PERSONALITY
TESTS AND REVIEWS

PERSONALITY
TESTS AND REVIEWS

Including an Index to
The Mental Measurements Yearbooks

Edited by
OSCAR KRISEN BUROS

THE GRYPHON PRESS
HIGHLAND PARK · NEW JERSEY

Table of Contents

Contributing Test Reviewers

HAROLD H. ABELSON   3:30, 3:105
C. J. ADCOCK   5:112
    5:147, 6:131, 6:143, 6:245
DAN L. ADLER   5:81, 5:117
MARY D. AINSWORTH   5:165, 5:166
LEWIS E. ALBRIGHT   6:58
ANNE ANASTASI   6:122
DWIGHT L. ARNOLD   4:90, 5:80
ALEXANDER W. ASTIN   6:58
FREDERIC L. AYER   4:66
ANDREW R. BAGGALEY   5:45, 5:96, 6:172
BENJAMIN BALINSKY   4:146, 5:135, 5:142
WARREN R. BALLER   5:104, 5:108
RICHARD S. BARRETT   6:97, 6:153
FRANK BARRON   5:47
HARRIET M. BARTHELMESS   1:929
ROBERT H. BAUERNFEIND   5:41, 5:100
BRENT BAXTER   5:29
KENNETH L. BEAN   5:124, 6:125
SAMUEL J. BECK   2:1200, 2:1240, 5:154
WESLEY C. BECKER   6:96, 6:157
RALPH C. BEDELL   3:67
H. R. BEECH   6:233
JOHN E. BELL   4:103, 4:105, 5:132
    5:163, 6:95, 6:146, 6:202
GEORGE K. BENNETT   5:29
P. M. BENTLER   6:127
ARTHUR L. BENTON   3:29, 3:60
    3:103, 4:71, 4:136, 4:144
ROBERT G. BERNREUTER   2:1252
ÅKE BJERSTEDT   5:33, 5:47
    6:162, 6:186, 6:238
JOHN D. BLACK   5:106, 6:133, 6:190
J. M. BLACKBURN   2:1220
C. B. BLAKEMORE   6:203, 6:212

HAROLD BORKO   6:149, 6:197
E. J. G. BRADFORD   3:95, 4:105, 4:132
FRANCIS F. BRADSHAW   1:915
ARTHUR H. BRAYFIELD   6:85
H. E. BROGDEN   4:47, 4:59
R. A. BROTEMARKLE   3:45
THOMAS C. BURGESS   6:66, 6:145
ALVIN G. BURSTEIN   6:63
DONALD T. CAMPBELL   4:46, 4:88
    5:116, 5:119, 6:168, 6:186
DUGAL CAMPBELL   6:60, 6:137
JOEL T. CAMPBELL   6:134
HAROLD D. CARTER   3:52
LAUNOR F. CARTER   4:56
RAYMOND B. CATTELL   2:1200, 2:1213
ROBERT C. CHALLMAN   4:116, 4:129
CHERRY ANN CLARK   5:131, 5:145
KENNETH E. CLARK   4:46, 4:52, 4:91
GLEN U. CLEETON   3:96
DOROTHY M. CLENDENEN   5:88
    6:111, 6:132
RICHARD W. COAN   6:217, 6:231
CHARLES N. COFER   4:130
    4:131, 5:134, 5:135
WILLIAM E. COFFMAN   3:59
BERTRAM D. COHEN   6:90, 6:160
JACOB COHEN   6:121, 6:124
W. D. COMMINS   2:1202
STEPHEN M. COREY   1:897, 2:1238, 2:1266
DOUGLAS COURTNEY   4:64, 4:79
WILLIAM J. E. CRISSY   4:63
JOHN O. CRITES   6:151
LYSLE W. CROFT   4:34, 4:96
LEE J. CRONBACH   3:35, 3:46
    3:52, 5:37, 6:118, 6:184

Richard Jessor	5:143, 5:145	H. Meltzer	3:48, 3:57
Cecil D. Johnson	5:71	Gerald A. Mendelsohn	6:99, 6:147
E. Harold Jones	1:918, 2:1214	T. R. Miles	5:52, 6:227, 6:228
	2:1222, 4:41, 4:73	Lorenz Misbach	3:48
Walter Kass	5:153, 5:161	Terence Moore	6:241
Walter Katkovsky	6:212, 6:220	G. A. V. Morgan	6:68, 6:81
E. Lowell Kelly	3:53, 3:54, 4:50	N. W. Morton	4:106
	4:76, 5:70, 6:71, 6:148	Charles I. Mosier	2:1234, 2:1239
Douglas T. Kenny	5:81, 5:126	C. Scott Moss	6:75, 6:178
Elaine F. Kinder	1:1143	Allyn M. Munger	6:84, 6:163
Forrest A. Kingsbury	2:1223	Bernard I. Murstein	6:206, 6:219
Philip M. Kitay	6:229	Theodor F. Naumann	6:84
Paul M. Kjeldergaard	6:124, 6:150	Theodore Newcomb	2:1202, 2:1239
Seymour G. Klebanoff	4:31, 4:51	Kenneth R. Newton	5:125, 5:161
Benjamin Kleinmuntz	6:189	Robert C. Nichols	6:99, 6:246
Milton V. Kline	6:178	Warren T. Norman	5:86, 6:57
Kate Levine Kogan	3:41, 4:35	Raymond C. Norris	5:68
William S. Kogan	4:35	Pedro T. Orata	2:1259
Morris Krugman	3:47, 3:73	David B. Orr	6:169
	4:29, 4:73, 5:102, 5:150	C. Robert Pace	4:45, 5:33, 5:116, 5:119
W. C. Kvaraceus	3:25, 3:35	Jerome D. Pauker	6:148, 6:175
Edward Landy	5:32, 5:92	R. W. Payne	6:101, 6:195
Theos A. Langlie	1:915	L. S. Penrose	3:60
Wilbur L. Layton	6:122, 6:132	Charles Clinton Peters	1:903
Richard Ledgerwood	1:916	Donald R. Peterson	6:160, 6:195
S. G. Lee	6:213, 6:240	John Pierce-Jones	5:100, 6:169, 6:190
Roger T. Lennon	4:66	Daniel A. Prescott	1:920, 1:928
Theodore F. Lentz	3:67, 3:70	M. L. Kellmer Pringle	6:68
Eugene E. Levitt	6:179, 6:231	Albert I. Rabin	4:113, 4:134, 5:126
Roy D. Lewis	5:92	John A. Radcliffe	5:58
John Liggett	6:207		5:59, 5:68, 6:87, 6:182
James C. Lingoes	6:93, 6:138, 6:143	Ralph M. Reitan	6:116, 6:177
Louis Long	3:70, 3:111	H. H. Remmers	1:899, 1:901, 1:902
Frank M. Loos	4:61	Gilbert J. Rich	3:113
Maurice Lorr	5:67	T. W. Richards	4:108
	5:82, 5:123, 6:114, 6:174	Carl R. Rogers	2:1237, 2:1240
C. M. Louttit	1:921, 1:922, 2:1200	Ephraim Rosen	4:105, 4:107
	2:1201, 2:1258, 3:59, 3:107, 4:76	Alan O. Ross	6:164, 6:241
Ardie Lubin	4:61, 4:87, 4:134	John W. M. Rothney	3:63, 3:107, 4:67
David T. Lykken	6:72, 6:172		4:79, 5:79, 5:122, 6:106, 6:142
Raymond J. McCall	5:154	Julian B. Rotter	3:60, 3:103
Boyd R. McCandless	6:129	Floyd L. Ruch	6:120
Louis L. McQuitty	4:63	David G. Ryans	4:93
Julius B. Maller	2:1237, 2:1252	H. Bradley Sagen	6:115, 6:153
Winton H. Manning	6:58	Bert R. Sappenfield	5:133
Ross W. Matteson	4:84		5:155, 6:204, 6:247
James Maxwell	3:59, 4:85	Irwin G. Sarason	6:208, 6:232
Arthur W. Meadows	5:45, 5:136	Theodore R. Sarbin	4:28, 4:60
Paul E. Meehl	3:53, 3:99, 3:112	Helen Sargent	4:117

PERSONALITY
TESTS AND REVIEWS

Preface

WHEN we initiated our cooperative test reviewing service for test users over thirty years ago, we greatly underestimated the difficulties [1] which we were to encounter in the years ahead. We were constantly faced with financing problems—we never knew whether or not we would be able to get out another *Mental Measurements Yearbook*. We found it impossible to publish a volume annually as originally planned. After repeated starts, we finally published *Tests in Print* in 1961—twenty years after we first decided to prepare this comprehensive test bibliography and master index to the contents of the MMY's.

In the Preface of *The 1940 Mental Measurements Yearbook* we announced plans for the publication of a series of monographs, each of which would cover a specific section of the MMY's. It took us over a quarter of a century before we were able to finance the publication of the first of these monographs, *Reading Tests and Reviews,* published in October 1968.

In the reading monograph we announced plans to publish in 1969 monographs in three more areas—personality, intelligence, and vocational aptitudes—to be followed by the 7th MMY in 1971. Again we underestimated the work involved; preparation of this personality monograph has been a much bigger task than we anticipated. As a result, publication of the intelligence and vocational aptitude monographs must be postponed until after the publication of *The Seventh Mental Measurements Yearbook* late in 1971.

The major purpose of this monograph is to make readily available to users of personality tests the wealth of information—original test reviews, excerpted test reviews, and references

on the construction, use, and validity of specific tests—to be found in the first six *Mental Measurements Yearbooks*. The volume also includes a great deal of new material on personality testing: a comprehensive bibliography of 513 personality tests; 7,116 new references dealing with the construction, use, and validity of specific tests; separate author indexes for all tests having 25 or more references; and a scanning index to all personality tests in this volume.

In addition to the material on personality tests, this monograph includes several other useful features: the MMY Test Index, a master index to the nonpersonality tests, reviews, and references in the first six MMY's; the MMY Book Review Index, an index to all reviews of measurement books excerpted in the first six MMY's; a reprinting of the APA-AERA-NCME *Standards for Educational and Psychological Tests and Manuals;* a title index which includes every test listed in an MMY, TIP, or RTR; and an analytical name index which includes the authors of all reviews and excerpts in the six MMY's.

Although approximately two-thirds of this volume has been reprinted from the MMY's, the labor and cost of the monograph's preparation and manufacture were actually greater than they were for the 6th MMY. Inflation and the excessive labor involved in the preparation of the analytical name index with over 27,000 entries more than offset the economies resulting from reprinting test reviews and bibliographies from the first six MMY's.

The literature explosion in recent years is making it increasingly difficult to present comprehensive bibliographies on specific tests. The number of new personality test references in this volume alone is greater than the total number of personality test references in the first five MMY's and very nearly as great as the number of references for all tests, both personality and nonpersonality, in the 6th MMY. In order to keep the 7th MMY within manageable size, it will not contain references for specific tests in the areas of intelligence, personality, and vocations. References in these three areas will, however, appear in the relevant monographs to be published after the publication of the 7th MMY.

In an effort to cope with the rapidly increasing output of tests, we also plan to introduce original test reviews in the monographs on intelligence and vocations and in the second monograph on personality. If the monographs are well received, we also plan to publish monographs in the subject areas of English, fine arts, foreign languages, mathematics, science, and social studies. A second edition of *Tests in Print,* planned for publication in early 1972, will again serve a dual purpose: to present a comprehensive bibliography of all standardized tests in print and to provide a master index to the reviews and references to be found in the MMY's and monographs published to date.

I have been most fortunate in having had the assistance of a competent and conscientious editorial and secretarial staff. It is difficult to express adequately my indebtedness to Miss Ethel Kersting, Editorial Associate, for her important contributions to this volume. She has been a dedicated right hand at every stage in the preparation of the manuscript and in seeing the book through the press. Mrs. Joan S. Paszamant, Editorial Assistant, has done excellent work in the preparation of test entries and in proofreading. Her competence and accuracy have been a great comfort to me. I also wish to express my appreciation and thanks for the able services of two editorial assistants: Mrs.

Shirle M. Hartley, who recently joined our staff, and Miss Elaine M. Negran, formerly of our staff. Copyreading, filing, index making, and typing were efficiently handled by Mrs. Doris G. McCan, Mrs. Augusta D. Fleagle, and Miss Natalie J. Rosenthal. Mrs. McCan, a veteran of the last four MMY's, was especially valuable in checking copy for style and in proofreading.

I wish to thank those publishers who have provided us with information and specimen sets of their tests for editorial processing and review. Our work would be greatly facilitated if all publishers would do likewise. We still have considerable difficulty in getting information from some test publishers—three small publishers even refuse to give or sell tests to us and ignore all our requests for information. Other publishers probably mean well but neglect to reply to our requests for information and specimen sets of tests or do so only after repeated letters and telephone calls.

Although numerous libraries have been used in the preparation of the bibliographies for specific tests, special acknowledgment should be made of our extensive use of the Rutgers University Library.

Finally, I wish to express my gratitude to the American Psychological Association for granting us permission to reprint the APA-AERA-NCME *Standards for Educational and Psychological Tests and Manuals.*

I hope that readers will inform us of errors and omissions which may be found in this volume.

OSCAR KRISEN BUROS

Highland Park, N.J.
September 4, 1969

1 For an informal discussion of some of our early difficulties, read "The Story Behind The Mental Measurements Yearbooks" published in the Summer 1968 issue of *Measurement and Evaluation in Guidance.* Reprints are available from the MMY office.

Introduction

PRIOR to 1938 there was no source to which test users could go to obtain information about the merits and limitations of the hundreds of standardized tests published for use by teachers, psychologists, and personnel specialists. Rarely were tests reviewed in the professional journals. Textbooks did little more than describe uncritically the most commonly used tests. Test manuals were generally much less informative than they are today. Poorly constructed tests having little or no validity could be marketed without fear of published criticism. There was a crying need for some sort of a bureau of standards to point out the weaknesses and strengths of competing tests.

SERVICE FOR TEST USERS

For a time, I hoped that I might be instrumental in the establishment of such a test-the-tests research organization back in the thirties. It was only after I failed in repeated attempts to get the financial support needed to launch a test consumers research organization that I conceived the idea of setting up a test reviewing service with the cooperation of hundreds of specialists in education, industry, and psychology who would contribute frankly critical reviews of tests for publication in a series to be called *The Mental Measurements Yearbooks.*

The first of the MMY's, *The 1938 Mental Measurements Yearbook,* was published thirty-one years ago. Some appreciation and understanding of the underlying philosophy and the crusading nature of our new cooperative test reviewing service may be gained by reading the following quotation from the Foreword written by Clarence E. Partch in *The 1938 Yearbook:*

The publication of *The 1938 Mental Measurements Yearbook....*is likely to prove a landmark of considerable importance in the history of tests and measurements. Heretofore, despite the obvious need of test users for frank evaluations of tests by competent reviewers, few standardized tests have been critically appraised in the professional journals and textbooks * Now, for the first time, a large number of frankly evaluative reviews by able test technicians, subject-matter specialists, and psychologists are available to assist test users in making more discriminating selections from among the hundreds of tests on the market.

An important outcome of the yearbook series will be the stimulative effect which the test reviews will have, and already are having, upon test authors, publishers, reviewers, and test users. Test authors and publishers will be impelled to construct fewer and better tests and to furnish a great deal more information concerning the construction, validation, use, and limitations of their tests. Test reviewers will not only benefit by the reviews of others, but will also be challenged to think through more carefully their own beliefs and values with respect to testing. Test users will be aided in setting up evaluation programs which will recognize the limitations and dangers associated with testing—and the lack of testing—as well as the possibilities.

The Editor is to be commended for taking the position that reviewers should be representative of all persons who are, or potentially are, test users. The yearbooks will not reflect any one school of thought or class of test users. Reviewers will be chosen from among persons who are considered especially able from the viewpoint of some particular group of test users. For example, no one person will consider all reviewers especially able from his own viewpoint, but every reviewer will be considered as having outstanding ability by some persons. Since the yearbook series is based upon the assumption that frankly critical reviews are badly needed, only persons who are likely to give their frank and honest evaluations will be asked to review tests. In editing the yearbooks, every effort will be made to obtain reviews which are fair to all concerned, namely, the test users, reviewers, authors, and publishers. However, at all times, the primary responsibility of the Editor will be to test users.

In the Preface and Introduction of *The 1938 Yearbook,* I wrote:

Up to the present time, test authors and publishers have been able to place on the market inadequately validated tests without fear of criticism. Test users have every right to demand that test authors and publishers present full particulars concerning the methods used in constructing and validating the tests which they place on the market. Tests not accompanied by detailed data on their construction, validation, uses, and limitations should be suspect. * *It is the responsibility of test authors and publishers to furnish in the test manual whatever data they wish to have considered by reviewers and test purchasers.* Test authors and publishers should devote less time and money to constructing new tests and more time to furnishing prospective test consumers with detailed information concerning the construction, validation, and use of the tests which they do publish.

The 1938 MMY was followed by "yearbooks" in 1941, 1949, 1953, 1959, and 1965—each MMY larger and more comprehensive than the previous volume. For the past thirty-one years, the *Mental Measurements Yearbooks* have been providing test users with critical information about the merits and limitations of tests of every description—achievement, aptitude, intelligence, personality, and vocational. Since each succeeding volume supplements rather than supplants earlier volumes, the six MMY's published to date present a tremendous amount of useful information for all who make, sell, buy, or use tests. Each of the yearbooks—published at intervals of three to eight years—consists of two major sections: "Tests and Reviews" and "Books and Reviews."

MMY OBJECTIVES

The objectives of the section Tests and Reviews—the heart of the MMY's—have remained essentially unchanged since this cooperative test reviewing service was first initiated thirty-one years ago. The major objectives of the test section are:

a) To provide comprehensive bibliographies of all standardized tests published in English-speaking countries.

b) To provide frankly critical evaluations of tests written by competent specialists representing a variety of viewpoints to assist test users in choosing the tests which will best meet their needs.

c) To provide comprehensive bibliographies of articles, books, and theses dealing with the construction, validity, use, and limitations of specific tests.

d) To impel test authors and publishers to place fewer but better tests on the market and to provide test users with detailed information on the validity and limitations of their tests at the time the tests are first published.

e) To suggest to test users better methods of arriving at their own appraisals of both standardized and nonstandardized tests in light of their own particular values and needs.

f) To stimulate contributing reviewers to reconsider and think through more carefully their own beliefs and values relevant to testing.

g) To inculcate upon test users a keener awareness of both the values and dangers involved in the use and non-use of standardized tests.

h) To impress test users with the desirability of suspecting all standardized tests—even though prepared by well-known authorities—unaccompanied by detailed data on their construction, validity, use, and limitations.

The two major objectives of the book section are:

a) To present bibliographies of recent books on measurements and closely associated fields published in all English-speaking countries.

b) To make readily available evaluative excerpts from hundreds of book reviews appearing in a great variety of journals in this country and abroad to assist test users in making more discriminating selections of books for study and purchase.

SIX MMY'S, TIP, AND RTR

One hundred and thirty-three specialists contributed 331 original test reviews to *The 1938 Mental Measurements Yearbook,*[1] the first publication to provide test users with critical information regarding standardized tests of every description. This 430-page volume was widely hailed as a landmark in the history of testing. Its publication marked the end of the days when tests having either no validity or unknown validity could be published without fear of criticism. *The 1938 Yearbook*—hereafter referred to as *The First Mental Measurements Yearbook*—presents information on 314 tests, most of which were published within the period of 1933–37. *The First Yearbook* also includes excerpts from 776 reviews of 241 books on testing and closely related subjects.

Two hundred and fifty cooperating reviewers contributed 503 original reviews to *The 1940*

1 BUROS, OSCAR KRISEN, EDITOR. *The Nineteen Thirty-Eight Mental Measurements Yearbook.* New Brunswick, N.J.: Rutgers University Press, 1938. Pp. xv, 415. Out of print. Xerographic prints are available from University Microfilms, Inc., Ann Arbor, Mich. 48106. Paper, $17.50; cloth, $19.75.

Mental Measurements Yearbook,[2] a 699-page volume published in 1941. *The 1940 Yearbook* —hereafter referred to as *The Second Mental Measurements Yearbook*—lists 524 tests, most of which were published in 1938–40. *The Second Yearbook* also includes excerpts from 13 test reviews first published in journals and excerpts from 735 reviews of 368 books on testing.

Comprehensive bibliographies—including a total of 1,511 references on the construction, validity, and use of specific tests—were introduced for the first time in *The Second Yearbook*. Except for unpublished theses, all references in the specific test bibliographies in this and later MMY's were examined at first hand to make sure that they were relevant and that the listings were accurate. The introduction of these comprehensive and carefully screened bibliographies added greatly to the usefulness of the series.

The Third Mental Measurements Yearbook,[3] a 1062-page volume published in 1949, presents buying information on 663 tests, most of which were published during the period 1941–47. Three hundred and twenty cooperating reviewers contributed 713 original reviews. *The Third Yearbook* also includes excerpts from 79 test reviews first published in journals, excerpts from 785 reviews of 549 books on testing, and 3,368 references on the construction, validity, and use of specific tests.

The Fourth Mental Measurements Yearbook,[4] a 1188-page volume published in 1953, lists 793 tests, most of which were published during the years 1948–51. Three hundred and eight specialists cooperated in the preparation of this volume by contributing 596 original test reviews. *The Fourth Yearbook* also presents excerpts from 53 test reviews, excerpts from 758 reviews of 429 books on testing, and 4,417 references in its bibliographies on specific tests.

The first three MMY's presented information on tests commercially available as separates in English-speaking countries. The scope of the fourth and later yearbooks was expanded to include tests available only as a part of highly restricted programs such as the tests of the College Entrance Examination Board.

The Fifth Mental Measurements Yearbook,[5] a 1321-page volume published in 1959, presents information on 957 tests, most of which were published in the years 1952–58. Three hundred and fifty reviewers contributed 698 original test reviews. *The Fifth Yearbook* also presents excerpts from 48 test reviews, excerpts from 535 reviews of 485 books on testing, and 6,468 references in the test bibliographies.

Since each yearbook supplements rather than supplants earlier volumes in the series, the publication of successive volumes made it necessary for the reader to search through several volumes to locate the information wanted. Despite the numerous cross references to reviews, excerpts, and bibliographic references in earlier volumes, it was becoming increasingly difficult to locate quickly the relevant material with the publication of each new volume. Furthermore, there was no way of knowing whether a test listed in an earlier volume but not in the latest MMY was still in print. Then again publishers and their addresses were constantly changing. Clearly, something needed to be done to facilitate the use of the five MMY's published through 1959.

Tests in Print,[6] a master index to the contents of the first five yearbooks and a comprehensive bibliography of standard tests, was published in 1961. This volume lists 2,967 tests, 2,126 of which were in print early in 1961. When information is wanted from the first five MMY's, the reader is well advised to consult *Tests in Print* first. TIP indicates which of the first five MMY's presents the most recent listing of a test along with information regarding its in print status, the number of reviews it received, the names of the reviewers, the number of references on its construction, validity, and use, and the number of excerpts reprinted from test reviews in journals. The dual function served by TIP—a comprehensive bibliography of tests in print and a master index to the wealth of material in the first five MMY's—makes it an indispensable tool for all who wish to derive the maximum benefit from the MMY's in the shortest possible time.

2 BUROS, OSCAR KRISEN, EDITOR. *The Nineteen Forty Mental Measurements Yearbook.* Highland Park, N.J.: Gryphon Press, 1941. Pp. xxv, 674. Out of print. Xerographic prints are available from University Microfilms, Inc., Ann Arbor, Mich. 48106. Paper, $28.00; cloth, $30.25.

3 BUROS, OSCAR KRISEN, EDITOR. *The Third Mental Measurements Yearbook.* Highland Park, N.J.: Gryphon Press, 1949. Pp. xv, 1047. $20.50.

4 BUROS, OSCAR KRISEN, EDITOR. *The Fourth Mental Measurements Yearbook.* Highland Park, N.J.: Gryphon Press, 1953. Pp. xxv, 1163. $22.50.

5 BUROS, OSCAR KRISEN, EDITOR. *The Fifth Mental Measurements Yearbook.* Highland Park, N.J.: Gryphon Press, 1959. Pp. xxix, 1292. $25.00.

6 BUROS, OSCAR KRISEN, EDITOR. *Tests in Print: A Comprehensive Bibliography of Tests for Use in Education, Psychology, and Industry.* Highland Park, N.J.: Gryphon Press, 1961. Pp. xxix, 479. $10.00.

The Sixth Mental Measurements Yearbook,[7] a 1751-page volume published in late 1965, presents information on 1,219 tests, most of which were published in the years 1959–64. Three hundred and ninety-six specialists prepared 795 original reviews for this volume. *The Sixth Yearbook* also includes excerpts from 377 book reviews, excerpts from 97 test reviews, and 8,001 references on the construction, validity and use of specific tests.

In addition to the 1,219 tests for which extensive information, references, and reviews are presented, the 6th MMY lists by title all other tests known to be in print as of mid-1964. Each of these tests listed by title only appears in both the Classified Index of Tests and in the Title Index with a cross reference to its listing in *Tests in Print.* Thus, used together, the 6th MMY and TIP provide a comprehensive bibliography of all tests known to be in print as of mid-1964.

In the Preface of *The Second Yearbook,* I first announced our plans for a series of monographs, each of which would cover a given area (e.g., intelligence, personality, reading, science) within the MMY's. The first monograph, to be devoted to English and reading, was announced for publication in late 1941 or early 1942. Considerable work was done on the manuscript, but we had to abandon the project because of our inability to finance the monograph. The first MMY monograph, *Reading Tests and Reviews,*[8] was finally published in 1968. This 542-page volume includes not only a reprinting of the reading sections of the first six MMY's but also a comprehensive bibliography of reading tests and the MMY Test Index, a classified listing of all tests listed in one or more MMY's.

PERSONALITY TESTS AND REVIEWS

This volume, *Personality Tests and Reviews,* is the second in the series of MMY monographs designed to serve special groups interested in only one or two sections of the yearbooks. The size of the monograph—very nearly as large as *The Sixth Mental Measurements Yearbook*—reflects the tremendous interest and activity of

psychologists in assessing personality. In no other area of testing has there been such an overwhelming flood of articles, books, dissertations, research monographs, and tests. Personality tests are generally long-lived and obsolesce very slowly. Paradoxically, the area of testing which has outstripped all others in the quantity of research over the past thirty years is also the area in which our testing procedures have the least generally accepted validity. The span of approximately forty years covered by this monograph will help readers to get a better historical perspective of developments and trends in personality assessment. In my own case, the preparation of this volume has caused me to become increasingly discouraged at the snail's pace at which we are advancing compared to the tremendous progress being made in the areas of medicine, science, and technology. As a profession, we are prolific researchers; but somehow or other there is very little agreement about what is the resulting verifiable knowledge.

This monograph consists of the following sections: (*a*) Personality Test Index, a comprehensive bibliography of personality tests; (*b*) Personality Test Reviews, a reprinting of corresponding test review sections in the first six MMY's; (*c*) MMY Test Index, a guide to all tests and test reviews in the six MMY's; (*d*) MMY Book Review Index, an index to excerpted book reviews in the six MMY's; (*e*) APA-AERA-NCME Standards, a reprinting of the *Standards for Educational and Psychological Tests and Manuals;* (*f*) Publishers Directory and Index; (*g*) Index of Titles, including all nonpersonality tests in the six MMY's, *Tests in Print,* and *Reading Tests and Reviews;* (*h*) Index of Names, including all persons who have reviewed a test—personality or otherwise—for an MMY; and (*i*) Scanning Index to Tests, an expanded table of contents to the personality tests in this volume.

PERSONALITY TEST INDEX

This 241-page chapter presents: (*a*) a comprehensive bibliography of personality tests known to be in print as of June 1, 1969; (*b*) a bibliography of personality tests now out of print but once listed, and possibly reviewed, in one or more MMY's; (*c*) cross references to the test reviews, excerpts, and references reprinted in the next chapter from the first six

7 BUROS, OSCAR KRISEN, EDITOR. *The Sixth Mental Measurements Yearbook.* Highland Park, N.J.: Gryphon Press, 1965. Pp. xxxvii, 1714. $35.00.
8 BUROS, OSCAR KRISEN, EDITOR. *Reading Tests and Reviews: Including a Classified Index to The Mental Measurements Yearbooks.* Highland Park, N.J.: Gryphon Press, 1968. Pp. xxii, 520. $15.00.

MMY's; (*d*) bibliographies on the construction, use, and validity of specific tests; and (*e*) author indexes for specific test bibliographies with 25 or more references.

The Personality Test Index lists a total of 513 tests—379 in print tests and 134 out of print tests. An analysis comparing nonprojective and projective tests is presented in Table 1.

TABLE 1

CLASSIFICATION OF PERSONALITY TESTS

Classification	In Print		Out of Print	
	Number	Percentage	Number	Percentage
Nonprojective	296	79.1	121	90.3
Projective	83	21.9	13	9.7
Total	379	100.0	134	100.0

Projective tests make up 21.9 per cent of the in print personality tests but only 9.7 per cent of the out of print tests. Over 75 per cent of the 513 personality tests developed over the past forty years are still being sold.

Table 2 presents information about new and revised or supplemented tests in this mono-

TABLE 2

NEW AND REVISED (OR SUPPLEMENTED) PERSONALITY TESTS

Classification	In Print	Percentage		
		New	Revised	Total
Nonprojective	296	31.4	14.5	45.9
Projective	83	20.5	18.1	38.6
Total	379	29.0	15.3	44.3

graph. Of the 379 in print tests, 110 (29.0 per cent) are new tests not previously listed in an MMY; 58 (15.3 per cent) tests have been either revised or supplemented since last listed in an MMY. A total of 168 (44.3 per cent) tests are new or have been revised or supplemented since the publication of the 6th MMY.

TEST ENTRIES

Long entries are presented for each of the 379 in print tests; short entries are presented for the 134 out of print tests. All entries were prepared in the MMY office from an actual examination of the test materials. It is our editorial policy to list nothing which we have not personally examined. We have tried to make these entries as informative as possible. Rarely are we able to complete an entry without requesting further information from the publisher —sometimes as many as five or six requests

must be made to get the information needed for an entry. Completed entries were submitted to publishers for checking. One publisher refused to check the entry prepared for his test; two others failed to reply to our repeated requests to check entries for their tests.

The short entries for out of print tests present the following information: title, population for which suitable, range of publication dates, number and description of scores, authors, and publisher. The long entries for in print tests include additional information: acronym; listing of all forms, levels, and accessories with pagination, copyright dates, and prices; absence of data on reliability and validity; available answer sheets and scoring services; and administration time. For both categories of tests, cross references are given to the reviews, excerpts, and references reprinted in the next chapter from the first six *Mental Measurements Yearbooks*.

To obtain the maximum information from the test entries, the following description of the kinds of information provided should be read:

a) TITLE. Test titles are printed in boldface type. Secondary or series titles are set off from main titles by a colon. Titles are always presented exactly as reported in the test materials. When the titles on the test booklet and manual differ, the better known title is given in boldface; the second title is generally given in italic type within the entry. Entry titles which differ from those reported in the test materials (generally because no definitive title is used) are enclosed in brackets. Stars (★) precede titles of tests which have never before been listed in an MMY; asterisks (*) precede titles of tests which have been revised or supplemented since their last MMY listing.

b) DESCRIPTION OF THE GROUPS FOR WHICH THE TEST IS INTENDED. Chronological age and school levels are the most common ways of describing the populations for which specific tests are suitable. The descriptions are usually self-explanatory. Commas are used to separate levels. "High school and college" denotes a single test booklet; "high school, college" denotes two test booklets, one for high school and one for college.

c) ACRONYM. An acronym is given for practically all tests. Usually, the acronym is formed from the initial of each word in the title. In a few instances, however, other letter sequences are used when they seem preferable.

d) DATE OF COPYRIGHT OR PUBLICATION. The inclusive range of copyright dates (or publication dates if not copyrighted) for the various forms, accessories, and editions of a test is reported. When the publication date differs from the copyright date, both dates are given; e.g., "1948, c1946–48" means that the test was copyrighted both in 1946 and in 1948 but was not published until 1948. When publication or copyright dates do not appear on the materials and the date has been secured through correspondence with the publisher, it is enclosed in brackets.

e) PART SCORES. The number of part scores is presented along with their titles or descriptions of what they presumably represent.

f) INDIVIDUAL OR GROUP TEST. All tests are group tests unless otherwise indicated.

g) FORMS, PARTS, AND LEVELS. All available forms, parts, and levels are listed with the number of pages and date of publication. Revised forms and manuals were systematically compared with earlier editions to determine the extent of the changes. Inconsequential and minor changes are so indicated. For example, in describing a booklet copyrighted in 1965, we might say : "1965, same as test copyrighted in 1960." Or we might say of a test : "the revised edition is identical to the original edition except for a minor change in the wording of one item."

h) PAGES. The number of pages on which print occurs is reported for test booklets, manuals, technical reports, profiles, and other nonapparatus accessories. Blank pages and pages containing only material not related to the test (e.g., advertising pages and pages containing only printer's marks) have not been counted. Self-covers have been counted only when the cover is not duplicated by a title page inside.

i) RELIABILITY AND VALIDITY. The complete absence of data in a test manual is indicated. It was originally intended to include in the entries the statement "reliability data for raw scores only" wherever appropriate. However, since it soon became apparent that almost all tests still report only raw score reliability data rather than data on reliability of normed scores, the idea of including such a statement was abandoned.

j) ANSWER SHEETS. In recent years, several electronic scoring machines have been developed and are now widely used. As a result, two, three, and even four kinds of answer sheets may be available for a given test. The test entries list all available answer sheets : Dela Data, Digitek, Hankes, IBM 805, IBM 1230, MRC, NCS, and Scribe.

k) COST. Price information is reported for test packages (usually 20 to 35 tests), answer sheets, scoring stencils, manuals, and specimen sets. A statement "$3 per 35 tests" means that all accessories are included unless otherwise indicated by the reporting of separate prices for accessories. Such a statement also means 35 tests of one level, one edition, or one part unless otherwise specified. Discounts that may be available for purchasing in large quantities and special discounts available to professional groups are not reported. Specimen set prices mean specimen sets of all levels, all editions, all parts—but not all forms—unless otherwise indicated. Information as to whether prices include postage is reported. Price information is believed to be correct as of early 1969. Although every precaution has been taken to ensure accuracy, some prices may be in error ; other prices will have increased in keeping with the current inflation. For full and up-to-date information on test prices, the latest catalogs of test publishers should be consulted.

l) SCORING AND REPORTING SERVICES. Scoring and reporting services obtainable from the publisher are reported in a test entry along with information on costs. Special computerized scoring and interpretation services are usually given a separate entry immediately following the test. Computer generated interpretative printouts represent a new development not previously listed in an MMY publication.

m) TIME. The number of minutes of actual working time allowed examinees and the approximate length of time needed for administering a test are reported whenever obtainable. The latter figure is always enclosed in parentheses. Thus, "50(60) minutes" indicates that the examinees are allowed fifty minutes of working time and that a total of sixty minutes is needed to administer the test. When the time necessary to administer a test is not reported or suggested in the test materials but has been obtained through correspondence with the test publisher or author, the time is enclosed in brackets.

n) AUTHOR. Authors' names are reported exactly as printed on the test booklets and manuals. An author of only part of the test materials is identified by listing the part authored in parentheses after his name.

o) PUBLISHER. The name of the publisher or distributor is reported for each test. For addresses of publishers and distributors, see the Publishers Directory and Index. Addresses are not reported for publishers with no tests currently in print. The asterisk following the publisher's name indicates that the entry was prepared in the MMY office from an actual examination of all test materials listed.

p) SUBENTRIES. Levels, editions, subtests, or parts of a test which are available in separate booklets are presented as subentries with titles set in small capitals. Sub-subentries are indented with titles set in italic type.

q) CROSS REFERENCES. The cross references serve as a key to the reviews, excerpts, and references reprinted in the next chapter from the first six *Mental Measurements Yearbooks*. Names of MMY reviewers, number of excerpted reviews, and number of references are reported for each test. The cross references list the yearbooks in reverse order of publication; i.e., references to material in the 6th are listed first, then the 5th, and so on. This reverse order will prompt the reader to look at the most recent material first. In using the cross references, it is important to note that the references are to entry numbers, not to page numbers. Entry numbers appear in the running heads next to the outside margins. Page numbers appear in the running heads next to the inside margins.

TEST BIBLIOGRAPHIES

Immediately following each test entry, references on its construction, use, and validity are presented. If references were presented in one of the first six MMY's, the earlier references are first cited ; e.g., "8–27. See 4 :48" means that references 8 through 27 appear in the next chapter under test 48 in the section reprinted from the 4th MMY. New references are arranged in chronological order by year of publication and alphabetically by authors within years. References are numbered consecutively through all

MMY volumes and monographs. The specific test bibliographies are believed to be fairly complete through November 1, 1968, with a few later references. In order to assist students who wish to do selected reading on a particular test, references are given to abstracts in *Dissertation Abstracts* and in *Psychological Abstracts*. For example, *"DA 33:6843"* refers to a thesis abstract beginning on page 6843 in volume 33 of *Dissertation Abstracts;* and *"PA 37:416"* refers to abstract number 416 in volume 37 of *Psychological Abstracts.*

Table 3 presents a breakdown of the 7,116 references reported for the first time in this

TABLE 3
PERSONALITY TEST REFERENCES IN THE FIRST SIX MENTAL MEASUREMENTS YEARBOOKS AND PERSONALITY TESTS AND REVIEWS

Volume	Total	Non-projective	Projective	Percentage Projective
PTR	7,116	4,976	2,140	30.0
6th	4,183	2,522	1,661	39.7
5th	3,431	1,388	2,043	59.5
4th	2,024	911	1,113	55.0
3rd	1,103	538	565	51.2
2nd	473	316	157	33.2
Total	18,330	10,651	7,679	41.9

monograph and the 11,214 references reprinted from the six MMY's. The extraordinary growth in the literature on personality testing is reflected by these statistics on references for specific tests. The number of new references in this monograph is 70.1 per cent greater than the number of personality test references in the 6th MMY. The new references outnumber all personality test references in the first five MMY's. Projective test references account for 41.9 per cent of the 18,330 references. The percentage of projective test references hit its peak in the 5th MMY with 59.5 per cent; since then, the percentage dropped to 39.7 in the 6th MMY and to 30.0 per cent in this volume.

A tabulation of the number of references by years is presented in Table 4 for the 30-year period 1939–68. Twenty years ago, there were about 370 references per year; 10 years ago it was approximately 660 references per year; the current output (estimated from data in this table and in our files) is running over 1,300 references per year! This is only for personality tests published as separates and consequently listed in this monograph.

The task of preparing these bibliographies is becoming very nearly overwhelming. Their

TABLE 4
PERSONALITY TEST REFERENCES BY YEARS, 1939–1968

Year	Total	Nonprojective	Projective	Percentage Projective
1968	895	625	270	30.2
1967	1,209	917	292	24.2
1966	1,070	742	328	30.7
1965	1,152	807	345	29.9
1964	1,028	720	308	30.0
1963	1,046	708	338	32.3
1962	929	634	295	31.8
1961	863	554	309	35.8
1960	784	462	322	41.1
1959	716	414	302	42.2
1958	683	370	313	45.8
1957	586	312	274	46.8
1956	636	265	371	58.3
1955	581	214	367	63.2
1954	557	196	361	64.8
1953	538	201	337	62.6
1952	628	250	378	60.2
1951	669	227	442	66.1
1950	551	197	354	64.2
1949	439	179	260	59.1
1948	353	160	193	54.7
1947	328	186	142	43.0
1946	217	95	122	56.0
1945	229	126	103	44.5
1944	143	81	62	43.1
1943	173	82	91	52.6
1942	185	110	75	40.3
1941	168	101	67	39.9
1940	155	105	50	32.3
1939	125	99	26	20.8
Earlier	689	510	179	26.0
Total	18,330	10,651	7,679	41.8

Note: Since all but a very few of the references were compiled only through October 1968, the counts for 1968—and to a much lesser extent, other recent years—are too low. Counting references in the MMY files as of May 1, 1969, the reference count for 1968 is: 1,275 for total, 925 for nonprojective, and 350 for projective with 27.5 per cent projective. The totals include 2 nonprojective and 3 projective test references published in 1969.

preparation has been extremely onerous and costly. The specific test bibliographies cover not only the literature of the English-speaking world, but also the literature published in non-English-speaking countries but written in English. Our goal is to include all published material—articles, books, chapters, and research monographs—as well as unpublished theses. Except for theses, only published material is listed as references. Research reports prepared for internal use within an organization and prepublication reports have not been included. All published references have been examined to make sure that they meet our criteria for a test reference and to permit us to prepare accurate listings. Secondary sources are never used as the basis for listing published references. Secondary sources may provide leads, but if we cannot locate the publication the reference is not used by us. Since we search dozens of libraries in this country and abroad, the number of not-seen references withheld is inappreciable.

Table 4 also presents interesting information on the rise and decline of the relative popularity of projective techniques. Twenty-six per cent of the 689 references published at least 30 years ago were for projective tests. This percentage increased fairly steadily reaching a peak of 66.1 per cent in 1951. In all but 3 of the 13 years between 1943 and 1956, more than half of the references were for projective tests. For six years, the percentage of projective references was continuously above 60 with an average of 63.5. Since 1955, the percentage has been decreasing fairly steadily and is now hovering about 27 per cent. The drop in the actual number of references is less than 15 per cent; during the same period the number of nonprojective references more than doubled. Although projective tests do not dominate the literature as they did up to 12 years ago, their 30 per cent share represents a sizable number—especially since fewer than one-fifth of the tests are projective.

Table 5 presents reference counts for the 89 personality tests with 25 or more references.

TABLE 5

TESTS WITH 25 OR MORE REFERENCES

Test (Rank)	References	
	Total	1964–68
Rorschach (1)	3,747	533
Minnesota Multiphasic Personality Inventory (2)	2,474	900
Thematic Apperception Test (3)	1,237	252
Edwards Personal Preference Schedule (4)	697	287
Study of Values (5)	475	153
Bender-Gestalt Test (6)	429	147
California Psychological Inventory (7)	398	218
Sixteen Personality Factor Questionnaire (8)	359	223
Personality Inventory (9)	340	13
Rosenzweig Picture-Frustration Study (10)	310	45
Guilford-Zimmerman Temperament Survey (11)	305	100
Maudsley Personality Inventory (12)	269	132
California Test of Personality (13)	242	54
Machover Draw-A-Person Test (14)	221	66
Szondi Test (15)	186	17
Adjustment Inventory (16)	172	7
Mooney Problem Check List (17)	136	39
H-T-P (18)	136	17
Vineland Social Maturity Scale (19)	135	17
Blacky Pictures (20)	118	27
Kent-Rosanoff Free Association Test (21)	116	33
Holtzman Inkblot Test (22)	112	77
Interpersonal Check List (23)	109	55
Adjective Check List (24)	102	69
Shipley Institute of Living Scale (25)	100	34
Lowenfeld Mosaic Test (26)	98	20
Goldstein-Scheerer Tests of Abstract and Concrete Thinking (27)	91	17
Inpatient Multidimensional Psychiatric Scale (28)	87	45
Stern Environment Indexes (29)	84	57
Guilford-Martin Inventory of Factors GAMIN (30)	83	9
Inventory of Factors STDCR (31)	82	7
Embedded Figures Test (32)	80	40
Cornell Medical Index (33)	77	37
Rotter Incomplete Sentences Blank (34)	76	28
Omnibus Personality Inventory (35)	71	59
Cornell Index (36)	70	7
Humm-Wadsworth Temperament Scale (37)	70	0
Guilford-Martin Personnel Inventory (38)	69	4
IPAT Anxiety Scale Questionnaire (39)	68	35
Stern Activities Index (40)	68	38
Myers-Briggs Type Indicator (41)	66	56
Personality Schedule (42)	66	0
A-S Reaction Study (43)	65	5
Gordon Personal Profile (44)	64	14
Kahn Test of Symbol Arrangement (45)	64	29

Test (Rank)	References	
	Total	1964–68
Spiral Aftereffect Test (46)	60	13
Survey of Interpersonal Values (47)	60	46
Babcock Test of Mental Efficiency (48)	59	4
Children's Apperception Test (49)	54	15
Eysenck Personality Inventory (50)	53	52
Social Distance Scale (51)	53	15
Social Intelligence Scale (52)	53	3
Jr.-Sr. High School Personality Questionnaire (53)	51	28
Make A Picture Story (54)	51	3
Structured-Objective Rorschach Test (55)	49	31
Thurstone Temperament Schedule (56)	49	12
Activity Vector Analysis (57)	48	16
Concept Formation Test (58)	47	5
Minnesota Counseling Inventory (59)	47	32
Purdue Master Attitude Scales (60)	47	1
FIRO Scales (61)	45	24
Vocational Preference Inventory (62)	44	28
Welsh Figure Preference Test (63)	44	20
Attitude-Interest Analysis Test (64)	41	3
IES Test (65)	41	25
College and University Environment Scales (66)	40	38
Memory-for-Designs Test (67)	38	11
Interaction Chronograph (68)	36	1
Minnesota Personality Scale (69)	36	0
Stanford Hypnotic Susceptibility Scale (70)	35	17
Washburne Social-Adjustment Inventory (71)	34	1
STS Youth Inventory (72)	33	2
Interaction Process Analysis (73)	32	9
Heston Personal Adjustment Inventory (74)	31	2
Wittenborn Psychiatric Rating Scales (75)	31	6
Empathy Test (76)	30	1
Tennessee Self-Concept Scales (77)	30	23
Kuder Preference Record-Personal (78)	29	6
Personality and Personal Illness Questionnaires (79)	29	22
Hoffer-Osmond Diagnostic Test (80)	28	18
Interpersonal Diagnosis of Personality (81)	28	6
KD Proneness Scale and Check List (82)	28	7
Multiple Affect Adjective Check List (83)	28	23
Personal Adjustment Inventory (84)	27	1
Gordon Personal Inventory (85)	26	8
Personal Orientation Inventory (86)	26	26
Pressey Interest-Attitude Tests (87)	26	0
Security-Insecurity Inventory (88)	26	9
It Scale for Children (89)	25	7
Total	16,152	4,642

The Rorschach leads with a staggering total of 3,747 references followed by the ever-gaining MMPI with 2,474 references. Together the Rorschach and the MMPI account for 6,221 references—33.9 per cent of all references in this volume. The 25 tests with 100 or more references have together 12,925 references, 67.1 per cent of the total. The 54 tests with 50 or more references account for 14,918 references, 81.4 per cent of the total. The 89 tests with 25 or more references have 16,152 references, 88.1 per cent of all references. The remaining 424 tests together have only 2,178 references, 11.9 per cent of the total.

The rate at which references are being currently published is also presented in Table 5. The MMPI leads with 900 references over the five years ending with 1968. Since very few references published in November and December 1968 are reported in this volume, it is safe to say that over 200 articles, books, and theses are currently being published each year on the MMPI alone. The output for the Rorschach is running approximately 120 references per year. Of the 3,811 references reported in this monograph for 1964–65, the MMPI has 23.6 per cent and the Rorschach has 14.0 per cent; together, they have 37.6 per cent of all references listed in this monograph for the past five years.

Table 6 lists the 18 tests which averaged at least 10 references per year for the 5 years end-

TABLE 6

TESTS WITH 50 OR MORE REFERENCES
IN THE FIVE YEARS, 1964–68
BY DATE OF FIRST PUBLICATION

Date	Test	References	Rank
1921	Rorschach	533	2
1931	Study of Values	153	7
1936	Thematic Apperception Test	252	4
1938	Bender-Gestalt	147	8
1939	California Test of Personality	54	17
1942	Minnesota Multiphasic Personality Inventory	900	1
1943	Myers-Briggs Type Indicator	56	15
1949	Guilford-Zimmerman Temperament Survey	100	10
1949	Machover Draw-A-Person Test	66	12
1949	Sixteen Personality Factor Questionnaire	223	5
1952	Adjective Check List	69	11
1953	Edwards Personal Preference Schedule	287	3
1955	Interpersonal Check List	55	16
1956	California Psychological Inventory	218	6
1957	Stern Environment Indexes	57	14
1959	Maudsley Personality Inventory	132	9
1959	Omnibus Personality Inventory	59	13
1963	Eysenck Personality Inventory	52	18
	Total	3,413	

ing 1968, arranged in order of their first publication. These 18 tests have 3,413 references for the past 5 years, 63.7 per cent of the total for all tests. Five of the tests were published in the 1930's or earlier. These 5 tests, all of which were published at least 30 years ago, have 1,139 references—21.3 per cent of the references listed in this volume for the last 5 years. The five tests published in the 1940's have a total of 1,345 references, 25.1 per cent of all references published during this five-year period. These 10 tests, first published 20 to 48 years ago, account for 46.5 per cent of all references published in recent years.

Table 7 presents a comparison of the percentages of references reported for the Rorschach and the MMPI for the years 1939 through 1968. The percentage of Rorschach references rose from 18.0 prior to 1939 to a high of 39.3 in 1943. During the 16-year period 1941–56 about one-third of all references were for the Rorschach; since then the percentage has dropped steadily to an average of 10.1 for the last five years. During this same 16-year period the percentage of references for the

TABLE 7

RORSCHACH AND MMPI REFERENCES BY YEARS
1939–1968

Year	Percentage of All References			Ratio of MMPI to Rorschach
	Rorschach	MMPI	Total	
1968	11.3	14.5	25.8	1.29
1967	8.3	16.9	25.1	2.04
1966	10.4	16.7	27.1	1.61
1965	9.8	18.3	28.1	1.87
1964	10.5	17.1	27.6	1.63
1963	12.6	15.3	27.9	1.21
1962	10.7	17.0	27.7	1.60
1961	13.2	16.7	29.9	1.26
1960	19.8	15.2	34.9	.77
1959	19.6	14.2	33.8	.73
1958	20.4	15.2	35.6	.75
1957	20.6	13.1	33.8	.64
1956	32.1	13.2	45.3	.41
1955	33.6	11.5	45.1	.34
1954	36.4	12.7	49.2	.35
1953	34.2	13.9	48.1	.41
1952	30.4	13.5	43.9	.45
1951	33.2	11.5	44.7	.35
1950	33.8	10.0	43.7	.30
1949	31.7	8.9	40.5	.28
1948	32.6	17.3	49.9	.53
1947	27.7	12.5	40.2	.45
1946	38.2	10.6	48.8	.28
1945	33.6	8.3	41.9	.25
1944	35.7	2.1	37.8	.06
1943	39.3	2.9	42.2	.07
1942	32.4	1.1	33.5	.03
1941	33.3		33.3	
1940	27.1	1.9	29.0	.07
1939	18.4		18.4	
Earlier	18.0		18.0	
Total	20.4	13.5	33.9	66.0

MMPI increased fairly steadily, passing the Rorschach in 1961, to an average of 16.7 for the last five years. One out of three references reported in this monograph are for these two tests. During the years 1950 through 1956 the Rorschach and MMPI together averaged 45.7 per cent of all references; since then, the combined percentage has dropped to an average of 26.7 for the last five years. Today, the Rorschach and MMPI account for one out of four references on the construction, use, and validity of published personality tests.

SOME REFLECTIONS

In this era of remarkable progress in science and technology, it is sobering to think that our most widely used instruments for personality assessment were published 20, 30, 40, and even more years ago. Despite the tremendous amount of research devoted to these old, widely used tests, they have not been replaced by instruments more acceptable to the profession. Nor has the research resulted in a consensus among psychologists concerning the validities of a particular test. The vast literature on personality testing has failed to produce a body of knowledge generally acceptable to psychologists. In fact, all personality instruments may be de-

scribed as controversial, each with its own following of devotees. Most psychologists interested in personality assessment appear to spe-
cialize in a single instrument rather than play
the field. This specialization certainly has some
advantages. On the other hand, it gives a person a vested interest in the test; it becomes advantageous for him to exploit the test; he is
likely to rely almost exclusively upon the one
test and to serve as its advocate and defender.
It probably would be better for the advancement of knowledge if, for example, the Mults [9]
and Rorschachers had vested interests which
coincided with personality assessment as a
whole.

It seems incredible, for example, that the
MMPI—now being researched at the rate of
200 articles, books, and theses per year—is still
the same instrument published 27 years ago.
The 2,474 references (over 400 are doctoral
dissertations) reported in this monograph apparently have not generated enough new knowledge to bring about a revision or replacement
of the test. Nor has this concentrated research
on the MMPI resulted in a consensus among
psychologists as to what it can and cannot do.
The search for correlates to MMPI responses,
scores, and patterns continues to be a favorite
research project for hundreds of psychologists
and others; despite this intensive study of the
MMPI, the inventory is probably just as controversial, if not more so, than it was ten or
twenty years ago. Nevertheless, the use of the
MMPI has been growing at a phenomenal
rate. Moreover, it is probable that its use will
continue to grow at an ever increasing pace,
especially now that computerized interpretive
printouts (see entries 167, 168, and 169) are
available at a nominal cost. These automated
services greatly simplify problems of scoring
and interpretation even for competent psychologists and psychiatrists. Unfortunately, it is
likely to increase sharply the use of the MMPI
among physicians and other professionals not
trained in personality assessment. An MMPI
user no longer needs to know how to score the
test or to interpret a profile. Electronic computers can generate narrative reports for him
which may very well be equal to or better than
those prepared by psychologists who are MMPI

9 The MMPI is commonly referred to as the "Mult" among
psychologists at the University of Minnesota. We are using it
here as a convenient designation for MMPI specialists.

specialists. Certainly, the computerized reports
are much less expensive.

The Rorschach, kingpin of all personality
tests judging by the vast amount of material
written on it, is another example. This monograph reports 3,747 references (over 530 are
doctoral dissertations) for the Rorschach, with
a current output of about 120 references per
year. This vast amount of writing and research has produced astonishingly little, if any,
agreement among psychologists regarding the
specific validities of the Rorschach. It is amazing to think that this voluminous research and
experiential writing over a period of nearly a
half a century has not produced a body of
knowledge generally accepted by competent
psychologists. Even among the Rorschach disciples, there are various schools of thought,
each with its own following. (A recent book
describes five "American Rorschach systems.")
It is easy to understand that we must expect
always to have believers among us—persons
who have the will to believe in a particular
instrument or theory—but it is difficult to understand why the research has been so unproductive.

The sterility of the research and experiential
writing on the Rorschach and the MMPI is
also applicable to other personality tests which
have generated fewer publications. In no case,
however, has the accumulated research produced an enduring body of generally accepted
knowledge concerning the validities of the test
under study. We are still at the stage where
every test, regardless of its merits and deficiencies, is considered useful by some and
useless by others.

NAME INDEXES FOR SPECIFIC TESTS

When a test has a fairly large number of
references scattered over two or more yearbooks, it is difficult to use the Index of Names
to locate what a particular individual has written on a specific test. To overcome this difficulty, we had hoped to introduce in the 4th
MMY name indexes for tests with 25 or more
references. We actually prepared these name
indexes for the 4th but pulled them at the last
minute to reduce printing costs. It is with a
sense of achievement that we have finally succeeded in providing name indexes for the 89
personality tests with 25 or more references.
Since these tests (see Table 5) together have
16,152 references, 88.1 per cent of all the ref-

erences in this monograph, the presentation of these 89 name indexes has more than doubled the labor involved in indexing authors of references.

To simplify indexing, forenames were reduced to initials and indexed exactly as so reduced. Authors who are not consistent in the way they report their names will find their publications under two or more entries. If John A. Doe sometimes dropped his middle initial, his publications will be found under J. Doe and J. A. Doe. Similarly, the references listed for J. Smith may include the publications of several persons. In all cases, however, the reference presents names exactly as they appear in the publication in question. A different practice was followed in the name index for the entire volume. In the Index of Names, entries were combined whenever we were reasonably confident that all the references were by the same person.

PERSONALITY TEST REVIEWS

This 1,104-page chapter presents a reprinting of the personality sections of the first six MMY's in the order of their original publication: 1st MMY, 17 pages; 2nd MMY, 52 pages; 3rd MMY, 168 pages; 4th MMY, 227 pages; 5th MMY, 239 pages; and 6th MMY, 400 pages. The sections from the last four yearbooks make up 1,034 pages, 93.7 per cent of the chapter.

This chapter presents 648 critical reviews of 386 personality tests by 291 specialists in

TABLE 8

Reviews, Excerpted Reviews, and References Reprinted From the First Six MMY's

MMY	Test Reviews	Test Excerpts	Book Excerpts	References
6	211	47		4,183
5	147	41		3,431
4	116	25	139	2,024
3	93	14	129	1,103
2	54	6		473
1	27	3		
Total	648	136	268	11,214

psychology and testing, 136 excerpts from personality test reviews originally published in professional journals, 268 excerpts from reviews of books dealing with specific personality tests, and 11,214 references on the construction, use, and validity of specific personality tests. Table 8 presents a breakdown by yearbooks. The great bulk of the material is from the last

four *Mental Measurements Yearbooks:* 87.5 per cent of the original test reviews, 93.4 per cent of the excerpted test reviews, 95.8 per cent of the references for specific tests, and all of the excerpted book reviews.

Because of the smaller page size and different design, copy for the personality section of the 1st MMY had to be reset; the remaining personality sections have been reproduced with only the running heads changed. Page numbers are given in the running heads next to the inside margin. Entry numbers of tests are given as catchwords next to the outside margins with the yearbook designation added; thus, 2:1244 refers to test 1244 in the 2nd MMY. To locate the reviews which a test has received, first consult the preceding chapter, Personality Test Index. The index is not only a comprehensive bibliography of all personality tests in print as of June 1, 1969, it is also a convenient guide to the reviews, excerpts, and references presented in this chapter.

The 291 contributing reviewers represent a wide range of interests and viewpoints. Every effort was made to select reviewers who would be considered highly competent by a sizable group of test users. The use of multiple reviews made it possible to have most tests evaluated independently from several viewpoints. Of the 291 reviewers, 114 reviewed only 1 personality test, 107 reviewed 2 tests, 26 reviewed 3 tests, 14 reviewed 4 tests, 10 reviewed 5 tests, 10 reviewed 6 tests, 2 reviewed 7 tests, 7 reviewed 8 tests, and 1 reviewed 11 tests. Five of the reviews were written jointly by two reviewers. Ten per cent of the reviewers are from outside of the United States: Great Britain has 20 reviewers, Australia 4, Canada 2, New Zealand 1, South Africa 1, and Sweden 1. The foreign reviewers contributed 76 reviews, 11.7 per cent of all reviews.

SUGGESTIONS TO REVIEWERS

A sheet entitled "Suggestions to Reviewers" was enclosed with each letter inviting a person to review for an MMY. The suggestions have been essentially the same for all six MMY's. To properly understand the viewpoint from which the test reviews were written, readers are urged to study the following suggestions which were sent to persons who reviewed for the 6th MMY.

1) Reviews should be written with the following major objectives in mind:

a) To provide test users with carefully prepared appraisals of tests for their guidance in selecting and using tests.

b) To stimulate progress toward higher professional standards in the construction of tests by commending good work, by censuring poor work, and by suggesting improvements.

c) To impel test authors and publishers to present more detailed information on the construction, validity, reliability, uses, and possible misuses of their tests.

2) Reviews should be concise, the average review running from 500 to 1,000 words in length. The average length of the reviews written by one person should not exceed 800 words. Except for reviews of achievement batteries, multi-factor batteries, and tests for which a literature review is to be made, longer reviews should be prepared only with the approval of the editor.

3) Reviews should be frankly critical, with both strengths and weaknesses pointed out in a judicious manner. Descriptive comments should be kept to the minimum necessary to support the critical portions of the review. Criticism should be as specific as possible; implied criticisms meaningful only to testing specialists should be avoided. Reviews should be written primarily for the rank and file of test users. An indication of the relative importance and value of a test with respect to competing tests should be presented whenever possible. If a reviewer considers a competing test better than the one being reviewed, the competing test should be specifically named.

4) If a test manual gives insufficient, contradictory, or ambiguous information regarding the construction, validity, and use of a test, reviewers are urged to write directly to authors and publishers for further information. Test authors and publishers should, however, be held responsible for presenting adequate data in test manuals—failure to do so should be pointed out. For comments made by reviewers based upon unpublished information received personally from test authors or publishers, the source of the information should be clearly indicated.

5) Reviewers will be furnished with the test entries which will precede their reviews. Information presented in the entry should not be repeated in reviews unless it is done for evaluative purposes.

6) The use of sideheads is optional with reviewers.

7) Each review should conclude with a paragraph presenting a concise summary of the reviewer's overall evaluation of the test. The summary should be as explicit as possible. Is the test the best of its kind? Is it recommended for use? If other tests are better, which of the competing tests is best?

8) A separate review should be prepared for each test. Each review should begin on a new sheet. The test and forms reviewed should be clearly indicated. Your name, title, position, and address should precede each review, e.g.: John Doe, Professor of Education and Psychology, University of Maryland, College Park, Maryland. The review should begin a new paragraph immediately after the address.

9) All reviews should be typed *double spaced* and *in triplicate. Two copies* of each review should be submitted to THE MENTAL MEASUREMENTS YEARBOOK; *one copy* should be retained by the reviewer.

10) If for any reason a reviewer thinks he is not in a position to write a frankly critical review in a scholarly and unbiased manner, he should request the editor to substitute other tests for review.

11) Reviewers may not invite others to collaborate with them in writing a review unless permission is secured from the editor.

12) Most tests will be reviewed by two or more persons in order to secure better representation of various viewpoints. Noncritical content which excessively overlaps similar material presented by another reviewer may be deleted. Reviews will be carefully edited, but no important changes will be made without the consent of the reviewer. Galley proofs (unaccompanied by copy) will be submitted to reviewers for checking.

13) The editor reserves the right to reject any review which does not meet the minimum standards of the yearbook series.

14) Each reviewer will receive a complimentary copy of THE SIXTH MENTAL MEASUREMENTS YEARBOOK.

MMY TEST INDEX

Most readers of this monograph will have occasion to consult *The Mental Measurements Yearbooks* for information about tests in areas other than personality such as achievement, aptitudes, intelligence, interests, reading, and sensory-motor. This chapter provides a master guide and classified index to the contents of the test sections in the first six MMY's. The MMY Test Index makes it possible for the reader to turn quickly to the appropriate MMY to learn where further information may be obtained about the tremendous wealth of information to be found in the test sections of the first six *Mental Measurements Yearbooks*.

Table 9 presents a summary of what is contained in the test sections of the first six

TABLE 9

Tests, Reviews, Excerpts, and References in the First Six MMY's by Major Classifications

Classification	Tests	Reviews	Excerpts	References
Achievement Batteries	54	174	5	462
Business Education	69	59	5	41
English	255	259	13	520
Fine Arts	43	72	2	288
Foreign Languages	164	156	5	191
Intelligence	290	483	64	5,494
Mathematics	247	312	6	181
Miscellaneous	297	177	25	713
Multi-Aptitude	25	77	10	680
Personality	386	648	136	11,214
Reading	224	351	31	601
Science	163	186	12	186
Sensory-Motor	60	29	11	467
Social Studies	160	154	4	75
Vocations	365	435	30	2,650
Total	2,802	3,572	359	23,763

MMY's: 2,802 tests, 3,572 original test reviews, 359 excerpted test reviews, and 23,763 references on the construction, validity, and use of specific tests.

Although the percentage of personality tests in the first six MMY's is only 13.8, the personality tests have 18.1 per cent of the original test reviews, 37.9 per cent of the excerpted test reviews, and 47.2 per cent of the test references.

The title last used in an MMY is presented for each test along with a listing of the names of persons who have reviewed the test in an MMY, the number of references on the construction, validity, and use of the test, and the number of reviews excerpted from journals. *The MMY Test Index does not indicate whether a test is currently in print; nor does it list tests published since the 6th MMY;* it is a master index to the tests, reviews, references, and excerpts to be found in the first six *Mental Measurements Yearbooks.* Within each classification, tests are listed in alphabetical order. If information is wanted about tests in a particular area, consult the key to the classification presented at the beginning of the MMY Test Index; if information is wanted about a particular test, consult the title index (superseded titles are also listed in the title index); if information is wanted about the tests reviewed by a particular person, consult the name index.

MMY BOOK REVIEW INDEX

This chapter is an index to 3,972 book review excerpts published in the first six *Mental Measurements Yearbooks* and in *Educational, Psychological, and Personality Tests of 1936.* A few books have been omitted—books in areas no longer considered eligible for inclusion in the book sections of the MMY's; for example, books on interviewing, research methods, social case records, and statistics.

The MMY Book Review Index lists 926 books published over a thirty-one year period, 1933 through 1963, with a few titles published in 1964. The Index serves as a guide to the published reviews of books on testing and closely related areas. Its primary purpose is to facilitate, for historical purposes, the retrieval of comments, criticisms, and viewpoints from among the thousands of review excerpts which have been published in the six MMY's and related publications.

The bibliographic information presented for each book has been compiled from the last listing in an MMY. No information is presented regarding prices, present name of publisher, or whether the book is still in print. The names of reviewers are presented along with references to the MMY's containing the reviews.

Titles are arranged alphabetically by authors with anonymous titles listed first. Although a classified index is presented at the beginning of the chapter, readers will probably want to skim over the titles looking for books of historical interest. All authors and reviewers are listed in the Index of Names and all book titles are listed in the Index of Titles.

The MMY's must be consulted for all book review excerpts in the 1st, 2nd, 5th, and 6th yearbooks. In some cases, review excerpts from the 3rd and 4th MMY's will be found in this monograph. In the 3rd and 4th yearbooks, all excerpted book reviews dealing with a specific personality test are presented as "Re" entries immediately following the test. This monograph includes from the 3rd and 4th MMY's 268 excerpted reviews of 50 books—157 of these excerpts are for 27 books on the Rorschach.

APA-AERA-NCME STANDARDS

One of the most important developments in testing in recent years was the 1954 publication of the *Technical Recommendations for Psychological Tests and Diagnostic Techniques* [10] and the 1955 publication of the derivative *Technical Recommendations for Achievement Tests.* [11] These two small monographs, commonly referred to as the Technical Recommendations, were jointly prepared by three professional organizations in education and psychology: American Psychological Association, American Educational Research Association, and National Council on Measurements Used in Education. The major objective of these two monographs was to persuade authors and publishers of tests to supply more information in their manuals concerning the construction, limitations, uses,

10 *Technical Recommendations for Psychological Tests and Diagnostic Techniques.* Prepared by a Joint Committee of the American Psychological Association, American Educational Research Association, and National Council on Measurements Used in Education. Supplement to the *Psychological Bulletin,* Vol. 51, No. 2, March 1954. Washington, D.C.: American Psychological Association, Inc., March 1954. Pp. ii, 38. (Reprinted in *Tests in Print.*)
11 *Technical Recommendations for Achievement Tests.* Prepared by the Committees on Test Standards of the American Educational Research Association and the National Council on Measurements Used in Education. Washington, D.C.: American Educational Research Association, 1955. Pp. 36. (Reprinted in *Tests in Print.*)

and validity of their tests. In 1966, the two monographs were replaced by a revised monograph, *Standards for Educational and Psychological Tests and Manuals*.[12] Since we believe that the Standards supplement and reinforce the MMY's, we are eager that they receive the widest possible circulation. For this reason and because we think that all readers of this monograph should be familiar with the Standards, we are reprinting the Standards with the kind permission of the American Psychological Association. Even persons who already have a copy of the Standards are likely to find it convenient to have them at hand in this monograph.

PUBLISHERS DIRECTORY AND INDEX

As an index, the Publishers Directory and Index is useful for locating both the in print and the out of print personality tests of a given publisher. As a directory, the Publishers Directory and Index provides: (a) the addresses of all publishers of personality tests currently in print, and (b) the addresses of publishers whose personality tests are now out of print but who have other tests in print. No addresses are reported for publishers with no in print tests.

All addresses have been checked by the publishers except in three instances where the publisher did not reply to repeated requests for checking. The 38 publishers issuing catalogs devoted entirely or in large part to tests are marked by a star (★).

The number of publishers of personality tests is surprisingly large. Considering only publishers of in print personality tests, there are 160 publishers: 138 in the United States, 10 in Great Britain, 4 in Canada, 3 in Holland, 2 in South Africa, 1 in Australia, 1 in India, and 1 in Switzerland.

One hundred and ten of the 160 publishers publish only 1 personality test; 22 publish 2 tests; 7, 3 tests; 5, 4 tests; 1, 5 tests; 4, 7 tests; 2, 8 tests; 2, 9 tests; 1, 10 tests; 1, 11 tests; 1, 14 tests; 1, 16 tests; 1, 20 tests; 1, 28 tests; and 1, 48 tests. The publishers with 7 or more personality tests are: Western Psychological Services, 48 tests; Consulting Psychologists Press, 28 tests; Psychometric Affiliates, 20 tests; Psy-

chological Corporation, 16 tests; Institute for Personality and Ability Testing, 14 tests; Educational and Industrial Testing Service, 11 tests; Science Research Associates, 10 tests; Educational Testing Service, 9 tests; Sheridan Psychological Services, 9 tests; Grune and Stratton, 8 tests; University of London Press, 8 tests; Family Life Publications, 7 tests; National Foundation for Educational Research in England and Wales, 7 tests; Psychological Test Specialists, 7 tests; and Springer Publishing Co., 7 tests. Together, these 15 publishers distribute 209 personality tests, more than the combined distribution of the other 145 publishers of in print personality tests.

INDEX OF TITLES

This title index lists the titles of: (a) 379 personality tests currently in print; (b) 134 personality tests now out of print but which were once listed in an MMY or TIP; (c) 926 books listed in the MMY Book Review Index; and (d) all nonpersonality tests listed in an MMY, TIP, or RTR. In addition, the Index of Titles reports acronyms for 348 of the in print personality tests and 54 of the more widely used nonpersonality tests.

References are to entry numbers, not to page numbers. Numbers not preceded by a letter or a yearbook designation refer to personality tests listed in the first chapter, the Personality Test Index. Numbers preceded by one of the letters A through O refer to nonpersonality tests listed in the third chapter, the MMY Test Index. Numbers preceded by the letter P refer to books in the MMY Book Review Index. Numbers preceded by TIP refer to tests in *Tests in Print*. Numbers preceded by RTR refer to tests in *Reading Tests and Reviews,* either new reading tests or tests revised since last listed in an MMY. Superseded or nonpreferred titles are followed by a "see" reference to the new or preferred title. In summary, the scope of this title index is much more inclusive than a mere listing of in print personality tests and their acronyms; it also lists all other tests (including out of print personality tests) which have been listed in an MMY, TIP, or RTR with a reference to the publication containing the most recent information.

INDEX OF NAMES

This gargantuan analytical name index lists and identifies authors of: (a) the 379 person-

12 *Standards for Educational and Psychological Tests and Manuals*. Prepared by a Joint Committee of the American Psychological Association, American Educational Research Association, and National Council on Measurement in Education. John W. French and William B. Michael, Cochairmen. Washington, D.C.: American Psychological Association, Inc., 1966. Pp. iii, 40.

ality tests currently in print and the 134 personality tests now out of print but which were once listed in an MMY or in TIP; (*b*) the 648 personality test reviews written for an MMY; (*c*) the 136 excerpted personality test reviews; (*d*) the 18,330 references reported in this monograph in the specific test bibliographies; (*e*) the 2,924 nonpersonality test reviews published in the six MMY's and referred to in the MMY Test Index; (*f*) the 926 books listed in the MMY Book Review Index; and (*g*) the 3,972 excerpted book reviews referred to in the MMY Book Review Index. Each citation is preceded by *rev, test, bk, exc,* or *ref* to indicate whether a person is author of an original test review written for the MMY (*rev*), a personality test (*test*), a measurements book (*bk*), an excerpted test or book review (*exc*), or a reference on the construction, use, and validity of a specific test (*ref*).

Forenames were reduced to initials in an effort to reduce the cost of indexing. In many cases when we were reasonably sure that two or more listings referred to the same person, we combined listings under one name, using, if possible, the author's preferred listing as reported in the *American Psychological Association 1968 Directory*. The reduction of forenames to initials means, of course, that two or more persons are more likely to be treated as though one person than would have been the case had the given names been reported in full.

Had we realized beforehand what it would cost to prepare and print an analytical index covering 27,549 separate items, we would never have started it. We mentioned above the specific name indexes which were prepared for the 89 tests with 25 or more references. Since the specific name indexes involved 16,152 references, we have indexed the equivalent of 43,701 publications in this monograph! We hope that readers will find the name indexes useful so that we may feel less badly about the cost in time and money spent in their preparation.

SCANNING INDEX TO TESTS

This Scanning Index is an expanded table of contents to the 513 personality tests listed in this monograph. The title, acronym (except for out of print tests), and entry number are reported for each test along with information as to whether it is a new test not previously listed in an MMY or whether it has been revised or supplemented since last listed in an MMY. Distinctive titles of subtests are also reported for in print tests. Stars (★) indicate new tests and scoring services; asterisks (*), revised or supplemented tests. Within each of the two categories—nonprojective and projective—in print tests are listed first followed by out of print tests set in smaller type size.

The major use of the Scanning Index will be to locate new, revised, and supplemented tests; to determine whether a test is currently in print; and to ascertain the acronym for a given test.

Personality Test Index

THIS chapter presents a comprehensive listing of all personality tests known to be in print in English-speaking countries as of June 1, 1969. In addition, the Personality Test Index lists all out of print tests which were once listed in one or more of the first six *Mental Measurements Yearbooks*. Consequently, the Index serves not only as a ready reference guide to the available personality tests, but also as an index to the personality sections reprinted in the next chapter, Personality Test Reviews, from the first six MMY's. For each of the 379 tests in print the following information is given: title; population for which suitable; range of publication dates; acronym; number and description of scores; forms with dates and paging; manuals and other accessories with dates and paging; absence of data on reliability and validity; absence or limitations of norms; available machine scorable answer sheets; prices of tests, accessories, specimen sets, and scoring services; administration time; authors; publisher; names of persons who have written original reviews of the test for an MMY; the number of references presented in the MMY's on the construction, use, and validity of the test; and the number of test reviews excerpted from other publications. Shorter entries, similar to those in *Tests in Print,* are presented for the 134 out of print tests.

Since the next chapter is a reprinting of the personality test sections of the first six MMY's, all the cross references to reviews, excerpts, and references in the MMY's are also cross references to the next chapter with a few exceptions. The citation 2:1205 refers to test 1205 in the second yearbook; this test may be located in the next chapter, Personality Test Reviews, by looking for the catchword, 2:1205, in the running heads. "See" references always refer to material in the next chapter; "consult" references refer to material which is not to be found in this volume. For example, "consult 6:682" means that the sixth yearbook must be consulted. All but ten of the cross references refer to material to be found in the next chapter.

A star preceding a test title denotes a new test which has not been listed in any of the first six MMY's; an asterisk indicates a test which has been revised or supplemented since its last listing in an MMY. Of the 379 personality tests currently in print, 110 (29.0 per cent) are new tests and 59 (15.6 per cent) have been revised or supplemented since last included in an MMY. The tests are listed in four alphabetical sequences by titles: (*a*) 296 nonprojective tests in print; (*b*) 121 nonprojective tests out of print; (*c*) 83 projective tests in print; and (*d*) 13 projective tests out of print.

NONPROJECTIVE

[1]

A-S Reaction Study: A Scale for Measuring Ascendance-Submission in Personality. College and adults; 1928–39; ASRS; separate forms for men ('28, 8 pages), women ('39, 8 pages); manual, second edition ('39, 16 pages); $3.90 per 35 tests; 75¢ per complete specimen set; postage extra; (20) minutes; Gordon W. Allport and Floyd H. Allport; Houghton Mifflin Co. *

For a review by Warren T. Norman, see 6:57 (11 references); see also 5:28 (15 references); for a review by William U. Snyder, see 3:23 (11 references); for a review by Doncaster G. Humm of the 1928 edition, see 2:1198 (19 references).

REFERENCES

1–19. See 2:1198.
20–30. See 3:23.
31–45. See 5:28.
46–56. See 6:57.
57. RAY-CHOWDHURY, K. "Allport's Ascendance-Submission Reaction Study in Indian Situation: 1, Study of Occupational Norms at the College Level and Correlations With Relevant Tests." *Indian Psychol B* 6:27-35 My '61. *
58. RAY-CHOWDHURY, K. "Allport's Ascendance-Submission Reaction Study in Indian Situation: 2, Occupational Group Differences in Ascendance-Submission Trait at the College Level." *Indian Psychol B* 6:37-40 My '61. *
59. RAY-CHOWDHURY, K. "Allport's Ascendance-Submission Reaction Study in Indian Situation: 3, Variation of Ascendance-Submission Trait With Age, Birth-Order, Locality and Region, Socio-Economic Status, and Religion." *Indian Psychol B* 6:41-7 S '61. *
60. PARAMESWARAN, E. G., and SANTHANAM, M. L. "Correlation of the A.S. Reaction Test Scores With Ratings on Ascendance-Submission Behaviour of Adolescents." *J Psychol Res* 6:90-2 My '62. * (*PA* 39:7793)
61. TILLMAN, KENNETH GENE. *The Relationship Between Physical Fitness and Selected Personality Traits.* Doctor's thesis, University of New Mexico (Albuquerque, N.M.), 1964. (*DA* 25:276)
62. HUNDAL, P. S. "Indian Version of Allport's A-S Reaction Study." *J Indian Acad Appl Psychol* 2:5-7 Ja '65. * (*PA* 39:12359)
63. TILLMAN, KENNETH. "Relationship Between Physical Fitness and Selected Personality Traits." *Res Q* 36:483-9 D '65. * (*PA* 40:4613)
64. DHILLON, P. K. "Item Analysis of Allport's A-S Reaction Study." *Indian Psychol R* 4:147-50 Ja '68. *
65. SINHA, J. N. "An Experimental Study of Prestige-Suggestion in Ascendant and Submissive Persons." *Psychol Studies* 13:108-10 Jl '68. *

NAME INDEX

Achilles, P. S.: 24
Allport, F. H.: 1
Allport, G. W.: 1-2, 4, 18
Barnette, W. L.: 34, 40
Beaver, A. P.: 44
Beckman, R. O.: 5
Bender, I. E.: 3, 38
Bronzaft, A.: 52-3
Broom, M. E.: 6
Brower, D.: 32
Brower, J. L.: 55
Carter, L.: 35
Chamberlain, F.: 17
Child, I. L.: 28
Decker, C. E.: 20
Dhillon, P. K.: 64
Dow, C. W.: 29
English, H. B.: 46
Farram, F.: 16
Flanagan, J. J.: 50
Gandhi, J. S.: 48
Hanna, J. V.: 8
Hardy, W. T.: 33
Hastorf, A. H.: 38
Hayes, R.: 52-3
Herr, V. V.: 50
Holcomb, G. W.: 10
Holmes, F. J.: 39
Holzberg, J. D.: 41
Horrall, B. M.: 36
Humm, D. G.: rev, 2:1198
Hundal, P. S.: 49, 62
Jersild, A.: 7
Koltuv, M.: 52-3
Laslett, H. R.: 10
Levine, M.: 5
Link, H. C.: 30
McGeoch, J. A.: 22

McKenna, F. S.: 42
Mann, R. D.: 51
Manzer, C. W.: 11
Moore, H.: 13
Nixon, M.: 35
Norman, W. T.: rev, 6:57
Oliver, A. G.: 54
Parameswaran, E. G.: 54, 56, 60
Perry, R. C.: 14
Posner, R.: 41
Ray-Chowdhury, K.: 48-9, 57-9
Reader, N.: 46
Reindl, M. O.: 45
Ruggles, R.: 18
Santhanam, M. L.: 60
Schultz, R. S.: 24, 26
Sheldon, W. H.: 28
Sinha, J. N.: 65
Skiff, S. C.: 47
Snyder, W. U.: rev, 3:23
Stagner, R.: 12, 23
Starer, E.: 43
Steele, I.: 13
Stevens, S. N.: 15
Sundaram, K.: 56
Thompson, C. E.: 31
Tillman, K.: 63
Tillman, K.: 61
Uhrbrock, R. S.: 37
Wang, C. K. A.: 9, 21
Wasson, M. M.: 19, 27
Weiss, L.: 25
Welch, L.: 52-3
Whitely, P. L.: 22
Williams, G. W.: 17
Wonderlic, E. F.: 15

[2]
Activity Vector Analysis. Ages 16 and over; 1945-63; AVA; test booklet is *Placement Analysis;* per-

sonality characteristics related to job success; 6 scores: aggressiveness, sociability, emotional adjustment, social adaptability, intelligent behavior, activity level; Forms A, B, C, ('62, 3 pages); 2 formats: standard, IBM punch card (Form A only); general information ('62, 15 pages); manual ('63, 43 looseleaf pages); directions for administering ['62, 1 page]; directions for scoring ['62, 1 page]; manual of correlation tables ('58, 161 looseleaf pages); profile ('62, 1 page) for each form; looseleaf Manual for Job Activity Rating includes separately copyrighted sections on job analysis ('56, 20 pages) and Jarsort procedure of job profile determination ('62, 9 pages), illustrative job analysis form ['56, 7 pages], 10 blank Jarsort profiles ('60, 2 pages), and 10 Jarsort correlation forms ('60, 2 pages); Jarsort cards ('60, 60 cards); distribution restricted to persons who have completed a training course offered by the publisher; quotations on course fee available on request; test materials must be purchased separately; postage extra; French, German, Italian, Portuguese, Puerto Rican, and Spanish editions available; (5-10) minutes; Walter V. Clarke Associates, Inc.; AVA Publications, Inc. *

For reviews by Lewis E. Albright, Alexander W. Astin, and Winton H. Manning, see 6:58 (21 references); for reviews by Brent Baxter and George K. Bennett, see 5:29 (11 references).

REFERENCES

1–11. See 5:29.
12–32. See 6:58.
33. MERENDA, PETER F. "Mr. K and the Ideal Self." *Percept & Motor Skills* 18:191-4 F '64. * (*PA* 39:1432)
34. MERENDA, PETER F. "Perception of Role of the President." *Percept & Motor Skills* 19:863-6 D '64. * (*PA* 39:7611)
35. MERENDA, PETER F. "Perception of Khrushchev One Year After His Retirement." *Percept & Motor Skills* 21:570 O '65. * (*PA* 40:2791)
36. MERENDA, PETER F., and CLARKE, WALTER V. "Self Description and Personality Measurement." *J Clin Psychol* 21:52-6 Ja '65. * (*PA* 39:12301)
37. MERENDA, PETER F., and MOHAN, JITENDRA. "Perception of Nehru and the Ideal Self in the Indian Culture." *Percept & Motor Skills* 22:865-6 Je '66. * (*PA* 40:11061)
38. WHITELEY, DONALD P. "Comparison of the Descriptive Validity of the Activity Vector Analysis and the Kuder Preference Record—Personal." *J Indus Psychol* 4(2):29-36 '66. *
39. CLARKE, WALTER V., and HASLER, KERMIT R. "Differentiation of Criminals and Non-Criminals With a Self-Concept Measure." *Psychol Rep* 20:623-32 Ap '67. * (*PA* 41:8145)
40. HASLER, KERMIT R., and CLARKE, WALTER V. "AVA Norms and Scores From General Population and Negro Population Samples." *Psychol Rep* 21:661-77 O '67. * (*PA* 42:4806)
41. HASLER, KERMIT R., and CLARKE, WALTER V. "An Experimental Measure of Personal Adjustment From a Self Concept Analysis." *J Clin Psychol* 23:467-9 O '67. * (*PA* 42:11407)
42. HASLER, KERMIT R., and CLARKE, WALTER V. "Personality Factors and Self-Concept Dimensions Associated With Proof Reading Ability." *Percept & Motor Skills* 24:1294 Je '67. * (*PA* 41:15258, title only)
43. MERENDA, PETER F., and MOHAN, JITENDRA. "Comparison of Indian Students' Perceptions of Nehru and Shastri." *Percept & Motor Skills* 24:1309-10 Je '67. * (*PA* 41:15169)
44. MERENDA, PETER F., and CLARKE, WALTER V. "Relationships Among AVA and ACL Scales as Measured on a Sample of College Students." *J Clin Psychol* 24:52-60 Ja '68. *
45. MERENDA, PETER F., and CLARKE, WALTER V. "Technique for Prediction of Outcome of Election of National Leaders." *Percept & Motor Skills* 26:1003-9 Je '68. * (*PA* 42:15380)
46. MERENDA, PETER F., and MOHAN, JITENDRA. "Indian Students' Perceptions of Mahatma Ghandi and Their Comparable American Ideal, Abraham Lincoln." *Percept & Motor Skills* 26:721-2 Je '68. * (*PA* 42:15327)
47. MERENDA, PETER F., and MOHAN, JITENDRA. "Perception of Ideal-Self, Nehru and Shastri." *Psychol Studies* 13:8-11 Ja '68. *
48. MERENDA, PETER F.; MOHAN, JITENDRA; CLARKE, WALTER V.; SCHULZ, HARTMUT; STREHSE, WOLFGANG; and WINNEKE, GERHARD. "Cross-Cultural Perceptions of Johnson and Kosygin." *Percept & Motor Skills* 26:843-7 Je '68. * (*PA* 42:15357)

NAME INDEX

Albright, L. E.: rev, 6:58
Astin, A. W.: rev, 6:58
Baxter, B.: rev, 5:29
Bennett, G. K.: rev, 5:29
Clarke, W. V.: 2-5, 7, 10-1,

14-27, 30-2, 36, 39-42, 44-5, 48
Dry, R. J.: 7
Dunnette, M. D.: 28
Farrington, A. D.: 12, 21

[3]

★Addiction Research Center Inventory. Drug addicts; 1961–67; ARCI; title on test booklet is *The ARC Inventory;* subjective effects of drugs and various dimensions of psychiatric disorders; 29 scales: carelessness, general drug, psychopathic deviate, alcohol withdrawal, opiate withdrawal, 7 empirical drug scales (alcohol, amphetamine, chlorpromazine, LSD, morphine, pentobarbital, pyrahexyl), 7 group pattern scales (alcohol, amphetamine, chlorpromazine, LSD, morphine, morphine-amphetamine, pentobarbital-chlorpromazine-alcohol), 10 factor scales (reactivity, efficiency, patience-impatience, sentimental, uncritical, immaturity, masculinity-femininity, inadequacy, impulsivity, neurotic sensitivity versus psychopathic toughness); 1 form ('61, 24 pages); temporary manual; separate answer sheets (IBM 805) must be used; test booklets free; standard answer sheets must be ordered from IBM; specimen set free; (60–120) minutes first testing, (45–75) minutes second testing; scoring service not available; Harris E. Hill, Charles A. Haertzen, and Richard E. Belleville; Addiction Research Center (Att. Charles A. Haertzen), National Institute of Mental Health. *

REFERENCES

1. HAERTZEN, CHARLES A. *A Test of a Basic Assumption of Causation in Factor Analytic Theory: Changes in Correlation Between Responses and Changes in Factor Composition Following the Administration of LSD.* Doctor's thesis, University of Kentucky (Lexington, Ky.), 1961.
2. HAERTZEN, CHARLES A., and HILL, HARRIS E. "Assessing Subjective Effects of Drugs: An Index of Carelessness and Confusion for Use With the Addiction Research Center Inventory (ARCI)." *J Clin Psychol* 19:407–12 O '63. * (PA 39:8418)
3. HAERTZEN, CHARLES A.; HILL, HARRIS E.; and BELLEVILLE, RICHARD E. "Development of the Addiction Research Center Inventory (ARCI): Selection of Items That Are Sensitive to the Effects of Various Drugs." *Psychopharmacologia* 4(3):155–66 '63. *
4. HILL, HARRIS E.; HAERTZEN, CHARLES A.; WOLBACH, ALBERT B., JR.; and MINER, EDWARD J. "The Addiction Research Center Inventory: Appendix: 1, Items Comprising Empirical Scales for Seven Drugs; 2, Items Which Do Not Differentiate Placebo From Any Drug Condition." *Psychopharmacologia* 4(3):184–205 '63. *
5. HILL, HARRIS E.; HAERTZEN, CHARLES A.; WOLBACH, ALBERT B., JR.; and MINER, EDWARD J. "The Addiction Research Center Inventory: Standardization of Scales Which Evaluate Subjective Effects of Morphine, Amphetamine, Pentobarbital, Alcohol, LSD-25, Pyrahexyl and Chlorpromazine." *Psychopharmacologia* 4(3):167–83 '63. *
6. HAERTZEN, C. A. "On the Addiction Research Center Inventory Scores of Former Addicts Receiving LSD and Untreated Schizophrenics." *Psychol Rep* 14:483–8 Ap '64. * (PA 39:2381)
7. HAERTZEN, CHARLES A. "Addiction Research Center Inventory (ARCI): Development of a General Drug Estimation Scale." *J Nerv & Mental Dis* 141:300–7 S '65. * (PA 40:4754)
8. HAERTZEN, CHARLES A. "Subjective Drug Effects: A Factorial Representation of Subjective Drug Effects on the Addiction Research Center Inventory." *J Nerv & Mental Dis* 140:280–9 Ap '65. * (PA 39:16115)
9. HAERTZEN, CHARLES A., and MINER, EDWARD J. "Effect of Alcohol on the Guilford-Zimmerman Scales of Extraversion." *J Personality & Social Psychol* 1:333–6 Ap '65. * (PA 39:10233)
10. HAERTZEN, CHARLES A. "Changes in Correlation Between Responses to Items of the Addiction Research Center Inventory Produced by LSD-25." *J Psycho-Pharmacol* 1(1):27–36 '66. * (PA 40:8258)
11. HAERTZEN, CHARLES A. "Development of Scales Based on Patterns of Drug Effects, Using the Addiction Research Center Inventory (ARCI)." *Psychol Rep* 18:163–94 F '66. * (PA 40:6376)
12. HAERTZEN, CHARLES A., and FULLER, GERALD. "Subjective Effects of Acute Withdrawal of Alcohol as Measured by the Addiction Research Center Inventory (ARCI)." *Q J Studies Alcohol* 28:454–67 S '67. * (PA 42:4215)
13. HAERTZEN, CHARLES A., and PANTON, JAMES H. "Development of a 'Psychopathic' Scale for the Addiction Research Center Inventory (ARCI)." *Int J Addictions* 2:115–27 sp '67. *
14. HAERTZEN, C. A., and MEKETON, M. J. "Opiate Withdrawal as Measured by the Addiction Research Center Inventory (ARCI)." *Dis Nerv System* 29:450–5 Jl '68. * (PA 43:1075)
15. HAERTZEN, C. A.; HOOKS, N. T.; MONROE, J. J.; FULLER, GERALD B.; and SHARP, HEBER. "Nonsignificance of Membership in Alcoholics Anonymous in Hospitalized Alcoholics." *J Clin Psychol* 24:99–103 Ja '68. * (PA 42:9182)

[4]

★The Adjective Check List. Grades 9–16 and adults; 1952–65; ACL; 24 scores: number of adjectives checked, defensiveness, favorable adjectives checked, unfavorable adjectives checked, self-confidence, self-control, lability, personal adjustment, achievement, dominance, endurance, order, intraception, nurturance, affiliation, hetero-sexuality, exhibition, autonomy, aggression, change, succorance, abasement, deference, counseling readiness; 1 form ('52); 4 formats; manual ('65, 34 pages); $2.50 per manual; $2.50 per specimen set; postage extra; (15–20) minutes; Harrison G. Gough and Alfred B. Heilbrun, Jr. (manual); Consulting Psychologists Press, Inc. *
a) BOOKLET FORMAT. Test booklet (3 pages); profile ('65, 1 page); $2.75 per 25 tests; $1.25 per 25 profiles; hand scoring stencils must be prepared by test user.
b) IBM FORMAT. IBM 1230 test-answer sheet (2 pages) labeled Parker Answer Sheet; $5 per 50 IBM 1230 test-answer sheets.
c) NCS FORMAT. NCS test-answer sheet (2 pages); $4.75 per 50 tests; NCS scoring service and duplicate profiles, 55¢ to 85¢ per test.
d) DELA DATA FORMAT. Mark sense test-answer cards (6 pages); $5 per 50 tests; Dela Data scoring service and duplicate profiles, 50¢ to 75¢ per test.

REFERENCES

1. MACKINNON, DONALD W. "The Development of Useful Tests for the Measurement of Non-Intellectual Functions," pp. 73–88. "Discussion of Professor MacKinnon's Paper," pp. 89–96 by John Dollard. General discussion, pp. 108–13. In *Proceedings of the 1951 Invitational Conference on Testing Problems, November 3, 1951.* Princeton, N.J.: Educational Testing Service, 1952. Pp. 119. *
2. BROWN, DONALD R., and BYSTRYN, DENISE. "College Environment, Personality, and Social Ideology of Three Ethnic Groups." *J Social Psychol* 44:279–88 N '56. *
3. GOWAN, J. C. "The Use of the Adjective Check List in Screening Teaching Candidates." *J Ed Res* 49:663–72 My '56. * (PA 31:3834)
4. HEILBRUN, ALFRED B., JR. "Validation of a Need Scaling Technique for the Adjective Check List." *J Consult Psychol* 23:347–51 Ag '59. * (PA 34:4072)
5. DiVESTA, FRANCIS J., and COX, LANDON. "Some Dispositional Correlates of Conformity Behavior." *J Social Psychol* 52:259–68 N '60. * (PA 35:4813)
6. GOUGH, HARRISON G. "The Adjective Check List as a Personality Assessment Research Technique." *Psychol Rep* 6:107–22 F '60. * (PA 34:7386)
7. GRIGG, AUSTIN E., and THORPE, JOSEPH S. "Deviant Responses in College Adjustment Clients: A Test of Berg's Deviation Hypothesis." *J Consult Psychol* 24:92–4 F '60. * (PA 34:7846)
8. HEILBRUN, ALFRED B., JR. "Personality Differences Between Adjusted and Maladjusted College Students." *J Appl Psychol* 44:341–6 O '60. * (PA 35:3893)
9. CROWNE, DOUGLAS P.; STEPHENS, MARK W.; and KELLY, RICHARD. "The Validity and Equivalence of Tests of Self-Acceptance." *J Psychol* 51:101–12 Ja '61. * (PA 35:6417)
10. HEILBRUN, ALFRED B., JR. "Client Personality Patterns, Counselor Dominance, and Duration of Counseling." *Psychol Rep* 9:15–25 Ag '61. *
11. HEILBRUN, ALFRED B., JR. "Male and Female Personality Correlates of Early Termination in Counseling." *J Counsel Psychol* 8:31–6 sp '61. * (PA 36:3KI31H)
12. PURCELL, JOHN FRANCIS. *Expressed Self Concept and Adjustment in Sexually Delinquent and Non-Delinquent Adolescent Girls.* Doctor's thesis, Fordham University (New York, N.Y.), 1961. (DA 22:918)

13. SPANNER, MARVIN. "Attribution of Traits and Emotional Health as Factors Associated With the Prediction of Personality Characteristics of Others." *J Consult Psychol* 25:210–5 Je '61. *

14. BROWN, ROBERT A., and GOODSTEIN, LEONARD D. "Adjective Check List Correlates of Extreme Scores on the MMPI Depression Scale." *J Clin Psychol* 18:477–81 O '62. * (*PA* 39:5168)

15. HEILBRUN, ALFRED B., JR. "Prediction of First Year College Drop-Out, Using ACL Need Scales." *J Counsel Psychol* 9:58–63 sp '62. * (*PA* 38:3199)

16. HEILBRUN, ALFRED B., JR., and SULLIVAN, DONALD J. "The Prediction of Counseling Readiness." *Personnel & Guid J* 41:112–7 O '62. * (*PA* 37:5289)

17. LANGER, PHILIP. "Sex Differences in Response Set." *J Psychol* 54:203–7 Jl '62. * (*PA* 37:3177)

18. LANGER, PHILIP. "Social Desirability and Acquiescence on the SORT." *Psychol Rep* 11:531–4 O '62. * (*PA* 37:8018)

19. LANGER, PHILIP. "Social Desirability and P Responses on the SORT." *J Clin Psychol* 18:472 O '62. * (*PA* 39:5205)

20. MACKINNON, DONALD W. "The Personality Correlates of Creativity: A Study of American Architects," pp. 11–39. (*PA* 37:4958) In *Personality Research*. Proceedings of the XIV International Congress of Applied Psychology, Vol. 2. Copenhagen, Denmark: Munksgaard Ltd., 1962. Pp. 229. *

21. SUINN, RICHARD M.; OSBORNE, DORENE; and WINFREE, PAGE. "The Self-Concept and Accuracy of Recall of Inconsistent Self-Related Information." Abstract. *J Clin Psychol* 18:473–4 O '62. * (*PA* 39:5009)

22. WEISER, JOHN CONRAD. *A Study of College of Education Students Divided According to Creative Ability.* Doctor's thesis, University of Missouri (Columbia, Mo.), 1962. (*DA* 23:4611)

23. WOOLINGTON, J. M., and MARKWELL, EARL D., JR. "The Influence of Hypnosis on Self-Attitudes." *Int J Clin & Exp Hyp* 10:109–13 Ap '62. * (*PA* 37:5248)

24. ANASTASIOW, NICHOLAS J. " 'Success' in First Grade as Seen by Teachers: Gough's Adjective Check List and Teachers' Ratings." *Psychol Rep* 13:403–7 O '63. * (*PA* 38:9213)

25. BOHN, MARTIN J., and STEPHENSON, RICHARD R. "Vocational Interests and Self-Concept." *Newsl Res Psychol* 5:21–2 Ag '63. * (*PA* 38:9336)

26. BROXTON, JUNE A. "A Test of Interpersonal Attraction Predictions Derived From Balance Theory." *J Abn & Social Psychol* 66:394–7 Ap '63. * (*PA* 37:7942)

27. ELDER, S. THOMAS; BUTLER, JOEL R.; and ADAMS, HENRY E. "Generality of Deviant Responses in Critical and Non-Critical Areas of Behavior." *Psychol Rep* 13:915–20 D '63. * (*PA* 38:8411)

28. HEILBRUN, A. B. "Evidence Regarding the Equivalence of Ipsative and Normative Personality Scales." *J Consult Psychol* 27:152–6 Ap '63. * (*PA* 37:7982)

29. JAMES, GRACE ROBBINS. *The Relationship of Teacher Characteristics and Pupil Creativity.* Doctor's thesis, University of North Carolina (Chapel Hill, N.C.), 1963. (*DA* 25:4544)

30. MARLOWE, DAVID. "Psychological Needs and Cooperation: Competition in a Two-Person Game." *Psychol Rep* 13:364 O '63. * (*PA* 38:8369)

31. SILLER, JEROME, and CHIPMAN, ABRAM. "Response Set Paralysis: Implications for Measurement and Control." *J Consult Psychol* 27:432–8 O '63. * (*PA* 38:4284)

32. TOMLINSON, JERRY RUDDICK. *Interactional Personality Factors Associated With Accuracy of Interpersonal Perception.* Doctor's thesis, State University of Iowa (Iowa City, Iowa), 1963. (*DA* 24:2568)

33. VACHER, CAROLE JEAN DOUGHTON. "The Self Concept of Underachieving Freshmen and Upperclass Women College Students." *J Col Stud Personnel* 5:28–31+ O '63. *

34. COSENTINO, FRED, and HEILBRUN, ALFRED B., JR. "Anxiety Correlates of Sex-Role Identity in College Students." *Psychol Rep* 14:729–30 Je '64. * (*PA* 39:5240)

35. COSTIN, FRANK. "Attitudinal Changes in Child Psychology Students Who Differ in Intensity of Personality Needs." *J Ed Res* 58:118–22 N '64. * (*PA* 39:9955)

36. HEILBRUN, ALFRED B., JR. "Social Value: Social Behavior Consistency, Parental Identification, and Aggression in Late Adolescence." *J Genetic Psychol* 104:135–46 Mr '64. *

37. HEILBRUN, ALBERT B., JR., and HALL, CHARLES L. "Resource Mediation in Childhood and Identification." *J Child Psychol & Psychiatry* 5:139–49 N '64. * (*PA* 39:7464)

38. LANGER, PHILIP, and McKAIN, CHARLES W. "Intertest Changes in Acquiescence." *Psychol Rep* 15:71–6 Ag '64. * (*PA* 39:1744)

39. LUCKY, ARTHUR W., and GRIGG, AUSTIN E. "Repression-Sensitization as a Variable in Deviant Responding." *J Clin Psychol* 20:92–3 Ja '64. * (*PA* 39:10058)

40. STOLLAK, GARY EDWARD. *The Conditioning and Transfer Effects of Verbally Reinforcing Choices of Personality Statements.* Doctor's thesis, Rutgers University (New Brunswick, N.J.), 1964. (*DA* 25:6771)

41. BIENEN, SANFORD M., and MAGOON, THOMAS M. "ACL Adjectives Associated With Differential Status on CPI Scales." *Personnel & Guid J* 44:286–91 N '65. * (*PA* 40:4245)

42. CARTER, FRANCES HELEN. *Selected Kinesthetic and Psychological Differences Between the Highly Skilled in Dance and in Sports.* Doctor's thesis, University of Iowa (Iowa City, Iowa), 1965. (*DA* 26:5850)

43. HEILBRUN, ALFRED B., JR. "Counseling Readiness: A Treatment—Specific or General Factor?" *J Counsel Psychol* 12:87–90 sp '65. *

44. HEILBRUN, ALFRED B., JR. "Personality Factors in College Dropout." *J Appl Psychol* 49:1–7 F '65. * (*PA* 39:7689)

45. HEILBRUN, ALFRED B., JR. "The Social Desirability Variable: Implications for Test Reliability and Validity." *Ed & Psychol Meas* 25:745–56 au '65. * (*PA* 40:2119)

46. HEILBRUN, ALFRED B., JR., and ORR, HELEN K. "Maternal Childrearing Control History and Subsequent Cognitive and Personality Functioning of the Offspring." *Psychol Rep* 17:259–72 Ag '65. * (*PA* 40:1438)

47. HOWELL, MARGARET AFFARENC. *Personality Factors in Medical Performance.* Doctor's thesis, University of California (Berkeley, Calif.), 1965. (*DA* 27:303B)

48. KREMER, BRUCE JAMES. *The Adjective Check List as an Indicator of Teachers' Stereotypes of Students.* Doctor's thesis, Michigan State University (East Lansing, Mich.), 1965. (*DA* 26:4451)

49. McDERMID, CHARLES D. "Some Correlates of Creativity in Engineering Personnel." *J Appl Psychol* 49:14–9 F '65. * (*PA* 39:7782)

50. McGURK, ETHEL. "Susceptibility to Visual Illusions." *J Psychol* 61:127–43 S '65. * (*PA* 40:4793)

51. MARKWELL, EARL D., JR. "Alterations in Self-Concept Under Hypnosis." *J Personality & Social Psychol* 1:154–61 F '65. * (*PA* 39:7848)

52. MASON, EVELYN P.; ADAMS, HENRY L.; and BLOOD, DON F. "Personality Characteristics of Gifted College Freshmen." *Proc Ann Conv Am Psychol Assn* 73:301–2 '65. * (*PA* 39:16316)

53. NICHOLS, ROBERT C. "Non-intellective Predictors of Achievement in College." *NMSC Res Rep* 1(6):1–19 '65. *

54. SHIPMAN, WILLIAM G. "Personality Traits Associated With Body-Image Boundary Concern." *Proc Ann Conv Am Psychol Assn* 73:271–2 '65. * (*PA* 39:15441)

55. STONE, GEORGE PRESTON. *Belated and Steady Achievers.* Doctor's thesis, University of Nebraska (Lincoln, Neb.), 1965. (*DA* 26:2062)

56. WARBURTON, MARY A. *An Investigation of Female Scholastic Achievement Utilizing the California Psychological Inventory and the Gough Adjective Check List.* Master's thesis, University of Kansas (Lawrence, Kan.), 1965.

57. WILLIAMS, ALLAN F. "Self-Concepts of College Problem Drinkers: 1, A Comparison With Alcoholics." *Q J Studies Alcohol* 26:586–94 D '65. * (*PA* 40:4401)

58. AARONSON, BERNARD S. "Personality Stereotypes of Aging." *J Gerontol* 21:458–62 Jl '66. *

59. BOHN, MARTIN J., JR. "Psychological Needs Related to Vocational Personality Types." *J Counsel Psychol* 13:306–9 f '66. * (*PA* 40:12644)

60. BOHN, MARTIN J., JR. "Vocational Maturity and Personality." *Voc Guid Q* 15:123–6 D '66. * (*PA* 41:12636)

61. BRUNKAN, R. J., and SHEN, F. "Personality Characteristics of Ineffective, Effective, and Efficient Readers." *Personnel & Guid J* 44:837–43 Ap '66. * (*PA* 40:8835)

62. BURKE, VIVIENNE BLACHE. *Development of Scientific and Artistic Creativity Scales for the Gough Adjective Check List.* Master's thesis, Fordham University (New York, N.Y.), 1966.

63. CASHDAN, SHELDON, and WELSH, GEORGE S. "Personality Correlates of Creative Potential in Talented High School Students." *J Personality* 34:445–55 S '66. * (*PA* 41:2876)

64. DAVIDS, ANTHONY. "Psychological Characteristics of High School Male and Female Potential Scientists in Comparison With Academic Underachievers." *Psychol Sch* 3:79–87 Ja '66. * (*PA* 41:2862)

65. FLYNN, JOHN T. "The Adjective Check List: A Device to Assess Perceived Self." Abstract. *J Teach Ed* 17:247–8 su '66. *

66. HOWELL, MARGARET A. "Personal Effectiveness of Physicians in a Federal Health Organization." *J Appl Psychol* 50:451–9 D '66. * (*PA* 41:3517)

67. MASON, EVELYN P.; ADAMS, HENRY L.; and BLOOD, DON F. "Personality Characteristics of Gifted College Freshmen." *Psychol Sch* 3:360–5 O '66. *

68. NICHOLS, ROBERT C. "Nonintellective Predictors of Achievement in College." *Ed & Psychol Meas* 26:899–915 w '66. * (*PA* 41:4953)

69. NIDORF, LOUIS J. "Variables Influencing the Cognitive Organization of the Self." *J Proj Tech & Pers Assess* 30:460–6 O '66. * (*PA* 41:582)

70. SCARR, SANDRA. "The Adjective Check List as a Personality Assessment Technique With Children: Validity of the Scales." *J Consult Psychol* 30:122–8 Ap '66. * (*PA* 40:6645)

71. SCARR, SANDRA. "The Origins of Individual Differences in Adjective Check List Scores." *J Consult Psychol* 30:354–7 Ag '66. * (*PA* 40:10901)

72. STEIN, KENNETH B., and LANGER, JONAS. "The Relation of Covert Cognitive Interference in the Color-Phonetic Symbol Test to Personality Characteristics and Adjustment." *J Personality* 34:241–51 Je '66. * (*PA* 40:12312)

73. STRATTON, JOHN R., and SPITZER, STEPHAN P. "Test Equivalence of Projective and Structured Self-Concept Instruments." *J Proj Tech & Pers Assess* 30:456–9 O '66. * (*PA* 41:583)

74. ALLEN, LEON R., and DOOTJES, INEZ. "Gough Adjective Checklist for an Alcoholic Population." *Psychol Rep* 21:972 D '67. * (*PA* 42:7474)

75. ANASTASIOW, NICHOLAS J. "Personality Traits of Teachers Nominated as Strong and Weak." *Psychol Rep* 20:1343–6 Je '67. * (*PA* 41:15854)

76. CLIZBE, JOHN ANTHONY. *A Multi-Dimensional Approach to Job Attitudes and Job Performance.* Doctor's thesis, Washington University (St. Louis, Mo.), 1967. (*DA* 28:4789B)

77. DOMINO, GEORGE. *Personality Patterns and Choice of Medical Specialty.* Doctor's thesis, University of California (Berkeley, Calif.), 1967. (*DA* 28:1694B)

78. DOWNES, SHELDON CANFIELD. *Attitudes Toward the Physically Disabled as Indicated in Rehabilitation and Non-Rehabilitation Groups.* Doctor's thesis, Pennsylvania State University (University Park, Pa.), 1967. (*DA* 29:120A)

79. GOWAN, JOHN CURTIS, and BRUCH, CATHERINE. "What Makes a Creative Person a Creative Teacher?" *Gifted Child Q* 11:157–9 au '67. * (*PA* 42:4533)

80. HALL, CHARLES C. *A Comparison of Peer Nominations and Other Variables of Student Teaching Effectiveness.* Doctor's thesis, North Texas State University (Denton, Tex.), 1967. (*DA* 28:2070A)

81. HELSON, RAVENNA. "Personality Characteristics and Developmental History of Creative College Women." *Genetic Psychol Monogr* 76:205–56 N '67. * (*PA* 42:3942)

82. HERSCH, PAUL D., and SCHEIBE, KARL E. "Reliability and Validity of Internal-External Control as a Personality Dimension." *J Consult Psychol* 31:609–13 D '67. * (*PA* 42:2581)

83. KAPLAN, MARTIN F. "Repression-Sensitization and Prediction of Self-Descriptive Behavior: Response Versus Situational Cue Variables." *J Abn Psychol* 72:354–61 Ag '67. * (*PA* 41:13644)

84. NEWBERRY, LAWRENCE A. "Defensiveness and Need for Approval." *J Consult Psychol* 31:396–400 Ag '67. * (*PA* 41:13622)

85. PARKER, GEORGE V. C., and MEGARGEE, EDWIN I. "Factor Analytic Studies of the Adjective Check List." *Proc Ann Conv Am Psychol Assn* 75:211–2 '67. * (*PA* 41:13653)

86. POLLACK, HERBERT BERNARD. *Change in Homogeneous and Heterogeneous Sensitivity Training Groups.* Doctor's thesis, University of California (Berkeley, Calif.), 1967. (*DA* 28:4762B)

87. SCHAEFER, CHARLES EUGENE. *Biographical Inventory Correlates of Scientific and Artistic Creativity in Adolescents.* Doctor's thesis, Fordham University (New York, N.Y.), 1967. (*DA* 28:1173B)

88. TOMLINSON, JERRY R. "Situational and Personality Correlates of Predictive Accuracy." *J Consult Psychol* 31:19–22 F '67. * (*PA* 41:4859)

89. WARR, PETER B., and KNAPPER, CHRIS. "Negative Responses and Serial Position Effects on the Adjective Check List." *J Social Psychol* 73:191–7 D '67. * (*PA* 42:3982)

90. WHITTAKER, DAVID NEIL EATON. *Psychological Characteristics of Alienated, Nonconformist, College-Age Youth as Indicated by AVL, OPI, ACL and SVIB-M/W Group Profiles.* Doctor's thesis, University of California (Berkeley, Calif.), 1967. (*DA* 28:3055B)

91. WILLIAMS, ALLAN F. "Self-Concepts of College Problem Drinkers: 2, Heilbrun Need Scales." *Q J Studies Alcohol* 28:267–76 Je '67. * (*PA* 42:691)

92. FOREMAN, MILTON E., and MARSH, MARION E. "Key Scoring the Adjective Check List." *Ed & Psychol Meas* 28:583–5 su '68. * (*PA* 42:18088)

93. HEILBRUN, ALFRED B., JR. "Counseling Readiness and the Problem-Solving Behavior of Clients." *J Consult & Clin Psychol* 32:396–9 Ag '68. * (*PA* 42:17696)

94. HEILBRUN, ALFRED B., JR. "Sex Role, Instrumental-Expressive Behavior, and Psychopathology in Females." *J Abn Psychol* 73:131–6 Ap '68. * (*PA* 42:8752)

95. KLINGER, ERIC. "Short-Term Stability and Concurrent Validity of TAT Need Scores: Achievement, Affiliation, and Hostile Press." *Proc Ann Conv Am Psychol Assn* 76:157–8 '68. * (*PA* 43:941, title only)

96. MEGARGEE, EDWIN I., and PARKER, GEORGE V. C. "An Exploration of the Equivalence of Murrayan Needs as Assessed by the Adjective Check List, the TAT and Edwards Personal Preference Schedule." *J Clin Psychol* 24:47–51 Ja '68. *

97. MERENDA, PETER F., and CLARKE, WALTER V. "Relationships Among AVA and ACL Scales as Measured on a Sample of College Students." *J Clin Psychol* 24:52–60 Ja '68. *

98. NORFLEET, MARY ANN WARBURTON. "Personality Characteristics of Achieving and Underachieving High Ability Senior Women." *Personnel & Guid J* 46:976–80 Je '68. * (*PA* 43:3130)

99. STIMSON, ROGER C., JR. "Factor Analytic Approach to the Structural Differentiation of Description." *J Counsel Psychol* 15:301–7 Jl '68. *

100. TAYLOR, ROBERT E., and EISENMAN, RUSSELL. "Birth Order and Sex Differences in Complexity-Simplicity, Color-Form Preference and Personality." *J Proj Tech & Pers Assess* 32:383–7 Ag '68. * (*PA* 42:18793)

101. WILLIAMS, ALLAN F. "Psychological Needs and Social Drinking Among College Students." *Q J Studies Alcohol* 29:355–63 Je '68. * (*PA* 42:15459)

102. ZUCKERMAN, MARVIN, and LINK, KATHRYN. "Construct Validity for the Sensation-Seeking Scale." *J Consult & Clin Psychol* 32:420–6 Ag '68. * (*PA* 42:16438)

NAME INDEX

Aaronson, B. S.: 58
Adams, H. E.: 27
Adams, H. L.: 52, 67
Allen, L. R.: 74
Anastasiow, N. J.: 24, 75
Bienen, S. M.: 41
Blood, D. F.: 52, 67
Bohn, M. J.: 25, 59–60
Brown, D. R.: 2
Brown, R. A.: 14
Broxton, J. A.: 26
Bruch, C.: 79
Brunkan, R. J.: 61
Burke, V. B.: 62
Butler, J. R.: 27
Bystryn, D.: 2
Carter, F. H.: 42
Cashdan, S.: 63
Chipman, A.: 31
Clarke, W. V.: 97
Clizbe, J. A.: 76
Cosentino, F.: 34
Costin, F.: 35
Cox, L.: 5
Crowne, D. P.: 9
Davids, A.: 64
DiVesta, F. J.: 5
Dollard, J.: 1
Domino, G.: 77
Dootjes, I.: 74
Downes, S. C.: 78
Eisenman, R.: 100
Elder, S. T.: 27
Flynn, J. T.: 65
Foreman, M. E.: 92
Goodstein, L. D.: 14
Gough, H. G.: 6
Gowan, J. C.: 3, 79
Grigg, A. E.: 7, 39
Hall, C. C.: 80
Hall, C. L.: 37
Heilbrun, A. B.: 4, 8, 10–1, 15–6, 28, 34, 36–7, 43–6, 93–4
Helson, R.: 81
Hersch, P. D.: 82
Howell, M. A.: 47, 66
James, G. R.: 29
Kaplan, M. F.: 83
Kelly, R.: 9
Klinger, E.: 95
Knapper, C.: 89
Kremer, B. J.: 48
Langer, J.: 72

Langer, P.: 17–9, 38
Link, K.: 102
Lucky, A. W.: 39
McDermid, C. D.: 49
McGurk, E.: 50
McKain, C. W.: 38
MacKinnon, D. W.: 1, 20
Magoon, T. M.: 41
Markwell, E. D.: 23, 51
Marlowe, D.: 30
Marsh, M. E.: 92
Mason, E. P.: 52, 67
Megargee, E. I.: 85, 96
Merenda, P. F.: 97
Newberry, L. A.: 84
Nichols, R. C.: 53, 68
Nidorf, L. J.: 69
Norfleet, M. A. W.: 98
Orr, H. K.: 46
Osborne, D.: 21
Parker, G. V. C.: 85, 96
Pollack, H. B.: 86
Purcell, J. F.: 12
Scarr, S.: 70–1
Schaefer, C. E.: 87
Scheibe, K. E.: 82
Shen, F.: 61
Shipman, W. G.: 54
Siller, J.: 31
Spanner, M.: 13
Spitzer, S. P.: 73
Stein, K. B.: 72
Stephens, M. W.: 9
Stephenson, R. R.: 25
Stimson, R. C.: 99
Stollak, G. E.: 40
Stone, G. P.: 55
Stratton, J. R.: 73
Suinn, R. M.: 21
Sullivan, D. J.: 16
Taylor, R. E.: 100
Thorpe, J. S.: 7
Tomlinson, J. R.: 32, 88
Vacher, C. J. D.: 33
Warburton, M. A.: 56
Warr, P. B.: 89
Weiser, J. C.: 22
Welsh, G. S.: 63
Whittaker, D. N. E.: 90
Williams, A. F.: 57, 91, 101
Winfree, P.: 21
Woolington, J. M.: 23
Zuckerman, M.: 102

[5–6]

The Adjustment Inventory. Grades 9–16, adults; 1934–63; AI; 1 form; 2 levels; postage extra; (20–30) minutes; Hugh M. Bell; Consulting Psychologists Press, Inc. *

a) REVISED (1962) STUDENT FORM. Grades 9–16; 1934–63; 6 scores: home, health, submissiveness, emotionality, hostility, masculinity; 1 form ('62, 4 pages); manual ('63, c1962, 27 pages); profile ('62, 2 pages); separate answer sheets (IBM 805) must be used; $3.25 per 25 tests; $4 per 50 answer sheets; $2 per set of hand or machine scoring stencils; $1.25 per manual; $1.50 per specimen set.

b) ADULT FORM. Adults; 1938–39; 6 scores: home, occupational, health, social, emotional, total; 1 form ('38, 4 pages); manual ['38, 4 pages]; $3 per 25 tests; separate answer sheets (IBM 805) may be used; $2.50 per 50 answer sheets; 75¢ per set of hand scoring stencil and manual; $1.75 per machine scoring stencil; 75¢ per specimen set.

For a review by Forrest L. Vance, see 6:59 (11 references, 1 excerpt); see also 5:30 (26 references); for reviews by Nelson G. Hanawalt and Theodore R. Sarbin, see 4:28 (104 references); for reviews by Raymond B. Cattell, John G. Darley, C. M. Louttit, and Percival M. Symonds of the original Student Form, and reviews by S. J. Beck, J. P. Guilford, and Doncaster G. Humm of the Adult Form, see 2:1200

(15 references, 1 excerpt) ; for a review by Austin H.
Turney of the Student Form, see 1:912.

REFERENCES

1–15. See 2:1200.
16–119. See 4:28.
120–145. See 5:30.
146–156. See 6:59.
157. SHAMES, GEORGE. "An Investigation of Prognosis and
Evaluation in Speech Therapy." *J Speech & Hearing Disorders*
17:386–92 D '52. * (*PA* 27:6652)
158. TARWATER, JESSE W. "Self-Understanding and the
Ability to Predict Another's Response." *Marriage & Family
Living* 15:126–8 My '53. * (*PA* 27:7797)
159. SHAW, MERVILLE C., and BROWN, DONALD J. "Scholastic Underachievement of Bright College Students." *Personnel
& Guid J* 36:195–9 N '57. * (*PA* 33:2191)
160. HUSAIN, M. Q., and RAY-CHOWDHURY, K. "Epigenetic
Factor Like Birth-Order Influencing Adjustment Patterns of
Criminals and Normals During Adolescence." *Indian Psychol
B* 6:53–7 S '61. *
161. JAMUAR, K. K. "Personality and Achievement." *Psychol Studies* 6:59–65 Jl '61. * (*PA* 38:3203)
162. RAY-CHOWDHURY, K. "Bell's Adjustment Inventory in
Indian Situation: 1, General Norms, Reliability and Validity."
Indian Psychol B 7:27–33 My '62. *
163. RAY-CHOWDHURY, K. "Bell's Adjustment Inventory in
Indian Situation: 2, Item Analysis by Phi-Co-Efficient Technique." *Indian Psychol B* 7:43–7 S '62. *
164. SERGEANT, RUSSELL LEWIS. *An Investigaton of Responses of Speech Defective Adults on Personality Inventories.*
Doctor's thesis, Ohio State University (Columbus, Ohio), 1962.
(*DA* 23:4020)
165. CHILDERS, PERRY ROBERT. *A Study of the Relationship
of Certain Factors to Fall Quarter Achievement by Freshman
Men at the University of Georgia.* Doctor's thesis, University
of Georgia (Athens, Ga.), 1963. (*DA* 24:4537)
166. JALOTA, S. "Psychological Adjustment and Industrial-
isation." *Indian Psychol B* 1:21–4 Jl '64. *
167. LUYSTER, RAYMOND JOHN. *Self-Concept of Fraternity
Members as Measured by the Bell Adjustment Inventory.*
Master's thesis, Ohio State University (Columbus, Ohio), 1964.
168. LINDGREN, HENRY CLAY, and MELLO, MARIA JORGIZA.
"Emotional Problems of Over- and Underachieving Children
in a Brazilian Elementary School." *J Genetic Psychol* 106:59–
65 Mr '65. * (*PA* 39:12980)
169. MAJUMDAR, A. K. "Adjustment Pattern of Adopters
and Non-Adopters." *Indian J Appl Psychol* 3:103 Jl '66. *
170. WEISS, AARON J., and DIAMOND, M. DAVID. "Psychologic Adjustment of Patients With Myelopathy." *Arch Phys
Med & Rehabil* 47:72–6 F '66. *
171. DERMAN, BRUCE IRVIN. *Adaptive Versus Pathological
Regression in Relation to Psychological Adjustment.* Doctor's
thesis. University of Georgia (Athens, Ga.), 1967. (*DA* 28:
4754B)
172. NATARAJ, P. "The Adjustment of Adolescent College
Girls." *Psychol Studies* 13:60–3 Ja '68. *

[7]

The Alcadd Test. Adults; 1949; AT; identification
of alcoholic addicts and individuals with alcoholic
problems; 6 scores: regularity of drinking, preference
for drinking over other activities, lack of controlled
drinking, rationalization of drinking, excessive emotionality, total; 1 form (4 pages); manual (2 pages);
no data on reliability of subscores; $7 per examiner's
kit of 25 tests, key, and manual; $6.50 per 25 tests;
$2 per specimen set; postpaid; (5–15) minutes; Morse
P. Manson; Western Psychological Services. *

For a review by Dugal Campbell, see 6:60 (6 references) ; for reviews by Charles H. Honzik and Albert
L. Hunsicker, see 4:30.

REFERENCES

1–6. See 6:60.
7. ARMSTRONG, RENATE GERBOTH. *Personality Structure in
Alcoholism.* Doctor's thesis, University of Colorado (Boulder,
Colo.), 1957. (*DA* 18:1851)
8. FOWLER, RAYMOND D., JR., and BERNARD, J. LAURENCE.
"Alternative Norms for the Alcadd Based on Outpatient Alcoholics." *J Clin Psychol* 21:29–33 Ja '65. * (*PA* 39:12283)
9. FOWLER, RAYMOND D., JR.; TEEL, SIDNEY K.; and COYLE,
F. A., JR. "The Measurement of Alcoholic Response to Treatment by Barron's Ego-Strength Scale." *J Psychol* 67:65–8 S
'67. * (*PA* 41:16841)

[8]

★**The Anxiety Scale for the Blind.** Ages 13 and
over (blind and partially sighted); 1966–68; ASB;
experimental form; orally administered; 1 form ('68,

4 pages); manual ('68, 7 pages plus test); mimeographed statistical data ['66, 12 pages, reprinted from research by author]; preliminary norms for high school students only; $1 per manual, postpaid; statistical data free on request from author (c/o School of Rehabilitation Counseling, Virginia Commonwealth University, Richmond, Va. 23220); (45–50) minutes; Richard E. Hardy; American Foundation for the Blind. *

REFERENCES

1. HARDY, RICHARD EARL. *A Study of Manifest Anxiety Among Blind Residential School Students Using an Experimental Instrument Constructed for the Blind.* Doctor's thesis, University of Maryland (College Park, Md.), 1966. (*DA* 27:3693A)
2. HARDY, RICHARD E. "Prediction of Manifest Anxiety Levels of Blind Persons Through the Use of a Multiple Regression Technique." *Int J Ed Blind* 17:51–5 D '67. * (*PA* 42:5916)
3. HARDY, RICHARD E. "A Study of Manifest Anxiety Among Blind Residential School Students." *New Outl Blind* 62:173–80 Je '68. *

[9]

Attitude-Interest Analysis Test. Early adolescents and adults; 1936–38; AIAT; also called *M-F Test;* masculinity-femininity; Form A ('36, 14 pages); manual ('38, 21 pages, out of print); $4.50 per 25 tests, postage extra; specimen set not available; (40–50) minutes; Lewis M. Terman and Catherine Cox Miles; McGraw-Hill Book Co., Inc. *

See 6:61 (16 references); for a review by Starke R. Hathaway, see 3:24 (20 references); for related book reviews not excerpted in this volume, consult the 2nd (B1094) and 1st (B498) MMY's.

REFERENCES

1–20. See 3:24.
21–36. See 6:61.
37. ZUCKMAN, LEONARD. *The Relationship Between Sex Differences in Certain Mental Abilities and Masculine-Feminine Sex Identification: An Analysis and Evaluation of Test Measures on Eighth Grade New York City Public School Students Equated as to Age, Intelligence, Health, Parent Rearage and Socio-Economic Status.* Doctor's thesis, New York University (New York, N.Y.), 1955. (*DA* 15:1251)
38. FRANZ, JACOB GEORGE. *Social Status and Masculinity-Femininity.* Doctor's thesis, Ohio State University (Columbus, Ohio), 1960. (*DA* 21:260)
39. ENGEL, ILONA M. "A Factor-Analytic Study of Items From Five Masculinity-Femininity Tests." Abstract. *J Consult Psychol* 30:565 D '66. * (*PA* 41:2880, title only)
40. SAPPENFIELD, BERT R., and BALOGH, BELA. "Stereotypical M-F as Related to Two Szondi Test Assumptions." *J Proj Tech & Pers Assess* 30:387–93 Ag '66. *
41. McCARTHY, DOROTHEA; SCHIRO, FREDERICK M.; and SUDIMACK, JOHN P. "Comparison of WAIS M-F Index With Two Measures of Masculinity-Femininity." *J Consult Psychol* 31:639–40 D '67. * (*PA* 42:2587)

NAME INDEX

Aronson, M. L.: 27
Balogh, B.: 40
Barnette, W. L.: 14
Beck, M. P.: 9
Bilsky, H. B.: 17
Bosselman, B.: 10
Botwinick, J.: 28
Bryson, G.: *exc,* consult 1:B498
Burger, F. E.: 15
Capwell, D. F.: 19
Carter, L.: 23
Cerf, A. Z.: 21
Child, I. L.: 11
de Cillis, O. E.: 24
Disher, D. R.: 7, 16
Dunlap, J. W.: 3
Durea, M. A.: 17
Edgerton, H. A.: 3
Engel, I. M.: 36, 39
Fisher, S.: 29
Flügel, J. C.: *exc,* consult 2:B1094
Ford, C. F.: 32
Forlano, G.: 19
Franz, J. G.: 38
Gilkinson, H.: 4, 8, 12

Hardy, V. T.: 22
Hartmann, G. W.: *exc,* consult 1:B498
Hathaway, S. R.: *rev,* 3:24
Hinds, E.: 29
Kelly, E. L.: 2–3
Knower, F. H.: 8, 12
Kurtz, A. K.: 3
Lee, M. C.: 25, 33
McAnulty, E. A.: 3
McCarthy, D.: 41
McCurdy, H.: *exc,* consult 1:B498
Machover, S.: 28
McNemar, Q.: 3
Merrill, M. A.: 3
Miles, C. C.: 1–3
Nemzek, C. L.: 15
Nixon, M.: 23
Orbison, W. D.: 24
Page, J.: 5
Parker, F. B.: 34
Pintner, R.: 18
Rosenzweig, S.: 6
Ross, R. T.: 26
Ruch, F. L.: 3
Sappenfield, B. R.: 40

Schiro, F. M.: 41
Schwesinger, G. C.: *exc,* consult 1:B498
Sheldon, W. H.: 11
Shepler, B. F.: 30
Silverberg, W. V.: *exc,* consult 2:B1094
Skorodin, B.: 10
Smith, J. H.: 20
Stanek, R. J.: 35
Stephenson, W.: *exc.* consult 1:B498
Sudimack, J. P.: 41

Terman, L. M.: 1–3
Tyler, L. E.: 32
Uhrbrock, R. S.: *exc,* consult 2:B1094
Vaccaro, J. J.: 31
Vaughn, C. L.: 15
Walker, E. L.: 13
Warkentin, J.: 5
Wyatt, H. G.: 3
Young, K.: *exc,* consult 1:B498
Zuckman, L.: 37

[10]

Attitudes Toward Industrialization. Adults; 1959; ATI; 1 form (1 page); manual (4 pages); $2.50 per 25 tests; $1 per specimen set (must be purchased to obtain manual); cash orders postpaid; (10) minutes; Donald E. Kaldenberg; Psychometric Affiliates. *

For a review by Marvin D. Dunnette, see 6:62.

[11]

Attitudes Toward Parental Control of Children. Adults; 1936; ATPCC; 1 form (1 page); manual [9 pages, reprint of 2:1205(2)]; $2 per 100 tests; postpaid; specimen set free; (15) minutes; Ralph M. Stogdill and Henry H. Goddard; Ralph M. Stogdill. *

See 2:1205 (2 references).

[12]

The Ayres Space Test. Ages 3 and over; 1962; AST; brain damage; 3 scores: accuracy, time, accuracy less adjustment for time; individual; 1 form; record booklet (4 pages); mimeographed manual (24 pages plus record booklet); no norms for ages 11 and over; $25 per set of test materials including two formboards, 25 record booklets, and manual; $6.50 per 25 record booklets; $3 per manual; postpaid; specimen set not available; (20–30) minutes; A. Jean Ayres; Western Psychological Services. *

For reviews by Alvin G. Burstein and Alfred B. Heilbrun, Jr., see 6:63 (2 references).

REFERENCES

1–2. See 6:63.
3. AYRES, A. JEAN. "Patterns of Perceptual-Motor Dysfunction in Children: A Factor Analytic Study." *Percept & Motor Skills* 20:335–68 Ag '65. * (*PA* 39:12639)
4. AYRES, A. JEAN. "Interrelations Among Perceptual-Motor Abilities in a Group of Normal Children." *Am J Occup Ther* 20:288–92 N–D '66. * (*PA* 41:5813)
5. AYRES, A. JEAN, and REID, WILLIAM. "The Self-Drawing as an Expression of Perceptual-Motor Dysfunction." *Cortex* 2:254–65 Ap '66. * (*PA* 41:665)

[13]

Babcock Test of Mental Efficiency. Ages 7 and over; 1930–62; BTME; formerly called *Babcock Test of Mental Deterioration;* record booklet title is *The Revised Examination for the Measurement of Efficiency of Mental Functioning;* individual; 10 scores: easy tests, repetition, initial learning, recall and recognition, motor A, motor B, perception time, easy continuous work, total efficiency (based on 8 previous scores), efficiency deviation; 1 form ('40); mimeographed manual ['62, 68 pages]; record booklet ('42, 8 pages); reliability data the same as reported in 1940; $14 per set of testing materials, 25 record booklets, and manual; $7 per 25 record booklets; $5 per set of testing materials; $5.50 per manual; postpaid; (70) minutes; Harriet Babcock and Lydia Levy (test); Western Psychological Services. *

See 6:64 (6 references); for reviews by D. Russell Davis and Seymour G. Klebanoff, see 4:31 (10 references); see also 3:71 (21 references) and 2:1248 (14 references); for excerpts from related book reviews, see 3:72.

REFERENCES

1–14. See 2:1248.
15–35. See 3:71.
36–45. See 4:31.
46–51. See 6:64.
52. McFie, J., and Piercy, M. F. "Intellectual Impairment With Localized Cerebral Lesions." *Brain* 75:292–311 S '52. * (PA 27:7649)
53. Warburton, J. W. "The Babcock Sentence in Clinical Practice." *Brit J Med Psychol* 36:351–3 pt 4 '63. * (PA 39: 1768)
54. Payne, R. W.; Caird, W. K.; and Laverty, S. G. "Overinclusive Thinking and Delusions in Schizophrenic Patients." *J Abn & Social Psychol* 68:562–6 My '64. * (PA 39:5763)
55. Foulds, G. A.; Hope, K.; McPherson, F. M.; and Mayo, P. R. "Paranoid Delusions, Retardation and Over-inclusive Thinking." *J Clin Psychol* 24:177–8 Ap '68. * (PA 42:12470)
56. Gonen, Yechiel. "Does Vocabulary Resist Mental Deterioration?" *J Clin Psychol* 24:341–3 Jl '68. * (PA 42: 17529)
57. Rapaport, David; Gill, Merton M.; and Schafer, Roy; edited by Robert R. Holt. Chap. 4, "The Babcock Story Recall Test," pp. 172–85. In their *Diagnostic Psychological Testing.* New York: International Universities Press, Inc., 1968. Pp. xi, 562. *

[14]

★**Baker-Schulberg Community Mental Health Ideology Scale.** Mental health professionals; 1967; CMHI; primarily intended for measuring groups; 1 form (4 pages); preliminary manual (12 pages, reprint of *1* below); norms consist of mean scores for various professional groups; $4.75 per 25 tests; 50¢ per set of scoring stencils; $1.50 per preliminary manual; $2.50 per specimen set; cash orders postpaid; [10–20] minutes; Frank Baker and Herbert C. Schulberg; Behavioral Publications, Inc. *

REFERENCE

1. Baker, Frank, and Schulberg, Herbert C. "The Development of a Community Mental Health Ideology Scale." *Commun Mental Health J* 3:216–25 f '67. * (PA 42:1399)

[15]

*****Barron-Welsh Art Scale: A Portion of the Welsh Figure Preference Test.** Ages 6 and over; 1959–63, c1949–63; a separate booklet printing of the art scale and revised art scale items from *Welsh Figure Preference Test, Research Edition;* 1 form ('49, 12 pages, published as a separate '63) ; no specific manual; instructions for administration, scoring, and interpretation contained in mimeographed preliminary manual ('59, 35 pages) for the parent test; manual supplement (no date, 1 page); reliability data, based on an earlier form, for revised art scale only; norms below adult level for ages 6–8 only; separate answer sheets (same as those used with parent test) must be used; $10.50 per 25 tests; $2.50 per 50 answer sheets; scoring stencils must be constructed locally; $1 per manual; $1.50 per specimen set; postage extra; (15–20) minutes; George S. Welsh and Frank Barron (test) ; Consulting Psychologists Press, Inc. *

For a review by Harold Borko of the *Welsh Figure Preference Test,* see 6:197 (1 excerpt).

REFERENCES

1. Barron, Frank, and Welsh, George S. "Artistic Perception as a Possible Factor in Personality Style: Its Measurement by a Figure Preference Test." *J Psychol* 33:199–203 Ap '52. * (PA 26:6844)
2. Rosen, John C. "The Barron-Welsh Art Scale as a Predictor of Originality and Level of Ability Among Artists." *J Appl Psychol* 39:366–7 O '55. * (PA 30:6932)
3. Raychaudhuri, Manas. "Some Perceptual Characteristics of Incipient Artists." *Indian J Psychol* 38:13–7 Mr '63. * (PA 38:6006)
4. Brown, George I. "Experiment in the Teaching of Creativity." *Sch R* 72:437–50 w '64. * (PA 39:7812)
5. Brown, George I. "Second Study in the Teaching of Creativity." *Harvard Ed R* 35:39–54 w '65. * (PA 39:10170)
6. Moyles, E. W.; Tuddenham, R. D.; and Block, J. "Simplicity/Complexity or Symmetry/Asymmetry? A Re-Analysis of the Barron-Welsh Art Scales." *Percept & Motor Skills* 20:685–90 Je '65. * (PA 39:15250)
7. Whittemore, Robert G., and Heimann, Robert A. "Originality Responses in Academically Talented Male University Freshmen." *Psychol Rep* 16:439–42 Ap '65. * (PA 39:10252)
8. Cashdan, Sheldon, and Welsh, George S. "Personality Correlates of Creative Potential in Talented High School Students." *J Personality* 34:445–55 S '66. * (PA 41:2876)
9. Howell, Margaret A. "Personal Effectiveness of Physicians in a Federal Health Organization." *J Appl Psychol* 50:451–9 D '66. * (PA 41:3517)
10. Keith, Berthe Wells. *An Analysis of the Barron-Welsh Art Scale as Used in the Third Grade.* Master's thesis, University of Utah (Salt Lake City, Utah), 1966.
11. Lucas, Frances H., and Dana, Richard H. "Creativity and Allocentric Perception." *Percept & Motor Skills* 22:431–7 Ap '66. * (PA 40:8858)
12. Raychaudhuri, Manas. "Perceptual Preference Pattern and Creativity." *Indian J Appl Psychol* 3:67–70 Jl '66. *
13. Hawthorne, Ruth Estella. *Aspects of Design Preference in Clothing: Aesthetic, Motivation, and Knowledge.* Doctor's thesis, Ohio State University (Columbus, Ohio), 1967. (DA 28:3769B)
14. Maitra, Amal K.; Mukherji, Kamal; and Raychaudhuri, Manas. "Artistic Creativity Among the Delinquents and the Criminals: Associated Perceptual Style." *B Council Social & Psychol Res* 9:7–10 Jl '67. *
15. Schaefer, Charles Eugene. *Biographical Inventory Correlates of Scientific and Artistic Creativity in Adolescents.* Doctor's thesis, Fordham University (New York, N.Y.), 1967. (DA 28:1173B)
16. Bradley, William Roger. *An Experimental Study of the Effect of Three Evaluation Techniques and Personal Orientation on Aesthetic Preference.* Doctor's thesis, University of Minnesota (Minneapolis, Minn.), 1968. (DA 29:1816A)
17. Helson, Ravenna. "Effects of Sibling Characteristics and Parental Values on a Creative Interest and Achievement." *J Personality* 36:589–607 D '68. * (PA 43:6923)
18. Pang, Henry, and Horrocks, Carol. "An Exploratory Study of Creativity in Deaf Children." *Percept & Motor Skills* 27:844–6 D '68. *
19. Pang, Henry, and Shillinger, Duane. "Barron-Welsh Art Scale Scores of Prison Inmates." *Percept & Motor Skills* 26:1054 Je '68. * (PA 42:11812)
20. Schaefer, Charles E. "The Barron-Welsh Art Scale as a Predictor of Adolescent Creativity." *Percept & Motor Skills* 27:1099–102 D '68. *
See also references for 287.

[16]

Behavior Cards: A Test-Interview for Delinquent Children. Delinquents having a reading grade score 4.5 or higher; 1941–50; BC; individual; 1 form ('41, 150 cards) ; mimeographed manual, third edition ('50, c1941, 20 pages); record sheet ('41, 2 pages) ; $5.62 per set of cards, 25 record sheets, and manual; $1 per 25 record sheets; postage extra; (15–30) minutes; Ralph M. Stogdill; distributed by C. H. Stoelting Co. *

See 6:65 (1 reference); for reviews by W. C. Kvaraceus and Simon H. Tulchin, see 3:25 (3 references).

[17]

Biographical Inventory for Students. Grades 12–13; 1955–62; BIS; for research use only; 10 scores: action, social activities, heterosexual activities, religious activities, literature-music-art, political activities, socioeconomic status, economic independence, dependence on home, social conformity; Form KDRD1 ('58, c1955–58, 14 pages); mimeographed manual ('62, c1955–58, 38 pages); separate answer sheets (IBM 805) must be used; $5 per 25 tests; 20¢ per single copy; $1 per 25 answer sheets; scoring stencils must be prepared locally; $1 per manual; postage extra; (55–60) minutes; Laurence Siegel; distributed by Educational Testing Service. *

See 6:67 (6 references).

[18]

Bonney-Fessenden Sociograph. Grades 4 and over; 1955; BFS; 1 form (4 pages); manual (20 pages); separate answer slips must be used; 90¢ per set of sociograph, 40 answer slips, and manual; 25¢ per sociograph; 15¢ per 40 answer slips; 50¢ per manual; 85¢ per specimen set; postage extra; administration time not reported; Merl E. Bonney and Seth A. Fessenden; California Test Bureau. *

For reviews by Åke Bjerstedt and C. Robert Pace, see 5:33.

[19]

A Book About Me. Grades kgn–1; 1952; BAM; workbook for gathering data about children's background, maturity, interests, and attitudes; 1 form (32 pages); manual (33 pages); analysis sheet (2 pages); norms for experimental form only; 69¢ per workbook; 79¢ per 20 analysis sheets; 60¢ per manual; $1 per specimen set; postage extra; Edith Sherman Jay; Science Research Associates, Inc. *

For a review by Florence M. Teagarden, see 5:34.

[20]

*****Bristol Social Adjustment Guides.** Ages 5–15; 1956–66; BSAG; ratings by teachers and others; adjustment score and an optional delinquency prediction score for boys; 1 form ('56, 4 pages); separate editions for children in school, residential care, and family; manual, third edition ('66, 69 pages); diagnostic form ('56, 1 page) for each scale; 7s. 6d. per 20 diagnostic forms; 30s. per manual; 3s. per specimen set of a–c (without manual); postage extra; (10–20) minutes per scale; D. H. Stott and E. G. Sykes (a, b); University of London Press Ltd. *

a) THE CHILD IN SCHOOL. 1956–66; separate editions for boys and girls; 11s. 6d. per 20 scales; 3s. 6d. per set of scoring stencils. [American edition: Ages 5–16; 1956–67; 1 form ('67, 4 pages, identical with the 1956 British edition except for minor changes in wording); preliminary manual ('67, 4 pages); diagnostic form ('67, 1 page); no data on reliability; no American norms; $4 per 25 scales; $1.50 per set of scoring stencils; $2 per 25 diagnostic forms; $2.25 per specimen set; postage, time, and authors same as for British edition; scoring service, 85¢ or less per test; Educational and Industrial Testing Service. *

b) THE CHILD IN RESIDENTIAL CARE. 1956–66; 11s. 6d. per 20 scales; 4s. per set of scoring stencils.

c) THE CHILD IN THE FAMILY. 1956–66; life history

chart ('56, 1 page); 17s. per 20 sets of scale and chart; 2s. 6d. per key.

d) DELINQUENCY PREDICTION INSTRUMENT. Boys ages 5–15; 1961–66; consists of a delinquency prediction key to be used with the diagnostic form for *The Child in School* scale and a teacher's questionnaire ('61, 1 page) for preliminary identification of pupils to be rated on the scale; no data on reliability; 5s. per 20 questionnaires; 1s. per scoring stencil; specimen set not available; (10–15) minutes. *

For reviews by G. A. V. Morgan and M. L. Kellmer Pringle, see 6:68 (13 references, 5 excerpts).

REFERENCES

1–13. See 6:68.
14. CHAZAN, MAURICE. "The Incidence and Nature of Maladjustment Among Children in Schools for the Educationally Subnormal." *Brit J Ed Psychol* 34:292–304 N '64. * (PA 39:8654)
15. STOTT, D. H. "Prediction of Success or Failure on Probation: A Follow-Up Study." *Int J Social Psychiatry* 10:27–9 w '64. * (PA 39:8447)
16. CRAFT, MICHAEL. Chap. 3, "Diagnosis and Aetiology Illustrated by an Analysis of Admissions to a Psychopathic Unit," pp. 32–54. In *Ten Studies Into Psychopathic Personality: A Report to the Home Office and the Mental Health Research Fund*. Bristol, England: John Wright & Sons Ltd., 1965. Pp. 133. *
17. FROST, BARRY P. "Some Personality Characteristics of Poor Readers." *Psychol Sch* 2:218–20 Ap '65. *
18. GREGORY, ROBIN E. "Unsettledness, Maladjustment and Reading Failure: A Village Study." *Brit J Ed Psychol* 35:63–8 F '65. * (PA 39:10791)
19. STOTT, D. H. *Studies of Troublesome Children*. London: Tavistock Publications Ltd., 1966. Pp. ix, 208. *

[21]

C-R Opinionaire. Grades 11–16 and adults; 1935–46, c1935; CRO; conservatism-radicalism; Forms J, K, ['46, 4 pages, test booklet contains both forms; identical with tests copyrighted in 1935 except for 8 revised items]; manual ('35, 4 pages); $2.50 per 25 double-form booklets; $1.50 per 25 single-form copies; 75¢ per specimen set; postpaid; (20 or 40) minutes; Theodore F. Lentz; Character Research Association. *

For a review by George W. Hartmann, see 4:39 (5 references); for a review by Goodwin Watson, see 2:1212 (5 references); for a review by H. H. Remmers, see 1:899.

REFERENCES

1–5. See 2:1212.
6–10. See 4:39.
11. *Normative Information: Manager and Executive Testing*. New York: Richardson, Bellows, Henry & Co., Inc., May 1963. Pp. 45. *
12. LEONARD, ELIZABETH W. "Attitude Change in a College Program of Foreign Study and Travel." *Ed Rec* 45:173–81 sp '64. * (PA 39:5840)
13. SPIERS, DUANE EDWIN. *A Study of the Predictive Validity of a Test Battery Administered to Theological Students*. Doctor's thesis, Purdue University (Lafayette, Ind.), 1965. (DA 26:1488)

[22]

★**CYR Youth Survey.** Ages 14 and over; 1958–67; prepared for use in Lutheran churches and schools; original 532-item edition called *LYR Youth Inventory;* LYR is acronym for Lutheran Youth Research, CYR is acronym for Church Youth Research; 28 scores: concerns (family unity, parental understanding, dating and emotions, life partner, spiritual doubts, personal assurance, lack of self-confidence, academic problems, relation to teachers, acceptance by classmates, personal faults, faults of adults, moral problems), attitudes (boy-girl relationships, personal faith, youth group participation, youth group spirit), interests (adventure goals, meaning in life, religious activities), church teachings (justification, human relations, traditional teachings, Christian concepts, forgiveness, certainty of belief), frankness (openness in admitting what is uncomplimentary, willingness to admit what is bothersome) ; 1 form ('66, 24 pages, except for slight changes in the wording of some items, this 1966 form consists of 400 of the 532 items in the 1958 form) ; manual ('64, 18 pages, manual for the superseded 532-item test) ; the 1966 form includes 28 of the 47 scores obtained from the original edition; publisher states that the 28 scores are based upon same items as the corresponding scores (12 of which have different titles) for the 1958 edition; all statistical data and technical information, most of which is presented in the author's *Profiles of Church Youth* ('63, see *2* below), reported are for the 1958 edition; distribution restricted to pastors; separate answer sheets (IBM 1230) must be used; $25 initial enrollment fee plus $2 per examinee for rental and scoring service; $1 for completed individual profile; postpaid; specimen set available on loan; (90) minutes; Merton P. Strommen; [Church Youth Research]. *

REFERENCES

1. STROMMEN, MERTON PETER. *A Comparison of Youth and Adult Reactions to Lutheran Youth Problems and Sources of Assistance.* Doctor's thesis, University of Minnesota (Minneapolis, Minn.), 1960. (*DA* 21:3364)
2. STROMMEN, MERTON P. *Profiles of Church Youth: Report on a Four-Year Study of 3,000 Lutheran High School Youth.* Saint Louis, Mo.: Concordia Publishing House, 1963. Pp. xxv, 356. *

[23]

Cain-Levine Social Competency Scale. Mentally retarded children ages 5–13; 1963; CLSCS; rating scale based upon information obtained from parents; 5 scores: self-help, initiative, social skills, communication, total; 1 form (7 pages) ; manual (19 pages) ; mimeographed supplementary data (24 pages) ; $3.85 per 25 tests; $1.35 per manual; $1.50 per specimen set; postage extra; supplementary data free on request; Leo F. Cain, Samuel Levine, and Freeman F. Elzey; Consulting Psychologists Press, Inc. *

For a review by Marshall S. Hiskey, see 6:69.

REFERENCES

1. GOLDSCHMID, MARCEL L., and DOMINO, GEORGE. "Some Para-Diagnostic Implications of the IQ Among Mentally Retarded Patients." *Training Sch B* 61:178–83 F '65. * (*PA* 39:10586)
2. LEVINE, SAMUEL; ELZEY, FREEMAN F.; and PAULSON, FLOYD L. "Social Competence of School and Non-School Trainable Mentally Retarded." *Am J Mental Def* 71:112–5 Jl '66. * (*PA* 40:11438)
3. ANDERSON, DONALD F., and ROSENTHAL, ROBERT. "Some Effects of Interpersonal Expectancy and Social Interaction of Institutionalized Retarded Children." *Proc Ann Conv Am Psychol Assn* 76:479–80 '68. * (*PA* 43:1258, title only)

[24]

★**The California Life Goals Evaluation Schedules.** Ages 15 and over; 1966; CLGES; 10 scores: esteem, profit, fame, power, leadership, security, social service, interesting experiences, self-expression, independence; 2 editions; preliminary manual (23 pages plus tests and profile) ; profile (2 pages) ; tentative norms; $6.50 per 25 tests; $3 per 25 profiles; $5 per manual; postpaid; (30–45) minutes; Milton E. Hahn; Western Psychological Services. *
a) [CONSUMABLE BOOKLET.] Experimental Form D-S (6 pages).
b) REUSABLE BOOKLET. Experimental Form D-M (4 pages) ; separate answer sheets must be used; $3 per 25 answer sheets; $2 per set of scoring stencils.

[25]

★**California Marriage Readiness Evaluation.** Premarital counselees; 1965; CMRE; 12 scores: personality (character, emotional maturity, marriage readiness, total), preparation for marriage (family experiences, dealing with money, planning ability, total), interpersonal compatibility (marriage motivation, compatibility, total), total; 1 form (4 pages) ; manual (4 pages plus test) ; no data on reliability; basis for profile not presented; $6.50 per 25 tests; $1.50 per manual; postage extra; (30–35) minutes; Morse P. Manson; Western Psychological Services. *

[26]

The California Medical Survey. Medical patients ages 10–18, adults; 1962; CMS; checklist of medical and psychological information; 18–23 scores: chronicity of illness, emotional conditions, familiar background, basic medical information, psychiatric symptoms, specific disorder, medical background, genitourinary, neuro-mus-skeletal, cardio-vas-blood, sensory, digestive, respiratory, 5 gynecologic scores (Form W only), anxiety-stress, psychiatric, habits-traits, sexualsocial, energy level; 2 levels; summary sheet (1 page) ; mimeographed manual (9 pages) ; no data on reliability and validity; no norms; $10 per examiner's kit of 30 forms (10 each for children, men, women), 30 summary sheets, and manual; $6.50 per 25 tests; $3.50 per 25 summary sheets; $1.50 per manual; $3.50 per specimen set; postpaid; (10–20) minutes; Harold L. Snow and Morse P. Manson; Western Psychological Services. *
a) CHILDREN'S FORM. Ages 10–18; Form C (4 pages).
b) ADULT FORMS. Adults; Forms M (for men), W (for women), (6 pages).

[27]

*★California Psychological Inventory.** Ages 13 and over; 1956–69; CPI; 18 scores: Dominance (Do), capacity for status (Ca), sociability (Sy), social presence (Sp), self-acceptance (Sa), sense of well-being (Wb), responsibility (Re), socialization (So), self-control (Sc), tolerance (To), good impression (Gi), communality (Cm), achievement via conformance (Ac), achievement via independence (Ai), intellectual efficiency (Ie), psychological-mindedness (Py), flexibility (Fx), femininity (Fe) ; 1 form ('56, 12 pages) ; revised manual ('69, c1957, 40 pages) ; profile ('57, 2 pages) ; separate answer sheets (hand scored, IBM 805, Dela Data, NCS) must be used; $6.25 per 25 tests; $3.75 per 50 sets of hand scored answer sheet and profile; $4.50 per set of hand scoring stencils; $4.25 per 50 sets of IBM 805 answer sheet and profile; $6 per set of IBM 805 scoring stencils; $3.50 per 50 Dela Data answer cards (scoring service, 45¢ and over per test) ; $3.25 per 50 NCS answer sheets (scoring service, 35¢ and over per test) ; $3 per manual; $1 per specimen set; postage extra; Dutch, French, German, Italian, and Japanese editions available; (45–60) minutes; Harrison G. Gough; Consulting Psychologists Press, Inc. *

For a review by E. Lowell Kelly, see 6:71 (111 references) ; for reviews by Lee J. Cronbach and Robert L. Thorndike, see 5:37 (33 references, 1 excerpt).

REFERENCES

1–33. See 5:37.
34–144. See 6:71.
145. POUNCEY, ANTHONY TRUMAN. *Psychological Correlates of Journalism Training Completion.* Doctor's thesis, University of Minnesota (Minneapolis, Minn.), 1954. (*DA* 14:1180)
146. KHANNA, JASWANT LAL. *A Study of the Relationship Between Some Aspects of Personality and Certain Aspects of Religious Beliefs.* Doctor's thesis, University of Colorado (Boulder, Colo.), 1956. (*DA* 17:2696)
147. STONER, WILLIAM GERALD. *Factors Related to the Underachievement of High School Students.* Doctor's thesis, Stanford University (Stanford, Calif.), 1956. (*DA* 17:96)
148. SHARMA, SOHAN LAL. *The Genesis of the Authoritarian Personality.* Doctor's thesis, University of Michigan (Ann Arbor, Mich.), 1957. (*DA* 18:1486)
149. BAUGHMAN, E. EARL; SHANDS, HARLEY C.; and HAWKINS, DAVID R. "Intensive Psychotherapy and Personality

Change: Psychological Test Evaluation of a Single Case."
Psychiatry 22:296–301 Ag '59. * (*PA* 34:6067)
150. BOGARD, HOWARD M. *Union and Management Trainees
—A Comparative Study of Personality and Occupational Choice.*
Doctor's thesis, Columbia University (New York, N.Y.), 1959.
(*DA* 20:1085)
151. MILLER, DANIEL LUDRICK. *Relationships Between Certain Personality Variables of Supervising Teachers and Their
Student Teachers and the Ratings Given the Student Teachers.*
Doctor's thesis, Indiana University (Bloomington, Ind.), 1960.
(*DA* 21:555)
152. MUNDY, JEAN. "Conformity to Group Judgment in
Relation to the Assumed Similarity of Members to Each
Other." *Newsl Coop Res Psychol* 2:15–8 Jl '60. *
153. NAKAMURA, CHARLES Y. "Measures of Over-Controlled
and Under-Controlled Behavior: A Validation." *J Clin Psychol*
16:149–53 Ap '60. * (*PA* 36:2HB49N)
154. BAILLIE, GORDON STUART. *An Investigation of Objective
Admission Variables as They Relate to Academic and Job
Success in One Graduate Library Education Program.* Doctor's thesis, Washington University (St. Louis, Mo.), 1961.
(*DA* 22:2804)
155. BLOCK, JACK. "Ego Identity, Role Variability, and
Adjustment." *J Consult Psychol* 25:392–7 O '61. * (*PA* 37:
3245)
156. CERBUS, GEORGE. *Personality Correlates of Picture
Preferences.* Doctor's thesis, Purdue University (Lafayette,
Ind.), 1961. (*DA* 22:319)
157. GORDON, CAROL ELIZABETH. *A Study of Susceptibility
to Influence as a Function of Personality Characteristics.* Doctor's thesis, University of Utah (Salt Lake City, Utah), 1961.
(*DA* 22:3921)
158. HARRILL, JAMES EDWARD. *An Investigation of the
Relationships Between Certain Personality Traits and Three
Levels of Achievement.* Doctor's thesis, University of North
Carolina (Chapel Hill, N.C.), 1961. (*DA* 23:531)
159. ALLER, FLORENCE D. "Role of the Self-Concept in Student Marital Adjustment." *Family Life Coordinator* 11:43–5
Ap '62. *
160. COMPTON, NORMA H. "Personal Attributes of Color and
Design Preferences in Clothing Fabrics." *J Psychol* 54:191–5
Jl '62. * (*PA* 37:3991)
161. COMPTON, NORMA HAYNES. *Clothing Fabric Preferences in Relation to Selected Physical and Personality Characteristics.* Doctor's thesis, University of Maryland (College
Park, Md.), 1962. (*DA* 23:1679)
162. GANTER, ROBERT LEWIS. *Some Relationships Between
a Measure of Self-Acceptance and Indications of the Acceptance of Others In a Nursing Education Program.* Doctor's
thesis, Catholic University of America (Washington, D.C.),
1962. (*DA* 23:1605)
163. HOIHJELLE, ANNE L. "Social Climate and Personality
Traits of Able Teachers in Relation to Reading Instruction."
Claremont Read Conf Yearb 26:114–21 '62. *
164. JAFFEE, LESTER D., and POLANSKY, NORMAN A. "Verbal Inaccessibility in Young Adolescents Showing Delinquent
Trends." *J Health & Hum Behav* 3:105–11 su '62. * (*PA*
37:5451)
165. PECK, ROBERT F. "Student Mental Health: The Range
of Personality Patterns in a College Population," pp. 161–99.
(*PA* 37:5614) In *Personality Factors on the College Campus:
Review of a Symposium.* Edited by Robert L. Sutherland and
others. Austin, Tex.: Hogg Foundation for Mental Health,
1962. Pp. xxii, 242. * (*PA* 37:5621)
166. AIKEN, LEWIS R., JR. "Personality Correlates of Attitude Toward Mathematics." *J Ed Res* 56:476–80 My–Je '63. *
(*PA* 39:9943)
167. BLOCK, JACK, and TURULA, EMILY. "Identification, Ego
Control, and Adjustment." *Child Develop* 34:945–53 D '63. *
(*PA* 38:10210)
168. BREAUX, ANGELINA. *Selected Personality Characteristics
and Their Relationship to Academic Achievement.* Doctor's
thesis, Ohio State University (Columbus, Ohio), 1963. (*DA*
26:1015)
169. COROTTO, LOREN V. "Personality Characteristics of
Patients Who Volunteer." *Calif Mental Health Res Dig* 1:13–
4 sp '63. * (*PA* 38:10352)
170. DUA, PREM SAKHI. *Identification of Personality Characteristics Differentiating Elected Women Leaders From Non-
Leaders in a University Setting.* Doctor's thesis, Pennsylvania
State University (University Park, Pa.), 1963. (*DA* 24:3145)
171. JAMES, GRACE ROBBINS. *The Relationship of Teacher
Characteristics and Pu+il Creativity.* Doctor's thesis, University
of North Carolina (Chapel Hill, N.C.), 1963. (*DA* 25:4544)
172. KURLAND, HOWARD D.; YEAGER, CHARLES T.; and
ARTHUR, RANSOM J. "Psychophysiologic Aspects of Severe
Behavior Disorders: A Pilot Study." *Arch Gen Psychiatry*
8:599–604 Je '63. * (*PA* 38:6368)
173. NICHOLS, ROBERT C., and HOLLAND, JOHN L. "Prediction of the First Year College Performance of High Aptitude
Students." *Psychol Monogr* 77(7):1–29 '63. * (*PA* 38:4693)
174. NUSSBAUM, HARVEY. *Systems and Non-Systems Engineers: An Exploratory Study of Discriminating Characteristics.* Doctor's thesis, Wayne State University (Detroit,
Mich.), 1963. (*DA* 25:6054)
175. VELDMAN, DONALD J., and PECK, ROBERT F. "Student-
Teacher Characteristics From the Pupils' Viewpoint." *J Ed
Psychol* 54:346–55 D '63. * (*PA* 38:6670)

176. ALLAN, THOMAS K. *The California Psychological Inventory and the Interpersonal Check List as Predictors of
Success in Student Teaching.* Master's thesis, University of
Maryland (College Park, Md.), 1964.
177. BENNETT, CARSON M., and HILL, ROBERT E., JR. "A
Comparison of Selected Personality Characteristics of Responders and Nonresponders to a Mailed Questionnaire Study."
J Ed Res 58:178–80 D '64. *
178. COBB, BART B. "Problems in Air Traffic Management:
5, Identification and Potential of Aptitude Test Measures for
Selection of Tower Air Traffic Controller Trainees." *Aerospace Med* 35:1019–27 N '64. * (*PA* 39:16518)
179. COROTTO, LOREN V. "The Excluded Research Subject's
Impact on Results." *J Nerv & Mental Dis* 139:581–7 D '64. *
(*PA* 39:10228)
180. CRITES, JOHN O. "The California Psychological Inventory: 1, As a Measure of the Normal Personality." *J Counsel
Psychol* 11:197–202 su '64. *
181. CRITES, JOHN O. "The California Psychological Inventory: 2, As a Measure of Client Personalities." *J Counsel
Psychol* 11:299–306 f '64. *
182. DARBES, ALEX, and MOTTESHEARD, NANCY. "A Validity
Check of Selected Cluster Scores of the California Psychological Inventory Tests of 239 College Students." *Proc W Va
Acad Sci* 36:191–4 S '64. * (*PA* 40:8251)
183. DEKKER, JAMES HERMAN. *A Comparative Study of the
Interests, Values, and Personality of Activity Leaders and
Non-Participating Students at Purdue University.* Doctor's
thesis, Purdue University (Lafayette, Ind.), 1964. (*DA* 25:
998)
184. DUA, PREM S. "Personality Characteristics Differentiating Women Leaders From Nonleaders in a University."
J Nat Assn Women Deans & Counselors 27:128–32 sp '64. *
185. DUNNETTE, MARVIN D.; WERNIMONT, PAUL; and
ABRAHAMS, NORMAN. "Further Research on Vocational Interest Differences Among Several Types of Engineers." *Personnel & Guid J* 42:484–93 Ja '64. * (*PA* 39:6640)
186. EDWARDS, ALLEN L., and WALSH, JAMES A. "Response
Sets in Standard and Experimental Personality Scales." *Am
Ed Res J* 1:52–61 Ja '64. * (*PA* 39:7754)
187. GOLDBERG, LEWIS R., and RORER, LEONARD G. "Test-
Retest Item Statistics." Abstract. *Psychol Rep* 15:413–4 O '64.
* (*PA* 39:5059)
188. GOLDBERG, LEWIS R., and RORER, LEONARD G. *Test-
Retest Item Statistics for the California Psychological Inventory.* ORI Research Monograph, Vol. 4, No. 1. Eugene, Ore.:
Oregon Research Institute, December 1964. Pp. 265. *
189. GOLDBERG, LEWIS R., and RUST, RALPH M. "Intra-
Individual Variability in the MMPI-CPI Common Item Pool."
Brit J Social & Clin Psychol 3:145–7 Je '64. *
190. GOUGH, HARRISON G. "Academic Achievement in High
School as Predicted From the California Psychological Inventory." *J Ed Psychol* 55:174–80 Je '64. * (*PA* 39:5970)
191. GOUGH, HARRISON G. "Achievement in the First Course
in Psychology as Predicted From the California Psychological Inventory." *J Psychol* 57:419–30 Ap '64. * (*PA* 39:2841)
192. GOUGH, HARRISON G. "A Cross-Cultural Study of
Achievement Motivation." *J Appl Psychol* 48:191–6 Je '64. *
(*PA* 39:4702)
193. GOUGH, HARRISON G., and HALL, WALLACE B. "Prediction of Performance in Medical School From the California
Psychological Inventory." *J Appl Psychol* 48:218–26 Ag '64. *
(*PA* 39:5980)
194. GOUGH, HARRISON G., and SANDHU, HARJIT S. "Validation of the CPI Socialization Scale in India." *J Abn &
Social Psychol* 68:544–7 My '64. * (*PA* 39:5150)
195. GRIFFIN, MARY LOUISE, and FLAHERTY, M. RITA.
"Correlation of CPI Traits With Academic Achievement." *Ed
& Psychol Meas* 24:369–72 su '64. * (*PA* 39:5993)
196. HAAS, RONALD FRANCIS. *Relationship Between Personality Adjustment of Low Ability High School Pupils and
Their Enrollment in the College Preparatory Curriculum.* Doctor's thesis, Rutgers University (New Brunswick, N.J.), 1964.
(*DA* 25:7078)
197. HARPER, FRANK B. W. "The California Psychological
Inventory as a Predictor of Yielding Behavior in Women."
J Psychol 58:187–90 Jl '64. * (*PA* 39:5177)
198. HELTON, WILLIAM BERNARD. *A Comparative Analysis
of Selected Characteristics of Intellectually Superior Male
Students Who Persist and Those Who Do Not Persist in an
Advanced Placement Program.* Doctor's thesis, North Texas
State University (Denton, Tex.), 1964. (*DA* 25:3394)
199. HEUSINKVELD, EDWIN DAVID. *A Study Comparing
Selected Characteristics of Academic Underachievers With
Normal Achieving Students at the State University of Iowa.*
Doctor's thesis, State University of Iowa (Iowa City, Iowa),
1964. (*DA* 25:1004)
200. JOHANNSEN, WALTER J.; REDEL, M. CONSTANCE; and
ENGEL, RONALD G. "Personality and Attitudinal Changes During Psychiatric Nursing Affiliation." *Nursing Res* 13:342–5
f '64. *
201. JOHNSON, DOROTHY ETHEL. *A Study of Interests and
Personality Characteristics of Counselor Trainees and Counseling Effectiveness.* Doctor's thesis, Purdue University (Lafayette, Ind.), 1964. (*DA* 26:2051)
202. JOHNSON, RONALD C., and LIM, DONALD. "Personality
Variables in Associative Production." *J General Psychol* 71:
349–50 O '64. * (*PA* 39:4989)

203. JOSHI, BHUWAN LAL. *Personality Correlates of Happiness.* Doctor's thesis, University of California (Berkeley, Calif.), 1964. (*DA* 25:2083)

204. KIRK, BARBARA A.; CUMMINGS, ROGER W.; and HACKETT, HERBERT R. "Correction to Their 'Personal and Vocational Characteristics of Dental Students' in the February 1963 Issue of the Journal." *Personnel & Guid J* 42:621 F '64. *

205. KNAPP, ROBERT R. "Value and Personality Differences Between Offenders and Nonoffenders." *J Appl Psychol* 48:59–62 F '64. * (*PA* 38:8364)

206. LOREI, THEODORE W. "Prediction of Length of Stay Out of the Hospital for Released Psychiatric Patients." *J Consult Psychol* 28:358–63 Ag '64. * (*PA* 39:5476)

207. LOVELL, VICTOR ROYAL. *Components of Variance in Two Personality Inventories.* Doctor's thesis, Stanford University (Stanford, Calif.), 1964. (*DA* 25:4258)

208. MEES, HAYDEN L.; GOCKA, EDWARD F.; and HOLLOWAY, HILDEGUND. "Social Desirability Values for California Psychological Inventory Items." *Psychol Rep* 15:147–58 Ag '64. * (*PA* 39:1841)

209. MORRIS, RUBY PEARL. *A Comparative Analysis of Selected Characteristics of Intellectually Superior Female Students Who Persisted and Those Who Did Not Persist in an Advanced Placement Program.* Doctor's thesis, North Texas State University (Denton, Tex.), 1964. (*DA* 25:3402)

210. NETSKY, MARTIN G.; BANGHART, FRANK W.; and HAIN, JACK D. "Seminar Versus Lecture and Prediction of Performance by Medical Students." *J Med Ed* 39:112–9 F '64. *

211. PURKEY, WILLIAM WATSON, SR. *An Investigation of Personality Characteristics of High School Students Testing at a Superior Level of Intelligence.* Doctor's thesis, University of Virginia (Charlottesville, Va.), 1964. (*DA* 25:3406) (Abstract: *Ed R* 2:66–8 '64. *)

212. SNIDER, J. G., and LINTON, T. E. "The Predictive Value of the California Psychological Inventory in Discriminating Between the Personality Patterns of High School Achievers and Underachievers." *Ont J Ed Res* 6:107–15 sp '64. * (*PA* 39:5918)

213. SPARROW, N. H., and ROSS, JOHN. "The Dual Nature of Extraversion: A Replication." *Austral J Psychol* 16:214–8 D '64. * (*PA* 39:10152)

214. SPRINGOB, H. KARL, and STRUENING, ELMER L. "A Factor Analysis of the California Psychological Inventory on a High School Population." *J Counsel Psychol* 11:173–9 su '64. * (*PA* 39:5183)

215. SWISDAK, BETSEY, and FLAHERTY, S. M. RITA. "A Study of Personality Differences Between College Graduates and Dropouts." *J Psychol* 57:25–8 Ja '64. * (*PA* 39:1688)

216. TRITES, DAVID K. "Problems in Air Traffic Management: 6, Interaction of Training-Entry Age With Intellectual and Personality Characteristics of Air Traffic Control Specialists." *Aerospace Med* 35:1184–94 D '64. * (*PA* 39:16533)

217. ULLMANN, LEONARD P.; KRASNER, LEONARD; and TROFFER, SUZANNE H. "A Contribution to FIRO-B Norms." *J Clin Psychol* 20:240–2 Ap '64. * (*PA* 39:7808)

218. VELDMAN, DONALD J., and PIERCE-JONES, JOHN. "Sex Differences in Factor Structure for the California Psychological Inventory." Abstract. *J Consult Psychol* 28:93 F '64. * (*PA* 38:8536, title only)

219. WESSELL, ALICE, and FLAHERTY, S. M. RITA. "Changes in CPI Scores After One Year in College." *J Psychol* 57:235–8 Ja '64. * (*PA* 39:1689)

220. WILCOCK, KEITH D. "Neurotic Differences Between Individualized and Socialized Criminals." *J Consult Psychol* 28:141–5 Ap '64. * (*PA* 39:2629)

221. BIENEN, SANFORD M., and MAGOON, THOMAS M. "ACL Adjectives Associated With Differential Status on CPI Scales." *Personnel & Guid J* 44:286–91 N '65. * (*PA* 40:4245)

222. BLANKENSHIP, JACOB W. "Biology Teachers and Their Attitudes Concerning BSCS." *J Res Sci Teach* 3(1):54–60 '65. *

223. BYRNE, DONN; GOLIGHTLY, CAROLE; and SHEFFIELD, JOHN. "The Repression-Sensitization Scale as a Measure of Adjustment: Relationship With the CPI." *J Consult Psychol* 29:586–9 D '65. * (*PA* 40:2935)

224. CARNEY, RICHARD E. "Research With a Recently Developed Measure of Achievement Motivation." *Percept & Motor Skills* 21:438 O '65. * (*PA* 40:2266, title only)

225. CORNISH, ROBERT L. "Predictors of College Students' Future Teaching Success." *Univ Kans B Ed* 19:56–9 F '65. *

226. DATEL, WILLIAM E.; HALL, FORREST D.; and RUFE, CHARLES P. "Measurement of Achievement Motivation in Army Security Agency Foreign Language Candidates." *Ed & Psychol Meas* 25:539–45 su '65. * (*PA* 39:16519)

227. DOLAN, FRANCES ANNE. *Personal Qualities and Characteristics Important in the Selection of Undergraduate Staff Members for Women's Residence Halls.* Doctor's thesis, Northwestern University (Evanston, Ill.), 1965. (*DA* 26:3124)

228. DONOVAN, GEORGE L., and OLSEN, LEROY C. "Personality Characteristics of Freshmen Women Applying for Positions in Activities." *J Col Stud Personnel* 6:236–9 Je '65. *

229. FLAHERTY, M. RITA, and REUTZEL, EILEEN. "Personality Traits of High and Low Achievers in College." *J Ed Res* 58:409–11 My–Je '65. * (*PA* 39:16304)

230. GAWRONSKI, DANIEL A., and MATHIS, CLAUDE. "Differences Between Over-Achieving, Normal Achieving, and Under-Achieving High School Students." *Psychol Sch* 2:152–5 Ap '65. *

231. GOLDSCHMID, MARCEL LUCIEN. *The Prediction of College Major in the Sciences and the Humanities by Means of Personality Tests.* Doctor's thesis, University of California (Berkeley, Calif.), 1965. (*DA* 26:4073)

232. GOUGH, HARRISON G. "Cross-Cultural Validation of a Measure of Asocial Behavior." *Psychol Rep* 17:379–87 O '65. * (*PA* 40:892)

233. GOUGH, HARRISON G.; WENK, ERNEST A.; and ROZYNKO, VITALI V. "Parole Outcome as Predicted From the CPI, the MMPI, and a Base Expectancy Table." *J Abn Psychol* 70:432–41 D '65. * (*PA* 40:3143)

234. HAAN, NORMA. "Coping and Defense Mechanisms Related to Personality Inventories." *J Consult Psychol* 29:373–8 Ag '65. * (*PA* 39:15352)

235. HASE, HAROLD DUANE. *The Predictive Validity of Different Methods of Deriving Personality Inventory Scales.* Doctor's thesis, University of Oregon (Eugene, Ore.), 1965. (*DA* 26:4807)

236. HATFIELD, JOHN S., and SHAPIRO, ALBERT M. "Dimensions Among Interview Ratings of Men: An Analysis of Their Meaning and Personality Inventory Correlates." *J Clin Psychol* 21:150–60 Ap '65. * (*PA* 39:12464)

237. HELSON, RAVENNA. "Childhood Interest Clusters Related to Creativity in Women." *J Consult Psychol* 29:352–61 Ag '65. * (*PA* 39:15292)

238. HOWELL, MARGARET AFFARENC. *Personality Factors in Medical Performance.* Doctor's thesis, University of California (Berkeley, Calif.), 1965. (*DA* 27:303B)

239. KIRCHNER, WAYNE K. "Relationships Between the Structured Objective Rorschach Test and the California Psychological Inventory." *J Indus Psychol* 3:24–30 Mr '65. * (*PA* 42:6192)

240. KNAFLE, JUNE D. "Personality Characteristics, Social Adjustment, and Reading Effectiveness in Low-Achieving, Prospective College Freshmen in a Reading Program." *J Ed Res* 59:149–53 D '65. * (*PA* 40:5902)

241. LICHTENSTEIN, EDWARD, and BRYAN, JAMES H. "California Psychological Inventory Correlates of the Need for Approval." *Proc Ann Conv Am Psychol Assn* 73:235–6 '65. * (*PA* 39:15361)

242. McDERMID, CHARLES D. "Some Correlates of Creativity in Engineering Personnel." *J Appl Psychol* 49:14–9 F '65. * (*PA* 39:7782)

243. McGURK, ETHEL. "Susceptibility to Visual Illusions." *J Psychol* 61:127–43 S '65. * (*PA* 40:4793)

244. MASON, EVELYN P.; ADAMS, HENRY L.; and BLOOD, DON F. "Personality Characteristics of Gifted College Freshmen." *Proc Ann Conv Am Psychol Assn* 73:301–2 '65. * (*PA* 39:16316)

245. MILLER, DORIS I. "Characteristics of Graduate Students in Four Clinical Nursing Specialties." *Nursing Res* 14:106–13 sp '65. *

246. MORDOCK, JOHN B., JR., and PATTERSON, C. H. "Personality Characteristics of Counseling Students at Various Levels of Training." *Voc Guid Q* 13:265–9 su '65. *

247. NICHOLS, ROBERT C. "Non-intellective Predictors of Achievement in College." *NMSC Res Rep* 1(6):1–19 '65. *

248. O'BRIEN, CYRIL C., and QUAN, JAMES. "Relapse and Non-Relapse in Alcoholic Patients." *Psychol Rep* 17:10 Ag '65. * (*PA* 40:1769, title only)

249. PLANT, W. T. "Personality Changes Associated With College Attendance." *Hum Develop* 8(2–3):142–51 '65. *

250. PLANT, WALTER T.; TELFORD, CHARLES W.; and THOMAS, JOSEPH A. "Some Personality Differences Between Dogmatic and Nondogmatic Groups." *J Social Psychol* 67:67–75 O '65. * (*PA* 39:15370)

251. RICHARDSON, HAROLD. "Utility of a New Method for Predicting College Grades." *J General Psychol* 72:159–64 Ja '65. * (*PA* 39:8693)

252. RICHARDSON, HAROLD, and ROEBUCK, JULIAN. "Minnesota Multiphasic Personality Inventory and California Psychological Inventory Differences Between Delinquents and Their Nondelinquent Siblings." *Proc Ann Conv Am Psychol Assn* 73:255–6 '65. * (*PA* 39:16142)

253. ROGERS, MILES S., and SHURE, GERALD H. "An Empirical Evaluation of the Effect of Item Overlap on Factorial Stability." *J Psychol* 60:221–33 Jl '65. * (*PA* 40:45)

254. SCHENDEL, JACK. "Psychological Differences Between Athletes and Nonparticipants in Athletics at Three Educational Levels." *Res Q* 36:52–67 Mr '65. * (*PA* 39:10248)

255. SCHNELL, RICHARD R. "Construction of Factor Scales for Personality Assessment." *Newsl Res Psychol* 7:61–2 My '65. *

256. SCOTT, LEON EDWARD. *Underachievers as Contrasted to Overachievers With Respect to Creative Ability, Achievement Motivation, Self-Control, and Parental Aspirations.* Doctor's thesis, University of Nebraska (Lincoln, Neb.), 1965. (*DA* 26:5881)

257. SPERRAZZO, G., and SCHURR, W. E. "Personality Changes and Efficient Reading." *J Clin Psychol* 21:65 Ja '65. * (*PA* 39:12370)

258. STROUP, ATLEE, and HUNTER, KATHERINE JAMISON. "Sibling Position in the Family and Personality of the Offspring." *J Marriage & Family* 27:65–8 F '65. * (*PA* 39:7462)

259. VAN DYKE, PAUL SHEPHERD. *Personality, Achievement*

and Social Acceptance Among Prospective Teachers. Doctor's thesis, University of Texas (Austin, Tex.), 1965. (*DA* 26: 7162)

260. VELDMAN, D. J., and KELLY, F. J. "Personality Correlates of a Composite Criterion of Teaching Effectiveness." *Alberta J Ed Res* 11:102–7 Je '65. * (*PA* 39:16482)

261. VINGOE, FRANCIS JAMES. *The Relationship Between Measures of Self-Awareness, Self-Acceptance and Hypnotizability.* Doctor's thesis, University of Oregon (Eugene, Ore.), 1965. (*DA* 26:7450)

262. WARBURTON, MARY A. *An Investigation of Female Scholastic Achievement Utilizing the California Psychological Inventory and the Gough Adjective Check List.* Master's thesis, University of Kansas (Lawrence, Kan.), 1965.

263. WHITTEMORE, ROBERT G., and HEIMANN, ROBERT A. "Originality Responses in Academically Talented Male University Freshmen." *Psychol Rep* 16:439–42 Ap '65. * (*PA* 39:10252)

264. WILSON, ROBERT LEE. *A Validity Study of the California Psychological Inventory.* Doctor's thesis, Indiana University (Bloomington, Ind.), 1965. (*DA* 26:5258)

265. ALLAN, THOMAS KENNETH. "Personality as a Predictor of Student Teaching Success." *SPATE* 5:12–6 f '66. *

266. ALLAN, THOMAS KENNETH. *The Relationship Between Supervisory Ratings and the Personality of Female Student Teachers.* Doctor's thesis, University of Maryland (College Park, Md.), 1966. (*DA* 27:2907A)

267. ALLEN, DANNY HARRISON. *Some Relationships Between Therapist Personality Characteristics and Techniques Employed in Therapy.* Doctor's thesis, University of Maryland (College Park, Md.), 1966. (*DA* 27:3280B)

268. ALLRED, GOLDEN HUGH. *A Study of the Personality Traits and Classroom Verbal Behavior of Senior High School Student Teachers.* Doctor's thesis, University of Oregon (Eugene, Ore.), 1966. (*DA* 27:2601A)

269. BECKER, GILBERT. "Visual Acuity and Motivational Patterns Underlying Achievement." *J Psychosom Res* 10: 275–9 D '66. * (*PA* 41:5989)

270. CANTER, FRANCIS M. "Personality Factors and Participation in Treatment by Hospitalized, Female Alcoholics." *Psychiatric Q Sup* 40:72–80 pt 1 '66. *

271. CARNEY, RICHARD E. "The Effect of Situational Variables on the Measurement of Achievement Motivation." *Ed & Psychol Meas* 26:675–90 au '66. * (*PA* 41:1939)

272. CARNEY, RICHARD E.; MANN, PHILIP A.; and McCORMICK, ROBERT P. "Validation of an Objective Measure of Achievement Motivation." *Psychol Rep* 19:243–8 Ag '66. * (*PA* 40:11662)

273. CARSON, GARY L., and PARKER, CLYDE A. "Leadership and Profiles on the MMPI and CPI." *J Col Stud Personnel* 7: 14–8 Ja '66. *

274. CRANDALL, VIRGINIA C. "Personality Characteristics and Social and Achievement Behaviors Associated With Children's Social Desirability Response Tendencies." *J Personality & Social Psychol* 4:477–86 N '66. * (*PA* 41:444)

275. DAVIDS, ANTHONY. "Psychological Characteristics of High School Male and Female Potential Scientists in Comparison With Academic Underachievers." *Psychol Sch* 3: 79–87 Ja '66. * (*PA* 41:2862)

276. DEMOS, GEORGE D., and WEIJOLA, MERRILL J. "Achievement-Personality Criteria as Selectors of Participants and Predictors of Success in Special Programs in Higher Education." *Calif J Ed Res* 17:186–92 S '66. * (*PA* 41:1923)

277. DE SALES, MARIE. *Relationship of Occupational Choice to Personality Traits of Women Students as Measured by the Sixteen Personality Factor Questionnaire and the California Psychological Inventory.* Master's thesis, Loyola University (Chicago, Ill.), 1966.

278. EHRLICH, HOWARD J., and BAUER, MARY LOU. "The Correlates of Dogmatism and Flexibility in Psychiatric Hospitalization." *J Consult Psychol* 30:253–9 Je '66. * (*PA* 40:8019)

279. ENGEL, ILONA M. "A Factor-Analytic Study of Items From Five Masculinity-Femininity Tests." Abstract. *J Consult Psychol* 30:565 D '66. * (*PA* 41:2880, title only)

280. FINNEY, JOSEPH C. "Programmed Interpretation of MMPI and CPI." *Arch Gen Psychiatry* 15:75–81 Jl '66. * (*PA* 40:11167)

281. GOTTESMAN, IRVING I. "Genetic Variance in Adoptive Personality Traits." *J Child Psychol & Psychiatry* 7:199–208 D '66. * (*PA* 41:8563)

282. GOUGH, HARRISON G. "Appraisal of Social Maturity by Means of the CPI." *J Abn Psychol* 71:189–95 Je '66. * (*PA* 40:8854)

283. GOUGH, HARRISON G. "A Cross-Cultural Analysis of the CPI Femininity Scale." *J Consult Psychol* 30:136–41 Ap '66. * (*PA* 40:6649)

284. GOUGH, HARRISON G. "Graduation From High School as Predicted From the California Psychological Inventory." *Psychol Sch* 3:208–16 Jl '66. * (*PA* 41:1942)

285. HILL, ARTHUR H. "Autobiographical Correlates of Achievement Motivation in Men and Women." *Psychol Rep* 18:811–7 Je '66. * (*PA* 40:10106)

286. HOWELL, MARGARET A. "Personal Effectiveness of Physicians in a Federal Health Organization." *J Appl Psychol* 50:451–9 D '66. * (*PA* 41:3517)

287. JURJEVICH, R. M. "The Regression Toward the Mean in MMPI, California Psychological Inventory and Symptom

Check List." *Ed & Psychol Meas* 26:661–4 au '66. * (*PA* 41: 1006)

288. JURJEVICH, R. M. "Short Interval Test-Retest Stability of MMPI, California Psychological Inventory, Cornell Index, and Symptom Check List." *J General Psychol* 74:201–6 Ap '66. * (*PA* 40:7209)

289. LAMB, ANN LEE. *The Relationship of Body Build, Motor Educability, and Personality.* Doctor's thesis, University of Utah (Salt Lake City, Utah), 1966. (*DA* 26:6503)

290. LANGE, GARRETT W. "Perceptual Defense and Manifest Anxiety." *Proc W Va Acad Sci* 37:278–82 F '66. * (*PA* 40:8839)

291. LEVENTHAL, ALLAN M. "An Anxiety Scale for the CPI." *J Clin Psychol* 22:459–61 O '66. * (*PA* 41:2260)

292. LICHTENSTEIN, EDWARD, and BRYAN, JAMES H. "CPI Correlates of the Need for Approval." *J Clin Psychol* 22: 453–5 O '66. * (*PA* 41:2900)

293. MAHAL, BARBARA KRUEGER. *Achievement and Rigidity.* Doctor's thesis, Rutgers—The State University (New Brunswick, N.J.), 1966. (*DA* 27:1661A)

294. MAHBOOB, SHAIKH GOLAM. *Personality Characteristics of Male County Extension Personnel in Wisconsin.* Doctor's thesis, University of Wisconsin (Madison, Wis.), 1966. (*DA* 27:925A)

295. MASON, EVELYN P., and BLOOD, DON F. "Cross-Validation Study of Personality Characteristics of Gifted College Freshmen." *Proc Ann Conv Am Psychol Assn* 74:283–4 '66. * (*PA* 41:6242)

296. MASON, EVELYN P.; ADAMS, HENRY L.; and BLOOD, DON F. "Personality Characteristics of Gifted College Freshmen." *Psychol Sch* 3:360–5 O '66. *

297. MEGARGEE, EDWIN I. "Estimation of CPI Scores From MMPI Protocols." *J Clin Psychol* 22:456–8 O '66. * (*PA* 41:2261)

298. MEGARGEE, EDWIN I.; BOGART, PATRICIA; and ANDERSON, BETTY J. "Prediction of Leadership in a Simulated Industrial Task." *J Appl Psychol* 50:292–5 Ag '66. * (*PA* 40: 11112)

299. MILLER, DORIS I. "Characteristics of Graduate Students Preparing for Teaching or Supervision in a Nursing Specialty." *Nursing Res* 15:168–71 sp '66. *

300. MORDKOFF, ARNOLD M. "Some Sex Differences in Personality Correlates of 'Autonomic Feedback.'" *Psychol Rep* 18:511–8 Ap '66. * (*PA* 40:8860)

301. NICHOLS, ROBERT C. "Nonintellective Predictors of Achievement in College." *Ed & Psychol Meas* 26:899–915 w '66. * (*PA* 41:4953)

302. NICHOLS, ROBERT C. "The Resemblance of Twins in Personality and Interests." *NMSC Res Rep* 2(8):1–23 '66. *

303. PLANT, WALTER T., and TELFORD, CHARLES W. "Changes in Personality for Groups Completing Different Amounts of College Over Two Years." *Genetic Psychol Monogr* 74:3–36 Ag '66. * (*PA* 40:12183)

304. PURKEY, WILLIAM WATSON. "Measured and Professed Personality Characteristics of Gifted High School Students and an Analysis of Their Congruence." *J Ed Res* 60:99–103 N '66. *

305. QUERY, WILLIAM T. "CPI Factors and Success of Seminary Students." *Psychol Rep* 18:665–6 Ap '66. * (*PA* 40:8864)

306. REXROAT, MELVIN EUGENE. *The Relationship of Personality Structure, Academic Ability, and Training in Flander's Interaction Analysis to Attitude Change of Prospective Elementary School Teachers.* Doctor's thesis, Utah State University (Logan, Utah), 1966. (*DA* 28:2915A)

307. RODGERS, DAVID A. "Estimation of MMPI Profiles From CPI Data." Abstract. *J Consult Psychol* 30:89 F '66. * (*PA* 40:4253, title only)

308. SNIDER, JAMES G. "Academic Achievement and Underachievement in a Canadian High School as Predicted From the California Psychological Inventory." *Psychol Sch* 3:370–2 O '66. * (*PA* 41:2055)

309. SNIDER, JAMES G. "The Canadian High School Achievement Syndrome as Indicated by the California Psychological Inventory." *Ont J Ed Res* 9:43–7 au '66. * (*PA* 41:5976)

310. STEIN, KENNETH B.; GOUGH, HARRISON G.; and SARBIN, THEODORE R. "The Dimensionality of the CPI Socialization Scale and an Empirically Derived Typology Among Delinquent and Nondelinquent Boys." *Multiv Behav Res* 1:197–208 Ap '66. * (*PA* 41:1015)

311. STEPHENSON, ROBERT W., and TREADWELL, YVONNE. "Personality Variables Related to the Effectiveness of a Creativity Training Program." *J Exp Ed* 35:64–75 w '66. *

312. THORESEN, CARL E. "Oral Non-Participation in College Students: A Study of Characteristics." *Am Ed Res J* 3:198–210 My '66. *

313. VINCENT, CLARK E. "Implications of Changes in Male-Female Role Expectations for Interpreting M-F Scores." *J Marriage & Family* 28:196–9 My '66. * (*PA* 40:7221)

314. VINCENT, MARY JANE PARKS. *A Study of Construct Validity in Self Concept Measurement.* Doctor's thesis, University of Idaho (Moscow, Idaho), 1966. (*DA* 27:3741A)

315. WAHL, CALVIN A. *California Psychological Inventory as a Variable for Predicting Success of Public School Principals in Montana.* Master's thesis, University of Montana (Missoula, Mont.), 1966.

316. ACEY, ALFRED EDWARD. *Time as a Relevant Variable When Personality Scores Are Used as Predictors of Achieve-*

ment. Doctor's thesis, University of Maryland (College Park, Md.), 1967. (*DA* 28:4439A)

317. BARCLAY, JAMES R. "Approach to the Measurement of Teacher 'Press' in the Secondary Curriculum." *J Counsel Psychol* 14:552–67 N '67. * (*PA* 42:4525)

318. BARON, ALVIN. *The Use of Personality Factors as Criteria for Grouping Pupils for Instruction With the Programed Material, English 2600.* Doctor's thesis, New York University (New York, N.Y.), 1967. (*DA* 28:4038A)

319. BOWLES, FRANCIS DOUGLAS. *An Exploratory Investigation of Certain Personality Characteristics at Grades Seven and Twelve in Selected Schools.* Doctor's thesis, University of Rochester (Rochester, N.Y.), 1967. (*DA* 28:1725A)

320. CHEN, MARTIN K.; PODSHADLEY, DALE W.; and SHROCK, JOHN G. "A Factorial Study of Some Psychological, Vocational Interest, and Mental Ability Variables as Predictors of Success in Dental School." *J Appl Psychol* 51:236–41 Je '67. * (*PA* 41:10970)

321. COLLINGS, DONALD J. "Psychological Selection of Drill Sergeants: An Exploratory Attempt in a New Program." *Mil Med* 132:713–5 S '67. * (*PA* 42:3024)

322. DICKEN, CHARLES, and FORDHAM, MICHAEL. "Effects of Reinforcement of Self-References in Quasi-Therapeutic Interviews." *J Counsel Psychol* 14:145–52 Mr '67. * (*PA* 41:7660)

323. DLABAL, JOHN J., JR., and HANSON, ROBERT L. "What Kind of Teacher for the Culturally Deprived?" *El Sch J* 67:218–23 Ja '67. * (*PA* 42:6125)

324. DOMINO, GEORGE. *Personality Patterns and Choice of Medical Specialty.* Doctor's thesis, University of California (Berkeley, Calif.), 1967. (*DA* 28:1694B)

325. EARL, ROBERT DUANE. *The Science Teacher's Inclusive Behavior as Related to Certain Personality Characteristics.* Doctor's thesis, Oklahoma State University (Stillwater, Okla.), 1967. (*DA* 28:4931A)

326. FELLOWS, THOMAS TOY, JR. *A Comparison of Multiple Regression Equations and Moderated Multiple Regression Equations in Predicting Scholastic Success.* Doctor's thesis, University of Utah (Salt Lake City, Utah), 1967. (*DA* 28:3020A)

327. FLAHERTY, M. RITA. "Personality Traits of College Leaders." *J Ed Res* 60:377–8 Ap '67. *

328. FREEDMAN, STEPHEN A.; ANTENEN, WAYNE W.; and LISTER, JAMES L. "Counselor Behavior and Personality Characteristics." *Counselor Ed & Sup* 7:26–30 f '67. * (*PA* 42:1154)

329. GOLDSCHMID, MARCEL L. "Prediction of College Majors by Personality Tests." *J Counsel Psychol* 14:302–8 Jl '67. * (*PA* 41:12452)

330. GREEN, DOROTHY D. "The Relationship of Psychometrically Determined Personality Variables to Perception of the Ames Trapezoidal Illusion: II." *J Psychol* 67:99–105 S '67. * (*PA* 41:16716)

331. HASE, HAROLD D., and GOLDBERG, LEWIS R. "Comparative Validity of Different Strategies of Constructing Personality Inventory Scales." *Psychol B* 67:231–48 Ap '67. * (*PA* 41:7340)

332. HELSON, RAVENNA. "Personality Characteristics and Developmental History of Creative College Women." *Genetic Psychol Monogr* 76:205–56 N '67. * (*PA* 42:3942)

333. HELSON, RAVENNA. "Sex Differences in Creative Style." *J Personality* 35:214–33 Je '67. * (*PA* 41:16700)

334. HERSCH, PAUL D., and SCHEIBE, KARL E. "Reliability and Validity of Internal-External Control as a Personality Dimension." *J Consult Psychol* 31:609–13 D '67. * (*PA* 42:2581)

335. HILL, ARTHUR H. "Use of a Structured Autobiography in the Construct Validation of Personality Scales." *J Consult Psychol* 31:551–6 D '67. * (*PA* 42:1408)

336. JONES, RICHARD R., and GOLDBERG, LEWIS R. "Interrelationships Among Personality Scale Parameters: Item Response Stability and Scale Reliability." *Ed & Psychol Meas* 27:323–33 su '67. * (*PA* 41:13618)

337. LAWLER, EDWARD E., III, and O'GARA, PAUL W. "Effects of Inequity Produced by Underpayment on Work Output, Work Quality, and Attitudes Toward the Work." *J Appl Psychol* 51:403–10 O '67. * (*PA* 42:1265)

338. LINTON, THOMAS E. "The C.P.I. as a Predictor of Academic Success." *Alberta J Ed Res* 13:59–64 Mr '67. * (*PA* 41:15878)

339. LUCAS, DONALD HERBERT. *Personality Correlates of Agreement and Nonagreement Between Measures of Ability and Interest for Two Groups of Institutionalized Males.* Doctor's thesis, University of Kansas (Lawrence, Kan.), 1967. (*DA* 28:2986A)

340. MASON, EVELYN P. "Comparison of Personality Characteristics of Junior High Students From American Indian, Mexican, and Caucasian Ethnic Backgrounds." *J Social Psychol* 73:145–55 D '67. * (*PA* 42:3947)

341. MIZUSHIMA, KEIICHI, and DeVOS, GEORGE. "An application of the California Psychological Inventory in a Study of Japanese Delinquency." *J Social Psychol* 71:45–51 F '67. * (*PA* 41:6089)

342. MOWRER, O. HOBART. "Civilization and Its Malcontents." *Psychol Today* 1:49–52 S '67. * (*PA* 42:935)

343. PATTERSON, C. H. "Effects of Counselor Education on Personality." *J Counsel Psychol* 14:444–8 S '67. * (*PA* 41:15294)

344. PLANT, WALTER T., and MINIUM, EDWARD W. "Differ-

ential Personality Development in Young Adults of Markedly Different Aptitude Levels." *J Ed Psychol* 58:141–52 Je '67. * (*PA* 41:10438)

345. SCHREIBER, ELLIOTT HAROLD. *The Relationship Between Personality Characteristics and Dental Disorders in Adolescents.* Doctor's thesis, West Virginia University (Morgantown, W. Va.), 1967. (*DA* 28:1313A)

346. SEVREN, MARION, and MENDELSON, LLOYD. "A Descriptive Study of Psycho-Social Characteristics of Caretakers in the California Family Care Program for the Adult Mentally Ill." *Calif Mental Health Res Dig* 5:243–4 au '67. * (*PA* 42:757)

347. SMITH, ROBERT J. "Explorations in Nonconformity." *J Social Psychol* 71:133–50 F '67. * (*PA* 41:5896)

348. STEIN, KENNETH B. "Correlates of the Ideational Preference Dimension Among Prison Inmates." *Psychol Rep* 21:553–62 O '67. * (*PA* 42:5757)

349. STEVENS, THOMAS GRANVILLE. *Congruency Between Diagnostic Dimensions of Personality Theories and Personality Tests.* Master's thesis, California State College at Fullerton (Fullerton, Calif.), 1967.

350. STUBBINGS, JOHN ROBERT, JR. *A Comparison of the Torrance Tests of Creative Thinking and Guilford's Measures of Creative Ability on Sex, Cognitive, and Personality Variables.* Doctor's thesis, University of Virginia (Charlottesville, Va.), 1967. (*DA* 28:4496A)

351. TRITES, DAVID K.; KUREK, ADOLPH; and COBB, BART B. "Personality and Achievement of Air Traffic Controllers." *Aerospace Med* 38:1145–50 N '67. *

352. WATSON, CHARLES G. "The California Psychological Inventory as a Predictor of Academic Achievement in Normal and Maladjusted College Males." *J Ed Res* 61:10–3 S '67. *

353. WORK, GERALD GEORGE. *Correlates of Academic Achievement for Female Sophomore Elementary Education Majors.* Doctor's thesis, Ohio University (Athens, Ohio), 1967. (*DA* 28:2926A)

354. YALOM, IRVIN D.; HOUTS, PETER S.; ZIMERBERG, SHELDON M.; and RAND, KENNETH H. "Prediction of Improvement in Group Therapy; An Exploratory Study." *Arch Gen Psychiatry* 17:159–68 Ag '67. * (*PA* 41:15391)

355. BALDRY, ARDIS INGALLS, and SARASON, IRWIN G. "Test Anxiety, Preliminary Instructions, and Responses to Personality Inventories." *J Clin Psychol* 24:67 Ja '68. *

356. BIELIAUSKAS, VYTAUTAS J.; MIRANDA, SIMON B.; and LANSKY, LEONARD M. "Obviousness of Two Masculinity-Femininity Tests." *J Consult & Clin Psychol* 32:314–8 Je '68. * (*PA* 42:13769)

357. BIGELOW, GORDON S., and EGBERT, ROBERT L. "Personality Factors and Independent Study." *J Ed Res* 62:37–9 S '68. *

358. BLANKENSHIP, JACOB W., and HOY, WAYNE K. "An Analysis of the Relationship Between Open- and Closed-Mindedness and Capacity for Independent Thought and Action." *J Res Sci Teach* 5(1):69–72 '68. *

359. BOTT, MARGARET M. "Measuring the Mystique." *Personnel & Guid J* 46:967–70 Je '68. * (*PA* 43:3012)

360. COTTLE, WILLIAM C. *Interest and Personality Inventories,* pp. 96–103. Guidance Monograph Series, Series 3, Testing, [No. 6]. Boston, Mass.: Houghton Mifflin Co., 1968. Pp. xi, 116. *

361. DOMINO, GEORGE. "Differential Prediction of Academic Achievement in Conforming and Independent Settings." *J Ed Psychol* 59:256–60 Ag '68. * (*PA* 42:16123)

362. EISENMAN, RUSSELL. "Birth Order, Insolence, Socialization, Intelligence, and Complexity-Simplicity Preferences." *J General Psychol* 78:61–4 Ja '68. * (*PA* 42:7314)

363. GOUGH, HARRISON G. Chap. 4, "An Interpreter's Syllabus for the California Psychological Inventory," pp. 55–79. In *Advances in Psychological Assessment, Vol. 1.* Edited by Paul McReynolds. Palo Alto, Calif.: Science & Behavior Books, Inc., 1968. Pp. xiii, 336. *

364. GOUGH, HARRISON G. "College Attendance Among High-Aptitude Students as Predicted From the California Psychological Inventory." *J Counsel Psychol* 15:269–78 My '68. * (*PA* 42:12689)

365. GOUGH, HARRISON G.; CHUN, KITAEK; and CHUNG, YANG-EUN. "Validation of the CPI Femininity Scale in Korea." *Psychol Rep* 22:155–60 F '68. * (*PA* 42:10605)

366. GOUGH, HARRISON G.; DE VOS, GEORGE; and MIZUSHIMA, KEIICHI. "Japanese Validation of the CPI Social Maturity Index." *Psychol Rep* 22:143–6 F '68. * (*PA* 42:10470)

367. GOUGH, HARRISON G.; DURFLINGER, GLENN W.; and HILL, ROBERT E., JR. "Predicting Performance in Student Teaching From the California Psychological Inventory." *J Ed Psychol* 59:119–27 Ap '68. * (*PA* 42:8096)

368. GRUPP, STANLEY; RAMSEYER, GARY; and RICHARDSON, JAY. "The Effect of Age on Four Scales of the California Psychological Inventory." *J General Psychol* 78:183–7 Ap '68. * (*PA* 42:12381)

369. JACKSON, DOUGLAS N., and LAY, C. H. "Homogeneous Dimensions of Personality Scale Content." *Multiv Behav Res* 3:321–37 Jl '68. * (*PA* 43:4030)

370. KIPNIS, DAVID. "Social Immaturity, Intellectual Ability, and Adjustive Behavior in College." *J Appl Psychol* 52:71–80 F '68. * (*PA* 42:6070)

371. KORMAN, MAURICE; STUBBLEFIELD, ROBERT L.; and MARTIN, LAWRENCE W. "Patterns of Success in Medical

School and Their Correlates." *J Med Ed* 43:405–11 Mr '68. *

372. LEFCOURT, HERBERT M. "Serendipitous Validity Study of Gough's Social Maturity Index." *J Consult & Clin Psychol* 32:85–6 F '68. * (*PA* 42:7357)

373. LEVENTHAL, ALLAN M. "Additional Technical Data on the CPI Anxiety Scale." Abstract. *J Counsel Psychol* 15:479–80 S '68. * (*PA* 42:18823)

374. LIPP, LELAND; ERIKSON, ROBERT; and SKEEN, DAVID. "Intellectual Efficiency: A Construct Validation Study." *Ed & Psychol Meas* 28:595–7 su '68. * (*PA* 42:18100)

375. McFADDEN, JACK D. "The Discrimination of Student Teaching Performance on the Basis of Psychological Attributes." *J Ed Res* 61:215–7 Ja '68. *

376. MILLER, JEAN M. *An Analysis of the Relationship Between California Psychological Inventory Profiles. Entrance Test Scores and College Success in a Group of Low-Achieving College Applicants.* Master's thesis, University of Maryland (College Park, Md.), 1968.

377. NORFLEET, MARY ANN WARBURTON. "Personality Characteristics of Achieving and Underachieving High Ability Senior Women." *Personnel & Guid J* 46:976–80 Je '68. * (*PA* 43:3130)

378. PIVIK, TERRY, and FOULKES, DAVID. "NREM Mentation: Relation to Personality, Orientation Time, and Time of Night." *J Consult & Clin Psychol* 32:144–51 Ap '68. * (*PA* 42:8252)

379. RAWLS, DONNA J. "The Use of the BIB in the Identification of College Seniors With Managerial Potential." *Proc Ann Conv Am Psychol Assn* 76:579–80 '68. * (*PA* 43:1563, title only)

380. ROSETT, HENRY L.; ROBBINS, HERBERT; and WATSON, WALTER S. "Physiognomic Perception as a Cognitive Control Principle." *Percept & Motor Skills* 26:707–19 Je '68. * (*PA* 42:14974)

381. RYBACK, DAVID. "The California Psychological Inventory and Scholastic Achievement." *J Ed Res* 61:225 Ja '68. *

382. SADLER, PAUL M. "Teacher Personality Characteristics and Attitudes Concerning PSSC Physics." *J Res Sci Teach* 5(1):28–9 '68. *

383. SCHWARTZ, MELVIN L.; DENNERLL, RAYMOND D.; and LIN, YI-GUANG. "Neuropsychological and Psychosocial Predictors of Employability in Epilepsy." *J Clin Psychol* 24:174–7 Ap '68. * (*PA* 42:12633)

384. SOUTHERN, MARA L., and PLANT, WALTER T. "Personality Characteristics of Very Bright Adults." *J Social Psychol* 75:119–26 Je '68. * (*PA* 42:13758)

385. STEIN, KENNETH B. "Motoric and Ideational Dimensions: A Study of Personality Styles Among Prison Inmates." *Psychol Rep* 22:119–29 F '68. * (*PA* 42:10824)

386. STUBBINGS, JOHN ROBERT, JR. "A Comparison of the Torrance Tests of Creative Thinking and Guilford's Measures of Creative Ability on Sex, Cognitive, and Personality Variables." *Ed R* 6:103–4 '68. *

387. VELDMAN, DONALD J.; PECK, ROBERT F.; and RICHEK, HERBERT G. "Personality Correlates of the High School Experiences of Prospective Teachers." *Personnel & Guid J* 46:473–7 Ja '68. * (*PA* 42:9489)

388. VINCENT, JANE. "An Exploratory Factor Analysis Relating to the Construct Validity of Self-Concept Labels." *Ed & Psychol Meas* 28:915–21 au '68. * (*PA* 43:4039)

389. VINGOE, FRANK J. "Note on the Validity of the California Psychological Inventory." *J Consult & Clin Psychol* 32:725–7 D '68. * (*PA* 43:4045)

390. VINGOE, FRANK J. "Validity of the Eysenck Extraversion Scale: Replication and Extension." *Psychol Rep* 22:706–8 Je '68. * (*PA* 42:12999)

391. VINGOE, FRANK J., and ANTONOFF, STEVEN R. "Personality Characteristics of Good Judges of Others." *J Counsel Psychol* 15:91–3 Ja '68. * (*PA* 42:5604)

392. VOSS, JACQUELINE RAE HOLM. *Perceived Parent-Child Relationships as a Determinant of Value Systems and Personality Development.* Doctor's thesis, University of Nebraska (Lincoln, Neb.), 1968. (*DA* 29:1796A)

393. WEINSTEIN, JOSHUA; AVERILL, JAMES R.; OPTON, EDWARD M., JR.; and LAZARUS, RICHARD S. "Defensive Style and Discrepancy Between Self-Report and Physiological Indexes of Stress." *J Personality & Social Psychol* 10:406–13 D '68. * (*PA* 43:6909)

NAME INDEX

[28]

The California Q-Set: A Q-Sort for Personality Assessment and Psychiatric Research. Adults; 1961; CQS; observer ratings; Form 3 (110 cards); manual (166 pages, see *I* below); record sheet (1 page); $8.75 per set of cards and manual; $2.25 per set of cards; $1.75 per 25 record sheets; $6.75 per manual; postage extra; administration time not reported; Jack Block; Consulting Psychologists Press, Inc. *

For reviews by Allen L. Edwards and David T. Lykken, see 6:72 (2 references, 3 excerpts).

REFERENCES

1–2. See 6:72.
3. JONES, MARY COVER. "Personality Correlates and Antecedents of Drinking Patterns in Adult Males." *J Consult & Clin Psychol* 32:2–12 F '68. * (PA 42:7477)

[29]

California Test of Personality, 1953 Revision. Grades kgn–3, 4–8, 7–10, 9–14, adults; 1939–53; CTP; 15 scores: self-reliance, sense of personal worth, sense of personal freedom, feeling of belonging, withdrawing tendencies, nervous symptoms, total personal adjustment, social standards, social skills, anti-social tendencies, family relations, school relations or occupation relations (adult level), community relations, total social adjustment, total adjustment; Forms AA, BB, ('53, 8 pages); 5 levels; manual ('53, 32 pages); profile ('53, 1 page); practice exercises ('64, 2 pages) for IBM answer sheets; $3.85 per 35 sets of test and profile; separate answer sheets (IBM 805 and 1230) may be used for grades 4 and over; $2.50 per 50 answer sheets; $2 per 100 practice exercises; 75¢ per hand scoring stencil; $3 per set of IBM 805 machine scoring stencils; postage extra; 75¢ per specimen set of any one level, postpaid; IBM 1230 scoring service, 15¢ and over per test; (45–60) minutes; Louis P. Thorpe, Willis W. Clark, and Ernest W. Tiegs; California Test Bureau. *

a) PRIMARY. Grades kgn–3; 1940–53.

b) ELEMENTARY. Grades 4–8; 1939–53.

c) INTERMEDIATE. Grades 7–10; 1939–53.

d) SECONDARY. Grades 9–14; 1942–53.

e) ADULT. Adults; 1942–53.

See 6:73 (49 references); for a review by Verner M. Sims, see 5:38 (93 references); for reviews by Laurance F. Shaffer and Douglas Spencer of the original edition, see 3:26 (24 references, 1 excerpt); for reviews by Raymond B. Cattell, Percival M. Symonds, and P. E. Vernon of the elementary and secondary levels, see 2:1213 (1 excerpt).

REFERENCES

1–24. See 3:26.
25–117. See 5:38.
118–166. See 6:73.
167. PERKINS, DOROTHY WILLOUGHBY. *An Item by Item Compilation and Comparison of the Scores of 75 Young Adult Stutterers on the California Test of Personality—Adult Form A.* Master's thesis, University of Michigan (Ann Arbor, Mich.), 1946. (Abstract: *Speech Monogr* 14:211.)
168. DAVIS, DAVID S. *An Investigation of the Relationship of Frustration Tolerance in Paraplegics and Degree and Rate of Success in Rehabilitation.* Doctor's thesis, New York University (New York, N.Y.), 1955. (DA 15:1262)
169. PHELPS, MORRIS OVERTON. *An Analysis of Certain Factors Associated With Under-Achievement Among High School Students.* Doctor's thesis, University of Georgia (Athens, Ga.), 1956. (DA 17:306)
170. STRAUS, MURRAY ARNOLD. *Child Training and Child Personality in a Rural and Urban Area of Ceylon.* Doctor's thesis, University of Wisconsin (Madison, Wis.), 1956. (DA 16:2230)

171. EMFINGER, WILLIAM EDWIN. *Effect of the Personal Maladjustment of the Mental Retardate Upon Special Class Placement and Test-Retest Gains.* Doctor's thesis, Florida State University (Tallahassee, Fla.), 1957. (*DA* 17:3082)

172. STRAUS, MURRAY A. "Anal and Oral Frustration in Relation to Sinhalese Personality." *Sociometry* 20:21–31 Mr '57. * (*PA* 32:290)

173. BROWNSTEIN, JEWELL BROWN. *A Study of Children With Contrasting Records of Social Adjustment in Relation to Certain School, Home and Community Factors.* Doctor's thesis, Indiana University (Bloomington, Ind.), 1958. (*DA* 19:1011)

174. McCONNELL, SHIRLEY. *A Study of Segregated Behavior-Problem Children in the Camden Public Schools.* Doctor's thesis, Temple University (Philadelphia, Pa.), 1959. (*DA* 20:3386)

175. WILSON, PAUL B., and BUCK, ROY C. "The Educational Ladder." *Rural Sociol* 25:404–13 D '60. * (*PA* 35:5334)

176. FARROW, BOBBY J., and SANTOS, JOHN F. "On Conditionability, Personality and Perception." *Percept & Motor Skills* 15:578 D '62. * (*PA* 38:2620)

177. GIBBONS, CARLOS WILBUR, SR. *Contribution of Selected Variables in Predicting Academic Achievement as Measured by Teacher Grades.* Doctor's thesis, University of Maryland (College Park, Md.), 1962. (*DA* 23:2805)

178. HENDERHAN, ROBERT CECIL. *The Relationship of Several Social-Psychological Variables to Empathic Ability.* Doctor's thesis, Ohio State University (Columbus, Ohio), 1962. (*DA* 23:3548)

179. JACKSON, VIOLET BURDEN. *Successful and Unsuccessful Elementary School Children: A Study of Some of the Factors That Contribute to School Success.* Doctor's thesis, Ohio State University (Columbus, Ohio), 1962. (*DA* 24:143)

180. LEUKEL, DEBORAH ANN. *The Psychogenic Tic in Childhood.* Doctor's thesis, University of Washington (Seattle, Wash.), 1962. (*DA* 23:2985)

181. MAHON, FLORENCE LUCY. *The Relationships of Certain Psychological Factors to Speech Development in Primary Grade Children.* Doctor's thesis, Boston University (Boston, Mass.), 1962. (*DA* 23:1610)

182. DACUS, WILFRED PENCE. *A Study of the Grade Organizational Structure of the Junior High School as Measured by Social Maturity, Emotional Maturity, Physical Maturity, and Opposite-Sex Choices.* Doctor's thesis, University of Houston (Houston, Tex.), 1963. (*DA* 24:1461)

183. IRWIN, ELEANOR CHIMA. *The Effect of a Program of Creative Dramatics Upon Personality as Measured by the California Test of Personality, Sociograms, Teacher Ratings and Grades.* Doctor's thesis, University of Pittsburgh (Pittsburgh, Pa.), 1963. (*DA* 24:2188)

184. ROBEY, DALE LEWIS. *A Differential Diagnosis of Low-Academic Ninth Grade Male Students as Compared With Average-Academic Ninth Grade Male Students.* Doctor's thesis, Indiana University (Bloomington, Ind.), 1963. (*DA* 24:5252)

185. SCHLUETER, MARY PETER. *The Role of Intelligence, Personality, and Selected Psychological Factors in Remedial Reading Progress.* Doctor's thesis, University of Rochester (Rochester, N.Y.), 1963. (*DA* 24:4088)

186. BAUER, NORMAN JAMES. *An Experimental Investigation of Differences in Selected Personality Traits Between Most Preferred and Least Preferred Adolescents in Grades Ten, Eleven and Twelve.* Doctor's thesis, Indiana University (Bloomington, Ind.), 1964. (*DA* 25:4471)

187. BLEDSOE, JOSEPH C. "A Factor Analytic Study of the Mental Health Domain at the Elementary School Level." *J Exp Ed* 33:99–102 f '64. * (*PA* 39:5535)

188. CHANSKY, NORMAN M. "Progress of Promoted and Repeating Grade I Failures." *J Exp Ed* 32:225–37 sp '64. * (*PA* 39:5902)

189. CHILTON, BRADLEY STUART. *The Relationship Between Certain Factors of Late and Regular Registrants.* Doctor's thesis, North Texas State University (Denton, Tex.), 1964. (*DA* 25:3344)

190. CHRONISTER, GLENN M. "Personality and Reading Achievement." *El Sch J* 64:253–60 F '64. *

191. DURR, WILLIAM K., and SCHMOTZ, ROBERT R. "Personality Differences Between High-Achieving and Low-Achieving Gifted Children." *Reading Teach* 17:251–4 Ja '64. *

192. ENGEL, WAYNE EMERSON. *Some Personality Functions Associated With Ability-Achievement Discrepancy Levels of Elementary School Children.* Doctor's thesis, University of Minnesota (Minneapolis, Minn.), 1964. (*DA* 25:4538)

193. HAMACHEK, DON E., and MORI, TAKAKO. "Need Structure, Personal Adjustment, and Academic Self-Concept of Beginning Education Students." *J Ed Res* 58:158–62 D '64. * (*PA* 39:10719)

194. SEITZ, THEODORE LEE. *The Relationship Between Creativity and Intelligence, Personality, and Value Patterns in Adolescence.* Doctor's thesis, University of Denver (Denver, Colo.), 1964. (*DA* 25:3679)

195. SNYDER, ROBERT THOMAS. *An Investigation of Personality Variability as a Major Determiner of the Degree of Academic Attainment Among Educable Retardates.* Doctor's thesis, Catholic University of America (Washington, D.C.), 1964. (*DA* 25:3409)

196. STEPHENS, HELEN BROWN. *The Relationship of Certain Psycho-Social Variables to Reading Achievement of Able Seventh Grade Students.* Doctor's thesis, Oklahoma State University (Stillwater, Okla.), 1964. (*DA* 26:1489)

197. TRAWEEK, MELVIN W. "The Relationship Between Certain Personality Variables and Achievement Through Programmed Instruction." *Calif J Ed Res* 15:215–20 N '64. * (*PA* 39:8635)

198. AIKMAN, ARTHUR L. *An Analytical Study of Attitudes and Other Selected Measures of Economically Depressed Children in Grades Five and Six.* Doctor's thesis, Southern Illinois University (Carbondale, Ill.), 1965. (*DA* 26:6435)

199. CONSTANTINIDES, PANAYIOTES DEMOSTHENOUS. *The Relationship of Critical Thinking Ability to Intelligence, to Personality, and to Teacher Evaluation of Pupil Personality.* Doctor's thesis, University of Virginia (Charlottesville, Va.), 1965. (*DA* 26:5861) (Abstract: *Ed R* 3:43–5 '65. *)

200. GIBBS, D. N. "Student Failure and Social Maladjustment." *Personnel & Guid J* 43:580–5 F '65. * (*PA* 39:10772)

201. GRAPKO, MICHAEL F. "The Construction of a Primary Form of the Institute of Child Study Security Test (The Story of Tommy)." *B Inst Child Study (Toronto)* 27:3–12 w '65. *

202. KEMP, C. GRATTON. "Parents' and Adolescents' Perceptions of Each Other and the Adolescents' Self-Perception." *Personnel & Guid J* 44:58–62 S '65. *

203. KING, PAUL T., and ROSS, DONALD R. "Test Transparency as Related to Test Response." *Personnel & Guid J* 43:669–73 Mr '65. * (*PA* 39:12292)

204. LOCKHART, HAZEL M. "Personality and Reading Readiness." *Ill Sch Res* 2:9–11 O '65. *

205. LoPRESTI, PETER LIBORIO JOSEPH. *Teachers' Appraisals of the Personal and Social Adjustment of Fourth, Fifth and Sixth Graders as Compared With Self-Evaluations by the Pupils.* Doctor's thesis, University of Connecticut (Storrs, Conn.), 1965. (*DA* 26:5134)

206. MATLIN, ARNOLD H., and MENDELSOHN, FRANCES A. "The Relationship Between Personality and Achievement Variables in the Elementary School." *J Ed Res* 58:457–9 Jl–Ag '65. * (*PA* 40:404)

207. RINGNESS, THOMAS A. "Emotional Adjustment of Academically Successful and Nonsuccessful Bright Ninth Grade Boys." *J Ed Res* 59:88–91 O '65. * (*PA* 40:3369)

208. SNYDER, ROBERT; JEFFERSON, WILLIAM; and STRAUSS, RUTH. "Personality Variables as Determiners of Academic Achievement of the Mildly Retarded." *Mental Retard* 3:15–8 F '65. * (*PA* 39:10599)

209. THOMSEN, VIRGINIA B. *Selected Teaching Implications Derived From Eighth Grade Mexican-American Pupils' Responses to the California Personality Inventory.* Master's thesis, Fresno State College (Fresno, Calif.), 1965.

210. WILLS, H. STANLEY. *A Comparison and Analysis of the Attitudes of Negro and White Junior High School Students as Revealed by the California Test of Personality.* Master's thesis, Millersville State College (Millersville, Pa.), 1965.

211. WILSON, JAMES JOHN, III. *The Relationship of Reading Achievement, Patterns of Eye Movements, and Emotional and Personality Adjustment.* Doctor's thesis, Arizona State University (Tempe, Ariz.), 1965 (*DA* 26:1999)

212. ZIMMERMAN, IRLA LEE, and ALLEBRAND, GEORGE N. "Personality Characteristics and Attitudes Toward Achievement of Good and Poor Readers." *J Ed Res* 59:28–30 S '65. * (*PA* 40:434)

213. DARBES, ALEX. "Some Test Characteristics of Female Student Beauticians." *Proc W Va Acad Sci* 37:286–8 F '66. * (*PA* 40:8250)

214. LAMBETH, HOSEA DeWOOD, JR. *The Self Concept of Mentally Retarded Children in Relation to Educational Placement and Developmental Variables.* Doctor's thesis, University of North Carolina (Chapel Hill, N.C.), 1966. (*DA* 27:3726A)

215. LOWE, JAY. "Prediction of Delinquency With an Attitudinal Configuration Model." *Social Forces* 45:106–13 S '66. * (*PA* 40:13339)

216. McREYNOLDS, GRACE MARIE. *A Study of the Usefulness of the California Test of Personality in the Placement of Student Teachers.* Doctor's thesis, University of Kansas (Lawrence, Kan.), 1966. (*DA* 28:910A)

217. STENNETT, RICHARD G. "Family Diagnosis: MMPI and CTP Results." *J Clin Psychol* 22:165–7 Ap '66. * (*PA* 40:7972)

218. TEIGLAND, JOHN J.; WINKLER, RONALD C.; MUNGER, PAUL F.; and KRANZLER, GERALD D. "Some Concomitants of Underachievement at the Elementary School Level." *Personnel & Guid J* 44:950–5 My '66. * (*PA* 40:10429)

219. TWINING, GERALDINE A. "The Relationship of Personality With Reading Achievement." *Ill Sch Res* 2:33–5 F '66. *

220. WILLIAMS, DALE E. *A Study of Selected Personality and Occupational Aspiration Variables Associated With Achievement Level.* Doctor's thesis, Oklahoma State University (Stillwater, Okla.), 1966. (*DA* 27:4143A)

221. BANSAVAGE, JUDITH CHASIN. *Social Acceptance in a Group of Orthopedically Impaired Adolescents.* Doctor's thesis, University of Pittsburgh (Pittsburgh, Pa.), 1967. (*DA* 28:5143A)

222. BEELER, ANN E. *The Applicability of the California Test of Personality to a Hearing-Impaired Population.* Master's thesis, Washington University (St. Louis, Mo.), 1967.

223. CRITES, JOHN O., and SEMLAR, IRA J. "Adjustment, Educational Achievement, and Vocational Maturity as Dimensions of Development in Adolescence." *J Counsel Psychol* 14:489–96 N '67. * (*PA* 42:3783)

224. GARDNER, WILLIAM I. "Use of the California Test of

Personality With the Mentally Retarded." *Mental Retard* 5:12–6 Ag '67. * (*PA* 41:15717)

225. HOLZINGER, MARGALITH. *Personality and Behavioral Characteristics of Able and Less Able Readers of Elementary School Age.* Doctor's thesis, University of Minnesota (Minneapolis, Minn.), 1967. (*DA* 28:4909A)

226. KENNEDY, LARRY D., and LARSON, ALFRED. "The Influence of Structural and of Traditional Grammatical Instruction Upon Language Perception and Writing Ability." *Ill Sch Res* 3:28–30 F '67. *

227. KEOUGH, BETTY J., and SCHURR, EVELYN. "Specific Aspects of Physical, Intellectual, and Personality Development of Gifted and Regular First Grade Children." *Ill Sch Res* 3:31–6 F '67. *

228. LESSING, ELISE E., and OBERLANDER, MARK. "Developmental Study of Ordinal Position and Personality Adjustment of the Child as Evaluated by the California Test of Personality." *J Personality* 35:487–97 S '67. * (*PA* 42:2413)

229. MARTIN, JUAN EFRAIN. *A Study of the Marginality Traits of a Group of Foreign Students at Catholic University of America, as Measured by Five Scales of the California Test of Personality.* Master's thesis, Catholic University of America (Washington, D.C.), 1967.

230. PRICE, THOMAS HUGH. *Psychological Case Studies of Successful Workers in the Field of Retailing.* Doctor's thesis, University of North Carolina (Chapel Hill, N.C.), 1967. (*DA* 28:4790B)

231. SCHREIBER, ELLIOTT HAROLD. *The Relationship Between Personality Characteristics and Dental Disorders in Adolescents.* Doctor's thesis, West Virginia University (Morgantown, W. Va.), 1967. (*DA* 28:1313A)

232. SMITH, JOHN T., JR.; RUTER, MAXINE D.; LACKNER, FRANK M.; and KWALL, DONNA S. "Academic, Sociometric and Personality Variables in the Prediction of Elementary School Achievement." *Proc Ann Conv Am Psychol Assn* 75:339–40 '67. * (*PA* 41:14225)

233. BANSAVAGE, JUDITH C. "Social Acceptance in a Group of Orthopedically Impaired Adolescents." *Proc Ann Conv Am Psychol Assn* 76:647–8 '68. * (*PA* 43:1199, title only)

234. BELL, LADDIE R., and SCHRIEBER, ELLIOTT H. "Psychological Adjustment and Verbal Ability of High School Seniors." *Penn Psychiatric Q* 8:57–62 sp '68. *

235. FLANAGAN, JOHN J., and LEWIS, GEORGE R. "Perception of Personal and Social Adjustment by Minor Offenders." *Correct Psychiatry & J Social Ther* 14:96–102 sp '68. *

236. GOLDMAN, BERT A. "Relationships Between Scores on the Mooney Problem Check List and the California Test of Personality." *J Ed Res* 61:307–10 Mr '68. *

237. LESSING, ELISE E. "Demographic, Developmental, and Personality Correlates of Length of Future Time Perspective (FTP)." *J Personality* 36:183–201 Je '68. * (*PA* 42:16947)

238. VEGELY, ANN BEELER, and ELLIOTT, LOIS L. "Applicability of a Standardized Personality Test to a Hearing-Impaired Population." *Am Ann Deaf* 113:858–68 S '68. * (*PA* 43:2921)

239. WOLF, WILLAVENE; KING, MARTHA L.; and HUCK, CHARLOTTE S. "Teaching Critical Reading to Elementary School Children." *Reading Res Q* 3:435–98 su '68. *

NAME INDEX

[30]

★**Cardiac Adjustment Scale.** Heart patients; 1964; CAS; research edition; "readiness for safe return to work"; 1 form (4 pages); preliminary manual (5 pages); $4.25 per 25 tests; $1 per key; $2.25 per specimen set; postage extra; (20) minutes; Duane M. Rumbaugh; Educational and Industrial Testing Service. *

REFERENCE

1. RUMBAUGH, DUANE M.; KNAPP, ROBERT R.; and McCARTY, CAROL J. "Prediction of Work Potential in Heart Patients Through Use of the Cardiac Adjustment Scale." Abstract. *J Consult Psychol* 29:597 D '65. * (*PA* 40:2562, title only)

[31]

★**Caring Relationship Inventory.** Marriage counselees; 1966; CRI; research edition; 7 scores: nurturing love, peer love, romantic love, altruistic love, self love, being love, deficiency love; 2 forms: male, female, (3 pages); preliminary manual (11 pages); profile (1 page); $6.50 per 25 tests; $3 per set of keys; $3.75 per 50 profiles; 50¢ per manual; $1 per specimen set; postage extra; scoring service, 85¢ or less per test; (40) minutes; Everett L. Shostrom; Educational and Industrial Testing Service. *

REFERENCE

1. PANG, HENRY, and FROST, LINDA JO. "College Couples on the Caring Relationship Inventory." *Psychol Rep* 22:956 Je '68. * (*PA* 42:13788)

[32]

The Cassel Group Level of Aspiration Test, 1957 Revision. Grades 5–16 and adults; 1952–57; CGLAT; 7 scores: clinical difference, Hausmann, aspiration difference, first goal, psychological response to failure, physiological response to failure, level of aspiration quotient; 1 form ('57, 4 pages); manual ('57, 26 pages); $7.50 per kit of 25 tests and manual; $6.50 per 25 tests; $2 per manual; $2.50 per specimen set; postpaid; Russell N. Cassel; Western Psychological Services. *

For reviews by W. Grant Dahlstrom, Harrison G. Gough, and J. P. Sutcliffe, see 5:39 (5 references, 2 excerpts).

REFERENCES

1–5. See 5:39.
6. SISKIND, GEORGE. "Level of Aspiration Task as a Selective Device for Psychiatric Aides." *Psychol Rep* 20:814 Je '67. * (*PA* 41:13870, title only)

[33]

The Cassel Psychotherapy Progress Record. Mental patients; 1953; CPPR; 3 ratings: emotional development, barrier vulnerability development, overall psychotherapy development; 1 form (8 pages); manual (41 pages); no data on reliability and validity; no norms; $7 per 25 record forms; $2 per specimen set; postpaid; Russell N. Cassel; Western Psychological Services. *

For a review by William Schofield, see 6:74.

[34]

★**Chapin Social Insight Test.** Ages 13 and over; 1967–68; CSIT; 1 form ('67, 4 pages); manual ('68, 15 pages); response booklet ('67, 4 pages); no norms; $3.75 per 25 tests; $6 per 50 response booklets; $3 per manual; $3.50 per specimen set; postage

extra; price of manual not available; specimen set not available; (20–30) minutes; F. Stuart Chapin (test) and Harrison G. Gough (manual); Consulting Psychologists Press, Inc. *

REFERENCES

1. CHAPIN, F. STUART. "Preliminary Standardization of a Social Insight Scale." Comment by George A. Lundberg. *Am Social R* 7:214–28 Ap '42. * (*PA* 16:3669)
2. GOUGH, HARRISON G. "A Validational Study of the Chapin Social Insight Test." *Psychol Rep* 17:355–68 O '65. * (*PA* 40:891)
3. McDERMID, CHARLES D. "Some Correlates of Creativity in Engineering Personnel." *J Appl Psychol* 49:14–9 F '65. * (*PA* 39:7782)

[35]

The Child Behavior Rating Scale. Grades kgn–3; 1960–62; CBRS; ratings by teachers or parents; 6 adjustment scores: self, home, social, school, physical, total; 1 form ('62, 4 pages); mimeographed manual ('62, 17 pages); no data on reliability of subscores; $7 per 25 tests and manual; $2 per manual; postpaid; specimen set not available; [5–10] minutes; Russell N. Cassel; Western Psychological Services. *

REFERENCE

1. CASSEL, RUSSELL N. "A Comparison of Teacher and Parent Ratings on the Child Behavior Rating Scale for 800 Primary Pupils." *J Ed Res* 57:437–9 Ap '64. *

[36]

Children's Embedded Figures Test. Ages 5–12; 1963; CEFT; revision of the Goodenough-Eagle modification (see 2 below) of the *Embedded Figures Test;* for research use only; 1 form (25 cards plus demonstration and practice materials); manual (15 pages); $6 per set of test materials, postage extra; [10–20] minutes plus practice session; Stephen A. Karp and Norma L. Konstadt; distributed by Consulting Psychologists Press, Inc. *

See 6:74b (2 references).

REFERENCES

1–2. See 6:74b.
3. CORAH, NORMAN L. "Differentiation in Children and Parents." *J Personality* 33:300–8 Je '65. * (*PA* 40:2895)
4. FIEBERT, MARTIN STEPHEN. *A Study of Cognitive Styles in the Deaf.* Doctor's thesis, University of Rochester (Rochester, N.Y.), 1965. (*DA* 26:3485)
5. MacCOBY, ELEANOR E.; DOWLEY, EDITH M.; HAGEN, JOHN W.; and DEGERMAN, RICHARD. "Activity Level and Intellectual Functioning in Normal Preschool Children." *Child Develop* 36:761–70 S '65. * (*PA* 39:14711)
6. BIGELOW, GORDON SHOEMAKER. *Global Versus Analytical Cognitive Style in Children as a Function of Age, Sex, and Intelligence.* Doctor's thesis, Brigham Young University (Provo, Utah), 1967. (*DA* 28:958A)
7. CAMPBELL, DONALD R.; DYER, FREDERICK N.; and BOERSMA, FREDERIC J. "Field Dependency and Picture Recognition Ability." *Percept & Motor Skills* 25:713–6 D '67. * (*PA* 42:8934)
8. DYE, GRETCHEN M. *Reliability Study of the Children's Embedded Figures Test.* Master's thesis, University of South Dakota (Vermillion, S.D.), 1967.
9. FIEBERT, MARTIN. "Cognitive Styles in the Deaf." *Percept & Motor Skills* 24:319–29 F '67. * (*PA* 41:9221)

[37]

The Children's Hypnotic Susceptibility Scale. Ages 5–12, 13–16; 1963, c1962; CHSS; downward extension of *Stanford Hypnotic Susceptibility Scale* (see 253), on which its content is based; individual; 2 levels; younger form, older form; manual ('63, c1962, 62 pages plus tests, and scoring and observation form); scoring and observation form (4 pages); no data on reliability; no norms; $5.50 per manual and 25 sets of scoring and observation forms; $6.50 per 50 scoring and observation forms; $2.25 per manual; $2.50 per specimen set; postage extra; (50–60) minutes; Perry London; Consulting Psychologists Press, Inc. *

For reviews by C. Scott Moss and John G. Watkins, see 6:75 (2 references, 1 excerpt).

REFERENCES

1–2. See 6:75.
3. LONDON, PERRY. "Developmental Experiments in Hypnosis." *J Proj Tech & Pers Assess* 29:189–99 Je '65. * (*PA* 39:12264)
4. COOPER, LESLIE M., and LONDON, PERRY. "Sex and Hypnotic Susceptibility in Children." *Int J Clin & Exp Hyp* 14:55–60 Ja '66. * (*PA* 40:4860)
5. MADSEN, CHARLES H., JR., and LONDON, PERRY. "Role Playing and Hypnotic Susceptibility in Children." *J Personality & Social Psychol* 3:13–9 Ja '66. * (*PA* 40:2665)
6. MOORE, ROSEMARIE K., and COOPER, LESLIE M. "Item Difficulty in Childhood Hypnotic Susceptibility Scales as a Function of Item Wording, Repetition, and Age." *Int J Clin & Exp Hyp* 14:316–23 O '66. * (*PA* 41:65)

[38]

*Children's Personality Questionnaire, 1963 Edition. Ages 8–12; 1959–68; CPQ; test booklet title is *What You Do and What You Think;* 14 scores: reserved vs. warmhearted (A), less intelligent vs. more intelligent (B), affected by feelings vs. emotionally stable (C), phlegmatic vs. excitable (D), obedient vs. assertive (E), sober vs. happy-go-lucky (F), expedient vs. conscientious (G), shy vs. venturesome (H), tough-minded vs. tender-minded (I), vigorous vs. circumspect individualism (J), forthright vs. shrewd (N), self-assured vs. apprehensive (O), undisciplined self-conflict vs. controlled (Q3), relaxed vs. tense (Q4); Forms A, B, ('63, 8 pages, authors recommend administration of both forms); taped edition also available; manual ('68, 16 pages); norms supplement ('68, 24 pages); technical handbook ('60, 54 pages) for 1959 edition; profile ('63, 1 page); $4 per 25 tests; $1.50 per set of keys; separate answer sheets may be used; $2.50 per 50 answer sheets; $2 per 50 profile sheets; $3 per 50 sets of answer sheet and profile; $1.80 per set of scoring stencils; $1.80 per technical handbook; 80¢ per norms supplement; 50¢ per manual; $25 per tape; $3.10 per specimen set; postage extra; German edition available; (60–100) minutes in 2 sessions; R. B. Porter and R. B. Cattell; Institute for Personality and Ability Testing. *

For reviews by Anne Anastasi, Wilbur L. Layton, and Robert D. Wirt, see 6:122 (2 references).

REFERENCES

1–2. See 6:122.
3. COLLINS, JAMES L. *A Comparative Study of the Personality Traits of Educable Mentally Retarded Children and Children of Average Intelligence.* Master's thesis, Indiana State College (Terre Haute, Ind.), 1962. (Abstract: *Teach Col J* 34:127–8)
4. BACHTOLD, LOUISE MARIE. *Differences in Personality, School Attitude, and Visual Motor Performance Among Specific Types of Underachievers.* Doctor's thesis, University of the Pacific (Stockton, Calif.), 1963. (*DA* 25:1730)
5. BERSON, MINNIE PERRIN. *Changes in Achievement and Personality in Children Functioning Below School Reading Norms in a Remedial Reading Program.* Doctor's thesis, Wayne State University (Detroit, Mich.), 1965. (*DA* 28:3496A)
6. FROST, BARRY P. "Some Personality Characteristics of Poor Readers." *Psychol Sch* 2:218–20 Ap '65. *
7. KARSON, SAMUEL. "Primary Factor Correlates of Boys With Personality and Conduct Problems." *J Clin Psychol* 21:16–8 Ja '65. * (*PA* 39:12765)
8. PORTER, RUTHERFORD B.; COLLINS, JAMES L.; and McIVER, M. RAYMOND. "A Comparative Investigation of the Personality of Educable Mentally Retarded Children and Those of a Norm Group of Children." *Excep Children* 31:457–63 My '65. * (*PA* 39:10598)
9. MUNDY, J. M. "Junior Children's Responses to the Murray Thematic Apperception Test and the Cattell Personality Questionnaire." Abstract. *Brit J Ed Psychol* 36:103–4 F 66. * (*PA* 40:6640, title only)
10. RUSHTON, JAMES. "The Relationship Between Personality Characteristics and Scholastic Success in Eleven-Year-Old Children." *Brit J Ed Psychol* 36:178–84 Je '66. * (*PA* 40:10426)
11. WERNER, EMMY E. "CPQ Personality Factors of Talented and Underachieving Boys and Girls in Elementary School." *J Clin Psychol* 22:461–4 O '66. * (*PA* 41:2890)
12. KOSIER, KENNETH P., and DeVAULT, M. VERE. "Effects of Teacher Personality on Pupil Personality." *Psychol Sch* 4:40–4 Ja '67. * (*PA* 41:4978)
13. LESSING, ELISE E., and SMOUSE, ALBERT D. "Use of the

Children's Personality Questionnaire in Differentiating Between Normal and Disturbed Children." *Ed & Psychol Meas* 27:657–69 au '67. * (*PA* 42:901)
14. ROSENBLATT, HOWARD STUART. *A Study of the Personality Dimensions of Disadvantaged Youth as Reflected by the Children's Personality Questionnaire.* Doctor's thesis, University of Southern Mississippi (Hattiesburg, Miss.), 1967. (*DA* 28:1311A)
15. BERK, T. J. C. "An Analysis of Personality Traits in a Group of Mildly Mentally Retarded Children With a Multivariate Personality Test." *J Mental Subnorm* 14:35–42 Je '68. *
16. HUNDLEBY, JOHN D., and CATTELL, RAYMOND B. *Personality Structure in Middle Childhood and the Prediction of School Achievement and Adjustment.* Monographs of the Society for Research in Child Development, Serial No. 121; Vol. 33, No. 5. Chicago, Ill.: University of Chicago Press, 1968. Pp. iv, 61. * (*PA* 43:6725)

[39]

Client-Centered Counseling Progress Record. Adults and children undergoing psychotherapeutic counseling; 1950–60; form for rating progress in up to 40 counseling visits; 1 form ('59, 4 pages); manual ('60, 8 pages); no norms; $2 per 25 records, postage extra; $1 per specimen set, postpaid; [3–5] minutes; Russell N. Cassel; Associated Publishers. *

For a review by William Schofield, see 6:76.

[40]

★Clinical Behavior Check List and Rating Scale. Clinical clients; 1965; 10 ratings: cooperation, activity level, intelligence, disposition, persistence, sociability, emotional stability, attention, communicativeness, relaxation-tension; 1 form (1 page); mimeographed manual (11 pages plus scale); no data on reliability; no norms; $2.50 per 20 scales; $1 per manual; postage extra; [10] minutes following interview; Psychological Research and Development Institute; Psychological Publications Press. *

[41]

★Clyde Mood Scale. Normals and schizophrenics; 1963; CMS; to measure changes produced by drugs by self ratings or ratings by others; 6 scores: friendly, aggressive, clear thinking, sleepy, unhappy, dizzy; 1 form; 2 formats: deck of 52 IBM cards, printed check list (1 page); manual (15 pages); $1 per deck of cards; 2¢ per check list; manual free; scales and scoring service free to investigators doing controlled experiments; [5–15] minutes; Dean J. Clyde; Biometrics Laboratory, University of Miami. *

REFERENCES

1. LEBOVITS, BINYAMIN Z.; VISOTSKY, HAROLD M.; and OSTFELD, ADRIAN M. "Lysergic Acid Diethylamide (LSD) and JB 318: A Comparison of Two Hallucinogens: 2, An Exploratory Study." *Arch Gen Psychiatry* 3:176–87 Ag '60. *
2. FRIEDMAN, ALFRED S., and GRANICK, SAMUEL. "A Note on Anger and Aggression in Old Age." *J Gerontol* 18:283–5 Jl '63. * (*PA* 38:4101)
3. CATTELL, RAYMOND B., and RICKELS, KARL. "Diagnostic Power of IPAT Objective Anxiety Neuroticism Tests With Private Patients." *Arch Gen Psychiatry* 11:459–65 N '64. * (*PA* 39:7935)
4. FRIEDMAN, ALFRED S. "Minimal Effects of Severe Depression on Cognitive Functioning." *J Abn & Social Psychol* 69:237–43 S '64. * (*PA* 39:5781)
5. KASL, STANISLAV, and COBB, SIDNEY. "Some Psychological Factors Associated With Illness Behavior and Selected Illnesses." *J Chronic Dis* 17:325–45 Ap '64. * (*PA* 39:10322)
6. KOLLAR, EDWARD J.; SLATER, GRANT R.; PALMER, JAMES O.; DOCTER, RICHARD F.; and MANDELL, ARNOLD J. "Measurement of Stress in Fasting Man: A Pilot Study." *Arch Gen Psychiatry* 11:113–25 Ag '64. * (*PA* 39:4233)
7. McKEEVER, WALTER F.; MAY, PHILIP R. A.; and TUMA, A. HUSSAIN. "Prognosis in Schizophrenia: Prediction of Length of Hospitalization From Psychological Test Variables." *J Clin Psychol* 21:214–21 Ap '65. * (*PA* 39:12856)
8. MILLER, CLARENCE K. "The Psychological Impact of Coronary Artery Disease." *Newsl Res Psychol* 7:21–2 Ag '65. *
9. KATZ, MARTIN M.; LOWERY, HENRI A.; and COLE, JONATHAN O. Chap. 10, "Behavior Patterns of Schizophrenics in the Community," pp. 209–30. In *Exploration in Typing Psychotics.* Edited by Maurice Lorr. London: Pergamon Press Ltd., 1966. Pp. viii, 241. *

10. LYERLY, SAMUEL B., and ABBOTT, PRESTON S. "Clyde Mood Scale," pp. 58–9. In their *Handbook of Psychiatric Rating Scales (1950–1964).* Public Health Service Publication No. 1495. Washington, D.C.: United States Government Printing Office, 1966. Pp. v, 69. *

11. RICKELS, KARL, and CLYDE, DEAN J. "Clyde Mood Scale Changes in Anxious Outpatients Produced by Chloridiazepoxide Therapy." *J Nerv & Mental Dis* 144:154–7 Ag '67. * (*PA* 42:4119)

12. KLEIN, HELEN P., and PARSONS, OSCAR A. "Self-Descriptions of Patients With Coronary Disease." *Percept & Motor Skills* 26:1099–107 Je '68. * (*PA* 42:19214)

[42]

College and University Environment Scales, Second Edition. College; 1962–69; CUES; an adaptation of the *College Characteristics Index* (see 256b); students' conceptions of "the prevailing atmosphere or climate of the campus"; 7 scores: practicality, community, awareness, propriety, scholarship, campus morale, quality of teaching and faculty-student relationships; Form X-2 ('69, 7 pages); directions for administration ['69, 3 pages]; technical manual ('69, 55 pages); separate answer sheets (Scribe) must be used; 35¢ per test; 5¢ per answer sheet; $2.50 per technical manual; $3 per specimen set; postage extra; scoring and reporting service, 80¢ and over per answer sheet ($50 minimum charge); reporting service includes a 16 page printout with number and percentage responding in the keyed direction to each of the 160 items, 10 local option questions, and 4 information questions along with scores on the 5 basic scales and 2 subscales for 4 mutually exclusive subgroups and the total group; no normative data on printouts; reports are mailed approximately 4 weeks after receipt of answer sheets; (30) minutes; C. Robert Pace; Educational Testing Service. *

REFERENCES

1. FISHER, M. SCOTT. *The Relationship of Satisfaction, Achievement, and Attrition to Anticipated Environmental Press.* Master's thesis, Brigham Young University (Provo, Utah), 1961.

2. STANDING, G. ROBERT. *A Study of the Environment at Brigham Young University as Perceived by Its Students and as Anticipated by Entering Students.* Master's thesis, Brigham Young University (Provo, Utah), 1962.

3. TUCKER, SYLVIA BOLTZ. *College and University Potential of Selected Junior College Students.* Doctor's thesis, University of California (Los Angeles, Calif.), 1964. (*DA* 25:5077)

4. EDSON, KENNETH CHARLES. *Factors Related to Changes in Environmental Expectations of College Freshmen.* Doctor's thesis, University of Minnesota (Minneapolis, Minn.), 1965. (*DA* 26:4441)

5. PACE, C. ROBERT. "When Students Judge Their College." *Col Board R* 58:26–8 w '65–66. *

6. BERDIE, RALPH F. "College Expectations, Experiences, and Perceptions." *J Col Stud Personnel* 7:336–48 N '66. *

7. CONNER, JOHN DOUGLAS. *The Relationship Between College Environmental Press and Freshman Attrition at Southern Methodist University.* Doctor's thesis, North Texas State University (Denton, Tex.), 1966. (*DA* 27:946A)

8. DEAN, GARY STEPHEN. *High School Seniors' Preferences and Expectations for College Environment in Relationship to High School Scholastic Achievement and Intellectual Ability and as a Predictor of College Success and Satisfaction.* Doctor's thesis, University of California (Los Angeles, Calif.), 1966. (*DA* 27:4099A)

9. DORWORTH, THOMAS R. *The Relationship Between the College and University Environment Scale (CUES) and Social Class.* Master's thesis, Marshall University (Huntington, W.Va.), 1966.

10. HARTSFIELD, KIRK FERNANDO. *The Perceived Environments of Selected Georgia Junior Colleges.* Doctor's thesis, University of Georgia (Athens, Ga.), 1966. (*DA* 27:3310A)

11. HASSENGER, ROBERT, and WEISS, ROBERT. "The Catholic College Climate." *Sch R* 74:419–45 w '66. * (*PA* 41:6221)

12. MCPEEK, BETH LEE. *College and University Environment Scales as a Measure of University Perceptions and Desired Environmental Conditions as Described by Students, Faculty and Administrators at Millikin University.* Doctor's thesis, Indiana University (Bloomington, Ind.), 1966. (*DA* 27:2051A)

13. SCHOEN, WALTER T., JR. "The Campus Climate: Student Perception and Faculty Idealism." *J Ed Res* 60:3–7 S '66. *

14. ABBOTT, CHARLES FRANKLIN. *An Investigation of the College Environmental Perceptions of Prospective College Freshmen and Their Relationships to the Choice of a College*

or University. Doctor's thesis, Michigan State University (East Lansing, Mich.), 1967. (*DA* 28:1673A)

15. BERDIE, RALPH F. "Some Psychometric Characteristics of CUES." *Ed & Psychol Meas* 27:55–66 sp '67. * (*PA* 41:9384)

16. BERDIE, RALPH F. "A University Is a Many-Faceted Thing." *Personnel & Guid J* 45:768–75 Ap '67. *

17. BODELSON, GERALD R. *Environmental Perceptions of Freshman College Students as Related to Selected Ability and Achievement Levels.* Doctor's thesis, Indiana University (Bloomington, Ind.), 1967. (*DA* 28:3966A)

18. FICK, DORCAS JANE. *A Comparison of Campus Climates of a Multi-Campus University as Measured by the College and University Environment Scales.* Doctor's thesis, Columbia University (New York, N.Y.), 1967. (*DA* 28:3412A)

19. GALLESSICH, JUNE MARIE. *Factors Associated With Academic Success of Freshmen Engineering Students of the University of Texas.* Doctor's thesis, University of Texas (Austin, Tex.), 1967. (*DA* 28:1677A)

20. HERRSCHER, BARTON ROBERT. *Patterns of Attainment and the Environmental Press of UCLA Student Groups.* Doctor's thesis, University of California (Los Angeles, Calif.), 1967. (*DA* 28:1705A)

21. JANSEN, DAVID GEORGE. *Characteristics of Student Leaders.* Doctor's thesis, Indiana University (Bloomington, Ind.), 1967. (*DA* 28:3768A)

22. KELLEY, DAVID BRANHAM. *Perceptions of College Environments of Freshman Students Enrolled in Three New Georgia Community Junior Colleges.* Doctor's thesis, University of Georgia (Athens, Ga.), 1967. (*DA* 28:4414A)

23. LINDAHL, CHARLES. "Impact of Living Arrangements on Student Environmental Perceptions." *J. Col Stud Personnel* 8:10–5 Ja '67. *

24. MOOMAW, ROBERT CLAYTON. *Need-Press Differences Among Community College Students.* Doctor's thesis, Ohio State University (Columbus, Ohio), 1967. (*DA* 28:2074A)

25. PACE, LAWLIS THERON. *Roommate Dissatisfaction in a College Residence Hall as Related to Roommate Scholastic Achievement, the College and University Environment Scales, and the Edwards Personal Preference Schedule.* Doctor's thesis, Colorado State College (Greeley, Colo.), 1967. (*DA* 28:2989A)

26. ROTTON, LENA BELLE. *An Environmental Study of Upper Iowa University.* Doctor's thesis, University of Mississippi (University, Miss.), 1967. (*DA* 28:2917A)

27. SHEMKY, ROBERT WILLIAM. "Catholic Higher Education: The Effect of the Academic Environment on the Stability of the Lay Faculty." *J Higher Ed* 38:70–7 F '67. *

28. BERDIE, RALPH F. "Changes in University Perceptions During the First Two College Years." *J Col Stud Personnel* 9:85–9 Mr '68. *

29. BOYER, ERNEST L., and MICHAEL, WILLIAM B. "Faculty and Student Assessments of the Environments of Several Small Religiously Oriented Colleges." *Calif J Ed Res* 19:59–66 Mr '68. *

30. CENTRA, JOHN A. "Student Perceptions of Residence Hall Environments: Living-Learning vs. Conventional Units." *J Col Stud Personnel* 9:266–72 Jl '68. *

31. CONNER, J. DOUGLAS. "The Relationship Between College Environmental Press and Freshman Attrition at Southern Methodist University." *Col & Univ* 43:265–73 sp '68. *

32. GELSO, CHARLES J., and SIMS, DAVID M. "Perceptions of a Junior College Environment." *J Col Stud Personnel* 9:40–3 Ja '68. *

33. JANSEN, DAVID G., and WINBORN, BOB B. "Perceptions of a University Environment by Social-Political Action Leaders." *Personnel & Guid J* 47:218–22 N '68. *

34. LEWIS, KATHRYN LUCETTA. *Correlates of College Choice Satisfaction.* Doctor's thesis, University of Southern California (Los Angeles, Calif.), 1968. (*DA* 29:2095A)

35. LOCKE, DONALD WILES. *A Comparison of College Environmental Expectations and Perceptions of Prospective and Enrolled Students at the University of Mississippi.* Doctor's thesis, University of Mississippi (University, Miss.), 1968. (*DA* 29:150A)

36. MARKS, EDMOND. "Personality and Motivational Factors in Responses to an Environmental Description Scale." *J Ed Psychol* 59:267–74 Ag '68. * (*PA* 42:15450)

37. RICHARDSON, THOMAS EDWARD. *The Relationship of Congruence Between Student Orientation Toward Higher Education and Campus Environment to Student Satisfaction on Selected Campuses.* Doctor's thesis, Florida State University (Tallahassee, Fla.), 1968. (*DA* 29:2360A)

38. RITLAND, MICHAEL DON. *A Study of Perceptions of Institutional Environment at Stout State University.* Doctor's thesis, Colorado State College (Greeley, Colo.), 1968. (*DA* 29:818A)

39. SIMMONS, HARRY EDWARD, JR. *Environmental Perceptions of Selected Groups of Reporters on a College Campus Committed to a Peer Group Concept.* Doctor's thesis, University of California (Los Angeles, Calif.), 1968. (*DA* 29:787A)

40. YONGE, GEORGE D. "Personality Correlates of the College and University Environment Scales." *Ed & Psychol Meas* 28:115–23 sp '68. * (*PA* 42:12723)

NAME INDEX

Dean, G. S.: 8
Dorworth, T. R.: 9
Edson, K. C.: 4
Fick, D. J.: 18
Fisher, M. S.: 1
Gallessich, J. M.: 19
Gelso, C. J.: 32
Hartsfield, K. F.: 10
Hassenger, R.: 11
Herrscher, B. R.: 20
Jansen, D. G.: 21, 33
Kelley, D. B.: 22
Lewis, K. L.: 34
Lindahl, C.: 23
Locke, D. W.: 35
McPeek, B. L.: 12
Marks, E.: 36

Michael, W. B.: 29
Moomaw, R. C.: 24
Pace, C. R.: 5
Pace, L. T.: 25
Richardson, T. E.: 37
Ritland, M. D.: 38
Rotton, L. B.: 26
Schoen, W. T.: 13
Shemky, R. W.: 27
Simmons, H. E.: 39
Sims, D. M.: 32
Standing, G. R.: 2
Tucker, S. B.: 3
Weiss, R.: 11
Winborn, B. B.: 33
Yonge, G. D.: 40

[43]
The College Inventory of Academic Adjustment.
College; 1949; CIAA; 7 scores: curricular adjustment, maturity of goals and level of aspiration, personal efficiency-planning and use of time, study skills
and practices, mental health, personal relations, total;
1 form (4 pages); manual (10 pages); $3 per 25 tests;
60¢ per set of manual and scoring stencils; 75¢ per
specimen set; postage extra; (15–25) minutes; Henry
Borow; [Consulting Psychologists Press, Inc.]. *
    For a review by Leonard D. Goodstein, see 6:77
(12 references); for reviews by Lysle W. Croft and
Harrison G. Gough, see 4:34 (3 references).

REFERENCES
1–3. See 4:34.
4–15. See 6:77.
16. JENSEN, VERN HARMON. *An Analysis and Comparison
of the Adjustment Problems of Nonachieving College Students of
Low Scholastic Ability and Other Groups of Achieving and Nonachieving Students.* Doctor's thesis, University of Colorado
(Boulder, Colo.), 1957. (*DA* 19:70)
17. BOND, PATRICIA JANE. *The Relationship Between Selected Nonintellective Factors and "Concealed Failure" Among
College Students of Superior Scholastic Ability.* Doctor's
thesis, Purdue University (Lafayette, Ind.), 1960. (*DA* 21:
121)
18. POOR, FREDERICK ALBERT. *The Similarities and Differences in the Successful and Unsuccessful Second-Semester Accounting Students at Northern Illinois University.* Doctor's
thesis, University of Minnesota (Minneapolis, Minn.), 1962.
(*DA* 23:2381)
19. CARMICHAEL, JACK JOE. *Some Relationships of Denominational Affiliation to Selected Personal Characteristics of Male
College Students.* Doctor's thesis, Ohio University (Athens,
Ohio), 1963. (*DA* 23:2787)
20. DE SENA, PAUL AMBROSE. *Identification of Non-Intellectual Characteristics of Consistent Over-, Under-, and Normal-
Achievers Enrolled in Science Curriculums at the Pennsylvania State University.* Doctor's thesis, Pennsylvania State
University (University Park, Pa.), 1963. (*DA* 24:3144)
21. DE SENA, PAUL A. "The Effectiveness of Two Study
Habits Inventories in Predicting Consistent Over-, Under- and
Normal Achievement in College." Comment by Henry Borow.
J Counsel Psychol 11:388–94 w '64. * (*PA* 39:8570)
22. DE SENA, PAUL A. "The Role of Consistency in Iden-
tifying Characteristics of Three Levels of Achievement." *Per-
sonnel & Guid J* 43:145–9 O '64. * (*PA* 39:10713)
23. GELSO, CHARLES J., and ROWELL, DAVID. "Academic
Adjustment and the Persistence of Students With Marginal
Academic Potential." *J Counsel Psychol* 14:478–81 S '67. *
(*PA* 41:15773)

[44]
★College Student Questionnaires. College entrants, students; 1965–68; CSQ; for research use
only; institutional self-study of student populations;
2 editions; for optional test, see *c* below; supervisor's
manual ['67, 21 pages]; technical manual, revised
('68, 64 pages); research prospectus ('68, 16 pages);
publisher recommends use of local norms; separate
answer sheets (Scribe) must be used; $2.50 per
technical manual; $3 per specimen set; postage extra;
scoring and reporting service, $1 and over per answer
sheet ($50 minimum charge); reporting service in-
cludes a 39 page printout with item statements (including the number and percentage checking each
item alternative), group statistics (mean, standard
deviation, and frequency distribution) for each scale,
and response frequency and percentage to 9 local op-

tion questions for 4 mutually exclusive subgroups
and total; normative data included on printout; reports are mailed approximately 4 weeks after receipt
of answer sheets; Richard E. Peterson (technical
manual); Educational Testing Service. *
a) PART 1. College entrants; 7 scores: motivation for
grades, family social status, family independence, peer
independence, liberalism, social conscience, cultural
sophistication; Form 200D ('65, 22 pages); 35¢ per
test; 5¢ per answer sheet; (55–65) minutes.
b) PART 2. College students end of academic year; 11
scores: family independence, peer independence, liberalism, social conscience, cultural sophistication, satisfaction with faculty, satisfaction with administration,
satisfaction with major, satisfaction with students,
study habits, extracurricular involvement; Form 200D
('65, 22 pages); 35¢ per test; 5¢ per answer sheet;
(55–65) minutes.
c) CONTROL TEST FOR ACADEMIC APTITUDE. CTAA;
group measure of academic aptitude used in tandem
with CSQ; test booklet title is *Control Test AA*;
Form NQA ('65, 4 pages); responses made on answer
sheets for Part 1 or Part 2; 15¢ per test; 12(20)
minutes.

REFERENCES
1. GRIFFEN, WILLIAM LAWRENCE. *Predictors of Freshman
College Students' Interest in Working on Major Social Problems.* Doctor's thesis, Cornell University (Ithaca, N.Y.), 1967.
(*DA* 28:2598A)
2. PETERSON, RICHARD E. "Predictive Validity of a Brief
Test of Academic Aptitude." *Ed & Psychol Meas* 28:441–4 su
'68. * (*PA* 42:19279)

[45]
★Community Adaptation Schedule. Normals and
psychiatric patients; 1965–68; CAS; for research
use only; self-report measure of subject's relationship
to the world outside of himself; primarily intended
for measuring groups; 45 scores: work (employment,
housework, family care, work potential, unemployment, volunteer, wage history, total), family (general
living, spouse, children, parents, other relatives, total),
social (general social, friends, dating, peers at work,
neighbors, total), larger community (recreation, religion, organizations, communications, education, moving, civic, total), commercial (finances, shopping,
transportation, modern technology, housing, total),
professional (social services, other services, individual
professionals, schools, total), affect, behavior, cognition, common question total, total, consistency; reliability data for an earlier form; norms consist of mean
scores on earlier forms for 3 groups: normals, outpatients, patients; Form 5A ('68, 23 pages); preliminary manual ('68, 24 pages); separate answer sheets
must be used; $10.90 per 25 tests; $4.25 per 50
answer sheets; $1.50 per set of scoring stencils; $2.25
per manual; $5.85 per specimen set; cash orders post-
paid; (30–50) minutes; Sheldon R. Roen and Alan J.
Burnes; Behavioral Publications, Inc. *

REFERENCES
1. ROEN, SHELDON R.; OTTENSTEIN, DONALD; COOPER, SAUL;
and BURNES, ALAN. "Community Adaptation as an Evaluative
Concept in Community Mental Health." *Arch Gen Psychiatry*
15:36–44 Jl '66. * (*PA* 40:11374)
2. BURNES, ALAN J., and ROEN, SHELDON R. "Social Roles
and Adaptation to the Community." *Commun Mental Health J*
3:153–8 su '67. * (*PA* 41:15086)

[46]
Community Improvement Scale. Adults; 1955;
CIS; community morale; 1 form (2 pages); hecto-
graphed manual (3 pages plus test); $2.50 per 25 tests;
$1 per specimen set (must be purchased to obtain
manual); postage extra; [5–10] minutes; Inez Fay
Smith; Psychometric Affiliates. *
    For a review by Wimburn L. Wallace, see 5:42.

[47]

Concept Formation Test. Normal and schizophrenic adults; 1940; CFT; also called *Vigotsky Test;* individual; 1 form (a set of blocks); mimeographed instructions ['40, 4 pages]; no data on reliability and validity; no norms; $17.85 per set of testing materials, postage extra; (10–60) minutes; Jacob Kasanin and Eugenia Hanfmann; C. H. Stoelting Co. *

See 6:78 (11 references); for a review by Kate Levine Kogan (with William S. Kogan), see 4:35 (8 references); for a review by O. L. Zangwill, see 3:27 (19 references); for excerpts from related book reviews, see 3:28.

REFERENCES

1–19. See 3:27.
20–27. See 4:35.
28–38. See 6:78.
39. MYDEN, WALTER DAVID. *An Interpretation and Evaluation of Certain Personality Characteristics Involved in Creative Production: An Investigation and Evaluation of Personality Structure and Characteristics of Creative Individuals in the Context of Psychoanalytic Theory and Ego Psychology.* Doctor's thesis, New York University (New York, N.Y.), 1956. (*DA* 17:897)
40. SEN, MYRA. "A New Method Scoring of Haufmann-Kasanin Test." *Manas* 8:21–7 '61. * (*PA* 37:1200)
41. ALLISON, ROSALIE NEWTON. *Children's Concepts of Form and Color in Relationship to Selected Variables.* Doctor's thesis, University of Georgia (Athens, Ga.), 1964. (*DA* 25:5721)
42. MEECE, R. SHERILYN, and ROSENBLUM, SIDNEY. "Conceptual Thinking of Sixth-Grade Children as Measured by the Vigotsky Block Test." *Psychol Rep* 17:195–202 Ag '65. * (*PA* 40:1418)
43. BROMLEY, DENNIS B. "Age and Sex Differences in the Serial Production of Creative Conceptual Responses." *J Gerontol* 22:32–42 Ja '67. *
44. SU, CHIEN-WEN. "A Study of Concept Formation in Children." *Psychol & Ed* 1:85–95 Ap '67. *
45. STONES, E., and HESLOP, J. R. "The Formation and Extension of Class Concepts in Primary School Children." *Brit J Ed Psychol* 38:261–71 N '68. *

NAME INDEX

Aldrich, C. K.: 15
Allison, R. N.: 41
Baker, C. A.: 27
Bolles, M. M.: 4
Bressler, M. B.: 33
Bromley, D. B.: 43
Brown, J. F.: 9
Cameron, N.: 6
Cook, C. H.: 22
Corter, H. M.: 29
Davidson, J. L.: 37
Des Lauriers, A.: 23
Diethelm, O.: *exc,* 3:28
Doehring, D. G.: 27
Draper, W. A.: 38
Dworsky, A.: 2
Edrington, T. C.: 34
Fisher, S.: 26
Fosberg, I. A.: 21, 24
French, T. M.: *exc,* 3:28
Gill, M.: 13, 17–8
Gillespie, W. H.: *exc,* 3:28
Goldstein, K.: *exc,* 3:28
Halpern, F.: 23
Hanfmann, E.: 3, 5, 5a, 7–8, 12, 20, 31
Hartmann, G. W.: *exc,* 3:28
Heslop, J. R.: 45
Kasanin, J.: 3, 5, 5a, 12
Kasanin, J. S.: 16
Knight, R. P.: 13
Kogan, K. L.: *rev,* 4:35
Kogan, W. S.: *rev,* 4:35
Kress, R. A.: 36

Laird, A. J.: 30
Landis, C.: 4
Lovibond, S. H.: 32
Lozoff, M.: 13
Maskin, M.: *exc,* 3:28
Mayman, M.: 19
Meece, R. S.: 42
Miller, E. O.: 35
Muncie, W.: *exc,* 3:28
Myden, W. D.: 39
Norman, R. D.: 27
O'Neill, J. J.: 37
Penny, R.: 28
Pickford, A. S.: *exc,* 3:28
Pickford, R. W.: *exc,* 3:28
Rapaport, D.: 9, 12a, 13–4, 17–8
Reichard, S.: 14
Rosen, G. P.: 4
Rosenblum, S.: 42
Schafer, R.: 17–8, 25
Semeonoff, B.: 30
Sen, M.: 40
Sengstake, C. B.: 38
Sonoda, B. C.: 38
Stones, E.: 45
Su, C. W.: 44
Thompson, C.: *exc,* 3:28
Thompson, J.: 10–1
Vigotsky, L. S.: 1
von Holt, H. W.: 38
Wright, D. G.: *exc,* 3:28
Zangwill, O. L.: *rev,* 3:27
Zubin, J.: 11

[48]

Cornell Index. Ages 18 and over; 1944–49; CI; revision for civilian use of the *Cornell Selectee Index Form N* and the *Cornell Service Index;* title on test is *C.I.—Form N2;* psychosomatic and neuropsychiatric symptoms; Form N2 ['45, 2 pages]; revised manual ('49, 8 pages); $1.75 per 25 tests; 50¢ per specimen set; postpaid; (5–15) minutes; Arthur Weider, Harold

G. Wolff, Keeve Brodman, Bela Mittelmann, and David Wechsler; Psychological Corporation. *

See 5:43 (7 references); for reviews by Hans J. Eysenck, Nelson G. Hanawalt, and Laurance F. Shaffer, see 4:37 (41 references).

REFERENCES

1–41. See 4:37.
42–48. See 5:43.
49. VONACHEN, HAROLD A.; MITTELMANN, BELA; KRONENBERG, MILTON H.; WEIDER, ARTHUR; and WOLFF, HAROLD G. "A Comprehensive Mental Hygiene Program at Caterpillar Tractor Co.: Improving Human Relationships in Industry." *Indus Med* 15:179–84 Mr '46. *
50. FRANKLE, A. H. "Psychometric Investigation of the Relationship Between Emotional Repression and the Occurrence of Psychosomatic Symptoms." *Psychosom Med* 14:252–5 Jl–Ag '52. * (*PA* 27:2911)
51. ARENTSEN, KAJ. "An Investigation of the Questionnaire Method by Means of the Cornell Index (Form N2): 1, Review of the Literature and Method; Results for a Group of Military Recruits." *Acta Psychiatrica et Neurologica Scandinavica* 32(3):231–56 '57. * (*PA* 33:1240)
52. ARENTSEN, KAJ. "An Investigation of the Questionnaire Method by Means of the Cornell Index (Form N2): 2, Results for a Group of Military Medical Patients." *Acta Psychiatrica et Neurologica Scandinavica* 32(3):257–79 '57. * (*PA* 33:1240)
53. ARENTSEN, KAJ. "An Investigation of the Questionnaire Method by Means of the Cornell Index (Form N2): 3, Results for Military Psychiatric Cases." *Acta Psychiatrica et Neurologica Scandinavica* 32(4):361–78 '57. * (*PA* 33:3895)
54. ARENTSEN, KAJ. "An Investigation of the Questionnaire Method by Means of the Cornell Index (Form N2): 4, Discriminative Ability; Clinical Use." *Acta Psychiatrica et Neurologica Scandinavica* 32(4):379–88 '57. * (*PA* 33:3895)
55. FULKERSON, SAMUEL C. "Individual Differences in Response Validity." *J Clin Psychol* 15:169–73 Ap '59. * (*PA* 35:4876)
56. GREEN, MAYER A. "Personality and Placebo Response in Hay Fever Patients." *Clin Med* 6:1367–8+ Ag '59. *
57. WISE, LEON M. "Abnormal Psychology as a Selective Factor: A Confirmation and Extension." *J Ed Psychol* 50:192–4 O '59. * (*PA* 36:1KD92W)
58. KANFER, FREDERICK H. "Verbal Rate, Eyeblink, and Content in Structured Psychiatric Interviews." *J Abn & Social Psychol* 61:341–7 N '60. * (*PA* 36:2HE41K)
59. THALLER, JACK L. "The Use of the Cornell Index to Determine the Correlation Between Bruxism and the Anxiety State: A Preliminary Report." *J Periodont* 31:138–40 Ap '60. *
60. MUELLER, ALFRED D.; LEFKOVITS, AARON, M.; BRYANT, JOHN E.; and MARSHALL, MAX L. "Some Psychological Factors in Patients With Rheumatoid Arthritis." *Arthr & Rheum* 4:275–82 Ap '61. *
61. CRUMBAUGH, JAMES C.; SHAPIRO, DAVID S.; MAHOLICK, LEONARD T.; and OAKEY, RUTH C. "The Bradley Center Mental Health Assessment Kit: An Analysis of Use in Group Testing." *J Clin Psychol* 18:431–6 O '62. * (*PA* 39:5047)
62. BOYD, ROBERT L. *An Analysis of the Cornell Index Form N2 for Proposed Use at the Veteran's Administration Hospital, Fort Bayard, New Mexico.* Master's thesis, Western New Mexico University (Silver City, N.M.), 1963.
63. GLADFELTER, JOHN H.; MARTIN, HARRY W.; LEON, ROBERT L.; and MAY, SOPHIA BELLE. "The Cornell Index and Social Dependency." *Tex Rep Biol & Med* 21:12–5 sp '63. * (*PA* 38:8851)
64. FEINBERG, M. R., and PENZER, W. N. "Factor Analysis of a Sales Selection Battery." *Personnel Psychol* 17:319–24 au '64. * (*PA* 39:8794)
65. HENRIKSON, LARS V. "Professed Anxiety and Related Factors in New Admissions to Maine State Prison." *Am J Correction* 26:22–3+ My–Je '64. *
66. CRUMBAUGH, JAMES C. "Critique of the 'Bradley Center Mental Health Assessment Kit' or 'Personal Data Kit.'" *Psychol Rep* 19:871–4 D '66. * (*PA* 41:3708)
67. JURJEVICH, R. M. "Short Interval Test-Retest Stability of MMPI, California Psychological Inventory, Cornell Index, and Symptom Check List." *J General Psychol* 74:201–6 Ap '66. * (*PA* 40:7209)
68. OSBORN, ROGER D. "Mental Health Screening at the Ohio State University." *J Sch Health* 37:278–85 Je '67. * (*PA* 42:936)
69. ROZAN, GERALD H.; FELDSTEIN, STANLEY; and JAFFE, JOSEPH. "'Denial Personality,' Reported Symptoms and the Clinical Course of an Inpatient Psychiatric Sample." *J Nerv & Mental Dis* 145:385–91 N '67. * (*PA* 42:9167)
70. LYLE, WILLIAM H., JR., and RAINEY, MICHAEL L. "The Cornell Index as a Screening Device With Institutionalised Offenders." *Brit J Criminol* 8:295–300 Jl '68. * (*PA* 43:1078)

NAME INDEX

Arentsen, K.: 51–4
Barnes, J. R.: 47
Birren, J. E.: 20
Boyd, R. L.: 62
Briggs, D. L.: 46
Broadbent, T. H.: 32, 39

Brodman, K.: 2, 4–5, 9, 15–6, 21–2, 32, 39
Bryant, J. E.: 60
Conrad, H. S.: 30
Crumbaugh, J. C.: 61, 66
Darke, R. A.: 28

[49]

Cornell Medical Index—Health Questionnaire.

Ages 14 and over; 1949–56; CMI; a questionnaire for use by physicians in collecting medical and psychiatric information from patients; separate forms ('49, 4 pages) for men and women; revised manual ('56, 15 pages including sample questionnaire and diagnostic sheet); diagnostic sheet ['53, 1 page]; no data on reliability; $3 per 50 questionnaires; $1.50 per 50 diagnostic sheets; postpaid; specimen set free; French Canadian and Spanish editions available; (10–30) minutes; Keeve Brodman, Albert J. Erdmann, Jr., and Harold G. Wolff; Cornell University Medical College. *

REFERENCES

1. BRODMAN, KEEVE; ERDMANN, ALBERT J., JR.; LORGE, IRVING; GERSHENSON, CHARLES P.; and WOLFF, HAROLD G.; with the technical assistance of Barbara Caples. "The Cornell Medical Index—Health Questionnaire: 3, The Evaluation of Emotional Disturbances." *J Clin Psychol* 8:119–24 Ap '52. * (*PA* 27:1951)

2. BRODMAN, KEEVE; ERDMANN, ALBERT J., JR.; LORGE, IRVING; GERSHENSON, CHARLES P.; and WOLFF, HAROLD G.; with the technical assistance of Todd H. Broadbent. "The Cornell Medical Index—Health Questionnaire: 4, The Recognition of Emotional Disturbances in a General Hospital." *J Clin Psychol* 8:289–93 Jl '52. * (*PA* 27:5858)

3. ERDMANN, A. J., JR.; BRODMAN, K.; LORGE, I.; and WOLFF, H. G. "Cornell Medical Index—Health Questionnaire: 5, Outpatient Admitting Department of a General Hospital." *J Am Med Assn* 149:550–1 Je 7 '52. *

4. BRODMAN, KEEVE. "Cornell Medical Index—Health Questionnaire," pp. 568–76. (*PA* 27:7756) In *Contributions Toward Medical Psychology: Theory and Psychodiagnostic Methods, Vol. II.* Edited by Arthur Weider. New York: Ronald Press Co., 1953. Pp. xi, 459–885. *

5. BRODMAN, KEEVE; ERDMANN, ALBERT J., JR.; LORGE, IRVING; and WOLFF, HAROLD G. "The Cornell Medical Index—Health Questionnaire: 6, The Relation of Patients' Complaints to Age, Sex, Race, and Education." *J Gerontol* 8:339–42 Jl '53. * (*PA* 28:7916)

6. BRODMAN, KEEVE; DEUTSCHBERGER, JEROME; ERDMANN, ALBERT J.; LORGE, IRVING; and WOLFF, HAROLD G. "Prediction of Adequacy for Military Service: Use of the Cornell Medical Index—Health Questionnaire." *U S Armed Forces Med J* 5:1802–8 D '54. * (*PA* 29:8052)

7. BRODMAN, KEEVE; ERDMANN, ALBERT J., JR.; LORGE, IRVING; DEUTSCHBERGER, JEROME; and WOLFF, HAROLD G. "The Cornell Medical Index—Health Questionnaire: 7, The Prediction of Psychosomatic and Psychiatric Disabilities in

Army Training." Discussion by Ruth Tolman. *Am J Psychiatry* 111:37–40 Jl '54. * (*PA* 29:2437)

8. ARNHOFF, FRANKLYN N.; STROUGH, LA VERN C.; and SEYMOUR, RICHARD B. "The Cornell Medical Index in a Psychiatric Outpatient Clinic." *J Clin Psychol* 12:263–8 Jl '56. * (*PA* 31:6055)

9. HOLMES, THOMAS H. Chap. 6, "Multidiscipline Studies of Tuberculosis," pp. 65–152. In *Personality, Stress, and Tuberculosis.* Edited by Phineas J. Sparer. New York: International Universities Press, Inc., 1956. Pp. xviii, 629. *

10. LAWTON, M. POWELL, and PHILLIPS, ROSWELL W. "The Relationship Between Excessive Cigarette Smoking and Psychological Tension." *Am J Med Sci* 232:397–402 O '56. * (*PA* 32:4327)

11. LEIGH, DENIS, and MARLEY, EDWARD. "A Psychiatric Assessment of Adult Asthmatics: A Statistical Study." *J Psychosom Res* 1:128–36 Je '56. * (*PA* 31:6482)

12. BARD, MORTON, and WAXENBERG, SHELDON E. "Relationship of Cornell Medical Index Responses to Postsurgical Invalidism." *J Clin Psychol* 13:151–3 Ap '57. * (*PA* 32:2884)

13. SUCHMAN, EDWARD A.; PHILLIPS, BERNARD S.; and STREIB, GORDON F. "An Analysis of the Validity of Health Questionnaires." *Social Forces* 36:223–32 Mr '58. *

14. WHITE, COLIN; REZNIKOFF, MARVIN; and EWELL, JOHN W. "Usefulness of the Cornell Medical Index—Health Questionnaire in a College Health Department." *Mental Hyg* 42:94–105 Ja '58. * (*PA* 33:8425)

15. BRODMAN, KEEVE; VAN WOERKOM, ANDRIANUS J.; ERDMANN, ALBERT J., JR.; and GOLDSTEIN, LEO S. "Interpretations of Symptoms With a Data-Processing Machine." *Arch Intern Med* 103:776–82 My '59. *

16. ERDMANN, ALBERT J., JR. "Experiences in Use of Self-Administered Health Questionnaire." *A.M.A. Arch Indus Health* 19:339–44 Mr '59. *

17. GORDON, CECIL; EMERSON, A. R.; and SIMPSON, J. "The Cornell Medical Index Questionnaire as a Measure of Health in Socio-Medical Research." *J Gerontol* 14:305–8 Jl '59. * (*PA* 34:4151)

18. LAWTON, M. POWELL. "The Screening Value of the Cornell Medical Index." *J Consult Psychol* 23:352–6 Ag '59. * (*PA* 34:4344)

19. ARNHOFF, F. N.; FREEMAN, L. C.; and PARLAGRECO, M. L. "Projected Symptoms of Old Age and Present Personal Assessment." *J General Psychol* 62:37–41 Ja '60. * (*PA* 34:7503)

20. CROOG, SYDNEY H. "Ethnic Origins, Educational Level, and Responses to a Health Questionnaire." *Hum Org* 20:65–9 su '61. *

21. MATARAZZO, RUTH G. "The Relationship Between Medical and Psychiatric Symptomatology in Medical and Psychiatric Patients." Abstract. *Acta Psychologica* 19:863–4 '61. *

22. MATARAZZO, RUTH G.; MATARAZZO, JOSEPH D.; and SASLOW, GEORGE. "The Relationship Between Medical and Psychiatric Symptoms." *J Abn & Social Psychol* 62:55–61 Ja '61. * (*PA* 36:3HI55M)

23. RHUDICK, PAUL J., and DIBNER, ANDREW S. "Age, Personality, and Health Correlates of Death Concerns in Normal Aged Individuals." *J Gerontol* 16:44–9 Ja '61. * (*PA* 35:6241)

24. BROWN, A. C., and FRY, JOHN. "The Cornell Medical Index—Health Questionnaire in the Identification of Neurotic Patients in General Practice." *J Psychosom Res* 6:185–90 Jl–S '62. * (*PA* 37:8200)

25. CHANCE, NORMAN A. "Conceptual and Methodological Problems in Cross-Cultural Health Research." *Am J Pub Health* 52:410–7 Mr '62. *

26. HAMILTON, M.; POND, D. A.; and RYLE, A. "Relation of C.M.I. Responses to Some Social and Psychological Factors." *J Psychosom Res* 6:157–65 Jl–S '62. * (*PA* 37:8030)

27. RYLE, ANTHONY, and HAMILTON, MADGE. "Neurosis in Fifty Married Couples: Assessed From General Practice Records, Interviews by a Psychiatric Social Worker and the Use of the Cornell Medical Index." *J Mental Sci* 108:265–73 My '62. * (*PA* 37:3725)

28. SKLAR, MAURICE, and EDWARDS, ALLAN E. "Presbycusis: A Factor Analysis of Hearing and Psychological Characteristics of Men Over 65 Years Old." *J Auditory Res* 2:194–207 Jl '62. *

29. DESROCHES, HARRY F., and LARSEN, ERNEST R. "The Cornell Medical Index as a Screening Device in a VA Population." *J Clin Psychol* 19:416–20 O '63. *

30. IMBODEN, JOHN B.; CANTER, ARTHUR; and CLUFF, LEIGHTON. "Separation Experiences and Health Records in a Group of Normal Adults." *Psychosom Med* 25:433–40 S–O '63. * (*PA* 38:9101)

31. KARK, E.; ZALANY, A.; and WARD, B. "Health of Undergraduate Students on Entry to the Hebrew University in Jerusalem." *Israel Med J* 22:147–55 My–Je '63. *

32. KASSARJIAN, HAROLD H. "Success, Failure, and Personality." *Psychol Rep* 13:567–74 O '63. * (*PA* 38:8591)

33. KNOX, STAFFORD J. "An Evaluation of C.M.I. Responses in the Identification of Psychiatric Illness Associated With Mitral Surgery." *J Psychosom Res* 7:35–9 Jl '63. * (*PA* 38:6365)

34. KNOX, STAFFORD J. "Psychiatric Aspects of Mitral Valvotomy." *Brit J Psychiatry* 109:656–68 S '63. * (*PA* 38:6366)

35. KOLE, DELBERT M., and MATARAZZO, J. D. "Intellectual

and Personality Characteristics of Medical Students." Abstract. *J Med Ed* 38:138–9 F '63. *

36. MATARAZZO, RUTH G.; BRISTOW, DAVID; and REAUME, RALPH. "Medical Factors Relevant to Psychological Reactions in Mitral Valve Disease." *J Nerv & Mental Dis* 137:380–8 O '63. *

37. POND, D. A.; RYLE, A.; and HAMILTON, MADGE. "Marriage and Neurosis in a Working-Class Population." *Brit J Psychiatry* 109:592–8 S '63. * (*PA* 38:6540)

38. POND, D. A.; RYLE, A.; and HAMILTON, MADGE. "Social Factors and Neurosis in a Working-Class Population." *Brit J Psychiatry* 109:587–91 S '63. * (*PA* 38:6539)

39. RUTTER, MICHAEL. "Psychosocial Factors in the Short-term Prognosis of Physical Disease: 1, Peptic Ulcer." *J Psychosom Res* 7:45–60 Jl '63. * (*PA* 38:6550)

40. SCOTCH, NORMAN A., and GEIGER, H. JACK. "An Index of Symptom and Disease in Zulu Culture." *Hum Org* 22:304–11 w '63–64. *

41. DESROCHES, HARRY F.; KAIMAN, BERNARD D.; and BALLARD, H. TED. "Factors Influencing Admission of Symptoms in the Aged." *Newsl Res Psychol* 6:24–5 N '64. *

42. KADRI, Z. N. "Personality Evaluation as a Part of Medical History (Analysis of the Cornell Medical Index Forms of 213 Psychologically Distressed Students)." *Med J Malaya* 19:15–24 S '64. *

43. KREITMAN, NORMAN. "The Patient's Spouse." *Brit J Psychiatry* 110:159–73 Mr '64. *

44. MATARAZZO, JOSEPH D.; ALLEN, BERNADENE V.; SASLOW, GEORGE; and WIENS, ARTHUR N. "Characteristics of Successful Policemen and Firemen Applicants." *J Appl Psychol* 48:123–33 Ap '64. * (*PA* 39:6047)

45. NELSON, L. G.; TADLOCK, L. D.; DAWES, J. W.; HIPPLE, J. L.; and JETMALANI, N. B. "Screening for Emotionally Disturbed Students in an Indian Boarding School: Experience With the Cornell Medical Health Questionnaire." *Am J Psychiatry* 120:1155–9 Je '64. *

46. URBAN, WILLIAM H. "The Cornell Medical Index-Health Questionnaire: A Possible Screening Psychodiagnostic Device." *J Am Osteopath Assn* 63:963–72 Je '64. *

47. ABRAMSON, J. H.; TERESPOLSKY, L.; BROOK, J. G.; and KARK, S. L. "Cornell Medical Index as a Health Measure in Epidemiological Studies: A Test of the Validity of a Health Questionnaire." *Brit J Prev & Social Med* 19:103–10 Jl '65. *

48. KOLE, DELBERT M., and MATARAZZO, JOSEPH D. "Intellectual and Personality Characteristics of Two Classes of Medical Students." *J Med Ed* 40:1130–44 D '65. *

49. MONROE, ROBERT T.; WHISKIN, FREDERICK E.; BONACICH, PHILIP; and JEWELL, WALTER O., III. "The Cornell Medical Index Questionnaire as a Measure of Health in Older People." *J Gerontol* 20:18–22 Ja '65. *

50. PILOWSKI, I. "The Relation of Cornell Medical Index Responses to a Measure of Interview Behaviour." *J Psychosom Med* 8:481–5 Mr '65. *

51. SILVERSTONE, J. TREVOR, and SOLOMON, TERENCE. "Psychiatric and Somatic Factors in the Treatment of Obesity." *J Psychosom Res* 9:249–55 D '65. * (*PA* 40:7938)

52. ABRAMSON, J. H. "The Cornell Medical Index as an Epidemiological Tool." *Am J Pub Health* 56:287–98 F '66. *

53. ARTHUR, RANSOM J.; GUNDERSON, E. K. ERIC; and RICHARDSON, JAMES W. "The Cornell Medical Index as a Mental Health Survey Instrument in the Naval Population." *Mil Med* 131:605–10 Jl '66. *

54. CALDBECK-MEENAN, JOHN. "Screening University Students With the C.M.I." *J Psychosom Res* 9:331–7 My '66. * (*PA* 40:11503)

55. CLUFF, LEIGHTON E.; CANTER, ARTHUR; and IMBODEN, JOHN B. "Asian Influenza: Infection, Disease, and Psychological Factors." *Arch Intern Med* 117:159–63 F '66. *

56. DENNEY, DUANE; QUASS, ROBERT M.; RICH, DEAN C.; and THOMPSON, JUDITH K. "Psychiatric Patients on Medical Wards: 1, Prevalence of Illness and Recognition of Disorders by Staff Personnel." *Arch Gen Psychiatry* 14:530–5 My '66. *

57. KOLE, DELBERT M. "A Cross-Cultural Study of Medical-Psychiatric Symptoms." *J Health & Hum Behav* 7:162–74 f '66. *

58. NAKAMOTO, KIMIAKI. "The Cornell Medical Index in Patients With Concave RS-T Elevation in Mid- and Left Precordial Leads and New Questionnaires Specially Designed for Actual Neurosis." *Jap Circ J* 30:1031–5, 1037–44 Ag '66. *

59. PAYKEL, E. S. "Abnormal Personality and Thyrotoxicosis: A Follow-Up Study." *J Psychosom Med* 10:143–50 S '66. * (*PA* 41:769)

60. RAWNSLEY, K. "Congruence of Independent Measures of Psychiatric Morbidity." *J Psychosom Res* 10:84–93 Jl '66. * (*PA* 40:13316)

61. RICHMAN, A.; SLADE, H. C.; and GORDON, G. "Symptom Questionnaire Validity in Assessing the Need for Psychiatrists' Care." *Brit J Psychiatry* 112:549–55 Je '66. * (*PA* 40:10236)

62. RYLE, ANTHONY. "A Marital Patterns Test for Use in Psychiatric Research." *Brit J Psychiatry* 112:285–93 Mr '66. * (*PA* 40:7970)

63. SHEPHERD, MICHAEL; COOPER, BRIAN; BROWN, ALEXANDER, C.; and KALTON, GRAHAM. Chap. 10, "Distribution of Medical Complaints in the General Population," pp. 106–27. In their *Psychiatric Illness in General Practice*. London: Oxford University Press, 1966. Pp. xvii, 220. *

64. DESROCHES, HARRY F.; KAIMAN, BERNARD D.; and BALLARD, H. TED. "Factors Influencing Reporting Physical Symp-

toms by the Aged Patient." *Geriatrics* 22:169–75 S '67. * (*PA* 42:6024)

65. GIBSON, H. B.; HANSON, RUTH; and WEST, D. J. "A Questionnaire Measure of Neuroticism Using a Shortened Scale Derived From the Cornell Medical Index." *Brit J Social & Clin Psychol* 6:129–36 Je '67. * (*PA* 41:12829)

66. HART, M. SYLVIA. *The Relationship Between Reported Satisfaction With Body Image, Anxiety and the Occurrence of Physiological Deviations Among Healthy College Females.* Doctor's thesis, New York University (New York, N.Y.), 1967. (*DA* 28:4376A)

67. KUNCE, JOSEPH; RANKIN, L. S.; and CLEMENT, ELAINE. "Maze Performance and Personal, Social, and Economic Adjustment of Alaskan Natives." *J Social Psychol* 73:37–45 O '67. * (*PA* 42:745)

68. LOVELL, R. R. H., and VERGHESE, A. "Personality Traits Associated With Different Chest Pains After Infarction." *Brit Med J* 3:327–30 Ag 5 '67. *

69. MARKS, ISAAC M. "Components and Correlates of Psychiatric Questionnaires: Observations on the Cornell Medical Index, Eysenck Personality Inventory, and Tavistock Self-Assessment Inventory in Phobic Patients." *Brit J Med Psychol* 40:261–72 S '67. * (*PA* 42:12362)

70. THALLER, JACK L.; ROSEN, GERALD; and SALTZMAN, STUART. "Study of the Relationship of Frustration and Anxiety to Bruxism." *J Periodont* 38:193–7 My–Je '67. *

71. CLUM, GEORGE A.; PLAG, JOHN; and KOLE, DELBERT. "Changes in Self-Reported Symptomatology During Recruit Training." *Proc Ann Conv Am Psychol Assn* 76:645–6 '68. * (*PA* 43:1567, title only)

72. DAVIES, BRIAN; MOWBRAY, R. M.; and JENSEN, DAMIEN. "A Questionnaire Survey of Psychiatric Symptoms in Australian Medical Students." *Austral & NZ J Psychiatry* 2:46–53 Mr '68. *

73. KENYON, F. E. "Studies in Female Homosexuality—Psychological Test Results." *J Consult & Clin Psychol* 32:510–3 O '68. * (*PA* 43:1121)

74. MARKS, ISAAC. "Measurement of Personality and Attitude: Applications to Clinical Research." *Postgrad Med J* 44:277–85 Ag '68. *

75. PENDERGAST, MARY CARITA. *Assessment of a Psychological Screening Program for Candidates to a Religious Congregation of Women.* Doctor's thesis, Fordham University (New York, N.Y.), 1968. (*DA* 29:2572A)

76. REDING, GEORGES R.; ZEPELIN, HAROLD; and MONROE, LAWRENCE J. "Personality Study of Nocturnal Teeth-Grinders." *Percept & Motor Skills* 26:523–31 Ap '68. * (*PA* 42:12085)

77. WAHLER, H. J. "The Physical Symptoms Inventory: Measuring Levels of Somatic Complaining Behavior." *J Clin Psychol* 24:207–11 Ap '68. * (*PA* 42:12127)

NAME INDEX

Reznikoff, M.: 14
Rhudick, P. J.: 23
Rich, D. C.: 56
Richardson, J. W.: 53
Richman, A.: 61
Rosen, G.: 70
Rutter, M.: 39
Ryle, A.: 26–7, 37–8, 62
Saltzman, S.: 70
Saslow, G.: 22, 44
Scotch, N. A.: 40
Seymour, R. B.: 8
Shepherd, M.: 63
Silverstone, J. T.: 51
Simpson, J.: 17
Sklar, M.: 28
Slade, H. C.: 61
Solomon, T.: 51
Streib, G. F.: 13
Strough, L. C.: 8

Suchman, E. A.: 13
Tadlock, L. D.: 45
Terespolsky, L.: 47
Thaller, J. L.: 70
Thompson, J. K.: 56
Tolman, R.: 7
Urban, W. H.: 46
van Woerkom, A. J.: 15
Verghese, A.: 68
Wahler, H. J.: 77
Ward, B.: 31
Waxenberg, S. E.: 12
West, D. J.: 65
Whiskin, F. E.: 49
White, C.: 14
Wiens, A. N.: 44
Wolff, H. G.: 1–3, 5–7
Zalany, A.: 31
Zepelin, H.: 76

(test), and Measurement Research Division, Industrial Relations Center, University of Chicago (manual) the Center. *

For reviews by Allyn Miles Munger and Theodor F. Naumann, see 6:84.

REFERENCES

1. KERR, WILLARD A., and ABRAMS, PETER. "Halstead Brain Impairment, Boldness, Creativity and Group Intelligence Measures." *J Clin Psychol* 18:115–8 Ap '62. * (*PA* 38:8458)
2. BOYCE, RICHARD W., and PAXSON, R. C. "The Predictive Validity of Eleven Tests at One State College." *Ed & Psychol Meas* 25:1143–7 w '65. * (*PA* 40:3563)
3. ALLRED, RAYMOND COYE. *The Relationship Between the Interaction of Two Anxiety Variables and Creative Production.* Doctor's thesis, North Texas State University (Denton, Tex.), 1967. (*DA* 28:2063A)

[53A]

★Current and Past Psychopathology Scales. Psychiatric patients and nonpatients; 1966–68; CAPPS; the *Psychiatric Evaluation Form—Diagnostic Version (PEF–D*, see 217) and the *Psychiatric History Schedule* (PHS, see 365A) have been stapled together and given a new title (the 2 component parts are no longer available as separates); rating scale and optional interview guide for use in diagnosing mental illness if any; judgments based upon various sources of information (subject, informant, case records, nurse's reports, etc.); the PEF–D section deals with the patient's current functioning over the past month, the PHS with his past functioning from age 12 up to the past month; computerized psychiatric diagnosis (DIAGNO II) produces for each subject 1 of 46 possible diagnoses, using the official nomenclature of the American Psychiatric Association for 44 of the diagnoses; Form C50 ('68, 11 pages, scales only); Form C51 ('68, 25 pages, scales and interview schedule); no manual; typewritten data sheets; for validity data, see *1* below; separate answer sheets must be used; 25¢ per test; 10¢ per answer sheet; postage extra; specimen set free; fee for editing, coding, key punching, and verifying protocol, 25¢ per subject; computerized psychiatric diagnosis (see *1* below) is available; (15–30) minutes for scales only, (60–120) minutes for scales with interview guide; Robert L. Spitzer and Jean Endicott; Biometrics Research, New York State Psychiatric Institute. *

REFERENCE

1. SPITZER, ROBERT L., and ENDICOTT, JEAN. "DIAGNO II: Further Developments in a Computer Program for Psychiatric Diagnosis." *Am J Psychiatry* 125(7, sup): 12–21 Ja '69. *

[54]

DF Opinion Survey. Grades 12–16 and adults; 1954–56; DFOS; 10 scores: need for attention, liking for thinking, adventure vs. security, self-reliance vs. dependence, aesthetic appreciation, cultural conformity, need for freedom, realistic thinking, need for precision, need for diversion; 1 form ('54, 7 pages); manual ('56, 3 pages); profile ('55, 1 page); separate answer sheets (IBM 805) must be used; $5 per 25 tests; 6¢ per answer sheet; 5¢ per profile; $2.50 per set of either hand or machine scoring stencils; 35¢ per manual; 60¢ per specimen set (complete test not included); postage extra; (45) minutes; J. P. Guilford, Paul R. Christensen, and Nicholas A. Bond, Jr.; Sheridan Psychological Services, Inc. *

For reviews by Andrew R. Baggaley, John W. French, and Arthur W. Meadows, see 5:45.

REFERENCES

1. ZOBERI, HASEENUDDIN. *The Relation of Evaluative Attitudes to Traits of Introversion and Extraversion.* Doctor's thesis, University of Southern California (Los Angeles, Calif.), 1960. (*DA* 21:1655)
2. HETHERINGTON, ELISABETH LEONE. *Personality Characteristics of College Women Students Majoring in Physical Edu-*

[50]

Cornell Word Form 2. Adults; 1946–55; title on test is *C.W.F.–2*; civilian edition of *Cornell Word Form* designed for use in military psychiatric screening; psychosomatic and neuropsychiatric symptoms; 1 form ['55, 2 pages]; manual ('55, 8 pages, see *11* below); $5 per 100 tests, postpaid; specimen set free; [5–15] minutes; Arthur Weider, Bela Mittelmann, David Wechsler, and Harold Wolff; Cornell University Medical College. *

For a review by S. B. Sells, see 6:80 (1 reference); see also 5:44 (11 references).

REFERENCES

1–11. See 5:44.
12. See 6:80.
13. VONACHEN, HAROLD A.; MITTELMANN, BELA; KRONENBERG, MILTON H.; WEIDER, ARTHUR; and WOLFF, HAROLD G. "A Comprehensive Mental Hygiene Program at Caterpillar Tractor Co.: Improving Human Relationships in Industry." *Indus Med* 15:179–84 Mr '46. *
14. CHERASKIN, E.; RINGSDORF, W. M.; SETYAADMADJA, A. T. S. H.; and BARRETT, R. A. "Psychological Testing (Controlled Association Test) and Protein-Nicotinic Acid Consumption." *Psychiatric Q* 42:313–20 Ap '68. *

[51]

Cotswold Personality Assessment P.A. 1. Ages 11–16; 1960; manual subtitle is *A Study of Preferences and Values for Use in Schools and Clubs;* 6 scores: 3 preference scores (things, people, ideas) and 3 attitude scores (using one's hands, being with other people, talking about school); 1 form ['60, 8 pages]; manual ['60, 6 pages]; no norms for attitude scores; 10*d.* per test; 1*s.* 3*d.* per manual; postage extra; (40) minutes; C. M. Fleming; Robert Gibson & Sons (Glasgow), Ltd. *

For reviews by Ralph D. Dutch and G. A. V. Morgan, see 6:81 (1 reference).

[52]

*A Courtship Analysis, [Revised]. Adults; 1961–66; unscored counseling and teaching aid for analysis of the attitudes and behavior traits of each partner as seen by the other; 1 form ('66, 8 pages); combined counselors' and teachers' guide ('66, 8 pages) for this test and test 55; no data on reliability; no norms; $1.25 per 10 forms; 35¢ per specimen set; cash orders postpaid; (30–35) minutes; Gelolo McHugh; Family Life Publications, Inc. *

For a review by William R. Reevy of the original edition, consult 6:675.

[53]

Cree Questionnaire. Industrial employees; 1957–59; CQ; creativity and inventiveness; 1 form ('57, 8 pages); manual ('59, 17 pages); no data on reliability; norms for males only; $5 per 20 tests, postage extra; $2 per specimen set, postpaid; (15–20) minutes; Thelma Gwinn Thurstone (test), John Mellinger *cation With a Concentrated Study in Contemporary Dance.* Doctor's research study No. 1, Colorado State College (Greeley, Colo.), 1961. (*DA* 22:4217)

3. PLITTMAN, JACK C. *The Influence of the Control of Personal Set Upon Prediction by Factored Tests of Temperament and Interest.* Doctor's thesis, University of Southern California (Los Angeles, Calif.), 1963. (*DA* 24:3833)

4. GRANGAARD, GEORGE HOWARD. *Factors Predicting Success of Students in Elementary Teacher Education.* Doctor's thesis, Ball State Teachers College (Muncie, Ind.), 1964. (*DA* 26:3162)

5. KNAPP, ROBERT R. "An Empirical Investigation of the Concurrent and Observational Validity of an Ipsative Versus a Normative Measure of Six Interpersonal Values." *Ed & Psychol Meas* 24:65–73 sp '64. * (*PA* 39:1806)

6. KNAPP, ROBERT R. "Value and Personality Differences Between Offenders and Nonoffenders." *J Appl Psychol* 48:59–62 F '64. * (*PA* 38:8364)

7. ABOU-GHORRA, I. M. "Dynamic Predictors of Production of Creative Novel Solutions in Counseling Among College Students." *Proc Ann Conv Am Psychol Assn* 73:353–4 '65. * (*PA* 39:15850)

8. LEEP, ALBERT GENE. *Selected Pre-Service Measures as Predictors of First Year Teaching Performance of Elementary Teachers.* Doctor's thesis, Ball State Teachers College (Muncie, Ind.), 1965. (*DA* 26:3163)

9. GIBBONS, BILLIE DWANE. *A Study of the Relationships Between Factors Found in Cattell's Sixteen Personality Factor Questionnaire and Factors Found in the Guilford Personality Inventories.* Doctor's thesis, University of Southern California (Los Angeles, Calif.), 1966. (*DA* 26:7438)

10. BRADFIELD, L. EUGENE. "College Adjustment and Performance of Low-Income Freshman Males." *Personnel & Guid J* 46:123–9 O '67. *

11. SINGER, ESTELLE, and ROBY, THORNTON B. "Dimensions of Decision-Making Behavior." *Percept & Motor Skills* 24:571–95 Ap '67. * (*PA* 41:9933)

12. CATTELL, RAYMOND B., and GIBBONS, B. D. "Personality Factor Structure of the Combined Guilford and Cattell Personality Questionnaires." *J Personality & Social Psychol* 9:107–20 My '68. * (*PA* 42:10588)

[55]

A Dating Problems Checklist. High school and college; 1961; DPC; unscored counseling and teaching aid; experimental form; 1 form (8 pages); combined counselors' and teachers' guide (7 pages) for this test and test 52; no data on reliability; no norms; $1.25 per 10 forms; 35¢ per specimen set; cash orders postpaid; [25–30] minutes; Gelolo McHugh; Family Life Publications, Inc. *

For reviews by Clifford R. Adams and Robert A. Harper, consult 6:676.

[56]

★**The Demos D Scale: An Attitude Scale for the Identification of Dropouts.** Grades 7–12; 1965; DDS; also called *Demos Dropout Scale;* 5 attitude scores: teachers, education, peers and parents, school behavior, total; 1 form (4 pages); manual (11 pages plus test); $6.50 per 25 tests; $1.50 per manual; postpaid; (15–40) minutes; George D. Demos; Western Psychological Services. *

[57]

★**Depression Adjective Check Lists.** Grades 9–16 and adults; 1967; DACL; Forms A, B, C, D, E, F, G, (1 page); manual (16 pages); $3.50 per 25 tests; 75¢ per scoring stencil; $1.75 per specimen set; postage extra; (3–5 minutes); Bernard Lubin; Educational and Industrial Testing Service. *

REFERENCES

1. LUBIN, BERNARD. "Adjective Check Lists for Measurement of Depression." *Arch Gen Psychiatry* 12:57–62 Ja '65. * (*PA* 39:7779)

2. HOLMES, J. STEVEN. "Relation of Depression and Verbal Interaction in Group Therapy." *Psychol Rep* 20:1039–42 Je '67. * (*PA* 41:15387)

3. LUBIN, BERNARD; DUPRE, VLADIMIR A.; and LUBIN, ALICE W. "Comparability and Sensitivity of Set 2 (Lists E, F, and G) of the Depression Adjective Check Lists." *Psychol Rep* 20:756–8 Je '67. * (*PA* 41:12833)

4. MARONE, JOSEPH, and LUBIN, BERNARD. "Relationship Between Set 2 of the Depression Adjective Check Lists (DACL) and Zung Self-Rating Depression Scale (SDS)." *Psychol Rep* 22:333–4 F '68. * (*PA* 42:10596)

[58]

Detroit Adjustment Inventory. Ages 5–8, grades 3–6, 7–12; 1942–54, c1940–54; DAI; title on tests for grades 3–6 and 7–12 is *Telling What I Do;* 3 levels; record blanks (no date, 4 pages); no data on reliability; no norms; $4.50 per 35 tests; 50¢ per specimen set; $1.50 per set of remedial leaflets; postage extra; Harry J. Baker; Bobbs-Merrill Co., Inc. *

a) DELTA FORM. Ages 5–8; 1954; 1 form (6 pages); manual (9 pages).

b) GAMMA FORM. Grades 3–6; 1950–52; 1 form ('52, 6 pages); manual ('52, 8 pages); (20–50) minutes.

c) ALPHA FORM. Grades 7–12; 1942, c1940–42; 1 form ('42, c1940–42, 8 pages); manual ('42, 16 pages); (20–40) minutes.

For a review by Laurance F. Shaffer, see 5:46 (1 reference); for a review by Albert Ellis of the form for grades 7–12, see 3:31.

REFERENCES

1. See 5:46.

2. WOLF, S. JEAN. "Comparison of the Woodworth-Cady Personal Data Sheet and Baker's Telling What I Do Test." *J Genetic Psychol* 53:353–63 D '38. * (*PA* 13:2741)

[59]

Developmental Potential of Preschool Children. Handicapped children ages 2–6; 1958–62; DPPC; title on record form is *Educational Evaluation of Preschool Children;* subtitle on report form is *Inventory of Developmental Levels;* level and pattern of intellectual, sensory, and emotional functioning and "readiness to profit from an educational program"; individual; 1 form (a series of objects, toys, and test cards); manual ('58, 297 pages); directions for assembling and constructing test kit ('62, 8 pages); recording form ('62, 7 pages, reprinted from manual); report form ('62, 4 pages); test cards ('62, 6 cards); no data on reliability; $5.50 per set of test cards; $5 per set of 20 recording forms and 20 report forms; $2.25 per manual for assembling test kit; $8.75 per manual; postage extra; test materials, except for cards, must be assembled locally; (45–120) minutes; Else Haeussermann; Grune & Stratton, Inc. *

For a related book review not excerpted in this volume, consult the 6th (B230) MMY.

[60]

★**Devereux Adolescent Behavior (DAB) Rating Scale.** Normal and emotionally disturbed children ages 13–18; 1967; also called *DAB Scale;* problem behaviors; 12 factor scores (unethical behavior, defiant-resistive, domineering-sadistic, heterosexual interest, hyperactive expansive, poor emotional control, need approval and dependency, emotional distance, physical inferiority-timidity, schizoid withdrawal, bizarre speech and cognition, bizarre action), 3 cluster scores (inability to delay, paranoid thought, anxious self-blame), 11 item scores (persecution, plotting, bodily concern, external influences, compulsive acts, avoids competition, withdrawn, socialization, peer dominance, physical coordination, distraction); 1 form (7 pages); manual (55 pages); $3.75 per 25 scales; $1 per manual; $4.50 per 25 scales and manual; sample copy of scale free; postpaid; (15 minutes); George Spivack, Jules Spotts, and Peter E. Haimes; The Devereux Foundation Press. *

REFERENCE

1. SPIVACK, GEORGE, and SPOTTS, JULES. "Adolescent Symptomatology." *Am J Mental Def* 72:74–95 Jl '67. * (*PA* 41:15075)

[61]

★**Devereux Child Behavior Rating Scale.** Emotionally disturbed and mentally retarded children ages

8–12; 1966; also called *DCB Scale;* ratings by clinicians, child care workers, parents, house parents, or others who have had "intimate living arrangement with the child over a period of time"; 17 scores: distractibility, poor self care, pathological use of senses, emotional detachment, social isolation, poor coordination and body tonus, incontinence, messinesssloppiness, inadequate need for independence, unresponsiveness to stimulation, proneness to emotional upset, need for adult contact, anxious-fearful ideation, "impulse" ideation, inability to delay, social aggression, unethical behavior; 1 form (8 pages); manual (34 pages); $3.75 per 25 scales; $1 per manual; $4.50 per 25 scales and manual; sample copy of scale free; postpaid; (10–20) minutes; George Spivack and Jules Spotts; The Devereux Foundation Press. *

REFERENCES

1. SPIVACK, GEORGE, and LEVINE, MURRAY. "The Devereux Child Behavior Rating Scales: A Study of Symptom Behaviors in Latency Age Atypical Children." *Am J Mental Def* 68:700–17 My '64. * (PA 39:1707)
2. SPIVACK, GEORGE, and SPOTTS, JULES. "The Devereux Child Behavior Scale: Symptom Behaviors in Latency Age Children." *Am J Mental Def* 69:839–53 My '65. * (PA 39:12758)
3. NALVEN, FREDRIC B. "Relationship Between Digit Span and Distractibility Ratings in Emotionally Disturbed Children." *J Clin Psychol* 23:466–7 O '67. * (PA 42:2731)

[62]

★**Devereux Elementary School Behavior Rating Scale.** Grades kgn–6; 1966–67; DESB; problem behaviors; 11 factor scores (classroom disturbance, impatience, disrespect-defiance, external blame, achievement anxiety, external reliance, comprehension, inattentive-withdrawn, irrelevant-responsiveness, creative initiative, need for closeness to the teacher), 3 item scores (unable to change, quits easily, slow work); 1 form ('67, 5 pages); manual ('67, 36 pages); $3.75 per 25 scales; $1 per manual; $4.50 per 25 scales and manual; sample copy of scale free; postpaid; (10) minutes; George Spivack and Marshall Swift; The Devereux Foundation Press. *

REFERENCES

1. SPIVACK, GEORGE, and SWIFT, MARSHALL S. "The Devereux Elementary School Behavior Rating Scales: A Study of the Nature and Organization of Achievement Related Disturbed Classroom Behavior." *J Spec Ed* 1:71–90 f '66. *
2. SWIFT, MARSHALL S., and SPIVACK, GEORGE. "The Assessment of Achievement-Related Classroom Behavior." *J Spec Ed* 2:137–53 w '68. * (PA 42:14468)

[63]

★**The Differential Value Profile.** College; 1963–67; DVP; 6 scores: aesthetic, humanitarian, intellectual, material, power, religious; Form A ('63, 4 pages); manual ('67, 35 pages); profile ['63, 1 page]; vocabulary sheet ['65, 1 page]; separate answer sheets must be used; 15¢ per test; 5¢ per answer sheet; 5¢ per profile; $1 per set of scoring stencils; $4 per manual; $5 per specimen set; postage extra; vocabulary sheet free; scoring service, 45¢ per test; (30–45) minutes; Walter L. Thomas; Educational Service Co. *

REFERENCES

1. BITTNER, JOHN R. "Student Value Profiles of State and Church-Related Colleges." *Col Stud Survey* 2:1–4 sp '68. * (PA 42:15989)
2. THOMAS, WALTER L. *The Initial Development of the Differential Value Profile.* Doctor's thesis, University of Tulsa (Tulsa, Okla.), 1968.

[64]

Diplomacy Test of Empathy. Business and industry; 1957–60; DTE; revision of *Primary Empathic Abilities* ('57); title on test is *Diplomacy Test of Empathic Ability;* 1 form ('60, 4 pages); manual

('60, 4 pages); separate answer sheets must be used; $5 per 25 tests; $2 per 25 answer sheets; $1 per specimen set (must be purchased to obtain manual and key); cash orders postpaid; (20–25) minutes; Willard A. Kerr; Psychometric Affiliates. *

For reviews by Arthur H. Brayfield and Richard S. Hatch, see 6:85 (1 reference); for a review by Robert L. Thorndike of the earlier test, see 5:99.

REFERENCES

1. See 6:85.
2. Ross, PAUL F., and DUNFIELD, NEIL M. "Selecting Salesmen for an Oil Company." *Personnel Psychol* 17:75–84 sp '64. *
3. KELLEHER, EDWARD J.; KERR, WILLARD A.; and MELVILLE, NORBERT T. "The Prediction of Subprofessional Nursing Success." *Personnel Psychol* 21:379–88 au '68. *

[65]

Dynamic Personality Inventory. Ages 15 or 17 and over with IQ's of 80 and over; 1956–61; DPI; for research and experimental use only (not so labeled in distributor's catalog); 33 scores: hypocrisy, passivity, seclusion-introspection, orality, oral aggression, oral dependence, emotional independence, verbal aggression, impulsiveness, unconventionality, hoarding behavior, attention to details, conservatism, submissiveness, anal sadism, insularity, phallic symbol interest, narcissism, exhibitionism, active Icarus complex, passive Icarus complex, sensuality, Icarian exploits, sexuality, tactile impression enjoyment, creative interests, masculine sexual identification, feminine sexual identification, social role seeking, social activity interest, need to give affection, ego defense persistence, initiative; 1 form ('56, 7 pages); also available, in abbreviated form and without scores for orality, phallic symbol interest, and sexuality, under the title *Likes and Interests Test* ('56, 6 pages) for use with apprentices and employee applicants ages 15 and over; mimeographed temporary manual ('61, 8 pages); the interpretive manual which the temporary manual says will be available "shortly" is not yet available as of spring 1969; DPI score-norms sheets ('56, 6 sheets, separate sheets for male students, female students, general population males, general population females, male neurotics, female neurotics); LIT score-norms sheets ('56, 2 sheets, separate sheets for male apprentices, female technical college students); separate answer sheets must be used; 15s. per 25 tests of either title; 8s. per 25 answer sheets; 83s. per set of DPI scoring keys; 41s. per set of LIT scoring keys; 30s. per 100 score-norms sheets for any one population; 4s. per manual; 8s. per specimen set; postage extra; (40) minutes; T. G. Grygier; distributed by National Foundation for Educational Research in England and Wales. *

For a review by S. B. Sells, see 6:86 (7 references).

REFERENCES

1–7. See 6:86.
8. BROWN, D. G., and YOUNG, A. J. "The Effect of Extraversion on Susceptibility to Disease: A Validatory Study on Contact Dermatitis." *J Psychosom Res* 8:421–9 Mr '65. *
9. GORDON, CAROL M. "Some Effects of Information, Situation, and Personality on Decision Making in a Clinical Setting." *J Consult Psychol* 30:219–24 Je '66. * (PA 40:9000)
10. HUBBARD, BETTY LEE. *An Attempt to Identify, by Psychometric and Peer Rating Techniques, Three Oral Character Types Described in Psychoanalytic Literature.* Doctor's thesis, University of North Carolina (Chapel Hill, N.C.), 1967. (DA 28:4757B)
11. STRINGER, PETER. "Masculinity-Femininity as a Possible Factor Underlying the Personality Responses of Male and Female Art Students." *Brit J Social & Clin Psychol* 6:186–94 S '67. * (PA 42: 759)
12. KLINE, PAUL. "The Validity of the Dynamic Personality Inventory." *Brit J Med Psychol* 41:307–13 S '68. * (PA 43:136)
13. SPRINGER, PETER, and TYSON, MOYA. "University Selection Interviewers' Ratings Related to Interviewee Self-Image." *Occup Psychol* 42:49–60 Ja '68. *

[66]

★Early School Personality Questionnaire. Ages 6–8; 1966, c1963–66; ESPQ; 13 first order factor scores (reserved vs. outgoing, less intelligent vs. more intelligent, affected by feelings vs. emotionally stable, phlegmatic vs. excitable, obedient vs. assertive, sober vs. happy-go-lucky, expedient vs. conscientious, shy vs. venturesome, self-reliant vs. dependent, vigorous vs. doubting, forthright vs. shrewd, placid vs. apprehensive, relaxed vs. tense), 2 second-order factor scores (extraversion, anxiety); orally administered; Form A, Parts A1 and A2 ('66, 4 pages, text for questions orally presented); answer booklets for either part ('66, 4 pages); profile ('66, 1 page); guidebook ('66, 19 pages); no data on reliability and validity; no instructions for computing second order factor scores; 25¢ per test; $5 per 25 sets of answer booklets; $2.50 per set of keys; $2 per 50 profiles; 50¢ per guidebook; tape available for administration; $2.35 per specimen set; postage extra; (60–100) minutes in 2 sessions; Richard W. Coan and Raymond B. Cattell; Institute for Personality and Ability Testing. *

REFERENCES

1. CATTELL, RAYMOND B., and COAN, RICHARD W. "Personality Factors in Middle Childhood as Revealed in Parents' Ratings." *Child Develop* 28:439–58 D '57. *
2. CATTELL, RAYMOND B., and COAN, RICHARD W. "Personality Dimensions in the Questionnaire Responses of Six- and Seven-Year-Olds." *Brit J Ed Psychol* 28:232–42 N '58. * (*PA* 34:2750)
3. CATTELL, RAYMOND B., and COAN, RICHARD W. "Objective-Test Assessment of the Primary Personality Dimensions in Middle Childhood." *Brit J Psychol* 50:235–52 Ag '59. * (*PA* 34:4056)
4. CATTELL, RAYMOND B., and PETERSON, DONALD R. "Personality Structure in Four and Five Year Olds in Terms of Objective Tests." *J Clin Psychol* 15:355–69 O '59. * (*PA* 36:1FF55C)
5. COAN, RICHARD W., and CATTELL, RAYMOND B. "The Development of the Early School Personality Questionnaire." *J Exp Ed* 28:143–52 D '59. * (*PA* 34:7374)
6. BAKER, HERBERT LASKEY. *A Comparison of the Personality Characteristics of Selected Third Grade Pupils From Three Socio-Economic Levels.* Doctor's thesis, University of Toledo (Toledo, Ohio), 1966. (*DA* 27:2383A)
7. KOSIER, KENNETH P., and DEVAULT, M. VERE. "Effects of Teacher Personality on Pupil Personality." *Psychol Sch* 4:40–4 Ja '67. * (*PA* 41:4978)

[67]

Edwards Personal Preference Schedule. College and adults; 1953–59; EPPS; 15 scores: achievement, deference, order, exhibition, autonomy, affiliation, intraception, succorance, dominance, abasement, nurturance, change, endurance, heterosexuality, aggression; 1 form ('54, 8 pages); revised manual ('59, 25 pages); separate answer sheets (Digitek, hand scoring, IBM 805 and 1230, NCS) must be used; no instructions on the use of specific answer sheets; $4 per 25 tests; $2.90 per 50 Digitek or IBM 1230 answer sheets; $2.70 per 50 hand scoring answer sheets; $2.60 per 50 IBM 805 answer sheets; $3.25 per 50 NCS answer sheets; set of manual and stencils: 60¢ with hand scoring stencil, $3 with set of IBM 805 hand scoring stencils, $4.75 with set of IBM 805 machine scoring stencils; Digitek and IBM 1230 scoring stencils not available; 75¢ per specimen set; postpaid; Digitek scoring service (available only from Optical Scanning Corporation), 5¢ per test; NCS scoring service (available only from National Computer Systems), 40¢ to $1.20 per test; (40–55) minutes; Allen L. Edwards; Psychological Corporation. *

For reviews by John A. Radcliffe and Lawrence J. Stricker, see 6:87 (284 references, 1 excerpt); for reviews by Frank Barron, Åke Bjerstedt, and Donald W. Fiske, see 5:47 (50 references, 2 excerpts).

REFERENCES

1–50. See 5:47.
51–326. See 6:87.

327. BOURESTOM, NORMAN CHARLES, JR. *The Interrelationships Between Two Personality Inventories and Other Behavioral Measures.* Doctor's thesis, University of Houston (Houston, Tex.), 1956. (*DA* 16:2208)
328. MAINORD, FLORENCE RITA. *Parental Attitudes in Schizophrenia.* Doctor's thesis, University of Washington (Seattle, Wash.), 1956. (*DA* 17:896)
329. NEWMAN, MICHAEL. *Personality Differences Between Volunteers and Non-Volunteers for Psychological Investigations: Self-Actualization of Volunteers and Non-Volunteers for Researches in Personality and Perception.* Doctor's thesis, New York University (New York, N.Y.), 1956. (*DA* 17:684)
330. DIENER, CHARLES L. *A Comparison of Over-Achieving and Under-Achieving Students at the University of Arkansas.* Doctor's thesis, University of Arkansas (Fayetteville, Ark.), 1957. (*DA* 17:1692)
331. STAFFORD, CURTIS RONALD. *Predicting Job Satisfaction of First Year Teachers.* Doctor's thesis, University of Illinois (Urbana, Ill.), 1957. (*DA* 18:951)
332. CADITZ, SYLVAN BERNARD. *The Effect of a Training School Experience on Delinquent Boys as Measured by Objective Personality Tests.* Doctor's thesis, University of Washington (Seattle, Wash.), 1958. (*DA* 19:1812)
333. CANNON, DEORE J. *The Concepts of Interest and Need Held by Two Occupational Groups.* Doctor's thesis, University of Texas (Austin, Tex.), 1958. (*DA* 19:2283)
334. ENDLER, NORMAN SOLOMON. *Conformity Analyzed and Related to Personality.* Doctor's thesis, University of Illinois (Urbana, Ill.), 1958. (*DA* 19:1114)
335. KIRMAN, WILLIAM JOSEPH. *The Relationship of Learning, With and Without Awareness, to Personality Needs.* Doctor's thesis, Columbia University (New York, N.Y.), 1958. (*DA* 19:362)
336. LANG, GERHARD. *Motives in Selecting Elementary and Secondary School Teaching.* Doctor's thesis, Columbia University (New York, N.Y.), 1958. (*DA* 18:1724)
337. LEVIN, JACOB JOSEPH. *Correlates of Intraception.* Doctor's thesis, Syracuse University (Syracuse, N.Y.), 1958. (*DA* 20:589)
338. SCHATZ, LOUIS. *An Evaluation of the Eysenck R and T Scales and Their Relation to Personality.* Doctor's thesis, American University (Washington, D.C.), 1958. (*DA* 19:589)
339. SHELDEN, MIRIAM A. *A Study of Certain Factors in Relation to Selection and Non-Selection of Sorority Members.* Doctor's thesis, New York University (New York, N.Y.), 1958. (*DA* 19:3197)
340. CARINO, OLIVA PALAFOX. *The Relationship Between Need Patterns of Student Nurses and Satisfaction With Nursing Education.* Doctor's thesis, University of Nebraska (Lincoln, Neb.), 1959. (*DA* 20:201)
341. HELLER, KENNETH. *Dependency Changes in Psychotherapy as a Function of the Discrepancy Between Conscious Self-Description and Projective Test Performance.* Doctor's thesis, Pennsylvania State University (University Park, Pa.), 1959. (*DA* 20:3378)
342. KEISLAR, EVAN R. "The Generalization of Prestige Among Adolescent Boys." *Calif Ed Res* 10:153–6 S '59. * (*PA* 34:7568)
343. MARSHALL, SIMONE VERNIERE. *Personality Correlates of Peptic Ulcer Patients.* Doctor's thesis, Columbia University (New York, N.Y.), 1959. (*DA* 20:759)
344. SAUTÉ, LOIS. *Judge Personality and Favorability Biases in Interpersonal Predictions.* Doctor's thesis, University of North Carolina (Chapel Hill, N.C.), 1959. (*DA* 20:3843)
345. SHIMABUKURO, SHINKICHI. *Personal Aggression and Other Correlates of the Attitude Toward the Use of Military Force in International Relations.* Doctor's thesis, Pennsylvania State University (University Park, Pa.), 1959. (*DA* 20:1645)
346. TREESH, EDWARD ORON. *Manifest Needs and Values as Related to Vocational Development.* Doctor's thesis, Purdue University (Lafayette, Ind.), 1959. (*DA* 20:370)
347. VAN DE CASTLE, ROBERT LEON. *The Relationship of Anxiety and Repression to Perceptual Predominance of Threatening Stimuli.* Doctor's thesis, University of North Carolina (Chapel Hill, N.C.), 1959. (*DA* 20:3847)
348. ABRAHAM, HANS HENRY LEO. *The Suggestible Personality: A Psychological Investigation of Susceptibility to Persuasion.* Doctor's thesis, Columbia University (New York, N.Y.), 1960. (*DA* 21:2810)
349. BABLADELIS, GEORGIA. *A Study of the Effects of a Personality Variable in Verbal Conditioning.* Doctor's thesis, University of Colorado (Boulder, Colo.), 1960. (*DA* 21:3160)
350. SCOTT, MARY HUGHIE. *An Analytic Study of Certain Motives and Needs of Prospective Women Teachers.* Doctor's thesis, University of Georgia (Athens, Ga.), 1960. (*DA* 21:2211)
351. SLUSSER, GERALD HERBERT. *Some Personality Correlates of Religious Orientation.* Doctor's thesis, University of Texas (Austin, Tex.), 1960. (*DA* 21:1654)
352. SOLDWEDEL, BETTE JEAN. *Attitudes Toward Discipline in College.* Doctor's thesis, New York University (New York, N.Y.), 1960. (*DA* 21:1114)
353. WEAVER, CHRISTINE PEARL. *A Study of Personality Characteristics of Obese Women of Two Age Groups as Compared With Paired Controls of Normal Weight.* Doctor's thesis, State University of Iowa (Iowa City, Iowa), 1960. (*DA* 21:1658)
354. WITHROW, CARLOS QUENTIN. *A Study of the Possible*

Correlation Between Theological Orientations and Certain Variables of Personality. Doctor's thesis, University of Southern California (Los Angeles, Calif.), 1960. (*DA* 21:1651)

355. WOO-SAM, JAMES MCDOWELL. *A Study of Selected Factors Related to Teaching Effectiveness of Mathematics Instructors at the College Level.* Doctor's thesis, Purdue University (Lafayette, Ind.), 1960. (*DA* 21:237)

356. DIPBOYE, W. J., and ANDERSON, W. F. "Occupational Stereotypes and Manifest Needs of High School Students." *J Counsel Psychol* 8:296–304 w '61. * (*PA* 37:3826)

357. DUNLAP, NAOMI GIBSON. *Alcoholism in Women: Some Antecedents and Correlates of Remission in Middle-Class Members of Alcoholics Anonymous.* Doctor's thesis, University of Texas (Austin, Tex.), 1961. (*DA* 22:1904)

358. MARTUCCI, LEO GEORGE. *Some Correlates of Responses to a Standard Interview Among High School Boys.* Doctor's thesis, Rutgers University (New Brunswick, N.J.), 1961. (*DA* 22:3266)

359. NEWMAN, WILLIAM HENRY. *Factors Affecting Leadership.* Doctor's thesis, Stanford University (Stanford, Calif.), 1961. (*DA* 21:3329)

360. PFEIFFER, MARIE STOLL. *Social and Psychological Variables Associated With Early College Marriages.* Doctor's thesis, Ohio State University (Columbus, Ohio), 1961. (*DA* 22:2381)

361. RISHEL, DARRELL FRED. *The Development and Validation of Instruments and Techniques for the Selective Admission of Applicants for Graduate Studies in Counselor Education.* Doctor's thesis, Pennsylvania State University (University Park, Pa.), 1961. (*DA* 22:2271)

362. BROOK, RUPERT RAMSAY. *Personality Correlates Associated With Differential Success of Affiliation With Alcoholics Anonymous.* Doctor's thesis, University of Colorado (Boulder, Colo.), 1962. (*DA* 23:1778)

363. CARR, JAMES GILES. *A Comparative Study of Aspirants to Secondary School Teacher Education.* Doctor's thesis, University of Florida (Gainesville, Fla.), 1962. (*DA* 24:619)

364. COVINGTON, JAMES DONALD. *A Study of Selected Personal Characteristics of Entering College Students.* Doctor's thesis, Auburn University (Auburn, Ala.), 1962. (*DA* 23:3197)

365. DIENER, ROBERT GEORGE. *The Prediction of Dependent Behavior and Dependency Related Anxiety From Psychological Tests.* Doctor's thesis, University of Colorado (Boulder, Colo.), 1962. (*DA* 23:3971)

366. GRANT, CHARLES O. *A Study of Personality Characteristics of Clients Self-Referred and Other-Referred to a Student Counseling Center.* Doctor's thesis, University of Buffalo (Buffalo, N.Y.), 1962. (*DA* 23:2204)

367. HOLT, FRED DUARD. *A Study of Change in Certain Personality Variables of Counselors in Training.* Doctor's thesis, University of Florida (Gainesville, Fla.), 1962. (*DA* 23:3775)

368. KOENIGSBERG, LEWIS ARNOLD. *An Investigation of Background Factors and Selected Personality Correlates of Achievement Motivation.* Doctor's thesis, Syracuse University (Syracuse, N.Y.), 1962. (*DA* 23:1067)

369. MARONEY, KENNETH AUSTIN. *Effectiveness of Short-Term Group Guidance With a Group of Transfer Students Admitted on Academic Probation.* Doctor's thesis, North Texas State University (Denton, Tex.), 1962. (*DA* 23:3238)

370. MASIH, LALIT KUMAR. *Career Saliency and Its Relation to Certain Personality and Environmental Variables.* Doctor's thesis, Syracuse University (Syracuse, N.Y.), 1962. (*DA* 24:181)

371. POOR, FREDERICK ALBERT. *The Similarities and Differences in the Successful and Unsuccessful Second-Semester Accounting Students at Northern Illinois University.* Doctor's thesis, University of Minnesota (Minneapolis, Minn.), 1962. (*DA* 23:2381)

372. REELING, GLENN EUGENE. *A Study of Undergraduate Student Characteristics as an Aid in Early Identification of Potential Counselors.* Doctor's thesis, Indiana University (Bloomington, Ind.), 1962. (*DA* 23:3784)

373. REITER, HENRY H. "A Note on the Inconsistency of Measures of Need Achievement. *J Psychol Studies* 13:170–1 S '62. *

374. ROBERTS, JOHN EDWARD. *An Investigation of Selected Personality Variables Among Elementary, Secondary, and Special Education Teachers.* Doctor's thesis, University of Denver (Denver, Colo.), 1962. (*DA* 23:2811)

375. SCHNITZEN, JOSEPH PETER. *Assessment of Certain Personality Potentials in Relation to Student Teaching.* Doctor's thesis, University of Minnesota (Minneapolis, Minn.), 1962. (*DA* 23:2426)

376. STERN, LUCETTA SMITH. *Ego Strength and Beliefs About the Cause of Illness.* Doctor's thesis, Columbia University (New York, N.Y.), 1962. (*DA* 23:1775)

377. SWANSON, PAUL REGINALD. *Some Effects of Clinical Pastoral Education on a Group of Theological Students and Pastors.* Doctor's thesis, Boston University (Boston, Mass.), 1962. (*DA* 23:1812)

378. TURGUT, MEHMET FUAT. *A Comparison Between Two Forced-Choice Personality Test Formats.* Doctor's thesis, Columbia University (New York, N.Y.), 1962. (*DA* 24:2118)

379. CARMICHAEL, JACK JOE. *Some Relationships of Denominational Affiliation to Selected Personal Characteristics of Male College Students.* Doctor's thesis, Ohio University (Athens, Ohio), 1963. (*DA* 23:2787)

380. COOK, ROBERT LEE. *The Relationship of Selected Factors to the Success of Student Teachers at the University of Arizona.* Doctor's thesis, University of Arizona (Tucson, Ariz.), 1963. (*DA* 24:3218)

381. CROOTOF, CHARLES. *Bright Underachievers' Acceptance of Self and Their Need for Achievement. A Study of Three Groups of High School Boys—Bright Achievers, Normal Achievers, and Bright Underachievers—to Determine the Relationship of Results Elicited From Them by Bills's Index of Adjustment and Values, Edwards's Personal Preference Schedule and McClelland's Picture Story Test for Measuring Achievement Motivation.* Doctor's thesis, New York University (New York, N.Y.), 1963. (*DA* 24:1695)

382. DANI, SHANKAR KRISHNA. *Level of Aspiration as a Function of Need for Achievement and Fear of Failure.* Doctor's thesis, State University of New York at Buffalo (Buffalo, N.Y.), 1963. (*DA* 24:4303)

383. FLINN, DON E.; HARTMAN, BRYCE O.; POWELL, DOUGLAS H.; and MCKENZIE, RICHARD E. "Psychiatric and Psychologic Evaluation," pp. 199–230. In *Aeromedical Evaluation for Space Pilots.* Edited by Lawrence E. Lamb. Brooks Air Force Base, Tex.: USAF School of Aerospace Medicine, July 1963. Pp. viii, 276. * (*PA* 38:4728)

384. GILBERT, ALGIE STEPHEN. *Relationships Between Patient Motivation for Physical Rehabilitation and Subscales on The Edwards Personal Preference Schedule.* Doctor's thesis, North Texas State University (Denton, Tex.), 1963. (*DA* 25:1319)

385. GOLDBERG, LEWIS R. *Test-Retest Item Statistics for the Edwards Personal Preference Schedule.* ORI Research Monograph, Vol. 3, No. 3. Eugene, Ore.: Oregon Research Institute, August 1963. Pp. 125. *

386. GUMESON, GEORGE GERALD. *A Comparative Analysis of the Needs, Values, Cognitive Abilities, and Other Personality Characteristics of High and Low Creative Junior College Students.* Doctor's thesis, University of Denver (Denver, Colo.), 1963. (*DA* 24:5527)

387. HILLIARD, ASA GRANT, III. *An Exploratory Study of Relationships Between Student Teacher Personality, Ability, Lower Division Grades, and the Student Teacher's Evaluation of Pupils.* Doctor's thesis, University of Denver (Denver, Colo.), 1963. (*DA* 24:5193)

388. HOFFMAN, STANLEY. *Occupational Preferences and Personality: A Study of Personality Needs Associated With Occupational Aspiration Group and Level.* Doctor's thesis, Yeshiva University (New York, N.Y.), 1963. (*DA* 25:295)

389. HOGAN, EARL EUGENE. *A Study of Differences in the Perception of Elementary Teacher Personality Structure.* Doctor's thesis, Michigan State University (East Lansing, Mich.), 1963. (*DA* 25:663)

390. JENNINGS, CHARLES L. "Psychologic Test Profiles of Special Groups." *Proc Ann Conf Air Force Clin Psychologists* 4:105–16 '63. *

391. JESSOT, RICHARD. "On Studying Autonomy: Without Deference." *Psychol Rep* 12:132–4 F '63. * (*PA* 38:2628)

392. LIPETZ, MILTON E. "Further Comments on the Prediction of Autonomy Behavior From the EPPS n Autonomy Scale." *Psychol Rep* 12:737–8 Je '63. * (*PA* 38:6091)

393. MESSMAN, WARREN BROWN. *Interest Patterns of Freshmen Industrial Arts Majors in Comparison With Personality Traits.* Doctor's research study No. 1, Colorado State College (Greeley, Colo.), 1963. (*DA* 25:314)

394. OSBORNE, DUNCAN. *The Relationship of Personality Factors to Academic Achievement in College.* Doctor's thesis, Columbia University (New York, N.Y.), 1963. (*DA* 24:3839)

395. PETERS, J.; BENJAMIN, F. B.; HELVEY, W. M.; and ALBRIGHT, G. A. "Study of Sensory Deprivation, Pain and Personality Relationships for Space Travel." *Aerospace Med* 34:830–7 S '63. *

396. POLAND, WILLIS DEAN. *An Exploration of the Relationships Between Self-Estimated and Measured Personality Characteristics in the Open and Closed Mind.* Doctor's thesis, Ohio State University (Columbus, Ohio), 1963. (*DA* 24:4804)

397. PRINCE, ALFRED JAMES, and BAGGALEY, ANDREW R. "Personality Variables and the Ideal Mate." *Family Life Coordinator* 12:93–6 Jl–O '63. *

398. REED, KENNETH EUGENE. *Psychological Testing in Supervision of Clinical Pastoral Training.* Doctor's thesis, Boston University (Boston, Mass.), 1963. (*DA* 24:2595)

399. SCHULZ, ESTHER FERNE DICKISON. *Desirable Personality Patterns for the Nursing Student: A Longitudinal, Comparative Study.* Doctor's thesis, Indiana University (Bloomington, Ind.), 1963. (*DA* 24:2791)

400. WARD, WILLIAM D. "Persuasibility as Related to Need Autonomy." *Psychol Rep* 13:357–8 O '63. * (*PA* 38:8509)

401. WEBER, ROBERT GENE. *Leadership Characteristics of Public School Business Administrators.* Doctor's research study No. 1. Colorado State College (Greeley, Colo.), 1963. (*DA* 25:259)

402. WILLIAMSON, HELEN M.; EDMONSTON, WILLIAM E., JR.; and STERN, JOHN A. "Use of the EPPS for Identifying Personal Role Attributes Desirable in Nursing." *J Health & Hum Behav* 4:266–75 w '63. * (*PA* 38:8537)

403. ASA, LELAND FORREST. *An Analysis of the Influence of Personality Variables as Measured by the Edwards Personal Preference Schedule on Guidance Students' Use of Counseling Leads.* Doctor's thesis, University of Wyoming (Laramie, Wyo.), 1964.

404. BACHMAN, JERALD G. "Prediction of Academic Achieve-

ment Using the Edwards Need Achievement Scale." *J Appl Psychol* 48:16–9 F '64. * (*PA* 38:9276)

405. BAKKER, CORNELIS B., and DIGHTMAN, CAMERON R. "Psychological Factors in Fertility Control." *Fertil & Steril* 15:559–67 S–O '64. *

406. BARBER, THEODORE XENOPHON, and CALVERLEY, DAVID SMITH. "Hypnotizability, Suggestibility, and Personality: 1, Two Studies With the Edwards Personal Preference Schedule, the Jourard Self-Disclosure Scale, and the Marlowe-Crowne Social Desirability Scale." *J Psychol* 58:215–22 Jl '64. *

407. BECKER, GILBERT. "The Complementary-Needs Hypothesis, Authoritarianism, Dominance, and Other Edwards Personal Preference Schedule Scores." *J Personality* 32:45–56 Mr '64. * (*PA* 39:5166)

408. BENDIG, A. W. "Factor Analytic Scales of Need Achievement." *J General Psychol* 70:59–67 Ja '64. * (*PA* 38:10111)

409. BLAZER, JOHN A. "The Male Signature as Related to Personality Characteristics." *Psychol* 1:14–8 N '64. * (*PA* 39:5189)

410. BLEDSOE, JOSEPH C., and MORRIS, KENNETH T. "A Comparative Study of Selected Needs, Values, and Motives of Science and Non-Science Teachers." *J Res Sci Teach* 2(2):123–31 '64. *

411. BRAZZIEL, WILLIAM F. "Correlates of Southern Negro Personality." *J Social Issues* 20:45–53 Ap '64. * (*PA* 39:4730)

412. CALIFF, JAMES IRVIN. *An Investigation of the Relationships Among the Ratings Given by Cooperating Teachers to Elementary and Secondary Student Teachers and Personality Scores of Student Teachers.* Doctor's thesis, University of Mississippi (University, Miss.), 1964. (*DA* 26:1494)

413. DOTY, CAROL N., and HOEFLIN, RUTH M. "A Descriptive Study of Thirty-Five Unmarried Graduate Women." *J Marriage & Family* 26:91–4 F '64. *

414. DOVE, VIRGINIA. *An Investigation Into Relationships Between Three Aspects of Achievement Motivation and Academic Achievement.* Doctor's thesis, University of Utah (Salt Lake City, Utah), 1964. (*DA* 25:1737)

415. DYE, HERSHEL ALLAN. *A Study of the Influence of Social Position, Ability and Personal Preferences Upon the Plans of High School Seniors.* Doctor's thesis, Purdue University (Lafayette, Ind.), 1964. (*DA* 26:3150)

416. EDWARDS, ALLEN L. "The Assessment of Human Motives by Means of Personality Scales." *Neb Symp Motiv* 12:135–62 '64. * (*PA* 39:12357)

417. ERICKSON, PAUL. *Selection Factors Relating to Success in a Counselor Education Program.* Doctor's thesis, University of Southern California (Los Angeles, Calif.), 1964. (*DA* 25:3391)

418. GOLDBERG, LEWIS R., and RORER, LEONARD G. "Test-Retest Item Statistics." Abstract. *Psychol Rep* 15:413–4 O '64. * (*PA* 39:5059)

419. GOODMAN, MARVIN. "Expressed Self-Acceptance and Interspousal Needs: A Basis for Mate Selection." *J Counsel Psychol* 11:129–35 su '64. * (*PA* 39:5522)

420. GORALSKI, PATRICIA SCHWARZ. *Creativity: Student Teachers' Perceptions of Approaches to Classroom Teaching.* Doctor's thesis, University of Minnesota (Minneapolis, Minn.), 1964. (*DA* 25:2851)

421. HAMACHEK, DON E., and MORI, TAKAKO. "Need Structure, Personal Adjustment, and Academic Self-Concept of Beginning Education Students." *J Ed Res* 58:158–62 D '64. * (*PA* 39:10719)

422. HEILBRUN, ALFRED B., JR. "Social Value: Social Behavior Consistency, Parental Identification, and Aggression in Late Adolescence." *J Genetic Psychol* 104:135–46 Mr '64. *

423. HEILIZER, FRED, and GERDINE, PHILIP V. "Comparison of Social Desirability Effects on the EPPS in Relation to Ratings of Compatibility or Incompatibility of the Needs." *Psychol Rep* 15:995–1001 D '64. * (*PA* 39:7862)

424. HEILIZER, FRED, and GERDINE, PHILIP V. "Social Desirability Effects in the EPPS." *Psychol Rep* 15:243–58 Ag '64. * (*PA* 30:1804)

425. HEISS, JEROLD S., and GORDON, MICHAEL. "Need Patterns and the Mutual Satisfaction of Dating and Engaged Couples." *J Marriage & Family* 26:337–8 Ag '64. * (*PA* 39:4798)

426. HENSCHEL, BEVERLY JEAN SMITH. *A Comparison of the Personality Variables of Women Administrators and Women Teachers in Education.* Doctor's thesis, University of Utah (Salt Lake City, Utah), 1964. (*DA* 25:6313)

427. HODDICK, NANCY ANNA. *Personality Correlates and Degree of Satisfaction With Undergraduate Field of Specialization.* Doctor's thesis, Ohio State University (Columbus, Ohio), 1964. (*DA* 25:1005)

428. JOHNSON, DOROTHY ETHEL. *A Study of Interests and Personality Characteristics of Counselor Trainees and Counseling Effectiveness.* Doctor's thesis, Purdue University (Lafayette, Ind.), 1964. (*DA* 26:2051)

429. JOSEPH, MICHAEL P. "Psychological Needs and Values of Entering College Freshman." *Nat Cath Guid Conf J* 9:67–8 f '64. *

430. JOSEPH, MICHAEL P., and MCDONALD, ARTHUR S. "Psychological Needs and Reading Achievement." *Yearb Nat Read Conf* 13:150–7 '64. *

431. KEMP, C. GRATTON. "Comparison of Manifest Needs of Open and Closed Minds." *J Res Sci Teach* 2(1):107–10 '64. *

432. KENNEDY, W. A.; COTTRELL, T. B.; and SMITH, A. H.

"EPPS Norms for Mathematically Gifted Adolescents." *Psychol Rep* 14:342 Ap '64. * (*PA* 39:1738, title only)

433. KNAPP, ROBERT H., and HOLZBERG, JULES D. "Characteristics of College Students Volunteering for Service to Mental Patients." *J Consult Psychol* 28:82–5 F '64. * (*PA* 38:8779)

434. KNOTT, THOMAS GARLAND. *Motivational Factors in Selected Women Candidates for the Master of Religious Education Degree.* Doctor's thesis, Boston University (Boston, Mass.), 1964. (*DA* 25:3140)

435. KOONS, PAUL B., JR., and BIRCH, ROBERT W. "Reevaluation of the EPPS Norms." *Psychol Rep* 14:905–6 Je '64. * (*PA* 39:5071)

436. LIBERTY, PAUL G.; PIERSON, JEROME S.; and BURTON, JIM G. "Cognitive and Non-Cognitive Aspects of Reading Ability." *Psychol Rec* 14:349–53 Jl '64. * (*PA* 39:5942)

437. LISKE, RALPH E.; ORT, ROBERT S.; and FORD, AMASA B. "Clinical Performance and Related Traits of Medical Students and Faculty Physicians." *J Med Ed* 39:69–80 Ja '64. *

438. LOVELL, VICTOR ROYAL. *Components of Variance in Two Personality Inventories.* Doctor's thesis, Stanford University (Stanford, Calif.), 1964. (*DA* 25:4258)

439. LUSTIG, PAUL. *Response Style and Personality.* Doctor's thesis, New York University (New York, N.Y.), 1964. (*DA* 25:1339)

440. McDAVID, JOHN W., and SISTRUNK, FRANK. "Personality Correlates of Two Kinds of Conforming Behavior." *J Personality* 32:420–35 S '64. *

441. MATARAZZO, JOSEPH D.; ALLEN, BERNADENE V.; SASLOW, GEORGE; and WIENS, ARTHUR N. "Characteristics of Successful Policemen and Firemen Applicants." *J Appl Psychol* 48:123–33 Ap '64. * (*PA* 39:6047)

442. MEADOW, LLOYD. "Assessment of Students for Schools of Practical Nursing." *Nursing Res* 13:222–9 su '64. *

443. MEDVEDEFF, EUGENE. *The Utility of Sub-Grouping Analysis in the Prediction of Sales Success.* Doctor's thesis, Purdue University (Lafayette, Ind.), 1964. (*DA* 26:1800)

444. NAKSHIAN, JACOB, and WIENER, MORTON. "Need Strength, Need Conflict and Adjustment." *J Social Psychol* 62:29–43 F '64. * (*PA* 39:1908)

445. NEIDT, CHARLES O., and DREBUS, RICHARD W. "Characteristics Associated With the Creativity of Research Scientists in an Industrial Setting." *J Ind Psychol* 2:102–12 D '64. * (*PA* 40:11550)

446. NELSON, REX ALBERT. *Personality Variables of College Students Who Signify Industrial Arts as a Major Field of Educational Preparation.* Doctor's research study No. 1, Colorado State College (Greeley, Colo.), 1964. (*DA* 25:300)

447. NICKESON, RICHARD CARROLL. *Five Approaches to Reducing Cognitive Dissonance in the Self Concept.* Doctor's thesis, St. Louis University (St. Louis, Mo.), 1964. (*DA* 25:6083)

448. PATTERSON, STANLEY DWIGHT. *A Psychological Study of Asthmatics and Former Asthmatics.* Doctor's thesis, Purdue University (Lafayette, Ind.), 1964. (*DA* 25:1342)

449. PETERSEN, DWAIN FRANKLIN. *Factors Common to Interest, Value, and Personality Scales.* Doctor's thesis, University of Nebraska (Lincoln, Neb.), 1964. (*DA* 25:5747)

450. QUINLAN, CLAIRE A. *The Prediction of Freshman Academic Success at Colorado State College by Means of Selected Standardized Tests and Admission Data.* Doctor's research study No. 1, Colorado State College (Greeley, Colo.), 1964. (*DA* 25:5124)

451. REITER, HENRY H. "Prediction of College Success From Measures of Anxiety, Achievement Motivation, and Scholastic Aptitude." *Psychol Rep* 15:23–6 Ag '64. * (*PA* 39:2805)

452. ROSENHAN, DAVID L., and TOMKINS, SILVAN S. "On Preference for Hypnosis and Hypnotizability." *Int J Clin & Exp Hyp* 12:109–14 Ap '64. * (*PA* 39:2199)

453. SCHUMACHER, CHARLES F. "Personal Characteristics of Students Choosing Different Types of Medical Careers." *J Med Ed* 39:278–88 Mr '64. *

454. SMITH, AMOS CHARLES. *A Comparison of Edwards Personal Preference Schedule Patterns of Doctoral Graduates in Guidance and Counseling With Other Doctoral Graduates in Education.* Doctor's thesis, Florida State University (Tallahassee, Fla.), 1964. (*DA* 25:2355)

455. SORBER, EVAN RALPH. *Classroom Interaction Patterns and Personality Needs of Traditionally Prepared First-Year Elementary Teachers and Graduate Teaching Interns With Degrees From Colleges of Liberal Arts.* Doctor's thesis, University of Pittsburgh (Pittsburgh, Pa.), 1964. (*DA* 26:3166)

456. STEFFLRE, BUFORD, and LEAFGREN, FREDERICK A. "Mirror, Mirror on the Wall: A Study of Preferences for Counselors." *Personnel & Guid J* 42:459–62 Ja '64. *

457. STOLLAK, GARY EDWARD. *The Conditioning and Transfer Effects of Verbally Reinforcing Choices of Personality Statements.* Doctor's thesis, Rutgers University (New Brunswick, N.J.), 1964. (*DA* 25:6771)

458. TUKEY, RUTH S. "Intellectually-Oriented and Socially-Oriented Superior College Girls." *J Nat Assn Women Deans & Counselors* 27:120–7 sp '64. *

459. VERDA, MARTHA MALIK. *A Comparison of Certain Characteristics of Undergraduate Women at Eastern Michigan University Who Remain in or Voluntarily Withdraw From the Physical Education Curriculum.* Doctor's thesis, University of Michigan (Ann Arbor, Mich.), 1964. (*DA* 25:7068)

460. WEATHERLEY, DONALD. "Some Personality Correlates of Authoritarianism." *J Social Psychol* 64:161–7 O '64. * (*PA* 39:5163)

461. WILLIAMS, CARL D. "Some Evidence for a Hierarchy of Needs." *J General Psychol* 70:85–8 Ja '64. *

462. ABOU-GHORRA, I. M. "Dynamic Predictors of Production of Creative Novel Solutions in Counseling Among College Students." *Proc Ann Conv Am Psychol Assn* 73:353–4 '65. * (*PA* 39:15850)

463. BAKER, SHELDON R. "The Relationship of Social Attitudes to Manifest Needs." *Nursing Res* 14:345–6 f '65. *

464. BECKER, GILBERT. "Visual Acuity, Birth Order, Achievement Versus Affiliation, and Other Edwards Personal Preference Schedule Scores." *J Psychosom Res* 9:277–83 D '65. * (*PA* 40:7743)

465. BHATNAGAR, R. P. "A Comparative Study of Personality Characteristics of Bright and Dull Students of Class 11." *Ed & Psychol R* 5:113–7 Ap '65. * (*PA* 40:2869)

466. BHATNAGAR, R. P. "A Review of Research on EPPS Variables as Related to Academic Achievement." *Ed & Psychol R* 5:218–21 O '65. * (*PA* 40:5923, title only)

467. BROWN, MAURICE BURTON. *Multiple Discriminant Analysis of the Edwards Personal Preference Schedule and the Study of Values Scores of Achieving and Non-Achieving Low Ability College Freshmen.* Doctor's thesis, Florida State University (Tallahassee, Fla.), 1965. (*DA* 26:1505)

468. BYERS, ALVAH PRATT. *A Study of Family Relations as Determinants of Vocational Choice Among Ministers of the American Lutheran Church: A Test of Anne Roe's Theory.* Doctor's thesis, University of North Dakota (Grand Forks, N.D.), 1965. (*DA* 26:5843)

469. CANNON, HAROLD LEE. *Personality Characteristics and Other Factors as Predictors of Achievement in College Elementary Accounting.* Doctor's thesis, University of Minnesota (Minneapolis, Minn.), 1965. (*DA* 26:153)

470. CAPUTO, DANIEL V., and HANF, CONSTANCE. "The EPPS Pattern and the 'Nursing Personality.'" *Ed & Psychol Meas* 25:421–35 su '65. * (*PA* 39:15343)

471. CAPUTO, DANIEL V.; PLAPP, JON M.; HANF, CONSTANCE; and ANZEL, ANNE SMITH. "The Validity of the Edwards Personal Preference Schedule (EPPS) Employing Projective and Behavioral Criteria." *Ed & Psychol Meas* 25:829–48 au '65. * (*PA* 40:2131)

472. CLARK, D. F. "The Psychometric Characteristics of an Adult Class in Psychology." *Brit J Psychiatry* 111:745–53 Ag '65. * (*PA* 40:1584)

473. COHEN, STUART J.; TREHUB, ARNOLD; and MORRISON, FRANK G. "Edwards Personal Preference Profiles of Psychiatric Nurses." *Nursing Res* 14:318–21 f '65. *

474. DIERS, CAROL JEAN. "Social-Desirability Ratings of Personality Items by Three Subcultural Groups." *J Social Psychol* 67:97–104 O '65. * (*PA* 39:14899)

475. DOLAN, FRANCES ANNE. *Personal Qualities and Characteristics Important in the Selection of Undergraduate Staff Members for Women's Residence Halls.* Doctor's thesis, Northwestern University (Evanston, Ill.), 1965. (*DA* 26:3124)

476. FLANDERS, JOHN N. *Selected Characteristics of Decided-Undecided Freshmen Students at Florida State University.* Doctor's thesis, Florida State University (Tallahassee, Fla.), 1965. (*DA* 26:1476)

477. GAURON, EUGENE F. "Changes in Edwards Personal Preference Schedule Needs With Age and Psychiatric Status." *J Clin Psychol* 21:194–6 Ap '65. * (*PA* 39:12358)

478. HARRINGTON, THOMAS FRANCIS, JR. *The Interrelation of Personality Variables and College Experiences of Engineering Students Over a Four Year Span.* Doctor's thesis, Purdue University (Lafayette, Ind.), 1965. (*DA* 26:1480)

479. HARRIS, DOROTHY VIRGINIA. *An Investigation of Psychological Characteristics of University Women With High and Low Fitness Indices.* Doctor's thesis, University of Iowa (Iowa City, Iowa), 1965. (*DA* 26:5851)

480. HEARN, JUNE L.; CHARLES, DON C.; and WOLINS, LEROY. "Life History Antecedents of Measured Personality Variables." *J Genetic Psychol* 107:99–110 S '65. * (*PA* 39:15324)

481. HEILIZER, FRED, and GERDINE, PHILIP V. "Comparison of How Two Content Variables Are Changed by the Special Format of the EPPS." *Psychol Rep* 16:3–15 F '65. * (*PA* 39:7763)

482. HOWARD, LORRAINE HARRIS. *A Comparison of Freshmen Attending Selected Oregon Community Colleges and Oregon State University in Terms of Interests, Values, and Manifest Needs.* Doctor's thesis, Oregon State University (Corvallis, Ore.), 1965. (*DA* 25:5738)

483. JENNINGS, CHARLES L. "A Psychologic Study of Klinefelter's Syndrome." *Proc Ann Conf Air Force Behav Sci* 11:185–95 Jl '65. *

484. KOLE, DELBERT M., and MATARAZZO, JOSEPH D. "Intellectual and Personality Characteristics of Two Classes of Medical Students." *J Med Ed* 40:1130–44 D '65. *

485. LAWTON, M. POWELL. "Personality and Attitudinal Correlates of Psychiatric-Aid Performance." *J Social Psychol* 66:215–26 Ag '65. * (*PA* 39:15809)

486. LENTZ, EDITH M., and MICHAELS, ROBERT G. "Personality Contrasts Among Medical and Surgical Nurses." *Nursing Res* 14:43–8 w '65. *

487. LEVITT, EUGENE E., and BRADY, JOHN PAUL. "Sexual Preferences in Young Adult Males and Some Correlates." *J Clin Psychol* 21:347–54 O '65. * (*PA* 40:1494)

488. LUBLIN, IRWIN. "Sources of Differences in Effectiveness Among Controllers of Verbal Reinforcement." *Proc Ann Conv Am Psychol Assn* 73:3–4 '65. * (*PA* 39:13927)

489. McGEHEARTY, LOYCE IVY DAWSON. *Factors Associated With the Probable Success of Prospective School Counselors as Evaluated by Their Peers and by Staff Members.* Doctor's thesis, University of Texas (Austin, Tex.), 1965. (*DA* 26:873)

490. MARCUS, ALAN S. "Obtaining Group Measures From Personality Test Scores: Auto Brand Choice Predicted From the Edwards Personal Preference Schedule." *Psychol Rep* 17:523–31 O '65. * (*PA* 40:1593)

491. MARZOLF, STANLEY S. "Parent Behavior as Reported by College Students." *J Clin Psychol* 21:360–6 O '65. * (*PA* 40:1459)

492. MILLS, DAVID H. "The Relationship of Abstraction to Selected Personality and Intellectual Variables." *Psychol* 2:10–5 N '65. * (*PA* 40:3091)

493. MOYERS, LAYMAN DEWITT. *A Comparison by Sex and Teaching Level of Prospective Teachers in Tennessee.* Doctor's thesis, University of Tennessee (Knoxville, Tenn.), 1965. (*DA* 26:5895)

494. MYERS, JESSE WOODROW. *The Personality Syndrome of Presbyterian University Pastors Using Need Characteristics and Based on a Stay-Leave Criterion.* Doctor's thesis, University of Maryland (College Park, Md.), 1965. (*DA* 27:4555B)

495. ORTENZI, ANGELO. *Establishment and Cross-Validation of Selection Criteria for Resident Counselors at the Pennsylvania State University.* Doctor's thesis, Pennsylvania State University (University Park, Pa.), 1965. (*DA* 26:6451)

496. POOL, DONALD A. "The Relation of Personality Needs to Vocational Counseling Outcome." *J Counsel Psychol* 12:23–7 sp '65. * (*PA* 39:10876)

497. PURCELL, THOMAS DAVID. *Motivation and Motivational-Relevance in the Linear and Non-Linear Prediction of Academic Performance.* Doctor's thesis, Southern Illinois University (Carbondale, Ill.), 1965. (*DA* 26:6160)

498. REILLY, ROBERT R.; YUFIT, ROBERT I.; and MATTSON, DALE E. "The Dental Student at the University of Illinois." *J Dental Ed* 29:162–74 Je '65. *

499. REITER, HENRY H. "Four Personality Correlates of Current Events Awareness." *Psychol Rep* 17:350 O '65. * (*PA* 40:1595, title only)

500. REITER, HENRY H. "Relation of Bodybuild and Personal Preference Among College Males." *Percept & Motor Skills* 21:34 Ag '65. * (*PA* 40:485, title only)

501. RICHARDSON, LA VANGE H., and WEITZNER, MARTIN. "The Relationship of Dependent, Acting Out, and Resistant Behavior to College Success." *Psychol Sch* 2:252–4 Jl '65. *

502. SAPER, BERNARD. "Motivational Components in the Interpersonal Transactions of Married Couples." *Psychiatric Q* 39:303–14 Ap '65. * (*PA* 39:15907)

503. SCHNELL, RICHARD R. "Construction of Factor Scales for Personality Assessment." *Newsl Res Psychol* 7:61–2 My '65. *

504. SCHULZ, ESTHER D. "Personality Traits of Nursing Students and Faculty Concepts of Desirable Traits: A Longitudinal Comparative Study." *Nursing Res* 14:261–4 su '65. *

505. SCOTT, GARY KUPER. *A Study of the Relationship Between Ratings of Counselor Success and Selected Personality Variables.* Doctor's thesis, University of Minnesota (Minneapolis, Minn.), 1965. (*DA* 26:5249)

506. SHIPMAN, WILLIAM G. "Personality Traits Associated With Body-Image Boundary Concern." *Proc Ann Conv Am Psychol Assn* 73:271–2 '65. * (*PA* 39:15441)

507. SMITH, GENE MARSHALL. "The Role of Personality in Nursing Education: A Comparison of Successful and Unsuccessful Nursing Students." *Nursing Res* 14:54–8 w '65. *

508. SPIES, CARL JOSEPH. *Some Non-Intellectual Predictors of Classroom Success.* Doctor's thesis, Washington University (St. Louis, Mo.), 1965. (*DA* 26:7442)

509. STAPLES, JOHN DIXON. *An Experimental Study to Identify the Basic Abilities Needed to Detect Typescript Errors With Implications for the Improvement of Instruction in Typewriting.* Doctor's thesis, University of North Dakota (Grand Forks, N.D.), 1965. (*DA* 27:1693A)

510. STOLLAK, GARY E. "EPPS Performance Under Social Desirability Instructions." *J Personality & Social Psychol* 2:430–2 S '65. * (*PA* 39:14996)

511. STOLLAK, GARY E. "EPPS Performance Under Social Desirability Instructions: College Females." *Psychol Rep* 16:119–22 F '65. * (*PA* 39:7802)

512. STOLLAK, GARY E. "Relationship Between EPPS and Marlowe-Crowne SD Scale." *Psychol Rep* 16:731–2 Je '65. * (*PA* 39:15374)

513. STONE, J. BLAIR. "The Edwards Personal Preference Schedule and Physically Disabled College Students." *Rehabil Counsel B* 9:11–3 S '65. *

514. STUFFLEBEAM, DANIEL LEROY. *Investigation of Individual Characteristics Associated With Guidance Competence Versus Individual Characteristics Associated With Counseling Competence.* Doctor's thesis, Purdue University (Lafayette, Ind.), 1965. (*DA* 26:1490)

515. TISDALE, JOHN R. "Comparison of Edwards Personal Preference Schedule Data for Three Groups." *Psychol Rec* 15:203–10 Ap '65. * (*PA* 39:10157)

516. TOLOR, ALEXANDER. "Social Competence and Personality

Needs in Psychiatric Patients." *J Clin Psychol* 21:97–8 Ja '65. * (*PA* 39:12596)

517. WAHLSTROM, MERLIN W. *A Comparison of EPPS and TAT Need for Achievement Scores and Academic Success.* Master's thesis, University of Alberta (Edmonton, Alb., Canada), 1965.

518. WEATHERLEY, DONALD. "Some Personality Correlates of the Ability to Stop Smoking Cigarettes." *J Consult Psychol* 29:483–5 O '65. * (*PA* 40:551)

519. WILLIAMS, ROBERT EVAN. *Teacher Role Expectations as Related to Manifest Needs and Selected Autobiographical Data of Educational Psychology Students at the University of Georgia.* Doctor's thesis, University of Georgia (Athens, Ga.), 1965. (*DA* 26:6521)

520. WINBORN, BOB, and MARONEY, KENNETH A. "Effectiveness of Short-Term Group Guidance With a Group of Transfer Students Admitted on Academic Probation." *J Ed Res* 58: 463–5 Jl–Ag '65. * (*PA* 40:772)

521. WOOLFOLK, EVA K. *The Relation of Certain Psychological Characteristics to Choice of a Type of Teacher Preparation Program.* Doctor's thesis, Syracuse University (Syracuse, N.Y.), 1965. (*DA* 26:886)

522. WORELL, JUDITH, and WORELL, LEONARD. "Personality Conflict, Originality of Response, and Recall." *J Consult Psychol* 29:55–62 F '65. * (*PA* 39:7718)

523. BERRIEN, F. KENNETH. "Japanese Values and the Democratic Process." *J Social Psychol* 68:129–38 F '66. * (*PA* 40:5306)

524. BHATNAGAR, R. P. "Development of the Edwards Personal Preference Schedule in Hindi." *Indian Psychol R* 2:103–8 Ja '66. * (*PA* 40:9422)

525. BISHOP, WILLIAM EDGAR. *Characteristics of Teachers Judged Successful by Intellectually Gifted, High-Achieving High School Students.* Doctor's thesis, Kent State University (Kent, Ohio), 1966. (*DA* 28:487A)

526. BLAZER, JOHN A. "Leg Position and Psychological Characteristics in Women." *Psychol* 3:5–12 Ag '66. * (*PA* 40:12361)

527. BRAY, DOUGLAS W., and GRANT, DONALD L. "The Assessment Center in the Measurement of Potential for Business Management." *Psychol Monogr* 80(17):1–27 '66. * (*PA* 41:850)

528. BROWN, ROBERT A., and POOL, DONALD A. "Psychological Needs and Self-Awareness." *J Counsel Psychol* 13:85–8 sp '66. * (*PA* 40:5459)

529. CAMERON, BERNARD, and MYERS, JEROME L. "Some Personality Correlates of Risk Taking." *J General Psychol* 74:51–60 Ja '66. * (*PA* 40:4884)

530. CAPUTO, DANIEL V.; PSATHAS, GEORGE; and PLAPP, JON M. "Test-Retest Reliability of the EPPS." *Ed & Psychol Meas* 26:883–6 w '66. * (*PA* 41:4590)

531. CUNNINGHAM, GROVER BENNETT, JR. *Prediction of Staff Ratings From Personality Variables of Counselors in Training and Prediction of Intelligence Test Scores of Children From Personality Variables of Parents.* Doctor's thesis, University of Texas (Austin, Tex.), 1966. (*DA* 27:3305A)

532. DANA, RICHARD H. "Eisegesis and Assessment." *J Proj Tech & Pers Assess* 30:215–22 Je '66. * (*PA* 40:9347)

533. DEMOS, GEORGE D., and ZUWAYLIF, FADIL H. "Characteristics of Effective Counselors." *Counselor Ed & Sup* 5:163–5 sp '66. *

534. FARLEY, FRANK H. "Individual Differences in Free Response-Speed." *Percept & Motor Skills* 22:557–8 Ap '66. * (*PA* 40:8851)

535. FARLEY, FRANK H. "Introversion and Achievement Motivation." *Psychol Rep* 19:112 Ag '66. * (*PA* 40:12340, title only)

536. FLYNN, JOHN T. "The Adjective Check List: A Device to Assess Perceived Self." Abstract. *J Teach Ed* 17:247–8 su '66. *

537. FOLDS, JONELL H., and GAZDA, GEORGE M. "A Comparison of the Effectiveness and Efficiency of Three Methods of Test Interpretation." *J Counsel Psychol* 13:318–24 f '66. * (*PA* 40:12332)

538. GANTZ, BENJAMIN SOULÉ, JR. *Predicting and Training Originality.* Doctor's thesis, Claremont Graduate School (Claremont, Calif.), 1966. (*DA* 28:1225B)

539. GAURON, EUGENE F., and ADAMS, JERRY. "The Relationship of the Edwards Personal Preference Schedule to the MMPI in a Patient Population." *J Clin Psychol* 22:206–9 Ap '66. * (*PA* 40:7206)

540. GHEI, S. N. "Needs of Indian and American College Females." *J Social Psychol* 69:3–11 Je '66. * (*PA* 40:9967)

541. GIANNELL, A. STEVEN. "Giannell's Criminosynthesis Theory Applied to Female Homosexuality." *J Psychol* 64:213–22 N '66. * (*PA* 41:1497)

542. GIANNELL, A. STEVEN. "Psychological Needs Characteristic of Four Criminal-Offender Groups." *J Social Psychol* 69:55–72 Je '66. * (*PA* 40:10254)

543. GIBBS, D. N. "A Cross-Cultural Comparison of Needs and Achievement of University Freshmen." *Personnel & Guid J* 44:813–6 Ap '66. * (*PA* 40:8744)

544. GOSS, ALLEN MILES. *Predicting Work Success for Patients on an Industrial Rehabilitation Ward in a Neuropsychiatric Setting.* Doctor's thesis, University of Texas (Austin, Tex.), 1966. (*DA* 27:2511B)

545. HAKEL, MILTON D. "Prediction of College Achievement From the Edwards Personal Preference Schedule Using Intellectual Ability as a Moderator." *J Appl Psychol* 50:336–40 Ag '66. * (*PA* 40:11489)

546. HALPERN, CHARLES, JR. *Situational Determinants of Authoritarian Attitudes.* Doctor's thesis, Temple University (Philadelphia, Pa.), 1966. (*DA* 27:3934A)

547. HINELY, REGINALD T.; GALLOWAY, CHARLES M.; COODY, BEN E.; SANDEFUR, WALTER S. "An Exploratory Study of Teaching Styles Among Student Teachers." *J Exp Ed* 35: 30–5 w '66. *

548. HURLEY, JOHN R., and SILVERT, DIANE M. "Mate-Image Congruity and Marital Adjustment." *Proc Ann Conv Am Psychol Assn* 74:219–20 '66. * (*PA* 41:6156)

549. JOHNSON, DAVIS G., and HUTCHINS, EDWIN B. "Doctor or Dropout? A Study of Medical Student Attrition: Chap. 4, 'The Student.'" *J Med Ed* 41:1139–56, 1263–5 D '66. *

550. JONES, REGINALD L., and GOTTFRIED, NATHAN W. "Psychological Needs and Preferences for Teaching Exceptional Children." *Excep Children* 32:313–21 Ja '66. * (*PA* 40:4615)

551. KISSINGER, R. DAVID. "The Edwards Personal Preference Schedule in a Psychiatric Setting." *J Proj Tech & Pers Assess* 30:149–52 Ap '66. * (*PA* 40:7210)

552. KO, YUNG–HO, and LIN, LI–HUEI. "The Relationships Between Personality and Ordinal Positions Among University Students." *Acta Psychologica Taiwanica* 8:29–37 Mr '66. * (*PA* 40:11168)

553. KOHLAN, RICHARD GEORGE. *Relationships Between Inventoried Interests and Inventoried Needs in a College Sample.* Doctor's thesis, University of Minnesota (Minneapolis, Minn.), 1966. (*DA* 27:2397A)

554. LANYON, RICHARD I. "A Free-Choice Version of the EPPS." *J Clin Psychol* 22:202–5 Ap '66. * (*PA* 40:7213)

555. LUNNEBORG, PATRICIA W., and LUNNEBORG, CLIFFORD E. "The Utility of EPPS Scores for Prediction of Academic Achievement Among Counseling Clients." *J Counsel Psychol* 13:241 su '66. * (*PA* 40:9252)

556. LYNCH, G. BERK, II. *The Edwards Personal Preference Schedule and Academic Performance.* Master's thesis, Marshall University (Huntington, W.Va.), 1966.

557. McKEE, NANCY ROBIN, and WILDMAN, ROBERT W. "EPPS Heterosexuality Scale and Dating Frequency." *J Clin Psychol* 22:464 O '66. * (*PA* 41:2883)

558. MASSY, WILLIAM F.; LODAHL, THOMAS M.; and FRANK, RONALD E. "Collinearity in the Edwards Personal Preference Schedule." *J Appl Psychol* 50:121–4 Ap '66. * (*PA* 40:4767)

559. MICHAEL, WILLIAM B.; HANEY, RUSSELL; and JONES, ROBERT A. "The Predictive Validities of Selected Aptitude and Achievement Measures and of Three Personality Inventories in Relation to Nursing Training Criteria." *Ed & Psychol Meas* 26:1035–40 w '66. * (*PA* 41:5117)

560. MILLAR, ANDREW CRAIG. *The Suitability of Using Non-Intellective Characteristics in the Selection of Honors Students at the University of North Dakota.* Doctor's thesis, University of North Dakota (Grand Forks, N.D.), 1966. (*DA* 27:1629A)

561. MILLS, DAVID H.; CHESTNUT, WILLIAM J.; and HARTZELL, JOHN P. "The Needs of Counselors: A Component Analysis." *J Counsel Psychol* 13:82–4 sp '66. * (*PA* 40:5808)

562. MOE, JOHN VALDORF. *An Identification of Some Personality Characteristics Associated With Reading Skill.* Doctor's thesis, Colorado State College (Greeley, Colo.), 1966. (*DA* 27:3631A)

563. MUSE, COREY J. *Personality and Need Characteristics as Predictors of Student Teacher and Inservice Teacher Ratings.* Doctor's thesis, Brigham Young University (Provo, Utah), 1966. (*DA* 27:987A)

564. NEWMAN, ALBERT. *Psychological Needs, Occupational Perceptions, and Occupational Preferences.* Doctor's thesis, Columbia University (New York, N.Y.), 1966. (*DA* 27:1293B)

565. NOWICKI, STEPHEN, JR. "Factor Analysis of Responses to Various Paper and Pencil Tests." *Newsl Res Psychol* 8:28–9 My '66. *

566. PHELPS, RICHARD E., and MEYER, MERLE E. "Personality and Conformity, and Sex Differences." *Psychol Rep* 18:730 Je '66. * (*PA* 40:10114)

567. PHILIPPUS, M. J., and NACMAN, M. "A Psychosocial and Vocational Follow-Up Study of Previously Hospitalized Asthmatic Patients." *Psychother & Psychosom* 14(3):171–9 '66. *

568. PLAPP, JON M.; PSATHAS, GEORGE; and CAPUTO, DANIEL V. "Effects of Nursing Training on Personality." *Proc Ann Conv Am Psychol Assn* 74:287–8 '66. * (*PA* 41:5974)

569. ROBBINS, PAUL R. "An Approach to Measuring Psychological Tensions by Means of Dream Associations." *Psychol Rep* 18:959–71 Je '66. * (*PA* 40:10237)

570. ROSEN, JULIUS. *The Predictive Value of Personal Characteristics Associated With Counselor Competency.* Doctor's thesis, New York University (New York, N.Y.), 1966. (*DA* 27:2408A)

571. SAMPSON, JACK BYRON. *A Comparison of Personality and Teacher Attitude Between Stout State University Undergraduate Fellows and Other Students Enrolled in Teacher Education.* Doctor's thesis, University of North Dakota (Grand Forks, N.D.), 1966. (*DA* 27:2089A)

572. SCHARLES, HENRY GODFREY, JR. *The Relationship of Selected Personality Needs to Participation, Drop-Out, and Achievement Among Adult Learners.* Doctor's thesis, Florida State University (Tallahassee, Fla.), 1966. (*DA* 27:3689A)

573. STANKOWSKI, WAYNE J. *Needs, as Measured by the Edwards Personal Preference Schedule Characteristic of*

Academically Successful and Unsuccessful Freshmen in Various Marquette University Colleges. Master's thesis, Marquette University (Milwaukee, Wis.), 1966.

574. STEINKAMP, STANLEY W. "Some Characteristics of Effective Interviewers." *J Appl Psychol* 50:487–92 D '66. * (PA 41:2868)

575. STOLLAK, GARY E. "Conditioning and Transfer Effects of Verbally Reinforcing Choices of Personality Statements." *Psychol Rep* 19:427–37 O '66. * (PA 41:208)

576. TISDALE, JOHN R. "Selected Correlates of Extrinsic Religious Values." *R Relig Res* 7:78–84 w '66. * (PA 41:7181)

577. TRAVIS, VAUD ANCIL, JR. *An Investigation of Selected Personality Need-Structure, Value and Attitude Characteristics of Student and Cooperating Teachers in Elementary Education at Oklahoma State University.* Doctor's thesis, Oklahoma State University (Stillwater, Okla.), 1966. (DA 27:4095A)

578. VOIGT, WALTER H. "Personality Variables in Rorschach Scoring." *J Proj Tech & Pers Assess* 30:153–7 Ap '66. * (PA 40:7740)

579. WATLEY, DONIVAN J. "Counselor Variability in Making Accurate Predictions." *J Counsel Psychol* 13:53–62 sp '66. * (PA 40:5817)

580. WATMAN, WALTER A. "The Relationship Between Acting Out Behavior and Some Psychological Test Indices in a Prison Population." *J Clin Psychol* 22:279–80 Jl '66. * (PA 40:11312)

581. WILLMAN, CAROL ELSIE. *A Comparison of Prospective Special Education and Elementary Teachers on Selected Personality Characteristics.* Doctor's thesis, University of Michigan (Ann Arbor, Mich.), 1966. (DA 28:100A)

582. WRIGHT, NANCY A., and ZUBEK, JOHN P. "Use of the Multiple Discriminant Function in the Prediction of Perceptual Deprivation Tolerance." *Can J Psychol* 20:105–13 Mr '66. * (PA 40:6647)

583. ABATE, MARIO, and BERRIEN, F. K. "Validation of Stereotypes: Japanese Versus American Students." *J Personality & Social Psychol* 7:435–8 O '67. * (PA 42:3863)

584. ASA, LELAND F. "Interview Behavior and Counselor Personality Variables." *Counselor Ed & Sup* 6:324–30 su '67. * (PA 41:14196)

585. BARE, CAROLE E. "Relationship of Counselor Personality and Counselor-Client Personality Similarity to Selected Counseling Success Criteria." *J Counsel Psychol* 14:419–25 S '67. * (PA 41:15844)

586. BERRIEN, F. K.; ARKOFF, ABE; and IWAHARA, SHINKURO. "Generation Difference in Values: Americans, Japanese-Americans, and Japanese." *J Social Psychol* 71:169–75 Ap '67. * (PA 41:8781)

587. BLANE, STEPHEN MARTIN. *Immediate Effect of Supervisory Experiences on Counselor Candidates.* Doctor's thesis, University of Florida (Gainesville, Fla.), 1967. (DA 29:116A)

588. BOOSE, BEATRICE J., and BOOSE, SIDNEY S. "Some Personality Characteristics of the Culturally Disadvantaged." *J Psychol* 65:157–62 Mr '67. * (PA 41:7331)

589. BROWN, GLEN JEWL. *A Social and Psychological Description of Externs in Educational Administration.* Doctor's thesis, Michigan State University (East Lansing, Mich.), 1967. (DA 28:2010A)

590. BURGE, EVERETT WADDELL. *The Relationship of Certain Personality Attributes to the Verbal Behavior of Selected Student Teachers in the Secondary School Classroom.* Doctor's thesis, North Texas State University (Denton, Tex.), 1967. (DA 28:139A)

591. CARDANY, ARTHUR THOMAS. *Selected Personal Needs of Public School Teachers and Attitudes Toward In-Service Education.* Doctor's thesis, State University of New York at Albany (Albany, N.Y.), 1967. (DA 28:4402A)

592. CHYLINSKI, JOANNE, and WRIGHT, MORGAN W. "Testing in Canada With the Minnesota Multiphasic Personality Inventory (MMPI) and the Edwards Personal Preference Schedule (EPPS)." *Can Psychologist* 8a:202–6 Jl '67. * (PA 42:755)

593. COODY, BEN E., and HINELY, REGINALD T. "A Validity Study of Selected EPPS Subscales for Determining Need Structure of Dominating and Submissive Student Teachers." *J Ed Res* 61:59–61 O '67. *

594. CUMMINGS, S. THOMAS, and CARSON, R. LAWRENCE. "Maternal Personality and the Externalizing-Internalizing Symptom Dimension in Neurotic Children." *Proc Ann Conv Am Psychol Assn* 75:181–2 '67. * (PA 41:13928)

595. DANIELSON, HARRY ALFRED. *Personality Variables of Prospective Elementary School Counselors.* Doctor's thesis, University of Florida (Gainesville, Fla.), 1967. (DA 29:118A)

596. DIENER, ROBERT G. "Prediction of Dependent Behavior in Specified Situations From Psychological Tests." *Psychol Rep* 20:103–8 F '67. * (PA 41:7320)

597. DOLEYS, ERNEST J.; OTTO, JOANN E.; OSBORNE, FLORENCE E.; HARRIS, CAROL D.; and SNYDER, DOROTHY. "Varying Amounts of Alcohol and Personality Inventory Performance." *J Clin Psychol* 23:484–6 O '67. * (PA 42:2597)

598. EBERLEIN, E. LARRY. *The Relationship Between School Climate and Edwards' Manifest Needs of the Elementary School Teacher.* Doctor's thesis, Michigan State University (East Lansing, Mich.), 1967. (DA 28:3994A)

599. ESCOTT, STANLEY BOSWORTH. *An Investigation Into the Predictive Value of Some Structured Observational Tools for Selection and Retention in Counselor Education.* Doctor's

thesis, Purdue University (Lafayette, Ind.), 1967. (DA 28:466A)

600. FINDLEY, DALE GENE. *Characteristics, Degree of Satisfaction and Personality Needs of Mobile Male Teachers in Iowa.* Doctor's thesis, University of Iowa (Iowa City, Iowa), 1967. (DA 28:2937A)

601. FITZGERALD, B. J.; PASEWARK, R. A.; and TANNER, C. E. "Use of the Edwards Personal Preference Schedule With Hospitalized Alcoholics." *J Clin Psychol* 23:194–5 Ap '67. * (PA 41:9100)

602. FRETZ, BRUCE R., and SCHMIDT, LYLE D. "Psychology Students' Graphic Expression of Need for Achievement." *Percept & Motor Skills* 25:647–8 O '67. * (PA 42:4801)

603. GOODMAN, CAROLYN. *A Study of Psychological Factors in Different Fertility and Family Planning Types.* Doctor's thesis, Columbia University (New York, N.Y.), 1967. (DA 28:3048B)

604. GOSS, ALLEN M., and PATE, KENTON D. "Predicting Vocational Rehabilitation Success for Psychiatric Patients With Psychological Tests." *Psychol Rep* 21:725–30 D '67. * (PA 42:7550)

605. GRIFFEN, WILLIAM LAWRENCE. *Predictors of Freshman College Students' Interest in Working on Major Social Problems.* Doctor's thesis, Cornell University (Ithaca, N.Y.), 1967. (DA 28:2598A)

606. HART, JAMES J. "Assessing Individual Differences in Motivation and Their Effect on Performance of Number Facility." *Psychol Rep* 20:55–9 F '67. * (PA 41:7299)

607. HEBERT, DAVID J. *The Counseling Relationship as a Function of Client-Counselor Personality Need and Sex Similarity.* Doctor's thesis, Kent State University (Kent, Ohio), 1967. (DA 28:4479A)

608. HWANG, CHIEN-HOU. "A Study of the Personal Preferences of Chinese Students by Edwards Personal Preference Schedule." *Psychol & Ed* 1:52–68 Ap '67. *

609. INGRAM, GILBERT LEWIS. *Personality Variables Associated With Successful Adaptation in Two Vocational Environments.* Doctor's thesis, University of Maryland (College Park, Md.), 1967. (DA 28:3060B)

610. JANUS, SAMUEL. *Personality Factors and Their Relationship to Adjustment in a Camping Situation.* Doctor's thesis, New York University (New York, N.Y.), 1967. (DA 29:147A)

611. JENKINS, JOHN MERVIN. *A Study of the Characteristics Associated With Innovative Behavior in Teachers.* Doctor's thesis, University of Miami (Coral Gables, Fla.), 1967. (DA 28:903A)

612. LADD, CLAYTON E., and LEVITT, EUGENE E. "The EPPS Heterosexual Scale and Marital Status." *J Clin Psychol* 23:192–4 Ap '67. * (PA 41:8924)

613. LECKART, BRUCE T.; WATERS, LAWRENCE K.; and TARPINIAN, JOHN. "Duration of Attention and Need for Affiliation." *Percept & Motor Skills* 25:817–24 D '67. * (PA 42:8982)

614. LEVITT, EUGENE E., and LUBIN, EDWARD. "Some Personality Factors Associated With Menstrual Complaints and Menstrual Attitude." *J Psychosom Res* 11:267–70 N '67. * (PA 42:10913)

615. LUNNEBORG, CLIFFORD E., and LUNNEBORG, PATRICIA W. "EPPS Patterns in the Prediction of Academic Achievement." *J Counsel Psychol* 14:389–90 Jl '67. * (PA 41:12573)

616. McCARY, ARTHUR DALE. *Personality Variables Associated With Five Levels of Academic Achievement Within Five Levels of Ability.* Doctor's thesis, University of Mississippi (University, Miss.), 1967. (DA 28:56A)

617. McGREEVY, C. PATRICK. "Factor Analysis of Measures Used in the Selection and Evaluation of Counselor Education Candidates." *J Counsel Psychol* 14:51–6 Ja '67. * (PA 41:3644)

618. MARTIN, JOHN DANIEL. *The Relationship of Responses to Geometric Designs to Inferiority Feelings and Certain Personality Variables.* Doctor's thesis, North Texas State University (Denton, Tex.), 1967. (DA 28:127A)

619. MELNICK, MURRAY. *Need Configurations and Evaluative Tendencies Toward Self and Others.* Doctor's thesis, New York University (New York, N.Y.), 1967. (DA 29:327A)

620. MINGE, M. RONALD, and BOWMAN, THOMAS F. "Personality Differences Among Nonclients and Vocational-Educational and Personal Counseling Clients." *J Counsel Psychol* 14:137–9 Mr '67. * (PA 41:7341)

621. MOOMAW, ROBERT CLAYTON. *Need-Press Differences Among Community College Students.* Doctor's thesis, Ohio State University (Columbus, Ohio), 1967. (DA 28:2074A)

622. MOOSBRUKER, JANE B. "Dental Assistants: Efficiency Ratings and Personality." *J Dental Ed* 31:471–93 D '67. *

623. MUMAW, CATHERINE RUTH. *Organizational Patterns of Homemakers Related to Selected Predispositional and Situational Characteristics.* Doctor's thesis, Pennsylvania State University (University Park, Pa.), 1967. (DA 29:1081B)

624. MURSTEIN, BERNARD I. "Empirical Tests of Role, Complementary Needs, and Homogamy Theories of Marital Choice." *J Marriage & Family* 29:689–96 N '67. * (PA 42:4359)

625. NOWICKI, STEPHEN, JR. "Birth Order and Personality: Some Unexpected Findings." *Psychol Rep* 21:265–7 Ag '67. * (PA 42:2755)

626. NOWICKI, STEPHEN, JR. "Use of the EPPS in a Psychiatric Population." *J Clin Psychol* 23:361–2 Jl '67. * (PA 41:15298)

627. OAKLAND, JAMES ALVIN. *The Performance of High*

School Students on the Edwards Personality Inventory and Its Relationship to Over- and Underachievement. Doctor's thesis, University of Washington (Seattle, Wash.), 1967. (*DA* 28:3882B)

628. O'SHEA, ARTHUR JOSEPH. *Differences in Certain Non-Intellective Factors Between Academically Bright Junior High School Male High and Low Achievers.* Doctor's thesis, Boston College (Chestnut Hill, Mass.), 1967. (*DA* 28:3515A)

629. PACE, LAWLIS THERON. *Roommate Dissatisfaction in a College Residence Hall as Related to Roommate Scholastic Achievement,* the College and University Environment Scales, and the Edwards Personal Preference Schedule. Doctor's thesis, Colorado State College (Greeley, Colo.), 1967. (*DA* 28:2989A)

630. PAYNE, MILTON ROBERT. *The Relationship of Student Teachers' Manifest Psychological Needs to Interpersonal Perception and Students' Self-Concepts.* Doctor's thesis, North Texas State University (Denton, Tex.), 1967. (*DA* 28:3533A)

631. PORTER, JANET B. *The Vocational Choice of Freshmen College Women as Influenced by Psychological Needs and Parent-Child Relationships.* Doctor's thesis, University of Oklahoma (Norman, Okla.), 1967. (*DA* 27:3730A)

632. REBSTOCK, CHARLES WESLEY. *Changes in the Personality, Values, Attitudes, and Verbal Behavior of Student Teachers Through the Use of Certain Objective Observational Techniques.* Doctor's thesis, University of Minnesota (Minneapolis, Minn.), 1967. (*DA* 28:4939A)

633. ROEMMICH, HERMAN. "The Need Structure of Public School Counselors." *J Ed Res* 61:24–6 S '67. *

634. ROSEN, JULIUS. "Multiple-Regression Analysis of Counselor Characteristics and Competencies." *Psychol Rep* 20:1003–8 Je '67. * (*PA* 41:12734)

635. ROSENBERG, C. M. "Personality and Obsessional Neurosis." *Brit J Psychiatry* 113:471–7 My '67. * (*PA* 41:12174)

636. SNYDER, JOHN ALLEN. *An Investigation of Certain Personality Needs and Relational Patterns in a Group of 70 Premaritally Pregnant Girls.* Doctor's thesis, University of Pennsylvania (Philadelphia, Pa.), 1967. (*DA* 28:3043A)

637. STABLER, JOHN R., and GOODRICH, ANN H. "Personality and Family Background Correlates of Students' Response to Physical Danger." *J Psychol* 67:313–8 N '67. * (*PA* 42:2557)

638. STEVENS, THOMAS GRANVILLE. *Congruency Between Diagnostic Dimensions of Personality Theories and Personality Tests.* Master's thesis, California State College at Fullerton (Fullerton, Calif.), 1967.

639. TOLOR, ALEXANDER, and MURPHY, VINCENT M. "Some Psychological Correlates of Subjective Life Expectancy." *J Clin Psychol* 23:21–4 Ja '67. * (*PA* 41:5954)

640. WALBERG, HERBERT J., and WELCH, WAYNE W. "Personality Characteristics of Innovative Physics Teachers." *J Creative Beh* 1:163–71 sp '67. * (*PA* 41:15285)

641. WATERS, L. K., and KIRK, WILLIAM E. "Birth Order and PPS Affiliation." *J Psychol* 67:241–3 N '67. * (*PA* 42:2603)

642. WEITZNER, MARTIN; STALLONE, FRANK; and SMITH, GENE M. "Personality Profiles of High, Middle, and Low MAS Subjects." *J Psychol* 65:163–8 Mr '67. * (*PA* 41:7350)

643. WILLIAMSON, JOHN ANDERSON. *Personality Characteristics of Effective Texas Teachers.* Doctor's thesis, University of Arkansas (Fayetteville, Ark.), 1967. (*DA* 28:67A)

644. WINK, RICHARD LEE. *Relationship of Self-Concept and Selected Personality Variables to Achievement in Music Student Teaching.* Doctor's thesis, Ohio State University (Columbus, Ohio), 1967. (*DA* 28:5100A)

645. WRIGHT, MORGAN W.; CHYLINSKI, JOANNE; SISLER, GEORGE C.; and QUARRINGTON, BRUCE. "Personality Factors in the Selection of Civilians for Isolated Northern Stations: A Follow-Up Study." *Can Psychologist* 8a:23–31 Ja '67. * (*PA* 41:7979)

646. YANG, KUO-SHU. "Need Patterns of Overseas Chinese Students in Taiwan From Different Southeast Asian Countries." *Acta Psychologia Taiwanica* 9:1–23 Mr '67. *

647. YORK, L. JEAN NETCHER. *Relationships Between Problems of Beginning Elementary Teachers, Their Personal Characteristics and Their Preferences for In-Service Education.* Doctor's thesis, Indiana University (Bloomington, Ind.), 1967. (*DA* 28:4037A)

648. YOUNG, FRANCIS A. "Myopia and Personality." *Am J Optom* 44:192–201 Mr '67. * (*PA* 41:8942)

649. ATKINSON, GILBERT, and LUNNEBORG, CLIFFORD E. "Comparison of Oblique and Orthogonal Simple Structure Solutions for Personality and Interest Factors." *Multiv Behav Res* 3:21–35 Ja '68. * (*PA* 42:11349)

650. BECKER, JAMES A. "Teacher Trainee Responses to Two Personality Inventories." *Psychol Rep* 22:609–10 Ap '68. * (*PA* 42:12781)

651. BERRIEN, F. K. "Cross-Cultural Equivalence of Personality Measures." *J Social Psychol* 75:3–9 Je '68. * (*PA* 42:13572)

652. BYERS, ALVAH P.; FORREST, GARY G.; and ZACCARIA, JOSEPH S. "Recalled Early Parent-Child Relations, Adult Needs, and Occupational Choice: A Test of Roe's Theory." *J Counsel Psychol* 15:324–8 Jl '68. * (*PA* 42:16181)

653. CALLAHAN, LUKE JAMES. *Characteristics of the Normative Group on the EPPS for a Minor Seminary.* Master's thesis, Loyola University (Chicago, Ill.), 1968.

654. CASELLA, CARMINE. "Need Hierarchies Among Nursing

and Nonnursing College Students." *Nursing Res* 17:273–5 My–Je '68. *

655. CONE, JOHN DRURY, JR. *The Married Person's Ability to Predict the Perception of Him by His Spouse on the Edwards Personality Inventory.* Doctor's thesis, University of Washington (Seattle, Wash.), 1968. (*DA* 29:1159B)

656. FARLEY, FRANK H. "Extraversion and the Self-Description of Endurance." *Brit J Social & Clin Psychol* 7:1–2 F '68. * (*PA* 42:8603)

657. FRAYN, DOUGLAS H. "A Relationship Between Rated Ability and Personality Traits in Psychotherapists." *Am J Psychiatry* 124:1232–7 Mr '68. *

658. GALBRAITH, GARY G.; HAHN, KENNETH; and LEIBERMAN, HARVEY. "Personality Correlates of Free-Associative Sex Responses to Double-Entendre Words." *J Consult & Clin Psychol* 32:193–7 Ap '68. * (*PA* 42:8954)

659. GEORGE, JANET A., and STEPHENS, MARGO D. "Personality Traits of Public Health Nurses and Psychiatric Nurses." *Nursing Res* 17:168-70 Mr–Ap '68. * (*PA* 42:17235)

660. GOLDSTEIN, GERALD; NEURINGER, CHARLES; REIFF, CAROLYN; and SHELLY, CAROLYN H. "Generalizability of Field Dependency in Alcoholics." *J Consult & Clin Psychol* 32:560–4 O '68. * (*PA* 43:1094)

661. GORDON, LEONARD V. "Comments on 'Cross-Cultural Equivalence of Personality Measures.'" *J Social Psychol* 75:11–9 Je '68. * (*PA* 42:13577)

662. GOSS, ALLEN. "Edwards Personal Preference Schedule Patterns in Psychiatric Populations." *J Proj Tech & Pers Assess* 32:173–6 Ap '68. * (*PA* 42:10592)

663. GOSS, ALLEN; MOROSKO, TOM; and SHELDON, ROBERT. "Use of the Edwards Personal Preference Schedule With Alcoholics in a Vocational Rehabilitation Program." *J Psychol* 68:287–9 Mr '68. * (*PA* 42:9288)

664. GOSS, ALLEN M. "Importance of Diagnostic Categories in Evaluating Psychological Data." *J Counsel Psychol* 15:476–8 S '68. *

665. HAKEL, MILTON D. "Task Difficulty and Personality Test Validity." *Psychol Rep* 22:502 Ap '68. * (*PA* 42:11405)

666. KOHLAN, RICHARD G. "Relationships Between Inventoried Interests and Inventoried Needs." *Personnel & Guid J* 46:592–8 F '68. * (*PA* 42:12126)

667. KORMAN, MAURICE; STUBBLEFIELD, ROBERT L.; and MARTIN, LAWRENCE W. "Patterns of Success in Medical School and Their Correlates." *J Med Ed* 43:405–11 Mr '68. *

668. LOWE, C. MARSHALL. "The Relationship Between Self-Report of Religious and Personality Needs Among Psychiatric Patients." *J Social Psychol* 75:261–8 Ag '68. * (*PA* 42:17084)

669. McCOLLUM, ROBERT EUGENE. *A Study of the Relationship Between Selected Personality Characteristics and the Reflective Method.* Doctor's thesis, Ohio State University (Columbus, Ohio), 1968. (*DA* 29:762A)

670. MALEY, ROGER F., and LEVINE, DAVID. "Differences Between Guidance Counselors Who Accept and Reject Psychological Consultation." Abstract. *Psychol Rep* 22:232 F '68. * (*PA* 42:11169)

671. MANNING, E. J. "'Personal Validation': Replication of Forer's Study." *Psychol Rep* 23:181–2 Ag '68. * (*PA* 43:6936)

672. MEGARGEE, EDWIN I., and PARKER, GEORGE V. C. "An Exploration of the Equivalence of Murrayan Needs as Assessed by the Adjective Check List, the TAT and Edwards Personal Preference Schedule." *J Clin Psychol* 24:47–51 Ja '68. * (*PA* 42:8603)

673. MILTON, G. ALEXANDER, and LIPETZ, MILTON E. "The Factor Structure of Needs as Measured by the EPPS." *Multiv Behav Res* 3:37–46 Ja '68. * (*PA* 42:11374)

674. PASEWARK, R. A.; DAVIS, F. G.; and FITZGERALD, B. J. "Utilization of the Edwards Personal Preference Schedule With Disturbed Adolescents." *J Clin Psychol* 24:451 O '68. * (*PA* 43:4162)

675. PERKINS, CHARLES W. "Patient Manifest-Need Hierarchies: Therapists' Formulations and EPPS Results Compared." *J Consult & Clin Psychol* 32:221–2 Ap '68. * (*PA* 42:8102)

676. RAWLS, DONNA J. "The Use of the BIB in the Identification of College Seniors With Managerial Potential." *Proc Ann Conv Am Psychol Assn* 76:579–80 '68. * (*PA* 43:1563, title only)

677. SCHULDT, W. JOHN, and SMEE, PATRICIA G. "Personal Needs of Graduate Students in Psychology." *Psychol Rep* 22:916 Je '68. * (*PA* 42:14491)

678. SCHWARTZ, MELVIN L.; DENNERLL, RAYMOND D.; and LIN, YI-GUANG. "Neuropsychological and Psychosocial Predictors of Employability in Epilepsy." *J Clin Psychol* 24:174–7 Ap '68. * (*PA* 42:12633)

679. SMITH, INEZ L. "Similarity of Psychological Needs Before and After a Program for the Preparation of Teachers for Emotionally Disturbed Children." *Excep Children* 34:754–5 su '68. *

680. SMITH, JEANNE E. "Personality Structure in Beginning Nursing Students: A Factor Analytic Study." *Nursing Res* 17:140–5 Mr–Ap '68. * (*PA* 42:17238)

681. STAUFFACHER, JAMES C., and NAVRAN, LESLIE. "The Prediction of Subsequent Professional Activity of Nursing Students by the Edwards Personal Preference Schedule." *Nursing Res* 17:256–80 My–Je '68. * (*PA* 42:18984)

682. TENNISON, JAMES C., and SNYDER, WILLIAM U. "Some Relationships Between Attitudes Toward the Church and Cer-

tain Personality Characteristics." *J Counsel Psychol* 15:187–9 Mr '68. * (*PA* 42:8845)

683. VACCHIANO, RALPH B.; STRAUSS, PAUL S.; and SCHIFFMAN, DAVID C. "Personality Correlates of Dogmatism." *J Consult & Clin Psychol* 32:83–5 F '68. * (*PA* 42:7323)

684. WALBERG, HERBERT J. "Personality Correlates of Factored Teaching Attitudes." *Psychol Sch* 5:67–74 Ja '68. *

685. WALBERG, HERBERT J. "Teacher Personality and Classroom Climate." *Psychol Sch* 5:163–9 Ap '68. *

686. WATERS, LAWRENCE K. "Stability of Edwards Personal Preference Schedule Need Scale Scores and Profiles Over a Seven-Week Interval." *Ed & Psychol Meas* 28:615–8 su '68. * (*PA* 42:18114)

687. WIGGINS, JERRY S.; WIGGINS, NANCY; and CONGER, JUDITH COHEN. "Correlates of Heterosexual Somatic Preference." *J Personality & Social Psychol* 10:82–90 S '68. *

688. WILLIAMS, CARL D., and BRUEL, IRIS. "Evidence for the Validity of the Construct of Intraception." *J Clin Psychol* 24:188–9 Ap '68. * (*PA* 42:12122)

689. ZUCKERMAN, MARVIN, and LINK, KATHRYN. "Construct Validity for the Sensation-Seeking Scale." *J Consult & Clin Psychol* 32:420–6 Ag '68. * (*PA* 42:16438)

NAME INDEX

[68]

★Edwards Personality Inventory. Grades 9–12 and adults; 1966–67; EPI; 53 scores listed below; 5 booklets; manual ('67, 54 pages); separate answer sheets (IBM 805, self scoring) must be used; $10 per 20 tests; $6.35 per 100 IBM 805 answer sheets for any one booklet; $3 per 20 self scoring answer sheets for any one booklet; $5 per specimen set; postage extra; (40–50) minutes per booklet; Allen L. Edwards; Science Research Associates, Inc. *

a) BOOKLETS 1A AND 1B. 1966; 14 scores: plans and organizes things, intellectually oriented, persistent, self-confident, has cultural interests, enjoys being the center of attention, carefree, conforms, is a leader, kind to others, worries about making a good impression on others, seeks new experiences, likes to be alone, interested in the behavior of others.

b) BOOKLET 2. 1966; 11 scores: anxious about his performance, avoids facing problems, is a perfectionist, absentminded, sensitive to criticism, likes a set routine, wants sympathy, avoids arguments, conceals his feelings, easily influenced, feels misunderstood.

c) BOOKLET 3. 1966; 15 scores: motivated to succeed, impressed by status, desires recognition, plans work efficiently, cooperative, competitive, articulate, feels superior, logical, assumes responsibility, self-centered, makes friends easily, independent in his opinions, is a hard worker, neat in dress.

d) BOOKLET 4. 1966; 13 scores: self-critical, critical of others, active, talks about himself, becomes angry, helps others, careful about his possessions, understands himself, considerate, dependent, shy, informed about current affairs, virtuous.

REFERENCES

1. OAKLAND, J. A. *The Performance of High School Students on Edwards Personality Inventory and Its Relationship to Over- and Underachievement.* Doctor's thesis, University of Washington (Seattle, Wash.), 1967.
2. LUNNEBORG, PATRICIA W. "Stereotypic Aspect to Masculinity-Femininity Measurement." *Proc Ann Conv Am Psychol Assn* 76:163–4 '68. * (*PA* 43:936, title only)

[69]

The Ego Strength Q-Sort Test. Grades 9–16 and adults; 1956–58; ESQST; 6 scores: ego-status, social

status, goal setting and striving, good mental health, physical status, total; 1 form ('58, 4 pages, essentially the same as form copyrighted in 1956); manual ('58, 53 pages); no data on reliability; $9 per examiner's kit of 25 tests, 2 item sheets (from which sort slips for 2 examinees may be prepared), manual, stencils, and sorting board; $3 per 25 tests; cash orders postpaid; (50–90) minutes; Russell N. Cassel; Psychometric Affiliates. *

For reviews by Allen L. Edwards and Harrison G. Gough, see 6:88 (3 references).

[70]

*The El Senoussi Multiphasic Marital Inventory. Premarital and marital counselees; 1963–68; SMMI; 10 scores: frustration and chronic projection, cumulative ego strain, adolescent hangover or immaturity, revolt against femininity, flight into rejection, early conditioning against marriage, will-o'-the-wisp, sex dissatisfaction, sex dissatisfaction and projection, total; 1 form ('63, 12 pages); manual ('63, 33 pages plus copy of test and protocol booklet); supplement ['68, 2 pages]; protocol booklet ('63, 4 pages); $15 per examiner's kit of 25 tests, 25 protocol booklets, and manual; $7.50 per 25 tests; $6.50 per 25 protocol booklets; $3 per manual; postpaid; (30–50) minutes; Ahmed El Senoussi; Western Psychological Services. *

[71]

*Embedded Figures Test. Ages 10 and over; 1950–69; EFT; individual; Forms A, B, ('69, 12 cards, identical with 24 cards published in 1957 as single form); temporary manual ['69, 8 pages, mimeographed]; simple figures and practice items ('69, 8 cards, identical with cards published in 1957); record sheet ('69, 1 page); $6 per complete set of testing materials and 50 record sheets; $2.25 per 50 record sheets; postage extra; (15–25) minutes; Herman A. Witkin; Consulting Psychologists Press. *

For reviews by Harrison G. Gough and Leona E. Tyler, see 6:89 (24 references); see also 5:49 (9 references).

REFERENCES

1–9. See 5:49.
10–33. See 6:89.
34. LINTON, HARRIET B. "Dependence on External Influence: Correlates in Perception, Attitudes and Judgement." *J Abn & Social Psychol* 51:502–7 N '55. * (*PA* 31:2374)
35. BIERI, JAMES, and MESSERLEY, SUSAN. "Differences in Perceptual and Cognitive Behavior as a Function of Experience Type." *J Consult Psychol* 21:217–21 Je '57. * (*PA* 32:5480)
36. FINK, DAVID MARTIN. *Sex Differences in Perceptual Tasks in Relation to Selected Personality Variables.* Doctor's thesis, Rutgers University (New Brunswick, N.J.), 1959. (*DA* 20:1428)
37. POLONI-DE LEVIE, ALETTA. *Cognitive and Personality Correlates of Reading Difficulty.* Doctor's thesis, New York University (New York, N.Y.), 1960. (*DA* 27:2144B)
38. ELLIOTT, ROGERS. "Interrelationships Among Measures of Field Dependence, Ability, and Personality Traits." *J Abn & Social Psychol* 63:27–36 Jl '61. * (*PA* 36:4HA27E)
39. STEELE, JAMES ROBERT, JR. *Personality Defense and Task Performance.* Doctor's thesis, University of Washington (Seattle, Wash.), 1961. (*DA* 23:3482)
40. SEVERSON, ROGER ALFRED. *Some Nonreading Correlates of Reading Retardation.* Doctor's thesis, State University of Iowa (Iowa City, Iowa), 1962. (*DA* 23:2798)
41. CRANDALL, VAUGHN J., and SINKELDAM, CAROL. "Children's Dependent and Achievement Behaviors in Social Situations and Their Perceptual Field Dependence." *J Personality* 32:1–22 Mr '64. * (*PA* 39:4592)
42. JACKSON, DOUGLAS N.; MESSICK, SAMUEL; and MYERS, CHARLES T. "Evaluation of Group and Individual Forms of Embedded-Figures Measures of Field-Independence." *Ed & Psychol Meas* 24:177–92 su '64. * (*PA* 39:3184)
43. SEITZ, ROBERT, JR. *An Examination of Visual Perceptual Performance by Retardates and Normals on Embedded Figures and Structural Analysis in Reading.* Doctor's thesis, Indiana University (Bloomington, Ind.), 1964. (*DA* 25:5750)
44. WILKINS, LEE GERTRUDE. *Some Correlates of Cognitive Controls, Personality Trait Factors, and n Achievement Motiva-*

tion. Doctor's thesis, New York University (New York, N.Y.), 1964. (*DA* 25:1327)

45. ZUCKERMAN, MARVIN; KOLIN, ELIZABETH A.; PRICE, LEAH; and ZOOB, INA. "Development of a Sensation-Seeking Scale." *J Consult Psychol* 28:477–82 D '64. * (*PA* 39:7735)

46. BLOOMBERG, MORTON. "Anagram Solutions of Field-Independent and Field-Dependent Persons." *Percept & Motor Skills* 21:766 D '65. * (*PA* 40:3786, title only)

47. BURDICK, J. ALAN. "Eye Movements During the Embedded Figures Test." *Percept & Motor Skills* 21:726 D '65. *

48. CORAH, NORMAN L. "Differentiation in Children and Parents." *J Personality* 33:300–8 Je '65. * (*PA* 40:2895)

49. FITZGIBBONS, DAVID; GOLDBERGER, LEO; and EAGLE, MORRIS. "Field Dependence and Memory for Incidental Material." *Percept & Motor Skills* 21:743–9 D '65. * (*PA* 40:3765)

50. KARP, STEPHEN A., and PARDES, HERBERT. "Psychological Differentiation (Field Dependence) in Obese Women." *Psychosom Med* 27:238–44 My–Je '65. * (*PA* 39:16278)

51. LEEDS, DAVID PAUL. *Personality Patterns and Modes of Behavior of Male Adolescent Narcotic Addicts and Their Mothers.* Doctor's thesis, Yeshiva University (New York, N.Y.), 1965. (*DA* 26:2861)

52. STUART, IRVING R. "Field Dependency, Authoritarianism, and Perception of the Human Figure." *J Social Psychol* 66:209–14 Ag '65. * (*PA* 39:15309)

53. STUART, IRVING R.; BRESLOW, A.; BRECHNER, S.; ILYUS, ROSEMARY B.; and WOLPOFF, M. "The Question of Constitutional Influence on Perceptual Style." *Percept & Motor Skills* 20:419–20 Ap '65. * (*PA* 39:11149)

54. THORPE, JOSEPH S. "A Cross-Cultural Study of Personality Development: Selection of Test Measures." *Congr Inter-Am Soc Psychol* 9(1964):242–9 ['65]. *

55. CHUNG, WON-SHIK. *Relationships Among Measures of Cognitive Style, Vocational Preferences, and Vocational Identification.* Doctor's thesis, George Peabody College for Teachers (Nashville, Tenn.), 1966. (*DA* 27:4110B)

56. LEVINSON, BORIS M. "Subcultural Studies of Homeless Men." *Trans N Y Acad Sci* 29:165–82 D '66. * (*PA* 41:16683)

57. McDONALD, ROBERT L., and HENDRY, CHARLES H. "Repression-Sensitization, Field-Dependence, and 'Adjustment.'" Abstract. *Psychol Rep* 19:558 O '66. * (*PA* 41:591)

58. WEISSENBERG, P., and GRUENFELD, L. W. "Relationships Among Leadership Dimensions and Cognitive Style." *J Appl Psychol* 50:392–5 O '66. * (*PA* 40:13595)

59. WITKIN, HERMAN A.; FATERSON, HANNA F.; GOODENOUGH, DONALD R.; and BIRNBAUM, JUDITH. "Cognitive Patterning in Mildly Retarded Boys." *Child Develop* 37:301–16 Je '66. * (*PA* 40:9184)

60. BLOOMBERG, MORTON. "An Inquiry Into the Relationship Between Field Independence-Dependence and Creativity." *J Psychol* 67:127–40 S '67. * (*PA* 41:16106)

61. CAMPBELL, DONALD R.; DYER, FREDERICK N.; and BOERSMA, FREDERIC J. "Field Dependency and Picture Recognition Ability." *Percept & Motor Skills* 25:713–6 D '67. * (*PA* 42:8934)

62. KARP, STEPHEN A. "Field Dependence and Occupational Activity in the Aged." *Percept & Motor Skills* 24:603–9 Ap '67. * (*PA* 41:10284)

63. LEVINSON, BORIS M. "Field Dependence in Homeless Men." *J Clin Psychol* 23:152–4 Ap '67. * (*PA* 41:8903)

64. LEWIS, LAURA HESTER. *Acquiescence Response Set: Construct or Artifact?* Doctor's thesis, University of Nebraska (Lincoln, Neb.), 1967. (*DA* 28:2626B)

65. PRESSEY, A. W. "Field Dependence and Susceptibility to the Poggendorff Illusion." *Percept & Motor Skills* 24:309–10 F '67. * (*PA* 41:8242)

66. REILLY, DAVID H., and SUGARMAN, A. ARTHUR. "Conceptual Complexity and Psychological Differentiation in Alcoholics." *J Nerv & Mental Dis* 144:14–7 Ja '67. * (*PA* 41:12143)

67. SCHWARTZ, DANIEL W., and KARP, STEPHEN A. "Field Dependence in a Geriatric Population." *Percept & Motor Skills* 24:495–504 Ap '67. * (*PA* 41:10285)

68. SPOTTS, JAMES V., and MACKLER, BERNARD. "Relationships of Field-Dependent and Field-Independent Cognitive Styles to Creative Test Performance." *Percept & Motor Skills* 24:239–68 F '67. * (*PA* 41:8892)

69. STUART, IRVING R. "Perceptual Style and Reading Ability: Implications for an Instructional Approach." *Percept & Motor Skills* 24:135–8 F '67. * (*PA* 41:8244)

70. THORNTON, CARL L., and BARRETT, GERALD V. "Methodological Note on n Achievement and Field Independence Comparisons." *J Consult Psychol* 31:631–2 D '67. * (*PA* 42:2591)

71. WEISS, A. A.; STEIN, B.; ATAR, H.; and MELNIK, N. "Rorschach Test Behaviour as a Function of Psychological Differentiation." *Israel Ann Psychiatry* 5:32–42 Ap '67. * (*PA* 42:3977)

72. BARRETT, GERALD V.; CABE, PATRICK A.; and THORNTON, CARL L. "Visual Functioning and Embedded Figures Test Performance." *Percept & Motor Skills* 26:40 F '68. * (*PA* 42:9780)

73. BUZBY, DALLAS E. "Precognition and Psychological Variables." *J Parapsychol* 32:39–46 Mr '68. *

74. CLARK, STEPHEN L. "Authoritarian Attitudes and Field Dependence." *Psychol Rep* 22:309–10 F '68. * (*PA* 42:10589)

75. HIGGINS, NORENE, and GAGE, GERALD. "Perceptual Mode and Reading Improvement of College Students." *Percept & Motor Skills* 26:1249–50 Je '68. * (*PA* 42:19305)

76. KIDD, ALINE H., and BEERE, DONALD B. "Relationship Between Kinaesthetic Figural Aftereffect and Certain Personality Variables." *Percept & Motor Skills* 26:577–8 Ap '68. * (*PA* 42:12082)

77. MINARD, JAMES G. "Embedded Figures and Frame Disappearance Tests (EFT and FDT) as Measures of 'Percept Maintenance': A Study and Its Replication." *Percept & Motor Skills* 27:118 Ag '68. * (*PA* 43:1818)

78. RHODES, ROBERT J., and YORIOKA, GERALD N. "Dependency Among Alcoholic and Non-Alcoholic Institutionalized Patients." *Psychol Rep* 22:1343–4 Je '68. * (*PA* 42:19025)

79. RHODES, ROBERT J.; CARR, JOHN E.; and JURJI, E. DAVID. "Interpersonal Differentiation and Perceptual Field Differentiation." *Percept & Motor Skills* 27:172–4 Ag '68. * (*PA* 43:2800)

80. ZUCKERMAN, MARVIN. "Field Dependency as a Predictor of Responses to Sensory and Social Isolation." *Percept & Motor Skills* 27:757–8 D '68. *

NAME INDEX

[72]

Emo Questionnaire. Adults; 1958–60; EQ; 14 scores; rationalization, inferiority feelings, fear and anxiety, N vector (total of preceding 3 scores), depression, projection, unreality, withdrawal, Z vector (total of preceding 4 scores), hostility, sex, organic response, total diagnostic, buffer score; 1 form ('58, 8 pages); manual ('59, 37 pages); report form ('60, 4 pages); no data on reliability of current form; $6 per 20 tests; postage extra; $2 per specimen set, postpaid; (20–30) minutes; George O. Baehr (test), Melany E. Baehr (test), and Measurement Research Division, Industrial Relations Center, University of Chicago (manual) ; the Center. *

For reviews by Bertram D. Cohen and W. Grant Dahlstrom, see 6:90 (1 reference).

[73]

The Empathy Test. Ages 13 and over; 1947–61; ET; Forms A ('47, 1 page), B Revised ('61, c1951, 1 page), C ('54, 1 page, adaptation of Form A for Canadian use) ; manual ('55, 4 pages) ; $2 per 25 tests; $1 per specimen set (must be purchased to obtain manual) ; cash orders postpaid; (10–15) minutes; Willard A. Kerr and Boris J. Speroff; Psychometric Affiliates. *

For a review by Wallace B. Hall, see 6:91 (9 references) ; for a review by Robert L. Thorndike, see 5:50 (20 references).

REFERENCES

1–20. See 5:50.
21–29. See 6:91.
30. SZPAK, MARY L. *A Study of the Relationship Between Communality of Thought on the Loyola Language Study and Empathic Ability on Kerr's Empathy Test.* Master's thesis, Loyola University (Chicago, Ill.), 1967.

[74]

Evaluation Modality Test. Adults; 1956; EMT; 4 scores: realism, moralism, individualism, total; 1 form (4 pages) ; manual (2 pages) ; no data on reliability ; $3 per 25 tests; $1 per specimen set (must be purchased to obtain manual) including 10 tests, manual, and scoring key; postage extra; (25–35) minutes; Hugo O. Engelmann; Psychometric Affiliates. *

For a review by Wilson H. Guertin, see 5:51.

[75]

Every-Day Life: A Scale for the Measure of Three Varieties of Self-Reliance. High school; 1941; EDL; 3 scores: independence, resourcefulness, responsibility; 1 form (4 pages) ; manual ['41, 1 page]; set of scoring weights (4 pages) ; $2.50 per 25 tests; separate answer sheets (IBM 805) may be used; 4¢ per answer sheet; $2.50 per set of either hand or machine scoring stencils; 25¢ per manual; 25¢ per set of scoring weights; 45¢ per specimen set (complete test not included) ; postage extra; (30) minutes; Leland H. Stott; Sheridan Psychological Services, Inc. *

For a review by Harold E. Jones, see 4:41; for a review by Albert Ellis, see 3:38 (6 references).

[76]

Examining for Aphasia, Revised Edition. Adolescents and adults; 1946–54; EA; 1 form ('54, 12 pages) ; manual ('54, 73 pages) ; no data on reliability and validity; no norms; $7 per set of 25 record booklets and manual; $3.75 per 25 record booklets;

$4 per manual; postpaid; (30–120) minutes; Jon Eisenson; Psychological Corporation. *

For a review by T. R. Miles, see 5:52 (3 references, 2 excerpts) ; for a review by D. Russell Davis, see 4:42 (2 excerpts) ; for a review by C. R. Strother, see 3:39 (1 excerpt).

REFERENCES

1–3. See 5:52.
4. TIKOFSKY, RONALD SHERWOOD. *An Investigation of Some Possible Relationships Between Neurologic and Psychologic Techniques in the Study of Aphasia.* Doctor's thesis, University of Utah (Salt Lake City, Utah), 1957. (*DA* 18:1903)
5. NELSON, LOIS AUDREY. *A Study of Certain Cognitive Aspects of the Speech of Multiple Sclerotic Patients.* Doctor's thesis, University of Wisconsin (Madison, Wis.), 1960. (*DA* 21:1666)

[77]

*Eysenck Personality Inventory. 1963–68; EPI; revision of *Maudsley Personality Inventory;* 2 editions: American, British (identical except for 3 words and directions) ; 3 scores: extraversion, neuroticism, lie; postage extra; [10–15] minutes; H. J. Eysenck and Sybil B. G. Eysenck. *

a) AMERICAN EDITION. Grades 9–16 and adults; 1963–68; Forms A, B, ('63, 2 pages) ; manual ('68, 27 pages) ; college norms sheet ['66, 2 pages] ; college norms only; $3.50 per 25 tests; $1.50 per set of scoring stencils; $1.25 per manual; $1.75 per specimen set; scoring service, 45¢ or less per test; a printing with title *Eysenck Personal Inventory* is available for industrial use; Educational and Industrial Testing Service.

b) BRITISH EDITION. Adults; 1963–64; Forms A, B, ('64, 4 pages) ; manual ('64, 24 pages) ; 6s. 6d. per 20 tests; 3s. per scoring stencil; 4s. 6d. per manual; 8s. 6d. per specimen set; University of London Press Ltd.

For a review by James C. Lingoes, see 6:93.

REFERENCES

1. See 6:93.
2. AL-ISSA, IHSAN. "Creativity and Its Relationship to Age, Vocabulary and Personality of Schizophrenics." *Brit J Psychiatry* 110:74–9 Ja '64. * (*PA* 39:2653)
3. AL-ISSA, IHSAN. "The Eysenck Personality Inventory in Chronic Schizophrenia." *Brit J Psychiatry* 110:397–400 My '64. * (*PA* 39:2654)
4. EYSENCK, H. J. "The Measurement of Personality: A New Inventory." *J Indian Acad Appl Psychol* 1:1–11 Ja '64. * (*PA* 39:1831)
5. EYSENCK, HANS J., and EYSENCK, SYBIL B. G. "An Improved Short Questionnaire for the Measurement of Extraversion and Neuroticism." *Life Sci* 3:1103–9 O '64. * (*PA* 39:5017)
6. EYSENCK, S. B. G., and EYSENCK, H. J. " 'Acquiescence' Response Set in Personality Inventory Items." *Psychol Rep* 14:513–4 Ap '64. * (*PA* 39:1832)
7. EYSENCK, SYBIL B. G., and EYSENCK, HANS J. "The Personality of Judges as a Factor in the Validity of Their Judgements of Extraversion-Intraversion." *Brit J Social & Clin Psychol* 3:141–8 Je '64. * (*PA* 39:7837)
8. HOLLAND, H. C. "The Spiral After-Effect and the Rigidity-Dysthymia Hypothesis." *Acta Psychologica* 22(2):100–8 '64. * (*PA* 39:10052)
9. EYSENCK, H. J., and LEVEY, A. "Alternation in Choice Behavior and Extraversion." *Life Sci* 4:115–9 Ja '65. * (*PA* 39:10194)
10. KNAPP, ROBERT R. "Relationship of a Measure of Self-Actualization to Neuroticism and Extraversion." *J Consult Psychol* 29:168–72 Ap '65. * (*PA* 39:10056)
11. KNOWLES, J. B., and KREITMAN, NORMAN. "The Eysenck Personality Inventory: Some Considerations." *Brit J Psychiatry* 111:755–9 Ag '65. * (*PA* 40:1592)
12. ROBINSON, J. T.; DAVIES, L. S.; KREITMAN, NORMAN; and KNOWLES, J. B. "A Double-Blind Trial of Oxypertine for Anxiety Neurosis." *Brit J Psychiatry* 111:527–9 Je '65. * Criticism by James McAllister, 111:1010–1 O '65. *
13. VINGOE, FRANCIS JAMES. *The Relationship Between Measures of Self-Awareness, Self-Acceptance and Hypnotizability.* Doctor's thesis, University of Oregon (Eugene, Ore.), 1965. (*DA* 26:7450)
14. BRAUN, JOHN R., and GOMEZ, BARBARA J. "Effects of Faking Instructions on the Eysenck Personality Inventory." *Psychol Rep* 19:388–90 O '66. * (*PA* 41:586)
15. FARLEY, FRANK H. "Introversion and Achievement

Motivation." *Psychol Rep* 19:112 Ag '66. * *(PA* 40:12340, title only)

16. FARLEY, FRANK H. "Social Desirability, Extraversion, and Neuroticism: A Learning Analysis." *J Psychol* 64:113–8 S '66. * *(PA* 40:12341)

17. KLINE, PAUL. "Extraversion, Neuroticism and Academic Performance Among Ghanaian University Students." *Brit J Ed Psychol* 36:92–4 F '66. * *(PA* 40:7050, title only)

18. MCEVEDY, COLIN P.; GRIFFITH, ALWYN; and HALL, THOMAS. "Two School Epidemics." *Brit Med J* 2:1300–2 N 26 '66. *

19. MOSS, PETER D., and MCEVEDY, COLIN P. "An Epidemic of Overbreathing Among Schoolgirls." *Brit Med J* 2:1295–300 N 26 '66. *

20. PAYKEL, E. S. "Abnormal Personality and Thyrotoxicosis: A Follow-Up Study." *J Psychosom Med* 10:143–50 S '66. * *(PA* 41:769)

21. SAVAGE, R. D. "Personality Factors and Academic Attainment in Junior School Children." *Brit J Ed Psychol* 36:91–2 F '66. * *(PA* 40:7057, title only)

22. VINGOE, F. J. "Validity of the Eysenck Extraversion Scale as Determined by Self-Ratings in Normals." *Brit J Social & Clin Psychol* 5:89–91 Je '66. * *(PA* 40:9443)

23. CAMERON, PAUL. "Introversion and Egocentricity Among the Aged." *J Gerontol* 22:465–8 O '67. *

24. COOPER, ROBERT, and PAYNE, ROY. "Extraversion and Some Aspects of Work Behavior." *Personnel Psychol* 20:45–57 sp '67. * *(PA* 41:10428)

25. EYSENCK, H. J. "Personality Patterns in Various Groups of Businessmen." *Occup Psychol* 41:249–50 O '67. * *(PA* 43:3186)

26. EYSENCK, H. J., and EYSENCK, SYBIL B. G. "On the Unitary Nature of Extraversion." *Acta Psychologica* 26(4):383–90 '67. * *(PA* 42:5263)

27. EYSENCK, SYBIL B. G., and EYSENCK, H. J. "Salivary Response to Lemon Juice as a Measure of Introversion." *Percept & Motor Skills* 24:1047–53 Je '67. * *(PA* 41:15327)

28. FARLEY, FRANK H. "On the Independence of Extraversion and Neuroticism." *J Clin Psychol* 23:154–6 Ap '67. * *(PA* 41:8919)

29. GOMEZ, BARBARA J., and BRAUN, JOHN R. "Effects of 'Salesman Candidate' Sets on the Eysenck Personality Inventory." *Psychol Rep* 20:192 F '67. * *(PA* 41:7337, title only)

30. KLINE, PAUL. "The Use of the Cattell 16 P.F. Test and Eysenck's E.P.I. With a Literate Population in Ghana." *Brit J Social & Clin Psychol* 6:97–107 Je '67. * *(PA* 41:13647)

31. LOVELL, R. R. H., and VERGHESE, A. "Personality Traits Associated With Different Chest Pains After Infarction." *Brit Med J* 3:327–30 Ag 5 '67. *

32. MCLAUGHLIN, R. J., and EYSENCK, H. J. "Extraversion Neuroticism and Paired-Associates Learning." *J Exp Res Personality* 2:128–32 My '67. * *(PA* 41:11909)

33. MARKS, ISAAC M. "Components and Correlates of Psychiatric Questionnaires: Observations on the Cornell Medical Index, Eysenck Personality Inventory, and Tavistock Self-Assessment Inventory in Phobic Patients." *Brit J Med Psychol* 40:261–72 S '67. * *(PA* 42:12362)

34. RICHARDSON, J. F. "Correlatons Between the Extraversion and Neuroticism Scales of the Eysenck Personality Inventory Under Australian Conditions." *Austral Mil Forces Res Rep* 12/67:1–12 D '67. * *(PA* 42:8809)

35. SALAS, R. G. "Some Characteristics of the Eysenck Personality Inventory (EPI) Found Under Australian Conditions." *Austral Mil Forces Res Rep* 6/67:1–11 Jl '67. * *(PA* 42:2602)

36. SALAS, R. G., and RICHARDSON, J. F. "A Further Note on Some Characteristics of the Eysenck Personality Inventory (EPI) Observed Under Australian Conditions." *Austral Mil Forces Res Rep* 11/67:1–8 D '67. * *(PA* 42:6392)

37. DAVIES, BRIAN; MOWBRAY, R. M.; and JENSEN, DAMIEN. "A Questionnaire Survey of Psychiatric Symptoms in Australian Medical Students." *Austral & NZ J Psychiatry* 2:46–53 Mr '68. *

38. DIMSDALE, ALAN. "Two Dimensional Dimensions of a Small Sample of British Athletes." *B Brit Psychol Soc* 21:171–2 Jl '68. *

39. FARLEY, FRANK H. "Extraversion and the Self-Description of Endurance." *Brit J Social & Clin Psychol* 7:1–2 F '68. * *(PA* 42:8603)

40. FARLEY, FRANK H. "Moderating Effects of Intelligence on the Independence of Extraversion and Neuroticism." *J Consult & Clin Psychol* 32:226–8 Ap '68. * *(PA* 42:8921)

41. GORMAN, BERNARD S. "Social Desirability Factors and the Eysenck Personality Inventory." *J Psychol* 69:75–83 My '68. * *(PA* 42:12125)

42. KENDELL, R. E., and DISCIPIO, W. J. "Eysenck Personality Inventory Scores of Patients With Depressive Illnesses." *Brit J Psychiatry* 114:767–70 Je '68. * *(PA* 42:18861)

43. KIDD, ALINE H., and BEERE, DONALD B. "Relationship Between Kinaesthetic Figural Aftereffect and Certain Personality Variables." *Percept & Motor Skills* 26:577–8 Ap '68. * *(PA* 42:12082)

44. MCKERRACHER, D. W.; LOUGHNANE, T.; and WATSON, R. A. "Self-Mutilation in Female Psychopaths." *Brit J Psychiatry* 114:829–32 Jl '68. * *(PA* 43:2787)

45. MOWBRAY, R. M., and DAVIES, B. M. "Scores Obtained by Australian Medical Students on the Eysenck Personality Inventory." *Austral J Psychol* 20:59–61 Ap '68. * *(PA* 42:13786)

46. MUNRO, HELLE. "Verbal Fluency in Test and Group Situations." *Brit J Proj Psychol & Pers Study* 13:25–9 Je '68. *

47. RICHARDSON, J. F. "Correlations Between the Extraversion and Neuroticism Scales of the E.P.I." *Austral J Psychol* 20:15–8 Ap '68. * *(PA* 42:12992)

48. RYLE, ANTHONY, and LUNGHI, MARTIN. "A Psychometric Study of Academic Difficulty and Psychiatric Illness in Students." *Brit J Psychiatry* 114:57–62 Ja '68. * *(PA* 42:9413)

49. SALAS, R. G. "Fakeability of Responses on the Eysenck Personality Inventory." *Austral J Psychol* 20:55–7 Ap '68. * *(PA* 42:12293)

50. SALAS, R. G., and RICHARDSON, J. F. "Some Australian Data on Forms A and B of the EPI." *Austral J Psychol* 20:11–3 Ap '68. * *(PA* 42:12994)

51. VINGOE, FRANK J. "Validity of the Eysenck Extraversion Scale: Replication and Extension." *Psychol Rep* 22:706–8 Je '68. * *(PA* 42:12999)

52. VINGOE, FRANK J., and ANTONOFF, STEVEN R. "Personality Characteristics of Good Judges of Others." *J Counsel Psychol* 15:91–3 Ja '68. * *(PA* 42:5604)

53. WHITE, JAMES H.; STEPHENSON, GEOFFREY M.; CHILD, SANDRA E. A.; and GIBBS, JANYCE M. "Validation Studies of the Eysenck Personality Inventory." *Brit J Psychiatry* 114:63–8 Ja '68. * *(PA* 42:8113)

NAME INDEX

[78]

★**The Eysenck-Withers Personality Inventory (For I.Q. 50–80 Range).** Institutionalized subnormal adults; 1965–66; EWPI; more than two thirds of the items are from the *Junior Eysenck Personality Inventory;* 3 scores: extraversion, neuroticism, lie; individual; 1 form ('65, 4 pages); manual ['65, 7 pages]; 6s. 6d. per 20 tests; 2s. 6d. per manual; 3s. per scoring stencil; postage extra; 6s. per specimen set; [20–30] minutes; Sybil B. G. Eysenck; University of London Press Ltd. *

REFERENCE

1. THORPE, J. G.; BARDECKI, A.; and BALAGUER, A. B. "The Reliability of the Eysenck-Withers Personality Inventory for Subnormal Subjects." *J Mental Def Res* 11:108–15 Je '67. * *(PA* 42:1061)

[79]

***The FIRO Scales.** Grades 9–16 and adults; 1957–67; 6 tests, of which all but FIRO-B are experimental tests; manual ('67, 19 pages); $3 per manual; $3.75 per set of tests and manual without keys; $5 per set of keys; postage extra; William C. Schutz; Consulting Psychologists Press, Inc. *

a) FIRO-B [FUNDAMENTAL INTERPERSONAL RELATIONS ORIENTATION—BEHAVIOR]. 1957–67; 6 scores of behavior toward others: inclusion (expressed, wanted), control (expressed, wanted), affection (expressed, wanted); 1 form ('67, 3 pages, identical with test copyrighted in 1957 except for directions and format); no high school norms; $3 per 25 tests; 50¢ per set of keys; $3.50 per specimen set; [8–15] minutes.

b) FIRO-F [FUNDAMENTAL INTERPERSONAL RELATIONS ORIENTATION—FEELINGS]. 1957–67; 6 scores of feelings toward others: inclusion (expressed, wanted), control (expressed, wanted), affection (expressed, wanted); 1 form ('67, c1957, 3 pages); no data on reliability; $3 per 25 tests; $1.50 per set of scoring stencils; $4.50 per specimen set; [8–15] minutes.

c) LIPHE [LIFE INTERPERSONAL HISTORY ENQUIRY]. 1962–67; retrospective childhood relationships with parents; 12 scores (6 scores for each parent): inclusion (behavior, feelings), control (behavior, feelings), affection behavior-feeling, perceived parental approval; 1 form ('62, 3 pages); no data on reliability; no norms; $3.25 per 25 tests; $1.25 per set of keys; $4.25 per specimen set; [20] minutes.

d) COPE [COPING OPERATIONS PREFERENCE ENQUIRY]. 1962–67; 5 scores: denial, isolation, projection, regression-dependency, turning-against-self; 1 form ('62, 4 pages); no data on reliability and validity; $3.25 per 25 tests; $3.25 per specimen set; [20] minutes.

e) MATE [MARITAL ATTITUDES EVALUATION]. 1967; 5 scores: inclusion (behavior, feelings), control (behavior, feelings), affection; separate forms for husbands and wives (3 pages); no data on reliability and validity; no norms; $4.25 per 25 tests; keys and specimen set not yet available; [8–15] minutes.

f) VAL-ED [EDUCATIONAL VALUES]. 1967; 14 scores: importance, mind, school-child control, teacher-child (control, affection), teacher-community (inclusion, control, affection), administrator-teacher (inclusion, control, affection), administrator-community (inclusion, control, affection); 1 form (4 pages); no data on reliability; no norms; $3.25 per 25 tests; $1.50 per set of keys; $4.50 per specimen set; [15] minutes.

See 6:94 (15 references); for related book reviews not excerpted in this volume, consult the 6th MMY (B432).

REFERENCES

1–15. See 6:94.
16. ALLEN, RONALD ROYCE. *The Effects of Interpersonal and Concept Compatibility on the Encoding Behavior and Achievement of Debate Dyads.* Doctor's thesis, University of Wisconsin (Madison, Wis.), 1960. (*DA* 21:1659)
17. WAXLER, NANCY. *Defense Mechanisms and Interpersonal Behavior.* Doctor's thesis, Harvard University (Cambridge, Mass.), 1960.
18. BACKNER, BURTON LEE. *"Attraction-to-Group," as a Function of Style of Leadership, Follower Personality, and Group Composition.* Doctor's thesis, University of Buffalo (Buffalo, N.Y.), 1961. (*DA* 22:628)
19. GILBERTS, ROBERT DUBOIS. *The Interpersonal Characteristics of Teaching Teams.* Doctor's thesis, University of Wisconsin (Madison, Wis.), 1961. (*DA* 22:1882)
20. KERCKHOFF, ALAN C., and DAVIS, KEITH E. "Value Consensus and Need Complementarity in Mate Selection." *Am Sociol R* 27:295–303 Je '62. * (*PA* 37:1536)
21. HUTCHERSON, DONALD ELLSWORTH, JR. *Relationships Among Teacher-Pupil Compatibility, Social Studies Grades, and Selected Factors.* Doctor's thesis, University of California (Berkeley, Calif.), 1963. (*DA* 24:5194)
22. ESTADT, BARRY K. *Interpersonal Compatibility and Intra-Group Choices.* Doctor's thesis, Catholic University of America (Washington, D.C.), 1964. (*DA* 25:3008)
23. GARD, JOHN G., and BENDIG, A. W. "A Factor Analytic Study of Eysenck's and Schutz's Personality Dimensions Among Psychiatric Groups." *J Consult Psychol* 28:252–8 Je '64. * (*PA* 39:5729)
24. GORLOW, LEON, and BAROCAS, RALPH. "Social Values and Interpersonal Needs." *Acta Psychologica* 22(3):231–40 '64. * (*PA* 39:14948)
25. HARTSOUGH, DONALD M. *Effects of Interpersonal Orientation and Language Similarity on Verbal Communication in Dyadic Interpersonal Relationships.* Doctor's thesis, University of Florida (Gainesville, Fla.), 1964. (*DA* 25:3726)
26. SAPOLSKY, ALLAN. "Utilization of the FIRO Scale With a Group Having Limited Interpersonal Contact." *J Hillside Hosp* 13:95–9 Ap '64. * (*PA* 39:7796)
27. ULLMAN, LEONARD P.; KRASNER, LEONARD; and TROFFER, SUZANNE H. "A Contribution to FIRO-B Norms." *J Clin Psychol* 20:240–2 Ap '64. * (*PA* 39:7808)
28. WEBSTER, STATEN W. "Parental Antecedents of Teacher-to-Pupil Behaviors: A Study of Identification." *J Exp Ed* 32:389–94 su '64. * (*PA* 39:6014)
29. SAPOLSKY, ALLAN. "Relationship Between Patient-Doctor Compatibility, Mutual Perception, and Outcome of Treatment." *J Abn Psychol* 70:70–6 F '65. * (*PA* 39:8034)
30. BIGGS, DONALD A.; HUNERYAGER, S. G.; and DELANEY, JAMES J. "Leadership Behavior: Interpersonal Needs and Effective Supervisory Training." *Personnel Psychol* 19:311–20 au '66. * (*PA* 41:872)
31. BRUMBAUGH, ROBERT B.; HOEDT, KENNETH C.; and BEISEL, WILLIAM H., JR. "Teacher Dogmatism and Perceptual Accuracy." *J Teach Ed* 17:332–5 f '66. * (*PA* 41:810, title only)
32. GUNDERSON, E. K. ERIC, and MAHAN, JACK L. "Cultural and Psychological Differences Among Occupational Groups." *J Psychol* 62:287–304 Mr '66. * (*PA* 40:8094)
33. GUNDERSON, E. K. ERIC, and NELSON, PAUL D. "Personality Differences Among Navy Occupational Groups." *Personnel & Guid J* 44:956–61 My '66. * (*PA* 40:10486)
34. KIKUCHI, AKIO, and GORDON, LEONARD V. "Evaluation and Cross-Cultural Application of a Japanese Form of the Survey of Interpersonal Values." *J Social Psychol* 69:185–95 Ag '66. * (*PA* 40:12212)
35. KNAPP, DEANNE E.; KNAPP, DAVID; and WEICK, KARL. "Interrelations Among Measures of Affiliation and Approval Motivation Under Stress and Nonstress Conditions." *J Social Psychol* 69:223–35 Ag '66. * (*PA* 40:12333)
36. SCHUTZ, WILLIAM C. *The Interpersonal Underworld.* Palo Alto, Calif.: Science & Behavior Books, Inc., 1966. Pp. xiii, 242. * (Originally published in 1958 under the title of *FIRO: A Three-Dimensional Theory of Interpersonal Behavior* by Holt, Rinehart & Winston, Inc.)
37. SOUTHARD, JERRY KERMIT. *Factors Affecting Teacher-Supervisor Compatibility.* Doctor's thesis, University of Denver (Denver, Colo.), 1966. (*DA* 28:884A)
38. BOWMAN, BENJAMIN PHILLIP, JR. *Teacher Interpersonal Behavior and Classroom Control.* Doctor's thesis, University of California (Berkeley, Calif.), 1967. (*DA* 29:162A)
39. KRAMER, ERNEST. "A Contribution Toward the Validation of the FIRO-B Questionnaire." *J Proj Tech & Pers Assess* 31:80–1 Ag '67. * (*PA* 41:14447)
40. PERKINS, EUGENE REED. *The Effect of Introducing Programmed Instruction in Interpersonal Relationship Techniques Into Counselor Practicum Training.* Doctor's thesis, Colorado State College (Greeley, Colo.), 1967. (*DA* 28:4450A)
41. POLLACK, HERBERT BERNARD. *Change in Homogeneous and Heterogeneous Sensitivity Training Groups.* Doctor's thesis, University of California (Berkeley, Calif.), 1967. (*DA* 28:4762B)
42. YALOM, IRVIN D.; HOUTS, PETER S.; ZIMERBERG, SHELDON M.; and RAND, KENNETH H. "Prediction of Improvement in Group Therapy: An Exploratory Study." *Arch Gen Psychiatry* 17:159–68 Ag '67. * (*PA* 41:15391)
43. INSEL, SHEPARD A.; REESE, CAROL SCHMIDA; and ALEXANDER, BARRETT B. "Self-Presentations in Relation to Internal and External Referents." *J Consult & Clin Psychol* 32:389–95 Ag '68. * (*PA* 42:17199)
44. TAYLOR, EVALYN W. "Interpersonal Orientation and Verbal Conditioning Effects." *Proc Ann Conv Am Psychol Assn* 76:541–2 '68. * (*PA* 43:830, title only)
45. WIGGINS, THOMAS WINFIELD. *Leader Behavior Characteristics and Organizational Climate.* Doctor's thesis, Claremont Graduate School and University Center (Claremont, Calif.), 1968. (*DA* 29:2504A)

NAME INDEX

[80]

Family Adjustment Test. Ages 12 and over; 1952–54; FAT; title on test is *Elias Family Opinion Survey;* 11 scores: attitudes toward mother, attitudes toward father, father-mother attitude quotient, oedipal, struggle for independence, parent-child friction-harmony, interparental friction-harmony, family inferiority-superiority, rejection of child, parental qualities, total; 1 form ('52, 6 pages); manual ('54, 4 pages); $5 per 25 tests; $1 per specimen set (must be purchased to obtain manual and key); cash orders postpaid; (35–45) minutes; Gabriel Elias; Psychometric Affiliates. *

For a review by John Elderkin Bell, see 6:95; for a review by Albert Ellis, see 5:53 (6 references).

REFERENCES

1–6. See 5:53.
7. McNEIL, ELTON B., and COHLER, J. ROBERT, JR. "The Effect of Personal Needs on Counselors' Perception and Behavior." *Papers Mich Acad Sci Arts & Letters* 42:281–8 pt 2 '57. * (*PA* 37:6924)

[81]

***Family Relations Test.** Ages 3–7, 7–15, adults; 1957–65; individual; 1 form ['57]; 3 levels; postage extra; (20–25) minutes; distributed by National Foundation for Educational Research in England and Wales. *

a) FAMILY RELATIONS TEST: AN OBJECTIVE TECHNIQUE FOR EXPLORING EMOTIONAL ATTITUDES IN CHILDREN. Ages 3–7, 7–15; 1957; 2 levels; manual (59 pages); 135*s.* per set of test materials; 20*s.* per specimen set; Eva Bene and James Anthony.

1) *Younger Children.* Ages 3–7; 40 item cards; 12*s.* 6*d.* per 25 record booklets.
2) *Older Children.* Ages 7–15; 86 item cards; 12*s.* 6*d.* per 25 record booklets; 12*s.* 6*d.* per 25 scoring blanks.

b) ADULT VERSION OF THE FAMILY RELATIONS TEST: AN OBJECTIVE TECHNIQUE FOR EXPLORING RECOLLECTED CHILDHOOD FEELINGS. Adults; 1965; 96 item cards; manual (30 pages); 107*s.* 6*d.* per set of test materials; 12*s.* 6*d.* per 25 record booklets; 12*s.* 6*d.* per 25 scoring blanks; 20*s.* per specimen set; Eva Bene.

For reviews by John E. Bell, Dale B. Harris, and Arthur R. Jensen of children's levels, see 5:132 (1 reference).

REFERENCES

1. See 5:132.
2. BENE, EVA. "The Family Relations Test." *Rorsch Newsl* 2:5–6 D '57. *
3. BENE, EVA. "The Objective Assessment of the Emotional Atmosphere in Which Children Live in Their Homes." Abstract. *Acta Psychologica* 15:495–6 '59. *
4. LINTON, HARRIET; BERLE, BEATRICE BISHOP; GROSSI, MARGARET; and JACKSON, ELSIE. "Reactions of Children Within Family Groups as Measured by the Bene-Anthony Tests." *J Mental Sci* 107:308–25 Mr '61. * (*PA* 36:2FG08L)
5. MEYER, HENRIETTA. "The Investigation of the Adopted Child by Means of the Bene-Anthony Test Compared With the Lowenfeld World Technique." *Rorsch Newsl* 6:20–31 D '61. *
6. MORROW, WILLIAM R., and WILSON, ROBERT C. "Family Relations of Bright High-Achieving and Under-Achieving High School Boys." *Child Develop* 32:501–10 S '61. * (*PA* 36:4FG01M)
7. WILLIAMS, JESSIE M. "Children Who Break Down in Foster Homes: A Psychological Study of Patterns of Personality Growth in Grossly Deprived Children." *J Child Psychol & Psychiatry* 2:5–20 Je '61. * (*PA* 36:FF05W)
8. GROSS, SEYMOUR Z. "Critique: Children Who Break Down in Foster Homes: A Psychological Study of Patterns of Personality Growth in Grossly Deprived Children." *J Child Psychol & Psychiatry* 4:61–6 Ap '63. *
9. MEYER, MORTIMER M. "Family Relations Test." *J Proj Tech & Pers Assess* 27:309–14 S '63. * (*PA* 38:4323)
10. BENE, EVA. "On the Genesis of Female Homosexuality." *Brit J Psychiatry* 111:815–21 S '65. * (*PA* 40:473)
11. BENE, EVA. "On the Genesis of Male Homosexuality: An Attempt at Clarifying the Role of Parents." *Brit J Psychiatry* 111:803–13 S '65. * (*PA* 40:472)
12. FRANKEL, JACOB JOSHUA. *The Relation of a Specific Family Constellation and Some Personality Characteristics of*

Children. Doctor's thesis, George Peabody College for Teachers (Nashville, Tenn.), 1965. (*DA* 28:2620B)
13. GRATTON, L., and MURRAY, JOSEPH D. "An Experimental Approach to the Study of Family Dynamics." *Proc Ann Conf Air Force Behav Sci* 13:124–41 S '66. *

[82]

Famous Sayings. Grades 9–16 and business and industry; 1958, c1957–58; FS; 4 scores: conventional mores, hostility, fear of failure, social acquiescence; Form 1 ('58, c1957–58, 4 pages); manual ('58, 19 pages, reprint of 6 below); $6.50 per set of test materials; $5 per 50 tests; $1.50 per manual; cash orders postpaid; specimen set not available; (15–30) minutes; Bernard M. Bass; Psychological Test Specialists. *

For reviews by Wesley C. Becker and Robert L. Thorndike, see 6:96 (17 references).

REFERENCES

1–17. See 6:96.
18. FEINBERG, M. R., and PENZER, W. N. "Factor Analysis of a Selection Battery." *Personnel Psychol* 17:319–24 au '64. * (*PA* 39:8794)
19. WALSH, T. MYRICK. "Responses on the Famous Sayings Test of Professional and Non-Professional Personnel in a Medical Population." *Psychol Rep* 18:151–7 F '66. * (*PA* 40:6646)
20. FISHER, SEYMOUR, and OSOFSKY, HOWARD. "Sexual Responsiveness in Women: Psychological Correlates." *Arch Gen Psychiatry* 17:214–26 Ag '67. * (*PA* 41:15149)
21. DARBES, ALEX, and PLATT, JEROME J. "Norms on the Famous Sayings Test for Student Beauticians." *Psychol Rep* 23:244 Ag '68. * (*PA* 23:6932)

[83]

Fatigue Scales Kit. Adults; 1944–54; FSK; 3 scales; hectographed manual ('54, 4 pages); $5 per set of 25 sets of the 3 scales and manual; $1.50 per 25 copies of any one scale; cash orders postpaid; specimen set not available; [10] minutes; [Willard A. Kerr]; Psychometric Affiliates. *

a) INDUSTRIAL SUBJECTIVE FATIQUE AND EUPHORIA SCALES. Adults; 1944–54; 2 scores: fatigue, unpleasantness; 1 form ('54, 1 page, identical with scale published in 1944).
b) RETROSPECTIVE WORK CURVE FEELINGS FOR NATIONAL RESEARCH PROGRAM ON EMPLOYEE FEELINGS AT WORK. Adults; 1954; 1 form (1 page).
c) STUDY OF DAY [MOTHER'S DAY FATIGUE SCALE]. Housewives; 1954; 1 form (1 page); no data on validity.

For a review by Richard S. Barrett, see 6:97 (1 reference).

[84]

Fels Parent Behavior Rating Scales. 1937–49; FPBRS; "for the use of the trained home visitor in appraising certain aspects of parent-child relationships"; 30 scores: adjustment of home, activeness of home, discord in home, sociability of family, coordination of household, child-centeredness of home, duration of contact with mother, intensity of contact with mother, restrictiveness of regulations, readiness of enforcement, severity of actual penalties, justification of policy, democracy of policy, clarity of policy, effectiveness of policy, disciplinary friction, quantity of suggestion, coerciveness of suggestion, accelerational attempt, general babying, general protectiveness, readiness of criticism, direction of criticism, readiness of explanation, solicitousness for welfare, acceptance of child, understanding, emotionality toward child, affectionateness toward child, rapport with child; 1 form (no date, 1–30 graphic rating scales); manual ('49, see *14* below); tabulation sheet ('41, c1939, 1 page); instructions ('41, c1939, 6 pages); $1 per set of scales; $1.50 per manual; postpaid; Alfred L. Baldwin, Joan Kalhorn, Fay Huffman Breese, and Horace Champney; Fels Research Institute. *

For a review by Dale B. Harris, see 4:43 (15 references).

REFERENCES

1-15. See 4:43.
16. LORR, MAURICE, and JENKINS, RICHARD L. "Three Factors in Parent Behavior." J Consult Psychol 17:306-8 Ag '53. * (PA 28:4087)
17. CRANDALL, VAUGHN J., and PRESTON, ANNE. "Patterns and Levels of Maternal Behavior." Child Develop 26:267-77 D '55. * (PA 30:6785)
18. BECKER, WESLEY C.; PETERSON, DONALD R.; HELLMER, LEO A.; SHOEMAKER, DONALD J.; and QUAY, HERBERT C. "Factors in Parental Behavior and Personality as Related to Problem Behavior in Children." J Consult Psychol 23:107-18 Ap '59. * (PA 34:1693)
19. SCHAEFER, EARL S. "A Circumplex Model for Maternal Behavior." J Abn & Social Psychol 59:226-35 S '59. * (PA 34:2572)
20. DONNELLY, ELLEN M. "The Quantitative Analysis of Parent Behavior Toward Psychotic Children and Their Siblings." Genetic Psychol Monogr 62:331-76 N '60. * (PA 35:3830)
21. CRANDALL, VAUGHN J., and PRESTON, ANNE. "Verbally Expressed Needs and Overt Maternal Behaviors." Child Develop 32:261-70 Je '61. * (PA 36:3FG61C)
22. MEDINNUS, GENE R. "The Relation Between Several Parent Measures and the Child's Early Adjustment to School." J Ed Psychol 52:153-6 Je '61. * (PA 38:3157)
23. WATERS, ELINOR, and CRANDALL, VAUGHN J. "Social Class and Observed Maternal Behavior From 1940 to 1960." Child Develop 35:1021-32 D '64. *

[85]

The Forty-Eight Item Counseling Evaluation Test. Adolescents and adults; 48 ICET; 1963; 7 problem area scores: anxiety-tension-stress, compulsive-obsessive-rigid behavior, depressive-defeatist thoughts and feelings, friendship-socialization, religious-philosophical goals, inadequacy feelings and behavior, total; 1 form (4 pages); manual (15 pages plus test); no data on reliability of subscores; $7 per examiner's kit of 25 tests, key, and manual; $6.50 per 25 tests; 50¢ per key; $1.50 per manual; postpaid; (10-20) minutes; Frank B. McMahon; Western Psychological Services. *

[86-7]

The Freeman Anxiety Neurosis and Psychosomatic Test. Mental patients; 1952-55; FANPT; title on test is *The Freeman AN and PS Test;* 9 scores: anxiety neurosis, psychosomatic syndrome, and 7 subscores; 1 form ('52, 10 pages); revised manual ('55, 11 pages); revised profile ('55, 1 page); no norms for subscores; $1.75 per 10 tests; $1.25 per manual; postage extra; specimen set not available; administration time not reported; M. J. Freeman; Grune & Stratton, Inc. *

For reviews by Gerald A. Mendelsohn and Robert C. Nichols, see 6:99 (4 references); see also 5:55 (3 references).

[88]

G. C. Personality Development Record. High school; 1959; GCPDR; ratings by teachers on 9 traits; adapted from a form used in the schools of Newark, N.J.; 1 form ['59, 1 page]; no manual or other accessories; no data on reliability and validity; no norms; 41¢ per pad of 50 records, postage extra; [5] minutes; Guidance Centre. *

[89]

★Getting Along. Grades 7-9; 1964-65; GA; Forms A, B ('64, 14 pages); 4 scores: self acceptance, acceptance by others, facing reality, total; manual ('65, 21 pages); no norms for part scores; separate answer sheets must be used; 20¢ per test; 1¢ per answer sheet; 10¢ per key; 25¢ per manual; postage extra; $1 per specimen set, postpaid; (50) minutes; Trudys Lawrence; the Author. *

REFERENCES

1. LAWRENCE, TRUDYS. An Appraisal Instrument for the Evaluation of the Emotional Health of Junior High School Pupils. Doctor's thesis, University of Southern California (Los Angeles, Calif.), 1964. (DA 25:3381)
2. LAWRENCE, TRUDYS. "Appraisal of Emotional Health at the Secondary School Level." Res Q 37:252-67 My '66. *

[90]

★The Gibson Spiral Maze. Ages 8.5 and over; 1965; c1961-65; psychomotor performance associated with maladjustment, delinquency, mental illness, and accident proneness; 2 scores: time, error; individual; 1 form ('61, 1 page); manual ('65, 12 pages); no data on reliability; 4s. per manual; 10s. per 20 tests; 4s. 6d. per specimen set; postage extra; (2) minutes; H. B. Gibson; University of London Press Ltd. *

REFERENCES

1. GIBSON, H. B. "The Spiral Maze: A Psychomotor Test With Implications for the Study of Delinquency." Brit J Psychol 55:219-25 My '64. * (PA 39:3656)
2. MAYO, P. R. "Speed and Accuracy of Depressives on a Spiral Maze Test." Percept & Motor Skills 23:1034 D '66. * (PA 41:6098)

[91]

Goldstein-Scheerer Tests of Abstract and Concrete Thinking. Brain damaged adults; 1941-51; individual; 1 form; 5 tests; manual ('41, 156 pages, see 9 below); supplementary manual ('47, 4 pages) for *a* and *e*; no data on reliability; no norms; $68 per complete set of test materials and manual; $3.50 per manual; postpaid; [30-60] minutes; Kurt Goldstein, Martin Scheerer, and Louis Rosenberg (*c*, record booklet); Psychological Corporation. *
a) GOLDSTEIN-SCHEERER CUBE TEST. 1941-45; separate record booklets ('45, 6 pages) for designs 1-6, 7-12; $5.75 per set of 2 design booklets and supplementary manual; $4.50 per set of Kohs' blocks; $3.75 per 50 copies of either record booklet.
b) GELB-GOLDSTEIN COLOR SORTING TEST. 1941-51; record booklet ('51, 4 pages); $15.50 per set of wool skeins; $4.50 per 50 record booklets.
c) GOLDSTEIN-SCHEERER OBJECT SORTING TEST. 1941-51; record booklet ('51, 8 pages); supplementary sheet ('51, 1 page) for experiment 3; $18.50 per set of objects; $4.20 per 50 record booklets; $1 per 50 supplementary sheets.
d) WEIGL-GOLDSTEIN-SCHEERER COLOR FORM SORTING TEST. 1941-45; record booklet ('45, 4 pages); $7.25 per set of blocks; $3 per 50 record booklets.
e) GOLDSTEIN-SCHEERER STICK TEST. 1941-45; record booklet ('45, 4 pages); $4.25 per set of sticks and supplementary manual; $3 per 50 record booklets.

For a review by R. W. Payne, see 6:101 (23 references); see also 5:57 (21 references); for reviews by Kate Levine Kogan, C. R. Strother (with Ludwig Immergluck), and O. L. Zangwill, see 3:41 (28 references); for an excerpt from a related book review, see 3:42.

REFERENCES

1-28. See 3:41.
29-49. See 5:57.
50-72. See 6:101.
73. SKLAR, MAURICE. "Psychological Test Scores, Language Disturbances, and Autopsy Findings in Aphasia Patients." Newsl Res Psychol 4:65-79 Ag '62. *
74. WEINBERG, NORRIS H. "Relativism, Self-Centering, and Conceptual Level." Child Develop 34:443-50 Je '63. * (PA 38:8067)
75. BALL, THOMAS S. "Perceptual Concomitants of Conceptual Reorganization." J Consult Psychol 28:523-8 D '64. * (PA 39:6824)
76. CARR, DONALD LEE. The Concept Formation and Psycholinguistic Abilities of Normal and Mentally Retarded Children of Comparable Mental Age. Doctor's thesis, State University of Iowa (Iowa City, Iowa), 1964. (DA 25:997)
77. HAWKS, D. V. "The Clinical Usefulness of Some Tests of Over-Inclusive Thinking in Psychiatric Patients." Brit J Social & Clin Psychol 3:186-95 O '64. * (PA 39:5730)

78. HOLTZMAN, WAYNE H.; GORHAM, DONALD R.; and MORAN, LOUIS J. "A Factor-Analytic Study of Schizophrenic Thought Processes." *J Abn & Social Psychol* 69:355–64 O '64. * (*PA* 39:8491)

79. KENNEDY, KIERAN, and KATES, SOLIS L. "Conceptual Sorting and Personality Adjustment in Children." *J Abn & Social Psychol* 68:211–4 F '64. * (*PA* 38:5786)

80. KIRSCHNER, DAVID. "Differences in Gradients of Stimulus Generalization as a Function of 'Abstract' and 'Concrete' Attitude." *J Consult Psychol* 28:160–4 Ap '64. * (*PA* 39:2389)

81. MICHAEL, JAMES. *A Developmental Study of Conceptual Performance on Words and on Objects.* Doctor's thesis, University of Massachusetts (Amherst, Mass.), 1964. (*DA* 26:2323)

82. ROSMAN, BERNICE; WILD, CYNTHIA; RICCI, JUDITH; FLECK, STEPHEN; and LIDZ, THEODORE. "Thought Disorders in the Parents of Schizophrenic Patients: A Further Study Utilizing the Object Sorting Test." *J Psychiatric Res* 2:211–21 O '64. * (*PA* 39:16236)

83. SILVERSTEIN, A. B., and MOHAN, PHILIP J. "A Re-analysis of the Color Form Sorting Test Performance of Mentally Retarded Adults." *Am J Mental Def* 69:402–4 N '64. * (*PA* 39:7799)

84. WEISS, A. A. "The Weigl-Goldstein-Scheerer Color-Form Sorting Test: Classification of Performance." *J Clin Psychol* 20:103–7 Ja '64. * (*PA* 39:10165)

85. SILVERSTEIN, A. B., and MOHAN, PHILIP J. "A Factor-Analytic Approach to Object-Sorting Behavior." Abstract. *J Consult Psychol* 29:89 F '65. * (*PA* 39:7708, title only)

86. STABENAU, JAMES R.; TUPIN, JOE; WERNER, MARTHA; and POLLIN, WILLIAM. "A Comparative Study of Families of Schizophrenics, Delinquents, and Normals." *Psychiatry* 28:45–59 F '65. * (*PA* 39:10490)

87. WHITE, WILLIAM F. "Personality and Cognitive Learning Among Alcoholics With Different Intervals of Sobriety." *Psychol Rep* 16:1125–40 Je '65. * (*PA* 39:16094)

88. BIRELEY, MARLENE BERGMAN. *A Comparison of the Responses of Neurologically Impaired, Psychogenic Emotionally Disturbed, and Normal, Well-Adjusted Children to the Goldstein-Scheerer Tests.* Doctor's thesis, Ohio State University (Columbus, Ohio), 1966. (*DA* 27:3716A)

89. SU, CHIEN-WEN. "A Study of Concept Formation in Children." *Psychol & Ed* 1:85–95 Ap '67. *

90. LOVIBOND, S. H., and HOLLOWAY, I. "Differential Sorting Behavior of Schizophrenics and Organics." *J Clin Psychol* 24:307–11 Jl '68. * (*PA* 42:17388)

91. RAPAPORT, DAVID; GILL, MERTON M.; and SCHAFER, ROY; edited by ROBERT R. HOLT. Chap. 5, "The Sorting Test," pp. 194–221. In their *Diagnostic Psychological Testing.* New York: International Universities Press, Inc., 1968. Pp. xi, 562. *

NAME INDEX

[92]

Gordon Personal Inventory. Grades 9–16 and adults; 1956–63, c1955–63; GPI; 4 scores: cautiousness, original thinking, personal relations, vigor; 1 form ('63, c1955–56, identical with 1956 form except for format and wording changes in directions); 2 editions: hand scored (3 pages), IBM 805 machine scorable (2 pages); revised manual ('63, c1956–63, 20 pages); mimeographed notes on the scoring system ['63, 5 pages] available upon request; tentative norms for high school students; $4.80 per 35 hand scored tests; $4 per 35 IBM 805 test-answer sheets; $2 per set of machine scoring stencils; $2 per specimen set including the complementary *Gordon Personal Profile;* postage extra; (15–20) minutes; Leonard V. Gordon; Harcourt, Brace & World, Inc. *

For reviews by Charles F. Dicken and Alfred B. Heilbrun, Jr., see 6:102 (13 references); for reviews by Benno G. Fricke and John A. Radcliffe, see 5:58 (1 reference, 2 excerpts).

REFERENCES

1–13. See 6:102.

14. LODATO, FRANCIS JOSEPH. *The Relationship Between Interest and Personality as Measured by the Kuder and the Heston and Gordon Inventories.* Doctor's thesis, St. John's University (Jamaica, N.Y.), 1955.

15. MEISGEIER, CHARLES HENRY. *Variables Which May Identify Successful Student Teachers of Mentally or Physically Handicapped Children.* Doctor's thesis, Pennsylvania State University (University Park, Pa.), 1962. (*DA* 23:3803)

16. PHELAN, JOSEPH G. "An Exploration of Personality Correlates to Business Risk-Taking Behavior." *J Psychol* 53:281–7 Ap '62. * (*PA* 37:2112)

17. DANIEL, KATHRYN LAVERNE BARCHARD. *A Study of Dropouts at the University of Alabama With Respect to Certain Academic and Personality Variables.* Doctor's thesis, University of Alabama (University, Ala.), 1963. (*DA* 25:1736)

18. LOCKE, EDWIN A. "Some Correlates of Classroom and Out-of-Class Achievement in Gifted Science Students." *J Ed Psychol* 54:238–48 O '63. * (*PA* 38:4649)

19. BRAUN, JOHN R. "Consistency of Cross-Test Individual Differences in Personality-Inventory Faking." *J Psychol* 58:313–6 O '64. * (*PA* 39:5167)

20. BECKER, PAUL W. "Some Correlates of Delinquency and Validity of Questionnaire Assessment Methods." *Psychol Rep* 16:217–7 F '65. * (*PA* 39:8431)

21. PRIEN, ERICH P., and BOTWIN, DAVID E. "The Reliability and Correlates of an Achievement Index." *Ed & Psychol Meas* 26:1047–52 w '66. * (*PA* 41:4998)

22. BARE, CAROLE E. "Relationship of Counselor Personality and Counselor-Client Personality Similarity to Selected Counseling Success Criteria." *J Counsel Psychol* 14:419–25 S '67. * (*PA* 41:15844)

23. DANIEL, KATHRYN BARCHARD. "A Study of College Dropouts With Respect to Academic and Personality Variables." *J Ed Res* 60:230–5 Ja '67. *

24. JONES, JOHN MARTIN. *The Relationship of Subject Area and Selected Personality Traits to the Preference to Teach by the Group or Lecture Method.* Doctor's thesis, North Texas State University (Denton, Tex.), 1967. (*DA* 28:2138A)

25. WELSCH, LAWRENCE A. *The Supervisor's Employee Appraisal Heuristic: The Contribution of Selected Measures of Employee Aptitude, Intelligence and Personality.* Doctor's thesis, University of Pittsburgh (Pittsburgh, Pa.), 1967. (*DA* 28:4321A)

26. JONES, JOHN E., and SCHOCH, EUGENE W. "Correlates of Success in MA-Level Counselor Education." *Counselor Ed & Sup* 7:286–91 sp '68. * (*PA* 42:17989)

NAME INDEX

Jones, J. M.: 24
Kriedt, P. H.: 8
Locke, E. A.: 18
Lodato, F. J.: 14
McKinney, E. D.: 2
Magaw, D. C.: 4
Meisgeier, C. H.: 15
Phelan, J. G.: 16
Prien, E. P.: 21

Radcliffe, J. A.: *rev*, 5:58
Ried, B. R.: 9
Schoch, E. W.: 26
Shaffer, L. F.: *exc*, 5:58
Siegel, L.: *exc*, 5:58
Weiss, R.: 6
Welsch, L. A.: 25
Willingham, W. W.: 13

[93]

Gordon Personal Profile. Grades 9–16 and adults; 1953–63, c1951–63; GPP; 4 scores: ascendancy, responsibility, emotional stability, sociability; 1 form ('63, c1951–53, identical with 1953 form except for format and wording changes in directions); 2 editions: hand scored (3 pages), IBM 805 machine scorable (2 pages); revised manual ('63, c1953–63, 27 pages); mimeographed notes on the scoring system ['63, 5 pages] available upon request; $4.80 per 35 hand scored tests; $4 per 35 IBM 805 test-answer sheets; $2 per set of machine scoring stencils; $2 per specimen set including the complementary *Gordon Personal Inventory;* postage extra; (15–20) minutes; Leonard V. Gordon; Harcourt, Brace & World, Inc. *

For reviews by Charles F. Dicken and Alfred B. Heilbrun, Jr., see 6:103 (25 references); for reviews by Benno G. Fricke and John A Radcliffe, see 5:59 (16 references, 1 excerpt).

REFERENCES

1–16. See 5:59.
17–41. See 6:103.
42. FRIEDMAN, JOSEPH. *Psychological Correlates of Overweight, Underweight and Normal Weight College Women.* Doctor's thesis, Temple University (Philadelphia, Pa.), 1958. (*DA* 19:3362)
43. SILBER, MARK BISCHOFF. *A Comparative Study of Three Methods of Effecting Attitude Change.* Doctor's thesis, Ohio State University (Columbus, Ohio), 1961. (*DA* 22:2488)
44. BARKER, RAYMOND FREDERICK. *A Test of the Validity of the Gordon Personal Profile as a Device to Isolate Members of the Do-It-Yourself Market in Fort Worth, Texas.* Doctor's thesis, University of Texas (Austin, Tex.), 1962. (*DA* 23:1541)
45. HOLLISTER, ALBERT VIRGIL. *Physical and Personality Measurements of Selected College Male Freshmen.* Doctor's thesis, George Peabody College for Teachers (Nashville, Tenn.), 1962. (*DA* 23:1999)
46. MISRA, R. G. "A Factorial Study of the Stability of Some Personality Factors." Comments by R. L. Thorndike. *Shiksha* 15:112–9 O '62. * (*DA* 37:8003)
47. DANIEL, KATHRYN LaVERNE BARCHARD. *A Study of Dropouts at the University of Alabama With Respect to Certain Academic and Personality Variables.* Doctor's thesis, University of Alabama (University, Ala.), 1963. (*DA* 25:1736)
48. FLINN, DON E.; HARTMAN, BRYCE O.; POWELL, DOUGLAS H.; and McKENZIE, RICHARD E. "Psychiatric and Psychologic Evaluation," pp. 199–230. In *Aeromedical Evaluation for Space Pilots.* Edited by Lawrence E. Lamb. Brooks Air Force Base, Tex.: USAF School of Aerospace Medicine, July 1963. Pp. viii, 276. * (*PA* 38:4728)
49. HINES, MARLIN POWELL. *The Relationship of Achievement Level to Certain Personality Factors Among High School Seniors.* Doctor's thesis, University of Arkansas (Fayetteville, Ark.), 1963. (*DA* 24:5193)
50. LOCKE, EDWIN A. "Some Correlates of Classroom and Out-of-Class Achievement in Gifted Science Students." *J. Ed Psychol* 54:238–48 O '63. * (*PA* 38:4649)
51. DOLE, ARTHUR A. "The Prediction of Effectiveness in School Counseling." Comment by Edward Landy. *J Counsel Psychol* 11:112–22 su '64. * (*PA* 39:5956)
52. ROSS, PAUL F., and DUNFIELD, NEIL M. "Selecting Salesmen for an Oil Company." *Personnel Psychol* 17:75–84 sp '64. *
53. SPITZER, MORTON EDWARD, and McNAMARA, WALTER J. "A Managerial Selection Study." *Personnel Psychol* 17:19–40 sp '64. * (*PA* 39:2945)
54. WELLS, WELDON STANLEY. *A Study of Personality Traits, Situational Factors, and Leadership Actions of Selected School Maintenance Supervisors.* Doctor's thesis, North Texas State University (Denton, Tex.), 1964. (*DA* 25:975)
55. BRAUN, JOHN R. "Effects of Specific Instructions to Fake on Gordon Personal Profiles Scores." *Psychol Rep* 17:847–50 D '65. * (*PA* 40:4228)
56. MARSCH, GAYLE G., and HALBERSTAM, JACOB L. "Personality Stereotypes of United States and Foreign Medical Residents." *J Social Psychol* 68:187–96 Ap '66. * (*PA* 40:7717)
57. PRIEN, ERICH P., and BOTWIN, DAVID E. "The Reliability and Correlates of an Achievement Index." *Ed & Psychol Meas* 26:1047–52 w '66. * (*PA* 41:4998)
58. ANTLER, LAWRENCE, and ZARETSKY, HERBERT H. "National Consciousness Among Foreign Physicians in the United States: Correlates in Attitude, Adjustment, Personality, and Demographic Variables." *J Social Psychol* 71:209–20 Ap '67. * (*PA* 41:8795)
59. ANTLER, LAWRENCE; ZARETSKY, HERBERT H.; and RITTER, WALTER. "The Practical Validity of the Gordon Personal Profile Among United States and Foreign Medical Residents." *J Social Psychol* 72:257–63 Ag '67. * (*PA* 41:14434)
60. BARE, CAROLE E. "Relationship of Counselor Personality and Counselor-Client Personality Similarity to Selected Counseling Success Criteria." *J Counsel Psychol* 14:419–25 S '67. * (*PA* 41:15844)
61. BLOOM, WALLACE. "Effectiveness of a Cooperative Special Education Vocational Rehabilitation Program." *Am J Mental Def* 72:393–403 N '67. * (*PA* 42:7625)
62. DANIEL, KATHRYN BARCHARD. "A Study of College Dropouts With Respect to Academic and Personality Variables." *J Ed Res* 60:230–5 Ja '67. *
63. JONES, JOHN MARTIN. *The Relationship of Subject Area and Selected Personality Traits to the Preference to Teach by the Group or Lecture Method.* Doctor's thesis, North Texas State University (Denton, Tex.), 1967. (*DA* 28:2138A)
64. JONES, JOHN E., and SCHOCH, EUGENE W. "Correlates of Success in MA-Level Counselor Education." *Counselor Ed & Sup* 7:286–91 sp '68. * (*PA* 42:17989)

[94]

*__The Grassi Block Substitution Test: For Measuring Organic Brain Pathology.__ Mental patients; 1947–66; GBST; formerly called *The Fairfield Block Substitution Test;* individual; 1 form ['47]; manual ('53, see 2 below, *out of print*); revised record form ('66, 4 pages); $15 per set of blocks; $3.50 per 35 record forms; postpaid; (20) minutes; Joseph R. Grassi; Child Development Products Co. *

See 5:60 (5 references, 2 excerpts).

REFERENCES

1–5. See 5:60.
6. STONESIFER, FRED A. *Intellectual and Perceptual Performance of Defective Idiopathic Epileptics and Familial Mental Defectives.* Doctor's thesis, Pennsylvania State University (University Park, Pa.), 1956. (*DA* 17:400)
7. JUSTISS, WILL ALAN. *The Electroencephalogram of the Frontal Lobes and Abstract Behavior in Old Age.* Doctor's thesis, University of Florida (Gainesville, Fla.), 1957. (*DA* 18:308)

8. PARSONS, OSCAR A.; STEWART, KENNETH D.; and AREN-
BERG, DAVID. "Impairment of Abstracting Ability in Multiple
Sclerosis." *J Nerv & Mental Dis* 125:221–5 Ap–Je '57. *
(*PA* 33:4478)
9. RHODES, HELEN E. *Normal Children's Performance on
the Grassi Test.* Master's thesis, Illinois State Normal University (Normal, Ill.), 1957.
10. RIBLER, RONALD IRWIN. *The Detection of Brain Damage Through Measurement of Deficit in Behavioral Functions.*
Doctor's thesis, Michigan State University (East Lansing,
Mich.), 1957. (*DA* 19:1810)
11. HAGUE, HARRIET RUTH. "An Investigation of Abstract
Behavior in Patients With Cerebral Vascular Accidents." *Am
J Occup Ther* 13:83–7 Mr–Ap '59. * (*PA* 34:1872)
12. MCLEOD, H. N. "My Two-Hour Psychological Test Battery." *O.P.A.Q.* 14:85–7 D '61. *
13. HIRT, MICHAEL L., and COOK, RICHARD A. "Use of a
Multiple Regression Equation to Estimate Organic Impairment
From Wechsler Scale Scores." *J Clin Psychol* 18:80–1 Ja
'62. * (*PA* 38:8421)
14. CRONHOLM, BORJE, and SCHALLING, DAISY. "Intellectual
Deterioration After Focal Brain Injury." *Arch Surgery* 86:
670–87 Ap '63. *
15. THOMAS, CHARLES A., JR. "An Application of the Grassi
Block Substitution Test in the Determination of Organicity."
J Clin Psychol 19:84–7 Ja '63. * (*PA* 39:2483)
16. ARCHIBALD, Y. M.; WEPMAN, J. M.; and JONES, L. V.
"Nonverbal Cognitive Performance in Aphasic and Nonaphasic
Brain-Damaged Patients." *Cortex* 3:275–94 S '67. * (*PA* 42:
9335)
17. ARCHIBALD, Y. M.; WEPMAN, J. M.; and JONES, L. V.
"Performance on Nonverbal Cognitive Tests Following Unilateral Cortical Injury to the Right and Left Hemisphere." *J
Nerv & Mental Dis* 145:25–36 Jl '67. * (*PA* 42:4382)
18. ARCHIBALD, Y. M., and WEPMAN, J. M. "Language
Disturbance and Nonverbal Cognitive Performance in Eight
Patients Following Injury to the Right Hemisphere." *Brain*
91:117–30 Mr '68. * (*PA* 42:19160)

[95]
The Grayson Perceptualization Test. Detection of
cortical impairment; 1950–57; Forms A, B, ('56, 4
pages); mimeographed manual ('57, 10 pages); no
data on reliability; no norms; $6.50 per 25 tests; $1.50
per manual; postpaid; specimen set not available;
(5–10) minutes; Harry M. Grayson; Western Psychological Services. *
For reviews by D. Russell Davis and William Schofield, see 5:61.

REFERENCE
1. FREED, EARL X. "Some Test Evidence of CNS Dysfunction in Psychiatric Patients Manifesting Alcoholism." *Newsl
Res Psychol* 9:26–7 Ag '67. *

[96]
★**Grid Test of Schizophrenic Thought Disorder.**
Adults; 1967; 2 scores: intensity, consistency; individual; set of 8 photographs; manual (21 pages); 5*s.*
per set of photographs; 10*s.* per 25 record sheets;
10*s.* per 25 analysis sheets; 10*s.* per manual; postage
extra; (15–25) minutes; D. Bannister and Fay Fransella; Psychological Test Publications. *

REFERENCES
1. BANNISTER, D. "Conceptual Structure in Thought Disordered Schizophrenics." *J Mental Sci* 106:1230–49 O '60.
* (*PA* 35:5235)
2. BANNISTER, D. "Personal Construct Theory: A Summary
and Experimental Paradigm." *Acta Psychologica* 20(2):104–
20 '62. * (*PA* 37:6671)
3. BANNISTER, D. "The Nature and Measurement of Schizophrenic Thought Disorder." *J Mental Sci* 108:825–42 N '62. *
(*PA* 37:5480)
4. BANNISTER, D. "The Genesis of Schizophrenic Thought
Disorder: A Serial Invalidation Hypothesis." *Brit J Psychiatry* 109:680–6 S '63. * (*PA* 38:6495)
5. BANNISTER, D. "The Genesis of Schizophrenic Thought
Disorder: Re-Test of the Serial Invalidation Hypothesis." *Brit
J Psychiatry* 111:377–82 My '65. * (*PA* 39:12834)
6. BANNISTER, D. "The Rationale and Clinical Relevance of
Repertory Grid Technique." *Brit J Psychiatry* 111:977–82 O
'65. * (*PA* 40:1622)
7. BANNISTER, D., and FRANSELLA, FAY. "A Grid Test of
Schizophrenic Thought Disorder." *Brit J Social & Clin Psychol*
5:95–102 Je '66. * (*PA* 40:10277)
8. MAIR, J. M. M., and BOYD, P. R. "A Comparison of Two
Grid Forms." *Brit J Social & Clin Psychol* 6:220–7 S '67. *
(*PA* 42:132)

[97]
Group Cohesiveness: A Study of Group Morale.
Adults; 1958, c1957–58; GC; title on test is *A Study
of Group Morale;* 5 scores: satisfaction of individual
motives, satisfaction of interpersonal relations, homogeneity of attitude, satisfaction with leadership, total;
1 form ('57, 1 page); manual ('58, 4 pages); no data
on reliability of subscores; $2.50 per 25 tests; $1 per
specimen set (must be purchased to obtain manual);
cash orders postpaid; (10–15) minutes; Bernard Goldman; Psychometric Affiliates. *
For reviews by Eric F. Gardner and Cecil A. Gibb,
see 6:104 (1 reference).

[98]
Group Dimensions Descriptions Questionnaire.
College and adult groups; 1956; GDDQ; for research
use only; 13 group dimensions scores: autonomy,
control, flexibility, hedonic tone, homogeneity, intimacy, participation, permeability, polarization, potency,
stability, stratification, viscidity; Form ERG (8
pages); manual (66 pages, see *4* below); tentative
norms; separate answer sheets (IBM 805) must be
used; 25¢ per test; 4¢ per answer sheet; scoring
stencils must be prepared locally; $3.50 per manual;
postage extra; [45–60] minutes; John K. Hemphill
and Charles M. Westie; distributed by Educational
Testing Service. *
See 6:105 (5 references).

REFERENCES
1–5. See 6:105.
6. HILL, THOMAS BARLOW, JR. *The Relationships Between
Teacher Morale and the Ability to Establish Rapport With
Pupils and Other Selected Variables.* Doctor's thesis, North
Texas State College (Denton, Tex.), 1961. (*DA* 22:789)
7. MORAN, GARY, and KLOCKARS, ALAN J. "Favorability of
Group Atmosphere and Group Dimensionality." *Psychol Rep*
22:3–6 F '68. * (*PA* 42:10532)

[99]
★**Group Psychotherapy Suitability Evaluation
Scale.** Patients in group therapy; 1965–68; SES; also
called *Suitability Evaluation Scale;* title on test is
Group Psychotherapy Evaluation Scale; ratings by
therapists; 6 ratings: amount of communication, quality of relatedness and communication, quality of content in relatedness, capacity for change and involvement, amount of therapist verbal activity, direction of
therapist verbal activity; 1 form ('65, 1 page); manual ['68, 15 pages plus scale, reprint of *1* below]; no
data on reliability; $2.50 per 100 tests; 35¢ per man-
ual; postpaid; [5] minutes; Clifton E. Kew; the Author. *

REFERENCE
1. KEW, CLIFTON E. "A Pilot Study of an Evaluating Scale
for Group-Psychotherapy Patients." *Pastoral Counselor* 6(2):
9–24 '68. *

[100]
Guidance Inventory. High school; 1960; GI; identification of problems related to underachievement and
need for counseling; 1 form (2 pages); manual (21
pages); no data on reliability; $20 per 200 tests and
manual; $1.75 per manual purchased separately; 50¢
per specimen set; postpaid; (50) minutes; Ralph
Gallagher; the Author. *
For a review by John W. M. Rothney, see 6:106.

[101]
Guilford-Holley L Inventory. College and adults;
1953–63; GHLI; leadership behavior; 5 scores: benevolence, ambition, meticulousness, discipline, aggressiveness; 1 form ('53, 4 pages); manual ('63, 6
pages); separate answer sheets (IBM 805) must be

used; $3.50 per 25 tests; 4¢ per answer sheet; $1.25 per scoring stencil; 4¢ per profile; 35¢ per manual; 55¢ per specimen set (complete test not included); postage extra; (25) minutes; J. P. Guilford and J. W. Holley; Sheridan Psychological Services, Inc. *

[102]
The Guilford-Martin Inventory of Factors GAMIN, Abridged Edition. Grades 12–16 and adults; 1943–48; GAMIN; 5 scores: general activity, ascendance-submission, masculinity-femininity, inferiority feelings, nervousness; 1 form ('43, 4 pages); revised manual ['48, 3 pages]; college norms only; $4 per 25 tests; $1.75 per scoring key; separate answer sheets (IBM 805) may be used; 5¢ per answer sheet; $2.50 per set of scoring stencils; 25¢ per manual; 40¢ per specimen set (complete test not included); postage extra; (30) minutes; [J. P. Guilford and H. G. Martin]; Sheridan Psychological Services, Inc. *

See 6:108 (11 references) and 5:63 (33 references); for a review by Hubert E. Brogden, see 4:47 (18 references); for a review by H. J. Eysenck, see 3:43 (7 references); for a review by R. A. Brotemarkle, see 3:45.

REFERENCES
1–7. See 3:43.
8–25. See 4:47.
26–58. See 5:63.
59–69. See 6:108.
70. WERNER, DONALD SEBASTIAN. *Personality, Environment and Decision Making: An Exploratory Investigation of the Influence of Personality and Environment on Decision Making, as Indicated by the Relation Between Leadership and Prediction Measures in Three Situations Differing in the Frequency of the Stimulus Event.* Doctor's thesis, New York University (New York, N.Y.), 1955. (*DA* 15:1265)
71. MANN, KENNETH WALKER. *Personality Correlates of Recognition and Recall of Faces.* Doctor's thesis, University of Michigan (Ann Arbor, Mich.), 1956. (*DA* 17:1388)
72. DESKINS, ANDREW JACKSON. *Magical Thinking, Superstition and Authoritarian Trends in Personality.* Doctor's thesis, University of Florida (Gainesville, Fla.), 1957. (*DA* 17:1123)
73. ABELES, NORMAN. *A Study of the Characteristics of Counselor Trainees.* Doctor's thesis, University of Texas (Austin, Tex.), 1958. (*DA* 18:2204)
74. ZOBERI, HASEENUDDIN. *The Relation of Evaluative Attitudes to Traits of Introversion and Extraversion.* Doctor's thesis, University of Southern California (Los Angeles, Calif.), 1960. (*DA* 21:1655)
75. HODGSON, RICHARD W. "Personality Appraisal of Technical and Professional Applicants." *Personnel Psychol* 17: 167–87 su '64. * (*PA* 39:6067)
76. DERMEN, DIRAN, and LONDON, PERRY. "Correlates of Hypnotic Susceptibility." *J Consult Psychol* 29:537–45 D '65. * (*PA* 40:2261)
77. BRAY, DOUGLAS W., and GRANT, DONALD L. "The Assessment Center in the Measurement of Potential for Business Management." *Psychol Monogr* 80(17):1–27 '66. * (*PA* 41:850)
78. GIBBONS, BILLIE DWANE. *A Study of the Relationships Between Factors Found in Cattell's Sixteen Personality Factor Questionnaire and Factors Found in the Guilford Personality Inventories.* Doctor's thesis, University of Southern California (Los Angeles, Calif.), 1966. (*DA* 26:7438)
79. IBRAHIM, HILMI. "Comparison of Temperament Traits Among Inter-Collegiate Athletes and Physical Education Majors." *Res Q* 38:615–22 D '67. *
80. McCARTHY, DOROTHEA; SCHIRO, FREDERICK M.; and SUDIMACK, JOHN P. "Comparison of WAIS *M-F* Index With Two Measures of Masculinity-Femininity." *J Consult Psychol* 31:539–40 D '67. * (*PA* 42:2587)
81. WINKLER, RONALD C., and MATHEWS, THEODORE W. "How Employees Feel About Personality Tests." *Personnel J* 46:490–2 Jl–Ag '67. *
82. CATTELL, RAYMOND B., and GIBBONS, B. D. "Personality Factor Structure of the Combined Guilford and Cattell Personality Questionnaires." *J Personality & Social Psychol* 9: 107–20 My '68. * (*PA* 42:10588)
83. GOLDSTEIN, GERALD; NEURINGER, CHARLES; REIFF, CAROLYN; and SHELLY, CAROLYN H. "Generalizability of Field Dependency in Alcoholics." *J Consult & Clin Psychol* 32:560–4 O '68. * (*PA* 43:1094)

NAME INDEX

[103]
The Guilford-Martin Personnel Inventory. Adults; 1943–46; GMPI; 3 scores: objectivity, agreeableness, cooperativeness; 1 form ('43, 4 pages); manual ['43, 2 pages]; mimeographed supplement ('46, 5 pages); $4 per 25 tests; $1.75 per scoring key; separate answer sheets (IBM 805) may be used; 4¢ per answer sheet; $2.50 per set of scoring stencils; 25¢ per manual; 40¢ per specimen set (complete test not included); postage extra; (30) minutes; [J. P. Guilford and H. G. Martin]; Sheridan Psychological Services, Inc. *

See 6:109 (9 references) and 5:64 (27 references); for a review by Neil Van Steenberg, see 4:48 (20 references); for a review by Benjamin Shimberg, see 3:44 (7 references); for a review by R. A. Brotemarkle, see 3:45.

REFERENCES
1–7. See 3:44.
8–27. See 4:48.
28–54. See 5:64.
55–63. See 6:109.
64. ABELES, NORMAN. *A Study of the Characteristics of Counselor Trainees.* Doctor's thesis, University of Texas (Austin, Tex.), 1958. (*DA* 18:2204)
65. JONES, J. B. "Some Personal-Social Factors Contributing to Academic Failure at Texas Southern University," pp. 135–6. (*PA* 37:5606) In *Personality Factors on the College Campus: Review of a Symposium.* Edited by Robert L. Sutherland and others. Austin, Tex.: Hogg Foundation for Mental Health, 1962. Pp. xxii, 242. * (*PA* 37:5621)
66. RONAN, W. W. "Evaluation of Skilled Trades Performance Predictors." *Ed & Psychol Meas* 24:601–8 f '64. * (*PA* 39:6074)
67. DERMEN, DIRAN, and LONDON, PERRY. "Correlates of Hypnotic Susceptibility." *J Consult Psychol* 29:537–45 D '65. * (*PA* 40:2261)
68. THUMIN, FRED J., and WITTENBERG, ANGELA. "Personality as Related to Age and Mental Ability in Female Job Applicants." *J Gerontol* 20:105–7 Ja '65. *
69. THUMIN, F., and GOLDMAN, SUE. "Comparative Test

Performance of Negro and White Job Applicants." *J Clin Psychol* 24:455-7 O '68. * (*PA* 43:4565)

NAME INDEX

[104]

The Guilford-Zimmerman Temperament Survey. Grades 12–16 and adults; 1949–55; GZTS; revision and condensation of *Inventory of Factors STDCR, Guilford-Martin Inventory of Factors GAMIN,* and *Guilford-Martin Personnel Inventory;* 10 scores: general activity, restraint, ascendance, sociability, emotional stability, objectivity, friendliness, thoughtfulness, personal relations, masculinity; 1 form ('49, 8 pages); manual ('49, 12 pages); norms ('55); profile ('55, 1 page); 3 *Falsification Scales* (gross-falsification, subtle falsification, carelessness-deviancy) and manual ('55, 3 pages) by Alfred Jacobs and Allan Schlaff; *G-Z Temperament Map* ('52, 2 pages) by Philip C. Perry; separate answer sheets (IBM 805) must be used; $5 per 25 tests; 6¢ per answer sheet; $2.50 per set of either hand or machine scoring stencils; 5¢ per profile; 50¢ per manual; $4.50 per set of scoring stencils and manual for falsification scales; 4¢ per copy of temperament map; 65¢ per specimen set (complete test not included); postage extra; (50) minutes; J. P. Guilford and Wayne S. Zimmerman; Sheridan Psychological Services, Inc. *

See 6:110 (120 references); for a review by David R. Saunders, see 5:65 (48 references); for reviews by William Stephenson and Neil Van Steenberg, see 4:49 (5 references, 1 excerpt).

REFERENCES

1–5. See 4:49.
6–53. See 5:65.
54–173. See 6:110.
174. WHITCOMB, JOHN CHARLES. *The Determination of the Relationship Between Personality Characteristics and the Nature and Persistence of Problems in the Protestant Ministry.* Doctor's thesis, University of Michigan (Ann Arbor, Mich.), 1954. (*DA* 14:1182)
175. HILTON, ANDREW C.; BOLIN, STANLEY F.; PARKER, JAMES W. JR.; TAYLOR, ERWIN K.; and WALKER, WILLIAM B. "The Validity of Personnel Assessments by Professional Psychologists." *J Appl Psychol* 39:287-93 Ag '55. * (*PA* 30:5294)
176. BURTON, ROGER V. *The Personality of the Contracted Studio Musician: An Investigation Using the Guilford-Zimmerman Temperament Survey.* Master's thesis, University of Southern California (Los Angeles, Calif.), 1956.
177. TANZER, WALTER L. *Vocational Choice and Personality:*

A Study of the Relationship of Personality to Choice of Vocational Field and Vocational Aspiration Level. Doctor's thesis, New York University (New York, N.Y.), 1956 (*DA* 17:890)
178. MAHONEY, WILLIAM MAY. *A Study to Determine the Differences in the Personal Characteristics and Certain Judgment Capacities of Effective and Ineffective Primary, Intermediate, and Secondary-School Teachers.* Doctor's thesis, Boston University (Boston, Mass.), 1957. (*DA* 17:2920)
179. SHAFFER, JOHN WHITCOMB. *Correlates of the Ability to Judge Children.* Doctor's thesis, Pennsylvania State University (University Park, Pa.), 1957. (*DA* 18:288)
180. SIDNEY, GEORGE PAUL. *A Study of Psychological Test and Biographical Variables as Possible Predictors of Successful Psychiatric Aide Performance.* Doctor's thesis, Pennsylvania State University (University Park, Pa.), 1957. (*DA* 18:289)
181. FRIEDMAN, JOSEPH. *Psychological Correlates of Overweight, Underweight and Normal Weight College Women.* Doctor's thesis, Temple University (Philadelphia, Pa.), 1958. (*DA* 19:3362)
182. KINNANE, JOHN FRANCIS. *The Relationship of Personal Adjustment to Realism of Expressed Vocational Preference.* Doctor's thesis, Columbia University (New York, N. Y.), 1958. (*DA* 19:172)
183. MURRAY, JOHN B. "Personality Study of Priests and Seminarians." *Homiletic & Pastoral R* 59:443-7 F '59. *
184. BELL, MYRTLE LEE. *The Relationship of Selected Variables to Success of Part-Time Recreation Personnel Employed as Summer Playground Leaders.* Doctor's thesis, University of Texas (Austin, Tex.), 1960. (*DA* 21:2528)
185. EIGENBRODE, CHARLES ROBERT. *An Empirical Derivation of Scales Designed to Predict a Theoretical Construct Using Motor Learning and Motor Reminiscence as Criteria.* Doctor's thesis, University of Pittsburgh (Pittsburgh, Pa.), 1960. (*DA* 21:679)
186. GABERMAN, FLORENCE KILGORE. *A Scale for Measuring Teacher Class Control and Its Relation to Personality.* Doctor's thesis, Pennsylvania State University (University Park, Pa.), 1960. (*DA* 21:1845)
187. GRAY, BENJAMIN GALBREATH. *Characteristics of High and Low Achieving High School Seniors of High Average Academic Aptitude.* Doctor's thesis, University of Southern California (Los Angeles, Calif.), 1960. (*DA* 21:1459)
188. ZOBERI, HASEENUDDIN. *The Relation of Evaluative Attitudes to Traits of Introversion and Extraversion.* Doctor's thesis, University of Southern California (Los Angeles, Calif.), 1960. (*DA* 21:1655)
189. CAMPBELL, ROBERT EDWARD. *Influence of the Counselor's Personality and Background on His Counseling Style.* Doctor's thesis, Ohio State University (Columbus, Ohio), 1961. (*DA* 22:3739)
190. HONIGFELD, GILBERT HOWARD. *A Factorial Study of "Neurological Efficiency," Perception and Personality.* Doctor's thesis, Temple University (Philadelphia, Pa.), 1961. (*DA* 22:908)
191. KENOYER, MARIE FRANCIS. *The Influence of Religious Life on Three Levels of Perceptual Processes.* Doctor's thesis, Fordham University (New York, N.Y.), 1961. (*DA* 22:909)
192. LUCAS, ANN F. *The Relationship Between Attitude of Student Nurses Toward Childbearing and Certain Selected Individual and Background Characteristics.* Doctor's thesis, Fordham University (New York, N.Y.), 1961. (*DA* 23:299)
193. NICKERSON, EILEEN TRESSLER. *Some Correlates of Adjustment of Paraplegics.* Doctor's thesis, Columbia University (New York, N.Y.), 1961. (*DA* 22:632)
194. SILBER, MARK BISCHOFF. *A Comparative Study of Three Methods of Effecting Attitude Change.* Doctor's thesis, Ohio State University (Columbus, Ohio), 1961. (*DA* 22:2488)
195. KEARNEY, HAROLD MORTON. *A Study of Certain Psycho-Social Factors Found in Female Rheumatoid Arthritis Patients as Compared With Non-Arthritic Sisters.* Doctor's thesis, Boston University (Boston, Mass.), 1962. (*DA* 23:1608)
106. MASIH, LALIT KUMAR. *Career Saliency and Its Relation to Certain Personality and Environmental Variables.* Doctor's thesis, Syracuse University (Syracuse, N.Y.), 1962. (*DA* 24:181)
197. MILES, JAMES BAKER. *An Analysis of Relationships Between Experiences in Correlated Courses in Art, Music, and Modern Dance, and Certain Behavioral Changes Related to Aesthetic Experience.* Doctor's thesis, North Texas State University (Denton, Tex.), 1962. (*DA* 23:3309)
198. LEACH, ALICE REA. *Prediction of Academic Success in College Freshmen at the University of Denver.* Doctor's thesis, University of Denver (Denver, Colo.), 1963. (*DA* 24:5199)
199. MAGEE, PAULINE CECILIA. *Cooperation, Background Factors, Personality, and Interests of Senior and Junior College Students in Three Achievement Categories.* Doctor's thesis, Fordham University (New York, N.Y.), 1963. (*DA* 24:630)
200. PLITTMAN, JACK C. *The Influence of the Control of Personal Set Upon Prediction by Factored Tests of Temperament and Interest.* Doctor's thesis, University of Southern California (Los Angeles, Calif.), 1963. (*DA* 24:3833)
201. RITCHEY, RONALD EUGENE. *Predicting Industrial Therapy Success and Hospital Progress in a Schizophrenic Population.* Doctor's thesis, University of Nebraska (Lincoln, Neb.), 1963. (*DA* 24:3426)
202. SCHINDLER, MARY DU PONT. *A Study of the Relationship of Temperament Variables to the Ability to Make Certain Judgments of Emotional Behavior.* Doctor's thesis, University

of Southern California (Los Angeles, Calif.), 1963. (*DA* 24: 3841)

203. THOMAN, MARY MUNDEN. *A Comparative Study of Personality Patterns and Attitudes Toward Mental Retardation and Child-Rearing Practices of Parents of Intellectually Normal and Educable and Trainable Mentally Retarded Children.* Doctor's thesis, University of Denver (Denver, Colo.), 1963. (*DA* 24:5209)

204. VAN BUREN, JOHN DEWEY. *An Assessment of the Relationship Between the Capacity to Empathize and the Emotional Maturity of a Group of Counselor-Trainees.* Doctor's thesis, Boston University (Boston, Mass.), 1963. (*DA* 25:1763)

205. VAUGHAN, GEORGE ELLIS, JR. *Some Characteristics of College Freshmen According to Sex and Ethnic Group and the Relationship of These Characteristics to Academic Achievement.* Doctor's thesis, North Texas State University (Denton, Tex.), 1963. (*DA* 25:1017)

206. BEHRMAN, ROBERT MARTIN. *A Study to Determine Whether There Are Distinguishing Personality Trait Differences Between Non-Swimmers and Those With Swimming Ability.* Doctor's thesis, Columbia University (New York, N.Y.), 1964. (*DA* 26:2040)

207. DEATHERAGE, DOROTHY. *Factors Related to Concepts of Sportsmanship.* Doctor's thesis, University of Southern California (Los Angeles, Calif.), 1964. (*DA* 25:3379)

208. ERICKSON, PAUL. *Selection Factors Relating to Success in a Counselor Education Program.* Doctor's thesis, University of Southern California (Los Angeles, Calif.), 1964. (*DA* 25: 3391)

209. FIELDER, DANIEL WILLIAM. *A Nomothetic Study of the Southern California School of Theology Seminarian.* Doctor's thesis, Southern California School of Theology (Claremont, Calif.), 1964. (*DA* 26:1192)

210. FOLEY, WALTER JAMES. *Empirical Derivation of Scales for the Selection of Counselor Trainees.* Doctor's thesis, University of Illinois (Urbana, Ill.), 1964. (*DA* 25:4540)

211. GILDSTON, HAROLD MAX. *Personality Changes Associated With Surgically Corrected Hypacusis.* Doctor's thesis, Columbia University (New York, N.Y.), 1964. (*DA* 25:5442)

212. GREENHOUSE, PHYLLIS FLOWERS. *A Comparison of Selected Personality Traits of Student Teachers and Supervising Teachers.* Doctor's thesis, University of Arkansas (Fayetteville, Ark.), 1964. (*DA* 25:5764)

213. HAND, JACK. "Measurement of Response Sets." *Psychol Rep* 14:907–13 Je '64. * (*PA* 39:5021)

214. HATTEM, JACK VICTOR. *The Precipitating Role of Discordant Interpersonal Relationships in Suicidal Behavior.* Doctor's thesis, University of Houston (Houston, Tex.), 1964. (*DA* 25:1335)

215. LEWIS, EDWIN C. "An Investigation of Student-Teacher Interaction as a Determiner of Effective Teaching." *J Ed Res* 57:360–3 Mr '64. *

216. LONG, JOHN M. "Sex Differences in Academic Prediction Based on Scholastic, Personality and Interest Factors." *J Exp Ed* 32:239–48 sp '64. * (*PA* 39:6058)

217. McDAVID, JOHN W., and SISTRUNK, FRANK. "Personality Correlates of Two Kinds of Conforming Behavior." *J Personality* 32:420–35 S '64. *

218. MATEJOWSKY, GLORIA F. *A Study of the Relation of Deviant Performance on the Guilford-Zimmerman Temperament Schedule to Certain Other Factors Within a Population of Counselor Candidates.* Master's thesis, University of Texas (Austin, Tex.), 1964.

219. PETERSEN, DWAIN FRANKLIN. *Factors Common to Interest, Value, and Personality Scales.* Doctor's thesis, University of Nebraska (Lincoln, Neb.), 1964. (*DA* 25:5747)

220. RONAN, W. W. "Evaluation of Skilled Trades Performance Predictors." *Ed & Psychol Meas* 24:601–8 f '64. * (*PA* 39:6074)

221. TROXEL, WILLIAM DEE. *An Investigation of Humor as a Dimension of Assessment of the Counselee.* Doctor's thesis, University of California (Los Angeles, Calif.), 1964. (*DA* 25:3409)

222. VETTER, LOUISE, and LEWIS, EDWIN C. "Some Correlates of Homemaking vs. Career Preference Among College Home Economics Students." *Personnel & Guid J* 42:593–8 F '64. * (*PA* 39:6057)

223. WAGNER, EDWIN E., and SOBER, KATHRYN A. "Effectiveness of the Guilford-Zimmerman Temperament Survey as a Predictor of Scholastic Success in College." *J Counsel Psychol* 11:94–5 sp '64. *

224. WATLEY, DONIVAN J. "The Effectiveness of Intellectual and Non-Intellectual Factors in Predicting Achievement for Business Students." *J Ed Res* 57:402–7 Ap '64. *

225. WATLEY, DONIVAN J., and MERWIN, JACK C. "The Effectiveness of Variables for Predicting Academic Achievement for Business Students." *J Exp Ed* 33:189–92 w '64. * (*PA* 39:8713)

226. WELLS, WELDON STANLEY. *A Study of Personality Traits, Situational Factors, and Leadership Actions of Selected School Maintenance Supervisors.* Doctor's thesis, North Texas State University (Denton, Tex.), 1964. (*DA* 25:975)

227. WOLAVER, KATHRYN EVANS. *A Longitudinal Study of the Stability of Teachers' Attitudes and Personality as Related to Teacher Education and Teaching Experience.* Doctor's thesis, Purdue University (Lafayette, Ind.), 1964. (*DA* 25:2866)

228. WYATT, LLOYD DOW. *The Significance of Emotional Content in the Logical Reasoning Ability of Schizophrenics.*

Doctor's thesis, Purdue University (Lafayette, Ind.), 1964. (*DA* 26:2330)

229. ALTLAND, NORMAN RICHARD. *Personality Correlates of Acute Myocardial Infarction.* Doctor's thesis, American University (Washington, D.C.), 1965. (*DA* 26:1157)

230. ANDERSON, JOHN MARTIN. *The Use of Musical Talent, Personality and Vocational Interest Factors in Predicting Success for Student Music Teachers.* Doctor's thesis, University of Southern California (Los Angeles, Calif.), 1965. (*DA* 26: 6523)

231. BARRATT, ERNEST S. "Factor Analysis of Some Psychometric Measures of Impulsiveness and Anxiety." *Psychol Rep* 16:547–54 Ap '65. * (*PA* 39:10087)

232. BAYTON, JAMES A.; AUSTIN, LETTIE J.; and BURKE, KAY R. "Negro Perception of Negro and White Personality Traits." *J Personality & Social Psychol* 1:250–3 Mr '65. * (*PA* 39:9864)

233. CARNEY, MELVIN EARL. *The Relationship Between Certain Personality Traits and Improvement in College Reading.* Doctor's thesis, Western Reserve University (Cleveland, Ohio), 1965. (*DA* 27:108A)

234. CRABTREE, BEVERLY DELES-DERNIER. *Predicting and Determining Effectiveness of Homemaking Teachers.* Doctor's thesis, Iowa State University (Ames, Iowa), 1965. (*DA* 26: 6013)

235. GUION, ROBERT M. "Synthetic Validity in a Small Company: A Demonstration." *Personnel Psychol* 18:49–63 sp '65. * (*PA* 39:16490)

236. HAERTZEN, CHARLES A., and MINER, EDWARD J. "Effect of Alcohol on the Guilford-Zimmerman Scales of Extraversion." *J Personality & Social Psychol* 1:333–6 Ap '65. * (*PA* 39: 10233)

237. HANNA, GERALD STANLEY. *An Investigation of Selected Ability, Aptitude, Interest, and Personality Characteristics Relevant to Success in High School Geometry.* Doctor's thesis, University of Southern California (Los Angeles, Calif.), 1965. (*DA* 26:3152)

238. HARRINGTON, THOMAS FRANCIS, JR. *The Interrelation of Personality Variables and College Experiences of Engineering Students Over a Four Year Span.* Doctor's thesis, Purdue University (Lafayette, Ind.), 1965. (*DA* 26:1480)

239. HUMMEL, RAYMOND, and SPRINTHALL, NORMAN. "Underachievement Related to Interests, Attitudes and Values." *Personnel & Guid J* 44:388–95 D '65. * (*PA* 40:4101)

240. JONES, KENNETH J. "Occupational Preference and Social Orientation." *Personnel & Guid J* 43:574–9 F '65. * (*PA* 39:10873)

241. McGEHEARTY, LOYCE IVY DAWSON. *Factors Associated With the Probable Success of Prospective School Counselors as Evaluated by Their Peers and by Staff Members.* Doctor's thesis, University of Texas (Austin, Tex.), 1965. (*DA* 26: 873)

242. McMILLIN, MARVIN REVELLE. *A Study of Certain High School Seniors Perceived as Growth-Facilitating by Their Peers.* Doctor's thesis, University of Florida (Gainesville, Fla.), 1965. (*DA* 26:5875)

243. MATHIS, JAMES OTTO. *Modes of Resolving Motor Conflict Situations, Certain Personality Variables, and Scholastic Achievement.* Doctor's thesis, North Texas State University (Denton, Tex.), 1965. (*DA* 26:3759)

244. METIVIER, LIONEL GERALD. *Selected Factors in Predicting Student Teaching Success in Grades Four, Five, and Six.* Doctor's thesis, University of Michigan (Ann Arbor, Mich.), 1965. (*DA* 26:3164)

245. OTTE, HAROLD WILLIAM. *Comparisons of Abilities, Motivations, and Personality Traits of Continuing and Non-Continuing Freshmen in Colleges of the Lutheran Church—Missouri Synod.* Doctor's thesis, University of Colorado (Boulder, Colo.), 1965. (*DA* 26:6480)

246. PILGRIM, MARY ALICE GUNN. *Relationships Among Guilford-Zimmerman Temperament Survey Profile, Choice of Field of Study in Business and Academic Performance of Upper-Classmen in Business Administration.* Doctor's thesis, North Texas State University (Denton, Tex.), 1965. (*DA* 26:4457)

247. SCHNELL, RICHARD R. "Construction of Factor Scales for Personality Assessment." *Newsl Res Psychol* 7:61–2 My '65. *

248. SCOTT, GARY KUPER. *A Study of the Relationship Between Ratings of Counselor Success and Selected Personality Variables.* Doctor's thesis, University of Minnesota (Minneapolis, Minn.), 1965. (*DA* 26:5249)

249. SHIPMAN, WILLIAM G. "Personality Traits Associated With Body-Image Boundary Concern." *Proc Ann Conv Am Psychol Assn* 73:271–2 '65. * (*PA* 39:15441)

250. SPIERS, DUANE EDWIN. *A Study of the Predictive Validity of a Test Battery Administered to Theological Students.* Doctor's thesis, Purdue University (Lafayette, Ind.), 1965. (*DA* 26:1488)

251. SPIES, CARL JOSEPH. *Some Non-Intellectual Predictors of Classroom Success.* Doctor's thesis, Washington University (St. Louis, Mo.), 1965. (*DA* 26:7442)

252. WATLEY, DONIVAN J. "Personal Adjustment and Prediction of Academic Achievement." *J Appl Psychol* 49:20–3 F '65. * (*PA* 39:8598)

253. WOFFORD, J. C. "Correcting Personality Test Scores for Defensiveness." *South Q* 3:151–4 Ja '65. *

254. CONGER, JOHN JANEWAY, and MILLER, WILBUR C.;

with the assistance of Robert V. Rainey and Charles R. Walsmith. *Personality, Social Class, and Delinquency.* New York: John Wiley & Sons, Inc., 1966. Pp. xi, 249. *

255. CUNNINGHAM, GROVER BENNETT, JR. *Prediction of Staff Ratings From Personality Variables of Counselors in Training and Prediction of Intelligence Test Scores of Children From Personality Variables of Parents.* Doctor's thesis, University of Texas (Austin, Tex.), 1966. (*DA* 27:3305A)

256. DeCENCIO, DOMINIC V. *Relationship Between Certain Interest and Personality Variables in a Sample of College Women.* Doctor's thesis, Temple University (Philadelphia, Pa.), 1966. (*DA* 27:1288B)

257. DOLLAR, ROBERT J. "Relationship Between Interpersonal Values and Temperament Traits." *Psychol Rep* 19:228 Ag '66. * (*PA* 40:11663, title only)

258. FINCO, ARTHUR ANTHONY. *Mathematics Majors and Transfers From the Mathematics Major at Purdue University: Temperament, Interest, Value, and Student Questionnaire Differences at the Exploratory Stage.* Doctor's thesis, Purdue University (Lafayette, Ind.), 1966. (*DA* 27:327A)

259. GIBBONS, BILLIE DWANE. *A Study of the Relationships Between Factors Found in Cattell's Sixteen Personality Factor Questionnaire and Factors Found in the Guilford Personality Inventories.* Doctor's thesis, University of Southern California (Los Angeles, Calif.), 1966. (*DA* 26:7438)

260. HUDSON, MARY MARLENE COE. *Interpersonal Values, Temperament Traits, and Interest Values of Elementary Education Students at the University of Oklahoma.* Doctor's thesis, University of Oklahoma (Norman, Okla.), 1966 (*DA* 27:1688A)

261. JOHNSON, CLARENCE JOY. *Personality Traits Affected by High School Football as Measured by the Guilford-Zimmerman Temperament Survey.* Doctor's thesis, University of Arkansas (Fayetteville, Ark.), 1966. (*DA* 27:658A)

262. KEIM, LAWRENCE. *A Study of Psychometric Profile Patterns of Selected Associate Degree Technology Majors.* Doctor's thesis, Purdue University (Lafayette, Ind.), 1966. (*DA* 27:2049A)

263. KELLY, EMMET EUGENE. "Member Personality and Group Counseling Interaction." *J Psychol* 63:89–97 My '66. * (*PA* 40:10180)

264. LEACH, JOHN JAMES. *A Semantic Differential Analysis of Four Selected Guilford-Zimmerman Temperament Survey Personality Scales.* Doctor's thesis, Purdue University (Lafayette, Ind.), 1966. (*DA* 27:4156B)

265. LEWIS, LESLIE. *A Multivariate Analysis of Variables Associated With Academic Success Within a College Environment.* Doctor's thesis, Oklahoma State University (Stillwater, Okla.), 1966. (*DA* 27:4134A)

266. PICKFORD, JOHN H.; SIGNORI, EDRO I.; and REMPEL, HENRY. "The Intensity of Personality Traits in Relation to Marital Happiness." *J Marriage & Family* 28:458–9 N '66. * (*PA* 41:1485)

267. PICKFORD, JOHN H.; SIGNORI, EDRO I.; and REMPEL, HENRY. "Similar or Related Personality Traits as a Factor in Marital Happiness." *J Marriage & Family* 28:190–2 My '66. * (*PA* 40:7688)

268. RYDER, ANN D. *An Inquiry Into the Kuder Preference Record-Vocational Verification Scale and the Guilford-Zimmerman Temperament Survey Falsification Scale.* Master's thesis, University of Richmond (Richmond, Va.), 1966.

269. SUINN, RICHARD M. "Personality and Grades of College Students of Different Class Ranks." *Ed & Psychol Meas* 26:1053–4 w '66. * (*PA* 41:5003)

270. TENOPYR, MARY L.; JACOBS, ALFRED; and MICHAEL, WILLIAM B. "A Dimensional Analysis of Guilford-Zimmerman Temperament Survey Scores Relative to Content and Response Style." *J Ed Meas* 3:45–51 sp '66. * (*PA* 41:69)

271. BECKER, GILBERT. "Ego-Defense Patterns in Extraverts and Introverts." *Psychol Rep* 20:387–92 Ap '67. * (*PA* 41:8913)

272. BEHRMAN, ROBERT M. "Personality Differences Between Nonswimmers and Swimmers." *Res Q* 38:163–71 My '67. (*PA* 41:12505)

273. CHAPPELL, JOHN SINGLEHURST. *Multivariate Discrimination Among Selected Occupational Groups Utilizing Self Report Data.* Doctor's thesis, Purdue University (Lafayette, Ind.), 1967. (*DA* 28:2620B)

274. DAVIS, KATHLEEN L. *The Sensitivity of Selected Instruments to Personality Changes Produced by Group Counseling.* Doctor's thesis, University of Georgia (Athens, Ga.), 1967. (*DA* 28:3968A)

275. ESCOTT, STANLEY BOSWORTH. *An Investigation Into the Predictive Value of Some Structured Observational Tools for Selection and Retention in Counselor Education.* Doctor's thesis, Purdue University (Lafayette, Ind.), 1967. (*DA* 28:466A)

276. FAGERBURG, JOAN EMELINE. *A Comparative Study of Undergraduate Women in Relation to Selected Personal Characteristics and Certain Effects of Educational Interruption.* Doctor's thesis, Purdue University (Lafayette, Ind.), 1967. (*DA* 28:4445A)

277. FOX, A. M. "Temperament and Attitude Correlates of Leadership Behavior." *Ed & Psychol Meas* 27:1167–8 w '67. * (*PA* 42:8953)

278. FREEDMAN, STEPHEN A.; ANTENEN, WAYNE W.; and LISTER, JAMES L. "Counselor Behavior and Personality Characteristics." *Counselor Ed & Sup* 7:26–30 f '67. * (*PA* 42:1154)

279. HANNA, GERALD S. "The Use of Students' Predictions of Success in Geometry and Year of High School to Augment Predictions Made From Test Scores and Past Grades." *J Ed Meas* 4:137–41 f '67. *

280. HARNEY, JAMES B. *A Validation Study of the Guilford-Zimmerman Temperament Survey.* Master's thesis, Loyola College (Chicago, Ill.), 1967.

281. JENNINGS, BETTY LEA. *A Comparison of Creative and Non-Creative Pre-Service Teachers on Scholastic Aptitude, Academic Achievement, Personality, and Item Sorts on Behavioral Classroom Situation Variables.* Doctor's thesis, University of Oklahoma (Norman, Okla.), 1967. (*DA* 28:987A)

282. LEVITT, EUGENE E., and LUBIN, EDWARD. "Some Personality Factors Associated With Menstrual Complaints and Menstrual Attitude." *J Psychosom Res* 11:267–70 N '67. * (*PA* 42:10913)

283. McLEMORE, MATTHEW HUNTER. *An Analysis of Interpersonal Group Structures and Personality Profiles of Team Members Representing Two Categories of Junior College Basketball Teams.* Doctor's thesis, North Texas State University (Denton, Tex.), 1967. (*DA* 28:3490A)

284. PICKFORD, JOHN H.; SIGNORI, EDRO I.; and REMPEL, HENRY. "Husband-Wife Differences in Personality Traits as a Factor in Marital Happiness." *Psychol Rep* 20:1087–90 Je '67. * (*PA* 41:15642)

285. SHAW, DALE J. "Personality Patterns Associated With Level of Adjustment to Psychiatric Affiliation." *J Clin Psychol* 23:222–3 Ap '67. * (*PA* 41:8926)

286. SINAY, RUTH DORIS. *Creative Aptitude Patterns of College Honors Students.* Doctor's thesis, University of Southern California (Los Angeles, Calif.), 1967. (*DA* 28:5212B)

287. SOREY, KENNETH ELDON. *A Study of the Distinguishing Personality Characteristics of College Faculty Who Are Superior in Regard to the Teaching Function.* Doctor's thesis, Oklahoma State University (Stillwater, Okla.), 1967. (*DA* 28:4916A)

288. STEVENS, THOMAS GRANVILLE. *Congruency Between Diagnostic Dimensions of Personality Theories and Personality Tests.* Master's thesis, California State College at Fullerton (Fullerton, Calif.), 1967.

289. STOEGBAUER, MARY KAY. "The Relationship of Psychometrically Determined Personality Variables to Perception of the Ames Trapezoidal Illusion: I." *J Psychol* 67:91–7 S '67. * (*PA* 41:16719)

290. WILLIAMSON, JERLYN F. *A Study of the Characteristics of Sorority Women and Non-Sorority Women as Measured by the Guilford-Zimmerman Temperament Survey.* Master's thesis, University of Kansas (Lawrence, Kan.), 1967.

291. WINDHOLZ, GEORGE. *Divergent and Convergent Abilities of Semantic Content as Related to Some Personality Traits of College Students.* Doctor's thesis, Columbia University (New York, N.Y.), 1967. (*DA* 28:2130B)

292. WINDHOLZ, GEORGE. "Divergent and Convergent Abilities of Semantic Content as Related to Some Personality Traits of College Students." *Ed & Psychol Meas* 27:1015–23 w '67. * (*PA* 42:8976)

293. BAYTON, JAMES A., and MULDROW, TRESSIE W. "Interacting Variables in the Perception of Racial Personality Traits." *J Exp Res Personality* 3:39–44 Je '68. * (*PA* 42:17106)

294. BECKER, JAMES A. "Teacher Trainee Responses to Two Personality Inventories." *Psychol Rep* 22:609–10 Ap '68. * (*PA* 42:12781)

295. CATTELL, RAYMOND B., and GIBBONS, B. D. "Personality Factor Structure of the Combined Guilford and Cattell Personality Questionnaires." *J Personality & Social Psychol* 9:107–20 My '68. * (*PA* 42:10588)

296. CATTELL, RAYMOND B., and NESSELROADE, JOHN R. "Note on Analyzing Personality Relations in Married Couples." *Psychol Rep* 22:381–2 Ap '68. * (*PA* 42:11996)

297. COMREY, ANDREW L.; JAMISON, KAY; and KING, NATHAN. "Integration of Two Personality Factor Systems." *Multiv Beh Res* 3:147–59 Ap '68. * (*PA* 42:14724)

298. GALLAGHER, ROBERT PATRICK. *Personality Characteristics of Counseling and Mathematics Institute Trainees, Changes That Occur During Training, and Relationships Between Counselor Characteristics and Counseling Potential.* Doctor's thesis, Rutgers—The State University (New Brunswick, N.J.), 1968. (*DA* 28:4908A)

299. GUPTA, G. C. "Normative Data for Guilford-Zimmerman Temperament Survey." *J Psychol Res* 12:37–44 Ja '68. * (*PA* 43:5370)

300. LEVENTHAL, D. B.; SHEMBERG, K. M.; and VAN SCHOELANDT, S. KAYE. "Effects of Sex-Role Adjustment Upon the Expression of Aggression." *J Personality & Social Psychol* 8:393–6 Ap '68. * (*PA* 42:8869)

301. LOWE, C. MARSHALL, and DAMANKOS, FREDERICK J. "Psychological and Sociological Dimensions of Anomie in a Psychiatric Population." *J Social Psychol* 74:65–74 F '68. * (*PA* 42:9031)

302. SCHNELL, RICHARD R., and HARNEY, JAMES. "Guilford-Zimmerman Temperament Survey and Peer Approval." *Proc Ann Conv Am Psychol Assn* 76:453–4 '68. * (*PA* 43:937, title only)

303. SIGNORI, EDRO I.; REMPEL, HENRY; and PICKFORD, JOHN H. "Multivariate Relationships Between Spouses' Trait Scores on the Guilford-Zimmerman Temperament Survey." *Psychol Rep* 22:103–6 F '68. * (*PA* 42:10480)

304. SINHA, AWADESH KUMAR. "On the Test-Retest Relia-

bility of First and Second Halves of Personality Questionnaires." *Psychol Studies* 13:29–37 Ja '68. *
305. WINDHOLZ, GEORGE. "The Relation of Creativity and
Intelligence Constellations to Traits of Temperament, Interest,
and Value in College Students." *J General Psychol* 79:291–9
O '68. * (*PA* 43:3998)

NAME INDEX

[105]

The Handicap Problems Inventory. Ages 16 and
over with physical disabilities; 1960; HPI; 4 scores:
personal, family, social, vocational; 1 form (4 pages);
manual (14 pages); $3 per 25 tests, postage extra;
$1 per specimen set, postpaid; (30–35) minutes;
George N. Wright and H. H. Remmers; [University
Book Store]. *

For a review by Dorothy M. Clendenen, see 6:111.

REFERENCES

1. WRIGHT, GEORGE NELSON. *An Investigation of Problems
Presented by Physically Handicapped Adults.* Doctor's thesis,
Purdue University (Lafayette, Ind.), 1959. (*DA* 20:371)
2. MEISSNER, ANN LORING WOODWORTH. *Adolescent Atti-*

tudes Toward Self and Toward Disabled People. Doctor's thesis, University of Wisconsin (Madison, Wis.), 1965. (*DA* 26:5572)

[106]

★The Hartman Value Inventory: Scales for Measuring the Capacity to Value. Grades 9–16 and adults; 1965–67; HVI; 10 main scores: intrinsic dimension, extrinsic dimension, systemic dimension, differentiation, dimension, integration, dissimilarity, value, self, balance; title on test sheets is *The Hartman Inventory;* for research use only; 1 form consisting of Parts 1, 2, ('66, 2 pages); directions for administering ('67, 4 pages); directions for scoring ('67, 8 pages); scoring form ('66, 1 page); report form ('66, 2 pages); $5 per 25 tests; $2.50 per 25 scoring forms; $5 per 25 report forms; $1.40 per directions for scoring; postage extra; $2 per specimen set, postpaid; (20–40) minutes; Robert S. Hartman and Mario Cardenas Trigos; Miller Associates. *

REFERENCES

1. HARTMAN, ROBERT S. "Formal Axiology and the Measurement of Values." *J Value Inquiry* 1:38–46 sp '67. *
2. HARTMAN, ROBERT S. *The Structure of Value: Foundations of Scientific Axiology.* Carbondale, Ill.: Southern Illinois University Press, 1967. Pp. xxi, 384. *

[107]

Harvard Group Scale of Hypnotic Susceptibility. College and adults; 1959–62; HGSHS; adaptation of Form A of the *Stanford Hypnotic Susceptibility Scale* for group administration; Form A ('62, 8 pages); manual ('62, 22 pages); no data on reliability; $6.50 per 25 tests; $2 per manual; $2.25 per specimen set; postage extra; (50–70) minutes; Ronald E. Shor and Emily Carota Orne; Consulting Psychologists Press, Inc. *

For a review by Seymour Fisher, see 6:112 (4 references).

REFERENCES

1–3. See 6:112.
4. COE, WILLIAM C. "Further Norms on the Harvard Group Scale of Hypnotic Susceptibility, Form A." *Int J Clin & Exp Hyp* 12:184–90 Jl '64. * (*PA* 39:5044)
5. FIELD, PETER B. "An Inventory of Experiences During Hypnosis." *Newsl Res Psychol* 6:31 N '64. *
6. O'CONNELL, DONALD NEIL. "An Experimental Comparison of Hypnotic Depth Measured by Self-Ratings and by an Objective Scale." *Int J Clin & Exp Hyp* 12:34–46 Ja '64. * (*PA* 38:8752)
7. ROSENHAN, DAVID L., and TOMKINS, SILVAN S. "On Preference for Hypnosis and Hypnotizability." *Int J Clin & Exp Hyp* 12:109–14 Ap '64. * (*PA* 39:2199)
8. DERMEN, DIRAN, and LONDON, PERRY. "Correlates of Hypnotic Susceptibility." *J Consult Psychol* 29:537–45 D '65. * (*PA* 40:2261)
9. FIELD, PETER B. "An Inventory Scale of Hypnotic Depth." *Int J Clin & Exp Hyp* 13:238–49 O '65. * (*PA* 40:107)
10. FIELD, PETER B.; EVANS, FREDERICK J.; and ORNE, MARTIN T. "Order of Difficulty of Suggestions During Hypnosis." *Int J Clin & Exp Hyp* 13:183–92 Jl '65. * (*PA* 39:15729)
11. HARTMAN, BERNARD J. "Hypnotic Susceptibility Assessed in a Group of Mentally Ill Geriatric Patients." *J Am Geriatrics Soc* 13:460–1 My '65. *
12. HARTMAN, BERNARD J. "Self-Scoring and Observer-Scoring Estimates of Hypnotic Susceptibility in a Group Situation." *Percept & Motor Skills* 20:452 Ap '65. * (*PA* 39:12547)
13. EVANS, FREDERICK J., and SCHMEIDLER, DEL. "Relationship Between the Harvard Group Scale of Hypnotic Susceptibility and the Stanford Hypnotic Susceptibility Scale: Form C." *Int J Clin & Exp Hyp* 14:333–43 O '66. * (*PA* 41:62)
14. MITCHELL, MEREDITH BURTON. *Hypnotic Susceptibility and Response to Distraction.* Doctor's thesis, Claremont Graduate School (Claremont, Calif.), 1967. (*DA* 29:774B)
15. BELAIR, ROBERT RALPH. *Selected Developmental Correlates of Hypnotic Susceptibility.* Doctor's thesis, Washington State University (Pullman, Wash.), 1968. (*DA* 29:765B)

[108]

★The Hellenic Affiliation Scale: An Inventory of Student Behavior and Beliefs for Use by School Personnel, Experimental Form. College; 1967; HAS; test title is H.A.S.; fraternity or sorority affiliation proneness; 1 form (2 mimeographed pages); mimeographed manual (12 pages plus test); 50¢ per test; $2.50 per manual; postpaid; test may be reproduced locally for research or experimental use; (3–8) minutes; LeRoy A. Stone, Marlo A. Skurdal, and David R. Skeen; LeRoy A. Stone. *

[109]

★Hill Interaction Matrix. Prospective members, members, and leaders of psychotherapy groups; 1954–68; HIM; matrix of 4 columns (topics, groups, personal, relationship) and 4 rows (conventional, assertive, speculative, confrontive) produces 16 scores, 8 marginal total scores, grand total, and other derivative scores; 3 editions; manual supplement ['68, 15 pages plus tests]; separate answer sheets must be used; $5 per 100 answer sheets; $5 per 100 tally sheets; $1.50 per manual supplement; training film may be rented ($6) or purchased ($65); postpaid; (20) minutes; Wm. Fawcett Hill; Sage Publications. *

a) HIM A AND B. Prospective and actual members of psychotherapy groups; 1954–68; 2 editions: HIM-A ['66, 9 pages, same as HIM-B except for simpler language in 31 of the 64 items], HIM-B ['61, 8 pages]; revised manual ('65, 119 pages); scoring manual ['63, 65 pages]; tally sheet (no date, 1 page); $1.50 per 10 tests; $2.50 per manual; $3 per specimen set of either edition.
b) HIM-G. Observers and leaders of psychotherapy groups; 1967–68; 1 form ['67, 13 pages]; no manual; no data on reliability; norms (mean scores) only for 8 marginal totals; $2 per 10 tests; $3.50 per specimen set.

[110]

★The Hoffer-Osmond Diagnostic Test. Mental patients; 1961–67; HOD; diagnosis of schizophrenia; 5 scores: perceptual, paranoid, depression, ratio, total; a short form score may also be determined; manual ('67, 33 pages plus test and record sheet); record sheet (no date, 1 page); Can $7.50 ($7.50) per set of stencils; Can $5.25 ($5.25) per 100 record sheets; Can $3.25 ($3.50) per manual; postage extra; [30–60] minutes; Harold Kelm (manual), Abraham Hoffer, and Humphry Osmond; Jules R. Gilbert Ltd. (Card Form only). (United States distributor: Bell-Craig, Inc.) * Also distributed in England by Psychological Test Publications.

a) [CARD FORM.] 1 form ['61, 145 cards]; statistical data in manual based on Card Form; Can $10.50 ($18) per set of cards, scoring stencils, 15 record sheets, and manual.
b) [BOOKLET FORM.] 1 form ('67, 7 pages); separate answer sheets must be used; 50¢ per test.

For reviews by Maurice Lorr and William Schofield, see 6:114 (6 references).

REFERENCES

1–5. See 6:114.
6. OSMOND, H., and HOFFER, A. "Commentary." *J Neuropsychiatry* 2:369–70 Ag '61. *
7. HOFFER, A., and OSMOND, H. "The Relationship Between Mood and Time Perception." *Psychiatric Q Sup* 36(1):87–92 '62. * (*PA* 39:2637)
8. HOFFER, A. "HOD Scores for Young Subjects." *J Neuropsychiatry* 4:279 Ap '63. *
9. HOFFER, A., and OSMOND, H. "A Question of Insight." *Dis Nerv System* 24:606–11 O '63. *
10. HOFFER, A. "A Comparison of Psychiatric Inpatients and Outpatients and Malvaria." *Int J Neuropsychiatry* 1:430–2 S–O '65. *
11. HOFFER, A. "Malvaria, Schizophrenia and the HOD Test." *Int J Neuropsychiatry* 2:175–8 Mr–Ap '65. *
12. KELM, H.. and HOFFER, A. "A Revised Score for the Hoffer-Osmond Diagnostic Test." *Dis Nerv System* 26:790–1 D '65. *
13. KELM, H.; GRUNBERG, F.; and HALL, R. W. "A Re-

Examination of the Hoffer-Osmond Diagnostic Test." *Int J Neuropsychiatry* 1:307–12 Jl–Ag '65. *

14. HOFFER, A. "Laboratory Tests for Following Progress of Schizophrenia." *Dis Nerv System* 27:466–9 Jl '66. *

15. HOFFER, A. "Malvaria and the Law." *Psychosomatics* 7:303–10 S–O '66. *

16. HOFFER, A. "Quantification of Malvaria." *Int J Neuropsychiatry* 2:559–61 N–D '66. * (*PA* 41:4744)

17. HOFFER, A., and OSMOND, H. "Some Psychological Consequences of Perceptual Disorder and Schizophrenia." *Int J Neuropsychiatry* 2:1–19 F '66. *

18. HOFFER, ABRAM. "Psychopathology and Galactic Forces." *Corrective Psychiatry & J Social Ther* 12:284–92 Jl '66. * (*PA* 40:13229)

19. KELM, H.; CHAMBERS, D. A.; and HALL, R. W. "An Evaluation of the Hoffer-Osmond Diagnostic Test." *J Clin Psychol* 22:120–2 Ja '66. * (*PA* 40:4234)

20. KELM, H., and HOFFER, A. "Age and the Hoffer-Osmond Diagnostic Test." *Int J Neuropsychiatry* 3:406–7 O '67. * (*PA* 42:7456)

21. KELM, H.; CALLBECK, M. J.; and HOFFER, A. "A Short Form of the Hoffer-Osmond Diagnostic Test." *Int J Neuropsychiatry* 3:489–90 N–D '67. * (*PA* 42:12356)

22. KELM, H.; HOFFER, A.; and HALL, R. W. "Reliability of the Hoffer-Osmond Diagnostic Test." *J Clin Psychol* 23:380–2 Jl '67. * (*PA* 41:14445)

23. KELM, HAROLD. "Hoffer-Osmond Diagnostic Test: A Review." *J Schizophrenia* 1(2):90–5 '67. * (*PA* 42–9161)

24. KELM, HAROLD, and HALL, R. W. "Hoffer-Osmond Diagnostic Test and Figural After-Effect." *J Nerv & Mental Dis* 144:305–7 Ap '67. * (*PA* 41:15289)

25. KOWALSON, B. "Metabolic Dysperception: Its Diagnosis and Management in General Practice." *J Schizophrenia* 1(3):200–3 '67. * (*PA* 42:7511)

26. SMITH, EUGENE R. "A Cursory Evaluation of HOD Test." *Proc Ann Conf Air Force Behav Sci* 14:314–9 D '67. *

27. WARD, JACK L. "Treatment of Neurotics and Schizophrenics Using Clinical and HOD Criteria." *J Schizophrenia* 1(3):140–9 '67. * (*PA* 42:7433)

NAME INDEX

[111]

*The Hooper Visual Organization Test. Ages 14 and over; 1957–66; HVOT; organic brain pathology; 1 form ('57, 4 pages); manual ('58, 16 pages plus test and protocol booklet); protocol booklet ('66, 4 pages); $17.50 per set of testing materials including manual, 25 tests for group administration, card material for individual administration, and 25 protocol booklets; $6.50 per 25 tests; $6.50 per 25 protocol booklets; $2 per manual; postpaid; (15–20) minutes; H. Elston Hooper; Western Psychological Services. *

For reviews by Ralph M. Reitan and Otfried Spreen, see 6:116 (4 references).

REFERENCES

1–4. See 6:116.

5. AUGER, RICHARD, and MASON, CHARLES F. "Differential Diagnosis With the Hooper Visual Organization Test: Brain Damage vs. Schizophrenia." *Newsl Res Psychol* 6:38–9 Ag '64. *

6. GANZLER, HENRY. "Motivation as a Factor in the Psychological Deficit of Aging." *J Gerontol* 19:425–9 O '64. *

7. MASON, CHARLES F., and GANZLER, HENRY. "Adult Norms for the Shipley Institute of Living Scale and Hooper Visual Organization Test Based on Age and Education." *J Gerontol* 19:419–24 O '64. *

8. EISENMAN, RUSSELL, and COYLE, F. A., Jr. "Absence of False Positives on the Hooper Visual Organization Test." *Psychol Rep* 17:417–8 O '65. * (*PA* 40:1587)

9. FREED, EARL X. "Some Test Evidence of CNS Dysfunction in Psychiatric Patients Manifesting Alcoholism." *Newsl Res Psychol* 9:26–7 Ag '67. *

10. NEWCOMB, WALDO BURKETT, JR. *Normal Achieving and Underachieving Hearing-Impaired Students' Performance on Raven's Progressive Matrices (1938) and the Hooper Visual Organization Test.* Master's thesis, University of Texas (Austin, Tex.), 1967.

11. COYLE, F. A., JR., and EISENMAN, RUSSELL. "Negro Performance on the Hooper Visual Organization Test: Impairment or Artifact?" *J Social Psychol* 75:269–71 Ag '68. * (*PA* 42:16406)

[112]

Hospital Adjustment Scale. Mental patients; 1951–53; HAS; 4 ratings: communication and interpersonal relations, self-care and social responsibility, work and recreation, total; 1 form ('53, 4 pages); manual ('53, 12 pages); $3.50 per 25 tests; 75¢ per set of scoring key and manual; $1 per specimen set; postage extra; (10–20) minutes; James T. Ferguson, Paul McReynolds, and Egerton L. Ballachey (test); Consulting Psychologists Press, Inc. *

For a review by Wilson H. Guertin, see 6:117 (3 references); for a review by Maurice Lorr, see 5:67 (5 references).

REFERENCES

1–5. See 5:67.
6–8. See 6:117.

9. ROBACK, HOWARD B., and SNYDER, WILLIAM U. "A Comparison of Hospitalized Mental Patients' Adjustment With Their Attitudes Toward Psychiatric Hospitals." *J Clin Psychol* 21:228–30 Ap '65. * (*PA* 39:12590)

10. LYERLY, SAMUEL B., and ABBOTT, PRESTON S. "Hospital Adjustment Scale," pp. 67–9. In their *Handbook of Psychiatric Rating Scales (1950–1964).* Public Health Service Publication No. 1495. Washington, D.C.: United States Government Printing Office, 1966. Pp. v, 69. *

11. LEWINSOHN, PETER M., and NICHOLS, ROBERT C. "Dimensions of Change in Mental Hospital Patients." *J Clin Psychol* 23:498–503 O '67. * (*PA* 42:2624)

12. LOWE, C. MARSHALL. "The Relationship Between Marital and Socioeconomic Status and In-Patient Impairment." *J Clin Psychol* 23:315–8 Jl '67. * (*PA* 41:15619)

13. ROBACK, HOWARD B. "Follow-Up Study of the Hospital Adjustment Scale." *J Abn Psychol* 72:110–1 Ap '67. * (*PA* 41:7478)

14. McREYNOLDS, PAUL. "The Hospital Adjustment Scale: Research and Clinical Applications." *Psychol Rep* 23:823–35 D '68. *

[113]

How Well Do You Know Yourself? High school, college, office and factory workers; 1959–61; HWDYKY; 19 scores: irritability, practicality, punctuality, novelty-loving, vocational assurance, cooperativeness, ambitiousness, hypercriticalness, dejection, general morale, persistence, nervousness, seriousness, submissiveness, impulsiveness, dynamism, emotional control, consistency, test objectivity; Form NE-21 ('61, 6 pages, identical with test copyrighted in 1959 except for two interchanges of items); 3 editions (identical except for profiles): secondary school, college, personnel; manual ('59, 28 pages); supplement ('61, 2 pages); $6.50 per 30 tests; $2 per set of scoring stencils; $1.10 per manual; $2.50 per specimen set; postage extra; (20) minutes; Thomas N. Jenkins, John H. Coleman (manual), and Harold T. Fagin (manual); Executive Analysis Corporation. *

For reviews by Lee J. Cronbach and Harrison G. Gough, see 6:118 (2 references, 2 excerpts).

[114]

Human Relations Inventory. Grades 9–16 and adults; 1954–59; HRI; social conformity; Form A ('54, 4 pages); manual ('59, 4 pages, identical with manual published in 1954 except for format and supplementary validity data and references); no data on reliability; $3 per 25 tests; $1 per specimen set (must be purchased to obtain manual); cash orders postpaid; (20) minutes; Raymond E. Bernberg; Psychometric Affiliates. *

See 6:119 (6 references); for reviews by Raymond C. Norris and John A. Radcliffe, see 5:68.

REFERENCES

1–6. See 6:119.

7. MUNDY, JEAN. "Conformity to Group Judgment in Relation to the Assumed Similarity of Members to Each Other." *Newsl Coop Res Psychol* 2:15–8 Jl '60. *

[115]

The Humm-Wadsworth Temperament Scale. Adults; 1934–60; HWTS; 47 scores: normal (4 subscores), hysteroid (6 subscores), manic (4 subscores), depressive (5 subscores), autistic (5 subscores), paranoid (3 subscores), epileptoid (4 subscores), response bias (2 subscores), self mastery (6 component control subscores plus integration index); 1 form ('34, 8 pages); mimeographed manual, 1954–55 revision ('55, 126 pages, with addendum copyrighted in 1960); profile-work sheet ('54, 1 page); qualitative analysis tables ('56, 8 pages); nomogram ('54), with response-bias corrector ('50) overleaf; distribution restricted; service fees for business organizations retaining publisher as consultant: $1,350 for first year (includes 3-week training course for 1–2 persons and consultation service), $10 per month thereafter; no service fees for psychologists; test materials rented to licensees only; $25 for the use of 25 tests and accessories for first year, $5 per year thereafter; separate answer sheets must be used; $2.50 per 25 additional tests; 25¢ per answer sheet; specimen set not available; postage extra; (45–90) minutes; Doncaster G. Humm and Kathryn A. Humm; Humm Personnel Consultants. *

For reviews by James R. Glennon and Floyd L. Ruch, see 6:120 (3 references); see also 5:69 (20 references); for reviews by H. J. Eysenck, H. Meltzer, and Lorenz Misbach, see 3:48 (31 references); for reviews by Forrest A. Kingsbury and P. E. Vernon, see 2:1223 (13 references); for a review by Daniel A. Prescott, see 1:920.

REFERENCES

1–13. See 2:1223.
14–44. See 3:48.
45–64. See 5:69.
65–67. See 6:120.

NAME INDEX

[116]

The IPAT Anxiety Scale Questionnaire. Ages 14 and over; 1957–63; IPAT ASQ; also called *IPAT Anxiety Scale;* title on test is *IPAT Self Analysis Form;* 6 scores: lack of self-sentiment development, ego weakness, protension or paranoid trend, guilt proneness, ergic tension, total anxiety; 1 form ('57, 4 pages); manual, second edition ('63, 16 pages); $3.30 per 25 tests; 50¢ per scoring stencil; $1.80 per manual; $2.40 per specimen set; postage extra; (5–10) minutes; Raymond B. Cattell and I. H. Scheier (manual); Institute for Personality and Ability Testing. *

For a review by Jacob Cohen, see 6:121 (23 references); for reviews by J. P. Guilford and E. Lowell Kelly, see 5:70 (1 excerpt).

REFERENCES

1–23. See 6:121.
24. FRIEDMAN, JOSEPH. *Psychological Correlates of Overweight, Underweight and Normal Weight College Women.* Doctor's thesis, Temple University (Philadelphia, Pa.), 1958. (*DA* 19:3362)
25. SCHEIER, IVAN HENRY. "To Be or Not To Be a Guinea Pig: Preliminary Data on Anxiety and the Volunteer for Experiment." *Psychol Rep* 5:239–40 Je '59. * (*PA* 34:3024)
26. PURCELL, JOHN FRANCIS. *Expressed Self Concept and Adjustment in Sexually Delinquent and Non-Delinquent Adolescent Girls.* Doctor's thesis, Fordham University (New York, N.Y.), 1961. (*DA* 22:918)
27. BARTA, JAMES. *A Study of the Concurrence of Anxiety and Hostility.* Doctor's thesis, Fordham University (New York, N.Y.), 1962. (*DA* 23:3471)
28. CATTELL, RAYMOND B. "The Nature and Measurement of Anxiety." *Sci Am* 208:96–104 Mr '63. * (*PA* 38:4346)
29. FEIN, LEAH GOLD. "Evidence of a Curvilinear Relationship Between IPAT Anxiety and Achievement at Nursing School." *J Clin Psychol* 19:374–6 Jl '63. * (*PA* 39:7954)
30. KENT, DERYCK RICHARD. *The Effectiveness of the Anxiety Differential as a Measure of Stress With Stutterers and Normals.* Doctor's thesis, University of California (Los Angeles, Calif.), 1963. (*DA* 24:3203)
31. McDONALD, ROBERT L.; GYNTHER, MALCOLM D.; and CHRISTAKOS, ARTHUR C. "Relations Between Maternal Anxiety and Obstetric Complications." *Psychosom Med* 25:357–63 Jl-Ag '63. * (*PA* 38:9104)
32. NHAN, NGUYEN. *Some Personality Determinants of the Effects of Role Pressures on the Interpersonal Behavior of Role Occupants.* Doctor's thesis, University of Michigan (Ann Arbor, Mich.), 1963. (*DA* 25:2084)
33. PURYEAR, HERBERT BRUCE. *Personality Characteristics of Reporters and Nonreporters of Dreams.* Doctor's thesis, University of North Carolina (Chapel Hill, N.C.), 1963. (*DA* 24:3425)
34. BONNEY, MERL E. "Some Correlates of a Social Definition of Normal Personality." *J Clin Psychol* 20:415–22 O '64. * (*PA* 39:12226)
35. GOLDING, LAWRENCE A., and HARVEY, VIRGINIA. "Relationship Between Anxiety and Serum Cholesterol." *Psychosom Sci* 1:149–50 Je '64. * (*PA* 38:10231)
36. LEVITT, EUGENE E.; PERSKY, HAROLD; and BRADY, JOHN PAUL. *Hypnotic Induction of Anxiety: A Psychoendocrine Investigation.* Springfield, Ill.: Charles C Thomas, Publisher, 1964. Pp. xvi, 134. *
37. LEWINSOHN, PETER M., and NICHOLS, ROBERT C. "The Evaluation of Changes in Psychiatric Patients During and After Hospitalization." *J Clin Psychol* 20:272–9 Ap '64. * (*PA* 39:8200)
38. OTTINGER, DONALD R., and SIMMONS, JAMES E. "Behavior of Human Neonates and Prenatal Maternal Anxiety." *Psychol Rep* 14:391–4 Ap '64. * (*PA* 39:1286)
39. SCHWAB, JOHN R., and IVERSON, MARVIN A. "Resistance of High-Anxious Subjects Under Ego Threat to Perception of Figural Distortion." *J Consult Psychol* 28:191–8 Je '64 * (*PA* 39:5001)
40. BARRATT, ERNEST S. "Factor Analysis of Some Psychometric Measures of Impulsiveness and Anxiety." *Psychol Rep* 16:547–54 Ap '65. * (*PA* 39:10087)
41. COOLEY, C. EWING, and HUTTON, JERRY B. "Adolescent Response to Religious Appeal as Related to IPAT Anxiety." *J Social Psychol* 67:325–7 D '65. * (*PA* 40:5478)
42. GRAFF, HAROLD. "Overweight and Emotions in the Obesity Clinic." *Psychosomatics* 6:89–94 Mr–Ap '65. *
43. KRAUS, J. "Cattell Anxiety Scale Scores and WAIS Attainment in Three Groups of Psychiatric Patients." *Austral J Psychol* 17:229–32 D '65. * (*PA* 40:5451)
44. LOMONT, JAMES F. "The Repression-Sensitization Dimension in Relation to Anxiety Responses." *J Consult Psychol* 29:84–6 F '65. * (*PA* 39:7959)
45. LUNDIN, ROBERT W., and SAWYER, CHARLES R. "The Relationship Between Test Anxiety, Drinking Patterns and Scholastic Achievement in a Group of Undergraduate College Men." *J General Psychol* 73:143–6 Jl '65. * (*PA* 39:16386)
46. RICKELS, KARL, and CATTELL, RAYMOND B. "The Clinical Factor Validity and Trueness of the IPAT Verbal and Objective Batteries for Anxiety and Regression." *J Clin Psychol* 21:257–64 Jl '65. * (*PA* 39:15261)
47. SLAYTON, WILFRED GEORGE. *A Comparison of Successful and Unsuccessful Bible College Students With Respect to Selected Personality Factors.* Doctor's thesis, University of Arizona (Tucson, Ariz.), 1965. (*DA* 26:1487)
48. BENDIG, A. W. "Reliability of and Intercorrelations Between Cattell's IPAT Anxiety and Neuroticism Scales." *J General Psychol* 75:1–7 Jl '66. * (*PA* 40:11661)
49. KNOWLES, J. B., and KREITMAN, N. "Trial of Oxypertime for Anxiety Neurosis." Letter. *Brit J Psychiatry* 112:104 Ja '66. *
50. LEY, P.; SPELMAN, M. S.; DAVIES, ANN D. M.; and RILEY, S. "The Relationships Between Intelligence, Anxiety,

Neuroticism and Extraversion." *Brit J Ed Psychol* 36:185–91 Je '66. * (*PA* 40:10100)

51. PETRUSICH, MARY MARGARET. *Some Relationships Between Anxiety and the Classroom Behavior of Student Teachers.* Doctor's thesis, University of Washington (Seattle, Wash.), 1966. (*DA* 27:1691A)

52. ALLRED, RAYMOND COYE. *The Relationship Between the Interaction of Two Anxiety Variables and Creative Production.* Doctors' thesis, North Texas State University (Denton, Tex.), 1967. (*DA* 28:2063A)

53. BONNEY, MERL E. "Interrelationships Between Content Analysis and Personality Self-Ratings in Studying *High* and *Low Normality* in a College Population." *J Social Psychol* 71:277–85 Ap '67. * (*PA* 41:8897)

54. BRADBURY, BEVERLY RAY. *A Study of Guilt and Anxiety as Related to Certain Psychological and Sociological Variables.* Doctor's thesis, North Texas State University (Denton, Tex.), 1967. (*DA* 28:2336A)

55. BROWN, L. B., and FERNALD, L. DODGE, JR. "Questionnaire Anxiety." *Psychol Rep* 21:537–40 O '67. * (*PA* 42:5593)

56. HOLM, JOY ALICE. *An Investigation of Some Relationships Among Components of Anxiety and Relation-Perceiving Functions as Represented in Perspective Drawings.* Doctor's thesis, University of Minnesota (Minneapolis, Minn.), 1967. (*DA* 28:4480A)

57. JACKSON, BARRIE T., and BARRY, W. F. "The Vasomotor Component of the Orientation Reaction as a Correlative of Anxiety." *Percept & Motor Skills* 25:514–6 O '67. * (*PA* 42:5251)

58. KRACHT, CONRAD RALPH. *The Relationship of Scores on the Minnesota Teacher Attitude Inventory and the IPAT Anxiety Scale Questionnaire to Evaluation of Student Teachers' Classroom Performance.* Doctor's thesis, Southern Illinois University (Carbondale, Ill.), 1967. (*DA* 28:3529A)

59. LEWINSOHN, PETER M. "Factors Related to Improvement in Mental Hospital Patients." *J Consult Psychol* 31:588–94 D '67. * (*PA* 42:2642)

60. LEWINSOHN, PETER M., and NICHOLS, ROBERT C. "Dimensions of Change in Mental Hospital Patients." *J Clin Psychol* 23:498–503 O '67. * (*PA* 42:2624)

61. SCHREIBER, ELLIOTT HAROLD. *The Relationship Between Personality Characteristics and Dental Disorders in Adolescents.* Doctor's thesis, West Virginia University (Morgantown, W.Va.), 1967. (*DA* 28:1313A)

62. WINK, RICHARD LEE. *Relationship of Self-Concept and Selected Personality Variables to Achievement in Music Student Teaching.* Doctor's thesis, Ohio State University (Columbus, Ohio), 1967. (*DA* 28:5100A)

63. ZUCKERMAN, MARVIN; PERSKY, HAROLD; ECKMAN, KATHERINE M.; and HOPKINS, T. ROBERT. "A Multitrait Multimethod Measurement Approach to the Traits (or States) of Anxiety, Depression and Hostility." *J Proj Tech & Pers Assess* 31:39–48 Ap '67. * (*PA* 41:13635)

64. FEIN, LEAH GOLD. "Non-Academic Personality Variables and Success at School." *Int Mental Health Res Newsl* 10:2+ sp '68. *

65. KROTH, JEROME A. "Relationship Between Anxiety and Menarcheal Onset." *Psychol Rep* 23:801–2 D '68. *

66. MEREDITH, GERALD M. "Personality Correlates to Religious Belief Systems." *Psychol Rep* 23:1039–42 D '68. *

67. PRIDE, L. FRANCES. "An Adrenal Stress Index as a Criterion Measure for Nursing." *Nursing Res* 17:292–303 Jl–Ag '68. *

68. SAMS, LAURANNE BROWN. *The Relationship Between Anxiety, Stress and the Performance of Nursing Students.* Doctor's thesis, Indiana University (Bloomington, Ind.), 1968. (*DA* 29:1456A)

NAME INDEX

[117]

IPAT Contact Personality Factor Test. High school and adults; 1954–56; title on test is *C.P.F.*; 2 scores: extroversion-introversion, distortion; Forms A, B, ('54, 3 pages); mimeographed sheets ['54–56, 21 pages] serving as manual; adult norms only; $2.90 per 25 tests; $2 per complete specimen set (must be purchased to obtain manual and key); postage extra; Form A also published, under the title *Employee Attitude Series: C.P.F.*, by Industrial Psychology, Inc.; (10) minutes; Raymond B. Cattell, Joseph E. King, and A. K. Schuettler; Institute for Personality and Ability Testing. *

See 6:123 (6 references); for reviews by Cecil D. Johnson and S. B. Sells, see 5:71.

REFERENCES

1–6. See 6:123.
7. BRAUN, JOHN R., and LA FARO, DOLORES. "Effects of Salesman Faking Instructions on the Contact Personality Factor Test." *Psychol Rep* 22:1245–8 Je '68. * (*PA* 42:18818)

[118]

IPAT 8-Parallel-Form Anxiety Battery. Ages 14 or 15 and over; 1960–62; 8PFAB; tests and answer sheets labeled *8-Form* and *8-Parallel-Form Battery,* respectively; Forms A, B, C, D, E, F, G, H, ('60, 7 subtests, each on a separate sheet); manual ('60, 6 pages); supplement ('62, 4 pages); $2.50 per 25 copies of any one subtest of any one form; $12.50 per 25 sets of all subtests of any one form; separate answer sheets may be used; $2.50 per pad of 50 answer sheets; 50¢ per set of manual and supplement; $8 per test kit consisting of single-booklet combination of manual and keyed copies of all subtests of all forms (must be purchased to obtain keys for certain subtests); postage extra; (10–15) minutes; Ivan H. Scheier and Raymond B. Cattell; Institute for Personality and Ability Testing. *

For reviews by Jacob Cohen and Paul M. Kjeldergaard, see 6:124 (4 references).

REFERENCES

1–4. See 6:124.
5. CATTELL, RAYMOND B., and RICKELS, KARL. "Diagnostic Power of IPAT Objective Anxiety Neuroticism Tests With Private Patients." *Arch Gen Psychiatry* 11:459–65 N '64. * (*PA* 39:7935)
6. OUTRIDGE, MARGARET. "Psycholinguistic Abilities of Five Children Attending a Brisbane Opportunity School." *Slow Learning Child* 11:165–75 Mr '65. * (*PA* 39:16419)
7. LANGER, PHILIP. "Varsity Football Performance." *Percept & Motor Skills* 23:1191–9 D '66. * (*PA* 41:5432)
8. PETRUSICH, MARY MARGARET. *Some Relationships Between Anxiety and the Classroom Behavior of Student Teachers.* Doctor's thesis, University of Washington (Seattle, Wash.), 1966. (*DA* 27:1691A)
9. RANKIN, RICHARD J., and BALFREY, WILLIAM R. "Impact of Delayed Auditory Feedback on the IPAT 8-Parallel-Form Anxiety Scales." *Psychol Rep* 18:583–6 Ap '66. * (*PA* 40:8865)
10. FORREST, GARY L.; BORTNER, TIMOTHY W.; and BAKKER, CORNELIS B. "The Role of Personality Variables in Response to Chlorpromazine, Dextroamphetamine and Placebo." *J Psychiatric Res* 5:281–8 Jl '67. * (*PA* 42:11814)
11. MILLER, NURAN B.; FISHER, WILLIAM P.; and LADD, CLAYTON E. "Psychometric and Rated Anxiety." *Psychol Rep* 20:707–10 Je '67. * (*PA* 41:13880)
12. SHEPPARD, CHARLES; FIORENTINO, DIANE; COLLINS, LOIS; and MERLIS, SIDNEY. "Performance Errors on Ravens Progressive Matrices (1938) by Sociopathic and Schizotypic Personality Types." *Psychol Rep* 23:1043–6 D '68. *

[119]

*IPAT Humor Test of Personality. High school and adults; 1949–66; test booklet title is *The IPAT Humor Test;* 13 scores: anxious considerateness vs. debonair sexual and general uninhibitedness, dry wit vs. good-natured play, compensation vs. tough self-composure, flirtatious playfulness vs. gruesomeness, urbane pleasantness vs. hostile derogation, impudent defiance of decency vs. resignation, theatricalism vs. cold realism, neat and lighthearted wit vs. ponderous humor, damaging retort vs. unexpected off-beat humor, cheerful independence vs. mistreatment humor, anxious concern vs. evasion of responsibility, rebound against feminine aggression vs. scorn of ineffectual male, dullness vs. general intelligence; Forms A, 1963 Edition ('63, 12 pages), B, Research Edition ('66, 12 pages); mimeographed manual with '66 supplementation ('63, 24 pages); profile ('64, 1 page); mimeographed norms supplement ['66, 5 pages] for Form A; no norms for Form B; separate answer sheets must be used; $7.50 per 25 tests; $2.50 per 50 answer sheets; $2 per 50 profiles; $1.25 per scoring stencil; $1.25 per manual; $2.25 per specimen set; postage extra; (30–45) minutes; Raymond B. Cattell and Donald L. Tollefson; Institute for Personality and Ability Testing. *

For reviews by W. Grant Dahlstrom, Ardie Lubin (with Frank M. Loos), and J. R. Wittenborn, see 4:61 (5 references).

REFERENCES

1–5. See 4:61.
6. CATTELL, R. B., and HOROWITZ, J. Z. "Objective Personality Tests Investigating the Structure of Altruism in Relation to Source Traits A, H, and L." *J Personality* 21:103–17 S '52. * (*PA* 26:5862)
7. YARNOLD, JAMES K., and BERKELEY, MARVIN H. "An Analysis of the Cattell-Luborsky Humor Test Into Homogeneous Scales." *J Abn & Social Psychol* 49:543–6 O '54. * (*PA* 29:5735)
8. PHILIPPUS, MARION JOHN. *A Study of Personality, Value and Interest Patterns of Student Teachers in the Areas of Elementary, Secondary and Special Education.* Doctor's thesis, University of Denver (Denver, Colo.), 1961. (*DA* 22:3926)
9. PHILIPPUS, MARION JOHN, and FLEIGLER, LOUIS. "A Study of Personality, Value and Interest Patterns of Student Teachers in the Areas of Elementary, Secondary, and Special Education." *Sci Ed* 46:247–52 Ap '62. *
10. LEE, JOAN C., and GRIFFITH, RICHARD M. "Forgetting of Jokes: A Function of Repression?" *J Indiv Psychol* 19:213–5 N '63. * (*PA* 38:6127)
11. HOWARD, KENNETH I. "Differentiation of Individuals as a Function of Repeated Testing." *Ed & Psychol Meas* 24:875–94 w '64. (*PA* 39:7863)
12. ADCOCK, C. J. *Humour Preferences and Personality.* Victoria University of Wellington Publications in Psychology No. 21. Wellington, New Zealand: Department of Psychology, the University, 1967. Pp. iii, 15. *
13. TAYLOR, A. J. W. "Prediction for Parole: A Pilot Study With Delinquent Girls." *Brit J Criminol* 7:418–24 O '67. *

[120]

IPAT Music Preference Test of Personality. "Adults and young adults"; 1952–63; MPTP; 11 scores of which the following 8 are profiled: adjustment vs. frustrated emotionality, hypomanic self-centeredness vs. self-distrust and doubt, tough sociability vs. tenderminded individuality, introspectiveness vs. social contact, anxiety and concern vs. paranoid imperiousness, complex eccentricity vs. stability-normality, resilience vs. withdrawn schizothymia, schizothyme tenacity vs. relaxed cyclothymia; Forms A, B, ['60, on one 12-inch, 33⅓ rpm record]; mimeographed manual ('60, c1954–60, 24 pages, identical with manual published in 1952 except for cover page); mimeographed supplement ('63, 4 pages); answer sheet-profile ('59, 1 page); separate answer sheets must be used; $13.50 per set of record, 100 answer sheets, scoring stencil, and manual; $2.50 per 50 answer sheets; $2 per specimen set without record; postage extra; (25–30) minutes; Raymond B. Cattell

and Herbert W. Eber; Institute for Personality and Ability Testing. *

For reviews by Kenneth L. Bean and Paul R. Farnsworth, see 6:125 (7 references); by Neil J. Van Steenberg, see 5:73 (4 references).

[121]

IPAT Neurotic Personality Factor Test. Grades 9–16 and adults; 1955; NPFT; for later version see *Neuroticism Scale Questionnaire* (see 178); test booklet title is N.P.F.; 2 scores: neuroticism, distortion; 1 form (3 pages); mimeographed manual (18 pages, issued in parts as separate bulletins); adult norms ['55] only; $2.90 per 25 tests; $2 per specimen set (must be purchased to obtain manual); cash orders postpaid; (10–15) minutes; R. B. Cattell, J. E. King, and A. K. Schuettler; published jointly by Institute for Personality and Ability Testing and Industrial Psychology, Inc. (Industrial Psychology, Inc. distributes the test under the title *Employee Attitude Series: N.P.F.*) *

For reviews by S. B. Sells and William Stephenson, see 5:74.

REFERENCES

1. BENDIG, A. W. "An Inter-Item Factor Analysis of Two 'Lie' Scales." *Psychol Newsl* 10:299–303 My–Je '59. * (*PA* 34:94)
2. BENDIG, A. W. "Factor Analyses of 'Anxiety' and 'Neuroticism' Inventories." *J Consult Psychol* 24:161–8 Ap '60. * (*PA* 34:8195)
3. BENDIG, A. W. "A Factor Analysis of Scales of Emotionality and Hostility." *J Clin Psychol* 17:189–92 Ap '61. * (*PA* 38:1034)
4. CATTELL, RAYMOND B., and SCHEIER, IVAN H. *The Meaning and Measurement of Neuroticism and Anxiety.* New York: Ronald Press Co., 1961. Pp. ix, 535. * (London: George G. Harrap & Co. Ltd.) (*PA* 36:1HK27C)
5. KEAR-COLWELL, J. J. "Studies of the I.P.A.T. Neuroticism Scale Questionnaire." *Brit J Social & Clin Psychol* 4:214–23 S '65. * (*PA* 40:893)
6. BENDIG, A. W. "Reliability of and Intercorrelations Between Cattell's IPAT Anxiety and Neuroticism Scales." *J General Psychol* 75:1–7 Jl '66. * (*PA* 40:11661)
7. KIDD, CECIL B., and WATT, KATIE I. M. "Neuroticism and Distribution of Lesions in Patients With Skin Diseases." *J Psychosom Res* 11:253–61 N '67. * (*PA* 42:11087)
See also references for 178.

[122]

★Independent Activities Questionnaire. High school and college; 1965–67; IAQ; for research use only; nonacademic achievement; 25 scores: 20 scale scores (agriculture, art and design, business, collecting, drama, electronics, exploring, games, handicraft, home responsibility, leadership, mathematics, mechanics, music, politics, public speaking, scholarship, science, sports, writing) and 5 derived scores (arts and crafts, speech, sciences, arts and sciences, social activities); 1 form ('65, 48 pages); manual ('67, 14 pages); 50¢ per test, postage extra; $1 per specimen set, postpaid; scoring involves local punching of IBM cards and computerized scoring by the publisher; (30–45) minutes; Stephen P. Klein (manual); Educational Testing Service. *

REFERENCES

1. SKAGER, RODNEY W.; SCHULTZ, CHARLES B.; and KLEIN, STEPHEN P. "Quality and Quantity of Accomplishments as Measures of Creativity." *J Ed Psychol* 56:31–9 F '65. *
2. SKAGER, R. W.; KLEIN, S. P.; and SCHULTZ, C. B. "The Prediction of Academic and Artistic Achievement at a School of Design." *J Ed Meas* 4:105–17 su '67. *

[123]

Individual and Marriage Counseling Inventory. Adult counselees; 1956; IMCI; a biographical data blank and record form; 1 form (4 pages); no manual; $1.25 per 20 inventories; 10¢ per single copy; postpaid; [15] minutes; Aaron L. Rutledge; Merrill-Palmer Institute. *

[124]

*Inpatient Multidimensional Psychiatric Scale (IMPS), 1966 Revision. Hospitalized mental patients; 1953–66; IMPS; revision of the *Multidimensional Scale for Rating Psychiatric Patients, Hospital Form* ('53–54) by Maurice Lorr, R. L. Jenkins, and J. Q. Holsopple, which was a revision of the *Northport Record* by Maurice Lorr, M. Singer, and H. Zobel; 10 scores based on ratings following an interview: excitement, hostile belligerence, paranoid projection, grandiose expansiveness, perceptual distortions, anxious intropunitiveness, retardation and apathy, disorientation, motor disturbances, conceptual disorganization; revised question booklet ('66, 8 pages, 14 new items have been added); revised answer-profile sheet ['66, 2 pages]; revised manual ('66, 19 pages); revised scoring booklet ['66, 4 pages]; separate answer-profile sheets must be used; $6 per 25 question booklets; $3.50 per 25 sets of scoring booklets and answer sheets; $1.75 per manual; $2 per specimen set; postage extra; (10–15) minutes following a 35–45 minute interview; original materials by Maurice Lorr, C. James Klett, Douglas M. McNair (scale), and Julian J. Lasky (scale); Consulting Psychologists Press, Inc. *

See 6:126 (26 references).

REFERENCES

1–26. See 6:126.
27. PAYNE, REED, and GUTHRIE, GEORGE M. "Symptom Syndromes Among Psychiatric Patients." *J Gerontol* 14:473–6 O '59. * (*PA* 34:4692)
28. CLEVELAND, SIDNEY E. "Body Image Changes Associated With Personality Reorganization." *J Consult Psychol* 24:256–61 Je '60. * (*PA* 35:6922)
29. BELL, ROBERT LOUIS, JR. *Factors Influencing Attitudes Toward Hospital Discharge in Neuropsychiatric Patients.* Doctor's thesis, University of Texas (Austin, Tex.), 1961. (*DA* 22:2067)
30. CASEY, J. F. "VA Cooperative Chemotherapy Studies in Psychiatry, Project 4: 3, Clinical Findings," pp. 15–22. In *Transactions of the Fifth Research Conference on Cooperative Chemotherapy Studies in Psychiatry and Research Approaches to Mental Illness.* Washington, D.C.: Veterans Administration, 1961. Pp. xxxv, 375. *
31. GORHAM, DONALD R. "VA Cooperative Chemotherapy Studies in Psychiatry: 5, A Report on the Attitude Measures Used in Project 4," pp. 28–31. In *Transactions of the Fifth Research Conference on Cooperative Chemotherapy Studies in Psychiatry and Research Approaches to Mental Illness.* Washington, D.C.: Veterans Administration, 1961. Pp. xxxv, 375. *
32. KLETT, C. JAMES. "Appendix A, VA Cooperative Studies of Chemotherapy in Psychiatry, Project Four: Statistical Supplement," pp. 309–31. In *Transactions of the Fifth Research Conference on Cooperative Chemotherapy Studies in Psychiatry and Research Approaches to Mental Illness.* Washington, D.C.: Veterans Administration, 1961. Pp. xxxv, 375. *
33. KURLAND, ALBERT A.; HANLON, THOMAS E.; TATOM, MARY H.; OTA, KAY Y.; and SIMOPOULOS, ARIS M. "The Comparative Effectiveness of Six Phenothiazine Compounds, Phenobarbital and Inert Placebo in the Treatment of Acutely Ill Patients: Global Measures of Severity of Illness." *J Nerv & Mental Dis* 133:1–18 Jl '61. * (*PA* 38:6183)
34. LASKY, JULIAN J. "VA Cooperative Chemotherapy Studies in Psychiatry, Project 4: 2, Research Design and Description of the Sample," pp. 10–4. In *Transactions of the Fifth Research Conference on Cooperative Chemotherapy Studies in Psychiatry and Research Approaches to Mental Illness.* Washington, D.C.: Veterans Administration, 1961. Pp. xxxv, 375. *
35. LORR, MAURICE. "Elements Central to Schizophrenia," pp. 217–20. In *Transactions of the Fifth Research Conference on Cooperative Chemotherapy Studies in Psychiatry and Research Approaches to Mental Illness.* Washington, D.C.: Veterans Administration, 1961. Pp. xxxv, 375. *
36. OVERALL, JOHN E.; GORHAM, DONALD R.; and SHAWVER, JOHN R. "Basic Dimensions of Change in the Symptomatology of Chronic Schizophrenics." *J Abn & Social Psychol* 63:597–602 N '61. * (*PA* 37:1803)
37. KURLAND, ALBERT A.; MICHAUX, MARY H.; HANLON, THOMAS E.; OTA, KAY Y.; and SIMOPOULOS, ARIS M. "The Comparative Effectiveness of Six Phenothiazine Compounds, Phenobarbital and Inert Placebo in the Treatment of Acutely Ill Patients: Personality Dimensions." *J Nerv & Mental Dis* 134:48–60 Ja '62. * (*PA* 38:6185)
38. OVERALL, JOHN E.; HOLLISTER, LEO E.; POKORNY, ALEX D.; CASEY, J. F.; and KATZ, GEORGE. "Drug Therapy in Depressions: Controlled Evaluation of Imipramine, Isocarboxazide, Dextroamphetamine-Amobarbital, and Placebo." *Clin Pharmacol & Therapeu* 3:16–22 Ja–F '62. *

39. GOLDBERG, SOLOMON C., and COLE, JONATHAN O. "Factor Analyses of Ratings of Schizophrenic Behavior." *Psychopharmacol Serv Center B* 2:23–8 F '63. *
40. KLEIN, DONALD F., and FINK, MAX. "Multiple Item Factors as Change Measures in Psychopharmacology." *Psychopharmacologia* 4(1):43–52 '63. *
41. LORR, MAURICE; KLETT, C. JAMES; and McNAIR, DOUGLAS M. *Syndromes of Psychosis.* New York: MacMillan Co., 1963. Pp. x, 286. *
42. OVERALL, J. E.; HOLLISTER, L. E.; HONIGFELD, G.; KIMBELL, I. H., JR.; MEYER, F.; BENNETT, J. L.; and CAFFEY, E. M., JR. "Comparison of Acetophenazine With Perphenazine in Schizophrenics: Demonstration of Differential Effects Based on Computer-Derived Diagnostic Models." *Clin Pharmacol & Therapeu* 4:200–8 Mr–Ap '63. *
43. AUERBACH, ARTHUR H., and EWING, JAMES H. "Some Limitations of Psychiatric Ratings Scales: The Clinician's Viewpoint." *Comprehen Psychiatry* 5:93–100 Ap '64. * (*PA* 39:5336)
44. CAFFEY, EUGENE M., JR.; DIAMOND, LEON S.; FRANK, THOMAS V.; GRASBERGER, JOSEPH C.; HERMAN, LOUIS; KLETT, C. JAMES; and ROTHSTEIN, CHARLES. "Discontinuation or Reduction of Chemotherapy in Chronic Schizophrenics." *J Chronic Dis* 17:347–58 Ap '64. * (*PA* 39:9583)
45. ELISEO, THOMAS S. "Delusions in Process and Reactive Schizophrenics." *J Clin Psychol* 20:352 Jl '64. * (*PA* 39:10652)
46. HUNDZIAK, MARCEL, and PASAMANICK, BENJAMIN. "Occupational and Industrial Therapy in the Treatment of Psychiatric Patients: A Controlled Study of Efficacy in an Intensive-Treatment Institution." *Genetic Psychol Monogr* 69:3–48 F '64. *
47. KATZ, MARTIN, M.; COLE, JONATHAN O.; and LOWERY, HENRI A. "Nonspecificity of Diagnosis of Paranoid Schizophrenia." *Arch Gen Psychiatry* 11:197–202 Ag '64. *
48. LEWINSOHN, PETER M., and NICHOLS, ROBERT C. "The Evaluation of Changes in Psychiatric Patients During and After Hospitalization." *J Clin Psychol* 20:272–9 Ap '64. * (*PA* 39:8200)
49. LORR, MAURICE. "A Simplex of Paranoid Projection." *J Consult Psychol* 28:378–80 Ag '64. * (*PA* 39:3187)
50. McNAIR, DOUGLAS M.; LORR, MAURICE; and HEMINGWAY, PETER. "Further Evidence for Syndrome-Based Psychotic Types." *Arch Gen Psychiatry* 11:368–76 O '64. *
51. National Institute of Mental Health Psychopharmacology Service Center Collaborative Study Group. "Phenothiazine Treatment in Acute Schizophrenia: Effectiveness." *Arch Gen Psychiatry* 10:246–61 Mr '64. *
52. SHERMAN, LEWIS J.; MOSELEY, EDWARD C.; GING, ROSALIE; and BOOKBINDER, LAWRENCE J. "Prognosis in Schizophrenia: A Follow-Up Study of 588 Patients." *Arch Gen Psychiatry* 10:123–30 F '64. * (*PA* 39:2712)
53. CURNUTT, ROBERT, and COROTTO, LOREN V. "Syndrome-Correlates of Bender-Gestalt Performance." *Calif Mental Health Res Dig* 3:79–80 sp '65. *
54. GOLDBERG, SOLOMON C.; KLERMAN, GERALD L.; and COLE, JONATHAN O. "Changes in Schizophrenic Psychopathology and Ward Behaviour as a Function of Phenothiazine Treatment." *Brit J Psychiatry* 111:120–33 F '65. *
55. HONIGFELD, GILBERT H.; ROSENBLUM, MARCUS P.; BLUMENTHAL, IRVING J.; LAMBERT, HENRY L.; and ROBERTS, ARTHUR J. "Behavioral Improvement in the Older Schizophrenic Patient: Drug and Social Therapies." *J Am Geriatrics Soc* 13:57–72 Ja '65. *
56. KLETT, C. JAMES, and MOSELEY, EDWARD C. "The Right Drug for the Right Patient." *J Consult Psychol* 29:546–51 D '65. * (*PA* 40:3051)
57. LORR, MAURICE, and KLETT, C. JAMES. "Constancy of Psychotic Syndromes in Men and Women." *J Consult Psychol* 29:309–13 Ag '65. * (*PA* 39:16162)
58. PETERS, PHYLLIS. *A Study of Clinical Judgment: Prediction of Patient Behavior From Projective, Self-Rating and Behavior Rating Instruments.* Doctor's thesis, Northwestern University (Evanston, Ill.), 1965. (*DA* 26:3489)
59. SEECH, PHYLLIS. "Factors Associated With Staff-Patient and Patient-Patient Interaction on Psychiatric Units." *Nursing Res* 14:69–71 w '65. *
60. GOLDBERG, SOLOMON C.; COLE, JONATHAN O.; and KLERMAN, GERALD L. Chap. 4, "Differential Prediction of Improvement Under Three Phenothiazines," pp. 69–84. In *Prediction of Response to Pharmacotherapy.* Edited by J. R. Wittenborn and Philip R. A. May. Springfield, Ill.: Charles C Thomas, Publisher, 1966. Pp. xii, 231. *
61. KATZ, MARTIN M. Chap. 5, "A Typological Approach to the Problem of Predicting Response to Treatment," pp. 85–101. In *Prediction of Response to Pharmacotherapy.* Edited by J. R. Wittenborn and Philip R. A. May, Springfield, Ill.: Charles C Thomas, Publisher, 1966. Pp. xii, 231. *
62. KATZ, MARTIN M.; LOWERY, HENRI A.; and COLE, JONATHAN O. Chap. 10, "Behavior Patterns of Schizophrenics in the Community," pp. 209–30. In *Exploration in Typing Psychotics.* Edited by Maurice Lorr. London: Pergamon Press Ltd., 1966. Pp. viii, 241. *
63. KLETT, C. JAMES. "A Study of Reliability Using Canonical Correlation." Abstract. *Psychol Rep* 18:830 Je '66. * (*PA* 40:9405, title only)
64. KLETT, C. JAMES, and LORR, MAURICE. Chap. 6, "Validity of the Acute Psychotic Types," pp. 93–127. In *Explora-*

tions in Typing Psychotics. Edited by Maurice Lorr. London: Pergamon Press Ltd., 1966. Pp. viii, 241. *

65. KLETT, C. JAMES, and McNAIR, DOUGLAS M. Chap. 5, "Reliability of the Acute Psychotic Types," pp. 76–92. In *Explorations in Typing Psychotics.* Edited by Maurice Lorr. London: Pergamon Press Ltd., 1966. Pp. viii, 241. *

66. LORR, MAURICE. Chap. 7, "Chronic Psychotic Types," pp. 128–50. In his *Explorations in Typing Psychotics.* London: Pergamon Press Ltd., 1966. Pp. viii, 241. *

67. LORR, MAURICE, and CAVE, RICHARD L. "The Equivalence of Psychotic Syndromes Across Two Media." *Multiv Behav Res* 1:189–95 Ap '66. * (*PA* 41:1756)

68. LORR, MAURICE; KLETT, C. JAMES; and McNAIR, DOUGLAS M. Chap. 4, "Acute Psychotic Types," pp. 33–75. In *Explorations in Typing Psychotics.* Edited by Maurice Lorr. London: Pergamon Press Ltd., 1966. Pp. viii, 241. *

69. LYERLY, SAMUEL B., and ABBOTT, PRESTON S. "The Inpatient Multidimensional Psychiatric Scale," pp. 47–50. In their *Handbook of Psychiatric Rating Scales (1950–1964).* Public Health Service Publication No. 1495. Washington, D.C.: United States Government Printing Office, 1966. Pp. v, 69. *

70. RASKIN, ALLEN; SCHULTERBRANDT, JOY G.; and REATIG, NATALIE. "Rater and Patient Characteristics Associated With Rater Differences in Psychiatric Scale Ratings." *J Clin Psychol* 22:417–23 O '66. * (*PA* 41:2947)

71. RICE, CHARLES E., and MATTSSON, NILS B. Chap. 8, "Types Based on Repeated Measurement," pp. 151–91. In *Explorations in Typing Psychotics.* Edited by Maurice Lorr. London: Pergamon Press Ltd., 1966. Pp. viii, 241. *

72. SHERMAN, LEWIS J.; ELDRED, STANLEY H.; BELL, NORMAN W.; and LONGABAUGH, RICHARD H. "A Revised Use of the Multidimensional Scale for Rating Psychiatric Patients." *J Clin Psychol* 22:248–51 Ap '66. * (*PA* 40:7710)

73. FIREMAN, JOSEPH, and TYNES, DALTON E. "Short-Term Withdrawal of Maintenance Medication." *Comprehen Psychiatry* 8:62–6 F '67. * (*PA* 41:10606)

74. GOLDBERG, SOLOMON C.; MATTSSON, NILS; COLE, JONATHAN O.; and KLERMAN, GERALD L. "Prediction of Improvement in Schizophrenia Under Four Phenothiazines." *Arch Gen Psychiatry* 16:107–17 Ja '67. * (*PA* 41:4710)

75. GOLDBERG, SOLOMON C.; SCHOOLER, NINA R.; and MATTSSON, NILS. "Paranoid and Withdrawal Symptoms in Schizophrenia: Differential Symptom Reduction Over Time." *J Nerv & Mental Dis* 145:158–62 Ag '67. * (*PA* 42:4115)

76. LEWINSOHN, PETER M. "Factors Related to Improvement in Mental Hospital Patients." *J Consult Psychol* 31:588–94 D '67. * (*PA* 42:2642)

77. LEWINSOHN, PETER M., and NICHOLS, ROBERT C. "Dimensions of Change in Mental Hospital Patients." *J Clin Psychol* 23:498–503 O '67. * (*PA* 42:2624)

78. LORR, MAURICE, and RADHAKRISHNAN, BELUR K. "A Comparison of Two Methods of Cluster Analysis." *Ed & Psychol Meas* 27:47–53 sp '67. *

79. LORR, MAURICE; KLETT, C. JAMES; and CAVE, RICHARD. "Higher-Level Psychotic Syndromes." *J Abn Psychol* 72:74–7 F '67. * (*PA* 41:4786)

80. MICHAUX, MARY HELEN; OTA, KAY Y.; HANLON, THOMAS E.; and ZWAAG, LETTIE VANDER. "Repeated Rater-Subject Contacts in Measurement of Change: Some Theoretical and Methodological Issues." *Psycho Rep* 21:697–707 D '67. * (*PA* 42:7388)

81. GALBRECHT, CHARLES R., and KLETT, C. JAMES. "Predicting Response to Phenothiazines: The Right Drug for the Right Patient." *J Nerv & Mental Dis* 147:173–83 Ag '68. * (*PA* 42:18958)

82. GALBRECHT, CHARLES R.; CAFFEY, EUGENE M., JR.; and GOLDMAN, DOUGLAS. "Pentothal-Activated Charges in the EEG of Schizophrenic Patients: Response to Phenothiazine Therapy and Relationship to Select Patient Variables." *Comprehen Psychiatry* 9:482–9 S '68. *

83. GOLDBERG, SOLOMON C.; SCHOOLER, NINA R.; and MATTSSON, NILS. "Paranoid and Withdrawal Symptoms in Schizophrenia Relationship to Reaction Time." *Brit J Psychiatry* 114:1161–5 S '68. *

84. KATZ, MARTIN M. "A Phenomenological Typology of Schizophrenia," pp. 300–22, discussion 322–52. In *The Role and Methodology of Classification in Psychiatry and Psychopathology.* Edited by Martin M. Katz and others. Public Health Service Publication No. 1584. Washington, D.C.: United States Government Printing Office, 1968. Pp. ix, 590. *

85. LORR, MAURICE. "A Typology for Functional Psychotics," pp. 261–77, discussion 322–52. In *The Role and Methodology of Classification in Psychiatry and Psychopathology.* Edited by Martin M. Katz and others. Public Health Service Publication No. 1584. Washington, D.C.: United States Government Printing Office, 1968. Pp. ix, 590. *

86. MEFFERD, ROY B., JR. "Technique for Minimizing the Instrumental Factor." *Multiv Behav Res* 3:339–54 Jl '68. * (*PA* 43:3299)

87. PRIEN, ROBERT F., and COLE, JONATHAN O. "High Dose Chlorpromazine Therapy in Chronic Schizophrenia." *Arch Gen Psychiatry* 18:482–95 Ap '68. *

NAME INDEX

[125]

Institute of Child Study Security Test. Grades 1–3, 4–8; 1957–68; 2 scores: consistency, security; $4.25 per 25 tests, postage extra; Michael F. Grapko; distributed by Institute of Child Study, University of Toronto. *

a) PRIMARY FORM. Grades 1–3; 1964–65; title on test is *The Story of Tommy;* 1 form ('64, 8 pages); mimeographed directions for administration ('64, 7 pages); $1 per specimen set; scoring service: 100 or more tests, 20¢ each; (20) minutes.

b) ELEMENTARY FORM. Grades 4–8; 1957–68; title on test is *The Story of Jimmy;* 1 form ('57, 8 pages); manual ('57, 25 pages); reliability data for grade 5 only; mimeographed norms ['68, 5 pages]; $1 per specimen set; scoring service: 100 or more tests, 30¢ each; (25) minutes.

For a review by Laurance F. Shaffer, see 5:75.

REFERENCES

1. GRAPKO, MICHAEL F. *The Relation of Certain Psychological Variables to Security: A Contribution to Theory.* Doctor's thesis, University of Toronto (Toronto, Ont., Canada), 1953.

2. FINE, MARVIN J. "The Security Patterns of Normal and Educable Mentally Retarded Boys." *B Inst Child Study (Toronto)* 27:13–8 w '65. *

3. FINE, MARVIN JERRY. *The Security of Educable Mentally Retarded Boys in Relation to Special Class Placement.* Doctor's thesis, Michigan State University (East Lansing, Mich.), 1965. (*DA* 26:4443)

4. GRAPKO, MICHAEL F. "The Construction of a Primary

Form of the Institute of Child Study Security Test (The Story of Tommy)." *B Inst Child Study (Toronto)* 27:3–12 w '65. *

[125A]

★**The Integration Level Test Series.** Adults; 1965–66; ILTS; for research use only; 8 tests; 1 form ('65, 4 pages); information sheets ('65, 9 pages); no manual or directions for administering or scoring (except for *Sex Inventory* and *Ideological Survey*); no data on reliability (except for *Sex Inventory*) and validity; no norms; $7.50 per 50 tests; $2.50 per sample set of the 8 tests, cash orders only; postpaid; (60) minutes per test; Frederick C. Thorne; Psychological Research Associates. *

a) PERSONAL HEALTH SURVEY. PHS; physical and mental symptoms related to mental health; 12 scores: general health, general development, gastro-intestinal system, cardio-vascular system, miscellaneous systems, central nervous system, neuro-muscular systems, anxiety-fear states, anger-frustration states, schizophrenia, affective psychoses, character disorders.

b) THE SEX INVENTORY. SI; separate editions for males and females; monograph ('66, 43 pages, reprint of *1, 3–7* below; $2.50 per monograph.

1) *Male Form.* 9 scores: sex drive and interest, sexual maladjustment and frustration, neurotic conflict associated with sex, sexual cathexes and fixations, repression of sexuality, loss of sex controls, homosexuality, sex role confidence, promiscuity and sociopathic tendency.

2) *Female Form.* 11 scores: sex drive and interest, sex maladjustment and frustration, neurotic conflict over sex, sexual cathexes and fixations, sexual repression, sex control, homosexuality, sex role confidence, sexual psychopathy, nymphomania, sexual frigidity.

c) THE IDEOLOGICAL SURVEY. IS; factors contributing to a person's conception of the place of man in the world; 13 scores: 5 scores reflecting individualism and capitalism (morality and reason, rational self-interest, self-sufficiency, self-responsibility, earning and creativity), 8 scores reflecting collectivism and socialism (altruism and morality, socialism, collectivism, insecurity and defensiveness, dependency, inadequacy, rationalizing failure, work attitudes); monograph ('68, 24 pages, reprint of *8–12* below); $4 per monograph.

d) SOCIAL STATUS STUDY. SSS; 10 role scores: citizen, social person, social class, parent and family, financial manager, sex partner, worker, marriage partner, leader-follower, political.

e) THE PERSONAL DEVELOPMENT STUDY. PDS; utilization of classical Freudian mechanisms in personality structure; 10 scores: repression, regression, projection, identification, rationalization, reaction formations, extrapunitiveness, intropunitiveness, impunitiveness, miscellaneous mechanisms.

f) THE EXISTENTIAL STUDY. EA; also called *Existential Analysis;* state of being in the world; 7 scores: self-status, self-actualization, existential morale, existential vacuum, humanistic identification, existence and destiny, suicide.

g) THE LIFE STYLE ANALYSIS. LSA; Adlerian life style patterns in relation to the Murray need systems; 30 scores: 10 characteristic life styles (normal coping, individual, exploitative, pampered-spoiled, defiant-resistive, domineering-authoritarian, conforming, escapist, oneupmanship, evasive-ignoring), 20 Murray needs (abasement, achievement, affiliation, aggression, autonomy, blame avoidance, counteraction, defendance, deference, dominance, exhibition, harm avoidance, inferiority avoidance, nurturance, order, play, rejection, sentience, succorance, understanding).

h) THE FEMININITY STUDY. FS; special situational

problems of women in modern culture; 11 scores: feminine social role, female parent role, feminine career role, female homemaker role, female role confidence, female sex identification, development and maturation, sex drive and interests, promiscuity, homosexuality, health and neurotic conflict.

REFERENCES

1. ALLEN, ROBERT M., and HAUPT, THOMAS D. "The Sex Inventory: Test-Retest Reliabilities of Scale Scores and Items." *J Clin Psychol* 22:375–8 O '66. * (*PA* 41:2244)
2. HAUPT, THOMAS D., and ALLEN, ROBERT M. "A Multivariate Analysis of Variance of Scale Scores on the Sex Inventory, Male Form." *J Clin Psychol* 22:387–95 O '66. * (*PA* 41:2257)
3. THORNE, FREDERICK C. "A Factorial Study of Sexuality in Adult Males." *J Clin Psychol* 22:378–86 O '66. * (*PA* 41:2268)
4. THORNE, FREDERICK C. "Scales for Rating Sexual Experience." *J Clin Psychol* 22:404–7 O '66. * (*PA* 41:2269)
5. THORNE, FREDERICK C. "The Sex Inventory." *J Clin Psychol* 22:367–74 O '66. * (*PA* 41:2270)
6. THORNE, FREDERICK C., and HAUPT, THOMAS D. "The Objective Measurement of Sex Attitudes and Behavior in Adult Males." *J Clin Psychol* 22:395–403 O '66. * (*PA* 41:2271)
7. GALBRAITH, GARY G.; KAPLAN, BURT E.; HIGGINS, J. DAVID; and TUTON, KAREN. "Subscale Intercorrelations of the Sex Inventory: Males and Females." *J Clin Psychol* 24:451–3 O '68. *
8. PISHKIN, VLADIMIR, and THORNE, FREDERICK C. "Analyses and Development of Ideological Survey Scales for Normal and Schizophrenic Subjects." *J Clin Psychol* 24:281–5 Jl '68. * (*PA* 42:16423)
9. PISHKIN, VLADIMIR, and THORNE, FREDERICK C. "A Factorial Study of Ideological Composition in Institutionalized Psychiatric Patients." *J Clin Psychol* 24:273–7 Jl '68. * (*PA* 42:17246)
10. PISHKIN, VLADIMIR, and THORNE, FREDERICK C. "Item Analysis of the Responses of Business Executives and Mental Hospital Patients on the Ideological Survey." *J Clin Psychol* 24:278–80 Jl '68. * (*PA* 42:16424)
11. THORNE, FREDERICK C., and PISHKIN, VLADIMIR. "A Factorial Study of Ideological Composition in Vocationally Successful Adults." *J Clin Psychol* 24:269–73 Jl '68. * (*PA* 42:17247)
12. THORNE, FREDERICK C., and PISHKIN, VLADIMIR. "The Ideological Survey." *J Clin Psychol* 24:264–8 Jl '68. * (*PA* 42:17248)

[126]

Interest Inventory for Elementary Grades: George Washington University Series. Grades 4–6; 1941; IIEG; 11 scores: reading, movies, radio, games and toys, hobbies, things to own, school subjects, people, occupations, activities, total; Form A (6 pages); mimeographed manual (3 pages); $1.50 per 25 tests; 25¢ per manual; 50¢ per specimen set; postage extra; (30–40) minutes; Mitchell Dreese and Elizabeth Mooney; Center for Psychological Service. *

For reviews by Harold D. Carter and Lee J. Cronbach, see 3:52 (1 reference).

REFERENCES

1. See 3:52.
2. TYLER, LEONA E. "The Development of 'Vocational Interests': 1, The Organization of Likes and Dislikes in Ten-Year-Old Children." *J Genetic Psychol* 86:33–44 Mr '55. * (*PA* 30:750)
3. TYLER, LEONA E. "A Comparison of the Interests of English and American School Children." *J Genetic Psychol* 88: 175–81 Je '56. * (*PA* 33:4615)
4. STEWART, LAWRENCE H. "'Occupational Level' Scale of Children's Interests." *Ed & Psychol Meas* 19:401–10 au '59. * (*PA* 34:6173)
5. STEWART, LAWRENCE H. "Relationship of Socioeconomic Status to Children's Occupational Attitudes and Interests." *J Genetic Psychol* 95:111–36 S '59. *

[127]

Interpersonal Check List. Adults; 1955–56; ICL; part of the *Interpersonal Diagnosis of Personality* (see 446); 1 form ['55, 3 pages]; battery manual ('56, 114 pages, see *2* below); $4 per 20 tests; $3 per scoring template; $7.50 per battery manual; (15–45) minutes depending on number of persons rated; Timothy Leary, Rolfe LaForge (test), Robert Suczek (test), and others (manual); Psychological Consultation Service. *

For a review by P. M. Bentler, see 6:127 (39 references); for related book reviews not excerpted in this volume, consult the 5th (B261) MMY.

REFERENCES

1–39. See 6:127.
40. EDWARDS, ALLEN L. "Social Desirability and the Description of Others." *J Abn & Social Psychol* 59:434–6 N '59. * (*PA* 34:5767)
41. LUCKEY, ELEANORE BRAUN. *An Investigation of the Concepts of the Self, Mate, Parents, and Ideal in Relation to Degree of Marital Satisfaction.* Doctor's thesis, University of Minnesota (Minneapolis, Minn.), 1959. (*DA* 20:396)
42. BOBGAN, MARTIN. *A Comparison of Variability in Identification and Self-Acceptance of Male Delinquents and Male Socially Acceptable School Students.* Doctor's thesis, University of Colorado (Boulder, Colo.), 1960. (*DA* 21:3355)
43. GOLDSTEIN, LAWRENCE. *Empathy and Its Relationship to Personality Factors and Personality Organization.* Doctor's thesis, New York University (New York, N.Y.), 1961. (*DA* 22:4402)
44. KING, ELSIE VIOLA. *Personality Characteristics—Ideal and Perceived in Relation to Mate Selection.* Doctor's thesis, University of Southern California (Los Angeles, Calif.), 1961. (*DA* 21:3882)
45. WHARTON, MARY CHARLOTTE. *Some Personality Characteristics of Frequent and Infrequent Visitors to a University Infirmary.* Doctor's thesis, University of Florida (Gainesville, Fla.), 1962. (*DA* 23:3483)
46. ALTROCCHI, JOHN, and PERLITSH, HILDA D. "Ego Control Patterns and Attribution of Hostility." *Psychol Rep* 12: 811–8 Je '63. * (*PA* 38:6009)
47. ARFFA, MARVIN SANFORD. *An Investigation of Some Criteria of Adjustive Behavior Among Chronic Female Psychiatric Patients in a State Mental Hospital.* Doctor's thesis, State University of New York at Buffalo (Buffalo, N.Y.), 1963. (*DA* 26:5544)
48. COOPER, BERNARD. *Parents of Schizophrenic Children Compared With the Parents of Non-Psychotic Emotionally Disturbed and Well Children: A Discriminant Function Analysis.* Doctor's thesis, Temple University (Philadelphia, Pa.), 1963. (*DA* 24:1694)
49. GALLIGAN, CAROL WOLFE. *Personality Correlates of Varying Degrees of Adherence to an Orthodox Structure.* Doctor's thesis, New York University (New York, N.Y.), 1963. (*DA* 24:3835)
50. JOSSE, JANE ZIEBOLD. *An Analysis of the Interpersonal Check List Responses of College Students.* Doctor's thesis, Southern Illinois University (Carbondale, Ill.), 1963. (*DA* 24:5195)
51. LAFORGE, ROLFE. *Research Use of the ICL.* ORI Technical Report, Vol. 3, No. 4. Eugene, Ore.: Oregon Research Institute, October 1963. Pp. iii, 49. * (Revision of *Supplementary Information on the Research Use of the Interpersonal Check List* by Rolfe LaForge and Robert F. Suczek.)
52. SEEGARS, JAMES E., JR., and McDONALD, ROBERT L. "The Role of Interaction Groups in Counselor Education." *J Counsel Psychol* 10:156–62 su '63. * (*PA* 38:10303)
53. SELLERS, DAVID JAY. *Effect of Threat on Self-Esteem, Esteem for Others and Anxiety in Well Adjusted and Poorly Adjusted Persons.* Doctor's thesis, Vanderbilt University (Nashville, Tenn.), 1963. (*DA* 24:5552)
54. TURNER, LYA NOEL. *The Certainty of Belief as a Variable of Personality.* Doctor's thesis, University of California (Berkeley, Calif.), 1963. (*DA* 24:5554)
55. ALLAN, THOMAS K. *The California Psychological Inventory and the Interpersonal Check List as Predictors of Success in Student Teaching.* Master's thesis, University of Maryland (College Park, Md.), 1964.
56. BARBER, THEODORE XENOPHON, and CALVERLEY, DAVID SMITH. "Hypnotizability, Suggestibility, and Personality: 4, A Study With the Leary Interpersonal Check List." *Brit J Social & Clin Psychol* 3:149–50 Je '64. * (*PA* 39:8140)
57. BOE, ERLING E., and KOGAN, WILLIAM S. "An Analysis of Various Methods for Deriving the Social Desirability Score." *Psychol Rep* 14:23–9 F '64. * (*PA* 39:1717)
58. GRAVATT, ARTHUR EUGENE. *Perception as a Factor in Mate Selection.* Doctor's thesis, Oregon State University (Corvallis, Ore.), 1964. (*DA* 25:684)
59. HATTEM, JACK VICTOR. *The Precipitating Role of Discordant Interpersonal Relationships in Suicidal Behavior.* Doctor's thesis, University of Houston (Houston, Tex.), 1964. (*DA* 25:1335)
60. HEISS, JEROLD S., and GORDON, MICHAEL. "Need Patterns and the Mutual Satisfaction of Dating and Engaged Couples." *J Marriage & Family* 26:337–8 Ag '64. * (*PA* 39: 4798)
61. KOGAN, KATE L., and JACKSON, JOAN K. "Perceptions of Self and Spouse: Some Contaminating Factors." *J Marriage & Family* 26:60–4 F '64. * (*PA* 38:8125)
62. KOGAN, WILLIAM S., and BOE, ERLING E. "Differential Responding to Items With High and Low Social Desirability Scale Values." *Psychol Rep* 15:586 O '64. * (*PA* 39: 5157)
63. LEE, ROBERT EDWARD. *An Investigation of Relationships Between Patient Self Perception and Hospital Ward Behavior.*

Doctor's thesis, University of Minnesota (Minneapolis, Minn.), 1964. (*DA* 25:2051)
64. LUCKEY, ELEANORE BRAUN. "Marital Satisfaction and Its Concomitant Perceptions of Self and Spouse." *J Counsel Psychol* 11:136–45 su '64. * (*PA* 39:5527)
65. LUCKEY, ELEANORE BRAUN. "Marital Satisfaction and Personality Correlates of Spouse." *J Marriage & Family* 26: 217–20 My '64. *
66. McDAVID, JOHN W., and SISTRUNK, FRANK. "Personality Correlates of Two Kinds of Conforming Behavior." *J Personality* 32:420–35 S '64. *
67. PARSONS, OSCAR A.; ALTROCCHI, JOHN; and SPRING, FAYE E. "Discrepancies in Interpersonal Perception, Adjustment and Therapeutic Skill." *Percept & Motor Skills* 18: 697–702 Je '64. * (*PA* 39:5239)
68. STANGER, WALTER. *An Investigation of the Relationship of Test-Taking Defensiveness to the Personality Dimension of Self-Responsibility.* Doctor's thesis, Temple University (Philadelphia, Pa.), 1964. (*DA* 25:1346)
69. BLANK, LEONARD. *Psychological Evaluation in Psychotherapy: Ten Case Histories.* Chicago, Ill.: Aldine Publishing Co., 1965. Pp. xii, 364. *
70. BOE, ERLING E.; GOCKA, EDWARD F.; and KOGAN, WILLIAM S. "The Effect of Group Psychotherapy on Interpersonal Perceptions of Psychiatric Patients." *Newsl Res Psychol* 7:32 N '65. *
71. BROOKS, MARJORY, and HILLMAN, CHRISTINE H. "Parent-Daughter Relationship as Factors in Nonmarriage Studied in Identical Twins." *J Marriage & Family* 27:383–5 Ag '65. * (*PA* 39:14605)
72. COOPER, G. DAVID; ADAMS, HENRY B.; and COHEN, LOUIS D. "Personality Changes After Sensory Deprivation." *J Nerv & Mental Dis* 140:103–18 F '65. * (*PA* 39:13642)
73. KOGAN, WILLIAM S.; BOE, ERLING E.; GOCKA, EDWARD F.; and JOHNSON, MERLIN H. "Personality Changes in Psychiatric Residents During Training." *Newsl Res Psychol* 7:33 N '65. *
74. LAWTON, M. POWELL. "Personality and Attitudinal Correlates of Psychiatric-Aid Performance." *J Social Psychol* 66:215–26 Ag '65. * (*PA* 39:15809)
75. McDONALD, ROBERT L. "Ego-Control Patterns and Attribution of Hostility to Self and Others." *J Personality & Social Psychol* 2:273–7 Ag '65. * (*PA* 39:15438)
76. McDONALD, ROBERT L., and GYNTHER, MALCOLM D. "Relations Between Self and Parental Perceptions of Unwed Mothers and Obstetric Complications." *Psychosom Med* 27:31–8 Ja–F '65. * (*PA* 39:12240)
77. McDONALD, ROBERT L., and GYNTHER, MALCOLM D. "Relationship of Self and Ideal-Self Descriptions With Sex, Race, and Class in Southern Adolescents." *J Personality & Social Psychol* 1:85–8 Ja '65. * (*PA* 39:7700)
78. RAWLINSON, MAY E. "Projection in Relation to Interpersonal Perception." *Nursing Res* 14:114–8 sp '65. *
79. TAYLOR, ALEXANDER BLAIR. *Role Perception, Empathy, and Marital Adjustment.* Doctor's thesis, University of Southern California (Los Angeles, Calif.), 1965. (*DA* 26:3527)
80. ADAMS, HENRY B.; ROBERTSON, MALCOLM H.; and COOPER, G. DAVID. "Sensory Deprivation and Personality Change." *J Nerv & Mental Dis* 143:256–65 S '66. * (*PA* 41: 6022)
81. ALLAN, THOMAS KENNETH. "Personality as a Predictor of Student Teaching Success." *SPATE* 5:12–6 f '66. *
82. KOGAN, WILLIAM S.; BOE, ERLING E.; GOCKA, EDWARD F.; and JOHNSON, MERLIN H. "Personality Changes in Psychiatric Residents During Training." *J Psychol* 62:229–40 Mr '66. * (*PA* 40:7812)
83. LUCKEY, ELEANORE BRAUN. "Number of Years Married as Related to Personality Perception and Marital Satisfaction." *J Marriage & Family* 28:44–8 F '66. * (*PA* 40:5824)
84. LUPTON, D. E. "A Preliminary Investigation of the Personality of Female Temporomandibular Joint Dysfunction Patients." *Psychother & Psychosom* 14(3):199–216 '66. * (*PA* 41:14004)
85. MEERS, MARJORIE. *The Emergence of Dependency as a Function of the Degree of Congruency Between Level I (Public Communication) and Level II (Self Concept) of the Leary Interpersonal Check List.* Master's thesis, University of Kansas (Lawrence, Kan.), 1966.
86. MURSTEIN, BERNARD I., and GLAUDIN, VINCENT. "The Relationship of Marital Adjustment to Personality: A Factor Analysis of the Inter-Personal Check List." *J Marriage & Family* 28:37–43 F '66. * (*PA* 40:5826)
87. PRESTON, CAROLINE E., and GUDIKSEN, KAREN S. "A Measure of Self-Perception Among Older People." *J Gerontol* 21:63–71 Ja '66. *
88. SAVAGE, CHARLES; FADIMAN, JAMES; MOGAR, ROBERT; and ALLEN, MARY HUGHES. "The Effects of Psychedelic (LSD) Therapy on Values, Personality, and Behavior." *Int J Neuropsychiatry* 2:241–54 My–Je '66. *
89. BOYD, HARRY S., and SISNEY, VERNON V. "Immediate Self-Image Confrontation and Changes in Self-Concept." *J Consult Psychol* 31:291–4 Je '67. * (*PA* 41:10493)
90. DIZNEY, HENRY F., and YAMAMOTO, KAORU. "Graduate Education Students' Preferences Among Professors." *Psychol Sch* 4:33–5 Ja '67. * (*PA* 41:5040)
91. GIBBY, ROBERT G., JR.; GIBBY, ROBERT G., SR.; and HOGAN, TERRENCE P. "Relationships Between Dominance Needs

and Decision-Making Ability." *J Clin Psychol* 23:450–2 O '67. * (*PA* 42:2546)

92. GRAFF, RICHARD LEE. *Identification as Related to Perceived Parental Attitudes and Powerlessness in Delinquents and Normals.* Doctor's thesis, Claremont Graduate School and University Center (Claremont, Calif.), 1967. (*DA* 29:369B)

93. GYNTHER, MALCOLM D., and BRILLIANT, PATRICIA J. "Marital Status, Readmission to Hospital, and Intrapersonal and Interpersonal Perceptions of Alcoholics." *Q J Studies Alcohol* 28:52–8 Mr '67. * (*PA* 41:9101)

94. McKEGNEY, F. PATRICK. "Psychological Correlates of Behaviour in Seriously Delinquent Juveniles." *Brit J Psychiatry* 113:781–92 Jl '67. * (*PA* 41:15508)

95. MEERS, MARJORIE, and NEURINGER, CHARLES. "A Validation of Self-Concept Measures of the Leary Interpersonal Checklist." *J General Psychol* 77:237–42 O '67. * (*PA* 42:134)

96. OLSSON, JAMES ERIC. *The Influence of the Personality of the Perceiver Upon Perception of Hostility in Other Persons.* Doctor's thesis, Catholic University of America (Washington, D.C.), 1967. (*DA* 28:2629B)

97. SANDS, PATRICK; ROTHAUS, PAUL; and OSBURN, HOBART G. "Application of the Interpersonal Problems Attitude Survey." *Newsl Res Psychol* 9:19–21 Ag '67. *

98. SIMON, WALTER B. "A Comparison Between Free and Forced Responding to Checklists: Assessment of the Social Desirability of Stereotypes." *J Clin Psychol* 23:475–9 O '67. * (*PA* 42:2473)

99. SMALLEY, NEAL STUART. *Implicit Personality Theory in Interpersonal Perception: A Study of Married Couples.* Doctor's thesis, Claremont Graduate School (Claremont, Calif.), 1967. (*DA* 29:762B)

100. SNYDER, JOHN ALLEN. *An Investigation of Certain Personality Needs and Relational Patterns in a Group of 70 Premaritally Pregnant Girls.* Doctor's thesis, University of Pennsylvania (Philadelphia, Pa.), 1967. (*DA* 28:3043A)

101. STRAHL, GLADYS TUXWORTH. *The Relationship of Centrality of Occupational Choice to Sex, Parental Identification, and Socioeconomic Level in University Undergraduate Students.* Doctor's thesis, Michigan State University (East Lansing, Mich.), 1967. (*DA* 28:4917A)

102. TAPLIN, JULIAN ROBERT. *Interpersonal Expectancies of Newly Hospitalized Psychiatric Patients.* Doctor's thesis, University of Oregon (Eugene, Ore.), 1967. (*DA* 28:2634B)

103. BELAIR, ROBERT RALPH. *Selected Developmental Correlates of Hypnotic Susceptibility.* Doctor's thesis, Washington State University (Pullman, Wash.), 1968. (*DA* 29:765B)

104. GOLDSTEIN, GERALD; NEURINGER, CHARLES; REIFF, CAROLYN; and SHELLY, CAROLYN H. "Generalizability of Field Dependency in Alcoholics." *J Consult & Clin Psychol* 32:560–4 O '68. * (*PA* 43:1094)

105. KOGAN, WILLIAM S.; BOE, EARLING E.; and GOCKA, EDWARD F. "Personality Changes in Unwed Mothers Following Parturition." *J Clin Psychol* 24:3–11 Ja '68. * (*PA* 42:8959)

106. McDONALD, ROBERT L. "Effects of Sex, Race, and Class on Self, Ideal-Self, and Parental Ratings in Southern Adolescents." *Percept & Motor Skills* 27:15–25 Ag '68. * (*PA* 43:2632)

107. McDONALD, ROBERT L. "Leary's Overt Interpersonal Behavior: A Validation Attempt." *J Social Psychol* 74:259–64 Ap '68. * (*PA* 42:10597)

108. SALAS, R. G., and JONES, P. R. "A Balanced Version of the Leary Interpersonal Check List." *Austral Mil Forces Res Rep* 2/68:1–9 F '68. * (*PA* 42:18106)

109. ZIMPFER, DAVID G. "Interpersonal Attitudes of Employment Service Supervisory Personnel." *Counselor Ed & Sup* 7:267–72 sp '68. *

See also references for 446.

NAME INDEX

[128]

★**Interpersonal Perception Method.** Married couples and other 2-person or 2-group situations; 1966; IPM; title used in publisher's catalog is *IPM Questionnaire;* 6 scores: interdependence and autonomy, warm concern and support, disparagement-disappointment, contentions, contradiction and confusion, extreme denial of autonomy; 5 booklets: he-she, she-he, he-he, she-she, we-they; manual (179 pages, see *1* below) ; score chart (2 pages, available in U.S. only) ; 52*s*. 6*d*. per 12 tests; 5*s*. per single copy; 35*s*. per manual; postage extra; ($10 per 20 tests; $2.50 per 10 charts; $4.75 per manual; postpaid; $6 per specimen set including manual, postage extra) ; (60–80) minutes; R. D. Laing, H. Phillipson, and A. R. Lee; distributed by National Foundation for Educational Research in England and Wales. * (United States distributor: Springer Publishing Co., Inc.)

REFERENCE

1. LAING, R. D.; PHILLIPSON, H.; and LEE, A. R. *Interpersonal Perception: A Theory and a Method of Research.* London: Tavistock Publications Ltd., 1966. Pp. 192. *

[129]

Inventory of Affective Tolerance. College and adults; 1942; IAT; 1 form (4 pages); manual (1 page) ; $2.50 per 25 tests; 35¢ per key; 25¢ per manual; 40¢ per specimen set (complete test not included) ; postage extra; (25) minutes; Robert I. Watson and V. E. Fisher; Sheridan Psychological Services, Inc. *

For reviews by Paul R. Farnsworth, E. Lowell Kelly, and William U. Snyder, see 3:54 (5 references).

REFERENCES

1–5. See 3:54.

6. HARDY, VIRGINIA T. "Relation of Dominance to Non-Directiveness in Counseling." *J Clin Psychol* 4:300–3 Jl '48. * (*PA* 23:179)

7. JONES, WORTH R. "Affective Tolerance and Typical Problems of Married and Unmarried College Students." *Personnel & Guid J* 37:126–8 O '58. * (*PA* 36:2KD26J)

[130]

An Inventory of Factors STDCR. Grades 9–16 and adults; 1934–45; STDCR; 5 scores: social introversion-extraversion, thinking introversion-extraversion, depression, cycloid disposition, rhathymia; 1 form ('40, 4 pages); revised manual ['45, 2 pages]; $4 per 25 tests; $1.75 per scoring key; separate answer sheets (IBM 805) may be used; 5¢ per answer sheet; $2.50 per set of either hand or machine scoring stencils; 25¢ per manual; 40¢ per specimen set (complete test not included); postage extra; (30) minutes; J. P. Guilford; Sheridan Psychological Services, Inc. *

See 6:128 (17 references) and 5:78 (28 references); for a review by Hubert E. Brogden, see 4:59 (17 references); for a review by H. J. Eysenck, see 3:55 (10 references); for a review by R. A. Brotemarkle, see 3:45.

REFERENCES

1–10. See 3:55.
11–27. See 4:59.
28–55. See 5:78.
56–72. See 6:128.
73. SHAMES, GEORGE. "An Investigation of Prognosis and Evaluation in Speech Therapy." *J Speech & Hearing Disorders* 17:386–92 D '52. * (*PA* 27:6652)
74. ABELES, NORMAN. *A Study of the Characteristics of Counselor Trainees.* Doctor's thesis, University of Texas (Austin, Tex.), 1958. (*DA* 18:2204)
75. JONES, J. B. "Some Personal-Social Factors Contributing to Academic Failure at Texas Southern University," pp. 135–6. (*PA* 37:5606) In *Personality Factors on the College Campus: Review of a Symposium.* Edited by Robert L. Sutherland and others. Austin, Tex.: Hogg Foundation for Mental Health, 1962. Pp. xxii, 242. * (*PA* 37:5621)
76. HODGSON, RICHARD W. "Personality Appraisal of Technical and Professional Applicants." *Personnel Psychol* 17:167–87 su '64. * (*PA* 39:6067)
77. BROWN, D. G., and YOUNG, A. J. "The Effect of Extraversion on Susceptibility to Disease: A Validatory Study on Contact Dermatitis." *J Psychosom Res* 8:421–9 Mr '65. *
78. DERMEN, DIRAN, and LONDON, PERRY. "Correlates of Hypnotic Susceptibility." *J Consult Psychol* 29:537–45 D '65. * (*PA* 40:2261)
79. SOUEIF, M. I. "Response Sets, Neuroticism and Extraversion: A Factorial Study." *Acta Psychologica* 24:29–40 My '65. * (*PA* 39:15272)
80. GIBBONS, BILLIE DWANE. *A Study of the Relationships Between Factors Found in Cattell's Sixteen Personality Factor Questionnaire and Factors Found in the Guilford Personality Inventories.* Doctor's thesis, University of Southern California (Los Angeles, Calif.), 1966. (*DA* 26:7438)
81. WINKLER, RONALD C., and MATHEWS, THEODORE W. "How Employees Feel About Personality Tests." *Personnel J* 46:490–2 Jl–Ag '67. *
82. CATTELL, RAYMOND B., and GIBBONS, B. D. "Personality Factor Structure of the Combined Guilford and Cattell Personality Questionnaires." *J Personality & Social Psychol* 9:107–20 My '68. * (*PA* 42:10588)

NAME INDEX

Abeles, N.: 74
Baehr, M. E.: 21, 32
Beach, L. R.: 66
Bessent, E. W.: 70
Bliss, J.: 59
Booth, M. D.: 57
Borg, W. R.: 24, 33, 47, 67
Brogden, H. E.: *rev,* 4:59
Brotemarkle, R. A.: *rev,* 3:45
Brown, D. G.: 77
Brueckel, J. E.: 28
Caron A. J.: 62
Carrigan, P. M.: 68
Carroll, J. B.: 34
Cattell, R. B.: 80, 82
Cerf, A. Z.: 11
Clark, E. J.: 14, 22
Cockrum, L. V.: 35
Coe, R. S.: 55
Cooper, M. N.: 48
Dermen, D.: 78
Dotson, E. J.: 56
Dunn, S.: 59
Erwin, E. F.: 15
Eysenck, H. J.: 9; *rev,* 3:55
Fisher, S.: 16
Fiske, D. W.: 17, 25
Franks, C. M.: 69
Gibbons, B. D.: 80, 82
Goche, L. N.: 45
Goldberg, H. D.: 44
Goldberg, L. R.: 64
Green, R. F.: 12, 23
Guilford, J. P.: 1–2, 4, 36, 46, 51–2, 63
Guilford, J. S.: 30, 37
Guilford, R. B.: 1–2
Hannum, T. E.: 72
Healy, I.: 24
Hodgson, R. W.: 76
Hollander, E. P.: 43, 49
Huffman, A. V.: 8
Izard, C. E.: 43, 49
Jenkin, N.: 60
Jones, J. B.: 75
Kelly, E. L.: 17, 25, 64
Kelty, E. J.: 65
Kornreich, M.: 42
Krasner, L.: 18
Kreitman, N.: 71
London, P.: 78
Loth, N.: 6
Lovell, C.: 7
Luborsky, L. B.: 10
McKenna, F. S.: 38
Manzano, I. B.: 31
Martin, H.: 4
Mathews, T. W.: 81
Maxwell, A. E.: 69
Neilen, G. C.: 39
Nelson, M. O.: 53
Neumann, T. M.: 29
North, R. D.: 13, 19
Panek, R. E.: 72
Pemberton, C. L.: 26
Richardson, L. H.: 5
Rosenberg, N.: 43, 49
Shames, G.: 73
Shames, G. H.: 40
Shea, S.: 53
Siipola, E.: 59
Sonohara, T.: 58
Soueif, M. I.: 79
Souieff, M. I.: 69
Spilka, B.: 54
Spivey, G. M.: 20
Stacey, C. L.: 44
Steinberg, D. L.: 3
Struening, E. L.: 54
Thomas, E. R.: 61
Thurston, D. R.: 50
Thurstone, L. L.: 27
Tomedy, F. J.: 41
Tsujioka, B.: 58
Wallach, M. A.: 62
Winkler, R. C.: 81
Wittman, M. P.: 3, 8
Yatabe, T.: 58
Young, A. J.: 77
Zimmerman, W. S.: 51–2

[131]

It Scale for Children. Ages 5–6; 1956; ITSC; for research use only; sex role preference; 1 form (37 cards); manual (20 pages, see 2 below); $15 per set of cards and manual, cash orders postpaid; (7–8) minutes; Daniel G. Brown; Psychological Test Specialists. *

For reviews by Philip L. Harriman and Boyd R. McCandless, see 6:129 (18 references).

REFERENCES

1–18. See 6:129.
19. HALL, MARJORIE, and KEITH, ROBERT A. "Sex-Role Preference Among Children of Upper and Lower Social Class." *J Social Psychol* 62:101–10 F '64. * (*PA* 39:1485)
20. SPENCER, T. D. "Sex-Role Learning in Early Childhood." *J Nursery Ed* 19:181–7 Ap '64. *
21. THOMAS, PAULA JEAN. *Sub-Cultural Differences in Sex Role Preference Patterns.* Doctor's thesis, Western Reserve University (Cleveland, Ohio), 1965. (*DA* 26:6894)
22. DURYEA, WALTER R. "Sex-Role Preference in Children: Individual and Group Administration of the It Scale for Children." *Psychol Rep* 21:269–74 Ag '67. * (*PA* 42:2605)
23. ENDSLEY, RICHARD C. "Effects of Concealing 'It' on Sex Role Preferences of Preschool Children." Abstract. *Percept & Motor Skills* 24:998 Je '67. * (*PA* 41:13615, title only)
24. REED, MAX R., and ASBJORNSEN, WILLOTTA. "Experimental Alteration of the It Scale in the Study of Sex-Role Preference." *Percept & Motor Skills* 26:15–24 F '68. * (*PA* 42:10600)
25. SCHELL, ROBERT E., and SILBER, JEAN WAGGONER. "Sex-Role Discrimination Among Young Children." *Percept & Motor Skills* 27:379–89 O '68. * (*PA* 43:5164)

NAME INDEX

Asbjornsen, W.: 24
Borstelmann, L. J.: 10
Brown, C. R.: 18
Brown, D. G.: 1–5, 11
Clark, E. T.: 13–4
Distler, L.: 7
Duryea, W. R.: 22
Endsley, R. C.: 23
Epstein, R.: 15
Hall, M.: 19
Harriman, P. L.: *rev,* 6:129
Hartup, W. W.: 9, 12, 16
Keith, R. A.: 19
Kobasigawa, A.: 6
Liverant, S.: 15
McCandless, B. R.: *rev,* 6: 129
Moore, S. G.: 16
Mussen, P.: 7, 17
Nickerson, R. S.: 18
Reed, M. R.: 24
Richardson, D. H.: 8
Rutherford, E.: 17
Sager, G.: 16
Schell, R. E.: 25
Silber, J. W.: 25
Spencer, T. D.: 20
Thomas, P. J.: 21
Zook, E. A.: 9

[132]

★**JIM Scale (Form F).** Grades 7–12; 1965–66; JIM; motivation toward school; 1 form ('65, 3 pages); mimeographed directions ['65, 1 page]; statistical data ('66, 2 pages); no data on validity; norms consist of means and standard deviations; $3.75 per 100 tests, postpaid; specimen set free; (30) minutes; Jack R. Frymier; Publications Sales and Distribution, Ohio State University. *

[133]

★**The Jesness Inventory.** Disturbed children and adolescents ages 8–18; 1966, c1962–66; 11 scores: social maladjustment, value orientation, immaturity, autism, alienation, manifest aggression, withdrawal, social anxiety, repression, denial, asocialization index; 1 form ('62, 4 pages); manual ('66, 32 pages); profile ('62, 2 pages); separate answer sheets must be used; $4 per 25 tests; $4 per 50 sets of answer sheet and profile; $1.75 per set of scoring stencils; $2 per manual; $2 per specimen set; postage extra;

scoring service, $1 per test; (20–30) minutes; Carl F. Jesness; Consulting Psychologists Press. *

REFERENCES

1. JESNESS, CARL F. *Redevelopment and Revalidation of the Jesness Inventory.* Research Report No. 35. Sacramento, Calif.: California Youth Authority, 1963. Pp. 90. *
2. DAVIES, MARTIN. *The Use of the Jesness Inventory on a Sample of British Probationers.* Home Office Studies in the Causes of Delinquency and the Treatment of Offenders 12. London: Her Majesty's Stationery Office, 1967. Pp. iv, 20. *
3. FISHER, ROBERT M. "Acquiescent Response Set, the Jesness Inventory, and Implications for the Use of 'Foreign' Psychological Tests." *Brit J Social & Clin Psychol* 6:1–10 F '67. * (*PA* 41:7531)

[134]

Jones Personality Rating Scale. Grades 9–12 and adults; 1939; 8 ratings: dependability, cultural refinement, leadership, industriousness, mental alertness, thoroughness, personal appearance, ability to get along with others; rating scale (2 pages); no data on reliability; no norms; $1.25 per 25 scales; 5¢ per single copy; postage extra; Harold J. Jones; Jones Teaching Aids. *

[135]

★**Junior Eysenck Personality Inventory.** Ages 7–16; 1963–65; JEPI; downward extension of *Eysenck Personality Inventory;* 3 scores: extraversion, neuroticism, lie; 2 editions: American and British (identical except for 2 words and directions); postage extra; [15–20] minutes; Sybil B. G. Eysenck. *
a) AMERICAN EDITION. 1963–65; 1 form ('65, 3 pages); preliminary manual ('63, 11 pages); no norms; $4 per 25 tests; $1.50 per set of scoring stencils; $1.75 per specimen set; scoring service, 45¢ or less per test; Spanish edition available; Educational and Industrial Testing Service.
b) BRITISH EDITION. 1965; 1 form ('65, 4 pages); manual ['65, 16 pages]; 6s. 6d. per 20 tests; 3s. per key; 3s. per manual; 6s. 6d. per specimen set; University of London Press Ltd.

REFERENCES

1. EYSENCK, SYBIL B. G. "A New Scale for Personality Measurements in Children." *Brit J Ed Psychol* 35:362–7 N '65. * (*PA* 40:2939)
2. RIM, Y. "Extraversion, Neuroticism and the Effect of Praise or Blame." *Brit J Ed Psychol* 35:381–4 N '65. *
3. EYSENCK, SYBIL B. G.; SYED, I. A.; and EYSENCK, H. J. "Desirability Response Set in Children." *Brit J Ed Psychol* 36:87–90 F '66. * (*PA* 40:6648)
4. ENTWISTLE, N. J., and CUNNINGHAM, SHIRLEY. "Neuroticism and School Attainment—A Linear Relationship?" *Brit J Ed Psychol* 38:123–32 Je '68. * (*PA* 42:17783)
5. EYSENCK, S. B. G., and PICKUP, A. J. "Teacher Ratings of Extraversion and Neuroticism and Children's Inventory Responses." *Brit J Ed Psychol* 38:94–6 F '68. * (*PA* 42:11956)
6. FROST, BARRY P. "Anxiety and Educational Achievement." *Brit J Ed Psychol* 38:293–301 N '68. * (*PA* 43:7368)
7. SHAMBERG, NEIL STEPHEN. *An Experimental Investigation of Eysenck's Theory With Respect to Four Adolescent Groups.* Doctor's thesis, Case Western Reserve University (Cleveland, Ohio), 1968. (*DA* 29:760B)

[136]

*****Jr.–Sr. High School Personality Questionnaire.** Ages 12–18; 1953–69; HSPQ; test booklet title is Jr.–Sr. H.S.P.Q.; 14 scores: reserved vs. warmhearted (A), dull vs. bright (B), affected by feelings vs. emotionally stable (C), undemonstrative vs. excitable (D), obedient vs. assertive (E), sober vs. enthusiastic (F), disregards rules vs. conscientious (G), shy vs. adventurous (H), tough-minded vs. tenderminded (I), zestful vs. circumspect individualism (J), self-assured vs. apprehensive (O), sociably group-dependent vs. self-sufficient (Q₂), uncontrolled vs. controlled (Q₃), relaxed vs. tense (Q₄); 2 editions; for computerized interpreting services, see 136A; (40–50) minutes per form.

a) [IPAT EDITIONS.] 1953–69; 2 editions; handbook ('69, 90 pages); separate answer sheets (hand scored, Digitek) must be used; $4 per 25 tests; $2.50 per 50 hand scored answer sheets; $3 per 50 hand scored answer-profile sheets; $3.75 per 50 Digitek answer sheets; $2 per 50 profiles; $1.90 per scoring stencil; 50¢ per manual; $4.50 per handbook; $3.20 per specimen set (without handbook); postage extra; Institute for Personality and Ability Testing. *
  1) *1963 Edition.* 1963–68; Forms A, B, second edition ('63, 8 pages, authors recommend administration of both forms); manual ['65, c1958–63, 15 pages]; norms supplement ('68, 16 pages); profile ('63, 1 page); tape recording is available for oral administration; 50¢ per norms supplement; $25 per tape; Raymond B. Cattell.
  2) *1968 Edition.* 1968–69; Forms A, B, C, D, ('68, 8 pages, authors recommend administration of 2 or more forms); manual ('68, 16 pages); profile ('68, 1 page); no norms; Raymond B. Cattell and Mary D. L. Cattell.
b) [BOBBS-MERRILL EDITION.] 1958–60; Forms A, B, ('60, 8 pages, identical with out of print 1958 IPAT edition except for format, title, and directions); manual ('60, c1958–60, 24 pages); norms supplement ('60, c1958–60, 4 pages, identical with IPAT edition except for format and title); profile ('60, 1 page); separate answer sheets must be used; $4.95 per 35 tests; $1.50 per 35 answer sheets; 40¢ per scoring stencil; $1.50 per 35 profiles; 75¢ per manual and norms supplement; $1 per specimen set (includes norms supplement but not manual); Raymond B. Cattell, Richard W. Coan, and Halla Beloff; Bobbs-Merrill Co., Inc. *

For reviews by C. J. Adcock and Philip E. Vernon, see 6:131 (17 references); see also 5:72 (4 references).

REFERENCES

1–4. See 5:72.
5–21. See 6:131.
22. SCHAIE, K. WARNER. "On the Equivalence of Questionnaire and Rating Data." *Psychol Rep* 10:521–2 Ap '62. * (*PA* 37:3160)
23. ABDEL-GHAFFAR, ABDEL-SALAM ABDEL-KADER. *Relationships Between Selected Creativity Factors and Certain Non-Intellectual Factors Among High School Students.* Doctor's thesis, University of Denver (Denver, Colo.), 1963. (*DA* 25:1728)
24. ASHE, MARGARET RUTH BERRY. *A Study of Change Measured Personality Adjustment and Release of Creativity Through Freedom of Expression in Writing.* Doctor's thesis, University of Texas (Austin, Tex.), 1964. (*DA* 26:860)
25. CATTELL, R. B.; BOUTOURLINE, N. YOUNG; and HUNDLEBY, J. D. "Blood Groups and Personality Traits." *Am J Hum Genetics* 16:397–402 D '64. * (*PA* 39:8006)
26. KARAS, SHAWKY FALTAOUS. *A Study of Personality and Socioeconomic Factors and Mathematics Achievement.* Doctor's thesis, Columbia University (New York, N.Y.), 1964. (*DA* 28:5191B)
27. MACDORMAN, CARROLL F.; RIVOIRE, JEANNE L.; GALLAGHER, PETER J.; and MACDORMAN, CLAUDIA F. "Size Constancy of Adolescent Schizophrenics." *J Abn & Social Psychol* 69:258–63 S '64. * (*PA* 39:5756)
28. PORTER, RUTHERFORD B. "A Comparative Investigation of the Personality of Sixth-Grade Gifted Children and a Norm Group of Children." *J Ed Res* 58:132–4 N '64. *
29. CATTELL, RAYMOND B. "A Cross-Cultural Check on Second Stratum Personality Factor Structure—Notably of Anxiety and Exvia." *Austral J Psychol* 17:12–23 Ap '65. * (*PA* 39:15456)
30. CLARK, CHARLES M.; VELDMAN, DONALD J.; and THORPE, JOSEPH S. "Convergent and Divergent Thinking Abilities of Talented Adolescents." *J Ed Psychol* 56:157–63 Je '65. * (*PA* 39:12317)
31. FORDEN, H. G. "A Study of the Use of the High School Personality Questionnaire as a Predictor of Grade 9 Academic Success in the Four-Year and Five-Year Courses at Kitchener-Waterloo Collegiate and Vocational School." *Ont J Ed Res* 8:195–206 w '65–66. * (*PA* 40:8852)
32. GOODWIN, WILLIAM L.; JOYCE, JULIANNE; ABRAMS, ALAN; BIAGGIO, ANGELA B.; and BIAGGIO, LUIS I. "Note: Relationships Between Matching Scales of the Cattell 16 Personality Factor Questionnaire and the High School Personality Questionnaire." *J Ed Meas* 2:220 D '65. *
33. KARSON, SAMUEL. "Primary Factor Correlates of Boys

With Personality and Conduct Problems." *J Clin Psychol* 21: 16–8 Ja '65. * (*PA* 39:12765)

34. HOOKE, JAMES FREDERICK. *Correlates of Adolescent Delinquent Behavior: A Multivariate Approach.* Doctor's thesis, University of Nebraska (Lincoln, Neb.), 1966. (*DA* 27:2136B)

35. NELSON, GENE W. *Predicting Seventh Grade School Achievement Using HSPQ Personality Dimensions, IQ, and Teacher Grades.* Master's thesis, St. Cloud State College (St. Cloud, Minn.), 1966.

36. PIERSON, GEORGE R.; CATTELL, RAYMOND B.; and PIERCE, JOHN. "A Demonstration by the HSPQ of the Nature of the Personality Changes Produced by Institutionalization of Delinquents." *J Social Psychol* 70:229–39 D '66. * (*PA* 41:2902)

37. ROACH, ARTHUR JAMES, JR. *Some Characteristics Differentiating Adolescent Religious Candidates Perceived as Superior From Those Perceived as Inferior: A Cross-Sectional, Exploratory Investigation Into Various Psychosocial Characteristics of Christian Brothers Candidates.* Doctor's thesis, University of Notre Dame (Notre Dame, Ind.), 1966. (*DA* 27:3732A)

38. SEALY, A. P., and CATTELL, R. B. "Adolescent Personality Trends in Primary Factors Measured on the 16 PF and the HSPQ Questionnaires Through Ages 11 to 23." *Brit J Social & Clin Psychol* 5:172–84 S '66. * (*PA* 40:13205)

39. CARDON, BARTELL W., and ZURICK, GEORGE T. "Personality Characteristics of High School Dropouts of High Ability." *Psychol Sch* 4:351–6 O '67. * (*PA* 42:2939)

40. HITTSON, ROBERT JOSEPH. *A Comparison of Certain Personality Characteristics of Selected Secondary Students in Special English Classes Who Score High on a Standardized Achievement Test With Those Who Score Low.* Doctor's thesis, North Texas State University (Denton, Tex.), 1967. (*DA* 28:3507A)

41. HUMPHREYS, LLOYD G. "Critique of Cattell's 'Theory of Fluid and Crystallized Intelligence: A Critical Experiment.'" *J Ed Psychol* 58:129–36 Je '67. * (*PA* 41:10447)

42. KURTZMAN, KENNETH A. "A Study of School Attitudes, Peer Acceptance, and Personality of Creative Adolescents." *Excep Children* 34:157–62 N '67. * (*PA* 42:8948)

43. PIERSON, GEORGE R.; MOSELEY, JOHN; and OLSEN, MARK. "The Personality and Character Structure of the Delinquent: Some Social Psychological Implications." *J Genetic Psychol* 110:139–47 Mr '67. * (*PA* 41:7536)

44. REGAN, GEORGE. "Personality Characteristics and Attitude to School." *Brit J Ed Psychol* 37:127–9 F '67. *

45. RIDDING, L. W. "An Investigation of Personality Measures Associated With Over and Under Achievement in English and Arithmetic." *Brit J Ed Psychol* 37:397–8 N '67. * (*PA* 42:6153) Abstract of master's thesis, University of Manchester (Manchester, England), 1966.

46. SLAVINSKA-NYLES, NONNA. *Time Sense in Relation to Personality Among Delinquent Adolescents.* Doctor's thesis, New York University (New York, N.Y.), 1967. (*DA* 28: 4495A)

47. FRENCH, JOSEPH L., and CARDON, BARTELL W. "Characteristics of High Mental Ability School Dropouts." *Voc Guid Q* 16:162–8 Mr '68. *

48. HUNDLEY, JOHN D. "The Trait of Anxiety, as Defined by Objective Performance Measures, and Indices of Emotional Disturbance in Middle Childhood," pp. 7–14. In *Progress in Clinical Psychology Through Multivariate Experimental Designs.* Edited by Raymond B. Cattell. Fort Worth, Tex.: Society of Multivariate Experimental Psychology, Inc., 1968. Pp. 168. *

49. LEE, KEY TON. *A Study of the Nature and Correlates of Pupil Adjustment in Seventh-Day Adventist Secondary Schools.* Doctor's thesis, University of Oklahoma (Norman, Okla.), 1968. (*DA* 29:2569A)

50. RENTZ, R. ROBERT; FEARS, EMORY B.; and WHITE, WILLIAM F. "Personality Correlates of Group Structure: A Canonical Correlation Analysis." *J Psychol* 70:163–7 N '68. * (*PA* 43:4036)

51. SATIR, KENNETH R., and CARDON, BARTELL W. "Personality Factors as Predictors of High Ability Dropouts." *J Sch Psychol* 7(1):22–5 '68. *

NAME INDEX

[136A]

★[Re Jr.–Sr. High School Personality Questionnaire.] The HSPQ Analytic Report. [1969]; computer interpretation of raw primary scores; a subject's sten or raw scores must be sent in to obtain a 2 page print-out presenting: a profile of the 14 scores plus narrative statements of "primary personality characteristics of special interest," "evaluation of second-stratum traits and criteria of general importance," and projections about the "individual's promise in the areas of academic achievement, leadership, creativity, and vocational success"; $3 or less per print-out plus $15 handling charge for less than 50 print-outs; reports are "normally" mailed within 1 week after receipt of sten or raw scores; postage extra; Institute for Personality and Ability Testing. *

[137]

KD Proneness Scale and Check List. Grades 7–12, ages 7 and over; 1950–56; revised manual ('53, 8 pages); supplement ('56, reprint of 6 below); $12 per examiner's kit of 25 scales, 25 check lists, scoring stencils, manual, and supplement; $1.50 per set of scoring stencils; $2.50 per manual and supplement; postpaid; William C. Kvaraceus; Western Psychological Services. *

a) KD PRONENESS SCALE. Grades 7–12; KDPS; also called *Delinquency Proneness Scale*; 1 form ('50, 6 pages); $6.50 per 25 scales; (15–25) minutes.

b) KD PRONENESS CHECK LIST, REVISED. Ages 7 and over; KDPCL; ratings by teachers; 1 form ('53, 2 pages); no data on reliability; norms for grades 5–8 only; $3.50 per 25 check lists; [6–25] minutes.

For a review by John W. M. Rothney, see 5:79 (6 references); for reviews by Douglas Courtney and Dale B. Harris, see 4:64.

REFERENCES

1–6. See 5:79.

7. DONAHUE, MARY C. *Further Validation of the K-D Proneness Scale.* Master's thesis, Boston University (Boston, Mass.), 1949.

8. EICHORN, JOHN R. *The Construction and Evaluation of a Non-Verbal Delinquency Proneness Scale.* Doctor's thesis, Boston University (Boston, Mass.), 1952.

9. WALTON, ARLINE J. *A Further Study of the Validity of the K-D Proneness Scale.* Master's thesis, Boston University (Boston, Mass.), 1953.

10. KVARACEUS, WILLIAM C. "A Partial Validation of the KD Proneness Check List via Case Records of Institutionalized Delinquents." *Forum Ed* 14:28–30 Jl '55. *

11. McGRATH, RICHARD L. *A Further Study of the KD Proneness Scale: Non-Verbal Form.* Master's thesis, Boston University (Boston, Mass.), 1957.

12. BALOGH, JOSEPH K. "A Study of Predictive Factors Involved in Delinquent Phenomena." *J Crim Law & Criminol* 48:615–8 Mr–Ap '58. * (*PA* 33:8726)

13. GARRISON, KARL C. "A Study of Student Disciplinarian Practices in Two Georgia High Schools." *J Ed Res* 53:153–6 D '59. * (*PA* 35:1180)

14. CLEMENTS, SAM D. *The Predictive Utility of Three Delinquency Proneness Measures.* Doctor's thesis, University of Houston (Houston, Tex.), 1960. (*DA* 20:3827)

15. WEATHERBY, JOHN H. *The Validation of the KD Proneness Scale (Non-Verbal): Trends in Prediction Study.* Master's thesis, Boston University (Boston, Mass.), 1960.

16. BALOGH, JOSEPH K., and FINN, PATRICIA. "A Methodological Study of Juvenile Delinquency Proneness Among Negroes." *Excep Child* 27:397–9 Mr '61. * (*PA* 36:4JO97B)

17. BORDUA, DAVID J. *Prediction and Selection of Delinquents.* Washington, D.C.: Children's Bureau, Social Security Administration, United States Department of Health, Education, and Welfare, 1961. Pp. ii, 29. *

18. KVARACEUS, WILLIAM C. "Forecasting Delinquency: A Three-Year Experiment." *Excep Child* 27:429–35 Ap '61. * (*PA* 36:4J029K)

19. PETERSON, DONALD R.; QUAY, HERBERT C.; and TIFFANY, THEODORE L. "Personality Factors Related to Juvenile Delinquency." *Child Develop* 32:355–72 Je '61. * (*PA* 36:3J055P)

20. BARNEY, ORVIN PAT. *The Use of the KD Proneness Scale and KD Proneness Check List in Identifying Pre-Delinquent Behavior in Selected Children in Grade Five.* Doctor's thesis, University of Oregon (Eugene, Ore.), 1962. (*DA* 23:526)

21. WING, JACK L. *A Study of the Differences Between Types of Students as Measured by the KD Proneness Scale.* Master's thesis, Arizona State College (Flagstaff, Ariz.), 1962.

22. BECHTOLD, MARY LEE. "Validation of K.D. Scale and Check List as Predictors of Delinquent Proneness." *J Exp Ed* 32:413–6 su '64. * (*PA* 39:5700)

23. COMA, ANTHONY S. *The Characteristics of Male Disciplinary Offenders and the Male Disciplinary Problem at a Large Urban High School.* Doctor's thesis, Temple University (Philadelphia, Pa.), 1964. (*DA* 25:986)

24. KILBURN, KENT LEE. *Further Validation and Refinement of the K.D. Proneness Scale (Verbal).* Doctor's thesis, Utah State University (Logan, Utah), 1964. (*DA* 26:200)

25. BOTHMAN, RICHARD W.; HARTINGER, WALTER; and RICHARDSON, HAROLD. "A Comparison of Two Delinquency Predicting Instruments." *J Res Crime & Del* 2:45–8 Ja '65. *

26. CHILES, DONNA R. "An Identification of the Characteristics of the Pre-Delinquent." *Ill Sch Res* 2:38–43 O '65. *

27. HARRIS, HAROLD R. *A Study to Determine If Pre-Delinquent Behavior Can Be Identified in a Group of Fifth Grade Students by Using the KD Proneness Scale and the KD Proneness Check List.* Master's thesis, Brigham Young University (Provo, Utah), 1965.

28. YINGST, CLARENCE E. *An Analysis of Delinquency-Proneness in Selected Groups of Elementary Students Using the KD Proneness Scale.* Master's thesis, Millersville State College (Millersville, Pa.), 1965.

NAME INDEX

[138]

★**Katz Adjustment Scales.** Normal and mentally disordered adults; 1961–64; KAS; adjustment and social behavior in the community; for research use only; separate booklets are used to obtain ratings by a close relative (Form R) and self-ratings by the patient (Form S); booklet titles are *KAS Behavior Inventories;* manual ('63, 33 pages, reprint of *2* below, coauthored with Samuel B. Lyerly); mimeographed instructions for administration ('61, 6 pages); dittoed supplemental instructions ('64, 6 pages, coauthored with M. Kathleen Herron, William W. Michaux, and Henri A. Lowery); mimeographed scoring instructions (no date, 1 page) for Forms R2–R5 and S1–S5; no data on reliability; no norms; [15–30] minutes; test materials supplied free and in some instances computer scoring to qualified researchers; Martin M. Katz; the Author. *

a) SCALES DESIGNED FOR RELATIVES RATINGS (R SCALES). Booklet ['63, 14 pages] includes the 5 scales listed below; 18 scores: 13 factor scores for Form R1, 1 score for each of Forms R2–R5 and 1 score (level of dissatisfaction with performance) based on differences between corresponding items on Forms R2 and R3.

1) *Form R1, Relative's Ratings of Patient's Symptoms and Social Behavior.* Primarily for use prior to hospitalization or following discharge; 13 factor scores: belligerence, verbal expansiveness, negativism, helplessness, suspiciousness, anxiety, with-drawal and retardation, general psychopathology, nervousness, confusion, bizarreness, hyperactivity, emotional stability; mimeographed scoring sheet (no date, 1 page).

2) *Form R2, Level of Performance of Socially Expected Activities.*

3) *Form R3, Level of Expectations for Performance of Social Activities.* Items are identical to those in Form R2.

4) *Form RS4, Level of Free Time Activities.* Adaptation of *Your Activities and Attitudes* (see 4:100).

5) *Form R5, Level of Satisfaction With Free Time Activities.* Items are identical to those in Form RS4.

b) SCALES DESIGNED FOR PATIENT'S SELF-RATINGS (S SCALES). Booklet ['63, 8 pages] includes the 5 scales listed below; 6 scores: 1 score for each of Forms S1, S2, S3, RS4, S5 and 1 score (level of dissatisfaction with performance) based on differences between corresponding items on Forms S2 and S3.

1) *Form S1, Symptom Discomfort.* Adaptation of *Johns Hopkins Symptom Distress Scale* (not published as a separate).

2) *Forms S2, S3, RS4, and S5.* Identical to the corresponding R scales except that they are adapted for self-rating.

REFERENCES

1. KATZ, MARTIN M., and COLE, JONATHAN O. "A Phenomenological Approach to the Classification of Schizophrenic Disorders." *Dis Nerv System* 24:147–54 Mr '63. *

2. KATZ, MARTIN M., and LYERLY, SAMUEL B. "Methods for Measuring Adjustment and Social Behavior in the Community: 1, Rationale, Description, Discriminative Validity and Scale Development." *Psychol Rep* 13:503–35 O '63. * (*PA* 38:8391)

3. KATZ, MARTIN M. Chap. 5, "A Typological Approach to the Problem of Predicting Response to Treatment," pp. 85–101. In *Prediction of Response to Pharmacotherapy.* Edited by J. R. Wittenborn and Philip R. A. May. Springfield, Ill.: Charles C Thomas, Publisher, 1966. Pp. xii, 231. *

4. KATZ, MARTIN M.; LOWERY, HENRI A.; and COLE, JONATHAN O. Chap. 10, "Behavior Patterns of Schizophrenics in the Community," pp. 209–30. In *Exploration in Typing Psychotics.* Edited by Maurice Lorr. London: Pergamon Press Ltd., 1966. Pp. viii, 241. *

5. LEFKOWITZ, MONROE M., and CANNON, JOHN. "Physique and Obstreperous Behavior." *J Clin Psychol* 22:172–4 Ap '66. * (*PA* 40:7886)

6. LYERLY, SAMUEL B., and ABBOTT, PRESTON S. "The Katz Adjustment Scales," pp. 53–7. In their *Handbook of Psychiatric Rating Scales (1950–1964).* Public Health Service Publication No. 1495. Washington, D.C.: United States Government Printing Office, 1966. Pp. v, 69. *

7. HOGARTY, GERARD E.; KATZ, MARTIN M.; and LOWERY, HENRI A. "Identifying Candidates From a Normal Population for a Community Health Program." *Psychiatric Res Rep Am Psychiatric Assn* 22:220–34 Ap '67. *

8. MICHAUX, WILLIAM W.; GANSEREIT, KATHLEEN H.; McCABE, OLIVER L.; and KURLAND, ALBERT A. "The Psychopathology and Measurement of Environmental Stress." *Commun Mental Health J* 3:358–72 w '67. * (*PA* 42:7553)

9. SCHOOLER, NINA R.; GOLDBERG, SOLOMON C.; BOOTHE, HELVI; and COLE, JONATHAN O. "One Year After Discharge: Community Adjustment of Schizophrenic Patients." *Am J Psychiatry* 123:986–95 F '67. * (*PA* 41:7602)

10. KATZ, MARTIN M. "A Phenomenological Typology of Schizophrenia," pp. 300–22, discussion 322–52. In *The Role and Methodology of Classification in Psychiatry and Psychopathology.* Edited by Martin M. Katz and others. Public Health Service Publication No. 1584. Washington, D.C.: United States Government Printing Office, 1968. Pp. ix, 590. *

[139]

*Kuder Preference Record—Personal.** Grades 9–16 and adults; 1948–63; KPR-P; 6 scores: group activity, stable situations, working with ideas, avoiding conflict, directing others, verification; 1 form; 2 editions; profile sheets: children ('49), adults ('52), (2 pages); profile leaflets for comparing vocational (see 6:1063) and personal scores: children ('53), adults ('54), (4 pages); manual, sixth edition ('63, 16 pages, same as fourth edition published in 1953 except for very slight changes); separate answer pads or answer sheets (IBM 805) must be used; 84¢ per 20 profile sheets; $1 per 20 profile leaflets; $1.50 per specimen set of either edition; postage extra; (40-45) minutes; G. Frederic Kuder; Science Research Associates, Inc. *

a) [HAND SCORING EDITION.] Form AH ('48, 16 pages); $13.65 per 20 tests; $3.15 per 20 answer pads.
b) [MACHINE SCORING EDITION.] Form AM ('48, 19 pages); $13.10 per 20 tests; $6.30 per 100 answer sheets; $4 per set of scoring stencils.

For reviews by Dorothy M. Clendenen and Wilbur L. Layton, see 6:132 (11 references); for a review by Dwight L. Arnold, see 5:80 (5 references); see also 4:65 (4 references, 1 excerpt).

REFERENCES

1-4. See 4:65.
5-9. See 5:80.
10-20. See 6:132.
21. ARMSTRONG, MARION ELIZABETH. *A Comparison of the Interests and Social Adjustment of Underachievers and Normal Achievers at the Secondary School Level.* Doctor's thesis, University of Connecticut (Storrs, Conn.), 1955. (DA 15:1349)
22. LEE, MARILYN CAIRNS. *Configural vs. Linear Prediction of Collegiate Academic Performance.* Doctor's thesis, University of Illinois (Urbana, Ill.), 1956. (DA 17:397)
23. CAMPBELL, ROBERT EDWARD. *Influence of the Counselor's Personality and Background on His Counseling Style.* Doctor's thesis, Ohio State University (Columbus, Ohio), 1961. (DA 22:3739)
24. CAINE, T. M. "Personality Tests for Nurses: An Experiment." *Nursing Times* 60:973-4 Jl 24 '64. *
25. SILVERMAN, PINCUS. *Characteristics of a Negro College Environment and Its Relationship to Student Value Systems.* Doctor's thesis, North Texas State University (Denton, Tex.), 1964. (DA 25:5125)
26. SCHROEDER, PEARL. "Relationship of Kuder's Conflict Avoidance and Dominance to Academic Accomplishment." *J Counsel Psychol* 12:395-9 w '65. * (PA 40:3381)
27. WHITELEY, DONALD P. "Comparison of the Descriptive Validity of the Activity Vector Analysis and the Kuder Preference Record—Personal." *J Indus Psychol* 4(2):29-36 '66. *
28. ATKINSON, GILBERT, and LUNNEBORG, CLIFFORD E. "Comparison of Oblique and Orthogonal Simple Structure Solutions for Personality and Interest Factors." *Multiv Behav Res* 3:21-35 Ja '68. * (PA 42:11349)
29. HARTMAN, BERNARD J. "Effect of Knowledge of Personality Test Results on Subsequent Test Performance." *Percept & Motor Skills* 26:122 F '68. * (PA 42:10593)

NAME INDEX

Anderson, M. E.: 15
Armstrong, M. E.: 21
Arnold, D. L.: rev, 5:80
Ash, P.: 14
Atkinson, G.: 28
Birge, W. R.: 2
Blocher, D. H.: 20
Bruce, M. M.: 8
Caine, T. M.: 24
Campbell, R. E.: 23
Clendenen, D. M.: rev, 6:132
Costello, C. G.: 15
Crites, J. O.: 19
Fjeld, H. A.: 5
Flowers, J. F.: 10, 17
Goshorn, W. M.: 3
Greene, J. E.: 9
Hartman, B. J.: 29
Iscoe, I.: 7
Kuder, G. F.: 1, 4
Layton, W. L.: rev, 6:132
Lee, M. C.: 22
Lucier, O.: 7
Lunneborg, C. E.: 28
McGuire, F. L.: 18
Mosier, M. F.: 1
Murray, L. E.: 8
Scholl, C. E.: 11
Schroeder, P.: 26
Shaffer, L. F.: exc, 4:65
Silverman, P.: 25
Smith, D. D.: 9, 12
Super, D. E.: 19
Wagner, E. E.: 16
Ward, P. L.: 13
Wardlow, M. E.: 6
Whiteley, D. P.: 27

[140]

★Kundu's Neurotic Personality Inventory. Adults; 1965; test booklet title is K.N.P.I.; 1 form (4 pages); manual (4 pages); separate answer sheets must be used; Rs. 9 per 10 tests; Rs. 7.50 per 25 answer sheets; Rs. 4 per specimen set; postage extra; (20-30) minutes; Ramanath Kundu; the Author. *

REFERENCES

1. KUNDU, RAMANATH. "A Brief Study of Reliability and Validity of a Neurotic Personality Inventory." *Psychol Studies* 8:08-101 Jl '63. *
2. KUNDU, RAMANATH. "Item-Analysis of a New Neurotic Personality Inventory." *J Psychol Res* 7:103-8 S '63. *
3. KUNDU, RAMANATH. "Standardization of the Kundu's Neurotic Personality Inventory." *Psychol Studies* 9:33-43 Ja '64. * (PA 39:1741)
4. KUNDU, RAMANATH. "A New Psychoneurotic Inventory for Adult." *Indian J Psychol* 41:17-22 Mr '66. *

5. KHANNA, ASHA, and KUNDU, RAMANATH. "A Comparison of Bernreuter Personality Inventory and Kundu Neurotic Personality Inventory." *Psychol Studies* 13:101-4 Jl '68. *

[141]

Language Modalities Test for Aphasia. Adults; 1961; LMTA; individual; Forms 1, 2, (26 pages); manual (91 pages); instruction manual (15 pages, reprinted from manual); record booklet (21 pages) for each form; medical history-scoring summary (4 pages); $35 per examiner's kit of 20 response booklets, 10 record booklets for each form, filmstrip for each form, 20 medical history-scoring summary forms, manual, and 4 instruction manuals; $4.50 per 10 response booklets; $4.50 per 10 record booklets; $7 per filmstrip; $1.75 per 10 medical history-scoring summary forms; $3 per manual; $2.50 per 4 instruction manuals; postage extra; 35 mm. filmstrip viewer or projector necessary for administration; a filmstrip viewer (DuKane Corporation Model 576-48A) may also be purchased through the publisher: $74.50 plus postage; (60-90) minutes in 1-3 sessions; Joseph M. Wepman and Lyle V. Jones; Education-Industry Service. *

For a review by T. R. Miles, consult 6:312.

REFERENCES

1. JONES, LYLE V., and WEPMAN, JOSEPH M. "Dimensions of Language Performance in Aphasia." *J Speech & Hearing Res* 4:220-32 S '61. * (PA 36:2JE20J) Comments by Hildred Schuell and James J. Jenkins. 4:295-9 S '61. *
2. GOODFELLOW, ROBERT L. *Administration of the Language Modalities Test for Aphasia to a Group of Junior High School Students With Undifferentiated Language Problems.* Master's thesis, University of Washington (Seattle, Wash.), 1963.
3. ZIGLER, EDWARD; JONES, LYLE V.; and KAFES, PATRICIA. "Acquisition of Language Habits in First, Second, and Third Grade Boys." *Child Develop* 35:725-36 S '64. * (PA 39:4580)
4. RADUS, LIBBY. *Dysphasia: Musical Perception as a Stimulus in Communication.* Doctor's thesis, University of Florida (Gainesville, Fla.), 1965. (DA 26:6230)
5. SPIEGEL, DOUGLAS K.; JONES, LYLE V.; and WEPMAN, JOSEPH M. "Test Responses as Predictors of Free-Speech Characteristics in Aphasia Patients." *J Speech & Hearing Res* 8:349-62 D '65. * (PA 40:7998)
6. ARCHIBALD, Y. M.; WEPMAN, J. M.; and JONES, L. V. "Nonverbal Cognitive Performance in Aphasic and Nonaphasic Brain-Damaged Patients." *Cortex* 3:275-94 S '67. * (PA 42:9335)
7. ARCHIBALD, Y. M.; WEPMAN, J. M.; and JONES, L. V. "Performance on Nonverbal Cognitive Tests Following Unilateral Cortical Injury to the Right and Left Hemisphere." *J Nerv & Mental Dis* 145:25-36 Jl '67. * (PA 42:4382)
8. ARCHIBALD, Y. M., and WEPMAN, J. M. "Language Disturbance and Nonverbal Cognitive Performance in Eight Patients Following Injury to the Right Hemisphere." *Brain* 91:117-30 Mr '68. * (PA 42:19160)

[142]

The Leadership Ability Evaluation. Grades 9-16 and adults; 1961; LAE; social climate created in influencing others; 5 scores: laissez faire, democratic-cooperative, autocratic-submissive, autocratic-aggressive, decision pattern; 1 form (8 pages); manual (18 pages plus test); supplement (4 pages); $7.50 per set of 25 tests and manual; $2 per manual; postpaid; [30] minutes; Russell N. Cassel and Edward J. Stancik; Western Psychological Services. *

For reviews by John D. Black and Cecil A. Gibb, see 6:133 (4 references).

[143]

The Leadership Q-Sort Test (A Test of Leadership Values). Adults; 1958; LQST; 7 scores: personal integrity, consideration of others, mental health, technical information, decision making, teaching and communication, total; 1 form (4 pages); manual (56 pages); no data on reliability of subscores; $9 per examiner's kit of 25 tests, 25 item sheets (must be cut up into sorting slips), set of keys, sorting board, and manual; $3 per 25 tests; $1 per set of keys; $2 per 25 item sheets; $1 per sorting board; $3 per

manual; cash orders postpaid; (40–50) minutes;
Russell N. Cassel; Psychometric Affiliates. *
    For reviews by Joel T. Campbell, Cecil A. Gibb,
and William Stephenson, see 6:134 (6 references).

[144]

★The Level of Aspiration Board. Mental ages 12.5
and over; 1940–50; LAB; 2 scores: mean difference
between performance and estimate, shifts; individual;
1 form ('40); mimeographed manual ['50, 6 pages];
no data on reliability; no norms; $39 per set of testing
materials (may also be constructed locally from
plans presented in 1 below); postpaid; manual free
on request; (20–25) minutes; J. B. Rotter; distributed by Edward Butler. *

REFERENCES

1. ROTTER, JULIAN B. "Level of Aspiration as a Method of
Studying Personality." J Exp Psychol 31:410–21 N '42. * (PA
17:598)
2. ROTTER, JULIAN B. "Level of Aspiration as a Method of
Studying Personality: 1, A Critical Review of Methodology."
Psychol R 49:463–74 S '42. * (PA 17:597)
3. ROTTER, JULIAN B. "Level of Aspiration as a Method of
Studying Personality: 4, The Analysis of Patterns of Re-
sponse." J Social Psychol 21:159–77 My '45. * (PA 19:2261)
4. WORTHINGTON, ANNA MAY LANGE. An Investigation of
the Relationship Between the Lipreading Ability of Congenitally
Deaf High School Students and Certain Personality Factors.
Doctor's thesis, Ohio State University (Columbus, Ohio), 1956.
(DA 16:2241)
5. ESHBAUGH, ROHE N., and FRIEDMAN, STANLEY R. "The
Rotter Level of Aspiration Task: A Validity Study." Psychon
Sci 1:341–2 N '64. *
6. COOPER, G. DAVID; ADAMS, HENRY B.; and COHEN, LOUIS
D. "Personality Changes After Sensory Deprivation." J Nerv
& Mental Dis 140:103–18 F '65. * (PA 39:13642)
7. CROWNE, DOUGLAS P. "Family Orientation, Level of
Aspiration, and Interpersonal Bargaining." J Personality &
Social Psychol 3:641–5 Je '66. * (PA 40:7587)
8. RAJESWARI, S. "A Study of Level of Aspiration of Delin-
quents and Non-Delinquents." Indian J Appl Psychol 4:35–40
Ja '67. *
9. LEFCOURT, HERBERT M.; LEWIS, LAWRENCE; and SILVER-
MAN, IRWIN W. "Internal vs. External Control of Reinforcement and Attention in a Decision-Making Task." J Personality
36:663–82 D '68. * (PA 43:6365)

[145]

The Life Adjustment Inventory. High school;
1951; LAI; 14 scores: adjustment to curriculum,
reading and study skills, communication and listening
skills, social skills and etiquette, boy-girl relationships,
religion-moral-ethics, functional citizenship, vocational
orientation and preparation, physical and mental
health, family living, orientation to science, consumer
education, art appreciation and creativity, use of leisure
time; 1 form (8 pages); manual (12 pages); $6 per
25 tests; $1 per specimen set; postage extra; (25)
minutes; J. Wayne Wrightstone and Ronald C. Doll;
Psychometric Affiliates. *
    For reviews by John W. M. Rothney and Helen
Shacter, see 4:67.

REFERENCE

1. ROWLEY, IRENE F. The Life Adjustment Inventory. Master's thesis, Boston College (Chestnut Hill, Mass.), 1953.

[146]

★M-Scale. College and adults; 1968; M-S; for experimental research, and discussion use only; integrative vs. separative attitudes toward black-white
relations in the United States; 1 form (3 pages,
mimeographed); mimeographed manual (1 page); no
data on reliability; no norms; $3 per 20 tests; $1 per
specimen set; postpaid; [15] minutes; James H. Morrison; the Author. *

[147]

The MACC Behavioral Adjustment Scale: An
Objective Approach to the Evaluation of Behavioral Adjustments of Psychiatric Patients.

Psychotic mental patients; 1957–62; MACC; Forms
1, 2, (4 pages); Form 2 is a revision of Form 1
rather than a parallel form; $6.50 per 25 scales, post-
paid; Robert B. Ellsworth; Western Psychological
Services. *
    a) FORM 1. 1957; 5 ratings: affect, cooperation, com-
munication, total adjustment, motility; mimeographed
manual (10 pages); $1.50 per manual; specimen set
not available.
    b) FORM 2. 1962; 5 ratings: mood, cooperation, com-
munication, social contact, total adjustment; mimeographed manual (17 pages); $2.50 per specimen set.
    For a review by Wilson H. Guertin, see 6:135 (2
references); for a review by Maurice Lorr, see 5:82.

REFERENCES

1–2. See 6:135.
3. ANKER, JAMES M., and WALSH, RICHARD P. "Group
Psychotherapy, a Special Activity Program, and Group Structure in the Treatment of Chronic Schizophrenics." J Consult
Psychol 25:476–81 D '61. * (PA 37:5175)
4. GIEDT, F. HAROLD. "Predicting Suitability for Group
Psychotherapy." Am J Psychother 15:582–91 O '61. * (PA
38:8712)
5. GOLDSTEIN, MICHAEL J., and JONES, ROBERT B. "The
Relationships Among Word Association Test, Objective Per-
sonality Test Scores and Ratings of Clinical Behavior in Psy-
chiatric Patients." J Proj Tech & Pers Assess 28:271–9 S '64.
* (PA 39:7840)
6. McKEEVER, WALTER F., and MAY, PHILIP R. A. "The
MACC Scale as a Predictor of Length of Hospitalization for
Schizophrenic Patients: A Cross Validation." Abstract. J
Consult Psychol 28:474 O '64. * (PA 39:5757, title only)
7. LYERLY, SAMUEL B., and ABBOTT, PRESTON S. "MACC
Behavioral Adjustment Scale (Form II)," pp. 19–24. In their
Handbook of Psychiatric Rating Scales (1950–1964). Public
Health Service Publication No. 1495. Washington, D.C.: United
States Government Printing Office, 1966. Pp. v, 69. *
8. WEEKS, LAYLE E. "Pilot Study Results and Recommendations for Department-Wide Use of the MACC Behavioral Adjustment Rating Scale." Calif Mental Health Res Dig 4:110–1
su '66. *
9. ELLSWORTH, ROBERT; ARTHUR, GILBERT; KROEKER,
DUANE; and CHILDERS, BARRY. "Comparative Validity of Staff
and Relatives' Assessment of Adjustment for Male Schizophrenic Patients." Proc Ann Conv Am Psychol Assn 75:219–20
'67. * (PA 41:13975)
10. ELLSWORTH, ROBERT; ARTHUR, GILBERT; KROEKER,
DUANE; and CHILDERS, BARRY. "Psychiatric Patients' Behavior
and Adjustment as Appraised in the Community and Hospital
Setting." Proc Ann Conv Am Psychol Assn 75:199–200 '67. *
(PA 41:13858)
11. DISTEFANO, M. K., JR., and PRYER, MARGARET W. "Relationship Between Severity of Emotional Impairment and Work-
Related Attitudes." J Clin Psychol 24:420–2 O '68. * (PA
43:4206)
12. ELLSWORTH, ROBERT B.; FOSTER, LESLIE; CHILDERS,
BARRY; ARTHUR, GILBERT; and KROEKER, DUANE. "Hospital
and Community Adjustment as Perceived by Psychiatric Patients, Their Families, and Staff." J Consult & Clin Psychol
Monogr Sup 32(5, part 2):1–41 O '68. * (PA 43:1140)

[148]

*M-B History Record: Self-Administered Form.
Psychiatric patients and penal groups; 1957–65;
MBHR; 7 scores: family disunity, conflict with parents, health awareness, introversion, school and job
failure, social misfit, breakdowns and addiction, 1 form
('65, 17 pages); no manual; 20 or more records, 15¢
each; specimen set free; postpaid; [60–90] minutes;
Peter F. Briggs; the Author. *

REFERENCES

1–2. See 6:136.
3. GUERTIN, WILSON H. "Are Differences in Schizophrenic
Symptoms Related to the Mother's Avowed Attitudes Toward
Child Rearing?" J Abn & Social Psychol 63:440–2 S '61. *
(PA 37:1791)
4. HOLMAN, THOMAS RANGER. A Factor Analytic Study of
the M-B History Record. Doctor's thesis, University of Minnesota (Minneapolis, Minn.), 1966. (DA 28:349B)
5. VESTRE, NORRIS D., and LOREI, THEODORE W. "Relationships Between Social History Factors and Psychiatric Symptoms." J Abn Psychol 72:247–50 Je '67. * (PA 41:10670)

[149]

The Male Impotence Test. Adult males; 1964;
title on test is MIT; 5 scores: reaction to female

rejection, flight from male role, reaction to male inadequacy, organic factor, total; 1 form (4 pages); manual (35 pages plus test); no data on reliability; $9 per 25 tests and manual; $6.50 per 25 tests; $3 per manual; postpaid; (10–30) minutes; Ahmed El Senoussi; Western Psychological Services. *

[150]

★The Manchester Scales of Social Adaptation. Ages 6–15; 1966; adaptation of *Vineland Social Maturity Scale;* 13 scores: social perspective (general, sport, current affairs, aesthetic, scientific, total), self-direction (socialisation of play, freedom of movement, self-help, handling of money, responsibility in home, total), total; individual; no reading by examinees; 1 form; manual (54 pages); scoring form (4 pages); 12*s.* 6*d.* per 25 scoring forms; 30*s.* per manual; 34*s.* per specimen set; postage extra; (30–40) minutes; E. A. Lunzer; National Foundation for Educational Research in England and Wales. *

[151]

★Mandel Social Adjustment Scale. Psychiatric patients and others; 1959; MSAS; 8 scores: occupational, family life, economic, health, religion, residence, community and social, total; individual; 1 form; mimeographed manual (16 pages) contains scale and profile; no data on reliability and validity; no norms; 20¢ per manual, postage extra; Nathan G. Mandel; the Author. *

REFERENCES

1. GOLDEN, JULES S.; SILVER, REUBEN J.; and MANDEL, NATHAN. "The Wives of 50 'Normal' American Men." *Arch Gen Psychiatry* 9:614–8 D '63. * (*PA* 38:8588)
2. BRIGGS, PETER F. "The Inter-Relationships of Seven Criteria of Adjustment Among Psychiatric Clients Seeking Vocational Counseling." *J Clin Psychol* 21:433–5 O '65. * (*PA* 40:1760)

[152]

The Manson Evaluation. Adults; 1948; ME; identification of alcoholics, potential alcoholics, and severely maladjusted adults; 8 scores: anxiety, depressive fluctuations, emotional sensitivity, resentfulness, incompletenesss, aloneness, interpersonal relations, total; 1 form (4 pages); manual (2 pages); no data on reliability of subscores; $7 per examiner's kit of 25 tests, key, and manual; $6.50 per 25 tests; $2 per specimen set; postpaid; (5–15) minutes; Morse P. Manson; Western Psychological Services. *
For a review by Dugal Campbell, see 6:137 (5 references); for reviews by Charles H. Honzik and Albert L. Hunsicker, see 4:68 (4 references).

REFERENCES

1–4. See 4:68.
5–9. See 6:137.
10. GAVALES, DANIEL. "Effects of Combined Counseling and Vocational Training on Personal Adjustment." *J Appl Psychol* 50:18–21 F '66. * (*PA* 40:4621)

[153]

Marital Roles Inventory. Marriage counselees; 1961; MRI; 4 derived scores: index of marital strain, index of deviation of role performances, index of deviation of role expectations, corrected index of marital strain; Forms H (2 pages, for men), W (2 pages, for women); husband and wife must both take inventory to obtain marital strain score; scoring-history form (4 pages); manual (17 pages plus tests and scoring form); no data on reliability; validity data based on an earlier form and scoring method; $13 per examiner's kit of 25 tests of each form, 25 scoring forms, and manual; $3 per 25 tests; $6.50 per 25 scoring forms; $3 per manual; postpaid; (20)

minutes; Nathan Hurvitz; Western Psychological Services. *
For a review by Robert A. Harper, consult 6:680.

REFERENCES

1. HURVITZ, NATHAN. "The Index of Strain as a Measure of Marital Satisfaction." *Sociol & Social Res* 44:106–11 N–D '59. * (*PA* 35:6683)
2. HURVITZ, NATHAN. "The Marital Roles Inventory and the Measurement of Marital Adjustment." *J Clin Psychol* 16:377–80 O '60. * (*PA* 37:3454)
3. HURVITZ, NATHAN. "The Measurement of Marital Strain." *Am J Sociol* 65:610–5 My '60. * (*PA* 35:6684)

[154]

A Marriage Adjustment Form. Adults; 1939–61; MAF; problems checklist; 1 form ['61, 8 pages, reprinted from *1* below]; combined manual ['61, 4 pages] for this test and test 158; no data on reliability; $1.25 per 10 tests; 35¢ per specimen set; cash orders postpaid; (30–50) minutes; Ernest W. Burgess; distributed by Family Life Publications, Inc. *
For a review by Lester W. Dearborn, consult 6:681.

REFERENCE

1. BURGESS, ERNEST W., and COTTRELL, LEONARD S., JR. *Predicting Success or Failure in Marriage.* New York: Prentice-Hall, Inc., 1939. Pp. xxiii, 472. * (*PA* 14:404)

[155]

The Marriage Adjustment Inventory. Marriage counselees; 1962; MAI; problems checklist; 52 scores: 4 scores (self-evaluation, spouse-evaluation, husband-wife evaluation, total) in each of 12 areas (family relationships, dominance, immaturity, neurotic traits, sociopathic traits, money-management, children, interests, physical, abilities, sexual, incompatibility) and total scores for self-evaluation, spouse-evaluation, husband-wife evaluation, total; Forms H (4 pages, for husbands), W (4 pages, for wives), identical except for booklet color; manual (16 pages plus tests); no data on reliability; $13 per examiner's kit of 25 tests of each form and manual; $6.50 per 25 tests; $2 per manual; postpaid; (10–30) minutes; Morse P. Manson and Arthur Lerner; Western Psychological Services. *
For reviews by Clifford R. Adams and Albert Ellis, consult 6:682.

[156]

★A Marriage Analysis. Married couples in counseling; 1966; 8 scores: role concepts, self image, feelings toward spouse, emotional openness, knowledge of spouse, sexual adjustment and security, common traits, meanings of marriage; experimental form (4 pages); counselor's guide (['66], 8 pages); profile (1 page); no data on reliability; $1.25 per 10 tests; 35¢ per specimen set; postage extra; Daniel C. Blazier and Edgar T. Goosman; Family Life Publications, Inc. *

[157]

★Marriage-Personality Inventory, Educational Research Edition. Individuals and couples; 1963–67; MPI; 24 profiled scores: items completed, satisfaction, growing up years (3 scores), life style preferences (2 scores), personality traits (2 scores), growth inviting (3 scores), life engaging (6 scores), flexibility (3 scores), dependability (3 scores); 4 booklets ('67, 16 pages) labeled forms, identical except for instructions to subjects; booklets essentially the same as *Clinical Research Edition* copyrighted in 1966; manual ('67, 39 pages); profile ('67, 1 page); individual guide ('67, 8 pages) for Forms 3 and 4; no data on reliability; separate answer sheets (NCS) must be used; $5 per 10 tests; $6 per 10 individual guides; scoring service, $17.50 per 10 tests; $8 per

specimen set (must be purchased to obtain manual);
cash orders postpaid; (60) minutes; Karl V. Schultz;
Psychological Services Press. *

a) FORM 1, INDIVIDUAL PERSONALITY. Responses in
terms of self-image, desired self-image, and satisfaction
with differences.

b) FORM 2, MATCH-MATE. Responses in terms of self-
image, desired mate image, importance of desired
mate image.

c) FORM 3, COURTSHIP PRE-MARRIAGE. Responses in
terms of self-image, prospective mate image, effect of
combination on marriage if married.

d) FORM 4, MARRIAGE. Responses in terms of self-
image, mate image, effect of combination on marriage.

[158]

A Marriage Prediction Schedule. Adults; 1939–61;
MPS; 1 form ['39, 8 pages, reprinted from *1* below];
combined manual ['61, 4 pages] for this test and test
6:681; no data on reliability and validity; $2.50 per
25 tests; 35¢ per specimen set; postage extra; (30–
50) minutes; Ernest W. Burgess; Family Life Publications, Inc. *

For a review by Lester W. Dearborn, consult 6:684;
consult also 5:84 (8 references).

[159]

Marriage Role Expectation Inventory. Adolescents
and adults; 1960–63; MREI; role expectations in 7
areas (authority, homemaking, care of children, personal characteristics, social participation, education,
employment and support) yielding an equalitarian-
traditional rating; Forms M (for males), W (for
females), ('63, 4 pages, identical except for wording
changes); originally published in *2* below; teacher's
and counselor's guide ('63, 7 pages); no data on reliability of subscores; no norms (author recommends
the use of local norms); $1.25 per 10 tests; 35¢ per
specimen set of both forms; cash orders postpaid;
(25–50) minutes; Marie S. Dunn; Family Life Publications, Inc. *

For a review by Robert C. Challman, consult 6:685.

REFERENCES

1. DUNN, MARIE S. *Marriage Role Expectations of Adolescents.* Doctor's thesis, Florida State University (Tallahassee,
Fla.), 1959. (DA 20:3277)
2. DUNN, MARIE S. "Marriage Role Expectations of Adolescents." *Marriage & Family Living* 22:99–111 My '60. *
3. MOSER, ALVIN J. *Marriage Role Expectations of High
School Students.* Master's thesis, Florida State University
(Tallahassee, Fla.), 1960.
4. GOULD, NORMAN S. *Marriage Role Expectations of Single
College Students as Related to Selected Social Factors.* Doctor's
thesis, Florida State University (Tallahassee, Fla.), 1961. (DA
22:2906)
5. MOSER, ALVIN J. "Marriage Role Expectations of High
School Students." *Marriage & Family Living* 23:42–3 F '61. *
(PA 36:3FH42M)
6. BUSBICE, JUANITA J. *Marriage Role Expectations and Personality Adjustments.* Master's thesis, Northwestern State
College (Natchitoches, La.), 1962.

[160]

★Maryland Parent Attitude Survey. Parents;
[1957–66]; MPAS; parental attitudes toward child
rearing; for research use only; 4 scores: disciplinarian,
indulgent, protective, rejecting; 1 form ['60, 8 pages,
mimeographed]; manual ('66, 6 pages, reprint of *3*
below); mimeographed norms (no date, 3 pages); $1
per set of test materials, postpaid; tests must be reproduced locally; [20–60] minutes; Donald K. Pumroy; the Author. *

REFERENCES

1. BRODY, GRACE F. *A Study of the Relationship Between
Maternal Attitudes and Mother-Child Interaction.* Doctor's
thesis, American University (Washington, D.C.), 1963. (DA
24:1728)
2. BRODY, GRACE F. "Relationship Between Maternal Attitudes

and Behavior." *J Personality & Social Psychol* 2:317–23 S '65.
* (PA 39:14604)
3. PUMROY, DONALD K. "Maryland Parent Attitude Survey:
A Research Instrument With Social Desirability Controlled."
J Psychol 64:73–8 S '66. * (PA 40:12165)
4. SCHWITZGEBEL, RALPH K., and BAER, DANIEL J. "Inten-
sive Supervision by Parole Officers as a Factor in Recidivism
Reduction of Male Delinquents." *J Psychol* 67:75–82 S '67. *
(PA 41:16993)
5. TOLOR, ALEXANDER. "An Evaluation of the Maryland
Parent Attitude Survey." *J Psychol* 67:69–74 S '67. * (PA
41:1072)
6. ALLAN, THOMAS KENNETH, and HODGSON, EDWARD W.
"The Use of Personality Measurements as a Determinant of
Patient Cooperation in an Orthodontic Practice." *Am J Orthodontics* 54:433–40 Je '68. *

[161]

Maudsley Personality Inventory. College and
adults; 1959–62; MPI; for revised edition, see *Eysenck Personality Inventory* (77); 2 scores: neuroticism, extraversion; H. J. Eysenck. *

a) BRITISH EDITION. 1959; 1 form (2 pages); manual
(8 pages); may be administered as a short scale;
6s. 6d. per 20 tests; 2s. per set of scoring stencils;
2s. 6d. per manual; 5s per specimen set; postage extra;
[5] minutes for short scale, [15] minutes for full scale;
University of London Press Ltd.

b) UNITED STATES EDITION. 1962; 1 form ('62, c1959–
62, 2 pages, items identical with British edition);
manual (21 pages); $3.50 per 25 tests; $1 per set of
scoring stencils; $1.25 per manual; $1.75 per specimen
set; postage extra; scoring service, 45¢ or less per
test; (10–15) minutes; Robert R. Knapp (manual);
Educational and Industrial Testing Service.

For reviews by Arthur R. Jensen, James C. Lingoes,
William Stephenson, and Philip E. Vernon, see 6:138
(120 references, 3 excerpts).

REFERENCES

1–117. See 6:138.
118. RAY, OAKLEY STERN. *Personality Factors in Motor
Learning and Reminiscence.* Doctor's thesis, University of
Pittsburgh (Pittsburgh, Pa.), 1958. (DA 19:1446)
119. EYSENCK, H. J. "Personality and Problem Solving."
Psychol Rep 5:592 D '59. * (PA 34:5611)
120. BENDIG, A. W.; VAUGHAN, C. J.; RAY, O.; and KLIONS,
H. L. "Attitude Toward Man-Into-Space: Development and
Validation of an Attitude Scale." *J Social Psychol* 52:67–75
Ag '60. * (PA 35:6313)
121. EYSENCK, S. B. G.; EYSENCK, H. J.; and CLARIDGE, G.
"Dimensions of Personality, Psychiatric Syndromes, and
Mathematical Models." *J Mental Sci* 106:581–9 Ap '60. *
(PA 35:6456)
122. DAS, J. P. "Some Correlates of Verbal Conditioning."
Psychol Studies 6:30–5 Ja '61. * (PA 37:367)
123. BANERJEE, DEBABRATA, and MALLICK, AMAL KUMAR.
"Form of Bengali Language as a Determinant of Ideas Contained in the Items of a Foreign Personality Inventory."
Indian J Psychol 37:23–6 pt 1 '62. * (PA 37:6729)
124. EYSENCK, H. J., and EYSENCK, SYBIL B. G. "A Factorial Study of an Interview-Questionnaire." *J Clin Psychol*
18:286–90 Jl '62. * (PA 39:175)
125. KENYON, F. E. "A Psychiatric Survey of a Random
Sample of Out-Patients Attending a Dermatological Hospital."
J Psychosom Res 6:129–35 Ap–Je '62. * (PA 37:5530)
126. MATTOON, PAUL F., II. "After-Contraction as a Function of Extraversion and Central Inhibition." *Acta Psychologica*
20(2):121–7 '62. * (PA 37:6734)
127. FISCHER, HERBERT LEON. *Personal Versus Impersonal
Test Administration as a Function of Various Subject Characteristics.* Doctor's thesis, Purdue University (Lafayette,
Ind.), 1963. (DA 24:5543)
128. FRANKS, CYRIL M. "Ocular Movements and Spontaneous Blink Rate as Functions of Personality." *Percept & Motor
Skills* 16:178 F '63. * (PA 38:188)
129. HAMMER, A. G. "Neuroticism, Extraversion and Hypnotizability." *Brit J Social & Clin Psychol* 2:185–91 O '63. *
(PA 38:6109)
130. KISSEN, D. M. "Aspects of Personality of Men With
Lung Cancer." *Acta Psychotherapeutica et Psychosomatica*
11(3–4):200–10 '63. * (PA 38:8638)
131. LUCAS, C. J., and OJHA, A. B. "Personality and Acne."
J Psychosom Res 7:41–3 Jl '63. * (PA 38:6159)
132. MARTIN, JOHN, and STANLEY, GORDON. "Social Desirability and the Maudsley Personality Inventory." *Acta Psychologica* 21(3):260–4 '63. * (PA 38:8526)
133. PAYNE, R. W.; EVESON, M. B.; and Sloane, R. B.
"The Relationship Between Blood Cholesterol Level and Objective Measures of Personality." *J Psychosom Res* 7:23–34 Jl
'63. * (PA 38:6160)

134. STERN, HERBERT. *Performance on Psychomotor Tasks as a Function of Extraversion and Neuroticism.* Doctor's thesis, Indiana University (Bloomington, Ind.), 1963. *(DA* 24:2990)

135. AL-ISSA, IHSAN. "The Effect of Attitudinal Factors on the Relationship Between Conditioning and Personality." *Brit J Social & Clin Psychol* 3:113–9 Je '64. * *(PA* 39:7571)

136. BENDIG, A. W. "Factor Analytic Scales of Need Achievement." *J General Psychol* 70:59–67 Ja '64. * *(PA* 38:10111)

137. BOLARDOS, A. C. "Validation of the Maudsley Personality Inventory in Chile." *Brit J Social & Clin Psychol* 3:148 Je '64. *

138. CAINE, T. M., and HOPE, K. "Validation of the Maudsley Personality Inventory E Scale." *Brit J Psychol* 55:447–52 N '64. * *(PA* 39:7743)

139. COOPER, GEORGE W., JR., and DANA, RICHARD H. "Hypnotizability and the Maudsley Personality Inventory." *Int J Clin & Exp Hyp* 12:28–33 Ja '64. * *(PA* 38:8745)

140. CROOKES, T. G., and HUTT, S. J. "A Note on the MPI: A Response Tendency in Neurotics Related to Intelligence." *Brit J Social & Clin Psychol* 3:137–8 Je '64. * *(PA* 39:7860)

141. DAS, J. P. "Hypnosis, Verbal Satiation, Vigilance, and Personality Factors: A Correlational Study." *J Abn & Social Psychol* 68:72–8 Ja '64. * *(PA* 38:8348)

142. EDWARDS, ALLEN L., and WALSH, JAMES A. "Response Sets in Standard and Experimental Personality Scales." *Am Ed Res J* 1:52–61 Ja '64. * *(PA* 39:7754)

143. EYSENCK, H. J. "Principles and Methods of Personality Description, Classification and Diagnosis." *Brit J Psychol* 55:284–94 Ag '64. * *(PA* 39:5225)

144. GARD, JOHN G., and BENDIG, A. W. "A Factor Analytic Study of Eysenck's and Schutz's Personality Dimensions Among Psychiatric Groups." *J Consult Psychol* 28:252–8 Je '64. * *(PA* 39:5729)

145. GIBSON, H. B. "Neuroticism, Extraversion, and 'Hypnotizability.'" *Brit J Social & Clin Psychol* 3:151–2 Je '64. *

146. HALL, JOHN DAVID. *An Investigation of Acquiescence Response Set, Extraversion, and Locus of Control as Related to Neuroticism and Maladjustment.* Doctor's thesis, George Peabody College for Teachers (Nashville, Tenn.), 1964. *(DA* 25:6060)

147. INGHAM, J. G., and ROBINSON, J. O. "Personality in the Diagnosis of Hysteria." *Brit J Psychol* 55:276–84 Ag '64. * *(PA* 39:5227)

148. JALOTA, S. "Some Data on the Maudsley Personality Inventory in Panjabi." *Brit J Social & Clin Psychol* 3:148 Je '64. *

149. KANTER, V. B., and HAZELTON, J. E. "An Attempt to Measure Some Aspects of Personality in Young Men With Duodenal Ulcer by Means of Questionnaires and a Projective Test." *J Psychosom Res* 8:297–309 D '64. * *(PA* 39:12455)

150. KISSEN, D. M. "The Use of Questionnaires in Personality Measurement in Psychosomatic Research." *J Psychosom Res* 8:293–6 D '64. *

151. KISSEN, DAVID M. "The Influence of Some Environmental Factors on Personality Inventory Scores in Psychosomatic Research." *J Psychosom Res* 8:145–9 S '64. * *(PA* 39:8551)

152. KREITMAN, NORMAN. "The Patient's Spouse." *Brit J Psychiatry* 110:159–73 Mr '64. *

153. LUOTO, KENNETH. "Personality and Placebo Effects Upon Timing Behavior." *J Abn & Social Psychol* 68:54–61 Ja '64. * *(PA* 38:8593)

154. MOFFAT, J., and LEVINE, S. "The Sedation Threshold of Psychoneurotic and Alcoholic Patients." *Brit J Med Psychol* 37:313–7 pt 4 '64. * *(PA* 39:10683)

155. RATH, R. "Attitudinal Direction Study-One Measurement." *J Madras Univ* 36:80–98 Jl '64 and Ja '65. *

156. ROBINSON, J. O. "A Possible Effect of Selection on the Test Scores of a Group of Hypertensives." *J Psychosom Res* 8:239–43 D '64. *

157. ROHRS, FREDERICK WILLIAM. *The Relationship of Sexual Symbol Identification and Preference to Neuroticism and Extraversion-Introversion.* Doctor's thesis, Michigan State University (East Lansing, Mich.), 1964. *(DA* 25:6769)

158. SAVAGE, R. D. "Electro-Cerebral Activity, Extraversion and Neuroticism." *Brit J Psychiatry* 110:98–100 Ja '64. *

159. SEVRANSKY, PAUL. *Extraversion and Neuroticism as Determinants of Vocational Level of Aspiration.* Doctor's thesis, Columbia University (New York, N.Y.), 1964. *(DA* 26:4817)

160. SHANMUGAN, T. E., and SANTHANAM, M. L. "Personality Differences in Serial Learning When Interference Is Presented at the Marginal Visual Level." *J Indian Acad Appl Psychol* 1:25–8 Ja '64. * *(PA* 39:660)

161. SMALHEISER, LAWRENCE. *Perceptual-Motor Behavior of Introverts and Extraverts.* Doctor's thesis, University of Miami (Coral Gables, Fla.), 1964. *(DA* 25:5410)

162. SPARROW, N. H., and ROSS, JOHN. "The Dual Nature of Extraversion: A Replication." *Austral J Psychol* 16:214–8 D '64. * *(PA* 39:10152)

163. STANLEY, GORDON. "Personality and Attitude Correlates of Religious Conversion." *J Sci Study Relig* 4:60–3 O '64. * *(PA* 39:9980)

164. TAUSS, W. "Maudsley Personality Inventory, Neurosis, and Stress." *Psychol Rep* 14:461–2 Ap '64. * *(PA* 39:2769)

165. BLACKBURN, R. "Denial-Admission Tendencies and the Maudsley Personality Inventory." *Brit J Social & Clin Psychol* 4:241–3 D '65. * *(PA* 40:4246)

166. BROWN, D. G., and YOUNG, A. J. "The Effect of Extraversion on Susceptibility to Disease: A Validatory Study on Contact Dermatitis." *J Psychosom Res* 8:421–9 Mr '65. *

167. CLARK, D. F. "The Psychometric Characteristics of an Adult Class in Psychology." *Brit J Psychiatry* 111:745–53 Ag '65. * *(PA* 40:1584)

168. COPPEN, ALEC. "The Prevalence of Menstrual Disorders in Psychiatric Patients." *Brit J Psychiatry* 111:155–67 F '65. * *(PA* 39:10636)

169. COPPEN, ALEC, and METCALFE, MARYSE. "Effect of a Depressive Illness on M.P.I. Scores." *Brit J Psychiatry* 111:236–9 Mr '65. * *(PA* 39:10227)

170. COPPEN, ALEC; COWIE, VALERIE; and SLATER, ELIOT. "Familial Aspects of 'Neuroticism' and 'Extraversion.'" *Brit J Psychiatry* 111:70–83 Ja '65. * *(PA* 39:10681)

171. HANNAH, F.; STORM, THOMAS; and CAIRD, W. K. "Sex Differences and Relationships Among Neuroticism, Extraversion, and Expressed Fears." *Percept & Motor Skills* 20:1214–6 Je '65. * *(PA* 39:15353)

172. HARE, E. H., and SHAW, G. K. "A Study in Family Health: 2, A Comparison of the Health of Fathers, Mothers and Children." *Brit J Psychiatry* 111:467–71 Je '65. * *(PA* 39:15894)

173. HAUN, KENNETH W. "Note on Prediction of Academic Performance From Personality Test Scores." *Psychol Rep* 16:294 F '65. * *(PA* 39:7687)

174. JALOTA, S. "A Study of the Maudsley Personality Inventory (in Hindi and Punjabi Versions)." *Indian Psychol R* 2:29–30 Jl '65. * *(PA* 40:2136)

175. JAMIESON, G. H. "Psychological Aspects of Craftsmanship in Pottery-Making at a Secondary School." *Brit J Ed Psychol* 35:179–82 Je '65. * *(PA* 39:16457)

176. KELVIN, R. P.; LUCAS, C. J.; and OJHA, A. B. "The Relation Between Personality, Mental Health and Academic Performance in University Students." *Brit J Social & Clin Psychol* 4:244–53 D '65. * *(PA* 40:4573)

177. KNAPP, BARBARA. "The Personality of Lawn Tennis Players." *B Brit Psychol Soc* 18:21–3 O '65. *

178. KNOWLES, JOHN B., and KRASNER, LEONARD. "Extraversion and Duration of the Archimedes Spiral Aftereffect." *Percept & Motor Skills* 20:997–1000 Je '65. * *(PA* 39:13503)

179. McPHERSON, FRANK M. "Comment on Eysenck's Account of Some Aberdeen Studies of Introversion-Extraversion and Eyeblink Conditioning." *Brit J Psychol* 56:483–4 N '65. * *(PA* 40:3733, title only)

180. MOHAN, JITENDRA, and MOHAN, VIDHU. "Personality and Variability in Aesthetic Evaluation." *Psychol Studies* 10:57–60 Ja '65. * *(PA* 39:10062)

181. MOHAN, JITENDRA, and MOHAN, VIDHU. "Personality and Variability in Aesthetic Evaluation." *Psychologia* 8:218–9 D '65. * *(PA* 41:1594)

182. PARDES, MORTON. *Eysenck's Introversion-Extraversion, Boredom, and Time Estimation.* Doctor's thesis, Columbia University (New York, N.Y.), 1965. *(DA* 26:3488)

183. RAFI, A. ABI. "The Maudsley Personality Inventory: A Cross-Cultural Study." *Brit J Social & Clin Psychol* 4:266–8 D '65. * *(PA* 40:4252)

184. SHANMUGAN, T. E. "Personality Severity of Conflict and Decision Time." *J Indian Acad Appl Psychol* 2:13–23 Ja '65. * *(PA* 39:11518)

185. SHAW, G. K., and HARE, E. H. "The Maudsley Personality Inventory (Short Form): Distribution of Scores and Test-Retest Reliability in an Urban Population." *Brit J Psychiatry* 111:226–35 Mr '65. * *(PA* 39:10151)

186. SIEGMAN, ARON WOLFE, and POPE, BENJAMIN. "Personality Variables Associated With Productivity and Verbal Influence in the Initial Interview." *Proc Ann Conv Am Psychol Assn* 73:273–4 '65. * *(PA* 39:15655)

187. SMART, REGINALD G. "The Relationships Between Intellectual Deterioration, Extraversion and Neuroticism Among Chronic Alcoholics." *J Clin Psychol* 21:27–9 Ja '65. * *(PA* 39:12771)

188. VENABLES, ETHEL C. "Differences Between Verbal and Non-Verbal Ability in Relation to Personality Scores Among Part-Time Day Release Students." *Brit J Social & Clin Psychol* 4:188–96 S '65. * *(PA* 40:1580)

189. BAKAN, PAUL, and LECKART, BRUCE T. "Attention, Extraversion, and Stimulus-Personality Congruence." *Percept & Psychophysics* 1:355–7 O '66. * *(PA* 41:566)

190. BARRETT, WILLIAM; CALDBECK-MEENAN, JOHN; and WHITE, JOHN GRAHAM. "Questionnaire Measures and Psychiatrists' Ratings of a Personality Dimension: A Note on the Congruent Validity of Caine's Self Description Questionnaire." *Brit J Psychiatry* 112:413–5 Ap '66. * *(PA* 40:10231)

191. DE, BIMALESWAR. "Questionnaire Measurement of Neuroticism and Extraversion in Normal Subjects." *Indian J Appl Psychol* 3:77–8 Jl '66. *

192. DEVADASAN, K. "Academic Achievement and Certain Selected Personality Variables." *J Voc & Ed Guid* 12:81–4 My '66. *

193. DEVADASAN, K. "Personality Factors and Bias in Ratiocination." *Indian J Psychol* 41:55–8 Je '66. *

194. FARLEY, FRANK H. "Individual Differences in Free Response-Speed." *Percept & Motor Skills* 22:557–8 Ap '66. * *(PA* 40:8851)

195. GUPTA, VED PRAKASH. "Persistence for Mental Task

Intraversion and Extraversion." *Indian J Psychol* 41:8–10 S '66. *

196. GUTMAN, GLORIA M. "A Note on the MPI: Age and Sex Differences in Extraversion and Neuroticism in a Canadian Sample." *Brit J Social & Clin Psychol* 5:128–9 Je '66. * (*PA* 40:9433, title only)

197. HOGAN, MARTIN J. "Influence of Motivation on Reactive Inhibition in Extraversion-Introversion." *Percept & Motor Skills* 22:187–92 F '66. * (*PA* 40:4873)

198. HUNT, WILLIAM A.; QUAY, HERBERT C.; and WALKER, RONALD E. "The Validity of Clinical Judgments of Asocial Tendency." *J Clin Psychol* 22:116–8 Ja '66. * (*PA* 40:4410)

199. INGHAM, J. G. "Changes in M.P.I. Scores in Neurotic Patients: A Three Year Follow-up." *Brit J Psychiatry* 112: 931–9 S '66. * (*PA* 41:694)

200. LEVY, PHILIP. "Effect of a Depressive Illness on M.P.I. Scores." Letter. *Brit J Psychiatry* 112:103–4 Ja 60. *

201. LEY, P.; SPELMAN, M. S.; DAVIES, ANN D. M.; and RILEY, S. "The Relationships Between Intelligence, Anxiety, Neuroticism and Extraversion." *Brit J Ed Psychol* 36:185–91 Je '66. * (*PA* 40:10100)

202. LUCAS, C. J.; KELVIN, R. P.; and OJHA, A. B. "Mental Health and Student Wastage." *Brit J Psychiatry* 112:277–84 Mr '66. * (*PA* 40:7958)

203. NOWICKI, STEPHEN, JR. "Factor Analysis of Responses to Various Paper and Pencil Tests." *Newsl Res Psychol* 8:28–9 My '66. *

204. OJHA, A. B.; KELVIN, R. P.; and LUCAS, C. J. "The Use of the Maudsley Personality Inventory on University Students." *Brit J Psychiatry* 112:543–8 Je '66. * (*PA* 40: 10123)

205. PAYNE, R. W.; DAVIDSON, P. O.; and SLOANE, R. B. "The Prediction of Academic Success in University Students: A Pilot Study." *Can J Psychol* 20:52–63 Mr '66. * (*PA* 40: 7054)

206. PUROHIT, ARJUN P. "Levels of Introversion and Competitional Paired-Associate Learning." *J Personality* 34: 129–43 Mr '66. * (*PA* 40:8863)

207. RADCLIFFE, J. A. "A Note on Questionnaire Faking With 16 PFQ and MPI." *Austral J Psychol* 18:154–7 Ag '66. * (*PA* 41:10479)

208. RAO, SHARADAMBA. "A Note on the Investigation of the MPI With Different Occupational Groups in India." *Brit J Social & Clin Psychol* 5:274–5 D '66. * (*PA* 41:4605, title only)

209. RAO, SHARADAMBA. "Occupational Role and Personality: A Comparative Study of a Few Occupational Groups in India." *Indian J Psychol* 41:59–64 Je '66. * (*PA* 41:2887)

210. SINGH, S. D.; GUPTA, V. P.; and MANOCHA, S. N. "Physical Persistence, Personality and Drugs." *Indian J Appl Psychol* 3:92–5 Jl '66. *

211. SINGH, UDAI PRATAP. "Another Study of a Hindi Version of the Maudsley Personality Inventory (MPI)." *Indian Psychol R* 3:57–8 Jl '66. * (*PA* 41:8167)

212. STANLEY, GORDON, and BOWNES, A. F. "Self-Disclosure and Neuroticism." *Psychol Rep* 18:350 Ap '66. * (*PA* 40: 8867, title only)

213. STERN, HERBERT, and GROSZ, HANUS J. "Personality Correlates of Patient Interactions in Group Psychotherapy." *Psychol Rep* 18:411–4 Ap '66. * (*PA* 40:8938)

214. STERN, HERBERT, and GROSZ, HANUS J. "Verbal Interactions in Group Psychotherapy Between Patients With Similar and With Dissimilar Personalities." *Psychol Rep* 19: 1111–4 D '66. * (*PA* 41:4691)

215. AL-ISSA, IHSAN, and KRAFT, TOM. "Personality Factors in Behaviour Therapy." *Can Psychologist* 8a:218–22 Jl '67. * (*PA* 42:832)

216. ARMSTRONG, HUBERT E., JR.; JOHNSON, MONTY H.; RIES, HAROLD A.; and HOLMES, DOUGLAS S. "Extraversion-Introversion and Process-Reactive Schizophrenia." *Brit J Social & Clin Psychol* 6:69 F '67. * (*PA* 41:7565, title only)

217. BROWN, L. B., and FERNALD, L. DODGE, JR. "Questionnaire Anxiety." *Psychol Rep* 21:537–40 O '67. * (*PA* 42:5593)

218. CHOUNGOURIAN, ASSADOR. "Introversion-Extraversion and Color Preferences." *J Proj Tech & Pers Assess* 31:92–4 Ag '67. * (*PA* 41:15303)

219. CLAEYS, WILLEM. "Conforming Behavior and Personality Variables in Congolese Students." *Int J Psychol* 2(1): 13–23 '67. * (*PA* 41:10427)

220. CLARIDGE, GORDON S. *Personality and Arousal: A Psychophysiological Study of Psychiatric Disorder.* Oxford, England: Pergamon Press, 1967. Pp. xviii, 274. *

221. DARR, RALPH FRANK, JR. *Psychological and Physiological Predictors of Semantic Conditioning.* Doctor's thesis, Southern Illinois University (Carbondale, Ill.), 1967. (*DA* 28:3894B)

222. DHAPOLA, T. S. "Adjustment and Extroversion-Neuroticism." *Indian Psychol R* 3:147–50 Ja '67. * (*PA* 41:8869)

223. DU PREEZ, P. "Field Dependence and Accuracy of Comparison of Time Intervals." *Percept & Motor Skills* 24: 467–72 Ap '67. * (*PA* 41:9686)

224. DUTT, N. K. "Adaption of M.P.I. on Indian Population." *Psychol Studies* 12:66–9 Ja '67. *

225. EVANS, FREDERICK J. "Field Dependence and the Maudsley Personality Inventory." *Percept & Motor Skills* 24: 526 Ap '67. * (*PA* 41:9711)

226. Feather, N. T. "Some Personality Correlates of External Control." *Austral J Psychol* 19:253–60 D '67. *

227. FENTON, GEORGE W., and SCOTTON, LEILA. "Personality and the Alpha Rhythm." *Brit J Psychiatry* 113:1283–9 N '67. * (*PA* 42:5799)

228. GOLIN, SANFORD; HERRON, E. WAYNE; LAKOTA, ROBERT; and REINECK, LINDA. "Factor Analytic Study of the Manifest Anxiety, Extraversion, and Repression-Sensitization Scales." *J Consult Psychol* 31:564–9 D '67. * (*PA* 42:1406)

229. KELLNER, R., and SHEFFIELD, B. F. "Symptom Rating Test Scores in Neurotics and Normals." *Brit J Psychiatry* 113:525–6 My '67. * (*PA* 41:12112)

230. LAKIE, WILLIAM L. "Relationship of Galvanic Skin Response to Task Difficulty, Personality Traits, and Motivation." *Res Q* 38:58–63 Mr '67. * (*PA* 41:6815)

231. MANGAN, GORDON L. "Studies of the Relationship Between Neo-Pavlovian Properties of Higher Nervous Activity and Western Personality Dimensions: 4, A Factor Analytic Study of Extraversion and Flexibility, and the Sensitivity and Mobility of the Nervous System." *J Exp Res Personality* 2: 124–7 My '67. * (*PA* 41:11908)

232. MANGAN, GORDON L., and FARMER, RONALD G. "Studies of the Relationship Between Neo-Pavlovian Properties of Higher Nervous Activity and Western Personality Dimensions: 1, The Relationship of Nervous Strength and Sensitivity to Extraversion." *J Exp Res Personality* 2:101–6 My '67. * (*PA* 41:11905)

233. NOWICKI, STEPHEN, JR. "Birth Order and Personality: Some Unexpected Findings." *Psychol Rep* 21:265–7 Ag '67. * (*PA* 42:2755)

234. OYAMADA, TAKAAKI. "Two Modes of the Self-Image." *Tohuko Psychologica Folia* 25(3–4):97–103 '67. *

235. PAYNE, ELSIE. "Musical Taste and Personality." *Brit J Psychol* 58:133–8 My '67. * (*PA* 42:10553)

236. PAYNE, R. W.; NETLEY, C. T.; and SLOANE, R. B. "Rigidity, Drive and Conditioning in Neurotics." *Brit J Psychol* 58:111–26 My '67. * (*PA* 42:10857)

237. PEMBERTON, D. A. "A Comparison of the Outcome of Treatment in Female and Male Alcoholics." *Brit J Psychiatry* 113:367–73 Ap '67. * (*PA* 41:10684)

238. RIDDING, L. W. "An Investigation of Personality Measures Associated With Over and Under Achievement in English and Arithmetic." *Brit J Ed Psychol* 37:397–8 N '67. * (*PA* 42:6153) Abstract of master's thesis, University of Manchester (Manchester, England), 1966.

239. ROSENBERG, C. M. "Personality and Obsessional Neurosis." *Brit J Psychiatry* 113:471–7 My '67. * (*PA* 41:12174)

240. SINGH, UDAI PRATAP. "Extraversion-Neuroticism: Their Distribution in Criminals." *Indian J Appl Psychol* 4:24–7 Ja '67. *

241. SINHA, AWADHESH K. "Psychology and Non-Psychology College Males: A Comparison on Some Personality Traits." *J Voc & Ed Guid (Bombay)* 13:13–7 F '67. *

242. SOLOMAN, EDITH. "Personality Factors and Attitudes of Mature Training College Students." *Brit J Ed Psychol* 37: 140–2 F '67. *

243. STEIN, STEVEN H., and HARRISON, ROBERT H. "Conscious and Preconscious Influences on Recall: A Reassessment and Extension." *Psychol Rep* 20:963–74 Je '67. * (*PA* 41: 13062)

244. SWIHART, PHILLIP J. *Dominance and Submission in Same- and Opposite-Sex Dyads.* Doctor's thesis, Purdue University (Lafayette, Ind.), 1967. (*DA* 28:4766B)

245. TAFT, RONALD. "Extraversion, Neuroticism, and Expressive Behavior: An Application of Wallach's Moderator Effect to Handwriting Analysis." *J Personality* 35:570–84 D '67. *

246. WATSON, DAVID L. "Introversion, Neuroticism, Rigidity, and Dogmatism." Abstract. *J Consult Psychol* 31:105 F '67. * (*PA* 41:4613, title only)

247. BLACKBURN, R. "The Scores of Eysenck's Criterion Groups on Some MMPI Scales Related to Emotionality and Extraversion." *Brit J Social & Clin Psychol* 7:3–12 F '68. * (*PA* 42:8978)

248. CAMERON, A., and HINTON, JOHN. "Delay in Seeking Treatment for Mammary Tumors." *Cancer* 21:1121–6 Je '68. * (*PA* 42:10843)

249. CLUM, GEORGE A. "Intervening Variables in Unaware Subjects in a Verbal Conditioning Task." *Psychol Rep* 22: 195–8 F '68. * (*PA* 42:10843)

250. FINE, BERNARD J., and SWEENEY, DONALD R. "Personality Traits, and Situational Factors, and Catecholamine Excretion." *J Exp Res Personality* 3:15–27 Je '68. * (*PA* 42:16867)

251. GELDER, M. G. "Verbal Conditioning as a Measure of Interpersonal Influence in Psychiatric Interviews." *Brit J Social & Clin Psychol* 7:194–209 S '68. *

252. GUPTA, VED PARKASH. "Persistence for Mental Task, Sex, Introversion and Extraversion." *Indian J Appl Psychol* 5:45–7 Ja '68. *

253. HUGGAN, R. R. "A Critique and Possible Reinterpretation of the Observed Low Neuroticism Scores of Male Patients With Lung Cancer." Comment by David M. Kissen. *Brit J Social & Clin Psychol* 7:122–8 Je '68. * (*PA* 42:17557)

254. HUNDLEBY, JOHN D., and CONNOR, WILLIAM H. "Interrelationships Between Personality Inventories: The 16 PF, the MMPI, and the MPI." *J Consult & Clin Psychol* 32:152–7 Ap '68. * (*PA* 42:8981)

255. JAWANDA, J. S. "Superstition and Personality." *J Psychol Res* 12:21–4 Ja '68. * (*PA* 41:5333)

256. KELLNER, R.; KELLY, A. V.; and SHEFFIELD, B. F.

"The Assessment of Changes in Anxiety in a Drug Trial: A Comparison of Methods." *Brit J Psychiatry* 114:863–9 Jl '68. *

257. KENYON, F. E. "Studies in Female Homosexuality—Psychological Test Results." *J Consult & Clin Psychol* 32:510–3 O '68. * (*PA* 43:1121)

258. KISSEN, DAVID M. "Some Methodological Problems in Clinical Psychosomatic Research With Special Reference to Chest Disease." *Psychosom Med* 30:324–35 My–Je '68. *

259. LESTER, DAVID. "Suicide as an Aggressive Act: A Replication With a Control for Neuroticism." *J General Psychol* 79:83–6 Jl '68. * (*PA* 42:17418)

260. LITTLE, J. CRAWFORD, and KERR, T. A. "Some Differences Between Published Norms and Data From Matched Controls as a Basis for Comparison With Psychiatrically-Disturbed Groups." *Brit J Psychiatry* 114:883–90 Jl '68. * (*PA* 43:1757)

261. MEGARGEE, EDWIN I., and SWARTZ, JON D. "Extraversion, Neuroticism, and Scores on the Holtzman Inkblot Technique." *J Proj Tech & Pers Assess* 32:262–5 Je '68. * (*PA* 42:15471)

262. MEYER, ADOLF-ERNST; GOLLE, RENATE; and WEITEMEYER, WOLFGANG. "Duration of Illness and Elevation of Neuroticism Scores: A Psychometric Correlation Study of Males With Bronchial Asthma, Pulmonary Tuberculosis or Cardiac Valve Lesions." *J Psychosom Res* 11:347–55 Mr '68. * (*PA* 42:15943)

263. POWER, R. P. "Simulation of Stable and Neurotic Personalities by Subjects Warned of the Presence of Lie Scales in Inventories." *Brit J Psychol* 59:105–9 My '68. * (*PA* 42:13787)

264. SHAPIRO, ARNOLD. *The Relationship Between Self Concept and Self Disclosure.* Doctor's thesis, Purdue University (Lafayette, Ind.), 1968. (*DA* 29:1180B)

265. SINGH, A. "Interests, Values and Personality Traits of Students Specializing in Different Fields of Study in University." *Ed R* 21:41–55 N '68. *

266. SINHA, AWADHESH KUMAR. "Psychology and Non-Psychology College Women: A Comparison on Some Personality Traits." *Psychol Studies* 13:94–7 Jl '68. *

NAME INDEX

[162]

Maxfield-Buchholz Scale of Social Maturity for Use With Preschool Blind Children. Infancy–6 years; 1958; revision of *Maxfield-Fjeld Adaptation of the Vineland Social Maturity Scale;* manual title is *A Social Maturity Scale for Blind Preschool Children;* individual; 1 form ['58, 6 pages]; manual ['58, 46 pages]; record form ['58, 7 pages]; no data on reliability; 10¢ per record form; 75¢ per manual; 75¢ per specimen set; postpaid; Kathryn E. Maxfield

and Sandra Buchholz; American Foundation for the Blind, Inc. *
See 6:139 (2 references).

[163]

Memory-For-Designs Test. Ages 8.5 and over; 1946–60; MFDT; brain damage; individual; 1 form ('60, 15 cards, identical with cards distributed by the authors in 1946); revised manual ('60, 43 pages, reprinted from 12 below); norms-scoring examples booklet (12 pages, reprinted from manual); $8.50 per set of test materials including manual; $2.50 per manual; cash orders postpaid; (5–10) minutes; Frances K. Graham and Barbara S. Kendall; Psychological Test Specialists. *

For a review by Otfried Spreen, see 6:140 (18 references); see also 4:69 (5 references).

REFERENCES

1–5. See 4:69.
6–23. See 6:140.
24. GALLAGHER, JAMES J. *A Comparison of Brain-Injured and Non-Brain-Injured Mentally Retarded Children on Several Psychological Variables.* Monograph of the Society for Research in Child Development, Vol. 22, No. 2. Lafayette, Ind.: Child Development Publications, 1957. Pp. 79. * (*PA* 33:1632)
25. ADLER, MILTON LEON. *Differences in Bright Low-Achieving and High-Achieving Ninth Grade Pupils.* Doctor's thesis, University of Illinois (Urbana, Ill.), 1963. (*DA* 24:5184)
26. KNOX, WILMA J., and WHALEY, DONALD. "Objective Scores of Non-Hospitalized Schizophrenic Veterans and Non-Hospitalized Psychotic Brain-Damaged Veterans on Selected Tests for Organic Involvement." *Newsl Res Psychol* 5:36–8 N '63. *
27. MACKIE, JAMES BENJAMIN. *A Comparative Study of Brain Damaged and Normal Individuals on Tests of Intelligence, Perception and Rigidity.* Doctor's thesis, University of Utah (Salt Lake City, Utah), 1963. (*DA* 24:1700)
28. RICHIE, JOAN, and BUTLER, ALFRED J. "Performance of Retardates on the Memory-for-Designs Test." *J Clin Psychol* 20:108–10 Ja '64. * (*PA* 39:10147)
29. ANGLIN, RAYMOND; PULLEN, MAXWELL; and GAMES, PAUL. "Comparison of Two Tests of Brain Damage." *Percept & Motor Skills* 20:977–80 Je '65. * (*PA* 40:12567)
30. NEWCOMBE, FREDA. "Memory-for-Designs Test: The Performance of Ex-Servicemen With Missile Wounds of the Brain." *Brit J Social & Clin Psychol* 4:230–1 S '65. * (*PA* 40:1101)
31. FJELD, STANTON P.; SMALL, IVER F.; SMALL, JOYCE G.; and HAYDEN, MARY P. "Clinical, Electrical and Psychological Tests and the Diagnosis of Organic Brain Disorder." *J Nerv & Mental Dis* 142:172–9 F '66. * (*PA* 40:11285)
32. KENDALL, BARBARA S. "Orientation Errors in the Memory-for-Designs Test: Tentative Findings and Recommendations." *Percept & Motor Skills* 22:335–45 Ap '66. * (*PA* 40:8260)
33. DAVIES, ANN D. M. "Age and the Memory-for-Designs Test." *Brit J Social & Clin Psychol* 6:228–33 S '67. * (*PA* 42:526)
34. BOURESTOM, NORMAN C., and HOWARD, MARY T. "Behavioral Correlates of Recovery of Self-Care in Hemiplegic Patients." *Arch Phys Med & Rehabil* 49:449–54 Ag '68. *
35. LYLE, J. G. "Performance of Retarded Readers on the Memory-for-Designs Test." *Percept & Motor Skills* 26:851–4 Je '68. * (*PA* 42:16017)
36. QUATTLEBAUM, LAWRENCE F. "A Brief Note on the Relationship Between Two Psychomotor Tests." *J Clin Psychol* 24:198–9 Ap '68. * (*PA* 42:12596)
37. STERNLICHT, MANNY; PUSTEL, GABRIEL; and SIEGEL, LOUIS. "Comparison of Organic and Cultural-Familial Retardates on Two Visual-Motor Tasks." *Am J Mental Def* 72:887–9 My '68. * (*PA* 42:14073)
38. WATSON, CHARLES G. "The Separation of NP Hospital Organics From Schizophrenics With Three Visual Motor Screening Tests." *J Clin Psychol* 24:412–4 O '68. * (*PA* 43:4168)

NAME INDEX

[164]

★**Mental Status Schedule.** Psychiatric patients and nonpatients; 1964–66; MSS; standardized interview schedule and matching inventory of present-absent items descriptive of pathological behavior; 3 macro scores (feelings-concern, confusion-retardation, delusions-hallucinations), 13 factor scores (inappropriate-bizarre, belligerence-negativism, agitation-excitement, retardation-withdrawal, speech disorganization, suspicion-persecution-hallucinations, grandiosity, depression-anxiety, suicide-self mutilation, somatic concerns, social isolation, disorientation-memory, denial of illness), and 22 supplemental scores (anxiety, auditory hallucinations, conversion reaction, depression-suicide, dissociation, elated mood, grandiosity non-delusional, grandiose psychoticism, guilt non-delusional, inappropriate-bizarre, incoherence, schizophrenic, nonspecific complaints, obsessions-compulsions, persecutory delusions, phobia, silliness, sociopath, somatic preoccupation, somatic delusions, somatic hallucinations, visual hallucinations); Form A ('64, 10 pages); manual ('66, 9 pages); inventory record sheet ('64, 2 pages); 50¢ per examiner's booklet; 5¢ per score sheet; 10¢ per inventory record sheet; 50¢ per manual; $3 per set of keys and teaching tape; specimen set free; fee for editing, coding, key punching, and verifying score sheets, 25¢ per subject; postage extra; scoring service with profile printout is available; (20–50) minutes; Robert L. Spitzer, Eugene I. Burdock (test), Anne S. Hardesty (test), Jean Endicott (manual), and George M. Cohen (manual); Biometrics Research, New York State Psychiatric Institute. *

REFERENCES

1. SPITZER, ROBERT L.; FLEISS, JOSEPH L.; BURDOCK, EUGENE I.; and HARDESTY, ANNE S. "The Mental Status Schedule: Rationale, Reliability and Validity." *Comprehen Psychiatry* 5:384–94 D '64. * (*PA* 39:12270)
2. FLEISS, JOSEPH L.; SPITZER, ROBERT L.; and BURDOCK, EUGENE I. "Estimating Accuracy of Judgment Using Recorded Interviews." *Arch Gen Psychiatry* 12:562–7 Je '65. * (*PA* 39:12410)
3. SPITZER, ROBERT L. "Immediately Available Record of Mental Status Exam: The Mental Status Schedule Inventory." *Arch Gen Psychiatry* 13:76–8 Jl '65. * (*PA* 39:15568)
4. SPITZER, ROBERT L.; FLEISS, JOSEPH; KERNOHAN, WILLIAM; LEE, JOAN C.; and BALDWIN, INGRAM T. "Mental Status Schedule: Comparing Kentucky and New York Schizophrenics." *Arch Gen Psychiatry* 12:448–55 My '65. *
5. DENNEY, DUANE; QUASS, ROBERT M.; RICH, DEAN C.; and THOMPSON, JUDITH K. "Psychiatric Patients on Medical Wards: 1, Prevalence of Illness and Recognition of Disorders by Staff Personnel." *Arch Gen Psychiatry* 14:530–5 My '66. *
6. SPITZER, ROBERT L. "Mental Status Schedule: Potential Use as a Criterion Measure of Change in Psychotherapy Research." *Am J Psychother* 20:156–67 Ja '66. *
7. SPITZER, ROBERT L.; ENDICOTT, JEAN; and FLEISS, JOSEPH L. "Instruments and Recording Forms for Evaluating Psychiatric Status and History: Rationale, Method of Development and Description." *Comprehen Psychiatry* 8:321–43 O '67. *
8. SPITZER, ROBERT L.; FLEISS, JOSEPH L.; ENDICOTT, JEAN; and COHEN, JACOB. "Mental Status Schedule: Properties of Factor-Analytically Derived Scales." *Arch Gen Psychiatry* 16:479–93 Ap '67. * (*PA* 41:10669)

[165]

Minnesota Counseling Inventory. High school; 1953–57; MCI; based on *Minnesota Multiphasic Personality Inventory* and *Minnesota Personality Scale*;

9 scores: family relationships, social relationships, emotional stability, conformity, adjustment to reality, mood, leadership, validity, question; 1 form ('53, 10 pages); profile ('57, 2 pages); manual ('57, 27 pages); no data on reliability of question score; separate answer sheets (IBM 805) must be used; $3.80 per 25 tests; $3.75 per 50 sets of answer sheet and profile; 90¢ per set of hand scoring stencils and manual; $1.50 per set of machine scoring stencils and manual; $1 per specimen set; postpaid; (50) minutes; Ralph F. Berdie and Wilbur L. Layton; Psychological Corporation. *

For reviews by Norman Frederiksen and John W. M. Rothney, see 6:142 (10 references); see also 5:85 (1 excerpt).

REFERENCES

1–10. See 6:142.
11. JONES, ELVET GLYN. An Analytical Study of the Relationship Between the Expression of Familial Conflict and the Presence of Potential Counseling Problems in Male Adolescents. Doctor's thesis, University of Minnesota (Minneapolis, Minn.), 1958. (DA 19:2852)
12. EGERMEIER, JOHN CARL. Construction and Validation of a College Dropout Predictor Scale for the Minnesota Counseling Inventory. Doctor's thesis, Oklahoma State University (Stillwater, Okla.), 1963. (DA 25:1000)
13. KETCHERSIDE, WILLIAM JOSEPH. Creative and Adjustive Factors Involved in Educational Development Beyond Expectancy. Doctor's thesis, University of Missouri (Columbia, Mo.), 1963. (DA 24:4545)
14. SAXON, SUE VIRGINIA. Test Profile Characteristics of Selected Behavioral Pattern Groups of Freshmen Women Residents on the Minnesota Counseling Inventory. Doctor's thesis, Florida State University (Tallahassee, Fla.), 1963. (DA 24:4553)
15. SINGLESTAD, ROBERT. A Comparative Study of the Structured Student Autobiography and the Minnesota Counseling Inventory. Master's thesis, Mankato State College (Mankato, Minn.), 1963.
16. BERDIE, RALPH F., and HOOD, ALBERT B. "Personal Values and Attitudes as Determinants of Post-High School Plans." Personnel & Guid J 42:754–9 Ap '64. * (PA 39:4764)
17. BERNAUER, CAMILLA R. A Validation Study of the Beck Word-Color Association Test With the Minnesota Counseling Inventory. Master's thesis, State College of Iowa (Cedar Falls, Iowa), 1964.
18. BIERMAN, RALPH; CARKHUFF, ROBERT R.; and LEPENDORF, STANLEY. "A Factor Analysis of the Minnesota Counseling Inventory for Adolescents." J Ed Res 58:186–7 D '64. *
19. KREGER, EUGENE C. Performance of Institutionalized Students on the Minnesota Counseling Inventory. Master's thesis, State College of Iowa (Cedar Falls, Iowa), 1964.
20. LARSON, ROLAND SIGWARD. A Study of Selected Personality Factors Associated With High School Dropout. Doctor's thesis, Michigan State University (East Lansing, Mich.), 1964. (DA 25:4544)
21. ROBB, HERBERT EDWARD. Factors Associated With Socio-Political Involvement of Suburban High School Youth. Doctor's thesis, New York University (New York, N.Y.), 1964. (DA 26:4111)
22. SALBER, EVA J., and ROCHMAN, JOAN E. "Personality Differences Between Smokers and Nonsmokers: A Study of School Children." Arch Environ Health 8:459–65 Mr '64. *
23. SMITH, ANITA PEARL. Differential Personality Characteristics Associated With Participation in High School Student Activities. Doctor's thesis, University of Minnesota (Minneapolis, Minn.), 1964. (DA 25:1759)
24. CRABTREE, BEVERLY DELES-DERNIER. Predicting and Determining Effectiveness of Homemaking Teachers. Doctor's thesis, Iowa State University (Ames, Iowa), 1965. (DA 26:6013)
25. SEYMOUR, PAUL JOHN. A Study of the Relationships Between the Communication Skills and a Selected Set of Predictors and of the Relationships Among the Communication Skills. Doctor's thesis, University of Minnesota (Minneapolis, Minn.), 1965. (DA 26:549)
26. SHOUKSMITH, GEORGE, and HARRISON, R. J. "A Note on a Scale for Measuring Student Adjustment." Austral J Psychol 17:140–2 Ag '65. * (PA 40:885)
27. SURETTE, RALPH FRANCIS. The Relationship of Personal and Work-Value Orientations to Career Versus Homemaking Preference Among Twelfth Grade Girls. Doctor's thesis, Catholic University of America (Washington, D.C.), 1965. (DA 26:4462)
28. WATLEY, DONIVAN J. "The Minnesota Counseling Inventory and Persistence in an Institute of Technology." J Counsel Psychol 12:94–7 sp '65. *
29. ZOOLALIAN, CHARLES H. "Factors Related to Differential Achievement Among Boys in Ninth-Grade Algebra." J Ed Res 58:205–7 Ja '65. *
30. BERDIE, RALPH F., and HOOD, ALBERT B. "How Effectively Do We Predict Plans for College Attendance?" Personnel & Guid J 44:487–93 Ja '66. * (PA 40:5899)
31. ELLIS, MIRIAM WEDGE. The Validation of the Minnesota Counseling Inventory for Freshmen in Residence Halls at the University of Arkansas. Doctor's thesis, University of Arkansas (Fayetteville, Ark.), 1966. (DA 27:670A)
32. HARRISON, R. J. "Predictive Validity of Some Adjustment Tests: A Research Note." Austral J Psychol 18:284–7 D '66. * (PA 41:4596)
33. LEWIS, LESLIE. A Multivariate Analysis of Variables Associated With Academic Success Within a College Environment. Doctor's thesis, Oklahoma State University (Stillwater, Okla.), 1966. (DA 27:4134A)
34. SAGE, ELLIS HENRY. The Development of Age Difference Scales by Sex From Item Response Change Between the Ninth Grade and Entrance Into College on the Minnesota Counseling Inventory. Doctor's thesis, University of Minnesota (Minneapolis, Minn.), 1966. (DA 28:1210B)
35. SCHWENK, LILLIAN CASLER. Personality Correlates of Accident Involvement Among Young Male Drivers. Doctor's thesis, Iowa State University (Ames, Iowa), 1966. (DA 27:3734A)
36. STEIN, JUNE BEVERLY. The Relation of Two Personality Traits to Some Measures of Socio-Economic Level and Student Plans After High School. Master's thesis, University of Minnesota (Minneapolis, Minn.), 1966.
37. BARRETT, JOSEPH ANTHONY. An Investigation of Social Desirability and Acquiescence in the Minnesota Counseling Inventory. Doctor's thesis, St. John's University (Collegeville, Minn.), 1967. (DA 28:4265A)
38. CREWE, NANCY LOUISE MOE. A Comparison of Factor Analytic and Empirically Derived Scales of the Minnesota Counseling Inventory. Doctor's thesis, University of Minnesota (Minneapolis, Minn.), 1967. (DA 29:754B)
39. CREWE, NANCY M. "Comparison of Factor Analytic and Empirical Scales." Proc Ann Conv Am Psychol Assn 75:367–8 '67. * (PA 41:12824)
40. FISCHER, ERBY CURTIS. A Study of the Relationship Between Selected Personality Factors and Special Disabilities in Mathematics. Doctor's thesis, University of Alabama (University, Ala.), 1967. (DA 28:2891A)
41. HOLM, KATHRYN LOUISE. Descriptive Adjectives Associated With Measured Personality Characteristics of Liberal Arts College Freshmen. Doctor's thesis, University of Minnesota (Minneapolis, Minn.), 1967. (DA 28:497A)
42. JOHNSON, DUANE ELDON. Characteristics of Entering Students as Measured by the Minnesota Counseling Inventory in Relation to Persistence in a Liberal Arts College. Doctor's thesis, University of Minnesota (Minneapolis, Minn.), 1967. (DA 28:2096A)
43. O'SHEA, ARTHUR JOSEPH. Differences in Certain Non-Intellective Factors Between Academically Bright Junior High School Male High and Low Achievers. Doctor's thesis, Boston College (Chestnut Hill, Mass.), 1967. (DA 28:3515A)
44. BERDIE, RALPH F. "Personality Changes From High School Entrance to College Matriculation." J Counsel Psychol 15:376–80 Jl '68. * (PA 42:15987)
45. COWDEN, JAMES E.; PETERSON, WILLIAM M.; and COHEN, MICHAEL F. "The 16 PF vs. the MCI in a Group Testing Program Within a Correctional Setting." J Clin Psychol 24:221–4 Ap '68. * (PA 42:12404)
46. SAGE, ELLIS H. "Developmental Scales for College Freshmen." J Counsel Psychol 15:381–5 Jl '68. * (PA 42:16004)
47. TRUAX, CHARLES B.; SCHULDT, W. JOHN; and WARGO, DONALD G. "Self-Ideal Concept Congruence and Improvement in Group Psychotherapy." J Consult & Clin Psychol 32:47–53 F '68. * (PA 42:7399)

NAME INDEX

[166]

*Minnesota Multiphasic Personality Inventory.
Ages 16 and over; 1942–67; MMPI; 14 scores: hypochondriasis (Hs, '43), depression (D, '43), hysteria
(Hy, '43), psychopathic deviate (Pd, '43), masculinity and femininity (Mf, '43), paranoia (Pa, '43),
psychasthenia (Pt, '43), schizophrenia (Sc, '43), hypomania (Ma, '43), social (Si, '51), question (?), lie
(L), validity (F, '43), test taking attitude (K, '46);
3 editions differing in format: individual, original
group, rearranged group; revised manual ('67, 36
pages); *An MMPI Handbook* ('60, see 6:B146) by
W. Grant Dahlstrom and George Schlager Welsh, an
essential supplement to manual; sections on scale
descriptions and interpretation of scores omitted from
1967 manual; normative and reliability data unchanged
since 1951; $1.50 per manual; $11.70 per MMPI
Handbook; $23 per set of tapes for nonreading ad-
ministration; postpaid; for computerized scoring and
interpreting services, see 167–9; Spanish edition available; Starke R. Hathaway and J. Charnley McKinley; Psychological Corporation. *
a) INDIVIDUAL FORM ("THE CARD SET"). 1942–51; 550
cards plus sorting guides ('43); record blank ('48,
2 pages); $29 per set of testing materials including
50 record blanks; $4 per 50 record blanks; (30–90)
minutes.
b) OLD GROUP FORM ("THE BOOKLET FORM"). 1943–51;
items same as in individual form; test ('43, 15 pages);
profile ('48, 2 pages); separate answer sheets (Hankes,
IBM 805 and 1230, NCS) must be used; $6.50 per
25 tests; $4.20 per 50 sets of IBM 805 answer sheets
and profiles; $4.60 per 50 sets of IBM 1230 answer
sheets and profiles; $3.30 per 50 Hankes answer
sheets; $3.50 per 50 NCS answer sheets; $6($7.50)
per set of manual and IBM 805 hand scoring (machine
scoring) stencils; $1.90 per specimen set; Hankes
scoring service, $1 to 48¢ per test; NCS scoring serv-
ice, 50¢ to 35¢ per test; NCS scoring and computer
interpretation printout, $3 to $1.40 per test; (40–90)
minutes.
c) NEW GROUP FORM (FORM R). 1965, c1943–66; new
sequence of items with the 399 items used to obtain
the 14 scores appearing first and the 167 research or
nonfunctioning items last; shortened versions consist
of the first 399 items or if K and Si scales are not
wanted, 366 items; hard cover booklet ('66, 23 step-
down pages) doubles as lapboard; separate NCS
answer sheets must be used; $2 to $1.50 per test; $4.50
per 50 answer sheets; $4.50 per set of manual and
hand scoring stencils; $3 per specimen set; NCS scor-
ing service same as for old group form; (40–90) minutes for complete form, (40–75) minutes for shortened
version.

For reviews by C. J. Adcock and James C. Lingoes,
see 6:143 (626 references); for reviews by Albert
Ellis and Warren T. Norman, see 5:86 (496 references); for a review by Arthur L. Benton, see 4:71
(211 references); for reviews by Arthur L. Benton,
H. J. Eysenck, L. S. Penrose, and Julian B. Rotter,
see 3:60 (72 references, 1 excerpt); for related book
reviews, see 4:72; for reviews not excerpted in this
volume, consult the 6th (B64, B113, B146, B159, B206,
B241, B414) and 5th (B199, B200, B467) MMY's.

REFERENCES

1–72. See 3:60.
73–283. See 4:71.
284–779. See 5:86.
780–1394. See 6:143.
1395. GOUGH, HARRISON G. "A New Dimension of Status:
3, Discrepancies Between the St Scale and 'Objective' Status."
Am Sociol R 14:275–81 Ap '49. * (*PA* 24:626)
1396. CLARK, JERRY H. "Interest Variability on the California Test of Mental Maturity in Relation to the Minnesota
Multiphasic Personality Inventory." *J Consult Psychol* 14:
32–4 F '50. * (*PA* 24:4112)

1397. GRIFFITH, RICHARD MARION. *Typical Dreams: A Statistical Study of Personality Correlates.* Doctor's thesis, University of Kentucky (Lexington, Ky.), 1950. (*DA* 18:1106)
1398. GROSSMAN, DONNA J. *A Study of the Parents of Stuttering and Non-Stuttering Children Using the Minnesota Multiphasic Personality Inventory and the Minnesota Scale of
Parents' Opinions.* Master's thesis, University of Wisconsin
(Madison, Wis.), 1951. (Abstract: *Speech Monogr* 19:193)
1399. WHITE, ASHER A. "Evaluation of Psychogenic Symptoms in General Medicine: Use of the Minnesota Multiphasic
Personality Inventory." *J Am Med Assn* 147:1521–6 D 15
'51. *
1400. HAND, THOMAS J. "Personality Characteristics of a
Tuberculosis Group." *Am J Phys Med* 31:95–101 Ap '52. *
(*PA* 27:2154)
1401. CROWELL, DAVID HARRISON. "Personality and Physical
Disease: A Test of the Dunbar Hypothesis Applied to Diabetes
Mellitus and Rheumatic Fever." *Genetic Psychol Monogr* 48:
117–53 Ag '53. * (*PA* 28:4710)
1402. MELTON, RICHARD S. "Studies in the Evaluation of
the Personality Characteristics of Successful Naval Aviators."
J Aviat Med 25:600–4+ D '54. * (*PA* 29:9038)
1403. JALKANEN, R. J. *The Personality Structure of Seminarians: The Use of Available MMPI Norms for Diagnosis.*
Master's thesis, Roosevelt University (Chicago, Ill.), 1955.
1404. KAHN, DOUGLAS MORTIMER. *The Relationship of Certain Personality Characteristics to Recovery From Tuberculosis.*
Doctor's thesis, New York University (New York, N.Y.), 1955.
(*DA* 15:1256)
1405. ALMOS, KERMIT ODELL. *A Study of Interrelationships
Between Measured Satisfaction With College and Certain
Academic and Personality Variables.* Doctor's thesis, University
of Minnesota (Minneapolis, Minn.), 1956. (*DA* 17:561)
1406. BOYCE, ERNEST MARSHALL. *A Comparative Study of
Overachieving and Underachieving College Students on Factors Other Than Scholastic Aptitude.* Doctor's thesis, University of Wisconsin (Madison, Wis.), 1956. (*DA* 16:2088)
1407. CHRISTENSEN, GEORGE MILFORD. *The Relationship Between Visual Discrimination and Certain Personality Variables.* Doctor's thesis, University of Minnesota (Minneapolis,
Minn.), 1956. (*DA* 17:901)
1408. KINGSLEY, LEONARD. *A Comparative Study of Certain Personality Characteristics of Psychopathic and Non-
Psychopathic Offenders in a Military Disciplinary Barracks:
With Reference to the Personality Characteristics of Immaturity, Impulsivity, Hostility, Avoidance, Superficiality, Shallowness, Anxiety, Guilt, Egocentricity, and Facility in Performance Tasks.* Doctor's thesis, New York University (New York,
N.Y.), 1956. (*DA* 16:2212)
1409. MILLER, SAMUEL CHARLES; THALLER, JACK L.; and
SOBERMAN, ALEXANDER. "The Use of the Minnesota Multiphasic Personality Inventory as a Diagnostic Aid in Periodontal
Disease: A Preliminary Report." *J Periodont* 27:44–6 Ja '56. *
1410. NORRIS, VERLYN L. *Relationships Between Susceptibility to Perceptual Interference and Personality Characteristics.* Doctor's thesis, Purdue University (Lafayette, Ind.),
1956. (*DA* 17:409)
1411. GLOTZBACH, CHARLES JEROME. *Intellectual and Non-
intellectual Characteristics Associated With Persistence of
Women in an Elementary and Nursery School Teacher-Education Program.* Doctor's thesis, University of Minnesota (Minneapolis, Minn.), 1957. (*DA* 18:146)
1412. HICKMAN, NORMAN WILLIAM. *The Role of Self-Related-Concept Discrepancies in Personal Adjustment.* Doctor's
thesis, University of Oregon (Eugene, Ore.), 1957. (*DA* 19:
2656)
1413. JENSEN, VERN HARMON. *An Analysis and Comparison
of the Adjustment Problems of Nonachieving College Students
of Low Scholastic Ability and Other Groups of Achieving and
Nonachieving Students.* Doctor's thesis, University of Colorado
(Boulder, Colo.), 1957. (*DA* 19:70)
1414. ROWE, FREDERICK B. *The Selection of Psychiatric
Aides: Criterion Development and Prediction.* Doctor's thesis,
University of Maryland (College Park, Md.), 1957. (*DA* 17:
2674)
1415. SNOW, BARBARA M. *An Analysis of the Relationship
of Certain Factors to the Social Acceptance Status of College
Freshman Women.* Doctor's thesis, Pennsylvania State University (University Park, Pa.), 1957. (*DA* 18:142)
1416. ABELES, NORMAN. *A Study of the Characteristics of
Counselor Trainees.* Doctor's thesis, University of Texas (Austin, Tex.), 1958. (*DA* 18:2204)
1417. BRANTNER, JOHN PATERSON. *Homeless Men, a Psychological and Medical Survey.* Doctor's thesis, University
of Minnesota (Minneapolis, Minn.), 1958. (*DA* 19:3018)
1418. BROŽEK, JOSEF, and TAYLOR, HENRY L. "Psychological Effects of Maintenance on Survival Rations." *Am J Psychol* 71:517–28 S '58. * (*PA* 34:1008)
1419. CADITZ, SYLVAN BERNARD. *The Effect of a Training
School Experience on Delinquent Boys as Measured by Objective Personality Tests.* Doctor's thesis, University of Washington (Seattle, Wash.), 1958. (*DA* 19:1812)
1420. DANSEREAU, RAYMOND A. "An Item Analysis of the
Responses of Private and Public High School Groups on the
MMPI." *Cath Counselor* 3:7–9+ f '58. *
1421. GRAYDEN, CHARLES. *The Relationship Between Neurotic Hypochondriasis and Three Personality Variables: Feeling of Being Unloved, Narcissism, and Guilt Feelings.* Doc-

tor's thesis, New York University (New York, N.Y.), 1958. (DA 18:2209)

1422. HILL, WALTER RAYMOND. *A Multivariate Comparison of College Freshmen With Adequate or Deficient Reading Comprehension*. Doctor's thesis, State University of Iowa (Iowa City, Iowa), 1958. (DA 19:3211)

1423. HOLDER, WAYNE B. "Value Conformity in Normal and Non-Normal Groups." *J Social Psychol* 48:147–54 Ag '58. * (PA 34:5722)

1424. JENSEN, VERN H., and CLARK, MONROE H. "Married and Unmarried College Students: Achievement, Ability, and Personality." *Personnel & Guid J* 37:123–5 O '58. * (PA 36:2KI23J)

1425. KOSA, JOHN; RACHIELE, LEO D.; and SCHOMMER, CYRIL O. "Psychological Characteristics of Ethnic Groups in a College Population." *J Psychol* 46:265–75 O '58. * (PA 34:3401)

1426. O'DONNELL, JERRY MYLES. *A Comparative Study of Rural and Urban Groups of College Freshmen*. Doctor's thesis, University of Alabama (University, Ala.), 1958. (DA 20:926)

1427. PINNEAU, SAMUEL R., and HOPPER, HAROLD E. "The Relationship Between Incidence of Specific Gastro-Intestinal Reactions of the Infant and Psychological Characteristics of the Mother." *J Genetic Psychol* 93:3–13 S '58. * (PA 35:1166)

1428. VOLKMAN, ARTHUR P. "A Matched-Group Personality Comparison of Delinquent and Nondelinquent Juveniles." *Social Probl* 6:238–45 w '58. * (PA 34:3252)

1429. WILKE, MARGUERITE M. *Experimentally Induced "Repression" as a Function of Personality Variables*. Doctor's thesis, New York University (New York, N.Y.), 1958. (DA 22:655)

1430. ANDERSON, ALICE VIRGINIA. *Predicting Response to Group Psychotherapy*. Doctor's thesis, University of Oklahoma (Norman, Okla.), 1959. (DA 20:1073)

1431. BAUGHMAN, E. EARL; SHANDS, HARLEY C.; and HAWKINS, DAVID R. "Intensive Psychotherapy and Personality Change: Psychological Test Evaluation of a Single Case." *Psychiatry* 22:296–301 Ag '59. * (PA 34:6667)

1432. BLOCK, DONALD S., and CALDWELL, WILLARD E. "Relationship Between Color and Affect in Paranoid Schizophrenics." *J General Psychol* 61:231–5 O '59. * (PA 35:1129)

1433. FINK, DAVID MARTIN. *Sex Differences in Perceptual Tasks in Relation to Selected Personality Variables*. Doctor's thesis, Rutgers University (New Brunswick, N.J.), 1959. (DA 20:1428)

1434. GREENFIELD, NORMAN S.; ROESSLER, ROBERT; and CROSLEY, ARCHER P., JR. "Ego Strength and Length of Recovery From Infectious Mononucleosis." *J Nerv & Mental Dis* 128:125–8 F '59. * (PA 34:4733)

1435. HEISKELL, CHARLES L.; RHODES, JOHN M.; and THAYER, KENT H. "Some Psychosomatic Aspects of Asthma." *J Am Med Assn* 170:1764–7 Ag 8 '59. *

1436. IMBODEN, JOHN B.; CANTER, ARTHUR; CLUFF, LEIGHTON E.; and TREVER, ROBERT W. "Brucellosis: 3, Psychologic Aspects of Delayed Convalescence." *A.M.A. Arch Intern Med* 103:406–14 Mr '59. * (PA 34:4734)

1437. LYON, JAMES BURKE. *A Study of Experiential Motivational, and Personality Factors Related to Vocational Decision Versus Indecision*. Doctor's thesis, University of Minnesota (Minneapolis, Minn.), 1959. (DA 20:1269)

1438. McPHERSON, JOE. "Some Comments About the Relationship Between the Industrial Research Laboratory 'Climate' and the Individual Scientist." *Univ Utah Res Conf Identif Creat Sci Talent* 3:94–103 '59. *

1439. MARTIN, BARCLAY. "The Measurement of Anxiety." *J General Psychol* 61:189–203 O '59. * (PA 35:792)

1440. MURRAY, JOHN B. "Personality Study of Priests and Seminarians." *Homiletic & Pastoral R* 59:443–7 F '59. *

1441. BARRY, WILLIAM A. *An MMPI Scale for Seminary Candidates*. Master's thesis, Fordham University (New York, N.Y.), 1960.

1442. BLAYLOCK, JOHN JOSEPH. *Verbal Conditioning Performance of Psychopaths and Non-Psychopaths Under Verbal Reward and Punishment*. Doctor's thesis, State University of Iowa (Iowa City, Iowa), 1960. (DA 21:1628)

1443. FINK, J. H. *A Psychophysiological Comparison of Brittle and Stable Diabetics*. Doctor's thesis, University of California (Los Angeles, Calif.), 1960.

1444. GABERMAN, FLORENCE KILGORE. *A Scale for Measuring Teacher Class Control and Its Relation to Personality*. Doctor's thesis, Pennsylvania State University (University Park, Pa.), 1960. (DA 21:1845)

1445. GRATER, HARRY. "Impulse Repression and Emotional Adjustment." *J Consult Psychol* 24:144–9 Ap '60. * (PA 34:8202)

1446. KANFER, FREDERICK H. "Verbal Rate, Eyeblink, and Content in Structured Psychiatric Interviews." *J Abn & Social Psychol* 61:341–7 N '60. * (PA 36:2HE41K)

1447. MATTHEWS, ROMINE ELLWOOD. *Certain Personality Variables Related to Success in Veterans' Rehabilitation Training in Clerical Occupations*. Doctor's thesis, University of Minnesota (Minneapolis, Minn.), 1960. (DA 21:127)

1448. NAKAMURA, CHARLES Y. "Measures of Over-Controlled and Under-Controlled Behavior: A Validation." *J Clin Psychol* 16:149–53 Ap '60. * (PA 36:2HB49N)

1449. QUEVILLON, NAOMI M. *Semantic Behavior of Three Different Personality Groups*. Doctor's thesis, University of Minnesota (Minneapolis, Minn.), 1960. (DA 21:242)

1450. ROSENSTEIN, ALBERT JULES. *A Comparative Study of the Role Conflict, Marital Adjustment, and Personality Configuration of Private Adoptive and Agency Adoptive Parents*. Doctor's thesis, University of Southern California (Los Angeles, Calif.), 1960. (DA 20:4208)

1451. SHAPIRO, GEORGE L. *An Inductive Investigation Into the Correlates of Ability to Predict Opinion*. Doctor's thesis, University of Minnesota (Minneapolis, Minn.), 1960. (DA 21:3196)

1452. VERTEIN, LESTER DALE. *A Study of the Personal-Social and Intellectual Characteristics of a Group of State College Students Preparing to Teach*. Doctor's thesis, University of Wisconsin (Madison, Wis.), 1960. (DA 21:1473)

1453. WERTS, CHARLES EARL, JR. *Multidimensional Analysis of Psychological Constructs*. Doctor's thesis, University of Minnesota (Minneapolis, Minn.), 1960. (DA 21:2008)

1454. ALOYSE, M. "Evaluation of Candidates for Religious Life." *Guild Cath Psychiat B* 8:199–204 O '61. *

1455. BAKER, ERNEST G.; CROOK, G. HAMILTON; and SCHWABACHER, ELSBETH D. "Personality Correlates of Periodontal Disease." *J Dent Res* 40:396–407 My–Je '61. *

1456. BELL, ROBERT LOUIS, JR. *Factors Influencing Attitudes Toward Hospital Discharge in Neuropsychiatric Patients*. Doctor's thesis, University of Texas (Austin, Tex.), 1961. (DA 22:2067)

1457. CERBUS, GEORGE. *Personality Correlates of Picture Preferences*. Doctor's thesis, Purdue University (Lafayette, Ind.), 1961. (DA 22:319)

1458. DUNLAP, NAOMI GIBSON. *Alcoholism in Women: Some Antecedents and Correlates of Remission in Middle-Class Members of Alcoholics Anonymous*. Doctor's thesis, University of Texas (Austin, Tex.), 1961. (DA 22:1904)

1459. FARAHMAND, SAIED SHAMLU. *Personality Characteristics and Child-Rearing Attitudes of Fathers of Schizophrenic Patients*. Doctor's thesis, Washington State University (Pullman, Wash.), 1961. (DA 22:1250)

1460. FIDDLEMAN, PAUL BARRY. *The Prediction of Behavior Under Lysergic Acid Diethylamide (LSD)*. Doctor's thesis, University of North Carolina (Chapel Hill, N.C.), 1961. (DA 22:2873)

1461. FOULDS, G. A. "Personality Traits and Neurotic Symptoms and Signs." *Brit J Med Psychol* 34:263–70 pt 4 '61. * (PA 37:1229)

1462. GIEDT, F. HAROLD. "Predicting Suitability for Group Psychotherapy." *Am J Psychother* 15:582–91 O '61. * (PA 38:8712)

1463. GOLDSTEIN, LAWRENCE. *Empathy and Its Relationship to Personality Factors and Personality Organization*. Doctor's thesis, New York University (New York, N.Y.), 1961. (DA 22:4402)

1464. HALBERSTAM, JACOB L. "Some Personality Correlates of Conditioning, Generalization, and Extinction." *Psychosom Med* 23:67–76 Ja–F '61. * (PA 36:3HF67H)

1465. HENRICHS, THEODORE FRED. *The Effect of Sensory Reduction and Personality Information on Self-Concept and Personal Adjustment*. Doctor's thesis, University of North Carolina (Chapel Hill, N.C.), 1961. (DA 22:2874)

1466. ILANIT, NATHAN. *Some Psychological Correlates of the Process-Reactive Concept of Schizophrenia*. Doctor's thesis, University of Southern California (Los Angeles, Calif.), 1961. (DA 21:3852)

1467. JORTNER, SIDNEY SELIG. *An Investigation of Certain Intellectual and Personality Characteristics of Multiple Sclerotics: A Comparison of the Psychological Functioning of Multiple Sclerotics With That of Brain-Damaged and Peptic Ulcer Patients as a Means of Testing the Psychosomatic Hypothesis of Multiple Sclerosis*. Doctor's thesis, New York University (New York, N.Y.), 1961. (DA 22:4406)

1468. LEREA, LOUIS, and GOLDBERG, ALVIN. "The Effects of Socialization Upon Group Behavior." *Speech Monogr* 28:60–4 Mr '61. * (PA 36:3GE60L)

1469. LICHTENSTEIN, EDWARD. *The Relation of Three Cognitive Controls to Some Perceptual and Personality Variables*. Doctor's thesis, University of Michigan (Ann Arbor, Mich.), 1961. (DA 22:2467)

1470. MULLER, BRUCE PAUL. *Personality Correlates of the Placebo Reaction*. Doctor's thesis, Columbia University (New York, N.Y.), 1961. (DA 21:3855)

1471. PHILLIPS, ALAN RICHARD. *The Dimension of Masculinity-Femininity as Related to Psychopathological Groups*. Doctor's thesis, Louisiana State University (Baton Rouge, La.), 1961. (DA 22:3268)

1472. RINGROSE, C. A. DOUGLAS. "Further Observations on the Psychosomatic Character of Toxemia of Pregnancy." *Can Med Assn J* 84:1064–5 My 13 '61. *

1473. RINGROSE, C. A. DOUGLAS. "Psychosomatic Influences in the Genesis of Toxemia of Pregnancy." *Can Med Assn J* 84:646–51 Mr 25 '61. *

1474. SINES, LLOYD K.; SILVER, REUBEN J.; and LUCERO, RUBEL J. "The Effect of Therapeutic Intervention by Untrained 'Therapists.'" *J Clin Psychol* 17:394–6 O '61. * (PA 38:8807)

1475. STEELE, JAMES ROBERT, JR. *Personality Defense and Task Performance*. Doctor's thesis, University of Washington (Seattle, Wash.), 1961. (DA 23:3482)

1476. AARONSON, BERNARD S., and ROTHMAN, IRIS. "A Key-Word Index to the Items of the MMPI." *J Psychol Studies* 13:121–51 S '62. * (PA 39:10068)

1477. ARCHIBALD, HERBERT C.; BELL, DOROTHY; MILLER, CHRISTINE; and TUDDENHAM, READ D. "Bereavement in Childhood and Adult Psychiatric Disturbance." *Psychosom Med* 24: 343–51 Jl–Ag '62. * (*PA* 37:5034)

1478. BRAATEN, LEIF J., and DARLING, C. DOUGLAS. "Suicidal Tendencies Among College Students." *Psychiatric Q* 36: 665–92 O '62. * (*PA* 38:6467)

1479. CARSON, ROBERT C., and HEINE, RALPH W. "Similarity and Success in Therapeutic Dyads." *J Consult Psychol* 26:38–43 F '62. * (*PA* 37:5165)

1480. CRADDICK, RAY A. "Selection of Psychopathic From Non-Psychopathic Prisoners Within a Canadian Prison." *Psychol Rep* 10:495–9 Ap '62. * (*PA* 37:3631)

1481. CROFT, GEORGE SEBASTIAN. *Time, Inquiry, and Discrepancy in Various Decision-Making Situations.* Doctor's thesis, Fordham University (New York, N.Y.), 1962. (*DA* 23:1780)

1482. DAVIS, CHARLES H., and JENKINS, C. DAVID. "Mental Stress and Oral Disease." *J Dental Res* 41:1045–9 S–O '62. * (*PA* 38:4489)

1483. EKMAN, PAUL; FRIESEN, WALLACE V.; and LUTZKER, DANIEL R. "Psychological Reactions to Infantry Basic Training." *J Consult Psychol* 26:103–4 F '62. * (*PA* 37:5746)

1484. FOWLER, BEVERLY DAVIS. *Relation of Teacher Personality Characteristics and Attitudes to Teacher-Pupil Rapport and Emotional Climate in the Elementary Classroom.* Doctor's thesis, University of South Carolina (Columbia, S.C.), 1962. (*DA* 23:1614)

1485. HENDERHAN, ROBERT CECIL. *The Relationship of Several Social-Psychological Variables to Empathic Ability.* Doctor's thesis, Ohio State University (Columbus, Ohio), 1962. (*DA* 23:3548)

1486. HERRON, WILLIAM G. "The Assessment of Ego Strength." *J Psychol Studies* 13:173–203 D '62. *

1487. HOLLOWAY, HILDEGUND, and GOCKA, EDWARD. "A Table for Obtaining Expected Scores of MMPI Scales From a Social Desirability Measure." *Newsl Res Psychol* 4:66–9 F '62. *

1488. JONES, J. B. "Some Personal-Social Factors Contributing to Academic Failure at Texas Southern University," pp. 135–6. (*PA* 37:5606) In *Personality Factors on the College Campus: Review of a Symposium.* Edited by Robert L. Sutherland and others. Austin, Tex.: Hogg Foundation for Mental Health, 1962. Pp. xxii, 242. * (*PA* 37:5621)

1489. LEACH, DOROTHY. *Meaning and Correlates of Peak-Experience.* Doctor's thesis, University of Florida (Gainesville, Fla.), 1962. (*DA* 24:180)

1490. LEUKEL, DEBORAH ANN. *The Psychogenic Tic in Childhood.* Doctor's thesis, University of Washington (Seattle, Wash.), 1962. (*DA* 23:2985)

1491. LEVINSON, BORIS M. "Yeshiva College Subcultural Scale: An Experimental Attempt at Devising a Scale of the Internalization of Jewish Traditional Values." *J Genetic Psychol* 101:375–99 D '62. * (*PA* 37:6576)

1492. LIEF, HAROLD I.; DINGMAN, JOSEPH F.; and BISHOP, MELVIN P. "Psychoendocrinologic Studies in Male With Cyclic Changes in Sexuality." *Psychosom Med* 24:357–68 Jl–Ag '62. * (*PA* 37:5514)

1493. MORRISON, JACK SHERMAN. *Four Hundred New Students in Theater Arts: An Experimental Study of Those Who Dropped Out and Those Who Achieved the B.A. Degree at UCLA.* Doctor's thesis, University of Southern California (Los Angeles, Calif.), 1962. (*DA* 23:3239)

1494. NEUBECK, GERHAD, and SCHLETZER, VERA M. "A Study of Extramarital Relationships." *Marriage & Family Living* 24:279–81 Ag '62. * (*PA* 38:2908)

1495. POWERS, JOHN HAMELIN. *Personality Correlates of Three Fine Motor Tasks.* Doctor's thesis, University of Minnesota (Minneapolis, Minn.), 1962. (*DA* 23:709)

1496. PRICE, JOHN RANDAL. *Relationship of the Hysteria-Psychasthenia Dimension to Stimulus Generalization Under Stress.* Doctor's thesis, University of Houston (Houston, Tex.), 1962. (*DA* 23:3480)

1497. ROME, HOWARD P. "Automation Techniques in Personality Assessment." *J Am Med Assn* 182:1069–72 D 8 '62. *

1498. ROME, HOWARD P.; SWENSON, WENDELL M.; MATAYA, PETE; McCARTHY, CHARLES E.; PEARSON, JOHN S.; KEATING, F. RAYMOND, JR.; and HATHAWAY, STARKE R. "Symposium on Automation Techniques in Personality Assessment." *Proc Staff Meetings Mayo Clinic* 37:61–82 Ja 31 '62. *

1499. SEEGARS, JAMES E., JR. "A Further Investigation of an M.M.P.I. Scale for Predicting College Achievement." *Personnel & Guid J* 41:251–3 N '62 * (*PA* 37:7202)

1500. SOARES, LOUISE MARIE GAVONI. *Adjustment of Music, Science, and Physical Education Majors in Teacher-Training.* Doctor's thesis, University of Illinois (Urbana, Ill.), 1962. (*DA* 23:4610)

1501. STELMACHERS, ZIGFRIDS TEODORS. *Stereotyped and Individualized Information and Their Relative Contribution to Predictive Accuracy.* Doctor's thesis, University of Minnesota (Minneapolis, Minn.), 1962. (*DA* 24:395)

1502. THORPE, J. G. "The Current Status of Prognostic Indicators for Electroconvulsive Therapy." *Psychosom Med* 24:554–68 N–D '62. * (*PA* 37:8055)

1503. ULLMANN, LEONARD P., and WIGGINS, JERRY S. "Endorsement Frequency and the Number of Differentiating MMPI Items To Be Expected by Chance." *Newsl Res Psychol* 4:29–34 My '62. *

1504. WAHBA, MICHEL. *A Multivariate Analysis of a Figure Preference Personality Test.* Doctor's thesis, University of North Carolina (Chapel Hill, N.C.), 1962. (*DA* 26:4821)

1505. WHITTINGTON, H. G. "Psychiatric Screening in the University: Methods and Rationale." *Stud Med* 10:351–62 F '62. *

1506. ALEXANDER, A. A.; ROESSLER, ROBERT; and GREENFIELD, NORMAN S. "Ego Strength and Physiological Responsivity: 3, The Relationship of the Barron Ego Strength Scale to Spontaneous Periodic Activity in Skin Resistance, Finger Blood Volume, Heart Rate, and Muscle Potential." *Arch Gen Psychiatry* 9:142–5 Ag '63. * (*PA* 38:2770)

1507. ALTROCCHI, JOHN, and PERLITSH, HILDA D. "Ego Control Patterns and Attribution of Hostility." *Psychol Rep* 12:811–8 Je '63. * (*PA* 38:6009)

1508. ANGERS, WILLIAM P. "Guidelines for Counselors for MMPI Interpretation." *Cath Counselor* 7:120–4 sp '63. *

1509. BOWERS, JOHN WAITE. "Language Intensity, Social Introversion, and Attitude Change." *Speech Monogr* 30:345–53 N '63. * (*PA* 38:8252)

1510. CARSSOW, KATHERINE P. *An Analysis of the Relationship of Deviant Minnesota Multiphasic Scores to Other Personality Measures Within a Counselor Population.* Master's thesis, University of Texas (Austin, Tex.), 1963.

1511. CLARK, DONALD LEWIS. *Prediction of Problem Behavior in Men's Residence Halls.* Doctor's thesis, University of Florida (Gainesville, Fla.), 1963. (*DA* 24:4081)

1512. COLLINS, DONALD JOSEPH. *Some Dimensions of Behavioral Control and Their Relation to MMPI Scales.* Doctor's thesis, University of North Carolina (Chapel Hill, N.C.), 1963. (*DA* 25:4812)

1513. COOPER, BERNARD. *Parents of Schizophrenic Children Compared With the Parents of Non-Psychotic Emotionally Disturbed and Well Children: A Discriminant Function Analysis.* Doctor's thesis, Temple University (Philadelphia, Pa.), 1963. (*DA* 24:1694)

1514. CUTTER, FRED. "Self Rejection Distress: A New MMPI Scale." *Calif Mental Health Res Dig* 1:33 sp '63. *

1515. DANIELSON, RICHARD HUGH. *A Pilot Study on the Relationships Among Ego-Strength, Motivation and Degree of Success in Rehabilitation Activity.* Doctor's thesis, Michigan State University (East Lansing, Mich.), 1963. (*DA* 24:2321)

1516. DE SENA, PAUL AMBROSE. *Identification of Non-Intellectual Characteristics of Consistent Over-, Under-, and Normal-Achievers Enrolled in Science Curriculums at the Pennsylvania State University.* Doctor's thesis, Pennsylvania State University (University Park, Pa.), 1963. (*DA* 24:3144)

1517. DEVRIES, ALCON GYSBERTUS. *Methodological Problems in the Identification of Suicidal Behavior by Means of Two Personality Inventories.* Doctor's thesis, University of Southern California (Los Angeles, Calif.), 1963. (*DA* 24:5541)

1518. DIGNA, M. "Uses of Information in a Screening Program." *R Relig* 22:300–6 My '63. *

1519. DUFF, FRANKLIN LEROY. *Item Subtlety in Personality Inventory Scales.* Doctor's thesis, Columbia University (New York, N.Y.), 1963. (*DA* 24:5190)

1520. EDWARDS, JOHN A. "Rehabilitation Potential in Prison Inmates as Measured by the MMPI." *J Crim Law & Criminol* 54:181–5 Je '63. * (*PA* 38:8517)

1521. FINE, BERNARD J., and COHEN, ALEXANDER. "Internalization Ratio, Accuracy, and Variability of Judgments of the Vertical." *Percept & Motor Skills* 16:138 F '63. * (*PA* 38:133)

1522. FINK, JOSEPHINE H. "Personality Variables in Brittle and Stable Diabetics." *Newsl Res Psychol* 5:8–9 Ag '63. * (*PA* 38:8587)

1523. FOWLER, ROY S., JR. *Predicting the MMPI From SD: A Comparative Study Using College Students and Neuropsychiatric Patients.* Master's thesis, University of Washington (Seattle, Wash.), 1963.

1524. GASTINEAU, C. F. "The Internist and the Minnesota Multiphasic Personality Inventory." *Proc IBM Med Symp* 4:347–53 ['63]. *

1525. GOLDBERG, LEWIS R., and RORER, LEONARD G. *Test-Retest Item Statistics for Original and Reversed MMPI Items.* ORI Research Monograph, Vol. 3, No. 1. Eugene, Ore.: Oregon Research Institute, March 1963. Pp. 299. *

1526. GOLDEN, JULES S.; SILVER, REUBEN J.; and MANDEL, NATHAN. "The Wives of 50 'Normal' American Men." *Arch Gen Psychiatry* 9:614–8 D '63. * (*PA* 38:8588)

1527. GRAVES, B. C. "Predicting Air Force Recidivism by the MMPI Test-Retest." *Proc Ann Conf Air Force Clin Psychol* 4:60–74 '63. *

1528. GREENFIELD, NORMAN S.; ALEXANDER, A. A.; and ROESSLER, ROBERT. "Ego Strength and Physiological Responsivity: 2, The Relationship of the Barron Ego Strength Scale to the Temporal and Recovery Characteristics of Skin Resistance, Finger Blood Volume, Heart Rate, and Muscle Potential Responses to Sound." *Arch Gen Psychiatry* 9:129–41 Ag '63. * (*PA* 38:2772)

1529. GREENFIELD, NORMAN S.; KATZ, DEBORAH; ALEXANDER, A. A.; and ROESSLER, ROBERT. "The Relationship Between Physiological and Psychological Responsivity: Depression and Galvanic Skin Response." *J Nerv & Mental Dis* 136:535–9 Je '63. * (*PA* 38:6157)

1530. HOFFMAN, HERBERT JACOB. *Ego Strength in Relation to Perception of Visual Illusions.* Doctor's thesis, Boston University (Boston, Mass.), 1963. (*DA* 24:2563)

1531. JAMES, BARBARA E. *Performance on the High Performance (HP) Scale of the Minnesota Multiphasic Inventory of Personality as a Function of Academic Productivity.* Master's thesis, Florida State University (Tallahassee, Fla.), 1963.

1532. JENKINS, ADELBERT HOWARD. *Tolerance for Unrealistic Experience as a Cognitive Control.* Doctor's thesis, University of Michigan (Ann Arbor, Mich.), 1963. (*DA* 24:834)

1533. JOY, VERNON LESTER. *Repression-Sensitization, Personality, and Interpersonal Behavior.* Doctor's thesis, University of Texas (Austin, Tex.), 1963. (*DA* 24:2976)

1534. KORNETSKY, CONAN. Chap. 13, "Minnesota Multiphasic Personality Inventory: Results on an Aged Population," pp. 253–6. In *Human Aging: A Biological and Behavioral Study.* Edited by James E. Birren, Robert N. Butler, Samuel W. Greenhouse, Louis Sokoloff, and Marian R. Yarrow. National Institute of Mental Health, Public Health Service Publication No. 086. Washington, D.C.: United States Government Printing Office, 1963. Pp. xiii, 328. * (*PA* 38:5821)

1535. LIGHTFOOT, FLORA L. *The Relation of Deviant Patterns of Scores on the Clinical Scales of MMPI to the Rated Promise of Counselor Candidates.* Master's thesis, University of Texas (Austin, Tex.), 1963.

1536. LUKER, WILLIAM ALLEN. *The Relationship Between Personality Integration and Creativity.* Doctor's thesis, North Texas State University (Denton, Tex.), 1963. (*DA* 25:940)

1537. LUTZ, WARREN WILLIAM. *The Personality Characteristics and Experiential Backgrounds of Successful High School Instrumental Music Teachers.* Doctor's thesis, University of Illinois (Urbana, Ill.), 1963. (*DA* 24:3781)

1538. LYKKEN, DAVID T., and ROSE, RICHARD. "Psychological Prediction From Actuarial Tables." *J Clin Psychol* 19:139–51 Ap '63. * (*PA* 39:3168)

1539. McCANTS, ALICE J. *A Study of the MMPI Profiles of Highly Rated Counselor Trainees at Atlanta University in 1962–63.* Master's thesis, Atlanta University (Atlanta, Ga.), 1963.

1540. McDONALD, ROBERT L., and CHRISTAKOS, ARTHUR C. "Relationship of Emotional Adjustment During Pregnancy to Obstetric Complications." *Am J Obst & Gynec* 86:341–8 Je '63. *

1541. McDONALD, ROBERT L.; GYNTHER, MALCOLM D.; and CHRISTAKOS, ARTHUR C. "Relations Between Maternal Anxiety and Obstetric Complications." *Psychosom Med* 25:357–63 Jl-Ag '63. * (*PA* 38:9104)

1542. MATHEWS, BLAIR HAROLD. *The Effect of Counseling Capable Students Experiencing Academic Difficulty.* Doctor's thesis, University of Florida (Gainesville, Fla.), 1963. (*DA* 24:4085)

1543. MULLANEY, ANTHONY JOSEPH. *Relationships Among Self-Disclosive Behavior, Personality, and Family Interaction.* Doctor's thesis, Fordham University (New York, N.Y.), 1963. (*DA* 24:4290)

1544. O'NEILL, JOHN PHILIP. *Prediction of College Women's Understanding of the Behavior of Preschool Children.* Doctor's thesis, Florida State University (Tallahassee, Fla.), 1963. (*DA* 24:4783)

1545. PESKIN, HARVEY. "Unity of Science Begins at Home: A Study of Regional Factionalism in Clinical Psychology." *Am Psychologist* 18:96–100 F '63. * (*PA* 38:2732)

1546. PETERS, J.; BENJAMIN, F. B.; HELVEY, W. M.; and ALBRIGHT, G. A. "Study of Sensory Deprivation, Pain and Personality Relationships for Space Travel." *Aerospace Med* 34:830–7 S '63. *

1547. PIGG, EVELYN E. *An Item Analysis of the Extended L and K Scales of the MMPI.* Master's thesis, University of Texas (Austin, Tex.), 1963.

1548. PORTER, KENNETH DUANE. *A Comparison of Three Methods for Developing MMPI Indicators of Psychosis and an Attempt to Demonstrate a "Bootstraps Effect."* Doctor's thesis, Purdue University (Lafayette, Ind.), 1963. (*DA* 24:5550)

1549. PURYEAR, HERBERT BRUCE. *Personality Characteristics of Reporters and Nonreporters of Dreams.* Doctor's thesis, University of North Carolina (Chapel Hill, N.C.), 1963. (*DA* 24:3425)

1550. RHODE, JACK FERDINAND. *A Pilot Study of the Prediction of Salesmen's Success in an Electronics Organization.* Doctor's thesis, University of Minnesota (Minneapolis, Minn.), 1963. (*DA* 25:2283)

1551. ROESSLER, ROBERT; ALEXANDER, A. A.; and GREENFIELD, NORMAN S. "Ego Strength and Physiological Responsivity: 1, The Relationship of the Barron Ego Strength Scale to Skin Resistance, Finger Blood Volume, Heart Rate, and Muscle Potential Responses to Sound." *Arch Gen Psychiatry* 8:142–54 F '63. * (*PA* 38:2774)

1552. ROME, HOWARD P. "Automation Technique in Personality Assessment: The Philosophy." *Proc IBM Med Symp* 4:335–46 ['63]. *

1553. ROSENTHAL, TED LEE. *Anxiety-Proneness and Susceptibility to Social Influence.* Doctor's thesis, Stanford University (Stanford, Calif.), 1963. (*DA* 24:3427)

1554. SLAWSON, PAUL F.; FLYNN, WILLIAM R.; and KOLLAR, EDWARD J. "Psychological Factors Associated With the Onset of Diabetes Mellitus." *J Am Med Assn* 185:166–70 Jl 20 '63. *

1555. SOURS, JOHN A.; FRUMKIN, PAUL; and INDERMILL, RICHARD R. "Somnambulism: Its Clinical Significance and Dynamic Meaning in Late Adolescence and Adulthood." *Arch Gen Psychiatry* 9:400–13 O '63. * (*PA* 38:6389)

1556. STEINER, FELIX. *Pictorial and Conceptual Thinking as Related to Personality.* Doctor's thesis, Yeshiva University (New York, N.Y.), 1963. (*DA* 25:2056)

1557. TURNER, LYA NOEL. *The Certainty of Belief as a Variable of Personality.* Doctor's thesis, University of California (Berkeley, Calif.), 1963. (*DA* 24:5554)

1558. VIAILLE, HAROLD D. *Prediction of Treatment Outcome of Chronic Alcoholics in a State Hospital.* Doctor's thesis, Texas Technological College (Lubbock, Tex.), 1963. (*DA* 24:5534)

1559. WILLIAMS, CECIL LEE. *A Study of the Strong Vocational Interest Blank and Scores From a Factor Analysis of the Minnesota Multiphasic Personality Inventory.* Doctor's thesis, University of Kansas (Lawrence, Kan.), 1963. (*DA* 25:1764)

1560. ZUCKERMAN, MARVIN; NURNBERGER, JOHN I.; GARDINER, SPRAGUE H.; VANDIVEER, JAMES M.; BARRETT, BEATRICE H.; and DEN BREEIJEN, ARIE. "Psychological Correlates of Somatic Complaints in Pregnancy and Difficulty in Childbirth." *J Consult Psychol* 27:324–9 Ag '63. * (*PA* 38:2751)

1561. AARONSON, BERNARD S. "Aging, Personality Change, and Psychiatric Diagnosis." *J Gerontol* 19:144–8 Ap '64. * (*PA* 39:5306)

1562. ADAIR, ALVIS V. *A Comparative Study of Performance on the PT Scale of the MMPI and a Visual Vigilance Task.* Master's thesis, Virginia State College (Petersburg, Va.), 1964.

1563. ALLEN, ROBERT M.; RICHER, HOWARD M.; and PLOTNIK, RODNEY J. "A Study of Introversion-Extroversion as a Personality Dimension." *Genetic Psychol Monogr* 69:297–322 My '64. * (*PA* 39:5143)

1564. ALTUS, WILLIAM D. "'Jewish' Names and MMPI Items." *Psychol Rep* 14:870 Je '64. * (*PA* 39:5035)

1565. ANDERSON, WAYNE, and ANKER, JAMES. "Factor Analysis of MMPI and SVIB Scores for a Psychiatric Population." *Psychol Rep* 15:715–9 D '64. * (*PA* 39:7831)

1566. ANGELO, JOSEPH ANDRIA, JR. *A Comparison of Factors Derived From R-Data With Those Derived From Ipsatized R-Data.* Doctor's thesis, University of Arizona (Tucson, Ariz.), 1964. (*DA* 25:2608)

1567. AZIMI, CYRUS. *Masculinity, Femininity and Perception of Warmth and Saliency in Parent-Son Relationships.* Doctor's thesis, Michigan State University (East Lansing, Mich.), 1964. (*DA* 25:2608)

1568. BAER, DANIEL J., and MOYNIHAN, JAMES F. "Stepwise Discriminant-Function Analysis of Seminary-Candidate MMPI Scores." *J Psychol* 58:413–9 O '64. * (*PA* 39:4976)

1569. BAKKER, CORNELIS B., and DIGHTMAN, CAMERON R. "Psychological Factors in Fertility Control." *Fertil & Steril* 15:559–67 S–O '64. *

1570. BARGER, BEN, and HALL, EVERETTE. "Personality Patterns and Achievement in College." *Ed & Psychol Meas* 24:339–46 su '64. * (*PA* 39:5989)

1571. BECKER, JOSEPH, and NICHOLS, CHARLES H. "Communality of Manic-Depressive and 'Mild' Cyclothymic Characteristics." *J Abn & Social Psychol* 69:531–8 N '64. * (*PA* 39:8532)

1572. BENDIG, A. W. "Factor Analytic Scales of Need Achievement." *J General Psychol* 70:59–67 Ja '64. * (*PA* 38:10111)

1573. BERDIE, RALPH F., and HOOD, ALBERT B. "Personal Values and Attitudes as Determinants of Post-High School Plans." *Personnel & Guid J* 42:754–9 Ap '64. * (*PA* 39:4764)

1574. BLUMENKRANTZ, JACK; DAHLGREN, HELEN; and BORUM, ELIZABETH. "The Effects of Chronic Physical Illness in the Aged on Personality." *Newsl Res Psychol* 6:16–7 N '64. *

1575. BOE, ERLING E. "Social Desirability Considerations in Separate Acquiescence Set and Content Scores." *Psychol Rep* 15:699–702 D '64. * (*PA* 39:7832)

1576. BOE, ERLING E., and KOGAN, WILLIAM S. "An Analysis of Various Methods for Deriving the Social Desirability Score." *Psychol Rep* 14:23–9 F '64. * (*PA* 39:1717)

1577. BOE, ERLING E., and KOGAN, WILLIAM S. "Effect of Social Desirability Instructions on Several MMPI Measures of Social Desirability." *J Consult Psychol* 28:248–51 Je '64. * (*PA* 39:5037)

1578. BOWLING, LLOYD SPENCER, SR. *Personality Characteristics of Veterans With Different Types of Hearing Losses.* Doctor's thesis, University of Maryland (College Park, Md.), 1964. (*DA* 25:4811)

1579. BROWN, FREDERICK G., and DUBOIS, THOMAS E. "Correlates of Academic Success for High-Ability Freshman Men." *Personnel & Guid J* 42:603–7 F '64. * (*PA* 39:5820)

1580. BROWN, L. B. "Anxiety in Pregnancy." *Brit J Med Psychol* 37:47–58 pt 1 '64. * (*PA* 39:1911)

1581. BUTCHER, JAMES; BALL, BRENDA; and RAY, EVA. "Effects of Socio-Economic Level on MMPI Differences in Negro-White College Students." *J Counsel Psychol* 11:83–7 sp '64. * (*PA* 38:8513)

1582. BUTCHER, JAMES NEAL. *Manifest Aggression: MMPI Correlates in Normal Boys and Their Parents.* Doctor's thesis, University of North Carolina (Chapel Hill, N.C.), 1964. (*DA* 25:6755)

1583. BYRNE, DONN. "Repression-Sensitization as a Dimension of Personality," pp. 169–220. In *Progress in Experimental Personality Research, Vol. 1.* Edited by Brendan A. Maher. New York: Academic Press, Inc., 1964. Pp. x, 368. *

1584. CANTOR, JOEL M. "All-or-None Style of Thinking as a Source of Test Bias." *Psychol Rep* 15:355–8 O '64. * (*PA* 39:5169)

1585. CHANSKY, NORMAN M. "A Note on the Validity of Reading Test Scores." *J Ed Res* 58:90 O '64. *

1586. CHATTERJEE, BISHWA B. "Masculinity-Femininity as Predictor of Job Satisfaction of Teachers." *Psychologia* 7:223–32 D '64. * (*PA* 41:2113)

1587. CLARK, DONALD L. "Exploring Behavior in Men's Residence Halls Using the MMPI." *Personnel & Guid J* 43: 249–51 N '64. * (*PA* 39:10226)

1588. COOKE, JANE WALKUP KLUTTZ. *The MMPI in Diagnosing Psychological Disturbance Among College Males.* Doctor's thesis, University of North Carolina (Chapel Hill, N.C.), 1964. (*DA* 26:1771)

1589. COOKE, ROBERT MURPHEY. *An "Internalization" Scale Based on the Minnesota Multiphasic Personality Inventory (MMPI).* Doctor's thesis, University of Washington (Seattle, Wash.), 1964. (*DA* 25:3106)

1590. CORAH, NORMAN L. "Neuroticism and Extraversion in the MMPI: Empirical Validation and Exploration." *Brit J Social & Clin Psychol* 3:168–74 O '64. * (*PA* 39:5171)

1591. CRADDICK, RAY A. "Psychological Correlates of Biodynamic Stress: Description of Six Subjects Sustaining Over 500 Accumulative 'G.' " *Aerospace Med* 35:40–2 Ja '64. *

1592. CRUMBAUGH, JAMES C., and MAHOLICK, LEONARD T. "An Experimental Study in Existentialism: The Psychometric Approach to Frankl's Concept of *Noogenic Neurosis*." *J Clin Psychol* 20:200–7 Ap '64. * (*PA* 39:8454)

1593. CUTTER, FRED. "Self-Rejection Distress: A New MMPI Scale." *J Clin Psychol* 20:150–3 Ja '64. * (*PA* 39:10229)

1594. DAVIS, KEITH G. "Correlates of the Fear of Insanity." *Newsl Res Psychol* 6:20–1 F '64. *

1595. DAVIS, KEITH GORDON. *Correlates of the Fear of Insanity.* Doctor's thesis, University of Colorado (Boulder, Colo.), 1964. (*DA* 25:6059)

1596. DEAN, ROBERT B., and RICHARDSON, HAROLD. "Analysis of MMPI Profiles of Forty College-Educated Overt Male Homosexuals." *J Consult Psychol* 28:483–6 D '64. * (*PA* 39:8407)

1597. DEMPSEY, PAUL. "Overall Performance on the MMPI as It Relates to Test-Taking Attitudes and Clinical Scale Scores." *J Clin Psychol* 20:154–6 Ja '64. * (*PA* 39:10224)

1598. DEMPSEY, PAUL. "Score vs. Performance on Certain MMPI Scales." *J Clin Psychol* 20:254–5 Ap '64. * (*PA* 39:7861)

1599. DEMPSEY, PAUL. "A Unidimensional Depression Scale for the MMPI." *J Consult Psychol* 28:364–70 Ag '64. * (*PA* 39:5049)

1600. DE SENA, PAUL A. "Comparison of Consistent Over-, Under-, and Normal-Achieving College Students on a MMPI Special Scale." *Psychol* 1:8–12 My '64. * (*PA* 39:1827)

1601. DE SENA, PAUL A. "The Role of Consistency in Identifying Characteristics of Three Levels of Achievement." *Personnel & Guid J* 43:145–9 O '64. * (*PA* 39:10713)

1602. DICKEN, CHARLES, and WIGGINS, JERRY S. "The Social Desirability Scale Is Not a Short Form of the MMPI: A Reply to Edwards and Walker." *Psychol Rep* 14:711–4 Je '64. * (*PA* 39:5172)

1603. DIERS, CAROL JEAN. "Social Desirability and Acquiescence in Response to Personality Items." *J Consult Psychol* 28:71–7 F '64. * (*PA* 38:8483)

1604. DORFMAN, MARCIA B. *Psychiatric Impairment as Measured by the Ego-Strength and Psychological Control Subscales of the MMPI.* Master's thesis, San Francisco State College (San Francisco, Calif.), 1964.

1605. DUNSTONE, JOHN J.; DZENDOLET, ERNEST; and HEUCKEROTH, OTTO. "Effect of Some Personality Variables on Electrical Vestibular Stimulation." *Percept & Motor Skills* 18:689–95 Je '64. * (*PA* 39:3355)

1606. EASTERBROOK, CAROLYN M. *Pursuit of a Quest: Mortalities Along the Way. A Study of a Selected Group of Variables Relative to the Holding Power of the Art Teaching Profession.* Doctor's thesis, Wayne State University (Detroit, Mich.), 1964. (*DA* 26:4478)

1607. EDWARDS, ALLEN L. "The Assessment of Human Motives by Means of Personality Scales." *Neb Symp Motiv* 12: 135–62 '64. * (*PA* 39:12357)

1608. EDWARDS, ALLEN L. "Prediction of Mean Scores on MMPI Scales." *J Consult Psychol* 28:183–5 Ap '64. * (*PA* 39:1829)

1609. EDWARDS, ALLEN L. "Social Desirability and Performance on the MMPI." *Psychometrika* 29:295–308 D '64. * (*PA* 39:10230)

1610. EDWARDS, ALLEN L., and WALSH, JAMES A. "Response Sets in Standard and Experimental Personality Scales." *Am Ed Res J* 1:52–61 Ja '64. * (*PA* 39:7754)

1611. EDWARDS, ALLEN L.; GOCKA, EDWARD F.; and HOLLOWAY, HILDEGUND. "The Development of an MMPI Acquiescence Scale." *J Clin Psychol* 20:148–50 Ja '64. * (*PA* 39:10231)

1612. EHRLE, RAYMOND A., and AUVENSHINE, CHARLES D. "Anxiety Level, Need for Counseling, and Client Improvement in an Operational Setting." *J Counsel Psychol* 11:286–7 f '64. *

1613. EICHER, IVAN LAWRENCE. *A Study of the Relation of Authoritarian Personalities to Course Achievement in Selected Classes in the School of Educaton at the University of Colo-*

rado. Doctor's thesis, University of Colorado (Boulder, Colo.), 1964. (*DA* 25:5730)

1614. ELVEKROG, MAURICE O. *The Development of Measures of Three Response Styles and Their Relationships to Test and Non-Test Variables.* Doctor's thesis, University of Minnesota (Minneapolis, Minn.), 1964. (*DA* 25:4814)

1615. ENDICOTT, NOBLE A., and ENDICOTT, JEAN. "Prediction of Improvement in Treated and Untreated Patients Using the Rorschach Prognostic Rating Scale." *J Consult Psychol* 28:342–8 Ag '64. * (*PA* 39:5345)

1616. ENDICOTT, NOBLE A., and ENDICOTT, JEAN. "The Relationship Between Rorschach Flexor and Extensor M Responses and the MMPI." *J Clin Psychol* 20:388–9 Jl '64. * (*PA* 39:10193)

1617. ERICKSON, PAUL. *Selection Factors Relating to Success in a Counselor Education Program.* Doctor's thesis, University of Southern California (Los Angeles, Calif.), 1964. (*DA* 25:3391)

1618. FIELDER, DANIEL WILLIAM. *A Nomothetic Study of the Southern California School of Theology Seminarian.* Doctor's thesis, Southern California School of Theology (Claremont, Calif.), 1964. (*DA* 26:1192)

1619. FINNEY, JOSEPH C. "A Factor Analysis of Mother-Child Influence." *J General Psychol* 70:41–9 Ja '64. * (*PA* 38:9968)

1620. FISHER, JEROME. "Some MMPI Dimensions of Physical and Psychological Illness." *J Clin Psychol* 20:369–75 Jl '64. * (*PA* 39:10232)

1621. FOLEY, WALTER JAMES. *Empirical Derivation of Scales for the Selection of Counselor Trainees.* Doctor's thesis, University of Illinois (Urbana, Ill.), 1964. (*DA* 25:4540)

1622. FORDYCE, WILBERT E. "Personality Characteristics in Men With Spinal Cord Injury as Related to Manner of Onset of Disability." *Arch Phys Med & Rehabil* 45:321–5 Jl '64. *

1623. FOULKES, DAVID, and RECHTSCHAFFEN, ALLAN. "Presleep Determinants of Dream Content: Effects of Two Films." *Percept & Motor Skills* 19:983–1005 D '64. * (*PA* 39:6627)

1624. FOX, WARREN IRVING. *Psychological Factors in Childbirth.* Doctor's thesis, New York University (New York, N.Y.), 1964. (*DA* 27:4121B)

1625. FREE, JOHN ELLSWORTH. *An Experiment to Show the Possible Contribution of Social Group Work to Counseling in Improving the Adjustment of Deviant High School Students.* Doctor's thesis, University of Minnesota (Minneapolis, Minn.), 1964. (*DA* 25:2849)

1626. GARD, JOHN G., and BENDIG, A. W. "A Factor Analytic Study of Eysenck's and Schutz's Personality Dimensions Among Psychiatric Groups." *J Consult Psychol* 28:252–8 Je '64. * (*PA* 39:5729)

1627. GEER, JAMES H. "Phobia Treated by Reciprocal Inhibition." *J Abn & Social Psychol* 69:642–5 D '64. * (*PA* 39:8130)

1628. GLOYE, EUGENE E. "A Note on the Distinction Between Social Desirability and Acquiescent Response Styles as Sources of Variance in the MMPI." *J Counsel Psychol* 11: 180–4 su '64. * (*PA* 39:5175)

1629. GOLDBERG, LEWIS R., and RORER, LEONARD G. "Test-Retest Item Statistics." Abstract. *Psychol Rep* 15:413–4 O '64. * (*PA* 39:5059)

1630. GOLDBERG, LEWIS R., and RUST, RALPH M. "Intra-Individual Variability in the MMPI-CPI Common Item Pool." *Brit J Social & Clin Psychol* 3:145–7 Je '64. *

1631. GOLDEN, MARK. "Some Effects of Combining Psychological Tests on Clinical Inferences." *J Consult Psychol* 28: 440–6 O '64. * (*PA* 39:5060)

1632. GOLDSTEIN, MICHAEL J., and JONES, ROBERT B. "The Relationships Among Word Association Test, Objective Personality Test Scores and Ratings of Clinical Behavior in Psychiatric Patients." *J Proj Tech & Pers Assess* 28:271–9 S '64. * (*PA* 39:7840)

1633. GONDA, THOMAS A. "Prediction of Short-Term Outcome of Electroconvulsive Therapy." *J Nerv & Mental Dis* 138:586–94 Je '64. * (*PA* 39:2034)

1634. GORMAN, JOHN ALFRED. *MMPI and Demographic Patterns for Discriminating Abnormal Behavior.* Doctor's thesis, University of North Carolina (Chapel Hill, N.C.), 1964. (*DA* 25:6759)

1635. GRACE, DAVID P. "Predicting Progress of Schizophrenics in a Work-Oriented Rehabilitation Program." Abstract. *J Consult Psychol* 28:560 D '64. * (*PA* 39:8489, title only)

1636. GRANGAARD, GEORGE HOWARD. *Factors Predicting Success of Students in Elementary Teacher Education.* Doctor's thesis, Ball State Teachers College (Muncie, Ind.), 1964. (*DA* 26:3162)

1637. GRANT, THEODORE FRANCIS, JR. *Personality Characteristics of Youthful Offenders Expressing Anxiety and Not Expressing Anxiety in the MMPI and Interview Situations.* Doctor's thesis, University of North Carolina (Chapel Hill, N.C.), 1964. (*DA* 25:7378)

1638. GROSS, SEYMOUR Z. "A Normative Study and Cross-Validation of MMPI Subtle and Obvious Scales for Parents Seen at a Child Guidance Clinic." *Psychol* 1:5–7 My '64. * (*PA* 39:1834)

1639. GYNTHER, MALCOLM D., and BRILLIANT, PATRICIA J. "Psychopathology and Attitudes Toward Mental Illness." *Arch Gen Psychiatry* 11:48–52 Jl '64. * (*PA* 39:4794)

1640. HAMMERSCHLAG, CARL A.; FISHER, SEYMOUR; DE COSSE, JEROME; and KAPLAN, EUGENE. "Breast Symptoms and Patient Delay: Psychological Variables Involved." *Cancer* 17: 1480–5 N '64. * *(PA* 39:10053)

1641. HANNUM, THOMAS E., and WARMAN, ROY E. "The MMPI Characteristics of Incarcerated Females." *J Res Crime & Del* 1:119–26 Jl '64. *

1642. HARDYCK, CURTIS D. "Sex Differences in Personality Changes With Age." *J Gerontol* 19:78–82 Ja '64. *

1643. HATHAWAY, STARKE R. "MMPI: Professional Use by Professional People." *Am Psychologist* 19:204–10 Mr '64. * *(PA* 39:1733)

1644. HEILBRUN, ALFRED B., JR. "Social-Learning Theory, Social Desirability, and the MMPI." *Psychol B* 61:377–87 My '64. * *(PA* 39:1835)

1645. HEILBRUN, ALFRED B., JR. "Social Value: Social Behavior Consistency, Parental Identification, and Aggression in Late Adolescence." *J Genetic Psychol* 104:135–46 Mr '64. * *(PA* 39:1834)

1646. HENRICHS, THEODORE. "Objective Configural Rules for Discriminating MMPI Profiles in a Psychiatric Population." *J Clin Psychol* 20:157–9 Ja '64. * *(PA* 39:10234)

1647. HEUSINKVELD, EDWIN DAVID. *A Study Comparing Selected Characteristics of Academic Underachievers With Normal Achieving Students at the State University of Iowa.* Doctor's thesis, State University of Iowa (Iowa City, Iowa), 1964. *(DA* 25:1004)

1648. HOLROYD, RICHARD GARRETT. *Prediction of Defensive Paranoid Schizophrenics Using the MMPI.* Doctor's thesis, University of Minnesota (Minneapolis, Minn.), 1964. *(DA* 25: 2048)

1649. HOSKINS, JOHN EMMETT. *A Study of Certain Characteristics Which Have Predictive Value for Vocational Adjustment in a Rehabilitation Workshop.* Doctor's thesis, Wayne State University (Detroit, Mich.), 1964. *(DA* 26:4797)

1650. HOVEY, H. BIRNET. "Brain Lesions and Five MMPI Items." *J Consult Psychol* 28:78–9 F '64. * *(PA* 38:8936)

1651. HOWARD, KENNETH I. "Differentiation of Individuals as a Function of Repeated Testing." *Ed & Psychol Meas* 24: 875–94 w '64. * *(PA* 39:7863)

1652. JOHNSON, DOROTHY ETHEL. *A Study of Interests and Personality Characteristics of Counselor Trainees and Counseling Effectiveness.* Doctor's thesis, Purdue University (Lafayette, Ind.), 1964. *(DA* 26:2051)

1653. JOHNSTON, JOSEPH ANDREW, JR. *Relationships Among Characteristics and Performance Ratings of Experienced Secondary School Counselors.* Doctor's thesis, University of Michigan (Ann Arbor, Mich.), 1964. *(DA* 25:7081)

1654. JOHNSTON, ROY, and MCNEAL, BENJAMIN F. "Combined MMPI and Demographic Data in Predicting Length of Neuropsychiatric Hospital Stay." *J Consult Psychol* 28:64–70 F '64. * *(PA* 38:8796)

1655. JOSHI, BHUWAN LAL. *Personality Correlates of Happiness.* Doctor's thesis, University of California (Berkeley, Calif.), 1964. *(DA* 25:2083)

1656. KATKIN, EDWARD S. "The Marlowe-Crowne Social Desirability Scale: Independent of Psychopathology?" *Psychol Rep* 15:703–6 D '64. * *(PA* 39:7864)

1657. KIDD, ALINE H., and RIVOIRE, JEANNE L. "The Correlation Between Level of Field-Dependence and the Elevation of MMPI Scale Scores." *J Clin Psychol* 20:256–7 Ap '64. * *(PA* 39:7865)

1658. KNAPP, ROBERT H., and GREEN, HELEN B. "Personality Correlates of Success Imagery." *J Social Psychol* 62: 93–9 F '64. * *(PA* 39:1807)

1659. KNAPP, ROBERT H., and HOLZBERG, JULES D. "Characteristics of College Students Volunteering for Service to Mental Patients." *J Consult Psychol* 28:82–5 F '64. * *(PA* 38:8779)

1660. KOBLER, FRANK J. "Screening Applicants for Religious Life." *J Relig & Health* 3:161–70 Ja '64. * *(PA* 40:1793)

1661. KOGAN, KATE L., and JACKSON, JOAN K. "Perceptions of Self and Spouse: Some Contaminating Factors." *J Marriage & Family* 26:60–4 F '64. * *(PA* 38:8125)

1662. KOGAN, KATE L., and JACKSON, JOAN K. "Personality Adjustments and Childhood Experiences." *J Health & Hum Behav* 5:50–4 sp '64. * *(PA* 39:5237)

1663. KOLLAR, EDWARD J.; SLATER, GRANT R.; PALMER, JAMES O.; DOCTER, RICHARD F.; and MANDELL, ARNOLD J. "Measurement of Stress in Fasting Man: A Pilot Study." *Arch Gen Psychiatry* 11:113–25 Ag '64. * *(PA* 39:4233)

1664. KREBS, DAVID O. *Perceptual Defense in the Delinquent Child.* Doctor's thesis, University of Denver (Denver, Colo.), 1964. *(DA* 25:5384)

1665. KRIPPNER, STANLEY. "The Identification of Male Homosexuality With the MMPI." *J Clin Psychol* 20:159–61 Ja '64. * *(PA* 39:10240)

1666. KRIPPNER, STANLEY. "The Relationship Between MMPI and WAIS Masculinity-Femininity Scores." *Personnel & Guid J* 42:695–8 Mr '64. * *(PA* 39:5072)

1667. KRUEGER, GEORGE RAYMOND. *A Study of the Personality Characteristics of a Group of Homosexual and Heterosexual Males Using the MMPI.* Master's thesis, MacMurray College (Jacksonville, Ill.), 1964.

1668. LAEDER, RONALD L. *Personality Differences of Adolescents With Hoarse, Harsh, Breathy Nasal and Normal Qualities as Measured by MMPI Clinical Scale.* Master's thesis, Central Michigan University (Mt. Pleasant, Mich.), 1964.

1669. LAHEY, THOMAS HAROLD. *Ego-Strength as a Variable in the Effects of Praise and Blame in One Learning Task on the Rate of Learning in a Subsequent Task.* Doctor's thesis, University of Virginia (Charlottesville, Va.), 1964. *(DA* 25: 3398)

1670. LEINER, MARVIN. *Changes in Selected Personality Characteristics and Persistence in the Career Choices of Women Associated With a Four Year College Education at One of the Colleges of the City University of New York.* Doctor's thesis, New York University (New York, N.Y.), 1964. *(DA* 25: 5636)

1671. LEWINSOHN, PETER M., and NICHOLS, ROBERT C. "The Evaluation of Changes in Psychiatric Patients During and After Hospitalization." *J Clin Psychol* 20:272–9 Ap '64. * *(PA* 39:8200)

1672. LIBERTY, PAUL G., JR.; LUNNEBORG, CLIFFORD E.; and ATKINSON, GILBERT C. "Perceptual Defense, Dissimulation, and Response Styles." *J Consult Psychol* 28:529–37 D '64. * *(PA* 39:7846)

1673. LOWE, C. MARSHALL. "The Equivalence of Guilt and Anxiety as Psychological Constructs." *J Consult Psychol* 28: 553–4 D '64. * *(PA* 39:7960)

1674. LUCERO, RUBEL J., and CURRENS, WILBUR C. "Effects of Clinical Training on Personality Functioning of the Minister." *J Clin Psychol* 20:147 Ja '64. * *(PA* 39:10057)

1675. MCDONALD, ROBERT L., and PARHAM, KENNETH J. "Relation of Emotional Changes During Pregnancy to Obstetric Complications in Unmarried Primigravidas." *Am J Obst & Gynec* 90:195–201 S '64. *

1676. MACDORMAN, CARROLL F.; RIVOIRE, JEANNE L.; GALLAGHER, PETER J.; and MACDORMAN, CLAUDIA F. "Size Constancy of Adolescent Schizophrenics." *J Abn & Social Psychol* 69:258–63 S '64. * *(PA* 39:5756)

1677. MCKENZIE, JAMES D., JR. "The Dynamics of Deviant Achievement." *Personnel & Guid J* 42:683–6 Mr '64. * *(PA* 39:5959)

1678. MCREYNOLDS, PAUL, and ULLMANN, LEONARD P. "Differential Recall of Pleasant and Unpleasant Words as a Function of Anxiety." *J Clin Psychol* 20:79–80 Ja '64. * *(PA* 39:10296)

1679. MARLOWE, DAVID, and GOTTESMAN, IRVING I. "The Edwards SD Scale: A Short Form of the MMPI?" *J Consult Psychol* 28:181–2 Ap '64. * *(PA* 39:1839)

1680. MARLOWE, DAVID, and GOTTESMAN, IRVING I. "Prediction of Mean Scores on MMPI Scales: A Reply." *J Consult Psychol* 28:185–6 Ap '64. * *(PA* 39:1840)

1681. MARTIN, CLYDE V., and CHANNELL, LAWRENCE H. "Personality and Social History Characteristics of Delinquents and Their Parents." *Correct Psychiatry & J Social Ther* 10: 93–107 Mr '64. * *(PA* 39:8439)

1682. MATARAZZO, JOSEPH D.; ALLEN, BERNADENE V.; SASLOW, GEORGE; and WIENS, ARTHUR N. "Characteristics of Successful Policemen and Firemen Applicants." *J Appl Psychol* 48:123–33 Ap '64. * *(PA* 39:6047)

1683. MEIER, MANFRED J., and FRENCH, LYLE A. "Caudality Scale Changes Following Unilateral Temporal Lobectomy." *J Clin Psychol* 20:464–7 O '64. * *(PA* 39:12362)

1684. MOGAR, ROBERT E., and SAVAGE, CHARLES. "Personality Change Associated With Psychedelic (LSD) Therapy: A Preliminary Report." *Psychotherapy* 1:154–62 f '64. * *(PA* 40:1700)

1685. MONROE, JACK J.; MILLER, JEROME S.; and LYLE, WILLIAM H., JR. "The Extension of Psychopathic Deviancy Scales for the Screening of Addict Patients." *Ed & Psychol Meas* 24:47–56 sp '64. * *(PA* 39:1677)

1686. MOOS, RUDOLF, and SOLOMON, GEORGE F. "Personality Correlates of the Rapidity of Progression of Rheumatoid Arthritis." *Ann Rheum Dis* 23:145–51 Mr '64. *

1687. MOOS, RUDOLF H., and SOLOMON, GEORGE F. "Minnesota Multiphasic Personality Inventory Response Patterns in Patients With Rheumatoid Arthritis." *J Psychosom Res* 8:17–28 Jl '64. * *(PA* 39:8553)

1688. MORROW, WILLIAM R., and BERGER, ANDREW. "Prejudice and the Offenses of Penal-Psychiatric Patients." *J Clin Psychol* 20:218–25 Ap '64. * *(PA* 39:8440)

1689. MYKLEBUST, HELMER R. *The Psychology of Deafness: Sensory Deprivation, Learning, and Adjustment,* Second Edition, pp. 133–58. New York: Grune & Stratton, Inc., 1964. Pp. xii, 423. *

1690. NALVEN, FREDERIC B., and O'BRIEN, JOHN F. "Personality Patterns of Rheumatoid Arthritic Patients." *Arthr & Rheum* 7:18–28 F '64. *

1691. NEAL, CAROLYN MAE. *A Study of the Relationship of Personality Variables to Reading Ability Utilizing Tests Administered College Freshmen.* Doctor's thesis, University of Illinois (Urbana, Ill.), 1964. *(DA* 25:4480)

1692. NEIDT, CHARLES O., and DREBUS, RICHARD W. "Characteristics Associated With the Creativity of Research Scientists in an Industrial Setting." *J Ind Psychol* 2:102–12 D '64. * *(PA* 40:11550)

1693. OLSON, RAY W. "MMPI Sex Differences in Narcotic Addicts." *J General Psychol* 71:257–66 O '64. * *(PA* 39:5687)

1694. ORB, VERGIL K. "A Study of Some Techniques Used for Predicting the Success of Teachers." *J Teach Ed* 15:67–71 Mr '64. *

1695. OSTFELD, A. M.; LEBOVITS, B. Z.; SHEKELLE, R. B.; and PAUL, O. "A Prospective Study of the Relationship Between Personality and Coronary Heart Disease." *J Chronic Dis* 17:265–76 Mr '64. * *(PA* 39:10326)

1696. PALMER, WILLIAM FISHER. *Relationships of Certain Personality, Attitude, and Classroom Behavior Factors of Classroom Supervisors and Student Teachers.* Doctor's thesis, University of North Carolina (Chapel Hill, N.C.), 1964. (*DA* 25:6411)

1697. PARSONS, OSCAR A.; ALTROCCHI, JOHN; and SPRING, FAYE E. "Discrepancies in Interpersonal Perception, Adjustment and Therapeutic Skill." *Percept & Motor Skills* 18:697–702 Je '64. * (*PA* 39:5239)

1698. PATTERSON, STANLEY DWIGHT. *A Psychological Study of Asthmatics and Former Asthmatics.* Doctor's thesis, Purdue University (Lafayette, Ind.), 1964. (*DA* 25:1342)

1699. PEPPER, LENNARD JAY. *The MMPI: Initial Test Predictors of Retest Changes.* Doctor's thesis, University of North Carolina (Chapel Hill, N.C.), 1964. (*DA* 26:1780)

1700. PERKINS, JULIA E., and GOLDBERG, LEWIS R. "Contextual Effects on the MMPI." *J Consult Psychol* 28:133–40 Ap '64. * (*PA* 39:1844)

1701. POOL, DONALD A. "Relation of Unrealistic Vocational Choices to Personality Characteristics in a Physically Handicapped Group." *Arch Phys Med & Rehabil* 45:466–8 S '64. *

1702. POOL, DONALD A., and BROWN, ROBERT A. "Kuder-Strong Discrepancies and Personality Adjustment." *J Counsel Psychol* 11:63–6 sp '64. * Supplementary letter to the editor. 11:387 f '64. *

1703. RAYGOR, ALTON L., and WARK, DAVID M. "Personality Patterns of Poor Readers Compared With College Freshmen." *J Read* 8:40–6 O '64. *

1704. RETTIG, SALOMON, and PASAMANICK, BENJAMIN. "Subcultural Identification of Hospitalized Male Drug Addicts: A Further Examination." *J Nerv & Mental Dis* 139:83–6 Jl '64. * (*PA* 39:5688)

1705. RIM, Y. "Personality and Group Decisions Involving Risk." *Psychol Rec* 14:37–45 Ja '64. * (*PA* 38:8376)

1706. ROTMAN, S. R., and VESTRE, NORRIS D. "The Use of the MMPI in Identifying Problem Drinkers Among Psychiatric Hospital Admissions." *J Clin Psychol* 20:526–30 O '64. * (*PA* 39:12366)

1707. SAVAGE, CHARLES; SAVAGE, ETHEL; FADIMAN, JAMES; and HARMAN, WILLIS. "LSD: Therapeutic Effects of the Psychedelic Experience." *Psychol Rep* 14:111–20 F '64. * (*PA* 39:2160)

1708. SCHUBERT, DANIEL S. P. "Arousal Seeking as a Motivation for Volunteering: MMPI Scores and Central-Nervous-System-Stimulant Use as Suggestive of a Trait." *J Proj Tech & Pers Assess* 28:337–40 S '64. * (*PA* 39:7706)

1709. SCHWARTZ, MILTON N.; COHEN, BERTRAM D.; and PAVLIK, WILLIAM B. "The Effects of Subject- and Experimenter-Induced Defensive Response Sets on Picture-Frustration Test Reactions." *J Proj Tech & Pers Assess* 28:341–5 S '64. * (*PA* 39:7852)

1710. SHAFFER, JOHN W.; OTA, KAY Y.; and HANLON, THOMAS E. "The Comparative Validity of Several MMPI Indices of Severity of Psychopathology." *J Clin Psychol* 20:467–73 O '64. * (*PA* 39:12367)

1711. SHERICK, IVAN GARY. *Body Image, Level of Ego Development and Adequacy of Ego Functioning.* Doctor's thesis, Washington University (St. Louis, Mo.), 1964. (*DA* 26:1782)

1712. SINGH, BEER. "Development of Some MMPI Scales in Indian Conditions (A Preliminary Report)." *Indian Psychol R* 1:75–80 Jl '64. * (*PA* 39:7875)

1713. SLATER, PHILIP, E., and SCARR, HARRY A. "Personality in Old Age." *Genetic Psychol Monogr* 70:229–69 N '64. * (*PA* 39:9861)

1714. SLUSHER, HOWARD S. "Personality and Intelligence Characteristics of Selected High School Athletes and Nonathletes." *Q Res* 35:539–45 D '64. * (*PA* 39:8594)

1715. SPIEGEL, DONALD E.; ACKER, CHARLES W.; and GRAYSON, HARRY M. "Associated Changes in MMPI and Autonomic Balance Scores in Hospitalized Depressives." *Newsl Res Psychol* 6:31–2 F '64. *

1716. STELMACHERS, ZIGFRIDS T., and McHUGH, RICHARD B. "Contribution of Stereotyped and Individualized Information to Predictive Accuracy." *J Consult Psychol* 28:234–42 Je '64. * (*PA* 39:5324)

1717. STONE, LEROY A. "Another Note on the Reliability of the MMPI Scatter Index." *Psychol Rep* 15:445 O '64. * (*PA* 39:5099)

1718. STONE, LEROY A. "Subtle and Obvious Response on the MMPI." *Psychol Rep* 15:721–2 D '64. * (*PA* 39:7876)

1719. SWEENEY, ROBERT H. *Testing Seminarians With MMPI and Kuder: A Report of Ten Years of Testing.* Master's thesis, Loyola University (Chicago, Ill.), 1964.

1720. SWEENEY, ROBERT HOWARD. "The Morality of Psychological Testing of Vocation Prospects." *Nat Cath Ed Assn B* 61:370–81 Ag '64. *

1721. SWENSON, W. M., and PEARSON, J. S. "Automation Techniques in Personality Assessment: A Frontier in Behavioral Science and Medicine." *Meth Inform Med* 3:34–6 Ja '64. *

1722. SWENSON, WENDELL M.; PEARSON, JOHN S.; and ROME, HOWARD P. "Automation Techniques in Personality Assessment: Fusion of Three Professions," pp. 149–56. In *Proceedings of Conference on Data Acquisition and Processing in Biology and Medicine, Vol. 2, Proceedings of the 1962 Rochester Conference.* Edited by Kurt Enslein. New York: Pergamon Press, Inc., 1964. Pp. ix, 367. *

1723. TELLEGEN, AUKE. Chap. 2, "The Minnesota Multiphasic Personality Inventory," pp. 30–48. In *Progress in Clinical Psychology, Vol. 6.* Edited by Lawrence Edwin Abt and Bernard F. Riess. New York: Grune & Stratton, Inc., 1964. Pp. xi, 252. * (*PA* 39:6295)

1724. TERWILLIGER, ROBERT F. "Sensitivity and Recall." *Psychol Rep* 14:217–8 F '64. * (*PA* 39:717)

1725. TETER, JEAN T., and DANA, RICHARD H. "Construct Validation of the Barron Ego Strength Scale." *Psychol Rep* 15:525–6 O '64. * (*PA* 39:5048)

1726. TEW, B. ORSON. *The Relationship of Measured Personality Variables to the Academic Success of College Students on Academic Probation.* Doctor's thesis, Brigham Young University (Provo, Utah), 1964. (*DA* 25:2328)

1727. THUMIN, F. J., and WITTENBERG, ANGELA. "Personality Characteristics and the Nonpayment of Bills." *J Clin Psychol* 20:234–5 Ap '64. * (*PA* 39:7855)

1728. TROXEL, WILLIAM DEE. *An Investigation of Humor as a Dimension of Assessment of the Counselee.* Doctor's thesis, University of California (Los Angeles, Calif.), 1964. (*DA* 25:3409)

1729. WATERFALL, RICHARD A. *An Evaluation of the Personality Characteristics of Institutionalized Narcotic Drug Addicts by Means of the MMPI.* Master's thesis, Immaculate Heart College (Los Angeles, Calif.), 1964.

1730. WHITE, ESTHER BOYD. *A Study of the Frequency of Use of the University Medical Services in Relation to Personality Factors and to Academic Achievement of Students at the University of North Carolina at Greensboro.* Doctor's thesis, Louisiana State University (Baton Rouge, La.), 1964. (*DA* 25:2358)

1731. WIGGINS, JERRY S. "Convergences Among Stylistic Response Measures From Objective Personality Tests." *Ed & Psychol Meas* 24:551–62 f '64. * (*PA* 39:5165)

1732. WIGGINS, JERRY S. "An MMPI Item Characteristic Deck." *Ed & Psychol Meas* 24:137–41 sp '64. * (*PA* 39:1850)

1733. WILCOCK, KEITH D. "Neurotic Differences Between Individualized and Socialized Criminals." *J Consult Psychol* 28:141–5 Ap '64. * (*PA* 39:2629)

1734. WINICK, CHARLES. "Personality Characteristics of Embalmers." *Personnel & Guid J* 43:262–6 N '64. * (*PA* 39:10222)

1735. WOGAN, MICHAEL. *A Study of the Relationship Between Personality Similarity in Psychotherapeutic Dyads and the Quality of the Therapeutic Experience.* Doctor's thesis, University of North Carolina (Chapel Hill, N.C.), 1964. (*DA* 26:1787)

1736. WOLF, SIDNEY; FREINEK, WILFRIED R.; and SHAFFER, JOHN W. "Comparability of Complete Oral and Booklet Forms of the MMPI." *J Clin Psychol* 20:375–8 Jl '64. * (*PA* 39:10253)

1737. ADAMS, DARRELL K., and HORN, JOHN L. "Nonoverlapping Keys for the MMPI Scales." Abstract. *J Consult Psychol* 29:284 Je '65. * (*PA* 39:12352, title only)

1738. ANDERSON, HARRY E., JR., and BARRY, JOHN R. "Occupational Choices in Selected Health Professions." *Personnel & Guid J* 44:177–84 O '65. * (*PA* 40:3419)

1739. BACH, GALE WINSTON. *Cognitive Functioning in Psychosomatic Illness.* Doctor's thesis, University of California (Berkeley, Calif.), 1965. (*DA* 27:960B)

1740. BARGER, BEN, and HALL, EVERETTE. "The Relationship of MMPI High Points and PIT Need Attitude Scores for Male College Students." *J Clin Psychol* 21:266–9 Jl '65. * (*PA* 39:15210)

1741. BECKER, SAMUEL L.; GOODSTEIN, LEONARD D.; and MITTMAN, ARTHUR. "Relationships Between the Minnesota Multiphasic Personality Inventory and the College Characteristics Index." *J Col Stud Personnel* 6:219–23 Je '65. *

1742. BECKETT, PETER G. S.; GRISELL, JAMES G.; and GUDOBBA, ROGER. "Psychiatric Attributes of MMPI Profiles." *Proc IBM Med Symp* 6:135–46 ['65]. *

1743. BERNARD, J. L.; KINZIE, W. B.; TOLLMAN, G. A.; and WEBB, R. A. "Some Effects of a Brief Course in the Psychology of Adjustment of a Psychiatric Admissions Ward." *J Clin Psychol* 21:322–6 Jl '65. * (*PA* 39:15211)

1744. BLACKBURN, R. "Emotionality, Repression-Sensitization, and Maladjustment." *Brit J Psychiatry* 111:399–404 My '65. * (*PA* 39:12887)

1745. BLACKMAN, SHELDON, and GOLDSTEIN, KENNETH M. "A Comparison of MMPI's of Enuretic With Non-Enuretic Adults." *J Clin Psychol* 21:282–3 Jl '65. * (*PA* 39:15340)

1746. BLANK, LEONARD. *Psychological Evaluation in Psychotherapy: Ten Case Histories.* Chicago, Ill.: Aldine Publishing Co., 1965. Pp. xii, 364. *

1747. BLAZER, JOHN A. "MMPI Interpretation in Outline: 1, The ? Scale." *Psychol* 2:23–4 My '65. * (*PA* 39:12354)

1748. BLAZER, JOHN A. "MMPI Interpretation in Outline: 2, The L Scale." *Psychol* 2:2–7 Ag '65. * (*PA* 15341)

1749. BLAZER, JOHN A. "MMPI Interpretation in Outline: 3, The F Scale." *Psychol* 2:2–9 N '65. * (*PA* 40:2933)

1750. BLOCK, JACK. *The Challenge of Response Sets: Unconfounding Meaning, Acquiescence, and Social Desirability in the MMPI.* New York: Appleton-Century-Crofts, 1965. Pp. ix, 142. * (*PA* 40:2934, title only)

1751. BODIN, ARTHUR M., and GEER, JAMES H. "Association Responses of Depressed and Non-Depressed Patients to Words of Three Hostility Levels." *J Personality* 33:392–408 S '65. * (*PA* 40:3231)

1752. BORGHI, JOHN HENRY. *An Investigation of Treatment*

Attrition in Psychotherapy. Doctor's thesis, University of Arizona (Tucson, Ariz.), 1965. (*DA* 26:1770)

1753. BOXHILL, CARLTON J. *A Special MMPI Scale Related to the Retention and Dismissal of Freshmen College Students on Academic Probation.* Doctor's thesis, Rutgers—The State University (New Brunswick, N.J.), 1965. (*DA* 27:384A)

1754. BRAATEN, LEIF J., and DARLING, C. DOUGLAS. "Overt and Covert Homosexual Problems Among Male College Students." *Genetic Psychol Monogr* 71:269–310 My '65. * (*PA* 39:16097)

1755. BRECKEL, MARY SUSANNE. *A Critical Analysis of Selected Research on the Minnesota Multiphasic Personality Inventory, 1951–1961.* Doctor's thesis, Boston College (Chestnut Hill, Mass.), 1965.

1756. BUTCHER, JAMES NEAL. "Manifest Aggression: MMPI Correlates in Normal Boys." *J Consult Psychol* 29:446–54 O '65. * (*PA* 40:548)

1757. CAINE, T. M. Chap. 13, "Changes in Symptom, Attitude, and Trait Measures Among Chronic Neurotics in a Therapeutic Community," pp. 262–91. In *Personality and Personal Illness.* By G. A. Foulds and others. London: Tavistock Publications Ltd., 1965. Pp. xii, 344. *

1758. CANTER, ARTHUR. "A Brief Note on Shortening Barron's Ego Strength Scale." *J Clin Psychol* 21:285–6 Jl '65. * (*PA* 39:15215)

1759. CARKHUFF, ROBERT R.; BARNETTE, W. LESLIE, JR.; and McCALL, JOHN N. *The Counselor's Handbook: Scale and Profile Interpretations of the MMPI.* Urbana, Ill.: R. W. Parkinson & Associates, 1965. Pp. 71. *

1760. CECIL, CARL EDWIN. *A Comparative Analysis of the Personality Patterns of Professional Education Personnel and Non-Education Personnel Using the Minnesota Multiphasic Personality Inventory.* Doctor's thesis, West Virginia University (Morgantown, W.Va.), 1965.

1761. CLARK, D. F. "The Psychometric Characteristics of an Adult Class in Psychology." *Brit J Psychiatry* 111:745–53 Ag '65. * (*PA* 40:1584)

1762. COHEN, LEON, and DAY, MERLE E. "Prediction of Performance of Nursing Assistant: Summary." *Newsl Res Psychol* 7:10 My '65. *

1763. COOPER, G. DAVID; ADAMS, HENRY B.; and COHEN, LOUIS D. "Personality Changes After Sensory Deprivation." *J Nerv & Mental Dis* 140:103–18 F '65. * (*PA* 39:13642)

1764. COROTTO, LOREN V. "Memory, Item Content, and MMPI Scale Test-Retest Reliability." *Calif Mental Health Res Dig* 3:81–3 sp '65. *

1765. COSTA, LOUIS D.; COX, MOLLY; and KATZMAN, ROBERT. "Relationship Between MMPI Variables and Percentage and Amplitude of EEG Alpha Activity." Abstract. *J Consult Psychol* 29:90 F '65. * (*PA* 39:7858, title only)

1766. COYLE, F. A., JR., and HEAP, ROBERT F. "Interpreting the MMPI L Scale." *Psychol Rep* 17:722 D '65. * (*PA* 40:3565)

1767. CRAFT, MICHAEL. Chap. 3, "Diagnosis and Aetiology Illustrated by an Analysis of Admissions to a Psychopathic Unit," pp. 32–54. In *Ten Studies Into Psychopathic Personality: A Report to the Home Office and the Mental Health Research Fund.* Bristol, England: John Wright & Sons Ltd., 1965. Pp. 133. *

1768. DANET, BURTON N. "Prediction of Mental Illness in College Students on the Basis of 'Nonpsychiatric' MMPI Profiles." *J Consult Psychol* 29:577–80 D '65. * (*PA* 40:2936)

1769. DICKEN, CHARLES F., and BLACK, JOHN D. "Predictive Validity of Psychometric Evaluations of Supervisors." *J Appl Psychol* 49:34–47 F '65. * (*PA* 39:8793)

1770. DUBNO, PETER. "Leadership, Group Effectiveness, and Speed of Decision." *J Social Psychol* 65:351–60 Ap '65. * (*PA* 39:15075)

1771. DUFF, FRANKLIN L. "Item Subtlety in Personality Inventory Scales." *J Consult Psychol* 29:565–70 D '65. * (*PA* 40:2938)

1772. EDWARDS, ALLEN L. "Correlation of 'A Unidimensional Depression Scale for the MMPI' With the SD Scale." *J Consult Psychol* 29:271–3 Je '65. * (*PA* 39:12356)

1773. EDWARDS, ALLEN L. "Measurement of Individual Differences in Ratings of Social Desirability and in the Tendency to Give Socially Desirable Responses." *J Exp Res Personality* 1:91–8 O '65. * (*PA* 40:2899)

1774. FAULS, LYDIA BOYCE. *Measurements of Interrelations Among Selected Suppression Factors, Anxiety, Impulse Expression, and Ego Strength.* Doctor's thesis, Florida State University (Tallahassee, Fla.), 1965. (*DA* 26:7446)

1775. FINNEY, JOSEPH C. "Development of a New Set of MMPI Scales." *Psychol Rep* 17:707–13 D '65. * (*PA* 40:4248)

1776. FINNEY, JOSEPH C. "Effects of Response Sets on New and Old MMPI Scales." *Psychol Rep* 17:907–15 D '65. * (*PA* 40:4249)

1777. FORSYTH, RALPH P., JR. "MMPI and Demographic Correlates of Post-Hospital Adjustment in Neuropsychiatric Patients." *Psychol Rep* 16:355–66 Ap '65. * (*PA* 39:10459)

1778. FOSSE, JOHN BENJAMIN. *The Prediction of Teaching Effectiveness: An Investigation of the Relationships Among High School Band Contest Ratings, Teacher Characteristics, and School Environmental Factors.* Doctor's thesis, Northwestern University (Evanston, Ill.), 1965. (*DA* 26:3391)

1779. FRANK, RUTH ESSER. *Changes in Classroom Interaction Patterns and Their Relationship to Scores on the Minnesota Multiphasic Personality Inventory of a Selected Group*

of Intern-Teachers During Their First Semester of Teaching. Doctor's thesis, Temple University (Philadelphia, Pa.), 1965. (*DA* 26:1476)

1780. FREEDMAN, MERVIN B. "The Sexual Behavior of American College Women: An Empirical Study and an Historical Survey." *Merrill-Palmer* 11:33–48 Ja '65. * (*PA* 39:9960)

1781. FRIBERG, RICHARD ROY. *A Study of Homosexuality and Related Characteristics in Paranoid Schizophrenia.* Doctor's thesis, University of Minnesota (Minneapolis, Minn.), 1965. (*DA* 26:491)

1782. FULLER, GERALD, and UYENO, ENSLEY. "Perception as a Function of Severity of Disturbance in Psychotics." *Percept & Motor Skills* 20:953–8 Je '65. * (*PA* 39:16155)

1783. GALLESSICH, JUNE M. *Interrelationships Between the Extended L and K Scales of the MMPI and Between These Scales and Other Measures Significant to Counseling Education.* Master's thesis, University of Texas (Austin, Tex.), 1965.

1784. GELSINGER, STEPHEN W. *The Value of the MMPI as a Screening Device for Boys' Baseball Programs.* Master's thesis, Occidental College (Los Angeles, Calif.), 1965.

1785. GILBERSTADT, HAROLD, and DUKER, JAN. *A Handbook for Clinical and Actuarial MMPI Interpretation.* Philadelphia, Pa.: W. B. Saunders Co., 1965. Pp. x, 134. * (*PA* 40:1589, title only)

1786. GILBERSTADT, HAROLD, and MALEY, MICHAEL. "GSR, Clinical State and Psychiatric Diagnosis." *J Clin Psychol* 21:235–8 Jl '65. * (*PA* 39:15553)

1787. GLUECK, BERNARD C., JR., and REZNIKOFF, MARVIN. "Comparison of Computer-Derived Personality Profile and Projective Psychological Test Findings." *Am J Psychiatry* 121:1156–61 Je '65. * (*PA* 39:15348)

1788. GOLDBERG, LEWIS R. "Diagnosticians vs. Diagnostic Signs: The Diagnosis of Psychosis vs. Neurosis from the MMPI." *Psychol Monogr* 79(9):1–28 '65. * (*PA* 39:12644)

1789. GOLDBERG, PHILIP A., and STARK, MILTON J. "Johnson or Goldwater?: Some Personality and Attitude Correlates of Political Choice." *Psychol Rep* 17:627–31 O '65. * (*PA* 40:1501)

1790. GOLDMAN, IRWIN J. "Acceptance of Sc Scale Statements by Visual Art Students." *Ed & Psychol Meas* 25:819–28 au '65. * (*PA* 40:2901)

1791. GOLDSCHMID, MARCEL LUCIEN. *The Prediction of College Major in the Sciences and the Humanities by Means of Personality Tests.* Doctor's thesis, University of California (Berkeley, Calif.), 1965. (*DA* 26:4073)

1792. GOLDSTEIN, GERALD, and CHOTLOS, JOHN W. "Dependency and Brain Damage in Alcoholics." *Percept & Motor Skills* 21:135–50 Ag '65. * (*PA* 40:608)

1793. GOLIN, SANFORD, and SOLKOFF, NORMAN. "Generality of the Repression-Sensitization Dimension: Threat of Nuclear War." *Psychol Rep* 16:385–6 Ap '65. * (*PA* 39:10293)

1794. GOUGH, HARRISON G.; WENK, ERNEST A.; and ROZYNKO, VITALI V. "Parole Outcome as Predicted From the CPI, the MMPI, and a Base Expectancy Table." *J Abn Psychol* 70:432–41 D '65. * (*PA* 40:3143)

1795. GRAHAM, JOHN ROBERT. *A Q-Sort Study of the Accuracy of Descriptions Based on the Minnesota Multiphasic Personality Inventory.* Doctor's thesis, University of North Carolina (Chapel Hill, N.C.), 1965. (*DA* 28:2623B)

1796. GRAVITZ, MELVIN A., and DAVIS, NORMAN W. "Procedures and Problems in Computer Analysis of the MMPI." *J Psychol* 61:171–6 N '65. * (*PA* 40:4742)

1797. GYNTHER, MALCOLM D., and SHIMKUNAS, ALGIMANTAS M. "Age, Intelligence, and MMPI F Scores." *J Consult Psychol* 29:383–8 Ag '65. * (*PA* 39:15351)

1798. GYNTHER, MALCOLM D., and SHIMKUNAS, ALGIMANTAS M. "More Data on MMPI F > 16 Scores." *J Clin Psychol* 21:275–7 Jl '65. * (*PA* 39:15350)

1799. HAAN, NORMA. "Coping and Defense Mechanisms Related to Personality Inventories." *J Consult Psychol* 29:373–8 Ag '65. * (*PA* 39:15352)

1800. HALL, CHARLES L., JR. "Maternal Control as Related to Schizoid Behaviors in Grossly Normal Males." *J Personality* 33:613–21 D '65. * (*PA* 40:4457)

1801. HANLEY, CHARLES. "Personality Item Difficulty and Acquiescence." *J Appl Psychol* 49:205–8 Je '65. * (*PA* 39:12286)

1802. HARE, ROBERT D. "Psychopathy, Fear Arousal and Anticipated Pain." *Psychol Rep* 16:499–502 Ap '65. * (*PA* 39:10640)

1803. HARRIS, JESSE G., JR., and BAXTER, JAMES C. "Ambiguity in the MMPI." *J Consult Psychol* 29:112–8 Ap '65. * (*PA* 39:10119)

1804. HATFIELD, JOHN S., and SHAPIRO, ALBERT M. "Dimensions Among Interview Ratings of Men: An Analysis of Their Meaning and Personality Inventory Correlates." *J Clin Psychol* 21:150–60 Ap '65. * (*PA* 39:12464)

1805. HAUN, KENNETH W. "Note on Prediction of Academic Performance From Personality Test Scores." *Psychol Rep* 16:294 F '65. * (*PA* 39:7687)

1806. HECK, EDWARD T., and DAWES, ROBYN MASON. "A Study of How Psychopathology Is Related to Attained Education and Occupational Class." *Newsl Res Psychol* 7:23–5 N '65. *

1807. HEDLUND, DALVA E. "A Review of the MMPI in Industry." *Psychol Rep* 17:875–89 D '65. * (*PA* 40:4629)

1808. HELSON, RAVENNA. "Childhood Interest Clusters Related to Creativity in Women." *J Consult Psychol* 29:352–61 Ag '65. * *(PA* 39:15292)

1809. HERRON, WILLIAM G.; GUIDO, STEPHEN M.; and KANTOR, ROBERT E. "Relationships Among Ego Strength Measures." *J Clin Psychol* 21:403–4 O '65. * *(PA* 40:1567)

1810. HIGGINS, JERRY; MEDNICK, SARNOFF A.; and PHILIP, FRANKLIN J. "The Schizophrenia Scale of the MMPI and Life Adjustment in Schizophrenia." *Psychol* 2:26–7 N '65. * *(PA* 40:3200)

1811. HILGARD, ERNEST R.; LAUER, LILLIAN W.; and CUCA, JANET MELEI. "Acquiescence, Hypnotic Susceptibility, and the MMPI." Abstract. *J Consult Psychol* 29:489 O '65. *

1812. HIMELSTEIN, PHILIP. "Validities and Intercorrelations of MMPI Subscales Predictive of College Achievement." *Ed & Psychol Meas* 25:1125–8 w '65. * *(PA* 40:3573)

1813. HINZMAN, JOHN L. *A Correlational Study of MMPI Non-Aptitude Traits and Guilford's Southern California Tests of Intellectual Abilities.* Master's thesis, Fort Hays Kansas State College (Hays, Kan.), 1965.

1814. HORNER, ALTHEA JANE. *An Investigation of the Relationship of Value Orientation to the Adaptive-Defensive System of the Personality.* Doctor's thesis, University of Southern California (Los Angeles, Calif.), 1965. *(DA* 26:1160)

1815. HOVEY, H. B. "Reply to Weingold, Dawson, and Kael." *Psychol Rep* 16:1122 Je '65. * *(PA* 39:15355)

1816. HOWELL, MARGARET AFFARENC. *Personality Factors in Medical Performance.* Doctor's thesis, University of California (Berkeley, Calif.), 1965. *(DA* 27:303B)

1817. HUFF, FREDERICK W. "Use of Actuarial Description of Abnormal Personality in a Mental Hospital." *Psychol Rep* 17:224 Ag '65. * *(PA* 40:1591, title only)

1818. JACOKES, LEE E. "MMPI Prediction of the Unwed Mother's Decision Regarding Child Placement." *J Clin Psychol* 21:280–1 Jl '65. * *(PA* 39:15356)

1819. JOHNSTON, ROY, and McNEAL, BENJAMIN F. "Residual Psychopathology in Released Psychiatric Patients and Its Relation to Readmission." *J Abn Psychol* 70:337–42 O '65. * *(PA* 40:550)

1820. JONES, NELSON F.; KAHN, MARVIN W.; and LANGSLEY, DONALD G. "Prediction of Admission to a Psychiatric Hospital." *Arch Gen Psychiatry* 12:607–10 Je '65. * *(PA* 39:12584)

1821. JORTNER, SIDNEY. "A Test of Hovey's MMPI Scale for CNS Disorder." *J Clin Psychol* 21:285 Jl '65. * *(PA* 39:15243)

1822. KANIA, WALTER. *An Investigation of the K Scale of the MMPI as a Measure of Defensiveness in Protestant Theological Seminary Students.* Doctor's thesis, Michigan State University (East Lansing, Mich.), 1965. *(DA* 26:6169)

1823. KEELER, MARTIN H., and DOEHNE, EDWARD F., III. "Consistency of Psilocybin Induced Changes in the Minnesota Multiphasic Personality Inventory." *J Clin Psychol* 21:284 Jl '65. * *(PA* 39:15358)

1824. KENNEDY, WALLACE A., and WALSH, JOHN. "A Factor Analysis of Mathematical Giftedness." *Psychol Rep* 17:115–9 Ag '65. * *(PA* 40:1553)

1825. KHATUN, SHAFIA. *A Comparative Study of Personality Characteristics of the Graduate Students Majoring in Educational Psychology and Guidance With the Graduate Students of Other Areas of Education at Colorado State College.* Doctor's research study No. 1, Colorado State College (Greeley, Colo.), 1965. *(DA* 26:868)

1826. KIDD, ALINE H., and RIVOIRE, JEANNE L. "Personality Variables and Attitudes Toward Traditional Cultural Fantasy." *J Clin Psychol* 21:377–80 O '65. * *(PA* 40:1569)

1827. KLETT, WILLIAM G. "An Investigation Into the Effect of Historically Based Inferences in Group Psychotherapy on the Behavior of Withdrawn Psychiatric Patients." *Newsl Res Psychol* 7:44–6 My '65. *

1828. KNUDSEN, ROBERT G. *A Study of the Relationship Between Personality as Measured by the Minnesota Multiphasic Personality Inventory and Interest as Measured by the Kuder Preference Record-Form C.* Master's thesis, Utah State University (Logan, Utah), 1965.

1829. KOGAN, KATE L., and JACKSON, JOAN K. "Some Concomitants of Personal Difficulties in Wives of Alcoholics and Nonalcoholics." *Q J Studies Alcohol* 26:595–604 D '65. * *(PA* 40:4396)

1830. LAFARGA, JUAN B. *An MMPI Study of Four Catholic College Groups.* Master's thesis, Loyola University (Chicago, Ill.), 1965.

1831. LANSDELL, H., and URBACH, NELLY. "Sex Differences in Personality Measures Related to Size and Side of Temporal Lobe Ablations." *Proc Ann Conv Am Psychol Assn* 73:113–4 '65. * *(PA* 39:14113)

1832. LAWTON, M. POWELL, and KLEBAN, MORTON H. "Prisoners' Faking on the MMPI." *J Clin Psychol* 21:269–71 Jl '65. * *(PA* 39:15359)

1833. LEE, RONALD REDVERS. *Theological Belief as a Dimension of Personality.* Doctor's thesis, Northwestern University (Evanston, Ill.), 1965. *(DA* 26:3510)

1834. LEEP, ALBERT GENE. *Selected Pre-Service Measures as Predictors of First Year Teaching Performance of Elementary Teachers.* Doctor's thesis, Ball State Teachers College (Muncie, Ind.), 1965. *(DA* 26:3163)

1835. LEVINSON, BORIS M. "Functioning on the Yeshiva College Subcultural Scale (YCSS) of Jewish Students Enrolled in a Jewish School of Social Work." *Psychol Rep* 17:744 D '65. * *(PA* 40:3579)

1836. LEVITT, HERBERT, and FELLNER, CARL. "MMPI Profiles of Three Obesity Subgroups." Abstract. *J Consult Psychol* 29:91 F '65. * *(PA* 39:7868, title only)

1837. LEWINSOHN, PETER M. "Dimensions of MMPI Change." *J Clin Psychol* 21:37–43 Ja '65. * *(PA* 39:12360)

1838. LIBERTY, PAUL G., JR. "Methodological Considerations in the Assessment of Acquiescence in the *MA* and *SD* Scale." *J Consult Psychol* 29:37–42 F '65. * *(PA* 39:7776)

1839. LIBERTY, PAUL G., JR.; VITOLA, BART M.; and PIERSON, JEROME S. "Set and Content Scores for Personality Scales and Response Styles in the MMPI." *J Appl Psychol* 49:326–31 O '65. * *(PA* 40:42)

1840. LICHTENSTEIN, EDWARD, and BRYAN, JAMES H. "Acquiescence and the MMPI: An Item Reversal Approach." *J Abn Psychol* 70:290–3 Ag '65. * *(PA* 39:15360)

1841. LOGUE, PATRICK E. *Concurrent Validation of Two Counselor Selection Inventories.* Doctor's thesis, University of North Dakota (Grand Forks, N.D.), 1965. *(DA* 26:6170)

1842. LOISELLE, ROBERT H., and MOLLENAUER, SANDRA. "Galvanic Skin Response to Sexual Stimuli in a Female Population." *J General Psychol* 73:273–8 O '65. * *(PA* 39:13691)

1843. LOMONT, JAMES F. "The Repression-Sensitization Dimension in Relation to Anxiety Responses." *J Consult Psychol* 29:84–6 F '65. * *(PA* 39:7959)

1844. MACANDREW, CRAIG. "The Differentiation of Male Alcoholic Outpatients From Nonalcoholic Psychiatric Outpatients by Means of the MMPI." *Q J Studies Alcohol* 26:238–46 Je '65. * *(PA* 40:2941)

1845. McDONALD, ROBERT L. "Ego-Control Patterns and Attribution of Hostility to Self and Others." *J Personality & Social Psychol* 2:273–7 Ag '65. * *(PA* 39:15438)

1846. McDONALD, ROBERT L. "Ego Control Patterns and Attributions of Hostility to Self, Parents, and Others." *Percept & Motor Skills* 21:339–48 O '65. * *(PA* 40:2944)

1847. McDONALD, ROBERT L. "Personality Characteristics, Cigarette Smoking, and Obstetric Complications." *J Psychol* 60:129–34 My '65. * *(PA* 39:15366)

1848. McDONALD, ROBERT L. "Personality Characteristics in Patients With Three Obstetric Complications." *Psychosom Med* 27:383–90 Jl–Ag '65. * *(PA* 39:15957)

1849. McDUFFIE, FREDERIC C., and McGUIRE, FREDERICK L. "Clinical and Psychological Patterns in Auto-Erythrocyte Sensitivity." *Ann Internal Med* 63:255–65 Ag '65. * *(PA* 39:15958)

1850. McGEHEARTY, LOYCE IVY DAWSON. *Factors Associated With the Probable Success of Prospective School Counselors as Evaluated by Their Peers and by Staff Members.* Doctor's thesis, University of Texas (Austin, Tex.), 1965. *(DA* 26:873)

1851. McGINNIS, CHARLES A., and RYAN, CHARLES W. "The Influence of Age on MMPI Scores of Chronic Alcoholics." *J Clin Psychol* 21:271–2 Jl '65. * *(PA* 39:15367)

1852. McKEEVER, WALTER F.; MAY, PHILIP R. A.; and TUMA, A. HUSSAIN. "Prognosis in Schizophrenia: Prediction of Length of Hospitalization From Psychological Test Variables." *J Clin Psychol* 21:214–21 Ap '65. * *(PA* 39:12856)

1853. McKEGNEY, F. PATRICK. "An Item Analysis of the MMPI F Scale in Juvenile Delinquents." *J Clin Psychol* 21:201–5 Ap '65. * *(PA* 39:12361)

1854. McMAHON, FRANK BORROMEO, JR. *Clinical Training: A Variable in Psychological Test Interpretation.* Doctor's thesis, Washington University (St. Louis, Mo.), 1965. *(DA* 26:4813)

1855. MANE, KAMAL LATHI. *An Experimental Investigation of the Relationship Between the MMPI and the Survey of Interpersonal Values.* Master's thesis, Loyola University (Chicago, Ill.), 1965.

1856. MARKWELL, EARL D. JR. "Alterations in Self-Concept Under Hypnosis." *J Personality & Social Psychol* 1:154–61 F '65. * *(PA* 39:7848)

1857. MARTIN, CLYDE V.; QUESNELL, JOHN G.; and ALVORD, JACK R. "Personality and Social History Characteristics of Enlisted Men Making Suicidal Gestures." *Proc Ann Conf Air Force Behav Sci* 11:72–91 Jl '65. *

1858. MARZOLF, STANLEY S. "Parent Behavior as Reported by College Students." *J Clin Psychol* 21:360–6 O '65. * *(PA* 40:1459)

1859. MEIER, M. J., and FRENCH, L. A. "Changes in MMPI Scale Scores and an Index of Psychopathology Following Unilateral Temporal Lobectomy for Epilepsy." *Epilepsia* 6:263–73 S '65. *

1860. MEIER, MANFRED J., and FRENCH, LYLE A. "Some Personality Correlates of Unilateral and Bilateral EEG Abnormalities in Psychomotor Epileptics." *J Clin Psychol* 21:3–9 Ja '65. * *(PA* 39:12693)

1861. MICHAEL, WILLIAM B.; HANEY, RUSSELL; and BROWN, STEPHEN W. "The Predictive Validity of a Battery of Diversified Measures Relative to Success in Student Nursing." *Ed & Psychol Meas* 25:579–84 su '65. * *(PA* 39:15247)

1862. MILLER, CLARENCE K. "The Psychological Impact of Coronary Artery Disease." *Newsl Res Psychol* 7:21–2 Ag '65. *

1863. MOOS, RUDOLF, and SOLOMON, GEORGE F. "Personality Correlates of the Degree of Functional Incapacity of Patients With Physical Disease." *J Chronic Dis* 18:1019–38 O '65. *

1864. MOOS, RUDOLF H., and SOLOMON, GEORGE F. "Psychologic Comparisons Between Women With Rheumatoid Arthritis and Their Nonarthritic Sisters: 1, Personality Test and Interview Rating Data." *Psychosom Med* 27:135–49 Mr–Ap '65. * (*PA* 39:12920)

1865. MOSBY, DORIS VIRGINIA PERRY. *Maternal "Identification" and Perceived Similarity to Parents in Adolescents as a Function of Grade Placement*. Doctor's thesis, Washington University (St. Louis, Mo.), 1965. (*DA* 26:6841)

1866. MULLER, BRUCE P. "Personality of Placebo Reactors and Nonreactors." *Dis Nerv System* 26:57–61 Ja '65. *

1867. MURRAY, JOHN B.; MUNLEY, M. JUDITH; and GILBART, THOMAS E. "The PD Scale of the MMPI for College Students." *J Clin Psychol* 21:48–51 Ja '65. * (*PA* 39:12364)

1868. MURTAUGH, JAMES J. *A Longitudinal Study Investigating the Predictability of the MMPI and Kuder for Diocesan Seminaries*. Master's thesis, Loyola University (Chicago, Ill.), 1965.

1869. MUTHARD, JOHN E. "MMPI Findings for Cerebral Palsied College Students." Abstract. *J Consult Psychol* 29:599 D '65. * (*PA* 40:3293, title only)

1870. MUZEKARI, LOUIS H. "The MMPI in Predicting Treatment Outcome in Alcoholism." Abstract. *J Consult Psychol* 29:281 Je '65. * (*PA* 39:12365, title only)

1871. NICHOLAS, D. JACK. *Guilt as Related to Self-Concept and Personality Adjustment*. Doctor's thesis, North Texas State University (Denton, Tex.), 1965. (*DA* 26:4080)

1872. PATTERSON, THOMAS STEPHEN. *An Investigation of MMPI Scale Mean Differences, Correlations and Profile Patterns of Low, Average, and High Reading Ability Males Attending Private, Catholic High Schools*. Doctor's thesis, Boston College (Chestnut Hill, Mass.), 1965.

1873. PAUKER, JEROME D. "MMPI Profile Stability in a Psychiatric, Inpatient Population." *J Clin Psychol* 21:281–2 Jl '65. * (*PA* 39:15369)

1874. PEARSON, JOHN S.; ROME, HOWARD P.; SWENSON, WENDELL M.; MATAYA, PETE; and BRANNICK, THOMAS L. "Development of a Computer System for Scoring and Interpretation of Minnesota Multiphasic Personality Inventories in a Medical Clinic." Discussion by Joseph Brožek. *Ann N Y Acad Sci* 126:684–95 Ag 6 '65. * (*PA* 40:2945)

1875. PEARSON, JOHN S.; SWENSON, WENDELL M.; and ROME, HOWARD P. "Age and Sex Difference Related to MMPI Response Frequency in 25,000 Medical Patients." *Am J Psychiatry* 121:988–95 Ap '65. * (*PA* 39:10244)

1876. PETERS, PHYLLIS G. *A Study of Clinical Judgment: Prediction of Patient Behavior From Projective, Self-Rating and Behavior Rating Instruments*. Doctor's thesis, Northwestern University (Evanston, Ill.), 1965. (*DA* 26:3489)

1877. PLYLER, SAMUEL AUSTIN. *Personality Differences as Measured by the MMPI Between Diagnosed Groups of Male Clients Seen at a College Counseling Bureau*. Doctor's thesis, University of Missouri (Columbia, Mo.), 1965. (*DA* 26:5243)

1878. POLLACK, DONALD. *Experimental Intoxication of Alcoholics and Normals: Some Psychological Changes*. Doctor's thesis, University of California (Los Angeles, Calif.), 1965. (*DA* 25:7383)

1879. POOL, DONALD A. "The Kuder Social Service Scale and Hospitalization." *Rehabil Counsel B* 9:47–52 D '65. *

1880. QUINN, ROBERT P., and LICHTENSTEIN, EDWARD. "Convergent and Discriminant Validities of Acquiescence Measures." *J General Psychol* 73:93–104 Jl '65. * (*PA* 39:13696)

1881. RAPOPORT, JUDITH L. "American Abortion Applicants in Sweden." *Arch Gen Psychiatry* 13:24–33 Jl '65. * (*PA* 39:14979)

1882. REILLY, HOWARD E. *A Comparative Analysis of Selected Characteristics of Admitted and Non-Admitted Students to the College of Education, Wayne State University*. Doctor's thesis, Wayne State University (Detroit, Mich.), 1965. (*DA* 27:988A)

1883. REZNIKOFF, MARVIN, and TOOMEY, LAURA C. "An Evaluation of Some Possible Prognostic Indicators of Response to Phenothiazine Treatment of Acute Schizophrenic Psychoses." *Int J Neuropsychiatry* 1:352–8 Jl–Ag '65. *

1884. RICHARDSON, HAROLD, and ROEBUCK, JULIAN. "Minnesota Multiphasic Personality Inventory and California Psychological Inventory Differences Between Delinquents and Their Nondelinquent Siblings." *Proc Ann Conv Am Psychol Assn* 73:255–6 '65. * (*PA* 39:16142)

1885. RICHARDSON, ROY LEWIS. *Parent-Child Relationships and the Divergent Student*. Doctor's thesis, University of Missouri (Columbia, Mo.), 1965. (*DA* 26:5542)

1886. RODGERS, DAVID A.; ZIEGLER, FREDERICK F.; ALTROCCHI, JOHN; and LEVY, NISSIM. "A Longitudinal Study of the Psycho-Social Effects of Vasectomy." *J Marriage & Family* 27:59–64 F '65. * (*PA* 39:8247)

1887. ROME, HOWARD P.; MATAYA, PETE; PEARSON, JOHN S.; and BRANNICK, THOMAS L. Chap. 21, "Automatic Personality Assessment," pp. 505–24. In *Computers in Biomedical Research, Vol. 1*. Edited by Ralph W. Stacey and Bruce D. Waxman. New York: Academic Press, Inc., 1965. Pp. xxii, 562. *

1888. RORER, LEONARD G. "The Great Response-Style Myth." *Psychol B* 63:129–56 Mr '65. * (*PA* 39:10064)

1889. RORER, LEONARD G., and GOLDBERG, LEWIS R. "Acquiescence and the Vanishing Variance Component." *J Appl Psychol* 49:422–30 D '65. * (*PA* 40:2946)

1890. RORER, LEONARD G., and GOLDBERG, LEWIS R. "Acquiescence in the MMPI?" *Ed & Psychol Meas* 25:801–17 au '65. * (*PA* 40:2143)

1891. ROSTON, RONALD A. "Some Personality Characteristics of Male Compulsive Gamblers." *Proc Ann Conv Am Psychol Assn* 73:263–4 '65. * (*PA* 39:16077)

1892. SALMON, PHILLIDA. "Fould's Punitiveness Scales in Relation to MMPI Validation and Diagnostic Scales." *Brit J Social & Clin Psychol* 4:207–13 S '65. * (*PA* 40:1572, title only)

1893. SANDS, PATRICK MERLIN. *Application of the Interpersonal Problems Attitude Survey in a Patients Training Laboratory*. Doctor's thesis, University of Houston (Houston, Tex.), 1965. (*DA* 26:2326)

1894. SCHUBERT, DANIEL S. P. "Arousal Seeking as a Central Factor in Tobacco Smoking Among College Students." *Int J Social Psychiatry* 11:221–5 su '65. * (*PA* 41:1596)

1895. SCOTT, GARY KUPER. *A Study of the Relationship Between Ratings of Counselor Success and Selected Personality Variables*. Doctor's thesis, University of Minnesota (Minneapolis, Minn.), 1965. (*DA* 26:5249)

1896. SHAW, DALE J., and MATTHEWS, CHARLES G. "Differential MMPI Performance of Brain-Damaged vs. Pseudo-Neurologic Groups." *J Clin Psychol* 21:405–8 O '65. * (*PA* 40:1892)

1897. SHEKELLE, R. B., and OSTFELD, ADRIAN M. "Psychometric Evaluations in Cardiovascular Epidemiology." *Ann N Y Acad Sci* 126:696–705 Ag 6 '65. *

1898. SHIPMAN, WILLIAM G. "Personality Traits Associated With Body-Image Boundary Concern." *Proc Ann Conv Am Psychol Assn* 73:271–2 '65. * (*PA* 39:15441)

1899. SHIPMAN, WILLIAM G. "The Validity of MMPI Hostility Scales." *J Clin Psychol* 21:186–90 Ap '65. * (*PA* 39:12368)

1900. SHURE, GERALD H., and ROGERS, MILES S. "Note of Caution on the Factor Analysis of the MMPI." *Psychol B* 63:14–8 Ja '65. * (*PA* 39:7872)

1901. SIEGMAN, ARON WOLFE, and POPE, BENJAMIN. "Personality Variables Associated With Productivity and Verbal Influence in the Initial Interview." *Proc Ann Conv Am Psychol Assn* 73:273–4 '65. * (*PA* 39:15655)

1902. SIKES, MELVIN P.; FAIBISH, GEORGE; and VALLES, JORGE. "Evaluation of an Intensive Alcoholic Treatment Program." *Newsl Res Psychol* 7:19–20 Ag '65. *

1903. SIKES, MELVIN P.; FAIBISH, GEORGE; and VALLES, JORGE. "Evaluation of an Intensive Alcoholic Treatment Program." *Proc Am Conv Am Psychol Assn* 73:275–6 '65. * (*PA* 39:16090)

1904. SILVERMAN, ALBERT J. "Psychophysiological Correlates of Perception." *Proc IBM Med Symp* 6:287–303 ['65]. *

1905. SILVERMAN, LLOYD H. "A Study of the Effects of Subliminally Presented Aggressive Stimuli on the Production of Pathologic Thinking in a Nonpsychiatric Population." *J Nerv & Mental Dis* 141:443–55 O '65. * (*PA* 40:5497)

1906. SINGH, BEER. "Development of MMPI Profiles for Different Academic Groups." *Indian Psychol R* 2:69–73 Jl '65. * (*PA* 40:2947)

1907. SINGH, BEER. *Development of Some MMPI Scales in Indian Conditions*, Doctor's thesis, Banaras Hindu University (Varanasi, India), 1965.

1908. SINGH, BEER. "Item-Analysis of the Indian Adaptation of Some MMPI Scales." *Psychol Studies* 10:61–5 Ja '65. * (*PA* 39:10249)

1909. SIVLEY, ROBERT B., and JOHNSON, DALE T. "Psychopathology and Locus of Control." *J Clin Psychol* 21:26 Ja '65. * (*PA* 39:12369)

1910. SOLOMON, GEORGE F., and MOOS, RUDOLF H. "The Relationship of Personality to the Presence of Rheumatoid Factor in Asymptomatic Relatives of Patients With Rheumatoid Arthritis." *Psychosom Med* 27:350–60 Jl–Ag '65. * (*PA* 39:16288)

1911. SOUEIF, M. I. "Response Sets, Neuroticism and Extraversion: A Factorial Study." *Acta Psychologica* 24:29–40 My '65. * (*PA* 39:15272)

1912. STONE, LeROY A. "Measured Personality Correlates of a Judged Prognosis Scale." *Proc Ann Conv Am Psychol Assn* 73:277–8 '65. * (*PA* 39:15444)

1913. STONE, LeROY A. "Relationships Between Response to the Marlowe-Crowne Social Desirability Scale and MMPI Scales." *Psychol Rep* 17:179–82 Ag '65. * (*PA* 40:1577)

1914. STONE, LeROY A. "Reliability Estimate for Favorability (Social Desirability) Ratings of MMPI Items." *Psychol Rep* 16:720 Je '65. * (*PA* 39:15274)

1915. STONE, LeROY A. "Social Desirability and Order of Item Presentation in the MMPI." *Psychol Rep* 17:518 O '65. * (*PA* 40:898)

1916. STONE, LeROY A. "Social Desirability Response Bias and MMPI Content Categories." *Psychol* 2:2–3 My '65. * (*PA* 39:12371)

1917. STONE, LeROY A. "Subtle and Obvious Response on the MMPI as a Function of Acquiescence Response Style." *Psychol Rep* 16:803–4 Je '65. * (*PA* 39:15275)

1918. STONE, LeROY A. "Test-Retest Stability of the MMPI Scales." *Psychol Rep* 16:619–20 Ap '65. * (*PA* 39:10155)

1919. STONE, LeROY A., and MARGOSHES, ADAM. "Verbal Embellishment Responses on the MMPI." *J Clin Psychol* 21:278–9 Jl '65. * (*PA* 39:15375)

1920. SUTTON-SMITH, B., and ROSENBERG, B. G. "Age Changes in the Effects of Ordinal Position on Sex-Role Identification." *J Genetic Psychol* 107:61–73 S '65. * (*PA* 39:14614)

1921. SWENSON, WENDELL M., and PEARSON, JOHN S. "Experience With Large-Scale Psychological Testing in a Medical Center." *Proc IBM Med Symp* 6:147–62 ['65]. *

1922. Swenson, Wendell M.; Rome, Howard P.; Pearson, John S.; and Brannick, Thomas L. "A Totally Automated Psychological Test: Experience in a Medical Center." *J Am Med Assn* 191:925–7 Mr 15 '65. * (*PA* 39:10251)

1923. Tellegen, Auke. "Direction of Measurement: A Source of Misinterpretation." *Psychol B* 63:233–43 Ap '65. * (*PA* 39:9003)

1924. Thumin, Frederick J. "Personality Characteristics of Diverse Occupational Groups." *Personnel & Guid J* 43:468–70 Ja '65. * (*PA* 39:10217)

1925. Truax, Charles B., and Carkhuff, Robert R. "Personality Change in Hospitalized Mental Patients During Group Psychotherapy as a Function of the Use of Alternate Sessions and Vicarious Therapy Pretraining." *J Clin Psychol* 21:225–8 Ap '65. * (*PA* 39:12530)

1926. Truax, Charles B.; Carkhuff, Robert R.; and Kodman, Frank. "Relationships Between Therapist-Offered Conditions and Patient Change in Group Psychotherapy." *J Clin Psychol* 21:327–9 Jl '65. * (*PA* 39:15702)

1927. Vaughan, Richard P. "The Influence of Religious Affiliation on the MMPI Scales." *J Clin Psychol* 21:416–7 O '65. * (*PA* 40:1491)

1928. Vitz, Paul C., and Johnston, Donald. "Masculinity of Smokers and the Masculinity of Cigarette Images." *J Appl Psychol* 49:155–9 Je '65. * (*PA* 39:13157)

1929. Wahler, H. J. "Item Popularity and Social Desirability in the MMPI." *J Appl Psychol* 49:439–45 D '65. * (*PA* 40:2948)

1930. Wallach, Martin S., and Schooff, Kenneth. "Reliability of Degree of Disturbance Ratings." *J Clin Psychol* 21:273–5 Jl '65. * (*PA* 39:15336)

1931. Waltmann, Robert H., and Birds, Valentine G. "Role of the Electronic Computer in Clinical Medicine." *Psychosomatics* 6:277–81 S–O '65. *

1932. Warman, Roy E., and Hannum, Thomas E. "MMPI Pattern Changes in Female Prisoners." *J Res Crime & Del* 2:72–6 Jl '65.

1933. Watley, Donivan J. "Performance and Characteristics of the Confident Student." *Personnel & Guid J* 43:591–6 F '65. * (*PA* 39:10782)

1934. Watson, Charles G. "A Test of the Relationship Between Repressed Homosexuality and Paranoid Mechanisms." *J Clin Psychol* 21:380–4 O '65. * (*PA* 40:1802)

1935. Weisgerber, Charles A. "Comparison of Normalized and Linear T Scores in the MMPI." *J Clin Psychol* 21:412–5 O '65. * (*PA* 40:1599)

1936. Weiss, Robert J.; Segal, Bernard E.; and Sokol, Robert. "Epidemiology of Emotional Disturbance in a Men's College." *J Nerv & Mental Dis* 141:240–50 Ag '65. * (*PA* 40:4431)

1937. Weiss, Robert L., and Moos, Rudolf H. "Response Biases in the MMPI: A Sequential Analysis." *Psychol B* 63:403–9 Je '65. * (*PA* 39:12372)

1938. Weiss, Stephen Marshall. *Psychological Adjustment Following Open Heart Surgery.* Doctor's thesis, University of Arizona (Tucson, Ariz.), 1965. (*DA* 26:1178)

1939. Welsh, George S. "MMPI Profiles and Factor Scales A and R." *J Clin Psychol* 21:43–7 Ja '65. * (*PA* 39:12373)

1940. Whittemore, Robert G., and Heimann, Robert A. "Originality Responses in Academically Talented Male University Freshmen." *Psychol Rep* 16:439–42 Ap '65. * (*PA* 39:10252)

1941. Wiggins, Jerry S., and Goldberg, Lewis R. "Interrelationships Among MMPI Item Characteristics." *Ed & Psychol Meas* 25:381–97 su '65. * (*PA* 39:15279)

1942. Wiggins, Jerry S., and Lovell, Victor R. "Communality and Favorability as Sources of Method Variance in the MMPI." *Ed & Psychol Meas* 25:399–412 su '65. * (*PA* 39:15280)

1943. Woolf, Maurice D. "Ego Strength and Reading Disability." *Yearb Nat Read Conf* 14:73–80 '65. *

1944. Woolfolk, Eva K. *The Relation of Certain Psychological Characteristics to Choice of a Type of Teacher Preparation Program.* Doctor's thesis, Syracuse University (Syracuse, N.Y.), 1965. (*DA* 26:886)

1945. Young, Rhodes C. "Effects of Differential Instructions on the Minnesota Multiphasic Personality Inventories of State Hospital Patients." *Proc Ann Conv Am Psychol Assn* 73:281–2 '65. * (*PA* 39:15431)

1946. Zimmerman, Irla Lee. "Residual Effects of Brain Damage and Five MMPI Items." *J Consult Psychol* 29:394 Ag '65. * (*PA* 39:16028)

1947. Zung, William W.; Richards, Carolyn B.; and Short, Marvin J. "Self-Rating Depression Scale in an Outpatient Clinic: Further Validation of the SDS." *Arch Gen Psychiatry* 13:508–15 D '65. * (*PA* 40:2144)

1948. Adams, Henry B.; Robertson, Malcolm H.; and Cooper, G. David. "Sensory Deprivation and Personality Change." *J Nerv & Mental Dis* 143:256–65 S '66. * (*PA* 41:6022)

1949. Adrian, Robert J.; Vacchiano, Ralph B.; and Gilbart, Thomas E. "Linear Discriminant Function Classification of Accepted and Rejected Adoptive Applicants." *J Clin Psychol* 22:251–4 Ap '66. * (*PA* 40:7716)

1950. Anderson, Harry E., Jr., and Bashaw, W. L.

"Further Comments on the Internal Structure of the MMPI." *Psychol B* 66:211–3 S '66. * (*PA* 40:11645)

1951. Anderson, Harry E., Jr.; Davis, Hugh C., Jr.; and Wolking, William D. "A Factorial Study of the MMPI for Students in Health and Rehabilitation." *Ed & Psychol Meas* 26:29–39 sp '66. *

1952. Apfeldorf, Max; Scheinker, J. L.; and Whitman, G. L. "MMPI Responses of Domiciliary Members With Disciplinary Records." *Newsl Res Psychol* 8:2 F '66. *

1953. Apfeldorf, Max; Scheinker, J. Leonard; and Whitman, Gloria L. "MMPI Responses of Aged Domiciled Veterans With Disciplinary Records." Abstract. *J Consult Psychol* 30:362 Ag '66. * (*PA* 40:11164, title only)

1954. Aronson, Arnold E.; Peterson, Herbert W., Jr.; and Litin, Edward M. "Psychiatric Symptomatology in Functional Dysphonia and Aphonia." *J Speech & Hearing Disorders* 31:115–27 My '66. * (*PA* 40:11388)

1955. Ayer, M. Jane; Thoreson, Richard W.; and Butler, Alfred J. "Predicting Rehabilitation Success With the MMPI and Demographic Data." *Personnel & Guid J* 44:631–7 F '66. * (*PA* 40:6913)

1956. Baggaley, Andrew R., and Riedel, Wolfgang W. "A Diagnostic Assembly of MMPI Items Based on Comrey's Factor Analyses." *J Clin Psychol* 22:306–8 Jl '66. * (*PA* 40:10622)

1957. Blank, Leonard, and Roth, Robert H. "Voyeurism and Exhibitionism." *Proc Ann Conv Am Psychol Assn* 74:225–6 '66. * (*PA* 41:5963)

1958. Blazer, John A. "MMPI Interpretation in Outline: 4, The K Scale." *Psychol* 3:4–11 My '66. * (*PA* 40:8247)

1959. Boe, Erling E., and Kogan, William S. "Social Desirability in Individual Performance on Thirteen MMPI Scales." *Brit J Psychol* 57:161–70 My '66. * (*PA* 40:11165)

1960. Boe, Erling E.; Gocka, Edward F.; and Kogan, William S. "A Factor Analysis of Individual Social Desirability Scale Values." *Multiv Behav Res* 1:287–92 Jl '66. * (*PA* 41:1615)

1961. Boxhill, Carlton J. "A Scale to Aid in the Retention or Dismissal Decision." *Personnel & Guid J* 45:53–5 S '66. * (*PA* 40:13471)

1962. Brick, Harry; Doub, W. H., Jr.; and Perdue, W. C. "Effects of Tybamate on Depressive and Anxiety States in Penitentiary Inmates: A Preliminary Report." *Int J Neuropsychiatry* 6:637–44 N–D '66. * (*PA* 41:4704)

1963. Briggs, Peter F., and Yater, Allan C. "Counseling and Psychometric Signs as Determinants in the Vocational Success of Discharged Psychiatric Patients." *J Clin Psychol* 22:100–4 Ja '66. * (*PA* 40:4472)

1964. Britton, P. G., and Savage, R. D. "The MMPI and the Aged—Some Normative Data From a Community Sample." *Brit J Psychiatry* 112:941–3 S '66. * (*PA* 41:587)

1965. Brown, Frederick G., and Scott, David A. "The Unpredictability of Predictability." *J Ed Meas* 3:297–301 w '66. *

1966. Brožek, Josef; Keys, Ancel; and Blackburn, Henry. "Personality Differences Between Potential Coronary and Noncoronary Subjects." *Ann N Y Acad Sci* 134:1057–64 F 28 '66. * (*PA* 40:10903)

1967. Burns, Neal M., and Ayers, Floyd W. "MMPI Profile Changes During an Eighteen-Day Confinement Study." *Percept & Motor Skills* 23:877–8 D '66. * (*PA* 41:7332)

1968. Butcher, James Neal, and Messick, David M. "Parent-Child Profile Similarity and Aggression: A Preliminary Study." *Psychol Rep* 18:440–2 Ap '66. * (*PA* 40:8722)

1969. Butcher, James Neal, and Tellegen, Auke. "Objections to MMPI Items." *J Consult Psychol* 30:527–34 D '66. * (*PA* 41:2891)

1970. Carr, John E.; Brownsberger, Carl N.; and Rutherford, Robert Carver. "Characteristics of Symptom-Matched Psychogenic and 'Real' Pain Patients on the MMPI." *Proc Ann Conv Am Psychol Assn* 74:215–6 '66. * (*PA* 41:6124)

1971. Carson, Gary L., and Parker, Clyde A. "Leadership and Profiles on the MMPI and CPI." *J Col Stud Personnel* 7:14–8 Ja '66. *

1972. Carson, Robert C., and Llewellyn, Charles E., Jr. "Similarity in Therapeutic Dyads: A Reevaluation." Abstract. *J Consult Psychol* 30:458 O '66. * (*PA* 40:13250, title only)

1973. Chu, Chen-Lin. *Object Cluster Analysis of the MMPI.* Doctor's thesis, University of California (Berkeley, Calif.), 1966. (*DA* 28:1158B)

1974. Cluff, Leighton E.; Canter, Arthur; and Imboden, John B. "Asian Influenza: Infection, Disease, and Psychological Factors." *Arch Intern Med* 117:159–63 F '66. *

1975. Cone, John D., Jr. "A Note on Marks' and Seeman's Rules for Actuarially Classifying Psychiatric Patients." *J Clin Psychol* 22:270 Jl '66. * (*PA* 40:11282)

1976. Crumpton, Evelyn; Wine, David B.; and Groot, Henriette. "MMPI Profiles of Obese Men and Six Other Diagnostic Categories." *Newsl Res Psychol* 8:39 Ag '66. *

1977. Crumpton, Evelyn; Wine, David B.; and Groot, Henriette. "MMPI Profiles of Obese Men and Six Other Diagnostic Categories." *Psychol Rep* 19:1110 D '66. * (*PA* 41:4592)

1978. Cruse, Daniel B. "Some Relations Between Minimal Content, Acquiescent-Dissentient, and Social Desirability Scales." *J Personality & Social Psychol* 3:112–9 Ja '66. * (*PA* 40:2896)

1979. Cunningham, Grover Bennett, Jr. *Prediction of*

Staff Ratings From Personality Variables of Counselors in Training and Prediction of Intelligence Test Scores of Children From Personality Variables of Parents. Doctor's thesis, University of Texas (Austin, Tex.), 1966. (*DA* 27:3305A)

1980. DACHOWSKI, MARJORIE McCORMICK. "Inconsistency Among Direct, Indirect and Projective Tests and General Neuroticism." *J Proj Tech & Pers Assess* 30:525–9 D '66. * (*PA* 41:3096)

1981. DANA, RICHARD H., and HOPEWELL, ELEANOR. "Repression and Psychopathology: A Cross-Validation Failure." *Psychol Rep* 19:626 O '66. * (*PA* 41:578)

1982. DEAN, ROBERT B., and RICHARDSON, HAROLD. "On MMPI High-Point Codes of Homosexual Versus Heterosexual Males." *J Consult Psychol* 30:558–60 D '66. * (*PA* 41:2892)

1983. DEVRIES, A. G. "Chance Expectancy, Sample Size, Replacement and Non-Replacement Sampling." *Psychol Rep* 18:843–50 Je '66. * (*PA* 40:9431)

1984. DEVRIES, A. G. "Demographic Variables and MMPI Responses." *J Clin Psychol* 22:450–2 O '66. * (*PA* 41:2893)

1985. DEVRIES, A. G. "Identification of Suicidal Behavior by Means of the MMPI." *Psychol Rep* 19:415–9 O '66. * (*PA* 41:683)

1986. DODD, JOHN M., and STRANG, HAROLD. "A Comparison of Prejudiced and Nonprejudiced Freshman Elementary Education Women." *J Ed Res* 59:424–6 My–Je '66. * (*PA* 40:11080)

1987. EDWARDS, ALLEN L. "A Comparison of 57 MMPI Scales and 57 Experimental Scales Matched With the MMPI Scales in Terms of Item Social Desirability Scale Values and Probabilities of Endorsement." *Ed & Psychol Meas* 26:15–27 sp '66. * (*PA* 40:8241)

1988. EISENMAN, RUSSELL, and TAYLOR, ROBERT E. "Birth Order and MMPI Patterns." *J Indiv Psychol* 22:208–11 N '66. * (*PA* 41:2894)

1989. ELMS, ALAN C., and MILGRAM, STANLEY. "Personality Characteristics Associated With the Obedience and Defiance Toward Authoritative Command." *J Exp Res Personality* 1:282–9 D '66. * (*PA* 41:4552)

1990. ENDICOTT, NOBLE A., and JORTNER, SIDNEY. "Objective Measures of Depression." *Arch Gen Psychiatry* 15:249–55 S '66. * (*PA* 40:11652)

1991. ENGEL, ILONA M. "A Factor-Analytic Study of Items From Five Masculinity-Femininity Tests." Abstract. *J Consult Psychol* 30:565 D '66. * (*PA* 41:2880, title only)

1992. ERIKSON, ROBERT V., and ROBERTS, ALAN H. "An MMPI Comparison of Two Groups of Institutionalized Delinquents." *J Proj Tech & Pers Assess* 30:163–6 Ap '66. * (*PA* 40:7884)

1993. FAUNCE, PATRICIA SPENCER. *Personality Characteristics and Vocational Interests Related to the College Persistence of Academically Gifted Women.* Doctor's thesis, University of Minnesota (Minneapolis, Minn.), 1966. (*DA* 28:338B)

1994. FINNEY, J. C. "Relations and Meaning of the New MMPI Scales." *Psychol Rep* 18:459–70 Ap '66. * (*PA* 40:8254)

1995. FINNEY, JOSEPH C. "Factor Structure With the New Set of MMPI Scales and the Formula Correction." *J Clin Psychol* 22:443–9 O '66. * (*PA* 41:2896)

1996. FINNEY, JOSEPH C. "Programmed Interpretation of MMPI and CPI." *Arch Gen Psychiatry* 15:75–81 Jl '66. * (*PA* 40:11167)

1997. FITZGERALD, E. T. "Measurement of Openness to Experience: A Study of Regression in the Service of the Ego." *J Personality & Social Psychol* 4:655–63 D '66. * (*PA* 41:2253)

1998. FOWLER, RAYMOND D., JR. *The MMPI Notebook: A Guide to the Clinical Use of the Automated MMPI.* Nutley, N.J.: Roche Psychiatric Service Institute, 1966. Pp. iv, 28. *

1999. FOX, JACK. "Social Desirability and the Prediction of MMPI Scores." Abstract. *J Consult Psychol* 30:460 O '66. * (*PA* 40:13200, title only)

2000. FULLER, GERALD B.; LUNNEY, GERALD H.; and NAYLOR, WILLIAM M. "Role of Perception in Differentiating Subtypes of Alcoholism." *Percept & Motor Skills* 23:735–43 D '66. * (*PA* 41:7521)

2001. GARSIDE, JAYNE GILLETTE. *A Cross-Cultural Comparison of Personality.* Doctor's thesis, Brigham Young University (Provo, Utah), 1966. (*DA* 26:5864)

2002. GAURON, EUGENE F., and ADAMS, JERRY. "The Relationship of the Edwards Personal Preference Schedule to the MMPI in a Patient Population." *J Clin Psychol* 22:206–9 Ap '66. * (*PA* 40:7206)

2003. GLUECK, BERNARD C., JR. "Current Personality Assessment Research." *Int Psychiatry Clin* 3:205–22 sp '66. *

2004. GOLD, STEVEN; DeLEON, PATRICK; and SWENSEN, CLIFFORD. "Behavioral Validation of a Dominance-Submission Scale." *Psychol Rep* 19:735–9 D '66. * (*PA* 41:4594)

2005. GOLDBERG, LEWIS R., and WERTS, CHARLES E. "The Reliability of Clinicians' Judgments: A Multitrait-Multimethod Approach." *J Consult Psychol* 30:199–206 Je '66. * (*PA* 40:8999)

2006. GOLDBERG, PHILIP A., and MILLER, SALLY J. "Structured Personality Tests and Dissimulation." *J Proj Tech & Pers Assess* 30:452–5 O '66. * (*PA* 41:589)

2007. GRAVITZ, MELVIN A. "MMPI Personality Patterns for Several Semi-Skilled and Unskilled Occupational Groups." *Psychol Rep* 19:1315–8 D '66. * (*PA* 41:4595)

2008. GREGORY, IAN. "Retrospective Data Concerning Childhood Loss of a Parent: 2, Category of Parental Loss by

Decade of Birth, Diagnosis, and MMPI." *Arch Gen Psychiatry* 15:362–7 O '66. * (*PA* 40:13226)

2009. GRUNDIG, MARILYN HIGHT. *Comparison of MMPI Profiles of Developmental and Reactive Overweight College Students—An Analysis of Important Personality Factors.* Doctor's thesis, University of Virginia (Charlottesville, Va.), 1966. (*DA* 27:2880A) (Abstract: *Ed R* 4:44–6 '66. *)

2010. GYNTHER, MALCOLM D., and SHIMKUNAS, ALGIMANTAS M. "Age and MMPI Performance." *J Consult Psychol* 30:118–21 Ap '66. * (*PA* 40:6650)

2011. HAMA, HARUYO. "Evaluation of Clinical Depression by Means of a Japanese Translation of the Minnesota Multiphasic Personality Inventory." *Psychologia* 9:165–76 S '66. * (*PA* 41:5972)

2012. HAMMER, FRANCES L. *A Comparison of Personality Characteristics of Congenitally, Adventitiously, Totally, and Legally Blind Men and Women on the MMPI.* Master's thesis, University of Kansas (Lawrence, Kan.), 1966.

2013. HARDYCK, CURTIS D.; CHUN, KITAEK; and ENGEL, BERNARD T. "Personality and Marital-Adjustment Differences in Essential Hypertension in Women." Abstract. *J Consult Psychol* 30:459 O '66. * (*PA* 40:13347, title only)

2014. HARRISON, R. J. "Predictive Validity of Some Adjustment Tests: A Research Note." *Austral J Psychol* 18:284–7 D '66. * (*PA* 41:4596)

2015. HEDSTROM, LLOYD JAMES. *Prediction of Duration of Psychotherapy by the MMPI and Ratings of Initial Interview Behavior and Socioeconomic Status.* Doctor's thesis, University of California (Los Angeles, Calif.), 1966. (*DA* 26:6848)

2016. HELLMUTH, GEORGE A.; JOHANNSEN, WALTER J.; and SORAUF, THOMAS. "Psychological Factors in Cardiac Patients: Distortion of Clinical Recommendations." *Arch Environ Health* 12:771–5 Je '66. *

2017. HENRICHS, THEODORE F. "A Note on the Extension of MMPI Configural Rules." *J Clin Psychol* 22:51–2 Ja '66. * (*PA* 40:4250)

2018. HERREID, CLYDE F., II, and HERREID, JANET R. "Differences in MMPI Scores in Native and Nonnative Alaskans." *J Social Psychol* 70:191–8 D '66. * (*PA* 41:2897)

2019. HIMELSTEIN, PHILIP, and LUBIN, BERNARD. "Relationship of the MMPI K Scale and a Measure of Self-Disclosure in a Normal Population." Abstract. *Psychol Rep* 19:166 Ag '66. * (*PA* 40:12343)

2020. HOVEY, H. B., and LEWIS, E. G. "Semiautomatic MMPI Interpretation." *Newsl Res Psychol* 8:33–4 Ag '66. *

2021. HOWELL, MARGARET A. "Personal Effectiveness of Physicians in a Federal Health Organization." *J Appl Psychol* 50:451–9 D '66. * (*PA* 41:3517)

2022. HUNDLEBY, JOHN D. "The Construct Validity of a Scale of Acquiescence." *Brit J Social & Clin Psychol* 5:290–8 D '66. * (*PA* 41:3711)

2023. HYDE, JOHN C. *Social Desirability Still Tenable? A Study of Block's Reinterpretation of the MMPI.* Master's thesis, Marshall University (Huntington, W.Va.), 1966.

2024. IBRAHIM, MICHEL A.; JENKINS, C. DAVID; CASSEL, JOHN C.; McDONOUGH, JOHN R.; and HAMES, CURTIS G. "Personality Traits and Coronary Heart Disease: Utilization of a Cross-Sectional Study Design to Test Whether a Selected Psychological Profile Precedes or Follows Manifest Coronary Heart Disease." *J Chron Dis* 19:255–71 Mr '66. *

2025. IRONSIDE, WALLACE. "The Incidence of Psychiatric Illness in a Group of New Zealand Medical Students." *J Am Col Health Assn* 15:50–3 O '66. *

2026. IVANOFF, JOHN M.; MONROE, GERALD D.; and MARITA, M. "Use of Intellective and Non-Intellective Factors in Classifying Female Elementary and Secondary Teacher Trainees." *J Exp Ed* 34:55–61 su '66. * (*PA* 40:11511)

2027. JOHNSON, RAY WENDELL. *Discrimination Between Diagnosed Vocational and Emotional Counseling Cases Through a Configural Scoring of the MMPI and the Graduation Rate of Diagnosed Groups.* Doctor's thesis, University of Missouri (Columbia, Mo.), 1966. (*DA* 27:957A)

2028. JOSHI, MOHAN C., and SINGH, BEER. "Age-Wise Score Constancy in MMPI." *Psychol Studies* 11:110–4 Jl '66. * (*PA* 40:12345)

2029. JOSHI, MOHAN C., and SINGH, BEER. "Construct Validity of Some MMPI Scales." *Indian Psychol R* 3:67–8 Jl '66. * (*PA* 41:8158)

2030. JOSHI, MOHAN C., and SINGH, BEER. "Influence of Socioeconomic Background on the Scores of Some MMPI Scales." *J Social Psychol* 70:241–6 D '66. * (*PA* 41:2898)

2031. JOSHI, MOHAN C., and SINGH, BEER. "Sex Difference on MMPI Scores." *Indian Psychol R* 2:150–2 Ja '66. * (*PA* 40:9436)

2032. JURJEVICH, R. M. "The Regression Toward the Mean in MMPI, California Psychological Inventory and Symptom Check List." *Ed & Psychol Meas* 26:661–4 au '66. * (*PA* 41:1006)

2033. JURJEVICH, R. M. "Short Interval Test-Retest Stability of MMPI, California Psychological Inventory, Cornell Index, and Symptom Check List." *J General Psychol* 74:201–6 Ap '66. * (*PA* 40:7209)

2034. JURJEVICH, RATIBOR M. "Personality Changes Concomitant With Institutional Training of Delinquent Girls." *J General Psychol* 74:207–16 Ap '66. * (*PA* 40:7811)

2035. KAMANO, DENNIS K., and CRAWFORD, CAROLE S. "Self-Evaluations of Suicidal Mental Hospital Patients." *J Clin Psychol* 22:278–9 Jl '66. * (*PA* 40:11305)

2036. KASSARJIAN, HAROLD H., and KASSARJIAN, WALTRAUD M. "Personality Correlates of Inner- and Other-Direction." *J Social Psychol* 70:281–5 D '66. * (*PA* 41:2899)

2037. KATKIN, EDWARD S. "Sex Differences and the Relationship Between the Marlowe-Crowne Social Desirability Scale and MMPI Indexes of Psychopathology." Abstract. *J Consult Psychol* 30:564 D '66. * (*PA* 41:2881, title only)

2038. KELLY, EMMET EUGENE. "Member Personality and Group Counseling Interaction." *J Psychol* 63:89–97 My '66. * (*PA* 40:10180)

2039. KLOPFER, WALTER G. "Correlation of Women's MF Scores on the MMPI and Strong VIB." *J Clin Psychol* 22:216 Ap '66. * (*PA* 40:7211)

2040. KNIEF, LOTUS M. "The Personality of Pre-Theological Majors." *J Exp Ed* 34:62–8 su '66. * (*PA* 40:11070)

2041. KROLL, WALTER, and PETERSEN, KAY H. "Cross-Validation of the Booth Scale." *Res Q* 37:66–70 Mr '66. * (*PA* 40:6118)

2042. LAND, MELVIN. "Management of Emotional Illness in Dental Practice." *J Am Dental Assn* 73:631–40 S '66. *

2043. LANYON, RICHARD I. "The MMPI and Prognosis in Stuttering Therapy." *J Speech & Hearing Disorders* 31:186–91 My '66. * (*PA* 41:11395)

2044. LEBOVITS, BINYAMIN Z., and OSTFELD, ADRIAN M. "Note on the Edwards Social Desirability Scale." *Psychol Rep* 19:1271–7 D '66. * (*PA* 41:4599)

2045. LEFKOWITZ, MONROE M. "MMPI Scores of Juvenile Delinquents Adjusting to Institutionalization." *Psychol Rep* 19:911–4 D '66. * (*PA* 41:4772)

2046. LEFKOWITZ, MONROE M., and CANNON, JOHN. "Physique and Obstreperous Behavior." *J Clin Psychol* 22:172–4 Ap '66. * (*PA* 40:7886)

2047. LEU, WEN-HUEY; KO, YUNG-HO; and CHEN, WEN-YEN. "A Preliminary Report of the Tryout of MMPI on the Freshmen of National Taiwan University." *Acta Psychologica Taiwanica* 8:79–84 Mr '66. * (*PA* 40:10631)

2048. LEWIS, LESLIE. *A Multivariate Analysis of Variables Associated With Academic Success Within a College Environment.* Doctor's thesis, Oklahoma State University (Stillwater, Okla.), 1966. (*DA* 27:4134A)

2049. LICHTENSTEIN, EDWARD, and BRYAN, JAMES H. "Short-Term Stability of MMPI Profiles." *J Consult Psychol* 30:172–4 Ap '66. * (*PA* 40:6651)

2050. LOEB, JANICE. "The Personality Factor in Divorce." Abstract. *J Consult Psychol* 30:562 D '66. * (*PA* 41:3184, title only)

2051. LOEB, JANICE, and PRICE, JOHN R. "Mother and Child Personality Characteristics Related to Parental Marital Status in Child Guidance Cases." *J Consult Psychol* 30:112–7 Ap '66. * (*PA* 40:6942)

2052. LOEVINGER, JANE. "The Meaning and Measurement of Ego Development." *Am Psychologist* 21:195–206 Mr '66. * (*PA* 40:8890)

2053. LUPTON, D. E. "A Preliminary Investigation of the Personality of Female Temporomandibular Joint Dysfunction Patients." *Psychother & Psychosom* 14(3):199–216 '66. * (*PA* 41:14004)

2054. McCORMICK, ALBERT GRANT. *An Investigation of Reading Skills, General Mental Ability and Personality Variables Used in the Selection of Practical Nursing Students.* Doctor's thesis, Oklahoma State University (Stillwater, Okla.), 1966. (*DA* 27:4136A)

2055. McDONALD, ROBERT L., and HENDRY, CHARLES H. "Repression-Sensitization, Field-Dependence, and 'Adjustment.'" Abstract. *Psychol Rep* 19:558 O '66. * (*PA* 41:591)

2056. MAINE, RICHARD F., and GOODSTEIN, LEONARD D. "Cross-Validation of the Aaronson Mf Index With a College Population." *Psychol Rep* 19:1141–2 D '66. * (*PA* 41:4600)

2057. MANDEL, NATHAN G., and BARRON, ALFRED J. "The MMPI and Criminal Recidivism." *J Crim Law & Criminol* 57:35–8 Mr '66. * (*PA* 40:9015)

2058. MARTIN, CLYDE V., and ALVORD, JACK R. "Long-Term Effects of Intensive Short-Term Treatment of the Character and Personality Disorder." *Correct Psychiatry & J Social Ther* 12:433–42 N '66. * (*PA* 41:10584)

2059. MATHEWS, C. G.; SHAW, D. J.; and KLØVE, H. "Psychological Test Performances in Neurologic and 'Pseudo-Neurologic' Subjects." *Cortex* 2:244–53 Ap '66. * (*PA* 41:672)

2060. MEGARGEE, EDWIN I. "The Edwards SD Scale: A Measure of Adjustment or of Dissimulation?" Abstract. *J Consult Psychol* 30:568 O '66. * (*PA* 41:2262, title only)

2061. MEGARGEE, EDWIN I. "Estimation of CPI Scores From MMPI Protocols." *J Clin Psychol* 22:456–8 O '66. * (*PA* 41:2261)

2062. MENSH, IVAN NORMAN. "Intellectual and Other Personality Adjustments to Aging." *Gerontologist* 6:104+ Je '66. *

2063. MICHAEL, WILLIAM B.; HANEY, RUSSELL; and JONES, ROBERT A. "The Predictive Validities of Selected Aptitude and Achievement Measures and of Three Personality Inventories in Relation to Nursing Training Criteria." *Ed & Psychol Meas* 26:1035–40 w '66. * (*PA* 41:5117)

2064. MILLAR, ANDREW CRAIG. *The Suitability of Using Non-Intellective Characteristics in the Selection of Honors Students at the University of North Dakota.* Doctor's thesis, University of North Dakota (Grand Forks, N.D.), 1966. (*DA* 27:1629A)

2065. MILLER, SALLY J. "Structured Personality Tests and Dissimulation." *Conn Col Psychol J* 3:20–4 sp '66. * (*PA* 40:8859)

2066. MILLER, WILLIAM EDGAR. *Factor Analytic Study of Perception of Self, Others, and the Environment.* Doctor's thesis, University of Kansas (Lawrence, Kan.), 1966. (*DA* 28:969A)

2067. MOORE, ROBERT A. *A Revised MMPI Scale for Measuring Psychopathy Among Prison Inmates.* Master's thesis, Marshall University (Huntington, W.Va.), 1966.

2068. MORDKOFF, ARNOLD M. "Some Sex Differences in Personality Correlates of 'Autonomic Feedback.'" *Psychol Rep* 18:511–8 Ap '66. * (*PA* 40:8860)

2069. MOSHER, DONALD L. "Some Characteristics of High- and Low-Frequency 'Cannot Say' Items on the MMPI." Abstract. *J Consult Psychol* 30:177 Ap '66. * (*PA* 40:6653, title only)

2070. MOSS, MIRIAM STEIN. *Reading, Personality, and Achievement: A Study of Relationships at the College Level.* Doctor's thesis, University of Florida (Gainesville, Fla.), 1966. (*DA* 27:3780A)

2071. MURRAY, JOHN B., and CONNOLLY, FRANCIS. "Follow-Up of Personality Scores of Seminarians: Seven Years Later." *Cath Psychol Rec* 4:10–9 sp '66. * (*PA* 40:10122)

2072. MUSE, COREY J. *Personality and Need Characteristics as Predictors of Student Teacher and Inservice Teacher Ratings.* Doctor's thesis, Brigham Young University (Provo, Utah), 1966. (*DA* 27:987A)

2073. NORMAN, RUSSELL P. "Dogmatism and Psychoneurosis in College Women." Abstract. *J Consult Psychol* 30:278 Je '66. * (*PA* 40:8861, title only)

2074. NOWICKI, STEPHEN, JR. "Factor Analysis of Responses to Various Paper and Pencil Tests." *Newsl Res Psychol* 8:28–9 My '66. *

2075. OETTING, E. R. "Examination Anxiety: Prediction, Physiological Response and Relation to Scholastic Performance." *J Counsel Psychol* 13:224–7 su '66. * (*PA* 40:9215)

2076. PAUKER, JEROME D. "Identification of MMPI Profile Types in a Female, Inpatient, Psychiatric Setting Using the Marks and Seeman Rules." Abstract. *J Consult Psychol* 30:90 F '66. * (*PA* 40:4369, title only)

2077. PAUKER, JEROME D. "Stability of MMPI Profiles of Female Psychiatric Inpatients." *J Clin Psychol* 22:209–12 Ap '66. * (*PA* 40:7718, title only)

2078. PAUKER, JEROME D. "Stability of MMPI Scales Over Five Testings Within a One-Month Period." *Ed & Psychol Meas* 26:1063–7 w '66. * (*PA* 41:4603)

2079. PEABODY, DEAN. "Authoritarianism Scales and Response Bias." *Psychol B* 65:11–23 Ja '66. * (*PA* 40:2916)

2080. PEDERSEN, FRANK A. "Relationships Between Father-Absence and Emotional Disturbance in Male Military Dependents." *Merrill-Palmer Q* 12:321–31 O '66. * (*PA* 41:5822)

2081. PEHLE, JOHN WILLIAM. *Repression-Sensitization and Psychological Adjustment.* Doctor's thesis, University of Florida (Gainesville, Fla.), 1966. (*DA* 27:1628B)

2082. PETERSON, CHARLES A. *The Prediction of Students' Success in College Accounting.* Doctor's thesis, University of Minnesota (Minneapolis, Minn.), 1966. (*DA* 28:61A)

2083. PHILIPPUS, M. J., and NACMAN, M. "A Psychosocial and Vocational Follow-up Study of Previously Hospitalized Asthmatic Patients." *Psychother & Psychosom* 14(3):171–9 '66. *

2084. RAE, JOHN B., and FORBES, ALAN R. "Clinical and Psychometric Characteristics of the Wives of Alcoholics." *Brit J Psychiatry* 112:197–200 F '66. * (*PA* 40:6810)

2085. RIES, HAROLD A. "The MMPI K Scale as a Predictor of Prognosis." *J Clin Psychol* 22:212–3 Ap '66. * (*PA* 40:7854)

2086. ROBINSON, BURTON W. "A Study of Anxiety and Academic Achievement." *J Consult Psychol* 30:165–7 Ap '66. * (*PA* 40:7044)

2087. RODGERS, DAVID A. "Estimation of MMPI Profiles From CPI Data." Abstract. *J Consult Psychol* 30:89 F '66. * (*PA* 40:4253, title only)

2088. ROSEN, ALBERT. "Stability of New MMPI Scales and Statistical Procedures for Evaluating Changes and Differences in Psychiatric Patients." *J Consult Psychol* 30:142–5 Ap '66. * (*PA* 40:6656)

2089. ROSMAN, RICHARD R.; BARRY, STANLEY M.; and GIBEAU, PHILIP J. "Problems in Atlas Classification of MMPI Profiles." *J Clin Psychol* 22:308–10 Jl '66. * (*PA* 40:10637)

2090. SANDNESS, DAVID GRIMSRUD. *The Minnesota Multiphasic Personality Inventory as a Predictor in Vocational Rehabilitation.* Doctor's thesis, University of North Dakota (Grand Forks, N.D.), 1966. (*DA* 27:3681B)

2091. SARASON, IRWIN G. *Personality: An Objective Approach,* pp. 148–61, passim. New York: John Wiley & Sons, Inc., 1966. Pp. xvi, 670. *

2092. SAVAGE, CHARLES; FADIMAN, JAMES; MOGAR, ROBERT; and ALLEN, MARY HUGHES. "The Effects of Psychedelic (LSD) Therapy on Values, Personality, and Behavior." *Int J Neuropsychiatry* 2:241–54 My–Je '66. *

2093. SCHILL, THOMAS. "The Effects of MMPI Social Introversion on WAIS PA Performance." *J Clin Psychol* 22:72–4 Ja '66. * (*PA* 40:4239)

2094. SCHOFIELD, WILLIAM. Chap. 31, "The Structured Personality Inventory in Measurement of Effects of Psychotherapy," pp. 536–50. In *Methods of Research in Psychotherapy.* Edited by Louis A. Gottschalk and Arthur H. Auerbach. New York: Appleton-Century-Crofts, 1966. Pp. xviii, 654. *

2095. SCHOFIELD, WILLIAM, and MERWIN, JACK C. "The Use of Scholastic Aptitude, Personality, and Interest Test Data in the Selection of Medical Students." *J Med Ed* 41:502–9 Je '66. *

2096. SHAW, DALE J. "Differential MMPI Performance in Pseudo-Seizure Epileptic and Pseudo-Neurologic Groups." *J Clin Psychol* 22:271–5 Jl '66. * (PA 40:11417)

2097. SHEPHEARD, DAVID C., and GOLDSTEIN, ROBERT. "Relation of Bekesy Tracings to Personality and Electrophysiologic Measures." *J Speech & Hearing Disorders* 9:385–411 S '66. *

2098. SHOSTROM, EVERETT L., and KNAPP, ROBERT R. "The Relationship of a Measure of Self-Actualization (POI) to a Measure of Pathology (MMPI) and to Therapeutic Growth." *Am J Psychother* 20:193–202 Ja '66. *

2099. SIMMONS, ALLAN D. "A Comparison of Repression-Sensitization Scores Obtained by Two Different Methods." *J Clin Psychol* 22:465 O '66. * (PA 41:2889)

2100. SINES, JACOB O. "Actuarial Methods and Personality Assessment." *Prog Exp Personal Res* 3:133–93 '66. *

2101. SKRZYPEK, GEORGE J., and WIGGINS, JERRY S. "Contrasted Groups Versus Repeated Measurement Designs in the Evaluation of Social Desirability Scales." *Ed & Psychol Meas* 26:131–8 sp '66. * (PA 40:8272)

2102. SOARES, ANTHONY T., and SOARES, LOUISE M. "Self-Description and Adjustment Correlates of Occupational Choice." *J Ed Res* 60:27–31 S '66. *

2103. STENNETT, RICHARD G. "Family Diagnosis: MMPI and CTP Results." *J Clin Psychol* 22:165–7 Ap '66. * (PA 40:7972)

2104. STONE, F. BETH; ROWLEY, VINTON N.; and MAC-QUEEN, JOHN C. "Using the MMPI With Adolescents Who Have Somatic Symptoms." *Psychol Rep* 18:139–47 F '66. * (PA 40:6904)

2105. STONE, LEROY, A. "Corrected (for Curtailment) Correlations Between the Marlowe-Crowne Social Desirability Scale and the MMPI." *Psychol Rep* 19:103–6 Ag '66. * (PA 40:11668)

2106. SWENSON, WENDELL M., and PEARSON, JOHN S. "Psychiatry—Psychiatric Screening." *J Chron Dis* 19:497–507 Ap '66. *

2107. SWORDS, IRBY RAY. *An Investigation of Personality Variables Associated With Specified Behaviors in Men's Residence Halls.* Doctor's thesis, University of Alabama (University, Ala.), 1966. (DA 27:1275A)

2108. TAMKIN, ARTHUR S. "Some Determinants of Rorschach Productivity." *Newsl Res Psychol* 8:6–7 Ag '66. *

2109. TAMKIN, ARTHUR S., and SONKIN, NATHAN. "Personality Factors in Psychogenic Somatic Complaints." *Newsl Res Psychol* 8:20–1 F '66. *

2110. TRYON, ROBERT C. "Unrestricted Cluster and Factor Analysis, With Applications to the MMPI and Holzinger-Harman Problems." *Multiv Behav Res* 1:229–44 Ap '66. * (PA 41:978)

2111. VANDERHOOF, ELLEN; CLANCY, JOHN; and ENGELHART, ROLAND S. "Relationship of a Physiological Variable to Psychiatric Diagnoses and Personality Characteristics." *Dis Nerv System* 27:171–7 Mr '66. *

2112. VAUGHAN, RICHARD P. "Personality Characteristics of Exceptional College Students." *Proc Ann Conv Am Psychol Assn* 74:281–2 '66. * (PA 41:6255)

2113. VINCENT, NICHOLAS M. P.; LINSZ, NORTON L.; and GREENE, MARTHA I. "The L Scale of the MMPI as an Index of Falsification." *J Clin Psychol* 22:214–5 Ap '66. * (PA 40:7722)

2114. WALIKE, B. CALEEN, and MEYER, BURTON. "Relation Between Placebo Reactivity and Selected Personality Factors: An Exploratory Study." *Nursing Res* 15:119–23 sp '66. *

2115. WATLEY, DONIVAN J. "Counselor Variability in Making Accurate Predictions." *J Counsel Psychol* 13:53–62 sp '66. * (PA 40:5817)

2116. WEST, KATHRYN L. *MMPI and Demographic Correlates of Ulcerative Colitis.* Doctor's thesis, University of Minnesota (Minneapolis, Minn.), 1966. (DA 27:4570B)

2117. WHISLER, R. HUGH, and CANTOR, JOEL M. "The Mac-Andrew Alcoholism Scale: A Cross-Validation in a Domiciliary Setting." *J Clin Psychol* 22:311–2 Jl '66. * (PA 40:10640)

2118. WIGGINS, JERRY S. "Social Desirability Estimation and 'Faking Good' Well." *Ed & Psychol Meas* 26:329–41 su '66. *

2119. WIGGINS, JERRY S. "Substantive Dimensions of Self-Report in the MMPI Item Pool." *Psychol Monogr* 80(22):1–42 '66. * (PA 41:1610)

2120. WIGGINS, NANCY, and HOFFMAN, PAUL J. "Models for Simulating Clinical Judgments of the MMPI." *Proc Ann Conv Am Psychol Assn* 74:237–8 '66. * (PA 41:5978)

2121. WOLKING, WILLIAM D.; QUAST, WENTWORTH; and LAWTON, JAMES J., JR. "MMPI Profiles of the Parents of Behaviorally Disturbed Children and Parents From the General Population." *J Clin Psychol* 22:39–48 Ja '66. * (PA 40:4089)

2122. WRIGHT, NANCY A., and ZUBEK, JOHN P. "Use of the Multiple Discriminant Function in the Prediction of Perceptual Deprivation Tolerance." *Can J Psychol* 20:105–13 Mr '66. * (PA 40:6647)

2123. YONGE, GEORGE D. "Certain Consequences of Applying the K Factor to MMPI Scores." *Ed & Psychol Meas* 26: 887–93 w '66. * (PA 41:4615)

2124. ZEISSET, RAY M. "Two 'Parallel' Short Forms of Welsh's A and R Scales." *Newsl Res Psychol* 8:11–2 My '66. *

2125. ZELEN, SEYMOUR L.; FOX, JACK; GOULD, EDWARD; and OLSON, RAY W. "Sex-Contingent Differences Between Male and Female Alcoholics." *J Clin Psychol* 22:160–5 Ap '66. * (PA 40:7873)

2126-7. ZUCKER, ROBERT A., and MANOSEVITZ, MARTIN. "MMPI Patterns of Overt Male Homosexuals: Reinterpretation and Comment on Dean and Richardson's Study." *J Consult Psychol* 30:555–7 D '66. * (PA 41:2903)

2128. ALDAG, JEAN, and CHRISTENSEN, CHERRYL. "Personality Correlates of Male Nurses." *Nursing Res* 16:375–6 f '67. * (PA 42:3978)

2129. ALEXANDER, JAMES FLOYD. *Perspectives of Psychotherapy Process: Dependency, Interpersonal Relationships, and Sex Differences.* Doctor's thesis, Michigan State University (East Lansing, Mich.), 1967. (DA 28:5197B)

2130. AL-ISSA, IHSAN, and KRAFT, TOM. "Personality Factors in Behaviour Therapy." *Can Psychologist* 8a:218–22 Jl '67. * (PA 42:832)

2131. ANTLER, LAWRENCE, and ZARETSKY, HERBERT H. "National Consciousness Among Foreign Physicians in the United States: Correlates in Attitude, Adjustment, Personality, and Demographic Variables." *J Social Psychol* 71:209–20 Ap '67. * (PA 41:8795)

2132. ARIMA, JAMES K. "Differentiation of Soldier Reactions to Severe Environmental Stress by MMPI and Other Variables." *Ed & Psychol Meas* 27:617–30 au '67. * (PA 42:446)

2133. ARMILLA, JOSE. "Predicting Self-Assessed Social Leadership in a New Culture With the MMPI." *J Social Psychol* 73:219–25 D '67. * (PA 42:3979)

2134. ARONSON, H., and WEINTRAUB, WALTER. "Verbal Productivity as a Measure of Change in Affective Status." *Psychol Rep* 20:483–7 Ap '67. * (PA 41:9073)

2135. ASHBROOK, JAMES B., and POWELL, ROGER K. "Comparison of Graduating and Nongraduating Theological Students on the Minnesota Multiphasic Personality Inventory." *J Counsel Psychol* 14:171–4 Mr '67. * (PA 41:7330)

2136. ATKINSON, ROLAND M., and RINGUETTE, EUGENE L. "A Survey of Biographical and Physical Features in Extraordinary Fatness." *Psychosom Med* 29:121–33 Mr-Ap '67. * (PA 41:11582)

2137. BAKER, JUANITA N. "Effectiveness of Certain MMPI Dissimulation Scales Under 'Real-Life' Conditions." *J Counsel Psychol* 14:286–92 My '67. * (PA 41:8929)

2138. BAKKER, CORNELIS B., and LEVENSON, ROBERT M. "Determinants of Angina Pectoris." *Psychosom Med* 29:621–33 N-D '67. * (PA 41:10907)

2139. BARRY, JOHN R.; ANDERSON, H. E., JR.; and THOMASON, O. BRUCE. "MMPI Characteristics of Alcoholic Males Who Are Well and Poorly Adjusted in Marriage." *J Clin Psychol* 23:355–60 Jl '67. * (PA 41:15636)

2140. BASHAW, W. L. "A Comparison of MMPI Profiles and Validity Scale Scores Obtained by Normal and Slide-Projected Administration." *Multiv Behav Res* 2:241–9 Ap '67. * (PA 41:11931)

2141. BERGMAN, PAUL; MALASKY, CHARLOTTE; and ZAHN, THEODORE P. "Relation of Sucking Strength to Personality Variables." *J Consult Psychol* 31:426–8 Ag '67. * (PA 41: 13637)

2142. BERNARD. J. L., and EISENMAN, RUSSELL. "Verbal Conditioning in Sociopaths With Social and Monetary Reinforcement." *J Personality & Social Psychol* 6:203–6 Je '67. * (PA 41:10696)

2143. BERNFELD, BENJAMIN. *MMPI Variables in the Prediction of Attrition of Students of Nursing in a Hospital School Program.* Doctor's thesis, New York University (New York, N.Y.), 1967. (DA 28:1690B)

2144. BLACK, WILLIAM GOBER. *The Description and Prediction of Recidivism and Rehabilitation Among Youthful Offenders by the Use of the Minnesota Multiphasic Personality Inventory.* Doctor's thesis, University of Oklahoma (Norman, Okla.), 1967. (DA 28:1691B)

2145. BLANK, LEONARD, and ROTH, ROBERT H. "Voyeurism and Exhibitionism." *Percept & Motor Skills* 24:391–400 Ap '67. * (PA 41:10708)

2146. BLUMBERG, STANLEY. "MMPI F Scale as an Indicator of Severity of Psychopathology." *J Clin Psychol* 23:96–9 Ja '67. * (PA 41:5971)

2147. BODENSTAB, ERNEST WILLIAM. *Personality Patterns and Heterogeneity Among Teaching Interest Areas.* Doctor's thesis, State University of New York at Buffalo (Buffalo, N.Y.), 1967. (DA 28:1715A)

2148. BOTWINICK, JACK, and THOMPSON, LARRY W. "Depressive Affect, Speed of Response, and Age." Abstract. *J Consult Psychol* 31:106 F '67. * (PA 41:4418, title only)

2149. BRIGGS. PETER F., and TELLEGEN, AUKE. "An Abbreviation of the Social Introversion Scale for 373-Item MMPI." *J Clin Psychol* 23:189–191 Ap '67. * (PA 41:8914)

2150. BRITTON, PETER G.; BERGMANN, KLAUS; KAY. DAVID W. K.; and SAVAGE, R. DOUGLASS. "Mental State, Cognitive Functioning, Physical Health, and Social Class in the Community Aged." *J Gerontol* 22:517–21 O '67. *

2151. CAHILL, CHARLES A. "Using the Computerized MMPI." *Hosp & Commun Psychiatry* 18:361 D '67. * (PA 42:5740)

2152. CAMPBELL, DONALD T.; SIEGMAN. CAROLE R.; and REES, MATILDA B. "Direction-of-Wording Effects in the Relationships Between Scales." *Psychol B* 68:293–303 N '67. * (PA 42:2571)

2153. CHAMBERS, EUGENE D. "Investigation of Invalid

MMPI Protocols Obtained in Group Testing." *Newsl Res Psychol* 9:10–3 My '67. *

2154. CHYLINSKI, JOANNE, and WRIGHT, MORGAN W. "Testing in Canada With the Minnesota Multiphasic Personality Inventory (MMPI) and the Edwards Personal Preference Schedule (EPPS)." *Can Psychologist* 8a:202–6 Jl '67. * (*PA* 42:755)

2155. CONE, JOHN D., JR. "Social Desirability and Marital Happiness." *Psychol Rep* 21:770–2 D '67. * (*PA* 42:7203)

2156. COOKE, JANE K. "Clinicians' Decisions as a Basis for Deriving Actuarial Formulae." *J Clin Psychol* 23:232–3 Ap '67. * (*PA* 41:9075)

2157. COOKE, JANE K. "MMPI in Actuarial Diagnosis of Psychological Disturbance Among College Males." *J Counsel Psychol* 14:474–7 S '67. * (*PA* 41:14405)

2158. COOKE, MARGARET K., and KIESLER, DONALD J. "Prediction of College Students Who Later Require Personal Counseling." *J Counsel Psychol* 14:346–9 Jl '67. * (*PA* 41:12484)

2159. DAVIS, KATHLEEN L. *The Sensitivity of Selected Instruments to Personality Changes Produced by Group Counseling.* Doctor's thesis, University of Georgia (Athens, Ga.), 1967. (*DA* 28:3968A)

2160. DERMAN, BRUCE IRVIN. *Adaptive Versus Pathological Regression in Relation to Psychological Adjustment.* Doctor's thesis, University of Georgia (Athens, Ga.), 1967. (*DA* 28:4754B)

2161. DEVRIES, A. G. "Control Variables in the Identification of Suicidal Behavior." *Psychol Rep* 20:1131–5 Je '67. * (*PA* 41:15486)

2162. DEVRIES, ALCON G., and FARBEROW, NORMAN L. "A Multivariate Profile Analysis of MMPIs of Suicidal and Nonsuicidal Neuropsychiatric Hospital Patients." *J Proj Tech & Pers Assess* 31:81–4 O '67. * (*PA* 42:756)

2163. DEVRIES, ALCON G., and SHNEIDMAN, EDWIN S. "Multiple MMPI Profiles of Suicidal Persons." *Psychol Rep* 21:401–5 O '67. * (*PA* 42:5775)

2164. DICKEN, CHARLES. "'Acquiescence' in the MMPI: A Method Variance Artifact?" *Psychol Rep* 20:927–33 Je '67. * (*PA* 41:13639)

2165. DICKEN, CHARLES, and VAN PELT, JOHN. "Further Evidence Concerning Acquiescence and the MMPI." *Psychol Rep* 20:935–41 Je '67. * (*PA* 41:13640)

2166. DIETZE, DORIS; STOTLAND, EZRA; and SPARKS, LARRY. "Experimental Manipulation of Sense of Competence." *Percept & Motor Skills* 24:785–6 Je '67. * (*PA* 41:13707)

2167. DILDY, LIONEL W., and LIBERTY, PAUL G., JR. "Investigation of Peer-Rated Anxiety." *Proc Ann Conv Am Psychol Assn* 75:371–2 '67. * (*PA* 41:13614)

2168. DOTY, BARBARA A. "Relationships Among Attitudes in Pregnancy and Other Maternal Characteristics." *J Genetic Psychol* 111:203–17 D '67. * (*PA* 42:5475)

2169. DRINKWATER, RUBY STRAUGHAN. *The Relationship Between Certain Factors and Academic Success in the School of Pharmacy at Southwestern State College.* Doctor's thesis, Oklahoma State University (Stillwater, Okla.), 1967. (*DA* 28:4871A)

2170. DUNLOP, EDWIN, and WALTMANN, ROBERT H. "The Emotional Temperature," pp. 195–7. In *Psychosomatic Medicine: Proceedings of the First International Congress of the Academy of Psychosomatic Medicine.* International Congress Series No. 134. Edited by E. Dunlop. Amsterdam, Netherlands: Excerpta Medica Foundation, 1967. Pp. viii, 273. *

2171. DUNTEMAN, GEORGE H., and BAILEY, JOHN P., JR. "A Canonical Correlational Analysis of the Strong Vocational Interest Blank and the Minnesota Multiphasic Personality Inventory for a Female College Population." *Ed & Psychol Meas* 27:631–42 au '67. * (*PA* 42:124)

2172. DUNTEMAN, GEORGE H., and WOLKING, WILLIAM D. "Relationship Between Marital Status and the Personality of Mothers of Disturbed Children." Abstract. *J Consult Psychol* 31:220 Ap '67. * (*PA* 41:7149, title only)

2173. EDWARDS, ALLEN L. "The Social Desirability Variable: A Review of the Evidence," pp. 48–70. In *Response Set in Personality Assessment.* Edited by Irwin A. Berg. Chicago, Ill.: Aldine Publishing Co., 1967. Pp. xi, 244. *

2174. ELLINWOOD, E. H., JR. "Amphetamine Psychosis: 1, Description of the Individuals and Process." *J Nerv & Mental Dis* 144:273–83 Ap '67. * (*PA* 41:15480)

2175. ELLS, EDWARD M. "MMPI Stability: Hospital Discharge vs. Outpatient Intake." *Newsl Res Psychol* 9:10–1 Ag '67. *

2176. ELMORE, THOMAS M., and CHAMBERS, EUGENE D. "Anomie, Existential Neurosis, and Personality: Relevance for Counseling." *Proc Ann Conv Am Psychol Assn* 75:341–2 '67. * (*PA* 41:13930)

2177. ENDICOTT, NOBLE A., and JORTNER, SIDNEY. "Correlates of Somatic Concern Derived From Psychological Tests." *J Nerv & Mental Dis* 144:133–8 F '67. * (*PA* 41:12111)

2178. EVANS, ROBERT R.; BORGATTA, EDGAR F.; and BOHRNSTEDT, GEORGE W. "Smoking and MMPI Scores Among Entering Freshmen." *J Social Psychol* 73:137–40 O '67. * (*PA* 42:769)

2179. FARBEROW, NORMAN L., and DEVRIES, ALCON G. "An Item Differentiation Analysis of MMPIs of Suicidal Neuropsychiatric Hospital Patients." *Psychol Rep* 20:607–17 Ap '67. * (*PA* 41:9113)

2180. FISHER, GARY. "The Performance of Male Prisoners on the Marlowe-Crowne Social Desirability Scale: 2, Differences as a Function of Race and Crime." *J Clin Psychol* 23:473–5 O '67. * (*PA* 42:2575)

2181. FISHER, SEYMOUR, and OSOFSKY, HOWARD. "Sexual Responsiveness in Women: Psychological Correlates." *Arch Gen Psychiatry* 17:214–26 Ag '67. * (*PA* 41:15149)

2182. FORD, LEROY H., JR., and HERSEN, MICHEL. "Need Approval, Defensive Denial, and Direction of Aggression in a Failure-Frustration Situation." *J Personality & Social Psychol* 6:228–32 Je '67. * (*PA* 41:9784)

2183. FORSYTH, RALPH P., and SMITH, SANDRA F. "MMPI Related Behavior in a Student Nurse Group." *J Clin Psychol* 23:224–9 Ap '67. * (*PA* 41:8920)

2184. FOWLER, RAYMOND D., JR. "Computer Interpretation of Personality Tests: The Automated Psychologist." *Comprehen Psychiatry* 8:455–67 D '67. * (*PA* 42:12352)

2185. FOWLER, RAYMOND D., JR. "MMPI Computer Interpretation for College Counseling." *Proc Ann Conv Am Psychol Assn* 75:363–4 '67. * (*PA* 41:14197)

2186. FOWLER, RAYMOND D., JR.; TEEL, SIDNEY K.; and COYLE, F. A., JR. "The Measurement of Alcoholic Response to Treatment by Barron's Ego-Strength Scale." *J Psychol* 67:65–8 S '67. * (*PA* 41:16841)

2187. FOX, JACK. "Social Desirability, Prediction Equation, Regression Equations, and Intrinsic Response Bias." *Psychol B* 67:391–400 Je '67. *

2188. FRANK, GEORGE H. "A Review of Research With Measures of Ego Strength Derived From the MMPI and the Rorschach." *J General Psychol* 77:183–206 O '67. * (*PA* 42:770)

2189. FREEMAN, EDITH H.; GORMAN, FRANK J.; SINGER, MARGARET T.; AFFELDER, MARILYN T.; and FEINGOLD, BEN F. "Personality Variables and Allergic Skin Reactivity: A Cross-Validation Study." *Psychosom Med* 29:312–22 Jl–Ag '67. * (*PA* 42:2768)

2190. FRIBERG, RICHARD R. "Measures of Homosexuality: Cross-Validation of Two MMPI Scales and Implications for Usage." *J Consult Psychol* 31:88–91 F '67. * (*PA* 41:4593)

2191. GILBERSTADT, HAROLD, and JANCIS, MARUTA. "'Organic' *vs.* 'Functional' Diagnoses From 1–3 MMPI Profiles." *J Clin Psychol* 23:480–3 O '67. * (*PA* 42:2598)

2192. GILBERSTADT, HAROLD, and SAKO, YOSHIO. "Intellectual and Personality Changes Following Open-Heart Surgery." *Arch Gen Psychiatry* 16:210–4 F '67. * (*PA* 41:7763)

2193. GILBERT, JEANNE G., and LOMBARDI, DONALD N. "Personality Characteristics of Young Male Narcotic Addicts." *J Consult Psychol* 31:536–8 O '67. * (*PA* 41:16843)

2194. GLOYE, EUGENE E., and ZIMMERMAN, IRLA LEE. "MMPI Item Changes by College Students Under Ideal-Self Response Set." *J Proj Tech & Pers Assess* 31:63–9 Ap '67. * (*PA* 41:13670)

2195. GOLDEN, JULES S.; MARCHIONNE, A. M.; and SILVER, REUBEN J. "Fifty Medical Students: A Comparison with 'Normals.'" *J Med Ed* 42:146–52 F '67. *

2196. GOLDSCHMID, MARCEL L. "Prediction of College Majors by Personality Tests." *J Counsel Psychol* 14:302–8 Jl '67. * (*PA* 41:12452)

2197. GOLDSTEIN, STEVEN G.; LINDEN, JAMES D.; and BAKER, THOMAS T. "7094 Template Programs for Scoring Dichotomous Response Format Tests With Special Reference to the Minnesota Multiphasic Personality Inventory." *Ed & Psychol Meas* 27:729–33 au '67. * (*PA* 42:107)

2198. GOLIN, SANFORD; HERRON, E. WAYNE; LAKOTA, ROBERT; and REINECK, LINDA. "Factor Analytic Study of the Manifest Anxiety, Extraversion, and Repression-Sensitization Scales." *J Consult Psychol* 31:564–9 D '67. * (*PA* 42:1406)

2199. GRAHAM, JOHN R. "A Q-Sort of the Accuracy of Clinical Descriptions Based on the MMPI." *J Psychiatric Res* 5:297–305 D '67. * (*PA* 42:12354)

2200. GRAVITZ, MELVIN A. "Frequency and Content of Test Items Normally Omitted From MMPI Scales." Abstract. *J Consult Psychol* 31:642 D '67. * (*PA* 42:2599)

2201. GRAVITZ, MELVIN A. "A New Computerized Method for the Fully Automated Printout of MMPI Graphic Profiles." *J Clin Psychol* 23:101–2 Ja '67. * (*PA* 41:5269)

2202. GREENWALD, ALLEN F. "Adjustment Patterns in First Year Theology Students." *R Relig* 26:483–8 My '67. *

2203. GUTHRIE, GEORGE M., and ZEKTICK, IDA N. "Predicting Performance in the Peace Corps." *J Social Psychol* 71:11–21 F '67. * (*PA* 41:6319)

2204. GYNTHER, MALCOLM D., and BRILLIANT, PATRICIA J. "Marital Status, Readmission to Hospital, and Intrapersonal and Interpersonal Perceptions of Alcoholics." *Q J Studies Alcohol* 28:52–8 Mr '67. * (*PA* 41:9101)

2205. GYNTHER, MALCOLM D., and PETZEL, THOMAS P. "Differential Endorsement of MMPI *F* Scale Items by Psychotics and Behavior Disorders." *J Clin Psychol* 23:185–8 Ap '67. * (*PA* 41:8921)

2206. HARRINGTON, MARY ANNE GEORGE. *Asthma: Psychological, Physical, and Historical Correlates; Asthma of Unknown Origin as a Psychological Group.* Doctor's thesis, University of Colorado (Boulder, Colo.), 1967. (*DA* 29:756B)

2207. HARRISON, ROBERT H., and KASS, EDWARD H. "Differences Between Negro and White Pregnant Women on the MMPI." *J Consult Psychol* 31:454–63 O '67. * (*PA* 41:16710)

2208. HARTMAN, BERNARD J. "Comparison of Selected Experimental MMPI Profiles of Sexual Deviates and Sociopaths

Without Sexual Deviation," *Psychol Rep* 20:234 F '67. * (*PA* 41:7516)

2209. HARWOOD, B. THOMAS. "Some Intellectual Correlates of Schizoid Indicators: WAIS and MMPI." Abstract. *J Consult Psychol* 31:218 Ap '67. * (*PA* 41:7339, title only)

2210. HEATH, HELEN A.; OKEN, DONALD; and SHIPMAN, WILLIAM G. "Muscle Tension and Personality: A Serious Second Look." *Arch Gen Psychiatry* 16:720–6 Je '67. * (*PA* 41:13932)

2211. HELSON, RAVENNA. "Personality Characteristics and Developmental History of Creative College Women." *Genetic Psychol Monogr* 76:205–56 N '67. * (*PA* 42:3942)

2212. HIMELSTEIN, PHILIP, and STOUP, DOUGLAS D. "Correlation of Three Mf Measures for Males." *J Clin Psychol* 23:189 Ap '67. * (*PA* 41:8922)

2213. HOLMES, DAVID S. "Male-Female Differences in MMPI Ego Strength: An Artifact." *J Consult Psychol* 31:408–10 Ag '67. * (*PA* 41:13642)

2214. HOLT, WILLIAM L., JR., and MARCHIONNE, A. M. "Personality Evaluation of Correctional Institution Inmates Awaiting Plastic Surgery and a Control Group of Inmates." *Int J Neuropsychiatry* 3:337–42 Jl–Ag '67. * (*PA* 42:9144)

2215. HOPE, K.; PHILIP, A. E.; and LOUGHRAN, J. M. "Psychological Characteristics Associated With XYY Sex-Chromosome Complement in a State Mental Hospital." *Brit J Psychiatry* 113:495–8 My '67. * (*PA* 41:12187)

2216. HOVEY, H. B. "MMPI Testing for Multiple Sclerosis." *Newsl Res Psychol* 9:21–2 My '67. *

2217. HOVEY, H. B. "MMPI Testing for Multiple Sclerosis." *Psychol Rep* 21:599–600 O '67. * (*PA* 42:5743)

2218. HOVEY, HENRY BIRNET, and LEWIS, EVAN GAYLE. "Semiautomatic Interpretation of the MMPI." *J Clin Psychol* 23:123–34 My '67. * (*PA* 41:8923)

2219. JACKSON, DOUGLAS N. "Acquiescence Response Styles: Problems of Identification and Control," pp. 71–114. In *Response Set in Personality Assessment*. Edited by Irwin A. Berg. Chicago, Ill.: Aldine Publishing Co., 1967. Pp. xi, 244. *

2220. JOHNSON, MONTY B., and HOLMES, DOUGLAS S. "An Attempt to Develop a Process-Reactive Scale for the MMPI." *J Clin Psychol* 23:191 Ap '67. * (*PA* 41:8154)

2221. JONES, RICHARD R., and GOLDBERG, LEWIS R. "Interrelationships Among Personality Scale Parameters: Item Response Stability and Scale Reliability." *Ed & Psychol Meas* 27:323–33 su '67. * (*PA* 41:13618)

2222. JORDAN, BRIAN T., and BUTLER, JOEL R. "GSR as a Measure of the Sexual Component in Hysteria." *J Psychol* 67:211–9 N '67. * (*PA* 42:1627)

2223. JURJEVICH, R. M. "Avoidable Errors on Raven Progressive Matrices and Psychopathological Indices." Abstract. *Psychol Rep* 21:364 O '67. * (*PA* 42:5803, title only)

2224. JURJEVICH, R. M. "Hostility and Anxiety Indices on the Rorschach Content Test, Hostility Guilt Index, and the MMPI." *Psychol Rep* 21:128 Ag '67. * (*PA* 42:2608, title only)

2225. KINCANNON, JAMES C. *An Investigation of the Feasibility of Adapting a Personality Inventory for Use in the Mental Status Exam.* Doctor's thesis, University of Minnesota (Minneapolis, Minn.), 1967. (*DA* 28:2625B)

2226. KING, FRANCIS W. "The MMPI F Scale as a Predictor of Lack of Adaptation to College." *J Am Col Health Assn* 15:261–9 F '67. *

2227. KISH, GEORGE B., and BUSSE, WILLIAM. "Correlates of Stimulus-Seeking Behavior." *Newsl Res Psychol* 9:1–3 Ag '67. *

2228. KISH, GEORGE B., and BUSSE, WILLIAM. "An Examination of the Hypothesis That Excessive Alcohol Consumption Is a Sensation-Seeking Activity." *Newsl Res Psychol* 9:29–31 Ag '67. *

2229. KLEINMUNTZ, BENJAMIN. *Personality Measurement: An Introduction*, pp. 216–37, 360–8. Homewood, Ill.: Dorsey Press, 1967. Pp. xiii, 463. *

2230. KLEINMUNTZ, BENJAMIN. "Sign and Seer: Another Example." *J Abn Psychol* 72:163–5 Ap '67. * (*PA* 41:7377)

2231. KLETT, WILLIAM G., and VESTRE, NORRIS D. "Demographic and Prognostic Characteristics of Psychiatric Patients Classified by Gross MMPI Measures." *Proc Ann Conv Am Psychol Assn* 75:205–6 '67. * (*PA* 41:13646)

2232. KLINE, PAUL. "Obsessional Traits and Emotional Instability in a Normal Population." *Brit J Med Psychol* 40:153–7 Je '67. * (*PA* 42:12358)

2233. KOENIG, RONALD; LEVIN, SAUL M.; and BRENNAN, MICHAEL J. "The Emotional Status of Cancer Patients as Measured by a Psychological Test." *J Chronic Dis* 20:923–30 N–D '67. *

2234. KRAUSS, HERBERT H., and RUIZ, RENE A. "Anxiety and Temporal Perspective." *J Clin Psychol* 23:340–2 Jl '67. * (*PA* 41:15617)

2235. KRAUSS, HERBERT H., and RUIZ, RENE A. "Anxiety and Temporal Perspective." *J Clin Psychol* 23:454–5 O '67. * (*PA* 42:2623)

2236. KRUG, RONALD S. "MMPI Response Inconsistency of Brain Damaged Individuals." *J Clin Psychol* 23:366 Jl '67. * (*PA* 41:15297)

2237. LAND, MELVIN. "Taking the Emotional Temperature of the Depressed Dental Patient," pp. 43–7. In *Psychosomatic Medicine: Proceedings of the First International Congress of the Academy of Psychosomatic Medicine*. International Congress Series No. 134. Edited by E. Dunlop. Amsterdam,

Netherlands: Excerpta Medica Foundation, 1967. Pp. viii, 273. *

2238. LANYON, RICHARD I. "Simulation of Normal and Psychopathic MMPI Personality Patterns." *J Consult Psychol* 31:94–7 F '67. * (*PA* 41:4598)

2239. LEBOVITS, BINYAMIN Z., and OSTFELD, ADRIAN M. "Personality, Defensiveness, and Educatonal Achievement." *J Personality & Social Psychol* 6:381–90 Ag '67. * (*PA* 41:13648)

2240. LEBOVITS, BINYAMIN Z.; SHEKELLE, RICHARD B.; OSTFELD, ADRIAN M.; and OGLESBY, PAUL. "Prospective and Retrospective Psychological Studies of Coronary Heart Disease." *Psychosom Med* 29:265–72 My–Je '67. * (*PA* 41:15752)

2241. LEVIS, DONALD J., and CARRERA, RICHARD. "Effects of Ten Hours of Implosive Therapy in the Treatment of Outpatients: A Preliminary Report." *J Abn Psychol* 72:504–8 D '67. * (*PA* 42:4099)

2242. LEWI, P. J., and PINCHARD, A. G. "An Automated Minnesota Multiphasic Personality Inventory Test." *Acta Psychologica* 27(4):397–9 '67. *

2243. LEWINSOHN, PETER M., and NICHOLS, ROBERT C. "Dimensions of Change in Mental Hospital Patients." *J Clin Psychol* 23:498–503 O '67. * (*PA* 42:2624)

2244. LEWIS, LAURA HESTER. *Acquiescence Response Set: Construct or Artifact?* Doctor's thesis, University of Nebraska (Lincoln, Neb.), 1967. (*DA* 28:2626B)

2245. LEWIS, MARGARET P. *MMPI Changes and Success or Failure in a Prevocational Rehabilitation Program.* Master's thesis, University of Washington (Seattle, Wash.), 1967.

2246. LOWE, C. MARSHALL. "Prediction of Posthospital Work Adjustment by the Use of Psychological Tests." *J Counsel Psychol* 14:248–52 My '67. * (*PA* 41:9197)

2247. LOWE, C. MARSHALL. "The Relationship Between Marital and Socioeconomic Status and In-Patient Impairment." *J Clin Psychol* 23:315–8 Jl '67. * (*PA* 41:15619)

2248. LOWRY, THOMAS P., and GOTTESMAN, IRVING J. Chap. 5, "The MMPI and Hyperventilation," pp. 118–27. In *Hyperventilation and Hysteria: The Physiology and Psychology of Overbreathing and Its Relationship to the Mind-Body Problem*. Edited by Thomas P. Lowry. Springfield, Ill.: Charles C Thomas, Publisher, 1967. Pp. xi, 192. *

2249. LUCAS DONALD HERBERT. *Personality Correlates of Agreement and Nonagreement Between Measures of Ability and Interest for Two Groups of Institutionalized Males.* Doctor's thesis, University of Kansas (Lawrence, Kan.), 1967. (*DA* 28:2986A)

2250. LUSHENE, ROBERT EDWARD. *Factor Structure of the MMPI Item Pool.* Master's thesis, Florida State University (Tallahassee, Fla.), 1967.

2251. LYONS, JOSEPH. "Whose Experience?" *J Proj Tech & Pers Assess* 31:11–6 Ag '67. * (*PA* 41:15313)

2252. MACANDREW, CRAIG. "Self-Reports of Male Alcoholics: A Dimensional Analysis of Certain Differences From Nonalcoholic Male Psychiatric Outpatients." *Q J Studies Alcohol* 28:43–51 Mr '67. * (*PA* 41:9105).

2253. McDONALD, ROBERT L. "The Effects of Stress on Self-Attribution of Hostility Among Ego Control Patterns." *J Personality* 35:234–45 Je '67. * (*PA* 41:16685)

2254. McGREEVY, C. PATRICK. "Factor Analysis of Measures Used in the Selection and Evaluation of Counselor Education Candidates." *J Counsel Psychol* 14:51–6 Ja '67. * (*PA* 41:3644)

2255. McKEGNEY, F. PATRICK. "Psychological Correlates of Behaviour in Seriously Delinquent Juveniles." *Brit J Psychiatry* 113:781–92 Jl '67. * (*PA* 41:15508)

2256. McKENZIE, RICHARD E.; SZMYD, LUCIAN; and HARTMAN, BRYCE O. "A Study of Selected Personality Factors in Oral Surgery Patients." *J Am Dental Assn* 74:763–5 Mr '67. *

2257. MAIER, LAWRENCE R. "Air Force Norms for the Thirty-One Harris and Lingoes MMPI Subscales." *Proc Ann Conf Air Force Behav Sci* 14:349–71 D '67. *

2258. MAIER, LAWRENCE R., and ABIDIN, RICHARD R. "Validation Attempt of Hovey's Five-Item MMPI Index for CNS Disorders." Abstract. *J Consult Psychol* 31:542 O '67. * (*PA* 41:16711)

2259. MAIER, LAWRENCE R., and ABIDIN, RICHARD R., JR. "A Validation Attempt of Hovey's 5-Item MMPI 'Index' for CNS Disorders." *Proc Ann Conf Air Force Behav Sci* 14:275–85 D '67. *

2260. MALMQUIST, CARL P.; KIRESUK, THOMAS J.; and SPANO, ROBERT M. "Mothers With Multiple Illegitimacies." *Psychiatric Q* 41:339–54 Ap '67. * (*PA* 42:4189)

2261. MANN, NANCY A. "The Relationship Between Defense Preference and Response to Free Association." *J Proj Tech & Pers Assess* 31:54–61 Ag '67. * (*PA* 41:15292)

2262. MARTIN, JOHN DANIEL. *The Relationship of Responses to Geometric Designs to Inferiority Feelings and Certain Personality Variables.* Doctor's thesis, North Texas State University (Denton, Tex.), 1967. (*DA* 28:127A)

2263. MEGARGEE, EDWIN I.; COOK, PATRICK E.; and MENDELSOHN, GERALD A. "Development and Validation of an MMPI Scale of Assaultiveness in Overcontrolled Individuals." *J Abn Psychol* 72:519–28 D '67. * (*PA* 42:4234)

2264. MENDELSOHN, GERALD A., and GRISWOLD, BARBARA B. "Anxiety and Repression as Predictors of the Use of Incidental Cues in Problem Solving." *J Personality & Social Psychol* 6:353–9 Jl '67. * (*PA* 41:11934)

2265. MENDOZA, BUENA FLOR H. *A Normative Analysis of*

Psychological Test Results of Graduate Students Selecting Counselor Education. Master's thesis, Western Michigan University (Kalamazoo, Mich.), 1967.

2266. MESSICK, SAMUEL J. "The Psychology of Acquiescence: An Interpretation of Research Evidence," pp. 115–45. In *Response Set in Personality Assessment.* Edited by Irwin A. Berg. Chicago, Ill.: Aldine Publishing Co., 1967. Pp. xi, 244. *

2267. MIDDENTS, GERALD JOHN. *The Relationship of Creativity and Anxiety.* Doctor's thesis, University of Minnesota (Minneapolis, Minn.), 1967. (*DA* 28:2562A)

2268. MILLER, NURAN B.; FISHER, WILLIAM P.; and LADD, CLAYTON E. "Psychometric and Rated Anxiety." *Psychol Rep* 20:707–10 Je '67. * (*PA* 41:13880)

2269. MOBLEY, EUGENIA L., and SMITH, STANLEY H. "Some Social and Economic Factors Relating to Periodontal Disease Among Negroes: 2, Observations on Personality Traits." *J Am Dental Assn* 75:104–10 Jl '67. *

2270. MORGAN, WILLIAM PATRICK. *Selected Physiological and Psychomotor Correlates of Depression in Psychiatric Patients.* Doctor's thesis, University of Toledo (Toledo, Ohio), 1967. (*DA* 28:2086A)

2271. MOWRER, O. HOBART. "Civilization and Its Malcontents." *Psychol Today* 1:49–52 S '67. * (*PA* 42:935)

2272. NEAL, CAROLYN M. "The Relationship of Personality Variables to Reading Ability." *Calif J Ed Res* 18:133–44 My '67. * (*PA* 41:12578)

2273. NEAL, CAROLYN M. "Student Ability: Its Effect on Reading-Personality Relationships." *Ed & Psychol Meas* 27:1145–53 w '67. * (*PA* 42:8985)

2274. NEWBERRY, LAWRENCE A. "Defensiveness and Need for Approval." *J Consult Psychol* 31:396–400 Ag '67. * (*PA* 41:13622)

2275. NORMAN, WARREN T. "On Estimating Psychological Relationships: Social Desirability and Self-Report." *Psychol B* 67:273–93 Ap '67. *

2276. NOWICKI, STEPHEN, JR. "Birth Order and Personality: Some Unexpected Findings." *Psychol Rep* 21:265–7 Ag '67. * (*PA* 42:2755)

2277. NYMAN, ARIE, and LE MAY, MORRIS L. "Differentiation of Types of College Misconduct Offenses With MMPI Subscales." *J Clin Psychol* 23:99–100 Ja '67. * (*PA* 41:6254)

2277a. OPTON, EDWARD M., JR., and LAZARUS, RICHARD S. "Personality Determinants of Psychophysiological Response to Stress: A Theoretical Analysis and an Experiment." *J Personality & Social Psychol* 6:291–303 Jl '67. * (*PA* 41:11579)

2278. OSKAMP, STUART. "Clinical Judgment From the MMPI: Simple or Complex?" *J Clin Psychol* 23:411–5 O '67. * (*PA* 42:2701)

2279. PEARSON, JOHN S., and SWENSON, WENDELL M. *A User's Guide to the Mayo Clinic Automated MMPI Program.* New York: Psychological Corporation, 1967. Pp. vi, 36. *

2280. PILLING, LORAN F.; BRANNICK, THOMAS J.; and SWENSON, WENDELL M. "Psychological Characteristics of Psychiatric Patients Having Pain as a Presenting Symptom." *Can Med Assn J* 97:387–94 Ag 19 '67. * (*PA* 41:15356)

2281. PISHKIN, VLADIMIR; PIERCE, CHESTER M.; and MATHIS, JAMES L. "Analysis of Attitudinal and Personality Variables in Relation to a Programmed Course in Psychiatry." *J Clin Psychol* 23:53–6 Ja '67. * (*PA* 41:6293)

2282. POPE, BENJAMIN, and SCOTT, WINFIELD. *Psychological Diagnosis in Clinical Practice: With Applications in Medicine, Law, Education, Nursing, and Social Work,* pp. 88–110. New York: Oxford University Press, 1967. Pp. xiii, 341. *

2283. POSTEMA, LEONARD J., and SCHELL, ROBERT E. "Aging and Psychopathology: Some MMPI Evidence for Seemingly Greater Neurotic Behavior Among Older People." *J Clin Psychol* 23:140–3 Ap '67. * (*PA* 41:8751)

2284. PRICE, ROBERT VIRGIL. *A Study of Personality Organization as It Relates to Work Behavior.* Doctor's thesis, University of Kansas (Lawrence, Kan.), 1967. (*DA* 28:2991A)

2285. RESNICK, ROBERT WILLIAM. *Personality Patterns and Psycholinguistic Differences in Response to Music.* Doctor's thesis, University of Florida (Gainesville, Fla.), 1967. (*DA* 29:1178B)

2286. REZNIKOFF, MARVIN, and HONEYMAN, MERTON S. "MMPI Profiles of Monozygotic and Dizygotic Twin Pairs." Abstract. *J Consult Psychol* 31:100 F '67. * (*PA* 41:4606, title only)

2287. RIFFEL, PIUS ANTHONY. *A Psychological Study of the Personality Characteristics of the Pastorally Scrupulous.* Doctor's thesis, Fordham University (New York, N.Y.), 1967. (*DA* 28:1207B)

2288. ROTH, HERBERT S. "Personal and Demographic Characteristics Associated With L-I-D Response Bias of Domiciled Veterans on an Institutional Interest Inventory." *Newsl Res Psychol* 9:19–21 F '67. *

2289. RUCH, FLOYD L., and RUCH, WILLIAM W. "The K Factor as a (Validity) Suppressor Variable in Predicting Success in Selling." *J Appl Psychol* 51:201–4 Je '67. * (*PA* 41:10486)

2290. RUIZ, RENE A.; THURSTON, HESTER I.; and POSHEK, NEILA A. "Intellectual Factors, Biographical Information, and Personality Variables as Related to Performance on the Professional Nurse Licensure Examination." *Nursing Res* 16:74–8 w '67. * (*PA* 42:4639)

2291. SANDS, PATRICK; ROTHAUS, PAUL; and OSBURN, HOBART G. "Application of the Interpersonal Problems Attitude Survey." *Newsl Res Psychol* 9:19–21 Ag '67. *

2292. SAVAGE, R. D., and BRITTON, P. G. "A Short Scale for the Assessment of Mental Health in the Community Aged." *Brit J Psychiatry* 113:521–3 My '67. * (*PA* 41:12119)

2293. SCHIRO, FREDERICK MICHAEL. *A Study of the Relationship Between Item Reversal Patterns on True-False Tests.* Doctor's thesis, St. John's University (Collegeville, Minn.), 1967. (*DA* 28:3884B)

2294. SHINOHARA, MUTSUHARU, and JENKINS, RICHARD L. "MMPI Study of Three Types of Delinquents." *J Clin Psychol* 23:156–63 Ap '67. * (*PA* 41:9132)

2295. SHODELL, MARGARET J. *Personalities of Mothers of Nonverbal and Verbal Schizophrenic Children.* Doctor's thesis, Yeshiva University (New York, N.Y.), 1967. (*DA* 28:1175B)

2296. SHULTZ, THOMAS R., and HARTUP, WILLARD W. "Performance Under Social Reinforcement as a Function of Masculinity-Femininity of Experimenter and Subject." *J Personality & Social Psychol* 6:337–41 Jl '67. * (*PA* 41:11193)

2297. SINGH, BEER. "Development of Some MMPI Scales in Indian Conditions." *Indian Psychol R* 3:151–3 Ja '67. * (*PA* 41:8166)

2298. SOLKOFF, NORMAN, and MARKOWITZ, JOAN. "Personality Characteristics of First-Year Medical and Law Students." *J Med Ed* 42:195–200 Mr '67. *

2299. SPIEGEL, DONALD E., and ACKER, CHARLES W. "Autonomic Balance and Reactivity in Relation to Indices of Psychopathology on the MMPI." *J Proj Tech & Pers Assess* 31:76–80 O '67. * (*PA* 42:758)

2300. STEIN, KENNETH B. "Correlates of the Ideational Preference Dimension Among Prison Inmates." *Psychol Rep* 21:553–62 O '67. * (*PA* 42:5757)

2301. STEIN, KENNETH B., and CHU, CHEN-LIN. "Dimensionality of Barron's Ego-Strength Scale." *J Consult Psychol* 31:153–61 Ap '67. * (*PA* 41:6464)

2302. STEIN, STEVEN H., and HARRISON, ROBERT H. "Conscious and Preconscious Influences on Recall: A Reassessment and Extension." *Psychol Rep* 20:963–74 Je '67. * (*PA* 41:13062)

2303. STEVENS, ROY ROBERT. *Sex Differences and Personality Correlates of Pain Experience.* Doctor's thesis, Washington State University (Pullman, Wash.), 1967. (*DA* 28:2633B)

2304. STEVENS, THOMAS GRANVILLE. *Congruency Between Diagnostic Dimensions of Personality Theories and Personality Tests.* Master's thesis, California State College at Fullerton (Fullerton, Calif.), 1967.

2305. STIX, DANIEL L. "Discrepant Achievement in College as a Function of Anxiety and Repression." *Personnel & Guid J* 45:804–7 Ap '67. * (*PA* 41:12494)

2306. STRAUSS, ROGER SMALL. *The MMPI and Types of Hospital Discharge.* Doctor's thesis, University of Michigan (Ann Arbor, Mich.), 1967. (*DA* 28:5196B)

2307. SULLIVAN, FRANK W.; GENTILE, KATHLEEN; and BOELHOUWER, CORNELIUS. "Relationship of Clinical Symptomatology to Abnormal EEG Findings: A Family Study." *Am J Psychiatry* 124:554–9 O '67. * (*PA* 42:4192)

2308. TAGGART, MORRIS. "Characteristics of Participants and Nonparticipants in Individual Test-Interpretation Interviews." *J Consult Psychol* 31:213–5 Ap '67. * (*PA* 41:7346)

2309. TAYLOR, A. J. W. "Prediction for Parole: A Pilot Study With Delinquent Girls." *Brit J Criminol* 7:418–24 O '67. *

2310. THALER, VICTOR HUGO. *Personality Dimensions Derived From Multiple Instruments.* Doctor's thesis, Columbia University (New York, N.Y.), 1967. (*DA* 28:509A)

2311. TRYON, ROBERT C. "Person-Clusters on Intellectual Abilities and on MMPI Attributes." *Multiv Behav Res* 2:5–34 Ja '67. * (*PA* 41:8928)

2312. TRYON, ROBERT C. "Predicting Individual Differences by Cluster Analysis: Holzinger Abilities and MMPI Personality Attributes." *Multiv Behav Res* 2:325–48 Jl '67. * (*PA* 41:16708)

2313. TUTHILL, EDWARD W.; OVERALL, JOHN E.; and HOLLISTER, LEO E. "Subjective Correlates of Clinically Manifested Anxiety and Depression." *Psychol Rep* 20:535–42 Ap '67. * (*PA* 41:9098)

2314. VAUGHAN, RICHARD P. "Academic Achievement, Ability, and the MMPI Scales." *Personnel & Guid J* 46:156–9 O '67. *

2315. VESTRE, NORRIS D., and LOREI, THEODORE W. "Relationships Between Social History Factors and Psychiatric Symptoms." *J Abn Psychol* 72:247–50 Je '67. * (*PA* 41:10670)

2316. WAGNER, EDWIN E., and DOBBINS, RICHARD D. "MMPI Profiles of Parishioners Seeking Pastoral Counseling." *J Consult Psychol* 31:83–4 F '67. * (*PA* 41:4611)

2317. WALKER, C. EUGENE. "The Effect of Eliminating Offensive Items on the Reliability and Validity of the MMPI." *J Clin Psychol* 23:363–6 Jl '67. * (*PA* 41:15300)

2318. WATSON, CHARLES G. "Relationships Between Certain Personality Variables and Overinclusion." *J Clin Psychol* 23:327–30 Jl '67. * (*PA* 41:15265)

2319. WEIGEL, RICHARD G., and PHILLIPS, MARYANN. "An Evaluation of MMPI Scoring Accuracy by Two National Scoring Agencies." *J Clin Psychol* 23:102–3 Ja '67. * (*PA* 41:5977)

2320. WERKMAN, SIDNEY L., and GREENBERG, ELSA S. "Personality and Interest Patterns in Obese Adolescent Girls." *Psychosom Med* 29:72–80 Ja–F '67. * (*PA* 41:5990)

2321. WILCOX, RONALD, and KRASNOFF, ALAN. "Influence

of Test-Taking Attitudes on Personality Inventory Scores." *J Consult Psychol* 31:188–94 Ap '67. * (*PA* 41:7351)

2322. WILSON, IAN C.; ALLTOP, LACOE B.; and BUFFALOE, W. J. "Parental Bereavement in Childhood: M.M.P.I. Profiles in a Depressed Population." *Brit J Psychiatry* 113:761–4 Jl '67. * (*PA* 41:15528)

2323. WOLFF, WIRT M. "Psychotherapeutic Persistence." Abstract. *J Consult Psychol* 31:429 Ag '67. * (*PA* 41:13757, title only)

2324. WOLKING, WILLIAM D.; DUNTEMAN, GEORGE H.; and BAILEY, JOHN P., JR. "Multivariate Analyses of Parents' MMPIs Based on the Psychiatric Diagnoses of Their Children." *J Consult Psychol* 31:521–4 O '67. * (*PA* 41:16714)

2325. WRIGHT, JOHN J. "Reported Personal Stress Sources and Adjustment of Entering Freshmen." *J Counsel Psychol* 14:371–3 Jl '67. * (*PA* 41:12496)

2326. WRIGHT, MORGAN W.; CHYLINSKI, JOANNE; SISLER, GEORGE C.; and QUARRINGTON, BRUCE. "Personality Factors in the Selection of Civilians for Isolated Northern Stations: A Follow-Up Study." *Can Psychologist* 8a:23–31 Ja '67. * (*PA* 41:7979)

2327. ZUCKERMAN, MARVIN; PERSKY, HAROLD; and LINK, KATHRYN. "Relation of Mood and Hypnotizability: An Illustration of the Importance of the State Versus Trait Distinction." *J Consult Psychol* 31:464–70 O '67. * (*PA* 41:16162)

2328. ZUCKERMAN, MARVIN; PERSKY, HAROLD; ECKMAN, KATHERINE M.; and HOPKINS, T. ROBERT. "A Multitrait Multimethod Measurement Approach to the Traits (or States) of Anxiety, Depression and Hostility." *J Proj Tech & Pers Assess* 31:39–48 Ap '67. * (*PA* 41:13635)

2329. ZUCKERMAN, MARVIN; SCHULTZ, DUANE P.; and HOPKINS, T. ROBERT. "Sensation Seeking and Volunteering for Sensory Deprivation and Hypnosis Experiments." *J Consult Psychol* 31:358–63 Ag '67. * (*PA* 41:12849)

2330. ZUNG, WILLIAM W. K. "Factors Influencing the Self-Rating Depression Scale." *Arch Gen Psychiatry* 16:543–7 My '67. * (*PA* 41:10722)

2331. AARONSON, BERNARD S. "Hypnosis, Time Rate Perception and Personality." *J Schizophrenia* 2(1):11–41 '68. *

2332. ADEVAI, GRETA; SILVERMAN, ALBERT J.; and McGOUGH, W. EDWARD. "MMPI Findings in Field-Dependent and Field-Independent Subjects." *Percept & Motor Skills* 26:3–8 F '68. * (*PA* 42:10604)

2333. ANDERSON, LORNA McLEOD. *Personality Characteristics of Parents of Neurotic, Aggressive and Normal Pre-Adolescent Boys.* Doctor's thesis, University of Minnesota (Minneapolis, Minn.), 1968. (*DA* 29:1165B)

2334. AUMACK, LEWIS. "MMPI Rational Subscales: A Question of Clinical Utility." *Newsl Res Psychol* 10:13–4 F '68. *

2335. BAXTER, JAMES C., and MORRIS, KATHRYN L. "Item Ambiguity and Item Discrimination in the MMPI." *J Consult & Clin Psychol* 32:309–13 Je '68. * (*PA* 42:12978)

2336. BERDIE, RALPH F. "Perhaps Mode of Response Does Not Explain Intra-Individual Variability." *Psychol Rep* 23:40–2 Ag '68. * (*PA* 23:6942)

2337. BERNARD, JACQUELINE HANRATTY. *Response Communalities of Specific Reference Groups as a Basis for Scoring Psychological Tests.* Doctor's thesis, University of Minnesota (Minneapolis, Minn.), 1968. (*DA* 29:1166B)

2338. BLACKBURN, R. "Emotionality, Extraversion and Aggression in Paranoid and Nonparanoid Schizophrenic Offenders." Abstract. *Brit J Psychiatry* 115:1301–2 O '68. *

2339. BLACKBURN, R. "Personality in Relation to Extreme Aggression in Psychiatric Offenders." *Brit J Psychiatry* 114:821–8 Jl '68. * (*PA* 43:2817)

2340. BLACKBURN, R. "The Scores of Eysenck's Criterion Groups on Some MMPI Scales Related to Emotionality and Extraversion." *Brit J Social & Clin Psychol* 7:3–12 F '68. * (*PA* 42:8978)

2341. BRADFORD, JEAN LOUISE. *Sex Differences in Anxiety.* Doctor's thesis, University of Minnesota (Minneapolis, Minn.), 1968. (*DA* 29:1167B)

2342. CARR, JOHN E., and WHITTENBAUGH, JOHN A. "Volunteer and Nonvolunteer Characteristics in an Outpatient Population." *J Abn Psychol* 73:16–7 F '68. * (*PA* 42:7378)

2343. COTTLE, WILLIAM C. *Interest and Personality Inventories*, pp. 70–95. Guidance Monograph Series, Series 3. Testing, [No. 6]. Boston, Mass.: Houghton Mifflin Co., 1968. Pp. xi, 116. *

2344. DAVID, KENNETH H. "Ego-Strength, Sex Differences, and Description of Self, Ideal, and Parents." *J General Psychol* 79:79–81 Jl '68. * (*PA* 42:17374)

2345. DAVIS, DAVID; KAUSCH, DONALD F.; and GOCHROS, HARVEY L. "Psycho-Social Characteristics of Check Offenders." *Comprehen Psychiatry* 9:474–81 S '68. *

2346. DeCENCIO, DOMINIC V.; LESHNER, MARTIN; and LESHNER, BONNIE. "Personality Characteristics of Patients With Chronic Obstructive Pulmonary Emphysema." *Arch Phys Med & Rehabil* 49:471–5 Ag '68. *

2347. DIES, ROBERT R. "Detection of Simulated MMPI Records Using the Desirability (DY) Scales." *J Clin Psychol* 24:335–7 Jl '68. * (*PA* 42:16409)

2348. DUBITZKY, MILDRED, and SCHWARTZ, JEROME L. "Ego-Resiliency, Ego-Control, and Smoking Cessation." *J Psychol* 70:27–33 S '68. * (*PA* 43:872)

2349. DUBLIN, JAMES E. "Perception of and Reaction to

Ambiguity by Repressors and Sensitizers: A Construct-Validity Study." *J Consult & Clin Psychol* 32:198–205 Ap '68. * (*PA* 42:8089)

2350. FAUNCE, PATRICIA SPENCER. "Personality Characteristics and Vocational Interests Related to the College Persistence of Academically Gifted Women." *J Counsel Psychol* 15:31–40 Ja '68. * (*PA* 42:6083)

2351. FAW, VOLNEY; SELLERS, DAVID J.; and WILCOCK, WARREN W. "Psychopathological Effects of Hypnosis." *Int J Clin & Exp Hyp* 16:26–37 Ja '68. *

2352. FENZ, WALTER D., and BROWN, MARVIN. "Betting Preferences and Personality Characteristics of Sport Parachutists." *Aerospace Med* 39:175–6 F '68. *

2353. FINE, BERNARD J., and SWEENEY, DONALD R. "Personality Traits, and Situational Factors, and Catecholamine Excretion." *J Exp Res Personality* 3:15–27 Je '68. * (*PA* 42:16867)

2354. FINNEY, JOSEPH C. "Normative Data on Some MMPI Scales." *Psychol Rep* 23:219–29 Ag '68. * (*PA* 43:6643)

2355. FISHER, GARY. "Human Figure Drawing Indices of Sexual Maladjustment in Male Felons." Abstract. *J Proj Tech & Pers Assess* 32:81 F '68. * (*PA* 42:9205)

2356. FISHER, GARY. "Human Figure Drawing Indices of Sexual Maladjustment in Male Felons." *Correct Psychiatry & J Social Ther* 14:48–53 sp '68. *

2357. FOWLER, R. D., JR.; STEVENS, SANDRA S.; COYLE, F. A., JR.; and MARLOWE, GUY H., JR. "Comparison of Two Methods of Identifying Maladjusted College Students." *J Psychol* 69:165–8 Jl '68. * (*PA* 42:15481)

2358. FOWLER, RAYMOND D., JR. "MMPI Computer Interpretation for College Counseling." *J Psychol* 69:201–7 Jl '68. * (*PA* 42:15479)

2359. FOWLER, RAYMOND D., JR., and COYLE, F. A., JR. "A Comparison of Two MMPI Actuarial Systems Used in Classifying an Alcoholic Out-Patient Population." *J Clin Psychol* 24:434–5 O '68. * (*PA* 43:4149)

2360. FOWLER, RAYMOND D., JR., and COYLE, F. A., JR. "Computer Application of MMPI Actuarial Systems With a College Population." *J Psychol* 69:233–6 Jl '68. * (*PA* 42:15480)

2361. FOWLER, RAYMOND D., JR., and COYLE, F. A., JR. "Overlap as a Problem in Atlas Classification of MMPI Profiles." *J Clin Psychol* 24:435 O '68. * (*PA* 43:4150)

2362. FOWLER, RAYMOND D., JR., and COYLE, F. A., JR. "Scoring Error on the MMPI." *J Clin Psychol* 24:68–9 Ja '68. * (*PA* 42:9159)

2363. FOWLER, RAYMOND D., JR.; COYLE, F. A., JR.; REED, P. C.; and WHITE, CHESTER A. "The MMPI Measurement of Phenotypic Anxiety: 1, Exploratory Study." *J Psychol* 68:305–12 Mr '68. * (*PA* 42:8092)

2364. FOX, BEATRICE, and DiSCIPIO, WILLIAM J. "An Exploratory Study in the Treatment of Homosexuality by Combining Principles From Psychoanalytical and Conditioning: Theoretical and Methodological Considerations." *Brit J Med Psychol* 41:273–82 S '68. * (*PA* 43:1120)

2365. FRAYN, DOUGLAS H. "A Relationship Between Rated Ability and Personality Traits in Psychotherapists." *Am J Psychiatry* 124:1232–7 Mr '68. *

2366. GALBRAITH, GARY G. "Reliability of Free Associative Sexual Responses." Abstract. *J Consult & Clin Psychol* 32:622 O '68. * (*PA* 43:130)

2367. GOLDSTEIN, GERALD; NEURINGER, CHARLES; REIFF, CAROLYN; and SHELLY, CAROLYN H. "Generalizability of Field Dependency in Alcoholics." *J Consult & Clin Psychol* 32:560–4 O '68. * (*PA* 43:1094)

2368. GOLDSTEIN, STEVEN GEORGE. *The Identification, Description and Multivariate Classification of Alcoholics by Means of the Minnesota Multiphasic Personality Inventory.* Doctor's thesis, Purdue University (Lafayette, Ind.), 1968. (*DA* 29:1170B)

2369. GONEN, JAY Y., and LANSKY, LEONARD M. "Masculinity, Femininity, and Masculinity-Femininity: A Phenomenological Study of the *Mf* Scale of the MMPI." *Psychol Rep* 23:183–94 Ag '68. * (*PA* 43:6944)

2370. GOTTHEIL, EDWARD; PAREDES, ALFONSO; and EXLINE, RALPH V. "Parental Schemata in Emotionally Disturbed Women." *J Abn Psychol* 73:416–9 O '68. * (*PA* 42:18851)

2371. GRAVITZ, MELVIN A. "Normative Findings for the Frequency of MMPI Critical Items." *J Clin Psychol* 24:220 Ap '68. * (*PA* 42:12107)

2372. GRAVITZ, MELVIN A. "Self-Described Depression and Scores on the MMPI *D* Scale in Normal Subjects." *J Proj Tech & Pers Assess* 32:88–91 F '68. * (*PA* 42:8979)

2373. GYNTHER, MALCOLM D., and BRILLIANT, PATRICIA J. "The MMPI *K+* Profile: A Reexamination." *J Consult & Clin Psychol* 32:616–7 O '68. * (*PA* 43:131)

2374. HAERTZEN, CHARLES A.; HILL, HARRIS E.; and MONROE, JACK J. "MMPI Scales for Differentiating and Predicting Relapse in Alcoholics, Opiate Addicts, and Criminals." *Int J Addiction* 3:91–106 sp '68. *

2375. HAMMER, MAX. "Differentiating 'Good' and 'Bad' Officers in a Progressive Rehabilitative Women's Reformatory." *Correct Psychiatry & J Social Ther* 14:114–7 sp '68. *

2376. HARRIS, ROBERT E.; FOGEY, EDWARD W.; ZUBIN, JOSEPH; NEULINGER, JOHN; SHAKOW, DAVID; and STEIN, MORRIS J. "Discussion of Papers on 'Systems Based on Patterns of Psychological Performance,'" pp. 404–18. In *The Role and Methodology of Classification in Psychiatry and*

Psychopathology. Edited by Martin M. Katz and others. Public Health Service Publication No. 1584. Washington, D.C.: United States Government Printing Office, 1968. Pp. ix, 590. *

2377. HEILBRUN, ALFRED B., JR. "Cognitive Sensitivity to Aversive Maternal Stimulation in Late-Adolescent Males." *J Consult & Clin Psychol* 32:326-32 Je '68. * (*PA* 42:13518)

2378. HOFFMAN, EDWARD LEE. *The Effect of Instructions to be "Accurate" on Responses to the MMPI.* Doctor's thesis, University of Illinois (Urbana, Ill.), 1968. (*DA* 29:757B)

2379. HONEYMAN, MERTON S.; RAPPAPORT, HERBERT; REZNIKOFF, MARVIN; GLUECK, BERNARD C., JR.; and EISENBERG, HENRY. "Psychological Impact of Heart Disease in the Family of the Patient." *Psychosomatics* 9:34-7 Ja-F '68. * (*PA* 42:12658)

2380. HORN, JOHN L., and STEWART, PATRICIA. "On the Accuracy of Clinical Judgments." *Brit J Social & Clin Psychol* 7:129-34 Je '68. * (*PA* 42:17385)

2381. HORN, JOHN L.; ADAMS, DARRELL K.; and LEVY, GEORGE. "On the Concept Validity of MMPI Scales." *J Ed Meas* 5:79-90 sp '68. * (*PA* 42:12984)

2382. HUNDLEBY, JOHN D., and CONNOR, WILLIAM H. "Interrelationships Between Personality Inventories: The 16 PF, the MMPI, and the MPI." *J Consult & Clin Psychol* 32:152-7 Ap '68. * (*PA* 42:8981)

2383. JACKSON, DOUGLAS N., and LAY, C. H. "Homogeneous Dimensions of Personality Scale Content." *Multiv Behav Res* 3:321-37 Jl '68. * (*PA* 43:4030)

2384. JONES, RICHARD R. "Differences in Response Consistency and Subjects' Preferences for Three Personality Inventory Response Formats." *Proc Ann Conv Am Psychol Assn* 76:247-8 '68. * (*PA* 43:935, title only)

2385. KIDD, ALINE H. "The Ego Strength Scale and the Goldberg Scale in Evaluating Clinic Outpatients." *J Clin Psychol* 24:438-9 O '68. * (*PA* 43:4156)

2386. KINCANNON, JAMES C. "Prediction of the Standard MMPI Scale Scores From 71 Items: The Mini-Mult." *J Consult & Clin Psychol* 32:319-25 Je '68. * (*PA* 42:12987)

2387. KLEINMUNTZ, BENJAMIN, and MCLEAN, ROBERT S. "Diagnostic Interviewing by Digital Computer." *Behav Sci* 13:75-80 Ja '68. * (*PA* 42:5744)

2388. KLETT, WILLIAM G., and VESTRE, NORRIS D. "Demographic and Prognostic Characteristics of Psychiatric Patients Classified by Gross MMPI Measures." *J Consult & Clin Psychol* 32:271-5 Je '68. * (*PA* 42:13811)

2389. KURLAND, HOWARD D., and HAMMER, MORTON. "Emotional Evaluation of Medical Patients." *Arch Gen Psychiatry* 19:72-8 Jl '68. * (*PA* 42:19005)

2390. LACHAR, DAVID. "MMPI Two-Point Code-Type Correlates in a State Hospital Population." *J Clin Psychol* 24:424-7 O '68. * (*PA* 43:4157)

2391. LANSDELL, H. "Effect of Extent of Temporal Lobe Surgery and Neuropathology on the MMPI." *J Clin Psychol* 24:406-12 O '68. * (*PA* 43:4324)

2392. LANSDELL, H., and POLCARI, A. R. "The Meaning of the Taulbee-Sisson Configurational Score on the MMPI With Neurosurgical Patients." *J Clin Psychol* 24:216-9 Ap '68. * (*PA* 42:12109)

2393. LEFKOWITZ, MONROE M. "Screening Juvenile Delinquents for Psychopathology by Use of the Z-Test." *J Proj Tech & Pers Assess* 32:475-8 O '68. * (*PA* 43:5574)

2394. LEVENTHAL, ALLAN M. "Additional Technical Data on the CPI Anxiety Scale." Abstract. *J Counsel Psychol* 15:479-80 S '68. * (*PA* 42:18823)

2395. LEVITT, HERBERT, and RICE, DAVID. "Sex and Verbal Proficiency on the Simulation of Normalcy Procedure." *J Clin Psychol* 24:440-3 O '68. * (*PA* 43:4058)

2396. LEWINSOHN, PETER M. "Characteristics of Patients With Hallucinations." Abstract. *J Clin Psychol* 24:423 O '68. * (*PA* 43:4223)

2397. LIEBERMAN, LEWIS R. "Further Efforts to Find Context Effects in Personality Inventories." *Percept & Motor Skills* 26:1277-8 Je '68. * (*PA* 42:18824)

2398. LIEBERMAN, LEWIS R., and WALTERS, WILLIAM M., JR. "Effect of Background Items on Responses to Personality Inventory Items." *J Consult & Clin Psychol* 32:230-2 Ap '68. *

2399. LOMBARDI, DONALD N.; O'BRIEN, BRIAN J.; and ISELE, FRANK W. "Differential Responses of Addicts and Non-Addicts on the MMPI." *J Proj Tech & Pers Assess* 32:479-82 O '68. * (*PA* 43:5586)

2400. LORR, MAURICE. "A Test of Seven MMPI Factors," pp. 151-6. (*PA* 42:15483) In *Progress in Clinical Psychology Through Multivariate Experimental Designs.* Edited by Raymond B. Cattell. Fort Worth, Tex.: Society of Multivariate Experimental Psychology, Inc., 1968. Pp. 168. *

2401. LORR, MAURICE; CAFFEY, EUGENE M., JR.; and GESSNER, THEODORE L. "Seven Symptom Profiles." *J Nerv & Mental Dis* 147:134-40 Ag '68. * (*PA* 42:19008)

2402. LOWE, C. MARSHALL, and DAMANKOS, FREDERICK J. "Psychological and Sociological Dimensions of Anomie in a Psychiatric Population." *J Social Psychol* 74:65-74 F '68. * (*PA* 42:9031)

2403. McCONAGHY, N., and CLANCY, M. "Familial Relationships of Allusive Thinking in University Students and Their Parents." *Brit J Psychiatry* 114:1079-87 S '68. * (*PA* 43:4286)

2404. McDONALD, ROBERT L. "Leary's Overt Interpersonal Behavior: A Validation Attempt." *J Social Psychol* 74:259-64 Ap '68. * (*PA* 42:10597)

2405. MASON, DONALD J., and HERRING, FRED H. "Hand Scoring Templates for the Roche Answer Sheet for the MMPI." *Newsl Res Psychol* 10:6 Ag '68. *

2406. MATTHEWS, CH. G., and KLØVE, H. "MMPI Performances in Major, Motor, Psychomotor and Mixed Seizure Classifications of Known and Unknown Etiology." *Epilepsia* 9:43-53 Mr '68. *

2407. MILLER, BYRON; POKORNY, ALEX D.; and HANSON, PHILIP G. "A Study of Dropouts in an In-Patient Alcoholism Treatment Program." *Dis Nerv System* 29:91-9 F '68. *

2408. MILLER, CHRISTINE; KNAPP, SARAH C.; and DANIELS, CLARA W. "MMPI Study of Negro Mental Hygiene Clinic Patients." *J Abn Psychol* 73:168-73 Ap '68. * (*PA* 42:9033)

2409. MILLER, J. PHILIP; BOHN, SUZANNE E.; GILDEN, JOANNE B.; and STEVENS, ED. "Anxiety as a Function of Taking the MMPI." *J Consult & Clin Psychol* 32:120-4 Ap '68. * (*PA* 42:8984)

2410. MOOS, RUDOLF H. "Differential Effects of Ward Settings on Psychiatric Patients: A Replication and Extension." *J Nerv & Mental Dis* 147:386-93 O '68. *

2411. MUNDAY, LEO A.; BRASKAMP, LARRY A.; and BRANDT, JAMES E. "The Meaning of Unpatterned Vocational Interests." *Personnel & Guid J* 47:249-56 N '68. * (*PA* 43:6022)

2412. NALVEN, FREDRIC B., and O'BRIEN, JOHN F. "On the Use of the MMPI With Rheumatoid Arthritic Patients." *J Clin Psychol* 24:70 Ja '68. * (*PA* 42:8997)

2413. NEAL, CAROLYN M. "Sex Differences in Personality and Reading Ability." *J Read* 11:609-14 My '68. * (*PA* 42:17204)

2414. NEWTON, JOSEPH R. "Clinical Normative Data for MMPI Special Scales: Critical Items, Manifest Anxiety, and Repression-Sensitization." *J Clin Psychol* 24:427-30 O '68. * (*PA* 43:4160)

2415. OLIVER, WAYNE A., and MOSHER, DONALD L. "Psychopathology and Guilt in Heterosexual and Subgroups of Homosexual Reformatory Inmates." *J Abn Psychol* 73:323-9 Ag '68. * (*PA* 42:17407)

2416. PARSONS, OSCAR A.; YOURSHAW, SARAH; and BORSTELMANN, LLOYD. "Self-Ideal-Self Discrepancies on the MMPI: Consistencies Over Time and Geographic Region." *J Counsel Psychol* 15:160-6 Mr '68. * (*PA* 42:8999)

2417. PEDERSEN, DARHL M., and WILLIAMS, BRIAN R. "Effects of the Interpersonal Game Upon Intra- and Interpersonal Concepts, Personality Characteristics, and Interpersonal Relationships." *Psychol Rep* 22:116-8 F '68. * (*PA* 42:10566)

2418. PIERCE, RICHARD M. "Comment on the Prediction of Posthospital Work Adjustment With Psychological Tests." *J Counsel Psychol* 15:386-7 Jl '68. * (*PA* 42:15539)

2419. PIVIK, TERRY, and FOULKES, DAVID. "NREM Mentation: Relation to Personality, Orientation Time, and Time of Night." *J Consult & Clin Psychol* 32:144-51 Ap '68. * (*PA* 42:8252)

2420. PTASNIK, JOSEPH ALBERT, JR. *A Diagnostic Use of the Minnesota Multiphasic Personality Inventory in a University Guidance Center.* Doctor's thesis, New Mexico State University (University Park, N.M.), 1968. (*DA* 29:817A)

2421. RANKIN, R. J. "Analysis of Items Perceived as Objectionable in the Minnesota Multiphasic Personality Inventory." *Percept & Motor Skills* 27:627-33 O '68. * (*PA* 43:5375)

2422. RAPPAPORT, HERBERT; REZNIKOFF, MARVIN; GLUECK, BERNARD C., JR.; HONEYMAN, MERTON S.; and EISENBERG, HENRY. "Smoking Behavior in Offspring of Heart Disease Patients: A Response to Cognitive Dissonance." *J Consult & Clin Psychol* 32:404-6 Ag '68. * (*PA* 42:17134)

2423. REDING, GEORGES R.; ZEPELIN, HAROLD; and MONROE, LAWRENCE J. "Personality Study of Nocturnal Teeth-Grinders." *Percept & Motor Skills* 26:523-31 Ap '68. * (*PA* 42:12085)

2424. REESE, PHYLLIS M.; WEBB, JAMES T.; and FOULKS, JIMMY D. "A Comparison of Oral and Booklet Forms of the MMPI for Psychiatric Inpatients." *J Clin Psychol* 24:436-7 O '68. * (*PA* 43:4163)

2425. REESE, PHYLLIS M.; WEBB, JAMES T.; and FOULKS, JIMMY D. "A Comparison of Oral and Booklet Forms of the MMPI for Psychiatric Inpatients." *Newsl Res Psychol* 10:7 F '68. *

2426. RESNICOFF, ARTHUR; SCHAUBLE, PAUL G.; and WOODY, ROBERT H. "Personality Correlates of Withdrawal From Smoking." *J Psychol* 68:117-20 Ja '68. * (*PA* 42:6911)

2427. RICE, DAVID G. "Rorschach Responses and Aggressive Characteristics of MMPI *F* > 16 Scorers." *J Proj Tech & Pers Assess* 32:253-61 Je '68. * (*PA* 42:15474)

2428. RITCHEY, RONALD E. "Evaluation of Schizophrenics on a Ward Halfway House Program." *Proc Ann Conv Am Psychol Assn* 76:499-500 '68. * (*PA* 43:1146, title only)

2429. ROSENBAUM, GERALD, and KATZ, JEROME. "Measures of Anxiety in Acute Schizophrenia: Test Anxiety and Reaction Time." *Proc Ann Conv Am Psychol Assn* 76:501-2 '68. * (*PA* 43:1169, title only)

2430. SCHROEDER, PEARL, and DOWSE, EUNICE. "Selection, Function, and Assessment of Residence Hall Counselors." *Personnel & Guid J* 47:151-6 O '68. *

2431. SERMAT, VELLO. "Dominance-Submissiveness and Competition in a Mixed-Motive Game." *Brit J Social & Clin Psychol* 7:35-44 F '68. * (*PA* 42:8872)

2432. SHEPPARD, CHARLES; FIORENTINO, DIANE; and MERLIS, SIDNEY. "Affective Differential: Comparison of Emotion Profiles Gained From Clinical Judgment and Patient Self-Report." *Psychol Rep* 22:809–14 Je '68. * (*PA* 42:14070)

2433. SHULTZ, TIMOTHY D.; GIBEAU, PHILIP J.; and BARRY, STANLEY M. "Utility of MMPI 'Cookbooks.'" *J Clin Psychol* 24:430–3 O '68. * (*PA* 43:4165)

2434. SIMMONS, DALE D. "Invasion of Privacy and Judged Benefit of Personality-Test Inquiry." *J General Psychol* 79: 177–81 O '68. * (*PA* 43:4038)

2435. SIMON, WERNER, and LUMRY, GAYLE K. "Suicide Among Physician-Patients." *J Nerv & Mental Dis* 147:105–12 Ag '68. * (*PA* 42:19040)

2436. SIMONO, RONALD B. "Personality Characteristics of Undergraduate Curricular Groups." *Psychol Sch* 5:280–2 Jl '68. * (*PA* 42:19280)

2437. SMITH, JAMES, and LANYON, RICHARD I. "Prediction of Juvenile Probation Violators." *J Consult & Clin Psychol* 32:54–8 F '68. * (*PA* 42:7496)

2438. SNORTUM, JOHN R. "Probability Learning and Gambling Behavior in the 'sychopathic Deviate." *J General Psychol* 79:47–57 Jl '68. * (*A* 42:17408)

2439. SOBOLIK, CLINTON F., and LARSON, HERBERT J. "Predicting Denture Acceptance Through Psychotechnics." *J Dental Ed* 32:67–72 Mr '68. *

2440. STEIN, KENNETH B. Chap. 5, "The TSC Scales: The Outcome of a Cluster Analysis of the 550 MMPI Items," pp. 80–104. In *Advances in Psychological Assessment, Vol. 1.* Edited by Paul McReynolds. Palo Alto, Calif.: Science & Behavior Books, Inc., 1968. Pp. xiii, 336. *

2441. STEIN, KENNETH B. "Motoric and Ideational Dimensions: A Study of Personality Styles Among Prison Inmates." *Psychol Rep* 22:119–29 F '68. * (*PA* 42:10824)

2442. TAMKIN, ARTHUR S., and SONKIN, NATHAN. "The Use of Psychological Tests in Differential Diagnosis." *Newsl Res Psychol* 10:24 Ag '68. *

2443. TAULBEE, EARL S., and LIBB, JOHN W. "Overt Sexual Responses in Personality Assessment and Alcoholism." *Newsl Res Psychol* 10:1–5 Ag '68. *

2444. THUMIN, FRED J. "MMPI Profiles as a Function of Chronological Age." *Psychol Rep* 22:479–82 Ap '68. * (*PA* 42:12868)

2445. THURSTON, JOHN R.; BRUNCLIK, HELEN L.; and FELDHUSEN, JOHN F. "The Relationship of Personality to Achievement in Nursing Education, Phase 2." *Nursing Res* 17:265–8 My–Je '68. * (*PA* 42:17997)

2446. TRUAX, CHARLES B.; SCHULDT, W. JOHN; and WARGO, DONALD G. "Self-Ideal Concept Congruence and Improvement in Group Psychotherapy." *J Consult & Clin Psychol* 32:47–53 F '68. * (*PA* 42:7399)

2447. TRYON, ROBERT C. "Comparative Cluster Analysis of Variables and Individuals: Holzinger Abilities and the MMPI." *Multiv Behav Res* 3:115–44 Ja '68. * (*PA* 42:12087)

2448. UPPER, DENNIS, and SEEMAN, WILLIAM. "Brain Damage, Schizophrenia and Five MMPI Items." *J Clin Psychol* 24:444 O '68. * (*PA* 43:4166)

2449. VAUGHAN, RICHARD P. "College Dropouts: Dismissed vs. Withdrew." *Personnel & Guid J* 46:685–9 Mr '68. * (*PA* 42:16144)

2450. VERY, PHILIP S., and IACONO, CARMINE. "Phenylthiourea Taste Blindness and MMPI Personality Patterns in Adult Caucasian Females." *J Clin Psychol* 24:187–8 Ap '68. * (*PA* 42:12120)

2451. WAGMAN, MORTON. "The Relationship of Types of Daydream Behavior to Selected MMPI Scales." *Psychiatry* 31:84–9 F '68. * (*PA* 42:9729)

2452. WAHLER, H. J. "Self-Evaluation With Favorable-Unfavorable Response Patterns: Reliability, Discriminative Validity and Changes With Instructions." *J Clin Psychol* 24: 319–23 Jl '68. * (*PA* 42:17403)

2453. WALES, BETH, and SEEMAN, WILLIAM. "A New Method for Detecting the Fake Good Response Set on the MMPI." *J Clin Psychol* 24:211–6 Ap '68. * (*PA* 42:12121)

2454. WATSON, CHARLES G. "Prediction of Length of Hospital Stay From MMPI Scales." *J Clin Psychol* 24:444–7 O '68. * (*PA* 43:4167)

2455. WATSON, CHARLES G., and THOMAS, RICHARD W. "MMPI Profiles of Brain-Damaged and Schizophrenic Patients." *Percept & Motor Skills* 27:567–73 O '68. * (*PA* 43:5583)

2456. WIGGINS, JERRY S.; WIGGINS, NANCY; and CONGER, JUDITH COHEN. "Correlates of Heterosexual Somatic Preference." *J Personality & Social Psychol* 10:82–90 S '68. *

2457. WIGGINS, NANCY, and HOFFMAN, PAUL J. "Three Models of Clinical Judgment." *J Abn Psychol* 73:70–7 F '68. * (*PA* 42:7467)

2458. WILLIAMS, ROBERT L., and COLE, SPURGEON. "A Study of MMPI Norms for College Students." *J Ed Res* 61:347 Ap '68. *

2459. WOLFF, WIRT M. "Personality Patterns of Private Clients." Abstract. *J Consult & Clin Psychol* 32:621 O '68. * (*PA* 43:955)

2460. WOODWARD, CHRISTEL ALMA GUNKEL. *Combining Methods of Description in Personality Assessment.* Doctor's thesis, Ohio State University (Columbus, Ohio), 1968. (*DA* 29:1851B)

[167]

★[Re Minnesota Multiphasic Personality Inventory.] A computerized scoring and interpreting service for physicians, psychiatrists, and psychologists; 1963–67; the interpretive report is a 4 or 5 page computer printout presenting an emotional disturbance score (called *Multiphasic Index,* MI), probabilities of disturbances, descriptive and interpretative statements (regarding ability to cope, suggestions for improving coping, special coping problems, most frequent diagnosis, critical items, salient clinical features), scores on 4 validity scales, 10 clinical scales, and 17 special research scales [anxiety index (AI), internalization ratio (IR), first factor (A), second factor (R), ego strength (Es), contradictory response (Tr), dissimulation index (F-K), dissimulation (Ds), positive malingering (Mp), control (Cn), ego defensiveness (Ed), severity of illness (FNF), manifest anxiety (At), low back (Lb), rigidity defense (Rg), dependency (Dy), social dominance (Do)], and a profile of the validity and clinical scores; reference guide ['66, 12 pages]; references guide abstract ['67, 15 pages]; special IBM 1230 answer sheets must be used; scoring and computerized report, $7.50 per test; reports are mailed within 2 days after receipt of answer sheets; postpaid; Institute of Clinical Analysis. *

REFERENCES

1. WALTMANN, ROBERT H., and BIRDS, VALENTINE G. "Role of the Electronic Computer in Clinical Medicine." *Psychosomatics* 6:277–81 S–O '65. *
2. DUNLOP, EDWIN, and WALTMANN, ROBERT H. "The Emotional Temperature," pp. 195–7. In *Psychosomatic Medicine: Proceedings of the First International Congress of the Academy of Psychosomatic Medicine.* International Congress Series No. 134. Edited by E. Dunlop. Amsterdam, Netherlands: Excerpta Medica Foundation, 1967. Pp. viii, 273. *

[168]

★[Re Minnesota Multiphasic Personality Inventory.] The Psychological Corporation MMPI Reporting Service. A computerized scoring and interpreting service for qualified users of the MMPI; 1967; the interpretive report is a 1 page computer printout presenting 6 to 15 interpretive statements (selected from a population of 73 statements), scores on 4 validity scales, 10 clinical scales, and 13 special scales [first factor (A), second factor (R), ego strength (Es), low back pain (Lb), caudality (Ca), dependency (Dy), dominance (Do), responsibility (Re), prejudice (Pr), status (St), control (Cn), tired housewife (Th), and worried breadwinner (Wb)], and a profile of the validity and clinical scores; none of the special scales are utilized in the computerized interpretive statements; manual ('67, 42 pages, entitled *A User's Guide to the Mayo Clinic Automated MMPI Program*); NCS answer sheets must be used; $3.50 per 50 answer sheets (Old Group Form); $4.50 per 50 answer sheets (Form R); scoring and computer interpretation service, $3 per single report; $2 each for 2–4; $1.50 each for 5–99 (by using prepaid report certificates, quantity prices apply even though for single reports); answer sheets must be sent to National Computer Systems; reports are mailed within 1 day after receipt of answer sheets; $1.50 per manual; postpaid; program and manual by John S. Pearson and Wendell M. Swenson; Psychological Corporation. *

REFERENCES

1. ROME, HOWARD P. "Automation Techniques in Personality Assessment." *J Am Med Assn* 182:1069–72 D 8 '62. *
2. GASTINEAU, C. F. "The Internist and the Minnesota Multiphasic Personality Inventory." *Proc IBM Med Symp* 4:347–53 ['63]. *
3. ROME, HOWARD P. "Automation Technique in Personality Assessment: The Philosophy." *Proc IBM Med Symp* 4:335–46 ['63]. *
4. SWENSON, W. M., and PEARSON, J. S. "Automation Techniques in Personality Assessment: A Frontier in Behavioral Science and Medicine." *Meth Inform Med* 3:34–6 Ja '64. *
5. SWENSON, WENDELL M.; PEARSON, JOHN S.; and ROME, HOWARD P. "Automation Techniques in Personality Assessment: Fusion of Three Professions," pp. 149–56. In *Proceedings of Conference on Data Acquisition and Processing in Biology and Medicine, Vol. 2, Proceedings of the 1962 Rochester Conference.* Edited by Kurt Enslein. New York: Pergamon Press, Inc., 1964. Pp. ix, 367. *
6. ROME, HOWARD P.; MATAYA, PETE; PEARSON, JOHN S.; and BRANNICK, THOMAS L. Chap. 21, "Automatic Personality Assessment," pp. 505–24. In *Computers in Biomedical Research, Vol. 1.* Edited by Ralph W. Stacey and Bruce D. Waxman. New York: Academic Press, Inc., 1965. Pp. xxii, 562. *
7. SWENSON, WENDELL M., and PEARSON, JOHN S. "Experience With Large-Scale Psychological Testing in a Medical Center." *Proc IBM Med Symp* 6:147–62 ['65]. *
8. SWENSON, WENDELL M., and PEARSON, JOHN S. "Psychiatry—Psychiatric Screening." *J Chron Dis* 19:497–507 Ap '66. *

[169]

★[Re Minnesota Multiphasic Personality Inventory.] Roche MMPI Computerized Interpretation Service. A computerized scoring and interpreting service for qualified users of the MMPI (clinical psychologists and psychiatrists for use in clinical practice and research); 1966–68; the interpretive report is a 3 page computer printout presenting a narrative report, scores on 4 validity scales, 10 clinical scales, and 14 special scales [first factor (A), second factor (R), ego strength (Es), low back pain (Lb), caudality (Ca), dependency (Dy), dominance (Do), responsibility (Re), prejudice (Pr), status (St), control (Cn), manifest anxiety (At), social desirability (So-R), maladjustment (Mt)], reproduction of critical items with responses, and a profile of the validity and clinical scores; only 3 (A, Pr, Es) of the 14 special scales are utilized in the computerized narrative report; new subscriber kits consist of test booklet, 20 answer sheets with preprinted identification numbers, *The MMPI Notebook* ('66, 44 pages, with additions issued periodically); instructions for administration ['67, 6 pages], instructions for patient ['68, 1 page], record of patient numbers ['67, 1 page], 2 pre-addressed envelopes, and 2 control cards; refill kits consist of test booklet and 20 answer sheets; $2.50 per new subscriber test kit (includes free reports on 2 patients); $1 per refill kit; scoring and computerized report, $2.50 per test; identification of subjects known only to test administrator; reports are mailed within 1 day after receipt of answer sheets; postpaid; program and manual by Raymond D. Fowler, Jr.; Roche Psychiatric Service Institute. *

REFERENCES

1. FOWLER, RAYMOND D., JR. *The MMPI Notebook: A Guide to the Clinical Use of the Automated MMPI*. Nutley, N.J.: Roche Psychiatric Service Institute, 1966. Pp. iv, 28. *
2. CAHILL, CHARLES A. "Using the Computerized MMPI." *Hosp & Commun Psychiatry* 18:361 D '67. * (PA 42:5740)
3. FOWLER, RAYMOND, D., JR. "Computer Interpretation of Personality Tests: The Automated Psychologist." *Comprehen Psychiatry* 8:455–67 D '67. * (PA 42:12352)
4. FOWLER, RAYMOND D., JR. "MMPI Computer Interpretation for College Counseling." *Proc Ann Conv Am Psychol Assn* 75:363–4 '67. * (PA 41:14197)
5. FOWLER, RAYMOND D., JR. "MMPI Computer Interpretation for College Counseling." *J Psychol* 69:201–7 Jl '68. *
6. FOWLER, RAYMOND D., JR., and COYLE, F. A., JR. "Computer Application of MMPI Actuarial Systems With a College Population." *J Psychol* 69:233–6 Jl '68. * (PA 42:15480)
7. FOWLER, RAYMOND D., JR., and COYLE, F. A., JR. "Scoring Error on the MMPI." *J Clin Psychol* 24:68–9 Ja '68. * (PA 42:9159)
8. FOWLER, RAYMOND D., JR., and MARLOWE, GUY H., JR. "A Computer Program for Personality Analysis." *Behav Sci* 13:413–6 S '68. * (PA 42:18075)
9. MASON, DONALD J., and HERRING, FRED H. "Hand Scoring Templates for the Roche Answer Sheet for the MMPI." *Newsl Res Psychol* 10:6 Ag '68. *

[170]

Minnesota Rating Scale for Personal Qualities and Abilities. College and adults; 1925–38; revision of Part 2 of *Rating Scale for Teachers of Home Economics;* 1 form ('38, 1 page); mimeographed manual ('38, 5 pages); no data on reliability; $1.75 per 100 scales; 25¢ per specimen set; postage extra; Clara M. Brown [Arny]; University of Minnesota Press. *

For a review by Dorothy M. Clendenen, see 5:88 (1 reference).

[171]

Minnesota T-S-E Inventory. Grades 13–16 and adults; 1942–57; TSE; for research use only; 3 introversion-extroversion scores; thinking, social, emotional; Experimental Form FETX ('42, 7 pages); revised manual ('57, 24 pages); separate answer sheets (IBM 805 scorable) must be used; $3.50 per 25 tests; 30¢ per single copy; $1 per 25 answer sheets; $1.50 per set of scoring stencils; $1 per manual; cash orders postpaid; (25–35) minutes; Catharine Evans and T. R. McConnell; distributed by Educational Testing Service. *

See 6:144 (5 references); for reviews by Philip Eisenberg and John W. French, see 3:62 (6 references).

REFERENCES

1–6. See 3:62.
7–11. See 6:144.
12. SIKKINK, DONALD E. *An Experimental Study of the Relationship Between Introversion-Extroversion (Minnesota T-S-E Scores) and Speech Improvement*. Master's thesis, Ohio State University (Columbus, Ohio), 1951. (Abstract: *Speech Monogr* 19:161)

[172]

★**Minnesota Test for Differential Diagnosis of Aphasia.** Adults; 1948–65, p1965; MTDDA; 47 tests (9 auditory, 9 visual and reading, 15 speech and language, 10 visuomotor and writing, and 4 numerical relations and arithmetic processes); used to classify subjects into 5 major and 2 minor categories of aphasia; individual; Form 8 ('65); administrative manual ('65, 26 pages); technical manual ('65, 110 pages, see 7 below); record booklet ('65, 7 pages); no data on reliability; $5 per set of cards; $3 per 25 record booklets; $1 per administrative manual; $4 per technical manual; postage extra; (60–180) minutes in two or more sessions; Hildred Schuell; University of Minnesota Press. *

REFERENCES

1. SCHUELL, HILDRED. "Diagnosis and Prognosis in Aphasia." *A.M.A. Arch Neurol & Psychiatry* 74:308–15 S '55. *
2. SCHUELL, HILDRED. "A Short Examination for Aphasia." *Neurology* 7:625–34 S '57. * (PA 33:1750)
3. CARROLL, VIRGINIA B. "Implications of Measured Visuospatial Impairment in a Group of Left Hemiplegic Patients." *Arch Phys Med & Rehabil* 39:11–4 Ja '58. *
4. HOHMAN, LESLIE B., and FREEDHEIM, DONALD K. "A Study of IQ Retest Evaluation on 370 Cerebral Palsied Children." *Am J Phys Med* 38:180–7 O '59. *
5. KNAPP, MILAND E. "Results of Language Tests of Patients With Hemiplegia." *Arch Phys Med & Rehabil* 43:317–20 Jl '62. *
6. SCHUELL, HILDRED; JENKINS, JAMES J.; and CARROLL, JOHN B. "A Factor Analysis of the Minnesota Test for Differential Diagnosis of Aphasia." *J Speech & Hearing Res* 5:349–69 D '62. * (PA 37:5358)
7. SCHUELL, HILDRED. *Differential Diagnosis of Aphasia With the Minnesota Test*. Minneapolis, Minn.: University of Minnesota Press, 1965. Pp. vi, 106. * (PA 40:1881, title only)
8. SCHUELL, HILDRED. "A Re-evaluation of the Short Examination for Aphasia." *J Speech & Hearing Disorders* 31:137–47 My '66. * (PA 40:11400)

[173]

Mooney Problem Check List, 1950 Revision. Grades 7–9, 9–12, 13–16, adults; 1941–50; MPCL; 4 levels; separate manuals for grades 7–16 ('50, 15 pages), adults ('50, 4 pages); no data on reliability for scores of individuals; no norms (authors recommend use of local norms); separate answer sheets (IBM 805) must be used with machine scorable forms; $2.20 per 25 tests of hand scored forms; $3 per 25 tests of machine scorable forms; $2.30 per 50 answer sheets; $1.10 per specimen set of hand scored forms; $1 per specimen set of machine scorable forms; 60¢ per specimen set of hand scored forms of any one level; postpaid; (20–50) minutes; Ross L. Mooney and Leonard V. Gordon (manuals, *c*, and *d*); Psychological Corporation. *

a) JUNIOR HIGH SCHOOL FORM. Grade 7–9; 1942–50; 7 scores: health and physical development, school, home and family, money-work-the future, boy and girl relations, relations to people in general, self-centered concerns; 2 editions: hand scored Form J ('50, 6 pages), machine scorable Form Jm ('50, 4 pages).
b) HIGH SCHOOL FORM. Grades 9–12; 1941–50; 11 scores: health and physical development, finances-living conditions-employment, social and recreational activities, social-psychological relations, personal-psychological relations, courtship-sex-marriage, home and family, morals and religion, adjustment to school work, the future—vocational and educational, curriculum and teaching procedures; 2 editions: hand scored Form H ('50, 6 pages), machine scorable Form Hm ('50, 4 pages).
c) COLLEGE FORM. Grades 13–16; 1941–50; 11 scores: same as for High School Form; 2 editions: hand scored Form C ('50, 6 pages), machine scorable Form Cm ('50, 4 pages).
d) ADULT FORM. Adults; 1950; 9 scores: health, economic security, self-improvement, personality, home and family, courtship, sex, religion, occupation; Form A (6 pages).

For a review by Thomas C. Burgess, see 6:145 (25 references); see also 5:89 (26 references); for reviews by Harold E. Jones and Morris Krugman, see 4:73 (13 references); for reviews by Ralph C. Bedell and Theodore F. Lentz, see 3:67 (17 references).

REFERENCES

1–17. See 3:67.
18–30. See 4:73.
31–56. See 5:89.
57–81. See 6:145.
82. ARJONA, ADORACION QUIJANO. *An Experimental Study of the Adjustment Problems of a Group of Foreign Graduate Students and a Group of American Graduate Students at Indiana University.* Doctor's thesis, Indiana University (Bloomington, Ind.), 1956. (*DA* 16:1838)
83. PHELPS, MORRIS OVERTON. *An Analysis of Certain Factors Associated With Under-Achievement Among High School Students.* Doctor's thesis, University of Georgia (Athens, Ga.), 1956. (*DA* 17:306)
84. SYLAR, JAMES ANDREW. *An Experimental Study to Determine the Effectiveness of the Freshman Orientation Lectures at the Arkansas State Teachers College.* Doctor's thesis, Indiana University (Bloomington, Ind.), 1956. (*DA* 17:1697)
85. CLINKER, BERNARD KEITH. *An Experimental Study of Selected Factors Important in Successful Teaching.* Doctor's thesis, Indiana University (Bloomington, Ind.), 1957. (*DA* 18:508)
86. JENSEN, VERN HARMON. *An Analysis and Comparison of the Adjustment Problems of Nonachieving College Students of Low Scholastic Ability and Other Groups of Achieving and Nonachieving Students.* Doctor's thesis, University of Colorado (Boulder, Colo.), 1957. (*DA* 19:70)
87. KIRVEN, JAMES ANNA ELMORE. *The Relationship Between Academic Achievement and Problems of Selected Eighth Grade Students in the Kealing Junior High School.* Doctor's thesis, Indiana University (Bloomington, Ind.), 1957. (*DA* 18:1722)
88. TOLLE, DONALD JAMES. *Identification of Troublesome Problems Affecting St. Petersburg Junior College Students, With Implications for Guidance Program Improvement.* Doctor's thesis, Florida State University (Tallahassee, Fla.), 1957. (*DA* 17:1262)
89. VILLEME, MELVIN G. *A Study of the Problems Associated With Various Types of Interest Patterns on the Kuder Preference Record as Indicated by the Mooney Problem Checklist.* Master's thesis, University of Kansas (Lawrence, Kan.), 1959.
90. HARRY, ORMSBY L. *A Study of the Student Personnel Services at Michigan College of Mining and Technology.* Doctor's thesis, Michigan State University (East Lansing, Mich.), 1960. (*DA* 21:1126)
91. RUTLEDGE, CHARLES WALTER. *Social Status and the Perception of Personal-Social Problems of a Selected Group of Early Adolescents.* Doctor's thesis, Michigan State University (East Lansing, Mich.), 1960. (*DA* 21:1112)
92. DAVE, INDU. "Personal Problems of Prospective Teachers." *J Voc & Ed Guid* 5:194–200 My '61. * (*PA* 37:7208)
93. BRAATEN, LEIF J., and DARLING, C. DOUGLAS. "Suicidal Tendencies Among College Students." *Psychiatric Q* 36:665–92 O '62. * (*PA* 38:6467)
94. HOLLON, THOMAS H., and ZOLIK, EDWIN S. "Self-Esteem and Symptomatic Complaints in the Initial Phase of Psychoanalytically Oriented Psychotherapy." *Am J Psychother* 16:83–93 Ja '62. * (*PA* 38:8685)
95. DE SENA, PAUL AMBROSE. *Identification of Non-Intellectual Characteristics of Consistent Over-, Under-, and Normal-Achievers Enrolled in Science Curriculums at the Pennsylvania State University.* Doctor's thesis, Pennsylvania State University (University Park, Pa.), 1963. (*DA* 24:3144)
96. LARSEN, ERNEST R., and DESROCHES, HARRY F. "The Mooney Problem Check List and the Domiciliary Member." *Newsl Res Psychol* 5:1–2 N '63. *
97. MARSHALL, JON C. *An Investigation of the Problems of Over-, Average, and Under-Achievers as Determined by the Mooney Problem Check List.* Master's thesis, University of Kansas (Lawrence, Kan.), 1963.
98. DE SENA, PAUL A. "The Role of Consistency in Identifying Characteristics of Three Levels of Achievement." *Personnel & Guid J* 43:145–9 O '64. * (*PA* 39:10713)
99. DESROCHES, HARRY F.; KAIMAN, BERNARD D.; and BALLARD, H. TED. "Factors Influencing Admission of Symptoms in the Aged." *Newsl Res Psychol* 6:24–5 N '64. *
100. ESPER, GEORGE. "Characteristics of Junior High School Students Who Seek Counseling." *Personnel & Guid J* 42:468–72 Ja '64. * (*PA* 39:5502)
101. FISHBURN, WILLIAM R., and KING, PAUL T. "The Relationship Between Values and Perceived Problems." *J Counsel Psychol* 11:288–90 f '64. *
102. HARTIK, LORRAINE M. *A Comparative Study of Problem Areas of Eighth and Ninth Grade Students, as Measured by the Mooney Problem Check List, in Two San Bernardino Junior High Schools.* Master's thesis, University of Redlands (Redlands, Calif.), 1964.
103. JOSHI, MOHAN C. "A Factorial Study of the Problems of Adjustment." *Indian Psychol R* 1:42–6 Jl '64. * (*PA* 39:7946)
104. KAKKAR, S. B. "A Study of Problems of Youth." *Manas* 11(1):1–9 '64. * (*PA* 39:1376)
105. KOBLER, FRANK J. "Screening Applicants for Religious Life." *J Relig & Health* 3:161–70 Ja '64. * (*PA* 40:1793)
106. LOOMIS, JAMES CLIFFORD. *A Study of the Differences in Problems Between Underachievers and Overachievers at Nallwood Junior High School as Indicated by the Mooney Problem Check List.* Master's thesis, University of Kansas (Lawrence, Kan.), 1964.
107. RAO, S. NARAYANA. "Problems of Adjustment and Academic Achievement." *J Voc & Ed Guid* 10:66–79 Ag '64. * (*PA* 39:5916)
108. SCHLOENER, CARL J. *The Effect of Intelligence and Anonymity in Problem Expression of 9th Grade Male Students in a Comparison of Autobiographies With the Mooney Problem Check List.* Master's thesis, Catholic University of America (Washington, D.C.), 1964.
109. TEW, B. ORSON. *The Relationship of Measured Personality Variables to the Academic Success of College Students on Academic Probation.* Doctor's thesis, Brigham Young University (Provo, Utah), 1964. (*DA* 25:2328)
110. YARROW, WALTER HARRY. *An Investigation of the Problems of Entering Freshmen at the University of Southern Mississippi.* Doctor's thesis, University of Southern Mississippi (Hattiesburg, Miss.), 1964. (*DA* 26:4351)
111. ABEL, HAROLD, and GINGLES, RUBY. "Identifying Problems of Adolescent Girls." *J Ed Res* 58:389–92 My–Je '65. * (*PA* 39:16365)
112. BRAATEN, LEIF J., and DARLING, C. DOUGLAS. "Overt and Covert Homosexual Problems Among Male College Students." *Genetic Psychol Monogr* 71:269–310 My '65. * (*PA* 39:16097)
113. CODER, JAMES F. *A Study of Problems Expressed on the Mooney Problem Check List by Tenth Grade Students at Topeka High School.* Master's thesis, University of Kansas (Lawrence, Kan.), 1965.
114. DESROCHES, HARRY F.; KAIMAN, BERNARD D.; and BALLARD, H. TED. "Problems of Living as Perceived by Domiciliary Veterans and Other Populations." *Newsl Res Psychol* 7:43 Ag '65. *
115. GAWRONSKI, DANIEL A., and MATHIS, CLAUDE. "Differences Between Over-Achieving, Normal Achieving, and Under-Achieving High School Students." *Psychol Sch* 2:152–5 Ap '65. *
116. KEMP, C. GRATTON. "Parents' and Adolescents' Perceptions of Each Other and the Adolescents' Self-Perception." *Personnel & Guid J* 44:58–62 S '65. *
117. McGARRY, NATHANIEL M. *A Study of Distortion on the Mooney Problem Check Lists.* Master's thesis, Catholic University of America (Washington, D.C.), 1965.
118. VITTENSON, LILLIAN KASS. *The Sources of Identification and Choice of Role Models by Selected White and Non-White College Students.* Doctor's thesis, Northwestern University (Evanston, Ill.), 1965. (*DA* 26:3158)
119. DE SENA, PAUL A. "Problems of Consistent Over-, Under-, and Normal-Achieving College Students as Identified by the Mooney Problem Check List." *J Ed Res* 59:351–5 Ap '66. * (*PA* 40:10436)
120. FREEMAN, TOM SCOTT. *Congruence of Student and Parent Perceptions of Adolescent Problems.* Doctor's thesis, Colorado State College (Greeley, Colo.), 1966. (*DA* 27:4125A)
121. GOLDBERG, PHILIP A., and MILLER, SALLY J. "Structured Personality Tests and Dissimulation." *J Proj Tech & Pers Assess* 30:452–5 O '66. * (*PA* 41:589)
122. McCALLUM, J. W. "The Mooney Problem Check List (C) With University Student Psychiatric Patients." *Can J Psychiatric Assn* 11:43–8 F '66. * (*PA* 40:4501)
123. MAYFIELD, RICHARD A. *Identifying Problem Areas of Adolescent Negro Boys Through Expression of the Mooney Problem Check List.* Master's thesis, University of Kansas (Lawrence, Kan.), 1966.
124. MILLER, SALLY J. "Structured Personality Tests and Dissimulation." *Conn Col Psychol* 3:20–4 sp '66. * (*PA* 40:8859)
125. NICOLAY, ROBERT C.; WALKER, RONALD E.; and RIEDEL, ROBERT G. "Anxiety as a Correlate of Personal Problems." *Psychol Rep* 19:53–4 Ag '66. * (*PA* 40:12346)
126. SANDEFUR, J. T., and BIGGE, JEANETTE. "An Investigation of the Relationship Between Recognized Problems of Adolescents and School Achievement." *J Ed Res* 59:473–4 Jl–Ag '66. * (*PA* 40:11481)
127. CLEMENTS, HUBERT M., and OELKE, MERRITT C. "Factors Related to Reported Problems of Adolescents." *Personnel & Guid J* 45:697–702 Mr '67. * (*PA* 41:8732)
128. HUMPHREY, MICHAEL. "Functional Impairment in Psychiatric Outpatients." *Brit J Psychiatry* 113:1141–51 O '67. * (*PA* 42:7453)
129. OTTOSON, JOSEPH WILLIAM. *A Longitudinal Study of the Expressed Problems of Students Attending a Midwestern Church-Related Liberal Arts College.* Doctor's thesis, Northwestern University (Evanston, Ill.), 1967. (*DA* 28:4007A)
130. SUINN, RICHARD M. "Types of Student Problems as a Function of Year in College for Males and Females." *Col & Univ* 42:221–30 w '67. *

131. TORGERSEN, DONALD T. *A Comparative Analysis of Student Problems of Negro and Caucasian Junior High School Students as Expressed Through the Mooney Problem Check List.* Master's thesis, Northern Illinois University (DeKalb, Ill.), 1967.

132. VITTENSON, LILLIAN K. "Areas of Concern to Negro College Students as Indicated by Their Responses to the Mooney Problem Check List." *J Negro Ed* 36:51–7 w '67. *

133. CUTSUMBIS, MICHAEL N. "The Relationship of Certain Sociological Factors to Self-Reported Anxiety as Revealed by the Mooney Problem Check List." *Ed & Psychol Meas* 28:577–81 su '68. * (*PA* 42:18779)

134. GOLDMAN, BERT A. "Relationships Between Scores on the Mooney Problem Check List and the California Test of Personality." *J Ed Res* 61:307–10 Mr '68. *

135. HARTMAN, BERNARD J. "Survey of College Students' Problems Identified by the Mooney Problem Check List." *Psychol Rep* 22:715–6 Je '68. * (*PA* 42:14480)

136. OLIVAS, ROMEO ARELLANO. *A Survey of the Problems of Students in Public Secondary Schools in the Province of Cagayan, Republic of the Philippines.* Doctor's thesis, Northwestern University (Evanston, Ill.), 1968. (*DA* 29:2533A)

NAME INDEX

[174]

The Mother-Child Relationship Evaluation. Mothers; 1961; MCRE; experimental form; 5 scores: 4 direct scores (acceptance, overprotection, overindulgence, rejection) and 1 derived score (confusion-dominance); 1 form (4 pages); manual (16 pages plus test); $7 per set of 25 tests and manual; $6.50 per 25 tests; $2 per manual; postpaid; (15–30) minutes; Robert M. Roth; Western Psychological Services. *

For reviews by John Elderkin Bell and Dale B. Harris, see 6:146.

[175]

*Motivation Analysis Test. Ages 17 and over; 1959–69; MAT; test booklet title is *MAT;* 45 scores: 4 motivation scores (integrated, unintegrated, total, conflict) for each of 5 drives (mating, assertiveness, fear, narcism-comfort, pugnacity-sadism) and each of 5 sentiment structures (superego, self-sentiment, career, home-parental, sweetheart-spouse), plus 5 optional scores (total integration, total personal interest, total conflict, autism-optimism, information-intelligence); Form A ('64, 17 pages); manual, second printing ('64, 53 pages, with 1969 supplementation); preliminary manual for individual assessment ('69, 45 mimeographed pages); profile ('64, 1 page); reliability data for total motivation scores only; separate answer sheets (hand scored, Digitek) must be used; $15 per 25 tests; $6 per 50 hand scored answer sheets; $5 per 50 Digitek answer sheets; $3 per set of scoring stencils; $4 per pad of 50 profiles; $1.70 per preliminary manual for individual assessment; $2 per manual; $4 per specimen set; postage extra; scoring service (available only from IPAT-Southern), $2 or less per test; (55–65) minutes; Raymond B. Cattell and John L. Horn with the assistance of Arthur B. Sweney and John A. Radcliffe; Institute for Personality and Ability Testing. *

REFERENCES

1. CATTELL, R. B.; HORN, J.; and BUTCHER, H. J. "The Dynamic Structure of Attitudes in Adults: A Description of Some Established Factors and of Their Measurement by the Motivational Analysis Test." *Brit J Psychol* 53:57–69 F '62. *

2. CATTELL, R. B.; RADCLIFFE, J. A.; and SWENEY, A. B. "The Nature and Measurement of Components of Motivation." *Genetic Psychol Monogr* 68:49–211 Ag '63. * (*PA* 39:10186)

3. HANSEN, JAMES C., and HARTLEY, HARRY J. "A Comparison of School Administration and School Counseling Students on the Motivation Analysis Test." *J Sec Ed* 41:353–7 D '66. *

4. SWENEY, ARTHUR. "Studies of Motivation." *Int Psychiatry Clin* 3:265–88 sp '66. *

5. DOOLEY, BOBBY JOE, and WHITE, WILLIAM F. "Motivational Patterns of a Select Group of Adult Evening College Students." *J Ed Res* 62:65–6 O '68. *

6. GUTSCH, KENNETH URIAL, and HARRIS, GEORGE. "Counseling: Exploring the Sensitivity Syndrome." *South J Ed Res* 2:201–11 Ag '68. *

[176]

★Multiple Affect Adjective Check List. Grades 8–16 and adults; 1965–66; MAACL; 3 scores: anxiety, depression, hostility; 2 formats: hand scoring ('65, 2 pages, Today Form for today's feelings and In General Form for general feelings with same items); IBM 1230 ('65, 1 page); manual ('65, 24 pages); addendum ('66, 27 pages); $12.50 per 100 hand scoring test-answer sheets; $1.50 per set of hand scoring stencils; $12.75 per 100 IBM 1230 test-answer sheets; $1.25 per manual; $2.25 per specimen set; postage extra; scoring service, 45¢ or less per test; (5–10) minutes; Marvin Zuckerman and Bernard Lubin; Educational and Industrial Testing Service. *

REFERENCES

1. ZUCKERMAN, MARVIN. "The Development of an Affect Adjective Check List for the Measurement of Anxiety." *J Consult Psychol* 24:457–62 O '60. * (*PA* 35:4853)

2. Zuckerman, Marvin, and Biase, D. Vincent. "Replication and Further Data on the Validity of the Affect Adjective Check List Measure of Anxiety." Abstract. *J Consult Psychol* 26:291 Je '62. * (*PA* 38:1048)

3. Siller, Jerome, and Chipman, Abram. "Response Set Paralysis: Implications for Measurement and Control." *J Consult Psychol* 27:432-8 O '63. * (*PA* 38:4284)

4. Winter, William D.; Ferreira, Antonio J.; and Ransom, Robert. "Two Measures of Anxiety: A Validation." *J Consult Psychol* 27:520-4 D '63. * (*PA* 38:8608)

5. Zuckerman, Marvin; Nurnberger, John I.; Gardiner, Sprague H.; Vandiveer, James M.; Barrett, Beatrice H.; and den Breeijen, Arie. "Psychological Correlates of Somatic Complaints in Pregnancy and Difficulty in Childbirth." *J Consult Psychol* 27:324-9 Ag '63. * (*PA* 38:2751)

6. Levitt, Eugene E.; Persky, Harold; and Brady, John Paul. *Hypnotic Induction of Anxiety: A Psychoendocrine Investigation.* Springfield, Ill.: Charles C Thomas, Publisher, 1964. Pp. xvi, 134. *

7. Zuckerman, Marvin; Kolin, Elizabeth A.; Price, Leah; and Zoob, Ina. "Development of a Sensation-Seeking Scale." *J Consult Psychol* 28:477-82 D '64. * (*PA* 39:7735)

8. Zuckerman, Marvin; Lubin, Bernard; Vogel, Lawrence; and Valerius, Elizabeth. "Measurement of Experimentally Induced Affects." *J Consult Psychol* 28:418-25 O '64. * (*PA* 39:3647)

9. Zuckerman, Marvin, and Lubin, Bernard. "Normative Data for the Multiple Affect Adjective Check List." *Psychol Rep* 16:438 Ap '65. * (*PA* 39:10167)

10. Zuckerman, Marvin; Lubin, Bernard; and Robins, Sidney. "Validation of the Multiple Affect Adjective Check List in Clinical Situations." Abstract. *J Consult Psychol* 29:594 D '65. * (*PA* 40:2932, title only)

11. Bringmann, Wolfgang G. "Awareness in Experimental Induction of Emotions." *Psychol Rep* 19:1188 D '66. * (*PA* 41:3830)

12. Datel, William E., and Engle, Elizabeth O. "Affect Levels in Another Platoon of Basic Trainees." *Psychol Rep* 19:407-12 O '66. * (*PA* 41:861)

13. Datel, William E.; Engle, Elizabeth O.; and Barba, Melvin A. "Affect Levels in a Company of Basic Trainees." *Psychol Rep* 19:903-9 D '66. * (*PA* 41:5114)

14. Datel, William E.; Gieseking, Charles F.; Engle, Elizabeth O.; and Dougher, Michael J. "Affect Levels in a Platoon of Basic Trainees." *Psychol Rep* 18:271-85 F '66. * (*PA* 40:7100)

15. Fogel, Max L.; Curtis, George C.; Kordasz, Florence; and Smith, William G. "Judges' Ratings, Self-Ratings and Checklist Report of Affects." *Psychol Rep* 19:299-307 Ag '66. * (*PA* 40:12450)

16. Hayes, Carol V. "The Measurement of Anxiety in Sophomore Nursing Students Using Zuckerman's AACL." *Nursing Res* 15:262-7 su '66. *

17. Lieberman, Lewis R. "Effects Upon Anxiety, Depression, and Hostility of Postponement of an Examination." *Percept & Motor Skills* 23:1051-4 D '66. * (*PA* 41:5421)

18. Tolor, Alexander, and Mabli, Jerome. "Stability of Schizophrenic Affect and Values." *Psychol Rep* 19:255-62 Ag '66. * (*PA* 40:12514)

19. Carrigan, William Clark. *Stress and Psychological Differentiation.* Doctor's thesis, State University of New York (Buffalo, N.Y.), 1967. (*DA* 28:1185B)

20. Knapp, Robert R.; Zimmerman, Wayne S.; Roscoe, Douglas L.; and Michael, William B. "The Suggested Effects of Experience With a College Entrance Examination on Measurable Affects of Anxiety, Depression, and Hostility." *Ed & Psychol Meas* 27:1121-6 w '67. * (*PA* 42:9423)

21. Lubin, Bernard, and Zuckerman, Marvin. "Affective and Perceptual-Cognitive Patterns in Sensitivity Training Groups." *Psychol Rep* 21:365-76 O '67. * (*PA* 42:5533)

22. Zuckerman, Marvin; Persky, Harold; and Link, Kathryn. "Relation of Mood and Hypnotizability: An Illustration of the Importance of the State Versus Trait Distinction." *J Consult Psychol* 31:464-70 O '67. * (*PA* 41:16162)

23. Zuckerman, Marvin; Persky, Harold; Eckman, Katherine M.; and Hopkins, T. Robert. "A Multitrait Multimethod Measurement Approach to the Traits (or States) of Anxiety, Depression and Hostility." *J Proj Tech & Pers Assess* 31:39-48 Ap '67. * (*PA* 41:13635)

24. Bloom, Paul M., and Brady, John Paul. "An Ipsative Validation of the Multiple Affect Adjective Check List." *J Clin Psychol* 24:45-6 Ja '68. * (*PA* 42:9158)

25. Bourne, Peter G.; Coli, William M.; and Datel, William E. "Affect Levels of Ten Special Forces Soldiers Under Threat of Attack." *Psychol Rep* 22:363-6 Ap '68. * (*PA* 42:11525)

26. Estrine, Steven Arnold. *Aggressive Drive Activation and Thought Disorder in Nonpsychiatric Subjects.* Doctor's thesis, University of Utah (Salt Lake City, Utah), 1968. (*DA* 28:5203B)

27. Herron, E. Wayne; Bernstein, Lewis; and Rosen, Harold. "Psychometric Analysis of the Multiple Affect Adjective Check List: MAACL-Today." *J Clin Psychol* 24:448-50 O '68. * (*PA* 43:3319)

28. Zuckerman, Marvin; Persky, Harold; Link, Katherine E.; and Basu, Gopal K. "Experimental and Subject

Factors Determining Responses to Sensory Deprivation, Social Isolation, and Confinement." *J Abn Psychol* 73:183-94 Je '68. * (*PA* 42:11527)

NAME INDEX

[177]

Myers-Briggs Type Indicator. Grades 9-16 and adults; 1943-62; MBTI; 4 scores: extraversion vs. introversion, sensation vs. intuition, thinking vs. feeling, judgment vs. perception; 2 editions (identical except for directions); manual ('62, 157 pages); 30¢ per test, postage extra; $3 per specimen set, postpaid (must be purchased to obtain manual); (50-55) minutes; Katharine C. Briggs (test) and Isabel Briggs Myers; Educational Testing Service. *

a) FORM F. 1 form ('57, c1943-57, 12 pages); separate answer sheets (IBM 805 scorable) must be used; $1 per 25 answer sheets; $7.50 per set of scoring stencils.

b) FORM FS. 1 form ('62, c1943-62, 12 pages); separate answer sheets (Scribe) must be used; answer sheet and scoring service, 60¢ per test.

For reviews by Gerald A. Mendelsohn and Norman D. Sundberg, see 6:147 (10 references, 1 excerpt).

REFERENCES

1-10. See 6:147.

11. Nichols, Robert C., and Holland, John L. "Prediction of the First Year College Performance of High Aptitude Students." *Psychol Monogr* 77(7):1-29 '63. * (*PA* 38:4693)

12. Peavy, Richard Vance. *A Study of C. G. Jung's Concept of Intuitive Perception and the Intuitive Type.* Doctor's thesis, University of Oregon (Eugene, Ore.), 1963. (*DA* 24:4551)

13. Ashbrook, James Barbour. *Protestant Ministerial Attributes and Their Implications for Church Organization.* Doctor's thesis, Ohio State University (Columbus, Ohio), 1964. (*DA* 25:7070)

14. Bradway, Katherine. "Jung's Psychological Types: Classification by Test Versus Classification by Self." *J Anal Psychol* 9:129-35 Jl '64. *

15. Hay, John Earl. *The Relationship of Certain Personality Variables to Managerial Level and Job Performance Among Engineering Managers.* Doctor's thesis, Temple University (Philadelphia, Pa.), 1964. (*DA* 25:3973)

16. Helton, William Bernard. *A Comparative Analysis of Selected Characteristics of Intellectually Superior Male Students Who Persist and Those Who Do Not Persist in an Advanced Placement Program.* Doctor's thesis, North Texas State University (Denton, Tex.), 1964. (*DA* 25:3394)

17. Joshi, Bhuwan Lal. *Personality Correlates of Happiness.* Doctor's thesis, University of California (Berkeley, Calif.), 1964. (*DA* 25:2083)

18. Michael, William B.; Baker, David; and Jones, Robert A. "A Note Concerning the Predictive Validities of Selected Cognitive and Non-Cognitive Measures for Freshman Students in a Liberal Arts College." *Ed & Psychol Meas* 24:373-5 su '64. * (*PA* 39:5984)

19. Morris, Ruby Pearl. *A Comparative Analysis of Selected Characteristics of Intellectually Superior Female Students Who Persisted and Those Who Did Not Persist in an Advanced Placement Program.* Doctor's thesis, North Texas State University (Denton, Tex.), 1964. (*DA* 25:3402)

20. Sease, William Andrew. *Perceived Congruence as an

Aspect of Counselor-Client Similarity. Doctor's thesis, University of Missouri (Columbia, Mo.), 1964. (*DA* 25:5749)

21. WEBB, SAM C. "An Analysis of the Scoring System of the Myers-Briggs Type Indicator." *Ed & Psychol Meas* 24:765–81 w '64. * (*PA* 39:7810)

22. WEBB, SAM C. "The Psychological Components of Scores for Two Tests of Report Writing Ability." *Ed & Psychol Meas* 24:31–46 sp '64. * (*PA* 39:1770)

23. BRAUN, JOHN R. "Note on a Faking Study With the Myers-Briggs Type Indicator." *Psychol Rep* 17:924 D '65. * (*PA* 40:4229)

24. CALDWELL, BILLY SIM, JR. *Task Situation and Personality Characteristics as Influences on the Consistency of Behavior in Learning and Problem Solving Tasks.* Doctor's thesis, University of Texas (Austin, Tex.), 1965. (*DA* 26:2047)

25. CHILD, IRVIN L. "Personality Correlates of Esthetic Judgment in College Students." *J Personality* 33:476–511 S '65. * (*PA* 40:2852)

26. CONARY, FRANKLIN MELVIN. *An Investigation of the Variability of Behavioral Response of Jungian Psychological Types to Select Educational Variables.* Doctor's thesis, Auburn University (Auburn, Ala.), 1965. (*DA* 26:5222)

27. EBERDT, MARY GERTRUDE. *An Analysis of Certain Characteristics of Secondary-School Teachers Rated as Most Approachable and Least Approachable by Secondary-School Students.* Doctor's thesis, University of Oregon (Eugene, Ore.), 1965. (*DA* 26:4327)

28. GOLDSCHMID, MARCEL LUCIEN. *The Prediction of College Major in the Sciences and the Humanities by Means of Personality Tests.* Doctor's thesis, University of California (Berkeley, Calif.), 1965. (*DA* 26:4073)

29. HELSON, RAVENNA. "Childhood Interest Clusters Related to Creativity in Women." *J Consult Psychol* 29:352–61 Ag '65. * (*PA* 39:15292)

30. KNAPP, ROBERT H., and LAPUC, PAUL S. "Time Imagery, Introversion and Fantasied Preoccupation in Simulated Isolation." *Percept & Motor Skills* 20:327–30 F '65. * (*PA* 39:10076)

31. LEVELL, JAMES PRESTON. *Secondary School Counselors: A Study of Differentiating Characteristics.* Doctor's thesis, University of Oregon (Eugene, Ore.), 1965. (*DA* 26:4452)

32. MENDELSOHN, GERALD A., and GELLER, MARVIN H. "Structure of Client Attitudes Toward Counseling and Their Relation to Client-Counselor Similarity." *J Consult Psychol* 29:63–72 F '65. * (*PA* 39:8221)

33. MILLER, PAUL VAN REED, JR. *The Contribution of Non-Cognitive Variables to the Prediction of Student Performance in Law School.* Doctor's thesis, University of Pennsylvania (Philadelphia, Pa.), 1965. (*DA* 26:7159)

34. RICHARDSON, ROY LEWIS. *Parent-Child Relationships and the Divergent Student.* Doctor's thesis, University of Missouri (Columbia, Mo.), 1965. (*DA* 26:5542)

35. ROSSI, ASCANIO M., and SOLOMON, PHILIP. "Note on Reactions of Extroverts and Introverts to Sensory Deprivation." *Percept & Motor Skills* 20:1183–4 Je '65. * (*PA* 39:13469)

36. STRICKER, LAWRENCE J.; SCHIFFMAN, HAROLD; and ROSS, JOHN. "Prediction of College Performance With the Myers-Briggs Type Indicator." *Ed & Psychol Meas* 25:1081–95 w '65. * (*PA* 40:3553)

37. WHITTEMORE, ROBERT G., and HEIMANN, ROBERT A. "Originality Responses in Academically Talented Male University Freshmen." *Psychol Rep* 16:439–42 Ap '65. * (*PA* 39:10252)

38. ANAST, PHILIP. "Similarity Between Self and Fictional Character Choice." *Psychol Rec* 16:535–9 O '66. * (*PA* 41:1607)

39. ANDERSON, C. C., and CROPLEY, A. J. "Some Correlates of Originality." *Austral J Psychol* 18:218–27 D '66. * (*PA* 41:4572)

40. BOWN, O. H.; FULLER, F. F.; and RICHEK, H. G. "Differentiating Prospective Elementary and Secondary School Teachers." *Alberta J Ed Res* 12:127–30 Je '66. * (*PA* 41:809)

41. FRETZ, BRUCE R. "Personality Correlates of Postural Movements." *J Counsel Psychol* 13:344–7 f '66. * (*PA* 40:12540)

42. LUCAS, FRANCES H., and DANA, RICHARD H. "Creativity and Allocentric Perception." *Percept & Motor Skills* 22:431–7 Ap '66. * (*PA* 40:8858)

43. MENDELSOHN, GERALD A. "Effects of Client Personality and Client-Counselor Similarity on the Duration of Counseling: A Replication and Extension." *J Counsel Psychol* 13:228–34 su '66. * (*PA* 40:9092)

44. RICHTER, ROBERT H., and WINTER, WILLIAM D. "Holtzman Inkblot Correlates of Creative Potential." *J Proj Tech & Pers Assess* 30:62–7 F '66. * (*PA* 40:5495)

45. ROSS, JOHN. "The Relationship Between a Jungian Personality Inventory and Tests of Ability, Personality and Interest." *Austral J Psychol* 18:1–17 Ap '66. * (*PA* 40:10116)

46. WRIGHT, JUDITH ANNE. *The Relationship of Rated Administrator and Teacher Effectiveness to Personality as Measured by the Myers-Briggs Personality Type Indicator.* Doctor's thesis, Claremont Graduate School (Claremont, Calif.), 1966. (*DA* 28:981A, title only)

47. ARAIN, AHMED ALI. *Relationships Among Counseling Clients' Personalities, Expectations, and Problems.* Doctor's

thesis, Rutgers—The State University (New Brunswick, N.J.), 1967. (*DA* 28:4903A)

48. BARTEE, GERALDINE MCMURRY. *The Perceptual Characteristics of Disadvantaged Negro and Caucasian College Students.* Doctor's thesis, East Texas State University (Commerce, Tex.), 1967. (*DA* 28:3455A)

49. CORLIS, R.; SPLAVER, G.; WISECUP, P.; and FISCHER, R. "Myers-Briggs Type Personality Scales and Their Relation to Taste Acuity." *Nature* 216:91–2 O 7 '67. * (*PA* 42:2572)

50. FRETZ, BRUCE R., and SCHMIDT, LYLE D. "Comparison of Improvers and Nonimprovers in an Educational Skills Course." *J Counsel Psychol* 14:175–6 Mr '67. * (*PA* 41:7880)

51. GIRARD, FRANCIS GEORGE. *The Interaction of Perceptual Discrimination, Aesthetic Preference and Personality Traits.* Doctor's thesis, Illinois State University (Normal, Ill.), 1967. (*DA* 28:2554A)

52. GOLDSCHMID, MARCEL L. "Prediction of College Majors by Personality Tests." *J Counsel Psychol* 14:302–8 Jl '67. * (*PA* 41:12452)

53. JONES, JANE HARDY. *Faculty Perceptions of University Students.* Doctor's thesis, Auburn University (Auburn, Ala.), 1967. (*DA* 27:4100A)

54. McNAMARA, THOMAS CHARLES. *A Study of Philosophical Identities in a Counseling Practicum.* Doctor's thesis, University of Illinois (Urbana, Ill.), 1967. (*DA* 28:4878A)

55. MENDELSOHN, GERALD A., and GELLER, MARVIN H. "Similarity, Missed Sessions, and Early Termination." *J Counsel Psychol* 14:210–5 My '67. * (*PA* 41:9416)

56. MILLER, PAUL VAN R. "Personality Differences and Student Survival in Law School." *J Legal Ed* 19(4):460–7 '67. *

57. STALCUP, DONNA LOU KILKER. *An Investigation of Personality Characteristics of College Students Who Do Participate and Those Who Do Not Participate in Campus Activities.* Doctor's thesis, Auburn University (Auburn, Ala.), 1967. (*DA* 28:4452A)

58. STEVENS, THOMAS GRANVILLE. *Congruency Between Diagnostic Dimensions of Personality Theories and Personality Tests.* Master's thesis, California State College at Fullerton (Fullerton, Calif.), 1967.

59. WALTER, JAMES I. *An Investigation of Prisoner Personality Types by Functions as Measured by the Myers-Briggs Type Indicator.* Master's thesis, Auburn University (Auburn, Ala.), 1967.

60. INSEL, SHEPARD A.; REESE, CAROL SCHMIDA; and ALEXANDER, BARRETT B. "Self-Presentations in Relation to Internal and External Referents." *J Consult & Clin Psychol* 32:389–95 Ag '68. * (*PA* 42:17199)

61. LONDON, PERRY, and BOWER, ROBERT K. "Altruism, Extraversion, and Mental Illness." *J Social Psychol* 76:19–30 O '68. * (*PA* 43:2763)

62. PARASKEVOPOULOS, IOANNIS. "How Students Rate Their Teachers." *J Ed Res* 62:25–9 S '68. *

63. POE, CHARLES A. "Assessment of Health's Model of Personality." *J Counsel Psychol* 15:203–7 My '68. * (*PA* 42:12116)

64. RICHEK, HERBERT G., and BOWN, OLIVER H. "Phenomenological Correlates of Jung's Typology." *J Anal Psychol* 13:57–65 Ja '68. * (*PA* 42:9728)

65. STEELE, FRED I. "Personality and 'Laboratory Style.'" *J Appl Behav Sci* 4:25–45 Ja–Mr '68. * (*PA* 42:17904)

66. TAYLOR, ROBERT ELLIS. *An Investigation of the Relationship Between Psychological Types in the College Classroom and the Student Perception of the Teacher and Preferred Teaching Practices.* Doctor's thesis, University of Maryland (College Park, Md.), 1968. (*DA* 29:2575A)

NAME INDEX

Ross, J.: 5, 7, 9-10, 36, 45
Rossi, A. M.: 35
Schiffman, H.: 36
Schmidt, L. D.: 50
Sease, W. A.: 20
Siegel, L.: *exc*, 6:147
Solomon, P.: 35
Splaver, G.: 49
Stalcup, D. L. K.: 57
Steele, F. I.: 65
Stevens, T. G.: 58

Stricker, L. J.: 7, 9-10, 36
Sundberg, N. D.: *rev*, 6:147
Taylor, R. E.: 66
Vaughan, J. A.: 8
Walter, J. I.: 59
Webb, S. C.: 21-2
Whittemore, R. G.: 37
Winter, W. D.: 44
Wisecup, P.: 49
Wright, J. A.: 46

[178]

The Neuroticism Scale Questionnaire. Ages 13 and over; 1961; NSQ; test booklet title is *NSQ;* the *IPAT Neurotic Personality Factor Test* (see 121), which is still available, is "an earlier version" of this test; 5 scores: depressiveness, submissiveness, over-protection, anxiety, total; 1 form (4 pages); manual (31 pages); $3.30 per 25 tests; 50¢ per key; $1.70 per manual; $2.30 per specimen set; postage extra; (5-10) minutes; Ivan H. Scheier and Raymond B. Cattell; Institute for Personality and Ability Testing. *

For reviews by E. Lowell Kelly and Jerome D. Pauker, see 6:148 (1 reference, 2 excerpts).

REFERENCES

1. See 6:148.
2. LUKENS, LOIS EILEEN. *Personality Patterns Related to Choice of Two Fields of Clinical Specialization in Nursing.* Doctor's thesis, University of Michigan (Ann Arbor, Mich.), 1964. (*DA* 25:3400)
3. RICKELS, K.; DOWNING, R.; and APPEL, H. "Some Personality Correlates of Suggestibility in Normals and Neurotics." *Psychol Rep* 14:715-9 Je '64. * (*PA* 39:5159)
4. KAPOOR, KAMLESH. "Hindi Version of the Neuroticism Scale Questionnaire (N.S.Q.)." *Indian J Psychol* 40:93-8 Je '65. *
5. KEAR-COLWELL, J. J. "Neuroticism in the Early Puerperium." *Brit J Psychiatry* 111:1189-92 D '65. * (*PA* 40:3163)
6. STANLEY, GORDON, and SALAS, R. G. "Simulation of Neurotic Responses on the Neuroticism Scale Questionnaire." *Austral J Psychol* 17:133-6 Ag '65. * (*PA* 40:1597)
7. GRAHAM, LOIS E. "Differential Characteristics of Graduate Students Preparing for Teaching or Supervision in Two Clinical Specialties." *Nursing Res* 16:182-4 sp '67. *
8. PHILIP, A. E., and McCULLOCH, J. W. "Social Pathology and Personality in Attempted Suicide." Abstract. *Brit J Psychiatry* 113:1405-6 D '67. * (*PA* 42:9200)
9. GUTSCH, KENNETH URIAL, and HARRIS, GEORGE. "Counseling: Exploring the Sensitivity Syndrome." *South J Ed Res* 2:201-11 Ag '68. *
10. KAPOOR, K., and KAPOOR, S. D. "Validation of the Neuroticism Scale Questionnaire Through Anxiety Manifestations." *J Psychol Res* 12:63-5 My '68. * (*PA* 43:5371)
11. PHILIP, ALISTAIR E., and McCULLOCH, J. W. "Some Psychological Features of Persons Who Have Attempted Suicide." Abstract. *Brit J Psychiatry* 114:1299-300 O '68. * (*PA* 43:4183)
See also references for 121.

[179]

★**The New Junior Maudsley Inventory.** Ages 9-16; 1961-67; NJMI; 3 scores: neuroticism, extraversion, lie; 2 editions; (10-15) minutes; W. D. Furneaux and H. B. Gibson. *

a) [BRITISH EDITION.] 1961-67; items are identical to those in the *Junior Maudsley Inventory* ('61, JMI) except for sequence and the addition of items for the lie scale; norms for neuroticism and extraversion were derived from the JMI; 1 form ('66, 4 pages); manual ('66, 16 pages); 7s. 6 d. per 20 tests; 12s. 6d. per set of keys; 5s. per manual; 18s. per specimen set; postage extra; University of London Press Ltd.

b) [UNITED STATES EDITION.] 1966-67; for research use only; 1 form ('67, 4 pages, items identical with British edition except for 2 wording changes); manual ('66, 16 pages, identical with British edition except for imprint and introductory paragraph); all statistical data and norms based on British populations; $4.00 per 25 tests; $1.50 per set of scoring stencils; $1.75 per specimen set; postage extra; Educational and Industrial Testing Service.

REFERENCES

1. FURNEAUX, W. D., and GIBSON, H. B. "A Children's Personality Inventory Designed to Measure Neuroticism and Extraversion." *Brit J Ed Psychol* 31:204-7 Je '61. * (*PA* 36: 3FF04F)
2. CALLARD, M. PAULINE, and GOODFELLOW, CHRISTINE L. "Three Experiments Using the Junior Maudsley Personality Inventory: 1, Neuroticism and Extraversion in Schoolboys as Measured by the Junior Maudsley Personality Inventory." *Brit J Ed Psychol* 32:241-50 N '62. * (*PA* 37:8239)
3. COSTELLO, C. G., and BRACHMAN, H. M. "Three Experiments Using the Junior Maudsley Personality Inventory: 3, Cultural and Sex Differences in Extraversion and Neuroticism Reflected in Responses to a Children's Personality Inventory." *Brit J Ed Psychol* 32:254-7 N '62. * (*PA* 38:7879)
4. GIBSON, H. B. "Acquiescence and Suggestibility in Children." *Ed & Psychol Meas* 22:737-46 w '62. * (*PA* 37:6469)
5. BRACHMAN, H. M., and COSTELLO, C. G. "The Relationship Between Persistence and Personality." *J Psychol* 55:299-306 Ap '63. * (*PA* 38:914)
6. CHILD, DENNIS. "The Relationships Between Introversion-Extraversion, Neuroticism and Performance in School Examinations." *Brit J Ed Psychol* 34:187-96 Je '64. * (*PA* 39:5904)
7. GIBSON, H. B. "The Validity of the Lie Scale of a Children's Personality Inventory." *Acta Psychologica* 22(3):241-9 '64. * (*PA* 39:15347)
8. CROPLEY, A. J., and D'AOUST, B. R. "Performance of Canadian School Children on the J.M.P.I." *Brit J Ed Psychol* 35:378-9 N '65. *
9. WHITING, H. T. A., and STEMBRIDGE, D. E. "Personality and the Persistent Non-Swimmer." *Res Q* 36:348-56 O '65. * (*PA* 40:2949)
10. YOUNG, GORDON C. "Personality Factors and the Treatment of Enuresis." *Behav Res & Ther* 3:103-5 S '65. * (*PA* 40:3109)
11. ANDERSON, C. C., and CROPLEY, A. J. "Some Correlates of Originality." *Austral J Psychol* 18:218-27 D '66. * (*PA* 41:4572)
12. CHILD, DENNIS. "Personality and Social Status." *Brit J Social & Clin Psychol* 5:196-9 S '66. * (*PA* 40:13199)
13. GIBSON, H. B. "Teachers' Ratings of Schoolboys' Behaviour Related to Patterns of Scores on the New Junior Maudsley Inventory." *Brit J Ed Psychol* 37:347-55 N '67. * (*PA* 42:5606)
14. MEHRYAR, A. H. "Some Evidence on the Validity of the Junior Maudsley Personality Inventory." *Brit J Ed Psychol* 37:375-8 N '67. * (*PA* 42:4816)
15. REGAN, GEORGE. "Personality Characteristics and Attitude to School." *Brit J Ed Psychol* 37:127-9 F '67. *
16. SHAMBERG, NEIL STEPHEN. *An Experimental Investigation of Eysenck's Theory With Respect to Four Adolescent Groups.* Doctor's thesis, Case Western Reserve University (Cleveland, Ohio), 1968. (*DA* 29:760B)
17. SHAPIRO, MARTIN ALLEN. *Relationships Among Extraversion, Neuroticism, Academic Reading Achievement and Verbal Learning.* Doctor's thesis, Rutgers—The State University (New Brunswick, N.J.), 1968. (*DA* 28:4915A)

[180]

Northampton Activity Rating Scale. Mental patients; 1951; NARS; "behavior exhibited by mental patients in rehabilitation and activity therapies of the hospital environment"; Form D (5 pages); manual (7 pages); no norms; $6.50 per 25 tests; 35¢ per specimen set; postpaid; Isidor W. Scherer; the Author. *

[181]

★**Object Sorting Scales.** Adults; 1966; OSS; modification of the *Goldstein-Scheerer Object Sorting Test* (see 91); 2 scores: schizotypy, brain damage; mimeographed interim manual ['66, 128 pages]; Aus $15 per set of test materials; 60¢ per 10 draft record sheets; $1 per manual; postpaid within Australia; test materials must be assembled locally; (20-45) minutes; S. H. Lovibond; Australian Council for Educational Research. *

[182]

*Objective-Analytic (O-A) Anxiety Battery.** Ages 14 and over; 1955-67; OAAB; *O-A Anxiety Battery;* revision of anxiety-to-achieve battery (U.I. 24) of out of print *Objective-Analytic Personality Test Batteries* (see 5:90); individual in part (tests 246-I and 2410-I); 1 form ('60); 10 tests from which user may select those appropriate to his needs: 241-G (susceptibility to annoyance, 4 pages), 242-G (honesty in admitting common frailties, 2 pages), 243-G (modesty in assuming skill in untried performance, 7 pages), 244-G (critical severity vs. indulgent standards, 3 pages), 245-G (number of friends recalled, 2 pages), 246-I (increase or recovery of pulse rate), 247-G (emotionality of comment, 4 pages), 248-G (acceptance of good aphorisms, 1 page), 249-G (susceptibility to embarrassment, 5 pages), 2410-I (systolic blood pressure); manual ('60, 15 pages); second norm supplement ('67, 4 pages); no data on reliability of 246-I and 2410-I; no norms for 246-I and 2410-I; prices per 25 tests: $4 for 241-G and 247-G, $2.40 for 242-G and 245-G, $5.60 for 243-G, $3.30 for 244-G, $1.25 for 248-G, $4.60 for 249-G; separate answer sheets may be used (except for 243-G, 245-G, 246-I, 2410-I); $2.70 per pad of 50 answer sheets; $2.50 per set of scoring stencils; $6 per test kit consisting of one copy of each test and administration and scoring instructions for each; $1.25 per manual; $7 per specimen set consisting of test kit and manual; postage extra; additional apparatus necessary for tests 246-I and 2410-I; (25–50) minutes for the complete battery; Raymond B. Cattell and Ivan H. Scheier; Institute for Personality and Ability Testing. *

For a review by Harold Borko, see 6:149 (5 references, 1 excerpt).

REFERENCES

1–5. See 6:149.
6. SCHEIER, IVAN H.; CATTELL, RAYMOND B.; and HORN, JOHN L. "Objective Test Factor U.I. 23: Its Measurement and Its Relation to Clinically-Judged Neuroticism." *J Clin Psychol* 16:135–45 Ap '60. * (*PA* 36:2HI35S)
7. CATTELL, RAYMOND B., and RICKELS, KARL. "Diagnostic Power of IPAT Objective Anxiety Neuroticism Tests With Private Patients." *Arch Gen Psychiatry* 11:459–65 N '64. * (*PA* 39:7935)
8. HUNDLEBY, JOHN D.; PAWLIK, KURT; and CATTELL, RAYMOND B. *Personality Factors in Objective Test Devices: A Critical Integration of a Quarter of a Century's Research.* San Diego, Calif.: Robert K. Knapp, Publisher, 1965. Pp. iii, 542. *
9. RICKELS, KARL, and CATTELL, RAYMOND B. "The Clinical Factor Validity and Trueness of the IPAT Verbal and Objective Batteries for Anxiety and Regression." *J Clin Psychol* 21:257–64 Jl '65. * (*PA* 39:15261)
10. CATTELL, RAYMOND B., and RICKELS, KARL. "The Relationship of Clinical Symptoms and IPAT-Factored Tests of Anxiety, Regression and Asthenia: A Factor Analytic Study." *J Nerv & Mental Dis* 146:147–60 F '68. * (*PA* 42:12351)
11. HUNDLEBY, JOHN D. "The Trait of Anxiety, as Defined by Objective Performance Measures, and Indices of Emotional Disturbance in Middle Childhood," pp. 7–14. (*PA* 42:15745) In *Progress in Clinical Psychology Through Multivariate Experimental Designs.* Edited by Raymond B. Cattell. Fort Worth, Tex.: Society of Multivariate Experimental Psychology, Inc., 1968. Pp. 168. *

[183]

★**Ohio College Association Rating Scale.** High school; no date; ratings by teachers; 1 form (1 page); no manual; no data on reliability; $5 per 100 scales; $1 per specimen set; postage extra; [5–15] minutes; [Herbert A. Toops]; distributed by Wilbur L. Layton. *

[184]

*****Omnibus Personality Inventory—Form F.** College; 1968, c1959–68; OPI; test booklet title is *OPI—Form F;* approximately 88 per cent of the items developed from over 13 other published and unpublished tests and research reports; 15 scores: thinking introversion (TI), theoretical orientation (TO), estheticism (Es), complexity (Co), autonomy (Au), religious orientation (RO), social extroversion (SE), impulse expression (IE), personal integration (PI), anxiety level (AL), altruism (Am), practical outlook (PO), masculinity-femininity (MF), response bias (RB), intellectual disposition category (IDC) based on average of first 4 scores; 1 form ('68, 11

pages); manual ('68, 71 pages); directions sheet ('68, 2 pages, reprinted from manual); norms for college freshmen only; separate answer sheets (MRC, NCS) must be used; $4.75 per 25 tests; $3.50 per 50 MRC or NCS answer sheets; $8 per set of NCS scoring stencils and manual; directions sheets free on request; $2.50 per manual; $3 per specimen set; postpaid; MRC scoring service, 45¢ or less per test; NCS scoring service, 33¢ to 85¢ per test; (45–60) minutes; Paul Heist, George Yonge, T. R. McConnell (test), and Harold Webster (test); Psychological Corporation. *

For reviews by Paul M. Kjeldergaard and Norman E. Wallen of earlier forms, see 6:150 (11 references, 1 excerpt).

REFERENCES

1–11. See 6:150.
12. HEIST, PAUL. "Diversity in College Students' Characteristics." *J Ed Sociol* 33:279–91 F '60. *
12a. AVILA, DONALD LEE. *An Inverted Factor Analysis of Personality Differences Between Career- and Homemaking-Oriented Women.* Doctor's thesis, University of Nebraska (Lincoln, Neb.), 1964. (*DA* 25:609)
13. CANON, HARRY J. "Personality Variables and Counselor-Client Affect." *J Counsel Psychol* 11:35–41 sp '64. * (*PA* 38:8829)
14. CHATER, SHIRLEY SEARS. *Differential Characteristics of Graduate Students in Nursing and Implications for Curriculum Development.* Doctor's thesis, University of California (Berkeley, Calif.), 1964. (*DA* 25:3965)
15. GRAVES, GRANT O., and INGERSOLL, RALPH W. "Comparison of Learning Attitudes." *J Med Ed* 39:100–11 F '64. *
16. McFALL, ROBERT W. "A Method for Differentiating Between High Scorers on Two of the Intellectual-Orientation Scales of the OPI." *J Psychol* 57:259–61 Ap '64. * (*PA* 39:1842)
17. MERRILL, KEITH ELMER. *The Relationship of Certain Non-Intellective Factors to Lack of Persistence of Higher-Ability Students and Persistence of Lower-Ability Students at the University of California, Berkeley.* Doctor's thesis, University of California (Berkeley, Calif.), 1964. (*DA* 25:3939)
18. STEWART, LAWRENCE H. "Change in Personality Test Scores During College." Comment by David V. Tiedeman. *J Counsel Psychol* 11:211–20 f '64. * (*PA* 39:5184)
19. STEWART, LAWRENCE H. "Factor Analysis of Nonoccupational Scales of the Strong Blank, Selected Personality Scales and the School and College Ability Test." *Calif J Ed Res* 15:136–41 My '64. * (*PA* 39:3201)
20. TUCKER, SYLVIA BOLTZ. *College and University Potential of Selected Junior College Students.* Doctor's thesis, University of California (Los Angeles, Calif.), 1964. (*DA* 25:5077)
21. WILLIAMS, PHOEBE ANN. *The Relationship Between Certain Scores on the Strong Vocational Interest Blank and Intellectual Disposition.* Doctor's thesis, University of California (Berkeley, Calif.), 1964. (*DA* 26:2863)
22. ELTON, CHARLES F. "A Comparative Study of Teacher Ratings, High School Average and Measures of Personality and Aptitude in Predicting College Success." *Psychol Sch* 2:47–52 Ja '65. *
23. FREEDMAN, MERVIN B. "The Sexual Behavior of American College Women: An Empirical Study and an Historical Survey." *Merrill-Palmer Q* 11:33–48 Ja '65. * (*PA* 39:9960)
24. GOLDSCHMID, MARCEL LUCIEN. *The Prediction of College Major in the Sciences and the Humanities by Means of Personality Tests.* Doctor's thesis, University of California (Berkeley, Calif.), 1965. (*DA* 26:4073)
25. GULUTSAN, METRO. "Teachers' Reactions to Procedures in Teaching Human Relations." *Alberta J Ed Res* 11:54–65 Mr '65. * (*PA* 39:16469)
26. INGERSOLL, RALPH W., and GRAVES, GRANT O. "Predictability of Success in the First Year of Medical School." *J Med Ed* 40:351–63 Ap '65. *
27. KEYTON, FREDERICK R. *Some Relationships Between a Measure of Self-Actualization and Various Aspects of Intermediate Grade Teacher Effectiveness.* Doctor's thesis, Catholic University of America (Washington, D. C.), 1965. (*DA* 26:4450)
28. RICHARDSON, LA VANGE H., and WEITZNER, MARTIN. "The Relationship of Dependent, Acting Out, and Resistant Behavior to College Success." *Psychol Sch* 2:252–4 Jl '65. *
29. ROSE, HARRIETT A. "Prediction and Prevention of Freshman Attrition." *J Counsel Psychol* 12:399–403 w '65. * (*PA* 40:3400)
30. WEISSMAN, HERBERT NATHANIEL. *The Disposition Toward Intellectuality: Its Composition and Its Assessment.* Doctor's thesis, University of California (Berkeley, Calif.), 1965. (*DA* 26:7451)
31. YONGE, GEORGE D., and HEIST, PAUL A. "The Influence of Suggested Contexts on Faking a Personality Test." *Am Ed Res J* 2:137–44 My '65. *
32. ALTUS, WILLIAM D. "Birth Order and the Omnibus

Personality Inventory, Form C." *Proc Ann Conv Am Psychol Assn* 74:279-80 '66. * (*PA* 41:5970)

33. BEACH, LESLIE R. "Personality Change in the Church-Related Liberal Arts College." *Psychol Rep* 19:1257-8 D '66. * (*PA* 41:4577)

34. DULING, JOHN LEON. *A Comparison of Certain Selected Personality and Performance Dimensions of Music Students in Three San Francisco High Schools.* Doctor's thesis, University of California (Berkeley, Calif.), 1966. (*DA* 27:2552A)

35. ELTON, CHARLES F. "The Relationship of Grades to Personality." *Psychol Sch* 3:180-3 Ap '66. *

36. ELTON, CHARLES F., and ROSE, HARRIETT A. "Personality Characteristics: Their Relevance in Disciplinary Cases." *J Counsel Psychol* 13:431-5 w '66. * (*PA* 41:3297)

37. ELTON, CHARLES F., and ROSE, HARRIETT, A. "Within-University Transfer: Its Relation to Personality Characteristics." *J Appl Psychol* 50:539-43 D '66. * (*PA* 41:3298)

38. GANTZ, BENJAMIN SOULÉ, JR. *Predicting and Training Originality.* Doctor's thesis, Claremont Graduate School (Claremont, Calif.), 1966. (*DA* 28:1225B)

39. GRUBERG, RONALD RAYMOND. *The Relationship of Counselor Interview Style and Rated Effectiveness of Response to Counselor Tolerance of Ambiguity [With] Supplement.* Doctor's thesis, State University of New York at Albany (Albany, N.Y.), 1966. (*DA* 28:536A)

40. JOHNSON, KENNETH WILLARD. *An Investigation Into Correlates of Increases in Impulse Expression Among College Students at Selected Institutions.* Doctor's thesis, University of California (Berkeley, Calif.), 1966. (*DA* 27:677A)

41. ROSE, HARRIETT A., and ELTON, CHARLES F. "Another Look at the College Dropout." *J Counsel Psychol* 13:242-5 su '66. * (*PA* 40:9217)

42. STEWART, LAWRENCE H. "Characteristics of Junior College Students in Occupationally Oriented Curricula." *J Counsel Psychol* 13:46-52 sp '66. * (*PA* 40:5475)

43. AVILA, DONALD L. "An Inverted Factor Analysis of Personality Differences Between Career- and Homemaking-Oriented Women." *J Ed Res* 60:416-8 My-Je '67. *

44. BEALER, JAMES EDWARD. *An Analysis of Personality and Demographic Factors Concerning Students Involved in Disciplinary Problems.* Doctor's thesis, Michigan State University (East Lansing, Mich.), 1967. (*DA* 28:4870A)

45. CHATER, SHIRLEY S. "Differential Characteristics of Graduate Students in Nursing." *Nursing Res* 16:146-57 sp '67. *

46. COPE, ROBERT GARY. *Differential Characteristics of Entering Freshmen, Environmental Presses and Attrition at a Liberal Arts College.* Doctor's thesis, University of Michigan (Ann Arbor, Mich.), 1967. (*DA* 28:2336A)

47. DISPENZIERI, ANGELO; KALT, NEIL C.; and NEWTON, DAVID. "A Comparison of Students at Three Levels of Ability and Three Levels of Achievement Using the Omnibus Personality Inventory." *J Ed Res* 61:137-41 N '67. *

48. ELTON, CHARLES F. "Male Career Role and Vocational Choice: Their Prediction With Personality and Aptitude Variables." *J Counsel Psychol* 14:90-105 Mr '67. * (*PA* 41:7870)

49. ELTON, CHARLES F., and ROSE, HARRIETT A. "Personality Characteristics of Students Who Transfer Out of Engineering." *Personnel & Guid J* 45:911-5 My '67. * (*PA* 41:17103)

50. ELTON, CHARLES F., and ROSE, HARRIET A. "Significance of Personality in the Vocational Choice of College Women." *J Counsel Psychol* 14:293-8 Jl '67. * (*PA* 41:12610)

51. ELTON, CHARLES F., and ROSE, HARRIETT A. "Traditional Sex Attitudes and Discrepant Ability Measures in College Women." *J Counsel Psychol* 14:538-43 N '67. * (*PA* 42:4471)

52. GOLDSCHMID, MARCEL L. "Prediction of College Majors by Personality Tests." *J Counsel Psychol* 14:302-8 Jl '67. * (*PA* 41:12452)

53. GRAVES, GRANT O.; INGERSOLL, RALPH W.; and EVANS, LLOYD R. "The Creative Medical Student: A Descriptive Study." *J Creative Behav* 1:371-82 f '67. *

54. HART, M. MAXINE, and BROWN, MARJORIE. "Dogmatism as Related to Accuracy of Student Teacher's Judgment of Students." *J Teach Ed* 18:429-37 w '67. * (*PA* 42:9481)

55. KEES, DONALD JOSEPH. *A Study of College Student Subcultures Using a Typology.* Doctor's thesis, Washington State University (Pullman, Wash.), 1967. (*DA* 28:2985A)

56. KISCH, JEREMY MAGNUS. *A Comparative Study of Patterns of Underachievement Among Male College Students.* Doctor's thesis, University of Michigan (Ann Arbor, Mich.), 1967. (*DA* 28:3461B)

57. LONSWAY, FRANCIS ANTHONY. *Background Characteristics and Personality Traits of Catholic First-Year Theological Students.* Doctor's thesis, University of Minnesota (Minneapolis, Minn.), 1967. (*DA* 28:4923A)

58. ROGERS, WILLIAM ALFRED. *Intellective-Nonintellective Characteristics and Academic Success of College Freshmen.* Doctor's thesis, State University of New York at Buffalo (Buffalo, N. Y.), 1967. (*DA* 28:973A)

59. SHRABLE, KENNETH, and STEWART, LAWRENCE H. "Personality Correlates of Achievement Imagery: Theoretical and Methodological Implications." *Percept & Motor Skills* 24:1087-98 Je '67. * (*PA* 41:15322)

60. SNYDER, BENSON. "'Creativity' Students in Science and Engineering." *Univ Q* 21:205-18 Mr '67. *

61. WALTON, H. J., and HOPE, KEITH. "The Effect of Age

and Personality on Doctors' Clinical Preferences." *Brit J Social & Clin Psychol* 6:43-51 F '67. * (*PA* 41:7383)

62. WHITTAKER, DAVID NEIL EATON. *Psychological Characteristics of Alienated, Nonconformist, College-Age Youth as Indicated by AVL, OPI, ACL and SVIB-M/W Group Profiles.* Doctor's thesis, University of California (Berkeley, Calif.), 1967. (*DA* 28:3055B)

63. ATHANASIOU, ROBERT. "Reliability and Validity of a Predictor of Engineering Student Attrition." *Proc Ann Conv Am Psychol Assn* 76:171-2 '68. * (*PA* 43:1351, title only)

64. BROWN, ROBERT D. "An Investigation of the Relationship Between the Intellectual and the Academic Aspects of College Life." *J Ed Res* 61:439-41 Jl-Ag '68. *

65. COPE, ROBERT G. "Selected Omnibus Personality Inventory Scales and Their Relationship to a College's Attrition." *Ed & Psychol Meas* 28:599-603 su '68. * (*PA* 42:19268)

66. ELTON, CHARLES F., and ROSE, HARRIETT A. "The Face of Change." *J Counsel Psychol* 15:372-5 Jl '68. * (*PA* 42:15994)

67. GORTNER, SUSAN R. "Western Majors in Twelve Western Universities: A Comparison of Registered Nurse Students and Basic Senior Students." *Nursing Res* 17:121-8 Mr-Ap '68. *

68. GOTTSDANKER, JOSEPHINE S. "Intellectual Interest Patterns of Gifted College Students." *Ed & Psychol Meas* 28:361-6 su '68. * (*PA* 42:19401)

69. YONGE, GEORGE D. "Personality Correlates of the College and University Environment Scales." *Ed & Psychol Meas* 28:1115-23 sp '68. * (*PA* 42:12723)

70. YONGE, GEORGE D., and SASSENRATH, JULIUS M. "Student Personality Correlates of Teacher Ratings." *J Ed Psychol* 59:44-52 F '68. * (*PA* 42:7758)

NAME INDEX

[185]

*Opinion, Attitude, and Interest Survey. High school seniors and college students; 1962-68, c1955-65; OAIS; factors related to academic success and educational interest; 14 scores: 3 response bias scores (set for true, infrequent response, social undesirability), 3 academic promise scores (achiever personality, intellectual quality, creative personality), 3 adjustment scores (social, emotional, masculine orientation), and 5 interest scores (business, humanities, social science, physical science, biological science); 1 form ('64, 16 pages, items identical to those copyrighted in 1955); handbook ('65, 301 pages, same as preliminary handbook published in 1963 except for addition of reprints of two articles by the author, see 9 below); student's guide ('67, 6 pages); counselor's guide ('68, 8 pages); profile ('67, 1 page); college reports ('67, 19 pages); self-descriptive check list ('68, 1 page) optional; separate answer sheets (MRC) must be used; NCS answer sheets no longer available; $12.50 per 50 tests;

$10.50 per 125 answer sheets; $8.50 per 125 profiles; scoring keys not available; $11.50 per 125 student's guides; $4.50 per 10 counselor's guides; $5.50 per 125 check lists; $4.50 per handbook; $8 per specimen set; postage extra; student's guide, counselor's guide, and profile may be reproduced locally; scoring service (available only from Measurement Research Center), 50¢ or less per test; (40–60) minutes; Benno G. Fricke; OAIS Testing Program. *

For reviews by John O. Crites and Harold Webster, see 6:151 (4 references).

REFERENCES

1–4. See 6:151.
5. WALKER, HOWARD EDGAR. *Relationships Between Predicted School Behavior and Measures of Creative Potential.* Doctor's thesis, University of Michigan (Ann Arbor, Mich.), 1963. (*DA* 24:636)
6. GRAVES, GRANT O., and INGERSOLL, RALPH W. "Comparison of Learning Attitudes." *J Med Ed* 39:100–11 F '64. *
7. MANGAN, JOHN CLIFFORD. *Personality Variables Among School Counselors, Graduate Students, and Secondary Education Students.* Doctor's thesis, Ohio State University (Columbus, Ohio), 1964. (*DA* 25:7027)
8. FRICKE, BENNO G. "The OAIS Test and Testing Program." *Sup Stud* 7:44–50 Mr–Ap '65. *
9. FRICKE, BENNO G. *Opinion, Attitude and Interest Handbook: A Guide to Personality and Interest Measurement.* Ann Arbor, Mich.: OAIS Testing Program, 1965. Pp. x, 301. * (Same as 1963 edition except for addition of reprints of two articles by the author.)
10. INGERSOLL, RALPH W., and GRAVES, GRANT O. "Predictability of Success in the First Year of Medical School." *J Med Ed* 40:351–63 Ap '65. *
11. LEPPER, ROBERT E. "Using the OAIS to Select Participants for High School Institutes." *J Res Sci Teach* 3 (4):346–7 '65. *
12. WEBB, SAM C. "Two Cross Validations of the Opinion, Attitude and Interest Survey." *Ed & Psychol Meas* 25:517–23 su '65. * (*PA* 39:16396)
13. DOHNER, CHARLES WESLEY. *The Relation of Non-Intellective Factors to the Academic Achievement of College Freshmen at the Ohio State University.* Doctor's thesis, Ohio State University (Columbus, Ohio), 1966. (*DA* 27:2826A)
14. DONNAN, HUGH HAWKINS. *An Evaluative Study of Selected Personality Measures in the Prediction of Achievement and Survival of Students at the University of North Carolina.* Doctor's thesis, University of North Carolina (Chapel Hill, N.C.), 1966. (*DA* 27:2388A)
15. STOHS, REUBEN VICTOR. *Comparative Analysis of Personality Variables Among Graduate Students in Guidance and Physical Education and Among School Counselors.* Doctor's thesis, Ohio State University (Columbus, Ohio), 1966. (*DA* 27:2410A)
16. BLANTON, GLORIA HORTENSE. *The Relationship of Opinion, Attitude and Interest Survey Interest Scales to Major Areas Selected, Academic Achievement, and Satisfaction With Choice of Major Areas Selected by College Males.* Doctor's thesis, University of North Carolina (Chapel Hill, N.C.), 1967. (*DA* 28:4441A)
17. GRAVES, GRANT O.; INGERSOLL, RALPH W.; and EVANS, LLOYD R. "The Creative Medical Student: A Descriptive Study." *J Creative Behav* 1:371–82 f '67. *
18. GUSSETT, RONALD LINCOLN. *A Study of Academic Achievement of Students in the College of Education Using the Opinion, Attitude and Interest Survey as a Predictive Device.* Doctor's thesis, Ohio State University (Columbus, Ohio), 1967. (*DA* 28:2070A)
19. HAUENSTEIN, FREDERICK BURT. *The Predictive Validity of the Opinion Attitude Interest Survey for a Junior College Population.* Doctor's thesis, Indiana University (Bloomington, Ind.), 1967. (*DA* 28:2071A)
20. KISCH, JEREMY MAGNUS. *A Comparative Study of Patterns of Underachievement Among Male College Students.* Doctor's thesis, University of Michigan (Ann Arbor, Mich.), 1967. (*DA* 28:3461B)
21. STEVENS, THOMAS GRANVILLE. *Congruency Between Diagnostic Dimensions of Personality Theories and Personality Tests.* Master's thesis, California State College at Fullerton (Fullerton, Calif.), 1967.
22. SORENSON, MOURITS A. "OAIS Adjustment Scales and Counselor Classification of Client Problem." *Ed & Psychol Meas* 28:605–7 su '68. * (*PA* 42:19281)
23. WIGGINS, NANCY; BLACKBURN, MARGARET; and HACKMAN, J. RICHARD. "Prediction of First-Year Graduate Success in Psychology." *Proc Ann Conv Am Psychol Assn* 76:237–8 '68. * (*PA* 43:1502, title only)

[186]

*Organic Integrity Test.** Ages 5 and over; 1960–65; OIT; also called *Tien's OIT;* form perception as an indication of brain deficit unrelated to intelligence; individual; 1 form ('60, 20 cards); manual ['67, c'65, 36 pages, includes reprints of *2, 3, 4,* and *7* below]; diagnostic chart ('60, 1 page); $25 per set of cards and manual, postpaid; (4–5) minutes; H. C. Tien; Psychodiagnostic Test Co. *

REFERENCES

1. See 6:152.
2. TIEN, H. C. "Organic Integrity Test (O.I.T.): A Quick Diagnostic Aid to Rule in Organic Brain Diseases." *A.M.A. Arch Gen Psychiatry* 3:43–52 Jl '60. *
3. TIEN, H. C., and CLARK, G. D. "Organic Integrity Test Confirmed." *Am J Psychiatry* 121:257–61 S '64. *
4. TIEN, H. C., and WILLIAMS, M. W. "Organic Integrity Test (OIT) in Children." *Arch Gen Psychiatry* 12:159–65 F '65. * (*PA* 39:7806)
5. LIN, JAMES YING. *The Clinical Use of the Organic Integrity Test as a Color-Form Perception Test With the Juvenile Delinquents.* Doctor's thesis, University of Oklahoma (Norman, Okla.), 1966. (*DA* 27:2139B)
6. PAUL, GERALD T. "Differential Performances of Chronic Schizophrenics and Organics on the Organic Integrity Test." *Newsl Res Psychol* 8:10 N '66. *
7. TIEN, H. C. "Use of the Organic Integrity Test (OIT) With Children Who Cannot Read." *Am J Psychiatry* 122:1165–71 Ap '66. * (*PA* 40:7198)
8. TIEN, H. C. "The AEIOU&Y Method of Reading: Theory and Technique." *J Spec Ed* 1:223–40 sp '67. * (*PA* 41:15896)
9. TIEN, H. C., and CLARK, G. D. "OIT as a Routine Neuro-Psychiatric Screening Test." *Mich Med* 66:302–7 Mr '67. *
10. REINEHR, ROBERT C., and GOLIGHTLY, CAROLE. "The Relationship Between the Bender Gestalt and the Organic Integrity Test." *J Clin Psychol* 24:203–4 Ap '68. * (*PA* 42:12384)
11. SNELBECKER, GLEN E.; SHERMAN, LEWIS J.; and SCHWAAB, EUGENE L., JR. "Validation Study of the Organic Integrity Test." *Percept & Motor Skills* 27:427–30 O '68. * (*PA* 43:5579)
12. TIEN, H. C. "Organic Integrity Test (OIT) as an Empirical Guide in the Treatment of Schizophrenia." *Brit J Psychiatry* 114:871–5 Jl '68. * (*PA* 43:2873)
13. TIEN, H. C. "Pattern Recognition in Mental Disorders and the Organic Integrity Tests (OIT)." *Psychosomatics* 10(1):29–35 Ja–F '69. *

[187]

The Orientation Inventory. College and industry; 1962; OI; kinds of satisfactions and rewards sought in jobs; 3 scores: self-orientation, interaction-orientation, task-orientation; 1 form (4 pages); mimeographed manual, research edition (21 pages); preliminary norms; $3 per 25 tests; $1 per set of manual and key; $1 per specimen set; postage extra; (20–25) minutes; Bernard M. Bass; Consulting Psychologists Press, Inc. *

For reviews by Richard S. Barrett and H. Bradley Sagen, see 6:153 (2 references).

REFERENCES

1–2. See 6:153.
3. DISTEFANO, M. K., JR., and PRYER, MARGARET W. "Task-Orientation, Persistence, and Anxiety of Mental Hospital Patients With High and Low Motivation." *Psychol Rep* 14:18 F '64. * (*PA* 39:2378, title only)
4. MARSTON, ALBERT R. "Personality Variables Related to Self-Reinforcement." *J Psychol* 58:169–75 Jl '64. * (*PA* 39:4992)
5. MARSTON, ALBERT R., and LEVINE, EDWARD M. "Interaction Patterns in a College Population." *J Social Psychol* 62:149–54 F '64. * (*PA* 39:1577)
6. BRAUN, JOHN R., and DUBÉ, C. S., II. "Faking Studies With the Orientation Inventory." *J Psychol* 59:207–10 Ja '65. * (*PA* 39:7857)
7. CAGLE, BERNADENE GARRETT. *Personality Orientation and Values of Teacher Trainees and Experienced Teachers in the Areas of Elementary and Special Education.* Doctor's thesis, University of Georgia (Athens, Ga.), 1965. (*DA* 26:2066)
8. MCGEHEARTY, LOYCE IVY DAWSON. *Factors Associated With the Probable Success of Prospective School Counselors as Evaluated by Their Peers and by Staff Members.* Doctor's thesis, University of Texas (Austin, Tex.), 1965. (*DA* 26:873)
9. DISTEFANO, M. K., JR.; PRYER, MARGARET W.; and RICE, DAVID P. "Orientation and Job Success of Mental Hospital Patients." *Psychol Rep* 19:113–4 Ag '66. * (*PA* 40:12536)
10. KNAPP, DEANNE E.; KNAPP, DAVID; and WEICK, KARL. "Interrelations Among Measures of Affiliation and Approval

Motivation Under Stress and Nonstress Conditions." *J Social Psychol* 69:223–35 Ag '66. * *(PA* 40:12333)

11. Bass, Bernard M. "Social Behavior and the Orientation Inventory: A Review." *Psychol B* 68:260–92 O '67. * *(PA* 42:611)

12. DiStefano, Michael Kelly, Jr. *Influence of Normal Development and Emotional Impairment on Work Related Attitudes.* Doctor's thesis, Louisiana State University (Baton Rouge, La.), 1967. *(DA* 28:3086B)

13. Barry, John R.; Dunteman, George H.; and Webb, Marvin W. "Personality and Motivation in Rehabilitation." *J Counsel Psychol* 15:237–44 My '68. * *(PA* 42:12535)

14. Braun, John R. "Effects of Salesman-Faking Instructions on the Orientation Inventory." *Psychol Rep* 22:1006 Je '68. * *(PA* 42:12980)

15. DiStefano, M. K., Jr., and Pryer, Margaret W. "Relationship Between Severity of Emotional Impairment and Work-Related Attitudes." *J Clin Psychol* 24:420–2 O '68. * *(PA* 43:4206)

[188]

The Orzeck Aphasia Evaluation. Mental and brain damaged patients; 1964; OAE; individual; 1 form; manual (9 pages plus sample copy of record booklet); record booklet (4 pages); no data on reliability and validity; no norms; $7 per set of 25 record booklets and manual; $6.50 per 25 record booklets; $1.50 per manual; postpaid; (30–40) minutes; Arthur Z. Orzeck; Western Psychological Services. *

[189]

Otto Pre-Marital Counseling Schedules. Adult couples; 1961, c1951–61; OPMCS; checklist for use as a discussion stimulator; 1 form ('61, c1951); 3 parts; manual ('59, 31 pages); no data on reliability; no norms; $8.75 per 25 sets of all 3 parts; $2 per manual; 75¢ per specimen set (includes descriptive summary but not manual); postage extra; (60) minutes; Herbert A. Otto; Consulting Psychologists Press, Inc. *

a) PRE-MARITAL SURVEY SECTION. 1 form (4 pages); $4.75 per 25 copies.

b) FAMILY FINANCE SECTION. 1 form (1 page); $2.25 per 25 copies.

c) SEXUAL ADJUSTMENT SECTION. 1 form (2 pages); $2.25 per 25 copies.

For reviews by Robert C. Challman and William R. Reevy, consult 6:686.

REFERENCES

1. Otto, Herbert A. *The Development, Application and Appraisal of Pre-Marital Counseling Schedules.* Doctor's thesis, Florida State University (Tallahassee, Fla.), 1956. *(DA* 16:795)

2. Otto, Herbert A. "The Use of Inter-Action Centered Schedules in Group Work With Pre-Marital Couples." *Group Psychother* 12:223–9 S '59. *

[190]

★PRADI Autobiographical Form. Clinical clients; 1966; PAF; 1 form (4 pages plus form and analysis sheet); analysis sheet (1 page); $3.50 per 20 forms; $2 per 20 analysis sheets; $1 per manual; postage extra; specimen set not available; (40–50) minutes; Psychological Research and Development Institute and Sheldon J. Lachman (manual); Psychological Publications Press. *

[190A]

★The Perceptual Maze Test. Children, adults; 1955–69; PMT; brain damage; 2 levels; no manual; no norms; 170s. per 100 tests; (30) minutes for individual administration, (12–20) minutes for group administration; Alick Elithorn; Medical Research Council. *

a) [CHILDREN'S EDITION.] Ages 6–16; 1969; test consists of 20 sheets; administration instructions (1 page); no data on reliability and validity.

b) [ADULT EDITION.] Adults; 1955–68; Forms VC 1 and VC 2 (referred to as Forms VO 1 and VO 2

when the solution numbers have been cut off); test consists of 21 sheets stapled together; individual and group versions identical except for instructions; no data on reliability; no data on validity except in the journal literature.

c) RECTANGULAR VERSION. Adults; 1955–63; "while this version....has some advantages it has in general been superseded by the triangular version" (*b* above); test consists of 21 sheets stapled together; no manual; no data on reliability; no data on validity except in the journal literature.

REFERENCES

1. Elithorn, Alick. "A Preliminary Report on a Perceptual Maze Test Sensitive to Brain Damage." *J Neurol Neurosurg & Psychiatry* 18:287–92 N '55. * *(PA* 31:1032)

2. Elithorn, Alick; Kerr, Myfanwy; and Mott, Joy. "A Group Version of a Perceptual Maze Test." *Brit J Psychol* 51:19–26 F '60. * *(PA* 34:6976)

3. Benton, A. L.; Elithorn, A.; Fogel, M. L.; and Kerr, M. "A Perceptual Maze Test Sensitive to Brain Damage." *J Neurol Neurosurg & Psychiatry* 26:540–4 D '63. * *(PA* 38:10333)

4. Buckingham, R. A.; Elithorn, A.; Lee, D. N.; and Nixon, W. L. B. "A Mathematical Model of a Perceptual Maze Test." *Nature* 199:676–8 Ag 17 '63. *

5. Elithorn, Alick; Kerr, Myfanwy; and Jones, David. "A Binary Perceptual Maze." *Am J Psychol* 76:506–8 S '63. * *(PA* 38:3454)

6. Elithorn, A. "Intelligence, Perceptual Integration and the Minor Hemisphere Syndrome." Abstract. *Revue Neurologique* 110:593–4 Je '64. *

7. Elithorn, Alick. "Intelligence, Perceptual Integration and the Minor Hemisphere Syndrome." *Neuropsychologia* 2:327–32 D '64. *

8. Elithorn, Alick; Jones, David; Kerr, Myfanwy; and Lee, David. "The Effects of the Variation of Two Physical Parameters on Empirical Difficulty in a Perceptual Maze Test." *Brit J Psychol* 55:31–7 F '64. * *(PA* 39:802)

9. Beard, R. M. "The Structure of Perception: A Factorial Study." *Brit J Ed Psychol* 35:210–22 Je '65. *

10. Davies, Ann D. M. "The Perceptual Maze Test in a Normal Population." *Percept & Motor Skills* 20:287–93 F '65. * *(PA* 39:10099)

11. Davies, Ann D. M., and Davies, M. G. "The Difficulty and Graded Scoring of Elithorn's Perceptual Maze Test." *Brit J Psychol* 56:295–302 Ag '65. * *(PA* 40:37)

12. Davies, M. G., and Davies, Ann D. M. "Some Analytical Properties of Elithorn's Perceptual Maze." *J Math Psychol* 2:371–80 Jl '65. * *(PA* 39:15222)

13. Elithorn, Alick. "Psychological Tests: An Objective Approach to the Problem of Task Difficulty." *Acta Neurologica Scandinavica* 41(sup 13):661–7 '65. *

14. Elithorn, Alick. "Subjective Difficulty as a Function of Complexity. (A Logical Approach to the Design of Tests of Intellectual Functions)." *Int Copenhagen Congr Sci Study Mental Retard* 1964:627–30 ['65]. *

15. Lee, David N. *A Psychological and Mathematical Study of Task Complexity in Relation to Human Problem Solving Using a Perceptual Maze Test.* Doctor's thesis, University of London (London, England), 1965.

16. Colonna, A., and Faglioni, P. "The Performance of Hemisphere-Damaged Patients on Spatial Intelligence Tests." *Cortex* 2:293–307 Ap '66. * *(PA* 41:4895)

17. Elithorn, A.; Jagoe, J. R.; and Lee, D. N. "Simulation of a Perceptual Problem-Solving Skill." *Nature* 211:1029–31 S 3 '66. *

18. Archibald, Y. M.; Wepman, J. M.; and Jones, L. V. "Nonverbal Cognitive Performance in Aphasic and Nonaphasic Brain-Damaged Patients." *Cortex* 3:275–94 S '67. * *(PA* 42:9335)

19. Archibald, Y. M.; Wepman, J. M.; and Jones, L. V. "Performance on Nonverbal Cognitive Tests Following Unilateral Cortical Injury to the Right and Left Hemisphere." *J Nerv & Mental Dis* 145:25–36 Jl '67. * *(PA* 42:4382)

20. Heron, Alastair, and Chown, Sheila. *Age and Function.* London: J. & A. Churchill Ltd., 1067. Pp. x, 182. *

21. Lee, David N. "Graph-Theoretical Properties of Elithorn's Maze." *J Math Psychol* 4:341–7 Je '67. * *(PA* 41:13089)

22. Archibald, Y. M., and Wepman, J. M. "Language Disturbance and Nonverbal Cognitive Performance in Eight Patients Following Injury to the Right Hemisphere." *Brain* 91:117–30 Mr '68. * *(PA* 42:19160)

23. Elithorn, Alick. "Computer-Aided Techniques for the Assessment of Cerebral Damage." *Proc Royal Soc Medicine* 61:855–8 S '68. *

[191]

Personal Adjustment Inventory. Ages 9–13; 1931–61; PAI; formerly called *Test of Personality Adjust-*

ment; title on test booklet is *P.A. Inventory;* 5 scores: personal inferiority, social maladjustment, family maladjustment, daydreaming, total; separate forms ('61, 8 pages, identical with tests copyrighted in 1931 except for four wording changes) for boys and girls; manual ('61, 17 pages, identical with 1931 manual except for introduction and minor revisions); $2.50 per 25 tests; 75¢ per specimen set; postage extra; (40–50) minutes; Carl R. Rogers; Association Press. *

For reviews by Norman D. Sundberg and Robert D. Wirt, see 6:154 (6 references); for reviews by Dan L. Adler and Harrison G. Gough, see 5:117 (19 references); for a review by C. M. Louttit, see 2:1258.

REFERENCES

1–19. See 5:117.
20–25. See 6:154.
26. CRAMER, WILLIAM F. *The Relation of Maturation and Other Factors to Achievement in Beginning Instrumental Music Performance at the Fourth Through Eighth Grade Levels.* Doctor's thesis, Florida State University (Tallahassee, Fla.), 1958. (*DA* 19:540)
27. NORRIS, NANCY PHILLIPS. *Parental Understanding, Parental Satisfaction, and Desirable Personality Characteristics in Pre-Adolescent Boys.* Doctor's thesis, University of South Carolina (Columbia, S. C.), 1967. (*DA* 28:4709A)

NAME INDEX

[192]

Personal Audit. Grades 9–16 and adults; 1941–45; PA; emotional adjustment; 2 forms; manual ('45, 16 pages); profile ('42, 1 page); 28¢ per manual; $1.08 per specimen set; postage extra; Clifford R. Adams and William M. Lepley; Science Research Associates, Inc. *

a) FORM SS (SHORT FORM). 1941; 6 scores: seriousness, firmness, frankness, tranquility, stability, tolerance; 1 form ('45, 8 pages); $3.65 per 20 tests; (40) minutes.

b) FORM LL (LONG FORM). 1941; 9 scores: 6 scores same as for the short form plus steadiness, persistence, contentment; 1 form ('45, 11 pages); $4.80 per 20 tests; (50) minutes.

For a review by William Seeman, see 4:75 (3 references); for a review by Percival M. Symonds, see 3:64 (9 references).

REFERENCES

1–9. See 3:64.
10–12. See 4:75.
13. WALCHER, HELEN ROSS. *A Study of the Adams-Lepley Personal Audit Scores Made by Parents of Children With Cerebral Palsy and Their Controls.* Master's thesis, University of Oklahoma (Norman, Okla.), 1950.
14. O'SHEA, JACK VERNON. *An Experimental Investigation of Two Specific Hypotheses Inferred From the Scoring Manual of the Adams-Lepley Personal Audit.* Master's thesis, University of Nebraska (Lincoln, Neb.), 1951.
15. SPANEY, EMMA. "Personality Tests and the Selection of Nurses." *Nursing Res* 1:4–26 F '53. *
16. SAWYER, JACK. *Self-Insight and Supervisory Performance.* Doctor's thesis, Purdue University (Lafayette, Ind.), 1955. (*DA* 15:1892)
17. JONES, WORTH R. "Affective Tolerance and Typical Problems of Married and Unmarried College Students." *Personnel & Guid J* 37:126–8 O '58. * (*PA* 36:2KD26J)
18. BECKER, JAMES A. "An Exploratory Factor Analytic Study of Interests, Intelligence, and Personality." *Psychol Rep* 13:847–51 D '63. * (*PA* 38:8399)

[193]

★Personal Orientation Inventory. Grades 9–16 and adults; 1962–68; POI; 12 scores: time competent, inner directed, self-actualizing value, existentiality, feeling reactivity, spontaneity, self regard, self acceptance, nature of man, synergy, acceptance of aggression, capacity for intimate contact; 1 form ('63, 8 pages); manual with 1968 supplementation ('66, 39 pages); profile ('65, 2 pages); separate answer sheets (hand scoring sheet, IBM 1230) must be used; $8.50 per 25 tests; $3.75 per 50 hand scoring answer sheets; $4.50 per 50 IBM 1230 answer sheets; $7 per set of scoring stencils; $3.75 per 50 profiles; $1.75 per manual; $2.25 per specimen set; postage extra; scoring service, 85¢ or less per test; (30–40) minutes; Everett L. Shostrom; Educational and Industrial Testing Service. *

REFERENCES

1. DANDES, HERBERT MARVIN. *The Relationship Between Measured Psychological Health and Certain Attitudes and Values of Teachers.* Doctor's thesis, Syracuse University (Syracuse, N.Y.), 1964. (*DA* 25:6386)
2. GUNNISON, HUGH, JR. *A Study of the Relationships of Psychological Health, Political and Economic Attitudes and Life Values.* Doctor's thesis, Syracuse University (Syracuse, N.Y.), 1964. (*DA* 25:5735)
3. SHOSTROM, EVERETT L. "An Inventory for the Measurement of Self-Actualization." *Ed & Psychol Meas* 24:207–18 su '64. * (*PA* 39:5031)
4. KNAPP, ROBERT R. "Relationship of a Measure of Self-Actualization to Neuroticism and Extraversion." *J Consult Psychol* 29:168–72 Ap '65. * (*PA* 39:10056)
5. McMILLIN, MARVIN REVELLE. *A Study of Certain High School Seniors Perceived as Growth-Facilitating by Their Peers.* Doctor's thesis, University of Florida (Gainesville, Fla.), 1965. (*DA* 26:5875)
6. BRAUN, JOHN R. "Effects of 'Typical Neurotic' and 'After Therapy' Sets on Personal Orientation Inventory Scores." *Psychol Rep* 19:1282 D '66. * (*PA* 41:3705)
7. DANDES, HERBERT M. "Psychological Health and Teaching Effectiveness." *J Teach Ed* 17:301–6 f '66. *
8. MASUCCI, MICHAEL JOSEPH. *Psychological Health and Occupational Perceptions in a Selected Sample.* Doctor's thesis, Syracuse University (Syracuse, N.Y.), 1966. (*DA* 27:4340A)
9. SHOSTROM, EVERETT L., and KNAPP, ROBERT R. "The Relationship of a Measure of Self-Actualization (POI) to a Measure of Pathology (MMPI) and to Therapeutic Growth." *Am J Psychother* 20:193–202 Ja '66. *
10. DAMM, VERNON JOHN. *The Relation of Ego-Strength to Creativity and Intelligence in High School Students.* Doctor's thesis, University of Oregon (Eugene, Ore.), 1967. (*DA* 28:3016A)
11. ELMORE, THOMAS M., and CHAMBERS, EUGENE D. "Anomie, Existential Neurosis, and Personality: Relevance for Counseling." *Proc Ann Conv Am Psychol Assn* 75:341–2 '67. * (*PA* 41:13930)
12. FISCHLE, MILDRED JULIA. *A Study of Attitude and Behavior Change of Teachers Attending an NDEA Institute for Teachers of Disadvantaged Children.* Doctor's thesis, Ball State University (Muncie, Ind.), 1967. (*DA* 28:4023A)
13. FOULDS, MELVIN LOUIS. *An Investigation of the Relationship Between Therapeutic Conditions Offered and a Measure of Self-Actualization.* Doctor's thesis, University of Florida (Gainesville, Fla.), 1967. (*DA* 20:120A)
14. GREEN, EDITH JOSEPHINE. *The Relationship of Self-Actualization to Achievement in Nursing.* Doctor's thesis, Indiana University (Bloomington, Ind.), 1967. (*DA* 28:2002A)
15. KLAVETTER, ROBERT E., and MOGAR, ROBERT E. "Stability and Internal Consistency of a Measure of Self-Actualization." *Psychol Rep* 21:422–4 O '67. * (*PA* 42:4810)
16. QUEENEY, DONNA SUSAN SUTIN. *A Study of Aesthetic Value and Aesthetic Sensitivity as Related to the Home.* Doctor's thesis, Pennsylvania State University (University Park, Pa.), 1967. (*DA* 28:3771B)
17. ROSENTHAL, JANE CHENOWETH. *A Study of the Self-Actualizing Process of Selected University Freshmen Women Students.* Doctor's thesis, Colorado State College (Greeley, Colo.), 1967. (*DA* 28:4451A)
18. VANCE, EDITH MYRLE BLACKMON. *Relationship of Self-Actualization to Mental Health.* Doctor's thesis, North Texas State University (Denton, Tex.), 1967. (*DA* 28:135A)
19. ZACCARIA, JOSEPH S., and WEIR, WILLIAM R. "A Comparison of Alcoholics and Selected Samples of Nonalcoholics in Terms of a Positive Concept of Mental Health." *J Social Psychol* 71:151–7 F '67. * (*PA* 41:6142)
20. CULBERT, SAMUEL A.; CLARK, JAMES V.; and BOBELE, H. KENNETH. "Measures of Change Toward Self-Actualization in Two Sensitivity Training Groups." *J Counsel Psychol* 15:53–7 Ja '68. * (*PA* 42:6063)

21. FISHER, GARY. "Performance of Psychopathic Felons on a Measure of Self-Actualization." Abstract. *Ed & Psychol Meas* 28:561–3 su '68. * (*PA* 42:19043)
22. FOX, JACK; KNAPP, ROBERT R.; and MICHAEL, WILLIAM B. "Assessment of Self-Actualization of Psychiatric Patients: Validity of the Personal Orientation Inventory." *Ed & Psychol Meas* 28:565–9 su '68. * (*PA* 42:18089)
23. ILARDI, ROBERT L., and MAY, W. THEODORE. "A Reliability Study of Shostrom's Personal Orientation Inventory." *J Humanistic Psychol* 8:68–72 sp '68. * (*PA* 42:12985)
24. LEIB, JERE W., and SNYDER, WILLIAM U. "Achievement and Positive Mental Health: A Supplementary Report." *J Counsel Psychol* 15:388–9 Jl '68. * (*PA* 42:16001)
25. LEMAY, MORRIS L., and DAMM, VERNON J. "The Personal Orientation Inventory as a Measure of the Self-Actualization of Underachievers." *Meas & Eval Guid* 1:110–4 su '68. *
26. STEWART, ROBERT A. C. "Academic Performance and Components of Self Actualization." *Percept & Motor Skills* 26:918 Je '68. * (*PA* 42:16143)

NAME INDEX

Bobele, H. K.: 20	Knapp, R. R.: 4, 9, 22
Braun, J. R.: 6	Leib, J. W.: 24
Chambers, E. D.: 11	LeMay, M. L.: 25
Clark, J. V.: 20	McMillin, M. R.: 5
Culbert, S. A.: 20	Masucci, M. J.: 8
Damm, V. J.: 10, 25	May, W. T.: 23
Dandes, H. M.: 1, 7	Michael, W. B.: 22
Elmore, T. M.: 11	Mogar, R. E.: 15
Fischle, M. J.: 12	Queeney, D. S. S.: 16
Fisher, G.: 21	Rosenthal, J. C.: 17
Foulds, M. L.: 13	Shostrom, E. L.: 3, 9
Fox, J.: 22	Snyder, W. U.: 24
Green, E. J.: 14	Stewart, R. A. C.: 26
Gunnison, H.: 2	Vance, E. M. B.: 18
Ilardi, R. L.: 23	Weir, W. R.: 19
Klavetter, R. E.: 15	Zaccaria, J. S.: 19

[194]
The Personal Preference Scale. Ages 15 and over; 1947–54; PPS; 10 scores: active-inactive, sociable-individualistic, permissive-critical, consistent-inconsistent, efficient-inefficient, self-effacing-egocentric, masculine-effeminoid, feminine-masculinoid, emotionally mature-emotionally immature, socially mature-socially immature; 1 form ('51, 4 pages); guide ('53, 4 pages); manual ('54, 47 pages, see *1* below); no norms below college level; 25¢ per test; $1.25 per specimen set (must be purchased to obtain manual); postpaid; (20) minutes; Maurice H. Krout and Johanna Krout Tabin; [Johanna Krout Tabin]. *
See 5:93 (2 references).

REFERENCES
1–2. See 5:93.
3. MCNEIL, ELTON B., and COHLER, J. ROBERT, JR. "The Effect of Personal Needs on Counselors' Perception and Behavior." *Papers Mich Acad Sci Arts & Letters* 42:281–8 pt 2 '57. * (*PA* 37:6924)
4. NIDORF, LOUIS. *A Study of the Krout Personal Preference Scale.* Master's thesis, University of Oregon (Eugene, Ore.), 1957.
5. SNIDER, MARVIN. "On the Adequacy of the Krout and Tabin Personal Preference Scale Standardization Group." *J Clin Psychol* 15:68–70 Ja '59. * (*PA* 34:3032)
6. HAWARD, L. R. C. "Krout Personal Preference Scale." *Psychometric Res B* (6):[12–4] su '60. *
7. LITTMAN, RICHARD A.; NIDORF, LOUIS J.; and SUNDBERG, NORMAN D. "Characteristics of a Psychosexual Scale: The Krout Personal Preference Scale." *J Genetic Psychol* 98:19–27 Mr '61. * (*PA* 35:6422)

[195]
★Personal Values Inventory (Student Form). Grades 12–13; 1941–67; PVI; for predicting academic achievement; 12 scores: high school self report, need for achievement, direction of aspirations, socio-economic status, peer influence, home influence, planning, persistence, self control, total of persistence and self control, faking, self insight; separate editions for men and women; 1 form ('64, 7 pages); mimeographed preliminary manual ('67, 68 pages); the test may currently be used only by colleges interested in carrying out validation research; separate answer cards must be used; $3 per manual; specimen set not available; postpaid; examination fee, 20¢ per student; fee

includes test booklet, answer card, scoring service, and research report on the validity of the test for predicting grades in the participating college; (50) minutes; George E. Schlesser, John A. Finger, and Thomas Lynch (manual only); Colgate University Testing Service. *

REFERENCES
1. SCHLESSER, GEORGE E. "Improving the Validity of Personality Measures by Use of Overrating." *Ed & Psychol Meas* 13:77–86 sp '53. * (*PA* 28:966)
2. D'HEURLE, ADMA; MELLINGER, JEANNE CUMMINS; and HAGGARD, ERNEST A. "Personality, Intellectual, and Achievement Patterns in Gifted Children." *Psychol Monogr* 73(13): 1–28 '59. * (*PA* 35:1234)
3. MCCORD, C. G. *Cautiousness: An Exploratory Investigation With Implications for Academic Motivation, the Prediction of Academic Success and Educational Guidance.* Master's project, Colgate University (Hamilton, N.Y.), 1961.
4. FINGER, JOHN A., and SCHLESSER, GEORGE E. "Academic Performance of Public and Private School Students." *J Ed Psychol* 54:118–22 Ap '63. * (*PA* 37:8282)
5. FORESMAN, C. S. *An Investigation of Self-Insight as Measured by the Personal Values Inventory.* Master's project, Colgate University (Hamilton, N.Y.), 1964.
6. BIDGOOD, FREDERICK E. *An Empirical Study of the Needs for Academic and Non-Academic Achievement, Mastery and Prestige.* Master's project, Colgate University (Hamilton, N.Y.), 1965.
7. FINGER, JOHN A., and SCHLESSER, GEORGE E. "Non-Intellective Predictors of Academic Success in School and College." *Sch R* 73:14–29 sp '65. * (*PA* 39:10832)
8. SMITH, COLIN L. *The Development and Evaluation of an Academic Skills Workshop Project.* Master's project, Colgate University (Hamilton, N.Y.), 1965.
9. STONE, DONALD BRADFORD. *Predicting Student Retention and Withdrawal in a Selected State University College of New York.* Doctor's thesis, Cornell University (Ithaca, N.Y.), 1965. (*DA* 26:5184)
10. FINGER, JOHN A., JR. "Academic Motivation and Youth-Culture Involvement: Their Relationships to School Performance and Career Success." *Sch R* 74:177–95 su '66. * (*PA* 40:10415)
11. FINGER, JOHN A., JR. "An Analysis of Some Research Methodology Through an Investigation and Reappraisal of Selected Research on Academic Motivation." *J Exp Ed* 35: 43–52 w '66. *
12. FINGER, JOHN A., JR., and SILVERMAN, MORTON. "Changes in Academic Performance in the Junior High School." *Personnel & Guid J* 45:157–64 O '66. * (*PA* 41:1885)
13. FINEGAN, ANN. "The Predictive Value of Measured Motivational Factors in Evaluating Nurse Candidates." *Psychiatric Q Sup* 41:77–85 pt 1 '67. *
14. GRANDE, PETER P., and SIMONS, JOSEPH B. "Personal Values and Academic Performance Among Engineering Students." *Personnel & Guid J* 45:585–8 F '67. *
15. GRANDE, PETER P.; SIMONS, JOSEPH B.; and PALLONE, NATHANIEL J. "The Perception of the College Experience and Academic Motivation." *J Ed Res* 61:65–7 O '67. *

[196]
★Personality and Personal Illness Questionnaires. Mental patients and normals; 1967–68; PPI; 3 tests; postage extra; University of London Press Ltd. *

a) HOSTILITY AND DIRECTION OF HOSTILITY QUESTIONNAIRE. Mental patients and normals; 1967; HDHQ; test booklet title is *Personality Questionnaire;* all items from *Minnesota Multiphasic Personality Inventory;* 7 scores: intropunitive (self criticism, guilt), extrapunitive (urge to act out hostility, criticism of others, projected delusional hostility), total hostility, direction of hostility; 1 form (4 pages); manual (20 pages); clinical diagram sheets for neurotics (1 page), psychotics (1 page); norms consist of means and standard deviations; 16s. 6d. per 20 tests; 4s. per scoring stencil; 9s. 6d. per 20 clinical diagrams; 4s. 6d. per manual; 10s. per specimen set; [15–20] minutes; T. M. Caine, G. A. Foulds, and K. Hope (diagrams and manual).

b) THE HYSTEROID-OBSESSOID QUESTIONNAIRE. Mental patients and normals; 1967; HOQ; test booklet title is *Self-Description Questionnaire;* 1 form (2 pages); manual (10 pages); norms consist of means and standard deviations; 6s. 6d. per 20 tests; 3s. per manual; 3s.

per scoring stencil; 6s. 6d. per specimen set; [10–15] minutes; T. M. Caine and K. Hope (manual).

c) SYMPTOM SIGN INVENTORY. Mental patients; 1968; orally administered; 2 editions; manual (35 pages); 8s. per set of keys; 7s. 6d. per manual; G. A. Foulds and K. Hope (manual).

1) [*Regular Edition.*] SSI; differential diagnosis among 8 categories (anxiety state, neurotic depression, hysteria, obsessional state, non-paranoid schizophrenia, paranoid schizophrenia, mania, psychotic depression) and 2 scales (personality disturbance, psychotic vs. neurotic); 1 form (4 pages); 12s. 6d. per 20 tests; [30–35] minutes.

2) *Short Version.* SSI/PD; consists of the 20 items of the personal disturbance scale of regular edition; may be used as a screening device; 1 form (1 page); 7s. 6d. per 20 tests; [10] minutes.

REFERENCES

1. ADAMS, ANNE, and FOULDS, G. A. "Depression and Personality." *J Mental Sci* 108:474–86 Jl '62. * (*PA* 37:3720)
2. FOULDS, G. A. "A Quantification of Diagnostic Differentiae." *J Mental Sci* 108:389–405 Jl '62. * (*PA* 37:3215)
3. ADAMS, ANNE, and FOULDS, G. A. "Personality and the Paranoid Depressive Psychoses." *Brit J Psychiatry* 109:273–8 Mr '63. * (*PA* 38:3034)
4. CAINE, T. M., and HAWKINS, L. G. "Questionnaire Measure of the Hysteroid/Obsessoid Component of Personality: The HOQ." *J Consult Psychol* 27:206–9 Je '63. * (*PA* 38:977)
5. FOULDS, G. A., and OWEN, ANNA. "Are Paranoids Schizophrenics?" *Brit J Psychiatry* 109:674–9 S '63. * (*PA* 38:6487)
6. HESELTINE, G. F. "The Site of Onset of Eczema and Personality Trait Differences: An Exploratory Study." *J Psychosom Res* 7:241–6 D '63. * (*PA* 38:8360)
7. HOPE, K. *The Structure of Hostility Among Normal and Neurotic Persons.* Doctor's thesis, University of London (London, England), 1963.
8. FOULDS, G. A. "Personal Continuity and Psychopathological Disruption." *Brit J Psychol* 55:269–76 Ag '64. * (*PA* 39:5226)
9. FOULDS, G. A., and OWEN, ANNA. "Speed and Accuracy on Mazes in Relation to Diagnosis and Personality." *Brit J Social & Clin Psychol* 3:34–5 F '64. * (*PA* 38:8870)
10. CAINE, T. M. Chap. 3, "Obsessoid and Hysteroid Components of Personality," pp. 30–55. In *Personality and Personal Illness.* By G. A. Foulds and Others. London: Tavistock Publications Ltd., 1965. Pp. xii, 344. *
11. CAINE, T. M. Chap. 13, "Changes in Symptom, Attitude, and Trait Measures Among Chronic Neurotics in a Therapeutic Community," pp. 262–91. In *Personality and Personal Illness.* By G. A. Foulds and others. London: Tavistock Publications Ltd., 1965. Pp. xii, 344. *
12. FOULDS, G. A. "The Significance of Intra-Individual Diagnostic Levels." *Brit J Psychiatry* 111:761–8 Ag '65. * (*PA* 40:1588)
13. FOULDS, G. A., and ADAMS, ANNE. Chap. 10, "The Melancholic-Depressive Continuum," pp. 210–28 and Chap. 11, "The Paranoid-Melancholic Continuum," pp. 229–40. In *Personality and Personal Illness.* By G. A. Foulds and others. London: Tavistock Publications Ltd., 1965. Pp. xii, 344. *
14. FOULDS, G. A., and OWEN, ANNA. Chap. 12, "Anaylsis of Results in Terms of the Clinical Diagnosis," pp. 241–61. In *Personality and Personal Illness.* By G. A. Foulds and others. London: Tavistock Publications Ltd., 1965. Pp. xii, 344. *
15. FOULDS, G. A.; in collaboration with T. M. Caine and with the assistance of Anne Adams and Anna Owen. *Personality and Personal Illness.* London: Tavistock Publications Ltd., 1965. Pp. xii, 344. *
16. FOULDS, G. A.; in collaboration with T. M. Caine and with the assistance of Anne Adams and Anna Owen. *Personality and Personal Illness,* pp. 100–209, 295–333. London: Tavistock Publications Ltd., 1965. Pp. xii, 344. *
17. BARRETT, WILLIAM; CALDBECK-MEENAN, JOHN; and WHITE, JOHN GRAHAM. "Questionnaire Measures and Psychiatrists' Ratings of a Personality Dimension: A Note on the Congruent Validity of Caine's Self Description Questionnaire." *Brit J Psychiatry* 112:413–5 Ap '66. * (*PA* 40:10231)
18. CAINE, T. M. "Response Consistency and Testing Levels." *Brit J Social & Clin Psychol* 6:38–42 F '67. * (*PA* 41:7319)
19. CAINE, T. M., and SMAIL, D. J. "Personal Relevance and the Choice of Constructs for the Repertory Grid Technique." *Brit J Psychiatry* 113:517–20 My '67. * (*PA* 41:12107)
20. FOULDS, G. A. "Some Differences Between Neurotics and Character Distorders." *Brit J Social & Clin Psychol* 6:52–9 F '67. * (*PA* 41:7336)
21. FOULDS, G. A., and MAYO, P. R. " 'Neurotic' Symptoms, Intropunitiveness, and Psychiatric Referral." *Brit J Med Psychol* 40:151–2 Je '67. * (*PA* 42:12419)
22. HOPE, K.; PHILIP, A. E., and LOUGHRAN, J. M. "Psychological Characteristics Associated with XYY Sex-Chromosome Complement in a State Mental Hospital." *Brit J Psychiatry* 113:495–8 My '67. * (*PA* 41:12187)
23. MAYO, P. R. "Some Psychological Changes Associated With Improvement in Depression." *Brit J Social & Clin Psychol* 6:63–8 F '67. * (*PA* 41:7562)
24. PHILIP, A. E., and McCULLOCH, J. W. "Social Pathology and Personality in Attempted Suicide." Abstract. *Brit J Psychiatry* 113:1405–6 D '67. * (*PA* 42:9200)
25. FOULDS, G. A. "Neurosis and Character Disorder in Hospital and in Prison." *Brit J Criminol* 8:46–9 Ja '68. * (*PA* 42:10847)
26. HOPE, K., and CAINE, T. M. "The Hysteroid Obsessoid Questionnaire: A New Validation." *Brit J Social & Clin Psychol* 7:210–5 S '68. * (*PA* 43:132)
27. MAYO, P. R. "Self-Disclosure and Neurosis." *Brit J Social & Clin Psychol* 7:140–8 Je '68. * (*PA* 42:17389)
28. PHILIP, ALISTAIR E. "The Constancy of Structure of a Hostility Questionnaire." *Brit J Social & Clin Psychol* 7:16–8 F '68. * (*PA* 42:8267)
29. PHILIP, ALISTAIR E., and McCULLOCH, J. W. "Some Psychological Features of Persons Who Have Attempted Suicide." Abstract. *Brit J Psychiatry* 114:1299–300 O '68. * (*PA* 43:4183)

NAME INDEX

Adams, A.: 1, 3, 13, 15–6
Barrett, W.: 17
Caine, T. M.: 4, 10–1, 15–6, 18–9, 26
Caldbeck-Meenan, J.: 17
Foulds, G. A.: 1–3, 5, 8–9, 12–6, 20–1, 25
Hawkins, L. G.: 4
Heseltine, G. F.: 6
Hope, K.: 7, 22, 26
Loughran, J. M.: 22
McCulloch, J. W.: 24, 29
Mayo, P. R.: 21, 23, 27
Owen, A.: 5, 9, 14–6
Philip, A. E.: 22, 24, 28–9
Smail, D. J.: 19
White, J. G.: 17

[197]

The Personality Evaluation Form: A Technique for the Organization and Interpretation of Personality Data. Ages 2 and over; 1955; PEF; 1 form; manual (8 pages plus evaluation form); $8 per kit of 25 evaluation forms and manual; $7.50 per 25 evaluation forms; $1.50 per manual; postpaid; Charlotte Buhler and Gertrude Howard; Western Psychological Services. *

For a review by Dorothy H. Eichorn, see 5:94 (1 excerpt).

[198]

The Personality Inventory. Grades 9–16 and adults; 1931–38; PI, also BPI; commonly called *Bernreuter Personality Inventory;* 6 scores: neurotic tendency, self-sufficiency, introversion-extroversion, dominance-submission, confidence, sociability; 1 form ('35, 4 pages); manual ('35, 7 pages); profile (no date, 1 page); tentative norms ('38, 2 pages); $3.25 per 25 tests; $1.25 per 50 profiles; 25¢ per manual; separate answer sheets (IBM 805, Hankes) may be used; $2.50 per 50 IBM answer sheets; $1.50 per 50 Hankes answer sheets (scored by Testscor only, consult 6:667); $2.50 per set of hand scoring stencils; $10 per set of IBM scoring stencils; 50¢ per specimen set; postage extra; (25) minutes; Robert G. Bernreuter; Consulting Psychologists Press, Inc. *

For reviews by Wesley C. Becker and Donald J. Veldman, see 6:157 (22 references); see also 5:95 (40 references); for a review by Leona E. Tyler, see 4:77 (188 references); for reviews by Charles I. Mosier and Theodore Newcomb, see 2:1239 (71 references); for related book reviews not excerpted in this volume, consult the 1st (B358) MMY.

REFERENCES

1–71. See 2:1239.
72–259. See 4:77.
260–299. See 5:95.
300–321. See 6:157.
322. WELLS, F. L. "Rorschach and Bernreuter Procedures With Harvard National Scholars in the Grant Study: Cases 3, 9, 10, 27, 28, 103–112." *J Genetic Psychol* 79:221–60 D '51. * (*PA* 26:5839)
323. SCHEUERMAN, EDWARD L. "The Use of the Bernreuter Personality Inventory in a Seminary Program of Personality Appraisal and Guidance." Abstract. *Nat Cath Ed Assn B* 55:93 Ag '58. *

324. SPRINGFIELD, FRANKLYN BRUCE. *Concept of Father and Ideal Self in a Group of Criminals and Non-Criminals.* Doctor's thesis, New York University (New York, N.Y.), 1960. (*DA* 21:1258)

325. RAY-CHOWDHURY, K. "Bernreuter's Personality Inventory in Indian Situation: 1, Development of Adjustment Scales With Indian Item Weight Scores." *Indian Psychol B* 7:7–21 Ja '62. *

326. RAY-CHOWDHURY, K. "Bernreuter's Personality Inventory in Indian Situation: 2, General Norms, Reliability and Validity." *Indian Psychol B* 7:35–42 S '62. *

327. SERGEANT, RUSSELL LEWIS. *An Investigation of Responses of Speech Defective Adults on Personality Inventories.* Doctor's thesis, Ohio State University (Columbus, Ohio), 1962. (*DA* 23:4020)

328. NHAN, NGUYEN. *Some Personality Determinants of the Effects of Role Pressures on the Interpersonal Behavior of Role Occupants.* Doctor's thesis, University of Michigan (Ann Arbor, Mich.), 1963. (*DA* 25:2084)

329. ALLEN, ROBERT M.; RICHER, HOWARD M.; and PLOTNIK, RODNEY J. "A Study of Introversion-Extroversion as a Personality Dimension." *Genetic Psychol Mongr* 69:297–322 My '64. * (*PA* 39:5143)

330. DE SENA, PAUL A. "The Role of Consistency in Identifying Characteristics of Three Levels of Achievement." *Personnel & Guid J* 43:145–9 O '64. * (*PA* 39:10713)

331. LYSAUGHT, JEROME P., and PIERLEONI, ROBERT G. "A Comparison of Predicted and Actual Success in Auto-Instructional Programing." *J Programed Instr* 3(4):14–23 '64. *

332. ODEN, WILLIAM BRYANT. *Preaching and Personality: A Functional Typology Related to Perceptions of Selected Pastors.* Doctor's thesis, Boston University (Boston, Mass.), 1964. (*DA* 25:6091)

333. STROM, LEONARD E. "Some Personality Dimensions of Doctors of Education." *J Exp Ed* 33:387–90 su '65. * (*PA* 39:12953)

334. WEISS, AARON J., and DIAMOND, M. DAVID. "Psychologic Adjustment of Patients With Myelopathy." *Arch Phys Med & Rehabil* 47:72–6 F '66. *

335. ANANT, SANTOKH S. "Belongingness, Anxiety and Self-Sufficiency: Pilot Study." *Psychol Rep* 20:1137–8 Je '67. * (*PA* 41:15286)

336. HINMAN, SUSAN LEE. *A Predictive Validity Study of Creative Managerial Performance.* Greensboro, N.C.: Creativity Research Institute of The Richardson Foundation, Inc., November 1967. Pp. vi, 124. *

337. KUNDU, RAMANATH. "Adaptation of Bernreuter Personality Inventory to Bengali Language." *Psychol Studies* 12:107–12 Jl '67. *

338. KUNDU, RAMANATH, and GHOSH, SADHANA. "Personality Pattern of Pharmaceutical Sales Personnel." *Indian J Appl Psychol* 4:51–5 Jl '67. *

339. MOFFIE, D. J., and GOODNER, SUSAN. *A Predictive Validity Study of Creative and Effective Managerial Performance.* Greensboro, N. C.: Creativity Research Institute of The Richardson Foundation, Inc., December 1967. Pp. 80. *

340. SABOURIN, GILLES JEAN. *A Study of Personality Differences Between Deaf and Blind High School Students as Revealed by the Bernreuter Personality Inventory Test.* Master's thesis, Catholic University of America (Washington, D.C.), 1968.

341. VERINIS, J. SCOTT. "Interview and the Bernreuter Personality Inventory for Screening Adjustment Problems in College Students." *Psychol Rep* 23:49–50 Ag '68. * (*PA* 43:7081)

NAME INDEX

[199]

Personality Rating Scale. Grades 4–12; 1944–62; PRS; test identical with *Child Personality Scale* ('51) except for format; originally called *22-Trait Personality Rating Scale;* modification for use with children of E. Lowell Kelly's *36-Trait Personality Rating Scale* [see 6:158(19)]; ratings by classmates and teachers or self-ratings; 22 ratings: pep, intelligence, sociability, nervousness-calmness, popularity, religiousness, punctuality, courtesy, cooperation, generosity, persistence, honesty, neatness, patience, interests, disposition, good sport, boisterous-quiet, entertaining, thoughtfulness, sense of humor, dependability; 1 form ('62, 7 pages); manual ('62, 25 pages); profile ['62, 1 page]; separate answer sheets must be used; $3.50 per 35 tests; 50¢ per specimen set; postpaid; (30–40) minutes for rating 10–15 classmates; S. Mary Amatora; Educators'-Employers' Tests & Services Associates. *

For a review by Laurance F. Shaffer, see 6:158 (4 references); for reviews by Robert H. Bauernfeind and Dale B. Harris, see 5:41 (18 references).

[200]

Personality Record (Revised). Grades 7–12; 1941–58; PR; also available in combination with either the *Secondary-School Record, Revised* or the *Junior High School Record;* 8 ratings by teachers: motivation, industry, initiative, influence and leadership, concern for others, responsibility, integrity, emotional stability; 1 form ('58, 2 pages); no manual; no data on reliability

and validity; $1.25 per 100 forms, cash orders postpaid; National Association of Secondary-School Principals. *

For a review by Verner M. Sims of the original edition, see 4:78 (1 reference).

REFERENCES

1. See 4:78.
2. ZINGLE, STANLEY A. *Prediction of Academic Success in High School From Personality Trait Ratings Obtained From the Personality Record.* Doctor's thesis, University of Pittsburgh (Pittsburgh, Pa.), 1959. (*DA* 20:1648)
3. CRITCHFIELD, JACK B., and HUTSON, PERCIVAL W. "Validity of the Personality Record." *Col & Univ* 40:41–8 f '64. *
4. HAAS, RONALD FRANCIS. *Relationship Between Personality Adjustment of Low Ability High School Pupils and Their Enrollment in the College Preparatory Curriculum.* Doctor's thesis, Rutgers University (New Brunswick, N.J.), 1964. (*DA* 25:7078)
5. IVEY, ALLEN E.; PETERSON, FLOYD E.; and TREBBE, E. STEWART. "The Personality Record as a Predictor of College Attrition: A Discriminant Analysis." *Col & Univ* 41:199–205 w '66. *

[201]

★**Personality Research Form.** College; 1965–67; PRF; 2 forms; 2 editions: standard, long; manual ('67, 31 pages); separate answer sheets (hand scored, Digitek) must be used; $8.75 per 25 tests; $1.90 per 25 answer sheets; $2.25 per hand scoring stencil; Digitek scoring stencils not available; $2.10 per 25 profiles; $4 per manual; $1.50 per specimen set, excluding manual and stencils; cash orders postpaid; Douglas N. Jackson; Research Psychologists Press, Inc. *

a) STANDARD EDITION. 15 scores: achievement, affiliation, aggression, autonomy, dominance, endurance, exhibition, harm avoidance, impulsivity, nurturance, order, play, social recognition, understanding, infrequency; Forms A, B, ('65, 6 pages); profile ('67, 2 pages); (30–45) minutes.

b) LONG EDITION. 22 scores: same as for Standard Edition plus abasement, change, cognitive structure, defendence, sentience, succorance, desirability; contains the 300 items of the Standard Edition plus 140 additional items intermixed; Forms AA, BB, ('65, 8 pages); profile ('67, 2 pages); (40–70) minutes.

REFERENCES

1. BENTLER, PETER M. *Response Variability: Fact or Artifact?* Doctor's thesis, Stanford University (Stanford, Calif.), 1964. (*DA* 25:6049)
2. JACKSON, DOUGLAS N. *A Modern Strategy for Personality Assessment: The Personality Research Form.* Research Bulletin No. 30. London, Ont., Canada: Department of Psychology, University of Western Ontario, October 1966. Pp. i, 42. *
3. ACKER, MARY BRYANT. *The Relation of Achievement Need, Time Perspective, and Field Articulation to Academic Performance.* Doctor's thesis, University of California (Berkeley, Calif.), 1967. (*DA* 29:1492B)
4. KUSYSZYN, IGOR. *The Objective Use of Judgmental Methods in Assessing Personality Traits.* Doctor's thesis, University of Western Ontario (London, Ont., Canada), 1967.
5. SIESS, THOMAS F., and JACKSON, DOUGLAS N. "A Personological Approach to the Interpretation of Vocational Interests." *Proc Ann Conv Am Psychol Assn* 75:353–4 '67. * (*PA* 41:14261)
6. TROTT, D. MERILEE, and JACKSON, DOUGLAS N. "An Experimental Analysis of Acquiescence." *J Exp Res Personality* 2:278–88 D '67. * (*PA* 42:8972)
7. JACKSON, DOUGLAS N., and GUTHRIE, GEORGE M. "Multitrait-Multimethod Evaluation of the Personality Research Form." *Proc Ann Conv Am Psychol Assn* 76:177–8 '68. * (*PA* 43:125, title only)
8. JACKSON, DOUGLAS N., and LAY, C. H. "Homogeneous Dimensions of Personality Scale Content." *Multiv Behav Res* 3:321–37 Jl '68. * (*PA* 43:4030)
9. JACKSON, DOUGLAS N., and LAY, CLARRY H. *Homogeneous Dimensions of Personality Scale Content.* Research Bulletin No. 74. London, Ont., Canada: Department of Psychology, University of Western Ontario, March 1968. Pp. i, 19. *
10. KUSYSZYN, IGOR. "Comparison of Judgmental Methods With Endorsements in the Assessment of Personality Traits." *J Appl Psychol* 52:227–33 Je '68. * (*PA* 42:12108)
11. KUSYSZYN, IGOR, and JACKSON, DOUGLAS N. "A Multimethod Factor Analytic Appraisal of Endorsement and Judg-

ment Methods in Personality Assessment." *Ed & Psychol Meas* 28:1047–61 w '68. *
12. KUSYSZYN, IGOR, and JACKSON, DOUGLAS N. *A Multimethod Factor Analytic Appraisal of Endorsement and Judgment Methods in Personality Assessment.* Research Bulletin No. 67. London, Ont., Canada: Department of Psychology, University of Western Ontario, January 1968. Pp. i, 15. *
13. MARKS, EDMOND. "Personality and Motivational Factors in Responses to an Environmental Description Scale." *J Ed Psychol* 59:267–74 Ag '68. * (*PA* 42:15450)

[202]

★**The Personnel Reaction Blank.** Adults; 1954–61; PRB; worker dependability and conscientiousness; 1 form ('54, 3 pages); mimeographed manual ('61, 6 pages); $15 per 100 tests; postage extra; specimen set free to psychologists; French, German, Italian, and Spanish editions available; major references are written in Italian and consequently are not eligible for listing in the MMY; (15) minutes; Harrison G. Gough; the Author. *

[203]

The Philo-Phobe. Ages 10 and over; 1943–50; PP; interview form for obtaining and analyzing data in 4 areas: aspiration, emotion, judgment and insight, ethicomoral development; individual; 1 form ('50, 4 pages); manual ('43, 8 pages, reprint of *1* below); no data on reliability and validity; no norms; $6.50 per 25 tests; $1 per manual; $1.50 per specimen set; postpaid; administration time not reported; John N. Buck; Western Psychological Services. *
For a review by Parker Davis, Jr., see 3:66 (3 references).

[204]

Pictorial Study of Values: Pictorial Allport-Vernon. Ages 14 and over; 1957; PSV; title on test is *The Pictorial Study;* 7 scores: aesthetic, economic, political, religious, social, theoretical, strength of liking things in general; 1 form (4 pages); manual (4 pages); preliminary norms; separate answer sheets must be used; $4 per 25 tests; $1.50 per 25 answer sheets; $1 per specimen set (must be purchased to obtain manual); cash orders postpaid; (20–30) minutes; Charles Shooster; Psychometric Affiliates. *
For reviews by Andrew R. Baggaley and Harrison G. Gough, see 5:96.

REFERENCE

1. KELLEHER, EDWARD J.; KERR, WILLARD A.; and MELVILLE, NORBERT T. "The Prediction of Subprofessional Nursing Success." *Personnel Psychol* 21:379–88 au '68. *

[205]

★**Polarity Scale, Fourth Edition.** College and adults; 1954–66; PS; 4 scores: humanistic, normative, both, neither; 1 form ('64, c1954–64, 5 pages); manual ('66, 4 pages); no data on reliability and validity; no norms; $8 per 50 tests, postage extra; (20–45) minutes; Silvan S. Tomkins; Springer Publishing Co., Inc. *

REFERENCE

1. TOMKINS, SILVAN S. Chap. 3, "Affect and the Psychology of Knowledge," pp. 72–97. In *Affect, Cognition, and Personality: Empirical Studies.* Edited by Silvan S. Tomkins and Carroll E. Izard. New York: Springer Publishing Co., Inc., 1965. Pp. vii, 464. * (*PA* 39:13287)

[206]

Polyfactorial Study of Personality. Adults; 1959; PSP; 11 scores: hypochondriasis, sexual identification, anxiety, social distance, sociopathy, depression, compulsivity, repression, paranoia, schizophrenia, hyperaffectivity; 1 form (7 pages); manual (12 pages); separate answer sheets (IBM 805) must be used; $6.25 per 20 tests; $2.75 per 20 answer sheets;

$2 per set of scoring stencils; $2.75 per 20 profiles; $1.75 per manual; $2.50 per specimen set; cash orders postpaid; (45–50) minutes; Ronald H. Stark; Martin M. Bruce. *
For reviews by Bertram D. Cohen and Donald R. Peterson, see 6:160 (1 excerpt).

[207–8]

★**Porch Index of Communicative Ability.** Adults; 1967; PICA; aphasia; 22 scores: gestural (8 unnamed subtest scores and total), verbal (4 unnamed subtest scores and total), graphic (6 unnamed subtest scores and total), total; 1 form; administration manual (100 pages); technical manual (62 pages); examiner's booklet (24 pages); set of profiles and score sheets (9 pages); $57 per set of testing materials, including 20 sets of profile and score sheet; $10 per 25 sets of profile and score sheet; $6.75 per administration manual; $4.25 per technical manual; specimen set not available; postage extra; testing materials may be assembled locally; [50–80] minutes; Bruce E. Porch; Consulting Psychologists Press, Inc. *

[209]

The Power of Influence Test. Grades 2–13; 1958; POIT; seating preference sociometric test; 1 form (1 page); manual (4 pages); no data on validity; norms for grades 5–11 only; $3 per examiner's kit of 50 tests, 3 report sheets, and manual; $1 per additional 25 tests; cash orders postpaid; specimen set not available; [10–15] minutes; Roy Cochrane and Wesley Roeder; Psychometric Affiliates. *
For reviews by Åke Bjerstedt and Eric F. Gardner, see 6:162 (1 reference).

[210]

Practical Policy Test. Adults; 1948; PPT; also called *Test of Cynicism;* Form C-S (7 pages); no manual; no data on reliability and validity; typewritten college norms only; 5¢ per test; 50¢ per sample copy and norms; postpaid; [10–20] minutes; Martin F. Fritz and Charles O. Neidt; Martin F. Fritz. *
See 5:98 (9 references).

[211]

Pre-Counseling Inventory. Ages 8–14; 1949; PCI; 2 scores: adjustment, tension; individual; Form R (4 pages); manual (13 pages); $1 per 20 tests; 25¢ per manual; 35¢ per specimen set; postage extra; (15–30) minutes; Alfred Schmieding; Concordia Publishing House. *
For a review by Charles H. Honzik, see 4:80 (1 reference).

REFERENCES

1. See 4:80.
2. SCHMIEDING, ALFRED. "Pre-Counseling Inventory, Form R," pp. 50–3. In *Tests and Measurements in Lutheran Education.* Edited by Arthur L. Miller. Lutheran Education Association, Fourteenth Yearbook, 1957. River Forest, Ill.: the Association, 1959. Pp. xi, 115. *

[212]

★**Preschool Self-Concept Picture Test.** Ages 4–5; 1966–68; PSCPT; comparison of self concept and ideal self concept; individual; 1 form ('66, 21 pages); a booklet showing Negro children is also available; mimeographed manual ['68, 6 pages); scoring sheet ['68, 1 page); no norms; $15 per set of booklets, manual and 25 scoring sheets, postage extra; specimen set not available; (10–20) minutes; Rosestelle B. Woolner; RKA Publishing Co. *

REFERENCE

1. WOOLNER, ROSESTELLE BACH. *Kindergarten Children's Self-Concepts in Relation to Their Kindergarten Experiences.* Doctor's thesis, University of Tennessee (Knoxville, Tenn.), 1966. (*DA* 27:2761A)

[213]

*The Press Test. Industrial employees; 1961–65; PT; ability to work under stress; 5 scores: reading speed, color-naming speed, color-naming speed with distraction, difference between color-naming speed with and without distraction, difference between reading speed and color-naming speed; 1 form ('65, 10 pages, identical with form copyrighted in 1961 except for slight modification in directions); manual ('61, 25 pages); reliability and validity data based on shorter time limits; norms for males only; $10 per 20 tests, postage extra; $2 per specimen set, postpaid; 4.5(15) minutes; Melany E. Baehr, Raymond J. Corsini, Richard Renck (manual), and Measurement Research Division, Industrial Relations Center, University of Chicago (manual); the Center. *

For reviews by William H. Helme and Allyn Miles Munger, see 6:163.

REFERENCE

1. KERR, WILLARD A., and McGEHEE, EDWARD M. "Creative Temperament as Related to Aspects of Strategy and Intelligence." *J Social Psychol* 62:211–6 Ap '64. * (*PA* 39:5126)

[214]

Problem Check List: Form for Rural Young People. Ages 16–30; 1946–48; adaptation of an earlier edition of *Mooney Problem Check List, 1950 Revision,* College Form (see 173); 10 scores: health and physical, relationship with people, citizenship, education, vocation and economic, morals and religion, personal temperament, courtship-sex-marriage, social and recreational, home and family; 1 form ('46, 4 pages); manual ('48, 31 pages); 5¢ per check list, postage extra; (30–50) minutes; Ralph E. Bender, Mary Alice Price, and Ross L. Mooney; Bureau of Educational Research, Ohio State University; distributed by Publications Sales and Distribution. *

See 4:81 (2 references).

REFERENCES

1–2. See 4:81.
3. WATERS, E. W. "Problems of Rural Negro High School Seniors on the Eastern Shore of Maryland: A Consideration for Guidance." *J Negro Ed* 22:115–25 sp '53. * (*PA* 28:1520)

[215]

A Process for In-School Screening of Children With Emotional Handicaps. Grades kgn–3, 3–6, 7–12; 1961–62; for research use only; 3 ratings: teacher, peer, and self; manual ('61, 49 pages); technical report ('61, 66 pages); pupil record folder ('62, 3 pages); no norms; 10¢ per screening summary form; 15¢ per pupil record folder; $2 per manual; $2.50 per technical report; postage extra; $10 per complete specimen set, postpaid; to be administered "over a period of two or three months"; Nadine M. Lambert and Eli M. Bower; distributor in California: Fiscal Office, State Department of Education; distributor in all other states: Educational Testing Service. *
a) BEHAVIOR RATINGS OF PUPILS. Grades kgn–12; ratings by teachers; 1 form ('62, 11 pages); no data on reliability; $1 per form; administration time not reported.
b) [PEER RATINGS.] Grades kgn–3, 3–7, 7–12; 3 levels; teacher's scoring instructions and worksheet ('62, 6 pages) for all 3 levels; 2) and 3) also include self-ratings; $1 per teacher's worksheet.
1) *The Class Pictures.* Grades kgn–3; individual; 1 form ('62, 12 cards); record form (1 page); no

data on reliability of current edition; $1 per set of pictures; 35¢ per pad of 30 record forms; (15–20) minutes.
2) *A Class Play.* Grades 3–7; 1 form ('62, 8 pages); 20¢ per test; (35–45) minutes.
3) *Student Survey.* Grades 7–12; 1 form ('62, 8 pages); no data on reliability; 20¢ per test; administration time not reported.
c) [SELF-RATINGS.] Grades kgn–3, 3–7, 7–12; 3 levels.
1) *A Picture Game.* Grades kgn–3; separate forms ('62, 66 cards) for boys and girls; $1.75 per set of cards; 15¢ per class record; (30) minutes.
2) *Thinking About Yourself.* Grades 3–7; Forms A (for boys), B (for girls), ('62, 6 pages); score sheet ('62, 1 page); 20¢ per test; 7¢ per score sheet; 15¢ per class record; administration time not reported.
3) *A Self Test.* Grades 7–12; 1 form ('62, 6 pages); score sheet ('62, 1 page); no data on reliability; 20¢ per test; 7¢ per score sheet; 15¢ per class record; administration time not reported.

For reviews by Alan O. Ross and J. Robert Williams, see 6:164 (3 references); for a related book review not excerpted in this volume, consult the 6th (B93) MMY.

REFERENCES

1–3. See 6:164.
4. KING, JOHN DOUGLAS. *An Evaluation of an In-School Method for Screening Children With Emotional Handicaps.* Doctor's thesis, University of Nebraska (Lincoln, Neb.), 1964. (*DA* 25:5741)

[216]

*Progress Assessment Chart of Social Development. Mentally handicapped children, mentally handicapped adults; 1962–69; behavior checklist for assessing progress in 4 areas: self-help, communication, socialisation, occupation; 3 levels; descriptive folder ['68, 4 pages]; no data on reliability; Norwegian, Portuguese, Spanish, and Swedish editions available; 20s. per 25 charts; 10s. per specimen set (without manual); postpaid; H. C. Gunzburg; SEFA (Publications) Ltd. *
a) PRIMARY PROGRESS ASSESSMENT CHART, FOURTH EDITION. Profoundly handicapped children and adults; 1966; PPAC; 1 form (4 pages); no manual; no norms.
b) PROGRESS ASSESSMENT CHART I, SEVENTH EDITION. Children unsuitable for education at school; 1962–67; PAC 1; 1 form ('65, 4 pages); manual ('64, 111 pages) for set of SEFA teaching aids and charts; mimeographed supplement ['65, 4 pages]; norms and record folder, second edition ('67, 4 pages, entitled *Progress Evaluation Index 1*); 32s. 6d. per 5 folders; 84s. per set of SEFA teaching materials (must be purchased to obtain manual).
c) PROGRESS ASSESSMENT CHART 2, FIFTH EDITION. Older mentally handicapped trainees; 1963–69; PAC 2; 1 form ('66, 4 pages); no manual; norms and record folder ('69, 4 pages, entitled *Progress Evaluation Index 2*); 32s. 6d. per 5 folders.

REFERENCES

1. GUNZBURG, H. C. "Symposium on Problems of Social Education: 1, Introduction: Identifying Weak Social Skills." *J Mental Subnorm* 9:3–7 Je '63.
2. GUNZBURG, H. C. "A New Method of Charting Social Skills Progress." *Mental Retard* 2:370–3 D '64. * (*PA* 39:10588)
3. GUNZBURG, H. C. "A 'Finishing School' for the Mentally Subnormal." *Med Officer* 114:99–102 Ag 13 '65. *
4. GUNZBURG, H. C. "Social Competence of the Imbecile Child: Landmarks and Directed Training." *Int Copenhagen Congr Sci Study Mental Retard* 1964:693–706 ['65]. *
5. GUNZBURG, H. C. Chap. 3, "Development of Social Competence," pp. 68–97; Appendix B, "The Use of the P-A-C and P-E-I," pp. 212–8. In his *Social Competence and Mental*

Handicap: An Introduction to Social Education. London: Baillière, Tindall & Cassell Ltd., 1968. Pp. x, 225. *

[216A]

★**Psychiatric Evaluation Form.** Psychiatric patients and nonpatients; 1967–68; PEF; an interview guide and rating scale for recording scaled judgments (based upon various sources of information: subject, informant, case records, nurses' notes, etc.) of a person's functioning over a one week period on 19 psychopathological dimensions and role impairment in 3 occupational roles and 2 social roles; Form R2 ('68, 20 pages); manual ('68, 20 pages); no norms; $1 per booklet; 10¢ per score sheet; 50¢ per manual; postage extra; specimen set free; fee for editing, coding, key punching, and verifying score sheets, 10¢ per subject; (2–4) minutes; Robert L. Spitzer, Jean Endicott, Alvin Mesnikoff, and George Cohen; Biometrics Research, New York State Psychiatric Institute. * [The Diagnostic Version, PEF-D ('68, 13 sheets, same as regular edition except for the addition of 12 scales and the coverage of a person's functioning over the past month) is available only as a part of *Current and Past Psychopathology Scales* (see 53A).]

[217]

★**The Psychiatric Status Schedules: Subject Form, Second Edition.** Psychiatric patients and nonpatients; 1966–68; PSS; a standardized interview schedule for gathering information from a subject needed to fill out a matching inventory designed to evaluate social and role functioning as well as mental status; most of the sections dealing with signs and symptoms of psychiatric disorder are from the *Mental Status Schedule* (see 164); 18 symptom scores (inappropriate affect-appearance-behavior, interview belligerence—negativism, agitation-excitement, retardation—lack of emotion, speech disorganization, grandiosity, suspicion-persecution-hallucinations, reported overt anger, depression-anxiety, suicide—self-mutilation, somatic concerns, social isolation, daily routine—leisure time impairment, antisocial impulses or acts, alcoholic abuse, drug abuse, disorientation memory, denial of illness), 5 role functioning scores (wage earner, housekeeper, student or trainee, mate, parent), 5 summary symptom and role scales (subjective distress, behavioral disturbance, impulse control disturbance, reality testing disturbance, summary role), and 20 supplemental scores (anxiety, auditory hallucinations, catatonic behavior, conversion reaction, delusions-hallucinations, depression-suicide, disassociation, elated mood, guilt, lack of emotion, obsessions-compulsions, persecutory delusions, phobia, psychomotor retardation, sex deviation, silliness, somatic delusions or hallucinations. visual hallucinations, miscellaneous, validity check); Subject Form, second edition ('68, 15 pages); manual, second edition ('68, 15 pages); norms based upon newly admitted psychiatric patients; $3 per booklet; 10¢ per score sheet; 50¢ per manual; $4 per set of keys and teaching tape; postage extra; specimen set free; fee for editing, coding, key punching, and verifying score sheet, 50¢ per subject; scoring service with either profile printout or a computerized psychiatric diagnosis (DIAGNO I) using standard American Psychiatric Association nomenclature is available; (25–50) minutes; Robert L. Spitzer, Jean Endicott, and George Cohen; Biometrics Research, New York Psychiatric Institute. *

[218]

★**Psychological Audit for Interpersonal Relations, Revised Edition.** Marriage counselees and

industrial personnel; 1964–66; PAIR; also called *The "PAIR" Test;* 20 scores: social status, intellectual rigidity, family cohesiveness, social extraversion, political conservatism, self-rejection, aggressive hostility, physical affection, monetary concern, change and variety, dominant leadership, nurturant helpfulness, order and routine, esthetic pleasures, submissive passivity, psychological support, emotional control, dependent suggestibility, health concern or outdoor interest, self-acceptance; 1 form ('66, 16 pages); manual ('66, 20 pages); profile ('66, 1 page); separate answer sheets (NCS) must be used; 50¢ per test; $1.50 per 10 answer sheets; $2 per manual; postage extra; scoring service, $10 per individual or couple; (60) minutes; Richard R. Stephenson; the Author. *

[219]

Psychometric Behavior Checklist. Adults; 1960; PBC; also called *Maryland Test Behavior Checklist;* for recording unusual test taking behavior; CC Form 19 ['60, 1 page, mimeographed]; instructions (4 pages, reprint of *1* below); specimen set free (checklist may be reproduced locally), postpaid; administration time varies with task rated; Bernard G. Berenson, Kathryn C. Biersdorf, Thomas M. Magoon, Martha J. Maxwell, Donald K. Pumroy, and Marjorie H. Richey; University Counseling Center. *
See 6:166 (1 reference).

[220]

Psycho-Somatic Inventory. Late adolescents and adults; 1938; PSI; 3 scores: physiological, psychological, total; title on test is P-S Experience Blank; 1 form (3 pages); mimeographed manual (5 pages); tests must be reproduced locally; $1 per specimen set, postpaid; (15–25) minutes; Ross A. McFarland and Clifford P. Seitz; Ross A. McFarland. *
For reviews by Doncaster G. Humm and Charles I. Mosier, see 2:1234 (2 references).

REFERENCES

1–2. See 2:1234.
3. PAGE, HOWARD E. "Detecting Psychoneurotic Tendencies in Army Personnel." *Psychol B* 42:645–58 N '45. * (PA 20:820)
4. FRENCH, VERA V. "The Structure of Sentiments: 2, A Preliminary Study of Sentiments." *J Personality* 16:78–108 S '47. *
5. KLUGMAN, SAMUEL F. "Test Scores of Psychoneurotic Returnees Before and After Convalescent Furlough." *J Clin Psychol* 4:195–200 Ap '48. * (PA 23:256)
6. CAUFFIEL, PAUL WENDELL. *A Comparison of the P-S Experience Blank With the Minnesota Multiphasic Personality Inventory.* Master's thesis, Pennsylvania State College (State College, Pa.), 1950.
7. CAUFFIEL, PAUL W., and SNYDER, WILLIAM U. "A Comparison of the Performance of a Randomly Selected College Population on the MMPI and the P-S Experience Blank." *J Clin Psychol* 7:267–70 Jl '61. *
8. WILLIAMS, MARIE E. *A Comparison of the Cornell Index, Form N2 With the Psycho-Somatic Experience Blank.* Master's thesis, Fordham University (New York, N.Y.), 1952.
9. DAVIDS, ANTHONY. "Relations Among Several Objective Measures of Anxiety Under Different Conditions of Motivation." *J Consult Psychol* 19:275–9 Ag '55. * (PA 30:4812)
10. DAVIDS, ANTHONY, and ERIKSEN, CHARLES W. "Some Social and Cultural Factors Determining Relations Between Authoritarianism and Measures of Neuroticism." *J Consult Psychol* 21:155–9 Ap '57. *
11. DAVIDS, ANTHONY, and PILDNER, HENRY, JR. "Comparison of Direct and Projective Methods of Personality Assessment Under Different Conditions of Motivation." *Psychol Monogr* 72(11):1–30 '58. * (PA 33:9937)
12. BROWN, D. G. "Psychosomatic Correlates in Contact Dermatitis: A Pilot Study." *J Psychosom Res* 4:132–9 D '59. * (PA 34:8214)
13. PRENTICE, NORMAN M. "Ethnic Attitudes, Neuroticism, and Culture." *J Social Psychol* 54:75–82 Je '61. * (PA 36:2HF75P)

[221]

*★**Psychotic Inpatient Profile.** Mental patients; 1961–68; PIP; ratings by nurses and psychiatric

aides; revision of still-in-print *Psychotic Reaction Profile* (see 221A); 12 scores: excitement, hostile belligerence, paranoid projection, anxious depression, retardation, seclusiveness, care needed, psychotic disorganization, grandiosity, perceptual disorganization, depressive mood, disorientation; 10 of the scores are "essentially equivalent" to the 10 scores obtained on the *Inpatient Multidimensional Psychiatric Scale* (see 124), the 2 new scores are seclusiveness and care needed; 1 form ('68, 6 pages); manual ('68, 15 pages plus test); $8.50 per 25 tests and manual; $7.50 per 25 tests; $2.75 per manual; postpaid; [10] minutes; Maurice Lorr and Norris D. Vestre; Western Psychological Services. *

For information regarding a review and references for the first edition, see 221A.

[221A]

The Psychotic Reaction Profile: An Inventory of Patient Behavior for Use by Hospital Personnel. Mental patients; 1961; PRP; for revised edition, see 221; ratings by nurses or psychiatric aides; 4 scores: withdrawal, thinking disorganization, paranoid belligerence, agitated depression; 1 form (4 pages); manual (8 pages plus test); $6.50 per 25 tests; 75¢ per manual; postpaid; (10–15) minutes; Maurice Lorr, James P. O'Connor (test), and John W. Stafford (test); Western Psychological Services. *

For a review by Wilson H. Guertin, see 6:167 (4 references).

REFERENCES

1–4. See 6:167.
5. CASEY, J. F. "VA Cooperative Chemotherapy Studies in Psychiatry, Project 4: 3, Clinical Findings," pp. 15–22. In *Transactions of the Fifth Research Conference on Cooperative Chemotherapy Studies in Psychiatry and Research Approaches to Mental Illness.* Washington, D.C.: Veterans Administration, 1961. Pp. xxxv, 375. *
6. GORHAM, DONALD R. "VA Cooperative Chemotherapy Studies in Psychiatry: 5, A Report on the Attitude Measures Used in Project 4," pp. 28–31. In *Transactions of the Fifth Research Conference on Cooperative Chemotherapy Studies in Psychiatry and Research Approaches to Mental Illness.* Washington, D.C.: Veterans Administration, 1961. Pp. xxxv, 375. *
7. KLETT, C. JAMES. "Appendix A, VA Cooperative Studies of Chemotherapy in Psychiatry, Project Four; Statistical Supplement," pp. 309–31. In *Transactions of the Fifth Research Conference on Cooperative Chemotherapy Studies in Psychiatry and Research Approaches to Mental Illness.* Washington, D.C.: Veterans Administration, 1961. Pp. xxxv, 375. *
8. LASKY, JULIAN J. "VA Cooperative Chemotherapy Studies in Psychiatry, Project 4: 2, Research Design and Description of the Sample," pp. 10–4. In *Transactions of the Fifth Research Conference on Cooperative Chemotherapy Studies in Psychiatry and Research Approaches to Mental Illness.* Washington, D. C.: Veterans Administration, 1961. Pp. xxxv, 375. *
9. LORR, MAURICE. "Elements Central to Schizophrenia," pp. 217–20. In *Transactions of the Fifth Research Conference on Cooperative Chemotherapy Studies in Psychiatry and Research Approaches to Mental Illness.* Washington, D.C.: Veterans Administration, 1961. Pp. xxxv, 375. *
10. KURLAND, ALBERT A.; MICHAUX, MARY H.; HANLON, THOMAS E.; OTA, KAY Y.; and SIMOPOULOS, ARIS M. "The Comparative Effectiveness of Six Phenothiazine Compounds, Phenobarbital and Inert Placebo in the Treatment of Acutely Ill Patients: Personality Dimensions." *J Nerv & Mental Dis* 134:48–60 Ja '62. * (*PA* 38:6185)
11. CAFFEY, EUGENE M., JR.; DIAMOND, LEON S.; FRANK, THOMAS V.; GRASBERGER, JOSEPH C.; HERMAN, LOUIS; KLETT, C. JAMES; and ROTHSTEIN, CHARLES. "Discontinuation or Reduction of Chemotherapy in Chronic Schizophrenics." *J Chronic Dis* 17:347–58 Ap '64. * (*PA* 39:9583)
12. LEE, ROBERT EDWARD. *An Investigation of Relationships Between Patient Self Perception and Hospital Ward Behavior.* Doctor's thesis, University of Minnesota (Minneapolis, Minn.), 1964. (*DA* 25:2051)
13. LORR, MAURICE; KLETT, C. JAMES; and McNAIR, DOUGLAS M. "Ward-Observable Psychotic Behavior Syndromes." *Ed & Psychol Meas* 24:291–300 su '64. * (*PA* 39:3188)
14. KLETT, WILLIAM G. "An Investigation Into the Effect of Historically Based Inferences in Group Psychotherapy on the Behavior of Withdrawn Psychiatric Patients." *Newsl Res Psychol* 7:44–6 My '65. *
15. PETERS, PHYLLIS G. *A Study of Clinical Judgment: Prediction of Patient Behavior From Projective, Self-Rating and Behavior Rating Instruments.* Doctor's thesis, Northwestern University (Evanston, Ill.), 1965. (*DA* 26:3489)
16. LORR, MAURICE. Chap. 9, "Ward Behavior Types," pp. 195–208. In his *Exploration in Typing Psychotics.* London: Pergamon Press Ltd., 1966. Pp. viii, 241. *
17. LORR, MAURICE, and CAVE, RICHARD L. "The Equivalence of Psychotic Syndromes Across Two Media." *Multiv Behav Res* 1::189–95 Ap '66. * (*PA* 41:1756)
18. LYERLY, SAMUEL B., and ABBOTT, PRESTON S. "Psychotic Reaction Profile," pp. 60–2. In their *Handbook of Psychiatric Rating Scales (1950–1964).* Public Health Service Publication No. 1495. Washington, D.C.: United States Government Printing Office, 1966. Pp. v, 69. *
19. VESTRE, NORRIS D. "Validity Data on the Psychotic Reaction Profile." *J Consult Psychol* 30:84–5 F '66. * (*PA* 40:4378)
20. GERBER, IRWIN. "Practitioners' Perceptions of Mental Patients' Psychotic and Nonpsychotic Behavioral Characteristics." *J General Psychol* 77:5–10 Jl '67. * (*PA* 41:13861)
21. GERBER, IRWIN. "Practitioners' Perceptual Consistency of Mental Patients' Behavioral Characteristics." *J Social Psychol* 72:129–34 Je '67. * (*PA* 41:11950)
22. MEFFERD, ROY B., JR. "Technique for Minimizing the Instrumental Factor." *Multiv Behav Res* 3:339–54 Jl '68. * (*PA* 43:3299)

[222]

★**Pupil Behavior Inventory.** Grades 7–12; 1966; PBI; a rating scale; 5 scores: classroom conduct, academic motivation, socio-emotional, teacher dependence, personal behavior; 1 form (1 page); manual (70 pages plus set of scoring stencils); $2.50 per 100 forms; $2.15 per manual; $2.15 per specimen set; postage extra; (5–10) minutes; Robert D. Vinter, Rosemary C. Sarri, Darrel J. Vorwaller, and Walter E. Schafer; Campus Publishers. *

[223]

The Purdue Master Attitude Scales. Grades 7–16; 1934–60; PMAS; series title for the first 8 scales was formerly listed as *Generalized Attitude Scales*; a–h have space for insertion of any 5 attitude variables; Forms A, B, ('60, 1 page, the 17 items of each scale were selected from the 37- to 50-item Forms A and B copyrighted in 1934–36); 9 scales; manual ('60, 7 pages); no data on reliability of current forms; $1 per 25 copies of any one scale, postage extra; 50¢ per specimen set of any one scale; $1 per complete specimen set; postpaid; (5–10) minutes per attitude variable; H. H. Remmers (editor and manual author); University Book Store. *

a) A SCALE TO MEASURE ATTITUDE TOWARD ANY SCHOOL SUBJECT. 1934–60; original forms by Ella B. Silance.

b) A SCALE FOR MEASURING ATTITUDES TOWARD ANY VOCATION. 1934–60; original forms by Harold E. Miller.

c) A SCALE FOR MEASURING ATTITUDE TOWARD ANY INSTITUTION. 1934–60; original forms by Ida B. Kelley.

d) A SCALE FOR MEASURING ATTITUDE TOWARD ANY DEFINED GROUP. 1934–60; revision of *A Scale for Measuring Attitude Toward Races and Nationalities;* original forms by H. H. Grice.

e) A SCALE FOR MEASURING ATTITUDES TOWARD ANY PROPOSED SOCIAL ACTION. 1935–60; original forms by Dorothy M. Thomas.

f) A SCALE FOR MEASURING ATTITUDES TOWARD ANY PRACTICE. 1934–60; original forms by H. W. Bues.

g) A SCALE FOR MEASURING ATTITUDE TOWARD ANY HOME-MAKING ACTIVITY. 1934–60; original forms by Beatrix Kellar.

h) A SCALE FOR MEASURING INDIVIDUAL AND GROUP "MORALE." 1936–60; original forms by Laurence Whisler.

i) HIGH SCHOOL ATTITUDE SCALE. 1935–60; original forms by F. H. Gillespie.

For a review by Donald T. Campbell, see 6:168; for reviews by Donald T. Campbell and Kenneth E. Clark of the original forms, see 4:46 (37 references); for reviews by W. D. Commins and Theodore Newcomb, see 2:1202 (9 references); for a review by Stephen M. Corey, see 1:897; for a review by Lee J. Cronbach of the earlier form of the High School Attitude Scale, see 3:46; for related book reviews not excerpted in this volume, consult the 2nd (B1050) MMY.

REFERENCES

1–9. See 2:1202.
10–46. See 4:46.
47. SNOW, ALEXANDRA, and COHEN, LOIS K. "Student Attitudes Toward the Sciences and the Humanities." *J Ed Res* 61:456–61 Jl–Ag '68. *

NAME INDEX

Bateman, R. M.: 44
Bues, H. W.: 12
Campbell, D. T.: *rev,* 4:46, 6:168
Clark, K. E.: *rev,* 4:46
Clouse, V. R.: 36
Cohen, L. K.: 47
Commins, W. D.: *rev,* 2:1202
Corey, S. M.: *rev,* 1:897
Cronbach, L. J.: *rev,* 3:46
Davidoff, M. D.: 45
Dimmitt, M.: 27–8
Dunlap, J. W.: 9, 37
Grice, H. H.: 13–4
Hadley, E.: 33
Hadley, J. E.: 29
Hancock, J.: 30
Hancock, J. W.: 38
Hoshaw, L. D.: 24, 31
Huffman, E. S.: 39
Jensen, J. A.: 46
Karslake, R. H.: 43
Kellar, B.: 15–6
Kelley, I. B.: 17–8

Kroll, A.: 9, 37
Likert, R.: 1
Miller, F. D.: 19–20
Miller, H. E.: 10, 21
Newcomb, T.: *rev,* 2:1202
Paterson, D. G.: 7
Prothro, E. T.: 46
Ramseyer, L. L.: *exc, consult* 2:B1050
Remmers, H. H.: 2–6, 8, 22–3, 32–3, 40
Schmidt, A. G.: *exc, consult* 2:B1050
Schneidler, G. G.: 7
Sigerfoos, C. C.: 25, 34
Silance, E. B.: 3, 11, 23
Snow, A.: 47
Thomas, D. M.: 26
Thomas-Baines, D. M.: 35
Tussing, L.: 41
Whisler, L.: 6
Whisler, L. D.: 40, 42
Williamson, E. G.: 7

[224]

The Purdue Rating Scale for Administrators and Executives. Administrators and executives; 1950–51; 36 ratings plus factor scores; 1 form ('50, 2 pages); 3 profile folders ('51, 4 pages) called Report Forms A, B, C; $2.50 per 25 sets of scale and a report form; 75¢ per specimen set; postage extra; (15–20) minutes; H. H. Remmers and R. L. Hobson; University Book Store, West Lafayette, Ind. *
a) REPORT FORM A. College administrators; 3 factor scores: fairness to subordinates, administrative achievement, democratic orientation.
b) REPORT FORM B. Business executives; 2 factor scores: social responsibility for subordinates and society, executive achievement.
c) REPORT FORM C. School administrators.
For reviews by John P. Foley, Jr. and Herbert A. Tonne, see 5:101 (1 reference); for a review by Kenneth L. Heaton, see 4:83 (7 references).

[225]

★**The Q-Tags Test of Personality.** Ages 6 and over, ages 12 and over; 1967–69; QTTP; individual; 2 forms; mimeographed manual ['69, 27 pages]; directions sheet ('69, 1 page); record form ('69, 1 page); norms consist of means and standard deviations; Can $4 per set of testing materials and 25 record forms; $1.50 per 25 record forms; postage extra; (60–80) minutes in 2 sessions; Arthur G. Storey and Louis I. Masson (manual); Institute of Psychological Research, Inc. *
a) [BIOGRAPHICAL FORM.] Ages 6 and over; 13 scores: 6 factor scores (affective, assertive, effective, hostility, reverie, social) in each of 2 areas (he or she is, he or she should be), correlation of self and idealself; 2 parts labeled Forms h, s, ('67, 54 cards plus paradigm); norms for ages 6–12 only.
b) [AUTOBIOGRAPHICAL FORM.] Ages 12 and over; 13 scores: 6 factor scores (same as *a* above) in each of

2 areas (I am, I wish I were), correlation of self and idealself; 2 parts labeled Forms i, w, ('67, 54 cards plus paradigm).

REFERENCES

1. STOREY, ARTHUR G. "Acceleration, Deceleration and Self Concepts." *Alberta J Ed Res* 13:135–42 Je '67. * (PA 41:15783)
2. DOOLEY, LILY BERNADETTE. *Self Concept of English and French-Speaking High School Canadians: A Comparative Study.* Master's thesis, University of Calgary (Calgary, Alta., Canada), 1968.
3. MASSON, L. I., and GOUGH, JOHN W. "Self-Concept of Adolescents in a Junior Academic Vocational School and in a Regular Junior High School." *Can Counsellor* 2:102–8 Ap '68. *
4. SAINTY, GEOFFREY EDWARD. *Some Predictors of Success in a Course for Academic Upgrading of Adults at a Canadian Vocational Training Centre.* Master's thesis, University of Calgary (Calgary, Alta, Canada), 1968.
5. STOREY, ARTHUR G., and CLARK, RONALD B. "The Self-Image and Wish Patterns of the Underachiever." *McGill J Ed* 3:56–62 sp '68. *

[226]

Rating Scale for Pupil Adjustment. Grades 3–9; 1950–53; RSPA; 1 form ('53, 2 pages); manual ('53, 4 pages); $1.20 per 20 scales; 10¢ per manual; postage extra; specimen set not available; [10] minutes; [Gwen Andrew, Samuel W. Hartwell, Max L. Hutt, and Ralph E. Walton]; Science Research Associates, Inc. *
For reviews by William E. Henry and Morris Krugman, see 5:102.

REFERENCES

1. SEMLER, IRA JACKSON. *Relationship Among Various Measures of Pupil Adjustment.* Doctor's thesis, State University of Iowa (Iowa City, Iowa), 1957. (DA 17:2923)
2. SEMLER, IRA J. "Relationships Among Several Measures of Pupil Adjustment." *J Ed Psychol* 51:60–4 Ap '60. * (PA 35:2741)
3. JACKSON, VIOLET BURDEN. *Successful and Unsuccessful Elementary School Children: A Study of Some of the Factors That Contribute to School Success.* Doctor's thesis, Ohio State University (Columbus, Ohio), 1962. (DA 24:143)
4. KENNEDY, DANIEL ARNOLD. *A Study of the Academic Achievement of Fourth Grade Boys Relative to Four Measures of Emotional Adjustment.* Doctor's thesis, University of Oregon (Eugene, Ore.), 1965. (DA 26:5869)

[227]

★**Rating Scales of Vocational Values, Vocational Interests and Vocational Aptitudes.** Grades 8–16 and adults; 1966; VIA; 3 scales for obtaining self ratings of aptitudes, interests, and values with regard to various vocational activities; 20 scores for each of the 3 scales: administrative, animal, artistic, athletic, clerical, commercial, computational, creative, dramatic, executive, literary, manual, mechanical, musical, organizing, plant, scholastic, scientific, service, socializing; 1 form (2 pages); manual (8 pages); profile (1 page); no adult norms; $3.50 per 25 tests; $3 per 25 profile sheets; 50¢ per manual; $1.50 per specimen set; postage extra; scoring service, 45¢ or less per scale; (45–50) minutes; George D. Demos and Bruce Grant; Educational and Industrial Testing Service. *
a) RATING SCALE OF VOCATIONAL APTITUDES.
b) RATING SCALE OF VOCATIONAL INTERESTS.
c) RATING SCALE OF VOCATIONAL VALUES.

[228–9]

★**The Richardson Emergency Psychodiagnostic Summary.** Mental patients; 1966; REP; checklist for making immediate reports of findings, impressions, and suggestions following diagnostic testing; 1 form (4 pages); manual (4 pages plus summary form); $6.50 per 25 summary forms; $1.50 per manual; postpaid; O. Roderick Richardson; Western Psychological Services. *

[230]

★**Russell Sage Social Relations Test.** Classroom groups in grades 3–6; [1956–59]; RSSRT; for research use only; group problem solving skills; 13 scores: planning stage (participation, communication, ideas, plan, involvement, autonomy, average), operations stage (involvement, atmosphere, activity, success, average), total; 1 form ['56]; manual ['56, 34 pages]; technical report ('59, 15 pages, reprint of 3 below); no data on reliability and validity; no norms; $2 per set of technical report and manual; postage extra; set of blocks and scoring profile sheets must be provided locally; [90] minutes; Dora E. Damrin; Educational Testing Service. *

REFERENCES

1. DAMRIN, DORA E. "The Russell Sage Social Relations Test: A Measure of Group Problem-Solving Skills in Elementary School Children." Abstract. *Yearb Nat Council Meas Used Ed* 12(pt 2):5 '55. *
2. DAMRIN, DORA E. "The Russell Sage Social Relations Test: A Measure of Group Problem-Solving Skills in Elementary School Children." *Proc Inv Conf Testing Probl* 1954: 75–84; discussion, 91–5 '55. * (*PA* 30:1615)
3. DAMRIN, DORA E. "The Russell Sage Social Relations Test: A Technique for Measuring Group Problem Solving Skills in Elementary School Children." *J Exp Ed* 28:85–99 S '59. * (*PA* 34:7538)

[231]

Rutgers Social Attribute Inventory. Adults; 1959; RSAI; perception of others (either real persons or generalized classes); 24 trait ratings: good natured-stubborn, intelligent-unintelligent, tense-relaxed, strong-weak, childish-mature, old fashioned-modern, dominating-submissive, thin-fat, adventurous-cautious, lazy-ambitious, optimistic-pessimistic, masculine-feminine, young-old, responsible-irresponsible, crude-refined, tall-short, suspicious-trusting, talkative-quiet, thrifty-wasteful, dependent-self reliant, unsympathetic-sympathetic, good looking-plain, conventional-unconventional, rich-poor; 1 form (1 page); manual (4 pages); no data on reliability; no norms; $2 per 25 tests; $2 per specimen set (must be purchased to obtain manual); cash orders postpaid; (30–60) minutes; William D. Wells; Psychometric Affiliates. *

For reviews by David B. Orr and John Pierce-Jones, see 6:169.

[232]

SAQS Chicago Q Sort. College and adults; 1956–57; SAQS; 1 form ['57, sheet of 50 adjectives to make 50 "cards" when cut]; manual ('56, 2 pages); profile ('57, 1 page); recording sheet ('56, 1 page); $2 per 25 tests; $2 per 25 profiles; $2 per 25 recording sheets; $3 per specimen set; cash orders postpaid; (15–20) minutes; Raymond Corsini; Psychometric Affiliates. *

For reviews by William Stephenson and Clifford H. Swensen, Jr., see 5:103 (2 references).

REFERENCES

1–2. See 5:103.
3. FOULKES, DAVID, and HEAXT, SUSAN. "Concept Attainment and Self Concept." *Psychol Rep* 11:399–402 O '62. * (*PA* 37:7625)
4. VAN DUSEN, WILSON, and RECTOR, WILLIAM. "A Q Sort Study of the Ideal Administrator." *J Clin Psychol* 19:244 Ap '63. * (*PA* 39:4845)

[232A]

★**STS Junior Inventory.** Grades 4–8; 1957–68; problems checklist; revision of the *SRA Junior Inventory* with the deletion of items construed by some as invading the personal privacy of the student and his family; Form G ('68, 7 pages); no manual; no data on reliability and validity; no norms; separate answer sheets (Digitek scorable) may be used; no instruc-

tions on the use of separate answer sheets; 17¢ per test; 10¢ per answer sheet; postage extra; scoring service, $7.50 and over per 100 tests; (35–40) minutes; H. H. Remmers and Robert H. Bauernfeind; Scholastic Testing Service, Inc. *

For a review by Warren R. Baller of the original edition, see 5:104 (2 excerpts); for a review by Dwight L. Arnold, see 4:90.

REFERENCES

1. BOMSE, GERARD C. *A Study to Determine the Degree of Similarity of Personality Problem Awareness Between Normal and Mentally Retarded Children.* Doctor's thesis, New York University (New York, N.Y.), 1957. (*DA* 18:1844)
2. BILLINGER, LOIS WHITE. *Relation of Empathy, Self Image, and Social Acceptance Among Gifted and Average Children of the Sixth Grade.* Doctor's thesis, University of Connecticut (Storrs, Conn.), 1959. (*DA* 20:1222)
3. CLARKE, H. HARRISON, and GREENE, WALTER H. "Relationships Between Personal-Social Measures Applied to 10-Year-Old Boys." *Res Q* 34:288–98 O '63. * (*PA* 38:5727)
4. HOWARD, DOUGLAS P. "The Needs and Problems of Socially Disadvantaged Children as Perceived by Students and Teachers." *Excep Children* 34:327–35 Ja '68. * (*PA* 42:9410)

[233]

★**STS Youth Inventory.** Grades 7–12; 1956–67; problems checklist; revision of the *SRA Youth Inventory* with the deletion of items construed by some as invading the personal privacy of the student and his family; Form G ('67, 7 pages); no manual; no data on reliability and validity; no norms; separate answer sheets (Digitek scorable) may be used; no instructions on the use of separate answer sheets; 17¢ per test; 10¢ per answer sheet; postage extra; scoring service, $7.50 and over per 100 tests; Spanish edition available; (30–35) minutes; H. H. Remmers and Benjamin Shimberg; Scholastic Testing Service, Inc. *

For a review by Forrest L. Vance of the original edition, see 6:170 (12 references, 1 excerpt); see also 5:105 (12 references); for reviews by Kenneth E. Clark and Frank S. Freeman, see 4:91 (7 references).

REFERENCES

1–7. See 4:91.
8–19. See 5:105.
20–31. See 6:170.
32. CHILES, DONNA R. "An Identification of the Characteristics of the Pre-Delinquent." *Ill Sch Res* 2:38–43 O '65. *
33. PAM, ELEANOR. *Ego Strength, Consistency in Problem Perception and Expectation of Counseling Assistance: A Study in Counselor Role Expectancy.* Doctor's thesis, New York University (New York, N.Y.), 1968. (*DA* 29:462A)

NAME INDEX

Barragan, M. F.: 21
Beckwith, A. V.: 22
Brown, C. P.: 8
Chiles, D. R.: 32
Clark, K. E.: *rev*, 4:91
Clarke, H. H.: 31
Coombs, R. W.: 15
de Lopategui, M. N.: 17
Drucker, A. J.: 9–10
Eugene, C. J.: 2
Fick, R. L.: 11
Freeman, F. S.: *rev*, 4:91
Greene, J. E.: 12
Greene, W. H.: 31
Hackett, C. G.: 7
Hudgins, B. B.: 25
Jacobs, R.: 5
Keislar, E. R.: 13
Kulkarni, S. S.: 28
Meyer, J. K.: 6

Milburn, D. J.: 29
Musselman, D. L.: 23
Nixon, W. W.: 20
Overn, A. V.: 2
Paisios, J. P.: 16
Pam, E.: 33
Pauley, B.: 19
Remmers, H. H.: 7, 9–10, 16, 30
Rice, D. L.: 24
Shimberg, B.: 1, 3–4
Siegel, L.: *exc*, 6:170
Smith, L. M.: 25
Spivak, M. L.: 18
Taliana, L. E.: 26
Vance, F. L.: *rev*, 6:170
Wardlow, M. E.: 12
Weimer, L. B.: 14
Weisbrodt, J. A.: 27

[234]

★**Scale of Socio-Egocentrism.** Grades 7–16; 1964; SSE; also called *S-E Scale;* 8 scores: 7 relationship scores (self, primary, peer group, boy-girl, secondary authority, impersonal, generalized), total; 1 form (6 pages); manual (3 pages); no data on reliability; no norms; $6.25 per 25 tests; 25¢ per single copy; $1 per manual; postpaid; (15–20) minutes; James S. Peters, II; Peters & Associates. *

[235]

*A Scale to Measure Attitudes Toward Disabled Persons. Disabled and nondisabled adults; 1957–66; ATDP; title on test is *ATDP Scale;* Forms O ('57, 1 page), A, B, ('64, 2 pages); revised manual ('66, 170 pages plus tests, see *10* below); manual free; tests may be reproduced locally; (10) minutes for Form O, [20] minutes for Forms A and B; Harold E. Yuker, J. R. Block, and Janet H. Younng; Human Resources Center. *

REFERENCES

1. BELL, A. HOWARD. "Attitudes of Selected Rehabilitation Workers and Other Hospital Employees Toward the Physically Disabled." *Psychol Rep* 10:183–6 F '62. * (*PA* 37:1589)
2. BLOCK, JULES RICHARD. *Motivation, Satisfaction and Performance of Handicapped Workers.* Doctor's thesis, New York University (New York, N.Y.), 1962. (*DA* 24:819)
3. KNITTEL, MARVIN GLENN. *A Comparison of Attitudes Toward the Disabled Between Subjects Who Had a Phsysically Disabled Sibling and Subjects Who Did Not Have a Physically Disabled Sibling.* Doctor's thesis, State University of South Dakota (Vermillion, S.D.), 1963. (*DA* 24:4084)
4. FREED, EARL X. "Opinions of Psychiatric Hospital Personnel and College Students Toward Alcoholism, Mental Illness, and Physical Disability: An Exploratory Study." *Psychol Rep* 15:615–8 O '64. * (*PA* 39:4782)
5. SILLER, JEROME, and CHIPMAN, ABRAM. "Factorial Structure and Correlates of the Attitudes Toward Disabled Persons Scale." *Ed & Psychol Meas* 24:831–40 w '64. * (*PA* 39:7873)
6. ANDERSON, HARRY E., JR., and BARRY, JOHN R. "Occupational Choices in Selected Health Professions." *Personnel & Guid J* 44:177–84 O '65. * (*PA* 40:3419)
7. BATES, ROBERT E.; ROTHAUS, PAUL; and VINEBERG, SHALOM E. "Limitations of the Term 'Disabled' in Attitude Measurement." *Newsl Res Psychol* 7:28–9 My '65. *
8. GENSKOW, JACK K., and MAGLIONE, FRANK D. "Familiarity, Dogmatism, and Reported Student Attitudes Toward the Disabled." *J Social Psychol* 67:329–41 D '65. * (*PA* 40:5363)
9. MEISSNER, ANN LORING WOODWORTH. *Adolescent Attitudes Toward Self and Toward Disabled People.* Doctor's thesis, University of Wisconsin (Madison, Wis.), 1965. (*DA* 26:5572)
10. YUKER, HAROLD E.; BLOCK, J. R.; YOUNNG, JANET H. *The Measurement of Attitudes Toward Disabled Persons.* Human Resources Study No. 7. Albertson, N.Y.: Human Resources Center, 1966. Pp. x, 170. * (*PA* 41:10814)
11. BELL, A. HOWARD. "Measure for Adjustment of the Physically Disabled." *Psychol Rep* 21:773–8 D '67. * (*PA* 42:7574)
12. DOWNES, SHELDON CANFIELD. *Attitudes Toward the Physically Disabled as Indicated in Rehabilitation and Non-Rehabilitation Groups.* Doctor's thesis, Pennsylvania State University (University Park, Pa.), 1967. (*DA* 29:120A)
13. FEINBERG, LAWRENCE B. "Social Desirability and Attitudes Toward the Disabled." *Personnel & Guid J* 46:375–81 D '67. *
14. WARR, PETER B.; FAUST, JUDITH; and HARRISON, GODFREY J. "A British Ethnocentrism Scale." *Brit J Social & Clin Psychol* 6:267–77 D '67. * (*PA* 42:6399)

[236]

*School Interest Inventory. Grades 7–12; 1966, c1959–66; SII; revision of *Life Adjustment Scale, Number 1* ('58); for identifying potential dropouts; 1 form (4 pages); manual (19 pages); $12 per 100 MRC test-answer booklets; 90¢ per set of hand scoring stencils; 48¢ per manual; 90¢ per specimen set; postage extra; scoring service, 33¢ per test; (20–30) minutes; William C. Cottle; Houghton Mifflin Co. *

REFERENCES

1. HAVENS, N. H. *A Study of the Answers, One Year in Advance, to the Life Adjustment Scale by Students Who Drop Out or Remain in Four Kansas High Schools.* Master's thesis, University of Kansas (Lawrence, Kan.), 1955.
2. HERRMAN, W. L. *Partial Validation of a Drop-Out Scale.* Master's thesis, University of Kansas (Lawrence, Kan.), 1957.
3. EPPS, MARGARET W., and COTTLE, WILLIAM C. "Further Validation of a Dropout Scale." *Voc Guid Q* 7:90–3 w '58. *
4. HERRMAN, LYNDON, and COTTLE, WILLIAM C. "An Inventory to Identify High School Dropouts." *Voc Guid Q* 6:122–3 sp '58. *
5. COTTLE, W. C. "The School Interest Inventory." *Psychol Rep* 9:66 Ag '61. *
6. COTTLE, WILLIAM C. "Dropout, Delinquent and Other Scales of the School Interest Inventory." *Yearb Nat Council Meas Ed* 19:94–6 '62. *
7. DAS, AJIT KUMAR. *The Effect of Counseling on the Vocational Maturity of a Group of Potential Drop-Outs From*

High School. Doctor's thesis, State University of Iowa (Iowa City, Iowa), 1962. (*DA* 23:2788)
8. CHILDERS, ROBERT DEWEY, SR. *The Identification of Potential School Dropouts by Discriminant Analysis.* Doctor's thesis, University of Georgia (Athens, Ga.), 1965. (*DA* 26:6506)
9. O'SHEA, ARTHUR JOSEPH. *Differences in Certain Non-Intellective Factors Between Academically Bright Junior High School Male High and Low Achievers.* Doctor's thesis, Boston College (Chestnut Hill, Mass.), 1967. (*DA* 28:3515A)

[237]

The School Inventory. High school; 1936; SI; attitudes toward teachers and school; 1 form (4 pages); manual (4 pages); tentative norms; author recommends use of local norms; $3.25 per 25 tests; 50¢ per scoring stencil and manual; 75¢ per specimen set; postage extra; (10–15) minutes; Hugh M. Bell; Consulting Psychologists Press, Inc. *

For a review by Ross W. Matteson, see 4:84 (3 references); for reviews by Robert G. Bernreuter and J. B. Maller, see 2:1252 (4 references); for related book reviews not excerpted in this volume, consult the 2nd (B842) and 1st (B309) MMY's.

REFERENCES

1–4. See 2:1252.
5–7. See 4:84.
8. WARDLOW, MARY E., and GREENE, JAMES E. "An Exploratory Sociometric Study of Peer Status Among Adolescent Girls." *Sociometry* 15:311–8 Ag–N '52. * (*PA* 27:7097)
9. SPEER, STANLEY CHARLES. *A Study of Dropouts Among Vocational High School Pupils With Respect to Attitude Toward School.* Doctor's thesis, University of Connecticut (Storrs, Conn.), 1964. (*DA* 25:4512)

[238]

The Science Research Temperament Scale. Grades 12–16 and adults; 1955; SRTS; test booklet title is *SRT Scale;* Form A (1 page); manual (5 pages); $2.50 per 25 tests; $1 per specimen set (must be purchased to obtain manual); cash orders postpaid; (10–30) minutes; William C. Kosinar; Psychometric Affiliates. *

For reviews by John D. Black and David R. Saunders, see 5:106 (1 reference).

REFERENCES

1. See 5:106.
2. MANSFIELD, NANCY S. *A Correlative Study of Creative Temperament.* Master's thesis, Illinois Institute of Technology (Chicago, Ill.), 1959.
3. KERR, WILLARD A., and ABRAMS, PETER. "Halstead Brain Impairment, Boldness, Creativity and Group Intelligence Measures." *J Clin Psychol* 18:115–8 Ap '62. * (*PA* 38:8458)
4. LOCKE, EDWIN A. "Some Correlates of Classroom and Out-of-Class Achievement in Gifted Science Students." *J Ed Psychol* 54:238–48 O '63. * (*PA* 38:4649)
5. KERR, WILLARD A., and MCGEHEE, EDWARD M. "Creative Temperament as Related to Aspects of Strategy and Intelligence." *J Social Psychol* 62:211–6 Ap '64. * (*PA* 39:5126)

[239]

Security-Insecurity Inventory. Grades 9–16 and adults; 1945–52; SII; title on test is *The S-I Inventory;* 1 form ('52, 4 pages); manual ('52, 11 pages); $3.25 per 25 tests; 50¢ per scoring stencil and manual; 75¢ per specimen set; postage extra; (15–25) minutes; A. H. Maslow, E. Birsh, I. Honigmann, F. McGrath, A. Plason, and M. Stein; Consulting Psychologists Press, Inc. *

For reviews by Nelson G. Hanawalt and Harold Webster, see 5:107 (10 references).

REFERENCES

1–10. See 5:107.
11. GROSS, HERBERT WILLIAM. *The Relationship Between Insecurity, Self-Acceptance, Other-Direction and Conformity Under Conditions of Differential Social Pressure.* Doctor's thesis, University of Buffalo (Buffalo, N.Y.), 1959. (*DA* 20:395)
12. MATHUR, KRISHNA. "Relationship of Socio-Economic Status to Personality Adjustment Among the High School Boys and Girls at Aligarh." *Indian Psychol B* 4:30–1 Ja '59. *

13. PYRON, BERNARD. "An Attempt to Test the Theory of Psychological Development." *Psychol Rep* 5:685–98 D '59. * (*PA* 34:4932)

14. KHALIQUE, NAZRE. "A Study of Insecurity Feeling and Anxiety in Step Children and Non-Step Children." *J Psychol Res* 5:114–5 S '61. * (*PA* 36:5FG14K)

15. STEWART, HORACE F., JR., *A Study of the Relationship Between Certain Personality Measures and Hallucinoidal Visual Imagery.* Doctor's thesis, University of Florida (Gainesville, Fla.), 1962. (*DA* 24:827)

16. HANAWALT, NELSON G. "Feelings of Security and of Self-Esteem in Relation to Religious Belief." *J Social Psychol* 59:347–53 Ap '63. * (*PA* 38:744)

17. WILLNER, ERIC. *The Adjustment of Jewish All-Day School Pupils Compared to That of Public School Pupils Attending Afternoon Hebrew Schools: As Determined by the Mooney Problem Check List, a Check List of "Problems Related to Religion," and an Adaptation of the Maslow S-I Inventory.* Doctor's thesis, New York University (New York, N.Y.), 1963. (*DA* 24:2794)

18. CHAMBERS, J. A. "Relative Personality and Biographical Factors to Scientific Creativity." *Psychol Monogr* 78(7):1–20 '64. * (*PA* 39:5113)

19. CHAMBERS, JACK ALLEN. *Relating Personality and Biographical Factors to Scientific Creativity.* Doctor's thesis, Michigan State University (East Lansing, Mich.), 1964. (*DA* 26:1762)

20. RATH, R. "Attitudinal Direction Study-One Measurement." *J Madras Univ* 36:80–98 Jl '64 and Ja '65. *

21. SUTHERLAND, BEVERLY V., and SPILKA, BERNARD. "Social Desirability, Item-Response Time, and Item Significance." *J Consult Psychol* 28:447–51 O '64. * (*PA* 39:5161)

22. MATHIS, JAMES OTTO. *Modes of Resolving Motor Conflict Situations, Certain Personality Variables, and Scholastic Achievement.* Doctor's thesis, North Texas State University (Denton, Tex.), 1965. (*DA* 26:3759)

23. DICKEY, LOIS EDITH. *Projection of the Self Through Judgments of Clothed-Figures and Its Relation to Self-Esteem, Security-Insecurity and to Selected Clothing Behaviors.* Doctor's thesis, Pennsylvania State University (University Park, Pa.), 1967. (*DA* 29:1080B)

24. SINHA, AWADHESH K. "Psychology and Non-Psychology College Males: A Comparison on Some Personality Traits." *J Voc & Ed Guid* (Bombay) 13:13–7 F '67. *

25. KAUR, RAJENDRA. "Study of Emotional Security-Insecurity, Home Adiustment and Family Size." *Indian Psychol R* 4:144–6 Ja '68. *

26. VINCENT, JANE. "An Exploratory Factor Analysis Relating to the Construct Validity of Self-Concept Labels." *Ed & Psychol Meas* 28:915–21 au '68. * (*PA* 43:4039)

NAME INDEX

[240]

Self-Analysis Inventory. Adults; 1945; SAI; title on test is *"How'm I Doin'?";* interviewing aid for locating maladjustment in 37 problem areas; 1 form ('45, 12 pages); manual ('45, 16 pages); record blank (no date, 4 pages); no data on reliability and validity; $4.50 per 35 tests; 50¢ per specimen set; postpaid; (30–60) minutes; Harry J. Baker; Bobbs-Merrill Co., Inc. *

For reviews by Warren R. Baller and John W. Gustad, see 5:108.

[241]

Self-Interview Inventory. Adult males; 1958; SII; 10 scores: current complaints, emotional insecurity, guilt feelings, composite neurotic (based on first 3 scores), prepsychotic or psychotic, behavior problems, childhood illness, composite maladjustment (based on previous 3 scores), validation (lack of carefulness, lack of truthfulness); 1 form (4 pages); manual (4 pages); profile ['58, 1 page]; no data on reliability; separate answer sheets must be used; $3 per 25 tests; $2 per 25 answer sheets; $1 per 25 profiles; scoring stencil must be constructed locally; $1 per specimen set (must be purchased to obtain manual and key); cash orders postpaid; administration time not reported; H. Birnet Hovey; Psychometric Affiliates. *

For reviews by Andrew R. Baggaley and David T. Lykken, see 6:172 (1 reference).

[242]

★**Self-Rating Depression Scale.** Adults; 1965–66; SDS; intensity of depression regardless of diagnosis; booklet entitled *The Measurement of Depression* ('66, 16 pages) presents directions, key, norms, and 12 scales; no charge for test materials; a 22 minute 16mm. sound and color film on the scale's use is available on loan without charge from Lakeside Laboratories, Inc. (Milwaukee, Wis. 53201); Czech, Dutch, French, German, Italian, Japanese, Slovak, Spanish, and Swedish editions of the scale are available; (5) minutes; William W. K. Zung; the Author. *

REFERENCES

1. ZUNG, WILLIAM W. K.; RICHARDS, CAROLYN B.; and SHORT, MARVIN J. "Self-Rating Depression Scale in an Outpatient Clinic: Further Validation of the SDS." *Arch Gen Psychiatry* 13:508–15 D '65. * (*PA* 40:2144)

2. ZUNG, WILLIAM W. K. "A Self-Rating Depression Scale." *Arch Gen Psychiatry* 12:63–70 Ja '65. * (*PA* 39:7736)

3. HUMPHREY, MICHAEL. "Functional Impairment in Psychiatric Outpatients." *Brit J Psychiatry* 113:1141–51 O '67. * (*PA* 47:453)

4. MORGAN, WILLIAM PATRICK. *Selected Physiological and Psychomotor Correlates of Depression in Psychiatric Patients.* Doctor's thesis, University of Toledo (Toledo, Ohio), 1967. (*DA* 28:2086A)

5. ZUNG, WILLIAM W. K. "Depression in the Normal Aged." *Psychosomatics* 8:287–92 S-O '67. * (*PA* 42:2431)

6. ZUNG, WILLIAM W. K. "Factors Influencing the Self-Rating Depression Scale." *Arch Gen Psychiatry* 16:543–7 My '67. * (*PA* 41:10722)

7. MARONE, JOSEPH, and LUBIN, BERNARD. "Relationship Between Set 2 of the Depression Adjective Check Lists (DACL) and Zung Self-Rating Depression Scale (SDS)." *Psychol Rep* 22:333–4 F '68. * (*PA* 42:10596)

8. WEINGOLD, HAROLD P.; LACHIN, JOHN M.; BELL, A. HOWARD; and COXE, RAYMOND C. "Depression as a Symptom of Alcoholism: Search for a Phenomenon." *J Abn Psychol* 73:195–7 Je '68. * (*PA* 42:12388)

[243]

The Sherman Mental Impairment Test. Adults; 1955–57; SMIT; 2 scores: letter finding, reaction time; 1 form ['57, 12 design cards]; manual ('56, 9 pages); scoring booklet ('57, 4 pages); no data on reliability for reaction time score; young adult norms only; $6.50 per 25 tests; $3 per set of cards; $2 per manual; $10 per set of 25 tests, cards, and manual; postpaid; specimen set not available; (10) minutes; Murray H. Sherman; Western Psychological Services. *

For reviews by D. Russell Davis and William Schofield, see 5:110 (1 reference).

REFERENCES

1. See 5:110.

2. WECKOWICZ, T. E., and BLEWETT, D. B. "Size Constancy and Abstract Thinking in Schizophrenic Patients." *J Mental Sci* 105:909–34 O '59. * (*PA* 34:6402)

[244]

Shipley-Institute of Living Scale for Measuring Intellectual Impairment. Adults; 1939–46; SILS; formerly called *Shipley-Hartford Retreat Scale for Measuring Intellectual Impairment;* 4 scores: vocabulary, abstractions, total, conceptual quotient; 1 form ('39, 2 pages); manual ('46, c1940–46, 4 pages, identical with manual copyrighted in 1940 except for title); $6.50 per 50 tests; $1 per specimen set; postpaid; 20(25) minutes; Walter C. Shipley; distributed by Mrs. John H. Boyle. *

See 6:173 (13 references) and 5:111 (23 references); for reviews by E. J. G. Bradford, William A. Hunt, and Margaret Ives, see 3:95 (26 references).

REFERENCES

1–25. See 3:95.
26–48. See 5:111.
49–61. See 6:173.
62. FINK, J. H. *A Psychophysiological Comparison of Brittle and Stable Diabetics.* Doctor's thesis, University of California (Los Angeles, Calif.), 1960.
63. ILANIT, NATHAN. *Some Psychological Correlates of the Process-Reactive Concept of Schizophrenia.* Doctor's thesis, University of Southern California (Los Angeles, Calif.), 1961. (*DA* 21:3852)
64. FINK, JOSEPHINE H. "Personality Variables in Brittle and Stable Diabetics." *Newsl Res Psychol* 5:8–9 Ag '63. * (*PA* 38:8587)
65. MASON, CHARLES F., and GANZLER, HENRY. "Adult Age Norms for the Shipley Scale." *Newsl Res Psychol* 5:30 Ag '63. * (*PA* 38:8942)
66. GANZLER, HENRY. "Motivation as a Factor in the Psychological Deficit of Aging." *J Gerontol* 19:425–9 O '64. *
67. LEWINSOHN, PETER M., and NICHOLS, ROBERT C. "The Evaluation of Changes in Psychiatric Patients During and After Hospitalization." *J Clin Psychol* 20:272–9 Ap '64. * (*PA* 39:8200)
68. MASON, CHARLES F., and GANZLER, HENRY. "Adult Norms for the Shipley Institute of Living Scale and Hooper Visual Organization Test Based on Age and Education." *J Gerontol* 19:419–24 O '64. *
69. PALMER, JAMES O. "A Restandardization of Adolescent Norms for the Shipley-Hartford." *J Clin Psychol* 20:492–5 O '64. * (*PA* 39:12304)
70. McKEEVER, WALTER F.; MAY, PHILIP R. A.; and TUMA, A. HUSSAIN. "Prognosis in Schizophrenia: Prediction of Length of Hospitalization From Psychological Test Variables." *J Clin Psychol* 21:214–21 Ap '65. * (*PA* 39:12856)
71. PHILLIPS, JAMES E.; JACOBSON, NAOMI; and TURNER, WM. J. "Conceptual Thinking in Schizophrenics and Their Relatives." *Brit J Psychiatry* 111:823–9 S '65. * (*PA* 40:649)
72. PRADO, WILLIAM M., and CANNON, ROBERT C. "Shipley-Hartford and Wechsler-Bellevue Intellectual Functioning: A Selection Screening Approach." *Psychol Rep* 16:853–6 Je '65. * (*PA* 39:15260)
73. SIEGMAN, ARON WOLFE, and POPE, BENJAMIN. "Personality Variables Associated With Productivity and Verbal Influence in the Initial Interview." *Proc Ann Conv Am Psychol Assn* 73:273–4 '65. * (*PA* 39:15655)
74. STONE, LeROY A. "Recent (1962–1964) Psychiatric-Patient Validation Norms for the Shipley-Institute of Living Scale." *Psychol Rep* 16:417–8 Ap '65. * (*PA* 39:10154)
75. STONE, LeROY A. "Test-Retest Stability of the Shipley Institute of Living Scale." *J Clin Psychol* 21:432 O '65. * (*PA* 40:1763)
76. STONE, LeROY A., and CHAMBERS, ANDREW, JR. "The Distribution of Measured Adult Intelligence in a State Psychiatric Hospital Population." *Psychol* 2:27–9 F '65. * (*PA* 39:10216)
77. STONE, LeROY A., and RAMER, JOHN C. "Estimating WAIS IQ From Shipley Scale Scores: Another Cross-Validation." *J Clin Psychol* 21:297 Jl '65. * (*PA* 39:15276)
78. ABRAMS, STANLEY, and NATHANSON, IRA A. "Intellectual Deficit in Schizophrenia: Stable or Progressive." *Dis Nerv System* 27:115–7 F '66. *
79. COROTTO, LOREN V. "Effects of Age and Sex on the Shipley-Institute of Living Scale." Abstract. *J Consult Psychol* 30:179 Ap '66. * (*PA* 40:6636, title only)
80. MONROE, KENTON L. "Note on the Estimation of the WAIS Full Scale IQ." *J Clin Psychol* 22:79–81 Ja '66. * (*PA* 40:4217)
81. PRADO, WILLIAM M., and TAUB, DANIEL V. "Accurate Prediction of Individual Intellectual Functioning by the Shipley-Hartford." *J Clin Psychol* 22:294–6 Jl '66. * (*PA* 40:11153)
82. SHAW, DALE J. "The Reliability of the Shipley-Institute of Living Scale." *J Clin Psychol* 22:441 O '66. * (*PA* 41:2888)
83. ZELEN, SEYMOUR L.; FOX, JACK; GOULD, EDWARD; and OLSON, RAY W. "Sex-Contingent Differences Between Male and Female Alcoholics." *J Clin Psychol* 22:160–5 Ap '66. * (*PA* 40:7873)
84. FREED, EARL X. "Some Test Evidence of CNS Dysfunction in Psychiatric Patients Manifesting Alcoholism." *Newsl Res Psychol* 9:26–7 Ag '67. *
85. KRAUS, J.; CHALKER, SUZANNE; and MACINDOE, I. "Vocabulary and Chronological Age as Predictors of 'Abstraction' on the Shipley-Hartford Retreat Scale." *Austral J Psychol* 19:133–5 Ag '67. * (*PA* 42:2583)
86. KRAUSS, HERBERT H., and RUIZ, RENE A. "Anxiety and Temporal Perspective." *J Clin Psychol* 23:340–2 Jl '67. * (*PA* 41:15617)
87. LEWINSOHN, PETER M. "Factors Related to Improvement in Mental Hospital Patients." *J Consult Psychol* 31:588–94 D '67. * (*PA* 42:2642)
88. LEWINSOHN, PETER M., and NICHOLS, ROBERT C. "Dimensions of Change in Mental Hospital Patients." *J Clin Psychol* 23:498–503 O '67. * (*PA* 42:2624)
89. MALMQUIST, CARL P.; KIRESUK, THOMAS J.; and SPANO, ROBERT M. "Mothers With Multiple Illegitimacies." *Psychiatric Q* 41:339–54 Ap '67. * (*PA* 42:4189)
90. RUIZ, R. A., and KRAUSS, H. H. "Test-Retest Reliability and Practice Effect With the Shipley-Institute of Living Scale." *Psychol Rep* 20:1085–6 Je '67. * (*PA* 41:14452)
91. BARRY, JOHN R.; DUNTEMAN, GEORGE H.; and WEBB, MARVIN W. "Personality and Motivation in Rehabilitation." *J Counsel Psychol* 15:237–44 My '68. * (*PA* 42:12535)
92. BARTZ, WAYNE R. "Relationship of WAIS, BETA and Shipley-Hartford Scores." *Psychol Rep* 22:676 Ap '68. * (*PA* 42:12089)
93. KISH, GEORGE B., and BALL, MARGARET E. "Low Educational Level as One Factor Producing a Verbal-Abstract Disparity on the Shipley Institute of Living Scale." *Newsl Res Psychol* 10:19–22 Ag '68. *
94. MATHAE, DAVID E. "Norms and Correlations of Scores From the Modified Alpha Examination Form 9 and the Shipley Institute of Living Scale for Hospitalized Female Neuropsychiatric Patients." *Newsl Res Psychol* 10:22–6 My '68. *
95. PRADO, WILLIAM M. "Shipley-Hartford Test as a Screening Instrument for Nursing School Applicants." *Newsl Res Psychol* 10:43–4 F '68. *
96. RITCHEY, RONALD E. "Evaluation of Schizophrenics on a Ward Halfway House Program." *Proc Ann Conv Am Psychol Assn* 76:499–500 '68. * (*PA* 43:1146, title only)
97. SCHALOCK, ROBERT L., and WAHLER, H. J. "Changes in Shipley-Hartford Scores With Five Repeated Test Administrations: Statistical Conventions vs. Behavioral Evidence." *Psychol Rep* 22:243–6 F '68. * (*PA* 42:10576)
98. WATSON, CHARLES G. "The Separation of NP Hospital Organics From Schizophrenics With Three Visual Motor Screening Tests." *J Clin Psychol* 24:412–4 O '68. * (*PA* 43:4168)
99. WATSON, CHARLES G., and KLETT, WILLIAM G. "Prediction of WAIS IQ's From the Shipley-Hartford, the Army General Classification Test and the Revised Beta Examination." *J Clin Psychol* 24:338–41 Jl '68. * (*PA* 42:16437)

NAME INDEX

Sines, L. K.: 48, 51
Sklar, M.: 57
Slater, P.: 11, 15, 26
Solomon, J. C.: 32
Spano, R. M.: 89
Stone, L. A.: 74-7
Suinn, R. M.: 53
Sydow, D. W.: 42
Taub, D. V.: 81
Tuma, A. H.: 70
Turner, W. J.: 71
Wahler, H. J.: 58, 97

Watson, C. G.: 98-99
Watson, L. S.: 58
Webb, M. W.: 91
Wesley, E. L.: 33
Wheeler, E. T.: 13, 29
Wiener, D. N.: 55
Wiens, A. N.: 54
Williams, S. B.: 25
Winfield, D. L.: 43
Wright, M. E.: 20
Yates, A. J.: 49
Zelen, S. L.: 83

[245]

*Sixteen Personality Factor Questionnaire. Ages 16 and over; 1949-69; 16 PF; 20 scores: 16 primary factor scores: reserved vs. outgoing (A), less intelligent vs. more intelligent (B), affected by feelings vs. emotionally stable (C), humble vs. assertive (E), sober vs. happy-go-lucky (F), expedient vs. conscientious (G), shy vs. venturesome (H), tough-minded vs. tender-minded (I), trusting vs. suspicious (L), practical vs. imaginative (M), forthright vs. shrewd (N), self-assured vs. apprehensive (O), conservative vs. experimenting (Q1), group-dependent vs. self-sufficient (Q2), undisciplined self-conflict vs. controlled (Q3), relaxed vs. tense (Q4), plus 4 second-order factor scores: introversion vs. extraversion (I), low anxiety vs. high anxiety (II), tenderminded emotionality vs. alert poise (III), subduedness vs. independence (IV); 3 levels; handbook, 1957 edition with 1964 supplementation ['64, c1962, 57 pages] for Forms A, B, and C; no norms for second-order factor scores; $2 per handbook; postage extra; for computerized scoring and interpreting service, see 246; Raymond B. Cattell and Herbert W. Eber; Institute for Personality and Ability Testing. *

a) FORMS A AND B. 1949-68; authors recommend that both forms (374 items) be used; 2 editions; manual ('62, 22 pages); profile ('67, 1 page); separate answer sheets (hand scored, Digitek, NCS) must be used; $12.50 per 25 tests; $4.50 per 50 hand scored answer sheets; $3.75 per 50 Digitek answer sheets; $3.25 per 50 NCS answer sheets; $5.50 per 50 combined hand scored answer sheet-profiles; $4 per 50 profiles; $2 per set of scoring stencils; 50¢ per manual; $3.50 per specimen set; NCS scoring service, 40¢ to $1.20 per test; (50-60) minutes.

1) *1961-62 Edition.* 1949-62; Forms A ('62, 10 pages), B ('61, 10 pages); norms supplement ('62, 23 pages); reliability data based upon the 1956-57 editions; 80¢ per norms supplement; experimental German and Spanish editions available.

2) *1967-68 Edition.* 1956-68; Forms A ('67, 10 pages), B ('67, 10 pages); manual not yet available for this edition; tentative norms ('68, 18 mimeographed pages); no data on reliability and validity.

b) FORMS C AND D. Reading levels grades 6 and over; 1954-69; short forms (105 items) using less difficult vocabulary; handbook supplement for Form C, second edition ('62, 25 pages); profile ('67, 1 page); separate answer sheets (hand scored, Digitek, NCS) must be used; $10 per 25 tests; answer sheet and profile prices same as for Forms A and B; $1.60 per scoring stencil; $1.20 per handbook supplement; $3 per specimen set; NCS scoring service, 40¢ to $1.20 per test; industrial edition published under title *Employee Attitude Series: 16P.F.*, by Industrial Psychology, Inc. (see 6:774b); (30-40) minutes.

1) [*1956 Edition.*] 1954-67; Form C ('56, 7 pages); authors recommend that all three forms (A, B, and C making a total of 479 items) be used for important research.

2) *1969 Edition.* 1954-69; Forms C, D, ('69, 7 pages, authors recommend administration of both forms); administration of all four forms (A, B, C, and D

making a total of 584 items) is recommended for important research; no data on reliability and validity; no norms.

c) FORM E. Reading levels grades 3-5; 1965-68; experimental edition; Form E ('67, 10 pages); mimeographed interim manual ['67, 8 pages, with 1968 norms]; profile ('67, 1 page); no data on reliability; no data on validity for subjects at reading levels grades 3-5; tape recording is available for oral administration to persons reading below the grade 3 level; separate answer sheets must be used; $12.50 per 25 tests; $4.50 per 50 answer sheets; $4 per 50 profiles; $1.50 per scoring stencil; $25 per tape; 50¢ per manual; $2.45 per specimen set; [20-30] minutes.

For a review by Maurice Lorr, see 6:174 (81 references); for a review by C. J. Adcock, see 5:112 (21 references); for reviews by Charles M. Harsh, Ardie Lubin, and J. Richard Wittenborn, see 4:87 (8 references).

REFERENCES

1-8. See 4:87.
9-29. See 5:112.
30-108. See 6:174.
109. DREVDAHL, JOHN E. *An Exploratory Study of Creativity in Terms of Its Relationships to Various Personality and Intellectual Factors.* Doctor's thesis, University of Nebraska (Lincoln, Neb.), 1954. (DA 14:1256)
110. WOOD, ROGER LEROY. *Prediction and Analysis of Attrition in Classes of a University Reading Service.* Doctor's thesis, University of Michigan (Ann Arbor, Mich.), 1957. (DA 18:2066)
111. BROŽEK, JOSEF, and TAYLOR, HENRY L. "Psychological Effects of Measurements on Survival Rations." *Am J Psychol* 71:517-28 S '58. * (PA 34:1008)
112. WILLIAMS, JOSEPH ROBERT. *The Definition and Measurement of Conflict in Terms of P-Technique: A Test of Validity.* Doctor's thesis, University of Illinois (Urbana, Ill.), 1958. (DA 19:2660)
113. CATTELL, RAYMOND B. "The Personality and Motivation of the Researcher From Measurements of Contemporaries and From Biography." *Univ Utah Res Conf Identif Creat Sci Talent* 3:77-93 '59. *
114. BOND, PATRICIA JANE. *The Relationship Between Selected Nonintellective Factors and "Concealed Failure" Among College Students of Superior Scholastic Ability.* Doctor's thesis, Purdue University (Lafayette, Ind.), 1960. (DA 21:121)
115. SITTS, MARVIN RALPH. *A Study of the Personality Differences Between a Group of Women Who Had Participated in Sewing Classes in an Adult Education Program and a Group of Their Friends and Neighbors Who Had Not Participated in Any Adult Education Activities.* Doctor's thesis, Michigan State University (East Lansing, Mich.), 1960. (DA 21:1120)
116. BARTH, GEORGE WILLIAM. *Some Personality and Temperament Characteristics of Selected School Music Teachers.* Doctor's thesis, University of Southern California (Los Angeles, Calif.), 1961. (DA 22:149)
117. HETHERINGTON, ELISABETH LEONE. *Personality Characteristics of College Women Students Majoring in Physical Education With a Concentrated Study in Contemporary Dance.* Doctor's research study No. 1, Colorado State College (Greeley, Colo.), 1961. (DA 22:4217)
118. STORLIE, THEODORE RUDOLPH. *Selected Characteristics of Teachers Whose Verbal Behavior Is Influenced by an In-Service Course in Interaction Analysis.* Doctor's thesis, University of Minnesota (Minneapolis, Minn.), 1961. (DA 22:3941)
119. BOSCO, JAMES SALVATORE. *The Physical and Personality Characteristics of Champion Male Gymnasts.* Doctor's thesis, University of Illinois (Urbana, Ill.), 1962. (DA 23:4211)
120. GALBO, CHARLES JOSEPH. *Personality and Influence in a Community Power Structure.* Doctor's thesis, University of Arizona (Tucson, Ariz.), 1962. (DA 23:3006)
121. HOLT, FRED DUARD. *A Study of Change in Certain Personality Variables of Counselors in Training.* Doctor's thesis, University of Florida (Gainesville, Fla.), 1962. (DA 23:3775)
122. JONFS, WYATT C.; MEYER, HENRY J.; and BORGATTA, EDGAR F. "Social and Psychological Factors in Status Decisions of Unmarried Mothers." *Marriage & Family Living* 24:224-30 Ag '62. * (PA 38:2907)
123. MEISGEIER, CHARLES HENRY. *Variables Which May Identify Successful Student Teachers of Mentally or Physically Handicapped Children.* Doctor's thesis, Pennsylvania State University (University Park, Pa.), 1962. (DA 23:3803)
124. MILLER, THEODORE KAY. *An Analysis of Critical Personality Factors in Helping and Non-Helping Relationship Behavior in a Residence Hall Situation.* Doctor's thesis, University of Florida (Gainesville, Fla.), 1962. (DA 23:3979)
125. MISRA, R. G. "A Factorial Study of the Stability of Some Personality Factors." Comments by R. L. Thorndike. *Shiksha* 15:112-9 O '62. * (PA 37:8003)

126. PECK, ROBERT F. "Student Mental Health: The Range of Personality Patterns in a College Population," pp. 161–99. (PA 37:5614) In *Personality Factors on the College Campus: Review of a Symposium.* Edited by Robert L. Sutherland and others. Austin, Tex.: Hogg Foundation for Mental Health, 1962. Pp. xxii, 242. * (PA 37:5621)

127. SWANSON, PAUL REGINALD. *Some Effects of Clinical Pastoral Education on a Group of Theological Students and Pastors.* Doctor's thesis, Boston University (Boston, Mass.), 1962. (DA 23:1812)

128. AIKEN, LEWIS R., JR. "Personality Correlates of Attitude Toward Mathematics." *J Ed Res* 56:476–80 My–Je '63. * (PA 39:9943)

129. ANDERSON, RODNEY EARL. *A Comparison of the Performance of College Freshmen Participants and Non-Participants in an Honors Program on Four Psychological Measures.* Doctor's research study No. 1, Colorado State College (Greeley, Colo.), 1963. (DA 25:279)

130. LAVELY, CAROLYN DECKER. *Non-Intellective Factors Relating to Academic Success in College or Withdrawal From College After One Year.* Master's thesis, Indiana State College (Terre Haute, Ind.), 1963. (Abstract: *Teach Col J* 35:68)

131. MATTHEWS, DOROTHY ROSE. *A Comparison of the Personality Traits of Teachers With Positive and Negative Influence on the School's Holding Power.* Doctor's thesis, University of Tennessee (Knoxville, Tenn.), 1963. (DA 24:5199)

132. NICHOLS, ROBERT C., and HOLLAND, JOHN L. "Prediction of the First Year College Performance of High Aptitude Students." *Psychol Monogr* 77(7):1–29 '63. * (PA 38:4693)

133. PEAVY, RICHARD VANCE. *A Study of C. G. Jung's Concept of Intuitive Perception and the Intuitive Type.* Doctor's thesis, University of Oregon (Eugene, Ore.), 1963. (DA 24:4551)

134. SANSON, WILLIAM EDWARD. *A Study of the Relationship Between Personality and Connotative Meaning.* Doctor's research study No. 1, Colorado State College (Greeley, Colo.), 1963. (DA 25:252)

135. BAKKER, CORNELIS B., and DIGHTMAN, CAMERON R. "Psychological Factors in Fertility Control." *Fertil & Steril* 15:559–67 S–O '64. *

136. CATTELL, RAYMOND B. "Reliability and Technical Meaning of Personality Questionnaire Scales." Letter. *Am Psychologist* 19:57–9 Ja '64. *

137. CATTELL, RAYMOND B.; TATRO, DONALD; and KOMLOS, ENDRE. "The Diagnosis and Inferred Structure of Paranoid and Non-Paranoid Schizophrenia From the 16 P.F. Profile: 1, The Status of Clinical Use of Factored Personality Measures." *Indian Psychol R* 1:52–61 Jl '64. * (PA 39:8475)

138. CHAMBERS, J. A. "Relative Personality and Biographical Factors to Scientific Creativity." *Psychol Mongr* 78(7):1–20 '64. * (PA 39:5113)

139. CHAMBERS, JACK ALLEN. *Relating Personality and Biographical Factors to Scientific Creativity.* Doctor's thesis, Michigan State University (East Lansing, Mich.), 1964. (DA 26:1762)

140. COAN, RICHARD W. "Factors in Movement Perception." *J Consult Psychol* 28:394–402 O '64. * (PA 39:3392)

141. CRONBACH, LEE J. "A Word on 16 PF and Reliability." Letter. *Am Psychologist* 19:417 Je '64. *

142. CROWELL, THOMAS ROLLA, JR. *A Comparative Study of Teacher Personalities, Attitudes, and Values in Relation to Student Nonpromotion in the Elementary Schools of Rockford, Illinois.* Doctor's research study No. 1, Colorado State College (Greeley, Colo.), 1964. (DA 25:2823)

143. CUNNINGHAM, DAVID FRANKLIN. *A Study of Background and Personality Characteristics of Teachers in Teaching Teams in Jefferson County, Colorado, Public Schools, 1962.* Doctor's thesis, University of Houston (Houston, Tex.), 1964. (DA 26:1496)

144. DAVIS, KEITH G. "Correlates of the Fear of Insanity." *Newsl Res Psychol* 6:20–1 F '64. *

145. DAVIS, KEITH GORDON. *Correlates of the Fear of Insanity.* Doctor's thesis, University of Colorado (Boulder, Colo.), 1964. (DA 25:6059)

146. DISTEFANO, M. K., JR., and PRYER, MARGARET W. "Task-Orientation, Persistence, and Anxiety of Mental Hospital Patients With High and Low Motivation." *Psychol Rep* 14:18 F '64. * (PA 39:2378, title only)

147. EBER, HERBERT W. "The Defense Rests?" Letter. *Am Psychologist* 19:287–8 Ap '64. *

148. FARE, DON EARL. *Teacher-Related Anxiety in Elementary School Children.* Doctor's thesis, Texas Technological College (Lubbock, Tex.), 1964. (DA 26:865)

149. HARBURG, E.; JULIUS, S.; MC GINN, N. F.; MC LEOD, J.; and HOOBLER, S. W. "Personality Traits and Behavioral Patterns Associated with Systolic Blood Pressure Levels in College Males." *J Chronic Dis* 17:405–13 My '64. * (PA 39:10321)

150. HASLER, KERMIT R. *Personality Characteristics and Psychological Satiation.* Doctor's thesis, New York University (New York, N.Y.), 1964. (DA 26:478)

151. HAY, JOHN EARL. *The Relationship of Certain Personality Variables to Managerial Level and Job Performance Among Engineering Managers.* Doctor's thesis, Temple University (Philadelphia, Pa.), 1964. (DA 25:3973)

152. HENDRIX, VERNON L. "Relationship Between Personnel Policies and Faculty Personality Characteristics in Public Junior Colleges." *Calif J Ed Res* 15:34–43 Ja '64. * (PA 38:9293)

153. HOWARD, KENNETH I. "Differentiation of Individuals as a Function of Repeated Testing." *Ed & Psychol Meas* 24:875–94 w '64. * (PA 39:7863) ..

154. KAPOOR, S. D. "The Personality Differences Between the Sexes." *Psychol Studies* 9:124–32 Jl '64. * (PA 39:5067)

155. KELLY, E. LOWELL. "Alternate Criteria in Medical Education and Their Correlates." *Proc Inv Conf Testing Probl* 1963:64–85 '64. *

156. KIMMEL, PANZE BUTLER. *Characteristics of Student Teachers as Correlates of Success in Student Teaching.* Doctor's thesis, Texas Technological College (Lubbock, Tex.), 1964. (DA 25:5765)

157. McCONNELL, CLAUDIA MAE. *Analysis of Socioeconomic, Achievement, and Personality Characteristics of Special Groups of Superior College Students.* Doctor's thesis, Indiana University (Bloomington, Ind.), 1964. (DA 26:5875)

158. MAZER, GILBERT EARNEST. *A Factor Analysis of Counseling Practices Reported by School Counselors.* Doctor's thesis, Arizona State University (Tempe, Ariz.), 1964. (DA 25:3977)

159. MEHROTRA, V. K. " 'Lie' Scores in the Sixteen Personality Factor Questionnaire." *Indian Psychol R* 1:47–51 Jl '64. * (PA 39:7849)

160. MEREDITH, GERALD M. "Personality Correlates of Pidgin English Usage Among Japanese-American College Students in Hawaii." *Jap Psychol Res* 6:176–83 D '64. * (PA 39:12363)

161. MOHAN, JITENDRA. "A Study of Scores on the 16 P.F. Test: A Study of Punjab College Students' Scores on the Sixteen Personality Factor Test." *Psychol Studies* 9:14–20 Ja '64. * (PA 39:1814)

162. MOULD, JOHN W. *A Comparison of the Personality Characteristics of Selected Underachieving and Achieving Engineering Students at the University of Toledo.* Doctor's thesis, University of Toledo (Toledo, Ohio), 1964. (DA 26:2574)

163. OSMON, WILLIAM R. *Factors Relevant to Groups of Predictable and Non-Predictable Freshman College Students.* Doctor's thesis, Indiana University (Bloomington, Ind.), 1964. (DA 25:5746)

164. OSTFELD, A. M.; LEBOVITS, B. Z.; SHEKELLE, R. B.; and PAUL, O. "A Prospective Study of the Relationship Between Personality and Coronary Heart Disease." *J Chronic Dis* 17:265–76 Mr '64. * (PA 39:10326)

165. REITER, HENRY H. "Prediction of College Success From Measures of Anxiety, Achievement Motivation, and Scholastic Aptitude." *Psychol Rep* 15:23–6 Ag '64. * (PA 39:2805)

166. SHIPMAN, WILLIAM G. "Age of Menarche and Adult Personality." *Arch Gen Psychiatry* 10:155–9 F '64. * (PA 39:1391)

167. SHIPMAN, WILLIAM G. "TAT Validity: Congruence With an Inventory." *J Proj Tech & Pers Assess* 28:227–32 Je '64. * (PA 39:5214)

168. STANLEY, WILLIAM HENRY. *The Relationship of Certain Conative Factors of Intellectually Gifted Children to Academic Success.* Doctor's thesis, North Texas State University (Denton, Tex.), 1964. (DA 25:4512)

169. TILLMAN, KENNETH GENE. *The Relationship Between Physical Fitness and Selected Personality Traits.* Doctor's thesis, University of New Mexico (Albuquerque, N.M.), 1964. (DA 25:276)

170. WHITE, WILLIAM FRANCIS. *Personality and Cognitive Learning Differences Among Alcoholics of Different Intervals of Sobriety.* Doctor's thesis, State University of New York at Buffalo (Buffalo, N.Y.), 1964. (DA 28:2106A)

171. WILKINS, LEE GERTRUDE. *Some Correlates of Cognitive Controls, Personality Trait Factors, and n Achievement Motivation.* Doctor's thesis, New York University (New York, N.Y.), 1964. (DA 25:1327)

172. BARRATT, ERNEST S. "Factor Analysis of Some Psychometric Measures of Impulsiveness and Anxiety." *Psychol Rep* 16:547–54 Ap '65. * (PA 39:10087)

173. BORROR, MERNA JANE, and CREEKMORE, ANNA M. "Relation of Physical Coloring and Personality Characteristics to Color Preferences for Clothing." *J Home Econ* 57:447–50 Je '65. *

174. BUTT, DORCAS SUSAN, and SIGNORI, EDRO I. "Personality Factors of a Canadian Sample of Male University Students." *Psychol Rep* 16:1117–21 Je '65. * (PA 39:15342)

175. BUTT, SUSAN DORCAS, and SIGNORI, EDRO I. "Relationship of Personality Factors to Conceived Values in Male University Students." *Psychol Rep* 16:609–17 Ap '65. * (PA 39:10223)

176. CATTELL, RAYMOND B.; TATRO, DONALD; and KOMLOS, ENDRE. "The Diagnosis and Inferred Structure of Paranoid and Non-Paranoid Schizophrenia From the 16 P.F. Profile: 2." *Indian Psychol R* 1:108–15 Ja '65. * (PA 39:10649)

177. COURT, J. H. "Anxiety Among Acute Schizophrenics and Temporal Lobe Patients." *Brit J Social & Clin Psychol* 4:254–8 D '65. * (PA 40:4471)

178. FEBINGER, GEORGE NORMAN. *A Study of the Personality*

Correlates and Other Variables Associated With the Open-ness and Closeness of the Belief Systems of Prospective Teachers at the University of Colorado. Doctor's thesis, University of Colorado (Boulder, Colo.), 1965. (*DA* 26:6511)

179. GOODMAN, JACK G. *The 16 P.F. Personality Test as an Aid in the Selection of Camp Counselors for the Physically Handicapped.* Master's thesis, Moorhead State College (Moorhead, Minn.), 1965.

180. GOODWIN, WILLIAM L.; JOYCE, JULIANNE; ABRAMS, ALAN; BIAGGIO, ANGELA B.; and BIAGGIO, LUIS I. "Note: Relationships Between Matching Scales of the Cattell 16 Personality Factor Questionnaire and the High School Personality Questionnaire." *J Ed Meas* 2:220 D '65. *

181. HENNING, WARREN DOUGLAS. *A Comparative Study of Personality Factors of 55 Business Teachers and 20 Business Students by Use of the Cattell 16 Personality Factor Questionnaire.* Master's thesis, University of Kansas (Lawrence, Kan.), 1965.

182. HERRON, WILLIAM G.; GUIDO, STEPHEN M.; and KANTOR, ROBERT E. "Relationships Among Ego Strength Measures." *J Clin Psychol* 21:403-4 O '65. * (*PA* 40:1567)

183. HOLT, NORMAN F. "A 16 PF Profile for Prisoners Convicted of 'Drunk and Disorderly' Behavior." *Brit J Criminol* 5:196-9 Ap '65. *

184. HOWARD, KENNETH I., and DIESENHAUS, HERMAN I. "Intra-Individual Variability, Response Set, and Response Uniqueness in a Personality Questionnaire." *J Clin Psychol* 21:392-6 O '65. * (*PA* 40:1568)

185. HOWARD, KENNETH I., and DIESENHAUS, HERMAN I. "Personality Correlates of Change-Seeking Behavior." *Percept & Motor Skills* 21:655-64 O '65. * (*PA* 40:2904)

186. HOWARD, KENNETH I., and DIESENHAUS, HERMAN. "16 PF Item Response Patterns as a Function of Repeated Testing." *Ed & Psychol Meas* 25:365-79 su '65. * (*PA* 39:15239)

187. JOSHI, MOHAN C. "Validity of Cattell's Source Trait 'B.'" *Indian Psychol R* 1:154-7 Ja '65. * (*PA* 39:10127)

188. KAPOOR, KAMLESH. "Preference for the Standard Ten-Point Scale (Sten) for the 16 P.F. Test (VKKJ) Norms." *Guid R (Delhi)* 3:18-20 Jl '65. *

189. KAPOOR, S. D. "Cross-validation of the Hindi Version of the 16 PF Test (VKKJ)." *Indian J Psychol* 40:115-20 S '65. *

190. KAPOOR, S. D. "Norms on the 16 PF Test: Forms A and B (VKKJ; KA and KHA)." *Indian J Psychol* 40:27-30 Mr '65. *

191. KROLL, WALTER, and PETERSEN, KAY H. "Personality Factor Profiles of Collegiate Football Teams." *Res Q* 36:433-40 D '65. * (*PA* 40:4610)

192. LEEDS, DAVID PAUL. *Personality Patterns and Modes of Behavior of Male Adolescent Narcotic Addicts and Their Mothers.* Doctor's thesis, Yeshiva University (New York, N.Y.), 1965. (*DA* 26:2861)

193. MARZOLF, STANLEY S. "Parent Behavior as Reported by College Students." *J Clin Psychol* 21:360-6 O '65. * (*PA* 40:1459)

194. METIVIER, LIONEL GERALD. *Selected Factors in Predicting Student Teaching Success in Grades Four, Five, and Six.* Doctor's thesis, University of Michigan (Ann Arbor, Mich.), 1965. (*DA* 26:3164)

195. MILLER, THEODORE K. "Characteristics of Perceived Helpers." *Personnel & Guid J* 43:687-91 Mr '65. * (*PA* 39:12242)

196. MURTHY, HOSUR NARAYANA. "Clinical Use of Sixteen Personality Factor Questionnaire." *Indian J Psychol* 40:7-11 Mr '65. *

197. NICHOLS, ROBERT C. "Personality Change and the College." *NMSC Res Rep* 1(2):1-27 '65. *

198. NULL, ELDON JAMES. *The Relationships Between the Organizational Climate of a School and Personal Variables of Members of the Teaching Staff.* Doctor's thesis, University of Minnesota (Minneapolis, Minn.), 1965. (*DA* 26:4392)

199. RAICHE, ALOISE. *Selected Teacher Characteristics and Verbal Behavior in the Classroom.* Doctor's thesis, University of Minnesota (Minneapolis, Minn.), 1965. (*DA* 26:4508)

200. REIMANIS, GUNARS. "Cattell 16 P.F. Study in a VA Domiciliary." *Newsl Res Psychol* 7:39-42 Ag '65. *

201. SCOTT, RUSSELL H.; PHIPPS, GRANT T.; and MORGART, HELEN S. "Prediction of Success in a Dental Assisting Course." *J Dental Ed* 29:348-57 D '65. *

202. SEMROW, JOSEPH JOHN. *Personal Variables and Their Relationship to Self-Role Conflict and Administrator Effectiveness.* Doctor's thesis, University of Wisconsin (Madison, Wis.), 1965. (*DA* 25:7053)

203. SHEKELLE, R. B., and OSTFELD, ADRIAN M. "Psychometric Evaluations in Cardiovascular Epidemiology." *Ann N Y Acad Sci* 126:696-705 Ag 6 '65. *

204. SIEGELMAN, MARVIN. "College Student Personality Correlates of Early Parent-Child Relationship." *J Consult Psychol* 29:558-64 D '65. * (*PA* 40:2705)

205. SMITH, GENE MARSHALL. "The Role of Personality in Nursing Education: A Comparison of Successful and Unsuccessful Nursing Students." *Nursing Res* 14:54-8 w '65. *

206. STEWART, HORACE. "The Relationship of Physical Illness to the IPAT 16 Personality Factors Test." *J Clin Psychol* 21:264-6 Jl '65. * (*PA* 39:15373)

207. SWERDLIN, RICHARD. *Demographic, Situational Per-*

ception, and Personality Correlates of Teacher Opinion. Doctor's thesis, University of Cincinnati (Cincinnati, Ohio), 1965. (*DA* 26:5140)

208. TARPEY, M. SIMEON. "Personality Factors in Teacher Trainee Selection." *Brit J Ed Psychol* 35:140-9 Je '65. * (*PA* 39:16480)

209. TILLMAN, KENNETH. "Relationship Between Physical Fitness and Selected Personality Traits." *Res Q* 36:483-9 D '65. * (*PA* 40:4613)

210. TSUJIOKA, BIEN, and CATTELL, RAYMOND B. "Constancy and Difference in Personality Structure and Mean Profile, in the Questionnaire Medium, From Applying the 16 P.F. Test in America and Japan." *Brit J Social & Clin Psychol* 4:287-97 D '65. * (*PA* 40:3590)

211. TSUJIOKA, BIEN, and CATTELL, RAYMOND B. "A Cross-Cultural Comparison of Second-Stratum Questionnaire Personality Factor Structures—Anxiety and Extraversion—in America and Japan." *J Social Psychol* 65:205-19 Ap '65. * (*PA* 39:14890)

212. WHITE, KINNARD. "Personality Characteristics of Educational Leaders: A Comparison of Administrators and Researchers." *Sch R* 73:292-300 au '65. *

213. WHITE, WILLIAM F. "Personality and Cognitive Learning Among Alcoholics With Different Intervals of Sobriety." *Psychol Rep* 16:1125-40 Je '65. * (*PA* 39:16094)

214. BUTT, DORCAS SUSAN. "Value and Personality Dimensions: Their Constancies and Their Relationships." *Psychol Rep* 19:1115-24 D '66. * (*PA* 41:4458)

215. CHILDERS, ROBERT D., and WHITE, WILLIAM F. "The Personality of Select Theological Students." *Personnel & Guid J* 44:507-10 Ja '66. * (*PA* 40:5927)

216. CORNWELL, HENRY G. "Personality Variables in Autokinetic Figure Writing." *Percept & Motor Skills* 22:731-5 Je '66. * (*PA* 40:11160)

217. de SALES, MARIE. *Relationship of Occupational Choice to Personality Traits of Women Students as Measured by the Sixteen Personality Factor Questionnaire and the California Psychological Inventory.* Master's thesis, Loyola University (Chicago, Ill.), 1966.

218. DRISCOLL, JOHN. *The Dimensions of Satisfaction With the Religious Life Among Scholastics in a Community of Teaching Brothers: A Descriptive Study.* Doctor's thesis, University of Notre Dame (Notre Dame, Ind.), 1966. (*DA* 27:1653A)

219. FINK, RUTH WASSERMAN. *An Inquiry Into the Possibility of Relationship Between Teacher Personality and Background Factors and Preference for or Assignment to Homogeneous or Heterogeneous Classes.* Doctor's thesis, Western Reserve University (Cleveland, Ohio), 1966. (*DA* 27:4152A)

220. GIBBONS, BILLIE DWANE. *A Study of the Relationships Between Factors Found in Cattell's Sixteen Personality Factor Questionnaire and Factors Found in the Guilford Personality Inventories.* Doctor's thesis, University of Southern California (Los Angeles, Calif.), 1966. (*DA* 26:7438)

221. HAERTZEN, CHARLES A., and HORINE, ILZE. "Noncomparability of the 1950 and 1956 Forms A of Cattell's Sixteen Personality Factor Questionnaire." *Psychol Rep* 18:342 Ap '66. * (*PA* 40:8259, title only)

222. HANDLEY, HERBERT MILTON. *Personal Characteristics of Influential Science Teachers, Regular Science Teachers and Science Research Students.* Doctor's thesis, University of Georgia (Athens, Ga.), 1966. (*DA* 27:3309A)

223. HARTMAN, BERNARD J. "Personality Factors of the Cattell '16 PF Test' and Hypnotic Susceptibility." *Psychol Rep* 19:1337-8 D '66. * (*PA* 41:4583)

224. HEALY, MARY MARGARET IRENE. *Assessment of Academic Aptitude, Personality Characteristics, and Religious Orientation of Catholic Sister-Teacher-Trainees.* Doctor's thesis, University of Minnesota (Minneapolis, Minn.), 1966. (*DA* 27:982A)

225. HENJUM, ARNOLD EUGENE. *The Relationships Between Certain Personality Characteristics of Student Teachers and Success in Student Teaching.* Doctor's thesis, University of Minnesota (Minneapolis, Minn.), 1966. (*DA* 28:316A)

226. HERSHEY, HARVEY. *Adult Education and Personality of Inmates of the State Prison of Southern Michigan.* Doctor's thesis, Michigan State University (East Lansing, Mich.), 1966. (*DA* 27:924A)

227. HUNDLEBY, JOHN D. "The Construct Validity of a Scale of Acquiescence." *Brit J Social & Clin Psychol* 5:290-8 D '66. * (*PA* 41:3711)

228. ISHIKAWA, AKIRA. "A Study of the Effects of Different Forms of Questionnaire Items on Factorial Validity." *Psychologia* 9:76-84 Je '66. * (*PA* 41:1002)

229. KENNEY, JAMES B., and WHITE, WILLIAM F. "Sex Characteristics in Personality Patterns of Elementary School Teachers." *Percept & Motor Skills* 23:17-8 Ag '66. * (*PA* 40:12635)

230. LANGER, PHILIP. "Varsity Football Performance." *Percept & Motor Skills* 23:1191-9 D '66. * (*PA* 41:5432)

231. LEY, P.; SPELMAN, M. S.; DAVIES, ANN D. M.; and RILEY, S. "The Relationships Between Intelligence, Anxiety, Neuroticism and Extraversion." *Brit J Ed Psychol* 36:185-91 Je '66. * (*PA* 40:10100)

232. LIU, PHYLLIS Y. H., and MEREDITH, GERALD M. "Personality Structure of Chinese College Students in Taiwan and

Hong Kong." *J Social Psychol* 70:165–6 O '66. * (*PA* 41:590)

233. MALUMPHY, THERESA MARY. *The Personality and General Characteristics of Women Athletes in Intercollegiate Competition.* Doctor's thesis, Ohio State University (Columbus, Ohio), 1966. (*DA* 27:2854A)

234. MEREDITH, GERALD M. "Amae and Acculturation Among Japanese-American College Students in Hawaii." *J Social Psychol* 70:171–80 D '66. * (*PA* 41:2901)

235. MEREDITH, GERALD M. "Comments on the Haertzen-Horine Paper on the Noncomparability of Forms A of Sixteen Personality Factor Questionnaire." *Psychol Rep* 18:581–2 Ap '66. * (*PA* 40:8266)

236. MEREDITH, GERALD M., and MEREDITH, CONNIE G. W. "Acculturation and Personality Among Japanese-American College Students in Hawaii." *J Social Psychol* 68:175–82 F '66. * (*PA* 40:5480)

237. MICHAEL, WILLIAM B.; HANEY, RUSSELL; and JONES, ROBERT A. "The Predictive Validities of Selected Aptitude and Achievement Measures and of Three Personality Inventories in Relation to Nursing Training Criteria." *Ed & Psychol Meas* 26:1035–40 w '66. * (*PA* 41:5117)

238. OSEAS, LEONARD. " 'Give the First Natural Answer.' " *J Counsel Psychol* 13:454–8 w '66. * (*PA* 41:2885)

239. RADCLIFFE, J. A. "A Note on Questionnaire Faking With 16 PFQ and MPI." *Austral J Psychol* 18:154–7 Ag '66. * (*PA* 41:10479)

240. SCHALOCK, ROBERT L., and MacDONALD, PATRICIA. "Personality Variables Associated With Reactions to Frustration." *J Proj Tech & Pers Assess* 30:158–60 Ap '66. * (*PA* 40:7708)

241. SEALY, A. P., and CATTELL, R. B. "Adolescent Personality Trends in Primary Factors Measured on the 16 PF and the HSPQ Questionnaires Through Ages 11 to 23." *Brit J Social & Clin Psychol* 5:172–84 S '66. * (*PA* 40:13205)

242. SIMS, NEIL B., and CLOWER, ROBERT P. "Correlation Between WAIS IQ's and 16 PF B Factor Scores of General Hospital Patients." *Newsl Res Psychol* 8:10–1 My '66. *

243. START, K. B. "The Relation of Teaching Ability to Measures of Personality." *Brit J Ed Psychol* 36:158–65 Je '66. * (*PA* 40:10482)

244. STEWART, HORACE. "Personality Characteristics of Student Nurses Having High and Low Frequency of Physical Illness." *Psychol Rep* 18:972 Je '66. * (*PA* 40:10143)

245. TAMKIN, ARTHUR S. "Correlation Between IQ and Factor B of the Sixteen Personality Factor Test With Psychiatric Patients." *Newsl Res Psychol* 8:1 N '66. *

246. TAMKIN, ARTHUR S., and SONKIN, NATHAN. "Personality Factors in Psychogenic Somatic Complaints." *Newsl Res Psychol* 8:20–1 F '66. *

247. TOWNES, BRENDA D., and WAGNER, NATHANIEL N. "Relation of Performance Ratings to Long Term Employment." *Nursing Res* 15:70–2 w '66. *

248. VINCENT, MARY JANE PARKS. *A Study of Construct Validity in Self Concept Measurement.* Doctor's thesis, University of Idaho (Moscow, Idaho), 1966. (*DA* 27:3741A)

249. WALKER, WENDY L. "A Preliminary Investigation of Personality Change in Depressed Patients Following ECT." *Austral J Psychol* 18:239–43 D '66. * (*PA* 41:4703)

250. WERNER, ALFRED C., and GOTTHEIL, EDWARD. "Personality Development and Participation in College Athletics." *Res Q* 37:126–31 Mr '66. * (*PA* 40:6658)

251. WILLIAMS, RICHARD CHARLES. *The Relationship Between Teacher Personality Factors and Selected Teacher Characteristics Including Membership in Teacher Organizations.* Doctor's thesis, University of Minnesota (Minneapolis, Minn.), 1966. (*DA* 27:2352A)

252. BAKKER, CORNELIS B., and LEVENSON, ROBERT M. "Determinants of Angina Pectoris." *Psychosom Med* 29:621–33 N–D '67. * (*PA* 42:10907)

253. BEHM, HARLEY DALE. *Characteristics of Community College Students: A Comparison of Transfer and Occupational Freshmen in Selected Midwestern Colleges.* Doctor's thesis, University of Missouri (Columbia, Mo.), 1967. (*DA* 28:3965A)

254. BERGMANN, ANNE MARIE WOERNER. *Identification of Differentiating Characteristics Among Delinquent Girls in a Correctional Institution.* Doctor's thesis, Indiana University (Bloomington, Ind.), 1967. (*DA* 28:3966A)

255. BLAIR, GARLAND EUGENE. *The Relationship of Selected Ego Functions and the Academic Achievement of Negro Students.* Doctor's thesis, Florida State University (Tallahassee, Fla.), 1967. (*DA* 28:3013A)

256. BONNEY, MERL E. "Interrelationships Between Content Analysis and Personality Self-Ratings in Studying *High* and *Low* Normality in a College Population." *J Social Psychol* 71:277–85 Ap '67. * (*PA* 41:8807)

257. BORTNER, RAYMAN W. "Measurement of Informal Selection Processes." *Percept & Motor Skills* 25:421–36 O '67. * (*PA* 42:5716)

258. BRYANT, G. PRESTON; TURNER, A. JACK; and LAIR, CHARLES V. "Word Familiarity as a Factor in Perceptual Defense Research." *Percept & Motor Skills* 25:229–34 Ag '67. * (*PA* 42:2544)

259. CATTELL, RAYMOND B., and KRUG, SAMUEL. "Personality Factor Profile Peculiar to the Student Smoker." *J Counsel Psychol* 14:116–21 Mr '67. * (*PA* 41:7334)

260. CATTELL, RAYMOND B., and NESSELROADE, JOHN R. "Likeness and Completeness Theories Examined by Sixteen Personality Factor Measures on Stably and Unstably Married Couples." *J Personality & Social Psychol* 7:351–61 D '67. * (*PA* 42:4348)

261. CLEERE, WILLIAM RAY. *A Comparative Analysis of Selected Psychological and Educational Characteristics of State Teacher Scholarship Recipients.* Doctor's thesis, University of Georgia (Athens, Ga.), 1967. (*DA* 28:2515A)

262. CROSS, PETER G.; CATTELL, RAYMOND B.; and BUTCHER, H. J. "The Personality Pattern of Creative Artists." *Brit J Ed Psychol* 37:292–9 N '67. * (*PA* 42:5564)

263. DEABLER, HERDIS L., and WILLIS, C. H. "Correlation Between Factor B of the 16 PF Test and the G Score of the GATB." *Newsl Res Psychol* 9:14–5 F '67. *

264. DeBLASSIE, RICHARD ROLAND. *Personality Variables as a Function of College Students Seeking Counseling.* Doctor's thesis, University of Arizona (Tucson, Ariz.), 1967. (*DA* 28:120A)

265. FORREST, GARY L.; BORTNER, TIMOTHY W.; and BAKKER, CORNELIS B. "The Role of Personality Variables in Response to Chlorpromazine, Dextroamphetamine and Placebo." *J Psychiatric Res* 5:281–8 D '67. * (*PA* 42:11814)

266. GEWINNER, MARCUS N. *A Study of the Results of the Interaction of Student Teachers With Their Supervising Teachers During the Student Teaching Period.* Doctor's thesis, Mississippi State University (State College, Miss.), 1967. (*DA* 29:165A)

267. GIRARD, FRANCIS GEORGE. *The Interaction of Perceptual Discrimination, Aesthetic Preference and Personality Traits.* Doctor's thesis, Illinois State University (Normal, Ill.), 1967. (*DA* 28:2554A)

268. GLESER, GOLDINE C., and GOTTSCHALK, LOUIS A. "Personality Characteristics of Chronic Schizophrenics in Relationship to Sex and Current Functioning." *J Clin Psychol* 23:349–54 Jl '67. * (*PA* 41:15553)

269. GORSUCH, RICHARD L., and CATTELL, RAYMOND B. "Second Stratum Personality Factors Defined in the Questionnaire Realm by the 16 P.F." *Multiv Behav Res* 2:211–23 Ap '67. * (*PA* 41:11935)

270. HARFORD, THOMAS C.; WILLIS, CONSTANCE H.; and DEABLER, HERDIS L. "Personality Correlates of Masculinity-Femininity." *Psychol Rep* 21:881–4 D '67. * (*PA* 42:7316)

271. HARFORD, THOMAS C.; WILLIS, CONSTANCE H.; and DEABLER, HERDIS L. "Personality, Values, and Intellectual Correlates of Masculinity-Femininity." *Newsl Res Psychol* 9:17–8 Ag '67. *

272. HASLER, KERMIT R., and CLARKE, WALTER V. "Personality Factors and Self-Concept Dimensions Associated With Proof Reading Ability." *Percept & Motor Skills* 24:1294 Je '67. * (*PA* 41:15258, title only)

273. HIRT, MICHAEL; KURTZ, RICHARD; and ROSS, W. DONALD. "The Relationship Between Dysmenorrhea and Selected Personality Variables." *Psychosomatics* 8:350–3 N–D '67. * (*PA* 42:8614)

274. HOCHMAN, LEONARD. *Level of Aspiration and Need Achievement in Employed and Unemployed Coronary Patients.* Doctor's thesis, Texas Technological College (Lubbock, Tex.), 1967. (*DA* 28:4757B)

275. HOWARD, KENNETH I., and DIESENHAUS, HERMANN I. "Direction of Similarity and Profile Similarity." *Multiv Behav Res* 2:225–37 Ap '67. * (*PA* 41:11134)

276. JANSEN, DAVID GEORGE. *Characteristics of Student Leaders.* Doctor's thesis, Indiana University (Bloomington, Ind.), 1967. (*DA* 28:3768A)

277. JENKINS, JOHN MERVIN. *A Study of the Characteristics Associated With Innovative Behavior in Teachers.* Doctor's thesis, University of Miami (Coral Gables, Fla.), 1967. (*DA* 28:903A)

278. JOSHI, MOHAN C., and ROY, SUBHRA. "Psychological Characteristics of Hypertension and Cardiac Cases." *Indian Psychol R* 4:62–7 Jl '67. *

279. KARSON, SAMUEL. "Second-Order Factors in Air Traffic Control Specialists." *Aerospace Med* 38:412–4 Ap '67. *

280. KENNEY, JAMES B.; WHITE, WILLIAM F.; and GENTRY, HAROLD W. "Personality Characteristics of Teachers and Their Perception of Organizational Climate." *J Psychol* 66:167–74 Jl '67. * (*PA* 41:14209)

281. KINGSTON, ALBERT J., and WHITE, WILLIAM F. "The Relationship of Reader's Self Concepts and Personality Components to Semantic Meanings Perceived in the Protagonist of a Reading Selection." *Reading Res Q* 2:107–16 sp '67. * (*PA* 41:11903)

282. KLINE, PAUL. "The Use of the Cattell 16 P.F. Test and Eysenck's E.P.I. With a Literate Population in Ghana." *Brit J Social & Clin Psychol* 6:97–107 Je '67. * (*PA* 41:13647)

283. KOSIER, KENNETH P., and DeVAULT, M. VERE. "Effects of Teacher Personality on Pupil Personality." *Psychol Sch* 4:40–4 Ja '67. * (*PA* 41:4978)

284. KROLL, WALTER. "Sixteen Personality Factor Profiles of Collegiate Wrestlers." *Res Q* 38:49–57 Mr '67. * (*PA* 41:7324)

285. KROLL, WALTER, and CARLSON, B. ROBERT. "Discriminant Function and Hierarchical Grouping Analysis of Karate

Participants' Personality Profiles." *Res Q* 38:405–11 O '67. * (*PA* 42:2600)

286. LEWIS, LAURA HESTER. *Acquiescence Response Set: Construct or Artifact?* Doctor's thesis, University of Nebraska (Lincoln, Neb.), 1967. (*DA* 28:2626B)

287. LOY, JOHN WILSON, JR. *Socio-Psychological Attributes of English Swimming Coaches Differentially Adopting a New Technology.* Doctor's thesis, University of Wisconsin (Madison, Wis.), 1967. (*DA* 28:3274A)

288. McCLAIN, EDWIN W. "Personality Characteristics of Negro College Students in the South—A Recent Appraisal." *J Negro Ed* 36:320–5 su '67. *

289. McQUAID, JOHN. "A Note on Trends in Answers to Cattell Personality Questionnaires by Scottish Subjects." *Brit J Psychol* 58:455–8 N '67. * (*PA* 42:12114)

290. MARSHALL, I. N. "Extraversion and Libido in Jung and Cattell." *J Anal Psychol* 12:115–36 Jl '67. * (*PA* 42:737)

291. MEOSKY, PAUL RICHARD. *A Study of the Relationship of Personality to Teaching Success in Industrial Arts at the Secondary School Level.* Doctor's thesis, University of Maryland (College Park, Md.), 1967. (*DA* 29:171A)

292. MEREDITH, GERALD M. "Observations on the Origins and Current Status of the Ego Assertive Personality Factor, U. I. 16." *J Genetic Psychol* 110:269–86 Je '67. * (*PA* 41:11910)

293. MEREDITH, GERALD M. "Personality Correlates of the Similes Preference Inventory." *Psychol Rep* 20:994 Je '67. * (*PA* 41:13651, title only)

294. MORRISON, W. LEE, and ROMOSER, R. C. " 'Traditional' Classroom Attitudes, the A.C.T. and the 16 P.F." *J Ed Res* 60:326–9 Mr '67. *

295. MORRISON, WAYLAND LEE. *Dimensions of Personality and Teacher Related Attitudes in Prospective Teachers.* Doctor's thesis, University of Denver (Denver, Colo.), 1967. (*DA* 28:502A)

296. NICHOLS, ROBERT C. "Personality Change and the College." *Am Ed Res J* 4:173–90 My '67. * (*PA* 41:13623)

297. OHNMACHT, FRED W. "Relationships Among Personality and Cognitive Referrents of Creativity." *Psychol Rep* 20:1331–4 Je '67. * (*PA* 41:15283)

298. OHNMACHT, FRED W., and MURO, JAMES J. "Self-Acceptance: Some Anxiety and Cognitive Style Relationships." *J Psychol* 67:235–9 N '67. * (*PA* 42:2601)

299. OLSON, HARRY, JR. *Relationships Between Certain Personality Characteristics of Distributive Education Teacher-Coordinators and Job Satisfaction.* Doctor's thesis, University of Minnesota (Minneapolis, Minn.), 1967. (*DA* 28:2900A)

300. PASHENZ, HOWARD SAMUEL. *The Relationship Between Self Conceptualized Group Task and Group Building and Maintenance Role Behavior and the Personality Variables of Masculinity-Femininity, Intelligence, and Assertiveness.* Doctor's thesis, New York University (New York, N.Y.), 1967. (*DA* 28:5195B)

301. PEMBERTON, D. A. "A Comparison of the Outcome of Treatment in Female and Male Alcoholics." *Brit J Psychiatry* 113:367–73 Ap '67. * (*PA* 41:10684)

302. PETERSON, SHERI L.; WEBER, JEROME C.; and TROUSDALE, WILLIAM W. "Personality Traits of Women in Team Sports vs. Women in Individual Sports." *Res Q* 38:686–90 D '67. *

303. REID, MARYANNE. *The Relationship of Identified Teacher Concerns and Personality Characteristics and Attitudes of Teachers of Disadvantaged Children.* Doctor's thesis, Texas Technological College (Lubbock, Tex.), 1967. (*DA* 28:3517A)

304. RENTZ, R. ROBERT, and WHITE, WILLIAM F. "Congruence of the Dimensions of Self-As-Object and Self-As-Process." *J Psychol* 67:277–85 N '67. * (*PA* 42:2555)

305. ROSENBERG, C. M. "Personality and Obsessional Neuosis." *Brit J Psychiatry* 113:471–7 My '67. * (*PA* 41:12174)

306. SCHULTZ, DUANE P. "The Volunteer Subject in Sensory Restriction Research." *J Social Psychol* 72:123–4 Je '67. * (*PA* 41:11781)

307. SIMMONS, MILTON DELBERT, JR. *The Relationship of Personality Characteristics to Attitudes of Ministerial Students.* Doctor's thesis, University of Oklahoma (Norman, Okla.), 1967. (*DA* 28:2522A)

308. SMITH, GENE M. "Personality Correlates of Cigarette Smoking in Students of College Age." *Ann N Y Acad Sci* 142:308–21 Mr 15 '67. * (*PA* 42:6913)

309. SOLOMON, EDITH. "Personality Factors and Attitudes of Mature Training College Students." *Brit J Ed Psychol* 37:140–2 F '67. *

310. SUMPTER, G. ROY, III. *Personality Adjustment and Family Surrogates of the Youthful Offender.* Doctor's thesis, Florida State University (Tallahassee, Fla.), 1967. (*DA* 28:3887B)

311. TAMKIN, ARTHUR S. "Correlation Between IQ and Factor B of the Sixteen Personality Factor Test With Psychiatric Patients." *J Clin Psychol* 23:486–8 O '67. * (*PA* 42:2565)

312. TAYLOR, A. J. W. "Prediction for Parole: A Pilot Study With Delinquent Girls." *Brit J Criminol* 7:418–24 O '67. *

313. THALER, VICTOR HUGO. *Personality Dimensions Derived From Multiple Instruments.* Doctor's thesis, Columbia University (New York, N.Y.), 1967. (*DA* 28:509A)

314. TILKER, HARVEY A. *Socially Responsible Behavior as a Function of Observer Responsibility and Victim Feedback.* Doctor's thesis, Michigan State University (East Lansing, Mich.), 1967. (*DA* 28:3887B)

315. TOWNES, BRENDA D., and WAGNER, NATHANIEL N. "Personality Variables and Length of Employment of Psychiatric Nurses." *Nursing Res* 15:354–6 f '67. * (*PA* 42:4635)

316. UDRY, J. RICHARD. "Personality Match and Interpersonal Perception as Predictors of Marriage. *J Marriage & Family* 29:722–5 N '67. * (*PA* 42:3856)

317. WEITZNER, MARTIN; STALLONE, FRANK; and SMITH, GENE M. "Personality Profiles of High, Middle, and Low MAS Subjects." *J Psychol* 65:163–8 Mr '67. * (*PA* 41:7350)

318. WHITE, WILLIAM F.; KINGSTON, ALBERT J.; and WEAVER, WENDELL W. "Affective Dimensions in Connotative Meaning in Reading." *J Psychol* 67:227–34 N '67. * (*PA* 42:2593)

319. WHITE, WILLIAM F.; ZIELONKA, ALFRED W.; and GAIER, EUGENE L. "Personality Correlates of Cheating Among College Women Under Stress of Independent-Opportunistic Behavior." *J Ed Res* 61:68–70 O '67. *

320. WINBORN, BOB B., and JANSEN, DAVID G. "Personality Characteristics of Campus Social-Political Action Leaders." *J Counsel Psychol* 14:509–13 N '67. * (*PA* 42:3956)

321. ALLMAN, THOMAS S., and WHITE, WILLIAM F. "Birth-Order Categories as Predictors of Select Personality Characteristics." *Psychol Rep* 22:857–60 Je '68. * (*PA* 42:13733)

322. AMRAM, FRED M., and WILLIAMS, FRANK E. "Creative Thinking Skills and Personality Traits: A Study of Their Relationship Among Young Adults." *J Nat Assn Women Deans & Counselors* 31:176–81 su '68. *

323. BALDRY, ARDIS INGALLS, and SARASON, IRWIN G. "Test Anxiety, Preliminary Instructions, and Responses to Personality Inventories." *J Clin Psychol* 24:67 Ja '68. *

324. BRAUN, JOHN R., and LaFARO, DOLORES. "Fakability of the Sixteen Personality Factor Questionnaire, Form C." *J Psychol* 68:3–7 Ja '68. * (*PA* 42:7342)

325. CAFFREY, BERNARD. "Reliability and Validity of Personality and Behavioral Measures in a Study of the Coronary Heart Disease." *J Chronic Dis* 21:191–204 Je '68. *

326. CATTELL, R. B.; EBER, H. W.; and DELHEES, K. H. "A Large Sample Cross Validation of the Personality Trait Structure of the 16 P.F. With Some Clinical Implications," pp. 107–31. (*PA* 42:14723) In *Progress in Clinical Psychology Through Multivariate Experimental Designs.* Edited by Raymond B. Cattell. Fort Worth, Tex.: Society of Multivariate Experimental Psychology, Inc., 1968. Pp. 168. *

327. CATTELL, RAYMOND B., and GIBBONS, B. D. "Personality Factor Structure of the Combined Guilford and Cattell Personality Questionnaires." *J Personality & Social Psychol* 9:107–20 My '68. * (*PA* 42:10588)

328. CATTELL, RAYMOND B., and NESSELROADE, JOHN R. "Note on Analyzing Personality Relations in Married Couples." *Psychol Rep* 22:381–2 Ap '68. * (*PA* 42:11996)

329. CATTELL, RAYMOND B.; KOMLOS, ENDRE; and TATRO, DONALD F. "Significant Differences of Affective, Paranoid, and Non-Paranoid Schizophrenic Psychotics on Primary Source Traits in the 16 P.F.," pp. 33–54. (*PA* 42:15761) In *Progress in Clinical Psychology Through Multivariate Experimental Designs.* Edited by Raymond B. Cattell. Fort Worth, Tex.: Society of Multivariate Experimental Psychology, Inc., 1968. Pp. 168. *

330. CHRISTENSEN, LARRY. "Intrarater Reliability." *South J Ed Res* 2:175–82 Ag '68. *

331. CORTIS, G. A. "Predicting Student Performance in Colleges of Education." *Brit J Ed Psychol* 38:115–22 Je '68. * (*PA* 42:17717)

332. COWDEN, JAMES E.; PETERSON, WILLIAM M.; and COHEN, MICHAEL F. "The 16 PF vs. the MCI in a Group Testing Program Within a Correctional Setting." *J Clin Psychol* 24:221–4 Ap '68. * (*PA* 42:12404)

333. DONNAN, HUGH H., and HARLAN, GRADY. "Personality of Counselors and Administrators." *Personnel & Guid J* 47:228–32 N '68. * (*PA* 43:5369)

334. EBER, HERBERT W. "Relation of Age, Education, and Personality Characteristics to Military Rank in an Army Reserve Unit." *J Counsel Psychol* 15:89–90 Ja '68. * (*PA* 42:6179)

335. HAMMER, MAX. "Differentiating 'Good' and 'Bad' Officers in a Progressive Rehabilitative Women's Reformatory." *Correct Psychiatry & J Social Ther* 14:114–7 sp '68. *

336. HANDLEY, HERBERT M., and BLEDSOE, JOSEPH C. "The Personality Profiles of Influential Science Teachers, Regular Science Teachers, and Science Research Students." *J Res Sci Teach* 5(1):95–103 '68. *

337. HUCKABEE, MALCOM W. "Cognitive and Personality Correlates of Performance in the General Psychology Course." *South J Ed Res* 2:221–5 Ag '68. *

338. HUNDLEBY, JOHN D., and CONNOR, WILLIAM H. "Interrelationships Between Personality Inventories: The 16 PF, the MMPI, and the MPI." *J Consult & Clin Psychol* 32:152–7 Ap '68. * (*PA* 42:8981)

339. KARSON, SAMUEL, and HAUPT, T. DOUGLAS. "Second-Order Personality Factors in Parents of Child Guidance Clinic Patients," pp. 97–106. (*PA* 42:15469) In *Progress in Clinical*

Psychology Through Multivariate Experimental Designs. Edited by Raymond B. Cattell. Fort Worth, Tex.: Society of Multivariate Experimental Psychology, Inc., 1968. Pp. 168. *

340. KLECKNER, JAMES H. "Personality Differences Between Psychedelic Drug Users and Nonusers." *Psychol* 5:66–71 My '68. *

341. McALLISTER, JAMES. "Foulds 'Continuum of Personal Illness' and the 16 P.F." *Brit J Psychiatry* 114:53–6 Ja '68. * (*PA* 42:9163)

342. McCLAIN, EDWIN W. "Sixteen P.F. Scores and Success in Student Teaching." *J Teach Ed* 19:25–32 sp '68. * (*PA* 42:17745)

343. OHNMACHT, FRED W. "Note on the Validity of the Sixteen Personality Factor Questionnaire Measure of Field Independence." *Percept & Motor Skills* 27:564 O '68. * (*PA* 43:5364)

344. PALLONE, NATHANIEL J., and BANKS, R. RICHARD. "Vocational Satisfaction Among Ministerial Students." *Personnel & Guid J* 46:870–5 My '68. *

345. PHADKE, K. M. "An Exploratory Study of the Personality Profile of Some Indian Scientific Researchers." *J Indian Acad Appl Psychol* 5:65–72 My '68. *

346. SCHEIER, IVAN; EBER, HERBERT; KARSON, SAMUEL; NOTY, CHARLES; PIERSON, GEORGE; and TATRO, DONALD. *Interpreting the 16 PF Profile: Some Case Studies.* Champaign, Ill.: Institute for Personality and Ability Testing, 1968. Pp. 29. *

347. SIMMONS, MILTON DELBERT, JR., and PARKER, HARRY J. "Attitude and Personality Traits of Ministerial Students: The Influence and Control of Reference Group Phenomena." *Relig Ed* 63:309–14 Jl '68. * (*PA* 42:17086)

348. START, K. B. "Rater-Ratee Personality in the Assessment of Teaching Ability." *Brit J Ed Psychol* 38:14–20 F '68. * (*PA* 42:12789)

349. TAMKIN, ARTHUR S., and SONKIN, NATHAN. "The Use of Psychological Tests in Differential Diagnosis." *Newsl Res Psychol* 10:24 Ag '68. *

350. THELEN, MARK H., and HARRIS, CHARLES S. "Personality of College Under-Achievers Who Improve With Group Psychotherapy." *Personnel & Guid J* 46:561–6 F '68. * (*PA* 42:12825)

351. TUCKER, WILLIAM VINCENT. *An Investigation of the Feasibility of Using the 16 PF Questionnaire to Identify the Personality Traits of Physically Handicapped College Students.* Doctor's thesis, University of South Dakota (Vermillion, S.D.), 1968. (*DA* 29:157A)

352. VACCHIANO, RALPH B.; STRAUSS, PAUL S.; and SCHIFFMAN, DAVID C. "Personality Correlates of Dogmatism." *J Consult & Clin Psychol* 32:83–5 F '68. * (*PA* 42:7323)

353. VINCENT, JANE. "An Exploratory Factor Analysis Relating to the Construct Validity of Self-Concept Labels." *Ed & Psychol Meas* 28:915–21 au '68. * (*PA* 43:4039)

354. WALTON, H. J. "Personality as a Determinant of the Form of Alcoholism." *Brit J Psychiatry* 114:761–6 Je '68. * (*PA* 42:19029)

355. WEAVER, WENDELL W.; WHITE, WILLIAM F.; and KINGSTON, ALBERT J., JR. "Affective Correlates of Reading Comprehension." *J Psychol* 68:87–95 Ja '68. * (*PA* 42:7878)

356. WHITE, KINNARD. "Anxiety, Extraversion-Intraversion, and Divergent Thinking Ability." *J Creative Behav* 2:119–27 sp '68. * (*PA* 42:17233)

357. WILSON, PHILIP KEITH. *Relationship Between Motor Achievement and Selected Personality Factors of Junior and Senior High School Boys.* Doctor's thesis, Colorado State College (Greeley, Colo.), 1968. (*DA* 29:1125A)

NAME INDEX

tain scoring services at 65¢ per test; $1 additional per order for the addition of a 4-line letterhead; reports are mailed within 1 day of receipt of answer sheets; postpaid; program by Herbert W. Eber; IPAT-Southern. *

[247]

★Sklar Aphasia Scale. Brain damaged adults; 1966; SAS; 5 scores: auditory verbal comprehension, reading comprehension, oral expression, graphic production, total; individual; 1 form; manual (24 pages plus record booklet); record booklet (4 pages); no data on reliability; no norms for subtest scores; no description of normative population; $6.50 per 25 record booklets; $6 per set of test materials; $4 per manual; postpaid; [30–60] minutes; Maurice Sklar; Western Psychological Services. *

REFERENCES

1. SKLAR, MAURICE. "Psychological Test Scores, Language Disturbances, and Autopsy Findings in Aphasia Patients." *Newsl Res Psychol* 4:65–79 Ag '62. *
2. REEVE, ROLLAND RALPH. *A Factor Analysis of the Responses of Brain-Damaged Adults to the Sklar Aphasia Evaluation Summary.* Doctor's thesis, University of Southern California (Los Angeles, Calif.), 1964. (DA 25:2104)

[248]

★Slosson Drawing Coordination Test (SDCT) for Children and Adults, 1967 Edition. Ages 1.5 and over; 1962–67; SDCT; brain dysfunction and perceptual disorders; 1 form ('67, 2 pages); manual ('67, 52 pages); 75¢ per 20 tests; $3.75 per 40 tests and manual; postpaid; (10–15) minutes; Richard L. Slosson; Slosson Educational Publications. *

[249]

*[Social Competence Inventories.] 1951–68; behavior checklist; 2 editions; no data on reliability; no description of normative population; $1.25 per 10 tests; 35¢ per specimen set of either form; postage extra; [30] minutes; Katharine M. Banham; Family Life Publications, Inc. *
a) A SOCIAL COMPETENCE INVENTORY FOR ADULTS. Adults (physically handicapped, mentally retarded, or senile); 1951–60; SCIA; 1 form ('60, 4 pages); manual ('60, 8 pages).
b) SOCIAL COMPETENCE INVENTORY FOR OLDER PERSONS. Ages 50 and over; 1951–68; SCIOP; except for the addition of 5 items, items are either same or revisions of items in earlier form; 5 scores: motor skills and control, perception and memory, self-care and self-help, social relationships and emotional control, total; 1 form ('68, 4 pages); manual ('68, 6 pages).
For reviews by William J. Eichman and Jerome D. Pauker of *A Social Competency Test for Adults*, see 6:175.

[246]

★[Re Sixteen Personality Factor Questionnaire.] 16 PF Computer Analysis and Reporting Service. A computerized interpreting (but not scoring) service for qualified users of the 16 PF; 1963–66; the interpretive report is a 2 page computer printout presenting a profile of estimated true factor scores (estimated by multiple regression techniques), and narrative statements under the headings broad influence patterns, psychopathological considerations, treatment considerations, and vocational considerations; tests normally scored locally by hand and scores are then submitted for computerized interpretation; reported scores may be for Forms A, B, C, D, A + B, C + D, or A + B + C + D; computerized report (6 copies), $5 per test; users of the service may also ob-

[250]

Social Intelligence Test: George Washington University Series, Revised Form. Grades 9–16 and adults; 1930–55; SIT; 3 editions; manual ('55, 5 pages); reliability data and norms for total scores only; $3.75 per 25 tests of *a* or *b*; $3.25 per 25 tests of *c*; 75¢ per specimen set of all 3 editions; postage extra; F. A. Moss, Thelma Hunt, K. T. Omwake, and L. G. Woodward (*a* and manual); Center for Psychological Service. *
a) SECOND EDITION. 1930–55; 6 scores: judgment in social situations, recognition of the mental state of the speaker, memory for names and faces, observation of human behavior, sense of humor, total; 1 form ('49, 11 pages); names and faces sheet ('48, 1 page); 49(55) minutes.

b) SHORT EDITION. 1944–55; 5 scores: same as for Second Edition except for omission of memory for names and faces; 1 form ('44, 6 pages); 40(45) minutes.

c) SP (SPECIAL) EDITION. 1947–55; 3 scores: judgment in social situations, observation of human behavior, total; 1 form ('47, 4 pages); 30(35) minutes.

See 6:176 (14 references) and 4:89 (7 references); for reviews by Glen U. Cleeton and Howard R. Taylor, see 3:96 (9 references); for a review by Robert L. Thorndike, see 2:1253 (20 references).

REFERENCES

1–20. See 2:1253.
21–29. See 3:96.
30–36. See 4:89.
37–50. See 6:176.
51. BECKER, GEORGE J. *Personality Characteristics of Good and Poor Judges of Religious-Moral Situations.* Doctor's thesis, New School for Social Research (New York, N.Y.), 1964. (*DA* 25:6049)
52. BOTTRILL, JOHN. "The Social Intelligence of Students." *J Psychol* 66:211–3 Jl '67. * (*PA* 41:13585)
53. HARTMAN, BERNARD J. "Hypnotic Susceptibility and Social Intelligence." *Am J Clin Hyp* 10:37–8 Jl '67. * (*PA* 42:233)

NAME INDEX

Abt, L. E.: 34
Aron, J.: 47
Bass, B. M.: 38
Becker, G. J.: 51
Bottrill, J.: 52
Broom, M. E.: 5, 8
Bruce, M. M.: 37, 39–40, 42–5
Burks, F. W.: 18
Cleeton, G. U.: *rev*, 3:96
Crane, W. J.: 48
Eimicke, V. W.: 33, 36
Fish, H. L.: 33
Flemming, C. W.: 29
Flemming, E. G.: 29
Garrett, H. E.: 30
Grosvenor, E. L.: 1
Harrell, W.: 27
Hartman, B. J.: 53
Hecht, R.: 45, 47
Herbert, N.: 50
Huddleston, E.: 32
Human Engineering Laboratory: 15, 20
Hunt, T.: 2–3, 6, 16, 22

Jackson, V. D.: 28
Juergenson, E. M.: 46
Kaess, W. A.: 41
Karstendiek, B.: 38
Kellogg, W. W.: 30
McClatchy, V. R.: 7
McCullough, G.: 38
Moss, F. A.: 3, 21–2
Pintner, R.: 4
Pruitt, R. C.: 38
Randolph, J. M.: 25
Raubenheimer, A. S.: 31
Rhinehart, J. B.: 13
Scudder, C. R.: 31
Smith, H. C.: 35
Stagner, R.: 11, 14, 24
Stein, S.: 19, 26
Strang, R.: 9–10, 12
Taylor, H. R.: *rev*, 3:96
Thorndike, R. L.: 17, 19; *rev*, 2:1253
Turnbull, G. H.: 50
Upshall, C. C.: 4
Wang, C. K. A.: 23
Witryol, S. L.: 41

[251]

Spiral Aftereffect Test. Ages 5 and over; 1958; SAT; brain damage; individual; 1 form (1 Archimedes spiral); manual (5 pages); supplementary data (8 pages, reprint of *23* below); record form (1 page); $75 per set of spiral, battery operated testing apparatus, record form, manual, and supplementary data; $1.25 per spiral; 75¢ per 50 record forms; $1 per manual and supplementary data; postage extra; [3–10] minutes; Psychological Research & Development Corporation. * [Many variations of the spiral aftereffect are in use. The following references relate to the procedure in general as well as to the specific test apparatus and accessories.]

For reviews by William J. Eichman and Ralph M. Reitan, see 6:177 (43 references).

REFERENCES

1–43. See 6:177.
44. STERN, ALEXANDER. *The Latency of the Spiral Effect and Aftereffect as a Function of Illumination and Speed of Rotation.* Doctor's thesis, University of Connecticut (Storrs, Conn.), 1959. (*DA* 20:1442)
45. HONIGFELD, GILBERT HOWARD. *A Factorial Study of "Neurological Efficiency," Perception and Personality.* Doctor's thesis, Temple University (Philadelphia, Pa.), 1961. (*DA* 22:908)
46. ANDERSSON, ALF L. "Adaptive Patterns in a Serial Spiral After-Effect Test as Related to a System of Personality Dimensions." *Scandinavian J Psychol* 3(4):205–14 '62. * (*PA* 38:1747)
47. ROEHRIG, WILLIAM C., and RUTSCHMANN, JACQUES. "Procedural Considerations of the Spiral Aftereffect Test." *Percept & Motor Skills* 17:551–7 O '63. * (*PA* 38:5077)
48. FRISK, GUY CARL. *Duration of the Archimedes Spiral*

Aftereffect Under Varied Stimulus Conditions. Doctor's thesis, University of Oklahoma (Norman, Okla.), 1964. (*DA* 24:2984)
49. SUEHS, JAMES ERNEST. *A Comparative Study of Brain-Damaged and Schizophrenic Subjects on Several Psychological Tests.* Doctor's thesis, University of Houston (Houston, Tex.), 1964. (*DA* 25:1347)
50. BAUMEISTER, ALFRED; SMITH, THOMAS E.; and URQUHART, DONALD. "Effects of Rotation Speed, Exposure Time, and Distance on the Spiral Aftereffect." *J General Psychol* 72:151–6 Ja '65. * (*PA* 39:6500)
51. ELLIOTT, JACOB J., III. "Response Bias in SAET Responses of Persons With Organic Brain Damage." *Percept & Motor Skills* 21:647–52 O '65. * (*PA* 40:3289)
52. GILBERT, JEANNE G., and LEVEE, RAYMOND F. "Age Differences in the Bender Visual-Motor Gestalt Test and the Archimedes Spiral Test." *J Gerontol* 20:196–200 Ap '65. *
53. HILDT, MICHAEL T., and VANLIERE, DAVID E. "Influence of Test Figure Depth Cues on the Spiral Aftereffect." *Percept & Motor Skills* 20:392 Ap '65. * (*PA* 39:11168, title only)
54. KNOWLES, JOHN B., and KRASNER, LEONARD. "Extraversion and Duration of the Archimedes Spiral Aftereffect." *Percept & Motor Skills* 20:997–1000 Je '65. * (*PA* 39:13503)
55. SMITH, JEAN P. "The Spiral Visual Aftereffect in Organic and Chronically Ill Patients With Control for Response Set and Communication." *J Clin Psychol* 21:13–5 Ja '65. * (*PA* 39:11171)
56. MORANT, RICARDO B., and EFSTATHIOU, AGLAIA. "The Archimedes Spiral and Diagnosis of Brain Damage." *Percept & Motor Skills* 22:391–7 Ap '66. * (*PA* 40:9003)
57. GILBERT, JEANNE G., and LEVEE, RAYMOND F. "Performances of Deaf and Normally-Hearing Children on the Bender-Gestalt and the Archimedes Spiral Tests." *Percept & Motor Skills* 24:1059–66 Je '67. * (*PA* 41:15063)
58. SNYDER, ROBERT T., and FREUD, SHELDON L. "Reading Readiness and Its Relation to Maturational Unreadiness as Measured by the Spiral Aftereffect and Other Visual-Perceptual Techniques." *Percept & Motor Skills* 25:841–54 D '67. * (*PA* 42:8736)
59. ADAM, JUNE, and RING, MARION. "Investigation of Interactions of Luminance Contrast and Temporal Factors in Figural Aftereffects." *Percept & Motor Skills* 27:287–91 Ag '68. * (*PA* 43:1800)
60. MINARD, JAMES G. "Embedded Figures and Frame Disappearance Tests (EFT and FDT) as Measures of 'Percept Maintenance': A Study and Its Replication." *Percept & Motor Skills* 27:118 Ag '68. * (*PA* 43:1818)

NAME INDEX

Aaronson, B. S.: 13
Adam, J.: 59
Allen, R. M.: 22
Alvord, A.: 42
Andersson, A. L.: 46
Baumeister, A.: 50
Beech, H. R.: 17
Berger, D.: 14
Blau, T. H.: 23
Blumberg, S.: 41
Bragg, R. A.: 43
Bryan, J. H.: 18, 27, 34
Claridge, G. S.: 39
Coons, W. H.: 29
Davids, A.: 6
Day, R. H.: 24
Deabler, H. L.: 3, 5, 8
Efstathiou, A.: 56
Eichman, W. J.: *rev*, 6:177
Elliott, J.: 51
Everson, R.: 14
Eysenck, H. J.: 7, 25–6
Eysenck, S. B. G.: 25
Freeman, E.: 1
Freud, S. L.: 35, 40, 58
Frisk, G. C.: 48
Gallese, A. J.: 4
Garrett, E. S.: 8
Gertz, B.: 12
Gilberstadt, H.: 15
Gilbert, J. G.: 52, 57
Glassman, S.: 9
Goldberg, L. R.: 16
Goldenberg, L.: 6
Gynther, M. D.: 12
Harding, G. F.: 9
Helz, W. C.: 9
Herrington, R. N.: 39
Hildt, M. T.: 53
Holland, H.: 7, 26
Holland, H. C.: 17
Honigfeld, G. H.: 45
Josey, W. E.: 1
Kaplan, H. K.: 10
Kaskoff, Y. D.: 14
Knowles, J. B.: 54
Korman, M.: 41
Krasner, L.: 54
Kurtzke, J. F.: 38

Laufer, M. W.: 6
Levee, R. F.: 52, 57
Levine, M.: 11, 21, 36
Loder, E.: 34
London, P.: 18, 27
McDonough, J. M.: 28
Mann, L.: 42
Mayer, E.: 29
Medlin, R. E.: 37
Metwally, A.: 33
Minard, J. G.: 60
Morant, R. B.: 56
Page, H. A.: 10
Philbrick, E. B.: 20
Price, A. C.: 3, 8
Price, H.: 42
Rakita, G.: 10
Reitan, R. M.: *rev*, 6:177
Ring, M.: 59
Ripke, R. J.: 31
Roehrig, W. C.: 47
Rosen, A.: 15
Rutledge, L.: 14
Rutschmann, J.: 47
Sappenfield, B. R.: 31
Saucer, R. T.: 5
Schaffer, R. E.: 23
Schein, J.: 15
Schein, J. D.: 19, 30
Scott, T. R.: 37, 43
Sindberg, R. M.: 32
Smarr, R. G.: 43
Smith, J. P.: 55
Smith, N. B.: 10
Smith, P. A.: 16
Smith, T. E.: 50
Snyder, R. T.: 58
Soueif, M. I.: 33
Spivack, G.: 11, 21, 36
Standlee, L. S.: 2
Stern, A.: 44
Stilson, D. W.: 12
Suehs, J. E.: 49
Trouton, D. S.: 7
Truss, C. V.: 22
Urquhart, D.: 50
VanLiere, D. E.: 53
Whitmyre, J. W.: 38

[252]

★**Stamp Behaviour Study Technique.** Preschool-kgn; 1968; BST; checklist for recording teacher's observation of behaviour in 12 areas: people, selfhood, demands of others, demands on others, frustration, stress, realistic fears, need for approval, communication, physical health, use of powers, general behaviour; 1 form (2 pages); teacher's guide (17 pages); psychologist's manual referred to in teacher's guide is not available; no data on reliability; Aus 30¢ per 10 tests; 75¢ per teacher's guide; postpaid within Australia; (15–45) minutes following observations; Isla M. Stamp; Australian Council for Educational Research. *

[253]

Stanford Hypnotic Susceptibility Scale. College and adults; 1959–62; SHSS; Forms A ('59), B ('59), C ('62); Form C, which is for research use only, contains more varied items and is not considered a parallel form; manual for Forms A and B ('59, 56 pages, including both forms and sample interrogatory and scoring blanks); manual for Form C ('62, 52 pages, including test and sample scoring booklet); separate scoring blanks ('59, 1 page) for Forms A, B; interrogatory blank ('59, 1 page) for Forms A and B; scoring booklet ('62, 6 pages) for Form C; norms for college students only; 75¢ per pad of 25 scoring blanks; $1 per pad of 50 interrogatory blanks; $2.75 per 25 scoring booklets; $2.25 per manual for Forms A and B; $1.50 per manual for Form C; $3.75 per specimen set of all 3 forms; postage extra; (40) minutes; André M. Weitzenhoffer and Ernest R. Hilgard; Consulting Psychologists Press, Inc. *

For reviews by Milton V. Kline and C. Scott Moss, see 6:178 (17 references).

REFERENCES

1–17. See 6:178.
18. FISHER, SEYMOUR. "Body Image and Hypnotic Response." *Int J Clin & Exp Hyp* 11:152–62 Jl '63. * (PA 38:6274)
19. COOPER, GEORGE W., JR., and DANA, RICHARD H. "Hypnotizability and the Maudsley Personality Inventory." *Int J Clin & Exp Hyp* 12:28–33 Ja '64. * (PA 38:8745)
20. EVANS, FREDERICK J., and SCHMEIDLER, DEL. "Reliability of Two Observers Scoring the Stanford Hypnotic Susceptibility Scale, Form C." *Int J Clin & Exp Hyp* 12:239–51 O '64. * (PA 39:5055)
21. KRAMER, ERNEST, and BRENNAN, EDWIN P. "Hypnotic Susceptibility of Schizophrenic Patients." *J Abn & Social Psychol* 69:657–9 D '64. * (PA 39:8496)
22. MELEI, JANET P., and HILGARD, ERNEST R. "Attitudes Toward Hypnosis, Self-Predictions, and Hypnotic Susceptibility." *Int J Clin & Exp Hyp* 12:99–108 Ap '64. * (PA 39:2195)
23. O'CONNELL, DONALD NEIL. "An Experimental Comparison of Hypnotic Depth Measured by Self-Ratings and by an Objective Scale." *Int J Clin & Exp Hyp* 12:34–46 Ja '64. * (PA 38:8752)
24. ROBERTS, MARY JOSEPHINE REINHARDT. *Attention and Cognitive Controls as Related to Individual Differences in Hypnotic Susceptibility.* Doctor's thesis, Stanford University (Stanford, Calif.), 1964. (DA 25:4261)
25. HILGARD, ERNEST R. *Hypnotic Susceptibility.* New York: Harcourt, Brace & World, Inc., 1965. Pp. xiii, 434. * (PA 39:15730)
26. HILGARD, JOSEPHINE R. Chap. 18, "Personality and Hypnotizability: Inferences From Case Studies." pp. 343–74. In *Hypnotic Susceptibility.* By Ernest R. Hilgard. New York: Harcourt, Brace & World, Inc., 1965. Pp. xiii, 434. * (PA 39:15730)
27. PEDERSEN, DARHL M., and COOPER, LESLIE M. "Some Personality Correlates of Hypnotic Susceptibility." *Int J Clin & Exp Hyp* 13:193–202 Jl '65. * (PA 39:15735)
28. VINGOE, FRANCIS JAMES. *The Relationship Between Measures of Self-Awareness, Self-Acceptance and Hypnotizability.* Doctor's thesis, University of Oregon (Eugene, Ore.), 1965. (DA 26:7450)
29. EVANS, FREDERICK J., and SCHMEIDLER, DEL. "Relationship Between the Harvard Group Scale of Hypnotic Susceptibility and the Stanford Hypnotic Susceptibility Scale: Form C." *Int J Clin & Exp Hyp* 14:333–43 O '66. * (PA 41:62)
30. O'CONNELL, DONALD N.; ORNE, MARTIN T.; and SHOR, RONALD E. "A Comparison of Hypnotic Susceptibility as Assessed by Diagnostic Ratings and Initial Standardized Test Scores." *Int J Clin & Exp Hyp* 14:324–32 O '66. * (PA 41:67)
31. VINGOE, FRANK J., and KRAMER, ERNEST F. "Hypnotic Susceptibility of Hospitalized Psychotic Patients: A Pilot Study." *Int J Clin & Exp Hyp* 14:47–54 Ja '66. * (PA 40:4864)
32. PALMER, ROBERT D. "Visual Imagery, Visual Complexity, and Susceptibility to Hypnosis." *Proc Ann Conv Am Psychol Assn* 75:185–6 '67. * (PA 41:12965)
33. SACHS, LEWIS B., and ANDERSON, WARREN L. "Modification of Hypnotic Susceptibility." *Int J Clin & Exp Hyp* 15:172–80 O '67. * (PA 42:4925)
34. PALMER, ROBERT D., and FIELD, PETER B. "Visual Imagery and Susceptibility to Hypnosis." *J Consult & Clin Psychol* 32:456–61 Ag '68. * (PA 42:16540)
35. THORNE, D. EUGENE, and BEIER, ERNST G. "Hypnotist and Manner of Presentation Effects on a Standardized Hypnotic Susceptibility Test." *J Consult & Clin Psychol* 32:610–2 O '68. * (PA 43:226)

NAME INDEX

[254]

★**Stanford Profile Scales of Hypnotic Susceptibility, Revised Edition.** College and adults; 1963–67; SPSHS; 25 scores: agnosia and cognitive distortion (4 item scores plus total), positive hallucinations (4 item scores plus total), negative hallucinations (4 item scores plus total), dreams and regressions (4 item scores plus total), amnesia and post-hypnotic compulsions (3 item scores plus total), total susceptibility; one of the item scores for amnesia and post-hypnotic compulsions is derived from Form A of the *Stanford Hypnotic Susceptibility Scale* (see 253) and provision is also made for profiling 3 additional scores (loss of motor coordination and 2 subscores) from this scale; Forms 1, 2; forms may be used separately but administration of both is recommended and profile is based upon administration of both; manual ('67, 83 pages, includes sample copy of scoring booklet for each form and stimulus cards for 2 subtests); scoring booklet ('67, 12 pages) for each form; $7.75 per 25 sets of scoring booklets for both forms; $2.50 per manual; $4 per specimen set; postage extra; administration time not reported; various equipment necessary for administration; Ernest R. Hilgard and André M. Weitzenhoffer (test), (revised standardization data by Ernest R. Hilgard, Leslie M. Cooper, Lillian W. Lauer, and Arlene H. Morgan); Consulting Psychologists Press, Inc. *

For reviews by Seymour Fisher and Eugene E. Levitt of the original edition, see 6:179.

REFERENCES

1. HILGARD, ERNEST R. "Profiles of Hypnotic Ability." *Am J Clin Hyp* 7:136–9 O '64. * (PA 39:8147)
2. HILGARD, ERNEST R. *Hypnotic Susceptibility.* New York: Harcourt, Brace & World, Inc., 1965. Pp. xiii, 434. * (PA 39:15730)
3. HILGARD, JOSEPHINE R. Chap. 18, "Personality and Hypnotizability: Inferences From Case Studies," pp. 343–74. In *Hypnotic Susceptibility.* By Ernest R. Hilgard. New York:

Harcourt, Brace & World, Inc., 1965. Pp. xiii, 434. * (PA 39:15730)
4. COOPER, LESLIE M.; BANFORD, SUZANNE A.; SCHUBOT, ERROL; and TART, CHARLES T. "A Further Attempt to Modify Hypnotic Susceptibility Through Repeated Individualized Experience." *Int J Clin & Exp Hyp* 15:118–24 Jl '67. * (PA 42:230)

[255]

*Stern Activities Index. Grades 7–16 and adults; 1950–69; SAI, also AI; also called *Activities Index;* personal needs (see 256 for related tests of environmental press covering the same areas) ; 48 scores: 30 need scores (abasement-assurance, achievement, adaptability-defensiveness, affiliation, aggression-blame avoidance, change-sameness, conjunctivity-disjunctivity, counteraction, deference-restiveness, dominance-tolerance, ego achievement, emotionality-placidity, energy-passivity, exhibitionism-inferiority avoidance, fantasied achievement, harm avoidance-risk taking, humanities and social science, impulsiveness-deliberation, narcissism, nurturance, objectivity-projectivity, order-disorder, play-work, practicalness-impracticalness, reflectiveness, science, sensuality-puritanism, sexuality-prudishness, supplication-autonomy, understanding), 12 factor scores (self-assertion, audacity-timidity, intellectual interests, motivation, applied interests, orderliness, submissiveness, closeness, sensuousness, friendliness, expressiveness-constraint, egoism-diffidence), 4 second-order factor scores (achievement orientation, dependency needs, emotional expressiveness, educability), 1 validity score, 1 academic aptitude score; also 5 composite culture factor scores (expressive, intellectual, protective, vocational, collegiate) based on combinations of needs scores with environmental press scores; Form 1158 ('58, 7 pages) ; research report entitled *People in Context: Measuring Person-Environment Congruence in Education and Industry* ('69, about 355 pages, John Wiley & Sons, Inc.) ; scoring and college norms manual ('63, 30 pages plus tests) for AI and *College Characteristics Index* (see 256b) ; NCS individual profile ('63, 1 page) for any norm group and for all scores ; need score profiles: individual ('63, 1 page), group ('66, 1 page) ; factor score profiles: individual ('66, 1 page), group ('63, 1 page) ; college culture need-press profile: individual ('66, 1 page), group ('66, 1 page) based upon AI and *College Characteristics Index;* separate answer sheets (IBM 1230, NCS) must be used; 25¢ per test; $3.25 per 50 NCS answer sheets; $6 per set of NCS hand scoring stencils ; $25 per 500 IBM 1230 answer sheets (available from author, Syracuse University, Syracuse, N.Y. 13210) ; $3.50 per scoring and norms manual; postpaid; scoring service, 40¢ to $1.20 per test; (20–90) minutes ; George G. Stern; distributed by National Computer Systems. *

REFERENCES

1–27. See 6:180.
28. BREWER, JUNE HARDEN. *An Ecological Study of the Psychological Environment of a Negro College and the Personality Needs of Its Students.* Doctor's thesis, University of Texas (Austin, Tex.), 1963. *(DA* 24:2777)
29. LANDIS, HOWARD LANDIS. *Dissonance Between Student and College Variables Related to Success and Satisfaction.* Doctor's thesis, Pennsylvania State University (University Park, Pa.), 1963. *(DA* 25:1047)
30. MUELLER, WILLIAM J. "The Influence of Self Insight on Social Perception Scores." *J Counsel Psychol* 10:185–91 su '63. * (PA 38:10135)
31. CAMPBELL, PAUL S. *Personality Needs of Community College and University Students and Their Perceptions of the Press of Their Institutions: An Experimental Investigation.* Doctor's thesis, Michigan State University (East Lansing, Mich.), 1964. *(DA* 25:2603)
32. CURETON, CHARLES BARTON. *The Relationship of the Student's Needs and the Teaching Environment to Academic Achievement.* Doctor's thesis, University of Tennessee (Knoxville, Tenn.), 1964. *(DA* 25:5105)
33. GILLIS, JOHN. "Personality Needs of Future Teachers." *Ed & Psychol Meas* 24:589–600 f '64. * (PA 39:6001)
34. GRADY, MICHAEL JOSEPH, JR. *The Interrelationships Between: (1) Each of Three Motivational Needs of Officer Students; (2) The Pattern of Scores on a Decision Making Test; and (3) Academic Success in One of Three Air University Resident Courses.* Doctor's thesis, University of Alabama (University, Ala.), 1964. *(DA* 25:3972)
35. GRIFFIN, WILLIAM MAXWELL. *A Study of the Relationship of Certain Characteristics of High School Seniors to Effectiveness in Independent Study.* Doctor's thesis, Syracuse University (Syracuse, N.Y.), 1964. *(DA* 25:5787)
36. KEITH, JAMES AUGUSTUS. *The Relationship of the Congruency of Environmental Press and Student Need Systems to Reported Personal Satisfaction and Academic Success.* Doctor's thesis, University of Alabama (University, Ala.), 1964. *(DA* 25:7081)
37. LOVELESS, EUGENE J. "Social Role Preferences and Responses to the Four Picture Test." *J Proj Tech & Pers Assess* 28:64–6 Mr '64. * (PA 39:1489)
38. LUKENS, LOIS EILEEN. *Personality Patterns Related to Choice of Two Fields of Clinical Specialization in Nursing.* Doctor's thesis, University of Michigan (Ann Arbor, Mich.), 1964. *(DA* 25:3400)
39. SCHWARTZ, RONALD M. *Congruence Between the Needs of Individuals and Environmental Press as Related to Performance and Adjustment in a Large Organization.* Doctor's thesis, New York University (New York, N.Y.), 1964. *(DA* 26:483)
40. WEBB, SAM C. "The Psychological Components of Scores for Two Tests of Report Writing Ability." *Ed & Psychol Meas* 24:31–46 sp '64. * (PA 39:1770)
41. GRADEL, DOROTHY V. *The Relationships Between Students' Needs—Environmental Press and Achievement in Nursing Education of Students in Selected Associate Degree Nursing Education Programs in Washington State.* Doctor's thesis, Washington State University (Pullman, Wash.), 1965. *(DA* 26:321)
42. LUKENS, LOIS GRAHAM. "Personality Patterns and Choice of Clinical Nursing Specialization." *Nursing Res* 14:210–21 su '65. *
43. MYERS, JESSE WOODROW. *The Personality Syndrome of Presbyterian University Pastors Using Need Characteristics and Based on a Stay-Leave Criterion.* Doctor's thesis, University of Maryland (College Park, Md.), 1965. *(DA* 27:4555B)
44. SPUHLER, LEE. *A Study of the Characteristics of the Academic Learning Climate of Montana State University.* Doctor's thesis, University of Montana (Missoula, Mont.), 1965. *(DA* 27:4140A)
45. STERN, GEORGE G. "Student Ecology and the College Environment." *J Med Ed* 40:132–54 F '65. *
46. STRICKER, GEORGE. "Intellective and Nonintellective Correlates of Grade-Point Average." *Proc Ann Conv Am Psychol Assn* 73:305–6 '65. * (PA 39:16460)
47. FURST, EDWARD J. "Validity of Some Objective Scales of Motivation for Predicting Academic Achievement." *Ed & Psychol Meas* 26:927–33 w '66. * (PA 41:4991)
48. HEALY, MARY MARGARET IRENE. *Assessment of Academic Aptitude, Personality Characteristics, and Religious Orientation of Catholic Sister-Teacher-Trainees.* Doctor's thesis, University of Minnesota (Minneapolis, Minn.), 1966. *(DA* 27:982A)
49. McCORMICK, FRED CHARLES. *Relation of Individual and Institutional Characteristics to Students' Personality Needs at Saint Louis University.* Doctor's thesis, University of Minnesota (Minneapolis, Minn.), 1966. *(DA* 28:56A)
50. McLAUGHLIN, ROGER JAMES. *The Process of Decision in College Selection and Its Relation to Student Achievement and Withdrawal.* Doctor's thesis, Syracuse University (Syracuse, N.Y.), 1966. *(DA* 28:805A)
51. MUELLER, WILLIAM J. "Need Structure and the Projection of Traits Onto Parents." *J Personality & Social Psychol* 3:63–72 Ja '66. * (PA 40:2914)
52. CALIFF, STANLEY NORMAN. *Perception of College Environment by Achieving and Non-Achieving Freshmen.* Doctor's thesis, Claremont Graduate School (Claremont, Calif.), 1967. *(DA* 29:751B)
53. D'AMICO, DONALD JOHN. *The Degree of Congruence Between Personality Needs and Environmental Press as a Basis for Discriminating Between Patterns of Teacher Behavior.* Doctor's thesis, Illinois State University (Normal, Ill.), 1967. *(DA* 28:4524A)
54. GRAHAM, LOIS E. "Differential Characteristics of Graduate Students Preparing for Teaching or Supervision in Two Clinical Specialties." *Nursing Res* 16:182–4 sp '67. *
55. GREENE, JAMES E., SR. "The 'Needs' of Enrollees in a 'Floating' University." *Sci Ed* 51:195–203 Mr '67. *
56. HAEFNER, DONALD ANDREW. *Levels of Academic Achievement as Related to Environmental Press and Psychological Needs of High Ability Liberal Arts Students.* Doctor's thesis, University of Tennessee (Knoxville, Tenn.), 1967. *(DA* 28:3998A)
57. HAMATY, GEORGE GREGORY. *Some Behavioral Correlates of Organizational Climates and Cultures.* Doctor's thesis, Syracuse University (Syracuse, N.Y.), 1967. *(DA* 28:4849A)
58. HERR, EDWIN L.; KIGHT, HOWARD R.; and HANSEN, JAMES C. "The Relation of Students' Needs to Their Per-

ceptions of a High School Environment." *J Ed Res* 61:51–2 O '67. *

59. JAMBURA, JOHN WAYNE. *An Analysis of Certain Relationships of Student Needs, College Environment, and College Choice.* Doctor's thesis, Washington State University (Pullman, Wash.), 1967. (*DA* 28:498A)

60. MERRITT, WILLIAM RAY. *A Study of the Relationship Between Grade Point Average and Certain Personality Characteristics in a Mississippi High School.* Doctor's thesis, University of Southern Mississippi (Hattiesburg, Miss.), 1967. (*DA* 28:1266A)

61. OLSON, GARY FRANKLIN. *Congruence and Dissonance in the Ecology of Educational Administrators as a Basis for Discriminating Between Patterns of Leadership Behavior.* Doctor's thesis, Illinois State University (Normal, Ill.), 1967. (*DA* 28:4422A)

62. SIMMONS, MILTON DELBERT, JR. *The Relationship of Personality Characteristics to Attitudes of Ministerial Students.* Doctor's thesis, University of Oklahoma (Norman, Okla.), 1967. (*DA* 28:2522A)

63. STABLER, JOHN R., and GOODRICH, ANN H. "Personality and Family Background Correlates of Students' Response to Physical Danger." *J Psychol* 67:313–8 N '67. * (*PA* 42:2557)

64. STEGMAN, WILBUR NUEL. *A Descriptive Study of Certain Socio-Psychological Characteristics of Selected Secondary School Environments.* Doctor's thesis, Oklahoma State University (Stillwater, Okla.), 1967. (*DA* 29:110A)

65. STERN, GEORGE G. *People in Context: The Measurement of Environmental Interaction in School and Society,* Vols. *1* and *2.* Syracuse, N.Y.: the Author, 1967. Pp. xxiv, 289; ii, 290–505, plus unnumbered appendices. *

66. STRICKER, GEORGE. "Interrelationships of Activities Index and College Characteristics Index Scores." *J Counsel Psychol* 14:368–70 Jl '67. * (*PA* 41:12504)

67. D'AMICO, DONALD J. "The Degree of Congruence Between Personality Needs and Environmental Press as a Basis for Discriminating Between Patterns of Teacher Behavior." *Ill Sch Res* 4:32–7 My '68. *

68. SIMMONS, MILTON DELBERT, JR., and PARKER, HARRY J. "Attitude and Personality Traits of Ministerial Students: The Influence and Control of Reference Group Phenomena." *Relig Ed* 63:309–14 Jl '68. * (*PA* 42:17086)

NAME INDEX

[256]

*Stern Environment Indexes. Grades 9–13, 13–16, adults, employees; 1957–69; SEI, also EI; environmental press (see 255 for a related test of personal needs covering the same areas); 30 press scores (abasement-assurance, achievement, adaptability-defensiveness, affiliation, aggression-blame avoidance, change-sameness, conjunctivity-disjunctivity, counteraction, deference-restiveness, dominance-tolerance, ego achievement, emotionality-placidity, energy-passivity, exhibitionism-inferiority avoidance, fantasied achievement, harm avoidance-risk taking, humanities and social science, impulsiveness-deliberation, narcissism,

nurturance, objectivity-projectivity, order-disorder, play-work, practicalness-impracticalness, reflectiveness, science, sensuality-puritanism, sexuality-prudishness, supplication-autonomy, understanding) for each index plus press factor scores and composite culture factor scores based on combinations of environmental press scores with needs scores specific to each edition as listed below; 4 editions; research report entitled *People in Context: Measuring Person-Environment Congruence in Education and Industry* ('69, about 355 pages, John Wiley & Sons, Inc.); separate answer sheets (IBM 1230, NCS) must be used; 25¢ per test; $3.25 per 50 NCS answer sheets; $6 per set of NCS hand scoring stencils; $25 per 500 IBM 1230 answer sheets (available from author, Syracuse University, Syracuse, N.Y. 13210); postpaid; scoring service, 40¢ to $1.20 per test; (20–90) minutes; distributed by National Computer Systems. *

a) HIGH SCHOOL CHARACTERISTICS INDEX. Grades 9–13; 1960; HSCI; Form 960 ('60, 7 pages); 40 scores: 30 press scores listed above, 7 factor scores (intellectual climate, expressiveness, group life, personal dignity, achievement standards, orderliness, practicalness) based on combinations of the press scores, and 3 second-order factor scores (development press, orderliness, practicalness); George G. Stern.

b) COLLEGE CHARACTERISTICS INDEX. Grades 13–16; 1957–63; CCI; Form 1158 ('58, 7 pages); 48 scores: 30 press scores listed above, 11 factor scores (aspiration level, intellectual climate, student dignity, academic climate, academic achievement, self-expression, group life, academic organization, social form, play-work, vocational climate) based on combinations of the press scores, 2 second-order factor scores (intellectual climate, non-intellectual climate), and 5 composite culture factor scores (expressive, intellectual, protective, vocational, collegiate) based on combinations of need scores with press scores; scoring and norms manual ('63, 30 pages plus tests) for CCI and *Stern Activities Index;* NCS profile ('63, 1 page) for any norm group; individual profile ('66, 1 page); group profile ('66, 1 page); factor score profiles: individual ('66, 1 page), group ('63, 1 page); $3.50 per scoring and norms manual; George G. Stern and C. Robert Pace.

c) EVENING COLLEGE CHARACTERISTICS INDEX, Adults; 1961; ECCI; Form 161 ('61, 7 pages); 30 press scores as listed above; George G. Stern, Clifford L. Winters, Jr., N. Sidney Archer, and Donald L. Meyer.

d) ORGANIZATIONAL CLIMATE INDEX. Employees; 1958–63; OCI; Form 1163 ('63, 7 pages); three norm groups; school districts: 47 scores: 30 press scores listed above, 6 factor scores (intellectual climate, achievement standards, practicalness, supportiveness, orderliness, impulse control) based on combinations of the press scores, 2 second-order factor scores (development press, control press), 6 composite culture factor scores (protective, achievement, development, emotional, friendliness, submissiveness) based on combinations of the need and press scores, 3 second-order composite culture factor scores (conventional, expressive, warmth); Peace Corps: 38 scores: 30 press scores listed above, 6 factor scores (group life vs. isolation, intellectual climate, personal dignity, achievement standards, orderliness, impulse control) based on combinations of the press scores, 2 second-order factor scores (development press, control press); Peace Corps factor score profile ('66, 1 page); industrial sites: 38 scores: 30 press scores listed above, 6 factor scores (intellectual climate, organizational effectiveness, personal dignity, orderliness, work, impulse control) based on combinations of the press scores, 2 second-order factor scores (development press, control press); George G. Stern and Carl R. Steinhoff.

REFERENCES

1–19. See 6:92.
20. PACE, C. ROBERT. Chap. 3, "Implications of Differences in Campus Atmosphere for Evaluation and Planning of College Programs," pp. 43–61. In *Personality Factors on the College Campus: Review of a Symposium.* Edited by Robert L. Sutherland and others. Austin, Tex.: Hogg Foundation for Mental Health, University of Texas, 1962. Pp. xii, 242. * (*PA* 37:5613)
21. PECK, ROBERT F. "Student Mental Health: The Range of Personality Patterns in a College Population," pp. 161–99. (*PA* 37:5614) In *Personality Factors on the College Campus: Review of a Symposium.* Edited by Robert L. Sutherland and others. Austin, Tex.: Hogg Foundation for Mental Health, 1962. Pp. xxii, 242. * (*PA* 37:5621)
22. HERR, EDWIN LEON. *An Examination of Differential Perceptions of "Environmental Press" by High School Students as Related to Their Achievement and Participation in Activities.* Doctor's thesis, Columbia University (New York, N.Y.), 1963. (*DA* 24:5078)
23. LANDIS, HOWARD LANDIS. *Dissonance Between Student and College Variables Related to Success and Satisfaction.* Doctor's thesis, Pennsylvania State University (University Park, Pa.), 1963. (*DA* 25:1047)
24. PRIOR, JOHN JOSEPH. *The College Characteristics Index as an Instrument for Identifying Areas of Self-Improvement in a Single University.* Doctor's thesis, Columbia University (New York, N.Y.), 1963. (*DA* 25:1666)
25. ROCK, ROBERT WILLIAM. *Features of the Pace College Image as Identified by the College Characteristics Index.* Doctor's thesis, Columbia University (New York, N.Y.), 1963. (*DA* 24:5146)
26. WINFREY, JAMES KING. *The Appraisal of Institutional Press as Perceived by Selected Groups of Minneapolis Area High School Students.* Doctor's thesis, University of Minnesota (Minneapolis, Minn.), 1963. (*DA* 25:2359)
27. WOOD, PAUL LESLIE. *The Relationship of the College Characteristics Index to Achievement and Certain Other Variables for Freshmen Women in the College of Education at the University of Georgia.* Doctor's thesis, University of Georgia (Athens, Ga.), 1963. (*DA* 24:4558)
28. CAMPBELL, PAUL S. *Personality Needs of Community College and University Students and Their Perceptions of the Press of Their Institutions: An Experimental Investigation.* Doctor's thesis, Michigan State University (East Lansing, Mich.), 1964. (*DA* 25:2603)
29. CURETON, CHARLES BARTON. *The Relationship of the Student's Needs and the Teaching Environment to Academic Achievement.* Doctor's thesis, University of Tennessee (Knoxville, Tenn.), 1964. (*DA* 25:5105)
30. KEITH, JAMES AUGUSTUS. *The Relationship of the Congruency of Environmental Press and Student Need Systems to Reported Personal Satisfaction and Academic Success.* Doctor's thesis, University of Alabama (University, Ala.), 1964. (*DA* 25:7081)
31. PATE, BART CARTER. *Colleges as Environmental Systems: Toward the Codification of Social Theory.* Doctor's thesis, Boston University (Boston, Mass.), 1964. (*DA* 25:3158)
32. RAMEY, WILLIAM EDWARD. *A Study of Selected Variables of the High School Characteristics Index.* Doctor's thesis, Arizona State University (Tempe, Ariz.), 1964. (*DA* 28:3035A)
33. SCHWARTZ, RONALD M. *Congruence Between the Needs of Individuals and Environmental Press as Related to Performance and Adjustment in a Large Organization.* Doctor's thesis, New York University (New York, N.Y.), 1964. (*DA* 26:483)
34. WALKER, WILLIAM JOHN. *Creativity and High School Climate.* Doctor's thesis, Syracuse University (Syracuse, N.Y.), 1964. (*DA* 25:5657)
35. BAKER, S. R. "Vocational Indecisiveness and Decisiveness, and Level of Grade Expectation as Related to Perception of University Environmental Press." *Percept & Motor Skills* 21:305–6 Ag '65. *
36. BECKER, SAMUEL L.; GOODSTEIN, LEONARD D.; and MITTMAN, ARTHUR. "Relationships Between the Minnesota Multiphasic Personality Inventory and the College Characteristics Index." *J Col Stud Personnel* 6:219–23 Je '65. *
37. BRUNING, CHARLES RICHARD. *Comparison of Institutional Press as Perceived by Selected Students in Church Related Schools.* Doctor's thesis, University of Minnesota (Minneapolis, Minn.), 1965. (*DA* 26:4356)
38. CREAMER, DON GENE. *An Analysis of the Congruence Between Perceived Environment and Reported Environment on a College Campus.* Doctor's thesis, Indiana University (Bloomington, Ind.), 1965. (*DA* 26:5808)
39. GRADEL, DOROTHY V. *The Relationships Between Students' Needs—Environmental Press and Achievement in Nursing Education of Students in Selected Associate Degree Nursing Education Programs in Washington State.* Doctor's thesis, Washington State University (Pullman, Wash.), 1965. (*DA* 26:321)

40. HERR, EDWIN L. "Differential Perceptions of 'Environmental Press' by High School Students." *Personnel & Guid J* 43:678–86 Mr '65. * (*PA* 39:12976)
41. KASPER, EUGENE C.; MUNGER, PAUL F.; and MYERS, ROGER A. "Student Perceptions of the Environment in Guidance and Non-Guidance Schools." *Personnel & Guid J* 43:674–7 Mr '65. * (*PA* 39:13003)
42. PADDACK, JERE DARRYL. *An Analysis of the Educational Characteristics of the University of North Dakota as Perceived by Residents of Social Fraternities and Residence Halls.* Doctor's thesis, University of North Dakota (Grand Forks, N.D.), 1965. (*DA* 26:5792)
43. SEYMOUR, WARREN RALPH. *Perceptions of College Environments Held by Students and Counselors.* Doctor's thesis, University of Missouri (Columbia, Mo.), 1965. (*DA* 26:5250)
44. SPUHLER, LEE. *A Study of the Characteristics of the Academic Learning Climate of Montana State University.* Doctor's thesis, University of Montana (Missoula, Mont.), 1965. (*DA* 27:4140A)
45. STERN, GEORGE G. "Student Ecology and the College Environment." *J Med Ed* 40:132–54 F '65. *
46. STONE, LEROY A. "Factor Analysis of the Stern Activities Index." Abstract. *Psychol Rep* 16:1223–4 Je '65. * (*PA* 39:15273)
47. VACCHIANO, RALPH B., and ADRIAN, ROBERT J. "The Interrelation Between the Picture Identification Test and the Activities Index." *J Psychol* 60:81–5 My '65. * (*PA* 39:15203)
48. WHITE, RICHARD EARL. *Patterns of Institutional Press Among Selected Groups of Minnesota Junior College Students.* Doctor's thesis, University of Minnesota (Minneapolis, Minn.), 1965. (*DA* 26:4411)
49. BAKER, SHELDON R. "A Comparative Study of Perceptions of a University Environment Between Honor and Nonhonor Freshmen Groups." *Ed & Psychol Meas* 26:973–6 w '66. * (*PA* 41:4988)
50. HASSENGER, ROBERT, and WEISS, ROBERT. "The Catholic College Climate." *Sch R* 74:419–45 w '66. * (*PA* 41:6221)
51. KASPAR, ELIZABETH ANN. *An Investigation of the Perception of College Climate Among Students of Varying Ability: Comparisons Within the Albion College Climate and Across Types of College Climate.* Doctor's thesis, Indiana University (Bloomington, Ind.), 1966. (*DA* 27:2071A)
52. KIGHT, HOWARD R., and HERR, EDWIN L. "Identification of Four Environmental Press Factors in the Stern High School Characteristics Index." *Ed & Psychol Meas* 26:479–81 su '66. *
53. LAUTERBACH, CARL G., and VIELHABER, DAVID P. "Need-Press and Expectation-Press Indices as Predictors of College Achievement." *Ed & Psychol Meas* 26:965–72 w '66. * (*PA* 41:4994)
54. McLAUGHLIN, ROGER JAMES. *The Process of Decision in College Selection and Its Relation to Student Achievement and Withdrawal.* Doctor's thesis, Syracuse University (Syracuse, N.Y.), 1966. (*DA* 28:805A)
55. PERVIN, LAWRENCE A. "Reality and Nonreality in Student Expectations of College." *J Psychol* 64:41–8 S '66. * (*PA* 40:12614)
56. STERN, GEORGE G. "Freshman Myth." *NEA J* 55:41–3 S '66. *
57. VACCHIANO, RALPH B., and ADRIAN, ROBERT J. "Multiple Discriminant Prediction of College Career Choice." *Ed & Psychol Meas* 26:985–95 w '66. * (*PA* 41:5006)
58. CALIFF, STANLEY NORMAN. *Perception of College Environment by Achieving and Non-Achieving Freshmen.* Doctor's thesis, Claremont Graduate School (Claremont, Calif.), 1967. (*DA* 29:751B)
59. D'AMICO, DONALD JOHN. *The Degree of Congruence Between Personality Needs and Environmental Press as a Basis for Discriminating Between Patterns of Teacher Behavior.* Doctor's thesis, Illinois State University (Normal, Ill.), 1967. (*DA* 28:4524A)
60. GREENE, JAMES E., SR. "The 'Needs' of Enrollees in a 'Floating' University." *Sci Ed* 51:195–203 Mr '67. *
61. HAEFNER, DONALD ANDREW. *Levels of Academic Achievement as Related to Environmental Press and Psychological Needs of High Ability Liberal Arts Students.* Doctor's thesis, University of Tennessee (Knoxville, Tenn.), 1967. (*DA* 28:3998A)
62. HERR, EDWIN L., and KIGHT, HOWARD R. "The High School Characteristics Index: A Study of Scale Reliabilities." *J Ed Res* 60:334–6 Mr '67. *
63. HERR, EDWIN L.; KIGHT, HOWARD R.; and HANSEN, JAMES C. "The Relation of Students' Needs to Their Perceptions of a High School Environment." *J Ed Res* 61:51–2 O '67. *
64. IVEY, ALLEN E.; MILLER, C. DEAN; and GOLDSTEIN, ARNOLD D. "Differential Perceptions of College Environment: Student Personnel Staff and Students." *Personnel & Guid J* 46:17–21 S '67. *
65. JAMBURA, JOHN WAYNE. *An Analysis of Certain Relationships of Student Needs, College Environment, and College Choice.* Doctor's thesis, Washington State University (Pullman, Wash.), 1967. (*DA* 28:498A)
66. KELLEY, DAVID BRANHAM. *Perceptions of College Environments of Freshman Students Enrolled in Three New Geor-*

gia Community Junior Colleges. Doctor's thesis, University of Georgia (Athens, Ga.), 1967. *(DA* 28:4414A)

67. LARKIN, JOSEPH M. *A Comparative Analysis of the Six Undergraduate College Environments at Oklahoma State University.* Doctor's thesis, Oklahoma State University (Stillwater, Okla.), 1967. *(DA* 28:4876A)

68. McGIBBENY, HERBERT G. *The Internal Images of a State College and Their Relationship to Certain Public Images of the Institution.* Doctor's thesis, University of Pittsburgh (Pittsburgh, Pa.), 1967. *(DA* 28:4449A)

69. MacLEAN, LOWE STANNARD. *Variant Perceptions of the Environmental Press.* Doctor's thesis, Indiana University (Bloomington, Ind.), 1967. *(DA* 28:1991A)

70. OLSON, GARY FRANKLIN. *Congruence and Dissonance in the Ecology of Educational Administrators as a Basis for Discriminating Between Patterns of Leadership Behavior.* Doctor's thesis, Illinois State University (Normal, Ill.), 1967. *(DA* 28:4422A)

71. STEGMAN, WILBUR NUEL. *A Descriptive Study of Certain Socio-Psychological Characteristics of Selected Secondary School Environments.* Doctor's thesis, Oklahoma State University (Stillwater, Okla.), 1967. *(DA* 29:110A)

72. STERN, GEORGE G. *People in Context: The Measurement of Environmental Interaction in School and Society, Vols. 1 and 2.* Syracuse, N.Y.: the Author, 1967. Pp. xxiv, 289; ii, 290–505, plus unnumbered appendices. *

73. STRICKER, GEORGE. "Interrelationships of Activities Index and College Characteristics Index Scores." *J Counsel Psychol* 14:368–70 Jl '67. * *(PA* 41:12504)

74. WEEDE, GARY DEAN. *Electronic Technician Personnel and Training Needs of Iowa Industries.* Doctor's thesis, Iowa State University (Ames, Iowa), 1967. *(DA* 28:3392A)

75. BENNETT, JAMES WELDON. *The Interrelationship of College Press, Student Needs, and Academic Aptitudes as Measured by Grade Point Average in a Southern Denominational College.* Doctor's thesis, North Texas State University (Denton, Tex.), 1968. *(DA* 29:474A)

76. D'AMICO, DONALD J. "The Degree of Congruence Between Personality Needs and Environmental Press as a Basis for Discriminating Between Patterns of Teacher Behavior." *Ill Sch Res* 4:32–7 My '68. *

77. BRAGG, EMMA W. "A Study of the College Campus as a Learning Environment." *J Negro Ed* 37:82–5 sp '68. *

78. EBERLY, CHARLES G., and CECH, EUGENE J. "Residence Hall Program and Perception of University Environment." *Col Stud Survey* 2:65–70 w '68. *

79. JONES, JOHN E. "Components of the High School Environment." *Personnel & Guid J* 47:40–3 S '68. * *(PA* 43:5889)

80. JONES, RONALD EVERETT. *Characteristics, Perceptions, and Values of Students Who Were Placed on Disciplinary Probation or Suspended at the University of Tennessee During the Academic Years 1964–65 and 1965–66.* Doctor's thesis, University of Tennessee (Knoxville, Tenn.), 1968. *(DA* 29:2481A)

81. MITCHELL, JAMES V., JR. "Dimensionality and Differences in the Environmental Press of High Schools." *Am Ed Res J* 5:513–30 N '68. *

82. SEYMOUR, WARREN R. "Student and Counselor Perceptions of College Environments." *J Col Stud Personnel* 9:79–84 Mr '68. *

83. SHAW, KENNETH A. "Accuracy of Expectations of a University's Environment as It Relates to Achievement, Attrition, and Change of Degree Objective." *J Col Stud Personnel* 9:44–8 Ja '68. *

84. TILLQUIST, PAUL FREDERICK. *A Study of Students' Perceptions of Their College Environment as Measured by the College Characteristics Index.* Doctor's thesis, Colorado State College (Greeley, Colo.), 1968. *(DA* 29:1112A)

NAME INDEX

[257]

★**Stockton Geriatric Rating Scale.** Hospital or nursing home patients 65 and older; 1964–66; SGRS; prediction of improvement; 5 scores: physical disability, apathy, communication failure, socially irritating behavior, total; 1 form ('65, 4 pages, referred to as Form 2 in manual); manual ('66, 12 pages, reprint of 1 below); no norms; separate answer sheets must be used; test materials free; Bernard Meer and Janet A. Baker; Department of Research, Stockton State Hospital. *

REFERENCES

1. MEER, BERNARD, and BAKER, JANET A. "The Stockton Geriatric Rating Scale." *J Gerontol* 21:392–403 Jl '66. *
2. KING, MOLLIE, and KRAG, CLETUS L. "The Use of the Stockton Geriatric Rating Scale in Evaluating Large Groups of Chronically Ill Geriatric Patients in a Psychiatric Hospital." Prepublication abstract. *Calif Mental Health Res Dig* 5:163–4 su '67. * *(PA* 42:2908)

[258]

★**Student Description Form.** Grades 9–12; 1964; SDF; ratings by teachers to be used on *Secondary-School Record—Student Description Summary;* 8 ratings: participation in discussion, involvement in classroom activities, pursuit of independent study, evenness of performance, critical and questioning attitude, depth of understanding, personal responsibility, consideration for others; 1 form (2 pages); no specific manual; instructions contained in manual for Secondary-School Record [1964 Edition] ('64, 18 pages); no data on reliability; no norms; $1.30 per 100 forms, cash orders postpaid; National Association of Secondary-School Principals. *

[259]

Study of Values: A Scale for Measuring the Dominant Interests in Personality, Third Edition. College and adults; 1931–60; SV, also AVL; for British adaptation, see 259A; 6 scores: theoretical, economic, aesthetic, social, political, religious; 1 form ('60, 12 pages, identical with test copyrighted in 1951); revised manual ('60, 19 pages); $4.20 per 35 tests; 75¢ per specimen set; postage extra; (20) minutes; Gordon W. Allport, Philip E. Vernon, and Gardner Lindzey; Houghton Mifflin Co. *

For reviews by John D. Hundleby and John A. Radcliffe, see 6:182 (137 references); for a review by N. L. Gage of the second edition, see 5:114 (57 references); for reviews by Harrison G. Gough and William Stephenson, see 4:92 (25 references, 1 excerpt); for a review by Paul E. Meehl of the original edition, see 3:99 (61 references).

REFERENCES

1–61. See 3:99.
62–86. See 4:92.
87–143. See 5:114.
144–280. See 6:182.
281. CARLTON, ROBERT L. *An Experimental Investigation of the Relationship Between Personal Value and Word Intelligibility.* Doctor's thesis, Ohio State University (Columbus, Ohio), 1953. *(DA* 18:1141)
282. HILTON, ANDREW C.; BOLIN, STANLEY F.; PARKER, JAMES W., JR.; TAYLOR, ERWIN K.; and WALKER, WILLIAM B. "The Validity of Personnel Assessments by Professional Psychologists." *J Appl Psychol* 39:207–93 Ag '55. * *(PA* 30:5294)

283. LILJEBLAD, MAYNARD T. *A Status and Personality Survey of Certain Persons Preparing for Educational Leadership.* Doctor's thesis, Northwestern University (Evanston, Ill.), 1956. (*DA* 17:2896)

284. LIVINGSTON, CHARLES DAVID. *The Personality Correlates of High and Low Identification With the Father Figure.* Doctor's thesis, University of Houston (Houston, Tex.), 1956. (*DA* 16:2525)

285. BORRIELLO, JOHN FRANCIS. *A Study of the Relationship Between Personal Value and the Selection of Words Presented Dichotically at a Supra Threshold Level.* Doctor's thesis, University of Minnesota (Minneapolis, Minn.), 1957. (*DA* 18: 283)

286. BOWIE, BLANCHE LUCILE. *Relationship of Teachers' Personal Values and Their Verbal Behavior.* Doctor's thesis, University of Maryland (College Park, Md.), 1957. (*DA* 17: 2508)

287. RAMÍREZ-LÓPEZ, RAMÓN. *A Comparative Study of the Values of Teachers, Students of Education, and Other University Students in Puerto Rico.* Doctor's thesis, University of Texas (Austin, Tex.), 1957. (*DA* 17:2503)

288. SHAW, MERVILLE C., and BROWN, DONALD J. "Scholastic Underachievement of Bright College Students." *Personnel & Guid J* 36:195-9 N '57. * (*PA* 33:2191)

289. SIROTA, LEON MICHAEL. *A Factor Analysis of Selected Personality Domains.* Doctor's thesis, University of Michigan (Ann Arbor, Mich.), 1957. (*DA* 18:1503)

290. ABELES, NORMAN. *A Study of the Characteristics of Counselor Trainees.* Doctor's thesis, University of Texas (Austin, Tex.), 1958. (*DA* 18:2204)

291. BROWN, MARION RHODES. *The Emergence of Group Members' Concepts of Each Other.* Doctor's thesis, Columbia University (New York, N.Y.), 1958. (*DA* 19:375)

292. BARKMAN, PAUL FRIESEN. *A Study of the Relationship of the Needs for Belonging and Conformity to Religious Beliefs and Values in a Christian College.* Doctor's thesis, New York University (New York, N.Y.), 1959. (*DA* 20:4196)

293. BLATT, SIDNEY J., and STEIN, MORRIS I. "Efficiency in Problem Solving." *J Psychol* 48:193-213 O '59. * (*PA* 35: 4971)

294. BOGARD, HOWARD M. *Union and Management Trainees —A Comparative Study of Personality and Occupational Choice.* Doctor's thesis, Columbia University (New York, N.Y.), 1959. (*DA* 20:1085)

295. MacDONALD, WILLIAM RUSSELL. *Personal Values and Visual Thresholds in a Complex Recognition Task.* Doctor's thesis, Boston University (Boston, Mass.), 1959. (*DA* 20:382)

296. PETERS, FRANK C. *A Comparison of Attitudes and Values Expressed by Mennonite and Non-Mennonite College Students.* Doctor's thesis, University of Kansas (Lawrence, Kan.), 1959. (*DA* 20:2680)

297. TREESH, EDWARD ORON. *Manifest Needs and Values as Related to Vocational Development.* Doctor's thesis, Purdue University (Lafayette, Ind.), 1959. (*DA* 20:370)

298. GARDNER, LARRY ALLAN. *Certain Religious Attitudes and Beliefs of Students in a Lutheran College, With Reference to Their Value Structures and Personal Variables.* Doctor's thesis, Boston University (Boston, Mass.), 1960. (*DA* 21:687)

299. HEIST, PAUL. "Diversity in College Students' Characteristics." *J Ed Sociol* 33:279-91 F '60. *

300. SPRINGFIELD, FRANKLYN BRUCE. *Concept of Father and Ideal Self in a Group of Criminals and Non-Criminals.* Doctor's thesis, New York University (New York, N.Y.), 1960. (*DA* 21:1258)

301. WEAVER, CHRISTINE PEARL. *A Study of Personality Characteristics of Obese Women of Two Age Groups as Compared With Paired Controls of Normal Weight.* Doctor's thesis, State University of Iowa (Iowa City, Iowa), 1960. (*DA* 21:1658)

302. ZOBERI, HASEENUDDIN. *The Relation of Evaluative Attitudes to Traits of Introversion and Extraversion.* Doctor's thesis, University of Southern California (Los Angeles, Calif.), 1960. (*DA* 21:1655)

303. CARMICAL, LaVERNE LATHROP. *The Identification of Certain Characteristics of Selected Achievers and Underachievers of Bellaire Senior High School.* Doctor's thesis, University of Houston (Houston, Tex.), 1961. (*DA* 22:2244)

304. KERN, KARL ROBERT. *Effects of Economic Value Orientation Upon Perceptual and Attitudinal Responses to a Persuasive Written Communication.* Doctor's thesis, University of Wisconsin (Madison, Wis.), 1961. (*DA* 22:2079)

305. NEWMAN, WILLIAM HENRY. *Factors Affecting Leadership.* Doctor's thesis, Stanford University (Stanford, Calif.), 1961. (*DA* 21:3329)

306. RISHEL, DARRELL FRED. *The Development and Validation of Instruments and Techniques for the Selective Admission of Applicants for Graduate Studies in Counselor Education.* Doctor's thesis, Pennsylvania State University (University Park, Pa.), 1961. (*DA* 22:2271)

307. BERNARDO, ROSE ANN. *Cultural Backgrounds of Students and Cooperating Teachers as Related to Attitudes Toward Children, Problems of Student Teaching, and Achievement of Student Teachers.* Doctor's thesis, Pennsylvania State University (University Park, Pa.), 1962. (*DA* 23:3791)

308. CAMPBELL, DORIS KLEIN. *Difference of Values Among College Students at Different Class Levels.* Doctor's thesis,

University of Florida (Gainesville, Fla.), 1962. (*DA* 23:3809)

309. COVINGTON, JAMES DONALD. *A Study of Selected Personal Characteristics of Entering College Students.* Doctor's thesis, Auburn University (Auburn, Ala.), 1962. (*DA* 23:3197)

310. FULLER, ALBERT DWANE. *The Values of Social Workers.* Doctor's thesis, University of Southern California (Los Angeles, Calif.), 1962. (*DA* 23:4779)

311. ROBERTS, JOHN EDWARD. *An Investigation of Selected Personality Variables Among Elementary, Secondary, and Special Education Teachers.* Doctor's thesis, University of Denver (Denver, Colo.), 1962. (*DA* 23:2811)

312. SWANSON, PAUL REGINALD. *Some Effects of Clinical Pastoral Education on a Group of Theological Students and Pastors.* Doctor's thesis, Boston University (Boston, Mass.), 1962. (*DA* 23:1812)

313. TERWILLIGER, JAMES SHAW. *Dimensions of Occupational Preference.* Doctor's thesis, University of Illinois (Urbana, Ill.), 1962. (*DA* 23:4424)

314. AIKEN, LEWIS R., JR. "Personality Correlates of Attitude Toward Mathematics." *J Ed Res* 56:476-80 My-Je '63. * (*PA* 39:9943)

315. CARMICHAEL, JACK JOE. *Some Relationships of Denominational Affiliation to Selected Personal Characteristics of Male College Students.* Doctor's thesis, Ohio University (Athens, Ohio), 1963. (*DA* 23:2787)

316. CHILDERS, PERRY ROBERT. *A Study of the Relationship of Certain Factors to Fall Quarter Achievement by Freshman Men at the University of Georgia.* Doctor's thesis, University of Georgia (Athens, Ga.), 1963. (*DA* 24:4537)

317. CROWELL, LAURA, and SCHEIDEL, THOMAS M. "A Study of Discussant Satisfaction in Group Problem Solving." *Speech Monogr* 30:56-8 Mr '63. * (*PA* 37:7943)

318. FRANCOEUR, THOMAS A. *A Study of Value Pattern of a Group of Franco-American Major Seminarians.* Master's thesis, University of Ottawa (Ottawa, Ont., Canada), 1963.

319. GERNER, HENRY LOUIS. *A Study of the Freedom Riders With Particular Emphasis Upon Three Dimensions: Dogmatism, Value-Orientation, and Religiosity.* Doctor's thesis, Pacific School of Religion (Berkeley, Calif.), 1963. (*DA* 25:1374)

320. GUMESON, GEORGE GERALD. *A Comparative Analysis of the Needs, Values, Cognitive Abilities, and Other Personality Characteristics of High and Low Creative Junior College Students.* Doctor's thesis, University of Denver (Denver, Colo.), 1963. (*DA* 24:5527)

321. HARRIS, PHOEBE TODD. *An Experimental Investigation of Joint Decision-Making by Husbands and Wives in Relation to Four Interest-Values.* Doctor's thesis, Pennsylvania State University (University Park, Pa.), 1963. (*DA* 24:5374)

322. KENNEDY, WALLACE A., and SMITH, ALVIN H. "Values of Future Scientists." *Percept & Motor Skills* 16:703-4 Je '63. * (*PA* 38:5864)

323. ANDERSON, ALVIN LEE. *Personal and Situational Factors Affecting the Choice Between College or Secondary Teaching.* Doctor's thesis, University of Oregon (Eugene, Ore.), 1964. (*DA* 25:2843)

324. BLAZER, JOHN A. "The Male Signature as Related to Personality Characteristics." *Psychol* 1:14-8 N '64. * (*PA* 39:5189)

325. BRAZZIEL, WILLIAM F. "Needs, Values, and Academic Achievement." *Improving Col & Univ Teach* 12:159-63 su '64. *

326. CARMICAL, LAVERNE. "Characteristics of Achievers and Under-achievers of a Large Senior High School." *Personnel & Guid J* 43:390-5 D '64. * (*PA* 39:10711)

327. CROWELL, THOMAS ROLLA, JR. *A Comparative Study of Teacher Personalities, Attitudes, and Values in Relation to Student Nonpromotion in the Elementary Schools of Rockford, Illinois.* Doctor's research study No. 1, Colorado State College (Greeley, Colo.), 1964. (*DA* 25:2823)

328. CRUMBAUGH, JAMES C., and MAHOLICK, LEONARD T. "An Experimental Study in Existentialism: The Psychometric Approach to Frankl's Concept of Noogenic Neurosis." *J Clin Psychol* 20:200-7 Ap '64. * (*PA* 39:8454)

329. DEATHERAGE, DOROTHY. *Factors Related to Concepts of Sportsmanship.* Doctor's thesis, University of Southern California (Los Angeles, Calif.), 1964. (*DA* 25:3379)

330. DEKKER, JAMES HERMAN. *A Comparative Study of the Interests, Values, and Personality of Activity Leaders and Non-Participating Students at Purdue University.* Doctor's thesis, Purdue University (Lafayette, Ind.), 1964. (*DA* 25: 998)

331. De SENA, PAUL A. "The Role of Consistency in Identifying Characteristics of Three Levels of Achievement." *Personnel & Guid J* 43:145-9 O '64. * (*PA* 39:10713)

332. DICK, WILLIAM W. *Vocational Self-Concept in Terms of the Vocational Interests and Values of Seminarians and Ministers.* Master's thesis, University of Ottawa (Ottawa, Ont., Canada), 1964.

333. DUA, PREM S. "Personality Characteristics Differentiating Women Leaders From Nonleaders in a University." *J Nat Assn Women Deans & Counselors* 27:128-32 sp '64. *

334. DUNNETTE, MARVIN D.; WERNIMONT, PAUL; and ABRAHAMS, NORMAN. "Further Research on Vocational Interest Differences Among Several Types of Engineers." *Personnel & Guid J* 42:484-93 Ja '64. * (*PA* 39:6040)

335. DUSTAN, LAURA C. "Characteristics of Students in Three Types of Nursing Programs." *Nursing Res* 13:159–66 sp '64. *

336. FEINBERG, M. R., and PENZER, W. N. "Factor Analysis of a Sales Selection Battery." *Personnel Psychol* 17:319–24 au '64. * (*PA* 39:8794)

337. FISHBURN, WILLIAM R., and KING, PAUL T. "The Relationship Between Values and Perceived Problems." *J Counsel Psychol* 11:288–90 f '64. *

338. FISHER, SEYMOUR. "Acquiescence and Religiosity." *Psychol Rep* 15:784 D '64. * (*PA* 39:7838)

339. GOODWIN, WILLIAM L. "Adjustment for Sex and Variability Differences on the Allport-Vernon-Lindzey *Study of Values* Profiles." *J Ed Meas* 1:55–8 Je '64. * (*PA* 39:7759)

340. HAVEN, GEORGE A., JR. *Creative Thought, Productivity, and the Self-Concept.* Doctor's thesis, University of Minnesota (Minneapolis, Minn.), 1964. (*DA* 25:2030)

341. HAYES, ALBERTINE BRANNUM. *Personal, Social and Academic Characteristics of Southern Education Foundation Fellows in Participating Colleges and Universities.* Doctor's thesis, University of Oklahoma (Norman, Okla.), 1964. (*DA* 25:3323)

342. HILTON, T. L., and KORN, J. H. "Measured Change in Personal Values." *Ed & Psychol Meas* 24:609–22 f '64. * (*PA* 39:4800)

343. JOSEPH, MICHAEL P. "Psychological Needs and Values of Entering College Freshmen." *Nat Cath Guid Conf J* 9:67–8 f '64. *

344. KNAPP, ROBERT H., and GREEN, HELEN B. "Personality Correlates of Success Imagery." *J Social Psychol* 62:93–9 F '64. * (*PA* 39:1807)

345. KNAPP, ROBERT H., and HOLZBERG, JULES D. "Characteristics of College Students Volunteering for Service to Mental Patients." *J Consult Psychol* 28:82–5 F '64. * (*PA* 38:8779)

346. LAUER, RACHEL M. *The Relationship Between Value Orientation and Primary Process Thinking.* Doctor's thesis, New York University (New York, N.Y.), 1964. (*DA* 25:1338)

347. LISKE, RALPH E.; ORT, ROBERT S.; and FORD, AMASA B. "Clinical Performance and Related Attitudes of Medical Students and Faculty Physicians." *J Med Ed* 39:69–80 Ja '64. *

348. LYSAUGHT, JEROME P., and PIERLEONI, ROBERT G. "A Comparison of Predicted and Actual Success in Auto-Instructional Programing." *J Programed Instr* 3(4):14–23 '64. *

349. LYSAUGHT, JEROME PAUL. *An Analysis of Factors Related to Success in Constructing Programmed Learning Sequences.* Doctor's thesis, University of Rochester (Rochester, N.Y.), 1964. (*DA* 25:1749)

350. McMAHON, WILLIAM JOSEPH. *Differential Analysis of Nonintellective Factors Associated With Identified Scholastic Talent in a High School.* Doctor's thesis, Fordham University (New York, N.Y.), 1964. (*DA* 26:873)

351. PETERSEN, DWAIN FRANKLIN. *Factors Common to Interest, Value, and Personality Scales.* Doctor's thesis, University of Nebraska (Lincoln, Neb.), 1964. (*DA* 25:5747)

352. RIGHTHAND, HERBERT. *A Comparison of Technical Institute Freshman Dropouts and Persisting Students With Respect to Sociological and Psychological Characteristics.* Doctor's thesis, University of Connecticut (Storrs, Conn.), 1964. (*DA* 25:4550)

353. RIZZO, JOHN R., and NAYLOR, J. C. "The Factorial Structure of Selected Consumer Choice Parameters and Their Relationship to Personal Values." *J Appl Psychol* 48:241–8 Ag '64. * (*PA* 39:3195)

354. SCHUMACHER, CHARLES F. "Personal Characteristics of Students Choosing Different Types of Medical Careers." *J Med Ed* 39:278–88 Mr '64. *

355. SILVERMAN, PINCUS. *Characteristics of a Negro College Environment and Its Relationship to Student Value Systems.* Doctor's thesis, North Texas State University (Denton, Tex.), 1964. (*DA* 25:5125)

356. SPRINTHALL, NORMAN A. "A Comparison of Values Among Teachers, Academic Underachievers, and Achievers." *J Exp Ed* 33:193–6 w '64. * (*PA* 39:8648)

357. STEWART, LAWRENCE H. "Change in Personality Test Scores During College." Comment by David V. Tiedeman. *J Counsel Psychol* 11:211–20 f '64. * (*PA* 39:5184)

358. STEWART, LAWRENCE H. "Factor Analysis of Nonoccupational Scales of the Strong Blank, Selected Personality Scales and the School and College Ability Test." *Calif J Ed Res* 15:136–41 My '64. * (*PA* 39:3201)

359. WILLIAMS, PHOEBE ANN. *The Relationship Between Certain Scores on the Strong Vocational Interest Blank and Intellectual Disposition.* Doctor's thesis, University of California (Berkeley, Calif.), 1964. (*DA* 26:2863)

360. WINICK, CHARLES. "Personality Characteristics of Embalmers." *Personnel & Guid J* 43:262–6 N '64. * (*PA* 39:10222)

361. ADAMS, HENRY L., and BLOOD, DON F. "Creative Potential in Honors Students." *Sup Stud* 7:41–3 Mr–Ap '65. *

362. BAICH, HENRY. *A Study of the Use of Value Analysis to Differentiate Between High and Low Scoring Administrators on the Purdue Rating Scale.* Doctor's thesis, University of Oregon (Eugene, Ore.), 1965. (*DA* 26:4434)

363. BLANKENSHIP, JACOB W. "Biology Teachers and Their Attitudes Concerning BSCS." *J Res Sci Teach* 3(1):54–60 '65. *

364. BROOKS, ROBERT DEAN. *An Investigation of the Relationship Between Personal Values and the Selection of Rhetorical Arguments.* Doctor's thesis, Cornell University (Ithaca, N.Y.), 1965. (*DA* 26:1213)

365. BROWN, MAURICE BURTON. *Multiple Discriminant Analysis of the Edwards Personal Preference Schedule and the Study of Values Scores of Achieving and Non-Achieving Low Ability College Freshmen.* Doctor's thesis, Florida State University (Tallahassee, Fla.), 1965. (*DA* 26:1505)

366. CAGLE, BERNADENE GARRETT. *Personality Orientation and Values of Teacher Trainees and Experienced Teachers in the Areas of Elementary and Special Education.* Doctor's thesis, University of Georgia (Athens, Ga.), 1965. (*DA* 26:2066)

367. CLARK, ALICE THOMPSON. *A Comparison of Measured Personality Change in Students at a Non-Denominational Public University and a Denominational Private University.* Doctor's thesis, Brigham Young University (Provo, Utah), 1965. (*DA* 26:1473)

368. CONLEY, NAOMI LEE. *Factors Related to Teacher Effectiveness of High School Distributive Education Teacher-Coordinators.* Doctor's thesis, University of Tennessee (Knoxville, Tenn.), 1965. (*DA* 26:6440)

369. DATTA, LOIS-ELLIN. "Value Conflict, Creativity, and the Study of Values." *Psychol Rep* 16:57–8 F '65. * (*PA* 39:7813)

370. DOLAN, FRANCES ANNE. *Personal Qualities and Characteristics Important in the Selection of Undergraduate Staff Members for Women's Residence Halls.* Doctor's thesis, Northwestern University (Evanston, Ill.), 1965. (*DA* 26:3124)

371. DOLL, PADDY ANN. *A Comparative Study of Top Level Male and Female Executives in Harris County.* Doctor's thesis, University of Houston (Houston, Tex.), 1965. (*DA* 26:6883)

372. EBERDT, MARY GERTRUDE. *An Analysis of Certain Characteristics of Secondary-School Teachers Rated as Most Approachable and Least Approachable by Secondary-School Students.* Doctor's thesis, University of Oregon (Eugene, Ore.), 1965. (*DA* 26:4327)

373. FLANDERS, JOHN N. *Selected Characteristics of Decided-Undecided Freshmen Students at Florida State University.* Doctor's thesis, Florida State University (Tallahassee, Fla.), 1965. (*DA* 26:1476)

374. HARRISON, JAMES HAYWOOD. *A Comparison of the Value Systems of Experienced Teachers and Prospective Secondary School Teachers in Inner-City Schools.* Doctor's thesis, University of Maryland (College Park, Md.), 1965. (*DA* 27:70A)

375. HAYES, DOROTHY D., and VARLEY, BARBARA K. "Impact of Social Work Education on Students' Values." *Social Work* 10:40–6 Jl '65. * (*PA* 39:14952)

376. HOWARD, LORRAINE HARRIS. *A Comparison of Freshmen Attending Selected Oregon Community Colleges and Oregon State University in Terms of Interests, Values, and Manifest Needs.* Doctor's thesis, Oregon State University (Corvallis, Ore.), 1965. (*DA* 25:5738)

377. HUMMEL, RAYMOND, and SPRINTHALL, NORMAN. "Underachievement Related to Interests, Attitudes and Values." *Personnel & Guid J* 44:388–95 D '65. * (*PA* 40:4101)

378. HUNTLEY, C. WILLIAM. "Changes in Study of Values Scores During the Four Years of College." *Genetic Psychol Monogr* 71:349–83 My '65. * (*PA* 39:14957)

379. KASSARJIAN, WALTRAUD M., and KASSARJIAN, HAROLD H. "Occupational Interests, Social Values and Social Character." *J Counsel Psychol* 12:48–54 sp '65. * (*PA* 39:10055)

380. KENNEDY, WALLACE A., and WALSH, JOHN. "A Factor Analysis of Mathematical Giftedness." *Psychol Rep* 17:115–9 Ag '65. * (*PA* 40:1553)

381. KROLL, WALTER, and PETERSEN, KAY H. "Study of Values Test and Collegiate Football Teams." *Res Q* 36:441–7 D '65. * (*PA* 40:4611)

382. KUMAR, PRAMOD. "A Study of Value-Dimensions in Student Leadership." *Psychol Studies* 10:73–9 Jl '65. * (*PA* 39:16385)

383. NASH, ALLAN N. "Vocational Interests of Effective Managers: A Review of the Literature." *Personnel Psychol* 18:21–37 sp '65. * (*PA* 39:16589)

384. PALMER, DENSLEY HARLEY. *A Comparison of the Consistency of the Self-Judgments of Physically Disabled and Non-Disabled Male College Students.* Doctor's thesis, University of Oregon (Eugene, Ore.), 1965. (*DA* 26:4456)

385. PLANT, W. T. "Personality Changes Associated With College Attendance." *Hum Develop* 8(2–3):142–51 '65. *

386. RIGHTHAND, HERBERT. "Identifying Technical Institute Dropouts." *Personnel & Guid J* 44:68–72 S '65. *

387. SLAYTON, WILFRED GEORGE. *A Comparison of Successful and Unsuccessful Bible College Students With Respect to Selected Personality Factors.* Doctor's thesis, University of Arizona (Tucson, Ariz.), 1965. (*DA* 26:1487)

388. TAGIURI, RENATO. "Value Orientations and the Relationship of Managers and Scientists." *Adm Sci Q* 10:39–51 Je '65. * (*PA* 39:16495)

389. VIVERS, BILLY B. *A Study of the Relationship Between Applicants Scores on the Thurstone Tests of Mental Alertness and the Allport, Vernon, Lindzey Study of Values and Subsequent Job Success as Psychiatric Aids.* Master's thesis, Kansas State College (Pittsburg, Kan.), 1965.

390. WHITTEMORE, ROBERT G., and HEIMANN, ROBERT A.

"Originality Responses in Academically Talented Male University Freshmen." *Psychol Rep* 16:439–42 Ap '65. * (*PA* 39: 10252)

391. ANDERSON, ALVIN L. "A Comparison of Study of Values Scores for Selected Secondary and College Teachers." *J Ed Res* 60:86–9 O '66. *

392. BLAZER, JOHN A. "Leg Position and Psychological Characteristics in Women." *Psychol* 3:5–12 Ag '66. * (*PA* 40:12361)

393. BRIGGS, KENNETH RAY. *Student Teacher Values and Behavior Patterns.* Doctor's thesis, North Texas State University (Denton, Tex.), 1966. (*DA* 27:2910A)

394. CONGER, JOHN JANEWAY, and MILLER, WILBUR C.; with the assistance of Robert V. Rainey and Charles R. Walsmith. *Personality, Social Class, and Delinquency.* New York: John Wiley & Sons, Inc., 1966. Pp. xi, 249. *

395. CORNWELL, HENRY G. "Personality Variables in Autokinetic Figure Writing." *Percept & Motor Skills* 22:731–5 Je '66. * (*PA* 40:11160)

396. DeCencio, DOMINIC V. *Relationship Between Certain Interest and Personality Variables in a Sample of College Women.* Doctor's thesis, Temple University (Philadelphia, Pa.), 1966. (*DA* 27:1288B)

397. DICK, WILLIAM W., and ISABELLE, LAURENT A. "Vocational Self-Concept in Terms of the Vocational Interests and Values of Seminarians and Ministers." *Can Psychologist* 7a: 8–16 Ja '66. *

398. DRISCOLL, JOHN. *The Dimensions of Satisfaction With the Religious Life Among Scholastics in a Community of Teaching Brothers: A Descriptive Study.* Doctor's thesis, University of Notre Dame (Notre Dame, Ind.), 1966. (*DA* 27:1653A)

399. FINCO, ARTHUR ANTHONY. *Mathematics Majors and Transfers From the Mathematics Major at Purdue University: Temperament, Interest, Value, and Student Questionnaire Differences at the Exploratory Stage.* Doctor's thesis, Purdue University (Lafayette, Ind.), 1966. (*DA* 27:327A)

400. GUNDERSON, E. K. ERIC, and MAHAN, JACK L. "Cultural and Psychological Differences Among Occupational Groups." *J Psychol* 62:287–304 Mr '66. * (*PA* 40:8094)

401. GUNDERSON, E. K. ERIC, and NELSON, PAUL D. "Personality Differences Among Navy Occupational Groups." *Personnel & Guid J* 44:956–61 My '66. * (*PA* 40:10486)

402. HARTSFIELD, KIRK FERNANDO. *The Perceived Environments of Selected Georgia Junior Colleges.* Doctor's thesis, University of Georgia (Athens, Ga.), 1966. (*DA* 27:3310A)

403. HOWELL, MARGARET A. "Personal Effectiveness of Physicians in a Federal Health Organization." *J Appl Psychol* 50:451–9 D '66. * (*PA* 41:3517)

404. HUDSON, MARY MARLENE COE. *Interpersonal Values, Temperament Traits, and Interest Values of Elementary Education Students at the University of Oklahoma.* Doctor's thesis, University of Oklahoma (Norman, Okla.), 1966. (*DA* 27: 1688A)

405. JOHNSON, DAVIS G., and HUTCHINS, EDWIN B. "Doctor or Dropout? A Study of Medical Student Attrition: Chap. 4, 'The Student.' " *J Med Ed* 41:1139–56, 1263–5 D '66. *

406. KEIM, LAWRENCE. *A Study of Psychometric Profile Patterns of Selected Associate Degree Technology Majors.* Doctor's thesis, Purdue University (Lafayette, Ind.), 1966. (*DA* 27:2049A)

407. KNAPP, THOMAS R. "Interactive Versus Ipsative Measurement of Career Interest." *Personnel & Guid J* 44:482–6 Ja '66. * (*PA* 40:5071)

408. MAY, W. THEODORE. "Differences Between Nursing Student Drop-Outs and Remainers on the Study of Values." *Psychol Rep* 19:902 D '66. * (*PA* 41:5102)

409. MILLAR, ANDREW CRAIG. *The Suitability of Using Non-Intellective Characteristics in the Selection of Honors Students at the University of North Dakota.* Doctor's thesis, University of North Dakota (Grand Forks, N.D.), 1966. (*DA* 27:1629A)

410. NIEMIEC, CARL J. *Specific Personality Values as Measured by the Allport-Vernon-Lindzey Study of Values Characteristic of Academically Successful and Unsuccessful Freshmen in Various Marquette University Colleges.* Master's thesis, Marquette University (Milwaukee, Wis.), 1966.

411. OBST, FRANCES. "A Comparison of Teacher Candidate Groups on the Allport-Vernon-Lindzey Aesthetic Scale." *Calif J Ed Res* 17:181–5 S '66. * (*PA* 41:2017)

412. PLANT, WALTER T., and TELFORD, CHARLES W. "Changes in Personality for Groups Completing Different Amounts of College Over Two Years." *Genetic Psychol Monogr* 74:3–36 Ag '66. * (*PA* 40:12183)

413. PLATT, ALEXANDER BRADFORD. *The Relationship of Values to Academic Goals, Attrition, Achievement, and Satisfaction.* Doctor's thesis, Columbia University (New York, N.Y.), 1966. (*DA* 28:1172B)

414. REDDY, K. MANORANJAN, and PARAMESWARAN, E. G. "Some Factors Influencing the Value Patterns of College Students." *Res B Dept Psychol Osmania Univ* 2:7–14 Mr '66. * (*PA* 40:7628)

415. REITER, HENRY H. "Relationship of Buying Preference and Certain Values of College Students." *Psychol Rep* 18:958 Je '66. * (*PA* 40:10124, title only)

416. ROSEN, JULIUS. *The Predictive Value of Personal Characteristics Associated With Counselor Competency.* Doctor's thesis, New York University (New York, N.Y.), 1966. (*DA* 27:2408A)

417. SCHARF, GEORGE CLIFTON, JR. *The Counselor Selection Scale: Design for an Experimental Test.* Doctor's thesis, University of Idaho (Moscow, Idaho), 1966. (*DA* 27:4103A)

418. SOUTHARD, JERRY KERMIT. *Factors Affecting Teacher-Supervisor Compatibility.* Doctor's thesis, University of Denver (Denver, Colo.), 1966. (*DA* 28:884A)

419. SPRINTHALL, NORMAN A., and BEATON, ALBERT E. "Value Differences Among Public High School Teachers Using a Regression Model Analysis of Variance Technique." *J Exp Ed* 35:36–42 w '66. *

420. WAGMAN, MORTON. "Interests and Values of Career and Homemaking Oriented Women." *Personnel & Guid J* 44: 794–801 Ap '66. * (*PA* 40:8782)

421. WEISGERBER, CHARLES A. "The Study of Values in Screening for a Religious Order." *J Relig & Health* 5:233–8 Jl '66. * (*PA* 41:585)

422. WHITE, WILLIAM F.; GAIER, EUGENE L.; and COOLEY, GARY M. "Selected Personality Characteristics and Academic Performance of Adult Evening College Students." *J Ed Res* 59:339–43 Ap '66. * (*PA* 40:10444)

423. DAVIS, KATHLEEN L. *The Sensitivity of Selected Instruments to Personality Changes Produced by Group Counseling.* Doctor's thesis, University of Georgia (Athens, Ga.), 1967. (*DA* 28:3968A)

424. FISHER, SEYMOUR, and OSOFSKY, HOWARD. "Sexual Responsiveness in Women: Psychological Correlates." *Arch Gen Psychiatry* 17:214–26 Ag '67. * (*PA* 41:15149)

425. GANGULY, ARUN K. "Dominance of Materialistic Trend in 'Values' Among the Students at the University Level." *Psychol Studies* 12:134–44 Jl '67. *

426. GORDON, JAMES H. "Value Differences Between Freshmen and Seniors at a State University." *Col Stud Survey* 1(3):69–70+ '67. * (*PA* 42:9409)

427. GORLOW, LEON, and NOLL, GARY A. "A Study of Empirically Derived Values." *J Social Psychol* 73:261–9 D '67. * (*PA* 42:3967)

428. GUTHRIE, GEORGE M., and ZEKTICK, IDA N. "Predicting Performance in the Peace Corps." *J Social Psychol* 71:11–21 F '67. * (*PA* 41:6319)

429. HARFORD, THOMAS C.; WILLIS, CONSTANCE H.; and DEABLER, HERDIS L. "Personality Correlates of Masculinity-Femininity." *Psychol Rep* 21:881–4 D '67. * (*PA* 42:7316)

430. HARFORD, THOMAS C.; WILLIS, CONSTANCE H.; and DEABLER, HERDIS L. "Personality, Values, and Intellectual Correlates of Masculinity-Femininity." *Newsl Res Psychol* 9:17–8 Ag '67. *

431. HELSON, RAVENNA. "Personality Characteristics and Developmental History of Creative College Women." *Genetic Psychol Monogr* 76:205–56 N '67. * (*PA* 42:3942)

432. HUNTLEY, C. W. "Changes in Values During the Four Years of College." *Col Stud Survey* 1:43–8 f '67. * (*PA* 42:7232)

433. McCLURE, GEORGE, and TYLER, FORREST. "Role of Values in the Study of Values." *J General Psychol* 77:217–35 O '67. * (*PA* 42:145)

434. MADAUS, GEORGE F., and O'HARA, ROBERT P. "Contrasts Between High School Boys Choosing the Priesthood as Their Occupational Choice and Boys Choosing Eight Other Occupational Categories." *Cath Psychol Rec* 5:41–51 sp '67. *

435. MARKING, KASPER CARROLL. *An Analysis of the Relationship of Student and Instructor Attitude and Personality Similarities and Student Achievement in a Public Junior College.* Doctor's thesis, Washington State University (Pullman, Wash.), 1967. (*DA* 28:500A)

436. MARTIN, JACKSON JAY. *Expressed Value Preferences for Types of Employment Opportunities by Male Elementary Teachers.* Doctor's thesis, University of California (Berkeley, Calif.), 1967. (*DA* 28:3425A)

437. MELLUM, DORETTA, and MEZZANO, JOSEPH. "Values of Graduate Students in Guidance: Self-Ranking and Score Ranking." *Col Stud Survey* 1:82–4 w '67. *

438. MOORE, ROBERT MILTON. *Value Change Among Junior College Students.* Doctor's thesis, University of Florida (Gainesville, Fla.), 1967. (*DA* 29:126A)

439. MUROV, HERMAN. *An Exploratory Study of the Psychological Meanings of Selected Occupations to Vocationally Committed, Male, College Students.* Doctor's thesis, New York University (New York, N.Y.), 1967. (*DA* 28:4489A)

440. O'HARA, ROBERT P. "Vocational Self Concepts of Boys Choosing Science and Non-Science Careers." *Ed & Psychol Meas* 27:139–49 sp '67. * (*PA* 41:9476)

441. PAIVIO, ALLAN, and STEEVES, RAY. "Relations Between Personal Values and Imagery and Meaningfulness of Value Words." *Percept & Motor Skills* 24:357–8 Ap '67. * (*PA* 41: 10418)

442. PAL, S. K. "Value Patterns of Engineering, Law, Medical and Teacher-Training Students in India." *Brit J Ed Psychol* 37:371–4 N '67. * (*PA* 42:5481)

443. PAL, S. K. "Values of Students in Four Professions Under Indian Conditions." *J Social Psychol* 72:297–8 Ag '67. * (*PA* 41:15779)

444. PLANT, WALTER T., and MINIUM, EDWARD W. "Differential Personality Development in Young Adults of Markedly

Different Aptitude Levels." *J Ed Psychol* 58:141–52 Je '67. * (*PA* 41:10438)

445. REBSTOCK, CHARLES WESLEY. *Changes in the Personality, Values, Attitudes, and Verbal Behavior of Student Teachers Through the Use of Certain Objective Observational Techniques.* Doctor's thesis, University of Minnesota (Minneapolis, Minn.), 1967. (*DA* 28:4939A)

446. REDMAN, BARBARA KLUG. "Predominant Values of Selected Intermediate Nursing Students and of Their Teachers." *Nursing Res* 15:348–50 f '67. * (*PA* 42:3877)

447. REILLY, DOROTHY ELIZABETH. *A Comparative Analysis of Selected Nonintellective Characteristics of College Graduate and Noncollege Graduate Women Who Entered a Collegiate Nursing Program.* Doctor's thesis, New York University (New York, N.Y.), 1967. (*DA* 28:4180B)

448. ROCHESTER, DEAN E. "Persistence of Attitudes and Values of NDEA Counselor Trainees." *J Counsel Psychol* 14:535–7 N '67. * (*PA* 42:3126)

449. ROGERS, WILLIAM ALFRED. *Intellective-Nonintellective Characteristics and Academic Success of College Freshmen.* Doctor's thesis, State University of New York at Buffalo (Buffalo, N.Y.), 1967. (*DA* 28:973A)

450. ROSEN, JULIUS. "Multiple-Regression Analysis of Counselor Characteristics and Competencies." *Psychol Rep* 20:1003–8 Je '67. * (*PA* 41:12734)

451. SERVIS, MARGERY, and FROST, REUBEN B. "Qualities Related to Success in Women's Physical Education Professional Preparation Program." *Res Q* 38:283–99 My '67. *

452. SHARPLESS, ELIZABETH A. *The LSSB Preference: A Test to Determine the Relative Merits of the Normative and Ipsative Measurement Techniques With the Allport-Vernon-Lindzey Study of Values.* Master's thesis, Teachers College, Columbia University (New York, N.Y.), 1967.

453. STEVENS, THOMAS GRANVILLE. *Congruency Between Diagnostic Dimensions of Personality Theories and Personality Tests.* Master's thesis, California State College at Fullerton (Fullerton, Calif.), 1967.

454. STROM, KENNETH R., and TRANEL, NED N. "An Experimental Study of Alcoholism." *J Relig & Health* 6:242–9 Jl '67. *

455. UHL, HAROLD JOHN. *Selected Personal Characteristics and Values of Participants in Secular and Religious Adult Education Programs in Mount Lebanon, Pennsylvania.* Doctor's thesis, University of Pittsburgh (Pittsburgh, Pa.), 1967. (*DA* 28:4504A)

456. WALBERG, HERBERT J., and WELCH, WAYNE W. "Personality Characteristics of Innovative Physics Teachers." *J Creative Beh* 1:163–71 sp '67. * (*PA* 41:15285)

457. WELSCH, LAWRENCE A. *The Supervisor's Employee Appraisal Heuristic: The Contribution of Selected Measures of Employee Aptitude, Intelligence and Personality.* Doctor's thesis, University of Pittsburgh (Pittsburgh, Pa.), 1967. (*DA* 28:4321A)

458. WHITTAKER, DAVID NEIL EATON. *Psychological Characteristics of Alienated, Nonconformist, College-Age Youth as Indicated by AVL, OPI, ACL and SVIB-M/W Group Profiles.* Doctor's thesis, University of California (Berkeley, Calif.), 1967. (*DA* 28:3055B)

459. WINDHOLZ, GEORGE. *Divergent and Convergent Abilities of Semantic Content as Related to Some Personality Traits of College Students.* Doctor's thesis, Columbia University (New York, N.Y.), 1967. (*DA* 28:2130B)

460. WINDHOLZ, GEORGE. "Divergent and Convergent Abilities of Semantic Content as Related to Some Personality Traits of College Students." *Ed & Psychol Meas* 27:1015–23 w '67. * (*PA* 42:8076)

461. ATKINSON, GILBERT, and LUNNEBORG, CLIFFORD E. "Comparison of Oblique and Orthogonal Simple Structure Solutions for Personality and Interest Factors." *Multiv Behav Res* 3:21–35 Ja '68. * (*PA* 42:11349)

462. GORTNER, SUSAN R. "Western Majors in Twelve Western Universities: A Comparison of Registered Nurse Students and Basic Senior Students." *Nursing Res* 17:121–8 Mr–Ap '68. *

463. HUNT, RICHARD A. "The Interpretation of the Religious Scale of the Allport-Vernon-Lindzey Study of Values." *J Sci Study Relig* 7:65–77 sp '68. * (*PA* 43:3869)

464. KIRCHNER, JOHN H., and HOGAN, ROBERT A. "Value Patterns of Future Teachers in Three Curricula." *J Teach Ed* 19:349–53 f '68. * (*PA* 43:3098, title only)

465. KLING, MARTIN. "Some Relationships Between Values and Reading Gains in College Programs." *Yearb Nat Read Conf* 17:156–61 '68. *

466. LATTA, WILLIAM S., and SEEMAN, WILLIAM. "The Wish Is Father to the Thought: Vocational Wish Fulfillment in Daydreams." *Proc Ann Conv Am Psychol Assn* 76:543–4 '68. * (*PA* 43:896, title only)

467. PALLONE, NATHANIEL J., and BANKS, R. RICHARD. "Vocational Satisfaction Among Ministerial Students." *Personnel & Guid J* 46:870–5 My '68. *

468. SADLER, PAUL M. "Teacher Personality Characteristics and Attitudes Concerning PSSC Physics." *J Res Sci Teach* 5(1):28–9 '68. *

469. SMITH, JEANNE E. "Personality Structure in Beginning Nursing Students: A Factor Analytic Study." *Nursing Res* 17:140–5 Mr–Ap '68. *

470. SOUTHERN, MARA L., and PLANT, WALTER T. "Personality Characteristics of Very Bright Adults." *J Social Psychol* 75:119–26 Je '68. * (*PA* 42:13758)

471. WALBERG, HERBERT J. "Personality Correlates of Factored Teaching Attitudes." *Psychol Sch* 5:67–74 Ja '68. *

472. WALBERG, HERBERT J. "Teacher Personality and Classroom Climate." *Psychol Sch* 5:163–9 Ap '68. *

473. WHITMORE, LOUIS CLYDE. *A Comparative Study of the Values of Teachers, Student Teachers, and Prospective Student Teacher Candidates.* Doctor's thesis, Colorado State College (Greeley, Colo.), 1968. (*DA* 29:1115A)

474. WINDHOLZ, GEORGE. "The Relation of Creativity and Intelligence Constellations to Traits of Temperament, Interest, and Value in College Students." *J General Psychol* 79:291–9 O '68. * (*PA* 43:3998)

475. YAMAMOTO, KAORU, and DIZNEY, HENRY F. "College Students' Preferences Among Four Types of Professors." *J Col Stud Personnel* 9:259–64 Jl '68. *

NAME INDEX

[259A]

★Study of Values: British Edition, 1965. College and adults; 1965; SV:B; adaptation of *Study of Values: A Scale for Measuring the Dominant Interests in Personality, Third Edition* (see 259); 6 scores: theoretical, economic, aesthetic, social, political, religious; 1 form (12 pages); manual (20 pages); 40s. per 25 tests; 15s. per manual; 19s. per specimen set; postage extra; (20) minutes; original test by Gordon W. Allport, Philip E. Vernon, and Gardner Lindzey; adaptation by Sylvia Richardson; National Foundation for Educational Research in England and Wales. *

[260]

Style of Mind Inventory: Trait, Value and Belief Patterns in Greek, Roman and Hebrew Perspectives. College and adults; 1958–61, c1957–61; SMI; formerly called *The Fetler Self-Rating Test;* 3 scores (Greek, Roman, Judeo-Christian) in each of 3 areas (traits, values, beliefs); 1 form ('61, 1 page); explanation sheet ['61, 1 page]; no data on reliability and validity; no norms; 5¢ per test; 3¢ per explanation sheet; postpaid; [60] minutes; Daniel Fetler; the Author. *

[261]

Survey of Interpersonal Values. Grades 9–16 and adults; 1960–63; SIV; 6 scores: support, conformity, recognition, independence, benevolence, leadership; 1 form ('60, 3 pages); preliminary manual ('60, 11 pages); revised mimeographed supplement ('63, 28 pages); $3.25 per 20 tests; 56¢ per scoring stencil; $1 per specimen set; postage extra; (15) minutes; Leonard V. Gordon; Science Research Associates, Inc. *

For reviews by Lee J. Cronbach, Leonard D. Goodstein, and John K. Hemphill, see 6:184 (12 references, 1 excerpt).

REFERENCES

1–12. See 6:184.
13. TOLLEFSON, THEODORE IVER. *The Relationship Between Attitudes, Personal Values, Biographical Data and Proficiency Ratings Obtained Upon Psychiatric Aides.* Doctor's thesis, Purdue University (Lafayette, Ind.), 1963. (DA 24:5553)
14. WHETSTONE, BOBBY DON. *A Differential Study of Some Personality Variables of Selected Counselors and Effective Teachers.* Doctor's thesis, University of Alabama (University, Ala.), 1963. (DA 24:4090)
15. BLEDSOE, JOSEPH C., and MORRIS, KENNETH T. "A Comparative Study of Selected Needs, Values, and Motives of Science and Non-Science Teachers." *J Res Sci Teach* 2(2): 123–31 '64. *
16. BRAUN, JOHN R. "Consistency of Cross-Test Individual Differences in Personality-Inventory Faking." *J Psychol* 58: 313–6 O '64. * (PA 39:5167)
17. HAY, JOHN EARL. *The Relationship of Certain Personality Variables to Managerial Level and Job Performance Among Engineering Managers.* Doctor's thesis, Temple University (Philadelphia, Pa.), 1964. (DA 25:3973)
18. KNAPP, ROBERT R. "An Empirical Investigation of the Concurrent and Observational Validity of an Ipsative Versus a Normative Measure of Six Interpersonal Values." *Ed & Psychol Meas* 24:65–73 sp '64. * (PA 39:1806)
19. KNAPP, ROBERT R. "Value and Personality Differences Between Offenders and Nonoffenders." *J Appl Psychol* 48:59–62 F '64. * (PA 38:8364)
20. LUBETKIN, ARVIN IRA. *The Relationship Between Response Consistency on a Vocational Interest Inventory and Certain Personality Attributes.* Doctor's thesis, Temple University (Philadelphia, Pa.), 1964. (DA 25:4817)
21. McDAVID, JOHN W., and SISTRUNK, FRANK. "Personality Correlates of Two Kinds of Conforming Behavior." *J Personality* 32:420–35 S '64. *
22. MEDVEDEFF, EUGENE. *The Utility of Sub-Grouping Analysis in the Prediction of Sales Success.* Doctor's thesis, Purdue University (Lafayette, Ind.), 1964. (DA 26:1800)
23. GORDON, LEONARD V., and MEDLAND, FRANCIS F. "Leadership Aspiration and Leadership Ability." *Psychol Rep* 17: 388–90 O '65. * (PA 40:1976)
24. HOSTETLER, DAVID KITCHEN. *An Analysis of the Differences in Selected Attitudes and Values of the College Student in the Eastern and Southern Part of the United States.* Doctor's thesis, University of Virginia (Charlottesville, Va.), 1965. (DA 27:126A) (Abstract: Ed R 3:89–91 '65. *)
25. MANE, KAMAL LATHI. *An Experimental Investigation of the Relationship Between the MMPI and the Survey of Interpersonal Values.* Master's thesis, Loyola University (Chicago, Ill.), 1965.
26. WHETSTONE, BOBBY D. "Personality Differences Between Selected Counselors and Effective Teachers." *Personnel & Guid J* 93:886–90 My '65. * (PA 39:15179)
27. DOLLAR, ROBERT J. "Relationship Between Interpersonal Values and Temperament Traits." *Psychol Rep* 19:228 Ag '66. * (PA 40:11663, title only)
28. GORDON, LEONARD V. "Values of the Peace Corps Volunteer." *Psychol Rep* 18:328 F '66. * (PA 40:6571)
29. GORDON, LEONARD V., and KAKKAR, S. B. "A Cross-Cultural Study of Indian and American Interpersonal Values." *J Social Psychol* 69:339–40 Ag '66. * (PA 40:12209)
30. GORDON, LEONARD V., and KIKUCHI, AKIO. "American Personality Tests in Cross-Cultural Research—A Caution." *J Social Psychol* 69:179–83 Ag '66. * (PA 40:12210)
31. GUNDERSON, E. K. ERIC, and MAHAN, JACK L. "Cultural and Psychological Differences Among Occupational Groups." *J Psychol* 62:287–304 Mr '66. * (PA 40:8094)
32. GUNDERSON, E. K. ERIC, and NELSON, PAUL D. "Life Status and Interpersonal Values." *Ed & Psychol Meas* 26:121–30 sp '66. * (PA 40:8855)
33. GUNDERSON, E. K. ERIC, and NELSON, PAUL D. "Personality Differences Among Navy Occupational Groups." *Personnel & Guid J* 44:956–61 My '66. * (PA 40:10486)
34. HOWELL, MARGARET A. "Personal Effectiveness of Physicians in a Federal Health Organization." *J Appl Psychol* 50:451–9 D '66. * (PA 41:3517)
35. HUDSON, MARY MARLENE COE. *Interpersonal Values, Temperament Traits, and Interest Values of Elementary Education Students at the University of Oklahoma.* Doctor's thesis, University of Oklahoma (Norman, Okla.), 1966. (DA 27:1688A)
36. KAKKAR, S. B., and GORDON, LEONARD V. "A Cross-Cultural Study of Teachers' Values." *Ed & Psychol R* 6: 172–7 O '66. * (PA 41:6266)
37. KAKKAR, S. B., and GORDON, LEONARD V. "The Interpersonal Values of Indian Teacher Trainees." *J Social Psychol* 69:341–2 Ag '66. * (PA 40:12211)
38. KIKUCHI, AKIO, and GORDON, LEONARD V. "Evaluation and Cross-Cultural Application of a Japanese Form of the Survey of Interpersonal Values." *J Social Psychol* 69:185–95 Ag '66. * (PA 40:12212)
39. LOGUE, JOHN JOSEPH. *A Comparison of Interest and Personality Variables in Two Job Categories.* Doctor's thesis, Temple University (Philadelphia, Pa.), 1966. (DA 27:1282B)
40. NEWCOMER, CHARLES ALFRED, JR. *The Relationship Between Certain Types of Aggressive Behavior and Selected Attitudes and Values.* Doctor's thesis, Temple University (Philadelphia, Pa.), 1966. (DA 27:3697A)
41. NORMAN, RALPH D. "The Interpersonal Values of Parents of Achieving and Nonachieving Gifted Children." *J Psychol* 64:49–57 S '66. * (PA 40:12163)
42. PRIEN, ERICH P., and BOTWIN, DAVID E. "The Reliability and Correlates of an Achievement Index." *Ed & Psychol Meas* 26:1047–52 w '66. * (PA 41:4998)
43. BRONZO, ANTHONY F., JR. "Preliminary Investigation of AFROTC Cadet Attrition." *J Psychol* 66:185–90 Jl '67. * (PA 41:11247)
44. GARSEE, JARRELL W., and GLIXMAN, ALFRED F. "Samoan Interpersonal Values." *J Social Psychol* 72:45–60 Je '67. * (PA 41:11855)
45. GORDON, LEONARD V. "Q-Typing of Oriental and American Youth: Initial and Clarifying Studies." *J Social Psychol* 71:185–95 Ap '67. * (PA 41:8782)
46. GRIFFITH, HARLEY JOSEPH, JR. *A Comparison of Leadership Motivation and Need for Recognition of Delegate Teachers With Selected Non-Delegate Teachers.* Doctor's thesis, Purdue University (Lafayette, Ind.), 1967. (DA 28:4374A)
47. HEATER, WILLIAM HENDERSON. *Attitudes of Michigan Clergymen Toward Mental Retardation and Toward Education: Their Nature and Determinants.* Doctor's thesis, Michigan State University (East Lansing, Mich.), 1967. (DA 28:4874A)
48. KREIDER, PAUL EDWARD. *The Social-Psychological Nature and Determinants of Attitudes Toward Education and Toward Physically Disabled Persons in Belgium, Denmark, England, France, the Netherlands, and Yugoslavia.* Doctor's thesis, Michigan State University (East Lansing, Mich.), 1967. (DA 28:1679A)
49. BACHTOLD, LOUISE M. "Interpersonal Values of Gifted Junior High School Students." *Psychol Sch* 5:368–70 O '68. *
50. BERRIEN, F. K. "Cross-Cultural Equivalence of Person-

ality Measures." *J Social Psychol* 75:3–9 Je '68. * (*PA* 42:13572)

51. BRONZO, ANTHONY F., and BAER, DANIEL J. "Leadership and Bureaucratic Tendency Measures as Predictors of Freshman Dropouts From AFROTC." *Psychol Rep* 22:232 F '68. * (*PA* 42:11233)

52. CLARK, WINIFRED BRADLEY. *An Empirical Study of Attitudes Toward Teaching Selected Values, and Demographic Information of Freshmen and Seniors.* Doctor's thesis, Auburn University (Auburn, Ala.), 1968. (*DA* 28:3992A)

53. FREED, EARL X. "Interpersonal Values of Hospitalized Alcoholic Psychiatric Patients." *Psychol Rep* 22:403–6 Ap '68. * (*PA* 42:12379)

54. GORDON, LEONARD V. "Comments on 'Cross-Cultural Equivalence of Personality Measures.' " *J Social Psychol* 75: 11–9 Je '68. * (*PA* 42:13577)

55. HARDESTY, D. L., and JONES, W. S. "Characteristics of Judged High Potential Management Personnel—The Operations of an Industrial Assessment Center." *Personnel Psychol* 21:85–98 sp '68. * (*PA* 42:16197)

56. McFADDEN, JACK D. "The Discrimination of Student Teaching Performance on the Basis of Psychological Attributes." *J Ed Res* 61:215–7 Ja '68. *

57. MORRIS, B. B. "Cross-Validation of the Gordon SIV." *Percept & Motor Skills* 27:44–6 Ag '68. * (*PA* 43:2633)

58. PARRY, MARY ELLEN. "Ability of Psychologists to Estimate Validities of Personnel Tests." *Personnel Psychol* 21: 139–47 su '68. * (*PA* 42:14727)

59. WADSWORTH, BARRY J.; RUNTE, RICHARD M.; and TOOKEY, THOMAS. "Values of Seminarians and Novices." *Psychol Rep* 23:870 D '68. *

60. WIGGINS, THOMAS WINFIELD. *Leader Behavior Characteristics and Organizational Climate.* Doctor's thesis, Claremont Graduate School and University Center (Claremont, Calif.), 1968. (*DA* 29:2504A)

NAME INDEX

[262]

*Survey of Personal Attitude "SPA" (With Pictures): Individual Placement Series. Adults; 1960–66; SPA; 3 scores: social attitude, personal frankness, aggressiveness; Form A ('60, 14 pages); no specific manual; series manual ('66, 107 pages); separate answer sheets must be used; $30 per 20 tests; $4 per 100 answer sheets; $1 per scoring stencil; $2.50 per series manual; $5.15 per specimen set; cash orders postpaid; [20–25] minutes; J. H. Norman; Personnel Research Associates, Inc. *

[263]

*Survey of Personal Values. High school and college; 1964–67; SPV; 6 scores: practical mindedness, achievement, variety, decisiveness, orderliness, goal orientation; 1 form ('65, 3 pages); manual ('67, 16 pages); $3.35 per 20 tests; 56¢ per key; $1 per

specimen set; postage extra; (15–20) minutes; Leonard V. Gordon; Science Research Associates, Inc. *

REFERENCES

1. GORDON, LEONARD V. "Values of the Peace Corps Volunteer." *Psychol Rep* 18:328 F '66. * (*PA* 40:6571)
2. BRONZO, ANTHONY F., JR. "Preliminary Investigation of AFROTC Cadet Attrition." *J Psychol* 66:185–90 Jl '67. * (*PA* 41:14247)
3. BRAUN, JOHN R., and COSTANTINI, ARTHUR. "Fakability and Control for Social Desirability of the Survey of Personal Values." *Proc Ann Conv Am Psychol Assn* 76:161–2 '68. * (*PA* 43:933, title only)

[263A]

*TAV Selection System. Adults; 1963–68; TAV; vocational selection and counseling; 7 tests; manual ('68, 65 pages); norms consist of means and standard deviations for 8 occupational groups (state traffic officers, municipal patrolmen, female high school teachers, male high school teachers, life insurance claims adjusters, life insurance salesmen, deputy sheriff cadets, and female probation counselors); 1–50 sets of test-answer sheets (IBM 805 scorable) for the battery, $1.10 per set; $4.25 per set of scoring stencils for the battery; $3.25 per manual; $8.10 per specimen set; postage extra; (180) minutes for the battery, (15–20) minutes for any one test; R. R. Morman; TAV Selection System. *

a) TAV ADJECTIVE CHECKLIST. 1963–68; 3 scores: toward people (T), away from people (A), versus people (V); 1 form ('63, 2 pages); 1–50 test-answer sheets, 15¢ each.

b) TAV JUDGMENTS. 1964–68; 3 scores as in *a*; 1 form ('64, 4 pages on 2 sheets); 1–50 sets of the 2 test-answer sheets, 18¢ per set.

c) TAV PERSONAL DATA. 1964–68; 3 scores as in *a*; 1 form ('64, 4 pages on 2 sheets); 1–50 sets of the 2 test-answer sheets, 18¢ per set.

d) TAV PREFERENCES. 1963–68; 3 scores as in *a*; 1 form ('63, 2 pages); 1–50 tests, 15¢ each.

e) TAV PROVERBS AND SAYINGS. 1966–68; 3 scores as in *a*; 1 form ('66, 3 pages on 2 sheets); 1–50 sets of the 2 test-answer sheets, 18¢ per set.

f) TAV SALESMAN REACTIONS. 1967–68; 3 scores as in *a*; 1 form ('67, 4 pages on 2 sheets); 1–50 sets of the 2 test-answer sheets, 18¢ per set.

g) TAV MENTAL AGILITY. 1965–68; 3 scores: follow directions and carefulness, weights and balances, verbal comprehension; 1 form ('65, 3 pages on 2 sheets); 1–50 sets of the 2 test-answer sheets, 18¢ per set.

REFERENCES

1. HANKEY, RICHARD O.; MORMAN, ROBERT R.; KENNEDY, PHYLISS; and HEYWOOD, HAROLD L. "Predicting State Traffic Officer Performance With TAV Selection System Theoretical Scoring Keys." *Police* 9:70–3 My–Je '65. *
2. HANKEY, RICHARD O.; MORMAN, ROBERT R.; KENNEDY, PHYLISS; and HEYWOOD, HAROLD L. "TAV Selection System and State Traffic Officer Job Performance." *Police* 9:10–3 Mr–Ap '65. *
3. MORMAN, ROBERT R.; HANKEY, RICHARD O.; HEYWOOD, HAL; and KENNEDY, PHYLISS K. "Multiple Relationships of TAV Selection System Predictors to State Traffic Officer Performance." *Police* 9:41–4 Jl–Ag '65. *
4. MORMAN, ROBERT R.; HEYWOOD, HAROLD L.; DUVLICK, JOHN; LIDDLE, L. ROGERS; and HANKEY, RICHARD O. "High School Teaching Effectiveness." *J Sec Ed* 40:270–4 O '65. *
5. MORMAN, R. R.; KENNEDY, P. K.; HEYWOOD, H. L.; and LIDDLE, L. R. "Predicting Automobile Insurance Adjuster Performance." *J Indus Psychol* 3(3):74–9 '65. * (*PA* 42: 4817)
6. MORMAN, ROBERT R.; LIDDLE, L. ROGERS; and HEYWOOD, HAROLD L. "Prediction of Academic Achievement of Nursing Students: A Theoretical Study Using the TAV Selection System." *Nursing Res* 14:227–30 su '65. *
7. MORMAN, ROBERT R.; HANKEY, RICHARD O.; HEYWOOD, HAROLD L.; and LIDDLE, L. ROGERS. "Predicting State Traffic Officer Cadet Academic Performance From Theoretical TAV Selection System Scores." *Police* 10:54–8 Ja–F '66. *
8. MORMAN, ROBERT R.; HANKEY, RICHARD O.; KENNEDY, PHYLISS K.; and JONES, ETHEL M. "Academy Achievement

of State Traffic Officer Cadets Related to TAV Selection System Plus Other Variables." *Police* 10:30–4 Jl–Ag '66. *

9. MORMAN, ROBERT R.; HANKEY, RICHARD O.; HEYWOOD, HAROLD L.; LIDDLE, L. ROGERS; and GOLDWHITE, MARIE. "Multiple Prediction of Municipal Police Officers' Ratings and Rankings Using Theoretical TAV Selection System and Certain Non-Test Data." *Police* 11:19–22 Ja–F '67. *

10. MORMAN, ROBERT; HEYWOOD, HAROLD; and LIDDLE, L. ROGERS. "Predicting College Academic Achievement From TAV Selection System on Fifty Male Elementary Teacher Trainees." *J Ed Res* 60:221–3 Ja '67. *

11. MORMAN, ROBERT R.; LIDDLE, L. ROGERS; HEYWOOD, HAROLD L.; and HANKEY, RICHARD O. "Predicting College Academic Achievement From TAV Selection System, Theoretical Scores and Age of Ninety-Five Female Elementary Teacher Trainees." *J Ed Res* 60:413–5 My–Je '67. *

[264]

Taylor-Johnson Temperament Analysis. Ages 17 and over; 1941–68; TJTA; revision of *Johnson Temperament Analysis;* individual, premarital, and marital counseling; 9 trait scores (nervous-composed, depressive-lighthearted, active/social-quiet, expressive/responsive-inhibited, sympathetic-indifferent, subjective-objective, dominant-submissive, hostile-tolerant, self-disciplined-impulsive) plus test taking attitude scale; 1 form ('67, 6 pages); manual ('68, 57 pages plus test materials); revised profile ('67, 1 page); sten profile ('67, 1 page); separate answer sheets must be used; $15 per counselor's kit (must be purchased to obtain manual); $5 per 25 tests; $2.50 per 50 answer sheets; $2.50 per 50 profiles; cash orders postpaid; (30–45) minutes; original edition by Roswell H. Johnson; revision by Robert M. Taylor and Lucile P. Morrison (manual); Psychological Publications, Inc. *

See 6:130 (10 references); for a review by Albert Ellis of the original edition, see 4:62 (6 references); for a review by H. Meltzer, see 3:57.

REFERENCES

1–6. See 4:62.
7–16. See 6:130.
17. BARNES, ALFRED CAVIS, JR. *Characteristics of Personality and Attitude Relationships of Selected Male Traffic Violators and Non-Violators.* Doctor's thesis, Indiana University (Bloomington, Ind.), 1962. (*DA* 22:4263)
18. PERDUE, WILLIAM C. "Screening of Applicants for Custodial Work by Means of a Temperament Test." *Am J Correction* 26:14–5+ N–D '64. *
19. PERDUE, WILLIAM C. "The Temperaments of Custodial Workers." *Am J Correction* 28:16–7+ Mr–Ap '66. *

[265]

Temperament Comparator. Adults; 1958–61; TC; identical with *Paired Comparison Temperament Schedule* ('58) except for format of presentation; 24 scores: 18 trait scores (calm, cautious, decisive, demonstrative, emotionally stable, energetic, enthusiastic, even-tempered, lively, persevering, prompt starter, quick worker, seeks company, self-confident, serious, socially at ease, steady worker, talkative), 5 factor scores (controlled vs. outgoing, stable vs. unstable, self-reliant vs. dependent, excitable vs. placid, sociable vs. solitary), and consistency; 1 form ('61, 2 pages); manual ('61, 51 pages); profile ('61, 1 page); administered with snap-on trait-pairing disc ('61); reliability data, validity data, and norms based on test in format of the earlier editions; $3 per 20 tests; $1.50 per set of reusable backing folder and disc; postage extra; $2 per specimen set, postpaid; (15–20) minutes; Melany E. Baehr and R. W. Pranis; Industrial Relations Center, University of Chicago. *

For reviews by Lawrence J. Stricker and Robert L. Thorndike, see 6:187 (1 reference).

[266]

★Tennessee Self Concept Scale. Ages 12 and over; 1956–65; TSCS; also called *Tennessee (Department of Mental Health) Self Concept Scale;* 2 scoring systems referred to as Counseling Form and Clinical

and Research Form; 1 form ('64, 6 pages); manual ('65, 31 pages); separate answer sheets must be used; 26¢ per test, 1–99 copies; 16¢ per answer sheet (including score and profile sheets), 1–99 copies; 90¢ per set of scoring keys for both forms; 70¢ per manual; 90¢ per specimen set; postage extra; scoring service, 50¢ per test; (10–20) minutes; William H. Fitts; Counselor Recordings and Tests. *

a) COUNSELING FORM. 15 profiled scores: self criticism, 9 self esteem scores (identity, self satisfaction, behavior, physical self, moral-ethical self, personal self, family self, social self, total), 3 variability of response scores (variation across first 3 of the self esteem scores, variation across the last 5 self esteem scores, total), distribution score, time score.

b) CLINICAL AND RESEARCH FORM. 30 profiled scores: the 15 scores in a above and the following 15: response bias, net conflict, total conflict, 6 empirical scales (defensive positive, general maladjustment, psychosis, personality disorder, neurosis, personality integration), deviant signs, 5 scores consisting of counts of each type of response made.

REFERENCES

1. ATCHISON, CALVIN O. *A Comparative Study of the Self-Concept of Behavior Problem and Non-Behavior Problem High School Boys.* Doctor's thesis, Indiana University (Bloomington, Ind.), 1958. (*DA* 19:1010)
2. CLAYE, CLIFTON MAURICE. *A Study of the Relationship Between Self-Concepts and Attitudes Toward the Negro Among Secondary School Pupils in Three Schools of Arkansas.* Doctor's thesis, University of Arkansas (Fayetteville, Ark.), 1958. (*DA* 19:587)
3. HAVENER, PHILIP H., and IZARD, CARROLL E. "Unrealistic Self-Enhancement in Paranoid Schizophrenics." *J Consult Psychol* 26:65–8 F '62. * (*PA* 37:5490)
4. BRASSARD, ELIANORA I. *Social Desirability and Self Concept Description.* Doctor's thesis, University of Nebraska (Lincoln, Neb.), 1963. (*DA* 24:3420)
5. DIMAYA, NATIVIDAD BONOAN. *An Analytical Study of the Self Concept of Hospitalized Patients With Hansen's Disease.* Doctor's thesis, Wayne State University (Detroit, Mich.), 1963. (*DA* 25:5729)
6. SEARLES, WARREN BARNHART. *The Relationship Between the Perceived Emotional Climate of the Home of College Students and Certain Variables in Their Functioning Related to Self-Concept and Academic Functioning.* Doctor's thesis, University of Maryland (College Park, Md.), 1963. (*DA* 24:5208)
7. WAYNE, STANLEY ROBERT. *The Relation of Self-Esteem to Indices of Perceived and Behavioral Hostility.* Doctor's thesis, Vanderbilt University (Nashville, Tenn.), 1963. (*DA* 24:5554)
8. ASHCRAFT, CAROLYN, and FITTS, W. H. "Self-Concept Changes in Psychotherapy." *Psychotherapy* 1:115–8 My '64. * (*PA* 40:1621)
9. HALL, JOHN DAVID. *An Investigation of Acquiescence Response Set, Extraversion, and Locus of Control as Related to Neuroticism and Maladjustment.* Doctor's thesis, George Peabody College for Teachers (Nashville, Tenn.), 1964. (*DA* 25:6060)
10. GREENBERG, GLORIA U., and FRANK, GEORGE H. "Response Set in the Tennessee Department of Mental Health Self Concept Scale." *J Clin Psychol* 21:287–8 Jl '65. * (*PA* 39:15236)
11. HARA, TADAO. *The Relationship Between Self-Concept of Foreign Students Measured by the Tennessee Self-Concept Scale and Their Academic Achievement.* Master's thesis, California State College at Long Beach (Long Beach, Calif.), 1965.
12. LEFEBER, JAMES ARTHUR. *The Delinquent's Self-Concept.* Doctor's thesis, University of Southern California (Los Angeles, Calif.), 1965. (*DA* 26:2052)
13. VINCENT, MARY JANE PARKS. *A Study of Construct Validity in Self Concept Measurement.* Doctor's thesis, University of Idaho (Moscow, Idaho), 1966. (*DA* 27:3741A)
14. BARTEE, GERALDINE McMURRY. *The Perceptual Characteristics of Disadvantaged Negro and Caucasian College Students.* Doctor's thesis, East Texas State University (Commerce, Tex.), 1967. (*DA* 28:3455A)
15. HALL, CHARLES C. *A Comparison of Peer Nominations and Other Variables of Student Teaching Effectiveness.* Doctor's thesis, North Texas State University (Denton, Tex.), 1967. (*DA* 28:2070A)
16. JENKINS, JOHN MERVIN. *A Study of the Characteristics Associated With Innovative Behavior in Teachers.* Doctor's thesis, University of Miami (Coral Gables, Fla.), 1967. (*DA* 28:903A)
17. RENTZ, R. ROBERT, and WHITE, WILLIAM F. "Congruence of the Dimensions of Self-as-Object and Self-as-Process." *J Psychol* 67:277–85 N '67. * (*PA* 42:2555)

18. RENTZ, R. ROBERT, and WHITE, WILLIAM F. "Factors of Self Perception in the Tennessee Self Concept Scale." *Percept & Motor Skills* 24:118 F '67. * *(PA* 41:8925)

19. SWIHART, PHILLIP J. *Dominance and Submission in Same- and Opposite-Sex Dyads.* Doctor's thesis, Purdue University (Lafayette, Ind.), 1967. *(DA* 28:4766B)

20. TRACY, GERALD TIMOTHY. *A Methodological Study of the Desirability Response Set on the Tennessee Department of Mental Health Self-Concept Scale.* Doctor's thesis, University of Miami (Coral Gables, Fla.), 1967. *(DA* 28:1179B)

21. FRANCIS, RAYMOND WALTER. *A Study of the Relationships Among Acceptance of Psychological Disability, Self Concept and Body Image.* Doctor's thesis, State University of New York at Buffalo (Buffalo, N.Y.), 1968. *(DA* 29:770B)

22. GUTSCH, KENNETH URIAL, and HARRIS, GEORGE. "Counseling: Exploring the Sensitivity Syndrome." *South J Ed Res* 2:201–11 Ag '68. *

23. HEBERT, DAVID J. "Reading Comprehension as a Function of Self-Concept." *Percept & Motor Skills* 27:78 Ag '68. * *(PA* 43:3015)

24. SCHALON, CHARLES L. "Effect of Self-Esteem Upon Performance Following Failure Stress." Abstract. *J Consult & Clin Psychol* 32:497 Ag '68. * *(PA* 42:17212)

25. VACCHIANO, RALPH B., and STRAUSS, PAUL S. "The Construct Validity of the Tennessee Self Concept Scale." *J Clin Psychol* 24:323–6 Jl '68. * *(PA* 42:16435)

26. VACCHIANO, RALPH B.; STRAUSS, PAUL S.; and SCHIFFMAN, DAVID C. "Personality Correlates of Dogmatism." *J Consult & Clin Psychol* 32:83–5 F '68. * *(PA* 42:7323)

27. VINCENT, JANE. "An Exploratory Factor Analysis Relating to the Construct Validity of Self-Concept Labels." *Ed & Psychol Meas* 28:915–21 au '68. * *(PA* 43:4039)

28. WENDLAND, MARILYN MARIE. *Self-Concept in Southern Negro and White Adolescents as Related to Rural-Urban Residence.* Doctor's thesis, University of North Carolina (Chapel Hill, N.C.), 1968. *(DA* 29:2642B)

29. WILLIAMS, ROBERT L., and BYARS, HARRY. "Negro Self-Esteem in a Transitional Society." *Personnel & Guid J* 47:120–5 O '68. *

30. WILLIAMS, ROBERT L., and COLE, SPURGEON. "Self-Concept and School Adjustment." *Personnel & Guid J* 46:478–81 Ja '68. * *(PA* 42:9415)

NAME INDEX

[267]

Test for Developmental Age in Girls. Girls ages 8–18; 1933–34; social maturity; also called *A Scale for Measuring Developmental Age in Girls;* 1 form ('33, 7 pages, must be reproduced locally); manual ('34, 69 pages, see *1* below); $1.50 per manual, postage extra; administration time not reported; Celestine Sullivan; Catholic University of America Press. *

For a related book review not excerpted in this volume, consult the 1st (B495) MMY.

REFERENCE

1. SULLIVAN, CELESTINE. *A Scale for Measuring Developmental Age in Girls.* Catholic University of America, Studies in Psychology and Psychiatry, Vol. 3, No. 4. Baltimore, Md.: Williams & Wilkins Co., May 1934. Pp. vii, 65. * *(PA* 8:5325)

[268]

*Test of Basic Assumptions. Adults; 1959–68; c1957–59; TBA; for experimental and research use only; 12 scores: 3 attitude scores (realist, idealist, pragmatist) for each of 4 "life areas" (organization of effort and problem solving, human abilities and the individual, general philosophy of life, economics and business); Form X ('59, 4 pages); manual ('59, 4

pages); supplement ('68, 1 page); score sheet (1 page); reliability data for total attitude scores only; no norms; $3.50 per 25 tests; $1 per specimen set; postpaid; (60) minutes; James H. Morrison and Martin Levit (test); James H. Morrison. *

[269]

Test of Behavioral Rigidity, Research Edition. Ages 21 and over; 1960, c1956–60; TBR; 4 scores: motor-cognitive rigidity, personality-perceptual rigidity, psychomotor speed, total; 1 form ('60, c1956, 8 pages); mimeographed preliminary manual ('60, 24 pages); no data on reliability; $4.75 per 25 tests; $1 per manual; $1.50 per specimen set; postage extra; (30) minutes; K. Warner Schaie; Consulting Psychologists Press, Inc. *

For reviews by Douglas P. Crowne and Benjamin Kleinmuntz, see 6:189 (9 references).

REFERENCES

1–9. See 6:189.

10. LANGER, PHILIP, and McKAIN, CHARLES W. "Rigidity and the SORT." *J Clin Psychol* 20:489–92 O '64. * *(PA* 39:12344)

11. ROSS, PAUL F., and DUNFIELD, NEIL M. "Selecting Salesmen for an Oil Company." *Personnel Psychol* 17:75–84 sp '64. *

12. LEWIS, LAURA HESTER. *Acquiescence Response Set: Construct or Artifact?* Doctor's thesis, University of Nebraska (Lincoln, Neb.), 1967. *(DA* 28:2626B)

13. SCHAIE, K. WARNER, and STROTHER, CHARLES R. "The Effect of Time and Cohort Differences on the Interpretation of Age Changes in Cognitive Behavior." *Multiv Behav Res* 3:259–93 Jl '68. * *(PA* 43:3834)

[270]

Test of Social Insight. Grades 6–12, 13–16 and adults; 1959–63; TSI; 6 scores: withdrawal, passivity, cooperation, competition, aggression, total; 1 form ('59, 8 pages); 2 levels (essentially the same except for wording changes): youth edition, adult edition; manual ('63, 19 pages); separate answer sheets (IBM 805) must be used; $6.25 per 20 tests; $2.75 per 20 answer sheets; $2 per set of scoring stencils; $2.75 per 20 profiles; $1.75 per manual; $2.50 per specimen set of either level; cash orders postpaid; French edition available; [20–25] minutes; Russell N. Cassel; Martin M. Bruce. *

For reviews by John D. Black and John Pierce-Jones, see 6:190 (4 references, 1 excerpt).

[271]

Test of Work Competency and Stability. Ages 21 and over; 1960–61, c1959–60; TWCS; for predicting work capacity and identifying persons psychologically incapable of work; individual; 1 form consisting of an interview questionnaire (no date, 5 pages, mimeographed, 1 or 2 scores: ego strength and, optionally, occupational stability) and 4 or 6 tests: 2 perceptual tests of intelligence (digits backward, picture arrangement), 2 psychomotor tests (tapping, steadiness), and (optionally) stress test (mirror drawing), digit symbol; manual ('61, c1959, 58 pages, English edition translated from the 1960 French edition which is also available); record booklet ('60, 4 pages); no data on reliability for interview questionnaire, digits backward, picture arrangement, or digit symbol; Can $110 per set of test materials including apparatus for tapping, steadiness, and mirror drawing tests, 25 record booklets, 25 questionnaires, 25 mirror tracing records, 25 tapping records, and manual; $3 per 25 questionnaires; $2 per 25 record booklets; $2.50 per manual; postage extra; (30–40) minutes; A Gaston Leblanc, Institute of Psychological Research. *

See 6:191 (2 references).

[272]

★**Tests of Social Intelligence.** High school and adults; 1965–66; TSI; 6 tests; 5 scores: implications (test *a*), classes (test *b*), systems (tests *c, d*), transformations (tests *e, f*), composite (tests *a, b, c, f*); manual ('66, 8 pages); norms for grade 10 only; separate answer sheets (IBM 805) must be used; 7¢ per answer sheet (space for all 6 tests); $2 per set of scoring stencils; 50¢ per manual; $2 per specimen set (complete test not included); postage extra; Maureen O'Sullivan, R. deMille (*c, d, e*), and J. P. Guilford; Sheridan Psychological Services, Inc. *

a) CARTOON PREDICTIONS. Form A ('65, 8 pages); $5 per 25 tests; 8(13) minutes.
b) EXPRESSION GROUPING. Form A ('65, 8 pages); $5 per 25 tests; 10(15) minutes.
c) MISSING CARTOONS. Form A ('65, 16 pages); $5 per 25 tests; 16(21) minutes.
d) MISSING PICTURES. Form A ('65, 12 pages); $5 per 25 tests; 12(17) minutes.
e) PICTURE EXCHANGE. Form A ('65, 12 pages); $5 per 25 tests; 12(17) minutes.
f) SOCIAL TRANSLATIONS. Form A ('65, 4 pages); $2.50 per 25 tests; 8(13) minutes.

REFERENCE

1. HOEPFNER, RALPH, and O'SULLIVAN, MAUREEN. "Social Intelligence and IQ." *Ed & Psychol Meas* 28:339–44 su '68. *

[273]

*Theological School Inventory.** Incoming seminary students; 1962–65; TSI; motivation for entering the ministry; 12 scores (definiteness, natural leading, special leading, concept of the call, flexibility, acceptance by others, intellectual concern, self-fulfillment, leadership success, evangelistic witness, social reform, service to persons) plus unscored sections on biographical information and reactions to demands of the ministry; Form C ('62, 14 pages); manual ('64, 110 pages); 5 research supplements ('64–'65, 6–25 pages each); separate answer sheets must be used; $1.50 per set of test and answer sheet; $6.50 per 25 additional answer sheets; $4 per set of scoring stencils; $5.50 per set of manual and supplements in a looseleaf binder; postage extra; (90–100) minutes; Educational Testing Service (test), James E. Dittes (manual and supplements), Frederick Kling (test and 1 supplement), Ellery Pierson (1 supplement), and Harry DeWire (1 supplement); Ministry Studies Board; distributed by Department of Publication Services, National Council of the Churches of Christ. *

REFERENCES

1. EMBREE, ROBERT ARTHUR. *A Factor Analytic Investigation of Motivations and Attitudes of College Students With Intentions for the Ministry and a Comparison of the Performance of Persisters and Non-Persisters on the Theological School Inventory.* Doctor's thesis, University of Denver (Denver, Colo.), 1964. (*DA* 25:7367)
2. KNOTT, THOMAS GARLAND. *Motivational Factors in Selected Women Candidates for the Master of Religious Education Degree.* Doctor's thesis, Boston University (Boston, Mass.), 1964. (*DA* 25:3140)
3. DITTES, JAMES E. *TSI Validity Studies: A Replication at Concordia Seminary (St. Louis).* Theological School Inventory Research Bulletin 5. Dayton, Ohio: Ministry Studies Board, 1965. Pp. 24. *
4. OTTE, HAROLD WILLIAM. *Comparisons of Abilities, Motivations, and Personality Traits of Continuing and Non-Continuing Freshmen in Colleges of the Lutheran Church—Missouri Synod.* Doctor's thesis, University of Colorado (Boulder, Colo.), 1965. (*DA* 26:6480)
5. SPIERS, DUANE EDWIN. *A Study of the Predictive Validity of a Test Battery Administered to Theological Students.* Doctor's thesis, Purdue University (Lafayette, Ind.), 1965. (*DA* 26:1488)

[274]

★**The Thomas Self-Concept Values Test.** Ages 3–9; 1967; TSCVT; experimental form; 19 scores: value scores (happiness, size, sociability, ability, sharing, male acceptance, fear of things, fear of people, strength, cleanliness, health, attractiveness, material, independence), self concept scores (self as subject, mother, teacher, peer, total); no reading by examinees; mimeographed manual (43 pages); answer-profile sheet (2 pages); no data on reliability and validity; 5¢ per answer-profile sheet; $4 per manual; postage extra; (10–20) minutes; Walter L. Thomas; Educational Service Co. *

[275]

★**The Thorman Family Relations Conference Situation Questionnaire.** Families receiving therapy; 1965; also called *Thorman Family Relations Evaluation;* 1 form (2 pages); record booklet (4 pages); manual (3 pages plus test and record booklet); family therapy handbook (22 pages plus manual); no data on reliability; $4 per 25 tests; $6.50 per 25 record booklets; $6 per handbook; $2.50 per manual; postpaid; (50–60) minutes; George Thorman; Western Psychological Services. *

[276]

★**Thorndike Dimensions of Temperament.** Grades 11–16 and adults; 1963–66; TDOT; 10 scores: sociable, ascendant, cheerful, placid, accepting, tough minded, reflective, impulsive, active, responsible; 1 form ('63, 7 pages); manual ('66, 35 pages); norms for grades 11–13 only; separate answer sheets (IBM 805) must be used; $3.50 per 25 tests; $2.60 per 50 answer sheets; $2 per set of hand scoring stencils and manual; $2.25 per set of machine scoring stencils and manual; $2.50 per specimen set; postpaid; (45–55) minutes; Robert L. Thorndike; Psychological Corporation. *

REFERENCES

1. HORN, DOROTHY MARIE. *A Comparison of Normative and Ipsative Measurements as Applied to Items From the Dimensions of Temperament Inventory.* Doctor's thesis, Columbia University (New York, N.Y.), 1966. (*DA* 27:3271B)
2. BRAUN, JOHN R., and LAFARO, DOLORES. "Effects of a Good Impression Set on the Thorndike Dimensions of Temperament." *J Ed Meas* 4:237–40 w '67. * (*PA* 42:9713)

[277]

Thurstone Temperament Schedule. Grades 9–16 and adults; 1949–53; TTS; 7 scores: active, vigorous, impulsive, dominant, stable, sociable, reflective; 2 editions; manual, second edition ('53, 14 pages); separate answer sheets (IBM 805) or pads must be used; $16.04 per 20 tests; $1.08 per specimen set; postage extra; (15–25) minutes; L. L. Thurstone; Science Research Associates, Inc. *

a) HAND SCORED EDITION. Form AH ('49, 7 pages); $3.20 per 20 answer pads.
b) MACHINE SCORABLE EDITION. Form AM ('49, 7 pages); $5 per 100 answer sheets; $2.50 per set of scoring stencils.

See 6:192 (17 references); for a review by Neil J. Van Steenberg, see 5:118 (12 references); for reviews by Hans J. Eysenck, Charles M. Harsh, and David G. Ryans, see 4:93 (1 excerpt).

REFERENCES

1–12. See 5:118.
13–28. See 6:192.
29. RAINIO, KULLERVO. *Leadership Qualities: A Theoretical Inquiry and an Experimental Study on Foremen.* Suomalaisen Tiedeakatemian Toimituksia, Annales Academiae Scientiarum Fennicae, Sarja-Ser. B, Nide-Tom. 95.1. Helsinki, Finland: Academiae Scientiarum Fennicae, 1955. Pp. 211. * (*PA* 31:1872)
30. GROTBERG, EDITH H. *An Experimental Investigation of Persistence.* Doctor's thesis, Northwestern University (Evanston, Ill.), 1958. (*DA* 19:1290)
31. BARTH, GEORGE WILLIAM. *Some Personality and Tem-*

perament Characteristics of Selected School Music Teachers. Doctor's thesis, University of Southern California (Los Angeles, Calif.), 1961. (*DA* 22:149)

32. CARMICAL, LAVERNE LATHROP. *The Identification of Certain Characteristics of Selected Achievers and Under-achievers of Bellaire Senior High School.* Doctor's thesis, University of Houston (Houston, Tex.), 1961. (*DA* 22:2244)

33. PURCELL, JOHN FRANCIS. *Expressed Self Concept and Adjustment in Sexually Delinquent and Non-Delinquent Adolescent Girls.* Doctor's thesis, Fordham University (New York, N.Y.), 1961. (*DA* 22:918)

34. CARR, JAMES GILES. *A Comparative Study of Aspirants to Secondary School Teacher Education.* Doctor's thesis, University of Florida (Gainesville, Fla.), 1962. (*DA* 24:619)

35. MEISGEIER, CHARLES HENRY. *Variables Which May Identify Successful Student Teachers of Mentally or Physically Handicapped Children.* Doctor's thesis, Pennsylvania State University (University Park, Pa.), 1962. (*DA* 23:3803)

36. WESTFALL, RALPH. "Psychological Factors in Predicting Product Choice." *J Marketing* 26:34–40 Ap '62. * (*PA* 37:2182)

37. BLYTH, CARL S., and LOVINGWOOD, BILL W. "Psycho-motor Responses and Their Relationship to Personality Traits of Young Men Performing in High Ambient Temperature (110 F)." *Res Q* 35:241–5 O '64. * (*PA* 39:4218)

38. BARRATT, ERNEST S. "Factor Analysis of Some Psychometric Measures of Impulsiveness and Anxiety." *Psychol Rep* 16:547–54 Ap '65. * (*PA* 39:10087)

39. BLUMENFELD, WARREN S., and BERRY, RICHARD N. "Rapidity of Test Completion and Level of Score Attained." *Psychol Rep* 16:327–30 F '65. * (*PA* 39:8682)

40. COATES, CHARLES ROBERT. *A Descriptive Analysis of School Dropouts, One to Three Years After Termination of School Attendance.* Doctor's thesis, University of Virginia (Charlottesville, Va.), 1965. (*DA* 26:5860)

41. CONLEY, NAOMI LEE. *Factors Related to Teacher Effectiveness of High School Distributive Education Teacher-Coordinators.* Doctor's thesis, University of Tennessee (Knoxville, Tenn.), 1965. (*DA* 26:6440)

42. LEON, HENRY V., and FRANK, GEORGE H. "Personality Correlates of Cognitive Disturbances in Short-Term Sensory Isolation." *J General Psychol* 74:273–7 Ap '66. * (*PA* 40:7274)

43. WRIGHT, NANCY A., and ZUBEK, JOHN P. "Use of the Multiple Discriminant Function in the Prediction of Perceptual Deprivation Tolerance." *Can J Psychol* 20:105–13 Mr '66. * (*PA* 40:6647)

44. FISHER, SEYMOUR, and OSOFSKY, HOWARD. "Sexual Responsiveness in Women: Psychological Correlates." *Arch Gen Psychiatry* 17:214–26 Ag '67. * (*PA* 41:15149)

45. HEATH, HELEN A.; OKEN, DONALD; and SHIPMAN, WILLIAM G. "Muscle Tension and Personality: A Serious Second Look." *Arch Gen Psychiatry* 16:720–6 Je '67. * (*PA* 41:13932)

46. HARTMAN, BERNARD J. "Effect of Knowledge of Personality Test Results on Subsequent Test Performance." *Percept & Motor Skills* 26:122 F '68. * (*PA* 42:10593)

47. HOWARD, DENNIS SCOTT. *Personality Similarity and Complementarity and Perceptual Accuracy in Supervisor-Subordinate Relationships.* Doctor's thesis, Illinois Institute of Technology (Chicago, Ill.), 1968. (*DA* 28:4789B)

48. NEWMAN, EARL N. "Personality Traits of Faster and Slower Competitive Swimmers." *Res Q* 39:1049–53 D '68. *

NAME INDEX

[278]

★**Trait Evaluation Index.** College and adults; 1967–68; TEI; 22 scores (social orientation, compliance, benevolence, elation, ambition, motivational drive, self confidence, dynamism, independence, personal adequacy, caution, self organization, responsibility, propriety, courtesy, verbal orientation, intellectual orientation, perception, self control, fairmindedness, adaptability, sincerity) plus 4 general supplementary scores (overall adjustment, masculinity, femininity, consistency) and 3 supplementary scores for engineers (employment stability, productivity-creativity, job satisfaction); 1 form ('67, 4 pages); manual ('68, 38 pages); supplement ['68, 4 pages]; profile ('67, 2 pages) for college; profile ('67, 2 pages) for adults; adult norms for males only; separate answer sheets (IBM 1230 scorable) must be used; $5 per 20 tests; $2.75 per 20 answer sheets; $6 per set of scoring stencils; $2.75 per 20 profiles; $2.75 per manual; $6.50 per specimen set; cash orders postpaid; (30–50) minutes; Alan R. Nelson; Martin M. Bruce. *

[279]

Triadal Equated Personality Inventory. Adult males; 1960–63; TEPI; 22 scores: dominance, self confidence, decisiveness, independence, toughness, suspiciousness, conscientiousness, introversion, restlessness, solemnity, foresight, industriousness, warmth, enthusiasm, conformity, inventiveness, persistence, sex drive, recognition drive, cooperativeness, humility-tolerance, self control; 1 form ('61, 4 pages); administration and technical manual ('63, 4 pages); norms manual ('61, 4 pages); profile ('61, 1 page); separate answer sheets must be used; $4 per 25 tests; $2 per 25 answer sheets; $2 per 25 profiles; $22 per specimen set (must be purchased to obtain manuals and scoring stencils); cash orders postpaid; scoring service, $1 per test; (60–80) minutes; Research Staff, United Consultants; Psychometric Affiliates. *

[280]

Tulane Factors of Liberalism-Conservatism. Social science students; 1946–55; TFLC; 5 scores: political, economic, religious, social, aesthetic; 1 form ('46, 2 pages); manual ('55, 1 page); college norms only; $2 per 25 tests; $1 per specimen set (must be purchased to obtain manual); cash orders postpaid; (25–35) minutes; Willard A. Kerr; Psychometric Affiliates. *

For reviews by Donald T. Campbell and C. Robert Pace, see 5:119 (2 references).

[281]

*Vineland Social Maturity Scale.** Birth to maturity; 1935–65; VSMS; individual; 1 form ('65, 4 pages, items identical with 1936 edition); condensed manual ('65, 35 pages, very nearly identical to 1947 edition); technical manual: *Measurement of Social Competence* ('53, 682 pages); $2 per 25 record blanks; $1.35 per condensed manual; $8 per technical manual; postage extra; $1.50 per specimen set, postpaid; (20–30) minutes; Edgar A. Doll; American Guidance Service, Inc. * (Australian edition: Australian Council for Educational Research.)

See 6:194 (20 references) and 5:120 (15 references); for reviews by William M. Cruickshank and Florence M. Teagarden, see 4:94 (21 references); for reviews by C. M. Louttit and John W. M. Rothney, see 3:107 (58 references, 1 excerpt); for reviews by Paul H. Furfey, Elaine F. Kinder, and Anna S. Starr, see 1:1143; for related book reviews not excerpted in this volume, consult the 5th (B121) MMY.

REFERENCES

1–58. See 3:107.
59–79. See 4:94.
80–94. See 5:120.
95–114. See 6:194.

115. RAIN, MARGARET E. "Development of Social Maturity in Familial and Non-Familial Mentally Deficient Children." *Training Sch B* 48:177–85 F '52. * (*PA* 26:4883)

116. HOHMAN, LESLIE B., and FREEDHEIM, DONALD K. "A Study of IQ Retest Evaluation on 370 Cerebral Palsied Children." *Am J Phys Med* 38:180–7 O '59. *

117. SANTOS, BERTHA. *A Comparison of Memory and Learning Ability With Social Competence and Social Participation in Aged Senile Dements in a Mental Institution.* Doctor's thesis, New York University (New York, N.Y.), 1959. (*DA* 20:1441)

118. BARKSDALE, MILDRED W. "Social Problems of Mentally Retarded Children." *Mental Hyg* 45:509–12 O '61. * (*PA* 36:4J109B)

119. KRIPPNER, STANLEY. "Relationship Between Reading Improvement and Ten Selected Variables." *Percept & Motor Skills* 19:15–20 Ag '64. * (*PA* 39:5941)

120. ALLEN, CLARK E., and TOOMEY, LAURA C. "Use of the Vineland Social Maturity Scale for Evaluating Progress of Psychotic Children in a Therapeutic Nursery School." *Am J Orthopsychiatry* 35:152–9 Ja '65. * (*PA* 39:8453)

121. GUNZBURG, H. C. "A 'Finishing School' for the Mentally Subnormal." *Med Officer* 114:99–102 Ag 13 '65. *

122. HUGHLEY, ROBERT CARL. *Some Factors Relating to the Vocational Adjustment of Special Class Graduates.* Doctor's research study No. 1, Colorado State College (Greeley, Colo.), 1965. (*DA* 26:5131)

123. MEIER, JOHN HENRY. *An Exploratory Factor Analysis of Psychodiagnostic and Case Study Information From Children in Special Education Classes for the Educable Mentally Handicapped.* Doctor's thesis, University of Denver (Denver, Colo.), 1965. (*DA* 26:3153)

124. RABIN, A. I. *Growing Up in the Kibbutz: Comparison of the Personality of Children Brought Up in the Kibbutz and of Family-Reared Children.* New York: Springer Publishing Co., Inc., 1965. Pp. x, 230. *

125. HOLROYD, RICHARD G. "A Profile Sheet to Facilitate Administration of the Vineland Social Maturity Scale." *J Clin Psychol* 22:197–9 Ap '66. * (*PA* 40:7195)

126. PEDRINI, DUILIO T., and PEDRINI, LURA N. "The Vineland Social Maturity Scale: Recommendations for Administration, Scoring and Analysis." *J Sch Psychol* 5:14–20 au '66. * (*PA* 41:3342, title only)

127. PRINGLE, M. L. KELLMER. *Social Learning and Its Measurement.* London: Longmans Green & Co., Ltd., 1966. Pp. viii, 100. *

128. WALL, W. D., and PRINGLE, M. L. KELLMER. "The Clinical Significance of Standard Score Discrepancies Between Intelligence and Social Competence." *Hum Develop* 9(3):121–51 '66. *

129. WERNER, EMMY, and SIMONIAN, KENNETH. "The Social Maturity of Preschool Children in Hawaii: Results of a Community Survey and a Review of Two Decades of Research." *J Social Psychol* 69:197–207 Ag '66. * (*PA* 40:12230)

130. ALPERN, GERALD D. "Measurement of 'Untestable' Autistic Children." *J Abn Psychol* 72:478–86 D '67. * (*PA* 42:4183)

131. BEHRLE, FREDERICK J. "Examiner Bias on the Vineland." *Training Sch B* 64:108–15 N '67. * (*PA* 42:11033)

132. HERIOT, JAMES T., and SCHMICKEL, CAROL A. "Maternal Estimate of IQ in Children Evaluated for Learning Potential." *Am J Mental Def* 71:920–4 My '67. * (*PA* 41:11917)

133. McHALE, A. "An Investigation of Personality Attributes of Stammering, Enuretic and School-Phobic Children." *Brit J Ed Psychol* 37:140–3 N '67. * (*PA* 42:5947) Abstract of doctor's thesis, University of Leicester (Leicester, England), 1966.

134. STERNLOF, R. E.; PARKER, H. J.; and McCOY, J. F. "Relationships Between the Goodenough DAM Test and the Columbia Mental Maturity Test for Negro and White Head-start Children." *Percept & Motor Skills* 27:424–6 O '68. *

135. WERNER, EMMY E.; SIMONIAN, KENNETH; and SMITH, RUTH S. "Ethnic and Socioeconomic Status Differences in Abilities and Achievement Among Preschool and School-Age Children in Hawaii." *J Social Psychol* 75:43–59 Je '68. * (*PA* 42:13553)

NAME INDEX

Allen, C. E.: 120
Allen, R. M.: 98
Alpern, G. D.: 130
Anderson, J. E.: *exc*, consult 5:B121
Anderson, M. L.: 60
Avery, C.: 69–70
Barclay, A.: 113–4
Barksdale, M. W.: 118
Bassett, D. M.: 23
Behrle, F. J.: 131
Blake, K. A.: 104
Bodman, F.: 55
Bradway, K. P.: 9–12, 19, 59
Brasell, W. N.: 72
Brodie, F. H.: 96
Brooks, J. J.: 42
Brower, D.: 56
Brower, J. F.: 56
Burchard, E. M. L.: 38, 68
Capobianco, R. J.: 104
Capwell, D. F.: 51–2
Carter, C. O.: 101
Cassel, M. E.: 82
Cassel, R. H.: 76
Croke, K.: 90
Cruickshank, W. M.: *rev*, 4:94; *exc*, consult 5:B121
Danenhower, H. S.: 76
Deacon, K. F.: 39
Doll, E. A.: 1–7, 13–7, 20–1, 24–5, 27–8, 40–2, 46, 53, 61, 71, 83–4, 95
Drexler, H. G.: 108
Dunsdon, M. I.: 57, 101
Fitch, K. A.: 20, 25
Fjeld, H. A.: 44
Francey, R. E.: 102
Freedheim, D. K.: 116
Furfey, P. H.: *rev*, 1:1143
Gambaro, P. K.: 48
Goldstein, H.: 85
Goodman, A. W.: 29
Gottsegen, M. G.: 93
Goulet, L. R.: 113–4
Gunzburg, H. C.: 121
Heriot, J. T.: 132
Herrick, C. J.: 33
Hohman, L. B.: 116
Hollinshead, M. T.: 81
Holroyd, R. G.: 125
Hughley, R. C.: 122
Hunter, M.: 33
Huntley, R. M. C.: 101
Hurst, J. G.: 111
Iscoe, I.: 94, 103; *exc*, consult 5:B121
Johnson, G. O.: 104
KaDell, M. B.: 105
Kellmer, M. L.: 77, 80
Kelly, E. M.: 73
Kenyon, E. L.: 86
Keyt, N. L.: 50
Kinder, E. F.: *rev*, 1:1143
Kirk, S. A.: 22
Kolstoe, O. P.: *exc*, consult 5:B121
Krause, A. L.: 67
Krippner, S.: 119
Krugman, M.: *exc*, consult 5:B121
Landisberg, S.: 58
Laslett, H. R.: 34
Lester, O. P.: 66
Levinson, B. M.: 109
Link, H. C.: 49
Longwell, S. G.: 16, 21, 23
Louttit, C. M.: 30; *rev*, 3:107
Lurie, L. A.: 31, 43
McCoy, J. F.: 134
McGee, E.: 89
McHale, A.: 133
McKay, B. E.: 8, 17
Maxfield, K. E.: 44, 86
Meier, J. H.: 123
Morales, N.: 45
Myklebust, H. R.: 38, 68
Newburger, M.: 31
Norris, M.: 96
Ordahl, G.: 50
Otness, H. R.: 32
Outcalt, L. C.: 31, 43
Parker, H. J.: 134
Patterson, C. H.: 47
Pedrini, D. T.: 126
Pedrini, L. N.: 126
Phillips, L.: 99
Pluhar, M.: 62
Porteus, S. D.: 33
Powell, L.: 34
Pringle, M. L. K.: 78, 106, 127–8
Rabin, A. I.: 124
Rain, M. E.: 115
Reile, P. J.: 87
Reingold, N.: 63
Riggs, M. M.: 82
Rosenthal, F. M.: 31, 43
Ross, G.: 88
Rothney, J. W. M.: *rev*, 3:107
Rudolf, G. de M.: 74–5
Saha, G. B.: 107
Santos, B.: 117
Satter, G.: 89, 91–2
Scherer, I. W.: 110
Schmickel, C. A.: 132
Shaffer, L. F.: *exc*, consult 5:B121
Shneidman, E. S.: *exc*, consult 5:B121
Simonian, K.: 129, 135
Smith, L. C.: 99
Smith, R. S.: 135
Spaulding, P. J.: 96
Springer, N. N.: 35
Starr, A. S.: *rev*, 1:1143
Steer, M. D.: 108
Sternlof, R. E.: 134
Streng, A.: 22
Teagarden, F. M.: *rev*, 4:94
Toomey, L. C.: 120
Troup, E.: 66
Trubin, B.: 64
Von Bulow, H.: 23
Wall, W. D.: 128
Watson, R.: 30
Watson, R. I.: 79
Watts, F. P.: 36
Werner, E.: 97, 129
Werner, E.: 135
Whitcomb, M. A.: 54
Wilson, M. T.: 26, 37, 65
Wolfensberger, W.: 117
Wright, C.: 50
Zuk, G. H.: 100

[282]

The Visual-Verbal Test: A Measure of Conceptual Thinking. Schizophrenic patients; 1959–60; VVT; individual; 1 form ['59, 46 cards]; manual ('59, 8 pages plus test); record booklet ('60, 4 pages); $12 per set of picture cards, 25 record booklets, and manual; $6.50 per 25 record booklets; $6 per set of picture cards; $2.50 per manual; postpaid; (30–130) minutes; Marvin J. Feldman and James Drasgow; Western Psychological Services. *

For reviews by R. W. Payne and Donald R. Peterson, see 6:195 (8 references).

[283]

*Vocational Preference Inventory, Sixth Revision. Grades 12–16 and adults; 1953–65; VPI; "a personality test employing occupational item content"; formerly called *Holland Vocational Preference Inventory;* 11 scores: realistic, intellectual, social, conventional, enterprising, artistic, self-control, masculinity, status, infrequency, acquiescence; 1 form ('65, 2 pages); manual ('65, 64 pages); profile (no date, 2 pages); $2 per 25 sets of test and profile; $1 per scoring stencil; $2 per manual; $2.50 per specimen set; postage extra; (15–30) minutes; John L. Holland; Consulting Psychologists Press. *

For reviews by Robert L. French and H. Bradley Sagen of an earlier edition, see 6:115 (13 references).

REFERENCES

1–13. See 6:115.
14. GONYEA, GEORGE GERALD. *Job Perception in Relation to Vocational Preference.* Doctor's thesis, University of Maryland (College Park, Md.), 1958. (*DA* 20:369)
15. LOPEZ, FELIX MANUAL, JR. *A Psychological Analysis of the Relationship of Role Consensus and Personality Consensus to Job Satisfaction and Job Performance.* Doctor's thesis, Columbia University (New York, N.Y.), 1962. (*DA* 23:1104)
16. NICHOLS, ROBERT C., and HOLLAND, JOHN L. "Prediction of the First Year College Performance of High Aptitude Students." *Psychol Monogr* 77(7):1–29 '63. * (*PA* 38:4693)
17. BRAUN, JOHN R. "Effects of a 'Good-Adjustment' Faking Set on the Holland Vocational Preference Inventory." *J Psychol* 57:303–6 Ap '64. * (*PA* 39:195)
18. BRAUN, JOHN R. "Relationship Between the Femininity Adjective Check List and the Vocational Preference Inventory M-F Scale." *Psychol Rep* 15:446 O '64. * (*PA* 39:5038)
19. HOLLAND, JOHN L., and NICHOLS, ROBERT C. "Prediction of Academic and Extracurricular Achievement in College." *J Ed Psychol* 55:55–65 F '64. * (*PA* 38:9279)
20. WALKER, HENRY ATCHINSON. *A Study of the Effectiveness of Holland's Vocational Preference Inventory in Identifying Academic Underachievers at the College Freshman Level.* Doctor's thesis, University of Maryland (College Park, Md.), 1964. (*DA* 25:4554)
21. ABE, CLIFFORD, and HOLLAND, JOHN L. "A Description of College Freshmen: 1, Students With Different Choices of Major Field." *ACT Res Rep* 3:1–53 My '65. *
22. ABE, CLIFFORD, and HOLLAND, JOHN L. "A Description of College Freshmen: 2, Students With Different Vocational Choices." *ACT Res Rep* 4:1–51 Je '65. *
23. HOLLAND, JOHN L., and RICHARDS, JAMES M., JR. "Academic and Nonacademic Accomplishment: Correlated or Uncorrelated?" *J Ed Psychol* 56:165–74 Ag '65. * (*PA* 39:15293)
24. McDERMID, CHARLES D. "Some Correlates of Creativity in Engineering Personnel." *J Appl Psychol* 49:14–9 F '65. * (*PA* 39:7782)
25. NICHOLS, ROBERT C. "Non-intellective Predictors of Achievement in College." *NMSC Res Rep* 1(6):1–19 '65. *
26. NICHOLS, ROBERT C. "Personality Change and the College." *NMSC Res Rep* 1(2):1–27 '65. *
27. HOLLAND, JOHN L. "A Psychological Classification Scheme for Vocations and Major Fields." *J Counsel Psychol* 13:278–88 f '66. * (*PA* 40:12651)
28. HOLLAND, JOHN L. *The Psychology of Vocational Choice: A Theory of Personality Types and Model Environments.* Waltham, Mass.: Blaisdell Publishing Co., 1966. Pp. xi, 132. *
29. JACOBS, STANLEY J. *An Investigation of the Effects of Sex, Intelligence, Guessing Habits and Test Modifications on Performance on the Holland Vocational Preference Inventory.* Master's thesis, University of Maryland (College Park, Md.), 1966.
30. NICHOLS, ROBERT C. "Nonintellective Predictors of Achievement in College." *Ed & Psychol Meas* 26:899–915 w '66. * (*PA* 41:4953)
31. NICHOLS, ROBERT C. "The Resemblance of Twins in Personality and Interests." *NMSC Res Rep* 2(8):1–23 '66. *
32. BARCLAY, JAMES R. "Approach to the Measurement of Teacher 'Press' in the Secondary Curriculum." *J Counsel Psychol* 14:552–67 N '67. * (*PA* 42:4525)
33. BARCLAY, JAMES R. "Effecting Behavior Change in the Elementary Classroom: An Exploratory Study." *J Counsel Psychol* 14:240–7 My '67. * (*PA* 41:9360)
34. BRAUN, JOHN R., and O'NEILL, LORNA. "Vocational Preference Inventory Fakability: Replication With the Sixth Revision." Abstract. *Psychol Rep* 21:384 O '67. * (*PA* 42:4793, title only)
35. HOLLAND, JOHN L., and LUTZ, SANDRA W. "Predicting a Student's Vocational Choice." *ACT Res Rep* 18:1–21 Mr '67. * (*PA* 41:9342)
36. NICHOLS, ROBERT C. "Personality Change and the College." *Am Ed Res J* 4:173–90 My '67. * (*PA* 41:13623)
37. REZLER, AGNES G. "Characteristics of High School Girls Choosing Traditional or Pioneer Vocations." *Personnel & Guid J* 45:659–65 Mr '67. * (*PA* 41:9472)
38. REZLER, AGNES G. "The Joint Use of the Kuder Preference Record and the Holland Vocational Preference Inventory in the Vocational Assessment of High School Girls." *Psychol Sch* 4:82–4 Ja '67. * (*PA* 41:5031)
39. BAIRD, LEONARD L. "The Indecision Scale: A Reinterpretation." *J Counsel Psychol* 15:174–9 Mr '68. * (*PA* 42:8086)
40. HOLLAND, JOHN L. "Explorations of a Theory of Vocational Choice: 6, A Longitudinal Study Using a Sample of Typical College Students." *J Appl Psychol Monogr Sup* 52 (1, pt 2):1–37 F '68. *
41. HOLLAND, JOHN L., and LUTZ, SANDRA W. "The Predictive Value of a Student's Choice of Vocation." Comment by David P. Campbell and reply by John L. Holland. *Personnel & Guid J* 46:428–36+ Ja '68. * (*PA* 42:9540)
42. HOLLAND, JOHN L., and WHITNEY, DOUGLAS R. "Changes in the Vocational Plans of College Students: Orderly or Random?" *ACT Res Rep* 25:1–44 Ap '68. * (*PA* 42:16184)
43. OSIPOW, SAMUEL H., and ASHBY, JEFFERSON D. "Vocational Preference Inventory High Point Codes and Educational Preferences." *Personnel & Guid J* 47:126–9 O '68. *
44. UHL, NORMAN P., and DAYTON, C. MITCHELL. "The Prediction of High School Academic Performance Using Vocational Inventory Scores." *J Ed Meas* 5:129–39 su '68. *

[284]

WLW Personal Attitude Inventory. Business and industry; 1954–60; 6 scores: emotional stability, friendliness, aggressiveness, humility and insight, reliability, leadership; 2 editions: third edition ('55, 3 pages), fifth edition ('60, 4 pages); mimeographed manual ['56, 13 pages] for third edition; mimeographed supplement ('56, 2 pages); profile ('56, 1 page); norms for men only; $17 per 100 tests, postpaid; [20] minutes; R. W. Henderson, W. E. Brown, T. L. Chappell, L. D. Edmonson, W. H. E. Geiger, R. L. Kaiser, L. C. Steckle, and L. E. Saddler; William, Lynde & Williams. *

[285]

★**Ward Behavior Inventory.** Mental patients; 1959–68; WBI; revision of *Ward Behavior Rating Scale;* ratings by ward nurses and attendants; 1 form ('68, 2 pages); manual ('68, 14 pages); $5.50 per 50 tests, postage extra; specimen set available on request; (5–15) minutes; Eugene I. Burdock, Anne S. Hardesty, Gad Hakerem (test), Joseph Zubin (test), and Yvonne M. Beck (test); Springer Publishing Co., Inc. *

REFERENCES

1. BURDOCK, E. I.; ELLIOTT, HELEN E.; HARDESTY, ANNE S.; O'NEILL, F. J.; and SKLAR, J. "Biometric Evaluation of an Intensive Treatment Program in a State Mental Hospital." *J Nerv & Mental Dis* 130:271–7 Ap '60. * (*PA* 35:6661)
2. BURDOCK, E. I.; HARDESTY, ANNE S.; HAKEREM, G.; and ZUBIN, JOSEPH. "A Ward Behavior Rating Scale for Mental Hospital Patients." *J Clin Psychol* 16:246–7 Jl '60. * (*PA* 36:2H146B)
3. BURDOCK, EUGENE I.; FLIESS, JOSEPH L.; and HARDESTY, ANNE S. "A New View of Inter-Observer Agreement." *Personnel Psychol* 16:373–84 w '63. * (*PA* 38:6902)
4. RASKIN, ALLEN, and CLYDE, DEAN J. "Factors of Psychopathology in the Ward Behavior of Acute Schizophrenics." *J Consult Psychol* 27:420–5 O '63. *
5. NATIONAL INSTITUTE OF MENTAL HEALTH PSYCHOPHARMACOLOGY SERVICE CENTER COLLABORATIVE STUDY GROUP. "Phenothiazine Treatment in Acute Schizophrenia: Effectiveness." *Arch Gen Psychiatry* 10:246–61 Mr '64. *
6. GOLDBERG, SOLOMON C.; KLERMAN, GERALD L.; and COLE, JONATHAN O. "Changes in Schizophrenic Psychopathology and Ward Behaviour as a Function of Phenothiazine Treatment." *Brit J Psychiatry* 111:120–33 F '65. *
7. SEECH, PHYLLIS. "Factors Associated With Staff-Patient and Patient-Patient Interaction on Psychiatric Units." *Nursing Res* 14:69–71 w '65. *
8. GOLDBERG, SOLOMON C.; COLE, JONATHAN O.; and KLERMAN, GERALD L. Chap. 4, "Differential Prediction of Improvement Under Three Phenothiazines," pp. 69–84. In *Prediction of Response to Pharmacotherapy.* Edited by J. R. Wittenborn and Philip R. A. May. Springfield, Ill.: Charles C Thomas, Publisher, 1966. Pp. xii, 231. *
9. KATZ, MARTIN M.; LOWERY, HENRI A.; and COLE,

JONATHAN O. Chap. 10, "Behavior Patterns of Schizophrenics in the Community," pp. 209–30. In *Exploration in Typing Psychotics*. Edited by Maurice Lorr. London: Pergamon Press Ltd., 1966. Pp. viii, 241. *

10. LYERLY, SAMUEL B., and ABBOTT, PRESTON S. "Ward Behavior Rating Scale," pp. 17–8. In their *Handbook of Psychiatric Rating Scales (1950–1964)*. Public Health Service Publication No. 1495. Washington, D.C.: United States Government Printing Office, 1966. Pp. v, 69. *

11. GOLDBERG, SOLOMON C.; MATTSSON, NILS; COLE, JONATHAN O.; and KLERMAN, GERALD L. "Prediction of Improvement in Schizophrenia Under Four Phenothiazines." *Arch Gen Psychiatry* 16:107–17 Ja '67. * (*PA* 41:4710)

12. RASKIN, ALLEN; SCHULTERBRANDT, JOY; REATIG, NATALIE; and RICE, CHARLES E. "Factors of Psychopathology in Interview, Ward Behavior, and Self-Report Ratings of Hospitalized Depressives." *J Consult Psychol* 31:270–8 Je '67. * (*PA* 41:10719)

13. GOLDBERG, SOLOMON C.; SCHOOLER, NINA R.; and MATTSSON, NILS. "Paranoid and Withdrawal Symptoms in Schizophrenia Relationship to Reaction Time." *Brit J Psychiatry* 114:1161–5 S '68. *

14. RASKIN, ALLEN. "High Dosage Chlorpromazine Alone and in Combination With an Antiparkinsonian Agent (Procyclidine) in the Treatment of Hospitalized Depressions." *J Nerv & Mental Dis* 147:184–95 Ag '68. *

[286]

A Weighted-Score Likability Rating Scale. Ages 6 and over; 1946; 10 ratings: honesty, cooperation, courtesy, responsibility, initiative, industry, attentiveness, enthusiasm, perseverance, willingness; 1 form (1 page); manual (2 pages); no data on reliability and validity; 10¢ per scale, postpaid; [1–2] minutes; A. B. Carlile; the Author. *

[287]

Welsh Figure Preference Test, Research Edition. Ages 6 and over; 1959, c1949–59; WFPT; 27 scores: don't like total, repeat, conformance, *Barron-Welsh Art Scale*, revised art scale, male-female, neuropsychiatric, children, movement, 5 sex symbol scores, and 13 figure-structure preference scores; 1 form ('59, c1949, 53 pages); mimeographed preliminary manual ('59, 35 pages); reliability data, based on earlier forms, for revised art scale and shortened versions of movement and don't like total only; norms below adult level for ages 6–8 only; separate answer sheets must be used; $8.50 per 10 tests; $2.50 per 50 answer sheets; scoring stencils must be constructed locally; $1 per manual; $1.75 per specimen set; postage extra; (50) minutes; George S. Welsh; Consulting Psychologists Press, Inc. *

For a review by Harold Borko, see 6:197 (20 references, 1 excerpt).

REFERENCES

1–20. See 6:197.

21. WAHBA, MICHEL. *A Multivariate Analysis of a Figure Preference Personality Test*. Doctor's thesis, University of North Carolina (Chapel Hill, N.C.), 1962. (*DA* 26:4821)

22. JAMES, GRACE ROBBINS. *The Relationship of Teacher Characteristics and Pupil Creativity*. Doctor's thesis, University of North Carolina (Chapel Hill, N.C.), 1963. (*DA* 25:4544)

23. PURYEAR, HERBERT BRUCE. *Personality Characteristics of Reporters and Nonreporters of Dreams*. Doctor's thesis, University of North Carolina (Chapel Hill, N.C.), 1963. (*DA* 24:3425)

24. RAYCHAUDHURI, MANAS. "Some Perceptual Characteristics of Incipient Artists." *Indian J Psychol* 38:13–7 Mr '63. * (*PA* 38:6006)

25. BROWN, GEORGE I. "Experiment in the Teaching of Creativity." *Sch R* 72:437–50 w '64. * (*PA* 39:7812)

26. WATSON, WILLIAM GENE. *An Analysis of Responses to the Welsh Figure Preference Test to Evaluate Its Effectiveness as a Measure of Mental Ability*. Doctor's thesis, University of North Carolina (Chapel Hill, N.C.), 1964. (*DA* 26:882)

27. BROWN, GEORGE I. "Second Study in the Teaching of Creativity." *Harvard Ed R* 35:39–54 w '65. * (*PA* 39:10170)

28. McDERMID, CHARLES D. "Some Correlates of Creativity in Engineering Personnel." *J Appl Psychol* 49:14–9 F '65. * (*PA* 39:7782)

29. MOYLES, E. W.; TUDDENHAM, R. D.; and BLOCK, J. "Simplicity/Complexity or Symmetry/Asymmetry? A Re-Analysis of the Barron-Welsh Art Scales." *Percept & Motor Skills* 20:685–90 Je '65. * (*PA* 39:15250)

30. WHITTEMORE, ROBERT G., and HEIMANN, ROBERT A. "Originality Responses in Academically Talented Male University Freshmen." *Psychol Rep* 16:439–42 Ap '65. * (*PA* 39:10252)

31. CASHDAN, SHELDON, and WELSH, GEORGE S. "Personality Correlates of Creative Potential in Talented High School Students." *J Personality* 34:445–55 S '66. * (*PA* 41:2876)

32. HOWELL, MARGARET A. "Personal Effectiveness of Physicians in a Federal Health Organization." *J Appl Psychol* 50:451–9 D '66. * (*PA* 41:3517)

33. KEITH, BERTHE WELLS. *An Analysis of the Barron-Welsh Art Scale as Used in the Third Grade*. Master's thesis, University of Utah (Salt Lake City, Utah), 1966.

34. LITTLEJOHN, MARY T. *A Comparison of the Responses of Ninth-Graders to Measures of Creativity and Masculinity-Femininity*. Doctor's thesis, University of North Carolina (Chapel Hill, N.C.), 1966. (*DA* 27:2399A)

35. LUCAS, FRANCES H., and DANA, RICHARD H. "Creativity and Allocentric Perception." *Percept & Motor Skills* 22:431–7 Ap '66. * (*PA* 40:8858)

36. McWHINNIE, HAROLD J. "Effects of a Learning Experience on Preference for Complexity and Asymmetry." *Percept & Motor Skills* 23:119–22 Ag '66. * (*PA* 41:1719)

37. MILLMAN, MARCIA, and CHANG, TERESA. "Inter-Correlations Among Three Widely Used Art Tests." *Percept & Motor Skills* 23:1002 D '66. * (*PA* 41:6434, title only)

38. WELSH, GEORGE S. "Comparison of D-48, Terman CMT, and Art Scale Scores of Gifted Adolescents." Abstract. *J Consult Psychol* 30:88 F '66. * (*PA* 40:4105)

39. HAWTHORNE, RUTH ESTELLA. *Aspects of Design Preference in Clothing: Aesthetic, Motivation, and Knowledge*. Doctor's thesis, Ohio State University (Columbus, Ohio), 1967. (*DA* 28:3769B)

40. KROGER, ROLF O. "Effects of Role Demands and Test-Cue Properties Upon Personality Test Performance." *J Consult Psychol* 31:304–12 Je '67. * (*PA* 41:10466)

41. LITTLEJOHN, MARY T. "Creativity and Masculinity-Femininity in Ninth Graders." *Percept & Motor Skills* 25:737–43 D '67. * (*PA* 42:8949)

42. MAITRA, AMAL K.; MUKHERJI, KAMAL; and RAYCHAUDHURI, MANAS. "Artistic Creativity Among the Delinquents and the Criminals: Associated Perceptual Style." *B Council Social & Psychol Res* 9:7–10 Jl '67. *

43. SCHAEFER, CHARLES EUGENE. *Biographical Inventory Correlates of Scientific and Artistic Creativity in Adolescents*. Doctor's thesis, Fordham University (New York, N.Y.), 1967. (*DA* 28:1173B)

44. KROGER, ROLF O. "Effects of Implicit and Explicit Task Cues Upon Personality Test Performance." *J Consult & Clin Psychol* 32:498 Ag '68. * (*PA* 42:17201)

NAME INDEX

[288]

The Western Personality Inventory. Adults; 1948–63; WPI; a combination in one booklet of *The Alcadd Test* (see 7) and *The Manson Evaluation* (see 152); identification of alcoholics and potential alcoholics; 1 form ('63, 6 pages); manual ('63, 4 pages, a combination, including identical norms and technical data, of the 1948 and 1949 manuals for the previously cited tests); $8 per 25 tests; $1.50 per specimen set; postpaid; (20–40) minutes; Morse P. Manson; Western Psychological Services. *

For a review by Dugal Campbell of *The Alcadd Test*, see 6:60 (6 references); for reviews by Charles

H. Honzik and Albert L. Hunsicker, see 4:30. For a review by Dugal Campbell of *The Manson Evaluation*, see 6:137 (5 references); for reviews by Charles H. Honzik and Albert L. Hunsicker, see 4:68 (4 references).

[289]
What I Like to Do: An Inventory of Children's Interests. Grades 4–7; 1954–58; WILD; 8 scores: art, music, social studies, active play, quiet play, manual arts, home arts, science; 1 form ('54, 14 pages); manual ('54, 15 pages); teacher's handbook ('58, 27 pages); profile ('54, 4 pages); no norms for grade 7; $4.60 per 20 tests; separate answer sheets (IBM 805) may be used; $6.30 per 100 answer sheets; $1.25 per 20 profiles; $1.50 per set of machine scoring stencils; 50¢ per handbook; 50¢ per manual; $2 per specimen set; postage extra; (60) minutes in 2 sessions for grade 4, (50) minutes for grades 5–7; Louis P. Thorpe, Charles E. Meyers, and Marcella Ryser Sea [Bonsall]; Science Research Associates, Inc. *

For reviews by John W. M. Rothney and Naomi Stewart, see 5:122 (1 excerpt).

REFERENCES

1. HENZE, MARY V. *An Analysis of Interests of Selected Sixth Grade Pupils as Determined by the "What I Like to Do" Inventory and a Study of the Relationship of Interests so Determined to Experience.* Master's thesis, Iowa State Teachers College (Cedar Falls, Iowa), 1957.
2. LOUDON, MARY LOU (SIMPSON). *The Interrelationships of Children's Interests, Achievement, and Social Adjustment.* Doctor's thesis, Louisiana State University (Baton Rouge, La.), 1961. (*DA* 22:3119)
3. BLEDSOE, JOSEPH C., and BROWN, IVA D. "The Interests of Preadolescents: A Longitudinal Study." *J Exp Ed* 33: 337–44 su '65. * (*PA* 39:11929)
4. CLAYPOOL, ARIANNA MARY. *A Study of the Relationships Between Children's Goals, Interests, and Feelings Inherent in Their Attitudes and the Lack of Scholastic Achievement.* Doctor's thesis, University of Maryland (College Park, Md.), 1965. (*DA* 26:6507)

[290]
William, Lynde & Williams Analysis of Personal Values, Second Edition. Business and industry; 1958–62; 6 scores: theoretical, practical, social, personal power, aesthetic, religious; 1 form ('60, 4 pages); mimeographed combined manual ('62, 8 pages) for this test and 6:1074; no data on reliability and validity; $12.50 per 100 tests, postpaid; [15] minutes; R. W. Henderson; William, Lynde & Williams. *

[291]
The Wishes and Fears Inventory. Ages 4–8, 8–16; 1949; WFI; 8 scores: wishes, positive identifications, negative identifications, desired activities, undesired activities, changes desired in oneself, fears, earliest recollection; individual; 1 form; 2 levels labeled Forms A (3 pages), B (1 page); mimeographed manual (6 pages); no data on reliability and validity; specimen set free; record blanks must be reproduced locally; (5–15) minutes; Martin L. Reymert; Child Guidance Clinic. *

REFERENCE

1. WINKER, JAMES B. "Age Trends and Sex Differences in the Wishes, Identifications, Activities, and Fears of Children." *Child Develop* 20:191–200 D '49. * (*PA* 24:5157)

OUT OF PRINT

[292]
The A-S Reaction Study: Revision for Business Use. Adult men; 1928–46; Gordon W. Allport and Floyd H. Allport, revision by R. O. Beckman; Psychological Corporation. * *Out of print.*

For additional information and a review by Doncaster G. Humm, see 2:1199 (4 references).

[292A]
Adjustment Questionnaire. Ages 12–17; 1951; AQ; 11 scores: self-confidence, sense of personal worth, sense of personal freedom, recognition, social relationships, nervous symptoms, moral attitudes, family relationships, school relationships, emotionality, total; National Bureau of Educational and Social Research. * *Out of print.*

For additional information, see 5:31.

[293]
Affectivity Interview Blank. Ages 7–12; 1951; child feelings; Elizabeth Mechem Fuller; Child Development Laboratories, University of Michigan. * *Out of print.*

For additional information and reviews by Morris Krugman and Verner M. Sims, see 4:29 (3 references).

[294]
Aspects of Personality. Grades 4–9; 1937–38; 3 scores: ascendance-submission, extroversion-introversion, emotionality; Rudolf Pintner, John J. Loftus, George Forlano, and Benjamin Alster; Harcourt, Brace & World, Inc. * *Out of print.*

For additional information and reviews by C. M. Louttit and P. E. Vernon, see 2:1201 (4 references); see also 1:913 (1 excerpt).

REFERENCES

1–4. See 2:1201.
5. WILSON, MARGARET T. *A Comparison of the 1937 Revision of the Stanford-Binet With the Vineland Social Maturity Scale.* Master's thesis, Fordham University (New York, N.Y.), 1939.
6. RIESS, BERNARD F., and DE CILLIS, OLGA E. "Personality Differences in Allergic and Non-Allergic Children." *J Abn & Social Psychol* 35:104–13 Ja '40. * (*PA* 14:3603)
7. PINTNER, R. "Some Personality Traits of Hard of Hearing Children." *J Genetic Psychol* 60:143–51 Mr '42. * (*PA* 16:3845)
8. PINTNER, R., and FORLANO, G. "Consistency of Response to Personality Tests at Different Age Levels." *J Genetic Psychol* 62:77–83 Mr '43. * (*PA* 17:2393)
9. PINTNER, R., and FORLANO, G. "Personality Tests of Partially Sighted Children." *J Appl Psychol* 27:283–7 Je '43. * (*PA* 17:3833)
10. YOUNG, LYLE L., and COOPER, DAN H. "Some Factors Associated With Popularity." *J Ed Psychol* 35:513–35 D '44. * (*PA* 19:1000)
11. VOLBERDING, ELEANOR. "Characteristics of Successful and Unsuccessful Eleven-Year-Old Pupils." *El Sch J* 49: 405–10 Mr '49. * (*PA* 23:5003)
12. BEEBE, EMILY NOYES. *A Study of Personality and Personality Deficiencies Among Intermediate Grade Pupils in Three New Orleans Public Schools.* Master's thesis, Tulane University (New Orleans, La.), 1950.
13. SMITH, ELMER LEWIS. "Personality Differences Between Amish and Non-Amish Children." *Rural Sociol* 23:371–6 D '58. * (*PA* 34:1239)
14. FURNEAUX, W. D., and GIBSON, H. B. "A Children's Personality Inventory Designed to Measure Neuroticism and Extraversion." *Brit J Ed Psychol* 31:204–7 Je '61. * (*PA* 36:3FF04F)
15. HALLWORTH, H. J. "Anxiety in Secondary Modern and Grammar School Children." *Brit J Ed Psychol* 31:281–91 N '61. * (*PA* 36:5KD81H)

[295]
[Attitude Scales for Measuring the Influence of the Work Relief Program.] College students and adults; 1940; 3 scales; E. D. Hinckley; University of Florida Press. * *Out of print.*
a) ATTITUDE TOWARD WORK RELIEF AS A SOLUTION TO THE FINANCIAL DEPRESSION.
b) ATTITUDE TOWARD EARNING A LIVING.
c) ATTITUDE TOWARD RECEIVING RELIEF.

For additional information, see 2:1203 (1 reference).

[296]

Attitudes Toward Child Behavior. Adults; 1936; Ralph M. Stogdill and Henry H. Goddard; Ralph M. Stogdill. * *Out of print.*

For additional information, see 2:1204 (2 references).

REFERENCES

1-2. See 2:1204.
3. STEDMAN, LOUISE A. *An Investigation of Knowledge of and Attitudes Toward Child Behavior.* Edited by H. H. Remmers. Purdue University, Division of Educational Reference, Studies in Higher Education [No.] 62. Lafayette, Ind.: the Division, March 1948. Pp. 66. *

[297]

BEC Personality Rating Schedule. Grades 7-16; 1936; 9 ratings by teachers: mental alertness, initiative, dependability, cooperativeness, judgment, personal impression, courtesy, health, final summary; Phillip J. Rulon, Elizabeth A. Nash, and Grace L. Woodward; distributed by Phillip J. Rulon. * *Out of print.*

For additional information and reviews by Francis F. Bradshaw and Theos A. Langlie, see 1:915.

REFERENCE

1. RULON, PHILLIP J. "A Personality Rating Schedule." *Harvard Ed R* 6:46-53 F '36. *

[298]

[The Baxter Group Tests of Child Feeling.] Grades 1-8, 7-9, (separate edition for parents and teachers of children in grades 1-9); 1935-46, c1935; a revision of *Baxter Group Test of Child Personality* (see 2:1206) and *Baxter Individual Tests of Child Personality* (see 2:1207); 3 tests; Edna D. Baxter; Baxter Foundation for Research in Education, Inc. * *Out of print.*

a) CHILD'S TEST: BAXTER GROUP STORY-TEST OF CHILD FEELINGS. Grades 1-8; 1935; 23 scores: friendliness, responsiveness, generosity (jealousy), respect (sarcasm), dependability, daydreaming, obedience, compliance, self-control, fairness (domineering), courage, studiousness, creativity, concentration, temperance (boisterousness), carefulness (destructiveness), grace (awkwardness), unselfishness, honesty, courtesy, cheerfulness, kindness, tidiness.

b) THE BAXTER TEST OF CHILD FEELINGS. Grades 7-9; 1935; 25 scores: same as above plus sociality, appearance.

c) THE BAXTER PARENT-TEACHER TEST OF CHILD FEELINGS. Parents and teachers of children in grades 1-9; 1935-46.

For additional information, see 4:32 (2 references).

[299]

Behavior Description. Grades 7-12; 1935; form for recording non-test-measured behavior characteristics; Reports and Records Committee of the Commission on the Relation of School and College, Progressive Education Association. * *Out of print.*

For additional information, see 1:898.

[300]

Behavior Maturity Blank. Grades 7-16 and adults; 1939; Walther Joël; Gutenberg Press. *Out of print.*

For additional information, see 2:1209 (2 references).

REFERENCES

1-2. See 2:1209.
3. HARTSON, MARY FRANCES, and CHAMPNEY, HORACE. "Parent Behavior as Related to Child Development: 2, Social Maturity." Abstract. *Psychol B* 37:583 O '40. * (*PA* 15:593, title only)
4. JOËL, WALTHER. "Behavior Maturity of High School and Junior College Students." Abstract. *Psychol B* 37:592 O '40. * (*PA* 15:597, title only)

[301]

Behavior Maturity Rating Scale for Nursery School Children. Ages 1.5-6; 1935; Walther Joël and Janet Joël; Walther Joël. * *Out of print.*

For additional information, see 2:1210.

REFERENCE

1. JOËL, WALTHER, " 'Behavior Maturity' of Children of Nursery School Age." *Child Develop* 7:189-99 S '36. * (*PA* 11:2009)

[302]

Behavior Preference Record: What Would You Do? (A Study of Some Home and School Problems). Grades 4-6, 7-9, 9-12; 1953; 6 scores: cooperation, friendliness, integrity, leadership, responsibility, critical thinking; Hugh B. Wood; California Test Bureau. * *Out of print.*

For additional information and reviews by J. Thomas Hastings and Edward Landy, see 5:32 (1 excerpt).

REFERENCES

1. PERRODIN, ALEX F. "Factors Affecting the Development of Cooperation in Children." *J Ed Res* 53:283-8 Ap '60. *
2. ROBEY, DALE LEWIS. *A Differential Diagnosis of Low-Academic Ninth Grade Male Students as Compared With Average-Academic Ninth Grade Male Students.* Doctor's thesis, Indiana University (Bloomington, Ind.), 1963. (*DA* 24:5252)
3. CHRONISTER, GLENN M. "Personality and Reading Achievement." *El Sch J* 64:253-60 F '64. *

[303]

Beliefs About School Life: Test 4.6. Grades 7-12; 1940; beliefs in 6 areas: school government, curriculum, grades and awards, school spirit, pupil-teacher relations, group life; Evaluation in the Eight Year Study, Progressive Education Association. * *Out of print.*

For additional information, see 2:1211.

[304]

Billett-Starr Youth Problems Inventory. Grades 7-9, 10-12; 1961, c1953-61; problems check-list; 12 scores: physical health and safety, getting along with others, boy-girl relationships, home and family life, personal finance, interests and activities, school life, personal potentialities, planning for the future, mental-emotional health, morality and religion, total; Roy O. Billett and Irving S. Starr; Harcourt, Brace & World, Inc. * *Out of print.*

For additional information and reviews by Thomas C. Burgess, J. Thomas Hastings, and Henry Weitz, see 6:66 (1 reference).

REFERENCES

1. See 6:66.
2. SCHUTZ, RICHARD EDWARD. *Patterns of Personal Problems of Adolescent Girls.* Doctor's thesis, Columbia University (New York, N.Y.), 1957. (*DA* 17:1808)
3. SCHUTZ, RICHARD E. "Patterns of Personal Problems of Adolescent Girls." *J Ed Psychol* 49:1-5 F '58. * (*PA* 36: 2FH01S)
4. UPHAM, ELIZABETH VESTA. *Parental Reactions to the Items in a Junior-High-School Youth Problems Inventory.* Doctor's thesis, Boston University (Boston, Mass.), 1963. (*DA* 25:5799)

[305]

Brown Personality Inventory for Children. Grades 4-9; 1935-46; Fred Brown; Public School Publishing Co. * *Out of print.*

For additional information, see 5:36 (10 references); for reviews by S. J. Beck and Carl R. Rogers, see 2:1240 (8 references).

REFERENCES

1-8. See 2:1240.
9-18. See 5:36.
19. NEUHAUS, EDMUND CONRAD. *A Personality Study of*

Asthmatic and Cardiac Children. Doctor's thesis, New York University (New York, N.Y.), 1954. (*DA* 15:1256)
20. ROSENBERG, B. G.; SUTTON-SMITH, B.; and MORGAN, E. "The Use of Opposite Sex Scales as a Measure of Psychosexual Deviancy." *J Consult Psychol* 25:221–5 Je '61. *
21. SUTTON-SMITH, B.; ROSENBERG, B. G.; and MORGAN, ELMER F., JR. "Historical Changes in the Freedom With Which Children Express Themselves on Personality Inventories." *J Genetic Psychol* 99:309–15 D '61. * (*PA* 36:3FF09S)

[306]

The Case Inventory. Grades 5–12; 1935–36; 5 scores: irrationality, adjustment, honesty, ethical judgment, total; J. B. Maller; Bureau of Publications. * *Out of print.*

For additional information and reviews by Harold E. Jones and E. G. Williamson, see 2:1214 (1 reference); for a review by Richard Ledgerwood, see 1:916.

REFERENCES
1. See 2:1214.
2. STOTT, LELAND H. *The Relation of Certain Factors in Farm Family Life to Personality Development in Adolescents.* University of Nebraska, College of Agriculture, Agricultural Experiment Station, Research Bulletin 106. Lincoln, Neb.: University of Nebraska, October 1938. Pp. 46. *
3. HARRIS, DALE B. "The Relation of Maller Case Inventory Scores to Institutional Adjustment of Delinquent Boys." *J Ed Psychol* 32:550–4 O '41. * (*PA* 16:2386)

[307]

Character and Personality Rating Scale. Grades 7–12; 1934; J. B. Maller; Bureau of Publications. * *Out of print.*

For additional information and a review by Bessie Lee Gambrill, see 2:1215.

[308]

Character Inventory Chart. Grades 6–12; 1931–33; 10 self ratings: health, honesty, loyalty, cheerfulness, courtesy, cooperation, moral courage, industry, self-control, leadership; B. L. Dougherty, F. L. O'Reilly, and M. Mannix; Public School Publishing Co. * *Out of print.*

For additional information, see 1:917 (1 excerpt).

[309]

Constant-Choice Perceptual Maze Attitude of Responsibility Test. Ages 4 and over; 1938–63; formerly called the *Line Centering Test;* "liking or disliking of required behavior"; 3 scores: intensity of quality (self-initiative), persistency of quality (self-importance), reaction tendencies (self-confidence); John C. Park; the Author. * *Out of print.*

For additional information, see 6:79.

[310]

The Cowan Adolescent Adjustment Analyzer: An Instrument of Clinical Psychology. Ages 12–18; 1935–49; revision of *Cowan Adolescent Personality Schedule;* 9 scores: fear, family emotion, family authority, feeling of inadequacy, non-family authority, immaturity, escape, neurotic, compensation; Edwina A. Cowan, Wilbert J. Mueller, Edra Weathers (test only), and Bentley Barnabas (manual); Bureau of Educational Measurements. * *Out of print.*

For additional information, see 4:38 (1 reference); for reviews by Harold H. Abelson and William U. Snyder, see 3:30; for a review by Goodwin Watson of an earlier edition, see 2:1217 (3 references); for a review by Harold E. Jones, see 1:918.

[311]

Cowell Personal Distance Scale. Grades 7–9; 1958–63; CPDS; title on scale is *Confidential Personal Distance Ballot;* social distance ratings of classmates; Charles C. Cowell; Tri-State Offset Co. * *Out of print.*

For additional information, see 6:82 (3 references).

REFERENCES
1–3. See 6:82.
4. MENZI, ELIZABETH ANNE. *Physical Fitness: Its Relation to Social Adjustment, Social Acceptability and Prestige, and Its Place in the Value Systems of Ninth and Twelfth Grade Girls of a Selected School System.* Doctor's thesis, University of Michigan (Ann Arbor, Mich.), 1964. (*DA* 25:7065)

[312]

Cowell Social Behavior Trend Index. Grades 7–9; 1958–61; CSBTI; social adjustment ratings by 3 teachers; Charles C. Cowell; Tri-State Offset Co. * *Out of print.*

For additional information, see 6:83 (2 references).

REFERENCES
1–2. See 6:83.
3. CLARKE, H. HARRISON, and GREENE, WALTER H. "Relationships Between Personal-Social Measures Applied to 10-Year-Old Boys." *Res Q* 34:288–98 O '63. * (*PA* 38:5727)
4. MENZI, ELIZABETH ANNE. *Physical Fitness: Its Relation to Social Adjustment, Social Acceptability and Prestige, and Its Place in the Value Systems of Ninth and Twelfth Grade Girls of a Selected School System.* Doctor's thesis, University of Michigan (Ann Arbor, Mich.), 1964. (*DA* 25:7065)

[313]

Detroit Scale of Behavior Factors. Grades 1–12; 1935–36; Harry J. Baker and Virginia Traphagen; Macmillan Co. *Out of print.*

For additional information, see 3:32 (1 reference); for an excerpt from a related book review, see 3:33; for reviews not excerpted in this volume, consult the 2nd (B835) and 1st (B306) MMY's.

[314]

Diagnosis and Treatment of Pupil Maladjustment. Grades kgn–12; 1938; T. L. Torgerson; E. M. Hale & Co. * *Out of print.*

For additional information and a review by Laurance F. Shaffer, see 3:34 (2 references).

[315]

Dunlap Academic Preference Blank. Grades 7–9; 1937–39; 10 scores: paragraph meaning, word meaning, history, language usage, geography, literature, arithmetic, general achievement, mental ability, intellectual alertness; Jack W. Dunlap; World Book Co. * *Out of print.*

For additional information and reviews by Lee J. Cronbach, W. C. Kvaraceus, and Edith I. M. Thomson, see 3:35 (6 references, 1 excerpt).

[316]

Environment Inventory for College and University Students. Grades 13–17; 1938; Robert H. Morrison and M. Ernest Townsend; Webster Publishing Co. * *Out of print.*

For additional information and a review by E. G. Williamson, see 2:1218 (1 reference).

[317]

Euphorimeter. Adults; 1940; Hornell Hart; Macmillan Co. * *Out of print.*

For additional information, see 3:36 (2 references); for excerpts from related book reviews, see 3:37.

[318]

Experience Variables Record: A Clinical Revision. Grades 13–16 and adults; 1928–38; Joseph Chassell; Sheppard & Enoch Pratt Hospital. * *Out of print.*

For additional information, see 2:1219 (2 references).

[319]

Gardner Behavior Chart. Mental patients; 1939; ratings on 15 aspects of behavior; Paul H. Wilcox; the Author. * *Out of print.*

For additional information, see 4:44 (2 references).

REFERENCES

1–2. See 4:44.
3. DAYAN, MAURICE, and McLEAN, JOEL. "The Gardner Behavior Chart as a Measure of Adaptive Behavior of the Mentally Retarded." *Am J Mental Def* 67:887–92 My '63. * (*PA* 38:1268)

[320]

General Goals of Life Inventory: General Education Series. College; 1942–50; 20 scores, each representing a "life goal"; developed by the Cooperative Study in General Education; Cooperative Test Division. * *Out of print.*

For additional information and reviews by C. Robert Pace and Leona E. Tyler, see 4:45 (10 references).

REFERENCES

1–10. See 4:45.
11. McKEACHIE, WILBERT, and GUETZKOW, HAROLD. "A Rating-Ranking Scale for Goals of Life." *Relig Ed* 47:25–7 Ja–F '52. *
12. PETERSEN, DWAIN FRANKLIN. *Factors Common to Interest, Value, and Personality Scales.* Doctor's thesis, University of Nebraska (Lincoln, Neb.), 1964. (*DA* 25:5747)

[321]

Haggerty-Olson-Wickman Behavior Rating Schedules. Grades kgn–12; 1930; 6 scores: behavior problems, behavior rating (intellectual, physical, social, emotional, total); M. E. Haggerty, W. C. Olson, and E. K. Wickman; Harcourt, Brace & World, Inc. * *Out of print.*

For additional information and a review by Harold E. Jones, see 2:1222 (8 references).

REFERENCES

1–8. See 2:1222.
9. KEYS, NOEL, and GUILFORD, MARGARET S. "The Validity of Certain Adjustment Inventories in Predicting Problem Behavior." *J Ed Psychol* 28:641–55 D '37. * (*PA* 12:2692)
10. SPRINGER, N. NORTON. "A Comparative Study of the Behavior Traits of Deaf and Hearing Children of New York City." *Am Ann Deaf* 83:255–73 My '38. * (*PA* 13:751)
11. VAN ALSTYNE, DOROTHY, and HATTWICK, LaBERTA A. "A Follow-Up Study of the Behavior of Nursery-School Children." *Child Develop* 10:43–72 Mr '39. * (*PA* 13:4423)
12. BROWN, FRED. "An Experimental Study of Parental Attitudes and Their Effects on Child Adjustment." *Am J Orthopsychiatry* 12:224–30 Ap '42. * (*PA* 16:3336)
13. BURCHARD, EDWARD M. L., and MYKLEBUST, HELMER R. "A Comparison of Congenital and Adventitious Deafness With Respect to Its Effect on Intelligence, Personality, and Social Maturity: Part 3, Personality." *Am Ann Deaf* 87:342–60 S '42. * (*PA* 17:200)
14. MITCHELL, JOHN C. "A Study of Teachers' and of Mental-Hygienists' Ratings of Certain Behavior Problems of Children." *J Ed Res* 36:292–307 D '42. * (*PA* 17:2188)
15. PUSEY, HARRIET CLOUGH. *The Relationship Between Mental, Physical and Achievement Levels and Certain Personality Traits as Measured by Tests.* Master's thesis, University of Kentucky (Lexington, Ky.), 1942.
16. MYKLEBUST, HELMER R., and BURCHARD, EDWARD M. L. "A Study of the Effects of Congenital and Adventitious Deafness on the Intelligence, Personality, and Social Maturity of School Children." *J Ed Psychol* 36:321–43 S '45. * (*PA* 20:2145)
17. HOLBROOKS, VIOLA COLLINS. *A Study of the Problems of Forty-Five Pupils in a Fifth Grade of the Florence Street School, Savannah, Georgia, as Revealed by the Ratings of Their Parents and Three of Their Teachers on the Haggerty-Olson-Wickman Behaviour Rating Schedule.* Master's thesis, Atlanta University (Atlanta, Ga.), 1946.
18. TINDALL, RALPH H. "Relationships Among Indices of Adjustment Status." *Ed & Psychol Meas* 15:152–62 su '55. * (*PA* 30:2330)
19. EMFINGER, WILLIAM EDWIN. *Effect of the Personal Maladjustment of the Mental Retardate Upon Special Class Placement and Test-Retest Gains.* Doctor's thesis, Florida State University (Tallahassee, Fla.), 1957. (*DA* 17:3082)

20. KAUL, MAN MOHINI. *Relationship Between Behavior Ratings by Teachers and Mental Age, Achievement, Physical Growth, and Total Growth of Children.* Doctor's thesis, University of Michigan (Ann Arbor, Mich.), 1958. (*DA* 19:1248)
21. AKERS, DOROTHY R. *A Study of the Prediction of Delinquency: The Effectiveness of the Haggerty-Olson-Wickman Behavior Rating Schedules in Predicting Delinquency in the Fresno (California) City Area.* Master's thesis, Fresno State College (Fresno, Calif.), 1959.

[322]

Heston Personal Adjustment Inventory. Grades 9–16 and adults; 1949; HPAI; 6 scores: analytical thinking, sociability, emotional stability, confidence, personal relations, home satisfaction; Joseph C. Heston; Harcourt, Brace & World, Inc. * *Out of print.*

For additional information, see 6:113 (14 references); see also 5:66 (11 references); for reviews by Albert Ellis, Hans J. Eysenck, and E. Lowell Kelly, see 4:50 (2 references, 1 excerpt).

REFERENCES

1–2. See 4:50.
3–13. See 5:66.
14–27. See 6:113.
28. CROSTHWAIT, CHARLES. *The Interrelationship of Secondary Student Teacher's Sociability, Teaching Field, and Method of Instruction.* Doctor's thesis, North Texas State University (Denton, Tex.), 1963. (*DA* 24:1490)
29. WOOD, PAUL LESLIE. *The Relationship of the College Characteristics Index to Achievement and Certain Other Variables for Freshmen Women in the College of Education at the University of Georgia.* Doctor's thesis, University of Georgia (Athens, Ga.), 1963. (*DA* 24:4558)
30. McMAHON, WILLIAM JOSEPH. *Differential Analysis of Nonintellective Factors Associated With Identified Scholastic Talent in a High School.* Doctor's thesis, Fordham University (New York, N.Y.), 1964. (*DA* 26:873)
31. ADEN, ROBERT C., and CROSTHWAIT, CHARLES. "Teaching Field Choice and Student Teacher Personality." *J Ed Res* 59:291–3 Mr '66. * (*PA* 40:10477)

NAME INDEX

Aden, R. C.: 31
Arbuckle, D. S.: 10, 15
Auble, D.: 11
Crane, W. J.: 24
Crosthwait, C.: 28, 31
Dotson, E. J.: 14
Durflinger, G. W.: 26–7
Ellis, A.: *rev,* 4:50
Eysenck, H. J.: *rev,* 4:50
Farber, R. H.: 3
Fick, D. J.: 6
Gingles, R. H.: 13
Heston, J. C.: 1
Holmes, J. A.: 7, 16
Hosford, P. McI.: 21
Kalish, R. A.: 22
Kelly, E. L.: *rev,* 4:50
Kiessling, R. J.: 22

Kingston, A. J.: 23
Lodato, F. J.: 8
McDaniel, E. D.: 18
McKenna, F. S.: 4
McMahon, W. J.: 30
Magnussen, M. G.: 19
Magnussen, M. H.: 19
Michaelis, J. U.: 2
Nichols, R. C.: 25
Scarborough, B. B.: 12
Shaffer, L. F.: *exc,* 4:50
Stephenson, H. W.: 18
Tindall, R. H.: 9
Tyler, F. T.: 2, 5
Welna, C. T.: 20
Wood, P. L.: 29
Wright, J. C.: 12, 17

[323]

Hunt-Minnesota Test for Organic Brain Damage. Chronological ages 16–70 and mental ages 8 and over; 1943; 16 tests grouped in 3 divisions: the vocabulary test of *Revised Stanford-Binet Intelligence Scale,* interpolated tests, learning and recall; Howard F. Hunt; University of Minnesota Press. * *Out of print.*

For additional information and a review by Seymour G. Klebanoff, see 4:51 (8 references); for reviews by Margaret Ives and O. L. Zangwill, see 3:49 (11 references).

REFERENCES

1–11. See 3:49.
12–19. See 4:51.
20. HUNT, HOWARD F. "Hunt-Minnesota Test for Organic Brain Damage," pp. 760–5. (*PA* 27:7775) In *Contributions Toward Medical Psychology: Theory and Psychodiagnostic Methods, Vol. II.* Edited by Arthur Weider. New York: Ronald Press Co., 1953. Pp. xi, 459–885. *
21. RAPPAPORT, SHELDON R. "Intellectual Deficit in Organics and Schizophrenics." *J Consult Psychol* 17:389–95 O '53. * (*PA* 28:6365)
22. YATES, AUDREY C. "The Validity of Some Psychological Tests of Brain Damage." *Psychol B* 51:359–79 Jl '54. *

23. RIBLER, RONALD IRWIN. *The Detection of Brain Damage Through Measurement of Deficit in Behavioral Functions.* Doctor's thesis, Michigan State University (East Lansing, Mich.), 1957. (*DA* 19:1810)

24. AVAKIAN, SONIA A. "The Applicability of the Hunt-Minnesota Test for Organic Brain Damage to Children Between the Ages of Ten and Sixteen." *J Clin Psychol* 17:45–9 Ja '61. * (*PA* 37:3524)

[324]

[Illinois Opinion Inventories.] Grades 6–8, 9–12, adults; 1948; opinion on schools; directions and interpretive procedures are presented in *What People Think About Their Schools* (see *1* below); Harold C. Hand, Gilbert C. Finlay, and Ardwin J. Dolio; [Harcourt, Brace & World, Inc.]. * *Out of print.*

a) ILLINOIS INVENTORY OF PUPIL OPINION: UPPER ELEMENTARY SCHOOL FORM. Grades 6–8.

b) ILLINOIS INVENTORY OF PUPIL OPINION: SECONDARY SCHOOL FORM. Grades 9–12.

c) ILLINOIS INVENTORY OF PARENT OPINION. Adults.

d) ILLINOIS INVENTORY OF TEACHER OPINION. Teachers.

For additional information and a review by Kenneth E. Clark, see 4:52 (1 reference); for an excerpt from a related book review, see 4:53.

REFERENCES

1. See 4:52.
2. MONTANDON, CARLOS MORRISON. *An Inventory of Parent Opinion in the Public Schools of Lynwood, California, Pertaining to Certain Aspects of the Elementary School Program.* Doctor's field study, Colorado State College of Education (Greeley, Colo.), 1953.
3. PHELPS, MORRIS OVERTON. *An Analysis of Certain Factors Associated With Under-Achievement Among High School Students.* Doctor's thesis, University of Georgia (Athens, Ga.), 1956. (*DA* 17:306)
4. SMITH, DOYNE M., and COOPER, BERNICE. "An Analysis of Certain Aspects of Teacher-Pupil Relationships as Determined by Teacher, Pupil, and Parent Opinions." *J Social Psychol* 66:191–9 Ag '65. * (*PA* 39:16393)

[325]

Information Blank EA: A Questionnaire on Emotional Adjustment, Provisional Form. Grades 10–16; 1938; H. T. Manuel, F. J. Adams, and Paul White; Steck Co. * *Out of print.*

For additional information and a review by Percival M. Symonds, see 3:50; for a review by Stanley G. Dulsky, see 2:1224.

[326]

Interaction Chronograph. All ages; 1944–57; device for recording interaction between 2 individuals; used in a standardized interview to obtain ratings on 29 personality characteristics; Eliot D. Chapple; E. D. Chapple Co., Inc. * *Out of print.*

For additional information and a review by Cecil A. Gibb, see 5:76 (20 references).

REFERENCES

1. CHAPPLE, ELIOT D. "The Measurement of Interpersonal Behaviour." *Trans N Y Acad Sci* 4:222–33 My '42. (*PA* 17:223)
2. LINDEMANN, ERICH; FINESINGER, JACOB E.; and CHAPPLE, ELIOT D. "The Measurement of Interaction During Psychiatric Examination." *Trans Am Neurol Assn* 70:174–5 '44. *
3. CHAPPLE, ELIOT D., and DONALD, GORDON, JR. "A Method for Evaluating Supervisory Personnel." *Harvard Bus R* 24:197–214 w '46. *
4. CHAPPLE, ELIOT D., and DONALD, GORDON, JR. "An Evaluation of Department Store Salespeople by the Interaction Chronograph." *J Marketing* 12:173–85 O '47. *
5. PIEL, GERARD. "Your Personality Sits for Its Photo." *Nation's Bus* 35:51–6 Ap '47. *
6–25. See 5:76.
26. PHILLIPS, JEANNE SHIRLEY. *The Relationship Between Two Measures of Interview Behavior Comparing Verbal Content and Verbal Temporal Patterns of Interaction.* Doctor's thesis, Washington University (St. Louis, Mo.), 1957. (*DA* 17:898)
27. GUZE, SAMUEL B., and MENSH, IVAN N. "An Analysis of Some Features of the Interview With the Interaction Chronograph." *J Abn & Social Psychol* 58:269–71 Mr '59. * (*PA* 34:1318)

28. SASLOW, GEORGE, and MATARAZZO, JOSEPH D. "A Technique for Studying Changes in Interview Behavior," pp. 125–59. In *Research in Psychotherapy: Proceedings of a Conference, Washington, D.C., April 9–12, 1958.* Edited by Eli A. Rubenstein and Morris B. Parloff. Washington, D.C.: American Psychological Association, Inc., 1959. Pp. viii, 293. *
29. CHAPPLE, ELIOT D.; CHAPPLE, MARTHA F.; WOOD, LUCIE A.; MIKLOWITZ, AMY; KLINE, NATHAN S.; and SAUNDERS, JOHN C. "Interaction Chronograph Method for Analysis of Differences Between Schizophrenics and Controls." *Arch Gen Psychiatry* 3:160–7 Ag '60. *
30. HARE, A. PAUL; WAXLER, NANCY; SASLOW, GEORGE; and MATARAZZO, JOSEPH D. "Simultaneous Recording of Bales and Chapple Interaction Measures During Initial Psychiatric Interviews." Abstract. *J Consult Psychol* 24:193 Ap '60. * (*PA* 34:7778)
31. PHILLIPS, JEANNE S.; MATARAZZO, RUTH G.; MATARAZZO, JOSEPH D.; and SASLOW, GEORGE. "Relationships Between Descriptive Content and Interaction Behavior in Interviews." *J Consult Psychol* 25:260–6 Je '61. *
32. TUASON, VICENTE B.; GUZE, SAMUEL B.; McCLURE, JAMES; and BEGUELIN, JERRY. "A Further Study of Some Features of the Interview With the Interaction Chronograph." *Am J Psychiatry* 118:438–46 N '61. *
33. WOOD, LUCIE A.; MIKLOWITZ, AMY; CHAPPLE, ELIOT D.; CHAPPLE, MARTHA F.; KLINE, NATHAN S.; and SAUNDERS, JOHN C. "The Effect of Phenothiazines on the Interactional Behavior of Schizophrenic Patients." *Am J Psychiatry* 117:825–9 Mr '61. *
34. CHAPPLE, E. D.; CHAMBERLAIN, A.; ESSER, A. H.; and KLINE, N. S. "The Measurement of Activity Patterns of Schizophrenic Patients." *J Nerv & Mental Dis* 137:258–67 S '63. * (*PA* 38:6496)
35. MATARAZZO, JOSEPH D.; WEITMAN, MORRIS; and SASLOW, GEORGE. "Interview Content and Interviewee Speech Durations." *J Clin Psychol* 19:463–72 O '63. * (*PA* 39:8028)
36. WIENS, ARTHUR N.; MATARAZZO, JOSEPH D.; and SASLOW, GEORGE. "The Interaction Recorder: An Electric Punched Paper Tape Unit for Recording Speech Behavior During Interviews." *J Clin Psychol* 21:142–5 Ap '65. * (*PA* 39:12474)

NAME INDEX

Arensberg, C. M.: 8
Beguelin, J.: 32
Brazier, M. A. B.: 11
Chamberlain, A.: 34
Chapple, E. D.: 1–4, 6–11, 13, 17, 29, 33–4
Chapple, M. F.: 29, 33
Donald, G.: 3–4
Esser, A. H.: 34
Finesinger, J. E.: 2, 11
Gibb, C. A.: *rev,* 5:76
Goldman-Eisler, F.: 15–6, 18
Goodrich, D. W.: 22
Guze, S. B.: 19–20, 27, 32
Hare, A. P.: 30
Houston, T. J.: 14
Kline, N. S.: 29, 33–4
Lindemann, E.: 2, 10–1
McClure, J.: 32

Matarazzo, J. D.: 19–21, 23–5, 28, 30–1, 35–6
Matarazzo, R. G.: 21, 23–5, 31
Mensh, I. N.: 27
Miklowitz, A.: 29, 33
Phillips, J. S.: 23–6, 31
Piel, G.: 5
Saslow, G.: 19–25, 28, 30–1, 35–6
Saunders, J. C.: 29, 33
Sharp, J. H.: 14
Stein, M.: 22
Tuason, V. B.: 32
Waxler, N.: 30
Weitman, M.: 35
Wiens, A. N.: 36
Wood, L. A.: 29, 33

[327]

Interaction Process Analysis. Groups of from 2–20 people (ages 4 and over); 1948–50; method of analyzing group character and processes; Robert F. Bales; Addison-Wesley Publishing Co., Inc. * *Out of print.*

For additional information and a review by Cecil A. Gibb, see 5:77 (10 references); for a review by Launor F. Carter, see 4:56 (3 references); for excerpts from related book reviews, see 4:57.

REFERENCES

1–3. See 4:56.
4–13. See 5:77.
14. TAKALA, MARTTI; PIHKANEN, TOIVO A.; and MARKKANEN, TOUKO. *The Effects of Distilled and Brewed Beverages: A Physiological, Neurological, and Psychological Study.* The Finnish Foundation for Alcoholic Studies, No. 4. Stockholm, Sweden: Almqvist & Wiksell, 1957. Pp. 195. * (*PA* 31:4890)
15. HARE, A. PAUL; WAXLER, NANCY; SASLOW, GEORGE; and MATARAZZO, JOSEPH D. "Simultaneous Recording of Bales and Chapple Interaction Measures During Initial Psychiatric Interviews." Abstract. *J Consult Psychol* 24:193 Ap '60. * (*PA* 34:7778)
16. PSATHAS, GEORGE. "Interaction Process Analysis of Two Psychotherapy Groups." *Int J Group Psychother* 10:430–45 O '60. *
17. BORGATTA, EDGAR F., and STIMSON, JOHN. "Some Formal

Properties of Groups." *J Psychol Studies* 12:211–24 S '61 [issued Ap '63]. *

18. HAMBLIN, ROBERT L., and MILLER, L. KEITH. "Variations in Interaction Profiles and Group Size." *Sociol Q* 2:105–17 Ap '61. * (*PA* 36:3GE05H)

19. PSATHAS, GEORGE. "Alternative Methods for Scoring Interaction Process Analysis." *J Social Psychol* 53:97–103 F '61. * (*PA* 35:6347)

20. SYDIAHA, DANIEL. "Bales' Interaction Process Analysis of Personnel Selection Interviews." *J Appl Psychol* 45:393–401 D '61. * (*PA* 37:2059)

21. BORGATTA, EDGAR F. "A Systematic Study of Interaction Process Scores, PEER and Self-Assessments, Personality and Other Variables." *Genetic Psychol Monogr* 65:219–91 My '62. * (*PA* 37:3030)

22. OAKES, WILLIAM F. "Reinforcement of Bales' Categories in Group Discussion." *Psychol Rep* 11:427–35 O '62. * (*PA* 37:7950)

23. HECKEL, R. V. "Comment on Oakes: 'Reinforcement of Bales' Categories in Group Discussion.'" *Psychol Rep* 13:301–2 Ag '63. * (*PA* 38:5306)

24. CHEEK, FRANCES E. "A Serendipitous Finding: Sex Roles and Schizophrenia." *J Abn & Social Psychol* 69:392–400 O '64. * (*PA* 39:8478)

25. FIELD, PETER B. "Bales Interaction Analysis of Hypnosis." *Int J Clin & Exp Hyp* 12:88–98 Ap '64. * (*PA* 39:2189)

26. AIKEN, EDWIN G. "Interaction Process Analysis Changes Accompanying Operant Conditioning of Verbal Frequency in Small Groups." *Percept & Motor Skills* 21:52–4 Ag '65. * (*PA* 40:489)

27. BALES, ROBERT F., and HARE, A. PAUL. "Diagnostic Use of the Interaction Profile." *J Social Psychol* 67:239–58 D '65. * (*PA* 40:4745)

28. CONANT, LUCY H. "Use of Bales' Interaction Process Analysis to Study Nurse-Patient Interaction." *Nursing Res* 14:304–9 f '65. *

29. WAXLER, NANCY E., and MISHLER, ELLIOT G. "Scoring and Reliability Problems in Interaction Process Analysis: A Methodological Note." *Sociometry* 29:28–40 Mr '66. * (*PA* 40:6542)

30. CHEEK, FRANCES E. "Parental Social Control Mechanisms in the Family of the Schizophrenic—A New Look at the Family Environment of Schizophrenia." *J Schizophrenia* 1(1):18–53 '67. * (*PA* 42:2748)

31. KINGSLEY, LEONARD. "Process Analysis of a Leaderless Countertransference Group." *Psychol Rep* 20:555–62 Ap '67. * (*PA* 41:8839)

32. WINTER, WILLIAM D., and FERREIRA, ANTONIO J. "Interaction Process of Analysis of Family Decision-Making." *Family Process* 6:155–72 S '67. * (*PA* 42:8827)

NAME INDEX

Aiken, E. G.: 26	Markkanen, T.: 14
Bales, R. F.: 1–4, 6–11, 27	Matarazzo, J. D.: 15
Borgatta, E. F.: 6, 10–1, 13, 17, 21	Miller, L. K.: 18
	Mills, T. M.: 3
Butler, W. R.: 5	Mishler, E. G.: 29
Carter, L. F.: *rev*, 4:56	Oakes, W. F.: 22
Cheek, F. E.: 24, 30	Osterberg, W.: *exc*, 4:57
Conant, L. H.: 28	Parsons, T.: 8
Cottrell, L. S.: 13	Pihkanen, T. A.: 14
Ferreira, A. J.: 32	Pringle, B. M.: *exc*, 4:57
Field, P. B.: 25	Psathas, G.: 16, 19
Fine, H. J.: 12	Roseborough, M. E.: 3
Foreman, P. B.: *exc*, 4:57	Saslow, G.: 15
Gerbrands, H.: 1	Shaffer, L. F.: *exc*, 4:57
Gibb, C. A.: *rev*, 5:77	Shils, E. A.: 8
Greenwood, E.: *exc*, 4:57	Stimson, J.: 17
Hamblin, R. L.: 18	Strodtbeck, F. L.: 3
Hare, A. P.: 15, 27	Sydiaha, D.: 20
Heckel, R. V.: 23	Takala, M.: 14
Heinicke, C.: 7	Waxler, N.: 15
Jensen, H. E.: *exc*, 4:57	Waxler, N. E.: 29
Kingsley, L.: 31	Winter, W. D.: 32
Lerner, D.: *exc*, 4:57	Zander, A.: *exc*, 4:57
Mann, J. H.: 13	Zimet, C. N.: 12

[328]

Interest Analysis, 1942 Revision. Ages 16 and over; 1938–42; Eugene J. Benge; Management Service Co. *Out of print.*

For additional information and a review by Edward B. Greene, see 3:51.

[329]

Interest Index: General Education Series. Grades 7–13; 1938–50; same as *Interest Index: Test 8.2a* ('39) which was a revision of *Test 8.2* ('38); original tests published by Evaluation in the Eight Year Study, Progressive Education Association; 30 scores: "like"

and "dislike" scores for English, foreign languages, mathematics, social studies, biology, physical sciences, music, fine arts, industrial arts, business courses, home economics, sports, manipulative, reading, total; Evaluation Staff of the Eight Year Study of the Progressive Education Association; published in 1950 by Cooperative Test Division. * *Out of print.*

For additional information, see 4:58 (2 references); see also 2:1226 (4 references).

REFERENCES

1–4. See 2:1226.
5–6. See 4:58.
7. SCHWARTZ, MILTON M. "The Relationship Between Projective Test Scoring Categories and Activity Preferences." *Genetic Psychol Monogr* 46:133–81 N '52. * (*PA* 27:4269)
8. COLLINS, CHARLES CORNELIUS. *The Relationship of Breadth of Academic Interest to Academic Achievement and Academic Aptitude.* Doctor's thesis, Stanford University (Stanford, Calif.), 1955. (*DA* 15:1782)
9. HALPERN, GERALD. "Scale Properties of the Interest Index." *Ed & Psychol Meas* 27:1085–9 w '67. * (*PA* 42:8956)

[330]

Interest Questionnaire: Games and Sports: Test 8.3. Grades 9–12; 1939; [W. H. Lauritsen]; Evaluation in the Eight Year Study, Progressive Education Association. *Out of print.*

For additional information, see 2:1227.

[331]

Interest-Values Inventory. Grades 9–16 and adults; 1939; 5 scores: theoretic, aesthetic, social, economic, emotional satisfaction; J. B. Maller and Edward M. Glaser; Bureau of Publications. * *Out of print.*

For additional information and reviews by E. Lowell Kelly and Paul E. Meehl, see 3:53 (5 references); see also 2:1228 (1 excerpt).

REFERENCES

1–5. See 3:53.
6. CERF, ARTHUR Z. "Maller-Glaser Interest Values Inventory, CE514A," pp. 611–3. In *Printed Classification Tests.* Edited by J. P. Guilford with the assistance of John I. Lacey. Army Air Forces Aviation Psychology Program Research Reports, Report No. 5. Washington, D.C.: United States Government Printing Office, 1947. Pp. xi, 919. * (*PA* 22:4145)
7. SPANEY, EMMA. "Personality Tests and the Selection of Nurses." *Nursing Res* 1:4–26 F '53. *
8. NICKERSON, EILEEN TRESSLER. *Some Correlates of Adjustment of Paraplegics.* Doctor's thesis, Columbia University (New York, N.Y.), 1961. (*DA* 22:632)

[332]

Interests and Activities: Tests 8.2b and 8.2c. Grades 7–12; 1939; 2 forms (both of which must be given); Evaluation in the Eight Year Study, Progressive Education Association. *Out of print.*

For additional information, see 2:1225 (7 references).

[333]

Inventory of Personal-Social Relationships: General Education Series. High school and college; 1941–50; a revision of the instrument developed in 1941 and described in *Student Personnel Services in General Education* by Paul J. Brouwer; 24 scores in each of 2 sections: activities and interests, concerns and difficulties; developed by the Cooperative Study in General Education; Cooperative Test Division. * *Out of print.*

For additional information and reviews by N. L. Gage and Theodore R. Sarbin, see 4:60 (2 references).

REFERENCES

1–2. See 4:60.
3. HOLLIS, ADELYN F. *Factors Related to Student Participation in Campus Activities in a Midwestern Teachers' College.* Doctor's thesis, University of Michigan (Ann Arbor, Mich.), 1953. (*DA* 13:337)

[334]

JNB Psychograph. Patients in mental hospitals; 1941; John N. Buck; the Author. *Out of print.*
For additional information, see 3:56 (1 reference).

[335]

Jurgensen Classification Inventory. Adults; 1947–50; Clifford E. Jurgensen; the Author. * *Out of print.*
For additional information and reviews by Robert G. Demaree (with Louis L. McQuitty) and William J. E. Crissy, see 4:63 (11 references).

[336]

Lewerenz-Steinmetz Orientation Test: Concerning Fundamental Aims of Education. High school and college; 1931–35; 10 scores: physical and mental health, education-general, education-specific, worthy home membership, vocation, civic education (government), civic education (industry and world), worthy use of leisure, ethical character, total; Alfred S. Lewerenz and Harry C. Steinmetz; California Test Bureau. * *Out of print.*
For additional information and reviews by Frederic L. Ayer and Roger T. Lennon, see 4:66 (3 references).

[337]

Life Experience Inventory. Ages 13 and over; 1957; 4 scores: childhood, social, emotional, total; Gilbert L. Betts and Russell N. Cassel; the Authors. * *Out of print.*
For additional information and reviews by Dan L. Adler and Douglas T. Kenny, see 5:81 (1 reference).

REFERENCES

1. See 5:81.
2. BETTS, GILBERT L. "Test Calibration for Categorical Classification." *Ed & Psychol Meas* 9:269–79 au '49. *

[338]

McCleery Scale of Adolescent Development. Grades 9–12; 1955; 11 scores: peer relations, social role, physique acceptance, independence of adults, economic independence, occupational preference, family life, civic competence, social responsibility, ethical system, total maturity; Robert L. McCleery; University of Nebraska Press. * *Out of print.*
For additional information and reviews by Eugene L. Gaier and John E. Horrocks, see 5:83 (1 reference).

[339]

Mental Health Analysis, 1959 Revision. Grades 4–8, 7–9, 9–16, adults; 1946–59; 13 scores: close personal relationships, interpersonal skills, social participation, satisfying work and recreation, adequate outlook and goals, total assets, behavioral immaturity, emotional instability, feelings of inadequacy, physical defects, nervous manifestations, total liabilities, total; Louis P. Thorpe and Willis W. Clark; California Test Bureau. * *Out of print.*
For additional information and a review by J. Robert Williams, see 6:141 (8 references); for reviews by William E. Coffman, Henry E. Garrett, C. M. Louttit, James Maxwell, and Douglas Spencer, see 3:59 (1 excerpt).

REFERENCES

1–8. See 6:141.
9. BLACKHAM, GARTH J. *A Clinical Study of the Personality Structures and Adjustments of Pupils Under-Achieving and Over-Achieving in Reading.* Doctor's thesis, Cornell University (Ithaca, N.Y.), 1954. (*DA* 15:1199)
10. ARNHOLTER, ETHELWYNE G. "School Persistence and Personality Factors." *Personnel & Guid J* 35:107–9 O '56. * (*PA* 31:8805)
11. STILES, GRACE ELLEN. *Relationships of Unmet Emotional Needs to Accident-Repeating Tendencies in Children.* Doctor's thesis, New York University (New York, N.Y.), 1957. (*DA* 17:2942)
12. TABARLET, BOBBY EUGENE. *A Study of Mental Health Status of Retarded Readers.* Doctor's thesis, Louisiana State University (Baton Rouge, La.), 1958. (*DA* 19:735)
13. GOLDSTEIN, SOLOMON NORMAN. *An Investigation of the Relationship of Perceptual Disparity and Mental Health Variables to Academic Achievement Disparity Among Elementary School Children.* Doctor's thesis, Syracuse University (Syracuse, N.Y.), 1963. (*DA* 24:5191)
14. BLEDSOE, JOSEPH C. "A Factor Analytic Study of the Mental Health Domain at the Elementary School Level." *J Exp Ed* 33:99–102 f '64. * (*PA* 39:5535)
15. BOWLING, LLOYD SPENCER, SR. *Personality Characteristics of Veterans With Different Types of Hearing Losses.* Doctor's thesis, University of Maryland (College Park, Md.), 1964. (*DA* 25:4811)
16. KRIPPNER, STANLEY. "Relationship Between Reading Improvement and Ten Selected Variables." *Percept & Motor Skills* 19:15–20 Ag '64. * (*PA* 39:5941)
17. WALTON, DONALD FLOYD. *Selected Mental Health Factors Significant to the Early Identification of Potential School Dropouts.* Doctor's thesis, Baylor University (Waco, Tex.), 1965. (*DA* 26:2597)
18. WILLINGHAM, GRADY WARNER. *The Mental Health of Prospective Elementary Teachers.* Doctor's thesis, North Texas State University (Denton, Tex.), 1965. (*DA* 26:3773)
19. CONGER, JOHN JANEWAY, and MILLER, WILBUR C.; with the assistance of Robert V. Rainey and Charles R. Walsmith. *Personality, Social Class and Delinquency.* New York: John Wiley & Sons, Inc., 1966. Pp. xi, 249. *
20. IVANOFF, JOHN M.; MONROE, GERALD D.; and MARITA, M. "Use of Intellective and Non-Intellective Factors in Classifying Female Elementary and Secondary Teacher Trainees." *J Exp Ed* 34:55–61 su '66. * (*PA* 40:11511)
21. NICKOLS, JOHN. "Self-Image Ratings of Normal and Disturbed Subjects." *J Health & Hum Behav* 7:28–36 sp '66. * (*PA* 40:7916)
22. VANCE, EDITH MYRLE BLACKMON. *Relationship of Self-Actualization to Mental Health.* Doctor's thesis, North Texas State University (Denton, Tex.), 1967. (*DA* 28:135A)

[340]

The Minnesota Inventory of Social Attitudes. College; 1937; 2 tests; E. G. Williamson and J. G. Darley; distributed by Psychological Corporation. * *Out of print.*
a) MINNESOTA INVENTORY OF SOCIAL BEHAVIOR. Form B.
b) MINNESOTA INVENTORY OF SOCIAL PREFERENCES. Form P.
For additional information and a review by Verner M. Sims, see 4:70 (12 references); for reviews by J. P. Guilford and George Hartmann, see 1:900.

REFERENCES

1–12. See 4:70.
13. HAHN, MILTON EDWIN. *An Investigation of Measured Aspects of Social Intelligence in a Distributive Occupation.* Doctor's thesis, University of Minnesota (Minneapolis, Minn.), 1942.
14. GUSTAD, JOHN W. "A Longitudinal Study of Social Behavior Variables in College Students." *Ed & Psychol Meas* 12:226–35 su '52. * (*PA* 27:6124)
15. SKEATH, JAMES MILTON. *Social Maladjustment as a Discrepancy Between Social Needs and Social Activities.* Doctor's thesis, Pennsylvania State College (State College, Pa.), 1952.
16. PANDEY, JAGADISH. "Hindi Adaptation of Williamson Darley's the Minnesota Inventory of Social Behaviour (MISB)." *J Voc & Ed Guid* 12:31–6 F '66. *
17. PANDEY, JAGADISH. "Influence of Response Set on Social Preferences." *Indian Psychol R* 3:39–42 Jl '66. * (*PA* 41:8907)
18. PANDEY, JAGADISH. "Effect of Response Set on the Scores of the Minnesota Inventory of Social Behaviour—Hindi Adaptation." *Indian J Appl Psychol* 4:14–6 Ja '67. *

[341]

Minnesota Personality Scale. Grades 11–16; 1941; 5 scores: morale, social adjustment, family relations, emotionality, economic conservatism; John G. Darley and Walter J. McNamara; Psychological Corporation. * *Out of print.*
For additional information, see 5:87 (22 references); for reviews by Philip Eisenberg and John W. French, see 3:61 (9 references).

REFERENCES

1–9. See 3:61.
10–31. See 5:87.
32. HYMAN, BERNARD. *The Relationship of Social Status and Vocational Interest.* Doctor's thesis, Columbia University (New York, N.Y.), 1955. (*DA* 15:1354)
33. SNOW, BARBARA M. *An Analysis of the Relationship of Certain Factors to the Social Acceptance Status of College Freshman Women.* Doctor's thesis, Pennsylvania State University (University Park, Pa.), 1957. (*DA* 18:142)
34. BURCHINAL, LEE G., and ROSSMAN, JACK E. "Relations Among Maternal Employment Indices and Developmental Characteristics of Children." *Marriage & Family Living* 23:334–40 N '61. * (*PA* 36:5FG34B)
35. WEBSTER, RAYMOND B. "The Effects of Hypnosis on Performance on the H-T-P and MPS." *Int J Clin & Exp Hyp* 10:151–3 Jl '62. * (*PA* 37:5245)
36. BURCHINAL, LEE G., and JACOBSON, PERRY E. "Migration and Adjustments of Farm and Urban Families and Adolescents in Cedar Rapids, Iowa." *Rural Sociol* 28:364–78 D '63. * (*PA* 38:5838)

[342]

Minnesota Scale for the Survey of Opinions. Ages 16–25; 1936; 7 scores: morale, inferiority feelings, family, law, economic conservatism, education, general adjustment; E. A. Rundquist and R. F. Sletto; University of Minnesota Press. * *Out of print.*

For additional information and reviews by H. H. Remmers and Goodwin Watson, see 1:901.

REFERENCES

1. RUNDQUIST, EDWARD A., and SLETTO, RAYMOND F. *Personality in the Depression: A Study of the Measurement of Attitudes.* University of Minnesota, Institute of Child Welfare, Monograph Series, No. 12. Minneapolis, Minn.: University of Minnesota Press, 1936. Pp. xxii, 398. * (*PA* 11:347)
2. DARLEY, JOHN G. *An Analysis of Attitude and Adjustment Tests: With Special Reference to Conditions of Change in Attitudes and Adjustments.* Doctor's thesis, University of Minnesota (Minneapolis, Minn.), 1937.
3. DARLEY, JOHN G. "Scholastic Achievement and Measured Maladjustment." *J Appl Psychol* 21:485–93 O '37. * (*PA* 12:2099)
4. DARLEY, JOHN G. "Tested Maladjustment Related to Clinically Diagnosed Maladjustment." *J Appl Psychol* 21:632–42 Ag '37. * (*PA* 12:3031)
5. DARLEY, JOHN G. "Changes in Measured Attitudes and Adjustments." *J Social Psychol* 9:189–99 My '38. * (*PA* 12:4833)
6. McNAMARA, WALTER J., and DARLEY, JOHN G. "A Factor Analysis of Test-Retest Performance on Attitude and Adjustment Tests." *J Ed Psychol* 29:652–64 D '38. *
7. SUKOV, MAY, and WILLIAMSON, E. G. "Personality Traits and Attitudes of Jewish and Non-Jewish Students." *J Appl Psychol* 22:487–92 O '38. * (*PA* 13:2658)
8. DARLEY, JOHN G., and McNAMARA, WALTER J. "Factor Analysis in the Establishment of New Personality Tests." *J Ed Psychol* 31:321–34 My '40. * (*PA* 15:922)
9. FERGUSON, LEONARD W. "A Study of the Likert Technique of Attitude Scale Construction." *J Social Psychol* 13:51–7 F '41. * (*PA* 15:2683)
10. GILKINSON, HOWARD, and KNOWER, FRANKLIN H. "A Study of Standardized Personality Tests and Skill in Speech." *J Ed Psychol* 32:161–75 Mr '41. * (*PA* 15:3888)
11. HARDING, JOHN. "A Scale for Measuring Civilian Morale." *J Psychol* 12:101–10 Jl '41. * (*PA* 15:5255)
12. DIGGS, E.; HANGER, E.; and MULL, H. K. "Morale in the College Situation in Relation to the Morale Scale of Rundquist and Sletto: Studies From the Psychological Lab-

oratory of Sweet Briar College, IV." *Am J Psychol* 55:561–2 O '42. * (*PA* 17:1640)

13. MENZIES, RODERICK. "Minnesota-Scale Morale and Adjustment of Young Men and Women as Related to Economic and Social Conditions in an Urban Environment." *J Psychol* 15:115–27 Ja '43. * (*PA* 17:1266)
14. SEWELL, WILLIAM H., and AMEND, ELEANOR E. "The Influence of Size of Home Community on Attitudes and Personality Traits." *Am Sociol R* 8:180–4 Ap '43. * (*PA* 17:3892)
15. CLARK, KENNETH E., and KRIEDT, PHILIP H. "An Application of Guttman's New Scaling Techniques to an Attitude Questionnaire." *Ed & Psychol Meas* 8:215–23 su '48. * (*PA* 23:3993)
16. BRAYFIELD, ARTHUR H.; WELLS, RICHARD V.; and STRATE, MARVIN W. "Interrelationships Among Measures of Job Satisfaction and General Satisfaction." *J Appl Psychol* 41:201–5 Ag '57. *

[343]

The Nebraska Personality Inventory. Grades 9–16 and adults; 1934; 3 scores: social introversion, emotionality, masculinity; J. P. Guilford; Sheridan Supply Co. * *Out of print.*

For additional information and reviews by John C. Flanagan and C. M. Louttit, see 1:922.

REFERENCES

1. GUILFORD, J. P., and GUILFORD, RUTH B. "Personality Factors S, E, and M, and Their Measurement." *J Psychol* 2:109–27 Jl '36. * (*PA* 10:4533)
2. EYSENCK, H. J. "Personality Factors and Preference Judgments." *Nature* 148:346 S 20 '41. * (*PA* 16:674)

[344]

Objective-Analytic Personality Test Batteries. Ages 11–16, adults; 1955; 18 single-factor batteries (plus 4 combinations as listed below): children and adults-competent assertiveness (U.I. 16), restraint-timidity (U.I. 17), hypomanic overcompensation (U.I. 18), critical-dominant exactness (U.I. 19), sociable willingness (U.I. 20), energetic decisiveness (U.I. 21), nervous-alert reactivity (U.I. 22), neural reserves vs. neuroticism (U.I. 23), anxiety to achieve (U.I. 24), accurate realism vs. psychoticism (U.I. 25), cultured introspective self-control (U.I. 26), apathetic temperament (U.I. 27), sociable-emotional evasiveness (U.I. 28), sympathetic mobilization of energy (U.I. 29), stolid superego satisfaction (U.I. 30), adults only-wary realism (U.I. 31), schizoid tenacity (U.I. 32), dourness (U.I. 33); for revision of the U.I. 24 battery, see *Objective-Analytic (O-A) Anxiety Battery* (182); Raymond B. Cattell, A. R. Baggaley, L. Checov, E. A. Cogan, D. Flint, W. Gruen, E. Husek, T. Meeland, D. R. Saunders, and H. Schiff; Institute for Personality and Ability Testing. * *Out of print.*

a) THE ADULT 18 0-A BATTERY. Ages 16 and over; 18 factors (U.I. 16–33).

b) THE ADULT 12 0-A BATTERY. Ages 16 and over; 12 factors (U.I. 16–27).

c) THE CHILDREN 14 0-A BATTERY. Ages 11–16; 14 factors (U.I. 16–26, 28–30).

d) THE CHILDREN 10 0-A BATTERY. Ages 11–16; 10 factors (U.I. 16, 17, 19–23, 26, 28, 29).

For additional information and a review by H. J. Eysenck, see 5:90 (6 references).

REFERENCES

1–6. See 5:90.
7. CATTELL, RAYMOND B., and SCHEIER, IVAN H. "The Objective Test Measurement of Neuroticism, U.I. 23 (—)." *Indian J Psychol* 33:217–36 pt 4 '58. * (*PA* 35:3427, title only)
8. MANGAN, GORDON L., and CLARK, JAMES W. "Rigidity Factors in the Testing of Middle-Aged Subjects." *J Gerontol* 13:422–5 O '58. * (*PA* 33:10073)
9. MOSHIN, S. M. "Plea for a Scientific Aptitude Test and a Preliminary Report of the Development of Such Test." *Indian J Psychol* 34:36–42 pt 1 '59. *
10. BORG, WALTER R. "Prediction of Small Group Role Behavior From Personality Variables." *J Abn & Social Psychol* 60:112–6 Ja '60. * (*PA* 34:7528)

11. CATTELL, RAYMOND B., and SCHEIER, IVAN H. *The Meaning and Measurement of Neuroticism and Anxiety.* New York: Ronald Press Co., 1961. Pp. ix, 535. * (London: George G. Harrap & Co. Ltd.) (*PA* 36:1HK27C)

12. KNAPP, ROBERT R. "Objective Personality Test and Sociometric Correlates of Frequency of Sick Bay Visits." *J Appl Psychol* 45:104–10 Ap '61. * (*PA* 36:3LD04K)

13. CATTELL, RAYMOND B. "Advances in the Measurement of Neuroticism and Anxiety in a Conceptual Framework of Unitary-Trait Theory." *Ann N Y Acad Sci* 93:815–39 O 10 '62. * (*PA* 37:6779)

14. KNAPP, ROBERT R. "The Validity of the Objective-Analytic Personality Test Battery in Navy Settings." *Ed & Psychol Meas* 22:379–87 su '62. * (*PA* 37:3109)

15. SCHEIER, IVAN H. "Experimental Results to Date From the Viewpoint of the Clinician." *Ann N Y Acad Sci* 93:840–50 O 10 '62. * (*PA* 37:6782)

16. PAWLIK, KURT, and CATTELL, RAYMOND B. "Third-Order Factors in Objective Personality Tests." *Brit J Psychol* 55: 1–18 F '64. * (*PA* 39:1819)

17. HUNDLEBY, JOHN D.; PAWLIK, KURT; and CATTELL, RAYMOND B. *Personality Factors in Objective Test Devices: A Critical Integration of a Quarter of a Century's Research.* San Diego, Calif.: Robert R. Knapp, Publisher, 1965. Pp. iii, 542. *

18. KNAPP, ROBERT R. "Delinquency and Objective Personality Test Factors." *J Appl Psychol* 49:8–10 F '65. * (*PA* 39:7845)

19. RICKELS, KARL, and CATTELL, RAYMOND B. "The Clinical Factor Validity and Trueness of the IPAT Verbal and Objective Batteries for Anxiety and Regression." *J Clin Psychol* 21:257–64 Jl '65. * (*PA* 39:15261)

20. CATTELL, RAYMOND B., and TATRO, DONALD F. "The Personality Factors, Objectively Measured, Which Distinguish Psychotics From Normals." *Behav Res Ther* 4:39–51 Mr '66. * (*PA* 40:7843)

21. CATTELL, R. B., and KILLIAN, L. R. "The Pattern of Objective Test Personality Factor Differences in Schizophrenia and the Character Disorders." *J Clin Psychol* 23:342–8 Jl '67. * (*PA* 41:15546)

22. FINE, BERNARD J., and SWEENEY, DONALD R. "Personality Traits, and Situational Factors, and Catecholamine Excretion." *J Exp Res Personality* 3:15–27 Je '68. * (*PA* 42:16867)

23. TATRO, DONALD F. "The Utility of Source Traits Measured by the O-A (Objective-Analytic) Battery in Mental Hospital Diagnosis," pp. 133–49. (*PA* 42:15694) In *Progress in Clinical Psychology Through Multivariate Experimental Designs.* Edited by Raymond B. Cattell. Fort Worth, Tex.: Society of Multivariate Experimental Psychology, Inc., 1968. Pp. 168. *

[345]

Occupational Personality Inventory. Applicants for sales positions; 1939; Arthur F. Dodge; Psychological Corporation. * *Out of print.*

For additional information, see 2:1232 (3 references).

[346]

Ohio Guidance Tests for Elementary Grades. Grades 4–6; 1944–46; manual by Wellington G. Fordyce, Wilbur A. Yauch, and Louis Raths; Ohio Scholarship Tests. * *Out of print.*

a) OHIO INTEREST INVENTORY FOR THE INTERMEDIATE GRADES.

b) OHIO INDIVIDUAL SUMMARY SHEET FOR COMMITTEE SELECTIONS.

c) OHIO SOCIAL ACCEPTANCE SCALE FOR THE INTERMEDIATE GRADES.

d) OHIO RECOGNITION SCALE FOR INTERMEDIATE GRADES: WHO'S WHO IN MY GROUP?

e) OHIO THINKING CHECKUP FOR INTERMEDIATE GRADES.

For additional information and reviews by M. H. Elliott and John W. M. Rothney, see 3:63 (8 references).

REFERENCES

1–8. See 3:63.
9. MCLENDON, IDA RUTH. *An Investigation of Factors Associated With the Social Acceptance of Children in the Intermediate Grades of Hamilton, Ohio.* Doctor's thesis, Ohio State University (Columbus, Ohio), 1947.
10. JUSTMAN, JOSEPH, and WRIGHTSTONE, J. WAYNE. "A Comparison of Three Methods of Measuring Pupil Status in the Classroom." *Ed & Psychol Meas* 11:362–7 au '51. * (*PA* 27:6126)
11. TAYLOR, EDWARD A. "Appraising and Developing Social

Acceptance in the Classroom." *Calif J Ed Res* 2:165–9 S '51. *
12. TAYLOR, EDWARD A. "Some Factors Relating to Social Acceptance in Eighth-Grade Classrooms." *J Ed Psychol* 43:257–72 My '52. * (*PA* 27:3770)
13. WARDLOW, MARY E., and GREENE, JAMES E. "An Exploratory Sociometric Study of Peer Status Among Adolescent Girls." *Sociometry* 15:311–8 Ag–N '52. * (*PA* 27:7097)
14. FORLANO, GEORGE, and WRIGHTSTONE, J. WAYNE. "Measuring the Quality of Social Acceptability Within a Class." *Ed & Psychol Meas* 15:127–36 su '55. * (*PA* 30:3404)
15. SEMLER, IRA JACKSON. *Relationship Among Various Measures of Pupil Adjustment.* Doctor's thesis, State University of Iowa (Iowa City, Iowa), 1957. (*DA* 17:2923)
16. SEMLER, IRA J. "Relationships Among Several Measures of Pupil Adjustment." *J Ed Psychol* 51:60–4 Ap '60. * (*PA* 35:2741)
17. CRITES, JOHN O., and SEMLER, IRA J. "Adjustment, Educational Achievement, and Vocational Maturity as Dimensions of Development in Adolescence." *J Counsel Psychol* 14:489–96 N '67. * (*PA* 42:3783)

[347]

P.Q. or Personality Quotient Test. Grades 7–13; 1936–38; test booklet title is *Inventory of Activities and Interests;* 5 scores: social initiative, self determination, economic self determination, adjustment to opposite sex, total; Henry C. Link, G. K. Bennett, Rose G. Anderson, Sydney Roslow, and P. G. Corby; Psychological Corporation. * *Out of print.*

For additional information and reviews by Douglas Spencer and Simon H. Tulchin, see 2:1233 (5 references); for reviews by C. M. Louttit and Edmund G. Williamson, see 1:921.

REFERENCES

1–5. See 2:1233.
6. PETERS, CHAS. C. "The Validity of Personality Inventories Studied by a 'Guess Who' Technique." Abstract. *Psychol B* 37:453 Jl '40. * (*PA* 14:5599)
7. ROSLOW, SYDNEY. "Nation-Wide and Local Validation of the P.Q. or Personality Quotient Test." *J Appl Psychol* 24:529–39 O '40. * (*PA* 15:931)
8. ROSLOW, SYDNEY. "The Nation-Wide Validation of a Personality Test." Abstract. *Psychol B* 37:520 Jl '40. * (*PA* 14:5600, title only)
9. MUSSELMAN, JOHN W. "Factors Associated With the Achievement of High School Pupils of Superior Intelligence." *J Exp Ed* 11:53–68 S '42. * (*PA* 17:1363)
10. LINK, HENRY C. "The Definition of Social Effectiveness and Leadership Through Measurement." *Ed & Psychol Meas* 4:57–67 sp '44. * (*PA* 18:3216)
11. SPINELLE, LEO, and NEMZEK, CLAUDE L. "The Relationship of Personality Test Scores to School Marks and Intelligence Quotients." *J Social Psychol* 20:289–94 N '44. * (*PA* 19:807)
12. JONES, RONALD DEVALL. "The Prediction of Teaching Efficiency From Objective Measures." *J Exp Ed* 15:85–99 S '46. * (*PA* 21:606)
13. JONES, RONALD D. *The Prediction of Teaching Efficiency.* Doctor's thesis, University of Wisconsin (Madison, Wis.), 1947.
14. LINK, HENRY C. "Significant Light on Personality." *Reader's Dig* 53:125–7 D '48. *
15. ZAKOLSKI, F. C. "Studies in Delinquency: 1, Personality Structure of Delinquent Boys." *J Genetic Psychol* 74:109–17 Mr '49. * (*PA* 23:4925)
16. LINK, HENRY C. Sect. 1, "Social Effectiveness and Leadership," pp. 3–10. In *Handbook of Applied Psychology,* Vol. I. Edited by Douglas H. Fryer and Edwin R. Henry. New York: Rinehart & Co., Inc., 1950. Pp. xxi, 380, ix. * (*PA* 25:8309)

[348]

Parents' Rating Scale. Parents; 1935; self ratings in 26 situations; Walther Joël and Janet Joël; Walther Joël. * *Out of print.*

For additional information, see 2:1235.

[349]

Personal Adaptability Test. Grades 11–13 and adults; 1957; 4 scores: botheredness, mental malfunctioning, physiological malfunctioning, total; Guy E. Buckingham; Public School Publishing Co. * *Out of print.*

For additional information and a review by Harold Webster, see 5:91 (1 reference).

[350]

The Personal and Social Development Program. Grades kgn–9; 1956; form for recording behavior incidents in 8 areas: personal adjustment, responsibility and effort, creativity and initiative, integrity, social adjustment, sensitivity to others, group orientation, adaptibility to rules and conventions; John C. Flanagan; Science Research Associates, Inc. * *Out of print.*

For additional information and reviews by Edward Landy and C. Gilbert Wrenn (with Roy D. Lewis), see 5:92.

[351]

Personal Data Scale. College entrants; 1937; prediction of college success; J. D. Heilman; Colorado State College of Education. * *Out of print.*

For additional information, consult 1:1119.

REFERENCE

1. CONGDON, NORA A. "New Weights for the Responses in the Heilman Personal Data Scale." *J Ed Psychol* 32:214–9 Mr '41. * *(PA* 15:3885)

[352]

Personal History Record, 1937 Revision. Grades 9–16 and adults; 1928–37; emotional stability; Lorin A. Thompson, Jr.; C. H. Stoelting Co. * *Out of print.*

For additional information, see 2:1236 (1 reference).

REFERENCES

1. See 2:1236.
2. NORTH, ROBERT D. "The Experimental Use of a Biographical Inventory in Four Public High Schools," pp. 77–83. In *1955 Fall Testing Program in Independent Schools and Supplementary Studies.* Educational Records Bulletin, No. 67. New York: Educational Records Bureau, February 1956. Pp. xii, 83. * *(PA* 31:3801)

[353]

Personal Index. Boys in grades 7–9; 1933; "detection of attitudes indicative of problem-behavior"; Graham C. Loofbourow and Noel Keys; Educational Test Bureau. * *Out of print.*

For additional information and reviews by J. B. Maller and Carl R. Rogers, see 2:1237 (5 references).

REFERENCES

1–5. See 2:1237.
6. MORGAN, DAVID H. "Emotional Adjustment of Visually-Handicapped Adolescents." *J Ed Psychol* 35:65–81 F '44. * *(PA* 18:3335)
7. BUTTIMORE, DENNIS J. *Some Aspects of the Personality of Male Juvenile Delinquents.* Doctor's thesis, New York University (New York, N.Y.), 1946.
8. PETERSON, DONALD R.; QUAY, HERBERT C.; and TIFFANY, THEODORE L. "Personality Factors Related to Juvenile Delinquency." *Child Develop* 32:355–72 Je '61. * *(PA* 36:3JO55P)

[354]

The Personal Preference Inventory: Student Form. College; 1947–49; 3 scores: economic background, social attitude, masculinity-femininity; Hugh M. Bell; Pacific Books. * *Out of print.*

For additional information and reviews by E. Lowell Kelly and C. M. Louttit, see 4:76.

REFERENCE

1. SHAW, MERVILLE C., and GRUBB, JAMES. "Hostility and Able High School Underachievers." *J Counsel Psychol* 5:263–6 w '58. * *(PA* 34:3413)

[355]

Personal Qualities Inventory. Business and industry; 1956–63; PQI; Richardson, Bellows, Henry & Co., Inc. * *Out of print.*

For additional information, see 6:155 (1 reference).

[356]

Personality and Interest Inventory: Elementary Form, Revised. Grades 4–8; 1935–59; PII; Gertrude Hildreth; Teachers College Press. * *Out of print.*

For additional information, see 6:156; for a review by Stephen M. Corey, see 2:1238 (3 references); for a review by Jack W. Dunlap, see 1:924.

[357]

Personality Index. Adults; 1945; 6 scores: job interest, social intelligence, leadership, planning, drive, follow through; Howard K. Morgan; La Rue Printing Co. * *Out of print.*

For additional information and a review by Benjamin Shimberg, see 3:65.

[358]

Personality Rating Chart for Preschool Children. Preschool children; 1938; 20 ratings in each of the areas: effective energy, mental effectiveness, emotional control, social adjustment, skill in work and play; Rachel Stutsman; Merrill-Palmer School. * *Out of print.*

For additional information, see 2:1241 (1 reference).

REFERENCES

1. See 2:1241.
2. GOLDSTEIN, HYMAN. "A Study of Introversion and Extroversion in a Group of Subnormal Children." *J Social Psychol* 5:238–44 My '34. * *(PA* 8:5994)
3. SHACTER, HELEN S. "Personality Tendencies and Sustained Attention in Preschool Children." *J Social Psychol* 5:313–28 Ag '34. * *(PA* 9:294)
4. RICHARDS, T. W. "Factors in the Personality of Nursery School Children." *J Exp Ed* 9:152–9 D '40. * *(PA* 15:2425)
5. POLLOCK, DOROTHY M. *A Personal Rating Scale as a Guidance Technique.* Doctor's thesis, University of Kansas (Lawrence, Kan.), 1942.

[359]

Personality Rating Scales. Preschool children; 1938; 9 scores: ascendance-submission, attractiveness of personality, compliance with routine, independence of adult affection or attention, physical attractiveness, respect for property rights, response to authority, sociability with other children, tendency to face reality; Katherine Elliott Roberts and Rachel Stutsman Ball; Merrill-Palmer School. * *Out of print.*

For additional information, see 2:1242 (1 reference).

[360]

Personality Schedule. Grades 13–16 and adults; 1928–30; neurotic tendencies; L. L. Thurstone and Thelma Gwinn Thurstone; University of Chicago Press. * *Out of print.*

For additional information, see 6:159 (38 references); for a review by J. P. Guilford, see 2:1243 (28 references).

REFERENCES

1–28. See 2:1243.
29–66. See 6:159.

NAME INDEX

Rosenbaum, B. B.: 47
Schott, E. L.: 21
Seagoe, M. V.: 63
Smith, H. N.: 8
Sperling, A.: 58
Stagner, R.: 4, 9, 35–6
Steele, I.: 12
Sung, S. M.: 20
Thurstone, L. L.: 2

Thurstone, T. G.: 2
Tryon, R. C.: 40
Wallin, P.: 62
Wesman, A. G.: 56
Whisler, L.: 25
Willoughby, R. R.: 5, 30, 33, 38
Zakolski, F. C.: 65
Zimmerman, M. A.: 61

[361]

Personality Sketches. Grades 4 and over; 1936; emotional adjustment; J. B. Maller; the Author. * *Out of print.*

For additional information and reviews by Henry E. Garrett and J. P. Guilford, see 1:925.

[362]

The Personality Survey. Grades 7–9; 1948; 9 scores: age, intelligence, reading comprehension, pupil questionnaire, teacher rating, sociometric rating, absence, school marks, total adjustment; Percival M. Symonds; Public School Publishing Co. * *Out of print.*

For additional information and reviews by Douglas Courtney and John W. M. Rothney, see 4:79 (2 references).

[363]

Pressey Interest-Attitude Tests. Grades 6–16 and adults; 1933–47; emotional maturity; 5 scores: things the subject considers wrong, things which interest him, things he worries about, characteristics of persons he admires, total; S. L. Pressey and L. C. Pressey; Psychological Corporation. * *Out of print.*

For additional information and a review by Douglas Spencer, see 2:1243.1 (5 references).

REFERENCES

1–5. See 2:1243.1.
6. PRESSEY, S. L., and PRESSEY, L. C. "A Study of the Emotional Attitudes of Indians Possessing Different Degrees of Indian Blood." *J Appl Psychol* 17:410–6 Ag '33. * *(PA* 8:513)
7. PRESSEY, SIDNEY L., and PRESSEY, LUELLA C. "A Comparative Study of the Emotional Attitudes and Interests of Indian and White Children." *J Appl Psychol* 17:227–38 Je '33. * *(PA* 8:512)
8. HARDIN, ROBERT ALLEN. *A Study of the Maturity of High School Seniors, Junior College, and University Students as Measured by the Ohio State University Psychological Test and the Pressey Interest-Attitude Test.* Doctor's thesis, University of Nebraska (Lincoln, Neb.), 1935.
9. DUREA, MERVIN A. "The Emotional Maturity of Juvenile Delinquents." *J Abn & Social Psychol* 31:472–81 Ja–Mr '37. * *(PA* 11:3834)
10. DUREA, MERVIN A. "Personality Characteristics of Juvenile Delinquents: 1, A Method for the Selection of Differentiating Traits." *Child Develop* 8:115–28 Jl '37. * *(PA* 11:4697)
11. JANNEY, J. E. "A Technique for the Measurement of Social Adjustment." *J Exp Ed* 7:203–5 Mr '39. * *(PA* 13:5835)
12. ODOROFF, M. E., and HARRIS, D. B. "A Study of the Interest-Attitude Test Scores of Delinquent Boys." Abstract. *Psychol B* 36:567–8 Jl '39. * *(PA* 13:6410, title only)
13. CHILD, IRVIN L. "The Relation Between Measures of Infantile Amnesia and Neuroticism." *J Abn & Social Psychol* 35:453–6 Jl '40. * *(PA* 14:5517)
14. KUHLEN, RAYMOND G. "The Pressey Interest-Attitude Test as a Measure of Personality at the College Level." Abstract. *Psychol B* 37:583 O '40. * *(PA* 15:337, title only)
15. DUREA, M. A., and FERTMAN, M. H. "Emotional Maturity of Delinquent Girls." *Am J Orthopsychiatry* 11:335–7 Ap '41. * *(PA* 15:4317)
16. DUREA, M. A., and FERTMAN, M. H. "Personality Characteristics of Juvenile Offenders." *J Crim Law & Criminol* 32:433–8 N–D '41. * *(PA* 16:1630)
17. DUREA, M. A., and HESTON, J. C. "Differential Diagnosis of Potential Delinquency: Additional Suggestions." *Am J Orthopsychiatry* 11:338–40 Ap '41. * *(PA* 15:4318)
18. DUREA, MERVIN A. "Personality Characteristics and Degree of Delinquency: 1, An Empirical Analysis of Blameworthy Circumstances and Anxiety States." *J Social Psychol* 13:329–39 My '41. * *(PA* 15:4757)
19. DUREA, MERVIN A. "Personality Characteristics and Degree of Delinquency: 2, An Empirical Analysis of Personal

Interests and Qualities Admired in Others." *J Social Psychol* 13:341–9 My '41. * *(PA* 15:4758)
20. KUHLEN, RAYMOND G. "Changes in the Attitudes of Students and Relations of Test Responses to Judgments of Associates." *Sch & Soc* 53:514–9 Ap 19 '41. * *(PA* 15:3513)
21. KUHLEN, RAYMOND GERHARDT. *An Analysis of Certain Personality Test Data With Reference to Cultural Backgrounds.* Doctor's thesis, Ohio State University (Columbus, Ohio), 1941.
22. DUREA, M. A. "A Comparison of Schizophrenia and Manic-Depressive With Reference to Emotional Maturity." *J Nerv & Mental Dis* 96:663–7 D '42. * *(PA* 17:850)
23. ODOROFF, M. E., and HARRIS, DALE B. "A Study of the Interest-Attitude Test Scores of Delinquent and Non-Delinquent Boys." *J Ed Psychol* 33:13–24 Ja '42. * *(PA* 16:3236)
24. CAPWELL, DORA F. "Personality Patterns of Adolescent Girls: 1, Girls Who Show Improvement in IQ." *J Appl Psychol* 29:212–28 Je '45. * *(PA* 19:3033)
25. CAPWELL, DORA F. "Personality Patterns of Adolescent Girls: 2, Delinquents and Non-Delinquents." *J Appl Psychol* 29:289–97 Ag '45. * *(PA* 20:191)
26. JACOBS, ALFRED. "Projection of Anxiety Aroused by Sexual Ideation in Mental Hospital Patients." *J Abn & Social Psychol* 46:160–4 Ap '51. * *(PA* 25:8202)

NAME INDEX

Capwell, D. F.: 24–5
Child, I. L.: 13
Durea, M. A.: 9–10, 15–9, 22
Fertman, M. H.: 15–6
Hardin, R. A.: 8
Harris, A. J.: 2
Harris, D. B.: 12, 23
Heston, J. C.: 17

Jacobs, A.: 26
Janney, J. E.: 11
Kuhlen, R. G.: 14, 20–1
Odoroff, M. E.: 12, 23
Pressey, L. C.: 1, 6–7
Pressey, S. L.: 1, 3, 6–7
Spencer, D.: *rev,* 2:1243.1
Thorndike, R. L.: 4–5

[364]

Primary Empathic Abilities. Grades 9–16 and adults; 1957–58; 7 scores: diplomacy, industrial, with insecure people, with conscientious middle class, with lower middle class, with stable young married people, with upper social levels; Willard Kerr; Psychometric Affiliates. * *Out of print.*

For additional information and a review by Robert L. Thorndike, see 5:99.

[365]

Problem Check List: Form for Schools of Nursing. Student nurses; 1945–48; adaptation of an earlier edition of *Mooney Problem Check List, 1950 Revision,* College Form (see 173); 13 scores: health and physical development, finances and living conditions, social and recreational activities, social-psychological relations, personal-psychological relations, courtship-sex-marriage, home and family, morals and religion, adjustment to school of nursing, the future-professional and educational, curriculum and school program, adjustment to human relationships in nursing, adjustment to administration of nursing care; Luella J. Morison, Mary Alice Price, and Ross L. Mooney; University Publication Sales, Ohio State University. * *Out of print.*

For additional information, see 4:82 (1 reference).

REFERENCES

1. See 4:82.
2. WILLMAN, MARILYN DAWN. *Attitudes and Problems of Student Nurses.* Doctor's thesis, University of Texas (Austin, Tex.), 1961. *(DA* 22:1953)

[365A]

★**Psychiatric History Schedule.** Psychiatric patients; 1968; PHS; an interview guide and rating scale dealing with aspects of a subject's history which are of importance for evaluating lifetime severity of psychiatric illness, prognosis and psychiatric diagnosis; available only as a part of *Current and Past Psychopathology Scales* (see 53A); Robert L. Spitzer, Jean Endicott, and George M. Cohen; Biometrics Research, New York State Psychiatric Institute. * *Out of print.*

[366]

Pupil Adjustment Inventory. Grades kgn–12; 1957; ratings in 7 areas: academic, social, emotional, physical, activities and interests, school's influence on pupil, home background; Houghton Mifflin Co. * *Out of print.*

For additional information and reviews by Robert H. Bauernfeind and John Pierce-Jones, see 5:100 (1 excerpt).

[367]

Pupil Portraits. Grades 4–8; 1934–38; R. Pintner, J. B. Maller, G. Forlano, and H. C. Axelrod; Bureau of Publications. * *Out of print.*

For additional information and a review by Simon H. Tulchin, see 2:1244 (2 references).

REFERENCES

1–2. See 2:1244.
3. PINTNER, R., and FORLANO, G. "Personality Tests of Partially Sighted Children." *J Appl Psychol* 27:283–7 Je '43. * (*PA* 17:3833)

[368]

Radio Checklist. Grades 9–12; 1939; Evaluation in the Eight Year Study, Progressive Education Association. *Out of print.*

For additional information, see 2:1245.

[369]

Recreation Inquiry. Grades 9–16; 1941; scores for knowledge, interest, membership, and activity in 10 areas: sports, games, social, hobbies, honoraries, literary, subject clubs, religious, music, total; Richard Wilkinson and Sidney L. Pressey; Psychological Corporation. * *Out of print.*

For additional information and reviews by Theodore F. Lentz and Louis Long, see 3:70 (2 references).

REFERENCES

1–2. See 3:70.
3. BEGELMAN, JACK. *Relationships of Body Build, Physical Performance, Intelligence, and Recreational Interests, to Occupational Choice.* Doctor's thesis, University of Michigan (Ann Arbor, Mich.), 1951.

[370]

Report Form on Temperament and Social Behavior. Ages 2–7; 1940; for recording observations; C. W. Valentine; the Author. * *Out of print.*

For additional information, see 2:1247 (1 reference).

[371–2]

[Rosander Social Attitude Scales.] Grades 7–16 and adults; 1937; 3 scales: *Democracy Scale, Federal Constitution Scale, Social Justice Scale;* A. C. Rosander; Association Press. * *Out of print.*

For additional information and reviews by H. H. Remmers and Goodwin Watson, see 1:902.

[373]

Scale for Evaluating the School Behavior of Children Ten to Fifteen. Ages 10–15; 1933; 9 scores: relation to others generally, respect for rights of others, relation to teacher, relation to other pupils, initiative, health habits, general interests, scholarship and study habits, total; Margaret L. Hayes; Psychological Corporation. * *Out of print.*

For additional information, see 1:926 (1 excerpt).

REFERENCES

1. HAYES, MARGARET. "A Scale for Evaluating Adolescent Personality." *J Genetic Psychol* 44:206–22 Mr '34. * (*PA* 8:4629)
2. POWELL, LEE, and LASLETT, H. R. "A Survey of the

Social Development of the 10th, 11th, and 12th Grade Pupils in a Small High School." *J Exp Ed* 9:361–3 Je '41. * (*PA* 15:4746)

[374]

Scale of Beliefs for Junior High School: Tests 4.4 and 4.5. Grades 7–9; 1940; adaptation of *Scale of Beliefs: Tests 4.21 and 4.31;* Evaluation in the Eight Year Study, Progressive Education Association. * *Out of print.*

For additional information, see 2:1251 (1 reference).

[375]

Scale of Beliefs: Tests 4.21 and 4.31. Grades 9–12; 1937–39; revision of Tests 4.2 and 4.3; 4 scores (liberalism, conservatism, uncertainty, consistency) in each of 6 areas (democracy, economic relations, labor and unemployment, race, nationalism, militarism) and the total; Evaluation in the Eight Year Study, Progressive Education Association. * *Out of print.*

For additional information, see 2:1250 (7 references).

REFERENCES

1–7. See 2:1250.
8. MURRAY, WALTER I. "A Study of an Aspect of Social Sensitivity of Some Negro High School Pupils." *J Negro Ed* 14:149–52 w '45. * (*PA* 19:2302)

[376]

Schrammel-Gorbutt Personality Adjustment Scale. Grades 7–16 and adults; 1943; H. E. Schrammel and Dorothy Gale Gorbutt; Bureau of Educational Measurements. * *Out of print.*

For additional information and reviews by Raleigh M. Drake and Nelson G. Hanawalt, see 3:92.

[377]

Selective Vocabulary Test. Ages 13 and over; 1944; a disguised test of masculinity-femininity; Patrick Slater; George G. Harrap & Co. Ltd. * *Out of print.*

For additional information and a review by James Maxwell, see 4:85 (2 references); for reviews by Jack W. Dunlap and Starke R. Hathaway, see 3:93.

[378]

A Self-Appraisal Schedule. Grades 9–16 and adults; 1937; a measure of persistence; C. K. A. Wang; C. H. Stoelting Co. * *Out of print.*

For additional information, see 1:927.

REFERENCE

1. WANG, CHARLES K. A. "A Scale for Measuring Persistence." *J Social Psychol* 3:79–90 F '32. * (*PA* 6:2049)

[379]

Self-Perception Inventory: An Adjustment Survey With Special Reference to the Speech Situation. High school and college; 1940–54; formerly called *Personal-Social Adjustment Inventory;* 8 scores: self-centered introversion, objective introversion, self-centered extroversion, objective extroversion, self-centeredness, objectivity, introversion, extroversion; Lawrence W. Miller and Elwood Murray; University of Denver Bookstores. * *Out of print.*

For additional information and a review by C. R. Strother, see 5:109.

[380]

Sense of Humor Test, Second Edition. Ages 16 and over; 1939–43; A. A. Roback; Sci-Art Publishers. * *Out of print.*

For additional information, see 3:94.

[381]

Social Distance Scale, Seventh Experimental Edition. Ages 15 and over; 1925–51; Emory S. Bogardus; the Author. * *Out of print.*

a) ETHNIC DISTANCE SCALE. 1925–51; formerly called *Racial Distance.*
b) OCCUPATION DISTANCE. 1925.
c) RELIGIOUS DISTANCE. 1925.
d) ECONOMIC DISTANCE. 1925.

For additional information and a review by Donald T. Campbell, see 4:88 (19 references).

REFERENCES

1–19. See 4:88.
20. BOGARDUS, EMORY S. "Scales in Social Research." *Sociol & Social Res* 24:69–75 S–O '39. *
21. BOGARDUS, EMORY S. "Measuring Changes in Ethnic Reactions." Discussion by Arnold M. Rose. *Am Sociol R* 16:48–53 F '51. *
22. CAMPBELL, DONALD T. "The Bogardus Social Distance Scale." *Sociol & Social Res* 36:322–6 My–Je '52. * (*PA* 27:5794)
23. LAMBERT, WALLACE E. "Comparison of French and American Modes of Response to the Bogardus Social Distance Scale." *Social Forces* 31:155–60 D '52. * (*PA* 27:5797)
24. CASSEL, RUSSELL N. "The Relationship of Certain Factors to the Level of Aspiration and Social Distance for Forty Four Air Force Prisoners." *J Crim Law & Criminology* 44:604–10 Ja–F '54. * (*PA* 29:1195)
25. PROTHRO, E. TERRY, and MELIKIAN, LEVON. "Social Distance and Social Change in the Near East." *Sociol & Social Res* 37:3–11 S–O '52. *
26. PROTHRO, E. TERRY, and MILES, OTHA KING. "Social Distance in the Deep South as Measured by a Revised Bogardus Scale." *J Social Psychol* 37:171–4 My '53. * (*PA* 28:2495)
27. BARDIS, PANOS D. "Social Distance Among Foreign Students." *Sociol & Social Res* 41:112–4 N–D '56. * (*PA* 32:881)
28. BEST, WALLACE H., and SOHNER, CHARLES P. "Social Distance Methodology in the Measurement of Political Attitudes." *Sociol & Social Res* 40:266–70 Mr–Ap '56. * (*PA* 31:4501)
29. SIEGEL, ARTHUR I., and GREER, F. LOYAL. "A Variation of the Bogardus Technique as a Measure of Perceived Prejudice." *J Social Psychol* 43:275–81 My '56. *
30. BOGARDUS, EMORY S. "Racial Distance Changes in the United States During the Past Thirty Years." *Sociol & Social Res* 43:127–35 N–D '58. * (*PA* 34:1208)
31. MURASKIN, JUDITH, and IVERSON, MARVIN A. "Social Expectancy as a Function of Judged Social Distance." *J Social Psychol* 48:11–4 Ag '58. * (*PA* 34:5825)
32. BARDIS, PANOS D. "Social Distance Among Gymnasium Students in Southern Greece." *Sociol & Social Res* 45:430–34 Jl '61. *
33. HARRIGAN, JOHN E.; DOLE, ARTHUR A.; and VINACKE, W. EDGAR. "A Study of Indignation-Bigotry and Extrapunitiveness in Hawaii." *J Social Psychol* 55:105–12 O '61. * (*PA* 36:4GD05H)
34. BARDIS, PANOS D. "Social Distance in a Greek Metropolitan City." *Social Sci* 37:108–11 Ap '62. *
35. SINHA, A. K. P., and UPADHYAYA, O. P. "Eleven Ethnic Groups on a Social Distance Scale." *J Social Psychol* 57:49–54 Je '62. * (*PA* 37:2993)
36. BRODY, EUGENE B., and DERBYSHIRE, ROBERT L. "Prejudice in American Negro College Students: Mental Status, Antisemitism and Antiforeign Prejudice." *Arch Gen Psychiatry* 9:619–28 D '63. * (*PA* 38:8253)
37. CARMICHAEL, JACK JOE. *Some Relationships of Denominational Affiliation to Selected Personal Characteristics of Male College Students.* Doctor's thesis, Ohio University (Athens, Ohio), 1963. (*DA* 23:2787)
38. MARTIN, JOHN W. "Social Distance and Social Stratification." *Sociol & Social Res* 47:179–86 Ja '63. * (*PA* 38:2535)
39. ADINARAYAN, S. P., and SWAMINATHAN, M. "Attitudes and Adjustment Problems of African Students in India." *J Social Psychol* 63:65–72 Je '64. * (*PA* 39:2838)
40. DERBYSHIRE, ROBERT L., and BRODY, EUGENE. "Social Distance and Identity Conflict in Negro College Students." *Sociol & Social Res* 48:301–14 Ap '64. * (*PA* 39:4733)
41. FAGAN, JOEN, and O'NEILL, MARION. "A Comparison of Social-Distance Scores Among College-Student Samples." *J Social Psychol* 66:281–90 Ag '65. * (*PA* 39:14943)
42. LEVER, H. "An Experimental Modification of Social Distance in South Africa." *Hum Relations* 18:149–54 My '65. * (*PA* 39:14964)
43. NATARAJ, P. "Social Distance Within and Between Castes and Religious Groups of College Girls." *J Social Psychol* 65:135–40 F '65. * (*PA* 39:12144)
44. RAO, T. NARAYANA, and PARAMESWARAN, E. G. "The

Effect of Duration of Hostel Stay on Social Distance Patterns." *Res B Dept Psychol Osmania Univ* 1:25–34 Mr '65. * (*PA* 39:14916)
45. LANDIS, JUDSON R.; DATWYLER, DARRYL; and DORN, DEAN S. "Race and Social Class as Determinants of Social Distance." *Sociol & Social Res* 51:78–86 O '66. * (*PA* 41:505)
46. BOGARDUS, EMORY S. *A Forty Year Racial Distance Study.* Los Angeles, Calif.: University of Southern California, 1967. Pp. iii, 49. *
47. BROWN, ROBERT L. "Social Distance and the Ethiopian Students." *Sociol & Social Res* 52:101–16 O '67. * (*PA* 42:693)
48. PRAKASH, JAI, and REDDY, B. G. "A Study of Social Distance and Order of Preferences Among Some Social and Caste Groups." *Indian J Social Work* 28:221–8 Jl '67. * (*PA* 42:5444)
49. AMES, RICHARD G.; MORIWAKI, SHARON Y.; and BASU, A. K. "Sex Differences in Social Distance: A Research Report." *Sociol & Social Res* 52:280–9 Ap '68. * (*PA* 42:12001)
50. BENTON, R. G.; SIEGEL, RISE; DERRICK, J.; and WALLACE, J. "Social-Distance Preferences Among Female and Male Medical Students and Cardiac Patients Toward Various Diseases and Disabilities." *Percept & Motor Skills* 27:512–4 O '68. * (*PA* 43:5803)
51. BOGARDUS, EMORY S. "Comparing Racial Distance in Ethiopia, South Africa and the United States." *Sociol & Social Res* 52:149–56 Ja '68. * (*PA* 42:8805)
52. LEVER, H. "Ethnic Preferences of White Residents in Johannesburg." *Sociol & Social Res* 52:157–73 Ja '68. * (*PA* 42:8841)
53. ZAIDI, S. M. HAFEEZ. "A Study of Social Distance as Perceived by Students of Karachi University." *J Social Psychol* 71:197–207 Ap '67. * (*PA* 41:8811)

NAME INDEX

Adinarayan, S. P.: 39	Landis, J. R.: 45
Ames, R. G.: 49	Lever, H.: 42, 52
Bardis, P. D.: 27, 32, 34	Martin, J. W.: 38
Basu, A. K.: 49	Melikian, L.: 25
Bell, H. V.: 13, 18	Miles, O. K.: 26
Benton, R. G.: 50	Moriwaki, S. Y.: 49
Best, W. H.: 28	Muraskin, J.: 31
Bogardus, E. S.: 1–3, 7, 9, 14–6, 20–1, 30, 46, 51	Nataraj, P.: 43
Brody, E.: 40	O'Neill, M.: 41
Brody, E. B.: 36	Parameswaran, E. G.: 44
Brooks, L. M.: 8	Prakash, J.: 48
Brown, R. L.: 47	Prothro, E. T.: 25–6
Campbell, D. T.: 22; rev, 4:88	Rao, T. N.: 44
	Reddy, B. G.: 48
Carmichael, J. J.: 37	Romney, A. K.: 19
Cassell, R. N.: 24	Rose, A. M.: 21
Datwyler, D.: 45	Sartain, A. Q.: 18
Davidoff, M. D.: 17	Schenk, Q. F.: 19
Derbyshire, R. L.: 36, 40	Siegel, A. I.: 29
Derrick, J.: 50	Siegel, R.: 50
Dole, A. A.: 33	Sinha, A. K. P.: 35
Dorn, D. S.: 45	Sohner, C. P.: 28
Fagan, J.: 41	Spoerl, D. T.: 12
Ford, R. N.: 11	Swaminathan, M.: 39
Greer, F. L.: 29	Upadhyaya, O. P.: 35
Harrigan, J. E.: 33	Vinacke, W. E.: 33
Hendrikson, G.: 4–6	Wallace, J.: 50
Iverson, M. A.: 31	Zaidi, S. M. H.: 53
Lambert, W. E.: 23	Zeligs, R.: 4–6, 10

[382]

Social Orientation. College students; 1935; attitudes toward problems involving social conflict; J. B. Maller and Harold S. Tuttle; the Authors. * *Out of print.*

For additional information and a review by Charles C. Peters, see 1:903.

[383]

Social Participation Scale, 1952 Edition. Adults; 1928–52; F. Stuart Chapin; University of Minnesota Press. * *Out of print.*

For additional information, see 5:113.

[384]

Social Personality Inventory for College Women. College women; 1937–42; self-esteem; A. H. Maslow; Consulting Psychologists Press, Inc. * *Out of print.*

For additional information and a review by Nelson G. Hanawalt, see 3:97 (10 references).

REFERENCES

1–10. See 3:97.
11. MASLOW, A. H. "Self-Esteem (Dominance-Feeling) and Sexuality." Abstract. *Psychol B* 37:504 Jl '40. * (*PA* 14:5596, title only)
12. READER, NATALIE, and ENGLISH, HORACE B. "Personality Factors in Adolescent Female Friendships." *J Consult Psychol* 11:212–20 Jl–Ag '47. * (*PA* 22:261)
13. SANFORD, NEVITT; WEBSTER, HAROLD; and FREEDMAN, MERVIN. "Impulse Expression as a Variable of Personality." *Psychol Monogr* 71(11):1–21 '57. * (*PA* 33:3336)
14. HANAWALT, NELSON G. "Feelings of Security and of Self-Esteem in Relation to Religious Belief." *J Social Psychol* 59:347–53 Ap '63.* (*PA* 38:744)
15. DICKEY, LOIS EDITH. *Projection of the Self Through Judgments of Clothed-Figures and Its Relation to Self-Esteem, Security-Insecurity and to Selected Clothing Behaviors.* Doctor's thesis, Pennsylvania State University (University Park, Pa.), 1967. (*DA* 29:1080B)

[385]

Social Problems: Test 1.42. Grades 9–12; 1938–40; revision of Tests 1.4 and 1.41; 16 scores in 4 areas: relation of principles to chosen courses of action, undesirable reasons for action choice, social values of action choice, social values of reasons; Evaluation in the Eight Year Study, Progressive Education Association. * *Out of print.*

For additional information, see 2:1254 (1 reference).

[386]

Straus Rural Attitudes Profile. Adults; 1956–59; SRAP; 5 scores: innovation proneness, rural life preference, primary group preference, economic motivation, total; Murray A. Straus; Washington State University. * *Out of print.*

For additional information, see 6:181 (1 reference, 1 excerpt).

[387]

Student Questionnaire. Grades 7–14; 1932–40; 8 adjustment scores: curriculum, social life of school, administration, teachers, other pupils, home and family, personal, total; Percival M. Symonds and Virginia Lee Block; Bureau of Publications. * *Out of print.*

For additional information and a review by Simon H. Tulchin, see 3:98.

[388]

Study of Attitudes Toward the Administration of Justice. College and adults; 1938; [F. C. Sumner]; the Author. * *Out of print.*

For additional information, see 2:1255 (1 reference).

[389]

Survey of Attitudes and Beliefs. Grades 9–12; 1954–55; 3 scores: society, education and work, sex-marriage-family; Leslie W. Nelson; Science Research Associates, Inc. * *Out of print.*

For additional information and reviews by Donald T. Campbell and C. Robert Pace, see 5:116.

[390]

Syracuse Scales of Social Relations. Grades 5–6, 7–9, 10–12; 1958–59; SSSR; pupil ratings of need interactions with classmates and others; Eric F. Gardner and George Thompson; Harcourt, Brace & World, Inc. * *Out of print.*

a) ELEMENTARY LEVEL. Grades 5–6; 4 scores: 2 ratings (made, received) for each of 2 needs (succorance, achievement-recognition).
b) JUNIOR HIGH LEVEL. Grades 7–9; 4 scores: 2 ratings (made, received) for each of 2 needs (succorance, deference).
c) SENIOR HIGH LEVEL. Grades 10–12; 4 scores: 2

ratings (made, received) for each of 2 needs (succorance, playmirth).

For additional information and reviews by Åke Bjerstedt and Donald T. Campbell, see 6:186 (16 references, 1 excerpt).

REFERENCES

1–16. See 6:186.
17. deJUNG, JOHN E. "Effects of Rater Frames of Reference on Peer Ratings." *J Exp Ed* 33:121–31 w '64. * (*PA* 39:7497)
18. NELSON, ROBERT EUGENE. *A Study of the Intra-Faculty Sociometric Position of the Teacher of the Educable Mentally Retarded.* Doctor's thesis, Syracuse University (Syracuse, N.Y.), 1964. (*DA* 25:5746)
19. ZIMPFER, DAVID GEORGE. *The Relationship of Self Concept to Certain Affective Dimensions in Multiple Counseling.* Doctor's thesis, State University of New York at Buffalo (Buffalo, N.Y.), 1964. (*DA* 25:3412)
20. KATZ, LYNN FRANCES. *The Prediction of Cooperative Behavior in Children Through the Use of Sociometric Scores.* Doctor's thesis, University of Pittsburgh (Pittsburgh, Pa.), 1965. (*DA* 27:1280B)
21. deJUNG, JOHN E. "Modification of the Syracuse Scales of Social Relations for Administration in the Third and Fourth Grades and in Special Classes for the Mentally Retarded." *Psychol Rep* 18:295–327 F '66. * (*PA* 40:6973)
22. WEATHERFORD, ROBERT R., and HORROCKS, JOHN E. "Peer Acceptance and Under- and Over-Achievement in School." *J Psychol* 66:215–20 Jl '67. * (*PA* 41:14185)
23. MEYER, WILLIAM J., and BARBOUR, MARY A. "Generality of Individual and Group Social Attractiveness Over Several Rating Situations." *J Genetic Psychol* 113:101–8 S '68. *

[391]

Teacher's Rating Scales for Pupil Adjustment. Grades kgn–14; 1937; 5 ratings: intellectual characteristics, work and study habits, emotional adjustment, social adjustment, scholastic achievement; Frank N. Freeman and Ethel Kawin; University of Chicago Press. * *Out of print.*

For additional information and a review by Bessie Lee Gambrill, see 2:1256.

[392]

Temperament and Character Test. College and adults; 1950–52; TCT; 11 scores: nervous, sentimental, choleric, passionate, sanguine, phlegmatic, amorphous, apathetic, emotivity, activity, perseveration; [Lidec, Inc.]. * *Out of print.*

For additional information, see 5:115.

[393]

Tentative Check List for Determining Attitudes on Fifty Crucial Social, Economic, and Political Problems. Grades 9–16 and adults; 1935–39; Herbert B. Bruner, Arthur V. Linden, and Hugh B. Wood; Bureau of Publications. * *Out of print.*

For additional information, see 2:1257.

[394]

Test of Social Attitudes. Grades 13–17; 1939; 8 scores: negro, war, economics and labor, social life and convention, government, religion, miscellaneous, total; E. C. Hunter; Psychological Corporation. * *Out of print.*

For additional information, see 2:1260.

REFERENCES

1. HUNTER, E. C. "Changes in General Attitudes of Women Students During Four Years in College." *J Social Psychol* 16:243–57 N '42. * (*PA* 17:901)
2. HUNTER, E. C. "Attitudes of College Freshmen, 1934–1949." *J Psychol* 31:281–96 Ap '51. * (*PA* 26:1091)

[395]

Tests of the Socially Competent Person. Grades 7–12; 1936–37; 5 scores: health, personal economics, family and community relationships, social-civic problems, total; Paul R. Mort, Ralph B. Spence, V. C. Arnspiger, and Laura K. Eads; Bureau of Publications. * *Out of print.*

For additional information and reviews by Alvin C. Eurich, Warren G. Findley, and Pedro T. Orata, see 2:1259 (1 reference); for reviews by Douglas E. Scates and Hilda Taba, consult 1:1154.

REFERENCES

1. See 2:1259.
2. RESNICK, JOSEPH. "A Study of Some Relationships Between High School Grades and Certain Aspects of Adjustment." *J Ed Res* 44:321–40 Ja '51. * (*PA* 25:8286)

[396]

[Torgerson's Inventories and Record Forms.] Grades kgn–12; 1947; "6 inventories and record forms"; Theodore L. Torgerson; the Author. *Out of print.*
a) CLASS SUMMARY OF BEHAVIOR SYMPTOMS AND DISABILITIES.
b) BEHAVIOR INVENTORIES.
c) HOME ENVIRONMENT INVENTORY.
d) SPEECH INVENTORY.
e) DEVELOPMENTAL INVENTORY OF BACKGROUND FACTORS.
f) CASE STUDY FORM.
For additional information and a review by Harold H. Abelson, see 3:105 (1 reference).

[397]

V.G.C. Personality Adjustment Indicator or Inventory. Grades 9–16; 1943–44; an adaptation of *Adjustment Inventory,* Student Form by Hugh M. Bell; 5 scores: home, health, social, emotional, total; M. D. Parmenter; Vocational Guidance Centre. * *Out of print.*
For references to reviews of the *Adjustment Inventory,* see 5.

[398]

Walther Social Attitudes Test. Grades 12–16; 1937; E. Curt Walther; the Author. *Out of print.*
For additional information, see 2:1261.

[399]

Washburne Social-Adjustment Inventory. Ages 12 and over; 1932–40; 9 scores: truthfulness, happiness, alienation, sympathy, purpose, impulse-judgment, control, wishes, total; John N. Washburne; Harcourt, Brace & World, Inc. * *Out of print.*
For additional information and a review by William Seeman, see 4:95 (12 references); see also 3:110 (11 references, 2 excerpts) and 2:1262 (4 references); for a review by Daniel A. Prescott, see 1:928.

REFERENCES

1–4. See 2:1262.
5–15. See 3:110.
16–27. See 4:95.
28. SMITH, BENJAMIN FRANKLIN. *A Critical Analysis of the Relationship Between Occupational Goals, Social Adjustment and Social Status of High School Seniors in Urban Negro High Schools in Two States.* Doctor's thesis, New York University (New York, N.Y.), 1951. (*DA* 12:162)
29. MITCHELL, IRVING EUGENE. *The Maturity of Delinquent and Non-Delinquent Adolescents as Defined by the Developmental Task Concept.* Doctor's thesis, Boston University (Boston, Mass.), 1957. (*DA* 19:593)
30. TOPETZES, NICK JOHN. "A Program for the Selection of Trainees in Physical Medicine." *J Exp Ed* 25:263–311 Je '57. * (*PA* 33:7024)
31. HARRELL, THOMAS W. "The Relation of Test Scores to Sales Criteria." *Personnel Psychol* 13:65–9 sp '60. * (*PA* 35:7192)
32. KORZI, JOHN R. "The Validity of *The Washburne Social Adjustment Inventory* in Measuring College Freshman Adjustment." *Personnel & Guid J* 40:462–6 Ja '62. * (*PA* 36:5KD62K)
33. ROHRS, DENNIS KERLIN. *Predicting Academic Success in a Liberal Arts College Music Education Program.* Doctor's thesis, State University of Iowa (Iowa City, Iowa), 1962. (*DA* 23:2937)
34. WALKER, FLOYD ALEXANDER. *The Social and Emotional*

Adjustment of Winning and Losing Football Teams. Doctor's thesis, University of Arkansas (Fayetteville, Ark.), 1966. (*DA* 27:1254A)

NAME INDEX

Burke, H. R.: 21
Capwell, D. F.: 9
Davidoff, P.: 7
Dillingham, H. I.: 17
Fessler, M. H.: 18
Flemming, C. W.: 14
Flemming, E. G.: 14
Forlano, G.: 10
Gordon, H. C.: 7
Gotham, R. E.: 11, 20
Gould, G.: 15
Green, M. E.: 25
Harrell, T. W.: 31
Husted, D.: 19
Kirkpatrick, F. H.: 10
Korzi, J. R.: 32
Lough, O. M.: 25
Marsh, C. J.: 8
Mitchell, I. E.: 29
Musselman, J. W.: 6
Patterson, R. E.: 16
Postel, H.: *exc*, 3:110
Prescott, D. A.: *rev*, 1:928
Rohrs, D. K.: 33
Rolfe, J. F.: 12
Rostker, L. E.: 13
Schmid, J.: 22, 26
Schwartz, A. N.: 27
Seeman, W.: *rev*, 4:95
Smith, B. F.: 28
Stepat, D. L.: 23
Topetzes, N. J.: 30
Walker, F. A.: 34
Washburne, J. N.: 1–5
Zakolski, F. C.: 24

[400]

Weitzman's Inventory of Social Behavior. Ages 16–25; 1941; personal competence and independence; Ellis Weitzman; Sheridan Supply Co. * *Out of print.*
For additional information and reviews by Louis Long and Goodwin Watson, see 3:111 (3 references).

[401]

What Do You Think? Grades 7–12; 1934–35; Victor H. Noll; Bureau of Publications. * *Out of print.*
For additional information and a review by Ralph K. Watkins, see 2:1263 (3 references, 1 excerpt); for a review by Francis D. Curtis, consult 1:1139.

[402]

What Should Our Schools Do? A Poll of Public Opinion on the School Program. Adults; 1938; Paul R. Mort, F. G. Cornell, and Norman H. Hinton; Bureau of Publications. * *Out of print.*
For additional information, see 2:1264 (1 excerpt).

[403]

What Would You Do? A Survey of Student Opinion. Grades 7–12; 1939; 2 parts; Ruth E. Eckert and Howard E. Wilson; Committee on Publications, Harvard Graduate School of Education. * *Out of print.*
a) PART I, SCHOOL AFFAIRS.
b) PART II, COMMUNITY AFFAIRS.
For additional information, see 2:1265 (1 reference).

[404]

Willoughby Emotional Maturity Scale. College and adults; 1931; Raymond R. Willoughby; Stanford University Press. * *Out of print.*
For additional information and a review by Lysle W. Croft, see 4:96 (7 references).

[405]

Wilson Scales of Stability and Instability. Grades 9–16 and adults; 1941; 2 scores: stability, instability; Matthew H. Wilson; Bureau of Educational Measurements. * *Out of print.*
For additional information and reviews by Paul E. Meehl and Katherine W. Wilcox, see 3:112.

[406]

Winnetka Scale for Rating School Behavior and Attitudes. Nursery school and grades 1–6; 1935–37; 5 scores: cooperation, social consciousness, emotional adjustment, leadership, responsibility; Dorothy Van Alstyne and the Winnetka Public School Faculty; Winnetka Educational Press. * *Out of print.*

For additional information and a review by Harriet M. Barthelmess, see 1:929.

REFERENCES

1. VAN ALSTYNE, DOROTHY. "A New Scale for Rating School Behavior and Attitudes in the Elementary School." *J Ed Psychol* 27:677–93 D '36. * (*PA* 11:1978)
2. VAN ALSTYNE, DOROTHY; HATTWICK, LABERTA WEISS; and TOTTEN, HELEN. "A New Scale for Rating School Behavior and Attitudes." *El Sch J* 37:115–21 O '36. * (*PA* 11:988)
3. ALSCHULER, ROSE H., and HATTWICK, LABERTA WEISS. "Measuring Social and Emotional Development." *Nat El Sch Prin* 16:502–7 Jl '37. *
4. LEON, DONALD A.; COLLINS, DWANE R.; and KOO, GLADYS Y. "Factor Analysis of the Winnetka Scale for Rating School Behavior." *J Exp Ed* 33:373–8 su '65. * (*PA* 39:12297)
5. GREENBERG, MARVIN, and MACGREGOR, BEATRIX. "Correlation of Musical Talents and Behavioral Traits." *Council Res Music Ed* 7:24–33 sp '66. * (*PA* 40:11155)

[407]

The Wishing Well. Grades 4–7; 1945–51; analysis of children's needs; 9 scores: belonging, achievement, economic security, fears, love and affection, guilt, sharing, world outlook, total; Evaluation Division, Bureau of Educational Research, Ohio State University. * *Out of print.*

For additional information, see 4:98 (1 reference).

[408]

Wittenborn Psychiatric Rating Scales. Mental patients; 1955; 9 ratings: acute anxiety, conversion hysteria, manic, depressed, schizophrenic, paranoid, paranoid schizophrenic, hebephrenic schizophrenic, phobic compulsive; J. Richard Wittenborn; Psychological Corporation. * *Out of print.* (A revised edition was prepared by the author in 1964 for use in his own research.)

For additional information and reviews by H. J. Eysenck and Maurice Lorr, see 5:123 (15 references, 1 excerpt).

REFERENCES

1–15. See 5:123.
16. WITTENBORN, J. R. "A New Procedure for Evaluating Mental Hospital Patients." *J Consult Psychol* 14:500–1 D '50. * (*PA* 26:938)
17. WITTENBORN, J. R., and LESSER, GERALD S. "Biographical Factors and Psychiatric Symptoms." *J Clin Psychol* 7:317–22 O '51. * (*PA* 26:3383)
18. WITTENBORN, J. R.; BELL, ELAINE G.; and LESSER, GERALD S. "Symptom Patterns Among Organic Patients of Advanced Age." *J Clin Psychol* 7:328–31 O '51. * (*PA* 26:3560)
19. WITTENBORN, J. R.; MANDLER, GEORGE; and WATERHOUSE, IAN K. "Symptom Patterns in Youthful Mental Hospital Patients." *J Clin Psychol* 7:323–7 O '51. * (*PA* 26:3561)
20. HOLZBERG, JULES D., and WITTENBORN, J. RICHARD. "The Quantified Multiple Diagnostic Procedure in Psychiatric Classification." *J Clin Psychol* 9:145–8 Ap '53. * (*PA* 28:2817)
21. WITTENBORN, J. R., and KLINE, NATHAN S. "Drive Strength and Symptom Manifestations." *J Abn & Social Psychol* 58:300–4 My '59. * (*PA* 34:5358)
22. WITTENBORN, J. R.; PLANTE, MARC; and BURGESS, FRANCES. "A Comparison of Physicians' and Nurses' Symptom Ratings." *J Nerv & Mental Dis* 133:514–8 D '61. *
23. WITTENBORN, J. R. "The Dimensions of Psychosis." *J Nerv & Mental Dis* 134:117–28 F '62. * (*PA* 37:1295)
24. SMITH, COLIN M.; McKERRACHER, D. G.; and McINTYRE, SHARON. "Care of the Certified Psychiatric Patient in the General Hospital: The Saskatoon Project." *Can Med Assn J* 88:360–4 F 16 '63. *
25. WITTENBORN, J. R., and PLANTE, MARC. "Patterns of Response to Placebo, Iproniazid and Electroconvulsive Therapy Among Young Depressed Females." *J Nerv & Mental Dis* 137:155–61 Ag '63. *
26. BRIGGS, PETER F. "The Inter-Relationships of Seven Criteria of Adjustment Among Psychiatric Clients Seeking Vocational Counseling." *J Clin Psychol* 21:433–5 O '65. * (*PA* 40:1760)
27. LEVEY, ARCHIBALD B., and SMITH, COLIN M. "Follow-Up and the Measurement of Change in Psychiatric Patients." *Acta Psychiatrica Scandinavica* 41(2):236–50 '65. * (*PA* 40:6712)
28. PETERS, PHYLLIS G. *A Study of Clinical Judgment:*
Prediction of Patient Behavior From Projective, Self-Rating and Behavior Rating Instruments. Doctor's thesis, Northwestern University (Evanston, Ill.), 1965. (*DA* 26:3489)
29. BRIGGS, PETER F., and YATER, ALLAN C. "Counseling and Psychometric Signs as Determinants in the Vocational Success of Discharged Psychiatric Patients." *J Clin Psychol* 22:100–4 Ja '66. * (*PA* 40:4472)
30. LYERLY, SAMUEL B., and ABBOTT, PRESTON S. "Wittenborn Psychiatric Rating Scales," pp. 32–6. In their *Handbook of Psychiatric Rating Scales (1950–1964).* Public Health Service Publication No. 1495. Washington, D.C.: United States Government Printing Office, 1966. Pp. v, 69. *
31. CRAIG, W. J. "Revised Scoring for the Wittenborn Psychiatric Rating Scales." *J Clin Psychol* 24:327–31 Jl '68. * (*PA* 42:16407)

NAME INDEX

[409]

Work Preference Inventory. Applicants for employment; 1946–50; 14 scores: reliability, creativeness, conservatism, ambition, masculinity, introversion, anxiety-depression, persuasive, social service, theoretical, artistic, mechanical, economic, scientific; Robert W. Henderson; the Author. * *Out of print.*

For additional information, see 4:99; for reviews by Edwin W. Davis, John C. Flanagan, and Gilbert J. Rich, see 3:113.

[410]

Wrightstone Scale of Civic Beliefs. Grades 9–12; 1938; J. Wayne Wrightstone; World Book Co. * *Out of print.*

For additional information and reviews by Stephen M. Corey and Harold Gulliksen, see 2:1266 (3 references).

[411]

Your Activities and Attitudes. Adults in later maturity; 1948–49; 2 scores: attitudes, activities; Ernest W. Burgess, Ruth S. Cavan, and Robert J. Havighurst; Science Research Associates, Inc. * *Out of print.*

For additional information, see 4:100 (4 references, 1 excerpt); for excerpts from related book reviews, see 4:101.

REFERENCES

1–4. See 4:100.
5. MOBERG, DAVID OSCAR. *Religion and Personal Adjustment in Old Age: A Study of Some Aspects of the Christian Religion in Relation to Personal Adjustment of the Aged in Institutions.* Doctor's thesis. University of Minnesota (Minneapolis, Minn.), 1952. (*DA* 12:341)
6. PAN, JU-SHU. "A Comparison of Factors in the Personal Adjustment of Old People in the Protestant Church Homes for the Aged and Old People Living Outside of Institutions." *J Social Psychol* 35:195–203 My '52. * (*PA* 27:3401)
7. BRITTON, JOSEPH H. "The Personal Adjustment of Retired School Teachers." *J Gerontol* 8:333–8 Jl '53. * (*PA* 28:8100)
8. PAN, JU-SHU. "Institutional and Personal Adjustment in Old Age." *J Genetic Psychol* 85:155–8 S '54. * (*PA* 29:5433)
9. LEPKOWSKI, J. RICHARD. "The Attitudes and Adjustments of Institutionalized and Non-Institutionalized Catholic Aged." *J Gerontol* 11:185–91 Ap '56. * (*PA* 31:713)

10. MOBERG, DAVID O. "Religious Activities and Personal Adjustment in Old Age." *J Social Psychol* 43:261–7 My '56. * (PA 33:3675)
11. NOLL, RACHEL PERKINS. *Insights of the Middle-Aged Child Concerning the Parent in a Home for Old People.* Doctor's thesis, Michigan State University (East Lansing, Mich.), 1959. (DA 21:314)
12. WOLFE, LLOYD MATHIAS. *A Study of the Relationship Between Lifelong Learning and Adjustment of Older People.* Doctor's thesis, University of Michigan (Ann Arbor, Mich.), 1963. (DA 24:603)

PROJECTIVE

[412]

The African T.A.T. Urban African adults; 1960–61; individual; 1 form ['60, 6 cards]; no manual; interpretive data presented in *1* below; no data on reliability; 100s. per set of cards, postage extra; [120] minutes; J. C. de Ridder; [Industrial Psychological Services]. *

For related book reviews not excerpted in this volume, consult the 6th (B153) MMY.

REFERENCES

1. See 6:200.
2. SHAW, LYNETTE. "The Practical Use of Projective Personality Tests as Accident Predictors." *Traffic Safety Res R* 9:34–72 Je '65. *

[413]

Association Adjustment Inventory. Normal and institutionalized adults; 1959; AAI; adaptation of *Kent-Rosanoff Free Association Test* (see 448); 13 scores: juvenility, psychotic responses, depressed-optimistic, hysteric-non-hysteric, withdrawal-sociable, paranoid-naive, rigid-flexible, schizophrenic-objective, impulsive-restrained, sociopathic-empathetic, psychosomapathic-physical contentment, anxious-relaxed, total; 1 form (4 pages); 2 editions: consumable, reusable; manual (15 pages); $5 per 20 tests; $4.50 per set of keys; separate answer sheets (IBM 805) must be used with reusable edition; $2.75 per 20 answer sheets; $4.50 per set of scoring stencils; $2.75 per 20 profiles; $1.75 per manual; $5 per specimen set; cash orders postpaid; (10–15) minutes; Martin M. Bruce; the Author. *

For reviews by W. Grant Dahlstrom and Bertram R. Forer, see 6:201 (1 excerpt).

[414]

The Auditory Apperception Test. Grades 9 and over; 1953; AAT; 1 form (10 sound-situations, each consisting of three sounds or dialogues) on five 7-inch records, 45 rpm; manual (23 pages); record booklet (8 pages); story booklet (11 pages); no data on reliability; $14.50 per set of records, 10 record booklets, 10 story booklets, and manual; $6.50 per 25 record booklets; $6.50 per 25 story booklets; $2 per manual; postpaid; specimen set not available; 50(80) or (50–80) minutes in 2 sessions; Western Psychological Services. *

For reviews by Kenneth L. Bean and Clifford H. Swensen, Jr., see 5:124 (3 references).

[415]

[Bender-Gestalt Test.] Ages 4 and over; 1938–69; individual; the original Bender-Gestalt is listed as *a* below; the modifications listed as *b-e* consist primarily of alterations in administration procedure, new scoring systems, or expanded interpretive procedures, rather than changes in the test materials; *b-e* use essentially the same administration procedure as the basic testing procedure; *c* and *d* provide, in addition,

for use of the materials as projective stimuli for associations.

a) VISUAL MOTOR GESTALT TEST. Ages 4 and over; 1938–46; VMGT; 1 form ('46, 9 cards); pictures are also available as 35 mm slides for group administration; manual ('38, see 5 below); directions for administering ('46, 8 pages); no data on reliability; $1.50 per set of cards and directions; $5.50 per manual; $10 per set of slides and manual; postpaid; [10] minutes; Lauretta Bender; American Orthopsychiatric Association, Inc. *
b) THE BENDER GESTALT TEST. Ages 4 and over; 1951; BGT; utilizes same test cards as *a;* scoring sheet ['51, 1 page]; manual ('51, see *41* below); $2.25 per pad of 50 scoring sheets; $8.25 per manual; postage extra; (10) minutes; Gerald R. Pascal and Barbara J. Suttell; Grune & Stratton, Inc. *
c) THE HUTT ADAPTATION OF THE BENDER-GESTALT TEST. Ages 7 and over; 1944–69; HABGT; formerly called *Revised Bender-Gestalt Test;* 1 form ['60, 9 cards, same as cards of *a* except for modification in 1 design and in drawing method throughout]; manual, second edition ('69, see *429* below); revised record form ('68, 4 pages); no data on reliability of scored factors; $1.25 per set of cards; $4 per 25 record forms; $6.75 per manual; postage extra; [45–60] minutes; Max L. Hutt; Grune & Stratton, Inc. *
d) THE BENDER VISUAL MOTOR GESTALT TEST FOR CHILDREN. Ages 7–11; 1962; utilizes same test cards as *a;* manual (72 pages); record form (4 pages); no data on reliability and validity; $2.50 per set of cards; $6.50 per 25 record forms; $6.50 per manual; postpaid; (10) minutes without associations; Aileen Clawson; Western Psychological Services. *
e) THE BENDER GESTALT TEST FOR YOUNG CHILDREN. Ages 5–10; 1964; a developmental scoring system; utilizes same test cards as *a;* manual (206 pages, see *259* below); $7.75 per manual, postage extra; administration time not reported; Elizabeth Munsterberg Koppitz; Grune & Stratton, Inc. *
f) THE VISUAL MOTOR GESTALT TEST TWO-COPY DRAWING FORM. 1964; 1 form (1 page plus backing sheet); $6.50 per 25 forms, postpaid; Western Psychological Services. *

For a review by C. B. Blakemore, see 6:203 (99 references, 1 excerpt); see also 5:172 (118 references); for reviews by Arthur L. Benton and Howard R. White, see 4:144 (34 references); see also 3:108 (8 references); for excerpts from related book reviews, see 4:145 and 3:109; for reviews not excerpted in this volume, consult the 6th (B268, B297, B487), 5th (B330), and 2nd (B843) MMY's.

REFERENCES

1–8. See 3:108.
9–42. See 4:144.
43–160. See 5:172.
161–259. See 6:203.
260. SULLIVAN, J. J., and WELSH, G. S. Chap. 9, "Results With the Bender Visual Motor Gestalt Test," pp. 31–5. In *Intelligence and Personality Factors Associated with Poliomyelitis Among School Age Children.* By E. Lakin Phillips, Isabel R. Berman, and Harold B. Hanson. Monographs of the Society for Research in Child Development, Serial No. 45; Vol. 12, No. 2. Washington, D.C.: the Society, 1948. Pp. vii, 60. *
261. POLITZER, FRANK. *An Exploratory Study of Ideomotor Action and Its Relation to Bender-Gestalt Performance.* Doctor's thesis, University of Pittsburgh (Pittsburgh, Pa.), 1951.
262. MALCOM, EDWARD VARTAN. *A Study of the Validity of Individual Personality Profiles Based on Each of Four Projective Techniques.* Doctor's thesis, University of Michigan (Ann Arbor, Mich.), 1952. (DA 12:221)
263. EAMES, THOMAS H. "Eye and Other Handicaps: Their Relation to Performance on a Visual Motor Gestalt Test." *Am J Ophthal* 36:112–4 Ja '53. * (PA 27:7572)
264. FELDMAN, IRVING S. "Psychological Differences Among Moron and Borderline Mental Defectives as a Function of Etiology: 1, Visual-Motor Functioning." *Am J Mental Def* 57:484–94 Ja '53. * (PA 27:6618)

265. FOSTER, ARTHUR LEE. *The Relationship Between EEG Abnormality, Psychological Factors and Delinquent Behavior.* Doctor's thesis, University of Houston (Houston, Tex.), 1956. (*DA* 16:2210)

266. MYDEN, WALTER DAVID. *An Interpretation and Evaluation of Certain Personality Characteristics Involved in Creative Production: An Investigation and Evaluation of Personality Structure and Characteristics of Creative Individuals in the Context of Psychoanalytic Theory and Ego Psychology.* Doctor's thesis, New York University (New York, N.Y.), 1956. (*DA* 17:897)

267. CONLIN, JOAN ELIZABETH. *Tactual Perception of the Blind: A Comparison of Reproductions by a Blind and Sighted Group to the Bender Gestalt Test.* Master's thesis, MacMurray College (Jacksonville, Ill.), 1957.

268. KAPLAN, HENRY KAY. *A Study of Relationships Between Handwriting Legibility and Perception Adjustment and Personality Factors.* Doctor's thesis, University of Wisconsin (Madison, Wis.), 1957. (*DA* 17:1950)

269. INGLIS, JAMES; COLWELL, CATHERINE; and POST, FELIX. "An Evaluation of the Predictive Power of a Test Known to Differentiate Between Elderly 'Functional' and 'Organic' Patients." *J Mental Sci* 106:1486–92 O '60. * (*PA* 35:5144)

270. FELDMANN, SHIRLEY CLARK. *Visual Perception Skills of Children and Their Relation to Reading.* Doctor's thesis, Columbia University (New York, N.Y.), 1961. (*DA* 22:1084)

271. CLEMENTS, SAM D., and PETERS, JOHN E. "Minimal Brain Dysfunction in the School-Age Child: Diagnosis and Treatment." *Arch Gen Psychiatry* 6:185–97 Mr '62. * (*PA* 37:3512)

272. SAFRIN, RENATE KERSTEN. *Differences in Visual Perception and in Visual-Motor Functioning Between Psychotic and Nonpsychotic Children.* Doctor's thesis, Columbia University (New York, N.Y.), 1962. (*DA* 23:1080)

273. SEVERSON, ROGER ALFRED. *Some Nonreading Correlates of Reading Retardation.* Doctor's thesis, State University of Iowa (Iowa City, Iowa), 1962. (*DA* 23:2798)

274. SKLAR, MAURICE. "Psychological Test Scores, Language Disturbances, and Autopsy Findings in Aphasia Patients." *Newsl Res Psychol* 4:65–79 Ag '62. *

275. SOLOMON, LILLIAN GREENBERG. *An Investigation of Visual Defect and Certain Cultural and Personality Factors in Juvenile Delinquency.* Doctor's thesis, University of Texas (Austin, Tex.), 1962. (*DA* 25:2617)

276. ABBOTT, ROBERT FRANKLIN. *The Prediction of First Grade Reading and Numbers Achievement by Means of Psychological Tests.* Doctor's thesis, University of Tennessee (Knoxville, Tenn.), 1963. (*DA* 25:1020)

277. BACHTOLD, LOUISE MARIE. *Differences in Personality, School Attitude, and Visual Motor Performance Among Specific Types of Underachievers.* Doctor's thesis, University of the Pacific (Stockton, Calif.), 1963. (*DA* 25:1730)

278. FLINN, DON E.; HARTMAN, BRYCE O.; POWELL, DOUGLAS H.; and McKENZIE, RICHARD E. "Psychiatric and Psychologic Evaluation," pp. 199–230. In *Aeromedical Evaluation for Space Pilots.* Edited by Lawrence E. Lamb. Brooks Air Force Base, Tex.: USAF School of Aerospace Medicine, July 1963. Pp. viii, 276. * (*PA* 38:4728)

279. FREED, EARL X. "The Group Bender-Gestalt Test as a Predictor of Length of Psychiatric Hospitalization." *Newsl Res Psychol* 5:9–10 F '63. *

280. FULLER, G. B., and LAIRD, J. T. "Comments and Findings About Rotations." *Percept & Motor Skills* 16:673–9 Je '63. * (*PA* 38:6107)

281. KEOGH, BARBARA K. "Form Copying Tests for Prediction of First Grade Reading." *Claremont Read Conf Yearb* 27:141–4 '63. *

282. KNAPP, PETER H., and BAHNSON, CLAUS BAHNE. "The Emotional Field: A Sequential Study of Mood and Fanstay in Two Asthmatic Patients." *Psychosom Med* 25:460–83 S–O '63. * (*PA* 38:9102)

283. KURLAND, HOWARD D.; YEAGER, CHARLES T.; and ARTHUR, RANSOM J. "Psychophysiologic Aspects of Severe Behavior Disorders: A Pilot Study." *Arch Gen Psychiatry* 8:599–604 Je '63. * (*PA* 38:6368)

284. BERG, WERNER. *The Effect of Aging on Tactual-Motor and Visual-Motor Performance.* Doctor's thesis, University of Tennessee (Knoxville, Tenn.), 1964. (*DA* 25:3105)

285. FREED, EARL X. "Frequencies of Rotations on Group and Individual Administrations of the Bender-Gestalt Test." *J Clin Psychol* 20:120–1 Ja '64. * (*PA* 39:10104)

286. FREED, EARL X. "Incidence of Bender-Gestalt Figure Rotations in Post-Lobotomy and Post-Leucotomy Psychiatric Patients." *Newsl Res Psychol* 6:17–8 N '64. *

287. FREED, EARL X. "The Use of a Bender-Gestalt Framing Stand." *Newsl Res Psychol* 6:38 My '64. *

288. GOLDFRIED, MARVIN R., and INGLING, JANE H. "The Connotative and Symbolic Meaning of the Bender Gestalt." *J Proj Tech & Pers Assess* 28:185–91 Je '64. * (*PA* 39:5148)

289. HAIN, JACK D. "The Bender Gestalt Test: A Scoring Method for Identifying Brain Damage." *J Consult Psychol* 28:34–40 F '64. * (*PA* 38:8416)

290. HARTMAN, WANDA L. *A Study of Some Factors in the Bender-Gestalt Reproductions of Demonstrable and Non-Demonstrable Brain Damaged Children.* Master's thesis, University of Tulsa (Tulsa, Okla.), 1964.

291. JAIN, K. S. PRABHACHANDRA. "An Organismic Study of Cognitive Errors." *Manas* 11(2):105–13 '64. * (*PA* 39:7392)

292. JERNIGAN, A. J. "Analyses of Bender Gestalt Figure Rotations in a GM&S Hospital Population." *Newsl Res Psychol* 6:14 N '64. *

293. LOVELL, K.; GRAY, E. A.; and OLIVER, D. E. "A Further Study of Some Cognitive and Other Disabilities in Backward Readers of Average Nonverbal Reasoning Scores." *Brit J Ed Psychol* 34:275–9 pt 3 '64. * (*PA* 39:8668)

294. MILLER, LOVICK C.; LOEWENFELD, RUTH; LINDER, RON; and TURNER, JACK. "Reliability of Koppitz' Scoring System for the Bender Gestalt." *J Clin Psychol* 19:211 Ap '64. * (*PA* 39:5081)

295. PASCAL, G. R., and THOROUGHMAN, J. C. "Relationship Between Bender-Gestalt Test Scores and the Response of Patients With Intractable Duodenal Ulcer to Surgery." *Newsl Res Psychol* 6:13 Ag '64. *

296. PASCAL, G. R., and THOROUGHMAN, J. C. "Relationship Between Bender-Gestalt Test Scores and the Response of Patients With Intractable Duodenal Ulcer to Surgery." *Psychosom Med* 26:625–7 S–O '64. * (*PA* 39:10697)

297. RUCKHABER, CHARLES J. "A Technique for Group Administration of the Bender Gestalt Test." *Psychol Sch* 1:53–6 Ja '64. *

298. SAFRIN, RENATE KERSTEN. "Differences in Visual Perception and in Visual-Motor Functioning Between Psychotic and Nonpsychotic Children." *J Consult Psychol* 28:41–5 F '64. * (*PA* 39:9025)

299. SCHORER, C. E. "Muscular Dystrophy and the Mind." *Psychosom Med* 26:5–13 Ja–F '64. * (*PA* 39:2402)

300. SILVER, ARCHIE A., and HAGIN, ROSA A. "Specific Reading Ability: Follow-Up Studies." *Am J Orthopsychiatry* 34:95–102 Ja '64. * (*PA* 39:2863)

301. VIITAMÄKI, R. OLAVI. "A Psychological Follow-up Study: Psychoses in Childhood, Part 2." *Acta Psychiatrica Scandinavica Supplementum* 40(174):33–93 '64. * (*PA* 39:8464)

302. WEINSTEIN, SIDNEY, and JOHNSON, LINDA. "The Bender-Gestalt Test in Differential Diagnosis of Temporal Lobectomy and Schizophrenia." *Percept & Motor Skills* 18:813–20 Je '64. * (*PA* 39:5107)

303. ANGLIN, RAYMOND; PULLEN, MAXWELL; and GAMES, PAUL. "Comparison of Two Tests of Brain Damage." *Percept & Motor Skills* 20:977–80 Je '65. * (*PA* 40:12567)

304. ARMSTRONG, RENATE GERBOTH. "A Re-evaluation of Copied and Recalled Bender-Gestalt Reproductions." *J Proj Tech & Pers Assess* 29:134–9 Je '65. * (*PA* 39:12276)

305. BENDER, LAURETTA. "On the Proper Use of the Bender Gestalt Test." *Percept & Motor Skills* 20:189–90 F '65. * (*PA* 39:10089)

306. CURNUTT, ROBERT, and COROTTO, LOREN V. "Syndrome-Correlates of Bender-Gestalt Performance." *Calif Mental Health Res Dig* 3:79–80 sp '65. *

307. DILLER, LEONARD, and WEINBERG, JOSEPH. "Bender Gestalt Test Distortions in Hemiplegia." *Percept & Motor Skills* 20:1313–23 Je '65. * (*PA* 39:15384)

308. DUBE, KUM S. "The Bender Gestalt Test." *Indian J Psychiatry* 7:47–9 Ja '65. *

309. EICHLER, MYRON, and NORMAN, JANET. "Repeated Use of the Bender Gestalt Test in a Study of an Induced Toxic State." *Percept & Motor Skills* 20:1033–6 Je '65. * (*PA* 39:14230)

310. EKLUND, SUSAN, and SCOTT, MYRTLE. "Effects of Bilingual Instruction on Test Response of Latin American Children." *Psychol Sch* 2:280 Jl '65. *

311. FLINT, FRIEDA SNYDOVER. *A Validation and Developmental Study of Some Interpretations of the Bender Gestalt Test.* Doctor's thesis, New York University (New York, N.Y.), 1965.

312. FREED, EARL X. "Incidence of Bender-Gestalt Figure Rotations Among Mentally Defective Psychiatric Patients." *Am J Mental Def* 69:514 Ja '65. * (*PA* 39:10510)

313. FREED, EARL X., and HASTINGS, KATHLEEN C. "A Further Note on the Stimulus Factor in Bender-Gestalt Test Rotations." *J Clin Psychol* 21:64 Ja '65. * (*PA* 39:12388)

314. FRIEDMAN, GLORIA. "A Case Study: Emotional Factors Contributing to the Test Performance and Behavior of a Brain-Damaged Child." *J Genetic Psychol* 106:89–99 Mr '65. * (*PA* 39:12695)

315. GARRON, DAVID C., and CHEIFETZ, DAVID I. "Comment on 'Bender Gestalt Discernment of Organic Pathology.'" *Psychol B* 63:197–200 Mr '65. * (*PA* 39:10109)

316. GILBERT, JEANNE G., and LEVEE, RAYMOND F. "Age Differences in the Bender Visual-Motor Gestalt Test and the Archimedes Spiral Test." *J Gerontol* 20:196–200 Ap '65. *

317. HARRIS, RUTHE M. *The Use of the Bender Gestalt Test in Differentiating Between Below and Above Average Reading Achievement.* Master's thesis, Long Beach State College (Long Beach, Calif.), 1965.

318. HERRON, WILLIAM G.; GUIDO, STEPHEN M.; and KANTOR, ROBERT E. "Relationships Among Ego Strength Measures." *J Clin Psychol* 21:403–4 O '65. * (*PA* 40:1567)

319. HUNTER, MILDRED CARSTARPHEN. *A Comparison of Bender Gestalt Test Performance of Caucasian-American With Chinese and Chinese-American Subjects.* Master's thesis, Furman University (Greenville, S.C.), 1965.

320. KEOGH, BARBARA K. "The Bender Gestalt as a Predictive and Diagnostic Test of Reading Performance." Abstract. *J Consult Psychol* 29:83–4 F '65. * (*PA* 39:8666, title only)

321. KEOGH, BARBARA K. "School Achievement Associated With Successful Performance on the Bender Gestalt Test." *J Sch Psychol* 3:37–40 sp '65. * (*PA* 39:15397)

322. KLONOFF, HARRY, and KENNEDY, MARGARET. "Memory and Perceptual Functioning in Octogenarians and Nonagenerians in the Community." *J Gerontol* 20:328–33 Jl '65. *

323. LIEBERMAN, MORTON A. "Psychological Correlates of Impending Death: Some Preliminary Observations." *J Gerontol* 20:181–90 Ap '65. *

324. MEADOWS, GUY D. *The Validity of the Pascal-Suttell Scoring Method for the Bender Gestalt Test.* Master's thesis, Marshall University (Huntington, W.Va.), 1965.

325. MEIER, JOHN HENRY. *An Exploratory Factor Analysis of Psychodiagnostic and Case Study Information From Children in Special Education Classes for the Educable Mentally Handicapped.* Doctor's thesis, University of Denver (Denver, Colo.), 1965. (*DA* 26:3153)

326. MOSHER, DONALD L., and SMITH, JEAN P. "The Usefulness of Two Scoring Systems for the Bender Gestalt Test for Identifying Brain Damage." *J Consult Psychol* 29:530–6 D '65. * (*PA* 40:2959)

327. PACELLA, MICHAEL J. "The Performance of Brain Damaged Mental Retardates on Successive Trials of the Bender-Gestalt." *Am J Mental Def* 69:723–8 Mr '65. * (*PA* 39:12745)

328. RHODES, ROBERT J. *The Bender-Gestalt Test as a Predictor of Left and Right Temporal Lobe Dysfunction.* Doctor's thesis, Wayne State University (Detroit, Mich.), 1965.

329. ROSENBERG, LEON A., and ROSENBERG, ANNA M. "The Effect of Tachistoscopic Presentation on the Hutt-Briskin Bender-Gestalt Scoring System." *J Clin Psychol* 21:314–6 Jl '65. * (*PA* 39:15262)

330. SALZMAN, LEONARD F., and HARWAY, NORMAN I. "Size of Bender Gestalt Drawings in Psychotic Depression." *Percept & Motor Skills* 20:1235–6 Je '65. * (*PA* 39:16249)

331. SCHULMAN, JEROME L.; KASPAR, JOSEPH C.; and THORNE, FRANCES M. *Brain Damage and Behavior: A Clinical-Experimental Study.* Springfield, Ill.: Charles C Thomas, Publisher, 1965. Pp. ix, 164. *

332. SINGH, BALWANT. "The Bender-Gestalt Test as a Group Test." *Ont J Ed Res* 8:35–45 au '65. * (*PA* 40:2125)

333. SMITH, LAURENCE C., JR. "The Effects of Heat Stroke on Cognitive Functioning." *Proc Ann Conf Air Force Behav Sci* 11:130–42 Jl '65. *

334. SNORTUM, JOHN R. "Performance of Different Diagnostic Groups on the Tachistoscopic and Copy Phases of the Bender-Gestalt." *J Consult Psychol* 29:345–51 Ag '65. * (*PA* 39:15333)

335. STERNBERG, DAVID, and LEVINE, ABRAHAM. "An Indicator of Suicidal Ideation on the Bender Visual-Motor Gestalt Test." *J Proj Tech & Pers Assess* 29:377–9 S '65. * (*PA* 39:15418)

336. STOER, LEOPOLD; COROTTO, LOREN V.; and CURNUTT, ROBERT H. "The Role of Visual Perception in the Reproduction of Bender-Gestalt Designs." *Calif Mental Health Res Dig* 3:80–1 sp '65. *

337. STOER, LEOPOLD; COROTTO, LOREN V.; and CURNUTT, ROBERT H. "The Role of Visual Perception in the Reproduction of Bender-Gestalt Designs." *J Proj Tech & Pers Assess* 29:473–8 D '65. * (*PA* 40:2923)

338. TAYLOR, JAMES B. "The Bender Gestalt as a Measure of Intelligence and Adjustment in the Lower Intellectual Range." Abstract. *J Consult Psychol* 29:595 D '65. * (*PA* 40:2875, title only)

339. TEMMER, HELENA W. "Wechsler Intelligence Scores and Bender-Gestalt Performance in Adult Male Mental Defectives." *Am J Mental Def* 70:142–7 Jl '65. * (*PA* 39:16070)

340. ALEXANDER, DUANE; EHRHARDT, ANKE A.; and MONEY, JOHN. "Defective Figure Drawing, Geometric and Human, in Turner's Syndrome." *J Nerv & Mental Dis* 142:161–7 F '66. * (*PA* 40:11185)

341. BLATT, BENJAMIN, and TSUSHIMA, WILLIAM. "A Psychological Study of Uremic Patients Being Considered for the Artificial Kidney Machine Program (Hemodialysis)." *Newsl Res Psychol* 8:17–8 F '66. *

342. BRENNER, MAY WOOLF, and GILLMAN, SELMA. "Visuomotor Ability in Schoolchildren: A Survey." *Develop Med & Child Neurol* 8:686–703 D '66. * (*PA* 41:4397)

343. CANTER, ARTHUR. "A Background Interference Procedure to Increase Sensitivity of the Bender-Gestalt Test to Organic Brain Disorder." *J Consult Psychol* 30:91–7 Ap '66. * (*PA* 40:6956)

344. CARLSON, LOUISE D. "A Comparison of Negro and Caucasian Performances on the Bender-Gestalt Test." *J Clin Psychol* 22:96–8 Ja '66. * (*PA* 40:4451)

345. CELLURA, A. RAYMOND, and BUTTERFIELD, EARL C. "Intelligence, the Bender-Gestalt Test, and Reading Achievement." *Am J Mental Def* 71:60–3 Jl '66. * (*PA* 40:11421)

346. CONNOR, JAMES PAUL. *The Relationship of Bender-Visual-Motor Gestalt Test Performance to Differential Reading*

Performance of Second Grade Children. Doctor's thesis, Kent State University (Kent, Ohio), 1966. (*DA* 28:491A)

347. COOPER, JOHN R., and BARNES, EDWARD J. "Technique for Measuring Reproductions of Visual Stimuli: 2, Adult Reproductions of the Bender-Gestalt." *Percept & Motor Skills* 23:1135–8 D '66. * (*PA* 41:5242)

348. CULBERTSON, FRANCES M., and GUNN, ROBERT C. "Comparison of the Bender Gestalt Test and Frostig Test in Several Clinical Groups of Children." *J Clin Psychol* 22:439 O '66. * (*PA* 41:2906)

349. DE HIRSCH, KATRINA; JANSKY, JEANNETTE JEFFERSON; and LANGFORD, WILLIAM S. *Predicting Reading Failure.* New York: Harper & Row, Publishers, Inc., 1966. Pp. xv, 144. *

350. EDGAR, MARGARET S. *The Bender-Gestalt Visual Motor Test as a Predictor of Success in First Grade.* Master's thesis, Stetson University (DeLand, Fla.), 1966.

351. EGELAND, BYRON RICKER. *The Relationship of Intelligence, Visual-Motor Skills and Psycholinguistic Abilities With Achievement in the First Grade.* Doctor's thesis, University of Iowa (Iowa City, Iowa), 1966. (*DA* 27:388A)

352. ERWIN, EDMOND F., and HAMPE, EDWARD. "Assessment of Perceptual-Motor Changes Following Electroshock Treatment." *Percept & Motor Skills* 22:770 Je '66. * (*PA* 40:11227)

353. FAUST, MARGARET, and FAUST, WILLIAM L. "Pathology or Immaturity: An Evaluation of Changes in Form Copying." *Claremont Read Conf Yearb* 30:95–110 '66. *

354. FJELD, STANTON P.; SMALL, IVER F.; SMALL, JOYCE G.; and HAYDEN, MARY P. "Clinical, Electrical and Psychological Tests and the Diagnosis of Organic Brain Disorder." *J Nerv & Mental Dis* 142:172–9 F '66. * (*PA* 40:11285)

355. FREED, EARL X. "Comparison on Admission and Discharge of Bender-Gestalt Test Performance by Hospitalized Psychiatric Patients." *Percept & Motor Skills* 23:919–22 D '66. * (*PA* 41:7467)

356. FREED, EARL X. "A Note on 'Alcoholic Signs' on the Bender-Gestalt Under Conditions of Stimulus Control." *Newsl Res Psychol* 8:45–7 My '66. *

357. FREED, EARL X. "Susceptibility of Individual Bender-Gestalt Test Designs to Rotation by Psychiatric Patients." *J Clin Psychol* 22:98–9 Ja '66. * (*PA* 40:3570)

358. FROMM, DAVID M. *A Study of Some Factors in the Bender Gestalt Reproductions of Well Adjusted and Poorly Adjusted Boys With Particular Emphasis Upon the Interpretative Process.* Doctor's thesis, University of Oklahoma (Norman, Okla.), 1966. (*DA* 27:2133B)

359. HARTLAGE, LAWRENCE. "Common Psychological Tests Applied to the Assessment of Brain Damage." *J Proj Tech & Pers Assess* 30:319–38 Ag '66. * (*PA* 40:12451)

360. HOFFMAN, STEVEN DAVID. *The Bender Gestalt Test: A Cross-Cultural Test(?).* Doctor's thesis, University of Oklahoma (Norman, Okla.), 1966. (*DA* 27:2136B)

361. HOLROYD, JEAN. "Cross Validation of the Quast and Koppitz Bender-Gestalt Signs of Cerebral Dysfunction." *J Clin Psychol* 22:200 Ap '66. * (*PA* 40:8005)

362. HOLROYD, RICHARD G. "The Koppitz Bender Gestalt Test for Young Children: A Scoring Guide." *J Clin Psychol* 22:440–1 O '66. * (*PA* 41:2913)

363. HUTTON, JERRY B. "Bender Recall of Children as Related to Age and Intelligence." *Percept & Motor Skills* 23:34 Ag '66. * (*PA* 40:12151)

364. KLONOFF, HARRY, and KENNEDY, MARGARET. "A Comparative Study of Cognitive Functioning in Old Age." *J Gerontol* 21:239–43 Ap '66. *

365. KRAMER, ERNEST, and FENWICK, JANET. "Differential Diagnosis With the Bender Gestalt Test." *J Proj Tech & Pers Assess* 30:59–61 F '66. * (*PA* 40:5657)

366. MOGIN, LENORE S. *Administration and Objective Scoring of the Bender Gestalt Test in Group Screening of Primary Grade Children for Emotional Maladjustment.* Doctor's thesis, Rutgers—The State University (New Brunswick, N.J.), 1966. (*DA* 27:1665A)

367. ORLOV, LELAND G. *The Effect of Intelligence on the Bender-Gestalt Performance in a Hospitalized Epileptic, Predominantly Brain-Damaged Population.* Master's thesis, Springfield College (Springfield, Mass.), 1966.

368. ROTHENBERG, HARRIET A. *A Study to Determine the Feasibility of Group Use of the Bender Gestalt Test in Kindergarten as an Aid in Predicting Success in Reading in Grade One.* Master's thesis, California State College at Long Beach (Long Beach, Calif.), 1966.

369. STONE, LEROY A. "A Cluster Analysis of the Bender Gestalt Test Designs." *J Clin Psychol* 22:94–6 Ja '66. * (*PA* 40:3588)

370. TAUBER, ROSALYN. "Identification of Potential Learning Disabilities." *Acad Ther Q* 2:116–9+ w '66–67. * (*PA* 41:5004)

371. TEETER, BARBARA SPEIER. *The Symbolic Meaning of the Bender-Gestalt.* Doctor's thesis, University of Minnesota (Minneapolis, Minn.), 1966. (*DA* 28:3069B)

372. WAGNER, EDWIN E., and EVANS, K. ANN. "A Brief Note on the Comparison of Two Grapho-Motor Techniques in Diagnosing Brain Damage." *J Proj Tech & Pers Assess* 30:54 F '66. * (*PA* 40:5660)

373. WHIPPLE, CLIFFORD I., and MAIER, LOUISE JO. "Perceptual-Motor Maturation and Language Development in

Young Children." *Percept & Motor Skills* 23:1208 D '66. * (*PA* 41:5794)

374. WIENER, GERALD. "The Bender-Gestalt Test as a Predictor of Minimal Neurologic Deficit in Children Eight to Ten Years of Age." *J Nerv & Mental Dis* 143:275–80 S '66. * (*PA* 41:6170)

375. WILE, DANIEL BLAHD. *Age and Pathology Differences in Bender-Gestalt Performance.* Doctor's thesis, University of California (Berkeley, Calif.), 1966. (*DA* 27:1298B)

376. ALLEN, ROBERT M. "Visual Perceptual Maturation and the Bender Gestalt Test Quality." *Training Sch B* 64:131–3 N '67. * (*PA* 42:11030)

377. BAER, DANIEL J., and GALE, RICHARD A. "Intelligence and Bender Gestalt Test Performance of Institutional and Noninstitutional School Children." *J Genetic Psychol* 111:119–24 S '67. * (*PA* 42:578)

378. BENDER, LAURETTA. "The Visual Motor Gestalt Function in 6- and 7-Year-Old Normal and Schizophrenic Children." *Proc Am Psychopath Assn* 56:544–63 '67. *

379. CHANG, THOMAS M. C., and CHANG, VIVIAN A. C. "Relation of Visual-Motor Skills and Reading Achievement in Primary-Grade Pupils of Superior Ability." *Percept & Motor Skills* 24:51–3 F '67. * (*PA* 41:8701)

380. COOPER, JOHN R.; DWARSHUIS, LOUIS; and BLECHMAN, GERALD. "Technique for Measuring Reproductions of Visual Stimuli: 3, Bender-Gestalt and Severity of Neurological Deficit." *Percept & Motor Skills* 25:506–8 O '67. * (*PA* 42:4751)

381. EGELAND, BYRON; RICE, JAMES; and PENNY, SUSAN. "Inter-Scorer Reliability on the Bender Gestalt Test and the Revised Visual Retention Test." *Am J Mental Def* 72:96–9 Jl '67. * (*PA* 41:15715)

382. EMBREE, ELTON DAVID. *The Behavioral Motor Gestalt Associated With Specific Brain Lesions.* Doctor's thesis, Louisiana State University (Baton Rouge, La.), 1967. (*DA* 28:349B)

383. FRIEDMAN, JOSEPH; STROCHAK, ROBERT D.; GITLIN, SIDNEY; and GOTTSAGEN, MITCHELL L. "Koppitz' Bender Scoring System and Brain Injury in Children." *J Clin Psychol* 23:179–82 Ap '67. * (*PA* 41:9240)

384. GILBERT, JEANNE G., and LEVEE, RAYMOND F. "Performances of Deaf and Normally-Hearing Children on the Bender-Gestalt and the Archimedes Spiral Tests." *Percept & Motor Skills* 24:1059–66 Je '67. * (*PA* 41:15063)

385. HAMMER, GLADYS TRIMBLE. *The Group Bender Gestalt Test as a Predictor of Academic Potential in First Grade, With Attention of Environmental Effects.* Doctor's thesis, University of California (Los Angeles, Calif.), 1967. (*DA* 28:964A)

386. HIRSCHENFANG, SAMUEL; BERMAN, DIANE; and BENTON, JOSEPH G. "Follow-Up Study of Bender-Gestalt Reproductions by Right and Left Hemiplegic Patients." *Percept & Motor Skills* 25:339–40 Ag '67. * (*PA* 42:2803)

387. HIRSCHENFANG, SAMUEL; SILBER, MAURYCY; and BENTON, JOSEPH G. "Comparison of Bender-Gestalt Reproductions by Patients With Peripheral Neuropathy." *Percept & Motor Skills* 24:1317–8 Je '67. * (*PA* 41:15671)

388. JERNIGAN, A. J. "Rotation Style on the Bender Gestalt Test." *J Clin Psychol* 23:176–9 Ap '67. * (*PA* 41:9080)

389. KEOGH, BARBARA K., and SMITH, CAROL E. "Visuo-Motor Ability for School Prediction: A Seven-Year Study." *Percept & Motor Skills* 25:101–10 Ag '67. * (*PA* 42:2402)

390. McCONNELL, OWEN L. "Koppitz's Bender-Gestalt Scores in Relation to Organic and Emotional Problems in Children." *J Clin Psychol* 23:370–4 Jl '67. * (*PA* 41:15315)

391. MURTHY, HOSUR NARAYANA. "Bender Gestalt Test and Its Use With Schizophrenics." *Indian J Appl Psychol* 4:1–5 Ja '67. *

392. NACHES, ARNOLD MARTIN. *The Bender Gestalt Test and Acting Out Behavior in Children.* Doctor's thesis, Colorado State College (Greeley, Colo.), 1967. (*DA* 28:2146B)

393. OGDON, DONALD P. Section 4, "The Bender-Gestalt Test," pp. 58–71, 82. In his *Psychodiagnostics and Personality Assessment: A Handbook.* Beverly Hills, Calif.: Western Psychological Services, 1967. Pp. v, 96. *

394. PLENK, AGNES M., and JONES, JEANNE L. "An Examination of the Bender Gestalt Performance of Three and Four Year Olds and Its Relationship to Koppitz Scoring System." *J Clin Psychol* 23:367–70 Jl '67. * (*PA* 41:15319)

395. PLENK, AGNES MERO. *Development of a Scoring System for the Bender Gestalt Test for Children of Preschool Age.* Doctor's thesis, University of Utah (Salt Lake City, Utah), 1967. (*DA* 28:2564A)

396. SAK, HELEN G.; SMITH, ALFRED A.; and DAVIES, JOSEPH. "Psychometric Evaluation of Children With Familial Dysautonomia." *Am J Psychiatry* 124:682–7 N '67. * (*PA* 42:5959)

397. SEIFERT, JOAN G. *The Relationship Between Visual Motor Perception and the Speed of Eye Movements by Selected Boys.* Doctor's thesis, Kent State University (Kent, Ohio), 1967. (*DA* 28:4493A)

398. SMITH, DONALD C., and MARTIN, ROBERT A. "Use of Learning Cues With the Bender Visual Motor Gestalt Test in Screening Children for Neurological Impairment." *J Consult Psychol* 31:205–9 Ap '67. * (*PA* 41:7702)

399. SNYDER, ROBERT T., and FREUD, SHELDON L. "Reading Readiness and Its Relation to Maturational Unreadiness as Measured by the Spiral Aftereffect and Other Visual-Perceptual Techniques." *Percept & Motor Skills* 25:841–54 D '67. * (*PA* 42:8736)

400. SUNDSTROM, DALE ALVIN. *The Influence of Parental Attitudes and Child-Parent Interaction Upon Remedial Reading Progress: A Re-Examination.* Doctor's thesis, University of Utah (Salt Lake City, Utah), 1967. (*DA* 28:2571A)

401. WERNER, EMMY E.; SIMONIAN, KEN; and SMITH, RUTH S. "Reading Achievement, Language Functioning and Perceptual-Motor Development of 10- and 11-Year-Olds." *Percept & Motor Skills* 25:409–20 O '67. * (*PA* 42:5403)

402. ALLEN, ROBERT M. "Experimental Variation of the Mode of Reproduction of the Bender-Gestalt Stimuli by Mental Retardates." *J Clin Psychol* 24:199–202 Ap '68. * (*PA* 42:12634)

403. BRENNER, M. W., and GILLMAN, S. "Verbal Intelligence, Visuomotor Ability and School Achievement." *Brit J Ed Psychol* 38:75–8 F '68. * (*PA* 42:12746)

404. CANTER, ARTHUR. "BIP Bender Test for the Detection of Organic Brain Disorder: Modified Scoring Method and Replication." *J Consult & Clin Psychol* 32:522–6 O '68. * (*PA* 43:128)

405. GARRON, DAVID C., and CHEIFETZ, DAVID I. "Electroshock Therapy and Bender-Gestalt Performance." *Percept & Motor Skills* 26:9–10 F '68. * (*PA* 42:10696)

406. GRAVITZ, HERBERT L., and HANDLER, LEONARD. "Effects of Different Modes of Administration on the Bender Visual Motor Gestalt Test." *J Consult & Clin Psychol* 32:276–9 Je '68. * (*PA* 42:13790)

407. HEINRICH, MAX JOSEPH. *Sources of Visual-Motor Dysfunctions Associated With Some Cases of Reading Disorder.* Doctor's thesis, Cornell University (Ithaca, N.Y.), 1968. (*DA* 29:370B)

408. HENDERSON, NORMAN B.; BUTLER, BRUCE V.; and GOFFENEY, BARBARA. "Is the Bender-Gestalt Test Effective in Predicting Arithmetic and Reading Achievement of Seven Year Old White and Nonwhite Children?" *Proc Ann Conv Am Psychol Assn* 76:589–90 '68. * (*PA* 43:1497, title only)

409. HIRSCHENFANG, SAMUEL; SILBER, MAURYCY; and BENTON, JOSEPH G. "Personality Patterns in Peripheral Neuropathy." *Dis Nerv System* 29:46–50 Ja '68. *

410. HUTT, MAX L. Chap. 13, "The Projective Use of the Bender-Gestalt Test," pp. 397–420. In *Projective Techniques in Personality Assessment: A Modern Introduction.* Edited by A. I. Rabin. New York: Springer Publishing Co., Inc., 1968. Pp. x, 638. *

411. KALIL, A. JOHN. *Bender Gestalt as a Test to be Included in a Counselor's General Readiness Battery for First Graders.* Master's thesis, Catholic University of America (Washington, D.C.), 1968.

412. KEOGH, BARBARA K. "Research Implications of the Bender-Gestalt for School Programs." *Proc Ann Conv Am Psychol Assn* 76:591–2 '68. * (*PA* 43:1356, title only)

413. KEOGH, BARBARA K., and SMITH, CAROL E. "Changes in Copying Ability of Young Children." *Percept & Motor Skills* 26:773–4 Je '68. * (*PA* 42:15288)

414. KOPPITZ, ELIZABETH MUNSTERBERG. Chap. 9, "Using HFD's in Combination With Other Psychological Tests," pp. 177–87. In her *Evaluation of Children's Human Figure Drawings.* New York: Grune & Stratton, Inc., 1968. Pp. x, 341. *

415. LIEBERMAN, LEWIS R. "Drawing Norms for the Bender-Gestalt Figures." *J Clin Psychol* 24:458–63 O '68. * (*PA* 43:4047)

416. NAWAS, M. MIKE, and WORTH, JAMES W. "Suicidal Configurations in the Bender-Gestalt." *J Proj Tech & Pers Assess* 32:392–4 Ag '68. * (*PA* 42:18838)

417. PHELPS, WILLIAM R. "Further Evidence on the Hain Scoring Method for the Bender-Gestalt Test." *J Learn Dis* 1:358–60 Je '68. *

418. POTEET, JAMES A. "Rotation or Reversal? A Proposed Definition." *Excep Children* 34:760–1 su '68. *

419. QUATTLEBAUM, LAWRENCE F. "A Brief Note on the Relationship Between Two Psychomotor Tests." *J Clin Psychol* 24:198–9 Ap '68. * (*PA* 42:12596)

420. REINEHR, ROBERT C., and GOLIGHTLY, CAROLE. "The Relationship Between the Bender Gestalt and the Organic Integrity Test." *J Clin Psychol* 24:203–4 Ap '68. * (*PA* 42:12834)

421. SABATINO, DAVID A.; assisted by R. L. Jones, Curtiss Brown, and W. M. Gibson. "The Relationship Between Twenty-Three Learning Disability Behavioral Variables," pp. 149–61. In *CEC Selected Convention Papers.* 46th Annual International Convention, 1968. Washington, D.C.: Council for Exceptional Children, [1968]. Pp. xii, 346. *

422. SABATINO, DAVID A.; WICKHAM, WILLIAM, JR.; and BURNETT, CALVIN W. "The Psychoeducational Assessment of Learning Disabilities." *Cath Ed R* 66:327–41 My '68. *

423. SAVERING, FRANCES ROSE. *Children's Bender Gestalt Drawings in Relation to Maturity and Behavior Rates.* Master's thesis, Southern Connecticut State College (New Haven, Conn.), 1968.

424. SILBER, MAURYCY; HIRSCHENFANG, SAMUEL; and BENTON, JOSEPH G. "Psychological Factors and Prognosis in Peripheral Neuropathy." *Dis Nerv System* 29:688–92 O '68. * (*PA* 43:5676)

425. SILBERBERG, NORMAN, and FELDT, LEONARD S. "Intel-

lectual and Perceptual Correlates of Reading Disabilities." *J Sch Psychol* 6:237–45 su '68. * (*PA* 42:3033)

426. STERNLICHT, MANNY; PUSTEL, GABRIEL; and SIEGEL, LOUIS. "Comparison of Organic and Cultural-Familial Retardates on Two Visual-Motor Tasks." *Am J Mental Def* 72:887–9 My '68. * (*PA* 42:14073)

427. TOLOR, ALEXANDER. "The Graphomotor Techniques." *J Proj Tech & Pers Assess* 32:222–8 Je '68. * (*PA* 42:15501)

428. WATSON, CHARLES G. "The Separation of NP Hospital Organics From Schizophrenics With Three Visual Motor Screening Tests." *J Clin Psychol* 24:412–4 O '68. * (*PA* 43:4168)

429. HUTT, MAX L. *The Hutt Adaptation of the Bender-Gestalt Test, Second Edition.* New York: Grune & Stratton, Inc., 1969. Pp. viii, 192. *

NAME INDEX

[416]

*The Blacky Pictures: A Technique for the Exploration of Personality Dynamics. Ages 5 and over; 1950-67; BP; psychosexual development; individual; 1 form ('50, 12 cards); manual ('50, 24 pages); research guide ('62, 27 pages, reprint of 74 below); inquiry cards ('50, 42 cards, separate sets for males and females); record blank ('50, 12 pages); factor scoring blank ['67, 4 pages] for males; dimensional scoring blank ['67, 4 pages] for males and females; no data on reliability and validity; no norms; $15 per set of test materials and 25 record blanks; $4 per 25 record blanks; $4 per 25 scoring blanks; $1.50 per research guide; $1.25 per manual; postpaid; (35-55) minutes; scoring blanks by Earl S. Taulbee and David E. Stenmark; Gerald S. Blum; Psychodynamic Instruments. *

For a review by Bert R. Sappenfield, see 6:204 (34 references); for a review by Kenneth R. Newton, see 5:125 (38 references, 1 excerpt); for a review by Albert Ellis, see 4:102 (7 references, 3 excerpts).

REFERENCES

1-7. See 4:102.
8-45. See 5:125.
46-79. See 6:204.
80. SEGAL, ALZIRE SOPHIA BLOCK. *The Prediction of Expressed Attitudes Toward the Mother.* Doctor's thesis, University of Michigan (Ann Arbor, Mich.), 1954. (*DA* 14:1259)
81. SHARMA, SOHAN LAL. *The Genesis of the Authoritarian Personality.* Doctor's thesis, University of Michigan (Ann Arbor, Mich.), 1957. (*DA* 18:1486)
82. SIROTA, LEON MICHAEL. *A Factor Analysis of Selected Personality Domains.* Doctor's thesis, University of Michigan (Ann Arbor, Mich.), 1957. (*DA* 18:1503)
83. FRIEDMAN, JOSEPH. *Psychological Correlates of Overweight, Underweight and Normal Weight College Women.* Doctor's thesis, Temple University (Philadelphia, Pa.), 1958. (*DA* 19:3362)
84. GRAYDEN, CHARLES. *The Relationship Between Neurotic Hypochondriasis and Three Personality Variables: Feeling of Being Unloved, Narcissism, and Guilt Feelings.* Doctor's thesis, New York University (New York, N.Y.), 1958. (*DA* 18:2209)
85. TRIPPE, MATTHEW JAMES. *A Study of the Relationship Between Visual-Perceptual Ability and Selected Personality Variables in a Group of Cerebral Palsied Children.* Doctor's thesis, Syracuse University (Syracuse, N.Y.), 1958. (*DA* 20:765)
86. MINKOWICH, ABRAM. *Correlates of Superego Functions.* Doctor's thesis, University of Michigan (Ann Arbor, Mich.), 1959. (*DA* 19:3356)
87. PERLOE, SIDNEY IRWIN. *An Experimental Test of Two Theories of Perceptual Defense.* Doctor's thesis, University of Michigan (Ann Arbor, Mich.), 1959. (*DA* 19:3358)
88. LEICHTY, MARY M. "The Effect of Father-Absence During Early Childhood Upon the Oedipal Situation as Reflected in Young Adults." *Merrill-Palmer Q* 6:212-7 Jl '60. * (*PA* 36:3FG12L)
89. LOGAN, NELL PAULINE. *Personality Correlates of Undergraduates Selecting Home Economics as an Area of Specialization in College.* Doctor's thesis, University of Tennessee (Knoxville, Tenn.), 1960. (*DA* 21:2268)
90. ORBACH, CHANNING HASKELL. *Perceptual Defense and Somatization: A Comparison of the Perceptual Thresholds of Obese and Peptic Ulcer Patients.* Doctor's thesis, University of Southern California (Los Angeles, Calif.), 1960. (*DA* 20:4440)
91. MARGOLIS, MARVIN. "The Mother-Child Relationship in Bronchial Asthma." *J Abn & Social Psychol* 63:360-7 S '61. * (*PA* 37:1840)
92. FIGETAKIS, NICK. *Process-Reactive Schizophrenia: Ego-Strength and Selected Psychosexual Dimensions.* Doctor's thesis, Michigan State University (East Lansing, Mich.), 1963. (*DA* 25:625)
93. LUTZKY, HARRIET L., and SCHMEIDLER, GERTRUDE R. "Perceptual Leveling in Institutional and Other Children." *J Genetic Psychol* 103:45-51 S '63. * (*PA* 39:1490)
94. MAES, JOHN L. *Identification of Male College Students With Their Fathers and Some Related Indices of Affect Expression and Psychosexual Adjustment.* Doctor's thesis, Michigan State University (East Lansing, Mich.), 1963. (*DA* 24:1245)
95. MARCUS, MARILYN MASAMED. *The Relation of Personality Structure to the Capacity for Memory Retention.* Doctor's thesis, University of Pittsburgh (Pittsburgh, Pa.), 1963. (*DA* 26:1779)
96. WEINGARTEN, LINDA LEE. *Correlates of Ambivalence Toward Parental Figures.* Doctor's thesis, University of Michigan (Ann Arbor, Mich.), 1963. (*DA* 24:840)
97. BLUM, GERALD S. "Defense Preferences Among University Students in Denmark, France, Germany, and Israel." *J Proj Tech & Pers Assess* 28:13-9 Mr '64. * (*PA* 39:241)
98. GIESZ, WILLIAM GEORGE. *Psychosexual Categories as*

Associated With Vocational Experience. Doctor's thesis, University of Maryland (College Park, Md.), 1964. (*DA* 25:4816)

99. KING, FRANCIS W., and KING, DOROTHY C. "The Projective Assessment of the Female's Sexual Identification, With Special Reference to the Blacky Pictures." *J Proj Tech & Pers Assess* 28:293–9 S '64. * (*PA* 39:7900)

100. NORMINGTON, CHERYL JOAN. *Some Aspects of Psychosexual Development in Process-Reactive Schizophrenia.* Doctor's thesis, Michigan State University (East Lansing, Mich.), 1964. (*DA* 25:5387)

101. POLLIE, DONALD M. "A Projective Study of Conflict and Defense in Peptic Ulcers and Bronchial Asthma." *J Proj Tech & Pers Assess* 28:67–77 Mr '64. * (*PA* 39:2779)

102. THELEN, MARK HERMAN. *Similarities of Defense Preferences Within Families, Within Sex Groups, and Their Relationship to Parental Identification in Adolescent Males.* Doctor's thesis, Michigan State University (East Lansing, Mich.), 1964. (*DA* 25:6772)

103. YELSKY, MIRIAM. *The Assessment of Several Personality Trait Responses of School Phobic Children: A Comparative Evaluation of the Responses to Psychological Tests of School Phobics, Emotionally Disturbed Children Who Attend School, and Normal Children.* Doctor's thesis, Yeshiva University (New York, N.Y.), 1964. (*DA* 25:2057)

104. CARPENTER, SUSANNE ILSE SCHUMANN. *Psychosexual Conflict, Defense, and Abstraction.* Doctor's thesis, University of Michigan (Ann Arbor, Mich.), 1965. (*DA* 26:7445)

105. DAWSON, JOSEPH G.; NOBLIN, CHARLES D.; and TIMMONS, EDWIN O. "Dynamic and Behavioral Predictors of Hypnotizability." *J Consult Psychol* 29:76–8 F '65. * (*PA* 39:8144)

106. FRIEDMAN, GLORIA. "A Case Study: Emotional Factors Contributing to the Test Performance and Behavior of a Brain-Damaged Child." *J Genetic Psychol* 106:89–99 Mr '65. * (*PA* 39:12695)

107. RABIN, A. I. *Growing Up in the Kibbutz: Comparison of the Personality of Children Brought Up in the Kibbutz and of Family-Reared Children.* New York: Springer Publishing Co., Inc., 1965. Pp. x, 230. *

108. KIMELDORF, CAROL, and GEIWITZ, P. JAMES. "Smoking and the Blacky Orality Factors." *J Proj Tech & Pers Assess* 30:167–8 Ap '66. * (*PA* 40:7831)

109. ROBINSON, SANDRA A., and HENDRIX, VERNON L. "The Blacky Test and Psychoanalytic Theory: Another Factor-Analytic Approach to Validity." *J Proj Tech & Pers Assess* 30:597–603 D '66. * (*PA* 41:2922)

110. SCHILL, THOMAS. "Sex Differences in Identification of the Castrating Agent on the Blacky Test." *J Clin Psychol* 22:324–5 Jl '66. * (*PA* 40:11177)

111. DE LUCA, JOSEPH N. "Performance of Overt Male Homosexuals and Controls on the Blacky Test." *J Clin Psychol* 23:497 O '67. * (*PA* 42:2697)

112. STRICKER, GEORGE. "Stimulus Properties of the Blacky to a Sample of Pedophiles." *J General Psychol* 77:35–9 Jl '67. * (*PA* 41:13691)

113. THELEN, MARK H. "The Relationship of Selected Variables to Intrafamily Similarity of Defense Preferences." *J Proj Tech & Pers Assess* 31:23–7 Je '67. * (*PA* 41:13656)

114. BLUM, GERALD S. Chap. 8, "Assessment of Psychodynamic Variables by the Blacky Pictures," pp. 150–68. In *Advances in Psychological Assessment,* Vol. 1. Edited by Paul McReynolds. Palo Alto, Calif.: Science & Behavior Books, Inc., 1968. Pp. xiii, 336. *

115. DELUCA, JOSEPH. "Psychosexual Conflict in Adolescent Enuretics." *J Psychol* 68:145–9 Ja '68. * (*PA* 42:7498)

116. KLINE, PAUL. "Obsessional Traits, Obsessional Symptoms and Anal Erotism." *Brit J Med Psychol* 41:299–306 S '68. * (*PA* 43:1061)

117. ROBINSON, SANDRA A. "The Development of a Female Form of the Blacky Pictures." *J Proj Tech & Pers Assess* 32:74–80 F '68. * (*PA* 42:9002)

118. TAULBEE, EARL S., and STENMARK, DAVID E. "The Blacky Pictures Test: A Comprehensive Annotated and Indexed Bibliography (1949–1967)." *J Proj Tech & Pers Assess* 32:105–37 Ap '68. * (*PA* 42:10627)

NAME INDEX

[417]

★**Braverman-Chevigny Auditory Projective Test.** Ages 4 and over; 1955–64; BCAPT; for research use only; intended to be an auditory equivalent of TAT; 1 form; 7½ ips tape recording ('55); mimeographed provisional manual ('64, 16 pages); no data on reliability or validity; no norms; tapes loaned only; manual free; [25–35] minutes; Sydell Braverman and Hector Chevigny; American Foundation for the Blind, Inc. *

REFERENCES

1. ABRAMSON, LEONARD S. "A Comparison of an Auditory and a Visual Projective Technique." *J Proj Tech* 27:3–11 Mr '63. * (*PA* 38:1005)
2. KRAMER, ERNEST, and ARONOVITCH, CHARLES D. "A Normative Study of an Auditory Projective Technique." *J Proj Tech & Pers Assess* 31:88–91 Ag '67. * (*PA* 41:15310)

[418]

Buttons: A Projective Test for Pre-Adolescent and Adolescent Boys and Girls. Grades 7–9; maladjustment; 1963; 3 scores: initial, content, total; 1 form (7 pages); manual (36 pages plus test and scoring booklet); scoring booklet (4 pages); no data on reliability of scores; $16 per examiner's kit of 25 tests, 25 scoring booklets, and manual; $4 per manual; postpaid; (45) minutes; Esther P. Rothman and Pearl H. Berkowitz; Western Psychological Services. *

[419]

★**Children's Apperception Test.** Ages 3–10; 1949–65; CAT; individual; 1 form; 3 editions; short form record booklet ('55, 5 pages) for use with *a* and *b* below and with test 484; checklist ('65, 2 pages, entitled *A Schedule of Adaptive Mechanisms in CAT Responses*); no data on reliability and validity; $8.50

per set of cards and manual for any one edition; $3 per 25 short form record booklets; $3 per 30 adaptive mechanisms schedules; $24.50 per set of cards and manuals for all 3 editions, 25 record blanks, and 30 adaptive mechanisms schedules; postage extra; [15–20] minutes; Leopold Bellak, Sonya Sorel Bellak, Mary R. Haworth (checklist), and Marvin S. Hurvich (manual for c); C.P.S., Inc. *

a) CHILDREN'S APPERCEPTION TEST. 1949–61; 1 form ('59, c1949, 10 cards, same as cards published in 1949 and 1951 except for finish); revised manual, fourth edition ('61, c1949, 16 pages, identical with 1959 third edition except for expanded bibliography).

b) CHILDREN'S APPERCEPTION TEST—SUPPLEMENT. 1952–55; 1 form ('52, 10 cards); manual ('52, 8 pages).

c) CHILDREN'S APPERCEPTION TEST (HUMAN FIGURES). 1965; 1 form ('65, 10 cards, designed to be "equivalent" to the regular CAT cards); manual ('65, 14 pages, including a copy of Haworth's *A Schedule of Adaptive Mechanisms in CAT Responses*).

For reviews by Bernard I. Murstein and Robert D. Wirt, see 6:206 (19 references); for reviews by Douglas T. Kenny and Albert I. Rabin, see 5:126 (15 references); for reviews by John E. Bell and L. Joseph Stone, see 4:103 (2 references, 5 excerpts); for related book reviews not excerpted in this volume, consult the 5th (B63) MMY. MMY

REFERENCES

1–2. See 4:103.
3–17. See 5:126.
18–36. See 6:206.
37. FITZSIMONS, RUTH. "Developmental Psychosocial, and Educational Factors in Children With Nonorganic Articulation Problems." *Child Develop* 29:481–9 D '58. * (*PA* 34:4639)
38. D'HEURLE, ADMA; MELLINGER, JEANNE CUMMINS; and HAGGARD, ERNEST A. "Personality, Intellectual, and Achievement Patterns in Gifted Children." *Psychol Monogr* 73(13):1–28 '59. * (*PA* 35:1234)
39. POWELL, KATHRYN SUMMERS. "Maternal Employment in Relation to Family Life." *Marriage & Family Living* 23:350–5 N '61. * (*PA* 36:5FG50P)
40. GUNN, ROBERT CONNER. *Some Personality Characteristics of Cerebral Palsied Children.* Doctor's thesis, University of Michigan (Ann Arbor, Mich.), 1964. (*DA* 25:7379)
41. HAWORTH, MARY R. "Parental Loss in Children as Reflected in Projective Responses." *J Proj Tech & Pers Assess* 28:31–45 Mr '64. * (*PA* 39:1857)
42. KOSIER, KENNETH P. *A Comparison CAT/TAT and Children's Drawings as Projective Stimuli.* Master's thesis, University of Wisconsin (Madison, Wis.), 1964.
43. GOOD, JUNE AMSDEN. *Some Relationships Between Hostility and Fantasy Production in Children.* Doctor's thesis, George Peabody College for Teachers (Nashville, Tenn.), 1965. (*DA* 26:6845)
44. BELLAK, LEOPOLD, and HURVICH, MARVIN S. "A Human Modification of the Children's Apperception Test (CAT-H)." *J Proj Tech & Pers Assess* 30:228–42 Je '66. * (*PA* 40:9427)
45. HAWORTH, MARY R. *The CAT: Facts About Fantasy.* New York: Grune & Stratton, Inc., 1966. Pp. xii, 322. * (*PA* 40:6667, title only)
46. LAWTON, MARCIA J. "Animal and Human CATs With a School Sample." *J Proj Tech & Pers Assess* 30:243–6 Je '66. * (*PA* 40:9437)
47. TSUJI, SHOZO, and KATO, NORIAKI. "Some Investigations of Parental Preference in Early Childhood: An Attempt to Obtain a Correspondence of Verbally Expressed Preference With Projectively Expressed Preference." *Jap Psychol Res* 8:10–7 My '66. * (*PA* 40:11027)
48. MATHUR, SHANTA, and KUMAR, B. "A Study of Delinquents and Non-Delinquents Through Children's Apperception Test." *Indian J Appl Psychol* 4:72–5 Jl '67. *
49. SIMMONS, DALE D. "Children's Preferences for Humanized Versus Natural Animals." *J Proj Tech & Pers Assess* 31:39–41 Je '67. * (*PA* 41:13446)
50. BELLAK, LEOPOLD. "Discussion: The Children's Apperception Test: Its Use in Developmental Assessments of Normal Children." *J Proj Tech & Pers Assess* 32:425–7 O '68. * (*PA* 43:5379)
51. HAWORTH, MARY R. "The Children's Apperception Test: Its Use in Developmental Assessments of Normal Children: Introduction." *J Proj Tech & Pers Assess* 32:405 O '68. * (*PA* 43:5387, title only)
52. MORIARTY, ALICE E. "Normal Preschoolers' Reactions to the CAT: Some Implications for Later Development." *J Proj Tech & Pers Assess* 32:413–9 O '68. * (*PA* 43:5392)
53. RABIN, A. I. "Children's Apperception Test Findings with Kibbutz and Non-Kibbutz Preschoolers." *J Proj Tech & Pers Assess* 32:420–4 O '68. * (*PA* 43:5393)
54. WITHERSPOON, RALPH L. "Development of Objective Scoring Methods for Longitudinal CAT Data." *J Proj Tech & Pers Assess* 32:406–12 O '68. * (*PA* 43:5397)

NAME INDEX

[420]

★Color Pyramid Test. Ages 6 and over; 1951–65 (English edition, 1964–65); CPT; nonverbal "technique for the study of the role of emotion and affect"; English revision of *Der Farbpyramiden-Test nach Max Pfister* (1951) by Robert Heiss and Hildegard Hiltmann; 1 form ('65); manual ('64, see 4 below); summary of administration and scoring instructions ('65, 6 pages); color code chart ('65, 1 card); record blank ('65, 1 page); separate profiles ('65, 1 page) for males, females; Fr. 20 per set of color chips; Fr. 8 per pad of 50 record blanks; Fr. 5 per 25 profile sheets for either sex; Fr. .80 per summary instructions; Fr. 1 per color code chart; Fr. 1.80 per set of 2 pyramid form cards; Fr. 40 ($10) per complete set of preceding test materials; Fr. 38 ($11) per manual; postage extra; (25–50) minutes; K. Warner Schaie and Robert Heiss; Hans Huber. * (United States distributor: Grune & Stratton, Inc.)

REFERENCES

1. SCHAIE, K. WARNER. "The Performance of Mentally Defective Children on the Color Pyramid Test." *J Proj Tech* 26:447–54 D '62. * (*PA* 37:6765)
2. SCHAIE, K. WARNER. "The Color Pyramid Test: A Nonverbal Technique for Personality Assessment." *Psychol B* 60:530–47 N '63. * (*PA* 38:4307)
3. DILTS, MARTHA, and TAYLOR, ROBERT E. "The Semantic Differential of Color Pyramid Test Instructions." *Percept & Motor Skills* 19:968–70 D '64. * (*PA* 39:7663)
4. SCHAIE, K. WARNER, and HEISS, ROBERT. *Color and Personality: A Manual for the Color Pyramid Test (Farbpyramiden-Test).* Berne, Switzerland: Hans Huber, 1964. Pp. 295. * (*PA* 39:15417)
5. HOLANCHOCK, GEORGE MICHAEL. *A Study of the Performance of Two Groups of Elementary School Children on the Color Pyramid Test.* Doctor's thesis, Temple University (Philadelphia, Pa.), 1965. (*DA* 26:3756)
6. SCHAIE, K. WARNER. "On the Relation of Color and

Personality." *J Proj Tech & Pers Assess* 30:512–24 D '66. * (*PA* 41:2867)
7. BURDICK, J. ALAN. "The Color Pyramid Test: A Critical Evaluation." *J Psychol* 70:93–7 S '68. * (*PA* 43:127)
8. HOOKE, JAMES F., and SCHAIE, K. WARNER. "A Group Administration Technique for the Color Pyramid Test." *J Clin Psychol* 24:99 Ja '68. * (*PA* 42:8995)
9. SCHAIE, K. WARNER. "Developmental Changes in Response Differentiation on a Color-Arrangement Task." *J Consult & Clin Psychol* 32:233–5 Ap '68. * (*PA* 42:8708)

[421]

*Curtis Completion Form. Grades 11–16 and adults; 1950–68; CCF; emotional maturity and adjustment; 1 form ('50, 4 pages); manual ('68, 9 pages plus English and foreign language editions of test, 1968 manual consists of the 1963 manual interspersed with reports on the use of the test); $6.50 per 25 tests; $2 per manual; postpaid; French and Spanish editions available; (30–35) minutes; James W. Curtis; Western Psychological Services. *

For reviews by Irwin G. Sarason and Laurance F. Shaffer, see 6:208 (2 references); for a review by Alfred B. Heilbrun, Jr., see 5:128.

REFERENCES

1–2. See 6:208.
3. PEARSON, DONALD RAYMOND. *A Comparative Study of the Curtis Completion Form.* Master's thesis, Illinois State University (Normal, Ill.), 1958.
4. HAMPTON, PETER J. "Application of the Dollard and Auld Content Analysis Method to Sentence Completion Material." *Psychol Rep* 15:67–70 Ag '64. * (*PA* 39:2936)
5. ROSETT, HENRY L.; ROBBINS, HERBERT; and WATSON, WALTER S. "Standardization and Construct Validity of the Physiognomic Cue Test." *Percept & Motor Skills* 24:403–20 Ap '67. * (*PA* 41:9639)

[422]

The Draw-A-Person. Ages 5 and over; 1963; DAP; 1 form (1 page plus backing sheet to be interleafed with carbon to make a 2-copy drawing form); manual (33 pages plus sample copies of protocol and interpretive booklets); protocol booklet (4 pages); interpretive booklet (4 pages); $22 per examiner's kit of 25 tests, 25 protocol booklets, 25 interpretive booklets, and manual; $6.50 per 25 copies of either test, protocol booklet, or interpretive booklet; $6 per manual; postpaid; (5–10) minutes; William H. Urban; Western Psychological Services. *

[423]

*Draw-A-Person Quality Scale. Ages 16–25; 1955–65; DPQS; level of intellectual functioning; 1 form ('65, 4 pages); manual ('55, 54 pages); 10¢ per test; $3 per manual; postage extra; Spanish edition available; [10–20] minutes; Mazie Earle Wagner and Herman J. P. Schubert; Herman J. P. Schubert. *

For a review by Philip L. Harriman, see 5:129 (3 references).

REFERENCES

1–3. See 5:129.
4. STRUMPFER, DEODANDUS JOHANN WILLHELM. *A Study of Some Communicable Measures for the Evaluation of Human Figure Drawings.* Doctor's thesis, Purdue University (Lafayette, Ind.), 1959. (*DA* 20:2910)
5. STRUMPFER, D. J. W. "The Relation of Draw-A-Person Test Variables to Age and Chronicity in Psychotic Groups." *J Clin Psychol* 19:208–11 Ap '63. * (*PA* 39:5102)
6. MARAIS, H. C., and STRUMPFER, D. J. W. "DAP Body-Image Disturbance Scale and Quality of Drawing." Abstract. *Percept & Motor Skills* 21:196 Ag '65. * (*PA* 40:43)

[424]

The Driscoll Play Kit. Ages 2–10; 1952; DPK; personality development and adjustment; individual; 1 form (5 dolls and 27 pieces of furniture); manual (6 pages); no scoring or interpretive procedure; $75 per set of materials, postpaid; manual free; adminis-

tration time not reported; Gertrude P. Driscoll; Psychological Corporation. *

See 6:210 (2 references).

[425]

The Eight Card Redrawing Test. Ages 7 and over; 1950–57; 8CRT; 1 form ('56, 9 pages); manual ('57, 161 pages, see 5 below); directions for administering ('56, 1 page); score sheet ('56, 1 page); no data on reliability; no norms; $6 per set of test materials for 35 administrations; $4 per manual; postpaid; (30–60) minutes; Leopold Caligor; 8CRT. *

See 6:211 (4 excerpts); for reviews by Cherry Ann Clark and Philip L. Harriman, see 5:131 (6 references, 1 excerpt).

REFERENCES

1–6. See 5:131.
7. SMITH, MARGUERITE ANDERSON. *Compliance and Defiance as It Relates to Role Conflict in Women.* Doctor's thesis, University of Michigan (Ann Arbor, Mich.), 1961. (*DA* 22:646)

[426]

★Evanston Early Identification Scale, Field Research Edition. Ages 5–0 to 6–3; 1967; EEIS; for identifying children who can be expected to have difficulty in school; 1 form (3 pages); manual (45 pages); $1.50 per 15 tests; $1.59 per manual; specimen set not available; postage extra; [10–45] minutes; Myril Landsman and Harry Dillard; Follett Educational Corporation. *

REFERENCE

1. DILLARD, HARRY K., and LANDSMAN, MYRIL. "The Evanston Early Identification Scale: Prediction of School Problems From the Human Figure Drawings of Kindergarten Children." *J Clin Psychol* 24:227–8 Ap '68. * (*PA* 42:12748)

[427]

*The Family Relations Indicator, Revised Edition. Emotionally disturbed children and their parents; 1962–67; FRI; intra-family relationships; 1 form ['67, 24 cards]; manual ('67, 31 pages); record sheet ['67, 1 page]; no data on reliability; 147s. per set of cards, 20 record sheets, and manual, postage extra; (60) minutes in 2 sessions; John G. Howells and John R. Lickorish; Oliver & Boyd Ltd. *

For reviews by C. B. Blakemore and Walter Katkovsky, see 6:212 (1 reference).

REFERENCES

1. See 6:212.
2. LICKORISH, JOHN R. "Evaluating the Child's View of His Parents." *J Proj Tech & Pers Assess* 30:68–76 F '66. * (*PA* 40:5491)

[428]

The Five Task Test: A Performance and Projective Test of Emotionality, Motor Skill and Organic Brain Damage. Ages 8 and over; 1955; FTT; 1 form; mimeographed manual (25 pages); scoring booklet (8 pages); no data on reliability; $10 per set of test materials; $2 per manual; postpaid; (15–20) minutes; Charlotte Buhler and Kathryn Mandeville; Western Psychological Services. *

For reviews by Dorothy H. Eichorn and Bert R. Sappenfield, see 5:133 (1 excerpt).

[429]

The Forer Structured Sentence Completion Test. Ages 10–18, adults; 1957; FSSCT; 1 form (4 pages); separate editions for boys, girls, men and women; mimeographed manual (16 pages); checklist (4 pages); no data on reliability; no norms; $6.50 per 25 tests; $6.50 per 25 checklists; $2 per manual; $10 per set of 20 tests, 20 checklists, and manual; postpaid;

specimen set not available; [30–45] minutes; Bertram R. Forer; Western Psychological Services. *

For reviews by Charles N. Cofer and Percival M. Symonds, see 5:134 (5 references).

REFERENCES

1–5. See 5:134.
6. CARR, ARTHUR C. Chap. 4, "The Psychodiagnostic Test Battery: Rationale and Methodology," pp. 28–39. In *Progress in Clinical Psychology, Vol. 3.* Edited by Daniel Brower and Lawrence E. Abt. New York: Grune & Stratton, Inc., 1958. Pp. vi, 249. * (*PA* 33:8255)
7. FORER, BERTRAM R. Chap. 11, "Word Association and Sentence Completion Methods," pp. 210–24. In *Projective Techniques With Children.* Edited by Albert I. Rabin and Mary R. Haworth. New York: Grune & Stratton, Inc., 1960. Pp. xiii, 392. * (*PA* 35:2229)
8. FORER, BERTRAM R. "Sentence Completions," pp. 6–17, 94–105. In *The Prediction of Overt Behavior Through the Use of Projective Techniques.* Edited by Arthur C. Carr. Springfield, Ill.: Charles C Thomas, Publisher, 1960. Pp. xiii, 177. * (*PA* 36:2HG77C)
9. KAREN, ROBERT L. "A Method for Rating Sentence Completion Test Responses." *J Proj Tech* 25:312–4 S '61. *

[430]

The Forer Vocational Survey. "Young adolescents"; 1957; FVS; vocational adjustment; Forms M (men), W (women), (4 pages); mimeographed manual (8 pages); record booklet (4 pages); no data on reliability and validity; no norms; $6.50 per 25 tests; $6.50 per 25 record forms; $2.50 per manual; postpaid; specimen set not available; [20–30] minutes; Bertram R. Forer; Western Psychological Services. *

For reviews by Benjamin Balinsky and Charles N. Cofer, see 5:135 (1 excerpt).

[431]

Four Picture Test (1930), Second Edition. Ages 10 and over; 1948–58; FPT; 1 form ('58, 4 cards); manual ('58, 15 pages); no data on reliability and validity; no norms; gld. 38 ($10) per set of cards and manual, postpaid; (30–45) minutes; D. J. van Lennep and R. Houwink (manual); publisher and distributor in Holland and Belgium: Netherlands Institute of Industrial Psychology; distributor in all other countries: Martinus Nijhoff. *

For reviews by S. G. Lee and Johann M. Schepers, see 6:213 (3 references); for reviews by John E. Bell, E. J. G. Bradford, and Ephraim Rosen of the original edition, see 4:105 (3 references, 1 excerpt).

REFERENCES

1–3. See 4:105.
4–6. See 6:213.
7. LOVELACE, EUGENE J. "Social Role Preferences and Responses to the Four Picture Test." *J Proj Tech & Pers Assess* 28:64–6 Mr '64. * (*PA* 39:1489)
8. KUNKE, TH. "Intellect and Creativity in Van Lennep's Four Picture Test." *Rorsch Newsl* 12:10–6 D '67. * (*PA* 42:17251)
9. THOMAS, EDWARD LLEWELLYN. "Eye Movements During Projective Testing." Abstract. *Int Congr Rorsch & Proj Meth* 6(3):325–6 '68. *

[432]

Franck Drawing Completion Test. Ages 6 and over; 1951–52; FDCT; masculinity-femininity; 1 form ['51, 4 pages]; mimeographed preliminary manual ['52, 7 pages]; scoring sheet ['51, 1 page]; no data on reliability and validity; Aus $1.40 per 10 tests; 35¢ per 10 scoring sheets; 50¢ per manual; $1.20 per specimen set; postpaid within Australia; (15–60) minutes; Kate Franck; Australian Council for Educational Research. *

For a review by Arthur W. Meadows, see 5:136 (5 references).

REFERENCES

1–5. See 5:136.
6. ENGEL, ILONA MARIA. *A Factor Analytic Study of Items From Five Masculinity-Femininity Tests.* Doctor's thesis,

University of Michigan (Ann Arbor, Mich.), 1962. (*DA* 23:307)
7. KETTERING, WALTER RICHARD. *The Use of Two Projective Drawing Techniques as Indices of Masculinity and Femininity With Children of Varying Levels of Intelligence.* Doctor's thesis, University of Pittsburgh (Pittsburgh, Pa.), 1965. (*DA* 27:956B)
8. ENGEL, ILONA M. "A Factor-Analytic Study of Items From Five Masculinity-Femininity Tests." Abstract. *J Consult Psychol* 30:565 D '66. * (*PA* 41:2880, title only)
9. SCHAEFER, CHARLES EUGENE. *Biographical Inventory Correlates of Scientific and Artistic Creativity in Adolescents.* Doctor's thesis. Fordham University (New York, N.Y.), 1967. (*DA* 28:1173B)
10. BIELIAUSKAS, VYTAUTAS J.; MIRANDA, SIMON B.; and LANSKY, LEONARD M. "Obviousness of Two Masculinity-Femininity Tests." *J Consult & Clin Psychol* 32:314–8 Je '68. * (*PA* 42:13769)

[433]

★The Graphoscopic Scale: A Projective Psychodiagnostic Method. Ages 5–16, 15 and over; 1953–69; author uses acronym PGS, denoting *Pikunas Graphoscopic Scale;* drawing completion technique; 5 scores: self-expressive balance, intelligence, creativity index, adjustment, total (called diagnostic and prognostic rating); 2 levels; mimeographed manual ('69, 44 pages plus tests and scoring blank); scoring blank ('69, 3 pages); no data on reliability; norms (consisting of means and standard deviations) for total score only; 50¢ per test; 10¢ per scoring blank; $2 per manual; postpaid; [30–50] minutes; Justin Pikunas; the Author. *

a) PGS 1. Ages 5–16; 1956–69; 1 form ('56, 1 page).
b) PGS 2. Ages 15 and over; 1963–69; 1 form ('63, 1 page).

REFERENCES

1. BUSHEY, J. T. *The Relation Between Intelligence as Shown on the PGS and School Success of Children Between the Ages of 7 and 9.* Master's thesis, University of Detroit (Detroit, Mich.), 1955.
2. DEMKO, D. *The Relation Between Adjustment as Shown on the PGS and Teachers' Ratings of Children Between the Ages of 10 and 12.* Master's thesis, University of Detroit (Detroit, Mich.), 1957.
3. PIKUNAS, JUSTIN, and CARBERRY, HUGH. "Standardization of the Graphoscopic Scale: The Content of Children's Drawing." *J Clin Psychol* 17:297–301 Jl '61. * (*PA* 38:8433)
4. WELTER, M. BORROMEO. *A Comparison of the California Test of Mental Maturity and the Pikunas Graphoscopic Scale as Measures of Intelligence and Academic Achievement.* Master's thesis, University of Detroit (Detroit, Mich.), 1961.
5. KUNTZ, PERPETUA. *The Pikunas Graphoscopic Scale as a Measure of Intelligence and Adjustment in the Testing of Mental Retardates.* Master's thesis, University of Detroit (Detroit, Mich.), 1962.
6. NEVILLE, HELEN ANN. *A Diagnostic Evaluation of the PGS II as Compared to the MMPI.* Master's thesis, University of Detroit (Detroit, Mich.), 1964.
7. GOLEN, M. EVARISTA. *A Comparison of WISC and the PGS in Prediction of School Achievement.* Master's thesis, University of Detroit (Detroit, Mich.), 1965.
8. MORRISSETTE, MARY PAULINE. *The Use of Categories by Bright, Normal, and Subnormal Preadolescent Girls on the Pikunas Graphoscopic Scale and the Stephens' Categorization Tasks.* Doctor's thesis, University of Oklahoma (Norman, Okla.), 1967. (*DA* 27:4565B)

[434]

The Group Personality Projective Test. Ages 11 and over; 1956–61; GPPT; formerly called *Kahn Stick Figure Personality Test;* 7 scores: tension reduction quotient, nurturance, withdrawal, neuroticism, affiliation, succorance, total; 1 form ('58, 17 pages); manual ('61, 20 pages, reprint of 4 below); directions for interpretation ('60, 2 pages); separate answer sheets (IBM 805) must be used; $13.50 per examiner's kit of 12 tests, 100 answer-profile sheets, set of scoring stencils, and manual; $2 per manual; cash orders postpaid; specimen set not available; (40–45) minutes; Russell N. Cassel and Theodore C. Kahn; Psychological Test Specialists. *

REFERENCES

1–7. See 6:214.
8. CASSEL, RUSSELL N., and KAHN, THEODORE C. "Development and Standardization of the Group Personality Projective Test." *J Proj Tech* 22:267–71 S '58. * (*PA* 33:9245)
9. BRAUN, JOHN R. "Group Personality Projective Test Fakability: A Re-Examination." *J Clin Psychol* 23:389–91 Jl '67. * (*PA* 41:15301)

[435]

Group Projection Sketches for the Study of Small Groups. Groups of 3–40 people (ages 16 and over) ; 1949 ; 1 form (5 pictures) ; manual [see 5:138 (1), *out of print*] ; no data on reliability and validity ; $3.50 per set of pictures, postage extra ; (60) minutes ; William E. Henry and Harold Guetzkow ; William E. Henry. *

For a review by Cecil A. Gibb, see 5:138 (1 reference) ; for reviews by Robert R. Holt and N. W. Morton, see 4:106.

[436]

★**HFD Test.** Ages 5–12 ; 1968 ; HFDT ; human figure drawing test, drawing of a whole person ; level of mental ability score and 30 emotional indicator signs ; manual (350 pages, see *1* below) ; no accessories ; no norms for total number of emotional indicators ; $9.75 per manual, postage extra ; (10–30) minutes ; Elizabeth Munsterberg Koppitz ; Grune & Stratton, Inc. *

REFERENCES

1. KOPPITZ, ELIZABETH M.; SULLIVAN, JOHN; BLYTH, DAVID D.; and SHELTON, JOEL. "Prediction of First Grade School Achievement With the Bender Gestalt Test and Human Figure Drawings." *J Clin Psychol* 15:164–8 Ap '59. * (*PA* 35:5372)
2. KOPPITZ, ELIZABETH MUNSTERBERG. "A Comparison of Pencil and Crayon Drawings of Young Children." *J Clin Psychol* 21:191–4 Ap '65. * (*PA* 39:12393)
3. KOPPITZ, ELIZABETH MUNSTERBERG. "Emotional Indicators on Human Figure Drawings and School Achievement of First and Second Graders." *J Clin Psychol* 22:481–3 O '66. * (*PA* 41:3432)
4. KOPPITZ, ELIZABETH MUNSTERBERG. "Emotional Indicators on Human Figure Drawings of Children: A Validation Study." *J Clin Psychol* 22:313–5 Jl '66. * (*PA* 40:10630)
5. KOPPITZ, ELIZABETH MUNSTERBERG. "Expected and Exceptional Items on Human Figure Drawings and IQ Scores of Children Age 5 to 12." *J Clin Psychol* 23:81–3 Ja '67. * (*PA* 41:5985)
6. DE MOREAU, MARGARET, and KOPPITZ, ELIZABETH M. "Relationship Between Goodenough Draw-A-Man Test IQ Scores and Koppitz Human Figure Drawing Scores." *Revista Interamericana de Psicología* 2:35–40 Mr '68. * (*PA* 42:13753)
7. KOPPITZ, ELIZABETH MUNSTERBERG. *Psychological Evaluation of Children's Human Figure Drawings.* New York: Grune & Stratton, Inc., 1968. Pp. x, 341. *
8. KOPPITZ, ELIZABETH M., and DE MOREAU, MARGARET. "A Comparison of Emotional Indicators on Human Figure Drawings of Children From Mexico and From the United States." *Revista Interamericana de Psicología* 2:41–8 Mr '68. * (*PA* 42:13579)

[437]

*****H-T-P: House-Tree-Person Projective Technique.** Ages 3 and over ; 1946–66 ; 1 form ['46, 4 pages] ; manual ('48, 115 pages) ; supplement ('64, 119 pages, including copies of drawing form, interrogation folders, and scoring folder) ; revised manual ('66, 356 pages) ; interrogation folder: adult form ('50, 4 pages), children's form ('56, 4 pages) ; scoring folder ('50, 4 pages) ; two copy drawing form ('64, 6 pages) may be used for group testing ; adult norms only ; $3 per 25 drawing forms ; $6.50 per 25 interrogation folders ; $6.50 per 25 scoring folders ; $6.50 per 25 two copy drawing forms ; $5.50 per manual ; $5 per supplement ; $12.50 per revised manual ; postpaid ; specimen set not available ; (60–90) minutes ; John N. Buck and Isaac Jolles (children's interrogation folder) ; Western Psychological Services. *

For a review by Mary R. Haworth, see 6:215 (32 references) ; for a review by Philip L. Harriman, see 5:139 (61 references) ; for reviews by Albert Ellis and Ephraim Rosen, see 4:107 (14 references, 1 excerpt ; for reviews by Morris Krugman and Katherine W. Wilcox, see 3:47 (5 references) ; for related book reviews not excerpted in this volume, consult the 5th MMY (B234).

REFERENCES

1–5. See 3:47.
6–19. See 4:107.
20–80. See 5:139.
81–112. See 6:215.
113. BRISTOW, M. ROBIN. *Formal Art Training and the H-T-P IQ's.* Master's thesis, Richmond Professional Institute (Richmond, Va.), 1957.
114. KELLY, J. J. *The Relationship Between Social Status and the H-T-P Drawings.* Master's thesis, Richmond Professional Institute (Richmond, Va.), 1957.
115. PIETY, KENNETH RALPH. *The Role of Defense in Reporting on the Self Concept.* Doctor's thesis, Vanderbilt University (Nashville, Tenn.), 1958. (*DA* 18:1869)
116. GRIMM, ELAINE R. "Psychological Tension in Pregnancy." *Psychosom Med* 23:520–7 N–D '61. * (*PA* 36:5JU20G)
117. LIEF, HAROLD I.; DINGMAN, JOSEPH F.; and BISHOP, MELVIN P. "Psychoendocrinologic Studies in Male With Cyclic Changes in Sexuality." *Psychosom Med* 24:357–68 Jl–Ag '62. * (*PA* 37:5514)
118. CAVANAGH, MICHAEL E. *The Validity of Some Qualitative Scoring Items on the Drawings of a House, Tree, and Person.* Master's thesis, University of Ottawa (Ottawa, Ont., Canada), 1963.
119. GOLDEN, JULES S.; SILVER, REUBEN J.; and MANDEL, NATHAN. "The Wives of 50 'Normal' American Men." *Arch Gen Psychiatry* 9:614–8 D '63. * (*PA* 38:8588)
120. AUSDENMOORE, R. J. *The Conventional Use of Color in Chromatic H-T-P Drawings.* Master's thesis, Xavier University (Cincinnati, Ohio), 1964.
121. JOLLES, ISAAC. *A Catalogue for the Qualitative Interpretation of the House-Tree-Person (H-T-P), Revised 1964.* Beverly Hills, Calif.: Western Psychological Services, Publishers, 1964. Pp. ii, 61. *
122. MABRY, MARIE. "Serial Projective Drawings in a Patient With a Malignant Brain Tumor." *J Proj Tech & Pers Assess* 28:206–9 Je '64. * (*PA* 39:5207)
123. NAAR, RAY. "An Attempt to Differentiate Delinquents From Non-Delinquents on the Basis of Projective Drawings." *J Crim Law & Criminol* 55:107–10 Mr '64. * (*PA* 39:1865)
124. WILLIAMS, L. A., JR. *An Evaluation of Selected Schizophrenic Signs in H-T-P Drawings.* Master's thesis, Xavier University (Cincinnati, Ohio), 1964.
125. WILLIAMS, PAUL J. *The Validity of Some Qualitative Scoring Items, in Terms of Hostility and Aggression, on the Drawings of a House, Tree and Person.* Master's thesis, University of Ottawa (Ottawa, Ont., Canada), 1964.
126. YAGODA, GERALD, and WOLFSON, WILLIAM. "Examiner Influence on Projective Test Responses." *J Clin Psychol* 20:389 Jl '64. * (*PA* 39:10276)
127. BIELIAUSKAS, VYTAUTAS J. *The House-Tree-Person (H-T-P) Research Review: A Bibliography and Research Review, 1965 Edition.* Beverly Hills, Calif.: Western Psychological Services, 1965. Pp. iii, 52. *
128. BIELIAUSKAS, VYTAUTAS J., and CLARKE, WALTER J. "The Problem of Shading in H-T-P Drawings: Its Internal Consistency and Relation to Personality Characteristics." *J General Psychol* 72:295–9 Ap '65. * (*PA* 39:12330)
129. CHOATE, M. S. *A Developmental Analysis of Details in H-T-P Drawings of the House.* Master's thesis, Richmond Professional Institute (Richmond, Va.), 1965.
130. BUCK, JOHN N. *The House-Tree-Person Technique: Revised Manual.* Beverly Hills, Calif.: Western Psychological Services, 1966. Pp. viii, 348. *
131. KUNCE, JOSEPH T., and WORLEY, BERT. "Projective Drawings of Brain-Injured Subjects." *Percept & Motor Skills* 22:163–8 F '66. * (*PA* 40:5129)
132. DOORBAR, RUTH RAE. "Psychological Testing of Transsexuals: A Brief Report of Results From the Wechsler Adult Intelligence Scale, the Thematic Apperception Test, and the House-Tree-Person Test." *Trans N Y Acad Sci* 29:455–62 F '67. * (*PA* 41:16827)
133. LATTAL, K. A., and LATTAL, ALICE D. "Student 'Gullibility': A Systematic Replication." *J Psychol* 67:319–22 N '67. * (*PA* 42:2490)
134. OFFORD, DAVID R., and APONTE, JOSEPH F. "A Comparison of Drawings and Sentence Completion Responses of Congenital Heart Children With Normal Children." *J Proj Tech & Pers Assess* 31:57–62 Ap '67. * (*PA* 41:13685)
135. WILDMAN, ROBERT W.; WILDMAN, ROBERT W., II; and SMITH, ROBERT D. "Expansiveness-Constriction on the H-T-P as Indicators of Extraversion-Introversion." *J Clin Psychol* 23:493–4 O '67. * (*PA* 42:2616)

136. JANSSEN, MARIA C. "A Psychological Study of the Emotional Implications of Pregnancy, Delivery and Puerperium." *Int Congr Rorsch & Proj Meth* 6(4)583-7 '68. *

NAME INDEX

[438]

*The Hand Test. Ages 6 and over; 1959-69; HT; 10 normed scores: interpersonal, environmental, maladjustive, withdrawal, affection-dependence-communication, direction-aggression, total responses, average initial response time, highest minus lowest response time, pathological; individual and group forms; postpaid; (10) minutes; Edwin E. Wagner. *
a) [INDIVIDUAL FORM.] 1959-69; 1 form ('59, 10 cards); scoring sheet ['62, 2 pages]; manual ('69, 72 pages, identical with 1962 manual with 7 additional pages of normative data and references); reliability data for pathological score only; $4.50 per set of cards; $6.50 per 100 scoring sheets; $4.50 per manual; Western Psychological Services.

b) [GROUP FORM.] 1959-65; for experimental use; 1 form ('65, 12 pages); no manual; no data on reliability and validity; no norms; 25¢ per test; the Author.

For a review by Goldine C. Gleser, see 6:216 (6 references, 1 excerpt); for a related book review not excerpted in this volume, consult the 6th MMY (B95).

REFERENCES

1-6. See 6:216.
7. HUBERMAN, JOHN. "A Failure of the Wagner Hand Test to Discriminate Among Workers Rated High, Average and Low on Activity Level and General Acceptability." *J Proj Tech & Pers Assess* 28:280-3 S '64. * (*PA* 39:8854)
8. SHAW, DALE J., and LINDEN, JAMES D. "A Critique of the Hand Test." *Ed & Psychol Meas* 24:283-4 su '64. * (*PA* 39:5090)
9. WAGNER, EDWIN E., and HAWKINS, ROGER. "Differentiation of Assaultive Delinquents With the Hand Test." *J Proj Tech & Pers Assess* 28:363-5 S '64. * (*PA* 39:7928)
10. DRUMMOND, FRANCES. "A Failure in the Discrimination of Aggressive Behavior of Undifferentiated Schizophrenics With the Hand Test." *J Proj Tech & Pers Assess* 30:275-9 Je '66. * (*PA* 39:9432)
11. HODGE, JAMES R.; WAGNER, EDWIN E.; and SCHREINER, FREDERICK. "Hypnotic Validation of Two Hand Test Scoring Categories." *J Proj Tech & Pers Assess* 30:385-6 Ag '66. * (*PA* 40:12355)
12. WAGNER, EDWIN E. "The Imaginary Lovers Delusion: A Diagnostic Case Study." *J Proj Tech & Pers Assess* 30:394-400 Ag '66. * (*PA* 40:12532)
13. WAGNER, EDWIN E., and CAPOTOSTO, MARY. "Discrimination of Good and Poor Retarded Workers With the Hand Test." *Am J Mental Def* 71:126-8 Jl '66. * (*PA* 40:11447)
14. BRODSKY, STANLEY L., and BRODSKY, ANNETTE M. "Hand Test Indicators of Antisocial Behavior." *J Proj Tech & Pers Assess* 31:36-9 O '67. * (*PA* 42:751)
15. OSWALD, MURRAY O., and LOFTUS, A. PATRICK. "A Normative and Comparative Study of the Hand Test With Normal and Delinquent Children." *J Proj Tech & Pers Assess* 31:62-8 Ag '67. * (*PA* 41:15318)
16. WETSEL, HARRIETTE; SHAPIRO, ROBERT J.; and WAGNER, EDWIN E. "Prediction of Recidivism Among Juvenile Delinquents With the Hand Test." *J Proj Tech & Pers Assess* 31: 69-72 Ag '67. * (*PA* 41:15514)
17. CAMPOS, LEONARD P. "The Hand Test," pp. 472-81. In *Projective Techniques in Personality Assessment: A Modern Introduction.* Edited by A. I. Rabin. New York: Springer Publishing Co., Inc., 1968. Pp. x, 638. *
18. ZUCKER, KARL B., and JORDAN, DANIEL C. "The Paired Hands Test: A Technique for Measuring Friendliness." *J Proj Tech & Pers Assess* 32:522-3 D '68. *

[439]

*The Holtzman Inkblot Technique. Ages 5 and over; 1958-66; HIT; 22 scores: reaction time, rejection, location, space, form definiteness, form appropriateness, color, shading, movement, pathognomic verbalization, integration, content (human, animal, anatomy, sex, abstract), anxiety, hostility, barrier, penetration, balance, popular; 2 formats; manual ('61, 423 pages, see 7 below) not adapted for group administration; $8 per manual, postpaid; for computerized scoring and interpreting service, see 440; (75) minutes; Wayne H. Holtzman, Joseph S. Thorpe (manual), Jon D. Swartz (manual), and E. Wayne Herron (manual); Psychological Corporation. *
a) [INDIVIDUAL TEST.] 1958-61; Forms A, B, ('58, 47 cards); administration and scoring guide ('61, c1958-61, 171 pages, reprinted in part from manual); record form ('58, 8 pages) for each form; summary sheet ('58, 2 pages); $29 per set of cards for either form, 25 record forms, and administration and scoring guide; $52 per set of cards and accessories for both forms; $2.75 per 25 record forms and summary sheets; $3.25 per administration and scoring guide.
b) [GROUP TEST.] 1958-66; Form A ('58, set of 35 mm. Kodaslides); no specific manual; group record form ('66, 2 pages); $55 per set of Kodaslides; $2.40 per 50 group record forms; for scoring service, see 440; Donald R. Gorham (record form).

For reviews by Richard W. Coan, H. J. Eysenck, Bertram R. Forer, and William N. Thetford, see 6:217 (22 references); for related book reviews not excerpted in this volume, consult the 6th MMY (B264).

REFERENCES

1–22. See 6:217.

23. HOLTZMAN, WAYNE H. Chap. 7, "Objective Scoring of Projective Tests," pp. 119–45. In *Objective Approaches to Personality Assessment.* Edited by Bernard M. Bass and Irwin A. Berg. New York: D. Van Nostrand Co., Inc., 1959. Pp. x, 233. * (*PA* 33:9926)

24. SIMKINS, LAWRENCE DAVID. *Behavioral Modification as a Function of Examiner Reinforcement and Situational Variables in a Projective Testing Situation.* Doctor's thesis, University of Houston (Houston, Tex.), 1959. (*DA* 20:1871)

25. CLEVELAND, SIDNEY E. "Body Image Changes Associated With Personality Reorganization." *J Consult Psychol* 24:256–61 Je '60. * (*PA* 35:6922)

26. CLEVELAND, SIDNEY E., and FISHER, SEYMOUR. "A Comparison of Psychological Characteristics and Physiological Reactivity in Ulcer and Rheumatoid Arthritis Groups: I, Psychological Measures." *Psychosom Med* 22:283–9 Jl–Ag '60. * (*PA* 35:5281)

27. STEFFY, RICHARD ALAN. *Measurement of the Process-Reactive Dimension in Schizophrenia by Means of the Holtzman Inkblot Test.* Master's thesis, University of Illinois (Urbana, Ill.), 1960.

28. THORPE, J. S. *Level of Perceptual Development as Reflected in Responses to the Holtzman Inkblot Technique.* Doctor's thesis, University of Texas (Austin, Tex.), 1960. (*DA* 21:2789)

29. HOLTZMAN, WAYNE H. "Measurement of Personality Change Through Inkblot Perception," pp. 220–4. In *Transactions of the Fifth Research Conference on Cooperative Chemotherapy Studies in Psychiatry and Research Approaches to Mental Illness.* Washington, D.C.: Veterans Administration, 1961. Pp. xxxv, 375. *

30. RUEBUSH, BRITTON K., and WAITE, RICHARD R. "Oral Dependency in Anxious and Defensive Children." *Merrill-Palmer Q* 7:181–90 Jl '61. * (*PA* 36:2FF81R)

31. CLEVELAND, SIDNEY E., and MORTON, ROBERT B. "Group Behavior and Body-Image: A Follow-Up Study." *Hum Relations* 15:77–85 F '62. * (*PA* 37:1094)

32. BARNES, CHARLES MANLY. *Prediction of Brain Damage Using the Holtzman Inkblot Technique and Other Selected Variables.* Doctor's thesis, State University of Iowa (Iowa City, Iowa), 1963. (*DA* 24:4789)

33. DORIS, JOHN; SARASON, SEYMOUR B.; and BERKOWITZ, LAWRENCE. "Test Anxiety and Performance on Projective Tests." *Child Develop* 34:751–66 S '63. * (*PA* 38:8546)

34. FERNALD, PETER SUTCLIFFE. *An Exploratory Study of the Human Content Response in the Holtzman Inkblot Technique.* Doctor's thesis, Purdue University (Lafayette, Ind.), 1963. (*DA* 24:5542)

35. OVERALL, JOHN E., and GORHAM, DONALD R. "A Pattern Probability Model for the Classification of Psychiatric Patients." *Behav Sci* 8:108–16 Ap '63. * (*PA* 38:1195)

36. DAW, RICHARD PATRICK. *An Assessment of the Holtzman and the Rorschach Inkblots Using the Semantic Differential.* Doctor's thesis, University of Denver (Denver, Colo.), 1964. (*DA* 26:488)

37. FISHER, SEYMOUR. "Body Image and Psychopathology." *Arch Gen Psychiatry* 10:519–29 My '64. * (*PA* 39:5749)

38. GRIGG, A. E.; LEFTWICH, W. H.; and GILMORE, MILDRED. "Connotative Associations of the Holtzman Inkblots." *Psychol* 1:11–3 N '64. * (*PA* 39:5202)

39. HARTLEY, RONALD BRYAN. *A Homonym Word Association Measure of the Barrier Variable and Its Comparison With the Inkblot Barrier Measure.* Doctor's thesis, University of Washington (Seattle, Wash.), 1964. (*DA* 25:3109)

40. HERRON, E. WAYNE. "Changes in Inkblot Perception With Presentation of the Holtzman Inkblot Technique as an 'Intelligence Test.'" *J Proj Tech & Pers Assess* 28:442–7 D '64. * (*PA* 39:7896)

41. HOLTZMAN, WAYNE H.; GORHAM, DONALD R.; and MORAN, LOUIS J. "A Factor-Analytic Study of Schizophrenic Thought Processes." *J Abn & Social Psychol* 69:355–64 O '64. * (*PA* 39:8491)

42. KOLLAR, EDWARD J.; SLATER, GRANT R.; PALMER, JAMES O.; DOCTER, RICHARD F.; and MANDELL, ARNOLD J. "Measurement of Stress in Fasting Man: A Pilot Study." *Arch Gen Psychiatry* 11:113–25 Ag '64. * (*PA* 39:4233)

43. LOPER, RODNEY GRANT. *The Influence of Prior Verbal Reinforcement on Inkblot Test Content.* Doctor's thesis, University of Minnesota (Minneapolis, Minn.), 1964. (*DA* 26:2870)

44. MURRAY, JOSEPH E., and JACKSON, DOUGLAS N. "Impulsivity and Color-Form Abstraction." *J Consult Psychol* 28:518–22 D '64. * (*PA* 39:7703)

45. VAN DE CASTLE, R. L., and SPICHER, ROBERT S. "A Semantic Differential Investigation of Color on the Holtzman." *J Proj Tech & Pers Assess* 28:491–8 D '64. * (*PA* 39:7926)

46. BLOCK, WILLIAM E., and GREENFIELD, LAWRENCE. "Adaptation to Inkblot Stimuli: Effects of Order of Presentation, Context and Stimuli Characteristics." *J Clin Psychol* 21:301–4 Jl '65. * (*PA* 39:15381)

47. CLARK, CHARLES M.; VELDMAN, DONALD J.; and THORPE, JOSEPH S. "Convergent and Divergent Thinking Abilities of Talented Adolescents." *J Ed Psychol* 56:157–63 Je '65. * (*PA* 39:12317)

48. CONNERS, C. KEITH. "Effects of Brief Psychotherapy, Drugs, and Type of Disturbance on Holtzman Inkblot Scores in Children." *Proc Ann Conv Am Psychol Assn* 73:201–2 '65. * (*PA* 39:15550)

49. DEROGATIS, LEONARD R. *Commonality in Perception Among Cultures as a Function of Degree of Stimulus Ambiguity: A Cross-Cultural Study With the Holtzman Inkblots.* Doctor's thesis, Catholic University of America (Washington, D.C.), 1965. (*DA* 27:4550B)

50. GORHAM, DONALD R. "The Development of a Computer Scoring System for Inkblot Responses." *Congr Inter-Am Soc Psychol* 9(1964):258–70 ['65]. *

51. HERRON, E. WAYNE. "Personality Factors Associated With the Acquisition of the Conditioned Eyelid Response." *J Personality & Social Psychol* 2:775–7 N '65. * (*PA* 40:2858)

52. MEGARGEE, EDWIN I. "The Performance of Juvenile Delinquents on the Holtzman Inkblot Technique: A Normative Study." *J Proj Tech & Pers Assess* 29:504–12 D '65. * (*PA* 40:3154)

53. MEGARGEE, EDWIN I. "Relation Between Barrier Scores and Aggressive Behavior." *J Abn Psychol* 70:307–11 Ag '65. * (*PA* 39:15404)

54. MILLER, HAROLD R. *Test Anxiety and the Holtzman Inkblot Technique.* Master's thesis, Ohio University (Athens, Ohio), 1965.

55. PETERS, PHYLLIS G. *A Study of Clinical Judgment: Prediction of Patient Behavior From Projective, Self-Rating and Behavior Rating Instruments.* Doctor's thesis, Northwestern University (Evanston, Ill.), 1965. (*DA* 26:3489)

56. SHIPMAN, WILLIAM G. "Personality Traits Associated With Body-Image Boundary Concern." *Proc Ann Conv Am Psychol Assn* 73:271–2 '65. * (*PA* 39:15441)

57. SPIEGEL, DOUGLAS KAY. *Relations Between Two Test Batteries.* Doctor's thesis, University of North Carolina (Chapel Hill, N.C.), 1965. (*DA* 27:296B)

58. SWARTZ, JON D. "Developmental Aspects of Perceptual-Cognitive Functioning: Preliminary Findings From the First Two Years of a Six-Year Longitudinal Study." *Congr Inter-Am Soc Psychol* 9(1964): 249–57 ['65]. *

59. SWARTZ, JON D. "Performance of High- and Low-Anxious Children on the Holtzman Inkblot Technique." *Child Develop* 36:569–75 Je '65. * (*PA* 39:12429)

60. THORPE, JOSEPH S. "A Cross-Cultural Study of Personality Development: Selection of Test Measures." *Congr Inter-Am Soc Psychol* 9(1964):242–9 ['65]. *

61. THORPE, JOSEPH S., and SWARTZ, JON D. "Level of Perceptual Development as Reflected in Responses to the Holtzman Inkblot Technique." *J Proj Tech & Pers Assess* 29:380–6 S '65. * (*PA* 39:15424)

62. ULLMANN, LEONARD P., and ECK, ROY A. "Inkblot Perception and the Process-Reactive Distinction." *J Clin Psychol* 21:311–3 Jl '65. * (*PA* 39:15425)

63. WHITAKER, LEIGHTON, JR. "The Rorschach and Holtzman as Measures of Pathognomic Verbalization." *J Consult Psychol* 29:181–3 Ap '65. * (*PA* 39:10275)

64. ALLARDICE, BARBARA S., and DOLE, ARTHUR A. "Body Image in Hansen's Disease Patients." *J Proj Tech & Pers Assess* 30:356–8 Ag '66. * (*PA* 40:12348)

65. DE ROO, WILLIAM MEERSE. *A Study of Relationships Between Counselor Personality and Counseling Behavior.* Doctor's thesis, Michigan State University (East Lansing, Mich.), 1966. (*DA* 27:1652A)

66. ENDICOTT, NOBLE A., and JORTNER, SIDNEY. "Objective Measures of Depression." *Arch Gen Psychiatry* 15:249–55 S '66. * (*PA* 40:11652)

67. FERNALD, PETER S., and LINDEN, JAMES D. "The Human Content Response in the Holtzman Inkblot Technique." *J Proj Tech & Pers Assess* 30:441–6 O '66. * (*PA* 41:507)

68. FISHER, SEYMOUR, and RENIK, OWEN D. "Induction of Body Image Boundary Changes." *J Proj Tech & Pers Assess* 30:429–34 O '66. * (*PA* 41:599)

69. HAMILTON, ROBERT, and ROBERTSON, MALCOLM. "Examiner Influence on the Holtzman Inkblot Technique." *Proc Ann Conv Am Psychol Assn* 74:245–6 '66. * (*PA* 41:5984)

70. HAMILTON, ROBERT G., and ROBERTSON, MALCOLM H. "Examiner Influence on the Holtzman Inkblot Technique." *J Proj Tech & Pers Assess* 30:553–8 D '66. * (*PA* 41:2912)

71. HILL, EVELYN F. "Affect Aroused by Color, a Function of Stimulus Strength." *J Proj Tech & Pers Assess* 30:23–30 F '66. * (*PA* 40:5487)

72. JORTNER, SIDNEY. "An Investigation of Certain Cognitive Aspects of Schizophrenia." *J Proj Tech & Pers Assess* 30:559–68 D '66. * (*PA* 41:3135)

73. KNUDSEN, ANN K; GORHAM, DONALD R.; and MOSELEY, EDWARD C. "Universal Popular Responses to Inkblots in Five Cultures: Denmark, Germany, Hong Kong, Mexico and United States." *J Proj Tech & Pers Assess* 30:135–42 Ap '66. * (*PA* 40:7731)

74. KRIPPNER, STANLEY. "Reading Improvement and Scores on the Holtzman Inkblot Technique." *Reading Teach* 19:519–22 Ap '66. * (*PA* 40:7732)

75. MEGARGEE, EDWIN I. "A Comparison of the Scores of

White and Negro Male Juvenile Delinquents on Three Projective Tests." *J Proj Tech & Pers Assess* 30:530–5 D '66. * (PA 41:2920)

76. MEGARGEE, EDWIN I. "The Relation of Response Length to the Holtzman Inkblot Technique." *J Consult Psychol* 30:415–9 O '66. * (PA 40:13208)

77. MEGARGEE, EDWIN I.; LOCKWOOD, VICKI; CATO, JERALDINE L.; and JONES, JOANNA K. "Effects of Differences in Examiner, Tone of Administration, and Sex of Subject on Scores of the Holtzman Inkblot Technique." *Proc Ann Conv Am Psychol Assn* 74:235–6 '66. * (PA 41:5986)

78. NORTON, ALBERTA K. *Validation of HIT Hostility Scorings System.* Master's thesis, Fort Hays Kansas State College (Hays, Kan.), 1966.

79. RICHTER, ROBERT H., and WINTER, WILLIAM D. "Holtzman Inkblot Correlates of Creative Potential." *J Proj Tech & Pers Assess* 30:62–7 F '66. * (PA 40:5495)

80. THORPE, JOSEPH S., and SWARTZ, JON D. "Perceptual Organization: A Developmental Analysis by Means of the Holtzman Inkblot Technique." *J Proj Tech & Pers Assess* 30:447–51 O '66. * (PA 41:604)

81. WELDON, PAUL I. *The Effect of Exposure to Symbolic Aggression on Aggressive Responses to the Holtzman Inkblot Test.* Master's thesis, Fort Hays Kansas State College (Hays, Kan.), 1966.

82. COLE, J. D.; MACHIR, D.; ALTMAN, I.; HAYTHORN, W. W.; and WAGNER, C. M. "Perceptual Changes in Social Isolation and Confinement." *J Clin Psychol* 23:330–3 Jl '67. * (PA 41:14581)

83. ENDICOTT, NOBLE A., and JORTNER, SIDNEY. "Correlates of Somatic Concern Derived From Psychological Tests." *J Nerv & Mental Dis* 144:133–8 F '67. * (PA 41:12111)

84. FISHER, SEYMOUR, and OSOFSKY, HOWARD. "Sexual Responsiveness in Women: Psychological Correlates." *Arch Gen Psychiatry* 17:214–26 Ag '67. * (PA 41:15149)

85. GORHAM, DONALD R. "Validity and Reliability Studies of a Computer-Based Scoring System for Inkblot Responses." *J Consult Psychol* 31:65–70 F '67. * (PA 41:4619)

86. GRAY, JAMES JOSEPH. *An Investigation of the Relationship Between Primary Process Thinking and Creativity.* Doctor's thesis, Fordham University (New York, N.Y.), 1967. (DA 28:5206B)

87. GREENWALD, ALLEN F. "Adjustment Patterns in First Year Theology Students." *R Relig* 26:483–8 My '67. *

88. HARTLEY, RONALD B. "The Barrier Variable as Measured by Homonyms." *J Clin Psychol* 23:196–203 Ap '67. * (PA 41:8931)

89. HEATH, HELEN A.; OKEN, DONALD; and SHIPMAN, WILLIAM G. "Muscle Tension and Personality: A Serious Second Look." *Arch Gen Psychiatry* 16:720–6 Je '67. * (PA 41:13932)

90. HIRT, MICHAEL; ROSS, W. DONALD; and KURTZ, RICHARD. "Construct Validity of Body-Boundary Perception." *Proc Ann Conv Am Psychol Assn* 75:187–8 '67. * (PA 41:12876)

91. JACKSON, DOUGLAS N. "The Holtzman Inkblot Technique in Graduate Clinical Training and Research." *J Psychol Studies* 15:39–48 Mr '67. *

92. KANTNER, LARRY ALLEN. *Commonality in the Use of Drawing Styles and Certain Ambiguous Stimuli.* Doctor's thesis, Pennsylvania State University (University Park, Pa.), 1967. (DA 29:185A)

93. KRIPPNER, STANLEY. "The Relationship of Reading Improvement to Scores on the Holtzman Inkblot Technique." *J Clin Psychol* 23:114–5 Ja '67. * (PA 41:6250)

94. MARWIT, SAMUEL J., and MARCIA, JAMES E. "Tester Bias and Response to Projective Instruments." *J Consult Psychol* 31:253–8 Je '67. * (PA 41:10483)

95. MEGARGEE, EDWIN I., and COOK, PATRICK E. "The Relation of TAT and Inkblot Aggressive Content Scales With Each Other and With Criteria of Overt Aggressiveness in Juvenile Delinquents." *J Proj Tech & Pers Assess* 31:48–60 F '67. * (PA 41:13683)

96. THALER, VICTOR HUGO. *Personality Dimensions Derived From Multiple Instruments.* Doctor's thesis, Columbia University (New York, N.Y.), 1967. (DA 28:509A)

97. ZUCKERMAN, MARVIN; PERSKY, HAROLD; ECKMAN, KATHERINE M.; and HOPKINS, T. ROBERT. "A Multitrait Multimethod Measurement Approach to the Traits (or States) of Anxiety, Depression and Hostility." *J Proj Tech & Pers Assess* 31:39–48 Ap '67. * (PA 41:13635)

98. DEROGATIS, LEONARD R.; GORHAM, DONALD R.; and MOSELEY, EDWARD C. "Structural vs. Interpretive Ambiguity: A Cross Cultural Study With the Holtzman Inkblots." *J Proj Tech & Pers Assess* 32:66–73 F '68. * (PA 42:8988)

99. FABREGA, HORACIO, JR., and SWARTZ, JON D. "Correlates of Personality Organization in Schizophrenic Patients." *J Nerv & Mental Dis* 146:127–35 F '68. * (PA 42:12129)

100. FREDE, MARTHA C.; GAUTNEY, DONALD B.; and BAXTER, JAMES C. "Relationships Between Body Image Boundary and Interaction Patterns on the MAPS Test." *J Consult & Clin Psychol* 32:575–8 O '68. * (PA 43:939)

101. GORHAM, DONALD R.; MOSELEY, EDWARD C.; and HOLTZMAN, WAYNE H. "Norms for the Computer-Scored Holtzman Inkblot Technique." *Percept & Motor Skills* 26:1279–305 Je '68. * (PA 42:18834)

102. HERRON, E. WAYNE; BERNSTEIN, LEWIS; ROSEN, HAROLD; and ROTHSTEIN, RALPH. "The Effects of Imminent Surgery on Responses to the Holtzman Inkblot Technique." *Int Congr Rorsch & Proj Meth* 6(4):781–6 '68. *

103. HOLTZMAN, WAYNE H. Chap. 6, "Holtzman Inkblot Technique," pp. 136–70. In *Projective Techniques in Personality Assessment: A Modern Introduction.* Edited by A. I. Rabin. New York: Springer Publishing Co., Inc., 1968. Pp. x, 638. *

104. MAYFIELD, DEMMIE G. "Holtzman Inkblot Technique in Acute Experimental Alcohol Intoxication." *J Proj Tech & Pers Assess* 32:491–4 O '68. *

105. MEGARGEE, EDWIN I., and SWARTZ, JON D. "Extraversion, Neuroticism, and Scores on the Holtzman Inkblot Technique." *J Proj Tech & Pers Assess* 32:262–5 Je '68. * (PA 42:15471)

106. MILLER, BYRON; POKORNY, ALEX D.; and HANSON, PHILIP G. "A Study of Dropouts in an In-Patient Alcoholism Treatment Program." *Dis Nerv System* 29:91–9 F '68. *

107. MORGAN, ANTONIA BELL. "Some Age Norms Obtained for the Holtzman Inkblot Technique Administered in a Clinical Setting." *J Proj Tech & Pers Assess* 32:165–72 Ap '68. * (PA 42:10620)

108. MUELLER, WILLIAM J., and DILLING, CAROLE A. "Therapist-Client Interview Behavior and Personality Characteristics of Therapists." *J Proj Tech & Pers Assess* 32:281–8 Je '68. * (PA 42:15537)

109. RENIK, OWEN D., and FISHER, SEYMOUR. "Induction of Body Image Boundary Changes in Male Subjects." *J Proj Tech & Pers Assess* 32:45–8 F '68. * (PA 42:9001)

110. ROSS, DONALD C. "Computer Processing of Inkblot Test Data." *J Sch Psychol* 6:200–5 sp '68. * (PA 42:17252)

111. SAILOR, PATRICIA J., and PONDER, HOYT, JR. "Use of Body Boundary Concept With Adolescent Retardates." *Am J Mental Def* 73:148–53 Jl '68. * (PA 42:19199)

112. SWARTZ, JON D., and SWARTZ, CAROL J. "Test Anxiety and Performance on the Holtzman Inkblot Technique." *J Clin Psychol* 24:463–7 O '68. * (PA 43:3804)

NAME INDEX

[440]

★[Re Holtzman Inkblot Technique.] Computer Scoring Service for the Holtzman Inkblot Technique. A computerized scoring and statistical service for qualified users of HIT; 1966–68; primarily for research and screening purposes where large numbers of subjects are being tested using the group method of administration developed by Donald R. Gorham; report consists of a printout listing subject's identification number, sex, age and 17 scores (compared with the 22 scores on the individually administered HIT): location, rejection, form definiteness, color, shading, movement, integration, human, animal, anatomy, sex, abstract, anxiety, hostility, barrier, penetration, popular; IBM summary cards for each subject are available upon request at no additional charge; the reported scores are raw scores, not normed scores; record form ('66, 1 page); User's Guide (no date, 7 pages); norms booklet ('68, 27 pages, reprint of 5 below); individual forms may be computer scored if first hand scored for location; minimum scoring order is 10 tests; $2.40 per 50 group record forms (must be purchased from Psychological Corporation); $2.60 per norms booklet; scoring service, $3.75 per test for handwritten records submitted on group form; lower prices for typed records, key punched records, and magnetic tape records; reports are mailed within 2 weeks after receipt of record sheets; postage extra; program by Donald R. Gorham; Institute for Behavioral Research. *

REFERENCES

1. MOSELEY, E. C.; GORHAM, D. R.; and HILL, EVELYN. "Computer Scoring of Inkblot Perceptions." Abstract. Percept & Motor Skills 17:498 O '63. * (PA 38:6097)
2. OVERALL, JOHN E., and GORHAM, DONALD R. "A Pattern Probability Model for the Classification of Psychiatric Patients." Behav Sci 8:108–16 Ap '63. * (PA 38:1195)
3. GORHAM, DONALD R. "The Development of a Computer Scoring System for Inkblot Responses." Congr Inter-Am Soc Psychol 9(1964):258–70 ['65]. *
4. GORHAM, DONALD R. "Validity and Reliability Studies of a Computer-Based Scoring System for Inkblot Responses." J Consult Psychol 31:65–70 F '67. * (PA 41:4619)
5. GORHAM, DONALD R.; MOSELEY, EDWARD C.; and HOLTZMAN, WAYNE H. "Norms for the Computer-Scored Holtzman Inkblot Technique." Percept & Motor Skills 26:1279–305 Je '68. * (PA 42:18834)

[441]

Horn-Hellersberg Test. Ages 3 and over; 1945–62; HHT; drawing completion test based on drawings adapted from Horn Art Aptitude Inventory (consult 5:242); "capacity to function or to adapt to a given surrounding"; 1 form ('45, 4 pages); mimeographed manual, third edition ('61, 16 pages, including 1962 instructions for interpreting spatial structures for determining developmental stages for ages 3–11); no data on reliability; no data on validity in manual; no description of normative population; $2 per 25 tests; 25¢ per manual; 35¢ per specimen set; postage extra; (30–90) minutes; Elisabeth F. Hellersberg; the Author. *

See 6:218 (1 reference); for reviews by Philip L.

Harriman and T. W. Richards, see 4:108 (5 references); for excerpts from related book reviews, see 4:109.

REFERENCES

1–5. See 4:108.
6. See 6:218.
7. DOSAJH, N. L. "Imagination and Maturity as Factors Indicative of Success in Teaching." Indian J Psychol 40:81–3 Je '65. * (PA 40:10478)

[442]

The Howard Ink Blot Tests. Adults; 1953–60; HIBT; individual; 1 form ('53, 12 cards); 1953 manual ('53, 47 pages, reprint of 1 below); 1960 manual ('60, 207 pages, see 4 below); no data on reliability; $12.50 per set of cards; $2 per 1953 manual; $5 per 1960 manual; cash orders postpaid; (90–105) minutes; James W. Howard; Journal of Clinical Psychology. *

For reviews by Jesse G. Harris, Jr. and Bernard I. Murstein, see 6:219 (1 reference, 1 excerpt); for a review by C. R. Strother, see 5:141 (3 references, 1 excerpt).

REFERENCES

1–3. See 5:141.
4. See 6:219.
5. MANNEN, GEORGE THOMAS. Examiner Influence and Control of Responses on the Howard Ink Blot Test. Doctor's thesis, University of Denver (Denver, Colo.), 1965. (DA 26:5874)

[442A]

★Human Figure Drawing Techniques. This is a dummy entry to serve as a catchall for references on the use of human figure drawings in general. References dealing with specific tests are listed under the relevant tests: Draw-A-Person Quality Scale, see 423 (6 references); The Eight Card Redrawing Test, see 425 (7 references); HFD Test, see 436 (8 references); H-T-P: House-Tree-Person Projective Technique, see 437 (136 references); Machover Draw-A-Person Test, see 451 (221 references); and Goodenough-Harris Drawing Test, consult 6:460 (137 references).

REFERENCES

1. BERRIEN, F. K. "A Study of the Drawings of Abnormal Children." J Ed Psychol 26:143–50 F '35. * (PA 9:2778)
2. MOTT, SINA M. "The Development of Concepts: A Study of Children's Drawings." J Genetic Psychol 48:199–214 Mr '36. * (PA 10:3789)
3. SPOERL, DOROTHY TILDEN. "Personality Drawing in Retarded Children." Char & Pers 8:227–39 Mr '40. * (PA 14:4317)
4. ANASTASI, ANNE, and FOLEY, JOHN P., JR. "A Survey of the Literature on Artistic Behavior in the Abnormal: 1, Historical and Theoretical Background." J General Psychol 25:111–42 Jl '41. * (PA 15:5114)
5. ANASTASI, ANNE, and FOLEY, JOHN P., JR. "A Survey of the Literature on Artistic Behavior in the Abnormal: 2, Approaches and Inter-Relations." Ann N Y Acad Sci 42:1–111 Ag 11 '41. * (PA 16:990)
6. ANASTASI, ANNE, and FOLEY, JOHN P., JR. "A Survey of the Literature on Artistic Behavior in the Abnormal: 4, Experimental Investigations." J General Psychol 25:187–237 Jl '41. * (PA 15:5115)
7. SPRINGER, N. NORTON. "A Study of the Drawings of Maladjusted and Adjusted Children." J Genetic Psychol 58:131–8 Mr '41. * (PA 15:4081)
8. SCHMIDL-WAEHNER, TRUDE. "Formal Criteria for the Analysis of Children's Drawings." Am J Orthopsychiatry 12:95–104 Ja '42. * (PA 16:3364)
9. ZIMMERMAN, JOSEPH, and GARFINKLE, LEONARD. "Preliminary Study of the Art Productions of the Adult Psychotic." Psychiatric Q 16:313–8 Ap '42. * (PA 16:3642)
10. WAEHNER, TRUDE S. "Interpretation of Spontaneous Drawings and Paintings." Genetic Psychol Monogr 33:3–70 F '46. * (PA 20:1610)
11. LEHNER, G. F. J., and SILVER, H. "Age Relationships on the Draw-A-Person Test." J Personality 17:199–209 D '48. * (PA 25:3171)
12. LEHNER, GEORGE F. J., and SILVER, HYMAN. "Some Relations Between Own Age and Ages Assigned on the Draw-

a-Person Test." Abstract. *Am Psychol* 3:341 Ag '48. * (*PA* 23:761, title only)

13. ALBEE, GEORGE W., and HAMLIN, ROY M. "An Investigation of the Reliability and Validity of Judgments Inferred From Drawings." *J Clin Psychol* 5:389–92 O '49. * (*PA* 24:3731)

14. BERK, NORMAN. *A Personality Study of Suicidal Schizophrenics.* Doctor's thesis, New York University (New York, N.Y.), 1949.

15. FIEDLER, FRED E., and SIEGEL, SAUL M. "The Free Drawing Test as a Predictor of Non-Improvement in Psychotherapy." *J Clin Psychol* 5:386–9 O '49. * (*PA* 24:3749)

16. GUNDERSON, ELLSWORTH K., and LEHNER, GEORGE F. J. "Reliability in a Projective Test (The Draw-A-Person)." Abstract. *Am Psychol* 4:387 S '49. * (*PA* 24:1887, title only)

17. MEYER, MORTIMER M. "Integration of Test Results With Clinical Observations: A Diagnostic Case Study." *Rorsch Res Exch & J Proj Tech* 13:325–40 S '49. * (*PA* 24:3202)

18. MORRIS, WOODROW W. "Methodological and Normative Considerations in the Use of Drawings of Human Figures as a Projective Method." Abstract. *Am Psychologist* 4:267 Jl '49. * (*PA* 23:6217, title only)

19. ROYAL, ROBERT E. "Drawing Characteristics of Neurotic Patients Using a Drawing-of-a-Man-and-Woman Technique." *J Clin Psychol* 5:392–5 O '49. * (*PA* 24:3817)

20. ALBEE, GEORGE W., and HAMLIN, ROY M. "Judgment of Adjustment From Drawings: The Applicability of Rating Scale Methods." *J Clin Psychol* 6:363–5 O '50. * (*PA* 25:8070)

21. GUNDERSON, E. K., and LEHNER, GEORGE F. J. "Height of Figure as a Diagnostic Variable in the Draw-a-Person Test." Abstract. *Am Psychol* 5:472 S '50. * (*PA* 25:4571, title only)

22. GÜNZBURG, H. C. "The Significance of Various Aspects in Drawings by Educationally Subnormal Children." *J Mental Sci* 96:951–75 O '50. * (*PA* 25:5413)

23. HARTOGS, RENATUS. "The Clinical Investigation and Differential Measurement of Anxiety." *Am J Psychiatry* 106:929–34 Je '50. * (*PA* 25:2553)

24. HOLZBERG, JULES D., and WEXLER, MURRAY. "The Validity of Human Form Drawings as a Measure of Personality Deviation." *J Proj Tech* 14:343–61 D '50. * (*PA* 26:3411)

25. LEVY, SIDNEY. "Figure Drawing as a Projective Test," pp. 257–97. (*PA* 25:2462) In *Projective Psychology: Clinical Approaches to the Total Personality.* Edited by Lawrence Edwin Abt and Leopold Bellak. New York: Alfred A. Knopf, Inc., 1950. Pp. xvii, 485, xiv. *

26. NOLLER, PAUL A., and WEIDER, ARTHUR. "A Normative Study of Human Figure Drawing for Children." Abstract. *Am Psychologist* 5:319–20 Jl '50. * (*PA* 25:1104, title only)

27. OPPENHEIM, SADI, and GOLDWASSER, MIRIAM L. "Psychological Report of the Cyprus Psychiatric Mission." *J Proj Tech* 14:245–61 S '50. * (*PA* 25:4547)

28. PRATER, G. F. *A Comparison of the Head and Body Size in the Drawing of the Human Figure by Hemiplegic and Non-Hemiplegic Persons.* Master's thesis, University of Kentucky (Lexington, Ky.), 1950.

29. SINGER, R. H. *A Study of Drawings Produced by a Group of College Students and a Group of Hospitalized Schizophrenics.* Master's thesis, Pennsylvania State University (University Park, Pa.), 1950.

30. WEIDER, ARTHUR, and NOLLER, PAUL A. "Objective Studies of Children's Drawings of Human Figures: 1, Sex Awareness and Socio-Economic Level." *J Clin Psychol* 6:139–25 O '50. * (*PA* 25:7985)

31. Wilson, Robert G. *A Study of Expressive Movements in Three Groups of Adolescent Boys, Stutterers, Non-Stutterers Maladjusted and Normals, by Means of Three Measures of Personality, Mira's Myokinetic Psychodiagnosis, the Bender-Gestalt, and Figure Drawing.* Doctor's thesis, Western Reserve University (Cleveland, Ohio), 1950. (*PA* 25:6584)

32. BERMAN, ABRAHAM B.; KLEIN, ALEXANDER A.; and LIPPMAN, ABBOTT. "Human Figure Drawings as a Projective Technique." *J General Psychol* 45:57–70 Jl '51. * (*PA* 26:4806)

33. DAVIS, J. E., JR. *A Comparative Study of the Projective Drawings of Hallucinated and Non-Hallucinated Schizophrenic Patients.* Master's thesis, George Washington University (Washington, D.C.), 1951.

34. GIEDT, F. HAROLD, and LEHNER, GEORGE F. J. "Assignment of Ages on the Draw-A-Person Test by Male Neuropsychiatric Patients." *J Personality* 19:440–8 Je '51. * (*PA* 26:3568)

35. HULSE, WILFRED C. "The Emotionally Disturbed Child Draws His Family." *Q J Child Behav* 3:152–74 Ap '51. *

36. KATZ, JOSEPH. *The Projection of Assaultive Aggression in the Human Figure Drawings of Adult Male Negro Offenders.* Doctor's thesis, New York University (New York, N.Y.), 1951.

37. BRADSHAW, D. H. *A Study of Group Consistencies on the Draw-A-Person Test in Relation to Personality Projection.* Master's thesis, Catholic University of America (Washington, D.C.), 1952.

38. ELKISCH, PAULA. "Significant Relationship Between the Human Figure and the Machine in the Drawings of Boys." *Am J Orthopsychiatry* 22:379–85 Ap '52. * (*PA* 27:2576)

39. FISHER, LILLIAN J. *An Investigation of the Effectiveness of the Human Figure Drawing as a Clinical Instrument for Evaluating Personality.* Doctor's thesis, New York University (New York, N.Y.), 1952. (*DA* 12:780)

40. FISHER, LILLIAN JAGODA. "An Investigation of the Effectiveness of Human Figure Drawings as a Clinical Instrument for Describing Personality." Abstract. *Am Psychol* 7:345–6 Jl '52. *

41. FISHER, SEYMOUR, and FISHER, RHODA LEE. "Style of Sexual Adjustment in Disturbed Women and Its Expression in Figure Drawings." *J Psychol* 34:169–79 O '52. * (*PA* 27:5216)

42. GÜNZBURG, H. C. "Maladjustment as Expressed in Drawings by Subnormal Children." *Am J Mental Def* 57:9–23 Jl '52. * (*PA* 27:3628)

43. GURVITZ, MILTON S., and MILLER, JOSEPH S. A. Chap. 11, "Some Theoretical and Practical Aspects of the Diagnosis of Early and Latent Schizophrenia by Means of Psychological Testing," pp. 189–207. (*PA* 27:571) Discussion by Paul H. Hoch, pp. 215–6. In *Relation of Psychological Tests to Psychiatry.* Edited by Paul H. Hoch and Joseph Zubin. The Proceedings of the Fortieth Annual Meeting of the American Psychopathological Association. New York: Grune & Stratton, 1952. Pp. viii, 301. *

44. GUTMAN, BRIGETTE. *An Investigation of the Applicability of the Human Figure Drawing in Predicting Improvement in Therapy.* Doctor's thesis, New York University (New York, N.Y.), 1952. (*DA* 12:722)

45. HULSE, WILFRED C. "Childhood Conflict Expressed Through Family Drawings." *J Proj Tech* 16:66–79 Mr '52. * (*PA* 27:429)

46. KATES, SOLIS L., and HARRINGTON, ROBERT W. "Authority Figure Perspective and Aggression in Delinquents." *J Genetic Psychol* 80:193–210 Je '52. * (*PA* 27:2866)

47. LEHNER, GEORGE F. J., and GUNDERSON, ERIC K. "Reliability of Graphic Indices in a Projective Test (The Draw-A-Person)." *J Clin Psychol* 8:125–8 Ap '52. * (*PA* 27:1971)

48. McDONALD, FRANKLIN RANDOLPH. *The Effect of Differential Cultural Pressures on Projective Test Performances of Negroes.* Doctor's thesis, University of Southern California (Los Angeles, Calif.), 1952.

49. RABINOWITZ, WILLIAM, and TRAVERS, ROBERT M. W. "The Use of a Drawing Technique for Studying Learning During Teacher Training." Abstract. *Am Psychol* 7:368–9 Jl '52. *

50. STONE, PHILIP M. *A Study of Objectively Scored Drawings of Human Figures in Relation to the Emotional Adjustment of Sixth Grade Pupils.* Doctor's thesis, Yeshiva University (New York, N.Y.), 1952. (*DA* 13:1265)

51. VERNIER, CLAIRE MYERS. *Projective Test Productions: I, Projective Drawings.* New York: Grune & Stratton, Inc., 1952. Pp. viii, 168. * (*PA* 27:447)

52. WEXLER, MURRAY, and HOLZBERG, JULES D. "A Further Study of the Validity of Human Form Drawings in Personality Evaluation." *J Proj Tech* 16:249–51 Je '52. * (*PA* 28:3042)

53. WIRTHS, CLAUDINE GIBSON. "A Simple Quantitative Measure of Pressure for Use in The Projective Techniques." *J Clin Psychol* 8:208–9 Ap '52. * (*PA* 27:1988)

54. BERMAN, SIDNEY, and LAFFAL, JULIUS. "Body Type and Figure Drawing." *J Clin Psychol* 9:368–70 O '53. * (*PA* 28:4412)

55. COHN, ROBERT. "Role of the 'Body Image Concept' in Pattern of Ipsilateral Clinical Extinction." *A.M.A. Arch Neurol & Psychiatry* 70:503–9 O '53. * (*PA* 28:5723)

56. DAVIDSON, ALENE J. *Cultural Differences in Personality Structure as Expressed in Drawings of the Human Figure.* Doctor's thesis, New York University (New York, N.Y.), 1953. (*DA* 14:394)

57. FEATHER, DON B. "An Exploratory Study in the Use of Figure Drawings in a Group Situation." *J Social Psychol* 37:163–70 My '53. * (*PA* 28:2629)

58. GOODMAN, MORRIS, and KOTKOV, BENJAMIN. "Predictions of Trait Ranks From Draw-A-Person Measurements of Obese and Non-Obese Women." *J Clin Psychol* 9:365–7 O '53. * (*PA* 28:4713)

59. KOTKOV, BENJAMIN, and GOODMAN, MORRIS. "The Draw-A-Person Tests of Obese Women." *J Clin Psychol* 9:362–4 O '53. * (*PA* 28:4716)

60. LEHNER, GEORGE F. J., and GUNDERSON, ERIC K. "Height Relationships on the Draw-a-Person Test." *J Personality* 21:392–9 Mr '53. * (*PA* 28:2648)

61. MACHOVER, KAREN. "Human Figure Drawings of Children." *J Proj Tech* 17:85–91 Mr '53. * (*PA* 28:2335)

62. SMITH, ELGIE. "A Study of Sex Differentiation in Drawings and Verbalizations of Schizophrenics." *J Clin Psychol* 9:183–5 Ap '53. * (*PA* 28:3032)

63. STEINMAN, KARL. *The Validity of a Projective Technique in the Determination of Relative Intensity in Psychosis: An Investigation of the Correlations Between the Human Figure Drawings of Diagnosed Psychotics and a Physiological Measurement Known to be Related to the Severity of the Psychotic Process.* Doctor's thesis, New York University (New York, N.Y.), 1953. (*DA* 14:717)

64. WEIDER, ARTHUR, and NOLLER, PAUL A. "Objective

Studies of Children's Drawings of Human Figures: 2, Sex, Age, Intelligence." *J Clin Psychol* 9:20–3 Ja '53. * (*PA* 27:7694)

65. WHITMYRE, JOHN W. "The Significance of Artistic Excellence in the Judgment of Adjustment Inferred From Human Figure Drawings." *J Consult Psychol* 17:421–4 D '53. * (*PA* 28:7563)

66. DE MARTINO, MANFRED F. "Human Figure Drawings by Mentally Retarded Males." *J Clin Psychol* 10:241–4 Jl '54. * (*PA* 29:2656)

67. HAMMER, EMANUEL F. "Relationship Between Diagnosis of Psychosexual Pathology and the Sex of the First Drawn Person." *J Clin Psychol* 10:168–70 Ap '54. * (*PA* 29:920)

68. KING, FRANCIS W. "The Use of Drawings of the Human Figure as an Adjunct in Psychotherapy." *J Clin Psychol* 10:65–9 Ja '54. * (*PA* 28:7603)

69. MITZEL, HAROLD E.; OSTREICHER, LEONARD M.; and REITER, SIDNEY R. *Development of Attitudinal Dimensions From Teachers' Drawings.* College of the City of New York, Division of Teacher Education, Office of Research and Evaluation, Publication No. 24. New York: Office of Research and Evaluation, the Division, October 1954. Pp. vi, 49. * (*PA* 29:7999)

70. WOODS, WALTER A., and COOK, WILLIAM E. "Proficiency in Drawing and Placement of Hands in Drawings of the Human Figure." *J Consult Psychol* 18:119–21 Ap '54. * (*PA* 29:2485)

71. GRAHAM, STANLEY R. "Relation Between Histamine Tolerance, Visual Autokinesis, Rorschach Human Movement, and Figure Drawing." *J Clin Psychol* 11:370–3 O '55. * (*PA* 30:6666)

72. MACHOVER, KAREN. "The Body Image in Art Communication as Seen in William Steig's Drawings." *J Proj Tech* 19:453–60 D '55. * (*PA* 30:7352)

73. MORRIS, W. W. "Ontogenetic Changes in Adolescence Reflected by the Drawing-Human-Figures Techniques." *Am J Orthopsychiatry* 25:720–8 O '55. * (*PA* 30:7216)

74. PLAUT, ERIKA, and CRANNELL, C. W. "The Ability of Clinical Psychologists to Discriminate Between Drawings by Deteriorated Schizophrenics and Drawings by Normal Subjects." *Psychol Rep* 1:153–8 S '55. * (*PA* 30:5477)

75. SWENSEN, CLIFFORD H. "Sexual Differentiation on the Draw-A-Person Test." *J Clin Psychol* 11:37–40 Ja '55. * (*PA* 29:7326)

76. TOLOR, ALEXANDER. "Teachers' Judgments of the Popularity of Children From Their Human Figure Drawings." *J Clin Psychol* 11:158–62 Ap '55. * (*PA* 30:1006)

77. TOLOR, ALEXANDER, and TOLOR, BELLE. "Judgment of Children's Popularity From Their Human Figure Drawings." *J Proj Tech* 19:170–6 Je '55. * (*PA* 30:2573)

78. ZIMMER, HERBERT. "Predictions by Means of Two Projective Tests of Personality Evaluations Made by Peers." *J Clin Psychol* 11:352–6 O '55. * (*PA* 30:6008)

79. CUTTER, FRED. "Sexual Differentiation in Figure Drawings and Overt Deviation." *J Clin Psychol* 12:369–72 O '56. * (*PA* 32:4320)

80. GRAHAM, STANLEY R. "A Study of Reliability in Human Figure Drawings." *J Proj Tech* 20:385–6 D '56. * (*PA* 32:1622)

81. HARE, A. PAUL, and HARE, RACHEL T. "The Draw-A-Group Test." *J Genetic Psychol* 89:51–9 S '56. *

82. REZNIKOFF, MARVIN, and MUNDY, LAURENCE. "Changes in Human Figure Drawings Associated With Therapy: A Case Study." *Am J Psychother* 10:542–9 Jl '56. * (*PA* 31:6121)

83. REZNIKOFF, MARVIN, and REZNIKOFF, HELGA R. "The Family Drawing Test: A Comparative Study of Children's Drawings." *J Clin Psychol* 12:167–9 Ap '56. * (*PA* 31:4708)

84. SILVERSTEIN, A. B., and ROBINSON, H. A. "The Representation of Orthopedic Disability in Children's Figure Drawings." *J Consult Psychol* 20:333–41 O '56. * (*PA* 31:8639)

85. VERNIER, CLAIRE M. Chap. 18, "Predictability in Treatment of Tuberculosis Patients," pp. 344–52. In *Personality Stress and Tuberculosis.* Edited by Phineas J. Sparer. New York: International Universities Press, Inc., 1956. Pp. xviii, 629. *

86. ZIMMER, HERBERT. "Validity of Sentence Completion Tests and Human Figure Drawings." *Prog Clin Psychol* 2:58–75 '56. * (*PA* 30:7239)

87. GOLDSTEIN, ARNOLD P., and RAWN, MOSS L. "The Validity of Interpretive Signs of Aggression in the Drawing of the Human Figure." *J Clin Psychol* 13:169–71 Ap '57. * (*PA* 32:2895)

88. LORAND, RHODA L. *Family Drawings and Adjustment.* Doctor's thesis, Columbia University (New York, N.Y.), 1957. (*DA* 17:1596)

89. PONZO, EZIO. "An Experimental Variation of the Draw-A-Person Technique." *J Proj Tech* 21:278–85 S '57. * (*PA* 33:1300)

90. RIBLER, RONALD I. "Diagnostic Prediction From Emphasis on the Eye and the Ear in Human Figure Drawings." *J Consult Psychol* 21:223–5 Je '57. * (*PA* 32:5524)

91. SINGER, ROLAND H. *Various Aspects of Human Figure Drawings as a Personality Measure With Hospitalized Psychiatric Patients.* Doctor's thesis, Pennsylvania State University (State College, Pa.), 1957. (*DA* 18:290)

92. DENNIS, WAYNE. "Handwriting Conventions as Determinants of Human Figure Drawing." *J Consult Psychol* 22:293–5 Ag '58. * (*PA* 34:710)

93. FOX, CYNTHIA; DAVIDSON, KENNETH; LIGHTHALL, FREDERICK; WAITE, RICHARD; and SARASON, SEYMOUR B. "Human Figure Drawings of High and Low Anxious Children." *Child Develop* 29:297–301 Je '58. * (*PA* 35:3256)

94. GLATTER, ANDREW M., and HAUCK, PAUL. "Sexual Symbolism in Line Qualities." *J Clin Psychol* 14:168–9 Ap '58. * (*PA* 33:6572)

95. HAMMER, EMANUEL F., Editor. *The Clinical Application of Projection Drawings.* Springfield, Ill.: Charles C Thomas, Publisher, 1958. Pp. xxii, 663. * (*PA* 33:1177)

96. LIEBERT, ROBERT S.; WERNER, HEINZ; and WAPNER, SEYMOUR. "Studies in the Effect of Lysergic Acid Diethylamide (LSD 25): Self- and Object-Size Perception in Schizophrenic and Normal Adults." *A.M.A. Arch Neurol Psychiatry* 79:580–4 My '58. * (*PA* 33:6398)

97. LORGE, IRVING; TUCKMAN, JACOB; and DUNN, MICHAEL B. "Human Figure Drawings by Younger and Older Adults." *J Clin Psychol* 14:54–6 Ja '58. * (*PA* 33:6259)

98. RABINOWITZ, WILLIAM, and ROSENBAUM, IRA. "A Failure in the Prediction of Pupil-Teacher Rapport." *J Ed Psychol* 49:93–8 Ap '58. *

99. REZNIKOFF, MARVIN, and NICHOLAS, ALMA L. "An Evaluation of Human-Figure Drawing Indicators of Paranoid Pathology." *J Consult Psychol* 22:395–7 O '58. * (*PA* 34:1413)

100. SHERMAN, L. J. "The Influence of Artistic Quality on Judgments of Patient and Non-Patient Status From Human Figure Drawings." *J Proj Tech* 22:338–40 S '58. * (*PA* 33:10362)

101. ZUCKER, LUISE J. *Ego Structure in Paranoid Schizophrenia: A New Method of Evaluating Projective Material.* Springfield, Ill.: Charles C Thomas, Publisher, 1958. Pp. x, 186. * (*PA* 33:1916)

102. ARBIT, JACK; LAKIN, MARTIN; and MATHIS, ANDREW G. "Clinical Psychologists' Diagnostic Utilization of Human Figure Drawings." *J Clin Psychol* 15:325–7 Jl '59. * (*PA* 35:3479)

103. FISHER, SEYMOUR. "Body Reactivity Gradients and Figure Drawing Variables." *J Consult Psychol* 23:54–9 F '59. * (*PA* 34:628)

104. HAMMER, EMANUEL F. "Critique of Swensen's 'Empirical Evaluations of Human Figure Drawings.'" *J Proj Tech* 23:30–2 Mr '59. * (*PA* 34:5950)

105. HOZIER, ANN. "On the Breakdown of the Sense of Reality: A Study of Spatial Perception in Schizophrenia." *J Consult Psychol* 23:185–94 Je '59. * (*PA* 34:4680)

106. MORGENSTERN, FRANCES BARZILAY. *The Effect of an Experimental Situation Involving Failure and Disparagement on Certain Features of Children's Figure Drawings.* Doctor's thesis, New York University (New York, N.Y.), 1959. (*DA* 20:3403)

107. ARMON, VIRGINIA. "Some Personality Variables in Overt Female Homosexuality." *J Proj Tech* 24:292–309 S '60. * (*PA* 35:818)

108. DENNIS, WAYNE, and RASKIN, EVELYN. "Further Evidence Concerning the Effect of Handwriting Habits Upon the Location of Drawings." *J Consult Psychol* 24:548–9 D '60. * (*PA* 36:1HE48D)

109. KAMANO, DENNIS K. "An Investigation of the Meaning of Human Figure Drawing." *J Clin Psychol* 16:429–30 O '60. * (*PA* 37:3147)

110. LAANE, CARL L. "Clinical Experience With the Figure Drawing Test." *J Clin & Exp Psychopathol* 21:129–41 Je '60. * (*PA* 35:6463)

111. LAKIN, MARTIN. "Formal Characteristics of Human Figure Drawings by Institutionalized and Non-Institutionalized Aged." *J Gerontol* 15:76–8 Ja '60. * (*PA* 35:6233)

112. TAYLOR, ROBERT E. "Figure Location in Student and Patient Samples." *J Clin Psychol* 16:169–71 Ap '60. * (*PA* 36:2HC69T)

113. BURTON, ARTHUR, and ADKINS, JOEL. "Perceived Size of Self-Image Body Parts in Schizophrenia." *Arch Gen Psychiatry* 5:131–40 Ag '61. *

114. KYLE, DAVID GEORGE. *The Relation of Performance in Drawing the Human Figure to Form Perception and Reading Achievement.* Doctor's thesis, University of Maryland (College Park, Md.), 1961. (*DA* 24:1479)

115. SILVERSTEIN, A. B., and ROBINSON, H. A. "The Representation of Physique in Children's Figure Drawings." *J Consult Psychol* 25:146–8 Ap '61. * (*PA* 36:4FC46S)

116. TOLOR, ALEXANDER, and COLBERT, JOHN. "Relationship of Body Image to Social Desirability." *J Mental Sci* 107:1060–1 N '61. * (*PA* 36:5HG60T)

117. COHEN, HASKEL. "Psychological Test Findings in Adolescents Having Ovarian Dysgenesis." *Psychosom Med* 24:249–56 My–Je '62. * (*PA* 37:5107)

118. GILBERT, JEANNE G., and HALL, MARION R. "Changes With Age in Human Figure Drawing." *J Gerontol* 17:397–404 O '62. * (*PA* 37:4775)

119. LAWTON, MARCIA J., and SECHREST, LEE. "Figure Drawings by Young Boys From Father-Present and Father-Absent Homes." *J Clin Psychol* 18:304–5 Jl '62. * (*PA* 39:1863)

120. WITKIN, H. A.; DYKE, R. G.; FATERSON, H. F.; GOODENOUGH, D. R.; and KARP, S. A. *Psychological Differentiation: Studies of Development.* New York: John Wiley & Sons, Inc., 1962. Pp. xii, 418. * (*PA* 37:819)

121. ABE, K.; TSUJI, K.; and SUZUKI, H. "The Significance of Birth Order and Age Difference Between Sibs as Observed in Drawings of Prekindergarten Children." *Folia Psychiatrica et Neurologica Japonica* 17:315–25 D '63. * (*PA* 39:4523)

122. BENNETT, VIRGINIA DAKIN CLIVER. *An Investigation of the Relationships Among Children's Self Concept, Achievement, Intelligence, Body Size, and the Size of Their Figure Drawing.* Doctor's thesis, Rutgers—The State University (New Brunswick, N.J.), 1963. (*DA* 24:2776)

123. CENTERS, LOUISE, and CENTERS, RICHARD. "A Comparison of the Body Images of Amputee and Non-Amputee Children as Revealed in Figure Drawings." *J Proj Tech & Pers Assess* 27:158–65 Je '63. * (*PA* 38:2933)

124. HANDLER, LEONARD. *The Effects of Stress on the Draw A Person Test.* Master's thesis, Michigan State University (East Lansing, Mich.), 1963.

125. LEVY, BERNARD I.; LOMAX, JAMES V., JR.; and MINSKY, RAPHAEL. "An Underlying Variable in the Clinical Evaluation of Drawings of Human Figures." *J Consult Psychol* 27:508–12 D '63. * (*PA* 38:8575)

126. ROSENBERG, CLARA Y. *An Assessment of the Comparative Validity of the Rorschach and Family Drawing Projective Tests in School Phobic and Normal Children.* Doctor's thesis, Yeshiva University (New York, N.Y.), 1963. (*DA* 25:2036)

127. STRUMPFER, D. J. W. "The Relation of Draw-A-Person Test Variables to Age and Chronicity in Psychotic Groups." *J Clin Psychol* 19:208–11 Ap '63. * (*PA* 39:5102)

128. WEINSTEIN, SIDNEY; JOHNSON, LINDA; and GUERRA, JOSEPH R. "Differentiation of Human Figure Drawings Made Before and After Temporal Lobectomy and by Schizophrenics." *Percept & Motor Skills* 17:687–93 D '63. * (*PA* 38:6392)

129. WILDMAN, ROBERT W. "The Relationship Between Knee and Arm Joints on Human Figure Drawings and Paranoid Trends." *J Clin Psychol* 19:460–1 O '63. * (*PA* 39:7931)

130. BADRI, MALIK B., and DENNIS, WAYNE. "Human-Figure Drawings in Relation to Modernization in Sudan." *J Psychol* 58:421–5 O '64. * (*PA* 39:4692)

131. BALDWIN, I. TRYON. "The Head-Body Ratio in Human Figure Drawings of Schizophrenic and Normal Adults." *J Proj Tech & Pers Assess* 28:393–6 D '64. * (*PA* 39:8467)

132. BENNETT, VIRGINIA D. C. "Does Size of Figure Drawing Reflect Self-Concept?" *J Consult Psychol* 28:285–6 Je '64. * (*PA* 39:4594)

133. CRADDICK, RAY A. "Size of Drawings-of-a-Person as a Function of Simulating 'Psychosis.'" *Percept & Motor Skills* 18:308 F '64. * (*PA* 39:2632)

134. GRAY, DAVID M., and PEPITONE, ALBERT. "Effect of Self-Esteem on Drawings of the Human Figure." *J Consult Psychol* 28:452–5 O '64. * (*PA* 39:5201)

135. PAUKER, JEROME D. "An Easily Constructed Scale for Rating Line Darkness of Drawings." *J Clin Psychol* 20:122 Ja '64. * (*PA* 39:10145)

136. SECHREST, LEE, and WALLACE, JOHN. "Figure Drawings and Naturally Occurring Events: Elimination of the Expansive Euphoria Hypothesis." *J Ed Psychol* 55:42–4 F '64. * (*PA* 38:8026)

137. TELDER, THOMAS VAN DOORN. *Utilization of the Draw-A-Teacher Technique in Studying Selected Dimensions in Teacher Education.* Doctor's thesis, Michigan State University (East Lansing, Mich.), 1964. (*DA* 26:216)

138. ZIMILES, HERBERT; BIBER, BARBARA; RABINOWITZ, WILLIAM; and HAY, LOUIS. "Personality Aspects of Teaching: A Predictive Study." *Genetic Psychol Monogr* 69:101–49 F '64. * (*PA* 39:2902)

139. CLARK, EDWARD T., and DEGENHARDT, FREDERICK J. "Ability of Females to Draw Sexually Undifferentiated Human Figures." *Percept & Motor Skills* 21:60 Ag '65. * (*PA* 40:556)

140. DENNIS, WAYNE, and URAS, ALEV. "The Religious Content of Human Figure Drawings Made by Nuns." *J Psychol* 61:263–6 N '65. * (*PA* 40:5484)

141. HANDLER, LEONARD; LEVINE, JOSEPH R.; and POTASH, HERBERT M. "Suggestions for More Accurate Measurement of Some Figure Drawing Variables." *J Clin Psychol* 21:316–7 Jl '65. * (*PA* 39:15390)

142. HILER, E. WESLEY, and NESVIG, DAVID. "An Evaluation of Criteria Used by Clinicians to Infer Pathology From Figure Drawings." *J Consult Psychol* 29:520–9 D '65. * (*PA* 40:2953)

143. JONES, LEONA W., and THOMAS, CAROLINE BEDELL. "Studies on Figure Drawings: Manual of Instructions for Coding Structural and Graphic Characteristics." *Psychiatric Q Sup* 39:241–67 pt 2 '65. * (*PA* 40:5489)

144. KETTERING, WALTER RICHARD. *The Use of Two Projective Drawing Techniques as Indices of Masculinity and Femininity With Children of Varying Levels of Intelligence.* Doctor's thesis, University of Pittsburgh (Pittsburgh, Pa.), 1965. (*DA* 27:956B)

145. KIDD, ALINE H., and CHERYMISIN, DIANA G. "Figure Reversal as Related to Specific Personality Variables." *Percept & Motor Skills* 20:1175–6 Je '65. * (*PA* 39:13447)

146. LIEBERMAN, MORTON A. "Psychological Correlates of Impending Death: Some Preliminary Observations." *J Gerontol* 20:181–90 Ap '65. *

147. LOURENSO, SUSAN V.; GREENBERG, JUDITH W.; and DAVIDSON, HELEN H. "Personality Characteristics in Drawings of Deprived Children Who Differ in School Achievement." *J Ed Res* 59:63–7 O '65. * (*PA* 40:2694)

148. McHUGH, ANN F. "Age Associations in Children's Figure Drawings." *J Clin Psychol* 21:429–31 O '65. * (*PA* 40:1399)

149. RICHEY, MARJORIE H. "Qualitative Superiority of the 'Self' Figure in Children's Drawings." *J Clin Psychol* 21:59–61 Ja '65. * (*PA* 39:12402)

150. ROSENBERG, LEON A. "Rapid Changes in Overt Behavior Reflected in the Draw-A-Person: A Case Report." *J Proj Tech & Pers Assess* 29:348–51 S '65. * (*PA* 39:15770)

151. WILDMAN, R. W. "Methodological Observations on an Incomplete Replication of Paranoid Indicants in Human Figure Drawings." *Percept & Motor Skills* 21:874 D '65. * (*PA* 40:4267)

152. APFELDORF, MAX, and SMITH, WALTER J. "The Representation of the Body Self in Human Figure Drawings." *J Proj Tech & Pers Assess* 30:283–9 Je '66. * (*PA* 40:10129)

153. APFELDORF, MAX; RANDOLPH, JOHN J.; and WHITEMAN, GLORIA L. "Figure Drawing Correlates of Furlough Utilization in an Aged Institutionalized Population." *J Proj Tech & Pers Assess* 30:467–70 O '66. * (*PA* 41:595)

154. BENNETT, VIRGINIA D. C. "Combinations of Figure Drawing Characteristics Related to the Drawer's Self Concept." *J Proj Tech & Pers Assess* 30:192–6 Ap '66. * (*PA* 40:7723)

155. CLOUSING, LOIS MOULTON. *The Effects of Stress on a Modified Form of the Draw-A-Family Test.* Master's thesis, San Jose State College (San Jose, Calif.), 1966.

156. COYLE, F. A., JR. "Knee and Arm Joints in Human Figure Drawings as Indicants of Paranoid Trends: Replication and Extension." *Percept & Motor Skills* 22:317–8 F '66. * (*PA* 40:5760)

157. DENNIS, WAYNE. *Group Values Through Children's Drawings.* New York: John Wiley & Sons, Inc., 1966. Pp. xiii, 211. *

158. HAMMER, MAX, and KAPLAN, ARTHUR M. "The Reliability of Children's Human Figure Drawings." *J Clin Psychol* 22:316–9 Jl '66. * (*PA* 40:11173)

159. HANDLER, LEONARD, and REYHER, JOSEPH. "Relationship Between GSR and Anxiety Indexes in Projective Drawings." *J Consult Psychol* 30:60–7 F '66. * (*PA* 40:4257)

160. LEVINGER, LEAH. *Children's Drawings as Indicators of Sexual Discrimination.* Doctor's thesis, New York University (New York, N.Y.), 1966. (*DA* 27:2873B)

161. ROBACK, HOWARD B., and WEBERSINN, ALFRED L. "Size of Figure Drawings of Depressed Psychiatric Patients." *J Abn Psychol* 71:416 O '66. * (*PA* 41:1624)

162. SILVERSTEIN, A. B. "Anxiety and Quality of Human Figure Drawings." *Am J Mental Def* 70:607–8 Ja '66. * (*PA* 40:5889)

163. THOMAS, CAROLINE BEDELL. *An Atlas of Figure Drawings: Studies on the Psychological Characteristics of Medical Students—III.* Baltimore, Md.: Johns Hopkins Press, 1966. Pp. xvi, 922. *

164. WEINER, IRVING B. *Psychodiagnosis in Schizophrenia.* New York: John Wiley & Sons, Inc., 1966. Pp. xiv, 573. * (*PA* 41:4753)

165. BLANK, LEONARD, and ROTH, ROBERT H. "Voyeurism and Exhibitionism." *Percept & Motor Skills* 24:391–400 Ap '67. * (*PA* 41:10708)

166. CHAPMAN, LOREN J., and CHAPMAN, JEAN P. "Genesis of Popular but Erroneous Psychodiagnostic Observations." *J Abn Psychol* 72:193–204 Je '67. * (*PA* 41:10653)

167. GRAVITZ, MELVIN A. "Marital Status and Figure Drawing Choice in Normal Young Adults." *J Proj Tech & Pers Assess* 31:86–7 Ag '67. * (*PA* 41:15257)

168. HANDLER, LEONARD. "Anxiety Indexes in the Draw a Person Test: A Scoring Manual." *J Proj Tech & Pers Assess* 31:46–52 Je '67. * (*PA* 41:13674)

169. MAJ, G.; GRILLI, A. T. SQUARZONI; and BELLETTI, M. F. "Psychologic Appraisal of Children Facing Orthodontic Treatment." *Am J Orthodontics* 53:849–57 N '67. *

170. SALZMAN, LEONARD F., and HARWAY, NORMAN I. "Size of Figure Drawings of Psychotically Depressed Patients." *J Abn Psychol* 72:205–7 Je '67. * (*PA* 41:10770)

171. STRICKER, GEORGE. "Actuarial, Naive Clinical, and Sophisticated Clinical Prediction of Pathology From Figure Drawings." *J Consult Psychol* 31:492–4 O '67. * (*PA* 41:16824)

172. WATSON, CHARLES G. "Interjudge Agreement of Draw-A-Person Diagnostic Impressions." *J Proj Tech & Pers Assess* 31:42–5 Je '67. * (*PA* 41:13694)

173. WATSON, CHARLES G.; FELLING, JAMES; and MACEACHERN, DONALD G. "Objective Draw-A-Person Scales: An Attempted Cross-Validation." *J Clin Psychol* 23:382–6 Jl '67. * (*PA* 41:14462)

174. BUZBY, DALLAS E. "Precognition and Psychological Variables." *J Parapsychol* 32:39–46 Mr '68. *

175. HAMMER, EMANUEL F. Chap. 12, "Projective Drawings," pp. 366–93. In *Projective Techniques in Personality Assessment: A Modern Introduction.* Edited by A. I. Rabin. New York: Springer Publishing Co., Inc., 1968. Pp. x, 638. *

176. KOPPITZ, ELIZABETH MUNSTERBERG. *Psychological Evaluation of Children's Human Figure Drawings.* New York: Grune & Stratton, Inc., 1968. Pp. x, 341. *

177. MOORE, WILLIAM BATEMAN. *Drawings of Human Figures in Relation to Psychopathology and Intellectual Functioning.* Doctor's thesis, George Washington University (Washington, D.C.), 1968. (*DA* 29:2657B)

178. ROSEN, ALBERT, and BOE, ERLING E. "Frequency of Nude Figure Drawings." *J Proj Tech & Pers Assess* 32:483–5 O '68. * (*PA* 43:4394)

179. SCHOEBERLE, ELIZABETH A., and CRADDICK, RAY A. "Human Figure Drawings by Freshman and Senior Student Nurses." *Percept & Motor Skills* 27:11–4 Ag '68. * (*PA* 43:2635)

180. ATTKISSON, C. CLIFFORD; HANDLER, LEONARD; and SHRADER, RAYMOND R. "The Use of Figure Drawings to Assess Religious Values." *J Psychol* 71:27–31 Ja '69. * (*PA* 43:5378)

181. SHEARN, CHARLES R., and RUSSELL, KENNETH R. "Use of the Family Drawing as a Technique for Studying Parent-Child Interaction." *J Proj Tech & Pers Assess* 33(1):35–44 F '69. *

NAME INDEX

[443]

The IES Test. Ages 10 and over and latency period girls; 1956–58; 14 scores: 3 scores each for *a–c* (impulses, ego, superego) plus 5 scores listed in *d* below; individual; 4 tests; manual ('58, 44 pages, reprint of *3* below); instructions ('58, 1 card) for each test; record form ('58, 1 page); norms for females based on fifth and sixth graders only; $28.50 per set of test materials including manual; $3 per manual; cash orders postpaid; (30) minutes; Lawrence A. Dombrose and Morton S. Slobin; Psychological Test Specialists. *

a) ARROW-DOT TEST. 1957–58; reaction to goal barriers; 1 form ('57, 5 pages).

b) PICTURE STORY COMPLETION TEST. 1956–58; conception of outside world; 1 form ('56, 71 cards).

c) PHOTO-ANALYSIS TEST. 1956–58; desired self-gratifications; 1 form ('56, 9 cards).

d) PICTURE TITLE TEST. 1956–58; recognition and acceptance of ego pressures; 5 scores: impulse, ego, superego, defense, superego plus defense; 1 form ('56, 12 cards).

For reviews by Douglas P. Crowne and Walter Katkovsky, see 6:220 (15 references, 1 excerpt).

REFERENCES

1–15. See 6:220.

16. HERRON, WILLIAM G. "The Assessment of Ego Strength." *J Psychol Studies* 13:173–203 D '62. *

17. BORTNER, RAYMAN W. "Personality Differences in Preferences for Skill- or Chance-Determined Outcomes." *Percept & Motor Skills* 18:765–72 Je '64. * (*PA* 39:4000)

18. BORTNER, RAYMAN W. "School Subject Preference and the Structure of Value Systems." *Percept & Motor Skills* 18:741–7 Je '64. * (*PA* 39:5145)

19. CANESTRARI, ROBERT E., JR. "Spatial Stimulus Generalization Gradients and Id, Ego, and Superego Strength." *Percept & Motor Skills* 19:51–5 Ag '64. * (*PA* 39:3390)

20. RANKIN, R. J., and WIKOFF, R. L. "The IES Arrow Dot Performance of Delinquents and Nondelinquents." *Percept & Motor Skills* 18:207–10 F '64. * (*PA* 39:2618)

21. SIGNORI, EDRO I.; SMORDIN, MARCELYN M.; REMPEL, HENRY; and SAMPSON, DONALD L. G. "Comparison of Impulse,

Ego, and Superego Functions in Better Adjusted and More Poorly Adjusted Delinquent Adolescent Girls." *Percept & Motor Skills* 18:485-8 Ap '64. * (*PA* 39:5160)

22. GOLIAS, GEORGE A., and ROBACK, HOWARD B. "IES Arrow-Dot Performance of Institutionalized Delinquents and Adolescent Patients in a Mental Hospital." *Percept & Motor Skills* 21:561-2 O '65. * (*PA* 40:2133)

23. ROBACK, HOWARD B. "Admission IES Arrow-Dot Performance of Mental Patients Presenting Management Problems at a State Hospital." *Percept & Motor Skills* 21:600-2 O '65. * (*PA* 40:3080)

24. WALKER, RONALD E.; FARRELL, GARY E.; McCARTHY, WINIFRED J.; and BAUR, LYNNE M. "Sex of Examiner as a Variable in IES Test Performance of College Males." *Percept & Motor Skills* 20:195-8 F '65. * (*PA* 39:10163)

25. BORTNER, RAYMAN W. "The IES Test and a Performance Measure of Intelligence." *Percept & Motor Skills* 22:171-5 F '66. * (*PA* 40:5449)

26. HERRON, WILLIAM G. "The IES 'Experiment.'" *Percept & Motor Skills* 23:279-90 Ag '66. * (*PA* 40:12354)

27. HOWARD, GAIL; SIGNORI, EDRO I.; and REMPEL, HENRY. "Further Research on the Picture Titles Subtest of the IES Test." *Percept & Motor Skills* 22:119-22 F '66. * (*PA* 40:5488)

28. LEVITT, EUGENE E.; LADD, CLAYTON E.; THADEN, MARCIA; and REASER, VIRGINIA. "An Empirical Study of the Validity of the Picture Story Completion Test of the IES Test." *J Proj Tech & Pers Assess* 30:143-8 Ap '66. * (*PA* 40:7214)

29. LIPPERT, JEROME J. *The Reliability of a Group Adapted I-E-S Test.* Master's thesis, Manhattan College (Bronx, N.Y.), 1966.

30. McCORMICK, CLARENCE C.; SCHNOBRICH, JANICE; and FOOTLIK, S. WILLARD. "IES Arrow-Dot Performance in Different Adolescent Populations." *Percept & Motor Skills* 22:507-10 Ap '66. * (*PA* 40:8875)

31. MANGOLD, K. M. "Comparison of Delinquents and Nondelinquents on the IES Test." *Percept & Motor Skills* 22:817-8 Je '66. * (*PA* 40:11175)

32. RANKIN, R. J., and THOMPSON, KENNETH. "A Factor Analytic Approach to Impulse as Measured by Arrow Dot I, Q, and SORT." *Percept & Motor Skills* 23:1239-45 D '66. * (*PA* 41:5262)

33. SIGNORI, EDRO I., and REMPEL, HENRY. "Research on the Picture Titles Subtest of the IES Test." *Percept & Motor Skills* 22:161-2 F '66. * (*PA* 40:5496)

34. TIWARI, J. G., and GAUTAM, R. P. "Personality Characteristics of Socially Neglected and Socially Neglected Junior High School Pupils." *Indian J Social Work* 27:211-7 Jl '66. *

35. BORTNER, RAYMAN W. "Measurement of Informal Selection Processes." *Percept & Motor Skills* 25:421-36 O '67. * (*PA* 42:5716)

36. SCOTT, JOHN MAURICE. *Interrelation of Impulses, Ego, and Superego in High Anxious and Low Anxious Male Adolescent Delinquents.* Doctor's thesis, University of Maryland (College Park, Md.), 1967. (*DA* 28:3066B)

37. SIGNORI, E. I. "The IES 'Experiment': Some Additional Perspective." *Percept & Motor Skills* 24:191-3 F '67. * (*PA* 41:8909)

38. SIGNORI, EDRO I. "Note on Response Tendencies to the Modified Picture Titles Subtest of the IES Test." *Percept & Motor Skills* 25:566 O '67. * (*PA* 42:4824)

39. SIGNORI, EDRO I., and REMPEL, HENRY. "Item Analysis of the Modified Picture Titles Subtest of the IES Test." *Percept & Motor Skills* 25:989-92 D '67. * (*PA* 42:8965)

40. SIGNORI, EDRO I., and REMPEL, HENRY. "Research on the Modified Picture Titles Subtest of the IES Test." *Percept & Motor Skills* 24:1255-8 Je '67. * (*PA* 41:15323)

41. TEWARI, J. G., and TEWARI, J. N. "On Extremes of Personality Adjustment as Measured by Adjustment Inventories." *J Psychol Res* 12:75-81 My '68. * (*PA* 43:5396)

NAME INDEX

[444]

An Incomplete Sentence Test. Employees, college; 1949-53; Forms M (for men), W (for women), (4 pages); 2 editions; no data on reliability; no norms; 15¢ per test; 25¢ per manual for *a;* 50¢ per specimen set; postpaid; (15-25) minutes; George Spache; [Reading Laboratory and Clinic]. *

a) AN INCOMPLETE SENTENCE TEST FOR INDUSTRIAL USE. Employees; 1949; 2 forms ('49); manual ['49, 8 pages].

b) AN INCOMPLETE SENTENCE TEST [COLLEGE EDITION]. College; 1953; 2 mimeographed forms ['53]; no manual; no data on validity.

For a review by Benjamin Balinsky, see 5:142.

[445]

The Industrial Sentence Completion Form. Employee applicants; 1963; ISCF; experimental form; 1 form (4 pages); no manual; no data on reliability and validity; no norms; [20-30] minutes; $5 per 20 tests, cash orders postpaid; specimen set not available; Martin M. Bruce; the Author. *

[446]

Interpersonal Diagnosis of Personality. Adults; 1955-58; a combination of assessment procedures consisting of the *Minnesota Multiphasic Personality Inventory,* the *Interpersonal Check List,* and the *Thematic Apperception Test* or the *Interpersonal Fantasy Test* (see *e* below); manual ('56, 114 pages, see *12* below); $7.50 per manual; specimen set (without manual) of *a-d* free; cash orders postpaid; Timothy Leary, Rolfe LaForge (*a*), Robert Suczek (*a*), and others (manual); Psychological Consultation Service. *

a) INTERPERSONAL CHECK LIST. [1955-56]; ICL; 1 form ['55, 3 pages]; $4 per 20 tests; $3 per scoring template; (15-45) minutes depending on number of persons rated.

b) RECORD BOOKLET FOR INTERPERSONAL DIAGNOSIS OF PERSONALITY. 1956-57; 1 form ('57, 4 pages); $5 per 20 booklets.

c) RECORD BOOKLET FOR INTERPERSONAL ANALYSIS OF GROUP DYNAMICS. 1956; 1 form ['56, 4 pages]; $5 per 20 booklets.

d) RECORD BOOKLET FOR INTERPERSONAL DIAGNOSIS OF FAMILY DYNAMICS. 1956; 1 form ['56, 6 pages]; $5 per 20 booklets.

e) INTERPERSONAL FANTASY TEST. 1957-58; 1 form ['57, 26 cards]; no data on reliability and validity; typewritten manual ('58, 5 pages); $15 per set of cards.

For a review by Jerry S. Wiggins, see 6:223 (10 references); see also 5:144 (11 references); for related book reviews not excerpted in this volume, consult the 5th (B261) MMY.

REFERENCES

1-11. See 5:144.
12-21. See 6:223.

22. TERRILL, JAMES McGUFFIN. *The Relationships Between Level II and Level III in the Interpersonal System of Personality Diagnosis.* Doctor's thesis, Stanford University (Stanford, Calif.), 1961. (*DA* 21:3529)

23. SULZER, WILMOT E. *An Investigation of the Relationship Between Conformity and Mental Health in Women Secondary School Teachers.* Doctor's thesis, New York University (New York, N.Y.), 1964. (*DA* 25:5755)

24. FRANZINI, BARBARA SCHILLINGER. *A Multilevel Assessment of Personality and Interpersonal Behavior of Mothers of Asthmatic Children as Compared With Mothers of Non-Asthmatic Children.* Doctor's thesis, New York University (New York, N.Y.), 1965. (*DA* 29:366B)

25. McDonald, Robert L. "Fantasy and the Outcome of Pregnancy." *Arch Gen Psychiatry* 12:602–6 Je '65. * (*PA* 39:12417)

26. Shore, Milton F.; Massimo, Joseph L.; Kisielewski, Julia; and Moran, Janet K. "Object Relations Changes Resulting From Successful Psychotherapy With Adolescent Delinquents and Their Relationship to Academic Performance." *J Am Acad Child Psychiatry* 5:93–104 Ja '66. * (*PA* 40:13268)

27. Harris, Frances W. *Personality Characteristics of Four Hospitalized Groups as Revealed by the Leary Interpersonal System.* Master's thesis, University of Kansas (Lawrence, Kan.), 1967.

28. Hurwitz, Jacob I., and Lelos, David. "A Multilevel Interpersonal Profile of Employed Alcoholics." *Q J Studies Alcohol* 29:64–76 Mr '68. * (*PA* 42:15709)

See also references for 127.

NAME INDEX

[447]

Kahn Test of Symbol Arrangement. Ages 6 and over; 1949–60; KTSA; individual; 1 form (16 plastic objects); record blank ('56, c1949–56, 4 pages); administrative manual ('56, 37 pages, reprint of *11* below); clinical manual ('57, 75 pages, reprint of *14* below); auxiliary evaluation guide ('60, 10 pages); $25 per complete set of test materials; $7.50 per 50 record blanks; $2 per administrative manual; $3 per clinical manual; cash orders postpaid; (15–30) minutes; Theodore C. Kahn; Psychological Test Specialists. *

See 6:224 (10 references); for reviews by Cherry Ann Clark and Richard Jessor, see 5:145 (16 references, 1 excerpt); for a review by Edward Joseph Shoben, Jr., see 4:110 (2 references).

REFERENCES

1–2. See 4:110.
3–18. See 5:145.
19–28. See 6:224.

29. Evans, W. R. *Performance of Delinquents and Non-Delinquents on the KTSA.* Master's thesis, Marshall College (Huntington, W.Va.), 1958.

30. Brodsly, W. J. *Comparative Performance of Epileptic and Non-Epileptic Children on a Projective Symbol Arrangement Test.* Master's thesis, University of Southern California (Los Angeles, Calif.), 1962.

31. Graves, B. C., and Hill, Larry K. "Explorations in the Performance of Air Force Prisoners on the KTSA." *Proc Ann Conf Air Force Clin Psychologists* 4:52–9 '63. * (*PA* 39:7892)

32. Hill, Larry K. "The Kahn Test of Symbol Arrangement: A Survey of Technic." *Proc Ann Conf Air Force Clin Psychologists* 4:9–21 '63. * (*PA* 39:7897)

33. Theiner, Eric C. "Interpretive Possibilities of Symbolic Thought Associations." *Proc Ann Conf Air Force Clin Psychologists* 4:22–34 '63. * (*PA* 39:7923)

34. Theiner, Eric C., and Giffen, Martin B. "A Comparison of Abstract Thought Process Among Three Cultures." *Proc Ann Conf Air Force Clin Psychologists* 4:35–51 '63. * (*PA* 39:7924)

35. Wyman, B. A. W. *The Effect of Sex Differences, Masculine-Feminine Interests, and Opposite Sex Roles on Performance on the Kahn Test of Symbol Arrangement.* Master's thesis, New Mexico State University (University Park, N.M.), 1963.

36. Craddick, Ray A. "Comment on Scorer Reliability and Validity of the Kahn Test of Symbol Arrangement." *Psychol Rep* 15:463–6 O '64. * (*PA* 39:5046)

37. Craddick, Ray A. "Psychological Correlates of Biodynamic Stress: Description of Six Subjects Sustaining Over 500 Accumulative 'G.'" *Aerospace Med* 35:40–2 Ja '64. *

38. Hedlund, James L., and Mills, David H. "Cross-validation of the KTSA With a Psychiatric Population." *J Clin Psychol* 20:100–3 Ja '64. * (*PA* 39:10121)

39. Hedlund, James L., and Mills, David H. "Scorer Reliability and the KTSA." *J Clin Psychol* 20:95–100 Ja '64. * (*PA* 39:10120)

40. Theiner, Eric C., and Giffen, Martin B. "A Comparison of Abstract Thought Processes Among Three Cultures." *Comprehen Psychiatry* 5:54–63 F '64. * (*PA* 39:1478)

41. Clack, Gerald S.; Guerin, Alan J.; and Latham, William R. "Interscorer Reliability of the KTSA." *Proc Ann Conf Air Force Behav Sci* 12:17–22 N '65. *

42. Craddick, Ray A., and Stern, Michael R. "Note on the Scorer Reliability on the Kahn Test of Symbol Arrangement." *J Clin Psychol* 21:197 Ap '65. * (*PA* 39:12385)

43. Kriegman, Lois S., and Kriegman, George. "The PaTE Report: A New Psychodynamic and Therapeutic Evaluative Procedure." *Psychiatric Q* 39:646–74 O '65. * (*PA* 40:3006)

44. L'Abate, Luciano, and Craddick, Ray A. "The Kahn Test of Symbol Arrangement (KTSA): A Critical Review." *J Clin Psychol* 21:115–35 Ap '65. * (*PA* 39:12294)

45. Nacewski, Richard M., and Byrne, Alfred E. "Considerations in Frontal-Lobe Evaluations With a Note on the KTSA." *Proc Ann Conf Air Force Behav Sci* 12:179–89 N '65. *

46. Smith, Laurence C., Jr. "The Effects of Heat Stroke on Cognitive Functioning." *Proc Ann Conf Air Force Behav Sci* 11:130–42 Jl '65. *

47. Abidin, Richard R. "Clinical Use of the KTSA With Children: A Critical Analysis." *Proc Ann Conf Air Force Behav Sci* 13:1–5 S '66. *

48. Abidin, Richard R. "KTSA Sorting Norms for School Age Children." *J Clin Psychol* 22:85–90 Ja '66. * (*PA* 40:4047)

49. Abidin, Richard R. "KTSA Symbolization Norms for School-Age Children." *J Proj Tech & Pers Assess* 30:474–8 O '66. * (*PA* 41:577)

50. Anderson, Laurence E., and Clack, Gerald S. "Interscorer Reliability and the KTSA." *Can Psychologist* 7a:213–5 Jl '66. *

51. Clack, Gerald S.; Guerin, Alan J.; and Latham, William R. "Scorer Reliability of the KTSA." *J Clin Psychol* 22:91–3 Ja '66. * (*PA* 40:3571)

52. Craddick, Ray A. "Some Personality Characteristics of Simulated Psychosis on the Kahn Test of Symbol Arrangement." *J Proj Tech & Pers Assess* 30:569–75 D '66. * (*PA* 41:2905)

53. Nevin, David A. *Performance of Cerebral Palsied and Normal Children on the Kahn Test of Symbol Arrangement.* Master's thesis, Fordham University (New York, N.Y.), 1966.

54. Craddick, Ray A. "Sorting and Arranging KTSA Objects According to Emotional Category and Preference Under Simulated 'Psychosis.'" *Percept & Motor Skills* 24:367–74 Ap '67. * (*PA* 41:10495)

55. Guerin, Alan J., and Abidin, Richard R., Jr. "The KTSA and Emotional Pathology in Children." *J Proj Tech & Pers Assess* 31:82–5 Ag '67. * (*PA* 41:15306)

56. Kipper, David A. "Diagnoses of Psychotic Patients With the Kahn Test of Symbol Arrangement." *Brit J Social & Clin Psychol* 6:70–1 F '67. * (*PA* 41:7323, title only)

57. Mann, Edward T. "The Symbolic Process of Recidivist and Non-Recidivist Children as Assessed by the Kahn Test of Symbol Arrangement." *J Proj Tech & Pers Assess* 31:40–6 O '67. * (*PA* 42:773)

58. Mann, Edward Thomas, III. *The Symbolic Process of Recidivist and Non-Recidivist Children as Assessed by the Kahn Test of Symbol Arrangement.* Doctor's thesis, University of Oklahoma (Norman, Okla.), 1967. (*DA* 28:1202B)

59. Shearn, Charles R., and Warren, Stacy L. "Performance of Hospitalized Male Alcoholics on the Kahn Test of Symbol Arrangement." *Percept & Motor Skills* 25:705–10 D '67. * (*PA* 42:9195)

60. Wyman, Barbara Walker, and Craddick, Ray A. "The Influence of Sex Related Variables on the Kahn Test of Symbol Arrangement." *J Psychol Studies* 15:130–5 Je '67. *

61. Abidin, Richard R., Jr. "Children's KTSA Performance: Research and Revision." *Proc Ann Conv Am Psychol Assn* 76:595–6 '68. * (*PA* 42:1350, title only)

62. Campos, Leonard P. "The Kahn Test of Symbol Arrangement (KTSA)," pp. 493–502. In *Projective Techniques in Personality Assessment: A Modern Introduction.* Edited by A. I. Rabin. New York: Springer Publishing Co., Inc., 1968. Pp. x, 638. *

63. Craddick, Ray A., and Levy, George. "Note on the Categorization, Recall and Preference of KTSA Objects by 'Aggressive' and 'Non-Aggressive' Prisoners." *Percept & Motor Skills* 27:26 Ag '68. * (*PA* 43:2818)

64. Kahn, Theodore C. "Signs of Creativity on the Kahn Test of Symbol Arrangement." *Percept & Motor Skills* 26:1065–6 Je '68. * (*PA* 42:18803)

NAME INDEX

[448]

Kent-Rosanoff Free Association Test. Ages 4 and over; 1910; K–R; for an adaptation, see 413; 1 form ['10, 2 pages]; hectographed manual ['10, 5 pages, reprinted from *Manual of Psychiatry*—seventh edition '38, original edition '05—formerly published by John Wiley & Sons, Inc. and now out of print]; no data on reliability; $4.73 per 50 tests, postage extra; specimen set not available; administration time not reported; G. H. Kent and A. J. Rosanoff; C. H. Stoelting Co. *

For a review by Jerry S. Wiggins, see 6:226 (82 references).

REFERENCES

1–82. See 6:226.
83. Volsky, Theodore C., Jr. *Modality of Word Association Test Responses as a Factor in Improving Counselor Predictions.* Doctor's thesis, University of Minnesota (Minneapolis, Minn.), 1958. (*DA* 19:881)
84. Milgram, Norman A. "Microgenetic Analysis of Word Associations in Schizophrenic and Brain-Damaged Patients." *J Abn & Social Psychol* 62:364–6 Mr '61. * (*PA* 36:4JQ64M)
85. Kincaid, Wendell D., Jr. *The Automatic and Selective Memory Process in Brain-Damaged, Schizophrenic, and Control Subjects.* Doctor's thesis, University of Connecticut (Storrs, Conn.), 1963. (*DA* 24:4798)
86. Jenkins, James J., and Palermo, David S. "A Note on Scoring Word Association Tests." *J Verbal Learning & Verbal Behav* 3:158–60 Ap '64. * (*PA* 39:3166)
87. Johnson, William Lawrence. *Relationships Between Variation in Choice of Types of Categorization and Variation in Personality Traits.* Doctor's thesis, Yeshiva University (New York, N.Y.), 1964. (*DA* 25:3676)
88. Klett, William G. "Geographical Differences in Word Associations." *Newsl Res Psychol* 6:12–3 N '64. *
89. Martin, James G. "Word-Association Frequency and the Proximity Effect." *J Verbal Learning & Verbal Behav* 3:344–5 Ag '64. * (*PA* 39:3820)
90. Osipow, Samuel H., and Grooms, Robert R. "Reciprocal Association to the Kent-Rosanoff Primary Associations." *Psychol Rep* 14:106 F '64. * (*PA* 39:304, title only)
91. Rosenzweig, Mark R. "Word Associations of French Workmen: Comparisons With Associations of French Students and American Workmen and Students." *J Verbal Learning & Verbal Behav* 3:57–69 F '64. * (*PA* 39:310)
92. Silverstein, A. B., and McLain, Richard E. "Associative Processes of the Mentally Retarded: 2, Effects of Selected Background Variables." *Am J Mental Def* 79:440–5 N '64. * (*PA* 39:8387)
93. Dokecki, Paul R.; Polidoro, Lewis G.; and Cromwell, Rue L. "Commonality and Stability of Word Association Responses in Good and Poor Premorbid Schizophrenics." *J Abn Psychol* 70:312–6 Ag '65. * (*PA* 39:16191)
94. Gerjuoy, Irma R., and Gerjuoy, Herbert. "Preliminary Word-Association Norms for Institutionalized Adolescent

Retardates." *Psychon Sci* 2:91–2 F 15 '65. * (*PA* 39:10583)
95. Henderson, John David. *The Relationship of Word Association Response Categories to Age: Response Category Shifts Under Stress.* Doctor's thesis, Syracuse University (Syracuse, N.Y.), 1965. (*DA* 26:6168)
96. Jenkins, James J., and Palermo, David S. "Further Data on Changes in Word-Association Norms." *J Personality & Social Psychol* 1:303–9 Ap '65. * (*PA* 39:10281)
97. Osipow, Samuel H., and Grooms, Robert R. "Norms for Chains of Word Associations." *Psychol Rep* 16:796 Je '65. * (*PA* 39:15257)
98. Palermo, David S., and Jenkins, James J. "Changes in Word Associations of Fourth- and Fifth-Grade Children From 1916 to 1961." *J Verbal Learning & Verbal Behav* 4:180–7 Je '65. * (*PA* 39:14660)
99. Palermo, David S., and Jenkins, James J. "Sex Differences in Word Associations." *J General Psychol* 72:77–84 Ja '65. * (*PA* 39:6421)
100. Restaino, Lillian C. R. Chap. 4, "Word Associations of Deaf Children," pp. 20–6. In *Research Studies on the Psycholinguistic Behavior of Deaf Children.* Edited by Joseph Rosenstein and Walter H. MacGinitie. CEC Research Monograph Series B, No. B-2. Washington, D.C.: Council for Exceptional Children, 1965. Pp. v, 40. *
101. Riegel, Klaus F. "Age and Cultural Differences as Determinants of Word Associations: Suggestions for Their Analysis." *Psychol Rep* 16:75–8 F '65. * (*PA* 39:7529)
102. Riegel, Klaus F., and Birren, James E. "Age Differences in Associative Behavior." *J Gerontol* 20:125–30 Ap '65. *
103. Shakow, David, and Jellinek, E. Morton. "Composite Index of the Kent-Rosanoff Free Association Test." *J Abn Psychol* 70:403–4 D '65. * (*PA* 40:2922)
104. Wolff, Craig. "Manifest Anxiety, Reaction Potential Ceiling, and Word Association." *J Personality & Social Psychol* 2:570–3 O '65. * (*PA* 40:552)
105. Wynne, Ronald D.; Gerjuoy, Herbert; and Schiffman, Harold. "Association Test Antonym-Response Set." *J Verbal Learning & Verbal Behav* 4:354–9 O '65. * (*PA* 40:1088)
106. Entwisle, Doris R. *Word Associations of Young Children.* Baltimore, Md.: Johns Hopkins Press, 1966. Pp. xiii, 599. * (*PA* 40:8685, title only)
107. Jung, John. "Experimental Studies of Factors Affecting Word Associations." *Psychol B* 66:125–33 Ag '66. * (*PA* 40:11127)
108. Nunnally, Jum C., and Blanton, Richard L. "Patterns of Word Association in the Deaf." *Psychol Rep* 18:87–92 F '66. * (*PA* 40:6945)
109. Silverstein, A. B., and McLain, Richard E. "Associative Processes of the Mentally Retarded: 3, A Developmental Study." *Am J Mental Def* 70:722–5 Mr '66. * (*PA* 40:6989)
110. Brenner, Arline R. "Effects of Prior Experimenter-Subject Relationships on Responses to the Kent-Rosanoff Word-Association List in Schizophrenics." *J Abn Psychol* 72:273–6 Je '67. * (*PA* 41:10733)
111. Canestrari, R. E., Jr., and Coppinger, N. W. "Age Changes in Free Association." *Newsl Res Psychol* 9:6–8 N '67. *
112. Koplin, James H.; Odom, Penelope B.; Blanton, Richard L.; and Nunnally, Jum C. "Word Association Test Performance of Deaf Subjects." *J Speech & Hearing Res* 10:126–32 Mr '67. * (*PA* 41:15651)
113. Wynne, Ronald D.; Gerjuoy, Herbert; Schiffman, Harold; and Wexler, Norman. "Word Association: Variables Affecting Popular-Response Frequency." *Psychol Rep* 20:423–32 Ap '67. * (*PA* 41:8391)
114. Dolinsky, Richard. "Estimating Word-Association Frequencies." *Psychol Rep* 22:512–4 Ap '68. * (*PA* 42:11626)
115. Ries, Harold A. "Commonality of Word Associations and Length of Hospitalization in Neurotics and Schizophrenics." *J Consult & Clin Psychol* 32:722–4 D '68. * (*PA* 43:4136)
116. Rosett, Henry L.; Robbins, Herbert; and Watson, Walter S. "Physiognomic Perception as a Cognitive Control Principle." *Percept & Motor Skills* 26:707–19 Je '68. * (*PA* 42:14974)

NAME INDEX

[449]

*The Lowenfeld Kaleidoblocs. Ages 2.5 and over; 1958–66; LK; individual; 1 form ['58]; mimeographed manual ('66, 13 pages); no data on reliability and validity; no norms; 125s. per set of testing materials, postpaid; specimen set not available; (60) minutes; Margaret Lowenfeld; Badger Tests Co., Ltd. *

For reviews by T. R. Miles and George Westby, see 6:227 (3 references).

[450]

Lowenfeld Mosaic Test. Ages 2 and over; 1930–58; LMT; individual; 1 form ['30]; 2 sets: standard (456 pieces), minor (228 pieces); directions for administering ['58, 9 pages, directions printed in English, French, German, and Spanish in same booklet]; manual ('54, 39 below); revised record booklet ['54, c1951, 4 pages]; no data on reliability; 490s. per standard set; 300s. per minor set; 25s. per tray; 50s. per 25 record booklets; 120s. per manual; postpaid; specimen set not available; (20–40) minutes; Margaret Lowenfeld; Badger Tests Co., Ltd. *

For reviews by T. R. Miles and George Westby, see 6:228 (20 references); for a review by C. J. Adcock, see 5:147 (43 references); see also 4:115 (13 references); for reviews not excerpted in this volume, consult the 6th (B51) and 5th (B274) MMY's.

REFERENCES

1–13. See 4:115.
14–56. See 5:147.
57–76. See 6:228.
77. LEVIN, MONROE LOUIS. *The Relationships Between Construction of Form-Color-Spatial Designs and Psychopathology.* Doctor's thesis, Columbia University (New York, N.Y.), 1954. (*DA* 14:1461)
78. MARQUIS, JOHN N. *A Comparison of Performance of Senile Dementia and Older Schizophrenic Patients on the Lowenfeld Mosaic Test.* Master's thesis, Ohio University (Athens, Ohio), 1954.
79. AMES, LOUISE BATES, and ILG, FRANCES L. "Age Changes in Children's Mosaic Responses From Five to Ten Years." *Genetic Psychol Monogr* 69:195–245 My '64. * (*PA* 39:4582)
80. AMES, LOUISE B., and ILG, FRANCES L. "Sex Differences in Test Performance of Matched Girl-Boy Pairs in the Five-to-Nine-Year-Old Age Range." *J Genetic Psychol* 104:25–34 Mr '64. * (*PA* 39:4582)
81. AMES, LOUISE BATES; ILG, FRANCES L.; and AUGUST, JUDITH. "The Lowenfeld Mosaic Test: Norms for Five-to-Ten-Year-Old American Public-School Children and Comparative Study of Three Groups." *Genetic Psychol Monogr* 70:57–95 Ag '64. * (*PA* 39:10085)
82. ROSE, DORIAN; SMITH, RUTH E.; and ROBLES, ALBERT. "Some Problems in Perceptual Handicap of Mentally Retarded Children." *J Genetic Psychol* 104:123–33 Mr '64. * (*PA* 39:5669)
83. SHARMA, S. N. "Behavioral Analysis of Three Projective Tests of Fantasy: the Mosaic, the Toy World and the MAPS Tests." *Manas* 2(2):81–5 '64. * (*PA* 39:7916)
84. SHARMA, S. N. "The Mosaic Test and Its Approach to Mental Evaluation." *Indian J Psychol* 39:81–6 Je '64. *
85. ABEL, THEODORA M. "Psychodynamics as Reflected in the Lowenfeld Mosaic Test." *J Social Psychol* 65:101–25 F '65. * (*PA* 39:12375)
86. CHASE, JOAN A. "Color Preference on the Lowenfeld Mosaic Test: Position Influence." *J Genetic Psychol* 106:259–63 Je '65. * (*PA* 39:15382)
87. ILG, FRANCES L., and AMES, LOUISE BATES. *School Readiness: Behavior Tests Used at the Gesell Institute*, pp. 243–52. New York: Harper & Row, Publishers, 1965. Pp. viii, 396. *
88. ILG, FRANCES L.; AMES, LOUISE BATES; and APELL, RICHARD J. "School Readiness as Evaluated by Gesell Developmental, Visual, and Projective Tests." *Genetic Psychol Monogr* 71:61–91 F '65. * (*PA* 39:12943)
89. KRANZ, PETER L. *Mosaic Designs of Children With Down's Syndrome.* Master's thesis, Utah State University (Logan, Utah), 1965.
90. AMES, LOUISE BATES, and AUGUST, JUDITH. "Comparison of Mosaic Response of Negro and White Primary-School Children." *J Genetic Psychol* 109:123–9 S '66. * (*PA* 40:13206)
91. BOWYER, RUTH; GILLIES, JOHN; and SCOTT, JENNIFER. "The Use of Projective Techniques With Deaf Children." *Rorsch Newsl* 11:3–6 D '66. * (*PA* 42:765)
92. KALDEGG, A. "Vocational Guidance in a Mental Hospital: With Particular Emphasis on the Mosaic Test." *Rorsch Newsl* 11:23–7 Je '66. * (*PA* 40:11365, title only)
93. KUMAR, PRAMOD. "The Mosaic Test in Normal and Schizophrenic Groups." *Indian J Psychol* 41:85–7 Je '66. *
94. AMES, LOUISE B., and ILG, FRANCES L. "Search for Children Showing Academic Promise in a Predominantly Negro School." *J Genetic Psychol* 110:217–31 Je '67. * (*PA* 41:11732)
95. SHARMA, SATYA N., and CHATTERJEE, BISHWA B. "Application of the Mosaic Test Upon Hindus and Muslims." *Acta Psychologica* 26:9–16 Ja '67. *
96. AMES, LOUISE BATES. "Academic Progress in Negro Schools." *J Learn Dis* 1:570–7 O '68. *
97. CAMPOS, LEONARD P. "Lowenfeld Mosaic Test," pp. 481–93. In *Projective Techniques in Personality Assessment: A Modern Introduction.* Edited by A. I. Rabin. New York: Springer Publishing Co., Inc., 1968. Pp. x, 638. *
98. SINGH, SATISH CHANDRA PRASAD. "Clinical Usefulness of the Lowenfeld Mosaic Test." *Psychol Studies* 13:115–7 Jl '68. *

NAME INDEX

[451]

Machover Draw-A-Person Test. Ages 2 and over; 1949; MDAP; also called *Machover Figure Drawing Test;* manual (192 pages, see 5 below); no accessories; $6.50 per manual, cash orders postpaid; (5-60) minutes without associations, (20-90) minutes with associations; Karen Machover; Charles C Thomas, Publisher. *

For a review by Philip M. Kitay, see 6:229 (84 references); see also 5:148 (39 references); for reviews by Philip L. Harriman and Naomi Stewart, see 4:111 (13 references); for excerpts from related book reviews, see 4:112.

REFERENCES

1-13. See 4:111.
14-52. See 5:148.
53-136. See 6:229.
137. EIGENBRODE, CHARLES R. *Effectiveness of the Machover Signs and Others in Differentiating Between a Normal Group and a Schizophrenic Group by Use of the Projective Drawing Test.* Master's thesis, George Washington University (Washington, D.C.), 1951.
138. MYDEN, WALTER DAVID. *An Interpretation and Evaluation of Certain Personality Characteristics Involved in Creative Production: An Investigation and Evaluation of Personality Structure and Characteristics of Creative Individuals in the Context of Psychoanalytic Theory and Ego Psychology.* Doctor's thesis, New York University (New York, N.Y.), 1956. (DA 17:897)
139. BODWIN, RAYMOND FRANKLIN. *The Relationship Between Immature Self-Concept and Certain Educational Disabilities.* Doctor's thesis, Michigan State University (East Lansing, Mich.), 1957. (DA 19:1645)
140. BRUCK, MAX. *A Study of Age Differences and Sex Differences in the Relationship Between Self-Concept and Grade-Point Average.* Doctor's thesis, Michigan State University (East Lansing, Mich.), 1957. (DA 19:1646)
141. YOUNG, HARL HENRY, JR. *Personality Test Correlates of Orientation to the Vertical: A Test of Witkin's Field-Dependency Hypothesis.* Doctor's thesis, University of Texas (Austin, Tex.), 1957. (DA 19:882)
142. POPPLESTONE, JOHN ARMSTRONG. *Male Human Figure Drawing in Normal and Emotionally Disturbed Children.* Doctor's thesis, Washington University (St. Louis, Mo.), 1958. (DA 19:573)
143. SAELENS, ELIZABETH A. *Reliability of Graphic Indices in the Draw-A-Person Test.* Master's thesis, Fordham University (New York, N.Y.), 1959.
144. WALLON, EDWARD J. *A Study of Criteria Used to Differentiate the Human-Figure Drawings of Normals, Neurotics, and Psychotics.* Doctor's thesis, Purdue University (Lafayette, Ind.), 1959. (DA 20:1873)
145. WISOTSKY, MORRIS. "A Note on the Order of Figure Drawing Among Incarcerated Alcoholics." *J Clin Psychol* 15:65 Ja '59. * (PA 34:3228)
146. BOOTH, GOTTHARD. "The Psychological Examination of Candidates for the Ministry," pp. 100-24. In *The Ministry and Mental Health.* Edited by Hans Hofmann. New York: Association Press, 1960. Pp. 251. *
147. FINK, J. H. A *Psychophysiological Comparison of Brittle and Stable Diabetics.* Doctor's thesis, University of California (Los Angeles, Calif.), 1960.
148. FISHER, GARY M. "Sexual Identification in Mentally Subnormal Females." *Am J Mental Def* 66:266-9 S '61. * (PA 36:3J166F)

149. CARKHUFF, ROBERT R. "The FACE Supplement: A Quick Index of Intelligence for Adult Subnormals." *J Clin Psychol* 18:346-7 Jl '62. * (PA 39:1721)
150. LAIRD, JAMES T. "A Comparison of Female Normals, Psychiatric Patients, and Alcoholics for Sex Drawn First." *J Clin Psychol* 18:473 O '62. * (PA 39:5074)
151. BACHTOLD, LOUISE MARIE. *Differences in Personality, School Attitude, and Visual Motor Performance Among Specific Types of Underachievers.* Doctor's thesis, University of the Pacific (Stockton, Calif.), 1963. (DA 25:1730)
152. CORAH, NORMAN L., and CORAH, PATRICIA LANEY. "A Study of Body Image in Children With Cleft Palate and Cleft Lip." *J Genetic Psychol* 103:133-7 S '63. * (PA 39:2414)
153. FINK, JOSEPHINE H. "Personality Variables in Brittle and Stable Diabetics." *Newsl Res Psychol* 5:8-9 Ag '63. * (PA 38:8587)
154. FLINN, DON E.; HARTMAN, BRYCE O.; POWELL, DOUGLAS H.; and McKENZIE, RICHARD E. "Psychiatric and Psychologic Evaluation," pp. 199-230. In *Aeromedical Evaluation for Space Pilots.* Edited by Lawrence E. Lamb. Brooks Air Force Base, Tex.: USAF School of Aerospace Medicine, July 1963. Pp. viii, 276. * (PA 38:4728)
155. LAWRENCE, STEPHEN BRUCE. *A Study of a Technique Used to Evaluate Achromatic and Chromatic Human Figure Drawings.* Doctor's thesis, Purdue University (Lafayette, Ind.), 1963. (DA 24:1700)
156. BRADFIELD, ROBERT H. "The Predictive Validity of Children's Drawings." *Calif J Ed Res* 15:166-74 S '64. * (PA 39:5194)
157. HAMMER, MAX, and KAPLAN, ARTHUR M. "Reliability of Profile and Front-Facing Directions in Children's Drawings." *Child Develop* 35:973-7 S '64. * (PA 39:4538)
158. HAMMER, MAX, and KAPLAN, ARTHUR M. "The Reliability of Sex of First Figure Drawn by Children." *J Clin Psychol* 20:251-2 Ap '64. * (PA 39:7894)
159. HAMMER, MAX, and KAPLAN, ARTHUR M. "The Reliability of Size of Children's Drawings." *J Clin Psychol* 20:121 Ja '64. * (PA 39:10118)
160. HANDLER, LEONARD, and REYHER, JOSEPH. "The Effects of Stress on the Draw-A-Person Test." *J Consult Psychol* 28:259-64 Je '64. * (PA 39:5063)
161. HERGER, JEAN. *A Test of Reliability of the Machover Draw-A-Person Test.* Master's thesis, Sacramento State College (Sacramento, Calif.), 1964.
162. JONES, LEONA WISE, and THOMAS, CAROLINE BEDELL. "Studies on Figure Drawings: Structural and Graphic Characteristics." *Psychiatric Q Sup* 38:76-110 pt 1 '64. * (PA 39:15434)
163. LEWINSOHN, PETER M. "Relationship Between Height of Figure Drawings and Depression in Psychiatric Patients." *J Consult Psychol* 28:380-1 Ag '64. * (PA 39:5785)
164. McHUGH, ANN F. "Children's Figure Drawings and School Achievement." *Psychol Sch* 1:51-2 Ja '64. *
165. PHELAN, HELEN M. "The Incidence and Possible Significance of the Drawing of Female Figures by Sixth-Grade Boys in Response to the Draw-A-Person Test." *Psychiatric Q* 38:488-503 Jl '64. * (PA 39:7911)
166. POLLITT, ERNESTO; HIRSCH, STEVEN; and MONEY, JOHN. "Priapism, Impotence and Human Figure Drawings." *J Nerv & Mental Dis* 139:161-8 Ag '64. * (PA 39:5210)
167. PRESTON, CAROLINE E. "Psychological Testing With Northwest Coast Alaskan Eskimos." *Genetic Psychol Monogr* 69:323-419 My '64. * (PA 39:4713)
168. SCHAEFFER, ROBERT W. "Clinical Psychologists' Ability to Use the Draw-A-Person Test as an Indicator of Personality Adjustment." Abstract. *J Consult Psychol* 28:383 Ag '64. * (PA 39:3246, title only)
169. SCHORER, C. E. "Muscular Dystrophy and the Mind." *Psychosom Med* 26:5-13 Ja-F '64. * (PA 39:2402)
170. WANDERER, ZEV WILLIAM. *The Validity of Diagnostic Judgments Based on "Blind" Machover Figure Drawings.* Doctor's thesis, Columbia University (New York, N.Y.), 1964. (DA 26:7163)
171. YAGODA, GERALD, and WOLFSON, WILLIAM. "Examiner Influence on Projective Test Responses." *J Clin Psychol* 20:389 Jl '64. * (PA 39:10276)
172. BLANK, LEONARD. *Psychological Evaluation in Psychotherapy: Ten Case Histories.* Chicago, Ill.: Aldine Publishing Co., 1965. Pp. xii, 364. *
173. GUINAN, JAMES F., and HURLEY, JOHN R. "An Investigation on the Reliability of Human Figure Drawings." *J Proj Tech & Pers Assess* 29:300-4 S '65. * (PA 39:15389)
174. HANDLER, LEONARD, and REYHER, JOSEPH. "Figure Drawing Anxiety Indexes: A Review of the Literature." *J Proj Tech & Pers Assess* 29:305-13 S '65. * (PA 39:15392)
175. KAHN, MARVIN W., and JONES, NELSON F. "Human Figure Drawings as Predictors of Admission to a Psychiatric Hospital." *J Proj Tech & Pers Assess* 29:319-22 S '65. * (PA 39:15396)
176. LEWINSOHN, PETER M. "Psychological Correlates of Overall Quality of Figure Drawings." *J Consult Psychol* 29:504-12 D '65. * (PA 40:2956)
177. LYMAN, HELENA WALKER. *The Relationship Between Speech Disability and Self-Concept as Measured by the Machover Draw-A-Person Test for Boys in Grades Three Through*

Six. Doctor's thesis, University of Portland (Portland, Ore.), 1965.

178. NANDY, ASHIS, and MITRA, SHIB K. "Economic Class and Images of Rich, Poor and Self in DAP." *J Psychol Res* 9:67–73 My '65. * (*PA* 39:14970)

179. OXHORN, JOSEPH LEWIS. *The Relation of Figure Drawings to Masculine-Feminine Orientation and Academic Achievement.* Doctor's thesis, Rutgers—The State University (New Brunswick, N.J.), 1965. (*DA* 27:601B)

180. RABIN, A. I. *Growing Up in the Kibbutz: Comparison of the Personality of Children Brought Up in the Kibbutz and of Family-Reared Children.* New York: Springer Publishing Co., Inc. 1965. Pp. x, 230. *

181. RICHARDSON, ROGER A. "The Effects of Hand Dominance on the Profile Orientation of Children's Human Figure Drawings." *Newsl Res Psychol* 7:53–4 Ag '65. *

182. RICHARDSON, ROGER A. "The Effects of Hand Preference on the Profile Orientation of Children's Human Figure Drawings." *Newsl Res Psychol* 7:59–60 My '65. *

183. WAIT, MARY ELEANOR. *Language Development, Anxiety, and Early Socialization Processes.* Doctor's thesis, Boston University (Boston, Mass.), 1965. (*DA* 26:5255)

184. WYSOCKI, BOLESLAW A., and WHITNEY, ELEANOR. "Body Image of Crippled Children as Seen in Draw-A-Person Test Behavior." *Percept & Motor Skills* 21:499–504 O '65. * (*PA* 40:3272)

185. APFELDORF, MAX; RANDOLPH, JOHN J.; and WHITMAN, GLORIA L. "Figure Drawing Correlates of Furlough Utilization in an Aged Institutionalized Population." *News Res Psychol* 8:17–9 N '66. *

186. BLATT, BENJAMIN, and TSUSHIMA, WILLIAM. "A Psychological Study of Uremic Patients Being Considered for the Artificial Kidney Machine Program (Hemodialysis)." *Newsl Res Psychol* 8:17–8 F '66. *

187. EVANS, FREDERICK J., and SCHMEIDLER, DEL. "Inter-Judge Reliability of Human Figure Drawing Measures of Field Dependence." *Percept & Motor Skills* 22:630 Ap '66. * (*PA* 40:8871)

188. GRAVITZ, MELVIN A. "Normal Adult Differentiation Patterns on the Figure Drawing Test." *J Proj Tech & Pers Assess* 30:471–3 O '66. * (*PA* 41:600)

189. HUISINGA, VIRGENIA N. *A Comparison of Normal and Mentally Retarded Children's Responses to the Machover Test.* Master's thesis, Illinois State University (Normal, Ill.), 1966.

190. KOPPITZ, ELIZABETH MUNSTERBERG. "Emotional Indicators on Human Figure Drawings of Shy and Aggressive Children." *J Clin Psychol* 22:466–9 O '66. * (*PA* 41:2915)

191. KRAJEWSKI, ROBERT JAMES. *Predicting 7th Grade Pupils' Adjustment by an Objective Interpretation of a Group Administration of the Draw-A-Person Test.* Doctor's thesis, Loyola University (Chicago, Ill.), 1966.

192. KURTZBERG, RICHARD L.; CAVIOR, NORMAN; and LIPTON, DOUGLAS S. "Sex Drawn First and Sex Drawn Larger by Opiate Addict and Non-Addict Inmates on the Draw-A-Person Test." *J Proj Tech & Pers Assess* 30:55–8 F '66. * (*PA* 40:5490)

193. LITT, SHELDON, and MARGOSHES, ADAM. "Sex-Change in Successive Draw-A-Person Tests." *J Clin Psychol* 22:471 O '66. * (*PA* 41:2917)

194. McHUGH, ANN F. "Children's Figure Drawings in Neurotic and Conduct Disturbances." *J Clin Psychol* 22:219–21 Ap '66. * (*PA* 40:7892)

195. MONEY, JOHN, and WANG, CHRISTINE. "Human Figure Drawing: 1, Sex of First Choice in Gender-Identity Anomalies, Klinefelter's Syndrome and Precocious Puberty." *J Nerv & Mental Dis* 143:157–62 Ag '66. * (*PA* 41:4622)

196. RIES, HAROLD A.; JOHNSON, MONTY H.; ARMSTRONG, HUBERT E., JR.; and HOLMES, DOUGLAS S. "The Draw-A-Person Test and Process-Reactive Schizophrenia." *J Proj Tech & Pers Assess* 30:184–6 Ap '66. * (*PA* 40:7737)

197. SHRY, STEPHEN A. "Relative Size of Same and Opposite Sex Drawings on the DAP as an Index of Dominance-Submissiveness." Abstract. *J Consult Psychol* 30:568 D '66. * (*PA* 41:2923, title only)

198. WANDERER, ZEV WILLIAM. "Validity of Clinical Judgments Based on Human Figure Drawings." *Proc Ann Conv Am Psychol Assn* 74:243–4 '66. * (*PA* 41:5988)

199. BROWN, L. B., and FERNALD, L. DODGE, JR. "Questionnaire Anxiety." *Psychol Rep* 21:537–40 O '67. * (*PA* 42:5593)

200. DOUBROS, STEVE G., and MASCARENHAS, JULIET. "Effect of Test Produced Anxiety on Human Figure Drawings." *Percept & Motor Skills* 25:773–5 D '67. * (*PA* 42:8989)

201. FRISCH, GIORA R., and HANDLER, LEONARD. "Differences in Negro and White Drawings: A Cultural Interpretation." *Percept & Motor Skills* 24:667–70 Ap '67. * (*PA* 41:10480)

202. GRIFFITH, ALBERT V., and LEMLEY, DOROTHY WEST. "Teeth and Threatening Look in the Draw-A-Person Test as Indicating Aggression." *J Clin Psychol* 23:489–92 O '67. * (*PA* 42:2607)

203. HARRIS, JAY E. "Elucidation of Body Imagery in Chronic Schizophrenia." *Arch Gen Psychiatry* 16:679–84 Je '67. * (*PA* 41:13979)

204. HERSHENSON, DAVID B. "Body-Image (Hand) and Arithmetic Ability." *Percept & Motor Skills* 25:967–8 D '67. * (*PA* 42:8994)

205. JACOBSON, HOWARD A., and HANDLER, LEONARD. "Extro-

version-Introversion and the Effects of Stress on the Draw-A-Person Test." Abstract. *J Consult Psychol* 31:433 Ag '67. * (*PA* 41:13677, title only)

206. JAMES, SARA L.; OSBORN, FRANCES; and OETTING, E. R. "Treatment for Delinquent Girls: The Adolescent Self-Concept Group." *Commun Mental Health J* 3:377–81 w '67. * (*PA* 42:7407)

207. REILLY, DAVID H., and SUGERMAN, A. ARTHUR. "Conceptual Complexity and Psychological Differentiation in Alcoholics." *J Nerv & Mental Dis* 144:14–7 Ja '67. * (*PA* 41:12143)

208. SOCCOLICH, CHRISTINA, and WYSOCKI, BOLESLAW A. "Draw-A-Person Protocols of Male and Female College Students." *Percept & Motor Skills* 25:873–9 D '67. * (*PA* 42:9006)

209. WATSON, CHARLES G. "Relationship of Distortion to DAP Diagnostic Accuracy Among Psychologists at Three Levels of Sophistication." *J Consult Psychol* 31:142–6 Ap '67. * (*PA* 41:7511)

210. CRADDICK, RAY A., and LEIPOLD, WILLIAM D. "Note on the Height of Draw-A-Person Figures by Male Alcoholics." *J Proj Tech & Pers Assess* 32:486 O '68. * (*PA* 43:5382)

211. DATTA, LOIS-ELLIN, and DRAKE, ANN K. "Examiner Sex and Sexual Differentiation in Preschool Children's Figure Drawings." *J Proj Tech & Pers Assess* 32:397–9 Ag '68. * (*PA* 43:3104)

212. EATON, MARY JAYNE. *An Investigation of Selected Personality Dimensions of Mothers Whose Children Have Severe Communication Problems.* Doctor's thesis, University of Alabama (University, Ala.), 1968. (*DA* 29:479A)

213. FISHER, GARY. "Human Figure Drawing Indices of Sexual Maladjustment in Male Felons." *Correct Psychiatry & J Social Ther* 14:48–53 sp '68. *

214. FISHER, GARY. "Human Figure Drawing Indices of Sexual Maladjustment in Male Felons." Abstract. *J Proj Tech & Pers Assess* 32:81 F '68. * (*PA* 42:9205)

215. GRAVITZ, MELVIN A. "The Height of Normal Adult Figure Drawings." *J Clin Psychol* 24:75 Ja '68. * (*PA* 42:8993)

216. LAPKIN, BENJAMIN; HILLABY, THELMA (GORDON); and SILVERMAN, LLOYD. "Manifestations of the Schizophrenic Process in Figure Drawings of Adolescents." *Arch Gen Psychiatry* 19:465–8 O '68. * (*PA* 43:4158)

217. ROBACK, HOWARD B. "Human Figure Drawings: Their Utility in the Clinical Psychologist's Armamentarium for Personality Assessment." *Psychol B* 70:1–19 Jl '68. * (*PA* 42:15692)

218. SINOWITZ, MELVIN, and BROWN, FRED. "Wechsler's MF Score as an Indicator of Masculinity and Femininity in a Psychiatric Population." *J Clin Psychol* 24:92–4 Ja '68. *

219. SWENSEN, CLIFFORD H. "Empirical Evaluations of Human Figure Drawings: 1957–1966." *Psychol B* 70:20–44 Jl '68. * (*PA* 42:15693)

220. TAULBEE, EARL S., and LIBB, JOHN W. "Overt Sexual Responses in Personality Assessment and Alcoholism." *Newsl Res Psychol* 10:1–5 Ag '68. *

221. WILKINSON, A. EARL, and SCHNADT, FREDERICK. "Human Figure Drawing Characteristics: An Empirical Study." *J Clin Psychol* 24:224–6 Ap '68. * (*PA* 42:12136)

NAME INDEX

[452]

Make A Picture Story. Ages 6 and over; 1947-52; MAPS; individual; 1 form ('47, 22 background pictures and 67 figure cutouts); figure location sheet ('48, 4 pages); manual ('25, 96 pages, see 27 below); no data on reliability and validity; $18 per set of test materials, 25 figure location sheets, and manual; $2.25 per 25 figure location sheets; $2.75 per manual; $18.50 per theater (optional) and carrying case; postpaid; (45-90) minutes; Edwin S. Shneidman; Psychological Corporation. *

For a review by Arthur R. Jensen, see 6:230 (10 references); see also 5:149 (19 references); for reviews by Albert I. Rabin and Charles R. Strother, see 4:113 (19 references); for excerpts from related book reviews, see 4:114.

REFERENCES

1-19. See 4:113.
20-38. See 5:149.
39-48. See 6:230.
49. NEYHUS, ARTHUR IRVIN. *The Personality of Socially Well Adjusted Adult Deaf as Revealed by Projective Tests.* Doctor's thesis, Northwestern University (Evanston, Ill.), 1962. (DA 23:2589)
50. SHARMA, S. N. "Behavioral Analysis of Three Projective Tests of Fantasy: the Mosaic, the Toy World and the MAPS Tests." *Manas* 2(2):81-5 '64. * (PA 39:7916)
51. FREDE, MARTHA C.; GAUTNEY, DONALD B.; and BAXTER, JAMES C. "Relationships between Body Image Boundary and Interaction Patterns on the MAPS Test." *J Consult & Clin Psychol* 32:575-8 O '68. * (PA 43:939)
52. NEURINGER, CHARLES, and ORR, SUSAN G. "Predictions of Pathology From Make-A-Picture Story (MAPS) Test Figures." *J Consult & Clin Psychol* 32:491-3 Ag '68. * (PA 42:17393)

NAME INDEX

[453]

The Marriage Adjustment Sentence Completion Survey. Marriage counselees; 1962-65; MASCS; Forms H ('65, 4 pages, for husbands), W ('65, 4 pages, for wives), identical except for sex references; manual ('65, 11 pages plus tests and protocol booklet) ; protocol booklet ('65, 4 pages) ; forms, manual, and protocol booklet identical with materials copyrighted in 1962 except for format of manual; no data on reliability and validity; no norms; $12 per set of 10 tests of each form, 20 protocol booklets, and manual; $6.50 per 25 tests; $6.50 per 25 protocol booklets; $2 per manual; postpaid; (20–40) minutes; Morse P. Manson and Arthur Lerner; Western Psychological Services. *

For a review by Albert Ellis, consult 6:683.

[454]

★The Measurement of Self Concept in Kindergarten Children. Kgn; 1967; MSCKC; experimental form; projective drawing technique; 3 scores: self concept, non-self concept, discrepancy; manual (101 pages) ; scoring manual ['67, 32 pages] ; $4.50 per 50 sets of score sheeets; $3 per scoring manual; $9 per manual; cash orders postpaid; [10] minutes for each of 16 weekly sessions; Lucienne Y. Levin and J. Clayton Lafferty; Research Concepts. *

[455]

The Michigan Picture Test. Ages 8–14; 1953; MPT; 8 scores: tension (4 subscores), verb tense (3 subscores), direction of forces (3 subscores), combined maladjustment, interpersonal relations (2 subscores), personal pronouns (2 subscores), psychosexual level (7 subscores), popular objects; individual; 1 form (16 cards, 4 for boys only and 4 for girls only) ; manual (117 pages, see 8 below) ; no data on reliability; $6.85 per set of cards; $1.90 per 20 record blanks; $2 per manual; $9 per specimen set including the complementary *Rating Scale for Pupil Adjustment* (see 226) ; postage extra; (60) minutes; Gwen Andrew, Samuel W. Hartwell, Max L. Hutt, and Ralph E. Walton; Science Research Associates, Inc. *

For reviews by William E. Henry and Morris Krugman, see 5:150 (7 references, 2 excerpts).

REFERENCES

1–7. See 5:150.
8. ANDREW, GWEN; HARTWELL, SAMUEL W.; HUTT, MAX L.; and WALTON, RALPH E. *The Michigan Picture Test: The Evaluation of Emotional Reactions of Children Eight to Fourteen Years of Age: An Introductory Symposium, a Research Report, and a Manual.* Chicago, Ill.: Science Research Associates, Inc., 1953. Pp. xviii, 108. *
9. BOLTON, RITA J. *A Comparison of the T.A.T. and the Michigan Picture Test With Adolescents.* Master's thesis, Cornell University (Ithaca, N.Y.), 1956.
10. COOK, MARY M. *The Use of the Michigan Picture Test in Evaluating the Emotional Adjustment of Children.* Master's thesis, Claremont College (Claremont, Calif.), 1957.
11. FLYNN, ANN PATRICE. *A Projective Picture Technique for Screening Emotionally Disturbed Children on the Junior High School Level.* Master's thesis, Immaculate Heart College (Los Angeles, Calif.), 1958.
12. WALL, HARVEY R. *A Differential Analysis of Some Intellective and Affective Characteristics of Peer Accepted and Rejected Preadolescent Children.* Doctor's thesis, University of Kansas (Lawrence, Kan.), 1960. (DA 21:2790)
13. ENGLISH, ROBERT HENRY. *Cleft Palate Children Compared With Non-Cleft Palate Children: A Personality Study.* Doctor's thesis, University of Oregon (Eugene, Ore.), 1961. (DA 23:2622)
14. McCULLY, ROBERT STEPHEN. *Fantasy Productions of Children With a Progressively Crippling and Fatal Illness.* Doctor's thesis, Columbia University (New York, N.Y.), 1961. (DA 22:643)
15. MASKIT, MAE LEE. *Management of Aggression in Preadolescent Girls: Its Effect on Certain Aspects of Ego Functioning.* Doctor's thesis, University of Michigan (Ann Arbor, Mich.), 1961. (DA 22:917)
16. MULLEN, F. A. "An Inductive Method for Determining Significant Aspects of the Responses of Mentally Handicapped Children to the Thematic Apperception Test and the Michigan Picture Test." Abstract. *Acta Psychologica* 19:861–2 '61. *
17. GOOD, JUNE AMSDEN. *Some Relationships Between Hostility and Fantasy Production in Children.* Doctor's thesis, George Peabody College for Teachers (Nashville, Tenn.), 1965. (DA 26:6845)
18. ALPER, THELMA G., and GREENBERGER, ELLEN. "Relation-

ship of Picture Structure to Achievement Motivation in College Women." *J Personality & Social Psychol* 7:362–71 D '67. * (PA 42:3964)

[456]

Miner Sentence Completion Scale. Adults, particularly managers and management trainees; 1961–64; MSCS; 1 form ('61, 4 pages) ; scoring guide ('64, 64 pages) ; scoring sheet ('61, 1 page) ; no data on reliability and validity; $8.50 per 50 sets of scale and scoring sheet; $2.75 per scoring guide; postage extra; specimen set not available; [30] minutes; John B. Miner; Springer Publishing Co., Inc. *

REFERENCES

1–2. See 6:230a.
3. MINER, JOHN B. "The Prediction of Managerial and Research Success." *Personnel Adm* 28:12–6 S–O '65. *
4. MINER, JOHN B. *Studies in Management Education.* New York: Springer Publishing Co., Inc., 1965. Pp. vii, 309. *
5. MINER, JOHN B. "The Early Identification of Managerial Talent." *Personnel & Guid J* 46:586–91 F '68. * (PA 42:12857)

[457]

*Minnesota Percepto-Diagnostic Test (Revised). Ages 5–16; 1962–69; MPDT; brain damages and emotional disturbances; individual; Forms A ('62, 6 cards and protractor), B (same stimulus cards presented in reverse order, '69) ; revised manual ('69, 83 pages) ; profile ('69, 1 page) for children; profile ('62, 1 page) for adults; $4.50 per set of testing materials; $3.50 per 50 profiles; $5 per manual; postpaid; (5–20) minutes; G. B. Fuller and J. T. Laird (test) ; Journal of Clinical Psychology. *

For reviews by Richard W. Coan and Eugene E. Levitt of the original edition, see 6:231 (2 references).

REFERENCES

1–2. See 6:231.
3. COBERLY, LUCILLE M. *A Reliability Study of the Minnesota Percepto-Diagnostic Test and the Usefulness as a Screening Device for Emotionally Disturbed Children.* Master's thesis, University of Kansas (Lawrence, Kan.), 1965.
4. FULLER, GERALD B. "The Objective Measurement of Perception in Determining Personality Disorganization Among Children." *J Clin Psychol* 21:305–7 Jl '65. * (PA 39:15232)
5. FULLER, GERALD B., and LUNNEY, GERALD H. "Relationship Between Perception and Body Image Among Emotionally Disturbed Children." *Percept & Motor Skills* 21:530 O '65. * (PA 40:2693)
6. FULLER, GERALD, and UYENO, ENSLEY. "Perception as a Function of Severity of Disturbance in Psychotics." *Percept & Motor Skills* 20:953–8 Je '65. * (PA 39:16155)
7. SWANEY, CHARLES W. "A Study of Certain Factors Related to Emotional Disturbances." *Ill Sch Res* 1:42–4 My '65. *
8. BURNETT, ALASTAIR, and FULLER, GERALD B. "Minnesota Percepto-Diagnostic Test Performance in Educable Mentally Retarded Children." *Psychol Sch* 3:176–80 Ap '66. *
9. FULLER, GERALD B. "A Comparison of Intelligence and Perception in Emotionally Disturbed Children." *J Clin Psychol* 22:193–5 Ap '66. * (PA 40:7890)
10. HARRISON, DONNA M., and CHAGNON, J. GILLES. "The Effect of Age, Sex and Language on the Minnesota Percepto-Diagnostic Test." *J Clin Psychol* 22:302–3 Jl '66. * (PA 40:10629)
11. KREITMAN, LEON. "A Note on the Use of the Minnesota Percepto-Diagnostic Test." *J Clin Psychol* 22:196 Ap '66. * (PA 40:7212)
12. KRIPPNER, STANLEY. "Diagnostic and Remedial Use of the Minnesota Percepto-Diagnostic Test in a Reading Clinic." *Psychol Sch* 3:171–5 Ap '66. *
13. L'ABATE, LUCIANO. "The Clinical Usefulness of the Minnesota Percepto-Diagnostic Test With Children." *J Clin Psychol* 22:298–9 Jl '66. * (PA 40:11290)
14. PAUL, SATINDER K. "The Clinical Validity of the Minnesota Percepto-Diagnostic Test With Adults in India." *J Clin Psychol* 22:299–301 Jl '66. * (PA 40:10634)
15. WATSON, CHARLES G., and UECKER, ALBERT E. "An Attempted Cross-Validation of the Minnesota Percepto-Diagnostic Test." Abstract. *J Consult Psychol* 30:461 O '66. * (PA 40:12785, title only)
16. BLUM, DONNA M., and CHAGNON, J. GILLES. "The Effect of Age, Sex, and Language on Rotation in a Visual-Motor Task." *J Social Psychol* 71:125–32 F '67. * (PA 41:5816)
17. ENDE, RUSSELL S. "An Application of a Visual Perceptual Test." *Ill Sch Res* 4:42–4 N '67. *

18. FULLER, GERALD B., and ENDE, RUSSELL. "The Effectiveness of Visual Perception, Intelligence and Reading Understanding in Predicting Reading Achievement in Junior High School Children." *J Ed Res* 60:280–2 F '67. *

19. FULLER, GERALD B.; SHARP, HEBER; and HAWKINS, WILLIAM F. "Minnesota Percepto-Diagnostic Test (MPD): Age Norms and IQ Adjustments." *J Clin Psychol* 23:456–61 O '67. * (*PA* 42:1404)

20. NOAK, JOHN ROBERT. *An Analysis of the Relationship Between Certain Intellectual, Perceptual, Personality, and Achievement Factors and Scores on the Minnesota Percepto Diagnostic Test.* Doctor's thesis, Loyola University (Chicago, Ill.), 1967.

21. FULLER, GERALD B. "Perceptual-Motor Characteristics of Dyslexia and Their Theoretical Implication." *Proc Ann Conv Am Psychol Assn* 76:587–8 '68. * (*PA* 43:1381, title only)

[458]
*The Object Relations Technique. Ages 11 and over; 1955–65; ORT; individual; 1 form ('55, 13 cards); manual ('55, see *3* below); protocol booklet not available; no data on reliability; 63s. per set of cards and manual, postage extra; (90) minutes; Herbert Phillipson; distributed by National Foundation for Educational Research in England and Wales. * [United States: protocol booklet ('65, 8 pages); $20.50 per set of cards, manual, and 25 protocol booklets; $7.50 per 25 protocol booklets; $7 per manual; postpaid; Western Psychological Services.]

For a review by H. R. Beech, see 6:233 (7 references, 1 excerpt); for a review by George Westby, see 5:151 (6 references); for related book reviews not excerpted in this volume, consult the 5th (B338) MMY.

REFERENCES
1–6. See 5:151.
7–13. See 6:233.
14. PHILLIPSON, H., and HOPKINS, JULIET. "An Experimental Approach to the Study of Personality Factors Operative in Perception." *Rorsch Newsl* 9:35–7 Je '64. * (*PA* 39:5209)
15. PHILLIPSON, H., and HOPKINS, JULIET. "Personality: An Approach to the Study of Perception." *Brit J Med Psychol* 37:1–15 pt 1 '64. * (*PA* 39:392)
16. RAYNER, E. H., and HAHN, H. "Assessment for Psychotherapy: A Pilot Study of Psychological Test Indications of Success and Failure in Treatment." *Brit J Med Psychol* 37:331–42 pt 4 '64. * (*PA* 39:10378)
17. TAKALA, K. Chap. 12, "Psychological Investigation and Its Results," pp. 444–525. In *The Family in the Pathogenesis of Schizophrenic and Neurotic Disorders.* By Yrjö O. Alanen and others. Acta Psychiatrica Scandinavica Supplementum 189. Copenhagen, Denmark: Munksgaard Ltd., 1966. Pp. 654. *
18. DAVIS, HAROLD. "Some Reaction Types Encountered in O.R.T. Practice." *Rorsch Newsl* 12:22–32 D '67. * (*PA* 42:17379)

[459]
★PRADI Draw-A-Person Test. Clinical clients; 1966; DAPT; 1 form; 2 parts: record leaflet 1 (2 pages) for drawings, record leaflet 2 (4 pages) for stories; mimeographed manual (13 pages); summary form (1 page); no norms; $7 per 20 sets of record leaflets; $3 per 20 summary forms; $1.25 per manual; postage extra; $1 per single copy of record leaflets or summary form, cash orders only; [20–40] minutes; Psychological Research and Development Institute; Psychological Publications Press. *

[460–1]
★Percept and Concept Cognition Test. High school and college; 1964–66; PCCT; identical with 1964 edition of *Percept Cognition Test* and *Concept Cognition Test* except for format; 3 scores: percept, concept, response achievement; 1 form ('66, 4 pages, mimeographed); mimeographed manual ('64, 8 pages); no data on reliability and validity; no description of normative population; $3 per 25 tests; $1.50 per specimen set; postage extra; (20–30) minutes; Martha Pingel [Taylor]; the Author. *

[462]
Pickford Projective Pictures. Ages 5–15; 1963; PPP; 1 form (120 cards); manual (130 pages, see *5* below); no data on reliability; 25s. ($5) per set of cards; 30s. ($4) per manual; 50s. per set of cards and manual; postage extra; to be administered about 6 pictures at a time over about 20 therapy sessions; R. W. Pickford with the assistance of Ruth Bowyer and John Struthers; distributed by National Foundation for Educational Research in England and Wales. (United States publisher: Springer Publishing Co., Inc.) *

For a review by Stanley J. Segal, see 6:234 (5 references, 3 excerpts).

[463]
★Picture Identification Test. High school and college; 1959–66; PIT; 3 scores (judgment, attitude, association) and an effectiveness rating for each of 21 needs (abasement, achievement, affiliation, aggression, autonomy, blame avoidance, counteraction, deference, defendence, dominance, exhibition, harm avoidance, inferiority avoidance, nurturance, order, play, rejection, sentience, sex, succorance, understanding); 2 forms: male, female, ['59, 6 cards]; no manual for examiners; manual ('65, 108 pages) to assist subjects in the interpretation of their scores; tests for males, females: part 1 ('59, 1 page), part 2 ('59, 6 pages); self-instructional manuals: book 1 ('66, 35 pages), books 2, 3, ('66, 89 pages); answer book for self-instructional manuals ['66, 23 pages]; no data on reliability; $1 per set of pictures, either sex; $3 per set of testing materials and scoring service; scoring service includes a printout of approximately 13 pages, 3 of which consist of a narrative interpretation; $5 per set of 3 self-instructional manuals and answer booklet (not a part of the test, used only to acquaint highly motivated subjects with the need concepts); postpaid; [30–50] minutes; Jay L. Chambers; Florida State University. *

REFERENCES
1. CHAMBERS, JAY L. "Identification With Photographs of People." *J Consult Psychol* 21:232–4 Je '57. * (*PA* 32:5462)
2. CHAMBERS, JAY L. "Trait Judgment of Photographs by Neuropsychiatric Patients." *J Clin Psychol* 13:393–6 O '57. * (*PA* 33:1921)
3. CHAMBERS, JAY L., and BROUSSARD, LOUIS J. "Need-Attitudes of Normal and Paranoid Schizophrenic Males." *J Clin Psychol* 16:233–7 Jl '60. * (*PA* 36:2JQ33C)
4. CHAMBERS, JAY L., and BROUSSARD, LOUIS J. "The Role of Need-Attitudes in Adjustment." *J Clin Psychol* 16:383–7 O '60. * (*PA* 37:3247)
5. CHAMBERS, JAY L. "Trait Judgment of Photographs and Adjustment of College Students." *J Consult Psychol* 25:433–5 O '61. * (*PA* 37:3248)
6. CHAMBERS, JAY L., and LIEBERMAN, LEWIS R. "Variability of Normal and Maladjusted Groups Attributing Needs to Best Liked and Least Liked People." *J Clin Psychol* 18:98–101 Ja '62. * (*PA* 38:8481)
7. COLE, J. K. *A Multidimensional Analysis of the Picture Identification Test.* Master's thesis, University of Kentucky (Lexington, Ky.), 1962.
8. LIEBERMAN, LEWIS R., and CHAMBERS, JAY L. "Differences Between Prisoners and Trade School Students on the Picture Identification Test." *Percept & Motor Skills* 17:355–61 O '63. * (*PA* 38:6060)
9. BARGER, BEN, and HALL, EVERETTE. "The Relationship of MMPI High Points and PIT Need Attitude Scores for Male College Students." *J Clin Psychol* 21:266–9 Jl '65. * (*PA* 39:15210)
10. CHAMBERS, JAY L., and LIEBERMAN, LEWIS R. "Differences Between Normal and Clinical Groups in Judging, Evaluating, and Associating Needs." *J Clin Psychol* 21:145–9 Ap '65. * (*PA* 39:12278)
11. CHAMBERS, JAY L.; BARGER, BEN; and LIEBERMAN, LEWIS R. "Need Patterns and Abilities of College Dropouts." *Ed & Psychol Meas* 25:509–16 su '65. * (*PA* 39:16372)
12. VACCHIANO, RALPH B., and ADRIAN, ROBERT J. "The Interrelation Between the Picture Identification Test and the Activities Index." *J Psychol* 60:81–5 My '65. * (*PA* 39:15203)
13. FISHER, JAMES RAWSON. *An Investigation of a Multifactor Approach to Predicting Achievement in College.* Doctor's

thesis, University of Florida (Gainesville, Fla.), 1966. (*DA* 27:1239A)

14. VACCHIANO, RALPH B., and ADRIAN, ROBERT J. "A Factor Analytic Study of the Picture Identification Test." *J Clin Psychol* 22:320–3 Jl '66. * (*PA* 40:10612)

15. LIEBERMAN, LEWIS R. "Picture-'Identification,' Self-Report, and Social Desirability Responses to Autobiographical and Non-Autobiographical Statements." *Percept & Motor Skills* 24:859–68 Je '67. * (*PA* 41:13680)

16. MUSSELMAN, GERALD C.; BARGER, BEN; and CHAMBERS, JAY L. "Student Need Patterns and Effectiveness in College." *J Clin Psychol* 23:108–11 Ja '67. * (*PA* 41:5968)

17. CHAMBERS, JAY L.; WILSON, WINSTON T.; and BARGER, BEN. "Need Differences Between Students With and Without Religious Affiliation." *J Counsel Psychol* 15:208–10 My '68. * (*PA* 42:12106)

[464]

*The Picture Impressions Test. Adolescents and adults; 1953–69; PIT; for investigating the patient-therapist relationship; individual; separate forms for men, women, ['56, 4 cards]; manual ('69, 17 pages); response sheet ['56, 1 page]; $2.50 per set of 8 cards; $3.75 per 25 response sheets; $1.75 per manual; $4.50 per specimen set; postage extra; (20–30) minutes; Lester M. Libo; Consulting Psychologists Press, Inc. *

See 5:152 (1 reference, 1 excerpt).

REFERENCES

1. See 5:152.
2. MULLEN, JOHN A., and ABELES, NORMAN. "The Projective Expression of College Students' Expectations With Regard to Psychotherapy." *J Clin Psychol* 23:393–6 Jl '67. * (*PA* 41:15317)

[465]

★The Picture Story Test Blank. Clinical clients; 1965–66; PSTB; manual title is *Picture Story Test Booklet;* for recording protocols of picture story tests; 1 form ('66, 12 pages); mimeographed manual ('65, 10 pages); $6.25 per 20 test blanks; $1 per single copy; $1 per manual; postage extra; [120] minutes; Psychological Research and Development Institute; Psychological Publications Press. *

[466]

*The Picture World Test. Ages 6 and over; 1955–65; PWT; 1 form ('56); record booklet ('56, 8 pages); revised manual ('65, 54 pages plus record booklet, same as the 1956 manual except for format, slight changes in wording, and the addition of 2 illustrative protocols); symbol sheet ('55); no data on reliability; $17.50 per 25 sets of testing materials including manual; $3.50 per manual; postpaid; (15–50) minutes; Charlotte Buhler and Morse P. Manson; Western Psychological Services. *

For a review by Walter Kass, see 5:153 (1 excerpt).

REFERENCE

1. BUHLER, CHARLOTTE, and MANSON, MORSE P. "The Picture World Test: A New Projective Technique." *J Psychol* 42:303–16 O '56. *

[467]

Psychiatric Attitudes Battery. Adults; 1955–61; PAB; attitudes toward mental hospitals, psychiatrists, and psychiatric treatment; 5 parts; directions for administration and scoring presented in 2 below; no data on reliability of scores; no data on validity; no norms; $4 per set of testing materials, postpaid; reprint of 6:235(2) free; test forms may be reproduced locally; Marvin Reznikoff, John Paul Brady, William W. Zeller, and Omneya Souelem (*d*); Institute of Living. *

a) PICTURE ATTITUDES TEST. 1 form ['59, 3 cards, separate cards for men and women and a general card]; [15] minutes.

b) SENTENCE COMPLETION ATTITUDES TEST. 4 attitude scores: psychiatrists, hospitals, treatment, outcome; 1 form ['59, 1 hectographed page]; revised scoring manual ('61, 17 hectographed pages); [10] minutes.

c) MULTIPLE CHOICE ATTITUDES QUESTIONNAIRE. 1 form ['59, 2 hectographed pages]; [5] minutes.

d) SOUELEM ATTITUDES SCALE. Forms A, B, ['55, 2 hectographed pages]; [10] minutes.

e) DEGREE OF IMPROVEMENT RATING SCALE. Ratings by psychiatrists; 1 form ['59, 1 hectographed page]; "a minute or two."

REFERENCES

1–10. See 6:235.
11. REZNIKOFF, MARVIN, and TOOMEY, LAURA C. "An Evaluation of Some Possible Prognostic Indicators of Response to Phenothiazine Treatment of Acute Schizophrenic Psychoses." *Int J Neuropsychiatry* 1:352–8 Jl–Ag '65. *
12. ROBACK, HOWARD, and SNYDER, WILLIAM U. "A Comparison of Hospitalized Mental Patients' Adjustment With Their Attitudes Toward Psychiatric Hospitals." *J Clin Psychol* 21:228–30 Ap '65. * (*PA* 39:12590)

[468]

Rock-A-Bye, Baby: A Group Projective Test for Children. Groups of 9–16 aged 5–10; 1959, c1951–56; sibling rivalry; 6 scores: self concept, jealousy index, aggression to parents, guilt index, anxiety index, index of obsessive trends; stimulus material presented by 35-minute 16 mm. sound film ('56, script previously published in 1951); 1 form ['59]; mimeographed manual ['59, 33 pages, containing record form and analysis sheet which must be reproduced locally]; no data on reliability of scores; no norms for self concept and aggression to parents; film may be rented ($10.20 per week) or purchased ($157); $1 per manual; monograph [see 6:236(1)] free with manual; postage extra; (60) minutes; Mary R. Haworth and Adolf G. Woltmann; Audio-Visual Services, Pennsylvania State University. *

See 6:236 (4 references).

[469]

Rohde Sentence Completions Test. Ages 12 and over; 1940–57; RSCT; test booklet title is *Sentence Completions;* revision of *Payne Sentence Completion Blank* ('29); 1 form ('53, 4 pages); manual ('57, 62 pages, reprint of chapters 2 and 3 of 4 below); scoring booklet ('47, 4 pages); reliability and validity data for 1940 form only; $6.50 per 25 tests; $6.50 per 25 scoring booklets; $4 per manual; $6 per specimen set; postpaid; (30–60) minutes; Amanda R. Rohde; Western Psychological Services. *

See 5:158 (1 reference); for reviews by Charles N. Cofer and Charles R. Strother of an earlier edition, see 4:131 (3 references, 1 excerpt); for a related book review not excerpted in this volume, consult the 5th (B358) MMY. MMY

REFERENCES

1–3. See 4:131.
4. See 5:158.
5. VERNIER, CLAIRE M.; STAFFORD, JOHN W.; and KRUGMAN, ARNOLD D. "A Factor Analysis of Indices From Four Projective Techniques Associated With Four Different Types of Physical Pathology." *J Consult Psychol* 22:433–7 D '58. * (*PA* 33:9360)
6. ENGLISH, ROBERT HENRY. *Cleft Palate Children Compared With Non-Cleft Palate Children: A Personality Study.* Doctor's thesis, University of Oregon (Eugene, Ore.), 1961. (*DA* 23:2622)
7. ZUCKERMAN, MARVIN; LEVITT, EUGENE E.; and LUBIN, BERNARD. "Concurrent and Construct Validity of Direct and Indirect Measures of Dependency." *J Consult Psychol* 25:316–23 Ag '61. * (*PA* 37:1326)
8. SMITH, ROBERT M. "Sentence Completion Differences Between Intellectually Superior Boys and Girls." *J Proj Tech & Pers Assess* 27:472–80 D '63. * (*PA* 38:8570)
9. VAUGHAN, RICHARD P. "A Psychological Assessment Program for Candidates to the Religious Life: Validation Study." *Cath Psychol Rec* 1:65–70 sp '63. * (*PA* 38:6715)

[470]

Rorschach. Ages 3 and over; 1921–66; variously referred to by such titles as Rorschach Method, Rorschach Test, Rorschach Ink Blot Test, Rorschach Psychodiagnostics; many variations and modifications are in use with no one method of scoring and interpreting generally accepted; unless otherwise indicated, the word Rorschach may be interpreted as referring to the use of the Psychodiagnostic Plates listed as *f* below.

a) BEHN-RORSCHACH TEST. 1941–56; a parallel set of inkblots; also called *The Bero-Test;* 1 form ('41, 10 cards); manual ('56, 198 pages, see *2156* below, translation of the German edition published in 1941); record blank ('51, 1 page); Fr. 19 ($11) per set of cards; Fr. 9 ($3.75) per pad of 100 record blanks; Fr. 25 ($8) per manual; postage extra; Hans Zulliger; Hans Huber. (United States distributor: Grune & Stratton, Inc.) *

b) ★THE DAVIS RORSCHACH MINIATURE LOCATION CHARTS IN COLOR (BRUNO KLOPFER SCORING AREAS). 1966; 1 card; $3.50 per card, postpaid; Julian C. Davis; Western Psychological Services. *

c) HARROWER'S GROUP RORSCHACH. Ages 12 and over; 1941–45; set of original Rorschach inkblots on 35 mm. slides; group blank (no date, 24 pages); $12.50 per set of slides; $6 per 25 group blanks; postpaid; (70–90) minutes; M. R. Harrower; distributed by Psychological Corporation. *

d) HARROWER'S MULTIPLE CHOICE TEST. Ages 12 and over; 1943–45; for use with either cards or slides; 1 form ('43, 4 pages); $3.60 per 25 record blanks, postpaid; M. R. Harrower; distributed by Psychological Corporation. *

e) ★HARROWER'S PSYCHODIAGNOSTIC INKBLOT TEST. Ages 16 and over; 1945–66; HPI; a parallel set of inkblots; formerly called *Psychodiagnostic Inkblots;* 1 form ('66, 10 cards, identical with set copyrighted in 1945 except for finish); expendable set of inkblots also available; manual, third edition ('66, 85 pages plus protocol booklet); protocol booklet ('66, 4 pages); $25 per examiner's kit of set of cards, 5 sets of expendable inkblots, 25 protocol booklets, and manual; $10 per set of cards; $3.50 per 5 sets of expendable inkblots; $6.50 per 25 protocol booklets; $7.50 per manual; postpaid; Molly R. Harrower; Western Psychological Services. *

f) PSYCHODIAGNOSTIC PLATES, FIFTH EDITION. 1921–54; 1 form ('54, 10 cards, identical with original edition copyrighted in 1921); manual, fifth edition ('51, 263 pages, translation of the 1942 German edition with the addition of a bibliography); record blank ('47, 1 page); Fr. 27 ($12.50) per set of cards; Fr. 8.50 ($3.75) per pad of 100 record blanks; Fr. 23 ($7) per manual; postage extra; Hermann Rorschach; Hans Huber. (United States distributor: Grune & Stratton, Inc.) *

g) ★THE REVISED RORSCHACH EVALOGRAPH. 1954–65; protocol booklet ('65, 16 pages); $3 per 10 booklets, postpaid; Morse P. Manson and George A Ulett; Western Psychological Services. *

h) RORSCHACH COMBINED LOCATION AND RECORD FORM. 1957; 1 form (12 pages); $2.75 per 25 booklets; 30¢ per specimen set; postpaid; Nicholas De Palma; the Author. *

i) ★THE RORSCHACH CONCEPT EVALUATION TECHNIQUE. Adults; 1965; CET; 3 conceptual scores: precision (J), conformity (V), deviance (C); manual (18 pages plus protocol booklet); protocol booklet (4 pages); $7.50 per examiner's kit of 25 protocol booklets and manual; $6 per 25 protocol booklets; $2 per manual; postpaid; set of Rorschach inkblots necessary for administration; (10–15) minutes for in-

dividuals, (20–30) minutes for groups; Paul McReynolds; Western Psychological Services. *

j) RORSCHACH LOCATION CHARTS (BECK'S SCORING AREAS). 1951–54; 1 form ('54, 12 cards, identical with set copyrighted in 1951); Fr. 9.50 ($3.25) per set of cards, postage extra; Julian C. Davis; Hans Huber. (United States distributor: Grune & Stratton, Inc.) *

k) RORSCHACH METHOD OF PERSONALITY DIAGNOSIS, REVISED EDITION. 1939–60; 1 form ('60, 4 pages); directions ('60, 4 pages); $4.20 per 35 blanks, postage extra; Bruno Klopfer and Helen H. Davidson; [Harcourt, Brace & World, Inc.]. *

l) ★THE RORSCHACH MINIATURE INKBLOTS IN COLOR: A LOCATION AND RECORD FORM. 1955–64; $6.50 per pad of 100 sheets, postpaid; Morse P. Manson; Western Psychological Services. *

m) STRUCTURED-OBJECTIVE RORSCHACH TEST: PRELIMINARY EDITION. See 477.

For reviews by Richard H. Dana, Leonard D. Eron, and Arthur R. Jensen, see 6:237 (732 references); for reviews by Samuel J. Beck, H. J. Eysenck, Raymond J. McCall, and Laurance F. Shaffer, see 5:154 (1078 references); for a review by Helen Sargent, see 4:117 (621 references); for reviews by Morris Krugman and J. R. Wittenborn, see 3:73 (451 references); see also 2:1246 (147 references); for excerpts from related book reviews, see 4:118–28 and 3:74–91; for reviews not excerpted in this volume, consult the 6th (B40, B52, B72-3, B91, B129, B152, B260, B295, B306–7, B344, B398, B409, B452, B526) and 5th (B32, B34, B40–1, B60, B73, B79, B190, B247–8, B337, B369, B372, B402) MMY's.

REFERENCES

1–147. See 2:1246.
148–598. See 3:73.
599–1219. See 4:117.
1220–2297. See 5:154.
2298–3030. See 6:237.

3031. SELINSKY, HERMAN; in collaboration with BRUNO KLOPFER and MARGUERITE EMERY. "Inferences Drawn From Rorschach Tests in Convulsive States." Abstract. Discussion by Zygmunt A. Piotrowski. *J Nerv & Mental Dis* 84:322–3 S '36. *

3032. SCHACHTEL, ANNA, and SCHACHTEL, ERNEST. Chap. 10, "The Rorschach Test," pp. 377–414. In *Child Life in School: A Study of a Seven-Year-Old Group.* By Barbara Biber and others. New York: E. P. Dutton & Co., Inc., 1942. Pp. xiv, 658. * *(PA* 16:4569)

3033. HARROWER-ERICKSON, M. R. "The Rorschach Method in the Study of Personality." Discussion by Ruth L. Munroe. *Ann N Y Acad Sci* 44:569–88 D 22 '43. *

3034. ENDACOTT, JOHN L. "A Rorschach Study of Symptomaniac Schizophrenia Following Brain Trauma." Discussion by Phyllis Wittman and C. A. Neymann. *Ill Med J* 90:187–93 S '46. *

3035. PIOTROWSKI, Z. A. "Differences Between Cases Giving Valid and Invalid Personality Inventory Responses." Discussion by F. L. Wells and Roy Schafer. *Ann N Y Acad Sci* 46:633–40 Jl 30 '46. * *(PA* 20:4677)

3036. STERN, KARL, and PRADOS, MIGUEL. "Personality Studies in Menopausal Women." *Am J Psychiatry* 103:358–68 N '46. * *(PA* 21:1485)

3037. KOGAN, KATE LEVINE. "The Personality Reaction Pattern of Children With Epilepsy: With Special Reference to Rorschach Method." *Res Publ Assn Nerv & Mental Dis* 26:616–30 '47. *

3038. PIOTROWSKI, ZYGMUNT A. "The Personality of the Epileptic." *Proc Am Psychopath Assn* 36:89–108 '47. * *(PA* 22:2272)

3039. ROCKWELL, FRED V.; SHERFEY, MARY JANE; and DIETHELM, OSKAR. "Epileptoid Psychopathologic Reactions." *Res Publ Assn Nerv & Mental Dis* 26:573–85 '47. *

3040. ROCKWELL, FRED V.; WELCH, LIVINGSTON; KUBIS, JOSEPH; and FISICHELLI, VINCENT. "Changes in Palmar Skin Resistance During the Rorschach Test: 1, Color Shock and Psychoneurotic Reactions." *Monatsschrift für Psychiatrie und Neurologie* 113:129–53 '47. *

3041. ROCKWELL, FRED V.; WELCH, LIVINGSTON; KUBIS, JOSEPH; and FISICHELLI, VINCENT. "Changes in Palmar Skin Resistance During the Rorschach Test: 2, The Effect of Repetition With Color Removed." *Monatsschrift für Psychiatrie und Neurologie* 116:321–45 '48. *

3042. RUST, RALPH MASON. "Some Correlates of the Movement Response." *J Personality* 16:369–401 Je '48. * *(PA* 23:2236)

3043. SIEGEL, MIRIAM G. "The Rorschach Test as an Aid in Selecting Clients for Group Therapy and Evaluating Progress." *Mental Hyg* 28:444–9 Jl '48. *

3044. MAHONEY, V. P.; BOCKUS, H. L.; INGRAM, MARGARET; HUNDLEY, J. W.; and YASKIN, J. C. "Studies in Ulcerative Colitis: 1, A Study of the Personality in Relation to Ulcerative Colitis." *Gastroenterology* 13:547–63 '49. * (PA 24:5991)

3045. ROSE, ALVIN W. "Projective Techniques in Sociological Research." *Social Forces* 28:175–83 D '49. * (PA 25:1723)

3046. ULETT, GEORGE. "Rorschach's Test as Used in the Psychiatric Interview." *Northw Med* 48:544–8 Ag '49. * (PA 24:651)

3047. BECK, SAMUEL J. Chap. 7, "Emotional Experience as a Necessary Constituent in Knowing," pp. 95–107. (PA 26:1988) In *Feelings and Emotions: The Mooseheart Symposium in Cooperation With the University of Chicago.* Edited by Martin L. Reymert. New York: McGraw-Hill Book Co., 1950. Pp. xxiii, 603. * (PA 26:2004)

3048. HUGHES, ROBERT M. "A Factor Analysis of Rorschach Diagnostic Signs." *J General Psychol* 43:85–103 Jl '50. * (PA 25:6214)

3049. MERCER, MARGARET, and WRIGHT, S. C. "Case Studies: Diagnostic Testing in a Case of Latent Schizophrenia." *J Proj Tech* 14:287–96 S '50. * (PA 25:4733)

3050. ORCHINIK, C.; KOCH, R.; WYCIS, H. T.; FREED, H.; and SPIEGEL, E. A. "The Effect of Thalamic Lesions Upon the Emotional Reactivity (Rorschach and Behavior Studies)." *Res Publ Assn Nerv & Mental Dis* 29:172–207 '50. * (PA 26:5040)

3051. RAPAPORT, DAVID. "Diagnostic Testing in Psychiatric Practice." *B N Y Acad Med* 26:115–25 F '50. * (PA 24:5250)

3052. STEPHENSON, WILLIAM. Chap. 47, "The Significance of Q-Technique for the Study of Personality," pp. 532–70. (PA 26:2040) In *Feelings and Emotions: The Mooseheart Symposium in Cooperation With the University of Chicago.* Edited by Martin L. Reymert. New York: McGraw-Hill Book Co., 1950. Pp. xxiii, 603. * (PA 26:2004)

3053. WEBER, GEORGE H. "Some Qualitative Aspects of an Exploratory Personality Study of 15 Juvenile Automobile Thieves." *Trans Kans Acad Sci* 53:548–56 '50. * (PA 25:7574)

3054. ALEXANDER, LEO, and AX, ALBERT F. "Rorschach Studies in Combat Flying Personnel." *Proc Am Psychopath Assn* 40:219–43 '51. * (PA 27:591)

3055. BACHRACH, ARTHUR J. "Some Factors in the Prediction of Suicide." *Neuropsychiatry* 1:21–7 w '51. * (PA 27:1268)

3056. BEIER, ERNST GUNTER. "The Effect of Induced Anxiety on the Flexibility of Intellectual Functioning." *Psychol Monogr* 65(9):i–v, 1–26 '51. * (PA 26:4653)

3057. DÖRKEN, HERBERT, JR. "Personality Factors Associated With Paraplegia and Prolonged Hospitalization: A Clinical Note." *Can J Psychol* 5:134–7 S '51. * (PA 26:2922)

3058. HIRE, A. WILLIAM. "Use of the Rorschach and Thematic Apperception Tests in the Counseling and Guidance of College Students." Thesis abstract. *Harvard Ed R* 21:65–8 w '51. *

3059. KRAL, V. ADALBERT, and DÖRKEN, HERBERT. "The Influence of Subcortical (Diencephalic) Brain Lesions on Emotionality as Reflected in the Rorschach Color Responses." *Am J Psychiatry* 107:839–43 My '51. * (PA 27:623)

3060. PIOTROWSKI, ZYGMUNT A., and LEWIS, NOLAN D. C. "An Experimental Criterion for the Prognostication of the Status of Schizophrenics After a Three-Year Interval Based on Rorschach Data." *Proc Am Psychopath Assn* 40:51–72 '51. * (PA 27:586)

3061. ROE, ANNE. "A Psychological Study of Physical Scientists." *Genetic Psychol Monogr* 43:121–235 My '51. * (PA 26:1756)

3062. SCHWARZ, WOLFGANG. "Correlation Between the Rorschach Test and the Lindberg Ring Test in Demonstration Personality Psychograms." *Acta Psychiatry et Neurologica Scandinavica* 26:199–212 '51. * (PA 26:5632)

3063. SHANKER, P. *A Comparative Study of the Educated and Uneducated Harijans as Regards Their Caste Hindu Attitude and Rorschach Personality Picture.* Master's thesis, Patna University (Patna, India), 1951.

3064. WELLS, F. L. "Further Notes on Rorschach and Case History in Harvard National Scholars: Cases 113–126." *J Genetic Psychol* 79:261–87 D '51. * (PA 26:5840)

3065. WELLS, F. L. "Rorschach and Bernreuter Procedures With Harvard National Scholars in the Grant Study: Cases 3, 9, 10, 27, 28, 103–112." *J Genetic Psychol* 79:221–60 D '51. * (PA 26:5839)

3066. ABEL, THEODORA M., and WEISSMANN, SERENA. "Psychological Aspects of Facial Disfigurement: A Rorschach Study." *Rorschachiana* 1(2):152–8 '52. * (PA 27:3740)

3067. BALLOCH, JOHN C. "The Effect of Degree of Shading Contrast in Ink Blots on Verbal Response." *J Exp Psychol* 43:120–4 F '52. * (PA 27:1947)

3068. BLEULER, M. "After Thirty Years of Clinical Experience With the Rorschach Test." *Rorschachiana* 1(1):12–24 '52. * (PA 27:2706)

3069. CROWN, SIDNEY. "An Experimental Study of Psychological Changes Following Prefrontal Lobotomy." *J General Psychol* 47:3–41 Jl '52. * (PA 27:6024)

3070. DÖRKEN, HERBERT, JR. "The Ink Blot Test: Clinical Application of a Brief Projective Technique." *Rorschachiana* 1(3):196–221 '52. * (PA 27:7192)

3071. FRIEDMAN, HOWARD. "Perceptual Regression in Schizophrenia: An Hypothesis Suggested by the Use of the Rorschach Test." *J Genetic Psychol* 81:63–98 S '52. * (PA 27:3693)

3072. GURVITZ, MILTON S. "World Destruction Fantasies in Early Schizophrenia: A Rorschach Study." *J Hillside Hosp* 1:7–20 Ja '52. * (PA 26:7144)

3073. KOTKOV, BENJAMIN, and MEADOW, ARNOLD. "Rorschach Criteria for Continuing Group Psychotherapy." *Int J Group Psychother* 2:324–33 O '52. * (PA 27:7828)

3074. LACEY, JOHN I.; BATEMAN, DOROTHY E.; and VAN LEHN, RUTH. "Autonomic Response Specificity and Rorschach Color Responses." *Psychosom Med* 14:256–60 Jl–Ag '52. * (PA 27:2736)

3075. MANSMANN, JAMES A. "Projective Psychological Test Applied to the Study of Bronchial Asthma." *Ann Allergy* 10:583–91 S–O '52. *

3076. MORRIS, WOODROW WILBERT. "Rorschach Estimates of Personality Attributes in the Michigan Assessment Project." *Psychol Monogr* 66(6):1–27 '52. * (PA 27:5155)

3077. SCHMEIDLER, GERTRUDE R. "Rorschach and ESP Scores of Patients Suffering From Cerebral Concussion." *J Parapsychol* 16:80–9 Je '52. * (PA 28:6438)

3078. SHAMES, GEORGE. "An Investigation of Prognosis and Evaluation in Speech Therapy." *J Speech & Hearing Disorders* 17:386–92 D '52. * (PA 27:6652)

3079. ZUCKER, LUISE. "The Psychology of Latent Schizophrenia: Based on Rorschach Studies." *Am J Psychother* 6:44–62 Ja '52. * (PA 26:5762)

3080. CROWELL, DAVID HARRISON. "Personality and Physical Disease: A Test of the Dunbar Hypothesis Applied to Diabetes Mellitus and Rheumatic Fever." *Genetic Psychol Monogr* 48:117–53 Ag '53. * (PA 28:4710)

3081. KAMMAN, GORDON R. "The Rorschach Test and Its Forensic Implications." *J Lancet* 73:325–7 Ag '53. *

3082. KAVAZANJIAN, THOMAS, and GURVITZ, MILTON S. "The W% on the Rorschach as Measure of Orality." *J Hillside Hosp* 2:213–8 O '53. * (PA 28:6033)

3083. LEVI, JOSEPH. "The Rorschach Test in Rehabilitation." *J Rehabil* 19:13–5+ Mr–Ap '53. * (PA 28:1438)

3084. PALM, ROSE. "The Psychodynamics of Enuresis: A Psychoanalytic Study in Rorschach Symbolism." *Am Imago* 10:167–80 su '53. * (PA 28:2926)

3085. POSER, E. G. "The Use of Psychological Tests in Psychosomatic Research." *Can J Psychol* 7:177–82 D '53. * (PA 28:6408)

3086. REITAN, RALPH M. "Intellectual Functions in Aphasic and Non-Aphasic Brain-Injured Subjects." *Neurology* 3:202–12 Mr '53. * (PA 28:3142)

3087. STEINER, M. E. "The Search for Occupational Personalities: The Rorschach Test in Industry." *Personnel* 29:335–43 Ja '53. * (PA 27:6810)

3088. BLACKHAM, GARTH J. *A Clinical Study of the Personality Structures and Adjustments of Pupils Under-Achieving and Over-Achieving in Reading.* Doctor's thesis, Cornell University (Ithaca, N.Y.), 1954. (DA 15:1199)

3089. CURNUTT, ROBERT H., and LEWIS, WILLIAM B. "The Relationship Between Z Scores on the Bender Gestalt and F+% on the Rorschach." *J Clin Psychol* 10:96–7 Ja '54. * (PA 28:7515)

3090. DEVOS, GEORGE. "A Comparison of the Personality Differences in Two Generations of Japanese-Americans by Means of the Rorschach Test." *Nagoya J Med Sci* 17:153–265 Ag '54. *

3091. DÖRKEN, HERBERT, JR. "A Psychometric Evaluation of Sixty-Eight Medical Interns." *Can Med Assn J* 70:41–5 Ja '54. *

3092. ELLENBERGER, HENRI. "The Life and Work of Hermann Rorschach (1884–1922)." *B Menninger Clinic* 18:173–219 S '54. * (PA 29:1839)

3093. LA FON, FRED E. "Behavior on the Rorschach Test and a Measure of Self-Acceptance." *Psychol Monogr* 68(10):1–14 '54. * (PA 29:5713)

3094. NEUHAUS, EDMUND CONRAD. *A Personality Study of Asthmatic and Cardiac Children.* Doctor's thesis, New York University (New York, N.Y.), 1954. (DA 15:1256)

3095. BRODY, HAROLD. *Psychologic Factors Associated With Infertility in Women: A Comparative Study of Psychologic Factors in Women Afflicted With Infertility Including Groups With and Without a Medical Basis for Their Condition.* Doctor's thesis, New York University (New York, N.Y.), 1955. (DA 15:1253)

3096. FOSTER, AUSTIN. "The Factorial Structure of the Rorschach Test." *Tex Rep Biol & Med* 13:34–61 sp '55. * (PA 30:2875)

3097. GOLDSMITH, HARRY. *The Contribution of Certain Personality Characteristics of Male Paraplegics to the Degree of Improvement in Rehabilitation.* Doctor's thesis, New York University (New York, N.Y.), 1955. (DA 16:1504)

3098. HALLOWELL, A. IRVING. Chap. 3, "The Rorschach Test in Personality and Culture Studies," pp. 32–74. (PA 30:2692) In his *Culture and Experience.* Philadelphia, Pa.: University of Pennsylvania Press, 1955. Pp. xvi, 434. * (PA 30:2645)

3099. JACOBSEN, ELDON ERNEST. *Assessment of Adjustment in Children and Adolescents: Reliabilities and Interrelationships Concerning Common Group Tests and Ratings and Their Relationships to Judgments From Clinical Tests.* Doctor's thesis, University of Washington (Seattle, Wash.), 1955. (*DA* 15:1653)

3100. KAHN, DOUGLAS MORTIMER. *The Relationship of Certain Personality Characteristics to Recovery From Tuberculosis.* Doctor's thesis, New York University (New York, N.Y.), 1955. (*DA* 15:1256)

3101. LINDNER, ROBERT. "The Clinical Uses of Content Analysis in Rorschach Testing." *Psychoanalysis* 3:12–7 sp '55. * (*PA* 30:7209)

3102. SHERMAN, MURRAY H. "A Psychoanalytic Definition of Rorschach Determinants." *Psychoanalysis* 3:68–76 w '55. * (*PA* 30:7225)

3103. SMOLINSKY, HAROLD JAY. *Sex Differences in Paranoid Schizophrenia: A Comparative Study of the Personality Characteristics of Male and Female Hospital Patients Diagnosed as Paranoid Schizophrenic.* Doctor's thesis, New York University (New York, N.Y.), 1955. (*DA* 15:1258)

3104. VON HOLT, HENRY WILLIAM, JR. *A Study of Personality Processes Operative Under Neutral, Failure, and Success Conditions.* Doctor's thesis, Clark University (Worcester, Mass.), 1955. (*DA* 15:1660)

3105. WALCOTT, WILLIAM O. *Memory and Personality: An Investigation of the Dynamics of Memory With the Rorschach and TAT Tests.* Doctor's thesis, Claremont College (Claremont, Calif.), 1955.

3106. FOSTER, ARTHUR LEE. *The Relationship Between EEG Abnormality, Psychological Factors and Delinquent Behavior.* Doctor's thesis, University of Houston (Houston, Tex.), 1956. (*DA* 16:2210)

3107. FREUDENBERGER, HERBERT J. *An Investigation Into Certain Personality Characteristics as They Relate to Improvement in Parkinsonism: The Influence of Submissiveness, Inactivity, Pessimism and Affective Relatedness on the Improvement of Parkinson Patients With the Pagitane Drug.* Doctor's thesis, New York University (New York, N.Y.), 1956. (*DA* 16:1944)

3108. KINGSLEY, LEONARD. *A Comparative Study of Certain Personality Characteristics of Psychopathic and Non-Psychopathic Offenders in a Military Disciplinary Barracks: With Reference to the Personality Characteristics of Immaturity, Impulsivity, Hostility, Avoidance, Superficiality, Shallowness, Anxiety, Guilt, Egocentricity, and Facility in Performance Tasks.* Doctor's thesis, New York University (New York, N.Y.), 1956. (*DA* 16:2212)

3109. MYDEN, WALTER DAVID. *An Interpretation and Evaluation of Certain Personality Characteristics Involved in Creative Production: An Investigation and Evaluation of Personality Structure and Characteristics of Creative Individuals in the Context of Psychoanalytic Theory and Ego Psychology.* Doctor's thesis, New York University (New York, N.Y.), 1956. (*DA* 17:897)

3110. PIOTROWSKI, ZYGMUNT A., and DUDEK, STEPHANIE Z. Chap. 11, "Research on Human Movement Responses in the Rorschach Examination of Marital Partners," pp. 192–207. In *Neurotic Interaction in Marriage.* Edited by Victor W. Eisenstein. New York: Basic Books, Inc., 1956. Pp. xv, 352. * (*PA* 31:890)

3111. SAI-HALÁSZ, A. "Psychic Alterations in Disseminated Sclerosis: A General, Statistical and Rorschach-Test Study on 200 Patients." *Monatsschrift für Psychiatry und Neurologie* 132:129–54 '56. *

3112. SCHWARG, WOLFGANG. *The Relation of Functional Periodicity to Changes in the Characteristics of Emotional Reactions and Personality.* Doctor's thesis, New York University (New York, N.Y.), 1956. (*DA* 19:3372)

3113. SIEGMAN, ARON W. "A 'Culture and Personality' Study Based on a Comparison of Rorschach Performance." *J Social Psychol* 44:173–8 N '56. * (*PA* 33:8403)

3114. STRAUS, MURRAY ARNOLD. *Child Training and Child Personality in a Rural and Urban Area of Ceylon.* Doctor's thesis, University of Wisconsin (Madison, Wis.), 1956. (*DA* 16:2230)

3115. VELTFORT, HELENE RANK. *Some Personality Correlates of Reading Disability.* Doctor's thesis, Stanford University (Stanford, Calif.), 1956. (*DA* 16:1947)

3116. DILLER, LEONARD, and RIKLAN, MANUEL. "Rorschach Correlates in Parkinson's Disease: M, Motor Inhibition, Perceived Cause of Illness, and Self-Attitudes." *Psychosom Med* 19:120–6 Mr–Ap '57. * (*PA* 32:3235)

3117. DUREMAN, INGMAR, and SALDE, HENRY. "The Question of a Possible Correlation Between Visual Autokinesis and the Amount of Human Movement Responses in the Rorschach Test." *Acta Societatis Medicorum Upsaliensis* 61(5–6):275–9 '57. *

3118. FELLEMAN, CARROLL ALFRED. *The Relationship Between Certain Personality Characteristics and Prognosis in Remedial Reading Instruction: An Investigation to Determine Whether Certain Personality Characteristics Found in Children With Reading Disabilities Can Be Predictive of Progress or Lack of Progress in Individual Remedial Reading Instruction.* Doctor's thesis, New York University (New York, N.Y.), 1957. (*DA* 17:1594)

3119. HICKMAN, NORMAN WILLIAM. *The Role of Self-Related-Concept Discrepancies in Personal Adjustment.* Doctor's thesis, University of Oregon (Eugene, Ore.), 1957. (*DA* 19:2656)

3120. HORRALL, BERNICE M. "Academic Performance and Personality Adjustments of Highly Intelligent College Students." *Genetic Psychol Monogr* 55:3–83 F '57. * (*PA* 33:4697)

3121. HUZIOKA, YOSINARU. "Report on the Result of Rorschach Test," pp. 363–96. In *Peoples of Nepal Himalaya: Scientific Results of the Japanese Expeditions to Nepal Himalaya 1952–1953, Vol. 3.* Edited by H. Kihara. Kyoto, Japan: Fauna and Flora Research Society, Kyoto University, 1957. Pp. xv, 477. *

3122. LEBOW, VICTOR SAMUEL. *A Study of Some Personality Factors Associated With Restructuring of Attitudes.* Doctor's thesis, Purdue University (Lafayette, Ind.), 1957. (*DA* 17:2066)

3123. STENBACK, ASSER, and VIITAMAKI, R. OLAVI. "Psychological Studies on a Patient Who Received 441 Electroconvulsive Treatments." *Acta Psychiatry et Neurologica Scandinavica* 32:473–578 '57. * (*PA* 33:4050)

3124. STRAUS, MURRAY A. "Anal and Oral Frustration in Relation to Sinhalese Personality." *Sociometry* 20:21–31 Mr '57. * (*PA* 32:290)

3125. YOUNG, HARL HENRY, JR. *Personality Test Correlates of Orientation to the Vertical: A Test of Witkin's Field-Dependency Hypothesis.* Doctor's thesis, University of Texas (Austin, Tex.), 1957. (*DA* 19:882)

3126. ADCOCK, C. J.; MCCREARY, J. R.; RITCHIE, J. E.; and SOMERSET, H. C. A. *Personality and Physique: A Rorschach Study of Maori and Europeans.* Victoria University of Wellington Publications in Psychology No. 12. Wellington, New Zealand: Department of Psychology, the University, 1958. Pp. 93. * (*PA* 34:1205)

3127. DAVIS, ARVILLE DEAN. *Physiological Correlates of the Body-Image.* Doctor's thesis, University of Texas (Austin, Tex.), 1958. (*DA* 18:2206)

3128. DEVOS, GEORGE, and MINER, HORACE. "Algerian Culture and Personality in Change." *Sociometry* 21:255–68 D '58. * (*PA* 34:1215)

3129. DREWES, HENRY WALTER. *An Experimental Study of the Relationship Between Electroencephalographic Imagery Variables and Perceptual-Cognitive Processes.* Doctor's thesis, Cornell University (Ithaca, N.Y.), 1958. (*DA* 19:87)

3130. GALLOWAY, JAMES RICHARD. *A Comparative Study of the Inhibition Process in Delinquent and Non-Delinquent Females.* Doctor's thesis, University of Oklahoma (Norman, Okla.), 1958. (*DA* 19:1290)

3131. KANTER, VICTOR B. Appendix 1, "A Comparison by Means of Psychological Tests: Young Men With Duodenal Ulcer and Controls," pp. 227–61. In *Family Influences and Psychosomatic Illness: An Inquiry Into the Social and Psychological Background of Duodenal Ulcer.* By E. M. Goldberg. London: Tavistock Publications, 1958. Pp. xii, 308. *

3132. MOLISH, HERMAN B., and BECK, SAMUEL J. "Further Explorations of the 'Six Schizophrenias': Type S-3." *Am J Orthopsychiatry* 28:809–27 O '58. *

3133. PRICE, RICHARD H. "The Rorschach Examination in Diagnosis and Treatment." *Delaware State Med J* 30:61–2 Mr '58. *

3134. TEMPLETON, GORDON, and SPRUIELL, VANN. "Methedrine Interviews: Clinical and Rorschach Studies." *Psychiatric Q* 32:781–95 O '58. * (*PA* 34:1577)

3135. TRIPPE, MATTHEW JAMES. *A Study of the Relationship Between Visual-Perceptual Ability and Selected Personality Variables in a Group of Cerebral Palsied Children.* Doctor's thesis, Syracuse University (Syracuse, N.Y.), 1958. (*DA* 20:765)

3136. VAN DEN BROEK, P. "Rorschach's Experience-Type and Jung's Attitudinal-Type." *Folia Psychiatrica Neurologica et Neurochirurgica Neerlandica* 61:55–61 '58. *

3137. VIITAMAKI, R. O. "The Features of the Mothers in the Schizophrenia Material in Comparison With the Control Materials in the Light of the Rorschach Variables," pp. 133–8, passim. In *The Mothers of Schizophrenic Patients.* By Yrjö O. Alanen. Copenhagen, Denmark: Ejnar Munksgaard, 1958. Pp. 361. *

3138. WILLIAMS, HERBERT H. *Some Aspects of Culture and Personality in a Lebanese Maronite Village.* Doctor's thesis, University of Pennsylvania (Philadelphia, Pa.), 1958. (*DA* 19:632)

3139. WINSTON, CARL M. *An Investigation of the Relationship Among Transference, Ego Strength and Age in Elementary School Boys.* Doctor's thesis, New York University (New York, N.Y.), 1958. (*DA* 19:2159)

3140. BAUGHMAN, E. EARL; SHANDS, HARLEY C.; and HAWKINS, DAVID R. "Intensive Psychotherapy and Personality Change: Psychological Test Evaluation of a Single Case." *Psychiatry* 22:296–301 Ag '59. * (*PA* 34:6667)

3141. BECK, SAMUEL J. "The Light-Dark Determinant in the Rorschach Test: A Survey of the Problems," pp. 179–93. In *Rorschachiana V.* Schweizerischen Zeitschrift für Psychologie, No. 34. Berne, Switzerland: Hans Huber, [1959]. Pp. 445. *

3142. BECK, SAMUEL J. "S-3, Schizophrenia Without Psychosis." *A.M.A. Arch Neurol & Psychiatry* 81:85–96 Ja '59. *

3143. BLANCHARD, W. H. "The Group Process in Gang Rape." *J Social Psychol* 49:259–66 My '59. * (*PA* 34:4170)

3144. CARTWRIGHT, ROSALIND DYMOND. "A Note on the Rorschach Prognostic Rating Scale." *J Counsel Psychol* 6: 160–2 su '59. * (*PA* 34:4371)

3145. D'HEURLE, ADMA; MELLINGER, JEANNE CUMMINS; and HAGGARD, ERNEST A. "Personality, Intellectual, and Achievement Patterns in Gifted Children." *Psychol Monogr* 73(13): 1–28 '59. * (*PA* 35:1234)

3146. FISHER, SEYMOUR. "Prediction of Body Exterior vs. Interior Reactivity From a Body Image Schema." *J Personality* 27:56–62 Mr '59. * (*PA* 34:4064)

3147. HOLTZMAN, WAYNE H. Chap. 7, "Objective Scoring of Projective Tests," pp. 119–45. In *Objective Approaches to Personality Assessment*. Edited by Bernard M. Bass and Irwin A. Berg. New York: D. Van Nostrand Co., Inc., 1959. Pp. x, 233. * (*PA* 33:9926)

3148. LABARRE, WESTON. "Religions, Rorschachs and Tranquilizers." *Am J Orthopsychiatry* 29:688–98 O '59. * (*PA* 34:5097)

3149. McCONNELL, SHIRLEY. *A Study of Segregated Behavior-Problem Children in the Camden Public Schools*. Doctor's thesis, Temple University (Philadelphia, Pa.), 1959. (*DA* 20:3386)

3150. VAN DE CASTLE, ROBERT LEON. *The Relationship of Anxiety and Repression to Perceptual Predominance of Threatening Stimuli*. Doctor's thesis, University of North Carolina (Chapel Hill, N.C.), 1959. (*DA* 20:3847)

3151. ZIMET, CARL N., and FINE, HAROLD J. "Perceptual Differentiation and Two Dimensions of Schizophrenia." *J Nerv & Mental Dis* 129:435–41 N '59. * (*PA* 34:6405)

3152. BELMONT, IRA, and BIRCH, HERBERT G. "Personality and Situational Factors in the Production of Rigidity." *J General Psychol* 62:3–17 Ja '60. * (*PA* 34:7364)

3153. BOOTH, GOTTHARD. "The Psychological Examination of Candidates for the Ministry," pp. 100–24. In *The Ministry and Mental Health*. Edited by Hans Hofmann. New York: Association Press, 1960. Pp. 251. *

3154. CLIFTON, JAMES A. *Explorations in Klamath Personality*. Doctor's thesis, University of Oregon (Eugene, Ore.), 1960. (*DA* 21:2072)

3155. EDELMAN, SHELDON KALMON. *Analysis of Some Stimulus Factors Involved in the Associative Response*. Doctor's thesis, Purdue University (Lafayette, Ind.), 1960. (*DA* 21: 1630)

3156. FINK, J. H. *A Psychophysiological Comparison of Brittle and Stable Diabetics*. Doctor's thesis, University of California (Los Angeles, Calif.), 1960.

3157. LIGGETT, JOHN. "The Simultaneous Use of Several Unstructured Human Portraits in the Study of Attitudes of Self and Other People: The 'Self-Evaluation Test,'" pp. 174–6. In *Rorschachiana VII*. Schweizerischen Zeitschrift für Psychologie, No. 40. Berne, Switzerland: Hans Huber, 1960. Pp. 187. *

3158. MUKHERJEE, M. *Normal Indian Personality as Projected in the Rorschach Test*. Doctor's thesis, Lucknow University (Lucknow, India), 1960.

3159. POLONI-DE LEVIE, ALETTA. *Cognitive and Personality Correlates of Reading Difficulty*. Doctor's thesis, New York University (New York, N.Y.), 1960. (*DA* 27:2144B)

3160. WERTS, CHARLES EARL, JR. *Multidimensional Analysis of Psychological Constructs*. Doctor's thesis, University of Minnesota (Minneapolis, Minn.), 1960. (*DA* 21:2008)

3161. BAUMBERGER, THEODORE SHRIVER. *Identification Differences Between Accepted and Rejected Children at One Critical Stage of Ego Development*. Doctor's thesis, University of Oklahoma (Norman, Okla.), 1961. (*DA* 21:2780)

3162. COOPER, ALLAN. *Correlates of Musical Creativity Obtained Under Standard and Additional Administration of the Rorschach Test*. Doctor's thesis, University of Rochester (Rochester, N.Y.), 1961.

3163. KAPLAN, BERT. Chap. 8, "Cross-Cultural Use of Projective Techniques," pp. 235–54. In *Psychological Anthropology: Approaches to Culture and Personality*. Edited by Francis L. K. Hsu. Homewood, Ill.: Homewood Press, Inc., 1961. Pp. ix, 520. *

3164. LEBO, DELL. "Mental Health and Occupation in the Rorschach Analysis of an Egyptologist." *Mental Hyg* 45: 180–4 Ap '61. * (*PA* 36:4IK80L)

3165. MULLER, BRUCE PAUL. *Personality Correlates of the Placebo Reaction*. Doctor's thesis, Columbia University (New York, N.Y.), 1961. (*DA* 21:3855)

3166. NOVICK, JACK ISRAEL. *The Effectiveness of Brief Psychotherapy as a Function of Ego Strength: An Investigation of the Contribution of Ego Strength to the Effectiveness of Brief Psychotherapy in the Adjustment of Mildly Disturbed Juveniles in Out-Patient Orthopsychiatric Clinics as Indicated by Behavioral Manifestations*. Doctor's thesis, New York University (New York, N.Y.), 1961. (*DA* 22:643)

3167. RABIN, ALBERT I. "Culture Components as a Significant Factor in Child Development: Symposium, 1960: 2, Kibbutz Adolescents." Discussion by Theodora M. Abel and Rogelio Diaz-Guerrero. *Am J Orthopsychiatry* 31:493–504, 512–20 Jl '61. * (*PA* 36:4FF81A)

3168. WOOD, WILLIAM WOODHULL. *Culture and Personality Aspects of the Pentecostal Holiness Religion*. Doctor's thesis,

University of North Carolina (Chapel Hill, N.C.), 1961. (*DA* 23:333)

3169. BANKS, HUGH CHRISTOPHER. *The Relationship of the Flexibility of Ego Defenses to the Rate of Recovery in Tuberculous Patients*. Doctor's thesis, New York University (New York, N.Y.), 1962. (*DA* 24:830)

3170. BLOCK, WILLIAM E. "Preliminary Study of Adaptation-Level Theory as a Framework for Projective Testing." *Percept & Motor Skills* 15:366 O '62. * (*PA* 37:8016)

3171. BRUELL, JAN H., and ALBEE, GEORGE W. "Higher Intellectual Functions in a Patient With Hemispherectomy for Tumors." *J Consult Psychol* 26:90–8 F '62. * (*PA* 37:5374)

3172. COBB, BEATRIX; DAMARIN, FRED; KRASNOFF, ALAN; and TRUNNELL, J. B. "Personality Factors and Stress in Carcinoma," pp. 738–65. In *Psychosomatic Obstetrics, Gynecology and Endocrinology*. Edited by William S. Kroger. Springfield, Ill.: Charles C Thomas, Publisher, 1962. Pp. xxv, 820. *

3173. COHEN, HASKEL. "Psychological Test Findings in Adolescents Having Ovarian Dysgenesis." *Psychosom Med* 24:249–56 Mr–Ap '62. * (*PA* 37:5107)

3174. DASTON, PAUL G., and McCONNELL, OWEN L. "Stability of Rorschach Penetration and Barrier Scores Over Time." *Newsl Res Psychol* 4:62–7 My '62. *

3175. HERRON, WILLIAM G. "The Assessment of Ego Strength." *J Psychol Studies* 13:173–203 D '62. *

3176. MURFETT, BETTY JEAN. *The Inhibition Process and the Handling of Humans and Humans in Movement*. Doctor's thesis, University of Oklahoma (Norman, Okla.), 1962. (*DA* 23:1785)

3177. NEYHUS, ARTHUR IRVIN. *The Personality of Socially Well Adjusted Adult Deaf as Revealed by Projective Tests*. Doctor's thesis, Northwestern University (Evanston, Ill.), 1962. (*DA* 23:2589)

3178. PIOTROWSKI, ZYGMUNT A. "Psychogenic Factors in Anovulatory Women: 2, Psychological Evaluation." *Fertil & Steril* 13:11–9 Ja–F '62. *

3179. RALSTON, HARRIETTE W. *Preferences of a Group of Schizophrenic Women for Style of Abstract Art as Related to the Rorschach Measure of Introversion-Extratension*. Master's thesis, George Washington University (Washington, D.C.), 1962.

3180. SACKS, HARRY. "The Effect of Preliminary Verbal Conditioning on Inkblot Test Responses." *J Proj Tech* 26:332–6 S '62. * (*PA* 37:3206)

3181. SCHMITT, WILLIAM CHARLES. *An Investigation of the Generality of Defense Mechanisms*. Doctor's thesis, University of Denver (Denver, Colo.), 1962. (*DA* 23:2987)

3182. SHRIFTE, MIRIAM L. "Toward Identification of a Psychological Variable in Host Resistance to Cancer." *Psychosom Med* 24:390–7 Jl–Ag '62. * (*PA* 37:5537)

3183. SKLAR, MAURICE. "Psychological Test Scores, Language Disturbances, and Autopsy Findings in Aphasia Patients." *Newsl Res Psychol* 4:65–79 Ag '62. *

3184. WETZEL, RITA JEANNE. *The Effect of a Marriage Course on the Personality Characteristics of Students*. Doctor's thesis, Florida State University (Tallahassee, Fla.), 1962. (*DA* 23:4012)

3185. ASTHANA, HARI SHANKER. "A Rorschach Study of the Indians," pp. 283–7. (*PA* 39:7881) In *Rorschachiana VIII*. Schweizerischen Zeitschrift für Psychologie, No. 45. Berne, Switzerland: Hans Huber, 1963. Pp. 300. *

3186. BAGGS, ROBERT EDWIN. *An Investigation of the Rorschach Movement Response as Related to Fantasy Activity and Other Behavior*. Doctor's thesis, Purdue University (Lafayette, Ind.), 1963. (*DA* 24:5537)

3187. BECK, SAMUEL J. "Rorschach's *Erlebnistypus*: An Empiric Datum," pp. 8–25. In *Rorschachiana VIII*. Schweizerischen Zeitschrift für Psychologie, No. 45. Berne, Switzerland: Hans Huber, 1963. Pp. 300. *

3188. BELMONT, IRA; POLLACK, MAX; WILLNER, ARTHUR; KLEIN, DONALD; and FINK, MAX. "The Effects of Imipramine and Chlorpromazine on Perceptual Analytic Ability, Perceptual Responsivity and Memory as Revealed in Rorschach Responses." *J Nerv & Mental Dis* 137:42–50 Jl '63. * (*PA* 38: 4587)

3189. BENDICK, MAUREEN RO-ANN. *Motor Inhibition. Sensory Deprivation and Rorschach Movements Responses*. Doctor's thesis, University of Portland (Portland, Ore.), 1963.

3190. CASELLA, CARMINE FRANK. *The Effects of Basal Ganglia Surgery (Chemopallidectomy) on Developmental Levels*. Doctor's thesis, Michigan State University (East Lansing, Mich.), 1963. (*DA* 25:1330)

3191. DESROCHES, HARRY F., and LARSEN, ERNEST R. "The Rorschach Test as an Index of Willingness and/or Ability to Communicate." *Newsl Res Psychol* 5:13–4 N '63. *

3192. FINK, JOSEPHINE H. "Personality Variables in Brittle and Stable Diabetics." *Newsl Res Psychol* 5:8–9 Ag '63. * (*PA* 38:8587)

3193. FISHER, SEYMOUR. "Body Image and Hypnotic Response." *Int J Clin & Exp Hyp* 11:152–62 Jl '63. * (*PA* 38:6274)

3194. FLINN, DON E.; HARTMAN, BRYCE O.; POWELL, DOUGLAS H.; and McKENZIE, RICHARD E. "Psychiatric and Psychologic Evaluation," pp. 199–230. In *Aeromedical Evaluation for Space Pilots*. Edited by Lawrence E. Lamb. Brooks

Air Force Base, Tex.: USAF School of Aerospace Medicine, July 1963. Pp. vii, 276. * (*PA* 38:4728)

3195. FRIEDMAN, ALICE R. "Rorschach Responses and Treatment Results Under Drug and Group Psychotherapy." *Acta Psychotherapeutica et Psychosomatica* 11(1):28–32 '63. * (*PA* 38:6094)

3196. GREENSTADT, WILLIAM MARTIN. *An Evaluation of Types of Drive and of Ego Strength Variables in Selected Problem and Non-Problem Elementary School Boys: Inter and Intra-Group Comparisons of Projective Test Variables of Seven-, Nine- and Eleven-Year-Old Boys Manifesting Certain Varieties of Classroom Behavioral Disturbances.* Doctor's thesis, New York University (New York, N.Y.), 1963. (*DA* 25:2610)

3197. HERTZ, MARGUERITE R. "Objectifying the Subjective," pp. 25–54. In *Rorschachiana VIII.* Schweizerischen Zeitschrift für Psychologie, No. 45. Berne, Switzerland: Hans Huber, 1963. Pp. 300. *

3198. HUZIOKA, YOSINARU. "Modal Personality of People in Nagir Through the Rorschach Technique," pp. 23–299. In *Personality and Health in Hunza Valley.* Edited by Kinji Imanishi. Results of the Kyoto University Scientific Expedition to the Karakoram and Hindukush, 1955, Vol. 5. Kyoto, Japan: Committee of the Kyoto University Scientific Expedition to the Karakoram and Hindukush, Kyoto University, 1963. Pp. xiii, 299. *

3199. JENNINGS, CHARLES L. "Psychologic Test Profiles of Special Groups." *Proc Ann Conf Air Force Clin Psychologists* 4:105–16 '63. *

3200. KAFKA, HELENE. *The Use of Color in Projective Tests and Dreams in Relation to the Theory of Ego Autonomy.* Doctor's thesis, New York University (New York, N.Y.), 1963. (*DA* 26:3487)

3201. KANEKO, ZIRO, and TAKAISHI, NOBORU. "Psychosomatic Studies on Chronic Urticaria." *Folia Psychiatrica Neurologica Japonica* 17:16–24 Jl '63. * (*PA* 38:6547)

3202. KRAUS, STEPHEN. "Rorschach-Type and Stress Response," pp. 196–200. In *Rorschachiana VIII.* Schweizerischen Zeitschrift für Psychologie, No. 45. Berne, Switzerland: Hans Huber, 1963. Pp. 300. *

3203. KUMAR, PRAMOD. "The Rorschach Test in Schizophrenic and Normal Groups." *Indian J Psychol* 38:121–4 Je '63. * (*PA* 39:10661)

3204. MCMICHAEL, ALLEN E., and GRAYBIEL, ASHTON. "Rorschach Indications of Emotional Instability and Susceptibility to Motion Sickness." *Aerospace Med* 34:997–1000 N '63. *

3205. MASSON, ROBERT LOUIS. *An Investigation of the Relationship Between Body-Image and Attitudes Expressed Toward Visibly Disabled Persons.* Doctor's thesis, State University of New York at Buffalo (Buffalo, N.Y.), 1963. (*DA* 24:2604)

3206. MOLISH, HERMAN B. "Rorschach's Test and Schizophrenia," pp. 247–65. In *Rorschachiana VIII.* Schweizerischen Zeitschrift für Psychologie, No. 45. Berne, Switzerland: Hans Huber, 1963. Pp. 300. *

3207. ŌYAMA, MASAHIRO. "Studies on Sensory Deprivation: 1, Preliminary Studies: Part 3, Rorschach Performance in Sensory Deprivation." *Tohoku Psychologica Folia* 22(1–2): 15–35 '63. *

3208. PESKIN, HARVEY. "Unity of Science Begins at Home: A Study of Regional Factionalism in Clinical Psychology." *Am Psychologist* 18:96–100 F '63. * (*PA* 38:2732)

3209. RAY, A. B. "Juvenile Delinquency Pattern by Rorschach Ink-Blots." *Psychologia* 6:190–2 D '63. * (*PA* 39:1868)

3210. ROSENBERG, CLARA Y. *An Assessment of the Comparative Validity of the Rorschach and Family Drawing Projective Tests in School Phobic and Normal Children.* Doctor's thesis, Yeshiva University (New York, N.Y.), 1963. (*DA* 25:2036)

3211. ROTHSCHILD, BERTRAM HAROLD. *Response Style: A Basis for Rorschach Construct Validity.* Doctor's thesis, Syracuse University (Syracuse, N.Y.), 1963. (*DA* 25:3116)

3212. ROTHSTEIN, RALPH. "Explorations of Ego Structures of Firesetting Children." *Arch Gen Psychiatry* 9:246–53 S '63. * (*PA* 38:4508)

3213. SINGER, MARGARET THALER. Chap. 12, "Personality Measurements in the Aged," pp. 217–49. In *Human Aging: A Biological and Behavioral Study.* Edited by James E. Birren, Robert N. Butler, Samuel W. Greenhouse, Louis Sokoloff, and Marian R. Yarrow. National Institute of Mental Health, Public Health Service Publication No. 986. Washington, D.C.: United States Government Printing Office, 1963. Pp. xiii, 328. * (*PA* 38:5821)

3214. SPYER, THEA C. *Test Retest Stability of Rorschach Content and Mode of Expression as a Function of Erlebnistyp and Examiner.* Doctor's thesis, Adelphi University (Garden City, N.Y.), 1963.

3215. ULLMANN, L. P.; WEISS, R. L.; and KRASNER, L. "The Effect of Verbal Conditioning of Emotional Words on Recognition of Threatening Stimuli." *J Clin Psychol* 19:182–3 Ap '63. * (*PA* 39:5162)

3216. WEINBERG, NORRIS H. "Relativism, Self-Centering, and Conceptual Level." *Child Develop* 34:443–50 Je '63. * (*PA* 38:8067)

3217. WEISS, A. A., and WINNIK, H. Z. "A Contribution to the Meaning of Anatomy Responses on the Rorschach Test." *Israel Ann Psychiatry* 1:265–76 O '63. * (*PA* 38:6103)

3218. ABRAMS, STANLEY. "A Validation of Piotrowski's Alpha Formula With Schizophrenics Varying in Duration of Illness." *Am J Psychiatry* 121:45–7 Jl '64. *

3219. ALLEN, ROBERT M.; RICHER, HOWARD M.; and PLOTNIK, RODNEY J. "A Study of Introversion-Extroversion as a Personality Dimension." *Genetic Psychol Monogr* 69:297–322 My '64. * (*PA* 39:5143)

3220. ALLISON, JOEL, and BLATT, SIDNEY J. "The Relationship of Rorschach Whole Responses to Intelligence." *J Proj Tech & Pers Assess* 28:255–60 S '64. * (*PA* 39:7879)

3221. AMES, LOUISE B., and ILG, FRANCES L. "Sex Differences in Test Performance of Matched Girl-Boy Pairs in the Five-to-Nine-Year-Old Age Range." *J Genetic Psychol* 104:25–34 Mr '64. * (*PA* 39:4582)

3222. AMES, LOUISE B., and WALKER, RICHARD N. "Prediction of Later Reading Ability From Kindergarten Rorschach and IQ Scores." *J Ed Psychol* 55:309–13 D '64. * (*PA* 39:8662)

3223. ARMSTRONG, HUBERT ELMER, JR. *The Relationship Between a Dimension of Body-Image and Two Measures of Conditioning.* Doctor's thesis, Syracuse University (Syracuse, N.Y.), 1964. (*DA* 25:1315)

3224. BARKER, G. B. "The Ganzer Syndrome—A Blind Rorschach Analysis." *Rorsch Newsl* 9:5–15 Je '64. * (*PA* 39:5188)

3225. BAUGH, V. S., and STANFORD, G. A. "Psychological Factors in Ulcer Patients." *Dis Nerv System* 25:553–7 S '64. *

3226. BECKER, GEORGE J. *Personality Characteristics of Good and Poor Judges of Religious-Moral Situations.* Doctor's thesis, New School for Social Research (New York, N.Y.), 1964. (*DA* 25:6049)

3227. BENDICK, MAURENE R., and KLOPFER, WALTER G. "The Effects of Sensory Deprivation and Motor Inhibition on Rorschach Movement Responses." *J Proj Tech & Pers Assess* 28:261–4 S '64. * (*PA* 39:7883)

3228. BINDER, ARNOLD. "The Rorschach Test: A Perceptual Bias." *Percept & Motor Skills* 18:225–6 F '64. * (*PA* 39:1851)

3229. BLOCK, WILLIAM E. "Adaptation Effects in Clinical Judgment of Projective Test Data." *J Clin Psychol* 20:448–54 O '64. * (*PA* 39:12380)

3230. BLOCK, WILLIAM E. "Adaptation-Level Theory: Paradigmatic Application to Profective Testing." *J Clin Psychol* 18:466–8 O '64. * (*PA* 39:5191)

3231. BOYER, L. BRYCE; BOYCE, RUTH M.; BRAWER, FLORENCE B.; KAWAI, HAYAO; and KLOPFER, BRUNO. "Apache Age Groups." *J Proj Tech & Pers Assess* 28:397–402 D '64. * (*PA* 39:7945)

3232. BOYER, L. BRYCE; KLOPFER, BRUNO; BRAWER, FLORENCE B.; and KAWAI, HAYAO. "Comparisons of the Shamans and Pseudoshamans of the Apaches of the Mescalero Indian Reservation: A Rorschach Study." *J Proj Tech & Pers Assess* 28:173–80 Je '64. * (*PA* 39:5193)

3233. BRAWER, FLORENCE B., and SPIEGELMAN, J. MARVIN. "Rorschach and Jung: A Study of Introversion-Extraversion." *J Anal Psychol* 9:137–49 Jl '64. *

3234. CASSWELL, WILFRED A. "A Projective Index of Body-Interior Awareness." *Psychosom Med* 26:172–7 Mr–Ap '64. * (*PA* 39:7888)

3235. COMPTON, NORMA H. "Body-Image Boundaries in Relation to Clothing Fabric and Design Preferences of a Group of Hospitalized Psychotic Women." *J Home Econ* 56:40–5 Ja '64. *

3236. CRADDICK, RAY A. "Psychological Correlates of Biodynamic Stress: Description of Six Subjects Sustaining Over 500 Accumulative 'G.'" *Aerospace Med* 35:40–2 Ja '64. *

3237. DAVIDS, ANTHONY, and TALMADGE, MAX. "Utility of the Rorschach in Predicting Movement in Psychiatric Casework." *J Consult Psychol* 28:311–6 Ag '64. * (*PA* 39:5469)

3238. DAW, RICHARD PATRICK. *An Assessment of the Holtzman and the Rorschach Inkblots Using the Semantic Differential.* Doctor's thesis, University of Denver (Denver, Colo.), 1964. (*DA* 26:488)

3239. DAWES, ROBYN MASON, and THALHOFER, NANCY N. "Regression of Intelligence on Rorschach Variables." *Newsl Res Psychol* 6:49–50 Ag '64. *

3240. DESROCHES, HARRY F., and LARSEN, ERNEST R. "The Rorschach Test as an Index of Willingness and/or Ability to Communicate." *J Clin Psychol* 20:384–6 Jl '64. * (*PA* 39:10259)

3241. DINCMEN, KRITON. "Rorschach Test and Questionnaire to Evaluate Character Changes in Tuberculous Patients." *Dis Nerv System* 25:487–90 Ag '64. *

3242. EDGERLY, JOHN. *An Exploratory Study of Rorschach Correlates of Initial Response Time.* Master's thesis, Springfield College (Springfield, Mass.), 1964.

3243. ENDICOTT, NOBLE A., and ENDICOTT, JEAN. "Prediction of Improvement in Treated and Untreated Patients Using the Rorschach Prognostic Rating Scale." *J Consult Psychol* 28:342–8 Ag '64. * (*PA* 39:5345)

3244. ENDICOTT, NOBLE A., and ENDICOTT, JEAN. "The Relationship Between Rorschach Flexor and Extensor M Responses and the MMPI." *J Clin Psychol* 20:388–9 Jl '64. * (*PA* 39:10193)

3245. EVANS, RAY B., and MARMORSTON, JESSIE. "Rorschach Signs of Brain Damage in Cerebral Thrombosis." *Percept & Motor Skills* 18:977–88 Je '64. * (*PA* 39:5199)

3246. FALK, GERTRUD. "Prognosis in a Case of School Phobia: George T. (aged 12.9/12)." *Rorsch Newsl* 9:27–31 D '64. *

3247. FIELDSTEEL, NINA DIAMOND. *The Value of the Rorschach Test for the Prediction of School Achievement.* Doctor's thesis, Columbia University (New York, N.Y.), 1964. (*DA* 25:3106)

3248. FISHER, SEYMOUR. "The Body Boundary and Judged Behavioral Patterns in an Interview Situation." *J Proj Tech & Pers Assess* 28:181–4 Je '64. * (*PA* 39:4982)

3249. FISHER, SEYMOUR, and FISHER, RHODA L. "Body Image Boundaries and Patterns of Body Perception." *J Abn & Social Psychol* 68:255–62 Mr '64. * (*PA* 38:8352)

3250. FRIEDMAN, HOWARD, and ORGEL, SIDNEY A. "Rorschach Developmental Scores and Intelligence Level." *J Proj Tech & Pers Assess* 28:425–8 D '64. * (*PA* 39:7889)

3251. GARMIZE, LEWIS M., and RYCHLAK, JOSEPH F. "Role-Play Validation of a Sociocultural Theory of Symbolism." *J Consult Psychol* 28:107–15 Ap '64. * (*PA* 39:1856)

3252. GOLDEN, MARK. "Some Effects of Combining Psychological Tests on Clinical Inferences." *J Consult Psychol* 28:440–6 O '64. * (*PA* 39:5060)

3253. GOLIN, SANFORD. "Anxiety and Color-Form Incongruity in Perception of Unstructured Stimuli." Abstract. *Psychol Rep* 15:738 D '64. * (*PA* 39:7891)

3254. HAAN, NORMA. "An Investigation of the Relationships of Rorschach Scores, Patterns, and Behavior to Coping and Defense Mechanisms." *J Proj Tech & Pers Assess* 28:429–41 D '64. * (*PA* 39:7893)

3255. HAFNER, A. JACK, and ROSEN, EPHRAIM. "The Meaning of Rorschach Inkblots, Responses and Determinants as Perceived by Children." *J Proj Tech & Pers Assess* 28:192–200 Je '64. * (*PA* 39:5203)

3256. HARROWER, MOLLY. *Appraising Personality: An Introduction to Projective Techniques, Revised Edition,* pp. 53–100. New York: Franklin Watts, Inc., 1964. Pp. xiv, 302. *

3257. HAWORTH, MARY R. "Parental Loss in Children as Reflected in Projective Responses." *J Proj Tech & Pers Assess* 28:31–45 Mr '64. * (*PA* 39:1857)

3258. HERZBERG, IRENE. "Can We Test Africans." *Rorsch Newsl* 9:16–26 D '64. *

3259. HEYDER, D. W., and WAMBACH, HELEN S. "Sexuality and Affect in Frogmen: An Investigation of Personality Factors in Resistance to Prolonged Stress." *Arch Gen Psychiatry* 11:286–9 S '64. * (*PA* 39:5152)

3260. JENSEN, ARTHUR R. "The Rorschach Technique: A Re-evaluation." *Acta Psychologica* 22(1):60–77 '64. * (*PA* 39:5204)

3261. JOHNSON, WILLIAM LAWRENCE. *Relationships Between Variation in Choice of Types of Categorization and Variation in Personality Traits.* Doctor's thesis, Yeshiva University (New York, N.Y.), 1964. (*DA* 25:3676)

3262. JORDAN, DAVID L. "Rorschach Systems and Brain Syndromes Associated With Metabolic Disorders." *Newsl Res Psychol* 6:23 F '64. *

3263. JUDSON, ABE J., and KATAHN, MARTIN. "Levels of Personality Organization and Production of Associative Sequences in Process-Reactive Schizophrenia." *J Consult Psychol* 28:208–13 Je '64. * (*PA* 39:5753)

3264. JURKO, MARION F., and ANDY, ORLANDO J. "Rorschach Study of Perceptual Changes Following Diencephalotomy." *Am J Psychiatry* 121:487–90 N '64. *

3265. KALDEGG, A. " 'Denial' in Hypomania." *Rorsch Newsl* 9:5–7 D '64. *

3266. KANTER, V. B., and HAZELTON, J. E. "An Attempt to Measure Some Aspects of Personality in Young Men With Duodenal Ulcer by Means of Questionnaires and a Projective Test." *J Psychosom Res* 8:297–309 D '64. * (*PA* 39:12455)

3267. KENNY, DOUGLAS T. "Stimulus Functions in Projective Techniques," pp. 285–354. In *Progress in Experimental Personality Research, Vol. 1.* Edited by Brendan A. Maher. New York: Academic Press, Inc., 1964. Pp. x, 368. *

3268. KIKUCHI, TETSUHIKO. "A Scoring Method of Rorschach Test and Levy Movement Test for Discrimination of Accident Proneness in Motor Driver." *Tohuko Psychologica Folia* 23(1–2):26–38 '64. *

3269. KLINGER, ERIC, and ROTH, IRVIN. "Diagnosing Schizophrenia With Rorschach Color Responses." *J Clin Psychol* 20:386–8 Jl '64. * (*PA* 39:10263)

3270. KRAUS, J. "Clinical Utility of Rorschach Anxiety Signs." *J Proj Tech & Pers Assess* 28:300–2 S '64. * (*PA* 39:7901)

3271. KRAUSER, EDWIN L. "The Couples Rorschach: An Approach to the Understanding of Marital Dynamics." *J Proj Tech & Pers Assess* 28:55–63 Mr '64. * (*PA* 39:1859)

3272. KUNTZ, KENNETH J. "Mass and Shading Effects on Masculine-Feminine Judgments on the Rorschach." *J Proj Tech & Pers Assess* 28:201–5 Je '64. * (*PA* 39:5206)

3273. LAUER, RACHEL M. *The Relationship Between Value Orientation and Primary Process Thinking.* Doctor's thesis, New York University (New York, N.Y.), 1964. (*DA* 25:1338)

3274. LEVITT, EUGENE E.; PERSKY, HAROLD; and BRADY, JOHN PAUL. *Hypnotic Induction of Anxiety: A Psychoendocrine*

Investigation. Springfield, Ill.: Charles C Thomas, Publisher, 1964. Pp. xvi, 134. *

3275. LEVY, JOSHUA, and EPSTEIN, NATHAN B. "An Application of the Rorschach Test in Family Investigation." *Family Process* 3:344–76 S '64. * (*PA* 39:7906)

3276. LOKANDER, SVEN, and MACHL, MARGARETA. "Sick Absence in a Swedish Company: 4, The Relationship Between Absence Due to Sickness and Psychological Status." *Acta Psychiatrica Scandinavica* 40(4):401–18 '64. * (*PA* 40:540)

3277. MACARI, LEOPOLD MICHAEL. *A Rorschach Study of the Relation Between Personality Traits and Culture Traits: A Cross-Cultural Comparison Between Two Groups of Similar Biological Descent.* Doctor's thesis, New York University (New York, N.Y.), 1964. (*DA* 25:2052)

3278. McGURK, WILLIAM N. *Rorschach Content of College Students.* Doctor's thesis, Loyola University (Chicago, Ill.), 1964.

3279. MATARAZZO, JOSEPH D.; ALLEN, BERNADENE V.; SASLOW, GEORGE; and WIENS, ARTHUR N. "Characteristics of Successful Policemen and Firemen Applicants." *J Appl Psychol* 48:123–33 Ap '64. * (*PA* 39:6047)

3280. MILTON, ROBERT GENE. *Prediction of Therapeutic and Intellectual Potential in Mentally Retarded Children.* Doctor's thesis, University of Southern California (Los Angeles, Calif.), 1964. (*DA* 25:3690)

3281. NICHOLSON, LISTON OLIVER. *The Relationship Between Self-Concept and Reading Achievement.* Doctor's thesis, New York University (New York, N.Y.), 1964. (*DA* 25:6063)

3282. OHYAMA, MASAHIRO. "The Changes of 'Body-Image Boundary Scores' Under Condition of Alcoholic Intoxication." *Tohuko Psychologica Folia* 22(3–4):100–7 '64. *

3283. ORME, J. E. "A Study of Weiner's Rorschach Schizophrenic Indicators." *J Clin Psychol* 20:531–2 O '64. * (*PA* 39:12400)

3284. PERDUE, WILLIAM C. "Rorschach Responses of 100 Murderers." *Correct Psychiatry* 10:323–8 N '64. * (*PA* 39:8428)

3285. PHELAN, JOSEPH G. "Analysis of the 'Good Errors' Made by Clinical Psychologists in Diagnostic Judgment." *J Psychol* 58:43–55 Jl '64. * (*PA* 39:5322)

3286. PHELAN, JOSEPH G. "Rationale Employed by Clinical Psychologists in Diagnostic Judgment." *J Clin Psychol* 20:454–8 O '64. * (*PA* 39:12469)

3287. PIOTROWSKI, ZYGMUNT A. "Digital-Computer Interpretation of Inkblot Test Data." *Psychiatric Q* 38:1–26 Ja '64. * (*PA* 39:7912)

3288. PRESTON, CAROLINE E. "Psychological Testing With Northwest Coast Alaskan Eskimos." *Genetic Psychol Monogr* 69:323–419 My '64. * (*PA* 39:4713)

3289. PRUITT, WALTER A., and SPILKA, BERNARD. "Rorschach Empathy-Object Relationship Scale." *J Proj Tech & Pers Assess* 28:331–6 S '64. * (*PA* 39:7913)

3290. RICKELS, K.; DOWNING, R.; and APPEL, H. "Some Personality Correlates of Suggestibility in Normals and Neurotics." *Psychol Rep* 14:715–9 Je '64. * (*PA* 39:5159)

3291. RIGHTMYER, NELSON WAITE. "The Harrower Multiple-Choice Test as a Prognosticating Device for Independent Secondary School Admissions." *J Ed Res* 57:380–1 Mr '64. *

3292. ROSE, DORIAN; SMITH, RUTH E.; and ROBLES, ALBERT. "Some Problems in Perceptual Handicap of Mentally Retarded Children." *J Genetic Psychol* 104:123–33 Mr '64. * (*PA* 39:5669)

3293. ROTHSCHILD, BERTRAM H. "Response Style: A Basis for Rorschach Construct Validity." *J Proj Tech & Pers Assess* 28:474–83 D '64. * (*PA* 39:7915)

3294. RYCHLAK, JOSEPH F., and MAIER, LAWRENCE R. "Rorschach Content Responses of Popular and Unpopular Junior High School Students." *J Clin Psychol* 20:381–4 Jl '64. * (*PA* 39:10269)

3295. SANDS, DAVID J. "The Personal Meaning of Rorschach Content." *Percept & Motor Skills* 19:57–8 Ag '64. * (*PA* 39:5212)

3296. SAPOLSKY, ALLAN. "An Effort at Studying Rorschach Content Symbolism: The Frog Response." *J Consult Psychol* 28:469–72 O '64. * (*PA* 39:5213)

3297. SCHULMAN, PAUL. *The Relationship of Certain Personality Factors to the Quantitative Ability of Gifted Male Adolescents.* Doctor's thesis, New York University (New York, N.Y.), 1964. (*DA* 25:2355)

3298. SHAPIRO, JAY N. "Comparison of Rorschach Score Patterns With Psychodrama Action Patterns." *Calif Mental Health Res Dig* 2:19–20 au '64. * (*PA* 39:12405, title only)

3299. SHAPIRO, JAY NOAH. *A Comparison of Certain Rorschach Score Patterns With Psychodrama Action Patterns.* Doctor's thesis, University of Arizona (Tucson, Ariz.), 1964. (*DA* 25:2615)

3300. SHERICK, IVAN GARY. *Body Image, Level of Ego Development and Adequacy of Ego Functioning.* Doctor's thesis, Washington University (St. Louis, Mo.), 1964. (*DA* 26:1782)

3301. SILVERMAN, LLOYD H., and SILVERMAN, DORIS K. "A Clinical-Experimental Approach to the Study of Subliminal Stimulation: The Effects of a Drive-Related Stimulus Upon Rorschach Responses." *J Abn & Social Psychol* 69:158–72 Jl '64. * (*PA* 39:5216)

3302. SPIVACK, GEORGE; LEVINE, MURRAY; and BRENNER,

BERNARD. "The Rorschach Index of Repressive Style and Scale Checking Style: A Study of Sex Differences." *J Proj Tech & Pers Assess* 28:484–90 D '64. * (*PA* 39:7919)

3303. SPIVACK, GEORGE; LEVINE, MURRAY; and GRAZIANO, ANTHONY. "Anxiety and Set in the Rorschach Test." Abstract. *J Consult Psychol* 28:189 Ap '64. * (*PA* 39:1871, title only)

3304. STARK, STANLEY. "Rorschach Movement and Bleuler's Three Kinds of Thinking: A Contribution to the Psychology of Creativity." *Percept & Motor Skills* 19:959–67 D '64. * (*PA* 39:6235)

3305. STEWART, LOUIS. "On the Existential Interpretation of the Rorschach Test." *J Proj Tech & Pers Assess* 28:350–6 S '64. * (*PA* 39:7920)

3306. STRICKER, GEORGE. "Stimulus Properties of the Rorschach to a Sample of Pedophiles." *J Proj Tech & Pers Assess* 28:241–4 Je '64. * (*PA* 39:5217)

3307. TAKAHASHI, SHIGEO. "A Comparative Study of the Rorschach Responses Between Juvenile Delinquent Groups and College Student Groups." Abstract. *Jap J Psychol* 34:180 O '64. * (*PA* 39:7921)

3308. TAKAHASHI, SHIGEO. "The Influence of Chromatic and Achromatic Colors on the Stimulus Value of the Rorschach Inkblots." Abstract. *Jap J Psychol* 34:274 F '64. * (*PA* 39:1872)

3309. TELTSCHER, HERRY O. *A Study of the Relationship Between the Perception of Movement on the Rorschach and Motoric Expression.* Doctor's thesis, Yeshiva University (New York, N.Y.), 1964. (*DA* 26:2317)

3310. VAN DE CASTLE, R. L. "Effect of Test Order Upon Rorschach Human Content." *J Consult Psychol* 28:286–8 Je '64. * (*PA* 39:5218)

3311. VANDENBERG, STEVEN G.; ROSENZWEIG, NORMAN; MOORE, KENNETH R.; and DUKAY, ALEXANDER F. "Diagnostic Agreements Among Psychiatrists and 'Blind' Rorschach Raters or the Education of an Interdisciplinary Research Team." *Psychol Rep* 15:211–24 Ag '64. * (*PA* 39:1899)

3312. VIITAMAKI, R. OLAVI. "A Psychological Follow-up Study: Psychoses in Childhood, Part 2." *Acta Psychiatrica Scandinavica Supplementum* 40(174):33–93 '64. * (*PA* 39:8464)

3313. VOIGT, WALTER H., and DANA, RICHARD H. "Inter- and Intra-Scorer Rorschach Reliability." *J Proj Tech & Pers Assess* 28:92–5 Mr '64. * (*PA* 39:1875)

3314. WAGONER, ROBERT A. "Comment: 'The Rorschach Test: A Perceptual Bias.'" *Percept & Motor Skills* 18:282 F '64. * (*PA* 39:1876)

3315. WEATHERLY, J. KENNY; CORKE, PATRICIA PERRY; and McCARY, J. L. "A Comparison of Rorschach Responses Between Negro and White College Students." *J Proj Tech & Pers Assess* 28:103–6 Mr '64. * (*PA* 39:1877)

3316. WEINER, IRVING B. "Differential Diagnosis in Amphetamine Psychosis." *Psychiatric Q* 38:707–16 O '64. * (*PA* 39:12831)

3317. WEINER, IRVING B. "Pure *C* and Color Stress as Rorschach Indicators of Schizophrenia." *Percept & Motor Skills* 18:484 Ap '64. * (*PA* 39:5219)

3318. WELTMAN, ROBERT, and WOLFSON, WILLIAM. "Rorschach S: Oppositional Tendencies or Mastery Strivings." *Percept & Motor Skills* 18:821–4 Je '64. * (*PA* 39:5221)

3319. WILKINSON, A. EARL. "Rorschach Body Image Content and the Prediction of Therapy Outcome." *Newsl Res Psychol* 6:42–3 Ag '64. *

3320. WILKINSON, NORMAN W. "Deprived Children and the Sense of Power." *Rorsch Newsl* 9:16–34 Je '64. * (*PA* 39:4622)

3321. WILLIAM, ROBERT L., and KRASNOFF, ALAN G. "Body Image and Physiological Patterns in Patients With Peptic Ulcer and Rheumatoid Arthritis." *Psychosom Med* 26:701–9 N–D '64. * (*PA* 39:12928)

3322. WILLNER, ARTHUR, and BELMONT, IRA. "Relation of Motor Performance to Perceived Movement in Rorschach Inkblots." *Percept & Motor Skills* 19:675–84 D '64. * (*PA* 39:7932)

3323. WINSLOW, CHARLES N., and RAPERSAND, ISAAC. "Postdiction of the Outcome of Somatic Therapy From the Rorschach Records of Schizophrenic Patients." *J Consult Psychol* 28:243–7 Je '64. * (*PA* 39:5777)

3324. YEN, YI-SHU. "The Diagnostic Indications of the Delusion of the Paranoid Schizophrenia in the Rorschach Test." *Acta Psychologica Taiwanica* 6:63–70 Mr '64. * (*PA* 39:5222)

3325. ALLEN, ROBERT M. "Perception and Personality Appraisal." *Rorsch Newsl* 10:15–23 D '65. * (*PA* 40:11170)

3326. AMES, LOUISE BATES. "Changes in the Experience-Balance Score on the Rorschach at Different Ages in the Life Span." *J Genetic Psychol* 106:279–86 Je '65. * (*PA* 39:15380)

3327. AMES, LOUISE BATES, and WALKER, RICHARD N. "A Note on School Dropouts in Longitudinal Research With Late Adolescents." *J Genetic Psychol* 107:277–9 D '65. * (*PA* 40:5482)

3328. AMIR, YEHUDA; KOHEN-RAZ, REUVEN; and RABINO-VITZ, GALIA. "Group Rorschach Technique for Screening Army Officers." Abstract. *J Consult Psychol* 29:598 D '65. * (*PA* 40:3425, title only)

3329. ARDHAPURKAR, INDU BALA, and DOONGAJI, DINSHAW R. "A Selective Study of Rorschach Records: 209 Cases." *Indian J Psychiatry* 7:287–91 O '65. *

3330. AUDUBON, JAMES J., and VANBUSKIRK, CHARLES. "Projection Across Sensory Modalities." *J Proj Tech & Pers Assess* 29:140–50 Je '65. * (*PA* 39:12376)

3331. BECK, SAMUEL J. *Psychological Processes in the Schizophrenic Adaptation.* New York: Grune & Stratton, 1965. Pp. ix, 421. * (*PA* 39:16176)

3332. BJORKSTEN, CHRISTEL. "Variability in Normal Ego-Structure During School Age." *Nordisk Psykologi* 17(6):371–424 '65. * (*PA* 40:5255)

3333. BLANK, LEONARD. *Psychological Evaluation in Psychotherapy: Ten Case Histories.* Chicago, Ill.: Aldine Publishing Co., 1965. Pp. xii, 364. *

3334. BLATT, SIDNEY J.; ALLISON, JOEL; and BAKER, BRUCE L. "The Wechsler Object Assembly Subtest and Bodily Concerns." *J Consult Psychol* 29:223–30 Je '65. * (*PA* 39:12225)

3335. BROWN, D. G., and YOUNG, A. J. "The Effect of Extraversion on Susceptibility to Disease: A Validatory Study on Contact Dermatitis." *J Psychosom Res* 8:421–9 Mr '65. *

3336. CLEVELAND, SIDNEY E.; REITMAN, E. EDWARD; and BREWER, EARL J., JR. "Psychological Factors in Juvenile Rheumatoid Arthritis." *Arthr & Rheum* 8:1152–8 D '65. *

3337. CLEVELAND, SIDNEY E.; SNYDER, REBECCA; and WILLIAMS, ROBERT L. "Body Image and Site of Psychosomatic Symptoms." *Psychol Rep* 16:851–2 Je '65. * (*PA* 39:16274)

3338. COOPER, G. DAVID; ADAMS, HENRY B.; and COHEN, LOUIS D. "Personality Changes After Sensory Deprivation." *J Nerv & Mental Dis* 140:103–18 F '65. * (*PA* 39:13642)

3339. COOPER, GEORGE W., JR.; BERNSTEIN, LEWIS; and HART, CYNTHIA. "Predicting Suicidal Ideation From the Rorschach: An Attempt to Cross-Validate." *J Proj Tech & Pers Assess* 29:168–70 Je '65. * (*PA* 39:12383)

3340. CRAFT, MICHAEL. Chap. 2, "Diagnosis and Aetiology Illustrated by an Analysis of Admissions to a Psychopathic Unit," pp. 32–54. In *Ten Studies Into Psychopathic Personality: A Report to the Home Office and the Mental Health Research Fund.* Bristol, England: John Wright & Sons Ltd., 1965. Pp. 133. *

3341. DAVIES, ROY, and BOWYER, RUTH. "The Effect of an Anxiety Arousing Situation on Some Rorschach Indicators of Anxiety." *Rorsch Newsl* 10:35–6 D '65. * (*PA* 40:10620)

3342. DE LUCA, JOSEPH N. "The Structure of Homosexuality." *Proc Ann Conv Am Psychol Assn* 73:205–6 '65. * (*PA* 39:16698)

3343. EFRON, HERMAN Y., and PIOTROWSKI, ZYGMUNT A. "A Factor Analytic Study of the Rorschach Prognostic Index." *Newsl Res Psychol* 7:15–6 My '65. *

3344. EISMAN, HOWARD DAVID. *Inhibition and the Human Movement Response in Children.* Doctor's thesis, Boston University (Boston, Mass.), 1965. (*DA* 26:2865)

3345. ELSTEIN, ARTHUR S. "Behavioral Correlates of the Rorschach Shading Determinant." *J Consult Psychol* 29:231–6 Je '65. * (*PA* 39:12389)

3346. FISCHER, HENRY LOUIS. *The Relationship of a Questionnaire Index of Fantasy Tendency to the Fantasy-Inhibition Hypothesis.* Doctor's thesis, University of Washington (Seattle, Wash.), 1965. (*DA* 27:302B)

3347. FISHER, SEYMOUR. "Body Sensation and Perception of Projective Stimuli." *J Consult Psychol* 29:135–8 Ap '65. * (*PA* 39:10260)

3348. FRANER, PAUL. "A Contribution to the Study of the Reliability and Validity of the Rorschach Test." *Rorsch Newsl* 10:31–4 D '65. * (*PA* 40:10626, title only)

3349. FRIEDMAN, GLORIA. "A Case Study: Emotional Factors Contributing to the Test Performance and Behavior of a Brain-Damaged Child." *J Genetic Psychol* 106:89–99 Mr '65. * (*PA* 39:12695)

3350. GAYLIN, NED L. *Psychotherapy and Psychological Health: A Rorschach Function and Structure Analysis.* Doctor's thesis, University of Chicago (Chicago, Ill.), 1965.

3351. GUTTENTAG, MARCIA, and DENMARK, FLORENCE. "Psychiatric Labelling: Role Assignment Based on the Projective Test Performance of In-migrants." *Int J Social Psychiatry* 11:131–7 sp '65. *

3352. HAMMOND, LEO KEITH. *Cognitive Structure and Clinical Inference.* Doctor's thesis, University of Colorado (Boulder, Colo.), 1965. (*DA* 26:6847)

3353. HERRON, WILLIAM G.; GUIDO, STEPHEN M.; and KANTOR, ROBERT E. "Relationships Among Ego Strength Measures." *J Clin Psychol* 21:403–4 O '65. * (*PA* 40:1567)

3354. HILTMANN, HILDEGARD, and STRAUCH, INGE. "Interpreting Texture Responses on the Rorschach: A Note on Dr. Linzer Schwartz' 'Note on Zulliger's Theory.'" Letter. *J Proj Tech & Pers Assess* 29:530–1 D '65. *

3355. HOLLEY, J. W.; FRÖBARJ, G.; and EKBERG, KERSTI. "On the Validity of the Rorschach Test." *Scandinavian J Psychol* 6(1):7–18 '65. * (*PA* 39:10123)

3356. HORNER, ALTHEA JANE. *An Investigation of the Relationship of Value Orientation to the Adaptive-Defensive System of the Personality.* Doctor's thesis, University of Southern California (Los Angeles, Calif.), 1965. (*DA* 26:1160)

3357. HUBERMAN, JOHN. "What Do We Really Measure in 'Testing the Limits' in the Rorschach?" *J Proj Tech & Pers Assess* 29:171–7 Je '65. * (*PA* 39:12390)

3358. ILG, FRANCES L., and AMES, LOUISE BATES. *School Readiness: Behavior Tests Used at the Gesell Institute,* pp.

372–4. New York: Harper & Row, Publishers, 1965. Pp. viii, 396. *

3359. ILG, FRANCES L.; AMES, LOUISE BATES; and APELL, RICHARD J. "School Readiness as Evaluated by Gesell Developmental, Visual, and Projective Tests." *Genetic Psychol Monogr* 71:61–91 F '65. * (*PA* 39:12943)

3360. JENNINGS, CHARLES L. "A Psychologic Study of Klinefelter's Syndrome." *Proc Ann Conf Air Force Behav Sci* 11:185–95 Jl '65. *

3361. JOHANNESSEN, FRITZ. "Some Aspects of Rorschach Responses in a Group of Norwegian Children at Three Age Levels." *Acta Psychologica* 24(5):371–86 '65. * (*PA* 40:2954)

3362. JOHNSON, DALE L., and SIKES, MELVIN P. "Rorschach and TAT Responses of Negro, Mexican-American, and Anglo Psychiatric Patients." *J Proj Tech & Pers Assess* 29:183–8 Je '65. * (*PA* 39:12392)

3363. KAHN, MARVIN W. "A Factor-Analytic Study of Personality, Intelligence, and History Characteristics of Murderers." *Proc Ann Conv Am Psychol Assn* 73:227–8 '65. * (*PA* 39:16125)

3364. KEELEY, TERRY DEAN. *A Comparison of the Rorschach Protocols of Selected Leaders and Nonleaders at the First Grade Level.* Doctor's research study No. 1, Colorado State University (Greeley, Colo.), 1965. (*DA* 26:1185)

3365. KISSEL, STANLEY. "A Brief Note on the Relationship Between Rorschach Developmental Level and Intelligence." *J Proj Tech & Pers Assess* 29:454–5 D '65. * (*PA* 40:2908)

3366. KLEBAN, MORTON H., and DICHTER, MARVIN. "The Role of Stimulus Properties in Rorschach Movement." *J General Psychol* 73:203–10 O '65. * (*PA* 39:15398)

3367. KLINGER, ERIC, and ROTH, IRVIN. "Diagnosis of Schizophrenia by Rorschach Patterns." *J Proj Tech & Pers Assess* 29:323–35 S '65. * (*PA* 39:15411)

3368. KNOBLOCK, PETER. "A Rorschach Investigation of the Reading Process." *J Exp Ed* 33:277–82 sp '65. * (*PA* 39:10723)

3369. KOSCHENS, RUBY L. "Body Image Boundary Constancy in Organ Transplant Cases." *Newsl Res Psychol* 7:3–4 My '65. *

3370. KOTTENHOFF, HEINRICH. "Reliability and Validity of the Animal Percentage in Rorschachs." *Acta Psychologica* 22(4):387–406 '65. * (*PA* 39:15399)

3371. KUMAR, PRAMOD. "The Rorschach Test in Some Mental Disorders: Manic Group." *Indian J Psychol* 40:13–7 Mr '65. *

3372. KURZ, RONALD B.; COHEN, ROBERT; and STARZYNSKI, SUSAN. "Rorschach Correlates of Time Estimation." *J Consult Psychol* 29:379–82 Ag '65. * (*PA* 39:15400)

3373. LA BARBA, RICHARD C. "Relation of Color Responses on the Rorschach to Qualitative Scores on the Porteus Maze Test." *Percept & Motor Skills* 21:61–2 Ag '65. * (*PA* 40:40)

3374. LANGER, PHILIP, and WOOD, CARLTON G. "Comparison of Two Multiple-Choice Rorschach Tests." *Percept & Motor Skills* 20:143–50 F '65. * (*PA* 39:10264)

3375. LEE, RONALD REDVERS. *Theological Belief as a Dimension of Personality.* Doctor's thesis, Northwestern University (Evanston, Ill.), 1965. (*DA* 26:3510)

3376. LEEDS, DAVID PAUL. *Personality Patterns and Modes of Behavior of Male Adolescent Narcotic Addicts and Their Mothers.* Doctor's thesis, Yeshiva University (New York, N.Y.), 1965. (*DA* 26:2861)

3377. LERNER, B. A. *Rorschach M and Dreams: A Validation Study Using Drug-Induced Dream-Deprivation.* Doctor's thesis, University of Chicago (Chicago, Ill.), 1965.

3378. LIEF, VICTOR F.; LIEF, HAROLD I.; and YOUNG, KATHLEEN M. "Academic Success: Intelligence and Personality." *J Med Ed* 40:114–24 F '65. *

3379. LIGHT, CAROLE S.; ZAX, MELVIN; and GARDINER, DWIGHT H. "Relationship of Age, Sex, and Intelligence Level to Extreme Response Style." *J Personality & Social Psychol* 2:907–9 D '65. * (*PA* 40:2911)

3380. McCAULEY, JOHN HOWARD, JR. *Rorschach, WISC, and ITBS Patterns of Nine-Year-Old School Boys With Labile and Stabile IQ Scores.* Doctor's thesis, University of Maryland (College Park, Md.), 1965. (*DA* 27:1663A)

3381. McCULLY, ROBERT S. "Process Analysis: A Tool in Understanding Ambiguity in Diagnostic Problems in Rorschach." *J Proj Tech & Pers Assess* 29:436–44 D '65. * (*PA* 40:2957)

3382. McKENZIE, RICHARD E. "Clinical Validity of the Rorschach and Szondi Tests." *Proc Ann Conf Air Force Behav Sci* 11:161–70 Jl '65. *

3383. McMAHON, FRANK BORROMEO, JR. *Clinical Training: A Variable in Psychological Test Interpretation.* Doctor's thesis, Washington University (St. Louis, Mo.), 1965. (*DA* 26:4813)

3384. McNAMARA, H. J., and FISCH, R. I. "Attributed Meaning of an Unstructured Stimulus." *Percept & Motor Skills* 20:853–7 Je '65. * (*PA* 39:15403)

3385. MASLING, JOSEPH. "Differential Indoctrination of Examiners and Rorschach Responses." *J Consult Psychol* 29:198–201 Je '65. * (*PA* 39:12396)

3386. MEIER, JOHN HENRY. *An Exploratory Factor Analysis of Psychodiagnostic and Case Study Information From Children in Special Education Classes for the Educable Mentally Handicapped.* Doctor's thesis, University of Denver (Denver, Colo.), 1965. (*DA* 26:3153)

3387. MEYER, MORTIMER M., and CARUTH, ELAINE. "Rorschach Indices of Ego Processes." *J Proj Tech & Pers Assess* 29:200–18 Je '65. * (*PA* 39:12397)

3388. MOLISH, H. B. Chap. 10, "Psychological Structure in Four Groups of Children," pp. 222–40. In *Psychological Processes in the Schizophrenic Adaptation.* By Samuel J. Beck. New York: Grune & Stratton, 1965. Pp. ix, 421. * (*PA* 39:16176)

3389. NEIGER, STEPHEN; SLEMON, ALAN G.; and QUIRK, DOUGLAS A. "Rorschach Scales of Regression in Psychosis." *Genetic Psychol Monogr* 71:93–136 F '65. * (*PA* 39:12399)

3390. NEURINGER, CHARLES. "The Rorschach Test as a Research Device for the Identification, Prediction and Understanding of Suicidal Ideation and Behavior." *J Proj Tech & Pers Assess* 29:71–82 Mr '65. * (*PA* 39:10267)

3391. NEURINGER, CHARLES; McEVOY, THEODORE L.; and SCHLESINGER, RICHARD J. "The Identification of Suicidal Behavior in Females by the Use of the Rorschach." *J General Psychol* 72:127–33 Ja '65. * (*PA* 39:8427)

3392. PARKER, ROLLAND S. "The Acceptability and Expression of Attitudes Associated to the Rorschach Human Movement Response." *J Proj Tech & Pers Assess* 29:83–92 Mr '65. * (*PA* 39:10268)

3393. PHELAN, JOSEPH G. "Use of Matching Method in Measuring Reliability of Individual Clinician's Diagnostic Judgment." *Psychol Rep* 16:491–6 Ap '65. * (*PA* 39:10283)

3394. PIOTROWSKI, ZYGMUNT A. Chap. 21, "The Rorschach Inkblot Method," pp. 522–61. In *Handbook of Clinical Psychology.* Edited by Benjamin B. Wolman. New York: McGraw-Hill Book Co., Inc., 1965. Pp. xv, 1596. *

3395. POULTON, I. A. "Paul M: Diagnostic and Prognostic Assessment of a 13-Year Old Boy." *Rorsch Newsl* 10:30–6 Je '65. *

3396. RABIN, A. I. *Growing Up in the Kibbutz: Comparison of the Personality of Children Brought Up in the Kibbutz and of Family-Reared Children.* New York: Springer Publishing Co., Inc., 1965. Pp. x, 230. *

3397. RAYCHAUDHURI, MANAS. "Personality Correlates of Creativity: A Review of Psychodynamic Studies." *Samiksa* 19(3):106–34 '65. *

3398. ROMANELLA, ALAN EUGENE. *Emotions in Adolescence and Response to Color on the Rorschach.* Doctor's thesis, St. John's University (Jamaica, N.Y.), 1965. (*DA* 28:344B)

3399. ROUTSONI, ALEXANDRA. "Rorschach Responses of Eight, Nine, Ten and Eleven Year Old Greek Children: A Preliminary Study." *Rorsch Newsl* 10:24–30 D '65. * (*PA* 40:11176, title only)

3400. RYCHLAK, JOSEPH F., and O'LEARY, LAWRENCE R. "Unhealthy Content in the Rorschach Responses of Children and Adolescents." *J Proj Tech & Pers Assess* 29:354–68 S '65. * (*PA* 39:15414)

3401. SAPPENFIELD, BERT R. "Perception of Attractive and Repelling Qualities in Rorschach Blots and Responses." *J Clin Psychol* 21:308–11 Jl '65. * (*PA* 39:15415)

3402. SAPPENFIELD, BERT R. "Perceptual Conformity and Ego Strength." *Percept & Motor Skills* 20:209–10 F '65. * (*PA* 39:10270)

3403. SATTLER, JEROME M. "Rorschach Popular, Word Association, and Social Desirability." *Percept & Motor Skills* 20:744 Je '65. * (*PA* 39:15416)

3404. SCHWARTZ, LITA LINZER. "A Note on Zulliger's Theory." *J Proj Tech & Pers Assess* 29:226–7 Je '65. * (*PA* 39:12403)

3405. SCOTT, BEATRICE. "Young Heroin and Cocaine Dependent Patients in Hospital—Aspects of the Rorschach and the Personality." *Rorsch Newsl* 10:12–29 Je '65. * (*PA* 40:3134, title only)

3406. SEGAL, STANLEY J. "The Use of Clinical Techniques for Structuring Feedback in Vocational Counseling." *Personnel & Guid J* 93:876–8 My '65. * (*PA* 39:16512)

3407. SHALIT, B. "Effects of Environmental Stimulation on the F, FM, and m Responses in the Rorschach." *J Proj Tech & Pers Assess* 29:228–31 Je '65. * (*PA* 39:12404)

3408. SILVERMAN, LLOYD H. "Psychology Research at Northport Utilizing a Clinical-Experimental Approach." *Newsl Res Psychol* 7:19–22 My '65. *

3409. SILVERMAN, LLOYD H. "Regression in the Service of the Ego: A Case Study." *J Proj Tech & Pers Assess* 29:232–44 Je '65. * (*PA* 39:12564)

3410. SILVERMAN, LLOYD H. "A Study of the Effects of Subliminally Presented Aggressive Stimuli on the Production of Pathologic Thinking in a Nonpsychiatric Population." *J Nerv & Mental Dis* 141:443–55 O '65. * (*PA* 40:5497)

3411. SINGER, MARGARET THALER, and WYNNE, LYMAN C. "Thought Disorder and Family Relations of Schizophrenics: 3, Methodology Using Projective Techniques." *Arch Gen Psychiatry* 12:187–200 F '65. * (*PA* 39:8516)

3412. SINGH, RAJ KANWAR JANMEJA. *Effects of Color on Associational and Perceptual Functions in Reference to Rorschach Color Shock.* Doctor's thesis, Boston University (Boston, Mass.), 1965. (*DA* 26:3491)

3413. SLEMON, ALAN G.; NEIGER, STEPHEN; and QUIRK, DOUGLAS A. "Adjustment for the Total Number of Responses in Calculating the Rorschach Apperception Type." *J Proj Tech & Pers Assess* 29:516–21 D '65. * (*PA* 40:2962)

3414. SPIELBERGER, CHARLES D.; BORGMAN, ROBERT; BECKER, JOSEPH; and PARKER, JOSEPH B. "Affective Expression in Manic-Depressive Reactions." *J Nerv & Mental Dis* 141:664–9 D '65. * (*PA* 40:7927)

3415. SPINDLER, GEORGE, and SPINDLER, LOUISE. "The Instrumental Activities Inventory: A Technique for the Study of the Psychology of Acculturation." *Southw J Anthrop* 21:1–23 sp '65. *

3416. STARK, STANLEY. "An Essay on Romantic Genius, Rorschach Movement, and the Definition of Creativity." *Percept & Motor Skills* 20:409–18 Ag '65. * (*PA* 39:12325)

3417. STARK, STANLEY. "Rorschach Movement Responses and Psychosurgery: Cautionary Note." *Percept & Motor Skills* 21:329–30 Ag '65. *

3418. STARK, STANLEY. "Toward a Psychology of Knowledge: Hypotheses Regarding Rorschach Movement and Creativity." *Percept & Motor Skills* 21:839–59 D '65. * (*PA* 40:4264)

3419. STEWART, KENNETH D., and DEAN, WAID H. "Perceptual-Cognitive Behavior and Autonomic Nervous System Patterns." *Arch Gen Psychiatry* 12:329–35 Ap '65. * (*PA* 39:10328)

3420. SULTAN, E. E. "A Quantitative Investigation of the Rorschach Inkblot Test as Applied to Student Teachers." *Brit J Social & Clin Psychol* 4:197–206 S '65. * (*PA* 40:1578)

3421. TAKAHASHI, SHIGEO. "Card Order and Stimulus Value of Rorschach Inkblots." Abstract. *Percept & Motor Skills* 20:480 Ap '65. * (*PA* 39:12311)

3422. TAKAHASHI, SHIGEO. "A Comparative Factorial Analysis of Semantic Structures of Rorschach Inkblots in University Students and Juvenile Delinquents." *Jap Psychol Res* 7:69–74 Jl '65. * (*PA* 40:1607)

3423. TAMKIN, ARTHUR S. "Determinants of Rorschach Card Rejection: A Replication." *Newsl Res Psychol* 7:16–7 N '65. *

3424. TERRIS, JAMES E. *The Group Rorschach as a Predictor of Standing in Education I at the University of Manitoba.* Master's thesis, University of Manitoba (Winnipeg, Man., Canada), 1965.

3425. THOMAS, CAROLINE BEDELL; ROSS, DONALD C.; and FREED, ELLEN S. *An Index of Responses to the Group Rorschach Test: Studies on the Psychological Characteristics of Medical Students—II.* Baltimore, Md.: Johns Hopkins Press, 1965. Pp. xlv, 502. * (*PA* 40:12407)

3426. TURNER, DALE ROBERT. *Predictive Efficiency as a Function of Amount of Rorschach Information and Level of Professional Experience.* Doctor's thesis, University of Portland (Portland, Ore.), 1965.

3427. VARMA, SHASHILATA. "Discrepancy Between Future and Past Performances as a Measure of Ego-Strength." *J Psychol Res* 9:35–8 Ja '65. * (*PA* 39:10219)

3428. WAGNER, EDWIN E. "Exhibitionistic Human Movement Responses of Strippers: An Attempt to Validate the Rorschach M." *J Proj Tech & Pers Assess* 29:522–4 D '65. * (*PA* 40:2966)

3429. WEINER, IRVING B. "Follow-Up Validation of Rorschach Tempo and Color Use Indicators of Schizophrenia." *J Proj Tech & Pers Assess* 29:387–91 S '65. * (*PA* 39:15428)

3430. WEINER, IRVING B. "Rorschach Color Stress as a Schizophrenic Indicator—A Reply." *J Clin Psychol* 21:313–4 Jl '65. * (*PA* 39:15427)

3431. WEISS, A. A. "Psychodiagnostic Follow-up of Eight Cases of Temporal Lobectomy." *Israel Ann Psychiatry* 3:259–66 O '65. * (*PA* 41:1820)

3432. WHITAKER, LEIGHTON, JR. "The Rorschach and Holtzman as Measures of Pathognomic Verbalization." *J Consult Psychol* 29:181–3 Ap '65. * (*PA* 39:10275)

3433. WHITE, WILLIAM F., and WASH, JAMES A., JR. "Prediction of Successful College Academic Performance From Measures of Body-Cathexis, Self-Cathexis, and Anxiety." *Percept & Motor Skills* 20:431–2 Ap '65. * (*PA* 39:13026)

3434. WITT, EUGENE LESTER, JR. *The Connotative Meaning of Selected "Forced" Rorschach Percepts as Measured by the Semantic Differential Technique.* Doctor's thesis, University of Houston (Houston, Tex.), 1965. (*DA* 26:4083)

3435. YANG, KUO-SHU; CHEN, WEN-YEN; and HSU, CHING-YUANG. "Rorschach Responses of Normal Chinese Adults: 4, The Speed of Production." *Acta Psychologica Taiwanica* 7:34–51 Mr '65. * (*PA* 39:14893)

3436. ZIMET, CARL N., and FINE, HAROLD J. "Primary and Secondary Process Thinking in Two Types of Schizophrenia." *J Proj Tech & Pers Assess* 29:93–9 Mr '65. * (*PA* 39:10673)

3437. ZUBIN, JOSEPH; ERON, LEONARD D.; and SCHUMER, FLORENCE. *An Experimental Approach to Projective Techniques,* pp. 166–393, passim. New York and London: John Wiley & Sons, Inc., 1965. Pp. xxi, 645. * (*PA* 39:15432)

3438. ABRAMSON, YITZCHOK, and RYCHLAK, JOSEPH F. "A Sociocultural Content Interpretation of Rorschach's Experience Balance." *J Proj Tech & Pers Assess* 30:407–14 O '66. * (*PA* 41:593)

3439. ALLEN, THOMAS WAKEFIELD. *Counselors in Training: A Study of Role Effectiveness as a Function of Psychological Openness.* Doctor's thesis, Harvard University (Cambridge, Mass.), 1966. (*DA* 27:4099A)

3440. AMES, LOUISE BATES. "Changes in Rorschach Response Throughout the Human Life Span." *Genetic Psychol Monogr* 74:89–125 Ag '66. * (*PA* 40:12349)

3441. AMES, LOUISE BATES; assisted by JUDITH AUGUST, "Rorschach Responses of Negro and White 5- to 10-Year-Olds." *J Genetic Psychol* 109:297–309 D '66. * (*PA* 41:4617)

3442. AMIR, YEHUDA; KOHEN-RAZ, REUVEN; and RABINOWITZ, GALIA. "The Effect of Non-Personality Factors on Ink-Blot Responses in a Cross Cultural Study." *J Proj Tech & Pers Assess* 30:247–9 Je '66. * (*PA* 40:10126)

3443. BAHNSON, CLAUS BAHNE, and BAHNSON, MARJORIE BROOKS. "Role of the Ego Defenses: Denial and Repression in the Etiology of Malignant Neoplasm." *Ann N Y Acad Sci* 125:827–45 Ja 21 '66. *

3444. BECK, SAMUEL J. Chap. 32, "The Rorschach Test, Communication, and Psychotherapy," pp. 551–72. In *Methods of Research in Psychotherapy.* Edited by Louis A. Gottshalk and Arthur H. Auerbach. New York: Appleton-Century-Crofts, 1966. Pp. xviii, 654. *

3445. BECK, SAMUEL J. "Emotions and Understanding." *Int Psychiatry Clin* 3:93–114 sp '66. *

3446. BENFARI, ROBERT. "Defense and Control: Further Indications." *Percept & Motor Skills* 22:736–8 Je '66. * (*PA* 40:10673)

3447. BLATT, BENJAMIN, and TSUSHIMA, WILLIAM. "A Psychological Study of Uremic Patients Being Considered for the Artificial Kidney Machine Program (Hemodialysis)." *Newsl Res Psychol* 8:17–8 F '66. *

3448. BORDIN, EDWARD S. "Personality and Free Association." *J Consult Psychol* 30:30–8 F '66. * (*PA* 40:4227)

3449. BOREHAM, JOHN. "Rorschach Test Prediction of Response to Psychotherapy." *Rorsch Newsl* 11:7–13 D '66. * (*PA* 42:763)

3450. BOURNE, GWEN. "The Cardiac Psychosis: A Case Study of Depersonalization Following Open Heart Surgery, Showing, by Use of the Rorschach, the Later Re-integration of the Ego." *Rorsch Newsl* 11:14–20 D '66. * (*PA* 42:764)

3451. BRAWER, FLORENCE B., and COHEN, ARTHUR M. "Global and Sign Approaches to Rorschach Assessment of Beginning Teachers." *J Proj Tech & Pers Assess* 30:536–42 D '66. * (*PA* 41:2904)

3452. CASSELL, WILFRED A. "A Tachistoscopic Index of Body Perception I Body Boundary and Body Interior Awareness." *J Proj Tech & Pers Assess* 30:31–6 F '66. * (*PA* 40:4774)

3453. CLARK, WARREN DONALD. *Quantification of Rorschach Content and Verbalizations to Predict Degree of Depression in Young Depressed Women.* Doctor's thesis, Rutgers—The State University (New Brunswick, N.J.), 1966. (*DA* 27:299B)

3454. CRUMPTON, EVELYN, and GROOT, HENRIETTE. "The 'Meaning' of Rorschach Color Cards as a Function of Color." *J Proj Tech & Pers Assess* 30:359–63 Ag '66. * (*PA* 40:12351)

3455. CRUMPTON, EVELYN, and GROOT, HENRIETTE. "Stimulus Value of Color on the Rorschach Color Cards." *News Res Psychol* 8:22–3 F '66. *

3456. DANA, RICHARD H., and HOPEWELL, ELEANOR. "Repression and Psychopathology: A Cross-Validation Failure." *Psychol Rep* 19:626 O '66. * (*PA* 41:578)

3457. DAVIDSON, HELEN H.; GREENBERG, JUDITH W.; and ALSHAN, LEONARD. "The Identification of Caution: A Correlate of Achievement Functioning." *J Proj Tech & Pers Assess* 30:381–4 Ag '66. * (*PA* 40:12352)

3458. DE LUCA, JOSEPH N. "The Structure of Homosexuality." *J Proj Tech & Pers Assess* 30:187–91 Ap '66. * (*PA* 40:7607)

3459. DESSAUER, BONNIE LIBBIN. *The M Component of the Rorschach as an Indicator of the Intellect.* Doctor's thesis, University of Oklahoma (Norman, Okla.), 1966. (*DA* 27:1279B)

3460. DOBBS, DARREL D., and GRIFFITH, RICHARD M. "An Experimental Manipulation of Rorschach Form: The Effect of Making Indistinct the Ambiguous." *J Consult Psychol* 30:151–7 Ap '66. * (*PA* 40:6663)

3461. DRAKE, ANN K., and RUSNAK, ALAN W. "An Indicator of Suicidal Ideation on the Rorschach: A Replication." *J Proj Tech & Pers Assess* 30:543–4 D '66. * (*PA* 41:2909)

3462. EFRON, HERMAN Y., and PIOTROWSKI, ZYGMUNT A. "A Factor Analytic Study of the Rorschach Prognostic Index." *J Proj Tech & Pers Assess* 30:179–83 Ap '66. * (*PA* 40:7727)

3463. EHRENWALD, JAN. "The Visual Distortion Test: A Study in Experimental Psychiatry." *Psychiatric Q* 40:429–48 Jl '66. * (*PA* 41:1735)

3464. EISENMAN, RUSSELL; BERNARD, J. L.; and HANNON, JOHN E. "Benevolence, Potency, and God: A Semantic Differential Study of the Rorschach." *Percept & Motor Skills* 22:75–8 F '66. * (*PA* 40:4748)

3465. ELKAN, GEOFFREY. "Serial Rorschach and Cognitive Tests in a Case of Mild Brain Injury: 'Robin' (Tested 5 Times Between the Ages of 16 and 21)." *Rorsch Newsl* 11:15–22 Je '66. * (*PA* 40:11411, title only)

3466. EVANS, RAY B., and MARMORSTON, JESSIE. "Race and Rorschach Signs of Brain Damage in Cerebral Thrombosis." *Percept & Motor Skills* 22:655–62 Ap '66. * (*PA* 40:8998)

3467. EXNER, JOHN E., JR. *A Workbook in the Rorschach*

Technique Emphasizing the Beck and Klopfer Systems. Springfield, Ill.: Charles C Thomas, Publisher, 1966. Pp. viii, 113. *

3468. FISHER, RHODA LEE. "Body Boundary and Achievement Behavior." *J Proj Tech & Pers Assess* 30:435–8 O '66. * (*PA* 41:598)

3469. FISHER, RHODA LEE. "Failure of the Conceptual Styles Test to Discriminate Normal and Highly Impulsive Children." *J Abn & Social Psychol* 71:429–31 D '66. * (*PA* 41:1423)

3470. GAYLIN, NED L. "Psychotherapy and Psychological Health: A Rorschach Function and Structure Analysis." *J Consult Psychol* 30:494–500 D '66. * (*PA* 41:2910)

3471. GEORGE, JANE, and PREMA, P. "Thought Disturbances of the Schizophrenics on Rorschach." *Trans All-India Inst Mental Health* 6:79–84 D '66. *

3472. GILL, H. S. "Delay of Response and Reaction to Color on the Rorschach." *J Proj Tech & Pers Assess* 30:545–52 D '66. * (*PA* 41:2911)

3473. GOLDBERG, LEWIS R., and WERTS, CHARLES E. "The Reliability of Clinicians' Judgments: A Multitrait-Multimethod Approach." *J Consult Psychol* 30:199–206 Je '66. * (*PA* 40:8999)

3474. GOLDFRIED, MARVIN R. "The Assessment of Anxiety by Means of the Rorschach." *J Proj Tech & Pers Assess* 30:364–80 Ag '66. * (*PA* 40:12353)

3475. GOLDFRIED, MARVIN R. "On the Diagnosis of Homosexuality From the Rorschach." *J Consult Psychol* 30:338–49 Ag '66. * (*PA* 40:11172)

3476. HAMMER, EMANUEL F. "Personality Patterns in Young Creative Artists." *Adolescence* 1:327–50 w '66–67. * (*PA* 42:748)

3477. HAMMER, MAX. "A Comparison of Responses by Clinic and Normal Adults to Rorschach Card III Human Figure Area." *J Proj Tech & Pers Assess* 30:161–2 Ap '66. * (*PA* 40:7729)

3478. HARGADON, KEVIN. "Psychological Requirements for Religious Vocations." *Nat Cath Guid Conf J* 10:271–9 su '66. *

3479. HARTLAGE, LAWRENCE. "Common Psychological Tests Applied to the Assessment of Brain Damage." *J Proj Tech & Pers Assess* 30:319–38 Ag '66. * (*PA* 40:12451)

3480. HIRSCHENFANG, SAMUEL, and BENTON, JOSEPH G. "Rorschach Responses of Paraplegic and Quadriplegic Patients." *Paraplegia* 4:40–2 My '66. *

3481. HOLT, ROBERT R. "Measuring Libidinal and Aggressive Motives and Their Controls by Means of the Rorschach Test," pp. 1–48. (*PA* 41:15307) In *Nebraska Symposium on Motivation, 1966.* Edited by David Levine. Lincoln, Neb.: University of Nebraska Press, 1966. Pp. ix, 209. *

3482. ICHIMURA, JUN. "Ten Year Follow-Up Study on the Early Prediction of Juvenile Delinquency by Means of the Rorschach Test." *Jap Psychol Res* 8:151–60 D '66. * (*PA* 41:16718)

3483. JACKSON, C. WESLEY, JR., and WOHL, JULIAN. "A Survey of Rorschach Teaching in the University." *J Proj Tech & Pers Assess* 30:115–34 Ap '66. * (*PA* 40:7172)

3484. JONES, JENNIE. "Characteristic Rorschach Records: 2, A Case of Long-Standing Schizophrenia in a Young Man of 22 (Mr. L. P. 30.8.63)." *Rorsch Newsl* 11:26–31 D '66. *

3485. KALDEGG, A. "Interaction Testing: An Engaged Couple of Drug Addicts Tested Separately and Together." *J Proj Tech & Pers Assess* 30:77–87 F '66. * (*PA* 40:5672)

3486. KAMANO, DENNIS K., and CRAWFORD, CAROLE S. "Self-Evaluations of Suicidal Mental Hospital Patients." *J Clin Psychol* 22:278–9 Jl '66. * (*PA* 41:11305)

3487. KENDRICK, SHERRILL R. *A Comparison of Certain Rorschach Indices Between Successful and Unsuccessful Students.* Master's thesis, North Texas State University (Denton, Tex.), 1966.

3488. KINSLINGER, HOWARD J. "Application of Projective Techniques in Personnel Psychology Since 1940." *Psychol B* 66:134–49 Ag '66. * (*PA* 40:11520)

3489. KLEINMAN, ROGER A., and HIGGINS, JERRY. "Sex of Respondent and Rorschach M Production." *J Proj Tech & Pers Assess* 30:439–40 O '66. * (*PA* 41:602)

3490. KNUDSEN, ANN K.; GORHAM, DONALD R.; and MOSELEY, EDWARD C. "Universal Popular Responses to Inkblots in Five Cultures: Denmark, Germany, Hong Kong, Mexico and United States." *J Proj Tech & Pers Assess* 30:135–42 Ap '66. * (*PA* 40:7731)

3491. KO, YUNG-HO, and YU, WEN-YUAN. "A Scoring System for the Evaluation of Degree of Mental Illness Through the Rorschach Responses." *Acta Psychologica Taiwanica* 8:17–28 Mr '66. * (*PA* 40:11174)

3492. KOHEN-RAZ, R., and ASSAEL, MARCEL. "EEG and Rorschach Findings in a Group of Juvenile Delinquents Suspect of Organic Brain Disorder." *Acta Paedopsychiatrica* 33:251–8 Ag '66. * (*PA* 41:687)

3493. KUMAR, P. "Rorschach Research With Mental Hospital Patients in an Indian Community." *Rorsch Newsl* 11:21–2 D '66. * (*PA* 42:649)

3494. LAMB, CHARLES WILLIAM. *Forms of Need for Variety: Differential Expression Following Arousal and Boredom.* Doctor's thesis, Ohio State University (Columbus, Ohio), 1966. (*DA* 27:3289B)

3495. LANG, ALFRED, Editor. *Rorschach-Bibliographie,*

Bibliographie Rorschach, Rorschach Bibliography, 1921–1964. Berne, Switzerland: Hans Huber, 1966. Pp. 191. *

3496. LERNER, BARBARA. "Rorschach Movement and Dreams: A Validation Study Using Drug-Induced Dream-Deprivation." *J Abn Psychol* 71:75–86 Ap '66. * (*PA* 40:6668)

3497. LEVINSON, BORIS M. "Subcultural Studies of Homeless Men." *Trans N Y Acad Sci* 29:165–82 D '66. * (*PA* 41:16683)

3498. LONG, ELEANOR, and MIEZITIS, SOLVEIGA. "Prediction of Aggressiveness in School Children From Clusters of Signs on the Rorschach Test." *Ont J Ed Res* 8:261–6 sp '66. * (*PA* 40:10133)

3499. LYTTON, H. "Children's Expression of Like-Dislike and Their Responses to Color in the Rorschach." *J Proj Tech & Pers Assess* 30:51–3 F '66. * (*PA* 40:5492)

3500. McREYNOLDS, PAUL. "A Comparison of Normals and Schizophrenics on a New Scale of the Rorschach CET." *J Proj Tech & Pers Assess* 30:262–4 Je '66. * (*PA* 40:9440)

3501. McREYNOLDS, PAUL. "The Concept Evaluation Technique: A Survey of Research." *J General Psychol* 74:217–30 Ap '66. * (*PA* 40:7197)

3502. MARGOSHES, ADAM, and LITT, SHELDON. "Projective Imagery in Shakespeare." *J Proj Tech & Pers Assess* 30:290–2 Je '66. * (*PA* 40:10134)

3503. MASLING, JOSEPH, and LEWIS, PHILIP. "The Social Psychology of the Use of Psychological Tests to Predict Brain Damage." *J Proj Tech & Pers Assess* 30:415–7 O '66. * (*PA* 41:581)

3504. MISCH, ROBERT C. "Impulse Control and Social Feeling." *Int Psychiatry Clin* 3:117–37 sp '66. *

3505. MUKHERJEE, KAMAL, and MAITRA, AMAL K. "Movement Responses in the Rorschach Protocols of Juvenile and Adult Offenders." *B Council of Social & Psychol Res* 6:5–11 Ja '66. * (*PA* 40:13210)

3506. MURPHY, H. B. "Personality and the Vermiform Appendix." *J Health & Hum Behav* 7:153–62 f '66. * (*PA* 40:13216)

3507. MURRAY, JOSEPH D., and RYCHLAK, JOSEPH F. "Healthy, Neutral, and Unhealthy Content in the Rorschach Responses of Schizophrenic and Normal Adults." *J Proj Tech & Pers Assess* 30:254–61 Je '66. * (*PA* 40:10135)

3508. NICKOLS, JOHN. "Self-Image Ratings of Normal and Disturbed Subjects." *J Health & Hum Behav* 7:28–36 sp '66. * (*PA* 40:7916)

3509. ORLINSKY, DAVID E. "Rorschach Test Correlates of Dreaming and Dream Recall." *J Proj Tech & Pers Assess* 30:250–3 Je '66. * (*PA* 40:10137)

3510. ORME, J. E. "A Further Comment on Weiner's Rorschach Color Indicators." *J Clin Psychol* 22:223 Ap '66. * (*PA* 40:7734)

3511. PATI, G. "Personality Pathology of the Delinquents." *Psychol Studies* 11:35–41 Ja '66. * (*PA* 40:6826)

3512. PEEBLES, RICHARD R. "Individual Differences in Childhood and Adolescence." *Int Psychiatry Clin* 3:163–201 sp '66. *

3513. PIOTROWSKI, ZYGMUNT A. "Evaluation of Outcome in Schizophrenia (The Long-Term Prognostic Test Index)." *Proc Am Psychopath Assn* 54:312–34 '66. *

3514. PRATAP, SARLA, and FILELLA, JAMES. "Rorschach Correlates of the Taylor's Manifest Anxiety Scale for a Group of Normal People." *J Psychol Res* 10:103–9 S '66. * (*PA* 41:7327)

3515. SARASON, IRWIN G. *Personality: An Objective Approach,* pp. 183–95, passim. New York: John Wiley & Sons, Inc., 1966. Pp. xvi, 670. *

3516. SCHACHTEL, ERNEST G. *Experiential Foundations of Rorschach's Test.* New York: Basic Books, Inc., Publishers, 1966. Pp. ix, 342. * (*PA* 40:13214, title only)

3517. SCHUBERT, JOSEF. "A Statistical Analysis of Rorschachs on Adolescent Approved School Girls." *Rorsch Newsl* 11:3–13 Je '66. * (*PA* 40:11178, title only)

3518. SHANKER, PREM. "Education and Rorschach Intelligence Factors of the Harijans." *Archivio di Psicologia Neurologia e Psichiatria* 27:167–75 Mr–Ap '66. * (*PA* 40:9975)

3519. SINGER, JEROME L. "Daydreaming and Planful Thought: A Note on Professor Stark's Conceptual Framework." *Percept & Motor Skills* 23:113–4 Ag '66. * (*PA* 40:11868)

3520. SINGER, MARGARET T., and WYNNE, LYMAN C. "Principles for Scoring Communication Defects and Deviances in Parents of Schizophrenics: Rorschach and TAT Scoring Manuals." *Psychiatry* 29:260–88 Ag '66. * (*PA* 41:10489)

3521. SINGER, MARGARET THALER, and WYNNE, LYMAN C. "Communication Styles in Parents of Normals, Neurotics, and Schizophrenics: Some Findings Using a New Rorschach Scoring Manual." Discussion by Stephen Fleck. *Psychiatric Res Rep Am Psychiatric Assn* 20:25–40 Ja '66. *

3522. SPRINTHALL, NORMAN A.; WHITELEY, JOHN M.; and MOSHER, RALPH L. "A Study of Teacher Effectiveness." *J Teach Ed* 17:93–106 sp '66. * (*PA* 40:9264, title only)

3523. STARK, STANLEY. "Autistic Thinking and Psychosurgery: A Conceptual Suggestion." *Psychol Rep* 18:247–50 F '66. * (*PA* 40:6339)

3524. STARK, STANLEY. "Role-Taking, Empathic Imagination, and Rorschach Human Movement Responses: A Review of Two Literatures." *Percept & Motor Skills* 23:243–56 Ag '66. * (*PA* 40:12337)

3525. STARK, STANLEY. "Rorschach Movement, Fantastic Daydreaming, and Freud's Concept of Primary Process: Interpretive Commentary." *Percept & Motor Skills* 22:523-32 Ap '66. * *(PA* 40:8879)

3526. STARK, STANLEY. "Toward a Psychology of Knowledge: 2, Two Kinds of Foresight and Foresight Theorizing." *Percept & Motor Skills* 23:547-74 O '66. * *(PA* 41:251)

3527. STELLERN, JOHN T. *The Susceptibility of the Rorschach Test to Faking.* Doctor's research study No. 1, Colorado State College (Greeley, Colo.), 1966. *(DA* 27:2146B)

3528. STERNBERG, DAVID, and SCHIFF, STANLEY. "Reality Checking Ability and Cognitive Functioning in Functional Psychiatric Disorders." *Psychiatric Q Sup* 40:306-14 pt 2 '66. * *(PA* 41:16823)

3529. TAKAHASHI, SHIGEO, and ZAX, MELVIN. "The Stimulus Value of Rorschach Inkblots: A Comparison of Japanese and American Students." *Jap Psychol Res* 8:38-45 My '66. * *(PA* 40:11180)

3530. TAKALA, K. Chap. 12, "Psychological Investigation and Its Results," pp. 444-525. In *The Family in the Pathogenesis of Schizophrenic and Neurotic Disorders.* By Yrjö O. Alanen and others. Acta Psychiatrica Scandinavica Supplementum 189. Copenhagen, Denmark: Munksgaard Ltd., 1966. Pp. 654. *

3531. TAMKIN, ARTHUR S. "The Determinants of Rorschach Card Rejection: A Replication." *J Clin Psychol* 22:469-70 O '66. * *(PA* 41:2925)

3532. TAMKIN, ARTHUR S. "Some Determinants of Rorschach Productivity." *Newsl Res Psychol* 8:2-3 N '66. *

3533. TAMKIN, ARTHUR S. "Some Determinants of Rorschach Productivity." *Newsl Res Psychol* 8:6-7 Ag '66. *

3534. TAMKIN, ARTHUR S., and SONKIN, NATHAN. "Personality Factors in Psychogenic Somatic Complaints." *Newsl Res Psychol* 8:20-1 F '66. *

3535. THUNE, JEANNE; TINE, SEBASTIAN; and CHERRY, NANCY. "Personality Characteristics of Successful Older Leaders." *J Gerontol* 21:463-70 Jl '66. *

3536. TSUJI, SHOZO, and KATO, NORIAKI. "Some Investigations of Parental Preference in Early Childhood: An Attempt to Obtain a Correspondence of Verbally Expressed Preference With Projectively Expressed Preference." *Jap Psychol Res* 8:10-7 My '66. * *(PA* 40:11027)

3537. TURNER, DALE R. "Predictive Efficiency as a Function of Amount of Information and Level of Professional Experience." *J Proj Tech & Pers Assess* 30:4-11 F '66. * *(PA* 40:5499)

3538. VERMA, S. K., and KUMAR, P. "Cross-Validation of an Objective Rorschach." *Indian J Psychol* 41:45-50 S '66. *

3539. VOIGT, WALTER H. "Personality Variables in Rorschach Scoring." *J Proj Tech & Pers Assess* 30:153-7 Ap '66. * *(PA* 40:7740)

3540. WAGNER, EDWIN E. "The Imaginary Lovers Delusion: A Diagnostic Case Study." *J Proj Tech & Pers Assess* 30:394-400 Ag '66. * *(PA* 40:12532)

3541. WARD, ALAN J. "The Meaning of the Movement Response and of Its Changes During Therapy: A Review." *J Proj Tech & Pers Assess* 30:418-28 O '66. * *(PA* 41:605)

3542. WEINER, IRVING B. *Psychodiagnosis in Schizophrenia.* New York: John Wiley & Sons, Inc., 1966. Pp. xiv, 573. * *(PA* 41:4753)

3543. WILCOX, RONALD M., and KRASNOFF, ALAN G. "Social Desirability and Multiple Choice Rorschach Responses." *J Clin Psychol* 22:61-5 Ja '66. * *(PA* 40:4266)

3544. WILK, XAVIER G. *Personality Differences Between the Underachievers and Overachievers According to Rorschach.* Master's thesis, St. Bonaventure University (St. Bonaventure, N.Y.), 1966.

3545. WRIGHT, NANCY A., and ZUBEK, JOHN P. "Use of the Multiple Discriminant Function in the Prediction of Perceptual Deprivation Tolerance." *Can J Psychol* 20:105-13 Mr '66. * *(PA* 40:6647)

3546. ZELEN, SEYMOUR L.; FOX, JACK; GOULD, EDWARD; and OLSON, RAY W. "Sex-Contingent Differences Between Male and Female Alcoholics." *J Clin Psychol* 22:160-5 Ap '66. * *(PA* 40:7873)

3547. ZIMMERMAN, IRLA LEE; LAMBERT, NADINE M.; and CLASS, LORETTA. "A Comparison of Children's Perceptions of Rorschach Cards III, IV and VII With Independent Ratings of Parental Adequacy, and Effectiveness of School Behavior." *Psychol Sch* 3:258-63 Jl '66. * *(PA* 41:1937)

3548. ZUERCHER, MARY C. *The Rorschach in Adolescence: A Longitudinal Study of Intellectually Superior Girls.* Master's thesis, Loyola University (Chicago, Ill.), 1966.

3549. AMES, LOUISE B., and ILG, FRANCES L. "Search for Children Showing Academic Promise in a Predominantly Negro School." *J Genetic Psychol* 110:217-31 Je '67. * *(PA* 41:11732)

3550. ARUNDALE, NALINI, and CHANDRA, SRI. "A Rorschach Study of Doctors." *Psychologia* 10:97-100 Je '67. * *(PA* 42:3984)

3551. AXTELL, BRYAN A., and HAASE, RICHARD F. "Expected Values of W, D, and Dd for Beck's Approach Score." *J Clin Psychol* 23:116-7 Ja '67. * *(PA* 41:5982)

3552. BAKAN, PAUL, and BROWN, RICHARD A. "On the Attention—Demand Value of Rorschach Stimuli." *J Proj Tech & Pers Assess* 31:3-6 Je '67. * *(PA* 41:3662)

3553. BAUGHMAN, E. EARL. "The Problem of the Stimulus

in Rorschach's Test." *J Proj Tech & Pers Assess* 31:23-5 O '67. * *(PA* 42:762)

3554. BECK, NORMA. *The Meaning of the Rorschach Cards for Children.* Doctor's thesis, St. John's University (Jamaica, N.Y.), 1967. *(DA* 28:4278B)

3555. BECK, SAMUEL J., and MOLISH, HERMAN B. *Rorschach's Test: 2, A Variety of Personality Pictures, Second Edition.* New York: Grune & Stratton, Inc., 1967. Pp. viii, 440. *

3556. BLOCK, WILLIAM E. "Adaptation Effects in Rorschach Testing and Their Theoretical Explanation." *Int Congr Rorsch & Proj Meth* 6(2):201-7 '67. *

3557. BOREHAM, JOHN. "The Prediction of Suicide." *Rorsch Newsl* 12:5-7 D '67. * *(PA* 42:17417)

3558. BOWYER, RUTH. "The Teaching of the Rorschach: 1, Teaching the Rorschach to Undergraduates Studying Experimental and Social Psychology." *Rorsch Newsl* 12:35-7 Je '67. * *(PA* 42:4592, title only)

3559. BOWYER, RUTH. "The Teaching of the Rorschach: 2, Teaching the Rorschach to M.Ed. Students." *Rorsch Newsl* 12:17-21 D '67. * *(PA* 42:16334)

3560. BOYER, L. BRYCE; BOYER, RUTH M.; KAWAI, HAYAO; and KLOPFER, BRUNO. "Apache 'Learners' and 'Nonlearners.'" *J Proj Tech & Pers Assess* 31:22-9 D '67. * *(PA* 42:5407)

3561. BROWN, L. B., and FERNALD, L. DODGE, JR. "Questionnaire Anxiety." *Psychol Rep* 21:537-40 O '67. * *(PA* 42:5593)

3562. BURNAND, G.; HUNTER, H.; and HOGGART, K. "Some Psychological Test Characteristics of Klinefelter's Syndrome." *Brit J Psychiatry* 113:1091-6 O '67. * *(PA* 42:7632)

3563. CLAEYS, WILLEM. "Conforming Behavior and Personality Variables in Congolese Students." *Int J Psychol* 2(1):13-23 '67. * *(PA* 41:10427)

3564. COLE, SPURGEON; WILLIAMS, ROGERT L.; and BOLEN, LARRY. "Symbolic Meaning of Card II." *Percept & Motor Skills* 24:66 F '67. * *(PA* 41:8930)

3565. COLEMAN, JOHN C. "Stimulus Factors in the Relation Between Fantasy and Behavior." *J Proj Tech & Pers Assess* 31:68-73 F '67. * *(PA* 41:13665)

3566. COOK, BARBARA FIETH. "An Approach to Use of Color on the Rorschach Through Individual Color Preferences." *J Proj Tech & Pers Assess* 31:48-53 Ag '67. * *(PA* 41:15304)

3567. COVEY, DIXIE SCOWCROFT. *Children's Rorschach Responses in Holiday Settings.* Master's thesis, University of Utah (Salt Lake City, Utah), 1967.

3568. DARBY, JOEL; HOFMAN, KEES; and MELNICK, BARRY. "Response Inhibition and the Rorschach 'M' Response." *J Proj Tech & Pers Assess* 31:29-30 O '67. * *(PA* 42:767)

3569. DASTON, PAUL G. "Applicability of a Rorschach Sign Approach to a British Suicide." *Rorsch Newsl* 12:19-20 Je '67. * *(PA* 42:3985)

3570. DE LUCA, JOSEPH N. "The Dynamic Structure of Homosexuality, Impotency, Exhibitionism, Pedophilia, Premature Ejaculation and Enuresis as Revealed by the Rorschach." *Int Congr Rorsch & Proj Meth* 6(1):115-7 '67. *

3571. DERMAN, BRUCE IRVIN. *Adaptive Versus Pathological Regression in Relation to Psychological Adjustment.* Doctor's thesis, University of Georgia (Athens, Ga.), 1967. *(DA* 28:4754B)

3572. DRAGUNS, JURIS G.; HALEY, E. MARIE; and PHILLIPS, LESLIE. "Studies of Rorschach Content: A Review of the Research Literature: Part 1, Traditional Content Categories." *J Proj Tech & Pers Assess* 31:3-32 F '67. * *(PA* 41:13666)

3573. EASTON, KAY, and FEIGENBAUM, KENNETH. "An Examination of an Experimental Set to Fake the Rorschach Test." *Percept & Motor Skills* 24:871-4 Je '67. * *(PA* 41:12985)

3574. EBLE, SELMA J. "A Guideline of Children's Popular Responses on the Group Zulliger Inkblot Test." *J Clin Psychol* 23:494-5 O '67. * *(PA* 42:2606)

3575. FAST, IRENE, and BROEDEL, JOHN W. "Intimacy and Distance in the Interpersonal Relationships of Persons Prone to Depression." *J Proj Tech & Pers Assess* 31:7-12 D '67. * *(PA* 42:5798)

3576. FEIRSTEIN, ALAN. "Personality Correlates of Tolerance for Unrealistic Experiences." *J Consult Psychol* 31:387-95 Ag '67. * *(PA* 41:13667)

3577. FISHER, SEYMOUR. "Projective Methodologies," pp. 166-76. *Ann R Psychol* 18:165-90 '67. * *(PA* 42:3986)

3578. FORREST, D. W., and DIMOND, S. J. "Association Between Galvanic Skin Response and Rorschach Performance." *Psychosom Med* 29:676-82 N-D '67. * *(PA* 42:10613)

3579. FRANK, GEORGE H. "A Review of Research With Measures of Ego Strength Derived From the MMPI and the Rorschach." *J General Psychol* 77:183-206 O '67. * *(PA* 42:770)

3580. GEORGAS, JAMES G., and VASSILIOU, VASSO. "A Normative Rorschach Study of Athenians." *J Proj Tech & Pers Assess* 31:31-8 Ag '67. * *(PA* 41:15305)

3581. GILL, WAYNE S. "Animal Content in the Rorschach." *J Proj Tech & Pers Assess* 31:49-56 Ap '67. * *(PA* 41:13669)

3582. GRISSO, J. THOMAS, and MEADOW, ARNOLD. "Test Interference in a Rorschach-WAIS Administration Sequence." *J Consult Psychol* 31:382-6 Ag '67. * *(PA* 41:13617)

3583. HAASE, RICHARD F., and AXTELL, BRYAN. "The Relationship of Rorschach F+% to Intelligence in College Students." *Psychol* 4:52–6 N '67. *

3584. HALEY, E. MARIE; DRAGUNS, JURIS G.; and PHILLIPS, LESLIE. "Studies of Rorschach Content: A Review of Research Literature: Part 2, Non-Traditional Uses of Content Indicators." *J Proj Tech & Pers Assess* 31:3–38 Ap '67. * (*PA* 41:13672)

3585. HEATH, HELEN A.; OKEN, DONALD; and SHIPMAN, WILLIAM G. "Muscle Tension and Personality: A Serious Second Look." *Arch Gen Psychiatry* 16:720–6 Je '67. * (*PA* 41:13932)

3586. HECKLER, VICTOR J. *The Inter- and Intrarater Reliability of the Rorschach Defense Checklist.* Master's thesis, Loyola College (Chicago, Ill.), 1967.

3587. HERDT, BERYL F. *The Relationship Between the Human Movement Factor in the Rorschach and Overt Motor Activity.* Doctor's thesis, St. John's University (Collegeville, Minn.), 1967. (*DA* 28:1163B)

3588. HOLLEY, J. W., and FRÖBARJ, G. "A Demonstration Study on the Validity of the Rorschach Test." *B Int Assn Appl Psychol* 16:30–50 sp '67. *

3589. HOLT, ROBERT R. "Discussion: On Using Experiential Data in Personality Assessment." *J Proj Tech & Pers Assess* 31:25–30 Ag '67. * (*PA* 41:15344)

3590. JAIN, K. S. PRABHACHANDRA, and PARIKH, BINDU S. "Linearity in Relations Between Sum R and Other Rorschach Score Variables: A Normative Study." *J General Psychol* 77:259–61 O '67. * (*PA* 42:772)

3591. JURJEVICH, R. M. "Hostility and Anxiety Indices on the Rorschach Content Test, Hostility Guilt Index, and the MMPI." *Psychol Rep* 21:128 Ag '67. * (*PA* 42:2608, title only)

3592. KAHN, MARVIN W. "Correlates of Rorschach Reality Adherence in the Assessment of Murderers Who Plead Insanity." *J Proj Tech & Pers Assess* 31:44–7 Ag '67. * (*PA* 41:15308)

3593. KAHN, PAUL. "Time Span and Rorschach Human Movement Responses." *J Consult Psychol* 31:92–3 F '67. * (*PA* 41:4620)

3594. KAPLAN, MARVIN L. "Ego Impairment and Ego Adaptation in Schizophrenia." *J Proj Tech & Pers Assess* 31:7–17 Je '67. * (*PA* 41:13981)

3595. KIKUCHI, TETSUHIKO, and SHIRAHATA, ETSUKO. "Single-Dosage of Chlorpromazine and Rorschach Performance." *Tohoku Psychologica Folia* 26(1–2):51–65 '67. * (*PA* 42:13791)

3596. KLEINMUNTZ, BENJAMIN. *Personality Measurement: An Introduction,* pp. 262–92. Homewood, Ill.: Dorsey Press, 1967. Pp. xiii, 463. *

3597. KURZ, RONALD B., and CAPONE, THOMAS A. "Cognitive Level, Role-Taking Ability and the Rorschach Human Movement Response." *Percept & Motor Skills* 24:657–8 Ap '67. * (*PA* 41:10220)

3598. LESTER, DAVID. "Attempted Suicide and Body Image." *J Psychol* 66:287–90 Jl '67. * (*PA* 41:13906)

3599. LEVENDAL, LÁZLÓ; MEZEI, ÁRPÁD; NEMES, LIVIA; and MEZEI-ERDÉLY, EVA. "Some Data Concerning the Personality Structure of Alcoholic Patients." *Brit J Addict* 62:317–30 D '67. *

3600. LOHRENZ, LEANDER J., and GARDNER, RILEY W. "The Mayman Form-Level Scoring Method: Scorer Reliability and Correlates of Form Level." *J Proj Tech & Pers Assess* 31:39–43 Ag '67. * (*PA* 41:15312)

3601. LOVELAND, NATHENE. "The Relation Rorschach: A Technique for Studying Interaction." *J Nerv & Mental Dis* 145:93–105 Ag '67. * (*PA* 42:3989)

3602. LOWE, C. MARSHALL. "Prediction of Posthospital Work Adjustment by the Use of Psychological Tests." *J Counsel Psychol* 14:248–52 My '67. * (*PA* 41:9197)

3603. LYONS, JOSEPH. "Whose Experience?" *J Proj Tech & Pers Assess* 31:11–6 Ag '67. * (*PA* 41:15313)

3604. MABRY-HALL, MARIE. "Aberrant Rorschach Perceptions of Alcoholics." *Q J Studies Alcohol* 28:255–66 Je '67. * (*PA* 42:907)

3605. McARTHUR, CHARLES. "The Contagious Poisson Distribution of Rorschach Scores." *J Proj Tech & Pers Assess* 31:34–44 D '67. * (*PA* 42:4781)

3606. McCULLY, ROBERT S. "Process Analysis: A Tool in Understanding Ambiguity in Diagnostic Problems in Rorschach." *Int Congr Rorsch & Proj Meth* 6(1):71–81 '67. *

3607. MAGNUSSEN, MAX G. "Effect of Test Order Upon Children's Rorschach Animal Content." *J Proj Tech & Pers Assess* 31:41–3 F '67. * (*PA* 41:13681)

3608. MAGNUSSEN, MAX G., and COLE, JAMES K. "Further Evidence of the Rorschach Card Stimulus Values for Children: A Partial Replication (and Generalizations)." *J Proj Tech & Pers Assess* 31:44–7 F '67. * (*PA* 41:13682)

3609. MALMQUIST, CARL P.; KIRESUK, THOMAS J.; and SPANO, ROBERT M. "Mothers With Multiple Illegitimacies." *Psychiatric Q* 41:339–54 Ap '67. * (*PA* 42:4189)

3610. MANN, NANCY A. "The Relationship Between Defense Preference and Response to Free Association." *J Proj Tech & Pers Assess* 31:54–61 Ag '67. * (*PA* 41:15292)

3611. MASLING, JOSEPH; RABIE, LILLIE; and BLONDHEIM, S. H. "Obesity, Level of Aspiration, and Rorschach and TAT

Measures of Oral Dependence." *J Consult Psychol* 31:233–9 Je '67. * (*PA* 41:10716)

3612. MAYMAN, MARTIN. "Object-Representations and Object-Relationships in Rorschach Responses." *J Proj Tech & Pers Assess* 31:17–24 Ag '67. * (*PA* 41:15314)

3613. MOLISH, HERMAN B. "Rorschach's Test, Ego Structure, and Assessment of Personality Change With Special Reference to Childhood Schizophrenia." *Int Congr Rorsch & Proj Meth* 6(2):155–75 '67. *

3614. NICKOLS, JOHN. "Effects of Group Projective Testing on Rorschach Scores." Abstract. *J Clin Psychol* 23:497 O '67. * (*PA* 42:2610)

3615. NICKOLS, JOHN. "Rorschach Z Scores on Outpatients." *J Clin Psychol* 23:111–4 Ja '67. * (*PA* 41:5987)

3616. OGDON, DONALD P. Section 3, "The Rorschach Test," pp. 10–38, 78–81. In his *Psychodiagnostics and Personality Assessment: A Handbook.* Beverly Hills, Calif.: Western Psychological Services, 1967. Pp. v, 96. *

3617. OSOFSKY, HOWARD J., and FISHER, SEYMOUR. "Psychological Correlates of the Development of Amenorrhea in a Stress Situation." *Psychosom Med* 29:15–23 Ja-F '67. * (*PA* 41:5686)

3618. PARLANTI, IDA A. *Rorschach Defense Checklist: Rationale and Validity.* Master's thesis, Loyola College (Chicago, Ill.), 1967.

3619. PIOTROWSKI, ZYGMUNT A. "Rorschach Inkblots and After." *Int Congr Rorsch & Proj Meth* 6(2):133–9 '67. *

3620. POPE, BENJAMIN, and SCOTT, WINFIELD. *Psychological Diagnosis in Clinical Practice: With Applications in Medicine, Law, Education, Nursing, and Social Work,* pp. 120–75. New York: Oxford University Press, 1967. Pp. xiii, 341. *

3621. PRABHU, G. G. "The Rorschach Technique With Normal Adult Indians." *Indian Psychol R* 3:97–106 Ja '67. *

3622. PRYOR, DAVID B. "A Comparison of the Occurrence of Oral and Anal Content on the Rorschach." *J Proj Tech & Pers Assess* 31:26–8 O '67. * (*PA* 42:775)

3623. RABIN, A. I., and LIMUACO, JOSEFINA A. "A Comparison of the Connotative Meaning of Rorschach's Inkblots for American and Filipino College Students." *J Social Psychol* 72:197–203 Ag '67. * (*PA* 41:15130)

3624. RAMOS, EDITH. "Rorschach's Test as an Instrument in Determining Attitudes and Adaptive Traits in a Group of 'Nisei' (Japanese Immigrant's Sons) in Brazil." *Psychologia* 10:155–8 N '67. *

3625. RAWLS, JAMES R., and BOONE, JERRY N. "Artistic Creativity and Rorschach Whole Responses." *J Proj Tech & Pers Assess* 31:18–22 Je '67. * (*PA* 41:13686)

3626. RICHMAN, JOSEPH. "Reporting Diagnostic Test Results to Patients and Their Families." *J Proj Tech & Pers Assess* 31:62–70 Je '67. * (*PA* 41:13733)

3627. ROEMER, GEORG A. "The Rorschach and Roemer Symbol Test Series." *J Nerv & Mental Dis* 144:185–97 Mr '67. * (*PA* 41:13687)

3628. ROHR, MICHAEL E. *An Exploratory Study of Selected Rorschach Variables in Artificially Shortened Rorschach Records.* Master's thesis, Springfield College (Springfield, Mass.), 1967.

3629. ROSANES, MARILYN BLITZER. "Psychological Correlates to Myopia Compared to Hyperopia and Emmetropia." *J Proj Tech & Pers Assess* 31:31–5 O '67. * (*PA* 42:776)

3630. RUSSELL, ELBERT W. "Rorschach Stimulus Modification." *J Proj Tech & Pers Assess* 31:20–2 O '67. * (*PA* 42:777)

3631. SAPOLSKY, ALLAN. "Comment on Drake and Rusnak." *J Proj Tech & Pers Assess* 31:95 Ag '67. *

3632. SCHACHTEL, ERNEST G. "Experiential Qualities of the Rorschach Ink Blots." *J Proj Tech & Pers Assess* 31:4–10 Ag '67. * (*PA* 41:15321)

3633. SCHAFER, ROY. *Projective Testing and Psychoanalysis: Selected Papers.* New York: International Universities Press, 1967. Pp. 229. *

3634. SHANAN, JOEL; COHEN, MARGALATI; and ADLER, EMIL. "Personality Features of Hemiplegics After Cerebrovascular Accidents (CVA)." *Int Congr Rorsch & Proj Meth* 6(2):177–80 '67. *

3635. SHODELL, MARGARET J. *Personalities of Mothers of Nonverbal and Verbal Schizophrenic Children.* Doctor's thesis, Yeshiva University (New York, N.Y.), 1967. (*DA* 28:1175B)

3636. SMITH, ROBERT J. "Explorations in Nonconformity." *J Social Psychol* 71:133–50 F '67. * (*PA* 41:5896)

3637. STRICKER, GEORGE; TAKAHASHI, SHIGEO; and ZAX, MELVIN. "Semantic Differential Discriminability: A Comparison of Japanese and American Students." *J Social Psychol* 71:23–5 F '67. * (*PA* 41:5877)

3638. TAMKIN, ARTHUR S. "Some Determinants of Rorschach Productivity." *J Clin Psychol* 23:496 O '67. * (*PA* 42:2614)

3639. TOLOR, ALEXANDER; BRESLOW, ADELE K.; and BRODIE, RICHARD E. "Rorschach Human Movement and Attitudes Toward Space Exploration." *Percept & Motor Skills* 24:787–91 Je '67. * (*PA* 41:13692)

3640. TOWNSEND, JEANNETTE K. "The Relation Between Rorschach Signs of Aggression and Behavioral Aggression in Emotionally Disturbed Boys." *J Proj Tech & Pers Assess* 31:13–21 D '67. * (*PA* 42:5811)

3641. UENO, HITOSHI. "Particular Way of Perceiving Body

in Persons Who Have Disease Image: From the Point of View of Body Boundary Theory." *Tohuko Psychologica Folia* 25(3–4):91–6 '67. *

3642. WALLEN, VINCENT. "A Research Design for Assessment of Personality Characteristics of Air Force Psychiatric Casualties in Southeast Asia." *Proc Ann Conf Air Force Behav Sci* 14:136–48 D '67. *

3643. WEISS, A. A. "Rorschach's Test as the Independent Variable in Research." *Int Congr Rorsch & Proj Meth* 6(1):91–4 '67. *

3644. WEISS, A. A.; STEIN, B.; ATAR, H.; and MELNIK, N. "Rorschach Test Behaviour as a Function of Psychological Differentiation." *Israel Ann Psychiatry* 5:32–42 Ap '67. * (*PA* 42:3977)

3645. WHITELEY, JOHN M., and BLAINE, GRAHAM R., JR. "Rorschach in Relation to Outcome in Psychotherapy With College Students." *J Consult Psychol* 31:595–9 D '67. * (*PA* 42:2650)

3646. WHITELEY, JOHN M.; SPRINTHALL, NORMAN A.; MOSHER, RALPH L.; and DONAGHY, ROLLA T. "Selection and Evaluation of Counselor Effectiveness." *J Counsel Psychol* 14:226–34 My '67. * (*PA* 41:9423)

3647. WILLIAMS, GERTRUDE J.; MONDER, RUTH; and RYCHLAK, JOSEPH F. "A One-Year Concurrent Validity Study of the Rorschach Prognostic Rating Scale." *J Proj Tech & Pers Assess* 31:30–3 D '67. * (*PA* 42:4831)

3648. WYATT, FREDERICK. "How Objective is Objectivity?: Reflections on Scope and Limitations of a Basic Tenet in the Study of Personality." *J Proj Tech & Pers Assess* 31:3–19 O '67. * (*PA* 42:742)

3649. ALLISON, JOEL; BLATT, SIDNEY J.; and ZIMET, CARL N. Chap. 4, "Rorschach Test," pp. 135–260, passim. In their *Interpretation of Psychological Tests.* New York: Harper & Row, Publishers, Inc., 1968. Pp. x, 342. *

3650. AMES, LOUISE BATES. "Academic Progress in Negro Schools." *J Learn Dis* 1:570–7 O '68. *

3651. AMES, LOUISE BATES, and WALKER, RICHARD N. "Prediction of Later Reading Ability From Kindergarten Rorschach and I.Q. Scores." *Int Congr Rorsch & Proj Meth* 6(4):609–15 '68. *

3652. APPELBAUM, STEPHEN A., and COLSON, DONALD B. "A Reexamination of the Color-Shading Rorschach Test Response and Suicide Attempts." *J Proj Tech & Pers Assess* 32:160–4 Ap '68. * (*PA* 42:10814)

3653. ARMSTRONG, HUBERT E., JR., and ARMSTRONG, DOLLIE C. "Relation of Physical Fitness to a Dimension of Body Image." *Percept & Motor Skills* 26:1173–4 Je '68. * (*PA* 42:18806)

3654. ASTHANA, H. S., and MOHAN, C. "Perceptual Development in the Indian Child: A Rorschach Study." *Int Congr Rorsch & Proj Meth* 6(4):593–608 '68. *

3655. BAUMAN, GERALD, and ROMAN, MELVIN. "Interaction Product Analysis in Group and Family Diagnosis." *J Proj Tech & Pers Assess* 32:331–7 Ag '68. * (*PA* 42:18828)

3656. BECK, SAMUEL J. Chap. 5, "Reality, Rorschach and Perceptual Theory," pp. 115–35. In *Projective Techniques in Personality Assessment: A Modern Introduction.* Edited by A. I. Rabin. New York: Springer Publishing Co., Inc., 1968. Pp. x, 638. *

3657. BENFARI, ROBERT C., and CALOGERAS, ROY C. "Levels of Cognition and Conscience Typologies." *J Proj Tech & Pers Assess* 32:466–74 O '68. * (*PA* 43:5398)

3658. BLANCHARD, W. H. "The Consensus Rorschach: Background and Development." *J Proj Tech & Pers Assess* 32:327–30 Ag '68. * (*PA* 42:18829)

3659. BLATT, SIDNEY J.; FEIRSTEIN, ALAN; and ALLISON, JOEL. "Adaptive Autonomic Arousal and Rorschach Color Scores." *Int Congr Rorsch & Proj Meth* 6(3):303–5 '68. *

3660. BOREHAM, JOHN. "A Theoretical Contribution to the Understanding of the Shading Responses." *Brit J Proj Psychol & Pers Study* 13:13–5 Je '68. *

3661. BOYER, L. BRYCE; BOYER, RUTH M.; KLOPFER, BRUNO; and SCHEINER, SUZANNE B. "Apache 'Learners' and 'Nonlearners': 2, Quantitative Rorschach Signs of Influential Adults." *J Proj Tech & Pers Assess* 32:146–59 Ap '68. * (*PA* 42:10468)

3662. BUTCHER, THOMAS; STEINAU, BERNIE; and CAMBIER, JOSEPH. "Rorschach as an Aid to Dynamic Group Psychotherapy." *Int Congr Rorsch & Proj Meth* 6(4):555–7 '68. *

3663. COLE, SPURGEON, and WILLIAMS, ROBERT L. "Age as a Determinant of Parental Interpretation of Rorschach Cards IV and VII." *Percept & Motor Skills* 26:55–8 F '68. * (*PA* 42:10609)

3664. COLEMAN, JOHN C. "Rorschach Content as a Means of Studying Child Development." *J Proj Tech & Pers Assess* 32:435–42 O '68. * (*PA* 43:5399)

3665. CUTTER, FRED. "Role Complements and Changes in Consensus Rorschachs." *J Proj Tech & Pers Assess* 32:338–47 Ag '68. * (*PA* 42:18830)

3666. CUTTER, FRED, and FARBEROW, NORMAN L. "Consensus Rorschach: Introduction to Theory and Clinical Applications." *Newsl Res Psychol* 10:33–5 My '68. *

3667. CUTTER, FRED, and FARBEROW, NORMAN L. "Serial Administration of Consensus Rorschachs to One Patient." *J Proj Tech & Pers Assess* 32:358–74 Ag '68. * (*PA* 42:18831)

3668. CUTTER, FRED; JORGENSEN, MARY; and FARBEROW, NORMAN L. "Replicability of Rorschach Signs With Known Degrees of Suicidal Intent." *J Proj Tech & Pers Assess* 32:428–34 O '68. * (*PA* 43:5400)

3669. DANA, RICHARD H. "Six Constructs to Define Rorschach M." *J Proj Tech & Pers Assess* 32:138–45 Ap '68. * (*PA* 42:10611)

3670. DANA, RICHARD H., and COCKING, RODNEY R. "Cue Parameters, Cue Probabilities, and Clinical Judgment." *J Clin Psychol* 24:475–80 O '68. * (*PA* 43:4046)

3671. DE LUCA, JOSEPH N. "A Rorschach Study of Adolescent Enuretics." *J Clin Psychol* 24:231–2 Ap '68. * (*PA* 42:12128)

3672. DOYLE, EDWARD D. *Rorschach Sex Responses, Norms and Defense Style of Normal Subjects.* Doctor's thesis, Loyola University (Chicago, Ill.), 1968.

3673. DRAGUNS, JURIS G.; HALEY, E. MARIE; and PHILLIPS, LESLIE. "Studies of Rorschach Content: A Review of Research Literature: Part 3, Theoretical Formulations." *J Proj Tech & Pers Assess* 32:16–32 F '68. * (*PA* 42:8990)

3674. DUDEK, S. Z. "M an Active Energy System Correlating Rorschach M With Ease of Creative Expression." *J Proj Tech & Pers Assess* 32:453–61 O '68. * (*PA* 43:5401)

3675. EFRON, HERMAN Y. "Comparison of Different Classes of Variables in Predicting Hospital Outcome for Schizophrenic Patients." *Proc Ann Conv Am Psychol Assn* 76:497–8 '68. * (*PA* 43:1161, title only)

3676. FARBEROW, NORMAN L. "Symposium: Consensus Rorschachs in the Study of Problem Behavior: Introduction." *J Proj Tech & Pers Assess* 32:326 Ag '68. * (*PA* 42:18833)

3677. FINN, JANE A., and NEURINGER, CHARLES. "Left-Handedness: A Study of Its Relation to Opposition." *J Proj Tech & Pers Assess* 32:49–52 F '68. * (*PA* 42:8992)

3678. FISHER, RHODA LEE. "Classroom Behavior and the Body Image Boundary." *J Proj Tech & Pers Assess* 32:450–2 O '68. * (*PA* 43:5857)

3679. FISHER, SEYMOUR. "Body Boundary and Perceptual Vividness." *J Abn Psychol* 73:392–6 Ag '68. * (*PA* 42:17195)

3680. FRANCIS, RAYMOND WALTER. *A Study of the Relationships Among Acceptance of Psychological Disability, Self Concept and Body Image.* Doctor's thesis, State University of New York at Buffalo (Buffalo, N.Y.), 1968. (*DA* 29:770B)

3681. FRIEDEMANN, A. "The History of Rorschach." *Brit J Proj Psychol & Pers Study* 13:3 Je '68. *

3682. GOODMAN, DAVID. "The Present State of Projective Testing or, Herman Rorschach Won't You Please Come Home?" *Int Congr Rorsch & Proj Meth* 6(3):481–4 '68. *

3683. GROVES, MARION H., and PETERSEN, PAUL A. "Effectiveness of Projective Techniques as Established by the Objective Agreement of Therapists With Diagnosticians." *Proc Ann Conv Am Psychol Assn* 76:459–60 '68. * (*PA* 43:940, title only)

3684. HARRIS, ROBERT E.; FOGEY, EDWARD W.; ZUBIN, JOSEPH; NEULINGER, JOHN; SHAKOW, DAVID; and STEIN, MORRIS J. "Discussion of Papers on 'Systems Based on Patterns of Psychological Performance,'" pp. 404–18. In *The Role and Methodology of Classification in Psychiatry and Psychopathology.* Edited by Martin M. Katz and others. Public Health Service Publication No. 1584. Washington, D.C.: United States Government Printing Office, 1968. Pp. ix, 590. *

3685. HEINEMANN, PETER O., and ZAX, MELVIN. "Extremeness in Evaluative Responses to Clinical Test Materials." *J Social Psychol* 75:175–83 Ag '68. * (*PA* 42:17384)

3686. HOLZBERG, JULES D. Chap. 2, "Psychological Theory and Projective Techniques," pp. 18–63. In *Projective Techniques in Personality Assessment: A Modern Introduction.* Edited by A. I. Rabin. New York: Springer Publishing Co., Inc., 1968. Pp. x, 638. *

3687. JANSSEN, MARIA C. "A Psychological Study of the Emotional Implications of Pregnancy, Delivery and Puerperium." *Int Congr Rorsch & Proj Meth* 6(4):583–7 '68. *

3688. KATZ, MELVYN M. "The Supplemental Use of Rorschach Performance as a Thematic Apperception Technique." *Int Congr Rorsch & Proj Meth* 6(3):523–6 '68. *

3689. KLOPFER, WALTER G. Chap. 7, "Current Status of the Rorschach Test," pp. 131–49. In *Advances in Psychological Assessment,* Vol. 1. Edited by Paul McReynolds. Palo Alto, Calif.: Science & Behavior Books, Inc., 1968. Pp. xiii, 336. *

3690. KLOPFER, WALTER G. Chap. 16, "Integration of Projective Techniques in the Clinical Case Study," pp. 523–52. In *Projective Techniques in Personality Assessment: A Modern Introduction.* Edited by A. I. Rabin. New York: Springer Publishing Co., Inc., 1968. Pp. x, 638. *

3691. KLOPFER, WALTER G. "Discussion: The Resurrection of the Rorschach as Consensus." *J Proj Tech & Pers Assess* 32:357 Ag '68. * (*PA* 42:18835)

3692. KLOPFER, WALTER G. "The Metamorphosis of Projective Methods." *J Proj Tech & Pers Assess* 32:402–4 O '68. * (*PA* 43:5388)

3693. LERNER, PAUL M. "Correlation of Social Competence and Level of Cognitive Perceptual Functioning in Male Schizophrenics." *J Nerv & Mental Dis* 146:412–6 My '68. * (*PA* 42:15788)

3694. LINGREN, RONALD H. "Child-Parent Attitudes: A Comparison of the Family Relations Test and Perceptions on

Rorschach Cards III, IV and VII." *Psychol Sch* 5:81–4 Ja '68. *

3695. LOISELLE, ROBERT H.; FISHER, VIRGINIA; and PARRISH, CATHERINE E. "Stimulus Value of Rorschach Inkblots and Percepts as Perceived by Children and Schizophrenics." *J Proj Tech & Pers Assess* 32:238–45 Je '68. * (*PA* 42:15789)

3696. McCULLY, ROBERT S.; GLUCKSMAN, MYRON L.; and HIRSCH, JULES. "Nutrition Imagery in the Rorschach Materials of Food-Deprived, Obese Patients." *J Proj Tech & Pers Assess* 32:375–82 Ag '68. * (*PA* 42:18837)

3697. MARTONOVA, F. "Rorschach Test Records Painted." *Int Congr Rorsch & Proj Meth* 6(4):713–4 '68. *

3698. MASLING, JOSEPH; WEISS, LILLIE; and ROTHSCHILD, BERTRAM. "Relationships of Oral Imagery to Yielding Behavior and Birth Order." *J Consult & Clin Psychol* 32:89–91 F '68. * (*PA* 42:7359)

3699. MONS, W. E. R. "Typology and the Rorschach." *Brit J Proj Psychol & Pers Study* 13:11–2 Je '68. *

3700. MURSTEIN, BERNARD I. "Discussion for Current Status of Some Projective Techniques." *J Proj Tech & Pers Assess* 32:229–32 Je '68. * (*PA* 42:15496)

3701. PAL, S. K. "Personality Patterns of Engineering, Law, Medical, and Teacher-Training Students: A Comparative Study." *J Social Psychol* 74:287–8 Ap '68. * (*PA* 42:10621)

3702. PARKER, ROLLAND S., and PIOTROWSKI, ZYGMUNT A. "The Significance of Varieties of Actors of Rorschach Human Movement Responses." *J Proj Tech & Pers Assess* 32:33–44 F '68. * (*PA* 42:8998)

3703. PARSONS, OSCAR A., and FULGENZI, LAWRENCE B. "Overt and Covert Hostility in Repressers and Sensitizers." *Percept & Motor Skills* 27:537–8 O '68. * (*PA* 43:5337)

3704. PIERCE, RICHARD M. "Comment on the Prediction of Posthospital Work Adjustment With Psychological Tests." *J Counsel Psychol* 15:386–7 Jl '68. * (*PA* 42:15539)

3705. PRYOR, DAVID B. "Correlates of the Mayman Form Level Scoring System." *J Proj Tech & Pers Assess* 32:462–5 O '68. * (*PA* 43:5365)

3706. RABIN, A. I. Chap. 19, "Adapting and Devising Projective Methods for Special Purposes," pp. 611–26. In his *Projective Techniques in Personality Assessment: A Modern Introduction.* New York: Springer Publishing Co., Inc., 1968. Pp. x, 638. *

3707. RAPAPORT, DAVID; GILL, MERTON M.; and SCHAFER, ROY; edited by ROBERT R. HOLT. Chap. 9, "The Rorschach Test," pp. 268–463. In their *Diagnostic Psychological Testing.* New York: International Universities Press, Inc., 1968. Pp. xi, 562. *

3708. RAWLS, JAMES R., and SLACK, GORDON K. "Artists Versus Nonartists: Rorschach Determinants and Artistic Creativity." *J Proj Tech & Pers Assess* 32:233–7 Je '68. * (*PA* 42:15498)

3709. RICE, DAVID G. "Rorschach Responses and Aggressive Characteristics of MMPI *F* > 16 Scorers." *J Proj Tech & Pers Assess* 32:253–61 Je '68. * (*PA* 42:15474)

3710. ROGOLSKY, MARYROSE M. "Artistic Creativity and Adaptive Regression in Third Grade Children." *J Proj Tech & Pers Assess* 32:53–62 F '68. * (*PA* 42:8104)

3711. ROSS, DONALD C. "Computer Processing of Inkblot Test Data." *J Sch Psychol* 6:200–5 sp '68. * (*PA* 42:17252)

3712. SACHS, KENNETH STEPHEN. *The Conditioning of Two Measures of Autonomic Reactivity Under Different Levels of Stress and the Relationship to a Dimension of the Body Image.* Doctor's thesis, Baylor University (Waco, Tex.), 1968. (*DA* 29:776B)

3713. SAITO, KUMIKO. "Relationship Between the Ego Functioning and the Phenomenal Self: A Study on Psychological Integration for Adjustment." *Psychologia* 11:59–66 Je '68. *

3714. SCHIMEK, J. G. "A Note on the Long-Range Stability of Selected Rorschach Scores." *J Proj Tech & Pers Assess* 32:63–5 F '68. * (*PA* 42:9003)

3715. SCHMID, FRED W. "Projective Tests in Vocational Counseling." *J Proj Tech & Pers Assess* 32:10–5 F '68. * (*PA* 42:9004)

3716. SCHUBERT, JOSEF. "Rorschachs of Asthmatic Children." *Brit J Proj Psychol & Pers Study* 13:17–23 Je '68. *

3717. SEMEONOFF, BORIS. "On the Equivalence of the Rorschach and Zulliger's." *Int Congr Rorsch & Proj Meth* 6(4):733–7 '68. *

3718. SHANAN, JOEL; LIVSON, YAEL; SHARON, MIRYAM; and FREUDENBERG, RACHEL. "Mental Health and Personality Change During the Adult Years (as Reflected in Projective Techniques in Israel)." *Int Congr Rorsch & Proj Meth* 6(3):273–6 '68. *

3719. SHANKER, PREM. "Education and Rorschach Affective Factors of the Harijans." *Indian Psychol R* 4:95–100 Ja '68. *

3720. SINGER, JEROME L. Chap. 18, "Research Applications of Projective Methods," pp. 581–610. In *Projective Techniques in Personality Assessment: A Modern Introduction.* Edited by A. I. Rabin. New York: Springer Publishing Co., Inc., 1968. Pp. x, 638. *

3721. SINGER, MARGARET THALER. "The Consensus Rorschach and Family Transaction." *J Proj Tech & Pers Assess* 32:348–51 Ag '68. * (*PA* 42:18839)

3722. SINOWITZ, MELVIN, and BROWN, FRED. "Wechsler's MF Score as an Indicator of Masculinity and Femininity in a Psychiatric Population." *J Clin Psychol* 24:92–4 Ja '68. *

3723. STANLEY, GORDON. "God in the Rorschach." *Percept & Motor Skills* 26:463–6 Ap '68. * (*PA* 42:12131)

3724. STAPLES, EDWARD A., and WILENSKY, HAROLD. "A Controlled Rorschach Investigation of Hypnotic Age Regression." *J Proj Tech & Pers Assess* 32:246–52 Je '68. * (*PA* 42:15500)

3725. STARK, STANLEY. "Experience, Rorschach Responses, and Role-Taking (Empathy): A Dualistic Suggestion." *Percept & Motor Skills* 26:287–94 F '68. * (*PA* 42:10625)

3726. STARK, STANLEY. "Historiography and the Rorschach Framework: 'Literary Skill' vs 'Literary Qualities.'" *Percept & Motor Skills* 26:1108–10 Je '68. * (*PA* 42:18840)

3727. STARK, STANLEY. "Inner Creation in Knower and Known, Observer and Observed, Theorist and Theorized: 1, Introduction." *Percept & Motor Skills* 27:371–8 O '68. * (*PA* 43:4628)

3728. STARK, STANLEY. "James' Mystic Consciousness and Rorschach's Inner Creation: A Suggestion on How to Regard Them." *Psychol Rep* 23:57–8 Ag '68. * (*PA* 43:6063)

3729. STARK, STANLEY. "On the Confounding of Creativity Contexts: Maslow's *Psychology of Science.*" *Psychol Rep* 23:88–90 Ag '68. * (*PA* 43:6926)

3730. STARK, STANLEY. "Suggestion Regarding Drama, Inner Creation, and Role-Taking (Empathy): 1, Dramatic Arts and Dramatic Dreaming." *Percept & Motor Skills* 26:1319–46 Je '68. * (*PA* 42:18841)

3731. STARK, STANLEY. "Toward a Psychology of Knowledge: 3, Speculations Regarding Philosophical Correlates of Rorschach Movement Responses." *Percept & Motor Skills* 26:67–93 F '68. * (*PA* 42:10626)

3732. STARK, STANLEY. "Toward a Psychology of Knowledge: 4, Further Illustrations of the Hypothesis Regarding Philosophical Conservatism and Rorschach Movement Responses." *Percept & Motor Skills* 26:455–60 Ap '68. * (*PA* 42:12132)

3733. STARK, STANLEY. "Toward a Psychology of Knowledge: 5, A Prefatory Note on Maurice Stein's 'Poetic Metaphors of Sociology.'" *Percept & Motor Skills* 26:1011–5 Je '68. * (*PA* 42:17977)

3734. STRAUSS, MILTON E. "Examiner Expectancy: Effects on Rorschach Experience Balance." *J Consult & Clin Psychol* 32:125–9 Ap '68. * (*PA* 42:9007)

3735. STRAUSS, MILTON E. "The Influence of Pre-testing Information on Rorschach Based Personality Reports." *J Proj Tech & Pers Assess* 32:323–5 Ag '68. * (*PA* 42:18842)

3736. STUART, I. R. "Rorschach Techniques and Political Art: Primary and Secondary Process as Symbols of Group Emotionality." *Int Congr Rorsch & Proj Meth* 6(4):565–7 '68. *

3737. TAMKIN, ARTHUR S., and SONKIN, NATHAN. "The Use of Psychological Tests in Differential Diagnosis." *Newsl Res Psychol* 10:24 Ag '68. *

3738. TAYLOR, ROBERT E., and EISENMAN, RUSSELL. "Birth Order and Sex Differences in Complexity-Simplicity, Color-Form Preference and Personality." *J Proj Tech & Pers Assess* 32:383–7 Ag '68. * (*PA* 42:18793)

3739. THOMAS, EDWARD LLEWELLYN. "Eye Movements During Projective Testing." Abstract. *Int Congr Rorsch & Proj Meth* 6(3):325–6 '68. *

3740. TOLOR, ALEXANDER, and JALOWIEC, JOHN E. "Body Boundary, Parental Attitudes, and Internal-External Expectancy." *J Consult & Clin Psychol* 32:206–9 Ap '68. * (*PA* 42:8931)

3741. TUCKER, G. J.; REINHARDT, R. F.; and CLARKE, N. B. "The Body Image of the Aviator." *Brit J Psychiatry* 114:233–7 F '68. * (*PA* 42:9009)

3742. VASSILIOU, VASSO, and GEORGAS, JAMES G. "Profile of the Athenian on the Rorschach." *Int Congr Rorsch & Proj Meth* 6(3):259–70 '68. *

3743. VASSILIOU, VASSO; GEORGAS, JAMES G.; and VASSILIOU, GEORGE. "An Exploration Study of Some Rorschach Variables and Performance in Paintings During Group Image Therapy." *Int Congr Rorsch & Proj Meth* 6(4):559–63 '68. *

3744. WAGNER, EDWIN E., and HODGE, JAMES R. "Transformations of Rorschach Content Under Two Hypnotic Trance Levels." *J Proj Tech & Pers Assess* 32:443–9 O '68. * (*PA* 43:5403)

3745. WAGNER, EDWIN E., and SLEMBOSKI, JEAN. "Psychological Reactions of Pregnant Unwed Women as Measured by the Rorschach." *J Clin Psychol* 24:467–9 O '68. * (*PA* 43:4049)

3746. WEINBERG, RITA MOHR. "Personality Characteristics of African Children: A Projective Analysis." *J Genetic Psychol* 113:65–77 S '68. * (*PA* 43:751)

3747. WILLIAMS, GERTRUDE J.; NAHINSKY, IRWIN D.; HALL, DEE M.; and ABRAMSON, YITZCHOK. "Frequency of the Rorschach Human-Movement Response in Negro and White Emotionally Disturbed Children." *J Consult & Clin Psychol* 32:158–63 Ap '68. * (*PA* 42:9226)

3748. WYNNE, LYMAN C. "Consensus Rorschachs and Related Procedures for Studying Interpersonal Patterns." *J Proj Tech & Pers Assess* 32:352–6 Ag '68. * (*PA* 42:18844)

3749. YARNELL, THOMAS D., and DAWSON, JOSEPH G. "Differential Responding to Achromatic and Chromatic Ror-

schach Stimuli." *J Clin Psychol* 24:228–30 Ap '68. * (*PA* 42:12137)
See also references for 477.

NAME INDEX

[471]

Rosenzweig Picture-Frustration Study. Ages 4–13, 14 and over; 1944–60; also called *Rosenzweig P–F Study;* 15 scores: direction of aggression (extrapunitive, intropunitive, impunitive), type of aggression (obstacle-dominance, ego-defense, need-persistence), 9 combinations of the preceding categories; 2 levels; record blank ('48, 1 page) for each level; $6 per 25 tests; $1.50 per 25 record blanks; postage extra; specimen set not available; [15–20] minutes; Saul Rosenzweig; the Author. *

a) FORM FOR CHILDREN. Ages 4–13; 1948–60; 1 form ('48, 7 pages); manual ('48, 53 pages, reprint of *21* below); supplementary data ('60, 29 pages, reprint of *222* below); tentative norms; $1.50 per manual; supplementary data free upon request.

b) REVISED FORM FOR ADULTS. Ages 14 and over; 1944–49; 1 form ('48, 7 pages); manual ('47, 48 pages, reprint of *15* below; includes 1949 revised norms); no data on reliability and validity; norms for ages 20–29 only; $1.50 per manual.

For a review by Åke Bjerstedt, see 6:238 (61 references); for reviews by Richard H. Dana and Bert R. Sappenfield, see 5:155 (109 references); for reviews by Robert C. Challman and Percival M. Symonds, see 4:129 (77 references).

REFERENCES

1–77. See 4:129.
78–186. See 5:155.
187–247. See 6:238.

248. HOLZBERG, JULES D., and HAHN, FRED. "The Picture-Frustration Technique as a Measure of Hostility and Guilt Reactions in Adolescent Psychopaths." Discussion by Goldie R. Kaback. *Am J Orthopsychiatry* 22:776–97 O '52. * (*PA* 27:5995)

249. DAVIS, DAVID S. *An Investigation of the Relationship of Frustration Tolerance in Paraplegics and Degree and Rate of Success in Rehabilitation.* Doctor's thesis, New York University (New York, N.Y.), 1955. (*DA* 15:1262)

250. DIAMOND, MORRIS DAVID. *A Comparison of the Interpersonal Skills of Schizophrenics and Drug Addicts.* Doctor's thesis, New York University (New York, N.Y.), 1955. (*DA* 15:1439)

251. FOSTER, ARTHUR LEE. *The Relationship Between EEG Abnormality, Psychological Factors and Delinquent Behavior.* Doctor's thesis, University of Houston (Houston, Tex.), 1956. (*DA* 16:2210)

252. LINDZEY, GARDNER, and TEJESSY, CHARLOTTE. "Thematic Apperception Test: Indices of Aggression in Relation to Measures of Overt and Covert Behavior." *Am J Orthopsychiatry* 26:567–76 Jl '56. * (*PA* 31:7943)

253. McKINLEY, DOUGLAS P. *A Study of Certain Relationships of Maternal Personality and Child-Rearing Attitudes to Children's Reading Performances.* Doctor's thesis, University of Florida (Gainesville, Fla.), 1958. (*DA* 19:3216)

254. SCHECKEL, ROSALIE. *An Analysis of the Frustration Pattern of Pupils in Day and Residential Schools for the Deaf as Revealed by Rosenzweig's Picture Frustration Study.* Master's thesis, Fordham University (New York, N.Y.), 1959.

255. WESSMAN, ALDEN E.; RICKS, DAVID F.; and TYL, MARY McILVAINE. "Characteristics and Concomitants of Mood Fluctuation in College Women." *J Abn & Social Psychol* 60:117–26 Ja '60. * (*PA* 34:7186)

256. ENGLISH, ROBERT HENRY. *Cleft Palate Children Compared With Non-Cleft Palate Children: A Personality Study.* Doctor's thesis, University of Oregon (Eugene, Ore.), 1961. (*DA* 23:2622)

257. TRIANDIS, LEIGH MINTURN, and LAMBERT, WILLIAM W. "Sources of Frustration and Targets of Aggression: A Cross-Cultural Study." *J Abn & Social Psychol* 62:640–8 My '61. * (*PA* 36:4GB4oT)

258. AINSWORTH, MARY D., and AINSWORTH, LEONARD H. "Acculturation in East Africa: 2, Frustration and Aggression." *J Social Psychol* 57:401–7 Ag '62. * (*PA* 37:4804)

259. BARTA, JAMES. *A Study of the Concurrence of Anxiety and Hostility.* Doctor's thesis, Fordham University (New York, N.Y.), 1962. (*DA* 23:3471)

260. COBB, BEATRIX; DAMARIN, FRED; KRASNOFF, ALAN; and TRUNNELL, J. B. "Personality Factors and Stress in Carcinoma," pp. 738–65. In *Psychosomatic Obstetrics, Gynecology and Endocrinology.* Edited by William S. Kroger. Springfield, Ill.: Charles C Thomas, Publisher, 1962. Pp. xxv, 820. *

261. SOLOMON, LILLIAN GREENBERG. *An Investigation of Visual Defect and Certain Cultural and Personality Factors*

in Juvenile Delinquency. Doctor's thesis, University of Texas (Austin, Tex.), 1962. (*DA* 25:2617)

262. ADLER, MILTON LEON. *Differences in Bright Low-Achieving and High-Achieving Ninth Grade Pupils.* Doctor's thesis, University of Illinois (Urbana, Ill.), 1963. (*DA* 24:5184)

263. HINES, MARLIN POWELL. *The Relationship of Achievement Level to Certain Personality Factors Among High School Seniors.* Doctor's thesis, University of Arkansas (Fayetteville, Ark.), 1963. (*DA* 24:5193)

264. STACK, JAMES JAY. *Individual Differences in the Reduction of Cognitive Dissonance: An Exploratory Study.* Doctor's thesis, Ohio State University (Columbus, Ohio), 1963. (*DA* 24:4806)

265. WHETSTONE, BOBBY DON. *A Differential Study of Some Personality Variables of Selected Counselors and Effective Teachers.* Doctor's thesis, University of Alabama (University, Ala.), 1963. (*DA* 24:4090)

266. ALTROCCHI, JOHN; SHRAUGER, SID; and McLEOD, MARY ANN. "Attribution of Hostility to Self and Others by Expressors, Sensitizers, and Repressors." *J Clin Psychol* 20:233 Ap '64. * (*PA* 39:7933)

267. BELL, ROBERT BRADDOCK. *Two Related Experimental Approaches to the Function of Projective Distance in Psychodiagnosis.* Doctor's thesis, Washington University (St. Louis, Mo.), 1964. (*DA* 26:486)

268. BERKUN, MITCHELL M., and BURDICK, HARRY A. "Effect of Preceding Rosenzweig's PF Test With the TAT." *J Clin Psychol* 20:253 Ap '64. * (*PA* 39:7884)

269. KUETHE, JAMES L. "Prejudice and Aggression: A Study of Specific Social Schemata." *Percept & Motor Skills* 18:107–15 F '64. * (*PA* 39:1522)

270. McDONOUGH, LEAH BROOKS. "Inhibited Aggression in Essential Hypertension." *J Clin Psychol* 20:447 O '64. * (*PA* 39:12418)

271. PAREEK, UDAI NARAIN. *Developmental Patterns in Reactions to Frustration.* New York: Asia Publishing House, 1964. Pp. xi, 182. * (*PA* 39:14882)

272. PRESTON, CAROLINE E. "Accident-Proneness in Attempted Suicide and in Automobile Accident Victims." *J Consult Psychol* 28:79–82 F '64. * (*PA* 38:8597)

273. SCHWARTZ, MILTON M.; COHEN, BERTRAM D.; and PAVLIK, WILLIAM B. "The Effects of Subject- and Experimenter-Induced Defensive Response Sets on Picture-Frustration Test Reactions." *J Proj Tech & Pers Assess* 28:341–5 S '64. * (*PA* 39:7852)

274. SEIDMAN, EMANUEL. *Some Relationships of Frustration Reaction to Aspects of Conscience and Social Reality.* Doctor's thesis, Yeshiva University (New York, N.Y.), 1964. (*DA* 26:2316)

275. BELL, ROBERT B., and ROSENZWEIG, SAUL. "The Investigation of Projective Distance With Special Reference to the Rosenzweig Picture-Frustration Study." *J Proj Tech & Pers Assess* 29:161–7 Je '65. * (*PA* 39:12379)

276. BROWN, L. B. "Aggression and Denominational Membership." *Brit J Social & Clin Psychol* 4:175–8 S '65. * (*PA* 40:1559)

277. GROSS, RUTH DORIS BRILL. *A Social Situations Test as a Measure of Adjustment Mechanisms.* Doctor's thesis, West Virginia University (Morgantown, W. Va.), 1965. (*DA* 28:2137B)

278. HERBERT, M. "Personality Factors and Bronchial Asthma: A Study of South African Indian Children." *J Psychosom Res* 8:353–64 Mr '65. *

279. KRIEGER, LESLIE, and SCHWARTZ, MILTON M. "The Relationship Between Sociometric Measures of Popularity Among Children and Their Reactions to Frustration." *J Social Psychol* 66:2–6 Ag '65. * (*PA* 39:15244)

280. MUSGROVE, WALTER JASON. *A Study of Type of Reaction to Frustration and Direction of Aggression in One Parent Families and in Two Parent Families.* Doctor's thesis, University of Maryland (College Park, Md.), 1965. (*DA* 26:6516)

281. PAREEK, UDAI, and DEVI, S. R. "Reliability of the Adult Form of the Indian Adaptation of the Rosenzweig P-F Study." *Indian J Psychol* 40:67–71 Je '65. * (*PA* 40:9442)

282. ROSENZWEIG, SAUL. "Note of Correction for Schwartz, Cohen and Pavlik's 'The Effects of Subject- and Experimenter-Induced Defensive Response Sets on Picture-Frustration Test Reactions.'" *J Proj Tech & Pers Assess* 29:352–3 S '65. * (*PA* 39:15410)

283. ROSS, EDWARD N. *Reactions to Frustration of Retardates in Special and in Regular Classes.* Doctor's thesis, Yeshiva University (New York, N.Y.), 1965. (*DA* 26:2316)

284. SALTZMAN, EARL SIDNEY. *A Comparison of Patterns of Identification as Shown by Family Members of Three Religious Denominations in Houston, Texas.* Doctor's thesis, University of Houston (Houston, Tex.), 1965. (*DA* 26:6857)

285. SCHWARTZ, ARTHUR N., and KLEEMEIER, ROBERT W. "The Effects of Illness and Age Upon Some Aspects of Personality." *J Gerontol* 20:85–91 Ja '65. *

286. SCHWARTZ, MILTON M., and LEVINE, HERBERT. "Union and Management Leaders: A Comparison." *Personnel Adm* 28:44–7 Ja–F '65. *

287. WEINER, IRVING B., and ADER, ROBERT. "Direction of Aggression and Adaptation to Free Operant Avoidance Con-

ditioning." *J Personality & Social Psychol* 2:426–9 S '65. * (*PA* 39:13785)

288. WHETSTONE, BOBBY D. "Personality Differences Between Selected Counselors and Effective Teachers." *Personnel & Guid J* 93:886–90 My '65. * (*PA* 39:15179)

289. ZAIDI, S. M. HAFEEZ, and SHAFI, KHALIDA. "An Objective Evaluation of Rosenzweig's Analysis of Subjective Reactions to Frustration in a Pakistani Cultural Setting." *Psychologia* 8:213–7 D '65. * (*PA* 41:1475)

290. LEVINSON, BORIS M. "Subcultural Studies of Homeless Men." *Trans NY Acad Sci* 29:165–82 D '66. * (*PA* 41:16683)

291. LUDWIG, DAVID JEROME. *Levels of Behavior in Reaction to Frustration as Related to the Self-Concept, With Special Reference to the Rosenzweig F-Battery.* Doctor's thesis, Washington University (St. Louis, Mo.), 1966. (*DA* 27:4578B)

292. MEGARGEE, EDWIN I. "A Comparison of the Scores of White and Negro Male Juvenile Delinquents on Three Projective Tests." *J Proj Tech & Pers Assess* 30:530–5 D '66. * (*PA* 41:2920)

293. PAREEK, UDAI, and KUMAR, V. K. "Establishing Criteria for Significance of Trends for the Adult Form of the Rosenzweig P-F Study." *Res B Dept Psychol Osmania Univ* 2:29–35 Mr '66. * (*PA* 40:7705)

294. SCHALOCK, ROBERT L., and MacDONALD, PATRICIA. "Personality Variables Associated With Reactions to Frustration." *J Proj Tech & Pers Assess* 30:158–60 Ap '66. * (*PA* 40:7708)

295. TIWARI, J. G., and GAUTAM, R. P. "Personality Characteristics of Socially Accepted and Socially Neglected Junior High School Pupils." *Indian J Social Work* 27:211–7 Jl '66. *

296. WEATHERLY, JAMES KENNY. *A Comparative Investigation of Frustration-Aggressive Patterns Shown by Adults and Children Within the Same Families of Three Religious Groups.* Doctor's thesis, University of Houston (Houston, Tex.), 1966. (*DA* 27:975B)

297. WHITMAN, JAMES R., and SCHWARTZ, ARTHUR N. "Relationship Between Social Desirability Scale Value and Probability of Endorsement for Responses in Social Situations." *J Proj Tech & Pers Assess* 30:280–2 Je '66. * (*PA* 40:9444)

298. WHITMAN, JAMES R., and SCHWARTZ, ARTHUR N. "Social Desirability Ratings of Selected Responses in the Rosenzweig P-F Study." Abstract. *Psychol Rep* 19:648 O '66. * (*PA* 41:606)

299. COLEMAN, JOHN C. "Stimulus Factors in the Relation Between Fantasy and Behavior." *J Proj Tech & Pers Assess* 31:68–73 F '67. * (*PA* 41:13665)

300. MITCHELL, KEVIN M. "The Rosenzweig Picture-Frustration Study as a Measure of Reaction to Personal Evaluation." *J Proj Tech & Pers Assess* 31:65–8 D '67. * (*PA* 42:5614)

301. ROSENZWEIG, SAUL. "Extending the Repressor-Sensitizer Dichotomy." *J Clin Psychol* 23:37–8 Ja '67. * (*PA* 41:5201)

302. ROSENZWEIG, SAUL. "Revised Criteria for the Group Conformity Rating of the Rosenzweig Picture-Frustration Study, Adult Form." *J Proj Tech & Pers Assess* 31:58–61 Je '67. * (*PA* 41:13688)

303. ROTH, ROBERT M., and PURI, PRABHA. "Direction of Aggression and the Nonachievement Syndrome." *J Counsel Psychol* 14:277–81 My '67. * (*PA* 41:9379)

304. SCHILL, THOMAS R., and BLACK, JOHN M. "Differences in Reaction to Frustration as a Function of Need for Approval." *Psychol Rep* 21:87–8 Ag '67. * (*PA* 42:2612)

305. THALLER, JACK L.; ROSEN, GERALD; and SALTZMAN, STUART. "Study of the Relationship of Frustration and Anxiety to Bruxism." *J Periodont* 38:193–7 My–Je '67. *

306. WHITMAN, JAMES R., and SCHWARTZ, ARTHUR N. "The Relationship Between Two Measures of the Tendency to Give Socially Desirable Responses." *J Proj Tech & Pers Assess* 31:72–5 O '67. * (*PA* 42:779)

307. FINE, BERNARD J., and SWEENEY, DONALD R. "Personality Traits, and Situational Factors, and Catecholamine Excretion." *J Exp Res Personality* 3:15–27 Je '68. * (*PA* 42:16867)

308. MORDKOFF, ARNOLD M., and GOLAS, RUTH M. "Coronary Artery Disease and Response to the Rosenzweig Picture-Frustration Study." *J Abn Psychol* 73:381–6 Ag '68. * (*PA* 42:17560) ·

309. TEWARI, J. G., and TEWARI, J. N. "On Extremes of Personality Adjustment as Measured by Adjustment Inventories." *J Psychol Res* 12:75–81 My '68. * (*PA* 43:5396)

310. WILSON, MILTON E., JR., and FRUMKIN, R. M. "Underlying Assumptions of the Rosenzweig Picture-Frustration Study: A Critical Appraisal." *Ed & Psychol Meas* 28:587–94 su '68. * (*PA* 42:18115)

NAME INDEX

[472]

The Rotter Incomplete Sentences Blank. Grades 9–12, 13–16, adults; 1950; RISB; test booklet title is *Incomplete Sentences Blank;* 1 form (2 pages); 3 levels; manual (86 pages); manual and standardization data based on college level only; $1.40 per 25 tests; $2.25 per manual; postpaid; specimen set not available; (20–40) minutes; Julian B. Rotter and Janet E. Rafferty (manual); Psychological Corporation. *

See 6:239 (17 references) and 5:156 (18 references); for reviews by Charles N. Cofer and William Schofield, see 4:130 (6 references, 1 excerpt).

REFERENCES

1–6. See 4:130.
7–24. See 5:156.
25–41. See 6:239.
42. HAMPTON, BARBARA J. *An Investigation of Personality Characteristics Associated With Self-Adequacy.* Doctor's thesis,

New York University (New York, N.Y.), 1955. (*DA* 15:1203)
43. ARNHOLTER, ETHELWYNE G. "School Persistence and Personality Factors." *Personnel & Guid J* 35:107–9 O '56. * (*PA* 31:8805)
44. WORTHINGTON, ANNA MAY LANGE. *An Investigation of the Relationship Between the Lipreading Ability of Congenitally Deaf High School Students and Certain Personality Factors.* Doctor's thesis, Ohio State University (Columbus, Ohio), 1956. (*DA* 16:2241)
45. KINNANE, JOHN FRANCIS. *The Relationship of Personal Adjustment to Realism of Expressed Vocational Preference.* Doctor's thesis, Columbia University (New York, N.Y.), 1958. (*DA* 19:172)
46. NEYHUS, ARTHUR IRVIN. *The Personality of Socially Well Adjusted Adult Deaf as Revealed by Projective Tests.* Doctor's thesis, Northwestern University (Evanston, Ill.), 1962. (*DA* 23:2589)
47. HEALY, BIGELOW CHANDLER. *Personality Factors in Level of Aspiration.* Doctor's thesis, University of Florida (Gainesville, Fla.), 1963. (*DA* 25:662)
48. STACK, JAMES JAY. *Individual Differences in the Reduction of Cognitive Dissonance: An Exploratory Study.* Doctor's thesis, Ohio State University (Columbus, Ohio), 1963. (*DA* 24:4806)
49. LEWINSOHN, PETER M., and NICHOLS, ROBERT C. "The Evaluation of Changes in Psychiatric Patients During and After Hospitalization." *J Clin Psychol* 20:272–9 Ap '64. * (*PA* 39:8200)
50. WALTER, DEAN; DENZLER, LORRAINE S.; and SARASON, IRWIN G. "Anxiety and the Intellectual Performance of High School Students." *Child Develop* 35:917–26 S '64. * (*PA* 39:5246)
51. FULKERSON, SAMUEL E., and GETTYS, VESTA C. "Validity of a Maladjustment Score From the Rotter Incomplete Sentences Blank." *J Clin Psychol* 21:422–4 O '65. * (*PA* 40:1761)
52. GOLDBERG, PHILIP A., and STARK, MILTON J. "Johnson or Goldwater?: Some Personality and Attitude Correlates of Political Choice." *Psychol Rep* 17:627–31 O '65. * (*PA* 40:1501)
53. KENNEDY, WALLACE A., and WALSH, JOHN. "A Factor Analysis of Mathematical Giftedness." *Psychol Rep* 17:115–9 Ag '65. * (*PA* 40:1553)
54. ROSE, HARRIETT A. "Prediction and Prevention of Freshman Attrition." *J Counsel Psychol* 12:399–403 w '65. * (*PA* 40:3400)
55. BRAY, DOUGLAS W., and GRANT, DONALD L. "The Assessment Center in the Measurement of Potential for Business Management." *Psychol Monogr* 80(17):1–27 '66. * (*PA* 41:850)
56. GARDNER, J. *A Study in the Reliability and Validity of the Qualitative Interpretation of the Sentence Completion Method.* Master's thesis, Hunter College (New York, N.Y.), 1966.
57. HARRISON, R. J. "Predictive Validity of Some Adjustment Tests: A Research Note." *Austral J Psychol* 18:284–7 D '66. * (*PA* 41:4596)
58. ROSE, HARRIETT A., and ELTON, CHARLES F. "Another Look at the College Dropout." *J Counsel Psychol* 13:242–5 su '66. * (*PA* 40:9217)
59. STRICKER, GEORGE, and DAWSON, DARRELL D. "The Effect of First Person and Third Person Instructions and Stems on Sentence Completion Responses." *J Proj Tech & Pers Assess* 30:169–71 Ap '66. * (*PA* 40:7730)
60. AARON, NORMA S. "Some Personality Differences Between Asthmatic, Allergic and Normal Children." *J Clin Psychol* 23:336–40 Jl '67. * (*PA* 41:15746)
61. BROWN, JANET R. *An Exploratory Study of Change in Self Concept.* Doctor's thesis, Case Western Reserve University (Cleveland, Ohio), 1967. (*DA* 28:3990A)
62. GARDNER, JAMES M. "The Adustment of Drug Addicts as Measured by the Sentence Completion Test." *J Proj Tech & Pers Assess* 31:28–9 Je '67. * (*PA* 41:13890)
63. GRANT, DONALD L.; KATKOVSKY, WALTER; and BRAY, DOUGLAS W. "Contributions of Projective Techniques to Assessment of Management Potential." *J Appl Psychol* 51:226–32 Je '67. * (*PA* 41:10481)
64. HERSCH, PAUL D., and SCHEIBE, KARL E. "Reliability and Validity of Internal-External Control as a Personality Dimension." *J Consult Psychol* 31:609–13 D '67. * (*PA* 42:2581)
65. LEWINSOHN, PETER M., and NICHOLS, ROBERT C. "Dimensions of Change in Mental Hospital Patients." *J Clin Psychol* 23:498–503 O '67. * (*PA* 42:2624)
66. McCONNELL, JOHN ALDEN. *The Prediction of Dependency Behavior in a Standardized Experimental Situation.* Doctor's thesis, University of Rochester (Rochester, N.Y.), 1967. (*DA* 28:2127B)
67. NEWBERRY, LAWRENCE A. "Defensiveness and Need for Approval." *J Consult Psychol* 31:396–400 Ag '67. * (*PA* 41:13622)
68. WALKER, C. EUGENE, and LINDEN, JAMES D. "Varying Degrees of Psychological Sophistication in the Interpretation of Sentence Completion Data." *J Clin Psychol* 23:229–31 Ap '67. * (*PA* 41:9090)
69. WOOD, FRANK A. "Tachistoscopic Vs. Conventional

Presentation of Incomplete Sentence Stimuli." *J Proj Tech & Pers Assess* 31:30-1 Je '67. * (*PA* 41:13695)

70. BARRY, JOHN R.; DUNTEMAN, GEORGE H.; and WEBB, MARVIN W. "Personality and Motivation in Rehabilitation." *J Counsel Psychol* 15:237-44 My '68. * (*PA* 42:12535)

71. FEIN, LEAH GOLD. "Non-Academic Personality Variables and Success at School." *Int Mental Health Res Newsl* 10:2+ sp '68. *

72. GETTER, HERBERT, and WEISS, STEPHAN D. "The Rotter Incomplete Sentences Blank Adjustment Score as an Indicator of Somatic Complaint Frequency." *J Proj Tech & Pers Assess* 32:266 Je '68. * (*PA* 42:15490)

73. GOLDBERG, PHILIP A. "The Current Status of Sentence Completion Methods." *J Proj Tech & Pers Assess* 32:215-21 Je '68. * (*PA* 42:15491)

74. NEURINGER, CHARLES, and ORWICK, PERRY O. "The Measurement of Anxiety on the Sentence Completion Test." *J General Psychol* 78:197-207 Ap '68. * (*PA* 42:12130)

75. SCHLICHT, WILLIAM J., JR.; CARLSON, HILMER J.; SKEEN, DAVID R.; and SKURDAL, MARLO A. "Screening Procedures: A Comparison of Self-Report and Projective Measures." *Ed & Psychol Meas* 28:525-8 su '68. * (*PA* 42:19012)

76. THURSTON, JOHN R.; BRUNCLIK, HELEN L.; and FELDHUSEN, JOHN F. "The Relationship of Personality to Achievement in Nursing Education, Phase 2." *Nursing Res* 17:265-8 My-Je '68. * (*PA* 42:17997)

NAME INDEX

[473]

★**School Apperception Method.** Grades kgn–9; 1968; SAM; individual; 1 form (22 cards); pictures are also available as 35 mm. transparencies for group administration; manual (35 pages); no directions for use of transparencies; no data on reliability and

validity; no norms; $10 per set of cards and manual; $12 per set of transparencies (without manual); postage extra; (30–45) minutes; Irving L. Solomon and Bernard D. Starr; Springer Publishing Co., Inc. *

REFERENCES

1. SOLOMON, IRVING L.; KLEIN, MILTON I.; and STARR, BERNARD D. "The School Apperception Method." *J Sch Psychol* 4:28-35 w '66. * (*PA* 40:7738)
2. SOLOMON, IRVING L., and STARR, BERNARD D. "New Developments in the School Apperception Method." *J Sch Psychol* 5:157-8 w '67. * (*PA* 41:9421)

[473A]

Self Valuation Test. Ages 7–15, adults; 1957; test booklet title is *S.V.T.*; verbal and non-verbal projective test employing several stimuli simultaneously; individual; 2 levels; mimeographed manual (21 pages); record booklet (4 pages); comparison sheet (1 page); no norms in manual; 126s. per set of test materials, 100 comparison sheets, and 50 record booklets, postpaid; 50s. per 100 record booklets; 20s. per 100 comparison sheets; postage extra; (5–25) minutes; John Liggett; J. & P. Bealls Ltd. *

a) [FORM FOR CHILDREN.] Ages 7–15; Form C ['57, 14 pictures]; specimen set not available.

b) [FORMS FOR ADULTS.] Adults; Forms F ['57, 14 pictures, for women], M ['57, 14 pictures, for men]; Form M (2 pages) also available under the title *Faces Test;* 42s. per 100 copies of *Faces Test* and manual; 10s. per specimen set of *Faces Test,* postpaid.

REFERENCES

1-2. See 5:157.
3. LIGGETT, J. "Self Valuation Test." *Psychometric Res B* (4):[16-20] Ag '59. *
4. LIGGETT, JOHN. "A Non-Verbal Approach to the Phenomenal Self: The Self Valuation Test." Abstract. *Acta Psychologica* 15:496-7 '59. *
5. LIGGETT, JOHN. "The Paired Use of Projective Stimuli." *Brit J Psychol* 50:269-75 Ag '59. * (*PA* 34:4391)

[473B]

★**Social Relations Test.** Adult males; 1960–66; test booklet title is *S.R.T.;* 1 form ('66, 10 pages); no manual; no data on reliability and validity; no norms; 10s. per test, postage extra; [45] minutes; [J. C. de Ridder and Lynette Shaw]; Industrial Psychological Services. *

REFERENCE

1. SHAW, LYNETTE. "The Practical Use of Projective Personality Tests as Accident Predictors." *Traffic Safety Res R* 9:34-72 Je '65. *

[474]

★**The Sound-Apperception Test.** Ages 16 and over; 1965; "unstructured sounds much like auditory equivalents of ink blots" and 16 "semi-structured sound effects that reveal fantasy and dynamics of interpersonal situations"; 10 scores: reality orientation, like-indifferent-dislike, loss of life, physical aggression, nonphysical aggression, internalized emotional stress, positive reassurance, total, failure, success; no reading by examinees; 1 form (33 1/3 rpm monaural record); manual (42 pages, reprint of 3 below); no data on reliability; $10 per record including manual, postpaid; (50–150) minutes; Kenneth L. Bean; Sound Apperception Test Distributor. *

REFERENCES

1. BEAN, KENNETH L., and MOORE, JACK R. "Music Therapy From Auditory Ink Blots." *J Music Ther* 1:143-7 D '64. * (*PA* 39:12254)
2. BEAN, KENNETH L. "Scoring and Interpreting Responses to Semi-Structured Sound Effects." *J Proj Tech & Pers Assess* 29:151-60 Je '65. * (*PA* 39:12378)
3. BEAN, KENNETH L. "The Sound-Apperception Test: Origin, Purpose, Standardization, Scoring and Use." *J Psychol* 59:371-412 Mr '65. *

[475]

The South African Picture Analysis Test. Ages 5–13; 1960, c1959; SAPAT; 8 interpretive categories: condition of hero, environmental pressure, needs, reactions, characteristics of stories (4 categories); individual; 1 form (12 cards, 8 for boys or girls and 2 for boys only and 2 for girls only); manual ('60, c1959, 71 pages); no data on reliability; gld. 31.50 per set of cards and manual; gld. 7.90 per manual purchased separately; postage extra; (60) minutes; B. F. Nel and A. J. K. Pelser; Swets & Zeitlinger. *

For reviews by S. G. Lee and Johann M. Schepers, see 6:240 (1 excerpt).

[476]

Structured Doll Play Test. Ages 2–6; 1959–60; SDPT; family and peer relationships; individual; 2 forms; 3 editions (identical except for test figures): Caucasian, Negroid, Oriental; no data on reliability and validity; $14 per set of all 3 editions including 5 record forms, general manual, and manual of instructions; $10 per Caucasian-figures edition including preceding accessories; $3.50 per 25 record forms; $1 per general manual; $3.50 per manual of instructions; postpaid; (30–45) minutes; David B. Lynn; Test Developments. *

a) [SERIES 1.] 1959; 1 form (12 cardboard figures and objects and 4 background cards); manual of instructions (18 pages); general manual (25 pages); record form (10 pages).

b) [SERIES 2.] 1959–60; for research use only; 1 form ['60, 10 cardboard figures and objects and 3 background cards]; manual of instructions ('60, 15 pages); general manual ('60, 4 pages); record form ('59, 8 pages); no norms.

For reviews by Terence Moore and Alan O. Ross, see 6:241 (6 references).

[477]

Structured-Objective Rorschach Test: Preliminary Edition. Adults; 1958; SORT; also called *S-O Rorschach Test;* 15 scores (for deriving 26 traits): whole-blot (W), major details (D), minor details (Dd), white space (S), form resemblance (F), poor form resemblance (F—), human movement (M), animal movement (FM), color and form resemblance (FC), color and poor form resemblance (CF), shading (Fch), animal figure (A), human figure (H), modal responses (P), rare responses (O); 1 form; 2 editions; preliminary manual (28 pages); separate answer sheets (IBM 805 and 1230) must be used; 10¢ per IBM answer sheet; $6 per set of hand scoring stencils; $1 per manual; postage extra; specimen set not available; (30–50) minutes; Joics B. Stone; [S-O Publishers]. *

a) ILLUSTRATED EDITION. 1 form (12 pages); $7.50 per test.

b) NON-ILLUSTRATED EDITION. 1 form (12 pages); to be used with slides or cards; 50¢ per test; $13 per set of inkblot cards; $12.50 per set of kodaslides.

For reviews by Jesse G. Harris, Jr. and Boris Semeonoff, see 6:242 (16 references, 2 excerpts).

REFERENCES

1–16. See 6:242.
17. BROE, JOHN RICHARD. *Prediction of Success in Training Among Electronics Technicians.* Doctor's thesis, University of Southern California (Los Angeles, Calif.), 1962. (*DA* 23:2417)
18. DOWNS, HARRY SIMS. *Temperament Trait Differences of Academically-Able College and Noncollege High School Graduates.* Doctor's thesis, Michigan State University (East Lansing, Mich.), 1962. (*DA* 23:1271)
19. BAILEY, ROBERT W. *The Structured-Objective Rorschach Test as a Measure of Over- and Underachievement.* Master's thesis, Utah State University (Logan, Utah), 1964.
20. CHANSKY, NORMAN M. "Stress, Personality and Visual Closure." *J Psychol* 57:289–301 Ap '64. * (*PA* 39:1852)
21. LANGER, PHILIP, and McKAIN, CHARLES W. "Rigidity and the SORT." *J Clin Psychol* 20:489–92 O '64. * (*PA* 39:12344)
22. MAHAN, THOMAS W., JR., and WICAS, EDWARD A. "Counselor Personality Characteristics: A Preliminary Exploration." *Counselor Ed & Sup* 3:78–83 w '64. *
23. CHANSKY, NORMAN M. "Aptitude, Personality, and Achievement in Six College Curricula." *Ed & Psychol Meas* 25:1117–24 w '65. * (*PA* 40:3564)
24. COOKE, NANCY B. *Personality Attributes as Measured by the Structured Objective Rorschach Test and Academic Achievement of Forestry Freshmen.* Master's thesis, North Carolina State University (Raleigh, N.C.), 1965.
25. HICK, THOMAS L. *Anxiety on the SORT.* Master's thesis, Utah State University (Logan, Utah), 1965.
26. KIRCHNER, WAYNE K. "Relationships Between the Structured Objective Rorschach Test and the California Psychological Inventory." *J Indus Psychol* 3:24–30 Mr '65. * (*PA* 42:6192)
27. LANGER, PHILIP, and HICK, THOMAS L. "Response Set on the SORT Revisited." *J Clin Psychol* 21:63 Ja '65. * (*PA* 39:12295)
28. LANGER, PHILIP, and HICK, THOMAS L. "The Structured-Objective Rorschach Test: A Question of Choice Frequency." *Percept & Motor Skills* 21:687–97 D '65. * (*PA* 40:3577)
29. LANGER, PHILIP, and NORTON, RON. "Structured-Objective Rorschach Test: A Question of Choice Location." *Percept & Motor Skills* 21:703–6 D '65. * (*PA* 40:3578)
30. LANGER, PHILIP, and WOOD, CARLTON G. "Comparison of Two Multiple-Choice Rorschach Tests." *Percept & Motor Skills* 20:143–50 F '65. * (*PA* 40:10264)
31. WEINLANDER, MAX M. "Alcoholics and the Validity of the Variables on the Structured-Objective Rorschach Test (SORT)." *J Psychol* 61:73–5 S '65. * (*PA* 40:5682)
32. WEINLANDER, MAX M. "Neurotics and the Validity of SORT Variables." *Percept & Motor Skills* 21:197–8 Ag '65. * (*PA* 40:629)
33. GOETZINGER, C. P.; ORTIZ, J. D.; BELLROSE, BETTY; and BUCHAN, L. G. "A Study of the S.O. Rorschach With Deaf and Hearing Adolescents." *Am Ann Deaf* 111:510–22 My '66. * (*PA* 40:10372)
34. LANGER, PHILIP, and HICK, THOMAS L. "The Structured-Objective Rorschach Test: A Question of Choice Intensity." *Percept & Motor Skills* 22:439–42 Ap '66. * (*PA* 40:8873)
35. LEWIS, JAMES NOLAN. *The Relationship of Attributes Measured by the Structured-Objective Rorschach Test and Success in Student Teaching.* Doctor's thesis, North Texas State University (Denton, Tex.), 1966. (*DA* 27:1282A)
36. PHILLIPS, BEEMAN N. "Defensiveness as a Factor in Sex Differences in Anxiety." *J Consult Psychol* 30:167–9 Ap '66. * (*PA* 40:6641)
37. RANKIN, R. J., and THOMPSON, KENNETH. "A Factor Analytic Approach to Impulse as Measured by Arrow Dot I, Q, and SORT." *Percept & Motor Skills* 23:1239–45 D '66. * (*PA* 41:5262)
38. WEINLANDER, ALBERTINA A. "Sex Differences in Scores on the Structured-Objective Rorschach Test." *Psychol Rep* 18:839–42 Je '66. * (*PA* 40:10140)
39. WEINLANDER, MAX M. "The SORT and Psychotic Patients." *J Clin Psychol* 22:224–5 Ap '66. * (*PA* 40:7741)
40. HARRIS, F. EDWARD. *Language Concepts and Personality Measurement in the Deaf Using the S-O Rorschach Test.* Doctor's thesis, Colorado State College (Greeley, Colo.), 1967. (*DA* 28:2984A)
41. STEINBERG, MARVIN; SEGEL, RUEBEN H.; and LEVINE, HARRY D. "Psychological Determinants of Academic Success: A Pilot Study." *Ed & Psychol Meas* 27:413–22 su '67. * (*PA* 41:14226)
42. WEINLANDER, MAX M. "Alcoholics and the Influence of Age on the Variables of the Structured-Objective Rorschach Test (SORT)." *J Psychol* 65:57–8 Ja '67. * (*PA* 41:4765)
43. WEINLANDER, MAX M. "Neurotics and the Influence of Age on SORT Variables." *Percept & Motor Skills* 24:125–6 F '67. * (*PA* 41:8939)
44. WEINLANDER, MAX M. "Psychotics and the Influence of Age on SORT Variables." *J Clin Psychol* 23:392–3 Jl '67. * (*PA* 41:15326)
45. WEINLANDER, MAX M. "SORT Relationships of Anxiety and Awareness for Alcoholics, Neurotics and Psychotics." *J Clin Psychol* 23:205–6 Ap '67. * (*PA* 41:8940)
46. WEINLANDER, MAX M. "Validity of the Variables on the Structured-Objective Rorschach Test (SORT) Among Alcoholics, Neurotics, and Psychotics." *J Genetic Psychol* 110:91–4 Mr '67. * (*PA* 41:7365)
47. BRADBERRY, RONALD DAVID. *Relationships Among Critical Thinking Ability, Personality Attributes, and Attitudes of Students in a Teacher Education Program.* Doctor's thesis, North Texas State University (Denton, Tex.), 1968. (*DA* 29:163A)
48. GALLAGHER, ROBERT PATRICK. *Personality Characteristics of Counseling and Mathematics Institute Trainees, Changes That Occur During Training, and Relationships Between Counselor Characteristics and Counseling Potential.*

Doctor's thesis, Rutgers—The State University (New Brunswick, N.J.), 1968. (*DA* 28:4908A)

49. WEINLANDER, ALBERTINA A. "Age Differences in Scores on the Structured-Objective Rorschach Test." *J Genetic Psychol* 112:27–36 Mr '68. * (*PA* 42:10631)

NAME INDEX

[478]

Symbol Elaboration Test. Ages 6 and over; 1950–53; SET; 1 form ('53 12 pages); manual ['50, 72 pages, see 5:160(1)]; $4.50 per 5 tests and manual; 35¢ per test; postpaid; [40–50] minutes; Johanna Krout [Tabin]; the Author. *

For a review by Richard H. Dana, see 5:160 (1 reference).

[479]

Symonds Picture-Story Test. Grades 7–12; 1948; SPST; individual; 1 form (20 cards); 2 parts (Sets A and B); Set B may be administered alone or Sets A and B together; no data on reliability; $6 per set of test materials, cash orders postpaid; (60–70) minutes per set; Percival M. Symonds; Teachers College Press. *

For reviews by Walter Kass and Kenneth R. Newton, see 5:161 (2 references); for a review by E. J. G. Bradford, see 4:132 (2 references, 1 excerpt); for excerpts from related book reviews, see 4:133.

REFERENCES

1–2. See 4:132.
3–4. See 5:161.
5. SHERMAN, RUTH LAUBGROSS. *A Study With Projective Techniques of Sociometrically High and Sociometrically Low Children.* Doctor's thesis, University of Maryland (College Park, Md.), 1958. (*DA* 20:767)
6. FARRELL, JAMES R. *An Investigation to Determine the Differences in the Need for Aggression and the Press of Coercion Between Readers and Retarded Readers by Means of the Symonds Picture-Story Test.* Master's thesis, Sacramento State College (Sacramento, Calif.), 1959.
7. STICKLER, JAMES IRWIN. *Some Personality Traits of Juvenile Delinquents as Indicated by a Rating Technique Utilizing the Symonds Picture Story Test.* Doctor's thesis, Temple University (Philadelphia, Pa.), 1961. (*DA* 22:919)
8. SYMONDS, PERCIVAL M.; with ARTHUR R. JENSEN. *From Adolescent to Adult.* New York: Columbia University Press, 1961. Pp. x, 413. * (*PA* 35:2021)
9. ANSARI, ANWAR. "A Study of Adolescent Fantasy." *Manas* 2(2):63–73 '64. * (*PA* 39:7475)

[480]

*Szondi Test. Ages 5 and over; 1937–65; ST; 8 factors, 4 vectors (each vector is a total of 2 factors); homosexual, sadistic, sexual vector, epileptic, hysteric, paroxysmal vector, catatonic, paranoic, schizophrenic vector, depressive, manic, contact vector; 1 form; 2 editions: individual, group; no data on reliability;

postage extra; Lipot Szondi; Hans Huber. * (United States publisher of English-language manual and distributor of the individual test: Grune & Stratton, Inc.; United States distributor of the group test: Intercontinental Medical Book Corporation.)

a) [INDIVIDUAL] SZONDI TEST. 1937–65; 1 form ('47, 48 pictures); manual ('52, translation by Gertrude Aull of 87 below, *out of print*); Szonditest-Tableau ('65, 6 pages); Fr. 44 per set of pictures and 10 Szonditest-Tableaux; $12.50 per set of pictures; $3.50 per 25 Szonditest-Tableaux; Grune & Stratton, Inc. sells, at $2 per 50 copies, an IBM 805 answer sheet, labeled Form D, designed by H. P. David, but there are no scoring stencils and no instructions for using the separate answer sheet; must be administered "at least six, preferably ten, times with at least one day intervals between administrations"; (10–15) minutes per administration.

b) THE GROUP SZONDI TEST. 1961; 1 form (12 slides, pictures identical with the 1947 pictures in the individual form); directions for administration (26 pages, containing instructions in English, French, and German); 10-profile form (1 page, labeled Form 2, identical with 1949 individual Form B); tendency tension quotient computing form (1 page, called form 6); record folder (3 pages, called form 1, identical with 1949 individual Form A); test behavior record (1 page, called form 5); computing form (1 page, called form 7); separate answer sheets (called form 3) must be used; Fr. 48 ($12) per set of 10 copies of form 1, 20 copies of Form 2, 100 copies of form 3, 100 copies of form 5, 100 copies of form 6, 10 copies of form 7, scoring templates, and directions; Fr. 52 ($13) per set of slides; 8–10 administrations are recommended with 2 administrations per day suggested; [15–30] minutes per administration; adapted for group administration by A. Friedemann.

See 6:243 (21 references) and 5:162 (74 references); for reviews by Ardie Lubin and Albert I. Rabin, see 4:134 (64 references); for a review by Susan K. Deri, see 3:100; for excerpts from related book reviews, see 4:135; for reviews not excerpted in this volume, consult the 6th (B474 and B501) and 5th (B418) MMY's.

REFERENCES

1–64. See 4:134.
65–138. See 5:162.
139–159. See 6:243.
160. FEAMSTER, JOHN HARRY, JR. *Preferences and Dislikes of Neuropsychiatric Patients and Normals for the Finger Paintings of Other Neuropsychiatric Patients.* Doctor's thesis, University of Kentucky (Lexington, Ky.), 1950. (*DA* 20:3829)
161. BOOTH, GOTTHARD. "The Psychological Examination of Candidates for the Ministry," pp. 100–24. In *The Ministry and Mental Health.* Edited by Hans Hofmann. New York: Association Press, 1960. Pp. 251. *
162. WEBB, MARVIN W., and LAWTON, ALFRED H. "Basic Personality Traits Characteristic of Patients With Primary Obstructive Pulmonary Emphysema." *J Am Geriatrics Soc* 9:590–610 Jl '61. *
163. FRIEDMAN, ERWIN, and WALLACE, JOHN L. "Comparative Studies of Szondi Profiles of Institutionalized Mentally Defectives: 1, The 'Sublimation' Phenomenon," pp. 137–41. In *Beiträge zur Diagnostic, Prognostik und Therapie des Schicksals.* Schweizerischen Zeitschrift für Psychologie, No. 43; Szondiana III. Berne, Switzerland: Hans Huber, 1962. Pp. 280. *
164. SASAKI, RYUZO. "Typological Study on Drive Structure of Juvenile Delinquents," pp. 153–66. In *Beiträge zur Diagnostic, Prognostik und Therapie des Schicksals.* Schweizerischen Zeitschrift für Psychologie, No. 43; Szondiana III. Berne, Switzerland: Hans Huber, 1962. Pp. 280. *
165. WEBB, MARVIN W., and LAWTON, ALFRED H. "Basic Personality Traits Characteristic of the Chronic Lung Disease, Emphysema," pp. 222–42. In *Beiträge zur Diagnostic, Prognostik und Therapie des Schicksals.* Schweizerischen Zeitschrift für Psychologie, No. 43; Szondiana III. Berne, Switzerland: Hans Huber, 1962. Pp. 280. *
166. DERI, SUSAN. "Genotripism in the Framework of a Unified Theory of Choice," pp. 39–74. In *Festschrift Leopold Szondi.* Schweizerischen Zeitschrift für Psychologie, No. 47;

Szondiana V. Berne, Switzerland: Hans Huber, 1963. Pp. 326. *

167. HARROWER, MOLLY. *Appraising Personality: An Introduction to Projective Techniques, Revised Edition,* pp. 53–100. New York: Franklin Watts, Inc., 1964. Pp. xiv, 302. *

168. KLOPFER, WALTER G. "Review of *Festschrift Leopold Szondi.*" *J Proj Tech* 28:248–50 Je '64. Reply by Susan K. Deri, 28:502–4 D '64. *

169. WEBB, MARVIN W., and IRVING, ROGER W. "Psychologic and Anamnestic Patterns Characteristic of Laryngectomees: Relation to Speech Rehabilitation." *J Am Geriatrics Soc* 12:303–22 Ap '64. *

170. McKENZIE, RICHARD E. "Clinical Validity of the Rorschach and Szondi Tests." *Proc Ann Conf Air Force Behav Sci* 11:161–70 Jl '65. *

171. SAPPENFIELD, BERT R. "Test of a Szondi Assumption by Means of M-F Photographs." *J Personality* 33:409–17 S '65. * (*PA* 40:2919)

172. DERI, SUSAN. "The Szondi Test as an Instrument for Reflecting Degrees of Split and Integration Within Personality," pp. 100–11. In *Beiträge zur Psychotherapie zu Ichstörungen und Ichentwicklung und zum Sozialen Verhalten.* Schweizerischen Zeitschrift für Psychologie, No. 50; Szondiana VI. Berne, Switzerland: Hans Huber, 1966. Pp. 284. *

173. RAYCHAUDHURI, MANAS, and MAITRA, AMAL K. "Szondi Test Signs of Delinquency: A Validational Study With Juvenile Subjects." *B Council Social & Psychol Res* 6:20–4 Ja '66. * (*PA* 40:13213)

174. SAPPENFIELD, BERT R., and BALOGH, BELA. "Stereotypical M-F as Related to Two Szondi Test Assumptions." *J Proj Tech & Pers Assess* 30:387–93 Ag '66. *

175. WEBB, MARVIN W., and IRVING, ROGER W. "Psychological Traits and Anamnestic Data Characteristic of Laryngectomees; Relation of These to Speech Rehabilitation," pp. 198–218. In *Beiträge zur Psychotherapie zu Ichstörungen und Ichentwicklung und zum Sozialen Verhalten.* Schweizerischen Zeitschrift für Psychologie, No. 50; Szondiana VI. Berne, Switzerland: Hans Huber, 1966. Pp. 284. *

176. BLUMER, DIETRICH. "The Temporal Lobes and Paroxysmal Behavior Disorders: A Study of Patients With Temporal Lobectomy for Epilepsy," pp. 273–85. In *Kriminalität Erziehung und Ethik.* Schweizerischen Zeitschrift für Psychologie, No. 51; Szondiana VII. Berne, Switzerland: Hans Huber, 1967. Pp. 354. *

177. COTTINGHAM, A. "The Szondi Test and Defense Organization of Personality," pp. 330–3. In *Kriminalität Erziehung und Ethik.* Schweizerischen Zeitschrift für Psychologie, No. 51; Szondiana VII. Berne, Switzerland: Hans Huber, 1967. Pp. 354. *

178. DERI, SUSAN. "Changing Concepts of Transference in Depth-Psychology," pp. 114–25. In *Kriminalität Erziehung und Ethik.* Schweizerischen Zeitschrift für Psychologie, No. 51; Szondiana VII. Berne, Switzerland: Hans Huber, 1967. Pp. 354. *

179. LESTER, M. "Developmental Aspects of the Dialectic Between Instinct and Education as Reflected in Different Vectors of the Szondi-Test," pp. 198–208. In *Kriminalität Erziehung und Ethik.* Schweizerischen Zeitschrift für Psychologie, No. 51; Szondiana VII. Berne, Switzerland: Hans Huber, 1967. Pp. 354. *

180. SATAKE, R. "The Basic Study Concerning the Objective Measurement of the Effects of Correctional Education: Centering the Observations of the Drive Construction of Juvenile Delinquents in the Light of the Szondi Test," pp. 150–91. In *Kriminalität Erziehung und Ethik.* Schweizerischen Zeitschrift für Psychologie, No. 51; Szondiana VII. Berne, Switzerland: Hans Huber, 1967. Pp. 354. *

181. WEBB, M. W. "Predicting Surgical Results in Intractable Duodenal Ulcer," pp. 252–72. In *Kriminalität Erziehung und Ethik.* Schweizerischen Zeitschrift für Psychologie, No. 51; Szondiana VII. Berne, Switzerland: Hans Huber, 1967. Pp. 354. *

182. CAMPOS, LEONARD P. "The Szondi Test," pp. 462–72. In *Projective Techniques in Personality Assessment: A Modern Introduction.* Edited by A. I. Rabin. New York: Springer Publishing Co., Inc., 1968. Pp. x, 638. *

183. THOMAS, EDWARD LLEWELLYN. "Eye Movements During Projective Testing." Abstract. *Int Congr Rorsch & Proj Meth* 6(3):325–6 '68. *

NAME INDEX

★**Tasks of Emotional Development Test.** Ages 6–11, adolescents; 1960–66; TED; individual; 2 levels; mimeographed directions for administration ['60, 16 pages]; mimeographed rating scales for pictures 1–6 ['61, 40 pages], 7–13 ['61, 43 pages]; no norms; $35 per set of testing materials, postpaid; (15–30) minutes; Haskel Cohen and Geraldine Rickard; Department of Psychiatry, Children's Hospital Medical Center. *

a) LATENCY. Ages 6–11; 5 scores (perception, outcome, affect, motivation, spontaneity) in each of 12 areas (peer socialization, trust, aggression toward peers, attitudes for learning, respect for property of others, separation from mother figure, identification with same-sex parent, acceptance of siblings, acceptance of need-frustration, acceptance of parents' affection to one another, orderliness and responsibility, self-image) ; 1 form ['62, 12 pictures for boys, 12 for girls] ; reliability and validity data ('66, reprint of 1 below).

b) ADOLESCENCE. 5 scores in each of 13 areas: same as for latency level plus heterosexual socialization; 1 form ('63, 13 pictures for boys, 13 for girls) ; no data on reliability and validity.

REFERENCE

1. RICKARD, GERALDINE, and COHEN, HASKEL. "Assessing the Emotional Development of Children." *Mental Hyg* 50:590–2 O '66. * (*PA* 41:4626)

[482]

Ten Silhouettes. Ages 5 and over; 1959–60; TS; individual; 1 form ['60, 10 cards] ; directions for administering ['60, 2 pages] ; no data on reliability and validity; no norms; 63s. per set of testing materials, postpaid; [45] minutes; B. E. Dockar-Drysdale; the Author. *

See 6:244 (4 references).

[483]

★**Test of Subjective and Objective Factors in Relationship to Communication Skills.** High school and college; 1964; 1 form (4 pages, mimeographed) ; mimeographed manual (8 pages) ; no data on reliability and validity; no description of normative population; $3 per 25 tests; $1.50 per specimen set; postage extra; (20–30) minutes; Martha Pingel [Taylor] ; the Author. *

[484]

Thematic Apperception Test. Ages 4 and over; 1936–43; commonly known as TAT; individual; 1 form ('43, 20 cards) ; manual ('43, 20 pages) ; no data on reliability; $6 per set of testing materials; 50¢ per manual; cash orders postpaid; 100(120) minutes in 2 sessions 1 day apart; Henry A. Murray; Harvard University Press. * [*Bellak TAT Blank.* 1947–51; 1 form ('47, 6 pages) ; analysis sheet ('47, 2 pages) ; manual ('51, 10 pages) ; $1.25 per 10 blanks; $2 per 100 analysis sheets; 35¢ per manual; 60¢ per specimen set of 1 blank, 10 analysis sheets, and manual; postpaid; Leopold Bellak; Psychological Corporation. *]

For a review by C. J. Adcock, see 6:245 (287 references) ; for reviews by Leonard D. Eron and Arthur R. Jensen, see 5:164 (311 references) ; for a review by Arthur L. Benton, see 4:136 (198 references) ; for reviews by Arthur L. Benton, Julian B. Rotter, and J. R. Wittenborn, see 3:103 (101 references, 1 excerpt) ; for excerpts from related book reviews, see 4:139–41, 3:104, and 3:104a; for reviews not excerpted in this volume, consult the 6th (B60, B326) and 5th (B63, B204, B395) MMY's.

REFERENCES

1–101. See 3:103.
102–299. See 4:136.
300–610. See 5:164.
611–897. See 6:245.

898. ROSE, ALVIN W. "Projective Techniques in Sociological Research." *Social Forces* 28:175–83 D '49. * (*PA* 25:1723)
899. WEBER, GEORGE H. "Some Qualitative Aspects of an Exploratory Personality Study of 15 Juvenile Automobile Thieves." *Trans Kans Acad Sci* 53:548–56 '50. * (*PA* 25:7574)
900. HIRE, A. WILLIAM. "Use of the Rorschach and Thematic Apperception Tests in the Counseling and Guidance of College Students." Thesis abstract. *Harvard Ed R* 21:65–8 w '51. *

901. ROE, ANNE. "A Psychological Study of Physical Scientists." *Genetic Psychol Monogr* 43:121–235 My '51. * (*PA* 26:1756)
902. WEBSTER, HAROLD D., JR. *The Prediction of Personality Data From Thematic Apperception Test Scores.* Doctor's thesis, University of California (Berkeley, Calif.), 1951.
903. MALCOM, EDWARD VARTAN. *A Study of the Validity of Individual Personality Profiles Based on Each of Four Projective Techniques.* Doctor's thesis, University of Michigan (Ann Arbor, Mich.), 1952. (*DA* 12:221)
904. POSER, E. G. "The Use of Psychological Tests in Psychosomatic Research." *Can J Psychol* 7:177–82 D '53. * (*PA* 28:6408)
905. BLACKHAM, GARTH I. *A Clinical Study of the Personality Structures and Adjustments of Pupils Under-Achieving and Over-Achieving in Reading.* Doctor's thesis, Cornell University (Ithaca, N.Y.), 1954. (*DA* 15:1199)
906. SEGAL, ALZIRE SOPHIA BLOCK. *The Prediction of Expressed Attitudes Toward the Mother.* Doctor's thesis, University of Michigan (Ann Arbor, Mich.), 1954. (*DA* 14:1259)
907. BRODY, HAROLD. *Psychologic Factors Associated With Infertility in Women: A Comparative Study of Psychologic Factors in Women Afflicted With Infertility Including Groups With and Without a Medical Basis for Their Condition.* Doctor's thesis, New York University (New York, N.Y.), 1955. (*DA* 15:1253)
908. ERVIN, SUSAN MOORE. *The Verbal Behavior of Bilinguals: The Effect of Language of Report Upon the Thematic Apperception Test Stories of Adult French Bilinguals.* Doctor's thesis, University of Michigan (Ann Arbor, Mich.), 1955. (*DA* 15:1664)
909. JACOBSEN, ELDON ERNEST. *Assessment of Adjustment in Children and Adolescents: Reliabilities and Interrelationships Concerning Common Group Tests and Ratings and Their Relationships to Judgments From Clinical Tests.* Doctor's thesis, University of Washington (Seattle, Wash.), 1955. (*DA* 15:1653)
910. KAHN, DOUGLAS MORTIMER. *The Relationship of Certain Personality Characteristics to Recovery From Tuberculosis.* Doctor's thesis, New York University (New York, N.Y.), 1955. (*DA* 15:1256)
911. SMOLINSKY, HAROLD JAY. *Sex Differences in Paranoid Schizophrenia: A Comparative Study of the Personality Characteristics of Male and Female Hospital Patients Diagnosed as Paranoid Schizophrenic.* Doctor's thesis, New York University (New York, N.Y.), 1955. (*DA* 15:1258)
912. VON HOLT, HENRY WILLIAM, JR. *A Study of Personality Processes Operative Under Neutral, Failure, and Success Conditions.* Doctor's thesis, Clark University (Worcester, Mass.), 1955. (*DA* 15:1660)
913. WALCOTT, WILLIAM O. *Memory and Personality: An Investigation of the Dynamics of Memory With the Rorschach and TAT Tests.* Doctor's thesis, Claremont College (Claremont, Calif.), 1955.
914. FREUDENBERGER, HERBERT J. *An Investigation Into Certain Personality Characteristics as They Relate to Improvement in Parkinsonism: The Influence of Submissiveness, Inactivity, Pessimism and Affective Relatedness on the Improvement of Parkinson Patients With the Pagitane Drug.* Doctor's thesis, New York University (New York, N.Y.), 1956. (*DA* 16:1944)
915. GROESBECK, BYRON LOU. *Personality Correlates of the Achievement and Affiliation Motives in Clinical Psychology Trainees.* Doctor's thesis, University of Michigan (Ann Arbor, Mich.), 1956. (*DA* 16:2513)
916. BERKOWITZ, HOWARD. *A Study of Psychological Attributes in the Second Half of Life.* Doctor's thesis, University of Texas (Austin, Tex.), 1957. (*DA* 17:2670)
917. FRIEDMAN, IRA. "Characteristics of the Thematic Apperception Test Heroes of Normal, Psychoneurotic, and Paranoid Schizophrenic Subjects." *J Proj Tech* 21:372–6 D '57. *
918. HORRALL, BERNICE M. "Academic Performance and Personality Adjustments of Highly Intelligent College Students." *Genetic Psychol Monogr* 55:3–83 F '57. * (*PA* 33:4697)
919. KAPLAN, MARTIN JEROME. *Unconscious Self Evaluation and Subliminal Familiarity: An Evaluation of the Wolff-Huntley Expressive Behavior Technique for Eliciting Self Concepts and Its Relationship to Subliminal Familiarity.* Doctor's thesis, New York University (New York, N.Y.), 1957. (*DA* 17:3083)
920. SAUER, R. E., and MARCUSE, F. L. "Overt and Covert Recording." *J Proj Tech* 21:391–5 D '57. *
921. ULLMANN, LEONARD P. "Productivity and the Clinical Use of TAT Cards." *J Proj Tech* 21:399–403 D '57. *
922. WEISSKOPF-JOELSON, EDITH. "Symposium: Research in Projective Techniques." *J Proj Tech* 21:347–9 D '57. *
923. WOHL, JULIAN. "A Note on the Generality of Constriction." *J Proj Tech* 21:410–3 D '57. *
924. YOUNG, HARL HENRY, JR. *Personality Test Correlates of Orientation to the Vertical: A Test of Witkin's Field-Dependency Hypothesis.* Doctor's thesis, University of Texas (Austin, Tex.), 1957. (*DA* 19:882)
925. BEARDSLEE, DAVID C., and FOGELSON, R. Chap. 9. "Sex Differences in Sexual Imagery Aroused by Musical Stimulation," pp. 132–42. In *Motives in Fantasy, Action, and Society: A Method of Assessment and Study.* Edited by John W. At-

kinson. Princeton, N.J.: D. Van Nostrand Co., Inc., 1958. Pp. xv, 873. * (PA 33:758)

926. FRIEDMAN, JOSEPH. Psychological Correlates of Overweight, Underweight and Normal Weight College Women. Doctor's thesis, Temple University (Philadelphia, Pa.), 1958. (DA 19:3362)

927. GOTTFRIED, NATHAN WOLF. Psychological Needs and Verbally Expressed Aggression of Adolescent Delinquent Boys. Doctor's thesis, Ohio State University (Columbus, Ohio), 1958. (DA 19:3352)

928. GROESBECK, BYRON L. Chap. 28, "Toward Description of Personality in Terms of Configuration of Motives," pp. 383–99. In Motives in Fantasy, Action, and Society: A Method of Assessment and Study. Edited by John W. Atkinson. Princeton, N.J.: D. Van Nostrand Co., Inc., 1958. Pp. xv, 873. * (PA 33:758)

929. JONES, MARY COVER, and MUSSEN, PAUL HENRY. "Self-Conceptions, Motivations, and Interpersonal Attitudes of Early- and Late-Maturing Girls." Child Develop 29:491–501 D '58. * (PA 34:4128)

930. KANTER, VICTOR B. Appendix 1, "A Comparison by Means of Psychological Tests: Young Men With Duodenal Ulcer and Controls," pp. 227–61. In Family Influences and Psychosomatic Illness: An Inquiry Into the Social and Psychological Background of Duodenal Ulcer. By E. M. Goldberg. London: Tavistock Publications, 1958. Pp. xii, 308. *

931. McNEIL, ELTON B., and COHLER, J. ROBERT, JR. "Adult Aggression in the Management of Disturbed Children." Child Develop 29:451–61 D '58. * (PA 34:3726)

932. REITMAN, WALTER R., and ATKINSON, JOHN W. Chap. 46, "Some Methodological Problems in the Use of Thematic Apperceptive Measures of Human Motives," pp. 664–83. In Motives in Fantasy, Action, and Society: A Method of Assessment and Study. Edited by John W. Atkinson. Princeton, N.J.: D. Van Nostrand Co., Inc., 1958. Pp. xv, 873. * (PA 33:758)

933. BAUGHMAN, E. EARL; SHANDS, HARLEY C.; and HAWKINS, DAVID R. "Intensive Psychotherapy and Personality Change: Psychological Test Evaluation of a Single Case." Psychiatry 22:296–301 Ag '59. * (PA 34:6067)

934. HELLER, KENNETH. Dependency Changes in Psychotherapy as a Function of the Discrepancy Between Conscious Self-Description and Projective Test Performance. Doctor's thesis, Pennsylvania State University (University Park, Pa.), 1959. (DA 20:3378)

935. HOLTZMAN, WAYNE H. Chap. 7, "Objective Scoring of Projective Tests," pp. 119–45. In Objective Approaches to Personality Assessment. Edited by Bernard M. Bass and Irwin A. Berg. New York: D. Van Nostrand Co., Inc., 1959. Pp. x, 233. * (PA 33:9926)

936. JUDSON, A. J., and WERNERT, CLAIRE. "Need Affiliation, Orality, and the Perception of Aggression." Psychiatric Q Sup 32:76–81 pt 1 '59. * (PA 34:3003)

937. KERCKHOFF, ALAN C. "Anomie and Achievement Motivation: A Study of Personality Development Within Cultural Disorganization." Social Forces 37:196–202 Mr '59. * (PA 34:1227)

938. LASKOWITZ, DAVID. The Effect of Varied Degrees of Pictorial Ambiguity on Fantasy Evocation: A Comparative Analysis of Two Techniques of Producing Gradated Ambiguity With Thematic Apperception Test Cards With Respect to the Amount of Fantasy Evoked. Doctor's thesis, New York University (New York, N.Y.), 1959. (DA 20:3379)

939. PHILIP, B. ROGER, and PEIXOTTO, HELEN E. "An Objective Evaluation of Brief Group Psychotherapy on Delinquent Boys." Can J Psychol 13:273–80 D '59. * (PA 36:5JO73P)

940. FINK, J. H. A Psychophysiological Comparison of Brittle and Stable Diabetics. Doctor's thesis, University of California (Los Angeles, Calif.), 1960.

941. REITMAN, WALTER R. "Motivational Induction and the Behavior Correlates of the Achievement and Affiliation Motives." J Abn & Social Psychol 60:8–13 Ja '60. * (PA 34:7171)

942. VEROFF, JOSEPH; ATKINSON, JOHN W.; FELD, SHEILA C.; and GURIN, GERALD. "The Use of Thematic Apperception to Assess Motivation in a Nationwide Interview Study." Psychol Monogr 74(12):1–32 '60. * (PA 36:1HG32V)

943. BERLEW, DAVID E. "Interpersonal Sensitivity and Motive Strength." J Abn & Social Psychol 63:390–4 S '61. * (PA 37:1298)

944. BYRNE, DONN. "Anxiety and the Experimental Arousal of Affiliation Need." J Abn & Social Psychol 63:660–2 N '61. * (PA 37:1329)

945. BYRNE, DONN. "Interpersonal Attraction as a Function of Affiliation Need and Attitude Similarity." Hum Relations 14:283–9 Ag '61. * (PA 37:1041)

946. DUNLAP, NAOMI GIBSON. Alcoholism in Women: Some Antecedents and Correlates of Remission in Middle-Class Members of Alcoholics Anonymous. Doctor's thesis, University of Texas (Austin, Tex.), 1961. (DA 22:1904)

947. FOULDS, G. A. "Personality Traits and Neurotic Symptoms and Signs." Brit J Med Psychol 34:263–70 pt 4 '61. * (PA 37:1229)

948. GOLDSTEIN, LAWRENCE. Empathy and Its Relationship to Personality Factors and Personality Organization. Doctor's thesis, New York University (New York, N.Y.), 1961. (DA 22:4402)

949. GRIMM, ELAINE R. "Psychological Tension in Pregnancy." Psychosom Med 23:520–7 N–D '61. * (PA 36:5JU2oG)

950. KAPLAN, BERT. Chap. 8, "Cross-Cultural Use of Projective Techniques," pp. 235–54. In Psychological Anthropology: Approaches to Culture and Personality. Edited by Francis L. K. Hsu. Homewood, Ill.: Homewood Press, Inc., 1961. Pp. ix, 520. *

951. McCULLY, ROBERT STEPHEN. Fantasy Productions of Children With a Progressively Crippling and Fatal Illness. Doctor's thesis, Columbia University (New York, N.Y.), 1961. (DA 22:643)

952. McKENZIE, MIRIAM TANZER. Flexibility and Mental Health: A T.A.T. Study. Doctor's thesis, New York University (New York, N.Y.), 1961. (DA 29:758B)

953. MUELLER, ALFRED D.; LEFKOVITS, AARON M.; BRYANT, JOHN E.; and MARSHALL, MAX L. "Some Psychological Factors in Patients With Rheumatoid Arthritis." Arthr & Rheum 4:275–82 Ap '61. *

954. POWELL, KATHRYN SUMMERS. "Maternal Employment in Relation to Family Life." Marriage & Family Living 23:350–5 N '61. * (PA 36:5FG50P)

955. RABIN, ALBERT I. "Culture Components as a Significant Factor in Child Development: Symposium, 1960: 2, Kibbutz Adolescents." Discussion by Theodora M. Abel and Rogelio Diaz-Guerrero. Am J Orthopsychiatry 31:493–504, 512–20 Jl '61. * (PA 36:4FF81A)

956. SHELLEY, ERNEST L. V., and JOHNSON, WALTER F., JR. "Evaluating an Organized Counseling Service for Youthful Offenders." J Counsel Psychol 8:351–4 w '61. * (PA 37:3650)

957. AINSWORTH, MARY D., and AINSWORTH, LEONARD H. "Acculturation in East Africa: 2, Frustration and Aggression." J Social Psychol 57:401–7 Ag '62. * (PA 37:4804)

958. COBB, BEATRIX; DAMARIN, FRED; KRASNOFF, ALAN; and TRUNNELL, J. B. "Personality Factors and Stress in Carcinoma," pp. 738–65. In Psychosomatic Obstetrics, Gynecology and Endocrinology. Edited by William S. Kroger. Springfield, Ill.: Charles C Thomas, Publisher, 1962. Pp. xxv, 820. *

959. COHEN, HASKEL. "Psychological Test Findings in Adolescents Having Ovarian Dysgenesis." Psychosom Med 24:249–56 Mr–Ap '62. * (PA 37:5107)

960. DIENER, ROBERT GEORGE. The Prediction of Dependent Behavior and Dependency Related Anxiety From Psychological Tests. Doctor's thesis, University of Colorado (Boulder, Colo.), 1962. (DA 23:3971)

961. HOWALD, BETTY LOU. An Investigation Into Anxiety Factors in Achieving and Underachieving Gifted Children at the Fifth Grade Level. Doctor's thesis, University of Maryland (College Park, Md.), 1962. (DA 25:1746)

962. HOWELL, MARY CATHERINE. Some Effects of Chronic Illness on Children and Their Mothers. Doctor's thesis, University of Minnesota (Minneapolis, Minn.), 1962. (DA 23:2976)

963. PECK, ROBERT F. "Student Mental Health: The Range of Personality Patterns in a College Population," pp. 161–99. (PA 37:5614) In Personality Factors on the College Campus: Review of a Symposium. Edited by Robert L. Sutherland and others. Austin, Tex.: Hogg Foundation for Mental Health, 1962. Pp. xxii, 242. * (PA 37:5621)

964. PIOTROWSKI, ZYGMUNT A. "Psychogenic Factors in Anovulatory Women: 2, Psychological Evaluation." Fertil & Steril 13:11–9 Ja–F '62. *

965. ROBIN, A. A. "The Psychological Changes of Normal Parturition." Psychiatric Q 36:129–50 Ja '62. * (PA 38:4343)

966. SILVERMAN, BEVERLY. Intra-Family Fantasy in Terms of Sexual Identification. Doctor's thesis, Yeshiva University (New York, N.Y.), 1962. (DA 25:2056)

967. WEINER, HERBERT; SINGER, MARGARET T.; and REISER, MORTON F. "Cardiovascular Responses and Their Psychological Correlates: 1, A Study in Healthy Young Adults and Patients With Peptic Ulcer and Hypertension." Psychosom Med 24:477–98 S–O '62. * (PA 37:5539)

968. WOOLF, MAURICE D. "The TAT and Reading Disability." Yearb Nat Read Conf 11:180–8 '62. *

969. ARFFA, MARVIN SANFORD. An Investigation of Some Criteria of Adjustive Behavior Among Chronic Female Psychiatric Patients in a State Mental Hospital. Doctor's thesis, State University of New York at Buffalo (Buffalo, N.Y.), 1963. (DA 26:5544)

970. ARTHUR, BETTIE. "Role Perceptions of Children With Ulcerative Colitis." Arch Gen Psychiatry 8:536–45 Je '63. * (PA 38:5720)

971. BURNSTEIN, EUGENE; MOULTON, R.; and LIBERTY, PAUL, JR. "Prestige vs. Excellence as Determinants of Role Attractiveness." Am Sociol R 28:212–9 Ap '63. * (PA 37:7903)

972. BYRNE, DONN; McDONALD, ROY DAVID; and MIKAWA, JAMES. "Approach and Avoidance Affiliation Motives." J Personality 31:21–37 Mr '63. * (PA 39:7833)

973. CHATTERJEE, TARIH K. "Study of Personality of an Epileptic Homicide." Samikas 17(4):207–23 '63. * (PA 39:2219)

974. CHORNY, HAROLD HERBERT. Fantasy Aggression and the Injuriousness of Induced Aggression. Doctor's thesis, Northwestern University (Evanston, Ill.), 1963. (DA 25:622)

975. FINK, JOSEPHINE H. "Personality Variables in Brittle

and Stable Diabetics." *Newsl Res Psychol* 5:8–9 Ag '63. * (*PA* 38:8587)

976. FLINN, DON E.; HARTMAN, BRYCE O.; POWELL, DOUGLAS H.; and McKENZIE, RICHARD E. "Psychiatric and Psychologic Evaluation," pp. 199–230. In *Aeromedical Evaluation for Space Pilots*. Edited by Lawrence E. Lamb. Brooks Air Force Base, Tex.: USAF School of Aerospace Medicine, July 1963. Pp. viii, 276. * (*PA* 38:4728)

977. GALLIGAN, CAROL WOLFE. *Personality Correlates of Varying Degrees of Adherence to an Orthodox Structure*. Doctor's thesis, New York University (New York, N.Y.), 1963. (*DA* 24:3835)

978. GREENSTADT, WILLIAM MARTIN. *An Evaluation of Types of Drive and of Ego Strength Variables in Selected Problem and Non-Problem Elementary School Boys: Inter and Intra-Group Comparisons of Projective Test Variables of Seven-, Nine- and Eleven-Year-Old Boys Manifesting Certain Varieties of Classroom Behavioral Disturbances*. Doctor's thesis, New York University (New York, N.Y.), 1963. (*DA* 25:2610)

979. HEALY, BIGELOW CHANDLER. *Personality Factors in Level of Aspiration*. Doctor's thesis, University of Florida (Gainesville, Fla.), 1963. (*DA* 25:662)

980. KANEKO, ZIRO, and TAKAISHI, NOBORU. "Psychosomatic Studies on Chronic Urticaria." *Folia Psychiatrica Neurologica Japonica* 17:16–24 Jl '63. * (*PA* 38:6547)

981. LAFFEY, JOHN JOSEPH. *Impulsivity and Temporal Experience in Prisoners*. Doctor's thesis, Michigan State University (East Lansing, Mich.), 1963. (*DA* 24:2564)

982. MAES, JOHN L. *Identification of Male College Students With Their Fathers and Some Related Indices of Affect Expression and Psychosexual Adjustment*. Doctor's thesis, Michigan State University (East Lansing, Mich.), 1963. (*DA* 24:1245)

983. SINGER, MARGARET THALER. Chap. 12, "Personality Measurements in the Aged," pp. 217–49. In *Human Aging: A Biological and Behavioral Study*. Edited by James E. Birren, Robert N. Butler, Samuel W. Greenhouse, Louis Sokoloff, and Marian R. Yarrow. National Institute of Mental Health, Public Health Service Publication No. 986. Washington, D.C.: United States Government Printing Office, 1963. Pp. xiii, 328. * (*PA* 38:5821)

984. WEISSMAN, STUART LEONARD. *Some Indicators of Acting Out Behavior From the Thematic Apperception Test*. Doctor's thesis, Yeshiva University (New York, N.Y.), 1963. (*DA* 25:636)

985. ALLISON, ROGER B., JR.; KORNER, IJA N.; and ZWANZIGER, MAX D. "Clinical Judgments and Objective Measures." *J Psychol* 57:451–6 Ap '64. * (*PA* 39:1878)

986. ANDERSON, LYNN R., and FIEDLER, FRED E. "The Effect of Participatory and Supervisory Leadership on Group Creativity." *J Appl Psychol* 48:227–36 Ag '64. * (*PA* 39:4903)

987. BECKER, GEORGE J. *Personality Characteristics of Good and Poor Judges of Religious-Moral Situations*. Doctor's thesis, New School for Social Research (New York, N.Y.), 1964. (*DA* 25:6049)

988. BERKUN, MITCHELL M., and BURDICK, HARRY A. "Effect of Preceding Rosenzweig's PF Test With the TAT." *J Clin Psychol* 20:253 Ap '64. * (*PA* 39:7884)

989. BROOTA, K. D. "A Preliminary Study of the Thematic Apperception Test." *Indian J Psychol* 39:51–8 Je '64. * (*PA* 40:2130)

990. CONGDON, ROBERT G. "Personality Factors and the Capacity to Meet Curriculum Demands." *Personnel & Guid J* 42:767–75 Ap '64. * (*PA* 39:5905)

991. DALACK, JOHN DONALD. *The Relationship Between TAT Hostility and Self-Report Hostility as a Function of Psychiatric Condition*. Doctor's thesis, Columbia University (New York, N.Y.), 1964. (*DA* 26:1772)

992. DANA, RICHARD H., and COOPER, GEORGE W., JR. "Susceptibility to Hypnosis and T.A.T. Card 12M." *Am J Clin Hyp* 6:208–10 Ja '64. * (*PA* 39:2180)

993. DAY, CHARLES WESLEY. *Thematic Hostility Responses of Repressors and Sensitizers as a Function of the Hostile Cue Characteristics of the Cards and an Aroused Hostile State*. Doctor's thesis, State University of Iowa (Iowa City, Iowa), 1964. (*DA* 25:5381)

994. EASTER, LAWRENCE V., and MURSTEIN, BERNARD I. "Achievement Fantasy as a Function of Probability of Success." *J Consult Psychol* 28:154–9 Ap '64. * (*PA* 39:1853)

995. EPSTEIN, MARILYN. *The Reliability and Internal Consistency of the Thematic Apperception Test*. Master's thesis, University of British Columbia (Vancouver, B.C., Canada), 1964.

996. ERVIN, SUSAN M. "Language and TAT Content in Bilinguals." *J Abn & Social Psychol* 68:500–7 My '64. * (*PA* 39:5198)

997. FOULDS, G. A. "Organization and Hostility in the Thematic Apperception Test Stories of Schizophrenics." *Brit J Psychiatry* 110:64–6 Ja '64. * (*PA* 39:2180)

998. FOULKES, DAVID, and RECHTSCHAFFEN, ALLAN. "Presleep Determinants of Dream Content: Effects of Two Films." *Percept & Motor Skills* 19:983–1005 D '64. * (*PA* 39:6627)

999. FRIEDMAN, C. JACK; JOHNSON, CARLETON A.; and FODE, KERMIT. "Subjects' Descriptions of Selected TAT Cards Via

the Semantic Differential." *J Consult Psychol* 28:317–25 Ag '64. * (*PA* 39:5058)

1000. GOLDEN, MARK. "Some Effects of Combining Psychological Tests on Clinical Inferences." *J Consult Psychol* 28:440–6 O '64. * (*PA* 39:5060)

1001. GUTMANN, DAVID L. Chap. 6, "An Exploration of Ego Configurations in Middle and Later Life," pp. 114–48. In *Personality in Middle and Late Life: Empirical Studies*. Edited by Bernice L. Neugarten. New York: Atherton Press, 1964. Pp. xxiii, 231. *

1002. HATTEM, JACK VICTOR. *The Precipitating Role of Discordant Interpersonal Relationships in Suicidal Behavior*. Doctor's thesis, University of Houston (Houston, Tex.), 1964. (*DA* 25:1335)

1003. HAWORTH, MARY R. "Parental Loss in Children as Reflected in Projective Responses." *J Proj Tech & Pers Assess* 26:31–45 Mr '64. * (*PA* 39:1857)

1004. KALIN, RUDOLF. "Effects of Alcohol on Memory." *J Abn & Social Psychol* 69:635–41 D '64. * (*PA* 39:6804)

1005. KANTER, V. B., and HAZELTON, J. E. "An Attempt to Measure Some Aspects of Personality in Young Men With Duodenal Ulcer by Means of Questionnaires and a Projective Test." *J Psychosom Res* 8:297–309 D '64. * (*PA* 39:12455)

1006. KENNY, DOUGLAS T. "Stimulus Functions in Projective Techniques," pp. 285–354. In *Progress in Experimental Personality Research, Vol. 1*. Edited by Brendan A Maher. New York: Academic Press, Inc., 1964. Pp. x, 368. *

1007. KOLLAR, EDWARD J.; SLATER, GRANT R.; PALMER, JAMES O.; DOCTER, RICHARD F.; and MANDELL, ARNOLD J. "Measurement of Stress in Fasting Man: A Pilot Study." *Arch Gen Psychiatry* 11:113–25 Ag '64. * (*PA* 39:4233)

1008. KOSIER, KENNETH P. *A Comparison CAT/TAT and Children's Drawings as Projective Stimuli*. Master's thesis, University of Wisconsin (Madison, Wis.), 1964.

1009. LEVITT, EUGENE E.; PERSKY, HAROLD; and BRADY, JOHN PAUL. *Hypnotic Induction of Anxiety: A Psychoendocrine Investigation*. Springfield, Ill.: Charles C Thomas, Publisher, 1964. Pp. xvi, 134. *

1010. MELIKIAN, LEVON H. "The Use of Selected T.A.T. Cards Among Arab University Students: A Cross-Cultural Study." *J Social Psychol* 62:3–19 F '64. * (*PA* 39:1472)

1011. MURSTEIN, BERNARD I. "A Normative Study of TAT Ambiguity." *J Proj Tech & Pers Assess* 28:210–8 Je '64. * (*PA* 39:5208)

1012. NEUGARTEN, BERNICE L. Chap. 9, "Summary and Implications," pp. 188–200. In her *Personality in Middle and Late Life: Empirical Studies*. New York: Atherton Press, 1964. Pp. xxiii, 231. *

1013. NEUGARTEN, BERNICE L., and GUTMANN, DAVID L. Chap. 3, "Age-Sex Roles and Personality in Middle Age: A Thematic Apperception Study," pp. 44–89. In *Personality in Middle and Late Life: Empirical Studies*. Edited by Bernice L. Neugarten. New York: Atherton Press, 1964. Pp. xxiii, 231. * Condensation of 654.

1014. NEUGARTEN, BERNICE L., and MILLER, DAVID L. Chap. 5, "Ego Functions in the Middle and Later Years: A Further Exploration," pp. 105–13. In *Personality in Middle and Late Life: Empirical Studies*. Edited by Bernice L. Neugarten. New York: Atherton Press, 1964. Pp. xxiii, 231. *

1015. NEUGARTEN, BERNICE L.; CROTTY, WILLIAM F.; and TOBIN, SHELDON S. Chap. 8, "Personality Types in an Aged Population," pp. 158–87. In *Personality in Middle and Late Life: Empirical Studies*. Edited by Bernice L. Neugarten. New York: Atherton Press, 1964. Pp. xxiii, 231. *

1016. PECK, ROBERT F., and BERKOWITZ, HOWARD. Chap. 2, "Personality and Adjustment in Middle Age," pp. 15–43. In *Personality in Middle and Late Life: Empirical Studies*. Edited by Bernice L. Neugarten. New York: Atherton Press, 1964. Pp. xxiii, 231. *

1017. PHELAN, JOSEPH G. "Analysis of the 'Good Errors' Made by Clinical Psychologists in Diagnostic Judgment." *J Psychol* 58:43–55 Jl '64. * (*PA* 39:5322)

1018. PHELAN, JOSEPH G. "Rationale Employed by Clinical Psychologists in Diagnostic Judgment." *J Clin Psychol* 20:454–8 O '64. * (*PA* 39:12469)

1019. POPE, BENJAMIN, and SIEGMAN, ARON W. "An Intercorrelational Study of Some Indices of Verbal Fluency." *Psychol Rep* 15:303–10 Ag '64. * (*PA* 39:1607)

1020. PRESTON, CAROLINE E. "Psychological Testing With Northwest Coast Alaskan Eskimos." *Genetic Psychol Monogr* 69:323–419 My '64. * (*PA* 39:4713)

1021. PYTKOWICZ, ANN ROTH. *An Experimental Study of the Relationship of Fantasy to the Reduction of Hostility*. Doctor's thesis, University of Washington (Seattle, Wash.), 1964. (*DA* 25:1323)

1022. REYNOLDS, DONALD. "Social Desirability in the TAT: A Replication and Extension of Reznikoff's Study." *J Proj Tech & Pers Assess* 28:78–80 Mr '64. * (*PA* 39:1869)

1023. ROSEN, JACQUELINE L., and NEUGARTEN, BERNICE L. Chap. 4, "Ego Functions in the Middle and Later Years: A Thematic Apperception Study," pp. 90–104. Addendum by Marc I. Lubin. In *Personality in Middle and Late Life: Empirical Studies*. Edited by Bernice L. Neugarten. New York: Atherton Press, 1964. Pp. xxiii, 231. * Adaptation of 743.

1024. ROSENWALD, GEORGE C. "The Relation of Drive Discharge to the Enjoyment of Humor." *J Personality* 32:682–98 D '64. * (*PA* 39:10290)

1025. RUBIN, SAMUEL S. "A Comparison of the Thematic Apperception Test Stories of Two I.Q. Groups." *J Proj Tech & Pers Assess* 28:81–5 Mr '64. * (*PA* 39:1870)

1026. SAWYIER, WILFRED GRENFELL. *A Study of the Effect of Group Counseling on the Antisocial Attitudes and Antisocial Behavior of Prison Inmates.* Doctor's thesis, Michigan State University (East Lansing, Mich.), 1964. (*DA* 25:5125)

1027. SCHWABE, ARTHUR G. *An Investigation of the Effect of Structuring of Stimuli on the Ambiguity of the Response Given by Subjects on the TAT.* Master's thesis, University of Portland (Portland, Ore.), 1964.

1028. SETHI, BRIJ B. "Relationship of Separation to Depression." *Arch Gen Psychiatry* 10:486–96 My '64. * (*PA* 39:5786)

1029. SHIPMAN, WILLIAM G. "TAT Validity: Congruence With an Inventory." *J Proj Tech & Pers Assess* 28:227–32 Je '64. * (*PA* 39:5214)

1030. SHORE, MILTON F.; MASSIMO, JOSEPH L.; and MACK, RONALD. "The Relationship Between Levels of Guilt in Thematic Stories and Unsocialized Behavior." *J Proj Tech & Pers Assess* 28:346–9 S '64. * (*PA* 39:7917)

1031. SHUKIN, ALEXEY, and NEUGARTEN, BERNICE L. Chap. 7, "Personality and Social Interaction," pp. 149–57. In *Personality in Middle and Late Life: Empirical Studies.* Edited by Bernice L. Neugarten. New York: Atherton Press, 1964. Pp. xxiii, 231. *

1032. SILVERMAN, LLOYD H. "Ego Disturbance in TAT Stories as a Function of Aggression-Arousing Stimulus Properties." *J Nerv & Mental Dis* 138:248–54 Mr '64. * (*PA* 39:5215)

1033. SPEER, STANLEY CHARLES. *A Study of Dropouts Among Vocational High School Pupils With Respect to Attitude Toward School.* Doctor's thesis, University of Connecticut (Storrs, Conn.), 1964. (*DA* 25:4512)

1034. SYDIAHA, D., and REMPEL, J. "Motivational and Attitudinal Characteristics of Indian School Children as Measured by the Thematic Apperception Test." *Can Psychologist* 5a:139–48 Jl '64. * (*PA* 39:4719)

1035. THOMPSON, PHYLLIS CONNELL. *Responses of White and Negro Subjects to M-TAT and T-TAT.* Doctor's thesis, Illinois Institute of Technology (Chicago, Ill.), 1964.

1036. VAN DE CASTLE, R. L. "Effect of Test Order Upon Rorschach Human Content." *J Consult Psychol* 28:286–8 Je '64. * (*PA* 39:5218)

1037. WEISSMAN, STUART L. "Some Indicators of Acting Out Behavior From the Thematic Apperception Test." *J Proj Tech & Pers Assess* 28:366–75 S '64. * (*PA* 39:7930)

1038. WELSH, RALPH SAMUEL. *Ambiguity and Response Richness in the TAT.* Doctor's thesis, University of Denver (Denver, Colo.), 1964. (*DA* 25:2619)

1039. WHITELEY, JOHN MINGUS. *A Method for Differentiating Between Superior Achievers and Underachievers and for Assessing the Effects of Ego-Counseling Using the Thematic Apperception Test.* Doctor's thesis, Harvard University (Cambridge, Mass.), 1964.

1040. WILKINS, LEE GERTRUDE. *Some Correlates of Cognitive Controls, Personality Trait Factors, and n Achievement Motivation.* Doctor's thesis, New York University (New York, N.Y.), 1964. (*DA* 25:1327)

1041. YELSKY, MIRIAM. *The Assessment of Several Personality Trait Responses of School Phobic Children: A Comparative Evaluation of the Responses to Psychological Tests of School Phobics, Emotionally Disturbed Children Who Attend School, and Normal Children.* Doctor's thesis, Yeshiva University (New York, N.Y.), 1964. (*DA* 25:2057)

1042. AGRAWAL, K. G. "A Study of Aggression on TAT Responses of a Group of Psychotics." *Indian J Appl Psychol* 2:74–6 Jl '65. *

1043. AXEL, GLENDA ROSLYN. *The Relationship Between Fantasy Hostility and Self-Report Hostility as a Function of Dependency in Orthopedically Handicapped Women.* Doctor's thesis, Columbia University (New York, N.Y.), 1965. (*DA* 26:4802)

1044. BARNES, DONALD J. "A Pilot Study in the Analysis of Thematic Apperception Test Protocols." *Proc Ann Conf Air Force Behav Sci* 12:1–8 N '65. *

1045. BERNSTEIN, LEWIS; TURRELL, EUGENE S.; and DANA, RICHARD H. "Motivation for Nursing." *Nursing Res* 14:222–6 su '65. *

1046. BLANK, LEONARD. *Psychological Evaluation in Psychotherapy: Ten Case Histories.* Chicago, Ill.: Aldine Publishing Co., 1965. Pp. xii, 364. *

1047. CHU, CHENG-PING. "A Comparison of Intellectual and Personality Characteristics of Poliomyelitis and Normal Children in an Orphanage Environment." *Acta Psychologica Taiwanica* 7:17–33 Mr '65. * (*PA* 39:14637)

1048. DANA, RICHARD H. "An NDEA Counseling and Guidance Institute: Prediction, Performance, and Follow-Up." *Genetic Psychol Monogr* 72:289–315 N '65. * (*PA* 40:5949)

1049. DOLL, PADDY ANN. *A Comparative Study of Top Level Male and Female Executives in Harris County.* Doctor's thesis, University of Houston (Houston, Tex.), 1965. (*DA* 26:6883)

1050. GOLDFRIED, MARVIN R., and ZAX, MELVIN. "The Stimulus Value of the TAT." *J Proj Tech & Pers Assess* 29:46–57 Mr '65. * (*PA* 39:10113)

1051. GREENBERGER, ELLEN. "Fantasies of Women Confronting Death." *J Consult Psychol* 29:252–60 Je '65. * (*PA* 39:12647)

1052. HALPIN, JOHN W. "An Attempt to Increase Verbal Productivity of the Mentally Retarded on the Thematic Apperception Test." *Training Sch B* 62:73–80 Ag '65. * (*PA* 40:722)

1053. HARRISON, ROSS. Chap. 22, "Thematic Apperception Methods," pp. 562–620. In *Handbook of Clinical Psychology.* Edited by Benjamin B. Wolman. New York: McGraw-Hill Book Co., Inc., 1965. Pp. xv, 1596. *

1054. HERBERT, M. "Personality Factors and Bronchial Asthma: A Study of South African Indian Children." *J Psychosom Res* 8:353–64 Mr '65. *

1055. HERRON, WILLIAM G.; GUIDO, STEPHEN M.; and KANTOR, ROBERT E. "Relationships Among Ego Strength Measures." *J Clin Psychol* 21:403–4 O '65. * (*PA* 40:1567)

1056. JOHNSON, AUGUST W., JR., and DANA, RICHARD H. "Color on the TAT." *J Proj Tech & Pers Assess* 29:178–82 Je '65. * (*PA* 39:12391)

1057. JOHNSON, DALE L., and SIKES, MELVIN P. "Rorschach and TAT Responses of Negro, Mexican-American, and Anglo Psychiatric Patients." *J Proj Tech & Pers Assess* 29:183–8 Je '65. * (*PA* 39:12392)

1058. JOSHI, VIDYA. "Personality Profiles in Industrial and Preindustrial Cultures: A TAT Study." *J Social Psychol* 66:101–11 Je '65. * (*PA* 39:14873)

1059. KALIN, RUDOLF; McCLELLAND, DAVID C.; and KAHN, MICHAEL. "The Effects of Male Social Drinking on Fantasy." *J Personality & Social Psychol* 1:441–52 My '65. * (*PA* 39:10262)

1060. KAPLAN, MARTIN F., and ERON, LEONARD D. "Test Sophistication and Faking in the TAT Situation." *J Proj Tech & Pers Assess* 29:498–503 D '65. * (*PA* 40:2906)

1061. LINDZEY, GARDNER. "Seer Versus Sign." *J Exp Res Personality* 1:17–26 Mr '65. * (*PA* 39:10203)

1062. MATHUR, SHANTA, and SHARMA, S. C. "Attitude Measurement by Two Projective Tests." *J Psychol Res* 9:39–40 Ja '65. * (*PA* 39:10265)

1063. MURSTEIN, BERNARD I. "New Thoughts About Ambiguity and the TAT." *J Proj Tech & Pers Assess* 29:219–25 Je '65. * (*PA* 39:12398)

1064. MURSTEIN, BERNARD I. "Projection of Hostility on the TAT as a Function of Stimulus, Background, and Personality Variables." *J Consult Psychol* 29:43–8 F '65. * (*PA* 39:7909)

1065. MURSTEIN, BERNARD I. "Scaling of the TAT for Achievement." Abstract. *J Consult Psychol* 29:286 Je '65. *

1066. MURSTEIN, BERNARD I., and EASTER, LAWRENCE V. "The Role of Achievement Motive, Anxiety, Stimulus, and Expectancy, on Achievement Motivation in Arithmetic and Thematic Tests." *J Proj Tech & Pers Assess* 29:491–7 D '65. * (*PA* 40:2915)

1067. MURSTEIN, BERNARD I., and WIENS, ARTHUR N. "Diagnostic and Actuarial Correlates of Thematic and Questionnaire Measures of Hostility." *J Proj Tech & Pers Assess* 29:341–7 S '65. * (*PA* 39:15406)

1068. NAWAS, M. MIKE. "Objective Scoring of the TAT: Further Validation." *J Proj Tech & Pers Assess* 29:456–60 D '65. * (*PA* 40:2961)

1069. OLANS, JEROME L. "The Dimensionality of Selected Thematic Apperception Test Cards." *Proc Ann Conv Am Psychol Assn* 73:247–8 '65. * (*PA* 39:15408)

1070. OLANS, JEROME LEON. *The Dimensionality of Selected Thematic Apperception Test Cards.* Doctor's thesis, George Washington University (Washington, D.C.), 1965.

1071. PERKINS, KENNETH ARTHUR. *Repression, Psychopathology, and Drive Representation: An Experimental Hypnotic Investigation of the Management of Impulse Inhibition.* Doctor's thesis, Michigan State University (East Lansing, Mich.), 1965. (*DA* 26:4815)

1072. PHELAN, JOSEPH G. "Use of Matching Method in Measuring Reliability of Individual Clinician's Diagnostic Judgment." *Psychol Rep* 16:491–6 Ap '65. * (*PA* 39:10283)

1073. PILOWSKY, I., and KAUFMAN, A. "An Experimental Study of Atypical Phantom Pain." *Brit J Psychiatry* 111:1185–7 D '65. * (*PA* 40:3270)

1074. RABAN, ROSEMARY. "Need Achievement in College Women: The Effects of Success or Failure." *Conn Col Psychol J* 2:24–48 f '65. * (*PA* 40:6642)

1075. RABIN, A. I. *Growing Up in the Kibbutz: Comparison of the Personality of Children Brought Up in the Kibbutz and of Family-Reared Children.* New York: Springer Publishing Co., Inc., 1965. Pp. x, 230. *

1076. RAYCHAUDHURI, MANAS. "Personality Correlates of Creativity: A Review of Psychodynamic Studies." *Samiksa* 19(3):106–34 '65. *

1077. SALTZMAN, EARL SIDNEY. *A Comparison of Patterns of Identification as Shown by Family Members of Three Religious Denominations in Houston, Texas.* Doctor's thesis, University of Houston (Houston, Tex.), 1965. (*DA* 26:6857)

1078. SCHMITZ, THOMAS JOSEPH. *A Factor Analytic Study of Stimulus Values of the Thematic Apperception Test.* Doctor's thesis, University of Colorado (Boulder, Colo.), 1965. (*DA* 26:6858)

1079. SEGAL, STANLEY J. "The Use of Clinical Techniques for Structuring Feedback in Vocational Counseling." *Personnel & Guid J* 93:876–8 My '65. * (*PA* 39:16512)

1080. SHANAN, JOEL, and SHARON, MIRIAM. "Personality and Cognitive Functioning of Israeli Males During the Middle Years." *Hum Develop* 8(1):2–15 '65. * (*PA* 39:14799)

1081. SINGER, MARGARET THALER, and WYNNE, LYMAN C. "Thought Disorder and Family Relations of Schizophrenics: 3, Methodology Using Projective Techniques." *Arch Gen Psychiatry* 12:187–200 F '65. * (*PA* 39:8516)

1082. SMAIL, D. J. *A Study of Aggression and Guilt in Psychiatric Patients.* Doctor's thesis, University of London (London, England), 1965.

1083. SPINDLER, GEORGE, and SPINDLER, LOUISE. "The Instrumental Activities Inventory: A Technique for the Study of the Psychology of Acculturation." *Southw J Anthrop* 21:1–23 sp '65. *

1084. STABENAU, JAMES R.; TUPIN, JOE; WERNER, MARTHA; and POLLIN, WILLIAM. "A Comparative Study of Families of Schizophrenics, Delinquents, and Normals." *Psychiatry* 28:45–59 F '65. * (*PA* 39:10490)

1085. STEKERT, ELLEN JANE. *Two Voices of Tradition: The Influence of Personality and Collecting Environment Upon the Songs of Two Traditional Folksingers.* Doctor's thesis, University of Pennsylvania (Philadelphia, Pa.), 1965. (*DA* 26:7251)

1086. TOWER, TEDDY ROGER. *An Experimental Study to Determine Perceptual Reactions to Conflict in Controlled Sub-Groups.* Doctor's thesis, University of Oklahoma (Norman, Okla.), 1965. (*DA* 26:2063)

1087. ULMER, RAYMOND ARTHUR. *An Objective Time-Dimensional Perception Measure Grouping Past, Present, and Future Time Concepts; an Empirical Existentialist Index of Personality Differences.* Doctor's thesis, Louisiana State University (Baton Rouge, La.), 1965. (*DA* 26:2329)

1088. VASSILIOU, G.; NASSIAKOS, MARIA; and VASSILIOU, VASSO. "Comparing Motivational Patterns of Normals and Patients With Psychophysiologic Cardiovascular Reactions." *Psychother & Psychosom* 13(6):401–9 '65. * (*PA* 40:7745)

1089. WAHLSTROM, MERLIN W. *A Comparison of EPPS and TAT Need for Achievement Scores and Academic Success.* Master's thesis, University of Alberta (Edmonton, Alb., Canada), 1965.

1090. WHITELEY, JOHN M., and HUMMEL, RAYMOND. "Adaptive Ego Functioning in Relation to Academic Achievement." *J Counsel Psychol* 12:306–10 f '65. * (*PA* 40:1946)

1091. WINTER, WILLIAM D.; FERREIRA, ANTONIO J.; and OLSON, JIM L. "Story Sequence Analysis of Family TATs." *J Proj Tech & Pers Assess* 29:392–7 S '65. * (*PA* 39:15430)

1092. ZUBIN, JOSEPH; ERON, LEONARD D.; and SCHUMER, FLORENCE. *An Experimental Approach to Projective Techniques*, pp. 394–604, passim. New York and London: John Wiley & Sons, Inc., 1965. Pp. xxi, 645. * (*PA* 39:15432)

1093. BECHTEL, ROBERT B., and ROSENFELD, HOWARD M. "Expectations of Social Acceptance and Compatibility as Related to Status Discrepancy and Social Motives." *J Personality & Social Psychol* 3:344–9 Mr '66. * (*PA* 40:5305)

1094. CARNEY, RICHARD E. "The Effect of Situational Variables on the Measurement of Achievement Motivation." *Ed & Psychol Meas* 26:675–90 au '66. * (*PA* 41:1939)

1095. CHAKRABARTI, P. K. "Personality of the Manic-Depressive Psychotics." *Indian J Psychol* 41:93–6 Je '66. *

1096. CHARLENS, ALAN M. "Need for Novelty and Occupational Preference." *Percept & Motor Skills* 22:697–8 Je '66. * (*PA* 40:11171)

1097. DACHOWSKI, MARJORIE MCCORMICK. "Inconsistency Among Direct, Indirect and Projective Tests and General Neuroticism." *J Proj Tech & Pers Assess* 30:525–9 D '66. * (*PA* 41:3096)

1098. DANA, RICHARD H. "Eisegesis and Assessment." *J Proj Tech & Pers Assess* 30:215–22 Je '66. * (*PA* 40:9347)

1099. DANA, RICHARD H., and HOPEWELL, ELEANOR. "Repression and Psychopathology: A Cross-Validation Failure." *Psychol Rep* 19:626 O '66. * (*PA* 41:578)

1100. DASS, S. L. "Comparison of Experienced and Inexperienced Judges' Assessment of Productivity of Movie Picture Projective Situations." *Psychol Studies* 11:42–51 Ja '66. * (*PA* 40:6662)

1101. DREYFUSS, F.; SHANAN, J.; and SHARON, MIRIAM. "Some Personality Characteristics of Middle-Aged Men With Coronary Artery Disease." *Psychother & Psychosom* 14(1):1–16 '66. * (*PA* 40:9761)

1102. DRYMAN, IRVING ARMIN. *The Relationship Between Personality and Orientation in an Interpersonal Game Situation.* Doctor's thesis, New York University (New York, N.Y.), 1966. (*DA* 27:823A)

1103. FERREIRA, ANTONIO H.; WINTER, WILLIAM D.; and POINDEXTER, EDWARD J. "Some Interactional Variables in Normal and Abnormal Families." *Family Process* 5:60–75 Mr '66. * (*PA* 40:9095)

1104. GREENBERGER, ELLEN. "'Flirting' With Death: Fantasies of a Critically Ill Woman." *J Proj Tech & Pers Assess* 30:197–204 Ap '66. * (*PA* 40:7943)

1105. GUTMANN, DAVID. "Mayan Aging: A Comparative

TAT Study." *Psychiatry* 29:246–59 Ag '66. * (*PA* 41:10321)

1106. HAMMER, EMANUEL F. "Personality Patterns in Young Creative Artists." *Adolescence* 1:327–50 w '66–67. * (*PA* 42:748)

1107. HOFFBERG, CAROLINE, and FAST, IRENE. "Professional Identity and Impulse Expression in Phantasy." *J Proj Tech & Pers Assess* 30:488–98 O '66. * (*PA* 41:601)

1108. HORROCKS, JOHN E., and GOTTFRIED, NATHAN W. "Psychological Needs and Verbally Expressed Aggression of Adolescent Delinquent Boys." *J Psychol* 62:179–94 Mr '66. * (*PA* 40:7885)

1109. HUNT, RAYMOND G., and SMITH, M. ESTELLIE. "Cultural Symbols and Response to Thematic Test Materials." *J Proj Tech & Pers Assess* 30:587–90 D '66. * (*PA* 41:2914)

1110. KLINGER, ERIC. "Fantasy Need Achievement as a Motivational Construct." *Psychol B* 66:291–308 O '66. * (*PA* 40:13207)

1111. KRAFT, ARTHUR. "Personality Correlates of Rebellion-Behavior in School." *Adolescence* 1:251–60 f '66. *

1112. LAMB, CHARLES WILLIAM. *Forms of Need for Variety: Differential Expression Following Arousal and Boredom.* Doctor's thesis, Ohio State University (Columbus, Ohio), 1966. (*DA* 27:3289B)

1113. LAZARUS, RICHARD S. "Story Telling and the Measurement of Motivation: The Direct Versus Substitutive Controversy." *J Consult Psychol* 30:483–7 D '66. * (*PA* 41:2916)

1114. LEFCOURT, HERBERT M. "Repression-Sensitization: A Measure of the Evaluation of Emotional Expression." *J Consult Psychol* 30:444–9 O '66. * (*PA* 40:13194)

1115. LEMAN, JOHN EDWARD, JR. *Aggression in Mexican-American and Anglo-American Delinquent and Non-Delinquent Males as Revealed in Dreams and Thematic Apperception Test Responses.* Doctor's thesis, University of Arizona (Tucson, Ariz.), 1966. (*DA* 27:3675B)

1116. LEVINSON, BORIS M. "Subcultural Studies of Homeless Men." *Trans N Y Acad Sci* 29:165–82 D '66. * (*PA* 41:16683)

1117. LUPTON, D. E. "A Preliminary Investigation of the Personality of Female Temporomandibular Joint Dysfunction Patients." *Psychother & Psychosom* 14(3):199–216 '66. * (*PA* 41:14004)

1118. MEGARGEE, EDWIN I. "A Comparison of the Scores of White and Negro Male Juvenile Delinquents on Three Projective Tests." *J Proj Tech & Pers Assess* 30:530–5 D '66. * (*PA* 41:2920)

1119. MISCH, ROBERT C. "Impulse Control and Social Feeling." *Int Psychiatry Clin* 3:117–37 sp '66. *

1120. MUNDY, J. M. "Junior Children's Responses to the Murray Thematic Apperception Test and the Cattell Personality Questionnaire." Abstract. *Brit J Ed Psychol* 36:103–4 F '66. * (*PA* 40:6640, title only)

1121. MURSTEIN, BERNARD I. "Sex Differences in TAT Ambiguity, Hostility, and Projection." *J Genetic Psychol* 108:71–80 Mr '66. * (*PA* 40:10136)

1122. NORTH, GEORGE E., and KEIFFER, ROBERT S. "Thematic Productions of Children in Foster Homes." *Psychol Rep* 19:43–6 Ag '66. * (*PA* 40:12357)

1123. PETERS, FRANCES G. *A Comparison of Certain Characteristics of the Responses of Tenth-Grade Boys to the Thematic Apperception Test.* Doctor's thesis, University of Oklahoma (Norman, Okla.), 1966. (*DA* 27:1667A)

1124. PRAKASH, JAI, and SARAN, MANJUL. "A T.A.T. Study of the Orphan Boys and Girls." *Indian J Appl Psychol* 3:43–5 Ja '66. *

1125. RAMSAY, R. W. "Personality and Speech." *J Personality & Social Psychol* 4:116–8 Jl '66. * (*PA* 40:10092)

1126. REITER, HENRY H. "The Effect of Group Participation on TAT Responses." *J Social Psychol* 68:249–51 Ap '66. * (*PA* 40:7736)

1127. SALMAN, ARTHUR R. "A Projective Test of Need for Social Approval." *Proc Ann Conf Air Force Behav Sci* 13:328–37 S '66. *

1128. SARASON, IRWIN G. *Personality: An Objective Approach*, pp. 197–204, passim. New York: John Wiley & Sons, Inc., 1966. Pp. xvi, 670. *

1129. SELLS, S. B. *Evaluation of Psychological Measures Used in the Health Examination Survey of Children Ages 6–11*, pp. 53–62. Public Health Service Publication No. 1000, Series 2, No. 15. Washington, D.C.: United States Government Printing Office, March 1966. Pp. viii, 67. * (*PA* 40:7217)

1130. SHERWOOD, JOHN J. "Self-Report and Projective Measures of Achievement and Affiliation." *J Consult Psychol* 30:329–37 Ag '66. * (*PA* 40:11179)

1131. SIEGMAN, ARON WOLFE, and POPE, BENJAMIN. "Ambiguity and Verbal Fluency in the TAT." *J Consult Psychol* 30:239–45 Je '66. * (*PA* 40:8877)

1132. SINGER, MARGARET T., and WYNNE, LYMAN C. "Principles for Scoring Communication Defects and Deviances in Parents of Schizophrenics: Rorschach and TAT Scoring Manuals." *Psychiatry* 29:260–88 Ag '66. * (*PA* 41:10489)

1133. SKOLNICK, ARLENE. "Motivational Imagery and Behavior Over Twenty Years." *J Consult Psychol* 30:463–78 D '66. * (*PA* 41:2924)

1134. SKOLNICK, ARLENE. "Stability and Interrelations of Thematic Test Imagery Over 20 Years." *Child Develop* 37:389–96 Je '66. * (*PA* 40:8878)

1135. SMAIL, D. J. "A Multiple-Choice Version of the TAT

as a Measure of Aggression in Psychiatric Patients." *Brit J Med Psychol* 39:163–9 Je '66. *

1136. SPRINTHALL, NORMAN A.; WHITELEY, JOHN M.; and MOSHER, RALPH L. "A Study of Teacher Effectiveness." *J Teach Ed* 17:93–106 sp '66. * (*PA* 40:9264, title only)

1137. TSUJI, SHOZO, and KATO, NORIAKI. "Some Investigations of Parental Preference in Early Childhood: An Attempt to Obtain a Correspondence of Verbally Expressed Preference With Projectively Expressed Preference." *Jap Psychol Res* 8:10–7 My '66. * (*PA* 40:11027)

1138. ULEMAN, JAMES STEPHEN. *A New TAT Measure of the Need for Power.* Doctor's thesis, Harvard University (Cambridge, Mass.), 1966. (*DA* 27:1934A)

1139. WALLACE, JOHN. "An Abilities Conception of Personality: Some Implications for Personality Measurement." *Am Psychol* 21:132–8 F '66. * (*PA* 40:7714)

1140. WEATHERLY, JAMES KENNY. *A Comparative Investigation of Frustration-Aggressive Patterns Shown by Adults and Children Within the Same Families of Three Religious Groups.* Doctor's thesis, University of Houston (Houston, Tex.), 1966. (*DA* 27:975B)

1141. WHITELEY, JOHN M. "A Method for Assessing Adaptive Ego Functioning Using the Thematic Apperception Test." *J Exp Ed* 34:1–21 sp '66. * (*PA* 40:7742)

1142. WINTER, WILLIAM D.; FERREIRA, ANTONIO J.; and OLSON, JIM L. "Hostility Themes in the Family TAT." *J Proj Tech & Pers Assess* 30:270–4 Je '66. * (*PA* 40:10141)

1143. WOLOWITZ, HOWARD M., and SHORKEY, CLAYTON. "Power Themes in the TAT Stories of Paranoid Schizophrenic Males." *J Proj Tech & Pers Assess* 30:591–6 D '66. * (*PA* 41:2927)

1144. YUDIN, LEE WILLIAM, and REZNIKOFF, MARVIN. "Color and Its Relation to Personality: The TAT." *J Proj Tech & Pers Assess* 30:479–87 O '66. * (*PA* 41:607)

1145. AARON, NORMA S. "Some Personality Differences Between Asthmatic, Allergic and Normal Children." *J Clin Psychol* 23:336–40 Jl '67. * (*PA* 41:15746)

1146. AHMED, SAMIR NAIM. *Patterns of Juvenile Drug Use.* Doctor's thesis, University of California (Berkeley, Calif.), 1967. (*DA* 28:4703A)

1147. BEGGS, JAMES JUDSON. *Personality Shift in Women at a Choice Point in Middle Life.* Doctor's thesis, University of Oregon (Eugene, Ore.), 1967. (*DA* 28:5188B)

1148. BRENDER, WILLIAM J., and KRAMER, ERNEST. "A Comparative Need Analysis of Immediately-Recalled Dreams and TAT Responses." *J Proj Tech & Pers Assess* 31:74–7 F '67. * (*PA* 41:13663)

1149. BROWN, JOSEPH EUGENE. *Motivational Factors in College Achievement.* Doctor's thesis, Catholic University of America (Washington, D.C.), 1967. (*DA* 28:3056B)

1150. CLAPPERTON, GILBERT, JR. *The Effects of Aggression Anxiety and Sex Differences on the Use of Repressing Defenses.* Doctor's thesis, Baylor University (Waco, Tex.), 1967. (*DA* 28:3467B)

1151. COLEMAN, JOHN C. "Stimulus Factors in the Relation Between Fantasy and Behavior." *J Proj Tech & Pers Assess* 31:68–73 F '67. * (*PA* 41:13665)

1152. COWAN, GLORIA, and GOLDBERG, FAYE J. "Need Achievement as a Function of the Race and Sex of Figures of Selected TAT Cards." *J Personality & Social Psychol* 5:245–9 F '67. * (*PA* 41:4618)

1153. CRAWFORD, ALFRED E., II. *The Thematic Apperception Test as a Method for the Identification of the Potentially Delinquent Junior High School Boy.* Master's thesis, Wichita State University (Wichita, Kan.), 1967.

1154. CUMMIN, PEARSON C. "TAT Correlates of Executive Performance." *J Appl Psychol* 51:78–81 F '67. * (*PA* 41:5141)

1155. DIENER, ROBERT G. "Prediction of Dependent Behavior in Specified Situations From Psychological Tests." *Psychol Rep* 20:103–8 F '67. * (*PA* 41:7320)

1156. DOORBAR, RUTH RAE. "Psychological Testing of Transsexuals: A Brief Report of Results From the Wechsler Adult Intelligence Scale, the Thematic Apperception Test, and the House-Tree-Person Test." *Trans N Y Acad Sci* 29:455–62 F '67. * (*PA* 41:16827)

1157. FISHER, SEYMOUR. "Projective Methodologies," pp. 176–83. *Ann R Psychol* 18:165–90 '67. * (*PA* 42:3986)

1158. FISHER, SEYMOUR, and OSOFSKY, HOWARD. "Sexual Responsiveness in Women: Psychological Correlates." *Arch Gen Psychiatry* 17:214–26 Ag '67. * (*PA* 41:15149)

1159. GOLDBLATT, MICHAEL. *The Effects of Fantasy Stimulation and Inhibition of Motor Response on Time Estimation in the Acting Out Adolescent.* Doctor's thesis, Temple University (Philadelphia, Pa.), 1967. (*DA* 28:1193B)

1160. GOLDRICH, JUDITH MARCH. "A Study in Time Orientation: The Relation Between Memory for Past Experience and Orientation to the Future." *J Personality & Social Psychol* 6:216–21 Je '67. * (*PA* 41:9687)

1161. GRANT, DONALD L.; KATKOVSKY, WALTER; and BRAY, DOUGLAS W. "Contributions of Projective Techniques to Assessment of Management Potential." *J Appl Psychol* 51:226–32 Je '67. * (*PA* 41:10481)

1162. HAMILTON, ROBERT; ROBERTSON, MALCOLM; and VODDE, THOMAS. "Three Variations in the Administration of

the TAT." *Proc Ann Conv Am Psychol Assn* 75:213–4 '67. * (*PA* 41:13673)

1163. HAMSHER, J. HERBERT, and FARINA, AMERIGO. " 'Openness' as a Dimension of Projective Test Responses." *J Consult Psychol* 31:525–8 O '67. * (*PA* 41:16717)

1164. HOCKETT, HARRY DONALD. *Aggressive Response Completion as a Function of Retaliation and TAT Exposure.* Doctor's thesis, University of Wisconsin (Madison, Wis.), 1967. (*DA* 28:3460B)

1165. KAPLAN, MARTIN F. "The Effect of Cue Relevance, Ambiguity, and Self-Reported Hostility on TAT Responses." *J Proj Tech & Pers Assess* 31:45–50 D '67. * (*PA* 42:5610)

1166. KLEINMUNTZ, BENJAMIN. *Personality Measurement: An Introduction*, pp. 295–319. Homewood, Ill.: Dorsey Press, 1967. Pp. xiii, 463. *

1167. McCONNELL, OWEN L. "Personality Correlates of Responsiveness to Social Reinforcement in Mental Retardates." *Am J Mental Def* 72:45–9 Jl '67. * (*PA* 41:15730)

1168. McGHEE, PAUL E., and TEEVAN, RICHARD C. "Conformity Behavior and Need for Affiliation." *J Social Psychol* 72:117–21 Je '67. * (*PA* 41:11777)

1169. MARTIN, JAMES G. "Hesitations in the Speaker's Production and Listener's Reproduction of Utterances." *J Verbal Learning & Verbal Behav* 6:903–9 D '67. * (*PA* 42:8907)

1170. MASLING, JOSEPH; RABIE, LILLIE; and BLONDHEIM, S. H. "Obesity, Level of Aspiration, and Rorschach and TAT Measures of Oral Dependence." *J Consult Psychol* 31:233–9 Je '67. * (*PA* 41:10716)

1171. MEGARGEE, EDWIN I. "Hostility on the TAT as a Function of Defensive Inhibition and Stimulus Situation." *J Proj Tech & Pers Assess* 31:73–9 Ag '67. * (*PA* 41:15316)

1172. MEGARGEE, EDWIN I., and COOK, PATRICK E. "The Relation of TAT and Inkblot Aggressive Content Scales With Each Other and With Criteria of Overt Aggressiveness in Juvenile Delinquents." *J Proj Tech & Pers Assess* 31:48–60 F '67. * (*PA* 41:13683)

1173. MELNICK, MURRAY. *Need Configurations and Evaluative Tendencies Toward Self and Others.* Doctor's thesis, New York University (New York, N.Y.), 1967. (*DA* 29:327A)

1174. MEYER, ROBERT G., and KARON, BERTRAM P. "The Schizophrenogenic Mother Concept and the TAT." *Psychiatry* 30:173–9 My '67. * (*PA* 41:15565)

1175. NAJJAR, BASIL EDWARD. *Differences in Motivational Patterns of Inadequate and Inept Psychopathic Deviant Prison Inmates as Revealed by TAT Story Sequence Analysis.* Doctor's thesis, Loyola University (Chicago, Ill.), 1967.

1176. PAL, SAMIR K. "Personality Needs of Engineering and Medical Students." *Psychologia* 10:48–50 Mr '67. * (*PA* 41:15293)

1177. POPE, BENJAMIN, and SCOTT, WINFIELD. *Psychological Diagnosis in Clinical Practice: With Applications in Medicine, Law, Education, Nursing, and Social Work*, pp. 175–86. New York: Oxford University Press, 1967. Pp. xiii, 341. *

1178. ROOKER, JAMES LEROY. *The Relationship of Need Achievement and Need Affiliation to Leader Behavior.* Doctor's thesis, University of Wisconsin (Madison, Wis.), 1967. (*DA* 28:4426A)

1179. SELLS, S. B.; COX, SAMUEL H.; and CHATHAM, LOIS R. "Scales of Language Development for the TAT." *Proc Ann Conv Am Psychol Assn* 75:171–2 '67. * (*PA* 41:13689)

1180. SIEGMAN, ARON WOLFE, and POPE, BENJAMIN. "Stimulus Factors in the TAT: Effects of Ambiguity on Verbal Fluency, Productivity and GSR." *Int Congr Rorsch & Proj Meth* 6(2):223–8 '67. *

1181. SMITH, STANLEY A. "The Effects of Color on Productivity of Protocols for Mentally Retarded Children." Abstract. *J Sch Psychol* 5:316–7 su '67. *

1182. THALER, VICTOR HUGO. *Personality Dimensions Derived From Multiple Instruments.* Doctor's thesis, Columbia University (New York, N.Y.), 1967. (*DA* 28:509A)

1183. TOOLEY, KAY. "Expressive Style as a Developmental Index in Late Adolescence." *J Proj Tech & Pers Assess* 31:51–9 D '67. * (*PA* 42:5616)

1184. VACCHIANO, RALPH B.; ADRIAN, ROBERT J.; LIEBERMAN, LEWIS R.; and SCHIFFMAN, DAVID C. "A Factor Analytic Comparison of TAT, Self-Description and Reputation Assessment Techniques." *J Clin Psychol* 23:416–9 O '67. * (*PA* 42:2615)

1185. VASSILIOU, GEORGE, and VASSILIOU, VASSO. "Transactional Story Sequence Analysis, a New Procedure on Family Diagnosis." *Int Congr Rorsch & Proj Meth* 6(1):99–107 '67. *

1186. WHITELEY, JOHN M.; SPRINTHALL, NORMAN A.; MOSHER, RALPH L.; and DONAGHY, ROLLA T. "Selection and Evaluation of Counselor Effectiveness." *J Counsel Psychol* 14:226–34 My '67. * (*PA* 41:9423)

1187. WINTER, WILLIAM D., and FERREIRA, ANTONIO J. "Interaction Process of Analysis of Family Decision-Making." *Family Process* 6:155–72 S '67. * (*PA* 42:8827)

1188. ZUCKERMAN, MARVIN; PERSKY, HAROLD; ECKMAN, KATHERINE M.; and HOPKINS, T. ROBERT. "A Multitrait Multimethod Measurement Approach to the Traits (or States) of Anxiety, Depression and Hostility." *J Proj Tech & Pers Assess* 31:39–48 Ap '67. * (*PA* 41:13635)

1189. ALLISON, JOEL; BLATT, SIDNEY J.; and ZIMET, CARL N. Chap. 3, "Thematic Apperception Test," pp. 89–134, passim. In their *Interpretation of Psychological Tests.* New York: Harper & Row, Publishers, Inc., 1968. Pp. x, 342. *

1190. BARROSO, MANUAL ANTONIO. *Study of Hostility and Maladjustment in Married Couples as Measured by the TAT and Its Correlation to the MAI.* Master's thesis, Loyola University (Chicago, Ill.), 1968.

1191. BERTHOLD, MICHAEL C. *A Predictive Study of High School Dropouts Using Story Sequence Analysis.* Master's thesis, Loyola University (Chicago, Ill.), 1968.

1192. BRADFORD, JEAN LOUISE. *Sex Differences in Anxiety.* Doctor's thesis, University of Minnesota (Minneapolis, Minn.), 1968. (*DA* 29:1167B)

1193. BROOTA, K. D., and BROOTA, ARUNA. "Personality and Social Status of Occupation." *Indian J Appl Psychol* 5:1–6 Ja '68. *

1194. BUTLER, GLORIA A. *A Critical Investigation of Several Measures of Achievement Motivation and Independence Training.* Doctor's thesis, Rutgers—The State University (New Brunswick, N.J.), 1968. (*DA* 28:5200B)

1195. CHAPMAN, GLORIA ORTNER. "The Thematic Apperception Test and the Diagnosis of Reading Problems." *Int Congr Rorsch & Proj Meth* 6(3):539–41 '68. *

1196. DANA, RICHARD H. "Thematic Techniques and Clinical Practice." *J Proj Tech & Pers Assess* 32:204–14 Je '68. * (*PA* 42:15488)

1197. DIES, ROBERT R. "Development of a Projective Measure of Perceived Locus of Control." *J Proj Tech & Pers Assess* 32:487–90 O '68. * (*PA* 43:5383)

1198. DORE, PATRICIA DIANE. *Attitudes on the TAT Characteristic of Petty Offenders and Reliefers.* Doctor's thesis, Loyola University (Chicago, Ill.), 1968.

1199. ESCHEL, HARRY GEORGE. *Personality Characteristics of the Alcoholic Derived From Story Sequence Analysis.* Doctor's thesis, Loyola University (Chicago, Ill.), 1968.

1200. FEFFER, MELVIN, and JAHELKA, MARION. "Implications of the Decentering Concept for the Structuring of Projective Content." *J Consult & Clin Psychol* 32:434–41 Ag '68. * (*PA* 42:17250)

1201. FINE, BERNARD J., and SWEENEY, DONALD R. "Personality Traits, and Situational Factors, and Catecholamine Excretion." *J Exp Res Personality* 3:15–27 Je '68. * (*PA* 42:16867)

1202. FRIEL, CHARLES M., and DE ABOITIZ, FREDERIC S. "Temporal Orientation in the Criminal Psychopath." *Proc Ann Conv Am Psychol Assn* 76:485–6 '68. * (*PA* 43:1110, title only)

1203. GROVES, MARION H., and PETERSEN, PAUL A. "Effectiveness of Projective Techniques as Established by the Objective Agreement of Therapists With Diagnosticians." *Proc Ann Conv Am Psychol Assn* 76:459–60 '68. * (*PA* 43:940, title only)

1204. HARRIS, ROBERT E.; FOGEY, EDWARD W.; ZUBIN, JOSEPH; NEULINGER, JOHN; SHAKOW, DAVID; and STEIN, MORRIS J. "Discussion of Papers on 'Systems Based on Patterns of Psychological Performance,'" pp. 404–18. In *The Role and Methodology of Classification in Psychiatry and Psychopathology.* Edited by Martin M. Katz and others. Public Health Service Publication No. 1584. Washington, D.C.: United States Government Printing Office, 1968. Pp. ix, 590. *

1205. HEINEMANN, PETER O., and ZAX, MELVIN. "Extremeness in Evaluative Responses to Clinical Test Materials." *J Social Psychol* 75:175–83 Ag '68. * (*PA* 42:17384)

1206. HOLZBERG, JULES D. Chap. 2, "Psychological Theory and Projective Techniques," pp. 18–63. In *Projective Techniques in Personality Assessment: A Modern Introduction.* Edited by A. I. Rabin. New York: Springer Publishing Co., Inc., 1968. Pp. x, 638. *

1207. KAPLAN, MARTIN F., and ERON, LEONARD D. "Test Sophistication and Faking in the TAT Situation." *Int Congr Rorsch & Proj Meth* 6(3):395–404 '68. *

1208. KEEPERS, TERRY DOUGLAS. *An Investigation of Some of the Relationships Between Test Protocols and Clinical Report Using a Computerized Analysis of Text.* Doctor's thesis, Case Western Reserve University (Cleveland, Ohio), 1968. (*DA* 29:771B)

1209. KLINGER, ERIC. "Short-Term Stability and Concurrent Validity of TAT Need Scores: Achievement, Affiliation, and Hostile Press." *Proc Ann Conv Am Psychol Assn* 76:157–8 '68. * (*PA* 43:941, title only)

1210. KLOPFER, WALTER G. Chap. 16, "Integration of Projective Techniques in the Clinical Case Study," pp. 523–52. In *Projective Techniques in Personality Assessment: A Modern Introduction.* Edited by A. I. Rabin. New York: Springer Publishing Co., Inc., 1968. Pp. x, 638. *

1211. LEVI, MARIO. "Use of Projective Methods in the Study and Treatment of Narcotic Addicts." *Int Congr Rorsch & Proj Meth* 6(3):311–7 '68. *

1212. McCLELLAND, DAVID C., and WATT, NORMAN F. "Sex-Role Alienation in Schizophrenia." *J Abn Psychol* 73:226–39 Je '68. * (*PA* 42:12486)

1213. McKEACHIE, W. J.; ISAACSON, ROBERT L.; MILHOLLAND, JOHN E.; and LIN, YI-GUANG. "Student Achievement Motives, Achievement Cues, and Academic Achievement." *J Consult & Clin Psychol* 32:26–9 F '68. * (*PA* 42:7865)

1214. MEGARGEE, EDWIN I., and PARKER, GEORGE V. C. "An Exploration of the Equivalence of Murrayan Needs as Assessed by the Adjective Check List, the TAT and Edwards Personal Preference Schedule." *J Clin Psychol* 24:47–51 Ja '68. *

1215. MITCHELL, KEVIN M. "An Analysis of the Schizophrenogenic Mother Concept by Means of the TAT." *Proc Ann Conv Am Psychol Assn* 76:461–2 '68. * (*PA* 43:944, title only)

1216. MURSTEIN, B. I. "An Analysis of Scoring Systems of TAT Hostility." *Int Congr Rorsch & Proj Meth* 6(3):413–6 '68. *

1218. MURSTEIN, BERNARD I. "Effect of Stimulus, Background, Personality, and Scoring System on the Manifestation of Hostility of the TAT." *J Consult & Clin Psychol* 32:355–65 Je '68. * (*PA* 42:13792)

1217. MURSTEIN, BERNARD I. "Discussion for Current Status of Some Projective Techniques." *J Proj Tech & Pers Assess* 32:229–32 Je '68. * (*PA* 42:15496)

1219. PAL, S. K. "Personality Needs of Engineering, Law, Medical, and Teacher-Training Students in an Indian University." *J Social Psychol* 74:135 F '68. * (*PA* 42:8930)

1220. PALMER, ROBERT D. "Psychological Factors in Visual Acuity." *Proc Ann Conv Am Psychol Assn* 76:539–40 '68. * (*PA* 43:904, title only)

1221. PALMER, ROBERT D. "Visual Acuity and Stimulus-Seeking Behavior." *Newsl Res Psychol* 10:5–7 My '68. *

1222. PIVIK, TERRY, and FOULKES, DAVID. "NREM Mentation: Relation to Personality, Orientation Time, and Time of Night." *J Consult & Clin Psychol* 32:144–51 Ap '68. * (*PA* 42:8252)

1223. RABIN, A. I. Chap. 19, "Adapting and Devising Projective Methods for Special Purposes," pp. 611–26. In his *Projective Techniques in Personality Assessment: A Modern Introduction.* New York: Springer Publishing Co., Inc., 1968. Pp. x, 638. *

1224. RAPAPORT, DAVID; GILL, MERTON M.; and SCHAFER, ROY; edited by ROBERT R. HOLT. Chap. 10, "The Thematic Apperception Test," pp. 464–521. In their *Diagnostic Psychological Testing.* New York: International Universities Press, Inc., 1968. Pp. xi, 562. *

1225. ROSENWALD, GEORGE C. Chap. 7, "The Thematic Apperception Test," pp. 172–221. In *Projective Techniques in Personality Assessment: A Modern Introduction.* Edited by A. I. Rabin. New York: Springer Publishing Co., Inc., 1968. Pp. x, 638. *

1226. SHAPIRO, DAVID. "Free Association and the Repression-Sensitization Continuum." *Newsl Res Psychol* 10:43–4 My '68. *

1227. SHEEHAN, PETER W. "Color Response to the TAT: An Instance of Eidetic Imagery?" *J Psychol* 68:203–9 Mr '68. * (*PA* 42:9005)

1228. SILBER, DAVID E., and COURTLESS, THOMAS F. "Measures of Fantasy Aggression Among Mentally Retarded Offenders." *Am J Mental Def* 72:918–23 My '68. * (*PA* 42:14426)

1229. SINGER, JEROME L. Chap. 18, "Research Applications of Projective Methods," pp. 581–610. In *Projective Techniques in Personality Assessment: A Modern Introduction.* Edited by A. I. Rabin. New York: Springer Publishing Co., Inc., 1968. Pp. x, 638. *

1230. SMITH, MARSHALL S. "The Computer and the TAT." *J Sch Psychol* 6:206–14 sp '68. * (*PA* 42:17255)

1231. STEWART, PATRICIA ANN. "The Use of Feedback in Training Clinical Diagnosticians." *Newsl Res Psychol* 10:31–3 Ag '68. *

1232. STIMSON, ROGER C., JR. "Factor Analytic Approach to the Structural Differentiation of Description." *J Counsel Psychol* 15:301–7 Jl '68. *

1233. TEWARI, J. G., and TEWARI, J. N. "On Extremes of Personality Adjustment as Measured by Adjustment Inventories." *J Psychol Res* 12:75–81 My '68. * (*PA* 43:5396)

1234. TSUSHIMA, WILLIAM T. "Responses of Irish and Italian Patients of Two Social Classes Under Preoperative Stress." *J Personality & Social Psychol* 8:43–8 Ja '68. * (*PA* 42:5451)

1235. VACCHIANO, RALPH B.; LIEBERMAN, LEWIS R.; ADRIAN, ROBERT J.; and SCHIFFMAN, DAVID C. "Relation of Photo-Trait-Attribution Method of Personality Assessment to Standard Assessment Techniques." *Psychol Rep* 22:95–102 F '68. * (*PA* 42:10628)

1236. WOHLFORD, PAUL. "Extension of Personal Time in TAT and Story Completion Stories." *J Proj Tech & Pers Assess* 32:267–80 Je '68. * (*PA* 42:15478)

NAME INDEX

[485]

Thematic Apperception Test for African Subjects. Ages 10 and over; 1953; 1 form (22 pages); manual (49 pages); no data on reliability; R 1.25 per set of test materials, postpaid; [60–120] minutes; S. G. Lee; University of Natal Press. *

For a review by Mary D. Ainsworth, see 5:165 (1 reference).

REFERENCES

1. See 5:165.
2. DE RIDDER, J. C. *The Personality of the Urban African in South Africa: A Thematic Apperception Test Study.* London: Routledge & Kegan Paul Ltd., 1961. Pp. xvi, 180. *

[486]

Thematic Apperception Test: Thompson Modification. Negroes ages 4 and over; 1949, c1943–49; individual; 1 form ['49, 30 cards, consists of 4 sets]; stimulus material (19 cards) based on sex and age; manual ('49, 11 pages); no data on reliability and validity; no norms; $6 per set of test materials, cash orders postpaid; (120) minutes in 2 sessions 1 day apart; Charles E. Thompson; Harvard University Press. *

For a review by Mary D. Ainsworth, see 5:166 (4 references); see also 4:138 (5 references, 3 excerpts).

REFERENCES

1–5. See 4:138.
6–9. See 5:166.
10. THOMPSON, PHYLLIS CONNELL. *Responses of White and Negro Subjects to M-TAT and T-TAT.* Doctor's thesis, Illinois Institute of Technology (Chicago, Ill.), 1964.

[487]

The Tomkins-Horn Picture Arrangement Test. Ages 10 and over; 1942–59; PAT; 1 form ('44, 30 pages); manual ('57, 399 pages, see 5 below); interpretation manual ('59, 191 pages, see 7 below); scoring materials ['57, 63 cards, 100 sheets, punch, board, and instructions, 8 pages, reprinted from manual]; profile ('58, 4 pages); $15 per 50 tests; $25 per set of scoring materials; $4.50 per 100 scoring sheets; $17.50 per 100 profiles; $10 per manual; $5.50 per interpretive manual; postage extra; (30–60) minutes; Silvan S. Tomkins, Daniel Horn, and John B. Miner (manuals); Springer Publishing Co., Inc. *

For a review by Robert C. Nichols, see 6:246 (7 references, 3 excerpts); for reviews by Donald W. Fiske, John W. Gittinger, and Wayne H. Holtzman, see 5:167 (6 references, 1 excerpt).

REFERENCES

1–6. See 5:167.
7–13. See 6:246.
14. DAVIS, MORRIS. "Results of Personality Tests Given to Negroes in the Northern and Southern United States and in Halifax, Canada." *Phylon* 25:362–8 w '64. *
15. MINER, JOHN B. Chap. 9, "A Statistical Model for the Study of Conformity," pp. 95–111. In *Mathematical Expectations in Behavioral Science.* Edited by Fred Massarik and Philburn Ratoosh. Homewood, Ill.: Richard D. Irwin, Inc., 1965. Pp. viii, 387. *
16. TOMKINS, SILVAN S. Chap. 3. "Affect and the Psychology of Knowledge," pp. 72–97. In *Affect, Cognition, and Personality: Empirical Studies.* Edited by Silvan S. Tomkins and Carroll E. Izard. New York: Springer Publishing Co., Inc., 1965. Pp. vii, 464. * (*PA* 39:13287)
17. FOSTER, PHILLIP BRYAN. *Conformity: A Construct Validation of the Tomkins-Horn Picture Arrangement Experiment.* Doctor's thesis, University of Oregon (Eugene, Ore.), 1968. (*DA* 29:2661B)

[488]

The Toy World Test. Ages 2 and over; 1941–55; TWT; formerly called *The World Test;* individual; kit of reusable toys ('49, 160 items); record blank ('55, 1 page); manual ('49, 12 pages); $130 per set of testing materials and 25 record blanks; $2 per 25 record blanks; $1.50 per manual; postage extra; (20–45) minutes; Charlotte Buhler; distributed by Joyce B. Baisden. *

For a review by L. Joseph Stone, see 5:168 (11 references); see also 4:147 (6 references).

REFERENCES

1–6. See 4:147.
7–17. See 5:168.
18. SHARMA, S. N. "Behavioral Analysis of Three Projective Tests of Fantasy: the Mosaic, the Toy World and the MAPS Tests." *Manas* 2(2):81–5 '64. * (*PA* 39:7916)

[489]

The Tree Test. Ages 9 and over; 1949–52; TT; 1 form ('52); manual ('52, see 1 below); no data on reliability and validity; Fr. 15.95 ($4.75) per manual, postage extra; [5–10] minutes; Charles Koch; Hans Huber. * (United States distributor: Grune & Stratton, Inc.)

For related book reviews not excerpted in this volume, consult the 5th MMY (B251).

REFERENCES

1–2. See 5:170.
3. STRAUB, RICHARD R. *The Representation of the Self in the Tree Test and the C-T-P: A Comparative Study.* Master's thesis, University of Detroit (Detroit, Mich.), 1961.
4. KUNKE, TH. "The Creative Situation in the Tree Test." *Rorsch Newsl* 12:5–14 Je '67. * (*PA* 42:3987)
5. WELMAN, A. J. "Brain Tumor and the Tree-Test." *Dis Nerv System* 29:592–8 S '68. * (*PA* 43:1245)

[490]

Twitchell-Allen Three-Dimensional Personality Test. Ages 3 and over (sighted and sightless); 1948–

60; TA3DPT; formerly called *Twitchell-Allen Three-Dimensional Apperception Test;* 1 form ('48); revised manual ('58, 22 pages); revised record booklet ('58, 8 pages); a copy of *The Three-Dimensional Personality Test: Reliability, Validity, and Clinical Implications* by Leah Gold Fein (see 4 below); $150 per set of testing materials, 50 record booklets, manual, Fein book, and carrying case; $2 per manual; postage extra; (60) minutes; Doris Twitchell-Allen; the Author. *

For a review by Edward Joseph Shoben, Jr., see 4:143.

REFERENCES

1–3. See 5:171.
4. FEIN, LEAH GOLD. *The Three-Dimensional Personality Test: Reliability, Validity and Clinical Implications.* New York: International Universities Press, Inc., 1960. Pp. xii, 324. * (*PA* 35:3393)
5. FEIN, LEAH GOLD. "Non-Academic Personality Variables and Success at School." *Int Mental Health Res Newsl* 10:2+ sp '68. *

[491]

Visual Apperception Test '60. Ages 6 and over; 1960–62; VAT '60; prevalent mood and clinical diagnosis; 1 form ('60, 14 pages); manual, third edition ('62, 30 pages); $10 per 12 tests and manual; $3.50 per manual; postage extra; 60¢ per test, postpaid; set of crayons necessary for administration; [10–35] minutes; Rafi Z. Khan; Midwest Psychological Services. *

For reviews by Bert R. Sappenfield and Stanley J. Segal, see 6:247.

REFERENCES

1. KHAN, RAFI ZAMAN. *A Comparative Study of the Development of Perceptual Patterns From Childhood to Adult Level Among American and Pakistani Subjects as Revealed by the Visual Apperception Test '60.* Doctor's thesis, University of the Panjab (Lahore, West Pakistan), 1965.
2. MONS, W. E. R. "The Visual Apperception Test 1960 of Prof. Rafi Khan, University of Chicago." *Rorsch Newsl* 12:8–9 D '67. * (*PA* 42:17392)

[492]

The Vocational Apperception Test: Advanced Form. College; 1949; VAT; individual; 2 forms; mimeographed manual (8 pages); no data on reliability in manual (for data presented elsewhere by the authors, see 1 below); publisher recommends use of local norms; $7.25 per set of testing materials, cash orders postpaid; (25–40) minutes; Robert B. Ammons, Margaret N. Butler, and Sam A. Herzig; Psychological Test Specialists. *

a) [FORM FOR MEN.] Preferences in 8 areas: teacher, executive or office worker, doctor, lawyer, engineer, personnel or social worker, salesman, laboratory technician; 1 form ['49, 8 pictures].
b) [FORM FOR WOMEN.] Preferences in 10 areas: laboratory technician, dietician, buyer, nurse, teacher, artist, secretary, social worker, mother, housewife; 1 form ['49, 10 pictures].

For reviews by Benjamin Balinsky and William E. Henry, see 4:146 (1 reference, 1 excerpt).

REFERENCES

1. See 4:146.
2. STOWE, EDWARD W. *The Relation of the Kuder Vocational Preference Record to Ammons' Apperception Test.* Master's thesis, Illinois State Normal University (Normal, Ill.), 1955.
3. GOLDSTEIN, ARNOLD P. "The Fakability of the Kuder Preference Record and the Vocational Apperception Test." *J Proj Tech* 24:133–6 Je '60. * (*PA* 35:1321)
4. CLARK, EDWARD T. "Children, People's Troubles, and the Image of Psychologists." *Percept & Motor Skills* 20:498–500 Ap '65. * (*PA* 39:12381)

OUT OF PRINT

[493]

Animal Puzzles. Pre-school and kgn; 1937; Gertrude Hildreth; Psychological Corporation. * *Out of print.*

For additional information, consult 1:1057.

[494]

The Behavioral Complexity Test: A Test for Use in Research. Ages 5 and over; 1955–61; revision of *The Adult-Child Interaction Test;* 9 scores: continuum (weighted total of scores for 5 complexity of response categories), symbolization (5 scores), emotional perceptional (positive, negative, total); Theron Alexander; distributed by Campus Stores. * *Out of print.*

For additional information and a review by John Elderkin Bell, see 6:202 (4 references).

[495]

Controlled Projection for Children, Second Edition. Ages 6–13; 1945–51; CPC; John C. Raven; H. K. Lewis & Co. Ltd. * (United States distributor: Psychological Corporation.) *Out of print.*

For additional information and a review by John Liggett, see 6:207; see also 5:127 (8 references, 3 excerpts); for reviews by Arthur L. Benton and Percival M. Symonds of the original edition, see 3:29 (5 excerpts).

[496]

The Drawing-Completion Test: A Projective Technique for the Investigation of Personality. Ages 5 and over; 1952; DCT; based on the *Wartegg Test Blank;* G. Marian Kinget; Grune & Stratton, Inc. * *Out of print.*

For additional information, see 5:130 (3 references, 4 excerpts).

REFERENCES

1–3. See 5:130.
4. JAMISON, PATRICIA M. *The Kinget Drawing-Completion Test: Comparison of Responses for Full-Blood Navajo and White Children in Grades Three and Six.* Master's thesis, University of Oklahoma (Norman, Okla.), 1959.
5. MURFETT, BETTY JEAN. *The Inhibition Process and the Handling of Humans and Humans in Movement.* Doctor's thesis, University of Oklahoma (Norman, Okla.), 1962. (*DA* 23:1785)
6. VIITAMAKI, R. OLAVI. *Psychoses in Children: A Psychological Follow-Up Study.* Annals of the Academia of Scientiarum Fennica, Series B, Vol. 125, Part 2. Helsinki, Finland: Suomalainen Tiedeakatemia, Academia Scientiarum Fennica, 1962. Pp. 52. * (*PA* 39:2650)
7. FRANKLIN, JULIA LAVINIA. *The Inhibition Process and the Handling of Humans and Humans in Movement on the Kinget.* Doctor's thesis, University of Oklahoma (Norman, Okla.), 1963. (*DA* 25:5110)
8. KEITH, JOHN PAUL. *Assessing Academic Achievement With Specific Variables of the Drawing Completion Test in Certain Sub-Saharan Tribal Groups: A Pilot Study.* Doctor's thesis, Michigan State University (East Lansing, Mich.), 1963. (*DA* 24:2783)
9. MATHENY, KENNETH B. *An Assessment of the Usefulness of the Wartegg Drawing Completion Test as a Measurement of Intelligence Among Children.* Doctor's thesis, Michigan State University (East Lansing, Mich.), 1963. (*DA* 24:1240)
10. LAIRD, ALBERT WALTER. *Differential Analysis of Creativity and Imagination Between Gifted and Non-Gifted High School Students as Ascertained by the Kinget Drawing-Completion Test.* Doctor's thesis, University of Oklahoma (Norman, Okla.), 1964. (*DA* 25:3399)
11. TAKALA, MARTTI; assisted by MATTI KAASINEN, ERKKI JANHUNEN, VOITTO VUORINEN, and SINIKKA OJANEN. *Studies of the Wartegg Drawing Completion Test: Studies of Psychomotor, Personality Tests II.* Annals of the Academia Scientiarum Fennica, Series B, Vol. 131, No. 1. Helsinki, Finland: Suomalainen Tiedeakatemia, Academia Scientiarum Fennica, 1964. Pp. 112. *
12. TANAKA, IRWIN ISAMU. *The Development of the Drawing Completion Test as a Cross-Cultural Non-Language Measurement of Academic Achievement Among Elementary School Children in Hawaii.* Doctor's thesis, Michigan State University (East Lansing, Mich.), 1964. (*DA* 26:880)

13. VIITAMAKI, R. OLAVI. "A Psychological Follow-up Study: Psychoses in Childhood, Part 2." *Acta Psychiatrica Scandinavica Supplementum* 40(174):33–93 '64. * (*PA* 39:8464)

14. GILBERT, OTTO ERNEST. *An Assessment of the Usefulness of the Wartegg Drawing Completion Test as a Cross-Cultural Non-Language Predictor of Academic Achievement Among Elementary School Children in Guatemala.* Doctor's thesis, Michigan State University (East Lansing, Mich.), 1965. (*DA* 26:4445)

15. KEITH, JOHN P.; JORDAN, JOHN E.; and MATHENY, KENNETH B. "Cross-Cultural Study of Potential School Dropouts in Certain Sub-Saharan Countries." *J Negro Ed* 35:90–4 w '66. *

16. SWINK, RICHARD HARLEN. *The Meaning of the Drawing Completion Test Stimuli and Its Relation to Stimulus Preference.* Doctor's thesis, University of Oklahoma (Norman, Okla.), 1966. (*DA* 27:2148B)

17. TAKALA, K. Chap. 12, "Psychological Investigation and Its Results," pp. 444–525. In *The Family in the Pathogenesis of Schizophrenic and Neurotic Disorders.* By Yrjö O. Alanen and others. Acta Psychiatrica Scandinavica Supplementum 189. Copenhagen, Denmark: Munksgaard Ltd., 1966. Pp. 654. *

18. CAMPOS, LEONARD P. "Drawing Completion Technique (DCT)," pp. 502–11. In *Projective Techniques in Personality Assessment: A Modern Introduction.* Edited by A. I. Rabin. New York: Springer Publishing Co., Inc., 1968. Pp. x, 638. *

19. KONTTINEN, RAIMO. *Relationships Between Graphic Expansivity and Extraversion as a Function of Anxiety and Defensiveness.* Annals Academia Scientiarum Fennica, Series B, No. 159. Helsinki, Finland: Suomalainen Tiedeakatemia, Academia Scientiarum Fennica, 1968. Pp. 108. *

[497]

Expressive Movement Chart. Ages 3–5; 1946–48; Werner Wolff; Grune & Stratton, Inc. * *Out of print.*

For additional information, see 4:104 (2 references); for a related book review not excerpted in this volume, consult the 3rd (1245) MMY.

[498]

"F" [Fluency of Association] Test. Ages 9 and over; 1938; Raymond B. Cattell, L. G. Studman, and C. A. Simmins; University of London Press Ltd. * *Out of print.*

For additional information and reviews by J. M. Blackburn, P. E. Vernon, and Ll. Wynn Jones, see 2:1220 (10 references, 1 excerpt).

[499]

The Graphomotor Projection Technique. Mental patients; 1948–54; Samuel B. Kutash and Raymond H. Gehl; C. H. Stoelting Co. * *Out of print.*

For additional information and a review by Philip L. Harriman, see 5:137 (7 references, 2 excerpts).

[500]

The Insight Test: A Verbal Projective Test for Personality Study. Adults; 1944–53; Helen D. Sargent; Grune & Stratton, Inc. * *Out of print.*

For additional information and a review by Richard Jessor, see 5:143 (8 references); for related book reviews not excerpted in this volume, consult the 5th MMY (B370).

REFERENCES

1–8. See 5:143.

9. SARGENT, HELEN DURHAM. *An Experimental Application of Projective Principles to a Paper and Pencil Personality Test.* Doctor's thesis, Northwestern University (Chicago, Ill.), 1944.

10. SARGENT, HELEN D. "Psychological Test Reporting: An Experiment in Communication." *B Menninger Clinic* 15:175–86 S '51. * (*PA* 26:4017)

11. VERRILL, BERNARD VICTOR. *An Investigation of the Concept of Impulsivity.* Doctor's thesis, University of Houston (Houston, Tex.), 1958. (*DA* 19:183)

12. SCHUMAN, ELLIOTT P. "A Scoring Rationale for the Sargent Test of Insight into Human Motives." *J Proj Tech* 26:462–8 D '62. * (*PA* 37:6693)

[501]

The Kell-Hoeflin Incomplete Sentence Blank: Youth-Parent Relations. College, adults; 1959;

KHISB; Ruth Hoeflin and Leone Kell; Child Development Publications, Society for Research in Child Development, Inc. * *Out of print.*

For additional information, see 6:225 (2 references).

REFERENCES

1–2. See 6:225.

3. SEARLES, WARREN BARNHART. *The Relationship Between the Perceived Emotional Climate of the Home of College Students and Certain Variables in Their Functioning Related to Self-Concept and Academic Functioning.* Doctor's thesis, University of Maryland (College Park, Md.), 1963. (*DA* 24:5208)

[502]

Myokinetic Psychodiagnosis. Ages 10 and over; 1951–58; MKP; expressive movement technique; English edition ('58, translated from the French edition, '51, by Mrs. Jacques Dubois); Emilio Mira y Lopez; Hoeber Medical Division, Harper & Row, Publishers, Inc. * *Out of print.*

For additional information and reviews by Philip L. Harriman and Irwin G. Sarason, see 6:232 (10 references); for related book reviews not excerpted in this volume, consult the 6th (B343) MMY.

REFERENCES

1–10. See 6:232.

11. GINSBERG, ANIELA MEYER; AZZI, ENZO; and PIRES, NELSON CAMPOS. "Projective and Experimental Methods in Personality Assessment." *Bulletin de l'Association Internationale de Psychologie Appliquée* 16:52–61 sp '67. * (*PA* 42:752)

[503]

Plot-Completion Test. Grades 9–12; 1946; a disguised personality test to be administered in an English class by an English teacher to elicit more honest answers; Sarah I. Roody; W. Wilbur Hatfield. * *Out of print.*

For additional information and reviews by Robert C. Challman and Percival M. Symonds, see 4:116 (2 references).

[504]

A Test of Family Attitudes. Ages 6–12; 1952; Lydia Jackson; Methuen & Co. Ltd. * *Out of print.*

For additional information and a review by John E. Bell, see 5:163 (2 references).

REFERENCES

1–2. See 5:163.

3. JACKSON, LYDIA. *Aggression and Its Interpretation.* London: Methuen & Co. Ltd., 1954. Pp. 237. *

4. JACKSON, LYDIA. "A Study of 200 School Children by Means of the Test of Family Attitudes." *Brit J Psychol* 55:333–54 Ag '64. * (*PA* 39:5066)

[505*]

The Travis Projective Pictures. Ages 4 and over; [1949–57]; revision of *The Travis-Johnston Projective Test: For the Exploration of Parent-Child Relationships;* [Lee E. Travis]; Griffin-Patterson Co., Inc. * *Out of print.*

For additional information and a review by Edwin S. Shneidman, see 5:169 (1 reference); for a review by Robert R. Holt of the original edition, see 4:142 (3 references).

REFERENCES

1–3. See 4:142.

4. See 5:169.

5. MEDINNUS, GENE R., and MEAD, D. EUGENE. "Comparison of a Projective and a Non-Projective Assessment of Parent Attitudes." *J Genetic Psychol* 107:253–60 D '65. * (*PA* 40:5494)

* Because of tests assigned double numbers (5–6, 86–7, 207–8, 228–9, 371–2, and 460–1) and tests assigned interpolated numbers (53A, 125A, 136A, 190A, 216A, 221A, 232A, 259A, 263A, 292A, 365A, 442A, 473A, and 473B), the total number of test entries is 513.

Personality Test Reviews

THE personality sections of the first six *Mental Measurements Yearbooks* are reprinted in this chapter in order of their original publication. The personality section of *The 1938 Mental Measurements Yearbook*—hereafter referred to as *The First Mental Measurements Yearbook*—appears first; the personality section of *The 1940 Mental Measurements Yearbook*—hereafter referred to as *The Second Mental Measurements Yearbook*—appears next; then the personality sections of the third, fourth, fifth, and sixth MMY's.

Because of different page sizes, copy for *The First MMY* had to be reset; the remaining personality sections have been reproduced by offset with only the running heads changed. The tests are arranged in alphabetical sequence by titles under the same headings and with the same entry numbers as in the corresponding yearbooks. The personality tests from the first MMY are listed under three headings: attitudes, personality, and social adjustment; the tests from the second and third MMY's are in a single sequence; the tests from the last three MMY's are listed under two headings: nonprojective and projective.

Page numbers are given in the running heads next to the inside margins; the entry numbers of tests are given in the running heads next to the outside margins. The entry numbers should be interpreted thus: 1:926 refers to the first yearbook, test number 926; 2:1238 refers to the second yearbook, test number 1238; and so forth. Consult the Introduction for information regarding the few cross references to publications other than the six *Mental Measurements Yearbooks*. All indexes and cross references in this monograph refer to entry numbers, not to page numbers. The right-hand running heads present the headings under which the tests from a given MMY are listed.

This chapter presents 648 original test reviews, 136 excerpted test reviews, 268 excerpted reviews of books dealing with specific tests, and 11,214 references on the construction, use, and validity of specific tests. More complete details on the contents of this chapter are presented in the Introduction.

References to the tests, reviews, and references in this chapter will be facilitated by first referring to the previous chapter, Personality Test Index. The Index lists all personality tests listed in the first six *Mental Measurements Yearbooks* and all other personality tests known to be in print as separates as of June 1, 1969. The Index gives cross references for each test to the reviews, excerpts, and references to be found in this chapter.

CHAPTER CONTENTS

REPRINTED FROM *The First Mental Measurements Yearbook*

PERSONALITY—FIRST MMY

REVIEWS BY *Harriet M. Barthelmess, Francis F. Bradshaw, Stephen M. Corey, Jack W. Dunlap, John C. Flanagan, Paul H. Furfey, Henry E. Garrett, J. P. Guilford, George W. Hartmann, Harold E. Jones, Elaine F. Kinder, Theos A. Langlie, Richard Ledgerwood, C. M. Louttit, Charles C. Peters, Daniel A. Prescott, H. H. Remmers, Anna S. Starr, Austin H. Turney, Goodwin Watson, and Edmund G. Williamson.*

ATTITUDES

[897]

[Attitude Scales.] Grades 7–16; c1934–36; each scale has space for indicating attitude toward five attitude variables; 2 forms; mimeographed; 1½¢ per test; 15¢ per specimen set of any one scale; 3(5) minutes per attitude variable; directed and edited by H. H. Remmers; [Division of Educational Reference].
a) SCALE FOR MEASURING ATTITUDE TOWARD ANY DISCIPLINARY PROCEDURE. p1936; V. R. Clouse.
b) SCALE FOR MEASURING ATTITUDE TOWARD ANY HOME-MAKING PROJECT. p1934; B. K. Vogel.
c) SCALE FOR MEASURING ATTITUDE TOWARD ANY INSTITUTION. p1934; T. B. Kelly.
d) SCALE FOR MEASURING ATTITUDE TOWARD ANY NATIONAL OR RACIAL GROUP. p1934; H. H. Grice.
e) SCALE FOR MEASURING ATTITUDE TOWARD ANY PRACTICE. p1934; H. W. Bues.
f) SCALE FOR MEASURING ATTITUDE TOWARD ANY SCHOOL SUBJECT. p1934; E. B. Silance.
g) SCALE FOR MEASURING ATTITUDE TOWARD ANY TEACHER. p1935; L. D. Hoshaw.
h) SCALE FOR MEASURING ATTITUDE TOWARD ANY VOCATION. p1934; H. E. Miller.
i) SCALE FOR MEASURING ATTITUDES TOWARD ANY PLAY. p1935; M. Dimmitt.
j) SCALE FOR MEASURING ATTITUDES TOWARD ANY PROPOSED SOCIAL ACTION. p1935; D. M. Thomas.
k) SCALE FOR MEASURING ATTITUDE TOWARD ANY SELECTION OF POETRY. p1935; J. E. Hadley.
l) SCALE FOR MEASURING INDIVIDUAL AND GROUP "MORALE." p1936; L. Whisler.

Stephen M. Corey, University of Wisconsin. Because no manual has as yet been published the reviewer was able to discover reliability and validity data for but 7 of the 15 scales sent to him. This information appeared in the Bulletin of Purdue University, Vol. 35, No. 4, written by Remmers and his students and entitled *Studies in Attitudes:* A Contribution to Social-Psychological Research Methods. This review is limited to an evaluation of the generalized attitude scales as described in this bulletin. Page references are to the bulletin.

Remmers and his students developed their method for measuring, on a single scale, attitudes toward many practices or objects or institutions because of the laboriousness of Thur-

stone's technique. The method they used most frequently to establish reliability was to determine the correlation between two forms of the same scale administered to the same population. Validity was established in terms of: (*a*) the logic underlying the construction of such scales taken in conjunction with the reliability determinations, (*b*) correlation with a specific scale as an external criterion, and (*c*) the extent to which groups known to differ in their attitudes through overt commitments are separated by the scales (p. 13). An attitude was defined as including "the sum total of an individual's beliefs, feelings, prejudices, notions, ideas and fears about any topic" (p. 18).

While it is true that Thurstone's technique is laborious, and needlessly so as Seashore, Hevner, Likert, and Remmers himself have shown, the fundamental difficulty with the generalized attitude scale is that one never knows how reliable and valid it is as a *generalized* scale. In use it is always *specific* and to determine its value as a measure of attitude toward a specific "object" (in Remmers' sense, p. 9) it is necessary to construct a *specific* scale for purposes of comparison in each instance. If this is not done, and to do so would appear to defeat the purpose of the generalized scale, the assumption is made that because a generalized scale measures rather reliably attitudes toward one, two, or three specific "objects" it will, therefore, measure reliably attitudes toward "twenty odd thousand" specific objects (p. 11). That would seem to be extrapolation of a very distinguished sort.

To illustrate this point specifically, a scale was developed by Miller to measure attitudes toward any occupation. The scale was "validated" by comparing the results obtained from it with results obtained from a single specific scale constructed to measure attitude toward teaching as a profession. The correlation between the two types of scales (found by averaging four other coefficients) was +.44 which in the judgment of the author, certainly not in the judgment of the reviewer, supports the conclusion: "The generalized attitude scale could be used in place of the specific scale for measuring attitudes, as the validity and reliability were high enough to indicate this" (p. 109).

Many of the statements in the generalized scales make very little sense if associated with certain *objects*. For example, consider the following statements from the *Generalized Scale to Measure Attitude Toward Any Institution* (p. 19) with respect to, let us say, the Interstate Commerce Commission. (1) Is the most beloved of institutions. (2) Is necessary to the very existence of civilization. (3) Gives real help in meeting moral problems. (4) Will destroy civilization if it is not radically changed. (5) Has done more for society than any other institution.

This criticism is increasingly apparent the more general the scales become. A scale measuring attitude toward any school subject is not so general (at present at least) as one measuring attitude toward any practice or any institution. It is in the latter that many of the statements appear irrelevant and sometimes humorous.

The monograph in which validity and reliability data for the generalized scale are reported leaves much to be desired statistically. Coefficients of correlation are averaged (pp. 42, 105), the critical ratio is misinterpreted (p. 67), scale values are tabulated for which there are no scale item equivalents (p. 106), differences between groups of 25 are subjected to careful statistical analysis (p. 66), and probable errors are computed for means based on groups as small as 14 (p. 80).

Whether or not the generalized attitude scale has many advantages over the specific scale which are not more than compensated for by disadvantages is still a question. Certainly the less general the scale the greater its reliability and validity. The reviewer is of the opinion that even the least general scales are little more than interesting questionnaires (hardly scales) which stand sorely in need of validation by some method other than a purely statistical one. The relationship of attitude scale scores to overt behavior, for example, has been rather completely neglected.

[898]

Behavior Description, Experimental Form. Grades 7–12; c1935; a Manila folder for recording non-test-measured behavior characteristics; 10¢ per folder; $3.50 per 50; $6 per 100; 40¢ per manual; 50¢ per specimen set; 50¢ per 100 "B Sheets" (one sheet is needed by each classroom teacher for making initial ratings before transposing to the individual folder forms); Reports and Records Committee (Eugene R. Smith, Chairman) of the Commission on the Relation of School and College, Progressive Education Association; Beaver County Day School, Chestnut Hill, Mass.

[899]

C-R Opinionaire. Advanced high school students, college students, and adults; c1935; a measure of conservatism-radicalism; 2 forms; the 2 forms are published as separates and combined in a single booklet; $1.25 per 25 double booklets; 75¢ per 25 of a single form; 25¢ per specimen set; (20) minutes per form; T. F. Lentz and colleagues of the Character Research Institute; Character Research Institute.

H. H. Remmers, Purdue University. This instrument made up of two forms of 120 agreement-disagreement items is designed to measure general conservatism or radicalism in regard to human values among reasonably literate individuals. That for college students relatively similar functions are measured by the two forms of instrument is indicated by reliability coefficients of .91 and .94 for the two forms respectively and of .94 for the combined scores. Factor analysis and genetic study of factors thus revealed could profitably be carried out. The items of the instrument to this reviewer are for the most part such as will continue to have cultural validity. A few will "date" rather soon. Ease of administration and scoring are commendable features. The manual of directions is informative concerning method of validation and uses of the instrument for research purposes. The standard error of estimate or of measurement would be a desirable feature, but is not provided.

[900]

Minnesota Inventory of Social Attitudes. Grades 13–16; c1937; 2 parts (labeled as forms); (15 to 20) minutes per part; 5¢ per test; 10¢ per specimen set; quantity discounts; E. G. Williamson and J. G. Darley; distributed by the Psychological Corporation.
a) FORM B, MINNESOTA INVENTORY OF SOCIAL BEHAVIOR.
b) FORM P, MINNESOTA INVENTORY OF SOCIAL PREFERENCES.

J. P. Guilford, University of Nebraska. The inventories appear in two forms, P and B. Of these the authors say, "Form P is called *Inventory of Social Preferences* and includes questions designed to measure preferences in the extent and type of desired social relationships, ranging from a desire to restrict one's social relationships to a very few contacts, to the opposite extreme of those who wish to experience relatively unrestricted social contacts. Form B is called *Inventory of Social Behavior* and includes questions which sample an individual's estimates of his own behavior and feelings in social situations, ranging from the extremely shy to the extremely active individual in social relationships."

Illustrative items from Form P are: "Likes to know a great many people intimately," "Likes to mix with people socially," and "Is indifferent to people." Illustrations from Form B are: "Is well poised in social contacts," "Is rather shy in contacts with people," "Has a fairly good time at parties." In both forms, beneath each item is a list of five judgments one of which the subject is to underline, for example, "Almost always [5] Frequently [4] Occasionally [3] Rarely [2] Almost never [1]." The digit after each judgment indicates the number of points to be added to the total score if that judgment is the one underlined. Sometimes, naturally, the numbers 1 to 5 will come in the order reversed to that in the above illustration. It seems very questionable, in spite of the great convenience to the scorer, to let the judgments be numbered lest this influence the response of the subject. At times, also the list of judgments as given above do not seem logical or natural responses to the item, for example the statement: "Neither seeks nor avoids social contacts." Each form contains 40 items.

The instructions seem not very pointed. Note that the form of statement describes a third person. The instructions read in part "Underline the phrase which best expresses your feeling about the statement." Will the subject take this as a self-rating problem, even if on a page preceding the instructions he is told, "The purpose of the survey is simply to see what is your usual behavior"?

The reliabilities of the two forms are exceptionally high, as such questionnaires go, lying in the range from .90 to .92. Correlations with the Thurstone *Psychological Examination* are about zero and also with school marks, for both forms. The use of the inventories therefore lies in the estimation of traits independent of intelligence and not important for scholastic success or failure. No coefficients of validity are given, but the test scores give highly significant differences between extreme groups distinguished as to social adjustment.

The correlation between the two forms is of the order .44 to .47, which is surprisingly low, considering the very great similarity in items in the two scales. In both scales the items were selected on the basis of Thurstone's method of scaling and Likert's technique, using the responses of 1000 students. Detailed percentile ranks are given for both forms.

George W. Hartmann, Columbia University. These paired self-estimates are issued in Form B (Social Behavior) and Form P (Social Preferences), consisting of 40 five-step multiple-choice ratings like these: (B) likes to be observed (almost always, frequently, occasionally, rarely, almost never) and (P) feels bored with people (ditto). One's first impression is that of a close kinship between the two measures and despite the authors' efforts to separate indices of "skill" from symptoms of "wishes," this impression is confirmed by the reported intercorrelation of .47. Both tests require about a half-hour to take and are designed for use in counseling college students, although the situations presented are general enough and constitute meaningful experiences for all persons beyond age twelve. Certainly they are far from subtle; many border on the naive.

The highest possible score in both instruments is 200 (40×5); the lowest, however, is not zero but 40 (40×1), a point which the authors should have emphasized when they stressed the necessity for answering every item. The self-correlation is .90 for both blanks. Clinically, these inventories should serve to reveal actual or potential over- or under-"socialization," provided the respondent is an individual of sufficient insight and probity; taken together—as they apparently must be—it would be highly significant if a score well beyond (or below) the mean in Form B were accompanied by one definitely below (or above) the mean in Form P. At the very least, the gap between desire and reality would be conspicuous.

The theoretical base upon which these measures rest is not readily seen in their contents. "Social" has apparently been restricted in meaning to poise in face-to-face contacts and pleasure in human association. Concern for others in the humanitarian sense of preventing war, eliminating poverty, etc., is not represented;

instead, attention is focused upon such terms as parties, conversation, games, entertainment, strangers, friends, mixing with people, etc. The underlying "construct" of the tests is ease versus embarrassment in group life—a shallow thing to some, but a matter of grave earnestness to many adolescents.

The validity has been established by substantial critical ratios between "well" versus "poorly" adjusted students, and by comparisons of the means of fraternity-sorority members and "unaffiliated" men and women. Cash evidently facilitates poise and "animal gregariousness" for the test scores are positively related to amount of spending money. Salesmen and politicians would certainly stand high on these measures; the unemployed and "frustrated" are certain to be low.

Although the tests are reasonably priced, the reviewer believes they could have been improved by consolidating the 80 items in sequence, thus producing one six-page rather than two four-page booklets. Appraisal of the two halves would have been helped rather than hindered by this step.

The absence of "critical scores" is regrettable. Most inventories seem to be helpful in guidance only when the upper and lower centiles are involved. Since the measures seem to be conventionally correct in other respects, this may be a question for further field experience to answer.

[901]

Minnesota Scale for the Survey of Opinions. Ages 16–25; c1936; 1 form; a battery of scales to measure certain phases of personality and social attitudes of significance for social adjustment; $5 per 100 tests, including scoring instructions and tabulation sheet; 10¢ per specimen set; (30–40) minutes; E. A. Rundquist and R. F. Sletto; University of Minnesota Press.

H. H. Remmers, Purdue University. This instrument is designed to measure "phases of personality and social attitudes that seem of fundamental significance for personal adjustment." Six separate scores for presumably as many different aspects of personality are obtained under the captions morale, inferiority feelings, family, law, economic conservatism and education. A general adjustment score is also yielded by sixteen of the 132 items from the various scales. The testing time required is between 30 and 40 minutes.

Norms for the seven different scales are

given in terms of T-scores, i.e., standard deviation scores multiplied by 10 and added to 50. These norms are based on a sampling of 1000 persons, 500 of each sex, which included 400 college students, 200 high school seniors and 400 youthful employed and unemployed persons in continuation classes at the high school level—all in Minneapolis. This sampling, as the authors admit, is rather severely restricted and rather heavily biased in terms of educational selection. One wonders how the norms would have been affected by the inclusion in the standardization group of negroes (northern and southern), various immigrant groups, share croppers, members of communistic religious sects and the like. Responses to many opinion items such as are included in the instrument under review are probably profoundly affected by *cultural* patterns. This, if true, would of course very decidedly affect norms to the extent that such patterns vary from group to group.

This is not to say that the instrument may not prove an effective device with such urban groups as were included in the study. In their monograph, *Personality in the Depression,* the authors have gone a long way toward furnishing a model of thinking and research of the kind requisite for the critical appraisal of a projected measuring instrument. Ingenuity and insight of a high order characterize their formulation and testing of hypotheses. For any worker who wishes to undertake any serious study or diagnosis by means of the Minnesota Survey of Opinions a careful reading of this monograph will be indispensable.

The most important desideratum concerning any measuring device is its validity. Bearing in mind the limitations of the standardizing population for the scales, the following quotation from *Personality in the Depression* is apropos:

Are the scales valid? Morale, being by definition a very general trait—it may, in fact, be the factor responsible for the covariation of the six scales—the evidence that it is the most generalized of the six scales may be considered as evidence for its validity. Morale has the highest multiple R against scores on the remaining scales, the morale items discriminate best in scales other than their own, and the scale is related to the largest number of outside variables * The inferiority scale is valid in the sense that it correlates well with another instrument designed to measure the same trait * Clear-cut validating evidence for the remaining scales is lacking. The nature of radicalism makes it highly probable that the economic conservatism scale will prove valid. The evidence points in the correct direction for the family scale, but is not completely convincing. The law scale....has no experimental support for its name * Precisely what the education scale is measuring is not indicated by anything except the apparent ideational content of the items (pp. 215–216).

Reliability coefficients between .78 and .88 estimated by means of correlations between equivalent forms and the Spearman-Brown formula are reported. The validity of the Spearman-Brown formula for this type of situation was assumed.

The scoring of the scales is rather laborious and might rather easily be made less so by means of stencils to obviate the need for transcribing all responses to a tabulation sheet for each individual.

Apparently only one form of the instrument is being made available in printed form.

Goodwin Watson, Columbia University. The blank is of the omnibus type, containing 132 statements on almost everything from "The future looks very black" to "One becomes nervous at home." Each is reacted to in a five-degree response from "strongly agree" to "strongly disagree." The statements are grouped for scoring, into those which appear to be related to: M—Morale versus insecurity and discouragement; I—Inferiority versus ease in social contacts; F—Family intimacy versus discord; L—Respect versus disrespect for law; EC—Economic conservatism versus "radicalism"; E—Value versus contempt for education; GA—General adjustment—much the same as morale.

No statements occur in more than one category except that the last named, "General Adjustment," includes seven repeated from the "Morale" group, three from "Education" and one or two from each other classification. Presumably "Morale" and "General Adjustment" scores will be artificially highly correlated.

Reliabilities between .80 and .90 are reported, with extensive data on standard deviations, intercorrelations, and item analyses. Statistically a very careful job has been done. The manual presents a table for translating raw scores on each scale into standard scores, based on a group of 1000 young people, 400 from college, 200 from high school and 400 from continuation schools.

Little has been done by the authors to eliminate the most serious error in such instruments —the desire to answer in such a way as to make a good impression. The directions ask for an "honest opinion" but the rest of the first page asks for data, including name, age, time since last regular employment, marital status, whether parents are living together and other items which would certainly constitute a serious threat to many subjects. Test-makers are so often good statisticians but poor psychologists.

In consequence, it is impossible to predict whether results from the test will accord with genuine opinion or not. Much will depend on the rapport between tester and subject, and on what the subject suspects the purpose of the test to be.

[902]

Social Attitude Scales. High school, college, and adults; c1937; 2 forms; $1.50 per set of 20 copies of each of the three scales in two forms and one manual; 75¢ per set of 20 copies of any one scale in two forms and one manual; 20¢ per specimen set of all scales; no time reported; A. C. Rosander; Association Press.

H. H. Remmers, Purdue University. These three social attitude scales are presumably constructed according to the Thurstone scaling technique. No directions for administering or scoring are given. A number of suggested uses accompany the scales. Data on validity and reliability are not given. From considerable experience with similar scales the present reviewer would judge that these scales would be adequately reliable for group comparisons.

Goodwin Watson, Columbia University. There are three social attitude scales, one on Democracy, one on the Federal Constitution, one on Social Justice. Each is prepared in two comparable forms. Form A and Form B, to facilitate "before" and "after" experimentation.

No manual accompanies the tests, so data on standardization, etc., are missing. If we may judge from his previous publications the author has probably used Thurstone's scaling technique. Statements are arranged in an approximate continuum from one extreme to the other.

A little mimeographed sheet on "suggested uses for social attitude scales" accompanies the tests. The author makes fairly obvious proposals such as comparing different groups, or shift due to educational influences, or stability of the attitude over time, or to plan discussions and remedial work.

The extent to which the answer is one given in order to make a favorable impression is not discussed. The point cannot be too often stressed that the essence of attitude testing must lie in the creation of psychological rapport facilitating frank communication. Lists of statements such as are here offered may or may not be valid, depending entirely upon conditions of use. It is to be regretted that the author failed to consider this crucial problem.

There is almost an implication in some of the statements about the tests that pupils who check statements like "What this nation needs is some of the good old frontier democracy" are really favorable to democratic practices while those who check "We are too eager to give everyone the right to vote" are deficient in democratic loyalties. The reverse may be true. Surely we are sufficiently sophisticated in our social psychology to know that the word "democracy" is a stereotype, and that response to it as a symbol may or may not be correlated with an attitude of approval for democratic practices in the schools, families, business and communities in which the individual lives. There is too much word-magic in such scales, and too little evidence of the exploration of actual differences in individual concepts, feelings and behavior.

[903]

Social Orientation. College students; c1935; 2 forms; $1.70 per 25 tests; 30¢ per specimen set; mimeographed manual; (30–40) minutes; J. B. Maller and H. S. Tuttle; published by the authors, Teachers College, Columbia University.

Charles C. Peters, Pennsylvania State College. According to the authors: "The test affords an opportunity for the expression of attitudes toward situations involving social conflict. These attitudes may range from extreme individualism to extreme social mindedness * One of the most puzzling aspects of contemporary education is the incongruity between the avowed *objectives* and the actual *criteria* used to determine academic success. Quite frequently the goals publicly announced are in the realm of personality and character development. Yet, examinations in secondary schools and colleges, for admission and promotion, deal almost exclusively with items of information and general intelligence" (*Manual of Directions,* page 1).

The test consists of four multiple-choice items involving forecast of probable consequences of societal behavior, ten true-false items about economic truths, nine news items calling for approval or disapproval, twenty-four words carrying pleasant or unpleasant suggestions, eight pairs of alternative "vital fac-

tors in civilization," three narratives with acceptable or inacceptable alternatives, and five groups in modern society to be evaluated as to their social characteristics.

All of the items are scored objectively. The reliability coefficient, between forms I and II, is given as .895. The test was validated by opinions of judges as to which was the answer revealing a liberal point of view, and by the ability of the test to differentiate groups known on other grounds to be widely separated in liberalism. The internal consistency of the test was assured by eliminating from it all items which did not correlate with the test as a whole at least .40 by the bi-serial technique. Tentative norms are given on the two forms, based on 300 college freshmen and high school seniors from institutions known to be liberal or progressive.

The test is intended definitely to be a test of liberalism. In some of its elements it would be more appropriately described as a test of radicalism rather than liberalism. In the last section of Form I the respondent must, to get credit for the item, list bankers, capitalists, and rugged individualists as "tends to undermine American institutions" and as "tends to create friction." In general, the alternatives are so widely spaced as to invite responses prompted by the slogans of radicalism rather than by the calmer thinking of liberalism, and this tendency is probably accentuated by the authors' suggestion in the instructions that the answers be checked rapidly and on first impression.

This is not meant at all as an adverse criticism of the test. It is a test of radical thought and such a test is valuable. Certainly any sincere effort to add to our testing techniques measures of attitudes and valuations to supplement the tests of factual information which have hitherto dominated the field is a commendable effort.

PERSONALITY

[912]

Adjustment Inventory. Grades 9–16; c1934; 1 form; $1.75 per 25 inventories; 25¢ per specimen set; (25) minutes; H. M. Bell; Stanford University Press.

Austin H. Turney, University of Kansas. This instrument purports to provide "four separate measures of personal and social adjustment," the four areas being home, health, social, and emotional adjustment. It is easy to give and score. The author presents tentative norms for high school and college by sexes on a relatively small number of cases. The principal methods of validation are those of contrasting groups and of correlation with other "scales."

Though the author gives coefficients of reliability of considerable size (.80 to .89) and presents correlations with other instruments (from .58 to .94), the reviewer views with skepticism their claim of utility. It must require considerable faith or temerity to believe that 140 items, averaging 35 items to a division of the kind in the scale, really measure adjustment in a satisfactory manner. The complexity of the "psychobiological environment" must have been grossly overestimated by a host of psychologists if we are mistaken about this.

[913]
Aspects of Personality. Grades 4–9; c1938; 1 form; $1.20 per 25 tests; 15¢ per specimen set; (30) minutes; R. Pintner, J. J. Loftus, G. Forlano, and B. Alster; World Book Co.

Sch 27:172–4 O '38. J. A. Long. This is an eight-page inventory, "constructed to meet the need for a personality inventory in the form of an easily used group test which would reveal maladjusted pupils in grades 4 to 9. Section I deals with ascendancy-submission; Section II with introversion-extroversion; and Section III with emotional stability." The inventory is objective, has a reliability coefficient of about .70 for children within an age-range of one year *

[914]
Attitude-Interest Analysis Test. Early adolescence and adults; c1936; a disguised test of mental masculinity and femininity; 2 forms; 10¢ per test; $1.50 per manual and scoring stencils; no time limit (40–60) minutes; L. M. Terman and C. C. Miles; McGraw-Hill Book Co.

[915]
BEC Personality Rating Schedule. Grades 7–16 and adults; c1936; 50¢ per 25 schedules; 10¢ per specimen set; prepared under the direction of the Business Education Council representing the National Office Management Assocation and the Eastern Commercial Teachers Association; P. J. Rulon, E. A. Nash, and G. L. Woodward with the assistance of G. G. Monks, R. H. Hawkins, J. T. Cook, G. E. Miles, and B. Feldman; Harvard University Press.

Francis F. Bradshaw, University of North Carolina. This scale represents an advance in scale construction in the following ways: (1) It includes mainly those traits or behavior characteristics which are not only significant but normally observable. (2) These trait scales are expressed in terms of actions to be observed rather than qualities to be inferred from behavior. (3) The scales contain five steps with possible rating between steps. (4) A definite procedure is suggested for systematic gathering of ratings without regard to special use to be made of them.

The scale continues the defects of previous scales as follows: (1) Teachers are requested to rate on twenty-nine aspects of behavior instead of five to ten. Experience with scales has indicated that such multiplication of ratings increases carelessness and decreases value of ratings. (2) The scales request ratings as qualities that can be better measured and recorded in other ways. Such traits are mental alertness and health. (3) The principal trait terms are less significant than the subscales since they slur over distinctions between kinds of behavior, e.g., including punctuality and honesty under the general heading of dependability. Therefore, the average of subscales is less significant than the separate items averaged. (4) The schedule form makes no provision for gathering from raters the behaviorgrams (sometimes called instances, anecdotes, or narratives) which not only justify the rating but convey more definitely the personal qualities involved. The behaviorgram also avoids the "error of generalization" involved in all ratings wherein a general uniformly operating trait is inferred from one or more specific responses to specific situations. (The justification for this statement appears in the research on the American Council on Education Rating Scale, printed as Archives of Psychology, 1930, No. 119, Columbia University, New York City.)

In summary, this scale, while including some of the improvements indicated by the experimentation of the last ten years, could probably be further improved by (1) greatly reducing the number of subscales, (2) discontinuing the averaging of subratings together, (3) arranging for gathering and transmitting to "the ultimate consumer" the behaviorgrams which really constitute the objective element in such scales, and (4) rewriting instructions to direct teachers' attention more definitely toward "observing and reporting" rather than "observing and inferring." In additon, space should be provided for a "no opportunity to observe" entry, since some traits would not be readily observable in classroom situations. Ratings secured without opportunity to observe will seriously dilute the reliability of the scale.

Theos A. Langlie, Wesleyan University. In a recent article published in the *Journal of Genetic Psychology* the writer stated:

the solution of the problem (of personality analysis) will not be hastened by the indiscriminate use of rating scales. Careful training of teachers in habits of observation, analysis, and judgment is necessary. Before such training can result in satisfactory measures of personality traits, definition of those traits is imperative. In fact, analysis of behavior components and formulation of definitions and specific descriptions would become the basis and furnish the content of a thorough plan for training teachers to observe, and enumerate significant phases of pupil behavior.[1]

The *BEC Personality Rating Schedule* seems to represent an attempt to achieve the above-quoted goal. The significant things about this rating schedule are not the multiplicity of traits to be rated (29 in number) nor the fact that the graphic method is used, but rather that each trait is described carefully and, in use, raters are trained and retrained when analysis indicates the need of retraining in the use of this rating schedule. In fact this is not the type of rating scale to be handed out once a year to a group of teachers with the expectation that valid ratings will be received from them. It is essentially a behavior trait description technique with frequent recordings of judgments on immediate observation of the students being judged. This last technique by itself would very likely result in all of the errors to which ratings in general incline, including the "halo" error, the "sex halo" error and tendencies to deviate from the average in making ratings. However, when the individual teacher's ratings are analyzed and the results of such analyses are reported at frequent intervals to the rater with suggestions for improving rating methods, we can expect to get more valid and more truly descriptive results than are obtained in the usual school situation. It must be remembered, however, that such methods are time consuming and may not be followed conscientiously by most school systems.

There are some traits included which might be measured in a more objective manner. Included among these would be: (I) mental alertness. (1) grasp of instructions; and (VIII) health, (1) illness *vs.* wellness. This is a very minor criticism, however, since it may be highly desirable to obtain a teacher's impressions of this characteristic in students.

It is to be hoped that machine scoring methods may be utilized in future editions of this rating schedule.

[916]

CASE Inventory, Third Edition. Grades 5 and above; c1935, p1936; 2 forms; $2.65 per 25 tests; $8.40 per 100; 30¢ per specimen set; (45) minutes; J. B. Maller; Bureau of Publications.

Richard Ledgerwood, Ohio State University. This is a battery of four short personality tests. The tests involve, respectively, word-association choice, self-description, over-statement, and ethical judgment. A questionnaire on background is included in the test blank. The first two tests contain 50 items each, the third and fourth 15 and 9 items, respectively, all selected for reliability and validity on the basis of previous experimental use. Reported reliability as determined by correlation of odd and even items, using both forms, ranges from .90 to .96. The test is self-administering at the high school and college level. Tentative norms based on the second edition of the test are provided.

[917]

Character and Inventory Chart. Grades 6–12; c1931–33; 1 form; self-rating; $5 per 100; 15¢ per Teacher's Handbook (c1933); B. L. Dougherty, F. L. O'Reilly, and M. Mannix; Public School Publishing Co.

Teach Col J 5:268 Jl '34. E. L. Abell. This chart is primarily for the purpose of stimulating among children an interest in self-improvement. It is attractively and cleverly arranged and ought to serve its purpose. The child first selects the word which best describes the degree to which he shows the given trait and writes the word in the proper place. This word is transferred by carbon to a second sheet which is so arranged as to give a profile of the child according to his own estimate in ten important traits. A study of the profile with the suggestions made is supposed to arouse in the child a desire to improve in those traits in which he is weak. The ten traits selected for use while admittedly very important apparently represent the authors' judgments rather than the result of scientific analyses of character traits. The chart ought to furnish opportunity for valuable remedial work.

[918]

Cowan Adolescent Personality Schedule, Revision 1. Ages 12 to 20; c1935–37; 1 form; $2 per

---

[1] LANGLIE, T. A. "Personality Ratings." *Journal of Genetic Psychology,* 50:339–59, 401–26; June 1937.

25 tests and record sheets; $7.50 per 100; 50¢ per specimen set; 15 minutes; E. A. Cowan; Wichita Child Research Laboratory.

Harold E. Jones, University of California. Modeled after the *Thurstone Personality Schedule for Adults,* this questionnaire consists of 201 items to be answered Yes, No, or ?. No attempt is made to utilize the newer types of items, such as those employed in the *Rogers Test of Personal and Social Adjustment.* Scoring of the items is on the basis of the author's judgment, checked by comparison of performance of 50 cases at each extreme of an experimental group of 648 children.[1] No data are reported concerning the validity of the individual items or of the total scale. Split-half reliability (corrected for length of test) is .84, but no retest coefficients are given. The question of reliability becomes particularly important in connection with the use of scores for individual categories (fears, inferiority, neurotic symptoms, etc.) which are based on from 18 to 35 items. The author has not attempted to justify these categories, although in another publication Brigden states that scores on "neurotic symptoms indicate a blockage of some basic desire .... maladjustment to responsibility indicates too much close parental supervision and lack of emotional maturity,"[2] etc. In this report, Brigden discusses the significance of the categories in rather definite terms. Scores on neurotic symptoms "indicate a blockage of some basic desire"; scores on maladjustment to responsibility "indicate too much close parental supervision and lack of emotional maturity," etc. Brigden is perhaps too confident in stating that in 15 minutes of testing and 5 minutes of scoring and profile construction it is possible to determine "the ground plan of a maladjustment." Until further statistical evidence and clinical support is obtained regarding this and similar tests, it would seem desirable to emphasize their provisional character, rather than to advocate their immediate widespread use for diagnostic and remedial purposes. The author wisely recommends that the inventory be regarded as preliminary to an interview rather than as offering final information in and of itself.

[1] COWAN, E. A.; McCLELLAN, M. C.; PRATT, B. M.; AND SKAER, M. "An Adolescent Personality Schedule." *Child Development,* 6:77-87; March 1935.
[2] BRIGDEN, R. L. "A Diagnostic Adolescent Personality Schedule," pp. 38-9. *Proceedings of the Second Biennial Meeting, Society for Research in Child Development.* Washington, D.C.: National Research Council, 1931.

[919]
"F" Test. Ages 10 and above; p1938; a temperament test of fluency of association "which reveals itself particularly in quickness of thinking, width and range in association and imagination"; group or individual test; 6*d.* per test; 5*s.* 6*d.* per 12 tests; 35*s.* per 100 tests; 15(20) minutes; R. B. Cattell in collaboration with G. L. Studman and C. A. Simmins; University of London Press Ltd.

[920]
Humm-Wadsworth Temperament Scale. Adults with I.Q.'s over 70, preferably over 80; c1934; 1 form; $2.50 per 25; $9 per 100; 50¢ per specimen set; 50¢ per report of research; 50¢ per copy of the booklet, *Analysis of Disposition or Temperament;* (30-90) minutes; D. G. Humm and G. W. Wadsworth, Jr.; published by D. G. Humm, 157½ N. Kenmore Ave., Los Angeles, Calif.

Daniel A. Prescott, Rutgers University. This scale is designed to make possible the rapid diagnosis and analysis of the temperament of adults and late adolescents. Temperament is regarded as the equivalent of disposition and refers to a person's characteristic affect in responding to situations. The scale does not evaluate intelligence, skill, or personality characteristics other than temperament.

The following hypotheses underlie the test: (1) that abnormal behavior is the uncontrolled manifestation of the same temperamental components as are found in normal persons; (2) that Rosanoff's older theory of personality gives an adequate description of the components of temperament. The content of the scale was developed from clinical experience and the methods of validation and standardization involved the use of clinical material.

The revised scale includes 318 questions designed to measure the following components of temperament: (1) "normal," which means capacity or habit of exercising self-control and self-discipline and of maintaining stability. The items referring to the "normal" component of personality were standardized by comparing the responses of persons rated self-controlled employees with those of abnormal, institutionalized subjects. The test appears to have been constructed carefully and its validity and usefulness depends entirely upon the soundness of the hypotheses upon which it is based. The authors claim that an adequate demonstration of validity and reliability has been made through an experimental study at the Southern Counties Gas Company in 1937. The reviewer concurs with the authors that any paper and pencil test should be regarded as a diagnostic aid rather than as a diagnostic criterion. Only the wide usage of this scale in functional situations in conjunction with careful ratings of behavior and case histories of the subjects will demonstrate its practical usefulness with college students and in industrial and commercial personnel work. It does deserve very much this experimental usage.

The authors point out that some subjects under particular circumstances tend to give an inordinate number of yes or no responses or to refuse cooperation, answering haphazardly or contrary to fact. They note that as high as 25 or 30 per cent of normal subjects may invalidate their tests under such circumstances. They have met this weakness by developing a table which makes it possible to evaluate the validity of the score of any subject. This is unique, valuable and highly commendable, and should be effective in preventing fallacious diagnoses and analyses of temperament.

The reviewer hails the development of scales based frankly upon specific hypotheses of personality structure, when such scales are constructed carefully. To wait for the slow accumulation of insights accidentally arrived at, and to continue clinical practice on the basis of hypotheses tested only subjectively, is much less scientific and wholesome than to construct and use widely with normal as well as abnormal subjects a series of valid instruments of measurement based upon the hypotheses currently held.

The reviewer feels that the availability of this scale offers a promising opportunity for the scientific evaluation of the truth which may underlie Rosanoff's theory; if the theory has holes in it the scale will not work well with normal subjects.

[921]

Inventory of Activities and Interests. Ages 12–19 and grades 7–12; c1936; also called *P.Q. or Personality Quotient Test;* separate forms for boys and girls; a disguised test to measure social initiative, self-determination, economic self-determination, adjustment to opposite sex, extroversion-introversion, and a personality quotient; (40) minutes; H. C. Link, P. G. Corby, G. K. Bennett, R. G. Anderson, and S. Roslow; Psychological Corporation.
a) INVENTORY OF ACTIVITIES AND INTERESTS (FOR BOYS AND YOUNG MEN).
b) INVENTORY OF ACTIVITIES AND INTERESTS (FOR GIRLS AND YOUNG WOMEN).

C. M. Louttit, Indiana University. On the theory that "personality is measured by the extent to which the individual has learned to convert his energy into habits and skills which influence and serve other people" the authors

have arranged a series of questions quite similar to those found on other personality inventories. These are said to measure five expressions of personality: extroversion, social aggressiveness, self-determination, economic self-determination, and sex adjustment. The score may be converted into a personality quotient which the authors feel is analogous to the IQ. For personality as thus narrowly defined this may be a useful scale. In general it is probably no better or no worse than the other scales which are now available.

Edmund G. Williamson, University of Minnesota. Separate inventories have been constructed for boys and girls, designed to measure five aspects of personality: extroversion, social aggressiveness, self-determination, economic self-determination and sex-adjustment. The measurement of personality is based upon the following five assumptions: (1) personality is the result of the individual's efforts "to convert his organic energies into habits or actions which successfully influence other people"; (2) these habits may be learned as are other types of skills; (3) emotional instability is a function of inadequate skills and habits; (4) many questions should be included in the (preliminary) test; and (5) the test questions may be grouped arbitrarily subject to regrouping following statistical analysis.

The test was administered to several large groups of students and careful item analyses were made. Each item was studied statistically in terms of each of the five scores (see above). Odd-even reliabilities (corrected) for these scores ranged from .70 (economic self-determination) to .88 (self-determination). The intercorrelations ranged from .289 to .785, uncorrected for attenuation. If the major interest of the authors is in the total personality and not in sub-traits, then these intercorrelations are not sufficiently high; if they are interested in measuring "significantly different habits, attitudes or skills," then these intercorrelations are too high for their purpose. But this test cannot be used to achieve both objectives except by ignoring all except any one score.

Out of this inventory the authors have derived a "personality quotient." This quotient has a mean value of 100 based upon the scores of students of any one sex and grade from the sixth grade through college. Actually this "PQ" is based upon the extroversion score alone, which in turn is derived by scoring all but a few of the items.

Thus far the inventory has been validated only by "flat" and by comparison of the scores of 1138 high school students from different schools, classified by their teachers in terms of scholarship and "leadership" (four categories in each variable).

The arbitrary restriction of this personality inventory to the use of habits and skills in the influencing of people may or may not be justified. Sufficient analysis has not yet been reported to determine the authors' achievement in this respect. Judging from the reported studies, it is not yet clearly established that a markedly different type of personality test has been produced. Comparison with standardized tests and more careful attempts to differentiate social groups are needed before this test can be accepted as valid. The invention of the "PQ" may have value as a catch-phrase but there is no indication of advantage over the standard practice of using percentiles.

[922]

Nebraska Personality Inventory. c1934; 1 form; $2.25 per 50 inventories; $4 per 100 inventories; J. P. Guilford; Sheridan Supply Co.

John C. Flanagan, Cooperative Test Service, New York City. This inventory aims to measure three of the five factors obtained from the factorial analysis of the responses to 36 questions of the type which has been traditionally used to diagnose tendencies toward introversion or extroversion. The present form contains 101 items, and furnishes scores on $S, E,$ and M. S is briefly characterized as social introversion: a tendency to withdraw from the social environment, shyness, seclusiveness. E is described as emotionality: a tendency to react with emotion to life situations, cycloid tendencies. M is labeled masculinity: a tendency to react to the test items in the manner characteristic of males.

The Spearman-Brown reliability coefficients reported for S and E range from .85 to .93, those for S being generally somewhat higher. The coefficients reported for M vary from .54 to .74, the median being .66. Some of the intercorrelations, which the authors hoped would be very close to zero, were disappointingly large, .46 and .40 for S with E and M respectively. The correlation between E and M was −.01. These results could hardly be considered unexpected since the authors made no attempt to take item intercorrelations into account in setting up their scoring weights. This test represents a very interesting approach to the problem, and the authors report further work in progress which it is anticipated will provide more satisfactory scoring weights for the various reponses.

About 50% of the items in this inventory sample specific points included in the *Bernreuter Personality Inventory* with slightly different wording. The other half represent items dealing mainly with such topics as temperament revealed in reaching decisions and work habits, interest in selling, and the ability to adapt oneself.

A stencil with the appropriate weights for each response for each of the three scales is provided. The present writer scored an inventory for all three scales in about 15 minutes. This could probably be decreased somewhat with practice. There is some doubt that the authors' use of as many as nine different weights is justified in view of the rather crude method used to obtain these scoring weights.

In summary, it may be said that this inventory in its present form should yield two fairly accurate and not highly intercorrelated scores which would appear to be useful in describing individuals. It does not seem at all certain that it would be worth while to score the inventories for M in most practical situations because of its ambiguity of definition, susceptibility to misinterpretation, and unreliability. How much additional knowledge one can expect to gain from the use of the M scale is perhaps suggested by the fact that answering the question, "Are you a male?" in the affirmative would change an individual's score from the 50th to the 70th percentile.

C. M. Louttit, Indiana University. The authors, on the basis of a factor analysis made on the responses of several hundred college students on 36 of the items in this schedule, have separated out three factors, which they feel are primary personality factors, measured by this scale. They suggest that further study might indicate more factors. The three they have found are social introversion, emotionality, and masculinity. The statistical analysis back of this schedule is thoroughly adequate but one wonders if the validity of any scale is adequately expressed in purely statistical terms. Does the index of reliability guarantee that the scale will validly diagnose personality patterns in individual cases?

[923]

Personal History Record (1937 Revision). College freshmen; c1937; a disguised test of emotional stability; $2.50 per 25 tests; $7.50 per 100 (catalog No. 24524); 25¢ per typewritten manual (No. 24524A); L. A. Thompson; C. H. Stoelting Co.

[924]

Personality and Interest Inventory. Grades 4–9, 9–12; c1935–36; 2 levels; 1 form; G. Hildreth; Bureau of Publications.
a) ELEMENTARY FORM. Grades 4–9; c1935; (45) minutes; $2.10 per 100 blanks; $18.90 per 100; 10¢ per specimen set.
b) HIGH SCHOOL FORM. Grades 9–12; c1936; (45) minutes; $4.20 per set of blanks (each set includes the List of Activities and Interests and the Information Blank); $37.80 per 1000; $2.10 per 100 information blanks; 15¢ per specimen set.

Jack W. Dunlap, University of Rochester. The elementary form has four sections containing respectively 24, 34, 24, and 53 items. Students are to underscore the three things they like most in each section in order of their real preference. However, they are not asked to indicate the order, so the examiner is unable to take advantage of this information. A fifth part consists of naming two books, two magazines, and the two friends that the student likes best.

No indication of the validity of the instrument is given. The author states that reliability can be determined in three ways, "by examining the inner consistency of the record, by comparing the record with the student's observed conduct, and by studying the change in trend of interest and activity in groups of different age and maturity." There seems to be a confusion here between reliability and validity. No evidence, objective or subjective, is given as to the reliability or validity of either the parts or of the entire instrument.

The high school form has 11 sections with a total of 409 items. The number of items in a section vary from 12 to 100. No attempt is made to designate which sections refer to interest and which refer to personality. The test is not scored, so norms are not given, making it difficult, if not impossible, to compare an individual with other subjects. The criticism against the elementary form concerning reliability and validity holds equally well for this form. These inventories have possibilities, but in their present form, their usefulness in practical work is questionable.

[925]

Personality Sketches: For Individual Diagnosis. Grade 4 and above; c1936; individual; a clinical test of emotional adjustment; form A is an inventory of social adjustment and form B is an inventory of personal adjustment; $1.75 per box of 50 cards of each form and manual; (20) minutes; J. B. Maller; the Author, Teachers College, Columbia University.

Henry E. Garrett, Columbia University. This variation of the author's *Character Sketches* (1932) is here introduced as an instrument for symptomatic diagnosis of simple maladjustments. Each of the 100 cards bears a single inventory item which the subject is directed to sort into either of two boxes designated "Yes, I am the same," and "No, I am different." The items themselves have been selected from the previous *Sketches* on the basis of high reliability on test and retest, consistency with total score, and some degree of differentiation value between normal and maladjusted groups. They are of the familiar "Are you sometimes afraid someone is watching you?"—"Do you often feel blue?" order which has previously been adopted by Woodworth, Thurstone, and others.

Although extensive analysis was carried on in deriving the test items, and pertinent statistical procedures have been duly regarded, the ultimate worth of the test as a clinical diagnostic measure is perhaps questionable. Composite groups of questionnaire responses are admittedly unreliable as true pictures of personality deviations. Further, while the author warns against attaching undue significance to specific item answers, at the same time he indicates that the examiner is to follow and interpret the subject's behavior, remarks, speed, and indecision as the test is given. Whatever good may be derived from this subjective activity on the part of the second person is certainly not measurable.

In the original *Sketches,* the author stressed the "indirect approach" of the item statements, going so far as to verify its preferability by experimentation. The present test has unaccountably not retained this feature, the questions reverting to the "Do you—" "Have you—" or "direct" type of approach. In the author's own opinion, the subject's rapport with the experimenter is somewhat impaired by this factor.

There is merit in the card-sorting method of presenting the test. Especially to children, this combination of physical and mental activity should prove an interest-stimulant. The cards are of a convenient size, and a two-color combination facilitates administration by the examiner. Aside from criticisms which are to be directed at the questionnaire method in general, the test, skillfully applied and interpreted, should prove useful.

J. P. Guilford, University of Nebraska. In the apt words of the author, "The *Personality Sketches* consist of 100 cards, each bearing one inventory item. The subject is directed to sort out the cards into two boxes, one marked 'Yes, I am the same,' and the other 'No, I am different.' Most of the items have been selected from the author's *Character Sketches* after extensive experimentation and item analysis." The items were selected according to the following criteria: reliabilities (test-retest) between .70 and 1.00; validities (correlations with total score) between .40 and 1.00; good discrimination between maladjusted and normal groups; and less than 50% but more than 1% of the normal population answering the item in the maladjusted manner.

The questions are printed in large lettering on 50 orange colored and 50 blue cards 2″ × 3″ and stated in language that a ten-year-old child can probably understand. No doubt they are thus made attractive to children in this way, but the author also states that "Both children and adults were found to be less irritated by the items when presented in this form than in the usual pencil and paper form." The reviewer will take his questions in paper and pencil form, but another advantage of the cards, it would seem, is that the subject can read only one or two questions at a time, and can thus give more complete attention to the one in hand and be less bothered by the effort to be self-consistent, except to the extent that he remembers previous questions.

The reliability (for 190 sixth grade children) is given as .91 (odd-even). The score is the number of maladjusted responses. Few individuals in a "normal" group give more than 45 maladjusted responses.

The validity rests upon the power of the total scores to discriminate significantly between exceptional groups, like probationary pupils, delinquents, problem boys, and psychiatric cases and other groups not regarded as abnormal. Pools of 7 to 20 items are selected as being most valid for discriminating specially maladjusted groups from the normal. But while

such diagnostic aid is possible with the test, its major purpose is to pick out the person with neurotic tendencies in normal groups.

Many investigations upon the inventory, and using the inventory, are cited. No percentile or decile norms are given. The rarity of the maladjusted response to every item is given in terms of the percentage of 302 sixth grade children who yield it. This may be a further guide, in addition to total score and to constellations of responses to pools of items, when dealing with the individual child. It is distinctly an individual test intended for individual diagnosis.

[926]
Scale for Evaluating the School Behavior of Children Ten to Fifteen. Ages 10–15; c1933; 1 form; primarily for ratings by teachers but may also be used by children for self-ratings; $1.50 per 25; 20¢ per specimen set; (30) minutes for self-rating; M. L. Hayes; Psychological Corporation.

J Abn & Social Psychol 29:349 O–D '34. Dorothea Johannsen. This scale is intended to help teachers analyze objectively the habit patterns of adolescents, as a basis for determining maladjustments and developmental needs. * There is no real criterion of validity save that arising from the fact that the items were selected on the basis of the pooled opinions of two groups of judges, but ratings upon pupils judged to have the most and the least desirable personalities indicated that the scale definitely discriminates between good and poor personalities. * The reviewer is unwilling to grant what the author of the scale suggests, that the individual being studied is himself best able to judge his own personality. * Granting that the present scale is attempting to evaluate only a specific part of the child's personality, i.e., his *school* behavior patterns, it is an approach from the right angle, for it is certain that a child's school behavior is frequently an index of the difficulties and maladjustments of personality which have their origin in the conflicts aroused by some other part of the environment. It is clear, however, that merely diagnosing the difficulties is insufficient—at least, from the standpoint of the child. We could wish that the author has indicated the technique of using the results as clearly as she indicated the method of giving and scoring the test.

[927]
Self-Appraisal Schedule. Grades 9–16 and adults; c1937; a disguised test of persistence; 1 form; $2.50

per 25 schedules; $7.50 per 100 (catalog No. 24535);
35¢ per mimeographed manual (No. 24535A); nontimed (20–25) minutes; C. K. A. Wang; C. H. Stoelting Co.

[928]
**Washburne Social Adjustment Inventory (Sapich
Edition).** Grades 9–16 and adults; [c1935]; 1 form;
$1 per 25 tests; 30¢ per specimen set; quantity dis-
counts; no time limit, (30–40) minutes; scoring, 4
minutes; John N. Washburne; the Author, Syracuse
University, Syracuse, N.Y.

Daniel A. Prescott, Rutgers University. The
dictates of common sense must cause any person examining a test to raise first the question
of its validity; yet most test makers supply but
meager relevant information on this matter.
John Washburne is a happy exception.

Washburne reports that his *Social Adjustment
Inventory* has been in preparation during almost
ten years. First he gave a large number of
questions, presumed to be discriminatory of
social and emotional adjustment, to populations
paired for intelligence, sex, and age but showing
marked contrast in social and emotional adjustment on the basis of court records, school
records, observations and ratings. From the
responses he discovered the questions showing
greatest discrimination, then he eliminated those
showing least discriminatory power, prepared
many new questions similar to the discriminatory ones, and tried out a new form of the test.
In this manner the test has gone through seven
or eight mimeographed editions and three
printed editions, most of them showing significant refinements over the preceding ones.
Well over 10,000 individuals have been tested
in this process of refinement and standardization. The result is that the difference between
the number of "adjusted" and "maladjusted"
individuals giving the "maladjusted" response
to each of the questions included is from 3 to
7 times the PE of the difference. The critical
ratio for the difference in the median test score
of well-adjusted and maladjusted high school
students (matched for age, sex, grade and IQ)
is 8.57. The biserial *r* coefficient of validity is
.90. In other words the test is valid and has
good discriminatory power.

Of course the power of these figures to
demonstrate genuine validity depends upon the
extent to which the groups measured were
paired accurately and contrasted validly by the
ratings. Washburne's carefulness in this respect
is illustrated by his study of the semifinal form
of the test, where it required the testing of

populations totaling 3114 persons to secure 468
paired and contrasted cases meeting his criteria.
In contrasting high school students he required
agreement among three judges (usually the
teacher, the principal, and the dean or psychologist) in selecting the exceptionally well-adjusted
and the exceptionally maladjusted. Third or
fourth offense prisoners were called socially
maladjusted on the basis of their records and
were contrasted with high school children left
unselected by the raters choosing the extremely
maladjusted and well-adjusted. The pairings
for age, sex, grade, and IQ were in all cases
based on objective data.

These populations yielded four groups representing significantly different levels of social
adjustment in the following order: prisoners,
very maladjusted pupils, average-adjusted pupils, markedly well-adjusted pupils. Washburne
reports that the plotted scores of these groups
yielded four overlapping, fairly normal curves,
arranged in exactly the above order with 75 per
cent of the highest group scoring above 90 per
cent of the lowest group. This is a further indication of validity.

The test is self-administering. Interpretative
tables are available. The correlation of total
test score with intelligence is negligible, being
.17. The coefficient of reliability is satisfactory,
being .92.

The reviewer believes that this test deserves
to be much more widely known and used: for
diagnosis in clinics, for guidance and counseling
in secondary schools and colleges, in scientific
investigations, and possibly in connection with
industrial personnel work.

[929]
**Winnetka Scale for Rating School Behavior and
Attitudes.** Nursery school through grade 6; c1937;
10¢ per copy; $4.50 per 50; $8 per 100; 2¢ per
direction sheet; D. Van Alstyne and the Winnetka
Public School Faculty; Winnetka Educational Press.

*Harriet M. Barthelmess, New York City
Public Schools.* This scale offers something new
in personality rating scales, since it is based
on incidents of behavior noted and recorded as a
result of thousands of actual classroom observations. The scale consists of thirteen classroom
situations (e.g., "When there is a group project
to be carried out"), each with five or more
specific responses (e.g., "Withdraws from
group and carries on non-valuable activity").
Scores assigned to given responses range from

10 to 0, based on percentile behavior scores of approximately 1200 pupils. A profile chart offers a means for seeing a pupil's assets in terms of five traits, into which the thirteen situations are grouped, viz., cooperation, social consciousness, emotional security, leadership, and responsibility.

The scale is particularly valuable because it can be used effectively by the teachers in the early diagnosis of personality, especially in the earliest school years, when habit patterns are being formed. Because the diagnosis is in terms of real situations, the problem of developing satisfactory behavior patterns is made specific.

A substantial correlation with the Haggerty-Olson-Wickman *Behavior Rating Schedule* is indicated.

SOCIAL ADJUSTMENT

[1140]

Scale for Developmental Age. Girls from 8 to 18 years of age; c1934; 1 form; mimeographed; C. Sullivan; Center for Research in Child Development, Catholic University of America.

[1141]

Social Participation Scale, 1937. Adults; c1938; 1 form; a scale to measure the degree of a person's or family's participation in community groups and institutions; $2.50 per 100; 10¢ per sample copy; F. S. Chapin; University of Minnesota Press.

[1143]

Vineland Social Maturity Scale: Experimental Form B. Infancy through adult life; c1936; previously published in two sections as Experimental Form A, now discontinued; Form B is published as a four-page folder; $3 per 100 record blanks; 25¢ per manual (revised and condensed) ; 30¢ per specimen set; E. A. Doll; Extension Department of the Training School, Vineland, N.J. (Also distributed by the Psychological Corp.)

Paul H. Furfey, Catholic University of America. This scale was originally announced by Doll in April 1935, while a first standardized revision has recently appeared. Its author conceives *social maturity* as a quality implying in children "a progressive capacity for looking after themselves and for participating in those activities which lead toward ultimate independence of adults." It is, therefore, a measure of social development, that is to say, of "development of social responsibility, or of independence of the help of family and society."

The scale itself consists of 117 items separated into age groups. The items also receive certain "categorical designations," that is, each item is assigned to one of the eight categories: self-help general, self-help eating, self-help dressing, self-direction, occupation, communication, locomotion, and socialization. It has the outer form made familiar to psychologists by the *Stanford-Binet* and similar intelligence tests. It differs from such tests, however, in that the testee does not himself necessarily make the responses which determine the score. On the contrary, the examiner, after obtaining such examination information as he can "regarding the behavioristic facts which reveal the manner and extent of the subject's actual performance on each item," makes the actual judgment upon which scoring depends. The informant need not necesarily be the testee himself. The subject may be "examined by proxy through an informant who is intimately familiar with his capacities." Thus the scale may be used even *in absentia*. The test, therefore, although not a rating scale (as Mr. Doll rightly says) nevertheless contains a slightly subjective element which is not found in the usual intelligence tests. This subjective element, however, is probably inevitable from the nature of the variable being tested. In any case, it is not a serious defect, as the reliability of the test shows.

The present standardization of the test rests upon the examination of 620 normal individuals, representing ten subjects of each sex from birth to 30 years of age, and obtained from the town of Vineland, New Jersey. The socioeconomic status of these subjects was controlled by paternal occupation. A Social Quotient (SQ) is computed according to the usual technique, Social Age (SA) being divided by life age. In contrast to the usual intelligence test, SA was found to increase through adolescence and to become stable only at the age of twenty-five years. The reliability of the scale was .92 by the test-retest method, the subjects being 125 individuals of various ages who were reexamined at intervals ranging from one day to nine months (Doll). Bradway reports a test-retest reliability of .94 on 144 mentally deficient subjects retested "at intervals sufficiently short to preclude growth or deterioration of competence."

A number of subsidiary studies have shown the usefulness of this scale in various areas. For example, Bradway found that a group of deaf subjects was twenty per cent inferior to a parallel group of hearing subjects on test score. Doll has studied the inheritance of social competence, while Doll and McKay examined 38 special-class children paired for M.A. and C.A. with children from an institution for the feeble-minded and found that the special-class children were noticeably superior on one-third of all items, especially on items emphasizing self-direction.

An especially promising feature of the test is the possibility it offers of distinguishing between the merely mentally subnormal and those in whom mental subnormality is accompanied by social incompetence. Many authorities feel, of course, that the term *feeble-minded* should be confined to the latter group.

Elaine F. Kinder, Letchworth Village. The *Social Maturity Scale* by Doll has been developed at The Training School at Vineland, whose laboratory has been a pioneer in the study of social adjustment. Earlier investigations in this field from the same laboratory have been reported by Porteus. The scale has appeared at a time when problems of social dependency and maladjustment are making unparalleled demands and invites serious consideration as an effort toward a more objective evaluation of social competence.

One hundred seventeen items dealing with activities classified under "self-help, self-direction, locomotion, occupation, communication and social relations" are arranged in age groups, the underlying principles involved in the construction of the scale, according to Doll, being "much the same as those employed by Binet and Simon in their scale for measuring intelligence." The author asserts that the scale "provides an objective schedule of developmental behavior which can be standardized normatively and comparatively in quantitative terms," and further, that each item "has been chosen to represent some major aspect of social competence which is normative for successive developmental age periods." Doll's Scale is thus clearly differentiated from the earlier "Social Ratings Scale" developed by Porteus. Unlike the *Stanford-Binet,* the *Social Maturity Scale* is not planned to be administered to the subject (though the subject may serve as informant). It is rather a basis for evaluating information about the subject, secured by an investigator from parents,

older siblings, close friends, housemothers in institutions, etc.—those who are in a position to know the subject's habitual activities. The reliability of the information upon which the rating is based, becomes, therefore, a matter of primary consequence, and the procedures for administration are prescribed with a view to eliciting specific, accurate, and adequate responses.

In the opinion of the present reviewer (based, however, upon limited use of the scale), these evaluations are less objective than is implied by the scoring method and can hardly be considered comparable in objectivity to the data secured through the standardized procedures of such scales as the *Stanford-Binet.* The reviewer also considers it unfortunate that the discriminative capacity of the test seems most limited in those middle age ranges where the clinical need for well-authenticated measures of social competence is particularly clear.

In spite of inevitable imperfections—which will invite revision or reformulation as data are accumulated—the Scale offers a clinical instrument of considerable importance for the social worker and mental hygienist. It also opens an avenue of research which may be profitably explored by careful investigators willing to enter a field in which assumptions still are numerous. Whatever the final answers to critics of the Scale may be (and it is unlikely that all of the claims which have been made for it will find full experimental support), its contribution may be expected to stand as an early investigative approach to some of the essential data in the field of social science.

Anna S. Starr, Rutgers University. Doll taps an entirely new field in the measurement of ability—that of the actual and customary behavior of the individual, not his isolated scholastic information or imaginary experiences in a test situation. He rates the specific responses in living situations made possible by one's ability, opportunity and emotional drive. The test is based upon the assumption that *if you can you will,* but then if you don't there is some restriction sapping your potential. In that case, your behavior remains as if you couldn't. However, most people do as soon as they actually can. A serious technical difficulty is that the examiner is left to his own devices in putting the questions by which he determines the subject's accomplishment. Difficulties may thus arise in the comparison of results.

As a by-product in clinical practice I find the test affords a standard of guidance for the parent-informant who may unwittingly be restricting or pushing a child because of mistaken standards of age attainment. The *Social Maturity Scale* promises much in evaluating how well an individual actually does "manage his affairs" without the restriction of a formal clinical setup.

PERSONALITY—SECOND MMY

Reviews by S. J. Beck, Robert G. Bernreuter, J. M. Blackburn, Raymond B. Cattell, W. D. Commins, Stephen M. Corey, John G. Darley, Stanley G. Dulsky, Alvin C. Eurich, Warren G. Findley, Bessie Lee Gambrill, J. P. Guilford, Harold Gulliksen, Doncaster G. Humm, Harold E. Jones, Forrest A. Kingsbury, C. M. Louttit, J. B. Maller, Charles I. Mosier, Theodore Newcomb, Pedro T. Orata, Carl R. Rogers, Douglas Spencer, Percival M. Symonds, Robert L. Thorndike, Simon H. Tulchin, P. E. Vernon, Goodwin Watson, Ralph K. Watkins, E. G. Williamson, and Ll. Wynn Jones.

[1198]

A-S Reaction Study: A Scale for Measuring Ascendance-Submission in Personality. College; 1928-39; 1 form, 2 editions; $1.80 per 25; single specimen set free; nontimed (20) minutes; Gordon W. Allport and Floyd H. Allport; Boston, Mass.: Houghton Mifflin Co.

a) FORM FOR MEN. 1928.

b) FORM FOR WOMEN, REVISED. 1928-39.

REFERENCES

1 ALLPORT, FLOYD H., AND ALLPORT, GORDON W. "Personality Traits: Their Classification and Measurement." *J Abn and Social Psychol* 16:6-40 Ap '21.

2 ALLPORT, GORDON W. "A Test for Ascendance-Submission." *J Abn and Social Psychol* 23:118-36 Jl-S '28.

3 BENDER, IRVING EDISON. "Ascendance-Submission in Relation to Certain Other Factors in Personality." *J Abn and Social Psychol* 23:137-43 Jl-S '28.

4 ALLPORT, GORDON W. "The Neurotic Personality and Traits of Self-Expression." *J Social Psychol* 1:524-7 N '30.

5 BECKMAN, R. O., AND LEVINE, MICHAEL. "Selecting Executives: An Evaluation of Three Tests." *Personnel J* 8:415-20 Ap '30.

6 BROOM, M. E. "A Study of a Test of Ascendance-Submission." *J Appl Psychol* 14:405-13 O '30.

7 JERSILD, ARTHUR. "A Study of Personality." *J Abn and Social Psychol* 25:115-20 Jl-S '30.

8 HANNA, JOSEPH V. "Reliability of Two Personality Questionnaires." *Psychol B* 28:621-2 O '31.

9 WANG, CHAS. K. A. "The Internal Consistency of the Allports' Ascendence-Submission Test (Form for Men)." *J Abn and Social Psychol* 26:154-61 Jl-S '31.

10 HOLCOMB, G. W., AND LASLETT, H. R. "A Prognostic Study of Engineering Aptitude." *J Appl Psychol* 16:107-15 Ap '32.

11 MANZER, CHARLES W. "The Effect of Self-Interest on Scores Made on the Allport Test for Measuring Ascendance-Submission." *Psychol Clinic* 21:268-70 D '32.

12 STAGNER, ROSS. "The Intercorrelation of Some Standardized Personality Tests." *J Appl Psychol* 16:453-64 O '32.

13 MOORE, HERBERT, AND STEELE, ISABEL. "Personality Tests." *J Abn and Social Psychol* 29:45-52 Ap-Je '34.

14 PERRY, RAYMOND CARVER. *A Group Factor Analysis of the Adjustment Questionnaire.* University of Southern California, Southern California Educational Monographs, 1933-34 Series, No. 5. Los Angeles, Calif.: University of Southern California Press, 1934. Pp. xi, 93. $1.50.

15 STEVENS, SAMUEL N., AND WONDERLIC, ELDON F. "The A-S Reaction Test. A Study of Beckman's Revision." *Personnel J* 13:222-4 D '34.

16 FARRAM, FREDA. "The Relation of Ascendance-Submission Tendencies to Neurosis." *Austral J Psychol and Philos* 13:228-32 S '35.

17 WILLIAMS, GRIFFITH W., AND CHAMBERLAIN, FLORENCE. "An Evaluation of the Use of the Allport Ascendance-Submission Test with High School Girls." *J Genetic Psychol* 49:363-75 D '36.

18 RUGGLES, RICHARD, AND ALLPORT, GORDON W. "Recent Applications of the A-S Reaction Study." *J Abn and Social Psychol* 34:518-28 O '39.

19 WASSON, MARGARET M. "The Agreements among Certain Types of Personality Schedules." *J Psychol* 9:351-63 Ap '40.

Doncaster G. Humm, Wadsworth-Humm Personnel Service, Los Angeles, California. [A review of the 1928 edition.] This behavior-study, according to the authors, aims to discover the disposition of an individual to dominate his fellows.

Its approximate reliability is reported as .74 for men and .78 for women. These figures represent respectively 33 and 37 per cent better than chance. In other words the chances are approximately 1.97 to 1 that a second test will return essentially the same results as the first in the case of men, and 2.20 to 1 in the case of women.

The validity obtained from ratings—the unreliability of which is mentioned by the authors—is reported as from .29 to .79, 4 and 29 per cent better than chance respectively. The chances accordingly are from 1.09 to 1 to 2.26 to 1 that the results will agree with ratings.

Statistical "certainty" is generally accepted as being 369 to 1.

In the light of these reported facts, it is very doubtful that the scale may be employed to advantage in obtaining self-knowledge, choosing a vocation, or in vocational selection and placement without considerable verification and supplementary information.

The authors are to be commended for their statement that the study "be used primarily as a basis of future research in the measurement of personality, rather than as a hard and fast criterion for social guidance."

Users of the *A-S Reaction Study* should interpret the results obtained in the light of a very high probable error, and should certainly not make recommendations without mentioning that probable error.

[1199]

A-S Reaction Study: Revision for Business Use. Adult men; 1928-32; 1 form; $5 per 100; 25¢ per specimen set; nontimed (20) minutes; the original form of the *A-S Reaction Study* was prepared by Gordon W. Allport and Floyd H. Allport; revision by R. O. Beckman; New York: Psychological Corporation.

REFERENCES

1 BECKMAN, R. O. "Ascendance-Submission Test—Revised." *Personnel J* 11:387-92 Ap '33.
2 ACHILLES, P. S., AND SCHULTZ, R. S. "Characteristics of Life Insurance Salesmen." *Personnel J* 12:260-3 F '34.
3 STEVENS, SAMUEL N., AND WONDERLIC, ELDON F. "The A-S Reaction Test: A Study of Beckman's Revision." *Personnel J* 13:222-4 D '34.
4 SCHULTZ, RICHARD S., AND ROSLOW, SYDNEY. "Restandardization of the A-S Reaction Study as a Personnel Form." *J Appl Psychol* 22:554-7 D '38.

Doncaster G. Humm, Wadsworth-Humm Personnel Service, Los Angeles, California. This is a revision for business use of the Allport *A-S Reaction Study*. The author has shortened the original questionnaire, has changed the language to that which would be more suitable to business, and has endeavored to provide more internal consistency for the test.

He has reported a distribution of scores by occupations which seems to establish that the test affords averages for various occupations which distinguish between the amount of ascendancy required for those occupations. There appears, however, to be large overlapping of ranges.

The correlation between the test and the success on the job of 35 store managers is reported as .27, or 3.7 per cent better than chance. In other words there is 52 per cent agreement and 48 per cent disagreement. One

is led to wonder if success as a manager is an adequate criterion for the tendency to be ascendant or vice versa.

There seems to be no direct measurement of reliability and validity for this scale. Until such is made the following recommendation of the author should be followed: "It is strongly urged that the scores obtained be regarded as suggestive rather than conclusive."

It does not seem established that there is justification for the author's statement: "That the present test may serve as a criterion for the selection of candidates for promotion or of applicants for executive and supervisory positions."

The test does appear to show differences in averages; but differences in individuals' scores is another matter.

[1200]

Adjustment Inventory. Grades 9-16 and adults; 1934-38; 1 form, 2 levels; $1.75 per 25; $1.75 per 100 machine-scorable answer sheets; nontimed (25) minutes; Hugh M. Bell; Stanford University, Calif.: Stanford University Press.

a) STUDENT FORM. Grades 9-16; 1934; 15¢ per specimen set.

b) ADULT FORM. Adults; 1938; 25¢ per specimen set.

REFERENCES

1 BELL, HUGH M. *The Theory and Practice of Student Counseling*: With Special Reference to the Adjustment Inventory. Stanford University, Calif.: Stanford University Press, 1935. Pp. 138. $1.00. Paper, lithotyped. (London: Oxford University Press. 4s. 6d.)
2 TURNEY, AUSTIN H., AND FEE, MARY. "An Attempt to Use the Bell Adjustment Inventory for High School Guidance." *Sch R* 44:193-8 Mr '36.
3 TYLER, HENRY T. "Evaluating the Bell Adjustment Inventory." *Jun Col J* 6:353-7 Ap '36.
4 DARLEY, JOHN G. "Tested Maladjustment Related to Clinically Diagnosed Maladjustment." *J Appl Psychol* 21:632-42 D '37.
5 FEDER, DANIEL D., AND MALLETT, DONALD R. "Validity of Certain Measures of Personality Adjustment." *J Am Assn Col Reg* 13:5-15 O '37.
6 KEYS, NOEL, AND GUILFORD, MARGARET S. "The Validity of Certain Adjustment Inventories in Predicting Problem Behavior." *J Ed Psychol* 28:641-55 D '37.
7 DARLEY, JOHN G. "Changes in Measured Attitudes and Adjustments." *J Social Psychol* 9:189-99 My '38.
8 DARLEY, JOHN G. "A Preliminary Study of Relations between Attitude, Adjustment, and Vocational Interest Tests." *J Ed Psychol* 29:467-73 S '38.
9 DROUGHT, NEAL E. "An Analysis of Eight Measures of Personality and Adjustment in Relation to Relative Scholastic Achievement." *J Appl Psychol* 22:597-606 D '38.
10 MCNAMARA, WALTER J., AND DARLEY, JOHN G. "A Factor Analysis of Test-Retest Performance on Attitude and Adjustment Tests." *J Ed Psychol* 29:652-64 D '38.
11 PATERSON, DONALD G.; SCHNEIDLER, GWENDOLEN G.; AND WILLIAMSON, EDMUND G. *Student Guidance Techniques*, pp. 185-9. New York: McGraw-Hill Book Co., Inc., 1938. Pp. xviii, 316. $3.00. (London: McGraw-Hill Publishing Co., Ltd., 18s.)
12 BELL, HUGH M. *The Theory and Practice of Personal Counseling*: With Special Reference to the Adjustment Inventory. A revision of *The Theory and Practice of Student Counseling*. Stanford University, Calif.: Stanford University Press, 1939. Pp. v, 167. $1.25. Paper, lithotyped. (London: Oxford University Press. 6s.)
13 GREENE, J. E., AND STATON, THOMAS F. "Predictive Value of Various Tests of Emotionality and Adjustment in a Guidance Program for Prospective Teachers." *J Ed Res* 32:653-9 My '39.
14 PALLISTER, HELEN, AND PIERCE, W. O'D. "A Comparison of Bell Adjustment Scores for American and Scottish Groups." *Sociometry* 2:54-72 Jl '39.
15 PEDERSEN, RUTH A. "Validity of the Bell Adjustment Inventory When Applied to College Women." *J Psychol* 9:227-36 Ap '40.

Raymond B. Cattell, G. Stanley Hall Professor of Genetic Psychology, Clark University. [Review of the Student Form.] To the writing of inventories there is no end, and one would think that today a very potent excuse would be necessary for putting a new one on the market. One looks in vain through this inventory and its equipment for any new research, improvement of technique or even some mere innovation which would justify its existence.

Most of the objections raised ten or fifteen years ago against the self-inventory as an objective measure of adjustment or personality apply to this example, as they have to most of the questionnaire approaches published in the interim, indeed the inventories tend if anything, to be less successful than the original and outstanding personal data sheets of Bernreuter, Woodworth, and Thurstone. What promised to be a passing phase in psychology, a temporary scaffolding to the structure of psychological research and the building of objective tests, threatens, through repeated publication such as this to become accepted as a permanent part of the landscape in applied psychology. One wonders what sort of a personnel is applying psychology.

The questionnaire abounds with questions requiring not only perfect self-knowledge and ruthless honesty but also a wide knowledge of humanity and its standards. Such are: "Are you troubled with shyness?" yes or no; "Are your feelings easily hurt?" yes or no; "Are you often sorry for the things you do?" yes or no; "Do you day-dream frequently?" yes or no (what is frequently?).

The inventory, we are told, has been "validated" in four ways. First, by item validation through internal consistency. Secondly, by being "checked during interviews with four hundred college students"; by what means checked, we are not told. Thirdly, by comparison with judgments of school administrators as to which students are well adjusted. Between groups of such students selected for good and bad adjustment it yields averages differing significantly. But there is no expression showing how effective the test is in differentiating individuals.

Lastly, the test is validated by comparison with a variety of other questionnaire totals. On a population of 39 the "Social Adjustment" pool of the inventory reached a correlation (corrected) of .90 with the B4-D scale [measure of dominance-submission] of Bernreuter's *Personality Inventory*. But it also correlated positively with the Allports' *A-S Reaction Study* (.72, corrected), a test of assertiveness of disposition. What is this inventory aiming at measuring?

Every care appears to have been taken to give the intending user of the test whatever data he might require. He is supplied with "validities" and consistencies, means and standard deviations for high school and college groups, and with an attractive scoring key in a special folder. Everything is given except that which justifies the test's existence—namely, its true validity. As to what the test measures there remains the completest confusion. It is divided into four distinct parts, one measuring home adjustment, one health adjustment (?), one social adjustment, and one emotional adjustment (general emotionality?). But these intercorrelate, so that it looks as if home and social adjustment are the only two measures that are in fact independent. And "emotional adjustment"—unfortunate term since all adjustment is emotional—correlates so much more with the other items than they do with one another that one suspects it is a better measure on its own of whatever tendency is being measured than the whole pool is.

If psychology is to improve in objectivity on psychoanalytic conceptions of adjustment and maladjustment it must find a more objective basis than this. Personal insight can only be abandoned for statistical treatment and measurement if measurement is based on adequate statistical research conceptions.

John G. Darley, Director of the University Testing Bureau and Assistant Professor of Psychology, The University of Minnesota. [Review of the Student Form.] The first two reviews of the *Adjustment Inventory* in *The 1938 Yearbook* were actually reviews of Bell's *School Inventory* [Editor's mistake]; the third review questioned the *Adjustment Inventory* on theoretical grounds. The present review stresses the clinical utility of the test. There are three general methods of validating instruments of this kind: correlation with already established personality tests; group difference techniques; methods based on internal consistency or homogeneity of content. Bell has used all three methods in his work. Data published independently elsewhere include extremely high test-retest correlations over intervals of six to nine months in high school and college age ranges. Such consistency is consonant with a "continuum of stability" concept in personality measurement wherein the more deep-seated personality characteristics presumably tapped by this test are relatively more stable aspects of personality.

In the systematic case study of an individual, personality characteristics are analyzed in four ways: anecdotal reports, rating scales, pencil-and-paper tests, and varying forms of interviewing. Where pencil-and-paper tests are used they are most wisely viewed as clues to identify deviations for more intensive analysis. Pragmatically a good personality test is one which identifies, in its additive score or in its individual items, areas of actual or potential maladjustment for further diagnosis and treatment. If a test picks out a high proportion of adjustment difficulties which a good clinician finds actually existed in the case, and if it misses a small proportion of such difficulties, it is useful in a personnel program. The *Adjustment Inventory* meets this criterion.

Factor analysis of this test as one of a battery of 13 attitude and adjustment test scores indicates that the health and emotional scales in combination may tap anxieties, neuroticism or hypochondriasis as personality characteristics.

The test seems most useful when used as part of a larger battery of personality measurements, thus permitting a cross-check in several areas of adjustment. Its published odd-even correlations have been reproduced in different samples, and these data, together with high test-retest correlations, may be taken as evidence of consistency of measurement.

The inventory yields four adjustment scores: home, health, social, and emotional. A fifth total score, summing all four, is not useful in interviewing or counseling since it lacks the specificity and meaning of the other four. Separate sex norms are provided for both high school and college populations. If the counselor uses these norms in conjunction with the published table of probable errors of measurement, interpretations of borderline cases will be more effective. Bell's selection of clinically well-defined extreme groups for purposes of determining critical ratios on each scale is an important

part of the supporting evidence for the utility of the test.

C. M. Louttit, Director of the Psychological Clinics and Associate Professor of Clinical Psychology, Indiana University. [Review of the Student Form.] This familiar schedule is arranged so that independent scores for home, health, social, and emotional adjustments may be secured, while the total score indicates general adjustment status. The possibility of breaking the scores down into four specific areas increases the usefulness of the scale for the purposes of guidance surveys, as well as for clinical study.

Norms are presented separately for high school and college men and women in terms of a five-point scale. The user is cautioned against overemphasis of the differences between adjacent groups. Reliabilities are high, and the validations are varied and consistent so that use of the schedule for individual analysis and prognosis is warranted.

As is so frequently true of personality schedules, the manual for this instrument is too incomplete. Except for a very brief statement of the meaning of high and low scores, the author fails to give the test user any help in interpreting either group or individual results. In fact there are not even references which might be helpful to the user. Perhaps this lack would be justified by saying that trained psychologists should be able to use the scale without special help. No matter how true this may be, an instrument such as this is freely available to anyone and therefore is open to serious misuse, or at least unintelligent use.

Percival M. Symonds, Professor of Education, Columbia University. [Review of the Student Form.] Bell's *Adjustment Inventory* consists of one hundred and forty simple incidents to be answered by encircling "Yes," "No," or "?." Four scores to serve as measures of home, health, social, and emotional adjustment can be secured as well as a total score. The questions belonging to each of these four special phases of adjustment are spaced at random through the test so that a special key is needed in order to select and score the items belonging to each of the four sections. The questionnaire has the merit of being very compact and simple for the student to answer.

One may question the reliability of the separate sections containing as they do thirty-five items. The manual which accompanies the test states that the coefficient of reliability of the separate sections ranges from .80 to .89. These reliability coefficients would seem to be higher than one would ordinarily expect with these few items.

Even if these scores were reliable enough for individual diagnosis, some skepticism should be exercised in taking the scores at face value as representing the names given to the various sections.

Norms are given in the manual for high school and college students. However, these norms instead of being percentile scores for various groups tested, describe levels on the test by such description as excellent, good, average, unsatisfactory, and very unsatisfactory. This would seem to be an unfortunate practice as it tends to place value judgment on the results of the test that certainly must be a matter for individual interpretation. The writer would prefer to leave to the counselor who is to use the test the privilege of deciding what range of scores he is to consider good and unsatisfactory.

The advantages of Bell's *Adjustment Inventory* are its compactness, simplicity, and the apparent careful selection of questions.

S. J. Beck, Head Psychologist, Michael Reese Hospital, Chicago, Illinois. [Review of the Adult Form.] This reviewer has not used the *Adjustment Inventory*. Critical comments that follow are, therefore, a reaction entirely to a study of the blank and the accompanying directions—reactions based on the reviewer's clinical experience.

This instrument consists of 160 items. The adjustment categories within which they are classified are home, health, social, emotional, and occupational. The directions allow for considerable flexibility, i.e., they make for an adaptability in application. Thus "questions about the meaning of words may be answered by the examiner." Again when subjects inquire concerning the purpose of the test "they should be answered frankly and honestly." This is a flexibility somewhat rare in studies statistically based and certainly commendable. The scoring requires stencils which come with the instructions. It is easy and quick. Norms were obtained from what looks like a good representation of individuals. They ranged in age from

20 to 50 with the majority between 25 and 40. They were taken from adult extension classes in California and in New Jersey, Counseling Service of the Seattle Y.M.C.A., a practice school of the Chicago Y.W.C.A., and adult classes in industrial psychology in Boston.

In fact one lays down this questionnaire with much more satisfaction than with most personality inventory efforts. The first reason is the evidence of much clinical sense in the questions themselves. The author, in other words, appears to have an interest in the entire personality. Confirmation of this is found in the method of validation. Counselors, each of whom had had five or more years of experience in working with maladjusted individuals were put on the alert for "individuals who evidenced during interviews, very good or very poor adjustment in any of the areas covered by the *Inventory*." To these extremes of adjustment the inventory was administered. A check, individual for individual was thus had on the instrument by a totally outside source. Validation, even if not as intensive as one is accustomed to in clinical experience, was real. The result is reflected both in the questions used and also in the subgroupings of adjustment areas. These, even if not elemental in personality or mutually exclusive, still give us a valid picture of the personality. This is not to say a dynamic picture. The questionnaire cannot do that. It can place the individual in a given position relative to the entire group in respect to certain personality tendencies. In turn this can be the starting point for more effective probing.

Some of the intercorrelations found by the author attract attention and certainly arouse interest. The highest positive correlations of reports are those between health and emotional adjustment; social and emotional; emotional and occupational; and home and emotional.

The inventory can be recommended to the clinician when, as, and if he finds himself in need of this type of instrument.

J. P. Guilford, Professor of Psychology, The University of Southern California. [Review of the Adult Form.] This is the familiar type of personality questionnaire, composed of 160 items to be answered by "Yes," "?," or "No." It is similar to the same author's inventory previously designed for students. The responses are scored for adjustment in five respects:

(a) Home Adjustment.—Whether the individual is satisfied with his home life, his living conditions, and his home associates. (b) Health Adjustment.—Whether he has been ill a great deal, having had operations or diseases, and minor ailments. (c) Social Adjustment.—Whether he is shy, retiring, and submissive in social contacts. (d) Emotional Adjustment.—Whether he is subject to emotional upsets of one kind or another; is nervous, or depressed. (e) Occupational Adjustment.—Whether he is satisfied with his job; the kind of work, his associates, his working conditions, and whether he is recognized for what he does.

Only 32 items are scored, with unweighted scoring, for each area of adjustment, no item being scored for more than one category of adjustment. This has the virtue of keeping the correlations among scores as low as possible (the intercorrelations range from −.06 to +.51) at the same time it places a heavy burden of discrimination upon a relatively small number of items. The reliability coefficients, as supplied by the author of the test for the five parts, range from .81 (Health Adjustment) to .91 (Home Adjustment and Emotional Adjustment) with probable errors of measurement between 1.74 (Occupational Adjustment) and 1.10 (Emotional Adjustment). The test items were selected on the basis of their power to discriminate between the upper and lower 15 per cent of an adult population who were selected on the basis of a preliminary scoring. The inventory scores have been found very discriminating between extreme groups that were selected by experienced counselors. A total score is used and though this is probably not as valuable as the part scores, it has a split-half reliability of .94 and a probable error of measurement of 3.14 for men and 3.42 for women.

The test will find its greatest value for the clinician who wishes in a systematic manner to locate the points at which the patient is at odds with the world. Three of the five areas explored—home, health, and occupation—are common places to look for sources of trouble. Incidentally, it will probably have to be determined whether a person with a significant "poor health" score needs medical attention or is merely a hypochondriac. Other areas of adjustment could have been added to make the survey more complete.

Norms are given for both men and women, though the sexes differ very little, as based upon a population ranging in age from 20 to 50, with the majority between 25 and 40. The occupational adjustment score can be obtained only for those who are employed or have recently been employed. Items indicating each type of adjustment in the inventory are labeled by letter so that the clinician may make further analysis within each category. The inventory is said to require not more than 25 minutes to fill out. A translucent scoring key permits complete scoring in about 4 minutes.

Doncaster G. Humm, Wadsworth-Humm Personnel Service, Los Angeles, California. [Review of the Adult Form.] The use of this inventory, as recommended by the author, is as an aid in counseling adults, with the total score indicative of general adjustment status.

The reliability of the inventory as reported is, for the total score, .94. This is 66 per cent better than chance, and indicates a chance of 4.86 to 1 that approximately the same score will be obtained when the test is repeated.

The validity of the inventory is reported in terms of how well it differentiates between a "Very well" adjusted group and a "Very poorly" adjusted group. These groups were selected by experienced counselors. The results clearly indicate that the inventory validly makes such distinction. The inventory seems to have the capability of distinguishing differences between well adjusted individuals and poorly adjusted individuals to the extent of a chance of from 19 to 1 in home adjustment to 499 to 1 in social adjustment. This indicates a high degree of certainty when inventory scores are either very high or very low, diminishing to a lesser degree, of course, in the intermediate classification of average adjustment. These data were collected in counseling situations. We do not know if the same figures hold in other situations, but it seems entirely safe to conclude that this is a valuable measuring instrument for counselors.

Contradictory standards seem to be presented in the suggested "Tentative Norms" presented in the manual and the means of the "Validating Groups Selected by Counselors." The latter would appear to be better standards of evaluation, especially for the counselor.

J Psychol 9:227-36 Ap '40. Ruth A. Pedersen. "Validity of the Bell Adjustment Inventory When Applied to College Women." *

this study was undertaken to determine the validity of the Bell *Adjustment Inventory* when applied to college women * The inventory was administered to . . . 380 freshman women * these individuals were rated by the writer with regard to home, health, social, and emotional adjustment, the categories of the Bell *Adjustment Inventory*. The bases of these ratings were: (*a*) the autobiography written before entrance to college, and (*b*) the Dean's files of the personal records of the students during their freshman year. In addition to these, the Social Advisor rated each subject as to social adjustment during her freshman year, and the Women's Director of Physical Education rated the subjects as to health adjustment. * due to the fact that, in general, both the Dean's files and the autobiographies gave evidence only of maladjustments . . . individuals were rated only "maladjusted" or "no information" * Obviously, many individuals among the "no information" group must have been maladjusted, but for one reason or another, their condition had not received official recognition. To this extent, then, any differences found between the "maladjusted" and the "no information" groups on the Bell will be too small. * By way of summary, it may be said: (*a*) The Bell *Adjustment Inventory* is valid in measuring home adjustment as indicated in the applicant's autobiography, but it does not predict home disturbances which are of sufficient importance to be called to the attention of the Freshman Dean and recorded in the personal records for the freshman year. (*b*) A high score on the health section of the *Inventory* is indicative of poor health as indicated by the autobiography, the personal records, and by the ratings of the Director of Physical Education. Further, individuals rated maladjusted to health tend to have significantly higher scores on the emotional section of the *Inventory* than do other individuals. (*c*) Individuals rated socially maladjusted by the Social Advisor tend to have higher scores on the social section of the Bell than do other individuals. Subjects rated maladjusted socially by other criteria did not, on the whole, have higher scores than the remaining individuals, but the numbers were so small that the results are inconclusive. (*d*) There is no real difference between the emotional scores of individuals rated emotionally maladjusted and other individuals. (*e*) In interpreting and

using these results, it should be kept in mind that any differences reported between the "maladjusted" and the "no information" groups have been attenuated due to the fact that there almost certainly are maladjusted individuals in the "no information" group.

For a review by Austin H. Turney, see 912. Although three reviews are listed under 912, only the review by Austin H. Turney is a review of Bell's Adjustment Inventory; the other two are reviews of Bell's School Inventory. See also B30, B309, and B842.

[1201]

Aspects of Personality. Grades 4-9; 1937-38; 1 form; $1.20 per 25; 15¢ per specimen set; nontimed (30-35) minutes; Rudolf Pintner, John J. Loftus, George Forlano, and Benjamin Alster; Yonkers, N. Y.: World Book Co.

REFERENCES

1 PINTNER, RUDOLF, AND FORLANO, GEORGE. "A Comparison of Methods of Item Selection for a Personality Test." *J Appl Psychol* 21:643-52 D '37.
2 PINTNER, RUDOLF, AND FORLANO, GEORGE. "Four Retests of a Personality Inventory." *J Ed Psychol* 29:93-100 F '38.
3 PINTNER, R., AND FORLANO, G. "Validation of Personality Tests by Outstanding Characteristics of Pupils." *J Ed Psychol* 30:25-32 Ja '39.
4 BROOKS, JAMES J. "A Technique for Determining the Degree of Behavior Maladjustment of Prison Inmates." *J Criminal Psychopathology* 1:339-53 Ap '40.

C. M. Louttit, Director of the Psychological Clinics and Associate Professor of Clinical Psychology, Indiana University. This personality schedule is one of the usual inventory type with the items adapted to the experiences of the school child and the vocabulary reduced to fourth grade level. The three sections of 35 items each refer to ascendance-submission, extroversion-introversion, and emotionality. This instrument is intended for group use by the classroom teacher. The authors suggest that the teacher give the test at the beginning of the school year "in order to acquaint the teacher as soon as possible with the personality make-up of her children." To the clinician this is unwise advice because it assumes that the inventory gives an accurate picture of the child's personality. This is a questionable assumption for any personality inventory, and in the present instance the manual gives no support for it. The validity depends entirely on factors intrinsic to the tests, e.g., selection of items from other instruments, the authors' judgment, an internal consistency of item correlations. Furthermore, the percentile norms given separately for grades 4-6 and for grades 7-9 are based upon an unrevealed number of cases.

Reliabilities by the split-half method for the subsections and for the whole scale by the re-test method range from .52 to .92 with a median of about .75. Consideration of reliability, validity, and the norms gives no reason for believing that teachers can safely depend upon an individual's score to reveal his personality.

It must not be understood from what has been written that this scale has no value. Used as a clinical tool we have found it very satisfactory because we can interpret the score in the light of a case history more extensive than anything the teacher usually has at the beginning of a term. We have also found that the individual responses are frequently valuable clues, and an interview with the child based on his responses is often most revealing.

P. E. Vernon, Lecturer in Psychology, University of Glasgow. The construction of the test and establishment of norms appear to have been competently carried out, though the numbers and types of children upon whom the norms were based are not stated. The average reliability coefficient (split-half and retest) for any one part of the test is close to .72. Though this figure is lower than those claimed for many personality inventories, it is, in the reviewer's opinion, adequate. Very high reliability usually means an over-long test. Scoring of the test blanks by means of a stencil should be both convenient and accurate.

The instructions appear very suitable for grades 4-5, but perhaps rather babyish for grades 8-9. The sample items, which are to be read and explained by the teacher, are not very happily chosen. They seem likely to suggest to the children that they should answer according to social respectability, or to what they think the teacher wants. No precautions for reducing this only too common attitude are mentioned.

A commendable feature of the test is that many of the items were worded by children themselves during preliminary trials. Another good point is the inclusion of many "positive" or socially desirable statements in the first two parts. It is a pity that almost all the third part (apart from a few "jokers") consists of "negative" or unattractive statements, which tend to arouse unfavourable attitudes in the subjects. The test shows another advantage over multiple tests like Bernreuter's *Personality In-*

ventory, namely that one of the criteria for the inclusion of an item in any one part was that the item should not correlate highly with the other two parts. No data are given as to the intercorrelations of total scores on the three parts. They are likely to be substantial, although lower than in the Bernreuter inventory owing to the application of this criterion.

In most respects the test seems to be a distinct advance on other personality inventories for children. Nevertheless the reviewer feels that the directions to teachers, and other users of the test, should have been more cautiously worded, in view of the well-known lack of validity of such inventories. A recent article [3] provided a certain amount of evidence of validity, but the correspondence with the criterion (ratings) was far from high. From the directions teachers are likely to suppose that they can apply the test and measure children's introversion, etc. as easily as their arithmetical disability. They are not even advised to supplement the test findings by careful observations of behaviour. Some useful advice is given on treatment of extremely ascendant, submissive, introverted or unstable children. In view of the assumption that those who fall into these categories require guidance, it is interesting to note small but significant correlations between introversion, emotional instability, and intelligence. The manual does not make clear the direction of these correlations, but apparently the better pupils tend to have more "undesirable" personalities.

See also 913.

[1202]

[**Attitude Scales.**] Grades 7-16; 1934-36; each scale has space for indicating attitude toward five attitude variables; 2 forms; mimeographed; 1½¢ per test; 15¢ per specimen set of any one scale; 3(5) minutes per attitude variable; directed and edited by H. H. Remmers; Lafayette, Ind.: Division of Educational Reference, Purdue University.

a) SCALE FOR MEASURING ATTITUDE TOWARD ANY DISCIPLINARY PROCEDURE. 1936; V. R. Clouse.
b) SCALE FOR MEASURING ATTITUDE TOWARD ANY HOMEMAKING PROJECT. 1934; B. K. Vogel.
c) SCALE FOR MEASURING ATTITUDE TOWARD ANY INSTITUTION. 1934; T. B. Kelly.
d) SCALE FOR MEASURING ATTITUDE TOWARD ANY NATIONAL OR RACIAL GROUP. 1934; H. H. Grice.
e) SCALE FOR MEASURING ATTITUDE TOWARD ANY PRACTICE. 1934; H. W. Bues.
f) SCALE FOR MEASURING ATTITUDE TOWARD ANY SCHOOL SUBJECT. 1934; E. B. Silance.
g) SCALE FOR MEASURING ATTITUDE TOWARD ANY TEACHER. 1935; L. D. Hoshaw.
h) SCALE FOR MEASURING ATTITUDE TOWARD ANY VOCATION. 1934; H. E. Miller.
i) SCALE FOR MEASURING ATTITUDES TOWARD ANY PLAY. 1935; M. Dimmitt.

j) SCALE FOR MEASURING ATTITUDES TOWARD ANY PROPOSED SOCIAL ACTION. 1935; D. M. Thomas.
k) SCALE FOR MEASURING ATTITUDES TOWARD ANY SELECTION OF POETRY. 1935; J. E. Hadley.
l) SCALE FOR MEASURING INDIVIDUAL AND GROUP "MORALE." 1936; L. Whisler.

REFERENCES

1 LIKERT, RENSIS. *A Technique for the Measurement of Attitudes.* Columbia University, Archives of Psychology, No. 140. New York: the University, 1932. Pp. 55. Paper. Out of print.
2 REMMERS, H. H., EDITOR. *Studies in Attitudes:* A Contribution to Social-Psychological Research Methods. Bulletin of Purdue University, Vol. 53, No. 4; Studies in Higher Education, No. 26. Lafayette, Ind.: the University, 1934. $1.25. Paper.
3 REMMERS, H. H., AND SILANCE, ELLA BELLE. "Generalized Attitude Scales." *J Social Psychol* 5:298-312 Ag '34.
4 REMMERS, H. H. "Measuring Attitude toward the Job." *Occupations* 14:945-8 Je '36.
5 REMMERS, H. H., EDITOR. *Further Studies in Attitudes, Series II.* Bulletin of Purdue University, Vol. 37, No. 4; Studies in Higher Education, No. 31. Lafayette, Ind.: the University, December, 1936. $2.25. Paper.
6 WHISLER, LAURENCE AND REMMERS, H. H. "A Scale for Measuring Individual and Group Morale." *J Psychol* 4:161-5 Jl '37.
7 PATERSON, DONALD G.; SCHNEIDLER, GWENDOLEN G.; AND WILLIAMSON, EDMUND G. *Student Guidance Techniques,* pp. 202-4. New York: McGraw-Hill Book Co., Inc., 1938. Pp. xviii, 316. $3.00. (London: McGraw-Hill Publishing Co. Ltd., 18s.)
8 REMMERS, H. H., EDITOR. *Further Studies in Attitudes, Series III.* Purdue University, Division of Educational Reference, Studies in Higher Education, No. 34. Lafayette, Ind.: the University, September, 1938. Pp. 151. $1.50. Paper.
9 DUNLAP, JACK W., AND KROLL, ABRAHAM. "Observations on the Methodology in Attitude Scales." *J Social Psychol* 10:475-87 N '39.

W. D. Commins, Assistant Professor of Psychology, The Catholic University of America. Generalized attitude scales represent an attempt to reduce the amount of preliminary labor and the technical difficulties involved in measuring attitudes. There is perhaps no question about the desirability of this. In using a generalized attitude scale (as in the case of one of the present scales which measures attitude toward any school subject), we are supplied a list of general statements of an evaluative nature both "pro" and "con," and these may be checked off against Latin, English, algebra, etc., in turn. We are able to employ the same list of statements in relation to each subject, the scale value of which has been determined for us in advance. This would mark an immense saving of time over having to devise a special list applicable to only one attitude object at a time. The authors are fully alive to the difficulties involved in this approach and present, in the relevant literature (there is no summary manual however), a comprehensive attempt to answer most of the questions that might be raised. They have, in certain instances, correlated the results of their generalized attitude scales with some of the Thurstone specific scales and have found the correlation to be high. This is offered in evidence of validity, and may be accepted in partial evidence of such, because the present question has to do with the justification of generalized scales and not with all attitude scales as such. Another interesting approach to validity is offered in the comparison of a number of different social groups, the results of which are favorable to the generalized scales. Reliability as determined by correlating equivalent forms is in general high, with some coefficients around .90.

The generalized attitude scales are as a rule longer than special scales, containing forty items or more. This should make for greater reliability if the statements represent variations along the same continuum. One, however, receives the impression that this increase in the number of items introduces a greater variety of "axes," thus compounding the result instead of necessarily making it more differential. For example, such an abstractive intellectual opinion as "Some people like to do this, but more of them dislike it" may not be tapping the same mental source as the personal preference item, "I don't care much about doing this," both items contained in the same scale. In order to make a generalized scale broad enough, moreover, we are likely to include items not universally applicable to all objects supposedly coming under the same general category. Thus, if we were to apply the scale "for any social activity" to dancing or playing baseball, we should be faced with such statements as, "is a destroyer of liberty," "destroys legitimate competition," "is out of focus with the times." This is an extreme instance but it represents one of the difficulties to be surmounted in devising generalized scales, which may reduce the number of effective items and perhaps their scale value.

The statements are arranged in a regular descending order of scale values, a departure from the random order of most special scales. This, according to the authors, results in an immense saving in the time required for scoring. More evidence however should be obtained on whether this innovation effects any change in the reliability and validity of the scale. The present scales are certainly worth a trial in a practical way. One might predict general satisfaction from the use of the less ambiguous ones, such as the scales for measuring attitude toward any school subject or toward any vocation. Many of the others need to be intelligently evaluated, and perhaps also independently checked as to relevance of statement and scale value, at the time of use. As a research technique they offer definite promise of eventually extending the field of attitude measurement.

Theodore Newcomb, Psychology Department, Bennington College. Remmers' generalized attitudes scales, being a modification of the Thurstone technique of equal-appearing intervals in scale construction, must first be examined in the light of Thurstone's general method, and then in the light of Remmers' specific modifications. As to the former, both criticisms of a theoretical nature and empirical evidence are now available in sufficient quantities so that a brief summary may be made with reasonable assurance.

The split-half reliabilities of Thurstone scales have repeatedly been shown to be less than when the same items (or even part of them) have been scored by the Likert method.[1] (It may be objected that the Likert method involves the measurement of strength as well as direction of attitude. This is true, but in every investigation known to the reviewer, correlations of scores obtained by the two methods have reached or exceeded the split-half reliabilities of either measure.) The Thurstone scales are based upon an assumption never realized in practice, namely, that an acceptance of a given scale position involves acceptance of all scale positions less extreme and in the same direction from the neutral position. Their validity is open to doubt except when they are given to the academically sophisticated, by whom the initial judgments (i.e., during the construction of the scales) must almost necessarily be made. Finally, the Thurstone method of scale construction is extremely laborious. In short, briefer scales of greater reliability and probably of greater validity can be constructed by simpler methods.

Remmers has extended Thurstone's work in the direction of mass production, an attempt begun largely because of the laboriousness of applying the Thurstone method anew to every conceivable attitude continuum. Remmers and his collaborators prepared master scales by the same methods. The statements were so worded that they could be applied to any institution, any defined group, any practice, any occupation, etc.—specific groups, occupations, etc., being filled in as the experimenter desires.

Their split-half reliability coefficients, when filled out for various specific attitudes, were almost or quite as satisfactory as those for comparable Thurstone scales; their reliability was somewhat increased, however, by the advantage of being somewhat longer than the Thurstone scales. Scores on those generalized scales, moreover, correlate highly in general with those for Thurstone scales on similar attitudes. The advantages are obvious: time-saving in construction, and ready applicability for a new purpose at a moment's notice. Remmers has also succeeded in using clear and simple language in his scaled statements—though this is not an advantage inherent in the method.

The generalized scales are subject to one disadvantage, however, which is inherent in the method. This is the danger of obtaining responses, not to the actual content of the issue in question, but to the symbol filled in at the top of the page. It has been experimentally demonstrated by others that many individuals whose reaction to such terms as "socialism" and "fascism" is consistently negative, actually accept a large part of what is commonly understood by those terms. The point is not simply that the generalized scales measure stereotyped attitudes evoked by symbols rather than the "true" issues involved, but rather that scores on the generalized scales are not truly comparable—each score represents the subject's reactions to whatever content the symbol evokes for him, whereas a scale specifically designed to measure a given set of issues can (though still dependent, of course, on meanings individually assigned to words) at least avoid the constant error which runs through all the items of the generalized scale.

If the Thurstone technique were clearly the best method of attitude measurement, the advantages of the generalized scale would, under some circumstances, outweigh the disadvantages. But the contrary seems pretty clearly demonstrated, and thus, in this reviewer's opinion, the disadvantages far outweigh the advantages. In view of the simplicity, reliability, and validity of attitude scales constructed by other methods, and in view of the fact that attitudes toward Japanese as a group (for example), or the medical profession as an occupation, do involve specific as well as general considerations, there seems to be no good reason why a scale should not be specifically constructed for any attitude continuum which it seems worth while to measure, rather than resorting to generalized scales.

For a review by Stephen M. Corey, see 897. See also B215, B216, and B1050.

[1203]

[**Attitude Scales for Measuring the Influence of the Work Relief Program.**] College students and adults; 1940; 1 form, 3 scales; 50¢ per 25; 10¢ per specimen set; nontimed (10-15) minutes; E. D. Hinckley; Gainsville, Fla.: University of Florida Press.
a) SCALE 1, ATTITUDE TOWARD WORK RELIEF AS A SOLUTION TO THE FINANCIAL DEPRESSION.
b) SCALE 2, ATTITUDE TOWARD EARNING A LIVING.
c) SCALE 3, ATTITUDE TOWARD RECEIVING RELIEF.

REFERENCES

1 HINCKLEY, ELMER DUMOND, AND HINCKLEY, MARTHA BROWN. "Attitude Scales for Measuring the Influence of the Work Relief Program." *J Psychol* 8:115-24 Jl '39.

[1204]

Attitudes Toward Child Behavior. Parents and others; 1936; 1 form; $1 per 100; 10¢ per specimen set; nontimed (15) minutes; Ralph M. Stogdill and Henry H. Goddard; Columbus, Ohio: Ralph M. Stogdill, 2280 W. Broad St.

REFERENCES

1 STOGDILL, RALPH M. *The Measurement of Attitudes toward Children.* Unpublished doctor's thesis, Ohio State University, 1934. Pp. 150
2 STOGDILL, RALPH M. "The Measurement of Attitudes toward Parental Control and the Social Adjustments of Children." *J Appl Psychol* 20:359-67 Je '36.

[1205]

Attitudes Toward Parental Control of Children. Parents and others; 1936; 1 form; $1 per 100; 10¢ per specimen set; nontimed (15) minutes; Ralph M. Stogdill and Henry H. Goddard; Columbus, Ohio: Ralph M. Stogdill, 2280 W. Broad St.

REFERENCES

1 STOGDILL, RALPH M. *The Measurement of Attitudes toward Children.* Unpublished doctor's thesis, Ohio State University, 1934. Pp. 150
2 STOGDILL, RALPH M. "The Measurement of Attitudes toward Parental Control and the Social Adjustments of Children." *J Appl Psychol* 20:359-67 Je '36.

[1206]

Baxter Group Test of Child Personality. Ages 4 through grade 8; 1935; 1 form; 4¢ per test; 25¢ per manual; nontimed (30-40) minutes; Edna Dorothy Baxter; Englewood, Colo.: the Author, Englewood Public Schools.

REFERENCES

1 BAXTER, EDNA DOROTHY. "The Baxter Child Personality Test." *J Appl Psychol* 21:410-30 Ag '37.

[1207]

Baxter Individual Tests of Child Personality. Children ages 4-13 and their mothers; 1935; 1 form; individual; 7¢ per test; 25¢ per manual; nontimed (40-70) minutes; Edna Dorothy Baxter; Englewood, Colo.: the Author, Englewood Public Schools.

REFERENCES

1 BAXTER, EDNA DOROTHY. "The Baxter Child Personality Test." *J Appl Psychol* 21:410-30 Ag '37.

[1208]

Behavior Cards: A Test-Interview for Delinquent Children. Delinquents having a reading grade score of 4.5 or higher; 1940; individual; 1 form; $2.25 per

testing outfit; nontimed (20-40) minutes; Ralph M. Stogdill; Columbus, Ohio: the Author, 2280 W. Broad St.

REFERENCES

1 PUSKIN, RUTH. *The Validation of a Test-Interview for Delinquent Boys.* Unpublished master's thesis, Ohio State University, 1938.
2 STOGDILL, RALPH M. "A Test-Interview for Delinquent Children." *J Appl Psychol* 24:325-33 Je '40.

[1209]

Behavior Maturity Blank. Grades 7-16 and adults; 1939; 1 form; $6 per 100; 10¢ per specimen set; nontimed (30) minutes; Walther Joël; Los Angeles, Calif.: Gutenberg Press.

REFERENCES

1JoËL, WALTHER. " 'Behavior Maturity' of Children of Nursery School Age." *Child Development* 7:189-99 S '36.
2 RICHARDS, T. W. "Note on the Joël Scale of 'Behavior Maturity.' " *J Genetic Psychol* 56:215-8 Mr '40.

[1210]

Behavior Maturity Rating Scale for Nursery School Children. Ages 1½ to 6; 1935; 1 form; $6 per 100; 10¢ per specimen set; (20-30) minutes; Walther Joël and Janet Joël; Los Angeles, Calif.: Walther Joël, Los Angeles City College.

[1211]

Beliefs About School Life: Test 4.6. Grades 7-12; 1940; 1 form; 5¢ per test; 1¢ per machine-scorable answer sheet; 5¢ per interpretation guide; $1 per set of stencils for machine scoring; nontimed (40) minutes; Chicago, Ill.: Evaluation in the Eight Year Study, Progressive Education Association.

[1212]

C-R Opinionaire. Grades 11-16 and adults; 1935; 2 forms; $1.25 per 25 double-form booklets; 75¢ per single-form booklets; 25¢ per specimen set; (20) minutes; Theodore F. Lentz and colleagues; St. Louis, Mo.: Character Research Institute, Washington University.

REFERENCES

1 LENTZ, THEODORE F., JR. "Utilizing Opinion for Character Measurement." *J Social Psychol* 1:536-42 N '30.
2 HANDY, UVAN, AND LENTZ, THEODORE F. "Item Value and Test Reliability." *J Ed Psychol* 25:703-8 D '34.
3 LENTZ, THEODORE F., JR. "Reliability of Opinionaire Technique Studied Intensively by the Retest Method." *J Social Psychol* 5:338-64 Ag '34.
4 LENTZ, THEODORE F. "Generality and Specificity of Conservatism-Radicalism." *J Ed Psychol* 29:540-6 O '38.
5 LENTZ, THEODORE F. "Personage Admiration and Other Correlates of Conservatism-Radicalism." *J Social Psychol* 10:81-93 F '39.

Goodwin Watson, Professor of Education, Columbia University. This questionnaire is a new arrangement of Lentz's items, most of which were previously used in Forms H and I, and all of which were included in Forms E and F. The characteristic measured is called "conservatism-radicalism" and means, in this instance, general tendency to oppose or to welcome cultural change. The items cover a wide range including possibility of cat meat diet, calendar reform, compulsory cremation, new inventions, and new religions. The trait is thus not identical with the contemporary political parties and doctrines commonly called "conservative" or "radical."

In his article on "generality and specificity of conservatism-radicalism" Lentz [4] reported a classification of items under headings of education, religion, government, sex, non-social, and general. Inter-correlations averaged .45 and the self-correlation within any one section .59, indicating almost as much variation in answers within any such classification, as from one to another. No factor analysis was made. On the basis of previous use of the items Lentz predicts a correlation of about .84 between Form J and Form K. Students who rated themselves as conservatives or median, who preferred Hoover to Smith, who had not changed their church affiliation and who were enrolled in small denominational colleges made relatively high scores.

A later study [5] shows "conservatives" favorable toward conventions, the church, moral prudishness, and the status quo. The test thus brings out agreement with the culture syndrome of what Mencken used to call the "Bible belt." The test does not distinguish between persons who accept these ideas because they have had no contact with any others, and those who have some bias toward the traditional.

There are test items (e.g., one concerning the work of Billy Sunday) which seem considerably outdated.

Lentz wisely suggests that the best use of the instrument is tentative experimentation by research experts, or as a springboard for group discussion.

For a review by H. H. Remmers, see 899.

[1213]

California Test of Personality: A Profile of Personal and Social Adjustment. Grades 4-9, 9-14; 1939; 1 form, 2 levels; $1 per 25; 1½¢ per machine-scorable answer sheet; 25¢ per specimen set of any one level; nontimed (45) minutes; Ernest W. Tiegs, Willis W. Clark, and Louis P. Thorpe; Los Angeles, Calif.: California Test Bureau.
a) ELEMENTARY SERIES. Grades 4-9.
b) SECONDARY SERIES. Grades 9-14.

Raymond B. Cattell, G. Stanley Hall Professor of Genetic Psychology, Clark University. These tests are in questionnaire form requiring "yes" or "no" answers. As far as the mechanics of test design are concerned these tests are admirably worked out. The psychometrist is supplied with efficient scoring keys, with will-spaced percentile norms, with probable errors and standard deviations, and with consistency coefficients corrected by the Spearman-Brown prophecy formula.

About validity, however, the handbook becomes persuasively vague. The detailed intention of the authors is, again, good. It is high time that other questionnaire designers should adopt, for example, their plan of disguising the real point of each question item. But it is with regard to the whole plan that one looks in vain for some substantiating research.

The total score is divided into two main parts, Self Adjustment and Social Adjustment. The first part, Self Adjustment, is divided into the following subdivisions: (*a*) Self-reliance, (*b*) Sense of Personal Worth, (*c*) Sense of Personal Freedom, (*d*) Feeling of Belonging, (*e*) Withdrawal Tendencies, and (*f*) Nervous Symptoms. The second part, Social Adjustment, is subdivided as follows: (*a*) Social Standards, (*b*) Social Skills, (*c*) Anti-social Tendencies, (*d*) Family Relations, (*e*) School Relations, and (*f*) Community Relations.

The broad bipartite division has some justification in the well-known clinical classification into personality and behavior disorders, but otherwise it is merely logical. A vein of maladjustment will cut right across these strata, manifesting itself now in personality disorders, now in antisocial behavior.

Moreover, what is this "Self Adjustment"? The notion of adjustment between an individual and his environment is a standard reference frame for analysis of personality; but is it possible to speak of an adjustment of the self to the self? It is possible to speak of adjustment between the ego and the id or the super-ego, or of conflict between some drive and the self-regarding sentiment. If "Self Adjustment" refers to this important internal aspect of adjustment, why then these particular six categories rather than many others which on clinical grounds might be considered equally important? And why is "Withdrawal Tendency" not among the "Social Adjustments"?

Seeking a research basis for such an ambitious application as a "Test of Personality" and especially for the reasoning behind the seemingly arbitrary and incomplete subdivisions, one encounters a small paragraph saying that factor analysis studies "have been in progress for some months." This sounds very promising, but "some months" are scarcely adequate for the whole factor analysis of personality, especially when they do not precede the publication of the test. Finally, we are told that the factor groupings which are emerging do not correspond with "the concepts which abound in the literature on personality and with which teachers are familiar," so that it is undesirable to regroup the items. Is it more important that psychology should be true or that it should avoid transcending the ideas of school teachers? This statement illuminates what is perhaps the real cause of applied psychology remaining at such a low technical level of efficiency.

With sublime indifference to consistency, the handbook follows this statement that the teacher is not trained to understand the complexities of scientific psychology, with some detailed "Suggestions for Treatment" on the basis of the personality analysis. Psychotherapy and remedial treatment are explained to the novice in five pages. To ponder on what may happen to children "treated" by a teacher with the aid of the handbook and the test profile is something of a nightmare. True, the writers remind the reader of the "wholeness" of the adjusting organism; but this is more in the mystical sense of gestalt and in defiance of their own principles of analysis into independent measurements, than with respect to the relativity of symptoms to a purposive whole, as understood by the clinician. If one were making an analysis into syndromes and symptom complexes with a view to remedial treatment it is very doubtful if one would adopt the subdivisions made here, in preference to the main neurotic and problem behavior patterns.

In so far as the questionnaire system can be used with children, and to the extent that a merely logically compartmentalised set of measurements can be useful in making decisions about personality maladjustment, this "test" has some value in routine work. In research, where group average differences in specific traits or social adjustments are being investigated, its value is more definite. After a factor analysis, and the treatment of children's responses not as answers to the questions but as symptomatic responses the meaning of which is to be determined, the test would have great value.

Incidentally, for any purpose, the value of the test is at present impaired by printing on the booklet, in full view of the child filling in the title page, a description of the adjustments in which he is being tested and an indication as to which set of questions determines the score on each.

Percival M. Symonds, Professor of Education, Columbia University. [Review of the Secondary Series.] The *California Test of Personality* appears to be a carefully worked out set of questions designed to reveal the quality of the individual's adjustments. Questions are divided into groups, one dealing with personal adjustment, the other with social adjustment, and each group is divided into six subsections of fifteen questions each. According to the manual of directions, the questions have been very carefully selected by reference to preceding studies and by actual item analysis with the present material. The scoring is objective and a helpful manual of directions accompanies the test.

A questionnaire of this kind furnishes teachers with worthy goals for personality development.

One question which occurs to the reviewer is whether the separate sections of which there are twelve in all can be considered sufficiently reliable to warrant their being scored separately. In the manual, reliability of the separate subsections is reported to range between .60 and .87 and these reliabilities are said to be "sufficiently high to locate more restricted areas of personality difficulty." The question is whether these reliabilities are high enough to do so for individuals.

Still more fundamental query concerns the significance of this questionnaire as a measure of adjustment. It is well known that adjustment is a term which has a variety of meanings. By asking pupils to answer questions about themselves one is securing evidence of only one kind of adjustment, namely the pupil's own attitudes. Adjustment may also mean the reputation that a person has with others, etc. Anyone using this questionnaire should recognize that it is perhaps more limited in its implications than its name, *Test of Personality*, would indicate.

The reviewer would question Part IX (pp. 6-12) in the manual which gives directions for interpreting profiles and guiding adjustment activities. It is his belief that it would be extremely dangerous to believe that simple questions of this kind would constitute a single diagnosis of a pupil's difficulties to serve as a basis for remedial treatment. One might ask whether questions which are asked and answered as part of a school requirement can be expected to reveal underlying trends which may be apparently unconscious in the personality. It is also open to question whether one should attempt to plan a program of treatment without knowing something about the developmental history and the family background of the pupil. This manual would imply that one deals in a rather uniform and stereotyped way with each problem without making inquiry as to the specific background factors which may have induced a given child to select this particular form of behavior or attitude as a way of meeting his frustration. These criticisms would apply with equal force to all personality inventories of this general type.

The *California Test of Personality* would appear to be one of the most carefully prepared questionnaires of this type.

P. E. Vernon, Lecturer in Psychology, University of Glasgow. Great masses of rather woolly verbiage are being published nowadays under the name of mental hygiene, and it seems unfortunate that many professional psychologists encourage and contribute to it. Certainly the ideal of helping teachers to understand their pupils' personalities, which presumably inspired this test, is a very worthy one, but equally certainly personality inventories have not yet been proved to give trustworthy information even to trained psychologists and psychiatrists, much less to untrained amateurs.

The manuals of these tests provide plenty of advice about treatment of pupils whose abnormalities the tests are said to diagnose, but contain a minimum of information about the technique of construction and standardization. In the Elementary Form the reliabilities of the total self- and social-adjustment scores, and the numbers of cases from whom the norms were derived, seem quite adequate. In the Secondary Form the reliabilities are even higher, but the numbers which provided the norms are not stated. Only one set of norms is given for each form, though it seems hardly credible that there should be no significant changes in average scores between 10 and 15, and between 15 and 20 years. One would also like to know the reliabilities of the twelve component parts and their intercorrelations before one can be sure that these components are rea-

sonably self-consistent and distinct from one another. Instead one is told that: "Some of the items of this profile touch relatively sensitive personal and social areas, and such student attitudes may change in a relatively short time," and that: "The obtained correlations among the components emphasize the unity or 'wholeness' of normal individuals." Such statements are not reassuring to psychologists, though they may impress teachers and other amateur testers. If the intercorrelations are high (relative to the reliabilities) this may be due more to halo effect than to "wholeness" of personality.

Wording and instructions appear satisfactory in the Elementary Form, and are suitable for younger pupils, but obviously most unsuitable for college students and adults, in the Secondary Form (e.g., "Are you allowed enough time to play and have a good time?"). It would have been better if, in certain sections, some of the items had been stated in the opposite direction, i.e., so as to suggest socially desirable rather than uniformly undesirable qualities. However, a good attempt has been made to disguise many of the items, so as to reduce their unattractiveness. The scoring will be somewhat lengthy (unless machine-scoring answer sheets are used), and will require careful checking. Since there are only twelve items for measuring each of the separate components—fifteen in the Secondary Form—the ranges of scores are small. The average interquartile range for any one component is only about 4. No evidence whatsoever is given of any correspondence between a pupil's scores and his actual behavior, or other people's impressions of his behavior.

Bus Ed World 20:826 My '40. Marion M. Lamb. It is a satisfaction to find in the California Test of Personality suggestions for curing personality ills as well as for identifying them. * The esoteric terms used by experts in tests and measurements are present for those who want them, but even to the nonexpert the California Test of Personality offers hope for improvement of the maladjusted. *

[1214]

Case Inventory, Third Edition. Grades 5-12; 1935-36; 2 forms; $2.65 per 25; 30¢ per specimen set; non-timed (25-35) minutes; J. B. Maller; New York: Bureau of Publications, Teachers College, Columbia University.

REFERENCES

1 HARRIS, D. B., AND DABELSTEIN, D. H. "A Study of the Maller and Boynton Personality Inventories." *J Ed Psychol* 29:279-86 Ap '38.

Harold E. Jones, Director of the Institute of Child Welfare and Professor of Psychology, The University of California. This personality schedule yields four subscores which are described as measuring (*a*) emotionalized response patterns, (*b*) adjustment, (*c*) honesty, and (*d*) ethical judgment and integration.

Test 1 consists of 50 key words with a choice of associations which are scored as either "rational" or "irrational." Test 2 consists of 50 self-description inventory items selected from Maller's *Character Sketches,* and referring to specific aspects of personal and social adjustment. Test 3 is an overstatement test disguised under the heading "What do you know about sports and hobbies?" Test 4 consists of 9 dual choice discrimination items, regarded as involving ethical judgment, and providing also a measure of integration between the subject's ethical judgment and his own code of behavior.

Two similar forms are available. The individual tests are reported as having a reliability of .90 or above, when odd-even items are correlated for both forms; no statement is made in the manual as to the sample used in the reliability study.

Validity was examined for each test (with the exception of Test 3) by the method of extreme groups, comparing "normals" with children on probation and delinquents. Although there is no statement as to the minimal degree of discrimination which was regarded as acceptable, all of the items included were said to be "valid." It is, of course, possible that items selected to differentiate normals and delinquents may be of restricted value for individual guidance within a relatively normal sample. In a Minnesota testing program a considerable overlapping was found between a normal and a "problem" group, the difference between the averages being in the expected direction but amounting to only about one-half the standard deviation of the normal group. At each age girls appear to be better adjusted than boys, the sex difference being about half as great as the difference between normal and "problem" boys. There is also an apparent age difference, with an improvement in the scores from age 10 to 16.

No attempt has been made to analyze validity in correlational terms, nor to allow for possible group differentials in intelligence, social status, etc. It would also be desirable to present validity data for the subscores as well as for the total scores, particularly in view of the fact that the author considers the individual tests to have greater meaning than the composite.

MERITS OF THE INVENTORY. It is conveniently organized, easy to administer, and in a form which is acceptable to subjects over a wide age range (from grade 4 or 5 to adults). In addition to the four tests, space is provided on the schedule for the recording of data concerning socio-economic background, recreational interests, wishes, fears, and worries.

PRINCIPAL DEFECT. Teachers or guidance workers who are unfamiliar with the sources of error in inventory techniques may attempt to use a schedule such as this for a direct and authoritative diagnosis of personality characteristics. To guard against unwise applications of the test, the manual of directions should include a specific discussion of its limitations.

E. G. Williamson, Coordinator of Student Personnel Services and Associate Professor of Psychology, The University of Minnesota. This inventory consists of four parts: (*a*) Controlled association test, two possible word associations (rational and irrational) with 50 stimulus words. Stereotypy of response is avoided by alternating the positions of the rational and irrational words. The rationality-irrationality score is the number of rational responses. (*b*) Adjustment test, 50 self-description questions involving personal and social adjustments. The adjustment score is the number of normal responses. (*c*) Self-scoring test, 15 questions providing a measure of honesty in classroom situations. The individual's trustworthiness is tested by his willingness to take credit for knowledge which he does not possess. The number of such items for which he has admitted ignorance multiplied by two is his score. (*d*) Ethical judgment test, 9 questions providing for a self-evaluation response in terms of knowledge of ethical standards. This part really yields two scores: E, the number of "correct" ethical discriminations; and I, the number of times the individual has indicated that he would act according to the ethical pattern. To get the total score for this part, the sum of E and I is multiplied by 2.

The third edition of the inventory includes a section on the student's socio-economic background, interests, preferences, forms of recreation, type of preferred radio and moving picture programs, minor physical complaints and occupational and educational plans.

The inventory is virtually self-administering, especially on the higher levels. In view of the fact that no validity coefficients are presented for the gross total score, the doubling of the part S and E scores seems unnecessary. Otherwise, the method of scoring is extremely simple.

The odd-even reliabilities for the four parts and the total score are: .9203, .9618, .9506, .9909, and .9365, respectively. But the age level of the group upon which these reliabilities were determined is not indicated.

Each question has been selected from the author's earlier forms and has been experimentally validated in several investigations. Items for the association test were selected from a list of 200 used to differentiate 108 patients in psychiatric clinics, an equated group of normal adults, 200 pupils in the New York Probationary Schools and an equated group of normal children.

Items for the adjustment test were selected from a list used to differentiate "well adjusted" children and adults from those exhibiting serious abnormalities. The author states that the "undesirable responses involve extreme introversion, lack of self-control, feeling of inadequacy and inferiority, and symptoms of psycho-neurotic tendencies."

The honesty test was constructed from an earlier test of sports and hobbies and supposedly measures "trustworthiness." The student's "acceptance of credit for these difficult items is evidence of over-statement. The validity of the measure may be considered as self-evident."

The ethical judgment test of 9 items was validated in terms of the extent to which each of a larger number of questions differentiated between delinquents, pupils in probation schools, and normal groups.

Incomplete norms, based upon the second edition, are presented with a table of revised norms and percentiles being promised for the future. The norms presented are based upon a study of 5214 pupils in Minnesota schools. These norms are very inadequate for interpretation of the test. For example, the means of total scores are presented for boys and girls at various age levels, but when deciles are presented, it is for all age groups combined. Since it is the part scores for which the validity is claimed, norms for them would be more useful.

The author does not refer in his manual to research studies reporting in detail his validating experiments. Stott reports an extensive investigation of 695 farm youth, 520 city youth, and 640 town youth in which the *Case Inventory* was used, with other tests, to determine what differences, if any, were, to be found among these three groups. On the adjustment test the urban group ranked, in average score, significantly above the town and farm groups. On the association test, the urban group was, on the average, significantly above the other two groups, the latter two having approximately equal mean scores. On the ethical judgment test, the town youth approximated the city youth in mean score and both groups exceeded the mean score of the farm group. The mean scores of the three groups were approximately the same on the honesty test.

The inventory has merit in that it is not completely dependent upon the subject's frank self-analysis. But the total score cannot be given serious consideration until more evidence is provided for its validity. The nature of the items is such as to raise some question as to its applicability for mature students. This is particularly true of the trustworthiness test. It is possible that more sophisticated subjects will "see through" the device. Studies using college freshmen and adults of various ages are mentioned, but neither data nor references to the literature are cited.

The inventory should be valuable for research studies of groups of cases and should provide valuable, though tentative, leads in the counseling of individuals.

For a review by Richard Ledgerwood, see 916.

[1215]

Character and Personality Rating Scale. 1934; 1 form, separate scales for boys and girls; $2.10 per 100 blanks; 25¢ per specimen set; J. B. Maller; New York: Bureau of Publications, Teachers College, Columbia University.

Bessie Lee Gambrill, Associate Professor of Elementary Education, Yale University. The scale includes fifty items, twenty-five under each of two general categories: I, Aspects of Character; II, Aspects of Personality. The first group includes attitudes, social adjustments and "fundamental habits of character," the summation of whose ratings the author believes will approximate an index of the totality of character. Under the second category, are items of emotional adjustment, "fundamental aspects of personality," and dominant forms of interest. Record blanks for the rating of twenty-five individuals are provided, with different colored cards for boys and girls.

Careful examination of the two divisions of the scale fails to reveal a consistent theory of character and personality underlying the selection of many of the items and their classification under the two major categories. For example, on what basis is a student's liking for school and his regard for teachers the first two items under character? Information as to these attitudes is desirable as a point of departure for further study—of pupil and school situation—but is it valid for rating character? Might a high rating in some situations merely indicate docility, or an uncritical mind? Again, a question arises as to why foresight, sense of humor, and responsiveness are classified under character, while intellectual interest, neatness, and social mindedness are grouped under personality. Since the sums of the ratings on each of the two parts of the scale are to be recorded as character rating and personality rating, such questions as these seriously affect the validity of the scale. The purpose of the scale is not defined further than the statement "intended primarily for classroom use, but may be found of value in work with young people's clubs or groups of employees." Obviously, a low rating on character or personality for any of these purposes, without interpretation of total scores in terms of the items of the scale itself, and without great care in safeguarding such criteria of validity as common understanding of separate scale items by all judges, opportunity and ability to secure reliable evidence on each item by the judges, etc., may lead to grave injustice.

The reliability of the scale was determined by the re-rating of 381 pupils in grades 7 and 8 by their respective teachers after an interval of six weeks, the correlation between the two

sets of total scores being .90. There is no information on the more important question of consistency of judgment on the individual items of the scale. Without this knowledge it is possible that the high correlation results from many shifts on single items which tend to balance each other. No evidence is offered on agreement of different judges. To guard against unreliability resulting from lack of opportunity to observe certain characteristics, raters are properly advised to omit these items. In the following paragraph, however, it is recommended that when comparison with norms is desired such items be given the intermediate rating of 2. This seems to recommend provision for statistical facilitation at the expense of reliability of judgment.

Norms for the test in terms of distribution of total scores of 1,219 junior high school pupils of New York City are given. In view of the facts: that this is a three-step scale; that the rating instructions recommend that in a normal group about one-fourth of the group be rated respectively *1* and *3* and the remaining fifty per cent be marked *2;* that a "normal group" for the qualities included in this scale has not been defined; that no information is given about the social-intellectual status of the group on which the standardization is based, use of the norms would be misleading. While the author states that the main value of the scale is for inter-group comparison, he is not emphatic in discouraging its use for group comparisons.

[1216]

Concept Formation Test. Normal and schizophrenic adults; 1940; 1 form; $15.50 per testing outfit (No. 36118); Jacob Kasanin and Eugenia Hanfmann; Chicago, Ill.: C. H. Stoelting Co.

REFERENCES

1 KASANIN, JACOB, AND HANFMANN, EUGENIA. "An Experimental Study of Concept Formation in Schizophrenia: I. Quantitative Analysis of Results." *Am J Psychiatry* 95:35-52 Jl '38.

[1217]

Cowan Adolescent Personality Schedule: Revision No. 2. Ages 12-18; 1935-37; 1 form; $2 per 25; 50¢ per specimen set; nontimed (10-30) minutes; Edwina A. Cowan; Wichita, Kan.: Wichita Child Research Laboratory.

REFERENCES

1 COWAN, EDWINA ABBOTT; McCLELLAN, MERNERVA CHURCH; PRATT, BERTHA M.; AND SKAER, MAE. "An Adolescent Personality Schedule." *Child Development* 6:77-87 Mr '35.
2 BRIGDEN, ROBERT L. "A Diagnostic Adolescent Personality Schedule," pp. 38-9. In *Proceedings, Second Biennial Meeting. Society for Research and Child Development.* Washington, D. C.: National Research Council, 1936.
3 BRIGDEN, R. L. "The Cowan Adolescent Personality Schedule: Its Function in Psychological Diagnosis." *Am J Med Jurisprud* 2:97-9 F '39.

Goodwin Watson, Professor of Education, Columbia University. This questionnaire on symptoms of maladjustment, to be answered by pupils in junior or senior high school, has developed refinements and improvements at every point except the fundamental ones. "Holy Gee!" said one thirteen-year-old boy, "I'm going to be careful how I answer this test!" It remains true of the Cowan schedule, as of its predecessors (Woodworth, Woodworth-Matthews, Thurstone, Colgate, Bernreuter, Bell, Symonds, Pinter, *et al.*), that a subject can answer it to give any impression that he may deem it advantageous to present. The directions take no account whatever of this basic limitation. Despite criticisms on this point in the literature for a decade or more, the authors fail to suggest that the validity of the test is a function of the rapport between examiner and adolescent. The "Instructions to be read or recited to the subject" seem to be based on the false assumption that no genuine relationship is necessary to persuade an adolescent to bare his soul with check marks.

Even granted the best will in the world, youngsters do not always mean what the author meant by his question. One boy read "People have told me 'scary' things," and checked "Yes" which is interpreted as a fear, but the boy hadn't been in the least disturbed by horror-tales which, as a matter of fact, he enjoys. Another answered "Yes" to "Have you ever been told that you were stupid?" because he and the other fellows often said such things in fun. This went mechanically into the profile as an inferiority score, although the boy usually rated tops in intellectual matters, and was well enough aware of it. One girl answered "Yes" to a feeling of smothering; what she meant was that sometimes it was hard to breathe when her nose was stopped up by a cold.

There are questions in the schedule which seem unnecessarily stupid. To answer a question mark to "I have a lot of friends" is supposed to show "childish immaturity." To answer a question mark to "I believe that most people are real good," gets one into the column "neurotic, keyed up emotionally, and frustrated." To answer that saying your prayers make you feel better is scored good adjustment—to answer "No" is interpreted as "avoids people and problems." A little hard on children not reared to orthodoxy!

One of the most untenable assumptions is that questions have the same value for boys and girls, in every culture group, and over the age range from 12 to 20. The statement "I like to fight" for example, is scored alike for both sexes, all ages, and every type of community atmosphere. Not having definite plans about what to do after finishing school is rated "irresponsibility" for the twelve-year-old in the same degree as for the boy of nineteen or twenty.

The instrument has the advantage of yielding nine scores (fear, family emotion, family authority, inferiority, nonfamily authority, responsibility, escapes, neurotic, and compensation) along lines that facilitate diagnosis. An ingenious scoring method, with a wire gadget, enables one quickly to strike an average and to observe "peaks" and "valleys." An "interpretation" of various combinations of peaks and valleys is furnished—complete almost to the point of being ridiculous. For example, "hypothyroid?" is suggested for an individual who has shown considerable "irresponsibility" by answering with a question mark such ambiguous queries as "Are you usually to blame for your mistakes?" and "Can you persuade other boys and girls to do things for you that you dislike to do yourself?"

The Cowan schedule is one more example of the delight of some psychologists in any kind of probe which purports to give insight into others by merely mechanical means, obviating the necessity for personal rapport, keen observation, broad experience, and common sense.

For a review by Harold E. Jones, see 918.

[1218]

Environment Inventory for College and University Students. 1938; 1 form; 5¢ per copy; sample copy free; Robert H. Morrison and M. Ernest Townsend; St. Louis, Mo.: Webster Publishing Co.

REFERENCES

1 TOWNSEND, M. E. "Environment Inventory in College Personnel Work," pp. 111-4. In *Research on the Foundations of American Education.* National Education Association, American Education Research Association, Official Report of the 1939 Meeting, Cleveland, Ohio, February 25-March 1, 1939. Washington, D. C.: the Association, 1939. Pp. 215. $1.50. Paper.

E. G. Williamson, Coordinator of Student Personnel Services and Associate Professor of Psychology, The University of Minnesota. This 15-page inventory is a special case-history form consisting of questions organized in the form of a questionnaire. On the basis of their counseling experiences, the authors selected items of information which they judged necessary for the work of the counselor. The inventory is to be filled out by the student before he is interviewed or during his interview with the counselor. It provides a convenient summary of important case data as reported by the student.

In addition to the usual identifying items (name, age, sex, etc.) the inventory includes questions on the following topics: usual ways of traveling to and from college; regular place of eating (e.g., home, campus, cafeteria, etc.); extent and ways of self-support and part-time employment; conditions and place of studying for each day of the week; name and extent of participation in extracurricular activities; educational and occupational plans; living, financial, and study conditions in the home; cultural aspects of the home and kind of furnishings of the home; education and occupation of parents; and 21 questions sampling the student's attitudes toward a number of socio-economic-political issues and problems.

A number of such inventories or case-history forms are now available and widely used. They are convenient methods of collecting directly from the student certain information necessary to effective counseling. To a certain extent the use of such an instrument makes unnecessary the long and tedious interview method of case history taking used by the doctor and the social worker. But there are some serious limitations in the use of such an inventory. The many unique and highly individual phases of each student's experiences and problems may be masked by the form of the general questions and statements. Such detailed and supplementary information must be collected in the personal interview. Secondly, it must be remembered by the counselor that such an inventory properly filled out constitutes but one part of a total and comprehensive case history. Many other sources of data must be tapped to round out the case history. Thirdly, the student's answers to questions in such an inventory as this one must be checked or verified. The student's reports cannot be accepted at face value unless they have been substantiated. This may be done incompletely in the personal interview but in many cases the counselor should seek verification from other counselors, parents, teachers and other individuals. When used with these limitations in mind, such an inventory can prove to be invaluable in providing the counselor with important information in advance of the interview, thereby making easier the task of establishing rapport and understanding and may also reduce to a minimum the routine collecting of information by the question and answer technique.

This particular inventory includes very important questions, well-phrased to elicit proper answers. It has the virtue of not requiring that the student attempt, through the dubious process of self-analysis, to diagnose his own capabilities and problems. Rather the student is asked to summarize for the counselor some of the important data by means of which the counselor and the student together may arrive at such an understanding of the latter's problems.

[1219]

Experience Variables Record: A Clinical Revision. College and adults; 1928-38; 1 form; individual; reprinted from the February 1938 issue of *Psychiatry*; 10¢ per copy; Joseph Chassell; Towson, Md.: Sheppard and Enoch Pratt Hospital.

REFERENCES

1 CHASSELL, J. O. *The Experience Variables*: A Study of the Variable Factors in Experience Contributing to the Formation of Personality. Bennington, Vt.: the Author, Bennington College, 1928. Pp. 42. $0.75. Paper.
2 CHASSELL, JOSEPH. "A Clinical Revision of the Experience Variables Record." *Psychiatry* 1:67-77 F '38.

[1220]

"F" Test. Ages 9 and over; 1938; 1 form; an individual test for ages 9-10 and group or individual for ages 11 and over; 5s. 6d. per 12; 15(20) minutes; Raymond B. Cattell with the assistance of L. G. Studman and C. A. Simmins; London: University of London Press, Ltd.

REFERENCES

1 BERNSTEIN, E. *Quickness and Intelligence*: An Enquiry Concerning the Existence of a General Speed Factor. British Journal of Psychology Monograph Supplements, Vol. 3, No. 7. London: Cambridge University Press, 1924. Pp. viii, 55. 7s. Paper.
2 HARGREAVES, H. L. The "Faculty" of Imagination: An Enquiry Concerning the Existence of a General "Faculty," or Group Factor, of Imagination. British Journal of Psychology Monograph Supplements, Vol. 3, No. 10. London: Cambridge University Press, 1927. Pp. viii, 55. 7s. Paper.
3 WYNN JONES, LL. "An Investigation into the Significance of Perseveration." *J Mental Sci* 74:653-9 '28.
4 KARVE, B. D. *An Experimental Investigation of 'Fluency' in School Children*. Unpublished master's thesis, University of Leeds, 1929.
5 STUDMAN, L. G. "Measurement of the Speed and Flow of Mental Activity." *Brit J Med Psychol* 14:124-31 '34.
6 WYNN JONES, LL. Chapter 10, "Fluency of Association and Imagination," pp. 112-7. In *An Introduction to Theory and Practice of Psychology*. London: Macmillan and Co., Ltd., 1934. Pp. x, 308. 12s. 6d.
7 STUDMAN, L. G. "The Factor Theory in the Field of Personality." *Char and Pers* 4:34-43 S '35.
8 STUDMAN, L. G. "Studies in Experimental Psychiatry: 'V', 'W' and 'F' Factors in Relation to Traits of Personality." *J Mental Sci* 81:107-37 '35.
9 CATTELL, RAYMOND B. *A Guide to Mental Testing*: For Psychological Clinics, Schools, and Industrial Psychologists, pp. 148-63. London: University of London Press, Ltd., 1936. Pp. xvi, 312. 10s. 6d.
10 CATTELL, RAYMOND B. "Temperament Tests in Clinical Practice." *Brit J Med Psychol* 16:43-61 pt 1 '36.

J. M. Blackburn, Lecturer in Social Psychology, London School of Economics. Is it overcompensation for an inferiority complex in relation to other sciences that has made so many—too many—psychologists the servants of statistics instead of remaining their masters? Do they think that the application of precise quantitative methods will endow indefinite data with a measure of exactitude, and thus allow them to hold up their heads again in the presence of workers from other sciences? Or can it be they sometimes feel that the presentation of complicated mathematical formulae will persuade many persons, who might otherwise be critically disposed, into a more ready acceptance of their views? Whatever the cause the principal result is a grotesque overemphasis on objectivity that ruins many tests for most clinical purposes. Subjects are hammered into the same objective situation regardless of their relative malleability; the responses of one subject are considered to be equivalent to the same responses of another in the same situation, although the attitudes of the two may be entirely different; and great emphasis is laid on arithmetical scores irrespective of how they are obtained. This great defect is to be found in most of the factorial tests, most acutely, perhaps, in those which are supposed to investigate p (so-called "perseveration"), because these are difficult to interpret other than quantitatively. Cattell's *"F" Test* has at least the advantage that one *can* ignore his method of scoring and interpret the results in a qualitative manner. Such interpretation is what the clinical worker finds most useful in filling in the picture of a subject's case history. Even from the most accurately standardised tests of intelligence it is the subject's grade of intelligence together with a knowledge of how the test was tackled that is of far greater importance to the clinical worker than a quantitative measure expressed in a single figure, the IQ. People are not condemned to permanent treatment in institutions for the mentally defective on the basis of one point of IQ alone, and it is to be hoped they never will be.

Cattell's test is useful to the clinician who ignores Cattell's instructions. In the Subtest 4, Topics, for example, the Cattell score is the number of significant words given in 30 seconds, omitting *a, the, and,* but counting the topic (man going up a ladder, dog barking, etc.) where repeated. This method of scoring is clearly somewhat arbitrary and it may, amongst other things, prejudice the results against a verbose though imaginative subject. It is certainly ridiculous to believe that an arithmetical score obtained in this way will represent with any fine degree of accuracy a subject's temperamental type. Thus, instead of counting the number of words, things, or drawings in estimating a subject's score and then solemnly looking in the appropriate table for an arithmetical figure to express his temperament—more valuable clinical material may be obtained by noting the kind of topics, drawings, etc., that the subject offers, paying not too strict attention to the timing of the test, and finally interpreting the results in terms of the kinds of topics, drawings, etc. mentioned, the relationship between them, and—most important—the way in which the subject gave them.

Cattell himself admits that the consistency of the *"F" Test* varies according to the subject's state of health, mood, fatigue, etc., and this provides all the stronger argument against an uncritical acceptance of the arithmetical scores. Instead, therefore, of concentrating his attention on the correlation coefficient between letters of the alphabet ($f, c, g,$ etc.) he might have been better advised to have developed his test as a useful clinical tool.

P. E. Vernon, Lecturer in Psychology, University of Glasgow. Fluency of association or "f-factor" is one of the group factors in mental operations which, with p and o, are stressed by Spearman and his followers. Cattell's battery of five tests depends on the speed of naming objects which might appear in certain pictures, the speed of associations with inkblots, speed of writing things which are "round," "eatable," "begin with S," and so on. The author discovered that such tests gave moderately high correlations with ratings of traits such as cheerfulness, sociability, humorousness, adaptability, quickness of apprehension, etc., i.e., traits which belong to the conventional extravert pattern. He gives this group of traits the name "surgency." Correlations of .60 to .65 between f tests and ratings on "surgent" traits have been obtained in three small groups of subjects. This leads the author to claim that the test is "of higher validity than any other yet discovered in the realm of temperament testing."

Though these results are as yet unconfirmed there is actually a good deal of evidence suggesting that such tests do correlate more highly with extraversion than do most objective personality tests (e.g., the June Downey or p tests) with the traits they are supposed to measure. They seem to be especially useful with mental hospital patients. Certainly f tests are worth more thorough study, and this battery should provide a good starting point, although its construction and norms are by no means satisfactory as yet.

The battery correlates about .30 with intelligence, and the author recommends a rough correction for high and low IQ. This needs to be worked out more accurately. The reliability is stated to be .78 with 14-year-olds; apparently the figure is based only on about 15 cases. The norms for 14 years are derived from 450 children, but for other ages the numbers are quite insufficient. Sex differences are not mentioned.

Ll. Wynn Jones, Senior Lecturer in Experimental Psychology, University of Leeds. The *"F" Test* is a temperament test of fluency of association and imagination and consists of five subtests: (1) Unfinished Pictures—Score: one point for each idea. (2) Word Series (things round, things to eat, words beginning with S)—Score: number of things or words. (3) Completing Forms—Score: number of drawings completed multiplied by three. (4) Topics—Score: number of significant words divided by two. (5) Ink Blots—Score: double the number of items conceived. Three periods of one minute are needed for each subtest, except Subtest 4 which needs six periods of half a minute. Fluency is a factor which has been extensively studied by the Spearman School.

The instructions for administering the *"F" Test* are given in Chapter 5 of Cattell's *Guide to Mental Testing.*[9] The f score was found to correlate about 0.3 with g (intelligence). Because of this, a correction for IQ has been empirically obtained for ages between 10 and 14 years. The results can then be converted to decile scores from the table given on page 162. Cattell found a correlation of 0.65 ± 0.07 between fluency and surgency and in his studies of temperament traits he prefers the terms surgent and desurgent to extravert and introvert. Cattell further claims that the *"F"*

Test remains the best objective test of a definite temperament so far discovered. Although the reviewer has not had experience in applying the above correction for IQ yet it appears to be a procedure which can be confidently recommended. The reviewer can also testify to the satisfactory reliabilities of such subtests.[4, 6] The reviewer's experience when similar tests were applied to manic and melancholic patients was also favourable to the view that such tests are objective tests of a definite temperament type.[8] It is, of course, essential to distinguish between fluency in the education of relations and correlates, that is, fluency in its noetic aspect and fluency in its reproductive aspect. The former figures in tests of g, the latter in tests of f. Thus the fluency of finding the fourth term of "soot : black :: snow : ————" is noetic, but the fluency in finding a large number of correlatives like salt, snow, note-paper, etc. which would form a fourth term of "black : soot :: white : ————" is reproductive.

Brit J Med Psychol 17:394 pts 3-4 '38. *J. C. Raven.* Cattell has . . . prepared in leaflet form his material for testing fluency or 'surgency' of ideas. The usual series of suggestive pictures, forms, ink blots, and stimulating phrases are employed. The only difference is that the subject is asked to write a list of his associations at the side of the test material. The psychological value of the material is naturally reduced. The leaflets are useful for experimental work but anyone who wishes to use them for practical purposes must bear in mind that they give low consistency coefficients.

[1221]
Fels Parent-Behavior Rating Scales. "For the use of the trained home visitor in appraising certain aspects of parent-child relationships"; 1939; 1 form, 30 parts; $1.50 per 30 sets; 25¢ per specimen set; Horace Champney; Yellow Springs, Ohio: Antioch Press.

REFERENCES

1 CHAMPNEY, HORACE. *Measurement of Parent Behavior as a Part of the Child's Environment.* Unpublished doctor's thesis, Ohio State University, 1939.
2 CHAMPNEY, HORACE, AND MARSHALL, HELEN. "Optimal Refinement of the Rating Scale." *J Appl Psychol* 23:323-31 Je '39.

[1222]
Haggerty-Olson-Wickman   **Behavior**   **Rating Schedules.** Kindergarten through grade 12; 1930; $1 per 25; 10¢ per specimen set; M. E. Haggerty, W. C. Olson, and E. K. Wickman; Yonkers, N. Y.: World Book Co.

REFERENCES

1 HAGGERTY, M. E. "The Incidence of Undesirable Behavior in Public School Children." *J Ed Res* 12:102-22 S '25.
2 WICKMAN, E. K. *Children's Behavior and Teachers' Attitudes.* New York: Commonwealth Fund, 1928. pp. ix, 247. $2.00. (London: George Allen & Unwin, Ltd. 9s.)

3 OLSON, WILLARD C. *Problem Tendencies in Children*: A Method for Their Measurement and Description. Minneapolis, Minn.: University of Minnesota Press, 1930. Pp. xi, 92. $2.00.
4 OLSON, WILLARD C. "The Clinical Use of Behavior Rating Schedules." *J Juvenile Res* 15:237-45 O '31.
5 OLSON, WILLARD C. "Utilization of the Haggerty-Olson-Wickman Behavior Rating Schedules." *Childh Ed* 9:350-9 Ap '33.
6 ELLIS, D. B., AND MILLER, L. W. "Teachers' Attitudes and Child Behavior Problems." *J Ed Psychol* 27:501-11 O '36.
6.1 KIRK, SAMUEL A. "Behavior Problem Tendencies in Deaf and Hard-of-Hearing Children." *Am Ann Deaf* 83:131-7 Mr '38.
7 DUREA, M. A. "Introversion-Extroversion and Problem Tendencies in Children." *Ed Res B* 18:103-6+ Ap '39.
8 BROOKS, JAMES J. "A Technique for Determining the Degree of Behavior Maladjustment of Prison Inmates." *J Criminal Psychopathology* 1:339-53 Ap '40.

Harold E. Jones, Director of the Institute of Child Welfare and Professor of Psychology, University of California. Schedule A, a behavior problem record, presents a list of 15 problems (such as defiance to discipline, speech difficulties etc.) to be checked in one of four columns according to frequency of occurrence in an individual. In summating for a total score, weights are assigned in terms of the frequency and seriousness of a given problem. It may be noted that these are standardized weightings and are not adjustable for variations in the significance of a problem for an individual.

Schedule B consists of a graphic 5-point rating scale for 35 traits classified in four groups—intellectual, physical, social, and emotional. For a given trait, each position on the scale is weighted in terms of its predictive relation to the problem tendency score on Schedule A. In general, extremes of a trait (such as quiet-talkative) receive higher problem-weightings than intermediate positions.

A re-rating correlation of .86 and a split-half correlation (raised) of .92 are reported for elementary school children on Schedule B. No reliability data are given in the manual for Schedule A.

A composite score on A and B has shown a correlation of .76 with frequency of referral for discipline or other action by the school principal. A comparison of normals with clinic cases has shown that only about ten per cent of the former equal or exceed the median of the latter.

The two schedules are printed conveniently in a single folder; a class record form and tally chart are provided on a separate sheet. Included in the manual of directions are tables for converting raw scores into percentile ranks; these apply to Schedules A and B, to the four divisions of Schedule B, and also to an abbreviated form of Schedule B recommended for use with preschool children. It is pointed out, however, that the percentile tables may not be equally applicable for all groups, and that scores should be taken as relative to the mean scores of the group which is being studied.

A sound understanding of the limitations of rating scales is shown in a cautioning statement which indicates the importance of using ratings, together with supplementary data, in a program of further study and guidance, rather than as a final classification.

[1223]

Humm-Wadsworth Temperament Scale, 1940 Edition. Adults; 1934-39; 1 form; sold only to qualified testers; $2.50 per 25; 50¢ per specimen set; non-timed (30-90) minutes; Doncaster G. Humm and Guy W. Wadsworth, Jr.; Los Angeles, Calif.: Wadsworth-Humm Personnel Service, 245½ South Western Ave.

REFERENCES

1 HUMM, DONCASTER G., AND WADSWORTH, GUY W., JR. "The Humm-Wadsworth Temperament Scale: Preliminary Report." *Personnel J* 12:314-23 Ap '34.
2 HUMM, DONCASTER G., AND WADSWORTH, GUY W., JR. "The Humm-Wadsworth Temperament Scale." *Am J. Psychiatry* 92:163-200 Jl '35.
3 WADSWORTH, GUY W., JR. "Temperament Tests as Personnel Aids." *Personnel J* 15:341-6 Mr '37.
4 HUMM, DONCASTER G. *The Analysis of Disposition or Temperament.* Los Angeles, Calif.: the Author, 416 West Eighth St., 1938. Pp. 20. $0.50. Paper.
5 KRUGER, BARBARA L. "A Statistical Analysis of the Humm-Wadsworth Temperament Scale." *J Appl Psychol* 22:641-52 D '38.
6 MOSIER, CHARLES I. "On the Validity of Neurotic Questionnaires." *J Social Psychol* 9:3-16 F '38.
7 PATERSON, DONALD G.; SCHNEIDLER, GWENDOLEN G.; AND WILLIAMSON, EDMUND G. *Student Guidance Techniques*, pp. 197-201. New York: McGraw-Hill Book Co., Inc., 1938. Pp. xviii, 316. $3.00. (London: McGraw-Hill Publishing Co., Ltd. 18s.)
8 DYSINGER, DON W. "A Critique of the *Humm-Wadsworth Temperament Scale*." *J. Abn and Social Psychol* 34:73-83 Ja '39.
9 HEMSATH, MARY ELIZABETH. "Theory and Practice of Temperament Testing." *Personnel J* 18:3-12 My '39.
10 HUMM, DONCASTER G. "Discussion of 'A Statistical Analysis of the Humm-Wadsworth Temperament Scale.'" *J Appl Psychol* 23:525-6 Ag '39.
11 HUMM, DONCASTER G. "Dysinger's Critique of the Humm-Wadsworth Temperament Scale." *J Abn and Social Psychol* 34:402-3 Jl '39.
12 HUMM, DONCASTER G.; STORMENT, ROBERT C.; AND IORNS, MARTIN E. "Combination Scores for the Humm-Wadsworth Temperament Scale." *J Psychol* 7:227-54 Ap '39.
13 WASSON, MARGARET M. "The Agreements among Certain Types of Personality Schedules." *J Psychol* 9:351-63 Ap '40.

Forrest A. Kingsbury, Associate Professor of Psychology, The University of Chicago. [Review of the Second Edition.] This is a profile scale, yielding scores on seven traits or "components of temperament." In general makeup it resembles neurotic questionnaires of the yes-no type, except for its greater length, 318 items, of which only 164 yield scores, the remaining 154 being padding. The authors, however, believe that these 154 help create "test atmosphere" and influence responses to the 164 valid questions, so they have declined thus far to publish a shortened form and thus risk invalidating the present norms.

In scoring and interpretation, however, the scale is distinctive in several ways. The seven components, taken from Rosanoff's theory of personality, are summarized in a recent article [12] as follows:

COMPONENT	SYMBOL	CONSTITUTED OF TRAITS ASSOCIATED WITH:
"Normal"	N	Self-control, self-improvement, inhibition, etc.
Hysteroid	H	Self-preservation, selfishness, crime, etc.
Manic Cycloid	M	Elation, excitement, sociability, etc.
Depressive Cycloid	D	Sadness, retardation, caution, worry, etc.
Autistic Schizoid	A	Daydreams, shyness, sensitiveness, etc.
Paranoid Schizoid	P	Fixed-ideas, restiveness, conceit, etc.
Epileptoid	E	Ecstasy, meticulousness, inspiration, etc.

Each significant yes- or no-response is assigned weighted log-scores of from 1 to 5 points on one or more components. These are totaled to make the 7 raw scores, which in turn are rated from "Very Strong" ($+3$) to "Very Weak" (-3), each rating being further divisible into upper, middle, and lower ranges.

Due to the tendency of many subjects to answer *No* too often while others mark too many items *Yes,* a validation device is provided by which questionnaires showing too many or too few no-responses can be identified and either rejected or accepted provisionally as doubtful. The 1939 article cited describes a new procedure for broadening this range of valid and semi-valid scores by taking into account "combination scores"; i.e., correcting each log-score in terms of scores on the other components.

Reliability coefficients (split-half, corrected) for the seven components range from .70 to .88. Validity, as determined by comparison of scores with case studies and clinical records of the original standardization group, is stated to be very high, "only .355 per cent of the cases showed discrepancy." This, of course, means merely that the weighting of this group's responses was done so carefully that their numerical scores describe them accurately. More impressive are the findings (1939 article) from 705 public service employees, college students, abnormals, and criminals. In one corporation, out of 185 engineering employees selected on the basis of temperament score, only 2 (of whom 1 had originally been rated doubtful) had been discharged for reasons arising out of temperamental maladjustment; 1500 other shop employees similarly selected lost only 18 (1.2 per cent) for like reasons. If these results are typical of what others can

do with this instrument, there can be no question of its high potential value; for the 7 characteristics measured are prima facie of great practical and theoretical importance.

A more explicit account might well have been given of the methods and criteria employed in obtaining the original standardization groups, beyond the bare statement that they were "selected" from state prison, state hospitals, homes for indigents, and private patients.

Scoring the Humm-Wadsworth—also taking it—is a time-consuming enterprise. This, of course, is a minor criticism, but it does affect the chances of error. More hazardous, perhaps, is the practice of employing distinctly pathological categories (even when valid), such as "Hysteroid," "Paranoid," "Manic," "Epileptoid," etc., in characterizing "normal" subjects. Even the qualifying "Border-line" or "Moderately Weak" does not altogether eliminate the stigma. The authors are justified in forbidding mention of these terms or giving out scores; but under pressure from advisees (curious, perhaps, about the large H, P, M, E, etc., on their blanks), or employers or others with a legitimate interest in the diagnoses, there is always the risk of unintentionally using aloud the terms in which one is thinking. Whether the answer lies in substituting more innocuous component-names, the reviewer does not know; but he feels the need of reassurance.

P. E. Vernon, Lecturer in Psychology, University of Glasgow. [Review of the Second Edition.] This test is, in the reviewer's opinion, much the best of the many questionnaires which are supposed to measure several different traits simultaneously. First, it is based on a logically worked out classification of normal and abnormal personalities, instead of being aimed at some ill-defined hotch-potch like introversion or psychoneurotic tendency. Rosanoff's seven-fold classification may or may not be widely accepted, but his components are clear-cut and should be fairly distinctive. These components are the normal or rational inhibition tendency, the hysteroid or antisocial tendency, the manic, depressive, autistic, paranoid, and epileptoid tendencies. One defect in the authors' presentation is that they do not tell us the actual amount of correlation between the scores of a normal group on these various components. However there should be far less overlapping than between introversion, emotionality, and submissiveness.

Secondly, the items of the questionnaire have been empirically validated. Each scorable response has been proved to differentiate persons who are high in one of the components from other persons, and the criterion for selecting the persons high in each component consisted of psychiatric case-studies. A complaint must, however, be raised here about the authors' data on validity. They fail to state the numbers of persons representing each component, with whom this validation was carried out. Almost certainly the numbers were too small, since the total for all seven components was only 436. Again we are told that the scale as a whole was validated by comparing its diagnoses with psychiatric case-studies of additional subjects, yielding a "coefficient of validity of +.98 ± .01." But the numbers of subjects and the extent of agreement with the case studies are not given. If the validity is as good as it is claimed, then to withhold such important details is stupid.

A third point is the admission that some 25 per cent of presumably normal persons and 45 per cent of abnormal patients produce invalid blanks, usually through being too negativistic or too suggestible. Checks are provided for determining when the blanks have been filled in sufficiently conscientiously to be accepted as valid. A recent article provides a new scoring method, again based on empirical investigations, which allows many of the previously unacceptable blanks to be scored. The scoring is, unfortunately, very elaborate; but this is justified by the usefulness of the results.

Another apparently unique feature is the retention in the scale of items which were proved invalid during the final standardization, on the grounds that the response to an item is not determined by that item alone, but also by the context in which it occurs. This means that half the items are not scored at all, and that the scale takes a very long time to answer. Again the trouble seems to be worth while.

Finally, we are particularly pleased to see restrictions imposed on the sale of the test. In the future it will only be supplied to members and associates of the American Psychological Association or the American Psychiatric Association, to qualified employment managers, and the like. There is far too much commercialism about present-day mental testing. It would be one of the greatest advances in the history of testing if psychologists would forego some of their royalties, and only sell intelligence, educational, and personality tests to persons competent to use them wisely.

For a review by Daniel A. Prescott, see 920.

[1224]

Information Blank EA: A Questionnaire on Emotional Adjustment, Provisional Form. Grades 10-16; 1938; 1 form; $1.00 per 50 machine-scorable test-answer sheets; 10¢ per specimen set; nontimed (10-20) minutes; H. T. Manuel, F. J. Adams, and Paul White; Austin, Tex.: Steck Co.

Stanley G. Dulsky, Chief Psychologist, Rochester Guidance Center, Rochester, New York. The *Information Blank EA* is "a questionnaire on emotional adjustment" designed for use with senior high school and college students and may be scored either by hand or by machine. It consists of thirty questions "of the type commonly used in inventories of emotional adjustment and of the type which psychiatric and clinical experience have found useful in dealing with personality difficulties." The questions are directed toward the individual's internal (as opposed to external) adjustment and are concerned mainly with feelings of anxiety, guilt, tension, and fantasy. Such questions are more difficult to answer than those applying to a person's overt behavior. "Its purpose is to direct attention to the emotional difficulties of students in school and college and to furnish a little of the personal information needed in student counseling."

It must be clearly understood that this blank is now only in provisional form. Correspondence with Mr. Manuel, one of the authors, revealed the following data: (*a*) Reliability of the test as determined by repetition of it to 98 college freshman after an interval of one to nine days is $r = .89$. (*b*) "The total score did *not* select freshmen who later became patients of the university psychiatrist." (*c*) "A psychiatric study . . . of a group of 14 students in a class in mental hygiene showed only moderate agreement with test scores."

It is obvious from the above that although the reliability is satisfactory the validity is not. To this reviewer the *raison d'être* of such a blank is its potentiality for selecting from a large group of students those who need psychiatric assistance. Did those students who made low scores (indicating emotional difficulty) need psychiatric help? This is another method of evaluating the efficacy of the blank. On this point we have no information.

Manuel stated that much of the information needed to evaluate the blank is still lacking. Further work is planned and is being done by the authors. It is too early to make a final judgment about the value of this blank and, therefore, it cannot now be recommended for use.

[1225]

Interests and Activities: Tests 8.2b and 8.2c. Grades 7-12; 1939; 2 forms (both of which must be given); an experimental edition; 3¢ per test; 1¢ per machine-scorable answer sheet; 15¢ per key to classification of items; nontimed (40) minutes; Chicago, Ill.: Evaluation in the Eight Year Study, Progressive Education Association.

REFERENCES

1 RATHS, LOUIS. "Evaluating the Program of Lakeshore School." *Ed Res B* 17:57-84 Mr 16 '38.
2 SHEVIAKOV, G. V., AND FRIEDBERG, JEAN. *Evaluation of Personal and Social Adjustment:* Report of Progress of the Study. Chicago, Ill.: Evaluation in the Eight Year Study, Progressive Education Association, 1939. Pp. iii, 65. $0.75. Paper, mimeographed.
3 AMSTUTZ, WADE S. "A Study of Characteristics of Education Freshmen Who Entered Ohio State University in 1938." *J Exp Ed* 8:289-92 Mr '40.
4 BITTNER, REIGN H., AND BORDIN, EDWARD. "The Study of an Interest Questionnaire." *J Exp Ed* 8:270-7 Mr '40.
5 CAHOW, ARTHUR C. "Relationships of Test Scores of Education College Freshmen to Grades in Selected Courses." *J Exp Ed* 8: 284-9 Mr '40.
6 SHEVIAKOV, G. V., AND FRIEDBERG, JEAN. "Use of Interest Inventories for Personality Study." *J Ed Res* 33:692-7 My '40.
7 SHEVIAKOV, G. V., AND FRIEDBERG, JEAN. "Use of Interest Inventories for Personality Study," pp. 87-90. In *Official Report of 1940 Meeting:* American Educational Research Association, A Department of the National Education Association, St. Louis, Missouri, February 24-27, 1940. Washington, D. C.: American Educational Research Association, May 1940. Pp. 192. $1.50. Paper.

[1226]

Interest Index: Test 8.2a. Grades 7-12; 1939; 1 form; revision of Test 8.2; 3¢ per test; 1¢ per machine-scorable answer sheet; 10¢ per key to classification of items; 5¢ per explanation sheet and interpretation guide; $2 per set of stencils for machine scoring; nontimed (40) minutes; Chicago, Ill.: Evaluation in the Eight Year Study, Progressive Education Association.

REFERENCES

1 RATHS, LOUIS. "Evaluating the Program of Lakeshore School." *Ed Res B* 17:57-84 Mr 16 '38.
2 SHEVIAKOV, G. V., AND FRIEDBERG, JEAN. *Evaluation of Personal and Social Adjustment:* Report of Progress of the Study. Chicago, Ill.: Evaluation in the Eight Year Study, Progressive Education Association, 1939. Pp. iii, 65. $0.75. Paper, mimeographed.
3 SHEVIAKOV, G. V., AND FRIEDBERG, JEAN. "Use of Interest Inventories for Personality Study." *J Ed Res* 33:692-7 My '40.
4 SHEVIAKOV, G. V., AND FRIEDBERG, JEAN. "Use of Interest Inventories for Personality Study," pp. 87-90. In *Official Report of 1940 Meeting:* American Educational Research Association, A Department of the National Education Association, St. Louis, Missouri, February 24-27, 1940. Washington, D. C.: American Educational Research Association, May 1940. Pp. 192. $1.50. Paper.

[1227]

Interest Questionnaire: Games and Sports: Test 8.3. Grades 9-12; 1939; an experimental form; 5¢ per test; 1¢ per machine-scorable answer sheet; $1.50 per set of stencils for machine scoring; [W. H. Lauritsen]; Chicago, Ill.: Evaluation in the Eight Year Study, Progressive Education Association.

[1228]

Interest-Values Inventory. Grades 9-16 and adults; 1939; 1 form; $7.20 per 100; 35¢ per record sheet; 20¢ per specimen set; nontimed (30) minutes; J. B. Maller and Edward M. Glaser; New York: Bureau of Publications, Teachers College, Columbia University.

REFERENCES

1 GLASER, E. M. *A Determination of Personality Patterns through Measurements of the Relative Dominance of Certain Basic Personality Interests.* Unpublished master's thesis, University of Kansas, 1936. Pp. 82.
2 GLASER, EDWARD M., AND MALLER, JULIUS B. "The Measurement of Interest Values." *Char and Pers* 9:67-81 S '40.

Loyola Ed Digest 15:9 N '39. Austin G. Schmidt. This inventory is designed to measure the relative dominance of four major types of interest or basic values within the individual: theoretic, esthetic, social, and economic. *

[1229]

Inventory of Factors STDCR. College; 1940; 1 form; $2.25 per 50; $1 per scoring key; 15¢ per specimen set; nontimed (30) minutes; J. P. Guilford; Beverly Hills, Calif.: Sheridan Supply Co.

REFERENCES

1 GUILFORD, J. P., AND GUILFORD, RUTH B. "Personality Factors D, R, T, and A." *J Abn and Social Psychol* 34:21-36 Ja '39.

[1230]

Jones Personality Rating Scale. High school; 1939; 1½¢ per scale; Harold J. Jones; New York: Gregg Publishing Co.

[1231]

Minnesota Rating Scale for Personal Qualities and Abilities, Fourth Revision. College students and adults; 1925-38; reprinted from the *Minnesota Rating Scale for Home Economics Teachers* (out of print); $1 per 100; 10¢ per specimen set; Clara M. Brown; Minneapolis, Minn.: University of Minnesota Press.

REFERENCES

1 BROWN, CLARA M. *An Evaluation of the Minnesota Rating Scale for Home Economics Teachers.* Minneapolis, Minn.: University of Minnesota Press, 1931. Pp. 29. $0.50. Paper.

[1232]

Occupational Personality Inventory. Applicants for sales positions in department stores; 1939; 1 form; $3 per 100; 15¢ per specimen set; nontimed (10) minutes; Arthur F. Dodge; New York: Psychological Corporation.

REFERENCES

1 DODGE, ARTHUR F. "Social Dominance and Sales Personality." *J Appl Psychol* 22:132-9 Ap '38.
2 DODGE, ARTHUR F. "What Are the Personality Traits of the Successful Sales-Person?" *J Appl Psychol* 22:229-38 Je '38.
3 DODGE, ARTHUR F. "Personality Measuring Stick." *Retailing* (Executive Edition) F 13'39.

[1233]

P. Q. or Personality Quotient Test, 1938 Revision. Grades 7-13; 1936-38; 2 editions; the title on the test booklet is *Inventory of Activities and Interests;* $5.00 per 100; 25¢ per specimen set; $2 per 100 machine-scorable answer sheets; nontimed (30-40) minutes; Henry C. Link with the assistance of G. K. Bennett, Rose G. Anderson, Sydney Roslow, and P. G. Corby; New York: Psychological Corporation.
a) FOR BOYS AND YOUNG MEN.
b) FOR GIRLS AND YOUNG WOMEN.

REFERENCES

1 LINK, HENRY C. "A Test of Four Personality Traits of Adolescents." *J Appl Psychol* 20:527-34 O '36.

1.1 LINK, HENRY C. "Personality Can Be Acquired." *Readers Digest* 29:1-4 D '36.
2 GIBBONS, CHARLES C. "A Short Scoring Method for the Link P.Q. Test." *J Appl Psychol* 22:653-6 D '38.
3 LINK, HENRY C. *The Rediscovery of Man*, pp. 55-90. New York: Macmillan Co., 1938. Pp. xi, 257. $1.75. (London: Macmillan & Co., Ltd., 1939. 7s. 6d.)
4 THOMSON, WILLIAM A. "An Evaluation of the P.Q. (Personality Quotient) Test." *Char and Pers* 6:274-92 Je '38.
5 DRAKE, MARGARET J.; ROSLOW, SYDNEY; AND BENNETT, GEORGE K. "The Relationship of Self-Rating and Classmate Rating on Personality Traits." *J Exp Ed* 7:210-3 Mr '39.

Douglas Spencer, Assistant Professor of Psychology, Queens College. The difficulties of personality measurement are so numerous and baffling that they invite a tolerant and respectful consideration for new attempts to overcome them when claims are limited by scientific caution and supporting data are made available.

The so-called "PQ Test," however, has little claim to such consideration. Probably no other test has been introduced to such a vast popular audience with such confident claims, before its promise could be verified. Witness: "The well-known 'IQ' or intelligence quotient is a measure of the kind of intelligence required in school—a test in terms of what a person *knows* about things and people. The 'PQ' or personality quotient is a new measure of what a person *does* about things and people. It is a yardstick of the traits required to get along in the world." [1.1]

If the popular reader were astonished at this great accomplishment, or a bit skeptical as to some of the confident directions for developing personality revealed as "findings," he was reassured by a note that "the scientific details of the construction of the test are described in the October (1936) Journal of Applied Psychology."

This citation is disappointing. Anticipating, on the basis of the claims, evidence of validity and trait isolation if not age-level norms comparable to the MA, one finds little more than a report of progress and promise. There is an interesting armchair discussion of the author's theory that personality is measured by "the extent to which the individual has learned to convert his energy into habits and skills which influence and serve other people." The test held to incorporate the assumptions underlying this theory is another self-report inventory. There are the usual stepped-up, odd-even reliability coefficients for the preliminary form. An item analysis is described. But the crucial question of validation is treated as follows: "If the general assumptions made in this study are correct then the validity of the scale

in terms of the conventional measures of validity is of secondary importance. The primary problem is a scale which reasonably exemplifies these fiats, both logically and statistically." [1]

Confident claims have been repeated in other popular articles and also in the publisher's catalogue (Catalogue of Test Division of the Psychological Corporation, 1939 Edition) : "By means of concrete questions five personality traits are measured: extroversion, social aggressiveness, self-determination, economic self-determination, adjustment to the opposite sex." If the test measures these or any other traits significant to personality functioning, this reviewer has been unable to find the evidence.

Nor can the manual of the 1938 revision be accused of understatement: "This test . . . is unique in that its validity has been demonstrated in a nation-wide study of 74 schools, as detailed on pages 11 and 12." Page 11 reports a classification of 1138 students from different high schools into four groupings of boys and girls based on teachers' ratings as to scholarship and leadership. Means and standard deviation of Scale X scores are given for these groupings and indicate that the groups rated high as leaders scored higher on Scale X on the average than those rated low in leadership. This rough comparison of an unvalidated instrument with a criterion as inadequate as teachers' ratings does not achieve validation. Since page 12 yields only a listing of schools "participating in the standardization," the evidence for the claim of nation-wide demonstration of validity is, after ten years, still unreported.

As to reliabilities, those reported are based on a tryout of an earlier form (1936) on 421 boys. The five scales yielded odd-even, corrected coefficients ranging from .73 to .87, according to the manual. These are too low for individual prediction. No evidence is found in the manual as to the reliability of the 1938 revision, which offers separate forms for boys and girls.

Of course the instrument is not a "test" in the strict sense of the term, and certainly does not "measure what a person does about things and people." It is a self-report blank inviting the subject, under his signature, to respond to highly vague and subjective questions many of which he may not be able or willing to answer. The first page offers an easy opportunity for the kind of deception revealed on other blanks of this kind. Here each subject can make a good impression by checking lists of group activities in which he has taken "an active part," hobbies at which he "spends a great deal of effort," games (athletics) in which he "practices hard and regularly," etc. The 150 items which follow are little different from those found in older self-report inventories. The manual describes them as "questions regarding habits and activities, rather than feelings and emotions." Nevertheless, there are many questions like the following : Does your temper occasionally explode? Do you cry when you are angry? Are you usually in a cheerful or happy frame of mind? Do you often get discouraged? Do your classmates often make remarks that hurt your feelings? Are you a rather nervous person? Are you planning to get married before you are 25?

The chief difference from other attempts of its kind is the introduction of the PQ score. PQ is derived from the scoring of only Scale X which the author assumes to be a measure of extroversion $[PQ = \dfrac{17}{\sigma}(X - M) + 100$, the mean PQ value for each sex and for each grade grouping being 100]. The promise of comparability with the IQ falls far short. Lacking evidence of validity, it is not easy to justify such a promising label as "Personality Quotient" except on the basis of market appeal.

Simon H. Tulchin, Consulting Psychologist, 136 East 57th St., New York, New York. This is a revision of an earlier test and consists of 150 questions which are intended to measure the personality of normal students in grades 7 to 13—ages 12 to 20. Separate inventories have been provided for boys and girls. These inventories are designed to measure five traits: personality, which includes nearly all the items ; social initiative, which includes items concerned with "habits" of taking initiative in dealing with people ; self-determination, or items representing "habits" of doing things considered desirable even if unpleasant ; economic self-determination, or those items which consist of "habits" of earning money ; and adjustment to the opposite sex, which includes "habits" of action toward members of the opposite sex.

Percentile norms based on 3,131 tests given to students in 74 schools throughout the country are recorded separately for each subtest for boys and for girls in grades 6, 7-8, 9-10,

11-12, and 13. Reliability has been determined from the 1936 edition administered to 421 boys. The reliability for each of the five scales was computed on the basis of the correlation between the odd and even scores, and the coefficients of reliability range between .73 and .88.

The definition of personality is a narrow and limited definition which considers personality in terms of "the possession of habits which interest and serve other people." "Personality is measured by the extent to which the individual has learned to convert his energies into habits and skills which *interest* and *serve* other people." "Our theory of personality assumes that it is the result of habits which can be developed just as education now develops the habits measured by scholastic tests." Having determined the weak points by means of the test, a personality building program can be developed for individuals and groups. The test "also lifts the subject of personality to the wholesome level of normal psychology and the practical problems of habit formation." The authors assert that habits and activities are stressed in the test questions rather than feelings and emotions, yet we find such questions as : "Do you frequently lose your temper?" "Do your classmates often make remarks which hurt your feelings?" "Do you often brood over your mistakes or hard luck?" A number of questions which seem significant carry no scoring value, as for example, "Do you often just sit and think or imagine things?" A number of questions which deal with adjustment to the opposite sex, such as, for example, "Have you had a steady girl friend for three months or more?" or, "Are you indifferent to girls?", certainly must have different meaning to a ten-year-old than to a twenty-year-old, but no attempt is made to consider this problem.

A table is presented for the purpose of converting the total score obtained on the personality test into a P.Q., or Personality Quotient, interpreted in the same way as the familiar intelligence quotient, with a P.Q. of 100 as average. Without presenting any evidence, it is claimed that the P.Q. indicates "the development or growth of the individual's personality," and is taken to be "valuable in giving a measure of effective personality."

Link evidently accepts replies to a questionnaire as factual data and seems satisfied in assigning Personality Quotients on admittedly partial sampling of personality traits. He attacks critics who demand that personality tests demonstrate their validity and suggests that "some of the criticism of the validity of personality scales should be directed rather at the situation which makes validation difficult." [1] On page one of the manual we find the statement that the test "is unique in that its validity has been demonstrated in a nationwide study of 74 schools, as detailed on pages 11 and 12." When we turn to these pages we find that only one attempt to validate the test is recorded by comparing scores made by 1,138 students who were classified by their teachers into four categories of leadership and scholarship. There follows merely a list of representative schools which participated in the standardization.

Determining the validity of a personality test is unquestionably difficult but it must remain its most essential requisite. It seems naive to assume that personality is but an aggregate of "habits" and activities which can be developed and modified by the simple process of habit training. It is equally dangerous to disregard the possibility that psychopathologic processes can be easily concealed by giving "proper" answers to test questions.

For reviews by C. M. Louttit and Edmund G. Williamson, see 921.

[1234]
P-S Experience Blank: Psycho-Somatic Inventory. Late adolescents and adults; 1938; 1 form; $1.25 per 25; 25¢ per specimen set; nontimed (20-60) minutes; Ross A. McFarland and Clifford P. Seitz; New York: Psychological Corp.

REFERENCES

1 McFarland, Ross A., and Seitz, Clifford P. "A Psycho-Somatic Inventory." *J Appl Psychol* 22:327-39 Ag '38.
2 Mosier, Charles I. "On the Validity of Neurotic Questionnaires." *J Social Psychol* 9:3-16 F '38.

Doncaster G. Humm, Wadsworth-Humm Personnel Service, Los Angeles, California. The authors state that the purpose of this inventory is to help physicians, clinicians, social workers, and school psychologists ascertain neurotic tendencies in late adolescents and adults.

Some objection may be had to the term "neurotic." This seems to be a euphemism which has gained currency as a substitute for "psychopathic." If psychoneuroses or neuroses are connoted by this term and findings are confined to hysteria, psychasthenia, neurasthenia, and the anxiety neuroses, this connota-

tion should be made plain. In such a case some distinction should be provided to differentiate between these four subclasses.

Reliability for the inventory was determined by the split-half method and found to be .87, or 51 per cent better than chance. This is about a 3 to 1 chance that retesting will give about the same result as the original testing. From retesting 52 males a reliability of .75 or 34 per cent better than chance was secured. This offers a retest chance of 2.02 to 1.

The inventory indicates trustworthy differences between the "normal group" and the "psychoneurotic group" in both males and females. For males the average chance seems to be 1.83 to 1 that it will differentiate between individuals; for females, 1.48 to 1. The high probable error for individual scores seems to be due to the selection of "normal" and "neurotic" subjects. There is considerable overlapping between these two control groups.

This inventory represents an excellent attack on the problem of determining individuals incapacitated by reason of personality. The methods used are sound. Probably the only weakness is in the selection of subjects, a weakness against which it is exceedingly difficult to guard.

Charles I. Mosier, Assistant Professor of Psychology and Assistant University Examiner, University of Florida. This inventory consists of two scales of forty-six questions each, to be answered "often," "at times," "seldom," or "never," designed to measure physiological dysfunction and psychological maladjustment, and to select those individuals in a normal group who exhibit excessive psychoneurotic tendency. The manual gives no description of construction, but does refer to such a description. It provides directions for administration and scoring, and percentile norms for each sex separately for normal and for psychoneurotic groups, based, except for the normal men, on less than two hundred subjects. The manual also reports reliability coefficients and validating evidence. Particularly noteworthy is the modesty of the manual's claim: "No questionnaire can be a final basis for classification, although it should direct attention to those cases which require further investigation."

The items composing the inventory were selected on the basis of their power to differentiate a group of psychoneurotics from a group of normal subjects. This mode of validation, granting the assumption that there is some single trait in which psychoneurotics differ from normal subjects, is superior to that used for many personality schedules. However, the work of Landis and his co-workers renders the validity of that assumption at least doubtful. The reported reliability coefficients by the Spearman-Brown method, based on only 100 normal subjects, were .86 and .80 respectively for Parts I and II, and .87 for the entire test. Test-retest coefficients based on only 52 subjects were .75. These reliabilities are not low by comparison with those of other similar tests, but are too low to justify much faith in the meaning of an individual score.

The validity of the scale is reported in terms of the differences between mean scores for normal and psychoneurotic groups. These differences were from thirteen to nineteen times their standard errors, and indicate, on the surface, unusually high validity, since workers with other inventories usually fail to find any difference of statistical significance. The fact that the validating groups were the same ones as those used in the selection of the items tends to produce, of course, a spuriously high validity, but this effect is mitigated by the fact that the scoring weights were computed on the basis of only a small part of the total number of subjects, and high critical ratios were also found for groups containing none of the individuals used to establish those scoring weights. In connection with validity, the authors' statement: "tubercular or cardiac patients might make equally low scores on the psycho-somatic inventory as the neurotics," [1] should be noted.

The correlation coefficient between the two parts of the scale as reported (but not in the manual) is of the order of the magnitude of .70, which, when corrected for the unreliability of the scales, is seen to approach unity. The scales do not measure two distinct traits, but only one, and that one, if the evidence of other workers with highly similar material is valid, a composite of a number of traits. (Seventeen of the items on the second scale were among the forty shown by Mosier [2] to be measuring six distinct traits. What combination of these traits is represented in any individual score on the *P-S Experience Blank* cannot be determined.) The distinction which the authors

claim between physiological dysfunction and psychological maladjustment is not maintained by their own reported results. Their suggestion, however, that "Experienced clinicians should find the separate items a good basis for further questioning," should be commended.

In general, the authors' modest claim (not repeated in the manual) that: "In a certain percentage of the cases, depending on the degree of cooperation of the subjects, such an inventory will detect the subject in the normal group who might profit by psychiatric guidance and treatment," [1] is probably justified. However, the words, "a certain percentage of cases," should be underscored, and the qualifying phrase, "depending on the degree of cooperation," should be extended to cover a number of other possible distorting factors.

[1235]
Parents Rating Scale. Self and mutual rating of parents; 1935; 1 form; $15 per 100; 25¢ per specimen set; nontimed (60) minutes; Walther Joël and Janet Joël, Los Angeles, Calif.: Walther Joël, Los Angeles City College.

[1236]
Personal History Record, 1937 Revision. Grades 9-16 and adults; 1928-37; a test of emotional stability; 1 form; $2.50 per 25 (No. 24524); 25¢ per manual (No. 24524A); nontimed (30) minutes; Lorin A. Thompson, Jr.; Chicago, Ill.: C. H. Stoelting Co.

REFERENCES

1 THOMPSON, LORIN A., JR. "Personal History, Intelligence, and Academic Achievement." *J Social Psychol* 5:500-7 N '34.

[1237]
Personal Index. Boys in grades 7-9; 1933; 1 form; 75¢ per 25; 25¢ per specimen set; nontimed, (30-40) minutes; Graham C. Loofbourow and Noel Keys; Minneapolis, Minn.: Educational Test Bureau, Inc.

REFERENCES

1 LOOFBOUROW, GRAHAM C. *Test Materials for Problem Behavior Tendencies in Junior High School Boys.* University of California Publications in Education, Vol. 7, No. 1. Berkeley, Calif.: the University, 1932. Pp. 62. $1.25. Paper.
2 LOOFBOUROW, GRAHAM C., AND KEYS, NOEL. "A Group Test of Problem Behavior Tendencies in Junior High School Boys." *J Ed Psychol* 24:641-53 D '33.
3 KEYS, NOEL, AND GUILFORD, MARGARET S. "The Validity of Certain Adjustment Inventories in Predicting Problem Behavior." *J Ed Psychol* 28:641-55 D '37.
4 RIGGS, WINIFRED C. *A Validation of the Loofbourow-Keys Personal Index.* Unpublished master's thesis, University of Denver, 1937. Pp. 47.
5 RIGGS, WINIFRED C., AND JOYAL, ARNOLD E. "A Validation of the Loofbourow-Keys Personal Index of Problem Behavior in Junior High Schools." *J Ed Psychol* 29:194-201 Mr '38.

J. B. Maller, Lecturer in Education, New York University. The test consists of four subtests: False Vocabulary—a test of overstatement; Social Attitudes—each key word or phrase is followed by one socially desirable and three undesirable alternatives (adapted from Raubenheimer); Virtues—(adapted from the moral knowledge tests of Hartshorne and May); Adjustment Questionnaire—(adapted from the psychoneurotic inventories of Woodworth, Mathews, Cady and Symonds).

The discrimination between the problem cases and normal groups on each of the four tests as reported by the authors is surprisingly high. Of particular interest is the evidence presented in the manual that the test results show a higher correlation with behavior ratings obtained after a lag of three years than with similar ratings of behavior obtained at the time the test was given. If this finding were substantiated by repeated studies and based on larger numbers of cases it would be considerable significance.

Numerous recent studies of problem cases reveal consistently that such behavior disorders are as a rule the result of environmental factors, teacher-pupil conflicts, and the like, rather than some inherent difficulty in the child himself. This finding would hardly lead one to expect that maladjustment could be predicted several years in advance on the basis of a series of highly specific pencil-and-paper responses such as those evoked by this test.

The authors indicate that its value might be "destroyed if the test were given in a way to arouse self-consciousness, suspicion, or open resentment." Therein lies the most serious weakness of tests of this type for the results will depend unduly upon the conditions under which the test is given and even upon the personality of the examiner. In spite of the authors' suggestion that the test results must be "interpreted with due scientific caution" it is likely that once such a test is placed in the open market it will be used under conditions quite different from those which prevailed in the process of validation. Diagnosis based on such indiscriminate usage and comparison with the "norms" will result in dubious value to the person using such tests as well as to the science of psychometrics.

A few words should be added about the subtests. Aside from the ethical problem involved in the inclusion of fictitious words there is of course a likelihood that many children will mistake these for similar words which they do know—for example: rettle for rattle, faline for feline, tromer for tremor, etc. It would be more desirable to include real but extremely difficult words. Of course, that involves the probability of an occasional child who may actually know the meaning of a difficult word but that, in the opinion of the reviewer, would be less hazardous than the presentation of fictitious words which differ from real and relatively easy words by a slight variation in spelling. In fact, children who are poor in spelling and who have a fairly good comprehension vocabulary are likely to appear very dishonest on this test.

Even more puzzling is the validity of the Virtues Test. Self-descriptions of a high degree of rectitude have been found in other studies to be indicative of untruthfulness, rather than of high moral standard. But this test is scored in such a way that in many items highly favorable self-descriptions are given positive weights.

Perhaps further research with the test on different groups will throw light on the surprisingly high degree of discrimination which this test yielded in the population upon which it was standardized.

Carl R. Rogers, Professor of Psychology, The Ohio State University. This test was designed primarily for boys, but is applicable both to boys and girls of junior high school age. It is intended to identify the individual who is or may become a serious disciplinary problem.

The test shows evidence of much careful preliminary work. Ten different types of paper-and-pencil tests were tried out on problem and control groups of boys and the degree to which they discriminated was determined. On the basis of this study all but four were discarded, and later one of these was discarded. The remaining tests have been evaluated item by item and only those showing a significant critical ratio have been retained. As revised, the test as a whole shows a critical ratio (difference divided by the standard error of the difference) of 16.8 between a group of 100 San Francisco disciplinary problems and a matched group of unselected high school boys. Between two groups chosen by the principal as the "best" and the "worst" boys in school the test gave a critical ratio of 25, with very little overlapping of score between the two groups. In another study institutionalized delinquent boys were compared with 500 nonproblem boys. Seventy-three per cent of the delinquent boys made scores over 35, while only 21 per cent of the nonproblem boys scored in this group.

An interesting further check on validity was

made by a follow-up study of 130 boys, three years after test scores and behavior ratings had first been obtained. It was discovered that the later behavior status of these boys was slightly more accurately predicted by the original scores on the *Personal Index* than by the original ratings of high school counselors and principals.

In its present form the test consists of three parts. First is a "vocabulary" test, essentially a test of falsification or tendency to make extravagant statements. The second portion is a measure of antisocial attitudes toward school, minor delinquencies, the law, and society. The third portion is a combination of a neurotic inventory (largely from the *Woodworth-Matthews Personal Data Sheet*) and a test of school adjustment. In general the questions are interestingly worded. The use of "yes-no" responses rather than multiple choice in Test 3 seems unfortunate. The manual gives adequate though not complete information regarding the construction and validation of the test.

The most serious drawback to the use of the test is that for the most part it would reveal only the obvious. The alert principal or counselor will know the problem individuals in his school. This test is sufficiently valid to confirm this knowledge, but it goes little further. It would discover a few problem individuals not recognized as such by the school counselor. It does not however, add very significantly to our knowledge of the causes of these tendencies. Even an inspection of the individual responses would give few clues to such causes, except for the twenty-one items on school adjustment in Test 3. The greatest possibility for usefulness would seem to lie in quickly identifying problems in a new group. Thus, given at the outset in a junior or senior high school, the test would select with considerable accuracy those individuals upon whom the personnel workers should concentrate their efforts.

[1238]

Personality and Interest Inventory. Grades 4-9, 9-12; 1935-36; 1 form, 2 levels; Gertrude Hildreth; New York: Bureau of Publications, Teachers College, Columbia University.
a) ELEMENTARY FORM. Grades 4-9; 1935; nontimed (45) minutes; $2.10 per 100; 10¢ per specimen set.
b) HIGH SCHOOL FORM. Grades 9-12; 1936; nontimed (45) minutes; $4.20 per 100; 15¢ per specimen set.

REFERENCES

1 HILDRETH, GERTRUDE. "Adolescent Interests and Abilities." *J Genetic Psychol* 43:65-93 S '33.
2 HILDRETH, GERTRUDE. "An Interest Inventory for High School Personnel Work." *J Ed Res* 27:11-9 S '33.
3 HILDRETH, GERTRUDE, AND KELLER, VICTORIA M. "Results of an Experience Inventory in the High School." *Teach Col Rec* 38:581-92 Ap '37.

Stephen M. Corey, Professor of Educational Psychology and Superintendent of the Laboratory Schools, The University of Chicago. In 1933 the author of the *Personality and Interest Inventory* wrote:

The objection to the questionnaire method when the record is made by the child and unchecked by other methods is that the child may be unable to give an accurate picture of himself with respect to the traits in question or he may intentionally falsify his record to make it fit the picture he wants his teachers and advisors to have of him.[2]

This is a profound criticism of inventories and led the reviewer to expect some research data that would indicate the extent to which the present questionnaires were free from such weakness. No such data were presented however. In a second article the author wrote:

Results from the present questionnaire indicate in the main a serious attitude on the part of the pupils responding, and little attempt to give an imaginary picture in place of the real one. The questionnaire results tally well with known facts about individual pupils.[1]

So far as the reviewer can judge, these were merely the author's casual impressions. No quantitative evidence was presented. As a matter of fact, the reviewer was unable to locate any data that would enable him to judge the value of the *Personality and Interest Inventory*. Inspection of the forms indicates that information of interest is called for and that the format of the sheets as well as the administrative procedures are satisfactory.

The manual of directions to accompany the *Personality and Interest Inventory* includes no data on reliability or validity. The author suggests that the "reliability of the inventory can be determined in three ways: by examining the inner consistency of the record, by comparing the written record with the student's observed conduct, and by studying the change in trend of interest and activity in groups of different age and maturity." No statement appears as to whether this had or had not been done for the inventory under consideration. No norms of any sort appear. No description is given of the source of the items which appear under headings such as: I, Activities; II, Games-Sports; III, School Subjects; IV, Types of Books, etc.

For a review by Jack W. Dunlap, see 924.

[1239]

Personality Inventory. Grades 9-16 and adults;
1931-38; 1 form, 6 scoring scales; $1.75 per 25; 25¢
per 25 individual report blanks; 25¢ per specimen
set; nontimed (25) minutes; Robert G. Bernreuter
(Scales F1-C and F2-S were prepared by John C.
Flanagan); Stanford, Calif.: Stanford University
Press.

REFERENCES

1 BERNREUTER, ROBERT G. *The Valuation of a Proposed New Method for Constructing Personality Trait Tests.* Unpublished doctor's thesis, Stanford University, 1931.
2 FINCH, F. H., AND NEMZEK, C. L. "The Relationship of the Bernreuter Personality Inventory to Scholastic Achievement and Intelligence." *Sch and Soc* 36:594-6 N 5 '32.
3 WELLES, HENRY HUNTER, 3RD. *The Measurement of Certain Aspects of Personality among Hard of Hearing Adults.* Columbia University, Teachers College, Contributions to Education, No. 545. Rudolf Pintner, faculty sponsor. New York: Bureau of Publications, the College, 1932. Pp. viii, 77.
4 BENNETT, WILHELMINA. *A Study of Several Well Known Personality Tests.* [New York: Psychological Corporation], October 1933. Pp. ii, 25. Paper, mimeographed. Out of print.
5 BERNREUTER, ROBERT G. "The Measurement of Self-Sufficiency." *J Abn and Social Psychol* 28:291-300 O-D '33.
6 BERNREUTER, ROBERT G. "The Theory and Construction of the Personality Inventory." *J Social Psychol* 4:387-405 N '33.
7 BERNREUTER, ROBERT G. "Validity of the Personality Inventory." *Personnel J* 11:383-6 Ap '33.
8 BROTEMARKLE, R. A. "What the Bernreuter Personality Inventory Does Not Measure." *J Appl Psychol* 17:559-63 O '33.
9 CAHOON, G. P. "The Use of the Bernreuter Personality Inventory in the Selection of Student Teachers." *Univ H Sch J* 13:91-103 D '33.
10 HARGAN, JAMES. "The Reaction of Native White Convicts to the Bernreuter Personality Inventory." *Psychol Clinic* 22:138-40 Je-Ag '33.
11 MARSHALL, HELEN. "Clinical Applications of the Bernreuter Personality Inventory." *Psychol B* 30:601-2 O '33.
12 BERNREUTER, ROBERT G. "The Imbrication of Tests of Introversion-Extroversion and Neurotic Tendency." *J Social Psychol* 5:184-201 My '34.
13 DARLEY, JOHN G., AND INGLE, DWIGHT J. "An Analysis of the Bernreuter Personality Inventory in Occupational Guidance," pp. 32-41. In *Research Studies in Individual Diagnosis.* Edited by D. G. Paterson. University of Minnesota, Bulletin of the Employment Stabilization Research Institute, Vol. 3, No. 4. Minneapolis, Minn.: University of Minnesota Press, August 1934. Pp. 55. Paper. Out of print.
14 GILLILAND, A. R. "What Do Introversion-Extroversion Tests Measure?" *J Abn and Social Psychol* 28:407-11 Ja-Mr '34.
15 JOHNSON, WINIFRED B. "The Effect of Mood on Personality Traits as Measured by Bernreuter." *J Social Psychol* 5:515-22 N '34.
16 KUZNETS, G. "Analysis of Bernreuter's Personality Inventory." (Abstract.) *Psychol B* 31:585 '34.
17 LANDIS, CARNEY, AND KATZ, S. E. "The Validity of Certain Questions Which Purport to Measure Neurotic Tendencies." *J Appl Psychol* 18:343-56 Je '34.
18 LASLETT, H. R., AND BENNETT, ELIZABETH. "A Comparison of Scores of Two Measures of Personality." *J Abn and Social Psychol* 28:459-61 Ja-Mr '34.
19 LAYCOCK, SAM R. "The Bernreuter Personality Inventory in the Selection of Teachers." *Ed Adm and Sup* 20:59-63 Ja '34.
20 LENTZ, THEODORE F., JR. "Reliability of Opinionaire Technique Studied Intensively by the Retest Method." *J Social Psychol* 5:338-64 Ag '34.
21 PERRY, RAYMOND CARVER. *A Group Factor Analysis of the Adjustment Questionnaire.* University of Southern California, Southern California Educational Monographs, 1933-34 Series, No. 5. Los Angeles, Calif.: University of Southern California Press, 1934. Pp. xi, 93. $1.50.
22 STAGNER, ROSS. "Validity and Reliability of the Bernreuter Personality Inventory." *J Abn and Social Psychol* 28:413-8 Ja-Mr '34.
23 BERGEN, GARRET L. *Use of Tests in the Adjustment Service,* pp. 51-2. Adjustment Service Series Report [No.] 4. New York: American Association for Adult Education, 1935. Pp. 70. Paper. Out of print.
24 BERNREUTER, ROBERT G. "Chance and Personality Inventory Scores." *J Ed Psychol* 26:279-83 Ap '35.
25 BLOOM, BENJAMIN S. *Further Validation of the Bernreuter Personality Inventory.* Unpublished master's thesis, Pennsylvania State College, 1935. Pp. 48.
26 BURNHAM, PAUL S., AND CRAWFORD, ALBERT B. "The Vocational Interests and Personality Test Scores of a Pair of Dice." *J Ed Psychol* 26:508-12 O '35.
27 DODGE, ARTHUR F. *Occupational Ability Patterns.* Columbia University, Teachers College, Contributions to Education, No. 658. Harry Dexter Kitson, faculty sponsor. New York: Bureau of Publications, the College, 1935. Pp. v, 97. $1.60.
28 FLANAGAN, JOHN C. *Factor Analysis in the Study of Personality.* Stanford University, Calif.: Stanford University Press, 1935. Pp. x, 103. $1.25. Paper, lithotyped. (London: Oxford University Press. 6s.)
29 FLANAGAN, JOHN C. "Technical Aspects of Multi-Trait Tests: A Reply to Dr. Lorge." *J Ed Psychol* 26:641-51 D '35.
30 FRANK, BENJAMIN. "Stability of Questionnaire Response." *J Abn and Social Psychol* 30:320-4 O-D '35.
31 LANDIS, CARNEY; ZUBIN, JOSEPH; AND KATZ, SIEGFRIED E. "Empirical Evaluation of Three Personality Adjustment Inventories." *J Ed Psychol* 26:321-30 My '35.
32 LINE, W., AND GRIFFIN, J. D. M. "The Objective Determination of Factors Underlying Mental Health." *Am J Psychiatry* 91:833-42 Ja '35.
33 LINE, W.; GRIFFIN, J. D. M.; AND ANDERSON, G. W. "The Objective Measurement of Mental Stability." *J Mental Sci* 81:61-106 Ja '35.
34 LORGE, IRVING. "Personality Traits by Fiat: [Part] I, The Analysis of the Total Trait Scores and Keys of the Bernreuter Personality Inventory." *J Ed Psychol* 26:273-8 Ap '35.
35 LORGE, IRVING. "Personality Traits by Fiat: [Part] II, A Correction." *J Ed Psychol* 26:652-4 D '35.
36 LORGE, IRVING; BERNHOLZ, ELNA; AND SELLS, SAUL B. "Personality Traits by Fiat: [Part] II, The Consistency of the Bernreuter Personality Inventory by the Bernreuter and by the Flanagan Keys." *J Ed Psychol* 26:427-34. S '35.
37 ZERILLI, VIRGINIA I. "Note on Scoring Tests of Multiple Weighted Items." *J Ed Psychol* 26:395-7 My '35.
38 BILLS, MARION A., AND WARD, L. W. "Testing Salesmen of Casualty Insurance." *Personnel J* 15:55-8 Je '36.
38.1 GUILFORD, J. P., AND GUILFORD, R. B. "Personality Factors S, E, and M and their Measurement." *J Psychol* 2:109-27 '36.
39 CONWAY, CLIFFORD B. "A New Scoring Apparatus for the Bernreuter Personality Inventory." *J Appl Psychol* 20:264-5 Ap '36.
40 JOHNSON, ELEANOR HOPE. "Objective Tests, Including the Bernreuter Personality Inventory, as Constructive Elements in a Counseling Technique." *Am J Orthopsychiatry* 6:431-6 Jl '36.
41 SHLAUDEMAN, KARL W. "A New Scale for Scoring the Bernreuter Personality Inventory." *J Social Psychol* 7:483-6 N '36.
42 SPEER, G. S. "The Use of the Bernreuter Personality Inventory as an Aid in the Prediction of Behavior Problems." *J Juvenile Res* 20:65-9 Ap '36.
43 DODGE, ARTHUR F. "Relation of 'Social Dominance' to General Intelligence." *J Ed Psychol* 28:387-90 My '37.
44 DODGE, ARTHUR F. "Social Dominance of Clerical Workers and Sales-Persons as Measured by the Bernreuter Personality Inventory." *J Ed Psychol* 28:71-3 Ja '37.
45 HOLLINGWORTH, LETA S., AND RUST, METTA MAUND. "Application of the Bernreuter Inventory of Personality to Highly Intelligent Adolescents." *J Psychol* 4:287-93 O '37.
46 KEYS, NOEL, AND GUILFORD, MARGARET S. "The Validity of Certain Adjustment Inventories in Predicting Problem Behavior." *J Ed Psychol* 28:641-55 D '37.
47 PINTNER, RUDOLF; FUSFELD, IRVING S.; AND BRUNSCHWIG, LILY. "Personality Tests of Deaf Adults." *J Genetic Psychol* 51:305-27 D '37.
48 ST. CLAIR, WALTER F., AND SEEGERS, J. CONRAD. "Certain Aspects of the Validity of the Bernreuter Personality Inventory." *J Ed Psychol* 28:530-40 O '37.
49 ANDERSON, ROSE G. "Some Technological Aspects of Counseling Adult Women." *J Appl Psychol* 22:455-69 O '38.
50 BAER, LENONA OPAL. *A Comparison of Ratings on the Bernreuter Personality Inventory with Case History Records.* Unpublished master's thesis, State University of Iowa, 1938.
51 BENNETT, GEORGE K. "A Simplified Scoring Method for the Bernreuter Personality Inventory." *J Appl Psychol* 22:390-4 Ag '38.
52 BILLS, MARION A., AND DAVIDSON, CHARLES M. "Study of Inter-relation of Items on Bernreuter Personality Inventory and Strong's Interest Analysis Test, Part VIII, and Their Relation to Success and Failure in Selling Casualty Insurance." *Psychol B* 35:677 N '38.
53 DODGE, ARTHUR F. "Social Dominance and Sales Personality." *J Appl Psychol* 22:132-9 Ap '38.
54 DODGE, ARTHUR F. "What Are the Personality Traits of the Successful Sales-Person?" *J Appl Psychol* 22:229-38 Je '38.
55 FARNSWORTH, PAUL R. "A Genetic Study of the Bernreuter Personality Inventory." *J Genetic Psychol* 52:3-13 Mr '38.
56 FARNSWORTH, PAUL R., AND FERGUSON, LEONARD W. "The Growth of a Suicidal Tendency as Indicated by Score Changes in Bernreuter's Personality Inventory." *Sociometry* 1:339-41 Ja-Ap '38.
57 HORSCH, ALFRED C., AND DAVIS, ROBERT A. "Personality Traits of Juvenile Delinquents and Adult Criminals." *J Social Psychol* 9:57-65 F '38.
58 JARVIE, L. L., AND JOHNS, A. A. "Does the Bernreuter Personality Inventory Contribute to Counseling?" *Ed Res B* 17:7-9+ Ja '38.
59 McQUITTY, LOUIS L. "An Approach to the Measurement of Individual Differences in Personality." *Char and Pers* 7:81-95 S '38.
60 MOSIER, CHARLES I. "On the Validity of Neurotic Questionnaires." *J Social Psychol* 9:3-16 F '38.
61 NEMZEK, CLAUDE L. "The Value of the Bernreuter Personality Inventory for Direct and Differential Prediction of Academic Success as Measured by Teachers' Marks." *J Appl Psychol* 22:576-86 D '38.

62 ST. CLAIR, WALTER F., AND SEEGERS, J. CONRAD. "Certain Aspects of the Validity of the F Scores of the Bernreuter Personality Inventory." J Ed Psychol 29:301-11 Ap '38.

63 STOGDILL, EMILY L., AND THOMAS, MINNIE E. "The Bernreuter Personality Inventory as a Measure of Student Adjustment." J Social Psychol 9:299-315 Ag '38.

64 TRAXLER, ARTHUR. The Use of Tests and Rating Devices in the Appraisal of Personality, pp. 15-7, 40-2. Educational Records Bulletin No. 23. New York: Educational Records Bureau, March 1938. Pp. vii, 80. $1.50. Paper, lithotyped.

65 COOK, P. H. "The Clinical Testing of Personality." Austral J Psychol and Philos 17:151-7 '39.

66 GREENE, J. E., AND STATON, THOMAS F. "Predictive Value of Various Tests of Emotionality and Adjustment in a Guidance Program for Prospective Teachers." J Ed Res 32:653-9 My '39.

67 HATHAWAY, S. R. "The Personality Inventory as an Aid in the Diagnosis of Psychopathic Inferiors." J Consulting Psychol 3:112-7 Jl-Ag '39.

68 KIRKPATRICK, FORREST H. The Measurement of Personality. Psychological Record, Vol. 3, No. 17. Bloomington, Ind.: Prinicipia Press, Inc., October 1939. Pp. 211-24. $0.30. Paper.

69 LAYCOCK, S. R., AND HUTCHEON, N. B. "A Preliminary Investigation into the Problem of Measuring Engineering Aptitude." J Ed Psychol 30:280-8 Ap '39.

70 ST. CLAIR, WALTER F. "The Relation of Scholastic Aptitude to 'Withdrawal' Personality." J Ed Psychol 30:295-302 Ap '39.

71 BABCOCK, HARRIET. "Personality and Efficiency of Mental Functioning." Am J Orthopsychiatry 10:527-31 Jl '40.

Charles I. Mosier, Assistant Professor of Psychology and Assistant University Examiner, University of Florida. The *Personality Inventory* is a multitrait test of the questionnaire type, designed to yield measures on six traits of personality adjustment, viz., neurotic tendency (B1-N), self-sufficiency (B2-S), introversion-extroversion (B3-I), dominance-submission (B4-D), self-confidence (F1-C), and sociability (F2-S). The manual provides a description of the construction and validation of the scales, and reports validity and reliability coefficients. Percentile norms are supplied for each sex at high school, college, and adult levels. The manual reports corrected split-halves reliabilities on college students for the B scales ranging from .85 to .91, and for the F scales of .86 and .78. Reliabilities obtained by other workers have been slightly lower. These reliabilities are rather low to warrant use in work with individuals. Validation was originally against other tests—Thurstone's *Personality Schedule,* Bernreuter's *Self-sufficiency Scale,* Laird's *C2 Introversion Test,* and the Allport's *A-S Reaction Study.* Since the items comprising the *Personality Inventory* were taken from or adapted from these tests originally,[16] it is not surprising that the author can report that "the four traits measured by the *Personality Inventory* are identical with four traits which have been measured by previously validated tests."[6] The validity of the Bernreuter test is thus seen to depend on the validity of these four scales.[60] Of the six personality traits measured, B3-I is identical with B1-N, and only one of the two scales need be used. The F scales were derived from the B scales by factorial analysis of the intercorrelations of total scores,[28] and reduces the four B scales to the two F scales. If the test is used, all of the information contained in the first four B scales, is obtained by use of the F scales only.

Other work by factor analysis of individual responses [38a, 60] indicates that the B1-N scale measures a composite of at least six identifiable traits, which may combine in any unknown proportions to yield a particular score. Attempts to validate the test clinically have, in general, been unsuccessful, due to the heterogeneity of the traits combined in a single total score. While Stagner[22] reports a subjectively observed agreement between scores and interview impressions (the interviews were made with knowledge of the scores) for selected cases, the general conclusion from clinical use is that while an extremely high score probably indicates maladjustment, a low score does not indicate adjustment. Landis and co-workers[17, 31] found that none of the Bernreuter scales would differentiate groups of normal college students from groups of hospitalized psychotic and psychoneurotic patients. Their conclusion concerning the validity of the test is probably the best guide to its use.

This analysis, together with the previous studies . . . indicates clearly the unsatisfactory nature of the personality inventories at present available. Until we have personality inventories which measure or at least indicate those factors in the life of the individual which the inventory purports to measure, psychologists can do no other than regard these questionnaires as instruments of research not yet ready for general application.[6] Even if the test does select the individual in need of psychiatric advice, the test user should remember that the assignment of the test title as a trait does not constitute a diagnosis of any value.

The *Personality Inventory* does, however, present an extremely useful checklist of symptoms, and without regard for the scales or scores from them, a study of the responses to individual questions should be far more revealing in the individual case than the total scores on all six scales.

The usefulness of the test as a group test to select those individuals most in need of mental hygiene is definitely limited. For this purpose the best single scale is probably F1-C. Even so, it must be remembered that while those individuals scoring extremely high are probably in need of assistance, those scoring low cannot be assumed to be adjusted, and some with low scores may be in as great or greater need of assistance as the individual with the highest score.

In the hands of the trained clinical psychologist, the *Personality Inventory* may be an extremely useful instrument, but for other users, even those with a course in "Tests and Measurements," the uncertainties in the field of personality measurement, particularly with the questionnaire type of test, make such tests, in the reviewer's opinion, of little value, and of some potential harm.

Theodore Newcomb, Psychology Department, Bennington College. Certain obvious disadvantages inhere in the method of asking direct yes-or-no questions of subjects who are bound to impute some personal significance to their replies, and who vary in the degree of their willingness to reveal whatever they imagine that significance to be. It is not difficult to prepare such schedules in such a manner that their split-half reliability can be demonstrated to be very satisfactory. But responses are determined by so many factors other than those necessarily involved in the trait ostensibly being measured that the validity of scores yielded by such methods is exceedingly doubtful. The rank order of scores obtained by a given population on a schedule of this type is thus of questionable significance. When given under favorable conditions, however, it is often true that either the high-scoring or the low-scoring individuals—rarely both, for one extreme of most scales is commonly considered more desirable than the other—will be found, following more exact study, actually to be characterized by a considerable degree of the trait in question.

Bernreuter's *Personality Inventory* must be evaluated in terms of this basic methodology, but it is in certain ways unique. As originally published, each reply (yes-no-?) to each of its 125 brief questions received a given score-value for each of four traits. These are neurotic tendency, self-sufficiency, introversion-extroversion, and dominance-submission, respectively labeled as B1-N, B2-S, B3-I, and B4-D. Each of the 125 items was initially selected as having high differentiating power, for one of the four traits, between high and low criterion groups as determined by previously existing

measures of those traits. Each item-response was then weighted for the other three traits, on the basis of empirical differentiating power for those traits.

The split-half reliabilities, as reported both by the author and by other investigators, are satisfactory by common standards, most of them ranging between .85 and .90 when corrected by the Spearman-Brown prophecy formula. But the validity of the several traits can scarcely be regarded as satisfactory, in view of their high intercorrelations. The correlation between B1-N and B3-I is actually higher (.95) than the reliability coefficient of either, and that between B1-N and B4-D (r's of $-.80$ and $-.83$ are reported by the author) is nearly as high as the reliability coefficient of either ($-.80$ and $-.83$). For all practical purposes it must be concluded that B1-N, B3-I, and B4-D are alternative measures of the same thing, whatever it be called. The author himself has proposed that either B1-N or B3-I be discarded.

It may be, of course, that neurotic tendency and introversion are actually indistinguishable, and that submissiveness (or nondominance) is almost equivalent to either of them. But few psychologists are prepared to concede this, and none have obtained such high intercorrelations by other measures. It is probable, therefore, that the method of differential weighting of the same responses is responsible for the apparent equivalence of these traits. For such reasons Flanagan,[28] using Hotelling's method of principal components, has more recently shown from an analysis of responses to the Bernreuter items, that by a revised weighting of item responses two unrelated scores can be obtained. These are tentatively labeled self-confidence and sociability. Self-confidence is by no means the same as Bernreuter's self-sufficiency, nor is sociability closely related to the constellation B1-N, B3-I, B4-D, judging from correlations presented.

If one starts with the assumption that the psychologist's task is to find important human traits which are not correlated, even though it is not quite clear what they represent, the Flanagan scores are certainly among the best personality measures available to date. It should not be forgotten, however, that his results depend upon the particular loading of items which Bernreuter happened to offer him. The only genuine validation of the measure is the empirical demonstration that they correspond to some significant human behavior, and this demonstration may yet be made. If one assumes that traits which it is important to measure may or may not be correlated, measures like the Bernreuter Schedule, which result in intercorrelations as a result of methodological artifacts, will be avoided. If one assumes, with this reviewer, that the results of yes-no-? questionnaires are valuable not for their rank-ordering of individuals but for their isolating of individuals for more intensive clinical or experimental study, one will wonder whether such crude means of obtaining data merit so much statistical refinement, and for one's own purposes (if one is to use such methods at all) will have recourse to briefer schedules which are equally reliable and perhaps more valid.

See also B108 and B358.

[1240]

Personality Inventory for Children. Ages 9-14; 1935; 1 form; $2.00 per 100; 15¢ per specimen set; nontimed (15) minutes; Fred Brown; New York: Psychological Corporation.

REFERENCES

1 BROWN, FRED. *An Experimental Study of the Psychoneurotic Syndrome in Childhood.* Unpublished doctor's thesis, Ohio State University, 1933. Pp. 175.
2 BROWN, FRED. "A Psychoneurotic Inventory for Children between Nine and Fourteen Years of Age." *J Appl Psychol* 18:566-77 Ag '34.
3 BROWN, FRED. "The School as a Subsidiary of the Psychological Clinic in the Prevention of Neuroticism in Childhood." *Ed Method* 13:254-8 F '34.
4 BROWN, FRED. "The Problem of Nervousness and Its Objective Verification in Children." *J Abn and Social Psychol* 31:194-207 Jl-S '36.
5 BROWN, FRED. "Neuroticism of Institution versus Non-Institution Children." *J Appl Psychol* 21:379-83 Ag '37.
6 BROWN, FRED. "Social Maturity and Stability of Non-Delinquents, Photo-Delinquents, and Delinquents." *Am J. Orthopsychiatry* 8:214-9 Ap '38.
7 SPRINGER, N. NORTON. "A Comparative Study of the Psychoneurotic Responses of Deaf and Hearing Children." *J Ed Psychol* 29:459-66 S '38.
8 SPRINGER, N. NORTON, AND ROSLOW, SYDNEY. "A Further Study of the Psychoneurotic Responses of Deaf and Hearing Children." *J Ed Psychol* 29:590-6 N '38.

S. J. Beck, Head Psychologist, Michael Reese Hospital, Chicago, Illinois. This reviewer has not used the inventory. The comments that follow are therefore a reaction entirely to a study of the blank and the accompanying directions.

This inventory consists of eighty items. In the directions accompanying the material the author classifies the items within five categories of personality area—home, school, physical symptoms, insecurity, and irritability. The questionnaire was standardized on "2,748 unselected cases between nine and fourteen years of age from the fourth to the ninth grade inclusive, and including equal distribu-

tion of both sexes." The scoring method has the advantage that it is simplified in the extreme, not even requiring the use of a key.

Examination of the eighty questions in the inventory reveals the difficulty so common in questionnaires. What does the question really mean? For example: "Are you very particular about the things you eat?" "Do your parents get angry with you often?" "Is your mother too strict with you?" The common experience when two or more persons get together to iron out the meanings of the questions in a questionnaire has been much time in mulling over the words and usually disagreement in the end. We are faced here with the old difficulty that the same experience cannot have the same meaning to two individuals. In this connection the author's dependence on unselected children deserves some comment. Unselected material is the lodestone of statistical studies. With intelligent adults having the difficulty they do in pinning down the content of the inventory items how intelligible could these questions have been to children at the average and lower end of the intelligence scale in the ninth, to say nothing of the fourth grades?

A second difficulty with inventories is the problem of how much faith can we put in the answers as speaking truth? This criticism must be asserted in spite of the effort at reassurance in the directions: "These questions have nothing to do with your regular school work. There are no right or wrong answers in this list. No one except the person giving this test will know how you answered the question. You will not be asked to explain your answers." The fact is that children are cagey and the number of untrue answers is pretty certain to vary with the amount of suspiciousness in the child. In other words, the one from whom we most need the truth is by the very fact of his emotional maladjustment, likely to cover it up. Anonymity is the one antidote; but that defeats, of course, the purpose of the questionnaire since it covers up the identity of the individual to be treated. The author's assurance to himself of "a tendency in children to regard the inventory as a sympathetic and unemotional recipient of confidences, which leads us to believe that questions are sometimes answered more truthfully in questionnaires than in person-to-person interviews," sounds a bit naive and inconsistent with clinical experience. The claim for the inventory's usefulness in treatment must again be challenged. The information obtained is at the best descriptive and static; not a presentation of the dynamics producing the overt behavior, i.e., not explanatory. And how can treatment be directed except by knowing the causative sequences? Does, for example, the fact that a child considers his work too hard (Item 66) or that he stutters (Item 7) have the same symptomatic value irrespective of the personality which produces this behavior? Then, too, why the five particular categories? Are they independent variables? The clinician must ask, for example, when is irritability (Category 5) an expression of insecurity (Category 1) or a physical symptom (Category 3)? Will the inventory answer these questions? Or again, when are the physical symptoms emotional reactions and when are they products of actual tissue pathology?

The big difficulty this reviewer senses throughout this questionnaire is the lack of clinical sense. This brings us to our chief criticism, namely the validation on which the author depends. This was based on the literature concerning the neurotic child and statistical technics for final selection of the items. There is no report of validation of findings in individuals' inventories with study of the same individual by other methods. The defect is one which the author, no doubt, shares with much present day study of personality. The fallacy it seems should be simple in its recognition, namely, statistics is a tool of science, an aid to it, but it is not a method of science. It cannot substitute for actual investigation. There is no more royal road to science than there is to any other learning.

A bibliography appended to the directions includes nine titles by the author and three other papers. The clinical literature is represented by its absence.

Carl R. Rogers, Professor of Psychology, The Ohio State University. It is difficult to know the purpose of this carelessly devised instrument. In the original published reference it is discussed as a measure of neurotic tendency, and this would seem to be its most accurate description. In the brief manual there seems to be complete confusion as to whether it is a measure of neuroticism or a measure of behavior maladjustment, and the norms are phrased to indicate the latter view. The fact that symptoms of nervousness, fear, guilt, hypochondria, and worry are not identical with behavior problems in children, is not even considered. Not every problem child is neurotic, nor does every neurotic exhibit behavior problems, but the author of the test seems unaware of this.

The questions are exceedingly direct and obvious, making evasion likely. Few children would give truthful answers to such a question as "Do you usually get headaches when you are told to do something which is disagreeable to you?" Likewise the "yes-no" technique, with no possibility of shaded or neutral responses, seems inexcusable. The questions are concerned primarily with neurotic physical symptoms, worries, fears, and irritability. There are a few questions regarding home and school adjustment.

There is little that can be commended in the construction of the test. The items were chosen from a review of the literature, and the scoring of the items is also based entirely on the literature. With this a priori choice of items, and an a priori method of scoring, the author proceeds to "validate" the test by comparing the group making high scores with those making low scores. This is lifting oneself by the bootstraps with a vengeance! Even this dubious type of validation is only mentioned, and not presented, in the manual.

This reviewer can see little usefulness in such an inventory. It is too blunt in its questions to be of very much help as a preliminary to interviewing. It is certainly not a valid measure of a child's maladjustment. It may be a measure of a child's neurotic tendencies, but no real study has been carried out to indicate whether it does discriminate between stable and neurotic children. The most that can be said for it is that it measures the degree to which children admit the existence of symptoms which are classed in the literature as neurotic.

[1241]
Personality Rating Chart for Preschool Children. Nursery school; 1938; 5¢ per chart; Rachel Stutsman; Detroit, Mich.: Merrill-Palmer School, 71 East Ferry Ave.

REFERENCES

1 WILSON, CHARLES A.; SWEENY, MARY E.; STUTSMAN, RACHEL; CHESIRE, LEONE E.; AND HATT, ELISE. *The Merrill-Palmer Standards of Physical and Mental Growth.* Detroit, Mich.: Merrill-Palmer School, 1930. Pp. ix, 121. $0.50. Paper.

[1242]
Personality Rating Scale for Preschool Children. Nursery school; 1938; 9 schedules; 20¢ per set of 9 schedules; 50¢ per reprint of article in the *Journal*

of Genetic Psychology; Katherine Elliott Roberts and Rachel Stutsman Ball; Detroit, Mich.: Merrill-Palmer School, 70 East Ferry Ave.

a) SCHEDULE 1, ASCENDANCE—SUBMISSION.
b) SCHEDULE 2, ATTRACTIVENESS OF PERSONALITY.
c) SCHEDULE 3, COMPLIANCE WITH ROUTINE.
d) SCHEDULE 4, INDEPENDENCE OF ADULT AFFECTION OR ATTENTION.
e) SCHEDULE 5, PHYSICAL ATTRACTIVENESS.
f) SCHEDULE 6, RESPECT FOR PROPERTY RIGHTS.
g) SCHEDULE 7, RESPONSE TO AUTHORITY.
h) SCHEDULE 8, SOCIABILITY WITH OTHER CHILDREN.
i) SCHEDULE 9, TENDENCY TO FACE REALITY.

REFERENCES

1 ROBERTS, KATHERINE ELLIOTT, AND BALL, RACHEL STUTSMAN. "A Study of Personality in Young Children by Means of a Series of Rating Scales." *J Genetic Psychol* 52:79-149 Mr '38.

[1243]

Personality Schedule, 1929 Edition. College and adults; 1928-30; 1 form; $1.25 per 25; 15¢ per specimen set; nontimed (30-40) minutes; L. L. Thurstone and Thelma Gwinn Thurstone; Chicago, Ill.: University of Chicago Press.

REFERENCES

1 ALLPORT, GORDON W. "The Neurotic Personality and Traits of Self-Expression." *J Social Psychol* 1:524-7 N '30.
2 THURSTONE, L. L., AND THURSTONE, THELMA GWINN. "A Neurotic Inventory." *J Social Psychol* 1:3-30 F '30.
3 HARVEY, O. L. "Concerning the Thurstone 'Personality Schedule.'" *J Social Psychol* 3:240-51 My '32.
4 STAGNER, Ross. "The Intercorrelation of Some Standardized Personality Tests." *J Appl Psychol* 16:453-64 O '32.
5 WILLOUGHBY, RAYMOND ROYCE. "Some Properties of the Thurstone Personality Schedule and a Suggested Revision." *J Social Psychol* 3:401-24 N '32.
6 HERTZBERG, OSCAR E. "Emotional Stability as a Factor in a Teachers College Administration and Training Program." *Ed Adm and Sup* 19:141-8 F '33.
7 HABBE, STEPHEN. "The Selection of Student Nurses." *J Appl Psychol* 17:564-80 O '33.
8 SMITH, HATTIE NESBIT. "A Study of the Neurotic Tendencies Shown in Dementia Praecox and Manic Depressive Insanity." *J Social Psychol* 4:116-28 F '33.
9 STAGNER, ROSS. "Improved Norms for Four Personality Tests." *Am J Psychol* 45:303-7 Ap '33.
10 HANNA, JOSEPH V. "Clinical Procedure as a Method of Validating a Measure of Psychoneurotic Tendency." *J Abn and Social Psychol* 28:435-45 Ja-Mr '34.
11 LANDIS, CARNEY, AND KATZ, S. E. "The Validity of Certain Questions Which Purport to Measure Neurotic Tendencies." *J Appl Psychol* 18:343-56 Je '34.
12 MOORE, HERBERT, AND STEELE, ISABEL. "Personality Tests." *J Abn and Social Psychol* 29:45-52 Ap-Je '34.
13 FARRAM, FREDA. "The Relation of Ascendance-Submission Tendencies to Neurosis." *Austral J Psychol and Philos* 13:228-32 S '35.
14 MORAN, THOMAS F. "A Brief Study of the Validity of a Neurotic Inventory." *J Appl Psychol* 19:180-8 Ap '35.
15 NEPRASH, J. A. "The Reliability of Questions in the Thurstone Personality Schedule." *J Social Psychol* 7:239-44 My '36.
16 CONKLIN, EDMUND S. *Three Diagnostic Scorings for the Thurstone Personality Schedule.* Indiana University Publications, Science Series, No. 6, Bloomington, Ind.: Indiana University Bookstore, 1937. Pp. 25. $0.50. Paper.
17 FEDER, DANIEL D., AND MALLETT, DONALD R. "Validity of Certain Measures of Personality Adjustment." *J Am Assn Col Reg* 13:5-15 O '37.
18 KIRKPATRICK, FORREST H. "The Validity of the Thurstone Personality Schedule." *Proc W Va Acad Sci* 10:204-9 S '37.
19 MOSIER, CHARLES I. "A Factor Analysis of Certain Neurotic Symptoms." *Psychometrika* 2:263-86 D '37.
20 PAI, T.; SUNG, S. M.; AND HSÜ, E. H. "The Application of Thurstone's Personality Schedule to Chinese Subjects." *J Social Psychol* 8:47-72 F '37.
21 SCHOTT, EMMETT, L. "Personality Tests in Clinical Practice." *J Abn and Social Psychol* 32:236-9 Jl-S '37.
22 HALL, MARGARET E. "Mental and Physical Efficiency of Women Drug Addicts." *J Abn and Social Psychol* 33:332-45 Jl '38.
23 KUZNETS, GEORGE M. "An Analysis of a Group of Most Differentiating Items of the Thurstone Personality Schedule. *Psychol B* 35:525 O '38.
24 MOSIER, CHARLES I. "On the Validity of Neurotic Questionnaires." *J Social Psychol* 9:3-16 F '38.
25 REMMERS, H. H.; WHISLER, LAURENCE; AND DUWALD, VICTOR F. " 'Neurotic' Indicators at the Adolescent Level." *J Social Psychol* 9:17-24 F '38.
26 McCANN, WILLIS H. "Responses of Psychotic Patients to the Thurstone Personality Schedule before and after Metrazol Treatment," pp. 187-9. In *Proceedings of the Indiana Academy of Science [for 1938]*, Vol. 48. Edited by Paul Weatherwax. Indianapolis, Ind.: the Academy, State Library, 1939. Pp. xxx, 253. $3.00. Paper.
27 McKINNEY, FRED. "Personality Adjustment of College Students as Related to Factors in Personal History." *J Appl Psychol* 23:660-8 D '39.
28 PINTNER, RUDOLF, AND FORLANO, GEORGE. "A Note on the Relation between Divergent Interests and Emotional Stability." *J Abn and Social Psychol* 34:539-41 O '39.

J. P. Guilford, Professor of Psychology, The University of Southern California. This extensive inventory of 223 questions was prepared in 1928 for the general purpose of singling out those college freshmen who were in need of special attention from psychologist or psychiatrist. Presumably, it is still of greatest value for that and similar purposes, although the variety of duties it has been asked to perform has been larger than that. Beginning with questions, gathered from all sources, that describe symptoms and causes of neurotic disorders of various kinds, the authors selected the final list on the basis of internal consistency, assuming that since the preliminary scoring was based upon every available common description of neurotic conditions, there was no better criterion than the test itself. The 50 highest and 50 lowest students in a population of nearly 700 were criterion groups, a latitude of difference that would result in few, if any, rejections if items are diagnostic at all.

The manual of instructions states that "thirty minutes is ample time for answering the questions" but in the reviewer's experience more time is required by many students. A single score is conveniently obtained in five to six minutes by means of a translucent stencil. No weights are used, which suggests that the schedule would be easily adaptable to machine scoring.

The reliability (split-half) for the total score is given as .95; and for one-half of the inventory as .90. The validity is more or less taken for granted, in view of the accepted symptomatic nature of the questions, assuming, of course, as the authors frankly do, that the student takes the test seriously and does his best to respond truthfully. They point out that only the very rare student would artificially raise his score toward the high (unfavorable) end, and that while an occasional neurotic is overlooked because of falsification, in this case we err on the side of safety.

In the light of factor-analysis studies of such test items since the time this inventory was published, and in view of the more analytical approaches of Bernreuter and Bell, it would seem that the Thurstone schedule would by now have some partial scorings. So extensive a list of questions should have the same analytical possibilities as are exploited in similar inventories. Perhaps such scorings have been developed; to the knowledge of the reviewer they have not yet been published.

The authors warn testers against comparing scores from different groups of individuals, lest the same diagnostic value of the items not obtain. Studies have shown that the same inventory that is validated on one population may not give the expected results when applied to another of different background and mental set. For example, lists of items validated with psychotic and psychopathic individuals may not give the expected differentation when applied to normals, and vice versa. The Thurstone schedule, and others like it, will fail to distinguish the mental patient from the normal in many cases. Furthermore, a high "neurotic tendency" score, no matter from what inventory it is obtained, may mean merely that the individual has indeed had numerous incidental factors that frequently "cause" neurotic breakdowns, but that because of a strong mental constitution he has not broken under them. Another individual with few such indicators has one of them to a severe degree and cracks under it. All we can say is that for a person with a high score the probability of a neurotic difficulty is greater than for a person with a low score. It is these probabilities that lead us to explore certain individuals further for expected trouble. A small amount of advance information that may serve as a warning is better than none at all.

The correlation of the schedule scores with college aptitude tests like the *American Council on Education Psychological Examination* is given as approximately zero. On the other hand, the correlation of the schedule scores with scholarship is positive, though low. This situation would make the inventory score an ally in the better prediction of scholarship. But it probably contributes much less to a multiple prediction than do other scores and so will rarely be included in a regression equation.

[1243.1]

Pressey Interest-Attitude Tests. Grades 6 to adults; 1933; 1 form; 75¢ per 25; 15¢ per specimen set; nontimed (30) minutes; S. L. Pressey and L. C. Pressey; New York: Psychological Corporation.

REFERENCES

1 PRESSEY, SIDNEY L., AND PRESSEY, LUELLA C. "Development of the Interest-Attitude Tests." *J Appl Psychol* 17:1-16 F '33.
2 HARRIS, A. J. "A Note on Three Recent Personality Tests." *J Social Psychol* 7:474-9 '36.
3 PRESSEY, SIDNEY L. "A Note on the Critical Note." *J Appl Psychol* 22:659-61 D '38.
4 THORNDIKE, ROBERT L. "Critical Note on the Pressey Interest-Attitudes Test." *J Appl Psychol* 22:657-8 D '38.
5 THORNDIKE, ROBERT L. "Responses of a Group of Gifted Children to the Pressey Interest-Attitude Test." *J Ed Psychol* 30:587-93 N '39.

Douglas Spencer, Assistant Professor of Psychology, Queens College. This reconstruction of the Pressey's *X-O Test* makes available in greatly improved form an instrument that has long proved an interesting addition to the clinician's battery. As heretofore, it has the advantage of being non-threatening to the subject because its purpose is disguised. Although many of the *X-O Test* items are retained, the mechanics of the old blank have been altered to simplify the administration and the scoring, and careful work has been done to reduce vocabulary difficulties and to eliminate insignificant items.

The new test, for use from the sixth grade to the adult level, "furnishes a simple and expedient way of investigating the maturity of the interests and attitudes of a group with respect to a large number of items," according to the authors.

Four subtests of 90 items each concern the following: (1) Things the subject considers wrong; (2) Things which interest him; (3) Things he worries about; and (4) Characteristics of persons he admires. He responds to each section by putting an X in front of words arranged in columns, and to register very strong feelings he can put two X's in front of any item. The 360 items were selected through a painstaking item analysis of 950 words, each item being retained on the basis of its power to differentiate between younger and older subjects. Separate norms are available for boys (2099 cases) and for girls (2088). The test is easy to give and to score.

Reliability by the split-half method for the entire test was found to vary for single grades from .94 to .96, and for the subtests varied from .85 to .96.

As to validity, while the authors stress the need for more research, the efforts thus far reported are encouraging. These findings include confirmation of expected differences between groups contrasting as to the apparent sophistication of their community, and also between groups of assumed contrast in racial maturity.

Correlation of scores with estimates of emotional maturity by various guidance workers are promising, varying from .66 to .72. Further research on clinically contrasting groups to reveal more clearly what the test measures, should prove worth the effort. More light needs to be thrown on the meaning of extreme high and low scores, especially when these occur in marked discrepancy with MA or CA. This would require a careful case study approach.

As on the older *X-O* blanks, the strong feeling responses often yield valuable clues for investigation through interviews. These may make the test well worth giving even when the numerical scoring is not taken seriously.

[1244]

Pupil Portraits. Grades 4-8; 1934; 2 forms; $2.10 per 100; 25¢ per specimen set; nontimed (25-40) minutes; R. Pintner, J. B. Maller, G. Forlano, and H. C. Axelrod; New York: Bureau of Publications, Teachers College, Columbia University.

REFERENCES

1 PINTNER, RUDOLF; MALLER, J. B.; FORLANO, G.; AND AXELROD, H. "The Measurement of Pupil Adjustment." *J Ed Res* 28:334-48 Ja '35.
2 PINTNER, RUDOLF. "An Adjustment Test with Normal and Hard of Hearing Children." *J Genetic Psychol* 56:367-81 Je '40.

Simon H. Tulchin, Consulting Psychologist, 136 East 57th St., New York, New York. The test consists of 100 items and is available in two forms. The items are phrased in language readily comprehended by pupils in grades 4 to 8 and include both positive and negative statements dealing with specific habits and attitudes presented in the form of impersonal descriptions of other children. For example, such statements as "This child thinks school helps children," "This child thinks everybody copies, so why shouldn't he," and "This child thinks his friends do not care much for him," etc., are made and the child is to draw a circle around the letter *S* if he thinks the same and around the letter *D* if he thinks he is different. The items are grouped into five subtests dealing with the relationship of the pupil to his school environment, to his teacher, to his classmates, to himself, and to his home and family. The score is the number of statements answered in agreement with the key. The scores show no definite relation to age. The correlations between total score and age are −.17 for 270 boys, and −.03 for 289 girls in grades 6 and 7. A wider age scatter would have been more desirable.

This test has been standardized on 1,720 boys and 1,434 girls in grades 4 to 8. Because the girls made significantly higher scores than the boys separate norms are given for the two sexes. No separate norms are given for the several subtests. However, norms are given for the first four subtests which are grouped under the heading of school adjustment and the last subtest under the heading of home adjustment as well as for total score on all items. Percentile equivalents have been calculated.

The reliability coefficient based on the correlation between the two forms administered to 600 pupils in grades 4 to 8 is .935 ± .004.

The authors employed several procedures [1] to determine the validity of the test. The test was given to a group of "problem" children in a probation school. The mean score of the normal group was 20 points higher than the mean score of the "problem" children and the difference was found to be statistically significant. However, this difference of 20 points was found during the preliminary study when 287 statements were used. Only items which differentiated between the two groups were included in the final form. In the article a table shows the correlation of each item with total test score, percentages of pupils who failed each item and the difference between percentages of failures in the normal and "problem" groups. The authors also had 36 matched pupils in each of two groups. In the one group were pupils who received C or D in conduct and in the other group those with the grade A. The difference in score was 9.25 in favor of the A group and this difference was more than 3 times its standard deviation. The correlation between the school adjustment items and Maller's *Character Sketches* is .46 ± .03. The correlation with intelligence quotients for 180 pupils is .13 ± .05 and with mental age on McCall's *Multi-Mental Scale* the correlations are .13 for 270 boys and .23 for 289 girls. The test also offers a series of 30 questions under the general heading of Background. Here questions dealing with the father's occupation, the home, and several miscellaneous items are scored and the result is considered a measure of socio-economic status. The correlation between this total score and score on the *Sims Score Card for Socio-Economic Status* is .86. A number of other items included in the background series are in the nature of an association test and the authors offer no discussion as to their relative significance. Some of these

items are "I wish ....," "I like ....,"
"I feel sad when ....," etc.

The authors of *Pupil Portraits* are fully
aware of the need for determining the validity
of their test. It is to be regretted that only
54 "problem" children and 36 matched conduct
grade children were studied. One would like
to see the use of more clinical material and
more investigations dealing with a great many
children whose adjustment in school and in
the home is known. Until the results of such
studies become available the test should be considered in an experimental stage.

[1245]

Radio Checklist. Grades 9-12; 1939; 4¢ per copy;
nontimed (30) minutes; Chicago, Ill.: Evaluation in
the Eight Year Study, Progressive Education Association.

[1246]

**Record Blank for the Rorschach Method of Per-
sonality Diagnosis,** Revised. Ages 3 and over; 1939-
40; individual; $1.75 per 25; 5¢ per blank, 100 or
more; 10¢ per sample blank; Bruno Klopfer and
Helen H. Davidson; New York: Rorschach Institute,
Inc., c/o Helen H. Davidson, Secretary of the Folder
Committee, 601 West 115th St.

REFERENCES

1 RORSCHACH, H., AND OBERHOLZER, E. "The Application of
the Interpretation of Form to Psychoanalysis." *J Nerv and
Mental Dis* 60:225-48, 359-79 '24.
2 BECK, SAMUEL J. "Personality Diagnosis by Means of the
Rorschach Test." *Am J Orthopsychiatry* 1:81-8 O '30.
3 BECK, S. J. "The Rorschach Test and Personality Diagnosis: I, The Feeble-Minded." *Am J Psychiatry* 10:19-52 Jl '30.
4 BECK, SAMUEL J. "The Rorschach Test and Personality
Diagnosis: The Feeble-minded," pp. 221-61. In *Institute for
Child Guidance Studies:* Selected Reprints. Edited by Lawson
G. Lowrey. New York: Commonwealth Fund, 1931. Pp. viii,
290. Out of print.
5 BECK, SAMUEL J. "The Rorschach Test in Problem Children." *Am J Orthopsychiatry* 1:501-11 O '31.
6 LEVY, D. M., AND BECK, S. J. "The Rorschach Test in
Manic Depressive Psychosis," pp. 167-81. In *Manic Depressive
Psychosis*. Proceedings of the Eleventh Annual Meeting of the
Association for Research in Nervous and Mental Disease held
in New York, December 29 and 30, 1930. Edited by W. A.
White, T. K. Davis, and A. M. Frantz. Baltimore, Md.:
Williams & Wilkins Co., 1931. Pp. xxix, 851. $10.00.
7 BECK, S. J. *The Rorschach Test as Applied to a Feeble-
Minded Group.* Columbia University, Archives of Psychology,
No. 136. New York: the University, 1932. Pp. 84. $1.00. Paper.
8 OESER, O. A. "Some Experiments on the Abstraction of
Form and Color: Rorschach Tests, Part II." *Brit J Psychol*
22:287-323 Ap '32.
9 WERTHAM, F., AND BLEULER, M. "Inconstancy of the
Formal Structure of the Personality: Experimental Study of
the Influence of Mescaline on the Rorschach Test." *Arch
Neurology and Psychiatry* 28:52-70 Jl '32.
10 BECK, SAMUEL J. "The Rorschach Method and Personality Organization: II, Balance in Personality." *Am J. Psychiatry* 13:519-32 N '33.
11 BECK, SAMUEL J. "Configurational Tendencies in Rorschach Responses." *Am J Psychol* 45:433-43 Jl '33.
12 BECK, SAMUEL J. "The Rorschach Method and the Organization of Personality: I. Basic Processes." *Am J Orthopsychiatry* 3:361-75 O '33.
13 BENNETT, WILHELMINA. *A Study of Several Well Known
Personality Tests.* [New York: Psychological Corporation],
October 1933. Pp. ii, 25. Paper, mimeographed. Out of print.
14 MACCALMAN, DOUGLAS R. "The Rorschach Test and Its
Clinical Application." *J Mental Sci* 79:419-24 Ap '33.
15 SHUEY, HERBERT. "A New Interpretation of the Rorschach Test." *Psychol R* 40:213-5 Mr '33.
16 VERNON, PHILIP E. "The Rorschach Ink-Blot Test: I."
Brit J Med Psychol 13:89-118 pt 2 '33.
17 VERNON, PHILIP E. "The Rorschach Ink-Blot Test: II."
Brit J Med Psychol 13:179-200 pt 3 '33.
18 VERNON, PHILIP E. "The Rorschach Ink-Blot Test: III."
Brit J Med Psychol 13:271-295 pt 4 '33.
19 BECK, SAMUEL J. "The Rorschach Method and Personality Organization: III, The Psychological and the Social
Personality." *Am J Orthopsychiatry* 4:290-7 Ap '34.
20 DIETHELM, O. "The Personality Concept in Relation to
Graphology and the Rorschach Test." *Proc Assn Res Nerv
Mental Dis* 14:278-86 '34.
21 HERTZ, MARGUERITE R. "The Reliability of the Rorschach
Ink-Blot Test." *J Appl Psychol* 18:461-77 Je '34.
22 KERR, MADELINE. "The Rorschach Test Applied to Children." *Brit J Psychol* 25:170-85 O '34.
23 LEVY, DAVID M., AND BECK, S. J. "The Rorschach Test
in Manic-Depressive Psychosis." *Am J Orthopsychiatry*
4:262-82 Ap '34.
24 MELTZER, H. "Personality Differences among Stutterers
as Indicated by the Rorschach Test." *Am J Orthopsychiatry*
4:262-82 Ap '34.
25 BECK, SAMUEL J. "Problems of Further Research in the
Rorschach Test." *Am J Orthopsychiatry* 5:100-15 Ap '35.
26 BLEULER, M., AND BLEULER, R. "Rorschach's Ink-Blot Test
and Racial Psychology: Mental Peculiarities of Moroccans."
Char and Pers 4:97-114 D '35.
27 DIMMICK, GRAHAM B. "An Application of the Rorschach
Ink-Blot Test to Three Clinical Types of Dementia Praecox."
J Psychol 1:61-74 Ja '35.
28 GUIRDHAM, ARTHUR. "On the Value of the Rorschach
Test." *J Mental Sci* 81:848-869 O '35.
29 GUIRDHAM, ARTHUR. "The Rorschach Test in Epileptics."
J Mental Sci 81:870-93 O '35.
30 HACKFIELD, A. W. "An Objective Interpretation by Means
of the Rorschach Test of the Psychobiological Structure Underlying Schizophrenia, Essential Hypertension, Graves' Syndrome,
etc." *Am J Psychiatry* 92:575-88 '35.
31 HARRIMAN, PHILIP LAWRENCE. "The Rorschach Test Applied to a Group of College Students." *Am J Orthopsychiatry*
5:116-20 Ap '35.
32 HERTZ, MARGUERITE R. "The Rorschach Ink-Blot Test:
Historical Summary." *Psychol B* 32:33-66 Ja '35.
33 HERTZ, MARGUERITE R. "Rorschach Norms for an Adolescent Age-Group." *Child Development* 6:69-76 Mr '35.
34 LINE, W., AND GRIFFIN, J. D. M. "The Objective Determination of Factors Underlying Mental Health." *Am J Psychiatry* 91:833-42 Ja '35.
35 LINE, W., AND GRIFFIN, J. D. M. "Some Results Obtained
with the Rorschach Test, Objectively Scored." *Am J Psychiatry*
92:109-14 '35.
36 LINE, W.; GRIFFIN, J. D. M.; AND ANDERSON, G. W.
"The Objective Measurement of Mental Stability." *J Mental
Sci* 81:61-106 Ja '35.
37 MELTZER, H. "Talkativeness in Stuttering and Non-
Stuttering Children." *J Genetic Psychol* 46:371-90 Je '35.
38 POWELL, MARJORIE. "Relation of Scholastic Discrepancy
to Free Associations on the Rorschach Tests." *Ky Personnel B*
14:3-4 My '35.
39 ROSENZWEIG, SAUL. "Outline of a Cooperative Project for
Validating the Rorschach Test." *Am J Orthopsychiatry* 5:121-3
Ap '35.
40 VERNON, P. E. "Recent Work on the Rorschach Test."
J Mental Sci 81:894-920 O '35.
41 VERNON, P. E. "The Significance of the Rorschach Test."
Brit J Med Psychol 15:199-217 '35.
42 WELLS, F. L. "Rorschach and the Free Association Test."
J Gen Psychol 13:413-33 O '35.
43 BECK, S. J. "Autism in Rorschach Scoring: A Feeling
Comment." *Char and Pers* 5:83-5 S '36.
44 BOOTH, GOTTHARD C., AND KLOPFER, BRUNO. "Personality
Studies in Chronic Arthritis." *Rorschach Res Exch* 1:40-8
N '36.
45 BOOTH, GOTTHARD C.; KLOPFER, BRUNO; AND STEIN-LEW-
INSON, THEA. "Material for a Comparative Case Study of a
Chronic Arthritis Personality." *Rorschach Res Exch* 1:49-54
N '36.
46 BRYN, DAG. "The Problem of Human Types: Comments
and an Experiment." *Char and Pers* 5:48-60 S '36.
47 GARDNER, G. E. "Rorschach Test Replies and Results in
100 Normal Adults of Avearge IQ." *Am J Orthopsychiatry*
6:32-60 Ja '36.
48 GUIRDHAM, ARTHUR. "The Diagnosis of Depression by the
Rorschach Test." *Brit J Med Psychol* 16:130-45 '36.
49 GUIRDHAM, ARTHUR. "Simple Psychological Data in Melancholia." *J Mental Sci* 82:649-53 S '36.
50 HERTZ, MARGUERITE R. *Frequency Tables to be Used in
Scoring the Rorschach Ink-Blot Test.* Cleveland, Ohio: the
Author, Brush Foundation, Western Reserve University, 1936.
Pp. v, 283. $3.50. Paper, mimeographed.
51 HERTZ, MARGUERITE R. "The Method of Administration of
the Rorschach Ink-Blot Test." *Child Development* 7:237-54
D '36.
52 KERR, MADELINE. "Temperamental Difference in Twins."
Brit J Psychol 27:51-9 Jl '36.
53 KLOPFER, BRUNO, AND SENDER, SADIE. "A System of
Refined Scoring Symbols." *Rorschach Res Exch* 1:19-22 N '36.
54 PIOTROWSKI, ZYGMUNT. "On the Rorschach Method and its
Application in Organic Disturbances of the Central Nervous
System." *Rorschach Res Exch* 1:23-39 N '36.
55 SENDER, SADIE, AND KLOPFER, BRUNO. "Application of the
Rorschach Test to Child Behavior Problems as Facilitated by a
Refinement of the Scoring Method." *Rorschach Res Exch*
1:5-17 S '36.
56 SUNNE, DAGNY. "Rorschach Test Norms of Young Children." *Child Development* 7:304-13 D '36.

57 THORNTON, GEORGE R. "A Note on the Scoring of Movement in the Rorschach Test." *Am J Psychol* 48:524-5 Jl '36.

58 THORNTON, GEORGE R., AND GUILFORD, J. P. "The Reliability and Meaning of Erlebnistypus Scores in the Rorschach Test." *J Abn and Social Psychol* 31:324-30 O-D '36.

59 VERNON, P. E. "Rorschach Bibliography No. III." *Rorschach Res Exch* 1:89-93 S '36.

60 BARRY, HERBERT, JR., EDITOR. "The Significance of the Rorschach Method for Consulting Psychology: Author's Abstracts of the Contributions to the Round-Table Conference at the Eighth Annual Meeting of the Association of Consulting Psychologists, May 7-8, 1937, at the New York State College for Teachers, Albany, New York." *Rorschach Res Exch* 1:157-66 Jl '37.

61 BECK, S. J. "Some Present Rorschach Problems." *Rorschach Res Exch* 2:15-22 S '37.

62 BECK, SAMUEL J. *Introduction to the Rorschach Method: A Manual of Personality Study.* Preface by F. L. Wells. Monograph No. 1 of the American Orthopsychiatric Association. New York: the Association, 1937. Pp. xi, 278. $4.00.

63 BECK, SAMUEL J. "Psychological Processes in Rorschach Findings." *J Abn and Social Psychol* 31:482-8 Ja-Mr '37.

64 BINDER, HANS. "The 'Light-Dark' Interpretations in Rorschach's Experiment." Translated by J. Jervis Carlson. *Rorschach Res Exch* 2:37-42 D '37.

65 BINDER, HANS; BLEULER, MANFRED; BENJAMIN, JOHN D.; BOOTH, GOTTHARD; HERTZ, MARGUERITE R.; KLOPFER, BRUNO; PIOTROWSKI, ZYGMUNT; AND SCHACHTEL, ERNST. "Discussion on 'Some Recent Rorschach Problems.'" *Rorschach Res Exch* 2:43-72 D '37.

66 BOOTH, GOTTHARD COHEN. "Personality and Chronic Arthritis." *J Nervous and Mental Dis* 85:637-62 Je '37.

67 GOLDSTEIN, KURT. "Personality Studies of Cases with Lesions of the Frontal Lobes: I, The Psychopathology of Pick's Disease." *Rorschach Res Exch* 1:57-64 Ja '37.

68 HERTZ, MARGUERITE R. "The Normal Details in the Rorschach Ink-Blot Test." Discussions by Sadie Sender and Bruno Klopfer. *Rorschach Res Exch* 1:104-20 Ap '37.

69 HUNTER, MARY. "Responses of Comparable White and Negro Adults to the Rorschach Test." *J Psychol* 3:173-82 Ja '37.

70 JACOBSEN, WILHELMINA E. "A Study of Personality Development in a High School Girl." *Rorschach Res Exch* 2:23-35 S '37.

71 KLOPFER, BRUNO. "The Present Status of the Theoretical Development of the Rorschach Method." *Rorschach Res Exch* 1:142-7 Jl '37.

72 KLOPFER, BRUNO. "The Technique of the Rorschach Performance." *Rorschach Res Exch* 2:1-14 S '37.

73 PIOTROWSKI, ZYGMUNT. "A Comparison of Congenitally Defective Children with Schizophrenic Children in Regard to Personality Structure and Intelligence Type." *Proc Am Assn Mental Def* 61:78-90 '37.

74 PIOTROWSKI, ZYGMUNT. "The M, FM, and m Responses as Indicators of Changes in Personality." *Rorschach Res Exch* 1:148-56 Jl '37.

75 PIOTROWSKI, ZYGMUNT. "Personality Studies of Cases with Lesions of the Frontal Lobes: II, Rorschach Study of a Pick's Disease Case." *Rorschach Res Exch* 1:65-76 Ja '37.

76 PIOTROWSKI, ZYGMUNT. "The Reliability of Rorschach's Erlebnistypus." *J Abn and Social Psychol* 32:439-45 O-D '37.

77 PIOTROWSKI, ZYGMUNT. "The Rorschach Inkblot Method in Organic Disturbances of the Central Nervous System." *J Nerv Mental Dis* 86:525-37 N '37.

78 PIOTROWSKI, ZYGMUNT. "Rorschach Studies of Cases with Lesions of the Frontal Lobes." *Brit J Med Psychol* 17:105-18 pt 1 '37.

79 "A Review of Rorschach Scoring Samples." *Rorschach Res Exch* 1:94-101 Ja '37.

80 SCHACHTEL, ERNST, AND HARTOCH, ANNA. "The Curve of Reactions in the Rorschach Test: A Contribution to the Theory and Practice of Rorschach's Psychodiagnostic Ink Blot Test." *Am J Orthopsychiatry* 7:320-48 Jl '37.

81 TALLMAN, GLADYS, AND KLOPFER, BRUNO. "Personality Studies of Cases with Lesions of the Frontal Lobes: III, Rorschach Study of Bilateral Lobectomy Case." *Rorschach Res Exch* 1:77-88 Ja '37.

82 TROUP, EVELYN, AND KLOPFER, BRUNO. "Sample Case Studies: from A Comparative Study of the Personality Development of Twenty Pairs of Monozygotic Twins by Means of the Rorschach Test." Summary and Records by Evelyn Troup; Scoring and Interpretations by Bruno Klopfer. *Rorschach Res Exch* 1:121-39 Ap '37.

83 VARVEL, W. A. "Suggestions toward the Experimental Validation of the Rorschach Test." *B Menninger Clinic* 1:220-26 '37.

84 BECK, SAMUEL J. *Personality Structure in Schizophrenia: A Rorschach Investigation in 81 Patients and 64 Controls.* Preface by C. MacFie Campbell. Nervous and Mental Disease Monograph No. 63. New York: Nervous and Mental Disease Publishing Co., 1938. Pp. 88. $2.00.

85 BENJAMIN, JOHN D., AND EBAUGH, FRANKLIN G. "The Diagnostic Validity of the Rorschach Test." *Am J Psychiatry* 94:1163-78 Mr '38.

86 CLAPP, HAZEL S.; MIALE, FLORENCE ROSENBLATT; AND KAPLAN, A. H. "Clinical Validation of a Rorschach Interpretation: The Case of Lillian K." *Rorschach Res Exch* 2:153-62 Je '38.

87 DAVIDSON, HELEN H., AND KLOPFER, BRUNO. "Rorschach Statistics: Part I, Mentally Retarded, Normal, and Superior Adults." *Rorschach Res Exch* 2:164-169 Je '38.

88 DAVIDSON, HELEN H., AND KLOPFER, BRUNO. "Rorschach Statistics: Part II, Normal Children." *Rorschach Res Exch* 3:37-43 O '38.

89 FOSBERG, IRVING ARTHUR. "Rorschach Reactions under Varied Instructions: On the Use of Chi-Squares as a Measure of the Reliability of the Rorschach Psychodiagnostic Technique." *Rorschach Res Exch* 3:12-30 O '38.

90 HERTZ, HELEN, compiler. "Binder's Shading Responses." Translated by Mary Hunter Sicha. *Rorschach Res Exch* 2:79-88 Mr '38.

91 HERTZ, MARGUERITE R. "The 'Popular' Response Factor in the Rorschach Scoring." *J Psychol* 6:3-31 Jl '38.

92 HERTZ, MARGUERITE R. "Scoring the Rorschach Ink-Blot Test." *J Genetic Psychol* 52:15-64 Mr '38.

93 HERTZ, MARGUERITE R. "Scoring the Rorschach Test with Specific Reference to 'Normal Detail' Category." *Am J Orthopsychiatry* 8:100-121 Ja '38.

94 KLOPFER, BRUNO. "A Further Rorschach Study of Mr. A." *Rorschach Res Exch* 3:31-35 O '38.

95 KLOPFER, BRUNO. "The Shading Responses." *Rorschach Res Exch* 2:76-79 Mr '38.

96 KLOPFER, BRUNO, AND MIALE, FLORENCE ROSENBLATT. "An Illustration of the Technique of the Rorschach Interpretation: The Case of Anne T." *Rorschach Res Exch* 2:126-52 Je '38.

97 PATTERSON, M., AND MAGAW, DAVID C. "An Investigation of the Validity of the Rorschach Technique as Applied to Mentally Defective Problem Children." *Proc Am Assn Mental Def* 62:179-85 '38.

98 PESCOR, M. J. "Age of Delinquents in Relationship to Rorschach Test Scores." *Pub Health Reports* 53:852-64 My '38.

99 PIOTROWSKI, Z. "Recent Rorschach Literature: Rorschach Bibliography No. IV." *Rorschach Res Exch* 2:172-5 Je '38.

100 PIOTROWSKI, ZYGMUNT. "Blind Analysis of a Case of Compulsion Neurosis." *Rorschach Res Exch* 2:89-111 Mr '38.

101 PIOTROWSKI, ZYGMUNT. "The Prognostic Possibilities of the Rorschach Method in Insulin Treatment." *Psychiatric Q* 12:679-89 O '38.

102 RICKERS-OVSIANKINA, MARIA. *Rorschach Scoring Samples.* Worcester, Mass.: Worcester State Hospital, 1938. Pp. [v, 166]. $3.00. Paper, mimeographed.

103 RICKERS-OVSIANKINA, MARIA. "The Rorschach Test as Applied to Normal and Schizophrenic Subjects." *Brit J Med Psychol* 17:227-57 pt 2 '38.

104 SHUEY, HERBERT. "Further Discussion on Some Recent Rorschach Problems." *Rorschach Res Exch* 2:170-1 Je '38.

105 SILL, JANE B. "A Case Study Comparing the Performance on the Binet and on the Rorschach." *Rorschach Res Exch* 2:112-124 Mr '38.

106 SUARES, NADINE. "Personality Development in Adolescence." *Rorschach Res Exch* 3:2-11 O '38.

107 TALLMAN, GLADYS. "Further Results of Retesting Mr. A." *Rorschach Res Exch* 3:35-6 O '38.

108 TROUP, EVELYN. "A Comparative Study by Means of the Rorschach Method of Personality Development in Twenty Pairs of Identical Twins." *Genetic Psychol Monogr* 20:461-556 N '38.

109 VAUGHN, JAMES, AND KRUG, OTHILDA. "The Analytic Character of the Rorschach Ink Blot Test." *Am J Orthopsychiatry* 8:220-9 Ap '38.

110 BECK, SAMUEL J. "Thoughts on an Impending Anniversary." *Am J Orthopsychiatry* 9:806-8 O '39.

111 BOOTH, G. C. "Objective Technics in Personality Testing." *Arch Neurology and Psychiatry* 42:514-30 S '39.

112 FRANK, LAWRENCE K. "Comments on the Proposed Standardization of the Rorschach Method." *Rorschach Res Exch* 3:101-5 My '39.

113 HERTZ, HELENE. "A Rorschach Comparison Between Best and Least Adjusted Girls in a Training School." *Rorschach Res Exch* 3:134-9 My '39.

114 HERTZ, MARGUERITE R. "On the Standardization of the Rorschach Method." *Rorschach Res Exch* 3:120-33 My '39.

115 HERTZ, MARGUERITE R., AND RUBENSTEIN, BORIS B. "A Comparison of Three 'Blind' Rorschach Analyses." *Am J Orthopsychiatry* 9:295-314 Ap '39.

116 HIRNING, L. C. "Case Studies in Schizophrenia." *Rorschach Res Exch* 3:66-90 F '39.

117 HUNTER, MARY. "The Practical Value of the Rorschach Test in a Psychological Clinic." *Am J Orthopsychiatry* 9:287-94 Ap '39.

118 KELLEY, DOUGLAS M. "Announcement of the Rorschach Institute." *Rorschach Res Exch* 3:92-100 My '39.

119 KELLEY, DOUGLAS M., AND KLOPFER, BRUNO. "Application of the Rorschach Method to Research in Schizophrenia." *Rorschach Res Exch* 3:55-66 F '39.

120 KELLEY, DOUGLAS M., AND RIETI, ETTORE. "The Geneva Approach to the Rorschach Method." *Rorschach Res Exch* 3:195-201 Ag '39.

121 KLOPFER, BRUNO. "Should the Rorschach Method Be Standardized?" *Rorschach Res Exch* 3:45-54 F '39.

122 KLOPFER, BRUNO; KRUGMAN, MORRIS; KELLEY, DOUGLAS M.; MURPHY, LOIS BARCLAY; AND SHAKOW, DAVID. "Shall the Rorschach Method Be Standardized? Round Table, 1939 Session [Rorschach Institute]." *Am J Orthopsychiatry* 9:514-28 Jl '39.

123 KLOPFER, BRUNO, IN COLLABORATION WITH EDWARD M. L.

BURCHARD, DOUGLAS M. KELLEY, AND FLORENCE R. MIALE. "Theory and Technique of Rorschach Interpretation." *Rorschach Res Exch* 3:152-94 Ag '39.
124 MIALE, FLORENCE R. "The Rorschach Forum at the Sixteenth Annual Meeting of the American Orthopsychiatric Association, February 23, 1939, in New York City." *Rorschach Res Exch* 3:106-19 My '39.
125 PESCOR, M. J. *Marital Status of Delinquents in Relationship to Rorschach Test Scores.* United States Public Health Service, Supplement No. 153 to the Public Health Reports. Washington, D. C.: Government Printing Office, 1939. Pp. 6. $0.05. Paper.
126 PIOTROWSKI, ZYGMUNT. "Rorschach Manifestations of Improvement in Insulin Treated Schizophrenics." *Psychosom Med* 1:508-26 O '39.
127 SARBIN, THEODORE R. "Rorschach Patterns under Hypnosis." *Am J Orthopsychiatry* 9:315-8 Ap '39.
128 WOLFSON, RUTH. "Scoring, Tabulation and Interpretation of the Two Sample Cases." *Rorschach Res Exch* 3:140-50 My '39.
129 BROSIN, H. W., AND FROMM, ERIKA OPPENHEIMER. "Rorschach and Color Blindness." *Rorschach Res Exch* 4:39-70 Ap '40.
130 HALLOWELL, A. IRVING. "Rorschach as an Aid in the Study of Personalities in Primitive Societies." Author's abstract. *Rorschach Res Exch* 4:106 Jl '40.
131 HARROWER-ERICKSON, M. R. "The Contribution of the Rorschach Method to Wartime Psychological Problems." *J Mental Sci* 86:366-77 My '40.
132 HARROWER-ERICKSON, M. R. "Personality Changes Accompanying Cerebral Lesions: I, Rorschach Studies of Patients with Cerebral Tumors." *Arch Neurology and Psychiatry* 43:859-90 My '40.
133 HARROWER-ERICKSON, M. R. "Personality Changes Accompanying Cerebral Lesions: II, Rorschach Studies of Patients with Focal Epilepsy." *Arch Neurology and Psychiatry* 43:1081-1107 Je '40.
134 HARROWER-ERICKSON, M. R., AND MIALE, F. R. "Personality Changes Accompanying Organic Brain Lesions: Pre- and Post-Operative Study of Two Pre-Adolescent Children." *Rorschach Res Exch* 4:8-25 Ja '40.
135 HERTZ, MARGUERITE R. "Problems on the Validity of the Rorschach Method." Author's abstract. *Rorschach Res Exch* 4:104-5 Jl '40.
136 HERTZ, MARGUERITE R. "The Shading Response in the Rorschach Ink-Blot Test: A Review of Its Scoring and Interpretation." *J Gen Psychol* 23:123-67 Jl '40.
137 HERTZ, M. R., AND KENNEDY, STEPHANIE. "The M Factor in Estimating Intelligence." Author's abstract. *Rorschach Res Exch* 4:105-6 Jl '40.
138 KELLEY, DOUGLAS M. "Survey of the Training Facilities for the Rorschach Method in the U. S. A." *Rorschach Res Exch* 4:84-7 Ap '40.
139 KELLEY, D. M., AND BARRERA, S. E. "The Present State of the Rorschach Method as a Psychiatric Adjunct." *Rorschach Res Exch* 4:30-6 Ja '40.
140 KLOPFER, BRUNO. "Personality Aspects Revealed by the Rorschach Method." *Rorschach Res Exch* 4:26-9 Ja '40.
141 KLOPFER, BRUNO, in collaboration with Helen Davidson, Evelyn Holzman, Douglas M. Kelley, Helen Margulies, Florence R. Miale, and Ruth Wolfson. "The Technique of Rorschach Scoring and Tabulation." *Rorschach Res Exch* 4:75-83 Ap '40.
142 KOGAN, WILLIAM. "Shifts in Rorschach Patterns During a Critical Period in the Institutional Experience of a Group of Delinquent Boys." *Rorschach Res Exch* 4:131-3 Jl '40.
143 KRUGMAN, MORRIS. "Out of the Ink Well: The Rorschach Method." *Rorschach Res Exch* 4:91-101 Jl '40.
144 MIALE, F. R. "Personality Structure in the Psychoneuroses." *Rorschach Res Exch* 4:71-4 Ap '40.
145 MUNROE, RUTH. "The Use of the Rorschach in College Guidance." *Rorschach Res Exch* 4:107-30 Jl '40.
146 ROSS, W. D. "The 'Anxiety Neurosis' Rorschach Record Compared with the Typical Basically Neurotic Record." *Rorschach Res Exch* 4:134-7 Jl '40.
147 TULCHIN, SIMON H. "The Pre-Rorschach Use of Ink-Blot Tests." *Rorschach Res Exch* 4:1-7 Ja '40.

[1247]

Report Form on Temperament and Social Behaviour. For recording observations of children ages 2-7; 1940; 4s. 6d. per 12; C. W. Valentine; Birmingham, England: Birmingham Printers, Ltd.

REFERENCES

1 VALENTINE, C. W. "The Specific Nature of Temperament Traits and a Suggested Report Form." *Brit J Ed Psychol* 10:25-48 F '40.

[1248]

Revision of the Babcock Examination for Measuring Efficiency of Mental Functioning. Ages 7 and over; 1940; a revision of *Babcock's Mental Deterioration Scale* (No. 37058); 1 form; $10 per test booklet and manual (No. 37058A); $2 per 25 record blanks (No. 37058R); 10¢ per *Color Naming Test*: Woodworth-Wells (No. 12309); $1.25 per *Cube Imitation Test*: Pintner (No. 33304); $1 per *Memory for Designs Test*: Army Performance Scale (No. 32317); nontimed (70+) minutes; Harriet Babcock and Lydia Levy; Chicago, Ill.: C. H. Stoelting Co.

REFERENCES

1 BABCOCK, HARRIET. *An Experiment in the Measurement of Mental Deterioration.* Columbia University, Archives of Psychology, No. 117. New York: the University, 1930. Pp. 105. $1.25. Paper.
2 BABCOCK, HARRIET. "Psychological Testing in Psychopathology." *J Appl Psychol* 15:584-9 D '31.
3 SCHWARZ, RUDOLPH. "Measurement of Mental Deterioration in Dementia Praecox." *Am J Psychiatry* 89:555-60 N '32.
4 BABCOCK, HARRIET. *Dementia Praecox: A Psychological Study.* Lancaster, Pa.: Science Press Printing Co., 1933. Pp. 167. $2.50.
5 WITTMAN, PHYLLIS. "The Babcock Deterioration Tests in State Hospital Practice." *J Abn and Social Psychol* 28:70-83 Ap-Je '33.
6 GILBERT, JEANNE G. *Mental Efficiency in Senescence.* Columbia University, Archives of Psychology, No. 188. New York: the University, July 1935. Pp. 60. $1.00. Paper.
7 SIMMONS, C. "Mental Incapacity: The Intelligence of Patients in Mental Hospitals." *Char and Pers* 4:25-33 S '35.
8 HARBINSON, M. R. "An Investigation of Deterioration of 'General Intelligence' or 'G' in Psychotic Patients." *Brit J Med Psychol* 16:146-8 '36.
9 ALTMAN, CHARLOTTE HALL, AND SHAKOW, DAVID. "A Comparison of the Performance of Matched Groups of Schizophrenic Patients, Normal Subjects, and Delinquents on Some Aspects of the Stanford-Binet." *J Ed Psychol* 28:519-29 O '37.
9.1 BOOKHAMMER, R. S., AND RUBIN, BEATRICE. "Babcock Test for Mental Deterioration." Discussion by Arthur P. Noyes, Frederick H. Allen, and J. C. Yaskin. *Arch Neurology and Psychiatry* 37:1204-6 My '37.
10 JASTAK, JOSEPH. "Psychometric Patterns of State Hospital Patients." *Del State Med J* 9:87-91 Ap '37.
11 BARNES, MARGARET R., AND FETTERMAN, JOSEPH L. "Mentality of Dispensary Epileptic Patients." *Arch Neurology and Psychiatry* 40:903-10 N '38.
12 HALL, MARGARET E. "Mental and Physical Efficiency of Women Drug Addicts." *J Abn and Social Psychol* 33:332-45 Jl '38.
12.1 CAPPS, HARRY MARCELLUS. *Vocabulary Changes in Mental Deterioration*: The Relationship of Vocabulary Functioning as Measured by a Variety of Word Meaning and Usage Tests to Clinically Estimated Degrees of Mental Deterioration in 'Idiopathic' Epilepsy. Columbia University, Archives of Psychology, No. 242. New York: the University, September 1939. Pp. 81. $1.25. Paper.
13 KENDIG, ISABELLE, AND RICHMOND, WINIFRED V. *Psychological Studies in Dementia Praecox,* pp. 14-22, and passim. Ann Arbor, Mich.: Edwards Brothers, Inc., 1940. Pp. x, 211. $0.50. Paper, lithotyped.
14 BABCOCK, HARRIET. "Personality and Efficiency of Mental Functioning." *Am J Orthopsychiatry* 10:527-31 Jl '40.

[1249]

Roback Sense of Humor Test. Adolescents and adults; 1939; 1 form; $1.25 per 25 (No. 24412); nontimed (15) minutes; A. A. Roback; Chicago, Ill.: C. H. Stoelting Co.

[1250]

Scale of Beliefs: Tests 4.21 and 4.31. Grades 9-12; 1939; 1 form, 2 parts (both of which must be given); revision of Tests 4.2 and 4.3; 5¢ per set of both parts; 1¢ per machine-scorable answer sheet; 5¢ per explanation sheet and interpretation guide; $2 per set of stencils for machine scoring; nontimed (40) minutes; Chicago, Ill.: Evaluation in the Eight Year Study, Progressive Education Association.

REFERENCES

1 GRIM, PAUL R. "A Technique for the Measurement of Attitudes in the Social Studies." *Ed Res B* 15:95-104 Ap '36.
2 RATHS, LOUIS. "Evaluating the Program of Lakeshore School." *Ed Res B* 17:57-84 Mr 16 '38.
3 *Social Sensitivity*: An Approach to Evaluation in Social Studies. Chicago, Ill.: Evaluation in the Eight Year Study, Progressive Education Association, March 1939. Pp. [34]. Paper, mimeographed. Out of print.
4 AMSTUTZ, WADE S. "A Study of Characteristics of Education Freshmen Who Entered Ohio State University in 1938." *J Exp Ed* 8:289-92 Mr '40.
5 CAHOW, ARTHUR C. "Relationships of Test Scores of Education College Freshmen to Grades in Selected Courses." *J Exp Ed* 8:284-9 Mr '40.
6 GIBBONS, C. C., AND SCHRADER, W. A. B. "Liberalism

and Consistency: A Study of Social Attitudes." *J Exp Ed* 8:259-67 Mr '40.

7 SCHRADER, W. A. B. "Analysis of Variance Applied to Liberalism Scores." *J Exp Ed* 8:267-70 Mr '40.

[1251]

Scale of Beliefs for Junior High School: Tests 4.4 and 4.5. Grades 7-9; 1940; an adaptation of *Scale of Beliefs*: Tests 4.21 and 4.31; 1 form, 2 parts (both of which must be given); 5¢ per set of both parts; 1¢ per machine-scorable answer sheet; 5¢ per explanation sheet and interpretation guide; $2 per set of stencils for machine scoring; nontimed (30) minutes; Chicago, Ill.: Evaluation in the Eight Year Study, Progressive Education Association.

REFERENCES

1 *Social Sensitivity*: An Approach to Evaluation in Social Studies. Chicago, Ill.: Evaluation in the Eight Year Study, Progressive Education Association, March 1939. Pp. [34]. Paper, mimeographed. Out of print.

[1252]

School Inventory. Grades 10-12; 1937; 1 form; $1.00 per 25; 15¢ per specimen set; nontimed (10-15) minutes; Hugh M. Bell; Stanford University, Calif.: Stanford University Press.

REFERENCES

1 BELL, HUGH M. *The Theory and Practice of Student Counseling*: With Special Reference to the Adjustment Inventory. Stanford, Calif.: Stanford University Press, 1935. Pp. 138. $1.00. Paper, lithotyped. (London: Oxford University Press. 4s. 6d.)

2 TYLER, HENRY T. "Evaluating the Bell Adjustment Inventory." *Jun Col J* 6:353-7 Ap '36.

3 BELL, HUGH M. *The Theory and Practice of Personal Counseling*: With Special Reference to the Adjustment Inventory. A revision of *The Theory and Practice of Student Counseling*. Stanford University, Calif.: Stanford University Press, 1939. Pp. v, 167. $1.25. Paper, lithotyped. (London: Oxford University Press. 6s.)

4 RYANS, DAVID G., AND PETERS, EDWIN F. "An Analysis and Adaptation of the Bell *School Inventory* with Respect to Student Adjustment in a Women's College." *J Appl Psychol* 24:455-62 Ag '40.

EDITOR'S NOTE: In *The 1938 Yearbook*, two reviews of Bell's *School Inventory* were incorrectly listed as reviews of Bell's *Adjustment Inventory*. These two reviews are herein reprinted under the correct test title.

Robert G. Bernreuter, Director of the Psycho-Educational Clinic and Associate Professor of Psychology, The Pennsylvania State College. The *Bell School Inventory* is intended to determine the attitude of pupils toward their school. According to the results obtained by the author, the inventory is sufficiently reliable to be used to determine the attitudes of individual students. Also, according to the data obtained by the author, the scores agree reasonably well with the ratings given pupils by their teachers.

An analysis of the items indicates that they fall into two major categories. One includes items expressing general attitude toward the school. The other includes attitudes toward such specific things as teachers, classmates, the curriculum, and extracurricular activities.

The only method of scoring developed by the author consists of finding the total number of items on which the student has expressed dissatisfaction regardless of whether the items are general or specific in nature. The inventory would be a more useful instrument if it could be scored to serve two purposes: first, to disclose dissatisfied pupils, and second, to disclose causes of dissatisfaction. The first is reasonably well done by the present scoring method but the second is not. The second purpose would be accomplished if the items were classified into subcategories on the basis of the types of specific items they involve and scored accordingly.

The inventory will need to be used with considerable caution and only after a good rapport has been established because it is particularly susceptible to invalidation through a desire on the part of the pupils to make a good showing before their teacher.

J. B. Maller, Lecturer in Education, New York University. This inventory directs the student to answer "honestly and thoughtfully" a number of questions about his school. He is asked to state whether some of his teachers are "bossy," narrow-minded, lazy, lack a sense of humor, lack enthusiasm for their work, nervous and easily excited, etc. Some of the questions are even more forceful. "Do you think that this school is run as if it were a prison? Do you dislike intensely certain teachers in this school?"

It is questionable whether high school students would have the courage and the desire to answer such questions honestly in a test which is given in school and which requires them to write their names on it. Furthermore, in schools which are poorly adapted to the needs and interests of their pupils would it be fair to label the outspoken students as "poorly adapted to the school"?

The inventory could hardly be used as a group test, if one is to follow the author's admonition that "the inventory should not be administered until the examiner has developed a feeling of cooperation among the students being tested."

The evidence of validity and the "norms" are based on the responses of 391 pupils in California high schools located at Chico, Yreka, Oroville, and Durham.

In view of the enormous differences between schools the norms are not only meaningless but also misleading. Even within one school the responses will probably vary from class to class, and from examiner to examiner. The statement in the directions that "your answers will be treated with the strictest confidence" will probably be of little reassurance for the directions also state that "the school will endeavor to improve the conditions which your answers indicate need improvement."

See also B842.

[1253]

Social Intelligence Test. High school, college, and adults; 1930; 1 form; $12.00 per 100; 20¢ per specimen set; 45(50) minutes; F. A. Moss, T. Hunt, and K. T. Omwake; Washington, D. C.: Center for Psychological Service, George Washington University.

REFERENCES

1 GROSVENOR, EDITH LOUISE. "A Study of the Social Intelligence of High School Pupils." *Am Physical Ed R* 32:649-57 N '27.
2 HUNT, THELMA. "What Social Intelligence Is and Where to Find It." *Industrial Psychol* 2:605-12 D '27.
3 MOSS, F. A., AND HUNT, T. "Are You Socially Intelligent? An Analysis of the Scores of 7,000 Persons on the George Washington University Social Intelligence Test." *Scientific Am* 137:108-10 Ag '27.
4 PINTNER, R., AND UPSHALL, C. C. "Some Results of Social Intelligence Tests." *Sch and Soc* 27:369-70 Mr 24 '27.
5 BROOM, M. EUSTACE. "A Note on the Validity of a Test of Social Intelligence." *J Appl Psychol* 12:426-8 Ag '28.
6 HUNT, THELMA. "The Measurement of Social Intelligence." *J Appl Psychol* 12:317-34 Je '28.
7 MCCLATCHY, VIVIENNE ROBISON. "A Theoretical and Statistical Critique of the Concept of Social Intelligence and of Attempts to Measure Such a Process." *J Abn and Social Psychol* 24:217-20 Jl-S '29.
8 BROOM, M. E. "A Further Study of the Validity of a Test of Social Intelligence." *J Ed Res* 22:403-5 D '30.
9 STRANG, RUTH. "Measures of Social Intelligence." *Am J Sociol* 36:263-9 S '30.
10 STRANG, RUTH. "Relation of Social Intelligence to Certain Other Factors." *Sch and Soc* 32:268-72 Ag 23 '30.
11 STAGNER, ROSS. "The Intercorrelation of Some Standardized Personality Tests." *J Appl Psychol* 16:453-64 O '32.
12 STRANG, RUTH. "An Analysis of Errors Made in a Test of Social Intelligence." *J Ed Sociol* 5:291-9 Ja '32.
13 RHINEHART, JESSE BATLEY. "An Attempt to Predict the Success of Student Nurses by the Use of a Battery of Tests." *J Appl Psychol* 17:277-93 Ap '33.
14 STAGNER, ROSS. "Improved Norms for Four Personality Tests." *Am J Psychol* 45:303-7 Ap '33.
15 Human Engineering Laboratory. *Revision of Form A of Worksample 169, Judgment in Social Situations.* Human Engineering Laboratory, Technical Report No. 6. Boston, Mass.: the Laboratory, 1936. Pp. xii, 56. $1.00. Paper, mimeographed.
16 HUNT, THELMA. *Measurement in Psychology,* pp. 335-51. New York: Prentice-Hall, Inc., 1936. Pp. xx, 471. $3.00.
17 THORNDIKE, ROBERT L. "Factor Analysis of Social and Abstract Intelligence." *J Ed Psychol* 27:231-3 Mr '36.
18 BURKS, FRANCES W. "The Relation of Social Intelligence Test Scores to Ratings of Social Traits." *J Social Psychol* 8:146-53 F '37.
19 THORNDIKE, ROBERT L., AND STEIN, SAUL. "An Evaluation of the Attempts to Measure Social Intelligence." *Psychol B* 34:275-85 My '37.
20 Human Engineering Laboratory. *Statistical and Graphic Analysis of Three Forms of Worksample 169, Judgment in Social Situations.* Human Engineering Laboratory, Technical Report No. 15. Boston, Mass.: the Laboratory, 1938. Pp. viii, 140. $1.00. Paper, mimeographed.

Robert L. Thorndike, Associate Professor of Education, Columbia University. Following up the suggestion made by E. L. Thorndike in 1920 that it might be profitable to make a tripartite division of intelligence into abstract, mechanical, and social intelligences, the authors of this test have endeavored to develop a paper-and-pencil technique of assaying differences in ability to respond to social situations.

The subtests require the individual to (a) select the best course of action in a briefly outlined social situation, (b) attach the appropriate emotional term to a brief quotation, (c) judge the truth or falsity of a number of statements about human behavior, (d) memorize names and faces and subsequently attach the right name to the right face, (e) choose the best completion of a series of jokes. All of these tests are in some degree verbal, and some of them seem to call for a high level of verbal comprehension. This being the case, it is not surprising to find that the test as a whole shows substantial correlation with tests of abstract intelligence. To what extent it measures abilities other than verbal abilities is not so easy to determine.

Hunt presents evidence for the validity of the test consisting of (a) the fact of marked occupational differences—executives, teachers, and salesmen scoring much higher than clerks and unskilled laborers, (b) the fact that students engaging in several extracurricular activities have a higher median score on the test than those engaging in few or none, (c) the fact that score on the test correlated rather well with rating by a superior executive in a large sales company. In none of these cases, however, was the effect of abstract intelligence partialled out. Whether these discriminations would hold up in groups equated in abstract verbal ability seems questionable to this reviewer. Other investigators have found very low correlations between test score and frequency of activity or rating for social adjustment.

In a factor analysis of the subtests of the *Social Intelligence Test* and the subtests of a general intelligence test, the writer was unable to find evidence of any clear-cut unity within the social intelligence test or differentiation between it and the general intelligence test.[17]

All in all, it seems to the reviewer that no satisfactory validation of this test has been presented. Until this has been done, he views it with suspicion, and doubts whether a test which is so predominantly verbal and abstract will give information about the individual's ability to actively handle social situations, except insofar as abstract comprehension is involved therein.

[1254]

Social Problems: Test 1.42. Grades 9-12; 1938-40; 1 form; revision of Tests 1.4 and 1.41; 5¢ per test; 1¢ per machine-scorable answer sheet; 5¢ per explanation sheet and guide; $1.50 per set of stencils for machine scoring; nontimed (90) minutes; Chicago, Ill.: Evaluation in the Eight Year Study, Progressive Education Association.

REFERENCES

1 *Social Sensitivity*: An Approach to Evaluation in Social Studies. Chicago, Ill.: Evaluation in the Eight Year Study, Progressive Education Association, March 1939. Pp. [34]. Paper, mimeographed. Out of print.

[1255]

Study of Attitudes toward the Administration of Justice. College and adults; 1938; 1 form; $1 per 25; 20¢ per specimen set; nontimed (60) minutes; [F. C. Sumner]; Washington, D. C.: the author, Howard University.

REFERENCES

1 SUMNER, F. C., AND CAMPBELL, ASTREA S. "Attitudes toward the Administration of Justice." *J Psychol* 8:23-52 Jl '39.

[1256]

Teacher's Rating Scales for Pupil Adjustment. Kindergarten through grade 14; 1937; 1 form; 25¢ per rating scale (only one copy is needed for a class of 40 students); 25¢ per 25 individual record blanks; 25¢ per specimen set; Frank N. Freeman and Ethel Kawin; Chicago, Ill.: University of Chicago Press.

Bessie Lee Gambrill, Associate Professor of Elementary Education, Yale University. Developed in the Laboratory Schools of the University of Chicago and in the public schools of Glencoe, Illinois, these rating scales are designed as a service instrument to help teachers in understanding and managing pupils rather than for research purposes. There are five scales, one for each of the following general categories: intellectual characteristics, work and study habits, emotional adjustment, social adjustment, scholastic achievement. While disclaiming any assumption that these are mutually exclusive categories and voicing the belief that a child's behavior is an expression of his total personality, the authors state that their experimentation indicates that teachers can discriminate among the categories and that pupils may show considerable variability on the five scales. To help the teacher define these five concepts a list of traits or characteristics is provided opposite each scale: three taken at random for illustration from the twelve which define *Intellectual Characteristics* are, "possession of average intelligence," "discrimination in selecting tasks," and "imagination." The ratings, from 1 to 5 in each scale division, are to be given, not in these defining terms, but in terms of the composite categories. A rough approximation to the normal curve of distribution in terms of percentages is sug-

gested as proper distribution of ratings for a large number of pupils. Provision is made on a separate sheet for a summary of individual ratings and a pupil graph, and for an anecdotal report on pupils who have been given a rating of 5 (lowest) on any scale. The purpose of this report is to serve as a background for study and understanding of the pupil. The individual sheets become a part of the student's cumulative record.

No attempt at establishing the reliability of the scales is attempted beyond the statement that in actual experimental use teachers do succeed in discriminating among the areas represented by the five scales. This seems sufficient in view of the stated purpose of the scales. The defining terms under each scale division should improve its validity in use. The authors' explanation of the effect of a teacher's own attitudes upon personality responses and personality ratings should operate in the same direction. Caution against halo effect and suggestions on how to reduce it are given.

Such an instrument as this has its greatest value as a supervisory device for helping teachers to form the habit of studying their children continuously and for developing skill in such study. The reviewer questions the value of emphasizing the general concept rating. Since the purpose is to improve the guidance given children, defining characteristics as given under each scale category would seem to be the focal points for teachers' attention. For this purpose, as well as for giving greater validity to any ratings undertaken, it is important that teachers should note and record adequate behavioral evidence for such defining categories as "Intellectual curiosity," "Being independent in one's work," "Has emotional reactions well controlled." The authors do not suggest this practice.

[1257]

Tentative Check List for Determining Attitudes on Fifty Crucial Social, Economic, and Political Problems. Grades 9-16 and adults; 1935-39; a revision of *A Tentative Check List for Determining the Positions Held by Students in Forty Crucial World Problems* (see 72); 1 form; 35¢ per check list; 35¢ per specimen set; nontimed (120) minutes; Herbert B. Bruner, Arthur V. Linden, and Hugh B. Wood; New York: Bureau of Publications, Teachers College, Columbia University.

[1258]

Test of Personality Adjustment. Ages 9-13; 1931; 1 form, separate editions for boys and girls; $1.75 per 20; 40¢ per specimen set; Carl R. Rogers; New York: Association Press.

REFERENCES

1 ROGERS, CARL R. *Measuring Personality Adjustment in Children Nine to Thirteen Years of Age.* Columbia University, Teachers College, Contributions to Education, No. 458. New York: Bureau of Publications, the College, 1931. Pp. v, 107. $1.50.

2 BABCOCK, MARJORIE E. *A Comparison of Delinquent and Non-Delinquent Boys by Objective Measures of Personality.* Ralph B. Spence, faculty sponsor. Honolulu, H. I.: the Author, 1932. Pp. 74. Paper.

C. M. Louttit, Director of the Psychological Clinics and Associate Professor of Clinical Psychology, Indiana University. Although this instrument for personality investigation of children is entirely different from the usual schedules, it is sufficiently familiar that a detailed description is unnecessary. It covers areas of personal inferiority, social maladjustment, family maladjustment, and daydreaming, by setting six tasks none of which are of the yes-or-no answer type. Our experience with the scale shows that children find it more interesting and game-like than schedules of the inventory type.

The statistician would frown upon this test because norms are based upon only 167 children, and the scoring is rather complicated. However Rogers carefully warns that, while the tests may be given to small groups, it is intended as a clinical tool. A section on interpretation of results in the manual is especially complete in that it suggests the many clues obtainable from a study of individual responses. In fact, the author does not seem to be particularly concerned about the numerical scores. This is a very refreshing attitude in a world filled with statistically minded psychometricians. Further help is given the test user in four case studies in which the significance of responses is related to items of the case history.

We have used this test in our clinics, and with the exception of the time-consuming method of scoring, have found it the most satisfactory instrument of personality measurement.

[1259]

Tests of the Socially Competent Person. Grades 7-12; 1936-37; 1 form; $6.30 per 25; 15¢ per specimen set; 75(80) minutes; Paul R. Mort, Ralph B. Spence, V. C. Arnspiger, and Laura K. Eads; New York, N. Y.: Bureau of Publications, Teachers College, Columbia University.

REFERENCES

1 SPENCE, RALPH B. "One Approach to the Appraisal of the Competence of High School Pupils." *Teach Col Rec* 40:507-20 Mr '39.

Alvin C. Eurich, Professor of Education, Stanford University. This test of the socially competent person is designed to measure reactions to situations in four areas of living: Health (Test I); Personal Economics (Test II); Family Community Relations (Test III); and Social-Civic Relations (Test IV). The items in Tests I and II call for reactions to generalizations on situations which a pupil can do something about as an individual; in Test III, to situations which a pupil can do something about with the cooperation of other members of his family or community; in Test IV, to situations which a pupil can do something about only as a member of a large group. Within each test the items are arranged in groups, each of which is preceded by a description of a situation. If the pupil agrees with an item he encircles an *A*; if he disagrees, he encircles a *D*.

Reliability coefficients for the total test, based on a single grade of about 300 cases, range from .83 to .94. Grade norms are provided for "typical schools" and for "superior curriculum schools." Validity is inferred from the value of the items and from the fact that children in superior curriculum schools make higher scores than pupils in typical schools.

The authors suggest that the test has three outstanding uses: (*a*) a broad check on the effectiveness of the school curriculum; (*b*) motivation of instruction through the presentation of practical problems to the pupils; and (*c*) individual diagnosis and guidance. They suggest also that individual problems might be prepared, although they fail to give the reliability of each part, so that the test user will know how much reliance he can place on the part scores.

A more accurate label for this test would be: A Test of Beliefs and Knowledge Concerning Four Areas of Living. The following is an example of a belief item: High school boys and girls should "have outdoor recreation or sports every day." The knowledge items may be illustrated by the following: "The differences in insurance rates for standard types of insurance from one company to another are small." If one agrees that beliefs and knowledge in the four areas of living determine whether or not a person is soundly competent, the test is a good one. If, however, one believes with the reviewer that social competence involves more than beliefs and knowledge—that it includes methods and habits of approaching and communicating with people, as well as other characteristics—the test is wholly inadequate as a measure of social competency, and a score is likely to be misleading.

Within the limited scope established by the nature of the items, the test is carefully prepared and should be useful for the purpose designated by the authors if the major limitation is kept in mind.

Warren G. Findley, Assistant Director, Division of Examinations and Testing, State Education Department, Albany, New York. The four parts of this test are designed to measure competence in four areas: health, personal economics, family and community relationships, and social-civic problems. The areas thus are arranged in ascending order of size of group through which the individual operates and by the same token in descending order of immediate personal control and responsibility.

The test is to be commended as an instrument which presents real situations for consideration. The claim that it may be used for "motivating instruction through the presentation of practical problems" seems wholly reasonable. It should be useful not only to the teacher who wishes to motivate pupils, but also to the supervisor who wishes to motivate teachers to relate their work to pupil problems.

Some credence may also be given to the claim that the test may be used to pick out for special attention pupils notably incompetent in the areas covered by the test.

On the other hand, the test cannot be recommended as a *measuring* instrument even for surveys. And the construction of individual pupil profiles from the scores on the various parts would be extremely dubious. In many places in the first three scales the correct answering of a single true-false item makes a difference of half a grade in the individual's rating. No matter how carefully these scales have been standardized, they are too coarse and unreliable for individual diagnosis.

Two factors combine to make the test a poor measuring instrument. First, the fact that it is a simple pencil-and-paper questionnaire of opinion makes its validity very doubtful. While the test exercises present real situations, the expression of agreement or disagreement with statements does not mean the making of real choices. Even though the situations are real and related especially to adolescents and though the answers allowed are as free from criticism as one can expect in such controversial areas,

the validity of a direct questionnaire for measuring social competence must be questioned.

The second source of weakness is the type of item that has been used. The agree-disagree or true-false item is the least reliable item in the test constructor's repertory. When one adds to this the fact that instructions about guessing and corrections for guessing are omitted, a greater degree of unreliability is certain. Moreover, the examination of individual questions leads to the conclusion that the negative answers do not reflect a clear position. In many comparative statements, of which there are 66 in the test, to disagree may mean that one believes the two items compared are equal or that the opposite comparison is true or that one does not know whether the two items compared are equal, or unequal in the opposite sense. Multiple-choice items would be better in most of these cases and, indeed, are generally better adapted to reflect the balanced "judgments characteristic of the socially competent person." One should also mention that of 33 statements which contain as *critical* words "all," "always," "every," "never," 29 are false. The effect of these and other items is to cause a preponderance of "disagree" answers on the scoring key for each part. If one were to mark all statements in the test "disagree," he would obtain a measurable score on the test.

In summary, then, the test should serve a very useful purpose in a "test-teach" plan but should not be considered adequate for objective appraisal of social competence or of effects of instruction on competence.

Pedro T. Orata, Special Consultant, Occupational Information and Guidance Service, United States Office of Education, Washington, D. C. The French naturalist, Cuvier, was once asked to pass judgment on the following definition: "A crab is a small red fish that walks backward." Cuvier replied: "The definition is entirely correct except at three points; the crab is not a fish, it is not red, and it does not walk backward." *Tests of the Socially Competent Person* is a perfect instrument except at three points: first, it is not a test, if by the term *test* is meant a valid measure of competent social behavior; second, it does not provide situations to which a person may act in a social way; and, third, it is entirely possible for a person to score perfectly in the test and still be a social misfit. As someone has so aptly put it, "Saying is not believing and believing is not behaving." A competent person is to be judged not by what he says or believes, but by what he does.

This weakness of the test is evidently recognized by the authors, because in the first paragraph of the manual of directions they state definitely that "The ultimate test of education is found in the behavior patterns produced in the pupils." Nevertheless, since to secure evidence for "behavior patterns" requires trained observers and the methods are very expensive of time, "A more practical method is to give pupils an opportunity to react to descriptions of situations similar to those which they face in everyday life."

The catch is in the meaning of the word *practical*. A test can be practical in the sense implied by the term *attainable* without being in the least useful. We have thousands of tests now that are practical in this sense whose validity, however, has been demonstrated to be very low indeed. The need is not more of the same kind. This world would be greatly benefited if we valued practicability less and usefulness more, especially in the field of tests and measurements, in which he who runs may make a test—and usually does.

Apart from the theoretical unsoundness of the test, it has manifest shortcomings in other respects. A careful reading of the items should enable one to classify an undue proportion of them under the following categories:

1) *Too Obviously Absurd or Wrong.* Test III, Problem I: "A group of high school boys and girls agreed that the people in the community should be actively interested in community problems." One of their reasons is: *"In order to reduce the free services for the poor."* Test II, Problem IV: "Harry's mother has always wanted him to be a lawyer. She worked hard sewing for a living, in order to send him to law school. Whenever he failed in an examination she provided private tutors for him. He tried the bar examination three times and finally passed them. He is now working as a clerk in a large law office. In general, persons like Harry probably: *Will be able to give better legal advice than most lawyers."*

2) *Too Obviously Right or May be Readily Granted.* Test II, Problem: "Jim is especially interested in bookkeeping and has decided that he would like to study to be an accountant.

To be well suited for this work he should rate high on . . .: *General intelligence."* Test I, Problem II: "High school boys and girls should plan their after-school hours wisely." One of the "sensible things that they might do" is: *"Carefully plan their recreation as well as their study."*

3) *Highly Ambiguous or Controversial, or Question-Begging.* Test IV, Problem XIII: "Following are some statements concerning present-day economic problems which are of particular importance to high school pupils today. Indicate those with which you agree and those with which you disagree: *If all people were consistently more thrifty there would be no poverty."* Test III, Problem III: "A group of high school boys and girls, disturbed by conflicting ideas concerning the value and importance of the home in American life today, decided to study this problem. As a result of their study they came to the conclusion that some of the following ideas were true and some were false. Indicate those with which you agree and those with which you disagree: *If all parents were well-educated, schools would be unnecessary."*

4) *Requiring Expert Information or Specific Knowledge.* Test IV, Problem IX: "Below are a few things, some of which have changed considerably within the last one thousand years and some of which have not. Indicate those you think have not: *Man's physical strength."* Test IV, Problem XII: "Because business depressions affect them and their futures so seriously high school pupils should understand the causes of such depressions. Among the factors contributing markedly to the occurrence of the depression in the United States during the years from 1929 on, were: *Unsound expansion of credit; increased government control of production; Lack of balance between production and distribution."*

In brief, it seems to the present reviewer that *Tests of the Socially Competent Person* lacks validity both in what it should measure according to the title and in what it is intended to measure according to the introductory statement of its makers. It may be highly practical from the point of view of the mechanical phases of execution and administration, but it may be practically useless from the point of view of the end to be served.

In spite of the shortcomings indicated the test has outstanding contributions to make toward the improvement of evaluation, among which may be mentioned the following: (*a*) seriously attempting to obtain evidence for one of the "intangibles" in education; (*b*) focusing attention upon the areas in life at the present time in which there exists the greatest need for emphasis—health, personal economics, family and community relationships, and social-civic problems; (*c*) suggesting a way of integrating school experiences in the various subjects around problems of personal and social concern; and (*d*) going one step forward in emphasizing "behavior patterns produced in the pupils" as "the ultimate test of education."

For reviews by Douglas E. Scates and Hilda Taba, see 1154.

[1260]
Test of Social Attitudes. Grades 13-17; 1939; 1 form; $1.25 per 25; 25¢ per specimen set; nontimed (25) minutes; E. C. Hunter; New York: Psychological Corporation.

[1261]
Walther Social Attitudes Test. Grades 12-16; 1937; 2 forms; 50¢ per 25; 15¢ per specimen set; nontimed (25-40) minutes; E. Curt Walther; Towson, Md.: the Author, State Teachers College.

[1262]
Washburne Social-Adjustment Inventory: Thaspic Edition. Age 12 and over; 1936-40; 1 form; $1.30 per 25; 20¢ per manual; 15¢ per specimen set (without manual); nontimed (45) minutes; John N. Washburne; Yonkers, N. Y.: World Book Co.

REFERENCES

1 WASHBURNE, JOHN N. "An Experiment in Character Measurement." *J Juvenile Res* 13:1-18 Ja '29.
2 WASHBURNE, JOHN N. "The Impulsions of Adolescents as Revealed by Their Written Wishes." *J Juvenile Res* 16:193-212 Jl '32.
3 WASHBURNE, JOHN N. "A Test of Social Adjustment." *J Appl Psychol* 19:125-44 Ap '35.
4 WASHBURNE, JOHN N. "The Social Adjustment of Adolescents," pp. 288-92. In *Reconstructing Education Thru Research.* Official Report, American Educational Research Association, A Department of the National Education Association, St. Louis, Missouri, February 22-26, 1936. Washington, D. C.: the Association, May 1936. Pp. 301. $1.50. Paper.

For a review by Daniel A. Prescott of an earlier edition, see 928.

[1263]
What Do You Think? Grades 7-12; 1934-35; 2 forms; $3.15 per 100; 35¢ per manual; 40¢ per specimen set; nontimed (35-45) minutes; Victor H. Noll; New York: Bureau of Publications, Teachers College, Columbia University.

REFERENCES

1 NOLL, VICTOR H. "Measuring Scientific Thinking." *Teach Col Rec* 35:685-93 My '34.
2 NOLL, VICTOR H. "Measuring the Scientific Attitude." *J Abn and Social Psychol* 30:145-54 Jl-S '35.
3 BLAIR, GLENN M. "The Validity of the Noll Test of Scientific Thinking." *J Ed Psychol* 31:53-9 Ja '40.

Ralph K. Watkins, Professor of Education, The University of Missouri. This is an attempt to measure scientific attitude and habits of thinking. The tests are intended for school pupils in grades 7-12.

Each form includes 75 true-false items, 15 added true-false items based upon the analysis of a diagram, and a final exercise requiring the numbering of 22 terms in alphabetical order.

The front page asks for certain personnel data concerning the pupil. There are some peculiar discriminations and lacks of discrimination in this. For example, there is a space for marking the number of years' experience in physical geography or general science as if these two courses were considered as of equivalent value in training in scientific attitudes. The space for recording training in history is marked "yrs. History (not U.S.)" as if training in United States history has not assumed training value for scientific attitudes and other history has.

One-half page at the front is devoted to questions concerning the likes and dislikes of pupils for various types of leisure activities. There is no apparent relationship between this material and the traits which the test purports to measure.

Of the first 75 true-false items in Form 1, 59 are keyed as false, 13 as questionable, and only 3 as true.

The tests may be considered useful as experimental tools for teachers interested in trying to train pupils in scientific attitudes. Teachers using the tests need to be cautious in forming conclusions concerning the exact status of the attitudes of their pupils as a result of scores on such tests.

Workers in education and in educational psychology are by no means in agreement upon the definition of scientific attitudes, nor of scientific habits of thinking. There is serious question on whether the "habit of accuracy of observation" can be attained as such, or whether accuracy of observation is always an attribute of definite situations or things. Is an individual accurate, or must he be accurate in *something*? This same type of question arises concerning all the other five "habits of thinking" which these tests purport to measure.

At least one other of the basic assumptions underlying the validity of the tests may be seriously questioned. In the handbook accompanying the tests the author says, "First, if the tests really measure habits of thinking, scores on them should be little dependent upon native mental capacity or intelligence." This, in effect, says that intelligence is little related to the formation of desirable habits of thinking or the formation of scientific attitudes. The writer of this review seriously questions the validity of this assumption.

Finally, the most important question concerning these tests is that of just what do they measure. Teachers may well restrict the use of these tests to experimental and tentative trials until this fundamental question can be more definitely answered.

J Ed Psychol 31:53-9 Ja '40. Glenn M. Blair. "The Validity of the Noll Test of Scientific Thinking." * The Noll test of scientific thinking has been devised to measure the extent to which school children can take an objective, scientific viewpoint toward a variety of problems. In brief, it purports to measure the scientific attitude. In order to check its validity, this test was given to sixteen top ranking scientists on the faculty of the University of Illinois. Each of these men holds the Ph.D. degree, and has a rank of associate professor or higher in the University. The branches of science represented by these scientists are: Bacteriology, botany, chemistry, entomology, physics, psychology, and zoology. The results of the investigation show that for many items of both forms of the test, the answers given by the scientists disagree with those given in the published scoring key. Several questions are found for which none of the sixteen scientists give acceptable answers according to the Noll key. There are twenty-six invalid items in Form 1 and twenty-five invalid items in Form 2, if it be held that for an item to be considered valid it must be answered according to the scoring key by three-fourths of the scientists. These facts cause one to question the validity of this test as a measure of scientific thinking. It is suggested, however, that the validity could be improved considerably by revising the scoring key so that it would fall in line with the answers of the group of scientists who took the tests. In a number of questions there is almost complete disagreement among the scientists as to what are the correct answers. It is suggested that these questions be eliminated from the tests altogether.

For a review by Francis D. Curtis, see 1139.

[1264]

What Should Our Schools Do? A Poll of Public Opinion on the School Program. Adults; 1938; 1 form; $2.10 per 100; 10¢ per specimen set; Paul R. Mort, F. G. Cornell, and Norman H. Hinton; New York: Bureau of Publications, Teachers College, Columbia University.

Loyola Ed Digest 14:12 Ap '39. Austin G. Schmidt. This is a questionnaire containing one hundred items, and is intended as a measure of the extent to which school authorities and the public are prepared to accept newer practices. One scores high if he says that children who do not know their subject matter should not be required to repeat the matter, if he denies that children have as much need for practicing restraint as they have for practicing freedom, and so forth. In justice to the authors it should be noted that they do not defend in the accompanying set of instructions these new and progressive ideas. Users of the questionnaire are at liberty to condemn as an undesirable citizen one who scores high in it. Not all the practices, of course, are equally extreme or radical.

[1265]

What Would You Do? A Survey of Student Opinion. Grades 7-12; 1939; 1 form, 2 parts; 75¢ per 25; 10¢ per specimen set; nontimed (15-20) minutes per part; Ruth E. Eckert and Howard E. Wilson; Cambridge, Mass.: Committee on Publications, Harvard Graduate School of Education.
a) PART I, SCHOOL AFFAIRS.
b) PART II, COMMUNITY AFFAIRS.

REFERENCES

1 WILSON, HOWARD E. *Education for Citizenship,* pp. 66-79. New York: McGraw-Hill Book Co., 1938. Pp. xii, 272. $2.75. (London: McGraw-Hill Publishing Co., Ltd., 1939. 15s.)

[1266]

Wrightstone Scale of Civic Beliefs. Grades 9-12; 1938; 2 forms; $1.00 per 25; 15¢ per specimen set; 15(20) minutes; J. Wayne Wrightstone; Yonkers, N. Y.: World Book Co.

REFERENCES

1 WRIGHTSTONE, J. WAYNE. "Appraising Newer Practices in Teaching Social Studies." *Sch R* 42:688-93 N '34.
2 WRIGHTSTONE, J. WAYNE. "Civic Beliefs and Correlated Intellectual and Social Factors." *Sch R* 42:53-58 Ja '34.
3 WRIGHTSTONE, J. WAYNE. "Measuring Some Major Objectives of the Social Studies." *Sch R* 43:771-9 D '35.

Stephen M. Corey, Professor of Educational Psychology and Superintendent of the Laboratory Schools, The University of Chicago. The most important single question that anyone can ask about a scale purporting to provide "a valid and reliable measure of civic attitudes" is: What hint do the scores give us as to the way the subjects will behave? This to the reviewer is the real test of the validity of attitude questionnaires. Some scale makers identify an attitude with a verbal statement checked on an inventory. Such an "attitude" has little significance psychologically or sociologically. The pragmatic justification of attitude questionnaires is the accuracy with which they make possible the prognostication of overt behavior. Especially is this true of scales such as Wrightstone's which are developed to measure attitudes because of "their importance as dynamic factors which exert a powerful influence on behavior." This concept of the validity of attitude scales is not emphasized in either the manual of directions or the three articles [1, 2, 3] the reviewer read which dealt with the scale. Wrightstone apparently believes that the validity of his scale was established by demonstrating that: (a) the items differentiated between liberals and conservatives, and (b) expert judges agreed that the items scored "liberal" and "conservative" were really so. No data were presented to indicate the degree to which the scale discriminated between the two groups (liberal and conservative) nor was there any description of the method employed to select the groups originally. The reliability coefficient between Forms A and B for 252 pupils in grades 10-12 inclusive was .90.

In the Catalog of Standard Tests (Spring 1940, p. 59) published by the World Book Company appears the statement: "This test [Wrightstone's] provides a measure of an individual's liberalism or conservatism with respect to social, economic, and political issues. It meets the need for a reliable index of the extent to which certain attitudinal or nonintellectual objectives of educational procedure are being attained." The reviewer doubts the accuracy of the second sentence. He has found no convincing evidence that scores on the Wrightstone Scale of Civic Beliefs are in any way related to the liberal or conservative behavior of children. It is the latter with which educators are primarily concerned. The scales are attractively put up, easy to administer, and economical of scoring time. The reviewer has found them interesting to children and provocative of much valuable classroom discussion.

Harold Gulliksen, Assistant Professor of Psychology and Examiner in the Social Sciences, The University of Chicago. From the viewpoint of the mechanics of administering and scoring, the test is well-constructed. The

directions to the student and examiner are clear. The test is completely objective, and a convenient scoring stencil is provided. Percentile norms are provided for a single form and for the combined score using both forms of the test. These norms are given separately for grades 9, 10, 11, and 12.

The reliability of the test is high, .90 for a single form and .94 for the combined score on both forms. However, we are told that the reliability was computed from a sample including pupils from grades 10 to 12 inclusive while norms are given for each grade separately. Since the "liberalism" score increases steadily from the ninth to the twelfth grade, the reliability for a single grade would certainly be less than .90, although in this case probably not much less. The best practice would be to give reliability figures for the same groups as those on which the norms are calculated. In addition to information on reliability, it should be common practice to give the standard error of measurement since this statistic probably is not as sensitive to changes in variability of the total population as is the reliability coefficient.

It is gratifying to note that when the author suggests the use of part scores on the test, he also points out that the reliability of these scores is low, that they are "not sufficiently reliable for accurate individual diagnosis."

The techniques used in selecting the test items and in validating the scale are described. These techniques, while indicating careful work, are not scaling techniques such as are now available. The need for scaling techniques can be illustrated. For example, agreement with either of the following statements adds the same amount to the "liberalism" score: "United States citizens have been jailed because of their political beliefs"; and "Business and industry increasingly need some government regulation"; whereas they should probably be weighted differently. Attitude measurement is a field in which factor analysis techniques could be used with considerable profit. There is no indication that they have been used or that the test items form a one-dimensional system. It would be desirable to take the precaution of determining this before constructing attitude scales, or to use a scaling technique which includes a test of linearity.

Some of the statements in the test seem to this reviewer to be so largely factual in nature that—barring considerable evidence to the contrary—they hardly constitute appropriate material for a scale of "liberalism." The following three statements will illustrate this point: "Democracy, unlike dictatorship, has certain limitations for dealing quickly with emergencies"; "Other nations approved our getting Panama from Colombia"; and "The United States is now entangled in European affairs." Also in view of our present knowledge of the precariousness of generalizations concerning nations, it seems somewhat unjustified to include the statement "German people are on the whole industrious and thrifty," and to score a person who agrees with this statement as more "liberal" than one who does not.

PERSONALITY—THIRD MMY

REVIEWS BY *Harold H. Abelson, Ralph C. Bedell, Arthur L. Benton, E. J. G. Bradford, R. A. Brotemarkle, Harold D. Carter, Glen U. Cleeton, William E. Coffman, Lee J. Cronbach, Edwin W. Davis, Parker Davis, Jr., Susan K. Deri, Raleigh M. Drake, Stanley G. Dulsky, Jack W. Dunlap, Philip Eisenberg, M. H. Elliott, Albert Ellis, H. J. Eysenck, Paul R. Farnsworth, John C. Flanagan, John W. French, Henry E. Garrett, Edward B. Greene, Nelson G. Hanawalt, Starke R. Hathaway, Thelma Hunt, William A. Hunt, Ludwig Immergluck, Margaret Ives, E. Lowell Kelly, Kate Levine Kogan, Morris Krugman, W. C. Kvaraceus, Theodore F. Lentz, Louis Long, C. M. Louttit, James Maxwell, Paul E. Meehl, H. Meltzer, Lorenz Misbach, L. S. Penrose, Gilbert J. Rich, John W. M. Rothney, Julian B. Rotter, Laurance F. Shaffer, Benjamin Shimberg, William U. Snyder, Douglas Spencer, C. R. Strother, Percival M. Symonds, Howard R. Taylor, Edith I. M. Thomson, Simon H. Tulchin, Goodwin Watson, Katherine W. Wilcox, J. R. Wittenborn, O. L. Zangwill.*

[23]

A-S Reaction Study: A Scale for Measuring Ascendance-Submission in Personality. College and adults; 1928–39; manual revised 1939; separate forms for men and women; $2.25 per 25; 15¢ per specimen set; nontimed (20) minutes; Gordon W. Allport and Floyd H. Allport; Houghton Mifflin Co.

a) FORM FOR MEN. 1928.
b) FORM FOR WOMEN, REVISED. 1928–39.

REFERENCES

1-19. *See* 40:1198.
20. DECKER, C. E. *An Experiment in the Use of Psychological Tests in the Selection of Life Insurance Agents.* Unpublished master's thesis, Dartmouth College, 1931.
21. WANG, CHARLES K. A. "The Significance of Early Personal History for Certain Personality Traits." *Am J Psychol* 44:768-74 O '32. * (PA 7:610)
22. McGEOCH, JOHN A., AND WHITELY, PAUL L. "Correlations Between Certain Measurements of Personality Traits and of Memorizing." *J Ed Psychol* 24:16-20 Ja '33. * (PA 7:1888)
23. STAGNER, ROSS. "The Relation of Personality to Academic Aptitude and Achievement." *J Ed Res* 26:648-60 My '33. * (PA 7:4857)
24. ACHILLES, P. S., AND SCHULTZ, R. S. "Characteristics of Life Insurance Salesmen." *Personnel J* 12:260-3 F '34. * (PA 8:2217)
25. WEISS, LEO. *The Allport A-S Reaction Study in Personality . . . Its Relation to Academic Performance and Participation in Extracurricular Activities.* Unpublished master's thesis, Brown University, 1934. Pp. 17.
26. SCHULTZ, RICHARD S. "Standardized Tests and Statistical Procedures in Selection of Life Insurance Sales Personnel." *J Appl Psychol* 20:553-66 O '36. * (PA 11:2899)
27. WASSON, MARGARET M. "The Agreements Among Certain Types of Personality Schedules." *J Psychol* 9:351-63 Ap '40. * (PA 14:4153)
28. CHILD, IRVIN L., AND SHELDON, WILLIAM H. "The Correlation between Components of Physique and Scores on Certain Psychological Tests." *Char & Pers* 10:23-34 S '41. * (PA 16:1040)
29. DOW, CLYDE W. "The Personality Traits of Effective Public Speakers." *Q J Speech* 27:525-32 D '41. * (PA 16:1590)
30. LINK, HENRY C. "The Definition of Social Effectiveness and Leadership Through Measurement." *Ed & Psychol Meas* 4:57-67 sp '44. * (PA 18:3216)

William U. Snyder, Associate Professor of Psychology and Associate Director, Psychological Clinic, The Pennsylvania State College, State College, Pennsylvania. This well-known test was designed to discover the disposition of an individual to dominate his fellows or to be dominated by them in face-to-face relationships. It thus tries to measure an individual's ascendance or submission, traits which have been placed at opposite poles in a continuum, although the authors are careful to indicate that they are not necessarily opposites, but really independent traits.

The test is widely used by clinical psychologists and also by college teachers and guidance counselors; it is frequently employed in industrial situations, for which there is a separate revision (*see* 40:1199). There are separate forms for men and women, independently standardized and not interchangeable. They consist of 41 and 43 items for which multiple-choice responses varying from two to four answers are provided. The items seem familiar, and that is largely because they have been copied on many later personality tests. They are written with a certain carefulness and qualification which makes answering simpler, because it reduces ambiguity. Scoring weights have been assigned to each response, and this makes scoring laborious if it occurs in any great quantity.

Norms for the test are given in deciles, based on scores of 2,578 men and 600 women. These subjects were college students, widely distributed geographically. Reliability quotients are reported as .85 for men and .90 for women. Numerous studies of validity of the test have been made in the nineteen years since its first publication. Using ratings and self-ratings as criteria of validity, the correlations have varied from .29 to .79. The authors state that using some of the better studies as typical, a suitable validity index would be .45. Thus, they do not make extensive claims of validity, holding that ultimate validity must depend on results obtained in a wide variety of clinical situations. Some external validation has been made in different studies. A correlation of .80 between this test and Bernreuter's dominance scale was found, but the authors deprecate this with the remark that a large number of Bernreuter items were taken from their own scale. In industrial situations an increasing incidence of ascendance was found in positions of increasing executive responsibility. It has also been shown that there is a steady increase in ascendance with increasing age in high school students. Howells demonstrated a correlation of .44 between ascendance and a tendency to "hang on" in an experimental situation. A correlation of .35 was found between teachers' ascendance and their rated teaching success.

As in most personality questionnaires, the authors recognize the possibility of errors of subjective evaluations and stipulate that cooperation and sincerity are necessary. That this cannot always be guaranteed is a weakness that the authors admit.

Perhaps one of the most effective validations of the test is the frequency with which it continues to be used. It is widely recognized as standard equipment in psychological clinics. As a test of total personality, it should not be exploited, but as a test of dominance, it is probably not excelled.

For a review by Doncaster G. Humm of the 1928 edition, see 40:1198; for his review of Beckman's revision for business use, see 40:1199.

[24]

Attitude-Interest Analysis Test. Early adolescents and adults; 1936; a disguised test of mental masculinity and femininity; also called M-F Test; Forms A, B; 10¢ per test; $1.75 per manual and scoring stencils; nontimed (40-60) minutes; Lewis M. Terman and Catharine Cox Miles; McGraw-Hill Book Co., Inc.

REFERENCES

1. MILES, CATHARINE COX, AND TERMAN, LEWIS M. "Sex Differences in the Association of Ideas." *Am J Psychol* 41:165-206 Ap '29. * (*PA* 3:2575)
2. KELLY, E. LOWELL; MILES, CATHARINE COX; AND TERMAN, LEWIS M. "Ability to Influence One's Score on a Typical Pencil-and-Paper Test of Personality." *Char & Pers* 4:206-15 Mr '36. * (*PA* 10:4111)
3. TERMAN, LEWIS M., AND MILES, CATHARINE COX; ASSISTED BY JACK W. DUNLAP, HAROLD A. EDGERTON, E. LOWELL KELLY, ALBERT K. KURTZ, E. ALICE McANULTY, QUINN McNEMAR, MAUD A. MERRILL, FLOYD L. RUCH, AND HORACE G. WYATT. *Sex and Personality: Studies in Masculinity and Femininity.* New York: McGraw-Hill Book Co., Inc., 1936. Pp. xii, 600. $4.50. * (London: McGraw-Hill Publishing Co., Ltd. 25s.) (*PA* 10:5879)
4. GILKINSON, HOWARD. "Masculine Temperament and Secondary Sex Characteristics: A Study of the Relationship Between Psychological and Physical Measures of Masculinity." *Genetic Psychol Monogr* 19:105-54 F '37. * (*PA* 11:3310)
5. PAGE, JAMES, AND WARKENTIN, JOHN. "Masculinity and Paranoia." *J Abn & Social Psychol* 33:527-31 O '38. * (*PA* 13:1486)
6. ROSENZWEIG, SAUL. "A Basis for the Improvement of Personality Tests With Special Reference to the M-F Battery." *J Abn & Social Psychol* 33:476-88 O '38. * (*PA* 13:1728)
7. DISHER, DOROTHY ROSE. "Attitude-Interest Analysis of Florida State College for Women Students." Abstract. *Psychol B* 36:616 O '39. * (*PA* 14:532, title only)
8. GILKINSON, HOWARD, AND KNOWER, FRANKLIN H. *Psychological Studies of Individual Differences Among Students of Speech.* Minneapolis, Minn.: Department of Speech; University of Minnesota, June 1939. Pp. iii, 196. Paper, mimeographed. Gratis. *
9. BECK, MAURICE P. "A Short Form of the Terman-Miles Masculinity-Femininity Test." Abstract. *Psychol B* 37:583 O '40. * (*PA* 15:313, title only)
10. BOSSELMAN, BEULAH, AND SKORODIN, BERNARD. "Masculinity and Femininity in Psychotic Patients: As Measured by the Terman-Miles Interest-Attitude Analysis Test." *Am J Psychiatry* 97:699-702 N '40. * (*PA* 15:1736)
11. CHILD, IRVIN L., AND SHELDON, WILLIAM H. "The Correlation Between Components of Physique and Scores on Certain Psychological Tests." *Char & Pers* 10:23-34 S '41. * (*PA* 16:1040)
12. GILKINSON, HOWARD, AND KNOWER, FRANKLIN H. "A Study of Standardized Personality Tests and Skill in Speech." *J Ed Psychol* 32:161-175 Mr '41. * (*PA* 15:3888)
13. WALKER, EDWARD L. "The Terman-Miles 'M-F' Test and the Prison Classification Program." *J Genetic Psychol* 59:27-40 S '41. * (*PA* 16:1120)
14. BARNETTE, W. LESLIE. "Study of an Adult Male Homosexual and Terman-Miles M-F Scores." *Am J Orthopsychiatry* 12:346-51 Ap '42. * (*PA* 16:4060)
15. BURGER, F. E.; NEMZEK, C. L.; AND VAUGHN, C. L. "The Relationship of Certain Factors to Scores on the Terman-Miles Attitude-Interest Analysis Test." *J Social Psychol* 16:39-50 Ag '42. * (*PA* 16:4945)
16. DISHER, DOROTHY ROSE. "Regional Differences in Masculinity-Femininity Responses." *J Social Psychol* 15:53-61 F '42. * (*PA* 16:3160)
17. DUREA, M. A., AND BILSKY, H. B. "An Exploratory Study of Personality Characteristics in Schizophrenia and Manic-Depressive Psychoses." *J General Psychol* 28:81-98 Ja '43. * (*PA* 17:1184)
18. PINTNER, R., AND FORLANO, G. "Some Measures of Dominance in College Women." *J Social Psychol* 19:313-5 My '44. * (*PA* 18:3815)
19. CAPWELL, DORA F. "Personality Patterns of Adolescent Girls: II, Delinquents and Non-Delinquents." *J Appl Psychol* 29:289-97 Ag '45. * (*PA* 20:191)
20. SMITH, JANE HARRIS. "The Relation of Masculinity-Femininity Scores of Sorority Girls on a Free Association Test to Those of Their Parents." *J Social Psychol* 22:79-85 Ag '45. * (*PA* 20:844)

Starke R. Hathaway, Professor and Clinical Psychologist, Department of Psychiatry and Neurology, University of Minnesota, Minneapolis, Minnesota. At the extreme, masculinity and femininity may be measured by the single item, "What is your sex?" This item would have a high reliability and would validate very favorably with the physical and physiological characteristics of the respondents. In a restricted way the *Attitude-Interest Analysis Test* could be criticized as being an unwarranted extension of this item; however, there are many reasons for attempts to distribute the variance of the masculinity-femininity variable. Whether the observed differences are attributable to nature or nurture is not so important as is the fact that the differences exist and probably contribute very materially to vocational and social adjustment.

The *Attitude-Interest Analysis Test* is unusually carefully developed and the authors have made available extensive data to indicate findings among various occupations, age levels, family relationships and the like. Its reliability is satisfactory but it is too long.

Item selection for the test was based upon

the differentiation of males from females. While some effort was made to avoid items that would be chiefly cultural or provincial, this type of test item is nearly impossible to free from these influences, and the statistics would have to be adjusted as one worked in a different cultural setting.

The purpose of the test as given by the authors is "to enable the clinician or other investigator to obtain a more exact and meaningful, as well as a more objective, rating of those aspects of personality in which the sexes tend to differ." This purpose must of course be evaluated against the manner in which the items were derived. Deviation is by that consideration defined in terms of the degree to which the individual's interests and attitudes vary from his sex norm on items showing a male-female differentiation experimentally. It is especially important to note that this definition of masculinity and femininity may be a restricted one. For example, it is not a priori to be accepted that the homoerotic or the "feminine" male would most usefully be identified by the same items or even the same variable that would differentiate males and females. In this regard, the authors state, "Most emphatic warning is necessary against the assumption that an extremely feminine score for males or an extremely masculine score for females can serve as an adequate basis for the diagnosis of homosexuality, either overt or latent." The findings of the authors indicate that while among female and male homosexuals the deviation in score is found toward the mean for the opposite sex, this can be interpreted no farther than that such deviation is present in affected persons. That the deviation in persons not known to be affected indicates similar possibilities is, of course, not proved. A special set of Form A item weights is given for a tentative homosexual invert scale. This scale is very cumbersome, and the groups contrasted to obtain the weights differ in too many respects other than in their sexual behavior.

The test, as shown by the authors' experiments, is subject to very considerable modification of score when the subjects are asked to attempt to simulate a strongly masculine or feminine score. Apparently the items are in large part identifiable as masculinity-femininity items when the subject is told that he is taking that type of test. On the other hand the authors point out that subjects did not appear to dis-cover spontaneously that they were taking a masculinity-femininity test. It nevertheless seems possible that a subject sensitized by knowing himself to be deviant might consciously or unconsciously modify his responses.

[25]

Behavior Cards: A Test-Interview for Delinquent Children. Delinquents having a reading grade score of 4.5 or higher; 1940; individual; 1 form: $2.75 per box of cards, postpaid; 75¢ per 25 record sheets postpaid; 35¢ per manual, postpaid; nontimed (15-30) minutes; Ralph M. Stogdill; distributed by Psychological Corporation.

REFERENCES
   1. PUSKIN, RUTH. The Validation of a Test-Interview for Delinquent Boys. Unpublished master's thesis, Ohio State University, 1938.
   2. STOGDILL, RALPH M. "A Test-Interview for Delinquent Children." Abstract. Psychol B 35:631 N '38. * (PA 13:1632, title only)
   3. STOGDILL, RALPH M. "A Test-Interview for Delinquent Children." J Appl Psychol 24:325-33 Je '40. * (PA 14:6139)

W. C. Kvaraceus, Associate Professor of Education, Boston University, Boston, Massachusetts. Those familiar with the field of juvenile delinquency in general and more particularly with the problem of identifying predelinquent tendencies or susceptibilities usually lament the paucity of available scientific tools and techniques that aim to define, diagnose, or treat cases of incipient or confirmed malbehavior. The author of *The Behavior Cards* presents a noteworthy and somewhat successful attempt to develop a useful test-interview aid in dealing with the delinquent child, particularly the boy delinquent.

The administration of this questionnaire-test calls for the subject's sorting of 150 items presented on individual cards describing specific behaviors. If the item describes the child's behavior, he is instructed to place the card in the box labeled YES; if the behavior described does not fit the subject, the card is placed in the NO box. The instrument, thus, runs the usual risk of items demanding categorical responses. While it is true that this mechanical sorting does get away from some of the evils of the usual paper and pencil instruments, it is doubtful whether the author's enthusiasm for any essential superiority of this technique in the rapport situation can be defended solely on the basis of the mechanics of test administration. The cards call for a minimum of mid-fourth-grade reading ability.

Validation of the cards is presented in terms of initial selection of items followed by an effective item analysis. Data are presented showing the tendency of the test to differentiate significantly between delinquent and nondelinquent boys, the internal consistency indexes of the items, and the validation coefficients for most of the items. Four hundred items were originally culled from the literature on delinquency, from case histories of delinquents, and from Hayward's *Family Inventory*. The final 150 items, for the most part, have met a reasonable criterion of acceptance before being incorporated in the questionnaire. The average validity coefficients of the items, using case study information as criterion data on items that the author was able to validate, are reported as .68 and .72 for two groups of male delinquents, 50 in each group. A similar study for 50 girl delinquents yielded a validity coefficient of .52. Although the validation and normative data are available on very small samples and although results are not available on a contrasting nondelinquent female group, sufficient information is presented by the author to suggest that this instrument is worthy of further study and use in clinical situations in which the individual follow-up technique will yield the best validation possible.

While the nature of the items is such as to render the questionnaire most allergic to inconsistencies in responses, the reported reliabilities of .92, .94, .83, and .85 are surprisingly high for this type of instrument.

Considering the multiplicity of problems presented by children popularly and perhaps too frequently mislabeled as delinquent, this type of instrument, when further refined, will prove a valuable supplement to the achievement, intelligence, and aptitude tests now commonly used in schools and clinics.

Simon H. Tulchin, Consulting Psychologist, 30 East 60th St., New York 22, New York. The test consists of 150 cards on which are printed questions relating to various areas of delinquent behavior and maladjustment. The subject is provided with two boxes and he is told to place those cards which describe him in the box marked YES and those cards which do not describe him in the box marked NO. All those who make fourth grade scores on reading tests require no assistance in sorting the cards. Others may have the items read to them. The test has been given to 200 delinquent boys who ranged in age from 10 to 18 years; 50 delinquent girls ages 12 to 18; 50 school boys ages 11 to 17; and 25 boy scouts ages 12 to 17. The average ages of the groups

ranged between 13.6 and 14.8 years. The score on the test is the number of cards placed in the YES box. Average scores are given for the four groups and percentile scores for the three larger groups.

The author of the test feels that the card sorting method has the advantage over the questionnaire method in that the child can consider each question separately and more objectively since no written record is made while he is in the room. A score of 50 is considered as suggestive of a disturbing conflict situation. A score of below 15 in a boy with a history of serious and repeated maladjustment is taken to be suggestive of schizophrenic tendencies. On the other hand, scores of below 20 in individuals who have previously shown good adjustment but who are brought into court on serious delinquency charges are given good prognosis for a successful adjustment on probation. As proof for the above conclusions, which should require a great deal of evidence, the author offers the following single sentence: "Follow-up studies indicate that this is a well founded observation."

Correlations of test score and IQ are zero while correlations of test score and age are negative, showing that younger delinquents make higher scores than older delinquents. Reliability is fairly high. Correlations of each question with information available in the histories of the groups of delinquent boys and girls show a wide range of coefficients.

While it may well be that for some children and adolescents answering direct personal questions by means of sorting cards is a less threatening experience than replying to questions in an interview, it is also true that sympathetic questioning makes possible an evaluation of responses which affords much greater insight into the personality of the subject and the nature of the maladjustment. The author recognizes, for example, that the delinquent girls responded less frankly than the boys. It is quite likely that this is in part due to the nature of their delinquency. No data are presented on a control group of girls.

For the delinquent boys fairly high agreement was found between the known behavior as reported in the case histories and the replies to the questions. High agreement is probably to be expected since all of these boys were committed to an agency for study and observation following their delinquencies and behavior maladjustment and recognized that certain facts about them were well known. No histories were available for the relatively small group of control boys, and no attempt was made to check their replies.

An examination of some of the questions reveals a lack of consistency in the replies. Thus to the question: "Do you tell lies sometimes?" 86 per cent of the delinquent boys, 56 per cent of the control boys, and 60 per cent of the delinquent girls answer in the affirmative as against 37, 23, and 16 per cent respectively to the question: "Do you say things that aren't true?" Are these differences due to the word "sometimes" or to the fact that eighty-three other questions intervene between these two? Similar discrepancies occur with other questions.

Apparently a great deal of further research on this test remains to be done.

[26]

California Test of Personality: A Profile of Personal and Social Adjustment. Grades kgn-3, 4-8, 7-10, 9-16, adults; 1939-43; IBM; 5 levels; Forms A, B; $1.25 per 25; 5¢ per copy of machine-scoring edition (grades 4 and over); 2¢ per copy of machine-scorable answer sheet; 25¢ per specimen set of any one level; nontimed (45) minutes; Louis P. Thorpe, Willis W. Clark, and Ernest W. Tiegs; California Test Bureau.
a) PRIMARY SERIES. Grades kgn-3; 1940.
b) ELEMENTARY SERIES. Grades 4-8; 1939.
c) INTERMEDIATE SERIES. Grades 7-10; 1939-40.
d) SECONDARY SERIES. Grades 9-16; 1942.
e) ADULT SERIES. 1942-43.

REFERENCES

1. DUNKERLEY, MARY DOROTHEA. A Statistical Study of Leadership Among College Women. Catholic University of America, Studies in Psychology and Psychiatry, Vol. 4, No. 7. Washington, D.C.: Catholic University of America Press, July 1940. Pp. vii, 65. Paper. $1.25. * (PA 14:5096)
2. MARTIN, M. FRANCES. "Personality Development and Social Adjustment of Mentally Retarded Children." Am J Mental Def 46:94-101 Jl '41. * (PA 16:209)
3. TIEGS, ERNEST W.; CLARK, WILLIS W.; AND THORPE, LOUIS P. "The California Test of Personality." J Ed Res 35:102-8 O '41. * (PA 16:656)
4. PUSEY, HARRIET CLOUGH. The Relationship Between Mental, Physical and Achievement Levels and Certain Personality Traits As Measured by Tests. Unpublished master's thesis, University of Kentucky, 1942. Pp. 80. (Theses in Education 1937-1943, 1943, pp. 40-1.)
5. ROSENWALD, ALAN. "The California Personality Scale As a Diagnostic Instrument." Abstract. Psychol B 39:599 O '42. * (PA 17:575, title only)
6. BONNEY, MERL E. "The Constancy of Sociometric Scores and Their Relationship to Teacher Judgments of Social Success and to Personality Self-Ratings." Sociometry 6:409-45 N '43. * (PA 18:2482)
7. SMALLENBURG, HARRY WALTER. Teachers' Knowledge of Pupil Characteristics in a Senior High School. Unpublished doctor's thesis, University of Southern California, 1943. (Abstracts of Dissertations . . . 1943, pp. 73-9.)
7a. TIEGS, ERNEST W. "Measuring Personality Status and Social Adjustment." Ed 63:631-5 Je '43. *
8. BONNEY, MERL E. "Sex Differences in Social Success and Personality Traits." Child Develop 15:63-79 Mr '44. * (PA 18:2987)
9. FLORY, CHARLES D.; ALDEN, ELIZABETH; AND SIMMONS, MADELINE. "Classroom Teachers Improve the Personality Adjustment of Their Pupils." J Ed Res 38:1-8 S '44. * (PA 19:797)
10. THOMPSON, CLAUDE EDWARD. "Personality and Interest Factors in Dental School Success." Ed & Psychol Meas 4:299-306 w '44. * (PA 20:332)
11. JACKSON, JOSEPH. "A Mutual Validation of Personality Traits." J Social Psychol 22:195-202 N '45. * (PA 20:1157)
12. KIMBER, MORRIS. "Insight of College Students Into the Items of a Personality Test." Psychol B 42:540 O '45. * (PA 20:199, title only)
13. KIMBER, JOHN ANTHONY MORRIS. The Insight of College Students Into the Items of a Personality Test. Unpublished doctor's thesis, University of Southern California, 1945. (Abstracts of Dissertations . . . 1945, pp. 64-6.)
14. RUCH, FLOYD. "Ability of Adults to Fake Desirable Responses on Two Personality Self-Inventories and an Attempt to Develop a 'Lie Detector' Key." Abstract. Psychol B 42:539-40 O '45. * (PA 20:206, title only)
14a. STOTT, LELAND H. "Family Prosperity in Relation to the Psychological Adjustments of Farm Folks." Rural Sociol 10:256-63 S '45. * (PA 20:258)
14b. STOTT, LELAND H. "Some Environmental Factors in Relation to Personality Adjustments of Rural Children." Rural Sociol 10:394-403 D '45. * (PA 20:1976)
15. ALEXANDRA, M. "Personality Adjustment and Leadership." Ed 66:584-90 My '46. * (PA 21:3489)
16. BLAIR, GLENN MYERS, AND CLARK, RONALD W. "Personality Adjustments of Ninth-Grade Pupils as Measured by the Multiple Choice Rorschach Test and the California Test of Personality." J Ed Psychol 37:13-20 Ja '46. * (PA 20:1956)
17. EDMISTON, R. W., AND HOLLAHAN, CATHERINE E. "Measures Predictive of First-Grade Achievement." Sch & Soc 63:268-9 Ap 13 '46. *
18. ENGLE, T. L. "Meanness in the Primary Grades." El Sch J 46:337-41 F '46. * (PA 20:2413)
19. JACKSON, JOSEPH. "The Relative Effectiveness of Paper-Pencil Test, Interview, and Ratings as Techniques for Personality Evaluation." J Social Psychol 23:35-54 F '46. * (PA 20:2397)
20. ANDERSON, W. E. "The Personality Characteristics of 153 Negro Pupils, Dunbar High School, Okmulgee, Oklahoma." J Negro Ed 16:44-8 w '47. * (PA 21:1922)
21. GRAHAM, ALVA WHITCOMB. "Personal and Social Adjustment of High-School Students." Sch R 55:468-73 O '47. *
22. KIMBER, J. A. MORRIS. "The Insight of College Students Into the Items on a Personality Test." Ed & Psychol Meas 7:411-20 au '47. *
23. KIMBER, J. A. MORRIS. "Interests and Personality Traits of Bible Institute Students." J Social Psychol 26:225-33 N '47. *
24. SEIDENFELD, MORTON A. "Behavior of Post-Polio School Children on the California Test of Personality." Abstract. Am Psychol 2:274 Ag '47. * (PA 21:4423, title only)

Laurance F. Shaffer, Professor of Education, Teachers College, Columbia University, New York, New York. The *California Test of Personality* consists of a series of five questionnaires for successive developmental levels, purporting to measure a number of components of personal and social adjustment. The components are uniform throughout the five series. The two principal components are Self Adjustment and Social Adjustment. Self Adjustment is further subdivided into six subtests called self-reliance, sense of personal worth, sense of personal freedom, feeling of belonging, withdrawing tendencies, and nervous symptoms. The score on Social Adjustment is based on six parts designated social standards, social skills, antisocial tendencies, family relations, school relations, and community relations. At the primary level there are 8 questions in each subtest; at the elementary level, 12; and at the intermediate, secondary, and adult levels, 15. The questionnaires may be given to groups, except that individual oral administration is recommended for the primary scale. Manuals of from 8 to 16 pages are provided for each series. All except the primary series are adapted to machine scoring.

Subjective evaluation of the questions gives the impression that they are skillfully worded and are well adapted to the developmental levels for which they are intended. Considerable use is made of indirectly worded questions, that might almost be designated as "projective" in character, in order to increase the likelihood of truthful and revealing responses. Thus, instead of asking "Do you cheat?" the authors ask "Are your tests so hard or unfair that it is all right to cheat?" Instead of asking "Do you quarrel?" the question is worded "Do your classmates quarrel with you?" Although the well-phrased questions give a presumption that misrepresentation will be held to a minimum, the questionnaires do not provide a means for estimating the truthfulness of an individual's responses, corresponding, for example, to the "L" score of the *Minnesota Multiphasic Personality Inventory*.

The reliabilities of the total scores on the tests range from .918 to .933, based on the split-half method, corrected by the Spearman-Brown formula, as determined for N's of from 237 to 792 for the various forms. The reliabilities of the principal component of Self Adjustment range from .888 to .904 and of Social Adjustment from .867 to .908. Subtest reliabilities are not given for two of the series; for the other three they are stated to be from .60 to .87. Although the latter reliabilities are as high as can be expected from 15-item subtests of this type, they are far too low for satisfactory individual diagnosis.

The low reliabilities of subtests are ignored in the instructions and illustrations on the interpretation of the test profile. Readers of the manual are encouraged to interpret subtest scores by descriptive phrases, such as that "Joan A. Doe . . . is low in self-reliance . . . is free from nervous symptoms . . . community relations are somewhat low." Thus, a personality picture is drawn from indicators based on scores whose reliabilities are as low as .60. The statistically unsophisticated user is almost certain to succumb to this attractive pitfall.

The manuals give no data on the validity of the *California Test of Personality,* other than to appeal to the face values of the items, and to make vague references to the use of teacher judgments, student reactions, and biserial r's. What was correlated with what in establishing validity is not stated. The manuals do not refer to any experimental studies of validity, not

even to such an obvious criterion as to whether selected groups of maladjusted children do or do not make scores significantly different from those of children in general. It must be concluded that the validity of these questionnaires is entirely unestablished.

Percentile norms are given for total scores, for the two principal components, and for each of the twelve subtests. These norms are said to be based on "over 1,000" cases for the primary and elementary tests, but no numbers are given for the higher series. All normative cases are from Los Angeles or its vicinity, which raises serious doubts concerning the applicability of the norms to persons in other subcultural areas. Because of the short range of the subtests, their percentile scales are unduly sharp. For example, on the "community relations" subtest of the Elementary Series, a raw score of 10 is equivalent to a percentile rank of 35, of 11 to one of 55, and of 12 to one of 85. Thus, a probably unreliable difference of two raw-score points may lead to an interpretative difference of from "very low" to "very high."

The manuals give extensive suggestions for the treatment of children who show deviations on test scores. Some of these are trite but unobjectionable, as illustrated by a technique for helping a child who lacks self-reliance to recite in class. Others are clearly contrary to good modern practice in counseling and therapy. One trembles at a suggested cure for a child who underestimates his own capacities: "explain his difficulties and show him his errors"!

On the whole, the faults of the *California Test of Personality* are those of personality questionnaires in general. Such devices vainly seek the pot of gold at the end of the rainbow: a simple, cheap, foolproof method for studying human personality. Teachers, administrators, and school counselors who are tempted to consider the use of such devices would be benefited by a psychological insight into the fact that their own great need to do something about personality problems leads them to the delusion of accepting instruments of very low objective value.

Douglas Spencer, Assistant Professor of Psychology, Queens College, Flushing, New York. This series of self-report, YES–NO response, group questionnaires—described in the publisher's catalogue as "designed to reveal the status of certain highly important factors in personality and social adjustment usually designated as intangible"—has now been extended to include two forms at each level from kindergarten to adulthood.

Unfortunately little has been done, it seems, to correct in these tests the serious weaknesses pointed out by reviewers (*see* 40:1213) of the earlier Elementary and Secondary forms. The elaborate manuals still offer no evidence of validity and but scant information as to construction and standardization. The stepped-up reliability coefficients, although fairly high, are of doubtful value. Factor analyses are again reported as "in progress," but no proof is offered that the two parts of the tests entitled Self Adjustment and Social Adjustment—with six alluringly labeled subsections under each— really measure personality functions that are separate and meaningful.

Like many older self-inventories, these tests involve the arbitrary scoring of highly subjective responses. Many items will prove ambiguous to even well-intentioned subjects of considerable insight. No less than earlier attempts of this sort, these tests appear to be invitations to overrating, haloing, and easy deception. This reviewer cannot agree with an earlier critic (40:1213) that the efforts to disguise the items have been successful. The authors point out that they do not ask, for instance, "Do you tell lies?" Instead, they ask, "Have you found that telling falsehoods is one of the easiest ways for people to get out of trouble?" Instead of asking "Do you play truant?" the test asks "Are things frequently so bad at school that you just naturally stay away?" The chance that such items, on a printed form administered by teachers, will obtain confessions by hitting upon the subject's personal rationalizations would seem to be rather tenuous. This reviewer finds few items in the entire series that an average subject at each age level could not "see through." Frankness may also be discouraged by the names of the twelve types of adjustment tested printed on the face of the test where the subject signs his name. These appear on both forms for three of the series. On the Adult and Secondary tests these labels have been abbreviated (for example, *Soc. Adj.* for *Social Adjustment*). But these older subjects should have little difficulty figuring them out, especially with the undisguised title of the test and the subtitle, "A Profile of Personal and Social

Adjustment," clearly printed above. It seems amazing that psychologists or business executives would expect job applicants to risk an unfavorable response to items in the Adult forms like the following: "Do you feel that most employers keep in mind the welfare of their workers?"; "Do you feel that many employers are unfair in their methods of making promotions?"; "Is it often your belief that it is difficult to gain promotions on the basis of merit?"; "Do you sometimes wonder whether people approve of your work?" Yet these forms are offered as instruments for selecting employees, for making job assignments, for salvaging unsatisfactory employees and for improving employee-management relations. In school use, truthful responses could be expected only if careful rapport were established with each student, and even then they would be difficult to interpret on the basis of the norms reported since we know nothing about the rapport conditions during standardization.

Discussions of validity in the manuals are vague. It is claimed that "many of these items had previously been validated by other workers." Items finally included were selected on the basis of judgments by teachers and principals, reactions by students, a study of the agreement between student responses and teacher appraisals, and a study of the relative significance of items by means of biserial r technique. No evidence is reported, so one still "looks in vain for some substantial research."

It is a doubtful service to clinical psychology to have given so much care and space in the manuals and in accompanying promotional bulletins to making the sales appeals of these tests so attractive, while omitting essential information about standardization and basic data needed to show what these tests are good for. The Adult series manual states vaguely that the "test is based on a study of several hundred ways adults respond. . . ." Manuals for the other four series state that they are based on a study of 1,000 specific adjustment patterns or modes of response.

"Percentile norms based on several thousand students for each series are given in the manual of directions," according to the sales catalogue. Actually, the number of cases is not given for the percentile norms in the manuals of the Adult, Secondary, and Intermediate tests; the Elementary and Primary norms are reported as based on "over a thousand pupils."

The groups on which the high split-halves, Spearman-Brown reliabilities are based are: Adult, 250 subjects; Secondary, 558 cases; Intermediate, 792; Elementary, 334; and Primary, 237 pupils. It is not stated which of the two forms for each series these data refer to nor how the forms were equated. Inspection of scoring keys reveals varying ratios of required YES to NO responses in the alternate forms and in the subtests of each, despite the fact that this has been found to influence validity of such schedules.*

Nothing is reported about the conditions of standardization or the age, sex, and IQ distribution or the social, racial, and economic background of the subjects, except that they were all in or near Los Angeles. Thus even the "California" in the title is open to question.

The worst features of the tests, in the opinion of this reviewer, are the elaborate suggestions to teachers for the treatment of conditions claimed to be revealed by the scores, profiles, and even individual item responses. When not clearly dangerous, these procedures are stereotyped, superficial, and lacking in clinical sense.

Clearing House 16:188 N '41. E(arl) R. G(abler). * Precautions were taken to insure validity, and the tryout reveals reasonable reliability. The format promises ease of scoring and interpretation—which is something we urgently need in tests of this sort. The individual and class profile chart speaks aloud and gives a diagnostic story of each person and class taking the test.

For reviews by Raymond B. Cattell, Percival M. Symonds, and P. E. Vernon of the Elementary and Secondary Series, see 40:1213.

[27]

Concept Formation Test. Normal and schizophrenic adults; 1940; 1 form; $12.00 per testing outfit; (10-60) minutes; Jacob Kasanin and Eugenia Hanfmann; C. H. Stoelting Co.

REFERENCES
1. VIGOTSKY, L. S. "Thought in Schizophrenia." Translated by J. Kasanin. *Arch Neurol & Psychiatry* 31:1063-77 My '34. * (PA 9:4668)
2. DWORSKY, ALEXANDER. *A Comparison of Conceptual Capacities of Noneducated and Educated Adults as Judged by Their Performances on the Vigotsky Concept-Formation Test.* Unpublished master's thesis, Columbia University, 1937.
3. HANFMANN, EUGENIA, AND KASANIN, JACOB. "A Method for the Study of Concept Formation." *J Psychol* 3:521-40 '37. * (PA 11:5006)
4. BOLLES, M. MARJORIE; ROSEN, GEORGE P.; AND LANDIS, CARNEY. "Pyschological Performance Tests as Prognostic Agents for the Efficacy of Insulin Therapy in Schizophrenia." *Psychiatric Q* 12:733-7 O '38. * (PA 13:2483)

* Lorge, Irving. "Gen-Like: Halo or Reality." Abstract. *Psychol B* 34:545-60 O '37.

5. KASANIN, JACOB, AND HANFMANN, EUGENIA. "An Experimental Study of Concept Formation in Schizophrenia: I, Quantitative Analysis of Results." *Am J Psychiatry* 95:35-48, discussion 48-52 Jl '38. * (PA 13:908)
5a. KASANIN, JACOB, AND HANFMANN, EUGENIA. "Disturbances in Concept Formation in Schizophrenia." Abstract. *Arch Neurol & Psychiatry* 40:1276-80, discussion 1280-2 D '38. *
6. CAMERON, NORMAN. "Schizophrenic Thinking in a Problem-Solving Situation." *J Mental Sci* 85:1012-35 S '39. * (PA 14:872)
7. HANFMANN, EUGENIA. "Personal Patterns in the Process of Concept Formation." Abstract. *Psychol B* 37:515 Jl '40. * (PA 14:5585, title only)
8. HANFMANN, EUGENIA. "A Study of Personal Patterns in an Intellectual Performance." *Char & Pers* 9:315-25 Je '41. * (PA 15:4277)
9. RAPAPORT, D., AND BROWN, J. F. "Concept Formation Tests and Personality Research." Abstract. *Psychol B* 38:597-8 Jl '41. * (PA 15:5222, title only)
10. THOMPSON, JANE. "The Ability of Children of Different Grade Levels to Generalize on Sorting Tests." *J Psychol* 11:119-26 '41. * (PA 15:2431)
11. ZUBIN, JOSEPH, AND THOMPSON, JANE. *Sorting Tests in Relation to Drug Therapy in Schizophrenia.* New York: New York State Psychiatric Institute, 1941. Pp. v, 23. Paper. Out of print. (PA 16:2715)
12. HANFMANN, EUGENIA, AND KASANIN, JACOB. *Conceptual Thinking in Schizophrenia.* Nervous and Mental Disease Monographs, No. 67. New York: Nervous and Mental Disease Monographs, 1942. Pp. viii, 115. Out of print. * (PA 16:2289)
12a. RAPAPORT, D. "Principles Underlying Projective Techniques." *Char & Pers* 10:213-9 Mr '42. * (PA 16:4668)
13. KNIGHT, ROBERT P.; GILL, MERTON; LOZOFF, MILTON; AND RAPAPORT, DAVID. "Comparison of Clinical Findings and Psychological Tests in Three Cases Bearing Upon Military Personnel Selection." *B Menninger Clinic* 7:114-28 My '43. * (PA 17:4241)
14. REICHARD, SUZANNE, AND RAPAPORT, DAVID. "The Role of Testing Concept Formation in Clinical Psychological Work." *B Menninger Clinic* 7:99-105 My '43. * (PA 17:4153)
15. ALDRICH, C. KNIGHT. "The Relationship of the Concept Formation Test to Drug Addiction and to Intelligence." *J Nerv & Mental Dis* 100:30-4 Jl '44. * (PA 18:3720)
16. KASANIN, J. S. "The Disturbances of Conceptual Thinking in Schizophrenia," pp. 41-9. In *Language and Thought in Schizophrenia.* Edited by J. S. Kasanin. Berkeley, Calif.: University of California Press, 1944. Pp. xiv, 133. $2.00. * (London: Cambridge University Press. 12s.) (PA 18:1428)
17. RAPAPORT, DAVID; WITH THE COLLABORATION OF ROY SCHAFER AND MERTON GILL. "Hanfmann-Kasanin Test," pp. 209-31. In their *Manual of Diagnostic Psychological Testing: I, Diagnostic Testing of Intelligence and Concept Formation.* Preface by Karl Menninger. Review Series, Vol. 2, No. 2. New York: Josiah Macy, Jr. Foundation, 1944. Pp. xiii, 239. Paper, lithotyped. Out of print. * (PA 19:3198)
18. RAPAPORT, DAVID; WITH THE COLLABORATION OF MERTON GILL AND ROY SCHAFER. Chap. 4, "The Hanfmann-Kasanin Test," pp. 462-77, 478-86. In their *Diagnostic Psychological Testing: The Theory, Statistical Evaluation, and Diagnostic Application of a Battery of Tests, Vol. I.* Chicago, Ill.: Year Book Publishers, Inc., 1945. Pp. xi, 573. $6.50. * (PA 20:929)
19. MAYMAN, MARTIN. "Review of the Literature on the Three Tests of Concept Formation," pp. 561-6. In *Diagnostic Psychological Testing: The Theory, Statistical Evaluation, and Diagnostic Application of a Battery of Tests, Vol. I.* By David Rapaport with the collaboration of Merton Gill and Roy Schafer. Chicago, Ill.: Year Book Publishers, Inc., 1945. Pp. xi, 573. $6.50. * (PA 20:929)

O. L. Zangwill, Assistant Director, Institute of Experimental Psychology, University of Oxford, Oxford, England. This test procedure serves to define, in an experimental setting, the peculiar disorder of thought and judgment characteristic of schizophrenia. It also provides a test, admittedly a somewhat difficult one, for the intellectual deficit states which may be associated with organic lesions of the brain cortex. It does not, however, enable a differential diagnosis to be made between organic and functional conditions or provide a quantitative measure of the degree of thought disturbance present in any given case.

The main value of the Hanfmann–Kasanin

technique lies in the opportunity it provides for the display and qualitative elucidation of conceptual disturbances. It should, at its present stage at least, be treated not as a strict psychometric test but as a flexible tool in research investigations. Thus, it should have real use in studying the vexed question of whether the thought disturbance in schizophrenia is primary or secondary to the affective disorganization. It should also prove of value in analyzing the conceptual disturbances associated with lesions of the frontal lobes and in examining patients treated by prefrontal leucotomy.

It would be an advantage if this test could be fully standardized for the different age and intelligence levels. At present, the clinical investigator is obliged to base his assessment very largely on crude empirical standards. It is therefore doubtful whether there is much to be gained by including it in a test battery for routine neuropsychiatric examination.

For related reviews, see 28.

[28]

★[*Re* Concept Formation Test.] HANFMANN, EUGENIA, AND KASANIN, JACOB. **Conceptual Thinking in Schizophrenia.** Nervous and Mental Disease Monographs, No. 67. New York: Nervous and Mental Disease Monographs, 1942. Pp. viii, 115. Out of print. * (*PA* 16:2289)

Am J Psychiatry 100:299–300 S '43. David G. Wright. * The authors....have done a praiseworthy thing in attempting an objective approach to this problem. However, they have fallen considerably short of this objective. They have dealt with a very small number of individuals, each group being an extremely heterogeneous one. Too many variables have been introduced, or have not been excluded, to allow for the validity of any of the conclusions. It is somewhat disappointing to find in this study yet another instance of psychiatric writing which purports to be objective, but must be said to draw conclusions that are not so justified.

Am J Psychol 60:146–8 Ja '47. George W. Hartmann. * The authors....were particularly concerned to check Vigotsky's contention that the essence of the schizophrenic disorder lies in a loss of ability to think in abstract concepts with regression to a more primitive level where objects are not viewed under general categories but are seen merely as individuals. This thesis appears to represent essentially an extension of Goldstein's position reached from his study of brain injuries. * The most apparent contribution of this study is that a reduction in the level of conceptual thinking occurs in *some* schizophrenics and is lacking in others. It is possible that patients so classified and exhibiting differing functional disorders have been grouped under a misleading common label, or conceivably the range of variation within the category *schizophrenia* is greater than ordinarily recognized. One wonders therefore why the authors declare they have confirmed Vigotsky's thesis. True, they propose three corrections, viz., (1) a trichotomy instead of a dichotomy of thought levels, (2) not normals but only college-educated adults typically reach the highest level, and (3) the presence of conceptual defect is rigorously demonstrable in no more than one-half of the schizophrenic cases. Moreover, in opposition to Cameron's position, they found their patients *unable* rather than *unwilling* to conceive of other possibilities of grouping than the one momentarily suggested to them by the material. A stimulating idea is the suggestion that the similarity in "conceptual loss" between schizophrenics and organics is sufficiently striking to point to the possibility of somatic origin for the disintegration often seen in the former. While the authors are plainly familiar with the basic experimental literature on 'the thought processes' since the pioneer work of Ach, it is a bit puzzling to see them, like the early behaviorists, disregard almost completely the interest or affect factor in their interpretations of problem-solving behavior, especially since they plainly state (p. 101) that "impairment of conceptual thinking is not the only, and certainly not the most, conspicuous disturbance found in the schizophrenic mentality." Emotional, attitudinal and valuational elements presumably must exist in effective combination with certain cognitive forces before the behavior on any of the three levels can occur. Excessive reliance upon a single test and insufficient use of genetically comprehensible 'frames of reference' constitute the chief limitations of this otherwise intensive analysis.

Arch Neurol & Psychiatry 49:321 F '43. * a close relationship was noted between performance at the highest conceptual level and high educational level. To this reviewer, the authors seem, at this point, to overlook the opportunity for clarifying the basic question as to whether this relationship is not actually one between intelligence level and high performance. * Unimpaired conceptual thinking was found most frequently in the group of patients characterized by prevalence of neurotic symptoms, while impairment was most evident in the groups showing (1) disturbance of intellectual function expressed in a tendency to incoherence and irrelevance, (2) marked dissociation with extensive fantastic elaboration of ideas and (3) a paranoid-hebephrenic trend with dull affectivity. While these observations seem to indicate that impairment in conceptual thinking is not, as Vigotsky claimed, the central disturbance in schizophrenic thinking, although it may be found in cases in which the personality is grossly affected, the authors formulate their conclusions rather confusingly by stating that their study "confirms" Vigotsky's thesis that conceptual thinking suffers impairment in schizophrenia. They take issue with Vigotsky's dichotomy of conceptual and "primitive" thinking, which they regard as inadequate, but do not comment on the factor of "regression," which he stresses. * This study is provocative and stimulating and represents an interesting contribution to the literature of schizophrenic thinking. *

Brit J Psychol 33:187–8 Ja '43. A. S. P(ickford) and R. W. P(ickford). * a valuable account of the use of Vigotsky's Concept Formation Test, originally due to Ach and modified by Saharov, in an investigation of the degree of impairment of thinking in schizophrenia * It would be of interest if the authors could find out exactly how performance of normals in the test is correlated with intelligence, and if possible what part emotional and other factors such as personal taste and prejudice play in hindering or assisting their performance. The method of scoring described by the authors is found to have many difficulties in practice by the reviewers.

Int J Psycho-Analysis 23:183 pts 3 & 4 '42. W. H. Gillespie. * presents the results of a careful and well-controlled piece of research * The authors....find that it is necessary to distinguish not less than three grades of thinking, as opposed to Vigotsky's simple division into conceptual and concrete ('complex') thinking. They find, in fact, that thinking in true abstract concepts is practically confined to the college-trained subjects; other normal subjects generally reach only the intermediate grade of

partially conceptual thinking. It is therefore essential to make allowance for a person's educational level * There is also a wide variation among schizophrenics of the same educational level, and further investigation led to the discovery that this variation is related to the different clinical forms of the disorder. * the results are not nearly so clear-cut as Vigotsky suggested, and they appear to rule out the possibility that this particular kind of thought disorder (which can reasonably be regarded as regressive, for a similar disability is found in children before puberty) is the essential change underlying all cases clinically diagnosed as schizophrenia. This result is scarcely surprising in view of the growing modern opinion that 'schizophrenia' is not a nosological entity. Researches such as the present should help to break it into its component parts, an important step towards a more satisfactory approach to the problem of schizophrenia.

J Am Med Assn 119:600 Je 13 '42. * For any one wishing to learn the fundamentals of the test the book is highly recommended.

J Nerv & Mental Dis 101:302–3 Mr '45. K. Goldstein. The book of Hanfmann and Kasanin comprises the well-known studies by these authors of the thinking processes in schizophrenics. There was much theoretical speculation in this field until the Russian psychologist, L. Vigotsky, began to analyze the behavior of schizophrenics by means of special performance tests. He came to the conclusion that the schizophrenic thought disorder is due to a "loss of ability to think in abstract concepts and a regression to a more primitive level of thinking in complexes." He used a concept formation test devised by Ach and later modified by Saharoff. The present authors in appreciation of the fruitfulness of Vigotsky's conception examined, by means of the Vigotsky test, a great number of different kinds of schizophrenic patients and compared the results with findings in patients with organic brain disease and normal subjects of different educational levels. * This book is excellently written and certainly cannot be overlooked by anyone who is interested in research in schizophrenics.

Mental Hyg 27:318–20 Ap '43. Wendell Muncie. * There are several important points to note about the findings: A shift from conceptual thinking to more concrete thinking often occurred under the stress of emotional frustration, which presupposes a certain grasp of the situation. Yet the authors deny Cameron's insistence on the emotional basis for the characteristic thinking disorders he discovered by use of the same and other tests. To the reviewer —who did not sit in on either set of experiments, but who has had acquaintance with many schizophrenics—it appears that accurate judgment on the emotional state of these subjects might be well-nigh impossible, certainly if based exclusively on their verbal comments. Can the authors assert that emotional factors have been excluded simply because those patients who showed the ordinary emotional expression were eliminated? The authors suggest that the performance of schizophrenics is qualitatively in many respects not unlike that of paretics and arteriosclerotics ("irreversible" cases), and this observation warrants the suggestion that deterioration in the thinking processes may proceed along a final common pathway, even when initiated by diverse factors. The authors mention the reviewer's clinical observations (among others) relative to the schizophrenic's misuse of metaphors. They omit the really pertinent item from this contribution: that such misuse is *spontaneous,* and always related *directly* in an *emotional* way to the dynamic factors in the illness. This was noted in the complete absence of similar distortions in the experimental situations of explaining metaphor, proverbs, and so forth. The reviewer finds it somewhat difficult to believe that an "impersonal" disease such as paresis or arteriosclerosis—if any disease is really impersonal—could bring about disturbance along such "lines of cleavage" of the personality. My view would fit in with certain of the authors' findings and with Cameron's—that the thinking disorder proceeds under the impetus of transitive emotions. Furthermore, I would not hold the view that experimental situations, in contrast to clinical observation, necessarily connote *"more* controlled observations." This is a good book, full of interesting detail, and providing a most helpful index to the use and interpretation of the Vigotsky test. The literature is covered in a welcome fashion.

Psychiatry 6:248–9 My '43. Meyer Maskin. * the authors conclude that conceptual thinking is significantly impaired in Schizophrenia, save in borderline states. * There will be little clinical denial that what is ordinarily termed conceptual thinking is altered in Schizophrenia. As in all experiments of this type, however, there

are inevitable and basic conundra: first, it is invariably difficult to evaluate precisely what part or parts of the mental apparatus actually operate in a given artificial test performance. Secondly, it may be quite incorrect to conclude that conceptual thinking is necessarily impaired as evidenced in test responses by schizophrenics. There are too many variables to permit this easy, happy conclusion. Since the schizophrenic is caught in a mighty web of feeling and thinking detached from prevailing reality, his response to such realities will vary. To establish definitively a lessened capacity to think abstractly, it should be demonstrated that such impairment exists within the domain of the schizophrenic's chief concerns. And clinically there is much reason to believe that the schizophrenic is fluently abstract in his symbolic formulations, neologisms and other-worldliness. The monograph is provocative, however, in suggesting continued research into the nature of thinking. There is a bibliography of 61 references.

Psychoanalytic Q 12:257–9 Ap '43. Thomas M. French. * an exceedingly painstaking and well thought out experimental study of thought disorders in schizophrenia. * The procedure is based upon experiments of the Russian psychologist, Vigotsky, whose methods are followed with slight modifications. The subjects are given twenty-two wooden blocks, varying in color, shape, height, and size. On the underside of each is written one of four nonsense words. The subject is told that there are four different kinds of blocks before him, that each kind has a name and that his task is to find and to separate these four kinds. The examiner then shows him the name of one block and asks him to pick out all blocks which he thinks might belong to the same kind. After he has attempted to do so the examiner turns up one of the wrongly selected blocks showing that this is a block of a different kind and then encourages the subject to continue trying. This procedure is repeated until it becomes clear whether he is able to complete the task of separating the four kinds. The subject is encouraged to think aloud and all comments are recorded in detail throughout the experiment. This test was given to three groups of subjects: schizophrenic patients, healthy adults and patients with an irreversible organic brain disease. * the authors offer the very tentative hypothesis that the similarities between the thinking of schizophrenics and that of organic patients 'are sufficiently striking to suggest the possibility of somatic origin of schizophrenic disorder or rather of some of its variants.' However, one of their findings is not given sufficient importance. In some cases the authors report that the performance of the subject deteriorated sharply upon the development of an emotional disturbance during the test. This fact is consistent with that view of schizophrenia which regards the disturbance of thought as a secondary result of disturbances in the emotional sphere rather than with the view which the authors seem cautiously to favor, that the disturbance of thought is primary.

Psychoanalytic R 33:383-4 Jl '46. *Clara Thompson.* * The test performance used is fully and clearly described and the formulation of the results is presented in a well-organized and simple manner. * The authors conclude that while their findings in general confirm Vigotsky, they cannot agree that conceptual thinking is a possession of every normal adult, and they have shown that some cases of schizophrenia are free from defect. The book is well organized and well written. The research seems carefully planned and executed and the conclusions are convincing. The only criticism is the one which can be made concerning the application of laboratory methods to human behavior generally. For example, on what basis was it determined that a subject was normal. Also is it not possible that the same schizophrenics at another stage of their illness would have shown different results!

Psychosomatic Med 5:202 Ap '43. *Oskar Diethelm.* The authors present....the results of their investigation of conceptual thinking by means of the Vigotsky test. After a brief review of the pertinent work of the Russian investigators, the test performance is analyzed under the headings of interpretation of the instructions by the subject, attempts at solution, and finding and mastering the correct solution. This chapter should be of interest to anyone wishing to use the Vigotsky test or to study conceptual thinking by any other method. * The discussion of the findings of other investigators in the field of conceptual thinking is highly informative. The authors accept educational standards as true indicators of intelligence. The results would be more valid if intelligence tests had been used. The normal findings in some schizophrenic patients bring

up the question whether a study of schizophrenic patients in general can give adequate results or whether these studies should not be related to carefully observed psychopathological reactions in general instead of to an involved and disputed "schizophrenia." The reviewer, however, agrees that "these studies and the possibilities of new approaches that they have uncovered are encouraging."

[29]

★**Controlled Projection (1944): A Standard Experimental Procedure.** Ages 6 and over, adults above average intelligence; 1945; J. C. Raven; H. K. Lewis & Co., Ltd. (The manual and a set of sketches are obtainable in the United States for $4, postpaid, from the Psychological Corporation.)
a) [INDIVIDUAL TEST.] Age 6 and over; individual.
b) [GROUP OR SELF-ADMINISTERED TEST.] Adults above average intelligence; separate forms for men and women.

Arthur L. Benton, Associate Professor of Psychology, University of Louisville School of Medicine, Louisville, Kentucky. An adult subject is shown a drawing of a person of the same sex as himself sitting at a table and writing on paper. The subject is asked to draw whatever he wishes and at the same time to answer questions concerning the interests, likes, dislikes, fears, etc., of the person in the picture. Children are also requested to draw whatever they wish but, instead of answering questions, are asked to complete items in a standard story presented to them.

The fundamental assumption underlying intrepretation of the subject's performance is that the statements of the subject about the picture refer primarily to himself and are therefore a projection and an unwitting self-evaluation. The test is still in an experimental stage in that its essential validity and clinical usefulness have not yet been established.

Percival M. Symonds, Professor of Education, Teachers College, Columbia University, New York, New York. This unpaged book describes a projective technique which combines drawing with storytelling. Raven calls his method "Controlled Projection," using the device of "projection pursuit." In brief, the method consists of asking the subject to draw a picture while plying him with questions as he is drawing. The author states that the method can be used with "almost everybody" over six years of age and provides simultaneously "two distinct and yet correlated forms of self-expression without disconcerting apparatus." He states the aim of projection pursuit to be "to discover not facts, but how people interpret the events of life to themselves; how they organise their thoughts and actions to their own satisfaction; how they regard other people, and imagine other people regard them; the motives they attribute to people's actions; and to reveal, as far as possible, the personal preferences, dislikes, desires and judgments by which their experience becomes organised and character is formed."

When the test is given to a child, he is told to draw anything he wants to. A standardized list of eleven questions are asked the child as he draws. The pursuit comes by "inducing a person to develop his ideas to his own satisfaction," and by following up answers with such questions as "Why?", "How?", "Yes?", "And then?", "What then?", and "What or who else?"

With adults a skeleton sketch of a road and of a box is given to the subject, and he is asked to sketch in what he might see walking along the road or what he imagines might be inside the box. A standard list of questions is provided to ask the subject while he sketches. In addition, for adults the materials include the picture of a person drawing. The subject is asked to sketch on paper what he thinks the person in the picture might be drawing or writing and a list of questions is asked the subject simultaneously.

The book contains a number of samples of children's and adults' drawings together with a "verbatim projection record" which consists of the answers given to the standardized questions. No interpretation of the pictures or of the answers is given.

The idea of distracting the subject by requiring him to do two things at the same time is novel, but no data or evidence are provided which indicate the value or strength of the method. There is considerable doubt as to whether a uniform set of questions can be made applicable to every case. The book provides nothing in the way of expectation or norms. The author believes that telling a person that his imagination is being tested is detrimental to the results. He believes that the method can be used as a self-administered or group test.

Undoubtedly within the next few years many different kinds of projective techniques will appear, but there is no way of knowing ahead of time what value each variation may have. Certainly much can be learned from stories and drawings told by a person no matter under what conditions they are obtained.

Am J Orthopsychiatry 17:548–9 Jl '47. * Although the author mentions H. M. Murray's *Explorations in Personality,* he leans very heavily on Spearman's *The Nature of Intelligence and Principles of Cognition.* * The book contains numerous records and drawings. Unfortunately, Dr. Raven does not go into the psychodynamic implications of these records, but keeps the reader hanging in mid-air after he has looked at the various pictures and read the stories which are not related to the drawings. The technique in itself is a very interesting one and warrants further experimental investigation.

Brit J Ed Psychol 16:48 F '46. * Unfortunately, although some detailed examples of cases are published, the author refrains from even a tentative evaluation which would have added immeasurably to the value of the book as a stimulus to further experimental work in a field where reliable techniques are urgently necessary. It is unfortunate too that there is neither the briefest table of contents nor even page numbering.

Brit J Psychol 36:177 My '46. * A series of illustrative case histories and the corresponding projected material is given. But neither these cases nor the general results of inquiry made by the techniques are discussed with sufficient clarity or detail to demonstrate how the projected material is used and interpreted. The answers may express the individual's conscious wishes and fears more clearly than would his answers to direct questioning, as at a psychiatric interview. But is it possible to use this technique to relate such wishes and fears to the personality as a whole, and to the individual's unconscious mental contents? Are the latter perhaps expressed in the drawings and 'doodlings'? If so, in what way? The method and its results need a more systematic exposition before it is possible to judge their value.

J Mental Sci 92:197–8 Ja '46. M. B. Brody. * Many records are given in full. The problem is real and important, and Raven's method promises to be richly productive. Time will tell if this promise will be fulfilled. Raven also makes some interesting general observations on the nature of projection, and on the factors which modify the drawings and replies to questions. The beauty of the reproductions cannot be passed without mention.

Nature 156:701–2 D '45. John Cohen. Recent developments in projective technique offer a new approach to the mind, the exploration of which is just beginning. The underlying concept of projection (attributing our own 'qualities' to others) owes its origin to Freud. It was postulated to explain the origin of delusions of persecution and ideas of reference in paranoia. Freud thus identified a distinctive mental process of which we had only been vaguely aware. Many proverbs embody the belief that projection enters into daily intercourse. Folk-knowledge recognizes that in judging others we judge ourselves, that in condemning or condoning the actions of others we betray our own private inclinations. In the narrower sense in which Freud understood it, however, projection is a mechanism of defence employed, as an alternative to repression, with the aim of ridding the mind of an intolerable burden of aggression or guilt. Some recent experiments have thrown further light on these alternative *extra-* or *intro*-punitive processes. Projection helps to shape our relationships with the outer world. We 'infer' from the dim or clear awareness of our own state of mind the state of mind of another person. It is not inference in the logical sense of inductive reasoning, but arguing by analogy from one particular to another. In Spearman's terminology, projection means educing correlates of our own social attitudes. Taken jointly, projection and correlate education are rich in explanatory value. Thus, to take one example, the late Prof. Aveling showed that ideas of cause and effect are generated (educed as correlates) by projecting on to external objects the experience of the self acting upon the organs and limbs of the body. The recognition that projection plays a major part in the organization of mind has led to its being exploited as a method of penetrating beneath the surface of personality. Indeed, the importance of projective techniques to the psychologist has been likened to that of the X-ray apparatus to the physician. A person's projections can be evoked so as to uncover his innermost impulses, wishes, fears and values. He will interpret an ambiguous social situation in a way which, unknown to himself, will disclose some of the hidden secrets of his mind. In choosing his invective he will most likely dip into his personal inventory of self-condemnation. In forecasting an event on inadequate data he will project himself into his predictions thus revealing what he *wants* to happen or what he privately fears *might* happen. He may perhaps project his own ignorance into the outside world. This last possibility was well exemplified by the Press in 1941 when ignorance of Japan's plans in regard to entering the war was projected on to the Japanese rulers, who were believed to be utterly uncertain of their own intentions. Projective techniques are methods of indirectly locating crucial foci of value and conflict. Just as a searchlight, in projecting its beams on to an object, discloses its own location, so the mind by projecting its own wishes, hostility, fears and values, reveals its key centers of activity. Projection is something more than a subjective mental process. It has a social quality inasmuch as it is the main avenue for the mind's interpretation of its environment, human and material. Hence its significance for the study of interpersonal relations. In England, projective techniques appear to have been first used by Wedeck in 1933 and described by him in a thesis deposited in the University of London library. His object was to inquire whether any 'group factor' existed which implied a special ability for understanding human character and relationships, whether, in other words, the interpretation of facial expression, gestures, social situations, proverbs and the like, required an ability statistically independent of general intelligence (Spearman's 'g' factor). Wedeck did, in fact, claim to have detected a special ability of estimating character uncorrelated with 'g.' The potentialities of projective techniques in the study of personality were first fully appreciated, however, in the United States. H. A. Murray seems to have been early in the field. He set out the methods in his "Explorations in Personality," which attracted curiously little attention in England when it was published in 1937. He had a different purpose in mind; not to find out whether the subjects were good judges of character or not (as measured by some agreed criterion), but to discover their general mental and social orientation. There is variety in projective techniques. The basic procedure requires that the subject should freely manipulate experimental materials presented to him. Alternatively he may be required to interpret the materials or situation, or he may be asked to carry out certain prescribed acts under observation. The underlying assumption is that the subject will employ the material or situation so as to express his inner values, his mental conflicts, his tendencies, aspirations and imaginary roles. He throws or projects himself into the medium of expression. Such techniques include the Rorschach Test, the Thematic Apperception Tests of Murray (briefly known as TAT), psychodramatic situations, and, in the case of children, play activities. Closely allied procedures are observations of expressive movement, posture, gait and physical activity of almost any kind. The fantasies projected by the subject or patient are not regarded as final indications of the trends in his mind but simply used as working hypotheses to be checked by other criteria. Murray's tests, which are the most important of these devices, were developed at the Harvard Psychological Clinic. In principle similar to the Rorschach Test, the material consists of reproductions of paintings instead of 'ink-blots.' The latest revision of the thematic apperception tests has just been published. Though originally devised for adults of normal intelligence, the tests have also been applied to mental defectives. The exigencies of war soon determined that, in the interests of military efficiency, methods should be adopted for the assessment of personality in selecting personnel for higher duties. As is now perhaps well known, the important step was taken in 1942 of introducing projective techniques into War Office Selection Board procedure as an aid in selecting candidates on grounds of 'officer quality' or leadership. Here the current tests of intellectual abilities were not appropriate and the new methods were of great help in detecting weakness and strength in the personality structure of candidates, and in the adequacy of their social adjustment. Similar methods are now being employed in selecting candidates for the higher grades of the Civil Service. Raven's work, stimulated by Murray's efforts and by the 'completion test' of a French investigator, M. Thomas, introduces new steps in testing procedure, part of which is common both to children and to adults. The subject is asked to draw, and while he is drawing, to imagine and describe a series of events. Since he is occupied with two tasks there is little residual energy left for self-observation or self-criticism. There are supplementary tests

suitable for adults only. Although best results are obtained with individual administration, an adaptation of the test material is also provided for administration to adult groups. Raven uses two kinds of material, verbal and spatial simultaneously, and he 'pursues' the subject's fantasies in a number of prescribed directions. There is thus a twofold pursuit of the subject's projections. In the result two distinct yet parallel forms of expression emerge side by side, one oral, the other pictorial; each is a check on the other. Both the verbal utterances and the drawings can be systematically followed, step by step, by the experimenter until he is satisfied that his explorations of the subject's personality are as complete as necessary. The materials used are simple and lack any structure of their own. The ambitious aims of 'projection pursuit' are clearly set out by Raven. It is not facts about the subject's past which are sought, but his interpretation of the events of life, how he organizes his thoughts and actions, how he regards other people and how he imagines other people regard him, what motives he attributes to the actions of others, what are his likes and dislikes, his wishes and judgments, and how, on the basis of these, his character is formed. The sample records given by Raven illustrate (they are not norms) what results are to be expected of children at different age- and ability-levels within the normal range of intelligence. Some records are also given of the projections of adults differing in age, sex and ability. Several criticisms of the present stage of Raven's techniques come to mind. The methods do not, as is claimed, appear to be appreciably subject to controlled variation. Nor do the results lend themselves at all easily to statistical treatment. Above all, to interpret the records is exceedingly difficult, and practically no guidance is offered on the subject. Raven admits that much has still to be learnt about the most informative questions to be put, about the best methods of pursuit, and about ways of recording the responses. These limitations the reader will readily concede. The value of the present arrangement of test material lies less in what it achieves than in what it foreshadows. It provides not so much a procedure ready for clinical application as a "method of enquiry suitable for experimental work"; it is therefore as a pioneer effort that the work is to be judged, and the reader must not be too critical, though there is much to criticize.

[30]

Cowan Adolescent Adjustment Analyzer: An Instrument of Clinical Psychology. Ages 12-18; 1935–46; revision of *Cowan Adolescent Personality Schedule* (*see* 40:1217) ; 1 form; $2.50 per 25; 50¢ per specimen set; nontimed (10-30) minutes; Edwina A. Cowan, Wilbert J. Mueller, and Edra Weathers; Cowan Research Project, Salina, Kansas.

REFERENCES

1-3. *See* 40:1217.

Harold H. Abelson, Associate Professor of Education and Director, Educational Clinic, The City College of New York, New York, New York. Despite its striking title, this instrument is simply a self-marking personality questionnaire with convenient arrangement for obtaining separate scores in nine categories: fear, family emotion, family authority, feeling of inadequacy, nonfamily authority, maturity, escape, neurotic, and compensation. Its value will depend largely on its use or misuse. While the authors do not intend that the "Analyzer" be used in lieu of a full array of clinical procedures, their ready use of illustrative clinical interpretations may encourage users to expect too much of the instrument, which is simply a source of data and not a diagnostic program.

Skeptical also must be one's reaction to the use of the "objective" validation procedure employed. Avoiding evidence from clinical sources as being too subjective, the authors resort to graphic comparisons of several deviate groups to show that the instrument is valid. A nonprecise inspection technique is used to ascertain whether there are differences in adjustment scores among the several groups. Moreover, while presumably validating the test, the authors slip into the fallacy of using the test findings as if they were already known to be valid. Thus, if one group is found to have lower "maturity" scores than another, the first group is said to be more mature ; if no difference is found, the groups are said to be the same. Instead of producing a rigid validation of the tests, the authors simply show that the test results of the several groups conform in general to what one may plausibly expect of these groups. On the basis of such observations, slight *group* trends are employed as supposedly reliable indications of *individual* characteristics.

Although the length of the questionnaire has been reduced to 90 items as compared with the 201 items of the original *Cowan Adolescent Personality Schedule,* and the score in each category is based on only 10 questions, the authors lay claim to the reliability of the obtained scores. The method of establishing reliability is a simple and specious one, namely, that of showing that the distribution graphs of groups from three towns in widely separated parts of Kansas "do not differ from each other in any category as much as they differ in some categories from distributions obtained with selected groups of children living under conditions presumed to foster maladjustment." No retest or split-half coefficients are quoted. The reliability of an individual's score on the test as a whole or in any of the nine categories clearly has not been established.

In making this revision, the authors have followed an elaborate procedure for selecting the questions to be retained. Simply put, an item was retained when it correlated with scores on the test as a whole but did not correlate too highly with scores in categories other than the one in which it fell. Apparently the original placement of an item in a category was not modified, such placement having the same subjective basis as on the original Cowan schedule. None of the objections previously voiced to possibly inadequate wordings of questions have been met in the revision. Although the subject is asked to indicate whether each parent lives at home and the number, age, and sex of siblings, no provision is made for correcting scoring when items relative to these are not applicable to a particular case. Another minor defect is found in the fact that while there are 77 YES's among the "maladjusted" answers, there are only 13 NO's. The effect of the uneven distribution is not clear. Norms are based on 500 high school pupils in one state and are not differentiated for age.

Despite its limitations, the new Cowan questionnaire, like its older counterpart, may well be the best available inventory for the adolescent range. Particularly significant is its recognition of two basic principles: (*a*) that admitting to few symptoms is likely to reveal maladjustment and (*b*) that the internal comparison of an individual's scores in the several categories may (in the hands of a clinically oriented person) lead to a preliminary understanding of certain aspects of the individual's adjustive processes. In its new form it certainly is a convenient and interesting device. Let us hope that those who use the instrument—and it warrants widespread use—will employ it with a full understanding of its merits and its limitations.

William U. Snyder, Associate Professor of Psychology and Associate Director, Psychological Clinic, The Pennsylvania State College, State College, Pennsylvania. This personality test is designed to assist the clinical psychologist to understand the fields of emotional and social maladjustment of the adolescent and to show the adjustive devices upon which the subject is depending. More specifically, it is a questionnaire which obtains scores for a given adolescent that are comparable to standard scores obtained on 500 Kansas high school children in response to 90 questions divided into groups of 10 each for the following nine traits: fear, family emotions, family authority, feeling of inadequacy, nonfamily authority, maturity, escape, neuroticism, and compensation.

The make-up of the test is in the form of three alternate answers to each question, viz., "YES," "NO," and "?." The test is self-scoring, like the *Henmon–Nelson Mental Ability Test.* Questions are so arranged that upon opening the folder the scorer finds parallel lines separating the nine sections and has only to count the number of encircled dots in each section and record the scores on a table which automatically provides standard scores and a profile of the subject's status in the nine traits. The questions themselves are also summarized inside the folder for easy reference by the clinician using the analyzer as an interview aid.

The wording of the questions is simple and appropriate for adolescents. The questions themselves show considerable care in selection and are not ambiguous. They are the items that proved most satisfactory of the 201 which were used in Cowan's former test, the *Cowan Adolescent Personality Schedule.* The reviewer found that test to have considerable merit in its field.

The selection of items was based on the results obtained from 1,150 questionnaires administered to unselected high school students. Two commendable techniques were utilized in this selection. The authors used the ten questions for each trait which best distinguished between the average score and the score of the upper quartile in maladjustment of a random sample of the total group. No question was included which showed less than 10 per cent difference, and most of them showed a much greater percentage of difference. The second technique was the avoidance of overlap between the nine

traits. Tables have been prepared to show that there is not a great deal of such overlap.

Reliability was based on 300 cases, used in the final norms, and while no reliability index appears in the literature for this test, the curves obtained for the three different populations of 100 look very similar on all traits but maturity. It would have been well if a test of goodness of fit had been used.

The test has some shortcomings. Most serious, as usual, is the question of validity. The authors reject the usual criteria of validity, clinical judgments of raters, but it is doubtful whether they have improved on that method. They have assumed that if the test is valid it should show a difference between an unselected population and adolescents living under special circumstances such as institutions, foster homes, or correctional schools. They compared their 500 unselected adolescents with 94 "broken home" and 145 delinquent children, classified into different subgroups. But the comparison is by inspection of frequency curves only, no predictive device being used. The authors seem occasionally to be reasoning after the facts, i.e., because a "difference" appears in two frequency curves an explanation is found to account for it.

Like all authors of questionnaires, the present authors have difficulty rationalizing the problem of subjective error. It has been suggested by Cowan and others that the true facts about a child are no more significant than the child's believing he is a deviate. But they do not answer the fact that by proper "lying" a child can obtain a normal answer although he is really abnormal. However, by allowing for deviation at both ends of the scale, they do greatly decrease this possibility.

Despite the care used in selecting the items, some question might be raised about the adequacy of the trait names. For example, it seemed to the reviewer that five of the ten questions on fear really pertain to inadequacy. The scoring of several items seems dubious, i.e., is talking to oneself about one's troubles a sign of escape or is it neuroticism?

One difficulty in administering the test is that some of the questions pertain to parents and siblings. The authors instruct the subject without parents to omit these items; but, if he does, he omits six items out of the ten relating to family emotion and *all ten* questions relating to family authority. Orphaned children might have good reason to skip these 16 questions, and children in foster homes might not know which of their different sets of foster parents, or real ones, they should refer to.

Sex differences are lightly treated; one hundred children of each sex from the same school were compared. Differences were found on at least two traits (fear and inadequacy feelings occurred more frequently for the girls), but the authors suggest that the clinician can allow for this fact and that the number of children compared was quite small, anyway.

Nothing is said about age of subjects, except that they were from high schools and were adolescents. The reviewer is also somewhat concerned about the use of children from only one state in the establishing of norms. And he wonders about the wisdom of using only ten questions to measure the incidence of any trait; a single error in the child's judgment would change his scores about half a standard deviation.

Despite the weaknesses mentioned it is the reviewer's opinion that this test is one of the better personality tests available for use with adolescents. Especially if used by a qualified child psychologist in the clinical situation, it should be a valuable tool.

For reviews by Harold E. Jones and Goodwin Watson of an earlier edition, see 38:918 and 40:1217.

[31]

★Detroit Adjustment Inventory: Alpha Form of "Telling What I Do." Grades 7-12; 1942; 1 form; $2.10 per 25; 42¢ per specimen set; nontimed (30-40) minutes; Harry J. Baker; Public School Publishing Co.

Albert Ellis, Consulting Psychologist, 2505 University Avenue, New York, New York. The distinguishing characteristics of the *Detroit Adjustment Inventory* are these: (*a*) Five choices of answers are provided instead of the common Yes-No scoring; and these are randomly assorted rather than being printed in systematic sequence. (*b*) The inventory is self-administering and can be given to one or more individuals. (*c*) The 120 items are divided into 24 major topics representing different diagnostic categories. (*d*) Each question is specific, and is worded in simple, popular style, making frequent use of the pronoun "I." (*e*) Twenty-four sets of remedial suggestions, one to cover each of the main topics of the test, are optionally provided for school use.

It will be noted that none of these distinguishing features of the inventory, except possibly the last one, is a radical departure from present-day practice in personality test construction. While the author must be commended at least for giving some careful consideration and discussion to the matter of remedial treatment as well as diagnosis, his questionnaire still suffers from most of the usual limitations of this kind of personality test. Specifically:

a) There is no indication that the test items were selected by methods other than the all too usual armchair technique. No preliminary item analyses are mentioned, nor any validating criteria for the individual items.

b) Validation is most inadequate. Although some 3,000 children are said to have taken the test, only 61 behavior problem and 27 non-behavior problem cases are used for validating purposes. The groups chosen are very maladjusted children on the one hand and very well-adjusted ones (according to teachers' ratings) on the other hand—with the great majority of presumably normally adjusted subjects excluded. The difference between the average scores of the two groups is said to be 6.1 times the standard error of the difference; and on the basis of this rather meaningless *group* difference both individual diagnosis and remedial treatment value are claimed for the test.

c) No reliability data are given for the inventory.

d) It is claimed that the respondents often give more objective answers to the questionnaire than they give in interviews and that honest answers are generally given to the test questions; but no adequate proof of this contention is provided. It is naïvely suggested that there is a large amount of inherent honesty in the great majority of people, despite overwhelming evidence to the contrary as far as personality questionnaire responses are concerned.

e) Diagnosis is made according to no less than 24 major categories. This kind of specifically detailed diagnosis is recommended in spite of the facts that only five questions are employed in each category and that, according to the author's own admission, several of the questions—particularly those about home and parents—"have been selected with great care so as not to emphasize bad features." This is akin to diagnosing an individual's marital adjustment by asking him a few innocuous questions about how he likes the hats his wife wears.

f) The remedial suggestions optionally provided with the test are of the pat-on-the-back exhortation type that put the entire remedial burden on the child—thus pleasantly relieving the school authorities from the necessity of finding out *why* the child possesses certain unfavorable symptoms and what may effectually be done to get at their roots.

g) The Teacher's Handbook accompanying the inventory is an odd mixture of its admitted limitations on the one hand and cagey circumlocutions of these on the other.

In sum: Baker's *Detroit Adjustment Inventory,* being little better or worse than the average personality questionnaire of its kind, makes up for none of the serious limitations still inherent in these instruments.

[32]

Detroit Scale of Behavior Factors. Grades 1-12; 1935–36; $3.85 per manual (*The Diagnosis and Treatment of Behavior-Problem Children*); 20¢ per case record form; Harry J. Baker and Virginia Traphagen; Macmillan Co.

REFERENCES

1. BAKER, HARRY J., AND TRAPHAGEN, VIRGINIA. *The Diagnosis and Treatment of Behavior-Problem Children.* New York: Macmillan Co., 1935. Pp. xiv, 393. $3.85. (London: Macmillan & Co. Ltd., 1936. 20s.) * (PA 10:2743)

For related reviews, see 33.

[33]

[*Re* Detroit Scale of Behavior Factors.] BAKER, HARRY J., AND TRAPHAGEN, VIRGINIA. Diagnosis and Treatment of Behavior-Problem Children. New York: Macmillan Co., 1935. Pp. xiv, 393. $3.85. (London: Macmillan & Co. Ltd., 1936. 20s.) * (PA 10:2743)

Fed Probation 3:38–9 My '39. Edw. H. Stullken. * gives recognition to the complexity of the problem of delinquency. The very length of the scale should make it more valid than most scales for discriminating between delinquent and non-delinquent types. The scale on a whole is well balanced and no particular school of thought predominates. The scale should act as a check on the user in overcoming any tendency to overemphasize any particular factor. The book gives publicity to some of the White House Conferences studies made in the *White House Conference on Child Health and Protection.* There may be a question whether the authors, who found personality and social factors more important than material and physical factors, give enough weight in the scale in this direction. The authors might have emphasized

more the attitude toward the school and toward satisfaction in school life and the importance of the influence of other members of the problem child's family. The statistical studies reported in the book of the constellation of factors in behavior problem cases are interesting and important. The book makes generalized suggestions for treatment, but does not give any specific results of what such treatment will do. Students of child nature and of behavior problems will find much of value in the volume concerning the intricacies of human motivation. The book is of value to clinical workers, teachers and administrators of special classes and special schools and to social workers and teachers in general. It is hoped that this volume will be followed by another giving more results of the use of the scale.

For additional reviews, see 36:B24, 38: B306, and 40:B835.

[34]

Diagnosis and Treatment of Pupil Maladjustment. Grades kgn-12; 1938; Part A, Pupil Adjustment Inventory, 50¢ per 40; Part B, Case Study Record, 15¢; Part C, Symptoms, Causes, and Remedies: A Handbook for Teachers, $1; Part D, Abbreviated Case Study Record, $4 per 100; Part E, Cumulative Pupil Adjustment Record, $4 per 100; Class Summary, free; $1.75 per specimen set; T. L. Torgerson; E. M. Hale & Co.

REFERENCES

1. RALPH, H. THOBURN. "The Measurement and Improvement of Pupil Adjustment." *Nat El Sch Prin* 16:508-13 Jl '37. *
2. WAHLSTROM, LAWRENCE F. *A Statistical Analysis of the Torgerson Pupil Adjustment Inventory.* Unpublished master's thesis, University of Wisconsin, 1937.

Laurance F. Shaffer, Professor of Education, Teachers College, Columbia University, New York, New York. Torgerson's materials for studying and treating maladjusted children consist of six items. The Pupil Adjustment Inventory is a single sheet on which each of ten supposed traits is rated on a four-point scale. The choice of traits and their description leave much to be desired. For example, the four rated degrees of "nervousness" are stated as "(1) calm and self-controlled; (2) uneasy, bites fingernails, etc.; (3) stammers, nervous, hyperactive; (4) afflicted with nervous disease." It is intended that the Pupil Adjustment Inventory be used to survey a class, the teacher rating each pupil, to identify the ones needing further study.

The Case Study Record is a sixteen-page form for the more detailed study of a child. It includes check lists for rating school history, study habits, physical efficiency and health status, interests and attitudes, and home environment. Space is provided for test results, and entirely blank pages are provided for "case history," "remedial treatment" (11 lines), and "results." Other forms include the Abbreviated Case Study Record and the Cumulative Pupil Adjustment Record, which are four-page manila folders, and a class summary form.

The heart of Torgerson's system is found in his handbook *Symptoms, Causes and Remedies*. The "symptoms," obtained from the Pupil Adjustment Inventory, are related by a chart to the "causes," which follow the outline of the Case Study Record. Thus, one has only to read a chart to locate the exact possible causes of any symptom. To give only a small sample, the chart shows that "laziness" may be caused by fatigue, malnutrition, poor posture, unsuitable curriculum, unwholesome motivation, overindulgent parents, or bad moral surroundings, among the twenty-six listed "causes."

Once one determines the "causes," treatment is almost automatic. Turning to page 19 of the handbook, one finds that for "over-indulgent parents," treatments 35, 60, 67, and 68 are indicated. These are found, in the section on remedial procedures, to be: "create a desire in the pupil to take part in extra-curricular activities," "suggest how family relationships can be improved," "urge the parents to give the child regular home duties," and "help the parents to encourage independence."

With the perspective attained in the years since its publication in 1938, one may view Torgerson's arrant nonsense with tolerant amusement. This system for handling the diagnosis and treatment of human maladjustments by a series of mechanical maneuvers is the *reductio ad absurdum* of all routinized guidance procedures. Those who have real professional training will not need a system. Those who lack psychological knowledge will help pupils more effectively by using simple human warmth and interest than by thumbing a handbook of oversimplified recipes.

[35]
★**Dunlap Academic Preference Blank.** Grades 7-9; 1937-39; IBM; Forms A, B; $1 per 25; 70¢ per set of scoring keys for one form; 35¢ per specimen set; non-timed (10-15) minutes; Jack W. Dunlap; World Book Co.

REFERENCES
   1. DUNLAP, JACK W. "Preferences as Indicators of Specific Academic Achievement." Abstract. *Psychol B* 31:706-7 N '34. * (PA 9:1396, title only)

   2. DUNLAP, JACK W. "Preferences as Indicators of Specific Academic Achievement." *J Ed Psychol* 26:411-5 S '35. * (PA 10:596)
   3. DUNLAP, JACK W. "The Predictive Value of Interest Test Items for Achievement in Various School Subjects." *J Appl Psychol* 19:53-8 F '35. * (PA 9:4800)
   4. DUNLAP, JACK W. "Relationships Between Constancy of Expressed Preferences and Certain Other Factors." *J Ed Psychol* 27:521-6 O '36. * (PA 11:338)
   5. CAHILL, GERTRUDE B. *A Study of the Constancy of Responses to the Items of the Dunlap Academic Preference Blank Over an Interval of One Year.* Unpublished master's thesis, Fordham University, 1938. (*Dissertations ...*, 1939, pp. 61-2.)
   6. SHARKEY, VINCENT J., AND DUNLAP, JACK W. "Study of the Reliability and Validity of the Academic Preference Blank." *J Ed Psychol* 31:103-10 F '40. * (PA 14:3785)

Lee J. Cronbach, Assistant Professor of Education, The University of Chicago, Chicago, Illinois. This blank has been constructed with unusual care and technical skill. This is its fifth revision; in each previous revision each item has been validated empirically.

The purpose of the blank is strikingly different from that of other interest tests. It does not attempt to describe the pupil's interests but rather predicts from them his academic achievement. Each paper may be scored on ten keys: paragraph meaning, word meaning, history, language usage, geography, literature, arithmetic, general achievement, mental age, and IQ. These scores predict the pupil's future achievement on the corresponding subtests of the *Metropolitan Achievement Tests* and the *New Stanford Achievement Test* and his score on the *Terman Group Test of Mental Ability*. That this is an effective predictor is evidenced by validity coefficients ranging well above .50. Mental ages estimated from interests correlate .49 to .70 with tested mental ages.

The uses of the test have not yet been adequately investigated. One can visualize situations where it might be profitable to estimate intelligence while seeming to test interest. Whether this test is useful as a predictor of achievement depends on whether it predicts better than an intelligence test or enhances a multiple correlation based on mental age. Unfortunately it predicts less well than the group mental test and enhances multiple r's by such negligible amounts as .02. Whether predicting scores on traditional achievement tests is important should also be examined further. These tests rarely measure all significant outcomes, and good performance on them may not be the major goal of many teachers.

The test is probably not usable for describing individual interests. Only 90 items are presented, and these do not sample interests broadly. In part, scores represent achievement, since the response "unknown" is usually penalized. The test may obtain spurious attitudes, since pupils may feel that they *should* like learning about Valley Forge or hyphens. Response sets may influence scores. The pupil who indiscriminately responds "like" to all these rather schoolish items will tend to get a better score than one who reports liking only for his strong interests. In this respect, the *Kuder Preference Record* uses a superior technique. Detchen has recently shown that the Kuder blank may be so adapted that it also predicts achievement.

W. C. Kvaraceus, Associate Professor of Education, Boston University, Boston, Massachusetts. This instrument is composed of 90 LIDU (Like, Indifferent, Dislike, Unknown) response items—10 were lopped off after the fourth revision as a concession to machine scoring. Predictive interest scores in terms of percentiles are available for each grade in the eight subject-matter areas patterned after the Stanford and the Metropolitan achievement tests. In addition, mental age and "intelligence alertness" may be estimated from the preference scores but not with any high degree of accuracy.

The author suggests the following general uses to which the instrument may be put: guidance, classification, and individual measurement. The author states, "the Blank gives valid estimates of the relative scholastic aptitude of students. Thus, measures of achievement in specific school subjects, general achievement, and intelligence or scholastic aptitude can be secured from a single test." This is a remarkable feat for a 90-item, 10-minute questionnaire. The potential test buyer should note that the author only claims that *estimates* of *relative* scholastic aptitude are yielded. He might have added that these estimates are rough and lack precision, as indicated by the validity coefficients which range from .28 to .73, using as criteria test results on the *Metropolitan Achievement Tests* and the *New Stanford Achievement Test,* and the *Terman Group Test of Mental Ability.*

An excellent description is provided of the item analysis starting with 435 items from which two nonequivalent blanks of 100 items each were derived in the fourth edition. The reported validity and reliability data appear to have been gathered on the fourth edition before the machine-scored edition of 90 items was issued. What happened to the validity and re-

liability of the instrument after 10 per cent of the questionnaire was discarded is not indicated.

For the guidance worker in the junior high school there is only limited value in the author's division of the questionnaire into the selected subject-matter elements since the choices to be made and the problems to be met do not correspond closely with his breakdown of school experiences. The results of achievement tests themselves, school marks in the different subject-matter areas, and intelligence test scores, which cannot be obtained, to be sure, in ten or fifteen minutes, individually and in composite, will yield the more precise data and information upon which classification, guidance, and individual measurement should be based. The naïve guidance worker who has little training but does have ten or fifteen minutes available for "testing" will find in this instrument a dangerous booby trap if he attempts to lean upon it in the learning, teaching, or guidance processes.

Edith I. M. Thomson, Lecturer in Education, University of Edinburgh, Edinburgh, Scotland. This blank examines "interests" at the junior high school stage by obtaining judgments of liking, indifference, dislike, or ignorance on 90 words, chosen as representing many fields of knowledge. The pupil spends about fifteen minutes in recording his responses, after which it is claimed the counselor can discover in which subjects he will do best, the principal can classify him, and "valid estimates of the relative scholastic aptitude of students" may be made. "Thus measures of achievement in specific school subjects, general achievement, and intelligence or scholastic aptitude can be secured from a single test." These are considerable claims for a 90-word test lasting 15 minutes.

The author certainly presents evidence of immense diligence in test preparation. The stimulus words were chosen from courses of study in New York and New Jersey, and for scoring purposes they are classified under the headings used in the *New Stanford* and *Metropolitan Achievement Tests.* The subjects in the standardising groups took those two tests, also the *Terman Group Test of Mental Ability,* and an elaborate item analysis was undertaken by means of biserial correlations between academic success and judgments on each item in the blank. Thus, the final choice of items was made, and a simple weighting system of scores was devised. Data on validity and reliability are given; it may be observed that median reliability coefficients between alternative versions are comparatively low, ranging from .83 to .70, though the self-correlations of the blanks, especially Form B are higher. Validity measured by correlation with subtests of the Stanford and Metropolitan tests is mostly in the neighbourhood of .5 and .6, with a tendency to drop in the higher grades. This decrease of correlation with age is also noticeable in the reliability scores. Thus, the "valid estimates" must be accepted with some caution.

Scoring is rapid and simple by means of perforated key sheets or, if special pencils are used, by a mechanical scoring device.

It is the actual content of the test and its scoring which leaves the critic sceptical. For example, let us look up certain items using the "General Achievement" key. "Liking" for certain arithmetical terms is not a favourable sign; to score points you must *dislike* "Multiplicands," "Drill in Addition," "Product in Multiplying"; to be "indifferent" gives you no mark; to "like" "Checking Problems" causes you to have a mark deducted; if you "like" London you get no mark, you ought to be "indifferent"; if you "dislike" "Expletives," you have a mark deducted—you should not know the meaning of the word. It will be said that the scoring has been experimentally determined; but after doing the test, one is left with the feeling that too much depends on how one happens to interpret "like" and that, while the score no doubt throws some light on "interests," more moderate claims should be made regarding its prognostic value.

Teach Col J 13:24 S '41. E. L. Abell. * Correlations were computed with intelligence scores and with subtests of the Metropolitan Achievement Test and the Stanford Achievement Test using the biserial-r technique. Correlations range from .52 to .72 and are thus high enough to suggest a strong relationship but not high enough to give accurate individual predictions. The blank should prove very useful in furnishing clues as to the subjects in which the pupil is likely to do best.

[36]

*Euphorimeter. Adults; 1940; $2 per manual (*Chart for Happiness*); Hornell Hart; Macmillan Co.

REFERENCES
1. HART, HORNELL. *Chart for Happiness.* New York: Macmillan Co., 1940. Pp. xi, 198. $2.00. * (*PA* 15:925)
2. HART, HORNELL, AND HART, ELLA B. *Personality and the Family,* Revised Edition, pp. 59-63. Boston, Mass.: D. C. Heath & Co., 1941. Pp. v, 526. $3.25. (*PA* 15:2688, title only)

For related reviews, see 37.

[37]

*[Re Euphorimeter.] HART, HORNELL. **Chart for Happiness.** New York: Macmillan Co., 1940. Pp. xi, 198. $2.00. * (*PA* 15:925)

Am J Psychol 56:158 Ja '43. J. W. Macmillan. * The fine disregard of the most elementary statistical precautions, the broad a priori statements, the positive examples cited as proof, the blatant appeal to the untrained layman and the obviously uncritical attitude of the author combine to make this a book which might better have been left unwritten, although considerable amusement may be derived from it by those familiar with the techniques used and the problems involved in the measurement of personality.

Am J Sociol 47:652-3 Ja '42. J. L. Moreno. * a book which should be of interest to sociologists, ministers, educators, and psychiatrists. * The book has a religious tinge. Professor Hart not only measures happiness but also tells the reader how to become happy. He measures happiness, diagnoses it, and builds it. The book contains tables for scoring "at-the-moment euphorimeters," a bibliography and an index. It seems to me that Professor Hart has published his findings prematurely. He might well have approached the complex problem of measuring a state of mind by means of other methods as well as that which he has chosen: by a more thorough analysis of the subjective aspect, for instance, by more intensive case studies, and by a larger number of them. This procedure might have avoided the suspicion of surface research and surface therapy.

J Abn & Social Psychol 36:449-50 Jl '41. Howard Davis Spoerl. The concept of happiness is rare in psychology, at least as a formal category. Thus it is with some degree of interest that one turns to a semi-technical study of the subject, such as the work under consideration. What is offered in this case is a means of testing happiness, either as a transitory state or as a protracted condition. The device employed, which was conceived and developed by the author, is called the "euphorimeter," and the quantitative index of happiness is a sum of weightings known as "euphor-units." The euphorimeters consist of a list of 48 adjectives to be selected as describing the subject's affective consciousness, some rating scales, and questions of the sort usually contained in adjustment inventories. * In the preface the euphorimeter is modestly classed with intelligence tests, the clinical thermometer, and the electrocardiograph, as a revolutionary diagnostic instrument. One chapter is devoted to its possible users; no field, from medical and ministerial activity to personnel management, appears to have been overlooked. * The author's definition of the quality which he hopes he is measuring is a semibehavioristic statement of hedonism * In simpler, and "operational" terms, happiness is "the state in which people are when they say sincerely, 'I am happy.'" No attempt is made to employ a standard psychological concept of pleasantness, and the definition seems, therefore, to lose distinctiveness. Moreover, since euphoria ordinarily refers either to bodily or to psycho-pathological states, the designations "euphor-unit" and "euphorimeter," apart from the linguistic shudders they induce, are not apt denotations. The general carelessness in characterizing delicate affective discriminations stigmatizes the crude superficiality of the book as a whole. It is divided into two parts entitled "The Pursuit of Happiness," and "How to Use the Euphorimeter Tests." The reader is invited, if he wishes "anything approaching scientific insight" into his adjustments and apparent satisfactions, to study the tests themselves before turning back to pursue happiness through play and work, love and home, vitality and success, sociability and religion. After determining whether or not he is happy, from a test based on his ability to state sincerely "I am happy," our scientifically reassured reader may thus proceed to absorb the array of pep-talks, barbershop diagnoses and remedies, temperance sermons, and advice to the lovelorn of which Chapters 3 to 10 consist. Later he may make liberal use of the "euphorimeter advice form" presented in Chapter 13, to derive therefrom all manner of suggestions such as "learn to meet life courageously" and "get out of debt—by heroic measures if necessary." Although he is long on advice couched in generalities of this kind, the author is short on concrete methods sufficiently profound to alter the motivation of the maladjusted. Indeed, the quest for happiness seems to consist in rearranging one's surface outlook while causing a minimum of disturbance to actual mechanisms of adjustment. * It is something of a shock, however, to encounter the results of the studies of Terman and of Burgess and Cottrell stated baldly in terms of euphor-units, nor is it made clear how the translation was achieved. The same dubious honor is paid to Shailer and to Goodwin Watson. The lay reader is almost certain to adopt the suggestion that these various authorities have already taken the euphorimeter to their collective bosom. * One further feature of the work should be mentioned—its potentiality for damage or at least its inevitable nuisance value. On the basis of the meager statistical account in the last chapter concerning the reliability of the tests, their widespread utilization is recommended, and the tests are commercially advertised. In the hands of untrained persons, or of zealous members of professions like the ministry, a considerable amount of harm might result from indiscriminate application and exaggerated pretensions, especially when one takes into account the present inordinate respect on the part of the digest-reading public for quasi-psychological mumbo-jumbo. The fact that the author frequently takes time out to caution the reader to seek only expert advice in sundry situations, seems more likely to silence by anticipation the protests of psychiatrists, than to inspire adequate caution in those who would voyage to salvation by this chart for happiness. Professor Hart has not succeeded in justifying one's interest in the psychological nature and possibilities of the concept.

Fed Probation 5:49 Ja-Mr '41. Dortha Williams Osborn. * The chief limitation of the.... [euphorimeter] appears to be its finite usefulness to those with less than two years' high school training. The author states that "persons who have quit school in the grades, or who have found high school work difficult, are likely to misunderstand the directions or to fail to know the meaning of important words." * this limitation is a serious one for social workers, particularly in the correctional field, as it will prevent its use as a formal test except in selected cases. However, the careful analysis of the fields of happiness and unhappiness, and the many suggestions for remedial work, cannot fail to be helpful to the correctional worker.

Mental Hyg 26:144 Ja '42. H. Neumann. * The book is careful to warn against self-treatment where expert consultation is needed; nor does it pretend to offer the results of new research. It serves a highly useful purpose in making available much that most readers would never come upon. For example, the score averages for couples who disagree chronically about friends, play, philosophy of life, are much lower than for cases in which either partner feels sexually starved. So, too, while extremely inadequate incomes are a handicap to happiness, more than enough scores indicate that amount of income is not the all-important factor some schools of philosophy would make it. *

Sci Ed 25:354 N '41. C(larence) M. P(ruitt).

Sociol & Social Res 25:579–80 Jl-Ag '41. E(mory) S. B(ogardus). It is in Part II that the author explains his euphorimeter tests and demonstrates that he is working upon a real human problem and is making headway. Part I is devoted largely to advice to people who for one reason or another are unhappy and are disturbed by their lack of happiness. A "long-run" test and an "at-the-moment" test of happiness are described, both to be used by the subject himself, who reports his own subjective reactions to life according to his feelings. The "long-run" test includes answers to a brief and selected list of questions, and the "at-the-moment" test relies on underlining and crossing out words in a series of forty-eight adjectives. The scoring methods are simple enough to be used by the subject. The ways in which the methods of scoring were derived are not fully explained or justified. Next the author develops a diagnostic test, whereby the subject may be expected to discover why he is unhappy if either the long-run or at-the-moment test indicates that he is below normal in the happiness that he enjoys. The diagnostic test is somewhat elaborate. It seeks to locate the subject's areas of happiness or unhappiness in such phases of life as recreation, work, love life, home, health, sense of success, mental harmony, economic status, friendships, loyalty to groups, religious adjustment, and altruism. The results of these subtests may be brought together, and the result is labeled the subject's "happiness spectrum." While many details will need to be perfected and vital changes made, yet the cause of scientific measurement and of prediction is furthered by the unique ways in which Dr. Hart has taken previous techniques and developed them and produced his euphorimeter tests.

[38]

★Every-Day Life: A Scale for the Measurement of Three Varieties of Self-Reliance. Grades 9-12;

1941; IBM; $1.75 per 25; machine-scorable answer sheets also available, 2¢ each; $3.50 per set of machine-scoring stencils; 40¢ per specimen set; nontimed (30) minutes; Leland H. Stott; Sheridan Supply Co.

REFERENCES

1. STOTT, LELAND H. "An Analysis of 'Self-Reliance'." Abstract. *Psychol B* 34:783 N '37. * (PA 12:1498, title only)
2. STOTT, LELAND H. "An Analytical Study of Self-Reliance." *J Psychol* 5:107-18 '38. *
3. STOTT, LELAND H. *The Relation of Certain Factors in Farm Family Life to Personality Development in Adolescents.* University of Nebraska, College of Agriculture, Agricultural Experiment Station, Research Bulletin 106. Lincoln, Neb.: University of Nebraska, October 1938. Pp. 46. Paper. *
4. STOTT, LELAND H. *Personality Development in Farm, Small-Town, and City Children.* University of Nebraska, College of Agriculture, Agricultural Experiment Station, Research Bulletin 114. Lincoln, Neb.: University of Nebraska, August 1939. Pp. 34. Paper. *
5. BROWN, PAUL A. "An Analysis of Sex Differences in Self-Reliance Among University Students." *Psychol Rec* 4:391-6 Jl '41. * (PA 15:5200)
6. STOTT, LELAND H. "Family Prosperity in Relation to the Psychological Adjustments of Farm Folks." *Rural Sociol* 10: 256-63 S '45. * (PA 20:258)

Albert Ellis, Consulting Psychologist, 2505 University Avenue, New York, New York. This questionnaire purports to measure three varieties of self-reliance: I, Independence in Personal Matters; II, Resourcefulness in Group Situations; and III, Personal Responsibility. The individual items of the inventory are of the conventional type but are more specific than the usual Woodworth–Bernreuter–Thurstone kind of question. Five categories of answers are provided for each question: YES (always), Yes (usually), ?, No (usually not), and NO (never). The advantages and disadvantages of the inventory are these:

a) The construction of the questionnaire was apparently empirically approached and carefully done, with adequate consideration being given to the statistical selection of the individual test items.

b) The split-half reliabilities of the three scales—ranging from .84 to .94—are satisfactorily high.

c) It is stated that "the validity of the scores as indicators of the 'factors' measured was insured by the methods of item selection employed. Every item scored for a particular factor was selected, first, because it was found to be very significantly correlated with a criterion score based upon the items highly loaded with that factor in the original analysis, and second, because it bore a *logical* relationship with the factor." At best, this statement means only that the test was shown to be valid for the groups on which it was standardized. Since no other validation attempts are reported for the inventory, the validity of this questionnaire has still not been established.

d) The correlation coefficients of .60 between factors I and II and of .64 between factors I and III raise the question whether this inventory is really measuring three independent traits as is claimed by the author.

In sum: Stott's *Every-Day Life* appears to be a well-constructed questionnaire, but its practical value still remains unproven.

[39]

★**Examining for Aphasia and Related Disturbances.** Ages 8 and over; 1946; individual; $5 per manual and 50 record forms, postpaid; $4 per 50 record forms, postpaid; $2 per manual, postpaid; (30-120) minutes; Jon Eisenson; Psychological Corporation.

C. R. Strother, Associate Professor of Clinical Psychology and Speech Pathology, The State University of Iowa, Iowa City, Iowa. Examining for Aphasia is designed primarily for the use of therapists who are concerned with planning and evaluating rehabilitation programs for aphasic patients. It does not purport to be a manual for comprehensive psychological examination.

The manual is divided into two sections. The first contains tests for receptive disturbances, and the second, tests to assess impairment of expression. Following Nielson, Eisenson includes tests for visual, auditory, and tactile agnosia and for apraxia. These tests should be useful in assisting the clinician to evaluate disabilities which present special problems in rehabilitation.

The tests for receptive disturbances include measures of auditory verbal comprehension and reading comprehension. The range of difficulty is limited. Since the items are multitple choice, they can be presented in such a manner as to avoid expressive difficulties. The tests for expressive difficulties include automatic speech, spelling, writing from dictation, calculations, oral reading, and clock setting. The brevity of the tests precludes much of a range of difficulty in the items and also constitutes a serious limitation on their use as a measure of improvement. The spelling test, for example, includes only six words. The method of administration is flexible, and no norms are provided, it being the author's intention that the tests be used as flexible clinical instruments rather than as rigid measuring devices.

The clinician should find the manual useful in obtaining an indication of the areas of difficulty presented by the patient and, perhaps, as a very gross measure of improvement. As Eisenson indicates, more extensive tests will be found necessary.

Arch Neurol & Psychiatry 56:244 Ag '46. * intended for the use of speech pathologists in planning a program of language rehabilitation for individual aphasic patients. The manual presents a comprehensive language examination in a clear form and should be useful for recording the progress in language function. The instructions for the various test items are specific and easily followed, and much of the test material is included in the manual. The author states that his interest is in speech therapy, and not in neurologic and neurosurgical implications of language dysfunctions; consequently, it is not a criticism of his work to point out that the examination is not entirely satisfactory for use by the clinical neurologist.

[40]

★**Furbay-Schrammel Social Comprehension Test.** Grades 9-16; 1941; $1.70 per 25, postpaid; 15¢ per specimen set, postpaid; 80(85) minutes; John H. Furbay and H. E. Schrammel; Bureau of Educational Measurements, Kansas State Teachers College of Emporia.

REFERENCES

1. BARKER, CLARENCE, JR. *A Comparative Study of the Social Comprehension of Selected Groups of College Freshmen.* Unpublished master's thesis, Kansas State Teachers College of Emporia, 1941. Pp. 31. (*An annotated Bibliography of Theses . . . 1939–1944,* 1944, p. 5.)

[41]

★**Goldstein-Scheerer Tests of Abstract and Concrete Thinking.** Adults; 1945; individual; $25.50 per testing outfit; Kurt Goldstein and Martin Scheerer; Psychological Corporation.
a) GOLDSTEIN-SCHEERER CUBE TEST. $3.25 per 50 record forms for Designs 1-6, postpaid; $3.25 per 50 record forms for Designs 7-12, postpaid.
b) WEIGL-GOLDSTEIN-SCHEERER COLOR FORM SORTING TEST. $2.50 per 50 record forms, postpaid.
c) GOLDSTEIN-SCHEERER STICK TEST. $2.50 per 50 record forms, postpaid.

REFERENCES

1. BOLLES, MARY MARJORIE. *The Basis of Pertinence: A Study of the Test Performance of Aments, Dements and Normal Children of the Same Mental Age.* Archives of Psychology, No. 212. Washington, D. C.: American Psychological Association, Inc., June 1937. Pp. 51. Paper. $1.00. * (*PA* 11:5549)
2. GOLDSTEIN, KURT, AND KATZ, SIEGFRIED E. "The Psychopathology of Pick's Disease." *Arch Neurol & Psychiatry* 38:473-90 S '37. * (*PA* 12:859)
3. BOLLES, MARJORIE, AND GOLDSTEIN, KURT. "A Study of the Impairment of 'Abstract Behavior' in Schizophrenic Patients." *Psychiatric Q* 12:42-65 Ja '38. * (*PA* 12:5302)
4. BOLLES, M. MARJORIE; ROSEN, GEORGE P.; AND LANDIS, CARNEY. "Psychological Performance Tests as Prognostic Agents for the Efficacy of Insulin Therapy in Schizophrenia." *Psychiatric Q* 12:733-7 O '38. * (*PA* 13:2483)
5. NADEL, AARON B. *A Qualitative Analysis of Behavior Following Cerebral Lesions Diagnosed as Primarily Affecting the Frontal Lobes.* Archives of Psychology, No. 224. Washington, D. C.: American Psychological Association, Inc., April 1938. Pp. 60. Paper. $1.00. * (*PA* 13:83)
6. GOLDSTEIN, KURT. "The Significance of Special Mental Tests for Diagnosis and Prognosis in Schizophrenia." *Am J Psychiatry* 96:575-88 N '39. * (*PA* 14:2424)
7. HANFMANN, EUGENIA. "Analysis of the Thinking Disorder in a Case of Schizophrenia." *Arch Neurol & Psychiatry* 41:568-79 Mr '39. *

8. BENTON, ARTHUR L., AND HOWELL, IRA L. "The Use of
Psychological Tests in the Evaluation of Intellectual Function
Following Head Injury: Report of a Case of Post-Traumatic
Personality Disorder." *Psychosom Med* 3:138-51 Ap '41. *
(*PA* 15:4206)
9. GOLDSTEIN, KURT, AND SCHEERER, MARTIN. *Abstract and
Concrete Behavior: An Experimental Study with Special Tests.*
Psychological Monographs, Vol. 53, No. 2, Whole No. 239.
Washington, D. C.: American Psychological Association, Inc.,
1941. Pp. vi, 151. Paper. $2.25. * (*PA* 16:1004)
10. RAPAPORT, D., AND BROWN, J. F. "Concept Formation
Tests and Personality Research." Abstract. *Psychol B* 38:597-8
Jl '41. * (*PA* 15:5222, title only)
11. THOMPSON, JANE. "The Ability of Children of Different
Grade Levels to Generalize on Sorting Tests." *J Psychol*
11:119-26 '41. * (*PA* 15:2431)
12. WEXBERG, ERWIN. "Testing Methods for the Differential
Diagnosis of Mental Deficiency in a Case of Arrested Brain
Tumor." *Am J Mental Def* 46:39-45 Jl '41. * (*PA* 16:369)
13. WEIGL, EGON. "On the Psychology of So-Called Processes
of Abstraction." Translated by Margaret J. Rioch. Edited by
Carney Landis and Kurt Goldstein. *J Abn & Social Psychol*
36:3-33 Ja '41. * (*PA* 15:2642)
14. ZUBIN, JOSEPH, AND THOMPSON, JANE. *Sorting Tests in
Relation to Drug Therapy in Schizophrenia.* New York: New
York State Psychiatric Institute, 1941. Pp. v, 23. Out of print.
* (*PA* 16:2715)
15. RAPAPORT, D. "Principles Underlying Projective Techniques." *Char & Pers* 10:213-9 Mr '42. * (*PA* 16:4068)
16. GOLDSTEIN, KURT. "Brain Concussion: Evaluation of the
After Effects of Special Tests." *Dis Nerv Sys* 4:325-34 N '43.
* (*PA* 18:478)
17. GOLDSTEIN, KURT. "The Significance of Psychological
Research in Schizophrenia," pp. 302-18. In *Contemporary Psychopathology: A Source Book.* Edited by Silvan S. Tomkins.
Cambridge, Mass.: Harvard University Press, 1943. Pp. xiv,
600. $5.00. * (*PA* 18:771) Reprinted from *J Nerv & Mental Dis*
97:261-79 Mr '43. (*PA* 17:1994)
18. REICHARD, SUZANNE, AND RAPAPORT, DAVID. "The Role
of Testing Concept Formation in Clinical Psychological Work."
B Menninger Clinic 7:99-105 My '43. * (*PA* 17:4153)
19. REICHARD, SUZANNE; SCHNEIDER, MARION; AND RAPA-
PORT, DAVID. "The Development of Concept Formation in Children." *Trans Kan Acad Sci* 46:120-3 '43. * (*PA* 18:3743)
20. CLEVELAND, SIDNEY E., AND DYSINGER, DON W. "Mental
Deterioration in Senile Psychosis." *J Abn & Social Psychol*
39:368-72 Jl '44. * (*PA* 18:3743)
21. GOLDSTEIN, KURT. "Methodological Approach to the
Study of Schizophrenic Thought Disorder," pp. 17-39. In *Language and Thought in Schizophrenia.* Edited by J. S. Kasanin.
Berkeley, Calif.: University of California Press, 1944. Pp. xiv,
133. $2.00. * (London: Cambridge University Press. 12s.)
(*PA* 18:1428)
22. KISKER, GEORGE W. "Abstract and Categorical Behavior
Following Therapeutic Brain Surgery." *Psychosom Med*
6:146-50 Ap '44. * (*PA* 18:3082)
23. NEEDHAM, NORMA R. "A Comparative Study of the
Performance of Feebleminded Subjects on the Goodenough
Drawing, the Goldstein-Scheerer Cube Test, and the Stanford-
Binet." *Am J Mental Def* 49:155-61 O '44. * (*PA* 19:2774)
24. RAPAPORT, DAVID; WITH THE COLLABORATION OF ROY
SCHAFER AND MERTON GILL. "The Sorting Test," pp. 162-209.
In their *Manual of Diagnostic Psychological Testing: I,
Diagnostic Testing of Intelligence and Concept Formation.*
Preface by Karl Menninger. Review Series, Vol. 2, No. 2. New
York: Josiah Macy, Jr. Foundation, 1944. Pp. xiii, 239. Paper,
lithotyped. Out of print. * (*PA* 19:3195)
25. REICHARD, SUZANNE; SCHNEIDER, MARION; AND RAPA-
PORT, DAVID. "The Development of Concept Formation in Chil-
dren." *Am J Orthopsychiatry* 14:156-61 Ja '44. * (*PA* 18:2327)
26. MAYMAN, MARTIN. "Review of the Literature on the
Three Tests of Concept Formation," pp. 561-6. In *Diagnostic
Psychological Testing: The Theory, Statistical Evaluation, and
Diagnostic Application of a Battery of Tests, Vol. I.* By David
Rapaport with the collaboration of Merton Gill and Roy Schafer. Chicago, Ill.: Year Book Publishers, Inc., 1945. Pp.
xi, 573. $6.50. * (*PA* 20:929)
27. RAPAPORT, DAVID; WITH THE COLLABORATION OF MERTON
GILL AND ROY SCHAFER. Chap. 4, "The Sorting Test," pp. 396-
461, 478-86, 533-47. In their *Diagnostic Psychological Testing:
The Theory, Statistical Evaluation, and Diagnostic Application
of a Battery of Tests, Vol. I.* Chicago, Ill.: Year Book Publishers, Inc., 1945. Pp. xi, 573. $6.50. * (*PA* 20:929)
28. ARMITAGE, STEWARD G. *An Analysis of Certain Psychological Tests Used for the Evaluation of Brain Injury.* Psychological Monographs, Vol. 60, No. 1, Whole No. 277. Washington, D. C.: American Psychological Association, Inc., 1946.
Pp. iii, 48. Paper. $1.25. *

*Kate Levine Kogan, Clinical Psychologist, 154
Chesterfield Road, Pittsburgh 13, Pennsylvania.*
These techniques, together with two other methods, are described in a monograph entitled *Ab-
tract and Concrete Behavior: An Experimental
Study With Special Tests* (9). A clear and thorough discussion of the concepts of abstract and
concrete behavior is provided, and the test procedures are depicted in great detail. Thus, the
purpose of the examinations is outlined explicitly, and a wealth of illustrative responses is
analyzed and discussed. The material presents
an aspect of behavior which has received little
attention elsewhere in the literature; furthermore, the concepts involved have been afforded
such clear delineation that they are readily applicable to, and recognizable in, the behavior of
patients in reaction to many other test items and
situations which are more commonly included
in clinical examinations.

The three procedures for which complete test
material can be purchased constitute only part
of a battery which the authors recommend be
used in its entirety. Since this recommendation
must be ignored because of the unavailability
of standard equipment, the methods will be
considered separately for brief evaluation of
their efficacy.

The Cube Test is of especial interest since it
is based on the block-design technique which
occurs in several of the intelligence scales most
widely used with both adults and children.
Hence, the occurrence of a marked deviation of
score on the block-design items as compared
with the remainder of the scores on the scale
would make an opportunity for more careful
analysis of the patient's approach to this task
both pertinent and desirable. The Cube Test,
therefore, has been proved useful in conjunction with other test procedures for obtaining
further, more qualitative, elaboration. The exactitude required by the two-pamphlet record
form, with a separate page for each test design,
is possibly somewhat out of proportion to the
broad, subjective evaluation of the data which
must be made.

One of the greatest values of the Color Form
Sorting Test lies in its brevity and simplicity.
Success or failure is clearly and objectively defined. Under most circumstances, less than five
minutes will suffice for administration. Intellectual level plays a small part, since most normal
children above the ages of seven or eight years
can achieve a solution. Motor disabilities, which
so often accompany cerebral pathology, interfere with effective response very little. Hence,
the absence of prompt solution in an adult
patient is likely to be significant. For this reason,

however, the technique is less likely to be discriminative in cases of mild or early brain pathology.

The Stick Test has been, in the writer's experience, the least effective of the three methods under discussion. Usually, only patients with fairly advanced and extensive cerebral pathology experience sufficient difficulty to make their productions significant. The first part of the test requires the patient to copy the structure. Other available techniques using paper and pencil offer less cumbersome administration and scoring and permit simpler permanent record of the performance; they also make use of more complex perceptual units and hence, are applicable to less severely impaired patients. The second portion of the test requires reproduction of designs from memory and has no discernible advantage over other more commonly used and better standardized techniques.

The entire battery used in this experimental study has achieved particular prominence as a method of determining and diagnosing organic brain disorder. This view of its use is a misconception in terms of actual experience and, apparently, in terms of the authors' intention. In the writer's opinion the authors offer a systematized description, analysis, and explanation of the test responses of a selected group of patients known to have cerebral pathology. Actually, many patients with various forms of cortical defect exhibit no "impairment of the abstract attitude" on these tests. For example, in an extensive research study of patients suffering from the late effects of mild concussive head injury, without focal lesion, no distinction could be made between the responses of the patients and members of normal and neurotic control series. Furthermore, it has been pointed out that some schizophrenics exhibit impairment analagous to that described for organics (3). Rapaport has made use of a modification of one of the techniques discussed in the study, Object Sorting, in his large-scale diagnostic study of functional disorders (26). It is regrettable, in terms of our interest here, that patients with organic disorders were not also included for comparative purposes.

It should be noted that this "experimental study" presents only qualitative results. There is no statement of the number or type of patient in whom the technique elicited the crucial behavior indicative of impairment. Not only are all data pertaining to standardization lacking,

but any definition of the extent to, or frequency with, which normal variability might introduce concrete elements into the responses of essentially healthy persons is omitted. There is no systematic method of scoring or evaluating test performance, and in this respect the methods fall slightly short even of the authors' statement that the tests enable the examiner "to determine whether a patient can or cannot assume the abstract attitude." For they offer incontrovertible evidence only in the very rare cases in which the subject experiences difficulty with all items presented. If one should obtain a record in which partial successes are present, no means has been offered whereby one may profit by the experience of the test authors in reaching a decision or interpretation; the material must be interpreted in the light of the more restricted past clinical experience of the particular examiner. Within these limits the techniques offer an opportunity for careful observation, clarification, and analysis of the patient's psychological approach as it is exhibited in a variety of situations.

Thus, in summary, these tests offer a means of evaluating aspects of behavior which are not treated adequately elsewhere; but they must be subjected to careful and well-planned standardization before they can make their fullest contribution to the studies of the clinician engaged in individual casework.

C. R. Strother, Associate Professor of Clinical Psychology and Speech Pathology; and Ludwig Immergluck, Research Assistant in Psychiatry; The State University of Iowa, Iowa City, Iowa. [Review of the monograph, *Abstract and Concrete Behavior*, which serves as a manual for the *Goldstein–Scheerer Tests*.] This 151-page monograph represents the results of extensive investigation of organic brain diseases and is intended to present a series of tests designed to evaluate these disorders.

The first part of the monograph consists of a theoretical discussion of the *nature* of thinking disorders. The authors base most of their discussion upon their extensive clinical experience. However, in spite of their impressive backgrounds as practicing clinicians, the reader cannot help but be struck by the lack of demonstrable evidence for many of the statements made. The authors conceive of behavior changes in the brain diseased, schizophrenic, ament, and dement in terms of an impairment of "abstract behavior." These findings are based on a series of investigations originally undertaken by Gelb and Goldstein. In their present monograph, Goldstein and Scheerer claim that the normal individual may assume two *distinct* types of behavior, the concrete and the abstract. These two types of behavior, in turn, are dependent upon two corresponding basic attitudes. The authors recognize that other investigators have made similar distinctions and have come to comparable conclusions. However, in defining the concrete and abstract attitude as basic "capacity levels of the total personality" they hope to distinguish themselves from previous investigators. Unfortunately, the authors take the opportunity to raise, on the basis of their own concepts, theoretical and systematic arguments against those psychologists who believe that concrete and abstract behavior is learned or acquired. Against this notion, Goldstein and Scheerer offer their own and, incidentally, vaguely defined concept of "capacity level." These reviewers, however, are at a loss to understand why the term "capacity level" necessarily precludes the concept of "learned" or "acquired." Furthermore, the authors imply a *qualitative distinction* between the abstract and concrete levels rather than, as many other investigators hold, conceiving of them as lying on a continuum.

Goldstein and Scheerer cite the following eight characteristics of the abstract attitude: (*a*) to detach our ego from the outer world or from inner experiences; (*b*) to assume a mental set; (*c*) to account for acts to oneself; to verbalize the account; (*d*) to shift reflectively from one aspect of the situation to another; (*e*) to hold in mind simultaneously various aspects of a situation; (*f*) to grasp the essentials of a given whole; to break up a given whole into parts; to isolate and synthesize them; (*g*) to abstract common properties reflectively; to form hierarchic concepts; (*h*) to plan ahead ideationally; to assume an attitude towards the "mere possible"; and to think or perform symbolically.

The concrete attitude, on the other hand, "does not imply conscious activity in the sense of reasoning, awareness or self-account of one's doing. We surrender to the experiences of an unreflective character: we are confined to the immediate apprehension of the given thing or situation in its particular uniqueness." Furthermore, the authors claim that concrete behavior

has none of the above-mentioned eight characteristics of the abstract attitude. Most investigators, however, would agree that even the most deteriorated organic or schizophrenic patient exhibits behavior which could not be characterized adequately in terms of the authors' strict definition of concreteness.

Following the introduction and discussion of basic concepts, the remainder of the monograph is devoted to a presentation and discussion of five tests designed to determine the extent of impairment of abstract thinking. The tests offered are: *The Goldstein–Scheerer Cube Test*— This is a modification of the *Kohs Block Design Test.* The modification consists essentially in presenting the subject who has failed under the usual procedure with card designs of the same size as the blocks, with designs with superimposed lines helping the subject perceptually to 'break down' the design, and, finally, with an actual block model of the design to be reproduced. *The Gelb–Goldstein Color Sorting Test* —The subject is presented with woolen skeins of different hues and shades and asked to sort them into groups. *The Gelb–Goldstein–Weigl–Scheerer Object Sorting Test*—This test consists of a set of objects which can be grouped according to material (e.g., metal, wood, porcelain, etc.), color, or form. The subject is asked to sort them into groups. Various groupings are possible and ability to shift is noted. *The Goldstein–Scheerer Stick Test*—By means of a series of sticks (3.5 inches and 5.5 inches long), the subject is required to reproduce from memory a series of figure designs.

Each test is carefully described and preceded by a discussion of its psychological rationale. The instructions to be used are presented verbatim, and each step is outlined in detail. However, no norms or standardization data are given, and these reviewers looked in vain for a description of the population on which these tests were developed. Instead of presenting norms, the authors content themselves with citing examples of typical failures of "patients." No evidence is presented which allows the reader to infer that there is any consistent relationship between test performance and *degree* of the patient's clinical impairment. Certainly, such information is of utmost importance for determining the usefulness of the test.

The seasoned practitioner may find these tests extremely useful as a qualitative tool and as an adjunct to his clinical judgment. The novice and student, on the other hand, are, in the absence of statistical data, deprived of the opportunity to evaluate the tests on their own merits. The authors' advice that "qualitative has to precede statistical analysis" is very well taken. Unfortunately, they have taken only the first of these steps.

O. L. Zangwill, Assistant Director, Institute of Experimental Psychology, University of Oxford, Oxford, England. These tests are well-adapted to elicit defects of abstract or "categorical" thinking of the type commonly, although by no means invariably, associated with injury or disease of the brain cortex. In using them with neuropsychiatric cases, however, it is important to bear the following points in mind:

a) The tests are essentially qualitative and standards of normal performance are somewhat problematical. As in the closely parallel case of the Rorschach test, it is most essential to gain experience in administering the tests before the results can be evaluated with any confidence.

b) The location of the cerebral lesion has some influence on test performance. Thus, gross defects on the Cube and Stick Tests with little or no impairment on the Color Form Sorting Test are quite common in patients with circumscribed lesions of the posterior parts of the brain cortex. In cases of this kind, the impairment is almost certainly due to specific agnostic or apraxic defects rather than to loss of "abstract attitude" in Goldstein's sense of the term. In patients with lesions of the frontal lobes, on the other hand, impairment in the categorical sphere is very common and may be predominantly displayed on the Sorting Test.

c) Some patients with ascertained cerebral lesions perform in an essentially normal fashion on these tests. This is by no means unusual in cases of traumatic brain injury and may be due to high previous intelligence level, to restitution of cortical function, or to a combination of these factors. In view of the possible influence of previous intelligence level on test performance, it would be most useful to have a suitably standardized series of abstraction tests of graded difficulty.

d) Certain cases of primary psychosis, in particular schizophrenia, show an impairment of conceptual understanding and thought somewhat similar to that of the organic case. It is also possible that psychogenic disturbances in patients of low intelligence may lead to patterns

of test performance easily confused with the reactions of organic patients.

e) The significance of abstraction defects from the point of view of occupational disability and problems of resettlement of the organic case is most difficult to assess. It is not uncommon to find patients with marked conceptual defects achieving adequate occupational readjustments. On the other hand, patients who perform well on the tests may display a marked impairment of practical judgment in daily life. Research on the significance of conceptual defects in relation to resettlement is needed before any but the most guarded opinion can be based on the test findings.

For related reviews, see 42.

[42]

★[*Re* Goldstein-Scheerer Tests of Abstract and Concrete Thinking.] GOLDSTEIN, KURT, AND SCHEERER, MARTIN. **Abstract and Concrete Behavior: An Experimental Study With Special Tests.** Psychological Monographs, Vol. 53, No. 2, Whole No. 239. Washington, D. C.: American Psychological Association, Inc., 1941. Pp. vi, 151. Paper. $2.25. * (PA 16: 1004)

Loyola Ed Digest 17:7 Je '42. Austin G. Schmidt. * Kurt Goldstein and his collaborators began as early as the first World War to develop certain sorting tests by means of which a subject's tendency to think in concrete terms when he might think in abstract terms could be measured. The present study, a most interesting one, is an analysis of the responses of abnormal subjects to the Goldstein–Scheerer Cube Test, the Gelb–Goldstein Color Sorting Test, the Gelb–Goldstein–Weigl–Scheerer Object Sorting Test, the Weigl–Goldstein–Scheerer Color Form Sorting Test, and the Goldstein–Scheerer Stick Test. The study is descriptive and qualitative rather than quantitative. It throws much light on how abnormal subjects think and on why they think as they do. The description (pp. 4–7) of the eight conscious and volitional modes of behavior of which the abstract attitude is the basis will be of interest to the teacher and the test-maker.

[43]

★**Guilford-Martin Inventory of Factors GAMIN, Abridged Edition.** College and adults; 1943–45; supersedes original edition; IBM; 1 form; $2.50 per 25; machine-scorable answer sheets also available, 2¢ each; $1.25 per set of plastic hand-scoring stencils for test booklet; $3.50 per set of machine-scoring stencils for answer sheet; $2.50 per set of hand-scoring stencils for answer sheet; 40¢ per specimen set; non-timed (30) minutes; J. P. Guilford and H. G. Martin; Sheridan Supply Co.

REFERENCES

1. GUILFORD, J. P., AND GUILFORD, RUTH B. "Personality Factors S, E, and M, and Their Measurements." *J Psychol* 2:109-27 '36. * (*PA* 10:4533)
2. GUILFORD, J. P., AND GUILFORD, RUTH B. "Personality Factors D, R, T, and A." *J Abn & Social Psychol* 34:21-36 Ja '39. * (*PA* 13:3185)
3. GUILFORD, J. P., AND GUILFORD, RUTH B. "Personality Factors N and GD." *J Abn & Social Psychol* 34:239-48 Ap '39. * (*PA* 13:4212)
4. LOVELL, CONSTANCE. "A Study of the Factor Structure of Thirteen Personality Variables." *Ed & Psychol Meas* 5:335-50 w '45. * (*PA* 20:2399)
5. MARTIN, HOWARD G. "The Construction of the Guilford-Martin Inventory of Factors G-A-M-I-N." *J Appl Psychol* 29:298-300 Ag '45. * (*PA* 20:201)
6. EYSENCK, H. J. *Dimensions of Personality*, pp. 38-9. A record of research carried out in collaboration with H. T. Himmelweit and W. Linford Rees with the help of M. Desai, W. D. Furneaux, H. Halstead, O. Marum, M. McKinlay, A. Petrie, and P. M. Yap. Foreword by Aubrey Lewis, London: Kegan Paul, Trench, Trübner & Co. Ltd., 1947. Pp. xi, 308. 25s. * (*PA* 22:210)
7. LUBORSKY, L. B., AND CATTELL, R. B. "The Validation of Personality Factors in Humor." *J Personality* 15:283-91 Je '47. * (*PA* 22:2072)

H. J. Eysenck, Senior Psychologist, Maudsley Hospital, London, England. This test consists of 186 questions of the Yes-?-No type and purports to measure five independent variables of temperament, viz., general pressure for overt activity, ascendancy in social situations, masculinity of attitudes and interests, lack of inferiority feelings, lack of nervous tenseness and irritability. Isolation of these variables was achieved by factorial analysis and subsequent item analysis. The original scale contained 270 items and used a more complicated scoring system; the abridged scale is no less reliable than the old. Norms are based on 80 male and 80 female university students.

The inventory is open to criticism on the following grounds: (*a*) There is no evidence of validity for any of the scales, excepting the masculine interests scale, which correlates .84 (phi coefficient) with sex of the subject filling in the inventory. The measurement is based on the assumption that the person who is suffering from nervous tenseness and irritability, for instance, will endorse the items grouped together in the factor analysis; there is no proof that there is any such correspondence. Clinical validation would appear to be a *sine qua non* for a scale of this type. (*b*) The factors measured by the inventory are not by any means independent; correlations between them range as high as .70. Thus, the factors themselves define a second-order factor which, judging from the figures given by Guilford, is responsible for a greater portion of the total variance than any of the factors given by the inventory. Yet no score or method of measurement for this "general factor" (presumably one of "general neu-

roticism") is provided, although this is the one factor for which there is good clinical evidence. (*c*) The suggestion is made in the manual that the test might play a part in the selection of industrial personnel. It does not appear likely, in the absence of any evidence, that an untried test would prove of great value in an industrial situation; here again what is lacking is evidence of validity.

As opposed to these criticisms, it should be said that in other respects the inventory has certain advantages over other well-known tests: (*a*) The statistical work is of a very high standard, and in particular the factorial approach to the problem of inventory construction, which is largely due to Guilford's original impetus, promises to result in much more analytical tests than we have known so far. (*b*) The inventory is not encumbered, as are the *Humm–Wadsworth Temperament Scale* and the *Minnesota Multiphasic Personality Inventory* by reliance on obsolescent psychiatric classifications not even widely accepted in psychiatric circles.

As a total summing up, it may be said that the test presents a distinct advance in technique of construction but lacks validation data; it is therefore a test for the experimenter rather than for the practician.

For a review by R. A. Brotemarkle, see 45.

[44]

★Guilford-Martin Personnel Inventory I. Adults; 1943; IBM; 1 form; $2.50 per 25; machine-scorable answer sheets also available, 2¢ each; $1.25 per set of plastic hand-scoring keys for test booklet; $3.50 per set of machine-scoring stencils for answer sheet; $2.50 per set of hand-scoring stencils for answer sheet; 40¢ per specimen set; nontimed (30) minutes; J. P. Guilford and H. G. Martin; Sheridan Supply Co.

REFERENCES

1. DORCUS, ROY M. "A Brief Study of the Humm-Wadsworth Temperament Scale and the Guilford-Martin Personnel Inventory in an Industrial Situation." *J Appl Psychol* 28:302-7 Ag '44. * (*PA* 18:3850) Abstract *Psychol B* 41:590 O '44. * (*PA* 19:220, title only)
2. MARTIN, HOWARD G. "Locating the Troublemaker With the Guilford-Martin Personnel Inventory." *J Appl Psychol* 28:461-7 D '44. * (*PA* 19:1323)
3. LOVELL, CONSTANCE. "A Study of the Factor Structure of Thirteen Personality Variables." *Ed & Psychol Meas* 5:335-50 w '45. * (*PA* 20:2399)
4. WESLEY, ELAINE. *Correlations Between the Guilford-Martin Personality Factors O, Ag, Co and the Minnesota Multiphasic Personality Inventory at the College Level.* Unpublished master's thesis, University of Minnesota, 1945.
5. ADAMS, CLIFFORD R. "The Prediction of Adjustment in Marriage." *Ed & Psychol Meas* 6:185-93 su '46. * (*PA* 21:177)
6. EYSENCK, H. J. *Dimensions of Personality*, pp. 38-9. A record of research carried out in collaboration with H. T. Himmelweit and W. Linford Rees with the help of M. Desai, W. D. Furneaux, H. Halstead, O. Marum, M. McKinlay, A. Petrie, and P. M. Yap. Foreword by Aubrey Lewis. London: Kegan Paul, Trench, Trubner & Co. Ltd., 1947. Pp. xi, 308. 25s. * (*PA* 22:210)
7. THOMPSON, CLAUDE EDWARD. "Selecting Executives by Psychological Tests." *Ed & Psychol Meas* 7:773-8 w '47. *

Benjamin Shimberg, Research Assistant, Division of Educational Reference, Purdue University, Lafayette, Indiana. This is a carefully prepared questionnaire which aims at detecting the potential "troublemaker" in business or industry. The traits measured are called O (objectivity), Ag (agreeableness), and Co (cooperation). The test actually seeks to identify persons low in these traits—those who show high tendencies toward personal reference, belligerence, and overcriticalness.

The inventory consists of 150 questions which may be answered by circling "Yes," "?," or "No" in the test booklet or by marking the appropriate space on the machine-scored answer sheet. The questions are applicable to most industrial and business situations and deal with experiences fairly common to workers. Since the questions are not of a highly personal nature, workers should not object to answering them.

The purpose of the test is thinly disguised and the validity of the responses depends on the willingness of the person taking the test to cooperate and reveal his true attitudes. In the initial study, which involved 500 California industrial workers of both sexes, and in subsequent validation studies, the test was given to persons already employed. No information is presented to show that applicants for jobs can be expected to cooperate to the same extent. If we could be sure that an undesirable job-applicant would answer the questions candidly, any strong tendency toward "troublemaking" would probably show up. Whether such persons are clever enough to "beat the test" is a problem which has not been investigated. It is possible that the use of the forced-choice type of item might be effective in reducing the tendency of job applicants to give the response which they think the examiner wants.

In constructing the test, items were selected by the criterion of internal consistency on a sample of 400 workers. Those items were retained which differentiated significantly between the upper and lower quartiles in terms of score for each trait on this test. In an effort to keep the intercorrelations among the traits as low as possible, only four of the items were weighted for more than one trait. Nevertheless, the scores for the three traits yielded fairly high intercorrelations: Co and O, .55; Co and Ag, .63; and O and Ag, .64. The weights were initially developed on the basis of subjective clinical information and later refined by statistical techniques devised by Guilford. There have been several studies which indicate that test scores for the three traits agree fairly well with employee ratings on these traits. Details of these studies may be obtained from the publisher.

Published validation reports on this test give some indication of promise, although they do not present any convincing evidence that the test has validity when used for employment purposes. The groups studied, thus far, have been employed persons whom management had rated as being either well-adjusted or maladjusted workers. In two of the studies, results showed that the test identifies approximately 80 per cent of those rated as "troublemakers," while at the same time erroneously classifying about 35 per cent of the satisfactory workers by placing them in the undesirable group. The authors recognize the fallibility of using the opinions of management as a sole criterion. It would be helpful if more information were given as to the number of judges used, how the ratings were made, and what standards were set to classify "troublemakers."

The norms which are published in the manual are based on the 500 cases used in the original study. Since this sample was not seeking employment or promotion, it is very likely that these norms would not hold for a group tested under other circumstances. The authors are themselves well aware of the methodological weaknesses of their instrument, and they advise prospective users to make validity studies to determine the usefulness of the test in their own employment situation. The publishers of the test offer technical assistance to those who wish to plan validity studies or to establish their own norms.

For a review by R. A. Brotemarkle, see 45.

[45]
★**Guilford-Martin Temperament Profile Chart.** College and adults; 1934–45; a profile chart for the following three inventories: *Guilford-Martin Inventory of Factors GAMIN, Abridged Edition* (*see* 43), *Guilford-Martin Personnel Inventory I* (*see* 44), and *Inventory of Factors STDCR* (*see* 55); 2¢ per chart; J. P. Guilford and H. G. Martin; Sheridan Supply Co.

REFERENCES
See references for 43, 44, and 55.

R. A. Brotemarkle, Professor of Psychology and Director of The Psychological Laboratory and Clinic, The University of Pennsylvania, Philadelphia, Pennsylvania. Guilford and Martin have developed three inventories for the measurement of thirteen variables of personality. Each inventory has been used and recommended for use in studies as a separate test and as one of a group for the construction of a temperament profile. We shall present the factors under each inventory as they are recorded on the profile chart and discuss the construction of the chart later.

Guilford's *Inventory of Factors STRDC* was developed on the basis of a factor analysis of items in personality questionnaires. Taken together, the factors probably cover the so-called introversion-extraversion syndrome. The factors represent dimensions of personality (with opposite poles) as follows: S, social introversion—shyness and withdrawal tendencies; T, thinking introversion—meditative, philosophizing, analyzing self and others; R, rhathymia—carefree disposition, liveliness, and impulsiveness; D, depression—feeling of unworthiness and guilt; C, cycloid—strong emotional reactions, fluctuation in mood, tending to instability. The 175 items were retained on the basis of internal consistency of responses of some 400 college students, predominantly of sophomore level. The Spearman-Brown estimated reliability (200 cases, 100 men and 100 women of original criterion group) are S .92, T .89, R .89, D .91, and C .91. These have been verified by other groups and statistical methods. Factorial studies revealed positive correlations among S, T, and D in the neighborhood of .50 and a small negative correlation between D and R. Centile norms are given, based on 388 University of Nebraska students.

The *Guilford–Martin ·Inventory of Factors GAMIN* measures five traits with operational definitions as follows: G—great pressure for overt activity; A—ascendancy in social situations, leadership; M—masculinity in attitudes and interests; I—lack of inferiority feelings, self-confidence; N—lack of nervousness and irritability. The 270 items were developed from 300 questionnaire items given to 500 (250 men and 250 women) Southern California college and university students, sophomores to seniors, ages 19 to 30. Items revealing heavy loadings, under item and factorial analyses, are used under each of the traits. Scoring keys were developed by the Guilford abac method for the highest and lowest quarters of original cases for G, A, I, and N. Item analysis was employed for M, using the 100 highest male scores and 100 **lowest female** scores. Reliability was tested on

the remainder of the group with random halves of items as follows, when corrected: G, .89; A, .88; M, .85; I, .91; N, .89. Intercorrelations are generally low enough to assume useful differences between trait scores for the same individual, with some question in the case of the I and N relationship. Scoring is facilitated by a five-column number giving the weight for each trait at a single glance on the key.

Due to the excessive length and difficulty of scoring the original *Guilford–Martin Inventory of Factors GAMIN,* it was abridged in 1945 with the reduction from 270 items to 186. Changes in reliability are reported as "merely of a random sample order." The scoring of the short form is greatly simplified, and norms based upon 160 University students, 80 men and 80 women, have been presented, and the C-scores changed for use on the new forms of the Temperament Profile Chart.

The *Guilford–Martin Personnel Inventory I* measures three traits of the syndrome more commonly called "paranoid" for the purpose of searching out discontented individuals who are likely to become "troublemakers." The traits, using the more favorable end of the two-pole concept, are O—objectivity as opposed to subjectivity; Ag—agreeableness as opposed to belligerence, dominance, and overreadiness to fight over trifles; Co—cooperativeness as opposed to faultfinding or overcriticalness of people and things. From 200 items used with 500 employees (250 men and 250 women) representing a diverse employment population, ages 20 to 45, 150 items were retained as significantly diagnostic as evidenced by correlation with the highest and lowest quarters of the sample. Scoring weights (Guilford method) were used with 100 (50 men and 50 women) to obtain split-half reliability as follows: O, .83; Ag, .80; Co, .91. Intercorrelations ranging from .55 to .64 were accepted as low enough to warrant use of separate scores. A validity study on 51 employees, using medians as criterion points, identified 73 per cent of those judged by employers as unsatisfactory and misplaced only 34 per cent in the satisfactory group.

Raw scores, for each of the 13 traits, obtained by keys are readily translated to C-scores (scaled scores) and are recorded on the *Guilford–Martin Temperament Profile Chart* on the following 11-point scale: 0 represents lowest 1% of 500 cases used for standardization; 1, next 3%; 2, next 7%; 3, next 12%; 4, next

17%; 5, middle 20%; 6, next 17%; 7, next 12%; 8, next 7%; 9, next 3%; and 10, the highest 1%. The reverse of the chart contains brief statements of interpretation of high, low, and middle-range scores, usually in terms of desirability for mental health, emotional adjustment, and work or social situations.

Most of the studies reported to date have presented the original report of construction of tests, scoring techniques, determination of reliability, validity, and interpretations.

In addition to the presentation articles, the authors and publishers have made available mimeographed information showing results with particular groups: troublemakers, purchasing and material-control employees, sales and service employees, engineers, and executive and administrative employees. In all of these, well-guarded statements of interpretation have been made. Particular emphasis has been given to the uniqueness of the separate traits and to the variable manner of clustering which necessitates continued study for specific groups before application of results.

One very significant study by Constance Lovell* shows cause for caution in interpretation and needed revision in specific traits C and D. A factor analysis (Thurstone and Guilford methods) based on results of 200 undergraduates in an elementary psychology class with so-called "normal" investigation set reveals four significant superfactors or trait clusters: I, drive-restraint (high loading on general drive, carefreeness, sociability, and social ascendance); II, realism (high loading on objectivity, masculinity, freedom from nervousness, and freedom from inferiority feelings); III, emotionality (high loading on stability of emotional reactions, freedom from depression, and extravertive orientation of thinking process); IV, social adaptability (high loadings on lack of quarrelsomeness and tolerance). Equations for predicting the above superfactors from the 13 C-scores were developed by the Doolittle method.

While this work is in line with recent research developments, especially the work of Raymond B. Cattell, it is unfortunate that Lovell should aid and abet any possible interpretation that the total structure of personality is revealed in the thirteen measures or in their clustering in four

* Lovell, Constance. "A Study of the Factor Structure of Thirteen Personality Variables." Ed & Psychol Meas 5:335-50 w '45.

superfactors by such a statement as "The results seem to picture the structure of personality as consisting of four general areas." This is true even with her protective statement that the study is based only on "the subjects used." It is self-evident that the complex structure of personality is not to be measured by any such brief series of trait measures as is found in the Guilford–Martin series or any other series at present.

For reviews by H. J. Eysenck and Benjamin Shimberg, see 43, 44, and 55.

[46]

High School Attitude Scale. Grades 7-16; 1935; Forms A, B; mimeographed; 1½¢ per test; 10¢ per sheet of directions and key; 15¢ per specimen set; F. H. Gillespie; directed and edited by H. H. Remmers; Division of Educational Reference, Purdue University.

Lee J. Cronbach, Assistant Professor of Education, The University of Chicago, Chicago, Illinois. This scale is one of the many Thurstone-type devices prepared by Remmers and his associates. It was constructed by the usual procedure and has the advantages and disadvantages to be expected in scales of this type. The scale requires little time and has adequate reliability for screening purposes. Parallel-form correlations are .753 and .727. Validity, as in all self-report devices, is open to question, but there is no doubt that a pupil reporting an unfavorable attitude toward school should be singled out for study. The scale may be said to measure attitude toward the value and pleasantness of high school. Statements are general and do not permit diagnosing specific causes of low morale.

The apparent weaknesses of the scale probably do not detract greatly from the accuracy of scores. Some statements are so extreme that it is doubtful if anyone could rationally agree with them: "A high school education is worth a million dollars to any young person," or "Any old fogy knows more than a high school graduate." The scale does not discriminate finely; in the preliminary trials of the test, only 4 pupils out of 168 fell in the half of the scale from 5.1 to 11.0. Statements do not always measure what the scale tries to test. Many statements are checked by those whose attitudes do not agree with the scale value of the statement. Such statements as the following dilute the validity of the test: "I like to go to school to be with other people"; "If one's parents need him at home he ought not to go to high school"; and "The kind-

est and best people I know don't have high
school educations."

Schools may find it important to use such a
test of morale as a means of identifying dissatisfied pupils and groups. The test would have
no value unless careful follow-up of such cases
were made. Research uses of the test may be
important, although the limited validity of self-
report must be borne in mind. The test is sufficiently sensitive to measure trends in group
morale with changing conditions. Such surveys
have proved useful in industrial personnel studies and might well be tried by school administrators. For this use norms would be of interest.

[47]

★H-T-P: House, Tree, and Person: A Measure of
Adult Intelligence and a Projective Device: Preliminary Edition. Adults; 1946-47; 1¢ per drawing
form; 2¢ per scoring folder (1946); 2¢ per interrogation folder (1947); John N. Buck; Steward's Office,
Lynchburg State Colony, Colony, Virginia.

REFERENCES
    1. BUCK, JOHN N. "The H-T-P, A Measure of Adult Intel-
ligence and a Projective Device." Abstract. Am Psychol 1:285-6
Jl '46. * (PA 20:3926, title only)
    2. BUCK, JOHN N. "The H-T-P: A Measure of Adult Intel-
ligence and a Projective Device." Va Mental Hyg Survey 9:3-5
O '46. *
    3. BUCK, JOHN N. "The H-T-P, A Projective Device." Am
J Mental Def 51:606-10 Ap '47. * (PA 22:1457)
    4. LANDISBERG, SELMA. "A Personality Study of Institution-
alized Epileptics." Am J Mental Def 52:16-22 Jl '47. * (PA
22:2267)
    5. LANDISBURG, SELMA. "A Study of the H-T-P Test."
Training Sch B 44:140-52 D '47. * (PA 22:1654)

*Morris Krugman, Assistant Superintendent
in Charge of Guidance, Public Schools, New
York, New York.* The *H-T-P* (House-Tree-
Person) purports to be an objective instrument
for measuring adult intelligence (more precisely,
conceptual level) as well as a projective technique
both for appraising personality and for determining the existence of various forms of psychopathology. The subject is asked, successively, to
draw a house, a tree, and a person; and in each
instance, spontaneous comments and behavior
during the performance are noted. An important
phase of the test is the "post-drawing interrogation," consisting of 46 specific questions and a
follow-up of any leads resulting from replies to
these.

The test was standardized on 120 adult subjects (C.A. 15 years and over), selected for intellectual level, 20 at each level from imbecile to
"above average." The coefficient of correlation
(Pearson) between the *H-T-P* and the full
Wechsler–Bellevue for 100 cases was found to
be .746 ± .029. The method of scoring the
H-T-P for intelligence is so complicated, however, that it seems doubtful whether anyone but

the author of the test can achieve so high a
correlation with a standardized intelligence
scale. Furthermore, the time required for scoring the objective part seems prohibitive, although extensive practice should reduce this
time. The test can be used either as a group or
an individual instrument, although, as Buck
states, it is not as productive when used as a
group test.

The more important aspect of the *H-T-P* is
its possibilities as a projective technique for
studying personality. Buck claims high validity
for the test, using hospital diagnoses, Rorschach
studies, and opinions of competent observers as
criteria for 60 cases; but no data are supplied in
the preliminary manual of 89 pages. Study of
this manual leads to the conclusion that this
phase of the test is still extremely subjective and
will depend largely upon the examiner's psychological orientation. The point of view of the
author of the test is partly Freudian. To this,
Buck adds much of his own symbol interpretation. One using the *H-T-P* as Buck evidently
intends it to be used should be well versed in
Freudian psychology. The type of qualitative
appraisal, or "inspectional analysis," of the
drawings and the replies to the questions will
thus depend upon the competence of the analyst
and upon his background in "dynamic" psychology.

It may be unfair to the author to cite examples
taken out of context, but in a brief review this is
unavoidable. Only a few samples are given to indicate Buck's approach to personality evaluation:

It should be further noted that the subject often
gives expression to his previously suppressed feelings
by the use of abnormal sequence of detail: for instance, he may find it impossible to draw the door of
his house until he had put in almost every other possible detail. In brief he does not wish to "open up." A
patient desirous of flight, however, might first draw
himself a side porch entrance before putting in any
other details; thus giving himself a means of escape
before committing himself further. Another might
draw a fireplace without a fire in it, but topped by a
chimney from which smoke is pouring forth in great
volume. This might be interpreted as indicative of a
feeling of recent coldness within the family relationship.
    The matter of force must always be considered: if
rain, or wind, or storm is shown, great stress may be
considered as being present.
    The tree appears most commonly to represent the
subject's felt ability to derive satisfaction from his
environment. It is belie ʌed that the trunk of the tree
represents the basic feeling of power within the self,
that the limb structure symbolizes the external self in
relation to the environment. It is believed that the
tree whose upper branches are "chopped off," so to
speak, by the paper's upper edge, represents a tendency

on the part of the individual to find satisfaction at the level of irreality.

The timid, anxious person tends to draw small, constricted trees. The uninhibited maladjusted child may show his lack of inhibition by drawing an enormous, expansive sort of tree.

The dead or dying tree must always be regarded as pathological unless proven otherwise.

Quite frequently the tree appears to represent the subject's psychosexual level. The child before puberty may draw for example, two trees, identifying one as the father, one as the mother. The juvenile young adult may indicate mother fixation by drawing a most maternal sheltering tree. Since the tree lends itself peculiarly well to expressions of masculinity or femininity and since the tree is a living object, subjects frequently project into it attitudes toward sex which they have previously been unable to verbalize.

The tree may also represent the subject's temporal relationship with his environment. When considering the aspect of time, the groundline is assumed to represent infancy; the growth upward from the groundline, the person's temporal progress through life, with the newest branches representing latest contact and growth. Occasionally it is possible to uncover psychic traumatic episodes of early life by close questioning concerning scars on the trunk or limbs that have obviously been chopped off. Withered or dead limbs frequently represent unpleasant episodes in the past.

A third aspect of the test is the rating of P, or pathological factors. These are of three levels of intensity and are ostensibly objective, but here, too, subjectivity is high. Buck believes that less experience is required for the rating of P factors than for the inspectional analysis, but this seems doubtful. P factors are intended to lead to a clinical diagnosis, and this should certainly not be left to the inexperienced.

The H-T-P has great possibilities as a projective technique, but, as Buck implies in his manual, the method needs much more work before it can be placed alongside the Rorschach or the TAT as a proven clinical instrument. For those well versed in the dynamics of behavior, the H-T-P should be useful even in its present state.

Katherine W. Wilcox, Chief Psychologist, Traverse City State Hospital, Traverse City, Michigan. The H-T-P is a nonstructured verbal and nonverbal projective test for clinical use in the evaluation of personality including intelligence. It consists of drawings by the subject of a House, a Tree, and a Person, followed by an interrogation period.

The quantitative scoring needed for the intelligence classification is based on the responses of a selected sample of population who, after a battery of other tests plus observation, were clinically judged to represent degrees of intelligence ranging from imbecile to superior with-

out marked personality deviation. Each item (analyzed characteristic), whether of detail, proportion, or perspective, receives a score on an eight-point scale of factor symbols: D3, very inferior; D2, imbecile; D1, moron; A1, borderline; A2, low average; A3, average; S1, above average; S2, superior. For example, D1 means that a particular item occurred in the drawings of at least 50 per cent of the persons of moron intelligence but in less than 50 per cent of all the combined higher levels. Each specific item analyzed in the drawings receives a weighted as well as a raw score. All average or superior scores are classified as G(Good). The percentage Raw G score and the weighted Good / weighted Flaw (ratio) score are obtained. These show the intelligence classification according to the author's norms. The analysis of the score pattern is often revealing in showing up some particularly good or poor responses in some fields. A certain amount of scatter is expected. A superior record containing several seriously low Flaw responses (D2 or D3) may be indicative of some malfunctioning. A difference of more than one intelligence classification level between the sum of the weighted Good and the sum of the weighted Flaw scores may be regarded as significant. Great scatter suggests some factor of repression or deterioration.

For the sake of qualitative analysis of the personality a complete record is kept of the subject's verbal responses, emotional manifestations, items of difficulty or blockage, and inter-item latencies together with when they occurred in relation to the drawing. In the interrogation an effort is made to get the subject's attitudes toward a dwelling place, a living thing, and a human being and his identification of others or himself with the respective wholes. For example, in the reviewer's series, a psychoneurotic with a reactive depression identified herself with a weeping willow tree completely bowed down by the weight of circumstances.

The qualitative analysis of the H-T-P drawings is based on selected samples of 60 adult patients at the University of Virginia Hospital plus 90 from the Lynchburg State Colony and its clinics. The P factors were postulated to be items which in most instances did not differentiate as to intelligence level and other items of concept, time, comments (spontaneous and induced), line quality, self-criticism, attitude, and drive which might serve to differentiate between drawings produced by persons of well-integrated and mature personalities and those produced by persons who were, on the other hand, maladjusted, psychopathic, psychoneurotic, or frankly psychotic. The P factors are graded P1, P2, and P3, according to whether they are judged to be a first-degree deviation from average, pathoformic, or pathological. There is no simple table by which such P items can be scored because each must be evaluated in its relationship to the entire configuration presented. Thus, the drawing of a person with the legs protruding from the head would merit a P3 rating if the subject were known to be or to have been recently of average intelligence; on the other hand, it might not even merit a P1 rating in the drawing of a congenital imbecile.

In favor of the employment of the *H-T-P* appear to be the following: (*a*) the relatively primitive method of expression, drawing, which aids the examiner in obtaining information from subjects who are withdrawn or who are of less than average intelligence; (*b*) its almost complete unstructuring during the nonverbal portion (the only constant stimulus is the printed word *House, Tree,* or *Person* at the top of the form sheet) which compels projection; (*c*) the fact that previously suppressed or repressed material can often be verbalized after the intensely emotion-producing drawings are completed; (*d*) the fact that the approach to the total personality is both nonverbal and verbal.

As the author himself points out, the major disadvantages at present appear to be: (*a*) the lack of objectivity of the qualitative scoring system and method of interpretation; hence the necessity for extensive clinical experience on the part of the examiner; (*b*) the absence of specific score patterns and response patterns identified as pathognomonic for specific syndromes; (*c*) the absence of quantitative and qualitative norms for children.

The *H-T-P* test is still in process of development and is now in use in selected hospitals and clinics by experienced clinicians who are interested in working with the author in its further development and refinement. When it becomes available to the profession in published form, it will undoubtedly prove to be a valuable projective technique complementary to the Rorschach and the *Thematic Apperception Test*.

[48]

Humm-Wadsworth Temperament Scale, 1940 Edition. Adults; 1934-43; 1 form; manual revised, 1942; supplementary manual, 1943; employee evaluation report form, 1939; qualitative evaluation sheet, 1942; quick-scoring sheet, 1943; work sheet, 1939; addenda 1-3, not dated; distributed on a restricted basis to authorized technicians only; nontimed (30-90) minutes; Doncaster G. Humm and Guy W. Wadsworth, Jr., Humm Personnel Service, 1219 West Twelfth St., Los Angeles, California.

REFERENCES

1-13. *See* 40:1223.
14. HUMM, DONCASTER G., AND WADSWORTH, GUY W., JR. "A Diagnostic Inventory of Temperament: Preliminary Report." Abstract. *Psychol B* 30:602 O '33. * (*PA* 8:1185, title only)
15. HUMM, DONCASTER G. "Intercorrelations of the Components of Temperament Measured by the Humm-Wadsworth Temperament Scale." Abstract. *Psychol B* 32:537 O '35. * (*PA* 10:468, title only)
16. WADSWORTH, GUY W., JR. "Tests Prove Worth to a Utility." *Personnel J* 14:183-7 N '35.
17. HOUTCHENS, H. MAX. "Temperament in Adolescent Groups," pp. 7-68. In *Studies in Emotional Adjustment II.* By H. Max Houtchens, Newell C. Kephart, and Delia Larson Sharp. University of Iowa Studies, Studies in Child Welfare, Vol. 15, No. 1. Iowa City, Iowa: the University, 1937. Pp. 196. Paper. $1.00. * (*PA* 12:3598)
18. KARLAN, SAMUEL C. "Symptoms and Previous Personality in Prison Psychoses." *Psychiatric Q* 13:514-20 Jl '39. * (*PA* 14:3012)
19. HUMM, DONCASTER G.; AS REPORTED TO JAMES H. COLLINS. "Can You Take a Salesman Apart to Find Out What Makes Him Tick?" *Sales Mgmt* 47:22-4+ N 15 '40. *
20. HUMM, DONCASTER G.; AS REPORTED TO JAMES H. COLLINS. "Selection of Employees for Good Public Relations." *Pub Util Fortn* 26:663-71 N '40. * (*PA* 15:4340)
20a. PRUDDEN, GEORGE H. "The Right Man for the Right Job," pp. 25-31. In *Selection and Development of Foremen and Workers.* Production Series, No. 127. New York: American Management Association, 1940. Pp. 43. Paper. $0.75. * (*PA* 15:2337)
21. STORMENT, ROBERT C.; AS REPORTED TO JAMES H. COLLINS. "We Find a Way to Select Better Employees." *Am Bus* 10:14-7+ Jl '40. * (*PA* 15:3557)
21a. BILLS, MARION A. "Tests That Have Failed—and Why," pp. 32-5. In *The Value of Psychology in Selecting Salesmen.* Marketing Series, No. 45. New York: American Management Association, 1941. Pp. 35. Paper. Out of print. * (*PA* 16:2023)
22. HUMM, DONCASTER G., AND WADSWORTH, GUY W., JR. "Using the Humm-Wadsworth Temperament Scale." *J Appl Psychol* 25:654-9 D '41. * (*PA* 16:1566)
23. VITELES, MORRIS S. "Getting Results from a Program of Testing for Sales Ability" (*see* pp. 23-5), pp. 18-31. In *The Value of Psychology in Selecting Salesmen.* By Thomas M. Stokes and others. American Management Association, Marketing Series, No. 45. New York: the Association, 1941. Pp. 35. Paper. Out of print. * (*PA* 16:2036)
23a. WADSWORTH, GUY W., JR. "The Humm-Wadsworth Temperament Scale at Work," pp. 58-61. In *Experience With Employment Tests.* Conference Board Reports, Studies in Personnel Policy, No. 32. New York: National Industrial Conference Board, Inc., 1941. Pp. 72. Paper. Out of print. (*PA* 15:3965)
24. ARNOLD, D. A. *The Clinical Validity of the Humm-Wadsworth Temperament Scale in Psychiatric Diagnosis.* Unpublished doctor's thesis, University of Minnesota, 1942.
25. GRIEDER, CALVIN, AND NEWBURN, HARRY K. "Temperament in Prospective Teachers." *J Ed Res* 35:683-93 My '42. * (*PA* 16:4172)
26. HUMM, DONCASTER, G. "Personality and Adjustment." *J Psychol* 13:109-134 Ja '42. * (*PA* 16:2318)
27. POOLE, F. E. "The Humm-Wadsworth Temperament Scale in Job Placement at Lockheed-Vega." *Ind Med* 2:260-3 Je '42. (*PA* 17:3230)
28. REED, PAUL H., AND WITTMAN, PHYLLIS. "'Blind' Diagnoses on Several Personality Questionnaires Checked With Each Other and the Psychiatric Diagnoses." Abstract. *Psychol B* 39:592 O '42. * (*PA* 17:573, title only)
29. HANSEN, ALICE VIOLA. *An Experimental Study of the Ability to Simulate Humm-Wadsworth Temperament Performance.* Unpublished master's thesis, University of Southern California, 1943.
30. HUMM, D. G., AND WADSWORTH, G. W., JR. "Temperament in Industry." *Personnel J* 21:314-22 Mr '43. * (*PA* 17:2130)
31. HUMM, DONCASTER G.; AS REPORTED TO JAMES H. COLLINS. "Tests for Hiring People—and After." *Trained Men* 23:3-9 My-Je '43. *
32. DORCUS, ROY M. "A Brief Study of the Humm-Wadsworth Temperament Scale and the Guilford-Martin Personnel Inventory in an Industrial Situation." *J Appl Psychol* 28:302-7 Ag '44. * (*PA* 18:3850) Abstract *Psychol B* 41:590 O '44. (*PA* 10:220, title only)
33. HUMM, DONCASTER G. "Discussion of Dorcus' Study of the Humm-Wadsworth Temperament Scale." *J Appl Psychol* 28:527-9 D '44. * (*PA* 19:1265)

34. Humm, Doncaster G. "The Validity of the Humm-Wadsworth Temperament Scale." Abstract. *Psychol B* 41:590 O '44. (*PA* 19:167, title only)

35. Humm, Doncaster G., and Humm, Kathryn A. "Validity of the Humm-Wadsworth Temperament Scale: With Consideration of the Effects of Subject's Response-Bias." *J Psychol* 18:55-64 Jl '44. * (*PA* 19:168)

36. Fulton, James L. "A Brief Statement Concerning the Effectiveness of the Humm-Wadsworth Temperament Scale." Abstract. *Psychol B* 42:539 O '45. * (*PA* 20:284, title only)

37. Humm, Doncaster G. "The Rationale of Temperament Testing." *Ed & Psychol Meas* 5:383-93 w '45. * (*PA* 20:2396)

38. Meehl, Paul E. *An Investigation of a General Normality or Control Factor in Personality Testing.* Psychological Monographs, Vol. 59. No. 4, Whole No. 274. Washington, D. C.: American Psychological Association, Inc., 1945. Pp. vi, 62. Paper. $1.50. * (*PA* 21:510)

39. Seagoe, May V. "Permanence of Interest in Teaching." *J Ed Res* 38:678-84 My '45. * (*PA* 19:3183)

40. Seagoe, May V. "Prognostic Tests and Teaching Success." *J Ed Res* 38:685-90 My '45 * (*PA* 19:3184)

41. Seagoe, May V. "Prediction of In-Service Success in Teaching." *J Ed Res* 39:658-63 My '46. (*PA* 20:4352)

42. Bluett, Charles G., and Beales, Ben B. "An Exemplification of Various Neuroses and Comparable Humm-Wadsworth Temperament Scale Profiles with Typical Case Briefs." *J Psychol* 23:133-49 Ap '47. * (*PA* 21:3475)

43. Humm, Doncaster G., and Humm, Kathryn A. "Compensations for Subjects' Response-Bias in a Measure of Temperament." Abstract. *Am Psychol* 2:305-6 Ag '47. * (*PA* 21: 4382, title only)

44. Super, Donald E. "The Validity of Standard and Custom-Built Personality Inventories in a Pilot Selection Program." *Ed & Psychol Meas* 7:735-44 w '47. *

H. J. Eysenck, Senior Psychologist, Maudsley Hospital, London, England. The Humm–Wadsworth scale was one of the first *analytic* scales; instead of assigning the individual a hodgepodge rating of "neuroticism" or "introversion" on the basis of his answers to questions which had practically never been properly validated, an attempt is made to investigate the temperamental constitution of the subject by means of a "profile," made up of seven components (normal, hysteroid, manic, depressive, autistic, paranoid, and epileptoid). These components are rated on a seven-degree scale, and the over-all picture considered.

The components were chosen on the basis of Rosanoff's psychiatric theory of personality structure. Scoring was derived from the following groups: hysteroids (habitual criminals in state prisons); cycloids, schizoids, and epileptoids from state hospitals for the insane. Four hundred and thirty-six subjects were studied. Reliabilities of the several components have been reported for various groups to be in the .80's; validity studies claim correlations of .94 and .98 between inventory scores and case history.

A special feature of the test is the "no-count"; records are rejected as probably invalid if the number of "no" answers varies far from the normal in either direction. As many as 30 per cent of normal subjects may invalidate their tests in this fashion. Recently introduced supplementary techniques have reduced the percentage of rejections, but the effect of these changes on the validity of the test is as yet unknown.

The scale is meant for use in industry, not in the clinic, although most of the validation data are culled from the clinic, not from industry. Scoring is complicated, although many aids are provided which reduce time of scoring and chances of error.

The scale would seem to embody a number of desirable features: (*a*) It is based on a definite theory of personality which may be empirically tested. (*b*) The scoring method is empirically validated on groups whose life histories show them to differ profoundly from each other, in the directions required by the theory. (*c*) Statistical treatment of the data is more adequate than is usual with scales of this type. (*d*) Widespread use of the scale in industry appears to have shown it to have a certain amount of validity. (*e*) The provision of the "no-count" counters one of the most usual criticisms of self-rating scales, viz., that people tend to suffer from "halo" effects as far as their personal qualities are concerned; the "no-count" excludes persons who too consistently give themselves favourable or unfavourable scores.

The scale is also subject to a number of criticisms: (*a*) The theory on which it is based is not widely held among psychiatrists or psychologists, and there appears to be little evidence in its favour. (*b*) For normal groups, such as those for whom the test is intended, the seven components correlate rather highly together (correlations of as high as .8 having been reported); this indicates that the components are not factorially pure and that a simpler scoring system might be devised by using factors derived from the intercorrelations between components rather than the components themselves. (*c*) While the "no-count" is useful, the number of blanks rejected on this account is so high that it may seriously restrict the usefulness of the whole test. (*d*) The evidence on which one may judge the test is not adequate. The reports in the literature are hardly ever full enough to make it possible for the critical student to evaluate them. Populations are seldom described in sufficient detail to identify them; numbers of cases are stated in such a way that considerable doubt remains as to the breakdown of the total number into the numbers concerned with each component; possible selective factors are not considered or discussed. (A validity coefficient of .98 is evidence of a very high degree of selectivity in the writer's experience and has little relevance to populations such as one encounters in normal life.)

In spite of these criticisms, it is doubtful if a better test exists for the particular purpose for which the Humm–Wadsworth scale was constructed. The proposed publication of further experimental detail in book form by the authors of the test will perhaps serve to allay such doubts as the reviewer still experiences.

H. Meltzer, Director, Psychological Service Center, St. Louis, Missouri. "I make mistakes all right but you are the one who makes the enemies." This is the response of a 19-year-old machine shop operator to a 35-year-old inspector. It illustrates the fact that temperamental differences do make their appearance in industrial situations and can play an important role in determining morale and productivity. It follows, therefore, that an instrument which measures temperament can be helpful in dealing with the human factor in industry. One outstanding fact about the Humm–Wadsworth is that it has been developed in industrial situations. Another is that, unlike other inventories, it is based on a definite theory of personality in the light of which items were selected, validated, and organized.

The test itself is composed of 318 questions to be answered *Yes* or *No*. Of these only 165 were discovered to be differentially worth while. The remaining 153, though not scored, were kept for context on the impression that they improved the test atmosphere. The questions included were picked from two thousand originally considered by Rosanoff. Items selected for each component and their weightings were standardized on fourteen groups of control subjects, two for each component. The seven components and the behavior tendencies associated with them are outlined as follows: *Normal*—integration, adjustment, and well-rounded development of the subject; *Hysteroid* —evidence of self-concern, self-interest, and possessiveness; *Manic*—evidence of cheerfulness, drive toward activity, alertness, and excitability; *Depressive*—evidence of depression, retardation, and indecision; *Autistic*—evidence of imaginativeness, retiring disposition, and tendency to flinch from social situations; *Paranoid*—evidence of tenacity of opinion and de-

fense of systematized ideas; and *Epileptoid*— tendencies toward projects and inspiration toward achievement.

To obtain a temperamental profile three systems of scores are used. First are the raw scores themselves, referred to as the "log scores." These are determined merely by adding the values of scored questions as indicated on scoring keys. Profile scores, obtained from a nomograph available to users of the test, provide profile points corrected to compensate for the no-response tendency. And there are regression scores provided for cases where the no-count is so extreme as not to provide an acceptable profile score. This at times is necessary because some people tend to overreport, others to underreport, and in standardizing the test it was discovered that the no-count is of significance in determining the acceptability of the scores. The degree of acceptability and validity of the scores can be obtained from a range of no-counts provided. Norms derived from the subjects on the original standardization and norms established from administering the scale to a large group of employed workers are furnished. A high no-score is interpreted as indicating defensiveness; a very low no-score, a tendency to overreport or suggestibility. Detailed instructions for determining the acceptability of the profile are given. By the use of supplementary techniques Humm has increased the number of temperamental scales found to be acceptable from 70 per cent reported in earlier studies to 90 or 95 per cent.

An abundant number of temperamental patterns to illustrate those which go with success and failure in certain positions are available in the literature furnished by the publishers of the test. Reports on the frequency of appearance of each component are also given. Emphasis is put on the need for considering temperamental integration from the profile, and warning is given to consider the total profile rather than the measures of each component in a segmented manner. Interpreted realistically, the temperamental pattern can furnish relevant information about the emotional load an individual can or cannot comfortably hold.

Reliability is reported to be higher on cases where there are acceptable no-counts. In cases of acceptable no-counts a correlation of .94 is reported, whereas for all cases the correlation given is .85. Studies of validity include the reports on a comparison of 548 employees selected by interview alone as against 550 selected by the use of the Humm and intelligence tests. Comparisons of the interview versus the use of the Humm range as follows: 29 per cent of the problems for the first group as against 5.58 per cent for the Humm group, 49 per cent satisfactory as against 61.5 per cent, and 22 per cent outstanding as against 33 per cent. This means five times as many problems were accepted by the use of the interview alone. Also given as measures of validity are the facts that many companies have had long continuous service histories through the use of the test and that some psychologists and psychiatrists have used it successfully over a long period of years.

As in any inventory, one questions the frankness of the subjects. Tiffin reports that when 65 college students were given the test with two sets of instructions, one to be as frank as possible and another to assume they were filling it out in an employment office when seeking a job, large changes occurred; the shift from clinical to employment ranged from +42 in Normal to −63 in Hysteroid. College students picked and instigated to mark tests in a certain way cannot be considered a very lifelike situation. For counseling and evaluating purposes in personnel evaluation programs of a staff already hired, the reviewer has generally found answers as frank as they are in clinical situations. Even in hiring, deviations are surprisingly small and infrequent; that is, the tendency to polish answers does not show up nearly so often as it does on shorter forms of inventories.

There is still room for more studies on the reliability and validity of this temperament scale. The scale has been criticized for using categories that are abnormal, which sound pathological, but they are less so than others and are susceptible to interpretation with the use of a more normal vocabulary load. One can question whether Rosanoff's categories will hold up in the long run. Rosanoff himself considered these components more or less as constitutional, inheritable traits. Humm definitely does not so consider them.

All in all, the reviewer would be willing to say from his years of experience with this instrument that he has found it to be very useful in industrial situations, particularly on a supervisory level; also at times he has found it useful in industrial counseling—he has found it advisable to use it more often in industrial

settings than in clinical work. Used well in known situations for known and well-defined purposes in connection with other relevant tests of skills and abilities and interpreted in the light of life stories, clinically evaluated, it has been and can be a worth-while aid to a realistic personnel evaluation program. So conceived, it has functional relevance and significance. It can profit from further research and knowledge of the relationship of temperament to definite situations; for example, the organization pattern of a company considered in terms of personalities and the organization of channels of communication implied.

Lorenz Misbach, Professor of Psychology, The University of Kansas City, Kansas City, Missouri. Peculiar merits of this scale appear to derive from the comprehensiveness of its theoretical grounds, its origin within an industrial situation, scoring techniques with reference to variations in frankness of subjects, and accumulation of statistical and qualitative evidence from extensive industrial use.

The dynamic character of Rosanoff's theory of temperament, which is basic to the scale, requires interpretation of profiles in terms of interrelations between forces, or components, of personality. This is an analytic rather than a typological enterprise. Familiarity with psychiatric concepts and considerable experience with the scale and related materials are necessary for use of it as intended by the authors.

Original standardization was sponsored by the Southern Counties Gas Company of California. For each of the seven preselected components—normal, hysteroid, manic, depressive, autistic, paranoid, and epileptoid—two groups of subjects were selected, from study of over 4,000 life histories, one group showing extreme manifestation of the subsumed traits and the other showing extreme deficiency in respect to these traits. Original work sheets show that the fourteen groups ranged in size from 23 to 62, totaling 436. Of these, 73 were from institutional populations and 383 were industrial employees.

From reinterviews with subjects concerning their attitude in taking the test, it was found that over- or under-frankness is reflected in the number of "no" answers (2, 35) and in the shape of the profile. In 1939 (12) a method of correcting scores with reference to frankness was described. Later research has resulted in a method of correction more practicable clerically. This newer method is derived from two equations for regression of no-count and profile-count, separately, with each of the seven components. The method of correction and the research from which it was developed are described in the 1943 manual.

Studies of validity, beyond initial standardization procedure, as with all tests, involve the difficulty of establishing trustworthy criteria. The highest coefficient of validity, .85, is given by Humm and Humm (35), with case studies as criterion. Seagoe (41) and Dorcus (32) report correlations of .65 and .55 respectively, with success ratings as criteria. These results seem to the reviewer to be surprisingly indicative of validity, in view of the known unreliability of ratings. In Dorcus' study, despite incompletenesses of method mentioned by Dorcus and by Humm (33), if correction is made on the assumptions that the validity of pooled ratings does not exceed .40 and that the best obtainable correlation of the scale with any criterion would be .85 (35), multiple correlation, with the standard multiple regression formula, would give a correction to .78 as the real validity. Reports by Wadsworth (16) and Fulton (36) concerning effectiveness of the scale in appraisal programs are still more impressive.

The authors of the scale urge clients to employ an essentially clinical approach to appraisal, with all available indices of fitness taken into consideration. The reviewer understands their position to be that although the final test of effectiveness of an instrument is experience with it, there are grave hazards in making predictions beyond statistically justified estimates of probability.

Office records of the Humm Personnel Service, which were made freely available to the reviewer, show that the scale has remained in continuous use by the corporation originally sponsoring its development and that over two million scorings have been made for employee selection and appraisal in a wide variety of industries. Major industrial users have insisted upon restrictions as to sale and use of the scale. However unfortunate the effect of these restrictions may be in the area of professional relations, a beneficial result for research purposes is the opportunity provided for accumulation of data in a central office.

The reviewer has used the scale for several years in clinical and guidance work and is well acquainted with the experience of a Midwestern industrial engineering firm which has used the scale, in selective and appraisal programs, for four years. In the reviewer's opinion, which he believes has been formed with due awareness of the limitations inherent in any questionnaire technique, the *Humm–Wadsworth Temperament Scale* is, if used within its proper limits, a remarkably effective instrument.

For reviews by Forrest A. Kingsbury, Daniel A. Prescott, and P. E. Vernon, see 38:920 and 40:1223.

[49]

★Hunt-Minnesota Test for Organic Brain Damage. Ages 16 and over; 1943; individual; $5 per set of testing materials and 25 record sheets; $1.25 per 25 record sheets; (15 or 30) minutes; Howard F. Hunt; University of Minnesota Press.

REFERENCES
1. HUNT, HOWARD F. "A Practical, Clinical Test for Organic Brain Damage." *J Appl Psychol* 27:375-86 O '43. * (PA 18:167)
2. HUNT, HOWARD FRANCIS. *A Psychological Examination for the Detection of Intellectual Deterioration in Organic Brain Disease.* Unpublished doctor's thesis, University of Minnesota, 1943.
3. HUNT, HOWARD F. "A Note on the Clinical Use of the Hunt-Minnesota Test for Organic Brain Damage." *J Appl Psychol* 28:175-8 Ap '44. * (PA 18:2808)
4. ARKOLA, A. *The Effect of Sodium Amytal Upon Performance on the Hunt-Minnesota Test for Organic Brain Damage.* Unpublished master's thesis, University of Minnesota, 1945.
5. AVAKIAN, SONIA A. *A Study of the Applicability of the Hunt-Minnesota Test for Organic Brain Damage to Children Between the Ages of Ten and Sixteen.* Unpublished master's thesis, Fordham University, 1945.
6. HUNT, HOWARD F. "A Note on the Problem of Brain Damage in Rehabilitation and Personnel Work." *J Appl Psychol* 29:282-8 Ag '45. * (PA 20:154)
7. ARMITAGE, STEWART G. *An Analysis of Certain Psychological Tests Used for the Evaluation of Brain Injury.* Psychological Monographs, Vol. 60, No. 1, Whole No. 277. Washington, D. C.: American Psychological Association, Inc., 1946. Pp. iii, 48. Paper. $1.25. *
8. MALAMUD, RACHEL F. "Validity of the Hunt-Minnesota Test for Organic Brain Damage." *J Appl Psychol* 30:271-5 Je '46. * (PA 20:4174)
9. MEEHL, PAUL E., AND JEFFERY, MARY. "The Hunt-Minnesota Test for Organic Brain Damage in Cases of Functional Depression." *J Appl Psychol* 30:276-87 Je '46. * (PA 20:4177)
10. AITA, J. A.; ARMITAGE, S. G.; REITAN, R. M.; AND RABINOVITZ, A. "The Use of Certain Psychological Tests in the Evaluation of Brain Injury." *J General Psychol* 37:24-44 Jl '47. * (PA 22:3044)
11. COLE, EDWIN M.; BAGGETT, MIRIAM P.; AND MACMULLEN, MARJORIE R. "Mental and Performance Testing of Neurologic Patients." Discussion by F. L. Wells. Abstract. *Arch Neurol & Psychiatry* 58:104-7 Jl '47. * (PA 22:1334, title only)

Margaret Ives, Psychologist, St. Elizabeths Hospital, Washington, D. C. This test, in contrast to others devised to measure intellectual deficit, is "specifically designed for routine clinical detection of organic brain damage" which has occurred after the subject has reached intellectual maturity. It consists of three parts— the 1937 Stanford–Binet vocabulary, "relatively insensitive to brain damage"; a series of verbal and nonverbal learning and recall tests, especially "sensitive to brain damage"; and a group of interpolated tests which supposedly "serve as validity indicators" by picking out those with emotional and motivational disturbances serious enough to invalidate the entire test.

Dr. Hunt makes allowance for normal retrogressive changes with age and includes a weighted age score subtracted from the vocabulary rating in calculating the half of the score to be compared with new learning efficiency. However, recently (3) he has reduced the range for which the test is maximally valid to persons between 20 and 55 years with Binet vocabularies from 12 to 32 words, although beyond these limits the test may be used cautiously by competent clinicians. At one end it is mathematically impossible for older persons with low vocabularies to have pathological scores. Conversely, above a certain level increased vocabulary does not accompany increased efficiency of new learning but only penalizes the subject. Shipley, in his *Shipley–Institute of Living Scale*, has circumvented this difficulty by granting no additional credit toward the "conceptual quotient" for vocabulary over 32 words.

The test is standardized and statistically evaluated so that the optimal level of learning can be predicted from the age and vocabulary scores. This predicted value is represented by a T-score of 50, and one standard error of estimate below this results in a T-score of 60. Dr. Hunt claims in a supplementary note (3) that T-scores over 66 indicate organic brain damage and that over 60 they justify suspicion of pathology.

In the attempt to make the test extremely delicate in detecting minimal defect, speed of recognition and response, timed to the half second, is all important on the crucial learning tests. It seems to this reviewer impossible, even with a stop watch, to score accurately such split-second intervals; but that difficulty is minor compared to the unfortute fact that although 21 neuropsychiatric patients were included in the standardization group, there was only one depressed psychotic and no catatonic schizophrenics. Yet these are the groups most likely to show retarded thinking even when superficially nearly recovered. Subsequent work with depressives at Minnesota shows that this group achieves a mean rating within the range considered indicative of organic brain damage. Thus, the test is not valid for differentiating organic damage from functional impairment involving slowed intellectual processes, perhaps temporary and reversible.

The test should nevertheless prove useful in detecting intellectual loss in persons within the age and vocabulary limits given, where there is no question of functional psychosis or neurotic depression. It seems probable that any test which will adequately differentiate functional from organic groups must be subject to qualitative as well as quantitative evaluation.

O. L. Zangwill, Assistant Director, Institute of Experimental Psychology, University of Oxford, Oxford, England. This test is based on the well-recognized clinical observation that the formation and retention of new associations is very generally impaired in organic affections of the brain. It comprises three major divisions: the Stanford–Binet vocabulary test, which is relatively insensitive to brain damage (except in cases of dysphasia); the learning and recall tests, utilizing both visual and auditory materials; and a group of interpolated tests, which serve *inter alia* as a means of filling the time intervals between the tests of recall in a uniform manner. Hunt has evaluated the discriminatory power of his tests by selecting 33 cases from a group of brain-damaged patients and a similar number of non-brain-damaged cases equated with the former on the basis of vocabulary and age. By applying the chi-squared test to check the significance of the differences in scores, it was found that the organic cases showed significant deterioration. The degree was assessed by obtaining each subject's predicted score on the deterioration tests by the use of regression weights determined from the statistics of the normal sample. The difference between this and the actual score furnishes an index of deterioration.

The test method is open to criticism on several counts: In the first place, more extensive control studies are required; R. F. Malamud (8) has shown that some normal persons give results indistinguishable from those of an organic case. In the second place, it has been shown by Meehl and Jeffery (9) that the test is not entirely specific to brain damage. Cases of affective disorder without known structural lesions are likely to give results strongly suggestive of organic damage. In the third place, all the patients in Hunt's original brain-damaged group were (with one exception) cases of *diffuse* cerebral disease. Preliminary research undertaken by the present reviewer suggests that the findings may be very different in cases of focal cerebral lesion. Thus cases with defects of visual or verbal learning associated with appropriately localized focal lesions but not with general cognitive deterioration show an impairment on the tests out of all proportion to the patient's mental status as assessed clinically. It is therefore essential that the test should be used with some care in the examination of cases with localized traumatic brain injuries. And in the fourth place, the prognostic significance of the milder grades of learning defect is difficult to assess in the absence of data bearing on the occupational competence of the patients tested.

From the diagnostic point of view, on the other hand, the test should be of some value in experienced hands, especially in detecting milder degrees of intellectual deficit associated with widespread cortical dysfunction. But it should not, at the present stage at least, be treated as a self-sufficient method for the detection and measurement of organic intellectual deterioration.

[50]

Information Blank EA: A Questionnaire on Emotional Adjustment, Provisional Form. Grades 10-16; 1938; IBM; 1 form; $1 per 50 machine-scorable test-answer sheets; 25¢ per specimen set; nontimed (10-20) minutes; H. T. Manuel, F. J. Adams, and Paul White; Steck Co.

Percival M. Symonds, Professor of Education, Teachers College, Columbia University, New York, New York. This 30-item psychoneurotic inventory prepared for use in the 1938-1939 testing program of the Texas Commission on Coordination in Education has been given the innocuous title *Information Blank EA.* It is designed not only to locate students with emotional difficulties but also to provide a counselor with some information concerning the specific nature of these difficulties. The blank is printed on an IBM machine-scoring sheet so that it is adapted for automatic scoring. A high score indicates favorable psychoneurotic adjustment. The reliability by the adjusted split-half method on a group of one hundred college students is .768.

As one peruses the items, he finds a judicious selection of questions representing neurotic symptoms. There are three psychosomatic items which were found in Army experience to be so significant in detecting neurotic poten-

tiality. However, questions with regard to headaches and dizziness, not included in the scale, may be of more significance than a feeling of tenseness in the forehead or neck, or sweaty hands. There would seem to be an overemphasis on questions relating to mood, and such questions as "Do you enjoy introducing someone to a person of high position?" or "Does the thought of your own sins or mistakes disturb you very much?" may not apply to all individuals. On the whole, however, it would appear that this brief collection of questions with regard to psychoneurotic and psychosomatic condition is effective for the purpose for which it was constructed.

For review by Stanley G. Dulsky, see 40: 1224.

[51]

★**Interest Analysis, 1942 Revision.** Ages 16 and over; 1938–42; $3 per introductory set including 10 tests, postpaid; 5¢ per extra test, postpaid; introductory sets may be ordered on approval; nontimed (10-15) minutes; Eugene J. Benge; Management Service Co.

Edward B. Greene, Chief, Personnel Training, Michigan Unemployment Compensation Commission, Detroit, Michigan; and Lecturer in Psychology, University of Michigan, Ann Arbor, Michigan. This form is a single sheet, printed on both sides, with five sections entitled: (*a*) School Interests (37 items), (*b*) Discussion of Topics of Interest to You (42 items), (*c*) Personal Activities (34 items), (*d*) Occupational Preferences (40 items), and (*e*) Personal Traits (40 items). In the first three sections you are asked to indicate your interest by a "plus" mark, a "minus" mark, or no mark at all if you neither disliked or liked an item. In the last two sections you are asked to indicate a choice between pairs of items by putting a "plus" mark in front of your preference. There is no apparent logical arrangement of items within sections, but rather they seem to have been arranged on a chance basis. It is also apparent that none of these sections attempt to be complete in covering a wide variety of items. The reason for this is that the test is not designed to be a measure of interest at all, but to indicate two personality traits, extraversion and dominance. For each of these traits a separate key is provided.

Dominance is indicated by such school interests as taking part in athletics, debating, playing hookey, dates with the opposite sex, dramatics. A negative aspect of dominance, or submission, is indicated by interest in algebra, English composition, civics, mechanical drawing, arithmetic, etc.

Extraversion is supposed to be indicated by taking part in athletics, debating, football games, choral singing, playing hookey, economics, civics, American history, amateur magic. Nearly all of the items which indicate dominance also indicate extraversion, but in addition a fairly large number of items are scored "positive" for extraversion.

The method of selecting these items and scoring them is not indicated, nor is there any definition of extraversion attempted.

In a short paragraph the author advises industrial concerns to establish standards for satisfactory workers in each distinct group, and then use these standards as passing grades for new employees coming into the group. "The interviewer should realize that many factors beside extraversion enter into success. Hence, the test should largely be used for rejective purposes—applicants who failed badly to meet the standard set should be excluded quickly. Those who pass should be subjected to further interview and examination." This last quotation indicates that the instrument is designed to be a quick screening procedure.

With regard to dominance, Mr. Benge writes, "Dominance is the characteristic of an individual whereby he desires to be ascendant in many situations. Most individuals are dominant in some situations, but the characteristic here referred to indicates a desire to be ascendant over other people, or dominant in most human relation situations." The author again advises company officials to set their own standards by selecting ten individuals who are dominant and ten who are submissive. If the blanks show that the ten selected for dominance average higher dominance scores than the ten submissive, then the scale may be used. If not, it should not be used for indicating dominance in the local situation. No figures are given for reliability, validity, or any indication of the sample of workers upon which the norms were secured.

The phrasing of individual items leaves considerable to be desired. Most of them are single words, although Section 5 (Personal Traits) uses equally vague, short phrases, such as "I like exciting amusements," or "Quiet amusements interest me most." Many persons are baffled by the fact that they like both exciting and quiet amusements in a reasonable but unknown mixture.

[52]

★Interest Inventory for Elementary Grades: George Washington University Series. Grades 4-6; 1941; Form A; 5¢ per test; 15¢ per manual; 25¢ per specimen set; nontimed (30-40) minutes; Mitchell Dreese and Elizabeth Mooney; Center for Psychological Service, George Washington University.

REFERENCES
1. MOONEY, ELIZABETH. *An Interest Inventory for Elementary Grades.* Unpublished master's thesis, George Washington University, 1940. Pp. 54.

Harold D. Carter, Associate Professor of Education, University of California, Berkeley, California. This inventory is intended for measurement of general interest patterns of boys and girls. It contains 250 items which elicit reactions to such things as movies, radio, things to read, games and toys, hobbies, things to own, school subjects, people, occupations, and activities. The items appear to have been well selected, on the basis of survey of children's activities.

The test is scored to measure normalcy of interest according to sex and grade. The scoring is such as to indicate the nature and extent of agreement between the interests of the individual and those of the group. It is intended that the test shall be useful in measurement and diagnosis, to aid the school in developing desirable interests among the children.

The test, containing 250 items, is probably fairly reliable. The evidence of reliability is inadequate; it consists of evidence that the item responses show marked consistency. There is no correlational evidence that the scores yielded by the test have satisfactory reliability. The validity of the test has apparently been taken for granted; the manual presents no evidence of validity.

The test has been carefully constructed and arranged for simple administration and scoring. Significant facts about a child's interest pattern are to be found through examination of the inventory. The test seems promising. Its guiding philosophy is constructive. One can imagine that research might show that the test can be used to measure various aspects of interests, such as ignorance, indecision, maturity, and concentration of interests.

As it now stands, the consumers must find out for themselves to what extent the test is useful. The manual does not provide the necessary evidence.

Lee J. Cronbach, Assistant Professor of Education, The University of Chicago, Chicago, Illinois. Elementary school teachers frequently wish to analyze the interests of pupils for curriculum planning and guidance. Most teachers use interviews and other informal methods to obtain this information. The *Interest Inventory* permits a more rapid but less flexible survey of interests in a group. It requires each pupil to respond Like, Indifferent, Dislike, or Unknown to 250 activities. The list is varied and probably as satisfactory as any standard checklist. Most items deal with interests significant to education, but the list may overlook interests important in a given child unless it is supplemented by an individual interview.

The only reported evidence of reliability is that fifty children retested after a few days changed only 15 per cent of their answers. Diagnosis on the basis of checked interests is likely to be correspondingly imperfect. There is no evidence that checked interests correspond to interests shown by behavior. The authors tend to regard responses of the child as unquestionably valid. Thus many likes "will show whether he is in general interested in most things." Such a pattern may as easily represent merely an acquiescent set toward suggestions, a desire to make a favorable impression on the teacher, or a tendency to say that he likes all activities that might appeal to him momentarily.

The authors recommend a scoring plan to rate each pupil on normality of interest. The purpose is to screen pupils having interests unusual for their grade and sex for special attention. This is equivalent to implying that interests of normal children do not require individual study, an idea which is thoroughly false. Scores are based on an empirically determined system of weights. There is no justification for such a time-consuming system as opposed to a mere count of "normal" responses. The weights are based, for any grade and sex, on an inadequate sample—an average of seventy cases, mostly suburban. There is no evidence of the reliability or empirical validity of scores.

The authors appear to have the false picture that the "normal child" has all the interests of his grade-sex group and no others. It is more likely that the "normal child" is advanced in some areas of interests and relatively undeveloped in others. The present scoring system penalizes such a pattern. The test would be improved if the maturity of the pupil in significant areas

rather than his normality were described. A concept of "interest age" could be profitably applied.

Minor faults also appear, such as a short and somewhat irrelevant set of preference items added at the end and a system of part scores based on brief and heterogeneous subtests. In general, the test appears useful as a checklist for item-by-item study and nearly worthless as a scored measuring instrument. The older *Pressey Interest-Attitude Tests* (*see* 40:1243.1) for grade 6 and over is a far sounder test.

[53]

Interest-Values Inventory. Grades 9-16 and adults; 1939; 1 form; $9.35 per 100; 25¢ per specimen set; nontimed (30) minutes; J. B. Maller and Edward M. Glaser; Bureau of Publications, Teachers College, Columbia University.

REFERENCES

1. GLASER, EDWARD M. *A Determination of Personality Patterns Through Measurement of the Relative Dominance of Certain Basic Personality Interests.* Unpublished master's thesis, City College of New York, 1936. Pp. 82. (*Abstracts of Theses . . . [School of Education] 1923-1939,* 1939, p. 92.)
2. GLASER, EDWARD M., AND MALLER, JULIUS B. "The Measurement of Interest Values." *Char & Pers* 9:67-81 S '40. * (*PA* 15:327)
3. DUFFY, ELIZABETH. "A Critical Review of Investigations Employing the Allport-Vernon *Study of Values* and Other Tests of Evaluative Attitude." *Psychol B* 37:597-612 O '40. * (*PA* 15:322)
4. GLASER, EDWARD M. *An Experiment in the Development of Critical Thinking.* Columbia University, Teachers College, Contributions to Education, No. 843. Goodwin Watson, faculty sponsor. New York: Bureau of Publications, the College, 1941. Pp. ix, 212. Out of print. * (*PA* 16:2057)
5. RUBISOFF, RHEA. "Interest-Values in Relation to Occupational Attitudes and Vocational Choice." Abstract. *Psychol B* 39:436-7 Je '42. * (*PA* 16:5032, title only)

E. Lowell Kelly, Professor of Psychology, University of Michigan, Ann Arbor, Michigan. This inventory was designed to measure the relative dominance of four of the six major interests or values proposed by Spranger and measured by the Allport–Vernon *Study of Values:* Theoretical, Aesthetic, Social, and Economic. It does not provide scores for religious or political values as does the Allport–Vernon scale.

The *Interest-Values Inventory* per se consists of four parts. Part I consists of 10 items, each composed of four words. The subject is asked to indicate which of the four words he likes best. Part II is composed of 10 items of the controlled association variety with four alternative response words. Part III consists of 12 questions or problems each of which is followed by four answers or comments. The subject is asked to rate each of the four alternatives on a 3-point (like-neutral-dislike) scale. Part IV consists of a list of 48 personality trait names. The subject is asked to rate himself on each of these traits by noting whether he is strong, average, or weak.

Each question in the inventory provides for the expression of any of the four types of interest which the scale purports to measure. Items which appear in the scale were retained on the basis of significantly different responses by four groups composed of 50 students, each chosen because of occupation or field of study to represent one of the four types of interests. Scoring is accomplished with the aid of a transparent stencil, and positive unit weights are counted successively to obtain each of the four scores.

Retest reliabilities of the resulting scores range from .87 to .93 for a ten-day interval and .70 to .87 for a three-month interval (N = 100 college students). Separate percentile norms are provided for high school students (N = 350) and adult graduate students (N not given).

As compared with Allport and Vernon's *Study of Values,* this instrument appears to require about the same time to administer, to be more easily scored, and to yield significantly higher reliabilities. Strangely, however, even though acknowledging their indebtedness to the previous work of Allport and Vernon, Maller and Glaser fail to report the correlation between the sets of four supposedly similar measures provided by the two instruments. And again, although the authors state that their classification of interests is based in part on Thurstone's factor analysis of Strong's *Vocational Interest Blank,* they fail to report a single correlation with any kind of vocational interest score. This omission is all the more pertinent when it is remembered that the four groups used for item validations were chosen on the basis of vocational or prevocational college interest.

To this reviewer, it would seem that persons who introduce a new test have a professional obligation to report correlations of scores on it with those on all widely used and related tests. Otherwise it is extremely difficult for the prospective user of the new test to judge its unique value (if any) over and above the instruments with which he is already familiar.

Part V of the test is in no sense a measure of interests but rather a supplementary inventory consisting of questions designed to distinguish between happy and unhappy persons. This part of the test is scored with apparently a priori weights to yield an "Emotional Satisfaction Score." No reliability is reported for this score, nor any indication of its validity. Just why this unvalidated instrument is printed in the same booklet is not clear. One can only surmise that it was felt its inclusion would make the test a more attractive instrument for student counseling!

Paul E. Meehl, Assistant Professor of Psychology, University of Minnesota, Minneapolis, Minnesota. This test is designed to measure relative dominance of theoretic, aesthetic, social, and economic interests or values. It was developed to be an improvement over Allport and Vernon's *Study of Values,* eliminating the "political" and "religious" scoring in the latter. An effort was made to improve the reliability of the "social" value score, which was highly unstable in the Allport–Vernon. The present test aims at somewhat greater subtlety by making use of the testee's preference for certain words over others and of his associations between words, in addition to his statement of preferred solution to a problem situation involving value conflict. The new items do not seem particularly subtle, but no evidence is available on this point.

The authors state that the items were selected empirically, on the basis of differentiation among college criterion groups defined by their chosen majors. It is not stated how large an initial item pool was involved, which makes it difficult to evaluate the critical ratios reported. It is to be presumed that differentiation would be reduced if the test were applied to a new "test" group other than those on which the items were selected. However, within the reported sample, there seems to be pretty good evidence for validity. The means of each of the four criterion groups run between 1.5 and somewhat over 2 standard deviations above the other three groups on the appropriate scale. On any given value, it would be possible to separate each major group from the other three from 25 to 34 per cent better than by chance, using the appropriate value score alone. Considering the numerous extra-value factors which influence a student's decision to major in one area or another, this seems fairly good evidence of validity. There are a number of important exceptions to the differentiation which the authors do not stress but which appear in their published material. For example, male students in the practical, economic area are not appreciably different in "social" value-interest from those majoring in the social-service area. There is also a numerical contradiction in both the manual and their published article (Table I, mean social value score for total economic criterion group) which tends to make the results look better than they are. Their validation data are given in terms of contingency coefficients, based upon the dominant value classification of students.

Norms are given for high school students only, except that the theoretical value norms are based upon adult graduate students, who are almost certainly atypical with respect to this particular value. It would seem desirable to have given sex norms separately, but this was not done. The description of the four value types is fairly adequate, although the lumping together of artistic and musical under Thurstone's "linguistic" interest factor would seem to be rather precarious. Scoring is medium in ease. There is the usual reference to "adults" together with high school and college students, with no evidence that the ordinary adult is validly testable. The directions and vocabulary make it at least questionable whether the run-of-mine adult is adequate to the task. However, the nature of the variables is such that this is not a serious drawback, since only rarely would this sort of measure become clinically relevant at the general adult level.

[54]

★Inventory of Affective Tolerance. College and adults; 1942; 1 form; $1.75 per 25; 40¢ per specimen set; nontimed (25) minutes; Robert I. Watson and V. E. Fisher; Sheridan Supply Co.

REFERENCES
1. FISHER, V. E., AND WATSON, ROBERT I. "An Inventory of Affective Tolerance." J Psychol 12:149-57 O '41. * (PA 16:1042)
2. WATSON, ROBERT I., AND FISHER, V. E. "An Inventory of Affective Potency." J Psychol 12:139-48 O '41. * (PA 16:1048)
3. WATSON, ROBERT I. "The Relationship of the Affective Tolerance Inventory to Other Personality Inventories." Ed & Psychol Meas 2:83-90 Ja '42. * (PA 16:2325)
4. WATSON, ROBERT I. "School and Sex Differences in Affective Tolerance." Ed & Psychol Meas 3:43-8 sp '43. * (PA 17:3169)
5. WATSON, ROBERT I. "Clinical Validity of the Inventory of Affective Tolerance." J Social Psychol 22:3-15 Ag '45. * (PA 20:419)

Paul R. Farnsworth, Professor of Psychology, Stanford University, Stanford, California. This personality inventory of 61 items (six-answer multiple-choice) purports to measure "sheer capacity to withstand or 'take' emotional disturbances." It also attempts to tap "the individual's ability to vent or discharge his affective tension, and his ability to give a subjectively appropriate form and direction to his release of tension." In the senior author's opinion this inventory has 30 items which are similar, or at least partially similar, to those of Bell's *Adjustment Inventory* and 29 quite like those of the Bernreuter *Personality Inventory.* Hence, it is not surprising that scores on this newer test correlate —.56

with total scores on the Bell and from —.56 to —.66 with the Bernreuter FIC (self-confidence) scores.

The taking of the *Inventory of Affective Tolerance* requires no more than 25 minutes at the most, and the hand scoring from two to three minutes. The weights of the items were figured by the t-ratio method. The test possesses a split-half reliability somewhere in the nineties. Centile norms for college students are offered which show that men, on the average, achieve slightly higher scores than do women. Validity data have been assembled through the matched pairing of normals and neurotics and by the study of cases with minor behavior difficulties.

Scrutiny of the available material on this test forces the conclusion that this work of R. I. Watson and V. E. Fisher is as good as, and perhaps a trifle better than, the general run of pencil-and-paper adjustment inventories. It will select out many individuals who should have clinical attention. But it will just as certainly fail to screen out many others who may have an equal need for mental therapy.

E. Lowell Kelly, Professor of Psychology, University of Michigan, Ann Arbor, Michigan. This instrument purports to measure "affective tolerance," defined by the authors in the Manual as "the capacity to deal with affective tensions or emotional excitements. The sheer capacity to withstand or 'take' emotional disturbances is the most basic aspect."

The inventory consists of 61 statements, typical of which are, "I do things in spite of myself and against my better judgment," "I have periods of anxiety," and "I experience feelings of hate," to which the testee responds by checking one of the adverbs which define a six-point scale: e.g., continuously, very frequently, frequently, occasionally, rarely, never.

The 61 items composing the inventory were selected from 150 original items on the basis of "F" and "t" values of total scores associated with individual item responses. Scoring weights ranging from 0 to +6 were assigned to each of the alternative responses of each item on the basis of t-ratios.

Reliability coefficients (split-half) are reported as .93, .94, and .93 for three different groups of college students. Because of significant sex differences in resulting scores, separate centile norms are provided, based on 270 men and 270 women students selected from four western state universities, one midwestern, and one eastern private college.

Just what this inventory measures is not easy to judge. Women score significantly lower (i.e., less tolerance) than men, and neurotics score lower than normals. Watson–Fisher scores correlate about −.60 with Bernreuter F1C scores and −.70 with scores on the *Thurstone Personality Schedule: Clark Revision*. Watson has also shown that college students who seek psychological counseling for emotional problems make significantly lower scores than those seeking assistance for nonemotional problems.

Since it is difficult to know what the instrument is measuring, it is also difficult to know where and how it might profitably be used. The manual suggests that it may be used "to select students in need of personal counseling, as a tool of guidance choice [*sic*] where such a measure may be significant and for purposes of research in the fields of personality and emotion." For the first and last of these suggested uses, this instrument would appear to be no better (or worse!) than several other so-called neurotic inventories. But just how it could be used as "a tool of guidance choice" this reviewer does not pretend to understand.

In summary, the *Inventory of Affective Tolerance* appears to be simply another personality test which yields fairly reliable measures of some as yet unidentified variable or variables. Thus it promises to provide uncritical investigators with one more set of relatively meaningless scores. Like similar inventories, responses to individual items may be of some use to the busy counselor or clinician in providing leads for the counseling interview.

William U. Snyder, Associate Professor of Psychology and Associate Director, Psychological Clinic, The Pennsylvania State College, State College, Pennsylvania. This test was designed to measure affective tolerance, or the ability of an individual to deal with emotional tensions. This appears to be the same as what Rosenzweig has described as frustration tolerance and is closely related to emotional adjustment.

The test consists of a questionnaire of 61 items, each of which may be answered by one of six possible choices, such as "never," "rarely," "occasionally," etc. Many of these items are the same ones that have been appearing in personality tests for thirty years. The publishers claim

that the test serves in much the same way as tests formerly called tests of neurotic tendency but with a new approach. About the only new aspect would seem to be the name of the test and possibly some of the items.

A favorable point regarding this test is the fact that only one aspect of personality is measured by the 61 items. This allows for some correction of subjective errors. But the publisher's dismissal of this problem is cavalier: "The inventory calls for the person's own evaluation of his affective tolerance. Hence, cooperation, honesty, and insight are necessary for valid results to be obtained." Assuming that the first two factors could be assured, no easy dismissal of the problem of insight is justified. On such questions as, "I possess self-confidence in my associations with members of the opposite sex" and "I am in fear of violating my own standard of morals," the aspect of opinion error must be quite high. Furthermore the discerning subject will quickly realize that the choices become increasingly favorable from "a" to "f" *in every case;* and even if he wants to be honest, he cannot then eliminate the subjective factor.

There is little doubt about the reliability of the test; it is in the nineties. But validity is a different matter. The publishers report that the discriminatory power of the test was measured by submitting it to a check with matched normals and neurotic adults. They do not report the numbers or the selection criteria of the groups mentioned, and this failure is indefensible. The trait of neuroticism is not adequately enough defined as yet to be taken for granted. Did the authors use only someone else's as-yet-unvalidated test of neuroticism as a criterion? This is answered in a published article. There were 25 neurotics and 25 normals matched for sex, age, marital status, rural-urban status, occupation, education, and income. The neurotics were so judged by Dr. Fisher in extensive interviews during clinical practice. There was virtually no overlap between neurotic and normal, i.e., college students, scores. A group of 93 psychotics scored between the normals and the neurotics and the authors attribute this to lack of insight.

A more recent study by the authors adds 40 more neurotic persons, of whom 16 were diagnosed after the scores on the inventory were available. There was no overlap with the normals' scores.

The norms for the test are based on scores obtained from 540 college students, equally divided as to sex, and selected from different colleges, three-quarters of which are in the northwest. The test is therefore significant for use only with college students.

Scoring of the test proves tedious with any sizable group. Each response is weighted, and the 61 weights must be summed. This sum may be interpreted on a table of centile norms. It is unfortunate that the authors of this relatively new test did not follow the request of the American Psychological Association regarding the use of standard scores instead of percentiles.

In general, it is the reviewer's opinion that the clinical psychologist need not be too concerned if he has not been using this test. Other tests, we believe, measure the same thing with equal or better validity and possibly with more originality.

[55]
Inventory of Factors STDCR. Grades 9-16 and adults; 1934-40; IBM; $2 per 25; machine-scorable answer sheets also available, 2¢ each; $1.25 per set of plastic hand-scoring keys for test booklet; $3.50 per set of machine-scoring stencils for answer sheet; $2.50 per set of hand-scoring stencils for answer sheet; 40¢ per specimen set; nontimed (30) minutes; J. P. Guilford; Sheridan Supply Co.

REFERENCES
1. GUILFORD, J. P., AND GUILFORD, RUTH B. "Personality Factors S, E, and M, and Their Measurements." J Psychol 2:109-27 '36. * (PA 10:4533)
2. GUILFORD, J. P., AND GUILFORD, RUTH B. "Personality Factors D, R, T, and A." J Abn & Social Psychol 34:21-36 Ja '39. * (PA 13:3185)
3. STEINBERG, DAVID LOUIS, AND WITTMAN, MARY PHYLLIS. "Etiologic Factors in the Adjustment of Men in the Armed Forces." War Med 4:129-39 Ag '43. * (PA 17:4248)
4. GUILFORD, J. P., AND MARTIN, HOWARD. "Age Differences and Sex Differences in Some Introvertive and Emotional Traits." J General Psychol 31:219-29 O '44. * (PA 19:445)
5. RICHARDSON, LAVANGE HUNT. The Personality of Stutterers. Psychological Monographs, Vol. 56, No. 7, Whole No. 260. Washington, D. C.: American Psychological Association, Inc., 1944. Pp. v, 41. Paper. $1.00. * (PA 18:3531)
6. LOTH, N. N. Correlations Between the Guilford-Martin Inventory of Factors STDCR and the Minnesota Multiphasic Personality Inventory at the College Level. Unpublished master's thesis, University of Minnesota, 1945.
7. LOVELL, CONSTANCE. "A Study of the Factor Structure of Thirteen Personality Variables." Ed & Psychol Meas 5:335-50 W '45. * (PA 20:2399)
8. WITTMAN, MARY PHYLLIS, AND HUFFMAN, ARTHUR V. "A Comparative Study of Developmental, Adjustment, and Personality Characteristics of Psychotic, Psychoneurotic, Delinquent, and Normally Adjusted Teen Aged Youths." J Genetic Psychol 66:167-82 Je '45. * (PA 20:617)
9. EYSENCK, H. J. Dimensions of Personality, pp. 38-9. A record of research carried out in collaboration with H. T. Himmelweit and W. Linford Rees with the help of M. Desai, W. D. Furneaux, H. Halstead, O. Marum, M. McKinlay, A. Petrie, and P. M. Yap. Foreword by Aubrey Lewis. London: Kegan Paul, Trench, Trubner & Co. Ltd., 1947. Pp. xi, 308. 25s. * (PA 22:210)
10. LUBORSKY, L. B., AND CATTELL, R. B. "The Validation of Personality Factors in Humor." J Personality 15:283-91 Je '47. * (PA 22:2072)

H. J. Eysenck, Senior Psychologist, Maudsley Hospital, London, England. This test consists of 175 questions of the Yes-?-No type and purports to measure five independent variables of temperament, viz., social introversion, thinking introversion, depression, cycloid disposition, and rathymia. Scores are given in terms of C-scores,

the norms being based on 800 senior high school students, 388 university students, and 80 adults (thus giving three sets of norms, not differentiated as to sex). The reliability of each of the separate five variables is high, both by the Spearman–Brown and by the Kuder–Richardson formulas.

The inventory is open to criticism on the following grounds: Evidence of validity is relatively weak, particularly for factors T and C (thinking introversion and cycloid disposition). In particular, little has been published regarding the practical use of the inventory in high school and college counseling services, in penal institutions, in family relations, and in hospitals, speech clinics, industrial plants, and so forth; while the inventory is known to have been widely used by these various agencies, the results still await publication. In the absence of such evidence, judgment must be withheld. The method of factorial analysis used, although orthodox, is open to criticism. The resulting rotated factors are not uncorrelated; correlations between scores of as high as .85 being reported. A factorial analysis of these correlations between scores has given rise to a second-order factor which accounts for a greater proportion of the variance than any of Guilford's five factors. In addition, clinical evidence for the validity of this "general factor of neuroticism" was presented (9); yet no score or method of measurement is given by Guilford for this second-order factor.

As opposed to these criticisms, it should be pointed out that Guilford's inventory has certain advantages over other well-known tests: (a) The statistical work is of the expected high standard, and in particular the factorial approach to the problem of inventory construction, which is largely due to Guilford's original impetus, promises to result in much more analytical tests than we have known so far. (b) The inventory is not encumbered, as are the *Humm–Wadsworth Temperament Scale* and the *Minnesota Multiphasic Personality Inventory*, by reliance on obsolescent psychiatric classifications not even widely accepted in psychiatric circles.

As a total summing up, it may be said that the published evidence regarding this test shows it to mark a distinct advance in test construction but to lack in validation data; it is therefore a test for the experimenter rather than for the practical tester in clinic or factory.

For a review by R. A. Brotemarkle, see 45.

[56]

★**JNB Psychograph.** Patients in mental hospitals; 1941; 2¢ per form; for manual, *see* (1) below; John N. Buck; Steward's Office, Lynchburg State Colony, Colony, Virginia.

REFERENCES

1. BUCK, JOHN N. "The JNB Psychograph." *J Appl Psychol* 27:65-74 F '43. * (PA 17:2708)

[57]

★**Johnson Temperament Analysis.** Grades 9-16 and adults; 1941–44; manual revised, 1944; IBM; $1.75 per 25; 2¢ per response record sheet; 1¢ per analysis profile; 60¢ per set of unweighted scoring stencils; $1.75 per set of weighted scoring stencils; 35¢ per specimen set; 7¢ per copy of machine-scoring edition; 2¢ per machine-scorable answer sheet; nontimed (40-50) minutes; Roswell H. Johnson; California Test Bureau.

REFERENCES

1. SEIBERT, EARL W. "An Evaluation of the Johnson Temperament Analysis." *J Clin Psychol* 1:193-5 Jl '45. * (PA 19:3411)

H. Meltzer, Director, Psychological Service Center, St. Louis, Missouri. An inventory for measuring temperament, to a large extent influenced by and to some extent patterned after the *Humm–Wadsworth Temperament Scale,* is the *Johnson Temperament Analysis.* It does have some differentiating features. For example, unlike the Humm–Wadsworth, it is not based on any distinct theory of personality but is, instead, organized around nine behavior tendencies considered important in the light of Dr. Johnson's family relations experience. Traits used by him are arranged in opposites and include: nervous–composed; depressive-gay-hearted; active–quiet; cordial–cold; sympathetic–"hard boiled"; subjective–objective; aggressive–submissive; critical–appreciative; and self-mastery–impulsive. Instead of 318 questions, there are 182. To avoid the error introduced by forcing a client to answer *yes* or *no,* he is advised to rate the subject in the highest 40 per cent, the middle 20 per cent, or the lowest 40 per cent. Another feature is that no single question is used to measure two traits.

The analysis profile resembles the Humm–Wadsworth profile except that it is shaded so that the user is protected from the grave danger of assuming that either an average or a maximum is necessarily the best condition. The traits selected show relationships to the Humm–Wadsworth list of components based on Rosanoff's personality analysis. This inventory has the disadvantage that it does not represent a distinct theory, but it does have the advantage of resembling more normal types of behavior patterns. There is very little published about the test, its reliability, validity, or usefulness.

In the manual there is a consideration of reliability, which is none too specific. The statistical reliability given for 300 cases for the various traits ranges from .57 to .77. Weighted norms are reported for high school girls and boys and for men and women. Most of the adult norms are given from cases reported at the American Institute of Family Relations. The high school weighted norms are based on 200 high school students, mostly seniors. Validity is reported for name agreement, and the use-validity is based on 100 spouses (50 men and 50 women) from the Institute as compared to 100 club and class people. Tetrachoric correlations for 100 men and 100 women are reported.

In the literature the reviewer has found only one article reporting the use of the test. This was at the Green Mountain Junior College for the freshman group of 1944–45. There is nothing in this article that would add to the literature on either the reliability or validity, or even the usefulness of the test. The results are reported in vague terms; the assumption is made that the test is valid because the nine traits were at or near the 50th percentile for the college freshman group. No more specific norms are reported, and the conclusion is made that the first evaluation of the test warrants its further use and further research as to its validity.

The crisscross method of scoring is advised for use in marriage cases. The most frequent use of the test to date has apparently been in marital counseling. The reviewer has not used this test and his reactions, therefore, are necessarily based solely on a review of written materials furnished by the author. On this basis it is the impression of the reviewer that the test is still too much in need of improved construction, improved description, and improved standardization in real situations before much can be said about its possibilities and limitations. Evidence to date is not too convincing.

[58]

★**Jurgensen Classification Inventory.** Adults; 1947; 1 form; separate answer sheets must be used; $5 per 25; 125 or more tests, $4.50 per 25; $1.90 per 100 answer sheets; 500 or more answer sheets, $1.71 per 100; single copies, 2½¢; 50¢ per specimen set, postpaid; test materials will be sold only to members of the American Psychological Association; score keys and norms are not provided as each user is expected to develop keys and norms to fit his own situation; (20-40) minutes; Clifford E. Jurgensen; the Author, Minneapolis Gas Light Co.

REFERENCES

1. JURGENSEN, CLIFFORD E. "Report on the 'Classification Inventory,' a Personality Test for Industrial Use." *J Appl Psychol* 28:445-60 D '44. * (PA 19:1320)

[59]

★Mental Health Analysis. Grades 4-8, 7-10, 9-16, adults; 1946; IBM; Form A; $1.75 per 25; 35¢ per specimen set, any one level; 7¢ per copy, machine-scoring edition; 2¢ per answer sheet; nontimed (50) minutes; Louis P. Thorpe and Willis W. Clark; Ernest W. Tiegs, consultant; California Test Bureau.
a) ELEMENTARY SERIES. Grades 4-8.
b) INTERMEDIATE SERIES. Grades 7-10.
c) SECONDARY SERIES. Grades 9-16.
d) ADULT SERIES. Adults.

William E. Coffman, Assistant in Psychological Foundations and Educational Research, Teachers College, Columbia University, New York, New York. With the publication of this inventory, the authors offer an instrument which avoids some of the more obvious defects of their *California Test of Personality*. The list of questions has been enlarged and refined. The categories under which responses are classified have been reduced from 12 to 10, and the number of questions in each has been increased from 12 to 20. The questions in each category are scattered throughout the inventory so that a pupil is less likely to perceive a pattern of "correct" responses. A coding system prevents him from discovering the exact nature of the analysis. The reliability coefficients (Kuder–Richardson) of the total score (.954) and of the two section scores, mental health liabilities (.924) and mental health assets (.906), are unusually high for a personality inventory. No evidence of reliability is offered with respect to separate category scores.

The prospective user of the inventory should give special attention to the list of limitations contained in Part 4 of the manual and to the suggestions for checking the validity of a profile given in Part 10. Concrete illustrations of these limitations were secured when the reviewer administered the inventory to a fifth grade class. The boy judged most maladjusted by the teacher made the highest score on the inventory. Some children asked the meaning of the words *contented, traits,* and *tense.* All responded "no" to the question, "Do you spend more time than you need to on your school work?" Evidently the authors intended this question as a disguised form of "Do you try to get by with as little school work as possible?" Several pupils were puzzled by the question, "Do you think that what people do is more important than who they are?" There appears to

be an error in the scoring key for Item 12. Any interpretation of an individual profile should be tentative and should be followed by a search for additional evidence.

The *Mental Health Analysis* is offered as an aid to "teachers, parents, and advisors in obtaining a better understanding of the subtle forces which condition and determine mental health." It appears to have special value as a device for calling the attention of teachers to the fact that elementary school children have such worries, fears, and feelings of inadequacy as are somemies revealed by answers to the questions contained in the section labeled *liabilities.* This aspect of adjustment is not necessarily evident from observations of overt behavior in the classroom. A careful study of the responses of a class to these items and an attempt to interpret each pupil's response should provide a body of concrete material contributing meaning to a study of mental hygiene principles.

The limitations of the suggestions for diagnosis and treatment given in Part 9 of the manual are not clearly indicated. The classroom teacher will need careful guidance and extensive study if she is to conduct satisfactory follow-up remedial work.

Henry E. Garrett, Professor of Psychology, Columbia University, New York, New York. This questionnaire consists of 200 items intended to assay the degree of mental health possessed by the examinee. Separate booklets have been prepared for four levels of maturity: for elementary grades, intermediate grades, secondary school–college, and adults. Each of the 200 questions at each level is to be answered by circling YES or NO.

Five sorts of personality "liabilities" are investigated by 100 of the questions. These liabilities are described as (a) behavioral immaturity, (b) emotional instability, (c) feelings of inadequacy, (d) physical defects, and (e) nervous manifestations. The other 100 questions are designed to estimate the examinee's personality "assets." These are designated as (a) close personal relationships, (b) interpersonal skills, (c) social participation, (d) satisfying work and recreation, and (e) adequate outlook and goals. The items of the questionnaire are so distributed that 20 apply to each specific classification.

High reliability is reported for the questionnaire, and the authors properly report the probable errors of their scores. Validity depends largely upon a consensus of experts. While many of the items are original, the authors have drawn upon the large amount of material available in other inventories and questionnaires. The use of queries designed to bring out specific attitudes rather than the use of questions dealing directly with general attitudes is to be commended.

While the various behavior classifications are useful practically, no evidence is given to show that these groupings are established upon any but an empirical or common sense basis. The diagnostic profile should be of some value in differential analysis, but I doubt if the total liability or asset score has any but the vaguest meaning. To know that a child answers many questions which indicate that he is socially immature is certainly valuable. But one cannot add such a "score" to other subscores and hope to determine the child's total personality liabilities unless he knows the relations among the categories being combined. Personality is a pattern of traits, not a sum or average of behavioral odds and ends.

C. M. Louttit, Professor of Psychology and Dean of the Undergraduate Division, University of Illinois, Galesburg, Illinois. The *Mental Health Analysis* is essentially a standard type of personality questionnaire in which the items are selected upon a more definitely systematic basis than is usually the case. Briefly, the instrument aims to reveal mental health liabilities (divided into five categories) which should be minimized or corrected and mental health assets (also divided into five categories) which should be sought or amplified. Each of the ten categories is carefully described, and percentile norms are provided for them. The performance may be delineated on a profile chart, and the authors have written independent discussion of clinical interpretation for each of the four levels. The reliabilities, based upon data from 1,000 or more subjects for each of the four forms, are represented by Kuder–Richardson formula correlations ranging from .890 to .967. In respect to the theory upon which the questionnaire is based, the care used in item selection and formulation, the mechanics of administration and scoring, and the statistical adequacy of norms and reliabilities, these instruments are equal or superior to similar instruments. However, we find the same faults here as are found elsewhere when validity is considered.

The authors rest the case for the validity of this instrument on a discussion of the adequacy of the selection of items, of the meaningfulness of their analysis of mental health categories, and of the cleverness in disguise of the items. However, no matter how weighty are the a priori arguments for validity, they are no proof that the instrument will serve the function which is claimed. There are no data, and no suggestion that any effort was made to secure data, which would show whether this instrument would even crudely select from a class those children, who by independent criteria would be judged of good or poor mental health. The extensive discussion of the use of scores presents illustrative case problems, but there is no indication that such problems were discovered by the instrument. The criticism of lack of validity studies against independent criteria cannot be directed against this questionnaire alone, but for a publication of 1946 not to have acknowledged the problem is almost inexcusable. For use in a clinic, the *Mental Health Analysis* may be useful in supplementing clinical study; for use in studying groups, it has all of the dangerous faults found in earlier questionnaires.

James Maxwell, Principal Lecturer in Psychology, Moray House, Edinburgh, Scotland. The Analysis is constructed on the proposition that mental health is divisible into certain "categories," not entirely discrete, which can be classified as either Liabilities or Assets. There are ten such categories, each being covered by 20 questions of the Yes-or-No type.

The accompanying manual contains rather wide claims about the value of the Analysis, but no objective evidence is offered in support either of its practical value or of its validity. The main evidence of validity is contained in the authors' claim that the Analysis is valid in virtue of the careful selection of items and that "the ten categories . . . represent functionally related groups of crucial, specific evidences of Mental Health assets or liabilities . . ." There is no evidence that the Analysis discriminates significantly between those whose mental health is good and those whose mental health is not.

Reliabilities for all four series are of the

order $r = .9$ or over, which is satisfactory for this type of test.

The most serious defect of the Analysis, however, is its failure to discriminate clearly. In the Adult Series, for example, the standard deviation is 31.5 for 200 items. For Liabilities and Assets (100 items each) S.D.'s are 16.5 and 15.0, respectively. These values are rather low for a test of this length.

A conversion table provides percentile norms for the various subdivisions of the test. Examination of this table confirms one's suspicions about the validity and discrimination of the Analysis. Throughout the table, scores of up to 50 per cent "correct" items fall almost entirely within the lowest ten percentile ranks, with the remaining scores spread thinly over the remaining 90 percentiles. In the Liabilities, for instance, the percentile rank of 1 includes all scores from 0 to 39, a range of nearly 10 P.E. of an observed score; at other score levels, on the other hand, an increase of 13 points of score (less than 4 P.E. of observed score) represents a movement from the 50th to the 90th percentile rank. In certain of the individual categories, also, a difference of 2 points of score may cause a shift from the 30th to the 70th percentile position. Over most of the table, in fact, a very slight variation in score may be reflected as a very considerable change in percentile rank. Nor are the other three series of the Analysis any better.

It is not possible to say whether this Analysis would function more satisfactorily as a qualitative clinical aid, but it does not on the surface appear to be more suitable than the various other inventories specifically devised for that purpose.

The test is well printed and well arranged, with adequate accessory material.

Douglas Spencer, Assistant Professor of Psychology, Queens College, Flushing, New York. This new test is offered as

an instrument, prepared for various levels of maturity, that provides an analysis of mental health liabilities and assets. Five types of liabilities to be minimized or corrected where present are included: (1) behavioral immaturity, (2) emotional instability, (3) feelings of inadequacy, (4) physical defects, and (5) nervous manifestations. Five types of . . . assets to be sought or amplified when not sufficiently present are included: (1) close personal relationships, (2) interpersonal skills, (3) social participation, (4) satisfying work and recreation, and (5) adequate outlook and goals.

Coming from the same source as the *California Tests of Personality,* this series reveals many of the same weaknesses. It is just another series of self-report, Yes-No response, group questionnaires that, however well intended, can be used to exploit urgent needs in education. With no evidence of validity, one may doubt the sales promises—despite reliability coefficients that are very high for such tests. Again, the title clearly reveals to subjects the purpose of the tests, and administration under signatures in school, college, or employment situations would seem to encourage concealment of liabilities and exaggeration of assets on many inadequately disguised items. As to the selection of the 200 items, there is but sketchy information and no data. The language employed, however, has been commendably evaluated by means of the Lewerenz Vocabulary formula to avoid reading difficulties at each level.

The tests have certain superiorities. The reliabilities (Kuder–Richardson formula) range from .93 to .96 and are based upon groups of from 980 to 2,075 subjects. Percentile norms derive from groups of adequate size: Elementary, 1,000 cases, from 9 school districts in 3 states (unnamed); Intermediate, 2,000 cases from 12 districts in California, Colorado, New York, and Oregon; Secondary, 2,000 cases from 14 schools in the same states; Adult, 1,200 cases from 8 communities (unlocated). Background information on these groups is not given, but it is stated that age and sex made no significant differences. Despite the more carefully derived norms and the reliabilities high enough for individual prediction, one may question the claimed adequacy of the tests for "individual diagnosis" in the absence of external validation and evidence that the components of the Liabilities and the Assets sections are separate and meaningful functions. Intercorrelations of the component scores with each other and with the total scores are not mentioned.

It is unfortunate that the superficial assets-liabilities approach, long outmoded in social case work, should now be deemed worthy of group psychometrics. Judged by the treatment, suggestions, and examples elaborated in the test manuals, a lot of school children—if unwisely frank on these tests—may well be the victims of zealous, stereotyped symptom treatment through the "talk-talk," "give 'em insight" methods that horrify experienced case workers, even those not devotees of the non-directive cult.

J Consult Psychol 11:156–7 My-Je '47. * The virtues of this blank are its emphasis on assets as well as shortcomings, and its well-worded items, many of which seem sufficiently disguised to penetrate superficial ego-involvements. The deficiencies of the questionnaire are numerous. Although the total scores have fair reliability (.89 to .97), almost all of the suggested interpretations use the subtest categories, which are of unknown and probably low reliability. On some categories, a probably insignificant difference of 3 score points may change a child from the 50th to the 99th, or from the 10th to the 50th, percentile. The intercorrelations of the 10 categories are not given, so that there are no data by which to judge their independence or relationships as factors. More serious than these technical considerations is the question of the real contribution of such questionnaires to individual mental health.

[60]

★Minnesota Multiphasic Personality Inventory, Revised Edition. Ages 16 and over; 1942–47; individual and group forms; 9 scales: hypochondriasis, depression, hysteria, psychopathic deviate, masculinity and femininity, paranoia, psychasthenia, schizophrenia, hypomania; 4 additional scores: question, lie, validity, and K; all prices postpaid; Starke R. Hathaway and J. Charnley McKinley; Psychological Corporation.
a) INDIVIDUAL FORM ("THE CARD SET"). $20 per testing outfit including 50 recording sheets; $2.50 per 50 record sheets; nontimed (30–90) minutes.
b) GROUP FORM ("THE BOOKLET FORM"). IBM; 25¢ per test; $1 per manual; $4 per set of scoring stencils (specify hand- or machine-scoring) with manual; $2.75 per 50 machine-scorable answer sheets including accompanying summary cards; nontimed (40–90) minutes.

REFERENCES

1. HATHAWAY, S. R., AND MCKINLEY, J. C. "The Measurement of Symptomatic Depression With the Minnesota Multiphasic Personality Schedule." Abstract. *Psychol B* 37:425 Jl '40. * (PA 14:5985, title only)
2. HATHAWAY, S. R., AND MCKINLEY, J. C. "A Multiphasic Personality Schedule (Minnesota): I, Construction of the Schedule." *J Psychol* 10:249-54 O '40. * (PA 15:926)
3. MCKINLEY, J. C., AND HATHAWAY, S. R. "A Multiphasic Personality Schedule (Minnesota): II, A Differential Study of Hypochondriasis." *J Psychol* 10:255-68 O '40. * (PA 15:887)
4. HATHAWAY, S. R., AND MCKINLEY, J. C. "A Multiphasic Personality Schedule (Minnesota): III, The Measurement of Symptomatic Depression." *J Psychol* 14:63-84 Jl '42. * (PA 16:4390)
5. MCKINLEY, J. C., AND HATHAWAY, S. R. "A Multiphasic Personality Schedule (Minnesota): IV, Psychasthenia." *J Appl Psychol* 26:614-24 O '42. * (PA 17:2766)
6. HEWITT, CHARLES C. "A Personality Study of Alcohol Addiction." *Q J Studies Alcohol* 4:368-86 D '43. * (PA 18:1753)
7. LEVERENZ, CARLETON W. "Minnesota Multiphasic Personality Inventory: An Evaluation of Its Usefulness in the Psychiatric Service of a Station Hospital." *War Med* 4:618-29 D '43. * (PA 18:1456)
8. MCKINLEY, J. C., CHARNLEY, AND HATHAWAY, STARKE R. "The Identification and Measurement of the Psychoneuroses in Medical Practice: The Minnesota Multiphasic Personality Inventory." *J Am Med Assn* 122:161-7 My 15 '43. * (PA 17:3428)
9. SCHIELE, B. C.; BAKER, A. B.; AND HATHAWAY, S. R. "The Minnesota Multiphasic Personality Inventory." *Journal-Lancet* 63:292-7 '43. (PA 18:3192)
10. VAN VORST, ROBERT B. "An Evaluation of Test Performances of a Group of Psychopathic Delinquents." Abstract. *Psychol B* 40:583 O '43. * (PA 18:192, title only)
11. ARTHUR, GRACE. "An Experience in Examining an Indian Twelfth-Grade Group With the Multiphasic Personality Inventory." *Mental Hyg* 28:243-50 Ap '44. * (PA 18:3526)
12. MCKINLEY, J. C., AND HATHAWAY, S. R. "The Minnesota Multiphasic Personality Inventory: V, Hysteria, Hypomania and Psychopathic Deviate." *J Appl Psychol* 28:153-74 Ap '44. * (PA 18:2845)
13. ROSEN H. *Correlations Between the Schellenberg Free Association Test and the Minnesota Multiphasic Personality Inventory.* Unpublished master's thesis, University of Minnesota, 1944.
14. ABRAMSON, HAROLD A. "The Effect of Alcohol on the Personality Inventory (Minnesota): Preliminary Report." *Psychosom Med* 7:184-5 My '45. * (PA 19:2635)
15. ABRAMSON, HAROLD A. "The Minnesota Personality Test in Relation to Selection of Specialized Military Personnel." *Psychosom Med* 7:178-84 My '45. * (PA 19:2634)
16. ALTUS, WILLIAM D., AND BELL, HUGH M. "The Validity of Certain Measures of Maladjustment in an Army Special Training Center." *Psychol B* 42:98-103 F '45. * (PA 19:1229)
17. BENTON, ARTHUR L. "The Minnesota Multiphasic Personality Inventory in Clinical Practice." *J Nerv & Mental Dis* 100:416-20 O '45. * (PA 20:836)
18. BIRNBERG, VITA K. *The Relationship Between Food Aversions and the Minnesota Multiphasic Personality Test for College Women.* Unpublished master's thesis, University of Minnesota, 1945.
19. BORTIN, AARON W., AND BRILL, ISIDORE. "Psychiatric Studies Based on New Personality Test." *Mil Surg* 96:497-503 Je '45. *
20. CAPWELL, DORA F. "Personality Patterns of Adolescent Girls: I, Girls Who Show Improvement in IQ." *J Appl Psychol* 29:212-28 Je '45. * (PA 19:3033)
21. CAPWELL, DORA F. "Personality Patterns of Adolescent Girls: II, Delinquents and Non-Delinquents." *J Appl Psychol* 29:289-97 Ag '45. * (PA 20:191)
22. CROSS, ORRIN H. *An Adaptation of the Minnesota Multiphasic Personality Inventory for Use With the Blind.* Unpublished master's thesis, University of Wisconsin, 1945.
23. HARMON, LINDSEY R., AND WIENER, DANIEL N. "Use of the Minnesota Multiphasic Personality Inventory in Vocational Advisement." *J Appl Psychol* 29:132-41 Ap '45. * (PA 19:2249)
24. HARRIS, R. E. "Measured Personality Characteristics of Convulsive Therapy Patients: A Study of Diagnostic and Prognostic Criteria." Abstract. *Psychol B* 42:535 O '45. * (PA 20:151, title only)
25. KAZAN, A. T., AND SHEINBERG, I. M. "Clinical Note on the Significance of the Validity Score (F) in the Minnesota Multiphasic Personality Inventory." *Am J Psychiatry* 102:181-83 S '45. * (PA 20:1568)
26. LOTH, N. N. *Correlations Between the Guilford-Martin Inventory of Factors STDCR and the Minnesota Multiphasic Personality Inventory at the College Level.* Unpublished master's thesis, University of Minnesota, 1945.
27. MEEHL, PAUL E. "The Dynamics of 'Structured' Personality Tests." *J Clin Psychol* 1:296-303 O '45. * (PA 20:482)
28. MEEHL, PAUL E. *An Investigation of a General Normality or Control Factor in Personality Testing.* Psychological Monographs, Vol. 59, No. 4, Whole No. 274. Washington, D. C.: American Psychological Association, Inc., 1945. Pp. vi, 62. Paper. $1.50. * (PA 21:510)
29. MICHAEL, J. C., AND BUHLER, C. "Experiences With Personality Testing in a Neuropsychiatric Department of a Public General Hospital." *Dis Nerv Sys* 6:205-11 '45. (PA 19:3038)
30. SCHMIDT, HERMANN O. "Test Profiles as a Diagnostic Aid: The Minnesota Multiphasic Inventory." *J Appl Psychol* 29:115-31 Ap '45. * (PA 19:2263)
31. VERNIAUD, WILLIE M. *Occupational Differences in the Minnesota Multiphasic Personality Inventory.* Unpublished master's thesis, University of Minnesota, 1945.
32. WESLEY, ELAINE. *Correlations Between the Guilford-Martin Personality Factors O, Ag, Co and the Minnesota Multiphasic Personality Inventory at the College Level.* Unpublished master's thesis, University of Minnesota, 1945.
33. ABRAMSON, HAROLD A. "The Effect of Alcohol on the Personality." Discussion by Rose G. Anderson and Arthur E. Traxler. *Ann N Y Acad Sci* 46:535-57, discussion 567-9 Jl 30 '46. * (PA 20:4651)
34. BENTON, ARTHUR L., AND PROBST, KATHRYN A. "A Comparison of Psychiatric Ratings With Minnesota Multiphasic Personality Inventory Scores." *J Abn & Social Psychol* 41:75-8 Ja '46. * (PA 20:1895)
35. BERDIE, RALPH F. "Range of Interests and Psychopathologies." *J Clin Psychol* 2:161-6 Ap '46. * (PA 20:3687)
36. BURTON, ARTHUR, AND BRIGHT, CHARLES J. "Adaptation of the Minnesota Multiphasic Personality Inventory for Group Administration and Rapid Scoring." *J Consult Psychol* 10:99-103 Mr-Ap '46. * (PA 20:4192)
37. DRAKE, LEWIS E. "A Social I.E. Scale for the Minnesota Multiphasic Personality Inventory." *J Appl Psychol* 30:51-4 F '46. * (PA 20:2390)
38. ELLIS, ALBERT. "The Validity of Personality Questionnaires." *Psychol B* 43:385-440 S '46. * (PA 21:502)

39. FERGUSON, ROBERT G. "A Useful Adjunct to the Minnesota Personality Inventory Scoring and Analysis." *J Clin Psychol* 2:248-53 Jl '46. * (*PA* 20:4665)

40. GOUGH, HARRISON G. "Diagnostic Patterns on the Minnesota Multiphasic Personality Inventory." *J Clin Psychol* 2:23-37 Ja '46. * (*PA* 20:1964)

41. GRANT, HARRY. "A Rapid Personality Evaluation: Based on the Minnesota Multiphasic Personality Inventory and the Cornell Selectee Index." *Am J Psychiatry* 103:33-41 Jl '46. * (*PA* 21:168)

42. HARRIS, ROBERT E., AND CHRISTIANSEN, CAROLE. "Prediction of Response to Brief Psychotherapy." *J Psychol* 21:269-84 Ap '46. * (*PA* 20:3212)

43. HATHAWAY, STARKE R. "Multiphasic Personality Inventory: A Study of Psychological Problems of Patients as an Aid to Clinic Efficiency." *Mod Hosp* 66:65-7 Ap '46. *

43a. HOUK, THEODORE W., AND ROBERTSON, YVONNE. "Diagnosis of Hypoglycemia-Neurosis With Minnesota Multiphasic Personality Inventory." *Northw Med (Seattle)* 45:923 '46. (*PA* 21:3049)

44. LATOURELLE, CURTIS WILBUR. *A Study of the Relationship of the Subtest Deviations on the Wechsler-Bellevue Intelligence Scale and Scores of the Minnesota Multiphasic Personality Inventory.* Unpublished master's thesis, University of Southern California, 1946.

45. LOUGH, ORPHA MAUST. "Teachers College Students and the Minnesota Multiphasic Personality Inventory." *J Appl Psychol* 30:241-7 Je '46. * (*PA* 20:4343)

46. MANSON, MORSE P., AND GRAYSON, HARRY M. "Keysort Method of Scoring the Minnesota Multiphasic Personality Inventory." *J Appl Psychol* 30:509-16 O '46. * (*PA* 21:509)

47. MEEHL, PAUL E. "Profile Analysis of the Minnesota Multiphasic Personality Inventory in Differential Diagnosis." *J Appl Psychol* 30:517-24. O '46. * (*PA* 21:481)

48. MEEHL, PAUL E., AND HATHAWAY, STARKE R. "The K Factor as a Suppressor Variable in the Minnesota Multiphasic Personality Inventory." *J Appl Psychol* 30:525-64. O '46. * (*PA* 21:511)

49. MORRIS, W. W. "A Preliminary Evaluation of the 'Diagnostic' Scales of the Minnesota Multiphasic Personality Inventory." Abstract. *Am Psychol* 1:264 Jl '46. * (*PA* 20:3710, title only)

50. RASHKIS, HAROLD A., AND SHASKAN, DONALD A. "The Effects of Group Psychotherapy on Personality Inventory Scores." *Am J Orthopsychiatry* 16:345-9 Ap '46. * (*PA* 20:3712)

51. ROSENZWEIG, SAUL. "The Dynamics of an Amnesic Personality." *J Personality* 15:121-42 D '46. * (*PA* 21:3062)

52. SHNEIDMAN, EDWIN S. "A Short Method of Scoring the Minnesota Multiphasic Personality Inventory." *J Consult Psychol* 10:143-5 My-Je '46. * (*PA* 21:171)

53. VERNIAUD, WILLIE MAUDE. "Occupational Differences in the Minnesota Multiphasic Personality Inventory." *J Appl Psychol* 30:604-13 D '46. * (*PA* 21:1534)

54. BROWER, DANIEL. "The Relation Between Intelligence and Minnesota Multiphasic Personality Inventory Scores." *J Social Psychol* 25:243-5 My '47. * (*PA* 22:1561)

55. BURTON, ARTHUR. "The Use of the Masculinity-Femininity Scale of the Minnesota Multiphasic Personality Inventory as an Aid in the Diagnosis of Sexual Inversion." *J Psychol* 24: 161-4 Jl '47. * (*PA* 21:4432)

56. CROSS, ORRIN H. "Braille Edition of the Minnesota Multiphasic Personality Inventory for Use With the Blind." *J Appl Psychol* 31:189-98 Ap '47. * (*PA* 21:2690)

57. DAVIS, CLIFFORD E. "The Minnesota Multiphasic Personality Inventory: A New Method of Scoring and Analysis." *J Clin Psychol* 3:298-301 Jl '47. * (*PA* 22:209)

57a. DRAKE, LEWIS E. "A Method for Machine Scoring the Card Form of the MMPI." *J Ed Res* 41:139-41 O '47. *

58. GOUGH, HARRISON G. "Simulated Patterns on the Minnesota Multiphasic Personality Inventory." *J Abn & Social Psychol* 42:215-25 Ap '47. * (*PA* 21:3140)

59. GULDE, CARL J., AND ROY, HOWARD L. "A Note on the Scoring of the Minnesota Multiphasic Personality Inventory." *J Consult Psychol* 11:221-2 Jl-Ag '47. * (*PA* 22:212)

59a. HATHAWAY, STARKE R. "A Coding System for MMPI Profile Classification." *J Consult Psychol* 11:334-7 N-D '47. *

60. HIBBELER, HELEN L. "Personality Patterns of White Adults With Primary Glaucoma." *Am J Ophthal* 30:181-6 F '47. * (*PA* 21:1883)

61. HUNT, HOWARD F.; CASS, WILLIAM A., JR.; CARP, ABRAHAM; AND WINDER, CLARENCE L. "A Study of the Effect of the K Correction on the Differential Diagnostic Efficiency of the Minnesota Multiphasic Personality Inventory." Abstract. *Am Psychol* 2:273 Ag '47. * (*PA* 21:4501, title only)

62. JENSEN, MILTON B., AND ROTTER, JULIAN B. "The Value of Thirteen Psychological Tests in Officer Candidate Screening." *J Appl Psychol* 31:312-22 Je '47. * (*PA* 21:4107)

63. KAMMAN, GORDON R. "Psychosomatic Diagnosis." *Journal-Lancet* 67:102-7 Mr '47.

64. LEWIS, JOHN A. "Kuder Preference Record and MMPI Scores for Two Occupational Groups." *J Consult Psychol* 11: 194-201 Jl-Ag '47. * (*PA* 22:349)

65. LOUGH, ORPHA MAUST. "Women Students in Liberal Arts, Nursing, and Teacher Training Curricula and the Minnesota Multiphasic Personality Inventory." *J Appl Psychol* 31: 437-45 Ag '47. * (*PA* 22:2201)

66. MODLIN, HERBERT C. "A Study of the Minnesota Multiphasic Personality Inventory in Clinical Practice: With Notes on the Cornell Index." *Am J Psychiatry* 103:758-69 My '47. * (*PA* 22:1657)

67. MORRIS, W. W. "A Preliminary Evaluation of the Minnesota Multiphasic Personality Inventory." *J Clin Psychol* (in press).

68. O'GORMAN, WILLIAM D., AND KUNKLE, E. CHARLES. "Study of the Relation Between Minnesota Multiphasic Personality Inventory Scores and 'Pilot Error' in Aircraft Accidents." *J Aviat Med* 18:31-8 F '47. * (*PA* 21:2328)

68a. PACELLA, B. L.; PIOTROWSKI, Z.; AND LEWIS, N. D. C. "The Effects of Electric Convulsive Therapy on Certain Personality Traits in Psychiatric Patients." *Am J Psychiatry* 104: 83-91 Ag '47. * (*PA* 22:2210)

69. PHILLIPS, E. L., AND WIENER, D. N. "Relationships Between Selected Disability and Disease Groups and the Minnesota Multiphasic Personality Inventory." Abstract. *Am Psychol* 2:274 Ag '47. * (*PA* 21:4505, title only)

70. SISK, HENRY L. "A Reply to Winfield's Study of the Multiple Choice Rorschach." *J Appl Psychol* 31:446-8 Ag '47. *

71. WIENER, DANIEL N. "Differences Between the Individual and Group Forms of the Minnesota Multiphasic Personality Inventory." *J Consult Psychol* 11:104-6 Mr-Ap '47. * (*PA* 21: 3488)

72. WIENER, DANIEL N. "Subtle and Obvious Keys for the Minnesota Multiphasic Personality Inventory." Abstract. *Am Psychol* 2:296 Ag '47. * (*PA* 21:4400, title only)

Arthur L. Benton, Associate Professor of Psychology, University of Louisville School of Medicine, Louisville, Kentucky. The inventory consists of 550 statements which the subject indicates as being true or false with respect to himself. Provision is made for placing items in a doubtful (?) category if the subject is not able to make a judgment concerning them. Different areas of life experience are covered by the items, e.g., somatic experiences, family relations, social-political attitudes, sexual attitudes, mood-tone, beliefs, etc. On the basis of the performance of patients in the various psychiatric diagnostic groupings, scoring scales (based on a total of 351 items) have been constructed for the following personality trends or structures: (*a*) hypochondriasis; (*b*) depression; (*c*) hysteria; (*d*) psychopathic deviate; (*e*) masculinity-femininity; (*f*) psychasthenia; (*g*) paranoia; (*h*) schizophrenia; (*i*) hypomania. Three scales designed to check the validity of the results are also part of the inventory: (*a*) a "lie" scale designed to show the extent to which the subject may be falsifying his answers to put himself in a socially favorable light, the essential effect of which is to tend to reduce the magnitude of abnormal scores; (*b*) an "F" scale, a high score on which raises the question as to whether the subject actually understands what he is reading; (*c*) a "?" scale, derived from the number of items placed in the "?" category, a high score on which tends to reduce the magnitude of abnormal scores. Both individual and group forms of the test have been devised. Since the reviewer's experience has been restricted to the use of the individual form, the remarks which follow should be taken to apply only to that form of the inventory.

The inventory purports to give an accurate measure, in terms of a score, of the strength of certain trends or components in the personality recognized in current psychiatric nosology. It was introduced to the medical profession as "an easily applicable measuring device which would identify and characterize the psychoneurotic patient with a minimum use of the time-consuming interview technique that is conventional in the psychiatric approach" (8). Cases are reported showing how the scores can be used in differential diagnosis, high scores definitely indicating significant psychiatric deviations even within the framework of established organic disease and low scores tending to exclude the possibility of an emotional etiology for somatic complaints with a consequent focusing of the clinician's attention on an organic basis for the complaints. Thus, Schiele, Baker and Hathaway (9) state: "a neurotic score indicates the presence of a neurotic temperament, but does not prove the absence of organic disease. Conversely....stable persons, even though suffering from widespread organic disease, score little higher on hypochondriasis or hysteria than do the normal." "The negative or normal profile....is a reassurance to the clinician, which relieves him in part from disturbing concern with psychological factors."

It is somewhat surprising, in view of the extensive utilization of the test by clinicians, to find how little work has been done to assess its validity as an analytic-diagnostic device. In this respect, it should be kept in mind that the inventory has been advanced as "the first inventory measuring common specific clinical syndromes, in contrast to the earlier schedules designed for either the more general concept of 'neuroticism' or special states like 'inferiority' " (9). Consequently, studies which report that the inventory is effective as a screening device for "abnormality in general" in mass selection situations cannot be considered as true assessments of the analytic-diagnostic validity of the inventory. Nor would such studies appear to have great clinical import in view of the demonstrated practical effectiveness for screening purposes of simple, abbreviated questionnaires. To utilize as elaborate an instrument as the inventory for screening purposes which are achieved as effectively by a twenty-item questionnaire is truly to "send a man to do a boy's work."

The studies that have been made on the va-

lidity and clinical usefulness of the inventory as an analytic-diagnostic device can be conveniently considered under two categories: (a) Studies assessing the validity of the scores derived from the separate scales; (b) Studies assessing the validity of "patterns" or "profiles" of scores.

Studies of the first type, i.e., evaluations of the validity of single scale scores by comparing such scores with established diagnoses, have been reported by Leverenz (7), Benton and Probst (17, 34), Michael and Buhler (29), and Morris (67). Leverenz found that in a group of normal soldiers, the *median* scores on all scales were within normal limits. Of 105 patients in surgical wards, only two showed "abnormal profiles." In a group of patients diagnosed as "psychoneurosis, hypochondriacal type," 96 per cent had T-scores greater than 70 on the hypochondriasis scale. In a group of patients clinically judged to be "depressed," 93 per cent made T-scores greater than 70 on the depression scale. It is stated, without citation of data, that similar results were found for patients judged to be cases of hysteria, psychasthenia, paranoid sensitivity, and psychopathic personality. It is further stated that "subjects with abnormal homosexual behavior invariably received an elevated score on the masculinity-feminity scale." A high proportion of a group of patients in whom the diagnosis of peptic ulcer was established made high scores on the "neurotic" scales. Leverenz concludes that the inventory is a highly valid analytic-diagnostic instrument of great clinical usefulness. In contrast to this favorable report of Leverenz are the findings of Benton, Probst, Michael, Buhler and Morris. Benton, working with small groups of selected patients in whom the diagnoses were established beyond reasonable doubt, secured the following results: (a) only about one-half of a group of hysterical patients made high scores on the hysteria scale; (b) only about one-half of a group of schizophrenics made high scores on the schizoprenia scale; (c) about four-fifths of a group of psychopathic delinquents made high scores on the psychopathic deviate scale; (d) virtually all of a group of *confessed* male homosexuals made high scores on the femininity scale. However, when these individuals were instructed to attempt to conceal the fact of their homosexuality, a majority of them were able to make normal scores on the femininity scale; (e) only a very small proportion of a group of patients suffering from diabetes mellitus made high scores on the "neurotic" scales; in contrast, a majority of a group of patients suffering from cardiovascular disease made high scores on the "neurotic" scales. Benton concludes that "in its present stage of development the Minnesota Inventory should not be regarded as a practical clinical test, the results of which can be accepted at face value by the practicing psychiatrist and the internist." Benton and Probst, comparing the ratings by psychiatrists of their patients with respect to the personality trends investigated by the Minnesota and the test scores themselves, found a significant degree of agreement between the psychiatric ratings and the test scores in respect to the psychopathic deviate, paranoia and schizophrenia scales. On the other hand there was no significant degree of agreement in respect to the other scales. Here, as in the earlier study of Benton, the over-all validity of inventory *scores* is called into serious question.

Michael and Buhler (29) found in 90 cases diagnosed in one of three broad categories (psychoneurosis, psychopathy, psychosis) that the Minnesota results agreed with the clinical diagnosis in only 45 per cent of the cases. They state that "the main problem which we found in the use of the Minnesota Multiphasic was that there were many unclear results in which the interpretation of the curve seemed doubtful."

Morris, comparing the mean scores of patients in various diagnostic categories (psychoneurosis, schizoid personality, constitutional psychopathic state–emotional instability) with those of a normal control group, found that the inventory readily distinguished the normal controls from the pathological groups. However, the mean score profiles of the abnormal groups were practically indistinguishable from each other, all having high hypochondriasis, depression and hysteria scores and all having femininity and hypomania scores within broad normal limits. The schizoid personalities had high schizophrenia scores but so did the emotionally unstable psychopaths. The anxious psychoneurotics had high psychasthenia scores but so did the schizoid personalities and the emotionally unstable psychopaths. The point is made that the emotionally unstable psychopaths scored within normal limits on the psychopathic deviate scale but it can be justly argued that this group

is not an adequate validating group for the psychopathic deviate scale which purports to assess delinquent and antisocial trends not "emotional instability." Morris concludes that the inventory "does differentiate borderline normals from serious pathological states but does not aid in the differential diagnosis among the pathological groups."

Studies of the second type, i.e., examination of the clinical validity of "profiles" or "patterns" of scores on the test have been reported by Schmidt (30), Gough (40) and Meehl (47). Schmidt's data, presented in terms of group means, show clearly that groups of patients in various psychiatric categories can be readily distinguished from a group of normal individuals. However, the situation is quite different in respect to comparisons between the abnormal groups (mild psychoneurosis, severe psychoneurosis, constitutional inadequacy, sexual psychopathy, psychosis) where relatively few statistically significant differences emerge. For example, even when dealing with group averages, there is not a single statistically significant difference in any scale score between the constitutionally inadequate personalities and the psychotics, between the constitutionally inadequate personalities and the severe psychoneurotics or between the severe psychoneurotics and the psychotics. Statistically significant differences do appear if the disorders are classified according to degree of severity, e.g., between mild and severe psychoneurosis and between psychosis and mild psychoneurosis. Schmidt describes what he feels to be characteristic differences in the profiles of the different groups. These differences are not statistically significant and would seem to have negligible clinical value in their application for classification purposes to an individual case.

Gough's paper, which includes a penetrating discussion of the sagacious use of the inventory, presents data purporting to show that psychoneurotic, psychopathic and psychotic subjects can be distinguished from each other on the basis of the relative predominance of the scores on the neurotic scales, psychopathic deviate scale and the psychotic scales. The reviewer's examination of these data fails to disclose the alleged discriminatory value of the score profiles. Particularly disturbing in this respect is the fact that the score profiles of severe psychoneurotics and psychotics appear to be practically identical. Gough's data, like

Schmidt's, do show a correlation between magnitude of scores in general and severity of disorder in general, but the findings on score profiles seem to lack any real qualitative differential-diagnostic significance.

Meehl evaluated the effectiveness of a rapid objective analysis of inventory scores by comparing the broad diagnostic category derived from such analyses with the established broad diagnostic category (psychosis, neurosis, conduct disorder). About two-thirds of the cases were placed in the correct category. It is concluded that "while the discriminations achieved are very much better than chance in the statistical sense....the proportion of false classifications is considerable."

It must be concluded that the claims of the authors of the *Minnesota Multiphasic Personality Inventory* in respect to the face validity of the inventory scores have not stood the test of critical examination. Recent publications of the Minnesota group contain many critical and incisive observations concerning the proper use of the inventory and indicate that they are well aware of the shortcomings of a naïve use of the test scores. The place for these observations would seem to be in the manual and in general articles in medical journals as well as in special articles in psychological journals.

As a detailed self-evaluation by the patient, the inventory has considerable potential usefulness both as a research instrument and a practical clinical aid. Continued experience with it suggests many values to the soundly trained clinical psychologist and appears to yield data of real clinical import. In utilizing the inventory in clinical situations, it would seem that the psychologist should report *his conclusions and clinical judgments,* supported by citation of the empirical data, rather than a mere score profile which, one can be sure, will be assessed at the face value it does not possess. But this potential usefulness of the inventory, it must be said, has been overshadowed to date by its gross *misuse,* which has tended to weaken clinical psychology in the eyes of critical psychiatrists and internists (who quickly learn that the inventory's performances fall far short of its claims) and which has made a "psychodiagnostician" of anyone who can score the test.

H. J. Eysenck, Senior Psychologist, Maudsley Hospital, London, England. This scale represents a further development of the old neuroti-cism-cum-introversion inventory along the two directions indicated first by Humm and Wadsworth: In the first place, there is not one over-all score, but a number of diagnostic indices are derived from the subject's answers, and in the second place, attempts are made to gain some information on the accuracy with which the questions have been answered.

The 550 questions included in this inventory are available either in booklet form or printed on cards for sorting into the usual "Yes," "?," "No" categories. From the answers, a profile chart is constructed which shows the deviation from the standardization group on the following scales: Hypochondriasis, Depression, Hysteria, Psychopathic Deviate, Masculine-Feminine Interests, Paranoia, Psychasthenia, Schizophrenia, and Hypomania. Items defining these various scales were derived from clinically diagnosed samples of patients exemplifying these various disorders.

Additional scores are provided on four scales: the Question score, the Lie score, the Validity score, and the K score. The Question score simply records the number of "?" answers; a high score is taken to mean that the true scores on the diagnostic categories would in all probability be further away from the mean than they are. The Lie score is made up from the answers to a number of questions which make the subject appear in a slightly unfavourable light; subjects claiming the favourable alternative in each case are presumed to have falsified their diagnostic scales also in the direction of greater favourableness. The Validity scale consists of items which are infrequently answered in the scored direction by either normal or abnormal subjects; high scores, with certain exceptions, indicate that great care is necessary in interpreting the record. The K scale acts as a *suppressor variable* and is claimed to sharpen the discriminatory power of the diagnostic scales.

The good points of this inventory are as follows: (*a*) The standardization has been done very carefully and conscientiously. (*b*) The statistical work is of a high quality and leaves little to be desired. (*c*) The four correction scores (Question, Lie, Validity, K) are a distinct improvement on the corresponding scale in the Humm–Wadsworth inventory (the No-count). (*d*) The whole scale is an "open" one; i.e., new diagnostic scoring categories can be added without necessitating a new set of questions. (e) The inventory is analytic and gets away from the simplicity of the neuroticism questionnaire. (f) Scoring is less laborious than on the Humm–Wadsworth scale and can be done in a relatively short time. (g) The method of having the subject sort cards, instead of fill in a questionnaire, is a distinct improvement with abnormal subjects.

Drawbacks are as follows: (a) The diagnostic groups are based on psychiatric classification, which is notoriously inaccurate and disputable. (b) Nothing is known about the intercorrelations of the diagnostic scales. (c) Reliability of the scales is not very high. (d) The number of items is excessive; the authors claim that the time taken for filling in the inventory is commonly as short as thirty minutes, but in our experience normal, and particularly abnormal, subjects take well over one hour, and at times as much as five hours.

Of its kind, this is probably the best inventory in existence; in the clinical situation, it is definitely preferable to the Humm–Wadsworth. In the industrial situation, however, I think the Humm–Wadsworth would probably have the stronger claims on the basis of better validation. Both these scales should ideally be based on factorial analyses, like the Guilford scales, but even in the absence of such analysis they have a definite contribution to make.

L. S. Penrose, Galton Professor of Eugenics, University College, London, England. The test material consists of a set of questions in the form of statements, to which the subject is exposed and required to determine if they are true or false. There are in all 566 statements and they are designed to give information about personality traits. The following examples indicate the range of reactions investigated:

I enjoy detective mystery stories.
I have a cough most of the time.
I am worried about sex matters.
Someone has been trying to influence my mind.
Policemen are usually honest.
I have no fear of spiders.

The questions can be presented either on a series of cards or in a booklet. If cards are used, the subject is asked to sort them into three piles according to whether he considers the statements printed on them true or false as applied to himself or whether he is unable to answer. Blank forms are supplied, on which a subject working from the booklet can record his decisions. Scoring is made as mechanical as possible and suitable for routine testing. Though the mechanizations makes the test remarkably easy to use, it conceals the force of individual items so well that it is difficult for the critical observer to appreciate how the result is obtained and, hence, to evaluate it.

The construction of the inventory is based on principles made well known by the work of Woodworth. The method of presentation is objective, in that the examiner need not enter into the picture as he must in any type of standardized interview. On the other hand, the fine points of clinical observation, which enable an experienced examiner to gain information about a subject at a personal interview, are eliminated also. The wording of the questions in the inventory is, on the whole, straightforward and independent of educational background but at times perhaps too colloquial. A few trivial alterations might have to be made if the test were to be widely used in the British Isles.

The inventory has the ambitious object of measuring specific clinical syndromes and not merely of deciding whether or not the subject is neurotic, as has been the case with some earlier schedules. Accordingly, the results of choices are scored on a number of different (though not necessarily independent) scales which purport to give quantitative measurements of hypochondriasis, depression, hysteria, psychopathy, paranoia, psychasthenia, masculinity or femininity, schizophrenia and hypomania. An ingenious device called "validity score" tends to show whether the subject is taking the test seriously and honestly giving his opinion or not. The final result is put in the form of a profile with standard scores which make the deviation from normality in each scale comparable. A standard score of 50 is average and every 10 points above or below represents one unit of standard deviation in the general population. Thus, standard scores above 70 are considered to indicate presence of abnormal amounts of the properties in question though, since the distributions of scores of some scales are far from being Gaussian, this criterion is questionable.

Much work has been done by experimenting with the test on various types of abnormal subjects and inevitably the scoring on various items has had to be altered from time to time as new information became available. The experimental results, however, indicate that some scales are much less reliable than others. In all cases there is, of course, an overlap between scores of known normal and known abnormal subjects and when the degree of overlapping is great, the test is less useful than when it is small. The best results appear to have been obtained on the scale of depression, where the overlap is such that only 12 per cent of cases would be misclassified, if the inventory were used to diagnose presence or absence of a depressive state (8). On the other hand, a state of acute depression is, from the psychiatric as well as from the common sense point of view, easy to appreciate and it is not clear whether the inventory will detect potential depression in a person who, for the time being, is reacting normally. The hypochondriacal scale seems to be also quite good in differentiating normal from abnormal subjects. On the other hand, the psychasthenic scale is almost useless, since diagnosis by this scale would classify one out of three symptomatic cases wrongly (5). Some other scales are of doubtful value. It is not to be expected that systems of scoring, standardized on the basis of a limited number of typical cases, will necessarily continue to be strongly discriminative when applied to fresh unknown populations.

The inventory will probably be widely used because of its attractive methods of presentation and scoring. In making "blind" diagnoses, its findings must be treated with reserve and laymen or psychologists without clinical experience might be encouraged by its use to make quite unwarranted inferences in individual cases. On the other hand it is claimed that, since the clinical impression obtained from psychiatric investigation is not always corroborated by the scores obtained on the inventory, this new instrument is capable of bringing to light hitherto unsuspected abnormal personality changes.

Julian B. Rotter, Associate Professor of Psychology, The Ohio State University, Columbus, Ohio. The *Minnesota Multiphasic Personality Inventory* is an attempt to provide in a single scale an objective appraisal of many of the major personality characteristics of interest to individuals working in the area of personality abnormality. As an inventory-type test, it has an advantage over other inventories in that it attempts to measure the validity of the test

for the particular individual with three different measures. One of these is the question score, which is dependent upon the number of items categorized as questionable by the subject. A second, the Lie score, attempts to measure falsification by the type of answer to crucial questions; and the third, the validity score, a measure of pertinency, rationality, and consistency, attempts to get at the subject's response to the whole testing situation. This attack on some of the usual criticisms of personality inventories is all to the good and is not lessened in value by the fact that some of these measures are related to the specific characteristics being studied by the test as a whole. The personality scales are Hypochondriasis, Hysteria, Psychopathic Deviate, Interest (masculinity-femininity), Paranoia, Psychasthenia, Schizophrenia, Depression, and Hypomania. The presence of several scales standardized on similar populations allows for studies of profiles and relationships rather than of unrelated entities.

Test-retest reliabilities for the separate scales are reported as ranging from .71 to .83. Validity measures are for single scales and are usually in terms of overlap between patients of a given nosology, unselected patients, and normals. Satisfactory differentiation is reported in most instances. In selecting subjects the important and extremely difficult factors such as severity and duration of illness and length of hospitalization are frequently neglected, but many controls which are not present in most personality-inventory validation groups, such as cultural factors, patient status, and socioeconomic level, are made. The number of cases for validation and cross-validation of some of the specific scales is still somewhat small. A new scale, the K scale, which attempts to act as a correction factor to increase the validity of several of the personality scales, has been published.

The test as used individually requires the subject to sort cards. The test may be scored by machine or by hand. The time for administration is usually from forty-five minutes to two hours and does not require supervision except as supervision of some psychotic patients is always necessary. Five hundred and fifty items are included.

In appraising the value of the test as a clinical instrument, stress should be placed on the fact that scoring standards were developed by determining the items in which a group of abnormal subjects "diagnosed" as belonging to some functional mental "disease entity" differentiated themselves from normals or from patients belonging to other disease entity groups. For cross-validation "the chief criterion....has been the valid prediction of clinical cases against the neuropsychiatric staff diagnosis." Herein lies the strengths and weaknesses of the test. Its reliability and validity are dependent upon the reliability and validity of diagnosis of disease entities themselves. This dependence is not only upon the diagnosis made at the University of Minnesota Hospital but at any place these diagnoses are made. That is, not only must it be true, to accept the found test validities, that such disease entities exist but also that they can be reliably determined from one psychiatrist to another. Many psychologists who have had experience in different hospitals would have grave doubts that either statement could be demonstrated to be wholly true. On the other hand, a major advantage of the test when working in mental hospitals and psychiatric clinics is that it speaks the language of the psychiatrist and gives him familiar variables with which to work.

Studies by Schmidt (30), Gough (40), and Benton and Probst (34) indicate how the validity of the subscales fare in hospitals other than the one where the standardization was made. A detailed analysis of the results of these studies taken together would indicate that a group diagnosed as belonging to one disease entity is more likely than not to have its highest subscore on a scale other than the one expected, and that profiles of all the scales differ more in terms of severity than of specific disease entity. Perhaps of particular significance is the fact that the depression scale tends to be highest for a great variety of clinical groups, and it may represent a general "complaint factor." The "complaint factor," although not isolated as such, appears to the reviewer as the significant variable which is being measured by most personality inventories. Although not specifically computed, the results of the above studies and the reviewer's experience with the test suggest that intercorrelations between some of the subtests may be fairly high.

The test at present utilizes only 391 of the 550 items (unless the K scale uses additional items). The test authors feel that the unused items should be left in because the test was standardized with them included and because they may be useful in scales to be developed in the future. The reviewer feels that the test might well be standardized without them and that further eliminations could be made of subscales which correlate highly with other scales and show no significant differences between groups when data is sampled from many psychiatric hospitals. The special attempts to cross-validate and to use measures of validity make this measure more valuable than most inventories, but the additional time needed for scoring and administration may restrict that value.

As a general screening test, it appears to be very valuable in psychiatric clinics and hospitals. At the present time, however, it appears to the reviewer that no great reliance may be placed in the belief that the subscales measure what their titles or manuals suggest they test. Perhaps some of the clinicians using the test interpret the separate scales in a more "categorical" fashion than the authors intended. This latter limitation is probably more a reflection of the lack of validity and of the limitations of the "disease entity" approach to personality than of the carefulness of test construction of the test authors.

J Am Med Assn 120:1441 D 26 '42. * This personality schedule, in the hands of properly trained psychiatrists and psychologists, would appear to be of considerable usefulness when large numbers of persons must come under observation, as in industry. Doubtless disturbed persons can be sifted out by proper use of devices such as those here offered. The fact that the schedule is easy to administer should not be permitted to lead to its use by persons untrained in psychiatry or psychology. The schedule is not intended to do more than help identify disturbed persons and does not offer material or direction for treatment.

[61]

★**Minnesota Personality Scale.** Grades 11-16; 1941; IBM; separate forms for men and women; $2.50 per 25; 3½¢ per answer sheet; 40¢ per set of hand-scoring stencils; $1 per set of machine-scoring stencils; 60¢ per specimen set, either form; nontimed (60) minutes; John G. Darley and Walter J. McNamara; Psychological Corporation.

REFERENCES

1. DARLEY, JOHN G. *An Analysis of Attitude and Adjustment Tests: With Special Reference to Conditions of Change in Attitudes and Adjustments.* Unpublished doctor's thesis, University of Minnesota, 1937.
2. DARLEY, JOHN G. "Scholastic Achievement and Measured Maladjustment." *J Appl Psychol* 21:485-93 O '37. * (PA 12:2099)

3. DARLEY, JOHN G. "Changes in Measured Attitudes and Adjustments." *J Social Psychol* 9:189-99 My '38. * (*PA* 12:4833)

4. McNAMARA, WALTER J., AND DARLEY, JOHN G. "A Factor Analysis of Test-Retest Performance on Attitude and Adjustment Tests." *J Ed Psychol* 29:652-64 D '38. * (*PA* 13:2747)

5. DARLEY, JOHN G., AND McNAMARA, WALTER J. "Factor Analysis in the Establishment of New Personality Tests." *J Ed Psychol* 31:321-34 My '40. * (*PA* 15:922)

6. HORNE, BETTY N., AND McCALL, W. C. "A Study of Some Local Factors Affecting Students' Scores on the Minnesota Personality Scale." *Ed & Psychol Meas* 2:257-66 Jl '42. * (*PA* 16:4874)

7. BENNETT, GEORGE K., AND GORDON, H. PHOEBE. "Personality Test Scores and Success in the Field of Nursing." *J Appl Psychol* 28:267-78 Je '44. * (*PA* 18:3184)

8. DUNCAN, MELBA HURD. "An Experimental Study of Some of the Relationships Between Voice and Personality Among Students of Speech." *Speech Monogr* 12:47-60 '45. * (*PA* 20:1961)

9. KIMBER, J. A. MORRIS. "Interests and Personality Traits of Bible Institute Students." *J Social Psychol* 26:225-33 N '47. *

Philip Eisenberg, Research Psychologist, Columbia Broadcasting System, New York, New York. An unusual amount of work was put into the construction and standardization of this scale. Originally four questionnaires, consisting of 368 items and yielding 13 different scores, were used. Factor analysis demonstrated that the 13 scores could be reduced to 5. Items which did not differentiate between high- and low-scoring individuals were weeded out. The use of factor analysis and item differentiation resulted in a high degree of internal consistency; the odd-even reliabilities for the various parts of the test are, with only one exception, above .90.

Another noteworthy feature of the test is that the authors reduced the ambiguity of the items by permitting five alternative answers to each question rather than the usual Yes-No-? variety. Thus, a person is less likely to be forced into an artificial dichotomy when he is asked to answer such a question as "Do you cross the street to avoid meeting people you know?" Also, the alternative of either hand or machine scoring is convenient.

As is usual with personality inventories, the major question is that of the validity of the scale. The scale purports to measure five aspects of individual adjustment: Morale (attitudes toward the legal system, to education, and general adjustment); Social Adjustment (feelings of inferiority, social behavior, social preferences, etc.); Family Relations (parent-child adjustment); Emotionality (health and emotional adjustment); and Economic Conservatism.

Judging from the names of the five parts of the scale, as well as the individual questions, it seems that the authors consider social adjustment an important aspect of individual adjustment. Counselors have found the scale useful in a college personnel adjustment program, and there is some evidence that the test can differentiate between students with adjustment problems and those with no such problems. But this is not completely convincing proof of validity. There is no doubt that any series of carefully selected questions will be useful to a counselor in the diagnosis of an individual case, yet the direct questionnaire method is bound to miss important problems.

It is also regrettable that such Herculean effort was devoted to the production of a test limited in use to high school and college students. While there is unquestionably a need for such instruments in educational institutions, there is a greater need for instruments which apply to a cross section of the adult American population.

John W. French, Research Associate, College Entrance Examination Board, Princeton, New Jersey. The test was constructed by using the best items from the *Minnesota Scale for the Survey of Opinions*, Bell's *Adjustment Inventory*, and the *Minnesota Inventory of Social Attitudes*. This is a commendable approach for two reasons: (*a*) Many existing personality inventories by themselves cover only a part of the total personality. (*b*) There are a great many personality inventories whose good items should be salvaged from their present mixture with useless items.

In selecting tests from which to construct their own tests, the authors might have chosen more wisely. They did not use enough tests to completely cover the personality picture, and some of the tests of attitude which they included do not contribute to the measurement of personality. The tests, however, were subjected to a factor analysis which shows that certain attitude items may properly be used in a personality test; e.g., attitudes toward the legal system and towards education are closely related to morale and general adjustment, and so they are properly used in composing a single score on morale. Economic conservatism, however, was not closely related with any personality tests and thus should be omitted. Consistently low correlations between economic conservatism and the other parts of the test as compared with the correlations of the other parts with each other is a further indication that economic conservatism does not belong in this personality group.

For item analysis, 25 high-scoring men and women and 25 low-scoring men and women were selected on the basis of their scores on each of the five parts of the test. Critical ratios showing the ability of each item to discriminate between the superior and inferior groups were computed. In two successive experiments with different groups of subjects the items with low critical ratios were eliminated, until only very few were left that did not have critical ratios of at least 3.0 for the men and for the women. This standard of internal consistency is high for tests of this type, although it seems surprising that a test of emotional stability should contain such items as "Do you have....athlete's foot?" and "Do your teeth seem to need dental attention?"

Two other characteristics of the test were selected on the basis of experimental evidence: (a) Five choices instead of the more usual three are used in spite of increasing the difficulty of scoring because reliability was shown to be appreciably higher with five choices than with three. (b) The items were written in the second person, like most items of this kind, instead of in the third person because the second person was preferred by 80 per cent of the subjects and yields the same reliability, though it also yields a somewhat more favorable mean score than was obtained by using items in the third person.

It must be borne in mind that personality inventories of this type are generally unsuitable for selective purposes when the subjects can gain by not answering the items frankly. Little effort has been made to disguise the purpose of this test. Satisfactory results can be obtained only in counseling or experimental situations where the subjects either are indifferent to the test results or desire an honest diagnosis of their personality.

[62]

★Minnesota T-S-E Inventory. Grades 10-16 and adults; 1942; preliminary manual, 1942; $2.15 per 25; 35¢ per set of scoring stencils; 50¢ per specimen set; nontimed (25) minutes; Catharine Evans and T. R. McConnell: Science Research Associates.

REFERENCES

1. EVANS, MARY CATHARINE. The Measurement of Different Types of Introversion-Extroversion and Their Relationships to Scholastic Achievement. Unpublished doctor's thesis, University of Minnesota, 1940.
2. EVANS, CATHARINE, AND McCONNELL, T. R. "A New Measure of Introversion-Extroversion." J Psychol 12:111-24 Jl '41. * (PA 15:5208)
3. EVANS, CATHARINE, AND WRENN, C. GILBERT. "Introversion-Extroversion as a Factor in Teacher-Training." Ed & Psychol Meas 2:47-58 Ja '42. * (PA 16:2446)
4. HAHN, MILTON E. An Investigation of Measured Aspects of Social Intelligence in a Distributive Occupation. Unpublished doctor's thesis, University of Minnesota, 1942.
5. ZIEGFELD, ERNEST. A Study of the Relation of Introversion-Extroversion to Picture Preferences. Unpublished master's thesis, University of Minnesota, 1942.
6. EVANS, M. CATHARINE. "Social Adjustment and Interest Scores of Introverts and Extroverts." Ed & Psychol Meas 7: 157-67 sp '47. * (PA 22:626)

Philip Eisenberg, Research Psychologist, Columbia Broadcasting System, New York, New York. This test was constructed to measure three types of introversion-extroversion: thinking, social, and emotional, which Guilford had isolated in a factor analysis of available I-E tests. They bear some relationship to, but are not the same as, Jung's types. Jung portrayed typologies of entire personality structures, while these tests measure only overt interests and actions. The overt interests may reflect deeper, underlying motives and needs, but this aspect of personality is not touched upon in the paper-and-pencil test items nor in the construction and validation of the test.

The separateness of the three types of I-E was demonstrated beyond Guilford's analysis by low intercorrelations between the three tests. The split-half and repeat reliabilities of each test lie within the high .80's, which according to the authors "seem to be sufficiently reliable for individual prediction." It seems to this reviewer, that a little better than 50 per cent prediction above chance is adequate for group, but not for individual, prediction.

The validation of the test has been mostly that of differentiation between groups with apparently different interests. Thus, physical education majors are more often thinking extroverts than English, art, mathematics and social studies majors. Sorority and fraternity members are more likely to be socially extroverted than students who do not belong to such groups. For the most part, college women tend to be more emotionally extroverted than college men. Also life insurance salesmen were found to be more extroverted on each of the three scales than men in general. There seems to be some differences in I-E between successful and unsuccessful air-line stewardesses. Thinking extroverts tend to prefer naturalistic pictures, and thinking introverts non-naturalistic pictorial representation. Some relationships have been found between scores on the *Minnesota T-S-E Inventory* and the *Minnesota Personality Scale* and the *Kuder Preference Record.*

These relationships suggest the usefulness of this test in situations where interests may be important as in choice of college major and in vocational guidance. However, such uses for this test have not yet been demonstrated by research. Beyond measurement of interests, this test seems to be limited as a diagnostic instrument. It is further limited by the fact that it can only be used with senior high school and college students.

John W. French, Research Associate, College Entrance Examination Board, Princeton, New Jersey. The test was constructed by gathering items about activities which were thought to discriminate introverts from extroverts in three fields of measurement: thinking, social, and emotional. Classification of the items into these three categories was done by judges. These three aspects of the introversion-extroversion problem are probably well chosen, since a factor analysis by Guilford brought out the factors "thinking introversion," "shyness," and "depression" which are similar to the three used here.

The manual gives an impressive table of validities. In each of the three fields groups of people having contrasting age, sex, or occupation are shown to differ significantly on the introversion-extroversion scale in the expected direction. However, the test uses direct questions about the interests and activities of groups of people similar to those used in the validity studies. For example, the tables show that the test will discriminate physical education majors from English majors. This is done by such questions as "Do you enjoy watching football, basketball, or baseball games?" and "Do you enjoy the plays of Henrik Ibsen?" Since the activities of English majors are associated with introversion, their activities are keyed for introversion in the test. Then the test is claimed to be valid, because it finds English majors to be an introverted group. This reasoning is dangerous unless it is known that English majors actually are an introverted group.

It must be borne in mind that personality inventories of this type are generally unsuitable for selective purposes when the subjects can gain by not answering the items frankly. No effort has been made to disguise the purpose of the test. What value the test may have can be realized only in counseling or experimental situations where the subjects either are indifferent to the test results or desire an honest diagnosis of their personality.

[63]
★Ohio Guidance Tests for Elementary Grades. Grades 4-6; 1944–46; 5 parts; 1 form; 25¢ per manual; 38¢ per specimen set; nontimed; manual prepared under the direction of Ohio Scholarship Tests and the Division of Elementary Supervision of the Ohio State Department of Education by Wellington G. Fordyce, Wilbur A. Yauch, and Louis Raths; tests developed by the Euclid, Ohio, elementary teachers in cooperation with the College of Education, Ohio State University; Ohio Scholarship Tests, Ohio State Department of Education.
a) OHIO INTEREST INVENTORY FOR THE INTERMEDIATE GRADES. Form G-1; 2¢ per test; nontimed (60) minutes.
b) OHIO INDIVIDUAL SUMMARY SHEET FOR COMMITTEE SELECTIONS. Form G-2; 2¢ per sheet.
c) OHIO SOCIAL ACCEPTANCE SCALE FOR THE INTERMEDIATE GRADES. Form G-3; 2¢ per scale.
d) OHIO RECOGNITION SCALE FOR INTERMEDIATE GRADES: WHO'S WHO IN MY GROUP? Forms G-4-A, G-4-B (both forms should be used); 4¢ per set; 1¢ per individual summary sheet.
e) OHIO THINKING CHECKUP FOR INTERMEDIATE GRADES. Form G-5; 2¢ per test.

REFERENCES
1. FORDYCE, WELLINGTON G. "Teachers Can Build a Test." *Ed Res B* 22:62-5 Mr 17 '43. *
2. RATHS, LOUIS. "The Development of a 'Guess Who' Type of Test." *Ed Res B* 22:70-2 Mr 17 '43. *
3. RATHS, LOUIS. "Identifying the Social Acceptance of Children." *Ed Res B* 22:72-4 Mr 17 '43. *
4. YAUCH, WILBUR. "The Committee Idea in Test Construction." *Ed Res B* 22:65-9 Mr 17 '43. *
5. RATHS, LOUIS E. "A Thinking Test." *Ed Res B* 23:72-5+ Mr 15 '44. *
6. RATHS, LOUIS, AND SCHWEICKART, E. F. "Social Acceptance Within Interracial School Groups." *Ed Res B* 25: 85-90 Ap 10 '46. * (PA 21:547)
7. RATHS, LOUIS. "Evidence Relating to the Validity of the Social Acceptance Test." *Ed Res B* 26:141-6+ S 17 '47. *
8. YOUNG, L. L. "Sociometric and Related Techniques for Appraising Social Status in an Elementary School." *Sociometry* 10:168-77 My '47. *

M. H. Elliott, Director of Research, Public Schools, Oakland, California. The *Ohio Guidance Tests* represent a desirable movement in the direction of developing instruments dealing with social and personal competence at the elementary school level. As such they constitute a break with the tradition of tests of academic skills and information.

The Ohio Interest Inventory contains 360 items ("To lead a class discussion," "To use a hammer and saw") to which children are to react by indicating a like or dislike. The items are classified into eighteen interest areas, such as: sports, school, helping others, music, movies, etc. This inventory bears an obvious relationship to the various vocational interest inventories in use at the secondary school level. The interest items and the vocabulary seem to be suitable for the ages for which it is intended.

The Ohio Individual Summary Sheet for Committee Selections deals with a sociometric technique. The class is asked to vote for members of a committee. The teacher uses the individual summary sheet to record who voted for each child and for whom he voted.

The Ohio Social Acceptance Scale consists of a six-point rating scale ranging as indicated by the following abbreviated descriptions from: "1. I would like to have this person as one of my very best friends," to "6. I do not like to work with this person and would rather not talk to this person." Each child uses this scale to rate every other member of the class.

The Ohio Recognition Scale—Who's Who in My Group contains 18 paragraph descriptions of behavior and personal characteristics. The children are asked to indicate under each paragraph the names of any members of the class to whom the description applies.

The Ohio Thinking Checkup, more nearly than the others, conforms to the usual conception of a "test." Essentially it is a test of interpretation of data and indicates tendencies to be overly cautious, to go beyond the data in drawing conclusions, etc.

The tests described above are developments or modifications of various instruments which have been rather widely used in research studies. Some of the original instruments were developed or utilized by Dr. Raths and numerous collaborators in the Eight-Year Study at the secondary level. Others are derived from the various developments of the "Guess Who" technique, and one stems from the sociometric work of Moreno.

The first four tests (excluding the Thinking Checkup for the moment) have their greatest usefulness in stimulating teachers to study children as individuals. No teacher can use instruments such as these without becoming more aware of differences. Furthermore, data of the kinds obtained will both challenge the teacher and suggest practical procedures to be followed in the classroom. Teachers are not always aware of the ramifications of the "peer culture" of the children. The natural tendency is to see children in terms of adult standards. These instruments reveal in various ways the children's judgments of each other.

The only statistical material furnished to the reviewer was a percentile table for scores on the Social Acceptance Scale. The number of children represented and their grade level was not indicated. However, on the first four of these tests wide-scale norms seem to the reviewer to be of relatively little importance at present. These four tests are of most significance for the training and sensitizing of teachers to the finer shades of social and personal

adjustment. For most purposes it is sufficient for the teacher to study and understand the range of differences within her own room. Furthermore, general norms would have little meaning. The scores on some of these tests would vary tremendously in a particular classroom with such factors as size of class, length of time which the class had been together as a unit, etc. The advent of a new and particularly attractive child could affect the scores obtained by a number of other children.

The Thinking Checkup belongs in a somewhat different category from the other four tests although it will in part reflect "personality" differences. On this particular test some sort of norms for different age groups might be interesting. This instrument would also fit into the orthodox pattern of determining reliability and validity more easily than the others.

These *Ohio Guidance Tests* should be considered as interesting instruments for teacher training and in-service training programs. Their use in this connection can be very stimulating. They are still in the experimental stage. The average teacher would not be able to make full use of them without much help and guidance.

One minor and probably unwarranted criticism of the presentation of this series is the possible implication that a teacher interested in guidance of her pupils should make use of the whole series. An interested teacher might profitably use the results of any one of the tests. However, the reviewer doubts that any of the busy elementary school teachers of his acquaintance could work out, comprehend, and fully utilize the results of the whole series of tests in one school term unless she had an assistant to carry on classroom instruction.

John W. M. Rothney, Associate Professor of Education, The University of Wisconsin, Madison, Wisconsin. By requiring children to mark as liked or disliked the 360 items of an interest inventory; by selecting committee members from among their classmates; by choosing children who fit certain classifications of acceptability; by naming pupils who fit descriptions of personality; and by interpreting paragraphs which reveal attitudes, the *Ohio Guidance Tests* attempt to provide an appraisal of social adjustment of intermediate school children. Suggestions for treatment of children whose characteristics are thus appraised are presented in the manual.

The tests provide good coverage of important characteristics. They do not attempt to "compare achievement of an individual with an established norm," but to provide information for his guidance. Percentile norms are, however, provided for the social acceptance scale. To this reviewer, it is unfortunate that this comparative aspect has been included since it invites possible misuse of the tests. The instruments would have been better named if the word "test" had been left out of the title.

The items of the scales have been carefully selected and the selection of vocabulary has been well done. Requiring the child to respond to 360 items on the interest inventory may result in the forcing of statement of preference where none really exists. While voting for committee members, the child is not given the opportunity to use a secret ballot and his choice may be influenced accordingly. The authors express proper doubt concerning the ability of children to make the discriminations required by the social acceptance scale, but use of the test may help to resolve the doubt.

The teachers who helped to build this scale should be able to use it effectively and those who know the field of child psychology will appreciate its value. To others, it will seem to demand a lot of extra work, and statements such as "the teacher will do this during recess or noon hour, or after school" will not make it seem less forbidding. The construction of these tests has shown what can be done by a concentrated and cooperative effort of a group of teachers and experts in the field of child study. Their work can be used very effectively as an example of what other school systems could do if they would attempt similar tasks. The *process* of development of such instruments will do more to make a group of teachers pupil-minded than the application of ready-made techniques. It is hoped that others will follow the example set by the Ohio group.

[64]

★Personal Audit. Grades 9-16 and adults; 1941–46; Forms SS (short form), LL (long form) ; Clifford R. Adams and William M. Lepley; Science Research Associates.
a) form ss. $2.65 per 25; 50¢ per specimen set; nontimed (35) minutes.
b) form ll. $3.65 per 25; 60¢ per specimen set; nontimed (45) minutes.

REFERENCES

1. Tubbs, William R. *A Study of the Interrelationships Between the Adams-Lepley Form D and the Bernreuter Personality Inventory.* Unpublished master's thesis, Pennsylvania State College, 1940.
2. Adams, Clifford R. "A New Measure of Personality." *J Appl Psychol* 25:141-51 Ap '41. * (PA 15:4271)
3. Gilliard, S. Bruce. *The Relationship of Certain Personal Characteristics to Leadership Ability in Advanced R.O.T.C. Students.* Unpublished master's thesis. Pennsylvania State College, 1942.
4. Lepley, William M. "A Comparison of Fraternity and Non-Fraternity Populations With Regard to Certain Personality Characteristics." *J Appl Psychol* 26:50-4 F '42. * (PA 16:2319)
5. Tubbs, William R. "A Study of the Interrelationships Between the Adams-Lepley Personal Audit and the Bernreuter Personality Inventory." *J Appl Psychol* 26:338-51 Je '42. * (PA 16:4070)
5a. Adams, Eris L. *The Validation and Standardization of The Personal Audit for the High School Level.* Unpublished master's thesis, Pennsylvania State College, 1944.
6. Reppert, Harold Curtis. *A Study of the Differentiating Values of Certain Personality Measures Applied to a Student and Registered Nurse Population.* Unpublished doctor's thesis, Pennsylvania State College, 1945. Pp. 83. (*Abstracts of Doctoral Dissertations . . . 1945, 1946,* pp. 117-25.)
7. Adams, Clifford R. "The Prediction of Adjustment in Marriage." *Ed & Psychol Meas* 6:185-93 su '46. * (PA 21:177)
8. Super, Donald E. "The Validity of Standard and Custom-Built Personality Inventories in a Pilot Selection Program." *Ed & Psychol Meas* 7:735-44 w '47. *
9. Thompson, Claude Edward. "Selecting Executives by Psychological Tests." *Ed & Psychol Meas* 7:773-8 w '47. *

Percival M. Symonds, Professor of Education, Teachers College, Columbia University, New York, New York. This is a self-administering personality test coming in an eleven-page folder. The test consists of nine separate questionnaires, each section containing 50 items. According to the manual, the *Personal Audit* measures the following personality characteristics: Part I, Seriousness–Impulsiveness; Part II, Firmness–Indecision; Part III, Tranquillity–Irritability; Part IV, Frankness–Evasion; Part V, Stability–Instability; Part VI, Tolerance–Intolerance; Part VII, Steadiness–Emotionality; Part VIII, Persistence–Fluctuation; Part IX, Contentment–Worry. Reliability for any part is stated to be .90 or above, based on the scores of 442 college students. Norms are given for high school students, college freshmen, general college, business and industrial, and general adult subjects.

It is the impression of this reviewer that claims are made for this instrument which go beyond the data which the authors present or have at their disposal. For instance, in Part I, high scores are said to indicate "a serious disposition characterized by quietness, ambition, and studiousness. Usually interests are specialized and stable resembling those of successful draftsmen, engineers, mathematicians, and chemists. Cautiousness is often present to some degree. Socializing tends to be confined to close friends. Agreeableness and cooperation may be present." In other words, one score is claimed to measure quietness, ambition, studiousness, cautiousness, agreeableness, and cooperation. The authors describe patterns of scores for the nine parts of individuals who are stubborn, delinquent, cooperative, agreeable, realistic, impulsive, happily married, but do not present the evidence on which these patterns are based.

The manual presents extensive validity data based on correlations of the *Personal Audit* with other tests and questionnaires. In general the correlations are low. Out of all those presented, few are .3 or above, indicating that the *Personal Audit* on the basis of the evidence presented is not related to other recognized personality scales. In order to validate the names assigned to the nine parts and the descriptions of what high and low scores for each part indicate. "Thirty psychologists, including twelve who had used the instrument, were asked to state what each part measured. The consensus of their judgments coincides with the descriptions which have been prepared for the various traits." This statement is extremely loose. It is impossible to believe that their free statements of what each part measures could coincide exactly with the descriptions provided for the scale by the authors. However, the degree of discrepancy is not stated in the manual.

A number of the parts represent new collections of items. For instance, Part III is a list of annoyances; Part V, a list of common fears; Part VI, a list of persons whom one might dislike; Part VIII, current social phenomena towards which the subject is asked to state changes in his feelings.

This reviewer is not convinced that the *Personal Audit* provides measures which correspond to the titles given to the separate parts.

[65]
★**Personality Index.** Adults; 1945; 1 form; $3 per 25; $1 per specimen set; nontimed (25) minutes; Howard K. Morgan; La Rue Printing Co., 906 Baltimore Ave., Kansas City 6, Missouri.

Benjamin Shimberg, Research Assistant, Division of Educational Reference, Purdue University, Lafayette, Indiana. This inventory represents an effort to "define personality in common business terms and not in psychological terms." The traits measured are called (*a*) job interest, (*b*) social intelligence, (*c*) leadership, (*d*) planning, (*e*) drive, and (*f*) follow through. These traits were supposedly educed by job analysis and from an extensive study of other tests and rating scales. In commenting on the table of intercorrelations given in the manual, the author states that the "intercorrelations are low enough to be satisfactory." Eight of the 15 intercorrelations are found to have values be-

tween .45 and .72, while only three are less than .20. Tests with intercorrelations of this magnitude seldom yield any noticeable increase from zero-order validity coefficients to multiple correlation coefficients.

The Index consists of 84 questions, about two-thirds of which deal with topics typical of most personality questionnaires. The other third are items concerning job interest, work habits, work attitudes, and the like. The answer to each question is selected from among three alternatives. Like the items in most questionnaires of this type, considerable ambiguity is present in the questions, making it difficult to give honest answers without knowing more about the circumstances involved.

Scoring the test must be done manually and is rather cumbersome. It involves aligning a score sheet with each column of the test booklet, indicating how the questions were answered by crossing out the alternatives which were not used, and then adding the appropriate numbers for each column to get the raw scores for the various traits. These may then be converted to percentile scores from a table, and a trait psychograph plotted on a card which is provided.

Only limited data are given in the manual as to the composition of the groups used in developing the weights or establishing norms. The author states that "normal industrial groups were used to set the test limits and averages" and that "persons from routine to important supervisory jobs were included," both sexes being represented about equally. The author has informed the writer that 75 cases were used in the initial study. Norms should be checked before use to make sure that the groups being tested are comparable to those used in developing this test.

Items for the test were selected by testing "known groups" and using only those items which differentiated the best from the poorest in the group with respect to a given trait. It appears, however, that the validation data reported as having been obtained by the use of the "small group method" utilized the same 75 individuals upon whom the items were initially evaluated. This factor would tend to make the validity coefficients spuriously high. Several of these coefficients were, in fact, .90 or greater. Another group, about twice the size of the first group, was used for an independent validation. Validity coefficients for the various traits on the second group ranged from .47 to .75. However, even these values seem unusually favorable for tests of this sort. It would be desirable to have more detailed information regarding the procedures and statistical methods employed. The small manual which is supplied with the test fails to provide this information. This writer would recommend caution in using this instrument until its worth has been more fully demonstrated.

[66]

★Philo-Phobe. Age 10 and over; 1943–47; individual; 3¢ per form sheet; John N. Buck; Steward's Office, Lynchburg State Colony, Colony, Virginia.

REFERENCES

1. BUCK, JOHN N. "Personality Appraisement by Use of the Philo-Phobe." *Am J Mental Def* 47:437-44 Ap '43. * (*PA* 17:3162)
2. FRENCH, VERA V. "The Structure of Sentiments: II, A Preliminary Study of Sentiments." *J Personality* 16:78-108 S '47. * (*PA* 22:2267)
3. LANDISBERG, SELMA. "A Personality Study of Institutionalized Epileptics." *Am J Mental Def* 52:16-22 Jl '47. *

Parker Davis, Jr., Assistant Professor of Psychology, Rutgers University, New Brunswick, New Jersey. This instrument is a semiformalized psychiatric examination which according to the author stands "somewhere between the 'free interview' and the stereotyped projective techniques—designed to help the examiner secure valuable information concerning the subject's personality integration and affective reactions." It is intended to be a "supplemental affair" to formal history and psychometric procedures. Buck states, "The examiner *must* know the relative parts played in the subject's development by his economic, social and cultural backgrounds; his heredity; and his physical disabilities, if he is to evaluate the responses accurately."

Administration is individual with examiner recording responses verbatim. Two or more sessions of one to two hours each are required. Considerable clinical experience is necessary for administration and analysis. Examination consists of a series of direct questions divided into four main groupings ("Aspiration," "Emotion," "Judgment and Insight," and "Ethico-moral Development") which serve as a basis for general analysis. Further analysis is made of "Response Patterns" from various points of view.

The character of the questions is illustrated by the following examples: "What would you like most to do?" "What worries you most?" "Whom do you like best in all the world?" "Do you think anyone is ever justified in telling a deliberate lie?"

According to the author, the instrument has been developed empirically with the theoretical structure eclectic. The primary purpose is the development of an objective-type research instrument in the field of personality dynamics based upon direct questions. No published research is available as yet.

In our opinion, the *Philo–Phobe* has its greatest usefulness as a guide and instrument for training in psychiatric interviewing. It should be particularly appealing to clinical psychologists who either are unfamiliar with the "free interview" or who have a strong positive bias for objective interview methods. As a research and clinical instrument it has a number of rather serious weaknesses: (*a*) Interpretation is essentially subjective and can only be made by an experienced clinician; (*b*) It is supplementary to, and requires for interpretation a vast amount of, other information regarding the subject; that is, the *Philo–Phobe* does not make any unique and independent contribution such as the structural diagnosis of the Rorschach; (*c*) It is highly dubious both in the light of previous attempts and in view of our present knowledge of psychodynamics whether any instrument whose basic approach consists of a standardized series of direct questions can ever be successful in depth analysis; for this reason, the *Philo–Phobe* will have slight appeal for Rogerian and projective technique psychologists.

[67]

★Problem Check List. Grades 7-9, 9-12, 13-16; 1941–47; 3 levels; 1 form; for adaptations, *see* 68 and 69; $1 per 25; 60¢ per manual for either the high school or college form; nontimed (20-40) minutes; Ross L. Mooney; Ohio State University Press.
a) JUNIOR HIGH SCHOOL FORM. 1942–47.
b) HIGH SCHOOL FORM. 1941–47.
c) COLLEGE FORM. 1941–47.

REFERENCES

1. COMBS, ARTHUR W. *The Problems of High School Students in a Typical American Community: A Survey of Major Problems, Trends, and Sex Differences.* Unpublished master's thesis, Ohio State University, 1941. Pp. 136.
2. COWAN, VERNON D. *Identifying Pupil Needs, Concerns and Problems as a Basis for Curriculum Revision in Stephens-Lee High School, Asheville, North Carolina.* Unpublished master's thesis, Ohio State University, 1942.
3. MARSH, CHARLES J. "The Worries of the College Woman." *J Social Psychol* 15:335-9 My '42. * (*PA* 16:4328)
4. MOONEY, ROSS L. "Surveying High-School Students' Problems by Means of a Problem Check List." *Ed Res B* 21:57-69 Mr 18 '42. * (*PA* 16:3795)
5. OUTLAND, RICHARD W. *Worry: A Common Problem of Elementary School Children.* Unpublished master's thesis, Ohio State University, 1942. Pp. 127.
6. ARNOLD, DWIGHT L., AND MOONEY, ROSS L. "A Students' Problem Check List for Junior High School." *Ed Res B* 22:42-8 F 17 '43. *
7. CONGDON, NORA A. "The Perplexities of College Freshmen." *Ed & Psychol Meas* 3:367-75 w '43. * (*PA* 18:2563)
8. MOONEY, ROSS L. "Community Differences in the Problems of High-School Students: A Survey of Five Communities by Means of a Problem Check List." *Ed & Psychol Meas* 3:127-42 su '43. * (*PA* 18:1890)

9. MOONEY, ROSS L. "Exploratory Research on Students' Problems." *J Ed Res* 37:218-24 N '43. * (*PA* 18:1240)
10. MOONEY, ROSS L. "Personal Problems of Freshman Girls: Reporting a Dormitory Survey by Means of a Problem Check List." *J Higher Ed* 14:84-90 F '43. * (*PA* 17:2189)
11. PRIEUR, MARJORIE. "Personal Guidance in Home Economics." *Ed Res B* 22:118-22 My '43. *
12. HIBLER, FRANCIS W., AND LARSEN, ARTHUR HOFF. "Problems of Upperclass Students in a Teachers College." *J Appl Psychol* 28:246-53 Je '44. * (*PA* 18:3289)
13. HOUSTON, V. M., AND MARZOLF, STANLEY S. "Faculty Use of the Problem Check List." *J Higher Ed* 15:325-8 Je '44. * (*PA* 18:3292)
14. PRIEUR, MARJORIE. "A Guidance Point of View and Its Practical Application." *Pract Home Econ* 22:328-9+ S '44. *
15. MARZOLF, STANLEY S., AND LARSEN, ARTHUR HOFF. "Statistical Interpretation of Symptoms Illustrated With a Factor Analysis of Problem Check List Items." *Ed & Psychol Meas* 5:285-94 au '45. * (*PA* 20:2905)
16. YOUNG, HARRY A. *The Personal-Social Problems of Youth in Relation to Curriculum Planning.* Unpublished doctor's thesis, University of Pittsburgh, 1945. Pp. 150.
17. FISCHER, ROBERT P. "Signed Versus Unsigned Personal Questionnaires." *J Appl Psychol* 30:220-5 Je '46. * (*PA* 20:4193)

Ralph C. Bedell, Professor of Educational Psychology and Measurements, The University of Nebraska, Lincoln, Nebraska. The *Problem Check Lists* consist of phrases intended to make it easy for students to express their troublesome problems. The arrangement is similar to that of interest inventories except that the items are problems rather than interests. The student underlines the problems that are of concern to him, circles the ones of most concern, answers a few general questions designed to help him organize his feelings about his problems and writes a summary in his own words. There are no time limits and directions are simple. Thirty to forty minutes represent the approximate maximum time needed.

All three forms are similar in arrangement with considerable duplication in content but designed to be most appropriate to the groups concerned. The two manuals for the College and High School Forms are similar and for many users either manual will suffice for both forms. Users of the Junior High School Form are referred to the High School or College manual. The available manuals are unusually complete, and all users are urged to make a careful study of at least one of them.

The items contained in the College and High School Forms are classified into eleven different general areas, with thirty items in each area. The Junior High School Form has seven general areas, with thirty items in each area. The areas employed in the College and High School Forms are indicative of those used in the other form: (*a*) health and physical development; (*b*) finances, living conditions and employment; (*c*) social and recreational activities; (*d*) social-psychological relations; (*e*) personal-psychological relations; (*f*) courtship, sex and marriage; (*g*) home and family; (*h*) morals and religion; (*i*) adjustment to college (school) work; (*j*) the future: vocational and educational; and (*k*) curriculum and teaching procedures.

The construction and use of the *Problem Check Lists* present many problems, most of which have been anticipated by the authors. Generally, the problems have been met on the basis of pragmatic criteria and much reliance has been placed on the judgments of those who use the check lists.

The technical development of these instruments differs in many respects from traditional methods of test construction; consequently many of the usual criteria for tests do not apply. In many respects Professor Mooney is correct when he states that "The Check List is not to be thought of as a test." There are no set scores to be placed on a continuum; the counting (or scoring) indicates only the number of problems marked in each general area. The lists provide means of indicating the behavior problems that occur in conjunction in any one individual or group of individuals; there is no attempt to arrive at categorical conclusions.

The traditional concepts of reliability and validity are not appropriately applied to the lists. Inconsistency in marking items is neither good nor bad, but merely presents new information to be used in following the changes in an individual or group. Repetition of markings with an interval of one week shows a fairly high stability in the number of problems marked in each general area (rank order coefficient, .90), which supports the author's clinical judgment that changes in the data from a check list function to add greater clarity to patterns and progressions.

The lists do not purport to represent some internal capacity or trait or to make categorical predictions. They do purport to give students an opportunity to express their problems and provide assistance in understanding the problems expressed. The evidence indicates that students can and do express the problems included. The average number of problems marked by students in most groups is thirty; one-fourth checked forty or more. A group of one hundred students will mark about 95 per cent of the different problems in the list. No check list can present definitively all problems, and users of this as well as other check lists should bear that fact in mind.

The principal contribution of the check lists is to be found in the extent to which they increase the understanding of the problems marked by students. These markings can best be understood by clinical evidence. The general areas presented in the check lists are primarily descriptive and the extent to which causal analyses may result is dependent on the skill of the user. It is to be hoped that further research will indicate those syndromes which occur as "central tendencies" and the variations which are to be expected under different conditions. Marzolf and Larsen (15) have done a preliminary study which indicates the probability that syndromes may be identified and, by further clinical study, explained. The judgment of experts in the classification of problems into general areas is to be respected as a valuable tool too infrequently used, but it is believed that the increased precision which results from statistical analysis is essential for maximum interpretative value.

The manuals devote much space to the uses of the lists, and ingenious personnel workers and teachers will find additional uses. The following are illustrative with suggested limitations: (a) As a point of departure in the interview, a list may be used either before or during the conference. The list is a means of exploring students' problems and is not diagnostic. (b) As a survey instrument to facilitate a personnel program, students may mark a list to assist in locating personnel agencies, or agencies may examine marked lists to assist in locating students in need of their special services. (c) As an instrument for educational surveys, the lists may be used to assist in locating needed adjustments in the school offerings, dissatisfactions with teaching methods or administrative procedures and general conditions of student morale. Young (16) has shown how the check lists may be used to differentiate curricula within a single metropolitan area. (d) As an aid to classroom teachers, the lists may be used as a basis for revising course content and modifying teaching procedures to meet individual needs, and as an aid in fusing teaching, counseling, and personnel work. (e) As an aid in the training of teachers and personnel workers, the lists provide a means of sensitizing trainees to the wide range of problems presented by individual students and serve as a point of departure in the development of increased precision in the description of students'

problems. (f) As an aid to research workers, the lists furnish educators an additional means of determining the influence of specific educational programs on the problems of pupils. Psychologists will find the check lists valuable in the many types of analyses designed to determine the extent to which problems appear in conjunction and the significance of the various syndromes thus discovered.

As a paramount precaution to users, it should be emphasized that the check lists are not diagnostic instruments; rather they are descriptive and to some extent analytical. Their interpretation depends upon a pragmatic analysis, the accuracy of which will be limited by the training of the user. The interviewer or counselor probably will use about the same qualities in interpreting the lists as he uses in his everyday contacts with students. The lists have the advantage of filling a gap between the use of the more precise diagnostic instruments and the skill of a naïve counselor. This reviewer takes vigorous exception to the author's statement that technical training in testing, psychometrics, and complex statistical processes is not required for interpretation of results in an individual case. The lists will be helpful to teachers and personnel workers at all levels of training, but they will be of greatest value in the hands of those most highly trained.

Theodore F. Lentz, Director, Attitude Research Laboratory and Associate Professor of Education, Washington University, St. Louis, Missouri. [Review of College and High School Forms.] COLLEGE FORM. This check list consists of 330 items (such as: being overweight, too little money for clothes, awkward in meeting people, losing friends, losing my temper, being in love, parents' drinking, losing faith in religion, slow in reading, not interested in any vocation, having unfair tests) classifiable in eleven areas: (a) health and physical development; (b) finances, living conditions, and employment; (c) social and recreational activities; (d) social-psychological relations; (e) personal-psychological relations; (f) courtship, sex, and marriage; (g) home and family; (h) morals and religion; (i) adjustment to college work; (j) the future: vocational and educational; and (k) curriculum and teaching procedures.

"The form is similar to that of interest inventories except that the items are problems rather than interests. The student goes through the list, underlines the problems which are of concern to him, circles the ones of most concern, and writes a summary in his own words." "The function of the *Problem Check List* is to help students in the expression of their personal problems."

The manual presents an immense amount of simple arithmetic data regarding students' reactions—emotional reaction to the exercise, relative frequency of problems, sex differences, grade progression, etc.

The author recommends two major subdivisions of function: (*a*) aid to individual interview; and (*b*) group projects to furnish guidance for students, personnel agencies, administrators, teachers, and research workers. In this second major division, the administered list and tabulated results yield scores per item and per area regarding the group, class, or campus as a whole. There is no set score for the individual. The author reports 90 per cent of students reacting positively and favorably to the exercise. The results aimed at are suggestive and not definitive.

The discussions of reliability and validity are only partially satisfying to this reviewer. As the author implies, the validity of the instrument is difficult to ascertain, since this is in part a function of the interpreter. To quote, "The interpreter himself is in the midst of the process."

All criticisms that occur to this reviewer inhere in the unfinished nature of the instrument's research. The data presented are best conceived as a progress report.

More data will surely be forthcoming on (*a*) the validity and reliability of the responses of the individual, (*b*) the validity of the scores per item, and (*c*) the cluster factors among the items, on which intriguing beginnings are reported. Very little data are presented on the "practice effect" of the exercise. When full data are forthcoming on this point, the most valuable feature of the check list may appear. The above considerations, and many others that could be mentioned, argue inescapably for a special "Bureau of Standards" for educational psychology, backed by unlimited funds for research.

The reviewer knows of no alternative or comparable instrument designed for the same purpose. It seems to constitute a unique contribution to our counseling aids and techniques. It is an instrument for an area of research

which must not be overlooked. As it stands, the instrument is highly commendable to the serious practitioner of guidance or the research scientist in social psychology.

With wider use, further verification, and extension, this instrument should have real effectiveness in upholding the morale of the philosophy of those who entertain the permissive in guidance and the democratic in school design.

HIGH SCHOOL FORM. Practically everything said about the college form can be said about this form: number of items, form, administration, functions, voluminousness of the manual, large quantity of, as well as demand for, more data, and significance as a contribution to practice and research instrumentation.

A number of the items are different to suit the age difference between high school and college students.

[68]
★**Problem Check List: Form for Rural Young People.** 1946–47; an adaptation of *Problem Check Lists* by Ross L. Mooney; $1 per 20; no manual; nontimed (20-40) minutes; Ralph E. Bender; Ohio State University Press.

REFERENCES
1. BENDER, RALPH E. "The Development of a Problem Check List and a Demonstration of Its Use in Planning Rural Youth Programs." *Agric Ed Mag* 20:116-7 D '47. *
2. BENDER, RALPH E. *The Development of a Problem Check List and a Demonstration of Its Use in Planning Rural Youth Programs.* Unpublished doctor's thesis, Ohio State University, 1947.

[69]
★**Problem Check List: Form for Schools of Nursing.** Student nurses; 1945–47; an adaptation of *Problem Check List, College Form* by Ross L. Mooney; $1 per 20; no manual; nontimed (20-40) minutes; Luella J. Morison; Ohio State University Press.

REFERENCES
1. MORISON, LUELLA J. "A Problem Check List: Its Use in Student Guidance." *Am J Nursing* 47:248-51 Ap '47. *

[70]
★**Recreation Inquiry.** Grades 9-16; 1941; 1 form; $2.25 per 25; 35¢ per specimen set; nontimed (50) minutes; Richard Wilkinson and Sidney L. Pressey; Psychological Corporation.

REFERENCES
1. CAVANAUGH, JEAN OGDEN. "The Relation of Recreation to Personality Adjustment." *J Social Psychol* 15:63-74 F '42. * (PA 16:3159)
2. HADLEY, LOREN S. *A Study of the Leisure-Time Activity Patterns of Adults.* Unpublished doctor's thesis, Ohio State University, 1942. (*Abstracts of Dissertations . . . Summer Quarter 1941*, 1942, pp. 87-92.)

Theodore F. Lentz, Director, Attitude Research Laboratory, and Associate Professor of Education, Washington University, St. Louis, Missouri. This inquiry contains 183 recreational items, such as football, bridge, campfire girls, leather craft, scholastic team, athletic honor societies, dramatics, history, church, orchestra

—grouped under nine heads: sports, games, social, hobbies, honoraries, literary, subject clubs, religious, and music. For each item the subject indicates his knowledge, interest, membership, and participation. In addition he indicates frequency of participation in ten activities and the hours per month at reading, radio, and automobiling. Further he lists activities wherein he is a leader and makes a self-evaluation of his total recreational life.

The instrument has two functions: (a) survey—valuable for study and appraisal of institutions and communities—and (b) individual guidance. An exceedingly brief manual includes norms for each section of the test for high school seniors, college freshmen, and college seniors—300 cases each. Along with some other instruments of this sort, these norms (probably like norms for any other community) furnish excellent challenge in the contrast between interest on one hand and participation on the other.

The authors claim comprehensiveness for the list and state that this has been experimentally determined. The data for this are not presented. One questions the presence of eight items under the classification "religious" and none under the classification "civics or politics," with the possible exception of such items as "public speaking" and "bull sessions." This would seem to be either a reflection on the instrument or a contradiction of the assumption that man is a political as well as a religious animal. In common with most studies and instruments for study of recreation, the instrument leaves out taboo items which would make a study more accurate but the instrument nonusable in certain situations. In view of the large place of recreational reading in our lives, reading has probably been given too little space.

Most observers will not blame the authors as much as our culture for the small amount of data presented with the test. When will our society give human relations, including research on behalf of recreational guidance, adequate consideration?

Louis Long, Director of Division of Testing and Guidance and Assistant Professor, Department of Student Life, The City College of New York, New York, New York. The manual states that the purpose of the *Recreational Inquiry* "is to provide a ready means for surveying the recreational and social life of the stu-

dent and to obtain a broad basis for consideration of his recreational and social needs." Certainly, the list of recreational activities is exhaustive, and the plan of having the student indicate the extent of his participation on a four-point scale (knowledge, interest, membership, or now-active) is a good one. It would seem that the most effective use of the inquiry would be in an interview situation, since a rapid scanning of the responses would give a good picture of the recreational and social life of the person.

The authors suggest that the form can also be used with groups. The interpretation of the results in a group situation presents a real problem, since the same total score for two individuals may be subject to very different interpretations. The form should be useful in making systematic surveys of local campuses where the investigator is interested primarily in determining whether the school's socio-recreational program is adequately fulfilling the needs of the student body.

Separate norms (in terms of quartile ratings) are presented for men and women, and each group is further subdivided into high school seniors, college freshmen, and college seniors. Whether or not the authors found statistically significant differences between the means of these groups is not indicated, nor is the exact number of subjects stated. The only reference to the number of subjects examined is that the "tentative norms are based on about 300 cases for each class." No information about the reliability of the form is included.

[71]

Revision of the Babcock Examination for Measuring Efficiency of Mental Functioning. Ages 7 and over; 1940; a revision of *Babcock's Mental Deterioration Scale* (No. 37057.5); 1 form; $8.40 per test booklet and manual (No. 30758A); $2.30 per 25 record blanks (No. 37058R); 15¢ per *Color Naming Test:* Woodworth-Wells (No. 12309); $1.40 per *Cube Imitation Test:* Pintner (No. 33304); $1.10 per *Memory for Designs Test:* Army Performance Scale (No. 32317); nontimed (70+) minutes; Harriet Babcock and Lydia Levy; C. H. Stoelting Co.

REFERENCES

1-14. *See* 40:1248.
15. SHARP, AGNES A. "A Statistical Analysis of the Validity of the Babcock Test of Mental Deterioration." Abstract. *Psychol B* 36:508 Jl '39. * (*PA* 13:6290, title only)
16. YACORZYNSKI, G. K. "An Evaluation of the Postulates Underlying the Babcock Deterioration Test." Abstract. *Psychol B* 37:425-6 Jl '40. * (*PA* 14:6034, title only)
17. BABCOCK, HARRIET. "The Level-Efficiency Theory of Intelligence." *J Psychol* 11:261-70 Ap '41. * (*PA* 15:3305)
18. BABCOCK, HARRIET. *Time and the Mind: Personal Tempo—The Key to Normal and Pathological Mental Conditions.* Cambridge, Mass.: Sci-Art Publishers, 1941. Pp. 304. $3.75. * (*PA* 15:3651)
19. GILBERT, JEANNE G. "Memory Loss in Senescence." *J Abn & Social Psychol* 36:73-86 Ja '41. * (*PA* 15:2541)
20. RAUTMAN, ARTHUR L. "The Measurement of Deterioration in Mental Deficiency." *Am J Mental Def* 46:220-4 O '41. * (*PA* 16:1718)

21. YACORZYNSKI, G. K. "An Evaluation of the Postulates Underlying the Babcock Deterioration Test." *Psychol R* 48: 261-7 My '41. * (*PA* 15:3879)

22. BRODY, M. B. "The Measurement of Dementia." *J Mental Sci* 88:317-27 Ap '42. * (*PA* 16:3324)

23. BRODY, M. B. "A Psychometric Study of Dementia." *J Mental Sci* 88:512-33 O '42. * (*PA* 17:1178)

24. HAYMAN, MAX. "A Rapid Test for 'Deterioration' With Comparison of Three Techniques." *J General Psychol* 29:313-7 O '43. * (*PA* 18:1423)

25. KNIGHT, ROBERT P.; GILL, MERTON; LOZOFF, MILTON; AND RAPAPORT, DAVID. "Comparison of Clinical Findings and Psychological Tests in Three Cases Bearing Upon Military Personnel Selection." *B Menninger Clinic* 7:114-28 My '43. * (*PA* 17:4241)

26. GILBERT, JEANNE G. "Measuring Mental Efficiency in Senescence." Discussion by David Shakow. *Am J Orthopsychiatry* 14:267-71, discussion 271-2 Ap '44. * (*PA* 18:3104, title only)

27. RAPAPORT, DAVID; WITH THE COLLABORATION OF ROY SCHAFER AND MERTON GILL. "The Bellevue Scale," pp. 121-52. In their *Manual of Diagnostic Psychological Testing: I, Diagnostic Testing of Intelligence and Concept Formation.* Preface by Karl Menninger. Review Series, Vol. 2, No. 2. New York: Josiah Macy, Jr. Foundation, 1944. Pp. xiii, 239. Paper, lithotyped. Out of print. * (*PA* 19:3195)

28. SCHAFER, ROY. "The Significance of Scatter in Research and Practice of Clinical Psychology." *J Psychol* 18:119-24 Jl '44. * (*PA* 19:147)

29. SEIDENFELD, MORTON A. "Measuring Mental Competency in the Aging." Discussion by F. H. Finch. *Am J Orthopsychiatry* 14:273-5, discussion 275-6 Ap '44. * (*PA* 18:3104, title only)

30. HUNT, HOWARD F. "A Note on the Problem of Brain Damage in Rehabilitation and Personnel Work." *J Appl Psychol* 29:282-8 Ag '45. * (*PA* 20:154)

31. MAYMAN, MARTIN. "Review of the Literature on the Babcock Test," pp. 558-61. In *Diagnostic Psychological Testing: The Theory, Statistical Application and Diagnostic Application of a Battery of Tests, Vol. I.* By David Rapaport with the collaboration of Merton Gill and Roy Schafer. Chicago, Ill.: Year Book Publishers, Inc., 1945. Pp. xi, 573. $6.50. (*PA* 20: 929)

32. RAPAPORT, DAVID; WITH THE COLLABORATION OF MERTON GILL AND ROY SCHAFER. Chap. 3. "The Babcock Test," pp. 319-81, 523-32. In their *Diagnostic Psychological Testing: The Theory, Statistical Evaluation, and Diagnostic Application of a Battery of Tests, Vol. I.* Chicago, Ill.: Year Book Publishers, Inc., 1945. Pp. xi, 573. $6.50. (*PA* 20:929)

33. SHOORE, AUDREY B. *A Study of Performance on the Babcock Test of a Group of Selected Manic Depressive Patients, Before and After Electric Shock.* Unpublished master's thesis, University of Iowa, 1945.

34. LANDISBERG, SELMA. "A Personality Study of Institutionalized Epileptics." *Am J Mental Def* 52:16-22 Jl '47. *

35. RABIN, ALBERT I. "Vocabulary and Efficiency Levels as Functions of Age in the Babcock Method." *J Consult Psychol* 11:207-11 Jl-Ag '47. * (*PA* 22:203)

For related reviews, see 72.

[72]

★[*Re* Revision of the Babcock Examination for Measuring Efficiency of Mental Functioning.] BABCOCK, HARRIET. **Time and the Mind: Personal Tempo—The Key to Normal and Pathological Mental Conditions.** Cambridge, Mass.: Sci-Art Publishers, 1941. Pp. 304. $3.75. * (*PA* 15:3651)

J Abn & Social Psychol 37:284–5 Ap '42. G. K. Yacorzynski. * Babcock's level-efficiency theory of mental functions has more promise and is an indication of more mature thinking than the theory which she used to explain the results of her first deterioration scale. Formerly she held that vocabulary remains unimpaired in cases of deterioration since it is an old habit, whereas recently acquired material or new associations (measured by the tests which are now purported to yield efficiency scores) deteriorate. With the author's emphasis on the time of mental functioning, and in contrast to her former deterioration scale, all the tests which are used at present to measure efficiency are timed. The author still maintains, however, that the primary value of using a vocabulary test to measure level is that "it draws on old, well-fixed learning which was acquired spontaneously because of natural interest and understanding" (p. 75), whereas, "Other reasons for its use are the fact that the responses do not depend upon time . . ." (p. 75). As a consequence the author devotes a great deal of space to the discussion of the disintegration of old and recently acquired materials. The reviewer feels that, as was true of the theoretical interpretation published in the first deterioration scale, Babcock has been interested in using many subjects and test items in order to standardize the procedure rather than attempting to analyze the mechanisms which are affected in deterioration. The author's theory is an addendum to the standardization of the test rather than the central core of her problem. This, of course, reflects the author's viewpoint embodied in the statement that, "Work in psychology . . . must be guided more than much of it has been by some utilitarian value . . ." (p. 241). The author's exposition suffers from the fact that there is little continuity in the presentation of the subject-matter and in the space of a few pages a number of unrelated topics may be discussed. Furthermore, the book is replete with analyses and statements which the reader will find very irritating. Some of these are: (1) Superficial categories such as, for example, dividing the "dimensions of the mind" into sensory discrimination, memory, level of intelligence, and mental tempo. Categories of this nature are used throughout the book in spite of the author's statement in the introductory chapters that the organism should be studied as a whole. (2) Use of mentalistic concepts, such as "psychic," without proper definitions. (3) Describing the cerebral cortex as an instinctive organ. (4) Emphasizing self-evident statements such as suggesting that psychology should use "scientific psychological analysis" (original italicized, p. 26), as if this is not an accepted truism in psychology; or that, "The human mind does not function without a human body" (p. 213), should be accepted as an axiom in psychology. (5) In the light of the present knowledge of frustration exactly the opposite may be held to the statement that, "When there is no expectation of sex gratification until a definite age or until marriage, sex is not so dominatingly forceful except for chance experience, and neuroses and other untoward manifestations of behavior are not apt to develop" (p. 258). (6) The fact that, "Correlations of the total efficiency score with mental level were higher than those which measure different phases of mental functioning" (p. 148), may mean that the reliability of parts of a test are lower than that of the whole test, rather than the interpretation given by the author that, "From this it is evident that the relation of the different phases to each other and the way in which different parts of mental process function together are of greater significance than either the total score or the different phases considered separately" (original italicized, p. 148). The above considerations vitiate the probability that an important theoretical contribution is made to the understanding of mental functions. The book also is not a manual for the revised form of the Babcock deterioration scale.

J Consult Psychol 6:270–2 S-O '42. Irving Lorge. * Operationally, the test, in its clumsy way, will yield a variety of patterns, and will yield a differential between level and efficiency which may be characterized as an efficiency index. But, such a function could be achieved by better tests better organized. It seems strange that with all the criticism of the mental age unit as applied to adults that Dr. Babcock has clung to it. Since Balinsky has shown that the factor pattern of the Bellevue–Wechsler at different ages lacks consistency, and since Jones and Conrad have shown that different subtests of the Army Alpha make different contributions to the total score at different ages, and since Lorge has shown the differential aspect of speed of performance in older ages, it seems strange that Dr. Babcock naively assumes that normal functioning should be appraised in terms of the performance of a group younger than 25 years. The contributions of speed, and of the various abilities measured will be different, particularly for persons aged 30 to 70. Certainly, in terms of the explicit statement "The only meaning to be attached to each test is what actually is done and what can be logically inferred from its relations to other results," Dr. Babcock's test must be criticized explicitly for at least two defects. The first is the failure to appreciate the relations of the test results to age, and second, the failure to show the intercorrelations among each of the

tests for the normal group at least. While Dr. Babcock looks askance on statistics, she does use them to make her point. She certainly had an obligation to show in how far the tests were measuring *validly* and *reliably* the performances she thinks are diagnostic of mental efficiency. * All in all, as a test to estimate mental efficiency, the Babcock–Levy examination will yield an estimate of mental functioning. It does so, however, despite the standardization of the selected tests, and at the expense of forcing a notion of intelligence which by this time might be more critically appraised. Vocabulary is not necessarily a measure of level or of older learning. * Dr. Babcock's notion that level of mental ability can be appraised by vocabulary, and that level of mental efficiency can be appraised by a battery of short, acceptable tests does not materially advance knowledge of intelligence or of its measurement. It, as a notion, suffers from the single score approach, particularly in assaying intellectual level, but just as specifically in estimating intellectual efficiency independent of age changes. In assaying intellectual or behavior deviates, the pattern approach might well be utilized, but it must be remembered that patterns need to be developed from very reliable tests, correlating rather low among each other. The task of reviewing Dr. Babcock's contributions has been made somewhat more burdensome by the lack of editorial supervision given her text. Terms, concepts, and definitions tend to get mixed up; table headings are ambiguous, and some of the tables of data do not check out. Dr. Babcock's contribution to psychology may be appraised incorrectly because of a lack of clarity in its presentation.

Psychol B 39:193 Mr '42. Arthur L. Benton. This book might well be considered as two books. "Book I" consists of the presentation.... of a revision of her well-known test battery * The revised test battery and the author's discussion of its applications will be of considerable interest not only to psychologists who are working with neurological and psychiatric material but also to those who are engaged in educational work and in vocational and personal counseling. "Book II" consists of the presentation of the author's opinions concerning a variety of psychological topics. Some of the section headings are: "Omissions in the Education of Academic Psychologists"; "Lack of Breadth in the Education of Leaders in Pathological Psychology"; "Sex and Education";

"Gestalt Psychology"; "Obstacles the Sustenance of Developing Character." As can be seen from even this meager sampling, much ground is covered.

Psychiatric Q 15:835–6 O '41. * [The author states,] "The praecox defect is usually constitutional," i.e., the patient is one of the damned. In speaking of borderland conditions, on the same page, she states, "It is a general mental weakness undoubtedly due to a neurological or somatic condition . . ." The use of words like "undoubtedly" is hardly permissible in science, and is entirely out of place in discussing the relationships of the psyche and soma, in the present state of our knowledge. If the facts are thus and so, an "undoubtedly" will not make them any more true. If they are not thus and so, an "undoubtedly" is subversive propaganda. Aside from her gratuitous remarks about the basic nature of mental illness, the author seems to have written a sound report concerning the results of the application of various batteries of tests to various groups of people, and to have reached sufficiently amiable conclusions as to their parolability, employability, etc., on the basis of these tests. Thus far, the report is useful, stimulating, and practical. However, having found that mental malfunctioning is almost uniformly associated with disturbances of mental tempo, which can be measured, the author seizes on this attribute of maladjustment and makes it the cause of maladjustment. That kind of thinking has led to great mistakes in the past, one example of which was national prohibition. Dr. Babcock has probably started something. There is a market for the exposition of any method which will attempt to settle psychiatric questions numerically or graphically. It saves thinking and shifts responsibility. Furthermore, research in mental tempo should serve to keep large numbers of students inoffensively occupied. They will not get any wrong ideas from "Time and the Mind." In a book which purports to be "The Key to Normal and Pathological Mental Conditions," there are two pages devoted, half-heartedly, to sex. On one of these (p. 258), there appear some remarkable statements. "The importance of sex has been well recognized since the dawn of history as is shown by the numerous taboos and customs, which seem to have been an intelligent way of handling the problem. People adjust to different customs because of unconscious acceptance of the right-

ness of the ideas inculcated by their society. These ideas preclude expectation and lessen mental stimulation to the sex impulse." The reviewer rests.

[73]

Rorschach. Ages 3 and over; 1921 to date; also commonly referred to as Rorschach Method, Rorschach Test, Rorschach Ink Blot Test, Rorschach Psychodiagnostics, and Rorschach Method of Psychodiagnosis; many variants have appeared such as Harrower-Erickson's Group Rorschach, Harrower-Erickson's Multiple-Choice Test, Monroe's Inspection Technique, Grassi's Graphic Rorschach, and Marseille Rorschach Mail Interview; many modifications of the variants are in use such as the Amplified Multiple-Choice Rorschach and the Ranking Rorschach Test; in addition to the Rorschach original Psychodiagnostic Plates, parallel plates have been prepared by Zulliger and Harrower and Steiner; Hermann Rorschach.

a) PSYCHODIAGNOSTIC PLATES, FOURTH EDITION. 1921-45; $6 per set of 10 cards mounted on heavy cardboard; $3 per pad of 100 record blanks; $5.75 per copy of the 1946 English translation of Rorschach's *Psychodiagnostics, Second Edition;* Hermann Rorschach; Grune & Stratton, Inc.

b) BEHN-RORSCHACH TEST. 1942; a parallel set of ink blots; $6 per set of 10 cards; $4 per manual; Hans Zulliger; Grune & Stratton, Inc.

c) PSYCHODIAGNOSTIC INKBLOTS. 1945; a parallel set of ink blots; $4.50 per set of 10 cards; $2 per manual; M. R. Harrower and M. E. Steiner; Grune & Stratton, Inc. (These ink blots on slides for use with standard projectors are distributed by Psychological Corporation at $20 per set, postpaid.)

d) HARROWER-ERICKSON'S GROUP RORSCHACH. Ages 12 and over; 1941-45; $8.50 per manual, *Large Scale Rorschach Technique* (published by Charles C. Thomas), postpaid; $20 per set of Rorschach ink blots on slides for standard projector, postpaid; $10.50 per set of ink blots on Kodaslides, postpaid; $3.75 per 25 record blanks, postpaid; (75-90) minutes; M. R. Harrower-Erickson and M. E. Steiner; distributed by Psychological Corporation.

e) HARROWER-ERICKSON'S MULTIPLE CHOICE TEST. Ages 12 and over; 1943-45; same manual and slides as for Harrower-Erickson's Group Rorschach; $1.75 per 25, postpaid; 30¢ per specimen set, postpaid; (45) minutes; M. R. Harrower-Erickson and M. E. Steiner; distributed by Psychological Corporation.

f) RORSCHACH METHOD OF PERSONALITY DIAGNOSIS. 1939-42; $1.50 per 25 record blanks; $3.50 per pad of 100 picture sheets; Bruno Klopfer and Helen H. Davidson; World Book Co.

g) MARSEILLE RORSCHACH MAIL INTERVIEW. Applicants for employment; 1945; $1 per booklet; Walter W. Marseille; the Author, 2145 California St., San Francisco 15, California.

REFERENCES

1-147. See 40:1246.
148. HERTZ, MARGUERITE R. *Concerning the Reliability and the Validity of the Rorschach Ink-Blot Test.* Unpublished doctor's thesis, Western Reserve University, 1932.
149. BLEULER, M. "The Delimitation of Influences of Environment and Heredity in Mental Disposition." *Char & Pers* 1:286-300 Je '33. * (PA 7:5198)
150. MELTZER, H. "Personality Differences Between Stuttering and Non-Stuttering Children as Indicated by the Rorschach Test." Abstract. *Psychol B* 30:726-7 N '33. * (PA 8:3659, title only)
151. BECK, S. J. "Psychological Processes, and Traits, in Rorschach Findings." Abstract. *Psychol B* 32:683-4 N '35. * (PA 10:1218, title only)
152. SHIENTAG, ISABEL. *A Study of Individual Responses in the Kent-Rosanoff and Rorschach Tests.* Unpublished master's thesis, Columbia University, 1935.

153. THORNTON, GEORGE RUSSELL. *The Erlebnistypus Factors in the Rorschach Test.* Unpublished master's thesis, University of Nebraska, 1935.

154. PIOTROWSKI, ZYGMUNT. "The Rorschach Method of Personality Analysis in Organic Psychoses." Abstract. *Psychol B* 33:795 N '36. * (*PA* 10:1336, title only)

155. NADEL, AARON B. "Rorschach Personality Studies Before and After Operation for Brain Tumor." Abstract. *Psychol B* 34:523-4 O '37. * (*PA* 12:355, title only)

156. WHITE, RALPH KIRBY. *A Factor Analysis of Tests Designed to Measure Fluency, Atypicality, and Intellectual Curiosity.* Unpublished doctor's thesis, Stanford University, 1937. (*Abstracts of Dissertations . . . 1936–37*, 1937, pp. 159-62.)

157. HUNTER, MARY. *A Study of the Rorschach Erlebnistypus of Comparable White and Negro Groups.* Unpublished doctor's thesis, Columbia University, 1938.

158. NADEL, AARON B. *A Qualitative Analysis of Behavior Following Cerebral Lesions Diagnosed as Primarily Affecting the Frontal Lobes.* Archives of Psychology, No. 224. Washington, D. C.: American Psychological Association, Inc., April 1938. Pp. 60. Paper. $1.00. * (*PA* 13:83)

159. STROBEL, MILDRED. *A Historical and Critical Survey of the Rorschach Tests.* Unpublished master's thesis, Columbia University, 1938.

160. DUNMIRE, HARRIETT. "An Evaluation of Beck's Norms as Applied to Young Children." Abstract. *Psychol B* 36:629 O '39. * (*PA* 14:608, title only)

161. KLOPFER, BRUNO. "The Interplay Between Intellectual and Emotional Factors in Personality Diagnosis," pp. 41-7. In *Progress of Scientific Research in the Field of the Exceptional Child: Proceedings of the Sixth Institute on the Exceptional Child of the Child Research Clinic of the Woods Schools.* Langhorne, Pa.: Woods Schools, October 1939. Pp. 62. Paper. *

162. KLOPFER, BRUNO. "Personality Differences Between Boys and Girls in Early Childhood." Abstract. *Psychol B* 36: 538 Jl '39. *

163. KRAFFT, MARGARET ROSENBERG. *Value of the Rorschach Test to Case Work.* Unpublished master's thesis, Smith College, 1939.

164. ARLUCK, EDWARD W. "A Study of Some Personality Differences Between Epileptics and Normals." *Rorschach Res Exch* 4:154-6 O '40. * (*PA* 15:1730)

165. BAKER, ELIZABETH. *Some Adolescent Personality Patterns as Revealed by the Rorschach Method.* Unpublished master's thesis, Western Reserve University, 1940. Pp. 134.

166. BARRERA, S. EUGENE. "Introductory Remarks to the Panel Discussion on Personality Studies in the Convulsive States." *Rorschach Res Exch* 4:152-3 O '40. *

167. BECK, S. J. "Sources of Error in Rorschach Test Procedures." Abstract. *Psychol B* 37:516-17 Jl '40. * (*PA* 14:5579, title only)

168. BIGELOW, R. BARRY. "The Evaluation of Aptitude for Flight Training: The Rorschach Method as a Possible Aid." *J Aviat Med* 11:202-9 D '40. * (*PA* 15:3102)

169. DAY, FRANKLIN; HARTOCH, ANNA; AND SCHACHTEL, ERNEST. "A Rorschach Study of a Defective Delinquent." *J Crim Psychopath* 2:62-79 Jl '40. * (*PA* 14:5653)

170. ENDACOTT, JOHN LAWRENCE. *The Rorschach Test and Juvenile Delinquency: A Sociopsychobiological Approach.* Unpublished master's thesis, University of Kansas, 1940. Pp. 139.

171. FOSBERG, IRVING ARTHUR. *An Experimental Study of the Reliability of the Rorschach Psychodiagnostic Technique.* Unpublished doctor's thesis, New York University, 1940.

172. HALPERN, FLORENCE. "Rorschach Interpretation of the Personality Structure of Schizophrenics Who Benefit From Insulin Therapy." *Psychiatric Q* 14:826-33 O '40. * (*PA* 15:2204)

173. HERTZ, MARGUERITE R. "Some Personality Changes in Adolescence as Revealed by the Rorschach Method." Abstract. *Psychol B* 37:515-6 Jl '40. * (*PA* 14:5587, title only)

174. HUNT, THELMA. "The Application of the Rorschach Test and a Word-Association Test to Patients Undergoing Prefrontal Lobotomy." Abstract. *Psychol B* 37:546 Jl '40. * (*PA* 15:266, title only)

175. JASTAK, JOSEPH. "Rorschach Performances of Alcoholic Patients." *Delaware State Med J* 12:120-3 My '40. * (*PA* 14:5993)

176. KELLEY, DOUGLAS M., AND LEVINE, KATE. "Rorschach Studies During Sodium Amytal Narcoses." Abstract. *Rorschach Res Exch* 4:146 O '40. *

177. KELLEY, DOUGLAS M., AND MARGULIES, HELEN. "Rorschach Case Studies in the Convulsive States." *Rorschach Res Exch* 4:157-90 O '40. * (*PA* 15:1772)

178. KRUGMAN, MORRIS. "Out of the Ink Well: The Rorschach Method." *Rorschach Res Exch* 4:91-101 Jl '40. * Same *Char & Pers* 9:91-110 D '40. * (*PA* 15:2267)

179. OBERHOLZER, EMIL. "The Rorschach Experiment." Abstract. *Arch Neurol & Psychiatry* 44:916-9 O '40. *

180. PIOTROWSKI, ZYGMUNT. "Positive and Negative Rorschach Organic Reactions." *Rorschach Res Exch* 4:147-51 O '40. *

181. PIOTROWSKI, ZYGMUNT. "A Simple Experimental Device for the Prediction of Outcome of Insulin Treatment in Schizophrenia." *Psychiatric Q* 14:267-73 Ap '40. * (*PA* 15:2239)

182. PIOTROWSKI, ZYGMUNT A., AND KELLEY, DOUGLAS M. "Application of the Rorschach Method in an Epileptic Case With Psychoneurotic Manifestations." *J Nerv & Mental Dis* 92:743-51 D '40. * (*PA* 15:1363)

183. ROBB, R. W.; KOVITZ, B.; AND RAPAPORT, D. "Histamine in the Treatment of Psychosis: A Psychiatric and Objective Psychological Study." *Am J Psychiatry* 97:601-10 N '40. * (*PA* 15:2631)

184. ROSS, W. D. "Anatomical Perseveration in Rorschach Records." *Rorschach Res Exch* 4:138-45 O '40. *

185. WILLIAMS, MARY GOSHORN. *Growth of Perception in Children as Revealed in Responses to the Rorschach Cards.* Unpublished master's thesis, University of Kansas, 1940. Pp. 54.

186. ARLUCK, EDWARD WILTCHER. Chap. 4, "Rorschach Test Results," pp. 33-49. In his *A Study of Some Personality Characteristics of Epileptics.* Archives of Psychology, No. 263. Washington, D. C.: American Psychological Association, Inc., July 1941. Pp. 77. Paper. $1.25. * (*PA* 16:1476)

187. BAKER, ELIZABETH. "Personality Changes in Adolescence as Revealed by the Rorschach Method." Abstract. *Psychol B* 38:705 O '41. * (*PA* 16:372, title only)

188. BENTON, ARTHUR L., AND HOWELL, IRA L. "The Use of Psychological Tests in the Evaluation of Intellectual Function Following Head Injury: Report of a Case of Post-Traumatic Personality Disorder." *Psychosom Med* 3:138-51 Ap '41. * (*PA* 15:4206)

189. CLARDY, E. R.; GOLDENSOHN, L. N.; AND LEVINE, KATE. "Schizophrenic-Like Reactions in Children: Preliminary Report: Studies by Electroencephalography, Pneumoencephalography and Psychological Tests." *Psychiatric Q* 15:100-16 Ja '41. * (*PA* 16:3569)

190. EARL, C. J. "A Note on the Validity of Certain Rorschach Symbols." *Rorschach Res Exch* 5:51-61 Ap '41. * (*PA* 15:3408)

191. ENDACOTT, JOHN L. "The Results of 100 Male Juvenile Delinquents on the Rorschach Ink Blot Test." *J Crim Psychopath* 3:41-50 Jl '41. * (*PA* 16:295)

192. FLEISCHER, RICHARD O., AND HUNT, J. McVICKER. "A Communicable Method of Recording Answers in the Rorschach Test." *Am J Psychol* 54:580-2 O '41. * (*PA* 16:1043, title only)

193. FOSBERG, IRVING ARTHUR. "An Experimental Study of the Reliability of the Rorschach Psychodiagnostic Technique." *Rorschach Res Exch* 5:72-84 Ap '41. * (*PA* 15:3470)

194. HALLOWELL, A. I. "The Rorschach Test as a Tool for Investigating Cultural Variables and Individual Differences in the Study of Personality in Primitive Societies." *Rorschach Res Exch* 5:31-4 Ja '41. * (*PA* 15:2264)

195. HALLOWELL, A. IRVING. "The Rorschach Method as an Aid in the Study of Personalities in Primitive Societies." *Char & Pers* 9:235-45 Mr '41. * (*PA* 15:3471)

196. HANFMANN, EUGENIA. "A Study of Personal Patterns in an Intellectual Performance." *Char & Pers* 9:315-25 Je '41. * (*PA* 15:4277)

197. HARROWER-ERICKSON, M. R. "Directions for Administration of the Rorschach Group-Test." *Rorschach Res Exch* 5: 145-53 Jl '41. * (*PA* 15:5212)

198. HARROWER-ERICKSON, M. R. "The Patient and His Personality: A Short Discussion of the Rorschach Method of Personality Evaluation and Its Use in Clinical Medicine." *McGill Med J* 11:25-40 O '41. * (*PA* 19:2608)

199. HARROWER-ERICKSON, M. R., AND STEINER, M. E. "Modification of the Rorschach Method for Use as a Group Test." *Rorschach Res Exch* 5:130-44 Jl '41. * (*PA* 15:5211)

200. HARROWER-ERICKSON, M. R.; WITH THE COLLABORATION OF F. R. MIALE. "Personality Changes Accompanying Organic Brain Lesions: III, A Study of Preadolescent Children." *J Genetic Psychol* 58:391-405 Je '41. * (*PA* 16:194)

201. HENRY, JULES. "Rorschach Technique in Primitive Cultures." *Am J Orthopsychiatry* 11:230-4 Ap '41. * (*PA* 15:3911)

202. HERTZ, MARGUERITE R. "Evaluation of the Rorschach Method in Its Application to Normal Childhood and Adolescence." *Char & Pers* 10:151-62 D '41. * (*PA* 16:2923)

203. HERTZ, MARGUERITE R. "Personality Changes in 35 Girls in Various Stages of Pubescent Development Based on the Rorschach Method." Abstract. *Psychol B* 38:705 O '41. * (*PA* 16:382, title only)

204. HERTZ, MARGUERITE R. "Pubescence and Personality." Abstract. *Psychol B* 38:598 Jl '41. * (*PA* 15:5424, title only)

205. HERTZ, MARGUERITE R. "Rorschach: Twenty Years After." *Rorschach Res Exch* 5:90-129 Jl '41. * (*PA* 15:5214)

206. HERTZ, MARGUERITE R. "Validity of the Rorschach Method." *Am J Orthopsychiatry* 11:512-9 Jl '41. * (*PA* 15:5213)

207. HERTZ, MARGUERITE, AND BAKER, ELIZABETH. "Personality Changes in Adolescence." Abstract. *Rorschach Res Exch* 5:30 Ja '41. * (*PA* 15:2413, title only)

208. HOLZMAN, GEORGE G., AND HOLZMAN, EVELYN E. "An Evaluation of Personality Analysis in the General Practice of Medicine." *Rorschach Res Exch* 5:67-71 Ap '41. * (*PA* 15:3423)

209. KELLEY, DOUGLAS M. "The Rorschach Method as a Means for the Determination of the Impairment of Abstract Behavior." *Rorschach Res Exch* 5:85-8 Ap '41. * (*PA* 15:3436)

210. KELLEY, DOUGLAS McG. "A Questionnaire for the Study and Possible Standardization of the Technique of the Rorschach Method." *Rorschach Res Exch* 5:62-6 Ap '41. * (*PA* 15:3473, title only)

211. KELLEY, DOUGLAS McG., AND BARRERA, S. EUGENE. "The Rorschach Method in the Study of Mental Deficiency: A Resumé." *Am J Mental Def* 45:401-7 Ja '41. * (*PA* 15:3437)

212. KELLEY, DOUGLAS McG., AND BARRERA, S. EUGENE. "Rorschach Studies in Acute Experimental Alcoholic Intoxication." *Am J Psychiatry* 97:1341-64 My '41. * (*PA* 16:1426)

213. KELLEY, DOUGLAS M.; LEVINE, KATE; PEMBERTON, WILLIAM; AND LILLIAN, KATZ K. "Intravenous Sodium Amytal Medication as an Aid to the Rorschach Method." *Psychiatric Q* 15:68-73 Ja '41. * (*PA* 16:3649)

214. KELLEY, DOUGLAS McG.; MARGULIES, HELEN; AND BARRERA, S. EUGENE. "The Stability of the Rorschach Method as Demonstrated in Electric Convulsive Therapy Cases." *Rorschach Res Exch* 5:35-43 Ja '41. * (*PA* 15:2217)

215. KISKER, GEORGE W., AND MICHAEL, NICHOLAS. "A Rorschach Study of Psychotic Personality in Uniovular Twins." *J Nerv & Mental Dis* 94:461-5 O '41. * (*PA* 16:203)

216. KLOPFER, BRUNO, AND MARGULIES, HELEN; WITH CONTRIBUTIONS BY LOIS B. MURPHY AND L. J. STONE. "Rorschach Reactions in Early Childhood, Part One." *Rorschach Res Exch* 5:1-23 Ja '41. * (*PA* 15:2417)

217. KRUGMAN, JUDITH I. *A Clinical Validation of the Rorschach Ink Blot Test as a Measure of Personality of Problem Children.* Unpublished doctor's thesis, New York University, 1941. Pp. 238. (*Abstracts of Theses . . . [School of Education] 1941*, pp. 141-4.)

218. KRUGMAN, MORRIS. "Rorschach Examination in a Child Guidance Clinic." *Am J Orthopsychiatry* 11:503-11 Jl '41. * (*PA* 15:5430)

219. MUNROE, RUTH. "Inspection Technique: A Modification of the Rorschach Method of Personality Diagnosis for Large Scale Application." *Rorschach Res Exch* 5:166-90 O '41. * (*PA* 16:1047)

220. MYERS, M. CLAIRE. "The Rorschach Method." Abstract. *Psychol B* 38:748-9 O '41. * (*PA* 16:649, title only)

221. PAULSEN, ALMA. "Rorschachs of School Beginners." *Rorschach Res Exch* 5:24-9 Ja '41. * (*PA* 15:2421)

222. PESCOR, M. J. "A Further Study of the Rorschach Test Applied to Delinquents." *Pub Health Reports* 56:381-95 F 28 '41. * (*PA* 15:3546)

223. PIOTROWSKI, ZYGMUNT A. "The Rorschach Method as a Prognostic Aid in the Insulin Shock Treatment of Schizophrenics." *Psychiatric Q* 15:807-22 O '41. * (*PA* 16:3617)

224. PORTEUS, STANLEY D.; WITH THE ASSISTANCE OF MARY HUNTER AND COLIN J. HERRICK. *The Practice of Clinical Psychology*, pp. 217-26. New York: American Book Co., 1941. Pp. ix, 579. $3.25. * (*PA* 15:4248)

225. ROSS, W. DONALD. "The Contribution of the Rorschach Method to Clinical Diagnosis." *J Mental Sci* 87:331-48 Jl '41. * (*PA* 15:4690)

226. RUESCH, JURGEN, AND FINESINGER, JACOB E. "The Relation of the Rorschach Color Response to the Use of Color in Drawings." *Psychosom Med* 3:370-88 O '41. * (*PA* 16:1959)

227. SCHACHTEL, ERNEST. "The Dynamic Perception and the Symbolism of Form: With Special Reference to the Rorschach Test." *Psychiatry* 4:79-96 F '41. * (*PA* 15:3479)

228. STAINBROOK, EDWARD J. "A Modified Rorschach Technique for the Description of Transitory Post-Convulsive Personality States." *Rorschach Res Exch* 5:192-203 O '41. * (*PA* 16:1026)

229. URBAITIS, JOHN C., AND WATERMAN, JOHN. "Application of the Rorschach Test to Practice in Mental Disease Hospitals." Abstract. *Arch Neurol & Psychiatry* 45:383-5 F '41. * (*PA* 16:3636, title only)

230. VARVEL, WALTER A. "The Rorschach Test in Psychotic and Neurotic Depressions." *B Menninger Clinic* 5:5-12 Ja '41. * (*PA* 15:2252)

231. VARVEL, WALTER A. "The Rorschach Test in Relation to Perceptual Organization and to Intelligence." Abstract. *Psychol B* 38:705 O '41. * (*PA* 16:238, title only)

232. WEIL, ANDRE A. "The Rorschach Test in Diagnosis of Psychoses and Psychoneuroses." *J Maine Med Assn* 32:35-9 F '41. * (*PA* 16:1555)

233. WILSON, MARGARET T. "Mental Ages and Social Ages of Normal and Defective Twins and Siblings." *Am J Mental Def* 45:374-9 Ja '41. * (*PA* 15:3648)

234. WOOD, AUSTIN; ARLUCK, EDWARD; AND MARGULIES, HELEN; COMPILERS. "Report of a Group Discussion of the Rorschach Method: Held Under the Auspices of the Josiah Macy, Jr. Foundation, April 19-20, 1941, New York City." *Rorschach Res Exch* 5:154-65 Jl '41. * (*PA* 15:5231)

235. ZUBIN, JOSEPH. "A Psychometric Approach to the Evaluation of the Rorschach Test." *Psychiatry* 4:547-66 N '41. * (*PA* 16:1580)

236. ZUBIN, JOSEPH. "A Quantitative Approach to Measuring Regularity of Succession in the Rorschach Experiment." *Char & Pers* 10:67-78 S '41. * (*PA* 16:1049)

236a. ZULLIGER, HANS. *Einführung in den Behn-Rorschach Test.* Berne, Switzerland: Verlag Hans Huber, 1941. Pp. 232. (New York: Grune & Stratton, Inc., 1942. $4.00. Accompanying plates, $6.00.) (*PA* 15:5232)

237. BECK, S. J. "Error, Symbol, and Method in the Rorschach Test." *J Abn & Social Psychol* 37:83-103 Ja '42. * (*PA* 16:2718)

238. BECK, S. J. "Stability of the Personality Structure." Abstract. *Psychol B* 39:512 Jl '42. * (*PA* 16:4863, title only)

239. BILLIG, OTTO, AND SULLIVAN, D. J. "Prognostic Data in Chronic Alcoholism." *Rorschach Res Exch* 6:117-25 Jl '42. * (*PA* 16:4788)

240. BOCHNER, RUTH, AND HALPERN, FLORENCE. *The Clinical Application of the Rorschach Test.* Introduction by Karl M. Bowman, New York: Grune & Stratton, Inc., 1942. Pp. x, 217. * (*PA* 16:2315) For latest edition, *see* (418) below

241. BROSIN, HENRY W., AND FROMM, E. "Some Principles of Gestalt Psychology in the Rorschach Experiment." *Rorschach Res Exch* 6:1-15 Ja '42. * (*PA* 16:2723)

242. BROWN, RALPH R. "The Effect of Morphine Upon the Rorschach Pattern in Post-Addicts." Abstract. *Psychol B* 39:512-3 Jl '42. * (*PA* 16:4735, title only)

243. BRUSSEL, JAMES A.; GRASSI, JOSEPH R.; AND MELNIKER, AARON A. "The Rorschach Method and Postconcussion Syndrome." *Psychiatric Q* 16:707-43 O '42. * (*PA* 17:537)

244. BRUSSEL, JAMES A., AND HITCH, KENNETH S. "The Rorschach Method and Its Uses in Military Psychiatry." *Psychiatric Q* 16:3-29 Ja '42. * (*PA* 16:3564)

245. CAMERON, DALE C. "The Rorschach Experiment—X-Ray of Personality." *Dis Nerv Sys* 3:374-6 N '42. * (*PA* 17:588)

246. COOK, P. H. "The Application of the Rorschach Test to a Samoan Group." *Rorschach Res Exch* 6:51-60 Ap '42. * (*PA* 16:4091)

247. COOK, P. H. "Mental Structure and the Psychological Field: Some Samoan Observations." *Char & Pers* 10:296-308 Je '42. * (*PA* 17:224)

248. DU BOIS, CORA, AND OBERHOLZER, EMIL. "Rorschach Tests and Native Personality in Alor, Dutch East Indies." *Trans N Y Acad Sci* 4:168-70 Mr '42. * (*PA* 16:2724)

249. FUNKHOUSER, JAMES B., AND KELLEY, DOUGLAS M. "The Rorschach Ink Blot Method." *Virginia Med Mo* 69:139-44 Mr '42. * (*PA* 16:3161)

250. GOLDFARB, WILLIAM. "Personality Trends in a Group of Enuretic Children Below the Age of Ten." *Rorschach Res Exch* 6:28-38 Ja '42. * (*PA* 16:2920)

251. GRASSI, JOSEPH R. "Contrasting Schizophrenic Patterns in the Graphic Rorschach." *Psychiatric Q* 16:646-59 O '42. * (*PA* 17:546)

252. HALLOWELL, A. I. "Acculturation Processes and Personality Changes as Indicated by the Rorschach Technique." *Rorschach Res Exch* 6:42-50 Ap '42. * (*PA* 16:4097)

253. HARROWER, GEORGE J. "Medical Technologists Group Personality Estimate." *Can J Med Tech* 4:177-8 D '42. * (*PA* 17:1625)

254. HARROWER, GEORGE J. "Personality Diagnosis and the Medical Technician." *Can J Med Tech* 4:34-7 Mr '42. *

255. HARROWER, GEORGE J., AND COX, KENNETH J. "The Results Obtained From a Number of Occupational Groupings on the Professional Level With the Rorschach Group Method." Abstract. *B Can Psychol Assn* 2:31-3 D '42. * (*PA* 17:1720, title only)

256. HARROWER-ERICKSON, M. R. "Group-Test Techniques: A Discussion of 'An Eclectic Group Method'." *Rorschach Res Exch* 6:147-52 O '42. * (*PA* 17:882)

257. HARROWER-ERICKSON, M. R. "The Value and Limitations of the So-Called 'Neurotic Signs'." *Rorschach Res Exch* 6:109-14 Jl '42. * (*PA* 16:4807)

258. HARTOG, ANNA, AND SCHACHTEL, ERNEST. "The Rorschach Test," pp. 377-408. In *Child Life in School: A Study of a Seven-Year-Old Group.* By Barbara Biber, Lois B. Murphy, Louise P. Woodcock, and Irma S. Block. New York: E. P. Dutton & Co., 1942. Pp. xvi, 658. $3.75.

259. HERTZ, MARGUERITE R. "Comments on the Standardization of the Rorschach Group Method." *Rorschach Res Exch* 6:153-9 O '42. * (*PA* 17:883)

260. HERTZ, MARGUERITE R. *Frequency Tables to Be Used in Scoring the Rorschach Ink-Blot Test, Revised Edition.* Cleveland, Ohio: Western Reserve University Bookstore, 1942. Pp. v, 275. Paper, mimeographed. $4.00. *

261. HERTZ, MARGUERITE R. "Personality Patterns in Adolescence as Portrayed by the Rorschach Ink-blot Method: I, The Movement Factors." *J General Psychol* 27:119-88 Jl '42. * (*PA* 16:5055)

262. HERTZ, MARGUERITE R. "Rorschach: Twenty Years After." *Psychol B* 39:529-72 O '42. * (*PA* 17:591)

263. HERTZ, MARGUERITE R. "The Scoring of the Rorschach Ink-Blot Method as Developed by the Brush Foundation." *Rorschach Res Exch* 6:16-27 Ja '42. * (*PA* 16:2729)

264. HERTZ, MARGUERITE R. "The Validity of the Rorschach Group Method." Abstract. *Psychol B* 39:514 Jl '42. * (*PA* 16:4871, title only)

265. HERTZMAN, MAX. "A Comparison of the Individual and Group Rorschach Tests." *Rorschach Res Exch* 6:89-108 Jl '42. * (*PA* 16:4872)

266. HERTZMAN, MAX, AND SEITZ, CLIFFORD P. "Rorschach Reactions at High Altitudes." *J Psychol* 14:245-57 O '42. * (*PA* 17:826)

267. HUNT, THELMA. Chap. 15, "Personality Profile Studies," pp. 164-81. In *Psychosurgery: Intelligence, Emotion and Social Behavior Following Prefrontal Lobotomy for Mental Disorders.* By Walter Freeman and James W. Watts. Springfield, Ill.: Charles C. Thomas, 1942. Pp. xiii, 337. $6.00. * (*PA* 16:4023)

268. KELLEY, DOUGLAS M. "Requirements for Rorschach Training." *Rorschach Res Exch* 6:74-7 Ap '42. * (*PA* 16:3864)

269. KISKER, GEORGE W. "A Projective Approach to Personality Patterns During Insulin-Shock and Metrazol-Convulsive Therapy." *J Abn & Social Psychol* 37:120-4 Ja '42. * (*PA* 16:2685)

270. KLOPFER, BRUNO, AND HIRNING, L. CLOVIS. "'Signs,' 'Syndromes,' and Individuality Patterns in Rorschach Reactions of Schizophrenics." Abstract. *Psychol B* 39:513 Jl '42. * (*PA* 16:4815, title only)

271. KLOPFER, BRUNO. *The Rorschach Technique: A Manual for a Projective Method of Personality Diagnosis.* With clinical

contributions by Douglas McGlashan Kelley. Yonkers, N. Y.: World Book Co., 1942. Pp. xi, 436. (London: Geo. G. Harrap & Co. Ltd.) * (PA 16:3170) For latest edition, see (519) below.

272. KRUGMAN, JUDITH I. "A Clinical Validation of the Rorschach With Problem Children." Rorschach Res Exch 6:61-70 Ap '42. * (PA 16:4211)

273. LEVINE, KATE N., AND GRASSI, JOSEPH R. "The Relation Between Blot and Concept in Graphic Rorschach Responses." Rorschach Res Exch 6:71-3 Ap '42. * (PA 16:4066)

274. LINDNER, R. M., AND CHAPMAN, K. W. "An Eclectic Group Method." Rorschach Res Exch 6:139-46 O '42. * (PA 17:884)

275. LINDNER, ROBERT M.; CHAPMAN, KENNETH W.; AND RINCK, EDWARD C. "The Development of a Group Rorschach Technique in a Federal Penal Institution, With Special Reference to the Problem of Psychopathic Personality." Abstract. Psychol B 39:513-4 Jl '42. * (PA 16:4953, title only)

276. LUKE, BROTHER. "The Rorschach Test Applied to Delinquent and Non-Delinquent Boys." Sch 30:917-8 Je '42. *

277. MARGULIES, HELEN. Rorschach Responses of Successful and Unsuccessful Students. Archives of Psychology, No. 271. Washington, D. C.: American Psychological Association, Inc., July 1942. Pp. 61. Paper. $1.00. * (PA 17:963)

278. MUNROE, RUTH L. "An Experiment in Large-Scale Testing by a Modification of the Rorschach Method." J Psychol 13:229-63 Ap '42. * (PA 16:3651)

279. PIOTROWSKI, ZYGMUNT A. "A Comparative Table of the Main Rorschach Symbols." Psychiatric Q 16:30-7 Ja '42. * (PA 16:3653)

280. PIOTROWSKI, ZYGMUNT A. "The Modifiability of Personality as Revealed by the Rorschach Method: Methodological Considerations." Rorschach Res Exch 6:160-7 O '42. * (PA 17:886)

281. PIOTROWSKI, ZYGMUNT A. "On the Rorschach Method of Personality Analysis." Psychiatric Q 16:480-90 Jl '42. * (PA 16:4882)

282. RAPAPORT, D. "Principles Underlying Projective Techniques." Char & Pers 10:213-9 Mr '42. * (PA 16:4068)

283. RICKERS-OVSIANKINA, MARIA. Rorschach Scoring Samples. Revised Edition. Norton, Mass.: the Author, Wheaton College, 1942. Pp. 197. Paper, mimeographed. $4.00. *

284. ROCHLIN, GREGORY N., AND LEVINE, KATE N. "The Graphic Rorschach Test I." Arch Neurol & Psychiatry 47:438-48 Mr '42. * (PA 16:3654)

285. RORSCHACH, HERMANN. Psychodiagnostics: A Diagnostic Test Based on Perception: Including Rorschach's paper, "The Application of the Form Perception Test" (Published Posthumously by Dr. Emil Oberholzer), Second Edition. Translation and English edition by Paul Lemkau and Bernard Kronenberg. Edited by W. Morgenthaler. Berne, Switzerland: Verlag Hans Huber, 1942. Pp. 238. (New York: Grune & Stratton, Inc. $5.75.) * (PA 16:4443, title only)

286. ROSS, W. D. "Notes on Rorschach 'Signs' in Diagnosis and Research." Rorschach Res Exch 6:115-6 Jl '42. * (PA 16:4840)

287. SARBIN, THEODORE R., AND MADOW, LEO W. "Predicting the Depth of Hypnosis by Means of the Rorschach Test." Am J Orthopsychiatry 12:268-70 Ad '42. * (PA 16:4008)

288. SCHACHTEL, ANNA HARTOCH; HENRY, JULES; AND HENRY, ZUNIA. "Rorschach Analysis of Pilagá Indian Children." Am J Orthopsychiatry 12:679-712 O '42. * (PA 17:630)

289. SHASKAN, DONALD; YARNELL, HELEN; AND ALPER, KAREN. "Physical, Psychiatric and Psychometric Studies of Post-Encephalitic Parkinsonism." J Nerv & Mental Dis 96:652-62 D '42. * (PA 17:872) Discussion Arch Neurol & Psychiatry 48:666-8 S '42. * (PA 17:871, title only)

290. STAVRIANOS, BERTHA. "An Investigation of Sex Differences in Children as Revealed by the Rorschach Method." Rorschach Res Exch 6:168-75 O '42. * (PA 17:1003)

291. STEINZOR, BERNARD. A Rorschach Study of Achieving and Nonachieving College Students of High Ability. Unpublished master's thesis. Ohio State University, 1942.

292. WEISSKOPF, EDITH A. "The Influence of the Time Factor on Rorschach Performances." Rorschach Res Exch 6:128-36 Jl '42. * (PA 16:4889, title only) Abstract Psychol B 39:515 Jl '42. * (PA 16:4888, title only)

293. YOUNG, ROBERT A., AND HIGGINBOTHAM, SIBLEY A. "Behavior Checks on the Rorschach Method." Am J Orthopsychiatry 12:87-94 Ja '42. * (PA 16:2527)

294. ABBOTT, WALTER D.; DUE, FLOYD O.; AND NOSIK, WILLIAM A. "Subdural Hematoma and Effusion as a Result of Blast Injuries." J Am Med Assn 121:739-41 Mr 6 '43. * (PA 17:3397)

295. BECK, SAMUEL J. "Effects of Shock Therapy on Personality, as Shown by the Rorschach Test." Discussion by Joseph Rheingold. Arch Neurol & Psychiatry 50:483, discussion 483-4 O '43. * (PA 18:515, title only)

296. BECK, SAMUEL J. "The Rorschach in Psychopathology." pp. 338-47. In Contemporary Psychopathology: A Source Book. Edited by Silvan S. Tomkins. Cambridge, Mass.: Harvard University Press. 1943. Pp. xiv, 600. $5.00. * (PA 18:771) Reprinted from J Consult Psychol 7:103-11 Mr-Ap '43. * (PA 17:2339)

297. BECK, SAMUEL J. "The Rorschach Test in Psychopathology." J Consult Psychol 7:103-111 Mr-Ap '43. * (PA 17:2339)

298. BILLIG, OTTO. "The Rorschach Test: An Important Aid in the Personality Diagnosis." N C Med J 4:46-50 F '43. * (PA 17:2036, title only)

299. BILLIG, OTTO, AND SULLIVAN, D. J. "Personality Structure and Prognosis of Alcohol Addiction: A Rorschach Study." Q J Studies Alcohol 3:554-73 Mr. '43. * (PA 17:2706)

300. BOYNTON, PAUL L., AND WALSWORTH, BARRIER M. "Emotionality Test Scores of Delinquent and Nondelinquent Girls." J Abn & Social Psychol 38:87-92 Ja '43. * (PA 17:3899)

301. BRENMAN, MARGARET, AND REICHARD, SUZANNE. "Use of the Rorschach Test in the Prediction of Hypnotizability." B Menninger Clinic 7:183-7 S-N '43. * (PA 18:1398)

302. BROWN, RALPH R. "The Effect of Morphine Upon the Rorschach Pattern in Post-Addicts." Am J Orthopsychiatry 13:339-42 Ap '43. * (PA 17:3452)

303. BUCKLE, D. F., AND COOK, P. H. "Group Rorschach Method: Technique." Rorschach Res Exch 7:159-65 O '43. * (PA 18:1116)

304. BUHLER, CHARLOTTE. "Father and Son." Rorschach Res Exch 7:145-58 O '43. * (PA 18:1117)

305. COLLIN, A. G. "European Rorschach Findings: An Abstract of an Article by Roland Kuhn entitled 'Der Rorschachische Formdeutversuch in der Psychiatrie' in the Monatschrift für Psychiatrie und Neurologie, Vol. 103, No. 1/2." Rorschach Res Exch 7:169-81 O '43. *

306. FOSBERG, IRVING A. "How Do Subjects Attempt Fake Results on the Rorschach Test?" Rorschach Res Exch 7:119-21 Jl '43. * (PA 17:4161)

307. FRANK, LAWRENCE K. "The Rorschach Method: Foreword." J Consult Psychol 7:63-6 Mr-Ap '43. * (PA 17:2385)

308. DERBY, ELIZABETH MARY. A Comparative Study in Projective Techniques Using the Rorschach and World Tests. Unpublished master's thesis, Clark University, 1943. (Abstracts of Dissertations . . . 1943, pp. 79-82.)

309. GOLDFARB, WILLIAM. "A Definition and Validation of Obsessional Trends in the Rorschach Examination of Adolescents." Rorschach Res Exch 7:81-108 Jl '43. * (PA 17:4162)

310. GOLDFARB, WILLIAM. "The Effects of Early Institutional Care on Adolescent Personality (Graphic Rorschach Data)." Child Develop 14:213-23 D '43. * (PA 18:2637)

311. GRASSI, JOSEPH R., AND LEVINE, KATE N. "The Graphic Rorschach Manual." Psychiatric Q 17:258-81 Ap '43. * (PA 17:3456)

312. HAMILTON, E. LOUISE. "The Rorschach Method in State Hospital Practice." Abstract. Arch Neurol & Psychiatry 49:306 F '43. *

313. HARRISON, ROSS. "The Thematic Apperception and Rorschach Methods of Personality Investigation in Clinical Practice." J Psychol 15:49-74 Ja '43. * (PA 17:1239)

314. HARROWER-ERICKSON, M. R. "Directions for Administration of the Rorschach Group-Test." J Genetic Psychol 62:105-17 Mr '43. * (PA 17:2388)

315. HARROWER-ERICKSON, M. R. "Diagnosis of Psychogenic Factors in Disease by Means of the Rorschach Method." Psychiatric Q 17:57-66 Ja '43. * (PA 17:2000)

316. HARROWER-ERICKSON, M. R. "Large Scale Investigation With the Rorschach Method." J Consult Psychol 7:120-6 Mr-Ap '43. * (PA 17:2387)

317. HARROWER-ERICKSON, M. R. "A Multiple Choice Test for Screening Purposes (For Use With the Rorschach Cards or Slides)." Psychosom Med 5:331-41 O '43. * (PA 18:1452)

318. HARROWER-ERICKSON, M. R. "Personality Testing in Penal Institutions." Probation 22:1-6 '43. (PA 18:2476)

319. HARROWER-ERICKSON, M. R., AND STEINER, M. E. "Modification of the Rorschach Method for Use as a Group Test." J Genetic Psychol 62:119-33 Mr '43. * (PA 17:2389)

320. HERTZ, MARGUERITE R. "Modification of the Rorschach Ink Blot Test for Large Scale Application." Am J Orthopsychiatry 13:191-211 Ap '43. * (PA 17:3165)

321. HERTZ, MARGUERITE R. "Personality Patterns in Adolescence as Portrayed by the Rorschach Ink-Blot Method: III. The 'Erlebnistypus' (A Normative Study)." J General Psychol 28:225-76 Ap '43. * (PA 17:3830)

322. HERTZ, MARGUERITE R. "Personality Patterns in Adolescence as Portrayed by the Rorschach Method: IV. The 'Erlebnistypus' (A Typological Study)." J General Psychol 29:3-45 Jl '43. * (PA 18:1752)

323. HERTZ, MARGUERITE R. "The Rorschach Method: Science or Mystery." J Consult Psychol 7:67-79 Mr-Ap '43. * (PA 17:2390)

324. HERTZ, MARGUERITE R., AND BAKER, ELIZABETH. "Personality Patterns in Adolescence as Portrayed by the Rorschach Ink-Blot Method: II, The Color Factors." J General Psychol 28:3-61 Ja '43. * (PA 17:1308)

325. HERTZMAN, MAX. "Recent Research on the Group Rorschach Test." Rorschach Res Exch 7:1-6 Ja '43. * (PA 17:2041)

326. HERTZMAN, MAX, AND MARGULIES, HELEN. "Developmental Changes as Reflected in Rorschach Test Responses." J Genetic Psychol 62:189-215 Je '43. * (PA 18:780)

327. HITCH, KENNETH S. "A Rorschach Diagnosis of Cerebral Arteriosclerosis." Psychiatric Q 17:81-6 Ja '43. * (PA 17:2002)

328. HITCH, KENNETH S. "Rorschach Examinations in Acute Psychiatric Admissions." J Nerv & Mental Dis 97:27-39 Ja '43. * (PA 17:1598)

329. KAY, LILLIAN WALD, AND VORHAUS, PAULINE G. "Rorschach Reactions in Early Childhood: Part II, Intellectual Aspects of Personality Development." Rorschach Res Exch 7:71-8 Ap '43. * (PA 17:3450)

330. KEMPLE, C. Chap. 11, "Contributions of the Rorschach Test to Psychosomatic Diagnosis." In Psychosomatic Diagnosis. By Helen F. Dunbar. Foreword by Leonard G. Rowntree. New

York: Paul B. Hoeber, Inc., 1943. Pp. xix, 741. $7.50. (PA 18:2434)

331. KLOPFER, BRUNO. "Instruction in the Rorschach Method." *J Consult Psychol* 7:112-9 Mr-Ap '43. * (PA 17:2255)

332. KNIGHT, ROBERT P.; GILL, MERTON; LOZOFF, MILTON; AND RAPAPORT, DAVID. "Comparison of Clinical Findings and Psychological Tests in Three Cases Bearing Upon Military Personnel Selection." *B Menninger Clinic*, 7:114-28 My '43. * (PA 17:4241)

333. KRAFFT, MARGARET R., AND VORHAUS, PAULINE G. "The Application of the Rorschach Method in a Family Case Work Agency." *Rorschach Res Exch* 7:28-35 Ja '43. * (PA 17:2073)

334. KRUGMAN, MORRIS. "The Rorschach in Child Guidance." *J Consult Psychol* 7:80-8 Mr-Ap '43. * (PA 17:2532)

335. LEVINE, KATE NATALIE. *A Comparison of Graphic Rorschach Productions With Scoring Categories of the Verbal Rorschach Record in Normal States, Organic Brain Disease, Neurotic and Psychotic Disorders.* Archives of Psychology, No. 282. Washington, D. C.: American Psychological Association, Inc., May 1943. Pp. 63. Paper. $1.25. * (PA 18:781)

336. LEVINE, KATE N.; GRASSI, JOSEPH R.; AND GERSON, MARTIN J. "Hypnotically Induced Mood Changes in the Verbal and Graphic Rorschach: A Case Study." *Rorschach Res Exch* 7:130-44 O '43. * (PA 18:1121)

337. LINDNER, ROBERT M. "A Further Contribution to the Group Rorschach." *Rorschach Res Exch* 7:7-15 Ja '43. * (PA 17:2044)

338. LINDNER, ROBERT M. "The Rorschach Test and the Diagnosis of Psychopathic Personality." *J Crim Psychopath* 5:69-93 Jl '43. * (PA 18:519)

339. LUKE, BROTHER. "The Rorschach Method Applied to Delinquent and Non-Delinquent Boys: Summary of Research." Abstract. *B Can Psychol Assn* 3:52-3 D '43. * (PA 18:1758)

340. MILLER, JOSEPH S., AND GAIR, MOLLIE. "A Traumatic Neurosis of World War I 23 Years After: Psychiatric and Rorschach Investigations." *J Nerv & Mental Dis* 97:436-46 Ap '43. * (PA 17:2741)

341. MORRIS, WOODROW W. "Prognostic Possibilities of the Rorschach Method in Metrazol Therapy." *Am J Psychiatry* 100:222-30 S '43. * (PA 18:1099) Abstract *Arch Neurol & Psychiatry* 49:927-8 Je '43. * (PA 16:4149)

342. MUNROE, RUTH. "Use of the Rorschach Method in College Guidance." *J Consult Psychol* 7:89-96 Mr-Ap '43. * (PA 17:2500)

343. PEMBERTON, W. H. "General Semantics and the Rorschach Test." *Papers Am Congr Gen Semant* 2:251-60 '43. (PA 18:1124)

344. PIOTROWSKI, ZYGMUNT A. "A Note on the 'Group Rorschach' and the 'Scoring Samples'." *Rorschach Res Exch* 7:182-4 O '43. * (PA 18:1125)

345. PIOTROWSKI, ZYGMUNT A. "Tentative Rorschach Formulae for Educational and Vocational Guidance in Adolescence." *Rorschach Res Exch* 7:16-27 Ja '43. * (PA 17:2191)

346. PIOTROWSKI, ZYGMUNT A. "Use of the Rorschach in Vocational Selection." *J Consult Psychol* 7:97-102 Mr-Ap. * (PA 17:2502)

347. RICKERS-OVSIANKINA, MARIA. "Some Theoretical Considerations Regarding the Rorschach Method." *Rorschach Res Exch* 7:41-53 Ap '43. * (PA 17:3461)

348. ROSS, W. D. "A Contribution to the Objectification of Group Rorschach Scoring." *Rorschach Res Exch* 7:70-8 Ap '43. * (PA 17:3462)

349. ROSS, W. D.; DANCEY, T. E.; AND BROWN, F. T. "Rorschach Scores of Parachute Troopers in Training." *B Can Psychol Assn* 3:26-7 Ap '43. * (PA 17:3231)

350. ST. CLAIR, WALTER F. "The Self-Recording Technique in Rorschach Administration." *Rorschach Res Exch* 7:109-18 Jl '43. * (PA 17:4165)

351. SCHACHTEL, ERNEST G. "On Color and Affect: Contributions to an Understanding of Rorschach's Test: II." *Psychiatry* 6:393-409 N '43. * (PA 18:2154)

352. SCHACHTEL, ERNEST G. "Some Notes on Fire-Setters and Their Rorschach Tests." *J Crim Psychopath* 5:341-50 O '43. * (PA 18:1459)

353. SCHNEIDMAN, EDWIN S. "A Note on the Experimental Study of the Appraisal Interview." *J Appl Psychol* 27:196-205 Ap '43. * (PA 17:3554)

354. SENDER, SADIE. "The Influence of Variations in the Rorschach Group Method Administration Upon the Scorability of Records." *Rorschach Res Exch* 7:54-69 Ap '43. * (PA 17:3463)

355. VAN BARK, BELLA, AND BARON, SAMUEL. "Neurotic Elements in the Rorschach Records of Psychotics." *Rorschach Res Exch* 7:166-8 O '43. * (PA 18:1109)

356. VENIAR, SEYMOUR. *The Reliability of the Rorschach Scales: A Study of the Agreement Between Judges' Ratings of Rorschach Responses on a Series of 24 Psychometric Scales.* Unpublished master's thesis, Columbia University. 1943.

357. YAWGER, NATHANIEL S. "The Rorschach Ink-Blot Tests." *Phil Med* 39:548-51 D 25 '43. * (PA 18:1761)

358. ZUBIN, JOSEPH; CHUTE, ELOISE; AND VENIAR, SEYMOUR. "Psychometric Scales for Scoring Rorschach Test Responses." *Char & Pers* 11:277-301 Je '43. * (PA 17:4170)

359. ABEL, THEODORA M.; PIOTROWSKI, ZYGMUNT; AND STONE, GERTRUDE. "Responses of Negro and White Morons to the Rorschach Test." *Am J Mental Def* 48:253-7 Ja '44. * (PA 18:2836)

360. APPELDORF, MAX. "Rorschach Theory and Psychoanalytic Theory." *Rorschach Res Exch* 8:189-91 O '44. *

361. BALINSKY, BENJAMIN. "A Note on the Use of the Rorschach in the Selection of Supervisory Personnel." *Rorschach Res Exch* 8:184-8 O '44. * (PA 19:1008)

362. BECK, S. J. "Errors in Perception and Fantasy in Schizophrenia," pp. 91-103. In *Language and Thought in Schizophrenia.* Edited by J. S. Kasanin. Berkeley, Calif.: University of California Press, 1944. Pp. xiv, 133. $2.00. * (London: Cambridge University Press. 12s.) (PA 18:1428)

363. BECK, S. J. "The Rorschach Test in a Case of Character Neurosis." *Am J Orthopsychiatry* 14:230-6 Ap '44. * (PA 18:3183)

364. BECK, SAMUEL J. *Rorschach's Test: I, Basic Processes.* Foreword by Willard L. Valentine. New York: Grune & Stratton, Inc., 1944. Pp. xiii, 223. $3.50. * (PA 18:2837)

365. CRANFORD, VICTORIA, AND SELIGER, ROBERT V. "A Practical Introduction to Rorschach Work." *South Med & Surg* 106:327-8 S '44. *

366-7. CRANFORD, VICTORIA, AND SELIGER, ROBERT V. "Understanding the Alcohol Patient: The Rorschach Analysis as a New Approach in Understanding and Treating the Alcohol Patient." *J Crim Psychopath* 6:323-34 O '44. * (PA 19:1688)

368. FORD, MARY ELIZABETH NESTLERODE. *The Application of the Rorschach Test to Young Children.* Unpublished doctor's thesis, University of Minnesota, 1944.

369. FREEMAN, H.; RODNICK, E. H.; SHAKOW, D.; AND LEBEAUX, THELMA. "The Carbohydrate Tolerance of Mentally Disturbed Soldiers." *Psychosom Med* 6:311-7 O '44. * (PA 19:714)

370. GAIR, MOLLIE. "Rorschach Characteristics of a Group of Very Superior Seven Year Old Children." *Rorschach Res Exch* 8:31-7 Ja '44. * (PA 18:2305)

371. GOLDFARB, WILLIAM. "Effects of Early Institutional Care on Adolescent Personality: Rorschach Data." *Am J Orthopsychiatry* 14:441-7 Jl '44. * (PA 18:3915)

372-3 GOLDFARB, WILLIAM, AND KLOPFER, BRUNO. "Rorschach Characteristics of 'Institution Children'." *Rorschach Res Exch* 8:92-100 Ap '44. * (PA 18:3100)

374. HARROWER-ERICKSON, M. R. "Developments of the Rorschach Test for Large Scale Application." *Rorschach Res Exch* 8:125-40 Jl '44. * (PA 19:165)

375. HARROWER-ERICKSON, M. R. "The Rorschach Test." *J Assn Am Med Col* 19:193-200 Jl '44. * (PA 18:3529)

376. HERTZ, MARGUERITE R., AND EBERT, ELIZABETH H. "The Mental Procedure of 6 and 8 Year Old Children as Revealed by the Rorschach Ink-Blot Method." *Rorschach Res Exch* 8:10-30 Ja '44. * (PA 18:2311)

377. HERTZMAN, MAX; ORLANSKY, JESSE; AND SEITZ, CLIFFORD P. "Personality Organization and Anoxia Tolerance." *Psychosom Med* 6:317-31 O '44. * (PA 19:715)

378. JACOB, ZOLTAN. "Some Suggestions on the Use of Content Symbolism." *Rorschach Res Exch* 8:40-1 Ja '44. * (PA 18:2138)

379. KAMMAN, GORDON R. "The Rorschach Method as a Therapeutic Agent." *Am J Orthopsychiatry* 14:21-7 Ja '44. * (PA 18:2140)

380. KENDIG, ISABELLE V. "Projective Techniques as a Psychological Tool in Diagnosis." *J Clin Psychopath* 6:101-10 Jl '44. * (PA 19:448)

381. KISKER, GEORGE W. "The Rorschach Analysis of Psychotics Subjected to Neurosurgical Interruption of the Thalamo-Cortical Projections." *Psychiatric Q* 18:43-52 Ja '44. * (PA 18:1754)

382. KLOPFER, BRUNO, AND DAVIDSON, HELEN H. "Form Level Rating: A Preliminary Proposal for Appraising Mode and Level of Thinking as Expressed in Rorschach Records." *Rorschach Res Exch* 8:164-77 O '44. * (PA 19:975)

383. LEVINE, KATE N.; GRASSI, JOSEPH R.; AND GERSON, MARTIN J. "Hypnotically Induced Mood Changes in the Verbal and Graphic Rorschach: A Case Study: Part II. The Response Records." *Rorschach Res Exch* 8:104-24 Jl '44. * (PA 19:169)

384. LINDNER, ROBERT M. "Some Significant Rorschach Responses." *J Crim Psychopath* 5:775-8 Ap '44. * (PA 18:3531)

385. MASLOW, PAUL. *Rorschach Theory.* Brooklyn 2, N. Y.: the Author, 16 Court St., 1944. Pp. ii, 89. Paper, mimeographed. For latest edition, *see* (573) below.

386. MELTZER, H. "Personality Differences Between Stuttering and Non-Stuttering Children as Indicated by the Rorschach Test." *J Psychol* 17:39-59 Ja '44. * (PA 18:1457)

387. MUNROE, RUTH. "The Inspection Technique: A Method of Rapid Evaluation of the Rorschach Protocol." *Rorschach Res Exch* 8:46-70 Ap '44. * (PA 18:3191)

388. MUNROE, RUTH; LEWINSON, THEA STEIN; AND WAEHNER, TRUDE SCHMIDL. "A Comparison of Three Projective Methods." *Char & Pers* 13:1-21 S '44. * (PA 19:1078)

389. MURPHY, LOIS BARCLAY. "Personality Development of a Boy From Age Two to Seven." Discussion by S. J. Beck and Percival M. Symonds. *Am J Orthopsychiatry* 14:10-6, discussion 17-20 Ja '44. * (PA 18:2319)

390. OBERHOLZER, EMIL. Chap. 22, "Rorschach's Experiment and the Alorese," pp. 588-640. In *The People of Alor: A Social-Psychological Study of an East Indian Island.* By Cora Du Bois. With analyses by Abram Kardiner and Emil Oberholzer. Minneapolis, Minn.: University of Minnesota Press, 1944. Pp. xvi, 654. $7.50. * (London: Oxford University Press. 45s. 6d.) (PA 18:3543)

391. PIOTROWSKI, Z.; CANDEE, B.; BALINSKY, B.; HOLTZBERG, S.; AND VON ARNOLD, B. "Rorschach Signs in the Selection of Outstanding Young Male Mechanical Workers." *J Psychol* 18:131-50 Jl '44. * (PA 19:229)

392. PRADOS, M. "Rorschach Studies on Artists and Painters: I, Quantitative Analysis." *Rorschach Res Exch* 8:178-83 O '44. * (*PA* 19:979)

393. RICHARDSON, LAVANGE HUNT. *The Personality of Stutterers.* Psychological Monographs, Vol. 56, No. 7, Whole No. 260. Washington, D. C.: American Psychological Association, Inc., 1944. Pp. v, 41. Paper. $1.00. * (*PA* 18:3531)

394. ROSENBERG, SEYMOUR J., AND FELDBERG, THEODORE M. "Rorschach Characteristics of a · Group of Malingerers." *Rorschach Res Exch* 8:141-58 Jl '44. * (*PA* 19:170)

395. ROSENZWEIG, SAUL. "A Note on Rorschach Pre-History." *Rorschach Res Exch* 8:41-2 Ja '44. * (*PA* 18:2150)

396. ROSS, W. D. "A Quantitative Use of the Rorschach Method: 'Instability' and 'Disability' Ratings Which Show Clinical and Psychometric Correlations." *Am J Psychiatry* 101:100-4 Jl '44. *

397. ROSS, W. D. "The Uses of the Rorschach Method in the Canadian Army." *Rorschach Res Exch* 8:159-61 Jl '44. * (*PA* 19:230)

398. ROSS, W. D., AND McNAUGHTON, F. L. "Head Injury: A Study of Patients With Chronic Post-Traumatic Complaints." *Arch Neurol & Psychiatry* 52:255-69 O '44. *

399. ROSS, W. D., AND ROSS, SALLY. "Some Rorschach Ratings of Clinical Value." *Rorschach Res Exch* 8:1-9 Ja '44. * (*PA* 18:2151)

400. SCHACHTEL, ANNA HARTOCH. "The Rorschach Test With Young Children." Discussion by S. J. Beck and Percival M. Symonds. *Am J Orthopsychiatry* 14:1-9, discussion 17-20 Ja '44. * (*PA* 18:2329)

401. SIEGEL, MIRIAM G. "The Rorschach Test as an Aid in Selecting Clients for Group Therapy and Evaluating Progress." *Mental Hyg* 28:444-9 Jl '44. * (*PA* 19:172)

402. STAINBROOK, EDWARD. "The Rorschach Description of Immediate Post-Convulsive Mental Function." *Char & Pers* 12:302-22 Je '44. * (*PA* 19:151)

403. STAINBROOK, EDWARD, AND SIEGEL, PAUL S. "A Comparative Group Rorschach Study of Southern Negro and White High School and College Students." *J Psychol* 17:107-15 Ja '44. * (*PA* 18:1461)

404. STEINZOR, BERNARD. "Rorschach Responses of Achieving and Nonachieving College Students of High Ability." *Am J Orthopsychiatry* 14:494-504 Jl '44. * (*PA* 19:174)

405. SWIFT, JOAN LOUISE WOODCOCK. *Application of the Rorschach Method to Preschool Children.* Unpublished doctor's thesis, University of Iowa, 1944.

406. SWIFT, JOAN W. "Matchings of Teachers' Descriptions and Rorschach Analyses of Preschool Children." *Child Develop* 15:217-24 D '44. * (*PA* 19:2265)

407. SWIFT, JOAN W. "Reliability of Rorschach Scoring Categories With Preschool Children." *Child Develop* 15:207-16 D '44. * (*PA* 19:2264)

408. VORHAUS, PAULINE G. "Rorschach Reactions in Early Childhood: Part 3, Content and Details in Pre-School Records." *Rorschach Res Exch* 8:70-91 Ap '44. * (*PA* 18:3341)

409. WITTSON, C. L.; HUNT, W. A.; AND OLDER, H. J. "The Use of the Multiple Choice Group Rorschach Test in Military Screening." *J Psychol* 17:91-4 Ja '44. * (*PA* 18:1523)

410. ABEL, THEODORA M. "Group Rorschach Testing in a Vocational High School." *Rorschach Res Exch* 9:178-88 D '45. * (*PA* 20:1955)

411. ABEL, THEODORA M. "The Relationship Between Academic Success and Personality Organization Among Subnormal Girls." *Am J Mental Def* 50:251-6 O '45. * (*PA* 20:2883)

412. ABEL, THEODORA M. "The Rorschach Test and School Success Among Mental Defectives." *Rorschach Res Exch* 9:105-10 S '45. * (*PA* 20:469)

413. BALINSKY, BENJAMIN. "The Multiple Choice Group Rorschach Test as a Means of Screening Applicants for Jobs." *J Psychol* 19:203-8 Ap '45. * (*PA* 19:1966)

414. BECK, S. J. "The Rorschach Experiment: Progress and Problems." *Am J Orthopsychiatry* 15:520-4 Jl '45. * (*PA* 20:187)

415. BECK, SAMUEL J. *Rorschach's Test: II, A Variety of Personality Pictures.* Foreword by Roy R. Grinker. New York: Grune & Stratton, Inc., 1945. Pp. xii, 402. $5.00. * (*PA* 20:1150)

416. BENTON, ARTHUR L. "Rorschach Performances of Suspected Malingerers." *J Abn & Social Psychol* 40:94-6 Ja '45. * (*PA* 19:1968)

417. BERGMANN, MARTIN S. "Homosexuality on the Rorschach Test." *B Menninger Clinic* 9:78-83 My '45. * (*PA* 20:124)

418. BOCHNER, RUTH, AND HALPERN, FLORENCE. *The Clinical Application of the Rorschach Test, Second Edition.* Introduction by Karl M. Bowman. New York: Grune & Stratton, Inc., 1945. Pp. xi, 331. $4.00. * (*PA* 20:472)

419. BURGEMEISTER, BESSIE B., AND TALLMAN, GLADYS. "Rorschach Patterns in Multiple Sclerosis." *Rorschach Res Exch* 9:111-22 S '45. * (*PA* 20:473)

420. CHALLMAN, ROBERT C. "The Validity of the Harrower-Erickson Multiple Choice Test as a Screening Device." *J Psychol* 20:41-8 Jl '45. * (*PA* 19:3399)

421. COWIN, MARION. "The Use of the Rorschach in Schools." *Rorschach Res Exch* 9:130-3 S '45. * (*PA* 20:474)

422. DUE, FLOYD O., AND WRIGHT, M. ERIK. "The Use of Content Analysis in Rorschach Interpretation: I, Differential Characteristics of Male Homosexuals." *Rorschach Res Exch* 9:169-77 D '45. * (*PA* 20:1960)

423. EGAS, EDUARDO O. *Components of the Intelligence and Erlebnistype in the Rorschach Method.* Unpublished master's thesis, Ohio State University, 1945. Pp. 146.

424. ENDACOTT, JOHN L. "The Rorschach Test in Post-Encephalitis." *Ill Med J* 88:256-8 N '45. * (*PA* 21:503)

425. EYSENCK, H. J. "A Comparative Study of Four Screening Tests for Neurotics." *Psychol B* 42:659-62 N '45. * (*PA* 20:794)

425a. FATERSON, HANNA F., AND KLOPFER, BRUNO. "A Survey of Psychologists' Opinions Concerning the Rorschach Method." *Rorschach Res Exch* 9:23-9 Mr '45. * (*PA* 19:2246)

426. GEIL, GEORGE A. "The Similarity in Rorschach Patterns of Adult Criminal Psychopaths and Pre-Adolescent Boys." *Rorschach Res Exch* 9:201-6 D '45. * (*PA* 20:1963)

427. GOLDFARB, WILLIAM. "The Animal Symbol in the Rorschach Test and an Animal Association Test." *Rorschach Res Exch* 9:8-22 Mr '45. * (*PA* 19:2247)

428. GOLDFARB, WILLIAM. "Organization Activity in the Rorschach Examination." *Am J Orthopsychiatry* 15:525-8 Jl '45. * (*PA* 20:476)

429. GOLDMAN, GEORGE S. AND BERGMANN, MARTIN S. "A Psychiatric and Rorschach Study of Adult Male Enuresis." *Am J Orthopsychiatry* 15:160-6 Ja '45. * (*PA* 19:1693)

429a. GOLDSTEIN, KURT, AND ROTHMANN, EVA. "Physiognomic Phenomena in Rorschach Responses." *Rorschach Res Exch* 9:1-7 Mr '45. * (*PA* 19:2248)

430. HALLOWELL, A. IRVING. "'Popular' Response and Cultural Differences: An Analysis Based on Frequencies in a Group of American Indian Subjects." *Rorschach Res Exch* 9:153-68 D '45. * (*PA* 20:1967)

431. HALLOWELL, A. IRVING. "The Rorschach Technique in the Study of Personality and Culture." *Am Anthrop* 47:195-210 Ap-Je '45. * (*PA* 19:3036)

432. HARROWER-ERICKSON, M. R., AND STEINER, M. E. *Large Scale Rorschach Techniques: A Manual for the Group Rorschach and Multiple Choice Test.* Springfield, Ill.: Charles C Thomas, Publisher, 1945. Pp. xi, 419. $8.50. * (*PA* 19:1720)

433. HARROWER, M. R., AND STEINER, M. E. *Manual for Psychodiagnostic Inkblots (A Series Parallel to the Rorschach Blots).* New York: Grune & Stratton, Inc., 1945. Pp. 112. Paper, lithotyped. $2.00. * Accompanying *Psychodiagnostic Inkblots,* $4.50. (*PA* 20:839)

434. HERTZ, MARGUERITE R. "The Role of the Rorschach Method in Planning for Treatment." *Rorschach Res Exch* 9:134-46 S '45. * (*PA* 20:478)

435. HILDRETH, GERTRUDE. "The Social Interests of Young Adolescents." *Child Develop* 16:119-21 Mr-Je '45. * (*PA* 20:236)

436. HUTT, MAX L. "The Use of Projective Methods of Personality Measurement in Army Medical Installations." *J Clin Psychol* 1:134-40 Ap '45. * (*PA* 19:2250)

437. JENSEN, M. B., AND ROTTER, J. B. "The Validity of the Multiple Choice Rorschach Test in Officer Candidate Selection." *Psychol B* 42:182-5 Mr '45. * (*PA* 19:2551)

438. KEMPLE, CAMILLA. "Rorschach Method and Psychosomatic Diagnosis: Personality Traits of Patients With Rheumatic Disease, Hypertensive Cardiovascular Disease, Coronary Occlusion, and Fracture." *Psychosom Med* 7:85-9 Mr '45. * (*PA* 19:2252)

439. KIMBLE, GREGORY A. "Social Influence on Rorschach Records." *J Abn & Social Psychol* 40:89-93 Ja '45. * (*PA* 19:1974)

440. KLOPFER, BRUNO. "Personality Diagnosis in Childhood." pp. 89-101. In *Modern Trends in Child Psychiatry.* Edited by Nolan D. C. Lewis and Bernard L. Pacella. New York: International Universities Press, 1945. Pp. 341. $6.00. * (*PA* 19:1919)

441. KLOPFER, WALTER G. "The Efficacy of Group Therapy as Indicated by Group Rorschach Records." *Rorschach Res Exch* 9:207-9 D '45. * (*PA* 20:1070)

442. MALAMUD, RACHEL F., AND MALAMUD, DANIEL. "The Validity of the Amplified Multiple Choice Rorschach as a Screening Device." *J Consult Psychol* 9:224-7 S-O '45. * (*PA* 20:1162)

443. MASLOW, PAUL. *Rorschach Psychology.* Brooklyn 2, N. Y.: the Author, 16 Court St., 1945. Pp. 149. Paper, mimeographed. (*PA* 19:3409) For latest edition, *see* (564) below.

444. MICHAEL, J. C., AND BUHLER, C. "Experiences With Personality Testing in a Neuropsychiatric Department of a Public General Hospital." *Dis Nerv Sys* 6:205-11 '45. (*PA* 19:3038)

445. MUNROE, RUTH L. "Considerations on the Place of the Rorschach in the Field of General Psychology." *Rorschach Res Exch* 9:30-40 Mr '45. * (*PA* 19:2254)

446. MUNROE, RUTH. "Objective Methods and the Rorschach Blots." *Rorschach Res Exch* 9:59-73 Je '45. * (*PA* 19:3041)

447. MUNROE, RUTH. "The Rorschach Test: A Report of Its Use at Sarah Lawrence College." *J Higher Ed* 16:17-23 Ja '45. * (*PA* 19:1725)

448. MUNROE, RUTH L. "Three Diagnostic Methods Applied to Sally." *J Abn & Social Psychol* 40:215-27 Ap '45. * (*PA* 19:2646)

449. MUNROE, RUTH LEARNED. *Prediction of the Adjustment and Academic Performance of College Students by a Modification of the Rorschach Method.* Foreword by Gardner Murphy. Applied Psychology Monographs of the American Association for Applied Psychology, No. 7. Stanford University, Calif.: Stanford University Press, 1945. Pp. 104. Paper. $1.25. * (London: Oxford University Press.) (*PA* 20:918)

450. PASTER, SAMUEL, AND GRASSI, JOSEPH R. "Clarification of Rorschach Responses by the Graphic Rorschach Method." *J Clin Psychol* 1:28-36 Ja '45. * (*PA* 20:2255)

451. PIOTROWSKI, ZYGMUNT A. "Experimental Psychological Diagnosis of Mild Forms of Schizophrenia." *Rorschach Res Exch* 9:189-200 D '45. * (*PA* 20:1937)

452. PIOTROWSKI, ZYGMUNT A. "Rorschach Records of Children With a Tic Syndrome." *Nerv Child* 4:342-52 Jl '45. * (*PA* 20:2529)

453. RABIN, ALBERT I. "Rorschach Test Findings in a Group of Conscientious Objectors." *Am J Orthopsychiatry* 15:514-9 Jl '45. * (*PA* 20:203)

454. RAPAPORT, DAVID, AND SCHAFER, ROY. "The Rorschach Test: A Clinical Evaluation." *B Menninger Clinic* 9:73-7 My '45. * (*PA* 20:204)

455. ROSS, W. DONALD. "The Rorschach Performance With Neurocirculatory Asthenia." *Psychosom Med* 7:80-4 Mr '45. * (*PA* 19:2259)

456. ROSS, W. D.; FERGUSON, G. A.; AND CHALKE, F. C. R. "The Group Rorschach Test in Officer Selection." *B Can Psychol Assn* 5:84-6 O '45. * (*PA* 20:1656)

457. ROSS, W. DONALD, AND McNAUGHTON, FRANCIS L. "Objective Personality Studies in Migraine by Means of the Rorschach Method." *Psychosom Med* 7:73-9 Mr '45. * (*PA* 19:2260)

458. ROTTERSMAN, WILLIAM, AND GOLDSTEIN, H. H. "Group Analysis Utilizing the Harrower-Erickson (Rorschach) Test." *Am J Psychiatry* 101:501-3 Ja '45. * (*PA* 19:3389)

459. SARASON, SEYMOUR B. "Projective Techniques in Mental Deficiency." *Char & Pers* 13:237-45 Mr-Je '45. * (*PA* 20:828)

460. SARGENT, HELEN. "Projective Methods: Their Origins, Theory, and Application in Personality Research." *Psychol B* 42:257-93 My '45. * (*PA* 19:2650)

461. SCHACHTEL, ANNA HARTOCH, AND LEVI, MARJORIE B. "Character Structure of Day Nursery Children in Wartime as Seen Through the Rorschach." *Am J Orthopsychiatry* 15:213-22 Ap '45. * (*PA* 19:2798)

462. SCHACHTEL, ERNEST G. "Subjective Definitions of the Rorschach Test Situation and Their Effect on Test Performance." *Psychiatry* 8:419-48 N '45. * (*PA* 20:1973)

463. SCHMIDL, FRITZ. "The Use of the Rorschach Method in Social Work Treatment of Adults." *Rorschach Res Exch* 9:123-5 S '45. * (*PA* 20:484)

464. SCHMIDT, HERMANN O. "Test Profiles as a Diagnostic Aid: The Rorschach." *J Clin Psychol* 1:222-7 Jl '45. * (*PA* 19:3410)

465. SCHNACK, GEORGE F.; SHAKOW, DAVID; AND LIVELY, MARY L. "Studies in Insulin and Metrazol Therapy: I, The Differential Prognostic Value of Some Psychological Tests." *J Personality* 14:106-24 D '45. * (*PA* 20:3669)

466. SELIGER, ROBERT V., AND CRANFORD, VICTORIA. "The Rorschach Analysis in the Treatment of Alcoholism." *Med Rec* 158:32-8 Ja '45. * (*PA* 19:1271)

467. SHAKOW, DAVID; RODNICK, ELIOT H.; AND LEBEAUX, THELMA. "A Psychological Study of a Schizophrenic: Exemplification of a Method." *J Abn & Social Psychol* 40:154-74 Ap '45. * (*PA* 19:2624)

468. SIEGEL, MIRIAM G. *The Diagnostic and Prognostic Validity of the Rorschach Test in a Child Guidance Clinic.* Unpublished doctor's thesis, New York University, 1945. (*Abstracts of Theses . . . [School of Education]* 1946, pp. 63-69.)

469. SIEGEL, MIRIAM G. "The Use of the Rorschach Test in a Treatment Program." *Rorschach Res Exch* 9:126-9 S '45. * (*PA* 20:485)

470. STERN, KARL, AND MacNAUGHTON, DOROTHY. "Capgras' Syndrome. A Peculiar Illusionary Phenomenon. Considered With Special Reference to the Rorschach Findings." *Psychiatric Q* 10:139-63 Ja '45. * (*PA* 19:3019)

471. STERN, KARL, AND MALLOY, HELGA TATT. "Rorschach Studies on Patients With Paranoid Features: With an Analysis of 35 Cases." *J Clin Psychol* 1:272-80 O '45. * (*PA* 20:486)

472. SWIFT, JOAN W. "Relation of Behavioral and Rorschach Measures of Insecurity in Preschool Children." *J Clin Psychol* 1:196-205 Jl '45. * (*PA* 10:3412)

473. SWIFT, JOAN W. "Rorschach Responses of Eighty-Two Preschool Children." *Rorschach Res Exch* 9:74-84 Je '45. * (*PA* 19:3046)

474. SYMONDS, PERCIVAL M., AND KRUGMAN, MORRIS. "Projective Methods in the Study of Personality." *R Ed Res* 14:81-98 F '44. * Reprinted in *Rorschach Res Exch* 9:85-101 Je '45. * (*PA* 19:175)

475. TULCHIN, SIMON H., AND LEVY, DAVID M. "Rorschach Test Differences in a Group of Spanish and English Refugee Children." *Am J Orthopsychiatry* 15:361-8 Ap '45. * (*PA* 19:3048)

476. WERNER, HEINZ. "Rorschach Method Applied to Two Clinical Groups of Mental Defectives." *Am J Mental Def* 49:304-6 Ja '45. * (*PA* 19:3413)

477. WERNER, HEINZ; WITH THE COLLABORATION OF DORIS CARRISON. *Perceptual Behavior of Brain-Injured, Mentally Defective Children: An Experimental Study by Means of the Rorschach Technique.* Genetic Psychology Monographs, Vol. 31, No. 2. Provincetown, Mass.: Journal Press, May 1945. Pp. 51-110. Paper. $4.00. * (*PA* 19:1083)

478. WILKINS, WALTER L., AND ADAMS, AUSTIN J. "The Use of the Rorschach Test Under Sodium Amytal and Under Hypnosis in Military Psychiatry." Abstract. *Psychol B* 42:538 O '45. * (*PA* 20:181, title only)

479. WITTMAN, PHYLLIS. "The Use of the Multiple Choice Rorschach as a Differential Diagnostic Tool." *J Clin Psychol* 1:281-7 O '45. * (*PA* 20:487)

480. ZANGWILL, O. L. "Observations on the Rorschach Test in Two Cases of Acute Concussional Head-Injury." *J Mental Sci* 91:322-36 Jl '45. * (*PA* 20:488)

481. ARMITAGE, STEWART G. *An Analysis of Certain Psychological Tests Used for the Evaluation of Brain Injury.* Psychological Monographs, Vol. 60, No. 1, Whole No. 277. Washington, D. C.: American Psychological Association, Inc., 1946. Pp. iii, 48. Paper. $1.25. *

482. BLAIR, GLENN MYERS. "Personality Adjustments of Teachers as Measured by the Multiple Choice Rorschach Test." *J Ed Res* 39:652-7 My '46. * (*PA* 20:4191)

483. BLAIR, GLENN MYERS, AND CLARK, RONALD W. "Personality Adjustments of Ninth-Grade Pupils as Measured by the Multiple Choice Rorschach Test and the California Test of Personality." *J Ed Psychol* 27:13-20 Ja '46. * (*PA* 20:1956)

484. BOOTH, GOTTHARD. "Organ Function and Form Perception: Use of the Rorschach Method With Cases of Chronic Arthritis, Parkinsonism and Arterial Hypertension." *Psychosom Med* 8:367-85 N-D '46. * (*PA* 21:1880)

485. BRADWAY, KATHERINE P.; LION, ERNEST G.; AND CORRIGAN, HAZLE G. "The Use of the Rorschach in a Psychiatric Study of Promiscuous Girls." *Rorschach Res Exch* 10:105-10 O '46. * (*PA* 21:806)

486. BURCHARD, EDWARD M. L. "A Ten-Year Bibliography: Rorschach Research Exchange 1937-1946." *Rorschach Res Exch* 10:173-83 D '46. * (*PA* 21:2680)

487. CHALKE, F. R. C. "The Harrower Stress Tolerance Test." *Psychosom Med* 8:215-6 My-Je '46. * (*PA* 20:4159)

488. CHIPMAN, CATHERINE E. "Psychological Variation Within a Homogeneous Psychometric Group." *Am J Mental Def* 51:195-205 O '46. * (*PA* 21:3000)

489. CLARKE, HELEN JANE. "The Diagnosis of a Patient With Limited Capacity." *J Personality* 15:105-12 D '46. * (*PA* 21:3001)

490. DERFMAN, ELAINE. *A Study of Rorschach Flexor and Extensor Movement Responses in Relation to Myokinetic Psychodiagnosis.* Unpublished master's thesis, Ohio State University, 1946. Pp. 61.

491. EISENDORFER, ARNOLD, AND BERGMANN, MARTIN S. "The Factor of Maturity in Officer Selection." *Psychiatry* 9:73-9 F '46. * (*PA* 20:2859)

492. ENGLE, T. L. "The Use of the Harrower-Erickson Multiple Choice (Rorschach) Test in Differentiating Between Well-Adjusted and Maladjusted High-School Pupils." *J Ed Psychol* 37:550-6 D '46. * (*PA* 21:1524)

493. EPSTEIN, HANS L., AND APPELDORF, MAX. "The Use of the Rorschach in a Groupwork Agency." *Rorschach Res Exch* 10:28-36 Mr '46. * (*PA* 20:2781)

494. FORD, MARY. *The Application of the Rorschach Test to Young Children.* University of Minnesota. The Institute of Child Welfare Monograph Series, No. 23. Minneapolis, Minn.: University of Minnesota Press, 1946. Pp. xii, 114. $2.00. (London: Oxford University Press. 12s.) * (*PA* 21:807)

495. GARFIELD, SOL L. "Clinical Values of Projective Techniques in an Army Hospital." *J Clin Psychol* 2:88-91 Ja '46. * (*PA* 20:1912)

496. GUSTAV, ALICE. "Estimation of Rorschach Scoring Categories by Means of an Objective Inventory." *J Psychol* 22:253-60 O '46. * (*PA* 21:808)

497. HACKBUSCH, FLORENTINE. "The Contribution of Projective Techniques to the Understanding and Treatment of Children Psychometrically Diagnosed as Feeble-Minded." With sample case studies by Bruno Klopfer. *Am J Mental Def* 51:15-34 Jl '46. * (*PA* 21:472)

498. HALPERN, FLORENCE. "The Rorschach Test and Other Projective Techniques," pp. 615-24. In *Progress in Neurology and Psychiatry, Vol. 1, 1946.* Edited by E. A. Spiegel. New York: Grune & Stratton, Inc., 1946. Pp. 308. $8.00. (*PA* 21:809)

499. HARRIS, ROBERT E., AND CHRISTIANSEN, CAROLE. "Prediction of Response to Brief Psychotherapy." *J Psychol* 21:269-84 Ap '46. * (*PA* 20:3212)

500. HARROWER-ERICKSON, M. R. "The Patient and His Personality: A Short Discussion of the Rorschach Method of Personality Evaluation and Its Uses in Clinical Medicine," pp. 685-701. In *Twentieth Century Psychology: Recent Developments in Psychology.* Edited by Philip Lawrence Harriman. New York: Philosophical Library, 1946. Pp. xv, 712. $6.00. * (*PA* 21:1337)

501. HARROWER, M. R., AND GRINKER, ROY R. "The Stress Tolerance Test: Preliminary Experiments With a New Projective Technique Utilizing Both Meaningful and Meaningless Stimuli." *Psychosom Med* 8:3-15 Ja-F '46. * (*PA* 20:1865)

502. HERTZ, MARGUERITE R. "The Rorschach Method and Its Significance in the Mental Hygiene Program," pp. 652-84. In *Twentieth Century Psychology: Recent Developments in Psychology.* Edited by Philip Lawrence Harriman. New York: Philosophical Library, 1946. Pp. xv, 712. $6.00. * (*PA* 20:1337)

503. HEUSER, KEITH D. "The Psychopathic Personality: The Rorschach Patterns of 28 Cases." *Am J Psychiatry* 103:105-12 Jl '46. * (*PA* 21:169)

504-5. HILDEN, ARNOLD H. "A Rorschach Succession Chart." *J Psychol* 22:53-8 Jl '46. * (*PA* 4194)

506. HUTT, MAX L., AND SHOR, JOEL. "Rationale for Routine Rorschach 'Testing-the-Limits'." *Rorschach Res Exch* 10:70-6 Je '46. * (*PA* 20:4195)

507. JACQUES, MARY GRIER. "A Comparison of Rorschach and Physiological Indications of Neurotic Disturbance." Abstract. *Am Psychol* 1:264 Jl '46. * (*PA* 20:3640, title only)

508. JANIS, MARJORIE G., AND JANIS, IRVING L. "A Supplementary Test Based on Free Associations to Rorschach Responses." *Rorschach Res Exch* 10:1-19 Mr '46. * (*PA* 20:2785)

509. KABACK, GOLDIE RUTH. "The Vocational Guidance Process and the Rorschach Method." *Occupations* 24:203-7 Ja '46. * (PA 20:1684)

510. KABACK, GOLDIE RUTH. *Vocational Personalities: An Application of the Rorschach Group Method.* Columbia University, Teachers College, Contributions to Education, No. 924. Harry D. Kitson, faculty sponsor. New York: Bureau of Publications, the College, 1946. Pp. xi, 116. $2.10. * (PA 21:1929)

511. KADINSKY, D. "Human Whole and Detail Responses in the Rorschach Test." *Rorschach Res Exch* 10:140-4 D '46. * (PA 21:2691)

512-3. KARLAN, SAMUEL C., AND HELLER, EUGENE. "Chronic Alcoholism: Psychiatric and Rorschach Evaluation." *J Clin Psychopath* 8:291-300 O '46. * (PA 21:2293)

514. KELLEY, DOUGLAS M. "Preliminary Studies of the Rorschach Records of the Nazi War Criminals." *Rorschach Res Exch* 10:45-8 Je '46. * (PA 20:4196)

515. KEMPLE, CAMILLA. "The Rorschach Method in Psychosomatic Problems: 1, A Case of Hypertensive Cardiovascular Disease." *Rorschach Res Exch* 10:130-9 D '46. * (PA 21:2641)

516. KLEBANOFF, SEYMOUR G. "A Rorschach Study of Operational Fatigue in Army Air Forces Combat Personnel." *Rorschach Res Exch* 10:115-20 D '46. * (PA 21:2629)

517. KLOPFER, BRUNO. "Rorschach Method," pp. 834-7. In *Encyclopedia of Psychology.* Edited by Philip Lawrence Harriman. New York: Philosophical Library, 1946. Pp. vii, 897. $10.00. * (PA 21:2325)

518. KLOPFER, BRUNO, AND DAVIDSON, HELEN H. *The Rorschach Technique: 1946 Supplement.* Yonkers, N. Y.: World Book Co., 1946. Pp. 431-75. Paper. $0.48. *

519. KLOPFER, BRUNO. *The Rorschach Technique: A Manual for a Projective Method of Personality Diagnosis.* With clinical contributions by Douglas McGlashen Kelley. With 1946 supplement by Bruno Klopfer and Helen H. Davidson. Yonkers, N. Y.: World Book Co., 1946. Pp. xi, 475. $4.80. *

520. KLOPFER, WALTER G. "Personality Patterns of Old Age." *Rorschach Res Exch* 10:145-66 D '46. * (PA 21:2692)

521. KOFF, SALMON A. "The Rorschach Test in the Differential Diagnosis of Cerebral Concussion and Psychoneurosis." *B U S Army Med Dept* 5:170-3 F '46. * (PA 20:1569)

522. KOGAN, KATE LEVINE. "The Diagnosis of a Patient With Organic Defect." *J Personality* 15:113-20 D '46. * (PA 21:3025)

523. KRUGMAN, MORRIS. "Psychosomatic Study of Fifty Stuttering Children: Round Table: IV. Rorschach Study." *Am J Orthopsychiatry* 16:127-33 Ja '46. * (PA 21:2525)

524. LE BAS, MARGARET. "Rorschacherel." Poem. *Rorschach Res Exch* 10:167 D '46. *

525. LINDNER, ROBERT M. "Content Analysis in Rorschach Work." *Rorschach Res Exch* 10:121-9 D '46. * (PA 21:2694)

526. LINDNER, ROBERT M., AND SELIGER, ROBERT V. "Content Analysis in Rorschach Work." Abstract. *Am Psychol* 1:286-7 Jl '46. * (PA 21:3708, title only)

527. LINN, LOUIS. "The Rorschach Test in the Evaluation of Military Personnel." *Rorschach Res Exch* 10:20-7 Mr '46. * (PA 20:2789)

528. MALAMUD, RACHEL F., AND MALAMUD, DANIEL I. "The Multiple Choice Rorschach: A Critical Examination of Its Scoring System." *J Psychol* 21:237-42 Ap '46. * (PA 20:3218)

529. MARKEY, OSCAR B., AND ZISSON, MILES M. "A Psychiatric Screening Aid for Pre-Combat Troops." *Am J Psychiatry* 103:377-80 N '46. * (PA 21:1514)

530. MONTALTO, FANNIE D. "An Application of the Group Rorschach Technique to the Problem of Achievement in College." *J Clin Psychol* 2:254-60 Jl '46. * (PA 20:4675)

530a. MUNROE, RUTH. "An Experiment With a Self-Administering Form of the Rorschach and Group Administration by Examiners Without Rorschach Training." *Rorschach Res Exch* 10:49-59 Je '46. * (PA 20:4200)

531. MUNROE, RUTH L. "Rorschach Findings on College Students Showing Different Constellations of Subscores on the A.C.E." *J Consult Psychol* 10:301-16 N-D '46. * (PA 21:3475)

532. RABIN, ALBERT I. "Homicide and Attempted Suicide: A Rorschach Study." Discussion by S. J. Beck. *Am J Orthopsychiatry* 16:516-23, discussion 523-4 Jl '46. * (PA 20:4202)

533. RAMZY, I. "Personality Tests: II, Rorschach Test." *Egypt J Psychol* 2:268-81 '46. (PA 21:1930)

534. RAPAPORT, DAVID, AND SCHAFER, ROY; WITH THE COLLABORATION OF MERTON GILL. "The Rorschach Test," pp. 26-72. In their *Manual of Diagnostic Psychological Testing: II, Diagnostic Testing of Personality and Ideational Content.* Review Series, Vol. 3, No. 1. New York: Josiah Macy, Jr. Foundation, 1946. Pp. 105. Paper. $0.75. * (PA 21:814)

535. RAPAPORT, DAVID; WITH THE COLLABORATION OF MERTON GILL AND ROY SCHAFER. Chap. 3, "The Rorschach Test," pp. 85-394, 472-91, 494-505. In their *Diagnostic Psychological Testing: The Theory, Statistical Evaluation, and Diagnostic Application of a Battery of Tests, Vol. II.* Chicago, Ill.: Year Book Publishers, Inc., 1946. Pp. xi, 516. $6.50. * (PA 20:1712)

536. RICHARDS, T. W. "Epileptic Seizure in the Rorschach Test Situation." *Rorschach Res Exch* 10:101-4 O '46. * (PA 21:785)

537. ROCKWELL, FRED V.; WELCH, LIVINGSTON; FISICHELLI, VINCENT; AND KUBIS, JOSEPH. "Changes in Palmar Skin Resistance During the Rorschach Experiment." Abstract. *Am Psychol* 1:287 Jl '46. * (PA 20:3713, title only)

538. ROE, ANNE. "Alcohol and Creative Work: Part I, Painters." *Q J Studies Alcohol* 6:415-67 Mr '46. * (PA 20:2793)

539. ROE, ANNE. "Painting and Personality." *Rorschach Res Exch* 10:86-100 O '46. * (PA 21:816)

540. ROE, ANNE. "The Personality of Artists." *Ed & Psychol Meas* 6:401-8 au '46. * (PA 21:817)

541. ROE, ANNE. "A Rorschach Study of a Group of Scientists and Technicians." *J Consult Psychol* 10:317-27 N-D '46. * (PA 21:3718)

542. ROSENZWEIG, SAUL. "The Dynamics of an Amnesic Personality." *J Personality* 15:121-42 D '46. * (PA 21:3062)

543. SARASON, SEYMOUR B., AND SARASON, ESTHER KROOP. "The Discriminatory Value of a Test Pattern in the High Grade Familial Defective." *J Clin Psychol* 2:38-49 Ja '46. * (PA 20:1940)

544. SIEGEL, MIRIAM G. "A Description of the Rorschach Method." *Family* 27:51-8 Ap '46. * (PA 21:172)

545. SIEGEL, MIRIAM G. "The Rorschach Test in Diagnosis and Prognosis." *Family* 27:102-9 My '46. * (PA 21:173)

546. SPRINGER, N. NORTON. "The Validity of the Multiple Choice Group Rorschach Test in the Screening of Naval Personnel." *J General Psychol* 35:27-32 Jl '46. * (PA 21:2641)

547. VORHAUS, PAULINE G. "Non-Reading as an Expression of Resistance." *Rorschach Res Exch* 10:60-9 Je '46. * (PA 20:4406)

548. WINFIELD, MARJORIE CASE. "The Use of the Harrower-Erickson Multiple Choice Rorschach Test With a Selected Group of Women in Military Service." *J Appl Psychol* 30:481-7 O '46. * (PA 21:514)

549. WITTMAN, PHYLLIS. "The Multiple Choice Rorschach Test as a Differential Diagnostic Test." Abstract. *Arch Neurol & Psychiatry* 55:154-6 Ja '46. * (PA 20:1980, title only)

550. WOLF, ELIZABETH B. "Investigation of the Meaning and Expression of the Movement Responses to the Rorschach Ink Blot Test in 216 Juvenile Delinquents." Abstract. *Am Psychol* 1:461 O '46. * (PA 21:515, title only)

551. ABT, LAWRENCE EDWIN. "The Efficiency of the Group Rorschach Test in the Psychiatric Screening of Marine Corps Recruits." *J Psychol* 23:205-17 Ap '47. * (PA 21:3705)

552. AITA, JOHN A.; REITAN, RALPH M.; AND RUTH, JANE M. "Rorschach's Test as a Diagnostic Aid in Brain Injury." *Am J Psychiatry* 103:770-9 My '47. * (PA 22:1661)

553. ALTABLE, JOSE PEINADO. "Rorschach Psychodiagnosis in a Group of Epileptic Children." *Nerv Child* 6:22-33 Ja '47. * (PA 21:2673)

554. BERGMANN, MARTIN S.; GRAHAM, HERBERT; AND LEAVITT, HARRY C. "Rorschach Exploration of Consecutive Hypnotic Chronological Age Level Regressions." *Psychosom Med* 9:20-8 Ja '47. * (PA 21:2313)

555. BOWLUS, D. E., AND SHOTWELL, ANNA M. "A Rorschach Study of Psychopathic Delinquency." *Am J Mental Def* 52:23-30 Jl '47. * (PA 22:2229)

556. BROWER, DANIEL. "The Relation Between Certain Rorschach Factors and Cardiovascular Activity Before and After Visuo-Motor Conflict." *J General Psychol* 37:93-95 Jl '47. * (PA 22:1661)

557. BUHLER, CHARLOTTE, AND LEFEVER, D. WELTY. "A Rorschach Study on the Psychological Characteristics of Alcoholics." *Q J Studies Alcohol* 8:197-260 S '47. * (PA 22:1232)

558. DUNKEL, HAROLD B. "The Effect of Personality on Language Achievement." *J Ed Psychol* 38:177-82 Mr '47. * (PA 22:832)

559. EYSENCK, H. J. *Dimensions of Personality,* pp. 212-25. A record of research carried out in collaboration with H. T. Himmelweit and W. Linford Rees with the help of M. Desai, W. D. Furneaux, H. Halstead, O. Marum, M. McKinlay. A. Petrie, and P. M. Yap. Foreword by Aubrey Lewis. London: Kegan Paul, Trench, Trubner & Co. Ltd., 1947. Pp. xi, 308. 25s. * (PA 22:210)

560. FRENCH, VERA V. "The Structure of Sentiments: II, A Preliminary Study of Sentiments." *J Personality* 16:78-108 S '47. * (PA 22:2512)

561. HANFMANN, EUGENIA; STEIN, MORRIS I.; AND BRUNER, JEROME S. "Personality Factors in the Temporal Development of Perceptual Organization—A Methodological Note." Abstract. *Am Psychol* 2:284 Ag '47. * (PA 21:1438, title only)

562. HERTZ, MARGUERITE R.; ELLIS, ALBERT; AND SYMONDS, PERCIVAL M. "Rorschach Methods and Other Projective Technics." *R Ed Res* 17:78-100 F '47. * (PA 21:3141)

563. HERTZMAN, MAX, AND PEARCE, JANE. "The Personal Meaning of the Human Figure in the Rorschach." *Psychiatry* 10:413-22 N '47. * (PA 22:3030)

564. HSU, E. H. "The Rorschach Responses and Factor Analysis." *J General Psychol* 37:129-38 O '47. * (PA 22:3031)

565. JENSEN, MILTON S., AND ROTTER, JULIAN B. "The Value of Thirteen Psychological Tests in Officer Candidate Screening." *J Appl Psychol* 31:312-22 Je '47. * (PA 21:4107)

566. JOLLES, ISAAC. "A Study of Mental Deficiency by the Rorschach Technique." *Am J Mental Def* 52:37-42 Jl '47. * (PA 21:2641)

567. KAMMAN, GORDON R. "Psychosomatic Diagnosis." *Journal-Lancet* 67:102-7 Mr '47. *

568. KEMPLE, CAMILLA. "A Comparative Study of Three Projective Methods: A Case of Rheumatic Heart Disease (Rorschach, Handwriting, Drawing)." *Rorschach Res Exch & J Proj Tech* 11(1):26-40 '47. * (PA 21:3767)

569. LAURIERS, AUSTIN DES, AND HALPERN, FLORENCE. "Psychological Tests in Childhood Schizophrenia." *Am J Orthopsychiatry* 17:57-67 Ja '47. *

570. LAWSHE, C. H., JR., AND FORSTER, MAX H. "Studies in Projective Techniques: I, The Reliability of a Multiple Choice

Group Rorschach Test." *J Appl Psychol* 31:199-211 Ap '47. * (*PA* 21:2693)

571. LUCHINS, ABRAHAM S. "Situational and Attitudinal Influences on Rorschach Responses." *Am J Psychiatry* 103:780-4 My '47. * (*PA* 22:1655)

572. MACHOVER, KAREN. "A Case of Frontal Lobe Injury Following Attempted Suicide (Drawings, Rorschach)." *Rorschach Res Exch & J Proj Tech* 11(1):9-20 '47. * (*PA* 22:3175)

573. MASLOW, PAUL. *The Analysis and Control of Human Experiences: The Individual Seen Through Rorschach, Volumes 1 and 2,* Brooklyn 2, N. Y.: the Author, 16 Court St., 1947. Pp. iii, 233; iv, 195. Paper, mimeographed. $3.50 per volume. * (*PA* 21:2326)

574. MAYMAN, MARTIN. "A Comparative Study of the Rorschach, Harrower, and Behn-Eschenberg Inkblot Tests." Abstract. *Am Psychol* 2:270-1 Ag '47. * (*PA* 21:4389, title only)

575. MERCER, MARGARET, AND FUNDERBURG, JOE. "A Case of Drug Addiction (Rorschach, TAT, Vocational Interests)." *Rorschach Res Exch & J Proj Tech* 11(1):41-5 '47. *

576. MUENCH, GEORGE A. *An Evaluation of Non-Directive Psychotherapy by Means of the Rorschach and Other Indices.* Foreword by Carl R. Rogers. Applied Psychology Monographs of the American Psychological Association, No. 13. Stanford University, Calif.: Stanford University Press, 1947. Pp. 163. Paper, lithotyped. $2.00. * (*PA* 22:320)

577. NORTHWAY, MARY L., AND WIGDOR, BLOSSOM T. "Rorschach Patterns Related to the Sociometric Status of School Children." *Sociometry* 10:186-99 My '47. *

578. PACELLA, B. L.; PIOTROWSKI, Z.; AND LEWIS, N. D. C. "The Effects of Electric Convulsive Therapy on Certain Personality Traits in Psychiatric Patients." *Am J Psychiatry* 104:83-91 Ag '47. * (*PA* 22:2210)

579. PHILLIPS, L., AND ELMADJIAN, F. "A Rorschach Tension Score and the Diurnal Lymphocyte Curve in Psychotic Patients." *Psychosom Med* 9:364-71 N-D '47. * (*PA* 22:2677)

580. PIOTROWSKI, ZYGMUNT A. "A Rorschach Compendium." *Psychiatric Q* 21:79-101 Ja '47. *

581. POTTER, ELMER H., AND SARASON, SEYMOUR B. "Color in the Rorschach and Kohs Block Designs." Abstract. *Am Psychol* 2:269-70 Ag '47. * (*PA* 21:4391, title only)

582. PRADOS, MIGUEL, AND FRIED, EDRITA G. "Personality Structure of the Older Age Groups." *J Clin Psychol* 3:113-20 Ap '47. * (*PA* 21:3326)

583. RABIN, A. I., AND SANDERSON, M. H. "An Experimental Inquiry Into Some Rorschach Procedures." *J Clin Psychol* 3:216-25 Jl '47. * (*PA* 22:218)

584. RASHKIS, HAROLD A. "The Psychometric Analysis of a Diagnostic Problem." *Am J Orthopsychiatry* 17:529-32 Jl '47. *

585. ROSENWALD, ALAN K. "A Comparison of the Rorschach and Behn Rorschach Tests Based on a Study of Chronic Alcoholic Subjects." Abstract. *Am Psychol* 2:270 Ag '47. * (*PA* 21:4441, title only)

586. SARASON, SEYMOUR B., AND POTTER, ELMER H. "Color in the Rorschach and Kohs Block Designs." *J Consult Psychol* 11:202-6 Jl-Ag '47. * (*PA* 22:205)

587. SARASON, SEYMOUR B., AND SARASON, ESTHER KROOP. "The Discriminatory Value of a Test Pattern With Cerebral Palsied, Defective Children. *J Clin Psychol* 3:141-7 '47. (*PA* 21:3029)

588. SCHMIDL, FRITZ. "The Rorschach Test in Juvenile Delinquency Research." *Am J Orthopsychiatry* 17:151-60 Ja '47. * (*PA* 21:2417)

589. SISK, HENRY L. "A Clinical Case Study Utilizing the Rorschach and the Murray Thematic Apperception Tests." *J Clin Psychol* 3:293-8 Jl '47. * (*PA* 22:310)

590. SISK, HENRY L. "A Reply to Winfield's Study of the Multiple Choice Rorschach." *J Appl Psychol* 31:446-8 Ag '47. *

591. SLOAN, WILLIAM. "Mental Deficiency as a Symptom of Personality Disturbance." *Am J Mental Def* 52:31-6 Jl '47. *

592. STEINER, MATILDA E. "The Use of Rorschach Method in Industry." *Rorschach Res Exch & J Proj Tech* 11(1):46-52 '47. * (*PA* 22:3233)

593. WEKSTEIN, LOUIS. "X-Raying the Personality: An Interpretative Evaluation of Two Projection Techniques." *Scientific Mo* 65:133-42 Ag '47. * (*PA* 22:220)

594. WILKINS, WALTER L., AND ADAMS, AUSTIN J. "The Use of the Rorschach Test Under Hypnosis and Under Sodium Amytal in Military Psychiatry." *J General Psychol* 36:131-8 Ap '47. * (*PA* 22:3041)

595. WILLIAMS, GERTHA. "The Possibilities of the Rorschach Technique in Industry." *Personnel* 24:224-31 N '47. * (*PA* 22:1897)

596. WILLIAMS, MEYER. "An Experimental Study of Intellectual Control Under Stress and Associated Rorschach Factors." *J Consult Psychol* 11:21-9 Ja-F '47. * (*PA* 21:2803)

597. ZUBIN, JOSEPH; LEVY, DAVID M.; AND RUST, RALPH. "Movement Responses in Normals. Schizophrenics and Neurotics on the Levy Movement Cards." Abstract. *Am Psychol* 2:269 Ag '47. * (*PA* 21:4401, title only)

598. STEINMETZ, HARRY C. "Obfuscating Personality." Letter. *Scientific Mo* 66:87 Ja '48. *

Morris Krugman, Assistant Superintendent in Charge of Guidance, Public Schools, New York, New York. The Rorschach method, in use since 1921, continues to be the most important single psychological instrument for the measurement of personality. Other projective techniques, notably the *Thematic Apperception Test* (TAT), have received considerable attention in recent years; but, as yet, not one of them has seriously challenged the place of the Rorschach in the clinical program. With further development, TAT should constitute an excellent supplement to the Rorschach, since the latter provides clues to the personality structure, while the former supplies the mental content and dynamics.

Although there is still considerable criticism of the Rorschach as a psychometric tool from some quarters, particularly from statisticians without clinical orientation, that criticism now amounts to a whisper when compared with the uproar against the method ten or twelve years ago. With the advance of more dynamic methods of diagnosis and therapy in clinical psychology, psychologists have come to recognize that a complex instrument like the Rorschach cannot yield a simple score that may be validated by the application of a Pearson or other correlation, but that the entire configuration must be compared with the clinical picture obtained from such procedures as the full case study or the psychiatric examination. In other words, validation must be by clinical rather than by mathematical processes. The Rorschach has stood the clinical test well throughout the years and has come out stronger for it; on the other hand, attempts at atomistic validation have been unsuccessful and will probably continue to be so. The test loses its value when broken down into its elements. It has meaning only when its elements are treated organismically in terms of their interrelationships.

Several schools of thought have arisen among Rorschach workers. Among the more important is that of Oberholzer, who follows Rorschach almost literally. Beck is a disciple of Oberholzer, but he deviates somewhat from the original. Klopfer has a very large following; his difference from the Psychodiagnostic lies in the designation of new scoring categories for some of the concepts which Rorschach originally discussed qualitatively. Rapaport claims that he follows Rorschach most closely, but actually, he deviates most of all. In the main, the differences among the various groups are in semantics and in symbols for the same concepts rather than in basic concepts.

The Rorschach method, as used in most psychological clinics, is an individual method. In 1941 Harrower–Erickson introduced the Group Rorschach and in 1945 the Multiple-Choice Rorschach. The Group Rorschach is administered by projecting the ten plates, one at a time, on a screen and having the subjects write their responses on given forms. In the Multiple-Choice Rorschach, the plates are projected in the same manner, but the responses are limited to choices among a given list for each plate. The group method seems to have some validity for screening purposes, although it cannot be used for individual clinical diagnosis in the way the individual test can. The multiple-choice test is of doubtful validity even as a screening method.

An objective method for evaluating factors of adjustment or maladjustment on the Rorschach was devised by Munroe and called the Inspection Technique. This consists essentially of a check list of Rorschach categories from which prediction of later adjustment can be made. This, too, is not equivalent to the complete Rorschach personality study, but it has merit when used for the purpose mentioned.

Two parallel sets of plates have been devised for use as an alternate series to the original Rorschach. One of these was developed in Europe—the Behn–Eschenberg series; the other was recently published in this country by Harrower–Erickson and Steiner. Although there is need for a duplicate series of plates, they are still used only occasionally.

J. R. Wittenborn, Assistant Professor of Psychology, Yale University, New Haven, Connecticut. Since the publication of Dr. Hermann Rorschach's *Psychodiagnostics* in 1921, this method of personality evaluation has gained steadily in popularity. Today graduate instruction in the Rorschach method is offered in departments of psychology where less than a decade ago more conservative phases of clinical psychology were shunned. At present, reservations concerning the ink blot test are rapidly becoming unfashionable. Since from the standpoint of relative progress little more is known now about the ink blots than was known by Rorschach, this rapid acceptance requires comment.

The enthusiasm for the Rorschach method manifested by almost all who have used it is an obvious factor in its growing popularity. The appearance of numerous publications suggesting new Rorschach practices and supporting old

ones has also encouraged this growth. The current trend in psychology and psychiatry toward replacing static, categorical concepts of personality with flexible, highly descriptive concepts of personality based on a dynamic view of behavior is also favorable to the acceptance of a flexible instrument such as the Rorschach. Underlying all of these developments, however, is a growing public consciousness of and tolerance for the emotional problems of the individual as a topic worthy of thorough study and sympathetic understanding. With this increase of public interest there arises a lively demand for new and powerful means of personality appraisal. For the gratification of these demands, no other single instrument now known appears to offer more promise than the Rorschach.

Despite the fact that there are many who hope that the Rorschach method may have a brilliant future, this method has neither the advantage of a theory worthy of the name nor, with certain exceptions, adequately designed research. What passes for research in this field is usually naïvely conceived, inadequately controlled, and only rarely subjected to usual standards of experimental rigor with respect to statistical tests and freedom from ambiguity. Despite these limitations, the test flourishes, its admirers multiply, and its claims proliferate.

This paradox may be partly understood in view of the tremendous difficulty of conceiving experimental designs appropriate to test the properties of an instrument of such remarkable power and flexibility. This difficulty is not lessened by the fact that several most eminent Rorschach authorities differ from each other with respect to details of scoring and interpretation (275, 364, 415, 535). Many Rorschach authorities have discouraged submitting the test to critical investigation. In some cases this reluctance may have been due to distrust of the capacity of usual methods of investigation to demonstrate the true quality of this complex instrument. In other cases, however, this suspicion of research is born of a convention that the Rorschach analysis is an intuitive analysis, an art, and not subject to scientific scrutiny. Finally, it is true that numerous enthusiastic would-be investigators of the Rorschach have found their way most difficult because of the dilemma inherent in attempting to study an instrument of personality appraisal when personality itself is as yet so little understood.

The Rorschach test, it will be remembered,

was developed in the atmosphere of a mental hospital, and it has won much of its popularity in the study of individuals for whom serious disturbance of affect, impulse, or character is suspected. This background combined with its common use in the differential diagnosis of psychotic groups and patients suspected of suffering from cerebral lesions causes it to be associated in the thoughts of many with the neuropsychiatric clinic, the mental hospital, and formal psychiatric work. Many workers, however, have found it to be extremely useful in vocational and educational guidance of college students as well as in primarily therapeutic work. In helping the individual plan his future it is frequently desirable to know the answer to such questions as: How does he control his affect? Is he prone to anxiety? Can he accept his needs and impulses? To what degree can he be assertive? Is he likely to seek dependent relations? Can he make a good sexual adjustment? Such questions as these and many similar ones may be answered much more readily through the aid of the Rorschach than without it. For these reasons alone, its wide use seems to be amply indicated.

The administration and interpretation of the Rorschach requires special training which many clinical psychologists have not had. Clinics or guidance bureaus contemplating the use of the Rorschach are confronted with several alternatives: securing the services of clinical psychologists experienced with the use of the Rorschach; providing for the training of present members of the staff in the Rorschach method; or hiring a Rorschach technician (a person trained in the Rorschach technique but with few if any of the other skills and experiences which are an important part of the psychologist's qualifications). The last alternative of depending on the services of the person trained only in Rorschach seems to be favored by two groups: one is the group which believes that the Rorschach method comprises a psychology in itself and that any person well trained in the Rorschach method is a competent psychologist; the other group is inclined to regard the mental tester as a technician and to feel that the Rorschach may be handled by a psychometrist at much the same level as the *American Council on Education Psychological Examination,* for example, is handled by a psychometrist. It is probable that a Rorschach worker at a technician level (i.e., an individual trained only in Rorschach) may

have an important place in mental hospital work and certain psychiatric clinics. In most guidance and minor therapy with adults, however, the writer has observed a difference between the quality of the Rorschach personality descriptions by workers who have a clinician's knowledge of people and those by workers who are regarded as good testers but who have had little or no responsible clinical experience.

One deterrent to the wider use of Rorschach in educational and vocational guidance is the expense of preparing a protocol. An hour is ordinarily required for merely eliciting the responses of the subject and conducting an inquiry. The actual scoring and interpretation of the responses may require several hours. For the administration, full scoring, and interpretation of the Rorschach, three hours is a moderate time allowance. For most guidance situations this is prohibitive. It is fortunate, therefore, that many important questions concerning an individual may be answered from a mere inspection of the responses. Factors usually of great importance in guidance and readily discerned from an inspection of the Rorschach responses are the level of psychosexual development, quality of affective control, level of ambition, efficiency and practicality in work, and others. As a logical expression of the increased interest in Rorschach, group methods of administration have been developed. The group procedures are at present subject to conflicting reports and justify separate **review.**

In general, it may be said that the Rorschach is one of the most promising of our methods for personality evaluation. When one considers, however, the vast cost of training and employing Rorschach workers as well as the guidance and care given individuals as a result of Rorschach evaluations, it is apparent that too little is known about this important instrument.

For related reviews, see 74–91.

[74]

[*Re* Rorschach.] BECK, SAMUEL J. **Personality Structure in Schizophrenia: A Rorschach Investigation in 81 Patients and 64 Controls.** Preface by C. Macfie Campbell. Nervous and Mental Disease Monographs, No. 63. New York: Nervous and Mental Disease Monographs, 1938. Pp. 88. Out of print. * (*PA* 13:277)

J Abn & Social Psychol 36:119–20 Ja '41. *D. Shakow.* * The author continues in this volume his pioneer work in the elucidation and application of the Rorschach test. The style is

lively and conservational—a tendency perhaps
pushed occasionally a trifle too far. This reviewer finds it difficult to become accustomed
to the use of "healthy" for the more generally
accepted "normal"; somehow a picture of an
Iowa 4–H contest winner persists in obtruding
itself at each such mention! Too, the reference
to the Rorschach "experiment" (more persistently used in others of the author's works) gives
the impression of a degree of control which the
test procedures do not ordinarily have. Although
the distinction between test and experimental
situations cannot clearly be drawn, the method
of administration used in the present study obviously falls into the former category. These are,
however, minor points. More important is the
fact that the author has not taken his own
recognition of the danger of lumping schizophrenics together (p. 14) seriously. An essential
methodological point is involved here. Paranoids
and hebephrenics (to take the most clearly dis-
guishable types and to accept a classification system which admittedly has its weaknesses) have
in a number of studies been shown to fall on
either side of the normal in certain characteristics. The combining of groups tends to wipe out
important differences by pushing towards uni-
modality tendencies which actually go in the
direction of bimodality. It is likely that a number of the negative results obtained in dealing
with schizophrenia may be due to such disregard
of fundamental syndromes. The personality
structure of schizophrenia which the author develops is in considerable harmony with clinical,
test, and experimental findings as well as with
the work of other Rorschach studies such as
those of Skalweit, Rickers-Ovsiankina, and
Rorschach himself. The monograph will undoubtedly take its place as one of the important
items in the Rorschach bibliography of schizophrenia and is, of course, essential to the Rorschacher. One must, however, admit that the
reader lays down the volume with a feeling of
incomplete satisfaction—due perhaps to the fact
that acquaintance with the extent of the experience and background of the author in psychopathology had led one to expect a much more
detailed and extensive consideration of the subject than is actually presented. Now that the
statistical aspects have been considered, cannot
we expect from him a supplementary essay relating clinical schizophrenic pictures in detail to
Rorschach findings?

For additional reviews, see 40:B841.

[75]

★[*Re* Rorschach.] Beck, Samuel J. **Rorschach's
Test: I, Basic Processes.** Foreword by Willard L.
Valentine. New York: Grune & Stratton, Inc., 1944.
Pp. xiii, 223. $3.50. * (*PA* 18:2837)

Am J Orthopsychiatry 15:178–9 Ja '45.
L(awson) G. L(owrey). * Beck demonstrates
thoroughly the processes used in evaluating responses in the Rorschach. * An especially interesting chapter is on "scoring problems," in
which the solutions for the questions involved in
scoring variable responses to Card I are presented. There is no interpretation in terms of
the whole personality structure. The effort
rather is to establish a stable manual of procedure. * For the Rorschach worker of some
experience this is certainly the most important
book yet to appear. While it presents a systematic analysis of each symbol, some familiarity with the test is desirable for most effective
use of the book. It is an entirely adequate suc-
cessor to Beck's *Introduction,* published by our
own Association in 1937, which is widely used
as a manual.

Am J Psychiatry 101:709–10 Mr '45. F. C.
Redlich. * The book....does not contain any new
fundamentals but includes much illustrative
material, a discussion of the many problems of
scoring, and consists chiefly of tables containing
thousands of responses which have been scored
by the author. This will be helpful to anyone
endeavoring to score a Rorschach record,
whether or not he accepts Beck's own refinements of the method or belongs to another
Rorschach "School." One criticism of these
tables is a certain lack of system which makes
it difficult to find the particular response one is
looking for; an alphabetic arrangement would
have been very helpful. The discussion advances
knowledge on some problems of scoring, e.g.,
the P response and the problem of "sequence"
and "approach." The problem of the scoring F
plus and F minus responses, as well as the
scoring of some M responses (e.g., animal
movement), are still far from being settled. The
reviewer agrees with Beck that the original (O)
response cannot be analysed in a quantitative
way; however, original and individual responses
as scored by Rorschach may still be of great
clinical significance. The old question arises as
to whether the Rorschach method can be made
an exact quantitative test. Attempts in this direction should be encouraged but the limitations of
such a procedure at the present stage of de-

velopment of the test ought to be kept constantly in mind. For instance, the reviewer is not convinced that Beck's elaborate method of scoring the organization (Z) response is worth the effort, although every Rorschach worker will agree as to the qualitative value of the (Z) response. The bibliography is short and does not do justice to other workers in the field. It is difficult to come to a definite opinion about this book without seeing its counterpart on interpretation or, as Beck optimistically says, "the correlation of clinical and Rorschach behavior." So far, our observation of both clinical [and Rorschach] behavior seems far too vague and uncertain to warrant such optimism; but it is stimulating to keep such endeavor in mind as a distant goal. Certainly agreements on scoring can be reached more easily than agreements on interpretation, just as agreements on grammar and syntax can be reached more easily than agreements on meaning; but scoring and interpretation are interdependent and the various elements should only be differentiated in the light of clinical meaning. Beck has made a real contribution with his first book, and much may be expected of the second, after the completion of the chapters on interpretation and clinical application. Generally speaking the present volume is a practical, helpful manual and in one respect constitutes a step ahead. The current books on the Rorschach method indicate the end of a period in which this valuable auxiliary technique ceases to be a secret cult which could be transmitted only to members of the tribe.

Am J Psychol 58:145–6 Ja '45. M. R. Harrower–Erickson. The Rorschach method can never be learned theoretically. Thus no basic text concerning it, no matter how clear, systematic or thorough it is, can provide a substitute for the collection of records which every experimenter must obtain before he is letter perfect in the technique. The chief criterion of a good text, therefore, is its ability to answer the maximal number of questions which the experimenter will inevitably ask once he is faced with the actual problems of scoring and interpreting specific records. * Beck's most outstanding contribution to the inkblot technique is developed in the chapter on Organizational Activity, where he makes explicit an idea merely hinted at by Rorschach; namely, that the manner and degree of the subject's ability to combine and synthesize various areas of the blots is important in the estimation of mental activity. Nu-

merical values have been given to various combinations of details in each of the ten cards, so that quantative scores for this activity can be obtained. Chapter vii (Approach and Sequence) demonstrates a very simple, but telling, manner of recording the sequence of responses, so that this aspect of the record can be appraised at a glance. * Beck has given us a valuable addition to the rapidly growing Rorschach literature. For while the detailed examples make for disconnected reading by the casual inquirer who is unfamiliar with the blots, the book undoubtedly answers many of the questions which arise inevitably for the serious student, and this is the main function of such a text.

Brit J Ed Psychol 14:168 N '44. W. D. W(all). For serious workers with the Rorschach Test this volume is indispensable. Rorschach's original scoring categories, conservatively developed in the light of much recent research and Dr. Beck's own extensive experience, are here very clearly illustrated and in some cases statistically evaluated. Thus the book here considered will do much to eliminate the subjective variations in scoring responses which have hindered validation experiments with Rorschach findings. In many categories the author parts company with other writers on the subject; but, although the symbols used differ, in most essentials he agrees with Klopfer and Kelley, whose book was previously reviewed in this *Journal.* With admirable candour he clearly differentiates those categories and scorings which are statistically justified from those in which subjective judgment is still paramount in the absence of reliable evidence. His lists of common and uncommon details, of F+ and F– responses and of sigma scores for organisation of details are of great practical use, as too are the discussion of approach and sequence and the list of popular responses. The complexity of scoring which necessitates so exhaustive a manual of illustrative material does, however, raise the question of whether the test itself is of more theoretic than practical value, whether the time consumed in administration and scoring produces a more accurate diagnosis than could be obtained by a well-directed clinical interview. The answer is, I think, that the test is a very useful clinical adjunct, especially with a suspicious or defensive patient.

Brit J Psychol 36:46 S '45. * This book would be of great use to anyone well acquainted with the Rorschach method, but useless to the beginner. No interpretations are given.

J Am Med Assn 126:927 D 2 '44. * a lucid, specific analysis of the way in which individual Rorschach responses are evaluated or "scored" * After employing scientific experimental procedure Dr. Beck has written a technical manual replete with countless examples * One of the unique contributions....is the chapter on the organization activity, wherein the author places a relatively unexplored significant mental process on a statistical basis. This manual should enable much wider use of the Rorschach test as it can be understood by beginners. It likewise can be utilized as a reference book for experienced testers and fulfils a concete need.

J Med Soc N J 41:453-4 D '44. F. W. O'Brien. A good deal of the confusion attendant to the Rorschach test is due to the fact that most of the writings on the subject reflect the individual interpretation of the examiner in which certain personal ramifications are necessarily included in order to explain such interpretations. This book is an important step forward in the use of the Rorschach test. It merely attempts to set up a stable and standard method of applying the test and cites verbatim reactions subsequently recording the reactions under standard Rorschach symbols. It should go far in setting up standards that will lead to a general understanding and greater usage of the test. It will also assist in providing a basis of comparison in evaluating the various techniques of the examiners. This should result in a higher standard generally in the application of the test. The book fills an important need in the literature relating to the Rorschach test.

Psychiatric Q 18:518-20 Jl '44. * seems to be the greatest collection of scoring samples available in print * To formalize the scoring of responses and make it as uniform as possible, Beck placed great emphasis on the wording of the responses. His attempts at standardization are in terms of the verbal form of the subject's responses rather than in terms of the visual images projected by the subjects into the blots. These projected visual images cannot be directly studied. The subjects have to describe them in order to make them accessible to the examiner. In the opinion of this reviewer, the verbal responses are indispensable but only as a means to a goal, not as the goal itself. Rorschach himself made this plain, and it is for this reason that he called his test a test of per-

ception. An exclusive reliance on the verbal form of the subject's response leads Beck, e.g., to score every "butterfly" response to Plate 1 as an F+ because "butterfly" is a frequent response of healthy persons, even when the subject's image of the butterfly is quite different from that of the healthy person's and incompatible with the real shape of a butterfly. * Fortunately for the beginner, for whom the book is intended, Beck is not consistent in his attitude of formalized standardization. Now and then, throughout the book, he departs from a rigid procedure and even overrules a subject. * Beck's feeling that interest in the psychological significance of the M is lacking is hardly justified in view of a number of articles by several authors on this very subject. Beck is occasionally polemical and somewhat inadequately presents the views of those he criticizes. E.g., Klopfer's FM or animal movement response and m or inanimate movement response are not "various forms of M" but are varieties of the F or form response. Beck justly warns against the "naïve largesse with this label M." However, he himself is rather generous with the symbol M and scores as human movement "a man sitting in an armchair" (projected in a tiny edge detail) or "the phallus, hanging down, not the erect position" (another tiny edge detail). There is no evidence of any motion or kinesthetic feeling in either of these responses which the reviewer sees as rather typical nongenuine, secondary movement responses, which are not scored as M. In these and similar examples, we are not dealing "with a movement sensed in the figure" for there is even no motion at all, and no kinesthetic feeling of tension or readiness of movement. The book will definitely aid the beginner in the acquisition of good scoring habits. Increased experience will guard the student against its shortcomings of formalized uniformity. Beck's "Basic Processes" is a welcome addition to the growing number of textbooks of the Rorschach method.

Psychoanalytic Q 13:508-12 O '44. Frederic S. Weil. * It was the reviewer's task to probe the clinical material and the statistical method, on which the scoring of the 'literally thousands of detailed and individual responses' is based. As sources of the responses the author used: patients in milder mental disturbance; adults in the community at large, comprising persons of average, high average and very superior intelligence, overtly in good mental health; adults in

psychoanalytic treatment; General Hospital patients; patients in acute schizophrenic disorganizations; a small group of patients with brain
pathology. Thus, the subjects whose records
were used represent a mixture of overtly sick
and of doubtfully healthy people in an unknown
proportion. Such clinical material used as a basis
for standardizing values of single factors is definitely objectionable, because standards which
are used for comparison must be based on normal clinical material. Out of Beck's six groups,
only one group (the second) represents overtly
mentally healthy and intelligent people. But how
many even intelligent persons, who 'overtly'
seem to be in good mental health, are neurotics!
A considerable number of our analytic patients
belong in this group. On the other hand, there
is not one factor in the Rorschach test which
may not be affected by even an inconspicuous
neurosis. A case in point is the differentiation
between Form responses, F+ and F−, in Chapter III. Beck realizes the definite need for
such a differentiation as well as the difficulty of
carrying it through. Roughly his criteria boil
down to the statement that intelligent persons
perceive good forms, unintelligent persons and
schizophrenics perceive poor forms. Thus in
Table 18 Beck classifies many poor responses
as F+, e.g., a good number of anatomical and
geographical interpretations. His criteria are debatable. Many neurotics score an alarmingly low
F+% in spite of a definite potentially good
intelligence. Another case in point is the author's
differentiation between Detail and Rare detail
responses, dealt with in Chapter III. Here, as
well as with the differentiation of Form responses, it stands to reason that the standards
should be derived from mentally healthy individuals. Furthermore it is unfortunate that in
this very important chapter Beck bases his conclusions on the statistics of someone else, Dr.
Ralph R. Brown; nor is it made clear on what
material these statistics are based. And, above
all, there is a lack of specifications as to the differentiation between D and Dd in each single
card. The same objections hold against the author's mode of dealing with the Approach in
Chapter VII. Beck cites Rorschach's incidental
statement in the latter's posthumously published
paper: 'A normal average distribution would
be 8 W, 23 D and 3 Dd.' Beck opposes this with
his own formula: 6 W, 20 D and 4 Dd, which he
considers as 'more consistently representative of
the validating facts.' However, he omits the

statistical proof. Had he started out with unquestionably mentally healthy and intelligent
subjects he would have discovered that the formula derived from such clinical material is
nearer to the original Rorschach formula than
to his own. In Chapter XIV the author doubles
the Popular responses. The statistics are again
Brown's. Unfortunately they are not appended
for reasons of space. In Chapter VIII, dealing
with Movement responses, Beck duly stresses
the subjective and objective difficulties in verifying M responses. He says about movement in
geometric figures and single lines: 'I myself
score such responses M as an act of faith in
Rorschach and Oberholzer rather than from
conviction based on validated findings'. He need
not have relied on faith, had he considered such
interpretations M responses only in persons who
have perceived many other clearcut M's. With
another less kinesthetic individual the same interpretation may be a definite F. This complication is apparently disliked by the author, nor
would it fit into his neat rubrics. But here, too,
Freud's *'Ça n'empêche pas d'exister'* holds.
Mutatis mutandis, the same is valid with regard
to the Color responses, which are dealt with and
listed in detail in Chapter IX. The author does
not point out that the same interpretation of the
same colored entity represents a pure Form with
one subject, a Form color response with another
subject, and even a Color form response with a
third subject. In Chapter X, devoted to the light
determined responses, it appears comforting and
convincing that the author differentiates only
between the Vista, i.e., the three-dimensional,
and the flat Grey interpretations. Grey, however,
is a color, more specifically a color visibly composed of black and white. Why, then, substitute
it for the Black white interpretations, which
Oberholzer has already described and qualified
as to their clinical significance in his paper on
post traumatic conditions (1931), and recently
in Dubois's book about the Aloris. Thus far the
author has adhered to Rorschach's original concepts. However, he has introduced changes concerning the factors as well as the testing procedure. The most striking one is that he has
omitted Rorschach's Original answer, and
wrongly so. In the reviewer's opinion no other
factor reflects the education and background of
a subject or hints at a neurosis as does the presence or absence of Original answers. In Chapter VI Beck introduces a new factor Z, the
Organization activity. Its justification is hard

to challenge as the discussion of its clinical significance is apparently reserved for a second volume. However, two objections can already be made. First, although Beck gives a list he omits the mode of derivation of the stated Organization values for the 10 figures. Secondly, Beck has already stated in his previous book, the Introduction, that 'Assoziationsbetrieb is essentially organization activity'. In the present volume he also translates Assoziationsbetrieb as 'combining or organizing activity' as 'organization drive', or as 'organizing activity'. However, to associate and to organize are not the same; and the question arises whether this is not more than just a linguistic misunderstanding. The English translators of Rorschach's Psychodiagnostics consistently translate Assoziationsbetrieb as 'associative activity' which is acceptable. As a third change Beck has modified the signature: Rorschach's Do becomes Hdx or Adx. The argument that anxiety rather than oligophrenia lies behind this reaction does not hold water. Did not Rorschach himself state that 'Do occur not only in oligophrenics but also in depressives and anxious subjects, as well as always in compulsives.' He could have added that they occur in subjects who do not see the forest for the trees. In other words they occur when an obviously specific form of inhibition of thought processes (Denkhemmung) is at work for whatever cause: stupidity, depression, anxiety or other factors. With regard to the same Chapter, XV, the reviewer wishes to add that not only should the sex interpretations be separated from the human detail and listed separately, but likewise the anal interpretations. So much for the author's modifications of test factors. Another of his modifications applies to the experimental procedure, namely the so-called inquiry, the repetition of the test in reverse in order to verify the entities and qualities of the single answers. Rorschach obviously did not consider such an inquiry necessary. Why should not the examiner, if any doubt arises, make the subject show the entity immediately after the response was given and induce him through neutral questions to verify or exclude the doubtful determinants? If, in a difficult response, the examiner's question should become too outspoken and thus risk a betrayal of possible determinants, one may postpone the clarification of this specific response until the end. But why, for this one instance, repeat the entire test? The immediate questioning, directly after a response is given,

offers the decisive advantage of reliability, a reliability which is lessened after a patient has gone through the entire test when he is likely to change his interpretations or even not to recognize them again or to see them in a different way. The last possibility, namely additional new interpretations, are explicitly disregarded even by Beck. One more remark about the author's technique: In Chapter IV, on Scoring, he says: '. . . for permanent recording of these very rare as well as of the poorly outlined Dd the best method is to use a facsimile of the Rorschach test card.' The reviewer still considers tracing the more exact method for this purpose. The facsimiles leaves out the most subtle details, and the fact that a Dd was seen may be much less decisive for the diagnosis than its specific type. A technical review of a technical book necessarily sounds more critical than it actually is. It is to be hoped that the second volume will appear soon.

Psychol B 43:379–80 Jl '46. Robert M. Lindner. It is unquestionably true that Dr. Beck has once more demonstrated his competence and scholarship by producing this book. The question, however, is just how much is contributed by it—and by other like material—to American psychology and psychiatry. From where this reviewer sits, the answer to the question is disappointing. Volume I of Beck's *Rorschach's Test* proposes to bring the presumptive reader up to date in Dr. Beck's cherished ambition to standardize and "demonstrate the processes used in evaluating Rorschach test responses." It fulfills its announced intention by painstakingly and deliberately detailing responses, rationalizing the use of the various symbols, explaining and cataloguing, arguing and justifying, through sixteen laborious chapters chaperoned by a brief bibliography, two appended tables, and ten disjointed schema of the blots. With commentary added to commentary, as one reads it, it takes on more and more the character of the Babylonian *Talmud*. To read such a book is obviously out of the question: to study it requires a fixity of purpose amounting almost to a dedication. Its real service will be as another standard reference work in a young but already needlessly over-complicated field. The practicing psychiatrist or psychologist is coming to rely upon the Rorschach as he does upon almost no other tool. It is a good technique, perhaps the best of the projective methods, and he appreciates what it can do for him by way of evaluating the personality and, indeed, for certain services nowhere else available. He regards it practically, as an invaluable instrument for diagnosis, as an index and guide to therapeusis, as a clue to treatment progress. Hence the cultism of Rorschachers, their allegiances, their bickerings and jealousies, bore and distract him; so also do their endless disputes over—let us say—the criteria of distinction between one F and another. What the clinician wants from the Rorschach worker and researcher are ways of increasing the sensitivity of the test, enlarging its scope, and making it more informative. The present book, on the other hand, leaves the field where it was before it was written. Perhaps the implied criticism of this review is unjustified in view of the fact that the volume under consideration really purports to do nothing more than reveal "basic processes." If this is so, however, then it must be taken as but another symptom of that compulsive over-zealousness to substitute cold hieroglyphs for warm humans that so diverts the stream of clinical endeavor in the behavior sciences. As for the volume itself, from the point of view of sheer book-making it is a satisfactory job of work. While the material could have been arranged in a manner more considerate of the reader and more sparing on his patience, it must be considered that merely setting up (much less proof reading) the text was a staggering accomplishment. For those who are preoccupied with scoring problems in Rorschach work and who adhere to the Beck method as exposited already in his *Manual* and other published works, this volume is an amplification and extension of what they already know. But for those who are seeking help in their efforts to help others, this is merely another book bound in blue.

Psychosom Med 6:342–3 O '44. Saul Rosenzweig. Any book concerned with the Rorschach test is inevitably of interest to the proponents of psychosomatic medicine. Few trustworthy and penetrating psychological tools are available for the study of the total personality and among these the Rorschach procedure is probably the most distinguished. In the present volume Beck continues his pioneer work with this test, which he first expertly represented in this country after an apprenticeship in Zurich with Oberholzer, himself a direct disciple of Rorschach. Against this historical background the title of the book is significantly laconic. Many "Rorschachers" have departed radically and, according to Beck's implication, dangerously from the original test. Some are self-styled experts and others have little adequate training or experience with the technique in its various clinical applications. Since the Rorschach of all tests is most technical and least adapted for popular use, Beck is concerned over its abuse. The title— *Rorschach's Test*—sets forth in a word what he hopes to achieve by the publication. * The scoring categories here included do not differ very much from those originally used by Rorschach himself. Beck is, in a sense, a defender of the faith though he admits readiness to accept new scoring categories and symbols once they have proved empirically to be an advance over the original test procedure. * Shading responses are given a somewhat novel treatment * The organization response—Z—represents Beck's most original contribution though based upon suggestions contained in Rorschach's own statements. When two or more parts of the blot figure are seen in relation to one another with a resultant emergence of new meaning the Z score is applied. This category aligns itself with the W and M factors as indicating creative or generalizing capacity but appears to reveal aspects of the personality which the other two categories less specifically indicate. On the basis of considerable research and careful statistical evaluation, examples for the scoring of Z in the various figures are given in the text and a table in the Appendices makes available the Z values for various types of organization encountered in the ten figures. An evaluation of the book must inevitably emphasize the positive features of which it has so many. The conservatism of the author will strike many users of the method as salutary. It is easy to be carried away by intuitive fancy in almost any projective procedure. By emphasizing the objective and, where possible, the statistical validation of the scoring categories Beck has done much to make the already-mentioned conservatism progressive. He has not, however, sacrificed psychological meaning by making clinical judgment secondary to statistical objectivity. On the whole the book will probably be easier for most students to use than the already available texts because, for one thing, it employs a minimum of scoring categories. It is true that the examples of responses given by Beck are not always easy to follow; that some of the discussions of the scoring categories, e.g., F+, could with profit be expanded; and that an occasional inconsistency mars the going. But such minor weaknesses are inevitable in a first edition. In future editions improvements may undoubtedly be expected. One such emendation that cannot be too strongly recommended is a longer and more complete discussion of how much constitutes one response for scoring purposes. The second volume of the present work, which will complete the discussion of the method by adding the all important principles of interpretation and provide representative examples of total records, will be awaited by many with eagerness.

Q R Biol 20:191 Je '45. Wendell Muncie. * will be found very useful to Rorschach testers. *For additional reviews, see 77.*

[76]

★[*Re* Rorschach.] BECK, SAMUEL J. **Rorschach's Test: II, A Variety of Personality Pictures.** Foreword by Roy R. Grinker. New York: Grune & Stratton, Inc., 1945. Pp. xii, 402. $5.00. * (*PA* 20:1150)

Am J Psychol 59:704–9 O '46. Donald E. Super. * in no scientific sense an experimental work * The work is refreshing, for the author appreciates that the last word has not been said on the subject and he makes some attempt to relate theory of personality as developed from Rorschach material to more general theories. One oriented to psychological theory and method is inclined, however, to wonder, upon reading the forword by Grinker, Beck's chief at Michael Reese Hospital, whether Beck was in a position to do scientific work. In this brief exposition of his views, Grinker demonstrates a disregard of scientific method and of psychological fact which psychologists associated with him in the Air Forces came to know and to distrust. Describing the Rorschach test as a "research tool" of great importance, he proceeds to attribute its improvement, not to the use of accepted scientific procedures but to clinical study by investigators who have used "every assistance from clinical psychiatry, psychoanalysis, and sociology . . ."—not, apparently, from psychology, with its emphasis upon avoiding the contamination of data, upon the use of experimental and control groups, upon the accumulation of facts in quantifiable form, the development of norms, and the use of tests of significance as illustrated in Rorschachean work by Munroe's fruitful research. Within the limits set by this unscientific dictatorship, Beck has produced a volume of considerable interest .to students of personality and of Rorschach's tech-

nique. In the opening chapter he outlines a theory of personality as background for his interpretation of data. This has been too rarely done by followers of Rorschach, despite their development of a certain type of theory from the inkblots. This chapter is very brief (9 pages) and sketchy, undocumented by evidence, and somewhat dogmatic. It is followed by a longer chapter on the psychologic (*sic*) significance of Rorschach test-factors, a discussion which helps Beck to achieve his translation of Rorschach into the language of the clinic. Here again are evidences of the conflict between unscientific orientation and a desire to conform to sound standards of investigation. * At times the variety of qualifying data to be kept in mind in interpretation is frightening. * it is clear that the interpretation of a single protocol is at least as complex a matter as the interpretation of a clinical case-history, making the Rorschach, as used by Beck, rather a diagnostic *method* than a *test*. * There is no hesitancy, it seems, in accepting ....[an] *opinion* of Rorschach's as evidence, despite a quarter-century of subsequent work with the inkblots, without citing evidence on the point. * Beck shows commendable caution when he refrains (pp. 32, 33) from attaching significance to the little understood phenomenon of colornaming * forty Rorschach records, each discussed at considerable length (331 pages in all) * It would have been helpful had each record been preceded by a systematic discussion of the condition, as seen, e.g., in Bochner and Halpern. There are no records of organic, psychopathic and various other categories. As detailed records and interpretations of cases in the categories covered, this part of the book will be useful to the student of Rorschach. It gives a clear picture of the interpretation of the Rorschach data and of the derivation of a description therefrom of personality. As a means of becoming familiar with the Rorschach technique this book, with its companion volume, is unexcelled in clarity and detail. As a source of information about, or demonstration of, the validity of the test, neither of which it purports to be, it is disappointing. A Rorschach 'manual' may in time be written with validities included. Or possibly—as in the case of the Revised Stanford Binet—a separate volume on validity will follow the manual. But the data must first be systematically gathered, tabulated, and analyzed—some brands of 'clinical psychiatry' to the contrary notwithstanding.

Brit J Psychol 36:177 My '46. * This volume continues with the interpretation of responses. A detailed discussion of the interpretation and its psychological significance, suitable for the Rorschach expert, is given first; and is followed by case histories to illustrate differences of intelligence, and studies of maladjusted adolescents, neurotic adults and schizophrenics. There are, however, no cases of normal children. A comprehensive bibliography is given.

J Abn & Social Psychol 41:233–6 Ap '46. Albert I. Rabin. The long-awaited volume on the interpretation of the Rorschach has finally appeared. Beck's first volume, in which the mechanics and techniques of scoring Rorschach records were given detailed exposition, appeared more than a year ago. It showed a considerable degree of crystallization of method and reflected the author's rich experience with the test, to some extent modulated by his experimental attitude. In the two volumes of the present series, the Rorschach has come of age; it is called a *test* rather than *method* or *experiment*, the terms with which Beck introduced it in his first manual, back in 1937. The feeling is implicit that the author now considers the Rorschach a more solidified and less tentative instrument in the evaluation of the human personality than he did eight years ago. The tremendous amount of work done with this method during recent years and the accumulated experience with it justify to a considerable degree such a viewpoint. The present volume is truly a "second" book in the study of the Rorschach test. Anyone attempting to read this book must be thoroughly familiar with the Rorschach "language," the scoring symbols, and the method of making a record summary. It is the author's assumption that the basic material of Volume I or its equivalent has been mastered and can be applied in following the personality analyses comprising the bulk of this book. * Part I is devoted to a general statement of principles and a description of personality components as related to the Rorschach, while the second part, which covers more than 80 per cent of the entire volume, is devoted to a detailed and masterful analysis of forty-seven Rorschach records representing a variety of diagnostic, normal and abnormal, groups. Though Beck disclaims any "effort at outlining any theory of personality," this is exactly what he is attempting to do in the first brief chapter of the book. It seems to be an attempt to bridge the gap between scientific, academic, and experimental psychology, on the one hand, and clinical psychology and psychiatry, on the other. The chapter is all too sketchy to accomplish such a task and leaves some dichotomies like "abstract" vs. "practical" intelligence, or "excitement" vs. "oppression," insufficiently clarified in terms of their relationship to the mass of scientific data compiled during many years of psychological research. Yet, it is difficult to find a better presentation in which the "island" of Rorschach personality theory approaches any closer to the "mainland" of the general psychology of personality. The admission that the Rorschach Test does not attempt to give a *"complete"* personality picture is quite evident; it selects personality factors and traits and shows their interrelationships. * A notable refinement in his new scoring as compared with his previous publications is the more precise differentiation between surface color (Y) and vista and perspective (V) in the black-grey cards. Different determination of rare and common details is also obvious. Even the "shading shock" (Klopfer), or, as Beck calls it, "grey-black shock," is given a place of prominence in the array of Rorschach factors. Throughout this part of the book, which draws considerably upon psychoanalytic theory, Beck remains the cautious and eclectic scientific experimentalist dealing, basically, with an empirical method of personality evaluation. Furthermore, it is quite apparent that Beck does not consider the Rorschach as a "closed and circumscribed system," but as an instrument which possesses a number of tentative and provisional aspects, and which is in need of further refinement, research, and validation. The alert reader will find, in this part of the book, a number of direct as well as indirect suggestions for further inquiry and investigation. Part II of this volume is devoted entirely to the detailed protocols and interpretations of the records of some forty individuals. The first ten records cover, in the author's words, the "intelligence curve." * It is understandable that the author was not at liberty to give full and adequate clinical personality characterizations of these individuals. Had he not been governed by the need for the anonymity of these subjects, a better understanding of the relationship between the Rorschach factors and the personality patterns would have been gained. The nine additional records of adolescents, within the normal range, are a particularly valuable contribution to the Rorschach literature. Their value is to be found especially in the aid they may provide in differential diagnosis. Many "normal" adolescent records resemble those of psychotic patients. Interpretative caution, therefore, is in order. The remaining records, with the exception of the last section, deal with "schizophrenic solutions" and "neurotic struggles." There, a wealth of material, including clinical notes, is presented. Beck brings into play abundant clinical experience as well as intuitive clinical sense and sheer artistic Rorschach empathy. The interpretations are penetrating and the constant reference to the factors and the records is very instructive. In the last section, four "before and after" Rorschach studies are analyzed. The clinician will find the analysis of the first case of special value. The occasionally difficult problem of differential diagnosis between schizophrenia and manic depressive psychosis is brought out and made salient. Unfortunately, the circular psychoses as such receive little attention in this book. The only other case dealing with this type of disorder may also be found in this section. The groupings of organic and convulsive disorders, psychopathic states, and behavior disorders and studies of the Rorschach in childhood are omitted. The reason for this omission is not clear. It may well become the subject of a third volume in the present series. In his 1937 monograph, Beck prefaced the records of each diagnostic group with a descriptive summary of Rorschach relationships and a quantitative table of Rorschach signs and their frequency of occurrence in the particular group under consideration. The student found these summaries very helpful, though occasionally misleading. It is to be questioned, however, whether the abandonment of this method of presentation is advisable. Lack of a reference point, especially for the beginner, makes the task of Rorschach mastery even more formidable than it would be otherwise. The inclusion of some "inadequate" records would also have been worthwhile. Every Rorschach worker has the misfortune of obtaining such records. How far the interpretation should or may go in these cases is a point worthy of consideration. The present volume represents the culmination of the author's work with the Rorschach method over a period of nearly twenty years. It represents the cumulative efforts of many investi-

gators, among whom the author is a pioneer. Dr. Beck's continuous efforts to integrate Rorschach's insights and empiricism with modern psychological and psychiatric views of personality have had a salutary effect upon many clinicians and are amply reflected in this book. No psychologist who is interested in the Rorschach, whether from the clinician's viewpoint or from the point of view of the investigator or research worker, can afford to overlook this volume. It is one of the most basic works in the entire Rorschach literature.

Psychoanalytic Q 15:383–6 Jl '46. Frederic S. Weil. * Beck convincingly offers a developmental exposition of the meaning of the Color responses and also discusses the Vista and Gray answers, the color shock ('neurosis'), and the gray-black shock ('anxiety') * Considering the great importance that Beck attributes to the associational contents, its richness and breadth, his insistence on discarding Rorschach's 'Original Response' seems even more surprising. His main argument, lack of frame of reference, can easily be refuted by quoting Rorschach's definition of Original Response: 'interpretations that are given in about one hundred experiments with *normal people* about once . . . according to their quality they are either good or poor. Original+ or Original− . . .' Beck begs the question in his polemic by substituting for Rorschach's clearly defined technical term Original Response the word 'original . . . as it is commonly understood.' However, in one respect he is right: apart from the example in his Psychodiagnostics, Rorschach did not leave a list of Original Responses. Yet lack of sufficient statistics is no reason for discarding a factor, and one wonders why Beck, who checked so many Rorschach factors statistically did not do so with the Original Response. The answer is that Rorschach's Original Response is derived from a healthy intelligent average, whereas Beck's statistical raw material, as criticized in the review of his previous book, represents a mixture of overtly sick and doubtfully healthy people in an unknown proportion, which could neither furnish nor check Rorschach's Original Response. This general disregard for the normality of his raw material in his first book is also conspicuously present in the records of this second volume. Thus the Intelligence Curve, that runs with ten records from most superior via middle range to feebleminded, includes one single case which is not complicated by a more or less severe neurosis, a possible psychosis, a psychopathy or immaturity, although all these additional clinical factors change the Intelligence factors in the Rorschach test. Of the eight cases of the Adolescent Years some are suspiciously schizophrenic and all are at least so neurotic that their pathology overshadows whatever may be characteristic of the adolescent years in the Rorschach test. Among the eleven records of the Schizophrenic Solutions, on the other hand, there are two from nonschizophrenic mothers of these patients. One mother, according to Beck's Rorschach interpretations, 'plays the rôle opposite that of her daughter' whereas 'passivity seen in the (other) mother progresses to its ultimate stage (in her daughter).' Neither 'playing of the opposite rôle' nor 'extreme passivity' make for a schizophrenia as far as we know, nor can the Rorschach prove it, even if Beck's title Schizophrenic Solutions suggests a psychogenic etiology of this still enigmatical psychosis. The short and insufficient Clinical Notes present another defect. The reader, presumably a Rorschach student, looks to them for crucial proof of the validity of the test, i.e., whether Rorschach's assumptions, deductions and connections are borne out or not. What he gets are interpretations of several pages which are verified not with a clinical description but with a few lines such as: 'The fact that this man is the president of a university is in itself a validation of the Rorschach findings,' or, 'This woman . . . is a professor . . .' Where the Clinical Notes are less laconic they show, with the exception of the records of schizophrenics and feebleminded, insufficient relation to the Rorschach interpretations—they are neither proof for nor against the interpretations, neither modifications nor qualifications of them. Beck seems to be aware of that deficiency; however, excuses such as: 'Conditions precluded using biographical information or inquiry,' are hardly admissible, since clinical pictures can be given without biographical data, or more suitable material could have been chosen instead. In this connection it should be said that the titles of the cases are misleading, as they epitomize the Clinical Notes throughout, regardless of whether or not the Rorschach interpretation bears out the Clinical Note. For instance, the case with the caption Compulsion in a Young Woman is according to Beck's interpretation a neurosis, although not a compul-

sive-obsessive one. Nor in A Male Homosexual, can Beck or anyone deduce homosexuality from the Rorschach record at all (as is often the case). More instances could be easily quoted. Incidentally, the presentation of each case in the following order: Response Summary—Interpretation of the Record—Clinical Note—Response Record, does not seem logical, as the interpretation refers again and again to the response record. Any attentive reader naturally will start reading the response record, then the summary, afterwards the interpretation which he will finally compare with the clinical note. It would go beyond the scope of a review to take up each of the interpretations. One symptom, however, which is contained in almost all of them should be singled out. With the exception of the few feebleminded and some schizophrenics there is hardly a record from which Beck does not infer anxiety. This ubiquity deprives the finding of a more specific significance. Even conceding that there is anxiety in the last analysis behind most psychopathological phenomena, clinically we are more interested in knowing whether anxiety is bound, for instance, by an obsessive-compulsive neurosis or is overt, and how it manifests itself—as free anxiety, or as part of a basic mood and so forth. Here adequate clinical notes could have demonstrated that the Rorschach can show more than unqualified anxiety. Beck's two volumes on the Rorschach test are conceived as a comprehensive textbook. Such an enterprise would serve its didactic purpose even better could some amendments be made in a future edition.

Psychosom Med 8:365–6 S-O '46. Saul Rosenzweig. * Beck has made a distinguished contribution in this second part of his work. While Chapter I is perhaps unduly impressionistic and will raise questions in the minds of more systematic thinkers than he, the second chapter provides a distinct compensation. In the latter, one finds within the compass of 50 pages the best existing exposition of the significance of the various Rorschach categories in their multiple relationships. The account is by no means uniform as to fullness of detail but this treatment is in agreement with the author's available information. He studiously admits, when necessary, the incompleteness of knowledge regarding one or another test factor. One misses, however, an exposition of some of the general principles in terms of which the Rorschach method—in common, to some degree, with other projective techniques—must be interpreted. The student could profit considerably from a better appreciation of the postulates upon which Rorschach interpretation proceeds: the nature of norms, the general significance of patterns in Rorschach results and the use of "signs," as well as the more general principles connected with the "analogizing" upon which Rorschach interpretations are founded. Obviously this omission can be supplied by an instructor using the text, but the inclusion of such a discussion would have helped the average student a good deal in his orientation to the less general discussion in Chapter II and to the concrete case presentations that follow. The second main portion of the work—the case illustrations—represents a unique contribution to Rorschach literature. Nowhere else is to be found a similar array of detailed Rorschach records with a full and, at times, bold interpretation of the entailed personality pictures. Regardless of whether every Rorschach examiner —let alone every psychologist—would agree with the interpretations made by Beck, the mere publication of these records, together with the full statement of conclusions from each, makes it possible for the method to undergo a critical examination at the hands of both the initiated and the uninitiated—an opportunity unparalleled in the literature to date. The selection of the cases is, on the whole, broad, there being included the various levels of intelligence, records from adolescent subjects, the varieties of schizophrenia, and the neuroses, as well as four paired records—before and after various critical experiences: psychosis and remission, murder and imprisonment, before and during psychoanalysis. Many readers will miss illustrative records from subjects younger than the adolescent group and some will regret the absence of cases of the organic and affective psychoses. But Beck was obviously not attempting to be exhaustive; he preferred apparently to present cases representing the stress of his own experience. Those acquainted with Beck's first book—*Introduction to the Rorschach Method*—will note a methodological change in the present volume which is at the same time both more and less conservative. While in the earlier work the various chapters, each devoted to a particular diagnostic category, were introduced by a page or two of general discussion, preceded by a

paradigm for the correlated Rorschach pattern, the present volume notably omits such schematizations. Each chapter is baldly empirical. Such conclusions as are to be drawn about the feebleminded, the neurotic or the schizophrenic individual, for example, must be drawn by induction from the individual case presentations as supplemented by the general comments in Chapter II. What one finds in these diagnostic chapters, instead of the omitted general characterizations, is an exhaustive employment of detail interpreted on the postulate of psychic determinism. The close relationship between the psychoanalytic approach and the Rorschach method—which was, of course, inherent in Rorschach's own original orientation—is evident in the present work. The style in which the case interpretations are written will at times pique the reader. An occasional flash of dogmatism—a conclusion drawn from evidence seemingly insufficient or, at least, insufficiently presented—is fortified by a too carefully chosen phrase. One is sometimes overconscious of the care with which the author has selected his words or phrases—as if he were attempting to avoid somewhat too conscientiously the repetition of some essential common expression. The defect is, however, not serious since, on the whole, the exposition is lucid and one almost always knows to which details of the record a particular interpretive statement owes its existence. In general, this second volume is superior to the first. It more nearly represents a unique contribution. The importance of the earlier volume is nonetheless very real—as was brought out in an earlier review. No reader of the total work can fail to appreciate the sincere effort of the author to establish the Rorschach method on a firm research basis, his willingness to present his interpretations—sound or unsound— for what they may be worth, and a certain evidence of liveliness in the understanding of the individual human being, which is all too infrequently encountered in textbooks of personality. Taken together Beck's two volumes constitute the best existing single work on the Rorschach method of personality diagnosis.

Rorschach Res Exch 10:37–9 Mr '46. Philip Lawrence Harriman. Forty-seven **complete** Rorschach records, with the subjects' own responses and with Beck's interpretations of the structures of personalities revealed therein, are a contribution of major importance not only to the specialist in Rorschach methodology but also to the general student of human psychology. Here, in fact, are the data which reveal the inadequacy of contemporary textbooks purporting to deal with personality from the standpoint of modern psychology. Though the title of this volume may deter many psychologists from reading it, actually the case materials are of such importance that they will justify thorough study by those who have never been convinced of the validity of the Rorschach technique. The responses, though occasionally a bit fragmentary and sometimes edited, are adequate for the experimental psychologist; and the stimuli are easily identified through Beck's exposition (Volume I, pp. 13–57). Apart, therefore, from the technicalities which are of particular interest to the student of the Rorschach method, here is a contribution which should be called to the attention of experimental psychologists who are concerned with perception or with individual differences as well as with explorations into personality. Consequently, the reviewer hopes that, after deleting Chapter I, his colleagues in the Rorschach group will urge all psychologists to put this book on their own list for required reading. As a matter of fact, it is somewhat perplexing to understand why Beck has developed no more tenable theory of personality than that which he expounds in Chapter I. The case materials are all here (pp. 63–392) from which one of the most substantial contributions to the theory of personality might be written. Unfortunately, Beck has expounded his theory of personality at the beginning of his book. In none of the seven footnotes to this chapter does he reveal an acquaintance with the extensive literature, particularly the major experimental findings and the newer points of view expounded in books and journals, that have been published in recent years. His own theory seems, at least to this reviewer, to be a hodgepodge of speculation and dogmatism. Does he lack a frame of reference for his appraisals of Rorschach records, or is he hesitant about expounding his views? Why does he first present a superficial theory, and then (p. 9) deny making "an effort at outlining any theory of personality"? The records and their interpretations (pp. 63–392) are ample illustrations of the fact that he has disappointed his readers with withholding the insights which he has developed during his years of research. Chapter II deals with the meanings of the various Ror-

schach factors as scored by the Beck method. Here in fifty-two pages, are compressed the discussions which must some day be expanded into a large volume, each major point being supported by reference to experimental or clinical evidence. Frankly, the reviewer would prefer to keep this material from the eyes of "academic" psychologists until more nearly conclusive proofs of Rorschach validity are available whereby to combat their scepticism. Nineteen separate references given in footnotes, one being a novel by Sigrid Undset and another being an article by Alfred Adler, are decidedly inadequate to represent the well-established principles now available for the interpretation of Rorschach factors. Though the experienced Rorschach investigator will read some of this material with benefit, the chapter disappoints the inquirer who can no longer be satisfied with mysticism, glib generalizations, and armchair theories. Were the chapter written twenty years ago, it might be regarded as a challenge to investigators. Now, however, many dependable principles have been established by Beck and others, and the literature abounds in reports which validate many procedures in interpretative work. Of course, much remains to be done in as thorough a manner, for example, as that which Beck has worked out for the feeble-minded and the schizophrenic. Curiously, he appears to be indifferent towards the contributions of many other investigators. This chapter, therefore, is by no means the best discussion of the psychological significance of Rorschach factors that could now be written. On the other hand, if the reader be motivated to embark upon the fascinating exploration of other literature on this subject, the chapter will serve a desirable purpose. That which really makes this volume a substantial contribution to the field of psychology is found in Part II. Here for the first time are the raw materials for a study of forty-three diverse personalities explored by means of the Rorschach technique. The reviewer hopes that Beck will publish more records in the years to come, particularly those of young children and of the aged, both of which types are not represented here. The response summaries are given in terms of Beck's own methods of scoring, interpretations of varying lengths follow, and then come the original responses and the scorings. The clinical notes on each case are too brief to satisfy the reader, and Beck would do a great service to the science of psychology if he would prepare cases for subsequent publication in which all pertinent data are given to help in evaluating the Rorschach findings. The third chapter presents records illustrating various grades of intelligence from that of a brilliant university president to the feeble-minded. Since many books of this type present only the records of deviates, it is a delight to find here four records of very superior persons and three of people in' the middle or average range of intelligence. Readers who deal with normal adolescents, either as parents or as teachers, are likely to raise an eyebrow when they come to Chapter IV, "The Adolescent Years." Each of the eight records presents the Rorschach test results for a maladjusted adolescent. Years ago psychologists exploded the myth that this period in the life span is marked by stress and strain, feelings of insecurity, conflict with parents, and stubbornness. Of course, Beck may have made an unwise selection from his files to represent the Rorschach findings of the years of adolescence. On the other hand, his own clinical experiences may have given him the "jaundiced eye." More than a quarter century of intimate association with large numbers of adolescents in school, on the athletic field, and at social gatherings make this reviewer question the wisdom of offering these records as "typical" of what Rorschach investigators find. Since Beck himself advocates the need for extensive acquaintance with various types of people on the part of the Rorschach expert, it would not be amiss to caution the reader to study modern youth before accepting these records as representative. Chapter V, which presents eleven records of schizophrenics, is excellent. It would be most enlightening to have Boisen review these cases in the light of his own experience and evaluate the interpretations which Beck has given. The clinical notes in this section are satisfyingly adequate. In short, this is the best chapter in the book. Chapter VI, "Neurotic Struggles," is rather disappointing because the writer has a limited concept of the neuroses. It is doubtful whether they can be interpreted, as Beck insists upon doing, *in vacuo,* with cavalier disregard of the milieu in which they occur. At any rate, here are the materials to enrich a course in mental hygiene as well as to interest the experienced student of the Rorschach method. One could wish that Beck had written at length on his concept of the neuroses, especially as he may differentiate the creative person from the individual

who is simply neurotic. This reviewer is left with an opinion that if Beck had a broader experience with "normal" people he might have given better interpretations of these records. The final chapter presents pairs of records for single individuals, the first pair being those before and after remission from a psychosis in which schizophrenia and hypomania are present. These records repay careful study. Excitement and depression are revealed in the next pair. Tests of a murderer, tested on entering prison and again after twenty-nine months of imprisonment, are given in full, together with interesting observations and interpretations by Beck. Finally, there are the records taken before and during the psychoanalysis of a nationally known psychiatrist. These records are of especial interest to all psychologists who followed the symposium published in the *Journal of Abnormal and Social Psychology.* In fact, they are among the best reports that have ever come from the author of this important book. After studying this volume carefully, one must agree that the Rorschach technique is largely an art, far less objective than the Terman-Merrill even in the hands of a neophyte. To be sure, the experiments in "blind diagnosis" have brought convincing proof of agreement among experts in the Rorschach test; but the interpretations of a beginner would inevitably be far removed from those of an experienced Rorschach worker. Beck has added little of value for the expert, and his procedures would be disastrous in the hands of one who would learn the method by self-study. The readable, fluent style in which he writes his interpretations is deceptively simple to the earnest but unqualified young student who would "practice" the method. On the other hand, the patient student can learn a great deal by taking a set of cards and working out each of the scorings which Beck has given. Only after a full year spent in this laborious research can he hope to be ready to piece the records together. Then, he must gain in knowledge of "reaction types" and "clinical pictures" before starting on the more stimulating task of interpretation. Beck's own weakness in the area of adolescent behavior should be construed as a warning against hasty ventures into meretricious interpretations, and his assurance in dealing with the Rorschach records of schizophrenics ought to inspire the student to acquire knowledge which makes interpretations valid and useful in clinical investigations.

War Med 8:436 N-D '45. This excellent book, essentially on personality, is written primarily, in the opinion of the reviewer, for the psychologist. Only a person well trained in psychiatric or psychologic behavior who has studied in detail the normal and intact personality in all its phases of development can understand the implications and meanings of the various processes found in the case reports of this book. Obviously a book of this kind lends itself to controversial interpretation because the text is that of "norms" for the normal and the abnormal personalities. This book is highly recommended to persons interested in personality and all its ramifications.

For additional reviews, see 77.

[77]

★[*Re* Rorschach.] BECK, SAMUEL J. **Rorschach's Test, Volumes I and II.** New York: Grune & Stratton, Inc., 1944–1945. Pp. xiii, 223; xii, 402. $3.50; $5.00. * (*PA* 18:2837, 20:1150)

J Clin Psychol 2:302–3 Jl'46. This two-volume work by the acknowledged master of Rorschach testing in the United States marks another milestone in the objectification of projective methods of personality study. Volume I demonstrates in minute detail the processes used in evaluating individual associations with little change in the theoretical orientation contained in Beck's *Introduction to the Rorschach Method* published in 1937. * The scoring precepts for each basic problem are clearly presented in separate chapters with numerous verbatim responses scored for each card to permit the reader to study the possible responses with maximum ease. A new scoring category, *organization* or Z responses, is introduced on the basis of previously reported studies indicating that not all organization responses are properly classified under Rorschach's W activity. * Volume II is devoted to an interpretation of the psychological significance of Rorschach test factors evaluated in light of the author's dynamic theory of personality. In contrast with other texts in this field, Beck has succeeded in presenting the theoretical implications of different types of activity in simple, easily-read style which makes the work useful to beginner as well as expert. The method is presented conservatively as an objective scientific instrument with no attempt to found a "school" or cult. The most important contribution of Volume II is the detailed presentation of 43 well selected cases with verbatim response records, response summaries and clinical interpretations. Included

are representative examples at all intelligence levels, in adolescence, in schizophrenia, in neurotic struggles, and, finally, records on four persons retested at significant periods of development. This work should be on the required book shelf of every clinical psychologist and psychiatrist since it is probably the most authoritative presentation in the field. It can be thoroughly recommended to all who are interested in the objective development of projective methods in psychological diagnosis.

J Consult Psychol 10:375–6 N-D '46. Zygmunt A. Piotrowski. These two volumes....constitute a very good manual for the use of beginners. The title, *Rorschach's Test,* apparently has been chosen advisedly. Beck decided to follow Rorschach faithfully, turning a deaf ear to the innovations and additions of the last quarter century on the ground that "examination of the published evidence does not result in conviction." Be that as it may, it is not necessary to include new developments in a text for beginners since none of the innovations are incompatible with any of Rorschach's important methodological principles. Many of the innovations enable us to infer more, and without a loss of validity, from a Rorschach record than Rorschach himself could infer (for example, from an analysis of the human and animal movement responses; cf. *The Nervous Child,* 1945, 4:344). However, this new type of inference about personality traits hitherto unmentioned in the Rorschach method does not clash with, and does not invalidate, the inferences from Rorschach's original method. It should be added that while Beck is uncompromising and orthodox in his preface and in a number of paragraphs, elsewhere he considers and admits the views of others besides Rorschach. Since Beck insists on following Rorschach closely, a comparison of Beck's work with Rorschach's *Psychodiagnostics* is natural. All text books on the Rorschach method are of course chiefly a paraphrase of the *Psychodiagnostics.* The latter (available in English since 1942) is written so concisely that it reads like a summary. It is difficult to use it as a textbook without the aid of an instructor. Thus the *Psychodiagnostics* requires amplification; its ideas must be made explicit and its principles illustrated more fully on a larger number of individual cases. Beck gives a particularly full exposition of the scoring of the subject's responses. * Beck publishes long lists of responses he personally classified as either good or poor forms. This seems to be the weakest portion of the *Basic Processes;* its weakness lies not so much in that it is based on the judgment of one man, no matter how experienced, but in its inconsistencies. Beck's lists seem to be based essentially on the statistical frequencies of the wording of a response and not on an analysis of the relation between the shape of the percept and the shape of the area of which the percept is an interpretation. Thus, for example, in Plate V "squashed animal," a percept of indeterminate shape, and for this reason alone not a good form, is scored by Beck as good form while "beetle" is scored as poor form; "insect" however is considered satisfactory. Certainly "beetle" is not a less plausible interpretation of Plate V than "insect" and therefore not a worse form than "insect." The emphasis should be placed on the percept, the visual image, and not on the words which convey the image. This emphasis upon the percept is implicit in Rorschach's own concept of the form response. Rorschach himself called his method a "diagnostic test based on perception"; his method obviously is not intended to be a word association test; words are necessary but merely as a means to a goal, not as the goal itself of the test procedure. In case of doubt, Oberholzer compares a patient's questionable response with the patient's unquestionably good and poor form responses and thus decides whether to score the questionable response as good or poor. This procedure is fraught with less danger than scoring rigidly according to a table and considering only the verbal form of the subject's response. In this connection it may be recalled that even such a common response as "butterfly" to Plate I can be a poor form; some patients with a psychosis or with brain damage "see" the "butterfly" in I in a very inexact and uncommon manner that does not resemble the shape of any real butterfly. The percentage of sharply conceived forms is a measure of the sense of reality and not of a verbal agreement with others. *Rorschach's Test* contains special chapters describing the psychological meaning of the scoring categories. These chapters are very restrained and in them Beck does not follow even Rorschach all the way. This is most noticeable in Beck's presentation of the shading responses. However in the long case presentations (the second volume contains forty-seven complete records and their interpretations) Beck is far less restrained and much freer. In the individual case

studies a great deal is made of the symbolic significance of the content, such as anatomy, of references to depressing happenings, etc. The case studies are the most instructive part of the textbook. They prove that the author not only has vast personal experience in the interpretation of Rorschach records but also knows and uses the literature well. There are sample records of healthy, feebleminded, neurotic and schizophrenic patients, including incidental remarks concerning specific diagnostic criteria. As far as the use of this method as a diagnostic aid is concerned Beck's second volume covers much less ground than Rorschach's book or other textbooks. Beck might have corrected Rorschach's error that color shock did not occur in psychosis. Color shock does occur in the functional psychoses and frequently is associated with brain damage. The repetition of Rorschach's error may lead to many clinically wrong diagnostic suggestions. The individual records are interpreted more fully than they were in the 1937 edition. In these interpretations Beck himself deviates from Rorschach in many points. He utilizes more than Rorschach ever did the content of the subject's responses. The case studies show that a great deal of personal skill is required in addition to intellectual knowledge in the practical application of the Rorschach method in its present phase of development. The "selected pertinent publications" which close the second volume are somewhat surprising. They include Plato's *Apologia* and several novels but do not contain any reference to Guirdham nor to the second of Rorschach's two long and important individual case studies (*see Zeitschrift Neurologie,* 1937). Ross' brief report on the uses of the Rorschach in the Canadian Army is mentioned but his more significant "Contribution of the Rorschach Method to Clinical Diagnosis" (*Journal of Mental Science,* 1941) is omitted. In spite of his demonstrative emphasis on orthodoxy Beck actually deviates from Rorschach in many instances with benefit to the reader. Many of these deviations need a fuller proof before they will be generally accepted. Beck included them because he had found them helpful in making individual case analyses. In conclusion, Beck's volumes cover less ground than Rorschach's *Psychodiagnostics.* However, they cover it in greater detail and in a manner that is easy to follow for a beginner. In the reviewer's opinion a careful study of the individual records and of their interpretations will be particularly profitable. These conscientiously written volumes are a definite contribution to psychological literature.

For additional reviews, see 75–6.

[78]

★[*Re* Rorschach.] BOCHNER, RUTH, AND HALPERN, FLORENCE. **The Clinical Application of the Rorschach Test.** Introduction by Karl M. Bowman. New York: Grune & Stratton, Inc., 1942. Pp. x, 217. * For latest edition, *see* 79. (*PA* 16:2315)

Am J Orthopsychiatry 14:186 Ja '44. L(awson) G. L(owrey). * The publishers say the book proves that the Rorschach is not "a cult in which only the initiated may serve." The latter point particularly seems to have caused a considerable emotional reaction among Rorschach specialists. Some reviews have dismissed the book as invalid and, in effect, useless. Some of the reaction seems dependent on an expressed belief that the book was hastily thrown together. Actually, the volume is a simple and unpretentious set of instructions for giving, scoring and interpreting the test. It will not make of any one a finished Rorschacher; there are errors and misinterpretations and it has not the value of Beck's or Klopfer's books; but it will be useful to the beginner and should be judged as such.

Am J Orthopsychiatry 16:731–2 O '46. Edna Mann. A newcomer to the Rorschach picks up many an article on the subject, reads it through, puts it down and sighs, "This is wonderful. I'll have to read it over again some time to see what it means." This book aims at being understandable, clear, simple, and practical. In its first edition, many army psychologists, with G. I. orders to become Rorschachers, found a road their everyday feet could follow. Several have mentioned that they found this book the best introduction to the Rorschach. The second edition ....contains twenty new case studies (making a total of 40), a new chapter on "Alcoholics" and one on "Behavior Problems." One of the most helpful aspects of the book, particularly for the relatively new Rorschacher (though it has much to interest the most experienced), is the meaningfulness and down-to-earth quality given to Rorschach symbols and concepts. * There is an attempt throughout to point up the first section of the book (on administration, scoring, analysis of determinants, etc.) by references to the actual cases in the second half. Incidentally, the cases do not always prove the point, showing perhaps that the Rorschach is too much like life itself. The poorest choice seems to be the three

records of compulsive neurotics which should be coarcted but turned out to be dilated in M:C relationship. The scoring follows Klopfer's, as does much of the book, but foregoes some valuable refinement. For example, where Klopfer and Davidson have elaborated the F score to 5 levels, Bochner and Halpern reduce it to the original two of Rorschach (F+ and F−). This reviewer feels that lumping true F+ along with crude F's beclouds the F+ rating. Of course, the psychologist can and will make a final qualitative evaluation of the record but why have scores if they do not "translate responses into most accurate symbols" —at least to the extent to 3 F levels (F+ carefully seen form; F− poorly perceived form; and F for noncommital or crude forms)? Other scoring simplifications, for better or worse, have apparently been a workaday response to the rush of the busy psychiatric clinics in which the authors have worked. Other clinic workers will understand the need to cut corners and streamline reports, reluctant as they may be to do so. They should also understand and hail with unmitigated enthusiasm the author's practical admonition on writing reports. When Rorschach workers recommend writing reports in English instead of Rorschachese, that should be welcome news to the social workers, and school and community people, who in the past have been heard to leave conferences muttering "What is that: labile affectivity"? In short, this is a good practical readable first book on the Rorschach which should not be a substitute for a course of careful training, but which might well follow or accompany it.

Am J Psychiatry 99:471 N '42. R. M. Finney. * a simple and understandable presentation of a very difficult psychological procedure, the Rorschach experiment. * Their explanation and instructions regarding scoring of the record are perhaps a little too simple, especially for research purposes. However, for practical, clinical use there is sufficient information given. The discussions of the meanings of the various symbols derived by scoring are perfectly adequate for orientation of the beginner in Rorschach work. The authors present a clear discussion of the test cards, although one cannot help feeling that reproductions of the cards in color would have enhanced the value of the text. One of the most commendable features of the book is the presentation of twenty actual Rorschach records with the interpretations appended. To research workers these interpretations might conceivably be thought too superficial, but for the practising psychiatrist they might be adequate and serve as guides in learning the method.

Am J Psychol 56:313–5 Ap '43. M. R. Harrower-Erickson. * One is not certain whether the authors have decided to put the clock back to where Rorschach left it, a perfectly legitimate procedure if adhered to conscientiously, or whether, in attempting to do this, they are actually unaware that their presentation of the Rorschach method incorporates, and is permeated with, certain systematic additions, and that even their terminology bears witness to the particular frame of reference on which they draw. * Another disconcerting feature is the manner in which reference to the articles in the *Rorschach Research Exchange* is handled, namely, by a blanket reference to the Journal in the index. Although work derived from this source is discussed, no citations are given. * Some features of the presentation, which, in the main, is clear and very readable, seem to show a fundamental lack of appreciation of the method, or else are careless slips. For example, the "average" and "above average" adult records (p. 80-81) both have *equal* FM, m, and K scores. This is in actual fact an unusual finding and far from "average." Or, again, there is the statement (p. 54) that when the number of responses in the last three cards exceeds 33 per cent there is an overdependence on external stimuli, but that fewer than 33 per cent of such responses indicates a withdrawal from the environment. Must we assume, therefore, that there is no middle ground, no way for the well-adjusted individual to show his adjustment along these lines? The book falls naturally into two parts, the discussion of the method per se and the clinical material derived from the authors' own experience. We have felt that, for various reasons, this theoretical discussion was disappointing. With the ideas which have prompted the authors to make available their case material, we are in complete sympathy. * The records, case histories, and discussions which are presented, although by no means all-inclusive, are an interesting cross-section of the clinical population which may be referred for Rorschach examination. Thus, while the book cannot provide the beginner with anything like the systematic treatment of the subject that can be found in Klopfer's *The Rorschach Technique,* and while the expert will not find in it much that is new to him, it may prove of interest and be somewhat of an eye-opener to psy-

chologists and physicians in various fields who have not as yet realized the applicability of the method to their particular sphere of interest.

Arch Neurol & Psychiatry 48:161–2 Jl '42. * Although....[the authors] state that their material is essentially derived from the literature, they neglect to include in their bibliography the two papers of Klopfer, "The Technique of the Rorschach Administration" and "Theory and Technique of the Rorschach Interpretation," from which most of their material might have been derived. This omission is surprising since some of the Klopfer theories have never been published elsewhere. Their handling of this material tends, unfortunately, toward oversimplification, and they are apparently unaware of certain changes which have been made since these articles were first published, some years ago. In addition, the authors themselves do not seem at all clear in their discussion of the more difficult problems. Their discussion of the M:Sum C ratio tends to be confused, and they contradict themselves concerning the meaning of the basic ratios on three consecutive pages. It requires more skill and experience than the average psychiatrist possesses to interpret these pages, 52, 53 and 54. The major difficulties with the work appear, however, when the authors approach the clinical field. Although the book purports to be a study of clinical application, it deals only with mental deficiency, neuroses, schizophrenia and "organic" disorders. Apparently the authors have had no experience with the affective psychosis or else consider this broad aspect of psychopathology as negligible. The clinical data given in the last half of the book are scant and filled with errors. An example of some of the misstatements is the interpretation of the value of popular responses of the mentally defective subject. Apparently the authors are unfamiliar with the work of Beck (the major investigator in this field), who stressed the significance of popular responses in indicating the ability of the defective person to get along in institutions. It is amusing to note in this connection that the sample record given for a mentally defective person has a high percentage of popular responses, in contradistinction to the authors' previous assertion, and that their records substantiate Beck's findings even though their theoretic statements do not. Concerning the rest of the theoretic discussion dealing with clinical entities, there is little to say except for enumeration of the frequent errors. The authors do not seem to be aware that there are no true pathognomic signs of schizophrenia or that their "neurotic indicators" are not only nonspecific but unsubstantiated by any type of research. Their failure to recognize variation in the quality of the performance in cases of damage to the brain is a serious oversight. The greatest drawback of the book, however, is its misleading oversimplification. The authors would have one believe that the technic is an easy one and that diagnoses can be made by simply scoring a record and then looking up the listed interpretation. Workers in the field are in complete agreement on the fact that there is no specific pattern or response for any psychopathic deviation. The Rorschach method gives only a personality pattern which clinicians must evaluate and interpret. A number of case records have been included, but the paucity of clinical material and the superficiality of the histories destroy any usefulness they might possess. In conclusion, one can only say that the large number of errata, the poor printing, the incomplete bibliography and the lack of an index make the physical structure of the book seem as unfinished as the content.

Brit J Ed Psychol 13:165 N '43. W. D. W(all). (Also a review of *The Rorschach Technique* by Bruno Klopfer and Douglas M. Kelley.) Continental and American psychologists in the last twenty years have widely used the Rorschach test as an instrument to investigate the psychoses, in vocational, delinquency, child and neurotic studies and more recently as a group technique. In England, Kerr has used it in studies of twins and of London school children; and Vernon in investigations with university students. Beyond the reports of these two investigators there are few references to English work with the test reported in the journals; and many English psychologists regard it rather as an esoteric cult than a practicable approach to personality diagnosis. The books at present under review, which contain the first full discussions of the method and summaries of research in book form, should do much to modify this view and lead to an urgently needed standardisation on English groups, by age and occupation, and statistical validation in fields other than the abnormal. At present, as the authors admit, the method is primarily clinical and individual; but it permits of wide group application in the study of normal and neurotic personalities and is superior to most in treating personality as a *gestalt*. * The scoring doubtless will be further simplified and standardised, and the diagnostic criteria more thoroughly validated and made wider in scope: but the basis of the test appears to be sound. * Unfortunately, although each book is provided with extensive references to the literature, neither cites precise figures of either the reliability or the validity of the method. The latter seems likely to be higher in skilful hands than that of personality inventories or even of experimental situations like those of May and Hartshorne. * How far poor visualisers are handicapped, the determination of what constitutes a popular response, what allowances must be made for intelligence level, and whether the artificiality of the situation is not such as to affect the responses of adult neurotics, are problems peculiar to the test which can be settled only by further research with large groups. Such research is made immeasurably more easy by these two books. The case records cited in Halpern and Bochner are extremely suggestive, particularly for those to whom the test is more than a curiosity. Klopfer and Kelley in their third and fourth parts deal, somewhat cursorily as is inevitable, with the whole field of application of the test. Best of all, both books provide an exhaustively clear account of the procedure and niceties of scoring. * At times, however, both sets of authors appear to forget that the test is in the nature of a series of miniature situations and that, without the most stringent statistical validation, rigidly detailed conclusions as to personality structure cannot safely be drawn from reactions to such things as nuances of shading and colour. *A priori* considerations should not blind us to the potentialities of the test, even if we regard it at present with caution. Its use as an adjunct and check upon subjective observation is obvious; Dr. Vernon goes so far as to say that he is "unable to call to mind any other test of personality or temperamental traits which will tell me so much about my subjects in so short a time," while Professor Burt has found it successful with neurotics: and its use in differential diagnosis of the organic and non-organic psychoses seems justified. It is to be hoped that these two books, ably written and soundly practical, will lead to an extensive use of and experiment with the test in this country.

Brit J Psychol 33:141–2 O '42. * may be recommended without hesitation to any student of psychology or medical practitioner who wishes to learn how to apply the test, or to any trained psychologist who desires to have data on which to form a reasonable opinion of the value and limitations of the Rorschach procedure. So far as we know there is no other book which covers the field as adequately and as fairly in so short a space. While the authors do not in any way disguise their belief in the test as a means of clinical examination, they exaggerate neither the strong nor the weak points of its use. They give very clear instructions in the matter of how to administer the test cards, they list and explain all the main categories of interpretation and the symbols by which these are expressed, they state the interrelations of the cards and why they have been placed in the order in which they are given, and they give a number of illustrative interpretations drawn from actual experiment. These interpretations cover records of normal people, of children, of mental defectives, of neurotics, of schizophrenic patients, and of people suffering from certain organic disorders. There is a very short and admittedly inadequate chapter dealing with recent developments which, however, ought not to be held up against the authors as a defect in their presentation, since they are perfectly clearly concerned with the procedure only as a basis for individual character diagnosis. What impression is the whole likely to make upon the interested, but undecided reader? It seems likely that he will be attracted and interested, and that however cautious he may wish to be he will have to admit that the test may have very great and expanding value for many purposes. He will also see that the technique may be very time-consuming, and that the possible interpretations are so various and the boundaries between one category and another so soft that it may become very difficult to strike a balance between individual judgment and conventional, perhaps esoteric, categorization. But whether he will regard this as an advantage or a disadvantage is likely to depend very much on his general psychological point of view and his personal predilections. However, any fair-minded reader is likely to agree that this admirable book does make out an impressive case.

J Am Med Assn 120:1347 D 19 '42. The avowed purpose of this book, as stated in the preface, is to make the Rorschach test "available to all psychologists and psychiatrists." It is therefore warrantable to evaluate it in terms of the degree to which it accomplishes this rather ambitious aim. Perhaps, however, we should question the possibility or, indeed, the desirability of attempting to put this tool in the hands of any total group, whether composed of physicians or psychologists. This is not at all to concede, as surprisingly enough the authors seem to, that the Rorschach has been a cult which only the initiated could serve but merely to recognize it as a technic fully as complicated as the reading of X-ray plates by the roentgenologist and therefore properly the function of the specialist. But, laying this question aside, how well does the book succeed in giving to any hitherto unenlightened person a working knowledge of the Rorschach test? Unfortunately it is not comprehensive enough or sufficiently precise for the beginning student and it is much too cluttered up with detail, too lacking in its presentation of underlying Rorschach philosophy, for the general reader. Not only for historical perspective but because it remains the single great classic in a rapidly growing literature, the student should begin with the Psychodiagnostik itself, now happily translated into English. This, followed with Oberholzer's article of twenty years ago in the *Journal of Nervous and Mental Disease,* will establish his firm foundation. Then if he keeps abreast of current material in the psychologic journals and the Rorschach exchange he will see both the many extensions in the use of the test and the new concepts which are being incorporated. Undoubtedly the best exposition of the subtleties and refinements of scoring which are used by members of the Rorschach Institute is embodied in another new book, *The Rorschach Technique,* by Klopfer and Kelley. The present book, then, like Beck's, which came out in 1937, is mainly useful in rounding out the picture with supplementary case material for those already familiar with Rorschach practice. What is still lacking and what the psychologist called on to present and defend Rorschach personality studies and diagnostic impressions longs for is a new Rorschach classic, a small book like Hart's on insanity. Such a book, stripped of the details that obscure the forest, should present the philosophy of personality organization on which Rorschach theory is based and which constitutes its unique contribution. This is what should be "available" to all psychologists and psychiatrists but, unhappily, it is yet unwritten.

J Consult Psychol 6:274–5 S-O '42. Morris Krugman. * a carelessly written work, replete with loose statements, contradictions, and misleading conclusions. Its generalizations are oversimplified to such an extent that a beginner in the Rorschach method, attempting to apply them, would become hopelessly confused. One can picture the confusion of the Rorschach learner who reads in the same paragraph (pp. 55–6) that "Ambiequal individuals are relatively rare," and then, "Thus we see why many neurotics fall in the ambiequal group." Then, to cite one more of many possible examples, let us follow that beginner to page 139, where he learns that, in the case of the compulsion neurotic, "The Rorschach protocol will show marked coarctation," but, when the reader examines the three cases illustrating compulsion neurosis (cases 11, 12, 13) all of them are markedly expanded. Some of the other illustrative cases likewise contradict the text, or are atypical. In the preface, the authors indicate that they have "organized and reworked" much of the Rorschach literature and have "given in brief and simplified form an exposition of the Rorschach Test." In reading the book, one is impressed by the small number of sources actually employed, and by the extent to which the authors leaned upon Klopfer, sometimes giving credit, and frequently not. The book was obviously compiled in great haste. The reviewer does not remember another book in which so many grammatical errors occur. The English is frequently so poor that it would not be acceptable in a freshman composition. The naïvete of the presentation is shown by some of the chapter headings. Chapter III is headed, "What the Symbols in Column I Mean," and Chapter IV, "What the Symbols in Column II Mean." On the other hand, the last chapter (XV) has a rather ambitious title: "Recent Developments of the Rorschach Test." This chapter consists of little more than three pages. No more apt commentary both on this chapter and on the entire book, can be made than that of the authors in the first sentence of the closing paragraph of the chapter and book: "This chapter in no way covered all the recent avenues of research, either as they relate to better understanding of the instrument or as they pertain to personality problems."

J Nerv & Mental Dis 101:88 Ja '45. A(rthur) N. F(oxe). * a very readable volume, something of a manual in the use of the Rorschach test. It is practical and excellent for the beginner. *

Mil Surg 93:226 Ag '43. Webb Haymaker. * The style of writing is clear, the explanations

easy to follow, its directions explicit. This book should serve well its purpose as a practical manual for psychologists. It should also be of interest to psychiatrists, but its value would be enhanced by illustrations of the test cards.

Occupational Psychol 16:149–50 Jl '42. C. J. C. Earl. In the field of personality testing the Rorschach method is in many ways the analogue of the Binet scale in the intellectual field. Both methods mark a sharp departure from anything which preceded them. Both methods abandon the precise and accurate measurement of strictly isolable or definable elements in favour of an approach to the problem as a whole. Both methods were devised primarily as practical clinical techniques, and both are certainly open to objections from the purely scientific point of view on this account. On the other hand both methods have such enormous clinical values that their place is assured. A grave difficulty in the case of the Rorschach which was absent in the case of the Binet scale is the difficulty in the technique of its scoring and interpretation. Rorschach's original book *Psychodiagnostik* was a brilliantly intuitive essay in the psychology of personality, but in no sense a manual for use in the actual administration and scoring of the test, and none of the very few books which have appeared since then has, in any considerable measure, filled the gap. Almost the whole of the extensive literature has appeared in the form of papers in journals of widely diverse character. Different authors have used different standards in scoring, and the very considerable improvements made by the American school are accessible only in the privately circulated journal of the Rorschach Institute. Most Rorschachists learnt their technique by personal training rather than by reading, and indeed the impression was fairly general that only by such training could the method be learnt. Even were this the case—as the present reviewer is convinced that it is not—the need for an elementary manual for practical use was very great, and this little book makes a brave attempt to meet this demand. The method of administration and scoring is fully and very simply set forth, the system of scoring being, in general, the orthodox American or 'Exchange' method. One unfortunate departure from the method is that in the tabulation of scores the chiaroscuro responses are listed with the achromatic colour responses, although the former undoubtedly represent introversive trends, while the latter have as certainly extratensive significance. The advantage of the orthodox listing of introversive and extratensive elements to the left and right respectively of the purely logical F scores is obvious, and this departure will tend to confuse beginners. Apart from this defect, the authors have been very successful in the difficult task of explaining the scoring method clearly and briefly. Numerous examples are given, but a discussion of complex responses and their scoring would have been helpful. The full discussion of the meaning of the scores, as also the final interpretation of a record, involves a very considerable discussion of the psychology of personality, etc. Rorschach's own essay on the *Erlebnistypus,* for example, is an important contribution to personology. Any such discussion is bound to be lengthy and perhaps tends to undue complication in a book intended for beginners. The authors have avoided the difficulty by omitting theoretical discussion and confining themselves to a few brief didactic statements and explanations, and the book is so much the poorer for this omission. The reader whose own knowledge of psychology is extensive will, however, be able to read much between the lines in this section; indeed, the authors in their preface, refer to the importance of the psychological background of the examiner for obtaining the fullest advantage from the test. In the last chapter of the book a number of records are given, together with their scoring and interpretation, and these should be helpful in clinical work with the test. * There is a brief mention of possible fields, other than the clinical, for the use of the test. The bibliography is fairly full but by no means complete, and the table of reciprocals will prove a boon in calculating percentages. The general lay-out of the book is so clear that the lack of an index will scarcely be felt. Though this book is guilty of over-simplification, there is no doubt that it fulfils a long felt need for the beginner with the method. A word of caution is, however, necessary on each of two points. The first of these is that any Rorschachist should be extremely cautious in his interpretation until his experience is fairly considerable. Secondly, and most importantly, efficiency with the method cannot be attained without a knowledge of the dynamic psychology of personality. The Rorschach method is an exquisitely sensitive clini-

cal technique; it cannot be expected to function as a penny in the slot machine.

Psychiatric Q 16:598–602 Jl '42. * this summer appears to mark an important turning point in development of the Rorschach method for psychiatric use in the United States. Two admirable introductory volumes on the technique have just been published; and the first authorized English translation of Rorschach's *"Psychodiagnostik"* has been brought out * For the first time, authoritative and readily comprehensible material in this field has become available for the beginner * While Dr. Bowman's introduction notes that "the beginner . . . will find the book well suited to his needs," the authors' treatment of their subject is from a somewhat different viewpoint than that of a training manual. Mrs. Bochner and Mrs. Halpern have devoted as much attention to what might be called the presentation of a birds-eye view of the Rorschach and its possibilities to the psychiatric profession as they have to the problem of teaching administration to beginners. * Mrs. Bochner and Mrs. Halpern ....illustrate the clinical application of the method by carefully chosen protocols, selected in a fashion to make plain to psychiatrist or student beginner the differences in the records of the commonly encountered mental states. Illustration and discussion of children's protocols, with emphasis on caution in accepting children's interpretations, seem of particular value. * [That the authors] do not consider their book complete equipment for administration and interpretation of the Rorschach examination is made plain in Dr. Bowman's introductory warning, "All tests . . . in the hands of the non-expert may do harm." * Both [Klopfer's *The Rorschach Technique* and this volume]....should be important contributions to greater knowledge and use of the Rorschach technique. The Bochner and Halpern work— based on much experience with the Rorschach at Bellevue Psychiatric Hospital—is unquestionably the easier to comprehend for a person wishing merely a general knowledge and understanding of the method; as the authors note, they have endeavored to present their material "in brief and simplified form." They follow, in general, the symbols and scoring methods developed by Dr. Klopfer at the Rorschach Institute, but with modifications, notably in their chiaroscuro scoring, in construction of personality graphs and in summation. It is, of course, testimony to the objectiveness and scientific validity of a method—administration of which is not only an examination but application of an art, and which, as Mrs. Bochner and Mrs. Halpern observe "cannot be scored against a stencil"—that such differences in technique do not prevent essential agreement on findings by all schools of Rorschach workers. The Bellevue workers' book is adequate for instruction of administrators, given at least a little personal supervision; and it gives an extraordinarily clear view of how the records of the various mental states compare. * The Bochner and Halpern volume also has an excellent bibliography, though a far less complete one; and it contains a useful table of reciprocals for calculating percentages of replies in any record of ordinary range. Regrettably, there is no index; and a specimen scoring chart and at least outline representations of the cards would have been desirable additions. Keeping in mind the somewhat different orientations of these two introductory books, either of them can be recommended without reservation as a better introduction to the study, practice and general evaluation of the Rorschach technique than has heretofore been available. The fact that a set of the cards is essential for serious study or comprehension of the Rorschach by use of either textbook is a matter which may not be entirely obvious to persons lacking any acquaintance whatever with the method. *

Psychiatry 5:606 N '42. Ernest G. Schachtel. * not quite free from errors in the rendition of Rorschach's as well as other Rorschach workers' teachings and it shows traces of being hastily written. It avoids, as the introduction declares, "lengthy discussions of the theoretical points." In fact, it avoids any discussion of such points. Consequently, it does not convey an adequate idea of Rorschach's work. This reviewer does not share the viewpoint, which the authors apparently hold, that it is possible to understand and use the Rorschach method without reference to theoretical concepts of personality and of the processes involved in the Rorschach test. The book contains a simple description of the technical categories used by Rorschach or by some of his followers, and some interesting case records.

Psychoanalytic Q 11:587–9 O '42. S. J. Beck. Having decided that 'a certain aura has gathered about the test, making of it a cult in which only the initiated may serve' (p. ix), these au-

thors are undertaking to make it 'available to all psychologists and psychiatrists.' They do so in chapters on How to Score a Record, What the Symbols in Column I Mean, and in a style reminiscent of the 'easy lessons' style of promotion. * To cite in full the numerous naïvetes committed in this small book would require far more space than is alloted this review. 'When the white space is used to indicate something missing, as a gap . . . in our experience this type of response is frequent in the records of children and adolescents from broken homes' (p. 30). Here the authors seem themselves to be doing some free associating of the *Klang* variety: 'broken blot', 'broken home'. Experience of other workers does not confirm this superficially simple working of the test. 'We feel that individuals of superior intelligence should not give an F— unless they are emotionally disturbed' (p. 38, n). Scientific method happens to be not a matter of feeling, but observation. The fact is that the healthy superiors always have some F—. They dare to make errors. That goes with superiority. With their highly endowed personalities they more than compensate for their errors as does also the rich Rorschach response pattern for the F—. Referring to the D (major detail) response: 'The shape of these details approximates reality more closely than does the shape of the whole blot' (p. 24). Here is a complete lack of understanding of the psychological processes in the Rorschach test factors. Reality in the test is totally independent of whole, detail, or rare detail. The 'butterfly' to Figure V (whole) is as real as 'muskrat' to the lateral red of Figure VIII. It is in F+, not D, that the individual reveals his loyalty to reality. Percentages and formulas are offered as though they represent well-established, quantitative measures of psychological processes (e.g., pp. 36–37, 41, 60–61). There is a too frequent use of quotations without quotation marks. The description on page 20 of the whole response as related to intelligence will be found in the *Psychodiagnostik,* p. 63 ff., 1932 edition; and the 'good form' discussion (p. 36) is a fairly faithful paraphrasing of Rorschach, pp. 60–61 *ibid.* Numerous other instances can be cited. Klopfer appears to be the chief sufferer in this respect, as in regard to 'testing the limits' (p. 4). The possible rationalization of such a practice is that the hitherto published material in a scientific field is the public property of all workers in it. This may be so in respect to the foundations of such an ancient science as, say, chemistry. But in a field so new as the psychology of personality and so specialized as the Rorschach test, it is small compensation for each worker to ask that his contribution be credited. The one merit of the book lies in the twenty complete Rorschach response records distributed in the several personality groups. It is the reviewer's teaching experience that the best way to get to know the test is to make comparative studies of the records of different clinical pictures. A valuable suggestion will be found on pages 34–35, regarding the *Suksez-zionstypus* as spatially determined (not only according to whether W, D, Dr follow in that order). The bibliography looks good but the omission of Skalweit's important monograph on schizophrenia looks like evidence of haste in preparing the manuscript. The book has no index—an inconvenience in a discipline so dependent on symbols peculiar to it. This work reflects no more than a shallow grasp by the authors of the psychological dynamics involved in the Rorschach experiment. It would have helped in judging their preparedness for writing such a book if they had informed us what is their background of direct experience with the test. A single, brief paper by one of the authors is their only other publication. Rorschach labored ten years before he published anything. Most conscientious workers today consider about three years' work a necessary minimum to enable them to grasp it solidly, let alone write a book. The introduction by Dr. Karl M. Bowman has a special interest in view of his own many years of association with the test. He not only has had the opportunity to observe it in use at Bellevue, but also in the Boston Psychopathic Hospital where he was chief medical officer in the years when it was receiving some of its early trials in the United States.

Psychol B 41:64 Ja '44. Ralph R. Brown. * Bochner and Halpern will at least convince psychologists that the test is not a cult or a religion, but this book will not serve to overcome the general objection to the test on the grounds of undemonstrated validity. * the authors....were principally concerned with presenting in a simple, condensed form the principles of administration, scoring and interpretation of the Rorschach. It is unfortunate that the authors did not include a chapter on validity.

Sufficient material is now available to convince most of us that the test is fundamentally sound, even though subject to misuse by over-enthusiastic proponents. For the beginner, the book offers a lucid and concise description of Rorschach testing. It is not sufficiently complete, however, to permit the beginner to score and interpret the test without consulting other references. There is no clear method of differentiating between major and minor details. The scoring of good and poor form quality is also left to the imagination. As an independent presentation, therefore, this book does not compare with Beck's "Introduction to the Rorschach Method," or "The Rorschach Technique" by Klopfer & Kelley. The advanced student of Rorschach will find much of interest in this book. The chapters dealing with interpretation of the symbols are well written and bring together under one heading the opinions of various Rorschach workers. Many of these interpretations are not from Rorschach and care must be exercised in the differentiation of well-established Rorschach principles from the more recent and less well-founded interpretations. The illustrative records are interesting and expertly interpreted. There are not sufficient records presented, however, to serve as a satisfactory background for "getting the feel" of records in various clinical categories. This book is recommended as supplementary reading for beginners. For the more experienced Rorschach worker, it offers a number of interesting records and interpretations.

Psychosom Med 6:277 Jl '44. Martin Grotjahn. * simple, clear and readable * Twenty records given in detail should be of special help for people using or learning to use this test.

War Med 3:111–2 Ja '43. * a handy little volume written by two psychologists who have had extensive experience in the use of the Rorschach test * so complex is the Rorschach technic that it is doubtful whether many, on the basis of this exposition alone and without some actual tutoring, would be able to start using it forthwith * In general the authors appear to have followed Klopfer....in the weighting and the interpretative significance which they assign to some of the test factors. While Rorschach's formulations are not necessarily final—certainly not to be accorded the uncritical acceptance of a "revealed religion"—neither can all of the more recent elaborations of the technic and the new meanings derived be accepted until a good deal more work has been done to validate them. They are extremely provocative for research but the authors make no effort to distinguish between the well-tested Rorschach principles of evaluation and the newer contributions to the theory. Despite these reservations the book should have a double usefulness. It provides a suggestive compendium for the neophyte to keep at hand. Also, though perhaps in somewhat too detailed a fashion, it gives any psychiatrist or psychologist hitherto unfamiliar with the Rorschach test an opportunity to learn the factors and the relations on which the often amazingly accurate character evaluations and clinical diagnoses of the experienced user are based. It should, therefore, do much to eradicate the feeling that the test is some sort of hocus-pocus and to increase the recognition of it as a valid and extremely delicate scientific tool.

[79]

★[Re Rorschach.] Bochner, Ruth, and Halpern, Florence. The Clinical Application of the Rorschach Test, Second Edition. Introduction by Karl M. Bowman. New York: Grune & Stratton, Inc., 1945. Pp. xi, 331. $4.00. * (PA 20:472)

Am J Psychiatry 103:429–30 N '46. Leslie Phillips. * Chapters have been added with Rorschach records of alcoholics and individuals who fit into the broad category of "behavior problems." The other chapters also have been filled out with many new records. * a brief, easily understandable introduction * The introductory chapters are little changed * A table of samples of good and poor form perception is not included, nor is there a list of common and rare details, although reference is made to where these may be obtained. These are unfortunate omissions, as they are needed, particularly by beginners, for practical work with the test. The variety of records chosen to illustrate those obtained in health and mental disorder is quite rich, although some records, particularly among the normals and "organic" cases, seem poorly chosen. However, they should be helpful in demonstrating how the test factors are pooled to obtain a picture of the personality. The interpretations are usually short and tend to be superficial, and the accompanying case histories seem particularly inadequate. No improvements have been made in this regard in the second edition, and consequently the book cannot lead to any deep appreciation of the Rorschach technique, nor is it adequate for advanced work. The addition of new material,

however, helps to increase its value as an elementary introduction to Rorschach testing.

Am J Psychol 59:704–9 O '46. Donald E. Super. * attempts to do in some 330 pages what Beck's two volumes do in twice that compass. In fact, more is here attempted * Covering so much in such limited space, this manual is of necessity too sketchy at many points. * The chapters on location, determinants, and content lack the helpful diagrams which Klopfer, Harrower–Erickson, and others, have popularized. Missing (as also in Beck's volume) are the frequency-tables which serve as useful reference points and give one confidence in Beck's earlier work and in that of a number of current publications. Psychoanalytical interpretations are frequent and are glibly incorporated into other statements with no citation of evidence to justify them. * There is occasional loose thinking of other types. * This book is characterized not only by an emphasis on psychoanalytical interpretation which seems to this sympathetic reviewer to go beyond the data, and by an allegiance to the old school of Rorschachers * It is refreshing and reassuring to find a note (p. 228) to the effect that "the necessity for confining the use of an instrument like the Rorschach test to professional workers who have had adequate training and experience in clinical psychology and psychiatry is clearly evident." It is to be hoped that the former is intended to include scientific procedure and research as well as practice. In view of this word of caution, one is inclined to question the place of this book, and others like it, in the professional literature. As a manual, it is too brief (Beck is much more detailed, supplemented by quantitative data from Harrower–Erickson and Steiner, Hertz and others). As an introduction, it is too sketchy for the critically or scientifically minded (Beck justifies his views somewhat more adequately, Munroe gives evidence) and oversimplified for the uncritical novice. (Beck points out more complexities and recognizes some unsolved problems.) One who knows something about the Rorschach but is not an expert may glean new insights from it and here and there, or a beginner may read it or Klopfer (if already grounded in the psychology of adjustment) as a first introduction before reading Beck's two volumes. He should then, with a critical eye, read Harrower–Erickson and Steiner, Munroe, and others, who have attempted more or less successfully to approach the Rorschach with scientific restraint. Such a reader will, it is hoped, then recognize that the Rorschach is still just one way among several of getting some tentative insights into the structure of a personality.

Brit J Psychol 36:177 My '46. This is an excellent manual for the use of the Rorschach ink-blot test. It is clear and intelligible to the beginner as well as to the expert, and the former could not do better than use it in learning how to administer the test. Good records and interpretations are given for normal adults and children, as well as for abnormals—mental defectives, neurotics, behaviour problems, schizophrenics, alcoholics and organic cases. There is an extensive bibliography of Rorschach literature.

J Abn & Social Psychol 41:233–6 Ap '46. Albert I. Rabin. * A little over 25 per cent of ....[the book] is devoted to the procedure, scoring, and meaning of the various test factors. In this section of the book, the authors endeavor to accomplish what Beck did in his entire first volume and in part of the second. It is a tall order; yet the authors have succeeded in filling it with some degree of success. The manner of presentation is simple and elementary, though it is taken too much for granted that the reader has a full understanding of the psychological correlates of the Rorschach factors. The personalities and traits of individuals in whom the given "signs" occur with some frequency are described in a rather naïve and common-sense manner without resorting to too much psychological sophistication. There is no attempt to "justify" the method or give it a theoretical foundation, or, as Beck attempts, to relate it more tangibly to the general psychological field. Neither is there the distinct "experimental attitude" with its implicit research interest and spirit of inquiry. It is a "manual" in the full sense of the word. It is a manual, of a "test," which as such also suffers from a number of weaknesses. In the first place, the section on form (F) in general and good form (F+) in particular leaves much to be desired. It is rather brief and leaves too much to the subjective judgment of the Rorschach worker. The theory of frequency as the determinant of good form is explained, but the beginner or even the advanced Rorschach worker who has not compiled his own frequency tables is left out on a limb. This manual does not give a set of ex-

pected responses, with or without their frequencies, which may be used as a standard of judgment of good or poor form. In the second place, the striking psychoanalytical and otherwise symbolic explanations of various answers and bits of independent content are sometimes over-dogmatic and not readily digestible by the experimentally minded clinician. The explanation of the isolated symbolism of bays and inlets "as a shelter or as an encircling menace," the suggestion that when details frequently seen as female genitalia are seen as vases and urns there is an indication of "a glorification of the female," or that the soft light quality of card VII gives "this card a feminine quality, frequently with maternal implications" (!), and that the denial of a detail in card IV is a situation in which "the whole problem of castration is involved," appear to this reviewer rather far-fetched and in need of better validation and substantiation. The remaining three-fourths of the volume are devoted to forty records of normal as well as abnormal individuals and their corresponding personality sketches. In addition to the usual schizophrenic, neurotic, and normal records, protocols and interpretations of Rorschach findings in some organic cases, alcoholics, and adolescent behavior problems, as well as those of young children, are included. Each group is prefaced by a general statement of the diagnostic features and how they are revealed in the test. These preliminary discussions are very helpful, especially to the beginning student. The scoring follows the standard procedures, with slight variations. One may question the usefulness of the multitude of percentages, for such factors as P, F, W, D, etc. The interpretations are comparatively brief, but bring out the essential features. In some cases one may wish that the authors were a bit more penetrating in their analysis and more generous with case-history notes and reference to them. Bochner and Halpern have written a readable, though somewhat oversimplified, Rorschach manual and have eliminated many of the errors included in its first edition. Along with Beck's somewhat erudite, basic two volumes, it may serve the student as a worthwhile reference book.

Psychiatry 9:411–2 N '46. Isabelle V. Kendig. The fact that a second edition of this book has been brought out undoubtedly attests its popularity as well as the widely extended use of the Rorschach test during the war years. This is both a more comprehensive presentation, especially of actual case material, and a somewhat wiser and more modest one. In the preface to the former edition, it was stated the purpose of the book was to make the Rorschach test "available to all psychologists and psychiatrists." This rather magniloquent goal seems to have been abandoned, and the present preface simply stresses the importance—and limitations—of the technique, concluding that it "must remain an instrument in the service of psychology and psychiatry." This is a commendable change, since to purport to teach the interpretation of Rorschach data in ten easy chapters is about as preposterous as to teach roentgenology by mail. * the authors are somewhat less fixed and dogmatic than formerly. A few new topics are discussed * the chief enrichment comes through the introduction of additional case material * Actual case material is always of interest to Rorschach workers but inevitably raises the question as to the comparability of the psychiatric nosology on which diagnosis is based. In the records presented here one wonders at the absence of samples of Rorschach production in the affective psychoses. The protocols taken from schizophrenics, while illuminating certain general characteristics, are unsatisfactory because no attempt is made to bring out the wholly different patterns shown in the various subtypes of the disorder. To the last record, that of an alcoholic, is appended the opprobrious term "psychopathic personality," and this term is also used for one of the cases presented as a "behavior problem." In both instances it is used quite uncritically although the concept of psychopathy is generally recognized as a most unsatisfactory one. Through the entire series, there is a lack of diagnostic specificity in the cases presented which diminishes their value and certainly implies that the Rorschach is a much less precise tool than it has proved itself to be in the hands of many workers.

Psychosom Med 8:290 Jl-Ag '46. Vernon Clark. * The value of the book will vary according to the use the reader means to make of it. The section devoted to technique and interpretation is clear, economically written and well organized, although the authors encounter the difficulties inherent in discussing piecemeal material which must be seen as a dynamic whole. The records selected for demonstration are rich and challenging, so rich that one is all

the more conscious of the fact that the analyses offered are often meagre and somewhat static. Moreover, the quest for typical patterns associated with the clinical entities leads to an oversimplification of the problem of differential diagnosis with the Rorschach. Thus, to the newcomer in the field, the book may seem to promise too much too soon. If its limitations are kept in mind, it will prove valuable to students interested in a general grounding in Rorschach testing and who wish to postpone complex theoretical questions until they have mastered the fundamentals of the technique.

U S Naval Med B 46:1309 Ag '46. * One gets the impression that the authors of this book, in their attempt to be clinically helpful, resort to rather rigid formulae in support of empty and rather arbitrary statements.

[80]

★[Re Rorschach.] FORD, MARY. The Application of the Rorschach Test to Young Children. University of Minnesota, The Institute of Child Welfare Monograph Series, No. 23. Minneapolis, Minn.: University of Minnesota Press, 1946. Pp. xii, 114. $2.00. (London: Oxford University Press. 12s.) * (PA 21:807)

Am J Orthopsychiatry 17:733 O '47. (Adolf G.) Woltmann. * This book fills a gap that has long been painfully noted by many Rorschach workers. The author's scholarly approach to the subject matter deserves high commendation. Her suggestions for future study should encourage research so that the application of the Rorschach test to young children becomes less a means of individual intuition and more a valid clinical tool. *

El Sch J 48:167-9 N '47. Lee J. Cronbach. * Ford gave the test to 123 children, ranging from three years to eight years in age. For many of the children, data were also available on other tests and rating scales. From this group, although it is in no sense considered an adequate sample of children, Ford derives norms which, for the first time, give a frame of reference for dealing with individual preschool test records. She explores thoroughly such questions as the changes in responses with age and sex. In an interesting section on stability, Ford finds that, for most scores, retests after one month correlate .65 or better with original scores. Ford also uses a split-half technique but contributes more by a sharp and highly accurate statement of the reasons why the split-half method is inappropriate, inadequate, and misleading with the Rorschach test. Two chapters on validity will have especial interest for all readers. One chapter studies the ability of the Rorschach test to estimate intelligence. It is assumed, without qualification, that the Stanford–Binet test is an adequate measure of intelligence. On these terms, Ford finds substantial relationships between mental age and the following scores: R—The total number of responses to the series of ten ink blots. Obj.—The total number of persons or objects mentioned in response to the series. F+—Response in which "good" form is the sole determinant of the interpretation. M—Response indicating an experience of felt movement. M+—Since M responses are *ipso facto* F responses, movement always being movement of forms, all M responses are either M+ or M— according to whether the form element is F+ or F—. These correlations are often around .70. There is little relation to the intelligence quotient, of course, because of the uncontrolled influence of chronological age, but it appears that reasonable estimates of the intelligence quotient could be made from Rorschach results. A more basic question is whether, when the two estimates disagree, the Rorschach scores may not be the more valid. The Maurer study [see 288] casts doubt on the meaning of certain items used in the Binet tests for early ages. Rorschach theory sets up a dynamic concept of intelligence in which attention is drawn to the interaction of drive, caution leading to self-criticism, imagination, experience background, and keenness of observation. If there is any validity to the assumptions commonly made from the Rorschach in clinical descriptions of mental functioning, it is unlikely that any single composite or quotient can adequately represent the information which it provides about these dimensions. If the Rorschach, treated mechanically, correlates with Binet performance as well as Ford finds, it should yield remarkable results when used in the objective but insightful manner for which it was designed. The chapter on validity of indicators of personality is inevitably disappointing, since Ford chooses in this study to consider single scores, whereas the meaningful contributions of Rorschach results to personality diagnosis lie in interpreting each individual's *pattern* of scores. Furthermore, criteria known to be valid are almost unobtainable. Ford has a few striking results. Teachers' ratings of emotional adjustment correlate .50 with the Rorschach ratings of adjustment—and again

one is faced with deciding which of the two is invalid! Ratings on the Marston Introversion-Extroversion Scale correspond with the Rorschach index of introversive-extroversive tendencies. Ford's characterization of the correspondence as "relatively low" is not surprising, because the traits bearing such deceptively similar names are differently defined by Rorschach and Marston. In general, one must conclude that Ford has made a superior contribution. She has gathered excellent data which can be reconsidered by persons who are not willing to accept her interpretations always. She has established beyond question that the ink-blot tests will work well with young children and has provided hints on administering the test at these ages, which will be widely appreciated. Where her data are inadequate or her methods conceal essential characteristics of Rorschach data, she can rightfully leave the development of fuller knowledge to subsequent studies. *

J Consult Psychol 11:154 My-Je '47.

J Ed Psychol 38:190–1 Mr '47. C. M. *Louttit.* In this monograph....Dr. Ford reports her investigations on the responses of children from three to eight years of age to the Rorschach test. The reader cannot help but be impressed at the evident objectivity and care with which this research has been planned and carried out. There were four major aims of the investigation: (1) the refinement and simplification of procedures adapting them to young children, (2) the study of variations in determinants as related to age, intelligence and sex, (3) the determination of reliability of determinants at young age levels, and (4) a check on the validity of claims as to the meaning of certain test determinants. The one hundred twenty-three children examined were attending nursery or elementary schools in Minneapolis and Ithaca, New York. Except for a restriction on rotating the cards, the administrative procedures were standard. There was no evidence that this one restriction influenced the responses. The results indicate that the Rorschach is definitely useful at the young ages studied; the children utilized all the ways of responding which are utilized by adults, but not to the same extent. The percentage rejecting at least one card decreased rapidly from thirty-two per cent at three years of age to none at six years of age. The monograph reviews the literature, especially of children, involved with work with inkblots. The procedures and results of the investigation are presented in detail, and illustrated with both tables and graphs. It is hardly necessary in this review to attempt to summarize the details. The important conclusions are that the test proves useful with children, although there is a great need for norms at young ages. The reliabilities varied, with some determinants showing high correlations between test and retest, and with others being low. The results with these young children do not always support certain validity claims based on work with adults. This study is an important contribution to the Rorschach literature. A particularly significant contribution for the Rorschach layman is a glossary of terms and symbols used in Rorschach interpretation.

Psychiatric Q 21:156 Ja '47. Dr. Ford....has made a very valuable contribution to the scientific literature on the Rorschach Test. Her concisely-written monograph summarizes the statistical findings obtained by other investigators and presents the author's own carefully gathered data from 123 boys and girls ranging in age from three to eight. On the whole, the author found that the data obtained by various investigators agree rather well. The differences noted appear to be due to intrinsic psychological differences among the various groups of children studied. The study throws light upon the problem of the influence of age, intelligence and maturity. Certain Rorschach components depend far more upon the age of the child than upon his intelligence. A clarification of this point is of great importance both practically and theoretically. The fact that during childhood the process of growth and maturation is intense complicates the interpretation of children's Rorschach records. There are essential differences between the records of children and of adults but there are also striking similarities. Dr. Ford's constructive study will enable psychologists to draw more valid and more complete conclusions from children's Rorschach records.

Psychol B 44:579–81 N '47. L. Joseph Stone. Dr. Ford's study was initiated in 1936; many of its goals and methods were set at that time. In the face of the enormous proliferation of Rorschach interest, Rorschach studies and Rorschach users (and misusers) in the past decade, what would once have been of pioneering significance is now more in the nature of confirmation, elaboration (or, occasionally, refutation) of studies published in the interim. The first problem Dr. Ford set herself, to refine and simplify Rorschach administration, was not resolved by research, but rather by preliminary experience. Most notable modifications are the use of a trial blot á la Hertz, a prohibition against turning the cards, and a certain amount of "prodding" for further responses. Undoubtedly there will be disagreement regarding the need for such changes. Although she appears to have been unusually successful in carrying through her inquiries, Ford, like others who have worked with young children, suggests the desirability of a brief inquiry at the time each card is shown. * Her second problem was the study of "variations in the test determinants" (scoring categories) and their relation to sex and age. No normative value is claimed because the 123 subjects "represent a highly selected group both in intelligence and in socioeconomic status" (p. 39). Existing adult and adolescent norms were used. This section cannot but remind the reader of the regrettable lack of final agreement on scoring nomenclature. In the few instances where the present study is at variance with the Klopfer–Margulies' findings this appears to have been a determining factor. (For example, including among whole responses the "cut-off whole," by Klopfer and Margulies but apparently not by Ford; or again, "One possible explanation for the low incidence of C responses in....the present study is the fact that Cn responses were not included in C responses" (p. 47) as is customary and was the case in the other report.) Certain other discrepancies raise the more serious question of disagreement on scoring. For example, the author points to the higher incidence of M in her study in spite of the fact that "all the investigators including the writer, use Rorschach's instructions in scoring M responses" (p. 54). Yet in the three sample protocols several instances appear to the reviewer in which movement was scored even though not "human or human-like." (E.g., "lots of bugs crawling around.") The reviewer would also quarrel with the scoring of some of the color responses. In general, sex differences appear unimportant. However, Ford shows that many important scoring categories bear a clear-cut relationship to chronological age between 3 and 8. These findings, along with others in the literature, point to the need of establishing norms perhaps for each year-level under 7 or 8. An attempt was made to validate the relationship between intelligence and certain specific determinants suggested by Rorschach. Satisfactory correlations were found for most of these but not for W and %A. These exceptions "make sense" in view of the fact that children's whole responses are often crude and undifferentiated, unlike the more structured W's of adults, and in view of the fact that animal concepts in children's thinking do not have the banality that they do for adults. A third contribution of the study was in establishing test-retest reliabilities for the specific determinants of the Rorschach with young children. * Her fourth major aim, the study of the "validity of some of the determinants of personality," Dr. Ford undertakes with great modesty, but it is difficult to evaluate because data so meticulously supplied in other sections of the monograph are inadequate here. As one example, in evaluating emotional adjustment on the Olson scale we are told that the subjects were "divided into three groups on the basis of emotional adjustment as indicated by the Rorschach Test" (p. 82), but we do not know how this was done. A new scoring concept of *organizational links* (OL) is tantalizing because it is always referred to allusively. Defined in the glossary as "The number of verbalized, logical connections within a response or within a record," this would appear to be a valuable indication of complexity of response. However, the sample protocols make it difficult to determine whether one counts links or items. "A man walking a fence" receives a score of 2 OL; "a partly burned tree trunk" is also scored 2 OL; while "a balanced snake" is scored 1 OL. For the clinician there is some disappointment in the mass treatment of data and the paucity of individual records or even scoring lists. However, he will find much of interest in the discussion of administration of the Rorschach and on the frequencies of locations, determinants and content. The student of personality development will discover certain interesting findings —and rather more interesting suggestions—for the use of the Rorschach to study development in general, and the development of the process of logical thinking in particular.

[81]

★[*Re* Rorschach.] HARROWER, M. R., AND STEINER, M. E. Manual for Psychodiagnostic Inkblots (A Series Parallel to the Rorschach Blots). New York: Grune & Stratton, Inc., 1945. Pp. 112. Paper, lithotyped. $2.00. * Accompanying *Psychodiagnostic Inkblots*, $4.50. * (*PA* 20:830)

Am J Orthopsychiatry 17:549 Jl '47. (Adolf G.) Woltmann. * Since a similarity exists between both sets of cards, retesting with inkblots can be achieved within a shorter time than would ordinarily be necessary in order to avoid carry-over or halo effects. In addition to the obvious similarities, a more carefully developed parallelism has been attempted in trying to reproduce the outstanding perceptual properties of each of the original Rorschach cards. The authors claim that this new series results in the giving of slightly more responses per record and a slightly greater incidence of form color answers. The scoring of records obtained with this new series follows that devised by Klopfer.

J Nerv & Mental Dis 104:231 Ag '46. (Zygmunt A.) Piotrowski. Rorschach examinations have become so frequent that for purposes of re-examination and validity the need for a new series of inkblots that would parallel Rorschach's original set of 10 plates has arisen. Dr. Harrower created the new parallel series and standardized it in collaboration with Miss Steiner. The data contained in the manual show that the Harrower blots elicit the same type of responses in practically the same proportions as do the original Rorschach plates. The authors should be complimented on their standardization. The new set of blots and the manual will be of great aid to clinical and research workers. *

Psychoanalytic Q 15:390–1 Jl '46. William F. Murphy. * All the various types of responses characteristic of the Rorschach record are found in their series. From a comparison with the original Rorschach series the authors feel that their series give rise to slightly more responses per record, and are more productive in FC responses, but as is pointed out, this is not necessarily a disadvantage and patients showing an absence of color responses to the Rorschach series might well be tested further with the Harrower–Steiner series.

Psychosom Med 7:384–5 N '45. Gotthard Booth. The authors have worked with a series of ten inkblots which look superficially different from the standard inkblots used by Rorschach. Actually the construction of the new cards follows carefully the course of systematic variations of gestalt and surface qualities underlying the original series. Statistical proof is given that the same types of scores are obtained with either series. This achievement should make the Harrower Blots most welcome to those who wish to objectivate changes of personality in subjects under prolonged clinical observation, because the new set allows for repeat performances which would not be affected by the influences of memory and past experience. The manual gives detailed statistical information on the responses obtained from 225 normal subjects and from 160 institutionalized patients. This makes it easy to use the new cards successfully without acquiring personal experience. The only difference between the old and the new series is found in the fact that the new series makes it easier to give form-color responses. This may be of practical value. Furthermore it raises again the theoretical question whether the original set is not unnecessarily limited in its usefulness by the personal bias of Rorschach himself. (See G. A. Roemer: Vom Rorschachtest zum Symboltest. Zentralblatt fuer Psychotherapie 10:310, 1937/38.) Aside from its main purpose the manual is valuable because it includes the results of a study of clerical workers and of engineers. It appears that different personality traits are required for success in each of the two groups. This reviewer feels that the reliability of technical aptitude tests could be greatly improved if used jointly with the projective ink blot technique.

[82]

★[Re Rorschach.] HARROWER-ERICKSON, M. R., AND STEINER, M.E. **Large Scale Rorschach Techniques: A Manual for the Group Rorschach and Multiple Choice Test.** Springfield, Ill.: Charles C Thomas, Publisher, 1945. Pp. xi, 419. $8.50. * (PA 19:1720)

Am J Orthopsychiatry 15:737 O '45. Louis A. Lurie. * If the conclusions of the authors are borne out by other workers, their technique will take its rightful place with the other objective psychological personality tests. For the present it must be remembered that the records of but 340 subjects provided the material for the analysis. * Not satisfied with the results of group Rorschach technique insofar as shortening and simplifying the procedure was concerned, the authors devised another modification of the Rorschach test which they call the multiple choice test. * The underlying assumption of the authors has been "that those individuals most likely to give certain types of responses when responding freely in the Rorschach method will pick such responses when confronted with them in a multiple choice situation." The weakness of this line of reasoning

is obvious. Among other things, no allowance is made for the effect of suggestion or the effect of confusion due to ability to choose. * Despite the need for further evaluation, this monograph is well worth reading, not only by those interested in the Rorschach technique but by everyone interested in objective psychological personality tests.

Am J Psychiatry 102:141–2 Jl '45. Fred V. Rockwell. * excellent organization * Specific directions for the administration and scoring of the group Rorschach are presented simply and clearly. * Eight thousand responses have been evaluated in a painstaking manner from the viewpoint of location, determinants and content. There is nothing in the literature to compare with these carefully worked-out and beautifully charted standards. The subjects include normal adults, psychotics, college age individuals and a group of prisoners. By comparison of these diverse groups, it has been possible to determine accurately the stimulus-producing properties of each individual card. Such standards are of fundamental and lasting importance both in the evaluation of group Rorschach tests and in connection with the original individual technique. * The multiple choice test was developed in an effort to permit tests to be given and scored by untrained persons. Here, in the opinion of this reviewer, the authors violate the fundamental principles involved in Rorschach interpretation by attempting to reduce the results to a numerical score. * Any person who has worked with the Rorschach technique is bound to experience a certain feeling of reverence and awe at the enormous amount of painstaking work which the authors have put into this most authoritative volume. The book is highly recommended as an essential part of any Rorschach reference library.

Am J Psychol 58:410–5 Jl '45. Donald E. Super. The sub-title of this volume and the descriptive material on the jacket will lead many clinical psychologists to look upon the appearance of this book as a hopeful indication that the Rorschachean techniques have now been adapted for their general use. The scientifically-minded psychologist may look upon it as a help in setting an estimate upon the test in its simpler forms. The table of contents and the introduction should confirm the reader's hopes. * Some readers may be more impressed by the possibilities of the method than by the inconclusive nature of much of the evidence, and some may note certain favorable, but subjective, valuations of the authors and of their authorities. The authors have at times—to be sure—successfully attempted to be scrupulous in their approach, with important results. For example, two careful and convincing studies of the value of the Group Rorschach in academic prediction, made by Harrower–Erickson at McGill and by Munroe at Sarah Lawrence, are described in some detail (pp. 18–27). In another section (p. 70 ff.), the stimulus values of each card were studied with the finding that the distribution of responses by location is relatively constant among normal and abnormal groups, but with slight group-differences. The incidence of anatomical responses in medical students, who might be expected to see such content more frequently than other groups as a result of training, was studied (p. 137), and the authors depart from traditional Rorschach theory in concluding, quite properly, that experience does affect the content of responses. But no consideration is given to other possible training effects, *e.g.* vista responses in persons trained in drawing. * [These] studies, despite lack here and there of statistical refinement, should interest the scientifically-minded reader in further research with large-scale Rorschach techniques. Unfortunately, however, these studies are in the minority. Despite the book's promise, its methods are frequently weak, its data sometimes inadequate, its statistical analyses often incomplete and unsophisticated, its conclusions generally colored by bias in favor of the techniques investigated, and cautious conclusions are too frequently discarded for clinical impressions and observations which smack of wishful thinking. The experimenters will be divided from the clinicians early in the book, where the statement is made (p. 8) ". . . it is clear that minor deviations in technique, in materials, in administration and scoring, will matter as little here as they do when the test is given individually." On the one hand, this attitude seems to involve a lack of scientific care and accuracy; on the other hand, it is clinical in its approach, attempting to maintain uniformity by adapting the situation to each patient rather than by standardizing the situation itself. Herein lies an old quarrel between clinicians and psychometricians. On pages 13 and 14, impressionistic conclusions reached by various users of the Group Rorschach are cited without quoting evidence

to justify the conclusions. For example, Krugman is quoted: "Although far from complete, preliminary results indicate that . . . the data yielded possess far greater usefulness for personality evaluation than any other pencil-paper 'personality' test now known to this writer and his colleagues." This is not evidence. In another place (pp. 85–86) trends "considered" typical by Klopfer are referred to and used as "well-recognized norms," thereby converting opinion into fact. It is stated (p. 36) that, in the group-test, the location of responses on cards by subjects is sometimes confused, but is sometimes spontaneously clearly delineated with varicolored pencils. No mention is made of the desirability of standardizing the method of locating the response to make possible more accurate scoring of locations; instead, in line with Rorschachean tradition, it is suggested that the method of locating responses be used as additional diagnostic material. It may be useful as such, but this unscorable material is gained at the sacrifice of the accuracy of the scoring of the more basic data on location. The authors decided to run a check (p. 190) on the identity of interpretations of group and individual responses in Rorschach. Forty subjects were therefore given an individual inquiry. Some general conclusions concerning the accuracy of scoring of data secured by group-methods and a number of examples of determinants scored for data gathered first by group and then by individual inquiries are presented. But there is no tabulation of data to justify the conclusions—nothing more than impressionistic judgment and selection of examples. Section viii (two pages) is entitled "Discussion of Content Categories," and is followed by eight pages of graphs and tables showing the distribution of responses according to content and clinical group. But there are no measures of the significance of the differences, and no discussion of the results. This leads the reviewer to wonder, with embarrassment, why it is that clinicians, and Rorschacheans particularly, have such strong leanings toward words without figures, on the one hand, and incompletely analyzed figures, without words, on the other? No critical ratios, chi-squares, or similar statistics are reported for any of the authors' distributions of responses, whether of clinical or occupational groups. This consistent failure to use measures of significance leads to overemphasis of differences of unknown significance. * The total percentages of failures seem, on the surface, to vary considerably from group to group: College Students 12 per cent, Adults 6 per cent, Prisoners 27 per cent, and Psychotics 54 per cent. But when reference is made to earlier sections of the book and it is ascertained that these groups consisted of 224, 34, 41, and 41 subjects respectively, one is inclined to wonder how significant these differences in total negative responses really are. Again, these figures tell only the percentage of negative responses in each group of subjects, instead of indicating the mean and standard deviation of the negative scores of each group. If the data were analyzed by the accepted method for comparisons of test-performances, and if critical ratios were computed, the differences might, or might not, seem "very striking." We do not know. Due, Wright and Wright also are guilty of unscientific methods and reasoning in their sections of the book, although they use occasional measures of significance. Their 731 psychiatric patients from the Navy are not comparable to their 369 "normal" recruits in age or education, and the authors state that officers "with frequent contact" with the normal group estimated, we are not told how, that from 20 to 30 per cent were moderately or severely maladjusted. No attempt was made, apparently, to weed out the maladjusted members to secure a truly normal group, or to match the two groups for age and education by dropping cases. The Naval authors report a significant difference between the mean introversiveness-extratension scores of their two groups (p. 198), but with so much overlapping as to make the scores "of little value." They then recommend a cut-off score of 54 which would single out 31 per cent of the patients and 19 per cent of the normals; whether these latter are the maladjusted members of the so-called normal group is not known, but "subsequent experience with the test at an embarkation center has strongly validated this inference." If the experience yielded evidence, the evidence could be statistically treated and analyzed. These high-scoring subjects are the extratensives; no mention is made of the low-scoring patients and normals who should, by definition, be introversive, obsessive, and repressed, and who are not differentiated at the lower ends of the distributions (Table I, p. 198) nor by the suggested critical score. These same authors report (pp. 199–200) that the distributions of negative scores of their psychiatric and normal

subjects overlap so much as to be nondifferentiating. This conflicts with Harrower–Erickson and Steiner's conclusion (pp. 157–161) that negative scores of 4 or more are indicative of maladjustment, but agrees with a study by Wittson, Hunt, and Older, referred to in the text. The only attempt to reconcile these conflicting findings is the suggestion that, in view of the possibility of maladjustment in some 20 per cent of the normal group, a critical score of 5 be used, thus selecting 37 per cent of the patients and 23 per cent of the normals. Statistical evidence failing, resort is again made to "clinical experience," which has "repeatedly demonstrated to the authors that an individual with 5 negative responses shows marked behavior disturbances." Again, if experience demonstrated this to the authors, the data would demonstrate it to the reader. That a recent study (M. B. Jensen and J. B. Rotter, The validity of the multiple choice Rorschach Test in officer candidate selection, *Psychol. Bull.* 42, 1945, 182–185) reports that 22 per cent of a group of Armored Force officers rated excellent by immediate supervisors made negative scores of 5 or more on this test, is perhaps an indication of the dangers of discarding objective evidence in favor of the impressions of clinical experience. In the light of these facts, even the positive results reported earlier in this review hardly justify the conclusion—or perhaps it is a hypothesis—of Due, Wright and Wright on page 212: "Experience with the test has shown that it may be useful in estimating the relative amenability or resistance of the patient to psychotherapeutic treatment. It is quite probable that the test can also be used as an objective evaluation of therapeutic progress." It seems to this reviewer that, as the result of too glib summaries of the results of research, leading by easy transitions to statements based on observations and impressions and from there to wishfully phrased hypotheses, the authors permit themselves to reach conclusions which have not actually been demonstrated for these two forms of the test. As a final illustration of the book's clinically oriented weaknesses, one might cite Section vii, an interesting and helpful discussion of interpretative principles for differential diagnosis. 'Helpful,' that is, *if true*. The material is all subjective, based on clinical impressions and on single-case illustrations. True, these interpretations are in line with Rorschach practice, and clinical experience suggests that they are sound. But unorganized experience, unanalyzed data, and tradition are often misleading. Validation should be accomplished by evidence gathered in controlled investigations and analyzed objectively, not by the opinions of authorities and the impressions of observers. A few defects and errors such as are found in most books might be mentioned. Tables are numbered serially in each section, thus making it necessary to identify tables by number and page; graphs are not numbered at all. The graphs on pages 188–189 have some unexplained hollow and broken-line extensions to otherwise solid bars. On page 31 the name "Snellen" is misspelled. Pages 101–103 are unnumbered. H. J. Older is referred to as "T. J." on page 239. Lt. Due is referred to as "(MC), USNR" on pages 195 and 205, but as "MC V–(S), USNR" on page 214, which, if true, should presumably be written "MC–V (S), USNR." But these are minor defects. Despite its major shortcomings, the book contains much valuable material, including norms for the distribution of responses by location, the frequency of determinants, content, popular responses, and rejections or negative responses. The beginning of the process of standardization, incomplete though it is, is important. Future studies will no doubt be made, building on the foundation laid by these investigations and leading to the development of a practical and well-validated instrument.

Arch Neurol & Psychiatry 54:72–3 Jl '45. In the first part of the book the authors deal extensively with the development of the group Rorschach method * Adequate directions for administration and for scoring are given, and numerous illustrations appear. The second part of the book, in which an analysis of the findings of an experimental investigation is presented, is much less convincing, from both the statistical and the clinical viewpoint. The statistical procedure open to most serious challenge is the small and poorly selected sample of subjects used for standardization purposes, involving, as it does, a college group in which more than one half are medical students and nurses. With the individual Rorschach method, such a professional group is generally conceded to report more than the usual number of anatomic responses. The authors recognize the need for contrasting control groups and include them, although a considerable amount of overlap-

ping appears to exist in their choices. Subjects consist of (1) unselected males, (2) patients (psychotic and psychopathic) and (3) two groups of prison inmates, composed of "sex offenders" or persons "serving terms for murder, burglary, grand larceny and forgery." The data do not suggest, however, that in the third group psychopathic personalities have been eliminated. Little attention is given to the basic problem of reliability of the group method itself, although it appears to be fairly sensitive to variations of administrative technic. Evidence is also lacking that qualitative aspects of the individual Rorschach test principles may not have been altered radically under group conditions. Nevertheless, interpretation is based primarily on principles of the individual Rorschach method, seemingly on the assumption that the two technics reveal personality patterns which are qualitatively similar. If, as the authors suggest, their book is to serve as a "manual" for the group Rorschach method, these theoretic considerations must be met before an adequate evaluation can be made of the method itself. Their statistical tabulation of responses is of value, inasmuch as it constitutes a new and genuine contribution to the literature. To date, no such analysis of responses obtained to the Rorschach cards presented by the group method has appeared. * Three sections of the book concern themselves with validation of the multiple choice test in terms of its effectiveness in the psychiatric differentiation of military personnel. The contributors....present evidence which, although favoring the use of the multiple choice test among trained workers, acknowledges its limitations when employed by persons unskilled in Rorschach interpretation. They qualify their endorsement of the test by stating that their "blind analyses were made from the interpretative principles of the individual Rorschach combined with subjective clinical hunches" (page 214). For a test which purports to objectify and quantify the Rorschach method to a degree which makes it usable by workers untrained in Rorschach interpretation, such evidence is not convincing. Some of the material in the section on the application of interpretative principles definitely suggests a need for further research. Clinicians experienced in the use of the individual Rorschach method will find it difficult to avoid feeling that much of qualitative significance has been sacrificed, from such statements as the following: "Organic and convulsive states are pooled in this discussion inasmuch as they are indistinguishable, interpretively, in the Multiple Choice Test" (page 231), or, "Three case records will be cited to illustrate this group, one with grand mal epilepsy and two cases demonstrating psychiatric evidences of organic intellectual impairment, one with post-traumatic encephalopathy and the other having nervous system syphilis with paresis" (page 232). From their grouping and interpretation, the contributors seem to suggest that organic damage to the brain is to be expected with convulsive disorders, a fact which has yet to be established. * The fourth, and last, part of the book contains classified lists of content obtained from group record responses based on the amplified version of the multiple choice test. This material is definitely of interest, although no conclusions are drawn from group records and no comparison made with individual records taken as a group. Throughout the entire book, administrative details and appraisal of them are handled by trained Rorschach workers, not by untrained laymen. There is evidence of considerable success with the use of the group Rorschach methods under these conditions. Much, however, remains to be done. In commenting on the book in a recent publication (Rorschach Research Exchange 9:46–53, 1945), Dr. Marguerite Hertz summarizes its contribution rather well when she says that " 'Large Scale Rorschach Techniques' is valuable as a pioneer effort," but that "it is still unsuited for widespread application." Just how far this falls short of the authors' intention is suggested by the publisher's statement on the jacket flap of the book, that the authors "have devised an entirely new test which can be readily used for screening out maladjusted persons by investigation *without extensive training in the Rorschach method.* They present evidence to show that by a simple procedure, taking a few minutes to administer and to evaluate, psychiatrist, psychologist, psychiatric social worker, educator, or counselor may now avail himself of the fruits of research of many years in the Rorschach method." Many Rorschach workers skilled in the use of the individual method will agree with Dr. Hertz when, in speaking of the group Rorschach and the multiple choice test, she further concludes: "Both tests may be used to advantage only by workers who are steeped in Rorschach methodology, who are willing to subject the tests to thorough study, and to treat their results with suspended judgment." Many will question the wisdom of attempting such oversimplification for the purpose of mass consumption and will regret that such a potentially dangerous weapon has already been placed at the disposal of the novice without proper validation.

Brit J Psychol 36:45–6 S '45. This book is intended mainly for those who already have a good knowledge of the Rorschach technique, though it will also be of considerable interest to psychologists in general. * a very interesting section by F. O. Due, M. E. Wright and B. A. Wright shows why a simple pass or fail score often gives inaccurate results. The particular responses of various maladjusted types, e.g. of different neurotic types, vary greatly; and it is the pattern of particular 'good' and 'bad' responses which is most likely to be really diagnostic. Although it requires the highly skilled Rorschach technician to work out these patterns, it seems possible that a trained psychologist might learn to use them in selection testing with less labour than is required to learn the whole Rorschach technique. The simple 'pass or fail' form of the Multiple Choice test can of course be given and scored by psychologically untrained personnel. It has the additional advantage over the older Rorschach techniques that it is less dependent on the verbal facility of the subject; but a possible disadvantage in that the choice of responses might be found unduly constricting by a highly imaginative subject. Moreover, the validity of both group techniques depends to a high degree on the subjects' co-operativeness. For one of the principal signs of emotional disorder is said to be the failure to respond (or the response "Nothing at all"). English subjects, often less amenable to testing than are Americans, might frequently fail to respond for reasons other than emotional disorder, e.g. because they "couldn't be bothered." However, it would of course be necessary to try out these new techniques on large representative groups of English subjects before deciding the best manner of using them in this country. They might be found exceedingly valuable if they could be used with a reasonable degree of accuracy by psychologists who had not the time for long periods of specialized training.

J Am Med Assn 127:955 Ap 7 '45. * a well written, comprehensive manual of large scale

Rorschach technics by writers who are well known and respected for their work in this field. Methods used for group testing and multiple choice tests....are clearly delineated. * The book is well indexed * The work represents an extremely valuable contribution to both military and civilian psychologic investigation.

J Consult Psychol 9:310–1 N-D '45. Bruno Klopfer. For the last four years the authors have been pioneering under the pressure of war demands for modifications of the Rorschach Technique which would make it feasible for use on a large scale. * The present volume is the first comprehensive account of these efforts previously only reported in articles and oral reports. The bulk of the volume....consists of tables containing the quantitative output of the experimentation with the modified techniques * The book is furthermore enriched by three original articles by F. O. Due, M. E. Wright, and B. A. Wright which contain some of the most stimulating experiments and thoughts in the whole volume. A variety of technical and typographical features deserve special mentioning: the use of figure and ground effects for the pictorial presentations of specific blot areas in the stimulus cards ('the areas under discussion appear as black blots on a lighter gray background); the large and easy-to-read print; the spacious tables; the careful index; the ample bibliographical references; and the simple and easy-to-understand chapter headings. The first part of the book deals with the modifications of the *administration* of the Rorschach Technique * The discussion covers quite adequately the important modifications of the recording of Rorschach responses: namely: (*a*) the substitution of slides for the ink-blot cards; (*b*) the substitution of self-recording techniques for the recording of the responses by the examiner; and (*c*) the substitution of a modified self-inquiry for the inquiry by the examiner as to how the subject arrived at his responses. The function of the volume as a "manual" is limited by the authors to this phase of the administration. For the scoring and interpretation of the responses thus collected, the reader is referred almost exclusively to *The Rorschach Technique.* * An ingenious technical device should be mentioned....which is used by the authors throughout Part II. The ten stimulus cards share the statistical spotlight with the group of

subjects. The distribution of scoring categories is shown for each card, thus highlighting its specific stimulus properties. Thorough familiarity with these stimulus properties is one of the most important prerequisites for a careful sequence analysis of Rorschach responses. * the multiple choice technique has added a new and extremely valuable tool for the experienced Rorschach worker. The articles by Due, Wright, and Wright give an amazing and convincing account (especially in the detailed analysis of multiple choice records published on pages 215–238) of the use an experienced clinician and Rorschach worker can make of the multiple choice technique; the same authors demonstrate that the mechanical quantitative evaluation of multiple choice records without Rorschach background and experience does not yield results of practical value. The responses chosen by different groups of subjects unquestionably reflect differences usually found in records of spontaneous responses, even to the extent of yielding statistically significant differences. However, the overlapping of such differences found in all experiments is sufficient to induce any blind interpreter to produce far too many false positive and false negative diagnoses, thus embarrassing himself and the method in the eyes of the clinician. The authors confirm these limitations of the multiple choice test * The modifications of the original multiple choice blank, described in the remaining sections of Part III, make it more valuable as a research tool for the Rorschach worker, but seem rather to accentuate than to change this shift of emphasis. (In view of this situation, it seems hardly justifiable that the publishers appraise the book on the jacket in the following sentences: ". . . they have devised an entirely new test which can be readily used for screening out maladjusted persons by investigation *without extensive training in the Rorschach method* (in bold type). They present evidence to show that by simple procedure, taking a few minutes to administer and evaluate, psychiatrist, psychologist, psychiatric social worker, educator, or counselor may now avail himself of the fruits of research of many years in the Rorschach method.")

J Nerv & Mental Dis 101:621–2 Je '45. Z. A. Piotrowski. * very carefully written book * The authors present their method and its results in a clear and straightforward manner. Their own results prove that the Multiple

Choice Test is too extreme an abbreviation of the Rorschach method to be of practical value. However, the authors' experience also demonstrates that the Rorschach, applied to groups, can be helpful provided these group records are interpreted in a way in which the individual Rorschach records are usually interpreted.

Nerv Child 5:276 Jl '46. * the subtitle....indicates that the attempt is made to use Rorschach plates to develop a means of mass testing, a task which must be considered most peripheric for a testing method with a great individual sensitivity. Since the Rorschach adherents are divided, the applicability of the test will cause much controversy among those who are most interested in it. It seems to us a mistake to use the word "group" as it is here applied; we should prefer the use of collective application of the Rorschach test as title.

Prison World 8:23 Mr-Ap '46.

Psychiatry 8:516 N '45. M. F. Ashley Montagu. * [This method for the group Rorschach] has been well tested by the authors and several other investigators whose independent reports are interestingly presented in this volume. The test works, and it works remarkably well. * The Group Rorschach is destined to be widely used; and its possibilities are great, particularly now that peace is restored to the world, for use in educational and industrial institutions. An entirely new group test, the multiple choice test, is also described in detail. * There are some remarkable reports on the results of the application of this test to naval personnel in which a 90 per cent accuracy in diagnosis was obtained, even down to organic brain lesions. Obviously this is a test full of the promise of immediate usefulness. The reader should be warned that some knowledge of the Rorschach technique is assumed for both tests.

Psychol B 43:285-7 My '46. Robert C. Challman. * This book purports to be a manual for the Group Rorschach (a technique of administering the Rorschach ink-blots to groups) and for the Multiple Choice Test (a technique in which the subject selects his responses to the Rorschach ink-blots from a list). * The literature on the Group Rorschach is well summarized, and a convincing case for the usefulness and merit of this approach is made. The authors contend on the basis of one study and a passing reference to two others that the group method yields essentially the same material as that yielded by the individual Rorschach. Ac-

cording to Dr. Marguerite Hertz, however, other studies not cited by the authors do not bear out this contention. In the section serving as a manual for the Group Rorschach, excellent directions for administration are given. The recommended methods for conducting the inquiry for determinants involve, however, what is tantamount to the use of leading questions—a practice which, for the individual Rorschach, both Beck and Klopfer strongly condemn. The chapter on scoring is not intended to aid the prospective scorer of the Group Rorschach since the authors believe that the scoring principles of the individual Rorschach apply. It seems likely, however, that all "F—" scores might not be the same with the two techniques and one might infer even from the authors' own data that "popular" responses and probably "usual detail" responses do not correspond entirely with their counterparts in the individual Rorschach. Over 200 pages are devoted to data concerning locations, determinants, and content—mostly in graphic and tabular form. Unfortunately the value of this material is seriously weakened by the following major and minor flaws. (1) No account of the procedure of administration of scoring is given. (2) The sampling is inadequate. Of the 340 subjects tested, 224 were of college age, and the rest consisted of relatively small groups of adult males, prisoners, and a mixed group of psychotics and psychopathic personalities. It is very doubtful whether any meaningful differences can be found between groups so heterogeneous within themselves. (3) No measures of dispersion or measures of reliability of differences are presented. (4) The authors state that their "main interest and concern [was in] providing norms for the college age group"...., but since their group is composed mainly of medical students and nurses, even this aim is not fulfilled. (5) Instead of attempting to ascertain what are the "usual details" from their own data, the authors use Klopfer's series and add other details which were seen by their subjects at least as often as the most infrequent one he lists. This results in their identifying as *usual* a large number of details whose actual frequencies are less than 1 per cent, i.e., *unusual* "usual details." (6) Although average figures for the different determinants would have been helpful in interpreting a Rorschach record, only percentages are given. * Although the original validating study of the authors [for the Multiple Choice Test] showed a very good discrimination between normals and abnormals, subsequent studies (one of which is presented in full in the book) have found such imperfect discrimination as to make its value as a screening instrument very dubious. The authors attempt to explain away these findings, but the more recent study of Jensen and Rotter showing that the test places 45 per cent of "actually excellent [Army] officers" in the abnormal group makes such attempts rather futile. In an effort to overcome some of the shortcomings of the test, the authors developed an amplified form. In this version, the number of items was tripled, objectivity of scoring was increased, differential weighting was introduced and a new critical score adopted. These changes were made on the basis of an analysis of "more than 50,000 test blanks," but only fragmentary data are presented to justify most of the innovations. The reliability and validity of the new instrument are not mentioned. Fortunately a recent study allows a tentative evaluation of this form. R. F. and D. I. Malamud, comparing the responses of 100 normals with those of 100 abnormals, found an almost complete overlapping of the two distributions. Item analysis, with the standard of C.R. of 2 or over, revealed only 10 per cent of the items as discriminative while 6 per cent discriminated in the wrong direction. Some material of value to those interested in experimental work can be gleaned from the book, but these hardly compensate for the many minor inaccuracies, the unsupported speculations, the overly optimistic attitude of the authors, the lack of organization of the material and the unduly low scientific standards employed. Since it is clear that both the Group Rorschach and the Multiple Choice Test are still in the experimental stage, the book offers little to the clinician.

U S Naval Med B 45:181–2 Jl '45. * The general reader who is not familiar with the Rorschach Test will be hopelessly lost among its professional intricacies, but the Rorschach specialist will find it a thorough and stimulating treatise which he will want on his reference shelves. *

War Med 7:274 Ap '45. * the group Rorschach test is a distinctly different test, and its usefulness is entirely different from that of the individual Rorschach test * The group procedure may be likened to a group mental test

procedure. The group Rorschach test is useful as a screening device and as a means of estimating in a rough sort of fashion personality adjustment, just as a group mental test measures mental ability. For a more accurate, precise measurement of mental ability an individual mental test administered by a trained examiner is preferred. For a more comprehensive, more accurate and more precise measurement of personality, the Rorschach test individually administered and interpreted is preferred. The book presents what is undoubtedly a forward step in personality testing. It is the feeling of this reviewer, however, that the book is for persons who have had training in the Rorschach technic, despite the fact that the authors state that they have written it for the psychologist, psychiatrist, educator, social worker or probation officer untrained in Rorschach interpretive principles.

[82a]

★[*Re* Rorschach.] KABACK, GOLDIE RUTH. **Vocational Personalities: An Application of the Rorschach Group Method.** Columbia University, Teachers College, Contributions to Education, No. 924. Harry D. Kitson, faculty sponsor. New York: Bureau of Publications, the College, 1946. Pp. xi, 116. $2.10. * (*PA* 21:1929)

Occupations 26:135–6 N '47. Joseph Zubin. This study attempted to determine whether the responses of two professional groups (accountants and pharmacists) differ significantly on the Group Rorschach Test and whether the students of these two professions also differ from each other in their Group Rorschach responses. This study marks a new departure for the Rorschach Test, since up to the present it has been largely limited to the clinical field. Its extension into this new field should be watched with interest both by Rorschach technicians as well as by students of personality and vocational guidance. Once before in the history of the Rorschach Test an attempt was made to use it technologically outside of the clinical field. After the first World War about 1921 when German psychologists began to reconvene and reorganize, the fame of the newly born test was spread by A Römer and many of the German psychologists lent a willing ear. It was Stern, however, who prevented a wholesale acceptance of the new test on the ground that it was not yet fully validated and depended upon artistic intuitive evaluation. The present study comes at a crucial time. We are now facing a somewhat similar situation in this country that

German psychology faced in 1921. Many of our applied psychologists, newly returned from their wartime experience, may not have had the experimental and academic training required for evaluating the validity and reliability of tests. For this reason it is high time that the Rorschach Test were subjected to a validation of its various claims, with special reference to its positive contributions as well as its limitations. The study itself takes an objective, neutral tone regarding the interpretive values of its findings. It generally maintains this dispassionate point of view despite its difficulty, except for one or two lapses. For example, on page 33 the author states that "data obtained from case histories, clinical records and psychoanalytical material confirm Rorschach's claim that human movement responses are representative of creative thinking, inventiveness, originality and imagination and that artists, imaginative subjects and abstract thinkers offer the largest number of M responses." This claim is not documented and furthermore some of our leading Rorschach experts freely admit that the meaning of the M response is still not settled. Only recently a study of outstanding artists failed to confirm Rorschach's claim. Several of the interpretations made on the basis of the Rorschach findings do not seem to fit into our general knowledge about the groups under investigation. On page 28 the finding that "Liberal Arts students are less inclined toward philosophic, theoretical or abstract thinking than the two other student groups" and that they also possess less aesthetic and ethical understanding seems somewhat strange. One wonders whether the Allport–Vernon Test of Values would have corroborated that finding. The statistical treatment of the data leaves little to be desired. In fact, in her attempt to squeeze out all the possible relationships, the author presents the same material in several guises. For example, not only are both the critical ratios as well as the chi squares for the same data computed, but a third measure of the same differential is provided by the point-bi-serial. This threefold presentation of the material leads to confusion rather than clarity, especially since the author does not seem to be aware of the fact that the three different methods should theoretically lead to identical results, and if they do not lead to the same results, some explanation on the basis of the sample structure should be made. Another difficulty is the author's interpretation of the correlation between

Original responses (O) and large details (D). A high correlation between these two needs not necessarily lead to the conclusion that "when an original concept (O) is perceived by the members of a group, it is quite likely to be based upon the interpretation of a large detail (D), etc." High correlation does not necessarily mean a high incidence of concurrence. Such a fact can be derived only from a pattern analysis, not from a correlation coefficient. * Finally, the use of the multiple r between the two professions regarded as a dichotomous variable and the twenty-four Rorschach Factors is somewhat of a puzzle. The exact method used is not indicated, but it sounds so much like the method of the discriminant function invented by Fisher that it is somewhat surprising that no mention is made of it. Despite the above critical comments, the study is well worth the reading. Out of the host of variables analyzed, no special pattern of personality characteristic of the two professions emerges. This holds true of both the men engaged in the profession as well as of the students. Apparently the interest and personality trait patterns for occupations discovered by Strong and his followers still remain the method of choice in vocational guidance. The personality trait differences observed by previous workers as characteristic of the two occupations need not be regarded as disproved by this study, for this study suffers from several basic difficulties inherent in the Rorschach Test which no experimental design can overcome. The first difficulty is the rather nebulously defined scoring categories with which the Rorschach worker contents himself. These are good enough for clinical usage but they can never serve to advantage in an experiment. We must provide some more rigorous psychometric frame of reference which will yield more systematic scores that can be operationally defined independently of their alleged personality correlates, if we are to use these scores experimentally. The second difficulty inheres in the undefined personality correlates of the Rorschach factors. Such personality traits as anxiety, creativity, etc., need some type of objective operational definition. How these two ends are to be achieved lies beyond the scope of the present study, but they are the foundations on which further attempts at studying personality via the Rorschach Test must be based.

Psychol B 44:581–2 N '47. Max Hertzman.
* The bulk of the monograph is devoted to a

meticulous statistical analysis of inter-group differences based on most of the large variety of scorable Rorschach factors that have been recognized to date. The statistical analysis is conscientiously performed and well presented but the scope of the study does not go much beyond statistically defined problems. A limitation is also placed on the data by dealing with the Rorschach factors in a purely quantitative fashion. The interpretations of the data are thus based only on the sheer number or the proportions of various significant items. The omission of qualitative considerations can at times be disastrous to an intensive character analysis. * A fuller understanding of the relationship between personality and vocational choice requires a broader investigation than the one reported here. Vocational choice is related to the prestige, economic reward, economic security afforded by the vocation as well as to the skills demanded by it. The prestige may vary with the social stratum from which an individual comes, as may the standards which determine adequate reward and adequate security. An analysis of what the appeals of given occupations are could be the basis of more sharpened hypotheses as to which personality factors to investigate. An attempt to obtain such information, in the present study, through a questionnaire was not very successful. When asked the reason for their choice of profession, over 60 percent of the 300 subjects either did not answer this question, or said they selected the profession because they liked it or were interested in it. Intensive interviews of a few subjects might have been more fruitful, perhaps yielding a picture of the relationship between self evaluation and occupational choice. Such findings as the greater anxiety among pharmacists could be clarified if there were greater understanding of the meaning of the profession as a way of life to the people in it. The discovery of a high degree of overlap between the pharmacists and the accountants, despite the wide differences in the nature of these professions, focusses attention on the limitations of a personality approach to vocational choice in present day society. As the author indicates, the present study cannot be taken as a final statement. She points to the need of a more diverse sample than was used and to the need for further experimentation with the Group Rorschach Method to clarify interpretations which were carried over bodily from the individual test. We would stress the value in future research of an intensive approach which would not limit personality description to the special characteristics of a single test and which would investigate motivational and social determinants as well as personality structure.

[83]

★[Re Rorschach.] KLOPFER, BRUNO, AND DAVIDSON, HELEN H. **The Rorschach Technique: 1946 Supplement.** Yonkers, N. Y.: World Book Co., 1946. Pp. 431-75. Paper. $0.48. *

J Consult Psychol 11:154 My-Je '47. * The first part of the supplement is a brief review of new trends in Rorschach development since 1942. A second part is a chapter on a method of form-level rating. This is of particular interest because of Klopfer's earlier rejection of Rorschach's F-plus per cent as a score. His new proposal rates each response for form on a new scale of from minus 2 to plus 2. A number of examples of scoring are given. *

[84]

★[Re Rorschach.] KLOPFER, BRUNO. **The Rorschach Technique: A Manual for a Projective Method of Personality Diagnosis.** With clinical contributions by Douglas McGlashan Kelley. Yonkers, N. Y.: World Book Co., 1942. Pp. xi, 436. (London: Geo. G. Harrap & Co., Ltd.) * For supplement, *see* 83. For latest edition, *see* 85. (PA 16:3170)

Am J Orthopsychiatry 12:739 O '42. (Ira S.) Wile. * As an interested and enthusiastic protagonist for this mode of analysis. [Klopfer] presents a well-organized discussion of its nature, technique, and problems of scoring. His enthusiasm is reflected in the section devoted to the general problems of interpretation and the nature of personality structure. When discussing the intellectual aspects of personality one notices an undercurrent of defensiveness. It is heartening to read: "It would naturally be absurd ever to expect to establish standardized tables based on statistical research which would enable one to determine whether a subject is schizophrenic, neurotic, or any other definite personality type—normal or abnormal." As personality diagnosis can only be made by inference, there is special interest attached to Part IV, dealing with clinical diagnoses, by Dr. Kelley. This section is not always clear nor is it very convincing. This may be exemplified by his reference to "the so-called *pathognomonic* signs" and then, "none of them is limited too exclusively to one single clinical entity." After referring to clinical entities that produce general constellations of Rorschach response, typically reflecting the personality structure, he states: "A quantitative validity is not to be expected from studies of these general signs, since, clinically, all that one may hope for is that a majority of patients showing the signs will be found to possess the disease entity in question and, conversely, that the majority of patients not suffering from the disease entity will not show these Rorschach responses." He is quite right in stating: "There is a grave danger of misusing such general Rorschach patterns by blindly applying them as diagnostic criteria without considering other qualitative factors and extenuating interrelationships which may be present." A careful analysis of the data derived from the Rorschach technique has meaning only to those thoroughly familiar with the scoring methods and their interpretation. Hence this volume has special value for Rorschach testers and clinicians. It will be useful also to those who are uncertain concerning the validity of the test as an instrument for diagnosis, prognosis or possible therapy.

Am J Orthopsychiatry 13:179–80 Ja '43. Edna Brand Mann. For anyone interested in Rorschach, this book is by so much the best in the field that it earns the rank of the authoritative text on the Rorschach. It does not sacrifice scholarship to simplicity. It does not minimize the living complexity of human nature to achieve a pseudo-simplicity. It is the outcome of rich clinical experience with the Rorschach in Europe, followed by seven years of "learning by teaching" in this country. When Klopfer started his first seminars, at a time when his English was as mystifying as the Rorschach still seems to a beginner, he attracted excited groups of select students who wished to follow him into the then artistic realms of his creative analyses. In those early days students thought, "This is wonderful, but is it Klopfer or Rorschach? Who else but Klopfer could get at an interpretation like that?" We longed for something less inspired and more usable. And now it is here, a beautiful job of logic, a neatly organized structure of thought; a practical, expertly written handbook which is safe for the beginner and illuminating for the Rorschach expert. Many of the questions we have been asking in our daily clinic work are here raised and answered. A few of the technical points this reviewer is particularly pleased to see emphasized in the scoring section are the differentiation in the Form (F) realm, e.g., the difference between a simple

popular or noncommittal F, the superior elaborated F (F plus), and the poor F (F –). Many clinical workers have found only confusion in lumping the two first F's into one F plus category or %, thus obscuring the significant diagnostic feature implicit in a genuinely high F plus, based in superior F. A similarly helpful discussion of Whole (W) responses, breaking the category down into the kind of helpless, unorganized Wholes characteristic of brain diseases, the vague noncommittal Wholes common among those who would put on a big front, and the carefully elaborated Whole showing genuine substance behind the Form. Only in the FC– refinement does there seem question as to whether the elaboration may not be too delicate for comfort. Would not such answers fit better under Cf or Cf–, where they can later be summated more appropriately under the CF than the FC category? An important section of the book is devoted to "Problems of Interpretation of Personality," based on the Major Scoring Categories. Included is a full case study to illustrate in neat detail just how the Rorschach is given, how the "Inquiry and Testing the Limits" are done, how each answer is located by the examiner on a location sheet and scored, and then how (and why) the finale is interpreted. The last section of the book, prepared by Dr. Douglas Kelley, will be of special interest to clinical psychologists and psychiatrists. It presents a well-documented account of Rorschach studies in the field of organic, psychotic and neurotic disorders and mental defectiveness. It contains a great deal of material which might be organized more tellingly. The final chapters introduce the reader to latest events in the Rorschach field, Dr. Harrower–Erickson's recently devised group method of administering the Rorschach, and its possibilities as an adjunct in military medicine and in selection of personnel. The book lives up to the hopes of early Rorschach and Klopfer enthusiasts for a text on the Rorschach that should be comprehensive and comprehensible.

Am J Psychiatry 99:901 My '43. R. Milton Finney. * the most comprehensive exposition of the Rorschach experiment published in English. * clearly and simply written, but such a wealth of detail and information is provided that repeated reading may be necessary by the student. On the other hand, the book will serve as an excellent reference for those familiar with the Rorschach technique. One would wish that the authors had felt free to use colored reproductions of the cards employed in the method, and the inclusion of more Rorschach records would probably have made the technique more intelligible to the beginner.

Am J Psychol 55:609–10 O '42. Z. A. Piotrowski. Of the several available books on the Rorschach method this volume best meets the needs of the beginner. * readable * presented in a clear and systematic manner * no exaggerated claims for the method are made * good index and a comprehensive bibliography * Klopfer gives a careful analysis of scoring. The differentiation between sharply and vaguely perceived forms is very difficult and yet important. Klopfer's treatment of this vexing problem is a definite contribution. His differentiation between F-plus and plain F-responses leads to a more valid estimate of the subjects' intelligence. He suggests that the F – % rather than the F + % be computed since the former possesses the same meaning for all investigators. It is this reviewer's considered opinion that Klopfer's tendency to super-refined scoring does not always achieve results commensurate with the effort expended on the scoring. Thus the chiaroscuro responses subdivided into as many as 12 categories are treated with disproportionately greater detail than other—perhaps even more important—types of response, e.g. the human movement-response. Furthermore, the numerous chiaroscuro categories create complicated problems of reliability and validity. Kelley ....gives a good survey of results obtained in various psychiatric categories of patients. * There are several....misstatements, but on the whole Kelley's review gives the reader a good idea of the type of problem encountered in the application of the Rorschach method to psychiatric diagnosis as well as of the results achieved to date. * Only those who will use the book as a guide in their work with the method will appreciate fully the many fine points which the authors raise. It must be borne in mind, however, that neither this nor any other book will enable the reader to use the method successfully. At least at the present time, the help of a qualified instructor seems indispensable, as Klopfer himself emphasizes, and as is attested by a number of articles in which half-baked views are offered in the naïve conviction that the method was used as Rorschach intended it to be used.

Am Sociol R 8:369–70 Je '43. M. R. Har-rower–Erickson. * a reliable and authentic textbook to which the enthusiastic would-be learner can turn, after his first contacts with the method through popular or pseudoscientific channels. *The Rorschach Technique*....is described by the senior author as follows "This book attempts for the first time to present the accumulated experience of twenty years of application (of the method) in terms of a technical description of the problems the beginner will encounter in his attempt to administer, score, and interpret a Rorschach record. While this book is hardly sufficient as a basis for self-training it is hoped that it will be of considerable help when used in conjunction with other training facilities." This is a modest statement, and the book more than measures up to the authors' hopes. * To [the] scoring system of Rorschach's, Klopfer, both as author and teacher, has done much not only to sharpen and refine it as a tool, but to make it understandable and significant to the bewildered beginner. Part III deals with the interpretation of the scored record * Klopfer's wide experience has enabled him to give to this phase much that is essential to the beginner, and of value to the expert. Part IV (Douglas Kelley) is an able presentation of the use made of the Rorschach method in clinical situations. * This section is obviously not intended to bring the completely uninitiated reader to the point where he can make a differential diagnosis between the patient with a brain tumor and the hysteric! It will be of great interest, however, to the clinical psychologist, and to the physician who has perhaps referred such patients for a Rorschach test, but whose knowledge of the actual characteristics of the personality, as revealed in the test, is scant. The psychiatric social worker, who may have felt the need for some objective method of estimating personality, will be amply rewarded by a study of the type of clinical problems which come within the scope of the test. All in all, the book is an important landmark in the development of a method of personality analysis which is showing that it has a vitally important contribution to make at the present time.

Arch Neurol & Psychiatry 49:930 Je '43. The Rorschach method of personality analysis is still a mystery to most neurologists and psychiatrists. It cannot be said that the present volume makes the matter simple, but the book does provide a great store of information about the test, which is far easier of access than that in Rorschach's original book or any others at present available. This history of the test is interestingly described; then precise directions are given for administering it. * an exhaustive bibliography * The test is useful in the differential diagnosis of various psychoses and neuroses. In addition, definite patterns of response are seen with certain types of structural disease of the brain. The specificity of the pattern in epilepsy is open to question. It would be difficult, but not impossible, to learn to give and to interpret the Rorschach test from this book alone. The manual will, however, be of great value to all those who are working with the procedure, or who are attempting to utilize its results.

Brit J Ed Psychol 13:165 N '43. For review, see 78.

J Abn & Social Psychol 37:572-3 O '42. Claire Myers. * the most thorough and complete summary of Rorschach material available * Although statisticians may disagree with many of the arguments advanced against standardization and validating statistics, nevertheless the authors make some sound objections to the routine application of statistical formulae and the development of a mechanical interpretative procedure. * In general the system of interpretation given is based on the use of formal scores, and the content of the responses is neglected. Many of the criticisms which might be made of this section are of the authors' theories of personality structure rather than of the system of interpretation *per se*. * One of the best features of the book is a complete bibliography of Rorschach publications. One important fault is an absence of statistical evidence for many of the statements made. Rorschach workers and students of the method will probably find the whole book of value. Psychologists and psychiatrists may find the two parts covering administration and interpretation too thorough and detailed, but the sections on history and clinical diagnosis should be of interest to them.

J Appl Psychol 27:209-11 Ap '43. Robert E. Harris. * the criteria for scoring are carefully enough defined so that the agreement between trained scorers should approach that on, say, the vocabulary items of the Revised Stanford–Binet. * A scoring category does not have a single interpretational significance; it may have different meanings in different records, depending on the values in each of the other categories. That every record has unique configurational aspects is continually emphasized, but in spite

of these recurring holistic strictures, Klopfer often seems to assume a one-to-one correspondence between a scoring category and a personality variable. For example, he says, "....the proportion of usual details may indicate the awareness of the obvious and the immediate problems of everyday life ..." (p. 203) * More commonly, though, the multiple interpretational possibilities of the variables and their ratios are discussed against the background of different kinds of records. It is unfortunate that this section [Part 3] contains no validating information of the kind usually found in the descriptions of more objective tests. Instead the reader must be satisfied with such statements as, "A predominance of human profiles, based on parts of the contours of all the blots, has been found in cases of anxiety neuroses, combined with a strongly introversial personality constellation" (p. 264). * Most of the interpretations assume a great deal more stimulus-equivalence and response-generalization than most experimental psychologists would be willing to grant without extensive empirical evidence. It is true that validating the interpretative significance of fifty to a hundred scoring categories, the meaning of each of which may vary with a change in the value of each of the others, presents a formidable task, logically and practically, and, indeed, some Rorschachists would claim, a work of supererogation. There are, however, many indications of the validity of the Rorschach in the clinical and experimental literature, and this section could have been made more convincing to the general reader and more useful to clinical and research workers if citations from these studies had been included. Such facts are an integral part of a technical manual. * Klopfer and Kelley have made a significant contribution to the study of personality. In offering a scheme for analyzing the projective material of the Rorschach which may well become standard, and summarizing what is known about interpretation and diagnosis, they have provided clinicians with an immediately useful tool. Research workers will be intrigued by the perplexing problems of validation, and they will be forced to use (or invent) more elaborate experimental designs than the simple measures of association used in validating tests of nomothetic abilities and traits. The field of personality measurement has been too long dominated by over-simplified conceptualizations of personality structure derived from methods successful in other areas of measurement; we have thought of personality as being made up of those things which we had the tools to measure and validate. It is good that Klopfer and Kelley have stated their conceptualization so clearly. It makes obvious the need for new methods.

J Consult Psychol 6:274–5 S-O '42. Morris Krugman. * a careful, scholarly presentation of a very difficult subject, and is extremely well written. The authors have presented a systematic, comprehensive exposition of the method and have added their own original contributions to the procedures. They have refined and elaborated many of the Rorschach concepts. Some Rorschach workers, including the reviewer, do not agree with all of these refinements and elaborations. However, the authors usually present opposing views, and are free to admit when their changes in scoring technique or interpretation are inconclusive or tentative. They have departed radically, for example, from Rorschach's original concept of "good form," or F+, and have eliminated the F+ per cent. The latter is so generally used that Klopfer and Kelley were forced, in discussing the Rorschach in connection with pathological conditions, to reintroduce this concept. The experienced Rorschach worker will find some of Klopfer's scoring refinements elaborated out of proportion to their importance. The beginner will probably find the very simple explanation of scoring symbols, included in the Record Blank attached to the end of the book, a more useful and concise treatment of scoring categories than the three chapters on that subject. Chapters V, VI, and VII could have been much clearer if some of the more technical and rarer aspects of scoring had been removed and placed in the appendix. The examination and scoring procedures also seem unnecessarily complicated, and very few experienced Rorschach workers would employ the full process as outlined in the book. The steps involved in performance, inquiry, testing the limits, location chart, scoring list, tabulation sheet, determinant graph, table of relationships among factors, and interpretation, have value for students. Most Rorschach workers adhere to the much simpler process of Rorschach's *Psychodiagnostik,* which places the responses, inquiry, and scoring adjacent to each other, followed by one summary tabulation of scoring factors. This simpler type of recording presents a single *gestalt* of the performance rather than a bewildering array of tabulations. Only one case is presented in the entire book. The reviewer feels that poor judgment was shown in selecting this case. It is atypical in many ways. Numerous pathological factors, admirably discussed elsewhere in the book, make their appearance in the sample case, but their significance is not pointed out. With the exception of the case, and some minor items, the treatment of the Rorschach method in this book is excellent. To say that it is the most complete manual on that method available in the English language would be saying very little indeed, since there are so few. It is difficult to see how a clearer manual can be compiled for years to come. One of the major merits of the book is the fact that the authors have not attempted to condense the complex, dynamic method into over-simplified, stagnant, magic formulae, so that he who runs may make snap judgments on personality. They present the substance of the method so that serious students of clinical psychology or psychiatry who are willing to put forth the necessary effort may learn to apply the method.

J General Psychol 30:105–11 Ja '44. Philip Lawrence Harriman. * ever since D. M. Levy acquainted the American psychiatrists and psychologists with the technique, and particularly after the publication of S. J. Beck's dissertation, interest in the Rorschach has increased with each passing year. Now the corpus of literature on Rorschach methodology rivals in bulk, if not in quality as well, the published research on the Binet-type of test. In part, no doubt, the increased attention is due to the novelty of the procedure; but a main contributory factor has been the rise of new theories of personality, especially those identified with Murphy and Jensen, G. W. Allport, Lewin, and others. These new views, emanating from the Gestalt protest against "atomistic psychology," have done much to raise questions about the serviceability of personality inventories and to pave the way for acceptance of a test which purports to measure the "total personality." Consequently, the publication of a book by the Director of the Rorschach Institute and by a psychiatrist who has contributed at least 13 research articles is an event of no little importance. * As all students of Rorschach technique know, there are three principle "schools" or methodologies in this country: the Beck, the Hertz, and the Klopfer. Unfortunately, there is little published research on the relative merits of these three groups; but some evidence supports the conclusion that "blind diagnoses" by each method bring unanimity of agreement in interpretations. Disagreements among the experts may pertain only to the superficial and mechanical phases of the procedure. At any rate, this book does not discuss the matter. It presents a direct and unambiguous exposition of the Klopfer technique. * In view of the current interest in the Harrower–Erickson and the Linder–Chapman experiments in group Rorschach testing, it is a little surprising to find only five short paragraphs devoted to this topic. Presumably, Klopfer, like many other exponents of the technique, believes that it should continue to be, what Rorschach intended, an individual examination. * Klopfer attaches a great deal of importance to the inquiry, which is the phase of the administration wherein the examiner learns how the subject arrived at the responses and wherein the subject has an opportunity to make elaborations. * Klopfer....agrees with Beck in postponing the inquiry until after all 10 cards have been presented. By the use of a location chart, the examiner records the response area. Some readers will have difficulty in appreciating the need for making precise localizations for each response discussed during the inquiry, since Klopfer seems to have little faith in tables of norms. Zubin has pointed out the need for statistical refinement in scoring Rorschach responses; Hertz has published elaborate scoring tables; and Beck appears to follow a somewhat rigorous method. On the other hand, Klopfer says that there is no likelihood of schematizing the method or of developing "foolproof, mechanical" tables. In fact, such a procedure obscures the "individual nuances and facets of any given record" and thus vitiates the basic purpose of the Rorschach. Of great importance is the phase of administration which is called testing-the-limits. At this time the examiner tries to elicit responses which were avoided during the initial administration of the cards and to clear up vague or evasive material. Especially is this phase of the administration to be conducted thoroughly if the record displays signs of blocking, "misunderstanding" the directions, absence of response to color, non-committal material, or failure to make the popular responses. In the sample record presented as an appendix to Part 3, the examiner had asked 12 brief questions in the testing-the-limits phase. No doubt, had the subject given a smaller number of responses, these notes (p. 308) would have been a less disappointing example of a technique which Klopfer considers to be an essential part of a Rorschach record. The scoring problems of the Rorschach investigator are infinitely complex. This book gives a great deal of help in the form of apposite comments, but it does not outmode Rickers–Ovsiankina's *Rorschach Scoring Samples* for a neophyte who wants to develop assurance in scoring responses. * One of the outstanding contributions which Klopfer has made....is to develop a detailed scoring plan which, presumably, reveals more of the subtleties in the responses than would appear in any other transmutation of associations into letter symbols. Each one of these symbols is, apparently, a logical development of the unfinished researches of Rorschach. One original addition is to discriminate the "cut-off whole" response, as to Cards III and VI, from a D (Beck) or a W. Responses to the entire figure must be carefully studied in order to estimate, qualitatively, their construction. Small details (d) are, of course, to be differentiated from usual details (D); and the only table in the book lists them in the approximate order of their frequency. Of particular interest is the account of tiny details (dd), edge details (de), and inside details (di). Kelley, unlike Beck, seems to regard the oligophrenic detail (do) as occurring in the records of feebleminded (p. 329), whereas Beck and Loosli–Usteri regard it as symptomatic of anxieties. Klopfer does not mention the do in his discussion of detail responses (pp. 91–105). Although it seems important to differentiate the exact type of detail response, neither the adequacy of the directions for scoring nor the exposition of interpretative significance is wholly satisfying to the careful reader. Probably there are advantages in going beyond the Beck procedure of scoring normal details, rare details, and the white space details (D's and Dr's); but as yet it seems a bit like *multa in parvo*. One possible danger is that revelatory material may become obscured when converted into symbols which have only a specious exactitude. Yet, the advantages in manipulating symbols rather than cumbersome and lengthy responses are obvious, and the diagnostic significance of various types of details seems to justify a tentative adherence to the Klopfer procedure rather than to the more general categories of Beck. In his discussion of the determinants, Klopfer makes a number of unique contributions to Rorschach methodology. First, he differentiates three types of "kinesthetic" responses: human or human-like movement (M), animal or animal-like action (FM), and minor movement (m). * In the section dealing with interpretations of Rorschach records, Klopfer does not include much information about the diagnostic value of minor movement, except to state that these responses are "an almost literal reflection of tensions within the personality structure....where the subject experiences his promptings from within as hostile and uncontrollable forces working upon him rather than as sources of energy at his disposal." In a sense, this quotation is representative of much of the presentation in the book. Broad generalizations and intuitive comments abound; but, except in the final part of the book, there is practically nothing in the way of experimental or statistical evidence to support them. No doubt, all these broad statements are the outgrowth of an extensive and varied experience with the Rorschach technique. Certainly, they are presented in a plausible manner, and they appear to have pragmatic justification. If the reader be an "academic psychologist" of the "old school," he may lift the quizzical eye-brow now and then during his perusal of the book. If, on the other hand, he has attempted to interpret a number of Rorschach records, he will be constantly delighted by Klopfer's argute, shrewd generalizations, even though they be clinical insights rather than conclusions based upon laboratory investigations. The scoring of the chiaroscuro responses (Beck's FY and Y) is the second important contribution in this textbook. * Unquestionably, this book presents the most elaborate plan for scoring these responses that has yet appeared in print. * The account of how to score the color determinants includes only a few novel contributions. * It is disappointing to find a very brief and inadequate chapter devoted to the *Record Blank*....which is one of the best devices for setting up a Rorschach report. Since the *gute Formen* responses are "really signs of the integrity of the Ego," some readers may wonder why Klopfer denies the value of tables of norms (such as Hertz, Beck, and Gardner have supplied) or why he does not furnish more examples of his own scoring plan. The outstanding merit of the exposition on how to score a Rorschach is that it provides symbols for almost every conceivable type of response. Whether or not each of these symbols stands for a definite referent is a troublesome ques-

tion. Since great diagnostic significance attaches to the sum of various symbols in the total configuration, inaccuracies in converting the responses into symbols could be disastrous. This reviewer feels a need for a book which will include every possible type of response, classified by experts, and which will provide practice material for the student. Klopfer gives an adequate exposition of the system of scoring now used by the Rorschach Institute, but he does not at all points furnish enough examples to illuminate his account. Neither does he present evidence to justify the extension of the conventional symbols which have been in use for the past 10 or 12 years. His plan for recording "secondary responses," trends, and refined differentiations is a distinctive contribution. The section of the book which is devoted to interpretations advances many hypotheses which will stimulate investigators for years to come. It may not be too extreme to say that this part is one of the finest examples of clinical insights to appear in recent years. Of course, the laboratory psychologist and the statistician will deplore the absence of experimental data and controlled investigatory evidence. * the serious inquirer about the Rorschach technique may be disappointed by one feature of this section— its comparative brevity. Whereas the intricacies of scoring methods take up about one-third of the text, only a quarter of the space is given over to interpretations. The sample interpretation presented as an appendix to Part Three makes the reader wish that the senior author had been less cautious and had included more examples of clinical insights. * the Rorschach method is not suitable to be introduced as a new course of study on the undergraduate level; hence the book is directed particularly to those psychologists and psychiatrists who want to learn more about the procedure. It might find a place as a parallel reading for advanced students in clinical psychology who wish to ascertain whether they have aptitude for specialized study in the Rorschach. For the instructor who is using the test in research, the publication of this book is an event fully as important as the issuance of a new revision of the Binet to a psychometrist. Unquestionably, this book, together with Beck's *Introduction,* will establish the Rorschach technique as one of the standard topics in psychology. Those who are interested in bringing the potentialities of this test to the attention of other psychologists find genuine satisfaction in being able to recommend these two excellent books. Except for a rather poor apportionment of space and for the use of "due to" in an adverbial sense, the Klopfer–Kelley book might also serve as a model for college classes in expository writing.

Psychiatric Q 16:598–602 Jl '42. * this summer appears to mark an important turning point in development of the Rorschach method for psychiatric use in the United States. Two admirable introductory volumes on the technique have just been published; and the first authorized English translation of Rorschach's *"Psychodiagnostik"* has been brought out * For the first time, authoritative and readily comprehensible material in this field has become available for the beginner * Klopfer notes modestly that "this book is hardly a basis for self-training," but expresses the entirely justified hope "that it will be of considerable help when used in conjunction with other training facilities." * Drs. Klopfer and Kelley, after presenting a thorough exposition of the problems of administration, have devoted their section on clinical diagnosis to material "of value primarily to the medically trained professional worker or to those readers who have had extensive experience in clinical psychopathological fields." Dr. Kelley's discussion of clinical findings, prepared during two years of research as Rockefeller Fellow at the New York State Psychiatric Institute and Hospital, is highly technical. It is intended for the expert and will be of use chiefly to the expert, an end deliberately sought by the authors to avert the possibility that inadequately trained workers would attempt to put the Rorschach to clinical use. The criteria of differential diagnosis are discussed thoroughly, but their application is not illustrated. * Dr. Klopfer feels that "Proficiency as a Rorschach administrator can be gained within a few months." To interpret, however, what has been administered and scored, he warns, requires "a wealth of general psychological experience" and the remaining in "a 'learning stage' for two or three years." * Both [Bochner and Halpern's *The Clinical Application of the Rorschach Test* and this volume] ....should be important contributions to greater knowledge and use of the Rorschach technique. * The Klopfer and Kelley volume is a far more complete training manual for any person who expects to do serious and continued work with the Rorschach. It covers the ground so comprehensively and so minutely that, despite Dr. Klop-

fer's expressed doubts, it might almost seem possible for a psychologist, by earnest study of the book and the cards to learn administration and scoring without personal instruction. The refined scoring system developed at the Rorschach Institute and through publication of the "Rorschach Research Exchange" is carefully and clearly explained, a protocol of a normal subject is presented in full, the standard "Individual Record Blank" printed for the Rorschach Institute is shown in facsimile, and the "location chart" with its gray, lithographed reproductions of the cards is reproduced and its use demonstrated. A bibliography of the Rorschach method through January, 1942, is included in the volume, and there is an excellent index. * Keeping in mind the somewhat different orientations of these two introductory books, either of them can be recommended without reservation as a better introduction to the study, practice and general evaluation of the Rorschach technique than has heretofore been available. The fact that a set of the cards is essential for serious study or comprehension of the Rorschach by use of either textbook is a matter which may not be entirely obvious to persons lacking any acquaintance whatever with the method. *

Psychiatry 5:604–6 N '42. Ernest G. Schachtel. Since the publication of Hermann Rorschach's *Psychodiagnostik* in 1921 quite a few manuals, textbooks, and introductions to his method have been published in various countries. Although varying in scope and thoroughness they all refrain from examining the psychological foundations of the Rorschach method. Klopfer's book is no exception to this rule and it is for this reason chiefly that—despite many valuable contributions and a painstaking thoroughness in technical details—it nowhere approaches the level of Rorschach's own presentation. Without an understanding of the psychological foundations of the Rorschach test and without clear concepts concerning the dynamisms of personality and interpersonal relations no amount of technical labor with regard to the descriptive scoring of a subject's interpretations of the Rorschach ink blots will add to the understanding of the human psyche. To contribute to such an understanding is the aim of all psychodiagnostics and certainly was the aim of Rorschach's Psychodiagnostics. That in his book the reader never loses sight of this aim, while in Klopfer's book it hardly ever comes into the field of the reader's vision, is a consequence of his partly vague, partly self-contradictory concepts regarding the nature of the Rorschach test and the nature of personality. Rorschach has given a prominent place to his inquiry into the psychic processes which constitute a subject's "Rorschach responses," and he has reached the conclusion that the interpretation of the ink blots is a perception in which the effort to integrate available memory pictures—engrams—with recent complexes of sensation—produced by the ink blots—is for most persons so great that it is consciously felt as an effort and that hence the interpretation of these chance forms "falls in the field of perception and apperception rather than imagination." This insight—although incomplete as an explanation and theoretical foundation of the test—is basic for an understanding of Rorschach's ideas and of the nature of his method. Klopfer does not even mention it. Instead he speaks on one occasion of an "interplay between the structural characteristics of the stimulus material and the personality structure of the subject" as reflected in concept formations, and a few pages further on—*page 12*—he follows Frank's and others' definition of the method as a "projective" procedure, adding, rather obscurely, that Rorschach's interest was in the person's personality structure and that "individual differences, as revealed by the ink blot method, were only incidental to this primary concern." It is never stated whether these two explanations of the test are offered as an alternative or what their relation to each other and to Rorschach's own explanation is. Both explanations, that of concept formation based on an interplay between stimulus material and personality and that of "projection" of the person into his interpretations of the test places, are less specific than Rorschach's, and the widely accepted projection theory is, in addition to that, misleading. Either the term "projection" is to be taken merely as another way of saying that every personal activity and feature is characteristic of the person engaging in this activity or having this feature and, thus, is a "projection" of his personality; in this case the use of the term "projection" would explain nothing which is specific to the Rorschach method—or to any other of the so-called projective techniques of personality testing—as distinguished from any other method of evaluation or interpretation of personal human behavior. Or else "projection" has the accepted psychiatric meaning that a person projects conscious or unconscious

attitudes, fears, desires on other persons or objects and assumes that the other person or object has this attitude, fear, desire. This frequent psychic dynamism plays an important rôle in the movement responses to the Rorschach ink blots and in some dynamic form responses, but it is quite insufficient as an explanation of the entire range of reactions to the Rorschach test, since the great majority of all responses do not show any such projection at all. An adequate explanation of the Rorschach test would have to analyze the complexity of the Rorschach situation, which changes considerably even during a single test, it would have to show the share that memory, perception, comprehension have in it, it would have to consider the test material, the tester, and the subject under the aspect of an *Aufgabe* and authority situation, it would have to describe the aspects of freedom and compulsion inherent in this situation or transferred to it by the subject, and it would have to examine the Rorschach categories and their significance which undergoes changes with the changing meaning of the test situation. Unless the Rorschach situation can be understood and analyzed in such a way, as a particular kind of human experience related to all other human experience, the test will become a sterile technique rather than the ingenious instrument for the exploration of man as which it was conceived and presented by Rorschach. It is obvious that the concept of personality in the mind of any student of human nature and personality will be of considerable importance for his insight into people, regardless of whether such a concept be articulate and explicit or vague and even unconscious. When dealing with a diagnostic tool for the exploration of the individual mind and personality it is impossible to make even a single statement without explicit or implicit reference to personality concepts, of which the person making such a statement may be aware or unaware. Klopfer thinks it unnecessary, for purposes of the Rorschach test, to have any theory of personality except the assumption that people are prompted "from without and from within" —*page 221*—and that the "susceptibility to be stimulated from within, or to be stimulated from without is distributed in mankind according to a normal curve"—*page 222*. But he constantly uses such concepts as spontaneity, inhibition, control, pseudo-control, repression, sublimation, some of which seem to stem from the psychoanalytic theory of personality which has influenced Rorschach's personality concept. Especially the term *control* is used freely throughout the book, a term which makes little sense unless at least two agencies are assumed within the human personality one of which controls the other, as they are assumed in Freud's theory of the ego and the id. Klopfer, then, makes many more assumptions concerning the human personality than he seems to be aware of—as most people do. But unfortunately in addition to that, he abrogates in one place even those concepts and assumptions which he uses quite explicitly in many other places. Also, he never clearly explains the two factors of his own avowed personality concept, the promptings from within and those from without and why they should be distributed according to a normal curve. While the basic concepts concerning the nature of the Rorschach method and of the "subjects" to whose benefit it is to be applied are thus vague, shaky, or absent, the merits of Klopfer's book lie chiefly in the accuracy of some of his descriptions of the properties of Rorschach's ink blots and in some of his elaborations of Rorschach's scoring categories, for instance the various stages of acuteness or dullness of form perception, and various ways to arrive at a "whole" interpretation of the ink blots. However, where the symptomatic and interpretative significance of Rorschach's scoring categories and of Klopfer's elaborations on them is concerned—and it is on this significance that the diagnostic picture of the personality rests—the lack or the opaqueness of the psychological concepts obstructs insight adequate to the labor spent on scoring or approaching the insights gained by Rorschach. Thus, for instance, Rorschach's description of the factors involved in acuteness of form perception, or his derivation of the significance of movement responses, is far richer in psychological content and insight than Klopfer's remarks on the same subjects, although he goes to much greater lengths than Rorschach in subdividing both movement and form responses. Altogether too often the reader has to be content with the mere assertion that certain scores have, or seem to have, certain symptomatic values, without any attempt by the author to prove his assertions. Klopfer succumbs to the same danger to which so many Rorschach workers before him have succumbed, namely of constructing a kind of immanent "Rorschach psychology" which uses the categories of scoring implicitly as categories of human behavior and human

psychology, without obtaining at first the necessary insight into their relation to the basic concepts of psychiatric and psychological theory and to the totality of human experience. It was the merit of Rorschach never to lose sight of these relations. A comparison of the one sample analysis of a Rorschach record in Klopfer's book with the three extensive analyses which have been published from Rorschach's own practical work shows that the elaboration of scoring categories in Klopfer's manner does not seem to yield as plastic and accurate diagnostic pictures as Rorschach achieved with less such elaboration, but with greater awareness of the relation between his—fewer—scoring categories and the general psychiatric and psychological categories on which his concept of the human personality was based. The fourth part of the book, written by Kelley, contributes a concise summary of the clinical diagnostic findings of Rorschach and others who have used his method. The best chapter of this part is that on intracranial organic pathology, while the chapter on psychoneuroses is confined to a symptomatology which does not penetrate to the present state of insight into the structure and core of neuroses. The difficult and interesting problem of the psychopathic personality is not discussed. A bibliography concludes the book.

Psychoanalytic Q 11:583–7 O '42. S. J. Beck.
* Klopfer's contribution....offers the latest and most complete description of the Rorschach test technique as he has been teaching it. The reader wishing to acquaint himself with the form that the test is taking under his molding can, therefore, do no better than read this book. From this point of view it is quite as authoritative as its advertisements announce it. However, this review is being written by a student trained in the Rorschach-Oberholzer discipline. Judged from that sphere of reference, Klopfer has superimposed on the Rorschach test so much that is strange to it as to make it, except for the broad outlines, essentially unrecognizable. With certain new emphases in interpretation, he has made of the test another instrument. Whether for better or for worse is another matter; the point is that it is something different. The first and most obvious transformation is in respect to the multiplicity of symbols which Dr. Klopfer has introduced. In the 'detail' category (responses to parts of the inkblot), Rorschach's two classifications, D, Dd, are expanded to six: D, d, dd, de, di, dr. This

is not to mention such inventions as D→S; or DS (apparently not identical with Rorschach's Dzw, the usual white space response). The variation becomes even more astonding in respect to movement, color and shading responses. In these categories, Rorschach was able to handle the material of his test with the simple M, C, CF, FC, and F(C) (translating his German letters), five symbols. The Klopfer repertory with M, FM, m, mF, Fm, k, kF, Fk, K, KF, FK, Fc, c, cF, FC', C'F, C', F/C, C/F, C, Cn, Cdes, Csym, is bewildering. As one studies the responses for which these Klopfer symbols are shorthand, there is no disputing their occurrence. They have been observed by various workers and commented upon. As precisely identifiable refinements, they are, however, too rare to warrant separate classificatory rubrics. They are those qualitative events which may overlay any Rorschach response record and help complete the diagnostic picture, the finer strokes that paint in the high-lights and the shadows once the structure itself has been established. The objection to designating them by special signs is that these symbols become part of the response summary which, in turn, becomes part of a formula; e.g., (p. 254) (Fm + m) : (Fc + c + C'). Or, (p. 229), 'there are several ways of measuring the degree of outer control with the aid of the quantitative Rorschach results' and several ratios are offered as: FC to (CF + C); (FC + CF + C) to (Fc + c + C'), by which to gauge 'outer control,' 'inner control,' 'crude control,' 'refined control,' 'extreme constriction,' 'modified constriction,' and others. This gives an impression of a quantitative foundation which simply does not obtain for the psychologic events tested. The few formulas which Rorschach and his followers use are not intended as a representation of exactly measured events. They are symbols of directions of psychic trends, not measurements. They do not presume to go further in interpreting psychologic events than is possible by inference from regularly occurring Rorschach response categories in clinical pictures of known dynamics. Rorschach's own ten years of careful labor, his psychologic insight backed by an experimenter's temperament, and Oberholzer's long experience with the test, on the background of his thoroughgoing clinical knowledge, are the bases for the personality interpretations that have been made from the Rorschach test. To offer formulas is to go much

further than is known experimentally concerning the symbols as referring to mental life. It is striking the pose of a quantitative method not warranted by the present state of knowledge. Deriving from this, is a second more serious objection. The creation of many symbols and formulas steers the examiner into a search for them. It encourages that superficial amateur psychologism which has been so much the bane of psychometrics, happily less so today than twenty years ago. It takes the student away from psychological dynamics, and leads him to hunt for signs and the magic of numbers. To make symbols—used by Rorschach only as a convenience in recording—so large a portion of the test is to lay the emphasis on sign at the expense of substance. This misplaced emphasis in turn leads to a third, and by far more fundamental, criticism. Klopfer informs us in his first sentence that the 'book grew out of seven years of "learning by teaching" '. He makes no statement of having first set his own foundation in study with any of the men who developed the test from its inception. Oberholzer is of course the most important of these and Zurich is not far from Bavaria where Dr. Klopfer lived. Now that both are in New York the distance is much less. Klopfer started his Rorschach work without profiting from the experience of those who devised and developed the test, and the results show it. This accounts for his fundamental error in regard to the all-important M, or movement (Rorschach's B or *Bewegung*) response, and particularly respecting movement in animal forms (pp. 114, ff). A single session with Oberholzer would have disabused Klopfer of the notion that 'the open mouth of a crocodile . . . devouring its victim' (pp. 115–116) has any M in the Rorschach sense; similarly with 'movement' in inanimate objects: 'something falling apart' (p. 117). The extreme to which this distortion of M may go is finding it in 'animal skin, nailed on a board . . . it is beginning to contract' (p. 119). The M response in the Rorschach test is something the individual does; it is of deep significance to him; it is something other than what he states in the manifest content of the association, in other words, it is the latent dream in the literal freudian sense. To designate any Rorschach association that has a verb in it as M is to apply this symbol to words, and miss its value for identifying events in the unconscious living of the individual. Some M responses obtained with the test have been shown to communicate the innermost personal needs of the individual. This value of M is what makes it so important a discovery and Rorschach's great contribution to the problem of objective ingress into personality. Accuracy in identifying it, therefore, is of the greatest importance. It makes the difference between the psychologist trained to search for subsurface mental activity, and the 'sign psychologist.' The merits of Klopfer's portion of the book are in the valuable suggestions for further exploration. One of the best is what he calls 'Testing the Limits.' In this he is making a regular rule of procedure of a practice that had formerly been employed only in those patients who had been extremely uncommunicative. Without doubt, this additional effort to elicit associations can also be used profitably in many instances where we now stop after obtaining that minimum set of responses considered essential for personality delineation. In extremely productive patients, Klopfer acknowledges the probability of adding little by 'testing the limits' (p. 52). The author devotes more space than have former publications—excepting, naturally, Binder's monograph—to the shading response. He makes some valuable suggestions as to possible significances of the different shading nuances. Especially important may be the lead that the 'surface' shading reaction (not the three dimensional, or vista percept) expresses a need for contact sensation. Beginners will be grateful for the considerable more space devoted to administration and recording than have earlier publications. The scoring blank (Klopfer and Davidson), which is a formal element in Klopfer's method, is pasted into the book. This author closes (Appendix to Part Three) with one sample Rorschach record, scored and interpreted. In this reviewer's opinion, teaching is best done by an abundance of illustrative material. The chapter on history includes some hitherto unpublished and valuable details. This reviewer regrets the omission of Campbell and Wells, in Boston, The American Orthopsychiatric Association, and Lawson Lowrey in New York. The first two were largely responsible for the early research with the test in this country. The Association was the forum before which the first reports were made, and Lowrey's persistent interest made possible many of the earlier American publications. * The best of [Kelley's] chapters are the ones on brain pathology

and schizophrenia, which is to be expected, these being the fields which have been most studied. The least satisfying is the one on psychoneuroses. The fault is due to the paucity of published reports on the Rorschach test in neurosis. It is indeed strange that this clinical group, which comprises so large a percentage of the population, should yield so few reports. Here is a big field, still to develop. The chapters by Kelley are much the most satisfying in the book. They reflect a caution born of clinical seasoning, and a balanced approach to Rorschach problems, unhappily missing in most of the rest. The book has a good bibliography, 370 titles, covering the literature through January 1942. It is well indexed and paginated, an important feature in any instruction manual. The introduction is appropriately by Doctor Nolan D. C. Lewis, one of the men whose support, material and moral, has done much toward developing this test in America.
Psychol B 40:144–6 F '43. S. J. Beck. [Practically the same as his review in *Psychoanalytic Quarterly,* excerpted above.]

[85]

★[*Re* Rorschach.] KLOPFER, BRUNO. **The Rorschach Technique: A Manual for a Projective Method of Personality Diagnosis.** With clinical contributions by Douglas McGlashan Kelley. With 1946 supplement by Bruno Klopfer and Helen H. Davidson. Yonkers, N.Y.: World Book Co., 1946. Pp. xi, 475. $4.80. * (London: George G. Harrap & Co. Ltd. 21s.)

[86]

★[*Re* Rorschach.] MASLOW, PAUL. **The Analysis and Control of Human Experiences: The Individual Seen Through Rorschach, Volumes 1 and 2.** Brooklyn 2, N. Y.: the Author, 16 Court St., 1947. Pp. iii, 233; iv, 195. Paper, mimeographed. $3.50 per volume. * (*PA* 21:2326)

Am J Psychother 1:529–30 O '47. Rose Palm. * Maslow has touched on most of the principal topics covering the field of human experience. Included in his discussion are psychology, psychoanalysis, philosophy, mythology, science, art, psychiatry, politics, sociology, ethics, culture, religion, anthropology and physiology. In addition, Maslow has ambitiously attempted to set up a new Rorschach system which would throw light on the topics under discussion and establish new uses for the Rorschach test as a future tool of social, cultural and political significance. Although it would appear that Maslow is in many respects an original and independent thinker, it is doubtful if this book will make its way as a guide for students of human nature in general or for Rorschach students in particular. To be certain, Maslow possesses a vast stock of information, a fact which has apparently misled him into covering too much ground. His statements tend to be too generalized and he is inclined to "over-interpret" his Rorschach material. * What is most lacking in Maslow's work is an empirical backlog of material to substantiate the many ideas which are proposed and developed. Maslow's presentation is subjective and speculative and is in many places contrary to established psychological or psychoanalytical concepts. * Another way in which Maslow stretches his point beyond the accepted limits is in the way he attempts to set up a Rorschach typology by picking out certain elements of a Rorschach record as representative of a type or of a group. * In interpreting the single features of a Rorschach record, it is necessary to remain within the framework of the total structure. Although the author himself stresses this point, he has often ignored his own teaching. The author's unorthodox use of the Rorschach symbols detracts greatly from the general merit and application of the book. It is true that....different schools are....using varying systems. While Maslow is thus perhaps justified in introducing his own symbols, he fails to prove in what way his system is preferable to the old ones. We feel that if the imaginative and creative faculties of this author were applied to certain more specialized areas of research and were backed by careful clinical experimentation, the results might afford valuable contributions to our knowledge of human nature and the use of the Rorschach test. We see the value of the book mainly in the way it may stimulate the reader to select some of the author's ideas as starting points for further investigation.

J Consult Psychol 11:155 My-Je '47. These volumes represent an attempt to explain all human characteristics and activities in terms of the Rorschach pattern. Problems of economics, war, fascism, politics and many other fields are subjected to a confused and usually inaccurate Rorschach appraisal.

[87]

★[Re Rorschach.] MASLOW, PAUL. Rorschach Psychology. Brooklyn 2, N. Y.: the Author, 16 Court St., 1945. Pp. ii, 149. Paper, mimeographed. For latest edition, see 86. (PA 19:3409)

Am J Psychol 59:330 Ap '46. D. R. Miller. * covers four topics. Present methods of interpreting the Rorschach test are summarized;

new additions are made to the interpretation of scoring symbols; a number of new scoring symbols are proposed, and an attempt is made to relate interpretation to social psychology. The summary of present methods of interpretation contains numerous misconceptions and careless generalizations. The attempt to relate interpretation to social psychology consists in the discussion of some strongly environmentalistic theories with occasionally interspersed 'Rorschach' terms; there is almost no attempt to relate these theories to the mechanics of interpreting the test. The proposed additions to interpretation are often so vaguely and incautiously phrased (the extravert "lives for and with the body, has the physical courage of might and the proud") that it would be almost impossible to apply them clinically. The proposed interpretations and scoring symbols have not been empirically obtained nor have they been objectively validated. The primary evidence offered in their support is a group of miscellaneous references in the fields of philosophy, art, literature, cinema, and theoretical and clinical psychology. Typical of the care with which many of these references have been chosen is the citation of Jung in the development of the author's conception of introversion-extraversion despite Rorschach's statement that the clinical picture of introversion obtained by the test has nothing in common with Jung's conception except the name. The carelessness with which the book has been organized, edited and published places many obstacles in the path of the reader. The book does not contain a statement of purposes and organization, nor does it contain an index. The grammar is often clumsy and occasionally incorrect. Finally, every two-pages average about one error in spelling or typing.

Nerv Child 5:276 Jl '46. This is the most thorough attempt so far at a philosophical and psychological evaluation of the Rorschach test. However, the author has failed to finally clarify his thoughts and reduce them to definite concepts. The manuscript therefore is more like an essay than a scientific treatise.

Psychiatry 8:517 N '45. Milton H. Erickson. In commenting on the author's book, *Rorschach Theory,* I suggested that the author secure an elementary textbook on the Rorschach Test and a competent instructor so that he might acquire some knowledge of the subject. Now he comes forth with a volume entitled, *Rorschach Psychology*, which is an even more pitiful demonstration of his tremendous desire to communicate something and his utter incompetency, at least in this field. The book is essentially a conglomeration of words, some new, some old, some especially adapted, arranged in phrases and sentences without regard for spelling, grammar, coherence, or relevancy, and expressing most often vague, unformulated ideas, sometimes related to the Rorschach Test. *

Psychoanalytic Q 15:387–90 Jl '46. William F. Murphy. * This manual is a perplexing and callow attempt to present the Rorschach Test as an all-revealing expression of the individual's personality to be used not only as the basis for a complete character analysis, but for psychotherapy, as a philosophy and even for social reform! It is exceedingly difficult to ascertain how much of the content of this book is the thought of the author and how much has been torn from the context of the one hundred and four items listed in the bibliography ranging from Freud's Collected Works to Ernie Pyle's Brave Men. The author begins by stating that the Rorschach test makes possible a quick and accurate insight into the total personality structure of the individual, and then goes on to say, "When we are quite sure of the subject's personality then we can make the proper recommendations with the hope that correct comprehension will be followed by therapeutic success". If only it were so! In the discussion of personality types, which he divides into intraverts and extraverts according to the amount, type and ratio of Movement to Color responses, Maslow confuses the Inner Living of Rorschach with the Introversion of Jung and frequently becomes involved in a vague, discursive and naive discussion of character traits. * Such confused thinking has not been helped by a liberal use of Rorschach symbols not ordinarily utilized. * At times the characteristics attached to the different types of responses are reminiscent of the fortunetelling cards that drop from the pennyweight machines. * Rationality, Anxiety, Emotionality, the Conscious, Unconscious and Foreconscious, Anal and Oral Complexes are all discussed with vague wordiness and superficial understanding. The most interesting chapters deal with the author's Social Psychology. After discussing shading and perspective responses indicative of sympathy and empathy he opines

that these qualities may be based on mental telepathy. * In another chapter we are introduced to "The Rorschach" who is apparently a combination of priest, analyst and social reformer. * As a therapist the "Rorschach," unlike the psychoanalyst who gives the patient "only the opportunity of seeing how bad he is," will "coolly reconnoiter the field before giving advice and then act quickly to restore a measure of objectivity by reducing mounting frightening ideas to their proper size." Similar absurdities can be found on practically any page. In conclusion, this book is useless for the student of Rorschach and embarrassing to those interested in the development of this excellent projection test. It is poorly printed in mimeograph form. Errors in spelling are numerous and pages are occasionally duplicated.

[88]

★[*Re* Rorschach.] MASLOW, PAUL. **Rorschach Theory.** Brooklyn 2, N. Y.: the Author, 16 Court St., 1944. Pp. ii, 89. Paper, mimeographed. For latest edition, *see* 86.

Psychiatry 8:257 My '45. Milton H. Erickson. This book purports to deal with the Rorschach Theory. Actually, however, it is essentially a disorderly, ungrammatical, uninformative, often irrelevant collection of polysyllabic phrases that demonstrates the author's need to study, under competent supervision, some elementary exposition of the Rorschach Test.

[89]

★[*Re* Rorschach.] MUNROE, RUTH LEARNED. **Prediction of the Adjustment and Academic Performance of College Students by a Modification of the Rorschach Method.** Foreword by Gardner Murphy. Applied Psychology Monographs of the American Association for Applied Psychology, No. 7. Stanford University, Calif.: Stanford University Press, 1945. Pp. 104. Paper. $1.25. * (*PA* 20:918)

Am J Orthopsychiatry 16:734 O '46. Marion Cowin. To find a carefully organized report of a research project maintaining a genuinely human and dynamic emphasis is a source of satisfaction to students of human behavior. * For years Rorschach workers have been debating the question of the extent to which the Rorschach should be standardized. Some have urged intensive efforts in this direction in the interests of objectivity, others have resisted too much statistical treatment of the data lest the essentially dynamic quality of the individual record be lost. Dr. Munroe's method to some extent reconciles these points of view. She does use a standardized check-list and obtains a nu-. merical rating, but her appreciation of the compensatory processes in individual behavior, her recognition of their important Rorschach equivalents, and her ingenious provision for them in the check-list reduce the danger of a mechanical or stereotyped concept of adjustment. * Appendices give detailed explanations of the check-list and instructions for use. The author believes that it may be used satisfactorily by persons with less background and experience than is usually required for Rorschach workers, though a good knowledge of scoring is essential. Whether it would prove true on protocols obtained from a less intelligent and cooperative group than at Sarah Lawrence is not certain, nor is it certain whether in this case the method itself could be applied with any such degree of success. Further experimentation in this direction would be of interest.

Am J Psychol 59:315–8 Ap '46. Donald E. Super. The history of the Rorschach 'psychodiagnostic technique' seems to parallel that of a successfully treated aggressive child, in that it first refused to conform to accepted standards (by becoming scientific and objective) while rejected by its family, but, having finally won a degree of acceptance and security, it is now proceeding to behave in a socially approved manner (by using quantitative techniques and scientific controls), apparently of its own volition * a slim but satisfying monograph which bears the earmarks of scientific endeavor. * As Munroe points out....she has 'demonstrated' that the Rorschach can be used as an ordinary psychological test, with a standard scoring technique requiring no more training than the Binet. That this was an unexpected outcome of the experiments makes it none the less significant, and perhaps somewhat more palatable to orthodox Rorschachers. * This review proposes to summarize some of the experimental procedures, results and conclusions, pointing out certain shortcomings and certain excellencies. Thirty-five freshmen were first tested with the standard technique, 'blind' personality descriptions were written and were then submitted, in groups of five and with a random list of the students' names to selected teachers for matching. The complete absence of matching errors demonstrates the reliability and validity of the technique when used by expert examiners and teachers who know their

students well. When the experiment was twice repeated, using the Inspection (briefer) Technique and more teachers, the results the first time yielded a *p* of less than .01, and, on the second repetition, "were not quite so good, though still clearly significant" (p. 15). Munroe has given her conclusion but has withheld the evidence upon which it is based, a type of error too frequently committed by clinicians. The reader, not knowing the probability of the last experiment, cannot judge for himself how much less good it was. Lack of sufficient care in presenting results is manifest again in the next paragraph, in which the author refers to the "1941" experiment, but does not tell the reader whether this is the first or second experiment with the Inspection Technique. * The occasional looseness of her experimental methods typified by....variations of procedure is subject to criticism, but they may have been the unavoidable concomitants of research in a practical situation (we are not told) ; that these variations in procedure are at other times glossed over or forgotten (e.g. Summary, p. 37.) typifies occasional careless reporting, although this study is on the whole a good example of experimenting and reporting, especially when compared to most Rorschach work. Unscientific methods and errors of the types too frequently committed by clinicians without experimental orientation occur in a few other places. *

J Appl Psychol 30:660–2 D '46. Paul E. Meehl. One of the facts about the Rorschach literature which is disturbing to those American psychologists who are interested but skeptical is the pitiably small number of studies which can really be called "validation" studies in any respectable sense, buried among a great mass of investigations whose titles would suggest that they were systematic studies of validity, but which turn out not to be so at all upon reading. It is, therefore, gratifying to come across this work of Dr. Munroe's, which is a contribution both to college guidance and to the case for the Rorschach. She presents data from three successive freshman classes, totalling 348 girls, at Sarah Lawrence College. Her aim was to determine the efficiency of the Rorschach in predicting "adjustment" and academic achievement. * Because of the nature of the criteria available, data are not presented in correlational form, but are expressed in terms of contingency tables. In one respect this turns out to be a decided advantage, since it brings out certain relationships which a Pearson *r* as ordinarily employed would possibly obscure. * The study is unfortunately marred by a few minor defects and deviations from perfect control which leave a way out for anyone who is adamantly skeptical about the Rorschach. For example, it would have been better had all of the tests been scored completely "blind," without any opportunity for clinical impressions to be formed in face-to-face contact. The author states that the results on those cases she tested personally were not "significantly" better than the others. The third freshman class might well have been excluded to increase the purity of design, since their records were filed and available to teachers before the year's close. Here, however, Dr. Munroe states that the results for the third year were not significantly better than those of the first two. One would like to have the data separately analysed for the middle year, when the most rigid control was exercised. On the whole, however, the study could be a pretty good model for other Rorschachers, and it certainly is an important contribution to Rorschach literature.

[89a]
★[*Re* Rorschach.] RICKERS-OVSIANKINA, MARIA. **Rorschach Scoring Samples: Compiled From Various Sources for Private Circulation.** [Revised Edition]. Norton, Mass.: the Author, Wheaton College, 1942. Pp. v, 197. Paper, mimeographed. $4.00, postpaid. *

Rorschach Res Exch 7:184 O '43. Zygmunt A. Piotrowski. * contains....over two thousand scored responses to the original Rorschach plates. The sample responses and their scores were taken from published case studies in English and other languages. The responses in foreign languages have been translated into English, and the English scoring symbols are used in the book. On each page there is an outline reproduction of the particular Rorschach card with the part to which the interpretations listed below refer, conspicuously marked. Sometimes there is doubt concerning scoring; the differentiation between F+ and F− responses is particularly troublesome in some cases. If the subject did not cooperate sufficiently to enable the examiner to decide about the quality of some of his form responses, the scoring samples by Dr. Rickers will assist in scoring and they have been collected for this purpose. A valid as well as an entirely objective method of distinguish-

ing F+ from F− responses in the Rorschach cards still remains a problem to be solved.

[90]
★[*Re* Rorschach.] RORSCHACH, HERMANN. **Psychodiagnostics: A Diagnostic Test Based on Perception: Including Rorschach's paper, "The Application of the Form Perception Test"** (Published posthumously by Dr. Emil Oberholzer), **Second Edition.** Translation and English edition by Paul Lemkau and Bernard Kronenberg. Edited by W. Morgenthaler. Berne, Switzerland: Verlag Hans Huber, 1942. Pp. 238. (New York: Grune & Stratton, Inc. $5.75.) * (*PA* 16:4443, title only)

J Am Med Assn 120:1076 N 28 '42. * The translators found the task of adequate translation exceedingly difficult, but it would appear that they have done an excellent piece of work. The Rorschach test was devised and organized by Hermann Rorschach, who was born in Zurich, Switzerland, in 1884 and died in 1922. His early death was a great loss to psychiatry in general and to Swiss psychiatry in particular. He was an extremely versatile man with a sound character and a practical grasp of scientific knowledge together with an inexhaustible interest in research. The Rorschach test, often referred to as the "ink blot test," is being used more and more for the differential diagnosis of personality problems. When given and evaluated by one who possesses a thorough knowledge of Rorschach's method and technic it offers an excellent guide relative to the prognosis and choice of treatment to be employed when some form of psychotherapy is indicated. The translation is intended primarily for students of the Rorschach Technic, but the book should prove of interest to all students of human behavior. * Anyone who is at all interested in attempts to measure or evaluate problems of human personality structure by means of academic laboratory methods is advised to study Rorschach's basic work very carefully. They seem to offer greater possibilities for accurate evaluation than any other method or methods that have been presented up to the present time. Improvements in the technic itself and evaluation of the material collected are constantly being worked out by Rorschach's followers.

J Consult Psychol 7:132–3 Mr-Ap '43. Bruno Klopfer. The English translation of this book, appearing twenty-one years after Hermann Rorschach first published his *Psychodiagnostik* in Switzerland, is the first authorized English translation. * Lemkau, one of

Adolph Meyer's co-workers in Baltimore.... should be congratulated at his admirable attempt "to present his (Rorschach) ideas adequately and at the same time preserve as much as possible of the personality of Rorschach as it is revealed in his choice of words, his sentence structure and his delicate shades of meanings." * the sometimes confusing double meaning of the word "interpretation" referring to the Rorschach responses of the subject as well as to the interpretation of these responses by the examiner might have been avoided. * This translation is much more faithful and adequate than previous attempts. * Rorschach's ....*Psychodiagnostik*....remains, even when evaluated in the light of more than four hundred books and papers published since that time, the most outstanding theoretical and practical contribution to the "Rorschach method" of personality diagnosis. Readers not thoroughly familiar with Rorschach work will be unable to comprehend the full importance and value of this book for the technical reason that it is anything but a manual. Even as an experimental report it might appear strange to many American trained psychologists and psychiatrists. Instead of statistically reliable data, arranged in the usual manner, they find a whole book full of rough quantitative estimates, hypothetical suggestions and theoretical hunches, interwoven with a most original and dynamic psychology of personality. On the other hand, twenty-one years of routine research have proven more than ninety per cent of his assumptions correct and even many of his hunches which seemed wrong at first glance proved to be pointing in the right direction on further scrutiny. * Taking for granted that the Psychodiagnostics are not meant to serve as a manual, one need not be concerned about such lack of the usual equipment for such books as an index. The third and fourth German editions contain valuable survey tables by Ewald Bohm, which substitute to some extent, for an index. They have not been included in the translation. The only new addition is a "Bibliography of the Important Contributions on the Rorschach Method." One-fourth of the 243 titles listed refer to non-Rorschach papers, dealing with related medical or psychological subjects or with similar methods like the "cloud picture test." Among the Rorschach listings are only 26 titles not contained in recent American Rorschach bibliographies. * On the other hand, all the Rorschach titles listed comprise just about half the titles to be found in other Rorschach bibliographies....covering about the same period and there doesn't seem [to be] any systematic selection. Rorschach's first report about a new kind of personality diagnosis is naturally most valuable as a historic document but most of his intuitive assumptions have proven so adequate that the Psychodiagnostics will point the way for research in the field of personality diagnosis for many years to come.

Psychiatric Q 16:598–602 Jl '42. * Hermann Rorschach published his original work *"Psychodiagnostik"* ("Psychodiagnostics") in 1921. The following year, his further important contribution on the subject was published by his friend and colleague, Emil Oberholzer, the psychoanalyst, shortly after Rorschach's own untimely death. This extraordinary "blind" Rorschach diagnosis of one of Oberholzer's analysands is included in the present English translation of the *"Psychodiagnostik"* under the title of "The Application of the Form Interpretation Test." ("To Psychoanalysis" might well have been added.) Despite a voluminous and still rapidly growing literature compiled by a large number of able and enthusiastic scientific workers in the past two decades, the original research of Rorschach remains by far the most important single contribution ever made to the understanding and application of the diagnostic method he devised —as fundamental to its theory and practice as the "Interpretation of Dreams" and the "Introductory Lectures" are to psychoanalysis. The translation by Drs. Lemkau and Kronenberg is the first authorized one and the first to be made generally available in English to students and Rorschach workers. For understanding of the development of the method, of the dynamic psychology involved in its operation, of the underlying concepts which account for its empiric validity, this work of the originator would still appear to be essential. Rorschach, in the "Psychodiagnostics," sets forth explicitly the conditions for conducting and interpreting his test; but his book is less a manual of instructions than a careful report of the astonishing results of an experiment; and the volume could not well be used for modern training, in view of the advances in application of the method which have taken place since Rorschach's death. What Rorschach reported and what the work here translated concerns is the application and theory of a procedure which must have seemed to many of his colleagues—as it does to many present-day psychiatrists—too absurdly simple for serious attention, let alone scientific usage. One may observe in Rorschach's text his extensive knowledge of psychoanalysis and his application of psychoanalytic principles in developing the theory of his inkblot method. Before he published *"Psychodiagnostik,"* he had studied results of the test as applied to patients before, during and after analysis. Here is a dynamic background for the method which is nowhere made clearer than in Rorschach's own writings and which is, perhaps, not sufficiently appreciated. It may be interesting to speculate whether it was not his psychoanalytic understanding which gave to Rorschach sufficient confidence to make public the results of his seemingly simple test. The publication is evidence of possession of insight which might justly be termed genius. It should not be overlooked that Rorschach, despite his youth—he was 37 when he died—was a psychiatrist of commanding reputation in Switzerland at the time he published his researches; and he must have known that he staked his repute on their scientific validity. The present long-overdue translation seems admirable. The volume includes a brief biographical sketch of the author and the introduction to the second German edition, both written by the editor * Typographical errors are comparatively few, considering that the volume was set by German-speaking compositors; and those undetected in this will doubtless be remedied in future editions. The original symbols of Rorschach are translated into generally used English forms. Both students and clinical workers will be interested to note that *Erlebnistyp,* which has given trouble to most translators, is rendered here as "experience type." The volume is eminently satisfactory and well calculated to take its place as a necessary part of every Rorschach worker's professional library. The translation will also perhaps bring home for the first time, to students and workers who are not familiar with German, Rorschach's repeated emphasis on the need for parallel series of figures to the plates used in "Psychodiagnostics" and all succeeding Rorschach work. Rorschach himself doubtless would have published such a series had he lived. It may or may not be coincidence that

publication of the translation of Rorschach's original work comes shortly after publication, also by Hans Huber, of *"Einfuerung in den Behn–Rorschach–Test"* by Hans Zulliger. This is the long-awaited test of 10 parallel plates which differ from the original and may be used for control purposes. The German text, 232 pages, is priced at $3.80, the new Zulliger plates at $3.75; the American distributors are Grune & Stratton. There is no announcement of an English translation. *

U S Naval Med B 46:771–2 My '46. * This translation is a fitting tribute to a brilliant pioneer.

[91]

★[*Re* Rorschach.] ZULLIGER, HANS. **Einführung in den Behn-Rorschach Test.** Berne, Switzerland: Verlag Hans Huber, 1941. Pp. 232. (New York: Grune & Stratton, Inc., 1942. $4.00. Accompanying plates, $6.00.) (*PA* 15:5232)

Psychiatric Q 17:715–6 O '43. When Rorschach published *"Psychodiagnostik,"* he already felt the need of another series of inkblots, which would parallel his own and would serve as a control series for reexamination. Behn-Eschenburg developed, with the aid of Rorschach himself, such a series in 1920. He used these blots in an experiment with school children and published his results in 1921; but the new series was not made available to the public until 1941. (H. Huber, Bern). In his "Einführung," Zulliger offers an excellent introduction to the Rorschach method, and specifically to the use of the new series of blots. Twenty-two pages of his book are given over to a presentation of some 500 sample interpretations of the new inkblots and include a description of the "normal details," without which a record could not be scored. More than half of the book consists of scored and interpreted Rorschach records obtained from 25 subjects. Both the original Rorschach plates and the new Behn–Rorschach plates were shown to most of these subjects. Zulliger suggests the abbreviated form, Bero, be used to designate the latter series. Zulliger proceeds on the assumption that there is an extremely close correspondence between the Rorschach and the Bero series and that consequently the same number of whole, detail, movement, color, form, etc., interpretations can be expected from both series. His own examples, however, frequently show a marked difference between the Rorschach and the Bero records. Invariably, Zulliger ascribes these differences to changes in the psychological condition of the subjects. This procedure does not appear justified, because Zulliger does not provide experimental evidence in support of his assumption that the two series of blots correspond perfectly. This observation, however, is not a very serious objection since the present norms appear to be satisfactory for most cases and since the correction of norms can be made relatively easily by anyone working regularly with the Rorschach and the Bero plates. Everything Zulliger writes about the administration and interpretation of records is equally applicable to the Rorschach and the Bero plates. His book is modelled after Rorschach's "Psychodiagnostics." Rorschach was very concise. Zulliger has succeeded in expressing explicitly many important ideas which Rorschach presented in a condensed and implicit form. Another significant contribution is the author's application of the Rorschach method to character analysis for educational and vocational purposes. Zulliger is known to have been very successful in using the Rorschach method as an aid in the solution of problems such as: "Why does John steal?" "Should Edward be placed in a reformatory or should he be given another chance?" "For what vocation is Mary best fitted?" "Is the testimony of Miss Smith trustworthy?" Zulliger has been able to answer these difficult questions well, not only because he has mastered the Rorschach technique but also because he has very wide and deep psychological and pedagogical experience. Never were the Rorschach findings the only basis for his recommendations. It is Zulliger's ability to link the Rorschach findings with sound psychological principles that accounts to a large degree for his success with the Rorschach method. His Rorschach record interpretations should be required reading for all Rorschach analysts. Zulliger is a Swiss educator, well known for his application of psychoanalysis to classroom situations. His articles on this subject appeared in the "American Journal of Orthopsychiatry." His previous contribution to Rorschach literature consists of a book on juvenile thieves and articles illustrating the use of the Rorschach method as an aid in education and vocational guidance. The author refrains in the present, as in his previous publications, from discussing the Rorschach as an aid in psychiatric diagnosis and prognosis, but concentrates on character or personality analysis. The present book belongs to the best works on the Rorschach method.

[92]

★Schrammel-Gorbutt Personality Adjustment Scale. Grades 7-16 and adults; 1943; Form A; 90¢ per 25, postpaid; 15¢ per specimen set, postpaid; nontimed (20) minutes; H. E. Schrammel and Dorothy Gale Gorbutt; Bureau of Educational Measurements, Kansas State Teachers College of Emporia.

Raleigh M. Drake, Professor of Psychology and Head of the Department, Kent State University, Kent, Ohio. This is a self inventory consisting of 117 items of the yes-no type constructed to discover and measure the neurotic personality. It was standardized on high school and college freshmen populations, the norms being based on 602 high school students, grades not stated, and 349 college freshmen. It is presumed that the population included both boys and girls in about equal proportions.

The authors report a correlation of .88 with Thurstone's *Personality Schedule.* Since it contains only 117 items as against 223 for the Thurstone test, its chief merit appears to be that it measures the same thing as this test but with an economy of almost half the items. The reviewer correlated the Schrammel–Gorbutt scale with the C-factor (cycloid disposition) in Guilford's *An Inventory of Factors STDCR* and obtained a correlation of .46 for thirty sophomore women in college. Author-reported reliability by the split-half method (corrected?) is given as .90 which seems satisfactory for so short an inventory.

It suffers, along with all other yes-no type inventories, in objectivity of representing life-like situations by forcing the testee to choose an all-or-none answer to a question. Degrees of response are provided in some cases by including the words "often" or "usually" in such questions as "Do you often feel you are someone else rather than yourself?" but many questions are categorically stated, e.g., "Can you listen to a lecture without fidgeting?"

Students taking the inventory complain that many of the questions are not realistic to them, that they cannot answer out of actual past experience and therefore must guess at what they would do under the circumstances. Such questions as "Do you think that you would be afraid to dive from a springboard?" is hard to answer if one has never tried diving. Others are ambiguous, such as, "Have you ever bitten your finger nails continually over a period of time?" or "When you are eating your meals, do you usually like to have someone eat with you?" One can hardly expect an objective answer from "Do you believe that you are selfish?" This inventory may not sin any more than similar inventories in this regard, but it is no better in this respect.

Nelson G. Hanawalt, Associate Professor of Psychology, New Jersey College for Women, Rutgers University, New Brunswick, New Jersey. This is just another test for neurotic tendencies. The reviewer can think of no reason for its publication or use. Although the reported reliability is as good as other tests of its kind, no attempt has been made to establish its validity beyond correlating it with Thurstone's *Personality Schedule* and testing the items for internal consistency. No test was made to determine whether or not it would differentiate between known adjusted and maladjusted groups of students. Yet the authors state that "because the interpretations are thus based on the distribution of over nine hundred representative cases, they possess a reasonable degree of validity and significance." This is quite misleading. The number of cases upon which the distribution of scores is based has nothing to do with its validity and significance as far as neurotic tendencies are concerned. If the test does not have these qualities to begin with, no amount of giving it will supply them.

The authors give the impression that a score made by the individual student on this test is as valid as a score made on an achievement test and that it can be of the same use to the student if he knows where he stands. They suggest that the mere knowledge that a student has a neurotic score is a valuable means of therapy and that he can improve his adjustment by this knowledge alone. Certainly no student should be given his rating on this test, nor on any other of its kind, unless it is supplemented by an adequate explanation of its meaning, limitations, etc.; and this is especially true for those in the lower brackets where the authors say that information of their standing will do the most good. The authors make a statement concerning the reliability of the individual score on the test. The assumption is made that this is a statement of the reliability of the adjustment of the individual, which is a different thing altogether from the reliability of the test score. No evidence of any kind is given of the relia-

bility of the adjustment score. Adjustment scores are given in terms of percentiles. The statements concerning degree of adjustment are made upon a statistical basis. No empirical test of the adjustment of students with the various scores is made. High school students and college freshmen are shown to have quite different distributions of scores, and yet they are combined in one distribution for the purpose of a verbal statement of adjustment.

The test is marked in terms of plus and minus. This is a great disadvantage on many of the items because it requires that natural yes-no questions be translated to plus and minus. It also allows for no question-mark answers. Just what effect forcing a true-false answer to all of the questions has on the results is unknown.

The only excuse for publishing another test of neurotic tendency in this day and age is increased validity over other tests in the field. This test is grossly lacking in this respect. It is unfortunate that the authors recommend its widespread use with or without the guidance of experienced and competent workers in the field. Such testing programs can only bring discredit upon the testing movement. If one has to test neurotic tendencies, it would be wise to stick to tests like Bernreuter's *Personality Inventory* and Bell's *Adjustment Inventory* which have a long list of research results available to assist in their interpretation.

[93]

★Selective Vocabulary Test. Ages 13 and over; 1944; a disguised test of masculinity–femininity; 1 form; 3s. 2d. per 25; 4d. per single copy; 3s. per manual; non-timed (15-30) minutes; Patrick Slater; George G. Harrap & Co. Ltd.

REFERENCES

1. SLATER, PATRICK. "Interpreting Discrepancies." *Brit J Med Psychol* 19:415-9 pts 3-4 '45. * (PA 17:3980)
2. SLATER, ELIOT, AND SLATER, PATRICK. "A Study of the Assessment of Homosexual Traits." *Brit J Med Psychol* 21:61-74 S 18 '47. * (PA 22:1238)

Jack W. Dunlap, Dunlap, Morris, and Associates, New York, New York. This test is designed to analyze the interests of individuals in such a manner as to give a measure of the masculinity-femininity of the subject. The test consists of 80 words, 40 of which are primarily familiar to boys and 40 of which are basically more familiar to girls than to boys. The subjects are required to write out a definition of each word. In scoring the test the examiner must consider whether the definition is sufficient and whether it is true. Correct answers are often falsified by unnecessary details, and sometimes these details reveal genuine misunderstandings of the meaning of a word. Therefore, answers must be both sufficient and true.

When the subject's answer sheet has been corrected, two scores are obtained, one for masculinity and one for femininity. For a boy it is necessary to determine whether he knows more or less feminine words than is usual for a boy of his age. In interpreting the results it is necessary to use both the masculine score and the feminine score in order to account for differences of vocabulary levels. The author has worked out detailed charts for evaluating the masculinity-femininity of individuals in various age groups.

This test is an ingenious method for measuring the masculinity-femininity and it seems to have been based on sound experimental work. However, like all such new instruments, further research is needed in order to establish more completely the reliability and the validity of the instrument. For anyone interested in measurements in this field it would be wise to examine carefully the *Selective Vocabulary Test*.

Starke R. Hathaway, Professor and Clinical Psychologist, Department of Psychiatry and Neurology, University of Minnesota, Minneapolis, Minnesota. Although this little test has been made available without adequate experimental background or clinical study, it is probably a good measure of male-female differentiation among school-age children in the cultural environment of that portion of England where it was developed. The subject is asked to write a short definition of each of 80 words and his definitions are scored correct or incorrect according to examples provided by the author. The vocabulary words that are used include such definitely English words as "scrum" and "googly" which illustrate the cultural factors involved.

The 80 words were chosen from among an original list of 365. Forty are characteristically defined correctly more frequently by males and 40 by females. The interpretation is based upon the relative number of feminine words correctly defined as contrasted to the number of masculine words.

It seems unfortunate to this reviewer that among the many ways in which we may differentiate male and female the author chose the subjective definition of words that in many cases are so obviously derived from a local culture. The departure from a simpler, more objective item would seem to be justified only on the basis that a particular variable could not be identified otherwise. No evidence is presented that this particular test variable is peculiar to this method of measurement.

It should be emphasized in all tests of this type in which the items have been derived from male-female differentiating items that, without experimental extension, the variable involved is no more than the extension of those differences into the interest field. The author provides no data on validity beyond the fact that the items correlate with sex.

The author is suitably cautious in warning users of the test against labeling subjects as excessively masculine or feminine. He emphasizes that extreme scores should merely indicate that ". . . a problem exists, for which some explanation should be sought. Abnormal sexual development is only one possible explanation." In another place he is not so clear on the point. He says, "We do not want to differentiate members of different sexes, but members of the same sex. This the test will do. It reveals abnormalities in the bias of an individual's interest towards subjects characteristic of one sex or the other: excessive masculinity and excessive femininity can be effectively differentiated in either sex." In the context it is clear that the author means only to say that the two sexes can each be sorted among themselves by scores on the test, but the use of the words "abnormalities" and "excessive" in the above sentences is clearly suggestive of something more.

[94]

★Sense of Humor Test, Second Edition. Ages 16 and over; 1939–43; 1 form; $4 per 10; 50¢ per single test; $1.50 per set of scoring sheets; (60) minutes; A. A. Roback; Sci-Art Publishers.

[95]

★Shipley-Institute of Living Scale for Measuring Intellectual Impairment. Adults; 1940–46; formerly entitled *Shipley-Hartford Retreat Scale for Measuring Intellectual Impairment;* 1946 copyright changed in title only; 1 form; limited distribution gratis; 20(25) minutes; Walter C. Shipley; Institute of Living, Hartford, Connecticut.

REFERENCES
1. SHIPLEY, WALTER C. "A Comparison of Two Techniques for Measuring Intellectual Impairment and Deterioration." Abstract. *Psychol B* 37:438-9 Jl '40. * (*PA* 14:5564, title only)
2. SHIPLEY, WALTER C. "A Self-Administering Scale for Measuring Intellectual Impairment and Deterioration." *J Psychol* 9:371-7 Ap '40. * (*PA* 14:3606)

3. Benton, Arthur L., and Howell, Ira L. "The Use of Psychological Tests in the Evaluation of Intellectual Function Following Head Injury: Report of a Case of Post-Traumatic Personality Disorder." *Psychosom Med* 3:138-51 Ap '41. * (*PA* 15:4206)

4. Shipley, Walter C., and Burlingame, C. Charles. "A Convenient Self-Administering Scale for Measuring Intellectual Impairment in Psychotics." *Am J Psychiatry* 97:1313-25 My '41. * (*PA* 16:1719)

5. Pollack, Benjamin. "The Validity of the Shipley-Hartford Retreat Test for 'Deterioration'." *Psychiatric Q* 16:119-31 Ja '42. * (*PA* 16:3619)

6. Abbott, Walter D.; Due, Floyd O.; and Nosik, William A. "Subdural Hematoma and Effusion as a Result of Blast Injuries: Second Preliminary Report: Diagnosis by Psychiatric Examination." *J Am Med Assn* 121:739-41 Mr 6 '43. * (*PA* 17:3397)

7. Fleming, G. W. T. H. "The Shipley-Hartford Retreat Scale for Measuring Intellectual Impairment." *J Mental Sci* 89:64-8 Ja '43. * (*PA* 17:2353)

8. Font, Marion McKenzie. "Psychological Techniques Applied to Selective Service Cases." *Am J Orthopsychiatry* 13:130-7 Ja '43. * (*PA* 17:2124)

9. Halstead, H. "An Analysis of the Matrix (Progressive Matrices) Test Results on 700 Neurotic (Military) Subjects, and a Comparison With the Shipley Vocabulary Test." *J Mental Sci* 89:202-15 Ap '43. * (*PA* 17:3794)

10. Hayman, Max. "A Rapid Test for 'Deterioration' With Comparison of Three Techniques." *J General Psychol* 29:313-7 O '43. * (*PA* 18:1423)

11. Slater, Patrick. "Interpreting Discrepancies." *Brit J Med Psychol* 19:415-9 pts 3-4 '43. * (*PA* 17:3080)

12. Ross, W. D., and McNaughton, F. L. "Head Injury: A Study of Patients With Chronic Post-Traumatic Complaints." *Arch Neurol & Psychiatry* 52:255-69 O '44. *

13. Wheeler, Erma Tilton. *A Validation Study of the Shipley-Hartford Scale.* Unpublished master's thesis, University of Pittsburgh, 1944.

14. Bradford, E. J. G. "Comments on the Shipley-Hartford Vocabulary Test." *J Mental Sci* 91:119-21 Ja '45. * (*PA* 19:2389)

15. Halstead, H., and Slater, Patrick. "An Experiment in the Vocational Adjustment of Neurotic Patients." *J Mental Sci* 92:509-15 Jl '45. * (*PA* 21:281)

16. Hunt, Howard F. "A Note on the Problem of Brain Damage in Rehabilitation and Personnel Work." *J Appl Psychol* 29:282-8 Ag '45. * (*PA* 20:154)

17. Armitage, Stewart G. *An Analysis of Certain Psychological Tests Used for the Evaluation of Brain Injury.* Psychological Monographs, Vol. 60, No. 1, Whole No. 277. Washington, D. C.: American Psychological Association, Inc., 1946. Pp. iii, 48. Paper. $1.25. *

18. Fecher, Irving Bernard. *The Efficacy of the Shipley-Hartford Retreat Scale for Measuring Mental Impairment in Relation to Age and Other Factors.* Unpublished master's thesis, University of Pittsburgh, 1946.

19. Lewinski, Robert J. "The Shipley-Hartford Scale as an Independent Measure of Mental Ability." *Ed & Psychol Meas* 6:253-9 su '46. * (*PA* 21:627)

20. Wright, M. Erik. "Use of the Shipley-Hartford Test in Evaluating Intellectual Functioning of Neuropsychiatric Patients." *J Appl Psychol* 30:45-50 F '46. * (*PA* 20:2386)

21. Aita, J. A.; Armitage, S. G.; Reitan, R. M.; and Rabinovitz, A. "The Use of Certain Psychological Tests in the Evaluation of Brain Injury." *J General Psychol* 37:25-44 Jl '47. * (*PA* 22:3044)

22. Garfield, Sol L. "The Shipley-Hartford Retreat Scale as a Quick Measure of Mental Status." *J Consult Psychol* 11:1480-50 My-Je '47. * (*PA* 22:303)

23. Kobler, Frank J. "The Measurement of Improvement Among Neuropsychiatric Patients in an Army Convalescent Facility." *J Clin Psychol* 3:121-8 Ap '47. * (*PA* 21:3098)

23a. Landisberg, Selma. "A Personality Study of Institutionalized Epileptics." *Am J Mental Def* 52:16-22 Jl '47. *

24. Manson, Morse P., and Grayson, Harry M. "The Shipley-Hartford Retreat Scale as a Measure of Intellectual Impairment for Military Prisoners." *J Appl Psychol* 31:67-81 F '47. * (*PA* 21:2494)

25. Williams, S. B., and Leavitt, H. J. "Prediction of Success in Learning Japanese." *J Appl Psychol* 31:164-8 Ap '47. * (*PA* 21:2796)

E. J. G. Bradford, Senior Lecturer in Education, The University of Sheffield, Sheffield, England. This pair of tests, devised originally to measure the deterioration of intellectual power resulting from mental illness, can be usefully employed in estimating the ability of persons in normal health. The American standardisation fits the British population fairly closely if the total score of the Abstraction Test, without the multiplication by two, is paired with the shortened Vocabulary Test recommended (by the reviewer) for use in Britain (14).

The Vocabulary Test differentiates well down to the mental age of eleven years, and the same can be said but with less confidence about the Abstraction Test. Since the ceiling for both tests would be 20 points, it is doubtful if scores above 18 have much differential significance. In a battery of seven tests, including reading, repetition of sentences, and performance tests, the Shipley tests work very well, but by themselves the difference in score between them would be very shaky evidence on which to base a verdict of mental illness. A difference between the reading test and the repetition test is as reliable and usually confirmatory, while in cases of neurosis the difference between reading or vocabulary and performance scores may be more suggestive of maladjustment. Thus, a random sample of five diabetic cases gave a mean Vocabulary–Abstraction difference of 1 year; five gastric cases, 4 years; 8 attempted suicides, 4 years. The corresponding Reading–Repetition differences were ½ year, 2 years, and 2½ years. For the Reading–Performance differences, 1½ years, 2½ years, and 4¾ years were obtained respectively. There is no doubt that age and sex play a part in producing these differences, for proneness to these illnesses varies with the age and sex of the person, just as the intelligence of the patient seems to be related to the type of syndrome which his maladjustment exhibits, whether it be obsessional, psychopath, anxiety, or hysteria.

Experience indicates that a reading (mechanical) test should, at a clinical interview, precede the vocabulary test, because a reading age of less than 11 years invalidates the vocabulary test as a test of intelligence. Indifferent or scanty schooling could through a weakness in reading result in vocabulary scores similar to those of a moron.

Responses to the Abstraction Test (Series Test would be a better name) when given orally often show that a dependence on auditory clues, meaning clues, or visual clues results in failures when clues of a different type are required. Full success at the test requires a flexibility of approach, the trial of alternative clues. This type of rigid or one-track mind is not disclosed in the self-administered use of the test. A suggestion such as "Read it aloud" will sometimes enable a patient who has been vainly struggling for a visual clue to give a correct solution from an auditory clue. Would a failure of this type be due to the decay of intelligence or to a bias which might be described as an unwillingness or inability to experiment, a lack of flexibility in other words?

William A. Hunt, Professor of Psychology, Northwestern University, Evanston, Illinois. This scale for measuring intellectual impairment or deficit is based upon the established tendency in such cases for a discrepancy to appear between vocabulary level and the ability to handle abstract thinking. Vocabulary level is measured by a 40-word, multiple-choice vocabulary test with a 10-minute time limit. Abstract reasoning is measured by a 20-item abstraction test in which the subject is asked to grasp the relationship involved in a progressive series of items and complete the final missing member of the series. This also has a 10-minute time limit. Mental age norms for vocabulary, abstraction, and total score are available based on a normative group of 1046 subjects on whom group intelligence test scores were available. Reliabilities of .87, .89, and .92, respectively, were obtained for vocabulary, abstraction, and total score. Intellectual impairment is expressed by a "Conceptual Quotient" or C.Q. based on the difference between vocabulary level and the level of abstract reasoning. The clinical value of the scale was established on a group of 374 mental patients.

Subsequent studies by other investigators here and abroad have confirmed the clinical value of the test as a measure of intellectual impairment within the usual limits of such tests. Correlations of .77 and .65 also have been reported between the Shipley total score and the Wechsler-Bellevue scale. This indicates that the test may serve satisfactorily as a quick measure of intelligence.

The reviewer has used the *Shipley-Institute of Living Scale* widely in both functional and organic mental disorders. In his experience it is as satisfactory as, if not more so than, the other available measures. Brevity and ease of administration are definitely in its favor. The answers on the Abstraction Test also offer relatively rich material for clinical interpretation despite the pencil-and-paper nature of the test. Some weakness develops at the lower ranges of intelligence,

suggesting the need for further extension at this level.

Margaret Ives, Psychologist, St. Elizabeths Hospital, Washington, D. C. This scale is intended to provide a sensitive but quick self-administering test which may be used by psychiatrists or even by general practitioners to aid in detecting early inefficient intellectual functioning. It is based upon the finding, first published by Babcock (1930) and now widely used, that, where there is intellectual decrement, vocabulary is usually least affected but that the capacity for conceptual thinking is among those abilities which decline rapidly. This concept, although it has proved highly useful, must be used with caution since frequently the vocabularies of chronic psychotics do vary in successive retests even as much as 5 years of mental age. It is doubtful, therefore, whether those who are not clinical psychologists should be encouraged to interpret results.

The Shipley vocabulary test is arranged in multiple-choice form with one explanatory sample. Additional explanation is allowed when necessary and although the 10-minute time limit is ample, the penalty for those whose thinking is unusually slow is minimized by allowing one point of credit for each four items not attempted.

Each item of the Abstraction Test requires the subject to "induce a general principle and from it to deduce a specific answer." There is no sample, but additional help is permitted including, at the examiner's discretion, explanation of the first, easiest item which cannot then be credited. Such a procedure seems to penalize those who are not well educated and test-wise, a discrimination which could be obviated by routine additional explanation including a sample. Also, although the time allowance is adequate, it is not nearly so generous as the vocabulary limit and there is no alleviation of the penalty for slowness. This tends to lower the conceptual quotient of those whose thinking has been slowed by their illness and introduces another factor in addition to impairment of ability to abstract.

The test provides four ratings—first, a vocabulary age to measure the patient's prepsychotic or original level; second, an abstraction age to measure the level of his abstract thinking; third, a total mental age which gives a rough estimate of the present functional level; and fourth, the "C.Q." or "conceptual quotient," which is the ratio of the patient's abstraction age to that of the "normal" person receiving his vocabulary score. A "C.Q." below 90 is suggestive of impairment; below 70 it indicates probable pathology.

Standardization is on 1046 individuals, all students from the fourth grade up through college who had had standardized group intelligence tests. One would expect such a group to set the norms somewhat higher than an unselected sample and at this hospital we find that the Binet vocabulary levels tend to run higher than the Shipley vocabulary ages; e.g., in a group of 12 paretics the median Binet vocabulary level was at 14 years as opposed to 11.7 on the Shipley. Since the test is not considered valid for those with a Shipley vocabulary age below 14 years, this excludes not only feebleminded and borderline individuals but the entire lower half of the general population, as measured by the Binet or Bellevue.

Also the standardization group includes no older people and therefore no allowance is made for normal retrogression. This is important in any patient population, but perhaps not so significant for verbal abstract thinking in a better than average group as it might be for a different kind of test (e.g., nonverbal new learning) or for a less intelligent population.

The results reported by Shipley (1941) show consistent differences in C.Q. between normals and mental hospital patients as well as among various diagnostic groups. The lowest C.Q.'s are reported for organics; next come the functional psychoses; while psychopathic personalities, psychoneurotics, and alcoholics fall within normal limits. The test does not claim to differentiate between functional and organic causes of decrement but unfortunately the interchangeable use of the words deterioration and impairment implies "irreversible diminution in intellectual capacity" in both types of cases (7).

This reviewer believes that wherever possible a complete psychological examination using a standard general intelligence test supplemented in doubtful cases by a Rorschach or other projective technique is preferable to any brief examination for special defect. However, for screening purposes or to supplement information from other tests, the Shipley scale provides valuable information regarding impairment in abstract thinking when restricted to the select group for which it is suited—above average in intelligence, reasonably well educated with no language handicap, test-sophisticated, not too disturbed to be cooperative, and preferably young.

[96]

Social Intelligence Test: George Washington University Series. Grades 9-16 and adults; 1930; 1 form; $12 per 100; 20¢ per specimen set; 49(55) minutes; F. A. Moss, T. Hunt, and K. T. Omwake; Center for Psychological Service, George Washington University.

REFERENCES

1-20. See 40:1253.
21. Moss, F. A. "Do you Know How to Get Along With People? Why Some People Get Ahead in the World While Others Do Not." Sci Am 135:26-7 Jl '26. *
22. Moss, F. A., and Hunt, Thelma. "Ability to Get Along With Others." Ind Psychol 1:170-8 Mr '26. *
23. Wang, Charles K. A. "The Significance of Early Personal History for Certain Personality Traits." Am J Psychol 44:768-74 O '32. * (PA 7:610)
24. Stagner, Ross. "The Relation of Personality to Academic Aptitude and Achievement." J Ed Res 26:648-60 My '33. * (PA 7:4857)
25. Randolph, Jane Marie. A Statistical Analysis of the Moss Social Intelligence Test. Unpublished master's thesis, University of New Mexico, 1934. (Abstracts of Theses . . . 1933-1937, 1946, p. 75.)
26. Stein, S. A Statistical Study of the George Washington University Social Intelligence Test and the George Washington University Mental Alertness Test. Unpublished master's thesis, George Washington University, 1935.
27. Harrell, Willard. "Testing Cotton Mill Supervisors." J Appl Psychol 24:31-5 F '40. * (PA 14:3709)
28. Jackson, Virgil Davis. "The Measurement of Social Proficiency." J Exp Ed 8:422-74 Je '40. * (PA 14:5106)
29. Flemming, Edwin G., and Flemming, Cecile White. "A Qualitative Approach to the Problem of Improving Selection of Salesmen by Psychological Tests." J Psychol 21:127-50 Ja '46. * (PA 20:1636)

Glen U. Cleeton, Director, Division of Humanistic and Social Studies, Carnegie Institute of Technology, Pittsburgh, Pennsylvania. Test administration is divided into two parts. Four minutes is allowed for preliminary study of a sheet containing twelve photographs. The photograph sheets are then collected, and the subjects are instructed that they will have 45 minutes to complete the examination. Except for preliminary study of photographs, the test is self-administering.

Percentile norms for college freshmen and upperclassmen are reported along with quartile scores for high school students, college freshmen, upper-class students, and college graduates. Quartile scores are also reported for industrial and commercial groups including administrative, secretarial, sales, engineering, clerical, and other office- and store-workers. A bibliography of twenty publications covering a period from 1920 to 1940 is included in the manual. No reliability or validity coefficients are reported in the manual.

Tests of social intelligence are open to two main criticisms, both of which apply to this test: (a) The results of such tests usually correlate highly with measures of abstract intelligence, indicating that evidence of existence of an independent factor of social intelligence has not been established, and (b) any measure or work sample in which the person is permitted to record the results of "thinking over" the thing to do in hypothetical situations rarely indicates how the person would respond in actual social situations.

Howard R. Taylor, Professor of Psychology and Head of the Department, University of Oregon, Eugene, Oregon. This test is an attempt to make the distinction suggested by E. L. Thorndike in 1920 between abstract, mechanical, and social intelligence. The revised form (1931) does not differ materially in organization or assumptions from the original test. The reliability of individual scores even in the limited range of college sophomores is high enough to identify with reasonable accuracy those who are superior, average and inferior in whatever the test measures. A retest with the same form gave a correlation of .89, and the estimated reliability coefficient based on self-correlation is .88. Unfortunately, however, as a means of differentiating between social and abstract intelligence the test has little or no validity. The results of two studies are fairly typical and conclusive.

Stein (26) reported that the intercorrelations of the five subtests of the *Social Intelligence Test* were of the order of .34; those of the *Mental Alertness Test* constructed and sold, by the same publisher, as a measure of abstract (verbal) intelligence were of the order of .39. But the intercorrelations of the mental alertness subtests with the social intelligence subtests were also of the order of .34. Thus these measures of two supposedly distinct kinds of intelligence have as much in common as the presumably similar samples of each ability comprising its subtests.

A factor analysis of the same set of intercorrelations (R. L. Thorndike, 1936) indicates that "the comprehension and use of words" accounts for most of whatever either test measures. The covariance of this general factor is nine times as great as that of a second factor which has small predominantly positive loadings with the subtests of the *Mental Alertness Test* and equally slight negative loadings with those of the *Social Intelligence Test.*

Clearly then, the test can only function as a somewhat disguised and to that extent imperfect measure of verbal intelligence. The differentiations between occupational and educational groups provided by the norms should be attributed primarily to selection in terms of such capacity instead of to some unique aptitude for dealing with people or social situations in general. If the ability to understand others and meet

social problems skillfully is not so specific to the individuals and situations involved as to be largely unmeasurable, some very different approach to the isolation of the generalities underlying it would seem to be called for.

For a review by Robert L. Thorndike, see 40:1253.

[97]

★Social Personality Inventory for College Women. 1942; 1 form; $1.50 per 25; 10¢ per specimen set; nontimed (20-30) minutes; A. H. Maslow; Stanford University Press.

REFERENCES

1. EISENBERG, PHILIP. *Expressive Movements Related to Feeling of Dominance.* Archives of Psychology, No. 211. Washington, D. C.: American Psychological Association, Inc., May 1937. Pp. 73. Paper. $1.00. * (PA 11:5780)
2. EISENBERG, PHILIP. "Factors Related to Feeling of Dominance." Abstract. *Psychol B* 34:527-8 O '37. * (PA 12:339, title only)
3. MASLOW, A. H. "Dominance-Feeling, Behavior, and Status." *Psychol R* 44:404-29 S '37. * (PA 11:5851)
4. MASLOW, A. H. "Dominance-Feeling, Behavior and Status in Women." Abstract. *Psychol B* 34:526-7 O '37. * (PA 12:354, title only)
5. CARPENTER, JUNE, AND EISENBERG, PHILIP. "Some Relations Between Family Background and Personality." *J Psychol* 6:115-36 Jl '38. * (PA 13:2590)
6. MASLOW, A. H. "Dominance, Personality, and Social Behavior in Women." *J Social Psychol* 10:3-39 F '39. * (PA 13:3793)
7. MASLOW, A. H. "A Test for Dominance-Feeling (Self-Esteem) in College Women." *J Social Psychol* 12:255-70 N '40. * (PA 15:1834)
8. MEADOW, ARNOLD. "A Relation Between Dominance-Feeling and a Classroom Situation." *J Psychol* 9:269-74 '40. * (PA 14:4146)
9. LINK, HENRY C. "The Definition of Social Effectiveness and Leadership Through Measurement." *Ed & Psychol Meas* 4:57-67 sp '44. * (PA 18:3216)
10. PINTNER, R., AND FORLANO, G. "Some Measures of Dominance in College Women." *J Social Psychol* 19:313-5 My '44. * (PA 18:3815)

Nelson G. Hanawalt, Associate Professor of Psychology, New Jersey College for Women, Rutgers University, New Brunswick, New Jersey. This inventory is based upon sound research and is recommended, provided it is used with due caution and only as directed by the author in the manual. Its chief use at the present stage of development should be as a research tool. In the experienced hands of a clinical worker it should be of great assistance in gaining insight into and understanding of the individual personality. The test measures one broad phase of personality, self-esteem or similar phases of personality, and is not intended as a measure of the personality as a whole. The name is a disguise to hide the real purpose of the test since the author has found that knowledge of purpose can change the results to a considerable extent. The test is not a measure of adjustment. The same score made by two individuals might mean adjustment for the one and maladjustment for the other. Adjustment depends upon the personality as a whole and, in the case of the amount of self-esteem, especially upon the feeling of security. With these facts in mind it is quite evident that for use with the individual an expert knowledge of the dynamics of personality is required.

The test is satisfactory from the point of reliability. Its validity is better established than that of most other tests in the field of personality. It has the advantage of being clinically derived and is validated against estimates made on the basis of careful interview by an expert in this phase of personality. It has stood the test of subsequent research by other investigators working in this field of personality. Nevertheless, it should be used with caution when applied to the individual case, for, as the author suggests, serious mistakes can be made in one out of twenty cases unless the test results are verified by personal interview. Another factor to bear in mind is the effect of culture upon the results. The test should be used only for college women unless research has established norms for other groups. Even among college women the average score varies from one school to another, from one locality to another, etc. Before it is used in a college clinic, it would probably prove a valuable asset to have it standardized on the group of women selected by that particular college. In any case it should be interpreted in the light of the background of the individual student.

Like other personality tests, the value of the test is dependent upon the research back of it. This test appears to measure something different from other personality tests. It is correlated to some extent with the Allports' *A–S Reaction Study* ($r = .55$) and with the self-sufficiency and dominance scales of Bernreuter's *Personality Inventory* ($r = .43$ and $.37$, respectively). These correlations are low enough to indicate that it is measuring something different from the other tests but high enough to substantiate the fact that it is not independent of them. The test is in its infancy. Self-esteem is an important aspect of personality. Future research will have to determine its ultimate usefulness and value.

[98]

Student Questionnaire. Grades 7-14; 1932–38; 1 form; $9.90 per 100; 35¢ per specimen set; nontimed (40) minutes; Percival M. Symonds and Virginia Lee Block; Bureau of Publications, Teachers College, Columbia University.

Simon H. Tulchin, Consulting Psychologist, 30 East 60th St., New York 22, New York. This questionnaire consists of 100 items which attempt to obtain data on the feelings and attitudes of students toward the curriculum, social life of the school, the administration, the teachers, other pupils, home and family, and a miscellaneous group of personal evaluations. For each item, the student is offered a selection of five statements and is to select the one which best expresses his own feelings. For the most part the choice can be made in terms of always, often, sometimes, seldom, or never. Depending on the item, however, the statements may be worded in more qualitative terms.

Two groups of high school seniors were used to establish the reliability of the test. The questionnaire was given to one group twice at an interval of two weeks and resulted in a coefficient of correlation of .83. With another group of seniors a correlation of .72 was obtained when the questionnaire was repeated after one week, and a correlation of .71 when it was repeated after three months. The correlation between the second questionnaire and the one given three months later was .80.

In order to establish validity the results of the questionnaire were checked against recorded statements of individual difficulties as well as check lists submitted by parents and teachers. Correlations of .72 and .70 were secured.

On the question of norms the authors take the position that general norms are not helpful and that "judgment must be made in the light of the standards of adjustment that the home, the school, and the community are setting." They feel that the adjustment of any particular group cannot be taken as "a valid basis for making an appraisal of the adjustment of any particular group of students in any other city." They feel that an item-by-item analysis is more important than total scores and that serious maladjustment in one or two areas may be covered up if only general scores are considered. However, the authors do state that in a study of 5,000 pupils in various parts of the country those who showed good general adjustment had scores between 76 and 85.

While it can be agreed that numerical scores on this type of questionnaire may be misleading, norms are essential in that they can serve as a background or standard for interpretation. Otherwise it is difficult to see the reason for calculating scores at all. Further questions are raised in relation to the wide range of ages covered by the test. A given statement must necessarily carry different connotations to different age groups. Some statements suitable for a seventh grade pupil are obviously out of place when presented to a college sophomore.

This test is also subject to the general criticism of all paper-and-pencil questionnaires. We do not know what motivates the choice of any given statement by any individual taking the test.

[99]

Study of Values: A Scale for Measuring the Dominant Interests in Personality. College and adults; 1931; $2.25 per 25; 15¢ per specimen set; nontimed (20) minutes; Gordon W. Allport and Philip E. Vernon; Houghton Mifflin Co.

REFERENCES

1. Decker, C. E. *An Experiment in the Use of Psychological Tests in the Selection of Life Insurance Agents.* Unpublished master's thesis, Dartmouth College, 1931.
2. Vernon, Philip E., and Allport, Gordon W. "A Test for Personal Values." *J Abn & Social Psychol* 26:231-48 O-D '31. * (*PA* 6:3417)
3. Cantril, H., and Allport, G. W. "Recent Applications of the *Study of Values.*" *J Abn & Social Psychol* 28:259-73 O-D '33. * (*PA* 8:3138)
4. Cantril, H.; Rand, H. A.; and Allport, G. W. "The Determination of Personal Interests by Psychological and Graphological Methods." *Char & Pers* 2:134-43 D '33. * (*PA* 8:1718)
5. Ford, C. A. "The Allport-Vernon 'Study of Values' Test Applied to Entering Freshmen." Abstract. *Psychol B* 30:557 O '33. * (*PA* 8:1178, title only)
6. Harris, D. "Group Differences in 'Values' Within a University." Abstract. *Psychol B* 30:555-6 O '33. * (*PA* 8:1182, title only)
7. Hartmann, George W. *Measuring Teaching Efficiency Among College Instructors.* Archives of Psychology, No. 154. Washington, D. C.: American Psychological Association, Inc., July 1933. Pp. 45. Paper. $0.80. * (*PA* 8:5229)
8. Meloun, Jan. "The Study of Values—Test and Graphology." *Char & Pers* 2:144-51 D '33. * (*PA* 8:1726)
9. Pintner, Rudolf. "A Comparison of Interests, Abilities and Attitudes." *J Abn & Social Psychol* 27:351-7 Ja-Mr '33. * (*PA* 7:5522)
10. Stone, Charles Leonard. "The Personality Factor in Vocational Guidance." *J Abn & Social Psychol* 28:274-5 O-D '33. (*PA* 8:3152)
11. Whitely, Paul L. "A Study of the Allport-Vernon Test for Personal Values." *J Abn & Social Psychol* 28:6-13 Ap-Je '33. * (*PA* 8:463)
12. Bowden, A. O. "Change—The Test of Teaching." *Sch & Soc* 40:133-6 Jl 28 '34. * (*PA* 8:5652)
13. Harris, Daniel. "Group Differences in Values Within a University." *J Abn & Social Psychol* 29:95-102 Ap-Je '34. * (*PA* 8:5576)
14. Hartmann, George W. "Sex Differences in Valuational Attitudes." *J Social Psychol* 5:106-12 F '34. * (*PA* 8:4153)
15. Rothney, John W. M. *Interests in Relation to School Success.* Unpublished doctor's thesis, Harvard University, 1934.
16. Hubbell, Marian Bellamy. *The Allport-Vernon Study of Values and Leisure-Time Activities.* Unpublished master's thesis, Columbia University, 1935.
17. Triplett, Richard J. "Interests of Commercial Students." *J Abn & Social Psychol* 29:409-14 Ja-Mr '35. * (*PA* 9:3798)
18. Hicks, Ethel M. *A Study of the Validity of the Allport-Vernon Scale A Study of Values With Students of the Twelfth Grade.* Unpublished master's thesis, Pennsylvania State College, 1936. Pp. 42.
19. Rothney, J. W. M. "Evaluative Attitudes and Academic Success." *J Ed Psychol* 27:292-8 Ap '36. * (*PA* 10:5992)
20. Schaefer, Benjamin R. "The Validity and Utility of the Allport-Vernon Study of Values Test." *J Abn & Social Psychol* 30:419-22 Ja-Mr '36. * (*PA* 10:4119)
21. Williams, Griffith W., and Chamberlain, Florence. "An Evaluation of the Use of the Allport Ascendance-Submission Test With High School Girls." *J Genetic Psychol* 49:363-75 D '36. * (*PA* 11:2812)
22. Lurie, Walter A. "A Study of Spranger's Value-Types by the Method of Factor Analysis." *J Social Psychol* 8:17-37 F '37. * (*PA* 11:4205)
23. Anderson, Rose G. "Some Technological Aspects of Counseling Adult Women." *J Appl Psychol* 22:455-69 O '38. * (*PA* 13:2669) Abstract *Psychol B* 35:631-2 N '38. * (*PA* 13:1655, title only)
24. Miller, Carroll H. "Value of Certain Standard Tests for a Study of Dramatic Talent." *J Social Psychol* 9:437-9 N '38. * (*PA* 13:1753)
25. Van Buskirk, W. L. "Some Educationally Significant Features of the Pharmaceutical Personality." *Am J Pharm Ed* 2:330-9 Jl '38. *
26. Whitely, Paul L. "The Constancy of Personal Values." *J Abn & Social Psychol* 33:405-8 Jl '38. * (*PA* 12:5979)

27. Duffy, Elizabeth, and Crissy, W. J .E. "Values Scores in Predicting Vocational Interest Scores and College Grades." Abstract. *Psychol B* 36:616-7 O '39. * (*PA* 14:588, title only)
28. Pintner, R., and Forlano, G. "Dominant Interests and Personality Characteristics." *J General Psychol* 21:251-60 O '39. * (*PA* 14:384)
29. Pintner, Rudolf, and Forlano, George. "A Note on the Relation Between Divergent Interests and Emotional Stability." *J Abn & Social Psychol* 34:539-41 O '39. * (*PA* 14:954)
30. Stump, N. Franklin. "Sense of Humor and Its Relationship to Personality, Scholastic Aptitude, Emotional Maturity, Height, and Weight." *J General Psychol* 20:25-32 Ja '39. * (*PA* 13:3759)
31. Van Dusen, A. C.; Wimberly, Stan; and Mosier, Charles I. "Standardization of a Values Inventory." *J Ed Psychol* 30:53-62 Ja '39. * (*PA* 13:3197)
32. Burgemeister, Bessie B. *The Permanence of Interests of Women College Students: A Study in Personality Development.* Archives of Psychology, No. 255. Washington, D. C.: American Psychological Association, Inc., July 1940. Pp. 59. Paper. $1.00. * (*PA* 15:3042)
33. Duffy, Elizabeth. "A Critical Review of Investigations Employing the Allport-Vernon Study of Values and Other Tests of Evaluative Attitude." *Psychol B* 37:597-612 O '40. * (*PA* 15:322)
34. Duffy, Elizabeth, and Crissy, W. J. E. "Evaluative Attitudes as Related to Vocational Interests and Academic Achievement." *J Abn & Social Psychol* 35:226-45 Ap '40. * (*PA* 14:4243)
35. Golden, Alfred L. "Personality Traits of Drama School Students." *J Speech* 26:564-75 D '40. * (*PA* 15:3045)
36. Sarbin, Theodore R., and Berdie, Ralph F. "Relation of Measured Interests to the Allport-Vernon Study of Values." *J Appl Psychol* 24:287-96 Je '40. * (*PA* 14:6227)
37. Sisson, E. Donald, and Sisson, Bette. "Introversion and the Aesthetic Attitude." *J General Psychol* 22:203-8 Ja '40. * (*PA* 14:2480)
38. Wickert, Frederic. "The Interrelationships of Some General and Specific Preferences." *J Social Psychol* 11:275-302 My '40. * (*PA* 14:5149)
39. Cohen, Jozef B. "A Scale for the Measurement of Attitude toward the Aesthetic Value." *J Psychol* 12:75-9 Jl '41. * (*PA* 15:5246)
40. Ferguson, Leonard W.; Humphreys, Lloyd G.; and Strong, Frances W. "A Factorial Analysis of Interests and Values." *J Ed Psychol* 32:197-204 Mr '41. * (*PA* 15:3887)
41. Todd, J. Edward. *Social Norms and the Behavior of College Students.* Columbia University, Teachers College, Contributions to Education, No. 833. Donald P. Cottrell, faculty sponsor. New York: Bureau of Publications, the College, 1941. Pp. xiii, 190. $2.00. * (*PA* 16:358)
42. McCarthy, Thomas J. *Personality Traits of Seminarians.* Catholic University of America, Studies in Psychology and Psychiatry, Vol. 5, No. 4. Washington, D. C.: Catholic University of America Press, July 1942. Pp. vii, 46. Paper. $2.00. * (*PA* 17:592)
43. Peters, Richarda. *A Study of the Intercorrelations of Personality Traits Among a Group of Novices in Religious Communities.* Catholic University of America, Studies in Psychology and Psychiatry, Vol. 5, No. 7. Washington, D. C.: Catholic University of America Press, December 1942. Pp. vii, 38. Paper. $1.00. * (*PA* 17:2047)
44. Young, A. W. *A Study of the Dominance of Six Basic Motives in Personality as Set Forth by Edward Spranger in His Book, Types of Men.* Unpublished master's thesis, Atlanta University, 1942.
45. Arsenian, Seth. "Change in Evaluative Attitudes During Four Years of College." *J Appl Psychol* 27:338-49 Ag '43. * (*PA* 18:525)
46. Arsenian, Seth. "The Relation of Evaluative Attitudes to Vocational Interest and Social Adjustment." *J Social Psychol* 17:17-24 F '43. * (*PA* 17:2154)
47. Fischer, Robert P. "Do the Interests of Students Indicate the Need of a Liberal Education?" *J Ed Res* 37:619-27 Ap '44. * (*PA* 18:3622)
48. Pintner, R., and Forlano, G. "Some Measures of Dominance in College Women." *J Social Psychol* 19:313-5 My '44. * (*PA* 18:3815)
49. Schultz, Richard S. "A Study of Values." *Personnel J* 22:308-12 F '44. * (*PA* 18:1791)
50. Barrett, Dorothy M. "Aptitude and Interest Patterns of Art Majors in a Liberal Arts College." *J Appl Psychol* 29:483-92 D '45. * (*PA* 20:1248)
51. Eagleson, Oran W., and Bell, Eleanor S. "The Values of Negro Women College Students." *J Social Psychol* 22:149-54 N '45. * (*PA* 20:1179)
52. Sartain, A. Q. "The Use of Certain Standardized Tests in the Selection of Inspectors in an Aircraft Factory." *J Consult Psychol* 9:234-7 S-O '45. * (*PA* 20:1241)
53. Seagoe, May V. "Permanence of Interest in Teaching." *J Ed Res* 38:678-84 My '45. * (*PA* 19:3183)
54. Seagoe, May V. "Prognostic Tests and Teaching Success." *J Ed Res* 32:685-90 My '45. * (*PA* 19:3184)
55. Evans, Chester Eugene. *Interrelations of Evidences of Vocational Interest.* Unpublished doctor's thesis, Ohio State University, 1946. (*Abstracts of Dissertations . . . Summer Quarter 1945-46,* 1946, pp. 51-7.)

56. Mandell, Milton M., and Adkins, Dorothy C. "The Validity of Written Tests for the Selection of Administrative Personnel." *Ed & Psychol Meas* 6:293-312 au '46. * (PA 21:905)

57. Wheatley, Luis Andrès, and Sumner, F. C. "Measurement of Neurotic Tendency in Negro Students of Music." *J Psychol* 22:247-52 O '46. * (PA 21:819)

58. Bruner, Jerome S.; Postman, Leo; and McGinnies, Elliott. "Personal Values as Determinants of Perceptual Selection." Abstract. *Am Psychol* 2:285-6 Ag '47. *

59. French, Vera V. "The Structure of Sentiments: II, A Preliminary Study of Sentiments." *J Personality* 16:78-108 S '47. * (PA 22:2512)

60. Seashore, Harold G. "Validation of the Study of Values for Two Vocational Groups at the College Level." *Ed & Psychol Meas* 7:757-63 w '47. *

61. Stefflre, Buford. "The Reading Difficulty of Interest Inventories." *Occupations* 26:95-6 N '47. * (PA 22:1722)

Paul E. Meehl, Assistant Professor of Psychology, University of Minnesota, Minneapolis, Minnesota. Considering its a priori method of construction, the problematic validity of its theoretical foundation (Spranger's types), and the relatively small number (45) of items which are used to measure six value dimensions, this seems to be a remarkably good test. It is administered either singly or in groups in around 20 minutes and is fairly easy to score. The reliabilities in the sense of internal consistency are not as high as are usually required, if this is taken to be of any great consequence; test-retest reliabilities range from around .70 to .90 with the exception of one score, the "social," which is reported by the authors and by numerous investigators as being of doubtful meaning and stability. Validity, as indicated by ratings, correlation with other tests, and differentiation of various academic and occupational groups, is fairly good when the many attenuating factors in such a situation are taken into account. Other investigators have reported normative data in fairly good agreement with those of the manual. The test scores have been shown to be related to field of college work, nature of the college itself, stated occupational preference, actual occupation, sex, religious affiliation, and various patterns of vocational interest as measured by the Strong and other vocational interest tests. Almost all of the trends which have been found are what the definitions of the five reliable value scores would lead one to expect theoretically. There is evidence of a slight relation to academic achievement.

The criticism has been made that it is impossible to value many things at once, since the items of the test force a choice between situations involving the "opposed" values of the subject. The manual has been quite explicit in pointing out that it is the *relative* strength of values which the test is supposed to get at, so this is hardly a real criticsm. There are reasons for believing that this pairing of valued alternatives is actu-

ally preferable to another method which, while allowing a subject to value two things equally strongly rather than being forced to choose, also introduces the new variables of differences among persons with regard to rating in general. While the norms compare one person with another, what they really compare is not the strength of a value in A versus its strength in B, but the extent to which the value competes with other values in A as contrasted with the corresponding extent in B.

As was mentioned above, there is considerable evidence for not paying much attention to the social value score, which is highly unreliable and in any case rather ambiguous in meaning. Factor analytic studies and other correlational work tends to indicate that the clearest case for primary component values is for the theoretical component. There seems to be a considerable overlap between the economic and political values, which some other investigators, using both this and other item sets, have referred to by various names such as "philistine," "practical," "business," and the like.

At Minnesota this test has proved itself useful and stimulating when administered in a class in personality. In some unpublished work with which the reviewer was connected, all of the investigators were very favorably impressed with the rather neat descriptive power of the values profile in some blind matching studies. In eliminating certain persons as possibilities for a matching, or in the final choice of one rather than the other, this instrument was often of crucial importance, even though in competition with several other fairly well-validated personality inventories. With suitable caution as to its use with the less educated and as to the untrustworthiness of the social value score, this test can be recommended as one of the few structured personality devices having considerable value.

[100]

★Szondi Test. Ages 4 and over; 1937; $7.50 per set of 48 picture cards; $6 per copy of manual, German edition; an English translation by Susan K. Deri is in preparation; L. Szondi; Grune & Stratton, Inc.

REFERENCES

1. Rapaport, David. "The Szondi Test." *B Menninger Clinic* 5:33-9 Mr '41. * (PA 15:3049)

2. Rapaport, D. "Principles Underlying Projective Techniques." *Char & Pers* 10:213-9 Mr '42. * (PA 16:4068)

3. Knight, Robert P.; Gill, Merton; Lozoff, Milton; and Rapaport, David. "Comparison of Clinical Findings and Psychological Tests in Three Cases Bearing Upon Military Personnel Selection." *B Menninger Clinic* 7:114-28 My '43. * (PA 17:4241)

Susan K. Deri, Visiting Lecturer in Psychology, The City College of New York, New York, New York. The *Szondi Test* is a projective technique originated by the Hungarian psychiatrist Lipot Szondi. The test has been in use in Europe since 1936. The test material consists of 48 photographs, representing various types of mental patients, grouped into six sets, each set consisting of eight photographs: a homosexual, a sadist, an epileptic, an hysteric, a catatonic schizophrenic, a paranoid schizophrenic, a manic-depressive depressive, and a manic-depressive manic.

The administration of the test requires about ten minutes. The subject is presented one set of pictures and asked to pick out the two he likes and the two he dislikes the most. This procedure is repeated with all six sets consecutively, finally resulting in the choice of twelve liked and twelve disliked pictures. These choices are recorded graphically on a scoring sheet. The test must be administered several times with at least one day of interval between administration in order to be able to give a valid clinical interpretation of the personality. For various research purposes, however, the use of one or two profiles for each subject is permissible.

The minimum age for which the *Szondi Test* can be given is approximately four years. It is administered individually although there are experiments under way trying it out as a group test by projecting the series on a screen. The same limitations which hold for the use of single test profiles hold for the group administration to an even greater extent. There are a limited number of research problems not entailing qualitative analysis of the individual profiles, in which cases the group administration is permissible.

Something has to be said about the psychological theory underlying this test although an adequate presentation of it is almost impossible within the framework of this short review. Szondi in his own theory contends that choices in the test are based on some kind of similarity between the hereditary factors (genes) of the choosing subject and the particular mental patient represented in the chosen picture. Actually one can very well work with the test without accepting this "gene-theory."

The eight different types of mental disorders have to be looked upon as extreme manifestations of psychological tendencies present to

greater or smaller extent in all of us. Thus we have an eight-dimensional concept of the personality. Depending on the state of tension in each of the eight "basic" psychological needs, the pictures representing the corresponding needs will be chosen in various proportions. To make it more concrete: more pictures of sadists will be chosen by a person whose aggression is pent up than by somebody who is able to find ways to discharge his aggression.

Whether the particular types of pictures are chosen as liked or as disliked depends upon the person's conscious or unconscious attitude towards the particular need in question. To continue our above example: the person whose aggression is dammed up and ready to be discharged as open aggression will choose a great number of pictures of sadists as *liked,* while somebody whose aggression is dammed up but strongly repressed, will choose the same amount of pictures of sadists as *disliked.* The psychological meaning of the choices in the remaining seven categories has to be interpreted according to the same dynamic principle but varying in the specific content of the needs represented by the various categories. Since all eight of these basic psychological tendencies ·have a wide range of potential manifestations ranging from the most normal psychological phenomena to psychotic or antisocial symptoms, the fields in which the test can be used are extremely wide.

Accordingly, the fields of application of the test include: clinical practice, normal personality testing, vocational guidance, experimental social psychology, and a variety of fields of research, for example, following up the effects of various psychiatric treatments such as psychotherapy, drug treatments, shock treatments, etc. It is particularly suited to follow up certain psychopathological processes such as the psychological changes during the paroxismal cycles of epileptics or the personality changes during the process of a developing psychosis.

From the above-mentioned points it follows that the test is not an instrument which is supposed to measure static traits of the personality but one which regards personality as a dynamic process. Therefore the usual criteria of reliability do not hold for this test since retesting is not supposed to show identical test profiles.

However, the degree and type of changes are the main diagnostic signs which indicate whether the person is psychologically adjusted, neurotic, or psychotic. The validity of the test was established against case histories and clinical data. Like in other projective techniques, the line of development followed detailed qualitative analysis of individual cases rather than collecting large-scale statistical data.

Another reason which makes statistical treatment of the data difficult lies again in a common characteristic of all projective techniques, namely in the fact that configurational patterns of the global profile have greater diagnostic value than the single factors. However, many tables with quantitative data are given in Szondi's new book *Experimentelle Trieblehre*. The data given in the tables are based on the test profiles of 2,237 subjects without any clinical symptoms ranging from the age of 3 to 90, and 1,880 subjects representing the various types of neuroses and psychoses. The tables indicate the frequency of the various configurations in different age groups, vocational groups, and pathological groups.

A critical appraisal was practically inherent in the above description. The very same aspects which make this test a unique instrument for the "measurement" of dynamic processes unapproachable for any of the other personality tests, account for the shortcomings of the method. To sum it up, the strength of the test lies in the following points: (a) Unlike most well-known projective techniques, the *Szondi Test* does not involve verbalization, thus excluding the possibility of certain types of verbal covering up or evasion well known to every Rorschachist. (b) Through the choice-reactions the subject reveals unconscious aspects of his personality which cannot be detected by any other projective test. (c) It is the only instrument which records the constantly fluctuating dynamisms of the personality.

Besides Szondi's theory about the role of the genes—which remains an hypothesis—the following points of criticism could be made: (a) More experimental work is needed to clarify the basic psychological processes involved in our reactions to the pictures. Not having a parallel series we do not exactly know the extent to which we react to these specific pictures or to the clinical entities as such. (b) In spite of all the aforementioned inherent difficulties, more statistical data are required for the purpose of standardization and validation. (c) A limitation or strong point of the test—depending from which angle we look at it—is the fact that a great deal of psychiatric and psychoanalytic

knowledge is required of the person who uses the test. Because of dealing with concepts originally derived from psychopathology, the danger of misinterpretation due to superficial knowledge is greater than in any other personality test.

[101]

★Test of Etiquette: George Washington University Series. Grades 10-16; 1941-42; 1 form; $8 per 100, postpaid; 15¢ per specimen set, postpaid; 50(55) minutes; Creelman Rowland and Mitchell Dreese; Center for Psychological Service, George Washington University.

[102]

Test of Knowledge of Social Usage, 1942 Edition. Grades 7-12; 1933-42; 1 form; $5.50 per 100; 25¢ per specimen set, postpaid; nontimed (30-60) minutes; Ruth Strang, Marion A. Brown, and Dorothy C. Stratton; Bureau of Publications, Teachers College, Columbia University.

REFERENCES

1. STRANG, RUTH. "Knowledge of Social Usage in Junior and Senior High Schools." *Sch & Soc* 34:709-12 N 21 '31. * (*PA* 6:1642)

[103]

★Thematic Apperception Test. Ages 7 and over; 1943; commonly known as TAT; individual; $5 per testing outfit; nontimed (120) minutes; Henry A. Murray; Harvard University Press. (28s. Oxford University Press, London, 1944.)

REFERENCES

1. MORGAN, CHRISTIANA D., AND MURRAY, HENRY A. "A Method for Investigating Phantasies: The Thematic Apperception Test." *Arch Neurol & Psychiatry* 34:289-306 Ag '35. * (*PA* 10:1347)
2. MURRAY, H. A. "Techniques for a Systematic Investigation of Fantasy." *J Psychol* 3:115-43 '37. * (*PA* 11:2803)
3. MASSERMAN, JULES H., AND BALKEN, EVA R. "The Clinical Application of Phantasy Studies." *J Psychol* 6:81-8 Jl '38. * (*PA* 13:2541)
4. MORGAN, CHRISTIANA D., AND MURRAY, H. A. "Thematic Apperception Test," pp. 530-45, passim. In *Explorations in Personality: A Clinical and Experimental Study of Fifty Men of College Age*. By Henry A. Murray and others. New York and London: Oxford University Press, 1938. Pp. xiv, 761. $7.50; 42s. *
5. SYMONDS, PERCIVAL M. "Criteria for the Selection of Pictures for the Investigation of Adolescent Phantasies." *J Abn & Social Psychol* 34:271-4 Ap '39. * (*PA* 13:4069) Abstract *Psychol B* 35:641 N '38. * (*PA* 13:2241, title only)
6. MASSERMAN, JULES H., AND BALKEN, EVA R. "The Psychoanalytic and Psychiatric Significance of Phantasy." *Psychoanalytic R* 26:343-79, 535-49 Jl, O '39. * (*PA* 13:5222, 14:294)
7. BALKEN, EVA RUTH, AND VANDER VEER, ADRIAN H. "The Clinical Application of the Thematic Apperception Test to Neurotic Children." Abstract. *Psychol B* 37:517 Jl '40. * (*PA* 14:5511, title only)
8. HARRISON, ROSS. "Studies in the Use and Validity of the Thematic Apperception Test With Mentally Disordered Patients: II, A Quantitative Validity Study." *Char & Pers* 9:122-33 D '40. * (*PA* 15:2206)
9. HARRISON, ROSS. "Studies in the Use and Validity of the Thematic Apperception Test With Mentally Disordered Patients: III, Validation by the Method of 'Blind Analysis'." *Char & Pers* 9:134-8 D '40. * (*PA* 15:2207)
10. ROTTER, JULIAN B. "Studies in the Use and Validity of the Thematic Apperception Test With Mentally Disordered Patients: I, Method of Analysis and Clinical Problems." *Char & Pers* 9:18-34 S '40. * (*PA* 15:299)
11. AMEN, ELISABETH W. "Individual Differences in Apperceptive Reaction: A Study of the Response of Preschool Children to Pictures." *Genetic Psychol Monogr* 23:319-85 My '41. * (*PA* 15:5409)
12. BENNETT, GEORGIA. "Structural Factors Related to Substitute Values of Activities in Normal and Schizophrenic Persons: I, A Technique for the Investigation of Central Areas of the Personality." *Char & Pers* 10:42-50 S '41. * (*PA* 16:992)
13. SANFORD, R. NEVITT. "Some Quantitative Results From the Analysis of Children's Stories." Abstract. *Psychol B* 38:749 O '41. * (*PA* 16:817, title only)

14. SLUTZ, MARGARET. "The Unique Contributions of the Thematic Apperception Test to a Developmental Study." Abstract. *Psychol B* 38:704 O '41. * (*PA* 16:237, title only)

15. BALKEN, EVA RUTH, AND VANDER VEER, ADRIAN H. "The Clinical Application of a Test of Imagination to Neurotic Children." *Am J Orthopsychiatry* 12:68-80 Ja '42. * (*PA* 16:2911)

16. BELLAK, LEOPOLD. "An Experimental Investigation of Projection." Abstract. *Psychol B* 39:489-90 Jl '42. * (*PA* 16:4864, title only)

17. BENNETT, GEORGIA. "Some Factors Related to Substitute Value at the Level of Fantasy." Abstract. *Psychol B* 39:488 Jl '42. * (*PA* 16:4787, title only)

18. BRENMAN, MARGARET. "The Recall of Fairy Tales in Normal and Hypnotic States." Abstract. *Psychol B* 39:488-9 Jl '42. * (*PA* 16:4772, title only)

19. RAPAPORT, D. "Principles Underlying Projective Techniques." *Char & Pers* 10:213-9 Mr '42. * (*PA* 16:4068)

20. RAPAPORT, D. "The Thematic Apperception Test: Qualitative Conclusions as to Its Interpretation." Abstract. *Psychol B* 39:592 O '42. * (*PA* 17:595, title only)

21. RODNICK, E. H., AND KLEBANOFF, S. G. "Projective Reactions to Induced Frustration as a Measure of Social Adjustment." Abstract. *Psychol B* 39:489 Jl '42. * (*PA* 16:4884, title only)

22. SARASON, SEYMOUR, AND ROSENZWEIG, SAUL. "An Experimental Study of the Triadic Hypothesis: Reaction to Frustration, Ego-Defense, and Hypnotizability: II, Thematic Apperception Approach." *Char & Pers* 11:150-65 D '42. * (*PA* 17:887)

23. TOMKINS, SILVAN S. "The Limits of Material Obtainable in the Single Case Study by Daily Administration of the Thematic Apperception Test." Abstract. *Psychol B* 39:490 Jl '42. * (*PA* 16:4887, title only)

24. WYATT, FREDERICK. "Formal Aspects of the Thematic Apperception Test." Abstract. *Psychol B* 39:491 Jl '42. * (*PA* 16:4893, title only)

25. BALKEN, EVA RUTH. "A Delineation of Schizophrenic Language and Thought in a Test of Imagination." *J Psychol* 16:239-71 O '43. * (*PA* 18:155)

26. BALKEN, EVA RUTH, AND MASSERMAN, JULES H. "The Language of Phantasy: III, The Language of the Phantasies of Patients With Conversion Hysteria, Anxiety State, and Obsessive-Compulsive Neuroses," pp. 244-53. In *Contemporary Psychopathology: A Source Book*. Edited by Silvan S. Tomkins. Cambridge, Mass.: Harvard University Press, 1943. Pp. xiv, 600. $5.00. * (*PA* 18:771) Reprinted from *J Psychol* 10:75-86 Jl '40. (*PA* 14:5510)

27. CHRISTENSON, JAMES A. "Clinical Application of the Thematic Apperception Test." *J Abn & Social Psychol* 38:104-6 Ja '43. * (*PA* 17:2713)

28. HARRISON, ROSS. "The Thematic Apperception and Rorschach Methods of Personality Investigation in Clinical Practice." *J Psychol* 15:49-74 Ja '43. * (*PA* 17:1239)

29. KNIGHT, ROBERT P.; GILL, MERTON; LOZOFF, MILTON; AND RAPAPORT, DAVID. "Comparison of Clinical Findings and Psychological Tests in Three Cases Bearing Upon Military Personnel Selection." *B Menninger Clinic* 7:114-28 My '43. * (*PA* 17:4241)

30. KORCHIN, SHELDON JEROME. *A Comparative Study of Three Projective Techniques in the Measurement of Frustration-Reaction Types.* Unpublished master's thesis, Clark University, 1943. (*Abstracts of Dissertations . . . 1943*, pp. 70-2.)

31. KUTASH, SAMUEL B. "Performance of Psychopathic Defective Criminals on the Thematic Apperception Test." *J Crim Psychopath* 5:319-40 O '43. * (*PA* 18:1454)

32. MURRAY, HENRY A., AND STEIN, M. "Note on the Selection of Combat Officers." *Psychosom Med* 5:368-91 '43. (*PA* 18:1515)

33. PROSHANSKY, HAROLD M. "A Projective Method for the Study of Attitudes." *J Abn & Social Psychol* 38:393-5 Jl '43. * (*PA* 17:3887)

34. RAPAPORT, DAVID. "The Clinical Application of the Thematic Apperception Test." *B Menninger Clinic* 7:106-13 My '43. * (*PA* 17:4164)

35. SANFORD, R. NEVITT. "Thematic Apperception Test," pp. 258-301. In *Physique, Personality and Scholarship: A Cooperative Study of School Children.* By R. Nevitt Sanford, Margaret M. Adkins, R. Bretney Miller, Elizabeth A. Cobb, and others. Monographs of the Society for Research in Child Development, Vol. 7, No. 1, Serial No. 34. Washington, D. C.: the Society, National Research Council, 1943. Pp. ix, 705. Paper, lithotyped. $2.50. * (*PA* 17:4319)

36. SARASON, SEYMOUR B. "The Use of the Thematic Apperception Test With Mentally Deficient Children: I, A Study of High Grade Girls." *Am J Mental Def* 47:414-21 Ap '43. * (*PA* 17:3150)

37. SARASON, SEYMOUR B. "The Use of the Thematic Apperception Test With Mentally Deficient Children: II, A Study of High Grade Boys." *Am J Mental Def* 48:169-73 O '43. * Same 50:272-6 O '45. * (*PA* 18:1740)

38. BALKEN, EVA R., AND VANDER VEER, ADRIAN H. "Clinical Application of the Thematic Apperception Test to Neurotic Children." *Am J Orthopsychiatry* 14:421-40 Jl '44. * (*PA* 18:3908)

39. BELLAK, LEOPOLD. "The Concept of Projection: An Experimental Investigation and Study of the Concept." *Psychiatry* 7:353-70 N '44. * (*PA* 19:1261)

40. CLARK, RUTH MILLBURN. *A Method of Administering and Evaluating the Thematic Apperception Test in Group Situations.* Genetic Psychology Monographs, Vol. 30, No. 1. Provincetown, Mass.: Journal Press, August 1944. Pp. 55. Paper, $4.00. * (*PA* 18:3777)

41. KENDIG, ISABELLE V. "Projective Techniques as a Psychological Tool in Diagnosis." *J Crim Psychopath* 6:101-10 Jl '44. * (*PA* 19:448)

42. PORTER, FLORENCE SWAN. *A Study of the Scoring and Interpretation of the Thematic Apperception Test Performance of a Selected Group of Problem Children.* Unpublished master's thesis, University of Iowa, 1944.

43. RICHARDSON, LAVANGE HUNT. *The Personality of Stutterers.* Psychological Monographs, Vol. 56, No. 7, Whole No. 260. Washington, D. C.: American Psychological Association, Inc., 1944. Pp. v, 41. Paper. $1.00. * (*PA* 18:3531)

44. SARASON, SEYMOUR B. "Dreams and Thematic Apperception Test Stories." *J Abn & Social Psychol* 39:486-92 O '44. * (*PA* 19:451)

45. SYMONDS, PERCIVAL M., AND KRUGMAN, MORRIS. "Projective Methods in the Study of Personality." *R Ed Res* 14:81-98 F '44. * (*PA* 19:175) Reprinted in *Rorschach Res Exch* 9:85-101 Je '45. *

46. ABEL, THEODORA M. "Responses of the Negro and White Morons to the Thematic Apperception Test." *Am J Mental Def* 49:463-8 Ap '45. * (*PA* 20:185)

47. BALKEN, EVA RUTH. "Thematic Apperception." *J Psychol* 20:189-97 O '45. * (*PA* 20:471)

48. HARRISON, ROSS, AND ROTTER, JULIAN B. "A Note on the Reliability of the Thematic Apperception Test." *J Abn & Social Psychol* 40:97-9 Ja '45. * (*PA* 19:1972)

49. HUTT, MAX L. "The Use of Projective Methods of Personality Measurement in Army Medical Installations." *J Clin Psychol* 1:134-40 Ap '45. * (*PA* 19:2250)

50. JAQUES, ELLIOTT. "The Clinical Use of the Thematic Apperception Test With Soldiers." *J Abn & Social Psychol* 40:363-75 O '45. * (*PA* 20:479)

51. JEFFRE, MARIA FREDERIKE DOROTHEA. *A Critical Study of the Thematic Apperception Test Performance of Normal Children.* Unpublished master's thesis, University of Iowa, 1945.

52. LOEBLOWITZ-LENNARD, HENRY, AND RIESSMAN, FRANK, JR. "Recall in the Thematic Apperception Test: An Experimental Investigation Into the Meaning of Recall of Phantasy With Reference to Personality Diagnosis." *J Personality* 14:41-6 S '45. * (*PA* 20:2398)

53. MICHAEL, J. C., AND BUHLER, C. "Experiences With Personality Testing in a Neuropsychiatric Department of a Public General Hospital." *Dis Nerv Sys* 6:205-11 '45. (*PA* 19:3038)

54. REEM, LINDA E. *A Comparison Between Individual and Group Methods of Administering and Scoring the Thematic Apperception Test.* Unpublished master's thesis, Stanford University, 1945.

55. SARGENT, HELEN. "Projective Methods: Their Origins, Theory, and Application in Personality Research." *Psychol B* 42:257-93 My '45. * (*PA* 19:2650)

56. SCHNACK, GEORGE F.; SHAKOW, DAVID; AND LIVELY, MARY L. "Studies in Insulin and Metrazol Therapy: I, The Differential Prognostic Value of Some Psychological Tests." *J Personality* 14:106-24 D '45. * (*PA* 20:3669)

57. SHAKOW, DAVID; RODNICK, ELIOT, H.; AND LEBEAUX, THELMA. "A Psychological Study of a Schizophrenic: Exemplification of a Method." *J Abn & Social Psychol* 40:154-74 Ap '45. * (*PA* 19:2624)

58. WELLS, HOWARD. "Differences Between Delinquent and Non-Delinquent Boys as Indicated by the Thematic Apperception Test." Abstract. *Psychol B* 42:534 O '45. * (*PA* 20:306, title only)

59. CHIPMAN, CATHERINE E. "Psychological Variation Within a Homogeneous Psychometric Group." *Am J Mental Def* 51:195-205 '46. (*PA* 21:3000)

59a. CLARK, RUTH MILLBURN. "Group Application of the Thematic Apperception Test." *Q J Speech* 32:343-9 O '46. *

60. COMBS, ARTHUR WRIGHT, JR. *An Evaluation of the Thematic Apperception Test for the Study of Certain Personality Factors by Comparison With Autobiography.* Unpublished doctor's thesis, Ohio State University, 1946. (*Abstracts of Dissertations . . . Summer Quarter 1945-46*, 1946, pp. 45-9.)

61. COMBS, ARTHUR W. "A Method of Analysis for the Thematic Apperception Test and Autobiography." *J Clin Psychol* 2:167-74 Ap '46. * (*PA* 20:3694)

62. COMBS, ARTHUR W. "The Use of Personal Experience in Thematic Apperception Test Story Plots." *J Clin Psychol* 2:357-63 O '46. * (*PA* 21:1156)

63. COMBS, ARTHUR W. "The Validity and Reliability of Interpretation From Autobiography and Thematic Apperception Test." *J Clin Psychol* 2:240-7 Jl '46. * (*PA* 20:4659)

64. EISENDORFER, ARNOLD, AND BERGMANN, MARTIN S. "The Factor of Maturity in Officer Selection." *Psychiatry* 9:73-9 F '46. * (*PA* 20:2859)

65. FLEMING, EDITH ENDSLEY. *A Descriptive Analysis of Responses in the Thematic Apperception Test.* Unpublished master's thesis, University of Pittsburgh, 1946.

66. FREED, HERBERT, AND ECCKER, WILLIAM F. "The Thematic Apperception Test: Its Value in Routine Psychiatric Practice." Abstract. *Dis Nerv Sys* 7:146-51 My '46. * (*PA* 20:3211) Same *Arch Neurol & Psychiatry* 56:600-2 N '46. * (*PA* 21:1525, title only)

67. GARFIELD, SOL. L. "Clinical Values of Projective Techniques in an Army Hospital." *J Clin Psychol* 2:88-91 Ja '46. * (*PA* 20:1912)

68. GERVER, J. M. *Level of Interpretation of Children on the Thematic Apperception Test.* Unpublished master's thesis, Ohio State University, 1946.

69. HACKBUSCH, FLORENTINE. "The Contribution of Projective Techniques to the Understanding and Treatment of Children Psychometrically Diagnosed as FeebleMinded." With sample case studies by Bruno Klopfer. *Am J Mental Def* 51: 15-34 Jl '46. * (*PA* 21:472)

70. LASAGA Y TRAVIESO, JOSE I.; IN COLLABORATION WITH CARLOS MARTINEZ-ARANGO. "Some Suggestions Concerning the Administration and Interpretation of the T.A.T." *J Psychol* 22:117-63 Jl '46. * (*PA* 20:4197)

71. MAYMAN, MARTIN. "Review of the Literature on the Thematic Apperception Test," pp. 496-506. In *Diagnostic Psychological Testing: The Theory, Statistical Evaluation, and Diagnostic Application of a Battery of Tests, Vol. II.* By David Rapaport with the collaboration of Merton Gill and Roy Schafer. Chicago, Ill.: Year Book Publishers, Inc., 1946. Pp. xi, 516. $6.50. * (*PA* 20:1712)

72. RAPAPORT, DAVID, AND SCHAFER, ROY; WITH THE COLLABORATION OF MERTON GILL. "The Thematic Apperception Test," pp. 72-96. In their *Manual of Diagnostic Psychological Testing: II, Diagnostic Testing of Personality and Ideational Content.* Review Series, Vol. 3, No. 1. New York: Josiah Macy, Jr. Foundation, 1946. Pp. 105. Paper. $0.75. * (*PA* 21:814)

73. RAPAPORT, DAVID; WITH THE COLLABORATION OF MERTON GILL AND ROY SCHAFER. Chap. 4, "The Thematic Apperception Test," pp. 395-459. In their *Diagnostic Psychological Testing: The Theory, Statistical Evaluation, and Diagnostic Application of a Battery of Tests, Vol. II.* Chicago, Ill.: Year Book Publishers, Inc., 1946. Pp. xi, 516. $6.50. * (*PA* 20:1712)

74. ROE, ANNE. "Alcohol and Creative Work: Part I, Painters." *Q J Studies Alcohol* 6:415-67 Mr '46. * (*PA* 20:2793)

75. ROE, ANNE. "Painting and Personality." *Rorschach Res Exch* 10:86-100 O '46. * (*PA* 21:816)

76. ROE, ANNE. "The Personality of Artists." *Ed & Psychol Meas* 6:401-8 au '46. * (*PA* 21:817)

77. ROSENZWEIG, SAUL. "The Dynamics of an Amnesic Personality." *J Personality* 15:121-42 D '46. * (*PA* 21:3062)

78. ROTTER, JULIAN B. "Thematic Apperception Tests: Suggestions for Administration and Interpretation." *J Personality* 15:70-92 S '46. * (*PA* 21:2332)

79. BELLAK, LEOPOLD; EKSTEIN, RUDOLF; AND BRAVERMAN, SYDELL. "A Preliminary Study of Norms for the Thematic Apperception Test." Abstract. *Am Psychol* 2:271 Ag '47. * (*PA* 21:4374, title only)

80. BETTELHEIM, BRUNO. "Self-Interpretation of Fantasy: The Thematic Apperception Test as an Educational and Therapeutic Device." *Am J Orthopsychiatry* 17:80-100 Ja '47. * (*PA* 21:2315)

81. COLEMAN, WILLIAM. "The Thematic Apperception Test: I, Effects of Recent Experience; II, Some Quantitative Observations." *J Clin Psychol* 3:257-64 Jl '47. * (*PA* 22:208)

82. COMBS, ARTHUR W. "A Comparative Study of Motivations as Revealed in Thematic Apperception Stories and Autobiography." *J Clin Psychol* 3:65-75 Ja '47. * (*PA* 21:2318)

83. DEABLER, HERDIS L. "The Psychotherapeutic Use of the Thematic Apperception Test." *J Clin Psychol* 3:246-52 Jl '47. * (*PA* 22:314)

84. ERICSON, MARTHA. "A Study of the Thematic Apperception Test as Applied to a Group of Disturbed Children." Abstract. *Am Psychol* 2:272 Ag '47. * (*PA* 21:4499, title only)

85. HENRY, WILLIAM E. "The Thematic Apperception Technique in the Study of Culture-Personality Relations." *Genetic Psychol Monogr* 35:3-135 F '47. * (*PA* 21:1957)

86. JENSEN, MILTON B., AND ROTTER, JULIAN B. "The Value of Thirteen Psychological Tests in Officer Candidate Screening." *J Appl Psychol* 31:312-22 Je '47. * (*PA* 21:4107)

87. KLEBANOFF, SEYMOUR G. "Personality Factors in Symptomatic Chronic Alcoholism as Indicated by the Thematic Apperception Test." *J Consult Psychol* 11:111-9 My-Je '47. * (*PA* 22:410)

88. LAURIERS, AUSTIN DES, AND HALPERN, FLORENCE. "Psychological Tests in Childhood Schizophrenia." *Am J Orthopsychiatry* 17:57-67 Ja '47. *

89. LEITCH, MARY, AND SCHAFER, SARAH. "A Study of the Thematic Apperception Tests of Psychotic Children." *Am J Orthopsychiatry* 17:337-42 Ap '47. * (*PA* 21:3632)

90. MAYMAN, MARTIN, AND KUTNER, BERNARD. "Reliability in Analyzing Thematic Apperception Test Stories." *J Abn & Social Psychol* 42:365-8 Jl '47. * (*PA* 22:1217)

91. ROSENZWEIG, SAUL, AND ISHAM, A. C. "Complementary Thematic Apperception Test Patterns in Close Kin." *Am J Orthopsychiatry* 17:129-42 Ja '47. * (*PA* 21:2331)

92. SISK, HENRY L. "A Clinical Case Study Utilizing the Rorschach and the Murray Thematic Apperception Tests." *J Clin Psychol* 3:293-8 Jl '47. * (*PA* 22:310)

93. SYMONDS, PERCIVAL M. "Interpreting the Picture-Story (TAT) Method." Abstract. *Am Psychol* 2:288-9 Ag '47. * (*PA* 21:4397, title only)

94. FRENCH, VERA V. "The Structure of Sentiments: II, A Preliminary Study of Sentiments." *J Personality* 16:78-108 S '47. * (*PA* 22:2512)

95. GOTHBERG, LAURA C. "A Comparison of the Personality of Runaway Girls With a Control Group as Expressed in the Themas of Murray's Thematic Apperception Test." *Am J Mental Def* 51:627-31 Ap '47. * (*PA* 22:1733)

96. LANDISBERG, SELMA. "A Personality Study of Institutionalized Epileptics." *Am J Mental Def* 52:16-22 Jl '47. *

97. MERCER, MARGARET, AND FUNDERBURG, JOE. "A Case of Drug Addiction (Rorschach, TAT, Vocational Interests)." *Rorschach Res Exch & J Proj Tech* 11(1):41-5 '47. *

98. TOMKINS, SILVAN S.; WITH THE COLLABORATION OF ELIZABETH J. TOMKINS. *The Thematic Apperception Test: The Theory and Technique of Interpretation.* New York: Grune & Stratton, Inc., 1947. Pp. xi, 297. $5.50. * (*PA* 22:1658)

99. WYATT, FREDERICK. "The Interpretation of the Thematic Apperception Test." *Rorschach Res Exch & J Proj Tech* 11(1): 21-5 '47. * (*PA* 22:1231)

100. WYATT, FREDERICK. "The Scoring and Analysis of the Thematic Apperception Test." *J Psychol* 24:319-30 O '47. *

101. WEKSTEIN, LOUIS. "X-Raying the Personality: An Interpretative Evaluation of Two Projection Techniques." *Scientific Mo* 65:133-42 Ag '47. * (*PA* 22:220)

Arthur L. Benton, Associate Professor of Psychology, University of Louisville School of Medicine, Louisville, Kentucky. The *Thematic Apperception Test* is a projective technique consisting of 20 pictures, the nature of which differs in certain instances according to the age and sex of the subject. The subject is requested to make up a story about each picture—to construct a plot about the characters indicating what they are doing, what events have led up to the pictured situation, how the situation is going to turn out, etc. The purpose of the test is to elicit the dominant "thema" in the subject's life, i.e., the drives, tensions, relationships, conflicts, and environmental pressures that have played a determining role in his behavior. These thema are inferred from analyses of the subject's stories, the fundamental assumption underlying the test being that the tensions, relationships, etc., projected in his stories represent actual past or present tensions, relationships, etc., of the subject.

This review will be for the most part a brief examination of some of the empirical data bearing upon this fundamental assumption. A sizable body of literature has accumulated on this topic, most of which provides favorable suggestive, rather than critical, evidence. Among the more critical assessments may be mentioned the reports of Harrison (8, 9), Murray and Stein (32), and Combs (61, 62, 63).

Harrison gave the test to 40 psychiatric patients whose backgrounds were unknown to him. Utilizing a personally developed method of analysis which "was eclectic and emphasized common-sense psychology," he found that a good deal of biographical and personality data could be inferred from the patients' performances (83 per cent agreement with case history data). In 39 of the 40 cases the test performances yielded sufficient information for the investigator to venture to offer a psychiatric diagnosis. The inferred diagnosis was correct in 30 cases (77 per cent). The validity of a "blind diagnosis" of the TAT records of 15 other patients was investigated. A slightly smaller amount of biographical and personality data was inferred (75 per cent agreement with case history data). In 11 of the 15 cases the inferred psychiatric diagnosis was correct (73 per cent).

Murray and Stein, using only 5 pictures which were adapted for group use by projection on a screen and having the subjects write their stories, report that it was possible to make judgments concerning the leadership qualifications of a group of officer candidates which correlated fairly well (rho = .65) with the judgments of the candidates' superior officers.

Combs, employing a method of analysis "which would be consistent with accepted psychological theory and in agreement with accepted clinical practice," compared TAT stories written by college students with their written autobiographies. He found that 31 per cent of the written stories included significant thema drawn from their own life experience, as indicated by autobiography. The individual pictures varied greatly in respect to their effectiveness in eliciting such thema, ranging from 58 per cent for Picture 2 to 5 per cent for Picture 11 (1943 edition).

The clinical significance of the various types of behavior elicited by the test and of the contextual and formal characteristics which may appear in the stories has been noted by many workers. Sound interpretation of a subject's performance requires considerable experience and skill and, above all, a sound, workable knowledge of psychology and psychopathology on the part of the examiner. Murray's (4) dictum that "one must know a lot to comprehend a little" applies with particular force to the problem of interpreting the segments of behavior elicited by a TAT or a Rorschach.

One can say that the general validity of the test is fairly well established if one means that in the hands of a competent examiner the test data permit true, meaningful inferences. At the present time the greatest hindrance to its usefulness is the lack of normative data on the test productions, and the collection of such data would seem to be a necessary step in the development of the test as a clinical tool.

Julian B. Rotter, Associate Professor of Psychology, The Ohio State University, Columbus, Ohio. The *Thematic Apperception Test* (TAT) is a projective device which purports to reveal the basic personality characteristics of individuals by interpreting the stories they tell or "imagine" about a series of pictures. It is expected to reveal to the trained interpreter the subject's more central conflicts, attitudes, and goals as well as underlying inhibited motivations which the subject cannot or will not admit as he is unaware of them. Unfortunately, these personality characteristics are not revealed in some simple or direct manner, but they appear mixed with cultural stereotypes, relatively unimportant recent events, and non-ego involved attitudes, and may reflect immediate emotional experiences.

The clinician or experimenter seeking to find basic personality characteristics has the problem of separating the basic or central characteristics from the more superficial, the immediate and specific from the more permanent and generalized, the cultural stereotypes from the idiosyncratic responses, and the directly reflected attitudes and conflicts from the distorted ones.

Like other projective devices dealing with content material, TAT stories may be analyzed in a variety of ways, and a number of articles have been published attesting to the value of the TAT by clinicians interested in divergent problems and with marked differences in personality theory. These differences include interest in "disease entity" diagnoses, in symbolic interpretations along freudian dream lines, and in "common sense" behavioral description. The method of reducing stories to a system of "needs and presses" advocated by Murray in the manual for the test is not followed by many clinicians. To the reviewer it appears to tend to mask important individual differences and to be too closely tied to a theory of personality which has not been fully validated. In addition to the test author's brief manual, somewhat different methods of analysis and procedure have been published by Rapaport (73), Henry (85), and Rotter (78) and still other manuals are in preparation.

Many investigators using projective techniques for clinical purposes are generally agreed that test-retest reliability is of little significance as the characteristics measured may change, the attitude towards the test and the stimulus-function of the material may change, or superficial content may change between testings. Split-half reliabilities are not appropriate as the tests are not made up of equivalent items which can be conveniently divided into comparable halves. Inter-scorer reliability is of greater concern as it tests the stability of interpretations from one investigator to another. Harrison and Rotter (48) found a reliability of .77 on a five-point rating scale for emotional stability of officer candidates for interpretations made from five written stories by two psychologists. Combs (61) using agreement between judges in determining the "needs" expressed in TAT stories from a list similar to Murray's found 50 to 60 per cent agreement.

Harrison (8, 9) has presented a statistical, controlled study of validity. He showed high validity for "blind guesses" regarding descriptive characteristics which could be checked against an adequate case history. Although this study established the validity of the hypothesis that people "projected" or reflected their personal experience in their stories, it did not wholly validate it for its more common use for "depth" interpretations. In this same study, guesses of IQ for 37 cases correlated .78 with obtained Stanford–Binet IQ's.

There are several different sets of pictures in use but the one in most common use is that of Murray's published in 1943. A number of investigators have felt that the more bizarre and abstract pictures in this set are less productive with children and adults of average and low ability than ones which contain real people with whom the subject can easily identify. An experimental study by Gerver (68) recently demonstrated this for children ages five to ten.

Although some crude attempts at collection of normative data which can serve as a background for interpretations have been made, the lack of standard methods of analysis and procedure for different investigators has prohibited combination of the results. Individuals have tended to use their own experience for implicit norms, and the beginning user is generally at a loss to understand in what way the subject's productions are unusual and significant.

In spite of the limitations of nonstandard procedure and lack of experimental evidence of reliability and validity for the different methods of analysis, this kind of technique reveals to many examiners the kind of information they find most helpful for making judgments regarding diagnosis and treatment, and its value as a clinical tool is considered unquestioned by those who have had sufficient practical experience with it.

However, in its present state of development the TAT cannot be considered as a clinical instrument apart from the person who uses it. The value, significance, nature, and validity of the tests are dependent upon the interpreter, his experience, and his approach to the field of personality. Different examiners may use the TAT as a source of material for finding characteristics of the subject which each thinks is important and significant. In one case the clinician may use the TAT solely for help in determining diagnostic characterizations of a subject's behavior; another may use it only to find what he considers to be the important emotional relationships of the subject to the world in which he lives. In all cases interpretations from the TAT should be considered as *hypotheses* or leads for further investigation.

J. R. Wittenborn, Assistant Professor of Psychology, Yale University, New Haven, Connecticut. The *Thematic Apperception Test,* a story-telling projective device, has been developed largely through the efforts of Henry A. Murray (4). The formal testing procedure recommended by him is set forth in a manual of directions which accompanies the set of twenty stimulus pictures. This procedure for the administration of the test requires both careful observation of the subject as he produces his stories and expert inquiry into the origins, implications, and extenuations of the responses. This is a time-consuming procedure, and the tester, if he is to profit both from his observations and the inquiry, should not only be an expert clinician but also be acquainted with the history of the subject.

Another procedure for administration is described by Rapaport (73), and in the literature there is indication that a variety of devices have been employed to secure responses to pictures in the form of stories or dramas. The story-telling technique is an extremely flexible device and the *Thematic Apperception Test* pictures may be used in a variety of ways. For example, the writer in his work with college students has found that the following procedure is not only economical of administration time but also highly rewarding in the quality of the stories produced: ten of the Murray pictures known to elicit clinically useful material are presented with instructions that they constitute a test of creative imagination and that the student is to write a highly dramatic incident about each. Invariably college students accept this as a challenge to their imagination and produce stories which usually exceed in richness those elicited through individual, formal administration.

Because of the all too prevalent limitations of time and clinically trained personnel, the use of the *Thematic Apperception Test* as Murray recommends is almost prohibitive. Nevertheless, because of the richness of the material which the pictures elicit and the useful insight which they afford, their general use in both vocational and educational guidance is to be recommended. For these reasons, the flexibility of the story-telling device should always be recognized, and local procedures devised which make its frequent application feasible.

The exhaustive interpretation of the productions described by Murray in the manual is not always employed by those who use his pictures. The sheer labor of his analysis or interpretation may in some instances exceed not only the time available for analysis but perhaps the demands of the case as well. His concepts of personality, moreover, are somewhat different from those held by many clinical workers. Accordingly, the procedures actually employed in interpretations are probably as varied as the procedures employed in administration.

The quality of the interpretations seems to this writer to be based on at least three characteristics of the interpreter: general knowledge of behavioral dynamics, including symbolism and other expressions of a dynamic unconscious; experience in guidance or therapy with the type of problems under investigation; and experience in observing the relationships between the content of the *Thematic Apperception Test* productions and the content of subjects' problems and their neurotic expressions.

The use made of TAT material naturally varies with the needs of the case, the habits and skill of the counselor, and the policy of the clinic or guidance bureau. The *Thematic Apperception Test* gives an expression of the content of the individual's problem, whereas the Rorschach expresses the structure of his personality. In this statement the word "content" should not be taken too literally, for the thematic productions not only give evidence of the nature of the individual's problems but also indicate his characteristic modes of reaction and the intensity of his conflicts. Such data have great value in guidance, short-term therapy, and psychiatric diagnosis (73). In almost any situation in which a serious effort is made to understand the individual, the *Thematic Apperception Test* in some of

its possible modifications will be found to be a genuinely good and useful technique.

Aside from their obvious value in the appraisal of an individual, the TAT stories may have exceptional value when employed in the interview as a means of guiding or facilitating the course of guidance or therapy. The writer has found in work with college students and adults numerous individuals who in the interview can read over, elaborate upon, and interpret their own *Thematic Apperception Test* productions. This procedure may have a supportive value for many cases and may be very useful for insight therapy.

There is little to be said about the standardization and objectification of a projective instrument such as the *Thematic Apperception Test*. Although it would be of academic interest and of probable clinical value to know how the thema vary with the society in which the individual lives, his age, his sex, and his status in society, true standardization of this device must wait for a theory of personality which is worthy of the name. In the meantime, norms for interpretation accrue from the experience of the clinician, and the chief validation of the test lies in the clinician's satisfaction with its use.

A recent review of the literature on the *Thematic Apperception Test* has been prepared by Martin Mayman and includes a useful bibliography (71).

Brit J Psychol 36:107 Ja '46. This revised form....consists of 30 pictures, and a manual of instructions and procedure. A brief description of methods of analysing the results is also given. The test is now suitable for use with men, women or children.

For related reviews, see 104 and 104a.

[104]

★[*Re* Thematic Apperception Test.] CLARK, RUTH MILLBURN. **A Method of Administering and Evaluating the Thematic Apperception Test in Group Situations.** Genetic Psychology Monographs, Vol. 30, No. 1. Provincetown, Mass.: Journal Press, August 1944. Pp. 55. Paper. $4.00. * (*PA* 18:3777)

J Consult Psychol 9:309 N-D '45. *Percival M. Symonds.* * There will undoubtedly be a number of attempts to find methods of scoring projective techniques. This reviewer, however, is of the opinion that not only will such methods prove of little value but that attempts to use the results of projective techniques along psychometric lines will bypass the more valuable methods of a direct analysis of the stories and the themes they contain. This study proves little because there is no reference to independent judgments of the individuals who are subjects in the study. It may be of interest to know that two different methods of evaluating the Thematic Apperception test lead to similar results. Of considerable more importance, however, would be to know that the Thematic Apperception test agrees with other and independent evidence concerning the personality characteristics of these same subjects. The student of projective techniques will be interested in the schedule for the analysis of the material which contains five headings. * This study is an honest attempt to find an objective method of evaluating the results of the Thematic Apperception test but its failure to measure the results against an independent criterion limits its value.

[104a]

★[Re Thematic Apperception Test.] TOMKINS, SILVAN S.; WITH THE COLLABORATION OF ELIZABETH J. TOMKINS. **The Thematic Apperception Test: The Theory and Technique of Interpretation.** New York: Grune & Stratton, Inc., 1947. Pp. xi, 297. $5.50. * (*PA* 22:1658)

J Consult Psychol 12:61 Ja-F '48. Tomkins' book is a substantial contribution to the literature of the TAT, perhaps the first sizable book intended primarily as a manual for this test. Chapters review the history and development of the TAT, administration, scoring (which departs somewhat from usual methods), and level analysis. The major part of the volume is then devoted to diagnosis in the regions of family, of love, sex and marriage, of social relationships, and of vocation. The final chapter explores the use of the TAT in therapy. Throughout, the book is exceptionally rich in clinical illustrations that will be of value both to the student and to the experienced worker. The bibliography has 110 entries, a tribute to the vitality of a technique scarcely twelve years old.

[105]

★[Torgerson's Inventories and Record Forms.] Grades kgn-12; 1947; these inventories and record forms appear in Theodore L. Torgerson's *Studying Children* (Dryden Press, 1947); until such time as they are published as separates, permission to mimeograph the inventories and record forms may be obtained by writing the author at the University of Wisconsin; Theodore L. Torgerson.
a) CLASS SUMMARY OF BEHAVIOR SYMPTOMS AND DISABILITIES.
b) BEHAVIOR INVENTORIES.
c) HOME ENVIRONMENT INVENTORY.
d) SPEECH INVENTORY.
e) DEVELOPMENTAL INVENTORY OF BACKGROUND FACTORS.
f) CASE STUDY FORM.

REFERENCES
1. TORGERSON, THEODORE L. *Studying Children: Diagnostic and Remedial Procedures in Teaching.* New York: Dryden Press, Inc., 1947. Pp. x, 230. $2.75. * (*PA* 21:4656)

Harold H. Abelson, Associate Professor of Education and Director, Educational Clinic, The City College of New York, New York, New York. In conjunction with his book, *Studying Children,* Dr. Torgerson has prepared a series of pupil-study forms which he claims "will enable teachers to make effective and objective observations of children with a view to discovering problems and identifying disabling factors, (provide) an objective rating scale for evaluating standardized tests, (result in) a cumulative record of the child's mental, educational, physical, personal, and social development, (and help) teachers to systematize and facilitate the writing of case histories." The inventories and record forms appear in Chapters 3, 6, 8, and 9 of the text. The forms are published separately as well.

a) The *Class Summary of Behavior Symptoms and Disabilities* is a form for indicating the number of specific symptoms or disabilities noted for each child under various subheadings arranged under the larger heading of scholarship, reading, spelling, arithmetic, vision, hearing, health, social behavior, and speech.

b) Used in connection with the foregoing Class Summary is a series of *Behavior Inventories,* corresponding to each of the major headings previously enumerated. In all, over two hundred characteristics are presented. No distinction is made in the tabulation as to the importance of the several items.

c) The *Home Environment Inventory* consists of a list of forty-three negatively expressed characteristics of such home factors as child training, parent-child relationships, child-to-child relationships, and socio-economic status. The record form itself makes provision for checking the statements that apply to each pupil.

d) The *Test Rating Scale* assigns numerical weight to "two major criteria: (1) validity and (2) reliability, and three minor criteria: (1) scoring, (2) norms, and (3) administration." A maximum of 50 points is given for validity, 25 for reliability, and so on down to 5 for administration. Detailed tables show just how many points to assign for such supposed indicators of the worth of the test as validity coefficients and reliability coefficients.

e) In the study of individual cases there is added a *Developmental Inventory of Back-*

ground Factors (case history) consisting of thirty-five items. This is to be used in addition to the *Behavior Inventories* previously described. In addition a *Case Study Form* is provided for summarizing various features of the case.

It should be added that the entire book explains how these various forms, along with such other approaches as anecdotal records, interview, and standard test procedures, can be used in a comprehensive program of child study in the school situation. The book concludes with an enumeration of 120 "practices and conditions essential in an effective child study program."

The forms developed by Dr. Torgerson will undoubtedly be appraised differently by persons with different backgrounds. Few clinically oriented child guidance workers whose concern is with dynamic relationships within the child will find palatable the atomic, enumerative approach implicit in the use of the inventories. The *Test Rating Scale,* with its almost indiscriminate application of numerical ratings to qualities that require finely differentiated interpretations, should have very little appeal to anyone. On the other hand, the beginning teacher may find the concrete aids developed by Dr. Torgerson helpful in directing attention to aspects of the child that might otherwise be overlooked and in encouraging active experimentation with child study procedures.

[106]

V.G.C. Personality Adjustment Indicator or Inventory. Grades 9-16; 1944; an adaptation of Hugh M. Bell's *Adjustment Inventory,* Student Form (40:1200); Form S; separate answer sheets must be used; $2.25 per 25; 40¢ per 25 answer sheets; 25¢ per specimen set; specimen sets must be purchased to obtain the manual; nontimed (25) minutes; adaptation by M. D. Parmenter; Vocational Guidance Centre.

For reviews of Bell's Adjustment Inventory by S. J. Beck, Raymond B. Cattell, John G. Darley, J. P. Guilford, Doncaster G. Humm, C. M. Louttit, Percival M. Symonds and Austin H. Turney, see 38:912 and 40:1200.

[107]

Vineland Social Maturity Scale. Birth to maturity; 1935-47; individual; 1 form; $1.25 per 25 record blanks; 72¢ per manual (1947); $1 per specimen set; 20(30) minutes; Edgar A. Doll; formerly published by Vineland Training School; Educational Test Bureau.

REFERENCES

1. DOLL, EDGAR A. "The Clinical Significance of Social Maturity." *J Mental Sci* 81:766-82 O '35. * (*PA* 10:2526)
2. DOLL, EDGAR A. "A Genetic Scale of Social Maturity." *Am J Orthopsychiatry* 5:180-90 Ap '35. * (*PA* 9:5808)
3. DOLL, EDGAR A. "The Measurement of Social Competence." *J Psycho-Asthenics* 40:103-26 '35. * (*PA* 10:1491)
4. DOLL, EDGAR A. "The Vineland Social Maturity Scale." *Training Sch B* 32:1-7, 25-32, 48-55, 68-74 Mr, Ap, My, Je '35. * (*PA* 9:3374, 5135)
5. DOLL, EDGAR A. "Mental Age Versus Social Age." *Proc Nat Conf Juvenile Agencies* 32(5) '36. (*PA* 11:1990, title only)
6. DOLL, EDGAR A. "Idiot, Imbecile, and Moron." *J Appl Psychol* 20:427-37 Ag '36. * (*PA* 11:266)
7. DOLL, EDGAR A. "Preliminary Standardization of the Vineland Social Maturity Scale." *Am J Orthopsychiatry* 6:283-93 Ap '36. * (*PA* 10:5471, title only)
8. MCKAY, B. ELIZABETH. "Social Maturity of the Pre-School Blind Child." *Training Sch B* 33:146-55 N '36. * (*PA* 11:1133)
9. BRADWAY, KATHERINE PRESTON. "The Social Competence of Deaf Children." *Am Ann Deaf* 82:122-40 Mr '37. * (*PA* 11:2819)
10. BRADWAY, KATHERINE PRESTON. "Social Competence of Exceptional Children: I, Measurements of Social Competence." *J Excep Child* 4:1-8+ O '37. * (*PA* 11:5987)
11. BRADWAY, KATHERINE PRESTON. "Social Competence of Exceptional Children: II, The Mentally Subnormal." *J Excep Child* 4:38-42 N '37. * (*PA* 12:1384)
12. BRADWAY, KATHERINE PRESTON. "Social Competence of Exceptional Children: III, The Deaf, the Blind, and the Crippled." *J Excep Child* 4:64-9 D '37. * (*PA* 12:1511)
13. DOLL, EDGAR A. "How Old Is Anne, Socially?" *Hygeia* 15:894-7 O '37. * (*PA* 12:384)
14. DOLL, EDGAR A. "The Inheritance of Social Competence." *J Hered* 28:153-65, discussion 165-6 My '37. * (*PA* 12:273)
15. DOLL, EDGAR A. "A Practical Method for the Measurement of Social Competence." *Eug R* 29:197-200 O '37. * (*PA* 12:1525)
16. DOLL, EDGAR A., AND LONGWELL, S. GERALDINE. "Social Competence of the Feeble-Minded Under Extra-Institutional Care." *Psychiatric Q* 11:450-64 Jl '37. * (*PA* 12:1397)
17. DOLL, EDGAR A., AND MCKAY, B. ELIZABETH. "The Social Competence of Special Class Children." *J Ed Res* 31:90-106 O '37. * (*PA* 12:274)
18. "Publications on the Vineland Social Maturity Scale." *Training Sch B* 35:57-9 Ap '38. * (*PA* 13:1039, title only)
19. BRADWAY, KATHERINE P. "Social Competence of Grade School Children." *J Exp Ed* 6:326-31 Mr '38. * (*PA* 12:5990)
20. DOLL, EDGAR A., AND FITCH, KATHRYN A. "Social Competence of Delinquent Boys." *J Psycho-Asthenics* 43:137-41 '38. * (*PA* 13:2664)
21. DOLL, EDGAR A., AND LONGWELL, S. GERALDINE. "Social Competence of Feeble-Minded in Family Care." *J Psycho-Asthenics* 43:211-6 '38. * (*PA* 13:2500)
22. STRENG, ALICE, AND KIRK, SAMUEL A. "The Social Competence of Deaf and Hard-of-Hearing Children in a Public Day School." *Am Ann Deaf* 83:244-54 My '38. * (*PA* 13:1286)
23. BASSETT, DOROTHY M.; LONGWELL, S. GERALDINE; AND VON BULOW, HARRY. "Social and Occupational Competence of Idiots." *J Psycho-Asthenics* 44:97-102 '39. * (*PA* 14:3500)
24. DOLL, EDGAR A. "Growth Studies in Social Competence." *J Psycho-Asthenics* 44:90-6 '39. * (*PA* 14:3631)
25. DOLL, EDGAR A., AND FITCH, KATHRYN A. "Social Competence of Juvenile Delinquents." *J Am Inst Crim Law & Criminol* 30:52-67 My-Je '39. * (*PA* 13:6397)
26. WILSON, MARGARET T. *A Comparison of the 1937 Revision of the Stanford-Binet With the Vineland Social Maturity Scale.* Unpublished master's thesis, Fordham University, 1939. (*Dissertations . . . ,* 1940, pp. 103-4)
27. DOLL, EDGAR A. "Annotated Bibliography on the Vineland Social Maturity Scale." *J Consult Psychol* 4:123-32 Jl-Ag '40. * (*PA* 14:5730)
28. DOLL, EDGAR A. "The Social Basis of Mental Diagnosis." *J Appl Psychol* 24:160-9, Ap '40. * (*PA* 14:4581)
29. GOODMAN, ALICE WHITEMAN. "Deviation of Social Competence in Selected Epileptics." *Am J Orthopsychiatry* 11:104-10 Ja '41.* (*PA* 15:1760)
30. LOUTTIT, C. M., AND WATSON, RUTH. "Vineland Social Maturity Scores of Entering First Grade Children." *Training Sch B* 38:133-7 N '41. * (*PA* 16:1272)
31. LURIE, LOUIS A.; NEWBURGER, MAURICE; ROSENTHAL, FLORENCE M.; AND OUTCALT, LOUISA C. "Intelligence Quotient and Social Quotient: Diagnostic and Prognostic Significance of Differences." *Am J Orthopsychiatry* 11:111-7 Ja '41. * (*PA* 15:2860)
32. OTNESS, H. ROBERT. "Educating for Social Competence." *Training Sch B* 38:21-32 Ap '41. * (*PA* 15:3597)
33. PORTEUS, STANLEY D.; WITH THE ASSISTANCE OF MARY HUNTER AND COLIN J. HERRICK. *The Practice of Clinical Psychology,* pp. 164-73. New York: American Book Co., 1941. Pp. ix, 579. $3.25. * (*PA* 15:4248)
34. POWELL, LEE, AND LASLETT, H. R. "A Survey of the Social Development of the 10th, 11th, and 12th Grade Pupils in a Small High School." *J Exp Ed* 9:361-3 Je '41. * (*PA* 15:4746)
35. SPRINGER, N. NORTON. "The Social Competence of Adolescent Delinquents: A Comparative Study of White and Negro First Offenders and Recidivists." *J Social Psychol* 14:337-48 N '41. * (*PA* 16:2395)
36. WATTS, FREDERICK P. "A Comparative Clinical Study of Delinquent and Non-Delinquent Negro Boys." *J Negro Ed* 10:190-207 Ap '41. * (*PA* 15:3550)
37. WILSON, MARGARET T. "Social Competence of Normal and Defective Twins." *Am J Orthopsychiatry* 11:300-3 Ap '41. * (*PA* 15:4313)
38. BURCHARD, EDWARD M. L., AND MYKLEBUST, HELMER R. "A Comparison of Congenital and Adventitious Deafness With Respect to Its Effect on Intelligence, Personality, and Social

Maturity: Part II, Social Maturity." *Am Ann Deaf* 87:241-51 My '42. * (*PA* 17:220)

39. DEACON, KATHRYN FITCH. "An Experiment in the Cottage Training of Low-Grade Defectives." *Am J Mental Def* 47:195-202 O '42. * (*PA* 17:849)

40. DOLL, EDGAR A. "Measurement of Social Maturity Applied to Older People," pp. 138-46. In *Mental Health in Later Maturity: Papers Presented at a Conference Held in Washington, D. C., May 23-24, 1941.* Supplement No. 168 to the Public Health Reports. Washington, D. C.: Government Printing Office, 1942. Pp. v, 147. Paper. $0.20. * (*PA* 20:3683)

41. DOLL, EDGAR A. "Social Age as a Basis for Classification and Training." *Am J Mental Def* 47:49-57 Jl '42. * (*PA* 16:5009)

42. DOLL, EDGAR A., AND BROOKS, JAMES J. "The Therapeutic Uses of the Vineland Social Maturity Scale and Its Application to Adult Prisoners." *J Crim Psychopath* 3:347-58 Ja '42. * (*PA* 16:2798)

43. LURIE, LOUIS A.; ROSENTHAL, FLORENCE M.; AND OUTCALT, LOUISA C. "Diagnostic and Prognostic Significance of the Differences Between the Intelligence Quotient and the Social Quotient: II, Relationship of Intelligence Quotient and Social Quotient to Age Level of Behavior Problem Children." *Am J Orthopsychiatry* 12:104-14 Ja '42. * (*PA* 16:2929)

44. MAXFIELD, KATHRYN ERROLL, AND FJELD, HARRIETT ANDERSON. "The Social Maturity of the Visually Handicapped Preschool Child." *Child Develop* 13:1-27 Mr '42. * (*PA* 16:2930)

45. MORALES, NOEMI. "The Social Competence of Idiots." *Am J Mental Def* 47:209-14 O '42. * (*PA* 17:867)

46. DOLL, EDGAR A. "Measurement of Social Maturity Applied to Older People." *Training Sch B* 40:69-77 Je '43. * (*PA* 17:3859)

47. PATTERSON (PETERSON), C. H. "The Vineland Social Maturity Scale and Some of Its Correlates." *J Genetic Psychol* 62:275-87 Je '43. * (*PA* 18:821)

48. GAMBARO, PROVIDENCE K. "Analysis of Vineland Social Maturity Scale." *Am J Mental Def* 48:359-63 Ap '44. * (*PA* 19:1996)

49. LINK, HENRY C. "The Definition of Social Effectiveness and Leadership Through Measurement." *Ed & Psychol Meas* 4:57-67 sp '44. * (*PA* 18:3216)

50. ORDAHL, GEORGE; KEYT, NELLIE L.; AND WRIGHT, CLARE. "The Social Competence of High-Grade Mental Defectives Determined by Self-Report." *Am J Mental Def* 48:367-73 Ap '44. * (*PA* 19:1952)

51. CAPWELL, DORA F. "Personality Patterns of Adolescent Girls: I, Girls Who Show Improvement in IQ." *J Appl Psychol* 29:212-28 Je '45. * (*PA* 19:3033)

52. CAPWELL, DORA F. "Personality Patterns of Adolescent Girls: II, Delinquents and Non-Delinquents." *J Appl Psychol* 29:289-97 Ag '45. * (*PA* 20:191)

53. DOLL, EDGAR A. "Influence of Environment and Etiology on Social Competence." *Am J Mental Def* 50:89-94 Jl '45. * (*PA* 20:2409)

54. WHITCOMB, MARIAN A. "A Comparison of Social and Intellectual Levels of 100 High-Grade Adult Mental Defectives." *Am J Mental Def* 50:257-62 O '45. * (*PA* 20:2850)

55. BODMAN, FRANK. "Social Maturity Test." *J Mental Sci* 92:532-41 Jl '46. * (*PA* 21:184)

56. BROWER, JUDITH F., AND BROWER, DANIEL. "The Relation Between Temporal Judgment and Social Competence in the Feebleminded." *Am J Mental Def* 52:619-23 Ap '47. * (*PA* 22:1728)

57. DUNSDON, M. I. "Notes on the Intellectual and Social Capacities of a Group of Young Delinquents." *Brit J Psychol* 38:62-6 D '47. *

58. LANDISBERG, SELMA. "A Personality Study of Institutionalized Epileptics." *Am J Mental Def* 52:16-22 Jl '47. *

C. M. Louttit, Professor of Psychology and Dean of the Undergraduate Division, University of Illinois, Galesburg, Illinois. The *Vineland Social Maturity Scale*, first published in 1935, has been so widely used that it hardly needs extended comment. As a means of evaluating social competency, this scale is a unique instrument, being neither test, nor rating scale, nor questionnaire. The present reviewer has used the scale both clinically and for research since its first publication and is particularly struck by the former function where four principle values may be enumerated: (*a*) In the differential diagnosis between mental deficiency and physical or personality conditions which

result in subnormal achievement in verbal learning which is commonly the criterion of psychological inadequacy. (*b*) The scale provides a systematic description of actual behavior as observed day by day in a variety of situations. Without some type of guide, the questioning of parents or other informants concerning a child's behavior is very apt to produce a picture colored by the informant's prejudices and by the interviewer's lapses or preconceived ideas. Further, in this respect, the use of the scale frequently helps to establish rapport with parents and to make it easier for them to describe behavior. (*c*) Both of the preceding values are pertinent in the study of children with personality and conduct problems. Comparison of responses given by mother and father or by other persons significant in the child's environment sometimes reveals differences in attitudes important in the etiology of the complained-of behavior. (*d*) Finally, the methodology of the scale provides a means of securing an evaluation of behavior level without subjecting the child to possibly disturbing conditions such as may be encountered in the usual type of test. Also, the data for evaluation may be secured by observation of the subject, or from reports of several observers who are in prolonged contact with the child.

There is a real need for a systematic analysis of the abundant literature on this scale. The present manual is primarily a guide only and needs extensive supplementation, especially in respect to the data on standardization and the empirically determined information for clinical interpretation. Such an enlarged manual has been in preparation for some time and it is hoped will appear shortly.

John W. M. Rothney, Associate Professor of Education, The University of Wisconsin, Madison, Wisconsin. This scale does not purport to be a psychometric test system although both point-scale and age-scale techniques are used. It is not intended to be a rating scale but rather a guided interview with someone who knows something about the behavior of some person between the ages of birth and twenty-five plus. The behavior is described in terms of self-help and self-direction generally, and particularly with respect to eating, dressing, locomotion, communication, social relations and occupation. The evidence is "hearsay" rather than the result of direct observation. Cautions

addressed to the interviewer about the possibilities of bias, or distortion by attitude and
questioning methods, suggest that only the
most skillful and thoroughly trained interviewers would obtain similar evidence about the
same subjects. Scoring is highly subjective and
there would be no objection to this if the standards were not as specific as those given in the
table of social-age values. These values are
based upon the appraisal of 620 subjects composed of ten normal persons of each sex from
ages birth to thirty.

There is need for a scale of this kind and
this reviewer is in sympathy with all the stated
objectives of the author. He also approves
highly of the attempt to get away from rating
which involves the making of observations and
judgments simultaneously. He does, however,
question the value of using standards which
suggest rather refined measurements when the
user of the scale, even if he is trained as fully
as the author suggests, is allowed so much
freedom in gathering the data.

The author promises a book with more data
and more information about his scale. Until it
appears it would seem desirable to restrict the
use of the scale to the purpose of getting supplementary materials for the preparation of
case histories. At present it appears that it
could be used very effectively in the discussion
of a person's behavior with parents, teachers,
and employers and in teaching them about general stages of development which can be expected at various age levels. The manual contains 59 references to articles about the scale
in which such uses are proposed. Study of
these references will convince the clinician that
he should have some forms of the scale available for use when the occasion arises.

J Consult Psychol 11:158 My-Je '47. * The
scale is neither a test nor a questionnaire, but
a series of behavioral observations, ranging
through "does not drool," "eats with fork,"
"bathes self assisted," "makes telephone calls,"
"buys all own clothing," to "advances general
welfare." The user of the scale is enjoined to
obtain in detail the facts on which to base the
scoring of each item. Herein lies a potential
weakness, not of the scale itself, but of those
who may use it to evaluate inadequate or unreliable observations and reports. The items
are subdivided into categories: self-help (general, eating, dressing), locomotion, occupation,

communication, self-direction, and socialization,
which permit some diagnostic use. The final
rating is a point score of the number of items
passed, which is converted to a Social Age by
means of a table. The scale is a valuable instrument for psychologists who recognize the wide
value of developmental studies, including aspects of personality in addition to intellect.

*For reviews by Paul H. Furfey, Elaine F.
Kinder, and Anna S. Starr of Experimental
Form B, see 38:1143.*

[108]

★Visual Motor Gestalt Test. Ages 4 and over; 1938–
46; individual; 1 form; $1 per set of cards and booklet
of instructions; $3.50 per copy of the complete manual
A Visual Motor Gestalt Test and Its Clinical Use;
(10) minutes; Lauretta Bender; American Orthopsychiatric Association, Inc.

REFERENCES
1. BENDER, LAURETTA. "Disturbances in Visuomotor Gestalt
Function in Organic Brain Disease Associated With Sensory
Aphasia." *Arch Neurol & Psychiatry* 30:514-37 S '33. * (PA
8:3581)
2. BENDER, LAURETTA. "Gestalt Function in Mental Defect."
J Psycho-Asthenics 38:88-104, discussion 104-6, 9 plates '33. *
(PA 8:1103)
3. SCHILDER, PAUL. "Space, Time and Perception." *Psyche*
14:124-38 '34. * (PA 9:4005)
4. BENDER, LAURETTA. "Gestalt Function in Visual Motor
Patterns in Organic Disease of the Brain: Including Dementia
Paralytica, Alcoholic Psychoses, Traumatic Psychoses and
Acute Confusional States." *Arch Neurol & Psychiatry* 33:
300-28, discussion 328-9 F '35. * (PA 9:5705)
5. BENDER, LAURETTA. *A Visual Motor Gestalt Test and Its
Clinical Use.* Preface by Paul Schilder. American Orthopsychiatric Association, Research Monographs, No. 3. New York:
the Association, 1938. Pp. xi, 176. $3.50. * (PA 13:1720)
6. SCHILDER, PAUL. "Notes on the Psychology of Metrazol
Treatment of Schizophrenia." *J Nerv & Mental Dis* 89:133-44
F '39. * (PA 14:356)
7. FABIAN, A. A. "Vertical Rotation in Visual-Motor Performance: Its Relationship to Reading Reversals." *J Ed Psychol* 36:129-54 Mr '45. * (PA 19:2363)
8. HUTT, MAX L. "The Use of Projective Methods of Personality Measurement in Army Medical Installations." *J Clin
Psychol* 1:134-40 Ap '45. * (PA 19:2250)

For related reviews, see 40:B843 and 109.

[109]

[*Re* Visual Motor Gestalt Test.] BENDER, LAURETTA.
A Visual Motor Gestalt Test and Its Clinical Use.
Preface by Paul Schilder. American Orthopsychiatric
Association, Research Monographs, No. 3. New York:
the Association, Inc., 1938. Pp. xi, 176. $3.50. * (*PA*
13:1720)

Am J Psychiatry 97:498–9 S '40. W. Line.
This monograph brings together some results
of the author's investigations previously published, and some new material. * The theoretical statements are hard to summarize, and at
this stage, to evaluate. The main facts are that
as children grow older their copies of presented
figures approach more and more closely those
of adults; that defective and abnormal subjects
often give primitive and bizarre performances;
that the variations from the original undoubtedly reflect phenomena that, if fully interpreted,
would be of great assistance to our psychologi-

cal understanding. But the procedure as adopted by the author as diagnostic, seeking differences in performance which characterize subjects of known and significant difference (e.g., age, degree of intelligence, pathology, etc.), and thence interpreting those differences by recourse to a somewhat elaborate story of perceptual unfolding. The validity and practical value of that story, as well as its clarification, must await further research. Undoubtedly, as Schilder affirms in his preface, it is clinically stimulating. It is too early, also, to comment very fully on the "Standardization of the Gestalt Function in a performance Test for Children" (chapter XI). The method is not reported in detail, and relatively few cases have as yet been used as subjects. The results to date are both interesting and promising. A final comment on the monograph as a whole. It is obviously ambitious in its scope, embracing as it does problems of development, deterioration and recovery. The general thesis is phenomenological, with frequent recourse to complex, broad and unclear concepts. The method is not rigidly experimental, and being diagnostic in its direction it leans heavily (for purposes of maintaining a "dynamic" rather than "static" outlook) on a great deal of somewhat speculative interpretation. The practical application or experimental verification of the theoretical formulations will accordingly be difficult. (The reviewer believes that the type of concept used does not lend itself to clear-cut investigation in these directions.) Nonetheless, the monograph represents a very stimulating contribution to a challenging and complex field.

J Abn & Social Psychol 36:128–9 Ja '41. M. A. Rickers–Ovsiankina. * Numerous reproductions of drawings offer very interesting material to those readers who are not familiar with these phenomena. Essentially they are not new, however, the novelty lying chiefly in very sweeping statements and theoretical generalizations made by the author. The theory expressed is certainly not a theory in the sense that it leads to predictions and conclusions or even factual statements of a specific nature. What is important to know is not that these influences exist but exactly in what way they are responsible for a particular perceptive phenomenon. The author forgets that psychologists themselves are very conscious of the fact that they have not yet mastered certain dynamic features of perception as well as of other fields of psychol-

ogy. More is needed, however, than just pointing this out. The clinical part of the book presents a contribution of greater value than the theoretical. One regrets only that so little use is made of statistics. Except for the chapter dealing with the standardization of the test on children, one never knows how frequent and consistent the described patterns of behavior are in the various clinical groups. The test gives an estimate of mental age in children and defectives in a way similar to the Goodenough test. The present test, however, since it employs meaningless figures, has the advantage that the picture of intelligence is not obscured by language and training. For the same reason it is valuable in following up the progress of transient states of mental disturbances, e.g. aphasia. With respect to malingering the study demonstrates the use of such drawing tests, when well standardized. In schizophrenia, manic-depressive psychosis, and psychoneurosis the subjects apparently behaved as one would expect a patient of that type to behave. On the whole, despite the criticisms which one might make especially of the theoretical section, the study is a stimulating one and the test has considerable promise for clinical purposes.

For additional reviews, see 40:B843.

[110]

Washburne Social-Adjustment Inventory, Thaspic Edition. Ages 12 and over; 1936–40; IBM; 1 form; separate answer sheets need not be used; $1.70 per 25; 20¢ per manual; 35¢ per specimen set, postpaid; $1.20 per 25 machine-scorable answer sheets; $2.40 per set of stencils for scoring answer sheets; nontimed (30-50) minutes; John N. Washburne; published in 1940 by the World Book Co.

REFERENCES

1-4. *See* 40:1262.
5. WASHBURNE, JOHN N. "Factors Related to the Social Adjustment of College Girls." *J Social Psychol* 13:281-9 My '41. * (*PA* 15:4721)
6. MUSSELMAN, JOHN W. "Factors Associated With the Achievement of High School Pupils of Superior Intelligence." *J Exp Ed* 11:53-68 S '42. * (*PA* 17:1363)
7. GORDON, HANS C., AND DAVIDOFF, PHILIP. "Honesty of Pupils in Answering Adjustment Questionnaires." *Sch & Soc* 57:54-6 Ja 9 '43. * (*PA* 17:1260)
8. MARSH, CHARLES J. "The Prognostic Value of the Washburne Social Adjustment Inventory." *J Social Psychol* 17:287-94 My '43. * (*PA* 17:3879)
9. CAPWELL, DORA F. "Personality Patterns of Adolescent Girls: I, Girls Who Show Improvement in IQ." *J Appl Psychol* 29:212-28 Je '45. * (*PA* 19:3033)
10. FORLANO, GEORGE, AND KIRKPATRICK, FORREST H. "Intelligence and Adjustment Measurements in the Selection of Radio Tube Mounters." *J Appl Psychol* 29:257-61 Ag '45. * (*PA* 20:283)
11. GOTHAM, R. E. "Personality and Teaching Efficiency." *J Exp Ed* 14:157-65 D '45. * (*PA* 20:2074)
12. ROLFE, J. F. "The Measurement of Teaching Ability: Study Number Two." *J Exp Ed* 14:52-74 S '45. * (*PA* 20:1268)
13. ROSTKER, L. E. "The Measurement of Teaching Ability: Study Number One." *J Exp Ed* 14:6-51 S '45. * (*PA* 20:1269)
14. FLEMMING, EDWIN G., AND FLEMMING, CECILE WHITE. "A Qualitative Approach to the Problem of Improving Selection of Salesmen by Psychological Tests." *J Psychol* 21:127-50 Ja '46. * (*PA* 20:1636)
15. GOULD, GEORGE. "The Predictive Value of Certain Selective Measures." *Ed Adm & Sup* 33:206-12 Ap '47. *

J Excep Child 7:212 F '41. Harold Postel. * will prove a valuable instrument for the secondary school or college counselor, dean, or psychologist that desires to secure a better adjustment for an individual, or that endeavors to select those students in need of psychiatric advice. The test is rather complicated in its administration and interpretation; the teacher not trained in testing and without some knowledge of mental hygiene would have difficulty in making proper use of the test. It is this reviewer's opinion that Dr. Washburne's inventory is best adapted for use by a specialist in the administration of an individual test, especially when it is used on the high school level. This psychometric scale is well constructed, the result of ten years of trial, revision, and improvement. It should find general favor in the secondary and college field, and will be a valuable aid in solving those problems of youth that are often responsible for serious social and academic maladjustments. The instrument will be increasingly used as teachers become more enlightened regarding the important role played by the use of mental hygiene in the development of a well-integrated personality.

J Nerv & Mental Dis 93:537–8 Ap '41. * an inventory designed to reveal in secondary school children divergences from the "norm" in social or affective maladjustment; thus calling the need for individual counsel and help to those charged with their guidance * If such necessarily rough classifications lead to the fulfillment of needed individual attention along mental hygiene lines, their use in group education is of value. But the whole approach of adjustment scales, tests, evaluations, etc., is so essentially superficial from the standpoint of the protean dynamic determinants of adjustment and maladjustment—to say nothing of the ever-present external social and economic determinants—that it is difficult to believe that any newcomer to the tribe is going to prove an exception to the rule.

For review by Daniel A. Prescott of the original edition, see 38:928.

[111]

★**Weitzman's Inventory of Social Behavior.** Ages 16-25; 1941; 1 form; $1.75 per 25; 40¢ per specimen set; nontimed (20) minutes; Ellis Weitzman; Sheridan Supply Co.

REFERENCES

1. WEITZMAN, ELLIS. *Test of Social Maturity and Its Use in Comparing People Sixteen Through Twenty-Four Years of Age.* Unpublished doctor's thesis, University of Nebraska, 1940. (*Abstracts of Doctoral Dissertations . . .*, 1940, pp. 94-100.)
2. WEITZMAN, ELLIS. "Note on a Test of Social Competence." *J Appl Psychol* 25:595-6 O '41. * (PA 16:1105)
3. WEITZMAN, ELLIS. "A Study of Social Maturity in Persons Sixteen Through Twenty-Four Years of Age." *J Genetic Psychol* 64:37-66 Mr '44. * (PA 18:2196)

Louis Long, Director of Division of Testing and Guidance and Assistant Professor, Department of Student Life, The City College of New York, New York, New York. An inventory, developed for the purpose of assessing the level of social maturity, and which consists of only 33 items, must necessarily sample a limited number of activities. Questions about the reliability and validity of the inventory cannot be satisfactorily answered by reading the manual. A test-retest reliability coefficient of .88, based upon 42 college students, is reported. A correlation of .55 between scores and chronological age is reported as indicative of the validity of the inventory. Further evidence of the validity is found in the fact that the mean score on the test is different for the following groups, equated as to chronological age: employed subjects, college students, Civilian Conservation Corps enrollees, and unemployed persons. The average score decreases (i.e., index of maturity drops) from the first to the fourth group. Of the six critical ratios between these groups two are below 2, two are below 3, and two are above 4 (unemployed vs. employed and unemployed vs. college). The use of such indices as the only measures of validity is questioned by the reviewer.

The inventory probably will find its greatest use as an interviewing aid. If, however, an interviewer wishes to use the total score, it would seem absolutely necessary for him to build up a set of norms for his own local population. Three different types of normative data are presented in the manual: centile ratings based upon total score, mean score for each year of chronological age from 16 through 25, and mean scores for first-, second-, third-, and fourth-year college students.

Goodwin Watson, Professor of Education, Teachers College, Columbia University, New York, New York. Dr. Ellis Weitzman, for his doctoral dissertation, prepared this inventory of 33 questions designed to measure social maturity (some items are from Doll's *Vineland Social Maturity Scale*) in young people 16 to 24 years of age. High scores are achieved by youth who report that they handle their own finances, go out nights without restriction, have regular health checkups, and make their own decisions. Items are weighted in accord with their capacity to differentiate older from younger adolescents.

Norms are based on 900 Nebraska young people during the 1930's, with young men at all ages scoring slightly higher than young women. No account is taken of the dependence of norms upon other factors such as urban vs. rural culture, economic status, foreign-born vs. native-born parents, or the particular time period. Reliability of .88 is reported (42 cases retested after one week), but the problem of accuracy of self-report on such items as "Do you follow current events?" or "How many evenings a week do you stay at home without guests or visitors?" or "Do you assume responsibilities beyond your own needs, which you might avoid?" or "Do you consider yourself the type of person who inspires the confidence of others in you?" is not discussed.

The inventory seems useful as a basis for group discussion among adolescents on the freedom they have or ought to have. Granted a desire to answer truthfully, it would enable an investigator to identify the more emancipated and the overprotected in a group of college or employed youth. Unemployed and underprivileged youth are penalized by several items requiring comfortable income.

[112]

★Wilson Scales of Stability and Instability. Grades 9-16 and adults; 1941; 1 form; $1.15 per 25, postpaid; 15¢ per specimen set, postpaid; nontimed (20-30) minutes; Matthew H. Wilson; Bureau of Educational Measurements, Kansas State Teachers College of Emporia.

Paul E. Meehl, Assistant Professor of Psychology, University of Minnesota, Minneapolis, Minnesota. This is a pair of tests printed in a single booklet but not to be combined into a single score as the title might seem to imply. The *stability* test consists of 42 items, each of which names or briefly describes some personal experience or situation, e.g., "animal pet," "picking own work," or "friends with high standards." The testee is asked to rate each of these experiences on a ten-point scale with respect to how much of a feeling of stability it gave him. The total score is the sum of these weighted ratings. The *instability* test consists of 38 items of an obviously adverse or unpleasant nature, e.g., "hurt in childhood," "restless," "family quarrels," on each of which he is asked to give a similar rating with respect to how much of a feeling of instability they

gave him. A short paragraph in the instructions briefly describes what is meant by the key words stability and instability.

Raw score distributions and percentile norms are given for 400 high school sophomores and 100 college freshmen. Phrases describing amounts of stability are coordinated with various percentile ranges. The test is supposed to be used with junior and senior high school and college students and "other adult groups." Corrected split-half reliabilities seem to be satisfactory (.91 to .95 for various groups).

No validation data are presented, nor have any appeared in the abstracted literature. The selection of items was from a larger pool, whose initial construction is not described in the manual. Basis of selection (which the author mistakenly considers evidence of "validity") was a self-judgment by the students as to the importance of each experience in determining their feelings of stability and instability. The items are uniformly of the obvious sort which abound in traditional personality inventories, and there is every reason to expect the usual influence of distortions in these self-ratings. The definition given to the testee of stability and instability is in the reviewer's opinion too vague to be of any real value. The author gives no consideration to the presumed effect of individual differences in constant rating tendencies on the scores. In the case of the instability subtest, large regions on the rating scale remain substantially unused, as might be expected from the nature of the situation presented. There is no accompanying definition of the measured variable for the use of the psychologist employing this test, and it is difficult to know what can be asserted about a person who achieves a deviant score, since no defined criterion groups of any sort are mentioned. It is not clear whether the terms *stability* and *instability* are to be conceived as extremes of a continuum; remarkably enough, although the same adjectival descriptions are used by the author to characterize deviates on each test, no correlation between the two is reported. Thus, a clinician would not know how to interpret a pair of scores indicating moderate stability on the first test and extreme instability on the second. The directions and the nature of the task itself are hardly appropriate to use with adults generally, although no caution regarding education or intelligence is included.

It is frankly difficult to say anything at all

favorable about this instrument. Although the complete absence of validity data makes it difficult to decide, there seems to be no reason for supposing that this is more than merely another "personality inventory" having all of the defects and none of the merits of the traditional variety. From everything available to us it would hardly seem justified to suggest anyone's using it except in an effort to determine whether any appreciable validity exists. Even this latter process would be quite a task since one does not get any clear idea of what sort of criterion ought to be used for the trait.

Katherine W. Wilcox, Chief Psychologist, Traverse City State Hospital, Traverse City, Michigan. These are self-rating scales intended to measure stability and instability. The items on the stability scale include such topics as "My love for my parents," "Friendliness," "Physical exercise," and "Work promotes independence" which are to be evaluated by the individual himself as to the degree to which these experiences contributed to his own sense of security and feeling of stability. On the instability scale the subject is asked to decide on such items as to what extent "Inferior" under the heading of emotional reactions and "Family relations" under the work and business heading contributed to feelings of insecurity.

These scales violate standard procedures of test construction in the following important ways: (*a*) The author assumes validation because of split-half reliability without any comparison of scores against any independent criterion. (*b*) The college data were from 100 freshmen attending 64 different colleges. Obviously there were some selective factors at work in the selection of cases which presumably influenced the results. The nature or direction of such influence is not considered. (*c*) The ratings are done on an eleven-point scale for material which is difficult to quantify at all and should certainly not be handled on more than a three-point scale. (*d*) The test items are briefly stated and are often ambiguous. (*e*) The author states his theory of stability of personality and expects the subject to have insight into his own longitudinal adjustment on the basis of the author's theory. The author does not give any consideration to the variability of results when such insight is lacking or defective. The arrangement of items by areas of experience, as in the instability scale,

increases the halo effect and tends to make the self-judgments more biased. The author concludes that adjustment in a life situation is the same thing as a score on a self-rating scale.

The only legitimate use of these scales in their present form is in bringing up topics for discussion between student and counselor.

[113]

★**Work Preference Inventory.** Applicants for employment; 1946; IBM; 1 form; separate answer sheets must be used; $25 per 100; $2 per 100 machine-scorable answer sheets; $2 per 100 profile sheets; $6 per set of 18 keys (personality traits: reliability, perseverance, emotional stability, creativeness, conservatism, ambition, masculinity, introversion, anxiety-depression, neurotic index; interests: persuasive, social service, theoretical, artistic, mechanical, economic, scientific); 35¢ per single copy; 25¢ per manual; nontimed (15-75) minutes; Robert W. Henderson: the Author, University Personnel Office, University of Kentucky, Lexington, Kentucky.

Edwin W. Davis, Director of Washington Counseling Center and Associate Professor of Psychology, The George Washington University, Washington, D. C. A hidden personality inventory within a regular vocational inventory makes this test about the most complete contribution to this technique of employee selection and vocational choice. The only question remaining for such an excellent idea is the effectiveness of this dual instrument. The ten personality traits are reliability, perseverance, emotional stability, creativeness, conservatism, ambition, masculinity, introversion, anxiety-depression, and neurotic index. The vocational interests are persuasive, social service, theoretical, artistic, mechanical, economic, and scientific. Although the test is mainly for adult employees and counselees, it can be used for adolescent youth.

Actual use of these tests on 25 cases in the Washington Counseling Center revealed the personality traits unreliable indicators for persons well known to the counselors. The occupational levels were a little more reliable when compared to the Kuder and to the revised Brainard.

The test would carry the technique of a combination personality-occupational inventory farther than any other test. Once this technique is perfected, it will be a great time-saver as well as provide a more acceptable personality test for over-sensitive clients. Immediate research should be undertaken to compare this test with the best comparable occupational inventory and personality inventory given to the same persons. The wording of the items in a few cases can be improved. A person giving too many neutral answers, as experienced adults seemed to do, tends not to give a very distinctive profile. The author reports fine acceptance of this test in industrial circles.

John C. Flanagan, Professor of Psychology, The University of Pittsburgh, Pittsburgh, Pennsylvania. This inventory consists of a list of 130 pairs of various types of activities. For each pair, the individual is asked to state his preference by marking on the answer sheet the first choice if he likes the first alternative much more than the second, the second choice if he likes the first a little more than the second, the third choice if he likes them both equally well, the fourth choice if he likes the second alternative a little better, and the fifth choice if he likes the second alternative much more than the first.

Items are listed under nine headings, the first five of which refer to preferences regarding kinds of work or work environment. The other categories involve other types of preferences. One section asks for choices regarding living conditions; another section, choices regarding reading materials; another section involves school subjects; and the last section is a miscellany consisting mainly of recreational activities.

The selection of specific items impressed this reviewer quite favorably. The general plan of the test seems good. The manual states,

The Work Preference Inventory gives ten personality scores and seven interest scores, although most testees will not realize that it is anything other than an interest test. Therefore it has the advantage of being partially disguised and will give a true personality picture in many employment situations.
The scoring keys for the components defined below were developed through item analysis. Clinical ratings were compared to test responses and the resultant keys include the majority of those who were rated high on a trait or interest and exclude the majority of those rated low.

The personality traits for which scoring keys are available include reliability, perseverance, emotional stability, creativeness, conservatism, ambition, masculinity, introversion, anxiety-depression, and neurotic index. The scoring keys available for obtaining information regarding an individual's interests include persuasive, social service, theoretical, artistic, mechanical, economic, and scientific.

Norms are provided for converting the scores obtained from each of the traits into the letter grades, A, B, C, D, and E. The corrected odd-even reliability coefficients based on 50 cases vary between .57 and .92, with a majority of them being in the .70's. Two illustrative individual profiles are given, one for a successful sales manager and the other for an individual discharged from the Army because of "anxiety state severe."

Biserial correlation coefficients are reported in a "validity table." These coefficients were obtained by correlating the test scores with the ratings of associates for the surface traits and interests and with clinical ratings for the other scales (introversion, masculinity, anxiety-depression, and neurotic index). In a letter to the reviewer Mr. Henderson states that in developing the scoring keys, "only those for whom there was agreement among the 2 to 4 raters were used. Consequently, in some cases, as few as 15 pairs of ratings were available. For example, 15 homosexuals versus 15 men rated as definitely masculine were compared item by item, and the items selected for the masculinity scoring key were those which differentiated the masculine from the nonmasculine. Sixty-five was taken as the lowest exclusion-inclusion percentage and the average for all items on all scales is about 77."

The "validity coefficients" reported in the table are based on between 25 and 85 individuals, the median number being 34. The biserial correlations range from .51 to .98, with seven of the coefficients reported above .90. The test author suggests that the high values may be due to the wide differences between the groups. This certainly seems to be a relevant explanation of part of the exceptionally high values obtained. It appears that it would have been more appropriate to have used the triserial correlation coefficient in this instance. In a communication to the reviewer the test author stated, "The validity *r*'s were not obtained from the same individuals (as used to develop the scoring keys), but the rating psychiatrists and clinicians were the same."

The test materials and method appear promising. However, the keys were developed on very small numbers of cases, and the norms currently available were also apparently based on a very small sample (the number was not reported). These facts raise serious doubt regarding the advisability of using this test in its present stage of development.

In order to obtain an impression regarding

the type of results provided by the inventory in its present form, scores were calculated on all 17 of the keys for the writer and eight of his associates. An indication of what appears to the reviewer as an inadequate basis for some of the scores obtained from the present blank is illustrated by the following finding. One girl obtained a score of 2 out of a possible score of 13 on Emotional Stability, which, according to the manual, indicated that she was in the last category of the scale and had strong tendencies toward being neurotic and unstable. This very low score was obtained by marking the following choices: a slight preference for clerical over mechanical work; a strong preference for criticizing, editing, and examining rather than planning, organizing, and creating; a strong preference for rewriting rather than writing rough drafts of reports; a slight preference for work which enables you to use hunches and intuition over work which requires you to think things out carefully; a slight preference for people who are very religious as compared with people who are not religious; a slight rather than a strong preference for people who are realistic over people who are impractical; a slight preference for living among poor people rather than among rich people; a slight rather than a strong preference for the comics or funnies over movie magazines; a slight preference for reading about the theater rather than reading about medicine; a slight preference for studying drama rather than accounting; and a slight preference for watching rather than playing your favorite game. It is suggested that the above constitutes very inadequate evidence on which to label a person as "emotionally unstable"; and it is believed that obtaining and reporting such scores may not only be of little value, but may actually do harm in some instances.

In conclusion, it is suggested that the inadequacy of the present test is primarily due to a lack of available resources for its development. It is believed that, for so important a topic as the diagnosing of personality, a very comprehensive and intensive research and development program is essential.

Although the materials and procedures used in the development of this test are superior to those used in most published tests in this field, the inadequate research basis for the present scoring keys suggests that it should be used only with full knowledge of its present limitations and by experienced psychologists.

Gilbert J. Rich, Director, Milwaukee County Guidance Clinic, Milwaukee, Wisconsin. This inventory attempts to serve both as a personality test and as an interest inventory. It consists of 130 paired items relating to the subject's preferences in regard to type of work, conditions of work, persons with whom one works, conditions of living, reading, studying, and leisure-time activities. On each pair of items, response is made upon a fivefold scale extending from one extreme through "liking both" to the opposite pole, with instructions to omit items where neither is liked. Scores are obtained for 10 personality characteristics: reliability, perseverance, emotional stability, creativeness, conservatism, ambition, masculinity, introversion, anxiety-depression, and neurotic index; and for 7 interests: persuasive, social service, theoretical, artistic, mechanical, economic, and scientific.

The individual questions were picked by a process of item analysis, but no information is available as to number of subjects used other than that it varied from one trait to another. Biserial correlation coefficients are given for groups of persons who either were rated high or low in the particular trait or interest or who fell into groups that could be so classified. This procedure yields coefficients varying from .51 to .98, but which are based upon small populations ranging from 25 to 85. Moreover, it must be noted that many of these were soldiers for whom such inexact criteria were used as lack of referral to a neuropsychiatric clinic (well-adjusted) and discharge from the army for neuropsychiatric reasons (neurotic). Anyone familiar with military referral procedures and military psychiatry will readily recognize the inadequacy of such classifications.

Moreover, a study of individual items likewise indicates the difficulties in selection of them within such a situation. Items chosen to indicate neurotic tendencies are heavily loaded with those which might unfit the subject only for military life, such as artistic and musical interests and unwillingness to accept responsibility.

There is a considerable degree of overlap between the items utilized to obtain different scores. For example, the scale for anxiety-depression contains 26 items, 25 of which are also found among the 36 items on the scale for neurotic index. Similarly, the definitions of emotional stability and neurotic index are exactly opposite, so that one should be the converse of the other. The inclusion of these three scales measuring the same characteristic (one in reverse) is a redundancy which gives to the inventory an appearance of exactness which is not there.

The plan of testing personality characteristics under the guise of work interests should have the definite advantage of lessening the tendency of the subject to describe himself as he wishes to be, but it involves a danger that he may try to show himself as he thinks his employer or the prospective job may require. On the whole, however, it would appear to be more advantageous than disadvantageous.

Taken as a whole, the inventory appears to be an effort to measure more characteristics than are justified upon a basis of 130 items. It also appears to be poorly standardized and to be validated upon too small a sample as well as upon inadequate criteria.

PERSONALITY—FOURTH MMY

REVIEWS BY *Dwight L. Arnold, Frederic L. Ayer, Benjamin Balinsky, John E. Bell, Arthur L. Benton, E. J. G. Bradford, Hubert E. Brogden, Donald T. Campbell, Launor F. Carter, Robert C. Challman, Kenneth E. Clark, Charles N. Cofer, Douglas Courtney, William J. E. Crissy, Lysle W. Croft, William M. Cruickshank, W. Grant Dahlstrom, D. Russell Davis, Robert G. Demaree, Albert Ellis, Hans J. Eysenck, Frank S. Freeman, N. L. Gage, Harrison G. Gough, Nelson G. Hanawalt, Philip L. Harriman, Dale B. Harris, Charles M. Harsh, George W. Hartmann, Kenneth L. Heaton, William E. Henry, Robert R. Holt, Charles H. Honzik, Albert L. Hunsicker, Harold E. Jones, E. Lowell Kelly, Seymour G. Klebanoff, Kate Levine Kogan, William S. Kogan, Morris Krugman, Roger T. Lennon, Frank M. Loos, C. M. Louttit, Ardie Lubin, Louis L. McQuitty, Ross W. Matteson, James Maxwell, N. W. Morton, C. Robert Pace, Albert I. Rabin, T. W. Richards, Ephraim Rosen, John W. M. Rothney, David G. Ryans, Theodore R. Sarbin, Helen Sargent, William Schofield, William Seeman, Helen Shacter, Laurance F. Shaffer, Edward Joseph Shoben, Jr., Verner M. Sims, William Stephenson, Naomi Stewart, L. Joseph Stone, Charles R. Strother, Percival M. Symonds, Florence M. Teagarden, Leona E. Tyler, Neil Van Steenberg, Howard R. White, and J. R. Wittenborn.*

NONPROJECTIVE

[27]

★**Activity Vector Analysis.** Adults; 1948; 5 scores: aggressiveness, sociability, emotional adjustment, social adaptability, total; 1 form; distribution is restricted to industrial firms using the Activity Vector Analysis Program of Human Relations and purchase is made by special arrangement with the publisher; nontimed 5(10) minutes; Walter V. Clarke; Walter V. Clarke Associates. *

[28]

The Adjustment Inventory. Grades 9–16 and adults; 1934–38; IBM; 2 levels; 1 form; tentative norms; 15¢ per specimen set; tissue paper stencil for hand scoring of test booklets supplied free; cash orders postpaid; nontimed (25) minutes; Hugh M. Bell; Stanford University Press. *

a) STUDENT FORM. Grades 9–16; 1934; 4 adjustment scores: home, health, social, emotional; 2 editions; manual ['34].

  1) [*Regular Edition.*] $1.75 per 25; separate answer sheets may be used; $1 per 50 IBM answer sheets; $1 per set of stencils for machine scoring of answer sheets; $1 per plastic stencil for hand scoring of test booklets.

  2) [*IBM Test-Answer Sheet Edition.*] $2.50 per 50; $1.50 per set of stencils for machine scoring of test-answer sheets.

b) ADULT FORM. Adults; 1938; 5 adjustment scores: home, occupational, health, social, emotional; manual ['38]; prices same as for Regular Edition; separate answer sheets may be used; plastic hand-scoring stencil not available.

REFERENCES

1–15. See 40:1200.
16. BELL, HUGH M. "Measurement of Student Adjustments." Abstract. *Psychol B* 31:587–8 O '34. * (*PA* 9:920, title only)
17. WILLIAMS, HAROLD M.; KEPHART, NEWELL C.; AND HOUTCHENS, H. MAX. "The Reliability of the Psychoneurotic Inventory With Delinquent Boys." Abstract. *Proc Iowa Acad Sci* 42:176 '35. * (*PA* 11:835)
18. BARTLETT, EDWARD R., AND HARRIS, DALE B. "Personality Factors in Delinquency." *Sch & Soc* 43:653–6 My 9 '36. * (*PA* 10:4108)
19. MALLETT, D. R. "A Validation of Certain Measures of Personality Adjustment at the College Level." *Proc Iowa Acad Sci* 43:299–302 '36. *
20. MALLETT, DONALD ROGER. *A Study of the Validity at*
the College Level of Certain Measures of Personality Adjustment.* Doctor's thesis, University of Iowa (Iowa City, Iowa), 1936. (*Programs Announcing Candidates for Higher Degrees....1936, 1937.*)
21. WILLIAMS, HAROLD M.; KEPHART, NEWELL C.; AND HOUTCHENS, H. MAX. "The Reliability of the Psychoneurotic Inventory With Delinquent Boys." *J Abn & Social Psychol* 31:271–5 O–D '36. * (*PA* 11:1861)
22. ANCONA, NINA M. *A Study of the Bell Adjustment Inventory.* Master's thesis, University of New Mexico (Albuquerque, N.M.), 1937. (*Abstracts of Theses....1933–37,* 1946, pp. 2–3.)
23. DARLEY, JOHN G. *An Analysis of Attitude and Adjustment Tests: With Special Reference to Conditions of Change in Attitudes and Adjustments.* Doctor's thesis, University of Minnesota (Minneapolis, Minn.), 1937.
24. DARLEY, JOHN G. "Scholastic Achievement and Measured Maladjustment." *J Appl Psychol* 21:485–93 O '37. * (*PA* 12:2099)
25. DROUGHT, NEAL EDWARD. *The Personality Adjustment of Freshmen Men at the University of Wisconsin.* Doctor's thesis, University of Wisconsin (Madison, Wis.), 1937. (*Summaries of Doctoral Dissertations....1937,* 1938, pp. 259–61.)
26. PALLISTER, HELEN, AND PIERCE, W. O'D. "The Bell Adjustment Inventory Applied to Scottish Subjects." Abstract. *Psychol B* 34:782–3 N '37. * (*PA* 12:1491, title only)
27. STUIT, DEWEY B. "Differential Characteristics of Superior and Inferior Students." *Sch & Soc* 46:733–6 D 4 '37. * (*PA* 12:1640)
28. ALTENEDER, LOUISE E. *The Value of Intelligence, and Vocational-Interest Tests in a Guidance Program.* Doctor's thesis, New York University (New York, N.Y.), 1938. Pp. 130. (*Abstracts of Theses....[School of Education] 1938,* pp. 41–4.)
29. McMORRIES, JAMES C. "A Study of New Students Admitted by a Negro College in 1936." *J Negro Ed* 7:535–9 O '38. * (*PA* 13:1089)
30. SUKOV, MAY, AND WILLIAMSON, E. G. "Personality Traits and Attitudes of Jewish and Non-Jewish Students." *J Appl Psychol* 22:487–92 O '38. * (*PA* 13:2658)
31. BEAL, A. ELIZABETH. "A Comparison of Personality Adjustment Scores of Rural and Urban Children in Ninth Grade." *Proc Iowa Acad Sci* 46:277–83 '39. *
32. GILKINSON, HOWARD, AND KNOWER, FRANKLIN H. *Psychological Studies of Individual Differences Among Students of Speech.* Minneapolis, Minn.: Department of Speech, University of Minnesota, June 1939. Pp. ii, 196. Paper, mimeographed. *
33. GITTINGER, JOHN WILLIAM, AND KRAMER, GEORGE ALLEN. *The Bell Adjustment Inventory as Predictive of College Success.* Master's thesis, University of Oklahoma (Norman, Okla.), 1939. Pp. xvi, 147. (*Abstracts of Theses....1939,* 1943, p. 131.)
34. HATHAWAY, S. R. "The Personality Inventory as an Aid in the Diagnosis of Psychopathic Inferiors." *J Consult Psychol* 3:112–7 Jl–Ag '39. * (*PA* 13:5704)
35. ALTENEDER, LOUISE E. "The Value of Intelligence, Personality, and Vocational Interest Tests in a Guidance Program." *J Ed Psychol* 31:449–59 S '40. * (*PA* 15:1480)
36. DARLEY, JOHN G., AND McNAMARA, WALTER J. "Factor Analysis in the Establishment of New Personality Tests." *J Ed Psychol* 31:321–34 My '40. * (*PA* 15:922)
37. ECKERT, RALPH G., AND KEYS, NOEL. "Public Speaking as a Cue to Personality Adjustment." *J Appl Psychol* 24:144–53 Ap '40. * (*PA* 14:4638)

38. GILKINSON, HOWARD, AND KNOWER, FRANKLIN. "Individual Differences Among Students of Speech as Revealed by Psychological Tests, I." *Q J Speech* 26:243–55 Ap '40. * (*PA* 15:326)

39. HACKMAN, RAY CARTER. *The Differential Prediction of Success in Two Contrasting Vocational Areas.* Doctor's thesis, University of Minnesota (Minneapolis, Minn.), 1940. (*Summaries of Ph.D. Theses,* 1949, pp. 100–5.)

40. PETERS, CHAS. C. "The Validity of Personality Inventories Studied by a 'Guess Who' Technique." Abstract: *Psychol B* 37:453 Jl '40. * (*PA* 14:5599)

41. FAIR, MARCELLA HYDE. *An Evaluation of the Bernreuter Personality Inventory, Bell Adjustment Inventory, and Willoughby (Clark-Thurstone) Personality Schedule on Emotional Stability of Ohio University Women.* Master's thesis, Ohio University (Athens, Ohio), 1941. Pp. 78. (*Abstracts of Masters' Theses....1941,* pp. 26–7.)

42. GILKINSON, HOWARD, AND KNOWER, FRANKLIN H. "A Study of Standardized Personality Tests and Skill in Speech." *J Ed Psychol* 32:161–75 Mr '41. * (*PA* 15:3888)

43. KRAUSE, LAWRENCE J. *The Correlation of Adjustment and Achievement in Delinquent Boys.* Catholic University of America, Studies in Psychology and Psychiatry, Vol. 5, No. 2. Washington, D.C.: Catholic University of America Press, July 1941. Pp. xiv, 74. Paper. * (*PA* 15:4764)

44. PETERS, EDWIN F. *The Construction of an Adjustment Inventory on the Basis of a Critical Analysis of the Factors as Measured by the Bell Inventories.* Doctor's thesis, New York University (New York, N.Y.), 1941. Pp. 156. (*Abstracts of Theses....[School of Education]* 1941, pp. 173–9.)

45. RYANS, DAVID G., AND PETERS, EDWIN F. "School Satisfaction Among First-Year Students in a Women's College." *Sch & Soc* 53:157–9 F 1 '41. * (*PA* 15:2383)

46. SMITH, JOSEPHINE M. "The Prognostic Value of Entrance Tests in a Junior College." *J Ed Psychol* 32:584–92 N '41. * (*PA* 16:2888)

47. SPERLING, ABRAHAM. *The Relationship Between Personality Adjustment and Achievement in Physical Education Activities.* Doctor's thesis, New York University (New York, N.Y.), 1941.

48. TRAXLER, ARTHUR E. "The Reliability of the Bell Inventories and Their Correlation With Teachers' Judgment." *J Appl Psychol* 25:672–8 D '41. * (*PA* 16:1576)

49. BERMAN, ABRAHAM B., AND KLEIN, ABRAHAM. "A Personality Study of Maladjusted Pupils of Superior Mentality." *High Points* 24:57–63 F '42. * (*PA* 16:2433)

50. CLARK, WILLIAM A., AND SMITH, LEO F. "Further Evidence on the Validity of Personality Inventories." *J Ed Psychol* 33:81–91 F '42. * (*PA* 16:3644)

51. McCARTHY, THOMAS J. *Personality Traits of Seminarians.* Catholic University of America, Studies in Psychology and Psychiatry, Vol. 5, No. 4. Washington, D.C.: Catholic University of America Press, July 1942. Pp. vii, 46. Paper. * (*PA* 17:592)

52. OBERHEIM, GRACE M. "The Prediction of Success of Student Assistants in College Library Work." *Ed & Psychol Meas* 2:379–85 O '42. * (*PA* 17:1364)

53. PETERS, RICHARDA. *A Study of the Intercorrelations of Personality Traits Among a Group of Novices in Religious Communities.* Catholic University of America, Studies in Psychology and Psychiatry, Vol. 5, No. 7. Washington, D.C.: Catholic University of America Press, December 1942. Pp. vii, 38. Paper. * (*PA* 17:2047)

54. SHEFFIELD, EDWARD F. "Achievement of Evening College Students." *J Am Assn Col Reg* 17:319–24 Ap '42. *

55. SPERLING, ABRAHAM. "A Comparison of the Human Behavior Inventory With Two Other Personality Measures." *Ed & Psychol Meas* 2:291–7 Jl '42. * (*PA* 16:4885)

56. TUSSING, LYLE. "An Investigation of the Possibilities of Measuring Personality Traits With the Strong Vocational Interest Blank." *Ed & Psychol Meas* 2:59–74 Ja '42. * (*PA* 16:2324)

57. WATSON, ROBERT I. "The Relationship of Affective Tolerance Inventory to Other Personality Inventories." *Ed & Psychol Meas* 2:83–90 Ja '42. * (*PA* 16:2325)

58. CRIDER, BLAKE. "A School of Nursing Selection Program." *J Appl Psychol* 27:452–7 O '43. * (*PA* 18:281)

59. KLUGMAN, SAMUEL F. "Test Scores and Graduation." *Occupations* 21:389–93 Ja '43. * (*PA* 17:1354)

60. MARSH, CHARLES J. "The Diagnostic Value of the Bell Adjustment Inventory for College Women." *J Social Psychol* 17:103–9 F '43. * (*PA* 17:2045)

61. SPOERL, DOROTHY TILDEN. "Bilinguality and Emotional Adjustment." *J Abn & Social Psychol* 38:37–57 Ja '43. * (*PA* 17:3837)

62. STEINBERG, DAVID LOUIS, AND WITTMAN, MARY PHYLLIS. "Etiologic Factors in the Adjustment of Men in the Armed Forces." *War Med* 4:129–39 Ag '43. * (*PA* 17:4248)

63. WOOLF, MAURICE D. "A Study of Some Relationships Between Home Adjustment and the Behavior of Junior College Students." *J Social Psychol* 17:275–86 My '43. * (*PA* 17:3976)

64. WOODRUFF, LOUISE, AND MULL, HELEN K. "The Relation of Home Adjustment to Social Adjustment in Northern and in Southern College Students: Studies From the Psychological Laboratory of Sweet Briar College." *Am J Psychol* 57:86 Ja '44. * (*PA* 18:1919)

65. ALTUS, WILLIAM D., AND BELL, HUGH M. "The Validity of Certain Measures of Maladjustment in an Army Special Training Center." *Psychol B* 42:98–103 F '45. * (*PA* 19:1229)

66. DUNCAN, MELBA HURD. "An Experimental Study of Some of the Relationships Between Voice and Personality Among Students of Speech." *Speech Monogr* 12:47–60 '45. * (*PA* 20:1961)

67. DYER, DOROTHY TUNELL. "Are Only Children Different?" *J Ed Psychol* 36:297–302 My '45. * (*PA* 19:3401)

68. FORLANO, GEORGE, AND KIRKPATRICK, FORREST H. "Intelligence and Adjustment Measurements in the Selection of Radio Tube Mounters." *J Appl Psychol* 29:257–61 Ag '45. * (*PA* 20:283)

69. GRIFFITHS, GEORGE R. "The Relationship Between Scholastic Achievement and Personality Adjustment of Men College Students." *J Appl Psychol* 29:360–7 O '45. * (*PA* 20:909)

70. SEAGOE, MAY V. "Prognostic Tests and Teaching Success." *J Ed Res* 38:685–90 My '45. (*PA* 19:3184)

71. WITTMAN, MARY PHYLLIS, AND HUFFMAN, ARTHUR V. "A Comparative Study of Developmental, Adjustment, and Personality Characteristics of Psychotic, Psychoneurotic, Delinquent, and Normally Adjusted Teen Aged Youths." *J Genetic Psychol* 66:167–82 Je '45. * (*PA* 20:617)

72. ELLIS, ALBERT. "The Validity of Personality Questionnaires." *Psychol B* 43:385–440 S '46. * (*PA* 21:502)

73. JONES, RONALD DeVALL. "The Prediction of Teaching Efficiency From Objective Measures." *J Exp Ed* 15:85–99 S '46. * (*PA* 21:606)

74. POWELL, VIRGINIA MARGARET. *An Analysis of Relationships Existent Among Current Health Practices, Personal and Social Adjustment, and Physical Performance.* Doctor's thesis, New York University (New York, N.Y.), 1946. (*Abstracts of Theses....[School of Education]* October 1946–June 1947, 1947, pp. 69–77.)

75. ROSE, ANNELIES ARGELANDER. "The Effect of the War on the Social and Emotional Adjustment of College Girls." *J Social Psychol* 24:177–85 N '46. * (*PA* 21:1579)

76. SEAGOE, MAY V. "Prediction of In-Service Success in Teaching." *J Ed Res* 39:658–63 My '46. * (*PA* 20:4352)

77. TUCKMAN, JACOB. "The Relationship Between Subjective Estimates of Personal Adjustment and Ratings on the Bell Adjustment Inventory." *J Appl Psychol* 30:488–92 O '46. * (*PA* 21:513)

78. BURKE, HENRY R. *Personality Traits of Successful Minor Seminarians.* Washington, D.C.: Catholic University of America Press, 1947. Pp. viii, 65. * (*PA* 22:848)

79. DAMRIN, DORA E. "A Study of the Truthfulness With Which High-School Girls Answer Personality Tests of the Questionnaire Type." *J Ed Psychol* 38:223–31 Ap '47. * (*PA* 22:625)

80. GOULD, GEORGE. "The Predictive Value of Certain Selective Measures." *Ed Adm & Sup* 33:208–12 Ap '47. *

81. JONES, RONALD D. *The Prediction of Teaching Efficiency.* Doctor's thesis, University of Wisconsin (Madison, Wis.), 1947. (*Summaries of Doctoral Dissertations....July, 1943 to June, 1947,* 1949, pp. 419–21.)

82. LOVELL, GEORGE D.; LAURIE, GLORIA; AND MARVIN, DORIS. "A Comparison of the Minnesota Personality Scale and the Bell Adjustment Inventory for Student Counseling." *Proc Iowa Acad Sci* 54:247–51 '47. * (*PA* 23:5524)

83. MUENCH, GEORGE A. *An Evaluation of Non-Directive Psychotherapy by Means of the Rorschach and Other Indices.* Foreword by Carl R. Rogers. Applied Psychology Monographs of the American Psychological Association, No. 13. Stanford University, Calif.: Stanford University Press, 1947. Pp. 163. Paper, lithotyped. * (*PA* 22:320)

84. SMITH, HENRY P. "The Relationship Between Scores on the Bell Adjustment Inventory and Participation in Extracurricular Activities." *J Ed Psychol* 38:11–6 Ja '47. * (*PA* 21:3275)

85. VAN DER MERWE, A. B., AND THERON, P. A. "A New Method of Measuring Emotional Stability." *J General Psychol* 37:109–23 O '47. * (*PA* 22:3040)

86. BROWER, DANIEL, AND SANDS, HARRY. "Relations Between Reaction Time and Personal Adjustment as Measured by the Bell Adjustment Inventory." *J General Psychol* 38:229–33 Ap '48. * (*PA* 23:1157)

87. COTTLE, WILLIAM C. "A Factorial Study of Selected Instruments for Measuring Personality and Interest." Abstract. *Am Psychol* 3:300 Jl '48. * (*PA* 22:5353, title only)

88. HAMLIN, ROY M., AND ALBEE, GEORGE W. "Muench's Tests Before and After Nondirective Therapy: A Control Group for His Subjects." *J Consult Psychol* 12:412–6 N–D '48. * (*PA* 23:2247)

89. NIMKOFF, MEYER F., AND WOOD, ARTHUR L. "Courtship and Personality." *Am J Sociol* 53:263–9 Ja '48. * (*PA* 22:1622)

90. PORTENIER, LILLIAN. "Personality Tests in a University Guidance Program." Abstract. *J Colo-Wyo Acad Sci* 3:51–2 S '48. *

91. SNYDER, WILLIAM U., AND SNYDER, BARBARA JUNE. "Implications for Therapy of Personality Changes Resulting From a Course in Mental Hygiene." Abstract. *Am Psychol* 3:286–7 Jl '48. * (*PA* 22:5456, title only)

92. STEWART, FRANK WALTER. *A Study of Changes in the Bell Adjustment Scores of High School Students in Relation to Sex and Intelligence.* Master's thesis, University of Southern California (Los Angeles, Calif.), 1948.

93. ARBUCKLE, DUGALD S. "Personality Tests as a Means of

Entry for Counseling." *Ed & Psychol Meas* 9:757–64 w '49. *
(*PA* 26:2726)

94. BATEMAN, RICHARD M. "The Effect of Work Experience on High-School Students as Revealed by the Bell Adjustment Inventory." *J Ed Res* 43:261–9 D '49. * (*PA* 24:3881)

95. CAPWELL, DORA F. *Psychological Tests for Retail Store Personnel.* Pittsburgh, Pa.: Research Bureau for Retail Training, University of Pittsburgh, 1949. Pp. 48. Paper. * (*PA* 25: 3449)

96. COHEN, DAVID. *Psychological Concomitants of Chronic Illness: A Study of Emotional Correlates of Pulmonary Tuberculosis, Peptic Ulcer, the Arthritides, and Cardiac Disease.* Doctor's thesis, University of Pittsburgh (Pittsburgh, Pa.), 1949. (*Abstracts of Doctoral Dissertations....1949,* 1950, pp. 277–90.)

97. COTTLE, WILLIAM C. *A Factorial Study of the Multiphasic, Strong, Kuder and Bell Inventories Using a Population of Adult Males.* Doctor's thesis, Syracuse University (Syracuse, N.Y.), 1949.

98. COTTLE, WILLIAM C. "Relationships Among Selected Personality and Interest Inventories." Abstract. *Am Psychol* 4:292–3 Jl '49. * (*PA* 23:6206, title only)

99. COTTLE, WM. C., AND POWELL, JACKSON O. "Relationship of Mean Scores on the Strong, Kuder and Bell Inventories With the MMPI M-F Scale as the Criterion." *Trans Kans Acad Sci* 52:396–8 '49. * (*PA* 24:2599)

100. DUNCAN, MELBA HURD. "Home Adjustment of Stutterers Versus Non-Stutterers." *J Speech & Hearing Disorders* 14:255–9 S '49. * (*PA* 24:5361)

101. JONES, ELVET GLYN. *A Critical Evaluation of the Bell Adjustment Inventory: Student Form.* Master's thesis, University of British Columbia (Vancouver, B.C., Canada), 1949. Pp. 130.

102. McALLISTER, ROBERT J. *The Relationship of Bell Adjustment Scores to Family Constellation.* Master's thesis, Catholic University of America (Washington, D.C.), 1949. (*PA* 24: 830, title only)

103. MACDONALD, GORDON LUNDY. *Predicting Collegiate Survival From Pre-Admission Data.* Doctor's thesis, New York University (New York, N.Y.), 1949. Abstract: *Microfilm Abstracts* 10:42–4 no 1 '50. * (*PA* 24:6063, title only)

104. ROSE, ANNELIES ARGELANDER. "Menstrual Pain and Personal Adjustment." *J Personality* 17:287–302 Mr '49. * (*PA* 25:3344)

105. SUPER, DONALD E. *Appraising Vocational Fitness By Means of Psychological Tests,* pp. 510–6. New York: Harper & Brothers, 1949. Pp. xxiii, 727. * (*PA* 24:2130)

106. WILSON, CLAUDE E. *Differences Between Personal Characteristics of Students Who Have Failed in High School and Those Who Have Not Failed.* Doctor's thesis, University of Southern California (Los Angeles, Calif.), 1949. (*Abstracts of Dissertations....1949,* 1950, pp. 195–7.)

107. ZAKOLSKI, F. C. "Studies in Delinquency: I, Personality Structure of Delinquent Boys." *J Genetic Psychol* 74:109–17 Mr '49. * (*PA* 23:4925)

108. BORG, WALTER R. "Some Factors Relating to Art School Success." *J Ed Res* 43:376–84 Ja '50. * (*PA* 24:4811)

109. BRYAN, J. R. *A Study of Personality Adjustment Differences of Delinquent and Non-Delinquent Groups as Measured by the Bell Adjustment Inventory and the California Test of Personality.* Master's thesis, University of Toronto (Toronto, Canada), 1950. Pp. 35.

110. COTTLE, WM. C. "A Factorial Study of the Multiphasic, Strong, Kuder, and Bell Inventories Using a Population of Adult Males." *Psychometrika* 15:25–47 Mr '50. * (*PA* 24: 4492)

111. COTTLE, WILLIAM C. "Relationships Among Selected Personality and Interest Inventories." *Occupations* 28:306–10 F '50. * (*PA* 24:4113)

112. KLUGMAN, SAMUEL F. "Spread of Vocational Interests and General Adjustment Status." *J Appl Psychol* 34:108–14 Ap '50. * (*PA* 25:1859)

113. POWELL, MARGARET. "Relationships Existent Between Adjustment Traits of College Freshmen Women: As Measured by the Bell Adjustment Inventory." *J Social Psychol* 31:145–9 F '50. * (*PA* 24:6048)

114. TAYLOR, M. V., JR., AND CAPWELL, DORA F. "High School Norms on the Bell Adjustment Inventory, Student Form." *Occupations* 28:376–80 Mr '50. * (*PA* 24:4613)

115. VAIL, JAMES P., AND STAUDT, VIRGINIA M. "Attitudes of College Students Toward Marriage and Related Problems: I, Dating and Mate Selection." *J Psychol* 30:171–82 Jl '50. * (*PA* 25:1266)

116. COWEN, EMORY L., AND THOMPSON, GEORGE G. "Problem Solving Rigidity and Personality Structure." *J Abn & Social Psychol* 46:165–76 Ap '51. * (*PA* 25:7940)

117. HURD, ARCHER W. *Evaluating Student Success in Medical Education,* pp. 35–9. Richmond, Va.: Bureau of Educational Research and Service, Medical College of Virginia, October 1951. Pp. vii, 69. Paper, mimeographed. *

118. POLLENS, BERTRAM. *The Relationship Between Psychological Data and Prognosis in Psychotherapy.* Doctor's thesis, New York University (New York, N.Y.), 1951. Abstract: *Microfilm Abstracts* 11:750–2 no 3 '51. (*PA* 26:1515 title only)

119. RESNICK, JOSEPH. "A Study of Some Relationships Between High School Grades and Certain Aspects of Adjustment." *J Ed Res* 44:321–40 Ja '51. * (*PA* 25:8286)

NELSON G. HANAWALT, *Associate Professor of Psychology, New Jersey College for Women, Rutgers University, New Brunswick, New Jersey.*

Since 1934 the Student Form has been a popular test in schools and clinics. Since 1938 an Adult Form has been available which adds occupational adjustment to the original measures of home, health, social, and emotional. Just how widely the Adult Form is used and to what purpose, the writer has been unable to ascertain. Only four published studies specifically referring to it have been found in our survey of the literature. Forlano and Kirkpatrick (*68*) combined the Social Scale score from the Adult Form with the Alienation score of the *Washburn Social Adjustment Inventory* for the purpose of selecting radio tube assemblers. In their validating study involving 20 girls on the job, all those scoring above average on the test were rated "good" by their supervisor and all those scoring below average were rated "fair." The supervisor had no knowledge of the test scores. The authors claim, but furnish no supporting data for the claim, that a composite of the social scores and intelligence ratings were effective in predicting the subsequent success of new tube mounters. Seagoe (*70, 76*) found that the Adult Form showed some predictive possibilities, especially long range ones, in selecting teachers. Her studies were based upon correlations of test scores with ratings of success of student teachers and teachers in service. No other study has been found where a prediction of occupational success has been attempted using the Bell.

Data on the Student Form are more abundant. In general these studies convey a favorable attitude toward the test; but some find it unsuited for a particular purpose, some express no opinion, and a few express a negative opinion.

Several surveys involving the inventory have been made. In 1936 Pallister [1] asked a number of psychologists to rate some vocational tests. Of the 38 psychologists responding, 14 rated the Bell: 11 rated it as efficient and 3 as not efficient. In 1946 Darley and Marquis [2] made a survey of tests used in 51 contract clinics for veteran guidance. Sixteen personality tests were mentioned by the respondents. The three most frequently mentioned were the *Minnesota Multi-*

1 Pallister, Helen. "American Psychologists Judge Fifty-Three Vocational Tests." *J Appl Psychol* 20:761–8 D '36. * (*PA* 11:2980)
2 Darley, John G., and Marquis, Donald G. "Veterans' Guidance Centers: A Survey of Their Problems and Activities." *J Clin Psychol* 2:109–16 Ap '46. * (*PA* 20:3885)

phasic Personality Inventory, use index 55; Bell's *Adjustment Inventory,* use index 35; and Bernreuter's *Personality Inventory,* use index 29. The same year Kornhauser[3] got replies from 67 well known test specialists to the question: "In the field of personality testing, how satisfactory or helpful for present practical use do you consider personality inventories and questionnaires (such as Bernreuter, Bell, Humm-Wadsworth, etc.)?" The results were: highly satisfactory, 1.5 per cent; moderately satisfactory, 13.5 per cent; doubtful, 36 per cent; rather unsatisfactory, 33 per cent; and highly unsatisfactory, 16 per cent. The clinical as compared to the nonclinical psychologists tended to rate the inventories more favorably. Only a slightly higher percentage of the raters considered the Rorschach more satisfactory than the inventories. There was some suggestion that those who consider the Rorschach satisfactory tend to consider the inventories unsatisfactory. In the few comments regarding particular blanks, the Bell and the MMPI received favorable mention.

In the same year Ellis (*72*) published a comprehensive survey of the literature concerning the validity of personality inventories and concluded that the evidence was largely negative. The Bell was one of four tests singled out for special study and made the poorest showing of the four. It is the writer's opinion that this study is misleading. Ellis assumed that the inventories were designed for the use to which the investigators put them, and that the validating data were unquestionable. In some of the 11 validating studies cited on the Bell by Ellis, the authors themselves pointed out the weakness of the validating data, and in others they should have done so. Intelligence tests would look a little sick if they were evaluated in a similarly *objective,* though indiscriminate, manner. We have analyzed the 11 studies cited by Ellis on the Bell and are not much impressed by his *objective* rating of them.

Also in 1946 Painter and Painter[4] made a survey of entrance tests used by a sample of colleges. Of the 42 replying, 14.3 per cent reported that they gave personality tests to incoming freshmen. Bell led the list of tests used for this purpose. Feder and Mallett (*5*) found

that the inclusion of the Bell in the entrance battery of tests left the prediction coefficient of scholastic success unchanged. Drought (*9*) and Griffiths (*69*) have both shown that there is no correlation with scholarship, either with the total score or with relevant subscales. Batemen (*94*) used the Bell to check the hypothesis that high school students who work for pay are better adjusted. The results were negative. However, Smith (*84*) found that students who participated in extracurricular activities were better adjusted as measured by the Social Scale. He interpreted this as validating data for the test.

A number of studies have checked the reliability coefficients of the Student Form (*2, 3, 7, 10, 48, 79*) and have found them satisfactory. Greene and Staton (*13*) and Eckert and Keys (*37*) have both found that there is no correlation between the Bernreuter-Flanagan Sociability Scale and the Bell Social Scale. Watson (*57*) reported correlations between his *Inventory of Affective Tolerance* and the Bell which range from —.60 for Social to —.11 for Health: for the total Watson and Bell, —.56. Tyler (*3*) and Sperling (*55*) have both verified Bell's intercorrelations of subscales and the total scale. The correlations reported by Bell in the manual appear to be well substantiated. Pallister (*14*) found that students in a Scottish University fell within the American norms, and Sukov and Williamson (*30*) found no difference in scores between Jews and non-Jews. Damrin (*79*) gave the test to 153 high school girls under signature and again anonymously but identified by an ingenious system. The correlations between the two administrations were high, ranging from .75 to .97; Damrin interpreted this as evidence both for the reliability of the test and the dependability of the answers. More responses on the anonymous tests were changed from poor to good adjustment than vice versa.

Validity is always a difficult problem. Unfortunately, only a few of the validating studies approach the care and scientific accuracy of Bell's original validating data. One of the better ones is that of Turney and Fee (*2*) with high school students. The reliability of teachers' ratings and the test were both checked by having them repeated after six months. Both were found to be reliable. The correlations between the two ranged from .18 for Home to .42 for Health. The second ratings correlated with the second Bell gave higher coefficients in three of the five measures. Traxler (*48*) found higher and lower

3 Kornhauser, A. "Replies of Psychologists to a Short Questionnaire on Mental Test Developments, Personality Inventories, and the Rorschach Test." *Ed & Psychol Meas* 5:3–15 sp '45. * (*PA* 20:343)
4 Painter, William I., and Painter, Helen Welch. "Orientation Testing Practices." *J Ed Res* 39:613–21 Ap '46. * (*PA* 20:4347)

correlations than the above: .64 for Social and zero for Home. He concluded that high school teachers do not know enough about home adjustments to rate them with any meaning. Clark and Smith (50) concluded that the test is not valid on the basis of teachers' ratings. However, we cannot take their findings too seriously, for the reliability of the teachers' ratings in the case of large departments was as low as .47. They found that the teachers tended to rate the students very much the same. Also the teachers' ratings were on more specific items than the Bell subtests.

Pederson (15) compared Bell test scores with data combed from college application autobiographies. Students who revealed home maladjustment showed a reliable difference on the Home Scale when compared with those not speaking of home maladjustment. However, these data were not very helpful in predicting the cases which would turn up at the dean's office on account of home difficulties. The Health score was found to be indicative of poor health as revealed in the autobiography, personnel records, and the health department. Individuals rated maladjusted by the social advisor tended to show maladjustment on the Social Scale. Aside from health, the dean's records appear to be sadly deficient concerning adjustment of college students and hence have limited value in validation studies. This is probably an important factor in Marsh's (60) conclusions that social and emotional maladjustment is best predicted from the Home Scale, and that this is not particularly sensitive to maladjustment until the case becomes "critical." This conclusion is based upon a comparison of 23 girls referred to the dean with 50 "normal" girls (i.e., girls not so referred). Keys and Guilford (6) found low but statistically significant correlations with problem behavior for the total score and three of the subtests. Spoerl (61) found the test useful in analyzing emotional difficulties of bilingual students.

Darley (4) found that roughly one third of the cases diagnosed clinically were picked up by the Social and the Emotional scales and that nearly one half of the cases diagnosed by the test as maladjusted were confirmed in clinical study. Darley found the subtest scores much more useful than the total score. Tuckman (77) found that self-ratings on a five point linear scale corresponding to the Bell subtests correlate high enough with the Bell scores that these ratings can be substituted for the Bell if the time is limited. These self-ratings would appear to be validating data for the Bell. In general, correlations between the subtests and outside ratings are highest where the raters are best qualified to rate (2, 15, 48, 50, 77).

Several item analyses have been made. Gilkinson and Knower (42) reported that good speakers as a group have better social adjustment as measured by the Social Scale; they found 19 items which differentiated between good and poor speakers, 15 of them from the Social Scale. Altus and Bell (65) found 22 items in the Student Form which discriminated between adjusted and nonadjusted illiterates in a special Army training center. These items, combined with some others, could be used to predict successful training. Marsh (60) found 14 items from the Home Scale which were useful in predicting social and emotional maladjustment. Woolf (63) found 12 items in the Home Scale which best discriminate between satisfactory and unsatisfactory adjustment in college.

Three studies have been found where an attempt has been made to use the Bell to discriminate between delinquents and nondelinquents. Bartlett and Harris (18) compared 119 delinquents with 148 school children and found no difference on the Social Scale but marked differences in Home and Emotional adjustment in the expected direction. Hathaway (34) found the test did not discriminate between his nine psychopaths (restricted usage) and the normal population. Wittman and Huffman (71), using the Adult Form, compared the scores of high school students, training school delinquents, and state hospital patients. Although the test showed rather marked differences on home adjustment and emotional adjustment, especially for the delinquent girls who were largely sex offenders, none of the differences were statistically significant due to the large standard deviations.

The Bell has been used in other special research projects. There has been some interest in measuring personality by means of interest tests. Tussing (56) found that he could predict the Bell Social scores by a rescoring of Strong's *Vocational Interest Blank,* but not the other scales. Klugman (112), however, found no relation between the *Kuder Preference Record* and the Bell. Cowen and Thompson (116) found no relation between the Bell and "rigid personality" as measured by the Luchins water jar test. Van der Merwe and Theron (85), however, found a substantial correlation between the Bell Emotional score and a finger plethysmograph record. This would appear to indicate that emotional stability as measured by the Bell has a physiological concomitant.

In conclusion it appears that there is no doubt concerning the correlations published in the manual of the *Adjustment Inventory*. The validity apparently is as good as any of the paper and pencil adjustment inventories and better established than most of them. The subtests furnish valuable data concerning adjustment in four areas. It has proved to be a valuable instrument in research, in schools, and in clinical work. Apparently its popularity over the years is well justified. There is no indication in the literature that it can be depended upon to pick out of a group all maladjusted individuals, nor that all "maladjusted" according to the score are actually maladjusted. Its greatest usefulness would appear to be as a guide to interview and as an aid in better understanding the individual. The quantitative scores furnish data of diagnostic value, but answers to specific items will often point the way to much more valuable data. In reviewing the literature one is impressed with the fact that the test results are very frequently more satisfying than the validating criteria. Some more studies involving the Adult Form would appear to be highly desirable.

THEODORE R. SARBIN, *Associate Professor of Psychology, University of California, Berkeley, California.*

The *Adjustment Inventory* began as a set of a priori scales intended to isolate persons who were maladjusted in four areas: home, health, social, and emotional. Later, an occupational scale was added to the adult form. The scales have satisfactory odd-even reliability coefficients, .80 to .89. Only those items which differentiated between extremes of the distribution on the standardizing group were retained. Empirical validation was achieved by comparing scores with ratings of counselors, personnel workers, etc. Critical ratios are all significant—demonstrating that the scores differentiate persons rated by counselors as "well-adjusted" from those rated as "poorly-adjusted" in a particular area, e.g., emotional adjustment.

A decade ago, this reviewer found the *Adjustment Inventory* useful in screening college students for mental hygiene interviews. The health, home, social, and emotional categories served as

a frame of reference for the counselor in organizing his impressions about the student. In the 1930's, when reliable knowledge of personality dynamics was in its infancy, these categories had descriptive utility for untrained or semitrained student personnel workers. Today, such rubrics as health adjustment, home adjustment, etc., seem anachronistic. More appropriate are scales that probe for specific variables, such as type of ego-defense, internalization, somatization, hysteria, etc. The *Minnesota Multiphasic Personality Inventory,* for example, is currently more useful as an instrument for personality diagnosis, especially when subject to coding, profile analysis, and configural scoring as advocated by G. S. Welsh.[1]

For reviews by Raymond B. Cattell, John G. Darley, C. M. Louttit, and Percival M. Symonds of the Student Form, and reviews by S. J. Beck, J. P. Guilford, and Doncaster G. Humm of the Adult Form, see 40:1200; for a review by Austin H. Turney of the Student Form, see 38:912 (although three reviews are listed under 38:912, only the review by Austin H. Turney is a review of Bell's Adjustment Inventory; *the other two are reviews of Bell's* School Inventory).

[29]
★**Affectivity Interview Blank.** Ages 7–12; 1951; a measure of child feelings; individual; 1 form ['51]; $1.40 per 25; 15¢ per specimen set; postpaid; (15) minutes; Elizabeth Mechem Fuller; Child Development Laboratories, University of Michigan. *

REFERENCES
1. MECHEM, MARY ELIZABETH. *The Relationship of Affectivity to Various Measures of Growth in Children.* Doctor's thesis, University of Michigan (Ann Arbor, Mich.), 1941. Abstract: *Microfilm Abstracts* 3:82–4 no 2 '41. *
2. MECHEM, ELIZABETH. "Affectivity and Growth in Children." *Child Develop* 14:91–115 Je '43. * (PA 17:3994)
3. FULLER, ELIZABETH MECHEM. "How do the Children Feel About It?" *Childhood Ed* 23:124–32 N '46. * (PA 21:3963)

MORRIS KRUGMAN, *Assistant Superintendent in Charge of Guidance, Board of Education, New York, New York.*

In its present stage, this instrument merits attention only because "The Affectivity Interview Blank was devised at the University of Michigan as a part of the child growth studies under the direction of Professor Willard C. Olson." Labeled an "interview blank," with the avowed purpose of contributing "to the problem of describing the feeling aspects of children's personalities," this blank could be accepted as an experimental subjective device.

1 Welsh, George S. "An Extension of Hathaway's MMPI Profile Coding System." *J Consult Psychol* 12:343–4 S–O '48. * (PA 23:1780)
Welsh, George S. "Some Practical Uses of MMPI Profile Coding." *J Consult Psychol* 15:82–4 F '51. *

The author, however, after considerable discussion of the tentativeness of the blank, proceeds to supply "norms," "evidence" of reliability, and scoring weights for each item, leaving the impression that we are dealing with an objective measuring instrument. This is definitely not the case.

The blank consists of 71 items of such diffuse nature that they do not seem, collectively, to make sense. Examples are: "Do you have a dog, cat, or other pet?" "Do you ever wish that you had never been born?" "Do you comb your own hair?" Each of these items has a weight of one. The 7-year-old (the 5-year-old also, according to the author) and the 12-year-old boy or girl achieves the same credit for saying "yes" to "Do you comb your own hair?" This is not an isolated example, but rather typical of the kind of "affectivity" measured by this blank.

"Norms" in terms of percentiles for children aged 7 to 12 (and applicable as low as age 5, according to the author) are based on 65 children in the original experimental group and 30 children added later. This is typical of the "standardization" procedure.

The author makes the following claim for the instrument: "In general, for the populations studied, the overt behavior of the children bore demonstrable relationship to their verbalized feelings about themselves." The manual does not supply the evidence for this conclusion.

In summary, the *Affectivity Interview Blank* does not give the impression of being an instrument that can measure affectivity in children, nor are the author's claims that it does so substantiated by the evidence presented in the manual.

VERNER M. SIMS, *Professor of Psychology, University of Alabama, University, Alabama.*

This blank is offered as a preliminary form of a structured interview blank from which it is possible to arrive at a quantitative expression of the "feeling aspects of children's personality." It is proposed for use with children prior to the mastery of reading, that is, from the ages 5 through 12 years. No serious effort is made by the author to define what the blank measures, but the description of its construction and an examination of the items indicate that it undertakes to measure what is generally comprehended under the term "personality adjustment." In fact, one of the two criteria used for the inclusion of items was "a minimum number

of five appearances in one or more....published personality tests, clinical findings, and textbook treatments of problems in the personality area."

Evidence of validity for the blank is contained in the method of selecting the items (which almost surely means some agreement with other such instruments); in the fact that items were retained only after an experimental tryout for "ambiguity or lack of understanding by the children" (the second criterion used in item selection); in the reported agreement among 150 adults, with advanced training in the psychology and education of young children, concerning the response to each question which was "indicative of a higher level of affectivity" (70 per cent or more of the judges agreed on all but 16 of the 69 scorable items in the blank); and in the finding that "for the population studied, the overt behavior of the children bore demonstrable relationship to their verbalized feelings about themselves" (although no data to support this conclusion are reported).

A split half reliability of .82 for 65 subjects, and a test-retest reliability of .70 for 44 subjects, with a school year intervening, suggest some stability for the quality or qualities measured by the test. The scoring of the blank is objective and relatively simple. Good suggestions for its administration and use are furnished in the manual. Percentile norms based on 65 elementary school children (a sample which is recognized by the author as inadequate) are given.

This interview blank seems to have promise. Accepted in the tentative spirit in which it is presented, it represents the beginnings of a worthwhile instrument. It is to be hoped that the author, or someone else, will undertake to carry on the work necessary if the blank is to become a tool useful in counseling and guidance. Particularly needed are more careful item analyses, better "outside" validation, and more extensive and representative norms.

[30]

★The Alcadd Test. Adults; 1949; a test for the measurement of alcoholic addiction and identification of individuals with alcoholic problems; 6 scores: regularity of drinking, preference for drinking over other activities, lack of · controlled drinking, rationalization of drinking, excessive emotionality, total; 1 form; $2.75 per 25; 35¢ per specimen set; postpaid; nontimed (5-15) minutes; Morse P. Manson; Western Psychological Services, Box 775, Beverly Hills, Calif. *

REFERENCES
1. MANSON, MORSE P. "A Psychometric Determination of Alcoholic Addiction." *Am J Psychiatry* 106:199–205 S '49. * (*PA* 24:3271)

CHARLES H. HONZIK, *Personal Counselor and Vocational Adviser, Veterans Administration, San Francisco, California.*

This test differs from the author's *The Manson Evaluation* in three respects: (*a*) *The Alcadd Test* items refer directly to drinking and drinking habits; (*b*) *The Alcadd Test* determines more closely the *degree* of alcoholic addiction; and (*c*) it attempts an objective recognition of such characteristics of alcoholic addiction as regularity of drinking, rationalization of drinking, etc. The existence of these two rather similar tests is valuable in large screening programs, such as may exist in Veterans Administration, federal and state hospitals, and clinics for alcoholics, where slightly differing practical questions may be better answered by one test than by the other. For example, in the cases where alcoholism or even moderate drinking is denied, *The Manson Evaluation* would be more likely to make the desired differentiation, as well as to indicate some of the personality characteristics of the testee; in those cases where there is no question of alcoholic addiction, the degree of addiction and some of the dynamics of the addiction, may be determined by *The Alcadd Test*.

The test consists of 65 items, 61 pertaining to drinking; examples are, "I drink only to join the fun," and "I often take a drink or two in the middle of the afternoon." Only 60 items are scored. An original battery of 160 such questions, obtained from observation of alcoholic addicts and from the literature on the overt behavior, attitudes, feelings, and other characteristics of alcoholics, was constructed and administered to comparable groups of male and female alcoholics and nonalcoholics. By item analysis 60 items were selected, each of which had a critical ratio of 2.7 or higher, for both male and female groups. These 60 items were then administered to 123 male and female alcoholics, and 159 male and female nonalcoholics. Using a cutting score of 12 for the male groups, it was found that 97.6 per cent of the alcoholics were correctly predicted, while a cutting score of 14 for the females gave 97.5 per cent correct predictions. The reliability coefficient of the test was found to be .92 for the male group, .96 for the female group.

A subjective analysis of the 65 items revealed five clusters which describe characteristics of alcoholic addiction and addicts. These are regularity of drinking, preference for drinking over other activities, lack of controlled drinking, rationalization of drinking, and excessive emotionality. Separate scores may be computed for these five characteristics, the differences between alcoholics and nonalcoholics on all the characteristics being statistically significant. Interesting differences were found between male and female alcoholics, the females showing less control, more rationalization, and more emotional immaturity than the males.

The test is easily administered to groups or individuals and takes from 5 to 15 minutes. Scoring is simple and can be done in 2 to 3 minutes. A profile is provided which is filled in as the scores are computed.

This test, like all questionnaires, is subject to the dangers of untrue scores through deliberate or unconscious falsification. A test in this area of human behavior would seem to be particularly vulnerable since many alcoholic addicts are known to deny stubbornly frequent drinking and other facts that are glaringly obvious to observers. For such addicts the test would give false scores. On this point, an interesting question arises: why were 2.4 per cent of the male alcoholics and 2.5 per cent of the female alcoholics incorrectly placed by the test? The tendency to falsify is probably responsible. Nevertheless, the reviewer believes that this test, discreetly used, can be a useful tool in screening programs and a valuable adjunct to clinical methods.

ALBERT L. HUNSICKER, *Supervising Psychologist, Galesburg State Research Hospital, Galesburg, Illinois.*

This yes-no questionnaire was designed to facilitate rapid identification of alcoholic addicts and to locate possible areas of their maladjustment. The 60 questions, obviously directed towards the evaluation of drinking habits and with no attempt to camouflage their purpose, were carefully selected from an original set of 160 questions administered to alcoholics and "normals" of essentially equivalent age, education, and social status.

The male scoring norms are based on results from 83 alcoholics in treatment for alcoholism, 61 social drinkers, and 17 abstainers. Female norms are based on 40 alcoholics in treatment, 58 social drinkers, and 23 abstainers. The shorter approximation of the Kuder-Richardson formula produced a reliability coefficient of .92 for the males and .96 for the females. The scores of the known alcoholic group and of the abstainers for either sex do not overlap, and very little overlapping is found between known alcoholics and social drinkers. This reviewer administered the *Alcadd Test* to 11 known alcoholics from an outpatient clinic and 18 hospital employees, who omitted all identifying information from their questionnaire. The results obtained were very similar to those found by the author.

From a *subjective analysis* of the 60 questions, the author finds five categories which are labeled (a) regularity of drinking, (b) preference for drinking over other activities, (c) lack of controlled drinking, (d) rationalization of drinking, and (e) excessive emotionality. The subjective breakdown of the 60 questions into these five arbitrary categories supposed to reveal areas of maladjustment would probably not stand up under a careful cluster or factor analysis of the questions.

When this questionnaire is used on known alcoholics in a treatment environment, results comparable to those discussed in the manual may be expected. However, could one expect the same results from the alcoholic addict if he were taking this test as one of a series of screening tests preparatory to a job which he wants badly? Or would he, as the reviewer feels certain, conceal the seriousness of his addiction in most situations where he becomes just another member of a "normal" population who takes this test?

The *Manson Evaluation,* by the same author, which is made up of 72 questions only remotely associated with drinking, will probably prove a better alcoholic screening test than this one. Still, this questionnaire remains a pioneer study in the field of alcoholic addiction and will prove useful to those institutions, clinics, and psychologists who are faced with the problem of evaluating and working with alcoholic addicts.

[31]

Babcock Test of Mental Deterioration. Ages 7–24; 1930–40; title on test booklet is *The Revised Examination for the Measurement of Efficiency of Mental Functioning;* 8 scores: easy questions, learning, repetition, motor, initial learning, easy continuous, total efficiency (total of six previous scores), verbal level; 1 form, '40; $13.75 per set of testing materials and 50 record blanks; $3.75 per 50 record blanks; $3 per specimen set (includes manual and pictures of testing materials); postage extra; nontimed in part (70+) minutes; Harriet Babcock and Lydia Levy; C. H. Stoelting & Co. *

REFERENCES

1–14. See 40:1248.
15–35. See 3:71.
36. PARTINGTON, J. EDWIN. "The Comparative Mental Efficiency of a Drug Addict Group." *J Appl Psychol* 24:48–57 F '40. * (PA 14:3567)
37. WESLEY, S. M. *A Study of the Use of Recent Memory Tests in the Measurement of Intellectual Deterioration.* Doctor's thesis, University of Minnesota (Minneapolis, Minn.), 1941.
38. BURR, EMILY. "Prime Factors in the Placement of the Below Normal." *Am J Mental Def* 51:429–34 Ja '47. * (PA 22:360)
39. SCHAFER, ROY. *The Clinical Application of Psychological Tests: Diagnostic Summaries and Case Studies.* Foreword by David Rapaport. The Menninger Foundation Monograph Series No. 6. New York: International Universities Press, Inc., 1948. Pp. 346. * (London: George Allen & Unwin Ltd., 1949.) (PA 23:778)
40. JASTAK, JOSEPH. "Problems of Psychometric Scatter Analysis." *Psychol B* 46:177–97 My '49. * (PA 24:188)
41. SCHERER, ISIDOR W. "The Psychological Scores of Mental Patients in an Individual and Group Testing Situation." *J Clin Psychol* 5:405–8 O '49. * (PA 34:2740)
42. FOX, CHARLOTTE, AND BIRREN, JAMES E. "Intellectual Deterioration in the Aged: Agreement Between the Wechsler-Bellevue and the Babcock-Levy." *J Consult Psychol* 14:305–10 Ag '50. * (PA 25:2344)
43. FOX, CHARLOTTE, AND BIRREN, JAMES E. "The Measurement of Intellectual Deterioration in the Aged." Abstract. *Am Psychol* 5:364 Jl '50. * (PA 25:980, title only)
44. NEWTON, RICHARD L. "A Comparison of Two Methods of Administering the Digit Span Test." *J Clin Psychol* 409–12 O '50. * (PA 25:8105)
45. BOTWINICK, JACK, AND BIRREN, JAMES E. "The Measurement of Intellectual Decline in the Senile Psychoses." *J Consult Psychol* 15:145–50 Ap '51. * (PA 26:6419)

D. RUSSELL DAVIS, *Reader in Clinical Psychology, University of Cambridge; and Honorary Consultant Research Psychiatrist, United Cambridge Hospitals; Cambridge, England.*

As early as 1914, B. Hart and C. E. Spearman studied the performance of psychotic patients on a large number of mental tests and compared it with that of normal subjects, but their findings were of little practical or theoretical value. A very useful advance was made in 1930 when Babcock first published her methods of examination, especially because she drew attention to the value of vocabulary tests as means of assessing the premorbid intelligence level of patients and, hence, by comparison between scores on vocabulary and on other tests, of measuring the deterioration that can be attributed to an illness. The theoretical views with which Babcock has tried to explain her original and her more recent results have been subjected to damaging criticism. That they are not acceptable need not detract, however, from the value placed on the essential features of her methods. Indeed, it is now generally agreed that the scores obtained on vocabulary and kindred tests are relatively unaffected either by psychological or by organic disease processes, and this fact has been made use of in most modern methods of psychological examination of patients.

Yet, however useful it may have been in the 1930's, Babcock's test battery is not now satisfactory for general use, and the present revision has done little or nothing to reduce the shortcomings which the all-round improvement in test methods in the last decade has revealed.

Four tests of the original battery have now

been omitted, seven new tests have been added, and changes have been made in eight tests. But the norms are inadequate by modern standards, and the manner of arriving at weighted scores and the efficiency index is an unnecessarily roundabout one. Some of the tests might still be useful for the many clinical purposes for which precise norms are not required and may survive for occasional use. Many of the tests are unsatisfactory, however, for too much emphasis is placed on speed in the scores; these scores are considerably influenced, therefore, by the "set" which the patient has been brought to adopt. Some of the material is inappropriate; for example, most examiners prefer to greet a patient by name at the first meeting and would dislike starting their testing with the words, "Now answer these questions as promptly as you can: what is your name?" In the reviewer's opinion, the counterparts in the *Wechsler-Bellevue Intelligence Scale* of the test of general information, substitution, and digits forward and reversed are better in every case, although it is debatable whether the Wechsler-Bellevue vocabulary test is superior to the Terman-Merrill vocabulary test.

The most useful tests in the battery are those of memory, which form an essential part of an examination when organic brain damage is suspected, and which the Wechsler-Bellevue scale lacks: especially useful are the paragraph reproduction test, which is a modification of the Terman-Merrill reading and report, and the sentence repetition test, now slightly revised. The paired associates test has been lengthened to include nine instead of seven pairs of words and is now too long. Also, learning is tested in two trials only, and there is now no chance of detecting failures to unlearn wrong responses—an interesting sign suggestive of an organic defect. The memory for designs test has something to be said in its favour, although many examiners may still prefer less formal and less standardised methods. The Knox cube test is a most suitable one for class demonstrations on patients.

SEYMOUR G. KLEBANOFF, *Chief Psychologist, Franklin Delano Roosevelt Veterans Administration Hospital, Montrose, New York.*

This examination consists of a group of sub-tests designed to measure three essential areas of mental functioning: learning ability, motor ability, and repetition ability. The final result is an obtained efficiency index which reflects the difference between capacity level of intellectual functioning and current efficiency.

Consideration of the principles underlying the construction of the test reveals certain significant problems. As Wesley has shown, the traditional concept that vocabulary consistently serves as a measure of capacity level must be challenged. More recent studies of the intellectual process indicate that vocabulary scores show a definite tendency to decline with increasing age as well as in the presence of significant personality pathology. Further, the assumption of Babcock that normal functioning can be evaluated optimally by the use of normal subjects of less than 25 years of age indicates a failure to consider the chronology of the population for whom the test was intended.

The revised Babcock test does not constitute a more novel or original contribution to the problem of intellectual deficit. It employs the longstanding thesis that discrepancy between vocabulary and recently acquired associations will serve as a measure of "deterioration." It appears that this clinical fact has been overly exploited in an effort to obtain a quantitative index of intellectual impairment and has impeded progress in understanding intellectual deficit. Continued corroboration of a clinical phenomenon does not advance knowledge of the intellectual process. It is time to direct energy toward qualitative analysis of those intellectual functions which reveal deficit with the end of determining the conditions under which impairment occurs. Further, the conditions underlying the reversibility of intellectual deficit constitute variables for concerted study.

In essence, the revision of the Babcock test approaches the problem of intellectual deficit with the same theoretical basis formulated by Wells and Kelley [1] in 1920. It remains, however, a useful technique when utilized by clinicians who are sensitive to its limitations.

For related reviews, see 3:72.

[32]

*[The Baxter Group Test of Child Feeling.]
Grades 1-8, 7-9 (separate edition available for parents and teachers of children in grades 1-9); 1935-46, c1935; a revision of *Baxter Group Test of Child Feelings* (see 40:1206) and *Baxter Individual Tests of Child Feelings* (see 40:1207); 2 levels; 2 editions; $1.50 per 25 of any one edition of any one level; 50¢ per manual for any one level of the children's tests; 60¢ per specimen set of any one edition of any one level; postage extra; (30-40) minutes; Edna D. Bax-

1 Wells, F. L., and Kelley, C. M. "Intelligence and Psychosis." *Am J Insanity* 77:17-45 Jl '20. *

ter; Baxter Foundation for Research in Education, Inc., 315 Central Park West, New York, N.Y. *

a) CHILD'S TEST: BAXTER GROUP STORY-TEST OF CHILD FEELINGS. Grades 1-8; 1935; 23 scores: friendliness, responsiveness, generosity (jealousy), respect (sarcasm), dependability, daydreaming, obedience, compliance, self-control, fairness (domineering), courage, studiousness, creativity, concentration, temperance (boisterousness), carefulness (destructiveness), grace (awkwardness), unselfishness, honesty, courtesy, cheerfulness, kindness, tidiness; 1 form; mimeographed manual ['35].

b) THE BAXTER TEST OF CHILD FEELINGS. Grades 7-9; 1935; 25 scores; same as above plus sociality, appearance; 1 form; mimeographed manual ['35].

c) THE BAXTER PARENT-TEACHER TEST OF CHILD FEELINGS. Parents and teachers of children in grades 1-9; 1935-46; 1 form, '46; no data on reliability and validity; no manual; no norms.

REFERENCES

1. BAXTER, EDNA DOROTHY. "The Baxter Child Personality Test." *J Appl Psychol* 21:410-30 Ag '37. * (PA 12:967)
2. BAXTER, EDNA DOROTHY. "Baxter Group Test of Child Personality." Abstract. *Psychol B* 36:629-30 O '39. * (PA 14:600, title only)

[33]

★Client Centered Counseling Progress Recording Chart. Adults and children undergoing psychotherapeutic counseling; 1950; individual; 1 form; $1 per 25; 35¢ per specimen set; postage extra; nontimed (20) minutes; Russell N. Cassel; the Author, 344 B St., Hayward, Calif. *

[34]

★The College Inventory of Academic Adjustment. College; 1949; 7 scores: curricular adjustment, maturity of goals and level of aspiration, personal efficiency-planning and use of time, study skills and practices, mental health, personal relations, total; 1 form; $2 per 25; 15¢ per specimen set; cash orders postpaid; nontimed (15-25) minutes; Henry Borow; Stanford University Press, Stanford, Calif. *

REFERENCES

1. BOROW, HENRY. *A Psychometric Study of Non-Intellectual Factors in College Achievement.* Doctor's thesis, Pennsylvania State College (State College, Pa.), 1945. (*Abstracts of Doctoral Dissertations....1945*, 1946, pp. 65-73.)
2. BOROW, HENRY. "The Measurement of Academic Adjustment." *J Am Assn Col Reg* 22:274-86 Ap '47. *
3. TROXEL, LEETHA LORETTA. *A Study of Three Vocational Interest Measures: Preference Record, Academic Interest Inventory, and Work Interest Analysis.* Master's thesis, University of Kentucky (Lexington, Ky.), 1949.

LYSLE W. CROFT, *Director of Personnel, University of Kentucky, Lexington, Kentucky.*

The inventory is "designed to identify certain attributes, apart from scholastic aptitude, which have been shown to be significantly related to the college student's academic performance." It consists of 90 items of the 3-choice type (yes, no, undecided), with from 12 to 21 items in each of the following six sections: Curricular Adjustment, Maturity of Goals and Levels of Aspiration, Personal Efficiency, Study Skills and Practices, Mental Health, and Personal Relations.

Percentile norms for the composite inventory are based on 237 male students at Pennsylvania State College and the University of Minnesota, and 454 women students at the Pennsylvania State College. The sampling procedure involved in selecting these normative characteristics of the two groups are specified. Means and standard deviations are given in lieu of percentile norms for each of the six sections.

Split half reliabilities, corrected by the Spearman-Brown formula, of .90 and .92 for groups of 155 men and 130 women students, respectively, are reported for the composite score of the inventory. The corrected test-retest reliability over a span of 10 days for a group of 130 women students is given as .92.

Items for the inventory were selected on the basis of their power to differentiate between groups of "under-achievers" and "over-achievers." The discussion in the manual of the validity of the inventory is based mainly upon the fact that section and total scores discriminate at the 1 per cent level between a group of 81 "under-achievers" and 67 "over-achievers." The author also reports the partial correlation between total scores on the inventory and the two-semester grade average is .32 with scholastic aptitude scores partialed out.

Considering the data presented in the manual, the inventory does not fulfil the reviewer's specifications for a useful diagnostic aid in counseling, although this is the expressed purpose of the inventory. In the first place, there is no direct evidence that cross-validation studies were made. In describing the various phases of the research, the author does not reveal the extent to which the population samples were independent. Unless the fact is established that the validity data were obtained on groups other than those used in the item selection process, the validity figures are severely open to question. In the second place, the evidence that the scores on the inventory discriminate significantly between groups of achievement deviates, and that the partial correlation of the composite scores with grade averages is .32, is not strong enough to justify the use of the inventory in individual counseling situations. "Cost and utility" data are more important than critical ratios and correlation coefficients for the uses for which this inventory is designed.

In summary, the author's claim that this inventory is a useful "diagnostic aid in counseling" is not supported by the data presented in the manual. Even the use of the inventory as a check list for locating the problem areas of the scholastic "under-achiever" is not justifiable until it is shown that the items have been cross validated.

This reviewer does not like the idea of the women overweighing the men in relation to the number of subjects. Follow-up research projects have not been accomplished, and it is rather doubtful that the results received by the author will follow in other institutions of higher learning.

HARRISON G. GOUGH, *Assistant Professor of Psychology, University of California, Berkeley, California.*

This is a 90-item inventory yielding part scores in each of six logically-derived categories. The test was developed at Pennsylvania State College by item analyzing the responses of over- and under-achievers (identified by·means of regression line deviations) to a specially written pool of 400 items. From those which survived the statistical analysis, a further choice was made using logical and subjective criteria. Each item included in the final version of the scale revealed differentiating power in both male and female samples, and satisfied requirements pertaining to clarity, meaningfulness, and consistency.

The main purpose of the test is to assess scholastic interest and potentiality, independently of intelligence and aptitude. The separate scores can also be used diagnostically for evaluating academic functioning in the areas specified. In a cross validating sample of 155 college men the following correlations with 2-semester grade averages were obtained: (*a*) curricular adjustment, .30; (*b*) maturity of goals and level of aspiration, .31; (*c*) personal efficiency: planning and use of time, .41; (*d*) study skills and practices, .22; (*e*) mental health, .27; (*f*) personal relations, .16; (*g*) total score, .36. Correlations for women were very similar, although somewhat lower.

Moreover, the test also shows almost no correlation with intellectual measures. This enhances its value as a predictor of academic achievement because it is tapping a domain not assessed by intellectual measures. Furthermore, the experienced counselor can examine the configurations of the six part scores to help gain an understanding of the reasons for academic accomplishment or difficulty.

The research methodology underlying the test's development impressed this reviewer as being basically sound. However, some doubts were raised concerning the criteria used for rejecting items that had satisfied the statistical requirements. The 90 selected items were culled from a pool of 246. The search for clarity and meaningfulness might have led the test developer to reject some highly valid, but subtle, items. Such an outcome would indeed be unfortunate for this kind of item is often the most significant product of an empirical inquiry, usually represents new knowledge, does not put a respondent on his guard, and is the most difficult kind of item to fake.

The language and style of the items is disturbingly cumbersome and awkward. The general flavor is of old fashioned written language with very little pacing and spontaneity. One of the properties of a good personality inventory item is its general resonance—the degree to which it sounds like "something people say." Such a quality encourages a response concerned with the question asked and the issues raised. The farther an item departs from this verisimilitude the greater is the opportunity for extraneous and complicating response sets to manifest themselves. In the extreme case an item may be consistently rejected merely because of the way it is worded rather than because of the question asked.

The reviewer also had some misgivings about the test directions. The first paragraph contains phrases like "high mental ability," "no better than average," "intellectually superior students," etc. Some students may be offended or annoyed by an introduction of this kind, and others may be made anxious. In any case, it would appear that an introductory paragraph could be written which did not put so much emphasis on superior and inferior achievement. One method would be merely to state that the test would inquire into study habits, personal reactions to college work, and general academic satisfaction.

The manual is thorough and systematic but suffers somewhat from intricacy and complexity. It is a good report on the test but not enough of an aid to a person who wants to use the test. No individual case material is presented, although the fundamental conception of the test recommends it for individual counseling and diagnostic application. No explanation is advanced for the use of weighted scores, as opposed to simpler methods. Some users may object to the labor involved in calculating weighted scores; a reference to the test's efficacy if unweighted scores are used would be helpful. The pages in the manual are not numbered, which is a mild annoyance to the reader.

The test does appear to fulfill a useful function—that of evaluating and specifying some of the nonintellectual factors contributing to academic achievement. It should be a useful device for college counselors. The limitations of the test do not appear to be critical, and can probably be overcome to a great extent in future editions.

[35]

Concept Formation Test. Normal and schizophrenic adults; 1940; individual; 1 form; no data on reliability and validity; no norms; mimeographed manual ['40]; $13 per set of testing materials, postage extra; (10–60) minutes; Jacob Kasanin and Eugenia Hanfmann; C. H. Stoelting Co. *

REFERENCES

1–19. See 3:27.
20. HANFMANN, EUGENIA. "Analysis of the Thinking Disorder in a Case of Schizophrenia." *Arch Neurol & Psychiatry* 41:568–79 Mr '39. *
21. FOSBERG, IRVING A. "Multiple Solutions to the Vigotsky Test." Abstract. *Am Psychol* 1:280 Jl '46. * (PA 20:3930, title only)
22. COOK, CHARLES HANNAFORD. *The Relation of Certain Factors of the Concept Formation Test to Scholastic Aptitude and to Scholastic Achievement.* Master's thesis, Clark University (Worcester, Mass.), 1947. (*Abstracts of Dissertations....* 1947, pp. 78–9.)
23. DES LAURIERS, AUSTIN, AND HALPERN, FLORENCE. "Psychological Tests in Childhood Schizophrenia." *Am J Orthopsychiatry* 17:57–67 Jl '47. * (PA 21:2226)
24. FOSBERG, IRVING ARTHUR. "A Modification of the Vigotsky Block-Test for the Study of the Higher Thought Processes." *Am J Psychol* 61:558–61 O '48. * (PA 23:4126)
25. SCHAFER, ROY. *The Clinical Application of Psychological Tests: Diagnostic Summaries and Case Studies.* Foreword by David Rapaport. The Menninger Foundation Monograph Series No. 6. New York: International Universities Press, Inc., 1948. Pp. 346. * (London: George Allen & Unwin Ltd., 1949.) (PA 23:778)
26. FISHER, SEYMOUR. *Patterns of Personality Rigidity and Some of Their Determinants.* American Psychological Association, Psychological Monographs: General and Applied, Vol. 64, No. 1, Whole No. 307. Washington, D.C.: the Association, Inc., 1950. Pp. v, 48. Paper. * (PA 24:6255)
27. NORMAN, RALPH D.; BAKER, CHARLES A.; AND DOEHRING, DONALD G. "The Hanfmann-Kasanin Concept Formation Test as a Measure of Rigidity in Relation to College Aptitude and Achievement." *J Clin Psychol* 6:365–9 O '50. * (PA 25:8256)

KATE LEVINE KOGAN, *Clinical Psychologist, 6034 44th Ave., N.E.; and* WILLIAM S. KOGAN, *Chief Psychologist, Veterans Administration Hospital; Seattle, Washington.*

This technique continues to be best characterized as an experimental device rather than a test method. The problem posed often serves to elicit certain forms of thinking disorder, which, when present, can be considered pathognomonic for schizophrenia. Other failures demonstrate interference with conceptual behavior whose exact character is not quite so clearly defined. It is generally agreed that poor performance on the test may be associated with both cortical lesions and the schizophrenias. Whether other groups do poorly in the same way has not been fully investigated. In all cases the judgment depends upon qualitative and subjective interpretation of the behavior and responses observed, and there are no quantitative norms or ratings upon which the inexperienced examiner may fall back.

None of these features detracts from the method's usefulness in clinical case studies where time permits the examiner to pursue investigations beyond the fewest number of most fully informative tests in the briefest time. The task which the test presents is sufficiently difficult to be challenging to subjects of the higher intellectual brackets and hence may highlight a breakdown in conceptual thinking which is still hidden behind the patient's façade of well-learned responses for dealing with more familiar problems. Moreover, because of its difficulty, it introduces certain elements analogous to "frustration" and "level of aspiration" experiments; in many instances one is permitted to witness the dynamic interplay of problem solving and emotional tensions as the subject proceeds toward solution. It might even prove to be worthwhile research to record and analyse verbatim productions in the test situation.

In essence, then, this concept formation test makes its contribution through its ingenious material and procedure which provide the examiner with a sample of behavior whose importance to him will be determined by his interests, the nature of the clinical problem, supporting data from other tests, and many other factors. It cannot be recommended for routine psychometric practice. It can be suggested as providing possible enrichment for full psychodiagnostic study.

For a review by O. L. Zangwill, see 3:27; for related reviews see 3:28.

[36]

★**Contemporary Problems.** Grades 7–9, 10–12; 1951–52; 2 levels; revised preliminary manual ('52); no norms; $5.25 per 35 sets of test and answer sheet of any one level; separate answer sheets must be used; 75¢ per 35 answer sheets; 75¢ per specimen set; postpaid; nontimed (20–40) minutes; Citizenship Education Project, Teachers College, Columbia University. *
a) JUNIOR HIGH SCHOOL. Grades 7–9; Form R ('51).
b) HIGH SCHOOL. Grades 10–12; Forms C ('51), D ('51).

[37]

★**Cornell Index.** Adults; 1944–49; a revision, for civilian use, of the Cornell Selectee Index Form N and the Cornell Service Index; title on test sheet is C.I.; psychosomatic and neuropsychiatric symptoms; Form N2 ['45]; revised manual ('49); $2.25 per 50; 35¢ per specimen set; postpaid; nontimed (5–15) minutes; Arthur Weider, Harold G. Wolff, Keeve Brodman, Bela Mittelmann, and David Wechsler; Psychological Corporation. *

REFERENCES

1. WOLFF, HAROLD G.; WEIDER, ARTHUR; MITTELMANN, BELA; AND WECHSLER, DAVID. "The Selectee Index: A Method for Quick Testing of Selectees for the Armed Forces." *Trans Am Neurol Assn* 69:126–9 '43. *
2. WEIDER, ARTHUR; MITTELMANN, BELA; WECHSLER, DAVID; BRODMAN, KEEVE; AND WOLFF, HAROLD G.; WITH THE TECHNICAL ASSISTANCE OF MARGARET MEIXNER. "The Cornell Service Index: A Method for the Assay of Neuropsychiatric and Psychosomatic Disturbances in Patients in Military Hospitals." *Trans Am Neurol Assn* 70:92–5 '44. * (PA 19:1259, title only)
3. WEIDER, ARTHUR; MITTELMANN, BELA; WECHSLER, DAVID; AND WOLFF, HAROLD G.; WITH THE TECHNICAL ASSISTANCE OF MARGARET MEIXNER. "The Cornell Selectee Index: A Method for Quick Testing of Selectees for the Armed Forces." *J Am Med Assn* 124:224–8 Ja 22 '44. *
4. MITTELMANN, BELA; WEIDER, ARTHUR; BRODMAN, KEEVE; WECHSLER, DAVID; AND WOLFF, HAROLD G.; WITH THE TECHNICAL ASSISTANCE OF MARGARET MEIXNER. "Personality and Psychosomatic Disturbances in Patients on Medical and Surgical Wards: A Survey of 450 Admissions." *Psychosom Med* 7:220–3 Jl '45. * (PA 19:3380)
5. MITTELMANN, BELA; WEIDER, ARTHUR; VONACHEN, HAROLD A.; KRONENBERG, MILTON; WEIDER, NORMA; BRODMAN, KEEVE; AND WOLFF, HAROLD G.; WITH THE TECHNICAL ASSISTANCE OF MARGARET D. MEIXNER. "Detection and Management of Personality and Psychosomatic Disorders Among Industrial Personnel." *Psychosom Med* 7:359–67 N '45. * (PA 20:1654)
6. WARNER, NATHANIEL, AND GALLICO, MARGARET WILSON. "Cornell Service Index: Report on Its Use in the Evaluation of Psychiatric Problems in a Naval Hospital." *War Med* 7:214–7 Ap '45. * (PA 19:2737)
7. WARNER, NATHANIEL, AND GALLICO, MARGARET WILSON. "Occurrence of Psychoneurotic Symptoms on the Various Services of a Naval Hospital." *U S Naval Med B* 45:1119–24 D '45. * (PA 20:2769)
8. WEIDER, ARTHUR. *Screening the Neuropsychiatrically Unfit Selectee From the Armed Forces.* Doctor's thesis. New York University (New York, N.Y.), 1945. Abstract: *Microfilm Abstracts* 7:76–9 no 1 '46–'47. *
9. WEIDER, ARTHUR; BRODMAN, KEEVE; MITTELMANN, BELA; WECHSLER, DAVID; AND WOLFF, HAROLD G. "The Cornell Service Index: A Method for Quickly Assaying Personality and Psychosomatic Disturbances in Men in the Armed Forces." *War Med* 7:209–13 Ap '45. * (PA 19:2738)
10. GRANT, HARRY. "A Rapid Personality Evaluation: Based on the Minnesota Multiphasic Personality Inventory and the Cornell Selectee Index." *Am J Psychiatry* 103:33–41 Jl '46. * (PA 21:168)
11. HARRIS, DANIEL H. "Questionnaire and Interview in Neuropsychiatric Screening." *J Appl Psychol* 30:644–8 D '46. * (PA 21:1511)
12. HARRIS, HAROLD J. "The Cornell Selectee Index: An Aid in Psychiatric Diagnosis." *Ann N Y Acad Sci* 46:593–603, discussion 603–5 Jl 30 '46. * (PA 20:4668)
13. LEAVITT, HARRY C. "A Comparison Between the Neuropsychiatric Screening Adjunct (NSA) and the Cornell Selectee Index (Form N)." *Am J Psychiatry* 103:353–7 N '46. * (PA 21:1512)
14. MANSON, MORSE P., AND GRAYSON, HARRY M. "The 'Sick Book Rider' in an Overseas Military Prison." *Psychosom Med* 8:414–6 N–D '46. * (PA 21:2243)
15. MITTELMANN, BELA, AND BRODMAN, KEEVE. "The Cornell Indices and the Cornell Word Form: 1, Construction and Standardization." *Ann N Y Acad Sci* 46:573–7, discussion 603–5 Jl 30 '46. * (PA 20:4674)
16. WEIDER, ARTHUR; BRODMAN, KEEVE; MITTELMANN, BELA; WECHSLER, DAVID; AND WOLFF, HAROLD G. "The Cornell Index: A Method for Quickly Assaying Personality and Psychosomatic Disturbances, to be Used as an Adjunct to Interview." *Psychosom Med* 8:411–3 N–D '46. * (PA 21:1020)
17. WEIDER, ARTHUR, AND WECHSLER, DAVID. "The Cornell Indices and the Cornell Word Form: 2, Results." *Ann N Y Acad Sci* 46:579–87, discussion 603–5 Jl 30 '46. * (PA 20:4684)
18. WEINSTOCK, HARRY I., AND WATSON, ROBERT I. "The Usefulness of the Cornell Selectee Index at the Neuropsychiatric Unit of a Naval Training Center." *U S Naval Med B* 46:1583–8 O '46. * (PA 21:175)
19. WOLFF, HAROLD G. "The Cornell Indices and the Cornell Word Form: 3, Application." *Ann N Y Acad Sci* 46:589–91, discussion 603–5 Jl 30 '46. * (PA 20:4688)
20. BIRREN, JAMES E., AND FISHER, M. BRUCE. "Susceptibility to Seasickness: A Questionnaire Approach." *J Appl Psychol* 31:288–97 Je '47. *
21. BRODMAN, KEEVE; MITTELMANN, BELA; WECHSLER, DAVID; WEIDER, ARTHUR; AND WOLFF, HAROLD G. "The Incidence of Personality Disturbances and Their Relation to Age, Rank and Duration of Hospitalization in Patients With Medical and Surgical Disorders in a Military Hospital." *Psychosom Med* 9:45–9 Ja–F '47. * (PA 21:2231)
22. BRODMAN, KEEVE; MITTELMANN, BELA; WECHSLER, DAVID; WEIDER, ARTHUR; AND WOLFF, HAROLD G. "The Relation of Personality Disturbances to Duration of Convalescence From Acute Respiratory Infections." *Psychosom Med* 9:37–44 Ja–F '47. * (PA 21:2237)

23. HEATHERS, GLEN L. "Cornell Selectee Index, Form N," pp. 64–8. In *The Psychological Program in AAF Convalescent Hospitals.* Edited by Sidney W. Bijou. Army Air Forces Aviation Psychology Program Research Reports, Report No. 15. Washington, D.C.: U.S. Government Printing Office, 1947. Pp. viii, 256. * (PA 22:4415)
24. KOBLER, FRANK J. "The Measurement of Improvement Among Neuropsychiatric Patients in an Army Convalescent Facility." *J Clin Psychol* 3:121–8 Ap '47. * (PA 21:3098)
25. LAZARUS, RICHARD S. *A Study of the Validity of the Cornell Selectee Index in the Prediction of Military Adjustment.* Master's thesis, University of Pittsburgh (Pittsburgh, Pa.), 1947.
26. MODLIN, HERBERT C. "A Study of the Minnesota Multiphasic Personality Inventory in Clinical Practice: With Notes on the Cornell Index." *Am J Psychiatry* 103:758–69 My '47. * (PA 22:1657)
27. MOORE, ROLAND C. "Psychiatric Screening Tests at a Precommissioning Center." *U S Naval Med B* 47:676–82 Jl–Ag '47. * (PA 22:3048)
28. DARKE, ROY A., AND GEIL, GEORGE A. "Homosexual Activity: Relation of Degree and Role to the Goodenough Test and to the Cornell Selectee Index." *J Nerv & Mental Dis* 108:217–40 S '48. * (PA 23:839)
29. DU MAS, FRANK M. "The Ability of the Cornell Selectee Index to Discriminate Between Physical and Mental Disorders." Abstract. *J Colo-Wyo Acad Sci* 3:62 Mr '48. *
30. ELLIS, ALBERT, AND CONRAD, HERBERT S. "The Validity of Personality Inventories in Military Practice." *Psychol B* 45:385–426 S '48. * (PA 23:1287)
31. WECHSBERG, FLORENCE ORIN, AND SPARER, PHINEAS J. "A Statistical and Profile Comparison of a Hospitalized Tuberculous Group With a Normal College Group Using the Cornell Index." *J Clin Psychol* 4:63–9 Ja '48. * (PA 22:5539)
32. BRODMAN, KEEVE; ERDMANN, ALBERT J., JR.; LORGE, IRVING; AND WOLFF, HAROLD G.; WITH THE TECHNICAL ASSISTANCE OF TODD H. BROADBENT. "The Cornell Medical Index: An Adjunct to Medical Interview." *J Am Med Assn* 140:530–4 Je 11 '49. *
33. FELTON, JEAN SPENCER. "The Cornell Index Used as an Appraisal of Personality by an Industrial Health Service: 1, The Total Score." *Ind Med* 18:133–44 Ap '49. * (PA 24:4869)
34. MANSON, MORSE P. "A Psychometric Analysis of Psychoneurotic and Psychosomatic Characteristics of Alcoholics." *J Clin Psychol* 5:77–83 Ja '49. * (PA 23:5627)
35. RABIN, ALBERT, AND GEISER, EUGENE. "Rorschach Checks on 'False Positives' of the Cornell Selectee Index Records of Student Nurses." *J General Psychol* 40:59–62 Ja '49. * (PA 23:3759)
36. MANN, WILLIAM A. *The Use of the Cornell Index With Freshman Students at Michigan State College.* Doctor's thesis, Michigan State College (East Lansing, Mich.), 1950.
37. MANN, WILLIAM A. "The Validation of the Cornell Index for Freshmen at Michigan State College." Abstract. *Am Psychol* 5:349–50 Jl '50. * (PA 25:1099, title only)
38. WICKERSHAM, FRANCIS MYRON. *A Factor Analysis of the Response of Psychopathic Personalities on the Cornell Selectee Index.* Doctor's thesis, Northwestern University (Evanston, Ill.), 1950. (*Summaries of Doctoral Dissertations.... June–September 1949, 1950,* pp. 435–7.)
39. BRODMAN, KEEVE; ERDMANN, ALBERT J., JR.; LORGE, IRVING; AND WOLFF, HAROLD G.; WITH THE TECHNICAL ASSISTANCE OF TODD H. BROADBENT. "The Cornell Medical Index-Health Questionnaire: II, As a Diagnostic Instrument." *J Am Med Assn* 145:152–7 Ja 20 '51. *
40. LEVINE, SOLOMON. *The Relationship Between Personality and Efficiency in Various Hospital Occupations.* Doctor's thesis, New York University (New York, N.Y.), 1951. Abstract: *Microfilm Abstracts* 11:741–2 no 3 '51. (PA 26:1736, title only)
41. NOLL, VICTOR H. "Simulation by College Students of a Prescribed Pattern on a Personality Scale." *Ed & Psychol Meas* 11:478–88 au '51. *

HANS J. EYSENCK, *Director, Psychology Department, Institute of Psychiatry, Maudsley Hospital, London, England.*

The Index has 101 Yes-No questions and is scored for general abnormality only. It has a Kuder-Richardson Reliability of .95. Regarding its validity, it may be said to discriminate between known neurotics and known normals with about the same degree of success as do most similar questionnaires. It is a trifle disingenuous of the authors to say, with respect to their Table 3, which shows the percentage of normal individuals and neurotics identified as rejects at various cutoff levels, that "since the *Index* is intended to identify the neuropsychiatric unfit, these tables are primary evidence of the instrument's validity." Presumably, the purpose of the Index is not to identify neurotics already diagnosed as such, but to predict neurotic breakdown in groups still psychiatrically undiagnosed. On this crucial point in the use of any psychological test for screening, no evidence is given. The fact that the *Cornell Index* correlates with the *Minnesota Multiphasic Personality Inventory* scales at a level of about .6 for the neurotic and psychotic triads, and .3 to .5 for individual scales, is presented as additional evidence of validity. Whether such correlations can be regarded as proof of validity is a doubtful question; the present writer would emphatically discourage this practice. Except for the use of "stop" questions this test contains little that is new and in some ways represents a return to the nonanalytic scales current in the 1920's. The Index's main use is probably the screening of potential neurotics for the Army, the field in which it was most extensively used. Even there, however, much shorter questionnaires have been shown to give equally good discrimination, for example the 40-item *Maudsley Medical Questionnaire.*

Four uses are suggested for the *Cornell Index:* (a) "Neurologic and Psychiatric Wards and Out Patient Departments." Here it seems certain that the *Minnesota Multiphasic Personality Inventory* would be a more useful and much better validated test. (b) "Medical and Surgical Wards and Out Patient Departments." Here again, evidence favours the MMPI; or if only a simple maladjustment quotient is required a much shorter type of index would be sufficient. (c) "Industry." In my experience, questionnaires are not really suitable instruments for use in industry; and the evidence quoted by the authors of this questionnaire is not sufficient to convince a critical reader that this view is not correct. (d) "Research." Any use of questionnaires in research altogether is of doubtful value; I do not feel that this particular questionnaire is an exception to that rule.

NELSON G. HANAWALT, *Associate Professor of Psychology, New Jersey College for Women, Rutgers University, New Brunswick, New Jersey.*

The purpose of the Index is to furnish a list of psychological symptoms "which would serve as a standardized psychiatric history and a guide to interview; and which, in addition, would statistically differentiate persons with serious personal and psychosomatic disturbances from the rest of the population." As an adjunct to interview, this test is probably as good as any other and has the added advantage of speed and simplicity in scoring. As to differentiating persons with serious personality difficulties from the normal population, it appears to be, like other inventories of its kind, not very valid for the individual case. The Index has been standardized on male military recruits. Under these conditions it has high reliability and good validity.

The list of 21 references in the manual contains only one based upon Form N2. Since there is quite a difference in the number of items and in the content of the various forms used in these studies (Form N, Service Index, Selectee Index), the extent to which the validating data can be transferred to the present Form N2 is unknown. The manual is not very helpful in enabling one to determine which form of the test was used for a particular reference. For instance, it is claimed that the Index is useful in hospitals, clinics, industry, and research. Thirteen references are given to buttress this claim, none of which report findings for Form N2. Another difficulty is the fact that most of these references are to military situations—a very special type of situation and quite different from the usual civilian situation. On the whole, the military reports are very favorable for the early forms of the Index. One exception is the report of Weinstock and Watson (*18*) who found the Selectee Index to be of little use in psychiatric screening at a Naval Induction Station. They found that the total score was practically valueless and that the stop questions, although "somewhat more valuable, resulted in very small additional identification." Your reviewer participated in a similar study at another naval station (unpublished), using the same test, with results more in line with those referred to in the manual. In this study the Selectee Index identified about 80 per cent of those eventually discharged and cut down the number of men who had to be interviewed to about one third (*19*).

If Form N2 turns out to be as good as the earlier forms (and there are good reasons to believe that it will), it should prove to be of great value in situations suggested in the manual. The authors' cautions for limitations of use should be very carefully followed. It was devised as "an adjunct to interview; not as a substitute unless an interview is impractical." In case an interview is impractical, one should be very careful in using the Index. In such a case an individual's fate should never be determined without additional corroborating data. The Index has been found to be better adapted to the man on the street than to the college graduate in an industrial situation (33).

The items on Form N2 are arranged according to various diagnostic categories. The authors do not suggest, and one should never attempt, a diagnosis on the basis of the test results alone.

During the past year we have done some research on Form N2 using 45 college women, mostly sophomores. Our results strengthen the suggestion in the manual that the test is probably useful for women although the standardization was based upon male military personnel. We found an r of .81 between Form N2 and the total score on Bell's *Adjustment Inventory*. Neither the Bell nor Form N2, however, showed a significant correlation with self-rating of adjustment on an 8-point rating scale. For Form N2 the mean was 6.62, the SD 6.26. This is lower than Mann's results (see manual) for freshman men and quite a bit lower than the average for freshman women. Our group was more selected and contained only five freshmen. We repeated the test after several weeks with the instructions to answer the questions in as favorable a light as possible, assuming that getting a job depended upon a low score. Under this condition the mean dropped to 1.80, the SD 3.04. This underlines the authors' warning that the Index should not be used for screening prospective employees. The girl with the highest score on the first testing, 28, reduced her score to zero under the second condition. This girl, by the way, was not seriously maladjusted. Her high score was partly due to a throat operation of some years past. The test also failed to pick out the most serious psychological case—the only one of the group who had to leave college because of her condition: her score was 12 with no stop answers.

In summary the reviewer would like to emphasize that Form N2 is an open questionnaire concerning clinical symptoms. It can be used effectively only under conditions where it is to the individual's advantage to report truthfully such as in a clinical or a military situation or for research purposes where the investigator has the full cooperation of the testee. The validating data are based upon military recruits. Some of the early forms of this test have proven their worth in clinics, industry, etc. The civilian use of this test should be checked for validity and usefulness in the particular situation. Where the individual is concerned, it should be used as an adjunct to the interview, not as a substitute for it. It fails to pick up certain types of maladjustment (see manual), and not all persons who are rated as seriously maladjusted by the test are really so.

LAURANCE F. SHAFFER, *Professor of Education, Teachers College, Columbia University, New York, New York.*

The *Cornell Index,* Form N2 is a revision, intended for civilian use, of a psychiatric screening questionnaire used widely during World War II. Its 100 yes-no items refer to neuropsychiatric and psychosomatic symptoms. The language is nontechnical, and most examinees with grade school education can answer it. Five to 15 minutes are required, depending mainly on the literacy of the examinee.

The reported Kuder-Richardson reliability is a satisfactory 95. The validity is not so readily established. In the construction of the original 64-item military form, items were analyzed against a criterion of neuropsychiatric discharge versus acceptance at an induction station after a brief psychiatric interview. Retained items had critical ratios exceeding 2.5. The manual states that the additional 36 items of Form N2 were "validated on civilian groups," but the nature of the groups and of the criteria is not specified. The only validation data presented in the manual spring from military sources. In view of the accumulated evidence that questionnaires were more effective under the controls and motivations of military life, the lack of evidence of validity for civilian applications is a serious fault.

Three methods are suggested for interpreting the scores of the Index. Method A, with a cutoff score of 23 unfavorably answered items, detects 50 per cent of psychiatric "rejects," while screening only 4 per cent of healthy persons. Method B, screening those who answer 13 or more items unfavorably, detects 74 per cent of the "rejects" but also falsely identifies 13 per cent of normal persons.

Method C for the interpretation of the Index uses the "stop questions" which were a novel feature of the military form. The stop questions (e.g., "Have you ever had a fit or convulsion?") were supposed to indicate such extreme pathology that an unfavorable response even to one of them would justify referring the examinee for further psychiatric diagnosis. Method C screens in terms of 13 or more unfavorable answers or one or more stop questions. In spite of the logical appeal of the stop questions, data in the manual show clearly that they are of no statistical value. At no cutoff point does the acceptance-rejection validity of Method C exceed that of Methods A or B which pay no special attention to the stop questions. Any critical reader of the manual may wonder why the authors still recommend the use of the stop questions, contrary to the evidence.

The manual contains percentile norms for 1,298 freshmen, 836 males and 462 females, at one college. There is also a table showing that the Index has moderate correlations, mainly from .30 to .50, with various scales of the *Minnesota Multiphasic Personality Inventory* when applied to a college population.

The available data do not permit a comprehensive evaluation of the *Cornell Index*. On the favorable side, it seems as thoughtfully compiled as are other instruments of its kind. Evidence shows that it does fairly well in predicting the acceptance-rejection behavior of psychiatrists at military induction stations. Its main shortcoming is a lack of validation against performance criteria in civilian situations. Educational or industrial applications should be preceded by searching experiments to test its value for the specific use proposed.

[38]

*The Cowan Adolescent Adjustment Analyzer: An Instrument of Clinical Psychology. Ages 12–18; 1935–49; a revision of *Cowan Adolescent Personality Schedule* (see 40: 1217); 9 scores: fear, family emotion, family authority, feeling of inadequacy, non-family authority, immaturity, escape, neurotic, compensation; Form 2 ('49—same as Form 1 copyrighted in 1946 except for slight changes in profile chart and format); manual ('49); $2.65 per 25; 40¢ per specimen set; postpaid; nontimed (10–30) minutes; Edwina A. Cowan, Wilbert J. Mueller, Edra Weathers (test only), and Bentley Barnabas (manual); Bureau of Educational Measurements, Kansas State Teachers College of Emporia. *

REFERENCES

1–3. See 40:1217.
4. ZAKOLSKI, F. C. "Studies in Delinquency: I, Personality Structure of Delinquent Boys." *J Genetic Psychol* 74:109–17 Mr '49. * (*PA* 23:4925)

For reviews by Harold H. Abelson and William U. Snyder, see 3:30; for a review by Goodwin Watson of an earlier edition, see 40:1217; for a review by Harold E. Jones of an earlier edition, see 38:918.

[39]

C-R Opinionaire. Grades 11–16 and adults; 1935; a disguised measure of conservatism and radicalism; Forms J, K; booklets containing both forms are also available; $1.50 per 25 double-form booklets; $1 per 25 single-form copies; postpaid; (20 or 40) minutes; Theodore F. Lentz and colleagues; Character Research Association, 946 Goodfellow, St. Louis 12, Mo. *

REFERENCES

1–5. See 40:1212.
6. DEXTER, EMILY S. "Personality Traits Related to Conservatism and Radicalism." *Char & Pers* 7:230–7 Mr '39. * (*PA* 13:3747)
7. ALPERT, R., AND SARGENT, S. S. "Conservatism-Radicalism Measured by Immediate Emotional Reactions." *J Social Psychol* 14:181–6 Ag '41. * (*PA* 16:1050)
8. SAPPENFIELD, BERT R. "Ideological Agreement and Disagreement Among Religious Groups." *J Abn & Social Psychol* 38:532–9 O '43. * (*PA* 18:827)
9. BROWER, DANIEL. "The Relations of Visuo-Motor Conflict to Personality Traits and Cardio-Vascular Activity." *J General Psychol* 38:69–99 Ja '48. * (*PA* 22:3383)
10. KLOSTOE, O. P. *The Relation of Serial Position on the Lentz Conservatism-Radicalism Scale to Affirmative Answers to General Domestic Acts.* Master's thesis, University of North Dakota (Grand Forks, N.D.), 1948.

GEORGE W. HARTMANN, *Professor of Psychology and Chairman of the Department, Roosevelt College, Chicago, Illinois.*

For a "social attitudes" measure developed in the Upper Mississippi Valley a score of years ago, this instrument contains remarkably few signs of obsolescence, a major peril from which such scales suffer when concrete contemporary controversial issues are incorporated as test items. If a specific quantification of so elusive a variable as political and economic "liberalism" is desired, better devices (cf. Thurstone) are available, but for a comprehensive estimate of an individual's disposition to welcome or resist rationally-grounded proposals for change in such diverse areas as science, technology, religious beliefs and practices, education, sex and family life, national and international organization, etc., this well seasoned Washington University product probably supplies as convenient and useful a composite score as any existing alternative.

Each available form consists of 60 symptomatic propositions, survivors of 437 original entries, such as "Cleanliness is a more valuable human trait than curiosity," and "It is not fitting that a statue of Einstein should occupy a niche in Dr. Fosdick's Riverside Drive Church." The respondent's agreement is then checked with a key that was validated beyond the prima facie stage as follows: "Experienced judges agree with regard to the key. People who call themselves conservative or middle-of-the-road and who have not changed their church or who did or would vote for Hoover or Smith or Roosevelt, or who are enrolled in the small denominational colleges, make respectively higher conservatism scores on the test than those who rate themselves as radical or who have changed their church or who would or did vote for Norman Thomas or who are enrolled in large universities." (Page 4 of Lentz's extensive and entertainingly-written manual.)

Among the advantages possessed by this test are its brevity, self-administering character, unpretentious but adequate format, percentile norms from 580 college students (Table I), adequate reliability with a self-*r* of .83, and a uniquely commendable Column 6 in Table II giving the substantial percentage of "reaction reversals" when retested. Noticeable limitations are: the questionable *disguised* nature of the variable, the apparent assumption that radicalism merely demands drastic and speedy institutional reconstruction stressing goals to the neglect of procedure, the paucity of items referring to war and violence (now a central cultural issue), a doubtful separation of the "acquiescent" or conformity tendency from conservative convictions as such, and in a very few propositions a failure to allow for the distinction between *pseudo-* or *partial-*radicalism and *authentic* or more *thorough-going* radicalism, thereby paradoxically giving the latter a conservative weight by default! Eliminating the ten weakest or most debatable items in each form would almost certainly strengthen both the inherent technical merit and the professional utility for "applied" social science inquiries of the remaining "streamlined" fifty.

In sum, this modest Opinionaire continues to serve a defensible and worthwhile function in those teaching and research situations where its content is relevant and mature interpretation is assured.

For a review by Goodwin Watson, see 40: 1212; for a review by H. H. Remmers, see 38:899.

[40]

★The Empathy Test. Ages 13 and over; 1947–51; Forms A ('47), B ('51); manual ('51), 2 mimeographed supplements ('51); $2.25 per 25; postage extra; $1 per specimen set; postpaid; nontimed (15) minutes; Willard A. Kerr and Boris J. Speroff; Psychometric Affiliates, Box 1625, Chicago 90, Ill. *

[41]

Every-Day Life: A Scale for the Measure of Three Varieties of Self-Reliance. High school; 1941; 3 scores: independence, resourcefulness, responsibility; IBM; 1 form; $1.75 per 25, postage extra;

50¢ per specimen set, postpaid; separate answer sheets may be used; 50¢ per 25 IBM answer sheets; $3.50 per set of stencils for machine scoring of answer sheets; $3.50 per set of stencils for hand scoring of answer sheets; postage extra; nontimed (30) minutes; Leland H. Stott; Sheridan Supply Co. *

REFERENCES

1–6. See 3:38.

HAROLD E. JONES, *Professor of Psychology, and Director, Institute of Child Welfare, University of California, Berkeley, California.*

This is a test of three aspects of "self-reliance," derived through a factor analysis of a preliminary list of items (patterned after those used by Maller in his *Character Sketches*), and an item validation of a series of subsequent forms. The test material as published consists of 150 questions such as "Is it hard to find something really interesting to do during your spare time?" and "Do you do extra work or unassigned reading in your courses?" Five alternative answers are given for each question, signifying a range in frequency from "always" to "never." A hand scoring key is provided for three scales: (*a*) independence in personal matters (autonomy, independence of decision); (*b*) resourcefulness in group activities (social initiative); and (*c*) personal responsibility (dependability, conscientiousness). "Centile norms" are given for each of these scales, but since they are based only on 380 cases from a single high school (in Lincoln, Nebraska) they must be regarded only as local norms, to be utilized elsewhere chiefly for the purpose of research comparisons. The estimated reliability of the scales, based on several determinations, ranges from .84 to .94, and their intercorrelations from .42 to .64. The latter values may be unexpectedly high, in view of the fact that they are regarded as representing factors which constitute an orthogonal system of dimensions. No correlations are reported with age, although it should be expected that a meaningful measure of self-reliance would exhibit age changes in the grade range (9 to 12) for which the test is designed and for which normative data are presented. A number of commendable features may be noted in the development of this test, but the manual provides no evidence of further standardization or of validation studies during the past decade. Additional research is needed to show whether the validity regarded as implicit in the three scales (resulting from the method of scale construction) is maintained against other criteria. Until such evidence is presented, together with more adequate norms, the instrument will be serviceable chiefly for a rather limited range of research purposes.

For a review by Albert Ellis, see 3:38.

[42]

Examining for Aphasia and Related Disturbances. Ages 8 and over; 1946; diagnostic ratings of 4 types of disturbances: agnosias, receptive aphasias, apraxias, expressive aphasias; individual; 1 form; no norms; $6.25 per manual and 50 record forms; $4.50 per 50 record forms; $2.75 per manual; postpaid; (30–120) minutes; Jon Eisenson; Psychological Corporation. *

REFERENCES

1. BLATT, BENJAMIN. *The Problem of Language Localization Into Specific Brain Areas: Psychological Tests as a Means of Localizing Brain Lesions in Patients With Aphasia.* Doctor's thesis, New York University (New York, N.Y.), 1950. (*Microfilm Abstracts....,* 1950, pp. 145-7.) (*PA* 25:454, title only)

D. RUSSELL DAVIS, *Reader in Clinical Psychology, University of Cambridge; and Honorary Consultant Research Psychiatrist, United Cambridge Hospitals; Cambridge, England.*

The careful testing of language and related functions may form an essential part of neurological examination or, a diagnosis having been made, may be necessary for the evaluation of a dysphasia in order to plan a course of retraining or to assess progress in retraining. Language disorders, however, vary so widely in degree and kind that, for whatever purpose they are required, tests have to be flexible. Rigidly standardised tests have no point. Scores are not required. As the author properly remarks, clinical judgments and not psychometric results are important, and this is not a field for the routine tester. In the reviewer's opinion, the author has gone about as far as is desirable in standardising the testing procedure.

The author's aims have been modest, but he has succeeded in assembling useful materials for a wide range of tests. Most of those who work with cases of aphasia will have assembled similar materials for themselves; Henry Head, as well as other more recent authorities, provides adequate instructions in his monograph for so doing. Yet, the author's contribution is useful, for he has provided a degree of standardisation and his materials are unobjectionable, whether the tests are applied to British or American patients. They contain no novel features and, perhaps, they are to be recommended as much for their convenience as for any other reason.

The tests cover a wide range of language functions and are intended more for the planning of retraining than for diagnosis. By their use an adequate *extensive* survey of the language functions can be carried out, but they do not form a complete examination in themselves; they do not excuse a more intensive and thorough study of the defects revealed in the survey. Again, they should only be resorted to after other less formal methods of examination. They can conveniently be used in conjunction with such other tests as the vocabulary test of the *Wechsler-Bellevue Intelligence Scale,* other vocabulary tests, and tests of abstraction.

J Nerv & Mental Dis 109:89 Ja '49. N(olan) D. C. L(ewis). * The method of evaluation and of recording the results is particularly useful in research work in this field, according to the reports the reviewer has had from those actively engaged in the study of aphasia.

Nerv Child 6:343 Jl '47. This is a well prepared test for aphasia, with directions for its use.

For a review by C. R. Strother and an excerpt from a review, see 3:39.

[43]

*****Fels Parent Behavior Rating Scales.** "For the use of the trained home visitor in appraising certain aspects of parent-child relationships"; 1937–49; 30 scores: adjustment of home, activeness of home, discord in home, sociability of family, coordination of household, child-centeredness of home, duration of contact with mother, intensity of contact with mother, restrictiveness of regulations, readiness of enforcement, severity of actual penalties, justification of policy, democracy of policy, clarity of policy, effectiveness of policy, disciplinary friction, quantity of suggestion, coerciveness of suggestion, accelerational attempt, general babying, general protectiveness, readiness of criticism, direction of criticism, readiness of explanation, solicitousness for welfare, acceptance of child, understanding, emotionality toward child, affectionateness toward child, rapport with child; 1 form ('37–'47); manual ('49—see reference *14* below); $1 per set of scales; $1.50 per manual; postpaid; manual by Alfred L. Baldwin, Joan Kalhorn, and Fay Huffman Breese; Horace Champney; Fels Institute, Yellow Springs, Ohio. *

REFERENCES

1. CHAMPNEY, HORACE. *Measurement of Parent Behavior as a Part of the Child's Environment.* Doctor's thesis, Ohio State University (Columbus, Ohio), 1939.
2. CHAMPNEY, HORACE. "Some Measurable Aspects of the Child's Home Environment." Abstract. *Psychol B* 36:628-9 O '39. * (*PA* 14:603, title only)
3. CHAMPNEY, HORACE, AND MARSHALL, HELEN. "Optimal Refinement of the Rating Scale." *J Appl Psychol* 23:323-31 Je '39. * (*PA* 13:5444)
4. HARTSON, MARY FRANCES, AND CHAMPNEY, HORACE. "Parent Behavior as Related to Child Development: II, Social Maturity." Abstract. *Psychol B* 7:583 O '40. * (*PA* 15:593, title only)
5. CHAMPNEY, HORACE. "The Measurement of Parent Behavior." *Child Develop* 12:131-66 Je '41. * (*PA* 15:4829)
6. CHAMPNEY, HORACE. "The Variables of Parent Behavior." *J Abn & Social Psychol* 36:525-42 O '41. * (*PA* 16:797)
7. BALDWIN, ALFRED L.; KALHORN, JOAN; AND BREESE, FAY HUFFMAN. *Patterns of Parent Behavior.* American Psychological Association, Psychological Monographs, Vol. 58, No. 3, Whole No. 268. Washington, D.C.: the Association, Inc., 1945. Pp. iii, 75. Paper. * (*PA* 19:3415)
8. BALDWIN, ALFRED L. "The Appraisal of Parent Behavior." Abstract. *Am Psychol* 1:251 Jl '46. * (*PA* 20:3724, title only)
9. BALDWIN, ALFRED L. "Differences in Parent Behavior

Toward Three-and-Nine-Year-Old Children." *J Personality* 15: 143–65 D '46. * (*PA* 21:3296)
10. KALHORN, JOAN C. "The Diagnosis of Parent Behavior." Abstract. *Am Psychol* 1:251–2 Jl '46. * (*PA* 20:3742, title only)
11. BALDWIN, ALFRED L. "Changes in Parent Behavior During Pregnancy: An Experiment in Longitudinal Analysis." *Child Develop* 18:29–39 Mr–Je '47. * (*PA* 22:2079)
12. RAY, MARGARET; CAMERON, EUGENIA S.; AND GILBERT, CHARLOTTE. "The Use of Behavior Rating Scales in the Analysis of Clinical Case Records." Abstract. *Am Psychol* 3:364 Ag '48. * (*PA* 23:769, title only)
13. BALDWIN, ALFRED L. "The Effect of Home Environment on Nursery School Behavior." *Child Develop* 20:49–61 Je '49. * (*PA* 24:467)
14. BALDWIN, ALFRED L.; KALHORN, JOAN; AND BREESE, FAY HUFFMAN. *The Appraisal of Parent Behavior.* American Psychological Association, Psychological Monographs, Vol. 63, No. 4, Whole No. 299. Washington, D.C.: the Association, Inc., 1949. Pp. vii, 85. Paper.
15. ROFF, MERRILL. "A Factorial Study of the Fels Parent Behavior Scales." *Child Develop* 20:29–45 Mr '49. * (*PA* 24: 2611)

DALE B. HARRIS, *Professor, Institute of Child Welfare, University of Minnesota, Minneapolis, Minnesota.*

Child development research has long needed a more adequate device than the case report for assessing parent behavior toward the child and psychological aspects of the home environment. Such a tool also should be of great help to clinicians, social workers, and others concerned with the description and evaluation of a home's impact on a child. The Fels scales go a long way toward supplying these needs.

Formulated by Champney as a result of an extensive analysis of the psychological aspects of child rearing, the 30 rating scales now offered have been carefully selected, revised, and proved over a period of 10 years. A considerable body of sound research is available to support their usefulness. The present scales require the rater to review systematically various aspects of the parent's relationship to a particular child and to record his estimates in terms of linear rating scales. A general description of each characteristic is offered, to set it apart from other characteristics. The rater registers his impression along a linear scale, aided by from five to seven verbal descriptions or "cue points" distributed along the continuum. A set of ratings ordinarily would be completed after two home visits and interviews of approximately two hours each.

The author's effort to make the scales objective and reliable may be seen in several additional features of the rating procedure. Space to rate 10 children appears on each sheet, so that comparisons from child to child as well as to the defined points of the scale may increase the meaningfulness of estimates. For each child the rater is required to indicate on the linear scale the limits within which he would accept the judgment of another rater as essentially agreeing with his own. He is further asked to estimate the limits of the parent's ordinary variation in behavior along the continuum indicated. In each case, he also rates the certainty of his judgment.

The manual furnishes a satisfying amount of evidence on validity and reliability. For the 30 scales, two sets of ratings by a relatively inexperienced rater on the same sample of approximately 100 families, separated by a six months interval, correlate from .53 to .85, half of the scales yielding correlations above .70. This same rater, after several years of experience in evaluating families, produced results which, over a period of six months, correlated from .62 to .90, nearly half of the correlations now exceeding .80. Two different raters evaluating independently a series of families during simultaneous visits agreed to the extent of correlations varying from .26 to .88 for the 30 scales; 22 of the 30 correlations exceeded .65. Means and standard deviations calculated from raw scores are gratifyingly similar among different raters, further indicating that some common basis of judgment is apparently operating.

Raw score norms are not available. The original research purpose for which these scales were devised embraced a longitudinal study of over 100 families, each to be rated twice a year. The authors of the manual suggest that where the scales are used to compare families, the ratings be accomplished by one person and the raw scores be reduced to standard measures in terms of the mean and standard deviations of raw scores for each scale separately. Thus, results from the several scales can be directly compared.

It should be clear that these scales are useful only in the hands of a skilled interviewer. It must be further pointed out that no interviewer or home visitor, no matter how skilled, can undertake these ratings without careful study of the manual and the scales themselves to familiarize himself with the cue points and to consolidate his "philosophy" of home evaluation. Furthermore, research evidence shows that a rater gradually shifts his interpretations and estimates of the several dimensions of family environment over a period of years—added evidence of the need for periodically reducing raw scores to standard scores.

All arguments point toward the soundness of such a standardized approach to the evaluation of complex phenomena. Research evidence indicates that, as the clinician systematizes his judgments, they improve in accuracy and value. Plenty of room remains for clinical art; the rater is encouraged to note down all qualifications, subjective impressions, and other evaluations which occur to him to clarify the basis for his judgment. Several research papers listed in the attached bibliography provide material on the interrelations of these dimensions of parent behavior and supply shrewd clinical appraisals of the impact of various "syndromes" of factors on child behavior.

The 30 scales for the rating of important aspects of parent behavior toward children afford not only important research tools but also useful clinical devices wherever a worker contacts a population of parents in order to describe or to evaluate the psychological "atmospheres" of homes. The scales are only devices for systematizing judgments—they are not tests or precise measures. Within the recognized limits of the rating method, they afford an exceedingly useful adjunct to the case report. While the scales record judgments essentially relative to the standards of a particular rater, research data suggest that they have fairly general meaning within a sample of lower and middle class occupational groups in the Midwest. This reviewer would like to see such devices used by child placement agencies and child guidance clinics as well as in researches on child development.

[44]

★Gardner Behavior Chart. Mental patients; 1939; ratings on 15 aspects of behavior; 1 form; $1 per 100, postpaid; specimen set not available; (5–10) minutes; Paul H. Wilcox; the Author, 526 West 10th St., Traverse City, Mich. *

REFERENCES

1. WILCOX, PAUL H. "The Gardner Behavior Chart." *Am J Psychiatry* 98:874–80 My '42. *
2. SCHRADER, PAUL J., AND ROBINSON, MARY FRANCES. "An Evaluation of Prefrontal Lobotomy Through Ward Behavior." *J Abn & Social Psychol* 40:61–9 Ja '45. * (PA 19:1956)

[45]

★General Goals of Life Inventory: General Education Series. College; 1942–50; 20 scores, each representing a "life goal"; 1 form, '50; no data on reliability and validity in manual (for data presented elsewhere, see 6 below); manual ('50); norms ['42]; separate answer sheets must be used; $2.50 per 25; 60¢ per 25 answer sheets; cash orders postpaid; 25¢ per specimen set, postpaid; nontimed (50) minutes; developed by the Cooperative Study in General Education (Ralph W. Tyler, Director); Cooperative Test Division, Educational Testing Service. *

REFERENCES

1. DUNKEL, HAROLD B. "An Inventory of Students' General Goals of Life." *Ed & Psychol Meas* 4:87–95 su '44. * (PA 19:467)
2. [WALTERS], ANNETTE, Sister. "An Investigation Into the Life Goals of College Students." *Cath Ed R* 45:475–82 O '47. *
3. CANNOM, C. W. "The Use of the Inventory in the Philosophy Classroom," pp. 55–62. In Harold Baker Dunkel's *General Education in the Humanities.* Washington, D.C.: American Council on Education, 1947. Pp. xix, 323. * (PA 22:434)
4. COOPERATIVE STUDY IN GENERAL EDUCATION, EXECUTIVE COMMITTEE, RALPH W. TYLER, DIRECTOR. "First Project: General Goals of Life," pp. 83–98. In *Cooperation in General Education.* Washington, D.C.: American Council on Education, 1947. Pp. xvii, 240. * (PA 22:432)
5. DUNKEL, HAROLD BAKER. *General Education in the Humanities,* pp. 21–78, 108–120, 267–89. Including sections by C. W. Cannom (pp. 55–62); Annette Walters (pp. 63–70); Pauline R. Hoeltzel, Gladys K. Brown and Dell Park McDermott (pp. 70–5); and Charles F. Sawhill Virtue (pp. 278–89). Foreword by Ralph W. Tyler. Washington, D.C.: American Council on Education, 1947. Pp. xix, 323. * (PA 22:434)
6. DUNKEL, HAROLD BAKER. Chap. 2, "Student's General Goals of Life," pp. 21–54, 75–8, 267–77. In his *General Education in the Humanities.* Washington, D.C.: American Council on Education, 1947. Pp. xix, 323. * (PA 22:434)
7. HOELTZEL, PAULINE R.; BROWN, GLADYS K.; AND McDERMOTT, DELL PARK. "The Use of the Inventory by the Department of English," pp. 75–8. In Harold Baker Dunkel's *General Education in the Humanities.* Washington, D.C.: American Council on Education, 1947. Pp. xix, 323. * (PA 22:434)
8. JONES, JAMESON M. "The Use of Inventories of Life-Goals and of Religious Concepts," pp. 107–20. In Harold Baker Dunkel's *General Education in the Humanities.* Washington, D.C.: American Council on Education, 1947. Pp. xix, 323. * (PA 22:434)
9. VIRTUE, CHARLES F. SAWHILL. Appendix B, "The Validity of the Inventory of General Life-Goals in Correlation With Other Inventories," pp. 278–89. In Harold Baker Dunkel's *General Education in the Humanities.* Washington, D.C.: American Council on Education, 1947. Pp. xix, 323. * (PA 22:434)
10. WALTERS, ANNETTE. "The Use of the Goals of Life Inventory," pp. 63–70. In Harold Baker Dunkel's *General Education in the Humanities.* Washington, D.C.: American Council on Education, 1947. Pp. xix, 323. * (PA 22:434)

C. ROBERT PACE, *Chairman, Department of Psychology, Syracuse University, Syracuse, New York.*

Twenty statements of life goals arranged in 190 paired comparisons constitute the substance of this inventory. The number of times each statement is preferred to all others is the score for that goal. The answer sheet contains a simple profile chart on which the student can summarize his own responses; the chart shows graphically how his rankings compare with the median and middle 50 per cent of 2,248 students in 16 colleges who took the inventory at the time when the Cooperative Study in General Education was in progress.

No statistics on reliability of the inventory are given in the manual. The reader is referred to Appendix A of Dunkel's *General Education in the Humanities* (6), where he will find test-retest coefficients on one group of 16 students and another group of 27 students. These reliabilities are generally in the .80's and .90's. Kuder-Richardson reliabilities of similar magnitudes are also reported. The reviewer's experience with paired comparison tests would lead him to conclude that students' responses to the inventory are probably quite reliable.

It is probable that the most appropriate use of the inventory is not so much as a testing instrument to compare one group with another but rather as a teaching device for promoting self-understanding among students. This use is clearly recognized by those who constructed the profile chart whereby each student can summarize and interpret his own rank order of preference, gaining self-insight in the process. The extent to which the inventory may be used in various colleges around the country will probably be small if it is thought of as a test; its use could be widespread and beneficial if professors would take the point of view that teaching and learning and evaluation are intimately related to one another and that the process of evaluation is in itself a significant teaching method and an effective learning experience. The inventory makes a useful contribution to the need for and importance of evaluating some of the more intangible goals of education.

Leona E. Tyler, *Associate Professor of Psychology, University of Oregon, Eugene, Oregon.*

This inventory was developed by the Cooperative Study in General Education. In connection with the evaluation of work in the humanities, it was thought desirable to develop an objective instrument which would accomplish with more precision the purpose which is served by having students write essays on their philosophies of life. The authors hoped that it would thus be possible to assess changes in students' philosophies growing out of educational influences and to compare various groups of students with each other. The inventory consists of 190 paired comparisons by means of which 20 life goals are ranked according to their importance for the individual.

The first question that might be raised is with regard to the choice of goals. Dunkel states only that the makers of the test drew heavily upon papers already written by students and on the experience of teachers, and that they included both statements of traditional philosophical and religious positions and expressions of "cracker-barrel" philosophy (6). It seems doubtful that an adequate representation of actual goals of life for college students can be obtained by these methods.

The best evidence presented as to the reliability of the inventory is based on two small groups of students, one class of 16 that was retested after two days and a class of 27 retested after 20 days. In general, the correlations would indicate that the reliability is high with the two-day interval, moderate with the longer lapse of time. Some students show much more consistency than others.

The case for the validity of the inventory is made on the basis of the correspondence between what it reveals and what shows up in other tests

developed for the study, the *Inventory of Beliefs About Postwar Reconstruction,* and the *Inventory of Religious Concepts.* The material as presented makes it difficult to judge just how much relationship there is, and the fact that the two other measuring instruments are at least as uncertain as the one being validated leaves the whole issue doubtful.

The most serious criticism of the inventory, however, is its unanalyzed assumption that we can accept these stated life goals at their face value without investigating the personality dynamics underlying them. Any one of these philosophical positions or any combination of them could be determined largely by rationalization, projection, identification, reaction formation, or any one of a number of well known psychological processes. Is any useful purpose to be served by obtaining these verbal statements by themselves? It would seem that the objectivity and comparability at which the authors aimed is a dubious gain, when we consider the greater flexibility of the essay type of expression the inventory was designed to replace. Perhaps the provision at the end of the inventory for a brief statement by the student is for the purpose of retaining some of these advantages.

The illustrations Dunkel gives of the use of the inventory in educational practice do not convince this reviewer that this test has a useful function in general education. Its wide use in colleges having clearly stated philosophies of their own could tend to produce in students hypocrisy rather than sincerity, conflict and anxiety rather than stability and integration.

[46]

[Generalized Attitude Scales.] Grades 7–16; 1934–38; each scale has space for indicating attitude toward five attitude variables; 13 scales; Forms A, B; mimeographed; no data on reliability and validity in manuals (for data presented elsewhere by authors, see references); 2¢ per scale; 15¢ per specimen set of any one scale; postpaid; 3(5) minutes per attitude variable; directed and edited by H. H. Remmers; Division of Educational Reference, Purdue University. *
a) A SCALE FOR MEASURING ATTITUDE TOWARD ANY ADVERTISEMENT. 1938; Form A, only; Ruth E. Henion.
b) A SCALE FOR MEASURING ATTITUDE TOWARD ANY DISCIPLINARY PROCEDURE. 1936; V. R. Clouse.
c) A SCALE FOR MEASURING ATTITUDE TOWARD ANY HOME-MAKING ACTIVITY. 1934; Beatrix Kellar.
d) A SCALE FOR MEASURING INDIVIDUAL AND GROUP "MORALE". 1936; Laurence Whisler.
e) A SCALE FOR MEASURING ATTITUDES TOWARD ANY PLAY. 1935; Mildred Dimmit.
f) A SCALE FOR MEASURING ATTITUDES TOWARD ANY PRACTICE. 1934; H. W. Bues.
g) A SCALE FOR MEASURING ATTITUDES TOWARD ANY PROPOSED SOCIAL ACTION. 1935; Dorothy M. Thomas.

h) A SCALE FOR MEASURING ATTITUDE TOWARD RACES AND NATIONALITIES. 1934; H. H. Grice.
i) A SCALE FOR MEASURING ATTITUDE TOWARD ANY SCHOOL SUBJECT. 1934; Ella B. Silance.
j) A SCALE FOR MEASURING ATTITUDE TOWARD ANY INSTITUTION. 1934; Ida B. Kelly.
k) A SCALE FOR MEASURING ATTITUDES TOWARD ANY SOCIAL SITUATION. 1938; Elna Huffman.
l) A SCALE FOR MEASURING ATTITUDE TOWARD ANY TEACHER. 1935; L. D. Hoshaw.
m) A SCALE FOR MEASURING ATTITUDES TOWARD ANY VOCATION. 1934; Harold E. Miller.

REFERENCES

1-9. See 40:1202.
10. MILLER, HAROLD E. *The Construction and Evaluation of a Scale of Attitudes Toward Occupations.* Master's thesis, Purdue University (Lafayette, Ind.), 1933.
11. SILANCE, ELLA B. *The Construction of a Scale for Measuring Attitude Toward High School Subject X.* Master's thesis, Purdue University (Lafayette, Ind.), 1933.
12. BUES, HARRY W. "The Construction and Validation of a Scale to Measure Attitude Toward Any Practice," pp. 64-7. (*PA* 9:3370) In *Studies in Attitudes: A Contribution to Social-Psychological Research Methods.* Edited by H. H. Remmers. Bulletin of Purdue University, Vol. 35, No. 4; Studies in Higher Education, No. 26. Lafayette, Ind.: Division of Educational Reference, Purdue University, December 1934. Pp. 112. Paper. *
13. GRICE, HENRY H. *The Construction and Validation of a Generalized Scale Designed to Measure Attitudes Toward Defined Groups.* Master's thesis, Purdue University (Lafayette, Ind.), 1934.
14. GRICE, H. H. "The Construction and Validation of a Generalized Scale Designed to Measure Attitudes Toward Defined Groups," pp. 37-46. (*PA* 9:3381) In *Studies in Attitudes: A Contribution to Social-Psychological Research Methods.* Edited by H. H. Remmers. Bulletin of Purdue University, Vol. 35, No. 4; Studies in Higher Education, No. 26. Lafayette, Ind.: Division of Educational Reference, Purdue University, December 1934. Pp. 112. Paper. *
15. KELLAR, BEATRIX. *The Construction and Validation of a Scale for Measuring Attitude Toward Any Home-Making Activity.* Master's thesis, Purdue University (Lafayette, Ind.), 1934.
16. KELLAR, BEATRIX. "The Construction and Validation of a Scale for Measuring Attitude Toward Any Home-Making Activity," pp. 47-63. (*PA* 9:3393) In *Studies in Attitudes: A Contribution to Social-Psychological Research Methods.* Edited by H. H. Remmers. Bulletin of Purdue University, Vol. 35, No. 4; Studies in Higher Education, No. 26. Lafayette, Ind.: Division of Educational Reference, Purdue University, December 1934. Pp. 112. Paper. *
17. KELLEY, IDA B. *The Construction and Evaluation of a Scale to Measure Attitudes Toward Any Institution.* Master's thesis, Purdue University (Lafayette, Ind.), 1934.
18. KELLEY, IDA B. "The Construction and Evaluation of a Scale to Measure Attitude Toward Any Institution," pp. 18-36. (*PA* 9:3394) In *Studies in Attitudes: A Contribution to Social-Psychological Research Methods.* Edited by H. H. Remmers. Bulletin of Purdue University, Vol. 35, No. 4; Studies in Higher Education, No. 26. Lafayette, Ind.: Division of Educational Reference, Purdue University, December 1934. Pp. 112. Paper. *
19. MILLER, FLOYD D. *The Validation of a Generalized Attitude Scaling Technique.* Master's thesis, Purdue University (Lafayette, Ind.), 1934.
20. MILLER, FLOYD D. "The Validation of a Generalized Attitude Scaling Technique," pp. 98-109. (*PA* 9:3406) In *Studies in Attitudes: A Contribution to Social-Psychological Research Methods.* Edited by H. H. Remmers. Bulletin of Purdue University, Vol. 35, No. 4; Studies in Higher Education, No. 26. Lafayette, Ind.: Division of Educational Reference, Purdue University, December 1934. Pp. 112. Paper. *
21. MILLER, HAROLD E. "The Construction and Evaluation of a Scale of Attitudes Toward Occupations," pp. 68-76. (*PA* 9:3346) In *Studies in Attitudes: A Contribution to Social-Psychological Research Methods.* Edited by H. H. Remmers. Bulletin of Purdue University, Vol. 35, No. 4; Studies in Higher Education, No. 26. Lafayette, Ind.: Division of Educational Reference, Purdue University, December 1934. Pp. 112. Paper. *
22. REMMERS, H. H. "Measuring Attitudes Toward Vocations," pp. 77-83. (*PA* 9:2948) In *Studies in Attitudes: A Contribution to Social-Psychological Research Methods.* Edited by H. H. Remmers. Bulletin of Purdue University, Vol. 35, No. 4; Studies in Higher Education, No. 26. Lafayette, Ind.: Division of Educational Reference, Purdue University, December 1934. Pp. 112. Paper. *
23. SILANCE, ELLA B., AND REMMERS, H. H. "An Experimental Generalized Master Scale: A Scale to Measure Attitude Toward Any School Subject," pp. 84-7. (*PA* 9:3458) In *Studies in Attitudes: A Contribution to Social-Psychological Research Methods.* Edited by H. H. Remmers. Bulletin of Pur-

due University, Vol. 35, No. 4; Studies in Higher Education, No. 26. Lafayette, Ind.: Division of Educational Reference, Purdue University, December 1934. Pp. 112. Paper. *
24. HOSHAW, LOYAL D. *The Construction and Evaluation of a Scale for Measuring Attitude Toward Any Teacher.* Master's thesis, Purdue University (Lafayette, Ind.), 1935. Pp. 68.
25. SIGERFOOS, CHARLES C. *The Validation and Application of a Scale of Attitude Toward Vocation.* Master's thesis, Purdue University (Lafayette, Ind.), 1935.
26. THOMAS, DOROTHY M. *The Construction and Evaluation of a Scale to Measure Attitude Toward Any Proposed Social Action.* Master's thesis, Purdue University (Lafayette, Ind.), 1935. Pp. 44.
27. DIMMITT, MILDRED. *The Construction and Evaluation of a Scale to Measure Audience Attitude Toward Any Play.* Master's thesis, Purdue University (Lafayette, Ind.), 1936. Pp. 80.
28. DIMMITT, MILDRED. "The Construction and Evaluation of a Scale to Measure Audience Attitude Toward Any Play," pp. 275-82. (*PA* 11:3324) In *Further Studies in Attitudes, Series II.* Edited by H. H. Remmers. Bulletin of Purdue University, Vol. 37, No. 4; Studies in Higher Education, No. 31. Lafayette, Ind.: Division of Educational Reference, Purdue University, December 1936. Pp. 298. Paper. *
29. HADLEY, J. EDWIN. *Measurement of Attitude Outcomes From the Teaching of Poetry.* Master's thesis, Purdue University (Lafayette, Ind.), 1936. Pp. 102.
30. HANCOCK, JOHN. "Reliability of Generalized Attitude Scales as Related to Length of Scale," pp. 291-5. (*PA* 11:3334) In *Further Studies in Attitudes, Series II.* Edited by H. H. Remmers. Bulletin of Purdue University, Vol. 37, No. 4; Studies in Higher Education, No. 31. Lafayette, Ind.: Division of Educational Reference, Purdue University, December 1936. Pp. 298. Paper. *
31. HOSHAW, LOYAL D. "The Construction and Evaluation of a Scale to Measure Attitude Toward Any Teacher," pp. 238-51. (*PA* 11:3415) In *Further Studies in Attitudes, Series II.* Edited by H. H. Remmers. Bulletin of Purdue University, Vol. 37, No. 4; Studies in Higher Education, No. 31. Lafayette, Ind.: Division of Educational Reference, Purdue University, December 1936. Pp. 208. Paper. *
32. REMMERS, H. H. "A Proposed Program Of Research in the Genetics of Attitudes." *Proc Ind Acad Sci* 45:241-4 '36. * (*PA* 11:828)
33. REMMERS, H. H., and HADLEY, EDWIN. "Curricular Material and Measuring Devices for Teaching Appreciation of Poetry," pp. 227-37. (*PA* 11:3444) In *Further Studies in Attitudes, Series II.* Edited by H. H. Remmers. Bulletin of Purdue University, Vol. 37, No. 4; Studies in Higher Education, No. 31. Lafayette, Ind.: Division of Educational Reference, Purdue University, December 1936. Pp. 298. Paper. *
34. SIGERFOOS, CHARLES C. "The Validation and Application of a Scale of Attitude Toward Vocations," pp. 177-91. (*PA* 11:3450) In *Further Studies in Attitudes, Series II.* Edited by H. H. Remmers. Bulletin of Purdue University, Vol. 37, No. 4; Studies in Higher Education, No. 31. Lafayette, Ind.: Division of Educational Reference, Purdue University, December 1936. Pp. 298. Paper. *
35. THOMAS-BAINES, DOROTHY M. "The Construction and Evaluation of a Scale to Measure Attitude Toward Any Proposed Social Action," pp. 252-8. (*PA* 11:3371) In *Further Studies in Attitudes, Series II.* Edited by H. H. Remmers. Bulletin of Purdue University, Vol. 37, No. 4; Studies in Higher Education. No. 31. Lafayette, Ind.: Division of Educational Reference, Purdue University, December 1936. Pp. 298. Paper. *
36. CLOUSE, VERL R. *Construction and Evaluation of a Scale to Measure Attitude Toward Any Disciplinary Procedure.* Master's thesis, Purdue University (Lafayette, Ind.), 1937. Pp. 58.
37. KROLL, ABRAHAM, and DUNLAP, JACK W. "The Arrangement of Statements in an Attitude Scale." Abstract. *Psychol B* 34:544-5 O '37. * (*PA* 12:347, title only)
38. HANCOCK, JOHN W. "An Experimental Study of Limiting Response on Attitude Scales," pp. 142-8. (*PA* 13:4759) In *Further Studies in Attitudes, Series III.* Edited by H. H. Remmers. Purdue University, Division of Educational Reference. Studies in Higher Education, No. 34. Lafayette, Ind.: the Division, September 1938. Pp. 151. Paper. *
39. HUFFMAN, ELAN STEWART. *The Construction and Evaluation of a Scale to Measure the Attitude of Stutterers Toward Any Social Situation.* Master's thesis, Purdue University (Lafayette, Ind.), 1938.
40. REMMERS, H. H., AND WHISLER, L. D. "Interrelationships of Attitudes of Parents and Children," pp. 114-25. (*PA* 13:4786) In *Further Studies in Attitudes, Series III.* Edited by H. H. Remmers. Purdue University, Division of Educational Reference, Studies in Higher Education, No. 34. Lafayette, Ind.: the Division, September 1938. Pp. 151. Paper. *
41. TUSSING, LYLE. "Studying Workers' Attitudes in Industry," pp. 46-67. (*PA* 13:4841) In *Further Studies in Attitudes, Series III.* Edited by H. H. Remmers. Purdue University, Division of Educational Reference, Studies in Higher Education, No. 34. Lafayette, Ind.: the Division, September 1938. Pp. 151. Paper. *
42. WHISLER, L. D. " 'Reliability' of Scores on Attitude Scales as Related to Scoring Method," pp. 126-9. (*PA* 13:4793) In *Further Studies in Attitudes, Series III.* Edited by H. H. Remmers. Purdue University, Division of Educational Refer-

ence, Studies in Higher Education, No. 34. Lafayette, Ind.: the Division, September 1938. Pp. 151. Paper. *
43. KARSLAKE, RUTH H. "A Technique for Measuring Consumer Attitude Toward Any Advertisement." *Ind Acad Sci Proc* 48:193-5 '39. * *(PA 13:6429)*
44. BATEMAN, RICHARD M. "The Construction and Evaluation of a Scale to Measure Attitude Toward Any Educational Program." *J Ed Res* 36:502-6 Mr '43. * *(PA 17:3237)*
45. DAVIDOFF, MELVIN D. *A Study of Empathy and Correlates of Prejudice Toward a Minority Group.* Edited by H. H. Remmers. Purdue University, Division of Educational Reference, Studies in Higher Education [No.] 67; Further Studies in Attitudes, Series 13. Lafayette, Ind.: the Division, 1949. Pp. 58. Paper. *
46. PROTHRO, E. TERRY, AND JENSEN, JOHN A. "Interrelations of Religious and Ethnic Attitudes in Selected Southern Populations." *J Social Psychol* 32:45-9 Ag '50. *(PA 25:3777)*

DONALD T. CAMPBELL, *Assistant Professor of Psychology, The University of Chicago, Chicago, Illinois.*

These tests were reviewed in *The 1940 Mental Measurements Yearbook.* They are being reviewed again primarily because they seem to be the only social attitude tests being published and sold since the Thurstone scales were allowed to go out of print. This should not be taken to mean, however, that they represent the most used tests. On the contrary, the present reviewer is aware of only one recent published use (*46*). In the flourishing area of research on attitudes toward minority groups, the general practice seems to be for the researcher to reduplicate all or parts of uncopyrighted tests, or to develop his own. Much used are the Bogardus *Social Distance Scale,*[1] the Likert test of attitudes toward Negroes,[2] and, recently, the Anti-Semitism and Ethnocentrism scales developed by Adorno, Frenkel-Brunswik, Sanford, and Levinson.[3]

Any person selecting attitude tests for research purposes should be aware of McNemar's[4] scathing review of the literature, even though he may not in the end agree with all of McNemar's evaluations. With regard to the Remmers scales, McNemar has this to say:

It is the writer's opinion that the comparability of scales constructed by the method of equal appearing intervals has not been sufficiently well demonstrated to permit the direct comparison of means based on different scales. Remmers and followers have been the most persistent in this practice. *

The Thurstone scaling method as used by him and his students has always involved scaling for some particular attitude. Remmers and Silance proposed in 1934 that the method could be adapted for the purpose of constructing "generalized attitude scales." * This assumes that a series of statements can be scaled as ap-

1 Bogardus, Emory S. *Immigration and Race Attitudes.* Foreword by Jerome Davis. Boston, Mass.: D. C. Heath & Co., 1928. Pp. xi, 268. * *(PA 2:3223)*
2 Likert, Rensis. *A Technique for the Measurement of Attitudes.* Archives of Psychology, No. 140. New York: Archives of Psychology, Columbia University, 1932. Pp. 55. Paper. *(PA 7:1885)*
3 Adorno, T. W.; Frenkel-Brunswik, Else; Levinson, Daniel J.; and Sanford, R. Nevitt; in collaboration with Betty Aron, Maria Hertz Levinson, and William Morrow. *The Authoritarian Personality.* New York: Harper & Brothers, 1950. Pp. xxxiii, 990. * *(PA 24:5796)*
4 McNemar, Quinn. "Opinion-Attitude Methodology." *Psychol B* 43:289-374 Jl '46. * *(PA 20:4703)*

plicable to a class of objects or phenomena, such as races, or school subjects, or proposed social changes * Thus one sorting and subsequent scaling provides a set of statements which serve for measuring attitude toward, for example, any institution such as war, marriage, communism, Sunday observance, and divorce. The advantage of the generalized scale is supposed to reside in the fact that many attitudes can be measured without great expenditure of time otherwise required for sorting and scale construction.

To make the scale applicable to any one of the phenomena in a class, the respondent is simply told that he is to keep in mind the particular attitude object as he checks the statements. That this procedure can become quite ridiculous is illustrated by the following items: "[war or marriage] does not consider individual differences"; "[marriage] gives too little service"; "[marriage] satisfies only the most stupid with its services"; "[marriage] offers opportunity for individual initiative"; "[war] is too conservative"; "[war] is too changeable in its policies"; "[marriage] appeals to man's lowest nature."

In order to establish the validity of the generalized attitude scaling technique, one of Remmers' students constructed a scale specifically for attitude toward teaching and then correlated the scores therefrom with scores based upon the generalized attitude toward any occupation checked for teaching. The correlation corrected for attenuation was only .58, but this is said to "show a satisfactory validity" for the generalized scaling scheme even though the validity of the specific scale is unknown. Remmers and his students have practically placed attitude scaling on a mass production basis, and have proceeded to use the scales as tools for research on a variety of topics. Individual citation of these studies would add more than 40 titles to a bibliography on attitude research. The fact that the dozens of reliability coefficients reported tend to have a median value of about .70 with values as frequently below .50 as above .80, and ranging down to .07, would indicate that a great deal of uncritical energy has been expended. These reliabilities are lower than those usually found for the Thurstone scales even though from 50% to 100% more items are included in the generalized scales. Evidently the latter scales contain dead timber.

In all fairness it must be said that McNemar's discussion, while accurate, accentuates the negative side of the picture. In the five instances reported in which Thurstone scales were studied in conjunction with Remmers scales, the reliabilities of the Remmers scales were higher in four (*14, 18*). For attitudes toward communism, the Remmers reliability was .89 and the Thurstone was .78. For other attitude topics the corresponding reliability coefficients were as follows: War, .77 and −.05; Sunday Observance, .98 and .90; the Negro, .84 and .87; the Chinese, .77 and .55 (*14, 18*). (Note the −.05 interform reliability coefficient obtained for the Thurstone-Peterson attitude toward war scale.) The low reliabilities which contribute the bulk of McNemar's tallies come mainly from grade and high school students, and their parents, where literacy and motivation might be low. They are also associated with topics about which attitudes may not exist, and for which any method might give low reliabilities. Such topics include attitudes toward vocations, attitudes toward various aspects of government regulation of farmers, etc. The two lowest values, .07 and .08, are for the attitudes of mothers and fathers toward the public school (*40*).

Most of the scales are now over 15 years old. In the interim, emphasis in test construction has shifted from the precise specification of item intensity to the more important problem of internal consistency (unidimensionality or single factoredness). Intensity scoring has tended to drop out as it became realized that the gross number of items endorsed in a favorable direction was functionally equivalent to the extremity of the endorsed items. These trends are epitomized in the Likert [2] and Guttman [5] scale construction methods. In Thurstone's full method of equal appearing intervals, internal consistency is taken care of by the coefficient of irrelevance.[6] However, this tedious procedure was rarely used even by Thurstone's own students, and there is no evidence that it was ever applied in the construction of any of the Remmers scales. Another important consideration which recent research has provided is the problem of response sets.[7] In these terms Remmers' procedure of reusing the same statements in measuring different attitudes might be expected to enhance reliability and correlations by adding consistent sources of variance irrelevant to the tester's purpose. In the most recent addition to the generalized scales, on "attitude toward any advertisement," another opportunity for irrelevant response sets is added through the use of seven levels of endorsement (from A! to D!) to each statement.

A more general question remains: Are any generalized attitude scales likely to be of use? On the one hand, general statements of liking and disliking are appropriate to almost any social object and can be found in almost every attitude test. These make appropriate ingredients for a generalized rating scale, or test, although con-

stant repetition of variations on this theme makes for dullness by the time one gets up to 20 or 40 items. Social distance preference statements are probably in this same category, and the Bogardus *Social Distance Scale* seems to be a meaningful generalized scale. The remainder of the items found in social attitude tests deal with stereotypes of a specific, quasi-factual nature. Such stereotypes have a way of aggregating around social objects in an opportunistic fashion, and attitude scales which use the public range of comments about the social object in question reflect this specificity. Thus an item about morality or intelligence is a much more useful item in a test of attitudes toward Negroes than in a test of attitudes toward Jews, and vice versa for an item dealing with sharp business practices. There is, however, one type of problem for which generalized scales are essential; this is the sociological problem of the relative reputational standing of social objects. In the Remmers series, this use is illustrated in the studies of attitudes toward school subjects, vocations, teachers, household activities, and ethnic groups. However, for this problem, one or a few questions, rather than 40, are probably sufficient, as shown in the work of Bogardus [1] and Thurstone.[8] For this purpose also, topical purity or specificity is extremely important— much more important than in the problem of measuring individual differences among the holders of the attitudes. For example, while the Negro has the most unfavorable position among U.S. minority groups when social distance items are used, Jews are most apt to be blamed for national difficulties and accused of misusing their power.[9] Such considerations limit the value of whole scale comparisons of ethnic group standings, as reported by Grice (*14*), and more recently by Prothro (*46*). Item by item comparisons would undoubtedly show exceptions to the overall picture.

KENNETH E. CLARK, *Associate Professor of Psychology, University of Minnesota, Minneapolis, Minnesota.*

The generalized attitude scale is a special type of Thurstone scale, designed to reduce the amount of labor ordinarily required to develop the latter type scale, and thus to make more readily available for general use instruments for

5 Stouffer, Samuel A.; Guttman, Louis; Suchman, Edward A.; Lazarsfeld, Paul F.; Star, Shirley A.; and Clausen, John A. *Studies in Social Psychology in World War II, Vol. 4.* Princeton, N.J.: Princeton University Press, 1950. Pp. x, 756. * (*PA* 25:3037)

6 Thurstone, L. L., and Chave, E. J. *The Measurement of Attitude: A Psychophysical Method and Some Experiments With a Scale for Measurement of Attitude Toward the Church.* Chicago, Ill.: University of Chicago Press, 1929. Pp. xii, 97. Paper. * (*PA* 3:4902)

7 Cronbach, Lee J. "Further Evidence on Response Sets and Test Design." *Ed & Psychol Meas* 10:3–31 sp '50. * (*PA* 25:681)

Cronbach, Lee. J. "Response Sets and Test Validity." *Ed & Psychol Meas* 6:475–94 w '46. * (*PA* 21:2489)

8 Thurstone, L. L. "An Experimental Study of National Preferences." *J General Psychol* 1:405–24 '28.

9 Campbell, Donald T. *The Generality of a Social Attitude.* Doctor's thesis, University of California (Berkeley, Calif.), 1947.

the measurement of attitudes. The assumption is made, and demonstrated to be reasonable, that a single set of items may be scaled by Thurstone methods and then used in the measurement of attitudes towards an entire class of objects. Thus, rather than develop a separate scale for each of hundreds of occupations, Remmers and his associates have developed a generalized attitude scale that may be used with any specified occupation.

The reduction in labor is the major advantage of the Remmers approach over the original Thurstone approach. In addition, however, Remmers includes a larger number of items, thus increasing reliability. He also ranges items in order of their scale values, which simplifies scoring at an unknown cost in reduced validity. Scores obtained through his methods do not always correlate highly with scores obtained on similar Thurstone scales (about .50 in one instance, for example). One disadvantage of his method—that all items must be interpreted in relation to a title added at the top of the sheet—does seem to reduce the value of the method. Response sheets, in addition, provide spaces for not one but five separate titles or subjects to be rated. The writer's experience is that only the most sophisticated students can make more than one or two sets of ratings on the same sheet without experiencing difficulty and confusion. Another difficulty arises when attitudes are measured with a generalized scale on two objects which differ in characteristics as much as, for example Communism and Marriage. Some items in Kelly's *Scale for Measuring Attitudes Toward Any Institution* ("Gives too little service," "Does not consider individual differences," "Is cordially hated by the majority for its smugness and snobbishness") obviously have entirely different meanings and implications in these two contexts, and hence either modify the scale value assigned the items or introduce irrelevant variance in the total score.

The need for generalized scales is not nearly as apparent today as it was in the middle 1930's. More reliable measurements may be obtained with less labor using Likert methods. A smaller number of more nearly homogeneous items may yield results more useful for many purposes through application of some of the contributions of Guttman. Certain of the generalized attitude scales (as those for vocations and school subjects) still retain their unique usefulness and will probably continue to be used. In general,

however, more recent developments which stress homogeneity of content and ease of scoring, show greater promise for most users of attitude measures.

For reviews by W. D. Commins and Theodore Newcomb, see 40:1202; for a review by Stephen M. Corey, see 38:897; for related reviews, see 40:B1050, 36:B215, and 36:B216.

[47]

*The Guilford-Martin Inventory of Factors GAMIN, Abridged Edition. Grades 9–16 and adults; 1943–48; supersedes original edition; 5 scores: general activity, ascendance-submission, masculinity-femininity, inferiority feelings, nervousness; IBM; 1 form, '43; manual ['48]; $2.50 per 25, postage extra; 60¢ per specimen set, postpaid; separate answer sheets may be used; 2¢ per IBM answer sheet; $3.50 per set of stencils for machine scoring of answer sheets; $2.50 per set of stencils for hand scoring of answer sheets; 2¢ per profile chart (also for tests 48 and 59); postage extra; nontimed (30) minutes; J. P. Guilford and H. G. Martin; Sheridan Supply Co. *

REFERENCES

1–7. See 3:43.
8. CERF, ARTHUR Z. "Inventory of Factors GAMIN, CE435A," pp. 595–9. In *Printed Classification Tests.* Edited by J. P. Guilford with the assistance of John I. Lacey. Army Air Forces Aviation Psychology Program Research Reports, Report No. 5. Washington, D.C.: U.S. Government Printing Office, 1947. Pp. xi, 919. * (*PA* 22:4145)
9. CLARK, ELMER J. *The Determination of the Relationship Between the Personality Traits of Teachers and Their Evaluation of Objectionable Pupil Behavior.* Doctor's thesis, University of Michigan (Ann Arbor, Mich.), 1949. Abstract: *Microfilm Abstracts* 9:78–9 no 2 '49. * (*PA* 24:4265)
10. GREEN, RUSSEL F. *The Validity of Certain Psychological Tests in the Selection and Classification of Juvenile Police Officers.* Master's thesis, University of Southern California (Los Angeles, Calif.), 1949.
11. NANCE, R. D. "Masculinity-Femininity in Prospective Teachers." *J Ed Res* 42:658–66 My '49. * (*PA* 24:320)
12. BRAY, DOUGLAS W. "The Prediction of Behavior From Two Attitude Scales." *J Abn & Social Psychol* 45:64–84 Ja '50. * (*PA* 24:4559)
13. CLARK, ELMER J. "The Mental Health of Elementary School Teachers as Measured by the Guilford-Martin Personality Battery," pp. 8–12. In *The Seventh Yearbook of the National Council on Measurements Used in Education, 1949–1950.* Fairmont, W.Va.: the Council, Fairmont State College, 1950. Pp. v, 56, ix. Paper, mimeographed. *
14. KELLY, E. LOWELL, AND FISKE, DONALD W. "The Prediction of Success in the VA Training Program in Clinical Psychology." *Am Psychol* 5:395–406 Ag '50. * (*PA* 25:2183)
15. KRASNER, LEONARD. *Personality Differences Between Patients Classified as Psychosomatic and as Non-Psychosomatic.* Doctor's thesis, Columbia University (New York, N.Y.), 1950. Abstract: *Microfilm Abstracts* 10:227–8 no 3 '50. *
16. TUPES, ERNEST C. "The Detection and Measurement of Faking on Personality Inventories." Abstract. *Am Psychol* 5:315 Jl '50. * (*PA* 25:1113, title only)
17. BAEHR, MELANY E. *A Factorial Study of Temperament.* University of Chicago, Psychometric Laboratory [Report] No. 63. Chicago, Ill.: the Laboratory, February 1951. Pp. 14. Paper, lithotyped. *
18. CLARK, ELMER J. "The Relationship Between the Personality Traits of Elementary School Teachers and Their Evaluation of Objectionable Behavior." *J Ed Res* 45:61–6 S '51. * (*PA* 26:3056)
19. FONDA, CHARLES P. "The Nature and Meaning of the Rorschach White Space Response." *J Abn & Social Psychol* 46:367–77 Jl '51. * (*PA* 26:2178)
20. GREEN, RUSSEL F. "Does a Selection Situation Induce Testees to Bias Their Answers on Interest and Temperament Tests?" *Ed & Psychol Meas* 11:503–15 au '51. *
21. HEALY, IRENE, AND BORG, WALTER R. "Personality Characteristics of Nursing School Students and Graduate Nurses." *J Appl Psychol* 35:275–80 Ag '51. * (*PA* 26:3088)
22. KELLY, E. LOWELL, AND FISKE, DONALD W. *The Prediction of Performance in Clinical Psychology.* Ann Arbor, Mich.: University of Michigan, 1951. Pp. xv, 311. Lithotyped. *
23. PEMBERTON, CAROL L. "Personality Inventory Data Related to Ace Subscores." *J Consult Psychol* 15:160–2 Ap '51. *
24. SILVERMAN, HIRSCH LAZAAR. *Relationships of Personality Factors and Religious Background Among College Students.*

Doctor's thesis, Yeshiva University (New York, N.Y.), 1951.
25. Thurstone, L. L. "The Dimensions of Temperament."
Psychometrika 16:11–20 Mr '51. * (PA 25:7327)

Hubert E. Brogden, *Personnel Research Section, The Adjutant General's Office, Department of the Army, Washington, D.C.*

In commenting on Guilford's *An Inventory of Factors STDCR* (see 59), this reviewer supported, in general, the development and use of a factor score inventory, but expressed doubts as to its usefulness for selection until more validity information became available. The need for control of over and under self-evaluation was also mentioned. These comments apply equally to the *Guilford-Martin Inventory of Factors GAMIN,* although somewhat more validity information is made available for this inventory.

The validity information provided relates to supervisory proficiency. High validities are reported for M and N respectively for a small group (N = 26) of branch managers and executives. However, these two scores gave negligible validity in predicting success of supervisors (N's of 289 and 120). A usefully high validity (eta) is reported for M when curvilinearity is taken into account. While these and other findings are interesting, they cover a rather narrow area and cannot yet be regarded as an adequate basis for the general usefulness of the inventory. As the authors themselves point out, users of the tests should undertake validity studies in order to establish which, if any, of the factor scores are useful for their particular selection purpose.

The intercorrelations of the several factor scores are, in some cases, higher than would seem desirable. However, it appears evident enough from examination of the reliabilities that each of the scores is sufficiently unique to allow independent contribution in a prediction problem. Since many of the factors basic to the scores are orthogonal to each other, the correlations between the scores is very likely due to the summated impurities of the individual scored items. Reduction of such intercorrelation is a difficult problem.

In spite of the several difficulties mentioned, the GAMIN inventory is likely to prove a useful tool. It is more likely to be useful to research workers willing to undertake validation for their own purposes than to individuals seeking an inventory for immediate application.

For reviews by R. A. Brotemarkle and H. J. Eysenck, see 3:43 and 3:45.

[48]
The Guilford-Martin Personnel Inventory.
Grades 9–16 and adults; 1943; 3 scores: objectivity, agreeableness, cooperativeness; IBM; 1 form; $2.50 per 25, postage extra; 50¢ per specimen set, postpaid; separate answer sheets may be used; 2¢ per IBM answer sheet; $3.50 per set of stencils for machine scoring of answer sheets; $2.50 per set of stencils for hand scoring of answer sheets; 2¢ per profile chart (also for tests 47 and 59); postage extra; nontimed (30) minutes; J. P. Guilford and H. G. Martin; Sheridan Supply Co. *

REFERENCES
1–7. See 3:44.
8. Cerf, Arthur Z. "The Guilford-Martin Personnel Inventory, CE436A," pp. 592–5. In *Printed Classification Tests.* Edited by J. P. Guilford with the assistance of John I. Lacey. Army Air Forces Aviation Psychology Program Research Reports, Report No. 5. Washington, D.C.: U.S. Government Printing Office, 1947. Pp. xi, 919. * (PA 22:4145)
9. Kahn, D. F. *An Analysis of Factors Related to Life Insurance Selling.* Doctor's thesis, Purdue University (Lafayette, Ind.), 1948. (PA 24:2884)
10. Clark, Elmer J. *The Determination of the Relationship Between the Personality Traits of Teachers and Their Evaluation of Objectionable Pupil Behavior.* Doctor's thesis, University of Michigan (Ann Arbor, Mich.), 1949. Abstract: *Microfilm Abstracts* 9:78–9 no 2 '49. * (PA 24:4265)
11. Hadley, J. M., and Kahn, D. F. "A Comment on Wallace's Note on 'Factors Related to Life Insurance Selling.'" *J Appl Psychol* 33:359–62 Ag '49. * (PA 24:2882)
12. Kahn, D. F., and Hadley, J. M. "Factors Related to Life Insurance Selling." *J Appl Psychol* 33:132–40 Ap '49. * (PA 24:357)
13. Wallace, S. Rains, Jr. "A Note on Kahn and Hadley's 'Factors Related to Life Insurance Selling.'" *J Appl Psychol* 33:356–8 Ag '49. * (PA 24:2884)
14. Belman, H. S., and Evans, R. N. "Selection of Students for a Trade and Industrial Education Curriculum," pp. 9–14. In *Motives and Aptitudes in Education: Four Studies.* Edited by H. H. Remmers. Purdue University, Division of Educational Reference, Studies in Higher Education, No. 74. Lafayette, Ind.: the Division, December 1950. Pp. iii, 63. Paper. * (PA 26:3010)
15. Clark, Elmer J. "The Mental Health of Elementary School Teachers as Measured by the Guilford-Martin Personality Battery," pp. 8–12. In *The Seventh Yearbook of the National Council on Measurements Used in Education, 1949–1950.* Fairmont, W.Va.: the Council, Fairmont State College, 1950. Pp. v, 56, ix. Paper, mimeographed. *
16. Ekstrom, Peter Richard. *An Attempt to Develop a Falsification Key for the Guilford-Martin Personnel Inventory.* Master's thesis, University of Southern California (Los Angeles, Calif.), 1950.
17. Gilbert, Claudia. "The Guilford-Zimmerman Temperament Survey and Certain Related Personality Tests." *J Appl Psychol* 34:394–6 D '50. * (PA 25:4567)
18. Krasner, Leonard. *Personality Differences Between Patients Classified as Psychosomatic and as Non-Psychosomatic.* Doctor's thesis, Columbia University (New York, N.Y.), 1950. Abstract: *Microfilm Abstracts* 10:227–8 no 3 '50. *
19. Weschler, Irving R. "The Personal Factor in Labor Mediation." *Personnel Psychol* 3:113–32 su '50. * (PA 25:2089)
20. Baehr, Melany E. *A Factorial Study of Temperament.* University of Chicago, Psychometric Laboratory [Report] No. 63. Chicago, Ill.: the Laboratory, February 1951. Pp. 14. Paper, lithotyped. *
21. Belman, H. S., and Evans, R. N. "Selection of Students for a Trade and Industrial Educational Curriculum." *J Ed Psychol* 42:52–8 Ja '51. * (PA 25:6486)
22. Clark, Elmer J. "The Relationship Between the Personality Traits of Elementary School Teachers and Their Evaluation of Objectionable Behavior." *J Ed Res* 45:61–6 S '51. * (PA 26:3056)
23. Fonda, Charles P. "The Nature and Meaning of the Rorschach White Space Response." *J Abn & Social Psychol* 46:367–77 Jl '51. * (PA 26:2178)
24. Healy, Irene, and Borg, Walter R. "Personality Characteristics of Nursing School Students and Graduate Nurses." *J Appl Psychol* 35:275–80 Ag '51. * (PA 26:3088)
25. Kelly, E. Lowell, and Fiske, Donald W. *The Prediction of Performance in Clinical Psychology.* Ann Arbor, Mich.: University of Michigan, 1951. Pp. xv, 311. Lithotyped. *
26. Pemberton, Carol L. "Personality Inventory Data Related to Ace Subscores." *J Consult Psychol* 15:160–2 Ap '51. *
27. Thurstone, L. L. "The Dimensions of Temperament." *Psychometrika* 16:11–20 Mr '51. * (PA 25:7327)

Neil Van Steenberg, *Research Psychologist, Personnel Research Section, The Adjutant Gen-*

eral's Office, Department of the Army, Washington, D.C.

The stated purpose of the inventory is to assist industrial, business, and similar establishments in obtaining evaluations of present and potential employees along a "paranoid" continuum. If fully effective, the test could be used to prevent the hiring of troublemakers and to spot those already employed in advance of overt difficulties.

The inventory consists of 150 statements in question form. To these the person investigated is instructed to answer by encircling one of three possible answers printed at the end of the question (an IBM sheet is enclosed and can be used instead). A sample is: "Do you get upset rather easily? Yes? No." The answers are indicative of certain attitudes toward and evaluation of jobs, society, human nature, and discipline together with some self-appraisal. The questions are not of such a nature as to cause a normal individual to be embarrassed by giving a truthful answer. The first six items are not scored but serve as orientation.

The concept of a "paranoid" space is derived from factor analysis and clinical studies. The space is defined by four factors, but in the present study, two of these were not sufficiently differentiated to be considered separately. The three factors used are named after the socially desirable poles of the continua as Objectivity, Agreeableness, and Cooperation. Each of the three factors is identified by a separate score.

Scoring is done with the aid of an overlay key of transparent paper on which the selected answers are indicated together with their scoring weights. A table on the "Direction and Norms" sheet enables the investigator to convert these to a "C" scale based on percentage of the experimentally investigated population achieving various raw scores. It enables the investigator to compare scores on the three factors with one another and with those of similar inventories.

Two hundred items were constructed together with a preliminary key based on "the best statistical and clinical evidence at hand." The inventory was then administered to 400 subjects chosen on a priori basis to represent a diversely employed population. The test of internal consistency was applied to each item, and 150 of them were found to be sufficiently differentiating between the highest and lowest fourths of scores to be retained.

The item construction, sampling of subject case, and development of scoring keys are all vaguely outlined, and in a negative way prevent any criticism; the users of the tests are forced to take the word of the inventory constructors.

On the other hand, the development of reliability is well detailed and regardless of whether any makeshift methods were involved in the construction, shows that the reliabilities of the finished products are very acceptable: .83 for O (Objectivity), .80 for Ag (Agreeableness), and .91 for Co (Cooperativeness), found by scoring 100 cases similar to those used for item selection, correlating scores on one random half against the other, and estimating reliabilities of the total score by the Spearman-Brown technique. The traits are not completely independent; the correlation between O and Ag is .64, between O and Co is .55, and between Ag and C is .63.

In assaying the validity of the inventory the story is not so favorable. The manual reports an attempt to differentiate between members of an industrial workers group of 51 cases, a number of whom had previously been rated as troublemakers and discontents. The criterion chosen for prediction of undesirables was arbitrarily chosen as below the median score on two of the traits. The results were as follows:

	Predicted as Unsatisfactory	Predicted as Satisfactory	Total
Rated as Unsatisfactory	16	6	22
Rated as Satisfactory	10	19	29
Total	26	25	51

(Equivalent to a tetrachoric r of .55 for 51 cases)

How good this discrimination is cannot be known without knowing more about the composition of the group. If the group is composed of the highest and lowest quarters of a population classed along a troublemaker continuum it means one thing, if it is an unselected group it would mean something else. The authors do not state how the experimental group was selected.

In evaluating the inventory, the general impression is that the items were carefully worked out and put together, and that the authors were satisfied when they found that the scores were very reliable. When 400 cases were used in selection of items and adjustment of the key, and 100 cases used for the establishment of coefficients of reliability, it would appear that a greater effort could have been exerted at validating the inventory.

The trouble would be one of criterion. The inventory will undoubtedly pick, better than chance, those who are grossly discontented with their work; among the potential employees, it will pick those who are likely to become discontented. It will not cull out those who, though they have a strong paranoid streak, are intelligent enough to know that their natural impulse to answer a question may not coincide with the socially accepted one. On the other hand, they may also be intelligent enough to stay out of serious trouble; thus from a practical point of view they should not be eliminated. (If they were, who would later develop into executives, superintendents, labor leaders and the like?)

Assuming that a large proportion of all malcontents could be spotted and eliminated, would it be desirable from a management point of view? The only way to find out is by correlating the scores on the inventory with an overall effectiveness on the job.

The inventory is probably as good for its stated purpose as one could be made with the present limited knowledge of personnel characteristics. It does not claim too much for itself, and when used in conjunction with other measures, it will tend to round out the estimation of the personality Gestalt of an employee, present or potential. As the inventory becomes more generally used, it can be hoped that a more extensive validation evaluation will be published.

For reviews by Benjamin Shimberg and R. A. Brotemarkle, see 3:44–5.

[49]

★The Guilford-Zimmerman Temperament Survey. Grades 9–16 and adults; 1949; a revision and condensation of *Inventory of Factors STDCR* ('34–'40), *Guilford-Martin Inventory of Factors GAMIN* ('43), and *Guilford-Martin Personnel Inventory* ('43); 10 scores: general activity, restraint, ascendance, sociability, emotional stability, objectivity, friendliness, thoughtfulness, personal relations, masculinity; IBM; 1 form; norms ('49); separate answer sheets must be used; $3.75 per 25; 75¢ per 25 IBM answer sheets; $2 per set of machine scoring stencils; $2 per set of hand scoring stencils; 25¢ per manual; 50¢ per 25 profile charts for men; 50¢ per 25 profile charts for women; postage extra; 60¢ per specimen set (does not include stencils), postpaid; nontimed (50) minutes; J. P. Guilford and Wayne S. Zimmerman; Sheridan Supply Co. *

REFERENCES

1. BENTLEY, MADISON. "Factors and Functions in Human Resources." *Am J Psychol* 61:286–91 Ap '48. * (*PA* 22:4711)
2. GILBERT, C. F. *A Comparison of the Guilford-Zimmerman Temperament Survey With Certain Related Personality Tests.* Master's thesis, Pennsylvania State College, (State College, Pa.), 1950.
3. GILBERT, CLAUDIA. "The Guilford-Zimmerman Temperament Survey and Certain Related Personality Tests." *J Appl Psychol* 34:394–6 D '50. * (*PA* 25:4567)
4. HARTER, AUBREY BAER. *Adjustment of High School Seniors and the Marital Adjustment of Their Parents in a Southern California City.* Doctor's thesis, University of Southern California (Los Angeles, Calif.), 1950. (*Abstracts of Dissertations ....1950*, 1951, pp. 226–8.)
5. EISELE, MARTHA C., AND COTTLE, WILLIAM C. "The Guil-ford-Zimmerman Temperament Survey: I, With Rural High School Students." *Univ Kans B Ed* 6:12–5 N '51.

WILLIAM STEPHENSON, *Visiting Professor of Psychology, The University of Chicago, Chicago, Illinois.*

This Survey puts into one schedule the 10 major "traits," GRASEOFTPM, that Guilford and others have variously identified by factor analysis, and which have hitherto been included in separate inventories: *Nebraska Personality Inventory* (SEM), *Guilford-Martin Inventory of Factors GAMIN, Guilford-Martin Personnel Inventory I* (OAgCo), and *Inventory of Factors STDCR.* It consists of 300 items, 30 for each of the "traits," each responded to with a yes, ?, or no. The responses are weighted only 0 or 1, and the layout lends itself to the standard IBM answer sheet. Only two stencils are needed for hand scoring.

The "traits" themselves are (G) general activity, (R) restraint, (A) ascendence, (S) sociability, (E) emotional stability, (O) objectivity, (F) friendliness, (T) thoughtfulness, (P) personal relations, and (M) masculinity respectively. The reliability with which each of the traits is assessed is shown to be of the order .80; and their intercorrelations are, as the authors say, "gratifyingly low," the implication being that all are approximately orthogonal in factor terms, that is, that "unique traits" are involved. Some consideration is given to possible biases which detract from the dependability of the schedule —everyone, for example, is apt to give himself favorable scores, although not on all the "traits." Finally, profile charts are provided for men and women for each of the 10 "traits."

As one would expect from Professor Guilford's laboratory, the Survey, its data and supporting norms are all adequate, thorough, and factually orientated. For the purposes for which these inventories are used it is probably better than most. We could raise, however, two methodological issues about it. Given 10 uncorrelated "traits," if each is used to indicate only two grades (*above average* for the trait, and *below* average), $2^{10} = 1,024$ possible classes of temperament can be indicated. This should either provide scope enough for almost anyone who believes in the relative uniqueness of temperamental qualities, or be the despair of those who find it difficult to believe that temperament can be as complex as all this! Moreover, given the premise of 10 uncorrelated traits, there must on the whole be an equal number of persons for each of the 1024 possibilities: is that not so? Thus, amongst 2048 college students there would have to be two of each class. These are interesting geometrical speculations, deductions from the Survey's nature. No doubt something is wrong, perhaps, to think of temperament as so nicely and geometrically allotted amongst college students, but so it must be if this Survey is as sound scientifically as it appears to be.

One wonders, however, whether someone could have a *theory* about temperament, somehow, and put this to test, if only to free us from a feeling that mankind is not ordered like squares on a chessboard with respect to its temperamental qualities. Temperament traits, after all, are in the happy position of being such as perhaps correspond to our behavior as observed by others—when we are *sad,* we *feel* it, and also others can see it in our demeanors. But when we save a life and are called *brave* by observers, we might feel in fact quite frightened and horrified and certainly not *brave-feeling.* There are those who wish to look at personality (and everything else) from the "internal frame of reference," and others who look at it only from the "external frame": temperament traits probably look the same both ways, or imply the same. Might not these, then, in relation to others of conduct as externally observed, provide interesting food for experimental speculation?

NEIL VAN STEENBERG, *Research Psychologist, Personnel Research Section, The Adjutant General's Office, Department of the Army, Washington, D.C.*

The stated purpose of this survey is to combine the findings of the Guilford series of personality inventories into a single battery and thus obtain scores on 10 personality traits from the administration of a single booklet.

This 8-page booklet contains instructions for marking and 300 items. The items are in the form of statements which the examinee marks as true, false, or indifferent; e.g., "You are a carefree individual. Yes ? No." (The fact that the sequence of numbers on the IBM sheet runs from left to right, instead of up and down as has become usual, is immediately noted or commented upon by test-technicians—it will probably never bother the average examinee because he has not acquired that particular reaction pattern.)

Overlay keys are provided for handscoring. Only one answer for each statement is keyed, and all keyed items are given equal weight. By spacing the statements so that every fifth one on the answer sheet gives a score on one particular trait, all the elements of the total score of each trait are in one column of the IBM sheet. This clever arrangement greatly facilitates hand scoring. There are 10 scores, one for each trait assayed, to be obtained with a maximum of 30 on each. A high score is in the direction of what is in general the socially desirable pole.

Previous inventories developed by the authors provided the raw materials from which the items were selected or reworked. By scoring each item on only one key, greater facility in scoring is achieved, though by limiting the possible score to 30 on any one trait, this facility has been achieved at some sacrifice of reliability of individual scores.

Norms for the survey were obtained for 9 of 10 traits on a college population of 523 men and 389 women. Norms for the remaining trait "T" were derived from a population of high school seniors and their parents. The authors state that various estimates of reliabilities were made, and a table is given showing the consensus. The coefficients vary between .75 and .85. The mean scores and the SD are given separately for men and women, but except on the trait of masculinity there are no substantial (certainly no significant) differences between the sexes.

The intercorrelations between the traits are generally small, one is as high as .61, some others are of the magnitude about .40, but most of them are small enough that there does not seem to be any question as to the existence of ten separate dimensions.

The validity of the scores is principally based on the factor analytic studies in which the traits were isolated. It is further indicated that a practical validation study has been carried out, but the details are not given.

The raw scores on the 10 traits are to be converted into "C" scores, which in turn are based on the percentage of the scores attained by the experimentally investigated population.

Interpretation of the 10 scores per individual is of course the real difficulty in a broad inventory of this kind. To assist the administrator of the survey, a very detailed and lucid description of the traits and clinical syndromes is given in the manual. But since evaluation is not only in terms of the 10 factors but also (rightly) in their interactions, the task demands a considerable amount of clinical sophistication on the part of the investigator if it is to be done adequately. The optimal scores for individuals who show supervisory promise are given in the manual.

There are some instructions given in the manual to which exceptions must be taken. It is stated that more than three question marks on an answer sheet is a probable indication either that the examinee does not know himself very well or that he has little confidence in whatever ideas he has about himself. The remedy recommended is to call the examinee into a conference and after orientation suggest that he change a substantial number of question marks to either "Yes" or "No." A number of mature psychologists in the office of this reviewer "took" the inventory and in most cases came up with more than three question marks on most traits. If a forced choice was desired by the authors, the question marks should not have been included among the choices.

The authors also indicate that there is in general a total bias toward the favorable pole. This is not surprising, and the personnel technician heeding the general warning given is able to adjust his evaluation by relating it to configuration of the profile rather than to individual scores. In this connection, the authors state that on the basis of probability theory the expectation of the score of a particular individual should not deviate widely from the mean in the same direction on many trait scores, since the traits are independent or almost so. In other words, if eight or nine of the ten traits are above (or below) the median, the whole set of ratings should be suspect. This line of reasoning would be valid if the traits were sampled independently but, of course, they are not. It is well known that favorable traits are positively correlated in individuals (a positive manifold), and it would be a source of surprise if an individual who was rated above normal in eight traits was not also found to be superior in the remaining two.

The survey gives a very favorable impression of a well rounded, carefully worked out method of evaluating an important portion of the total personality. It is easy to administer and to score, and if interpretation of the obtained measures is difficult, it is a function of the complexity of personalities rather than a function of the survey. It will be particularly useful in counseling at the upper high school and college levels as well as in organizations employing a large number of young people and having in their employ psychologists with enough experience and competence to interpret the results.

J Consult Psychol 14:162 Ap '50. Laurance F. Shaffer. * As the outstanding omnibus instrument based primarily on factor analyses, the *Survey* will have usefulness for screening, rapid evaluation and research.

[50]

★Heston Personal Adjustment Inventory. Grades 9–16 and adults; 1949; 6 scores: analytical thinking, sociability, emotional stability, confidence, personal relations, home satisfaction; IBM; 1 form; $2.40 per 25; 30¢ per manual; postage extra; 35¢ per specimen set, postpaid; separate answer sheets may be used; $1.10 per 25 IBM answer sheets; 40¢ per set of stencils for scoring answer sheets; postage extra; nontimed (40–60) minutes; Joseph C. Heston; World Book Co. *

REFERENCES
1. HESTON, JOSEPH C. "A Comparison of Four Masculinity-Femininity Scales." *Ed & Psychol Meas* 8:375-87 au '48. * (PA 23:4256)
2. MICHAELIS, JOHN U., AND TYLER, FRED T. "Diagnostic and Predictive Value of the Heston Inventory Used in Student Teaching." *J Teacher Ed* 1:40-3 Mr '50. *

ALBERT ELLIS, *Consulting Psychologist, 56 Park Ave., New York 16, New York.*

Compared to other personality inventories, this inventory is a better than average instrument which possesses most of the advantages which its author and publisher claim for it. It independently measures—or at least provides a score for—traits of personal adjustment; "it affords adequate statistical reliability of measurement"; it has been validated by several methods; it is usable at both the college and high school level; it provides fairly stable and representative norms; and "it is simple to administer and convenient to score." Having duly noted these advantages of the test, it is now in order to examine its main, and somewhat less well publicized, shortcomings:

a) It is claimed that "clinical experience with many individual cases during the last three years has demonstrated the value of the inventory approach," but no confirmatory evidence is given in the extensive test manual. Apparently, moreover, no attempt is being made to check, experimentally, this "clinical experience." The writer suspects that it is the same kind of "clinical experience" which has been offered, for many years, in support of orthodox Freudianism, dianetics, the *Szondi Test,* and many other as yet experimentally unvalidated hypotheses. This type of "clinical experience" normally consists of making a tremendous fuss about one case which supports the hypothesis in question—and conveniently forgetting about the other nine cases which do not.

b) The six "personality traits" scored on the Heston inventory differ widely in clinical usability. One of them, analytical thinking, is hardly a personality trait at all, but belongs more with descriptions of mental processes. Three of the other traits—sociability, personal relations, and home satisfaction—are largely the effects of personality traits, rather than the traits themselves. Moreover, they are fairly easily determined by almost any type of inventory or, much better, by a brief psychological interview. The only truly important personality traits that the inventory appears to measure are confidence and emotional stability which turn out to have an intercorrelation coefficient of .73.

c) When outside criteria were employed to test the validity of the scales, low coefficients of correlation were generally found between the inventory scores and the ratings of acquaintances. Thus, *r*'s were found of only .24 for emotional stability and .36 for confidence.

d) The author unfortunately uses many of the vaguely worded, confusing questions from some of the oldest personality inventories, instead of constructing unequivocally worded new ones. Questions like, "Do you daydream often?," which have time and again been found to be of the meaningless armchair variety, have been retained. And many questions to which *all* truly honest and conscientious respondents would necessarily have to answer yes have often been included. For example: "Do you ever wish you were more attractive?" "Do you ever feel too self-conscious?" "Do you sometimes become angry?" "Are your nerves ever raw or on edge?" "Are there some people you dislike?" A *no* answer to most of these questions is, according to the scoring sheet, distinctly rewarded, which, apparently, means that only those who lie to themselves or to others are considered to be well adjusted in our society.

e) The author writes that "it is the writer's firm persuasion that such tests [as the Heston] do have valuable practical utility and that most forward-looking counselors would rather use a tool with some admitted difficulties than rely solely on subjective judgment." If this is a correct belief, then counseling is certainly in a sad state today. While it may be true that the majority of contemporary counselors still favor old-fashioned inventory techniques instead of getting down to modern clinical methods of per-

sonality evaluation, it is a little hard to believe that most *forward-looking* counselors may also be included in this diehard group. Personality inventories may of course have real value as screening instruments, to be used prior to counseling or psychotherapeutic processes; but it is discouraging to believe that well trained, forward-looking clinicians would for a moment think of spending valuable time giving and scoring inventories for use with disturbed individuals who have come for some form of counseling or treatment.

In sum: the *Heston Personal Adjustment Inventory,* while as good as most of the similar tests of this type, seems to have only a screening usefulness; and it is depressing to see counselors being encouraged to use any instrument of this sort in dealing with individual counselees who have gone beyond a screening process. All contemporary personality inventories, including this one, have dubious individual diagnostic value. Any counselor who, in a 15- or 20-minute interview with a counselee, cannot obtain more concrete and valid information than can be obtained with these instruments had better return to tests and measurements or other more academic applications of psychology.

HANS J. EYSENCK, *Director, Psychology Department, Institute of Psychiatry, Maudsley Hospital, London, England.*

This inventory claims to test six basic components of an individual's adjustment: analytical thinking, sociability, emotional stability, confidence, personal relations, and home satisfaction. Norms are provided for high school and college groups but not for adults. The inventory comprises 270 questions in all. Scores are converted into percentiles and may be represented on a profile chart. Split half reliabilities of the individual scales are reasonably satisfactory, ranging from .80 to .91. Validity is claimed on three grounds: (*a*) *Internal Consistency.* This is based on item analysis, not as might have been preferable, on factor analysis. (*b*) *Psychological Meaningfulness.* This is difficult to appraise in view of the differences between individual judges as to what precisely is psychologically meaningful. (*c*) *Independent Criteria.* Correlations are presented here showing moderately sized correlations between inventory traits and ratings by counselors and other psychologically trained persons. Differences were found between college men and reformatory inmates, but not between high school boys and boys in a juvenile correction institution.

Intercorrelations are given between the scales which are high enough—.73, .61, .58, .44, .39, .38, .38, .32, .31, .26, .03, .01, −.08, −.17, and −.18—to make it quite clear that the six traits measured have no separate entity. A factorial analysis is necessary before these six traits can be regarded as independently useful. There is little in this scale to set it apart from the many others on the market, and from the point of view of intercorrelation of scores, it is clearly inferior to the other scales.

It is difficult to know the extent to which this type of questionnaire can be used because there is no evidence presented that the alleged areas measured have any meaningful existence or, if they do, that they can be measured by questionnaires of this type. The path of research in personality measurement is much more thorny and difficult than is suggested by the authors of inventories and questionnaires; and, until they face more realistically the problems of taxonomy and validity, their products will be of doubtful scientific value.

E. LOWELL KELLY, *Professor of Psychology, and Director, Bureau of Psychological Services, University of Michigan, Ann Arbor, Michigan.*

This is a self-report inventory of 270 yes-no items designed to evaluate six aspects of an individual's personal adjustment. Like other self-report inventories, it is administered without a time limit: most persons complete the form in 40 to 50 minutes. Scoring is facilitated by the use of a separate answer sheet. Percentile norms are provided for college men (884), college women (597), high school senior men (216) and high school senior women (251). The reverse side of the answer sheet contains a profile chart for use in preparing a profile of the individual scores. As a means of emphasizing the greater significance of percentile differences as the score deviates from the mean at the extremes of the scales, the percentile scale used on the profile chart has been made to correspond to z-score units.

Test items were selected from a pool of 450 items on the basis of internal consistency: each item used has a minimum discrimination index of 30; the mean index for the items on each scale is 45 or higher. In addition, the author used the criterion of face validity: regardless of its discrimination index, an item was not included in

a scale unless the term was "psychologically meaningful" for the variable. Unit scoring weights are used and no item contributes to more than one of the six scores. Corrected split half reliability coefficients for the six scores are: .86, .91, .86, .84, .80, and .87. The intercorrelations between the six scores are low with the exception of those between emotional stability, confidence, and personal relations (.73, .61, and .58). All show correlations of .50 to .75 with the MMPI scales for depression, psychasthenia, and schizophrenia. The author regards the differences between the reliabilities and intercorrelations of these scales great enough to justify separate scoring keys and separate reporting of scores. However, these three scores are plotted sequentially on the profile chart. Scores on analytical thinking (thinking introversion) correlate .31 with ACE scores and .36 with first-semester college grades.

Evidence of the validity of the several scores includes: reasonably good agreement between the scores and the judgments of counselors based on more extended contact; correlations of .26 to .59 between scores and trait ratings of acquaintances; correlations of .31 to .63 with self-ratings; and the fact that for five of the six traits, the correlation of the scores with both of these criteria is higher than the intercriterion correlation.

The inventory impresses this reviewer as being a good instrument for the purposes for which it was designed: to *assist* the busy counselor in identifying students in need of attention and to provide a *preliminary* assessment of the student. The author is to be commended for the generally superior and unusually complete manual. It reflects not only a considerable amount of research but thoughtful consideration of the problems underlying the design and use of any personality inventory. In this connection, it is noted that the author states that the reliability coefficients "are all large enough for very satisfactory use in group situations," yet the inventory is designed and recommended for use in the evaluation of individuals. The manual warns the user of the test to be cautious in the interpretation of the scores of individuals, but this word of caution may not be sufficient.

The author is quite insistent that whatever correlations exist between the several scales represent true relationships between the variables, since each is "measured *entirely independently,* by a separate set of items." Whether or not one accepts this contention is of course a matter of the meaning attached to the phrase, "measured entirely independently." To be sure, the scores are based on different items, but some of the items appearing in the emotional stability scale would certainly have high enough discrimination indices to have been included in one of the other scales with which emotional stability is highly correlated. Just because intelligence may be measured by two tests with no common items would not lead to the conclusion that the two tests are measuring different variables. The author apparently chose to build a test with six scales. Three of these—analytical thinking, sociability, and home satisfaction—are relatively independent of each other and of whatever is being measured by the other three scales which have high intercorrelations.

In addition to detailed instructions for the use of the inventory, the manual contains all essential technical data, makes but modest claims for the instrument, and offers wise counsel with respect to its appropriate use in student personnel programs.

*J Consult Psychol 13:224 Je '49. Laurance F. Shaffer. * Although there are many objections to the questionnaire approach to the study of personality, Heston's contribution is not "just another" inventory, but a workmanlike job with a number of areas of potential usefulness, including the selection of students for more individual guidance.*

[51]

Hunt-Minnesota Test for Organic Brain Damage. Chronological ages 16-70 and mental ages 8 and over; 1943; 16 tests grouped in 3 divisions: the vocabulary test of *Revised Stanford-Binet Scale,* interpolated tests, learning and recall; individual; 1 form; no data on reliability and validity in manual (for data presented elsewhere by the author, see *1*); tentative norms; $5 per set of testing materials and 25 record blanks; $1.25 per 25 record blanks; postage extra; (30) minutes; abbreviated test (15) minutes; Howard F. Hunt; University of Minnesota Press. *

REFERENCES

1-11. See 3:49.
12. BROOKS, LEAH E. *The Application of the Hunt-Minnesota Test for Organic Brain Damage and the Wechsler-Bellevue Test to Psychotic Patients Before and After Shock Therapy.* Master's thesis, Fordham University (New York, N.Y.), 1946.
13. ARKOLA, AUDREY L. "An Experimental Study of the Effects of Sodium Amytal Upon Performance on the Hunt-Minnesota Test for Organic Brain Damage." *J Clin Psychol* 3:392-6 O '47. * (PA 22:4305)
14. BROWN, MARY MORROW. "A Study of Performance on a Deterioration Test as Related to Quality of Vocabulary and Rigidity." Abstract. *Am Psychol* 3:372 Ag '48. * (PA 23:669, title only)
15. FANELLI, GLORIA C. *An Evaluation and Comparison of the Wechsler Memory Scale and the Hunt-Minnesota Test for Organic Brain Damage.* Master's thesis, Fordham University (New York, N.Y.), 1948.
16. JUCKEM, HARRIET, AND WOLD, JANE A. "A Study of the Hunt-Minnesota Test for Organic Brain Damage at the Upper

Levels of Vocabulary." *J Consult Psychol* 12:53-7 Ja-F '48. * (PA 22:3033)
17. PHILLIPS, E. LAKIN; BERMAN, ISABEL R.; AND HANSON, HAROLD B. *Intelligence and Personality Factors Associated With Poliomyelitis Among School Age Children.* Monographs of the Society for Research in Child Development, Vol. 12, No. 2, Serial No. 45. Evanston, Ill.: Child Development Publications, the Society, 1948. Pp. vii, 60. Paper, lithotyped. *
18. SCHERER, ISIDOR W. "The Psychological Scores of Mental Patients in an Individual and Group Testing Situation." *J Clin Psychol* 5:405-8 O '49. * (PA 24:3740)
19. BARNES, T. CUNLIFFE. "Electroencephalographic Validation of the Rorschach, Hunt and Bender Gestalt Tests." Abstract. *Am Psychol* 5:322 Jl '50. * (PA 25:1088, title only)

SEYMOUR G. KLEBANOFF, *Chief Psychologist, Franklin Delano Roosevelt Veterans Administration Hospital, Montrose, New York.*

This test was designed to detect and measure intellectual impairment as seen in patients with organic brain damage. Hunt utilized the general clinical observation that recently acquired associations are impaired in the presence of organic brain dysfunction while old habits show relatively little deficit. The test thus consists of the 1937 Stanford-Binet vocabulary, which should reveal little impairment; a group of timed verbal and nonverbal tests involving learning and recall, which should be sensitive to organic brain damage; and a group of interpolated tasks which serve the purposes of providing uniform intervals between tests of recall and also of detecting significant personality disturbances.

The test is statistically standardized so that T scores may be obtained. These constitute predictions of the maximal level of learning as based upon age and vocabulary scores. Hunt studied the significance of difference in scores between a standardizing group of brain damaged cases and a matched control group of patients without brain damage. This permitted the determination of a T score cutoff beyond which the diagnosis of organic brain damage may be made.

The literature reveals definite weaknesses associated with the test which indicate the need for further investigation. A primary difficulty involves the relatively limited number of patients employed in the initial standardizing group. Further standardization utilizing a large number of patients with organic brain damage seems indicated. In addition, there is a need for comparison between normal and psychiatric groups. This would serve to clarify the problem of "false-positive" selection which is a frequent criticism of this technique as pointed out by Malamud (*8*), Meehl and Jeffery (*9*), and Juckem and Wold (*16*). The last two have demonstrated that in a normal population of superior vocabulary level, 60 per cent of the subjects obtain T scores indicative of organic brain damage. Extreme caution must therefore be exercised in the use of this test with superior individuals. Further, the basic difficulty of differentiating organic deficit from types of impairment due to chronic psychogenic illness persists in the strictly quantitative use of this technique.

Strict adherence to the quantitative aspects of the test findings can produce spurious interpretation. However, the test remains a valuable tool in the evaluation of intellectual efficiency despite weaknesses in the determination of the etiology of the intellectual impairment. The test would appear to be of greatest value when utilized by an experienced clinician with emphasis upon the qualitative aspects of the test results.

For reviews by Margaret Ives and O. L. Zangwill, see 3:49.

[52]

★[Illinois Opinion Inventories.] Grades 6–8, 9–12, adults; 1948; a survey form for use by school administrators in sampling parent and student opinion on schools; 4 inventories (only 2 published as separates); 1 form; no manual; no data on reliability and validity; directions and the complete inventories are presented in *What People Think about Their Schools* (see *1* below); Harold C. Hand, Gilbert C. Finlay, and Ardwin J. Dolio; World Book Co. *

a) ILLINOIS INVENTORY OF PARENT OPINION. Adults; $1.80 per 25, postage extra; 20¢ per specimen set, postpaid; (50) minutes.

b) ILLINOIS INVENTORY OF PUPIL OPINION; SECONDARY SCHOOL FORM. Grades 9–12; $1.40 per 25, postage extra; 20¢ per specimen set, postpaid; (30–50) minutes.

c) ILLINOIS INVENTORY OF PUPIL OPINION: UPPER ELEMENTARY SCHOOL FORM. Grades 6–8; may be produced by individual school systems with permission from publisher.

d) ILLINOIS INVENTORY OF TEACHER OPINION. Teachers; may be reproduced by individual school systems with permission from publisher.

REFERENCES

1. HAND, HAROLD CURTIS. *What People Think About Their Schools: Values and Methods of Public-Opinion Polling as Applied to School Systems.* Yonkers, N.Y.: World Book Co., 1948. Pp. iv, 219. *

KENNETH E. CLARK, *Associate Professor of Psychology, University of Minnesota, Minneapolis, Minnesota.*

These inventories are designed to provide: (*a*) school superintendents and boards of education with information about parents' attitudes towards their children's schools; (*b*) teachers and administrators with information about students' attitudes and opinions toward their schools; and (*c*) administrators with information about teachers' attitudes towards their schools and jobs. These are types of opinions "which school-board members, superintendents, principals, and teachers must secure if they are

to know instead of guess (1) how well they are succeeding in their public-relations or personnel practices, (2) at what specific points they are succeeding or failing, and (3) what their consequent top priorities actually are."

Each of the four separate inventories is reported to have been developed and carefully pretested, used in city wide polls, and modified on the basis of experience in its use. The final forms presented for use give evidence of this work. The generally well phrased questions cover very well the important issues and look as though they would give useful results. Some questions do show a need for additional work, however, being either too long and involved, or failing to distinguish between the differences in opinions of informed and uninformed respondents. Sample findings for one school system are presented. Neither normative data nor evidence of the sensitivity of the measures for reflecting changes in school practices over a period of time are presented, although these would seem to be rather important points. The lack of evidences of reliability and validity is less serious since the meaning of these concepts for an inventory of this sort is obscure.

Two of the four forms of the inventories (the parent form and the secondary school form) are printed and available from the publisher. The other forms must be reproduced locally by the institution wishing to use them. When used for nonprofit purposes and with the publisher's permission, the two printed inventories may also be reproduced locally without charge. Thus the vast amount of work ordinarily required in preparing surveys of opinions about schools is greatly reduced by the easy availability of these inventories. The school administrator or teacher who is interested in surveying the attitudes of his associates or students will do well to consult Hand's monograph, *What People Think About Their Schools.*

For a related review, see 53.

[53]

★[*Re* Illinois Opinion Inventories.] HAND, HAROLD C. **What People Think About Their Schools: Values and Methods of Public-Opinion Polling as Applied to School Systems.** Yonkers, N.Y.: World Book Co., 1948. Pp. iv, 219. $2.52. *

El Sch J 49:477–8 Ap '49. John Withall. Are you a school administrator? Are you interested in getting fairly accurate information about parents', teachers', and pupils' attitudes toward the school and its administrations? Since a "yes" to the first question makes an affirmative reply to the second almost inevitable, Harold C. Hand's book, *What People Think about Their Schools,* may be of value to you. The publication presents techniques for procuring more reliable and valid data than are customarily available to school administrators with respect to the satisfactions and dissatisfactions of the three groups mentioned above. Primarily a manual, the book describes the rationale behind the Opinion Inventories presented by the author and enlarges in detail on the methodology of administering the inventories and of processing and interpreting the resulting data. One of the major themes of this slim volume (the book comprises 149 pages of text proper) is the delineation of the dangers confronting the administrator who depends on guesswork and hearsay for assessing the likes and dislikes of any of the groups of persons with whom he works. In Hand's opinion, guesswork and the pitfalls it brings to administrative practice can be eliminated by careful polling of the school's patrons and teachers. This polling can be done through the use of the Illinois Opinion Inventories * In the main, the inventories are composed of strength-of-feeling check items and a few write-in answers. * The questions in the inventories are unusually clear and straightforward. There seems to be only one item which evidences some ambiguity. This item revolves around the parents' and pupils' interpretations of the phrase "social problems." The question is aimed at assessing their opinions of the effectiveness of the school's efforts in helping pupils with problems of personal adjustment. Will the phrase "Social problems" connote adjustive problems to them? Furthermore, judging from the amount of attention and space devoted to the two problems, assessing the parents' and pupils' opinions about the value of the school's guidance and counseling program appears to be of less moment to the authors than obtaining reactions to the problem raised by the exclusion of some pupils from extra-curriculum activities because of the prohibitive cost. The authors of the inventories seem to be on secure ground in all instances in which they ask for an individual's attitudes or opinions on the *existing* school situation. In Part II of the parents' inventory, however, they leave their more secure pastures by attempting to plumb parents' attitudes about matters such as federal aid for education; extending the formal

period of education upward; society's responsibility for insuring basic needs—food, shelter, clothing, health services—which will render education effective; the operational reality of educational opportunity for all; and so on. The language throughout the book is refreshingly clear and simple. In some respects it may seem to the reader that the author sets out in too much detail suggestions regarding sampling procedures, types of data sheets, steps and procedures in processing the data, and even the types of tables to be used. If one realizes, however, that the book is primarily a manual to accompany the Illinois Inventories of Opinion, the meticulous descriptions of ways of collecting and interpreting data seem justifiable.

[54]

★**Industrial Subjective Fatigue and Euphoria Scales: Present Feelings.** Ages 14 and over; 1944; Forms A, B; manual ('44—see *1* below); $2 per 25; $1 per specimen set; postpaid; (1) minute; Willard A. Kerr; Psychometric Affiliates, Box 1625, Chicago 90, Ill. *

REFERENCES

1. MIDDLETON, W. C.; FAY, P. J.; KERR, W. A.; AND AMFT, F. "The Effect of Music on Feelings of Restfulness-Tiredness and Pleasantness-Unpleasantness." *J Psychol* 17:299–318. '44. * (*PA* 18:3451)

[55]

★**Industrial Subjective Fatigue Scale: Retrospective Work Curve Feelings: National Research Program on Employee Feelings at Work.** Ages 14 and over; 1950–51; Form A ['51]; mimeographed; manual ('50—see *1* below); $2 per 25; $1 per specimen set; postpaid; (2) minutes; Willard Kerr and Ivan Lippitz: Psychometric Affiliates, Box 1625, Chicago 90, Ill. *

REFERENCES

1. GRIFFITH, JOHN W.; KERR, WILLARD A.; MAYO, THOMAS B., JR.; AND TOPAL, JOHN R. "Changes in Subjective Fatigue and Readiness for Work During the Eight-Hour Shift." *J Appl Psychol* 34:163–6 Je '50. * (*PA* 25:4014).

[56]

★**Interaction Process Analysis.** Groups of from 2 to 20 people (ages 4 and over); 1948–50; a method of analyzing group character and processes; $3 per 250 interaction scoring forms ['50]; $6 per manual, *Interaction Process Analysis: A Method for the Study of Small Groups* ('50—see *2* below); postage extra; the *Interaction Recorder,* an optional instrument which facilitates the recording of observations in sequence, is described in *1* below; Robert F. Bales; Addison-Wesley Press Inc. *

REFERENCES

1. BALES, ROBERT F., AND GERBRANDS, HENRY. "The 'Interaction Recorder': An Apparatus and Check List for Sequential Content Analysis of Social Interaction." *Human Relations* 1: 456–63 no 4 '48. * (*PA* 23:2012)
2. BALES, ROBERT F. *Interaction Process Analysis: A Method for the Study of Small Groups.* Cambridge, Mass.: Addison-Wesley Press, Inc., 1950. Pp. xi, 203. * (*PA* 24:4553)
3. BALES, ROBERT F.; STRODTBECK, FRED L.; MILLS, THEODORE M.; AND ROSEBOROUGH, MARY E. "Channels of Communication in Small Groups." *Am Sociol R* 16:461–8 Ag '51. *

LAUNOR F. CARTER, *Director of Research, Army Field Forces Human Research Unit No. 2, Fort Ord, California.*

Bales' form is printed on an 8 by 11½ inch sheet of paper and is used for recording the behavior of individuals in a group situation. On the left-hand side are 12 categories for classifying individuals' behavior and the remaining area is ruled into boxes for tallying the frequency of occurrence of each behavior. There are 12 rows to correspond to the categories and 20 columns which can be used for successive time intervals. Extensive instructions for the use of the form, detailed definitions of the categories, and suggestions for training observers are contained in the book, *Interaction Process Analysis.*

One of the serious problems of interaction recording is the nature of the categories to be used. Bales' categories have been evolved both from theoretical considerations and as a result of considerable empirical refinement. The 12 categories are, in order, (1) shows solidarity, (2) shows tension release, (3) agrees, (4) gives suggestion, (5) gives opinion, (6) gives orientation, (7) asks for orientation, (8) asks for opinion, (9) asks for suggestion, (10) disagrees, (11) shows tension, and (12) shows antagonism. In Bales' theoretical formulation categories 6 and 7 have to do with problems of communication, 5 and 8 with problems of evaluation, 4 and 9 with problems of control, 3 and 10 with problems of decision, 2 and 11 with tension reduction, and 1 and 12 with reintegration. Thus different groups can be compared with respect to the relative proportion of time devoted to these various activities. An extensive theoretical discussion of the meaning and implication of the various categories is contained in Bales' book.

While it is contended that this system of categorizing is widely applicable, it is this reviewer's experience that it is best adapted to discussion groups and is not entirely appropriate for groups engaged in work on tasks requiring manipulation of material.

The question of the reliability and validity of interaction scoring procedures usually refers to the total process of the recording technique and the performance of the observers. One chapter of Bales' book is devoted to the problem of appraising observer reliability. In general, an attempt to demonstrate reliability is made by comparing the frequency of observed behavior for a given time interval recorded as falling into each category when observations of the same group are made by independent observers. In this reviewer's opinion Bales' demonstrations

of reliability are unsatisfactory, since they are largely based on an inappropriate use of chi-square. However, using different statistical techniques, others have shown that such observations can be adequately reliable. In a sense the validity of the technique is self-evident since it allows the recording of immediately perceived behavior; whether the behavior categories recorded are appropriate for a particular study depends on the problem being investigated.

The *Interaction Scoring Form* and *Interaction Process Analysis* represent pioneer efforts in a complicated but rapidly growing field. The scoring form will prove valuable as a convenient device for scoring interaction in discussion groups and for the introductory training of observers. For some group behavior studies more complex techniques will be needed such as are involved in the use of the *Interaction Recorder,* the *Interaction Chronograph,* or the modified stenograph.

For related reviews, see 57.

[57]

★[*Re* Interaction Process Analysis.] BALES, ROBERT F. **Interaction Process Analysis: A Method for the Study of Small Groups.** Cambridge, Mass.: Addison-Wesley Press, Inc., 1950. Pp. xi, 203. $6.00. * (*PA* 24:4553)

Am Sociol R 15:693–4 O '50. Ernest Greenwood. * [The book's] chief contribution lies in demonstrating the utility of a system of twelve basic, general-purpose categories whereby small group interaction, regardless of setting, might be observed, recorded and analyzed * represents a faltering but encouraging step toward the development of an experimental social psychology worthy of that name. Studies of....[this type] promise eventually to crack open some of the heretofore imposing obstacles blocking the development of experimentation in our discipline. Two such problems, to which the author himself all too briefly alludes, are relevant here, viz. how to translate crudely derived a priori generalizations into operational hypotheses, and how to standardize observations over time and space. We already know so much about why we behave as human beings and still we know so little about how to control ourselves. We shall persist in our inability to shape the macrocosm until we have learned to manipulate the microcosm. Therefore principles of group behavior that we already have discovered must be made concrete, anchored to observable and manipulatable referents. The twelve general-purpose categories developed by the author represent an attempt to impart handles to group interaction so that we might get hold of and see it in settings sufficiently circumscribed to be manageable. The other of our difficulties has been our inability to render our observations additive, to impart to them the cumulative property which is the *sine qua non* of scientific progress. Thus we have had no way of guaranteeing comparability among a series of observations of the same observer of the same group or among the observations of many scattered observers of similar groups. The author's suggested minimal set of interaction categories, with his scheme for their observation and recording, is a step toward a long sought for standardization. The author is apparently well aware of the crudity of his attempts and invites critical appraisal of them. Whatever may be the shortcomings of his efforts, they deserve encouragement. It is from such beginnings that we shall transform social science from a catalogue of mere truisms into a kit of workable tools.

J Abn & Social Psychol 45:786–8 O '50. Alvin Zander. * a stimulating progress report * The format is good and the writing style is interesting and clear. There is no doubt that this volume is creating a great deal of interest. It is a stimulating and provocative aid for some types of research on groups which many are sure to find helpful. One wonders if its appearance will encourage descriptive research similar to that which blossomed not many years ago with the first appearance of psychological tests. If so, to what end? This reviewer knows of several group practitioners who have tried to use the observation schedule with their groups and then wondered what to do with their data. Similarly, what will be done with an accumulation of group-descriptions made in terms of standard-categories? Apparently the author is ambivalent concerning the range of applicability of this observation scheme. At one point he states that his aspiration is to develop a standard set of general-purpose categories which should be able to encompass every act by anyone in a group. In another place he asserts that the categories might best be used as a supplement to other research methods or observation categories. Only experience will show whether or not this short set of observation categories, built in terms of a very definite theoretical system, will be a useful supplement for studies employing quite a different theoretical framework. This reviewer is skeptical about its ready integration into many

studies, especially experimental research. Skeptical, because the *standard* nature of the categories will almost certainly be changed under the influence of different experimental situations. The significance and interpretations of "asking for opinions" or "showing tension release," for example, might be quite different when varying leadership styles as compared to, say varying group homogeneity of membership. The author states that he hopes this approach will make it possible for him to develop more adequate theories about full-scale social systems. His theoretical framework which proposes that each act of a group member is part of an interaction system gives promise that small group behavior may be found to be isomorphic to the behavior of larger social systems. We hope that later revisions, which are promised from time to time, will report progress on this problem. At present the book is mainly concerned with the behavior of members. There is relatively little on group phenomena, and almost none on the influence of the institutions of which the group is a part, or the society into which the institution fits. Certainly much of the behavior of the group or the members can best be understood by some measurement of these influences external to the group. We will wait with interest for reports on improvements in this methodology—and with even greater impatience for the findings of research studies using these procedures. In the meantime, students of person-person interaction whether they be clinical psychologists, social psychologists, sociologists, or anthropologists, will find this a most worthwhile and informative discussion of an intriguing methodology.

J Appl Psychol 35:220–1 Je '51. Wesley Osterberg. * The task which the author took upon himself in writing this book was probably no less complex and difficult than the problem—objectifying and quantifying behavior—itself. He is to be commended for his attempt, but not, however, for his presentation. Excursions down theoretical byroads which lead nowhere are frequent. As one example, the relationship the author attempts to establish between his concepts and those of psychoanalysis (p. 46) is extremely tenuous and apparently irrelevant. In addition, much of the material is difficult to read, and unnecessarily so. Sentences with over sixty words are commonplace; some have more than one hundred. The reliability design, which involves a sequence of six phases and a number of tests is illustrated by a chart which itself presents an interesting challenge to the reader in the way of interpretation. Even when the design and results are understood, conclusions regarding reliability cannot be drawn because of the way in which Chi Square is used. For example, when the expected frequency contributes one-half of the variance of the observed frequency, as in the example cited of two observers, a limit is imposed on the Chi Square value obtained. Furthermore, there is no indication that the scores recorded are of the same behavior. Although Observer A and Observer B both recorded five scores under category 10 during a twelve minute recording (Table 2), there is no assurance that they were observing the same behavior when they did so. Interaction process analysis is applicable to a wide variety of groups and inter-personal situations where an objective method of behavior analysis is badly needed. Because of the presentation, however, the use of the method here will probably be limited—even among other researchers in the field, to whom the book is addressed. This is regrettable because the author has provided at least a foundation for further development, and possibly considerable superstructure.

J Consult Psychol 14:235 Je '50. Laurance F. Shaffer. A detailed description of the methods used by the Laboratory of Social Relations at Harvard University for the recording and analysis of the interactions in small groups. Itself a product of interdisciplinary contacts between sociology and psychology, the method of analysis is one of the most promising tools for the advancement of the study of many interpersonal areas: psychotherapy, education, social action, and politics. No recent development has shown more clearly the rewards that follow the quantification of observations that previously have been made only qualitatively and crudely.

Pub Opinion Q 14:588–90 fall '50. Daniel Lerner. There is a style of talk which makes extensive use of dichotomies and dilemmas. Its staple ingredient is the forced choice. Sometimes enlightening, as when paired comparisons are used to elicit hypothetical preferences, the technique is more often obscurantist in actual situations. There may be no earthly reason, in "real life," to choose one of a given pair—e.g., if both can be had or neither is wanted. Few dilemmas are inescapable and many dichotomies are false. Against this sterile mode of discussion in social science, Dr. Bales is a powerful ally.

His book shows up the vacuity of the Theorist-Empiricist dichotomy which too often allows scientific controversy to degenerate into mere controversialism. His contribution is the more valuable because it quickly passes beyond pious exegesis of why it is virtuous to integrate theory and research, and gives us a usable demonstration of how to do it. It will be suggestive to the student of opinion and content analyst, as well as to the empirical sociologist. The core of Bales' method for studying interaction as a process in small groups is "a way of classifying direct, face-to-face interaction as it takes place, act by act, and a series of ways of summarizing and analyzing the resulting data so that they yield useful information" (pp. 5–6). Methodology here is emphasized in the sense of conceptualized technique, the empirical focus within a theoretical context. Technique thus becomes an instrument of knowledge, a better way of getting answers to meaningful questions. Although his method makes use of elaborate new gadgetry—one-way mirrors, concealed microphones, Interaction Recorders—Bales is not ridden by his machines. He says: "By memorizing the categories and the numbers he assigns to subjects, [a trained] observer might even dispense with prepared forms and require only a pencil and paper" (p. 5). The most striking feature of the book is its carefully articulated conception of a method for stabilizing observation and objectifying interpretation in complex observational situations. It deals first with the inevitable problem of eliminating "observer bias" from the observational situation. Three standard ways of doing this are: (1) to observe without letting the observed know; (2) to handle the observed so that being observed makes no difference in their behavior; (3) to find out the difference and account for it in evaluating the data. The author apparently uses all three, although we are left in the dark between the second and third method when he tells us only that "it appears that the knowledge of observation is not a particularly disrupting factor" (p. 1). He eliminates observer bias from the gathering and processing data by content analysis—i.e., by specifying the verbal and non-verbal items of behavior which are to be coded and the categories under which they are to be arranged. This represents a promising application of content analytic technique to observational problems of small-group interaction. (Curiously, he does not mention the wartime work of Lasswell, the pioneer in content analysis, and his associates on the Library of Congress project. The development of the equations in Chapters V and VI surely would be aided by the preliminary work of the Lasswell group on a "coefficient of imbalance," reported by Janis and Fadner in *Language of Politics,* and on "reliability" reported by Kaplan, Goldsen and others in the same volume.) To preside over the wedding, where a technique heretofore mainly applied to verbal behavior in mass media is adapted to the observation of problem-solving behavior in small groups, Bales introduces the concept of sequential analysis (the temporal succession of events, not the statistical method recently developed by Wald). This conceptual innovation justifies Dr. Bales' claim that he is interested in analyzing the *process of interaction,* rather than merely in arranging selected characteristics by frequency of occurrence or other such criteria. The concept is worked into a research tool by means of a new and interesting apparatus—the Interaction Recorder. * The ....two chapters, on training observers and appraising their reliability, will be useful to those interested in trying out the Bales method or in applying what he has learned to other content analytic methods involving variant readings of the same data. * The final chapter, on problems of analysis and interpretation, is a sustained effort to present a synthesis of the method : "how to give operational content to the referents of our theoretical variables, and how to give theoretical meaning to the empirical uniformities in our data" (p. 116). As a final statement, this does not quite come off. There are several excellent points : e.g., his exposition of the "flip-flop" problem (pp. 117ff)—the temptation, when results appear to demonstrate the reverse of the original hypothesis, simply to reverse the hypothesis to conform with the data—and his concise statement of the logical role of inference (p. 120). These should be read by all who work with statistically controlled data. The technical presentation is straightforward and competent (although the equation for Generalized Status Index on page 168 is likely to prove so misleading, if taken at all seriously, that it should be abandoned and no statistical treatment of this index attempted until some reliable weighting can be worked out of accumulated empirical data). What weakens the presentation is the final section (pp. 172–6). As *axiomata media,* the hypotheses here formulated are not inspiring. In part, they suffer from the malady that afflicts all

such general-purpose categories as Bales here proposes : they appear too obvious—not in the vulgar sense that everybody "knows" these hypotheses to be true, but in the policy sense that they do not seem in urgent need of investigation. Also, at this final point, the author gives us technical propositions where we want (and have a right to expect) behavioral hypotheses. The listed assertions, all beginning with the phrase "There is a fluctuation about an unstable balance between tendencies toward...." (pp. 173–5), are not genuine hypotheses and they are not about behavior. The outcome of such propositions, even when indexed and tested, will be to show that it is technically feasible to define "unstable balance" so that "fluctuations," when measured, will turn out to be within a given area of the graph. At the very end, Bales does propose several interesting hypotheses by specifying certain regularities that occur in the "fluctuations about an unstable balance": (1) as the group grows older, (2) as its size increases, (3) as its membership changes (mixing old and new members), (4) as its membership becomes more heterogeneous, (5) as it confronts increasingly difficult problems of adapting to the external situation. But these are the last five sentences, and one is left to wait for clarification and data in the next book. In fairness to the author, it must be said that he has asked us to read this book as "a working manual, not a finished product." The above comments are intended to suggest possible directions, or redirections, of effort that may be useful in developing the finished product. Meanwhile, the book serves as a progress report on efforts to date. Viewed this way, it gives us a fine demonstration of how to wed theory and research in concrete situations. We look forward to the next report, when sufficient data on the interactive sequences of "Adaptive-Instrumental" and "Integrative-Expressive" behavior in small groups will have been accumulated.

Psychiatric Q 24:620 Jl '50. * The book.... is well organized and is written in a way to capture and excite the esoteric reader. The subject matter is worthy of consideration by social science and psychiatry.

Social Forces 29:329–30 Mr '51. Howard E. Jensen. Ever since Le Play a continuing tradition in sociology has stressed the intensive study of small groups as an indispensable inductive basis for generalizations about the structure and process of society at large. But such studies have been based upon no consensus as to what the unit phenomena of social interaction are, and they have lacked a practically workable system of simple and clearly defined categories in terms of which the units could be observed and effective techniques by which observations could be quickly and accurately recorded. The results have consequently been lacking in precision and comparability, and have contributed much less than their earlier promise to a cumulative body of dependable social science. Dr. Bales' volume represents a notable attempt to supply this lack. He and his colleagues....have devised a method for breaking up social interaction into unit acts which can be recorded separately, have formulated a small number of categories into which they can be classified, and have constructed an instrument by means of which each unit act can be recorded as it occurs, and properly attributed to both its originator and the person or persons to whom it is directed. The aspects of social interaction with which the method can deal are admittedly limited. Only its formal structural and functional features can be taken into account. Any reference to the nature, significance and concrete content of the behavior, or any interpretation based on the temporal sequence of its constituent units, is ruled out. The concentration of the observer upon recognizing, categorizing, attributing and recording the unit acts as they occur is so intense that he often misses the larger implications of the activity as a whole and is at the end "not able to give a very coherent account of what went on." The importance of these aspects of activity, which the author calls "the ideosyncratic (*sic*) or 'topical' content," is, however, not ignored, but is recorded by sound or typescript for supplementary analysis. In the last chapter the author writes convincingly of the wide range of possible applications of the method. "Many of the most important generalizations of social science," he thinks, "have already been discovered." The most important future advances will probably come, not from "brand new, high level generalizations," but from discovering the obscure implications of the generalizations already known, from identifying more specifically the concrete referents of their terms, from delimiting the range of their application and of the psychological, cultural and structural conditions under which they are valid. As the foregoing quotation implies, the theoretical orientation of the research is not new. It builds solidly upon the work of such pioneers as Dewey, Mead, Cooley,

Thomas, and others, supplemented by the better established results of more recent work in social psychology and psychiatry. It is clear gain that sociology, after wandering in the wilderness of barren factfinding, should return to the germinal insights of its founders, which alone can give significance to facts and direction to their accumulation. But it is regrettable that the sections dealing with these general notions have not been done with the lucidity which characterizes the descriptive and interpretative sections. These sections read as if they were the work of another hand. That both the culture and structure of the group arise out of the interaction of its members; that once in being they provide the patterns which condition further interaction; that individuals in social interaction do not respond to one another's acts as momentary and isolated units; that they do not consider themselves as homogeneous group members but are conscious of themselves as differentiated personalities and react to one another as such; that their acts are related to both the past and the future and either contribute to a behavioral sequence leading to satisfactions or disrupt such a sequence; that the collective behavior of a group is impaired if its members do not share a sufficient body of common thoughts, feelings and intentions—all this and much more has often been briefly, simply and clearly stated. It gains nothing in scientific precision and rational intelligibility by being restated in an esoteric language that goes far to justify the time-worn jibe that "sociology is what everybody knows told in language that nobody understands." Mead's treatment of role-taking as the method whereby the self acquires the group patterns, for example, is not helped by restatement as a process in which the "elements are regarded as present 'inner' surrogates of the structured influence of factors which also are, or were, 'outer.'" In these days of little books at big prices, the reader would be better served were these sections rewritten in a third their present compass, were numerous repetitions eliminated (page 9 reappearing as page 59 down to the last comma), were a list of charts and tables added to the Table of Contents, and were the analyses and interpretations in Chapter 5 cross-referenced to the pages in Chapter 1 which contain the raw data discussed.

Sociol & Social Res 34:392 My–Je '50. Bruce M. Pringle. * Instructions for training observers and for determining and improving reliability are....not so clear or so detailed as might be desired by those who wish to use the method * A well-developed rationale for the twelve categories is given, together with a number of hypotheses which can be tested by the method. * The book is noteworthy as an example of the *rapprochement* between theory and research that has been so much talked about recently.

Southw Social Sci Q 31:57–8 Je '50. Paul B. Foreman. * a major contribution to the small fund of concise research reports—the studies of Dorothy Swaine Thomas, Kurt Lewin, Ronald Lippitt and others—which have sought close-checked empirical knowledge about immediate group relations * What marks this progress report as essential for any student of inter-personal relations is that it invites further study—study which with little cost can be conducted anywhere by anyone with some ingenuity and mastery of the basic statistical techniques necessary for this sort of research design. Following the leads expressed in this monograph or focused by it would seem to be much more acute use of time than devoting a similar amount of energy to more attitude tests and more sociograms. If this suggestion is the essential why behind publication of this progress report, it is probably true that interested researchers will—as they should anyway—have to orient work largely in terms of their own theory. It is more than pleasing to note Bales' acknowledgment to Jameson of Oregon for arousing interest in measuring social interaction. Jameson for at least a score of years has been maintaining that sociologists should measure when they have something to measure and that meanwhile the quest for the what is equal in importance to knowing how.

[58]

*Interest Index: General Education Series. Grades 7–13; 1938–50; same as *Interest Index: Test 8.2a* ('39) which was a revision of Test 8.2 ('38); original tests published by Evaluation in the Eight-Year Study, Progressive Education Association; 30 scores: "like" and "dislike" scores for English, foreign languages, mathematics, social studies, biology, physical sciences, music, fine arts, industrial arts, business courses, home economics, sports, manipulative, reading, total; 1 form, '50; interpretation leaflet ('50); no data on validity in manual (for data presented elsewhere, see 5 below); manual ('50); separate answer sheets must be used; $2.25 per 25; $1 per 25 interpretative leaflets containing answer sheet and profile chart; cash orders postpaid; 50¢ per specimen set, postpaid; nontimed (40) minutes; Evaluation Staff (Ralph W. Tyler, Director) of the Eight-Year Study of the Progressive Education Association; published in 1950 by Cooperative Test Division, Educational Testing Service. *

REFERENCES

1–4. See 40:1226.
5. HARRIS, CHESTER WILLIAM; EBERHART, WILFRED; AND BLOCK, JEAN FRIEDBERG. "The Interest Index 8.2a," pp. 838–48. In *Appraising and Recording Student Progress.* By Eugene R. Smith, Ralph W. Tyler, and the Evaluation Staff. Progressive Education Association Publications, Commission on the Relation of School and College, Adventure in American Education, Vol. 3. New York: Harper & Brothers, 1942. Pp. xxiii, 550. * (PA 16:5033)
6. SMALLENBURG, HARRY WALTER. *Teachers' Knowledge of Pupil Characteristics in a Senior High School.* Doctor's thesis, University of Southern California (Los Angeles, Calif.), 1943. (*Abstracts of Dissertations....1943,* pp. 73–9.)

[59]

An Inventory of Factors STDCR. Grades 9–16 and adults; 1934–45; 5 scores: social introversion-extraversion, thinking introversion-extraversion, depression, cycloid tendencies, rhathymia; IBM; 1 form, '40; revised manual ['45]; $2.50 per 25; 50¢ per specimen set, postpaid; separate answer sheets may be used; 2¢ per IBM answer sheet; $3.50 per set of stencils for machine scoring of answer sheets; $2.50 per set of stencils for hand scoring of answer sheets; 2¢ per profile chart (also for tests 47 and 48); postage extra; nontimed (30) minutes; J. P. Guilford; Sheridan Supply Co. *

REFERENCES

1–10. See 3:55.
11. CERF, ARTHUR Z. "An Inventory of Factors STDCR, CE434A," pp. 589–92. In *Printed Classification Tests.* Edited by J. P. Guilford with the assistance of John I. Lacey. Army Air Forces Aviation Psychology Program Research Reports, Report No. 5. Washington, D.C.: U.S. Government Printing Office, 1947. Pp. xi, 919. * (PA 22:4145)
12. GREEN, RUSSEL F. *The Validity of Certain Psychological Tests in the Selection and Classification of Juvenile Police Officers.* Master's thesis, University of Southern California (Los Angeles, Calif.), 1949.
13. NORTH, ROBERT D., JR. "An Analysis of the Personality Dimensions of Introversion-Extroversion." *J Personality* 17:352–67 Mr '49. * (PA 25:2913)
14. CLARK, ELMER J. "The Mental Health of Elementary School Teachers as Measured by the Guilford-Martin Personality Battery," pp. 8–12. In *The Seventh Yearbook of the National Council on Measurements Used in Education, 1949–1950.* Fairmont, W.Va.: the Council, Fairmont State College, 1950. Pp. v, 56, ix. Paper, mimeographed. *
15. ERWIN, EDMOND FRANCIS. *Objective and Projective Measures of Withdrawal Behavior.* Doctor's thesis, Columbia University (New York, N.Y.), 1950. Abstract: *Microfilm Abstracts* 11:418–9 no 2 '51. (PA 26:2275, title only)
16. FISHER, SEYMOUR. *Patterns of Personality Rigidity and Some of Their Determinants.* American Psychological Association, Psychological Monographs: General and Applied, Vol. 64, No. 1, Whole No. 307. Washington, D.C.: the Association, Inc., 1950. Pp. v, 48. Paper. * (PA 24:6255)
17. KELLY, E. LOWELL, AND FISKE, DONALD W. "The Prediction of Success in the VA Training Program in Clinical Psychology." *Am Psychol* 5:395–406 Ag '50. * (PA 25:2183)
18. KRASNER, LEONARD. *Personality Differences Between Patients Classified as Psychosomatic and as Non-Psychosomatic.* Doctor's thesis, Columbia University (New York, N.Y.), 1950. Abstract: *Microfilm Abstracts* 10:227–8 no 3 '50. *
19. NORTH, ROBERT D., JR. *An Analysis of the Personality Dimensions of the Introversion-Extroversion.* Doctor's thesis, Columbia University (New York, N.Y.), 1950.
20. SPIVEY, GORDON MAURICE. *The Relationship Between Temperament and Achievement of a Selected Group of John Muir College Students.* Doctor's thesis, University of Southern California (Los Angeles, Calif.), 1950. (*Abstracts of Dissertations....1950,* 1951, pp. 298–300.)
21. BAEHR, MELANY E. *A Factorial Study of Temperament.* University of Chicago, Psychometric Laboratory [Report] No. 63. Chicago, Ill.: the Laboratory, February 1951. Pp. 14. Paper, lithotyped. *
22. CLARK, ELMER J. "The Relationship Between the Personality Traits of Elementary School Teachers and Their Evaluation of Objectionable Behavior." *J Ed Res* 45:61–6 S '51. * (PA 26:3056)
23. GREEN, RUSSEL F. "Does a Selection Situation Induce Testees to Bias Their Answers on Interest and Temperament Tests?" *Ed & Psychol Meas* 11:503–15 au '51. *
24. HEALY, IRENE, AND BORG, WALTER R. "Personality Characteristics of Nursing School Students and Graduate Nurses." *J Appl Psychol* 35:275–80 Ag '51. * (PA 26:3088)
25. KELLY, E. LOWELL, AND FISKE, DONALD W. *The Prediction of Performance in Clinical Psychology.* Ann Arbor, Mich.: University of Michigan, 1951. Pp. xv, 311. Lithotyped. *
26. PEMBERTON, CAROL L. "Personality Inventory Data Re-

lated to Ace Subscores." *J Consult Psychol* 15:160–2 Ap '51. *
27. THURSTONE, L. L. "The Dimensions of Temperament."
Psychometrika 16:11–20 Mr '51. * (*PA* 25:7327)

HUBERT E. BROGDEN, *Personnel Research Section, The Adjutant General's Office, Department of the Army, Washington, D.C.*

The several inventories of Guilford and Martin are among the first based on factorial techniques. They should, because of their basic rationale, have certain advantages. The traits measured should be more basic than those conventionally evaluated through personality questionnaires; the scores should be relatively independent of each other; and by avoiding the overlap resulting from minor variations in or redefinitions of traits, they should provide the beginnings of a conceptually simpler system for a systematic understanding and treatment of validity data in the personality area.

The question as to whether the advantages expected in theory will be borne out in practice can only be decided through extended empirical tests of the factorial as opposed to other approaches. This reviewer is of the opinion that the factor score approach is well worth a trial.

Questionnaire measurement, as a technique, has long been regarded as questionable. Until other practicable measures of personality traits yielding higher validity are developed, much of such criticism does not seem profitable and will not be attempted here. It is pertinent to note, however, that techniques have been developed which appear successful in minimizing the effect of tendencies of the respondent to overevaluate or underevaluate himself. While it seems inappropriate here to review the evidence on such techniques, both forced choice techniques and use of suppressors (as in the *Minnesota Multiphasic Personality Inventory*) appear promising.

Little validity information against external criteria is available in the manual. For this reason, *An Inventory of Factors STDCR* can hardly be regarded as competing with the questionnaires such as the MMPI if considered for clinical diagnosis. Both the validity information provided on the MMPI and the control of exaggeration by suppressor keys seem to give a clear advantage to the *Minnesota Multiphasic Personality Inventory* for use in clinical diagnosis.

One technical point on factorial basis of the scores is worthy of comment. The intercorrelations of the scores show high correspondence between D and C scores. The use of both of these

scores is, on this account, questionable. Review of the original factor studies suggests to this reviewer that the two factors in question were not, in any event, established as independent primary traits.

The general advantage of the *Inventory of Factors STDCR* seems to be based, then, on the future promise of the general factorial approach. Regardless of the general promise of this approach, data are not yet available showing the practical utility of this inventory.

For reviews by R. A. Brotemarkle and H. J. Eysenck, see 3:45 and 3:55.

[60]
★**Inventory of Personal-Social Relationships: General Education Series.** High school and college; 1941–50; a revision of the instrument developed in 1941 and described in *Student Personnel Services in General Education* by Paul J. Brouwer; 24 scores in each of 2 sections: activities and interests, concerns and difficulties; 1 form, '50; no data on reliability and validity in manual (for data presented elsewhere, see 2 below); no norms—publishers recommend the use of local norms; manual ('50) $2.50 per 25; 75¢ per 25 individual interpretative sheets; cash orders postpaid; 25¢ per specimen set, postpaid; nontimed (50) minutes; developed by the Cooperative Study in General Education (Ralph W. Tyler, Director); Cooperative Test Division, Educational Testing Service. *

REFERENCES

1. COOPERATIVE STUDY IN GENERAL EDUCATION, EXECUTIVE COMMITTEE, RALPH W. TYLER, DIRECTOR. Chap. 8, "Major Projects in Student Personnel," pp. 158–79. In *Cooperation in General Education.* Washington, D.C.: American Council on Education, 1947. Pp. xvii, 240. * (*PA* 22:432)
2. BROUWER, PAUL J.; with the collaboration of John L. Bergstresser. "Appraising the Personal-Social Needs of Students: First Project, The Self-Inventory of Personal-Social Relations," pp. 173–216. In Paul J. Brouwer's *Student Personnel Services in General Education.* Washington, D.C.: American Council on Education, 1949. Pp. xix, 317. * (*PA* 23:3440)

N. L. GAGE, *Associate Professor of Education, University of Illinois, Urbana, Illinois.*

This inventory consists of two lists, the first of 100 activities, and the second of 100 difficulties which a student may experience. The student is asked to mark each activity in the first list according to whether he participates in it (A), does not participate in it but would like to (U), or does not participate and is indifferent to it (D). The second list is to be marked in terms of whether the difficulty is of important concern to him, of mild concern to him, or of no concern to him. The inventory, like the *Mooney Problem Check List* and the *SRA Youth Inventory* which it resembles, is essentially intended to facilitate the counseling process through setting up a standardized channel of communication from the client to the counselor. Its underlying theory seems to be sociological rather than psychological; the items thus fall into such categories as "opposite sex," "family," "school or college faculty," etc.

The inventory is intended as an aid to counselors, who are to interpret the results to their students, and is not to be used by students without guidance. The scoring, which consists of counting the number of each of the three kinds of responses to each of the eight categories of items in both parts, has a logical, a priori, basis. Whether the scores thus defined would hold up under the application of techniques for estimating internal consistency is a question that critical users of the inventory might want answered before they paid much attention to these scores.

The form of item used is likely to elicit response sets, so that the replies a student makes may reflect overall tendencies to check A, U, or D more than they reflect the psychological states with which the items are ostensibly concerned. Such response sets would result in a spurious kind of internal consistency; they might also indeed be related to the psychological states at which the inventory is aimed, but empirical studies are needed to establish any such hypothesized relationships between number of A, U, or D responses and actual interests and concerns.

The inventory is also recommended for use in describing groups of students or the social environment of activities, interests, concerns, and difficulties in which an individual student finds himself when associated on a given campus with a group of fellow students. Here the inventory would yield percentages of students in a given group responding in various ways to the individual items and categories of items. Using the inventory in this way involves the interpreter of group results in dangerous assumptions concerning the absolute significance of such percentages unless he has the results either from a sample of other comparable high schools or colleges or from a series of such surveys in a single school. In other words, the interpretation of group results needs to be enhanced with norms in the same way that the interpretation of achievement or intelligence test responses needs norms. The manual, and Brouwer's supporting text (2), provide no cautioning influence on this matter; users of group results from the inventory can easily find themselves attaching psychological or social significance to results which should more properly be considered reflections of the particular wording of the items.

The inventory was developed in full awareness of the nondirective or "permissive" approach to counseling. How practicing counselors of the nondirective school view inventories of this kind is, however, a major question. It seems likely that such counselors, opposed to asking direct questions or formulating by themselves the significant questions that need to be raised, would view the inventory as a violation of the essence of their approach to counseling. The mere administration of the inventory implies that the counselor, by inspection of the responses and patterns of scores, will identify possible needs of the student. The student may expect that, since a diagnosis has been made, a prescription will be forthcoming. This is exactly the expectation that nondirective counselors want to combat from the very start. Consequently, it is difficult to see how the inventory can be used in nondirective counseling. Brouwer sees a place for both permissive and "prescriptive" methods and recognizes that most faculty members typically take the prescriptive approach to counseling. If we are willing to grant the desirability in some cases of the prescriptive approach, this inventory may be useful in establishing rapport, revealing student's problems, and providing a basis for counseling interviews.

A word should be said concerning the items themselves. Any list of activities, interests, concerns and difficulties must inevitably be a sample which reflects the biases of the authors. This list was developed by the central staff of the Cooperative Study in General Education and perhaps reflects the biases of "student personnel workers" in small liberal arts colleges. The flavor of the items, the general impression they create, is one in which the well adjusted student is "well rounded," a "good Joe" of a wholesome, "decent," congenial sort—in short, a middle class adolescent bent on self-improvement and unafflicted with divine discontent, passionate intellectual thirsting or any similar imbalance. There are colleges and high schools, and even more certainly individual high school or college students who might be disturbed by finding themselves so poorly embraced by the items of this inventory. And yet it is not impossible that the leaders of the significant intellectual and social movements of our time might be the very same students. In short, students who do not fit the middle class, well rounded, wholesome stereotype set up by the items of this inventory might be needlessly disturbed by it.

THEODORE A. SARBIN, *Associate Professor of Psychology, University of California, Berkeley, California.*

This inventory, in common with others that have been constructed on a rationalistic basis, suffers from the absence of empirical validity. The inventory purportedly samples students' "activities and interests" and "concerns and difficulties." The items were selected on the basis of two preliminary inventories administered to a group of students. The results were "exhaustively studied by an intercollegiate committee whose members went through the inventories item by item, eliminating some, adding others, revising many * The basic assumptions regarding human behavior that were implicit in the selection of items were questioned, analyzed, and clarified." (*2*) Such a procedure seems inexcusable in the light of experience with hundreds of inventories constructed on a priori lines beginning with Woodworth's *Personal Data Sheet.* What does any score on this inventory mean? Only that a student's answers to questions were combined according to the "basic assumptions about human behavior" of an intercollegiate committee.

Procedurally, the student answers the one hundred items in Part I (activities and interests) in one of three ways: participation in activity (coded "A"); nonparticipation in an activity "but would like to," an unfulfilled interest (coded "U"); does not participate and is indifferent to the activity in question (coded "D"). Thus a total score is derived in which the number of A, U, and D responses are summed. The same procedure is followed for Part II (concerns and difficulties) except that each question is answered as an *important* concern or difficulty, a *mild* concern or difficulty, or *no* concern or difficulty.

The 100 items in each part of the inventory are divided among eight categories of logically related items. For Part I these are opposite sex, family, faculty, belonging, social skills, intellectual and esthetic, social service, and leadership and initiative. For Part II the categories are opposite sex, family (home), faculty, belonging, social skills, physical well-being, likeness-to-others, and social experience. The mere listing of these categories raises questions for the reviewer as to the independence of the categories, their meaning in terms of actual behavior, and their relative weighting in a total adjustment index.

The author of the test recommends the use of local norms and making cautious interpretations on the basis of significant deviation from the median score for any subcategory. This procedure only means that a student has been singled out for attention because he has checked certain items more or less frequently than the median student in his group. It does not necessarily mean that his deviation from the mean is a sign of maladjustment. Although the author warns against regarding deviation and maladjustment as synonyms, there is an implicit assumption here: the deviant on this rationally derived scale is somehow bad or maladjusted. The recommended approach to the interpretation of the inventory is reminiscent of unstandardized projective tests. The counselor is advised to analyze responses to specific items and to pay attention to the individual patterns of responses. Then why bother with scores at all?

The inventory will probably be used by guidance officers in high schools and smaller colleges where psychologically trained personnel are not available and where there is a basic philosophy of adjustment by conformity.

[61]

★The IPAT Humor Test of Personality. Grades 9–16 and adults; 1949–52; title on test booklet is *The IPAT Humor Test (A Humor Rating Quiz)*; formerly called *The C-L Humor Test (A Humor Rating Quiz)*; 10 scores: debonair sexual and general uninhibitedness vs. anxious considerateness, good-natured play vs. dry wit, tough self-composure vs. reassurance in embarrassment, gruesomeness vs. flirtatious playfulness, hostile derogation vs. urbane pleasantness, resignation vs. impudent defiance of decency, cold realism vs. theatricalism, ponderous humor vs. neat and light-hearted wit, whimsical retort vs. damaging retort, mistreatment humor vs. cheerful independence; IBM; Forms A ('52), B ('52); [revised] manual ['52]; $3.50 per 25 of Form A; $3 per 25 of Form B; $6 per 25 sets of both forms; 50¢ per manual; 85¢ per sample set of every form; separate answer sheets may be used; $1.50 per 50 IBM answer sheets for any one form; design for machine scoring stencils included in manual; 50¢ per set of stencils for hand scoring of answer sheets; cash orders postpaid; (30–40) minutes; R. B. Cattell and L. B. Luborsky; Institute for Personality and Ability Testing. *

REFERENCES

1. CATTELL, RAYMOND B. "Projection and the Design of Projective Tests of Personality." *Char & Pers* 12:177–94 Mr '44. * (PA 18:3185)
2. CATTELL, RAYMOND B., AND LUBORSKY, L. B. "Personality Factors in Response to Humor." *J Abn & Social Psychol* 42:402–21 O '47. * (PA 22:1564)
3. LUBORSKY, L. B., AND CATTELL, R. B. "The Validation of Personality Factors in Humor." *J Personality* 15:283–91 Je '47. * (PA 22:2072)
4. SCHWARTZ, ANTHONY NICHOLAS. "A Study of the Discriminating Efficiency of Certain Tests of the Primary Source Personality Traits of Teachers." *J Exp Ed* 19:63–93 S '50. * (PA 25:4864)
5. SMITH, NATHALIE VAN ORDER, AND VINACKE, W. EDGAR. "Reactions to Humorous Stimuli of Japanese, Chinese, and Caucasians in Hawaii." *J Social Psychol* 34:69–96 Ag '51. *

W. Grant Dahlstrom, *Visiting Assistant Professor of Psychology, State University of Iowa, Iowa City, Iowa.*

The authors of this test feel that repressed material is as important diagnostically as that produced by any other ego-defensive mechanism, such as projection or rationalization. The "action" in a joke which a subject finds humorous presumably mirrors the response trends of that individual. The authors do not specify how complete a picture of a particular personality is obtained in this sample; conceivably, some important characteristics which have not undergone repression would not appear within responses to the test. This instrument does not provide a measure of any trait relating to sense of humor except indirectly in Form B in terms of number of items rated as funny.

The authors use two ways of sampling humor appreciation. The subject rates the humor in each joke on a 2-point scale in Form B. In Form A, the subject expresses preferences for items in a paired comparison design. Although the authors are aware that incidental factors may distort these measures, they do not seem to have given them proper consideration. Most importantly, they underevaluate the effect of novelty of the item. Within their own research they find important changes in a subject's ratings upon reexposure to the same jokes; it would seem desirable to provide some check on the variation attributable to this source of distortion.

Since the authors' aim is to measure stable traits, this question of reliability is crucial. The information for evaluating the reliability of the instrument is somewhat contradictory. The manual mentions a test-retest study with a lapse of a month, but no precise summary of the findings is offered. The coefficients ranged from .10 to .60 for the various clusters; presumably, the small number of items in each contributes to this low stability. An estimate of the equivalence cannot legitimately be made from a study of the two forms since the subject makes quite different types of responses to the two tests. The lack of agreement between the two forms has led the authors to recommend the use of both forms in evaluating a particular individual. The authors seem to have avoided the error of weighting both directions of the response to one item— a procedure which could act to force artificially low scores in some components when a few high component scores are obtained.

Evaluation of the validity of this instrument rests upon the adequacy of the closely related program of research in personality measurement carried out by the Institute for Personality and Ability Testing. The most important result of these analyses has been the *Sixteen Personality Factor Questionnaire.* The Humor Test has been validated against this scale, the *Guilford-Martin Inventory of Factors GAMIN* and the *Inventory of Factors STDCR,* and some ratings and psychiatric diagnoses. However, neither the articles by Cattell and Luborsky (*2, 3*), to which the test purchaser is referred nor the manual itself provides sufficient information on which to judge the practical value of the present humor scales. For instance, Cluster 10 (Silly Good Humor vs. Dry Comment) is said to have separated successfully the mean of a group of psychotics from the mean of a group of normals, but no particulars of this study are provided. In regard to validity in general, the authors consider publication of the test as only one stage of a long research program to accumulate data relating to both its theoretical implications and its practical applications.

Similarly, only sketchy information is given about the norm groups on which the modified standard score tables were constructed. Presumably, the authors advance this material as representative of a cross section of the general population who have adequate intelligence and reading ability to respond to these items. For instance, they report that a little less than 10 per cent of their 1,044 cases could be regarded as neurotics, which proportion they consider close to the existing ratio. Actually, all of their subjects were university undergraduates.

The basic mechanics of the test in its present form are deficient. The test is on green paper and lacks attractiveness, legibility, and convenience of response. The scoring (until an IBM form becomes available) involves destruction of the test booklet, which greatly hinders filing for research purposes. To apply the scoring stencil, the pages must be restapled, and even time-consuming care will not insure a proper fit. The stencil itself is mimeographed and so arranged that it is confusing and likely to generate errors in accumulating the component scores.

This test must be considered to be of research interest only. If the user is in a position to administer it and learn about its possible contributions, it should be of definite interest. If the purchaser needs an instrument to gather information, it is not sufficiently well developed to be dependable.

ARDIE LUBIN, *Statistical Psychologist; and* FRANK M. LOOS, *Research Psychologist; Institute of Psychiatry, Maudsley Hospital, London, England.*

"Psychologists, from smoking-room amateurs to Freud, have long been aware that some of the more profound aspects of a man's personality may be revealed by observing the things at which he laughs" (*2*). Cattell and Luborsky, stimulated by the work of T. G. Andrews [1] and the Freudian theory of humor,[2] have attempted to devise a test of humor which will "reveal deeper aspects of personality." (They believe that only "relatively superficial personality data" can be obtained from other paper and pencil personality tests.) The authors recommend their test for clinical diagnosis and personnel work because: (*a*) it does not depend "upon the insight and honesty of the subject," (*b*) the humorous content makes it attractive to the subject, and (*c*) it is easy to administer and to score.

Form A includes 91 pairs of jokes of which the subject is asked to choose the funnier. Each of the 112 jokes making up Form B is to be classified as funny or dull. The 11 scores obtainable from each form are based on 11 clusters of jokes gathered from three successive researches. "The jokes put together in one cluster have had to meet the criterion of correlating above .25 with every joke therein, on at least two sample populations." The manual states that both forms measure "the same eleven personality dimensions." This equating of clusters (rather than factors) to dimensions is in contradiction to Cattell's previous work and to the usual definitions given in factor analysis.

The actual reliabilities for each cluster are not quoted, but it is stated that the correlations between Forms A and B "over a one month interval range from .10 to .60." This unsatisfactory result leads the authors to conclude that "the present test must therefore be used tentatively with that combination of measurement and clinical insight necessary with all clinical or misperceptive ('projective') tests today."

Figures for correlations between cluster scores

1 Andrews, T. Gaylord. "A Factorial Analysis of Responses to the Comic as a Study in Personality." *J General Psychol* 28: 209–224 Ap '43. *
2 Freud, Sigmund. *Wit and Its Relation to the Unconscious.* New York: Moffat, Yard & Co., 1916. Pp. ix, 388. *

and various "source traits" scores are given for three clusters; actual figures are not presented in the handbook for any other clusters. Not mentioned in the handbook is the authors' discovery of near zero correlations between 13 cluster scores from a 69 item joke test and 10 factor scores from the *Guilford-Martin Inventory of Factors GAMIN* and the *Inventory of Factors STDCR* (*3*). The only suggestion that the test has diagnostic validity comes from the statement in the handbook that one cluster "both on the A and B forms has been shown to distinguish psychotics from normals at the one percent level of confidence." It is stated that only one other cluster tends to distinguish psychotics from normals. Although it is indicated that the *IPAT Humor Test* was designed in accordance with the Freudian postulates which experimental evidence obtained by use of the test tends to confirm, we cannot find any factual evidence that this is true.

In summary we may note the following points. It is not possible to rely on the published articles (*2, 3*) for information about the Humor Test because at most only 69 jokes of those mentioned in these articles are included in the 294 jokes making up the test. The handbook gives little useful information on construction, standardization, and validity. However, the vague statement about reliabilities (quoted earlier) shows, if the usual standards of reliability are accepted, that the two forms are not measuring the same variables. There is no evidence that the test can be used for the prediction of human behavior.

The test might serve as a novel basis for interesting research in personality, but at the present stage of its development, it is not definitely known to be of any practical use whatsoever.

J. R. WITTENBORN, *Research Associate in Psychology, Yale University, New Haven, Connecticut.*

This test is related to a "Freudian hypothesis that the 'tendency' in wit is an expression of needs normally repressed in everyday life." The jokes which comprise the two forms of the Humor Test are each relevant to 1 of 11 clusters of jokes. Evidence for the clusters is based on three successive researches but the samples of jokes and subjects employed in these researches are not specified. The validity claims for some of the cluster scores are based on correlations with certain of the basic personality factors which provide the scores for Cattell's *Sixteen Personality Factor Test* scores. The manual does not provide such validity evidences for all of the humor cluster scores, however, and for the prospective examiner the possible validity of most of the humor clusters remains a matter of speculation.

The evidence for cluster score reliability is not altogether reassuring. Retest correlations vary from cluster score to cluster score and range from .10 to .60. Whether this is a result of an intrinsic unreliability or evidence that humor expressed by appreciation of jokes is an unstable phenomenon is not known. If this aspect of humor is not stable, however, the question arises as to how scores for clusters of jokes may best be used in the evaluation of personality, if they may be so used at all. It is reported in the manual that there is some variation in ability to recognize and that in a given situation this ability may vary inversely with the period of time spent reading jokes (adaptation). This possibility has certain implications for the manner in which the test may best be used. The score for Form A of the test is based on a comparison of jokes whereas the score for Form B of the test is based on a judgment as to the funniness of the jokes. Accordingly, Form B permits a determination of a score for general readiness to rate jokes as funny. Since there is an adaptation factor, it would seem desirable to specify whether Form A or the Form B should be given first. Otherwise, the Form B score on general readiness to rate as funny may not have a uniform significance.

The norms provided are based on undergraduates and the test is considered to be appropriate for the general population. The scoring procedure involves counting items from different pages and combining them on the basis of a path marked on a stencil. Such use of a stencil is, of course, convenient and familiar; unfortunately, however, the paths for all the humor cluster scores are indicated on the same stencil, and this saving of paper may prove expensive in terms of the energies of the scorer. An additional handicap was experienced by the reviewer who found that the stencil was prepared on a smaller scale than the answer sheet.

In general, the possibility of assessing personality by an employment of jokes is pleasant to contemplate. Perhaps, as the authors claim,

the subject does not know the personal significance of his sense of humor but the possibility exists that the subject's judgments will be influenced by his familiarity with the jokes. Quite often there is something decidedly unhumorous about a hackneyed joke. This is no idle criticism because if jokes are related to personality, the subject's familiarity with jokes may suffer from a selective bias as a result of his personality and, accordingly, the use of familiar jokes on a test may yield scores which are not truly representative of the subject's preference for jokes.

Despite the rather discouraging lack of reliability, the fact that the manual does not indicate the degree to which the cluster scores are correlated, and the fact that the evidence for validity is incomplete and consists of occasional correlations with other factors, the idea of a humor test for personality is a good one and the clusters appear to be plausible (the only implausible aspect of the clusters is that they are all of a bipolar nature suggesting that every form of humor sampled by the jokes has a singular and specifiable antithesis). In conclusion, it seems distinctly possible that this approach can elicit clinically relevant factors which may not be forthcoming by an employment of questionnaire or rating procedures.

[62]

Johnson Temperament Analysis. Grades 12–16 and adults; 1941–45; 9 scores: nervous-composed, depressed-cheery, active-quiet, cordial-cold, sympathetic-hard, subjective-objective, aggressive-submissive, critical-appreciative, self-mastery-impulsive; IBM; Form A ('41); Form B ('44) discontinued; manual ('44); separate answer sheets must be used; $2 per 25; 2¢ per response record sheet; 1¢ per revised analysis profile ('45); 60¢ per set of unweighted scoring stencils; $1.75 per set of weighted scoring stencils; 35¢ per specimen set, postpaid; 2¢ per IBM answer sheet; postage extra; nontimed (40–50) minutes; Roswell H. Johnson; California Test Bureau. *

REFERENCES

1. SEIBERT, EARL W. "An Evaluation of the Johnson Temperament Analysis." *J Clin Psychol* 1:193–5 Jl '45. * (PA 19: 3411)
2. RAINES, SHIRLEY. *Personality Traits of Remarried-Divorced Individuals as Measured by the Johnson Temperament Analysis.* Master's thesis, University of Southern California (Los Angeles, Calif.), 1949.
3. TYLER, F. T. "Personality Tests and Teaching Ability." *Can J Psychol* 3:30–7 Mr '49. * (PA 23:4443)
4. JOHNSON, ROSWELL H., AND WAAGE, LILLIAN. "Temperament Syndromes and Temperament Values." Abstract. *Am Psychol* 5:461 S '50. * (PA 25:4424, title only)
5. RAINES, SHIRLEY. "The Temperament of the Divorced." Abstract. *Am Psychol* 5:462 S '50. * (PA 25:4521, title only)
6. TYLER, FRED T., AND MICHAELIS, JOHN U. "Diagnostic and Predictive Values of the Johnson Temperament Analysis Used in Student Teaching." *J Teach Ed* 2:18–20 Mr '51. *

ALBERT ELLIS, *Consulting Psychologist, 56 Park Ave., New York 16, New York.*

Aside from the fact that the *Johnson Temperament Analysis* is no worse than most conventional personality inventories, there is little that can be said in its favor. Its shortcomings, some of the most important of which are listed as follows, come much easier to mind than its advantages:

a) The language and indirect phrasing of the questions make difficult reading and answering. A typical question reads: "Is S very eager to have his own business, or be an independent professional man, or if in an organization to be in a position to give orders rather than to take them?"

b) The temperament traits which the test purportedly measures are hardly of uniform usefulness or importance, and include vague traits like active, cordial, sympathetic, and subjective. Moreover, the traits are all stated in bipolar terms; according to recent researches of Thomas N. Jenkins and his associates, this type of dichotomization of traits has dubious validity.

c) The reliabilities of the nine scores obtained on the test range from .57 to .78, rather low for this type of inventory.

d) The latest (1944) manual for the test contains no adequate validity reports. The one validity study using an independent criterion and reported in detail was done with groups who had voluntarily come for marriage counseling and who, unlike unselected groups of subjects, could be expected to give relatively honest test protocols. Even with this type of subject, the test reliably distinguished unhappily married from about-to-be-married individuals only in extreme (and presumably few) instances.

e) According to the author's published data, respondents tend to overrate themselves, in an appreciably biased manner, on seven of the nine traits tested.

f) The test manual shows no comprehension of modern clinical psychological methods or of the psychodynamics of normal or exceptional human behavior. The manual belittles clinical interviewing, cavalierly attempts to give a 3-page course in personal and marital counseling, glosses over the serious shortcomings of all personality inventories, implies wide-ranging diagnostic accuracy which the test most certainly does not seem to possess, and makes special claims for industrial uses of the test which are highly unrealistic.

In summary, the *Johnson Temperament Analysis* and its accompanying manual attempt to show, in all seriousness, (*a*) that personality inventories now constitute one of the best techniques for the deep exploration of human personality and for the uncovering and treatment of serious emotional problems, and (*b*) that the *Johnson Temperament Analysis,* in particular, is one of the most reliable and valid instruments of its type. In neither of these claims or implications does the author appear to approximate even remotely factual reality.

For a review by H. Meltzer, see 3:57.

[63]

*Jurgensen Classification Inventory.** Adults; 1947–50; 1 form, '47; norms and scoring keys are not provided as each user is expected to develop keys and norms to fit his own situation; manual ('50); separate answer sheets must be used; $5 per 25; $1.90 per 100 answer sheets; postage extra; 50¢ per specimen set, postpaid; test materials will be sold only to members of the American Psychological Association; (20–40) minutes; Clifford E. Jurgensen; the Author, 4741 Elliot Ave. South, Minneapolis 7, Minn. *

REFERENCES

1. JURGENSEN, CLIFFORD E. "Report on the 'Classification Inventory,' a Personality Test for Industrial Use." *J Appl Psychol* 28:445–60 D '44. * (PA 19:1320)
2. ADAMS, EDWARD B. *An Investigation of the Validity of the Jurgensen Classification Inventory as a Predictor of Academic Achievement of Purdue University Students.* Master's thesis, Purdue University (Lafayette, Ind.), 1948. Pp. 24.
3. PRED, GORDON D. *A Comparison of the Test Performance of "Good" and "Poor" Industrial Supervisors.* Master's thesis, Purdue University (Lafayette, Ind.), 1948.
4. BOSWELL, CHARLES ALAN. *The Consistency of Responses to Forced-Choice Items in a Preference Inventory.* Master's thesis, State University of Iowa (Iowa City, Iowa), 1949. Pp. iv, 42.
5. KIRKPATRICK, JAMES J. *Validity of the Jurgensen Classification Inventory as a Predictor of College Achievement.* Master's thesis, University of Tennessee (Knoxville, Tenn.), 1949.
6. KNAUFT, EDWIN B. "A Selection Battery for Bake Shop Managers." *J Appl Psychol* 33:304–15 Ag '49. * (PA 24:2850)
7. LAWSHE, C. H. "How Can We Pick Better Supervisors?" *Personnel Psychol* 2:69–73 sp '49. * (PA 23:5071)
8. OLSON, MARJORIE. *Validation of the Forced-Choice Technique in Personality Measurement.* Doctor's thesis, University of Minnesota (Minneapolis, Minn.), 1949. Pp. x, 143.
9. MAIS, ROBERT DALE. *A Study of the Effectiveness With Which the Jurgensen Classification Inventory Counteracts Falsifying.* Master's thesis, University of Colorado (Boulder, Colo.), 1950.
10. KIRKPATRICK, JAMES J. "Cross-Validation of a Forced-Choice Personality Inventory." *J Appl Psychol* 35:413–7 D '51. * (PA 27:431)
11. MAIS, ROBERT D. "Fakability of the Classification Inventory Scored for Self Confidence." *J Appl Psychol* 35:172–4 Je '51. * (PA 26:924)

ROBERT G. DEMAREE, *Assistant Professor of Psychology,* and LOUIS L. MCQUITTY, *Professor of Psychology, University of Illinois, Urbana, Illinois.*

DESCRIPTION AND PURPOSE OF THE TEST. This inventory, first reported in 1944, represents one of the first, if not the first, personality inventories which utilizes the forced-choice technique as it is known today. The inventory was devised explicitly for situations such as personnel selection where an incentive exists for an individual to depict himself favorably.

The test consists of 72 triads, each composed of three descriptive phrases from which the subject selects the phrase most and least descriptive of him, and 36 paired items from which the subject makes a preference and indicates whether it is strong or weak.

Forty-five triads refer to irritating types of persons; 17 triads refer to reputations, and the remaining 10 triads refer to personal likes and dislikes. Twenty pairs require choices in activities and the remaining 16 pairs refer to types of disliked persons.

The inventory is self-administering and no time limits are specified.

The test booklet is stapled together, and has the disadvantage that it will not lie flat when opened. However, when the answer sheet is inserted into the rear of the test booklet, the right-hand margin of the page of items is conveniently matched by the column on the answer sheet into which responses are to be placed.

The instructions for the first part do not specify whether the subject is to use himself as a referrent in making choices, or whether he should respond in the way he conceives that some group, such as his acquaintances, would respond. Choices must be made, in each triad, of the type of person which the subject thinks is "most irritating" and "least irritating." Irritating to whom? The available interpretations of the latter by the respondent is a feature of this part of the inventory which deserves explicit consideration.

SCORING. The test presumes that those who use it will develop weighted scoring keys appropriate to the particular situations.

The manual offers practical procedures for item analysis and validation which are quite commendable, except for two points. Contrary to a statement in the manual, "Level of significance" is not equal to the "Chances of a true difference." Instead, it is the times in a hundred that chance alone would produce a difference as large as the one obtained when the true difference is zero. Another error is the listing of levels of significance appropriate to unidirectional differences without warning that this is appropriate only when the direction of the difference can be specified in advance. The responses to the item by the criterion groups must be specified on an a priori basis. This does not appear possible in the case of most items.

RESULTS IN THE USE OF THE TEST. (a) Reliability. Several studies have evidenced reliabilities adequate for the uses proposed for this test. Test-retest reliability (N = 23) was .78 in one study. (b) Validity. Excluding studies without cross-validation, the test showed some validity for selection of bakeshop managers (correlation of .39 for 33 cases with a composite criterion, significant at the 5 per cent level of confidence), but failed to distinguish between 176 "good" and "poor" industrial supervisors in 45 plants.

Tailor-made scoring keys revealed significant differences between engineering students and journalism students. Studies using items from this test for predicting academic achievement have given negative results.

OVERALL EVALUATION. This inventory offers an approach with more promise in personnel selection than the conventional personality inventories. In many situations, however, it would seem to be preferable to build items especially adapted to the situation, rather than restrict oneself to the items of this inventory.

WILLIAM J. E. CRISSY, *Assistant Professor of Psychology, Queens College; and Lecturer on Applied Psychology, Fordham University; New York, New York.*

This personality questionnaire samples the following aspects of the examinee's adjustment: the kinds of persons he finds most and least irritating, the ways in which he would most prefer and least prefer to be thought of by others, personal likes and dislikes, preferred activities or modes of behavior, and, finally, the kinds of persons he dislikes. The instructions for administration are contained in the test booklet proper and are clearly and explicitly written; the test may be self-administered.

The test does *not* purport to measure specific personality traits, nor does it claim *general* validity. The author intends that each prospective user try it out on his own group or groups, evolve his own scoring key based upon an item analysis against available criteria, and cross validate the test on a second appropriate group. In summary, it is Jurgensen's thesis that in the employment situation specific validity is the prime consideration. Therefore, each user must determine whether this test is appropriate for the solution of his particular testing problems.

The author furnishes a miscellany of highly useful aids to facilitate the experimental use of the test. Specifically, he furnishes easy-to-understand directions and work sheet layouts for doing various kinds of item analyses and statistical tables for various levels of confidence. These aids are well within the comprehension of any-one with an elementary knowledge of test theory and statistical methods.

Although no validity or reliability data as such are reported in the manual, Jurgensen and others have elsewhere reported such informa-tion. The validity data show promise for the test, especially for use with sales groups. In the case of one study (*1*) using various scoring keys, the obtained validity coefficients range from .77 to .81 for a sales group and from .67 to .72 for a graduate student group. However, these co-efficients are computed on the same sample as was used for constructing the scoring keys used and are therefore open to question as to stability. Jurgensen has reported to the reviewer that in a sequel study involving additional small groups, the validity coefficients remained relatively stable (.71 for the sales personnel, .64 for the students). The reliability data are reported in terms of modified, stepped-up, split half coefficients. They range from .90 to .97 on the sales group and from .80 to .98 on the student group. While the writer does not report standard errors of meas-urement, the reviewer has estimated these from the dispersions reported in the paper and they are relatively small and generally satisfactory.

The test appears to have potential usefulness in the screening and selection of employees for all white collar positions. Each prospective user must determine experimentally whether this is a good test for his purposes. The individual items in the test appear to have "face validity," that is, they seem to be sampling the aspects of ad-justment the prospective employer would con-sider relevant in connection with almost any job. The more usual personality inventories which purport to measure specific traits have not proved very valid in industrial usage. It re-mains to be seen whether a test that makes no such pretensions will prove to be a more efficient kind of measure. At this writing, the validity data are too sparse to warrant drawing general conclusions with regard to the applicability and usefulness of the test.

[64]

★KD Proneness Scale and Check List. Grades 7–12; 1950; also called *Delinquency Proneness Scale;* 2 parts; 1 form; distribution is restricted and purchase is made by special arrangement with the publisher; William C. Kvaraceus; World Book Co. *
a) KD PRONENESS SCALE. Nontimed (15–25) minutes.
b) KD PRONENESS CHECKLIST. Ratings made by teach-ers; nontimed (6–25) minutes.

DOUGLAS COURTNEY, *Program Director, In-stitute for Research in Human Relations, Phila-delphia, Pennsylvania.*

This test consists of two parts: a scale of 75 multiple choice questions designed to detect "de-linquency proneness" in children in grades 6–12 to be answered by the child himself, and a 58-item checklist to be filled in by the social worker or other professional person evaluating the behaviour of a group of children. The items concern those aspects of the person, his home, and his school which appear to be related to delinquency. Each item on the checklist is an-swered by checking yes, no, or ?.

The scale is well printed; the items appear to be well and thoughtfully constructed. The man-ual is prepared with the usual thoroughness of the World Book Company. In a letter to the reviewer, the World Book Company indicated that the present materials are being used on a limited basis only. The company indicated that they were "awaiting the outcome of several studies now in process to obtain additional normative data." Since the authors and pub-lishers are apparently taking every precaution in the preparation of this scale and checklist it would seem neither appropriate, helpful, nor prudent to be overly critical at this time.

One or two considerations might be borne in mind by both publishers and potential users as they work toward further validation of the meas-ure, especially the scale.

a) It would seem appropriate to balance more closely the various criterion groups. There is no indication whether the "Public School Boys" represent a sample from the same public schools that produced the "Delinquent Boys." If they are not from the same population the interpreta-tion derived from these comparative data (Table 1 in the manual) would appear to be heavily "loaded" in favor of the desired predictions. It may well be that only three or four of the 98 "Delinquent Boys" (Table 1) could have been removed from the 156 "Public School Boys" on the same table. Where those delinquent boys actually fell in relation to the 156 other boys would have a lot to do with our interpretation of the validity of the KD Scale as a discriminating predictor in a real situation.

b) The section entitled "Correlations with other measures" with its accompanying Table 3, has the same elusive statistical quality. The correlations all appear to be done with one or the other end of the KD distribution. If this proves to be true the negative intercorrelations between segments of the KD distribution and the *Otis Self-Administering Tests of Mental Ability,* for example, are very high and would be much higher if the entire distribution were to be used. The test of this assumption would be to obtain an intercorrelation between the Otis and the KD scale for all of the persons involved pooled into a single group. It is an old trick of test makers to expand the range when they wish to push up intercorrelations. This is a new one directed at pushing down the intercorrelation. In saying this the reviewer is imputing neither goodness nor badness to the author or publisher. He is merely saying that interrelationships should be computed at the level at which predictions are to be made and used. If we wish to discriminate between boys who are in public school and boys who are in "reform" school, we need only look at the roster of the two schools without the use of a predictor. If we wish to discriminate within a neighborhood between those children who are going to reform school and those who are not, we need validity coefficients derived from neighborhood data. The author and publisher are aware of this and state in the manual that studies are in progress to determine the instrument's predictive value for unselected groups. It has been necessary to use a much rougher validating technique at this stage in the development than might be wished for.

The area of delinquency predictions is a complex, socially valuable area of research. The outcomes of the studies on this scale and checklist are awaited with keen interest for they appear to be a promising development in a sparse field.

DALE B. HARRIS, *Professor, Institute of Child Welfare, University of Minnesota, Minneapolis, Minnesota.*

The first item, the *KD Proneness Scale,* taps children's attitudes and interests and presumably indicates trends toward delinquent behavior. The nature of the instrument appears to be sufficiently concealed. Although a sophisticated person could affect his score in the direction of socially acceptable answers, this is not likely to happen in the junior high age range. While the concepts included in the Scale are well within the understanding of children in the seventh grade and above, the vocabulary of the Scale may present some difficulties for poor readers.

One distinct advantage of this test is that it is applicable to girls as well as to boys. However, data contained in the manual indicate that the test does not discriminate as successfully between known delinquent girls and unselected girls as it does between delinquent and nondelinquent boys.

The one criticism which must be made is that the manual fails to report cross validation material. Tests from the same delinquent group were used both for obtaining the score distributions reported in the manual and for selecting the original items. However, data supplied to this reviewer by the author indicate that in further studies, a biserial correlation of the order of .85 was obtained between test scores and a dichotomous grouping composed of delinquent boys and boys with high moral reputations. The comparable figure for girls is .46. In still other groups, correlations between 5-point ratings of behavior (undefined) and scale scores run between .10 and .49, values being higher for boys. It is clear from these data, too, that mean scores are significantly higher (i.e., indicative of delinquency) for younger than for older children.

The criterion groups of delinquents and nondelinquents were apparently not matched with respect to such factors as age, socio-economic status, and intelligence. Published research on delinquency shows that differentials between delinquent and nondelinquent groups on attitude type material frequently are minimized when such factors as socio-economic status and intelligence are controlled. The manual reports that for a variety of groups the correlation of scale scores with results of a group intelligence test run between $-.26$ and $-.42$. Thus, intelligence is not unassociated with results of the measure. One correlation of $-.24$ is reported with the *Personal Index,* a scale for the detection of potential behavior problem cases (this scale is otherwise unidentified).

The author states in the manual that, "It is to be noted that no 'norms,' in the customary sense are furnished for interpreting scores on the Scale, nor are any needed for the use of results here proposed." He provides a threshold or "cutting score" presumptive of delinquency. However, he has published several distributions of scores which the discriminating test user is likely to consult to give meaning to his work. Even though the legal code considers delinquency to exist or not to exist in terms of presence or absence of specific acts, most school people are trained to think of maladjustment as a variable, existing in greater and lesser degrees. Undoubtedly this thinking will apply to obtained scores on this test, even though a "cutting score" is offered as the most meaningful way of interpreting results.

A second instrument, the checklist, provides a list of descriptive characteristics which have apparently been drawn from research literature as being significantly associated with delinquency. It has obvious "face validity" to anyone familiar with the sociological and psychological literature of delinquency, but the manual affords no real knowledge of how the items were selected. Certain items are especially designated as having "the greatest bearing on potential delinquent behavior"; again no basis for the author's selection is afforded. The checklist is to be marked by a teacher or professional worker on the basis of his knowledge of a particular child. Ranges of scores presumed to indicate conditions of "vulnerable" and "extreme exposure" to delinquency are tentatively offered. While the author recommends that the two instruments be used together, he gives no information concerning the correlation of the measures except to say, "there will not always be complete agreement between the two instruments in identifying a given youngster as probably delinquent, but even children for whom the scale and check list do not agree should receive further attention from the appropriate professional worker."

From research data available, it would appear that this test is comparable or perhaps somewhat superior to several other paper and pencil instruments purporting to predict delinquency. All such instruments suffer from the poor definition provided by the socio-legal basis of the criterion group. The KD Scale, used with considerable caution, will indicate some of the children needing the special attention of guidance workers. The checklist will probably do as much as the scale, by systematizing facts already known about the child, and will not require the child's time to obtain a record of his attitudes. The author and publishers are to be highly commended for restricting the distribution of the test. Such limitation should be used more widely to prevent poorly considered judgments being passed on children, especially in cases where an instrument is still in process of development.

[65]

★Kuder Preference Record—Personal. Grades 9–16 and adults; 1948–49; 6 scores: sociable, practical, theoretical, agreeable, dominant, verification; IBM; 2 editions; 1 form, '48; preliminary manual, second revision ('49); separate answer pads or answer sheets must be used; 55¢ per 25 profile sheets for men and women or boys and girls; 75¢ per specimen set of either edition; cash orders postpaid; nontimed (40–45) minutes; G. Frederic Kuder; Science Research Associates, Inc. *
a) FORM AH (HAND SCORING EDITION). 49¢ per test and answer pad; $2.15 per 25 answer pads.
b) FORM AM (MACHINE SCORING EDITION). 39¢ per test; $2.90 per 100 IBM answer sheets; $4 per set of scoring keys.

REFERENCES
1. MOSIER, MARY F., AND KUDER, G. FREDERIC. "Personal Preference Differences Among Occupational Groups." J Appl Psychol 33:231-9 Je '49. * (PA 24:1926)
2. BIRGE, WILLIAM R. "Preferences and Behavior Ratings of Dominance." Ed & Psychol Meas 10:392-4 au '50. * (PA 25:2987)
3. GOSHORN, WENONAH MARJORIE. A Study of the Relationships Between the Kuder Preference Record—Personal and Certain Sociometric Ratings. Doctor's thesis, Indiana University (Bloomington, Ind.), 1950. (Thesis Abstract Series....1950, 1951, pp. 37–43.) (PA 25:7107, title only)
4. KUDER, G. FREDERIC. "Identifying the Faker." Personnel Psychol 3:155-67 su '50. * (PA 25:1791)

J Consult Psychol 13:67 F '49. Laurance F. Shaffer. * A wide use may be predicted for this convenient and soundly-developed questionnaire.

[66]

Lewerenz-Steinmetz Orientation Test: Concerning Fundamental Aims of Education. High school and college; 1931–35; 10 scores: physical and mental health; education-general, education-specific, worthy home membership, vocation, civic education (government), civic education (industry and world), worthy use of leisure, ethical character, total; 1 form, '35; manual ('35); $2.50 per 25, postage extra; 25¢ per specimen set, postpaid; nontimed (60) minutes; Alfred S. Lewerenz and Harry C. Steinmetz; California Test Bureau. *

REFERENCES
1. ROLFE, J. F. "The Measurement of Teaching Ability: Study Number Two." J Exp Ed 14:52-74 S '45. * (PA 20:1268)
2. ROSTKER, L. E. "The Measurement of Teaching Ability: Study Number One." J Exp Ed 14:6-51 S '45. * (PA 20:1269)
3. RESNICK, JOSEPH. "A Study of Some Relationships Between High School Grades and Certain Aspects of Adjustment." J Ed Res 44:321-40 Ja '51. * (PA 25:8286)

FREDERIC L. AYER, *Head, Division of Evaluation and Research, Citizenship Education Project, Teachers College, Columbia University, New York, New York.*

The purpose of this test is to measure "beliefs likely to condition attitudes." The general pattern is a list of statements ranging from superstition to fact; the respondent is asked to mark those statements which are absolutely true. High reliability is reported in the manual. The validity report may be summed up in these words of the authors: "The Orientation Test appears to be valid in that with individuals the test results seem to check with subjective expectations." This statement is based on the fact that individuals of different educational attainment made sharp differences in scores. Standardization was done on separate samples of college instructors, graduate students, public school teachers, college upperclassmen, miscellaneous tradesmen, city policemen, city jail prisoners, and 372 white adults who were "probably above the average of a typical population." These groups, with the exception of the last, are listed in the rank order of their median scores. It is the opinion of this reviewer that this test is a reasonably good measure of educational attainment which does not necessarily measure superstition and dogma. This opinion is supported by such items as the following, which constitute more of a vocabulary test than an attitude questionnaire: "Revolt against equitable authority, if an habitual response, is a manifestation of a pathological mental condition"; "Inevitably involving renunciation, marriage is essentially tragic, though not necessarily unhappy"; and "Most cinematographic performances have a deleterious effect on adolescent minds." Contrast those with items like these: "A square jaw is a sign of will power"; "In divorce the man is always most to blame"; and "Motion picture plays vary in merit."

True to the claims of the authors, high school students (in the suburban area surrounding New York City) did not attain as high scores as Columbia University graduate students who, being older, had had time to develop more prejudices than the younger students. Although the test is intended for use in high schools and colleges, this reviewer doubts whether the test would serve any purpose in a high school and probably only limited purpose in college.

Even if reasonably well informed college students do not know the difference between superstition and fact, they would be able to figure out the scoring pattern after the first two pages if they are at all testwise, since the "absolutely true" responses are in an identical pattern on each page. This makes for ease in scoring, it is true, but also may leave the truthfulness of the responses open to question.

In the opinion of this reviewer, the test lacks validity as an attitude test, and is not sufficiently comprehensive to make an efficient test of educational achievement.

ROGER T. LENNON, *Director, Division of Test Research and Service, World Book Company, Yonkers, New York.*

This test is intended "as a measure of beliefs likely to condition attitudes." The beliefs are those having to do with "fundamental aims of education." The test consists of 475 items, organized into seven subtests, two of which are divided into two parts. Thus, nine scores are derived as indicated in the description above, together with a total score. The number of items per subtest varies from 25 to 75.

The items include statements of fact ("A titmouse is a small bird"); common beliefs either false or unsupported by adequate evidence ("The genius is likely to be unbalanced"; "It is better to tell your troubles to your friends than to keep them to yourself"); and value judgments ("Hard work deserves a high school-mark"). The examinee is directed to mark those statements which he thinks are "absolutely true." Two scores are derived for each subtest: a "True" score, which is the number of statements keyed as true and marked true by the subject; and a "Doubtful" score, which is the number of statements keyed as doubtful but marked as true by the subject. On the whole, the statements are clear, although the phrasing of a few of them might be criticized—e.g., Section IV, Item 21; V, 50; VI, 25; VII, 7. The reviewer did not, in every instance, find himself in agreement with the keying. The "absolute" truth of statements such as I, 21 and 46; II, 51; III, 28; IV, 21 may be questioned.

Information on validity is confined to the statements that the test "appears to be valid in that with individuals the test results seem to check with subjective expectations," and that there are "sharp differences in score existing between certain groups of individuals of varying educational attainment." These latter data (included as part of the normative material) are scarcely unambiguous evidences of validity. The nine areas into which the test is organized are represented as a classification of "commonly accepted objectives of education," a not unreasonable claim; but there is no indication of the manner in which the individual items in the subtests were constructed, selected, or validated.

Estimates of reliability of the total test reported in the manual include a coefficient of .89 (N = 152 adults, otherwise undefined), derived by the "split-half method on average per-

centile score," and corrected by the Spearman-Brown formula; and corrected odd-even
coefficients of .951 for True scores and .958 for
Doubtful scores (N = "100 cases of college students and adults"). These latter coefficients are
described, rather puzzlingly, as indicating the
"agreement between odds and evens of items
answered correctly." *No reliability data are provided for subtest scores,* a serious omission in
view of the fact that use of subtest scores of
individual examinees is encouraged both in the
manual and by the provision on the test booklet
of a profile chart on which these scores are to
be charted. No data are furnished concerning
subtest intercorrelations.

Materials for interpretation of scores include
tables of percentile ranks and adjective ratings,
for subtest and total scores, for a mixed adult
population and for a population of high school
seniors and college freshmen. For adults, the
percentile rank and the rating for each subtest
is derived from a combination of the Doubtful
score and the True score. Occasionally, the combinations lead to peculiar results: e.g., in Section I, for a given Doubtful score, an examinee
with a True score of 14 has a percentile rank
of 6 and is rated as Inferior, whereas an examinee
with the presumably better True score of 15
receives a percentile rank of 3 and is rated Very
Inferior. For high school and college students,
percentiles are calculated separately for the
Doubtful and the True score on each subtest;
these two percentiles are then summed and this
sum of percentiles is itself converted to a percentile rank. For both students and adults percentile ranks for all nine subtests are totaled
and divided by 9 to yield an average percentile
rank for the entire test, which is converted to
still another percentile rank and rating. The well
known lack of equivalence of percentile units
appears not to have discouraged the authors
from adding and averaging percentiles; but the
reviewer regards this system of interpretation
as needlessly crude and inexact, and not to be
defended on grounds of apparent simplicity.
Further, presumably because of the small standard deviation of subtest scores, very small differences in raw score are frequently associated
with extremely large differences in percentile
rank.

The adult "standards" are based on a population described as "almost entirely made up of
superior adults" and "largely....university gradu-

ates" but otherwise unspecified. Percentile ranks
for average percentile scores are also furnished
for seven different groups of adults (N from 19
to 119); it is not clear from the manual whether
the adult standard population included any or
all of the cases in these latter groups. The population from which the high school senior and
college freshman norms were derived is not
described. No distributions of scores, means, or
standard deviations of either subtest or total
scores are presented.

From the standpoint of format, the test is
adequate. Administration is simple, though
likely to require somewhat more than the 60
minutes suggested. Scoring is by means of a
strip key. Suggestions for "diagnosis" and use
of the results are limited to brief generalities.

The authors, in developing this test some 20
years ago, apparently had in mind the provision
of an instrument intended to get at some of the
important attitudinal outcomes of education,
certainly a praiseworthy aim. The reviewer is
disposed to feel, however, (*a*) that the nature of
the items and of the task set for the examinee
are such as to make the test very largely a measure of achievement or knowledge in the various
areas rather than an attitude measure; and (*b*)
that in the absence of data beyond that provided
in the manual, particularly with respect to validity, reliability, intertest correlations, and norms,
the test is of but limited usefulness for the purposes it was designed to serve.

[67]

★The Life Adjustment Inventory. High school;
1951; 14 scores: adjustment to curriculum, reading and
study skills, communication and listening skills, social
skills and etiquette, boy-girl relationships, religion-
moral-ethics, functional citizenship, vocational orientation and preparation, physical and mental health, family living, orientation to science, consumer education,
art appreciation and creativity, use of leisure time;
1 form; $2.25 per 25; 50¢ per manual; 75¢ per speci-
men set; postage extra; nontimed (25) minutes; edited
by J. Wayne Wrightstone; Ronald C. Doll; Acorn
Publishing Co. *

JOHN W. M. ROTHNEY, *Professor of Education,
University of Wisconsin, Madison, Wisconsin.*

This is just another one of those toss-a-
circle-around-the-symbol-for-your-problem inventories which holds no promise of contributing any more to our understanding of pupils'
problems than the scores of others which represent the lowest form of the testmaker's art. In
25 minutes the student encircles numbers at the
end of 180 problems to indicate whether they

are big, medium or small ones to him. The student is asked to give his "honest and sincere opinions"; this request should be warning enough that not much can be expected from the instrument. Many studies have shown that answers to this type of question can be faked consciously or unconsciously, and no check is provided in this inventory as to the sincerity and honesty of the students' opinions. The very fact that the student is asked to be honest and sincere may even suggest to those who had not thought about being insincere or dishonest that they could answer in that way.

The authors state, "The validity of an inventory of this sort is difficult to establish concretely." Then they say, "The present Inventory has been validated by administering it to thirty-four random-selected freshmen, sophomores, juniors, and seniors in a public high school and then making case studies of the thirty-four pupils." Note the number. A total of 34 cases spread over four grades! It is well established statistically and scientifically that validation on so few cases is entirely inadequate. After showing that the inventory and case study results are somewhat similar, the authors conclude that the "early attempts at validation appear, therefore, to have brought encouraging results," and they give the usual promise to determine and substantiate the validity of the inventory some time in the future. This reviewer would not recommend purchase of the inventory until we have seen the results of the determination and substantiation processes.

The usual long, detailed, impressive but almost meaningless tables of norms commonly provided for adjustment inventory scores are given. When the 2,005 cases are broken down by sex and grade, the groups range in number from 212 to 307. Fortunately the authors do not urge the user of the inventory to employ the norms extensively. It is suggested that norms may be used as general guides but that attention be focused on the local situation because "each local school community has its own peculiar conditions which may affect the way pupils respond." Then, why not use a locally constructed inventory which can be adapted to those peculiar conditions? Drawing up lists of statements similar to those used in this inventory could be done by a faculty committee as competently as it is done here.

Since this reviewer sees *no* merit whatever in the procedure used in this inventory and such similar devices as the *Mooney Problem Check List* and the *SRA Youth Inventory,* comparisons between them seem valueless. It is hoped that we will soon pass that naive stage in educational and psychological thought in which we expect to get at important problems by a hurried mass approach. Perhaps these inventories will find their best use in bonfires celebrating our emergence from the ruts that the personality and adjustment testers, ably abetted by high pressure salesmen, have carved out for us.

Caveat emptor.

HELEN SHACTER, *Consulting Psychologist; and Lecturer in Psychology, Northwestern University; Chicago, Illinois.*

As defined by the author, the purpose of the *Life Adjustment Inventory* is broad and the uses to which it may be put are very varied. A fourfold aim is the stated objective: (*a*) to survey the extent to which a high school curriculum meets the needs of its pupils; (*b*) to assist teachers toward better understanding of pupils' problems, needs, and interests; (*c*) to aid guidance workers in individual counseling; and (*d*) to carry out research in both guidance and curriculum problems.

It would be naive to believe that so diversified a goal could indeed be achieved through one paper and pencil approach. While the inventory can probably contribute in some degree to parts of its broad objective if it is used judiciously and if its findings are considered in an investigation which utilizes the instrument as one of a battery, the reviewer believes that the most promising utilization of the inventory would be in a guidance program of individual counseling.

The inventory is presented in the form of 180 statements to which the respondent is asked to react by encircling 1, 2, or 3 after each statement, indicating that he considers the item either a BIG problem, a problem of MEDIUM importance, or one of SMALL or NO importance. There is no time limit; 20 to 25 minutes are said to be sufficient to complete the inventory.

The items are classified into 14 areas of learning considered significant because of emphasis "to greater or lesser extent by youth commissions, curriculum committees, and individual educators, as well as by young people themselves." (None of the commissions or committees is identified.) Fourteen scores are obtained from reactions to 24 items relative to curriculum adjustment, and to 12 items each for 13 other problem areas as listed in the bibliographic entry above.

The wording of the statements is simple and brief; a few examples can illustrate the general tone:

> I'd like to quit school now.
> I'd like to know how to cook.
> I often wonder just how well I'm doing in my school work.
> I seem to have trouble in working with other people.
> I'd like to know more about dating.
> I wonder how to select a college.
> I know too little about local and state government to become a good voting citizen.

Not nearly so simple, however, are the implications of the reactions to these items. The manual accompanying the inventory differentiates interpretation for *survey* purposes and for *individual diagnosis*. A scoring sheet is provided and also standardization data giving (*a*) the average number of BIG problem items by areas; (*b*) the percentage of pupils, identified by sex and grade, marking each item in each area; and (*c*) the rank order of learning areas in which the standardization group felt the curricula of their schools most inadequate.

The standardization group numbered 2,005 pupils in 8 high schools in 5 states of the East and Middle West. It is not noted whether urban or suburban or rural populations (or all three) were included. Nor is it stated whether public or private schools (or both) were studied.

Reliability coefficients of .91 for boys and .92 for girls are quoted for the inventory as a whole. These findings may be misleading, for they are based on responses of only 85 boys and 95 girls to whom the inventory was readministered six weeks after the original administration. These were unselected pupils from the three upper classes of a four-year high school.

The manual states frankly that the validity of an inventory such as this is "difficult to establish concretely," but adds that "encouraging results" have come from early attempts at validation through making nondirective studies of 34 high school pupils to whom the inventory had been administered. However, results are detailed relative to three only of the total of 14 problem areas considered. It seems to the reviewer that more comprehensive and extensive data would be desirable.

The *Life Adjustment Inventory* does not appear to be well named nor well established statistically. Neither does it seem well adapted to the fourfold goal sought through its use. It is highly questionable that high school students differentiate between their personal needs and dearth in curriculum provisions. It is debatable that high school teachers would have the opportunity, even if there were the inclination, to utilize data in 14 areas of pupil response concerning problems, needs and interests.

Nevertheless, the inventory does offer an interesting extension to studies of student viewpoint relative to curricula and guidance in the high school, although findings should probably be considered suggestive rather than specific. It provides, too, an approach which can be utilized in individual guidance as an additional instrument of investigation which is relatively brief to administer, interesting to record, and productive of a variety of reactions in several areas of importance in the adjustment of high school boys and girls. For such use it can serve the counselor both in direct pupil contacts and also in teacher contacts concerning individual pupils.

[68]

★The Manson Evaluation. Adults; 1948; a test for the identification of alcoholics, potential alcoholics and severely maladjusted adults; 8 scores: anxiety, depressive fluctuations, emotional sensitivity, resentfulness, incompleteness, aloneness, interpersonal relations, total; 1 form; $2.75 per 25; 35¢ per specimen set; postpaid; nontimed (5-15) minutes; Morse P. Manson; Western Psychological Services, Box 775, Beverly Hills, Calif. *

REFERENCES

1. MANSON, MORSE P. *A Psychometric Differentiation of Alcoholics From Nonalcoholics.* Doctor's thesis, University of Southern California (Los Angeles, Calif.), 1948.
2. MANSON, MORSE P. "A Psychometric Differentiation of Alcoholics From Non-Alcoholics." *Q J Studies Alcohol* 9:175-206 S '48. * (*PA* 23:1384)
3. MANSON, MORSE P. "A Psychometric Analysis of Psychoneurotic and Psychosomatic Characteristics of Alcoholics." *J Clin Psychol* 5:77-83 Ja '49. * (*PA* 23:5627)
4. MANSON, MORSE P. "A Psychometric Analysis of Psychopathic Characteristics of Alcoholics." *J Consult Psychol* 13:111-8 Ap '49. * (*PA* 23:4893)

CHARLES H. HONZIK, *Personal Counselor and Vocational Adviser, Veterans Administration, San Francisco, California.*

The test author states that, although it is not difficult for the practitioner or therapist to make the clinical diagnosis of alcoholic addiction, a brief, objective, paper and pencil test for the determination of alcoholism has the advantage of saving valuable time of clinically trained people through the avoidance of time-consuming consultations, histories, and examinations and has the further usefulness of objectively reinforcing the clinical diagnosis of alcoholic addiction. *The Manson Evaluation* consists of 72 questions of the type used in personality tests, such as the *Minnesota Multiphasic Personality Inventory,* all remotely associated with drinking.

The test is well standardized and validated and probably differentiates the alcoholic from the nonalcoholic as effectively as any test of this sort could be expected to do.

The author states that four methods of validation were used. Of these, only the method that determined the effectiveness of the test in separating alcoholics from nonalcoholics solely through test scores is of practical importance to the prospective test user. This was done by presenting the percentages of correct predictions as follows: male alcoholics, 79 per cent; female alcoholics, 80 per cent; male nonalcoholics, 79 per cent; and female nonalcoholics, 85 per cent. This means that incorrect predictions run for four groups from 15 to 21 per cent, the poorest prediction being for male alcoholics and male nonalcoholics. In other words, the test differentiates alcoholics from nonalcoholics 29 to 35 per cent better than chance. The practical question confronting the prospective test user is whether for his purposes it is worth while to give the test for such an amount of additional assurance.

The test is easily given and scored. An interesting and potentially valuable feature of the test for clinical purposes is the provision of scores which indicate the extent of an alcoholic's psychoneurotic and psychopathic traits; that is, how closely he resembles the neurotic or the psychopathic individual. The traits of anxiety, depressive fluctuations, and emotional sensitivity, for which differentiating scores may be obtained, are designated psychoneurotic; feelings of resentment, failure to complete social objectives, feelings of aloneness, and poor interpersonal relationships are called psychopathic.

This carefully validated test can be a useful diagnostic tool in clinical work with alcoholics. It must, of course, be used with discretion and with awareness of its limitations. Since, as noted above, incorrect predictions run from 15 to 21 per cent, some alcoholics will be placed in the class of nonalcoholics, and vice versa. Since one never knows from the test alone which particular individuals have been so misplaced, further checking through clinical methods is essential.

ALBERT L. HUNSICKER, *Supervising Psychologist, Galesburg State Research Hospital, Galesburg, Illinois.*

This questionnaire of 72 yes-no questions is designed to identify (a) individuals addicted to alcohol, (b) individuals possessing the personality structure characteristically found in alcoholics, (c) areas of personality disorder frequently associated with alcoholism. The questions, only remotely associated with drinking, were selected from a series of 470 questions administered to 126 alcoholics and 157 nonalcoholics. An attempt was made to match groups for age, education, and social status; one set of scoring keys with separate norms for males and females is offered. The shorter approximation of the Kuder-Richardson formula yielded a reliability of .94 for both the male and the female groups. Correct prediction of known alcoholics in treatment is claimed for 79 per cent of the male group and 89 per cent of the female group studied. This reviewer administered the questionnaire to 11 known alcoholics in therapy for alcoholism at an outpatient clinic and to 18 hospital employees, who omitted all identifying information; he, like the author, found five overlapping scores.

The author reports that a subjective analysis of the 72 questions resulted in establishing seven neurotic or psychopathic traits. These are (a) anxiety, (b) depressive fluctuations, (c) emotional sensitivity, (d) feelings of resentment, (e) failure to complete social objectives, (f) feelings of aloneness, and (g) poor interpersonal relationships.

It has been this reviewer's experience that the results from questionnaires of this type will vary with the circumstances under which they are taken. When administered to a known clinical group in treatment for failure to adjust because of the clinical symptoms, one can almost always expect more valid results. These subjects, in the treatment situation, are willing to be self critical and to record this self criticism. However, these same subjects when taking the same test in a situation where their symptoms and failures are unknown (e.g. when applying for a job) can be expected to perform more like the control (normal) group than like the experimental (alcoholic) group. The author's suggestion that this test may prove useful in identifying alcoholics or potential alcoholics prior to employment or training is one that will have to be carefully evaluated, for it is not yet demonstrated. Furthermore, the subjective breakdown of the 72 questions into seven categories will probably not stand up under a careful cluster or factor analysis or under the test of differentiating psychiatric groups. However, unlike the *Alcadd Test* by the same author, which consists of 60 frank drinking questions, this test may prove an excellent research tool for screening alcoholics or possible alcoholics. More work needs to be done with known alcoholics in testing situations where they believe themselves to be considered members of the "normal" population.

[69]

★**Memory-for-Designs Test.** Ages 8.5 and over; 1946–48; a test for the presence of brain damage; individual; 1 form, '46; no data on reliability and validity in manual (for data presented elsewhere by the authors, see references below); manual ('46); supplementary manual ('48); $2 per set of testing materials, postpaid; (3½–15) minutes; Frances Graham and Barbara Kendall; Department of Neuropsychiatry, Washington University School of Medicine, St. Louis, Mo. *

REFERENCES

1. GRAHAM, FRANCES K., AND KENDALL, BARBARA S. "Performance of Brain-Damaged Cases on a Memory-for-Designs Test." *J Abn & Social Psychol* 41:303–14 Jl '46. * (*PA* 20: 4616)
2. GRAHAM, FRANCES K., AND KENDALL, BARBARA S. "Note on the Scoring of the Memory-for-Designs Test." *J Abn & Social Psychol* 42:253 Ap '47. * (*PA* 21:3022)
3. KENDALL, BARBARA S. "A Note on the Relation of Retardation in Reading to Performance on a Memory-for-Designs Test." *J Ed Psychol* 39:370–3 O '48. * (*PA* 23:1698)
4. KENDALL, BARBARA S., AND GRAHAM, FRANCES K. "Further Standardization of the Memory-for-Designs Test on Children and Adults." *J Consult Psychol* 12:349–54 S–O '48. * (*PA* 23:1773)
5. WATSON, ROBERT I. *The Clinical Method in Psychology*, pp. 353–7. New York: Harper & Brothers, 1951. Pp. xii, 779. *

[70]

The Minnesota Inventory of Social Attitudes. College; 1937; 2 tests; $1.50 per 25 of any one test; 35¢ per specimen set; postpaid; (15–20) minutes per test; E. G. Williamson and J. G. Darley; distributed by Psychological Corporation. *
a) MINNESOTA INVENTORY OF SOCIAL BEHAVIOR. Form B.
b) MINNESOTA INVENTORY OF SOCIAL PREFERENCES. Form P.

REFERENCES

1. DARLEY, JOHN G. *An Analysis of Attitude and Adjustment Tests: With Special Reference to Conditions of Change in Attitudes and Adjustments.* Doctor's thesis, University of Minnesota (Minneapolis, Minn.), 1937.
2. DARLEY, JOHN G. "Scholastic Achievement and Measured Maladjustment." *J Appl Psychol* 21:485–93 O '37. * (*PA* 12: 2099)
3. DARLEY, JOHN G. "Tested Maladjustment Related to Clinically Diagnosed Maladjustment." *J Appl Psychol* 21:632–42 Ag '37. * (*PA* 12:3031)
4. WILLIAMSON, E. G., AND DARLEY, J. G. "The Measurement of Social Attitudes of College Students: I, Standardization of Tests and Results of a Survey." *J Social Psychol* 8:219–29 My '37. * (*PA* 11:5277)
5. WILLIAMSON, E. G., AND DARLEY, J. G. "The Measurement of Social Attitudes of College Students: II, Validation of Two Attitude Tests." *J Social Psychol* 8:231–42 My '37. * (*PA* 11:5278)
6. DARLEY, JOHN G. "Changes in Measured Attitudes and Adjustments." *J Social Psychol* 9:189–99 My '38. * (*PA* 12: 4833)
7. MCNAMARA, WALTER J., AND DARLEY, JOHN G. "A Factor Analysis of Test-Retest Performance on Attitude and Adjustment Tests." *J Ed Psychol* 29:652–64 D '38. *
8. DARLEY, JOHN G., AND MCNAMARA, WALTER J. "Factor Analysis in the Establishment of New Personality Tests." *J Ed Psychol* 31:321–34 My '40. * (*PA* 15:922)
9. GILKINSON, HOWARD, AND KNOWER, FRANKLIN H. "A Study of Standardized Personality Tests and Skill in Speech." *J Ed Psychol* 32:161–175 Mr '41. * (*PA* 15:3888)
10. JOHNSON, A. P. *The Prediction of Scholastic Achievement for Freshman Engineering Students at Purdue University.* Purdue University, Division of Educational Research, Studies in Engineering Education II. Lafayette, Ind.: the Division, May 1942. Pp. 22. Paper. * (*PA* 16:5020)

11. JOHNSON, A. P. *The Relationship of Test Scores to Scholastic Achievement for 244 Engineering Freshmen Entering Purdue University in September, 1939.* Doctor's thesis, Purdue University (Lafayette, Ind.), 1942.
12. BENDER, I. E., AND HASTORF, A. H. "The Perception of Persons: Forecasting Another Person's Responses on Three Personality Scales." *J Abn & Social Psychol* 45:556–61 Jl '50. * (*PA* 25:988)

VERNER M. SIMS, *Professor of Psychology, University of Alabama, University, Alabama.*

Judged in terms of the conventional standards, the Minnesota Inventories would appear to rank high. Considerable effort at validating the inventories was made, their reliability is high, they are simple to administer and score, the manual is adequate, and norms based upon a relatively large college population (although all from the University of Minnesota) are reported.

There are, however, a few questions concerning the inventories which the reviewer would like to raise. Although the directions given the testee state there are no right or wrong answers to the statements, actually for each possible answer, score values (ranging from one to five) are printed on the inventory along with the answer. This is done for convenience in scoring, but it seems to be an open invitation to the bright, "high-score" conscious subject to make a "good" score. Thus it would demand unnecessarily high rapport with the testee if the answers are to be valid. Some other scoring arrangement should increase the usefulness of the inventories.

Again, the effort to fit the response to all questions into a standard 5-choice pattern (almost always, frequently, occasionally, rarely, almost never) often results in clumsy sentence structure which seems unnecessary and may well reduce the validity of the inventories particularly if they are used with subjects who are not too verbally facile. In the case of nine items, for example, the choice "almost never" results in a double negative, such as, "Does not like to take the initiative ·in making friends" and "almost never." Other items are almost as difficult to interpret: "Has about the average fear of making blunders before people" and the choice "rarely"; "Neither seeks nor avoids social contacts" and the choice "occasionally." More natural question forms would seemingly lead to better understanding on the part of many subjects.

The authors do not seem to have studied or even considered the possible interdependence of the items within either inventory. Inspection shows cases where there would appear to be high interdependence. In Form B, for instance, Item 4 reads, "Is reluctant to meet important people," Item 28 reads, "Has no hesitancy about meeting important people"; in Form P, Item 16 reads, "Prefers being with other people rather than being alone," Item 18, "Prefers to be alone as much as possible." Such cases (and the reader who will examine the inventories can find several others) appear to be no more than repetitions of the same questions. To the extent that this is true, the effectiveness of the measurement is reduced.

A final, and perhaps more serious, question has to do with the two "personality traits" which the authors claim the inventories measure: "preferences in the extent and type of desired social relationships," and "an individual's estimates of his own behavior and feelings in social situations." In the reviewer's opinion, the authors have not even established the existence of two such unitary traits, let alone proven that their inventories measure them. They report uncorrected coefficients between the two forms of .47 for men and .44 for women, and inspection of the items in the two forms show many cases of great similarity. For example, Item 30 in Form B reads, "Has a fairly good time at most parties," while Item 3, Form P, reads, "Has the time of his life at social affairs" and Item 40 in the same form, "Is annoyed by social activities." It is difficult to accept as a fact that the first of these items is indicative of one personality trait while the other two indicate another trait. The reader who cares to investigate will find other striking illustrations. In fact, five items in Form B (10, 16, 25, 30, and 39) ask directly for preferences in social relationships, and at least three items in Form P (3, 8, and 32) inquire directly concerning overt social behavior. It is possible, of course, that more careful investigation would establish the fact that "social preferences" and "self-estimate of social behavior" are different traits, but there is considerable doubt in the reviewer's mind that there is any essential difference in what these two inventories measure.

In spite of the questions we have raised, scores on the inventories should be helpful in counseling students where some information on social adjustment is needed. These criticisms, if valid, indicate only need for further work with the inventories, not that they are without worth as they stand.

For reviews by J. P. Guilford and George W. Hartmann, see 38:900.

[71]

*Minnesota Multiphasic Personality Inventory, Revised Edition.** Ages 16 and over; 1942–51; 13 scores: hypochondriasis, depression, hysteria, psychopathic deviate, masculinity and femininity, paranoia, psychasthenia, schizophrenia, hypomania, question, lie, validity, K; individual and group forms; manual ('51); postpaid; Starke R. Hathaway and J. Charnley McKinley; Psychological Corporation. *
a) INDIVIDUAL FORM ("THE CARD SET"). $23 per set of testing materials including 50 recording sheets; $2.90 per 50 recording sheets; nontimed (30–90) minutes.
b) GROUP FORM ("THE BOOKLET FORM"). IBM; for Engineers Northwest scoring service and Hankes Answer Sheets, see 466; separate answer sheets must be used; $5.50 per 25; $1.50 per manual; $3.50 per 50 IBM answer sheets and case summary cards; $4.50 per set of machine scoring stencils with manual; $4.50 per set of hand scoring stencils with manual; nontimed (40–90) minutes.

REFERENCES

1–72. See 3:60.
73. BROWER, DANIEL. "The Relations of Visuo-Motor Conflict to Personality Traits and Cardiovascular Activity." Abstract. Am Psychol 1:244 Jl '46. * (PA 20:3690, title only)
74. BLUM, LAWRENCE PHILIP. "A Comparative Study of Students Preparing for Five Selected Professions Including Teaching." J Exp Ed 16:31–65 S '47. * (PA 22:1881)
75. BROWER, DANIEL. "The Relations Between Minnesota Multiphasic Personality Inventory Scores and Cardiovascular Measures Before and After Experimentally Induced Visuo-Motor Conflict." J Social Psychol 26:55–60 Ag '47. * (PA 22:2539)
76. BROWN, HUGH S. An Investigation of the Validity of the Minnesota Multiphasic Personality Inventory for a College Population and the Relationship of Certain Personality Traits to Achievement. Doctor's thesis, University of Minnesota (Minneapolis, Minn.), 1947.
77. CERF, ARTHUR Z. "The Minnesota Multiphasic Personality Inventory, CE437A," pp. 599–601. In Printed Classification Tests. Edited by J. P. Guilford with the assistance of John I. Lacey. Army Air Forces Aviation Psychology Program Research Reports, Report No. 5. Washington, D.C.: U.S. Government Printing Office, 1947. Pp. xi, 919. * (PA 22:4145)
78. HAMPTON, PETER J. "The Minnesota Multiphasic Personality Inventory as a Psychometric Tool for Diagnosing Personality Disorders Among College Students." J Social Psychol 26:99–108 Ag '47. * (PA 22:2624)
79. HARRIS, R. E., AND IVES, V. M. "A Study of the Personality of Alcoholics." Abstract. Am Psychol 2:405 O '47. * (PA 22:1282, title only)
80. HENDERSON, CHARLES R.; WHEELER, NORMAN C.; JOHNSON, HOWARD C.; COGSWELL, ROBERT C., JR.; BERRYMAN, GEORGE H.; IVY, ANDREW C.; FRIEDMANN, THEODORE E.; AND YOUMANS, JOHN B. "Changes in Personality Appraisal Associated With a Restricted Intake of B Vitamins and Protein." Am J Med Sci 213:488–93 Ap '47. *
81. HUNT, EDWARD L., AND LEHNER, GEORGE F. J. "Relationships of the Hildreth Feeling and Attitude Scales to the Minnesota Multiphasic Personality Inventory." Abstract. Am Psychol 2:417 O '47. * (PA 22:1108, title only)
82. HUNT, HOWARD F.; CASS, WILLIAM A., JR.; CARP, ABRAHAM; AND WINDER, CLARENCE L. "A Study of the Diagnostic Utility of the Minnesota Multiphasic Personality Inventory." Abstract. Am Psychol 2:417 O '47. * (PA 22:1234, title only)
83. JEFFERY, MARY E. Some Factors Influencing Answers on the Multiphasic K Scale. Doctor's thesis, University of Minnesota (Minneapolis, Minn.), 1947.
84. KALHORN, JOAN. "Personality and Parent Behavior." Abstract. Am Psychol 2:425 O '47. * (PA 22:1109, title only)
85. KRISE, E. MORLEY. "A Short Method of Scoring the Minnesota Multiphasic Personality Inventory." J Clin Psychol 3:386–92 O '47. * (PA 22:4421)
86. MORRIS, WOODROW W. "A Preliminary Evaluation of the Minnesota Multiphasic Personality Inventory." J Clin Psychol 3:370–4 O '47. * (PA 22:4430)
87. PAGE, ROGER B. Application of the Minnesota Multiphasic Personality Inventory to Tuberculosis Patients. Doctor's thesis, University of Minnesota (Minneapolis, Minn.), 1947.
88. SHACTER, HELEN. "Personality Profiles of Psychoneurotics Before and After Treatment." Abstract. Am Psychol 2:420 O '47. * (PA 22:1319, title only)
89. SHERMAN, ARTHUR W., JR. "Personality Factors in the Psychological Weaning of College Women." Abstract. Am Psychol 2:423 O '47. * (PA 22:1369, title only)
90. WALCH, A. E., AND SCHNEIDER, ROBERT A. "The Minnesota Multiphasic Personality Inventory: An Evaluation of Its Use in Private Practice." Minn Med 30:753–8 Jl '47. * (PA 22:1665)
91. WHEELER, ERMA T. A Study of Certain Aspects of Per-

sonality as Related to the Electroencephalogram. Doctor's thesis, University of Pittsburgh (Pittsburgh, Pa.), 1947. (*Abstracts of Doctoral Dissertations...., 1948,* pp. 183–96.)

92. WINBERG, WILMA C. "Some Personality Traits of Collegiate Underachievers." *Proc Iowa Acad Sci* 54:267–70 '47. * (*PA* 23:5759)

93. ALTUS, W. D. "Correlates of Certain M.M.P.I. Scales Found in the Group Rorschach for 100 'Normal' College Students." Abstract. *Am Psychol* 3:349 Ag '48. * (*PA* 23:741, title only)

94. ALTUS, W. D. "Some Correlates of the Group Rorschach and the Schizophrenia Scale of the Group MMPI Among Two Groups of 'Normal' College Students." *J Consult Psychol* 12: 375–8 N–D '48. * (*PA* 23:2225)

95. ALTUS, WILLIAM D. "A College Achiever and Non-Achiever Scale for the Minnesota Multiphasic Personality Inventory." *J Appl Psychol* 32:385–97 Ag '48. * (*PA* 23:1438)

96. APPLEZWEIG, MORTIMER H. "A Statistical Analysis of the Influence of Age, Education, and Intelligence on the Scales of the Minnesota Multiphasic Personality Inventory." Abstract. *J Colo-Wyo Acad Sci* 3:59 Mr '48. *

97. AXTELL, S. B. *Diagnostic Patterns on the Minnesota Multiphasic Personality Inventory.* Master's thesis, University of California (Berkeley, Calif.), 1948.

98. BARNABAS, BENTLEY. "Validity of Personality and Interest Tests in Selection and Placement Situations." *Trans Kans Acad Sci* 51:335–9 S '48. * (*PA* 23:2432)

99. BIER, WILLIAM C. *A Comparative Study of a Seminary Group and Four Other Groups on the Minnesota Multiphasic Personality Inventory.* Washington, D.C.: Catholic University of America Press, 1948. Pp. xi, 107. Paper. * (*PA* 22:5609)

100. BROWER, DANIEL. "The Relations of Visuo-Motor Conflict to Personality Traits and Cardio-Vascular Activity." *J General Psychol* 38:69–99 Ja '48. * (*PA* 22:3383)

101. BROWN, HUGH S. "Similarities and Differences in College Populations on the Multiphasic." *J Appl Psychol* 32:541–9 O '48. * (*PA* 23:2703)

102. BROZEK, JOSEF, AND ERICKSON, NANCY KEELY. "Item Analysis of the Psychoneurotic Scales of the Minnesota Multiphasic Personality Inventory in Experimental Semistarvation." *J Consult Psychol* 12:403–11 N–D '48. * (*PA* 23:2227)

103. BROZEK, JOSEF, AND SCHIELE, BURTRUM C. "Clinical Significance of the Minnesota Multiphasic F Scale Evaluated in Experimental Neurosis." *Am J Psychiatry* 105:259–66 O '48. *

104. CARP, ABRAHAM. *Psychological Test Performance and Insulin Shock Therapy.* Doctor's thesis, Stanford University (Stanford, Calif.), 1948. (*Abstracts of Dissertations....1947–48,* 1948, pp. 180–3.) (*PA* 23:354, title only)

105. CLARK, JERRY H. "Application of the MMPI in Differentiating A.W.O.L. Recidivists From Non-Recidivists." *J Psychol* 26:229–34 Jl '48. * (*PA* 23:1391)

106. CLARK, JERRY H. "Clinical Use of the Altus Thirty-Six Point Adjustment Test in Screening Army A.W.O.L.'s." *J Consult Psychol* 12:276–9 Jl–Ag '48. * (*PA* 23:1286)

107. CLARK, JERRY H. "Some M.M.P.I. Correlates of Certain Color Responses in the Group Rorschach Test." Abstract. *Am Psychol* 3:349 Ag '48. * (*PA* 23:747, title only)

108. CLARK, JERRY H. "Some MMPI Correlates of Color Responses in the Group Rorschach." *J Consult Psychol* 12: 384–6 N–D '48. * (*PA* 23:2228)

109. COTTLE, WILLIAM C. "A Factorial Study of Selected Instruments for Measuring Personality and Interest." Abstract. *Am Psychol* 3:300 Jl '48. * (*PA* 22:5353, title only)

110. DEANE, MAURICE ALLEN. *A Factorial Study of the Minnesota Multiphasic Inventory.* Master's thesis, University of Utah (Salt Lake City, Utah), 1948.

111. DRAKE, L. E., AND THIELE, W. B. "Further Validation of the Social I. E. Scale for the Minnesota Multiphasic Personality Inventory." *J Ed Res* 41:551–6 Mr '48. * (*PA* 22:4609)

112. ELLIS, ALBERT. "The Relationship Between Personality Inventory Scores and Other Psychological Test Results." *J Social Psychol* 28:287–9 N '48. * (*PA* 23:2705)

113. ELLIS, ALBERT, AND CONRAD, HERBERT S. "The Validity of Personality Inventories in Military Practice." *Psychol B* 45:385–426 S '48. * (*PA* 23:1287)

114. FELDMAN, MARVIN J. "A Prognosis Scale for Shock Therapy." Abstract. *Am Psychol* 3:348 Ag '48. * (*PA* 23:788, title only)

115. GOUGH, HARRISON G. "A New Dimension of Status: I, Development of a Personality Scale." *Am Sociol R* 13:401–9 Ag '48. * (*PA* 24:523)

116. GOUGH, HARRISON G. "A New Dimension of Status: II, Relationship of the St Scale to Other Variables." *Am Sociol R* 13:534–7 O '48. * (*PA* 24:524)

117. GOUGH, HARRISON G. "A Note on the Security-Insecurity Test." *J Social Psychol* 28:257–61 N '48. * (*PA* 23:2706)

118. GOUGH, HARRISON G. "Personality Correlates of Socio-Economic Status." Abstract. *Am Pyschol* 3:360 Ag '48. * (*PA* 23:637, title only)

119. HALES, WILLIAM M., AND WERNER, SIMON. "Minnesota Multiphasic Personality Inventory Patterns Before and After Insulin Shock Therapy: A Preliminary Report." *Am J Psychiatry* 105:254–8 O '48. * (*PA* 23:4333)

120. HARRIS, ROBERT E.; BOWMAN, KARL M.; AND SIMON, ALEXANDER. "Studies in Electronarcosis Therapy: III, Psychological Test Findings." *J Nerv & Mental Dis* 107:371–6 Ap '48. * (*PA* 22:4448)

121. HESTON, JOSEPH C. "A Comparison of Four Masculinity-Femininity Scales." *Ed & Psychol Meas* 8:375–87 au '48. * (*PA* 23:4256)

122. HOVEY, H. BIRNET. "Detection of Circumvention in the Minnesota Multiphasic Personality Inventory." *J Clin Psychol* 4:97 Ja '48. * (*PA* 22:5429)

123. HUNT, EDWARD L., AND LEHNER, GEORGE F. J. "Relationships of the Hildreth Feeling and Attitude Scales to the Minnesota Multiphasic Personality Inventory." *J Clin Psychol* 4:412–4 O '48. * (*PA* 23:5521)

124. HUNT, HOWARD F. "The Effect of Deliberate Deception on Minnesota Multiphasic Personality Inventory Performance." *J Consult Psychol* 12:396–402 N–D '48. * (*PA* 23:2232)

125. HUNT, HOWARD F. "The Effect of Deliberate Deception on Minnesota Multiphasic Personality Inventory Profiles." Abstract. *Am Psychol* 3:349–50 Ag '48. * (*PA* 23:756, title only)

126. HUNT, HOWARD F.; CARP, ABRAHAM; CASS, WILLIAM A., JR.; WINDER, C. L.; AND KANTOR, ROBERT E. "A Study of the Differential Diagnostic Efficiency of the Minnesota Multiphasic Personality Inventory." *J Consult Psychol* 12:331–6 S–O '48. * (*PA* 23:1782)

127. JENNINGS, L. SHERMAN. "Minnesota Multiphasic Personality Inventory: Differentiation of Psychologically Good and Poor Combat Status Among Flying Personnel." *J Aviat Med* 19:222–6+ Ag '48. * (*PA* 23:167)

128. JOHNSON, GERALD KENNETH. *Personality Patterns Peculiar to Theological Students.* Master's thesis, University of North Dakota (Grand Forks, N.D.), 1947. Review: *Sch Ed Rec Univ N Dakota* 33:200–3 Ap '48. *

129. McCRORY, ANITA TAYLOR. *The Minnesota Multiphasic Personality Inventory: A Tool for Detecting Personality Problems Among Senior High School Students.* Master's thesis, University of Southern California (Los Angeles, Calif.), 1948.

130. McKINLEY, J. C.; HATHAWAY, S. R.; AND MEEHL, P. E. "The Minnesota Multiphasic Personality Inventory: VI, The K. Scale." *J Consult Psychol* 12:20–31 Ja–F '48. * (*PA* 22: 3035)

131. MORTON, MARY A. "The Army Adaptation of the Minnesota Multiphasic Personality Inventory." Abstract. *Am Psychol* 3:271–2 Jl '48. * (*PA* 22:5432, title only)

132. MULLEN, FRANCES A. "The Minnesota Multiphasic Personality Inventory: An Extension of the Davis Scoring Method." *J Clin Psychol* 4:86–8 Ja '48. * (*PA* 22:5433)

133. OWENS, WILLIAM A., AND JOHNSON, WILMA C. "Some Measured Personality Traits of Collegiate Under-Achievers." Abstract. *Am Psychol* 3:363 Ag '48. * (*PA* 23:934, title only)

134. PORTENIER, LILLIAN. "Personality Tests in a University Guidance Program." Abstract. *J Colo-Wyo Acad Sci* 3:51–2 S '48. *

135. RUBIN, HAROLD. "The Minnesota Multiphasic Personality Inventory as a Diagnostic Aid in a Veterans Hospital." *J Consult Psychol* 12:251–4 Jl–Ag '48. * (*PA* 23:1300)

136. SCHIELE, BURTRUM C., AND BROZEK, JOSEF. "'Experimental Neurosis' Resulting from Semistarvation in Man." *Psychosom Med* 10:31–50 Ja '48. * (*PA* 22:5075)

137. SCHMIDT, HERMANN O. "Notes on the Minnesota Multiphasic Personality Inventory: The K-Factor." *J Consult Psychol* 12:337–42 S–O '48. * (*PA* 23:1785)

138. SCHNECK, JEROME M. "Clinical Evaluation of the F Scale on the Minnesota Multiphasic Personality Inventory." *Am J Psychiatry* 104:440–2 Ja '48. *

139. SCHNECK, JEROME M. "The Double-Spike Pattern of the Minnesota Multiphasic Personality Inventory." *Am J Psychiatry* 104:445–5 Ja '48. *

140. SCHOFIELD, WILLIAM. *Minnesota Multiphasic Personality Inventory Response Changes With Certain Therapies.* Doctor's thesis, University of Minnesota (Minneapolis, Minn.), 1948. (*PA* 23:1012, title only)

141. SNYDER, WILLIAM U., AND SNYDER, BARBARA JUNE. "Implications for Therapy of Personality Changes Resulting From a Course in Mental Hygiene." Abstract. *Am Psychol* 3:286–7 Jl '48. * (*PA* 22:5456, title only)

142. STAUDT, VIRGINIA M. "The Relationship of Certain Personality Traits to Errors and Correct Responses in Several Types of Tasks Among College Women Under Varying Test Conditions." Abstract. *Am Psychol* 3:273–4 Jl '48. * (*PA* 22: 5360, title only)

143. SWEETLAND, ANDERS. "Hypnotic Neuroses: Hypochondriases and Depression." *J General Psychol* 39:91–105 Jl '48. * (*PA* 23:3354)

144. THOMPSON, GRACE. "M.M.P.I. Correlates of Movement Responses in the Rorschach." Abstract. *Am Psychol* 3:348–9 Ag '48. * (*PA* 23:772, title only)

145. THOMPSON, GRACE M. "M.M.P.I. Correlates of Certain Movement Responses in the Group Rorschachs of Two College Samples." *J Consult Psychol* 12:379–83 N–D '48. * (*PA* 23: 2238)

146. WELSH, GEORGE S. "An Extension of Hathaway's MMPI Profile Coding System." *J Consult Psychol* 12:343–4 S–O '48. * (*PA* 23:1780)

147. WIENER, DANIEL N. "Personality Characteristics of Selected Disability Groups." *J Clin Psychol* 4:284–90 Jl '48. * (*PA* 23:299)

148. WIENER, DANIEL N. "Selecting Salesmen With Subtle-Obvious Keys for the Minnesota Multiphasic Personality Inventory." Abstract. *Am Psychol* 3:364 Ag '48. * (*PA* 23:972, title only)

149. WIENER, DANIEL N. "Subtle and Obvious Keys for the

Minnesota Multiphasic Personality Inventory." *J Consult Psychol* 12:164–70 My–Je '48. * (*PA* 22:4966)
150. WIENER, D. N., AND PHILLIPS, E. L. "A Study of Progress in Psychotherapy." *J Clin Psychol* 4:201–6 Ap '48. * (*PA* 23:200)
151. ANDERSEN, A. LLOYD. "Personality Changes Following Prefrontal Lobotomy in a Case of Severe Psychoneurosis." *J Consult Psychol* 13:105–7 Ap '49. * (*PA* 23:4936)
152. BIRKNER, EDWARD C. *The Relationship of Personality Characteristics to the Seeking of Medical Advice.* Master's thesis, Ohio University (Athens, Ohio), 1949. Pp. 65. (*Abstracts of Masters' Theses…, 1948*, pp. 60–1.)
153. BURTON, ARTHUR. "The Use of Psychometric and Projective Tests in Clinical Psychology." *J Psychol* 28:451–6 O '49. * (*PA* 24:2595)
154. CHYATTE, CONRAD. "Personality Traits of Professional Actors." *Occupations* 27:245–50 Ja '49. * (*PA* 23:3483)
155. CLARK, JERRY H. "The Adjustment of Army AWOL'S." *J Abn & Social Psychol* 44:394–401 Jl '49. * (*PA* 24:1321)
156. COFER, C. N.; CHANCE, JUNE; AND JUDSON, A. J. "A Study of Malingering on the Minnesota Multiphasic Personality Inventory." *J Psychol* 27:491–9 Ap '49. * (*PA* 23:4252)
157. COFER, CHARLES N.; JUDSON, A. J.; AND WEICK, D. V. "On the Significance of the Psychogalvanic Response as an Indicator of Reaction to Personality Test Items." *J Psychol* 27:347–54 Ap '49. * (*PA* 23:4253)
158. COHEN, DAVID. *Psychological Concomitants of Chronic Illness: A Study of Emotional Correlates of Pulmonary Tuberculosis, Peptic Ulcer, the Arthritides, and Cardiac Disease.* Doctor's thesis, University of Pittsburgh (Pittsburgh, Pa.), 1949. (*Abstracts of Doctoral Dissertations….1949*, 1950, pp. 277–90.)
159. CORSINI, RAYMOND J. "A Time and Motion Study of Hand Scoring the Individual Minnesota Multiphasic Personality Inventory." *J Consult Psychol* 13:62–3 F '49. * (*PA* 23:3747)
160. COTTLE, WILLIAM C. *A Factorial Study of the Multiphasic, Strong, Kuder and Bell Inventories Using a Population of Adult Males.* Doctor's thesis, Syracuse University (Syracuse, N.Y.), 1949.
161. COTTLE, WILLIAM C. "Relationships Among Selected Personality and Interest Inventories." Abstract. *Am Psychol* 4:292–3 Jl '49. * (*PA* 23:6206, title only)
162. COTTLE, WM. C., AND POWELL, JACKSON O. "Relationship of Mean Scores on the Strong, Kuder and Bell Inventories With the MMPI M-F Scale as the Criterion." *Trans Kans Acad Sci* 52:396–8 '49. * (*PA* 24:2599)
163. DANIELS, E. E., AND HUNTER, W. A. "MMPI Personality Patterns for Various Occupations." *J Appl Psychol* 33:559–65 D '49. * (*PA* 24:4153)
164. FEIL, MADELEINE HOFFMAN. *A Study of Leadership and Scholastic Achievement in Their Relation to Prediction Factors.* Doctor's thesis, Ohio State University (Columbus, Ohio), 1949. (*Abstracts of Dissertations….Summer Quarter 1948–49*, 1950, pp. 151–5.) (*PA* 24:6522, title only)
165. FRY, FRANKLYN D. "A Study of the Personality Traits of College Students, and of State Prison Inmates as Measured by the Minnesota Multiphasic Personality Inventory." *J Psychol* 28:439–49 O '49. * (*PA* 24:2565)
166. GLENN, ROBERT. *A Study of Personality Patterns of Male Defective Delinquents as Indicated by the Minnesota Multiphasic Personality Inventory.* Master's thesis, Pennsylvania State College (State College, Pa.), 1949. (*PA* 24:5546, title only)
167. GORDON, THOMAS. "The Airline Pilot's Job." *J Appl Psychol* 33:122–31 Ap '49. * (*PA* 24:331)
168. GOUGH, HARRISON G. "Factors Relating to the Academic Achievement of High-School Students." *J Ed Psychol* 40:65–78 F '49. * (*PA* 24:2058)
169. GOUGH, HARRISON G. "A Research Note on the MMPI Social I.E. Scale." *J Ed Psychol* 43:138–41 O '49. * (*PA* 24:2807)
170. HANVIK, LEO J. *Some Psychological Dimensions of Low Back Pain.* Doctor's thesis, University of Minnesota (Minneapolis, Minn.), 1949.
171. HOLZBERG, JULES D., AND ALESSI, SALVATORE. "Reliability of the Shortened Minnesota Multiphasic Personality Inventory." *J Consult Psychol* 13:288–92 Ag '49. * (*PA* 24:1200)
172. HOVEY, H. BIRNET. "Somatization and Other Neurotic Reactions and MMPI Profiles." *J Clin Psychol* 5:153–7 Ap '49. * (*PA* 24:1888)
173. KAHN, HARRIS, AND SINGER, ERWIN. "An Investigation of Some of the Factors Related to Success or Failure of School of Commerce Students." *J Ed Psychol* 40:107–17 F '49. * (*PA* 24:2062)
174. KIRKWOOD, JAMES W. *Incidence, Contributory Etiological Factors, and Use of the Minnesota Multiphasic Personality Inventory as a Prognostic and Diagnostic Instrument of Psychopathological Conditions Among Public School Teachers in California.* Doctor's thesis, University of California (Los Angeles, Calif.), 1949.
175. KRISE, E. MORLEY. "A Common Error in Scoring the Minnesota Multiphasic Personality Inventory." *J Clin Psychol* 5:180–1 Ap '49. * (*PA* 24:1889)
176. LEHMAN, CHARLES F., JR. *A Comparative Study of Instrumental Musicians on the Basis of the Kwalwasser Dykema Music Tests, the Otis I.Q. Intelligence Test and the Minnesota Multiphasic Personality Inventory.* Doctor's thesis, Syracuse University (Syracuse, N.Y.), 1949.
177. LITTLE, JAMES WILLIAM. *An Analysis of the Minnesota*

Multiphasic Personality Inventory. Master's thesis, University of North Carolina (Chapel Hill, N.C.), 1949. (*Research in Progress, January, 1949–December, 1949*, 1950, p. 186.) (*PA* 25:5343, title only)
178. MANSON, MORSE P. "A Psychometric Analysis of Psychopathic Characteristics of Alcoholics." *J Consult Psychol* 13:111–8 Ap '49. * (*PA* 23:4893)
179. MOCHEL, MARGUERITE. *The Minnesota Multiphasic Personality Inventory as a Factor in the Selection and Guidance of Physical Education Major Students.* Doctor's thesis, University of Southern California (Los Angeles, Calif.), 1949. (*Abstracts of Dissertations….1949*, 1950, pp. 49–51.)
180. NANCE, R. D. "Masculinity-Femininity in Prospective Teachers." *J Ed Res* 42:658–66 My '49. * (*PA* 24:320)
181. OWENS, WILLIAM A., AND JOHNSON, WILMA C. "Some Measured Personality Traits of Collegiate Underachievers." *J Ed Psychol* 40:41–6 Ja '49. * (*PA* 23:5014)
182. ROSENZWEIG, SAUL; WITH THE COLLABORATION OF KATE LEVINE KOGAN. *Psychodiagnosis: An Introduction to Tests in the Clinical Practice of Psychodynamics*, pp. 96–103, 203–5. New York: Grune & Stratton, Inc., 1949. Pp. xii, 380. * (*PA* 23:3761)
183. SCHMID, JOHN, JR. *Factor Analyses of Prospective Teachers' Differences.* Doctor's thesis, University of Wisconsin (Madison, Wis.), 1949. (*Summaries of Doctoral Dissertations ….July 1949 to June 1950*, 1951, pp. 337–9.)
184. SIMON, WERNER, AND HALES, WILLIAM M. "Note on a Suicide Key in the Minnesota Multiphasic Personality Inventory." *Am J Psychiatry* 106:222–3 S '49. * (*PA* 24:3274)
185. STAUDT, VIRGINIA M. "The Relationship of Certain Personality Traits to Errors and Correct Responses in Several Types of Tasks Among College Women Under Varying Test Conditions." *J Psychol* 27:465–78 Ap '49. * (*PA* 23:4109)
186. STOUT, MARJORY. *An Analysis of the Structure of the Minnesota Multiphasic Personality Inventory.* Master's thesis, Pennsylvania State College (State College, Pa.), 1949. (*PA* 24:5568, title only)
187. SUPER, DONALD E. *Appraising Vocational Fitness By Means of Psychological Tests*, pp. 499–510. New York: Harper & Brothers, 1949. Pp. xxiii, 727. * (*PA* 24:2130)
188. VARVA, FRANK. *A Study of Deception on the Minnesota Multiphasic Personality Inventory.* Master's thesis, Pennsylvania State College (State College, Pa.), 1949. (*PA* 24:5572, title only)
189. AARONSON, BERNARD S., AND WELSH, GEORGE S. "The MMPI as Diagnostic Differentiator: A Reply to Rubin." *J Consult Psychol* 14:324–6 Ag '50. * (*PA* 25:2444)
190. ABRAMS, ELIAS NELSON. *A Comparative Factor Analytic Study of Normal and Neurotic Veterans: A Statistical Investigation of the Interrelationships of Intellectual and Emotional Factors as Disclosed in the Primary Mental Abilities Examination and the Minnesota Multiphasic Personality Inventory.* Doctor's thesis, New York University (New York, N.Y.), 1950. Abstract: *Microfilm Abstracts* 10:94–5 no 3 '50. * (*PA* 25:4555, title only)
191. ANDERSEN, A. LLOYD, AND HANVIK, LEO J. "The Psychometric Localization of Brain Lesions: The Differential Effect of Front and Parietal Lesions on MMPI Profiles." *J Clin Psychol* 6:177–80 Ap '50. * (*PA* 24:6475)
192. BARRETT, ALBERT M. *Personality Characteristics Under the Stress of High Intensity Sound.* Doctor's thesis, Pennsylvania State College (State College, Pa.), 1950. (*Abstracts of Doctoral Dissertations….1950*, 1951, pp. 388–91.) (*PA* 26:2029, title only)
193. BLAIR, W. R. N. "A Comparative Study of Disciplinary Offenders and Non-Offenders in the Canadian Army, 1948." *Can J Psychol* 4:49–62 Je '50. * (*PA* 24:6428)
194. BLAKE, ROBERT R., AND WILSON, GLEN P., JR. "Perceptual Selectivity in Rorschach Determinants as a Function of Depressive Tendencies." *J Abn & Social Psychol* 45:459–72 Jl '50. * (*PA* 25:142)
195. BRADFIELD, ANNE FREDERIKSEN. *Predicting the Success in Training of Graduate Students in School Administration.* Doctor's thesis, Stanford University (Stanford, Calif.), 1950. (*Abstracts of Dissertations….1949–50*, 1950, pp. 294–7.)
196. BRODY, DAVID S. "A Genetic Study of Sociality Patterns of College Women." *Ed & Psychol Meas* 10:513–20 au '50. * (*PA* 25:6418)
197. BROTHERS, WILBUR LEO. *The Relationship of Certain Factors to Effectiveness in Student Teaching in the Secondary Schools.* Doctor's thesis, Indiana University (Bloomington, Ind.), 1950. (*Thesis Abstract Series….1950*, 1951, pp. 12–8.)
198. BROWN, M. A. "Alcoholic Profiles on the Minnesota Multiphasic." *J Clin Psychol* 6:266–9 Jl '50. * (*PA* 25:1894)
199. BROWN, MANUEL N. "Evaluating and Scoring the Minnesota Multiphasic 'Cannot Say' Items." *J Clin Psychol* 6:180–4 Ap '50. * (*PA* 24:6348)
200. CALIGOR, LEOPOLD. *The Determination of the Individual's Unconscious Conception of His Own Masculinity-Femininity Identification.* Doctor's thesis, New York University (New York, N.Y.), 1950. Abstract: *Microfilm Abstracts* 10:292–3 no 4 '50. * (*PA* 25:4418, title only)
201. CANNING, WILLIAM; HARLOW, GEORGE; AND REGELIN, CLINTON. "A Study of Two Personality Questionnaires." *J Consult Psychol* 14:414–5 O '50. * (*PA* 25:4561)
202. CARP, ABRAHAM. "MMPI Performance and Insulin Shock Therapy." *J Abn & Social Psychol* 45:721–6 O '50. * (*PA* 25:2594)

203. CAUFFIEL, PAUL WENDELL. *A Comparison of the P-S Experience Blank With the Minnesota Multiphasic Personality Inventory.* Master's thesis, Pennsylvania State College (State College, Pa.), 1950. *(PA 24:5540, title only)*

204. COOK, ELLSWORTH B., AND WHERRY, ROBERT J. "A Factor Analysis of MMPI and Aptitude Test Data." *J Appl Psychol* 34:260–6 Ag '50. * *(PA 25:6208)*

205. COTTLE, WM. C. "A Factorial Study of the Multiphasic, Strong, Kuder, and Bell Inventories Using a Population of Adult Males." *Psychometrika* 15:25–47 Mr '50. * *(PA 24:4492)*

206. COTTLE, WM. C. "Card Versus Booklet Forms of the MMPI." *J Appl Psychol* 34:255–9 Ag '50. * *(PA 25:6209)*

207. COTTLE, WILLIAM C. "Relationships Among Selected Personality and Interest Inventories." *Occupations* 28:306–10 F '50. * *(PA 24:4113)*

208. ELKIN, ALBERT. *Personality as a Variable in Serial Verbal Learning.* Doctor's thesis, Northwestern University (Evanston, Ill.), 1950. *(Summaries of Doctoral Dissertations ....June–September 1950, 1951, pp. 596–8.)*

209. FARBEROW, NORMAN L. "Personality Patterns of Suicidal Mental Hospital Patients." *Genetic Psychol Monogr* 42: 3–79 Ag '50. * *(PA 25:4722)*

210. FEATHER, DON B. "The Relation of Personality Maladjustments of 503 University of Michigan Students to Their Occupational Interests." *J Social Psychol* 32:71–8 Ag '50. * *(PA 25:3796)*

211. FRANCEY, RUTH. "A Study on the 'Epileptic Personality.'" *Can J Psychol* 4:81–7 Je '50. * *(PA 24:6476)*

212. GOUGH, HARRISON G. "The F Minus 'K Dissimulation Index for the Minnesota Multiphasic Personality Inventory." *J Consult Psychol* 14:408–13 O '50. * *(PA 25:4569)*

213. GUTHRIE, GEORGE M. "Six M.M.P.I. Diagnostic Profile Patterns." *J Psychol* 30:317–23 O '50. * *(PA 25:3164)*

214. HANVIK, LEO J. "Some Comparisons and Correlations Between MMPI and Rosenzweig P-F Study Scores in a Neuropsychiatric Hospital Sample." Abstract. *J Colo-Wyo Acad Sci* 4:70 O '50. * *(PA 25:5339, title only)*

215. HAWKES, GLENN R. "Use of the Minnesota Multiphasic Personality Inventory in Screening College Students for Counseling Purposes." *J Ed Psychol* 41:116–21 F '50. * *(PA 24:4607)*

216. JAMES, RICHARD WARREN. *Selection of Graduate Students: (1) The Adequacy of Certain Measures for Differentiating Between Two Groups of Master Candidates (2) The Value of These Measures in Prognosing Graduate Academic Achievement.* Doctor's thesis, New York University (New York, N.Y.), 1950. Abstract: *Microfilm Abstracts* 11:53–4 no 1 '51. * *(PA 26:2428, title only)*

217. KAUFMANN, PETER. "Changes in the Minnesota Multiphasic Personality Inventory as a Function of Psychiatric Therapy." *J Consult Psychol* 14:458–64 D '50. * *(PA 26:950)*

218. LEHMAN, CHARLES F. "A Comparative Study of Instrumental Musicians on the Basis of the Otis Intelligence Test, the Kwalwasser-Dykema Music Test, and the Minnesota Multiphasic Personality Inventory." *J Ed Res* 44:57–61 S '50. * *(PA 25:2927)*

219. LEHNER, GEORGE F. J.; WHEELER, WILLIAM MARSHALL; AND LITTLE, KENNETH B. "A Factor Analysis of the MMPI." Abstract. *Am Psychol* 5:471 S '50. * *(PA 25:4577, title only)*

220. LEVINSON, MARIA HERTZ. "Ethnocentrism in Relation to the Minnesota Multiphasic Personality Inventory," pp. 910–7. In *The Authoritarian Personality.* By T. W. Adorno, Else Frenkel-Brunswik, Daniel J. Levinson, and R. Nevitt Sanford in collaboration with Betty Aron, Maria Hertz Levinson, and William Morrow. New York: Harper & Brothers, 1950. Pp. xxxiii, 990. * *(PA 24:5796)*

221. LOUGH, ORPHA M., AND GREEN, MARY E. "Comparison of the Minnesota Multiphasic Personality Inventory and the Washburne S-A Inventory as Measures of Personality of College Women." *J Social Psychol* 32:23–30 Ag '50. * *(PA 25:3812)*

222. MEEHL, PAUL E. "Configural Scoring." *J Consult Psychol* 14:165–71 Je '50. * *(PA 25:366)*

223. MONACHESI, ELIO D. "Personality Characteristics of Institutionalized and Non-Institutionalized Male Delinquents." *J Crim Law & Criminology* 41:167–79 Jl–Ag '50. * *(PA 25:3892)*

224. MONACHESI, ELIO D. "Personality Characteristics and Socio-Economic Status of Delinquents and Non-Delinquents." *J Crim Law & Criminology* 40:570–83 Ja–F '50. *

225. NAFFZIGER, JOSEPH VALENTINE. *A Study of the Personality Characteristics of Juniors in a Teacher Education Program as Revealed by the Minnesota Multiphasic Personality Inventory.* Master's thesis, Illinois State Normal University (Normal, Ill.), 1950. *(PA 25:4087, title only)*

226. PATTEN, JACK. *Personality Patterns and Written Expression.* Doctor's thesis, Stanford University (Stanford, Calif.), 1950.

227. PEARSON, JOHN S. "Prediction of the Response of Schizophrenic Patients to Electro-Convulsive Therapy." *J Clin Psychol* 6:285–7 Jl '50. * *(PA 25:1954)*

228. POTTER, C. STANLEY. Chap. 10, "A Method for Using the Minnesota Multiphasic Personality Inventory With the Blind," pp. 130–6. *(PA 26:503)* In *Psychological Diagnosis and Counseling of the Adult Blind: Selected Papers From the Proceedings of the University of Michigan, Conference for the Blind, 1947.* Edited by Wilma Donahue and Donald Dabelstein.

New York: American Foundation for the Blind, Inc., 1950. Pp. vii, 173. *

229. RENAUD, HAROLD R. *Clinical Correlates of the Masculinity-Femininity Scale of the Minnesota Multiphasic Personality Inventory.* Doctor's thesis, University of California (Berkeley, Calif.), 1950.

230. ROSEN, E. *Some Personality and Attitude Differences Between Volunteers and Non-Volunteers for a Psychological Experiment.* Doctor's thesis, University of California (Berkeley, Calif.), 1950. *(PA 25:4097, title only)*

231. RUBIN, HAROLD. "A Note on 'Reply to Rubin.'" *J Consult Psychol* 14:327–8 Ag '50. * *(PA 25:2467)*

232. SANDERS, MERRITT WILLIAM. *The Prediction of Academic Success Among University Freshmen in a School of Education.* Doctor's thesis, New York University (New York, N.Y.), 1950. Abstract: *Microfilm Abstracts* 11:63–4 no 1 '51. * *(PA 26:2430, title only)*

233. SCHMID, JOHN, JR. "Factor Analyses of Prospective Teachers' Differences." *J Exp Ed* 18:287–319 Je '50. * *(PA 25:2060)*

234. SCHOFIELD, WILLIAM. *Changes in Responses to the Minnesota Multiphasic Inventory Following Certain Therapies.* American Psychological Association, Psychological Monographs: General and Applied, Vol. 64, No. 5, Whole No. 311. Washington, D.C.: the Association, Inc., 1950. Pp. v, 33. Paper. *(PA 25:3223)*

235. SPIAGGIA, MARTIN. "An Investigation of the Personality Traits of Art Students." *Ed & Psychol Meas* 10:285–93 su '50. * *(PA 25:6429)*

236. THORN, KATHERINE F. *A Study of the Personality of Stutterers as Measured by the Minnesota Multiphasic Personality Inventory.* Doctor's thesis, University of Minnesota (Minneapolis, Minn.), 1950.

237. WAUCK, LE ROY A. "Schizophrenia and the MMPI." *J Clin Psychol* 6:279–82 Jl '50. * *(PA 25:1959)*

238. WHEELER, WILLIAM MARSHALL. "The Internal Structure of Three Clinical Instruments." Abstract. *Am Psychol* 5:470 S '50. * *(PA 25:4599, title only)*

239. WIENER, DANIEL N., AND SIMON, WERNER. "Personality Characteristics of Embalmer Trainees." *J Appl Psychol* 34: 391–3 D '50. * *(PA 25:4649)*

240. WINNE, JOHN FREY. *The Factorial Composition of Normal and Neurotic Responses to an Adaptation of "The Minnesota Multiphasic Personality Inventory."* Doctor's thesis, University of Pennsylvania (Philadelphia, Pa.), 1950. Abstract: *Microfilm Abstracts* 10:311–3 no 4 '50. * *(PA 25:4601, title only)*

241. ARONSON, MARVIN LUCIUS. *A Study of the Freudian Theory of Paranoia by Means of a Group of Psychological Tests.* Doctor's thesis, University of Michigan (Ann Arbor, Mich.), 1951. Abstract: *Microfilm Abstracts* 11:443–4 no 2 '51. *(PA 26:2316, title only)*

242. BARRON, EMERSON M., AND DONOHUE, H. H. "Psychiatric Aide Selection Through Psychological Examinations: A Preliminary Report of the Screening of Applicants at the Arkansas State Hospital." *Am J Psychiatry* 107:859–65 My '51. *

243. BENARICK, STANLEY J.; GUTHRIE, GEORGE M.; AND SNYDER, WILLIAM U. "An Interpretive Aid for the *Sc* Scale of the MMPI." *J Consult Psychol* 15:142–4 Ap '51. * *(PA 26:6250)*

244. BLANTON, RICHARD, AND LANDSMAN, THEODORE. "An Examination of the Retest Reliability of the 'Group' Rorschach and Some Relationships to the MMPI." Abstract. *Am Psychol* 6:379 Jl '51. *

245. BROZEK, JOSEF, AND KEYS, ANCEL. "Personality Changes With Age: An Item Analysis of the Minnesota Multiphasic Personality Inventory." Abstract. *Am Psychol* 6:397 Jl '51. *

246. CALIGOR, LEOPOLD. "The Determination of the Individual's Unconscious Conception of His Own Masculinity-Femininity Identification." *J Proj Tech* 15:494–509 D '51. * *(PA 26:6228)*

247. CANTER, AARON H. "MMPI Profiles in Multiple Sclerosis." *J Consult Psychol* 15:253–6 Je '51. * *(PA 26:6480)*

248. CAUFFIEL, PAUL W., AND SNYDER, WILLIAM U. "A Comparison of the Performance of a Randomly Selected College Population on the MMPI and the P-S Experience Blank." *J Clin Psychol* 7:267–70 Jl '51. * *(PA 26:908)*

249. CLARK, GEORGE C., AND ALLEN, ROBERT M. "Item Analysis Aid for the Minnesota Multiphasic Personality Inventory." *J Consult Psychol* 15:262 Je '51. * *(PA 26:6256)*

250. COTTLE, WILLIAM C., AND POWELL, JACKSON O. "The Effect of Random Answers to the MMPI." *Ed & Psychol Meas* 11:224–7 su '51. * *(PA 26:2744)*

251. DOBSON, W. R., AND STONE, D. R. "College Freshman Responses on the Minnesota Multiphasic Personality Inventory." *J Ed Res* 44:611–8 Ap '51. *

252. GILLILAND, A. R. "The Humm-Wadsworth and the Minnesota Multiphasic." *J Consult Psychol* 15:457–9 D '51. * *(PA 26:6998)*

253. GILLILAND, A. R., AND COLGIN, RUSSELL. "Norms, Reliability, and Forms of the MMPI." *J Consult Psychol* 15:435–8 O '51. * *(PA 26:6999)*

254. GLASER, ROBERT. "Predicting Achievement in Medical School." *J Appl Psychol* 35:272–4 Ag '51. * *(PA 26:3046)*

255. GLASER, ROBERT. "The Validity of Some Tests for Predicting Achievement in Medical School." Abstract. *Am Psychol* 6:298 Jl '51. *

256. Gough, Harrison G. "Studies of Social Intolerance: II, A Personality Scale for Anti-Semitism." *J Social Psychol* 33: 247–55 My '51. * (*PA* 26:6194)

257. Gough, Harrison G. "Studies of Social Intolerance: III, Relationship of the *Pr* Scale to Other Variables." *J Social Psychol* 33:257–62 My '51. * (*PA* 26:6195)

258. Gough, Harrison G. "Studies of Social Intolerance: IV, Related Social Attitudes." *J Social Psychol* 33:263–9 My '51. * (*PA* 26:6196)

259. Gough, Harrison G.; McClosky, Herbert; and Meehl, Paul E. "A Personality Scale for Dominance." *J Abn & Social Psychol* 46:360–6 Jl '51. * (*PA* 26:2181)

260. Grayson, Harry. Chap. 21, "The Minnesota Multiphasic Personality Inventory," pp. 220–1. In *Thematic Test Analysis.* By Edwin S. Shneidman with the collaboration of Walther Joel and Kenneth B. Little. Foreword by Henry A. Murray. New York: Grune & Stratton, Inc., 1951. Pp. xi, 320. *

261. Hampton, Peter J. "Differences in Personality Traits Between Alcoholic and Nonalcoholic Subjects." Abstract. *Am Psychol* 6:313 Jl '51. *

262. Hanvik, Leo J. "MMPI Profiles in Patients With Low-Back Pain." *J Consult Psychol* 15:350–3 Ag '51. * (*PA* 26:6472)

263. Hathaway, Starke R., and Meehl, Paul E. *An Atlas for the Clinical Use of the MMPI.* Minneapolis, Minn.: University of Minnesota Press, 1951. Pp. xliv, 799. * (London: Oxford University Press.) (*PA* 25:7468)

264. Hathaway, Starke R., and Meehl, Paul E. Sect 9, "The Minnesota Personality Inventory," pp. 71–111. In *Military Clinical Psychology.* Department of the Army Technical Manual TM 8:242; Department of the Air Force Manual AFM 160–45. Washington, D.C.: U.S. Government Printing Office, 1951. Pp. iv, 197. Paper. *

265. Hathaway, Starke R., and Monachesi, Elio D. "The Prediction of Juvenile Delinquency Using the Minnesota Multiphasic Personality Inventory." *Am J Psychiatry* 108:469–73 D '51. * (*PA* 26:4130)

266. Holzberg, Jules D.; Cahen, Eleanor R.; and Wilk, Edward K. "Suicide: A Psychological Study of Self-Destruction." *J Proj Tech* 15:339–54 S '51. *

267. Kelly, E. Lowell, and Fiske, Donald W. *The Prediction of Performance in Clinical Psychology.* Ann Arbor, Mich.: University of Michigan, 1951. Pp. xv, 311. Lithotyped. *

268. Levine, Solomon. *The Relationship Between Personality and Efficiency in Various Hospital Occupations.* Doctor's thesis, New York University (New York, N.Y.), 1951. Abstract: *Microfilm Abstracts* 11:741–2 no 3 '51. (*PA* 26:1736, title only)

269. Lough, Orpha Maust. "Correction for 'Women Students in Liberal Arts, Nursing, and Teacher Training Curricula and the MMPI.'" *J Appl Psychol* 35:125–6 Ap '51. * (*PA* 25:8283)

270. McClelland, William A. "A Preliminary Test of Role-Playing Ability." *J Consult Psychol* 15:102–8 Ap '51. * (*PA* 26:6277)

271. Michaelis, John U., and Tyler, Fred T. "MMPI and Student Teaching." *J Appl Psychol* 35:122–4 Ap '51. * (*PA* 25:8288)

272. Patten, Jack. "Personality Patterns and Written Expression." *Calif J Ed Res* 2:119–23 My '51. *

273. Pearson, John S., and Swenson, Wendell M. "A Note on Extended Findings With the MMPI in Predicting Response to Electro-Convulsive Therapy." *J Clin Psychol* 7:288 Jl '51. * (*PA* 26:928)

274. Rosen, Ephraim. "Differences Between Volunteers and Non-Volunteers for Psychological Studies." *J Appl Psychol* 35: 185–93 Je '51. * (*PA* 26:625)

275. Shepler, Bernard F. "A Comparison of Masculinity-Femininity Measures." *J Consult Psychol* 15:484–6 D '51. * (*PA* 26:7011)

276. Smykal, Anthony, and Thorne, Frederick C. "Etiological Studies of Psychopathic Personality: II, Asocial Type." Case Study. *J Clin Psychol* 7:299–316 O '51. * (*PA* 26:3532)

277. Tyler, Fred T. "A Factorial Analysis of Fifteen MMPI Scales." *J Consult Psychol* 15:541–6 D '51. * (*PA* 26:7015)

278. Vidor, Martha. "Personality Changes Following Prefrontal Leucotomy as Reflected by the Minnesota Multiphasic Personality Inventory and the Results of Psychometric Testing." *J Mental Sci* 97:159–73 Ja '51. * (*PA* 25:6390)

279. Weisgerber, Charles A. "The Predictive Value of the Minnesota Multiphasic Personality Inventory With Student Nurses." *J Social Psychol* 33:3–11 F '51. * (*PA* 26:1162)

280. Welsh, George S. "Some Practical Uses of MMPI Profile Coding." *J Consult Psychol* 15:82–4 F '51. * (*PA* 26: 6304)

281. Wheeler, William Marshall; Little, Kenneth B.; and Lehner, George F. J. "The Internal Structure of the MMPI." *J Consult Psychol* 15:134–41 Ap '51. * (*PA* 26:6307)

282. Wiener, Daniel N. "A Control Factor in Social Adjustment." *J Abn & Social Psychol* 46:3–8 Ja '51. * (*PA* 25: 7589)

283. Winne, John F. "A Scale of Neuroticism: An Adaptation of the Minnesota Multiphasic Personality Inventory." *J Clin Psychol* 7:117–22 Ap '51. * (*PA* 25:8117)

Arthur L. Benton, *Professor of Psychology, State University of Iowa, Iowa City, Iowa.*

The major development in recent years with respect to this instrument has been the introduction of the *K* score (*130*). This score is not intended to be a "clinical" index although it appears that it may have interesting clinical correlates. Rather it is a validating device designed to assess "test-taking attitude" along a "defensiveness-frankness" continuum, the extremes of the continuum being frank simulation at the one end and deliberate dissimulation at the other. The clinical application of the *K* score consists in its use as a correction to some of the Inventory scale scores (Hs, Pd, Pt, Sc, Ma) with the aim of augmenting the discriminative value of these scales and of the Inventory in general. Attempts to verify this purported usefulness of the *K* score have yielded generally negative results (*124, 125, 126*). However, there is evidence suggesting that an index involving both the *F* and *K* scores possesses some merit in detecting simulation of mental abnormality (*124, 212*). This lead should be followed up in view of both the practical need for instruments designed to disclose malingering in clinical and military settings and the theoretical importance of an understanding of malingering as a personality reaction.

The Inventory continues to enjoy extensive and interesting investigation of its psychological implications by the Minnesota group, with the new Hathaway-Meehl *Atlas* (*263*) being the most significant single product. There is an obvious tendency in this recent investigative work to get away from the simple empirical validation against clinical diagnoses based upon official psychiatric nosology which was demanded by the names of the scales and the initial claims made for their efficacy in classifying patients. In the new *Atlas,* for example, the scales are referred to by number rather than by name (a practice which its users are advised to follow) and the comment that "it would probably have been better to have used numbers....from the first" is made.

As reviews of the Inventory in *The Third Mental Measurements Yearbook* indicated, these scale scores (or combinations of them in "profile" form) demonstrated little utility in differential diagnosis. A more recent validation study (*126*), employing more "sophisticated" criteria, has yielded similarly negative results. In this respect, the statement in the new manual that "a high score on a scale has been found to predict positively the corresponding final clinical diagnosis or estimate in more than 60 per cent of new psychiatric admissions," while no doubt factually true in the sense that a majority of patients in the various nosologic categories will show high scores in the corresponding scales (and in many a noncorresponding scale), is, in the reviewer's opinion, definitely misleading in its implication that a true differential prediction can be attained in this manner.

Much exploratory work on the application of the Inventory to a variety of psychosomatic, neurological and psychosocial problems has been done in recent years. Whether the results of this work will survive cross-validation is still largely an open question but the initial findings have been in some instances most provocative.

For reviews by Arthur L. Benton, H. J. Eysenck, L. S. Penrose, and Julian B. Rotter and an excerpt from a review, see 3:60; for related reviews, see 72.

[72]

★[*Re* Minnesota Multiphasic Personality Inventory, Revised Edition.] HATHAWAY, STARKE R., AND MEEHL, PAUL E. **An Atlas for the Clinical Use of the MMPI.** Minneapolis, Minn.: University of Minnesota Press, 1951. Pp. xliv, 799. $9.75. * (London: Oxford University Press. 78s.) (*PA* 25:7468)

J Clin Psychol 7:387 O '51. * Students and clinical psychologists will find this a valuable source book for use with the MMPI.

J Consult Psychol 15:355 Ag '51. *Laurance F. Shaffer.* The *Atlas* is a most unusual volume, consisting of 968 short histories of a wide variety of psychiatric cases, arranged by their coded profiles on the Minnesota Multiphasic Personality Inventory. Each case summary is mainly factual, describing the patient as he entered the hospital, his pertinent history, and how he appeared to the therapist or hospital staff. There is a minimum of dynamic interpretation. The cases were taken without reference to MMPI profiles, except for a few selected in the last stages of the preparation of the volume to provide examples of rare patterns. Although the authors, quite wisely, make no claim that the case studies validate the MMPI, reading the cases does suggest that the profiles group them according to their main behavioral trends. The aim of the *Atlas* is to provide supplementary clinical training for users of the Inventory. It assumes that the reader already has some knowledge of the MMPI and of the research underlying its construction. The *Atlas* makes readily available a wider variety of case pictures than

most workers would meet in their clinical experience. The volume has shortcomings that the authors recognize, including the brevity of the case citations and their limited source, mostly from one hospital. As a new experiment in clinical training, however, the *Atlas* will be of wide interest.

[73]

*Mooney Problem Check List: 1950 Revision. Grades 7-9, 9-12, 13-16, adults; 1941-50: earlier edition published by Ohio State University Press; 4 levels; no norms—authors recommend the use of local norms; manual ('50); $1.65 per 25 of any one level; 35¢ per specimen set of any one level; postpaid; Ross L. Mooney and Leonard V. Gordon (College and Adult Forms); Psychological Corporation. *
a) JUNIOR HIGH SCHOOL FORM. Grades 7-9; 1942-50; 7 scores: health and physical development, school, home and family, money-work-the future, boy and girl relations, relations to people in general, self-centered concerns; Form J ('50); (35-50) minutes.
b) HIGH SCHOOL FORM. Grades 9-12; 1941-50; 11 scores: health and physical development, finances-living conditions-employment, social and recreational activities, social-psychological relations, personal-psychological relations, courtship-sex-marriage, home and family, morals and religion, adjustment to school work, the future-vocational and educational, curriculum and teaching procedures; Form H ('50); nontimed (35-50) minutes.
c) COLLEGE FORM. Grades 13-16; 1941-50; 11 scores: same as for High School Form; Form C ('50); nontimed (35-50) minutes.
d) ADULT FORM. Adults; 1950; 9 scores: health, economic security, self-improvement, personality, home and family, courtship, sex, religion, occupation; Form A ('50); nontimed (20-30) minutes.

REFERENCES

1-17. See 3:67.
18. KUHLEN, RAYMOND G., AND BRETSCH, HOWARD S. "Sociometric Status and Personal Problems of Adolescents." *Sociometry* 10:122-32 My '47. * (*PA* 23:659)
19. PFLIEGER, ELMER F. "Pupil Adjustment Problems and a Study of Relationships Between Scores on the California Test of Personality and the Mooney Problem Check List." *J Ed Res* 41:265-78 D '47. * (*PA* 22:2746)
20. KOHR, MILDRED CHAPIN. "Personal Problems of College Students." *J Home Econ* 40:447-8 O '48. * (*PA* 23:2909)
21. STONE, L. GORDON. "Student Problems in a Teachers College." *J Ed Psychol* 39:404-16 N '48. * (*PA* 23:2911)
22. GORDON, LEONARD V. "The Evaluation of Personality by Population Judgments." *J Social Psychol* 30:305-9 N '49. * (*PA* 24:4115)
23. GORDON, LEONARD V. "The Reflection of Problem Changes by the Mooney Problem Check List." *Ed & Psychol Meas* 9:749-52 w '49. * (*PA* 26:4748)
24. GORDON, LEONARD V., AND MOONEY, ROSS L. "A Note on the Organization of the Mooney Problem Check List." *Ed Res B* 28:212-4 N 9 '49. *
25. HORRALL, BERNICE MOODY. "Relationships Between College Aptitude and Discouragement-Buoyancy Among College Freshmen." *J Genetic Psychol* 74:185-243 Je '49. * (*PA* 24:2090-1)
26. SCHMID, JOHN, JR. *Factor Analyses of Prospective Teachers' Differences.* Doctor's thesis, University of Wisconsin (Madison, Wis.), 1949. (*Summaries of Doctoral Dissertations ....July 1949 to June 1950, 1951, pp. 337-9.*)
27. STEPAT, DOROTHY L. *A Study of Clothing and Appearance Problems in Relation to Some Aspects of Personality and Some Cultural Patterns in a Group of College Freshman Girls.* Doctor's thesis, New York University (New York, N.Y.), 1949. Pp. 181. Abstract: *Microfilm Abstracts* 10:64-5 no 1 '50. * (*PA* 24:6049, title only)
28. SCHMID, JOHN, JR. "Factor Analyses of Prospective Teachers' Differences." *J Exp Ed* 18:287-319 Je '50. * (*PA* 25:2060)
29. SCHOENFELD, HENRY, JR. *A Method of Free-Response Interviewing for Determining the Role of Faculty Advisers in College Student Adjustment.* Doctor's thesis, University of Wisconsin (Madison, Wis.), 1950. (*Summaries of Doctoral Dissertations....July 1949 to June 1950, pp. 341-2.*)

30. SELDERS, GILBERT R. W. *A Study of the Academic, Social and Personal Needs of Students of the Pennsylvania State College for the Years 1948–1950 Through an Analysis of Instruments Administered in Education 105.* Doctor's thesis, Pennsylvania State College (State College, Pa.), 1950. (*Abstracts of Doctoral Dissertations....1950*, 1951, pp. 289–97.) (*PA* 26:2405, title only)

HAROLD E. JONES, *Professor of Psychology, and Director, Institute of Child Welfare, University of California, Berkeley, California.*

In its present form, the *Mooney Problem Check List* is based on the analysis of brief statements written by 4,000 high school students describing their personal problems, and on a number of other sources including case records and counseling interviews. Repeated revisions have utilized data from various parts of the country. The authors state that in the choice of items they have attempted to select problems which are either commonly checked, or which are "serious enough to be important in an individual case." This latter criterion would seem to have very little restrictive value. Illustrative items (High School Form) follow: being overweight, being talked about, being treated like a child at home, not getting along with a teacher, wanting to be more popular, and giving in to temptations.

In the Junior High School Form, 30 items are presented in each of 7 "problem areas": Health and Physical Development; School; Home and Family; Money, Work and the Future; Boy and Girl Relations; Relations to People in General; and Self-Centered Concerns. The High School and College Forms are expanded to 11 areas and 330 items. A form for adults is also provided, with a separate manual.

The Check List is designed primarily as an aid to counseling: to acquaint the counselee with topics that may be discussed, to help him in reviewing his own problems, and also to give counselors some preliminary notion as to matters of concern. In using the list with college students Marsh (*3*) reports: "This check list was felt to be valuable at Stephens because it helped to locate areas of student problems, gave a quick overview of students' felt difficulties, and offered a good basis for an opening conference." Similar advantages are mentioned by Congdon (*7*) who points out also that the absence of scores, classificatory labels, and threatening psychological terms is an aid in establishing a good relationship with students.

The Check List, in various forms, has had such extensive use that it should be possible to give more information than is now available as to its value in counseling programs. Under what conditions, and for what level of counseling expertness, is it most serviceable? Does this abrupt and peripheral approach to problems sometimes set up a barrier to effective counseling?

Since the list is not designed to produce "scores" and no normative or correlational data are supplied, it cannot be assessed with regard to the usual concepts of reliability and validity. Chief attention is directed to the individual items as the significant data. Persons who mark an exceptionally large number of items may be likely candidates for counseling, but the selection of such cases rests upon local conditions and not on adjustment norms, which the authors regard as inapplicable. Similarly, problem area data (the term "category score" is avoided) are described as useful in the referral of cases to special programs, but not as having diagnostic significance.

The authors are to be commended for the limited claims made for this instrument. They caution that it should not be expected to disclose problems that the individual is unwilling to admit, either to himself or others. Some inconsistencies, however, occur in statements about the Check List, as in the instructions on the Adult Form: "Mark the list honestly and sincerely and you will obtain a representative inventory of your problems." It should be added that such an inventory can only be representative of self-perceived and self-reported foci of difficulty, and that the manifest report is often likely to provide a distorted as well as an incomplete representation of underlying sources of conflict.

In an application of the College Form, Congdon (*7*) found that the most frequent *reported* problems were in the area of adjustments to college. Low frequencies were obtained in areas involving courtship, sex, marriage, home and family. It may be questioned if these data closely reflect the actual distribution of problems which would be elicited by other approaches.

The use of the Check List for surveys (unsigned) is advocated as a means of discovering topics for discussion, to throw light on educational needs, and to study problem clusters, trends, and differences among groups. If the list is to be used for research purposes, it would be desirable to supply item frequencies for various samples; the interpretation of group differences is by no means simple, but the availability of data would at least assist in forming hypotheses. The authors may be fully justified in withholding normative data from counselors, in view of the possibly misleading nature of "adjustment" scores and of scores in pseudo-diagnostic categories. For other purposes, however, it is appropriate to look for some degree of statistical organization of results from schedules which have been so extensively used.

If the *Mooney Problem Check List* is of genuine value in counseling, it is legitimate to hope that the data which it furnishes can in some way be utilized for serious research purposes. If this is not possible without destroying the service value of the instrument, it may be questioned whether the instrument will stand the test of continued practical use.

MORRIS KRUGMAN, *Assistant Superintendent in Charge of Guidance, Board of Education, New York, New York.*

The *Mooney Problem Check List* is not a test, and therein lies its strength. Psychologists, guidance workers, industrial personnel workers and educators have been searching for years for a simple way to evaluate personality, but simple ways in a complex field have a disagreeable habit of yielding little. Most of the pencil and paper tests of personality have been extremely disappointing. The *Mooney Problem Check List* has not been in that category because it promised little and produced much.

It is refreshing to find authors of a psychological instrument whose claims are modest to the point of understatement. They say,

At all times the counselor must keep in mind that the *Problem Check List* is not a test. It does not yield scores on traits or permit any direct statements about the adjustment status of the person who made the responses. Rather, the *Problem Check List* is a form of simple communication between the counselee and counselor designed to accelerate the process of understanding the student and his real problems.

The check list is not considered a substitute for the interview or for the clinical approach, but an aid to them. It functions well under some conditions, and not under others. Its strengths and limitations are well described in the manuals, and a brief section on counseling with the check list in the manual is clinically sound.

Although validity, reliability, and norms are discussed in the manual, the authors are careful to point out that the usual criteria for these do not obtain for this type of instrument. This makes good sense, since the authors do not emphasize objectivity in this instrument. Instead, the uses to which it can be safely put are de-

scribed: facilitate counseling interviews; conduct group surveys leading to plans for individualized action; serve as a basis for group guidance; increase teacher understanding; and conduct research on problems of youth and adults.

The present forms are revisions of the check lists that have been in use for ten years. The sound suggestions for the use of this instrument are based on these years of experience.

The *Mooney Problem Check List* is a valuable aid in guidance for adjustment if used in conjunction with the interview. As an independent instrument it has value mainly for research purposes.

For reviews by Ralph C. Bedell and Theodore F. Lentz, see 3:67.

[74]

★Northampton Activity Rating Scale. Mental patients; 1951; Form D; no normative data; manual ['51]; $5.50 per 25; 30¢ per specimen set; postpaid; Isidor W. Scherer; Meed Scientific Apparatus Co., P.O. Box 658, Springfield, Mass. *

[75]

Personal Audit. Grades 9–16 and adults; 1941–45; 2 editions, 1 form, '45; manual ('45); 50¢ per specimen set of any one edition; cash orders postpaid; Clifford R. Adams and William M. Lepley; Science Research Associates, Inc. *
a) FORM LL (LONG FORM). 1941; emotional adjustment in 9 areas: seriousness, firmness, frankness, tranquillity, stability, tolerance, steadiness, persistence, contentment; $3.65 per 25; nontimed (45) minutes.
b) FORM SS (SHORT FORM). 1941; emotional adjustment in 6 areas: seriousness, firmness, frankness, tranquillity, stability, tolerance; $2.65 per 25; nontimed (35) minutes.

REFERENCES

1–9. See 3:64.
10. CERF, ARTHUR Z. "The Personal Audit, CE431A," pp. 585–8. In *Printed Classification Tests.* Edited by J. P. Guilford with the assistance of John I. Lacey. Army Air Forces Aviation Psychology Program Research Reports, Report No. 5. Washington, D.C.: U.S. Government Printing Office, 1947. Pp. xi, 919. * (PA 22:4145)
11. GIESE, WILLIAM JAMES. "A Tested Method for the Selection of Office Personnel." *Personnel Psychol* 2:525–45 w '49. * (PA 24:4278)
12. LIFTON, WALTER M. *A Study of the Changes in Self Concept and Content Knowledge in Students Taking a Course in Counseling Techniques.* Doctor's thesis, New York University (New York, N.Y.), 1950. Abstract: *Microfilm Abstracts* 11:55–6 no 1 '51. * (PA 26:2164, title only)

WILLIAM SEEMAN, *University of Minnesota, Minneapolis, Minnesota.*

This structured personality inventory has the advantage that it is self-administering in character, is easily and quickly scored, and (in the use of a profile pattern rather than a single score) takes some cognizance of the "Gestalt" properties of personality. The odd-even reliability is stated as .90 or above and the test-retest reliability .90 to .97. There are nine parts to the long

form: seriousness-impulsiveness, firmness-inde-
cision, tranquility-irritability, frankness-evasion,
stability-instability, tolerance-intolerance, stead-
iness-emotionality, persistence-fluctuation, con-
tentment-worry. The short form consists of the
first six parts.

It seems probable, on the basis of the item
analysis, that high scores and low scores on the
inventory differentiate individuals on the basis
of *something,* but one may have serious misgivings about what useful information is revealed
by such differences and by profile differences. It
is by no means clear that the 18 labels for the
nine parts actually constitute *dimensions* along
which meaningful measurements may be made.
Definition of the criterion in each part is either
not attempted or is left in the vague terms of
popular language. This reviewer is frankly puzzled, also, about the meaning of the statement
that the consensus of judgements of 30 psychologists "coincides with the descriptions which have
been prepared for the various traits." No information is given to indicate how this consensus
was determined nor how it was decided that the
consensus "fit" the descriptions. Incidentally,
since such a method of consensus is a form of
"face" validity, one wonders how "deception
has been nearly eliminated." (No evidence is
submitted to support this statement.) The point
is that such a method virtually eliminates "subtle" items which alone defy deception.

Another feature which puzzled this reviewer
lies in the correlations presented in Tables 1 and
4 of the manual, in the section on validation. The
correlations in Table 1 are regarded as "evidence
1or validation by negation, since the nine parts
do not overlap." In other words, this set of correlations is interpreted as showing that the nine
parts are *different.* Table 4 presents correlations
with the Bernreuter which are supposed to show
how parts of the inventory are *like* another personality scale. Yet, by the chi-square test, these
two sets of correlations may be said to be homogeneous. It does not seem to be misrepre-
senting the state of affairs to say that two relatively homogeneous sets of correlations are
interpreted in opposite directions.

In summary, one may say that this is an easily
administered, easily .scored, inexpensive structured inventory which yields a profile rather than
a single score. However, there is some doubt
about the nature of the dimensions and hence
about the value of the information which the test
yields. It would be desirable to have more ade-

quate empirical or experimental definitions of
the criteria for the various scales.

*For a review by Percival M. Symonds, see
3:64.*

[76]

★The Personal Preference Inventory: Student
Form. College; 1947–49; 3 scores: economic background, social attitude, masculinity-femininity; 1 form,
'47; manual ['49]; tentative norms—author recommends use of local norms; $2 per 25, postage extra;
15¢ per specimen set, postpaid; nontimed (10–20) minutes; Hugh M. Bell; Pacific Books, P.O. Box 558,
Palo Alto, Calif. *

E. LOWELL KELLY, *Professor of Psychology,
and Director, Bureau of Psychological Services,
University of Michigan, Ann Arbor, Michigan.*

This inventory is composed of 90 yes-no-?
items printed on the inner pages of a four-page
folder. Each of the three scales is composed of
30 items, scored with unit weights with the aid
of a semitransparent stencil. As with the Bell
Adjustment Inventory, each of the items is
preceded by a letter designating the scale to
which the item belongs. The items are arranged
in a cyclical order, that is, every third item
belongs to the same scale.

This inventory is said to provide three separate measures of students' attitude and adjustment: (*a*) Economic Background: "The individual who scores high tends to feel that others
have been more fortunate than he in their economic backgrounds." (*b*) Social Attitude:
"High scores indicate that a student possesses
a strong critical attitude toward people....is cautious and self-defensive." (*c*) Masculinity-Femininity: "For men, high scores indicate masculinity of interests * for women, low scores
indicate marked femininity of interests."

Corrected split half reliabilities of the three
scales are reported as .80, .85, and .84, based on
99 freshmen and sophomores, presumably of
both sexes. Selection of the items for each of the
scales was based on "the degree to which they
differentiated between extreme groups"; the
specific procedure used is not reported. The
three scales show relatively low intercorrelations
(−.23 to +.36); similarly low correlations are
reported with the four scales of the author's *Adjustment Inventory.*

The only evidence of the validity of the scales
is a statement that in using the scale in counseling 650 students, "marked agreement" was
found between the scores and the judgment of
both students and counselors. Separate norms

are provided for college men (186) and college women (144).

This instrument is obviously an attempt on the part of the author to construct a supplement to his *Adjustment Inventory* for use in the counseling of college students. For some reason, he has chosen to publish the new scales as a separate inventory rather than to add the items to the other inventory. Furthermore, he has chosen to publish the instrument with what appear to be decidedly inadequate norms, based as they are on relatively few students at one college in California. The criticism seems especially relevant with respect to the variable, economic background, although there would seem to be little excuse for not obtaining more representative normative data for all scales. The manual admits that the inventory has not been used with high school students, and that "nothing is known concerning its effectiveness" with them.

This inventory was designed for use in college counseling, and its validity rests solely on the counselors' report of its usefulness. Has anyone demonstrated that the counselors do a better job with the instrument than without it? The counselors' feeling about this matter may be significant, and it may even be correct, but this reviewer would be happier if there were some relevant evidence. In the same vein, if it is true that the scores are in "marked agreement" with the student's evaluation of himself on these variables, why should we not simply ask the student to rate himself directly on the variables concerned?

This reviewer is also concerned about the extremely provincial nature of this instrument. The brief manual has no bibliography and reflects no awareness on the part of the author of related developments in the measurement of adjustment variables. The only other test mentioned and the only intercorrelations reported are with the author's other inventory. Is masculinity-femininity as measured by this scale the same as measured by Strong's *Vocational Interest Blank,* the *Guilford-Martin Inventory of Factors GAMIN,* or the *Minnesota Multiphasic Personality Inventory?* One is left with the impression that the author not only does not know the answers to such questions, but worse still, does not care.

C. M. LOUTTIT, *Assistant to the Provost, University of Illinois, Urbana, Illinois.*

This inventory is intended to provide information for the clinical counselors on the college student's attitudes toward his economic background, his attitude toward people, and his position on the masculinity-femininity continuum. It follows the usual format of inventories in presenting 90 yes-no-? questions. Inasmuch as the inventory may be taken individually or in a group and seldom requires more than 15 minutes, it is a convenient way of exploring these particular areas of the students' attitudes. While tentative norms based on 186 men and 144 women are presented, the author advises that norms be developed in each local situation. Coefficients of reliability based on 99 cases are .80 for economic background, .85 for social attitude, and .84 for masculinity-femininity. Intercorrelations among the three sections of the scale are low as are the correlations between the three sections and the four parts of Bell's *Adjustment Inventory*. It is questionable whether numerical scores on this instrument can be taken as of too great meaning. The reliabilities would seem to be rather low for use in individual prediction; however, the author is quite explicit in considering the instrument as an aid in exploring certain aspects of the college student client. Used as a means of securing information with economy of time, it promises to have a clinical usefulness.

[77]

The Personality Inventory. Grades 9–16 and adults; 1931–38; 6 scores: neurotic tendency, self-sufficiency, introversion-extroversion, dominance-submission, confidence, sociability; IBM; 1 form, '35; manual ('35); tentative norms ('38); $1.75 per 25; 2¢ per norm sheet; 40¢ per specimen set; separate answer sheets may be used; $1 per 50 IBM answer sheets; $1 per 100 Hankes answer sheets (see 466); $2.50 per set of stencils for machine scoring of IBM answer sheets; 25¢ per 25 individual report blanks; postage extra; nontimed (25) minutes; Robert G. Bernreuter (scales measuring sociability and confidence were prepared by John C. Flanagan); Stanford University Press. *

REFERENCES

1–71. See 40:1239.
72. DeAngelis, Louis. *A Study of the Bernreuter Test With Psychiatric Cases.* Master's thesis, Columbia University (New York, N.Y.), 1932.
73. Pintner, R. "Neurotic Tendency and Its Relation to Some Other Mental Traits." *Sch & Soc* 36:765–7 D 10 '32. * (*PA* 7:1375)
74. Bernreuter, R. G. "The Imbrication of Tests of Intro-version-Extroversion and Neurotic Tendency." Abstract. *Psychol B* 30:665–6 N '33. * (*PA* 8:3135, title only)
75. Campbell, Albert A. "A Study of the Personality Adjustments of Only and Intermediate Children." *J Genetic Psychol* 43:197–206 S '33. * (*PA* 8:1717)
76. Farnsworth, Paul R. "The Study of Bernreuter Profiles." Abstract. *Psychol B* 30:600–1 O '33. * (*PA* 8:1177, title only)
77. Hartmann, George W. *Measuring Teaching Efficiency Among College Instructors.* Archives of Psychology, No. 154. Washington, D.C.: American Psychological Association, Inc., July 1933. Pp. 45. Paper. * (*PA* 8:5229)
78. Rhinehart, Jesse Batley. "An Attempt to Predict the Success of Student Nurses by the Use of a Battery of Tests." *J Appl Psychol* 17:277–93 Je '33. * (*PA* 8:567)
79. Roberts, Charles S., and Fisher, V. E. "Another Attempt at Measures of Extraversion-Introversion." *Psychol Clin* 22:88–93 Je–Ag '33. * (*PA* 8:4635)
80. Stagner, Ross. "The Relation of Personality to Aca-

demic Aptitude and Achievement." *J Ed Res* 26:648–60 My '33. * (*PA* 7:4857)

81. FARNSWORTH, P. R. "A Genetic Study of the Bernreuter Inventory and the Peterson War Scale." Abstract. *Psychol B* 31:586 O '34. * (*PA* 9:767, title only)

82. YU, POE EENG. "A Personality (Bernreuter) Study of Two Groups of Psychotics." Abstract. *Psychol B* 31:586–7 O '34. * (*PA* 9:761, title only)

83. DIERENFIELD, HAROLD. *A Study to Determine the Personality Adjustment in Athletes as Measured by the Bernreuter Personality Inventory.* Master's thesis, University of Michigan (Ann Arbor, Mich.), 1935.

84. JOHNSON, ELEANOR HOPE. "The Bernreuter Personality Inventory as an Interviewing Device." *Consulting Psychologist* 2:8–11 D '35. *

85. SHAPLAND, DOROTHY. *A Study of Personality Tests as They May Be Used in Vocational Guidance, Including an Experiment With the Bernreuter Personality Inventory Test.* Master's thesis, University of Michigan (Ann Arbor, Mich.), 1935.

86. SWARD, KEITH. "Patterns of Jewish Temperament." *J Appl Psychol* 19:410–25 Ag '35. * (*PA* 10:1050)

87. SWARD, KEITH, AND FREEDMAN, MEYER B. "Jewish Temperament." *J Appl Psychol* 19:70–84 F '35. * (*PA* 9:4684)

88. TERMAN, LEWIS M., AND BUTTENWIESER, PAUL. "Personality Factors in Marital Compatibility." *J Social Psychol* 6:143–71, 267–89 My, Ag '35. * (*PA* 10:1649, 2149)

89. BARTLETT, MARION W. "Relation of Suggestibility to Other Personality Traits." *J General Psychol* 15:191–6 Jl '36. * (*PA* 11:334)

90. COPELAND, HAROLD W. *A Study of the Reliability of the Bernreuter Personality Inventory as Determined by the Spearman-Brown Formula Through Various Grouping Methods.* Master's thesis, University of Colorado (Boulder, Colo.), 1936.

91. LABARRE, EMMA DOROTHY. *A Measure of the Extent to Which Scores on the Bernreuter Personality Inventory are Influenced by Reticence.* Master's thesis, Pennsylvania State College (State College, Pa.), 1936. Pp. 26.

92. RICE, MARGARET E. *The Reliability of the Bernreuter Personality Scores Obtained From Institutionalized Criminals.* Master's thesis, University of Colorado (Boulder, Colo.), 1936.

93. ST. CLAIR, WALTER. *A Study of the Validity of the Bernreuter Personality Inventory.* Master's thesis, Temple University (Philadelphia, Pa.), 1936. Pp. 41.

94. SHLAUDEMAN, KARL WHITMAN. *A Correlational Analysis of Idiosyncrasy of Response to Tests of Association, Interest, and Personality.* Doctor's thesis, Stanford University (Stanford, Calif.), 1936. (*Abstracts of Dissertations....1936–37*, 1937, pp. 22–6.)

95. STAMBAUGH, CHARLES J., JR. *A Study of the Correlation of Pre-Competitive Excitement and the Bernreuter Personality Inventory.* Master's thesis, Pennsylvania State College (State College, Pa.), 1936. Pp. 28.

96. NEMZEK, CLAUDE LAWRENCE. *The Value of Intelligence Quotients, Personality, and Other Factors for Differential Prediction of Scholastic Success in High School.* Doctor's thesis, University of Minnesota (Minneapolis, Minn.), 1937. (*Summaries of Ph.D. Theses.....*, 1939, pp. 131–4.)

97. ANDERSON, ROSE G. "Some Technological Aspects of Counseling Adult Women." Abstract. *Psychol B* 35:631–2 N '38. * (*PA* 13:1655, title only)

98. BRYAN, ALICE I., AND PERL, RUTH E. "A Comparison of Woman Students Preparing for Three Different Vocations." *J Appl Psychol* 22:161–8 Ap '38. * (*PA* 13:2673)

99. CHRISTENSEN, ARNOLD M. "Traits of College-Going, Employed, and Unemployed High School Graduates." *Sch R* 46:597–601 O '38. * (*PA* 13:4344)

100. COLLIER, R. M., AND EMCH, MINNA. "Introversion-Extraversion: The Concepts and Their Clinical Use." *Am J Psychiatry* 94:1045–75 Mr '38. * (*PA* 12:5381)

101. McMORRIES, JAMES C. "A Study of New Students Admitted by a Negro College in 1936." *J Negro Ed* 7:535–9 O '38. * (*PA* 13:1089)

102. MILLER, CARROLL H. "Value of Certain Standard Tests for a Study of Dramatic Talent." *J Social Psychol* 9:437–9 N '38. * (*PA* 13:1753)

103. ROSE, FORREST H. *Training in Speech and Changes in Personality.* Doctor's thesis, University of Wisconsin (Madison, Wis.), 1938. (*Summaries of Doctoral Dissertations....1938*, pp. 281–3.)

104. SAPPENFIELD, BERT REESE. *The Relation Between Personality and High School Achievement: the Value of Bernreuter Personality Inventory Scores in the Division of Groups Upon Which Aptitude-Scholarship Correlations Are Based.* Master's thesis, New York University (New York, N.Y.), 1938.

105. GARRISON, K. C. "The Use of Psychological Tests in the Selection of Student-Nurses." *J Appl Psychol* 23:461–72 Ag '39. * (*PA* 13:6426)

106. GILKINSON, HOWARD, AND KNOWER, FRANKLIN H. *Psychological Studies of Individual Differences Among Students of Speech.* Minneapolis, Minn.: Department of Speech; University of Minnesota, June 1939. Pp. ii, 196. Paper, mimeographed. *

107. HENRY, MAX. *A Study of the Predictive Validity of Certain Keys of the Bernreuter Personality Inventory.* Master's thesis, Pennsylvania State College (State College, Pa.), 1939. Pp. 78.

108. MARICLE, LeCLAIRE ROBERT. *The Relationship of Cer-

tain Personality Traits to Patterns of Interest.* Master's thesis, University of Oklahoma (Norman, Okla.), 1939. Pp. vi, 56. (*Abstracts of Theses....1939*, 1943, p. 132.)

109. MINTZER, A., AND SARGENT, S. S. "The Relationship Between Family Economic Status and Some Personality Traits of College Students." *Sch & Soc* 49:322–4 Mr 11 '39. * (*PA* 13:3188)

110. RYANS, DAVID G. "A Tentative Statement of the Relation of Persistence Test Scores to Certain Personality Traits as Measured by the Bernreuter Inventory." *J Genetic Psychol* 54:229–34 Mr '39. * (*PA* 13:5265)

111. STONUM, MARY McCAULEY. *An Item Analysis of the Bernreuter Personality Inventory as Related to Speaking Performance.* Master's thesis, University of Iowa (Iowa City, Iowa), 1939.

112. STRAYER, FLOYD J. *A Study of Certain Teacher's Personality Traits as Measured by a Teaching-Situations Questionnaire and the Bernreuter Personality Inventory.* Master's thesis, University of Michigan (Ann Arbor, Mich.), 1939.

113. BROWN, J. E. *The Relationship of Personality Traits and Vocational Interest to Success in Teaching Vocational Agriculture.* Master's thesis, Virginia Polytechnic Institute (Blacksburg, Va.), 1940. Pp. 88.

114. CHENOWETH, EUGENE C. "The Adjustment of College Freshmen to the Speaking Situation." *Q J Speech* 26:585–8 D '40. * (*PA* 15:3066)

115. CHILD, IRVIN L. "The Relation Between Measures of Infantile Amnesia and Neuroticism." *J Abn & Social Psychol* 35:453–6 Jl '40. * (*PA* 14:5517)

116. DODGE, ARTHUR F. "What Are the Personality Traits of the Successful Clerical Worker?" *J Appl Psychol* 24:576–86 O '40. * (*PA* 15:994)

117. DUNKERLEY, MARY DOROTHEA. *A Statistical Study of Leadership Among College Women.* Catholic University of America, Studies in Psychology and Psychiatry, Vol. 4, No. 7. Washington, D.C.: Catholic University of America Press, July 1940. Pp. vii, 65. Paper. * (*PA* 14:5096)

118. ECKERT, RALPH G., AND KEYS, NOEL. "Public Speaking as a Cue to Personality Adjustment." *J Appl Psychol* 24:144–53 Ap '40. * (*PA* 14:4638)

119. HAMPTON, PETER. "Is There a 'Grocer' Personality?" *Occupations* 19:184–7 D '40. * (*PA* 15:924)

120. PETERS, CHAS. C. "The Validity of Personality Inventories Studied by a 'Guess Who' Technique." Abstract: *Psychol B* 37:453 Jl '40. * (*PA* 14:5599, title only)

121. RARICK, HAROLD J. *Professional Prognostic Value of College Objective Testing With Special Reference to the Bernreuter Personality Inventory and Thurstone's Psychological Examination for College Freshmen.* Master's thesis, Ball State Teachers College (Muncie, Ind.), 1940. Pp. 62.

122. REED, HOMER B. "The Relation of Bernreuter Personality and Thurstone Vocational Interest Scores to Each Other and to Scholastic and Mechanical Achievement." Abstract. *Psychol B* 37:449–50 Jl '40. * (*PA* 14:5716, title only)

123. SISSON, E. DONALD, AND SISSON, BETTE. "Introversion and the Aesthetic Attitude." *J General Psychol* 22:203–8 Ja '40. * (*PA* 14:2480)

124. EISENBERG, PHILIP. "Individual Interpretation of Psychoneurotic Inventory Items." *J General Psychol* 25:19–40 Jl '41. * (*PA* 15:5205)

125. FAIR, MARCELLA HYDE. *An Evaluation of the Bernreuter Personality Inventory, Bell Adjustment Inventory, and Willoughby (Clark-Thurstone) Personality Schedule on Emotional Stability of Ohio University Women.* Master's thesis, Ohio University (Athens, Ohio), 1941. Pp. 78. (*Abstracts of Masters' Theses....1941*, pp. 26–7.)

126. FEDER, D. D., AND BAER, L. OPAL. "A Comparison of Test Records and Clinical Evaluations of Personality Adjustment." *J Ed Psychol* 32:133–44 F '41. * (*PA* 15:3886)

127. FISHER, WILLIS, AND HAYES, SAMUEL P., JR. "Maladjustment in College, Predicted by Bernreuter Inventory Scores and Family Position." *J Appl Psychol* 25:86–96 F '41. * (*PA* 15:3043)

128. GILKINSON, HOWARD, AND KNOWER, FRANKLIN H. "A Study of Standardized Personality Tests and Skill in Speech." *J Ed Psychol* 32:161–175 Mr '41. * (*PA* 15:3888)

129. HAMPTON, PETER. "A Comparative Study of Certain Personality Traits and Success in Retail Selling." *J Appl Psychol* 25:431–46 Ag '41. * (*PA* 15:5321)

130. HAMPTON, PETER. "Language Difficulties of the Bernreuter Personality Inventory." *J Ed Psychol* 32:471–3 S '41. * (*PA* 16:1044)

131. HAMPTON, PETER. "Personality Scores of Grocers and Their Success Ratings." Abstract. *B Can Psychol Assn* 1:41–3 O '41. * (*PA* 16:640)

132. JOHNSON, H. M. "Analysis of Bernreuter's Inventory as a Predictor of Success in Certain Vocations: A Problem in Scientific Method." Abstract. *Psychol B* 38:694 O '41. * (*PA* 16:343, title only)

133. McQUITTY, LOUIS L. "An Approach to the Nature and Measurement of Personality Integration." *J Social Psychol* 13:3–14 F '41. * (*PA* 15:2654)

134. MIDDLETON, WARREN C. "The Relation of Height and Weight Measurements to Certain Personality Traits as Measured by the Bernreuter Inventory." *J Psychol* 11:143–49 Ja '41. * (*PA* 15:2270)

135. MIDDLETON, WARREN C. "The Relation of Height and Weight Measurements to Certain Personality Qualities as Meas-

ured by the Bernreuter Inventory: Some Errata." *J Psychol* 11:421–2 Ap '41. * *(PA* 15:3047)

136. PETERSON, C. H. "The Relationship of Bernreuter Personality Scores to Other Parent Characteristics, Including Parent-Child Behavior." Abstract. *Psychol B* 38:704 O '41. * *(PA* 16:236, title only)

137. REED, HOMER B. "The Place of the Bernreuter Personality, Stenquist Mechanical Aptitude, and Thurstone Vocational Interest Tests in College Entrance Tests." Abstract. *Psychol B* 38:711 O '41. * *(PA* 16:351, title only)

138. REED, HOMER B. "The Place of the Bernreuter Personality, Stenquist Mechanical Aptitude, and Thurstone Vocational Interest Tests in College Entrance Tests." *J Appl Psychol* 25:528–34 O '41. * *(PA* 16:1205)

139. SHAFFER, J. *Pleasant and Unpleasant Memory Recall as Related to the Bernreuter Personality Inventory.* Master's thesis, Pennsylvania State College (State College, Pa.), 1941.

140. THOMPSON, CHARLES E. "The Personality of the Teacher as a Factor Not Only in the Total Learning Situation But Also in Developing the Personality of the Child." *Proc Okla Acad Sci* 21:133–6 '41. * *(PA* 16:1215)

141. ACHARD, FRANCIS H. *The Selection of Supervisory Employees in Business and Industry.* Doctor's thesis, New York University (New York, N.Y.), 1942. Pp. 337. *(Abstracts of Theses....[School of Education]* 1943, pp. 1–7.)

142. BRYAN, ALICE I. "Grades, Intelligence and Personality of Art School Freshmen." *J Ed Psychol* 33:50–64 Ja '42. * *(PA* 16:3186)

143. CAVANAUGH, JEAN OGDEN. "The Relation of Recreation to Personality Adjustment." *J Social Psychol* 15:63–74 F '42. * *(PA* 16:3159)

144. COBLENTZ, IRVING. *Prognosis of Freshman Academic Achievement at the Pennsylvania State College.* Doctor's thesis, Pennsylvania State College (State College, Pa.), 1942. Pp. 245. *(Abstracts of Doctoral Dissertations....1942,* 1943, pp. 386–92.)

145. COGGINS, K.; HENSLEY, R.; AND MULL, H. K. "Introversion and the Appreciation of Literature: Studies From the Psychological Laboratory of Sweet Briar College, III." *Am J Psychol* 55:560–1 O '42. * *(PA* 17:1622)

146. GOODMAN, CHARLES H. "A Comparison of the Interests and Personality Traits of Engineers and Liberal Arts Students." *J Appl Psychol* 26:721–37 D '42. * *(PA* 17:2486)

147. HAMPTON, PETER. "Objections of a Group of Grocers to Taking the Bernreuter Personality Inventory." *J Social Psychol* 15:159–61 F '42. * *(PA* 16:3166)

148. JOHNSON, ELEANOR HOPE. "Personality and Religious Work." *Am J Orthopsychiatry* 12:317–23 Ap '42. * *(PA* 16:4064)

149. LINDSAY, CHARLES, AND MULL, HELEN K. "Introversion-Extraversion in Northern and Southern College Students: Studies From the Psychological Laboratory of Sweet Briar College, I." *Am J Psychol* 55:109–10 Ja '42. * *(PA* 16:1973)

150. MCCARTHY, THOMAS J. *Personality Traits of Seminarians.* Catholic University of America, Studies in Psychology and Psychiatry, Vol. 5, No. 4. Washington, D.C.: Catholic University of America Press, July 1942. Pp. vii, 46. Paper. *

151. MUNROE, RUTH L. "An Experiment in Large-Scale Testing by a Modification of the Rorschach Method." *J Psychol* 13:229–63 Ap '42. * *(PA* 16:3651)

152. PETERS, RICHARDA. *A Study of the Intercorrelations of Personality Traits Among a Group of Novices in Religious Communities.* Catholic University of America, Studies in Psychology and Psychiatry, Vol. 5, No. 7. Washington, D.C.: Catholic University of America Press, December 1942. Pp. vii, 38. Paper. * *(PA* 17:2047)

153. REINING, HENRY, JR., AND STROMSEN, KARL E. "Mental Abilities and Personality Traits." *Personnel Adm* 5:14–8 S '42. *

154. RUCH, FLOYD L. Chap. 12, "A Technique for Detecting Attempts to Fake Performance on the Self-Inventory Type of Personality Test," pp. 229–34. In *Studies in Personality: Contributed in Honor of Lewis M. Terman.* Edited by Quinn McNemar and Maude A. Merrill. New York: McGraw-Hill Book Co., Inc., 1942. Pp. x, 351. * *(PA* 16:2742)

155. ST. CLAIR, WALTER F. *Identification of Personality Patterns Through the Use of a Specially Constructed Inventory.* Doctor's thesis, Temple University (Philadelphia, Pa.), 1942. *(Abstracts of Dissertations....[Teachers College]* 1940–1949, 1951, pp. 205–11.)

156. SUPER, DONALD E. "The Bernreuter Personality Inventory: A Review of Research." *Psychol B* 39:94–125 F '42. * *(PA* 16:1977)

157. THOMPSON, CHARLES E. "The Personality of the Teacher as It Affects the Child." *Ed Forum* 6:261–4 Mr '42. * *(PA* 17:329)

158. TUBBS, WILLIAM R. "A Study of the Interrelationships Between the Adams-Lepley Personal Audit and the Bernreuter Personality Inventory." *J Appl Psychol* 26:338–51 Je '42. * *(PA* 16:4070)

159. TUSSING, LYLE. "An Investigation of the Possibilities of Measuring Personality Traits With the Strong Vocational Interest Blank." *Ed & Psychol Meas* 2:59–74 Ja '42. * *(PA* 16:2324)

160. WARD, LEWIS B., AND KIRK, SAMUEL A. "Studies in the Selection of Students for a Teachers College." *J Ed Res* 35:665–72 My '42. * *(PA* 16:4194)

161. WATSON, ROBERT I. "The Relationship of Affective Tolerance Inventory to Other Personality Inventories." *Ed & Psychol Meas* 2:83–90 Ja '42. * *(PA* 16:2325)

162. BOYNTON, PAUL L., AND WALSWORTH, BARRIER M. "Emotionality Test Scores of Delinquent and Nondelinquent Girls." *J Abn & Social Psychol* 38:87–92 Ja '43. * *(PA* 17:3899)

163. BROGDEN, HUBERT E., AND THOMAS, WILLIAM F. "The Primary Traits in Personality Items Purporting to Measure Sociability." *J Psychol* 16:85–97 Jl '43. * *(PA* 17:4159)

164. DURFLINGER, GLENN W. "Scholastic Prediction in a Teachers College." *J Exp Ed* 11:257–67 Je '43. * *(PA* 17:4263)

165. HANAWALT, NELSON G.; RICHARDSON, HELEN M.; AND HAMILTON, R. JANE. "Leadership as Related to Bernreuter Personality Measures: II, An Item Analysis of Responses of College Leaders and Non-Leaders." *J Social Psychol* 17:251–67 My '43. * *(PA* 17:3954)

166. PATTERSON, C. H. "A Note on Bernreuter Personality of Mothers and Some Measures of Child Personality." *J Social Psychol* 17:89–92 F '43. * *(PA* 17:2225)

167. PINTNER, R., AND FORLANO, G. "Consistency of Response to Personality Tests at Different Age Levels." *J Genetic Psychol* 62:77–83 Mr '43. * *(PA* 17:2393)

168. RICHARDSON, HELEN M., AND HANAWALT, NELSON G. "Leadership as Related to the Bernreuter Personality Measures: I, College Leadership in Extracurricular Activities." *J Social Psychol* 17:237–49 My '43. * *(PA* 17:3968)

169. ROACH, PATRICIA PALMER. "An Experimental Study of the Pl ('Plodding') Characteristics of Persistence." *J Appl Psychol* 27:458–68 D '43. * *(PA* 18:205)

170. ZALMAN, WILLIAM ROBERT. *The Relationship of the Bernreuter Personality Inventory Ratings to Traits Exhibited by Students in College Courses.* Master's thesis, University of Nebraska (Lincoln, Neb.), 1943.

171. BENNETT, GEORGE K., AND GORDON, H. PHOEBE. "Personality Test Scores and Success in the Field of Nursing." *J Appl Psychol* 28:267–78 Je '44. * *(PA* 18:3184)

172. DORCUS, ROY M. "A Brief Study of the Humm-Wadsworth Temperament Scale and the Guilford-Martin Personnel Inventory in an Industrial Situation." *J Appl Psychol* 28:302–7 Ag '44. * *(PA* 18:3850)

173. HANAWALT, NELSON G., AND RICHARDSON, HELEN M. "Leadership as Related to the Bernreuter Personality Measures: IV, An Item Analysis of Responses of Adult Leaders and Non-Leaders." *J Appl Psychol* 28:397–411 O '44. * *(PA* 19:446)

174. KEMPFER, HOMER. "Simplifying the Scoring Technique of the Bernreuter Personality Inventory." *J Appl Psychol* 28:412–3 O '44. * *(PA* 19:447)

175. MCCLELLAND, DAVID C. "Simplified Scoring of the Bernreuter Personality Inventory." *J Appl Psychol* 28:414–9 O '44. * *(PA* 19:450)

176. MARCUSE, F. L.; HILL, A.; AND KEEGAN, M. "Identification of Posthypnotic Signals and Responses." *B Can Psychol Assn* 4:74 D '44. * *(PA* 19:1220)

177. MARTIN, HOWARD G. "Locating the Troublemaker With the Guilford-Martin Personnel Inventory." *J Appl Psychol* 28:461–7 D '44. * *(PA* 19:1323)

178. PINTNER, R., AND FORLANO, G. "Some Measures of Dominance in College Women." *J Social Psychol* 19:313–5 My '44. * *(PA* 18:3815)

179. RICHARDSON, HELEN M., AND HANAWALT, NELSON G. "Leadership as Related to the Bernreuter Personality Measures: III, Leadership Among Adult Men in Vocational and Social Activities." *J Appl Psychol* 28:308–17 Ag '44. * *(PA* 18:3818)

180. SAINTE-LAURE, *Sister.* "Un Premier Essai du Questionnaire de la Personnalité Bernreuter-Ottawa." Text in English. *B Can Psychol Assn* 4:75–6 D '44. * *(PA* 19:1270, title only)

181. ACHARD, F. H., AND CLARKE, FLORENCE H. "You *Can* Measure the Probability of Success as a Supervisor." *Personnel* 21:353–73 My '45. *

182. BURTON, MARTHA V. "The Effect of College Attendance Upon Personality as Measured by the Bernreuter Personality Inventory." *J Ed Res* 38:708–11 My '45. * *(PA* 19:3150)

183. GOTHAM, R. E. "Personality and Teaching Efficiency." *J Exp Ed* 14:157–65 D '45. * *(PA* 20:2074)

184. MULL, H. K.; KEDDY, M.; AND KOONCE, M. "Some Personality Differences in Northern and Southern College Students." *Am J Psychol* 58:555–7 O '45. * *(PA* 20:843)

185. PAGE, HOWARD E. "Detecting Psychoneurotic Tendencies in Army Personnel." *Psychol B* 42:645–58 N '45. * *(PA* 20:820)

186. PATTERSON, CECIL H. *The Relationship of Bernreuter Scores to Parent Behavior, Child Behavior, Urban-Rural Residence, and Other Background Factors in 100 Normal Adult Parents.* Master's thesis, University of Minnesota (Minneapolis, Minn.), 1945.

187. ROLFE, J. F. "The Measurement of Teaching Ability: Study Number Two." *J Exp. Ed* 14:52–74 S '45. * *(PA* 20:1268)

188. ROSTKER, L. E. "The Measurement of Teaching Ability: Study Number One." *J Exp Ed* 14:6–51 S '45. * *(PA* 20:1269)

189. SCHMIDT, HERMANN O., AND BILLINGSLEA, FREDERICK Y. "Test Profiles as a Diagnostic Aid: The Bernreuter Inventory." *J Abn & Social Psychol* 40:70–6 Ja '45. * *(PA* 19:1979)

190. SEAGOE, MAY V. "Prognostic Tests and Teaching Success." *J Ed Res* 38: 685–90 My '45. * *(PA* 19:3184)

191. SHULTZ, IRVIN T., AND BARNABAS, BENTLEY. "Testing for Leadership in Industry." *Trans Kan Acad Sci* 48:160–4 S '45. * (*PA* 20:896)

192. TIMMONS, WILLIAM M. "Personality Changes From Acting in a Play." *J Social Psychol* 21:247–55 My '45. * (*PA* 19:2266)

193. ZALMAN, WILLIAM R. "The Relationship of the Traits of the Bernreuter Personality Inventory to Academic Success." *J Am Assn Col Reg* 21:81–4 O '45. * (*PA* 20:1981)

194. CORSINI, RAYMOND. "Bernreuter Patterns of a Group of Prison Inmates." *J Clin Psychol* 2:283–5 Jl '46. * (*PA* 20:4660)

195. ELLIS, ALBERT. "The Validity of Personality Questionnaires." *Psychol B* 43:385–440 S '46. * (*PA* 21:502)

196. FLEMMING, EDWIN G., AND FLEMMING, CECILE WHITE. "A Qualitative Approach to the Problem of Improving Selection of Salesmen by Psychological Tests." *J Psychol* 21:127–50 Ja '46. * (*PA* 20:1636)

197. KILLINGER, GEORGE G., AND ZUBIN, JOSEPH. "Psychobiological Screening Procedures in the War Shipping Administration." Discussion by Rose G. Anderson and Arthur E. Traxler. *Ann N Y Acad Sci* 46:559–67, discussion 567–9 Jl 30 '46. * (*PA* 20:4808)

198. PATTERSON, CECIL H. "The Relationship of Bernreuter Scores to Parent Behavior, Child Behavior, Urban-Rural Residence, and Other Background Factors in 100 Normal Adult Parents." *J Social Psychol* 24:3–49 Ag '46. * (*PA* 21:1528)

199. SARTAIN, A. Q. "Predicting Success in a School of Nursing." *J Appl Psychol* 30:234–40 Je '46. * (*PA* 20:4350)

200. SARTAIN, A. Q. "Relation Between Scores on Certain Standard Tests and Supervisory Success in an Aircraft Factory." *J Appl Psychol* 30:328–32 Ag '46. * (*PA* 21:250)

201. SARTAIN, A. Q. "A Study of Bernreuter Personality Inventory Scores Made by Candidates for Supervisory Positions in an Aircraft Factory." *J Social Psychol* 24:255–9 N '46. * (*PA* 21:1532)

202. WHEATLEY, LUIS ANDRÈS, AND SUMNER, F. C. "Measurement of Neurotic Tendency in Negro Students of Music." *J Psychol* 22:247–52 O '46. * (*PA* 21:819)

203. WILLIAMS, ROGER K. *A Comparison of College Students Classified By a Psychological Clinic as Personality Maladjustment Cases and as Vocational Guidance Cases.* Doctor's thesis, Pennsylvania State College (State College, Pa.), 1946. (*Abstracts of Doctoral Dissertations....1946,* 1947, pp. 118–22.)

204. ANDERSON, ROSE G. "Abbreviated Forms of the Bernreuter Personality Inventory." *J Consult Psychol* 11:310–4 N-D '47. * (*PA* 22:2146)

205. CAWLEY, ANNE MARY. *A Study of the Vocational Interest Trends of Secondary School and College Women.* Washington, D.C.: Catholic University of America Press, 1947. Pp. 185–247. Paper. Reprinted from *Genetic Psychol Monogr* 35: 185–247 Mr '47. * (*PA* 22:2290)

206. CERF, ARTHUR Z. "The Bernreuter Personality Inventory, CE433A," pp. 588–9. In *Printed Classification Tests.* Edited by J. P. Guilford with the assistance of John I. Lacey. Army Air Forces Aviation Psychology Program Research Reports, Report No. 5. Washington, D.C.: U.S. Government Printing Office, 1947. Pp. xi, 919. * (*PA* 22:4145)

207. DAMRIN, D. E. "A Study of the Truthfulness With Which High School Girls Answer Personality Tests of the Questionnaire Type." *J Ed Psychol* 38:223–31 Ap '47. * (*PA* 22:625)

208. FRENCH, VERA V. "The Structure of Sentiments: II, A Preliminary Study of Sentiments." *J Personality* 16:78–108 S '47. * (*PA* 22:2267)

209. HELLFRITZSCH, ALVIN GUSTAV. *A Factor Analysis of Teacher Abilities.* Doctor's thesis, University of Wisconsin (Madison, Wis.), 1947. (*Summaries of Doctoral Dissertations ....July, 1943 to June, 1947,* 1949, pp. 414–7.)

210. JOHNSON, GERALD KENNETH. *Personality Patterns Peculiar to Theological Students.* Master's thesis, University of North Dakota (Grand Forks, N.D.), 1947. Review: *Sch Ed Rec Univ N Dakota* 33:200–3 Ap '48. *

211. LENNON, LAWRENCE J. *Predicting Student Nursing Aptitude in Eight Pennsylvania Nursing Schools.* Doctor's thesis, Pennsylvania State College (State College, Pa.), 1947. Pp. vii, 155. (*Abstracts of Doctoral Dissertations....1947,* 1948, pp. 230–7.) (*PA* 23:2462, title only)

212. McCLELLAND, DAVID C. "Further Application of Simplified Scoring of the Bernreuter Personality Inventory." *J Appl Psychol* 31:182–8 Ap '47. * (*PA* 21:2695)

213. MARTIN, GLENN C. "A Factor Analysis of the Bernreuter Personality Inventory." *Am Psychol* 2:418 O '47. * (*PA* 22:1112, title only)

214. MOSS, MARY FRANCES. *Bernreuter Personality Inventory Scores of Neurotic and Physically Disabled Veterans.* Master's thesis, Southern Methodist University (Dallas, Tex.), 1947. (*Abstracts of Theses....1946,* 1947, [no date], pp. 71–2.)

215. ONARHEIM, JAMES. "Scientific Selection of Sales Engineers." *Personnel* 24:24–34 Jl '47. *

216. SCHWARTZ, L. *Changes in Stability Rating From First to Eighth Semesters Between General and Psychology Students as Measured by the Bernreuter Personality Inventory.* Master's thesis, Pennsylvania State College (State College, Pa.), 1947.

217. WAGNER, P. *The Results of Factor Analysis Applied to the Personality Inventory.* Master's thesis, Pennsylvania State College (State College, Pa.), 1947.

218. WALTON, WILLIAM E. "A New Method of Scoring the Bernreuter Personality Inventory." *Personnel* 24:200 N '47. * (*PA* 22:1568)

219. BARNABAS, BENTLEY. "Validity of Personality and Interest Tests in Selection and Placement Situations." *Trans Kans Acad Sci* 51:335–9 S '48. * (*PA* 23:2432)

220. EIMICKE, VICTOR W., AND FISH, HERMAN L. "A Preliminary Study of the Relationships Between the Bernreuter Personality Inventory and Performances on the Army Alpha Examination and the George Washington Social Intelligence Test." *J Psychol* 25:381–7 Ap '48. * (*PA* 22:4418)

221. ELLIS, ALBERT, AND CONRAD, HERBERT S. "The Validity of Personality Inventories in Military Practice." *Psychol B* 45:385–426 S '48. * (*PA* 23:1287)

222. ESPENSCHADE, ANNA. "Selection of Women Major Students in Physical Education." *Res Q* 19:70–6 My '48. * (*PA* 22:4635)

223. FAW, VOLNEY. "Situational Variations of Neurotic Scores Measured by the Bernreuter Inventory." *J Consult Psychol* 12:255–8 Jl–Ag '48. * (*PA* 23:1186)

224. KELLEY, RAY K., AND JOHNSON, PAUL E. "Emotional Traits in Pacifists." *J Social Psychol* 28:275–86 N '48. * (*PA* 23:2646)

225. MARQUART, DOROTHY IRENE. "The Pattern of Punishment and Its Relation to Abnormal Fixations in Adult Human Subjects." *J General Psychol* 39:107–44 Jl '48. * (*PA* 23:3099)

226. MARTIN, GLENN C. "A Factor Analysis of the Bernreuter Personality Inventory." *Ed & Psychol Meas* 8:85–92 sp '48. * (*PA* 22:3947)

227. PORTENIER, LILLIAN. "Personality Tests in a University Guidance Program." Abstract. *J Colo-Wyo Acad Sci* 3:51–2 S '48. *

228. POWELL, MARGARET G. "Comparisons of Self-Rating, Peer-Ratings, and Expert's-Ratings of Personality Adjustment." *Ed & Psychol Meas* 8:225–34 su '48. * (*PA* 23:4248)

229. RICHARDSON, HELEN M. "Adult Leadership Scales Based on the Bernreuter Personality Inventory." *J Appl Psychol* 32:292–303 Je '48. * (*PA* 23:1236)

230. SHERMAN, ARTHUR W., JR. "Personality Factors in the Psychological Weaning of College Women." *Ed & Psychol Meas* 8:249–56 su '48. * (*PA* 23:4420)

231. SPEER, GEORGE S. "The Interest and Personality Patterns of Fire Protection Engineers." Abstract. *Am Psychol* 3:364 Ag '48. * (*PA* 23:822, title only)

232. SUMNER, F. C. "Neurotic Tendency and Socio-Economic Status of Negro College Women." *J Social Psychol* 28:291 N '48. * (*PA* 23:241)

233. WINGFIELD, ROBERT C. "Bernreuter Personality Ratings of College Students Who Recall Having Had Imaginary Playmates During Childhood." *J Child Psychiatry* 1:190–4 sect a '48. * (*PA* 23:2282)

234. ABT, LAWRENCE EDWIN. "A Test Battery for Selecting Technical Magazine Editors." *Personnel Psychol* 2:75–91 sp '49. * (*PA* 23:5099)

235. DONCEEL, JOSEPH F.; ALIMENA, BENJAMIN S.; AND BIRCH, CATHERINE M. "Influence of Prestige Suggestion on the Answers of a Personality Inventory." *J Appl Psychol* 33: 352–5 Ag '49. * (*PA* 24:2601)

236. KOTASH, WILLIAM E. *Relationship Between Scores Obtained by Bennett and Bernreuter Systems of Scoring the Bernreuter Inventory.* Master's thesis, University of Alberta (Edmonton, Alberta, Canada), 1949. Pp. 35.

237. LANDY, J. C. *A Study of the Relationships Between the Verbal Summator (Tautophone) and Two Questionnaire-Type Personality Tests.* Master's thesis, Pennsylvania State College (State College, Pa.), 1949. (*PA* 24:5552, title only)

238. McQUITTY, LOUIS L. "Diversity of Self Endorsements as a Measure of Individual Differences in Personality." *Ed & Psychol Meas* 9:3–14 sp '49. * (*PA* 23:5325)

239. MOREY, ELWYN A. "Vocational Interests and Personality Characteristics of Women Teachers." *Austral J Psychol* 1:26–37 Je '49. * (*PA* 26:1111)

240. RINSLAND, HENRY D. "The Prediction of Veterans' Success From Test Scores at the University of Oklahoma." Part 1, pp. 59–72. In *The Sixth Yearbook of the National Council on Measurements Used in Education, 1948–1949.* Fairmont, W.Va.: the Council, Fairmont State College, 1949. Pp. v, 140 (variously numbered). Paper, mimeographed. *

241. ROSENZWEIG, SAUL; WITH THE COLLABORATION OF KATE LEVINE KOGAN. *Psychodiagnosis: An Introduction to Tests in the Clinical Practice of Psychodynamics,* pp. 95–6. New York: Grune & Stratton, Inc., 1949. Pp. xii, 380. * (*PA* 23:3761)

242. SHUPP, FRANKLIN M. *A Study of the Relationship Between the Bernreuter Personality Inventory and the Rosenzweig Picture-Frustration Study in Testing High School Students.* Master's thesis, Pennsylvania State College (State College, Pa.), 1949. (*PA* 24:5565, title only)

243. SUPER, DONALD E. *Appraising Vocational Fitness By Means of Psychological Tests,* pp. 488–99. New York: Harper & Brothers, 1949. Pp. xxiii, 727. * (*PA* 24:2130)

244. UHRBROCK, RICHARD STEPHEN. "Construction of a Selection Test for College Graduates." *J General Psychol* 41:153–93 O '49. * (*PA* 24:4874)

245. WHITLOCK, JOHN B., JR., AND CRANNELL, CLARKE W. "An Analysis of Certain Factors in Serious Accidents in a Large Steel Plant." *J Appl Psychol* 33:494–8 O '49. * (*PA* 24:3467)

246. ZAKOLSKI, F. C. "Studies in Delinquency: I, Personality

Structure of Delinquent Boys." *J Genetic Psychol* 74:109–17 Mr '49. * (*PA* 23:4925)

247. DEAN, CHARLES W. *An Investigation of Relationships Between Several Scholastic Aptitude Components and Certain Bernreuter Personality Scores.* Master's thesis, University of Pittsburgh (Pittsburgh, Pa.), 1950.

248. GILBERT, C. F. *A Comparison of the Guilford-Zimmerman Temperament Survey With Certain Related Personality Tests.* Master's thesis, Pennsylvania State College (State College, Pa.), 1950.

249. GILBERT, CLAUDIA. "The Guilford-Zimmerman Temperament Survey and Certain Related Personality Tests." *J Appl Psychol* 34:394–6 D '50. * (*PA* 25:4567)

250. IVES, KENNETH H. "A Note on the Presentation of Personality Inventory Scores." *J Clin Psychol* 6:415–6 O '50. * (*PA* 25:8098)

251. JARECKE, WALTER H. *A Study of the Professional Characteristics of Teachers.* Doctor's thesis, Pennsylvania State College (State College, Pa.), 1950. (*Abstracts of Doctoral Dissertations....1950*, 1951, pp. 255–8.) (*PA* 26:2438, title only)

252. JOHNSON, J. *The Relationship Between Discomfort-Relief Quotients and Scores on the B1-N (Neurotic Tendency) Scale of the Bernreuter Personality Inventory.* Master's thesis, Pennsylvania State College (State College, Pa.), 1950.

253. MACNEIL, VINCENT ALFRED. *Relationship Between Scores Obtained by Bennett and Bernreuter Systems of Scoring Bernreuter Inventory.* Master's thesis, University of Alberta (Edmonton, Alberta, Canada), 1950. Pp. 25.

254. NAIR, RALPH KENNETH. *Predictive Value of Standardized Tests and Inventories in Industrial Arts Teacher Education.* Doctor's thesis, University of Missouri (Columbia, Mo.), 1950. Abstract: *Microfilm Abstracts* 10:77–8 no 3 '50. * (*PA* 25:4862, title only)

255. PRED, ANNE L. SLESSER. *The Relationship of the Bernreuter Test of Personality to Opinion Judgments of Personality.* Master's thesis, Purdue University (Lafayette, Ind.), 1950. (*PA* 24:4930, title only)

256. EIMICKE, VICTOR WILLIAM. *A Study of the Effect of Intensive Sales Training Experience Upon the Measured Abilities and Personality Characteristics of Salesman-Candidates.* Doctor's thesis, New York University (New York, N.Y.), 1951. Abstract: *Microfilm Abstracts* 11:951–2 no 4 '51.

257. HUMPHREY, ELIZABETH M. "Relationship of the Bernreuter Introversion-Extraversion Ratings and Scores in Extra-Sensory Perception Tests." Abstract. *Am Psychol* 6:338–9 Jl '51. *

258. SPARKS, CHARLES P. "Limitations of the Bernreuter Personality Inventory in Selection of Supervisors." *J Appl Psychol* 35:403–6 D '51. * (*PA* 26:6570)

259. TERMAN, L. M.; WITH THE ASSISTANCE OF NANCY BAYLEY, HELEN MARSHALL, OLGA W. MCNEMAR, MELITA H. ODEN, AND ELLEN B. SULLIVAN. "Correlates of Orgasm Adequacy in a Group of 556 Wives." *J Psychol* 32:115–72 O '51. * (*PA* 26:3373)

LEONA E. TYLER, *Associate Professor of Psychology, University of Oregon, Eugene, Oregon.*

The advantage that this test has over many others is that information based on 20 years of experience has accumulated around it. Thus, it is now possible to say with some assurance what it will and will not accomplish, to map out the areas in which it is useful, and to sum up its principal limitations.

First, it can be used legitimately only in situations where the testee has no reason to attempt to get a better score than he deserves. There is abundant evidence that a difference in the set with which a person takes the test can and does affect his score. This means that the Bernreuter is of doubtful value in most if not all selection programs, but is much more satisfactory when used by educational or vocational counseling agencies. Similarly it could be used in an outpatient clinic, but not in a mental hospital situation where patients are attempting to appear well in order to be released. The Bernreuter worked fairly well as a screening technique in certain of the armed forces programs; this was,

however, largely because men in the armed services are more willing to admit their maladjustments in order to avoid unpleasant duties.

In the second place, the test identifies general personality inadequacies better than it evaluates an individual's suitability for particular jobs or life situations. Evidence accumulates that, although it is possible to score the blank for six traits, the nature of the inter-correlations is such that actually only two characteristics are being measured, those which Flanagan (*28*) named self-confidence and solitariness. Since the first of these correlates highly with the Bernreuter scale for neuroticism, it would perhaps be more meaningful to think of it as having to do with general emotional stability. The second deals with the sociability or the self-sufficiency of the individual. While there has been some work showing significant group differences on Bernreuter scales between salesmen and nonsalesmen, campus leaders and nonleaders, successful and unsuccessful practice teachers, etc., none of these differences are large enough to support decisions about *individual* cases. Correlations with various indicators of educational and vocational success have been too low to furnish a basis for any individual prediction. It is to be noted also that the "unfavorable" scores furnish more evidence for maladjustment than the apparently "good" scores furnish for superior adjustment.

In the third place, the test as now scored is designed to distinguish between the degrees of adjustment *within the normal range*. There is empirical evidence that psychiatric patients answer many of the items in ways that are in an opposite direction to that indicated by the scoring weights. (This phenomenon has also been noted in connection with the development of the *Minnesota Multiphasic Personality Inventory*, where empirical differences formed the basis for item weights.) It is true that in spite of this, groups of patients do obtain average scores deviating significantly from the norms, but there are numerous individual exceptions. Thus, educational and guidance situations seem to be the places in which a test of this type is of most value. When used in such settings, only the anxious withdrawing types of maladjustment are assessed by this test. There is considerable evidence that behavior problems and psychopathic tendencies are not identified by the Bernreuter. The large amount of overlapping which validity studies have consistently shown between adjusted and maladjusted groups should, of course, always be kept in mind when studying the individual case.

With these limitations and qualifications, *The Personality Inventory* can still be a useful instrument. It would be still more useful if it could be restandardized with only two keys and a simplified scoring system. There is ample statistical justification for these changes.

For reviews by Charles I. Mosier and Theodore Newcomb, see 40:1239; for related reviews, see 38:B358 and see 36:B108.

[78]

★**Personality Record.** A rating scale for pupils in grades 7–14; 1941; 7 ratings: seriousness of purpose, industry, initiative, influence, concern for others, responsibility, emotional stability; 1 form; no data on reliability and validity; no manual; 1–99, 5¢ each; 100–499, $2 per 100, 500–999, $1.50 per 100; also available in combination with the *Secondary-School Record;* cash orders postpaid; National Association of Secondary-School Principals. *

REFERENCES

1. ELICKER, PAUL E. "Record Forms for Secondary Schools." *B Nat Assn Sec Sch Prin* 31:39–48 N '47. *

VERNER M. SIMS, *Professor of Psychology, University of Alabama, University, Alabama.*

The *Personality Record* is one of a series of forms "designed by Committees of School Administrators for Secondary Schools" and "adopted by the National Association of Secondary-School Principals" for use in maintaining permanent records of high school pupils. It is a standard form on which teachers record for each pupil confidential information concerning the pupil's personal characteristics, with space for recording teacher judgements of the pupil's school activities, interests and abilities, and physical, social, and mental limitations.

Before considering the Record, let us raise a question concerning whether the Association should sponsor such an undertaking. Consciously or unconsciously, the committee responsible for the *Personality Record* has tried to define for thousands of teachers the ideal personality for high school pupils. In other words, through identifying seven aspects of personality (no more, no less) and setting up for each of these a hierarchy of five levels of behavior, the committee has decided for American education that the ideal American youth is "purposeful," is industrious to the point where he "seeks additional work," is "actively creative"; in influence, is "strongly controlling" but "deeply and generally concerned for others"; "assumes much

responsibility"; and, is "exceptionally stable" emotionally. These all seem good, middle class American virtues; but the reviewer has considerable doubt that a committee of high school principals, however able they may be, should be vested with power for making such decisions.

The Record itself is clearly a rating scale of the absolute type, where, for each of the traits included, the pupil is to be matched with the most appropriate of several described levels of performance. The authors, however, deny this fact and claim that these "are not ratings." The only satisfactory explanation which the reviewer can find for the failure of the authors to recognize the Record as a rating scale is their lack of familiarity with rating scales and their construction. This ignorance may also account for the fact that they have managed to violate most of the rules for the construction of such scales.

The descriptive material accompanying the Record reports that it was adopted "after extensive research and tryout in school systems," but if any effort was made to validate the scale, or to test its objectivity and reliability, it is not reported. Inspection of the scale suggests that had such investigation been carried out, the authors would probably have been sorely disappointed.

Three basic rules for constructing such scales are: (*a*) carefully define the aspects of personality which are to be rated; (*b*) describe the levels of performance in terms of objectively observable behaviors; and (*c*) develop directions for using the scale which will help the user to standardize the procedure. None of these rules are observed in the Record. Intangible aspects of personality such as industry, influence, responsibility and emotional stability go undefined. Levels of performance are described in such vague terms as purposeless, conscientious, somewhat socially concerned, usually dependable, hyperemotional, and well-balanced. And, finally, there are *no* instructions for users of the scale.

Recording such information as this instrument yields on the permanent records of pupils may well do many of them permanent harm. The reviewer would recommend that the Association of Secondary-School Principals withdraw its support of the *Personality Record* until such time as, first, the Association has consciously faced the issue of whether it should sponsor such an enterprise, and secondly, should the answer above be yes, has reconsidered whether it cares to sponsor a scale of such doubtful worth.

[79]

★The Personality Survey. Grades 7-9; 1948; 9 scores: age, intelligence, reading comprehension, pupil questionnaire, teacher rating, sociometric rating, absence, school marks, total adjustment; scores in intelligence and reading comprehension must be obtained from *Traxler Silent Reading Test for Grades 7 to 10;* 1 form ['48]; no data on reliability; manual ['48]; author recommends use of local norms; 2¢ per pupil's report; 2¢ per teacher's report; 2¢ per table for transmuting scores; 2¢ per class record sheet; 12¢ per manual; postage extra; 20¢ per specimen set, postpaid; Percival M. Symonds; Public School Publishing Co. *

REFERENCES

1. SYMONDS, PERCIVAL M., AND SHERMAN, MURRAY. "A Personality Survey of a Junior High School." *Sch R* 55:449-61 O '47. * (PA 23:1460)
2. SYMONDS, PERCIVAL M., AND SHERMAN, MURRAY. "Personality Survey of a Junior High School," pp. 23-50. In *The Measurement of Student Adjustment and Achievement.* Edited by Wilma T. Donahue, Clyde H. Coombs, and Robert M. W. Travers. Ann Arbor, Mich.: University of Michigan Press, 1949. Pp. xiv, 256. * (PA 23:6416)

DOUGLAS COURTNEY, *Program Director, Institute for Research in Human Relations, Philadelphia, Pennsylvania.*

The author states that the *Personality Survey* is

designed to furnish evidence regarding basic personality traits and personal attitudes from several sources—tests of proficiency taken by the pupil himself, and testimony from teachers, fellow pupils, and from each pupil himself * is designed to provide a profile and also a single measure of the pupil's adjustment * is designed to indicate which pupils in a school are in greatest need for specialized help, not only with regard to school progress, but also with regard to their social relations and their personal adjustment * is also designed to reveal those who are making the best adjustments in school; those with the best academic record, with the greatest capacity for leadership, with the most acceptable social attitudes and relationships and with emotional stability and freedom from feelings of inferiority and inadequacy. Such a survey should reveal those with the greatest promise on whom the school can well concentrate its efforts to produce leaders.

Eight "factors" are used in the Survey: (1) chronological age, (2) intelligence, (3) reading ability, (4) pupil self-rating, (5) teacher-rating, (6) rating by associates, (7) attendance, and (8) school marks. These "factors" are really variables in accepted research usage.

Variable 1 is chronological age. A table is provided to simplify the computation of chronological age. Each child is given a decile ranking from 1 to 10. The author suggests that these decile rankings be based on half grades. On page 10 of the manual, however, he uses the words "your class" as though he were talking to an individual teacher. In a reported application of the Survey (1), Symonds uses distributions based on half-grade ranges across the junior

high school. Four different normative bases are suggested to or inferred by the reader; the use of a shifting normative base is quite indefensible if the average teacher is to come out with anything but a hodgepodge.

Variable 2, named intelligence by the author, would be more appropriately named reading vocabulary since it is the vocabulary section of the *Traxler Silent Reading Test.* A table is provided to convert these vocabulary scores into mental ages based on correlations obtained with 61 children who had been given both the vocabulary tests and the *Wechsler-Bellevue Intelligence Scale,* a scale for the measurement of adult intelligence. Such a conversion is quite inappropriate but since it is not necessary for the use of the Survey, the table can be ignored safely.

Variable 3, named reading ability, is the Test of Paragraph Comprehension, Part 3 of the *Traxler Silent Reading Test.*

Variable 4 is a 30-item questionnaire in which the children answer questions about themselves. Certain answers, based apparently on the a priori judgment of the author, are considered favorable. The form is not suitable for girls. Decile ratings are based on decile norms for the entire school rather than either the classroom or the grade level.

Variable 5 is a rating by teachers of those children in the school, not just in their own homerooms, who indicate certain stated physical and personality assets and handicaps. The positive mentions are balanced against the negative mentions, and the algebraic sum for each child is converted into a decile ranking based on school wide norms.

Variable 6 is a sociometric rating in which each child matches certain descriptions with the names of other children chosen from the classroom. The children also make certain social choices. A score is derived in the same manner as for the teacher rating. There is no form for girls.

Variable 7 is a record of absences based on the entire school over a given period of time.

Variable 8 is that of school marks. They are averaged for each pupil and a decile ranking obtained. For some reason not specified, the extremely important areas of physical education, music, and the arts are excluded.

The author suggests the computation of three composite scores for each child: (*a*) median of the eight scores, (*b*) median of the three scores on variables 1–3, and (c) the median of the five scores on variables 4–8. Symonds suggests that the last two composite scores indicate promise or child potential and fulfillment or achievement, respectively; the author refers to the difference between these scores as the gap between potential and fulfillment. He suggests that the children with much greater potential than fulfillment (a high minus difference score) "are those on whom the school might well turn its searchlight of individual study, for these are the pupils who have the greatest promise but who have failed to meet expectations."

The manual refers to an article (1) by the author for data on the validity of this technique. The validity data presented in the article consists of five cases chosen at random and clinically described. Here we bump into certain semantic difficulties. These eight variables have been called criteria by the author. The further "criteria" which are chosen to validate the first eight are a series of unspecified clinical judgments of five cases chosen at random. Only the most unsophisticated reader would accept such evidence although it is provocative and could be used as the basis for more rigorous research.

The *Personality Survey* is a very good technique, in one way, in that it offers a method whereby a teacher or administrator may look at the differences that exist among his pupils. This is good because it provides a base for individual instruction. Provision for individual differences in the school situation is about the only sensible resultant that can come from an extensive consideration of individual differences. All eight variables appear to be important variables in the study of children. The methods suggested for measuring these important variables appear to be sensible and appropriate. The only notable exception is the absence of forms applicable to girls for variables 4 and 6.

The recommended statistical manipulations of these variables appear to involve statistical techniques which are not appropriate to the underlying assumptions. There are four different normative bases from which decile rankings are derived. One is the individual classroom; one is the half-grade range within the classroom; one is the half-grade range within the school; and one is the entire school (3-grade range). The fact that different teachers know and are rating different and overlapping groups of children provides an unknown but suspected large number of additional normative bases. The reviewer

suggests that this is unnecessary. If the individual classroom is the actual stage on which children compete in school, it is on this stage that all comparisons should be made. If the teacher would take the variables suggested by Symonds, measure her 30 or 40 children on each of them and then merely rank the children in her own classroom she would be operating on a single base. Median ranks could then be obtained for a total composite score as well as the difference scores which Symonds suggests. This reviewer feels that the composite scoring will prove less useful in actual practice than a study of the separate variables in relation to each other in a given child.

The reviewer disagrees with the philosophy implied in the author's interpretation of the *Personality Survey*. The author's suggestion that children with high minus differences should be the focal point for individual study implies a philosophy that is repugnant to the reviewer. A survey designed to outline individual differences should result in each child's receiving equal attention from the school to make the most of his capacities. Neither the fool, nor the genius, nor the genius acting like a fool should receive undue attention at the expense of the others.

JOHN W. M. ROTHNEY, *Professor of Education, University of Wisconsin, Madison, Wisconsin.*

This instrument proposes to furnish evidence about *basic* (!) personality traits and personal attitudes from tests, testimony from teachers, fellow pupils, and from the pupil himself. The manual states that it is intended for use in grades 7 through 9 and, although no data are given for other grade levels, it is suggested that it may be used in the sixth grade and the senior high school. When you are using the shot gun approach, you may just as well spread the shot to get any game within reach.

The test is designed more specifically to reveal those pupils who are "making the best adjustments in school: those with the best academic records, with the greatest capacity for leadership, with the most acceptable social attitudes and relationships and with emotional stability and freedom from feelings of inferiority and inadequacy." All this is to be done by assembling data on eight factors at the rate of 17 minutes per pupil. The millennium has arrived. Now, at last we will have time to work with pupils! The assembly line is out of the factory and into a social institution. But wait.

Factor 1, *chronological age,* is used on the assumption that, other things being equal, the older the pupil in a junior high school the less well adjusted he is.

Factors 2 and 3, *intelligence* and *reading ability,* are obtained from scores on the *Traxler Silent Reading Test.* Both factors are obtained from a reading test. Just why you should use the *Personality Survey* up to this point is not clear. Give the Traxler and look up the pupil's age and you have factors 1, 2, and 3.

Factor 4, *pupil self-rating,* is another version of the common, "Are your feelings easily hurt?" type of item. The author *believes* (but presents no evidence) that a battery of 30 such questions "will discriminate effectively between boys and girls who are happy, adequate and well-adjusted socially and those who are not happy." Many persons of course will *not* believe it. A distribution of scores on this factor for 770 pupils in a New York junior high school is given. In the manual it is stated that, "It is not known how representative this distribution is of junior high school pupils in general." Until such data are presented the norms are of no value.

Factor 5, *teacher rating,* is obtained by having teachers write names of pupils under such headings as, "insolent, smart alecky" and "sensitive, touchy, hurt by criticism." The invitation to call pupils names is there for those who like to do so. The author points out difficulties in use of ratings but adds, "such discrepancies in rating will occur to no greater degree by this method than by some other method." No evidence is offered.

Factor 6, *sociometric ratings,* is a combination of the common "guess who" and sociometric procedures. The combination is not a happy one.

Factor 7, *absence,* is taken from the school register on the theory that regularity in attendance is one index of good adjustment.

Factor 8, *school marks,* is taken from school records and is the average of the pupil's marks in 4 or 5 major subjects because, "It is generally recognized that school marks represent an important index of a pupil's adjustment to his work in school."

Decile positions on the eight factors are to be computed locally.

Note that this *Personality Survey,* designed to get evidence about basic *personality* traits, is obtained from your own records by noting age, absences, and marks, by giving one reading test, by using questionable ratings, by asking the pupils to answer 30 questions, and by speeded up guess who and sociometric procedures.

In the reviewer's opinion this is the worst of all the very bad ways of studying pupils so far devised.

[80]

★**Pre-Counseling Inventory.** Ages 8–14; 1949; individual; 2 scores: adjustment, tension; Form R; $1 per 20; 35¢ per specimen set; postpaid; (15–30) minutes; Alfred Schmieding; Concordia Publishing House. *

REFERENCES

1. SCHMIEDING, ALFRED. *Parent-Child Relationships in the Christian Home.* Foreword by Herbert H. Gross. River Forest, Ill.: Lutheran Education Association, 1949. Pp. vii, 22. Paper. *

CHARLES H. HONZIK, *Personal Counselor and Vocational Adviser, Veterans Administration, San Francisco, California.*

This inventory is designed "to bring to the surface the feelings, emotions, anxieties, and tensions of children often difficult to isolate or to define by ordinary observation or by the commonly used methods of interview." It is intended as a precounseling device to uncover the possible causes of maladjustment and behavior difficulties of children. The basic idea of the inventory is a comparison of responses given to statements about an imaginary boy or girl (the Story Projection) and responses given to the same statements directed in question form to the boy or girl being interviewed (the Questionnaire). There are 30 such statements, chosen from a larger battery by trial and error for their diagnostic value. Examples from the Story Projection are: "John Sumner likes to play with other boys and girls" and "John likes his father and mother about the same." These are repeated later in the Questionnaire as questions: "Do you like to play with other boys and girls?" and "Do you like your father and mother about the same?"

The child's affirmative responses are given a value of one; negative, zero. This allows a comparison of responses in the Story Projection as against responses to the same items in the Questionnaire. The number of disagreements gives what is termed the Tension Score. The number of favorable responses minus the number of disagreements is called the Adjustment Score.

The validation of the inventory, as described in the manual, and its theoretical foundations do not appear adequate. It is stated that, "In a tabulation of 77 cases the Adjustment Score was correlated with judgment. The judgment of the child's adjustment was in each case secured independently by a competent judge." But how and under what circumstances the independent judgments were obtained is not described. Though the Tension Score is the distinctive feature of the inventory and is considered valuable, the correlation between it and "independent judgment" was only .55. The author cautions against its unqualified use but states that "the Tension Score is of such value that it has been included if for no other reason than experimental purposes." On the theoretical side, the significance of disagreements between responses in the Story Projection and responses in the Questionnaire is not made clear, nor is it clear that the term "tension" adequately describes the presumably complex psychological factors that cause the differences in response.

An interesting feature of the inventory is the emphasis on religious attitudes. Five of the 30 items refer to religious matters, such as, "Do you often feel that you have many unforgiven sins?" The author states, "The Christian counselor will from time to time calmly and objectively call the child's attention to the great source of help the Bible offers him." It is evident that this feature will limit the general use of the inventory since the religious atmosphere and indoctrination implied by these items are not common to many schools and communities. The author remarks that frequently the religious items "serve the purpose of opening up some maladjusted religious emotions, which may then be explored more fully, to the benefit of the child." And, "Occasionally, a child would indicate that Jesus may have saved others from sin, but he was not sure that this applied to him." The impression one gets is that maladjustment has been manufactured by unfortunate religious attitudes and indoctrination, and more religion is to be used to undo the maladjustment. There may be some truth in this, but in this reviewer's opinion a much more fundamental and radical revision of religious education is required than is implied by the author's comments.

Aside from the Adjustment and the Tension Scores, the author believes that each item has its own value in revealing emotions and attitudes that may be the sources of conflict and maladjusted behavior. In this respect, the Inventory may be a distinctly helpful tool. Though the Tension Score is not statistically reliable the disagreements in the child's responses may be significant and exploration may reveal the source of the conflict, this being the first necessary step in the job of resolving the conflict.

[81]
*Problem Check List: Form for Rural Youth.
Ages 16–30; 1946–48; an adaptation of the *Mooney Problem Check List;* 10 scores: health and physical, relationship with people, citizenship, education, vocation and economic, morals and religion, personal temperament, courtship-sex-marriage, social and recreational, home and family; 1 form, '46; manual ('48); $1.50 per 25; 20¢ per specimen set; postage extra; nontimed (30–50) minutes; Ralph E. Bender, Mary Alice Price (manual), and Ross L. Mooney (manual); Ohio State Unversity Press. *

REFERENCES
1. BENDER, RALPH E. "The Development of a Problem Check List and a Demonstration of Its Use in Planning Rural Youth Programs." *Agric Ed Mag* 20:116–7 D '47. *
2. BENDER, RALPH E. *The Development of a Problem Check List and a Demonstration of Its Use in Planning Rural Youth Programs.* Unpublished doctor's thesis, Ohio State University (Columbus, Ohio), 1947.

[82]
*Problem Check List: Form for Schools of Nursing. Student nurses; 1945–48; an adaptation of the *Mooney Problem Check List;* 13 scores: health and physical development, finances and living conditions, social and recreational activities, social-psychological relations, personal-psychological relations, courtship-sex-marriage, home and family, morals and religion, adjustment to school of nursing, the future-professional and educational, curriculum and school program, adjustment to human relationships in nursing, adjustment to administration of nursing care; 1 form, '45; manual ('48); $1.50 per 25; 20¢ per specimen set; postage extra; nontimed (35–50) minutes; Luella J. Morison, Mary Alice Price (manual), and Ross L. Mooney (manual); Ohio State University Press. *

REFERENCES
1. MORISON, LUELLA J. "A Problem Check List: Its Use in Student Guidance." *Am J Nursing* 47:248–51 Ap '47. *

[83]
★The Purdue Rating Scale for Administrators and Executives. Administrators and executives; 1950–51; 3 levels; 1 form, '50; manual ('51); 3¢ per scale; 5¢ per profile chart for any one level ('51); 25¢ per manual; 35¢ per specimen set; postpaid; H. H. Remmers and R. L. Hobson; Personnel Evaluation Research Service, Division of Educational Reference, Purdue University. *
a) REPORT FORM A. College administrators. 3 scores: fairness to subordinates, administrative achievement, democratic orientation.
b) REPORT FORM B. Business executives; 2 scores: social responsibility for subordinates and society, executive achievement; no norms for part scores.
c) REPORT FORM C. School administrators.

REFERENCES
1. HOBSON, ROBERT L. "Some Psychological Dimensions of Academic Administrators." Abstract. *Proc Okla Acad Sci* 28: 131 '48. * (*PA* 25:1288, title only)
2. HOBSON, ROBERT L. *Some Psychological Dimensions of Academic Administrators.* Doctor's thesis, Purdue University (Lafayette, Ind.), 1948.
3. HOBSON, ROBERT L. "Some Psychological Dimensions of Academic Administrators," pp. 7–64. In *Further Studies in Attitudes, Series XVIII.* Edited by H. H. Remmers. Purdue University. Division of Educational Reference, Studies in Higher Education, [No.] 73. Lafayette, Ind.: the Division, [1950]. Pp. 95 Paper. * (*PA* 25:6490)
4. KIRK, BRUCE. *A Study of Subordinates' Attitudes Toward Public School Administrators.* Master's thesis, Purdue University (Lafayette, Ind.), 1950.
5. RUPE, JESSE C. *Some Psychological Dimensions of Business and Industrial Executives.* Doctor's thesis, Purdue University (Lafayette, Ind.), 1950. (*PA* 24:4933, title only)
6. RUPE, JESSE C. "Some Psychological Dimensions of Business and Industrial Executives," pp. 65–95. In *Further Studies in Attitudes, Series XVIII.* Edited by H. H. Remmers. Purdue

University, Division of Educational Reference, Studies in Higher Education, [No.] 73. Lafayette, Ind.: the Division, [1950]. Pp. 95. Paper. * (*PA* 25:6499)
7. RUPE, J. C. "When Workers Rate the Boss." *Personnel Psychol* 4:271–89 au '51. * (*PA* 26:3637)

KENNETH L. HEATON, *Richardson, Bellows, Henry and Co., Inc., Philadelphia, Pennsylvania.*

The scale is designed for use in the rating of administrative or executive personnel in business, industry, school or college. It presents 36 traits or characteristics on which the administrator is to be rated by his subordinates. A variety of items are included: "Possesses specific knowledge in his own field," "Is emotionally poised and calm," "Makes plans carefully and adequately," and so forth.

The authors claim that "the extensive statistical researches" done on this scale support the conclusions: "(1) There are basic aspects of administration common to all administrative work, and this scale measures at least some of the important aspects. (2) The scale is satisfactorily reliable and valid. (3) The scale does not have a serious general halo effect."

Reliability coefficients for each item were obtained by a modified split half method for business and industry and for colleges, and by the Horst technique for schools. By the split half method the range is from .54 to .98 with few items below .75. By the Horst method there was a range from .40 to .80 for public school administrators.

The authors assumed that there was no better method of validation than to compare the ratings of one subordinate with those of another subordinate, as indicated on the scale itself. Thus, they assumed that the reliability and validity coefficients were identical. These assumptions are surely open to serious question.

Normative data are based on 823 ratings of 54 administrators in nine colleges and universities, 702 ratings of 113 business and industrial executives, and 1,153 ratings of 88 superintendents and principals in 25 public schools.

Factor analysis has been applied and norms developed for the general factors "Fairness to Subordinates," "Administrative Achievement," and "Democratic Orientation" for university and college administrators.

A carefully prepared manual discusses matters of administration, scoring, and interpretation. Separate tally sheets and profile charts are provided for each of the three groups of executives.

If used by the administrator to encourage criticism on the part of his subordinates and to prepare the way for frank discussion of administrative weaknesses and failures, this can be a helpful instrument. It should often help the administrator to locate the general areas in which there is greatest dissatisfaction with his functioning. However, to use the scale as a diagnostic instrument would be unfortunate. Because of its very nature, it can not be expected to provide the specificity of information which the administrator must secure before he knows what is wrong and what improvements can be made.

[84]

The School Inventory. High school; 1936; 1 form; tentative norms—author recommends the use of local norms; $1 per 25; 10¢ per specimen set; 60¢ per plastic scoring stencil; cash orders postpaid; nontimed (10–15) minutes; Hugh M. Bell; Stanford University Press. *

REFERENCES

1–4. See 40:1252.
5. PETERS, EDWIN F. *The Construction of an Adjustment Inventory on the Basis of a Critical Analysis of the Factors as Measured by the Bell Inventories.* Doctor's thesis, New York University (New York, N.Y.), 1941. Pp. 156. (*Abstracts of Theses....[School of Education]* 1941, pp. 173–9.)
6. RYANS, DAVID G., AND PETERS, EDWIN F. "School Satisfaction Among First-Year Students in a Women's College." *Sch & Soc* 53:157–9 F 1 '41. * (*PA* 15:2383)
7. RYANS, DAVID G., AND PETERS, EDWIN F. "Factors Affecting the School-Satisfaction of Students in a Women's College." *Sch & Soc* 55:26–8 Ja 3 '42. * (*PA* 16:1691)

ROSS W. MATTESON, *Counselor, Michigan State College, East Lansing, Michigan.*

This inventory, used in high schools for the past 16 years, consists of 76 questions aimed at discovering what things about their school students may or may not consider satisfactory. Space is provided on the last page for the listing of any specific suggestions a student may have for the improvement of his school.

Approximately two thirds of the items seek to determine the student's opinions as to teacher personality and efficiency and teacher-student relationships. The remaining questions have to do with school subjects, classes, grades, and such general factors as school organization, discipline, physical facilities, and relationships with fellow students.

Students are instructed to answer each question by drawing a circle around yes, no, or ?. The instrument is practically self-administering; however, as suggested in the manual, it probably should not be administered until a "feeling of cooperation among the students" has been established.

Scoring the inventory consists simply of superimposing a transparent stencil on the answer columns and counting the number of items indicated. The higher the score the more "unsatisfactory" the attitude toward the school. Since the items are not classified, this score in itself gives no indication as to sources of dissatisfaction.

Norms for the inventory, based on a limited number of high school students, provide descriptions ranging from "excellent" to "very unsatisfactory" for the various score ranges. Perhaps the most valid use of the questionnaire lies in the information about the individual student that a detailed analysis may provide for subsequent counseling interviews.

Although the student is assured that his answers "will be treated with the strictest confidence," caution is definitely indicated both in the instrument's administration and in its interpretation. Scores of different students are more likely to reflect comparative outspokenness than comparative lack of adaptation to the school. The inventory's chief value appears to lie in its use, where indicated, with individual students and in connection with the counseling process.

For reviews by Robert G. Bernreuter and J. B. Maller, see 40:1252; for related reviews, see 40:B842, 38:B309, and 36:B30.

[85]

Selective Vocabulary Test. Ages 13 and over; 1944; a disguised test of masculinity-femininity; 1 form; no data on reliability; 2s. 6d. per 25; 3d. per single copy; 3s. per manual; purchase tax (British purchasers only) and postage extra; nontimed (15-30) minutes; Patrick Slater; George G. Harrap & Co. Ltd. *

REFERENCES

1. SLATER, PATRICK. "Interpreting Discrepancies." *Brit J Med Psychol* 19:415-9 pts 3-4 '45. ² (PA 17:3980)
2. SLATER, ELIOT, AND SLATER, PATRICK. "A Study of the Assessment of Homosexual Traits." *Brit J Med Psychol* 21:61-74 S 18 '47. * (PA 22:1238)

JAMES MAXWELL, *Principal Lecturer in Psychology, Moray House, Edinburgh, Scotland.*

This test is based on the principle that the different interests of men and women lead to their acquiring different types of vocabulary; hence masculine and feminine tendencies can be differentiated by vocabulary. The test requires the subject to define 80 words, 40 of which represent masculine interests, and 40 feminine. No words, of course, are exclusively the property of one sex, and the selection of words for the test is made on the correlation between knowledge of the word and sex, these correlations ranging from .34 to .99. No further statistical data are given.

The scoring is not entirely objective, but a number of specimen definitions are given for each word. At times the scoring appears rather arbitrary. For the word "muff" for instance, only the meaning of a hand warmer is accepted; and of the 10 definitions of "fillet" in the *Oxford Dictionary,* only one is accepted, the definitions as a headband or as a supporting strip of wood not being mentioned. By its nature the test reflects the interests of the group on whom it was validated, and it is rather English in bias. Of the sports mentioned, cricket is represented by two items, Rugby football, golf, and polo by one each. The feminine words are of more general application.

The test is primarily intended as a personality test and as a pointer to abnormalities in sexual development and attitudes. Though the author, in a rather discursive manual, appears to have the clinical applications of the test mainly in mind, a fairly comprehensive set of norms is provided for children aged 13 and 15. For each sex, for each score in the vocabulary appropriate to the sex, are given the 1, 2, 5, 10, 30, 50, 70, 90, 95, 98, and 99 percentiles for the scores in the opposite-sexed words. As the average number of cases on which each of the four sets of norms is based is about 80, this high degree of discrimination is probably not justified.

There is no doubt that further development of the test is required before it can be considered as soundly established. Of this the author is aware, and he states that he has published the test to enable further data to be obtained. To what extent the publication of an admittedly incomplete test, with comprehensive norms, etc., is justified, is a matter of opinion.

For reviews by Jack W. Dunlap and Starke R. Hathaway, see 3:93.

[86]

★**Self Analysis Inventory.** Adults; 1945; title on test booklet is "How'm I Doin'?"; an interviewing aid for locating maladjustment in 37 problem areas; 1 form; no data on reliability and validity; $9.60 per 100; 54¢ per specimen set, postpaid; 2¢ per leaflet of remedial suggestions for any one area; 48¢ per combined booklet of remedial suggestions for the 37 areas; postage extra; nontimed (30-60) minutes; Harry J. Baker; Public School Publishing Co. *

[87]

★**The Sixteen Personality Factor Questionnaire.** Adults; 1949-50; formerly called *The 16 P.F. Test;* 16 scores: cyclothymia vs. schizothymia, general intelligence vs. mental defect, emotional stability vs. general neuroticism, dominance vs. submission, surgency vs. desurgency, positive character vs. immature dependent character, adventurous cyclothymia vs. inherent withdrawn schizothymia, emotional sensitivity vs. tough maturity, paranoid schizothymia vs. trustful accessibility, bohemianism vs. practical concernedness, sophistication vs. rough simplicity, worrying suspiciousness vs. calm trustfulness, radicalism vs. conservatism, independent self-sufficiency vs. lack of resolution, will control and character stability, nervous tension; IBM; Forms A ('49), B ('49); authors recommend the use of both forms; manual ['50]; $3 per 25; $5.50 per 25 of both forms; 85¢ per specimen set of every form; separate answer sheets may be used; $2 per 50 IBM answer sheets; design for machine scoring stencils included in manual; $2 per set of stencils for hand scoring of answer sheets; 90¢ per scoring key; cash orders postpaid; (30–40) minutes for any one form; R. B. Cattell and G. Stice; Institute for Personality and Ability Testing. *

REFERENCES

1. CATTELL, RAYMOND B. "The Description of Personality: Principles and Findings in a Factor Analysis." *Am J Psychol* 58:69–90 Ja '45. * (PA 19:1511)
2. CATTELL, RAYMOND B. "Interpretation of the Twelve Primary Personality Factors." *Char & Pers* 13:55–91 S '45. * (PA 19:1971)
3. CATTELL, RAYMOND B. "Personality Traits Associated With Abilities: II, With Verbal and Mathematical Abilities." *J Ed Psychol* 36:475–86 N '45. * (PA 20:2389)
4. CATTELL, RAYMOND B. "Confirmation and Clarification of Primary Personality Factors." *Psychometrika* 12:197–220 S '47. *
5. CATTELL, RAYMOND B. "Primary Personality Factors in the Realm of Objective Tests." *J Personality* 16:459–87 Je '48. * (PA 23:2154)
6. CATTELL, RAYMOND B. "The Primary Personality Factors in Women Compared With Those in Men." *Brit J Psychol, Stat Sect* 1:114–30 Jl '48. * (PA 23:4670)
7. CATTELL, RAYMOND B. "The Main Personality Factors in Questionnaire Self-Estimate Material." *J Social Psychol* 31:3–38 F '50. * (PA 24:5722)
8. CATTELL, R. B., AND SAUNDERS, D. R. "Inter-Relation and Matching of Personality Factors From Behavior Rating, Questionnaire, and Objective Test Data." *J Social Psychol* 31:243–60 My '50. * (PA 25:2902)

CHARLES M. HARSH, *Research Psychologist, U.S. Navy Electronics Laboratory, San Diego, California.* *

The authors claim that, among personality tests, this is as pure a product of factor analysis as can be found, in that each item has appreciable saturation by one of the 16 "source traits" of ability, temperament, and character integration. Twelve of the factors were isolated by factor analysis of observers' ratings of traits, the other four were found in questionnaire responses. The printed test directions are brief, with freedom for amplification by the administrator. Items are of two types, each with three alternate answers:

Do you tend to get angry with
 people rather easily? . . . . .   In
Would you prefer the life of: Yes Between No
 (a) an artist?
 (b) a Y.M.C.A. secretary? (a) Uncertain (b)

Many of the items look familiar to users of older personality and interest inventories, but the manual does not indicate the method of derivation of items or the method whereby observer-rating factors were translated into questionnaire items. Many of the items have the objectionable ambiguity which was criticized in older questionnaires, thus arousing a rather uncooperative attitude among college students, to whom this

reviewer has administered the test. In general the items seem less subtle and penetrating than items of the *Guilford-Martin Inventory of Factors GAMIN* or of the revised *Kuder Preference Record*. This is only a superficial judgment, of course, but it points to the need for objective evidence of the superiority of *The 16 P.F. Test*.

The parallel Forms A and B have identical rotation of 187 items, with 3 buffer items and 10 or 13 items measuring each factor. On a general population sample of 200, the corrected split half reliabilities of the factor scores from Forms A and B combined range from .50 to .88 (Md = .71). No reliabilities are reported for the separate forms, but the manual implies that they are too unreliable for most purposes since it recommends that both forms be given as a single test. Hand scoring by transparencies involves repositioning and stapling the sheets of the test booklet. A separate answer sheet can be machine scored with six sets of keys which fit either Form A or B. Positions on the answer sheet do not line up with items on the test booklet. Raw scores are converted to standard scores on a 10-point scale, based on the responses of 293 college students plus 50 other adults.

The manual claims that the items represent an even sampling from the personality sphere with a minimum of overlapping of factor scores, but no objective evidence is presented to support these claims. The manual gives no information concerning either the factor saturations of the items or the intercorrelation of factor scores. Neither is there any indication of the correlation of factor scores with other personality measures. It is implied that no other measures are pure enough to use for validating the 16 personality factors, which are merely described verbally and defended on the grounds that they, or apparently closely related factors, have shown up in many different factorial studies of personality and even in clinical studies. To this reviewer it seems very desirable to know how factor B (general intelligence) is related to recognized measures of intelligence, how factor E (ascendance-submission) is related to the Allports' *A-S Reaction Study,* how Q_1 (radicalism-conservatism) is related to other radicalism tests, and how the other factors are related to somewhat similarly named factors in the tests of Kuder, Guilford, Thurstone, and others who have assembled fairly "pure factor" subtests. Such information will neither validate nor invalidate *The 16 P.F. Test,* but it will help to orient psychometrists who wish to evaluate the alleged distinction between the 16 source traits and the personality factors previously revealed in other factor studies.

The 16 P.F. Test is presented as a research instrument with possible applied psychology uses. In its present form it seems unlikely that it can give an assessment of personality much superior to that of other multifactor paper tests. Cattell has suggested the factorial determinants of various life situations, and the test may be useful in investigating hunches concerning the composition of psychometric classifications or clinical syndromes. But, in general, the utility of the 16 factor scores remains to be demonstrated, and the neutral observer will probably want better evidence of the purity of the factor scores before he starts using *The 16 P.F. Test* as an analytical research instrument.

ARDIE LUBIN, *Statistical Psychologist, Institute of Psychiatry, Maudsley Hospital, London, England.*

This personality questionnaire contains items such as "Do you think that most of us have so many faults that unless people are charitable to one another life would be intolerable? Yes. In Between. No." The subject picks one of the three alternatives.

The split half reliabilities for scores on *the two forms combined* based on 200 cases range from .50 to .88 for the various factors. The standardisation given in the handbook is casually described as "based on 293 men and women college students, averaging 22 years of age, plus some 50 men and women from other walks of life." Means and standard deviations are given. Within the handbook, various references are made to "peripheral standardisation" in terms of means and standard deviations for "occupations, clinical syndromes, social, educational, sex and age classes, etc." This information, if it existed, would make the test unique; this reviewer, however, has been unable to find any such data either in the handbook or in published articles. The test user is invited to substitute, for the actual validation data, a mental estimate of how important the given factors are in the given situation where prediction is needed which is to be based on an "understanding of the intrinsic meaning of each of" the 16 scores. The test user presumably obtains this understanding by reading descriptions presented in the handbook such as the following:

FACTOR F. SURGENCY AND DESURGENCY. * It is well known and frequently confirmed that the factor is a powerful component in what used to be called extraversion-introversion. Eysenck's study in the abnormal range shows that it is associated with a basic temperamental difference which causes some individuals (the surgent individuals) to show *conversion hysteria* responses in emotional difficulties while the desurgent individuals tend to show free floating anxiety and depression as in typical *anxiety hysteria*.

The reviewer found that he and other psychologists reading this passage tended to interpret it as meaning that Eysenck had found that scores on Factor F differentiated conversion hysteria from anxiety hysteria. At present, neither Eysenck nor any other psychologist has published evidence showing that Factor F discriminates between any two groups of mental patients. This free, though unwarranted, linking of factor scores to mental illnesses is found throughout the handbook. "As far as resemblance to clinical diagnostic categories are concerned it will be readily seen that A and H are two factors in schizophrenia, O corresponds to free anxiety or neurasthenia, F differentiates conversion hysteria and manic conditions from anxiety neurosis and depression, Q_3 is the pattern of the obsessional character, L is the paranoid component and C is a measure of general neuroticism." Again, no published evidence can be found that shows that these factor scores actually do discriminate in this manner between the specified groups of mental patients. Presumably, these clinical terms are used as hypotheses, possible explanations of the factors. But to make this clear to the test user, the handbook would have to be entirely rewritten.

We conclude that *The 16 P.F. Test* could be used in a harmful manner. Either the statements about the diagnostic value of the factor scores should be confirmed, or the present handbook withdrawn and rewritten. At present the test has no known validated use.

J. RICHARD WITTENBORN, *Research Associate in Psychology, Yale University, New Haven, Connecticut.*

This questionnaire is based on a factorial approach to the study of personality. Accordingly, the virtues and the limitations to be considered should include a review of the virtues and limitations of both a factorial approach and of a questionnaire method. When items are scored on the basis of their factorial composition, it in effect means that their intercorrelations have determined the manner in which they are grouped for scoring, and on this basis it may be claimed that all the items which comprise a given factor score are to some degree or another measuring the same thing, i.e., that is they tend to distinguish between people in a similar way. Scores based on this kind of behavioral homogeneity have certain advantages. (*a*) Scores of different magnitudes are likely to have the same kind of behavioral significance (the distinction between individuals is on the basis of *degree* rather than *kind*). (*b*) The person who interprets the score has a better chance of knowing what the score means than a person who is forced to interpret scores which represent heterogeneous and unspecified behavior. (*c*) Because of their behavioral homogeneity, it is possible that such scores may have an exceptional validity for homogeneous criteria of similar content and reduced validity for criteria which are heterogeneous in content. Ordinarily, this should mean that factor scores can be combined more economically in the multiple prediction of criteria than can scores which have no particular claim to behavioral homogeneity.

According to the manual, the authors aim *"to leave out no important aspect of the total personality"* (and apparently they assume that the basic aspects are limited in number and for the most part have been discovered by their studies). This is a notable aim inasmuch as important aspects of the personality may be defined ad infinitum on the basis of an almost countless variety of desiderata. It should be emphasized, however, that factors are based on patterns of intercorrelation. Inasmuch as the pattern of intercorrelation among items is determined by the habits which the sample of items may represent and by the habits which are present in the sample of subjects employed, factors cannot be claimed to have a significance which transcends time, place, and circumstance. As a matter of fact, they may have no significance at all which is relevant to the purposes of testing and as a consequence they are best regarded as a kind of economy or shortcut in describing a sample of behavior; the practical value of the economy is relative and dependent upon a correspondence between the sampling considerations which determined the selection of items and subjects and the anticipated practical testing situation. In any event, it seems unwarranted for the test users to accept naively the label which the factor analyst applies to his factor scores. Before factor scores can be used intelligently, the reader should ex-

amine the items which contribute to the factor and compare his own inference concerning the basis for their homogeneity with the inference provided by the factor analyst. He should next refine his inference by a scrutiny of the items which do not form a part of the factor score in question. This type of scrutiny is particularly desirable when no external validity is provided for the factor score.

The examiner's use of the factor scores obviously cannot be dependable until he knows their reliability; just as important and perhaps less obvious is the desirability of the examiner's knowing the manner in which the factor scores are intercorrelated. Even though the factor analyst may claim that his factors are relatively independent, their actual dependence or independence of the factors must be empirically determined.

The reliabilities of the factor scores for Forms A and B combined range from .50 to .88. The intercorrelations among the factor scores are not found in the manual. Although it is claimed that the traits inferred by the authors and measured by the questionnaire are based on a variety of studies employing different kinds of material, the manual offers the examiner no specific information concerning the samples of subjects and data employed in making the inferences or concerning the manner in which the nature of a trait was inferred. The norms are based primarily on college students.

From the information provided by the manual it may be remarked that the reliabilities of the scores are rather low for the study of the individual, that the samples (subjects and variables) on which the factors are based are not specified, that the interdependence of the scores is not given, and that the possible practical validity of the scores is for the most part a matter for speculation. Despite these limitations (which may be limitations in the preparation of the manual), it is quite probable that the questionnaire may be valuably employed in a variety of personnel research undertakings. The questionnaire as it stands is not a finished tool. It represents a very worthwhile and ambitious beginning, however, and this reviewer takes pleasure in suggesting its use wherever trial approaches to the evaluations of new aspects of personality are desired.

[88]
★**Social Distance Scale, Seventh Experimental Edition.** Ages 15 and over; 1925–51; 4 scales listed

below; mimeographed; no data on reliability and validity; no manual; 20 or more sets of the 4 scales, 8¢ per set; 2¢ per copy of any one scale; postage extra; 10¢ per specimen set, postpaid; 20(25) minutes; Emory S. Bogardus; the Author, 3518 University Ave., Los Angeles 7, Calif. *
a) ETHNIC DISTANCE SCALE. 1925-51; formerly called *Racial Distance;* 1 form, '51.
b) OCCUPATION DISTANCE. 1925.
c) RELIGIOUS DISTANCE. 1925.
d) ECONOMIC DISTANCE. 1925.

REFERENCES

1. BOGARDUS, EMORY S. "Measuring Social Distances." *J Appl Sociol* 9:299-308 My-Je '25. *
2. BOGARDUS, EMORY S. "Social Distance and Its Origins." *J Appl Sociol* 9:216-26 Ja-F '25. *
3. BOGARDUS, EMORY S. "A Social Distance Scale." *Sociol & Social Res* 17:265-71 Ja-F '33. * (*PA* 9:3965)
4. ZELIGS, ROSE, AND HENDRIKSON, GORDON. "Racial Attitudes of Two Hundred Sixth-Grade Children." *Social & Social Res* 18:26-36 S-O '33. * (*PA* 8:2384)
5. ZELIGS, ROSE, AND HENDRIKSON, GORDON. "Checking the Social Distance Technique Through Personal Interviews." *Sociol & Social Res* 18:420-30 My-Je '34. * (*PA* 9:2899)
6. ZELIGS, ROSE, AND HENDRIKSON, GORDON. "Factors Regarded by Children as the Basis of Their Racial Attitudes." *Sociol & Social Res* 19:225-33 Ja-F '35. * (*PA* 9:6056)
7. BOGARDUS, EMORY S. *Introduction to Social Research,* pp. 96-103. University of Southern California School of Research Series, No. 14; Social Science Series, No. 17. Los Angeles, Calif.: Suttonhouse Ltd., 1936. Pp. xiii, 237. *
8. BROOKS, LEE M. "Racial Distance as Affected by Education." *Sociol & Social Res* 21:128-33. N-D '36. *
9. BOGARDUS, EMORY S. "Social Distance and Its Practical Implications." *Sociol & Social Res* 22:462-76 My-Je '38. * (*PA* 8:3201)
10. ZELIGS, ROSE. "Racial Attitudes of Children As Expressed by Their Concepts of Races." *Sociol & Social Res* 21:361-71 Mr-Ap '38. *
11. FORD, ROBERT N. *Techniques for Scaling Experiences: A Study of White-Negro Contacts.* Doctor's thesis, University of Pittsburgh (Pittsburgh, Pa.), 1940. (*Abstracts of Theses.... 1940,* 1941, pp. 113-22.)
12. SPOERL, DOROTHY TILDEN. "Bilinguality and Emotional Adjustment." *J Abn & Social Psychol* 38:37-57 Ja '43. * (*PA* 17:3837)
13. BELL, HAROLD VERNON, JR. *An Evaluation of the Bogardus Scale of Social Distance by the Method of Equal-Appearing Intervals.* Master's thesis, Southern Methodist University (Dallas, Texas), 1947.
14. BOGARDUS, EMORY S. "Changes in Racial Distances." *Int J Opin & Attit Res* 1:55-62 D '47. * (*PA* 22:4367)
15. BOGARDUS, EMORY S. "Measurement of Personal-Group Relations." *Sociometry* 10:306-11 N '47. * (*PA* 23:1246)
16. BOGARDUS, EMORY S. "The Intercultural Workshop and Racial Distance." *Sociol & Social Res* 32:798-802 Mr-Ap '48. * (*PA* 22:3424)
17. DAVIDOFF, MELVIN D. *A Study of Empathy and Correlates of Prejudice Toward a Minority Group.* Edited by H. H. Remmers. Purdue University, Division of Educational Reference, Studies in Higher Education [No.] 67; Further Studies in Attitudes, Series 13. Lafayette, Ind.: the Division, 1949. Pp. 58. Paper. $0.75. *
18. SARTAIN, A. Q., AND BELL, HAROLD V., JR. "An Evaluation of the Bogardus Scale of Social Distance by the Method of Equal-Appearing Intervals." *J Social Psychol* 29:85-91 F '49. * (*PA* 23:4201)
19. SCHENK, QUENTIN F., AND ROMNEY, A. KIMBALL. "Some Differential Attitudes Among Adolescent Groups as Revealed by Bogardus' Social Distance Scale." *Sociol & Social Res* 35:38-45 S-O '50. * (*PA* 25:6071)

DONALD T. CAMPBELL, *Assistant Professor of Psychology, The University of Chicago, Chicago, Illinois.*

The Bogardus *Social Distance Scale* is probably the most used single test of social attitudes, with a popularity that shows no signs of waning after 27 years. It is also one of the oldest tests. Only Harper's *A Social Study* [1] is older among attitude tests that have been used beyond the

research in which they were originally presented. The *Social Distance Scale* provides the backbone of Bogardus' outstanding research on race attitudes in the United States.[2] It is also a major instrument in Hartley's recent research,[3] that of Murphy and Likert,[4] Zeligs and Hendrikson (4, 5, 6), and of many others we have made no attempt to cite here. Perhaps even more outstanding is the fact that such subsequent research has reinforced Bogardus' main conclusions as to the generality within the United States of a hierarchy of preferences for nationality and ethnic groups, a hierarchy which even minority groups share in its essential outline.[2,3] The test has also been used to measure social distance toward professions, religious groups, conscientious objectors, etc. It is probably the most frequent illustration of attitude measurement cited in social psychology texts.

The test itself is simple. While the various users have modified the instructions, and occasionally the items, the general format has usually been kept. In its original version it went like this: "According to my first feeling reactions, I would willingly admit members of each race (as a class, and not the best I have known nor the worst members) to one or more of the classifications under which I have placed a cross: (1) To close kinship by marriage. (2) To my club as personal chums. (3) To my street as neighbors. (4) To employment in my occupation in my country. (5) To citizenship in my country. (6) As visitors only to my country. (7) Would exclude from my country." Under the 7 points as column headings were spaces to rate a large number of ethnic and nationality groups (1).

In spite of this general acceptance, the test has had a cinderella-like history in its reputation for scientific respectability within the test and measurement fraternity. Some 10 months after Bogardus first published the scale in 1925, Allport and Hartman published their article [5] which is often cited as the beginning of scientific attitude measurement. (Actually efforts at attitude testing date back to 1920, at least.) Taking

1 Harper, Manly H. *Social Beliefs and Attitudes of American Educators.* Columbia University, Teachers College, Contributions to Education, No. 294. New York: Bureau of Publications, the College, 1927. Pp. v, 91. * (*PA* 2:1295)

2 Bogardus, Emory S. *Immigration and Race Attitudes.* Foreword by Jerome Davis. Boston, Mass.: D. C. Heath & Co., 1928. Pp. xi, 268. * (*PA* 2:3223)
3 Hartley, Eugene L. *Problems in Prejudice.* New York: King's Crown Press, 1946. Pp. x, 124. (*PA* 20:3231)
4 Murphy, Gardner, and Likert, Rensis. *Public Opinion and the Individual: A Psychological Study of Student Attitudes on Public Questions, With a Retest Five Years Later.* New York: Harper & Brothers, 1938. Pp. ix, 316. * (*PA* 12:5448)
5 Allport, Floyd H., and Hartman, D. A. "The Measurement and Motivation of Atypical Opinion in a Certain Group." *Am Pol Sci R* 19:735-60 N '25. *

off from this article, L. L. Thurstone [6] threw the elaborate machinery of the psychophysical methods into the problem of attitude test construction. The weight of this tradition and its greater claims for mathematical sophistication gave the Thurstone scales a superior prestige that today seems largely specious. (In general, the preponderant emphasis of the Thurstone methods was on the precise scaling of item intensity, a nonessential by current standards. Item homogeneity is today the main objective.[7,8]) So dominating was this aura of scientific respectability that even Bogardus himself felt its weight, and in 1933 (3) published a revision of his scale with "equal" steps, as established by processing some 60 social distance steps through the equal-appearing-intervals method.[9] The items of this scale are as follows: "(1) Would marry. (2) Would have as regular friends. (3) Would work beside in an office. (4) Would have several families in my neighborhood. (5) Would have merely as speaking acquaintances. (6) Would have live outside my neighborhood. (7) Would have live outside my country." So far as the present reviewer is aware, this revision has not been extensively used. Hartley, for instance, used the original scale, adding an additional step "to my school as classmates" between Bogardus' steps 3 and 4. So far did the reputation for scientific respectability of the Bogardus scale slip that McNemar [10] was able to ignore it completely in his otherwise thorough review of the literature.

Fads in attitude measurement have, however, changed, and today the apex of respectability is occupied by a specialized language of internal consistency known as Guttman Scale Analysis,[8] with its criteria of unidimensionality and reproducibility. The 20 or 30 Thurstone scales of social attitude are made obsolete by this criterion (and incidentally also by Thurstone's own later criterion of interitem factor analysis). And although Guttman has not expressly stated so,

the old Bogardus scale is a perfect illustration of the hierarchical unidimensional set of items that scale analysis requires. (For scale analysis purposes, slight rewording would be required of Item 6 in the original scale, so that it would read "As visitors to my country," and thus avoid the double-endedness of its original wording. In the 1933 revised scale, Item 5 would have to drop the "merely.") Two very recent research reports have explicitly confirmed this, finding that in larger batteries of items dealing with attitudes toward Negroes, only items in the social distance domain "scaled." [11,12]

The *Social Distance Scale* shares, of course, the difficulties of all measuring instruments depending upon voluntary self-description by the population under study. This weakness is to be found in all published attitude tests, and in all interest tests except those utilizing differential information profiles. In spite of this limitation, much valuable research has been done with such techniques, characteristically using anonymity as a substitute for disguise. Another note of caution seems indicated where, as in the studies of Hartley [3] and Murphy and Likert,[4] the social distance test involving a large number of out-groups is scored to get one general ethnocentrism or xenophobia score. As Cronbach [13] has so ably pointed out, any repetitive response required of the respondent may create "response sets," which in an irrelevant way increase the internal consistency of the test. Both Murphy and Likert, and Hartley report split half reliabilities, corrected, in the range .94 to .97 with the social distance test involving 21 to 32 social groups to be judged. This reliability for a test taking but 10 minutes is so high as to cause suspicion rather than comfort. The present reviewer would also tend to interpret as evidence of response set rather than validity Hartley's finding that the social distance expression to three nonsuch ethnic groups (e.g., Pireneans) correlated .80 with the composite social distance score based on 32 actual ethnic and nationality groups. These qualifications are minor, however, and do not affect the more sociological use of the test for ranking social groups in popular favor. Among social attitude tests, the *Social Distance Scale*

6 Thurstone, L. L. "The Method of Paired Comparisons for Social Values." *J Abn & Social Psychol* 21:384–400 '27. (PA 1:1216)

7 Likert, Rensis. *A Technique for the Measurement of Attitudes.* Archives of Psychology, No. 140. New York: Archives of Psychology, Columbia University, 1932. Pp. 55. Paper. (PA 7:1885)

8 Stouffer, Samuel A.; Guttman, Louis; Suchman, Edward A.; Lazarsfeld, Paul F.; Star, Shirley A.; and Clausen, John A. *Studies in Social Psychology in World War II, Vol. 4.* Princeton, N.J.: Princeton University Press, 1950. Pp. x, 756. * (PA 25:3037)

9 Thurstone, L. L., and Chave, E. J. *The Measurement of Attitude: A Psychophysical Method and Some Experiments With a Scale for Measuring Attitude Toward the Church.* Chicago, Ill.: University of Chicago Press, 1929. Pp. xii, 97. Paper. * (PA 3:4902)

10 McNemar, Quinn. "Opinion-Attitude Methodology." *Psychol B* 43:289–374 Jl '46. * (PA 20:4703)

11 Schuessler, K. F. "Item Analysis in Scale Analysis." Paper read at the 46th Annual Meeting of the American Sociological Society, Chicago, September 7, 1951.

12 Suchman, Edward A. "Attitude Research in the Elmira Study." Paper read at the 46th Annual Meeting of the American Sociological Society, Chicago, September 6, 1951.

13 Cronbach, Lee J. "Further Evidence on Response Sets and Test Design." *Ed & Psychol Meas* 10:3–31 sp '50. * (PA 25:681)

Cronbach, Lee J. "Response Sets and Test Validity." *Ed & Psychol Meas* 6:475–94 w '46. * (PA 21:2489) is so good, and so naturally suited to its purpose, that if Bogardus had not invented it, some one else would have. Such a situation is rare indeed in the social sciences.

[89]

*Social Intelligence Test: George Washington University Series, Revised Form. Grades 9–16 and adults; 1930–49; 3 editions; 1 form; no data on reliability and validity in manual; no norms for part scores; manual ('49); names and faces sheet ('48); 50¢ per specimen set; postpaid; F. A. Moss, Thelma Hunt, and K. T. Omwake; Center for Psychological Service, George Washington University. *
a) SECOND EDITION. 1930–49; 6 scores: judgment in social situations, recognition of the mental state of the speaker, memory for names and faces, observation of human behavior, sense of humor, total; 1 form, '49; $3.75 per 25; 49(55) minutes; prepared with the assistance of L. G. Woodward.
b) SHORT EDITION. 1944; 5 scores: same as for *Second Edition* except for memory for names and faces; $3.75 per 25; 40(45) minutes.
c) SP (SPECIAL) EDITION. 1947; 3 scores: judgment in social situations, observation of human behavior, total; $3 per 25; 30(35) minutes.

REFERENCES

1–20. See 40:1253.
21–29. See 3:96.
30. GARRETT, H. E., AND KELLOGG, W. W. "The Relation of Physical Constitution to General Intelligence, Social Intelligence, and Emotional Instability." *J Exp Psychol* 11:113–29 Ap '28. *
31. SCUDDER, CHARLES ROLAND, AND RAUBENHEIMER, A. S. "Are Standardized Mechanical Aptitude Tests Valid?" *J Juvenile Res* 14:120–3 Ap '30. * (*PA* 5:897)
32. HUDDLESTON, EDITH. *Construction and Preliminary Study of a Revised Student Form of the Social Intelligence Test.* Master's thesis, George Washington University (Washington, D.C.), 1940.
33. EIMICKE, VICTOR W., AND FISH, HERMAN L. "A Preliminary Study of the Relationships Between the Bernreuter Personality Inventory and Performances on the Army Alpha Examination and the George Washington Social Intelligence Test." *J Psychol* 25:381–7 Ap '48. * (*PA* 22:4418)
34. ABT, LAWRENCE EDWIN. "A Test Battery for Selecting Technical Magazine Editors." *Personnel Psychol* 2:75–91 sp '49. * (*PA* 23:5099)
35. SMITH, HENRY CLAY. "Psychometric Checks on Hypotheses Derived From Sheldon's Work on Physique and Temperament." *J Personality* 17:310–20 Mr '49. * (*PA* 25:2916)
36. EIMICKE, VICTOR WILLIAM. *A Study of the Effect of Intensive Sales Training Experience Upon the Measured Abilities and Personality Characteristics of Salesman-Candidates.* Doctor's thesis, New York University (New York, N.Y.), 1951. Abstract: *Microfilm Abstracts* 11:951–2 no 4 '51.

For reviews by Glen U. Cleeton and Howard R. Taylor, see 3:96; for a review by Robert L. Thorndike, see 40:1253.

[90]

★SRA Junior Inventory. Grades 4–8; 1951; 5 scores: my health, getting along with other people, about me and my school, about myself, about me and my home; IBM; 1 form; separate answer pads or answer sheets must be used; $1.15 per 25 profiles; 75¢ per specimen set; cash orders postpaid; nontimed (30–40) minutes; H. H. Remmers and Robert H. Bauernfeind; Science Research Associates, Inc. *
a) FORM AH (HAND SCORING EDITION). 49¢ per test and answer pad; $1.90 per 25 answer pads.
b) FORM AM (MACHINE SCORING EDITION). 39¢ per test; $2.90 per 100 IBM answer sheets; $1.50 per set of scoring stencils.

REFERENCES

1. BAUERNFEIND, ROBERT H. *The Development of a Needs and Problems Inventory for Elementary School Children.* Doctor's thesis, Purdue University (Lafayette, Ind.), 1951.

DWIGHT L. ARNOLD, *Professor of Education, and Director of Guidance Testing, Kent State University, Kent, Ohio.*

The development of problem check lists for use in the high school and elementary school is a promising step in developing guidance programs and educational programs more nearly geared to the actual living problems of boys and girls. The publication of instruments in this area and the addition of further data are definitely desirable.

Basic procedures indicated in the development of this inventory seem sound and thorough. The items in the inventory were developed from statements of pupils. The inventory has been given to a sufficiently large number of pupils representing various regions and types of schools so that the norms must be recognized as being not only adequate but well presented. Table 7, giving the percentage of children checking each item from the various subgroups by sex, grade, community, region, and social economic status, is a very significant table. In fact, it greatly enhances the value of such an inventory and answers a number of questions which may properly be raised about this instrument. These data show that such a device is usable in the fourth and fifth grades. They show the extent to which the grade level and type of community influence the number of items checked by these children. The data in this table are so significant that its value may easily be overlooked. This and similar studies can well be the source of significant information for curriculum development as well as for suggesting types of guidance programs and activities needed. This table also suggests an important use that may be made of such instruments.

The suggestions given in the manual for use are well stated and helpful. No caution is found in the manual about the possibility of negative reactions from parents and children in the use of the inventory. Although this does not occur frequently in using such problem check lists in the school, users should be cautioned to prepare the students adequately and to have a reasonably favorable attitude in the community before such an instrument is extensively used. It is probably a desirable suggestion that such an inventory should be used on a voluntary basis unless it is used without names for research purposes. There should be some caution in the use of these inventories regarding the danger that users may get into psychological problems of greater depth than they are prepared to handle. It is true of all personality inventories and check lists that harm may be done by attempting to deal with problems at a much deeper level than these instruments allow. The major emphasis should be on the recognition of problems as normal and on the common sense ways of dealing with these problems or of talking them through with trained persons who are working in areas where they have had adequate background and training.

A profile chart for a problem check list seems to be entirely out of place. For example, what does it mean to indicate that a child who marks one item stands at the 14th percentile in the number of problems checked about himself whereas a student who marks four items is at the 50th percentile? This profile violates the generally accepted principle that high points on the profile should represent desirable scores.

Failure to give credit to the extensive and excellent work done by Ross Mooney at Ohio State University in the development of problem check lists points either to negligence or to intentional omission, neither of which is defensible.

The form of the inventory using several different sheets and a special carbon answer pad is a needlessly complicated and much more expensive instrument than is needed for scoring which involves simply counting items checked. According to prices from the 1951 catalogue the *SRA Junior Inventory* will cost a minimum of 16¢ a pupil whereas the *Mooney Problem Check List* available for grades 7–9 is available for 6 to 7 cents apiece.

While this inventory seems to function satisfactorily at the junior high school level, the wording of items seems decidedly more appropriate for grades 4 to 6 than for junior high school. For grades 7–9, the *Mooney Problem Check List,* Junior High Form, is decidedly more appropriate. Aside from high cost and needless complexity, the *SRA Junior Inventory* seems a satisfactory instrument for the purpose intended, especially for grades 4–6.

[91]

★SRA Youth Inventory. Grades 7–12; 1949–50; 9 scores: my school, looking ahead, about myself, getting along with others, my home and family, boy meets girl, health, things in general, basic difficulty; IBM; 2 editions; 1 form, '49; manual for grades 9–12 ('49); supplementary manual for grades 7–9 ('50); separate answer sheets must be used; $1.15 per 25 profiles; 75¢ per specimen set; cash orders postpaid; nontimed (35–45) minutes; H. H. Remmers, Benjamin Shimberg, and A. J. Drucker; Science Research Associates, Inc. *
a) FORM AH (HAND SCORING EDITION). 49¢ per test and

answer pad; $1.90 per 25 answer pads; 50¢ per scoring stencil.
b) FORM AM (MACHINE SCORING EDITION). 39¢ per test; $2.90 per 100 IBM answer sheets; $2.50 per set of scoring stencils.

REFERENCES

1. SHIMBERG, BENJAMIN. *The Development of a Needs and Problems Inventory for High School Youth.* Doctor's thesis, Purdue University (Lafayette, Ind.), 1949.
2. EUGENE, CHESTER J. *The Nature and Extent of Worries of North Dakota High School Pupils.* Master's thesis, University of North Dakota (Grand Forks, N.D.), 1950. Review: A. V. Overn. *Sch Ed Rec Univ N Dak* 36:245–8 My '51. *
3. SHIMBERG, BENJAMIN. *The Development of a Needs and Problems Inventory for High-School Youth.* Foreword by H. H. Remmers. Purdue University, Division of Educational Reference, Studies in Higher Education [No.] 72; Further Studies in Attitudes, Series 17. Lafayette, Ind.: the Division, 1950. Pp. 75. Paper. * (PA 25:4836)
4. SHIMBERG, BENJAMIN. "The Development of a 'Youth Inventory' for Use in Guidance and Curriculum Planning." Abstract. *Am Psychol* 5:354 Jl '50. * (PA 25:1271, title only)
5. JACOBS, ROBERT. "A Report on Experimental Use of the SRA Youth Inventory in the Fall Testing Program of the Educational Records Bureau," pp. 47–60. (PA 25:6442) In *1950 Fall Testing Program in Independent Schools and Supplementary Studies.* Foreword by Ben D. Wood. Educational Records Bulletin, No. 56. New York: Educational Records Bureau, January 1951. Pp. xiii, 89. Paper, lithotyped. *
6. MEYER, JOHN K. *An Experimental Study of Response Set in the SRA Youth Inventory.* Master's thesis, Purdue University (Lafayette, Ind.), 1951.
7. REMMERS, H. H., AND HACKETT, C. G. *What Are Your Problems?* Chicago, Ill.: Science Research Associates, Inc., 1951. Pp. 48. Paper. * (PA 26:2653)

KENNETH E. CLARK, *Associate Professor of Psychology, University of Minnesota, Minneapolis, Minnesota.*

This checklist of 298 questions "has been designed as a tool to help teachers, counselors, and school administrators to identify quickly the problems that young people say worry them most. Its results should also prove useful to students and their parents."

Items for the eight major areas of problems tapped by the inventory came from analysis of "hundreds of essays" obtained by asking students in more than 100 high schools throughout the country to state anonymously in their own words "what things bothered them most." Questions prepared to cover as wide a range of the problems as possible were then administered to "thousands of high school students in every section of the country." The resulting inventory covers in very satisfactory fashion the problems young people consider to be most important.

Responses to items are either check marks (if the statement "expresses something that has been a problem to you") or blanks. A self-scoring answer sheet is provided in addition to separate machine scorable answer sheets. Scoring of the responses in the eight areas may be done by the student himself but scoring of the Basic Difficulty items is reserved for the counselor or teacher. The general wording of questions, methods of scoring, and methods of translating raw scores into percentile scores are carefully planned and make the instrument exceedingly easy to administer.

The interpretation of scores is not easy. The authors suggest that the high points on a profile of scores be used by students to stimulate them to solve their own problems and that teachers use the inventory to learn more about their students and their problems. Counselors would want to interview first those persons with high Basic Difficulty scores and should consider that any score above, say, the 75th percentile indicates a need for counseling. In counseling, item responses for an individual or for a class may be discussed. The authors caution that the use of scores by themselves to indicate maladjustment is not warranted—that these scores merely indicate the relative frequency, not the intensity or severity, of problems. The manual is devoted in large part to discussion of appropriate uses of the inventory.

Items in the inventory are divided into eight areas, on a judgmental basis, checked by internal consistency analysis. Evidence presented indicates that each of the eight areas is sufficiently homogeneous to warrant use of a single score for it. Intercorrelations of area scores are reported as ranging from .20 to .67 with a median intercorrelation of .46. No test-retest reliabilities of area scores are presented: hence, the user cannot estimate whether area scores are relatively stable indicators of problems over a long time interval. No evidences of longitudinal time changes in scores of any individual or group are presented. The reliabilities of the area scores, estimated by Kuder-Richardson methods, seem high enough for individual use with the possible exception of the health area key.

The norms are more adequate than those for most instruments of this sort. The normative sample is large, spread across the entire country, and stratified to approximate known population characteristics. Separate norms are presented for sexes, and condensed norms are provided for 16 subgroups broken on sex, grade, and rural-urban distribution. In addition, the percentages of young people checking each item are provided, broken down by sex, grade, geographic region, rural-urban distribution, religion, and family income.

It is apparent that the authors consider this instrument to be both a measure of adjustment and an aid in the counseling interview. Thus, "the inventory is supposed to provide an indication of what a student *thinks* are his problems."

Used for this purpose, no validation is possible. The authors do expect, however, that the inventory will have external validity. Preliminary evidence on this point, presented in the manual, indicates that 22 out of 35 students independently rated as well adjusted scored above the median on the Basic Difficulty key, and that 36 of 57 poorly adjusted students had scores below the median. This validity evidence is not striking, perhaps because of the unreliability of the independent ratings of adjustment, and is practically useless to the teacher or counselor, since interpretations of profiles will presumably be made using the 75th percentile as the cut-off point (at the authors' suggestion) rather than the median.

This inventory thus shows promise of being useful as a screening or diagnostic instrument in school counseling situations, but is not currently ready for such use, except in the hands of a carefully trained person. It may be used as an aid to interviewing, but again, only if the person doing the interviewing is well qualified. For experimental or survey purposes it is probably as good as any available device of its kind.

FRANK S. FREEMAN, *Professor of Psychology and Education, Cornell University, Ithaca, New York.*

This checklist of 298 questions, subdivided as indicated above, is intended to assist school personnel, parents, and the pupils themselves in identifying problems that junior and senior high school pupils indicate as worrying them most.

Original materials for the inventory were obtained by having high school pupils write unstructured, anonymous essays on problems of greatest concern to them. Essays were obtained from "more than 500" respondents in "about 40 schools." The content of these was analyzed; earlier investigations and inquiries regarding teen-age problems were surveyed; and on the basis of the analyses and surveys, the preliminary list of items was devised. These items were then edited by members of the staff in Psychology and Education of Purdue University. Thus, the items arrived at had the benefit of direct contribution from the persons primarily concerned, professional evaluation, and comparative study. The preliminary inventory was administered to approximately 15,000 pupils in grades 9–12 and about 4,000 in grades 7 and 8, widely distributed geographically. Actual statistical analysis of the test results was made upon a stratified sampling of 2,500 cases, stratification being based upon sex, school grade, religion, urban or rural residence, and economic level.

The manuals accompanying the inventory were carefully prepared; they give a complete descriptive background and a full statistical account of the results, as well as a discussion by the authors of the possible uses which may be made of the inventory's results by educators, psychologists, and parents. The authors are properly cautious in discussing the interpretation of an individual's scores and responses, pointing out that these must be used together with other information about that individual. As in the case of all other pencil and paper personality inventories, there is always the danger that in this inventory, too, the nonprofessional persons in psychology or counseling will be too much impressed and guided by scores, norms, and percentile ranks in interpreting an individual's responses. The authors, however, have done well to caution repeatedly against mechanical use of the results and against failure to distinguish between items that suggest concern with relatively superficial problems and those that suggest basic difficulties requiring interview or therapy with one who is professionally qualified to deal with problems of personality and adjustment.

Reliability coefficients of this inventory were calculated separately for each of the eight areas, using the Kuder-Richardson Case II formula. These coefficients varied from .75 (Health) to .94 (My Home and Family), the median being .88. It is doubtful that the areas and individual items of this instrument satisfy the conditions and assumptions specified for the use of this method of estimating reliability. And even if the inventory did satisfy the specified conditions and assumptions, we may seriously question whether this is the most appropriate procedure for estimating reliability of this type of testing device. The procedure employed yields an index of the test's internal consistency at the particular moment the individuals were answering the questions, as the authors themselves recognize. In using an inventory like this one, however, we should be more interested, as psychologists and counselors, in how consistent and persistent each individual's concerns are from day to day, over a length of time, rather than how an individual feels at a particular moment. The practical difficulties of determining reliability by the test-retest method, here being suggested, are considerable. One such study has been reported by Jacobs (5) with a small number of cases (N = 48) retested after an interval of one month. The reliability coefficients ranged from .72 (Health) to .88 (My Home and Family), with a median of .82.

Estimation of validity of a personality inventory is always difficult; and this inventory is no exception. In the first place, we may agree with the authors that since the worries, concerns, and problems included in the inventory were initially specified by the teen-age groups themselves, the items undoubtedly have a degree of face validity. In addition, a biserial coefficient of correlation was calculated for each item with the total score of its own area (N = 1,000). For the eight areas the range of the medians is from .50 to .70; the median of these medians being approximately .55. The range of r's between items and their respective area scores is great, in one instance having an approximate range from .95 to .25. Clearly, then, the degree of internal homogeneity of items is, on the whole, moderate and varies considerably between items. Another validating procedure used was to intercorrelate total scores of the eight problems areas. The median coefficients for the eight areas varied from .39 to .51; and the median of the medians is approximately .46. These would indicate a moderate, but, under the circumstances, not excessive, amount of communality between areas. Other tentative validating procedures were used: such as judgment of psychologists and guidance counselors regarding diagnostic value of items, comparisons of counselors' ratings with inventory scores, and comparisons of scores obtained by "known groups." These results offer some support for the inventory, but they are at present tentative.

On the whole, this inventory appears to be one of the sounder instruments in its field. The authors describe in detail and with care their procedures in deriving the items and in standardizing them. They present sufficient data to enable prospective users of the inventory to evaluate it for themselves. They have drawn their raw materials from a wide area and from large numbers of subjects. They recognize the present limitations of the inventory and are properly cautious in discussing its possible uses. In the hands of professional psychologists and counselors this instrument should be useful and more valid than some others of the same type in facilitating the discovery of areas of difficulty and maladjustment as a basis for subsequent counseling or therapy.

[92]

*Study of Values: A Scale for Measuring the Dominant Interests in Personality, Revised Edition. College and adults; 1931–51; 6 scores: theoretical, economic, aesthetic, social, political, religious; 1 form, '51; manual ('51); $2.50 per 25; 40¢ per specimen set, postpaid; nontimed (20) minutes; Gordon W. Allport, Philip E. Vernon, and Gardner Lindzey; Houghton Mifflin Co. *

REFERENCES

1–61. See 3:99.
62. ARSENIAN, SETH. "Changes in Attitude of College Students." Psychol B 39:483–4 Jl '42. * (PA 16:4999, title only)
63. TUSSING, LYLE. "An Investigation of the Possibilities of Measuring Personality Traits With the Strong Vocational Interest Blank." Ed & Psychol Meas 2:59–74 Ja '42. * (PA 16:2324)
64. SPOERL, DOROTHY TILDEN. "Bilinguality and Emotional Adjustment." J Abn & Social Psychol 38:37–57 Ja '43. * (PA 17:3837)
65. UHRBROCK, RICHARD STEPHEN. "The Expressed Interests of Employed Men," pp. 364–7. Am J Psychol 57:317–70 Jl '44. * (PA 18:3602)
66. BURKE, HENRY R. Personality Traits of Successful Minor Seminarians. Doctor's thesis. Washington, D.C.: Catholic University of America Press, 1947. Pp. viii, 65. * (PA 22:848)
67. FISCHER, ROBERT P., AND ANDREWS, AVONNE L. "A Study of the Effect of Conformity to Social Expectancy on Evaluative Attitudes." Ed & Psychol Meas 7:331–5 su '47. * (PA 22:1365)
68. FRENCH, VERA V. "The Structure of Sentiments: III, A Study of Philosophicoreligious Sentiments." J Personality 16:209–44 D '47. * (PA 22:4840)
69. ANDERSON, ROSE G. "Subjective Ranking Versus Score Ranking of Interest Values." Personnel Psychol 1:349–55 au '48. * (PA 23:1326)
70. PORTENIER, LILLIAN. "Personality Tests in a University Guidance Program." Abstract. J Colo-Wyo Acad Sci 3:51–2 S '48. *
71. POSTMAN, LEO; BRUNER, JEROME S.; AND McGINNIES, ELLIOTT. "Personal Values as Selective Factors in Perception." J Abn & Social Psychol 43:142–54 Ap '48. * (PA 22:4254)
72. CARTER, LAUNOR, AND NIXON, MARY. "Ability, Perceptual, Personality, and Interest Factors Associated With Different Criteria of Leadership." J Psychol 27:377–88 Ap '49. * (PA 23:4183)
73. ROSENZWEIG, SAUL; with the collaboration of Kate Levine Kogan. Psychodiagnosis: An Introduction to Tests in the Clinical Practice of Psychodynamics, pp. 103–7. New York: Grune & Stratton, Inc., 1949. Pp. xii. 388. * (PA 23:3761)
74. SMITH, HENRY CLAY. "Psychometric Checks on Hypotheses Derived From Sheldon's Work on Physique and Temperament." J Personality 17:310–20 Mr '49. * (PA 25:2916)
75. SUPER, DONALD E. Appraising Vocational Fitness By Means of Psychological Tests, pp. 465–71. New York: Harper & Brothers, 1949. Pp. xxiii, 727. * (PA 24:2130)
76. CLARK, WALTER HOUSTON. "The Psychology of Religious Values," pp. 45–62. In Values in Personality Research. Personality-Symposium No. 1. Edited by Werner Wolff. New York: Grune & Stratton, Inc., April 1950. Pp. 74. * (PA 25:6814)
77. JOHNSON, JAMES MYRON. Student Interests and Values and Curricular Satisfaction in Engineering. Master's thesis, Clark University (Worcester, Mass.), 1950. (Abstracts of Dissertations & Theses....1950, pp. 136–8.) (PA 25:5463, title only)
78. KELLY, E. LOWELL AND FISKE, DONALD W. "The Prediction of Success in the VA Training Program in Clinical Psychology." Am Psychol 5:395–406 Ag '50. * (PA 25:2183)
79. KLEHR, HAROLD. An Investigation of Some Personality Factors in Women With Rheumatoid Arthritis. Doctor's thesis, Northwestern University (Evanston, Ill.), 1950. (Summaries of Doctoral Dissertations...June–September 1950, 1951, pp. 605–6.)
80. EIMICKE, VICTOR WILLIAM. A Study of the Effect of Intensive Sales Training Experience Upon the Measured Abilities and Personality Characteristics of Salesman-Candidates. Doctor's thesis, New York University (New York, N.Y.), 1951. Abstract: Microfilm Abstracts 11:951–2 no 4 '51.
81. KELLY, E. LOWELL, AND FISKE, DONALD W. The Prediction of Performance in Clinical Psychology. Ann Arbor, Mich.: University of Michigan, 1951. Pp. xv, 311. Lithotyped. *
82. MITCHELL, PHILIP HAROLD. An Evaluation of the Relationship of Values to Sociometric Selection. Doctor's thesis, University of Michigan (Ann Arbor, Mich.), 1951. Abstract: Microfilm Abstracts 11:304–5 no 2 '51. (PA 26:2402, title only)
83. PEMBERTON, CAROL J. "Personality Inventory Data Related to Ace Subscores." J Consult Psychol 15:160–2 Ap '51. * (PA 26:6569)
84. PUGH, THOMAS J. "A Comparative Study of the Values of a Group of Ministers and Two Groups of Laymen." J Social Psychol 33:225–35 My '51. * (PA 26:5532)
85. SILVERMAN, HIRSCH LAZAAR. Relationships of Personality Factors and Religious Background Among College Students. Doctor's thesis, Yeshiva University (New York, N.Y.), 1951.
86. STANLEY, JULIAN C. "Insight Into One's Own Values." J Ed Psychol 42:399–408 N '51. * (PA 26:4811)

HARRISON G. GOUGH, Assistant Professor of Psychology, University of California, Berkeley, California.

This is a 1951 revision of one of the better known and more widely used personality tests. The items have been somewhat streamlined and modernized, and an attempt has been made to sharpen the conceptions underlying the social scale. The result is a test similar to the earlier version in all important aspects, but of more pleasing format, more clearly differentiated dimensions, and improved statistical reliability.

Evidence is cited in the manual showing the degree to which the various scales reflect group differences. These citations, and an abundance of evidence from the research literature, indicate that the six value scores do relate in the manner specified by the type-theory to a wide variety of criteria. For example, clergymen attain high scores on the religious scale, business administration students on the economic scale, and medical students on the theoretical scale.

The manual also presents an interesting and useful section on research applications of the test. This section is helpful in indicating the possible range of application of the instrument, and in providing hints concerning the authors' convictions about the general utility and meaningfulness of the test.

The test does not seek to measure the absolute strength of each of the six values, but rather the relative intensity. Thus, a high score on one value must be compensated for by a lower score elsewhere. This mode of scoring may not be a deficiency, as some users claim, but it may lead to serious interpretational difficulty if the user thinks in terms of absolute levels. It would appear to the reviewer that a modification of scoring could be achieved which would permit an assessment of both relative and absolute strength.

The six values are based on Spranger's theory of types. The definitions appear to be somewhat invidious and judgmental, to a greater degree than is required by the "ideal type" approach. The definitions, and perhaps to an equal extent the questions in the test, tend to make the theoretical and aesthetic values "good" ones, and the political and economic values "bad." The danger in this is that later research concerned with adjustmental and personological correlates of value preferences, as measured by this test, will necessarily rediscover the relationships already built into the *Study of Values*. Biases of this kind would almost seem to be an inherent defect of tests constructed by a priori methods. It is an interesting theoretical question to ask how such bias can be avoided in a test where the test maker decides, by himself, what questions will be asked and which answers will be considered "correct."

The test is suitable for high school and college groups. The language is too academic and involved for use in groups very far removed from a scholastic environment. There may be some question, too, as to whether the notion of value orientations of the kind invoked here has much applicability outside the realm of highly educated groups.

The test is also fairly transparent in meaning and import. There are no internal checks on response validity, dissimulation, or on less conscious response sets. Useful results with the test are thus predicated upon the interest and cooperation of the subject.

One feature which is sorely missing from the manual is a discussion of the use of the test with individual cases. This is a somewhat surprising omission in view of the senior author's identification with the idiographic point of view in psychology. The test does have interesting and useful properties in individual guidance and assessment, and it is to be regretted that the manual does not include some reference to this kind of use, and a few examples of individual interpretation.

In summary, the *Study of Values* would appear to be a dependable and informative instrument. It has a definite, if questionable, theoretical basis, its statistical properties are adequate, and it yields scores which possess utility for both group and individual interpretation. The range of application of the test is somewhat limited, and the variables themselves may not have wide relevance. However, within the appropriate context the test possesses considerable merit and utility.

WILLIAM STEPHENSON, *Visiting Professor of Psychology, The University of Chicago, Chicago, Illinois.*

This revised edition offers improvements over the original 1931 edition without changing the test in any essential respects. New questions have been introduced, the wording simplified, the scoring procedures streamlined, and fresh norms have been prepared. A major change in the basic feature of the test is the restriction of Spranger's "social" value to altruism or philanthropy, to the exclusion of more mundane forms of conjugal, familial, and religious affections. The norms are also far less extensive for the revised edition.

It is scarcely necessary for the reviewer to affirm or to question the general usefulness of this well-known test. It has been used in many researches and has had some indirect validation in several directions, e.g., in studies of seminarians, novices in religious communities, college students, married couples, and the like. As is well known, the test was based upon Spranger's *Types of Men* which specifies six types of persons: theoretical, economic, aesthetic, social, political, and religious. Assuming that personality is best known through a study of such values, the test attempts to indicate in which of these classes a person most dominantly belongs.

But twenty years have elapsed since this test was first introduced, and it is perhaps the occasion for evaluating it as a research tool, before it sets out in its revived condition. It has always seemed an anomaly to the reviewer that one of the great critics of nomothesis and advocates of the ideographic approach to the study of personality should take part in the production of a test of this kind without fostering its supposed theoretical formulations on their own account. One need not deny a certain very crude testability, along these test lines, of some of Spranger's notions, but it should not at this time be taken on faith, or because definitive norms are available for it, or because external validations can be reported for it. After all, the ability to stand on one leg might provide similar norms and similar external validities. Some researches which are intrinsic to Spranger's theory and which seem to us to be essential have yet to be attempted, although methods now exist for such studies. Spranger's types were far more than averages of persons of a kind; a group or class of persons did not define them. Rather, the *types* were theoretical formulations that *preceded* the possible demarcation of classes of persons. It is important, therefore, to represent these theoretical matters; and although Spranger is not easy to understand, it is possible to construct balanced block designed samples of statements for Spranger's theory as such, at least with respect to what could reasonably be the independencies for his theory. Propositions can then be asserted about, say, any experimental subject, and empirical tests made of these. A theory like Spranger's cannot be proved or disproved for its "general implications" (everywhere involved in the test under review). Instead, we can test propositions about or in relation to it. Thus, when the present reviewer uses this test, its questions are cut to pieces and divided into briefer units; a structured design is made of these, following R. A. Fisher's well known devices; experiments are then conducted about a single curate, seminarian, or college student to see what Spranger's theory as such can bring to light. We would suggest, therefore, that the time has come for those who issue tests of this kind to provide evidence that the theory they purport to be employing has intrinsic points of interest and value.

Spranger was undoubtedly a subtle psychologist, the first of Dilthey's breed: it would be pleasant to see even one study, along the methodological lines for which Dilthey stood preeminent in his day, pursued in terms of singular propositional tests of the theory itself. Otherwise there will be more decades of studies, finding little bits of fact here and there through the test but never any advance upon its elementary nomothetical formulations, against which, it so happens, Dilthey, Spranger, and Allport have all objected, and, we believe, correctly so.

J Consult Psychol 15:515 D '51. Laurance F. Shaffer. After twenty years of wide and varied use, the *Study of Values* has been revised thoroughly. There are changes both in content and in format. The old "social" value, which had proved unreliable because of adherence to Spranger's excessively broad definition, has been redefined in terms of altruistic or philanthropic interest. Most of the items have been revised, to simplify wordings, and to eliminate outdated and overspecific cultural references. The new items give the impression that they are likely to maintain their meanings with the passage of time. The manual gives an extensive report of the statistical characteristics of the revision. New and revised items were selected by three successive item analyses, and each scale is internally consistent. Scale reliabilities are substantially improved, ranging from .87 to .92 on a one-month retest. Scale intercorrelations are mainly low.

Norms are supplied in terms of the means and SD's of 1,816 college students, and are further analyzed in terms of sex and of occupational groups. The new format simplifies the process of scoring and eliminates the need for a separate score sheet. In its excellent new revision, the *Study of Values* seems destined to several more decades of service as a tool for guidance and for research.

For a review by Paul E. Meehl of the first edition, see 3:99.

[93]

★**Thurstone Temperament Schedule.** Grades 9–16 and adults; 1949–50; 7 scores: active, vigorous, impulsive, dominant, stable, sociable, reflective; IBM; 2 editions; 1 form, '49; manual ('50); separate answer sheets must be used; 75¢ per specimen set of any one edition; cash orders postpaid; nontimed (10–20) minutes; L. L. Thurstone; Science Research Associates, Inc. *
a) FORM AH (HAND SCORING EDITION). 49¢ per test and answer pad; $1.90 per 25 answer pads.
b) FORM AM (MACHINE SCORING EDITION). IBM; 39¢ per test; $2.90 per 100 IBM answer sheets; $2.50 per set of machine-scoring stencils.

REFERENCES
1. THURSTONE, L. L. "The Dimensions of Temperament." *Psychometrika* 16:11–20 Mr '51. * (PA 25:7327)

HANS J. EYSENCK, *Director, Psychology Department, Institute of Psychiatry, Maudsley Hospital, London, England.*

This inventory contains 140 "Yes" "?" "No" questions, which measure seven areas of personality: active, vigorous, impulsive, dominant, stable, sociable, and reflective. These seven areas were derived from a factorial analysis not yet reported in print, so that it is impossible to express an opinion regarding the basis of this questionnaire. It is disturbing to know, however, that although this factorial analysis included the various factors isolated by Guilford, the result is only very superficially like Guilford's set of factors. While the reviewer believes that factor analysis is indispensable in arriving at useful and fundamental dimensions of personality, he feels that divergent results of this kind must make one very careful of accepting any particular solution unless it is strongly supported by the evidence. Intercorrelations among some of the seven traits are surprisingly high, correlations of .71 and .52 being reported, so that one of the main advantages of factorial design, namely, the independence of factors, is clearly sacrificed. Reliabilities for the seven areas are not very high for any of the standardised groups (men, women, boys, and girls). Coefficients of .45, .48, .46, occurring quite frequently, with the highest coefficient .86, are still well below the .9 level. An ingenious argument is presented in the manual to show that even with a reliability as low as .4, not more than one sixth of the population will be misclassified as being in the highest quarter when their true scores are below the mean. This, of course, is true, but such a gross misclassification of almost 20 per cent of the population is a serious matter if any action is taken on the basis of the results. Also, of course, it should be borne in mind that like the proverbial dying man grasping at a straw, the user of a questionnaire, whether he be counselor or clinical psychologist, frequently interprets even very slight differences in profile scores, and he is unlikely to be dissuaded from this practice by any amount of statistical argument regarding lack of reliability of the scores.

No follow-up data are reported, except the failure of the schedule to discriminate between good and poor office workers.

As a research instrument, no doubt, this schedule has a place. Its clinical and industrial use, however, must await proper validation studies. It should be added that in a text dependent for its appraisal so much on statistical details of factorial analysis, more information should be given in the manual to enable the reader to form an adequate opinion.

CHARLES M. HARSH, *Research Psychologist, U.S. Navy Electronics Laboratory, San Diego, California.*

This 140-item self-administering questionnaire is designed to give a brief appraisal of seven relatively permanent aspects of temperament in persons who are fairly well adjusted. The simple items calling for "yes," "?," "no" responses are suitable for high school students or average adults. Instructions are clear and items are well spaced. The separate answer sheet is easy to use, the appropriate column always being aligned with the items on the successively narrower pages of the test booklet, each page revealing one more column of the answer sheet. Raw scores may be plotted directly on the normative profile forms printed on the back of the separate answer sheet, or the scores may be evaluated relative to office worker norms printed in the examiner's manual. Each set of norms is based on a sample of from 400 to 1,200 persons.

Split half reliabilities for the seven subscores, determined for five different samples of high school students or adults, vary from .45 to .86.

Retest reliabilities on a male executive group range from .61 to .82. The manual has a good discussion of the reliability of a profile, which for this type of schedule is more important than the reliability of the subscores. Tables of intercorrelation of subscores (for men and women separately) show that most of the scores are statistically independent, although two correlations are above .50.

The seven aspects of temperament were determined by refactoring of Lovell's scoring of Guilford's three personality inventories. Items derived from several personality and preference tests were tentatively scored for these seven aspects of temperament, leaving out any implication of maladjustment, and the twenty most discriminating items in each area were selected for the present schedule. For various sample populations, the manual presents tables of intercorrelations between the subscores and the subscores of the Guilford-Martin questionnaires, the *Study of Values,* the *Kuder Preference Record—Vocational,* the *Kuder Preference Record—Personal,* and the *Thurstone Interest Schedule.* This statistical information will give helpful orientation until there is more direct evidence of the validity of the *Thurstone Temperament Schedule* as a supplementary aid to vocational guidance or placement. The manual frankly admits the need of validity studies and discusses the failure of the schedule to discriminate between good and poor office workers in one study. The excellence and clarity of the manual encourages a favorable attitude on the part of prospective users who could contribute to validation studies of this little test, which may be of use in prescreening for longer or more discriminating specialized tests.

DAVID G. RYANS, *Director, Teacher Characteristics Study, American Council on Education; and Professor of Education, University of California, Los Angeles, California.*

This questionnaire was designed to describe normal, well adjusted individuals from the standpoint of important and stable personality traits. It is not intended to reflect psychotic or neurotic tendencies. Seven areas of temperament are appraised: Active (referring to the tendency to hurry and be "on the go"); Vigorous (relating to the liking of physical activities and outdoor occupations); Impulsive (referring to the tendency to make quick decisions and ability to change easily from one task to another); Dominant (referring to the desire for leadership, and for taking initiative and responsibility) ; Stable (referring to the tendency to be relaxed and to remain calm) ; Sociable (referring to the liking for other people and the ability to get along with others) ; and Reflective (referring to liking for quiet work and reflective thinking).

The 140 items covering these seven areas are presented in question form. They are printed in a 6-page step-down booklet which can be used with either a self-scoring carbon answer pad or a machine-scorable answer sheet. Profile charts are provided for adults, with separate normative data for men and women, and for high school youth, with separate norms for boys and girls.

Preliminary to development of the *Thurstone Temperament Schedule* the intercorrelations among 13 personality scores yielded by the Guilford and Guilford-Martin schedules were factor analyzed by the centroid method, with scale reliabilities in the diagonal cells of the matrix, to determine the number of factors that seemed to be represented by questionnaire materials pertaining to normal persons. Nine factors were extracted and then rotated to oblique simple structure. Two factors were regarded as residual factors. The remaining seven formed the framework for the present instrument. All available interest and personality questionnaires were surveyed and 320 adapted items chosen as representative of the seven personality factors. Subsequent item analysis against the upper and lower thirds of each area resulted in the selection of 140 items.

The norms available in 1950 were contributed to by 694 freshman men and 161 freshman women at the University of Illinois (Navy Pier), 540 male and 496 female office workers, and Chicago high school students consisting of 419 boys and 504 girls of ages 14 to 18.

Odd-even reliabilities reported in the manual range from .45 for the Reflective scale to .86 for the Dominant scale, based upon the scores of 106 subjects. Odd-even reliabilities given for five samples cluster around an *r* of .65. Test-retest reliability coefficients, based upon the scores of 81 male executives, range from .61 to .82 (median = .78) for the several scales.

Intercorrelations of the scores on the seven scales are generally positive and relatively low. For 338 college freshmen the intercorrelation coefficients ranged from −.16 between the Sociable and Reflective scales to .60 between the

Dominant and Sociable scales, .58 between the Impulsive and Dominant scales, and .53 between the Impulsive and Sociable scales. The tendency for the Impulsive, Dominant, and Sociable scales to be significantly correlated also was noted in studies based upon 694 freshman men students and 161 freshman women students at the University of Illinois. The only sizeable negative correlation reported was one of −.41 between the Sociable and Reflective scales, based upon the scores of 161 college freshman women.

Of particular interest are intercorrelations between scores on the scales of the *Thurstone Temperament Schedule* and scores on other personality and interest inventories. Correlations between the scales of the *Thurstone Temperament Schedule* and the *Kuder Preference Record—Personal* are generally low positive and range from −.37 between the Impulsive scale (Thurstone) and Practical (Kuder) to .57 between Dominant (Thurstone) and Sociable (Kuder). Correlations between the scales of the *Thurstone Temperament Schedule* and those of the *Kuder Preference Record—Vocational* are generally low, although there is a suggestion that the Vigorous scale (Thurstone) and the Clerical scale (Kuder) and the Reflective scale (Thurstone) and the Mechanical scale (Kuder) are significantly *negatively* correlated, whereas the Dominant scale (Thurstone) and Persuasive scale (Kuder), the Sociable scale (Thurstone) and the Persuasive (Kuder), and the Vigorous scale (Thurstone) and the Mechanical scale (Kuder) are significantly positively correlated. Correlations between scores on scales of the *Thurstone Temperament Schedule* and scores on the *SRA Primary Mental Abilities* are generally of zero order, the only exceptions being *r*'s of .25 and .28 respectively between Dominant and Sociable (*Thurstone Temperament Schedule*) and Word Fluency (*PMA*).

Although the reliabilities of these scales are none too high, probably due to their shortness, and although the empirical intercorrelations of the scales clearly indicate they are not independent (no claim for independence has been made by the author or publisher; rather, the factor analysis indicated oblique structure) the construction procedure followed appears to have been sound; and the author and publishers have been particularly attentive to the supply of information about the instrument and interpretive data.

J Consult Psychol 15:170 Ap '51. *Laurance F. Shaffer.* A distinctive and perhaps valuable feature of this questionnaire is its emphasis on normality. There are no items describing neurotic symptoms, and the seven scores that are obtained from it are all designated by trait terms descriptive of ways in which normal people may vary—active, vigorous, impulsive, dominant, stable, sociable, and reflective. The seven clusters in which the 140 items are arranged were obtained from factor analyses by Thurstone and Guilford. The actual items were selected for internal consistency within each cluster. The reliabilities are moderate, .48 to .77 for the adult male group, the intercorrelations between trait scores are generally low, and the norms are based on adequately large groups. Despite all these statistical virtues, the interpretation of the schedule is almost surely subject to abuses. Many users will be tempted to follow the intriguing suggestions for using it in vocational guidance, without paying enough attention to the cautious footnote that calls attention to the need for validation.

[94]

Vineland Social Maturity Scale. Birth to maturity; 1935–47; individual; 1 form, '46, c1936; manual ('47); $1.50 per 25; $1 per manual; postage extra; $1 per specimen set, postpaid; (20–30) minutes; Edgar A. Doll; Educational Test Bureau, Educational Publishers, Inc. *

REFERENCES

1–58. See 3:107.
59. BRADWAY, KATHERINE P. "Scale Calibration by the Thomson Method." Abstract. *Psychol B* 34:748 N '37. * (PA 12:1650, title only)
60. ANDERSON, META L. "Administrative Uses of the Social Maturity Scale." *Binet R* 6:7–8 Mr '39. *
61. DOLL, EDGAR A. *Your Child Grows Up.* Boston, Mass.: John Hancock Mutual Life Insurance Co., 1939. Pp. 32. Paper. *
62. PLUHAR, MARCELLA. "Vineland Social Maturity Scale: Given to 24 Children in Normal Group." *Binet R* 6:27–32 Mr '39. *
63. REINGOLD, NETTIE. "Social Maturity Scale Analysis." *Binet R* 6:38–41 Mr '39. *
64. TRUBIN, BEATRICE. "Social Maturity Scale Results and Analysis." *Binet R* 6:33–7 Mr '39. *
65. WILSON, MARGARET T. "Mental Ages and Social Ages of Normal and Defective Twins and Siblings." *Am J Mental Def* 45:374–9 Ja '41. * (PA 15:3648)
66. TROUP, EVELYN, AND LESTER, OLIVE P. "The Social Competence of Identical Twins." *J Genetic Psychol* 60:167–75 Mr '42. * (PA 16:3712)
67. KRAUSE, ARNOLD L. "The Relationship of Mental and Social Quotients and Ages to Program Reading and Recitation Performances." *Training Sch B* 41:41–7, 69–79 My, Je '44. * (PA 19:551)
68. MYKLEBUST, HELMER R., AND BURCHARD, EDWARD M. L. "A Study of the Effects of Congenital and Adventitious Deafness on the Intelligence, Personality, and Social Maturity of School Children." *J Ed Psychol* 36:321–43 S '45. * (PA 20:2145)
69. AVERY, CHARLOTTE. *A Study of Pre-School Acoustically Handicapped Children.* Master's thesis, Northwestern University (Evanston, Ill.), 1947.
70. AVERY, CHARLOTTE. "Social Competence of Pre-School Acoustically Handicapped Children." *J Excep Child* 15:71–3+ D '48. *
71. DOLL, EDGAR A. "What Is a Moron?" *J Abn & Social Psychol* 43:495–501 O '48. * (PA 23:1839)
72. BRASELL, WAYMAH NORRIS. *Social Maturity of the Deaf: Its Nature and Correlates.* Doctor's thesis, Temple University (Philadelphia, Pa.), 1949. (*Abstracts of Dissertations....[Teachers College]* 1940–1949, 1951, pp. 167–73.)
73. KELLY, ELIZABETH M. "Educational Implications in the Public School Special Class of the Endogenous-Exogenous Classification." *Am J Mental Def* 54:207–11 O '49. * (PA 24:2677)
74. RUDOLF, G. DE M. "Comparison of the Intelligence Quotient With Behaviour." *J Mental Sci* 95:703–5 Jl '49. * (PA 24: 1944)
75. RUDOLF, G. DE M. "Re-Testing of the Intelligence Quotient and the Social Age." *J Mental Sci* 95:696–702 Jl '49. * (PA 24:1945)
76. CASSEL, ROBERT H., AND DANENHOWER, HAROLD S. "Mental Subnormality Developmentally Arrested: Social Competence." *Am J Mental Def* 54:282–9 Ja '50. * (PA 24:3779)
77. KELLMER, M. L. "Intelligence, Social Maturity, and Environment." Abstract. *Adv Sci* 8:89–90 Je '51. *
78. PRINGLE, M. L. KELLMER. "Social Maturity and Social Competence." *Ed R* 3:113–28 F '51. *
79. WATSON, ROBERT I. Chap. 11, "The Vineland Social Maturity Scale," pp. 313–29. In his *The Clinical Method in Psychology.* New York: Harper & Brothers, 1951. Pp. xii, 779. * (PA 26:5577)

WILLIAM M. CRUICKSHANK, *Director, Education for Exceptional Children, School of Education, Syracuse University, Syracuse, New York.*

Since it is essential that clinical testing keep in step with theoretical advances in personality description, it is fortunate that the clinician has available a scale such as the Vineland which can offer vital information on the results of the individual's maturational interaction with his social milieu. Although there are no direct measurements of the influence of interpersonal contacts, most of the items of the scale indirectly bear the impact of the developing organism's response to the socialization process.

The categories of adequacy which the author has set up to facilitate evaluation reflect very well the processes involved in the maturation of social competence. The areas of occupation, locomotion, communication, and socialization delineate the instruments available for moving toward people while those of self-help and self-direction (the latter concerning itself mainly with the measurement of the individual's competent use of money) point up the necessity for the development of independence and freedom which enable one to move more confidently and thus more competently among others.

The test does not follow the usual procedure of laboratory measurement since it employs the method of report, rather than examination or observation. A person intimately familiar with the subject, such as parent, nurse, or institutional guardian, responds to careful interviewing by the examiner on the subject's demonstrated performance of the 117 items covered by the scale. The danger inherent in utilizing the potentially biased observation of untrained and perhaps emotionally involved reporters has been pointed out by some as a critical shortcoming of the instrument. However, the author's claim that it demands administration by clinically trained examiners, and that the careful basis for scoring items and questioning the respondee allows for a minimum of inaccurate evaluation as to whether a behavior is or is not evidenced by the subject, seems to adequately handle these objections.

The final score is computed from the total number of items successfully performed, with consideration given in scoring for lack of opportunity and for performances which are in a transitional stage. The score can be converted very simply into a social age and thence, if desired, into a social quotient. Studies by the author have revealed that, on the average, the social quotient tends to be higher than the intelligence quotient and, further, that when the IQ is low, the SQ tends to be higher and when the IQ is high, the SQ tends to fall below it. The latter may be due to the fact that there is a rather definite cutting off point above which one cannot become any more socially competent.

It would appear that a person's social age provides a more effective basis of classification for purposes of care and training than would the mental age. Allied to this, the scale has demonstrated its ability to differentiate between true mental defectives who are socially inadequate and people who are merely of subnormal intellect but who are quite competent in managing their personal and social lives. It has also been found valuable as a measure of therapeutic improvement; for intercultural comparison, i.e., Negro and white, Jewish and non-Jewish; in evaluation of the acoustically, visually, and other physically handicapped individuals; and as an index for the measurement of growth or change.

The author has indicated that a new manual containing more detailed analysis of the behavior required for each item, additional standardization data, and clinical experimentation in which the instrument was utilized to produce empirical evidence is in the process of development. This should encourage even more widespread use of the scale by practicing clinicians.

FLORENCE M. TEAGARDEN, *Professor of Psychology, University of Pittsburgh, Pittsburgh, Pennsylvania.*

This is a point and age scale combination of 117 items of performances "in respect to which children show a progressive capacity for looking after themselves and for participating in those activities which lead toward ultimate independence as adults." It is scaled to test these capacities from birth through age 25 plus and gives *social ages* through year 30 plus. *Social quotients* may also be derived. The functions tested are self-help (general, eating, dressing), self-direction, locomotion, occupation, communication, and social relations. The manual of directions suggests that each of these functions be tested "serially." Each item within the age range involved is scored either plus, plus F (temporary failure under certain conditions), plus N.O. (no opportunity), minus N.O., plus-minus, or minus. Determination of "no opportunity" scoring is sometimes quite difficult.

Standardization data were obtained from "ten normal subjects of each sex at each year from birth to thirty years of age, or a total of 620 subjects." Extensive research has been done with the scale, the manual itself reporting 59 studies selected as being "representative." Any one familiar with the literature in this field realizes that research on the Vineland scale has continued since the publication of the manual in 1947.

Information with which to score items and to derive ratings of social maturity may be obtained from the subject himself, in the case of older subjects, or from parents and other adults in the case of children. Clinical use of the scale shows that it is perhaps even better as an *interviewing device* with parents than as a measuring scale for the child. Often information secured from the mother and from the father does not agree at all at certain points. The clinician thus gets a valuable "lead" even if he is not sure how the particular item should be scored. Frequently also parents will say, when asked for information on some item of the scale, "Oh, I believe the child *could* do that himself but I have always done it for him." Excellent counseling data! Or again parents sometimes say, "Well, we never do that in our home ("Plays simple table games?") but I guess maybe we *should* play with the children."

Constant use of the scale leads one naturally enough to see some weaknesses. For example, certain items frequently have to be juggled somewhat in the case of young children living in city apartment houses and others living in residential districts or rural areas directly along through highways. Again "Gets drink unassisted?" (age level 2–3) is usually answered negatively by parents of children of this age as they say, "He can't reach it himself." "Brushes or combs hair acceptably without help?" (age level 7–8) appears to be one thing for boys with short hair and quite another thing for girls who may have long hair that needs considerable dressing. Girls seem likewise to be penalized somewhat on the item "Does small remunerative work?" (age level 10–11) since many girls have no opportunity for earning money. Parents seem a little doubtful sometimes as to how they should truthfully reply to the standardized questions "Washes hands unaided?" (age level 3–4) and "Washes face unassisted?" (age level 4–5). Scoring directions for some items of the "locomotion" category such as "Goes about home town freely?" (age level 9–10) and "Goes to nearby places alone?" (age level 15–18) do not require that any social caution be displayed. This leaves the examiner in a considerable scoring quandary at times in the case, for example, of unmarried mothers who get around town all right so far as "locomotion" is concerned. "Self direction" is, however, required at other points in the scale.

In spite of these experiential difficulties, in spite of the clinician's reluctance to report social ages carried to the second decimal place, and in spite of his unwillingness to do much statistical handling of data of uncertain accuracy, the scale has undoubted value, particularly for interview and counseling purposes. Mentally deficient children in superior homes often display amazingly high *social quotients,* thereby giving clues as to possible social development and as to supervision. Contrariwise, the clinician often finds a child whose IQ on intelligence tests seems spuriously high. The social quotient of such a child may give the answer; he may be socially less developed than we would have a right to expect from his intelligence. He may be the square peg in the round hole or the bull in the china shop or the bungler. One hundred and seventeen items such as Doll has scaled for us are valuable adjuncts to the clinician who is attempting to appraise the strengths and weaknesses of his client. Social ages and social quotients can often be reported with considerable conviction. Even when special circumstances make the use of such mathematical measures unwise, the incidental data elicited by the scale and the informant's reactions to the questions often far outweigh these deficiencies. When used wisely, the *Vineland Social Maturity Scale* adds greatly to our clinical insights.

For reviews by C. M. Louttit and John W. M. Rothney and an excerpt from a review, see 3:107; for reviews by Paul H. Furfey, Elaine F. Kinder, and Anna S. Starr of Experimental Form B, see 38:1143.

[95]
Washburne Social-Adjustment Inventory, Thaspic Edition. Ages 12 and over; 1932–40; a revision of *The Washburne Social Adjustment Inventory, Sapich Edition* (see 40:1262); 9 scores: truthfulness, happiness, alienation, sympathy, purpose, impulse-judgment, control, wishes, total; IBM; 1 form, '40; manual ('40); $2 per 25; 30¢ per manual ('40); 35¢ per specimen set (does not include manual), postpaid; separate answer sheets may be used; $1.10 per 25 IBM answer sheets; $2.40 per set of stencils for machine-scoring of answer sheets; postage extra; nontimed (30–50) minutes; John N. Washburne; World Book Co. *

REFERENCES
1–4. See 40:1262.
5–15. See 3:110.
16. PATTERSON, RUTH E. *A Study of the Social Adjustment of Orphanage Children.* Master's thesis, Syracuse University (Syracuse, N.Y.), 1937.
17. DILLINGHAM, HOWARD IRVING. *The Relationship of Certain Factors of Social Adjustment to Academic Success.* Doctor's thesis, Syracuse University (Syracuse, N.Y.), 1938. Pp. 87.
18. FESSLER, MARIANNE HAWLEY. *The Social Adjustment of High School Children With Employed and Unemployed Mothers.* Master's thesis, Syracuse University (Syracuse, N.Y.), 1939. Pp. 95.
19. HUSTED, DOROTHEA. *The Relationship Between Physical Characteristics and Social Adjustment of High School Girls.* Master's thesis, Syracuse University (Syracuse, N.Y.), 1941.
20. GOTHAM, RAYMOND E. *The Personality Factor in Teaching Success.* Doctor's thesis, University of Wisconsin (Madison, Wis.), 1943. (*Summaries of Doctoral Dissertations.... July, 1942–June, 1943,* pp. 171–3.)
21. BURKE, HENRY R. *Personality Traits of Successful Minor Seminarians.* Doctor's thesis. Washington, D.C.: Catholic University of America Press, 1947. Pp. viii, 65. Out of print. * (PA 22:848)
22. SCHMID, JOHN, JR. *Factor Analyses of Prospective Teachers' Differences.* Doctor's thesis, University of Wisconsin (Madison, Wis.), 1949. (*Summaries of Doctoral Dissertations ....July 1949 to June 1950,* 1951, pp. 337–9.)
23. STEPAT, DOROTHY L. *A Study of Clothing and Appearance Problems in Relation to Some Aspects of Personality and Some Cultural Patterns in a Group of College Freshman Girls.* Doctor's thesis, New York University (New York, N.Y.), 1949. Pp. 181. Abstract: *Microfilm Abstracts* 10:64–5 no 1 '50. * (PA 24:6049, title only)
24. ZAKOLSKI, F. C. "Studies in Delinquency: I, Personality Structure of Delinquent Boys." *J Genetic Psychol* 74:109–17 Mr '49. * (PA 23:4925)
25. LOUGH, ORPHA M., AND GREEN, MARY E. "Comparison of the Minnesota Multiphasic Personality Inventory and the Washburne S-A Inventory as Measures of Personality of College Women." *J Social Psychol* 32:23–30 Ag '50. * (PA 25:3812)
26. SCHMID, JOHN, JR. "Factor Analyses of Prospective Teachers' Differences." *J Exp Ed* 18:287–319 Je '50. * (PA 25:2060)
27. SCHWARTZ, ANTHONY NICHOLAS. "A Study of the Discriminating Efficiency of Certain Tests of the Primary Source Personality Traits of Teachers." *J Exp Ed* 19:63–93 S '50. * (PA 25:4864)

WILLIAM SEEMAN, *University of Minnesota, Minneapolis, Minnesota.*

This questionnaire type personality inventory consists of an 8-page booklet which includes an answer sheet for the 122 items, most of which are answered by "yes" or "no." The items appear to be of a rather obvious character (e.g., "Do you sometimes enjoy the sight of an animal or a person being hurt?" and "Did you ever act greedily by taking more than your share of anything?") such as are found in the majority of personality inventories. The purpose of the test as stated in the directions for administering is "to determine the degree of social and emotional adjustment." The keys are scored for Truthfulness, Happiness, Alienation, Sympathy, Purpose, Impulse-Judgment, and Control. There is also a "Wishes" subtest the scoring of which is, however, stated to be "not absolutely necessary." There is a 4-page manual of directions for administration; to interpret the test results, however, it is necessary to order the manual of interpretation separately, which the reviewer regards as unjustifiable. It does not appear too much to ask of a testmaker that he make his instrument as compact and economical as possible for purposes of meaningful use.

To the extent that this instrument has been used in the differentiation of criterion cases of maladjustment which have required help in a mental hygiene clinic and "normals" who have required no such assistance, it takes a salutary cognizance of the need for empirical meaning in adjustment inventories. However, the distinction between "social" adjustment and "emotional" adjustment is by no means clear to this reviewer. It is also not clear whether Happiness, Alienation, Sympathy, Purpose, or the other concepts tested are to be regarded as trait concepts; nor is there any attempt at experimental or empirical definition of these concepts. Although mental hygiene cases may legitimately furnish a criterion group for the vague concept of "maladjustment," it is not equally clear what criterion groups could be obtained to give experimental or empirical meaning to these subtests. Purpose, Impulse-Judgment, and Control are abstract concepts the experimental definition of which is no simple task. Since the criterion groups for "adjusted" and "maladjusted" are so broadly defined it is difficult to see what information is gleaned from deviant scores other than the knowledge that they indicate "poor adjustment." It is by no means suggested that such knowledge is useless; however, the test would appear to be most useful as a crude screening device. It should also be noted that the obvious character of the items renders them susceptible to distortion both intentional and unintentional.

The biserial correlation coefficient of validity is given as .90; the test-retest reliability for college students is .92 when the administrations are separated by a school semester.

For a review by Daniel A. Prescott of the original edition, see 38:928; for excerpts from reviews, see 3:110.

[96]

Willoughby Emotional Maturity Scale. College and adults; 1931; title on test booklet is *Willoughby EM Scale;* 1 form; $1.50 per 25; 10¢ per specimen set; cash orders postpaid; nontimed (20) minutes; Raymond R. Willoughby; Stanford University Press. *

REFERENCES
1. WILLOUGHBY, RAYMOND R. "The Emotional Maturity of Some Religious Attitudes." *J Social Psychol* 1:532–6 N '30. * (PA 5:1976)
2. WILLOUGHBY, RAYMOND R. "A Scale of Emotional Maturity." *J Social Psychol* 3:3–36 F '32. * (PA 6:2052)
3. BROOKS, ESTHER. "The Value of Psychological Testing." *Am J Nursing* 37:885–90 Ag '37. *
4. FARNSWORTH, PAUL R. "The Measure of Emotional Maturity." *J Social Psychol* 9:235–7 My '38. * (PA 12:4836)
5. GREENE, J. E., AND STATON, THOMAS F. "Predictive Value of Various Tests of Emotionality and Adjustment in a Guidance Program for Prospective Teachers." *J Ed Res* 32:653–9 My '39. * (PA 13:4211)
6. STUMP, N. FRANKLIN. "Sense of Humor and Its Relationship to Personality, Scholastic Aptitude, Emotional Maturity, Height, and Weight." *J General Psychol* 20:25–32 Ja '39. * (PA 13:3759)
7. WASSON, MARGARET M. "The Agreements Among Certain Types of Personality Schedules." *J Psychol* 9:351–63 Ap '40. * (PA 14:4153)

LYSLE W. CROFT, *Director of Personnel, University of Kentucky, Lexington, Kentucky.*

This scale was developed to indicate the individual's degree of freedom from childish emotional attitudes and immature motives and to reveal the extent to which he can make adjustments to his environment. Each of the 60 items describes, in terms of a hypothetical subject, a type of situation and a reaction to it. The rater attempts to rate the real subject by checking those items which equal a fair description of characteristic behavior, actual or probable. The manual states a subject may rate himself with only a small loss of precision—a rather rash claim when presented without qualification.

The scoring of the scale is simple—a total score of weighted items which have been checked is averaged and multiplied by 10. The manual states that this represents the pooled judgment of 100 *expert* students of personality as to the amount or degree of emotional maturity.

The claimed reliability of rating (which is the agreement between two raters) is .54 for college student raters. Certainly the use of the scale is somewhat limited in view of the reported reliability. The author indicates there is "reason to believe that the services of raters experienced in the estimation of personality will be considerably increased, possibly to .70 or .80." No research is offered which has any bearing on the statement, and it should have no bearing on the proven reliability of the scale.

Tentative results on a small group of college

students indicate that correlations with instruments *alleged* to measure emotional stability will be in the neighborhood of .60 or .70. Evaluation of the validity of the scale depends upon the degree to which one accepts the author's statement that "There is probably no better criterion of the trait in question in existence at present than the judgment of experts." First, one could ask, just who are the experts and on what basis were they selected as experts. This statement alone causes one to look upon the scale with caution.

The norms for the scale are based on 70 students, equally divided as to sex. If the scale is of value in counseling, why has not the author expanded these norms of 1931?

The statement is made that the self-ratings do not show the usual tendency to overestimation, but this statement is not explained further.

The author points out in his journal article, in response to the criticism that the language is too involved, that "while the scale is not intended to be restricted to use by psychiatrists, it cannot be used by naive or uneducated persons." This limitation is not incorporated into the manual, which is itself far too brief and does not do justice to the amount of statistical work involved in the development of the scale, as described in the journal article.

Practically no research has been reported on the scale and certainly the original research with 70 college students, each rating himself and two fellow students, is insufficient to warrant the use of the scale as a counseling tool. The elaborate claims made as to the uses of the scale, such as an aid in selecting industrial workers, teachers, lawyers, and administrators, rather than using references, certainly have not been proven valid; and until additional researches are completed and published in a more complete manual, it is rather doubtful that this scale can be considered a reliable instrument for counseling.

[97]

★**The Wishes and Fears Inventory.** Ages 4–8, 8–16; 1949; 8 scores: wishes, positive identifications, negative identifications, desired activities, undesired activities, changes desired in oneself, fears, earliest recollection; individual; 1 form, 2 levels (labeled Forms A and B); 1 form ['49]; mimeographed; manual ['49]; (Forms A, B); no data on reliability and validity; 25¢ per specimen set, postage extra; record blanks must be reproduced by test user; (5–15) minutes; Martin L. Reymert; The Mooseheart Laboratory for Child Research, Mooseheart, Ill. *

[98]

★**The Wishing Well.** Grades 4–7; 1945–51; an analysis of children's needs; 9 scores: belonging, achievement, economic security, fears, love and affection, guilt, sharing, world outlook, total; 1 form, '49; mimeographed manual ('51); withdrawn from publication; nontimed (30) minutes; Evaluation Division, Bureau of Educational Research, Ohio State University. *

REFERENCES
1. RATHS, LOUIS, AND METCALF, LAWRENCE. "An Instrument for Identifying Some Needs of Children." *Ed Res B* 24:169–77+ O 17 '45. *

[99]

★**Work Preference Inventory.** Applicants for employment; 1946–50; 14 scores: reliability, creativeness, conservatism, ambition, masculinity, introversion, anxiety-depression, persuasive, social service, theoretical, artistic, mechanical, economic, scientific; IBM; 1 form, '46; manual ['50]; separate answer sheets must be used; $30 per 100; $2 per 100 IBM answer sheets; $7 per set of 14 machine scoring stencils (revised '50); $3 per 100 profile sheets; 20¢ per manual; 75¢ per specimen set (does not include scoring stencils); postpaid; nontimed (15–75) minutes; Robert W. Henderson; the Author, 940 Eighth St., N.E., Massillon, Ohio. *

For reviews by Edwin W. Davis, John C. Flanagan, and Gilbert J. Rich, see 3:113.

[100]

★**Your Activities and Attitudes.** Adults in later maturity; 1948–49; 2 scores: attitudes, activities; 1 form, '48; preliminary manual ('49); $2.75 per 25; 50¢ per specimen set; cash orders postpaid; nontimed (60–90) minutes; Ernest W. Burgess, Ruth S. Cavan, and Robert J. Havighurst; Science Research Associates, Inc. *

REFERENCES
1. CAVAN, RUTH SHONLE; BURGESS, ERNEST W.; HAVIGHURST, ROBERT J.; AND GOLDHAMER, HERBERT. *Personal Adjustment in Old Age.* Chicago, Ill.: Science Research Associates, Inc., 1949. Pp. xiii, 204. * (PA 25:2340)
2. HAVIGHURST, ROBERT J., AND SHANAS, ETHEL. "Adjustment to Retirement: The Fossils—A Case Study." *Sociol & Social Res* 34:169–76 Ja–F '50. * (PA 25:981)
3. SHANAS, ETHEL. "The Personal Adjustment of Recipients of Old Age Assistance." *J Geront* 5:249–53 Jl '50. * (PA 25:1670)
4. HAVIGHURST, ROBERT J. "Validity of the Chicago Attitude Inventory as a Measure of Personal Adjustment in Old Age." *J Abn & Social Psychol* 46:24–9 Ja '51. * (PA 25:7469)

J Consult Psychol 13:385 O '49. Laurance F. Shaffer. The first standardized inventory intended specifically for elderly adults * It consists of three parts, an adult activities inventory measuring reported social participations, an attitude inventory, and questions on background information. *

For related reviews, see 101.

[101]

★**[Re Your Activities and Attitudes.]** CAVAN, RUTH SHONLE; BURGESS, ERNEST W.; HAVIGHURST, ROBERT J.; AND GOLDHAMER, HERBERT. **Personal Adjustment in Old Age.** Chicago, Ill.: Science Research Associates, Inc., 1949. Pp. xiii, 204. $3.25. * (PA 25:2340)

J Appl Psychol 34:217 Je '50. Albert R. Chandler. The distinctive contribution of this book to applied psychology lies in its detailed account of the development, testing and application of an Attitude Inventory and an Activity

Inventory for the study of persons past sixty years of age. The aim of these inventories is to secure data on activities and attitudes in various areas including health, family, friends, work and economic security. In testing the validity of these inventories, interesting auxiliary schedules were developed: a checklist of personal characteristics which an interviewer might observe, a set of word portraits, and a list of symptoms supposed to indicate senility (Appendixes D, E, F). * Tables 7 to 17 (pp. 48 to 59) are based on a smaller "study group" of 499 men and 759 women (pp. 46–48 and Appendix C). The relation between the "study group" and the total group is not made clear in the text. Replying to a query from this reviewer Dr. Havighurst states: "The 'study group' consisted of all the respondents except the two major occupational groups, namely the retired teachers and the retired ministers and their wives. Thus, the 'study group' consists of the people who are described on pages 170 and 171 under paragraphs (d) and (e), and the groups described in the first few paragraphs on page 171." * The authors have made an exceptionally valuable contribution by their thorough, cautious, and critical development of the two inventories and by using them in a study of a large number of cases.

Sociol & Social Res 34:218 Ja–F '50. Arthur Chen. * an important....[volume] by distinguished figures in American sociology. *

PROJECTIVE

[102]

★The Blacky Pictures: A Technique for the Exploration of Personality Dynamics. Ages 5 and over; 1950; a measure of psychosexual development; individual; 1 form; $10.50 per set of testing materials and 25 record blanks; $3.50 per 25 record blanks; postpaid; (35–55) minutes; Gerald S. Blum; Psychological Corporation.

REFERENCES
1. BLUM, GERALD S. *A Study of the Psychoanalytic Theory of Psychosexual Development.* Doctor's thesis, Stanford University (Stanford, Calif.), 1949. (*Abstracts of Dissertations.... 1948–49,* 1949, pp. 202–4.) (*PA* 25:4952, title only)
2. BLUM, GERALD S. "A Study of the Psychoanalytic Theory of Psychosexual Development." *Genetic Psychol Monogr* 39: 3–99 F '49. * (*PA* 23:3650)
3. BLUM, GERALD S. "A Reply to Seward's 'Psychoanalysis, Deductive Method, and the Blacky Test.'" *J Abn & Social Psychol* 45:536–7 Jl '50. * (*PA* 25:644)
4. KLEHR, HAROLD. *An Investigation of Some Personality Factors in Women With Rheumatoid Arthritis.* Doctor's thesis, Northwestern University (Evanston, Ill.), 1950. (*Summaries of Doctoral Dissertations....June–September 1950,* 1951, pp. 605–6.)
5. SEWARD, JOHN P. "Psychoanalysis, Deductive Method, and the Blacky Test." *J Abn & Social Psychol* 45:529–35 Jl '50. * (*PA* 25:653)
6. ARONSON, MARVIN LUCIUS. *A Study of the Freudian Theory of Paranoia by Means of a Group of Psychological*

Tests. Doctor's thesis, University of Michigan (Ann Arbor, Mich.), 1951. Abstract: *Microfilm Abstracts* 11:443–4 no 2 '51.
7. MICHAL-SMITH, H.; HAMMER, EMANUEL; AND SPITZ, HERMAN. "Use of the Blacky Pictures With a Child Whose Oedipal Desires Are Close to Consciousness." *J Clin Psychol* 7:280–2 Jl '51. * (*PA* 26:927)

ALBERT ELLIS, *Consulting Psychologist, 56 Park Ave., New York 16, New York.*

The *Blacky Pictures* constitute an interesting projective technique of personality evaluation which was originally devised to test several specific Freudian hypotheses. The object of the test is to discover whether the subject has acquired, in the course of his psychosexual development, a significantly high degree of oral eroticism, oral sadism, anal sadism, oedipal intensity, masturbation guilt, castration anxiety (males), penis envy (females), positive identification, sibling rivalry, guilt feelings, positive ego ideal, and love-object relationships. The test consists of eleven cartoons depicting a dog, Blacky, going through various sexuo-amative experiences with other dogs representing Blacky's papa, mama, and sibling. Test responses consist of (a) spontaneous TAT-like stories about the cartoons; and (b) answers to specific questions, many of which are stated in multiple choice form, about the cartoons.

Unfortunately, the *Blacky Pictures* manual provides virtually no information on the reliability or validity of the test; nor does the article, "A Study of the Psychoanalytic Theory of Psychosexual Development" (2), which contains the author's main study of the test. Instead of being properly standardized, the Pictures have been used to test several specific hypotheses— namely, Freudian assumptions that boys and girls in our culture react differently in their psychosexual developments. Over and above this, a kind of internal consistency study of the test has been made, in that tetrachoric correlations have been computed to show the relationship between how subjects react to one aspect of the test and how they react to another aspect of it. The obtained coefficients of correlation are rarely above .40.

The only true validity study of the test that is mentioned in the manual is one in the course of which *Blacky Picture* ratings on a single subject who was under psychoanalysis were checked with the analyst's ratings of the subject, and were found substantially to agree. To check this single validity study, the present reviewer administered the test to one of his patients who had had some 200 hours of psychoanalysis, and then presented her test protocol to more than 30 clinical psychologists and psychological interns. This study is still in progress; but so far the results show that while the writer's ratings of the patient, based on his knowledge of her as an analysand, correspond closely to her ratings of herself, there are wide discrepancies between these ratings and those of the clinical psychologists and interns who rated the subject's Blacky protocol.

The writer's experience with the *Blacky Pictures* has thus far indicated the following shortcomings of the test:

a) Some of the cartoons are not in the least clear, and may easily confuse many subjects. This is particularly true in the case of the Masturbation Guilt and Castration Anxiety cartoons.

b) The practice of giving the test Inquiry, consisting of structured questions, after each card has been spontaneously evaluated, rather than reserving the Inquiry until after *all* spontaneous stories have been given (as is usually done in Rorschach inquiries), invites biased responses to all but the first cartoon.

c) The multiple choice questions in the Inquiry are often transparent; so that the intelligent and sophisticated subject can easily figure out the "good" responses.

d) The test seems to be more adaptable for use with children and with unsophisticated adults than with the college students with whom it was originally employed and partly standardized.

e) The manual encourages psychologists first to interpret the test with a minimum of background information on the subject, and independently from other test data; and, considering the present status of psychoanalytic theory in general and the test theory in particular, this may easily lead to dangerous diagnostic practices.

f) As stated above, reliability and validity studies in connection with the *Blacky Pictures* are at present virtually nonexistent, and consequently all test interpretations must be made with the utmost caution and reserve.

In sum: the *Blacky Pictures* make an intriguing projective technique of personality evaluation which appears to have some good possibilities of aiding in the uncovering of some of the subjects' specific sexuo-amative problems. At the present time, however, the test is sadly in need of supporting validational studies, and until these appear its diagnostic employment should be more experimental than routine.

J Consult Psychol 14:332–3 Ag '50. Laurance F. Shaffer. * Although the manual and the research monograph....suggest the purposes and uses of the test, no attempt is made to provide full training for its interpretation. The author wisely suggests that it be used only by clinical psychologists with general competence in other projective tests and with a broad knowledge of psychoanalytic theory.

J Proj Tech 15:109–11 Mr '51. Ephraim Rosen. Although projective techniques stem indirectly from psychoanalytic theory, the majority of them are not closely tied to psychoanalytic or to any other definite personality formulation. Usually one does not find a clear statement of either the theoretical concepts which have guided the construction of the test or of the conceptual system to be used as an aid in test interpretation. The Blacky Pictures are unique in attempting to evaluate the subject's status in terms of a number of specified psychoanalytic variables. * The evidence for the validity of the technique is avowedly incomplete. As of the present, evidence for validity is drawn from two sources— the feeling of clinicians who have used the test that it is extremely helpful, and an investigation by the author into sex differences in psychosexual development and interrelations between psychoanalytic dimensions as manifested by Blacky Picture protocols of a fairly large number of college students. This investigation showed that a large majority of the significant quantitative differences in test performance between male and female students and of the dimensional intercorrelations found were derivable from psycho analytic theory. Parenthetically, it may be noted that the methodology of this study has been attacked by Seward, primarily on the basis of Blum's procedure of looking for Freudian explanations for all empirically found relationships. A more stringent deductive method would involve prediction of the relationships from the theory rather than consideration of only those relationships empirically found. A second possible criticism of the study is that the lack of formal clarity in much of psychoanalytic theory makes it difficult to assess the subjective probability that the relationships found by Blum *do* flow logically from psychoanalytic tenets. Nevertheless, Seward has challenged only a few of Blum's specific findings and interpretations. To this extent, at least, there is evidence for test validity. The evidence does not necessarily imply usefulness and validity in the *clinical* setting, but it contrasts with the lack of objective validity evidence of any type in the case of a number of other projective techniques. In summary, the Blacky Pictures constitute a simple and ingenious device which promises to contribute to future clarification of systematic problems of personality and to take its place as a welcome addition to practical clinical instruments. Not the least of the favorable prognostic indications for it is the author's sophisticated awareness of such problems as the identification of the levels of personality tapped by a projective technique, the nature of interpretation, and the effect of partial structuring in a projective technique. The manual communicates a clarity of thinking about these issues that is refreshing by contrast with the muddled state of much past and some present work in projective psychology.

Q J Child Behavior 2:474–6 O '50. M. M. Genn. * The author deals ably with a problem which has troubled many users of projective tests. All projective tests, though the stimuli are relatively unstructured, usually contain stimuli which are intended to elicit responses to particular areas. For example, the Rorschach Plate VI is purported to contain the male sexual symbol. Frequently, examiners "get the subject coming and going." If he ignores the stimulus, he is said to be repressing strong feelings about it. If he deals with the stimulus, he is said to be overconcerned about it. The author of the Blacky Test (which contains highly structured situations) handles this problem as follows: "Interpretation of spontaneous stories is dynamically oriented, with emphasis upon latent, rather than manifest content. Particular attention is paid to emotional intensity, ego defense mechanisms, blocking, evasiveness, symbolism, artificiality, significant slips, and so forth. The fact that a patient responds to Cartoon VIII, for example, with a sibling rivalry story, is not in itself an indication of strong disturbance in the area, since the stimulus situation is loaded in that direction. Instead the degree of sibling involvement is judged primarily in terms of *intensity* and *how* the rivalry theme is handled, not simply, whether or not it is present." The author then gives examples of so-called "Strong" and "Not Strong" stories. These examples should prove extremely helpful to users of the test in deciding whether there is a problem in a particular area. * The test has not been tried out on children. Although it seems likely that the test is appro-

priate for children, it still remains to be seen whether children's productions will lend themselves to the same levels of interpretation, as those set up for adults. * the validity of the *Blacky Test* has been established to some extent. However, the reliability, or the extent to which a protocol is actually representative of the subject's psychosexual development, has not as yet been demonstrated. This problem, however, exists in relation to all projective tests.

[103]

★**Children's Apperception Test, Revised Edition.** Ages 3–10; 1949–50; also called CAT; individual; 1 form, '49; [revised] picture 2 ['51]; revised manual ('50); [revised] record sheet ('50); $6 per set of 10 pictures in folder and manual; $6 per set of 30 record analysis booklets; $11 per set of pictures, manual, and 30 record analysis booklets; postage extra; (15–50) minutes; Leopold Bellak and Sonya Sorel Bellak; C.P.S. Co., P.O. Box 42, Gracie Station, New York 28, N.Y. *

REFERENCES

1. BELLAK, LEOPOLD, AND BELLAK, SONYA S. "An Introductory Note on the Children's Apperception Test (CAT)." *J Proj Tech* 14:173–80 Je '50. * (*PA* 25:4152)
2. GUREVITZ, SAUL, AND KLAPPER, ZELDA S. "Techniques for and Evaluation of the Responses of Schizophrenic and Cerebral Palsied Children to the Children's Apperception Test (C.A.T.)." *Q J Child Behavior* 3:38–65 Ja '51. * (*PA* 26:4809)

JOHN E. BELL, *Associate Professor of Psychology, Clark University, Worcester, Massachusetts.*

The materials of this test were designed to provide pictures for children about which stories might be told; the test complements, then, the *Symonds Picture Story Test* for adolescents and the *Thematic Apperception Test* for adults. The CAT differs from these two tests in having animals as the characters. The assumption underlying this choice of animals is that children will identify themselves more readily with animals than with human beings and will reveal in their stories the "dynamic meaningfulness of the individual differences of perception of standard stimuli." The range of situations presented permits expression of fantasies relating to such problems as those of feeding, other oral activity, sibling rivalry, parent-parent and parent-child interrelationships, aggression, acceptance by the adult world, night fears, toileting, masturbation, and growth.

The administration is similar to that used in the TAT, but the instructions are less formal. The authors suggest adapting the procedure to the particular age and spontaneity of the child. A story is sought about each picture under as good conditions of rapport between the examiner and the child as possible.

Interpretation based on the symbolic meaning

of the content of the fantasies is emphasized in the brief manual, which describes typical themes that may be elicited by each of the 10 pictures. As may be surmised from the situations portrayed, the themes relate primarily to problems suggested by psychoanalytic theory. Four case illustrations with selected stories amplify the authors' technique of interpretation. Interpretation is facilitated by an analysis sheet for checking 10 possible variables in each story: main theme, main hero (heroine), attitudes to parental figures, family roles and identifications, figures or objects or external circumstances introduced, objects or figures omitted, nature of anxieties, significant conflicts, punishment for crime, and outcome.

Since the major contribution of the Bellaks in introducing this test has been to develop a new set of pictures, the evaluation of their work at this point must depend upon the potential usefulness of the plates in calling forth fantasies. A limited number of trials of the test with children in the suggested age range indicates that fantasies *are* called forth by the pictures. Most children appear to respond enthusiastically to the pictures and to warm up readily to the task of story telling. The pictures are sufficiently simple that most older children, at least, understand their content, yet ambiguous enough to stimulate a variety of response from different subjects. Unfortunately the pictures are printed on a matt finish cardboard that soils easily, even though it duplicates (more adequately) the artistic qualities of the original drawings by Violet Lamont, an illustrator of children's books. While others, such as Balken and Masserman, and Le Shan and Le Shan, have used projective story telling to pictures as a research and diagnostic method, they have not published their pictures and have made it difficult for others to replicate their experiments or to apply their insights in diagnosis. The Bellaks have thus done a real service in making available a standard set of pictures which now may be widely used and studied—and, from all appearances, the representation of children's problems through animal characters was a touch of genius.

L. JOSEPH STONE, *Professor of Child Study, Vassar College, Poughkeepsie, New York.*

The basic procedure and method of interpretation of this test derives from the *Thematic Apperception Test:* its plan to use various animals in humanly family-centered action stems from a suggestion by Dr. Ernst Kris that "we could expect children to identify much more readily with animals than with humans." The manual states that "ideally, we should like to see the C.A.T. used for children from three to 10; Symonds Picture-Story Test, for adolescents; and the T.A.T. for adolescents and adults." There are 10 picture stimulus cards "loaded" to produce material in certain directions determined by the authors' theoretical and clinical orientation; the reviewer feels that caution must be used in interpreting the fact that a particular protocol *does* supply material of the expected sorts; it follows, too, that the user must bear in mind that other aspects of childhood activity—and possibly other aspects of child personality—are neglected.

The pictures were designed to elicit responses to "feeding problems specifically, and oral problems generally; to [investigate] problems of sibling rivalry; to illuminate the attitude toward parental figures and the way in which these figures are apperceived; to learn about the child's relationship to the parents as a couple—technically spoken of as the oedipal complex and its culmination in the primal scene: namely, the child's fantasies about seeing the parents in bed together. Related to this, we wish to elicit the child's fantasies about aggression; about acceptance by the adult world, and its fear of being lonely at night with a possible relation to masturbation, toilet behavior and the parents' response to it." In our own use of the test we have observed only partial approximation of these stress areas.

No information has yet been published on the standardization or validation of the CAT although reference is made to preliminary "experience," on the basis of which the 10 published cards were selected from an initial series of 18, and "typical" themes (with no indication, as yet, of their actual typicality) are offered. However, it is the reviewer's understanding from correspondence with the authors that they and others are carrying on active research on the attributes of the test which includes investigation of the suitability of adding cards to extend stimulation especially in the direction of peer and school relations and attitudes.

As with the TAT (and many other projective devices) the stories elicited by the CAT cards may be evaluated in various ways, depending upon the purpose of administration and upon the tastes and training of the administrator. The

CAT Blank for Recording and Analysis may properly be considered separately from the test materials themselves: it is the reviewer's opinion that the test will be strengthened (though standardization may be retarded) if there is independent study of the stimulus cards and of the efficacy of various methods of interpretation and analysis, including that of the blank. Moreover, the richness of thematic material produced in response to stimuli like the CAT is never satisfactorily reducible to any single set of rubrics to be applied for all purposes. Hence, Bellak's blank is better regarded as *one* guide to analysis, just as he has supplied a very similar one for the TAT. The reviewer's personal experience in (unsystematic) use of the method has been that the blank's categories omit much that he has found most fruitful in understanding a particular child.

One further remark is prompted by the manual's claim "that the CAT is relatively culture-free." Seven of the 10 cards include objects or utensils (flowered hats, pipes, cereal bowls, furniture, plumbing, etc.) which not only are not "culture free" but also bear a certain middle class stamp. Moreover, the style of drawing and the selection of animals portrayed are such that the pictures are congenial to young American children and to our stereotypes of certain "personality traits" of specific animal species: by this very token the test cannot be "culture free."

At its present stage of development the CAT is a very promising tool for the experimental student of children's attitudes and personality development and for the clinician who is ready to use the results of this test, like those of the TAT or interview material, to build up a clinically shrewd and (hopefully) consistent concept of a personality; it is not ready for those who wish quantitative or even qualitative guideposts to normative status or to differential diagnosis.

Am J Orthopsychiatry 20:844–5 O '50. Adolf G. Woltmann. * an important milestone in our search for better and more suitable test materials for children. The test is based upon the fact that children identify more readily with animals than with human figures. The pictures were....chosen in such a way as to elicit stories which constitute projections revealing the basic problems of children from three to ten years. By placing animals in social situations, reactions can be elicited to parents, siblings, eating habits, fear of loneliness,

anxieties, oedipal situations, aggression, cleanliness, masturbation, sexual curiosity, etc. The test consists of only ten cards, which are applicable to both boys and girls. This eliminates constant sorting and shortens the testing time. The test administration is the same as for the T.A.T. A special analysis sheet aids in the scoring and final interpretation of the stories obtained. Each story is analyzed in terms of the main theme, the main hero, attitudes to parental figures, family constellations, the introduction of figures, objects or external circumstances (friend, enemy, punisher, etc.), figures or objects omitted, the nature of anxiety, significant conflicts, attitudes toward punishment and the final outcome. The C.A.T. is a very valuable and important addition to the clinical tools now available for the understanding of the child's personality, and this reviewer sincerely believes that in years to come it will occupy a selected place among projective methods.

Am J Psychiatry 108:317–8 O '51. Herbert Herman. It is gratifying to know that now.... we....have a projective technique that may be applied to the age-group of 3 to 10. * may be profitable in the hands of psychiatrists, psychologists, social workers, and teachers as well as psychologically trained pediatricians. * The C.A.T. is well on its way toward finding for itself an important role in the field of projective techniques in child psychiatry. It may be well to point out, however, that, since it is a projective technique, its value in this field is directly proportional to the ability of the individual attempting its interpretation. When such limitations are recognized, the C.A.T. may be used to good advantage.

J Consult Psychol 14:161 Ap '50. Laurance F. Shaffer. A most appealing thematic apperception test for young children, the C.A.T. presents animal characters in situations significant to the problems of childhood. A little bear helps one of two bigger bears in a tug-of-war. A lion sits with pipe and cane while a mouse views him from a mousehole. An adult spaniel spanks a young one, the background a very obvious bathroom. Suggestive protocols in the brief manual seem to show that the animal figures are sufficiently human-like to evoke identification, but enough unlike humans to free the child from inhibitions against expression. The analysis sheet provides for an interpretation mainly in terms of content: theme, hero, attitudes to parental figures, family roles, anxieties, conflicts, and the like. The C.A.T. is a ready and needed clinical tool, and also a provocative research instrument for future studies of age, socioeconomic, intellectual and ethnic groups.

Q J Child Behavior 2:469–70 O '50. M. M. Genn. * The pictures were drawn by Viola Lamont, a children's illustrator. While these pictures might do very well for illustrations in a children's book, they have some limitations as test material. Picture #6 which contains animals sleeping or hibernating in a cave, is very dimly drawn, and some young children to whom the reviewer exposed the picture in the clinical situation could not determine what it was and were unable to fabricate anything. Picture #3 is a large lion seated in a chair, with a small mouse in the corner. This picture is intended to elicit stories about the relationship with the father-figure. However, the mouse is so tiny and indistinctly drawn that some children miss it. The vagueness of some of the stimuli might be justified if it were the intention to elicit responses to unstructured forms, as in the Rorschach. However, since the purported aim is to elicit dynamic story-telling based on concrete stimuli, some of these pictures are inadequate. Picture #10 appears to be "overstructured" for diagnostic differentiation. This is a picture of a small puppy apparently being spanked by an older puppy in a bathroom. Some children simply tell that the child is being spanked for not going to the toilet. One wonders if a picture of the two figures simply standing near the toilet would elicit a story more clearly related to the child's own experience. The manual does not provide instructions for the introductory steps in the administration. Presumably it is assumed that the clinician will use the same instructions as recommended for Murray's *Thematic Apperception Test*. The manual does give some useful hints for interpretation. The check-list containing points to be noted is especially helpful. In spite of the above-mentioned shortcomings with respect to some of the art work and the content of some of the pictures, the C.A.T. meets a long-felt need for pictured stimuli containing figures with which children could easily identify. The author acknowledges the fact that the publication of the test does not necessarily imply that the technique is fully standardized, and points out the need for the accumulation of further data.

TAT Newsletter 4:5–7 su '50. Robert R. Holt. The standard set of TAT plates issued by Murray contains three pictures specifically for boys and girls, two of them suggested by Sanford on the basis of his experience with the children of the Shady Hill study. Using these to substitute for a couple of the adult series, the set is supposed to be adaptable for use with children of seven years or younger. Sarah Schafer and Mary Leitch have demonstrated that some of the pictures have a limited usefulness even with nursery school children. Why, then, a special set of cards for children? The primary practical reason is that the TAT is rarely a very productive instrument with preadolescent or younger children. Though the material it provokes is often scanty, it is useful enough to be employed routinely by a number of persons working with children. But if a picture-story test could really tap the rich fantasy life of the child it might have far more usefulness for diagnostic and therapeutic work, and for research. It looks as if the Bellaks may have provided us with such a test. The principal theoretical reason for designing a new set of pictures was suggested by Ernst Kris, the manual tells us. "Theoretically, we had reason to assume that animals might be preferred identification figures from three years up to possibly ten," the authors say, "and thus we set out to create, pictorially, situations vital to this age range." A further advantage cited of using animals is that they make the test easily usable with Negro children and almost any others within the Western-European cultural framework. The pictures themselves were drawn by Violet Lamont, an illustrator of children's books, and show a sure professional touch. The sprightly animal figures, some naturalistic, some with human accessories like hats or a pipe, have style and charm, and certainly appealed to a complete sample of one population, the reviewer's own children. These little girls, aged four and a half and three years, fell to the game of making up stories with relish, and seemed to identify themselves with the animal children with great ease and naturalness. Of course, such a miniature try-out cannot show anything more than the fact that it *is* possible for very young children to take to the test and to produce usable material freely. Eighteen pictures were used by the authors and a number of other clinicians in preliminary try-outs, and the ten most useful retained. They seem to have been well chosen to touch upon the most significant problems and conflicts that most children in our society are likely to encounter. * the authors state their feeling that when one is dealing with projective techniques, all that is necessary by way of standardization is to try a new one out and see that it gives useful material. For the rest, one relies upon "the basic hypothesis of projective—or apperceptive—phenomena," and "the individual case can stand by itself." They do not wholly side-step the problem of norms, however, saying that it would be very desirable to assemble them for different age levels, but too difficult a task for a single team of investigators. The fact that this seems to be S.O.P. for the production of new projective tests does not make it any more desirable. The authors do go a good deal beyond what is usual, however, in their generous offer to cooperate with all users of their test, "to organize all available findings and make it available to users of the C.A.T., upon request" and to act "as an informal clearing house." * Persons who are unskilled in analysis of thematic materials will probably find the examples of interpreted stories more helpful. The orientation given is sound, but of course no one should expect to learn interpretation from reading a manual, short or long. Taken as a whole, the test (and particularly the manual, which is rife with minor errors and carelessness) show signs of being put out in a little too much of a hurry—compare the Four Picture Test, published after 18 years and the experience of thousands of administrations. Nevertheless, the C.A.T. is a very promising-looking addition to the available instruments for testing young children.

[104]

★Expressive Movement Chart. Ages 3–5; 1946–48; individual; revised recording form ('48); examiner's guide ('48); $3.50 per set of figure cards, examiner's guide, and 25 recording forms; $1 per set of figure cards and guide; 15¢ per recording form; $5 per copy of *The Personality of the Preschool Child* ('46—see 3:1245) which serves as the manual; postage extra; (45) minutes; Werner Wolff; Grune & Stratton. *

REFERENCES

1. WOLFF, WERNER. "Projective Methods for Personality Analysis of Expressive Behavior in Preschool Children." *Char & Pers* 10:309–30 Je '42. * (PA 17:362)
2. WOLFF, WERNER. *The Personality of the Preschool Child: The Child's Search for His Self.* New York: Grune & Stratton, Inc., 1946. Pp. xvi, 341. * (London: William Heinemann, Ltd., 1947.) (PA 21:1706)

For a related review, see 3:1245.

[105]

★Four-Picture Test (1930). Ages 12 and over; 1948; also called FPT; individual; 1 form; manual ('48); $16.90 (65 guilders) per set of testing materials (bound), postage extra; nontimed (15–70) minutes; D. J. van Lennep; publisher and distributor in Netherlands and Belgium: National Institute of Industrial Psychology, Utrecht, Netherlands; distributor in all other countries: Martinus Nijhoff, The Hague, Netherlands.

REFERENCES

1. BELL, JOHN ELDERKIN. "The Case of Gregor: Psychological Test Data." *Rorsch Res Exch & J Proj Tech* 13:155–205 no 2 '49. * (PA 24:2589)
2. SHNEIDMAN, EDWIN S. "Some Comparisons Among the Four Picture Test, Thematic Apperception Test, and Make A Picture Story Test." *Rorsch Res Exch & J Proj Tech* 13:150–4 no 2 '49. * (PA 24:2614)
3. VAN LENNEP, D. J. Chap. 6, "The Four-Picture Test," pp. 149–80. In *An Introduction to Projective Techniques.* Edited by Harold H. Anderson and Gladys L. Anderson. New York: Prentice-Hall, Inc., 1951. Pp. xxiv, 720. *

JOHN E. BELL, *Associate Professor of Psychology, Clark University, Worcester, Massachusetts.*

This test, designed in 1930, is based on the principle of storytelling to pictures. Four subtly colored pictures are provided which represent four different situations: (*a*) being together with one other person (a room with two persons talking across a long table); (*b*) being personally alone (a bedroom); (*c*) being socially alone (a street scene with a single figure under a lamppost); (*d*) being together with many others in a group (a tennis match, with observers). The pictures are sufficiently ambiguous (or polyvalent) to permit highly personalized interpretations.

A unique feature of the technique is the demand that the subject produce a continuous story that incorporates all four pictures. Neither order nor time limit is prescribed; most examinees take about 35 minutes. Stories may be oral or written. The examiner may present the pictures for one minute, remove them, and then ask for written stories. If the story is banal, he may request another story; if only three pictures are combined, he may urge the subject to try to incorporate the fourth or he may remove the fourth picture and ask the subject to imagine the picture needed to complete the series; if the subject cannot combine the pictures, the examiner may ask for a separate description of each picture and then attempt to combine two or more.

Interpretation follows the two basic patterns for projective analysis: the formal, and the contentual. Study of the content for its personality significance follows the patterns used in the analysis of the TAT or other storytelling projective techniques. It is in the formal analysis that one of the advantages of this method is most clearly revealed. Study of such formal elements as the order and span of combination and number of pictures used gives data not ordinarily obtained from most picture-story methods. From such factors the examiner may be helped in arriving at conclusions about the level and manner of intellectual functioning.

A new interpretative suggestion to be applied to the study of story materials is also contained in the test blank and elaborated in the manual—the use of the time quality of the fantasy for interpretation. The author points out the difficulty schizophrenics have in giving a coherent time quality to the figures in the story; the successive (after each other) time sequences in the stories of depressives; and the *final,* or future, emphasis in the productions of hysterics. He follows Hugenholtz in dividing time into four forms—physical, vital, animal, and human—and in suggesting the interpretative value of each by itself, when combined, and when interrupted. The application of concern about the time is a principle that may be applied equally well to other types of story materials, but it is especially appropriate here because of the demand for a continuous story.

In general, the technique has the following advantages: (*a*) a brief administration time; (*b*) suggestiveness of the stimulus materials; (*c*) an aesthetically pleasing quality to the color and composition of the pictures; (*d*) the values implicit in the necessity of combining the pictures to produce a story; and (*e*) the wide age range of subjects with whom the method may be used.

One of the advantages (the brevity) may appear also as a disadvantage. The risk in interpreting such limited productions is that over-emphasis upon minor details may lead to invalid conclusions that cannot be checked within other parts of the response. Perhaps when one has used the technique as extensively as the author, dependence upon information from other diagnostic methods for validation is less important. Without such a background, an interpreter should probably regard conclusions from the method as hypotheses of a most tentative nature. This would suggest that the two major uses of the test will be as a rough screening device and as a contribution with some unique elements to a larger battery of projective techniques.

E. J. G. BRADFORD, *Senior Lecturer in Education, The University of Sheffield, Sheffield, England.*

The four pictures which form the basis of this test are coloured reproductions of scenes painted in an "impressionist" style. In one picture, a bedroom, no human form is depicted; in another is a solitary figure in a dark, damp, and otherwise deserted street; in a third, two people in a room are presumably in conversation; the remaining picture depicts a social occasion on a tennis court, a game in progress and four seated onlookers, male and female. The subject is required to construct one story incorporating all four scenes. The scenes are well chosen to disclose the subject's general attitudes to society, its values, and moral standards. The scenes may be incorporated in any order, and the order chosen may in itself have definite significance. In the resulting stories, dependent, aggrieved, depressed, aggressive, and hysterical personality types can usually be recognised with little difficulty.

Unfortunately, and this applies to most projection tests, only about one third of adult subjects will produce really adequate material, and it is rare to get satisfactory responses from male juvenile delinquents. In the experience of this reviewer, with those whose command of language is below average, as is the case with many delinquents, the material produced is so meagre that the time spent is not worthwhile. Hence a preliminary reading and vocabulary test is advisable. However, the blindness to details and even to whole pictures is very revealing.

The reviewer's experience supports the author's claim that better results are obtained if the pictures are withdrawn after a minute or two for inspection, and the story is then dictated by the subject. Well educated, intelligent subjects are less self-conscious if allowed to write out the story in a room by themselves. Both in hospital work and in vocational selection, the reviewer has found this test to assist materially in the interpretation of the results of an intelligence battery (incorporating verbal and performance tests) applied individually, the *Four Picture Test* following the battery during the course of the interview.

EPHRAIM ROSEN, *Assistant Professor of Psychology, University of Minnesota, Minneapolis, Minnesota.*

This projective technique consists of four ambiguous water color pictures, varying in size from 4 by 5½ to 5 by 6 inches, designed to represent "four very general and existential situations." Picture I depicts two figures, of ambiguous sex and age, conversing in a room. It is intended to represent "being together with one other person." Picture II shows a bed on which the outline of a head on a pillow can be very dimly made out. It symbolizes "being personally alone." The third picture, intended to symbolize "being socially alone," is of a figure standing under a lamppost in a dark and rainy atmosphere. Picture IV depicts a tennis match watched by several spectators and symbolizes "being together with many others in a group."

The four pictures are placed on a table close together so as to form a square. The subject is then instructed to make up a story combining them and relating them to each other. He may start where he wishes and follow any order. The examiner makes a verbatim record of the story. There are several alternative modes of administration: The subject may tell his story after looking at the pictures for one minute, after which they are removed; the subject may write his story (thus making group administration possible) ; or combinations of these variations may be used.

A flexible procedure analogous to testing the limits on the Rorschach may then be employed. The examiner may ask for a new story related to anywhere from one to all four of the pictures, depending on the subject's performance in the test proper. Thus, if one of the four pictures is only loosely connected to the other three in the original story, the subject may be asked to tell a new story incorporating all four or to describe a substitute picture that he could include in his story.

The manual provides a guide for formal analysis in terms of such variables as order of pictures in the story; extent of differentiation within a picture; use made of time, space, and thoughts and dreams of a figure to connect the pictures; conflicts; and themes. Such formal analysis is considered to be only the beginning of interpretation, for the examiner must then proceed clinically and intuitively. Four protocols and interpretations are presented in the manual to illustrate formal and clinical interpretation.

The technique is ingenious and original. A priori, it would seem to provide a method of inquiry into many areas not easily approached by most projective techniques. Thus rigidity versus flexibility can be evaluated by the subject's success in shifting to a new story. Insight into the subject's social relations can be obtained by observing his response to the many figures in Picture IV. The analysis of the use made of time and causality in connecting the pictures—for example, connection by making each event the result of the preceding event versus connection by making each event a function of a goal to be reached by the performer—is an original approach to dimensions of personality hitherto little studied.

On the other hand, the *Four Picture Test* suffers from certain deficiencies. The test, perhaps due to the difficulty of reproducing the water colors, is quite expensive. More important, norms have not been compiled as an aid to that part of interpretation based on formal analysis. Apparently Dr. van Lennep worked on the technique for 18 years before making it public, thus accumulating an immense number of protocols. Analysis of these protocols, however, has not been presented statistically. We do not know what sort of stories are typical of various groups, what the effects of various administrative procedures are, nor what validation data exist. Dr. van Lennep is not concerned with standardization. In line with a tradition stronger in European psychology than in the United States, he seems to imply that emphasis on interpreter skill is incompatible with emphasis on objective norms. Understanding, intuition, and internal consistency are sought, rather than objective evidences of validity. Thus, though a skilled examiner may find the test very useful, we have no scientific indications of where its limitations and greatest usefulness lie.

TAT Newsletter 2:2–4 Mr '49. Robert R. Holt. In America, the production of new tests is so prolific that a special section of the Psychological Abstracts is devoted to them and every month sees a goodly crop. Typically, these are brain-children of no long gestation; the bright idea is materialized in the form of test materials which are tried out long enough to show some promise, and forthwith published. Our Dutch colleague puts us to shame with his Four Picture Test (FPT), conceived in 1930 and brought forth into the light of commercial distribution only after 18 years of careful work. One thinks of the European tradition of patient hand-work by master craftsmen, as compared to American assembly-line mass production. There are of course advantages to our own way; most conspicuously, we are more concerned than is the author of the FPT to present normative data and summarize our experience with a test statistically so that others may be helped a little over the initial stages of building up their own fund of experience. But it does not take more than a reading of the manual and a few trials of the test itself to convince one that Dr. van Lennep has produced a small but firmly-wrought masterpiece. The pictures, manual, and a half a dozen test blanks indicating the variables used in analyzing stories, are all done up nicely between boards in the manner of the Rorschach plates, making a slim light volume indeed for the price. The author assures me, however, that the unusual cost of producing exact duplicates of the original watercolor pictures makes it impossible to market the test for less. The reproductions do indeed seem to be excellent, being nearly indistinguishable from actual watercolors. They are done chiefly in brownish greens, except for the contrasting russet of the tennis court in IV. In size they range from four by five and a half inches (I) to slightly over five by six inches (IV)....I is an interior scene; two persons are in a room with a table between them and bookshelves in the background; one is standing, gesturing towards the other. II, a bedroom, contains a bed with a window behind it and the very dim indication of a head on the pillow. III depicts a rainy night in which someone is leaning against a lamp-post. IV is a scene at a tennis court, showing two players and in the foreground two couples looking on and conversing. In the first three pictures, the figures are all fairly ambiguous as to sex and age and all expressions are indeterminate due to the deliberately sketch-like, somewhat slap-dash style of the paintings. These four pictures were planned to represent "the four existential situations: being personally alone (i.e., in the kind of solitude one seeks, as in II), being socially alone (i.e., rejected, as in III), being together with one other person (I), and being together with many others in a group (IV)." The unique feature of the test is that "the subject has not only to give a meaning to each of the four pictures, but must do it in such a manner that the interpreted pictures can be combined in one story. This demands, in addition to a higher intellectual function, the imagining of connecting links in which projections occur easily and almost necessarily." The subject is told that the pictures are unrelated in the way they are laid out, and that he is to make up a story which combines all four of them in any order he likes, starting or finishing with any one. Clinicians who have had experience with the Picture Arrangement subtest of the Wechsler-Bellevue scale will rightly expect that many psychotics and persons of inferior mental ca-

pacities (particularly, those with defects in the function of *anticipation*) will be unable to perform the task as thus presented. As a result of experiences with such patients and with children, van Lennep suggests a variety of altered techniques of administration. In general, their essence is to accept whatever the patient can produce on however low a level, and then to urge and lead him to produce on higher levels of story production (instead of description) and combination (instead of separate consideration of the pictures). In addition, various methods of "testing the limits" by requiring stories for combinations different from the one spontaneously chosen are outlined. The author indicates that many valuable protocols have been obtained by having subjects write out their own stories. Finally, he recommends the variation of allowing one minute's inspection of the cards, then taking them away before the subject writes or tells his story. By means of this admirable flexibility and ingenuity of administrative methods, the FPT's creator has found ways to use it with all kinds of subjects, and allows for its free adaptive utilization. With the gain in freedom there is a corresponding loss in standardization; there are no indications of systematic differences in the results according to the particular variation employed. Presumably the tester builds up his own norms, and the assumption is made that the data may be used in roughly the same way no matter how they are obtained. And while this assumption is undoubtedly true within limits, it is uncertain just how broad the limits are. The little manual contains, besides a brief theoretical introduction, description of the pictures and instructions for administration, 20 pages on interpretation and four protocols with detailed analyses. Van Lennep introduces the reader to the interpretation of his test in this manual in much the same way Tomkins does for the TAT in his book: by extensive cataloguing of obtained form-varieties of each significant aspect of the stories. Thus we are prepared for the variety of protean forms the material may take somewhat at the expense of direct help in getting at the meaning of the stories. Still, considering the brevity of the manual and the probably inevitable difficulties of translation, the author has done a fine job of communicating some of his insights relative to the interpretation of thematic material. There is grist here not just for the clinician who wants to learn the use of this test, but also for those who want to extend their proficiency with the TAT. One of the most interesting and original contributions to interpretation is van Lennep's treatment of *time* as it is used in stories. Almost nothing has been written about the significance of the kind of time in which the subject lives as projected in TAT stories; judging by what the Hollanders seem to have been doing, we have been missing a subtle but revealing dimension. Building on the work of P. Th. Hugenholtz, van Lennep distinguishes the following principal kinds of time: *physical* time (e.g., "eight o'clock") which occurs seldom and is of little importance; *vital* time, "when an event is aimed from the past at the future"; *animal* time: "the future is brought towards the moment"; and *human* time, in which man unfolds his own boundless future. Depressives, we are told, "live in the after-each-other of things"; they tend to picture events as *due to* preceding events in the form: "something happened *because of* something else in the past." Hysterics, on the other hand, have a *final* or future-oriented quality to their temporal relations: one does something *in order to* bring about a desired state of affairs. The similar analysis of the use of space is less transferable to the TAT, being closely related to the problem of organizing four separate pictures. What other features of the FPT differentiate it from the TAT? First, we learn more about the organizational abilities of the subject, from the way in which he combines the scenes into a connected narrative. Second, there is the additional variable, the particular order of pictures chosen. One looks in vain for indications of possible significances of the different orders, however, beyond the statement that particular ones are common or rare. Third, by asking for another story with a different order of pictures from that chosen by the subject, one can learn about the flexibility vs. rigidity of his thought, the ease with which he is able to shift. Fourth, it does seem that the author is right in claiming that projective material is more easily got out of certain subjects through the transitional material they must introduce to provide continuity between the four pictures. It looks as if these particular pictures make it possible to tell more than the TAT usually does about a person's broader social relationships—those beyond his contacts with the few significant persons in his life. This last fact is probably attributable to the fact that picture IV (the tennis court) contains more people than does any TAT picture and in a different type of activity; indeed, it is the only one for which a pretty good analogue cannot be found in one of the editions of the TAT. To sum up the difference in a (somewhat oversimplified) word, there are richer possibilities for *formal* analysis in the FPT than in the TAT, while the latter provides more by way of personal *content*. Of course, the last fact is due in large part to the greater length of the TAT. The Four Pictures are remarkably well chosen for their possibilities of bringing out significant material about sexual, passive, affiliative and aggressive needs, the latter particularly in terms of rivalry—a striving not much touched off by the TAT. For all these reasons, one can probably learn more from a single FPT story than from one TAT story; minute for minute, van Lennep's test may be more productive than Murray's. Certainly the author has trained himself to a great sensitivity and resourcefulness in working with a minimum of material, by sticking to an essentially one-story test. But it seems to be inherently limited. My feeling after a very insufficient trial of the FPT is that after the first spontaneous story, more could be learned by using other pictures than by using the same ones in recombination. Where time is not at a premium, and when one wants to go as deeply as possible into personality dynamics, the TAT would have the edge every time—in the opinion of a grossly prejudiced party!

[106]

★**Group Projection Sketches for the Study of Small Groups.** Groups of from 3 to 40 people (ages 16 and over); 1949; 20 scores: grouped under 3 categories (sociodynamics, group structure, outcome of group process): communication clarity, content-procedure ratio, information providing, goal concentration, problem source, value orientation, tension level, tension direction, pacing level, personal interdependence, personal affect, participation spread, role differentiation, in-group feeling, individuality of members, quality of group product, organization of outcome, creativity of group product, group satisfaction with outcome, motivation to execute outcome; 1 form; no data on reliability and validity; $2.50 per set of 5 pictures and mimeographed manual (content same as *J Social Psychol* 33:77–102 F '51), postpaid; (60) minutes; William E. Henry and Harold Guetzkow; University of Michigan Press. *

REFERENCES

1. HENRY, WILLIAM E., AND GUETZKOW, HAROLD. "Group Projection Sketches for the Study of Small Groups." *J Social Psychol* 33:77–102 F '51. * (PA 26:917)

ROBERT R. HOLT, *Director, Psychological Staff, The Menninger Foundation, Topeka, Kansas.*

Starting with the assumption that groups have unique personality-like properties and characteristic ways of functioning, which might be studied by methods similar to those for studying individual personalities, Horwitz and Cartwright created a "Group TAT" a few years ago. Henry and Guetzkow have, with permission, taken the idea up and developed it into the present test. The result is a promising-appearing instrument, which rather regrettably has been published before much work has been done to actualize its apparent potentialities.

There are five pictures about each of which a group is asked to write a story, taking about 10 minutes for each: a conference group of men, a single man, two men of different ages, an older woman and a man, and an informal group of men. It seems unfortunate that there is no equivalent form for women, or at least a few more pictures offering all-female and mixed groups. There are many feminine and mixed groups that might well be studied by a technique such as this, and some essential features of their "group personality" may not come through clearly because of the masculine nature of the present pictures. The pictures are, however, attractively drawn and are large enough (21 by 18 inches) to be seen easily by all members of a moderate sized group.

The technique of administration (which in many ways is similar to that for the individual TAT) is carefully presented in the manual, with enough detail to cover most problems the user is likely to encounter. Several protocols from different kinds of groups are accompanied by detailed interpretations which make it clear how a variety of group characteristics may show themselves in the stories. The authors also offer 20 rating scales for aspects of group dynamics, structure and process which may be assessed from the set of five stories as a whole. These scales seem to be well chosen to quantify significant facts about a group; scorings on the scales are offered for two sets of stories, and there are some brief comments with each to indicate the kinds of inferences from stories that may be made in making the ratings. The ratings and "freehand" analyses, however, can be done only by clinically trained persons who are already competent in interpreting the individual TAT, and who in addition have a good understanding of group dynamics and structure.

No data are given on the validity of inferences drawn from the test nor on the reliability of the scoring categories, though some are promised for the future. The authors are careful to state that the illustrative cases in the manual, each with a brief statement from independent sources

about the group concerned, do not constitute validation and are not presented as such. Nevertheless, they do convey a strong impression of the validity of the blind analyses, and suggest ways in which validation research could easily be done.

The authors have used the *Group Projection Sketches* with white-collar staff workers in industry, adult academic groups, and the like. Apparently the test may be used with even quite psychologically sophisticated persons, but it is not at all clear how well adapted it would be to subjects with less than college education. In its present state of development, it is primarily a test for use in research on small groups, where it should provide very useful data. One can think of a number of situations where it might prove useful: diagnosing difficulties in conference groups, comparing the functioning of seminars or of different clinical teams, perhaps following the progress of therapeutic groups, or locating trouble spots in certain kinds of business or industrial setups where people must work together in moderate numbers. For a test of this character, it would be most useful to know how groups respond to retesting: whether the test is sensitive enough to reflect changes in group structure and functioning after attempts have been made to bring them about. If so, it might be a very useful aid to the diagnosis and treatment of group difficulties.

That branch of social psychology and sociology known as *group dynamics* has been developing rapidly in recent years and shows distinct promise of great social usefulness. The present test is to my knowledge the only instrument of its kind available to this new discipline for aiding in the diagnostic study of groups, and though too little work has been done with it for a proper evaluation at this time, it seems worthy of wide experimental trial in the hands of persons with the requisite interpretative skills.

N. W. MORTON, *Director, Operational Research Group, Defense Research Board, Ottawa, Canada.*

These five 21- by 18-inch pencil sketches were prepared as a basis for a group product which may reveal some of the characteristics of the group and its mode of functioning. The product is a story about the human figures in each picture or at least an interpretation of the scene presented. This story or written interpretation produced by the group is formally comparable with a written TAT response from an individual.

While there appears to be no reason why observations of the behaviour of the members of the group while engaged in the production of its stories may not be made if desired, the intention of the authors is to provide an instrument which will not require such a direct assessment. That is, the evaluation of the group is entirely in terms of its products.

Two forms of analysis of the stories are suggested. It is emphasized by the authors that these are provisional only, being based on preliminary experience rather than on extensive experimental study or validation.

The two methods of analysis consist of a clinical type appreciation, wholly verbal in form, and a series of ratings conceived more or less systematically to assess the way the group works, its formal characteristics, and the nature of its product. In both methods projection appears to this reviewer to be treated very literally; that is, that the most plausible hypothesis about the group—the proposition concerning it most likely to be true—is that its various characteristics will each be mirrored directly in the respective features of its interpretation of the pictures. This is as if one were calling a series of shots with each individual outcome (i.e., the particular characteristic of the group) uncertain, but the long term odds in one's favor. Probably without further evidence about the test, this is the most reasonable thing to do.

The three main divisions of ratings, on the group's sociodynamics, structure, and product, seem to the reviewer to be obviously of quite different face validity. The last is a more or less direct assessment, certain features of the first (e.g., value orientation) are fairly so, while the judgments about group structure involve a considerable and thereby rather uncertain process of inference.

In achieving the economy of recording and using only the final story produced by the group about each picture rather than the necessarily detailed account of how it arrived at its conclusions, it is judged that the chief loss is in direct information about the relationships of individuals to the group and within it. A principal effect is to transfer emphasis from description of individuals interacting in the group to evaluation of the group as a whole. One gains the impression that a further result may be the assumption of a considerable degree of homogeneity in the group. Thus the method may be better adapted to the description of a well defined group having certain settled and homogeneous qualities than to groups more heterogeneously or temporarily composed.

The sketches are well drawn. The selection of subject matter appears to the reviewer to represent some degree of bias toward the younger male urban academic or white collar level type of interest or experience. In this respect, and in the clarity rather than vagueness of the drawings, the material is thought to be more definitely oriented and structured than has been true of other TAT pictures.

[107]

*H-T-P: A Projective Device and a Measure of Adult Intelligence. Adults; 1946–50; individual; drawing form ('46); scoring folder ('50); post-drawing interrogation form ('50); manual ('47); $1.25 per 25 drawing forms; $2 per 25 scoring folders; $2 per 25 interrogation forms; $2.25 per manual; postpaid; (60–90) minutes; John N. Buck; Western Psychological Services, Box 775, Beverly Hills, Calif. *

REFERENCES

1–5. See 3:47.
6. BUCK, JOHN N. The H-T-P Technique: A Qualitative and Quantitative Scoring Manual. Appendix, "Comments on the Analysis of Chromatic Drawings," by John T. Payne. Journal of Clinical Psychology Monograph Supplement No. 5. Burlington, Vt.: Journal of Clinical Psychology, October 1948. Pp. 120. Paper. * (Reprinted from J Clin Psychol 5:37–76 Ja '49.) (PA 23:5135, 5516, 5529)
7. BUCK, JOHN N. "The H-T-P Test." J Clin Psychol 4: 151–9 Ap '48. * (PA 23:8)
8. BUCK, JOHN N. "The Use of the H-T-P in Personality Analysis." Abstract. Am Psychol 3:284 Jl '48. * (PA 22:5420, title only)
9. SLOAN, WILLIAM, AND GUERTIN, WILSON H. "A Comparison of H-T-P and Wechsler-Bellevue IQ's in Mental Defectives." J Clin Psychol 4:424–6 O '48. * (PA 23:5532)
10. BUCK, JOHN N. "The H-T-P Technique." J Clin Psychol 5:37–74 Ja '49. * (PA 23:5516)
11. PAYNE, JOHN T. "Comments on the Analysis of Chromatic Drawings." J Clin Psychol 5:75–6 Ja '49. * (PA 23:5529)
12. REAGAN, BRUCE V., JR. "The HTP Test: a Reading Aid," pp. 154–6. In Claremont College Reading Conference, Fourteenth Yearbook, 1949: Conference Theme: The Problems and Techniques Involved in Reading Social Relationships. Claremont, Calif.: Claremont College Curriculum Laboratory, 1949. Pp. viii, 191. Paper. *
13. BUCK, JOHN N. "The Use of the House-Tree-Person Test in a Case of Marital Discord." J Proj Tech 14:405–34 D '50. * (PA 26:3366)
14. BUCK, JOHN N., Editor. Administration and Interpretation of the H-T-P Test: Proceedings of the H-T-P Workshop Held at Veterans Administration Hospital, Richmond 19, Virginia, March 31, April 1, 2, 1950. [Beverly Hills, Calif.: Western Psychological Services, 1950.] Pp. 67. Paper, mimeographed. *
15. PAYNE, JOHN T. Observations on the Use of Color With the H-T-P. Morganton, N.C.: State Hospital, October 1950. Pp. ii, 17. Paper, mimeographed. *
16. SCHWARTZ, ARTHUR A. "Some Interrelationships Among Four Tests Comprising a Test Battery: A Comparative Study." J Proj Tech 14:153–72 Je '50. * (PA 25:4592)
17. BUCK, JOHN N. "Directions for Administration of the Achromatic-Chromatic H-T-P." J Clin Psychol 7:274–6 Jl '51. * (PA 26:905)
18. BUCK, JOHN N. "The Quality of the Quantity of the H-T-P." J Clin Psychol 7:352–6 O '51. * (PA 26:3401)
19. SMYKAL, ANTHONY, AND THORNE, FREDERICK C. "Etiological Studies of Psychopathic Personality: II, Asocial Type." Case Study. J. Clin Psychol 7:299–316 O '51. * (PA 26:3532)

ALBERT ELLIS, Consulting Psychologist, 56 Park Ave., New York 16, New York.

Buck's original manual for the H-T-P is certainly one of the worst horrors ever perpetrated in the field of clinical psychology. For deriving IQ's and other quantitative scores from the *H-T-P,* the standardization data presented in the manual are inadequately based on only 140 cases, evenly spread over 7 mental levels from imbecile to superior intelligence. The standardization group for qualitative personality interpretation is also most inadequate, based on the study of only 150 disturbed individuals, ranging from adult maladjustment and psychoneurosis to psychopathy, epilepsy, and psychosis. If any specific facts on the reliability or validity of the *H-T-P* were obtained from these two standardization studies, they are conspicuously missing from the manual. Considering that, at the time this manual was published in 1948, Buck had admittedly had "ten years of study and clinical usage" of the *H-T-P,* the manual displays incredible naïveté, fanaticism, and arrant disregard for any attempt at scientific validation of the material presented.

Fortunately for Buck, however, the manual appears to be as unreliable as a projective test of its author's personality as many of its dogmatic maxims prove to be when employed in the projective testing of patients and other individuals. For Buck has recently followed up the manual with complete mimeographed proceedings (*14*) of the *H-T-P* workshop held at the Veterans Administration Hospital, Richmond, Virginia in the spring of 1950; and these proceedings indicate that he is a reasonably open-minded psychologist who is still learning a good deal about his own test and who is willing to revise many of his originally rash pronouncements in the light of subsequently gained experience with, and criticism of, the *H-T-P* technique. Since the new mimeographed material seems to supersede much of the material in the original manual, the present review will be limited to a discussion of the *H-T-P* as used in conjunction with the new material and with John T. Payne's supplementary mimeographed paper, *Observations on the Use of Color with the H-T-P.* (*15*)

The *H-T-P* technique is unquestionably a valuable addition to the clinical psychologist's battery of projective tests of personality evaluation. Two vitally important questions quickly arise, however, in connection with its employment: (*a*) *How* shall it be administered? and (*b*) How shall its results be *interpreted?*

Buck's method of administering the *H-T-P* includes several basic steps: (*a*) individual administration of the test; (*b*) postdrawing inter-

rogation; (*c*) individual administration of the chromatic *H-T-P* (the drawing of the house, tree, and person with various colored pencils instead of with regular pencils); (*d*) postdrawing interrogation of the chromatic drawings; (*e*) quantitative and qualitative scoring of the test, including the estimation of specific IQ's; and (*f*) general qualitative interpretation of the test, particularly in relation to the personality evaluation of the subject and his differential diagnosis. This procedure is a thoroughgoing one that is likely, under ideal testing circumstances, to provide maximum material for test interpretation. The present reviewer, on the basis of much experience with the *H-T-P,* is skeptical, however, about the *practical* value of this involved procedure, for several reasons:

a) When done in the orthodox manner as outlined in the new mimeographed manual, the administration, scoring, and interpretation of the *H-T-P* takes several hours. Considering the unknown reliability and, especially, validity of the *H-T-P* intelligence estimations and personality interpretations at the present time, and considering the time available to the psychologist in a normal clinical situation, it is unlikely that the *H-T-P* is normally worth this many hours of a busy psychologist's time.

b) The standard administration procedure does not provide for the drawing of persons of both sexes by the subject. The writer has found it most valuable to administer the test so that the subject first draws a house, then a tree, then a person, and then a second person of the sex opposite to the one drawn first. This combines the advantages of the *H-T-P* and the Machover figure drawing technique and often adds valuable material for interpretative purposes.

c) The present writer sees no particular value in employing the standard *H-T-P* booklets for the actual drawings. Any ordinary size white paper serves the same purpose.

d) The quantitative scoring of the *H-T-P,* and particularly the obtaining of specific IQ's, has been found to be of relatively little value, considering the time and effort involved.

e) In practice it has been quite feasible to gather *H-T-P* drawings on a group rather than an individual basis; much of the interpretative value of the tests can be obtained from such group-gathered drawings.

f) The postdrawing interrogation may also be done on a group basis; or it may be omitted entirely. The time and effort spent in making this postdrawing interrogation on an individual basis is questionably expended, as against utilizing this time for a general psychological interview of the subject, in which reference to the drawings may play some part.

For the foregoing reasons, this reviewer would strongly advise clinical psychologists who use the *H-T-P* to take Buck's administration and scoring procedures with decided skepticism and to adapt testing methodology to their own realistic work schedules. Used in this freer manner, the test may yield, for an expenditure of relatively little time and effort, some extremely useful interpretative material—albeit not nearly as much as Buck would like us to believe that it normally yields.

Regarding the manner of interpreting personality evaluations and making differential diagnoses from *H-T-P* protocols, Buck is to be especially commended for his recently found skepticism about attributing specific meanings to specific aspects of the figures drawn by the subjects. Thus, he continually warns us in the new mimeographed manual, "you don't want to put too much weight on any one or two isolated items"; "nothing (if one can make such a general statement about anything in the *H-T-P)* always and necessarily represents any one thing"; "colors do not have any absolute and universal meaning"; "nothing in the quantitative scoring system can be taken automatically at face value"; "no specific patterns need ever be expected on the H-T-P"; "no single sign is of and by itself conclusive evidence of anything; it is the total constellation that matters." These are salient warnings long overdue from overenthusiastic exponents of drawing interpretation and are to be taken most seriously by the sound clinical psychologist who uses this test.

Unfortunately, Buck frequently contradicts his own warnings and makes rash general and specific interpretative statements about the *H-T-P* which, as yet, are not backed up by any factual evidence whatever. He presents, in fairly dogmatic form, hypothesis after hypothesis which may, logically, seem to be true but which have not yet been psychologically and scientifically established. For example:

Each drawn whole, the House, the Tree, and the Person, is to be regarded as a self-portrait. * You can use the H-T-P in blind analysis without any information about the patient and arrive at a fairly accurate diagnosis in the majority of cases. * If the ground line is spontaneously drawn it appears to be because the patient, himself, feels insecure * If it is drawn going up-

ward to the right of the page, the subject probably feels he has a pretty uphill row to hoe in the future.

When the perspective score is depressed we assume that the subject is losing insight. * Inadequate detailing....definitely suggests withdrawal tendencies. * A subject who makes sparing and unemphasized use of shading....is sensitive to....his relationship with other people. * Placement to the left of the vertical midline tends to emphasize immediate satisfaction of impulses *

The House drawn with the side wall only visible.... connotes very serious withdrawal and oppositional tendencies. * The wall (or walls) of the House seems to depict the Ego of the subject and its strength or weakness to symbolize the corresponding strength or weakness of the Ego. * If there are no panes drawn in the window, we presume that the subject has definite oppositional tendencies. * The Tree appears to be the best subconscious portrait of the Self of the three wholes. * The disproportionately small head is....the obsessive's expression of a desire to deny the site of painful thoughts and guilt feelings. An overly large mouth implies oral eroticism. *

These are all interesting hypotheses; it is possible that some of them may eventually be proved factually true. At the present time, however, Buck presents no objective evidence in their support. As Payne notes in his *Observations on the Use of Color with the H-T-P:* "These observations will have to be proven, or disproven, as the case may be, by additional research. Certainly more questions have been raised than answered." It must be sadly noted, however, that at the date of their 1950 presentations, Payne had been experimenting with the chromatic *H-T-P* for 5 years, and Buck with the achromatic *H-T-P* for more than 15 years. Under the circumstances, it is surely reasonable to expect considerably less speculation and more factual supporting material from both these authors. But, as yet, we are given literally hundreds of speculative statements—and virtually not a single fact—on personality interpretation through *H-T-P* analysis.

In sum: the *H-T-P* technique appears to be a valuable addition to the projective testing battery of the clinical psychologist under the following conditions: when the test is used in a nonrigid, practical manner; when the time devoted to its administration, scoring, and interpretation is reduced considerably below that advocated by Mr. Buck; when interpretations are made on a cautious, distinctly realistic basis, and the interpreter endeavors to get a little valid material rather than a mass of speculative meanderings; when the *H-T-P* interpretations are made in the light of considerable other information known about the subject; and when these interpretations are backed by wide experience with clinical psychological procedures in general, and projective drawing techniques in particular. The sooner Buck gives us some factual data in support of his several hundred speculations concerning *H-T-P* personality interpretations, the sooner we shall be able to take these speculations more seriously.

EPHRAIM ROSEN, *Assistant Professor of Psychology, University of Minnesota, Minneapolis, Minnesota.*

New developments in administration, scoring, and interpretation of the *H-T-P* have occurred since the test was reviewed in *The Third Mental Measurements Yearbook:* (*a*) A chromatic form of the test, in which the subject has a choice of eight colored crayons with which to draw, has been devised. Choice of colors and methods of using them are believed to point to a variety of personality factors. (*b*) To the original scoring modes have been added some new approaches, particularly one with the striking name "Quality of the Quantity." This approach qualitatively evaluates scores and discrepancies between intratest scores by clinical interpretation of the pattern into which the scores fall. (*c*) On the basis of cumulative test records, the test author and other *H-T-P* users have added further suggestions as to the meaning of specific qualitative "signs."

Most of the criticisms of the test made by the reviewers in *The Third Mental Measurements Yearbook* seem to have retained their validity. Quantitative scoring is as complex and time-consuming as ever. The qualitative scoring system and interpretation are, on the whole, as subjective as before. Validity data, in general, are meager. However, it is equally true, as the earlier reviewers pointed out, that the *H-T-P,* like many other projective devices, may well be useful in the hands of skilled clinicians and that with further work it may develop into a proved instrument.

Psychiatric Q Sup 23:376 pt 2 '49. * The administration of the test is relatively simple; however, the scoring is so complex that it seems doubtful whether anyone except the author can achieve adequate results. This reviewer has used the test and found rather poor correlations with other standard intelligence tests. In addition, its power as a diagnostic tool is questionable. Clinicians versed in Freudian concepts will derive useful material concerning personality dynamics from the subjects' drawings. There is no doubt that the test has possibilities as a projective technique; but as the author implies in his manual, it needs much more work before it can be considered a proved clinical instrument and take its place alongside the T.A.T. and/or the Rorschach. However, for clinicians well versed in personality dynamics, the H-T-P test should be useful even in its present state of development.

For reviews by Morris Krugman and Katherine W. Wilcox, see 3:47.

[108]

★**Horn-Hellersberg Test.** Ages 3 and over; 1945-49; based upon drawings taken from *Horn Art Aptitude Inventory* (see 3:171); a measure of "capacity to function or to adapt to a given surrounding"; 1 form, '45; no data on reliability; no data on validity in manual (for data presented elsewhere by the author, see 5 below); no description of normative population; mimeographed manual, second edition ('49); $2 per 25 tests; 25¢ per manual; 35¢ per specimen set; postage extra; (30–90) minutes; Elizabeth F. Hellersberg; the Author, 641 Whitney Ave., New Haven, Conn. *

REFERENCES
1. HELLERSBERG, ELIZABETH F. "The Horn-Hellersberg Test and Adjustment to Reality." *Am J Orthopsychiatry* 15:690–710 O '45. * (*PA* 20:1277)
2. AMES, LOUISE BATES, AND HELLERSBERG, ELIZABETH. "The Horn-Hellersberg Test: Responses of Three to Eleven Year Old Children." *Rorsch Res Exch & J Proj Tech* 13:415–32 D '49. * (*PA* 24:3732)
3. BELL, JOHN ELDERKIN. "The Case of Gregor: Psychological Test Data." *Rorsch Res Exch & J Proj Tech* 13:155–205 no 2 '49. * (*PA* 24:2589)
4. HELLERSBERG, ELIZABETH F. "Horn-Hellersberg Test: The Case of Gregor: Interpretation of Test Data: Symposium Presented at American Psychological Association Meeting, Denver, 1949." *Rorsch Res Exch & J Proj Tech* 13:461–3 D '49. (*PA* 24:3734)
5. HELLERSBERG, ELIZABETH F. *The Individual's Relation to Reality in Our Culture: An Experimental Approach by Means of the Horn-Hellersberg Test.* Springfield, Ill.: Charles C Thomas, Publisher, 1950. Pp. x, 128. * (*PA* 25:2131)

PHILIP L. HARRIMAN, *Professor of Psychology and Head of the Department, Bucknell University, Lewisburg, Pennsylvania.*

Hellersberg has developed a psychological technique based upon a section of the *Horn Art Aptitude Test.* Twelve small rectangles, each of which contains portions of lines taken from well known pictures, and a blank rectangle are presented to the subject. A picture is drawn in each rectangle, a title is written beneath, and the subject is interviewed at length to determine the significance of each drawing. Since the pictures are drawn in pencil, erasures may be made during the test. Careful notes are taken by the examiner during the entire performance, and a complete record of the interview must be made. Supplemental material for graphological inferences may be obtained from a 5- to 10-line pen-and-ink description the subject writes on one of the productions.

The pictures are studied for themes and items. In the population tested by Hellersberg and her associates, certain picture elements were found to be of frequent occurrence; others occurred rarely. Pictures related to daily life, for instance, indicate a good social rapport. Those with morbid or horror elements are assumed to indicate dysphoria and loss of contact with reality. Attempts to imitate Charles Addams, however, might occur in the drawings of pseudo sophisticates. The examiner must probe carefully to determine whether the productions indicate a sense of reality. Bizarre horror-drawings, for instance, might be plotted on Chart A as lying in the "Danger Zone" and in the column indicating "Loss of Reality Contact." Percentages are calculated from this chart. These indicate the positions of items and themes in the following zones: objective, expressive-emotional, repressive-rationalization, and danger. Mere scribbling by an adult would lie completely outside these zones and indicate loss of the sense of reality. Normal individuals have a flexibility in their productions. On the stereotypy-individuality dimension, they vary between objective representational drawings and those expressive of wholesome affects.

Table B is provided for including data about form elements. For instance, a drawing might be done in bold, heavy strokes; it might depict a scene of violence; it might be original or trite. The clinician's notes taken during the test and the interview are used to arrange form elements in this table. Tempo of work, erasures, mood fluctuations, ego-involvements, signs of pleasure or frustration—these are examples of data included in the table. In particular, the use of symbols must be determined. Many of them are obvious to the experienced clinical psychologist. A thorough inquiry is required in order to work up the material to be included in this table.

At least an hour is needed for administering the test and conducting the interview. Though the manual contains some examples of scoring problems, the labor of working out the chart and the table is arduous. Subjective criteria must be employed. Great skill is needed in eliciting from the subject his interpretation of each production. Both the verbalizations and the pictures must then be evaluated. Apparently, there are as yet no scoring tables or samples analogous to those available to users of the Rorschach. Experience, common sense, and intuitive clinical judgment must guide the examiner. In our culture, with its emphasis upon individuality, a wide variety of items and themes is to be expected. Pueblo Indians who were tested by the Horn-

Hellersberg technique were relatively easy subjects compared to the urban groups Hellersberg and her colleagues have examined. Nevertheless, the test yields "an effective yardstick of the individual's present capacity to function in the adult world of our American civilization."

The rationale of the *Horn-Hellersberg Test* is inadequately, though plausibly, set forth. No statistical evidence is offered to demonstrate the validity or the reliability of this test. Both the chart and the table do present an array of data that are impressive. How can the examiner be at all certain that these data are of value in assessment of the sense of reality? Behavior data of importance, no doubt, are brought into expression by means of this technique. Affirmations, specious generalizations, and brief case notes are included to justify the assumption that they reveal the individual's degree of rapport with reality. Nevertheless, Hellersberg does state that the test is still in its experimental stages. Perhaps objective validating evidence will be forthcoming. It may be, indeed, that this test will "complement other personality tests such as the Rorschach Ink Blots, Thematic Aperception [*sic*] Test, Bender Gestalt, Drawing of Human Figure, Handwriting Analysis, etc." At present, no valid data are offered to support this hope.

A Rorschach, if intelligently administered and cautiously interpreted, might yield data about an individual's sense of contact with reality. At the same time, it might bring into expression many other facets of the personality. On the grounds of economy of time alone, it is doubtful whether clinical psychologists will have much use for the *Horn-Hellersberg Test*. It does, however, offer many possibilities for research investigations. There are opportunities for establishing norms for scoring, quantifying data, and comparing the results with those obtained from other projective techniques. Certainly, there is a need for an objective assessment of the individual's status on the objectivity-subjectivity continuum. This technique may mark the beginning of research in this area. In short, further research is certainly to be encouraged. The clinical serviceability of the test at its present stage of development is rather doubtful.

After a conscientious perusal of this monograph, together with a little experience in trying to score a few tests, the reviewer came to three conclusions. First, there is a need for a clearly written, explicit manual with adequate scoring samples, norms, and instructions for interpretation. Secondly, "the whole problem of reality deserves far greater consideration than it has thus far received." This test should be an influential stimulus to further attacks on the problem. Thirdly, the results of *Horn-Hellersberg Test* reported in this monograph derive their value from Hellersberg's enthusiasm, clinical experience, and proficiency in making shrewd inferences. Perhaps, had she appraised the sense of reality through the use of any other worth while technique, she might have obtained material that would be equally convincing. This fact, however, does not warrant the assumption that other clinical psychologists will be able to employ this technique in its present form with similar proficiency.

T. W. RICHARDS, *Professor of Psychology, Northwestern University, Evanston, Illinois.*

This test, like the *Geosign Test* of Reichenberg-Hackett, presents the subject with partially structured graphic figures which he is asked to complete in any way he chooses. These represent "reality," apparently, and what the subject does is interpreted as bringing to light "the concrete manner in which the individual realizes his inner strength *in a life situation.*" Hellersberg feels that in this sense the H-H Test is a *complement* of tests such as the Rorschach, Bender-Gestalt, Drawing of the Human Figure, and so forth.

The manual presents several illustrative cases, but no normative sample of productions. There are no data on reliability or validity, though she does refer to analysis of 40 cases of adolescents followed up after a year's work experience in which she was able to "predict which subject was prepared for adult life and which was lagging in maturity."

After the 13 drawings of this test are obtained, together with a handwriting sample, productions are discussed with the subject, and he indicates preferences. His total performance for each picture is evaluated according to an interpretive scheme which leans heavily on principles of "depth" psychology or psychodynamics. This scoring yields a pattern by which the drawings are considered as varying between the "Objective Zone" through intermediary zones to "Loss of Reality Contact." This classification of responses requires the exercise of considerable judgment by the scorer.

It should be evident that the H-H Test (as proposed by its author) offers (*a*) a technique for eliciting productions and (*b*) a scheme for interpreting the significance of these productions. In the opinion of this reviewer, the first of these contributions is worth further exploration; by completing a partial structure the subject may well reveal his individuality in important areas. The second offering of the test—its interpretive scheme—requires theoretical assumptions which themselves need to be tested at a much more basic level. This reviewer does not feel that the assumptions are invalid, but that, since they are assumptions, they do not justify the formal structure of the scoring system here proposed by the author of the test.

For related reviews, see 109.

[109]

★[*Re Horn-Hellersberg Test.*] HELLERSBERG, ELIZABETH F. **The Individual's Relation to Reality in Our Culture: An Experimental Approach by Means of the Horn-Hellersberg Test.** Springfield, Ill.: Charles C Thomas, Publisher, 1950. Pp. x, 128. $3.25. * (*PA* 25 : 2131)

B Menninger Clinic 15:155 Jl '51. Walter Kass. The title of this monograph could more accurately be: An Introduction to the Horn-Hellersberg Test. This test is a semi-structured projective drawing completion technique in which various given lines within a series of squares are the basis of drawings freely made by the subject. After an interview with the subject about the meaning of the title and content of each drawing, personality analysis and diagnosis of psychopathology is made from the individual ways of dealing with reality revealed in the drawings. It is regrettable that Dr. Hellersberg did not have space to develop her culture-reality, acculturation concepts, and document them more liberally from the ample source materials she has. This test has rich psychodiagnostic possibilities. It is recommended as a diagnostic tool for clinical psychologists, a research tool for anthropologists, sociologists and other investigators of personality expression.

J Clin Psychol 7:295 Jl '51. * The author claims to identify several signs which may be taken as indicators of a breakdown of contact and adaptability to reality. These signs probably have suggestive significance but there is no objective data in this monograph in support of the author's intuitions.

J Consult Psychol 15:168–9 Ap '51. E. Lowell Kelly. * essentially a manual for the Horn-Hellersberg Test. Although the ten-page Appendix is entitled "Instructions for administration and interpretation," it is in itself a very inadequate manual, so it is fortunate that the body of the text is devoted largely to further instructions and to discussions of a series of illustrative cases with whom the instrument has been used. The Horn-Hellersberg Test is a projective device in which the subject is instructed to finish incomplete line drawings. This task is followed by an interview inquiry structured by the examiner to provide the necessary information for scoring and interpreting the subject's test behavior. Although responses are scored on many determinants—sequence, movement originality, etc.—the author regards the test as primarily useful in evaluating a subject's relation to reality, and has derived a method of content scoring to provide an index of reality adjustment regardless of the subject's cultural background. It would appear to be a useful technique. The author states that she has used the test with 2500 cases and has "found that if 36 per cent of all drawn items are placed in the Objective Zone, the individual is still able to function normally as an adult in our civilization." Unfortunately, however, no normative data are provided, and there is no indication as to what may be expected by way of test-retest reliability or interexaminer agreement in scoring and interpretation.

Psychol Service Center J 2:250–2 S '50. Alfred Jacobs. * "Relation to reality," as measured by the test, appears to be based on a comparison of the content and the associations connected with the drawings of one individual to the drawings of other individuals in the culture. However, no norms are presented in the monograph. The author states that if 36% of the responses fall in an "Objective Category," the individual is able to function normally as an adult in our culture, so that a criterion measure of adjustment to society is implied. It might be disputed, considering the failure of the author to submit relevant evidence, that neither the test score nor a measure of adjustment to society are highly related to what the psychiatrist considers "sense of reality." Also absent are tests of the significance of the assumed relationship between scores on the Horn-Hellersberg Test and whatever operations were used to define adjustment to society. The author describes the validity of the test as depending on "inner and qualitative consistency, a concept which more and more displaces that of a proof by mere quantitative methods" (p. 52). The reviewer is not convinced that current

psychological literature provides any evidence for the increasing popularity or acceptance of a non-quantitative definition of validity. Despite the lack of communicable reliability and validity statements, the author states that "vocational counsellors, teachers, guidance agents, social workers, who must make certain decisions regarding an individual's training, placement or vocational choice, can use such a test to help control and supervise the effect of any new arrangement made by or for the subject." (p. 102). The test appears to be capable of eliciting varied responses which are scored in terms of dimensions developed by the author, and in terms of categories previously used in the scoring of such tests as the Rorschach and the Bender-Gestalt. Assuming that the scoring has reasonable reliability, which would appear questionable for some of the complex dimensions, the test should prove a promising one for personality investigation. Aside from sampling drawing behavior, the test does not appear to differ appreciably from other commonly used projective techniques. In view of the recent deluge of projective materials in clinical psychology, the question may be raised at this point as to whether it will be more fruitful to extend the validation of accepted tests rather than looking for new projective devices, and, as in the case of the Horn-Hellersberg Test, whether it is legitimate to insist that new tests support their claims of being improvements or of being different by the type of evidence which is demanded for all types of psychological research. As in the case of other projective techniques, the Horn-Hellersberg Test seems to elicit responses which give information about both associative and motivational factors. Because of the lack of previously established responses to the ambiguous test stimulus, the responses which are elicited are frequently widely generalized and characteristic of the individual in many other situations. Since responses which are strongly motivated also seem to generalize more widely than less strongly motivated responses, strongly motivated responses appear to be more easily elicited by the ambiguous test stimulus, and information about motivation is obtained from the test. In view of the lack of reliability and validity data, the use of the test as a clinical instrument at this time might be premature. In view of the quantifiability of some of the scoring dimensions, the test would provide an interesting and amenable area of investigation.

Q J Child Behavior 3:114–5 Ja '51. Joseph Katz. * The author has developed a systematic scoring scheme which is intended to serve as a measure for evaluating the normality of an individual's relation to reality. This consists of classifying the subject matter drawn according to a check list of 40 topics under 9 degrees of subjective relatedness of these topics to the individual. The tabulation of the items drawn are then seen to distribute themselves to form a scatter which normally falls, for the most part, into the Objective Zone, which is the zone of closest contact with reality. * The author categorically states that by repeated experimentation she has found that if 36 per cent of all drawn items are placed in the Objective Zone, the individual is still able to function normally as an adult in our civilization. However, no details or data as to the scope or nature of the experimentation is presented; nor is mention made of the possibility of so called normals who might conceivably fall below this 36 per cent objectivity or of some schizophrenics who may very well attain higher than this rigid criterion score. Later in the book, the author herself correctly states that the qualitative verbalizations, fluctuations in performance, general approach, and most important, the pertinent background of the individual, are all indispensable factors which have to be considered before passing judgment on the individual's relation to reality. Again, the author speaks glibly of the high reliability of diagnosis and prediction made by means of this test in the past, without presenting ample substantiating proof. The book is very well illustrated with drawings, interpretations, and brief case histories of a variety of normal and abnormal subjects presented. The interpretation of some of the drawing features and symbolizations are at times somewhat speculative but in general are treated cautiously and within a sound framework of personality development. The present investigation, while leaving much to be desired, nevertheless helps to establish the Horn-Hellersberg Test as a valuable contribution to projective psychology and as a very useful tool for the experimental study of such a vital but neglected concept as the individual's relation to reality in our culture.

[110]

★The Kahn Test of Symbol Arrangement. Grades 3–16 and adults; 1949; a projective technique for differential personality diagnosis; $18.50 per set of testing materials, postpaid; nontimed (25–30) minutes;

Theodore C. Kahn; Guidance Tools, P.O. Box 802, Wilmington, Calif. *

REFERENCES

1. FILS, DAVID HENRI. *Comparative Performance of Schizophrenics and Normals on a Projective Object Symbol Arrangement Test.* Doctor's thesis, University of Southern California (Los Angeles, Calif.), 1950. (*Abstracts of Dissertations....1950,* 1951, pp. 118–20.)
2. KAHN, THEODORE C. "An Original Test of Symbol Arrangement Validated on Organic Psychotics." *J Consult Psychol* 15:439–44 O '51. * (*PA* 26:7147)

EDWARD JOSEPH SHOBEN, JR., *Associate Professor of Education, Teachers College, Columbia University, New York, New York.*

While it has much in common with certain of the projective techniques, the *Kahn Test of Symbol Arrangement* (KTSA) differs in that it uses essentially well structured stimulus objects, such as hearts, stars, dogs, an anchor, etc., rather than amorphous ones. The rationale for this is not completely clear but seems to lie in the assertion that in the selection and manipulation of symbols the individual "reacts holistically with all of his dynamics concentrated at a given point at a given time." Thus, in the selection and manipulation of the symbols of the *Kahn Test of Symbol Arrangement,* the subject is presumed to reveal his typical modes of approach to the various symbols impinging upon him in his daily life.

However that may be, this test presents an interesting and easily administered task, apparently suitable to a wide range of subjects. It consists simply of 15 plastic objects which the subject is required to line up on a strip of felt marked off into 15 consecutively numbered segments of equal size. He is then asked to verbalize his arrangement. This is gone through twice. The next step involves having the subject interpret each of the objects symbolically in the sense that the American flag is symbolic of the United States as a nation. When this is done, he must recall the second of his arrangements. A final procedure has the subject line up the objects in order of his preference or "liking" for them. There are some interpolated tasks in which the subject must superimpose one object on another, but these do not (as yet, at least) enter into the scoring in any significant way.

Scoring is in terms of categories descriptive of the subject's approach to the "line-up," "symbolization," and "preference" tasks. Inter-scorer reliabilities of the order of .97 are reported. This impressive coefficient is buttressed by a reported retest reliability of about .95, indicating that not only are the categories amenable to independent evaluation among judges, but that the behavior that the test elicits tends to be stable from administration to administration.

The only evidence for validity lies in a study of the KTSA's power to discriminate a group of brain-damaged psychotics from a nonpsychotic control group. The differentiation was successful, but a number of cautionary notes must be sounded. First, the control group exceeded the brain-damaged psychotics in IQ, educational attainment, and occupational status; these, rather than "personality factors," may have determined the performance differences. Second, while the overlap in scores is not great, there is no information as to the number of false positives or false negatives picked up by the test. Third, studies of this sort are by no means conclusive until cross-validational investigations have eliminated the possibility that sampling fluctuations did not account for differences. Finally, with such extreme groups as these, one may legitimately wonder if the test improves diagnostic prediction at all. Would not the same amount of time spent in an interview result in the same separation of the diagnostic categories?

Another point must be made relative to the use of the instrument in its present stage of development. While the scoring categories seem to promise much in terms of their objectivity, there is as yet no indication of how they are related to specific nontest aspects of behavior. Until such evidence is gathered, it must remain a tenable hypothesis, especially in the light of the relatively uncontrolled educational and intelligence factors in the only available validation study, that cognitive rather than psychodynamic factors are being tapped by the KTSA.

On the other hand, the KTSA is a simpler, more widely applicable situation than most instruments at hand for investigating developmental patterns and various attributes of psychopathological behavior. On a research basis, its use should be strongly encouraged. As a test, it is still essentially unproven.

[111]

★Machover Draw-A-Person Test. Ages 2 and over; 1949; also called *Machover Figure Drawing Test;* individual; $3.50 (17s. 6d.) per manual, *Personality Projection in the Drawing of the Human Figure: A Method of Personality Investigation* (see 5 below), which contains directions for administering and interpreting and associations record sheet; associations record sheets must be reproduced by individual test users; cash orders postpaid; (5–60) minutes without associations, (20–90) minutes with associations; Karen Machover; Charles C Thomas, Publisher, 301–327 East Lawrence Ave., Springfield, Ill. * (English publisher: Blackwell Scientific Publications, Ltd., Oxford, England.)

REFERENCES

1. MACHOVER, KAREN, AND WEXLER, ROCHELLE M. "A Case of Manic Excitement." *Rorsch Res Exch & J Proj Tech* 12: 179–201 no 4 '48. * (PA 24:1351)
2. MARGOLIS, MURIEL FRANKLIN. "A Comparative Study of Figure-Drawing at Three Points in Therapy." *Rorsch Res Exch & J Proj Tech* 12:94–105 no 1 '48. * (PA 23:4843)
3. BELL, JOHN ELDERKIN. "The Case of Gregor: Psychological Test Data." *Rorsch Res Exch & J Proj Tech* 13:155–205 no 2 '49. * (PA 24:2589)
4. MACHOVER, KAREN. "Human Figure Drawings: The Case of Gregor: Interpretation of Test Data: Symposium Presented at American Psychological Association Meeting, Denver, 1949." *Rorsch Res Exch & J Proj Tech* 13:447–50 D '49. (PA 24:3734)
5. MACHOVER, KAREN. *Personality Projection in the Drawing of the Human Figure: A Method of Personality Investigation.* Springfield, Ill.: Charles C Thomas, Publisher, 1949. Pp. ix, 183. * (Oxford, England: Blackwell Scientific Publications, Ltd.) (PA 23:3217)
6. MODELL, ARNOLD H., AND POTTER, HOWARD W. "Human Figure Drawing of Patients With Arterial Hypertension, Peptic Ulcer, and Bronchial Asthma." *Psychosom Med* 11:282–92 S–O '49. * (PA 24:3214)
7. COPELAND, LYNN PRESTON. *Personality Differences Between a Group of Adolescents With Behavior Disorders and Normally Well-Adjusted Children as Revealed on the Machover Draw-A-Person Projective Test.* Master's thesis, Catholic University of America (Washington, D.C.), 1950. (PA 25:4057, title only)
8. FISHER, SEYMOUR, AND FISHER, RHODA. "Test of Certain Assumptions Regarding Figure Drawing Analysis." *J Abn & Social Psychol* 45:727–32 O '50. * (PA 25:2454)
9. GOLDWORTH, SAMUEL. *A Comparative Study of the Drawings of a Man and a Woman Done by Normal, Neurotic, Schizophrenic, and Brain-Damaged Individuals.* Doctor's thesis, University of Pittsburgh (Pittsburgh, Pa.), 1950. (*Abstracts of Doctoral Dissertations....1950,* 1951, pp. 282–9.) (PA 24:5547, title only)
10. GURVITZ, MILTON S. *The Dynamics of Psychological Testing: A Formulation and Guide to Independent Clinical Practice.* Foreword by Joseph S. A. Miller. New York: Grune & Stratton, Inc., 1951. Pp. xv, 396. *
11. MACHOVER, KAREN. Chap. 22, "Draw A Person," pp. 222–6. In *Thematic Test Analysis.* By Edwin S. Shneidman with the collaboration of Walther Joel and Kenneth B. Little. Foreword by Henry A. Murray. New York: Grune & Stratton, Inc., 1951. Pp. xi, 320. *
12. MACHOVER, KAREN. Chap. 12, "Drawing of the Human Figure: A Method of Personality Investigation," pp. 341–69. In *An Introduction to Projective Techniques.* Edited by Harold H. Anderson and Gladys L. Anderson. New York: Prentice-Hall, Inc., 1951. Pp. xxiv, 720. *
13. MODELL, ARNOLD H. "Changes in Human Figure Drawings by Patients Who Recover from Repressed States." *Am J Orthopsychiatry* 21:584–96 Jl '51. * (PA 26:3552)

PHILIP L. HARRIMAN, *Professor of Psychology and Head of the Department, Bucknell University, Lewisburg, Pennsylvania.*

Complex in its interpretation, the technique of personality investigation through drawings of the human figure is simple to administer. Only 10 or 20 minutes are needed to have the individual draw a person and then to draw another of the opposite sex to that first drawn. The examiner obtains useful clinical data from the associations which are given at the end of the test. In a future publication there is to be a full discussion of the significance of information elicited by free associations and directive questions.

Interpretations of "salient characteristics" of the individual require but 10 or 15 minutes. More complete analysis of the personality, of course, takes a much longer time. Nevertheless, the method is recommended because of its ease of administration, its economy in time, and its interest-value for both the individual who is tested and the clinical psychologist who knows how to interpret the material. The Machover monograph is in the nature of a report-of-progress. Fifteen years of work have been devoted to the development of the technique, principally in improvements of the drawing analysis as "a valuable supplementary clinical method." That the method is not overly difficult to master is apparent from this quotation: "With proper training and experience....facility in the use of the method may be gained in a relatively brief time * graduate psychology students have been able to acquire a grasp of basic principles....after some orientation lectures."

The monograph is divided into three parts. Part I is the least rewarding section of the book. Although she does mention some of the literature on creative drawings, Machover does not yet appear to have developed a satisfactory theoretical basis for her procedures. It is only fair to state that she realizes this weakness and that future publications are in the making. In the 29 references given at the end, there are many suggestions for a lucid and convincing rationale, but they are not utilized in her disappointing introductory section. Many discussions of expressive art are readily available, and it should not be hard to locate them. It is rather arrestive to observe that Viktor Lowenfeld's analyses [1] of expressive drawings were overlooked. Similarly, she takes no cognizance of recent investigations into the psychological aspects of creative art. In familiar territory of creative literary work, such scholars as Lowes would have much to contribute to a better understanding of expressive activity in almost any form. The vast amount of folklore connected with various parts of the human figure is completely ignored. Even a hasty perusal of Frazer's *Golden Bough* or of a good commentary on Hebrew folklore in the Old Testament would seem to be of great assistance in establishing a more convincing basis of theory. Certainly, an extensive reading of references listed by Goodenough [2] and by Anastasi and Foley [3] would be of value in working out a co-

herent, logical theory for the figure-drawing test.

The basic assumption is that an individual's experience with his own body results in symbolic investments of various parts of the human figures which he draws in the test period. He becomes profoundly ego-involved in the task, and deep conflictual needs and tensions come into expression. Thousands of drawings collected in psychological clinics are said to confirm this assumption. It is asserted that the technique may prove to be as valuable in locating personality assets as it has already been proved to be in appraising deficits of personality. Not only do the separate parts of the drawing have significance, but also the structural and the formal aspects reveal a great deal.

Whether or not similar findings might be found among normal individuals goes unmentioned. When this reviewer tried out the Machover technique on college students, he found that the better adjusted ones either took the test facetiously or became irked by inability to reach their level of aspiration in pencil drawings. Badly adjusted students did become ego-involved and exhibited symptoms of dysphoria, not only in their drawings and associations but also during the test itself. Normal women seemed to be preoccupied with depicting current fashions in clothing and hairdo for their own sex and in humorous caricatures of "Joe College" males. The normal men labored to produce Vargas-type females. When normal males drew their own sex, they became deeply involved, and a wide variety of significant drawings was produced. This little excursion into a use of the Machover technique is what made the reviewer disappointed with Part I.

Part II is written with convincing enthusiasm. No doubt, many a stimulating discussion lies behind the innumerable hypotheses and inferences in this section. The symbolic investments of each part of the human figure are described in a style that never departs from ebullience. Naturally, the writer's sincere conviction about the value of figure drawing as a method of personality investigation carries weight with the reader. Here and there a bold generalization is supported by case notes, and then the case notes

1 Lowenfeld, Viktor. *Creative and Mental Growth: A Textbook on Art Education.* New York: Macmillan Co., 1947. Pp. xv, 304.

2 Goodenough, Florence L. *Measurement of Intelligence by Drawings.* Yonkers, N.Y.: World Book Co., 1926. Pp. xiv, 177.

3 Anastasi, Anne, and Foley, John P., Jr. "A Survey of the Literature on Artistic Behavior in the Abnormal: I, Historical and Theoretical Background." *J General Psychol* 25:111–42 Jl '41. * (*PA* 15:5114)

Anastasi, Anne, and Foley, John P. "A Survey of the Literature on Artistic Behavior in the Abnormal: II, Approaches and Interrelationships." *Ann NY Acad Sci* 42:1–112 Ag 11 '41. * (*PA* 16:990)

Anastasi, Anne, and Foley, John P. *A Survey of the Literature on Artistic Behavior in the Abnormal: III, Spontaneous Productions.* American Psychological Association, Psychological Monographs, Vol. 52, No. 6, Whole No. 237. Washington, D.C.: the Association, Inc., 1940. Pp. iii, 71. * (*PA* 15:3387)

Anastasi, Anne, and Foley, John P., Jr. "A Survey of the Literature on Artistic Behavior in the Abnormal: IV, Experimental Investigations." *J General Psychol* 25:187–237 Jl '41. * (*PA* 15:5115)

are cited as justification of the generalization. Just as an eloquent orator can obfuscate his auditors, so does Machover succeed in keeping the reader from asking such questions as: What is the evidence? Are there any objective proofs? Why, for instance, is the Adam's apple sometimes indicative of sexual weakness (p. 58)? The style often becomes fervent and exhortatory, as if to induce a sort of religious conversion to the Machover technique. Only by re-reading the section with zealous devotion to the ideals of scientific expository writing can one escape being "sold on" the test. Though evidence and proof are lacking, the discussion of interpretation is decidedly worth study. Shrewd clinical observations abound. Hypotheses worthy of experimental investigation illuminate almost every page. Like many other proponents of ingenious projective techniques, Machover is a facile, convincing writer and an experienced clinical psychologist. Were she to "sell" a technique for the investigation of personality by any other worth-while method, she would, no doubt, succeed in establishing it in "many progressive clinical units throughout the country." Likewise, no doubt, the questions about rationale and about validation would still be pertinent. In its present stages of development, Part II may be of greatest use in stimulating objective research, not in personality investigations where human welfare is involved.

Part III includes seven brief illustrative examples of the method. Clinical histories, reproductions of the drawings, and full interpretations are given. These furnish useful data for one who would understand the method of interpretation and the underlying concepts of the technique. They also bring out the fact that the procedure is challenging, worth while, and plausible as a supplementary clinical tool. In its present stage of development, it will attract a great deal of attention and stimulate further study. This little book is of great importance to the psychologist who is concerned to keep up-to-date in psychodiagnostics. Machover is to be commended for making a report of progress. Nevertheless, drastic improvements are needed before the draw-a-person technique should be employed in personality appraisals. This preliminary report offers substantial hope that they will be effected.

NAOMI STEWART, *Educational Testing Service, Princeton, New Jersey.*

Drawings of the human figure, along with other projective devices, have been used in clinical evaluations for a number of years, and a certain amount of "figure-drawing lore," varying in content from installation to installation, has accumulated. However, no detailed exposition of figure-drawing analysis such as that presented in Machover's *Personality Projection in the Drawing of the Human Figure* has been hitherto available.

The method of administration is similar to that often followed in figure-drawing analysis. The subject is given a letter-size sheet of paper, a medium-soft lead pencil with eraser, and asked to "draw a person." Neither the sex of the figure to be drawn, nor its age, attire, nor attitude is specified. It is made clear that the drawing of a whole person is desired. When one drawing is completed, the subject is given another sheet of paper and asked to draw another figure of the opposite sex from the first. The drawing process is inconspicuously observed and notes made concerning sex of figure drawn first, sequence of parts, omissions rectified only at the examiner's suggestion or urging, approximate time required, and so forth. At the option of the examiner, the subject may also be asked to reply to various questions concerning each person drawn. Ostensibly "associations" to the figures, the questions are actually designed to elicit the subject's attitude toward himself and others. The "associations" data, however, are regarded by Machover as providing useful *adjunct* information only. They are not an essential part of the technique.

Using only the drawings, it is presumably possible "in a significant proportion of cases" to make accurate judgments covering the subject's "emotional and psychosexual maturity, his anxiety, guilt, aggression, and a host of other traits," and to arrive at a comprehensive understanding of his personality and behavior dynamics. The proportion of cases in which accurate judgments of this sort may be made is not indicated. No specific information is given concerning the extent of agreement among different analysts attempting to make such judgments on the basis of a given pair of drawings, nor concerning the extent of agreement among judgments based on different pairs of drawings by the same individual. Machover states that her interpretative principles have been reasonably verified in clinical application to thousands of drawings studied in coordination with individual case records over a period of 15 years, and that numerous studies involving the "blind" interpretation of drawings have repeatedly validated the method, but data and details are not furnished.

Although the Machover principles of interpretation are frankly empirical in origin, an attempt is made to provide a basic rationale for the method. Machover holds that the drawing of a person, in involving a projection of the "body image," furnishes a natural vehicle for the expression of one's body needs and conflicts. Her technique of interpretation is essentially an attempt to reconstruct the major features of this "self-projection."

The Machover method involves a careful and detailed examination of both the content of the drawings—the manner in which each part of the body and the clothing is drawn—and the structural and formal aspects of the drawings—absolute and relative size of the male and female figure, placement on the page, symmetry, perspective, type of line, shading, erasures, etc. In the interpretation, considerable emphasis is placed on the overall mood or tone conveyed by the figure through its facial expression and postural attitude. Considerable attention is also paid to "conflict indicators"—differential treatment given to any area of the figure by conspicuous omissions, subtle breaks, dimming out or reinforcement of line, erasures, or shading. Interpretation of the particular graphic treatment is based upon the functional significance of the part stressed.

The essential character of the Machover method is perhaps best conveyed by quoting the author:

The process of drawing the human figure is for the subject, whether he realizes it or not, a problem not only in graphic skill, but one of projecting himself in all of the body meanings and attitudes that have come to be represented in his body image. Consequently, the drawing analyst should feel free to extract from the graphic product what the subject has put into it. He should feel free to interpret directly aspects which, with striking literalness, often reflect real life problems and behavior of the individual who is drawing. The figure is, in a way, an introduction to the individual who is drawing. Thus, when a subject erases his arms and changes the position of them several times, it may be literally interpreted that the subject does not know what to do with his arms in his behavior. If the fist is clenched, he may literally be expressing his belligerence. If the eye of the figure has a pensive, furtive, or bewildered gaze, it may often be characteristic of the individual who is projecting.

The theme of "striking literalness" does indeed loom large throughout the interpretation, and where the system is not directly literal it is indirectly so, through the mediation of various psychoanalytic equivalences which are assumed to exist. It is stated, for example, that overemphasis of the mouth is frequently tied up with food fadism and gastric symptoms, profane language, and temper tantrums; that the individual who is quick to take offense and is resistive to authority may show moderate ear accentuation on that basis; that hair emphasis, whether it occurs on the head, on the chest, as a beard, or a mustache, may be regarded as an indication of virility strivings. Button emphasis, it is pointed out, occurs mainly in the drawings of mother-attached individuals, suggesting that the psychological significance of buttons may be connected with the umbilical symbol of mother-dependence; ties are described as varying from "the uncertain, tiny, and debilitated-looking tie of the individual who is despairingly aware of his weak sexuality, to the long and conspicuous tie, sometimes decorated with phallic like details, of the sexually aggressive individual who is driven to excessive compensation by fear of impotence." Similarly, the stance of the figure is regarded in the same light as the stance of a real person, so that "insecurity of footing" shown in a drawing is taken as indicative of possible "insecurity of footing" on the part of the subject. By the same token, it is held that drawings characterized by a certain type of stance quite directly indicate fear of sexual assault on the part of a female subject, or anticipation of resistance to fantasied assault on the part of a male subject.

Although undeniably literal, the technique of interpretation is not, however, as atomistic as these scattered excerpts may suggest. Machover stresses that the meaning of specific drawing traits must be considered in the context of their interrelation and cautions that a grasp of the mechanical details of drawing analysis cannot substitute for the knowledge of personality dynamics and clinical syndromes which is indispensable to the proper use of the method. Nevertheless, despite this emphasis on the importance of context and interrelationships, she gives very little explicit attention to the possible influence on drawing behavior of cultural and socio-economic background and educational level. Sex differences, adult-adolescent-child differences, and gross intelligence differences (feebleminded versus normal) are considered, but the possible effects of age differences among adults or of differences in intelligence among adults are almost completely ignored. (Differences in artistic skill, it might also be noted here, are held to be unimportant so far as the interpretation of figure-drawings is concerned.)

From a theoretical standpoint, an additional question arises. As Goldworth (9) has pointed out, Machover, in emphasizing the projection of body needs and conflicts, appears largely to disregard the role of visual, objectively determined stimuli in the formation of the subject's body image. Yet from the work of Ross,[1] Schilder,[2] and Lowenfeld,[3] it would appear that visual as well as tactile and kinesthetic experiences are involved. Particularly from Lowenfeld's work, it would, in fact, appear that there are basic differences among individuals with respect to the predominance of the two kinds of components in their body image. If so, it would seem that to whatever extent the "body image" is projected in the subject's drawing of a human figure, the resulting product cannot be interpreted in the same manner for all individuals.

Because it has been available in published form only since 1949, not much research has to date been reported concerning the Machover technique as distinct from other methods of figure drawing analysis, and very little of this has been on a sufficiently large number of cases to assure even a modicum of reliability. In the study already mentioned, Goldworth investigated the incidence of "conflict indicators," using the Machover criteria, in the drawings of normal, neurotic, schizophrenic, and brain damaged subjects. His data fail to substantiate Machover's formulations with respect to "conflict indicators." To a certain extent, however, other data he reports may be taken as affording corroborative evidence for her statements regarding the significance of size differences between the male and the female figure and concerning the meaning of breast emphasis in drawings of the female figure. They may perhaps also be considered to confirm certain of Machover's observations regarding the interpretation of facial expression and stance.

On the other hand, a study by Fisher and Fisher (8), designed to test the validity of certain "paranoid signs" mentioned by Machover, fails entirely to support her formulations in this area. Further, Fisher and Fisher find rather poor agreement among trained raters as well as among untrained raters attempting to describe facial expression and stance, both of which figure prominently in the Machover technique.

Until a considerable amount of additional evidence becomes available, it would seem unwise to rely on judgments based solely on interpretation of the figure drawings. This does not preclude the possibility of using such drawings to furnish additional cues or otherwise to help clarify particular problems relating to individual cases, provided this is done in light of a great deal of more objective information.

The few studies of the Machover technique, or selected aspects of it, which have been made to date have differed considerably in their orientation and their methodology. The findings—some possibly confirmatory, others apparently failing to confirm—may perhaps indicate that certain of the Machover formulations are more promising than others, both with respect to operational reliability and with respect to fundamental validity. Perhaps it will be possible eventually to rationalize the various specific findings and reformulate the basic hypotheses accordingly. At the present time it would appear that the greatest value of the Machover technique lies in the focus for research in the figure-drawing area which it affords.

For related reviews, see 112.

[112]

★[*Re* Machover Draw-A-Person Test.] MACHOVER, KAREN. **Personality Projection in the Drawing of the Human Figure: A Method of Personality Investigation.** Springfield, Ill.: Charles C Thomas, Publisher, 1949. Pp. ix, 183. $3.50. * (Oxford, England: Blackwell Scientific Publications, Ltd. 17s. 6d.) (PA 23: 3217)

Am J Psychiatry 106:395 N '49. T. W. Richards. This contribution to the literature on projective techniques will be received enthusiastically by those to whom the theoretical assumptions of dynamic psychology are congenial, and examined with suspicion, probably, by those who look for statistical or other quantitative evidence of validity for a test of personality. * the author relies for verification for her hypotheses regarding personality almost entirely on clinical evidence. She seems to expect that her discussion will seem plausible with only this. * As a report of methodology....Dr. Machover's book is a stimulating contribution. We need just such qualitative discussions to generate scientific

1 Ross, Nathaniel. "The Postural Model of the Head and Face in Various Positions (Experiments on Normals)." *J General Psychol* 7: 144–62 '32. * (PA 7: 451)
2 Schilder, Paul. *The Image and Appearance of the Human Body: Studies in the Constructive Energies of the Psyche.* London: Kegan Paul, Trench, Trubner & Co., Ltd., 1935. Pp. 353. (PA 5: 5693)
3 Lowenfeld, Viktor. *Creative and Mental Growth: A Textbook on Art Education.* New York: Macmillan Co., 1947. Pp. xv, 304. *

study of personality. As a contribution to the facilities of the clinician, it is to be expected that one's experience with the method in work with individual cases will confirm or contradict Dr. Machover's evaluation of her own experience. It is hoped that someone—Dr. Machover, perhaps—will bring together the several contributions to the analysis of personality through drawings, and develop an integration with the theoretical principles which seem implicit in each or all of them. This task has been ignored in the present volume. It would be unfortunate if the author's failure to integrate her work with that of Goodenough, Buck, and others served in any way to foster the notion of a "Machover technique" such as the illusion of specificity which was created for the Rorschach. It is the reviewer's opinion that essential contribution to our understanding of personality will come not from some new technique, but from the study of what communality is revealed in the use of various techniques of appraisal.

Am J Psychol 62:312–3 Ap '49. * The bibliography....[suggests] the psychiatrical and clinical bent of the book. * The book, which is intelligently and well written, offers agreeable relief from the new grist of divinations upon the hand-writing of the great.

Am J Psychother 4:174–5 Ja '50. John G. Watkins. * interesting and readable little book * One who has not been previously acquainted with this method of picture analysis will be amazed at the wealth of clinical impressions that can be obtained by the technique. * The book concludes with a brief bibliography and a rather thorough index. Excellently bound, the printing is on a high grade of paper. The interpretations are psychoanalytically oriented, and one cannot help but be impressed with the extensive experience which the author has obviously had in the use of the method and with the shrewd clinical insight she shows in her interpretations. However, the work suffers, as do so many other methods in the field of projective testing, with inadequate objective validation. The various interpretations given different features are offered without statistical results to support them. There is vague mention that these are based on a large number of cases, but the author does not share with us the exact findings from these data. Because of this severe limitation, objective and experimental-minded clinicians will find much to criticize in the work and will tend to use the interpretations presented

with great caution and reserve until they are more universally proven. In this respect the reader will find it interesting to compare the subjective method of drawing-analysis utilized by Machover with the more objective, but also more cumbersome, techniques used by John N. Buck in his development of the HTP (House-Tree-Person) test. The psychiatrist, the psychoanalyst and the clinical psychologist will find the book highly stimulating and well-worth reading. They will be grateful to the author for giving us the benefit of her experience and insight in the use of the method. They will use it themselves, many times with excellent results, supplementing other psychodiagnostic techniques. But still, they will probably exhibit a cautious and healthy skepticism in its use and consider its findings as tentative and subjective to confirmation by other diagnostic methods which have been more widely and thoroughly validated. I feel certain the author, herself, would want her methods to grow into wider use in this conservative and scientific way. The method is no substitute for clinical insight. Rather it provides the shrewd and experienced psychodiagnostician with many valuable clues and leads into the underlying assets and liabilities of a human personality and into the dynamics of its functioning. As such the method of analyzing personality through its projection into drawings of the human figure deserves a place among the diagnostic weapons in the arsenal of the modern clinician.

Am J Sociol 57:205–6 S '51. Olive Westbrooke Quinn. Karen Machover has admirably delineated the uncertain stance of a relatively new technique for investigating personality. She obviously did not intend this little volume as a manual for administering and analyzing the "draw a person" test but rather for showing the potentialities and present shortcomings of a projective technique for personality analysis. The author states forthrightly that she has no intention of trying to communicate the method to the reader; one hopes, however, that, if this technique is as useful as its advocates claim, someone will present the principles clearly, stating the criteria for analysis and the underlying rationale. The author suggests that such a work must await the outcome of experimentation now in progress or proposed; certainly, experimental verification of the present tentative hypotheses must be undertaken if social scientists are to have confidence in the method. There are some omissions, however, which make the book unsatisfactory. In general, the treatment of the-oretical considerations is adequate, but the con-ceptual framework has sometimes been neglected. While the author suggests a concept of the "nor-mal" personality and mentions "normality or adjustment indicators," the latter are not speci-fied, and the implication is clear that the "nor-mal" configuration is not one which can be ascertained in positive terms but simply one which is comparatively free from the indicators of abnormality. Mrs. Machover obviously recog-nizes this lack but seems to consider it relatively unimportant: "the differentiation of normal from abnormal by drawing analysis is a less real problem than the effectiveness of the method in determining the personality and dynamics of the behavior of the individual." It is true, how-ever, that at the present time clinical psycholo-gists are using this particular technique for making judgments that differentiate the normal and the abnormal. A further shortcoming is that, although it is quite clear that the sexes are ex-pected to draw differently, there is no firm statement of the varying significance of the indicators for the two sexes. Mrs. Machover points out that her data are more nearly complete for males than for females and that most of the interpretative data relate to drawings made by males, but the occasional mention of alternative explanations when drawings are made by female subjects becomes a distracting feature which contributes little to understanding the test. Omitting interpretation for female subjects com-pletely would have been better than this wholly inadequate treatment of the subject. Configura-tions of indicators are stated to be the proper basis for analysis; yet careful study of the sam-ple analyses fails to reveal these patterns and leaves the reader with a strong suspicion that conclusions are based upon a simple additive process rather than a weighing and balancing of indicators. A technique should not be aban-doned or refused recognition because it does not do everything. What the author succinctly calls "economy of method" makes it imperative that every effort be made to determine the valid-ity and reliability of the test and to perfect the technique if it can be shown to be dependable. A method of personality investigation which so simplifies problems of administration would be invaluable if it could be made precise and clearly communicable.

B Menninger Clinic 15:75 Mr '51. Irene Hol-lingsworth. * a more organized presentation of personality analysis through interpretation of drawings of the human figure than has yet been available * While there may be doubt as to the validity of some of the particular findings, this book is an excellent way for the interested cli-nician to become further acquainted with ways of using a very useful tool, after which he can adapt it to his own particular needs.

Brit J Psychol, Gen Sect 40:47–8 S '49. M(agdalen) D. V(ernon). * as the author her-self states, she has started from a particular the-oretical position, mainly psycho-analytic, with regard to the significance of many of the features of the drawings, for instance, as to their phallic symbolism. Working then largely from cases upon the nature of whose personalities and per-sonality disorders she has already decided, the author proceeds to conclude that particular fea-tures of the drawings demonstrate personality characteristics the existence of which she has already postulated. In this way she has, it is true, reached a fair agreement between drawing interpretation and clinical diagnosis. But it seems likely that it would be equally possible to start with some other theory as to the nature of the personality, and demonstrate with equal clarity its projection into the drawings. Nor is there any indication how far the drawing is actually carried out in accordance with schematic ideas originating within the individual; or how far in an attempt, varying with the individual's sophis-tication and skill, to make a representational drawing. Again, a determining effect may be exerted by social customs as to how the human figure should be drawn—differing surely in dif-ferent cultural groups. Considerations such as these must be taken into account in making ac-curate interpretations. Thus, however useful this method may be to the individual clinician in indicating particular characteristics of his pa-tients, its use as a general projection method for personality analysis is fraught with difficulty.

Can J Psychol 3:242 D '49. Noël Mailloux. [Review in French; editor's English abstract follows.] * this book is very useful for clinical psychology, from the technical point of view. Remarkable for its fullness and for the extreme simplicity of its treatment, it contains data sup-ported by observations accumulated over a period of fifteen years. Its greatest merit lies in the fact that the author has tried to formulate his explanations in dynamic terms.

J Abn & Social Psychol 45:785–6 O '50. John E. Bell. This handsomely printed monograph

....contains....many suggestions for clinical research * The least satisfactory part....is the theoretical discussion with which it begins. While the author manifests a sincere theoretical interest, and indicates that research to answer theoretical questions is in progress, she seems in a hurry to proceed to the technical aspects of her method, and even in the section on theory introduces an illustration of interpretation which is nearly as lengthy as the discussion of theory. The basic theorem that drawing serves a functional purpose for the individual who is making the drawing is briefly noted. The author then dismisses previous literature in the subject with a few generalizations and two specific references and advances to the rewarding part of her monograph, the discussion of her clinical method. It is in the second part of the volume, the discussion of principles of interpretation, that the author hits her stride. * The author wisely and conscientiously makes use of the verb "may" to indicate the tentativeness of her conclusions, since she has not here quoted any statistical basis for her interpretative cues. On several occasions she points out that her work is based upon patient comparison of drawing indicators and case history material over a period of fifteen years. It is to be hoped that the details of such study may be presented at a future time in such a manner that independent evaluation of her conclusions may be accomplished. * Until validation studies are published it cannot be expected that this simple clinical tool will reach its full usefulness. As a guide for clinical experimentation with a promising and expedient diagnostic method this monograph amply justifies its publication.

J Consult Psychol 13:223 Je '49. Laurance F. Shaffer. Because of the simplicity of its administration and the scope of its claimed usefulness, the draw-a-person projective test is rapidly gaining a wide recognition. * There can be little question of the merit of the projective theory on which the test is based, that "the human figure drawn by an individual....relates intimately to the impulses, anxieties, conflicts and compensations characteristic of that individual. In some sense, the figure drawn *is* the person...." On the other hand, psychologists may rightly demand that authors supply them with more public evidence about a new method than the reassurance that it was "developed....in the course of studying thousands of drawings in clinical contexts." The monograph—alas, like many others in the projective field—abounds with de-

tailed interpretive hypotheses unsupported by research data. In many instances quantitative criteria are not impossible to obtain, and real validation could be accomplished. Further, the cry against "atomistic" validation is unjustified when the interpretive suggestions are given in terms of the relationships of specific picture qualities to specific personality characteristics. "Disproportionately large heads will often be given by individuals suffering from organic brain disease...." [*How often?*] "Full lips, given to the male figure, are regarded as an effeminacy indicator...." [*What is the x^2 with some reasonable criterion of masculinity-femininity?*] "....the paranoid individual....gives much graphic emphasis to the eyes...." [*What is the overlap of paranoid and non-paranoid groups when judged independently by this feature?*] One may hope that the future of this promising technique will be marked, not by slavish adherence to formulas, but by sound research to determine its validity—and its limitations.

J Crim Law & Criminology 40:782 Mr–Ap '50. Robert H. Gault. * The present book includes analyses of drawings made by several persons who had been charged with crime. The layman, on reading them, will naturally be puzzled by such a statement as the following relating to a drawing that had been made by a young man who was a car thief (Page 131) : "The omission of hands would relate to the patient's guilt regarding his car stealing and also regarding his lack of achievement. (Guilt aggravated by the demands of his guardians.) He had never made an adequate adjustment to people or things." Couldn't hands be omitted from the drawing merely because the drawer found it difficult to include them? In another case "Regression and collapse of judgment are seen in....the confusion of profile and full face.... (Page 119)." Could this peculiarity, also, be due to lack of skill in drawing? Somewhat analogous questions were asked years ago when the Binet Tests were new. Untiring research has answered them, or submerged them in practical results. It is to be hoped that such an outcome will be forthcoming in relation to Projective tests.

Psychol B 47:84–5 Ja '50. Lillian Wald Kay. It would be unfortunate if we came to feel that our techniques in personality study were apart from our theories. If theories are valid, they should be demonstrable. If techniques are valid, it must be because they stem from some hypothesis which is basically true. This should hold for all aspects of our research even when practical considerations are most important, as it is understandable that they should be for the clinician whose primary concern is for the patient's welfare. It is, therefore, to be deplored that a prominent clinician, describing an important projective device, should state that: "Incentive for, and primary focus of, investigation centered around perfection of the drawing technique as a clinical tool for personality analysis, rather than around any theoretical hypotheses" (p. 20). The statement is, of course, not adequately descriptive of the content of the book. The first part, "Personality Projection in the Drawing of the Human Figure," actually has a section on theoretical considerations. The second part, "Principles of Interpretation," draws heavily on psychoanalytic theory, as well as on empirical clinical experience. The third part, "Illustrative Case Studies," is an attempt to relate the theory of projection in drawing the human figure to examples of drawings accompanied by case histories. * [Nevertheless] the method seems to have considerable validity in clinical procedure. As one reads the illustrative cases, Dr. Machover's analyses can be followed without much argument. The question which often arises in connection with new projective techniques— "Would I see that if I didn't know the case history?"—is answered by her report on "blind" interpretations (pp. 25 to 27). The drawing of the human figure is an extremely intriguing projective device. It is, admittedly, still in its infancy and communication of method is limited, as for most techniques which emphasize patterns of relationship rather than "scoring." It is very much to be hoped that readers will be stimulated by this book to further study and research. Dr. Machover introduces some challenging experimental problems. In spite of the format of the book, it is a progress report rather than a manual. It would be undesirable, with so many people working on this new method, to accept this report as a manual and mark the problem solved.

Psychosom Med 12:138–9 Mr–Ap '50. Samuel Waldfogel. * The assumption underlying this method as stated by the author (page 35) is "....that the human figure drawn by an individual who is directed to 'draw a person' relates intimately to the impulses, anxieties, conflicts, and compensations characteristic of that individual." Support for this assumption is presented in the form of some eight case histories where clinical material is presented side by side with the drawings and their interpretation. While these do not lack conviction, they cannot be accepted as sufficient validating data. The only deference to accepted methods of test validation is made (p. 26) where the author refers to a brief experiment conducted by herself and another competent judge, in which an attempt was made to match drawings with case records. We are told that "....a degree of accurate matching was achieved that was much better than chance." No specific figures are given. In regard to test reliability the author assures us that drawings from the same individuals obtained over long periods may be so much alike as to constitute personal signatures. Again no supporting data are given and no mention is made of the degree of consistency among interpreters. Allusions are made to studies in progress that should ultimately supply this information but it would seem that at our present stage of methodological sophistication in personality measurement, an introduction to a new test should contain at least preliminary data of this sort. * Each characteristic of the drawing is considered separately and its implications are enumerated. Many of the statements made have an almost glib quality and some are startling in their resemblance to physiognomic stereotypes. This similarity exists, we are told, because the average individual has been exposed to these stereotypes and has either consciously or unconsciously adopted them. Again the argument would be more convincing if supported by precise and detailed documentation. A fair idea of the writer's method of exposition may be gained by the following excerpts which are typical: "The concave or orally receptive mouth is frequently encountered in the drawings of infantile, dependent individuals...." (p. 44); "The eyes are the chief point of concentration of the feeling of 'self' and the vulnerability of the self," (p. 47); "The Adams apple ....has been seen mostly in the drawings of young males as an expression of a strong virility or masculinity drive," (page 58); and "Severely shaded or reinforced fingers are generally regarded as guilt indicators." (page 64). To some, these statements will have a high degree of plausibility; to others, they will sound like nonsense. However, regardless of their truth or falsity, it is certain that such generalities are more easily made than proved. Although one may quarrel with the nature of the evidence that Dr. Machover presents to support her assertions, there can be no question of her ingenuity and originality. She has, through the careful observation of a very ordinary phenomenon, laid down a new path in the field of personality investigation. While it is too early to say where this will eventually lead, it beckons us to explore it further. Practitioners, in the meantime, are proffered another instrument to assist them in their work. While this technique will not give them the precision in personality description and measurement that is so sorely needed and so sadly lacking, it will provide them with an additional projective method for supporting their diagnostic impressions.

Q R Psychiatry & Neurol 4:252–3 Jl '49. Isabelle V. Kendig. The significance of this book hinges upon the validation of the basic hypothesis upon which it is developed, viz., that drawings of the human figure represent projections of the subject's own attitudes, particularly his conception of the body image. To be sure, there has been general validation, by Allport and others, that all expressive movements, whether in gait, gesture, or handwriting, reveal intrapsychic tensions, conflicts, and formulations, compensatory or otherwise, of the Ego role. To this extent the body-image of the individual may reasonably be expected to emerge in response to the directive to "draw a person." Where validation is specifically lacking....in regard to the meaning to be attached to any given detail, for instance, that a concave mouth indicates fixation at the oral level, that buttons signify mother-dependence, and elongated feet or a conspicuous neck-tie are phallic symbols. In general, psychoanalysis, of which such drawing interpretation must be considered at least in part derivative, has escaped from its bondage to fixed symbols. While formerly all long, narrow objects—swords, guns, sceptres, etc., were wont to be accepted as symbols of the male sex organ and all broad objects —bowls, boxes, rooms, etc., as symbols of the female genitalia, no longer are such generic meanings accepted. Instead, there has been a growing realization of the extremely individualistic language of symbolization. Long antedating psychoanalytic doctrine, however, are the theories of constitutional typology which in our own culture may be traced from the speculations of Hippocrates and Galen through the French, German, Italian and Swiss schools to the recent work of Sheldon in this country. Running through them all is the assumption that physique and character are inextricably related.

Tending to substantiate these typological theories, essentially akin however differently verbalized, we find an underlying belief of men everywhere that certain specific features are expressive of significant personality traits—thin, compressed lips of cruelty, a broad forehead and well-spaced eyes of frankness, generosity and nobility, a strutting gait of braggadocio. Upon the virtually universal acceptance of such "stereotypes" do literature and drama depend to convey meaning swiftly and economically. Given such consensus as to the meaning of various physical features on the one hand, and the psychoanalytical concept of projection and symbolization, with such general psychological validation as has been given to "expressive movement," on the other, the twin supports upon which this experimental drawing technique rests become clear. The book itself should be regarded only as a progress report. Recurrently it is stated that research is going on to answer questions as to the constancy of projection, the significance of mood, and, through the use of associative material, the meaning to the individual of the stereotypes employed. To date the chief validation, as in psychoanalysis, and in such other projective techniques as the Thematic Apperception Test, has come from success in personality evaluation and diagnosis especially in so-called "blind" analysis and from the improvement following treatment based upon it. The detailed presentation of the interpretive concepts utilized by the writer gives other workers an opportunity to test their usefulness and thus the publication of the book at this time seems justified.

Rorsch Res Exch & J Proj Tech 12:259–60 no 4 '48. Hanna F. Faterson. Fifteen years of research have preceded the publication of Mrs. Machover's book * Obliged because of requirements laid down by the publishers....the author was forced to condense her presentation. She concentrates on the basic formulations of interpretative principles. Those who look for tables of intercorrelations, levels of confidence, and traditional data on reliability and validity will be disappointed. But those who are clinically oriented and who are experienced in the use of projective techniques will appreciate this invaluable addition to methodology which enables us to understand what the patient tells us about himself in his graphic projections. The fundamental working hypothesis underlying the analysis of drawings is "that the human figure drawn by the individual who is directed to 'draw a person' relates intimately to the impulses, anxieties, conflicts, and compensations characteristic of that individual" (p. 35). The data consists of the drawings of a male and a female figure in the order determined by the subject, and of a fairly detailed list of questions, amplified and modified as needed. The questions are introduced with the instructions to "make up a story about the person as if he were a character in a novel or a play." The author's observation that resistance to these tasks is likely to be a function of timidity on the part of inexperienced examiner is born out by the experience of many who have used this and other projective methods. * The volume is divided into three parts—introductory material, principles of interpretation, and illustrative cases. The didactic section on interpretative principles is necessarily "fragmented" into analysis of specific items. In a sense, such a presentation may be thought of as parallel to the teaching of Rorschach scoring as part of Rorschach interpretation. Actually, mastery of these items no more guarantees success in drawing analysis than mastery of scoring and interpretation of individual scoring symbols guarantees skillful use of the Rorschach method. In neither case can a list of "signs" yield either diagnostic impressions, or insight into personality. "As with....all projective tools, grasp of mechanical details....cannot substitute for the knowledge of personality dynamics and clinical syndromes which is so indispensable to the proper use of the method (p. 22)." The case studies, which take up fully one third of the book, are presented with related clinical history, and with clear reproductions of the drawings. In analyzing these, the author goes far beyond the preceding text, showing the method at work. Anyone seriously interested in using the technique would do well to study these analyses carefully, since they constitute the "meat" of the book. These eight cases also illustrate the validity of the method, since they contain a detailed demonstration of the relationship between graphic projection and clinical data. A detailed index of twenty-one pages will prove a boon to anyone who actually works with drawings, and who is constantly running into a snag with such items as "symmetry," "reinforced line," "hair emphasis," "evasiveness," or any other feature under consideration. * in the experience of the reviewer and many colleagues who have used the method for several years, the Machover Figure Drawing Test has already established

itself as an indispensable part of a battery of projective methods used in personality evaluation. Drawings invariably make their unique contribution to the total personality picture: answering questions raised by other tests, calling attention to factors underplayed or not manifested elsewhere, clarifying or corroborating, by means of a different medium of expression, evidence from other tests, and, like the Rorschach, varying in richness, clarity, and eloquence from case to case.

[113]

★Make A Picture Story. Adolescents and adults; 1947–48; commonly called MAPS; a measure of formal psycho-social aspects of fantasy production; individual; figure cards ('47); background pictures ('47); figure location sheets ('47); manual ('48; see 7 below); $13 per complete set of testing materials and 25 figure location sheets; $11 per set of testing materials, excluding manual, and 25 figure location sheets; $1.50 per 25 figure location sheets; theatre and carrying case (optional) $13.50 when ordered with set, $15 when ordered separately; postpaid; nontimed (45–90) minutes; Edwin S. Shneidman; Psychological Corporation. *

REFERENCES

1. FANTEL, ERNEST, AND SHNEIDMAN, EDWIN S. "Psychodrama and the Make a Picture Story (MAPS) Test." *Rorsch Res Exch & J Proj Tech* 11:42–67 nos 2–4 '47. * (PA 22: 4963)
2. SHNEIDMAN, EDWIN S. "The Make-a-Picture-Story (Maps) Projective Personality Test: A Preliminary Report." *J Consult Psychol* 11:315–25 N–D '47. * (PA 22:1945)
3. SHNEIDMAN, EDWIN S. "Prospectus of the Make-a-Picture-Story (MAPS) Projective Personality Test." Abstract. *Am Psychol* 2:407 O '47. * (PA 22:931, title only)
4. FINE, REUBEN. *The Personality of the Asthmatic Child.* Doctor's thesis, University of Southern California (Los Angeles, Calif.), 1948. (*Abstracts of Dissertations....1948,* 1949, pp. 165–9.) (PA 23:4855)
5. JOEL, WALTHER. "The Use of the Make-a-Picture-Story (MAPS) Test With Disturbed Adolescents." Abstract. *Am Psychol* 3:340–1 Ag '48. * (PA 23:757, title only)
6. JOEL, WALTHER. "The Use of the Make-a-Picture-Story (MAPS) Test with Disturbed Adolescents." *Rorsch Res Exch & J Proj Tech* 12:155–64 no 3 '48. * (PA 23:4824)
7. SHNEIDMAN, EDWIN S. "Schizophrenia and the MAPS Test: A Study of Certain Formal Psycho-Social Aspects of Fantasy Production in Schizophrenia as Revealed by Performance on the Make a Picture Story (MAPS) Test." *Genetic Psychol Monogr* 38:145–223 N '48. * (PA 23:2816)
8. SHNEIDMAN, EDWIN S. "Some Objective Aspects of Fantasy Production in Schizophrenia on the Make-a-Picture-Story (MAPS) Test." Abstract. *Am Psychol* 3:340 Ag. '48. * (PA 23:881, title only)
9. SHNEIDMAN, EDWIN S. *A Study of Certain Formal Psychosocial Aspects of Fantasy Production in Schizophrenia as Revealed by Performance on the Make-a-Picture-Story (Maps) Test.* Doctor's thesis, University of Southern California (Los Angeles, Calif.), 1948. (*Abstracts of Dissertations....1948,* 1949, pp. 181–5.)
10. BELL, JOHN ELDERKIN. "The Case of Gregor: Psychological Test Data." *Rorsch Res Exch & J Proj Tech* 13:155–205 no 2 '49. * (PA 24:2589)
11. JOEL, WALTHER, AND SHAPIRO, DAVID. "A Genotypical Approach to the Analysis of Personal Interaction." *J Psychol* 28:9–17 Jl '49. * (PA 24:657)
12. SHNEIDMAN, EDWIN S. "Make A Picture Story Test: The Case of Gregor: Interpretation of Test Data: Symposium Presented at American Psychological Association Meeting, Denver, 1949." *Rorsch Res Exch & J Proj Tech* 13:461 D '49. (PA 24:3734)
13. SHNEIDMAN, EDWIN S. "Some Comparisons Among the Four Picture Test, Thematic Apperception Test, and Make A Picture Story Test." *Rorsch Res Exch & J Proj Tech* 13:150–4 no 2 '49. * (PA 24:2614)
14. FARBEROW, NORMAN L. "Personality Patterns of Suicidal Mental Hospital Patients." *Genetic Psychol Monogr* 42:3–79 Ag '50. * (PA 25:4722)
15. WALKER, ROBERT G. *A Comparison of Clinical Manifestations of Hostility With Rorschach and MAPS Test Performances.* Doctor's thesis, University of Southern California (Los

Angeles, Calif.), 1950. (*Abstracts of Dissertations....1950*, 1951, pp. 196-7.)

16. GOLDENBERG, HERBERT C. "A Resume of Some Make-A-Picture-Story (MAPS) Test Results." *J Proj Tech* 15:79-86 Mr '51. * (*PA* 26:297)

17. HARROW, GERTRUDE S. "The Effects of Psychodrama Group Therapy on Role Behavior of Schizophrenic Patients." *Group Psychother* 3:316-20 Mr '51. * (*PA* 26:440)

18. SHNEIDMAN, EDWIN S.; WITH THE COLLABORATION OF WALTHER JOEL AND KENNETH B. LITTLE. *Thematic Test Analysis.* Chapters by Magda Arnold, Betty Aron, Leopold Bellak, Leonard Eron, Reuben Fine, A. Arthur Hartman, Robert R. Holt, Walther Joel, David Shapiro, Seymour Klebanoff, Sheldon Korchin, Jose J. Lagasa, Julian B. Rotter, Shirley Jessor, Helen D. Sargent, Percival M. Symonds, and Ralph K. White. Foreword by Henry A. Murray. New York: Grune & Stratton, Inc., 1951. Pp. xi, 320. * (*PA* 26:3422)

19. WALKER, ROBERT G. "A Comparison of Clinical Manifestations of Hostility With Rorschach and MAPS Test Performances." *J Proj Tech* 15:444-60 D '51. * (*PA* 26:6241)

ALBERT I. RABIN, *Associate Professor of Psychology, and Director, Psychological Clinic, Michigan State College, East Lansing, Michigan.*

This instrument is a variation upon the *Thematic Apperception Test.* Whereas TAT consists of some populated and some unpopulated pictures, MAPS gives the subject an opportunity to construct his own dramatic situation with a given supply of backgrounds and people and to tell his story about them.

The test material includes 22 background pictures, some of which are highly structured (livingroom, bathroom, etc.), while others are unstructured and vague (dream, stage, etc.). One blank background is included. Sixty-seven cardboard cutout figures (about 5 inches in height) in various poses and with different facial expressions (including several with blank faces) make up the population from which the testee may select his dramatis personnae. The 67 figures fall in the following categories: males (19 figures), females (11), indeterminate as to sex (2), children (12), legendary and fictitious (6), animals (2), minority figures (10), and blank faces (5). The examinee is instructed to place one or more of the figures on the given background and to tell a story about it. The rest of the instructions concerning the story are similar to those given with TAT. A special Figure Location Sheet with reproductions of the backgrounds is used for the recording of the subject's choice of figures and their placement in the picture.

Investigation of "psycho-social aspects of fantasy production" is the chief aim of the author of MAPS. Consequently, formal scoring categories which bear upon the problem of interpersonal relationships have been devised. The scoring categories deal with such questions as the number of figures used by the testee, the number of times the same figure was used, the actual figures selected, the activity and interaction of the figures, their meaning, and so on. Out of a total of about eight hundred "signs" derived from the scoring categories some several dozen differentiate to a statistically significant degree between schizophrenics and normals. In addition to the "formal" sign approach, it is also recommended that the stories obtained be treated like TAT stories, for the interpretation of personality dynamics.

For clinical use, usually, only 11 background pictures are used. It is advocated that they include some of the unstructured pictures as well as the blank one. Flexibility in the choice of backgrounds to fit the particular case being studied is recommended.

So far, the use of MAPS has been rather limited. The sign approach for differential diagnosis is time-consuming; in addition to the hour and a half that it takes to administer the test, some time must be spent in sign counting. Moreover, the range of psychopathologic populations upon whom such data have been obtained is limited. No material on women is available at present. If the less "formal" story-interpretation TAT-like approach is used, no distinct advantage over the more time-honored test is evident or has been reported.

Though it is questionable whether MAPS, at its present stage of development, offers much that is new to the busy clinician that may reward him for his time, further research with it may uncover greater potential. The opportunity that the subject is given to construct his own dramatic situation may be an advantage over TAT, facilitating the projection of an "inner world" and leading the clinician to deeper insights.

CHARLES R. STROTHER, *Professor of Clinical Psychology, University of Washington, Seattle, Washington.*

The MAPS test was developed initially as a method of studying schizophrenic phantasy. The subject selects one or more of 67 cutout figures, which he places on one of 22 background pictures selected by the examiner. The subject then constructs a story, as in the *Thematic Apperception Test.* A record blank is provided, on which each of the background pictures is duplicated and provision is made for noting the choice and placement of the figures used with each background. The instructions and inquiry follow the usual TAT form and the story protocols are recorded verbatim.

In addition to modifying the TAT materials, Shneidman has developed a method of "formal analysis" to supplement the conventional analysis of thematic content. Formal analysis is defined as "analysis....in terms of which figures are chosen, how many are chosen, where they are placed on the background, how they are handled by the subject and what relationship they bear to each other." For purposes of the formal analysis, a comprehensive list of 800 "signs" (i.e., categories of number, selection, placement, activity and interaction of figures, etc.) was drawn up on an a priori basis. The frequency of occurrence of each of these signs in the records of an experimental group of 50 psychotics (mainly paranoid schizophrenics) was compared with a rather carefully screened and reasonably well matched group of "normal" controls. The significance of the difference between percentages of the two groups was determined for each of the 800 signs. Sixty-four of the signs were significant at the 10 per cent level—42 "normal signs" and 22 "psychotic signs." These signs were weighted plus one and minus one respectively and "difference scores" were then computed for each of the 100 subjects.

In an attempt to validate the signs, both groups were split in half and a new critical ratio for the difference in proportions was determined for each of the 64 signs which had been found significant for the group as a whole. Differences were significant (10 per cent level) for 51 of the 64 signs. These 51 signs were then applied to the second halves of the two groups and significant differences were found on 29 signs (22 normal and 7 psychotic signs). "Difference scores" discriminated significantly between both experimental and both control groups, with nonsignificant differences between the two experimental groups and between the two control groups. This is, of course, validation in a very restricted sense and the manual carefully states the limitations of the sign approach and of the data presented. No attempt is made to present an analysis of thematic content, which would probably have been of more interest to prospective users than the formal analysis.

The MAPS is somewhat more difficult to administer than the TAT because of the necessity for manipulation of the figures and for formal as well as content recording. With many individuals, however, this disadvantage is outweighed by the fact that the MAPS test is more stimulating than the TAT. This is particularly true of adolescents and insecure or inhibited patients. There is the further advantage that the materials may be used as "miniature psychodrama" for therapeutic purposes.

For related reviews, see 114.

[114]

★[*Re* Make A Picture Story Test.] SHNEIDMAN, EDWIN S. "Schizophrenia and the *MAPS* Test: A Study of Certain Formal Psycho-Social Aspects of Fantasy Production in Schizophrenia as Revealed by Performance on the Make a Picture Story (*MAPS*) Test." *Genetic Psychol Monogr* 38: 145–223 N '48. * (*PA* 23:2816)

J Personality 18:385-7 Mr '50. Robert R. Holt. * Enough evidence is presented to support the contention that the MAPS Test really has something that the TAT does not, and thus to justify it as a contribution to the only too rapidly growing heap of devices available to the clinical psychologist. After reading through the monograph, one feels that the test itself remains the author's most solid contribution. As a manual to accompany the test....*Schizophrenia and the MAPS Test* suffers from its attempt to be a research report. Considered under the latter heading, it is painstakingly clear and comprehensive—so much so that its deficiencies of method are readily apparent. Only a few of its nearly 80 pages present the kinds of information one wishes from a manual, although in this space it does provide more useful information than one usually gets with a new projective technique these days. There are norms for many formal aspects of the test performance, based on 50 schizophrenics and 50 nonneurotic veterans temporarily hospitalized for somatic conditions. (The selection of these normal controls was unusually well handled, and may serve as a model for similar studies.) The materials are carefully described; there are a few pages on the principal aspects of administration, and brief mention of uses other than in psychodiagnosis—principally as an aid in psychotherapy. The unique feature of the MAPS Test is that the subject participates actively in structuring the scene about which he builds a story. * this requirement of an incitation to active participation would appear to be an important asset of the test. It is regrettable that the monograph is devoted entirely to the formal features of the test performance. It is acknowledged that the thematic content of the stories that result is the most important aspect of the test, but we are told nothing about the ways the author would suggest that content should be analyzed or interpreted. There are only a very few indications of the "popular" stories told to a few particular backgrounds, and nothing about "popular" interpretations of the numerous figures. The variety of materials will probably make it difficult to assemble useful norms. Nevertheless, it is to be hoped that normative studies of the kinds mentioned will appear soon, to shorten the otherwise lengthy period of groping on the part of the clinician who attempts to use the technique. A few words about the book as research: The design is adequate enough, if conventional, and well carried out. Limited as it was to the attempt to find test "signs" which would differentiate normal from schizophrenic subjects, the study could hardly contribute much to our understanding of schizophrenic fantasy. * It is in the use of statistics to demonstrate the differentiation of the groups that the research is weakest. The decision to treat the data in terms of percentages and their standard errors was not a happy one; it had the result that the significance of many differences involving extreme proportions was underestimated; that of differences between proportions near 50 per cent was often seriously overestimated. The calculation of direct probability via binomial expansions would have avoided these difficulties. The procedure was to identify all signs which gave even a slight degree of differentiation, then to combine them (without weighting) into a total score. The distributions of the resulting scores show an impressive amount of overlap, considering the extreme nature of the groups in question. In the range where the scores of the two groups overlap fall 46 per cent of the "normals" and 68 per cent of the schizophrenics. Of course, much of this result is due to a few atypical extremes in both groups; their medians are still quite significantly differentiated—if one assumes that the sign-scores constitute an equal-interval scale. The author admits, however, that they do not; he gives this inequality as a reason for working with medians instead of means, but then goes on to perform the same operations (in obtaining a critical ratio) that he forbade himself in getting a measure of central tendency. Other examples of faulty statistical reasoning could be cited, but would not greatly affect the general picture of the research. Despite the weakness of the original research in the context of which it is presented, the MAPS Test shows distinct signs of being an important contribution to psy-

chological testing. The fact that so young a technique could have been the basis for a special group of papers at the 1949 APA meetings is testimony to the vigor of Dr. Shneidman's brain child. We may confidently expect to see it used in more significant researches in the future, as well as in diagnostic and therapeutic work.

TAT Newsletter 4:7–9 su '50. John E. Bell. Under normal circumstances, a monograph of this dimension would scarcely merit independent review. As a report of a single clinical experiment, it follows the traditional pattern of carefully defining a problem, reviewing previous literature, describing procedures and populations, presenting data, and arriving at conclusions, which in this instance are not of singular importance. Because the monograph also serves as the manual for a new and important projective method, the Make-A-Picture Story (MAPS) Test, it becomes worthy, however, of especial attention. It is the chapter on materials and procedure (III) and that on quantitative results containing the MAPS Test Signs (V) that will have the most interest for the clinician. * the author has focused his attention on formal analysis of the protocols of matched groups of 50 psychotic patients, primarily paranoid schizophrenics, and 50 hospitalized non-psychotic patients. By formal analysis he means the study of "which figures are chosen, how many are chosen, where they are placed on the background, how they are handled by the subject, and what relationship they bear to each other." He has developed a list of signs, or objective scores (800 in this study) by which such analysis might progress. While recognizing that contentual analysis, after the manner of TAT interpretations, would probably provide the major diagnostic value of the MAPS Test, he bases his study on the objective aspects of the fantasy creations, claiming rather broadly that "the unique contribution of this study lies in the interpretation of the *formal* aspects of fantasy production." While the MAPS Test does permit of ready analysis by formal techniques, it is to be recognized that this is not a unique property of this test. Formal analysis is a characteristic, if not always explicit, interpretative method of all projective techniques, including all those which are based on fantasy productions. While formal analysis in the MAPS Test is not a unique interpretative method, the monograph illustrates that it may be possible to develop it here with greater ease than in other techniques because of the large number of quantifiable results. It must be stressed, however, as the author has stated, that use of the MAPS Test for formal analysis will depend upon the multiplication of normative studies with many clinical groups. This is one of the handicaps in using formal analysis in any projective device, a limitation that applies with as much force to the MAPS Test as to any other. The MAPS Test, as Klopfer has indicated in his Preface to this monograph, adds "information not easily revealed by existing techniques"; and lends "itself readily for inclusion in a well integrated battery." One of the advantages observed in the use of the Test is that the subject, in telling a story about a picture he has created, has potentially less stress in revealing fantasy than when he is required to associate to a more ordered stimulus as in the TAT. This may lead to greater productivity in fantasy; it may, however, be disadvantageous in not reflecting as readily a subject's reactions under pressure. The freedom of choice of figures would seem also to enhance "the possibilities....for personal identification and interpersonal projections." The inclusion of figures representing minority groups serves to make the Test of usefulness in the study of racial attitudes and tensions. The materials are of wide enough interest to make them applicable to the study of children, adolescents and the total adult range. Further uses of the materials for a sorting test and for a "miniature psychodrama" have been suggested by the author. Dr. Shneidman's study well illustrates another potential use of the Test. In his final chapter he has attempted to generalize on the characteristics of schizophrenic fantasy and behavior on the basis of the signs that significantly (i.e., in this study below the 10% level of confidence) differentiate schizophrenics from normals. Thus he tentatively concludes that schizophrenic fantasy is marked by "(a) intra-group variability; (b) self-identification; (c) variability of identification; (d) social isolation; (e) over-inclusion; (f) inappropriateness; (g) symbolization; (h) desire for environmental simplification; (i) inhibition of fantasied violences; (j) punitive conscience; (k) lack of identification with normal masculine role; (l) religiosity; and (m) debasement of women." While he has overextended his conclusions by failure to qualify that his groups of schizophrenics is a paranoid group, and has spoken of his conclusions as relevant to "schizophrenia," he has demonstrated that as a tool for research into the nature of fantasy behavior the

MAPS Test may be of more than considerable value. The monograph has thus served to introduce effectively a new technique that appears distinctly worthy of further experimentation and clinical application.

[115]

★The Mosaic Test. Ages 4–adults; 1930–51; 1 form ['30]; no data on reliability and validity; no manual; no norms; [revised] directions for administering ['51]; $37.50 per complete double set of testing materials; $24 per complete single set; postpaid; nontimed (20) minutes; Margaret Lowenfeld; distributed by Psychological Corporation. *

REFERENCES

1. KERR, MADELINE. "The Validity of the Mosaic Test." Am J Orthopsychiatry 9:232–6 Ja '39. * (PA 13:4393)
2. WERTHAM, FREDERIC, AND GOLDEN, LILI. "A Differential-Diagnostic Method of Interpreting Mosaics and Colored Block Designs." Am J Psychiatry 98:124–31 Jl '41. * (PA 16:1035)
3. DIAMOND, BERNARD L., AND SCHMALE, HERBERT T. "The Mosaic Test: I, An Evaluation of Its Clinical Application." Am J Orthopsychiatry 14:237–50 Ap '44. * (PA 18:3147)
4. HIMMELWEIT, H. T., AND EYSENCK, H. J. "An Experimental Analysis of the Mosaic Projection Test." Brit J Med Psychol 20:283–94 O '45. * (PA 20:1156)
5. BELL, JOHN ELDERKIN. Chap. 20, "The Mosaic Test," pp. 410–20. In his Projective Techniques: A Dynamic Approach to the Study of the Personality. New York: Longmans, Green & Co., Inc., 1948. Pp. xvi, 533. * (London: Longmans, Green & Co. Ltd., 1949.) (PA 23:1284)
6. COLM, HANNA. "The Value of Projective Methods in the Psychological Examination of Children: The Mosaic Test in Conjunction With the Rorschach and Binet Tests." Rorsch Res Exch & J Proj Tech 12:216–37 no 4 '48. * (PA 24:1194)
7. GORMAN, MARY MARGARET. An Evaluation of the Mosaic Test With Grade School Children. Master's thesis, Catholic University of America (Washington, D.C.), 1948. (PA 23:2990, title only)
8. BELL, JOHN ELDERKIN. "The Case of Gregor: Psychological Test Data." Rorsch Res Exch & J Proj Tech 13:155–205 no 2 '49. * (PA 24:2589)
9. McCULLOCH, THOMAS L., AND GIRDNER, JOHN B. "Use of the Lowenfeld Mosaic Test With Mental Defectives." Am J Mental Def 53:486–96 Ja '49. * (PA 23:3271)
10. MORAN, MAURICE J. An Experimental Inquiry Into Two Mosaic Procedures to Determine Which Method Has the Greater Diagnostic Utility. Master's thesis, Catholic University of America (Washington, D.C.), 1949. (PA 24:834, title only)
11. REIMAN, M. GERTRUDE. "The Mosaic Test: Its Applicability and Validity." Discussion by Anni Weiss Frankl. Am J Orthopsychiatry 20:600–14, discussion 614–15 Jl '50. * (PA 25:3181)
12. WERTHAM, FREDERIC. "The Mosaic Test: Technique and Psychopathological Deductions," pp. 230–56. (PA 25:2471) In Projective Psychology: Clinical Approaches to the Total Personality. Edited by Lawrence Edwin Abt and Leopold Bellak. New York: Alfred A. Knopf, Inc., 1950. Pp. xvii, 485, xiv. *
13. SHOTWELL, ANNA M., AND LAWRENCE, ERNEST S. "Mosaic Patterns of Institutionalized Mental Defectives." Am J Mental Def 21:161–8 Jl '51. * (PA 26:2263)

[116]

★Plot-Completion Test. Grades 9–12; 1946; a disguised personality test to be administered in an English class by an English teacher to elicit more honest answers; 1 form ['46]; manual ['46]; $1.50 per 25; 10¢ per manual; 15¢ per specimen set; postpaid; nontimed (45) minutes; Sarah I. Roody; W. Wilbur Hatfield, 211 West 68th St., Chicago 21, Ill. *

REFERENCES

1. ROODY, SARAH I. "The Plot-Completion Test: For Use in High Schools by Guidance Counselors, School Psychiatrists, and Teachers of Literature." J Exp Ed 12:45–7 S '43. * (PA 18:1263)
2. ROODY, SARAH I. "Plot-Completion Test." Engl J 34:260–5 My '45. * (PA 19:2760)

ROBERT C. CHALLMAN, Clinical Psychologist, 301 Kenwood Parkway, Minneapolis, Minnesota.

This test consists of 10 incomplete stories about high school pupils who get involved in minor conflict situations. Five endings are given for each story and the testee is asked to rank each ending having in mind its trueness to life and the extent to which it is in line with expectations based on the personalities of the characters. Two of the endings to each story are realistic, one contradictory to the facts, one a fortunate coincidence, and one "morbid or sadistic." It is expected that the pupil will identify himself with the central character and thus reveal his personality. The fact that it is to be given in an English class by an English teacher is thought to reduce the wariness of the testees.

The split half reliability is reported as .84 though there is no indication as to the group upon which this figure was obtained. Its validity was assessed by correlating the scores of 91 pupils with their scores on Noll's *What Do You Think? A Test of Scientific Thinking* (r "between .14 and .78 on the one percent level").

The incomplete stories appear to the reviewer as being interesting to high school pupils and the endings are apparently in keeping with the author's intention. Whether the test has any merit as a personality test cannot be assessed since the only evidence of validity given is the relatively low correlation with a test which can hardly be considered a criterion. The idea upon which the test is based is good, but unfortunately many ideas which appear to be good turn out to be valueless when put to the proof.

PERCIVAL M. SYMONDS, *Professor of Education, Teachers College, Columbia University, New York, New York.*

This test is essentially a measure of certain outcomes in English instruction, but its author recognizes that the test also has some projective possibilities. It may be used either as a teaching device, by having pupils discuss the several alternatives, or as a measure of improvement, in which case the test naturally should not be discussed.

The test consists of 10 brief unfinished incidents, episodes, or plots with five possible endings for each. The subject is asked to rank each of these endings "according to how probable you think it is as an outcome of the given situation." It is suggested that those who finish the test early go through it again marking with a star the ending that would make the best story for each of the 10 plots and with a check the ending that seems to be the most advisable course of action. The difficulty that most individuals have in

ranking five items (as contrasted with selecting best and worst or even rating) seems not to have been considered by the author.

In every story, two of the endings are "not only possible but highly probable." One ending disregards some of the facts in the story, another presents an "extraordinarily fortunate coincidence." In several of the stories a closing "violates some fundamental law of nature in order to bring about a happy ending." Some alternatives represent "morbid or sadistic" outcomes. A "morbid" ending is one in which a person becomes ill, receives a severe punishment or indulges in strong aggression.

A split half reliability coefficient of .7168 (sic!), raised to .8350 by the Spearman-Brown formula, is reported for an u..defined group. The author reports that errors made on the test tend to be similar to those made in short stories actually written by the same subjects. This reviewer is mystified by the statement that the test serves as a measure of adjustment to life because it correlates with Noll's *What Do You Think? A Test of Scientific Thinking* (see 40: 1263). The only norms presented are median scores for a twelfth grade group. The size and composition of this normative group are not reported.

This test undoubtedly has some value for an English teacher in indicating how realistic and logical a student is in creating the structure for a short story. Its value as a projective technique remains to be demonstrated. Cursory inspection leads one to believe that the several alternatives are so concerned with logical and moral factors that the test would have only limited usefulness as an instrument for revealing personality trends or the quality of a pupil's "adjustment to life."

[117]

Rorschach. Ages 3 and over; 1921 to date; also commonly referred to as Rorschach Method, Rorschach Test, Rorschach Ink Blot Test, Rorschach Psychodiagnostics, and Rorschach Method of Psychodiagnosis; many variants have appeared such as Harrower Group Rorschach, Harrower Multiple Choice Test, Monroe's Inspection Technique, Grassi's Graphic Rorschach, and Marseille Rorschach Mail Interview; many modifications of the variants are in use, such as the Amplified Multiple-Choice Rorschach and the Ranking Rorschach Test; in addition to the Rorschach original Psychodiagnostic Plates, parallel plates have been prepared by Zulliger and Harrower and Steiner; Hermann Rorschach.
a) PSYCHODIAGNOSTIC PLATES, FOURTH EDITION. 1921–45; $10 per set of 10 cards mounted on heavy cardboard; $3 per pad of 100 record blanks; $6.50 per copy of the 1949 English translation of Rorschach's *Psychodiagnostics, Fourth Edition;* Hermann Rorschach; Grune & Stratton, Inc.
b) BEHN-RORSCHACH TEST. 1942; a parallel set of ink

blots; $10 per set of 10 cards; $3 per pad of 100 record blanks; $4.75 per manual; Hans Zulliger; Grune & Stratton, Inc.

c) PSYCHODIAGNOSTIC INKBLOTS. 1945; a parallel set of ink blots; $5.70 per set of 10 cards; $2.10 per manual; M. R. Harrower and M. E. Steiner; Grune & Stratton, Inc. (These ink blots on slides for use with standard projectors are distributed by Psychological Corporation at $20 per set, postpaid, for glass slides and $10.50 per set, postpaid, for Kodaslides.)

d) HARROWER'S GROUP RORSCHACH. Ages 12 and over; 1941-45; $20 per set of the original Rorschach ink blots on slides for standard projector, postpaid; $10.50 per set of ink blots on Kodaslides, postpaid; $3.75 per 25 record blanks, postpaid; (75-90) minutes; M. R. Harrower and M. E. Steiner; distributed by Psychological Corporation.

e) HARROWER'S MULTIPLE CHOICE TEST. Ages 12 and over; 1943-45; same slides as for Harrower's Group Rorschach; $1.75 per 25, postpaid; 30¢ per specimen set, postpaid; (45) minutes; M. R. Harrower and M. E. Steiner; distributed by Psychological Corporation.

f) RORSCHACH METHOD OF PERSONALITY DIAGNOSIS. 1939-42; $1.60 per 25 record blanks; Bruno Klopfer and Helen H. Davidson; World Book Co.

REFERENCES

1-147. See 40:1246.
148-598. See 3:73.
599. STROMWELL, G. EVA LINNIA. *The Study of Values and the Rorschach Ink-Blot Test.* Master's thesis, Columbia University (New York, N.Y.), 1934.
600. INGEBREGTSEN, ERLING. "Some Experimental Contributions to the Psychology and Psychopathology of Stutterers." *Am J Orthopsychiatry* 6:630-49 O '36. * (*PA* 11:1874)
601. HARROWER-ERICKSON, M. R. "Personality Studies in Patients With Cerebral Lesions." Abstract. *B Can Psychol Assn* 1:9-10 D '40. * (*PA* 15:3420, title only)
602. HARROWER-ERICKSON, M. R. "Personality Studies in Cases of Focal Epilepsy." Abstract. *B Can Psychol Assn* 1:19-21 F '41. * (*PA* 15:3421, title only)
603. ROSS, W. D. "The Incidence of Some Signs Elicited by the Rorschach Method." Abstract. *B Can Psychol Assn* 1:21-2 F '41. * (*PA* 15:3457, title only)
604. SCHATIA, VIVA. "The Incidence of Neurosis in Cases of Bronchial Asthma as Determined by the Rorschach Test With Psychiatric Examination." *Psychosom Med* 3:157-69 Ap '41. * (*PA* 15:4253)
605. SCHMIDL-WAEHNER, TRUDE. "Formal Criteria for the Analysis of Children's Drawings." *Am J Orthopsychiatry* 12:95-103 Ja '42. * (*PA* 16:3364)
606. RICHARDS, THOMAS W. "The Appraisal of Naval Psychiatric Casualties by the Rorschach Method." *U S Naval Med B* 41:788-99 My '43. * (*PA* 17:3815)
607. SCHMIDL, FRITZ. "The Rorschach Personality Test in Family Case Work." *Family* 24:83-90 My '43. *
608. CATTELL, RAYMOND B. "Projection and the Design of Projective Tests of Personality." *Char & Pers* 12:177-94 Mr '44. * (*PA* 18:3185)
609. HARROWER-ERICKSON, M. R.; WASHBURNE, ANNETTE C.; AND JACOBS, JAMES S. L. "A Preliminary Screening Test for Disturbances in Personality." *B Can Psychol Assn* 4:4-6 F '44. * (*PA* 19:2643)
610. KORNHAUSER, ARTHUR. "Replies of Psychologists to a Short Questionnaire on Mental Test Developments, Personality Inventories, and the Rorschach Test." *Ed & Psychol Meas* 5:3-15 sp '45. * (*PA* 20:343)
611. MALLOY, HELGA. "Rorschach Interpretation." Abstract. *B Can Psychol Assn* 5:79-80 Ap '45. * (*PA* 20:841, title only)
612. RAINES, GEORGE N., AND BROOMHEAD, ELIZABETH. "Rorschach Studies on Combat Fatigue." *Dis Nerv Sys* 5:250-6 Ag '45. * (*PA* 19:3440)
613. STERN, KARL, AND MALLOY, HELGA TAIT. "Rorschach Studies of Patients With Paranoid Features." Abstract. *B Can Psychol Assn* 5:82-3 Ap '45. * (*PA* 20:486)
614. ALVAREZ-TOSTADO, VEE JANE HOLT. *Rigidity Theory in the Light of the Rorschach Performances of Bright, Normal, and Dull Children.* Doctor's thesis, Stanford University (Stanford, Calif.), 1946. (*Abstracts of Dissertations....1946-47,* 1947, pp. 120-4.) (*PA* 23:107, title only)
615. BROWER, DANIEL. "The Relations of Visuo-Motor Conflict to Personality Traits and Cardiovascular Activity." Abstract. *Am Psychol* 1:244 Jl '46. * (*PA* 20:3690, title only)
616. COOK, P. H. "Criteria for the Selection of Personnel Officers." *B Ind Psychol & Personnel Prac* 2:28-37 Je '46. * (*PA* 20:4761)
617. FRENKEL-BRUNSWIK, ELSE. "Personality and Prejudice in Women." Abstract. *Am Psychol* 1:239 Jl '46. * (*PA* 20:3696, title only)
618. HALPERN, FLORENCE. "Studies of Compulsive Drinkers: Psychological Test Results." *Q J Stud Alcohol* 6:468-79 Mr '46. * (*PA* 20:2747)
619. HARROWER-ERICKSON, M. R. Chap. 33, "Modification of the Rorschach Method for Large Scale Investigations," pp. 340-4. (*PA* 21:3478) In *Military Neuropsychiatry:* Proceedings of the Association, December 15 and 16, 1944, New York. Association for Research in Nervous and Mental Disease, Research Publications, Vol. 25. Baltimore, Md.: Williams & Wilkins Co., 1946. Pp. xviii, 366. *
620. HERTZ, MARGUERITE R. *Frequency Tables to Be Used in Scoring Responses to the Rorschach Ink-Blot Test: Revised Edition With Code Charts for Locating Responses, Lists of Normal Details, Lists of F+ and F− Responses, Lists of Popular Responses, Indications of Original Responses.* Cleveland, Ohio: Western Reserve University Bookstore, 1946. Pp. iii, 160. Paper, spiral binding, lithotyped. *
621. LEVY, DAVID M. "The German Anti-Nazi: A Case Study." *Am J Orthopsychiatry* 16:507-15 Jl '46. * (*PA* 20:4219)
622. PRASAD, KALI, AND ASTHANA, H. S. "An Experimental Study of Meaning by Rorschach Method." Abstract. *Proc 34th Indian Sci Congr, Delhi, 1947* 34:3 '46. *
623. ROE, ANNE. "Artists and Their Work." *J Personality* 15:1-40 S '46. * (*PA* 21:2330)
624. ROE, ANNE. "Personality Studies of Scientists and Technicians." Abstract. *Am Psychol* 1:241-2 Jl '46. * (*PA* 20:3715, title only)
625. WOLF, ELIZABETH B. *An Investigation of the Meaning and Expression of the Rorschach "M" Response in 216 Juvenile Delinquents.* Doctor's thesis, Western Reserve University (Cleveland, Ohio), 1946.
626. ABT, LAWRENCE E. *The Efficiency of the Group Rorschach Test in Predicting Success in Marine Corps Recruit Training.* Doctor's thesis, New York University (New York, N.Y.), 1947.
627. ALTABLE, JOSE PEINADO. "The Rorschach Psychodiagnostic as Applied to Deaf-Mutes." *Rorsch Res Exch & J Proj Tech* 11:74-9 no 2-4 '47. * (*PA* 22:5094)
628. BILLIG, OTTO; GILLIN, JOHN; AND DAVIDSON, WILLIAM. "Aspects of Personality and Culture in a Guatemalan Community: Ethnological and Rorschach Approaches, Part I." *J Personality* 16:153-87 D '47. * (*PA* 22:4899)
629. BLAIR, GLENN MYERS, AND HOEHN, ARTHUR J. "The Use of the Multiple Choice Rorschach Test With Adolescents." *J Ed Res* 41:297-304 D '47. * (*PA* 22:2620)
630. BLAKE, ROBERT R. *Ocular Activity During the Administration of the Rorschach Test.* Doctor's thesis, University of Texas (Austin, Tex.), 1947.
631. BRUSSEL, JAMES A., AND HITCH, KENNETH S. *An Introduction to Rorschach Psychodiagnostics in Military and Civilian Psychiatry: With Color Illustrations of the Rorschach Cards, [Second Edition].* Including "A Rorschach Compendium" by Zygmunt A. Piotrowski. Revisions of papers from *Psychiatric Quarterly,* January 1942. Utica, N.Y.: State Hospitals Press, 1947. Pp. i, 51. Paper. *
632. BUHLER, CHARLOTTE. "Rorschach Studies on Alcoholism." Abstract. *Am Psychol* 2:405-6 O '47. * (*PA* 22:1277, title only)
633. CERF, ARTHUR Z. "The Rorschach Test, CE701A," pp. 625-37. In *Printed Classification Tests.* Edited by J. P. Guilford with the assistance of John I. Lacey. Army Air Forces Aviation Psychology Program Research Reports, Report No. 5. Washington, D.C.: U.S. Government Printing Office, 1947. Pp. xi, 919. * (*PA* 22:4145)
634. COFER, CHARLES N. "Psychological Test Performance Under Hyoscine: A Case of Post-Infectious Encephalopathy." *J General Psychol* 36:221-8 Ap '47. * (*PA* 22:3028)
635. DES LAURIERS, AUSTIN, AND HALPERN, FLORENCE. "Psychological Tests in Childhood Schizophrenia." *Am J Orthopsychiatry* 17:57-67 Ja '47. * (*PA* 21:2226)
636. EPSTEIN, HANS L., AND SCHWARTZ, ARTHUR. "Psychodiagnostic Testing in Group Work: Rorschach and Painting Analysis Technique." *Rorsch Res Exch & J Proj Tech* 11:23-41 no 2-4 '47. * (*PA* 22:4945)
637. EYSENCK, H. J. "Screening-Out the Neurotic." *Lancet* 252:530-1 Ap 19 '47. * (*PA* 22:408)
638. GARFIELD, SOL L. "The Rorschach Test in Clinical Diagnosis." *J Clin Psychol* 3:375-81 O '47. * (*PA* 22:4429)
639. GRASSI, JOSEPH R. "The Graphic Rorschach as a Supplement to the Rorschach in the Diagnosis of Organic Intracranial Lesions." *Psychiatric Q Sup* 21:312-27 pt 2 '47. * (*PA* 23:5710)
640. HALPERN, FLORENCE. Chap. 29, "The Rorschach Test and Other Projective Technics," pp. 425-34. In *Progress in Neurology and Psychiatry: An Annual Review, Vol. II.* Edited by E. A. Spiegel. New York: Grune & Stratton, Inc., 1947. Pp. xii, 541. *
641. HARRIS, R. E., AND IVES, V. M. "A Study of the Personality of Alcoholics." Abstract. *Am Psychol* 2:405 O '47. * (*PA* 22:1282, title only)
642. JOLLES, ISAAC. "The Diagnostic Implications of Rorschach's Test in Case Studies of Mental Defectives." *Genetic Psychol Monogr* 36:89-197 N '47. * (*PA* 22:2655)
643. KLEBANOFF, SEYMOUR GEORGE. *The Rorschach Test in an Analysis of Personality Changes in General Paresis.* Doctor's thesis, Northwestern University (Evanston, Ill.), 1947. (*Summaries of Doctoral Dissertations....June-September 1947,* 1948, pp. 262-5.)
644. KURTZ, ALBERT K. "Selection of Managers." [*Proc*

Annual Mtg Assn Life Agency Officers & Life Ins Sales Res Bur, 1946, 1946:196–212 '47. *

645. LEAVITT, HARRY C.; WITH THE TECHNICAL ASSISTANCE OF MARTIN S. BERGMANN. "A Case of Hypnotically Produced Secondary and Tertiary Personalities." *Psychoanalytic R* 34: 274–95 Jl '47. * (*PA* 22:4841)

646. LEFEVER, D. WELTY. "An Attempt to Quantify Rorschach Responses." Abstract. *Am Psychol* 2:406 O '47. * (*PA* 22:1215, title only)

647. LEVY, JEANNE R. *Changes in the Galvanic Skin Response Accompanying the Rorschach Test*. Master's thesis, University of Alabama (University, Ala.), 1947.

648. LIBERTHSON, LEO. "Thoughts Around a Rorschach Analysis." Poem. *J Clin Psychopath* 8:816 Jl–O '47. *

649. LINDNER, ROBERT M. "Analysis of the Rorschach Test by Content." *J Clin Psychopath* 8:707–19 Ap '47. * (*PA* 23: 2708)

650. McCANDLESS, BOYD R. "The Rorschach as a Differential Predictor of Academic Success for Matched Groups of Highly Superior Men." Abstract. *Am Psychol* 2:414–5 O '47. * (*PA* 22:1384, title only)

651. MARTIN, ANNA Y. *The Rorschach Pattern of Non-Deteriorated Epileptics*. Doctor's thesis, University of Texas (Austin, Tex.), 1947.

652. MAYMAN, M. *A Comparative Study of the Rorschach, Harrower, and Behn-Eschenberg Ink-Blot Tests*. Master's thesis, New York University (New York, N.Y.), 1947.

653. MIALE, FLORENCE R. "Rorschach Sequence Analysis in a Case of Paranoid Schizophrenia." *Rorsch Res Exch & J Proj Tech* 11:3–22 nos 2–4 '47. * (*PA* 22:5063)

654. MONS, W. *Principles and Practice of the Rorschach Personality Test*. London: Faber & Faber Ltd., 1947. Pp. 164. * (*PA* 22:4424)

655. OSTRANDER, JESSIE M. "Rorschach Record From a Patient After Removal of a Tumor From the Frontal Lobe." Abstract. *Am Psychol* 2:406 O '47. * (*PA* 22:1335, title only)

656. PRASAD, KALI, AND ASTHANA, H. S. "An Experimental Study of Meaning by Rorschach Method." *Indian J Psychol* 22:55–8 nos 1–4 '47. * (*PA* 24:5877)

657. PUZZO, FRANK S. *A Study of the Psychometric Signs of Anxiety in the Wechsler-Bellevue Intelligence Scale and the Rorschach Test*. Master's thesis, Fordham University (New York, N.Y.), 1947.

658. ROE, ANNE. "Personality and Vocation." *Trans N Y Acad Sci* 9:257–67 My '47. * (*PA* 21:4392)

659. SUTTON, DOROTHY M. *A Study of the Rorschach Test as a Test of Intelligence for Young Children Five-, Six-, and Seven-Years of Age*. Doctor's thesis, University of Kansas (Lawrence, Kan.), 1947.

660. THOMPSON, GRACE M. "Non-Intellective Factors and Grades: The Group Rorschach." Abstract. *Am Psychol* 2:415 O '47. * (*PA* 22:1390, title only)

661. WHEELER, ERMA T. *A Study of Certain Aspects of Personality as Related to the Electroencephalogram*. Doctor's thesis, University of Pittsburgh (Pittsburgh, Pa.), 1947. (*Abstracts of Doctoral Dissertations....*, 1948, pp. 183–96.) * (*PA* 22:5361, title only)

662. WISCHNER, GEORGE J.; ROTTER, JULIAN B.; AND GILLMAN, ROBERT D. Chap. 9, "Projective Techniques," pp. 144–57. In *The Psychological Program in AAF Convalescent Hospitals*. Edited by Sidney W. Bijou. Army Air Forces Aviation Psychology Program Research Reports, Report No. 15. Washington, D.C.: U.S. Government Printing Office, 1947. Pp. viii, 256. *

663. ZUCKER, LUISE. "Rorschach Patterns of a Group of Hard of Hearing Patients." *Rorsch Res Exch & J Proj Tech* 11:68–73 no 2–4 '47. * (*PA* 22:5109)

664. ABEL, THEODORA M. "The Rorschach Test in the Study of Culture." *Rorsch Res Exch & J Proj Tech* 12:79–93 no 1 '48. * (*PA* 23:4742)

665. ALDRICH, C. KNIGHT, AND COFFIN, MABEL. "Clinical Studies of Psychoses in the Navy: I, Prediction Values of Social Histories and the Harrower-Erickson Test." *J Nerv & Mental Dis* 108:36–44 Jl '48. * (*PA* 23:171)

666. ALDRICH, C. KNIGHT, AND COFFIN, MABEL. "Clinical Studies of Psychoses in the Navy: II, Prognosis." *J Nerv & Mental Dis* 108: 142–8 Ag '48. * (*PA* 23:242)

667. ALLEN, ROBERT M. "A Simple Method of Validating Color and Shading Shock." *J Consult Psychol* 12:360 S–O '48. * (*PA* 23:1768)

668. ALTUS, W. D. "Correlates of Certain M.M.P.I. Scales Found in the Group Rorschach for 100 'Normal' College Students." Abstract. *Am Psychol* 3:349 Ag '48. * (*PA* 23:741, title only)

669. ALTUS, W. D. "Some Correlates of the Group Rorschach and the Schizophrenia Scale of the Group MMPI Among Two Groups of 'Normal' College Students." *J Consult Psychol* 12: 375–8 N–D '48. * (*PA* 23:2225)

670. ANDERSEN, IRMGARD, AND MUNROE, RUTH. "Personality Factors Involved in Student Concentration on Creative Painting and Commercial Art." *Rorsch Res Exch & J Proj Tech* 12:141–54 no 3 '48. * (*PA* 23:467)

671. BECK, S. J. "Trends in Orthopsychiatric Therapy: II, Rorschach F Plus and the Ego in Treatment." *Am J Orthopsychiatry* 18:395–401 Jl '48. * (*PA* 23:1302)

672. BECK, SAMUEL J. "Rorschach's Test in This Anniversary Year." pp. 422–55. In *Orthopsychiatry, 1923–1948: Retrospect and Prospect*. Lawson G. Lowrey and Victoria Sloane, Editors.

New York: American Orthopsychiatric Association, Inc., 1948. Pp. viii, 623. *

673. BELL, JOHN ELDERKIN. Chap. 6. "The Rorschach Technique," pp. 75–201. In his *Projective Techniques: A Dynamic Approach to the Study of the Personality*. New York: Longmans, Green & Co., Inc., 1948. Pp. xvi, 533. * (London: Longmans, Green & Co. Ltd., 1949.) (*PA* 23:1284)

674. BENJAMIN, EDWARD. *A Psychobiological Approach to the Color-Shock Phenomena on the Rorschach Test*. Master's thesis, University of Chicago (Chicago, Ill.), 1948. (*PA* 23:345, title only)

675. BILLIG, OTTO; GILLIN, JOHN; AND DAVIDSON, WILLIAM. "Aspects of Personality and Culture in a Guatemalan Community: Ethnological and Rorschach Approaches: Part II." *J Personality* 16:326–68 Mr '48. * (*PA* 23:2185)

676. BLACKWELL, ERNESTINE B. *The Use of the Rorschach in the Validation of the Criteria of Normalcy and Illness*. Doctor's thesis, University of Texas (Austin, Texas), 1948.

677. BLAKE, ROBERT R. "Ocular Activity During Administration of the Rorschach Test." *J Clin Psychol* 4:159–69 Ap '48. * (*PA* 23:165)

678. BRENER, ROY. "A Preliminary Study on Form Evaluation in the Rorschach." Abstract. *Am Psychol* 3:362 Ag '48. * (*PA* 23:744, title only)

679. BROSIN, HENRY. "Clinical Aspects of Rorschach Testing." Abstract. *Dig Neurol & Psychiatry* 16:214 Ap '48. *

680. BROWER, DANIEL. "The Relations of Visuo-Motor Conflict to Personality Traits and Cardio-Vascular Activity." *J General Psychol* 38:69–99 Ja '48. * (*PA* 23:383)

681. BROWN, RALPH R. "The Rorschach in Industry." *Personnel* 24:434–6 My '48. * (*PA* 22:5163)

682. BRUNER, JEROME S. "Perceptual Theory and the Rorschach Test: IV, The Problems of Quantification and Objectification in Personality: A Symposium." *J Personality* 17:157–68 D '48. * (*PA* 25:2801)

683. BUHLER, CHARLOTTE; BUHLER, KARL; AND LEFEVER, D. WELTY. *Development of the Basic Rorschach Score With Manual of Directions*. Rorschach Standardization Studies, No. 1. Los Angeles 46, Calif.: Charlotte Buhler (1127 North Sweetzer Ave.), 1948. Pp. ix, 190. Paper, mimeographed. * (*PA* 23:745)

684. BUHLER, CHARLOTTE, AND LEFEVER, D. WELTY. *A Rorschach Study on the Psychological Characteristics of Alcoholics*. Yale University, Laboratory of Applied Physiology, Memoirs of the Section of Studies on Alcohol, No. 6. New Haven, Conn.: Quarterly Journal of Studies on Alcohol, 1948. Pp. viii, 64. Paper. * (*PA* 22:1232)

685. CALABRESI, RENATA A. "Interpretation of Personality With the Szondi Test." *Rorsch Res Exch & J Proj Tech* 12: 238–53 no 4 '48. * (*PA* 24:1192)

686. CARP, ABRAHAM. *Psychological Test Performance and Insulin Shock Therapy*. Doctor's thesis, Stanford University (Stanford, Calif.), 1948. (*Abstracts of Dissertations....1947–48*, 1948, pp. 180–3.) (*PA* 23:354, title only)

687. CARP, FRANCES MERCHANT. "Constriction as Rated on Three Productions." Abstract. *Am Psychol* 3:284 Jl '48. * (*PA* 22:5421, title only)

688. CASTELNUOVO-TEDESCO, PETER. "A Study of the Relationship Between Handwriting and Personality Variables." *Genetic Psychol Monogr* 37:167–220 My '48. * (*PA* 23:1185)

689. CHRISTENSON, JAMES A., JR., AND JOHNSON, LAWRENCE C. "Indications for Use of the Rorschach in Mental Hygiene Clinics." *J Abn & Social Psychol* 43:555 O '48. * (*PA* 23:1781)

690. CLARK, JERRY H. "Some M.M.P.I. Correlates of Certain Color Responses in the Group Rorschach Test." Abstract. *Am Psychol* 3:349 Ag '48. * (*PA* 23:747, title only)

691. CLARK, JERRY H. "Some MMPI Correlates of Color Responses in the Group Rorschach." *J Consult Psychol* 12:384–6 N–D '48. * (*PA* 23:2228)

692. COLM, HANNA. "The Use of the Rorschach for Children in Diagnosing Interrelationship Difficulties Between Parents and Children." *J Child Psychiatry* 1:247–65 sect 3 '48. * (*PA* 24:1193)

693. COLM, HANNA. "The Value of Projective Methods in the Psychological Examination of Children: The Mosaic Test in Conjunction With the Rorschach and Binet Tests." *Rorsch Res Exch & J Proj Tech* 12:216–37 no 4 '48. * (*PA* 24:1194)

694. COX, KENNETH J. "Can the Rorschach Pick Sales Clerks?" *Personnel Psychol* 1:357–63 au '48. * (*PA* 23:1481)

695. CUTTS, RICHARD A. "Evaluation of a Short Form of Rorschach." Abstract. *Am Psychol* 3:282 Jl '48. * (*PA* 22:5423, title only)

696. DOUGAN, CATHERINE, AND WELCH, LIVINGSTON. "A Study of Elation, Making Use of the Rorschach Test and an Association Test." *J Psychol* 26:363–6 O '48. * (*PA* 23:1660)

697. ELONEN, ANNA S., AND KORNER, ANNELIESE FRIEDSAM. "Pre- and Post-Operative Psychological Observations on a Case of Frontal Lobectomy." *J Abn & Social Psychol* 43:532–43 O '48. * (*PA* 23:1821)

698. EVANS, HARRISON S., AND COLLET, GRACE M. "The Rorschach Test in Clinical Psychiatry." *Ohio State Med J* 44:482–6 My '48. * (*PA* 23:1288)

699. FINE, REUBEN. *The Personality of the Asthmatic Child*. Doctor's thesis, University of Southern California (Los Angeles, Calif.), 1948. (*Abstracts of Dissertations....1948*, 1949, pp. 165–9.) (*PA* 23:4855)

700. FRANKLE, ESTHER ALPERN. *The Relationship Between Quantified Group Rorschach Scores and Sociometric Adjustment Ratings of a Freshman College Group*. Master's thesis, University of Chicago (Chicago, Ill.), 1948. (*PA* 23:365, title only)

701. FROST, CARL F., AND RODNICK, ELIOT H. "The Relationship Between Particular Rorschach Determinants and the Concomitant Galvanic Skin Responses for Schizophrenic and Normal Subjects." Abstract. *Am Psychol* 3:277 Jl '48. * (*PA* 22:5511, title only)

702. GARRISON, MORTIMER, JR. "Relationships Between Rorschach Scores and Clinical Changes in Mental Patients: II, The Problems of Quantification and Objectification in Personality: A Symposium." *J Personality* 17:146–52 D '48. * (*PA* 25:3163)

703. GLIK, EDWARD E. "Involutional Psychosis With Alcoholism: A Brief Case Study." *Rorsch Res Exch & J Proj Tech* 12:168–70 no 3 '48. * (*PA* 23:4927)

704. HALPERN, FLORENCE. Chap. 32, "The Rorschach Test and Other Projective Technics," pp. 549–62. (*PA* 22:5427) In *Progress in Neurology and Psychiatry: An Annual Review, Vol. III.* Edited by E. A. Spiegel. New York: Grune & Stratton, Inc., 1948. Pp. xiv, 661. *

705. HAMLIN, ROY M., AND ALBEE, GEORGE W. "Muench's Tests Before and After Nondirective Therapy: A Control Group for His Subjects." *J Consult Psychol* 12:412–6 N–D '48. * (*PA* 23:2247)

706. HAMLIN, ROY M., AND KOGAN, WILLIAM S. "Objectification in Rorschach Interpretation: VI, The Problems of Quantification and Objectification in Personality: A Symposium." *J Personality* 17:177–81 D '48. * (*PA* 25:3165)

707. HARRIS, THOMAS M. "The Use of Projective Techniques in Industrial Selection," pp. 40–51. In *Exploring Individual Differences: A Report of the 1947 Invitational Conference on Testing Problems, New York City, November 1, 1947.* Henry Chauncey, Chairman. American Council on Education Studies, Vol. 12, Series 1, No. 32. Washington, D.C.: the Council, October 1948. Pp. vii, 110. Paper. *

708. HERTZ, MARGUERITE R. "Further Study of Suicidal Configurations in Rorschach Records." Abstract. *Am Psychol* 3:283–4 Jl '48. * (*PA* 22:5491, title only)

709. HERTZ, MARGUERITE R. "Suicidal Configurations in Rorschach Records." *Rorsch Res Exch & J Proj Tech* 12:3–58 no 1 '48. * (*PA* 23:4818)

710. HILDEN, ARNOLD H. "Repeated Annual Rorschach Records on a Single Child Over a Period of Years." Abstract. *J Colo-Wyo Acad Sci* 3:61–2 Mr '48. *

711. HUGHES, ROBERT M. "Rorschach Signs for the Diagnosis of Organic Pathology." *Rorsch Res Exch & J Proj Tech* 12:165–7 no 3 '48. * (*PA* 23:4820)

712. HUGHES, ROBERT MOORE. *A Factor Analysis of Rorschach Diagnostic Signs.* Doctor's thesis, University of North Carolina (Chapel Hill, N.C.), 1948. (*Research in Progress, October, 1945–December, 1948,* 1949, pp. 335–6.) (*PA* 23:1008, title only)

713. JACQUES, MARY G. *A Comparison of Indications of Emotional Response and of Neurotic Disturbance in Physiological Reactions and in the Rorschach Test.* Doctor's thesis, University of Chicago (Chicago, Ill.), 1948. Pp. 144.

714. JOHNSON, C. EARLE, JR., AND SHERMAN, JAMES E. "The Clinical Significance of the Rorschach Test." *Am J Psychiatry* 104:730–7 My '48. * (*PA* 23:758)

715. KALINKOWITZ, BERNARD NATHAN. *An Attempt to Differentiate Paranoid Schizophrenic Patients From Brain-Damaged Patients by Use of Psychological Test Procedures.* Doctor's thesis, New York University (New York, N.Y.), 1948. Abstract: *Microfilm Abstr* 9:175–6 no 2 '49. * (*PA* 24:4197, title only)

716. KENDIG, ISABELLE V., AND VERNIER, CLAIRE M. "Rorschach Patterns in Involutional Melancholia." Abstract. *Am Psychol* 3:283 Jl '48. * (*PA* 22:5513, title only)

717. KESSLER, CHARLES RICHARDS. *A Comparison of Rorschach Records With Performance on Tests of Deterioration in a Group of Aged People.* Master's thesis, University of Southern California (Los Angeles, Calif.), 1948.

718. KIMBALL, ALICE JAMES. *Evaluation of Form-Level in the Rorschach.* Doctor's thesis, University of California (Berkeley, Calif.), 1948.

719. KLEBANOFF, SEYMOUR G. "The Rorschach Test in an Analysis of Personality Changes in General Paresis." Abstract. *Am Psychol* 3:362–3 Ag '48. * (*PA* 23:898, title only)

720. KRUG, JOHN E. *The Projective Technique of Personality Study as Illustrated by the Rorschach Test, Its History, Its Methods, and Its Status.* Master's thesis, Indiana State Teachers College (Terre Haute, Ind.), 1948. Pp. 94. Abstract: *Teach Col J* 20:37 N '48. *

721. KURTZ, ALBERT K. "A Research Test of the Rorschach Test." *Personnel Psychol* 1:41–51 sp '48. * (*PA* 22:4152)

722. LANE, BARBARA M. "A Validation Test of the Rorschach Movement Interpretations." *Am J Orthopsychiatry* 18:292–6 Ap '48. * (*PA* 22:5431)

723. LANTZ, HERMAN. "Rorschach Testing in Pre-Literate Cultures." *Am J Orthopsychiatry* 18:287–91 Ap '48. * (*PA* 22:4372)

724. LAZARUS, RICHARD S. *An Experimental Analysis of the Influence of Color on the Protocol of the Rorschach Test.* Doctor's thesis, University of Pittsburgh (Pittsburgh, Pa.), 1948. (*Abstracts of Doctoral Dissertations....1948,* 1949, pp. 244–9.) (*PA* 23:384, 24:1202; title only)

725. LAZARUS, RICHARD S. "An Experimental Analysis of the Influence of Color on the Protocol of the Rorschach Test: VII, The Problems of Quantification and Objectification in Personality: A Symposium." *J Personality* 17:182–5 D '48. * (*PA* 25:3169)

726. LEDWITH, NETTIE HERRINGTON. *The Performance of Six Year Old Children on the Rorschach Ink Blot Test: A Normative Study.* Doctor's thesis, University of Pittsburgh (Pittsburgh, Pa.), 1948. (*Abstracts of Doctoral Dissertations....1948,* 1949, pp. 250–5.) (*PA* 23:385, 24:1203; title only)

727. LEVINE, EDNA SIMON. *An Investigation Into the Personality of Normal Deaf Adolescent Girls.* Doctor's thesis, New York University (New York, N.Y.), 1948. Abstract: *Microfilm Abstracts* 9:103–5 no 1 '49.

728. LEVY, JEANNE R. "Changes in the Galvanic Skin Response Accompanying the Rorschach Test." Abstract. *Am Psychol* 3:335 Ag '48. * (*PA* 23:762, title only)

729. LINN, LOUIS. "A Note on 'Manner of Approach' in the Rorschach Test as a Measure of Psychic Energy." *Psychiatric Q* 22:634–40 O '48. * (*PA* 23:6214)

730. LISANSKY, EDITH SILVERGLIED. "Convulsive Disorder and Personality." *J Abn & Social Psychol* 43:29–37 Ja '48. * (*PA* 22:3574)

731. LUBAR, GERALD H. "Rorschach Content Analysis." *J Clin Psychopath* 9:146–52 Ja '48. *

732. MCFARLAND, ROBERT LEO. *An Investigation of Differences in Form-Determined Responses to the Rorschach Psychodiagnostik Test Between Schizophrenic and Normal Subjects.* Master's thesis, University of Chicago (Chicago, Ill.), 1948. (*PA* 23:389, title only)

733. MACHOVER, KAREN, AND WEXLER, ROCHELLE M. "A Case of Manic Excitement." *Rorsch Res Exch & J Proj Tech* 12:179–201 no 4 '48. * (*PA* 24:1351)

734. MUNROE, RUTH L. "Academic Success and Personal Adjustment in College," pp. 30–42. In *Exploring Individual Differences: A Report of the 1947 Invitational Conference on Testing Problems, New York City, November 1, 1947.* Henry Chauncey, Chairman. American Council on Education Studies, Vol. 12, Series 1, No. 32. Washington, D.C.: the Association, October 1948. Pp. vii, 110. Paper. *

735. MUNROE, RUTH L. "The Use of Projective Methods in Group Testing." *J Consult Psychol* 12:8–15 Ja–F '48. * (*PA* 22:3036)

736. NIKOLAISEN, KATHERINE. "The Rorschach Performance of 10-Year-Old Children—A Normative Study." Abstract. *Am Psychol* 3:362 Ag '48. * (*PA* 23:767, title only)

737. OPPENHEIM, SADI, AND BROWER, DANIEL. "The Effects of Electric Shock Therapy as Revealed by the Rorschach Technique." *Psychiatric Q Sup* 22:318–25 pt 2 '48. * (*PA* 25:1827)

738. ORR, FRANCES G. *Age Changes and Constancy of Rorschach Test Variables During Adolescence.* Doctor's thesis, University of California (Berkeley, Calif.), 1948.

739. OSTRANDER, JESSIE M. "A Report of Rorschach and Wechsler-Bellevue Records of a Man After the Removal of Tumor From the Frontal Lobes." *Rorsch Res Exch & J Proj Tech* 12:65–71 no 1 '48. * (*PA* 23:4950)

740. PITRELLI, FERDINAND R. "Psychosomatic and Rorschach Aspects of Stuttering." *Psychiatric Q* 22:175–93 Ap '48. * (*PA* 23:5640)

741. READER, NATALIE. *An Investigation Into Some Personality Changes Occurring in Individuals Undergoing Client-Centered Therapy.* Doctor's thesis, University of Chicago (Chicago, Ill.), 1948.

742. REDMOUNT, ROBERT S. "Description and Evaluation of a Corrective Program for Reading Disability." *J Ed Psychol* 39:347–58 O '48. * (*PA* 23:1930)

743. REICHARD, SUZANNE. "Rorschach Study of Prejudiced Personality." *Am J Orthopsychiatry* 18:280–6 Ap '48. * (*PA* 22:4377)

744. RICHARDS, T. W. "The Individual Child's Development as Reflected by the Rorschach Performance." *Rorsch Res Exch & J Proj Tech* 12:59–64 no 1 '48. * (*PA* 23:4707)

745. ROOK, LEROY H. "A Comparison of the Methods of Scoring the Rorschach Method: Beck, Hertz, Klopfer." *Proc Okla Acad Sci* 29:113–7 '48 (published Mr '50). * (*PA* 25:1106)

746. ROSENWALD, ALAN KENNETH. *A Comparison of the Rorschach and Behn-Rorschach Tests.* Doctor's thesis, Northwestern University (Evanston, Ill.), 1948. Pp. 54 (*Summaries of Doctoral Dissertations....June–September 1948,* 1949, pp. 404–5.)

747. ROTTER, JULIAN B. "The Present Status of the Rorschach in Clinical and Experimental Procedures." *J Personality* 16:304–11 Mr '48. * (*PA* 23:2235)

748. RUST, RALPH M. "The Levy Movement Cards: EPA Round Table: III, The Problems of Quantification and Objectification in Personality: A Symposium." *J Personality* 17:153–6 D '48. * (*PA* 25:3187)

749. SCHAFER, ROY. *The Clinical Application of Psychological Tests: Diagnostic Summaries and Case Studies.* Foreword by David Rapaport. The Menninger Foundation Monograph Series No. 6. New York: International Universities Press, Inc., 1948. Pp. 346. * (London: George Allen & Unwin Ltd., 1949.) (*PA* 23:778)

750. SCHAFER, SARAH, AND LEITCH, MARY. "An Exploratory Study of the Usefulness of a Battery of Psychological Tests With Nursery School Children." *Am J Psychiatry* 104:647–52 Ap '48. * (*PA* 23:813)

751. SEARS, RICHARD. "Castration Anxiety in an Adult as Shown by Projective Tests." Abstract. *Am Psychol* 3:281 Jl '48. * (*PA* 22:5371, title only)

752. SHAW, BARRIE. "'Sex Populars' in the Rorschach Test." *J Abn & Social Psychol* 43:466–70 O '48. * (*PA* 23:1777)

753. SIEGEL, MIRIAM G. "The Diagnostic and Prognostic Validity of the Rorschach Test in a Child Guidance Clinic." *Am J Orthopsychiatry* 18:119–33 Ja '48. * (*PA* 22:3087)

754. SIPLE, HOWARD LEROY. *Physiological Correlates of Color Shock in the Rorschach Test.* Doctor's thesis, Northwestern

University (Evanston, Ill.), 1948. (*Summaries of Doctoral Dissertations....June–September 1948*, 1949, pp. 406–7.)

755. SLOAN, WILLIAM. "Prediction of Extramural Adjustment of Mental Defectives by Use of the Rorschach Test." *J Consult Psychol* 12:303–9 S–O '48. * (*PA* 23:1846)

756. SOLOMON, JOSEPH C. "Adult Character and Behavior Disorders." *J Clin Psychopath* 9:1–55 Ja '48. *

757. STEINER, MATILDA E. "The Use of Projective Techniques in Industry (A Review of Published Material)." *Rorsch Res Exch & J Proj Tech* 12:171–4 no 3 '48. * (*PA* 23:5073)

758. SYMONDS, PERCIVAL M. "Survey of Projective Techniques," pp. 3–18. In *Exploring Individual Differences: A Report of the 1947 Invitational Conference on Testing Problems, New York City, November 1, 1947*. Henry Chauncey, Chairman. American Council on Education Studies, Vol. 12, Series 1, No. 32. Washington, D.C.: the Council, October 1948. Pp. vii, 110. Paper. *

759. THOMPSON, GRACE. "M.M.P.I. Correlates of Movement Responses in the Rorschach." Abstract. *Am Psychol* 3:348–9 Ag '48. * (*PA* 23:772, title only)

760. THOMPSON, GRACE M. "College Grades and the Group Rorschach." *J Appl Psychol* 32:398–407 Ag '48. * (*PA* 23:1448)

761. THOMPSON, GRACE M. "M.M.P.I. Correlates of Certain Movement Responses in the Group Rorschachs of Two College Samples." *J Consult Psychol* 12:379–83 N–D '48. * (*PA* 23:2238)

762. THURSTONE, L. L. "The Rorschach in Psychological Science." *J Abn & Social Psychol* 43:471–5 O '48. * (*PA* 23:1779)

763. VAN WATERS, RALPH O., AND SACKS, JEROME G.; WITH THE COLLABORATION OF PAUL G. MYERSON. "Rorschach Evaluation of the Schizophrenic Process Following a Prefrontal Lobotomy." *J Psychol* 25:73–88 Ja '48. * (*PA* 22:3146)

764. WALLEN, RICHARD. "The Nature of Color Shock." *J Abn & Social Psychol* 43:346–56 Jl '48. * (*PA* 23:773)

765. WIKLER, ABRAHAM, AND DAINGERFIELD, MARY. "Practical Use of the Rorschach Test." *Dis Nerv Sys* 9:42–5 F '48. *

766. WISHNER, JULIUS. "Rorschach Intellectual Indicators in Neurotics." *Am J Orthopsychiatry* 18:265–79 Ap '48. * (*PA* 22:4427)

767. YOUNG, REGINALD J. "The Value of the Rorschach Test in Differential Diagnoses." *Am J Psychiatry* 105:381–2 N '48. * (*PA* 23:4261)

768. ZUBIN, JOSEPH; IN COLLABORATION WITH KATHLEEN M. YOUNG. *Manual of Projective and Cognate Techniques*, Chaps. 3, 4, 5A, 6, 8, 9. Madison, Wis.: College Typing Co., 1948. Pp. 175. Paper, mimeographed. For latest edition, see 1063.

769. ZUCKER, LUISE. "A Case of Obesity: Projective Techniques Before and During Treatment." *Rorsch Res Exch & J Proj Tech* 12:202–15 no 4 '48. * (*PA* 24:1414)

770. ZUCKERMAN, STANLEY B. "A Research Suggestion in Large-Scale Rorschach." *J Consult Psychol* 12:300–2 S–O '48. * (*PA* 23:1787)

771. INTERNATIONAL PSYCHOLOGICAL SERVICE CENTER, MEDICOPSYCHOLOGICAL RESEARCH STAFF. "A Standard Method for Recording Rorschach Test Administration and Computation Procedures." *Psychol Service Center J* 1:21–8 S '49. * (*PA* 24:3211)

772. ABEL, THEODORA M., AND HSU, FRANCIS L. K. "Some Aspects of Personality of Chinese as Revealed by the Rorschach Test." Abstract. *Rorsch Res Exch & J Proj Tech* 13:242 no 2 '49. * (*PA* 24:2496, title only)

773. ABEL, THEODORA M., AND HSU, FRANCIS L. K. "Some Aspects of Personality of Chinese as Revealed by the Rorschach Test." *Rorsch Res Exch & J Proj Tech* 13:285–301 S '49. * (*PA* 24:3163)

774. ALTUS, WILLIAM D. "The Group Rorschach as a Measure of Intelligence at the College Level." Abstract. *Am Psychol* 4:388 S '49. * (*PA* 24:1876, title only)

775. ALTUS, W. D., AND THOMPSON, GRACE M. "The Rorschach as a Measure of Intelligence." *J Consult Psychol* 13:341–7 O '49. * (*PA* 24:2587)

776. AMOROSO, MARIE D. "The Rorschach Test as an Aid to Electroencephalographic Analysis." Abstract. *Federation Proc* 8:4 Mr '49. * (*PA* 25:6865, title only)

777. ANDERSON, ROSE C. "Rorschach Tests Results and Efficiency Ratings of Machinists." *Personnel Psychol* 2:513–24 W '49. * (*PA* 24:4275)

778. ANDERSON, THOMAS E., JR. *Rorschach Determinants in Ulcer Patients*. Master's thesis, Catholic University of America (Washington, D.C.), 1949. (*PA* 24:801, title only)

779. BAKER, LAWRENCE M., AND HARRIS, JANE S. "The Validation of Rorschach Test Results Against Laboratory Behavior." *J Clin Psychol* 5:161–4 Ap '49. * (*PA* 24:1877)

780. BECK, SAMUEL J. *Rorschach's Test: I, Basic Processes, Second Edition*. Foreword to first edition by W. L. Valentine; foreword to second edition by James G. Miller. New York: Grune & Stratton, Inc., 1949. Pp. xiii, 227. * (*PA* 24:2588)

781. BELL, JOHN ELDERKIN. "The Case of Gregor: Psychological Test Data." *Rorsch Res Exch & J Proj Tech* 13:155–205 no 2 '49. * (*PA* 24:2589)

782. BERK, NORMAN. *A Personality Study of Suicidal Schizophrenics*. Doctor's thesis, New York University (New York, N.Y.), 1949. Abstract: *Microfilm Abstracts* 10:155–6 no 2 '50. (*PA* 25:479, title only)

783. BERSADSKY, LEONA. *A Study of the Validity of the Intelligence Determinants in the Rorschach Test on Seven-Year-Old Children*. Master's thesis, Tulane University (New Orleans, La.), 1949. (*Abstracts of Theses 1949*, pp. 84–5.)

784. BLACKWELL, TOM B. *College Vocational Guidance and Group Rorschach Personality Patterns*. Doctor's thesis, University of Texas (Austin, Tex.), 1949.

785. BOURKE, WILLIAM THEODORE. *The Incidence of Schizophrenic Signs in Tuberculous and Schizophrenic Hospital Patients as Measured by the Rorschach Test*. Master's thesis, Tulane University (New Orleans, La.), 1949. (*Abstracts of Theses 1949*, p. 85.)

786. BUHLER, CHARLOTTE. "Personality Integration Levels in Rorschach Analysis." Abstract. *Rorsch Res Exch & J Proj Tech* 13:243–4 no 2 '49. * (*PA* 24:2593, title only)

787. BUHLER, CHARLOTTE; GRAYSON, HARRY M.; LEFEVER, D. WELTY; MEYER, MORTIMER M.; WESLEY, S. M.; AND WHEELER, WILLIAM MARSHALL. "Symposium on a 'Basic Rorschach Score.'" *Rorsch Res Exch & J Proj Tech* 13:6–24 no 1 '49. *

788. BURNHAM, CATHERINE A. "A Study of the Degree of Relationship Between Rorschach H% and Wechsler-Bellevue Picture Arrangement Scores." *Rorsch Res Exch & J Proj Tech* 13:206–9 no 2 '49. * (*PA* 24:2594)

789. BURTON, ARTHUR. "The Use of Psychometric and Projective Tests in Clinical Psychology." *J Psychol* 28:451–6 O '49. * (*PA* 24:2595)

790. CARR, ARTHUR C. "An Evaluation of Nine Nondirective Psychotherapy Cases by Means of the Rorschach." *J Consult Psychol* 13:196–205 Je '49. * (*PA* 24:197)

791. CHESROW, EUGENE J.; WOSIKA, PAUL H.; AND REINITZ, ARTHUR H. "A Psychometric Evaluation of Aged White Males." *Geriatrics* 4:169–77 My–Je '49. * (*PA* 24:540)

792. COOPER, JAMES G., III. *Quantitative Rorschach Factors in the Evaluation of Teacher Effectiveness*. Doctor's thesis, Stanford University (Stanford, Calif.), 1949. (*PA* 25:5697, title only)

793. CRONBACH, LEE J. "'Pattern Tabulation': A Statistical Method for Analysis of Limited Patterns of Scores, With Particular Reference to the Rorschach Test." *Ed & Psychol Meas* 9:149–71 su '49. * (*PA* 24:18)

794. CRONBACH, LEE J. "The Rorschach Test," pp. 434–46. In his *Essentials of Psychological Testing*. New York: Harper & Brothers, 1949. Pp. xiii, 475. * (*PA* 24:647)

795. CRONBACH, LEE J. "Statistical Methods Applied to Rorschach Scores: A Review." *Psychol B* 46:393–429 S '49. * (*PA* 24:1883)

796. DICKSON, LOIS P. *The Rorschach Test as an Indicator of Prognosis in Psychoneurosis*. Master's thesis, Catholic University of America (Washington, D.C.), 1949. (*PA* 24:814, title only)

797. DORKEN, HERBERT, JR., AND TUNIS, MARTIN M. "Projective Technique With Narcosis." *Am J Psychiatry* 106:216–21 S '49. * (*PA* 24:3296)

798. DUMAS, LEONORE R. "Can Brain-Injured Children Be Evaluated by the Rorschach Test?" Abstract. *Am Psychol* 4:250 Jl '49. * (*PA* 23:6347, title only)

799. ELIZUR, ABRAHAM. "Content Analysis of the Rorschach With Regard to Anxiety and Hostility." *Rorsch Res Exch & J Proj Tech* 13:247–84 S '49. * (*PA* 24:3208)

800. FITZGERALD, JEAN C. *A Study of Rorschach Color Factors as Indicators of Social Acceptance*. Doctor's thesis, Iowa State College of Agriculture and Mechanic Arts (Ames, Iowa), 1949. Pp. 70.

801. FROST, CARL FREDERICK. *The Relationship Between the Verbal and Galvanic Skin Responses to the Rorschach Test for Schizophrenic and Normal Subjects*. Doctor's thesis, Clark University (Worcester, Mass.), 1949. Pp. 118. (*Abstracts of Dissertations....1948*, 1949, pp. 36–9.) (*PA* 23:3214, title only)

802. GOLDFARB, WILLIAM. "Rorschach Test Differences Between Family-Reared and Institution-Reared, and Schizophrenic Children." *Am J Orthopsychiatry* 19:624–33 O '49. * (*PA* 24:4147)

803. GOODMAN, HOWARD WILLIAM. *An Experimental Investigation of the Affective Value of Color on the Rorschach Test*. Doctor's thesis, University of Pittsburgh (Pittsburgh, Pa.), 1949. (*Abstracts of Doctoral Dissertations....1949*, 1950, pp. 298–304.)

804. GRIFFITH, R. M., AND DIMMICK, G. B. "Differentiating Rorschach Responses of Alcoholics." *Q J Studies Alcohol* 10:430–3 D '49. * (*PA* 24:2694)

805. HALPERIN, SIDNEY L. "A Study of the Personality Structure of the Prisoner in Hawaii." Abstract. *Rorsch Res Exch & J Proj Tech* 13:243 no 2 '49. * (*PA* 24:2707, title only)

806. HARRIS, WILLIAM E. *A Study of Rorschach Factors in Paranoid Schizophrenia*. Doctor's thesis, University of Kentucky (Lexington, Ky.), 1949.

807. HECHT, IRVING. *The Differentiation of Certain Psychosomatic Groups in Terms of Psychometric Patterns: An Evaluation of the Wechsler-Bellevue Intelligence Scale and the Rorschach Projective Technique to Differentiate Among the Ulcer, Colitis, and Hypertension Groups*. Doctor's thesis, New York University (New York, N.Y.), 1949. Abstract: *Microfilm Abstracts* 10:148–9 no 2 '50. (*PA* 25:361, title only)

808. HENRY, WILLIAM E., AND GARDNER, BURLEIGH B. "Personality Evaluation in the Selection of Executive Personnel." *Pub Personnel R* 10:67–71 Ap '49. * (*PA* 23:6481)

809. HERSHENSON, JEANNE R. "Preference of Adolescents for Rorschach Figures." *Child Develop* 20:101–18 Je '49. * (*PA* 24:4116)

810. HERTZ, MARGUERITE R. "Further Study of 'Suicidal' Configurations in Rorschach Records." *Rorsch Res Exch & J Proj Tech* 13:44–73 no 1 '49. * (*PA* 24:1198)

811. HERTZMAN, MAX; SMITH, G. MILTON; CLARK, KENNETH B. "The Relation Between Changes in the Angioscotoma and Certain Rorschach Signs Under Prolonged Mild Anoxia." *J General Psychol* 41:263-71 O '49. * (*PA* 24:4387).

812. HILZIM, EUGENIE SARRÉ. *Use of the Rorschach Technique With Young Children: A Survey of Normative Studies.* Master's thesis, Tulane University (New Orleans, La.), 1949. (*Abstracts of Theses 1949*, p. 87.)

813. HIRE, A. WILLIAM. *Use of the Rorschach and Thematic Apperception Tests in the Counseling and Guidance of College Students.* Doctor's thesis, Harvard University (Cambridge, Mass.), 1949. Abstract: *Harvard Ed R* 21:65-8 w '51. *

814. HOHNE, H. H. "The Prediction of Academic Success." *Austral J Psychol* 1:38-42 Je '49. * (*PA* 26:1103)

815. HUTT, M. L.; GIBBY, R.; MILTON, E. O.; AND POTTHARST, K. "The Effect of Varied Experimental 'Sets' Upon Rorschach Test Performance." Abstract. *Rorsch Res Exch & J Proj Tech* 13:240-1 no 2 '49. * (*PA* 24:2605, title only)

816. KAHN, HARRIS, AND SINGER, ERWIN. "An Investigation of Some of the Factors Related to Success or Failure·of School of Commerce Students." *J Ed Psychol* 40:107-17 F '49. * (*PA* 24:2062)

817. KAMMAN, GORDON R. "The Value of the Rorschach Test." *Minn Med* 32:621-4+ Je '49. * (*PA* 24:4608)

818. KATES, SOLIS L. "Rorschach Responses of New York City Patrolmen Related to Their Vocational Interests and Job Satisfaction." Abstract. *Rorsch Res Exch & J Proj Tech* 13:238-9 no 2 '49. * (*PA* 24:2849, title only)

819. KELLMAN, SAMUEL. "A Proposed Revision of the Multiple-Choice Rorschach: Theoretical and Methodical Problems." Abstract. *Rorsch Res Exch & J Proj Tech* 13:244 no 2 '49. * (*PA* 24:2607, title only)

820. KENDIG, ISABELLE V. "Rorschach Indications for the Diagnosis of Schizophrenia." *Rorsch Res Exch & J Proj Tech* 13:142-0 no 2 '49. * (*PA* 24:2713)

821. KENNEDY, RUBY ELDER. *The Performance of Five-Year-Old Children on the Rorschach Ink-Blot Test.* Master's thesis, Tulane University (New Orleans, La.), 1949. (*Abstracts of Theses 1949*, p. 88.)

822. KITZINGER, HELEN; ARNOLD, DeVERE G.; CARTWRIGHT, ROBERT W.; AND SHAPIRO, DAVID. "A Preliminary Study of the Effects of Glutamic Acid on Catatonic Schizophrenics." *Rorsch Res Exch & J Proj Tech* 13:210-8 no 2 '49. * (*PA* 24:2714)

823. KLEBANOFF, SEYMOUR G. "The Rorschach Test in an Analysis of Personality Changes in General Paresis." *J Personality* 17:261-72 Mr '49. * (*PA* 25:3313)

824. KLOPFER, BRUNO. "Rorschach Method: The Case of Gregor: Interpretation of Test Data: Symposium Presented at American Psychological Association Meeting, Denver, 1949." *Rorsch Res Exch & J Proj Tech* 13:458-60 D '49. * (*PA* 24:3724)

825. KLOPFER, WALTER G. *Suggestions for the Systematic Analysis of Rorschach Records.* Los Angeles, Calif.: U.C.L.A. Student's Store, University of California, September 1949. Pp. 16. Paper, mimeographed. *

826. KUTASH, SAMUEL B. "Recent Developments in the Field of Projective Techniques." *Rorsch Res Exch & J Proj Tech* 13:74-86 no 1 '49. * (*PA* 24:1201)

827. LANTANGE, JOSEPH E. *An Analysis of Health Interests of 3,000 Secondary School Students of California.* Doctor's thesis, Stanford University (Stanford, Calif.), 1949.

828. LAZARUS, RICHARD S. "The Influence of Color on the Protocol of the Rorschach Test." *J Abn & Social Psychol* 44:506-15 O '49. * (*PA* 24:2608)

829. LINDER, THELMA D. *The Personality of Arrested Tuberculous Subjects as Indicated by the Rorschach Test.* Master's thesis, Catholic University of America (Washington, D.C.), 1949. (*PA* 24:829, title only)

830. LISANSKY, EDITH S. *Inter-Examiner Reliability of Scoring and Interpretation in the Rorschach Test.* Doctor's thesis, Yale University (New Haven, Conn.), 1949.

831. LORD, EDITH ELIZABETH. *The Influence of Negative and Positive Rapport Conditions on Rorschach Performance.* Doctor's thesis, University of Southern California (Los Angeles, Calif.), 1949. (*Abstracts of Dissertations....1949, 1950*, pp. 88-91.)

832. McCAMBELL, ROBERT H. "Reading Others Through the Rorschach," pp. 144-8. In *Claremont College Reading Conference, Fourteenth Yearbook, 1949: Conference Theme: The Problems and Techniques Involved in Reading Social Relationships.* Claremont, Calif.: Claremont College Curriculum Laboratory, 1949. Pp. viii, 101. Paper. *

833. McCANDLESS, BOYD ROWDEN. "The Rorschach as a Predictor of Academic Success." *J Appl Psychol* 33:43-50 F '49. * (*PA* 23:3915)

834. MACE, NORMAN C.; KOFF, SALMON A.; CHELNEK, IRVING; AND GARFIELD, SOL L. "Diagnostic Problems in Early Schizophrenia." *J Nerv & Mental Dis* 110:336-46 O '49. * (*PA* 24:2715)

835. McFATE, MARGUERITE Q., AND ORR, FRANCES G. "Through Adolescence With the Rorschach." *Rorsch Res Exch & J Proj Tech* 13:302-19 S '49. * (*PA* 24:3111)

836. McGOVERN, JOSEPH D. *Validity of Rorschach Components as Measures of Intellectual Efficiency in the Psychoneuroses.* Master's thesis, Catholic University of America (Washington, D.C.), 1949. (*PA* 24:832, title only)

837. McREYNOLDS, PAUL. "The Rorschach Concept Evaluation

Technique." Abstract. *Am Psychol* 4:270 Jl '49. * (*PA* 23:6216, title only)

838. McREYNOLDS, PAUL W. *Development and Evaluation of a New Rorschach Technique.* Doctor's thesis, Stanford University (Stanford, Calif.), 1949. (*PA* 25:5344, title only)

839. MATHIEU-FORTIN, CLAIRE. "L'Usage du Test Rorschach dans L'Etude Anthropologique d'une Societe Paysanne." Includes English abstract. *Can J Psychol* 3:226-30 D '49. * (*PA* 24:3166)

840. MERCER, MARGARET. "Diagnostic Testing in Two Cases of Schizophrenic Depression." *J Psychol* 28:147-60 Jl '49. * (*PA* 24:712)

841. MEYER, MORTIMER M. "Integration of Test Results With Clinical Observations: A Diagnostic Case Study." *Rorsch Res Exch & J Proj Tech* 13:325-40 S '49. * (*PA* 24:3202)

842. MILTON, E. OHMER, JR. *The Influence of Varied Experimental Sets Upon Certain Rorschach Variables: I, Stability of the Human Movement Variable.* Doctor's thesis, University of Michigan (Ann Arbor, Mich.), 1949.

843. MILTON, E. OHMER, JR. *The Influence of Varied Experimental Sets Upon Certain Rorschach Variables: II, Stability of the Human Movement Variable.* Doctor's thesis, University of Michigan (Ann Arbor, Mich.), 1950. Abstract: *Microfilm Abstracts* 10:127-8 no 1 '50. * (*PA* 24:5873, title only)

844. MORRIS, WOODROW WILBERT. *The Prediction of Personality Attributes by Means of the Rorschach Method.* Doctor's thesis, University of Michigan (Ann Arbor, Mich.), 1949. Abstract: *Microfilm Abstracts* 9:176-7 no 3 '50. (*PA* 24:4611, title only)

845. NEWTON, RICHARD LEE. *A Comparison of the Rorschach Test Records of Far Advanced Tuberculosis Patients With Those of Minimally and Moderately Advanced Tuberculosis Patients.* Master's thesis, University of Pittsburgh (Pittsburgh, Pa.), 1949.

846. OSBORNE, R. T., AND SANDERS, WILMA B. "Multiple-Choice Rorschach Responses of College Achievers and Non-Achievers." *Ed & Psychol Meas* 9:685-91 w '49. * (*PA* 26:2976)

847. PALMER, JAMES O. "Two Approaches to Rorschach Validation." Abstract. *Am Psychol* 4:270-1 Jl '49. * (*PA* 23:6219, title only)

848. PEDIGO, LOUISE. *Creative Writing and the Rorschach Test.* Doctor's thesis, Stanford University (Stanford, Calif.), 1949. (*PA* 25:5184, title only)

849. POSER, ERNEST G. *Personality Factors in Patients With Duodenal Ulcer: A Rorschach Study.* Master's thesis, Queen's University (Kingston, Ont., Canada), 1949.

850. PRINCE, SIDNEY DAVID. *A Comparative Study of Personality Characteristics in Bronchial Asthma and Peptic Ulcer Patients as Revealed by the Rorschach Test.* Doctor's thesis, University of Southern California (Los Angeles, Calif.), 1949. (*Abstracts of Dissertations....1949, 1950*, pp. 92-5.)

851. RABIN, ALBERT, AND GEISER, EUGENE. "Rorschach Checks on 'False Positives' of the Cornell Selectee Index Records of Student Nurses." *J General Psychol* 40:59-62 Ja '49. * (*PA* 23:3759)

852. RABIN, ALBERT I. "Statistical Problems Involved in Rorschach Patterning." Abstract. *Biometrics* 5:77-8 Mr '49. * (*PA* 23:3760)

853. RAMZY, I., AND PICKARD, P. M. "A Study in the Reliability of Scoring the Rorschach Ink Blot Test." *J General Psychol* 40:3-10 Ja '49. * (*PA* 23:3760)

854. RASHKIS, HAROLD A. "Projective Techniques as Psychotherapy." *J Clin Psychol* 5:418-21 O '49. * (*PA* 24:3756)

855. REECE, MICHAEL MAURICIO. *Color Shock in the Rorschach Test: The Effect of Achromatic Reproductions.* Master's thesis, Stanford University (Stanford, Calif.), 1949.

856. REITZELL, JEANNE MANNHEIM. "A Comparative Study of Hysterics, Homosexuals and Alcoholics Using Content Analysis of Rorschach Responses." *Rorsch Res Exch & J Proj Tech* 13:127-41 no 2 '49. * (*PA* 24:2698)

857. RIEGER, AUDREY F. "The Rorschach Test in Industrial Selection." *J Appl Psychol* 33:569-71 D '49. * (*PA* 24:4286)

858. RIEGER, AUDREY F. *The Rorschach Test and Occupational Personalities.* Doctor's thesis, University of Chicago (Chicago, Ill.), 1949. Pp. 96.

859. RIEGER, AUDREY F. "The Rorschach Test and Occupational Personalities." *J Appl Psychol* 33:572-8 D '49. * (*PA* 24:4285)

860. RIOCH, MARGARET J. "The Use of the Rorschach Test in the Assessment of Change in Patients Under Psychotherapy." *Psychiatry* 12:427-34 N '49. * (*PA* 24:3757)

861. ROE, ANNE. "Analysis of Group Rorschachs of Biologists." *Rorsch Res Exch & J Proj Tech* 13:25-43 no 1 '49. * (*PA* 24:1524)

862. ROE, ANNE. "Psychological Examinations of Eminent Biologists." *J Consult Psychol* 13:225-46 Ag '49. * (*PA* 24:1525)

863. ROSENZWEIG, SAUL; WITH THE COLLABORATION OF KATE LEVINE KOGAN. *Psychodiagnosis: An Introduction to Tests in the Clinical Practice of Psychodynamics*, pp. 115-39. New York: Grune & Stratton, Inc., 1949. Pp. xii, 380. * (*PA* 23:3761)

864. SANAI, M., AND PICKARD, P. M. "The Relation Between Politico-Economic Radicalism and Certain Traits of Personality." *J Social Psychol* 30:217-27 N '49. * (*PA* 24:4004)

865. SAPPENFIELD, BERT R., AND BUKER, SAMUEL L. "Validity of the Rorschach 8-9-10 Per Cent as an Indicator of Re-

sponsiveness to Color." *J Consult Psychol* 13:268–71 Ag '49. * (*PA* 24:1206)

866. SARASON, SEYMOUR B. "The Rorschach Test," pp. 223–52. In his *Psychological Problems in Mental Deficiency.* New York: Harper & Brothers, 1949. Pp. xi, 366. *

867. SCHERER, ISIDOR W. "The Psychological Scores of Mental Patients in an Individual and Group Testing Situation." *J Clin Psychol* 5:405–8 O '49. * (*PA* 24:3740)

868. SCHMEIDLER, GERTRUDE R. "Personality Correlates of ESP as Shown by Rorschach Studies." *J Parapsychol* 13:23–31 Mr '49. * (*PA* 24:526)

869. SCHMIDT, HERMANN O. "A Case of Folie A Deux." *J Abn & Social Psychol* 44:402–10 Jl '49. * (*PA* 24:1361)

870. SCHMIDT, HERMANN O. "The Rorschach Test in a Case of a Paranoid Reaction." *J Consult Psychol* 13:134–43 Ap '49. * (*PA* 23:4933)

871. SCHUMER, FLORENCE C. *Some Behavioral Correlations of Rorschach Human Movement Responses.* Doctor's thesis, Yale University (New Haven, Conn.), 1949.

872. SCHWARTZ, MILTON M. *The Relationships Between Projective Test Scoring Categories and Activity Preferences.* Doctor's thesis, New York University (New York, N.Y.), 1949.

873. SCOLLON, ROBERT. *A Study to Determine the Effect of Popular Information About the Rorschach Test on Test Results.* Master's thesis, Pennsylvania State College (State College, Pa.), 1949. (*PA* 24:5563, title only)

874. SEN, AMYA. *A Study of the Rorschach Test.* Doctor's thesis, University of London (London, England), 1949. Abstract: *Brit J Ed Psychol* 19:142–3 Je '49. *

875. SINGER, ERWIN. *Personality Structure of Chronic Alcoholics.* Doctor's thesis, New York University (New York, N.Y.), 1949. Abstract: *Microfilm Abstracts* 10:153–4 no 2 '50. (*PA* 25:448, title only)

876. SMITH, DOROTHEA M. *An Experimental Analysis of Human Movement on the Rorschach Test.* Master's thesis, University of Pittsburgh (Pittsburgh, Pa.), 1949. (*PA* 23:3002, title only)

877. SMITH, HENRY CLAY. "Psychometric Checks on Hypotheses Derived From Sheldon's Work on Physique and Temperament." *J Personality* 17:310–20 Mr '49. * (*PA* 25:2916)

878. STEIN, MORRIS I. *Personality Factors in the Temporal Development of Rorschach Responses.* Doctor's thesis, Harvard University (Cambridge, Mass.), 1949. (*PA* 25:5785, title only)

879. STEIN, MORRIS I. "Personality Factors Involved in the Temporal Development of Rorschach Responses." *Rorsch Res Exch & J Proj Tech* 13:355–414 D '49. (*PA* 24:3742)

880. STEINBERG, ARTHUR. *An Experimental Investigation of the Relation of Galvanic Skin Response to Rorschach Shock.* Doctor's thesis, Boston University (Boston, Mass.), 1949. (*PA* 24:841, title only)

881. STEISEL, I. *An Experimental Investigation of the Relationships Between Some Measures of the Rorschach Test and Certain Measures of Suggestibility.* Doctor's thesis, University of Iowa (Iowa City, Iowa), 1949.

882. STEPHENSON, WILLIAM. "A Statistical Approach to Typology." Abstract. *Biometrics* 5:78–9 Mr '49. *

883. SUPER, DONALD E. *Appraising Vocational Fitness By Means of Psychological Tests,* pp. 516–24. New York: Harper & Brothers, 1949. Pp. xxiii, 727. * (*PA* 24:2130)

884. TATOM, MARY H. *Relationships Between Wechsler-Bellevue Sub-Test Scores and Certain Rorschach Test Factors in Clinical Patients.* Master's thesis, Catholic University of America (Washington, D.C.), 1949. (*PA* 24:842, title only)

885. THOMPSON, GRACE M. "Personality Factors Characterizing the Achieving College Student as Revealed by the Rorschach: A Follow-Up Study." Abstract. *Am Psychol* 4:388–9 S '49. * (*PA* 24:2079, title only)

886. TUCKER, JOHN. *The Rorschach Movement Factor in 100 Male-Neurotic Veterans.* Master's thesis, Pennsylvania State College (State College, Pa.), 1949. (*PA* 24:5571, title only)

887. WATROUS, BLANCHE G. *A Personality Study of Ojibwa Children.* Doctor's thesis, Northwestern University (Evanston, Ill.), 1949. (*Summaries of Doctoral Dissertations....June–September 1949,* 1950, pp. 139–41.)

888. WELLISCH, E. "Auditory, Olfactory-Gustatory and Thermic Rorschach Responses." *J Mental Sci* 95:667–72 Jl '49. * (*PA* 24:1894)

889. WELLISCH, E. "The Rorschach Method as an Aid to the Psychotherapy of an Asthmatic Child." *Brit J Med Psychol* 22:72–87 pts 1–2 '49. * (*PA* 24:5995)

890. WELLISCH, E. "A Rorschach Study in Folie à Deux of Mother and Son." *J Mental Sci* 95:467–76 Ap '49. * (*PA* 24:286)

891. WELLISCH, E. "The Use of Projective Paintings in the Rorschach Method." *Brit J Med Psychol* 22:66–71 pts 1–2 '49. * (*PA* 24:5889)

892. WHEELER, WILLIAM M. *An Analysis of Rorschach Indices of Male Homosexuality as Compared With Clinical Data.* Doctor's thesis, University of California (Los Angeles, Calif.), 1949.

893. WHEELER, WILLIAM MARSHALL. "An Analysis of Rorschach Indices of Male Homosexuality." *Rorsch Res Exch & J Proj Tech* 13:97–126 no 2 '49. * (*PA* 24:2701)

894. WITTENBORN, J. R. "Certain Rorschach Response Categories and Mental Abilities." *J Appl Psychol* 33:330–8 Ag '49. * (*PA* 24:2615)

895. WITTENBORN, J. R. "A Factor Analysis of Discrete Responses to the Rorschach Ink Blots." *J Consult Psychol* 13:335–40 O '49. * (*PA* 24:2616)

896. WITTENBORN, J. R. "Statistical Tests of Certain Rorschach Assumptions: Analyses of Discrete Responses." *J Consult Psychol* 13:257–67 Ag '49. * (*PA* 24:1211)

897. WITTENBORN, J. R., AND SARASON, SEYMOUR B. "Exceptions to Certain Rorschach Criteria of Pathology." *J Consult Psychol* 13:21–7 F '49. * (*PA* 23:3764)

898. ZUCKER, LUISE. "The Use of the Rorschach Test in an Out-Patient Clinic." *Am J Psychother* 3:34–45 Ja '49. * (*PA* 23:4848)

899. ZULLIGER, HANS. "Psycho-Analysis and Ink-Blot Test." Abstract. *Int J Psycho-Analysis* 30:208 pt 3 '49. * (*PA* 25:3196, title only)

900. ABRAMSON, LEONARD S. *The Effects of Experimentally Induced Sets With Regard to Area on the Rorschach Test Results.* Doctor's thesis, University of Pittsburgh (Pittsburgh, Pa.), 1950. (*PA* 24:5536, title only) (*Abstracts of Doctoral Dissertations....1950,* 1951, pp. 239–44.)

901. AX, ALBERT F. *The Effect of Combat Fatigue on Imaginal Processes: An Evaluation of Leo Alexander's Rorschach Tests on Flying Personnel.* Doctor's thesis, Harvard University (Cambridge, Mass.), 1950. (*PA* 25:5751, title only)

902. BALLOCH, J. C. *An Experimental Investigation of the Effect of the Degree of Shading Contrast in Ink-Blots on Verbal and Physiological Responses.* Doctor's thesis, Michigan State College (East Lansing, Mich.), 1950.

903. BARNES, T. CUNLIFFE. "Electroencephalographic Validation of the Rorschach, Hunt and Bender Gestalt Tests." Abstract. *Am Psychol* 5:322 Jl '50. * (*PA* 25:1088, title only)

904. BARNETT, IRVING. *The Influence of Color and Shading on the Rorschach Test.* Doctor's thesis, University of Pittsburgh (Pittsburgh, Pa.), 1950. (*Abstracts of Doctoral Dissertations....1950,* 1951, pp. 251–5.) (*PA* 25:4047, title only)

905. BARON, SAMUEL. *The Constancy of Human Movement and Color Responses in the Rorschach Test.* Doctor's thesis, New York University (New York, N.Y.), 1950. Abstract: *Microfilm Abstracts* 10:212–4 no 3 '50. *

906. BECK, SAMUEL J.; RABIN, ALBERT I.; THIESEN, WARREN G.; MOLISH, HERMAN; AND THETFORD, WILLIAM N. "The Normal Personality as Projected in the Rorschach Test." *J Psychol* 30:241–98 O '50. * (*PA* 25:3157)

907. BELLAK, LEOPOLD. "The Rorschach Test," pp. 529–32. In *Progress in Neurology and Psychiatry: An Annual Review, Vol. V.* Edited by E. A. Spiegel. New York: Grune & Stratton, Inc., 1950. Pp. xiv, 621. * (*PA* 24:1286)

908. BENTON, ARTHUR L. "The Experimental Validation of the Rorschach Test." *Brit J Med Psychol* 23:45–58 pts 1–2 '50. * (*PA* 25:4558)

909. BIALICK, IRVING. *A Method of Applying Clinical Judgment to Problems of Rorschach Validation: The Quality of Rorschach Whole Responses and Intelligence.* Master's thesis, University of Pittsburgh (Pittsburgh, Pa.), 1950.

910. BLAKE, ROBERT R., AND WILSON, GLEN P., JR. "Perceptual Selectivity in Rorschach Determinants as a Function of Depressive Tendencies." *J Abn & Social Psychol* 45:459–72 Jl '50. * (*PA* 25:142)

911. BOLIN, BYRON J. *The Relationship of Duration of Birth to Childhood Anxieties as Reflected in the Rorschach Test.* Doctor's thesis, University of Kentucky (Louisville, Ky.), 1950. (*PA* 25:4054, title only)

912. BRADFIELD, ANNE FREDERIKSEN. *Predicting the Success in Training of Graduate Students in School Administration.* Doctor's thesis, Stanford University (Stanford, Calif.), 1950. (*Abstracts of Dissertations....1949–50,* 1950, pp. 294–7.)

913. BRODY, ABRAHAM BARNET. *A Factorial Study of Intellectual Functioning in Normal and Abnormal Adults.* Doctor's thesis, Columbia University (New York, N.Y.), 1950. Abstract: *Microfilm Abstracts* 11:445–6 no 2 '51. (*PA* 26:2171, title only.)

914. BROWN, MALCOLM; BRESNAHAN, T. J.; CHALKE, F. C. R.; PETERS, BARBARA; POSER, E. G.; AND TOUGAS, R. V. "Personality Factors in Duodenal Ulcer." *Psychosom Med* 12:1–5 Ja–F '50. * (*PA* 24:6458)

915. BUHLER, CHARLOTTE. "The Concept of Integration and the Rorschach Test as a Measurement of Personality Integration." *J Proj Tech* 14:315–9 S '50. * (*PA* 25:4417)

916. CARP, ABRAHAM L., AND SHAVZIN, ARTHUR R. "The Susceptibility to Falsification of the Rorschach Psychodiagnostic Technique." *J Consult Psychol* 14:230–3 Je '50. * (*PA* 25:356)

917. CARP, FRANCES MERCHANT. "Psychological Constriction on Several Projective Tests." *J Consult Psychol* 14:268–75 Ag '50. * (*PA* 25:2327)

918. CASS, WILLIAM A., JR. *Quantitative Rorschach Patterns: A Methodological Study.* Doctor's thesis, Stanford University (Stanford, Calif.), 1950.

919. CASSEL, RUSSELL N. *An Experimental Investigation of the "Reality-Strata" of Certain Objectively Defined Groups of Individuals by Use of the Level of Aspiration Technique.* Doctor's thesis, University of Southern California (Los Angeles, Calif.), 1950. (*Abstracts of Dissertations....1950,* 1951, pp. 288–90.)

920. CLAYTON, THOMAS E. *The Personality Adjustment Status of Teachers in Relation to Evaluation by Pupils.* Doctor's thesis, University of Southern California (Los Angeles, Calif.), 1950. (*Abstracts of Dissertations....1950,* 1951, pp. 291–4.)

921. CLEVELAND, SIDNEY EARL. *The Relationship Between Examiner Anxiety and Subjects' Rorschach Scores.* Doctor's thesis, University of Michigan (Ann Arbor, Mich.), 1950. Abstract: *Microfilm Abstracts* 11:415–6 no 2 '51. (*PA* 26:2172, title only)

922. COUNTS, ROBERT M., AND MENSH, IVAN N. "Personality Characteristics in Hypnotically-Induced Hostility." *J Clin Psychol* 6:325–30 O '50. * (*PA* 25:7939)

923. COX, S. M. "The Rorschach Test in Children," p. 50. Abstract. In *Proceedings and Papers of the Twelfth International Congress of Psychology Held at the University of Edinburgh, July 23rd to 29th, 1948.* Edinburgh, Scotland: Oliver & Boyd Ltd., 1950. Pp. xxviii, 152. Paper. *

924. CRONBACH, LEE J. "Studies of the Group Rorschach in Relation to Success in the College of the University of Chicago." *J Ed Psychol* 41:65–82 F '50. * (*PA* 24:4844)

925. CROSBY, MARION JOSEPHINE. *Personality Adjustment, Academic Achievement and Job Satisfaction.* Doctor's thesis, Columbia University (New York, N.Y.), 1950. Abstract: *Microfilm Abstracts* 10:99–101 no 3 '50. * (*PA* 25:4819, title only)

926. CUMMINGS, S. THOMAS. *An Investigation of the Reliability and Validity of Judgments of Adjustment Inferred From Rorschach Test Performance.* Doctor's thesis, University of Pittsburgh (Pittsburgh, Pa.), 1950 (*Abstracts of Doctoral Dissertations....1950,* 1951, pp. 273–81.) (*PA* 25:4059, title only)

927. DAVIDSON, G. M., AND CONKEY, RUTH C. "The Rorschach Test and the Questions of 'Prognosis' and 'Recovery' in Syphilitic Meningo-Encephalitis." *Psychiatric Q* 24:243–67 Ap '50. * (*PA* 26:6481)

928. DAVIDSON, HELEN H. "A Measure of Adjustment Obtained From the Rorschach Protocol." *J Proj Tech* 14:31–8 Mr '50. * (*PA* 25:1092)

929. DILLON, KATHERINE M. *Rating Adolescent Adjustment by Rorschach and Casework Methods.* Master's thesis, Smith College School for Social Work (Northampton, Mass.), 1950. Abstract: *Smith Col Studies Social Work* 21:153 F '51. *

930. DÖRKEN, HERBERT, JR. "The Ink Blot Test as a Brief Projective Technique: A Preliminary Report." *J Am Orthopsychiatry* 20:828–33 O '50. * (*PA* 25:4976)

931. DREGER, RALPH MASON. *Some Personality Correlates of Religious Attitudes as Determined by Projective Techniques.* Doctor's thesis, University of Southern California (Los Angeles, Calif.), 1950. (*Abstracts of Dissertations....1950,* 1951, pp. 202–5.) (*PA* 26:170, title only)

932. DUBROVNER, RAPHAEL J.; VON LACKUM, WILLIAM J.; AND JOST, HUDSON. "A Study of the Effect of Color on Productivity and Reaction Time in the Rorschach Test." *J Clin Psychol* 6:331–6 O '50. * (*PA* 25:8081)

933. DULSKY, STANLEY G., AND KROUT, MAURICE H. "Predicting Promotion Potential on the Basis of Psychological Tests." *Personnel Psychol* 3:345–51 au '50. * (*PA* 25:3452)

934. EICHLER, ROBERT M. *The Influence of a Stress-Produced Anxiety on Alleged Rorschach Indices of Anxiety.* Doctor's thesis, University of Iowa (Iowa City, Iowa), 1950.

935. ELLIS, ROBERT W., AND BROWN, GLADYS G. "The Nature of Rorschach Responses From Pulmonary Tuberculosis Patients." *J Clin Psychol* 6:298–300 Jl '50. * (*PA* 25:1972)

936. ERWIN, EDMOND FRANCIS. *Objective and Projective Measures of Withdrawal Behavior.* Doctor's thesis, Columbia University (New York, N.Y.), 1950. Abstract: *Microfilm Abstracts* 11:418–9 no 2 '51. (*PA* 26:2275, title only)

937. FARLEY, ROBERT EDWARD. *Rorschach Studies in Conversion Hysteria.* Master's thesis, Stanford University (Stanford, Calif.), 1950.

938. FEIN, LEAH GOLD. "Rorschach Signs of Homosexuality in Male College Students." *J Clin Psychol* 6:248–53 Jl '50. * (*PA* 25:1895)

939. FICCA, SYLVESTER C. *Relationship of "Autonomic" Blood Pressure Pattern Types of Subject's Performance on the Wechsler-Bellevue and the Rorschach Test.* Doctor's thesis, Pennsylvania State College (State College, Pa.), 1950. (*Abstracts of Doctoral Dissertations....1950,* 1951, pp. 398–400.) (*PA* 26:2177, title only)

940. FISHER, SEYMOUR. *Patterns of Personality Rigidity and Some of Their Determinants.* American Psychological Association, Psychological Monographs: General and Applied. Vol. 64, No. 1, Whole No. 307. Washington, D.C.: the Association, Inc., 1950. Pp. v, 48. Paper. * (*PA* 24:6255)

941. FISHER, SEYMOUR, AND SUNUKJIAN, HELEN. "Intellectual Disparities in a Normal Group and Their Relationship to Emotional Disturbance." *J Clin Psychol* 6:288–90 Jl '50. * (*PA* 25:1786)

942. FONDA, CHARLES P. *The Nature and Meaning of the Rorschach White Space Response.* Doctor's thesis, Johns Hopkins University (Baltimore, Md.), 1950. (*PA* 25:629)

943. FONT, MARION. "Some Clinical Applications of the Rorschach Technique in Cases of Borderline Deficiency." *Am J Mental Def* 54:507–11 Ap '50. * (*PA* 25:359)

944. FORER, BERTRAM R. "The Latency of Latent Schizophrenia." *J Proj Tech* 14:297–302 S '50. * (*PA* 25:4724)

945. FREEMAN, FRANK S. *The Theory and Practice of Psychological Testing,* pp. 402–17. New York: Henry Holt & Co., 1950. Pp. xxiii, 518. * (London: Sir Isaac Pitman & Sons, Ltd., 1951.) (*PA* 24:4344)

946. FRIEDMAN, HOWARD. *Perceptual Regression in Schizophrenia, An Analysis by Means of the Rorschach Test.* Doctor's thesis, Clark University (Worcester, Mass.), 1950. (*Abstracts of Dissertations & Theses....1950,* pp. 37–40.) (*PA* 25:5494, title only)

947. GIBBY, ROBERT GWYN. *The Influence of Varied Experimental Sets Upon Certain Rorschach Variables: I, Stability of the Intellectual Variables.* Doctor's thesis, University of Michigan (Ann Arbor, Mich.), 1950. Abstract: *Microfilm Abstracts* 10:125–6 no 1 '50. * (*PA* 24:5866, title only)

948. GLAD, DONALD D., AND HAMMACK, BARBARA W. "An Interest Validation and Normative Study of the Rorschach and TAT with Schizophrenia." Abstract. *J Colo-Wyo Acad Sci* 4:65–6 O '50. * (*PA* 25:5495, title only)

949. GLIK, EDWARD E. "The Relationship of Emotional Control as Measured on the Rorschach to Morally Dichotomous Thinking." Abstract. *Am Psychol* 5:301 Jl '50. * (*PA* 25:911, title only)

950. GLUECK, SHELDON, AND GLUECK, ELEANOR. *Unraveling Juvenile Delinquency.* Foreword by Erwin N. Griswold. New York: Commonwealth Fund, 1950. Pp. xv, 399. (London: Oxford University Press.) (*PA* 25:2578)

951. GOLDMAN, GEORGE DAVID. *An Investigation of the Similarities in Personality Structure of Idiopathic Epileptics, Hysterical Convulsives, and Neurological Patients.* Doctor's thesis, New York University (New York, N.Y.), 1950. Abstract: *Microfilm Abstracts* 11:176–7 no 1 '51. * (*PA* 26:2368, title only)

952. GOLDMAN, LEO. *Relationship Between Aptitude Scores and Certain Rorschach Indices.* Doctor's thesis, Columbia University (New York, N.Y.), 1950. Abstract: *Microfilm Abstracts* 11:421–3 no 2 '51. (*PA* 26:2180, title only)

953. GOODMAN, HOWARD W. *An Experimental Investigation of the Affective Value of Color on the Rorschach Test.* Doctor's thesis, University of Pittsburgh (Pittsburgh, Pa.), 1950. (*Abstracts of Doctoral Dissertations....1949, 1950,* pp. 298–304.)

954. GOODMAN, HOWARD W. "An Experimental Investigation of the Affective Value of Color on the Rorschach Test." Abstract. *Am Psychol* 5:321–2 Jl '50. * (*PA* 25:1095, title only)

955. GRASSI, JOSEPH R. "Impairment of Abstract Behavior Following Bilateral Prefrontal Lobotomy." *Psychiatric Q* 24:74–88 Ja '50. * (*PA* 26:6478)

956. HAMLIN, ROY M.; ALBEE, GEORGE W.; AND LELAND, EARL M. "Objective Rorschach 'Signs' for Groups of Normal, Maladjusted and Neuropsychiatric Subjects." *J Consult Psychol* 14:276–82 Ag '50. * (*PA* 25:2457)

957. HANEY, HAROLD RUSSELL. *Motives Implied by the Act of Stuttering as Revealed by Prolonged Experimental Projection.* Doctor's thesis, University of Southern California (Los Angeles, Calif.), 1950. (*Abstracts of Dissertations....1950,* 1951, pp. 16–9.) (*PA* 25:8183, title only)

958. HARRIS, FRANK J. "Can Personality Tests Identify Accident-Prone Employees?" *Personnel Psychol* 3:455–9 w '50. * (*PA* 25:3984)

959. HARRIS, LESTER LEE. *A Clinical Study of Nine Stuttering Children in Group Psychotherapy.* Doctor's thesis, University of Southern California (Los Angeles, Calif.), 1950. (*PA* 25:8184, title only)

960. HARROWER, M. R. "Group Techniques for the Rorschach Test," pp. 146–84. (*PA* 25:2458) In *Projective Psychology: Clinical Approaches to the Total Personality.* Edited by Lawrence Edwin Abt and Leopold Bellak. New York: Alfred A. Knopf, Inc., 1950. Pp. xvii. 485, xiv. *

961. HERTZ, MARGUERITE R. "The First International Rorschach Conference." *J Proj Tech* 14:39–51 Mr '50. * (*PA* 25:711)

962. HIRE, A. WILLIAM. "A Group Administration of the Rorschach: Method and Results." *J Consult Psychol* 14:496–9 D '50. * (*PA* 26:918)

963. HOLTZMAN, WAYNE H. "Validation Studies of the Rorschach Test: Impulsiveness in the Normal Superior Adult." *J Clin Psychol* 6:348–51 O '50. * (*PA* 25:8096)

964. HOLTZMAN, WAYNE H. "Validation Studies of the Rorschach Test: Shyness and Gregariousness in the Normal Superior Adult." *J Clin Psychol* 6:343–7 O '50. * (*PA* 25:8097)

965. HOLTZMAN, WAYNE HAROLD. *The Rorschach Test in the Assessment of the Normal Superior Adult.* Doctor's thesis, Stanford University (Stanford, Calif.), 1950. (*Abstracts of Dissertations....1949–50,* 1950, pp. 215–8.)

966. HOLZBERG, JULES D., AND WEXLER, MURRAY. "The Predictability of Schizophrenic Performance on the Rorschach Test." *J Consult Psychol* 14:395–9 O '50. * (*PA* 25:4729)

967. HOWARD, THOMAS WILLIAM. *The Hughes Diagnostic Technique Applied to Rorschach Protocols: A Reliability Study on Neuropsychiatric Patients.* Master's thesis, Tulane University (New Orleans, La.), 1950. (*Abstracts of Dissertations and Theses 1950,* p. 120.)

968. HUTT, M. L.; GIBBY, R.; MILTON, E. O.; AND POTTHARST, K. "The Effect of Varied Experimental 'Sets' Upon Rorschach Test Performance." *J Proj Tech* 14:181–7 Je '50. * (*PA* 25:4572)

969. KALDEGG, ANN, AND O'NEILL, DESMOND. "Rorschach Pattern in Duodenal Ulcer." *J Mental Sci* 96:190–8 Ja '50. * (*PA* 25:5404)

970. KATES, SOLIS L. "Objective Rorschach Response Patterns Differentiating Anxiety Reactions From Obsessive-Compulsive Reactions." *J Consult Psychol* 14:226–9 Je '50. * (*PA* 25:365)

971. KATES, SOLIS L. *Rorschach Responses Related to Vocational Interests and Job Satisfaction.* American Psychological Association, Psychological Monographs: General and Applied,

Vol. 64, No. 3, Whole No. 309. Washington, D.C.: the Association, Inc., 1950. Pp. v, 34. Paper. * (PA 25:2689)

972. KATES, SOLIS L. "Rorschach Responses, Strong Blank Scales, and Job Satisfaction Among Policemen." *J Appl Psychol* 34:249–54 Ag '50. * (PA 25:6495)

973. KELLY, E. LOWELL, AND FISKE, DONALD W. "The Prediction of Success in the VA Training Program in Clinical Psychology." *Am Psychol* 5:395–406 Ag '50. * (PA 25:2183)

974. KIMBALL, ALICE JAMES. "Evaluation of Form-Level in the Rorschach." *J Proj Tech* 14:219–44 S '50. * (PA 25:4573)

975. KIMBALL, ALICE JAMES. "History of Form-Level Appraisal in the Rorschach." *J Proj Tech* 14:134–52 Mr '50. * (PA 25:4574)

976. KLEIN, GEORGE S., AND SCHLESINGER, HERBERT J. "Perceptual Attitudes of 'Form-Boundedness' and 'Form-Liability' in Rorschach Responses." Abstract. *Am Psychol* 5:321 Jl '50. * (PA 25:1097, title only)

977. KORNER, ANNELIESE FRIEDSAM. "Theoretical Considerations Concerning the Scope and Limitations of Projective Techniques." *J Abn & Social Psychol* 45:619–27 O '50. * (PA 25:2460)

978. LAWRENCE, RAY MARGARET. *An Investigation of Selected Physical, Psychological and Sociological Factors Associated With Migraine and Psychogenic Headache.* Doctor's thesis, New York University (New York, N.Y.), 1950. Abstract: *Microfilm Abstracts* 11:171–2 no 1 '51. * (PA 26:2355)

979. LEVI, JOSEPH. "Rorschach Patterns as a Tool in Predicting Success or Failure in the Rehabilitation of the Physically Handicapped." Abstract. *Am Psychol* 5:320–1 Jl '50. * (PA 25:1223, title only)

980. LEVY, JEANNE R. "Changes in the Galvanic Skin Response Accompanying the Rorschach Test." *J Consult Psychol* 14:128–33 Ap '50. * (PA 24:5871)

981. LINDNER, ROBERT M. "The Content Analysis of the Rorschach Protocol," pp. 75–90. (PA 25:2463) In *Projective Psychology: Clinical Approaches to the Total Personality.* Edited by Lawrence Edwin Abt and Leopold Bellak. New York: Alfred A. Knopf, Inc., 1950. Pp. xvii, 485, xiv. * (PA 25:2445)

982. LORD, EDITH. *Experimentally Induced Variations in Rorschach Performance.* American Psychological Association, Psychological Monographs: General and Applied, Vol. 64, No. 10, Whole No. 316. Washington, D.C.: the Association, Inc., 1950. Pp. v, 34. Paper. * (PA 25:6217)

983. LORD, EDITH. "Two Sets of Rorschach Records Obtained Before and After Brief Psychotherapy." *J Consult Psychol* 14:134–9 Ap '50. * (PA 24:5898)

984. McLEOD, HUGH. "A Rorschach Study With Pre-School Children." *J Proj Tech* 14:453–63 D '50. * (PA 26:3323)

985. MALLINGER, BETTY R. *The Value of the Rorschach Test in Predicting Academic Achievement of Students in the Research Bureau for Retail Training.* Doctor's thesis, University of Pittsburgh (Pittsburgh, Pa.), 1950.

986. MEER, BERNARD, AND SINGER, JEROME L. "A Note on the 'Father' and 'Mother' Cards in the Rorschach Inkblots." *J Consult Psychol* 14:482–4 D '50. * (PA 26:925)

987. MENSH, IVAN NORMAN. "Personality Structure in Folie A Deux." *Am J Orthopsychiatry* 20:806–16 O '50. * (PA 25:5509)

988. MENSH, IVAN NORMAN. "Rorschach Study of the Gifted Child." *J Excep Child* 17:8–14 O '50. *

989. MERCER, MARGARET, AND GIBSON, R. W. "Rorschach Content in Hypnosis: Chronological Age Level Regression." *J Clin Psychol* 6:352–8 O '50. * (PA 25:8104)

990. MILLER, DANIEL R.; SANDERS, RICHARD; AND CLEVELAND, SIDNEY E. "The Relationship Between Examiner Personality and Obtained Rorschach Protocols: An Application of Interpersonal Relations Theory." Abstract. *Am Psychol* 5:322–3 Jl '50. * (PA 25:1101, title only)

991. MILTON, E. OHMER, JR. *The Influence of Varied Experimental Sets Upon Certain Rorschach Variables: II, Stability of the Human Movement Variable.* Doctor's thesis, University of Michigan (Ann Arbor, Mich.), 1950. Abstract. *Microfilm Abstracts* 10:127–8 no 1 '50. * (PA 24:5873, title only)

992. MORRIS, WOODROW WILBERT, AND NICHOLAS, ALMA L. "Intrafamilial Personality Configurations Among Children With Primary Behavior Disorders and Their Parents: A Rorschach Investigation." *J Clin Psychol* 6:309–19 O '50. * (PA 25:8138)

993. MUELLER, PAUL FREDERICK CHARLES. *The Comparability of Scoring and Interpretation on the Rorschach and Behn-Rorschach Tests.* Master's thesis, Stanford University (Stanford, Calif.), 1950.

994. MUNROE, RUTH L. "The Inspection Technique for the Rorschach Protocol," pp. 91–145. (PA 25:2464) In *Projective Psychology: Clinical Approaches to the Total Personality.* Edited by Lawrence Edwin Abt and Leopold Bellak. New York: Alfred A. Knopf, Inc., 1950. Pp. xvii, 485, xiv. *

995. MURRAY, V. F., AND JOSEPH, A. "The Rorschach Test as a Tool in Action Research: A Study of Acculturation Phenomena in a Group of Young Chamorro Women." *J Proj Tech* 14:362–84 D '50. * (PA 26:3362)

996. ODOM, CHARLES L. "A Study of the Time Required to Do a Rorschach Examination." *J Proj Tech* 14:464–8 D '50. * (PA 26:3419)

997. OPPENHEIM, SADI, AND GOLDWASSER, MIRIAM L. "Psy-

chological Report of the Cyprus Psychiatric Mission." *J Proj Tech* 14:245–61 S '50. * (PA 25:4547)

998. OSBORNE, R. TRAVIS, AND SANDERS, WILMA B. "Rorschach Characteristics of Duodenal Ulcer Patients." *J Clin Psychol* 6:258–62 Jl '50. * (PA 25:1977)

999. OSBORNE, R. TRAVIS; SANDERS, WILMA B.; AND GREENE, JAMES E. "The Prediction of Academic Success by Means of 'Weighted' Harrower-Rorschach Responses." *J Clin Psychol* 6:253–8 Jl '50. * (PA 25:2053)

1000. PALMER, BARBARA. *Rorschach Data Associated With Psychiatric Evaluations of Prognostic Personality Factors.* Master's thesis, Vanderbilt University (Nashville, Tenn.), 1950. (Abstracts of Theses....1949–1950, 1950, p. 132.)

1001. PALMER, JAMES O. *Two Approaches to the Validation of a Projective Technique: The Rorschach.* Doctor's thesis, University of California (Berkeley, Calif.), 1950.

1002. PASCAL, G. R.; RUESCH, H. A.; DEVINE, C. A.; AND SUTTELL, B. J. "A Study of Genital Symbols on the Rorschach Test: Presentation of a Method and Results." *J Abn & Social Psychol* 45:286–95 Ap '50. * (PA 24:5874)

1003. PICKERING, WILLIAM DONALD. *A Comparison of Predominant Verbal Levels on the Thematic Apperception Test With the Rorschach Experience Balance.* Doctor's thesis, University of Pittsburgh (Pittsburgh, Pa.), 1950. (Abstracts of Doctoral Dissertations....1950, 1951, pp. 309–16.)

1004. PIOTROWSKI, Z. A. "Principles Underlying the Projective Technics of Personality Measurement." Abstract. *Arch Neurol & Psychiatry* 64:478–9 S '50. * (PA 25:5346, title only)

1005. PIOTROWSKI, ZYGMUNT A. "A Rorschach Compendium, Revised and Enlarged." *Psychiatric Q* 24:543–96 Jl '50. *

1006. PIOTROWSKI, ZYGMUNT A., AND LEWIS, NOLAN D. C. "A Case of Stationary Schizophrenia Beginning in Early Childhood With Remarks on Certain Aspects of Children's Rorschach Records." *Q J Child Behavior* 2:115–39 Ap '50. *

1007. PIOTROWSKI, ZYGMUNT A., AND LEWIS, NOLAN D. C. "An Experimental Rorschach Diagnostic Aid for Some Forms of Schizophrenia." *Am J Psychiatry* 107:360–6 N '50. * (PA 25:6334)

1008. POTTHARST, KARL EDWARD. *The Influence of Varied Experimental Sets Upon Certain Rorschach Variables: III, The Influence of a Complex Set.* Doctor's thesis, University of Michigan (Ann Arbor, Mich.), 1950. Abstract: *Microfilm Abstracts* 10:304–5 no 4 '50. * (PA 25:4582, title only)

1009. RABIN, ALBERT I. "Statistical Problems Involved in Rorschach Patterning." *J Clin Psychol* 6:19–21 Ja '50. * (PA 25:368)

1010. RABIN, ALBERT I., AND BECK, SAMUEL J. "Genetic Aspects of Some Rorschach Factors." *Am J Orthopsychiatry* 20:595–9 Jl '50. * (PA 25:3180)

1011. RANZONI, JANE H.; GRANT, MARGUERITE Q.; AND IVES, VIRGINIA. "Rorschach 'Card-Pull' in a Normal Adolescent Population." *J Proj Tech* 14:107–33 Mr '50. * (PA 25:4585)

1012. RIEMAN, GLENN WALKER. *An Investigation to Determine Which Rorschach Elements Reveal Group Differences Between Neurotic and Ambulatory Schizophrenic Subjects.* Doctor's thesis, University of Pittsburgh (Pittsburgh, Pa.), 1950. (Abstracts of Doctoral Dissertations....1950, 1951, pp. 317–25.)

1013. ROE, ANNE. "Analysis of Group Rorschachs of Physical Scientists." *J Proj Tech* 14:385–98 D '50. * (PA 26:3679)

1014. ROSS, W. DONALD. "Relationships Between Rorschach Interpretations and Clinical Diagnoses." *J Proj Tech* 14:5–14 Mr '50. * (PA 25:1110)

1015. ROSS, W. DONALD, AND BLOCK, STANLEY L. "The Use of Projective Techniques in the Evaluation of Neurosurgical Approaches to Psychiatric Treatment." *J Proj Tech* 14:399–404 D '50. * (PA 26:3446)

1016. ROYAL, ROBERT E. *An Experimental Investigation of the Relationship Between Questionnaire and Rorschach Measures of Introversion.* Doctor's thesis, University of Pittsburgh (Pittsburgh, Pa.), 1950. (Abstracts of Doctoral Dissertations ....1950, 1951, pp. 326–33.) (PA 25:4098, title only)

1017. SACKS, JOSEPH M., AND LEWIN, HERBERT S. "Limitations of the Rorschach as Sole Diagnostic Instrument." *J Consult Psychol* 14:479–81 D '50. * (PA 26:934)

1018. SALFIELD, D. "The Usefulness of the Rorschach Test for Diagnosis, Prognosis, and Epicrisis in Child Guidance Treatment," p. 111. Abstract. In *Proceedings and Papers of the Twelfth International Congress of Psychology Held at the University of Edinburgh, July 23rd to 29th, 1948.* Edinburgh, Scotland: Oliver and Boyd Ltd., 1950. Pp. xxviii, 152. Paper. *

1019. SALFIELD, D. J. "An Attempt at a Numerical Evaluation of Rorschach Test Results." *J General Psychol* 43:305–11 O '50. * (PA 25:5818)

1020. SANAI, M., AND PICKARD, P. M. "Relation Between Political Radicalism and Some Personality Traits," p. 112. Abstract. In *Proceedings and Papers of the Twelfth International Congress of Psychology Held at the University of Edinburgh, July 23rd to 29th, 1948.* Edinburgh, Scotland: Oliver and Boyd Ltd., 1950. Pp. xxviii, 152. Paper. *

1021. SANDERS, JOSEPH ROBERT. *Verbal Concept Formation in Relation to Personal Adjustment.* Doctor's thesis, Columbia University (New York, N.Y.), 1950. Abstract: *Microfilm Abstracts* 11:431–3 no 2 '51. (PA 26:2006, title only)

1022. SANDLER, J. "A Factor Analysis of the Rorschach Test in Adult Mental Patients," p. 112–3. Abstract. In *Proceedings and Papers of the Twelfth International Congress of Psychol-

ogy Held at the University of Edinburgh, July 23rd to 29th, 1948. Edinburgh, Scotland: Oliver & Boyd Ltd., 1950. Pp. xxviii, 152. Paper. *

1023. SANDLER, JOSEPH. *Rorschach Content Analysis.* Doctor's thesis, University of London (London, England), 1950.

1024. SARASON, ESTHER KROOP. *The Discriminatory Value of the Rorschach Test Between Two Etiologically Different, Mentally Defective Groups.* Doctor's thesis, Clark University (Worcester, Mass.), 1950. *(Abstracts of Dissertations and Theses....1950,* pp. 44–8.) (PA 25:5418, title only)

1025. SCHACHTEL, ERNEST G. "Projection and Its Relation to Character Attitudes and Creativity in Kinesthetic Responses: Contributions to an Understanding of Rorschach's Test, IV." *Psychiatry* 13:69–100 F '50. * (PA 24:5259)

1026. SCHACHTEL, ERNEST G. Appendix E, "Some Notes on the Use of the Rorschach Test," pp. 363–85. In *Unraveling Juvenile Delinquency.* By Sheldon Glueck and Eleanor Glueck. Foreword by Erwin N. Griswold. New York: Commonwealth Fund, 1950. Pp. xv, 399. (London: Oxford University Press.) *

1027. SCHAFER, ROY. *Selective Response to Oral Content: A Study of Inter-Function Reliability.* Doctor's thesis, Clark University (Worcester, Mass.), 1950. *(Abstracts of Dissertations and Theses....1950,* pp. 49–52.) (PA 25:5149, title only)

1028. SCHNEIDER, LEONARD I. "Rorschach Validation: Some Methodological Aspects." *Psychol B* 47:493–508 N '50. * (PA 25:3189)

1029. SCHWARTZ, ARTHUR A. "Some Interrelationships Among Four Tests Comprising a Test Battery: A Comparative Study." *J Proj Tech* 14:153–72 Je '50. * (PA 25:4592)

1030. SEN, AMYA. "A Statistical Study of the Rorschach Test." *Brit J Psychol, Stat Sect* 3:21–39 Mr '50. * (PA 24:5260)

1031. SHASKAN, DONALD A.; CONRAD, DOROTHY C.; AND GRANT, J. DOUGLAS. "Prediction of Behavior in Group Psychotherapy From Rorschach Protocols (Preliminary Report)." *Group Psychother* 3:218–30 Ag–D '50. * (PA 25:5375)

1032. SIIPOLA, ELSA M. "The Influence of Color on Reactions to Ink Blots." *J Personality* 18:358–82 Mr '50. * (PA 25:3190)

1033. SIIPOLA, ELSA; KUHNS, FLORENCE; AND TAYLOR, VIVIAN. "Measurement of the Individual's Reactions to Color in Ink Blots." *J Personality* 19:153–71 D '50. * (PA 25:6881)

1034. SINGER, MARTIN. *The Validity of a Multiple-Choice Projective Test in Psychopathological Screening.* American Psychological Association, Psychological Monographs: General and Applied, Vol. 64, No. 8, Whole No. 314. Washington, D.C.: the Association, Inc., 1950. Pp. v, 40. Paper. * (PA 25:6221)

1035. SPANER, FRED E. *An Analysis of the Relationship Between Some Rorschach Test Determinants and Subtest Scores on the Wechsler Bellevue Adult Scale.* Doctor's thesis, Purdue University (Lafayette, Ind.), 1950. (PA 24:4938, title only)

1036. STARER, EMANUEL. *An Analysis of the Type and Direction of Aggression and Sources of Frustration as Shown by the Results of the Rosenzweig Picture-Frustration Study, Rorschach Findings, and Case History for a Group of Anxiety Neurotic and a Group of Paranoid Schizophrenic Patients.* Doctor's thesis, New York University (New York, N.Y.), 1950. Abstract: *Microfilm Abstracts* 11:178–9 no 1 '51. * (PA 26:2342, title only)

1037. STERLING, MAC E. *Color Shock on the Rorschach Test.* Doctor's thesis, University of Kentucky (Louisville, Ky.), 1950. (PA 25:4110, title only)

1038. STEWART, BARBARA MACMICHAEL. *A Study of the Relationship Between Clinical Manifestations of Neurotic Anxiety and Rorschach Test Performance.* Doctor's thesis, University of Southern California (Los Angeles, Calif.), 1950. *(Abstracts of Dissertations....1950,* 1951, pp. 184–7.)

1039. STONE, GIDEON BARTO, II. *A Study of Parent-Child Relationships in Patients With Peptic Ulcer and Bronchial Asthma, as Revealed by Projective Techniques.* Doctor's thesis, University of Southern California (Los Angeles, Calif.), 1950. *(Abstracts of Dissertations....1950,* 1951, pp. 188–91.)

1040. SUTHERLAND, EDWIN H.; SCHROEDER, H. G.; AND TORDELLA, C. L. "Personality Traits and the Alcoholic: A Critique of Existing Studies." *Q J Studies Alcohol* 11:547–61 D '50. * (PA 25:5452)

1041. THEAMAN, MILTON. *The Performance of Post-Traumatics, Post-Traumatic Epileptics, and Idiopathic Epileptics on Psychological Tests: A Study of the Relative Influence of Symptom and Etiology Upon Psychological Performance.* Doctor's thesis, New York University (New York, N.Y.), 1950. Abstract: *Microfilm Abstracts* 10:232–3 no 3 '50. *

1042. THOMPSON, GRACE M. "Rorschach Populars as a Function of Length of Record." Abstract. *Am Psychol* 5:470 S '50. * (PA 25:4595, title only)

1043. THOMPSON, GRACE M. "Rorschach 'Populars' as a Function of the Length of Record." *J Consult Psychol* 14:287–9 Ag '50. * (PA 25:2469)

1044. TUCKER, J. E. "Rorschach Human and Other Movement Responses in Relation to Intelligence." *J Consult Psychol* 14:283–9 Ag '50. * (PA 25:2470)

1045. ULETT, GEORGE. *Rorschach Introductory Manual: A Primer for the Clinical Psychiatric Worker: With Interpretative Diagram to Permit Clinical Use While Learning the Ink-Blot Technique.* St. Louis, Mo.: Educational Publishers, Inc., 1950. Pp. 48. * (PA 24:5262)

1046. ULETT, GEORGE A.; MARTIN, DONALD W.; AND MCBRIDE, JOHN R. "The Rorschach Findings in a Case of Suicide." *Am J Orthopsychiatry* 20:817–27 O '50. * (PA 25:5453)

1047. VALENTINE, MAX, AND ROBIN, ASHLEY A. "Aspects of Thematic Apperception Testing: Paranoid Schizophrenia." *J Mental Sci* 96:869–88 O '50. * (PA 25:5524)

1048. WALKER, ROBERT G. *A Comparison of Clinical Manifestations of Hostility With Rorschach and MAPS Test Performances.* Doctor's thesis, University of Southern California (Los Angeles, Calif.), 1950. *(Abstracts of Dissertations....1950,* 1951, pp. 196–7.)

1049. WATSON, DONALD T. *An Evaluation of the Personality of Neurotic Patients with Migraine Symptoms by Means of the Rorschach Test.* Master's thesis, Catholic University of America (Washington, D.C.), 1950. (PA 25:4112, title only)

1050. WELLISCH, E. "Active Imagination During the Use of the Rorschach Method." *J Ment Sci* 96:476–83 Ap '50. * (PA 25:5350)

1051. WENTWORTH-ROHR, IVAN. *A Study in the Differential Diagnosis of Idiopathic and Symptomatic Epilepsy Through Psychological Tests.* Doctor's thesis, New York University (New York, N.Y.), 1950. Abstract: *Microfilm Abstracts* 11:180–1 no 1 '51. * (PA 26:2374, title only)

1052. WHEELER, WILLIAM MARSHALL. "The Internal Structure of Three Clinical Instruments." Abstract. *Am Psychol* 5:470 S '50. * (PA 25:4599, title only)

1053. WHITE, MARY ALICE, AND TANZER, MIRIAM. "Rorschach Differences and Electroshock: A Case Report." *Psychol Service Center J* 2:46–54 Mr '50. * (PA 25:6224)

1054. WILSON, DONALD MURRAY. *A Study of the Personalities of Stuttering Children and Their Parents as Revealed Through Projection Tests.* Doctor's thesis, University of Southern California (Los Angeles, Calif.), 1950. (PA 25:8189)

1055. WILSON, GLEN P., JR. "Techniques for Obtaining a Constant Number of Responses in Rorschach Protocols." Abstract. *Am Psychol* 5:282 Jl '50. * (PA 25:1115, title only)

1056. WILSON, GLEN P., JR., AND BLAKE, ROBERT R. "A Methodological Problem in Beck's Organizational Concept." *J Consult Psychol* 14:20–4 F '50. * (PA 24:4121)

1057. WISHNER, JULIUS. *Neurosis, Anxiety, and Tension: An Exploratory Study of the Relationship of Physiological and Rorschach Measures.* Doctor's thesis, Northwestern University (Evanston, Ill.), 1950. *(Summaries of Doctoral Dissertations....June–September 1950,* 1951, pp. 612–3.)

1058. WITTENBORN, J. R. "A Factor Analysis of Rorschach Scoring Categories." *J Consult Psychol* 14:261–7 Ag '50. * (PA 25:2472)

1059. WITTENBORN, J. R. "Level of Mental Health as a Factor in the Implications of Rorschach Scores." *J Consult Psychol* 14:469–72 D '50. * (PA 26:937)

1060. WITTENBORN, J. R. "Statistical Tests of Certain Rorschach Assumptions: The Internal Consistency of Scoring Categories." *J Consult Psychol* 14:1–19 F '50. * (PA 24:4122)

1061. YOUNG, REGINALD J. "The Rorschach Diagnosis and Interpretation of Involutional Melancholia." *Am J Psychiatry* 106:748–9 Ap '50. * (PA 25:1961)

1062. ZELEN, SEYMOUR L. "Level of Aspiration and Rigidity on the Rorschach Compared With Operationally Determined Measures." *Am Psychol* 5:470 S '50. * (PA 25:4603, title only)

1063. ZUBIN, JOSEPH. *Quantitative Techniques and Methods in Abnormal Psychology,* Chaps. 11, 13, 14A, 14B, 15. New York, N.Y.: Columbia University Bookstore, 1950. Pp. 220. Paper, mimeographed. * (PA 25:6933)

1064. ZUCKER, LUISE. "The Clinical Significance of the Mosaic and Rorschach Methods." *Am J Psychother* 4:473–87 Jl '50. *

1065. ZULLIGER, HANS. "Personality Dynamics as Revealed in the Rorschach and Behn Test of a 15-Year-Old Girl." Translated by V. J. Lowenbach. *J Proj Tech* 14:52–60 Mr '50. * (PA 25:1199)

1066. ZULLIGER, HANS. "Psycho-Analysis and the Form-Interpretation Test." Translated by Joseph Sandler. *Int J Psycho-Analysis* 31:152–5 pts 1–2 '50. * (PA 25:2474)

1067. ABRAMSON, LEONARD S. "The Influence of Set for Area on the Rorschach Test Results." *J Consult Psychol* 15:337–42 Ag '51. * (PA 26:6245)

1068. ADCOCK, CYRIL J. "A Factorial Approach to Rorschach Interpretation." *J General Psychol* 44:261–72 Ap '51. * (PA 26:4802)

1069. AINSWORTH, MARY D. "Some Problems of Validation of Projective Techniques." *Brit J Med Psychol* 24:151–61 S 11 '51. * (PA 26:2166)

1070. ALDEN, PRISCILLA, AND BENTON, ARTHUR L. "Relationship of Sex of Examiner to Incidence of Rorschach Responses With Sexual Content." *J Proj Tech* 15:231–4 Je '51. * (PA 26:3395)

1071. ALLEN, ROBERT M. "The Influence of Color in the Rorschach Test on Reaction Time in a Normal Population." *J Proj Tech* 15:481–5 D '51. * (PA 26:6246)

1072. ALLEN, ROBERT M. "A Longitudinal Study of Six Rorschach Protocols of a Three-Year-Old Child." *Child Develop* 22:61–9 Mr '51. * (PA 25:6733)

1073. ALLEN, ROBERT M.; MANNE, SIGMUND H.; AND STIFF, MARGARET. "The Role of Color in Rorschach's Test: A Preliminary Normative Report on a College Student Population." *J Proj Tech* 15:235–42 Je '51. * (PA 26:3396)

1074. ARNHEIM, RUDOLF. "Perceptual and Aesthetic Aspects of the Movement Response." *J Personality* 19:265–81 Mr '51. * (PA 26:3397)

1075. ARONSON, MARVIN L. "A Study of the Freudian Theory of Paranoia by Means of the Rorschach Test." Abstract. *Am Psychol* 6:349 Jl '51. *

1076. Aronson, Marvin Lucius. *A Study of the Freudian Theory of Paranoia by Means of a Group of Psychological Tests.* Doctor's thesis, University of Michigan (Ann Arbor, Mich.), 1951. Abstract: *Microfilm Abstracts* 11:443–4 no 2 '51. (PA 26:2316, title only)

1077. Baron, Samuel. "Suggestions for an Improved M-Limits Technique." *J Proj Tech* 15:371–5 S '51. * (PA 26:4002)

1078. Barrell, Robert Poindexter. *The Relationship of Various Types of Movement Responses in the Rorschach Test to Personality Trait Ratings.* Doctor's thesis, University of Michigan (Ann Arbor, Mich.), 1951. Abstract: *Microfilm Abstracts* 11:407–9 no 2 '51. (PA 26:2167, title only)

1079. Baughman, Emmett E. "Rorschach Scores as a Function of Examiner Difference." *J Proj Tech* 15:243–9 Je '51. * (PA 26:3398)

1080. Baughman, Emmett E., Jr. *A Comparative Study of Rorschach Forms With Altered Stimulus Characteristics.* Doctor's thesis, University of Chicago (Chicago, Ill.), 1951.

1081. Beck, Samuel J. Chap. 4, "The Rorschach Test: Multi-Dimensional Test of Personality," pp. 101–22. In *An Introduction to Projective Techniques and Other Devices for Understanding the Dynamics of Human Behavior.* Edited by Harold H. Anderson and Gladys L. Anderson. New York: Prentice-Hall, Inc., 1951. Pp. xxiv, 720. *

1082. Blanton, Richard, and Landsman, Theodore. "An Examination of the Retest Reliability of the 'Group' Rorschach and Some Relationships to the MMPI." Abstract. *Am Psychol* 6:379 Jl '51. *

1083. Blatt, Benjamin, and Hecht, Irving. "The Personality Structure of the Multiple Sclerosis Patient as Evaluated by the Rorschach Psychodiagnostic Technique." *J Clin Psychol* 7:341–4 O '51. * (PA 26:3586)

1084. Bradway, Katherine. "Rorschach Records of a Schizophrenic Patient Before, During and After Electric Shock and Insulin Treatment." *J Proj Tech* 15:87–97 Mr '51. * (PA 26:435)

1085. Brown, Malcolm; Chalke, F. C. R.; Peters, Barbara; Poser, E. G.; and Quarrington, Mary. "Some Rorschach Findings in Cases of Duodenal Ulcer: A Quantitative Study." *Can J Psychol* 5:1–8 Mr '51. * (PA 25:7019)

1086. Buckle, D. F., and Holt, N. F. "Comparison of Rorschach and Behn Inkblots." *J Proj Tech* 15:486–93 D '51. * (PA 26:6253)

1087. Buker, Samuel L., and Williams, Meyer. "Color as a Determinant of Responsiveness to Rorschach Cards in Schizophrenia." *J Consult Psychol* 15:196–202 Je '51. * (PA 26:6420)

1088. Calden, George, and Carp, Abraham. "A Comparison of Three Projective Techniques in a Longitudinal Study of a Post-Lobotomized Patient." Abstract. *Am Psychol* 6:343–4 Jl '51. *

1089. Callahan, Robert, and Berger, David. "Differentiation of Acute and Chronic Schizophrenic Patients on the Basis of Rorschach Test Patterns." Abstract. *Am Psychol* 6:348 Jl '51. *

1090. Canter, Arthur. *An Investigation of the Psychological Significance of Reactions to Color on the Rorschach and Other Tests.* Doctor's thesis, University of Iowa (Iowa City, Iowa), 1951.

1091. Cass, William A., Jr., and McReynolds, Paul. "A Contribution to Rorschach Norms." *J Consult Psychol* 15:178–84 Je '51. * (PA 26:6254)

1092. Christensen, Arden Hans. *A Quantitative Study of Personality Dynamics in Stuttering and Nonstuttering Siblings.* Doctor's thesis, University of Southern California (Los Angeles, Calif.), 1951.

1093. Cooper, James G., and Lewis, Roland B. "Quantitative Rorschach Factors in the Evaluation of Teacher Effectiveness." *J Ed Res* 44:703–7 My '51. * (PA 26:1722)

1094. Cowen, Emory L., and Thompson, George G. "Problem Solving Rigidity and Personality Structure." *J Abn & Social Psychol* 46:165–76 Ap '51. * (PA 25:7940)

1095. Cox, Shelagh M. "A Factorial Study of the Rorschach Responses of Normal and Maladjusted Boys." *J Genetic Psychol* 79:95–113 S '51. * (PA 26:2745)

1096. Curtis, Henry S., and Wolf, Elizabeth B. "The Influence of the Sex of the Examiner on the Production of Sex Responses on the Rorschach." Abstract. *Am Psychol* 6: 345–6 Jl '51. *

1097. Diers, Wallace C., and Brown, Clinton C. "Rorschach 'Organic Signs' and Intelligence Level." *J Consult Psychol* 15:343–5 Ag '51. * (PA 26:6262)

1098. Dunn, Wesley A. *A Comparison Between Certain Rorschach Factors, Orientation Scores, and College Grades.* Doctor's thesis, Purdue University (Lafayette, Ind.), 1951.

1099. Eichler, Robert M. "A Comparison of the Rorschach and Behn-Rorschach Inkblot Tests." *J Consult Psychol* 15: 185–9 Je '51. * (PA 26:6263)

1100. Eichler, Robert M. "Experimental Stress and Alleged Rorschach Indices of Anxiety." *J Abn & Social Psychol* 46:344–55 Jl '51. * (PA 26:2176)

1101. Eichler, Robert M. "Some Comments on the Controlling of Differences in Responses on the Rorschach Test." *Psychol B* 48:257–9 My '51. * (PA 26:911)

1102. Farnum, Hollis B. *An Investigation of the Psychological Meaning of Selected Signs on the Rorschach Test.* Doctor's thesis, Pennsylvania State College (State College, Pa.), 1951. (PA 26:4270, title only)

1103. Ferguson, George A. "Approaches to the Experimental Study of the Rorschach Test." *Can J Psychol* 5:157–66 D '51. *

1104. Filmer-Bennett, Gordon T. *A Study of Prognostic Indices in the Rorschach Records of Hospitalized Patients.* Doctor's thesis, University of Pittsburgh (Pittsburgh, Pa.), 1951.

1105. Fisher, Seymour. "Rorschach Patterns in Conversion Hysteria." *J Proj Tech* 15:98–108 Mr '51. * (PA 26:459)

1106. Fisher, Seymour. "The Value of the Rorschach for Detecting Suicidal Trends." *J Proj Tech* 15:250–4 Je '51. * (PA 26:3545)

1107. Fonda, Charles P. "The Nature and Meaning of the Rorschach White Space Response." *J Abn & Social Psychol* 46:367–77 Jl '51. * (PA 26:2178)

1108. Fromm, Erika O., and Elonen, Anna S. "The Use of Projective Techniques in the Study of a Case of Female Homosexuality." *J Proj Tech* 15:185–230 Je '51. * (PA 26:3498)

1109. Gardner, Riley W. "Impulsivity as Indicated by Rorschach Test Factors." *J Consult Psychol* 15:464–8 D '51. * (PA 26:6997)

1110. Gibby, Robert G. "The Influence of the Stimulus Value of the Examiner on the Inquiry of the Rorschach Test." Abstract. *Am Psychol* 6:346 Jl '51. *

1111. Gibby, Robert Gwyn. "The Stability of Certain Rorschach Variables Under Conditions of Experimentally Induced Sets: I, The Intellectual Variables." *J Proj Tech* 15:3–26 Mr '51. * (PA 26:296)

1112. Gillenson, Gertrude. *A Study of the Effects of Color on the Rorschach.* Doctor's thesis, Columbia University (New York, N.Y.), 1951.

1113. Goldman, Leo. "Relationships Between Aptitude Test Scores and Certain Rorschach Indices." Abstract. *Am Psychol* 6:300 Jl '51. *

1114. Grassi, Joseph R. "Suggested Refinement of Rorschach Scoring." *J Proj Tech* 15:255–62 Je '51. * (PA 26:3406)

1115. Grauer, David. *The Prognostic Value of the Rorschach Test in Paranoid Schizophrenia.* Doctor's thesis, University of Chicago (Chicago, Ill.), 1951.

1116. Griffith, Richard M. "Test-Retest Similarities of the Rorschachs of Patients Without Retention, Korsakoff." *J Proj Tech* 15:516–25 D '51. * (PA 26:6271)

1117. Gurvitz, Milton S. *The Dynamics of Psychological Testing: A Formulation and Guide to Independent Clinical Practice.* Foreword by Joseph S. A. Miller. New York: Grune & Stratton, Inc., 1951. Pp. xv, 396. * (PA 26:4007)

1118. Gurvitz, Milton S. "A Forerunner of Rorschach." *J Consult Psychol* 15:120–1 Ap. '51. * (PA 26:6273)

1119. Hallow, William C. *Effects of Intravenous Sodium Amytal Medication on Rorschach Performance.* Doctor's thesis, Duke University (Durham, N.C.), 1951.

1120. Hallowell, A. I. "The Use of Projective Techniques in the Study of the Socio-Psychological Aspects of Acculturation." *J Proj Tech* 15:27–44 Mr '51. * (PA 26:232)

1121. Halpern, Florence Cohn. *An Investigation Into the Nature and Intensity of the Anxiety Experienced by Three Clinical Groups of Children at Two Different Age Levels and of the Defenses They Develop Against Their Anxiety.* Doctor's thesis, New York University (New York, N.Y.), 1951. Abstract: *Microfilm Abstracts* 11:1094–6 no 4 '51.

1122. Hammond, Kenneth R. "A Tabulation Method for Analyzing Combinations of Rorschach Scores." *J Clin Psychol* 7:276–9 Jl '51. * (PA 26:915)

1123. Harrow, Gertrude S. "The Effects of Psychodrama Group Therapy on Role Behavior of Schizophrenic Patients." *Group Psychother* 3:316–20 Mr '51. * (PA 26:440)

1124. Harrower, M. R. "Visual Aids in the Presentation of Test Findings." *J Proj Tech* 15:380–4 S '51. * (PA 26:4008)

1125. Harrower, M. R., and Steiner, M. E. *Large Scale Rorschach Techniques: A Manual for the Group Rorschach and Multiple Choice Tests, Second Edition.* With contributions by Floyd O. Due, Beatrice A. Wright, and M. Erik Wright. Springfield, Ill.: Charles C Thomas, Publisher, 1951. Pp. xx, 353. * (Oxford, England: Blackwell Scientific Publications, Ltd.) (PA 26:2183)

1126. Hays, William; Gellerman, Saul; and Sloan, William. "A Study of the Relationship Between the Verb-Adjective Quotient and the Rorschach Experience Balance." *J Clin Psychol* 7:224–7 Jl '51. * (PA 26:916)

1127. Hemmendinger, Larry. *A Genetic Study of Structural Aspects of Perception as Reflected in Rorschach Test Responses.* Doctor's thesis, Clark University (Worcester, Mass.), 1951. (*Abstracts of Dissertations and Theses,* 1951, pp. 50–3.)

1128. Hertz, Marguerite R. "Current Problems in Rorschach Theory and Technique." *J Proj Tech* 15:307–38 S '51. * (PA 26:4009)

1129. Hertz, Marguerite R. "Evaluating Adjustment in Terms of the Rorschach Record: Reliability of Different Test-Interpreters." Abstract. *J Proj Tech* 15:416–7 S '51. *

1130. Holzberg, Jules D.; Cahen, Eleanor R.; and Wilk, Edward K. "Suicide: A Psychological Study of Self-Destruction." *J Proj Tech* 15:339–54 S '51. * (PA 26:4096)

1131. Hughes, Halcyon; Epstein, Leon J.; and Jost, Hudson. "The Relationship Between Certain Measurable Functions of Autonomic Nervous System Activity and Color Responses on the Rorschach Test." *J Clin Psychol* 7:244–9 Jl '51. * (PA 26:919)

1132. Kaldegg, A. "A Study of German and English Teacher-Training Students by Means of Projective Techniques." *Brit J Psychol, Gen Sect* 42:56–113 Mr, My '51. * (*PA* 26:550)

1133. KATZ, JOSEPH. *The Projection of Assaultive Aggression in the Human Figure Drawings of Adult Male Negro Offenders: A Study of Inmates Convicted of Homicide or Assault by Means of Human Figure Drawings, Rorschach, Thematic Apperception Test, and Szondi.* Doctor's thesis, New York University (New York, N.Y.), 1951. Abstract: *Microfilm Abstracts* 11:1096–8 no 4 '51.

1134. KELLEY, DOUGLAS M. "Clinical Reality and Projective Technique." *Am J Psychiatry* 107:753–7 Ap '51. * (*PA* 26:300)

1135. KELLY, E. LOWELL, AND FISKE, DONALD W. *The Prediction of Performance in Clinical Psychology.* Ann Arbor, Mich.: University of Michigan, 1951. Pp. xv, 311. Lithotyped. *

1136. KEYES, EDWARD J. *An Experimental Investigation of Some Sources of Variance in the Whole Response to the Rorschach Ink Blots.* Doctor's thesis, University of Iowa (Iowa City, Iowa), 1951.

1137. KIRKNER, F. J., AND WISHAM, WAYNE. "A Preliminary Report on the Predictability of the Rorschach Prognostic Rating Scale." Abstract. *J Proj Tech* 15:421–2 S '51. *

1138. KLEIN, GEORGE S., AND SCHLESINGER, HERBERT J. "Perceptual Attitudes Toward Instability: I, Prediction of Apparent Movement Experiences From Rorschach Responses." *J Personality* 19:289–302 Mr '51. * (*PA* 26:3412)

1139. KLOPFER, BRUNO. "Introduction: The Development of a Prognostic Rating Scale." Abstract. *J Proj Tech* 15:421 S '51. *

1140. KLOPFER, BRUNO. Sect. 7, "The Rorschach Technique," pp. 39–54, 169–71. In *Military Clinical Psychology.* Department of the Army Technical Manual TM 8–242; Department of the Air Force Manual AFM 160–45. Washington, D.C.: U.S. Government Printing Office, 1951. Pp. iv, 197. Paper. *

1141. KLOPFER, BRUNO. Chap. 19, "Rorschach Test," pp. 203–10. In *Thematic Test Analysis.* By Edwin S. Shneidman with the collaboration of Walther Joel and Kenneth B. Little. Foreword by Henry A. Murray. New York: Grune & Stratton, Inc., 1951. Pp. xi, 320. * (*PA* 26:3422)

1142. KLOPFER, BRUNO; KIRKNER, FRANK J.; WISHAM, WAYNE; AND BAKER, GERTRUDE. "Rorschach Prognostic Rating Scale." *J Proj Tech* 15:425–8 S '51. *

1143. KORCHIN, SHELDON J.; MELTZOFF, JULIAN; AND SINGER, JEROME L. "Motor Inhibition and Rorschach Movement Responses." Abstract. *Am Psychol* 6:344 Jl '51. *

1144. KORNETSKY, CONAN H. "A Possible Relationship of Personality Factors to Development of a Psychosis During Abstinence From Barbiturates." Abstract. *Am Psychol* 6:333 Jl '51. *

1145. KROUT, MAURICE H.; KROUT, JOHANNA; AND DULIN, THEODORE J. "Rorschach Test-Retest as Gauge of Progress in Psychotherapy." Abstract. *J Proj Tech* 15:417–8 S '51. *

1146. KUHLMANN, FRIEDA M., AND ROBINSON, HELEN P. "Rorschach Tests as a Diagnostic Tool in Adoption Studies." *Social Casework* 32:15–22 Ja '51. * (*PA* 26:280)

1147. KUTASH, SAMUEL B. "The Rorschach Examination and Psychotherapy." *Am J Psychother* 5:405–10 Jl '51. * (*PA* 26:1511)

1148. LEVI, JOSEPH. "Rorschach Patterns Predicting Success or Failure in the Rehabilitation of the Physically Handicapped." *J Abn & Social Psychol* 46:240–4 Ap '51. * (*PA* 25:8100)

1149. LIPTON, MORTIMER BENJAMIN. *The Differentiation of Mild Schizophrenia From Psychoneurosis by Means of the Rorschach Test.* Doctor's thesis, Columbia University (New York, N.Y.), 1951. Abstract: *Microfilm Abstracts* 11:1110–1 no 4 '51.

1150. LIPTON, M. B.; TAMARIN, S.; AND LOTESTA, P. "Test Evidence of Personality Change and Prognosis by Means of the Rorschach and Wechsler-Bellevue Tests on 17 Insulin-Treated Paranoid Schizophrenics." *Psychiatric Q* 25:434–44 Jl '51. * (*PA* 26:5755)

1151. LUNDIN, WILLIAM H. *Projective Techniques and Psychotherapy: Examination of a Therapy Process Through the Use of the Projective Movement Sequence and Rorschach Technique.* Projective Technique Monographs, No. 1. New York: Society for Projective Techniques and Rorschach Institute, Inc. September 1951. Pp. i, 39. Paper. * (*PA* 26:6335)

1152. McCALL, RAYMOND JOSEPH. *Psychometric Evaluation of Rorschach Records in Brain-Operated Patients.* Doctor's thesis, Columbia University (New York, N.Y.), 1951. Abstract: *Microfilm Abstracts* 11:1098–1100 no 4 '51.

1153. McFIE, J.; PIERCY, M. F.; AND ZANGWILL, O. L. "The Rorschach Test in Obsessional Neurosis With Special Reference to the Effects of Pre-Frontal Leucotomy." *Brit J Med Psychol* 24:162–79 pt 3 '51. * (*PA* 26:2349)

1154. McREYNOLDS, PAUL. "Perception of Rorschach Concepts as Related to Personality Deviations." *J Abn & Social Psychol* 46:131–41 Ap '51. * (*PA* 25:8101)

1155. MARTIN, A. W., AND WEIR, A. J. "A Comparative Study of the Drawings Made by Various Clinical Groups." *J Mental Sci* 97:532–44 Jl '51. *

1156. MASLOW, PAUL. *The Individual Through the Rorschach: Volume 1 of The Life of Science.* Brooklyn, N.Y.: the Author, 16 Court St., 1951. Pp. iii, 134. Paper, spiral binding, mimeographed. * (*PA* 26:305)

1157. MERCER, MARGARET, AND HECKER, A. O. "The Rorschach Human Movement Response in Paranoid Schizophrenia." Abstract. *J Proj Tech* 15:418 S '51. *

1158. MEYER, BILL T. "An Investigation of Color Shock in the Rorschach Test." *J Clin Psychol* 7:367–70 O '51. * (*PA* 26:3415)

1159. MINDESS, HARVEY. "Application of the Scale to a Group of Psychiatric Patients." Abstract. *J Proj Tech* 15:422 S '51. *

1160. MOLISH, H. B. "The Popular Response in Rorschach Records of Normals, Neurotics, and Schizophrenics." *Am J Orthopsychiatry* 21:523–31 Jl '51. * (*PA* 26:3418)

1161. MOSAK, HAROLD H. "Performance on the Harrower-Erickson Multiple Choice Test of Patients With Spinal Cord Injuries." *J Consult Psychol* 15:346–9 Ag '51. * (*PA* 26:6490)

1162. NEFF, WALTER S., AND LIDZ, THEODORE. "Rorschach Pattern of Normal Subjects of Graded Intelligence." *J Proj Tech* 15:45–57 Mr '51. * (*PA* 26:310)

1163. ORNE, MARTIN T. "The Mechanisms of Hypnotic Age Regression: An Experimental Study." *J Abn & Social Psychol* 46:213–25 Ap '51. * (*PA* 25:7886)

1164. PALMER, JAMES O. *A Dual Approach to Rorschach Validation: A Methodological Study.* American Psychological Association, Psychological Monographs: General and Applied, Vol. 65, No. 8, Whole No. 325. Washington, D.C.: the Association, Inc., 1951. Pp. iii, 27. Paper. * (*PA* 26:7007)

1165. PERLMAN, JANET A. "Color and Validity of the Rorschach 8–9–10 Per Cent." *J Consult Psychol* 15:122–6 Ap '51. * (*PA* 26:6280)

1166. PERLMAN, JANET A. *The Effects of Color on Rorschach Test Responses: An Experimental Study.* Doctor's thesis, Cornell University (Ithaca, N.Y.), 1951.

1167. PHILLIPS, LESLIE. "Case Studies of Two Schizophrenic Patients." *J Proj Tech* 15:355–70 S '51. * (*PA* 26:4147)

1168. PLESCH, EGON. "A Rorschach Study of Rosacea and Morbid Blushing." *Brit J Med Psychol* 24:202–5 S 11 '51. * (*PA* 26:2356)

1169. POLLENS, BERTRAM. *The Relationship Between Psychological Data and Prognosis in Psychotherapy.* Doctor's thesis, New York University (New York, N.Y.), 1951. Abstract: *Microfilm Abstracts* 11:750–2 no 3 '51. (*PA* 26:1515, title only)

1170. POSER, ERNEST G. "Personality Factors in Patients With Duodenal Ulcer: A Rorschach Study." *J Proj Tech* 15:131–43 Je '51. * (*PA* 26:3582)

1171. RABIN, ALBERT I. Chap. 5, "Validating and Experimental Studies with the Rorschach Method," pp. 123–46. In *An Introduction to Projective Techniques.* Edited by Harold H. Anderson and Gladys L. Anderson. New York: Prentice-Hall, Inc., 1951. Pp. xxiv, 720. *

1172. RAV, JEHUDA. "Anatomy Responses in the Rorschach Test." *J Proj Tech* 15:433–43 D '51. * (*PA* 26:6282)

1173. REICHARD, SUZANNE. "Some Contributions of Psychological Tests to Therapeutic Planning." Discussion by Anneliese F. Korner. *Am J Orthopsychiatry* 21:532–41, discussion 541–2 Jl '51. * (*PA* 26:3445)

1174. REITAN, RALPH M. "Relationships of Certain Rorschach Test Indicators to the Abstraction and Power Factors of Biological Intelligence." Abstract. *Am Psychol* 6:345 Jl '51. *

1175. REITAN, RALPH M. *Relationships of Certain Rorschach Test Indicators to the Abstraction and Power Factors of Biological Intelligence.* Doctor's thesis, University of Chicago (Chicago, Ill.), 1951.

1176. ROBERTS, LYNN K. *The Predictive Significance of the Rorschach Technique in Relation to the Outcome of Psychotherapy.* Doctor's thesis, University of Iowa (Iowa City, Iowa), 1951.

1177. ROE, ANNE. "Psychological Tests of Research Scientists." *J Consult Psychol* 15:492–5 D '51. * (*PA* 26:7292)

1178. ROGERS, LAWRENCE S.; KNAUSS, JOANNE; AND HAMMOND, KENNETH R. "Predicting Continuation in Therapy by Means of the Rorschach Test." *J Consult Psychol* 15:368–71 O '51. * (*PA* 26:7010)

1179. ROSEN, EPHRAIM. "Symbolic Meanings in the Rorschach Cards: A Statistical Study." *J Clin Psychol* 7:239–44 Jl '51. * (*PA* 26:931)

1180. RYAN, FRANCIS JOSEPH. *Personality Differences Between Under- and Over-Achievers in College.* Doctor's thesis, Columbia University (New York, N.Y.), 1951. Abstract: *Microfilm Abstracts* 11:967–8 no 4 '51.

1181. SALFIELD, D. J. "The Usefulness of the Rorschach Test for Diagnosis, Prognosis and Epicrisis, Mainly in Child Guidance Treatment." *J Mental Sci* 97:84–9 Ja '51. * (*PA* 25:6247)

1182. SANDERS, RICHARD. *The Relationship Between Examiner Hostility and Subjects' Rorschach Scores.* Doctor's thesis, University of Michigan (Ann Arbor, Mich.), 1951. Abstract: *Microfilm Abstracts* 11:433–4 no 2 '51. (*PA* 26:2195, title only)

1183. SANDERSON, HERBERT. "Norms for 'Shock' in the Rorschach." *J Consult Psychol* 15:127–9 Ap. '51. * (*PA* 26:6288)

1184. SANDLER, JOSEPH, AND ACKNER, BRIAN. "Rorschach Content Analysis: An Experimental Investigation." *Brit J Med Psychol* 24:180–201 S 11 '51. * (*PA* 26:2196)

1185. SCHACHTEL, ERNEST G. "Notes on Rorschach Tests of 500 Juvenile Delinquents and a Control Group of 500 Non-Delinquent Adolescents." *J Proj Tech* 15:144–72 Je '51. * (*PA* 26:3531)

1186. SEWARD, GEORGENE H.; MORRISON, LESTER M.; AND FEST, BEVERLY; WITH THE ASSISTANCE OF NELLIE M. YOUNG AND VANCE BOILEAU. *Personality Structure in a Common Form of Colitis.* American Psychological Association, Psychological Monographs: General and Applied, Vol. 65, No. 1, Whole No. 318. Washington, D.C.: the Association, Inc., 1951. Pp. v, 26. Paper. * (*PA* 25:7024)

1187. SHATIN, LEO. *Relationships Between the Rorschach Test and the Thematic Apperception Test.* Doctor's thesis, Harvard University (Cambridge, Mass.), 1951.

1188. SHEEHAN, JOSEPH, AND SPIEGELMAN, MARVIN. "Application of the Scale to a Group of Stutterers." Abstract. *J Proj Tech* 15:422 S '51. *

1189. SIEGEL, EDWARD LOUIS. *Genetic Parallels of Perceptual Structurization in Paranoid Schizophrenia: An Analysis by Means of the Rorschach Technique.* Doctor's thesis, Clark University (Worcester, Mass.), 1951. (*Abstracts of Dissertations and Theses*, 1951, pp. 53–6.)

1190. SIEGEL, MAX. *The Personality Structure of Children With Reading Disabilities as Compared With Children Presenting Other Clinical Problems.* Doctor's thesis, New York University (New York, N.Y.), 1951. Abstract: *Microfilm Abstracts* 11:1100–1 no 4 '51.

1191. SIEGEL, SAUL M. "Personality Factors in Psychotherapeutic Improvement as Identified by the Rorschach Test." Abstract. *Am Psychol* 6:341–2 Jl '51. *

1192. SIEGEL, SAUL M. *Prediction of Psychotherapeutic Improvement in Psychoneurotics by Means of the Rorschach Test.* Doctor's thesis, University of Chicago (Chicago, Ill.), 1951.

1193. SLOTE, WALTER HAROLD. *The Personality of the Psychogenic Hard of Hearing Adult: A Comparative Study of the Personality Characteristics of Psychogenic Hard of Hearing Adults Through the Media of Objective and Projective Psychological Procedures.* Doctor's thesis, New York University (New York, N.Y.), 1951. Abstract: *Microfilm Abstracts* 11:1102–3 no 4 '51.

1194. SMITH, SYDNEY, AND GEORGE, C. E. "Rorschach Factors Related to Experimental Stress." *J Consult Psychol* 15:190–5 Je '51. * (*PA* 26:6293)

1195. SMYKAL, ANTHONY, AND THORNE, FREDERICK C. "Etiological Studies of Psychopathic Personality: II, Asocial Type." Case Study. *J Clin Psychol* 7:299–316 O '51. * (*PA* 26:3532)

1196. SNIDER, LOUIS B. "A Rorschach Study of High School Achievement." Abstract. *Am Psychol* 6:374 Jl '51. *

1197. STEIN, HARRY. "Scoring Movement Responses on the Rorschach." *J Proj Tech* 15:526–33 D '51. * (*PA* 26:6296)

1198. STEIN, MORRIS I. "Clinical Psychology and the Propaedeutic Science." *J Proj Tech* 15:401–4 S '51. * (*PA* 26:4019)

1199. STERLING, MAC E. *Color Shock on the Rorschach Test.* Doctor's thesis, University of Kentucky (Lexington, Ky.), 1951.

1200. STOTSKY, BERNARD ALEXANDREVICH. *Factors in Remission of Schizophrenics: A Comparative Study of Personality and Intellectual Variables Among Schizophrenics.* Doctor's thesis, University of Michigan (Ann Arbor, Mich.), 1951. Abstract: *Microfilm Abstracts* 11:758–9 no 3 '51. (*PA* 26:1618, title only)

1201. SUESSMILCH, FREDERICK L. "A Long-Term Maladjustment Culminating in Catatonic Episodes During Adolescence." Case Study. *J Proj Tech* 15:461–79 D '51. *

1202. TARLAU, MILTON, AND SMALHEISER, IRWIN. "Personality Patterns in Patients With Malignant Tumors of the Breast and Cervix: An Exploratory Study." *Psychosom Med* 13:117–21 Mr–Ap '51. * (*PA* 25:7609)

1203. THETFORD, WILLIAM N.; MOLISH, HERMAN B.; AND BECK, SAMUEL J. "Developmental Aspects of Personality Structure in Normal Children." *J Proj Tech* 15:58–78 Mr '51. *

1204. THIESEN, J. WARREN. "A Pattern Analysis of Structural Characteristics of the Rorschach Test in Schizophrenia." Abstract. *Am Psychol* 6:348–9 Jl '51. *

1205. THOMPSON, GRACE M. "College Grades and the Group Rorschach: A Follow-Up Study." *J Genetic Psychol* 78:39–46 Mr '51. * (*PA* 25:8262)

1206. TUNIS, M. MARTIN, AND DÖRKEN, HERBERT, JR. "A Case of Reactive Depression Suffering From Ulcerative Colitis: Serial Psychological Investigation." *Psychiatric Q Sup* 25:22–39 '51. *

1207. VALENTINE, MAX. "Experimental Abridgement of the Rorschach Test." *J Clin & Exp Psychopathol* 12:157–69 Je '51. * (*PA* 26:4814)

1208. VERNIER, CLAIRE M., AND KENDIG, ISABELLE V. "Analysis of the Relationships Between Various Measures of Creative Productivity in Two Projective Tests." Abstract. *Am Psychol* 6:349–50 Jl '51. *

1209. WALDMAN, MARVIN. "Personality Factors and Performance Under Stress in Schizophrenics." Abstract. *Am Psychol* 6:314 Jl '51. *

1210. WALKER, ROBERT G. "A Comparison of Clinical Manifestations of Hostility With Rorschach and MAPS Test Performances." *J Proj Tech* 15:444–60 D '51. * (*PA* 26:6241)

1211. WARNER, SAMUEL J. "An Evaluation of the Validity of Rorschach Popular Responses as Differentiae of Ambulatory Schizophrenia." *J Proj Tech* 15:268–75 Je '51. * (*PA* 26:3559)

1212. WISHNER, JULIUS. "Neurosis and Tension: An Exploratory Study of the Relationship of Physiological and Rorschach Measures." Abstract. *Am Psychol* 6:351 Jl '51. *

1213. WITTENBORN, J. R. "An Evaluation of the Use of Difference Scores in Prediction." *J Clin Psychol* 7:108–11 Ap '51. * (*PA* 25:7797)

1214. WITTENBORN, J. R., AND HOLZBERG, JULES D. "The Rorschach and Descriptive Diagnosis." *J Consult Psychol* 15:460–3 D '51. * (*PA* 26:7018)

1215. WITTENBORN, J. R., AND METTLER, FRED A. "A Lack of Perceptual Control Score for the Rorschach Test." *J Clin Psychol* 7:331–4 O '51. * (*PA* 26:3427)

1216. YERBURY, EDGAR C.; HOLZBERG, JULES D.; AND ALESSI, SALVATORE L. "Psychological Tests in the Selection and Placement of Psychiatric Aides." *Am J Psychiatry* 108:91–7 Ag '51. *

1217. YORK, RICHARD H. *The Effect of Color in the Rorschach Test and in Selected Intellectual Tasks.* Doctor's thesis, Boston University (Boston, Mass.), 1951.

1218. ZEHRER, FREDERICK A. "Investigation of Rorschach Factors in Children Who Have Convulsive Disorders and in Those Who Present Problems of Adjustment." *Am J Orthopsychiatry* 21:292–302 Ap '51. * (*PA* 26:2200)

1219. ZIMMERMAN, FREDERIC T.; BURGEMEISTER, BESSIE B.; AND PUTNAM, TRACY J. "Intellectual and Emotional Makeup of the Epileptic." *AMA Arch Neurol & Psychiatry* 65:545–56 My '51. * (*PA* 25:8236)

HELEN SARGENT, *Chief Psychologist, Winter VA Hospital, Topeka, Kansas.*[1]

DESCRIPTION AND HISTORY. A critical appraisal of the Rorschach Test must take into consideration the popularity and prestige which it has won in spite of still unsettled questions of technique, scoring, rationale, and standardization. On the other hand, its limitations despite extensive experience amassed through its use, must also be recognized. These paradoxes can best be understood and evaluated in the setting of its history and development.

The Rorschach has, in recent years, become the best known and most widely used projective method for the description of personality, both normal and abnormal, in terms of dynamic processes. The test, which consists of a set of 10 inkblots (5 achromatic and 5 in which color is combined in part or all of the blot) was originated by a Swiss psychiatrist, Herman Rorschach, who published a monograph on the method in 1922 shortly before his death. In spite of the incompleteness of his own work (or perhaps because of it), his originality in devising the method itself and his penetrating thinking on problems of interpretation have exerted a strong and continuing influence upon subsequent research. In spite of hundreds of published studies which have appeared in increasing numbers since the first English publication by Oberholzer in 1924 (*1*) the *Psychodiagnostik* (*285*) itself is still the basic reference and the arbiter of many questions.

Although in the 1930's a few pioneer workers with a small but active following introduced the test in this country and began important research, not only experimental psychologists but the then more orthodox and behavioristically oriented clinical psychologists viewed the method with cold skepticism and active antagonism. Although controversy has by no means died out, the issues now center around

1 Sponsored by the VA and published with the approval of the Chief Medical Director. The statements and conclusions published by the author are a result of her own study and do not necessarily reflect the opinion or policy of the Veterans Administration.

questions of research methodology, problems of establishing reliability and validity, and alarm over the widespread and uncritical acceptance of inferences drawn from the Rorschach alone. Its admission to the armamentarium of the clinical psychologist is no longer debated: the problem now is, rather, *how* it shall be used, by whom, and in what way. Kelley (*1134*) has recently compared certain Rorschach reports to 35-cent horoscopes (a just attack upon abuse of the test, though unfair to its demonstrated effectiveness when properly used by qualified clinicians).

The increased status of the test in clinical work began with the publication of the first treatise by Beck in 1937 (*62*). Until 1942, when the Klopfer-Kelley (*271*) and Bochner-Halpern (*240*) texts appeared almost simultaneously, the Beck work was the only reference in book form other than Rorschach's own monograph. Klopfer and Kelley has remained a standard volume. Beck's earlier book, now supplemented by a more recent two volume work (*364, 415*) and the extensive discussions in Rapaport (*535*) and in Schafer (*749*) are the most complete resources now available for the practicing clinician. Rorschach examining is, however, not a skill which can be acquired by reading, but only through instruction and experience. Until after World War II, training was carried out mainly through the seminars and workshops offered by Beck at Michael Reese in Chicago, by Klopfer at the Rorschach Institute founded at Columbia in 1939, and by Marguerite Hertz at the Brush Foundation in Cleveland. In addition, since the war, an increasing number of courses are being offered at universities and in clinical training centers.

AREA OF USEFULNESS. The Rorschach is used in almost every conceivable situation requiring the psychological appraisal of individuals, including child guidance, vocational selection, and college counseling as well as clinical diagnosis. It has been administered to individuals and groups in such widely varied settings as industrial concerns, schools, military installations, clinics and hospitals. Although for research purposes diversified application is to be encouraged, the limitations of the test for applied use in such an assortment of problems must be recognized. By far the largest body of experience with the Rorschach has been accumulated in the clinical setting. It is in the area of mental illness, therefore, that we can place relatively greater confidence in what the data can reveal. Even

here, however, it is important to distinguish fact from theory and evidence from proof. Rorschach findings like the findings from any other clinical method (whether this is a testing device, an interview, or an observation) depend upon the knowledge, experience, sensitivity, and sound judgment of the clinician more than upon the eliciting power of the inkblot stimuli themselves. This decidedly limits the value of the instrument in the hands of the untrained or unqualified worker.

The skilled Rorschach examiner, on the basis of experience (still considerably in advance of experimental methodology to demonstrate crucially what is believed to be clinically valid), uses the test chiefly for what it can contribute, in conjunction with other psychological methods, to the understanding of certain important aspects of personality. The test offers a means not only for appraising capacity, both intellectual and emotional, but for analyzing the way in which capacity is used in problem solving, in adaptation, and in control of thinking and impulse. Thus it offers an index of the extent to which normal functioning is preserved, disturbed, disorganized, or destroyed.

The test is expected to yield not a catalogue of traits or predispositions, and certainly not even a list of signs of abnormality or impairment, but a view of personality processes as they function. The theory which supports the use of ambiguous stimuli (such as the inkblots) to elicit a response which is then interpreted in terms of an individual's idiosyncratic imposition of structure upon a perceptual stimulus field having only rudimentary structure of its own is the "projective hypothesis" (Rapaport, *535*). This theory, that perception is individually motivated, selective, and organized in terms of the person's needs, experiences, and habitual patterns of response, as well as by properties of the stimulus itself, is an extension of Freud's concept of projection as a mechanism of defense. It has been elaborated by Frank,[2] Bellak,[3] and others as a rationale for the projective tests. Because ambiguous stimuli are unfamiliar problems to be solved, they set in motion processes of perceiving, associating, or-

---

[2] Frank, Lawrence K. *Projective Methods.* Springfield, Ill.: Charles C Thomas, Publisher, 1948. Pp. vii, 86. * (*PA* 23: 1771)

[3] Bellak, Leopold. "Concept of Projection: An Experimental Investigation and Study of the Concept." *Psychiatry* 7:353–70 N '44. * (*PA* 19:1261)
Bellak, Leopold. "On the Problems of the Concept of Projection," pp. 7–32. (*PA* 25:2307) In *Projective Psychology: Clinical Approaches to the Total Personality.* Edited by Lawrence Edwin Abt and Leopold Bellak. New York: Alfred A. Knopf, Inc., 1950. Pp. xvii, 485, xiv. *

ganizing, selecting, and rejecting which provide the opportunity to study these processes in action. Since, furthermore, the unfamiliar situation is anxiety instigating, the adequacy or mismanagement of function under stress may be observed.

Some of the questions with which the Rorschach analyst approaches the response record are of the following nature: How accurately or arbitrarily does this person perceive what is seen by most others? How rich is the experience and knowledge he brings to bear on it? How much anxiety is aroused in the face of the problem of responding to vagueness? What is his way of handling anxiety and to what extent can he get it under control? How responsive is he to stimuli from the outer world which normally excite, please, or threaten? What does he do when impulse is aroused—does he try for escape, become cautious, or show disorganization, or is he resourceful enough to delay and direct the impulse into an appropriate response? How productive, flexible, and adaptive is he? How much tension and drive does he experience?

It is, of course, in the disturbance of processes such as the above (which are inferred from their verbal end products) that abnormality and impairment are most evident, and it is on this basis that special kinds of pathology characteristic of various nosological groupings of mentally ill patients have been studied through their reflection in the patterns of response found in the Rorschach. A large body of evidence is available (though poorly systematized) which describes the typical performance in the psychoses (schizophrenic and affective) and neuroses (hysteria, obsessional neuroses, anxiety states, etc.), in organically impaired patients, and in character disorders. Diagnostic criteria for distinguishing these and other groups range from Rorschach indications which are so universally agreed upon by clinicians as to be considered pathognomonic to a variety of signs either so over-specific and unsupported by adequate research, or so diffuse and general, as to be differentially meaningless.

CONTROVERSIES OVER ADMINISTRATION TECHNIQUE. There are several different procedures for the administration of the Rorschach method, all of which have enthusiastic adherents and severe critics. All techniques are based on agreement on the following points: (a) that the purpose of the experiment is to get the subject to react to the blots (telling what they look like to him) in his own way with a minimum of sugges-

tion from the examiner, (b) that a full verbatim record of all the subject's verbalization is essential, (c) that time to the first response on each card and total time for the experiment be recorded, and (d) that responses must be followed up by inquiry to determine to what part of the blot the response refers, what aspects of the card determine it, and how the percept is conceived and organized.

On the last point there is general acceptance of a division of the test into two parts, the first of which is known variously as the Association (Beck), the Performance (Klopfer), or the Test (Rapaport) and the second of which is called the Inquiry. It is on the handling of the inquiry that "schools" differ most sharply. Beck and Klopfer advocate going through the entire series of ten cards without interrupting the subject by questions. At the end of this period, the cards are re-presented, responses are read back to the subject, and questions are asked to elicit the additional information necessary for scoring. Rapaport, however, has introduced a "blindfold" inquiry (535) which follows the presentation of each card. Without showing the card again (except when absolutely necessary to clear up confusion in regard to location), the subject is queried on those responses which are not readily identifiable or scorable on the basis of the spontaneous verbalization. Most workers also advocate additional probing (after the initial inquiry), a procedure which Klopfer introduced and termed "testing the limits." Answers to the more leading questions in this period are not allowed to influence scoring, but yield fuller information for qualitative interpretation. Both immediate and delayed inquiry are proposed by their advocates to minimize suggestion. Beck and his followers hold that card-by-card inquiry alters the experiment in that it influences the response to subsequent cards. Rapaport, on the contrary, insists that questioning after the remainder of the test has intervened reveals less of the original response determinants and requires more suggestive questioning. The Beck method does play down the interpersonal relationship between examiner and subject during the association, thus reducing examiner influence and making the *objective* conditions of testing more nearly equal in the hands of different examiners. The Rapaport technique, in the hands of skilled examiners, provides a rich and fresh material on a subject's immediate experience and allows the clinician to establish better rapport which, in a sense, means equating the *subjective* conditions of testing. The main objection to the latter method is the unpredictable effect which even minimal examiner-attention to certain responses and not to others exerts upon the subject who is quick to detect what the examiner thinks is important. The method of choice, however, depends largely upon the clinician's preference for a controlled method by which individual behavior in an objectively standardized situation can be compared or for a less controlled technique which allows richer observational data and more leeway for intuitive interpretation.

There are other variations in administration technique among the leading experts with regard to wording of instructions, amount of pressure exerted to elicit response, position of subject in relation to examiner (Beck's subject sits with back turned and is handed cards over his shoulder), handling of the cards, and the like. Only the instructions, or manner of presenting the task, is of much importance. Beck and Klopfer both offer an initial explanation about the inkblot test, Beck utilizing a standardized introductory statement in contrast to a less formal introduction by Klopfer. Rapaport uses only Rorschach's original question "What might this be?", answering requests for more information as they arise, rather than seeking to anticipate them. The latter procedure has much to recommend it. Initial explanations may be useful in quieting the anxiety and guilt feelings of the examiner for the task he imposes, but they have a variable effect on the subject and ordinarily are not so helpful as dealing with questions, confusion, or uneasiness at the time they become manifest. The selection of administration method must be guided largely by the examiner's training and preference. No systematic research has been carried out to demonstrate which is best. Even the criteria of "best" would be in doubt.

The above discussion refers only to individual Rorschach testing. Various methods for the group administration of the test have also been devised. The Harrower group method, using slides and booklets in which responses are written, produces protocols which can be scored and interpreted in much the same way as if the test were individually administered (*199, 316*). The material elicited suffers only from lack of detailed inquiry data on doubtful responses. Beck calls this method "a test but not a Rorschach." However, experience suggests that the situational variables and the mode of presentation do not seriously alter the meaning of response. Harrower's multiple choice form is not recommended, since it limits response possibilities in a way which is incompatible with the principles of projective test construction and is less well standardized than the better established non-projective inventories.

SCORING SYSTEMS. The variety of scoring systems is at first bewildering to the beginner in Rorschach. Actually, the difference is in symbol and method of tabulation, rather than in the test variables they represent. The clinician familiar with one "shorthand" (Beck's term to describe the reduction of complex response material to symbols for purposes of analysis) can easily learn to translate from one to another.

In all systems the following are represented in scoring: (*a*) the proportion of responses to the card as a whole, to prominent detail, and to various small or unusual details; (*b*) the determinant of each response according to the influence of qualities inherent in the figures themselves, such as form, color, movement, and chiaroscuro or shading; (*c*) content classified into various categories; and (*d*) various quantitative relationships and percentages derived from the above scores, plus qualitative aspects of verbalization, organization, form level, originality, or commonality.

The beginner will be annoyed to find different ratios and indices computed in each system and will discover that a determinant such as shading is called Y in one system, K in another, and Ch in a third, for reasons known only to the symbol originators. As indicated above, these differences are not as important as they may at first seem.

Somewhat more disquieting, but also more apparent than real, are differences in interpretation which strike at the core of the problem of validity to be discussed below. M (movement) for example, has been thought to represent intelligence, native endowment, creativity, wealth and flexibility, phantasy activity, unconscious wish, amount of inner resource, and control of impulse. Beck emphasizes the wish fulfilling and creative character of M (which he calls the wish or "waking dream"), whereas Rapaport stresses its implications for wealth of intellectual resource and ideational control, depending on form quality. Beck has emphasized certain types of shading response as indicative of self-appraisal, self-criticism, special forms of anxiety. Rapaport points to the relation of chiaroscuro to anxiety, but more particularly to the manner in which it is handled. Klopfer and Hertz each utilize interpretations peculiar to their own systems. The several experts, moreover, have different lists of "popular" responses and different standards for evaluating the good or poor quality of form.

A system of scoring less widely known, and too new to be evaluated at this time, is an elaborate sign approach by Charlotte Buhler (*787*). Its major purpose is to provide for more adequate quantitative evaluation of protocols and a more objective appraisal of the level of personality integration. A method which aids in the rapid evaluation of large numbers of records for research or screening purposes is the Munroe Check List (*219*).

RELIABILITY AND VALIDITY. From the standpoint of objectivity, the above variations and differences between schools of Rorschach are a weakness of the test but are also a strength in that they show flexibility and almost unlimited possibilities for development. At the same time the complexity of the test variables and the comprehensiveness of rationale for their interpretation create for the Rorschach the same problems in establishing reliability and validity that other projective methods encounter. Variables are interrelated and interdependent, and "results" are not simply the product of the test, but of the interpreter who reads and organizes them. Scores are only a step toward interpretation rather than the interpretation itself as is the case with more objective tests. For example, in an inventory which purports to distinguish neurotic from non-neurotic subjects by comparison with established cutting scores, the obtained score *is* the diagnosis. The score itself may thus be checked for agreement with a criterion measure. No Rorschach score, singly or in combination, has any such meaning except as the interpreter considers it in relation to the entire record. Furthermore, various scores have different meanings according to the setting in which they appear. Methods for dealing with patterns of scores proposed by Cronbach (*795*), Buhler (*787*), Zubin (*358*), and others are hopeful, but these still form only the basis for conclusions and cannot be directly read.

In addition to the validation problems which are inherent in the nature of the instrument and its use, there is the difficulty of establishing valid criteria for those aspects of personality with which the test deals. There are virtually no sound measures for internal states (which may or may not be manifest in behavior). The very existence of these is an inference whether drawn from Rorschach or other evidence. It is a strange paradox that the psychiatric interview, the case history, and the unstructured clinical observation (bases of inferences which are equally complex and equally invalid as scientific evidence) have been so frequently used as diagnostic and descriptive criteria with which the Rorschach and other projective test findings are correlated. We demand of projective tests an accuracy of prediction which cannot be demonstrated for other clinical methods, yet we use the latter to judge whether Rorschach conclusions are "right" or "wrong." While agreement may be viewed as evidence in the direction of validation, disagreement is a negative datum not subject to explanation.

Validity studies on the Rorschach may be roughly classified into three groups: (*a*) "sign" studies in which contrasting groups of known composition are compared in terms of difference on various scores; (*b*) matching or correlation of diagnoses and/or total personality descriptions with clinical or history data, and (*c*) verification of one-dimensional Rorschach interpretations (intellectual control, anxiety, impulsivity, etc.) by comparison with other measures of the same variable.

The difficulties in the first two procedures have been cited above. The first type of research has normative value in that it has helped to establish expectancies for groups and for the range of variation in the scores themselves; this, however, is not validation. The second approach has been valuable in those studies in which criteria have been carefully chosen. The third method is promising but has only begun to be exploited. One study of intellectual control (Williams, *596*) and one of impulsivity (Gardner, *1109*) show a promising agreement between Rorschach judgments and external measures of the same inferred characteristic. Williams' study is unique in that an experimental method for producing a phenomenon predicted from the Rorschach (good or poor intellectual control under stress) was devised. Gardner showed satisfactory correlation between Rorschach measures of impulsivity and impulsivity rated on the basis of another test and on direct acquaintance and observation. Both of these studies, although they are interpretation rather than score oriented, fall back upon correlations of scores and score patterns with the criteria, rather than upon interpretations (the basis of which may be interchangeable). A promising method for validating interpretations, utilizing the Q technique, has been developed by Kobler in a study of Szondi, Rorschach, and full battery inferences in relation to therapists' judgments. Benton has recently reviewed a number of validation studies, the results of which are conflicting (908).

The reliability of the Rorschach, defined as consistency of measurement, can be judged only by agreement between interpreters, since the self-agreement of a single Rorschach protocol (split half) is affected by variations in the stimulus value of the ten cards, and agreement between Rorschachs administered to the same patient after an interim is disrupted to an unknown degree by changes in the subject. Although two series of alternate cards, the Behn Rorschach and the Harrower set, are available, the published studies are so few in number that results are inconclusive.

SUMMARY. The Rorschach test is a clinical technique, not a psychometric method. As such it has the advantages, and is subject to the limitations, of other complex, flexible clinical tools. In its present stage of development it is an aid to psychological investigation and interpretation, the usefulness of which depends upon the clinician who applies it. It is to be hoped that differences in regard to administration, scoring, and interpretation will be reconciled through research rather than argument. It is to be hoped also that validation studies in which care is exercised in the choice of criteria, and in which the interpretation rather than the score will be the candidate for proof, will be forthcoming. The test has no magic; vital diagnosis and treatment planning should not rest on its results alone. At present as much critical attention should be directed to the processes engaged in by the clinician who interprets it as to the validation of the test itself. Within these limits, the Rorschach is a method for the study of personality which has no threatening competition today.

For reviews by Morris Krugman and J. R. Wittenborn, see 3:73; for related reviews, see 118–28.

[118]

★[Re Rorschach.] BRUSSEL, JAMES A.; HITCH, KENNETH S.; AND PIOTROWSKI, ZYGMUNT A. **A Rorschach Training Manual, [Third Edition].** Utica, N.Y.: State Hospitals Press, 1950. Pp. 86. Paper. $0.75. * (*PA* 25:4560, 4581)

Am J Psychiatry 108:236 S '51. George A. Ulett. * a helpful manual for Rorschach training

consisting of 2 articles that appeared first in the *Psychiatric Quarterly* in 1942. Other brief Rorschach manuals have since appeared, but this reprinting is timely owing to the present increasing tempo of neuropsychiatric training. The manual contains pictures of the Rorschach cards in miniature and helpful summary tables. Dr. Piotrowski's article contains a brief but very interesting historical account and developmental sketch of Rorschach theory. His discussion of the meaning of the separate scoring symbols is excellent and reflects a wide background of clinical experience. The book suffers from want of organization, as both articles cover, in part, the same material. Combining the 2 sections could have prevented duplication of material and produced greater clarity. The use of a somewhat different scoring system in the 2 papers will be confusing to the beginner. An attempt to simplify the scoring of shading responses is commendable, but the inexperienced trainee who will wish for a means to understand current Rorschach literature should be given a clearer comparison of the author's system with standard accepted terminologies. Considerable space is used to convince the reader that the Rorschach test is a valuable procedure, and to this end there is included a study of 50 patients in whom the Rorschach and clinical diagnoses are compared. The manual as a whole contains much worthwhile information but, as the writers themselves state, it cannot serve as the "sole armamentarium" with which to plunge into Rorschach administration and interpretation.

B Menninger Clinic 15:192 S '51. Walter Kass. * It is regrettable that assumptions, rationale, interpretive speculation are undifferentiated. Too meager for introductory teaching and too elementary for advanced students, when used alone, it is recommended as supplementary reading by all Rorschach students.

Q J Child Behavior 3:111 Ja '51. M. M. Genn. This manual is a re-printing under one cover of two previously published monographs *An Introduction to Rorschach Psychodiagnostics in Psychiatry* by Brussel and Hitch and *A Rorschach Compendium* by Piotrowski. The section by Brussel and Hitch explains in simple, readable form, what the Rorschach is and how it is administered. There are colored reproductions of the plates and a comprehensive form containing all the tabulations the Rorschach examiner might make. The authors give concise and careful descriptions of all the scoring symbols, what they are usually considered to mean, and what significance can be attached to an excess or deficit of the various signs in any one protocol, especially as related to the various diagnostic entities. Finally, this section includes a report of the Fort Dix study in which a close agreement was found between the Rorschach diagnoses and the psychiatric diagnoses of 50 patients with a variety of mental ailments. This section by Brussel and Hitch is a good, brief introduction to the Rorschach method. Piotrowski in his section covers not only the administration technique, but the history of the Rorschach and the theory behind it. The latter discussion is particularly valuable for potential users of the test. The most important contribution Piotrowski makes is an excellent and comprehensive redefinition of each scoring symbol. These definitions go beyond what is usually found in most training manuals, for they are closely tied to dynamic principles. Piotrowski defines and discusses these symbols in relation to the everyday functioning of individuals, and this frees the trainee from the confinement of interpreting Rorschachs in terms that only another Rorschach examiner can understand. Both sections would be extremely useful to beginners. Piotrowski's section should be useful even to those examiners who have already had some experience with the Rorschach. As the authors themselves indicate, it is understood that a reading of this manual alone will not provide proficiency in Rorschach interpretation. The potential Rorschach examiner should have also a sound understanding of dynamic principles of personality, as well as considerable supervised experience and training.

[119]

★[Re Rorschach.] BUHLER, CHARLOTTE; BUHLER, KARL; AND LEFEVER, D. WELTY. **Development of the Basic Rorschach Score With Manual of Directions.** Rorschach Standardization Studies, No. 1. Los Angeles 46, Calif.: Charlotte Buhler (1127 North Sweetzer Ave.), 1948. Pp. ix, 190. Paper, mimeographed. $4.95. * (PA 23:745)

Am J Orthopsychiatry 19:722–3 O '49. Herman Molish. * The Rorschach records were obtained through individual administrations in which questionable deviations from the usual procedures occurred: (1) "Total time of the test is not measured because it is affected by the subject's verbosity, a factor irrelevant to diagnosis." (2) "The subject is told to give three to five responses per card....subjects who see very little on certain cards and suddenly a great deal

on others are always allowed to continue because the difference in responsiveness is significant." One wonders, however, if increased responsiveness can be obtained in all cases if the examiner has originally induced a mental set by instructing the subject to give only three to five responses per card. (3) "It is best to rely as little as possible on the subject's opinion of what determined his perceptual process." This statement is made to defend the unorthodox series of alternative questions employed during the inquiry period. As justification for this method the authors state that individual Rorschach records given "in the usual way" compare favorably with group Rorschachs. True, the group Rorschach method can also suggest certain determinants by the printed instructions, but this cannot be comparable to the situation where the examiner employs suggestion by such questions as those cited by the authors. * The statistical treatment is extensive; but the selection of sizes of groups within the population upon which these statistics are based invites criticism. The thirty normals who comprise the criterion group in establishing the Basic Rorschach Score are very possibly one of *superior* adults. Especially small, are the normal and schizophrenic groups. After the authors accept their weighted scores, we are informed, "In a number of instances the scoring weights from this chart were modified in the light of the clinical experience of the two authors." It thus appears that the authors already have lost faith in their original hypothesis that "typical personality pictures in Rorschach terms can be described statistically." They do not discuss to any extent their reasons for these changes based on their clinical experience. One does not deny the value of clinical experience, but to conveniently accept statistical findings on the one hand when they agree with hypotheses and discard them on the other certainly cannot be justified in scientific method. An important step in this research is the formulation of four levels of personality integration. These levels are determined statistically by the distribution of the Basic Rorschach Scores in the various clinical groups. The rationale of these levels of integration is to be commended. It stresses the need of functional classification rather than the traditional clinical categories. These levels are: adequacy, conflict, impairment, and reality loss. The problem of overlapping between clinical groups and the so-called "blurring effect" within the four levels, recognized by the authors, is not attacked in the present study but is left for further research. Just how useful these levels are in terms of their present description is doubtful. Personality structure, whatever its clinical classification, is too complex to be fitted into levels described by a series of terms as "unabsorbed and defective reality awareness," "over-wide aspiration focus," etc. For the present, this study will be found valuable not in terms of its application to Rorschach analysis, but only as a beginning point in the understanding of the extensive problem at hand in quantifying Rorschach data, and describing personality structure on a statistical basis.

Am J Psychiatry 106:558–9 Ja '50. Douglas M. Kelley. * The book is quite technical, based primarily on Klopfer's work, and a knowledge of his scoring system is essential for its understanding. Some Rorschach experts will certainly disapprove the changes which are presented primarily in Chapter 10 of the book and which, taken as a whole, in spite of the discussion of these authors, yield a definitely different approach with different results from those achieved by a Rorschach given in the accustomed fashion. Such deviations are not new but must be emphasized particularly in a book of this type which is quantitatively oriented. From this point of view, it is not especially important as to whether the changes in technique are good or bad since the results presented can be assumed to hold good only when the authors' technique is employed. This means that, unless all workers agree to accept this new method of administration and inquiry, little gain is to be had from the volume as a clinical work except the indication that it seems to be successful in the hands of the present workers. It is, of course, highly interesting as a research project but a great deal of validation by other workers must be presented before the changes introduced can be generally accepted. It does, however, represent an excellent example of the type of study which can be done in this complicated field and certainly as such is of interest to all experts. The statistical data seem adequate as far as they go. The book....introduces a system of clinical groups or ranks which can be discriminated by the modifications of the technique. Four ranks are indicated: level I represents essentially variations of normality; level II represents neurotics; III contains depressions, manics, alcoholics and nonpsychotic organics; and IV, schizophrenic categories. This method of evaluation deviates markedly from the usual nosological approach but may be of some practical value. The Rorschach sign list which consists of the usual Rorschach symbols alone or in combined form is well worked out and may prove of use along with ordinary Rorschach procedures. In addition to a comprehensive discussion of their method of administration, the authors have provided ample data explaining their specific modifications in the scoring system. They also present interesting discussions on the psychodynamics of Rorschach signs and, of course, include a wealth of statistical data with a vast area of tables which will hopelessly confuse the nonstatistically trained clinician but serve toward validation of their theory. A number of case presentations are given depicting examples of various types of psychopathology and are of real value. The book should certainly be provocative of considerable argument among Rorschach workers and as such may perhaps provoke some clarification of this complicated but most useful technique.

Arch Neurol & Psychiatry 63:677–8 Ap '50. Mortimer M. Meyer. * a real contribution * Although the study is essentially a statistical one, and will have most direct meaning to Rorschach workers familiar with statistics, it has importance for the clinical psychiatric and psychologic fields, both for its further objective, statistical examination of this widely used instrument and for the new technic—"the basic Rorschach score." * Since the tables and figures are referred to only in a general way, it might have been more helpful if the tables had been placed in the appendix, as they tend to interrupt the reading for the many who are not statisticians. Although the book is mimeographed, rather than printed, it is an excellent publication.

B Menninger Clinic 14:35–6 Ja '50. Walter Kass. * The content and treatment....are geared to the understanding of the more experienced Rorschacher.

J Abn & Social Psychol 45:173–6 Ja '50. Maria A. Rickers-Ovsiankina. * an ambitious and, in many ways, an impressive attempt at standardizing the diagnostic significance of quantitative aspects of the Rorschach Test. The procedure employed for this purpose is the development of a statistically validated sign list, consisting of over one hundred signs....based on the Klopfer scoring system. Although no mention of origin is made, the similarity between this list and the so-called "check list" of Ruth Munroe is evident. The newness of the present approach lies in the systematic application of this list to a large variety of clinical subjects (518 all told, ranging from normal to schizophrenic) and in the careful statistical testing of each item with respect to its usefulness in differentiating one clinical group from another. According to the relative incidence of these signs in the various clinical groups they were assigned numerical weights, ranging from +5 to −5, the plus signs indicating frequency of this sign in groups "more nearly normal," whereas the minus signs reveal an association with the less adjusted groups. The algebraic summation of all weighted signs occurring in a specific record constitutes its Basic Rorschach Score—the focal contribution of this investigation. * the frequent occurrence of a certain Rorschach sign in a particular clinical group or on a certain integration level, as well as its tendency to appear in conjunction with some signs and not with others, in turn throws additional light upon the psychodynamics of the chief Rorschach categories. It is this latter material which seems to the present reviewer to be of most immediate interest to Rorschach workers. The value of an overall measure of adjustment, as the BRS purports to be, is readily appreciated by everyone in research. The usefulness of the BRS, however, at the present stage of the investigation is limited by evidence of wide overlap in scores obtained from the different clinical groups. One therefore doubts that many clinicians will be ready to discard the more conventional psychiatric classifications for the sake of this new measuring device, although there is in principle a good deal of truth in the statement "To predict a patient's chances for recovery with reference to his job, his family, and his practical affiliations, it would be a more functional classification to determine the patient's disintegration level rather than to call him a psychopath or a psychoneurotic." (p. 13) Confidence in the clinical usefulness of the proposed scale also suffers from the employment of precariously crude gradations within the scale, a jump from −3 to +3 being assigned to such minor changes in raw scores as R = 24 vs R = 25, F% = 20 vs F% = 21, sum C = 2½ vs sum C = 3. With respect to the theoretical aspects of the study, our main dissent is with the concepts employed and with their implications. The central concept of integration, e.g., seems to be used interchangeably with that of adjustment. Although it cannot be denied that these two concepts are often linked, they are by no

means synonymous, if only because of their disparity in semantic area of discourse. The promise of quantifiable integration levels within the personality organization presents stimulating potentialities both theoretically and practically. A difficulty arises, however, in trying to think of conflict, defect and reality loss as real levels or relative degrees of some one function, such as integration. It is hard to imagine how these concepts, referring to totally different psychological phenomena, can be related in linear fashion either to each other or to the highest level in the hierarchy, that of adequacy of integration. To return now to the discussion of the psychodynamics of individual Rorschach signs. Categories such as *FM* (animal movement), *m* (movement of inanimate objects), and *C'* (achromatic color), the psychological meaning of which hitherto had not been demonstrated very convincingly in the literature, gain in interpretative clarity. Somewhat new light is thrown upon *F%* (percentage of form responses), *C sum* (weighted total of color responses) and the various shading categories. Although not everybody would agree with all inferences drawn, this analysis is quite enlightening and will no doubt enhance our understanding of these problems, within certain limitations of technique to be discussed later. In a few categories, however, the conclusions seem more misleading than constructive, as e.g., the blanket assertion that "*W* increase is a negative sign." (p. 38) In cases like this one senses the difficulty in trying to deal with Rorschach factors in a crudely quantitative fashion without consideration not only for qualitative aspects of the response, but even for objective discriminations of a finer nature like the "instantaneous whole" or *Wv* response vs the more complex *W's,* analysis of *W's* by cards, etc. Part II of this study describes the authors' technique of administering the test. It involves important departures from the established procedure. Informing the subject of the purpose of the examination, prodding for specific responses, requesting 3–5 interpretations per card, introducing alternatives during the inquiry and so forth, are sufficiently drastic changes to necessitate a good deal of caution in applying the findings of this study to data obtained by a more conventional method. E.g., the novel observation that the peak for *S* (space responses) and *Dd* (small detail) falls into the normal group might very well be a result of prodding for responses. It seems safe to predict that these technical innovations will be the part of the investigation most widely discussed in the Rorschach world, but since such dissection is by nature highly specialized, a mere mention of its implications will suffice here. Part III presents separately the statistics of this investigation, by elucidating in detail (1) the different steps of analysis which led ultimately to the development of the BRS; (2) the establishment of its reliability and validity and finally (3) a variance analysis of the individual Rorschach signs. It is a commendable piece of work, well organized, clearly and comprehensively written, and may be recommended to anyone interested in the problem of quantification in projective techniques. When the Rorschach Test first became popular in this country two schools of thought emerged, one stressing the need for objectivity and norms and the other favoring a qualitative and more wholistic approach. In recent years this opposition has fortunately diminished with both sides explicitly or implicitly admitting the indispensability of either method for a truly valid Rorschach analysis. It is therefore a noteworthy development to see within the same year the publication of two books which not only are reviving the gap, but actually make it deeper than ever: L. K. Frank's so decisively individual-centered interpretation of projective techniques at the one pole and the present volume at the other extreme. Clearly, the latter is the most vigorous and bold champion of making the test "as objective, as simplified and as brief as possible" (p. 50) that has appeared in the literature, aside from Harrower's multiple choice variation. To be sure, we are warned repeatedly not to interpret the concentration upon quantitative aspects of the analysis as an indication of rejection of its qualitative side. And yet, after having made this laudable avowal, the authors soon forget about it and permit themselves to be carried away by their statistical findings. At least such appears to be the case when it is asserted e.g., that no information regarding moral qualities or super ego functions could be elicited from a Rorschach test (p. 32), or when diagnostic inferences are made solely on the basis of the sign list (pp. 164 ff.). Last but not least, it is regrettable that in a publication which sets itself such broad aims, there is a conspicuous absence of reference to the vast Rorschach literature here and abroad. Except for reliance on Klopfer's work, one finds almost no mention of the numerous clinical investigations which have built up over the years the reputation of the Rorschach Test. Even the standardization studies of Beck and of Hertz receive no citation here. Whatever the reason for this "isolationism," it is surely as deplorable in research as it is in any other field.

J Consult Psychol 13:64–5 F '49. Laurance F. Shaffer. Clinical acumen and statistical discipline combined to procure this study of the quantification of the Rorschach. A list of 102 diagnostic signs was developed in an attempt to differentiate among groups ranging from normals to schizophrenics. By statistical procedures, positive and negative weights were attached to each sign, yielding an algebraic total designated as the Basic Rorschach Score (BR). Such scores appear to discriminate significantly among clinical groups, and further, to rank the groups in the order of the severity of personality disturbance shown. * While BR scores cannot be used for individual diagnosis, they may serve to exclude syndromes that do not apply, and may assist in gauging the level of adjustment. If further study sustains the validity of the BR scores, their convenience will increase the utility of the Rorschach in research. Despite minor flaws, the BR represents a forward stride in the difficult task of expressing significant aspects of personality function in quantitative terms. *

J Nerv & Mental Dis 3:173 F '50. (Zygmunt A.) Piotrowski. * The authors introduce a change in the administration of the test limiting the freedom of the association of the individual. "Our procedure makes the test administration more independent of the individual talents of the examiner and examinee." One wonders whether making the test "more independent of the examinee" might not lower its validity. * This is clearly and deliberately a book for the specialist who uses the Rorschach for a diagnostic aid. Everyone actively engaged in Rorschach practice will wish to acquaint himself with this contribution. It is a highly technical book and, for this reason, might discourage the general reader.

Nerv Child 8:71 Ja '49. This is the preliminary edition of a book destined to be the basis of all sound Rorschach work in the future. * The folly of overestimating the Rorschach results is emphasized and a sound evaluation established.

Occupations 27:425–6 Mr '49. Goldie Ruth Kaback. * Personality analysis based on Rorschach signs is not new. The particular weighting of these signs, however, marks a new departure for clinical diagnosis. * Part I....includes an excellent discussion of the psychodynamics of Rorschach signs. However, this discussion is not for the novice. A thorough background in psychoanalytic theory and familiarity with psychopathology are needed in order to differentiate between the interpretations presented here and those held by other Rorschach workers. Part II consists of a Manual of Directions. The procedure is recommended for use for diagnostic purposes only, and if and when objective results are considered essential. The original presentation limits the subject to not more than five responses to each card. The authors apparently have not considered the stimulus value, which differs from card to card. The inquiry also marks a new departure in Rorschach testing. The examiner asks direct questions regarding movement, posture, color, texture, etc. The authors, however, present good logical reasoning for the inquiry changes advocated. Testing the limits procedure is abandoned. Part III presents the Statistical Development of the Basic Rorschach Score. The statistical treatment of the data leaves little to be desired. Figures and tables are clearly explained and can easily be followed. The basis for determining the weights assigned to each BRS is fully described. * The authors warn Rorschach workers that the mechanical use of the diagnostic sign list is to be avoided. The list will probably be most useful for quick personality appraisal. Content analysis is still an important technique for good psychological diagnosis. This manual is not for the newcomer to the Rorschach field. It can best be used by those who have had extensive Rorschach training and experience with a variety of clinical subjects.

[120]

★[Re Rorschach.] BUHLER, CHARLOTTE, AND LEFEVER, D. WELTY. **A Rorschach Study on the Psychological Characteristics of Alcoholics.** Yale University, Laboratory of Applied Physiology, Memoirs of the Section of Studies on Alcohol, No. 6. New Haven, Conn.: Quarterly Journal of Studies on Alcohol, 1948. Pp. viii, 64. Paper. $0.75. * (PA 22: 1232) (Reprinted from Q J Studies Alcohol 8: 197–260 S '47. *)

Am J Psychiatry 106:78–9 Jl '49. *Albert Ax and Milton Greenblatt.* This interesting and provocative monograph attempts to define characteristics of patients suffering from chronic alcoholism by relating Rorschach findings in 100 alcoholics with findings for other groups * The authors are well aware of the complexity of their

problem, and the fact that alcoholics represent a wide diversity of types. Their differentiation between superficial and deep-level conflicts, however, makes one pause to wonder whether acute pressures are not highly selective phenomena related to deeper problems even in the alcoholic. Further difficulty is encountered in comprehending what is meant by a "a physiological factor underlying alcoholism." "The reasonableness of such an assumption is strengthened by our finding that there are striking similarities in the response patterns of the alcoholic group and the nonpsychotic group. Further support for this assumption may be seen in the fact that educational, moral, religious, and social influences, as well as manipulation of the environment, are more effective in some cases of alcoholism than formal psychotherapy alone." In dealing with human behavior, can we ever neglect a *physiological factor?* And does the supposed lack of effectiveness of psychotherapy in alcoholism argue in favor of an "organic" disease? The authors' objective and statistical method of setting up a comprehensive list of discriminative signs empirically evaluated on clinical groups is an effective approach to Rorschach diagnosis. Doing a "Discriminant Function" analysis would probably be the ideal method as it would take into consideration the intercorrelations of the various signs, but the work would be prohibitive for more than a few signs. The charting of the signs and marking their discriminative reliability by the 5% confidence level is excellent. Of course with 99 signs, at least 5 signs significant at the 5% level should occur by chance. Significant differences between groups can only be claimed when the number of significant signs exceeds 5. The crucial problem arises as to which of the significant signs are the *real* discriminative ones and which are the spurious 5 that occurred by chance. The only way to separate satisfactorily the sheep from the goats is to apply the set of empirically determined discriminative signs on a new group of subjects and see which signs stand up to their discriminative task. The old problem of regression toward the mean is especially dangerous here where there are so many signs to select from. While very likely some of the signs here found discriminative may hold up on a new group, it is very probable that some will lose all, and others a great part, of their discriminative value. Even more vulnerable is the weighting of signs, regardless by what method. The arbitrary weights, as used here, may be as good as any but when tried out on a new group the weights will nearly all be changed. Most experimenters with such data have found that the weights are so radically changed when applied to a new group as to be worthless. The net effect of weighting seems to be to exaggerate the discrimination as found on the original groups and actually to reduce the discriminative value of the signs when tried on new groups. They tend to exaggerate the effect of regression to the mean and at the same time exaggerate the researcher's disappointment when verification is attempted. The obvious answer to the above criticism is to apply the identical set of discriminative signs to a new group of subjects and verify the predictive signs. Even without increasing the number of subjects, possibly a more rigorous method would have been to select randomly one half of the cases and pick the discriminative signs on the basis of the first half, then apply them to the second half and retain only those signs that discriminate for the new groups. A dubious trend in this monograph is the definition in clinical terms of a Rorschach sign (like *m*) on the basis of the clinical groups here used, then using the presence or absence of the sign as descriptive of the diagnostic group. Thus they arrive at the novel meaning of *m* as "tension tolerance" presumably from clinical observations (since the standard Rorschach authorities do not thus define *m*) and then proceed to use the low *m* for alcoholics as indicative of low tension tolerance in the group. If they have other sources for this definition of *m*, they fail to specify them. Certainly external definitions of all the Rorschach signs are required if they are to be used for describing the personalities of the diagnostic groups. On the other hand, it is perfectly legitimate to use clinically described groups to give new meaning to the Rorschach signs, but one cannot do both on the same material. The above criticisms do not significantly detract from the value of this excellent monograph which represents a definite advance in Rorschach diagnosis.

B Menninger Clinic 14:38 Ja '50. Laura Malkenson. * Before this approach can yield fruitful results, a better understanding of what such signs mean in terms of personality must be gained. The larger research which the authors are conducting may further such understanding, rendering the study they present here more meaningful.

J Am Med Assn 138:786 N 6 '48. * The monograph does not include a sample of the original Rorschach test records. A report on a Rorschach test investigation, without a sample of original test records, amounts to asking a reviewer to accept interpretations on faith, without the raw material that was interpreted. The authors do promise (page 13) that "detailed reports will be made elsewhere," since the present study is part of a larger one. Perhaps when these other reports are published, some Rorschach test records will be included. Until then the report is incomplete.

Psychiatric Q 22:770 O '48. The authors.... report "a pattern of signs significant for the alcoholic of every clinical group." * However, one non-alcoholic group composed of non-psychotic epileptics and non-psychotic organics, had the same pattern. These signs, then, would be of little value in differentiating between the two groups. * The authors have conducted an excellent study which may well contribute to a better understanding of the Rorschach records of alcoholics and the results may be of some value in differentiating the alcoholic types. This well-written book should be of definite interest to all Rorschach workers whether or not they agree with the findings.

Psychosom Med 11:393 N–D '49. Gotthard Booth. * interesting * The procedure is based on the frequency of 99 "signs" in different clinical groups. Most of the "signs" are derived from the scoring system of Klopfer and Kelley, and carefully differentiated and quantified. Some of the "signs," however, appear to be arbitrary combinations of incongruous contents, e.g. #77 "Confabulation, contamination" and #93 "Dead, injured animals, corpses, snakes, spiders, gorillas, monsters, ghosts or frightening fantasy figures = 3+." No attempt is made to consider the gestalt character of the inkblots in general, and its specific variations in the ten cards. Thanks to the very rigorous statistical evaluation of the sign frequencies the questionable signs do not appear among those which the authors found significant. * The syndrome shared by the alcoholics and the neurological cases is the combination of low tension tolerance and high anxiety, despite immediate discharge of tensions. This character of the alcoholic personality is not the result of secondary alcoholic deterioration, since it is most outspoken among the younger patients. The authors point out that the presence of a "primary organic factor" in alcoholism explains that alcoholism manifests itself first when the patient has to meet the demands of society as an adult, that he is benefited by social support rather than by individual psychotherapy. Without such external help the alcoholic "feels up against a wall....and escapes....in forgetting by means of alcohol" (p. 41). Perhaps it would be more pertinent to say that the organically overemphasized dependent needs of the alcoholic can be satisfied on the level of strong group relationship. Only if the latter fails does the alcoholic experience the need for the chemical crutch of alcohol.

Q R Psychiatry & Neurol 3:364–5 Jl'48. Isabelle V. Kendig. The questions which this study was designed to answer were framed by L. K. Frank as follows: "What in the alcoholic leads him, or drives him to utilize alcohol instead of all the other neurotic, psychotic or psychosomatic patterns of defense or escape or release equally available?" and "How does it happen that the individual develops craving for alcohol only at adolescence or in adult years, as contrasted with the early development of the neurotic and psychotic patterns, many of which derive from infancy or preschool years?" The answers were sought by the authors in Rorschach studies of alcoholics and contrasting normal and clinical groups. * the dependence of this study on such ill-defined concepts as psychopathy, psychoneurosis, schizophrenia, etc., must be considered a limiting factor. After a brief review of three recent Rorschach studies of alcoholism, in which the findings show an almost perfect negative correlation (!), the authors set forth in some detail their own statistical procedures. Their scoring is based on the principles developed by Klopfer and Davidson but they themselves have devised an exhaustive check list of diagnostic criteria (99 items) in terms of which their data is expressed. * Interpreting their data, the authors find "a pattern of signs significant for the alcoholic of every clinical group." They are distinguished from nonalcoholics in general by significantly high anxiety (k plus K plus FK) in conjunction with low tension tolerance (low m). The only nonalcoholic group showing a similar pattern are organic cases (including epileptics) without psychosis, which tends to strengthen the assumption of an underlying physiologic factor. The alcoholic differs from the psychopath in showing better functioning rationality (F per cent), greater self criticism (FK), greater sensitivity (Fc), and better emotional responsiveness (Sum C). The answer to Frank's first

question is not explicitly given by the authors but presumably is to be found in the intolerance of tension (low m) which differentiates the alcoholic from the psychoneurotic and from most other clinical groups. The onset of his symptomatology in adolescence is a direct result for he is unable to meet the new demands which arise at that time involving the choice and pursuit of a career and responsibility for a family. With a great deal of ambition or wishful thinking (high W) but lacking directivity (low M), the painfulness of his failures in perseverance accentuates his difficulties. As already indicated, this study is weakened by its uncritical acceptance of our present purely descriptive nomenclature but the approach is otherwise sound and the results fruitful to the extent that they uncover the dynamics of well-recognized behavioral patterns, whatever may be their ultimate status as psychiatric entities.

[121]

[*Re* Rorschach.] FORD, MARY. **The Application of the Rorschach Test to Young Children.** University of Minnesota, Institute of Child Welfare Monograph Series, No. 23. Minneapolis, Minn.: University of Minnesota Press, 1946. Pp. xii, 114. $2.00. (London: Oxford University Press. 16*s.*) * (*PA* 21:807)

Brit J Psychol, Gen Sect 38:42–3 S'47. T. A. Although much has been published about the Rorschach test as applied to adults and adolescents, the literature regarding its use with young children is comparatively scanty, and to this Dr Ford's book makes a welcome addition. She presents a careful analysis of the responses given by 123 children of ages between 3 and 8 years with whom she had wisely established previously a friendly relationship, so making the test situation easier. Another aid to good co-operation was probably the high intelligence of the children, whose average I.Q. was 124–35—not a typical sample of the population, as the author recognizes. In administering the test Dr Ford made a deviation from the standard Rorschach procedure by restricting the use of each card to the upright position, so decreasing markedly the normal range of perceptual stimuli—a simplification which she found necessary with very young children, but which makes comparison difficult between her results and those of other investigators. To many Rorschach workers it may seem a pity that the modern Research Exchange scoring has been ignored in favour of the less differentiated original, though to the latter there is added a new category described as OL., "Organizational Link," which seems to deserve further investigation as a factor in estimating the intellectual development of young subjects. Interesting tables are given of determinants compared with age, sex, and intelligence quotients, and an appendix contains three sample records scored by the author. In the study of these 123 tests there is perhaps too much stress laid upon the points value of isolated determinants and too little upon the interrelation of components and the general personality structure. It is, however, clear that Dr Ford combines a scientific approach with an excellent contact with small children, and it may be hoped that this book will prove to be a trial trip before her fuller exploration of this field of enquiry.

Can J Psychol 1:214–16 D '47. Frances S. Alexander. As a contribution to the scientific investigation of the Rorschach test applied to young children, this volume merits consideration. * No one will doubt the usefulness of Dr. Ford's study in exploring the use of the Rorschach with young children. The reviewer feels that certain considerations must be kept in mind in accepting her data. These relate primarily to sampling and statistical treatment of results. In making comparisons with respect to sex and age, the number of cases is often too small to give valid age and sex trends. In fact, trends are made much of and the impression is given that these trends point to valid conclusions even though the critical ratios reported are below the limit of statistical reliability or omitted entirely. In this respect, great confusion exists in the discussion of colour determinants (pages 47, 48, and 54). Sometimes the data are analyzed on the basis of the average number of a particular determinant in relation to an age group, at other times, on the basis of the percentage of the determinant in the total R. The results drawn by these two methods are sometimes diametrically opposed (pages 45 and 73). It would have made for clarity to have kept the comparisons in terms of proportions since R shows variation with age. The author presents a list of suggestions for further study which indicates that she realizes the limitations of her data. A useful glossary of Rorschach terminology is appended.

Fed Probation 13:54 Mr '49. Z. A. Piotrowski. * Ford studied 123 children, 57 boys and 66 girls, with an age range from 2½ to 8 years. This is the largest single group of children ever reported. However, the group is not representa-

tive because its average IQ was 124 with a range from 90 to 157. The fathers of more than two-thirds of the children were professional people; only 10 percent of the fathers belong to the average socioeconomic group. * An extensive and helpful bibliography of 154 items closes the monograph. The interpretation of children's records is more difficult than that of adults for two main reasons: First, the intensive process of growth and maturation which takes place in childhood complicates the interpretation of Rorschach records. We should have different norms for different age groups. It would be easier to differentiate pathology from inadequacy due to the immaturity of young age. Furthermore an adult examiner finds it more difficult to understand children than adults. Therefore it is more difficult for him to translate children's Rorschachs in terms of real psychological experiences than to explain adults' Rorschachs in terms of attitudes and real feelings. It will take a great deal of effort to obtain adequate norms for all ages and intellectual levels in childhood. Dr. Ford's contribution is an important step toward this desirable goal.

Nerv Child 7:344 Jl '48. This short study, which has been almost completely ignored, seems to us to have a very sound viewpoint, avoiding the mechanization of the Rorschach test which is unfortunately so prevalent today and which will eventually destroy its usefulness.

Q R Biol 22:369 D '47. Helen Hewitt Arthur. * a careful exploratory study done to evaluate the use of the Rorschach test as it is now applied to very young children. It is a most provocative subject and one which the author....has dealt with in a scholarly but never pedantic fashion. * She aptly stresses the need for standardizing this test for more intelligent and valuable usage with the pre-school child. In addition to making these original observations, Mary Ford has compared her results minutely with the conclusions reached in the few previous studies of a similar nature. Of especial importance to clinical workers with children are not so much the formal conclusions which Mary Ford draws so ably as rather the implications of the insight to be gained into child thinking through the use of a properly standardized projective test. It is to be hoped that serious Rorschach students will take up some or all of the author's twelve suggestions for future research in this area.

Rorschach Res Exch & J Proj Tech 11:53–5 no 1 '47. This book promises to be of great interest to Rorschach workers because of the paucity of published material in this field. Unfortunately, the promise is not completely borne out, for reasons inherent in the author's approach. * Ford is chiefly concerned with the statistical and non-clinical aspects of the method, hence she has stressed especially those studies whose results were quantitatively expressed. * the scoring method....is an eclectic combination of the original Rorschach symbols with certain additions suggested by Beck, Hertz and Rickers. The concept of small usual details (d) was not utilized, and the author states that she made no distinction between animal and human movement. This, however, is later contradicted by a breakdown (in Tables 6 and 11) into M, FM, and m responses. One new scoring category, that of "organizational links" (OL) or "number of logical connections," is introduced. * With respect to the general pattern of responses, the earlier work of Klopfer and Margulies is substantially corroborated. To these authors' three patterns of early Rorschach reactions, Dr. Ford suggests the addition of a fourth. This is the so-called "perseverated-logic" stage, occurring most frequently with 3- and 4-year-olds, in which "magic repetition" occurs in response to *details* rather than to the whole card. In the color area, the author's findings disagree with Klopfer and Margulies, in that she finds that CF exceeded other color responses at all levels except at age 5, where FC predominated. Many factors might contribute to this discrepancy, including differences in scoring standards, which are difficult to apply at the preschool level, or differences in emotional maturity between the subjects used in the two studies. Since this is a crucial area for interpretation, the need for further careful normative research is emphasized. To provide data on reliability, 55 of the children were retested and correlation coefficients computed for the major categories. Also, the split-half technique was used for selected determinants. The test-retest coefficients were all positive, ranging from +.38 to +.86 with a majority above +.70. The split-half method gave reliabilities of +.47 to +.84 on the original test. This method is obviously inappropriate in Rorschach research since the different potentialities of the cards prevent their division into two equal groups. Despite this, it is encouraging to note the size of the coefficients. * Of major interest to many Rorschach workers will be the findings with respect to the validity of intelligence and personality diagnosis. The au-

thor investigated Rorschach's original contention that W, M, and F+% were related positively and A% was related negatively to intelligence, and that O% and C increased with increase in the intellectual level, but also increased as it declined. The highest correlations found were between MA and OL (+.684), number of items mentioned (+.680), and R(+.634). W correlated only to a slight degree (+.108). F+ M, M+, and O+% were all positively related to MA. Color responses as a group showed a slight but positive relationship to MA, and A% (in agreement with Beck but in disagreement with Rorschach) correlated slightly but positively (+.070) with MA. In evaluating these findings, it is necessary to consider two factors. Most of the determinants vary with *both* CA and MA, a factor which immensely complicates the determination of such statistical relationships among young children whose mental ability is growing very rapidly. Also, it will be remembered that Rorschach's findings were based largely on work with adults and that Beck's study was of feeble-minded children; thus, differences from both their results might well be expected in a homogeneous group of superior young children. Once again, this reviewer wishes to point out that adequate norms are needed at each year level before completely valid theories can be established beyond cavil. The section on the validity of the determinants of personality, which is a crucial issue in Rorschach work, is very disappointing. As criteria, Dr. Ford used scores on the Marston Introversion-Extraversion Scale and on four selected items from the Olson Behavior Rating Scale, the ratings being made by nursery school teachers. The M : Sum C and R (VIII–X) : R ratios were utilized as a measure of introversion-extraversion. In this superior group of young children, introversion was positively related to MA. In average or inferior groups, a different result might well occur. Comparison of the M : Sum C ratio with scores on the Marston for 30 children showed a contingency ratio of 60%. Combination with R(VIII–X) : R increased the ratio to 73%. This finding supports Klopfer and Kelley's claim as to the value of this ratio and, at the same time, indicates the extent to which determinants taken out of context lose their value. * The subject matter of this book is potentially of great importance. Very few studies of Rorschach reactions of young children have been published and none other to the reviewer's knowledge in which such a painstaking, statistical analysis has been made. In the light of Dr. Ford's stated aims, she has fulfilled her commitments in all except the fourth. Here, the reader is disappointed to find such a vital problem as that of the validity of the determinants of personality dismissed with a statement of coefficients of correlation with an Introversion-Extraversion Scale and four items (!) selected from the Olson Behavior Rating Scale. This same coldly non-clinical viewpoint pervades the entire volume and dilutes the enthusiasm with which the reader might otherwise greet it. If the author's laborious statistical treatment had only been leavened with some attempt to delineate also the qualitative aspects of the records and to consider these in relation to more full-bodied criteria of adjustment, how much more valuable a study this might have been! Among its positive contributions, however, are the following: discovery that forbidding card rotation assists in administration to young children without decreasing the number of responses; description of a new stage in the appearance of characteristic early reaction patterns to the test; verification of the earlier use of movement by boys and of color by girls; establishment of the reliability of the major determinants; last but not least, underlining the necessity for normative studies of young children of varying intellectual, social and economic status.

For additional reviews, see 3:80.

[122]

★[*Re* Rorschach.] HARROWER, M. R., AND STEINER, M. E. **Large Scale Rorschach Techniques: A Manual for the Group Rorschach and Multiple Choice Tests, Second Edition.** With contributions by Floyd O. Due, Beatrice A. Wright, and M. Erik Wright. Springfield, Ill.: Charles C Thomas, Publisher, 1951. Pp. xx, 353. $8.50. * (Oxford, England: Blackwell Scientific Publications, Ltd. 63*s*.) (*PA* 26: 2183)

J Am Med Assn 147: 1718 D 22 '51. * To fully understand the group procedures and their results it is advisable that the reader have some previous knowledge of scoring and interpretative principles for the individual Rorschach, since they are not given in the book. This edition contains several studies not found in the first edition (1944). The most valuable is a statistical comparison between the group and individual Rorschach methods as to the locations, determinants, and contents "pulled" by each card for normal persons. This, together with the studies of frequency of rejection and distri-

bution of anatomic answers on each of the 10 cards and the list of popular answers, can be a great aid even to the clinician interested only in the individual Rorschach. The section on interpretative principles in differential diagnosis provides a good review of pathognomonic indicators, for they are presented in a clearer and more condensed form than in the more basic texts by Klopfer and Beck. It tends to be dogmatic, however, and over-generalized, so that one who is unfamiliar with the Rorschach may be led to accept them without qualification. This is not intended to be the last word on the group Rorschach and multiple choice tests, but rather it is meant to point the way to future research. Clear in its presentation of experimental design and the statistical methods used, this book is an excellent example of the scientific approach to a study of personality.

J Consult Psychol 15:513 D '51. Laurance F. Shaffer. * The main body of the original book is unchanged, save for the deletion of numerous pages of superfluous graphs, and for a few minor editorial corrections. The principal new material is confined to a 53-page added section on "recent developments," which does scant justice to its topic. Of the 34 "new" studies cited, 26 are dated 1947 or earlier. Moreover, the section's poor organization gives evidence of hasty and careless preparation. A really up-to-date annotated bibliography would have been more serviceable. There is also a supposedly new section on "card-pull" that turns out to be a rearrangement of some old data on the relative frequencies of locations, determinants, and content categories. The second edition does not give nearly as good support as it might to the genuinely useful Group Rorschach. On the other hand, it maintains the unduly optimistic attitude of the first edition toward the Multiple Choice Test, in spite of the bulk of adverse evidence.

For reviews of the first edition, see 3:82.

[123]

[*Re* Rorschach.] KABACK, GOLDIE RUTH. **Vocational Personalities: An Application of the Rorschach Group Method.** Columbia University, Teachers College, Contributions to Education, No. 924. Harry D. Kitson, faculty sponsor. New York: Bureau of Publications, the College, 1946. Pp. xi, 116. $2.10. * (*PA* 21:1929)

J Appl Psychol 33:612-3 D '49. Boyd McCandless. * The author is to be commended for a type of study greatly needed. It seems however, first, that such a study can hardly attain highly reliable or valid results as long as socio-economic pressures, family predilections, etc., determine the chosen career, often quite without regard to the personal wishes or capabilities of the individual involved; and that, second, a Rorschach study is difficult if not impossible when scoring categories of the test are considered (as is almost necessary) without the benefit of refinements in statistics of percentages, ratios, and sub-relationships. The most ardent proponent of the Rorschach would probably not regard it as infallible when adapted as a group method and scored for means, using isolated scoring categories. In the hands of a competent technician, used to illuminate other data, it often seems to be of great use in vocational counseling; more "clinical" validations along the rather promising lines shown by the author may result from this interesting, carefully done, but practically not too useful study, the final conclusion of which is necessarily that there are all types of persons who enter or study in the fields of accountancy and pharmacy.

For additional reviews, see 3:82a.

[124]

★[*Re* Rorschach.] KLOPFER, WALTER G. **Suggestions for the Systematic Analysis of Rorschach Records.** Los Angeles, Calif.: U.C.L.A. Student's Store, University of California, September 1949. Pp. 16. Paper, mimeographed. $0.35. *

J Proj Tech 14:79 Mr '50. Winafred Lucas. This brief but comprehensive manual begins with a delineation of personality areas in which the Rorschach is able to contribute hypotheses and information. A succinct review of the analysis of quantitative Rorschach data begins the actual discussion of interpretative clues. This is followed by a sequence analysis of the ten cards. In this analysis both the inter-relationships of the cards and their content symbolism are discussed in a practical way, valuable in the sketching out of norms for the various cards so that the new Rorschach worker will have some idea what to expect before, instead of after, his first hundred records. The manual closes with an outline of relevant quantitative and qualitative aspects from which hypotheses concerning various areas of the personality may be drawn, as, for example, intellectual potentials or the availability of inner resources as an aid in adjustment. These "Suggestions" have been in experimental use by graduate students for the last

academic year and have proven very useful in closing the gap between the interpretative hypotheses published in the literature and the many additional interpretative clues used by most experienced workers in actual clinical practice. The author would appreciate receiving information on any differences in findings or on any further clues in content analysis for the various cards. A revision of the manual will be made taking cognizance of such contributions.

[125]

[*Re* Rorschach.] MASLOW, PAUL. **The Analysis and Control of Human Experiences: The Individual Seen Through Rorschach, Volumes 1 and 2.** Brooklyn 2, N.Y.: the Author, 16 Court St., 1947. Pp. iii, 233; iv, 195. Paper, mimeographed. Out of print. * (*PA* 21:2326)

Am J Orthopsychiatry 18:180–1 Ja '48. * a revision and an expansion of the author's *Rorschach Psychology,* which appeared in 1945, and constitutes the philosophy rather than the clinical knowledge of one not a psychologist, who mastered the Rorschach technique autodidactically. The bibliography of 212 items testifies to the author's extensive reading, done in a few years. Personal contact with Mr. Maslow made it clear that he does not expect anyone to learn Rorschach technique from these two volumes. Yet even the trained Rorschach worker will find it hard to digest their contents. The author is as radical as he is revolutionary in some of his philosophical speculations and conclusions. Basically, he is in opposition to many of the tenets of modern psychology, psychiatry, and psychoanalysis. He attempts to find his own system or formulation. Hence he tries to cover the whole realm of human behavior, from both micro- and macro-scopic angles. Generalizations are then presented as they might appear in a Rorschach setting. The books contain no case records analyzed and explained in terms of personality constellations. Rather, items such as reason, dialectics of thinking, cultural frame of reference, constriction, anxiety, formation of ideas, and many others are discussed in general terms and then related to Rorschach language. Maslow finds the present systems of Rorschach scoring inadequate. He substitutes his own individual scoring, thus adding many over-refined combinations to the already comprehensive series of Rorschach symbols. For instance, he breaks down human movement (M) into EAM (active), LAM (living), RAM (restrained) and FAM (flexor). Not only does such an over-elaboration lead to confusion, it serves no practical purpose. To this reviewer it appears almost pathological to attempt to explore every crevice and niche of possible human behavior with philosophical speculation in which clinical reality is not considered.

Am J Psychiatry 104:510–1 Ja '48. W. Donald Ross. * Maslow's book....contains neither preface nor summary to indicate the audience for whom it is intended or the function it is expected to fulfill. It contains many ideas which might be of interest to Rorschach specialists, but these are diluted by ambitious generalizations and mixed with discussions on social philosophy which seem hardly relevant to the starting point of the book. The Rorschach data which are included suggest that the author has a considerable knowledge of the technique and a profound understanding of people, but he presents these data dogmatically, without evidence, and makes constant use of an apparently original and almost neologistic scoring system, with no explanation of its origins. Many of his sociological ideas are also profound, and his future prophecies are indicative of a most fertile imagination. However, the connections of these with the Rorschach method are extremely tenuous, and the route by which they have been reached most circuitous. If there is a contribution from the Rorschach method to social science, the author has obscured it by circumstantiality and excessive ambition. There are many typographical errors, suggesting a hasty printing, and the footnote on the very first page of Volume One makes reference to a bibliography supposed to be presented in that volume but not appearing until the second volume dated in the following year. The book was apparently not conceived as a whole nor finished with care toward a definite purpose. There are two reasons for printing a review of it. One is to warn others that its pearls can be gleaned only at the expense of much wasted reading. The other is to give recognition to the brilliance of the author, which requires harnessing into more useful channels. There is much in the book which could profitably be printed if it were rewritten several times to eliminate the circumlocution of the author's spontaneity. Some of the chapters could be published, with some revision, as essays on a great variety of topics. Better still, collaboration with someone of a different temperament might enable the author to make a unique contribution to the integration of the Rorschach technique with

psychopathology. At present the volumes are unique, but their contribution is not clear.

Am J Sociol 53:318 Ja '48. Alfred R. Lindesmith. The reviewer finds it almost impossible to comment adequately upon the ruminations included in these two volumes, with their one hundred and eight chapters. The ostensible purpose of the books is to describe the inner workings of the human personality as revealed by the Rorschach technique. The author, however, uses the Rorschach test as a springboard from which he plunges into discussions not only of personality but also of such subjects as war, business, profits, science, fascism, and countless others, whose relevance to the central purpose is not adequately indicated. Comments specifically directed at the Rorschach technique are vague, and the evidence upon which statements are made is lacking. The work itself may best be described as a kind of Rorschach test for the reader. The readability of the volumes is reduced by the prevalence of typographical errors, awkward and incorrect sentences, poor type, and by the use of a superfluous system of alphabetical symbols. If these faults were corrected and the entire study were condensed and made more compact by being limited to matters definitely connected with the Rorschach test, something of value might emerge.

Nerv Child 6:475 O '47. A few years ago this author offered a philosophical discussion of the Rorschach method. He now adds an extensive study of the same type which attempts to apply Rorschach diagnosis to the total personality and to the various concepts most commonly known in modern psychology. Since not too many Rorschach signs are applied, the uninitiated can also get something out of the intensive study.

Psychiatric Q 21:701 O '47. Only small parts of these two volumes deal directly with the Rorschach method. Mr. Maslow touches on a very wide variety of topics, great and small, in an unexpected order. The topics include various mental mechanisms, religion, the OPA, communism, fascism, psychotherapy, recent socioeconomic changes in the United States, the unity of sciences, an outline of a future "empathetic" society, and many others. The author criticizes psychology for seeing only the bad in man. Psychoanalysis "is the single science that attempts to fill the breach left by a rejected church in the lives of irreligious people. Were it not for this stepchild [psychoanalysis], science would have absolutely nothing to offer to the spirit of mankind." Mr. Maslow's work is rambling, vague, and almost incomprehensible in parts. Its quality level is very uneven; it lacks synthesis and lucidity. Whatever unity there is, is due to the author's fervent and exalted appeal for "empathy" and for the recognition of the good in man.

For additional reviews, see 3:86.

[126]

★[*Re* Rorschach.] Mons, W. **Principles and Practice of the Rorschach Personality Test.** London: Faber & Faber Ltd., 1947. Pp. 164. * (*PA* 22:4424) For latest edition, see 127.

Am J Psychiatry 105:556 Ja '49. Fred V. Rockwell. This short book....is based upon his lectures on the Rorschach method given in the British army during the last war. It was compiled in the field, without benefit of textbooks or even the author's own notes. The book, designed to serve as an introduction for the study of more advanced works, contains brief sections on administration, scoring, interpretation of the separate scores, and assessment of personality, in a style very similar to Klopfer and Kelley's presentation, of which it might be termed a synopsis. As such it could serve a useful purpose to the reader who is already familiar with the more detailed productions of various earlier writers. For anyone not acquainted with the Rorschach method, this book at best offers a rather one-sided orientation to a highly controversial field of investigation.

Austral J Philos 26:132–3 S '48. I. K. Waterhouse. * the author claims "freedom from dogmatism where the method is concerned" and proposes its "reduction to a basis of logic and common sense." In the text, however, there is little to justify this claim: it is clear from the outset that he follows most of the established procedures of administration, scoring, and interpretation and accepts the test as offering a valid and reliable assessment of various personality traits. Although the Rorschach technique has been so frequently criticised on these very points of reliability and validity, he provides no satisfactory evidence or discussion to support the assumptions involved in these procedures. Again, the author remarks that when he began to use the Rorschach technique he had hoped it would be an "empirically standardised instrument," but that trial and error and considerable reading had revealed disagreement between workers and freedom in their definitions and

interpretations. But despite the author's claim to eschew dogma and rely on logic and common sense, none of this disagreement is presented in this book. * The opening chapter, on *The Theory of the Test,* does not give....a critical examination of underlying theory, but a superficial account of the origin of the test, a sound warning that the technique will not automatically provide a diagnosis, that much depends on the skill and experience of its user, a cursory description of the ten standard cards and a short statement on the results of retests. * This book is an introductory sketch for beginners: the author has leant heavily on material already recorded in available literature. * The neophyte who wishes to use the test will not be adequately equipped by a perusal of this book. He will need to take the author's prescription seriously and embark on a liberal and critical study of more advanced works, and also to receive some initial supervision from practised Rorschach workers.

Brit J Psychol, Gen Sect 39:69 S '48. Anybody who is proposing to use the Rorschach test will find this a very good practical manual. No attempt is made to present the method as easy or short; there is no suggestion that success is likely to be achieved by "blind" trial or in the absence of a considerable amount of information which cannot be contributed by the test itself. Rorschach is in fact presented as a useful tool for the psychologist or psychiatrist—especially the latter—who is well equipped in other ways. The volume is the outcome of a large amount of practical experience. It is clearly presented and is mercifully concise. Nothing better concerning this technique has been published in this country.

Brit Med J 4595:184–5 Ja 29 '49. Eliot Slater. Though the Rorschach test has become firmly established and is widely used in Britain, no really elementary textbook has been published until now, and the test remains largely in the hands of the expert. One unfortunate result of this is that its potentialities are not always realized as fully as they might be. The tester is seldom a clinician and so does not select his subjects, and the clinician does not know how to select those patients for whom the test can most appropriately be used. Both classes of reader will welcome this book. Dr. Mons gives an account of the theoretical basis and of the actual technique of the test, and provides the clinician with information about the indications for its use and about its limitations.

He emphasizes the fact that this is an introduction only; he is writing for beginners, and does not take for granted in his readers any previous acquaintance with the test. He has evolved his own technique of interpretation, and this he describes minutely and clearly. The reader will have little difficulty in following the instructions, and will find that most of his difficulties and questions have been answered. Although for so small a book it is remarkably comprehensive, it is by no means an exhaustive description of all the theories and techniques which have grown up round the Rorschach test, especially in recent years. It is rather an account of the views and practice of one exponent, evolved by him from an extensive acquaintance with the literature and wide personal experience. It is to be recommended as a most readable introduction to the subject.

J Consult Psychol 13:309 Ag '49. Laurance F. Shaffer. * The author makes a few original contributions to scoring, including *Wv* for inferior "cheap" wholes, and *Mm* for "expressive poses." * While it offers little that is novel, the book is a clear and simple text, quite adequate for an introductory course.

J Nerv & Mental Dis 109:281 Mr '49. (Zygmunt A.) Piotrowski. * The presentation of the results which can be expected from the use of the test is reserved and testifies better than any other part of the book to the wide and sound experience of the author. Dr. Mons has given us a lucid, lively and very informative introductory text for beginners. The book is very readable and can be highly recommended.

Lancet 254:600 Ap 17 '48. * Mons's account is thoroughly intelligible: it does not conceal the difficulties of using the test, nor introduce unnecessary complications. On the other hand, it does not offer convincing evidence on the test's reliability or validity. This is not a criticism of Dr. Mons, however, since the extremely wide scope allowed for personal interpretations of results makes it impossible to produce general evidence of that kind. Some will feel that the use of the Rorschach test is as far removed from scientific psychology as palmistry or graphology; but this implies no disrespect, for the practitioner who has made an extensive study of human hands can learn a great deal about a man's character from the pair presented to him, especially if he is skilful in the conversation he makes in the meantime. The Rorschach expert conducts his test in the same way, using all the

additional information he can assemble to help him in interpreting the result. Can we then, safely attribute to the test the successes achieved by the skilled practitioner, or blame it for the failures and indiscretions of the unskilled? Is it not, perhaps, a measure of the examiner rather than the examined?

Mental Health 8:81 F '49. T. A. In common with other pioneer Rorschach workers in this country, Dr. Mons learnt the hard way, teaching himself by reading, experience, and comparison of notes with colleagues. With his own past tribulations in mind he sets out to smooth the path of beginners in this complex method of personality assessment, and does so with much skill. * To produce a simple handbook on so elaborate a diagnostic instrument is a formidable task. Dr. Mons' courage is especially worthy of honour because, as noted in the preface, his book was compiled during the war, on active foreign service, having "neither textbooks at hand nor access to my notes stored in England." It is an amazing feat to have produced so good a book under such conditions, with only a rare slip for lack of references. Dr. Mons modestly describes his work as an introduction to more advanced studies, but in addition to describing the mechanism of the test, he puts forward a number of original views and interesting suggestions upon the basis of a very wide range of cases. Besides adult work, Dr. Mons has given the Rorschach test to over a thousand children of ages between 4 and 16 years, an experience probably unique in this country. It is to be hoped that he will later find time to publish his norms for various ages. This book is admirably practical in plan and content, with excellent advice upon methods of recording. A chapter entitled "The Practice of the Test" supplies a long-felt want in setting the student on the right road, while later chapters on scoring and assessment are clearly set out and exemplified. The significance of separate signs in the various categories are lucidly described, with the use of familiar modes of reasoning and examples from everyday life to illustrate points which are further demonstrated by case records. It may be that too great stress is laid upon isolated signs as diagnostic factors instead of upon the balance of all factors in the total record; it may be that some of Dr. Mons' opinions will be challenged; but any criticism should be far outweighed by appreciation, with respectful congratulations to the author on producing the first British textbook upon the Rorschach method.

Mind 57:389 Jl '48. B. A. Farrell. * a helpful manual for the beginner * The tone....is cautious and undogmatic. But because the validity of the Test is not discussed, the significance assigned to some of the responses may strike the beginner and the outsider as rather arbitrary, and much of the procedure for assessing the personality as mere rules of thumb. In spite of all the careful help it provides, the book serves to reinforce the point that training and skill are required for the adequate use of the Rorschach Test, and that scoring and assessment are partly a matter of personal interpretation by the tester. The book ends with three examples which are scored and interpreted. These are useful in view of the difficulties of scoring and the vagueness of the terms used in interpretation. More examples could have been included with profit to help the beginner through his apprenticeship.

Nature 162:87 Jl 17 '48. John Cohen. * It is refreshing....to read Dr. Mons' clear and restrained account of the techniques and interpretation of the Rorschach "ink-blot" test, an account based on extensive experience with Service and civilian patients and on the examination of a thousand clerical records. With the difficulties of the novice in mind, Dr. Mons painstakingly explains how to administer the test, how to classify the responses according to a widely used, though somewhat pretentious, notation, and how to evaluate the significance of the responses so as to yield an assessment of the personality, particularly its "structural" features. Several new formulae useful for diagnostic purposes are suggested. It is to be hoped that this useful manual will stimulate workers to pursue much more rigorously than hitherto methods of validating the test which could greatly improve its potential value as a diagnostic tool.

Psychiatric Q 23:405–6 Ap '49. * clearly-written * Its main value seems to lie in its simplicity and concise form: It expresses no original views or thought and makes no significant additions to the more comprehensive texts of Klopfer and Kelley, Beck, Bochner and Halpern and others. * He practically achieves his stated aim of sticking to reason and logic in his explanations, and remaining free from the dogmatic setting forth of principles. And therefore we find, for example, that the section on scoring is not a rigid system, but simply a necessary convenience clearly outlined as an anchoring point

for understanding of the total personality picture. Dr. Mons does slight in his book an important aspect of the test, the inquiry period, which has been highly developed and perfected as a sensitive adjunct to the examination proper for bringing out meanings and undercurrents of the subject's original responses; he also barely mentions the testing-the-limits period in which the clinician can determine whether the subject will accept popular concepts or possibly be able to utilize color or shading determinants that had been neglected in the original protocol, or will be able to project movement to the blots. He does make the "helpful" suggestion of preserving the cards by wrapping them in a cellophane covering, a procedure which has been looked upon with horror by experts here, (It adds a shiny quality to the cards which may be distracting or may bring out new determinants in the record.) Another small point on which Dr. Mons' teachings differ from the findings of the accepted Rorschach authorities is his inclusion of the statement, "You may turn the cards any way you like" in his original instructions to the test subject. This is generally held to be unnecessarily suggestive and it has been found better to say nothing about card-turning at the beginning but to be encouraging when the subject questions on this matter. The book is possibly adequate for one who is interested in the very barest principles of the Rorschach test that can be digested in short order. For those who will spend more time and effort, or who plan to go further into the subject, other published texts would be more satisfactory and give a more substantial understanding.

Psychosom Med 12:66–7 Ja-F '50. Peter H. Knapp. "A fool uttereth all his mind." This quotation appears on the cover of a new manual by W. Mons on the Rorschach. One wonders about the choice of quotation. Does it just refer to the ink-blot method? Is there a conscious intent to be modest, which, in many ways, the writer is? Or is there a still deeper, unwitting confession? For there are vulnerable points in this small work of 164 pages. The author introduces it as a manual for beginners on the *practice* of the Rorschach technique. As such it has useful features. It gives a clear description of the test, a diagrammatic representation of the cards to facilitate location of responses and an adequate statement of the major scoring categories. There are convenient summaries of work done by some leaders in the field—Hertz's indicators of hysteria, Piotrowski's "organic signs," and, above all, many of the statements of the Klopfer school. Sometimes the tenets of the Rorschach Research Exchange group are presented to the exclusion of other viewpoints; some names of importance figure only fleetingly, such as Binder, Oberholzer, Beck, indeed Rorschach himself; and considered as a practical guide the book has dubious aspects. For instance, the paragraph of instructions to be given to a test subject contains two outspoken suggestions, one that the cards are made of "Indian ink," two, that "you may turn the card as much as you like." One might ask if the work is more valuable than other instructional aids, such as that of Beck or that of Klopfer, from which it stems in such great part. Still, as a handbook, it has the virtue of compactness. However, it goes further. "We have to establish fundamental principles which can be checked by any experimenter, and lay a foundation of common sense upon which to build up theory and practice." This laudable statement on page 15 carries with it the implication that the author will attempt to clarify such basic *principles* of the method. At times he tries conscientiously to do this. Some of his thoughts on the significance of chiaroscuro response are cautious and stimulating. At other times, for instance in the discussion of black and white used as color, C', (page 75), the text seems to be merely a restatement of what others have said—which is both glib and arbitrary. Dogmatism dominates the interpretation of responses embodying "vista" (page 68), and responses to the whole card (page 57). At times the thinking appears perplexed, as in the discussion of responses to the white areas (pages 59–60). Similarly his categorial acceptance of FC responses as a sign of "manual dexterity" seems slipshod. The style is often loose. For example, on page 44 he refers to anatomy, blood, fire, and clouds as "pathognomic responses." "Pathognomic" of what? He does not say. Certainly little confidence is inspired in his deep understanding of clinical phenomena by statements such as the one on page 86: "The Schizoid response expresses a schism in the personality which enables it to live at one and the same time in reality and in fiction." On page 96 we find a remark about rare detail responses; they "arouse the suspicion that the person is trying to find an escape from the real problems of life by courting petty interests." Such turgid phraseology might be forgiven, but some state-

ments are downright wrong. Examples are his definition of "Confabulation" on page 46, and his statement on page 14 that Rorschach got color responses "mainly from elated manics," whereas the "movement response, such as a 'running man,' occurred mainly in the depressives." The *Psychodiagnostik,* and subsequent studies report as a uniform and significant feature in depressions the constriction of both color *and* movement responses. Three sample test protocols close the book. Many mathematical ratios are worked out. The responses themselves are not accurately delineated, far less the personalities of the subjects. The Rorschach method attempts to derive information about a person from his apperception of a complex group of *gestalten.* Its use depends upon careful observation of the process of apperception in any given subject, and cautious testing of his production according to certain working hypotheses. There is, indeed, a need for "fundamental principles." These will come only from careful comparison of Rorschach data with clinical data. To speculate, a guess is that the clinical data will have to reach deep back into personal development, possibly to preverbal levels. My own preference for investigation is along the lines of clinicians who have attempted such comparisons, Rorschach himself, Binder, and Oberholzer. However, one cannot criticize attempts at statistical validation on large groups of "types," if the attempts are honest. Although this work stems from a "collection of over a thousand selected records" the statistical effort is not even made. What is left often seems naive, facile, or oracular. The author states that he is compiling the book in the field, in response to requests that he publish some instructions for beginners. Yet it is hard to see how his work serves much purpose as a guide in this difficult field. With this manual as a tool beginners might be poorly armed. They should be told not only that "A fool uttereth all his mind" but that "A little learning is a dangerous thing"—to avoid the risk of rushing in where angels fear to tread.

Rorsch Res Exch & J Proj Tech 12:258 no 4 '48. Edward M. L. Burchard. This little book by a British psychiatrist is meant to serve as an introduction to the more advanced works of Klopfer and Kelley, Beck, Binder, and Rorschach. The author further states in his preface that he compiled it during the war when he had neither notes nor textbooks available. This circumstance perhaps explains the very meager documentation and one reference to this Journal as the *Rorschach Exchange Research* (p. 15). However, this reviewer is also puzzled by such statements as: "the movement response, such as 'a running man,' occurred mainly in depressives" (p. 14); responses given during testing for limits should be added in brackets as additional responses; and "Responses which cannot be fitted with confidence into any of the score groups outside F, should be scored, either F, F+, or F−. *The end results will not be materially affected.*" (p. 43—reviewer's italics.) Similar seeming confusions or important divergences from usual procedure occur frequently without any documentation to back them up. The book is logically organized as a manual —discussing in turn—administration, inquiry, recording, scoring, tabulation, significance of separate scoring categories, and interpretation or assessment of the total personality. A ten-page section then sets forth "some useful elaborations of the method." Here are included refinements in scoring from diverse sources— Beck's "Z" and "Po," the "Mm" score for expressive poses, Earl's "F/C" and "C/F," "Hdx" and "Adx" for Rorschach's oligophrenic details, etc. The book closes with a nine-page discussion of Rorschach diagnosis of the normal personality, neurosis, psychosis, mental defect, epilepsy, enuresis, and juvenile delinquency; followed by a detailed analysis of three cases. This last is perhaps the most valuable portion of the book, since here the author does illustrate rather fully the manner in which he scores and interprets. The book is handsomely printed in two colors on good paper; the author has an excellent reputation in England; and it is thus with some regret that this reviewer must state that, in his opinion, the book serves little useful purpose. The dilettante should not be encouraged to use the Rorschach method at all, and the serious student has little need for such a primer. Instead, he should be advised to begin his studies with the more complete and better-documented manuals of Klopfer and Kelley, Rapaport, or Beck. As *obiter dicta* the reviewer cannot resist stating his disapproval of the inclusion of the motto, "Thus are the secrets of his heart made manifest," on the dust jacket of what purports to be a serious, scientific book; and his delight in Mons' perhaps unconscious humor in warning of the dangers of blind diagnosis on page 17: "Neglect of this precaution can otherwise lead to socially embarrassing situ-

ations, as in the case of a young Rorschach worker who practiced "blind" diagnosis and wrote "Schizophrenic with Homicidal tendencies" underneath the anonymous record of his Superintendent; *this method is so informative that one should never test one's friends or colleagues*" (reviewer's italics).

Sociol & Social Res 33:241–2 Ja–F '49. Emory S. Bogardus. * succinct and incisive treatise * Mons makes his main contribution in his organization and interpretation of the symbols and in pointing out the structuring of personality that certain reactions to the test seem to indicate. The author has strengthened the role of Rorschach as one method of approach to the study of certain types of personality.

[127]

★[*Re* Rorschach.] Mons, W. **Principles and Practice of the Rorschach Personality Test, Second Edition.** London: Faber & Faber Ltd., 1950. Pp. 176. 12s. 6d. (Philadelphia, Pa.: J. B. Lippincott Co., 1951. $4.00. *)

J Consult Psychol 15:447 O '51. Laurance F. Shaffer. The second edition of this compact and clear British text differs little from the first edition....except that civilian cases have been substituted for the military examples.

Psychiatric Q 25:704 O '51. * differs only in minor points from the first edition. It is still intended for the beginner, presenting the Rorschach method in a clear and simplified manner. Possible criticism may be directed to the discussion of determinants, in which oversimplification suggests a possible injustice to the technique. In general, however, it is a compact little volume and may be recommended to those beginning the study of this test.

Psychol Service Center J 2:145–6 Je '50. Mary Morrow. The author's purpose....was to provide a much-needed primer for beginners in the use of the Rorschach technique, as well as a guide to better understanding of the test for people in allied fields or interested laymen. The book, itself, is a commentary on the fact that this is a difficult feat to perform. Although written in a clear and readable style, with the use of interesting clinical material, it falls short of its ultimate intentions. The reasons are not readily determined, for what seems a lack to one individual may not seem so at all to another who reads a book for a different purpose. As a text for neophyte Rorschachers, there are several aspects of the book which would seem to encourage poor methodological habits. For example, the author does not stress the inquiry part of the test, which is generally regarded as a delicate and exacting operation, stating only that inquiry is unnecessary except in the case of responses which confuse the administrator. In helping others learn the Rorschach test, one of the major difficulties encountered is the inadequacy of inquiry made by the beginner. With them it is necessary to emphasize that the apparent scoring of a response often does not include the determinants actually utilized by the subject. The author also implies that the test can be readily self-taught and that the scoring of responses comes largely from one's own experience with many and varied kinds of records. Although one cannot gainsay the value of experience, this thinking tends to place the administrator on an island of self-decision, whereas he should be encouraged from the beginning to attempt to objectify his use of the test by careful reference to the research done for this very purpose. This tendency is clearly reflected in the author's own writing in which few references are cited for the many dogmatic statements. One is never certain whether these conclusions are gleaned from the author's experience or the summarizing of other investigators. For example, in determining intellectual level from the Rorschach, the author states, "The I.Q. in records without gross abnormality can be worked out to within 5% of the Stanford-Binet Test as applied by Terman and Merrill." This method is not concretely defined, nor are references cited from which one might gain a more satisfactory explanation. No student should be asked to accept such statements as fact without sufficient foundation. He should be encouraged to ask, "Why is this so? What is the basis for this conclusion?" And, his questions should be answered as fully as possible. As a text for the student, it does not seem to be sufficiently objective in its approach to the Rorschach test. For the allied worker or the interested layman, its exposition is too ambiguous and obscure, and therefore it is likely to increase his confusion. Therefore, although this book provides interesting reading and a great deal of informative material, in a field where much is needed, it does not attain its stated goal.

For reviews of the first edition, see 126.

[128]

★[*Re* Rorschach.] ULETT, GEORGE. **Rorschach Introductory Manual: A Primer for the Clinical Psychiatric Worker: With Interpretative Diagram to Permit Clinical Use While Learning the Ink-Blot Technique.** St. Louis, Mo.: Educational Publishers, Inc., 1950. Pp. 48. $3.00. * (*PA* 24: 5262)

Am J Psychiatry 108:158 Ag '51. W. Donald Ross. This is a most ingenious "short cut" to the Rorschach method for clinical psychiatrists. It describes in a very simple manner how any psychiatrist can proceed to use the test on his own patients. It provides valuable tables and a quite inspired scoring template for dealing with the test performance. It gives enough of interpretative and diagnostic guidance to stimulate interest in using the method to develop one's own interpretative skill with practice and the help of the suggested further reading. It is oversimplified. It cuts many corners. It presents many valuable compromises, however, between the various scoring systems which are extant. It is too glib on the subject of clinical diagnosis, although this aspect is mitigated somewhat by the explanatory text. There is a danger that it may be used by psychiatrists as if they were in possession of the sensitive instrument provided by the more complicated use of the test materials in the hands of a well-trained and experienced worker. Such psychiatrists might blame the failures on the technique rather than on their own rough use of it. It is to be hoped, however, that it may become widely used as an initiation into Rorschach possibilities, to be followed up by more intensive study and supervision with the method, or by a more judicious use of referrals to clinical psychologists for Rorschach examinations than the psychiatrists previously could have made. * This reviewer is in agreement with Karl Menninger, who is quoted in the foreword as follows: "This is the most practical manual to serve as a primer to the psychiatrist that I have seen." Why Dr. Menninger's name is enclosed in quotes, while his statement has quotation marks only at the beginning, is something that remains for the author to explain!

Am J Psychother 5:475–6 Jl '51. Lily H. Gondor. * There is no doubt that the author has used his excellent capacity for organization and his ingenuity to simplify the learning process of the test. It is as though the whole Rorschach method were served on a tray, so to speak, in palatable portions, ready for use—and this is exactly where the danger of this manual lies. The author himself emphasizes that he is aware of the incompleteness and the almost naive oversimplification of his presentation of the Rorschach. * the oversimplification of the method in this manual, the chart and the checking-device are indeed a great temptation for any student of the Rorschach who wants to take a shortcut rather than devote the time necessary for the intensive study which proficiency in this technique requires. There is no doubt that there is a lack of psychologically trained personnel, in comparison to the number of psychiatric patients. These patients and their doctors, however, are poorly served when the psychological report consists mainly of slogans and technical phrases. Unfortunately such reports are not rare. One suspects that the authors often do not know themselves what they are writing about and only use the terminology of Rorschach textbooks without deeper understanding of the personality they have tested. This manual was originally devoted as a teaching device. As such it may render a good service as a primer for beginners who are learning the Rorschach technique under the supervision of an expert in projective tests.

Brit J Med Psychol 24:148–9 pt 2 '51. T. Alcock. It is difficult to reconcile Dr. Ulett's reference to "the long training required for mastery" of the Rorschach test with his claim that his monograph is designed to "bring this valuable diagnostic test within the reach of many who are not otherwise familiar with (psychological) testing"...."*without the otherwise wasted time of learning technique.*" (Italics are the reviewer's.) This beautifully printed short book aims at providing for the psychiatrist, unlearned in test procedure, a more than royal road to learning-as-you-go. The novice is advised that the author's technique "permits almost immediate interpretation of personality trends and suggests clinical diagnoses." While administering the test he is recommended to score as he receives each response, searching for the appropriate symbol in a table of scoring kept open before him; this in addition to the already arduous task of recording responses verbatim, with notes of observed behaviour and of timing in terms of seconds. To "facilitate the conversion of the subject's scored responses into terms of a personality diagnosis" there is devised a visual aid in the form of a multicoloured circle whose segments are severally labelled imagination, deep inner feelings, emotions, associations, intellectual control, orderliness and apperception. Factors towards the centre of the circle are said to represent normality, decreasing towards the periphery. In this circle are punched holes into which scores are entered and the personality is then read off—(It is tempting to say "clocked out")—with the aid of interpretive descriptions around each hole and tables of diagnostic points. It is comforting to read in the chapter on Clinical Diagnosis that "further verification of such Rorschach diagnoses on clinical material is necessary," and it is also noted that "it will be obvious to a trained Rorschach worker that the interpretations suggested will not be complete." It is to be feared that they might also be misleading. Since this work is specifically directed to its use by psychiatrists, it is perhaps taken for granted that the human relationship of tester and testee will not be disregarded, but there is a striking omission of any consideration of the test from the patient's point of view, or of the means by which an optimal situation may be brought about and a maximum amount of valid material obtained. The theory of personality as a dynamic process of interacting forces, which underlies the Rorschach method, is brushed aside. Of the four stages of the test, the introduction and inquiry are only lightly touched upon, while the valuable stage of limit testing is disregarded. Of his simplified Rorschach Dr. Ulett writes clearly and with conviction, but as the famous couturier said "Simplicity is always expensive." And oversimplicity in diagnostic methods may prove dangerously expensive to the patient.

J Nerv & Mental Dis 112:177 Ag '50. * The text is arranged in a way to be understood by any psychiatrist and will orient him in the use of this valuable diagnostic tool. * the author has rendered a valuable service to psychiatry by his clear presentation of the fundamentals of the test, of the technical procedures and of a simplified scheme of interpretation. This manual may be recommended with the satisfaction that the reader will be well repaid for his efforts. *

J Proj Tech 15:279–80 Je '51. L. Joseph Stone. This is a highly condensed manual of Rorschach procedure—rather eclectic, although its scoring principles are closest to the Klopfer system. The first half summarizes administration (without testing the limits) and scoring (with estimation of form level according to the F+ and F− method); the latter half is a fairly complete but extremely abbreviated statement of essential interpretive principles. The core of the contribution is a circular chart or diagram placing before the user all the scoring categories with their major interpretive significance indicated in small type. * There is obvious value—particularly in the process of Rorschach learning—in any device which holds the multifarious Rorschach variables before one, which permits crosscomparison between them, and which serves constantly to suggest interpretive meanings and interrelations: this is the value claimed by the author. It is equally obvious that any kind of interpretive code sheet invites misuse by the unskilled who are also unscrupulous. Precisely because the device is handy it is subject to this misuse. However, it is doubtful whether the author—who disclaims all uses save that of a more or less temporary crutch in the process of acquiring Rorschach skill—should be held responsible for possible misapplications. His manual is intended for the psychiatrist and the clinical psychologist in training and assumes some sophistication regarding personality organization and its disorganizations. As far as the structure of the chart is concerned, many Rorschach workers will wonder why the F segment of the chart does not lie between the segments pertaining to diffusion and to texture instead of falling quite apart from these. This would appear to be a more logical placement and would also make it easier for the student to go from Ulett's circular chart to the Klopfer-Davidson profile. As a handy condensation of the gist of much Rorschach material, there is much to recommend this manual. It is useful for the worker already reasonably sophisticated in clinical understanding who has not yet passed from the initial Rorschach stage of understanding scoring principles to the stage of full mastery of many variables and their interpretive values. It is not—and does not appear to be intended as—a substitute for adequate intensive training. There is always the danger, however, that such devices will serve as "dream books" and the profession should be on guard against such misuse. Unfortunately, the ingenious dial-diagram itself, the essential contribution, is marred by some misprints.

Psychiatric Q 24:617–8 Jl '50. The main purpose of this manual is to enable psychiatrists to use the Rorschach method as a rapid diagnostic tool. The essential parts of the procedure—administration, scoring and interpretation—are presented in concise and oversimplified form. A neat and colorful circular diagram serves as a visual aid for personality interpretation and for rapid recognition of "abnormal" areas. Major Rorschach "signs" found in different clinical entities are combined in a well-organized and comprehensive table, and there is a second table which includes short definitions of scoring symbols as well as the popular and other frequently-encountered responses. In his introduction Dr. Ulett states: "It is our purpose to present an aid to learning the Rorschach test that will facilitate its more rapid mastery." If by "mastery" the author means learning basic Rorschach symbols and their individual meaning, then he has succeeded remarkably well in his purpose. However, it is doubtful if persons unfamiliar with the Rorschach will be able to interpret a record adequately, or come to a diagnostic decision, on the basis of the information contained in this manual alone. One can easily visualize, for example, a person unfamiliar with the technique trying to fit his results into one of the constellations of "signs" and finding to his disappointment that his record does not correspond to any one of the clinical subgroups. After a number of such experiences, he may disregard the method as unsuitable for diagnostic purposes. And this is really not the case. The basic error lies in using statistically discriminative points, which are indicative of group trends only, for individual diagnosis. A small number of cases, usually those presenting extreme conditions, may be diagnosed by signs, but there are many others where only one or two—or even none—of the classical signs can be found. The author feels that the manual "allows some clinical application during the otherwise wasted period of learning technique." Perhaps such a learning period, enabling a real understanding of the basic personality structure revealed by the Rorschach, would not be so "wasted" in the long run. Recalling that the originator of this test was a psychiatrist himself it seems only appropriate that as many psychiatrists as possible should use the Rorschach. However, to the present day no magic short-cut for interpreting records has been found. This book cannot replace standard works on the Rorschach technique for anyone interested in interpreting a record, but will serve as an excellent introduction to the basic principles involved. It will also prove useful as an adjunct in courses where this method is taught, or if read in combination with some of the standard source books on the Rorschach.

[129]

★**Rosenzweig Picture-Frustration Study.** Ages 4–13, 14 and over; 1944–48; also called *Rosenzweig P-F Study;* 2 levels; 1 form, '48; $4 per 25 examination blanks; $1 per 25 record blanks; specimen set not available; postage extra; Saul Rosenzweig; the Author, 8029 Washington St., St. Louis 14, Mo. *
a) FORM FOR CHILDREN. Ages 4–13; 1948; manual ('48); $1 per manual (reprinted from *J Psychol* 26: 141–91 Jl '48; see *21* below); nontimed (20) minutes.
b) REVISED FORM FOR ADULTS. Ages 14 and over; 1944–48; manual ('47); $1 per manual (reprinted from *J Psychol* 24: 165–208 O '47; see *15* below); nontimed (15) minutes.

REFERENCES

1. ROSENZWEIG, SAUL, AND SARASON, SEYMOUR. "An Experimental Study of the Triadic Hypothesis: Reaction to Frustration, Ego-Defense and Hypnotizability: I, Correlational Approach." *Char & Pers* 11:1–19 S '42. * *(PA* 17:887)
2. BURNHAM, CATHARINE ANNETTE. *Preliminary Experiments With the Rosenzweig F(rustration)–Reaction Study.* Master's thesis, Clark University (Worcester, Mass.), 1943. *(Abstracts of Dissertations....1943,* pp. 75–6.)
3. KORCHIN, SHELDON JEROME. *A Comparative Study of Three Projective Techniques in the Measurement of Frustration–Reaction Types.* Master's thesis, Clark University (Worcester, Mass.), 1943. *(Abstracts of Dissertations....1943,* pp. 70–2.)
4. ROSENZWEIG, SAUL. "The Picture-Association Method and Its Application in a Study of Reactions to Frustration." *J Personality* 14:3–23 S '45. * *(PA* 20:2401)
5. SHAKOW, DAVID; RODNICK, ELIOT H.; AND LEBEAUX, THELMA. "A Psychological Study of a Schizophrenic: Exemplification of a Method." *J Abn & Social Psychol* 40:154–74 Ap '45. * *(PA* 19:2624)
6. CLARKE, HELEN JANE. "The Diagnosis of a Patient With Limited Capacity." *J Personality* 15:105–12 D '46. * *(PA* 21: 3001)
7. KOGAN, KATE LEVINE. "The Diagnosis of a Patient With Organic Defect." *J Personality* 15:113–20 D '46. * *(PA* 21: 3025)
8. PATTERSON, VIRGINIA LOUISE. *An Exploratory Study of Reaction to Frustration by Means of the Rosenzweig Picture-Frustration Test.* Master's thesis, Stanford University (Stanford, Calif.), 1946.
9. ROSENZWEIG, SAUL. "The Dynamics of an Amnesic Personality." *J Personality* 15:121–42 D '46. * *(PA* 21:3062)
10. ROSENZWEIG, SAUL; CLARKE, HELEN JANE; GARFIELD, MARJORIE S.; AND LEHNDORFF, ANNEMARIE. "Scoring Samples for the Rosenzweig Picture-Frustration Study." *J Psychol* 21: 45–72 Ja '46. * *(PA* 20:1570)
11. BROWN, J. F. "A Modification of the Rosenzweig Picture-Frustration Test to Study Hostile Interracial Attitudes." *J Psychol* 24:247–72 O '47. * *(PA* 22:928)
12. BROWN, MARTHA MARLIN. *An Investigation of the Validity of the Rosenzweig Picture-Frustration Study.* Master's thesis, University of Pittsburgh (Pittsburgh, Pa.), 1947.
13. CLARKE, HELEN JANE; ROSENZWEIG, SAUL; AND FLEMING, EDITH E. "The Reliability of the Scoring of the Rosenzweig Picture-Frustration Study." *J Clin Psychol* 3:364–70 O '47. * *(PA* 22:4416)
14. LANDISBERG, SELMA. "A Personality Study of Institutionalized Epileptics." *Am J Mental Def* 52:16–22 Jl '47. * *(PA* 22:2267)
15. ROSENZWEIG, SAUL; FLEMING, EDITH E.; AND CLARKE, HELEN JANE. "Revised Scoring Manual for the Rosenzweig Picture-Frustration Study." *J Psychol* 24:165–208 O '47. * *(PA* 22:1221)
16. BELL, JOHN ELDERKIN. Chap. 11, "Rosenzweig Picture-Frustration Study," pp. 264–8. In his *Projective Techniques: A Dynamic Approach to the Study of the Personality.* New York: Longmans, Green & Co., Inc., 1948. Pp. xvi, 533. * (London: Longmans, Green & Co. Ltd., 1949.) *(PA* 23:1284)
17. FALLS, ROBERT P., AND BLAKE, ROBERT R. "A Quantitative Analysis of the Picture-Frustration Study." *J Personality* 16:320–5 Mr '48. * *(PA* 23:2230)
18. FRANKLIN, JOSEPH C., AND BROZEK, JOSEF. "The Rosenzweig Picture-Frustration Study as a Measure of Frustration Response." Abstract. *Am Psychol* 3:357 Ag '48. * *(PA* 23:751, title only)
19. FRENCH, ROBERT L., AND PICKETT, BETTY J. "Changes in Performance on the Rosenzweig Picture-Frustration Test Following Experimentally Induced Frustration." Abstract. *Am Psychol* 3:357–8 Ag '48. * *(PA* 23:752, title only)
20. HARDY, VIRGINIA T. "Relation of Dominance to Non-Directiveness in Counseling." *J Clin Psychol* 4:300–3 Jl '48. * *(PA* 23:179)
21. ROSENZWEIG, SAUL; FLEMING, EDITH E.; AND ROSENZWEIG, LOUISE. "The Children's Form of the Rosenzweig Pic-

ture-Frustration Study." *J Psychol* 26:141–91 Jl '48. * *(PA* 23:1046)
22. BARRETT, RUTH EVELYN. *Some Effects on the "Job-Testing" Attitude on Performance on the Rosenzweig Picture-Frustration Test.* Master's thesis, University of Pittsburgh (Pittsburgh, Pa.), 1949. *(PA* 24:363, title only)
23. BELL, JOHN ELDERKIN. "The Case of Gregor: Psychological Test Data." *Rorsch Res Exch & J Proj Tech* 13:155–205 no 2 '49. * *(PA* 24:2589)
24. BERK, NORMAN. *A Personality Study of Suicidal Schizophrenics.* Doctor's thesis, New York University (New York, N.Y.), 1949. *(Microfilm Abstracts....,* 1950, pp. 155–6.) *(PA* 25:479, title only)
25. BERNARD, JACK. "The Rosenzweig Picture-Frustration Study: I, Norms, Reliability, and Statistical Evaluation." *J Psychol* 28:325–32 O '49. * *(PA* 24:2590)
26. BERNARD, JACK. "The Rosenzweig Picture-Frustration Study: II, Interpretation." *J Psychol* 28:333–43 O '49. * *(PA* 24:2591)
27. COHEN, DAVID. *Psychological Concomitants of Chronic Illness: A Study of Emotional Correlates of Pulmonary Tuberculosis, Peptic Ulcer, the Arthritides, and Cardiac Disease.* Doctor's thesis, University of Pittsburgh (Pittsburgh, Pa.), 1949. *(Abstracts of Doctoral Dissertations....1949,* 1950, pp. 277–90.)
28. FRANKLIN, JOSEPH C., AND BROZEK, JOSEF. "The Rosenzweig P-F Test as a Measure of Frustration Response in Semistarvation." *J Consult Psychol* 13:293–301 Ag '49. * *(PA* 24: 1195)
29. FRY, FRANKLYN D. "A Study of Reactions to Frustration in 236 College Students and in 207 Inmates of State Prisons." *J Psychol* 28:427–38 O '49. * *(PA* 24:2566)
30. RICCIUTI, EDWARD A. *A Study of Listeners and Non-Listeners to Various Types of Radio Programs in Terms of Selected Ability, Attitude and Behavior Measures.* Doctor's thesis, Fordham University (New York, N.Y.), 1949. *(Dissertations....,* 1949, pp. 140–9.)
31. ROBERTSON, MARY. *An Investigation of the Responses of Forty Adult Female Offenders on the Rosenzweig Picture-Frustration Test.* Master's thesis, University of Toronto (Toronto, Canada), 1949. Pp. 35.
32. ROSENZWEIG, SAUL; WITH THE COLLABORATION OF KATE LEVINE KOGAN. *Psychodiagnosis: An Introduction to Tests in the Clinical Practice of Psychodynamics,* pp. 167–80. New York: Grune & Stratton, Inc., 1949. Pp. xii, 380. * *(PA* 23:3761)
33. SCHWARTZ, MILTON M. *The Relationships Between Projective Test Scoring Categories and Activity Preferences.* Doctor's thesis, New York University (New York, N.Y.), 1949.
34. SHUPP, FRANKLIN M. *A Study of the Relationship Between the Bernreuter Personality Inventory and the Rosenzweig Picture-Frustration Study in Testing High School Students.* Master's thesis, Pennsylvania State College (State College, Pa.), 1949. *(PA* 24:5565, title only)
35. SINAIKO, H. WALLACE. "The Rosenzweig Picture-Frustration Study in the Selection of Department Store Section Managers." *J Appl Psychol* 33:36–42 F '49. * *(PA* 23:3945)
36. VERNALLIS, FRANCIS FLORENZ. *Some Relationships Between a Level of Aspiration Situation and the Picture Frustration Study.* Master's thesis, University of Pittsburgh (Pittsburgh, Pa.), 1949.
37. WILLIAMS, HERBERT HOWARD. *An Investigation of Extra Punitiveness as Measured by the Rosenzweig Picture Frustration Study and the California Scale of the Antidemocratic Personality.* Master's thesis, University of Pittsburgh (Pittsburgh, Pa.), 1949. *(PA* 23:3006, title only)
38. ALBEE, GEORGE W., AND GOLDMAN, ROSALINE. "The Picture Frustration Study as a Predictor of Overt Aggression." *J Proj Tech* 14:303–8 S '50. * *(PA* 25:4676)
39. CASSEL, RUSSELL N. *An Experimental Investigation of the "Reality-Strata" of Certain Objectively Defined Groups of Individuals by Use of the Level of Aspiration Technique.* Doctor's thesis, University of Southern California (Los Angeles, Calif.), 1950. *(Abstracts of Dissertations....1950,* 1951, pp. 288–90.)
40. COLEMAN, JAMES C.; WITH THE ASSISTANCE OF CHARLES J. SERET. "The Role of Hostility in Fingernail Biting." *Psychol Service Center J* 2:238–44 S '50. * *(PA* 26:2703)
41. DREGER, RALPH MASON. *Some Personality Correlates of Religious Attitudes as Determined by Projective Techniques.* Doctor's thesis, University of Southern California (Los Angeles, Calif.), 1950. *(Abstracts of Dissertations....1950,* 1951, pp. 202–5.) *(PA* 26:170)
42. DuBOIS, PHILIP H., AND WATSON, ROBERT I. "The Selection of Patrolmen." *J Appl Psychol* 34:90–5 Ap '50. * *(PA* 25:2076)
43. FARBEROW, NORMAN L. "Personality Patterns of Suicidal Mental Hospital Patients." *Genetic Psychol Monogr* 42:3–79 Ag '50. * *(PA* 25:4722)
44. FRENCH, ROBERT L. "Changes in Performance on the Rosenzweig Picture-Frustration Study Following Experimentally Induced Frustration." *J Consult Psychol* 14:111–5 Ap '50. * *(PA* 24:5865)
45. HANVIK, LEO J. "Some Comparisons and Correlations Between MMPI and Rosenzweig P-F Study Scores in a Neuropsychiatric Hospital Sample." Abstract. *J Colo-Wyo Acad Sci* 4:70 O '50. * *(PA* 25:5339, title only)

46. HARRIS, FRANK J. "Can Personality Tests Identify Accident-Prone Employees?" *Personnel Psychol* 3:455–9 w '50. * (PA 25:3984)

47. JACKSON, PATRICIA LEE. *Frustration Tolerance in Social Situations as a Factor in Successful Retail Salesmanship.* Doctor's thesis, Columbia University (New York, N.Y.), 1950. Abstract: *Microfilm Abstracts* 10:225–7 no 3 '50. *

48. KEHEW, DAVID L. *The Effect of Revising the Instructions on the Rosenzweig Picture-Frustration Study.* Master's thesis, University of Pittsburgh (Pittsburgh, Pa.), 1950. (PA 24:5551, title only)

49. LINDZEY, GARDNER. "An Experimental Test of the Validity of the Rosenzweig Picture-Frustration Study." *J Personality* 18:315–20 Mr '50. * (PA 25:3172)

50. McCARY, J. L. "Ethnic and Cultural Reactions to Frustration." *J Personality* 18:321–6 Mr '50. * (PA 25:3066)

51. OLSTEAD, MARGERY. *Performance on the Children's Form of the Rosenzweig Picture-Frustration Test as Related to Sociometric Status.* Master's thesis, University of Toronto (Toronto, Canada), 1950. Pp. 29.

52. ROSENZWEIG, SAUL. "Frustration Tolerance and the Picture-Frustration Study." *Psychol Service Center J* 2:109–15 Je '50. * (PA 26:965)

53. ROSENZWEIG, SAUL. "Levels of Behavior in Psychodiagnosis With Special Reference to the Picture-Frustration Study." *Am J Orthopsychiatry* 20:63–72 Ja '50. * (PA 24:5258)

54. ROSENZWEIG, SAUL. "Revised Norms for the Adult Form of the Rosenzweig Picture-Frustration Study." *J Personality* 18:344–6 Mr '50. * (PA 25:3183)

55. ROSENZWEIG, SAUL. "Some Problems Relating to Research on the Rosenzweig Picture-Frustration Study." *J Personality* 18:303–5 Mr '50. * (PA 25:3184)

56. ROSENZWEIG, SAUL. "The Treatment of Humorous Responses in the Rosenzweig Picture-Frustration Study: A Note on the Revised (1950) Instructions." *J Psychol* 30:139–43 Jl '50. * (PA 25:1109)

57. ROSENZWEIG, SAUL, AND MIRMOW, ESTHER LEE. "The Validation of Trends in the Children's Form of the Rosenzweig Picture-Frustration Study." *J Personality* 18:306–14 Mr '50. * (PA 25:3186)

58. ROSS, R. W. *An Examination of Normal and Psychotic Responses on the Rosenzweig P-F Study.* Master's thesis, University of Toronto (Toronto, Canada), 1950. Pp. 31.

59. SCHMEIDLER, GERTRUDE R. "Some Relations Between Picture-Frustration Ratings and ESP Scores." *J Personality* 18:331–43 Mr '50. * (PA 25:3188)

60. SIMOS, IRVING. "The Picture-Frustration Study in the Psychiatric Situation—Preliminary Findings." *J Personality* 18:327–30 Mr '50. * (PA 25:3192)

61. SIMOS, IRVING. *The Rosenzweig PF Study as Used With Psychiatric Patients.* Doctor's thesis, University of Minnesota (Minneapolis, Minn.), 1950.

62. SPACHE, GEORGE. "Differential Scoring of the Rosenzweig Picture-Frustration Study." *J Clin Psychol* 6:406–8 O '50. * (PA 25:8111)

63. STARER, EMANUEL. *An Analysis of the Type and Direction of Aggression and Sources of Frustration as Shown by the Results of the Rosenzweig Picture-Frustration Study, Rorschach Findings, and Case History for a Group of Anxiety Neurotic and a Group of Paranoid Schizophrenic Patients.* Doctor's thesis, New York University (New York, N.Y.), 1950. Abstract: *Microfilm Abstracts* 11:178–9 no 1 '51. * (PA 26:2342, title only)

64. WALKER, ROBERT G. *A Comparison of Clinical Manifestations of Hostility With Rorschach and MAPS Test Performances.* Doctor's thesis, University of Southern California (Los Angeles, Calif.), 1950. (Abstracts of Dissertations.... 1950, 1951, pp. 196–7.)

65. ANGELINO, HENRY R. *The Validity of the Rosenzweig Picture-Frustration Study (Children's Form).* Doctor's thesis, University of Nebraska (Lincoln, Neb.), 1951.

66. CLARKE, HELEN JANE. Chap. 10, "The Rosenzweig Picture-Frustration Study," pp. 312–23. In *An Introduction to Projective Techniques.* Edited by Harold H. Anderson and Gladys L. Anderson. New York: Prentice-Hall, Inc., 1951. Pp. xxiv, 720. *

67. HOLZBERG, JULES D.; CAHEN, ELEANOR R.; AND WILK, EDWARD K. "Suicide: A Psychological Study of Self-Destruction." *J Proj Tech* 15:339–54 S '51. * (PA 26:4096)

68. HOLZBERG, JULES D., AND POSNER, RITA. "The Relationship of Extrapunitiveness on the Rosenzweig Picture-Frustration Study to Aggression in Overt Behavior and Fantasy." *Am J Orthopsychiatry* 21:767–79 O '51. * (PA 26:5619)

69. KRALL, VITA. "Personality Factors in Accident Prone and Accident Free Children." Abstract. *Am Psychol* 6:375–6 Jl '51. *

70. McCARY, JAMES L. "Reactions to Frustration by Some Cultural and Racial Groups." *Personality* 1:84–102 Ja '51. * (PA 25:6799)

71. RUSSELL, MAXTON A. *A Comparative Investigation of Repression in Normal and Neurotic Subjects as Measured by the Rosenzweig P-F Study.* Doctor's thesis, Washington University (St. Louis, Mo.), 1951.

72. SEWARD, GEORGENE H.; MORRISON, LESTER M.; AND FEST, BEVERLY; WITH THE ASSISTANCE OF NELLIE M. YOUNG AND VANCE BOILEAU. *Personality Structure in a Common Form of Colitis.* American Psychological Association, Psychological Monographs: General and Applied, Vol. 65, No. 1, Whole No. 318. Washington, D.C.: the Association, Inc., 1951. Pp. v, 26. Paper. * (PA 25:7024)

73. SPACHE, GEORGE. "Sex Differences in the Rosenzweig P-F, Children's Form." Abstract. *Am Psychol* 6:372–3 Jl '51. *

74. SPACHE, GEORGE. "Sex Differences in the Rosenzweig P-F Study, Children's Form." *J Clin Psychol* 7:235–8 Jl '51. * (PA 26:936)

75. TAYLOR, MAHLON V., JR., AND TAYLOR, O. M. "Internal Consistency of the Group Conformity Rating of the Rosenzweig Picture-Frustration Study." *J Consult Psychol* 15:250–2 Je '51. * (PA 26:6300)

76. WATSON, ROBERT I. Chap. 15, "The Rosenzweig Picture-Frustration Study," pp. 416–35. In his *The Clinical Method in Psychology.* New York: Harper & Bros., 1951. Pp. xii, 779. *

77. WECHSBERG, FLORENCE O. *An Experimental Investigation of Levels of Behavior With Special Reference to the Rosenzweig Picture-Frustration Study.* Doctor's thesis, Washington University (St. Louis, Mo.), 1951.

ROBERT C. CHALLMAN, *Clinical Psychologist, 301 Kenwood Parkway, Minneapolis, Minnesota.*

Both forms of the P-F Study consist of 24 crudely drawn cartoon-like pictures involving two central characters. One of the characters is placed in a mildly frustrating situation while the other is shown saying something which frustrates the first or helps to define the frustrating situation. The adult subject is asked to write in the blank caption box what the person would answer, "the very *first* reply that comes into your mind." Children are given a simpler formulation of the instructions. Two thirds of the pictures involve a directly frustrating obstacle; in the remainder one of the characters is accused of a minor offense.

Responses are scored for direction of aggression: i.e., extrapunitiveness—aggression expressed against the environment; intropunitiveness—aggression turned inward on the subject himself; and impunitiveness—"aggression is evaded in an attempt to gloss over the frustration." Responses are also scored for type of reaction: i.e., obstacle dominance, ego-defense, and need-persistence, in accordance with the response being concerned with the barrier, the subject's ego, or with a solution for the problem. Instructions are also given for detecting certain "trends" in the subject's responses: i.e., shifting from one type or direction of response to another in the course of the test. A group conformity rating (GCR) may also be obtained by comparing the subject's scores with typical reactions to 12 of the items.

The Revised Form for Adults is standardized on 236 males and 224 females in the age group 20–30. Although this group included a relatively small number of skilled and unskilled laborers, the vast majority were middle class with a fairly high educational level (a mean length of schooling of 13.5 years). It is not clear whether the norms based on this group are to be used for any adult since this point is not mentioned in the manual; in fact, the norms were bound into the already printed manual and follow directly after a normative table labeled "Revised Figures." In another place (*54*) the author comments that the norms are only slightly different from the original tentative norms, and Bernard's norms (*25*) based on 175 college students of both sexes are also very similar to the original norms. In any case, caution would dictate their use only with people whose class and educational status is similar to that of the standardizing group.

The manual does not include mention of reliability although the manual for the children's form asserts that the adult form has a retest reliability of from .60 to .80. Bernard in the above mentioned study found retest r's of .50 to .75, the retests being made about four months after the original tests. He also found the reliability of the GCR to be .45. These reliabilities are rather low for individual diagnosis. A special study (*13*) showed the reliability of scoring to be adequate, since two scorers, after a series of discussions with each other, were able to increase their agreement from about 74 to 85 per cent. It is unlikely, however, that the average user of the test could achieve that level of reliability.

Validity is not mentioned in the manual, although in a previous article (*4*) the author claims that validity "has been repeatedly examined on a clinical basis." He also mentions a comparison of extrapunitiveness on the P-F Study and on the TAT as yielding an r of .74. Other studies of validity (*28, 44, 49, 60*) have shown results varying from negative to slightly positive. All these studies were group centered, however, and cast little light on the individual. Perhaps special mention should be called to a study of Bernard (*26*) in which he concluded that "blind" analysis of the P-F Study was of value with normal cases and of still greater value when used in combination with other tests. The GCR, however, was found to be of little value.

Extensive examples are offered in the manual as an aid in scoring, but even so it is not an easy test to score; the distinctions between some of the responses placed in different catagories is often difficult to understand. The meticulous scoring of trends also appears to the reviewer as possibly attempting to get more out of one's data than there is in it.

It is assumed that the subject "unconsciously or consciously identifies himself with the frus-

trated individual....and projects his own bias in the replies given." Yet the author frankly admits (in the children's manual) that there is no way of deciding whether the subject's replies reflect what he would actually say or whether he is censoring his answers or whether they "disclose a more covert or latent basis of the subject's manifest behavior." An inquiry is suggested after completion of the test to clarify "responses which are too brief or ambiguous" and to permit a judgment from "the tone of voice or additional remarks" of the subject. In the reviewer's opinion it would be better to follow the procedure advised for children and have the subject read all his replies aloud. Or still better, to have the subject respond orally in the first place. This would also permit some judgment on self-censorship since the time before replying could be measured and it would permit a correct scoring of remarks apparently easy to classify but in reality ironic, or meant in some other special way.

Other possible imperfections are: (*a*) the tacit assumption that response to mild frustration is predictive of response to strong frustration especially when a threat to the personality is involved; (*b*) the absence of any assessment of intensity of reaction although one might expect that to be very important; (*c*) the lack of clarity in the interpretation of the results after they have been obtained. Suppose a subject is more impunitive and less extrapunitive than the norm. Does this mean he inhibits normal aggression or avoids blaming someone when he should do so? Not necessarily, since Schmeidler (*59*), for example, found that the subjects in her impunitive group tended to be split into two subgroups, one of them composed of gentle and helpful people and the other composed of restrained and cold persons.

The Form for Children was standardized on 131 boys and 125 girls with approximately equal numbers of each sex at each age from 4 to 13. The children at age 7 and below were drawn from private schools and the rest from public schools—a class difference which might affect the obtained norms is reflected here. No reliability is reported and the only comment on validity in the manual is "the clinical indications of validity....are promising but systematic results must await the completion of a study now in progress." Presumably one aspect of this study was reported in 1950 by Rosenzweig and Mirmow (*57*) in which 79 per cent of a group of 19 4–7 year-old children classified (on the basis of teachers' detailed records of their adjustment in school) as socially inadequate had one or more "trends" in their records. On the other hand, the socially adequate and the socially uninterested children had percentages very similar to each other and lower than that for socially inadequate children—about 56. This group difference of 23 per cent at the .07 level of confidence can hardly be considered very adequate validation.

The instructions for administering this form are in general similar to those for the adult form, the most notable exception being that the younger children are required to give their responses orally. Older children are asked to read all their responses aloud when they have finished the Study and explicit directions are given as to how to conduct the inquiry. Scoring is similar to that of the adult form and as with that form very complete scoring samples are given. Norms are given for each two-year age span between 4 and 14. An illustrative record of an 11-year-old child is presented, scored, and given a rather superficial interpretation.

At present it appears to the reviewer that the clinical use of both forms of the P-F Study except in relation to other tests or case history material is rather hazardous. The data on reliability, validity and to some extent the norms themselves are inadequate. As the authors mention, the fundamental problem of the projective level on which the subject approaches the test has not been solved, and the possible different meanings of similar records with respect to personality has not been sufficiently explored. On the other hand, if given individually and orally together with an extensive and judicious inquiry and with an attitude of readiness to disregard it if it contradicts other more valid material, the P-F Study may often yield valuable insights.

PERCIVAL M. SYMONDS, *Professor of Education, Teachers College, Columbia University, New York, New York.*

This test is recognized today as one of the established projective techniques with its own unique method for obtaining the responses of an individual to frustrating situations. The author describes the test as consisting of a

series of 24 cartoonlike pictures, each depicting two persons who are involved in a mildly frustrating situation of common occurrence. The figure at the left of each picture is shown saying certain words which either help to describe the frustration of the other individual, or which are themselves actually frustrating to him. The person on the right is always shown with a blank caption box above. * The subject is instructed to examine the situations one at a time and write in the blank box the first appropriate reply which enters his mind.

These responses must be classified by the examiner to indicate the direction of aggression, and the reaction type. Aggression can be directed in one of three ways; outwardly on the environment—extrapunitiveness; inwardly on the subject himself—intrapunitiveness; or evasively to avoid the frustration—impunitiveness. Three types of reaction are recognized; obstacle-dominance, in which the response concentrates on the barrier occasioning the frustration; ego-defense, in which attention is turned to the self of the subject; and need-persistence, in which the solution of the frustrating problem is emphasized. All combinations of the six categories give nine scoring factors (plus two additional variants). To assist scoring, Rosenzweig has prepared elaborate scoring samples for each of the 24 situations. He suggests the use of an inquiry, as in the Rorschach, following the responses in order to clarify the intention behind the responses.

A record blank is provided for recording the scoring of the responses. In addition to entering the classification of each response, certain additional comparisons are suggested. The possible significance of these additional items in the record blank has not been demonstrated, and they add considerably to the task of analyzing a given record. First, there is a group conformity rating which indicates the extent to which a subject conforms with or departs from expectation as determined by the responses of normal subjects. Second, there is a set of boxes called "profiles" in which the scores and percentages of responses of each of the six types can be recorded. Third, there is a space for summarizing the relative order of direction of aggression apart from type of reaction and of type of response apart from direction of aggression. Finally, there is a calculation of trends of the change of the direction of type of response during the course of a given test. In one study using the children's form, Rosenzweig has demonstrated that the presence of a trend in a record is an index of personal instability and of low frustration tolerance.

The author has met expectations in standardizing the test and making it usable and useful by providing standardized instructions for administration and a helpful manual for scoring and interpretation and supplying norms on both the adult and children's forms. The adult norms are based on responses from 236 males and 224 females between the ages of 20 and 29 with an average of 13.5 years of schooling. The children's norms are based on the records of 256 boys and girls broken down into five age levels between the ages of 4 and 13. He has tested the reliability of the scoring and found in his trial 85 per cent agreement between independent scorers, which seems satisfactory in view of the fact that tests in this experiment were administered without determining the meaning of the responses or of revised scoring samples.

In spite of all the care that the author has taken in making his test useful, he is still unable to tell the worker how to interpret the results. But this is a difficulty that the *Rosenzweig Picture-Frustration Study* shares with all other projective techniques, and Rosenzweig is fully aware of the difficulties. For instance, in spite of the fact that the instructions tell the subject to write the first appropriate reply which enters his mind, the examiner does not know whether the response is what the subject *would* do in a similar situation as depicted in the test, what he thinks he *ought* to do, or what he *feels* like doing but would not actually do. The examiner knows, for example, that the subject has extrapunitive tendencies, but he does not know where or how these will be expressed by the subject in actual life. Rosenzweig says that eventually experimental investigation will answer this question. This reviewer believes that scores on the P-F Study cannot be interpreted blindly. The test has value only when interpreted in the light of other facts known about the subject; hence its main value should be in helping to understand the meaning of behavior and personality in terms of the underlying modes of response to frustration. Rosenzweig suggests that, in the absence of experimentally determined meanings for the responses, one assumes that what an individual writes on the test indicates how he will respond in real life; but this is an untenable assumption, for one never knows whether it applies in a given case.

The *Rosenzweig Picture-Frustration Study* is one of the recognized projective techniques. It is carefully prepared, and its author has done all that could reasonably be expected in making the test useful.

[130]

★**The Rotter Incomplete Sentences Blank.** Grades 9–12, 13–16, adults; 1950; also called ISB; 3 levels, 1 form; manual and standardization data for use with college level only; $1.25 per 25; $1.90 per manual; specimen set not available; postpaid; (20–40) minutes; Julian B. Rotter and Janet E. Rafferty (manual); Psychological Corporation. *

REFERENCES

1. MORTON, R. B. *A Controlled Experiment in Psychotherapy Based on Rotter's Social Learning Theory of Personality.* Doctor's thesis, Ohio State University (Columbus, Ohio), 1949.
2. ROTTER, JULIAN B. "The Incomplete Sentence Test as a Method of Studying Personality." Abstract. *Am Psychol* 1:286 Jl '46. * (*PA* 20:3715, title only)
3. ROTTER, JULIAN B., AND WILLERMAN, BENJAMIN. "The Incomplete Sentences Test as a Method of Studying Personality." *J Consult Psychol* 11:43–8 Ja–F '47. * (*PA* 21:2697)
4. WISCHNER, GEORGE J.; ROTTER, JULIAN B.; AND GILLMAN, ROBERT D. Chap. 9, "Projective Techniques," pp. 144–57. In *The Psychological Program in AAF Convalescent Hospitals.* Edited by Sidney W. Bijou. Army Air Forces Aviation Psychology Program Research Reports, Report No. 15. Washington, D.C.: U.S. Government Printing Office, 1947. Pp. viii, 256. *
5. BELL, JOHN ELDERKIN. "The Case of Gregor: Psychological Test Data." *Rorsch Res Exch & J Proj Tech* 13:155–205 no 2 '49. * (*PA* 24:2589)
6. ROTTER, JULIAN B.; RAFFERTY, JANET E.; AND SCHACHTITZ, EVA. "Validation of the Rotter Incomplete Sentences Blank for College Screening." *J Consult Psychol* 13:348–56 O '49. * (*PA* 24:2613) Correction: *J Consult Psychol* 13:454 D '49. *

CHARLES N. COFER, *Professor of Psychology, University of Maryland, College Park, Maryland.*

This blank is designed for use as a gross screening instrument for maladjustment. It appears to be simple to administer to either individuals or groups. The manual contains a rather extensive set of examples, presented as guides for scoring; adequate scoring reliability, even on the basis of familiarity with the manual alone, is reported.

Specific validity studies of the Rotter blank have been performed. Although one may doubt the ultimate value of the criteria employed and deplore the small number of cases used in the validity studies, there is, nevertheless, some clearly presented evidence that the test has some validity as an indicator of maladjustment. The authors are to be complimented for their presentation of validity data in a form that clearly illustrates how their validity studies were performed, an unusual occurrence in the case of projective tests. Norms are presented for 85 female and 214 male college freshmen at Ohio State University. Unfortunately, the validity studies are reported for samples that are not strictly comparable to those for which the norms are presented, and it is therefore not certain that the tentative cutting scores suggested on the basis of the validity studies would be applicable to the norm group. It is probably unwise to discuss specific cutting scores in the manual at all, since, as the authors point out, such cutting scores should be developed in the light of the purposes for, and the groups on, which the test is to be used.

There are separate scoring examples and norms for male and female subjects. In view of this, it seems quite likely that for noncollege groups the norms and the conclusions concerning validity are inapplicable. No norms or other information are presented for the Adult Form and the High School Form, which differ slightly in wording from the College Form. I would seriously criticise the publication and distribution of these two forms for which there are no data, since this seems to invite the use of the college norms with results obtained for the adult and high school groups.

Another feature of the test is its clinical interpretation, designed to obtain information of value in planning initial treatment interviews. Six case records are presented with a fairly detailed clinical interpretation. It is to be hoped that the users of the manual will exercise the same restraint and caution in their interpretations as the authors apparently do.

On the whole, this reviewer is well impressed with the prospects of this test as a useful screening instrument. On the other hand, it should be emphasized that present data permit its use only for college groups and that even here the norms and cutting scores will need considerable revision before they have wide utility. It is unfortunate that the authors have not considered developing a scoring system for the thematic characteristics of the test responses, rather than being content with clinical interpretation alone.

WILLIAM SCHOFIELD, *Associate Professor, Departments of Psychiatry and Psychology, University of Minnesota, Minneapolis, Minnesota.*

Of this instrument one might indeed remark: "E pluribus unum!" Sets of incomplete sentences have been sired so prolifically that the question of parenthood has drawn amusing attention. The *Rotter Incomplete Sentences Blank, College Form* is a revision of a revision by Rotter and Willerman of an Army instrument devised by Shor and others. The authors had two objectives: the provision of a technique having experimental and screening potential and the obtaining of information pertinent to diagnosis and treatment.

The ISB, College Form presents 40 incomplete items on two sides of a simple record form which includes blanks for identifying informa-

tion—age, sex, marital status, etc. Each item has a single line, between 5 and 6 inches in length. This might seem to impose certain undesirable restrictions on those persons whose graphomotor personality projections assume the form of rather expansive hieroglyphics. The authors mention the possibility of the subject crowding words on the single line or writing a double line within this space; the scoring system takes such behavior into account.

An advantage claimed for the ISB is that the time required for scoring and analysis is generally shorter than that for most projective techniques. Though the manual does not indicate the usual time required for scoring, the claim seems reasonable. The scoring examples for each item have been empirically selected so as to represent a 7-step scale covering a continuum from extremely good adjustment to need for psychotherapy as manifested in relatively small samples of male and female college students. Scoring examples are presented separately for the two sexes. It is possible for an inexperienced scorer to score a single record with good accuracy in as little as 15 minutes.

Interscorer reliabilities of .91 and .96 are reported for *trained* scorers, using 50 male and 50 female records respectively. Spearman-Brown reliability coefficients of .84 and .83 are reported for 124 male and 71 female college student records respectively. No test-retest coefficients are reported. Such data would be very desirable in view of the probability that temporary moods and reactive states might serve to alter greatly the overall adjustment rating yielded by this instrument.

For the most part the validity data are not impressive. Scores for each sex are reported separately for students in effective study and mental hygiene classes who were rated by their instructors as "adjusted" or "maladjusted" under a "forced choice" technique (Group I). A group of 10 (!) females were rated by "advanced student clinicians" as definitely well or poorly adjusted. Finally, data are reported for 46 males which were either self-referrals to a psychological clinic for treatment or cases referred for personal counseling by vocational counselors. The authors are to be commended for reporting the complete score distributions of all of these groups rather than resorting to the misleading statement only of mean scores and critical ratios. The distributions clearly depict a considerable overlap of adjusted and maladjusted groups. Selection of an appropriate cutting score permitted good identification of the adjusted, and considerably poorer identification of the maladjusted students. The Group I distributions yielded biserial coefficients of .50 and .62 for the females and males respectively between ISB scores and classification as adjusted or maladjusted.

Normative data are provided in the form of actual frequency and cumulative per cent distributions of the scores of 85 female and 214 male college freshmen. The manual, which is very well organized and generally thorough in its coverage, includes a discussion of scoring procedures, six practice cases illustrating scoring, and six cases illustrating clinical interpretation. The High School and Adult Forms of the ISB are identical with the College Form in 34 and 36 of their 40 items respectively. However, the authors correctly caution against unreserved use of the college norms with these forms.

Though more validity data with better clinical criteria are needed, the authors have produced an excellent model for the conservative, objective standardization of instruments of this kind. The ISB certainly has much experimental potential and should prove useful as a gross screening instrument for college students.

Am J Orthopsychiatry 21:649–50 Jl '51. Adolf G. Woltmann. * differs from others in that it allows the testee to include humorous answers. Most tests of this kind make no allowance for the scoring of humor and often specifically request the subject to refrain from answering humorously. Such omissions fail to recognize that humor is a healthy way to meet frustrating situations. * Like all test instruments of this kind, the Rotter ISB is not as well disguised as other projective methods. This might enable the sophisticated subject to fake answers in order to appear better adjusted than he may actually be. On the other hand, the general intent of what constitutes a good or bad answer is not readily apparent to most subjects. This test should not be scored in a purely mathematical manner. Interpretation depends on the examiner's general clinical experience, skill and awareness of personality dynamics. In this way the Incomplete Sentences Blank is less of a straight paper and pencil personality test, but must be viewed essentially as a projective technique. As such it is comparatively easy to administer and takes less time to give and to score

than most projective tests. * This test is warmly recommended to clinical psychologists and also to psychiatrists or analysts who want to gain information about their patients in a minimum of time.

[131]

★Sentence Completions Test. Ages 12 and over; 1940–47; a revision of *Payne Sentence Completions Blank* ('28) ; 1 form, '40; manual ('47) ; $1.50 per 25 ; $1.50 per 25 scoring and interpretation forms ; $1.80 per manual (contains the test and interpretation form) ; specimen set not available ; postpaid ; nontimed (45–50) minutes ; Amanda R. Rohde and Gertrude Hildreth ; distributed by Psychological Corporation. *

REFERENCES
1. ROHDE, AMANDA R. "Explorations in Personality by the Sentence Completion Method." *J Appl Psychol* 30:169–81 Ap '46. * (*PA* 20:3222)
2. ROHDE, AMANDA R. "A Note Regarding the Use of the Sentence Completions Test in Military Installations Since the Beginning of World War II." *J Consult Psychol* 12:190–3 My-Je '48. * (*PA* 22:4956)
3. STEIN, MORRIS I. "The Record and a Sentence Completion Test." *J Consult Psychol* 13:448–9 D '49. * (*PA* 24:3217)

CHARLES N. COFER, *Professor of Psychology, University of Maryland, College Park, Maryland.*

This test was developed to provide an instrument simpler than other projective tests but preserving their advantages. Apparently it may be interpreted clinically to estimate maladjustment. There is also an elaborate scoring system which yields values for each of a large number of needs, environmental press, and other variables derived from the work of H. A. Murray.

The test is simple to administer and is intended for persons whose mental age is at least 12 years. Although the author (the manual is by Rohde alone) apparently believes that it may be used for adults, the only data presented come from studies of ninth grade students from one high school in New York City and one in Fort Lee, New Jersey. That extreme caution should be exercised in the use of the norms is indicated by the fact that the parents of only 30 per cent of the children were American born.

In the reviewer's opinion, it would be impossible to score a record on the basis of the instructions given in the manual with assurance that the scoring was properly done so as to permit comparisons of scores with the norms. Although each need, environmental press, and inner state is presumably to be scored in terms of its frequency of occurrence and its strength (3-point scale), criteria for counting the occurrence and for rating the strength of a variable are not presented. Similarly, it is not apparent how the frequency and strength estimates are combined to give a single score for each variable, although the norms given indicate that this is done. In none of the examples cited in the manual is a numerical score listed; the analysis usually is clinically oriented and the completed sentences are simply listed for the various needs they presumably indicate. Percentage of agreement among different scorers is reported to be fairly high but variable; however, they must have been trained by methods not indicated in the manual. A test-retest reliability check is reported for some of the subjects over an eight-month period. The average test-retest correlations for the various variables were .68 and .64 for girls and boys, respectively. These are reported as .80 and .76 when corrected for attenuation; the reviewer is unable to understand why they were corrected for attentuation.

Unusually high correlations are reported between scores on the test variables and a composite rating on each of the same variables (average for girls .79; for boys, .82). These were averages of ratings made by teachers and the investigator. Insufficient information is given concerning the distribution of the original scores or of the ratings to permit an interpretation of the correlations, and the validity study was restricted to but a part of the original norm group.

In its basic characteristics this test is essentially the same as other sentence completion tests. The scoring system is so poorly described, however, that it cannot be used, and the norms are inadequate. On this basis, the *Rotter Incomplete Sentences Blank* seems to be a better instrument, although it is applicable only to college students at present. Clinicians may, however, prefer this somewhat longer test and, with experience, may find it useful.

CHARLES R. STROTHER, *Professor of Clinical Psychology, University of Washington, Seattle, Washington.*

This test consists of a list of 64 single words or short phrases, intended as the beginnings of sentences which are to be completed as rapidly as possible by the examinee. The items were selected so as to: (*a*) sample as many phases of personality as possible; (*b*) cover various areas of conflict; (*c*) be intelligible to persons with an MA of ten years or over; and (*d*) allow maximal latitude of response. The test was standardized on 180 ninth grade students in two junior high schools.

For scoring and interpretation, the test blank provides a check list of attitudes toward parents, siblings, self, friends, associates, religion, education, etc., and tabulation sheets on which are entered the frequency and strength of various "needs," "inner states and traits," "inner integrates," "press," and "cathexes," according to Murray's system of personality analysis. The manual gives abbreviated but reasonably adequate definitions of these terms. The checklist and needs-press scores are to be filled out by the examiner on the basis of inspection of the record as a whole, rather than by tabulation of responses to individual items.

The manual provides a distribution of "needs," "inner state," and "inner integrate" scores only for a sample of 180 ninth grade cases. Because of the restricted nature of this population these norms are of very limited value. Interscorer agreement, for judges familiar with Murray's system, was .95 for two judges and .78 among five judges. Test-retest correlations for ratings (not for particular items) for 44 cases retested after an 8-month interval, ranged from .44 to .98 (corrected for attenuation) for specific needs. The validity criterion was the pooled judgments of several teachers and the investigator, who interviewed each of 100 students and had access to their school records. Correlations of scores and ratings averaged .79 for girls and .82 for boys, with a range of .30 to .96.

The clinician will find frequent use for a sentence-completion test, particularly for screening purposes and in out-clinic work. The Rohde-Hildreth test is to be preferred for adolescents, with or without the Murray scoring, and the *Sacks Sentence Completion Test* [1] will be preferred for adult subjects. The possibility of substituting or adding items for special purposes increases the usefulness of this method.

J Consult Psychol 12:284 Jl–Ag '48. Laurance F. Shaffer. The recent publication of the scoring form and manual has increased the potential usefulness of the well-known incomplete sentences technique. The scoring form provides a framework for evaluating the needs, inner states and presses shown by the sentence completions according to a classification scheme adapted from H. A. Murray. There is also a more informal analysis of the examinees' attitudes, interests, values and emotional problems. The manual defines and illustrates the concepts

1 Sacks, Joseph M., and Levy, Sidney. "The Sentence Completion Test," pp. 357–402. (*PA* 25: 2468) In *Projective Psychology: Clinical Approaches to the Total Personality.* Edited by Lawrence Edwin Abt and Leopold Bellak. New York: Alfred A. Knopf, Inc., 1950. Pp. xvii, 485. xiv. *

used in scoring, and gives normative data based on 680 ninth-grade students. Reliability is discussed in connection with the problems of repeated scoring by different examiners, and of repeated administration after various intervals of time. Validity is studied by means of teachers' ratings of the pupils. Case studies illustrate diagnostic and clinical applications of the test.

[132]

★Symonds Picture Story Test. Grades 7–12; 1948; individual; 2 parts (Sets A and B); 1 form; Set B may be administered alone or Sets A and B together; $5.25 per set of testing materials, postpaid; nontimed (60–70) minutes per set; Percival M. Symonds; Bureau of Publications, Teachers College, Columbia University. *

REFERENCES

1. SYMONDS, PERCIVAL M. "Survey of Projective Techniques," pp. 3–18. In *Exploring Individual Differences: A Report of the 1947 Invitational Conference on Testing Problems, New York City, November 1, 1947.* Henry Chauncey, Chairman. American Council on Education Studies, Vol. 12, Series 1, No. 32. Washington, D.C.: the Council, October 1948. Pp. vii, 110. Paper. *
2. SYMONDS, PERCIVAL M. *Adolescent Fantasy: An Investigation of the Picture-Story Method of Personality Study.* New York: Columbia University Press, 1949. Pp. xii, 397. $6.00. * (London: Oxford University Press. 32s. 6d.) (PA 24:650)

E. J. G. BRADFORD, *Senior Lecturer in Education, The University of Sheffield, Sheffield, England.*

The chief limitations of the projection technique based upon pictures as the primary or initial stimulus are undoubtedly: (a) the intellectual efficiency of the person tested; (b) the culture pattern within which that person has developed his personality; and (c) the strength of the inhibitive forces as they influence that person's freedom to give rein to his imagination. These limitations apply whether the investigator is concerned primarily with making a diagnosis or obtaining a psychometric estimate of the strength of the dynamic forces or merely using such tests as a preliminary screening to determine whether psychotherapy in any form is called for.

It is the opinion of the reviewer, based admittedly on limited experience, that the schools in the U.S.A. encourage, and succeed in developing among the pupils, a greater readiness to the free oral expression of their thoughts than is achieved among the pupils in British schools: the American pupil is also more "test conscious" than his British contemporary. Both these factors may contribute to a more copious supply of material being obtained in response to the pictures. Consequently, it is of the utmost importance that for psychometric purposes specific norms should be worked out to correspond to the different culture patterns. Actual pictures

themselves may need modification; e.g., picture 1 of series A is liable to be interpreted as a youth amidst an enormous industrial plant because the pupil's experience does not lead him to think of skyscrapers as so many "homes." Picture 2 prompts the reaction "What on earth is it?" because it does not fit neatly into the concept of letterbox, sweet machine, or first-aid outfit.

The manual says "stories and case material were collected from 40 normal adolescent boys and girls." Reference to the author's book *Adolescent Fantasy,* which gives a very full account of all the work which culminated in the construction of the test, shows that these 40 pupils include 7 only children, 8 children from broken homes, 4 children with foreign parents. The medical histories include one of vomiting attacks over a period of 3 years, one of severe migraine for 9 years, one of infantile paralysis. Does "normal" in this context mean "representative sample"? If it does, is it related to a particular culture pattern?

Although the results reported in *Adolescent Fantasy* have been examined statistically with care and insight, the author's caution has lapsed when he published the table of norms in the manual. These norms appear to have been reproduced from pages 97–98 of *Adolescent Fantasy.* Norms derived from the responses to 42 pictures do not apply to a *selected* group of 20 drawn from the original 42. If one examines the frequency of themes for each picture, given in Appendix D of the same book, with a view to discovering whether the 20 pictures of the shorter version call forth similar themes to the discarded 22 pictures, the impression gained is that they do not. If one sums the positive (+5 and over) and the negative (−4 and over) deviations from independence separately for each group of 20 and the 22 pictures, one finds that the shortened version is much more likely to produce erotic and economic themes or categories of response, is more likely to produce family themes, less likely to produce aggressive themes, and much less likely to produce punishment themes than do the 22 rejected pictures. These differences suggest that revised norms are required.

In spite of the above criticisms, the reviewer is impressed by the possibilities of the test and believes it will become a valuable addition to the present small company of projection tests. One specially useful feature is to be found in the instructions, which attempt (but significantly may fail) to focus attention upon features that will have diagnostic importance: e.g., What happened before the scene depicted and what followed from it? What are the characters thinking, doing, and saying?

Though more time consuming than the van Lennep *Four Picture Test,* in which the subject is required to weave one story out of four pictures, *Symonds Picture Story Test* is better suited to persons of lower intellectual calibre. The reviewer has found that used in conjunction, these two tests furnish information which is confirmatory to a degree which inspires some confidence in the method of projection.

Rorsch Res Exch & J Proj Tech 13:347–9 S '49. Robert R. Holt. The publication, after about 10 years, of the TAT pictures which Dr. Symonds had drawn by Lynd Ward raises again the important question: how are pictures for a thematic test to be chosen? * The original idea that stimulated Symonds' research seems....to have been a sound one: that pictures might be found or designed which would be better suited for clinical use with adolescents than Murray's and Morgan's. But it is unfortunate that the research was designed in such a way that it could lead only to a competing set of pictures, not a systematic supplement to the original test, replacing those cards which were shown to be of less value. For after all the years of work of Symonds, Milton Wexler and others on the Adolescent Fantasy Project, there is only the original assumption, in place of any proof, that the nicely gotten-out little pictures are in any way superior to Murray's set for their avowed purpose. In fact, Symonds makes statements about the ease with which adolescents can identify themselves with figures of any age or sex, even with objects and abstract ideas; these are results which cast doubt on the necessity of a special set of pictures. The method by which the 20 pictures were arrived at seems to be a sound one. * the author....had a well-known artist make a set of 42 wash drawings to his specifications, representing a wide variety of situations and interpersonal relations of concern to adolescents, most of them with figures of teen-age boys and girls in them. Then after analysis of all the stories told by 20 boys and 20 girls to all pictures, the latter were rank ordered separately according to four criteria: "(1) those pictures which yielded the largest number of themes in the stories told about them; (2) those pictures

which yielded stories with the most important themes; (3) those pictures which were judged best (on a five-point scale) by examiners who used them; (5) those pictures which yielded stories used for illustrative purposes in the report of the investigation." A final combined rank order was made up, giving equal weight to each criterion (why the last was weighted so heavily is an obscure but perhaps unimportant point), and the 20 pictures with the lowest mean ranks were chosen for publication. Now if one were starting from scratch without any other basis on which to make a choice of test materials, a procedure such as this would be quite in order. But to think to supplant the set of TAT pictures, with which many clinicians have the experience of many scores of administrations and interpretations, by virtue of a study involving only 40 subjects seems unrealistic. When this much criticism has been made, there is a good deal to be said for the new pictures. A picture which suggests the topic of sibling rivalry, (B4) is one which is sorely missed in Murray's test; jealousy (A3) and a variety of parent-child situations look also as if they might be quite useful. On the other hand, as a group they look as if they have more uniformity of style and mood than is desirable—the figures in successive pictures look enough alike to encourage perseverative carry-over stories. With one exception all are on the plane of daily reality. My impression (unbacked by any systematic evidence) is that it is stimulating to subjects' imagination to have a variety of styles, media, types of characters, and degrees of imaginativeness in the pictures. Of course, such an off-the-cuff evaluation without any experience with the pictures is not worth much; the acid test is experience. As for the manual which accompanies the pictures, it says hardly anything that is not in Murray's. Procedure and instructions are very similar, even to the stress on imagination in introducing the test to the subject. An extremely non-directive approach is urged, "mild encouragement" being recommended only for "unusual cases in which material is produced very slowly." Symonds routinely includes a final period of association to each story as it is read back to the subject—a good idea where feasible. * Analysis and interpretation of content and form are given brief treatment, again along rather conventional lines. The main task of content-analysis is "to tabulate the principal psychological forces which are indicated in the stories"; a list of 14 are suggested. It is a rather miscellaneous group of needs, defenses and what Murray calls inner states. Eleven formal aspects are also described, but their significance is left entirely unclarified. In general, Symonds has some sober and sensible things to say about interpretation, but he seems so eager to prevent anyone from going off the deep end that he leans over backwards to deny the test any usefulness except in the context of much corroborating case data. One thing this manual has that is nowhere to be found in Murray's publications: a table of norms. The author deserves some sort of an A for effort, but for the effort only—the norms (Q_1, Mdn. and Q_3 percentile points for 28 miscellaneous themes) are of questionable usefulness. They are no better than the representativeness of the original tiny sample of 40 on which they are based; and there are no instructions for identifying the 28 themes, which do not even include all of the 14 themes listed in the section on analysis of content. There is nothing in the manual to indicate that Dr. Symonds has accumulated any clinical experience with his pictures, or indeed that they were ever used with any subjects other than the original group of high school volunteers. Perhaps his sizeable volume, *Adolescent Fantasy,* has favorable answers to these doubting questions; at any rate, the pictures are now available to others who may give them the kind of clinical try-out in simultaneous comparison with Murray's TAT that is very much needed at this point. It is devoutly to be hoped that comparative studies will be made, and that they will use as systematic and explicit a method for deciding the relative merits of all the pictures as Dr. Symonds has in his own research.

For related reviews, see 133.

[133]

★[*Re* Symonds Picture Story Test.] SYMONDS, PERCIVAL M. **Adolescent Fantasy: An Investigation of the Picture-Story Method of Personality Study.** New York: Columbia University Press, 1949. Pp. xii, 397. $6.00. * (London: Oxford University Press. 32s. 6d.) (*PA* 24: 650)

Am J Orthopsychiatry 20:845–6 O '50. Leo Kanner. * original, meaty, and highly informative study * painstaking and carefully organized investigation * Symonds....has a way of letting the reader in on his plans and deliberations in a lucid style and with unswerving scientific honesty. His review of the literature, with its concise emphasis on essentials, gives a good basic orientation and leads to an understanding of

the problems and areas of inquiry which have preoccupied the author in the course of his undertaking. * A number of problems arose during the investigation. Symonds discusses these thoughtfully, never yielding to the temptation of drawing hasty conclusions. * Some of the author's conclusions are extremely important: For the psychotherapist, a knowledge of the patient's fantasy is of the utmost significance. Telling the stories "is a real growth experience out of which a boy or girl gains slightly more courage to express his aggressions, goals, and ambitions, to assert his independence, to learn that his fears are trivial, to reduce in some small measure his burden of guilt, and to become more self-assured and confident." * a good bibliography * a most valuable addition to the literature on the psychology of adolescents. This reviewer wishes it a wide circulation.

Am J Psychol 63:160 Ja '50. Madison Bentley. * The "fantasy pictures" used are well reproduced in the attractive and well-written volume, which is a major addition to the rapidly growing literature of this method. Two of the cases are fully "analyzed" in the text. A casual remark may be added upon the possible change from one generation to the next in a subject administered in Columbia's Teachers College (*cf. sup.,* a review of Thorndike's *Selected Writings from a Connectionist's Psychology*).

B Int Bur Ed 24:74 q 2 '50. A thorough study * The pictures....take into account the American background. Used with a similar age group elsewhere, they might not yield the same results.

B Menninger Clinic 14:187 S '50. John A. Grimshaw. This study....should interest the clinical psychologist. For reasons that the author did not make clear, he found it necessary to prepare a complete new set of pictures. * The pictures which are given in an appendix of the book are in general rather morose, gloomy, tragic in mood and seem to lack the variability and flexibility seen in the pictures used in the familiar Murray Thematic Apperception Test.

Brit J Psychol, Gen Sect 40:229–30 Je '50. M. Powell. * A conscientious account is given of the exhaustive analysis made of the stories obtained, including an inventory of themes, tables of norms, and a section on quantitative relations among groups of themes and relations between the themes and the other variables of the study. In the light of his extensive experience with efforts to work out objective methods for scoring the stories, the author's conclusion about the value of such methods should carry considerable weight: "I am more than ever convinced that the value of a projective technique is lost by any attempt to analyse or score it psychometrically—its value resides in the degree to which the interpreter is able to build up from the trends and the themes in the stories a dynamically integrated picture of the individual being studied." He is aware, of course, that interpretations derived in this way are subjective, governed as they are by the factors to which the experimenter is at the moment most sensitive; but this limitation, he suggests, may be one of incompleteness rather than of inaccuracy. In contrast with some workers in this field, who advocate blind analysis of the TAT, Symonds emphatically denies the possibility of deducing facts in the real life of the subjects from their stories, and would emphasize that the proper purpose of the TAT and similar techniques in personality study is not to yield precise facts and information, but to reveal background motives and tendencies which help to show the meaning and motivational significance of other facts known about the person. Perhaps the most interesting section of the book is a discussion of fantasy and character, which includes a comparison of the stories with the life-history material. There is a useful account of problems connected with the process of identification of the subject with the characters in his stories, and one rather startling conclusion made by the author is that sex lines are no barrier whatever to identification: "Apparently boys can tell stories in which a girl is the hero as easily as those in which the boy is the hero—and vice versa for girls. Consequently there is no reason for having separate sets of pictures for boys and girls." The author is refreshingly cautious in relating the fantasy material to the overt behaviour of his subjects. He found, for example, but a negligible correlation between the nature of the fantasy material and "adjustment," and concludes that this would indicate that the picture-story method does not have diagnostic value, that is, does not help to distinguish between normal and pathological subjects. "The same fantasies are produced by normal and by pathological individuals; this means that the same dynamic forces help to make a person normal that help to make him pathological." It is difficult to find meaningful connexions between fantasy and overt behaviour, he adds, because these two forms of expression may par-

allel or oppose one another in a given individual. This relation in turn would seem to depend in each case upon the degree to which the fantasy need and the manifest expression of it are both expressions of some more general factor or disposition. The section of the book which tabulates the norms for the themes obtained in the stories, although making a needed contribution to the literature in this field, may be of but little practical value to the English reader: e.g. many of the individual items may reflect the "mom" culture in which American adolescents are often said to live. This objection does not appear to apply, however, to the full discussions given of two individual cases, one of a well-adjusted boy and one of a boy with delinquent tendencies; for here the interest lies in the relations that are traced among all the variables which were considered in an effort to obtain a "dynamically integrated" picture of the two boys. The richness of these two pictures suggests that the author has been perhaps too modest in the claims for the value of his method.

Cath Ed R 48:70–1 Ja '50. F. J. Houlahan. * Unfortunately, all of the pictures....are "on the whole gloomy, severe, morose, mournful and tragic." Despite the obvious critical importance of the pictures for this study, the artist's own interpretation is ignored except to say: "It is possible that the record of adolescent fantasy which this study yields is influenced to some extent by the fantasy life of the artist who drew the pictures, but it is not believed that this is a very important factor, even though a constant factor." * A tremendous amount of work went into the study. It is a very good illustration of a method, and of a report of an investigation. However, in this reviewer's opinion, there is little validity to it. The pictures are admittedly of one general type. Whatever statistical formulas may show, generalizations based on 20 boys and 20 girls are of dubious representativeness, particularly when the two sexes are compared. It appears that the psychological preconceptions of the investigators must have had much influence in classifying the themes. On the other hand, the authority of the author and of his collaborators is such as to compensate for much of what the study lacks.

J Consult Psychol 13:310–1 Ag '49. Laurance F. Shaffer. Symonds' work is a skillful blend of objective and dynamic approaches, applied to the development of a picture-story technique for exploring the personalities of adolescents. *

Several chapters are of general value in giving insight into adolescent needs, stresses and fantasies, apart from the particulars of the test itself. * The volume is an indispensable background and aid in the use of the Symonds *Picture-Story Test* *

J Proj Tech 15:276–9 Je '51. Eva Ruth Balken. In this decade of intoxication with the merits of projective techniques as the psychologist's *sine qua non* of psychotherapy and psychodiagnostics, it is refreshing to find a book which deals specifically with methodology and rationale and does not transcend the data to make generalizations about either psychodiagnostics or psychotherapy. *Adolescent Fantasy: An Investigation of the Picture-Story Method* is what its title claims it to be. It summarizes the results of a ten-year research project. Dr. Symonds' earlier investigations of adolescent fantasy are not only the first application of the TAT, but the most important methodological contribution in this area. With the meteoric rise of clinical psychology and the ascendancy of the TAT-and-its-derivatives cult, the implications of this early study have been overlooked and the "criteria" exploited into: "Given the right set of pictures, the rest follows," "Anything Goes," and "Anybody can do anything and everything." This in turn has been exploited into an equation of fantasy with symbolism, symbolism with the fantastic, the unreal, the impossible, the improbable, and of the fantastic with penetration to "deeper layers of the personality." It is hoped that this book will not also be exploited in similar fashion and that it will serve to establish a new trend in clinical psychology—the investigation of fundamentals—and to serve as a model in methodology and rationale. The subtitle does more justice than does the main title to the contents of the book and its twofold purpose: "to prepare a set of pictures for general use as a projective technique," and "to learn how the picture-story method operates." A set of 20 pictures is now available and the book, as its table of contents reveals, is a faithful presentation of how the picture-story method operates with a given methodology and with a given rationale: "Exploration of the problem of classification of projective responses....The question posed in personality diagnosis (at present, at any rate) is not how much of this or that trait or function does a person possess, but what are his characteristic attitudes and responses." If only Dr. Symonds did not distrust his own intuitions and

observations and formulate the problems in terms of the structure of personality, the quantitative element, so clearly brought out in his data, would not have to be subordinated to the finality of classification. Chapter XVI presents 21 conclusions. This reviewer has selected conclusions 2 and 3 as an orientation: "(2) Stories must successfully reveal personality when interpreted dynamically. Themes in the stories are those which would be expected from the findings of dynamic psychology and psychoanalytic theory. (3) The same dynamic principles which explain the personalities of poorly adjusted individuals also help us to understand the personalities of well adjusted individuals." The review of the literature is restricted to The Thematic Apperception Test and its antecedents in free-association tests. There is no discussion of the nature of fantasy, no indication that fantasy is an activity, a mental activity, and hence no comparison with day-dreaming and imagination. There is no indication that fantasy represents the fulfilment of a wish and improves on unsatisfactory reality, that the impelling wishes vary with the character, sex, and circumstances, that with growing into adulthood and with the adult they are concealed with so much secretiveness that some of the wishes from which the growing-into-adulthood and the adult's fantasies spring are such as to be entirely hidden from its creator, that the activity of fantasy covers the three periods of ideation and is linked up with some current impression, occasioned by some event in the present, which has the power to arouse an intense desire. Above all, there is no stressing of the quantitative element, the decisive element, and no description of the psychoanalytic findings regarding adolescence. In fact, there is no reference to either Sigmund Freud or Anna Freud. So the reader has no idea of what "findings of dynamic psychology and psychoanalytic theory" and what "dynamic principles" the author is referring to in conclusions 2 and 3. The 42 pictures used in this study were reproduced from sketches in black and white crayon made in accordance with two criteria: "A minimum of detail and characters with whom the subject can identify himself" and in accordance with content specifications. The pictures have a sameness, a shadowy and unreal quality which they might not have had if the artist had not been bound by restrictions. They are easily identifiable as the productions of one artist and have the effect of a continued story, which may account for the "warming-up effect" noted. Experience has shown that drawing upon sources such as magazines provides greater opportunity for displacement and hence greater permissiveness for communicating the story. As so often happens when the nature of fantasy is not appreciated, the dynamic interaction of unconscious and conscious not recognized, and the distinction between internal and external history not grasped, fantasy eventually becomes equated with symbolism and symbolism indiscriminately equated with the symbolic. So the Section: "Equations-Symbolism," while very informative, is still misleading with its equations: (1) "love-acceptance-place in family-food-job." (2) "clothes-poverty-riches-old-young-aspects of self." (3) "poverty-deprivation, without desirable characteristics, mean." (4) "job-affection-belonging and clothes-self-esteem." (5) "being crazy-death wishes." (6) "school-mother." The fantasies have not been related to the totality of the research situation; hence the ubiquitous phenomena of transference and resistance have not been unfolded. A careful examination of the overtones and undertones of this book reveals that Dr. Symonds has never been motivated by a belief in the magical powers of the research techniques and in the omniscience of the investigator and the examiner. It also reveals that again and again—as in the instance of the equations and in the discussion of Implications of Fantasy for Counseling and Psychotherapy—he is on the verge of recognizing the defenses against anxiety and finding the clues for their identification. But the failure to consider the importance of the directions has prevented appreciation of the extent to which a conflict had been created by the conditions of the research situation itself—a *sine qua non* in any investigation which claims to be an application of psychoanalysis—which would then delineate the individual's mode of reacting to a conflictful situation. The subject not only takes a test of creative imagination. He is also required to take a double role: actor and playwright—"imagine yourself a story writer"; then his freedom is checked by various admonitions and specifications: "Please don't feel....," and before the second picture the further check: "That was pretty good, but I am sure that you can do better. Perhaps you are afraid to say just what you are thinking about. It is all right to tell me anything you think of." "Better" is equated with the "fantastic," perhaps the im-

probable and impossible. The population consisted of 20 boys and 20 girls from a suburban city, all but one "well-adjusted" without observable conflict. (The 40 sketches show that discounting age and the like, they still were far from being a homogeneous group.) An initial conference preceded the testing. The 42 stories were obtained in a school period of 40 minutes, taking an average of 5.5 periods. At the completion of the 42 stories came the association period in which the stories were read back to the subject. An interview with the parent (preferably the mother), one with the teacher, and an autobiography were obtained. The autobiographies were among the most helpful parts of the study. In addition, there were Sheviakov-Friedberg Questionnaire, pupil ratings by the teachers, school records, and rankings for adjustment. But it is not indicated how they and the biographical material were utilized in the delineation of fantasy. The Sheviakov-Friedberg Questionnaire merits special discussion. This is the first and sole instance, to the reviewer's knowledge, in which it has been included in the methodology of investigations of projective techniques. It is scored for 26 categories; in this study 24 were scored, but only five used in the quantitative relationship study: aggression, family, authority, identification, and opposite sex. (Chapter IX). It is regretted that the ratings were not scrapped so as to utilize the other scored categories. The quantitative and the qualitative analyses of the data were restricted to the identifying and classification of themes. There is a count of theme production by individuals and by pictures. Only those themes were listed which had occurred three or more times. The total number was 1850—an average of 46.25 per individual. The total number per picture was 257, average 6.42, ranging from 150 (average 3.98) for card 7 to 319 (average 7.98) for card 38. The peak is at age 15, confirming by inference that with growing into adulthood there is the growing tendency to be secretive about day-dreams, etc. Whether the peak is really at 15 is obscured by the conditions and circumstances of the research as is also the significance of the finding that the boys are more productive than the girls. The 1850 themes were then classified into three large "natural" groups: "(1) those of a psychological nature, (2) those of environmental nature, and (3) those derived from stylistic qualities of the stories," no attempt being made "to analyze the grammatical and other structural features of the stories." Such a classification involves much overlapping and leads to such label impasses as "special fantasies" and "equation-symbolism." This inventory led to the establishment of norms for "only 30 main themes." To really comprehend the scope and promises of this contribution, the appendices must be referred to constantly: A. Sketches of the forty cases, B. Personality traits of the 40 cases as inferred from the stories and as observed in real life, C. Theme headings, D. Frequency of norms by pictures, and E. Correlation tables. This reviewer has found A. and E. most helpful, instructive, and suggestive of problems for further research. A −.01 correlation of anxiety (Symonds) with I.Q. as contrasted with a −.27 of guilt (Symonds) with I.Q., a −.34 of repentance with I.Q., and a +.26 of depression with I.Q. certainly justifies further investigation, as do also the sketches, especially the skillful summation of the case data. This review may seem to many readers impertinent. So also will seem the cautionings of the author, which are too numerous to cite out of context, and his constant reminder that the analysis of the data is restricted to content, to identifying and classifying themes. The reader is especially apt to disregard Dr. Symonds' remarks regarding the riding of "hobbies." This is an age in which science is being travested into "hobbies" and subordinated to their furtherance and sustenance. The relation between science and techniques is a reciprocal one and appreciation of this relation is an art: "It is a man's imagination that devises experiments." It is the problem of technique, which brings about specialization in the unity which is science. A technique cannot create a science. Under the aegis of the projective techniques cult, especially the TAT-and-its-derivatives cult (because of the belief that the effect must resemble the cause) various hobbies are being ridden and masked by a benevolent skepticism regarding theories, facts and principles which must then await acceptance, rejection, or indifference until the constantly enlarging jury has passed its verdict. Fantasy, the reality of fantasy, is still on trial. The significance of Dr. Symonds' contribution lies in his demonstration of the reality, the existence of fantasy. It is hoped that it will serve to terminate the endless controversies and riding of "hobbies."

Jun Col J 20:230–3 D '49. Robert R. Blake. * the report of a piece of research....[which] might very well serve as a basic text....in the relatively unexplored realm of adolescent fantasy life * While the investigation seems to have been conducted with care, some possibility of bias is present since the same investigator who had administered the Picture-Story Method occasionally participated in the collection of the other information as well. This allows the danger that the investigator would look for and consequently see what he thought "should be there." The hazards from this source are probably not too great, however, because the investigators do not appear to have had preconceived notions as to what the data should mean in the final analysis and interpretation. * No direct demonstration of validity is provided for the interpretations that are given. The conclusions drawn are numerous and important. * This report....should prove to be of value to those investigators who are concerned with the deeper mainsprings of behavior as well as to those who teach, counsel, and advise adolescents.

Psychoanalytic Q 19:431–3 Jl '50. Hyman S. Lippman. * a painstaking effort to penetrate the personality and conflicts of the adolescent * a good deal of significant material was stimulated by the pictures which could be very useful in psychotherapeutic interviews. The tests would be more revealing in psychotherapy because the therapist is in a position to elicit associations and to trace the source of the fantasy, after having obtained a trusting relationship with the subject. In spite of the fact that there were so many revealing fantasies in this study, this test has not the advantages of the Rorschach Test in which the subject is totally unaware of the nature of the material he is revealing. Its advantage is the stimulation to discuss subjects generally avoided which produce conflict. * In several instances references to the dynamics involved in the stories seem forced and unclear. This may be due to the fact that material is omitted for brevity. It would seem to the reviewer, however, that such references should not be made unless the evidence for them is clear and unmistakable. The author wisely states in his conclusions that the interpretations at best are hypothetical, and subject to revision. When the master of a technique concludes with such a statement, it is to be hoped that his less well-trained followers will use correspondingly greater caution. Adolescent Fantasy is a book well worth reading. The picture method will probably be used extensively and, as time goes on, may help to reveal important factors con-

cerning the complex fantasy life of young people.
Q R Biol 26:111 Mr '51. *Helen Arthur.* *
impressive study * exceedingly careful and detailed approach * Throughout the book there
is a nice balance between the statistical use of
the data and a reporting of the actual clinical
material. *

[134]

Szondi Test. Ages 4 and over; 1937–51; 8 "factors"
and 4 "vectors" (each vector is the total of 2 factors):
homosexual, sadistic, sexual vector, epileptic, hysteric,
paroxysmal vector, catatonic, paranoic, schizophrenic
vector, depressive, manic, contact vector; individual;
IBM; 1 form, '47; $5 per manual, *Introduction to the
Szondi Test* ('49—see 11 below); $11 per set of 48
test pictures ('47); separate answer sheets may be
used; $1.80 per 50 IBM answer sheets ('51—labeled
Form D); $3 per 100 profile sheets ('49—labeled
Form B); $3 per 100 table-of-tendencies sheets
('49—labeled Form C); $3 per 50 folders containing
the preceding two sheets ('49—labelled Form A);
postage extra; test must be administered "at least six,
preferably ten, times with at least one day intervals
between administrations"; (10–15) minutes per administration; English manual by Susan K. Deri; L.
Szondi; Grune & Stratton, Inc. *

REFERENCES

1. DERI, SUSAN K. *The Psychological Effects of Electric
Shock Treatments on Depressive Patients.* Master's thesis,
State University of Iowa (Iowa City, Iowa), 1943.
2a. RAPAPORT, DAVID. "The Szondi Test." *B Menninger
Clinic* 5:33–9 Mr '41. * (*PA* 15:3049)
2b. RAPAPORT, D. "Principles Underlying Projective Techniques." *Char & Pers* 10:213–9 Mr '42. * (*PA* 16:4068)
2c. KNIGHT, ROBERT P.; GILL, MERTON; LOZOFF, MILTON;
AND RAPAPORT, DAVID. "Comparison of Clinical Findings and
Psychological Tests in Three Cases Bearing Upon Military Personnel Selection." *B Menninger Clinic* 7:114–28 My '43. * (*PA*
17:4241)
2d. DERI, SUSAN KOROSY. "Description of the Szondi Test: A
Projective Technique for Psychological Diagnosis." Abstract.
Am Psychol 1:286 Jl '46. * (*PA* 20:3695, title only)
3. DERI, OTTO. *Musical Taste and Personality.* Master's
thesis, Columbia University (New York, N.Y.), 1947.
4. BALINT, MICHAEL. "On Szondi's 'Schicksalsanalyse' and
'Triebdiagnostik.'" *Int J Psycho-Analysis* 29:240–9 pt 4 '48. *
(*PA* 24:3207)
5. BELL, JOHN ELDERKIN. Chap. 12, "The Szondi Test," pp.
269–72. In his *Projective Techniques: A Dynamic Approach to
the Study of the Personality.* New York: Longmans, Green &
Co., Inc., 1948. Pp. xvi, 533. * (London: Longmans, Green &
Co. Ltd., 1949.) (*PA* 23:1284)
6. CALABRESI, RENATA A. "Interpretation of Personality
With the Szondi Test." *Rorsch Res Exch & J Proj Tech* 12:
238–53 no 4 '48. * (*PA* 24:1192)
7. BELL, JOHN ELDERKIN. "The Case of Gregor: Psychological Test Data." *Rorsch Res Exch & J Proj Tech* 13:155–205
no 2 '49. * (*PA* 24:2589)
8. CALABRESI, RENATA A., AND HELME, WILLIAM H. "Analysis of Personality Configuration of Outpatients in Psychotherapy by the Use of the Szondi Test." Abstract. *Rorsch Res
Exch & J Proj Tech* 13:239–40 no 2 '49. * (*PA* 24:2596, title
only)
9. DAVID, H. P. *An Evaluation of Repeated Administrations
of the Szondi Test.* Master's thesis, University of Cincinnati
(Cincinnati, Ohio), 1949.
10. DAVIDSON, WILLIAM N.; MURPHY, MAXINE M.; AND
NEWTON, BERNAUER W. "Experimental Analysis of the Szondi
Test." Abstract. *Am Psychol* 4:388 S '49. * (*PA* 24:1884, title
only)
11. DERI, SUSAN. *Introduction to the Szondi Test: Theory
and Practice.* Foreword by Lipot Szondi. New York: Grune &
Stratton, Inc., 1949. Pp. xiv, 354. * (*PA* 23:3748)
12. DERI, SUSAN K. "The Szondi Test." *Am J Orthopsychiatry* 19:447–54 Jl '49. * (*PA* 24:1885)
13. DERI, SUSAN K. "Szondi Test: The Case of Gregor: Interpretation of Test Data: Symposium Presented at American
Psychological Association Meeting, Denver, 1949." *Rorsch Res
Exch & J Proj Tech* 13:438–43 D '49. (*PA* 24:3734)
14. KLOPFER, WALTER G. "An Investigation of the Szondi
Test by the Association Method." Abstract. *Am Psychol* 4:269
Jl '49. * (*PA* 23:6213, title only)
15. SCHERER, ISIDOR W. "The Psychological Scores of Mental Patients in an Individual and Group Testing Situation."
J Clin Psychol 5:405–8 O '49. * (*PA* 24:3740)

16. BLESSING, HAROLD D.; BEDFORD, GEORGE STEWART; AND
GLAD, DONALD D. "An Experimental Investigation of Some Incidental Features of the Szondi Test." Abstract. *J Colo-Wyo
Acad Sci* 4:65 O '50. * (*PA* 25:5337, title only)
17. BORSTELMANN, LLOYD JOSEPH. *Affective Stimulus Values
of the Szondi Pictures.* Doctor's thesis, University of California
(Berkeley, Calif.), 1950. (*PA* 25:5755, title only)
18. BORSTELMANN, L. J., AND KLOPFER, W. G. "Do the
Szondi Choices Reflect Individuality?" Abstract. *Am Psychol*
5:470 S '50. * (*PA* 25:4559, title only)
19. COLE, DAVID, AND ROBERTS, EUGENE. "Szondi Results in
Group Testing With College Students." *J Clin Psychol* 6:381–6
O '50. * (*PA* 25:8075)
20. DAVID, HENRY P. "An Inquiry Into the Szondi Pictures."
J Abn & Social Psychol 45:735–7 O '50. * (*PA* 25:2449)
21. DAVID, HENRY P. "A Szondi IBM Form." *J Consult
Psychol* 14:502 D '50. * (*PA* 26:910)
22. DERI, SUSAN K. "The Szondi Test: Its Application in a
Research Study of Depressive Patients Before and After
Electric-Shock Treatment," pp. 298–321. (*PA* 25:2450) In
*Projective Psychology: Clinical Approaches to the Total Per-
sonality.* Edited by Lawrence Edwin Abt and Leopold Bellak.
New York: Alfred A. Knopf, Inc., 1950. Pp. xvii, 485, xiv. *
23. FOSBERG, IRVING ARTHUR. "A Study of the Sensitivity
of the Szondi Test in the Sexual and Paroxysmal Vectors." Abstract. *Am Psychol* 5:326–7 Jl '50. * (*PA* 25:1093, title only)
24. GALLAGHER, JAMES JOHN. *Use of the Szondi Test in Differentiating Three Diagnostic Groups of Prison Inmates.* Master's thesis, Pennsylvania State College (State College, Pa.),
1950. (*PA* 24:5544, title only)
25. GOLDMAN, GEORGE DAVID. *An Investigation of the Similarities in Personality Structure of Idiopathic Epileptics, Hysterical Convulsives, and Neurological Patients.* Doctor's thesis,
New York University (New York, N.Y.), 1950. Abstract:
Microfilm Abstracts 11:176–7 no 1 '51. * (*PA* 26:2368, title
only)
26. GUERTIN, WILSON H. "A Consideration of Factor Loadings on the Szondi Test." *J Clin Psychol* 6:262–6 Jl '50. * (*PA*
25:1782)
27. GUERTIN, WILSON H. "A Test of a Basic Assumption of
the Szondi." *J Consult Psychol* 14:404–7 O '50. * (*PA* 25:
4570)
28. HOLT, ROBERT R. "An Approach to the Validation of
the Szondi Test Through a Systematic Study of Unreliability."
J Proj Tech 14:435–44 D '50. * (*PA* 26:3410)
29. KLOPFER, WALTER G. *An Investigation of the Associative Stimulus Value of the Szondi Pictures.* Doctor's thesis,
University of California (Berkeley, Calif.), 1950. (*PA* 25:4073,
title only)
30. KLOPFER, WALTER G., AND BORSTELMANN, LLOYD J. "The
Associative Valences of the Szondi Pictures." *J Personality*
19:172–88 D '50. * (*PA* 25:6874)
31. MERCER, MARGARET, AND WRIGHT, S. C. "Diagnostic
Testing in a Case of Latent Schizophrenia." *J Proj Tech* 14:
287–96 S '50. * (*PA* 25:4733)
32. PAINE, HAROLD E. *Association of Measurable Changes
in Szondi Test Profiles With Measurable Factors in Behavior
of Psychotics.* Doctor's thesis, Western Reserve University
(Cleveland, Ohio), 1950. (*PA* 25:6572, title only)
33. PRELINGER, ERNST. "On the Reliability of the Szondi
Test." *Psychol Service Center J* 2:227–30 S '50. * (*PA* 26:5626)
34. RABIN, ALBERT I. "Szondi's Pictures: Effects of Formal
Training on Ability to Identify Diagnoses." *J Consult Psychol*
14:400–3 O '50. * (*PA* 25:4584)
35. RABIN, ALBERT I. "Szondi's Pictures: Identification of
Diagnoses." *J Abn & Social Psychol* 45:392–5 Ap '50. * (*PA*
24:5878)
36. WELLS, STEPHEN. *Szondi Test Constellations of Fifty
Students of Music and Fifty Students of Technology.* Master's
thesis, College of the City of New York (New York, N.Y.),
1950.
37. WHITEMAN, PAUL H. *An Experimental Investigation of
Inter-Series Changes as a Diagnostic Factor in the Szondi Test.*
Master's thesis, Western Reserve University (Cleveland,
Ohio), 1950. (*PA* 25:6583)
38. WHITMYRE, JOHN WARREN. *A Comparison of Szondi Ego
Stage and Chronological Age in Children.* Master's thesis, University of Pittsburgh (Pittsburgh, Pa.), 1950.
39. BORSTELMANN, LLOYD J. *Affective Stimulus Values of
the Szondi Pictures.* Doctor's thesis, University of California
(Berkeley, Calif.), 1951. (*PA* 25:5755, title only)
40. BORSTELMANN, LLOYD J., AND KLOPFER, WALTER G.
"Does the Szondi Test Reflect Individuality? The Affective
Valences of the Szondi Pictures." *J Personality* 19:421–39 Je
'51. * (*PA* 26:3400)
41. CAHILL, ROBERT F. "The Role of Intelligence in Changes
Within the Szondi Test Profiles." *J Clin Psychol* 7:379–81 O
'51. * (*PA* 26:3402)
42. COHEN, JACOB. "The Chance Distribution of Szondi Valences." *J Consult Psychol* 15:130–3 Ap. '51. * (*PA* 26:6257)
43. COHEN, JACOB. "A Note on Fosberg's 'Four Experiments
with the Szondi Test.'" *J Consult Psychol* 15:511 D '51. * (*PA*
26:6992)
44. COLE, DAVID. "The Reliability of a Single Szondi Profile." *J Clin Psychol* 7:383–4 O '51. * (*PA* 26:3403)
45. DAVID, HENRY PHILIP. *Relationships of Szondi Picture
Preferences to Personality.* Doctor's thesis, Columbia University (New York, N.Y.), 1951. Abstract: *Microfilm Abstracts*
11:1091–2 no 4 '51.

46. DAVID, HENRY P. "The Szondi Test in Idiopathic Epilepsy and Overt Homosexuality." Abstract. *Am Psychol* 6:338 Jl '51. *

47. DAVID, HENRY P., AND RABINOWITZ, WILLIAM. "The Development of a Szondi Instability Score." *J Consult Psychol* 15:334–6 Ag '51. * (*PA* 26:6260)

48. FEIGENBAUM, LOUIS. *An Investigation of Some Aspects of the Szondi Test.* Doctor's thesis, University of Kentucky (Lexington, Ky.), 1951.

49. FOSBERG, IRVING ARTHUR. "Four Experiments With the Szondi Test." *J Consult Psychol* 15:39–44 F '51. * (*PA* 26:6267)

50. FROMM, ERIKA O., AND ELONEN, ANNA S. "The Use of Projective Techniques in the Study of a Case of Female Homosexuality." *J Proj Tech* 15:185–230 Je '51. * (*PA* 26:3498)

51. GUERTIN, WILSON H. "A Comparison of the Stimulus Value of Szondi's Pictures With Those of Normal Americans." *J Clin Psychol* 7:163–6 Ap '51. * (*PA* 25:8091)

52. GUERTIN, WILSON H. "A Factor Analysis of Some Szondi Pictures." *J Clin Psychol* 7:232–5 Jl '51. * (*PA* 26:914)

53. GUERTIN, WILSON H., AND MCMAHAN, HERBERT G. "A Survey of Szondi Research." *Am J Psychiatry* 108:180–4 S '51. *

54. KALDEGG, A. "An Account of the Szondi Test." *J Mental Sci* 97:555–66 Jl '51. * (*PA* 26:2185)

55. KATZ, JOSEPH. *The Projection of Assaultive Aggression in the Human Figure Drawings of Adult Male Negro Offenders: A Study of Inmates Convicted of Homicide or Assault by Means of Human Figure Drawings, Rorschach, Thematic Apperception Test, and Szondi.* Doctor's thesis, New York University (New York, N.Y.), 1951. Abstract: *Microfilm Abstracts* 11:1096–8 no 4 '51.

56. LUBIN, A., AND MALLOY, M. "An Empirical Test of Some Assumptions Underlying the Szondi Test." *J Abn & Social Psychol* 46:480–4 O '51. * (*PA* 26:4013)

57. MERCER, MARGARET. "Clinical Uses of and Evaluation of the Szondi Test." Abstract. *AMA Arch Neurol & Psychiatry* 65:126–7 Ja '51. * (*PA* 25:5345, title only)

58. RABIN, ALBERT I. Chap. 17, "The Szondi Test," pp. 498–512. In *An Introduction to Projective Techniques.* Edited by Harold H. Anderson and Gladys L. Anderson. New York: Prentice-Hall, Inc., 1951. Pp. xxiv, 720. *

59. REICHARD, SUZANNE. "Some Contributions of Psychological Tests to Therapeutic Planning." Discussion by Anneliese F. Korner. *Am J Orthopsychiatry* 21:532–41, discussion 541–2 Jl '51. * (*PA* 26:3445)

60. SANDLER, JOSEPH, AND LUBIN, ARDIE. "A Note on the Reliability of the Szondi Test." *Brit J Med Psychol* 24:141–3 Je '51. * (*PA* 26:935)

61. SCHERER, I. W.; WINNE, J. F.; PAGE, H. A.; AND LIPTON, H. "An Analysis of Patient-Examiner Interaction With the Szondi Pictures." Abstract. *J Proj Tech* 15:419–20 S '51. *

62. SZOLLOSI, E.; LAMPHIEAR, D. E.; AND BEST, H. L. "The Stimulus Values of the Szondi Pictures." *J Consult Psychol* 15:419–24 O '51. * (*PA* 26:7014)

63. WALLEN, RICHARD. "Factors Affecting the Choice of Certain Szondi Test Pictures." *J Consult Psychol* 15:210–5 Je '51. * (*PA* 26:6301)

64. WHITEMAN, PAUL H. "An Experimental Investigation of Inter-Series Change as a Diagnostic Factor in the Szondi Test." Abstract. *Am Psychol* 6:342 Jl '51. *

ARDIE LUBIN, *Statistical Psychologist, Institute of Psychiatry, Maudsley Hospital, London, England.*

The aim of this review is to persuade psychologists to use the *Szondi Test* only for those purposes for which it has been shown to be valid. Since the published data to date have not shown the Szondi to be unequivocally valid for any of its stated purposes, this aim resolves itself into a warning that the Szondi must be used for research purposes only.

Deri states that the purpose of the *Szondi Test* is "to reflect the personality as a functioning dynamic whole. * Its field of application is ....similar to that of other projective technics; in other words, as a diagnostic instrument for clinical use or for the interpretation of the so-called normal personality, vocational guidance, experimental social psychology and a variety of fields of research" (*11*). Deri claims that the

Szondi is particularly valuable for demonstrating changes in personality.

THE VALIDITY OF THE SZONDI FOR PSYCHODIAGNOSIS. Studies by David (*9, 45*), Fosberg (*49*), and Whiteman (*64*) give, on the whole, negative results. Deri concludes that psychotics can be distinguished from normals because of the greater stability of the normals (*22*). However, when her data were analysed by the reviewer, the results were not wholly consistent with her conclusions.

From the data available, it seems that the diagnostic signs given by Deri and Szondi are invalid. Although David and Whiteman have shown that certain empirically derived scores do discriminate, David points out that so many scores were tested, that some would be expected to pass the 5 per cent level by chance alone. Obviously the Szondi cannot be used for clinical diagnosis without further verification.

THE VALIDITY OF DERI'S NEED-SYSTEM THEORY. Deri has elaborated a theory about the Szondi which makes use of the concept of "need-systems." The essence of the theory is that each of the eight factors represents a need, and that a lack of choice in a factor (known as an "open" reaction) reflects a weakness of the particular need or indicates that the drive has been "lived out" through adequate activity. Conversely, a large number of choices in a factor (known as a "loaded" reaction) indicates an unsatisfied need. For example, an open reaction in the sexual vector would ordinarily mean that there had been sexual activity.

Fosberg (*49*) has produced the most extensive and best designed tests of Deri's theory. Although his statistical technique is not the best that could have been used, his data show that the *Szondi Test* is not sensitive to sexual activity or electrically induced seizures. (Deri specifically states that the Szondi should be a good measure of the tensions and discharges in these need-systems.) Deri's data (*22*) suggest that the *s, hy,* and *k* factors are affected by a complete course of electric shock treatment. But the changes in the *hy* and *k* factors had not been predicted by Deri and contradicted the general theory that discharges of need tensions should result in decreased loadings.

CHANCE AND THE SZONDI TEST. The question has been raised whether the responses to the Szondi are the same ones that would occur by chance. Researches by Cohen (*42*), David (*45*), Fosberg (*49*) and Guertin (*27*) show that chance is not the sole determiner of Szondi responses. This is necessary but not sufficient for establishing the validity of the Szondi technique.

THE VALIDITY OF THE LABELS ON SZONDI'S PICTURES. What is the relation of Szondi's pictures to the eight types of mental patient they are supposed to represent? The studies by Klopfer and Borstelmann (*30*), Rabin (*34–5*) and Fosberg (*49*) seem to show that psychiatrists and psychologists, as well as other subjects having some psychological training, can classify the photographs into Szondi's eight categories with considerably better than chance success.

THE INTERNAL CONSISTENCY OF THE SZONDI. Studies by Ancelin, Duchene and Schützenberger,[1] Lubin and Malloy (*56*), and Guertin (*27, 52*) show that photographs bearing the same Szondi labels do not (except by chance) measure the same trait.

THE TEST-RETEST RELIABILITY OF THE SZONDI. Lubin and Sandler (*60*) found that the test-retest correlations ranged from .20 to .65 for the 16 like and dislike scores. (The interval between test and retest was 5 to 7 days.) All correlations, except the lowest, are significantly different from zero. It was found that the test profile of Szondi responses could be matched to the retest profile with 96 per cent accuracy.

SUMMARY AND CONCLUSIONS. The Szondi is a highly structured, easily administered test; however, it must be given over at least six days, and it requires a long time for interpretation. Szondi's "genotropic" theory has been rejected by Deri, who has substituted a need-system set of assumptions. Empirical attempts to validate the need-system theory have resulted in observations which contradict the theory (except for Deri's results which were ambivalent). Szondi's and Deri's diagnostic signs cannot be trusted for use in clinical diagnosis, but other scores not mentioned by Szondi or Deri may be of some use. The observed relations between the photographs are not in accordance with the theory on which the test was constructed, and it is highly probable that the majority of photographs measure traits other than those indicated by the labels they bear. The Szondi has a low internal consistency but a high test-retest reliability (presumably due to memory).

Because there is no positive evidence of the Szondi's theoretical validity, practical usefulness, or superiority over other widely used tests,

such as the Rorschach, it is *not* recommended.

If further research is to be carried out on the Szondi, the reviewer feels that the most fruitful approach would be to substitute classification by the clinician for the single quantitative scores and repeat the studies on the diagnostic utility of the Szondi as well as on the validity of Deri's theories.

ALBERT I. RABIN, *Associate Professor of Psychology, and Director, Psychological Clinic, Michigan State College, East Lansing, Michigan.*

This test is a projective technique which does not involve any verbal responses. The test material consists of six sets of photographs of mental patients in European hospitals. In each set there are eight pictures representing the following diagnostic categories: homosexuality, sadism, epilepsy, hysteria, catatonic schizophrenia, paranoid schizophrenia, depression, and mania. Each set is placed before the testee who is asked to select the two pictures he "likes most" and the two he "dislikes most." Thus, the final selections consist of 12 liked and 12 disliked pictures, out of the total of 48. For clinical purposes it is recommended that the test be administered at least six times with one-day intervals between testing sessions. It usually takes about 15 minutes to give the test.

The basic assumption of this device is that the photographs have meanings which correspond to need-systems characteristic of all persons. The selection or rejection of the photographs is indicative of the relative tension reduction in the need systems which they represent. The test profile that is obtained indicates the relative tension present in each need system represented by the factors which are named after the diagnoses represented in the photographs (homosexual, sadist, etc.). A related assumption is also the equal valence of pictures within the same diagnostic category.

The interpretation is a rather complex process since it does not involve only the relative "loading" (selection and rejection) of the factors, but also the interplay of the need systems and their integration within the personality. Moreover, the "process" of the changes from one administration to another further complicates the task. The result is not a cross sectional static analysis, but a dynamic interpretation in the temporal dimension.

1 Ancelin, A. E.; Duchene, H.; and Schützenberger, M. P. "Recherches Critiques sur la Theorie et le Test de L. Szondi." *Enfance* 3: 65–73 '50. (*PA* 25: 3155)

Since the publication of the English manual, a number of investigations with the Szondi have been reported. The acceptance of this test as a clinical tool is not widespread at the present time. Contrary to the historical trend of other projective techniques, clinical reports are few. The bulk of the investigations deal with a critical examination of the basic assumptions and theoretical foundations of the test.

Some studies have demonstrated that psychologically trained persons without familiarity with the test are able to identify the diagnoses represented in the pictures better than is expected by chance (*34, 35, 49*). This is an indication of the "meaningfulness" of the pictures. They are not merely neutral stimuli. It was also found that the pictures have "a demonstrable associational valence" similar to that described by the author of the test (*30*). However, another study (*63*) showed no differences between the catatonic and paranoid pictures in traits assigned them by several judges. Muscular contractions and expressions of friendliness in the pictures seem to be important determiners in picture selection. Some doubt is, therefore, cast upon the picture representation of particular need systems. That the pictures are not selected on a chance basis and that sex differences may be seen in the selection of some of them has been demonstrated in another study (*19*). Yet, artifacts other than the "foreign" appearance (*20*) of the patients must be operating.

The assumption of equivalence of pictures within the same diagnostic categories does not hold up in any of the investigations dealing with the problem (*26, 27, 49, 51, 52*).

There is ample evidence that the Szondi does not differentiate readily between groups of psychotics and normals (*64*) or between different psychopathological groups such as homosexuals and epileptics (*46*). Lack of relationship between sexual discharge, convulsive seizures, and changes in Szondi factor loading has also been shown (*49*). Some positive relations between Szondi choices and fluctuations on other tests in a single case have also been reported (*28*).

Many difficulties in the statistical treatment of Szondi data have been encountered. Some of the reported suggestions (*42*) may be useful in further validation studies.

Thus far, the evidence shows that the cautious approach to the Szondi as a diagnostic tool has been amply justified. Pending more positive statistical and clinical validating findings, it will have to continue its precarious position in the field of projective techniques.

For a review by Susan K. Deri, see 3:100; for related reviews, see 135.

[135]

★[*Re* Szondi Test.] DERI, SUSAN. **Introduction to the Szondi Test: Theory and Practice.** Foreword by Lipot Szondi. New York: Grune & Stratton, Inc., 1949. Pp. xiv, 354. $5.00. * (*PA* 23:3748)

Am J Orthopsychiatry 20:650–1 Jl '50. Joseph P. Lord. This book, strongly endorsed by Szondi as a valuable "supplement to and elaboration" of his *Experimentelle Triebdiagnostik* stems from a well-qualified background; its author has had eleven years of clinical experience with this projective technique and worked with its originator for four years during its inception. * Supporters of Freudian psychoanalysis or Lewin's vector psychology will note the inclusion of many of their principles; the statistically minded will writhe at the large amount of nonquantitatively supported data and at the necessity of "suspending judgment" until employing the technique, although Deri partially precludes this objection by reference to the appendix of Szondi's cited work; the clinician in search of a rapidfire personality prober will derive satisfaction from the objectivity of the scoring and from the ease of a single administration, but must accept the limitations inherent in the necessity for six to preferably ten day-spaced administrations to the same Subject, as well as in the complexities involved in the wide range of possible factor and vector combinations. Of great import, if the author's claim is valid, is the test's capacity for delineating levels of functioning in the personality.

Am J Psychiatry 107:237 S '50. Paul E. Meehl. This important book appears opportunely, as the Szondi test is arousing increasing interest among American clinicians, most of whom will probably not work their way through Dr. Szondi's two volumes in German. * The book is clearly an attempt to teach clinicians how to *use* the test, and not in any sense a study of its validity or an effort to produce conviction about the latter. She says "....acceptance of practically any of my statements about the....constellations is left to the good-will of the reader" (p. xi). This remark will strike most American psychologists as rather odd, unless the purpose of the book is kept in mind. * On the negative side, it is dangerous to speak pending satisfactory validity studies. There is a good deal of the "now-you-see-it-now-you-don't" type of discussion, in which the interpretations are loaded with enough qualification and references to the "rest of the pattern" so that we approach empirical emptiness. Although an isomorphism with the psychoanalytic vocabulary is denied, the constant use of it with subtly altered meanings produces a certain vagueness. In the attempt to get across the "feel" of a personality, enough words are used so that the picture becomes uncomfortably general. There is some statistical-psychometric naiveté (or else careless formulation). For example, we are told that "....these changes always imply *some* change in the subject's attitude toward a particular drive" (p. 40). Here we see no apparent recognition of the existence of "uniqueness" in the factor-analytic sense—each picture is free of any contribution from specificity or error. Again, the question is not raised of how much of the temporal shifting found in schizophrenics could be attributable simply to the variability found in almost any kind of repeated performance obtained from these patients. Again, the threshold value for the various pictures is not discussed; it is apparently assumed that each picture is located at the same "difficulty" level on its own factor, and that no other variables produce differences in its stimulus properties. Hence, we are asked to accept differences among picture sets (absolute values) as confirmatory of the theory, *e.g.*, "....minus *s* is not very frequent because it implies ability to sublimate aggression which is not common...." (p. 77), or "the frequency of minus *p* in the general population.... is much higher than that of plus *p*....this would mean that most people act according to their emotional needs...." (p. 179). In general, all responses and shifts in responses are attributed to real changes in the named factors, as if perfect validity and factorial purity were established. The factor matrix of the Szondi must be unique among all psychological tests ever built, if this is true. Finally, even though it is unfair to criticize a book for not achieving aims explicitly repudiated by the author, it is perhaps fair to ask why *no* systematic validity data are presented? This reviewer would gladly have exchanged Chapter III, on "factorial association," for a section of similar length presenting some validation material. After all, the book is not easy to read, and will be a lot of work to really master. Surely the reader is entitled to a few pages devoted to establishing validity, before taking on such a task. It is not a question of his lacking "good-will," since the best will in the world *could* not convince the scientific clinician on the basis of this book. Should we be asked to accept "....proving it pragmatically by the use of the test...." (p. ix) or "....the increasing demands for Szondi reports...." (p. xi) as substitutes for validation studies, to the point of embarking on a learning task which will only *then* be able to tell us, from our own experience with it, whether we spent our time well or not? I do not think so.

Am J Psychol 63:141–2 Ja '50. B. L. Margolet. * The....book runs from a description of the test and the proper mode of its administration to a polemic upon its significance, a polemic which occupies a good part of the eleven chapters (Chaps. iv–xi). The point of departure for the argument is the test-subject's selections of "liked" and "disliked" pictures from among 48 serially arranged photographs of "mental patients" (8–16). The tenets of the argument would be the transition between these selections and a divination of the mainsprings of the subject's "personality." But they are tenets neither convincing nor plausible. As here conceived "personality" seems to represent a centrifuged mixture of orthodox freudian mechanisms and forces, psychiatric "malignancies," lewinian vectors and tensions, some of Szondi's factorial postulates, and certain products of Deri's own clinical and pedagogical experiences (2–4, 7–8, 25–28, 65–66, 88, 118–120, 167–172, 287). Sanction and documentation for this strange product are wanting. The author, who has been pressed to write now through suspicion of misuse of Szondi's work (ix, xi), notes that her exposition rests upon assumption and postulate (3, 26, 38, 45, 66, 286) and states that, because of "the lack of rigorous quantitative validating data....the acceptance of practically any of my statements about the meaning of the various factorial constellations [the main concern of the book] is left to the good-will of the reader" (xi). Some three-hundred pages of these "statements" make a heavy draft upon "good-will" standing in the account of a critical reader. The volume seems to be making headway among some clinicians in this country. Possibly a simplified Szondi, largely relieved of statistics and written in English, might be expected to arouse hopes among clinical testers of personality.

B Menninger Clinic 15:34 Ja '51. Walter

Kass. * There is much intuitive material of interest to clinicians. But those who look for validational data will see only large claims and little evidence.

J Abn & Social Psychol 45:184–8 Ja '50. Roy Schafer. The formal introduction of a new personality test of any complexity is an extremely demanding task. Mrs. Deri's book, based on 11 years' participation in the development and application of the test, meets some of the demands but falls far short of meeting many others. Unfortunately, limitations of space in this review will make it impossible to cover adequately all of the author's claims for the test or to document all the criticisms to be advanced. * basic definitions [are] given on pages 55–56; and pages 57–285 are devoted to elaborating their general implications as well as their specific meanings in different factorial and vectorial configurations of choices. This task is carefully and thoroughly carried out, with due respect for the shifting psychological implications of specific sub-patterns depending on the total contexts in which they occur. Frequently only lip-service or a little more is paid in publications to the problems of interpretation-within-context, but Mrs. Deri takes this quite seriously. * The book is easily readable and has a helpful index. There are three main headings under which this book will be criticized: specific test rationale, validation, and the general handling of personality dynamics in the interpretive process. *Rationale:* There is a minimum of rationale in the strict sense of the word, i.e., the elucidation of mediating processes between the stimulus and the response. Pertinent mediational processes would include all the stimulation of thoughts, attitudes, values, and feelings by global and/or fragmentary perception of the photographs, how these are integrated, how the level of attention fluctuates from one picture to the next, etc. The author loosely refers to the principles of interpretation as "rationale" and otherwise pretty much limits herself to the basic assumption that the psychopathological dynamics in the members of the various diagnostic categories are somehow communicated to and perceived by the subjects through the photographs used. This assumption actually embraces or conceals a number of assumptions. (1) The dynamics of patients in each psychiatric category are well established, and (2) are identical in all patients with the same diagnosis. (3) These deep dynamics are expressed in the faces of the patients, and (4) these

facial expressions are adequately "caught" in the pictures used. (5) The underlying dynamics are expressed equally well in all six representatives of each diagnostic category, pattern analysis being a purely quantitative matter and remaining independent of particular choices; thus (6) the sexual identity of these pictured patients makes no differences in one's response to them, (7) the more or less striking cultural differences in appearance (hair-do, clothing, beard) make no difference to American subjects, and (8) there are no "popular" reactions (pictures "liked" or "disliked" with very high frequency) which, by being "popular," require some modification of interpretation; this reviewer's experience with the test indicates that there are "populars." (9) The expressed dynamics on the faces of the patients are equally well perceived by all subjects, so that for each picture the "likes" or "dislikes" of all subjects have essentially the same qualitative implications and quantitative weights. (10) Varying choices from day to day reflect basic shifts in the subject's need-tensions and have little or nothing to do with factors of satiation, superficial mood changes, interest or disinterest in consistency of reaction, and other ego attitudes. (11) The fate of every factorial distribution in the test is independently determined, and the limited number of choices (12 plus, 12 minus) has no real bearing on the results; thus, for example, given special sensitivity to pictures in two or three factors with resulting loaded distributions in these factors, the remaining more or less open distributions in the other factors can still be directly interpreted as if they were left open by conscious or unconscious intent alone. All of these assumptions are more or less doubtful. The uniqueness of individual perception, particularly in interpersonal matters, one of our most valuable clinical psychological insights, is implicitly dismissed when the above assumptions are made, although its superficial expression is acknowledged. *Validation:* It goes without saying that in the introduction of a new test with as bold and deep interpretations as are made from this, careful presentation of validating techniques and data is indispensable. The author frequently mentions interfactorial correlations or significant group differences with no mention of the size and selection of the samples, the statistical techniques used, or the magnitude and reliability of the results obtained. Strict validation of psychological interpretations of test results is admittedly an extremely complex, uncertain, and as yet by no means satisfactorily worked out procedure, but when big claims are made, one would like to know more about their justification. With regard to her presentation of the genetic and occupational studies as validational material, even if it were adequately presented, it would not be entirely satisfactory as validation, because (1) it makes the dubious assumptions that there are common dynamics in the members of any occupation or age level and that these dynamics are well established, and (2) since the "established" test patterns do not cover all the members of the group, it must be, but has not been, demonstrated that the interpretations apply to just those members of the group who have the patterns in question. Indirect validation of the type attempted, even when statistically significant differences are obtained, does not truly validate the deep interpretations. The author claims, however, that pragmatically the test works, that is, skillful interpretation produces a personality description that corresponds closely with the clinical picture as derived from case history and psychiatric or psychoanalytic study of the individual. Indeed, in discussing the absence of formal validational material in the book, the author asks for the reader's "good will" acceptance of the interpretive principles, and assures the reader that he will convince himself of their validity by the use of the test. It is here that the basic weakness of the entire presentation is found. It is difficult to imagine how, at the present stage of sophistication in clinical psychological validation techniques, one can validate the claims made for the test. The author acknowledges this difficulty but then claims convincing pragmatic validation— as if this could be something other than a more or less systematic correlation and ordering of experience and still retain meaning. The extreme difficulty of validation comes about, first of all, because scant attention is paid by the author to the phenotypical referents of many of the deep dynamic trends. Without carefully specifying these referents, and as would probably be necessary, the context or configuration of referents from which the underlying genotype may be inferred or ruled out, the author's claims are not subject to validational tests. In this regard, the author treats variables like "need to fuse into environmental objects" relatively casually, as if their observation is a more or less routine matter to any psychoanalytically sophisticated observer. Altogether an atmosphere of certainty is cre-

ated around a loose mixture of clinical psychoanalytic findings and hypotheses, which though highly provocative and penetrating, are often equally abstract and speculative. The author writes as if always presenting clinical facts, while the fact of the matter is that on theoretical points, on the general dynamic characterizations of diagnostic entities, and on the interpretation of specific case material, there is as a rule quite a bit of variation of emphasis if not outright disagreement in the field, even when those concerned are numbered among the more orthodox Freudians. A second source of validational difficulty, related to the difficulty of establishing concrete indications and contra-indications, is that if one proceeds to a sufficiently abstract level of dynamic description and does not strictly and consistently define corresponding behavioral referents one reaches a point where all things are true of all people; that is to say, we all have impulses or aspects of impulses which may be characterized as oral or clinging, anal or possessive, homoerotic, narcissistic, exhibitionistic, repressive, projective, hostile, and the like. The life of a human being is so complex that by the proper selection or interpretation one can set out, if he wishes, and find behavior items to confirm almost any interpretation. Case material of any detail is enormously plastic and not to be trusted in a clinical experiment unless there are guarantees of independence of validating criteria and techniques, the precise nature of which are stated, and unless weighted estimates or predictions, however gross, are made and then checked. Careful reading of the chapter on the "experiment of factorial association," in which some randomly selected descriptions of pictures by different types of subjects are presented as tentative validation material, will illustrate how blurred the line can become between careful, controlled analysis and facile, often glib interpretations which smack of sophisticated psychological fortunetelling. The same can be said for the author's hasty and omniscient rationalization of the genetic, occupational and diagnostic findings presented all through the 228 pages on interpretation. Further mistrust is engendered by the hedging, I'm-never-wrong quality in statements to the effect that indications of lack of tension in any need-system do not mean that there is no such tension in the subject, but only that such tension is not indicated in the test results. *Theoretical aspects:* (1) Though the author leans heavily on Freudian psychoanalytic knowledge and theory to support her arguments, in many places she comments on the happy coincidence of Szondi Test and psychoanalytic findings as if these were two independent systems, and in still other places she indicates that the Szondi Test has an independent psychology of its own, though it overlaps much with psychoanalysis. This shifting use of personality theory is confusing, and the introduction of a relatively independent psychology of personality and psychopathology as a frame of reference for a new test inevitably implies a closed, instrument-centered system: personality becomes what the Szondi Test measures. Although the book generally adheres to the Freudian psychoanalytic viewpoint of the last 30 years, it also refers frequently to Lewinian concepts and sometimes, where this is convenient for her argument, to Jungian and Rankian concepts, and even to some early ideas of Freud's which, as the author acknowledges, he subsequently repudiated. There is a quality of opportunistic eclecticism and selectivity in all this. Further material of this sort includes relatively frequent, casual, and in the main unacknowledged revisions of accepted psychoanalytic theory, as where she maintains that introjection and repression are dynamic opposites, and, as in the test report quoted above, that what she considers to be an essentially orally fixated and apparently quite neurotic patient has "basically healthy heterosexual drives." (2) It is a questionable proposition that it is the tensions in the loaded factors which underlie the symptom formation or overt behavioral characteristics indicated in the open factors; this principle implies, for example, that tension indicated by a loaded paranoid factor may underlie symptom formation in the oral area, or vice versa. (3) It is a questionable proposition that the distributions in the ego vector reflect dynamics (the general mode of handling needs) at a more general level than those of the other three vectors. That the mediational processes can vary so (reaching different levels of personality organization) while the stimulus situations remain the same (photographs) requires considerably more explanation and validation than we find. The same point holds for the paroxysmal vector which has to do chiefly with defenses, while the sexual and contact vectors have more to do with specific needs. (4) There is a tendency to reify some of the constructs used, particularly those in the ego vector. (5) There is a questionably expansive and fluid use of the key terms "subli-

mation" and "projection." The author ends by promising a second volume to follow soon with more detailed case illustrations. It is to be hoped that there will be a third and less omniscient book presenting discussion and data pertaining to rationale and particularly to sound validational techniques and their results; the magnificent claims made for the test are badly in need of support. A convincing validational technique for this test and for the variables described by the author will represent a great methodological contribution to clinical psychology and psychiatry. It is to be doubted that this will be forthcoming: a test in which *process* is so concealed and only the end results observable is inherently weak as a projective technique; interpretation is inevitably dictionary-style. It is difficult to see what aspects of the response process the interpreter can project himself into—a psychological act, according to the author, indispensable in adequate interpretation.

J Consult Psychol 13:307 Ag'49. Laurance F. Shaffer. The long-awaited text on the Szondi method contains the instructions for its administration, which are simple, and those for its interpretation, which are not simple at all. * The most astonishing aspect of the book is the total absence of evidence attesting to the method's value other than by reference to the experience of the author, and the lack of any reference to research literature beyond Szondi's three books in German. The absence of public evidence for the test's merit is a matter of preference or philosophy, rather than of neglect or ignorance. Mrs. Deri appeals to *private* evidence. The acceptance of her statements is "left to the good-will of the reader," who should keep his judgment "suspended until he can convince himself about the clinical validity....of the test." But, alas, the personal feeling of validity has been an unhappy guide since Mesmer; most of us prefer more public and communicable testimony. It may be hoped that skillful and hard-headed research workers will not be repelled by the implausibility of the Szondi until it has been given a thorough and public evaluation.

J Ed Psychol 41:447–8 N'50. George K. Bennett. * To the reader who is accustomed to look for experimental data in support of claims of usefulness or validity, this volume is wholly inadequate. Elaborate explanations of the significance of various factors are given without even frequency tables. Sums, differences and ratios are computed and interpreted without thought for the problems of reliability involved. Shifts in type preference or aversion from one day to the next are regarded as indications of changes in the needs and tensions of the subject rather than errors of measurement. Validity in the usual sense appears to be dismissed in the following paragraph:

> The superficial appearance of normalcy is responsible for the extreme difficulties inherent in the problem of validating studies on the basis of observable behavior or verbal or written questionnaires. Many basically unhappy individuals who are unable really to become emotionally attached to any person or object would rate extremely high on a written adjustment inventory, or on the basis of observation.

This reviewer can only conclude that, on the basis of Mrs. Deri's book, the Szondi test is one more unproven instrument proposed as an aid in personality diagnosis. Pending the publication of adequate supporting evidence, the psychologist using this method is proceeding on the basis of faith and should be willing to recognize the peril of his course.

Psychoanalytic Q 19:112–4 Ja '50. William F. Murphy. * Criticism of this book cannot be separated from criticism of the test and it is difficult to know where to begin. Szondi's theories of the genesis of mental disorders are omitted, and to this reviewer they appear to be simply a variation of the universally accepted belief that constitutional factors play an extremely important role in determining the strength of the instinctual needs. The main bone of contention, however, is whether or not these needs are expressed in a photograph and are responded to in the test situation. The author expresses the problem very well: "Without the assumption that these eight types of mental disturbances imply well definable extreme manifestations of generally known psychological mechanisms, the functioning of the test would be inconceivable. We also have to assume that the presence of these extreme and exaggerated psychologic drives is somehow expressed through the corresponding photographs and further that the subject's liking or rejection of the pictures is based on an unconscious identification or counteridentification with the processes depicted." She appears to be perfectly well aware that all of this is somewhat dubious and nonvalidated and spends a great deal of time and energy digging into psychoanalytic literature in an effort to make it sound plausible. There appear to be some doubts as to whether or not this has been accomplished, and she begs the reader's indulgence: "As it is, the acceptance of prac-

tically any of my statements about the meaning of the various factorial constellations is left to the good will of the reader....until he can convince himself about the clinical validity of the statements by the actual use of the test." With the leeway given an examiner with this type of test, any connection between results and validity is purely coincidental. The author feels that the coincidence of the student's interpretations with independent clinical evidence is a constant source of validation as is also the increasing demand for Szondi reports. In connection with this, another of her statements is interesting. "I am fully aware of the autistic nature of this reasoning since actually in this manner I am the only one who has received the accumulative evidence of all these individual clinical validations." This type of reasoning does not need criticism. She feels that the fact that the test works has to be accepted anyway as a pragmatic proof that something essentially characteristic is expressed and reacted to in the picture used as a stimulus material. No one will quarrel with this statement. However, one wonders what the subject is reacting to. An individual's reactions are so unique and complicated that a great deal of work must be done fully to comprehend his likes and dislikes, which may turn more on a dislike for a beard or a bald head than on the fact that the subject is a catatonic praecox, more on the size of the nose or the presence or absence of teeth than whether the subject is hysteric or epileptic. The subject may repeatedly choose adjacent photographs. Some may be interested in small details in the pictures and react to them accordingly. Others consider the picture as a whole as in the Rorschach Test. As yet, these reactions have not been integrated into the text. The administration of the test is adequately described and, despite the theoretical deficiencies, the material and clinical examples are interesting enough to warrant reading by those interested in research in the evaluation of personality.

Psychol B 47:360–1 Jl '50. Helen D. Sargent. The publication of Susan Deri's long awaited book on the Szondi method will, in the opinion of this reviewer, be to the Szondi what Beck's *Manual* was to the Rorschach in 1937. Both books were written by ardent disciples of a master; both bear the stamp of their author's original extension of a creative idea; and both were produced in response to the intense interest of a few at a stage of apparent readiness for sharing with the many. Since Deri began her seminars in

1945, research under her leadership has grown in an atmosphere of mingled fascination and skepticism. American psychologists have found it impossible to take seriously Szondi's theory of choice based on affinity between the genes of a subject and the genes of a patient whose photograph is selected as "liked" or "disliked." The test has nevertheless had strong appeal, not only because of its ease and simplicity of administration and recording, but because the experience of many clinicians suggests that clinically valid interpretations of choice profiles can be derived even without fully acceptable explanation of the assumptions developed from this theory. In her book, Deri loyally states Szondi's views, including the typology which appears in his own untranslated book. Then, with a tact which is unusual in professional writing, she sets his theory aside and proceeds to the description of her own rationale of interpretation. To this task she brings her experience as a practicing analyst, and her training under Lewin. The determinants of choice are discussed not in terms of genetic characteristics of pictured patients falling in eight nosological categories, but rather in terms of stereotypes which the pictures represent to subjects who select or reject them in terms of their own needs. Choice, according to Deri, is the result of tension or satiation in eight need-tension systems, grouped into four vectors, which provide "an octagonal gauge for the understanding of personality dynamics." Although the need systems are reconciled both with Freudian constructs and with topological conceptualization of personality structure, the vectorial approach offers a new set of dimensions within which to conceive the dynamic processes of sexuality and aggression, cycles of control and discharge, ego structure and function, and object relationship. To the extent that the clinical validity of the test proves verifiable, the Szondi test, as Deri describes it, promises several unique contributions. Through serial administration, it is possible to study test-retest change, thus capitalizing on a form of unreliability which in more cumbersome methods is an obstacle. Second, the interpretation of "loaded" and "open" factors, in terms of discharge and discharge readiness, allows the prediction of symptoms and overt behavior patterns in relation to stable, "root" factors in which may be sought the deeper, inner springs of action. Although Deri's book does not in itself clear the mystery of why the test appears to "work," it offers a clear formulation of assumptions which should lend themselves to experiment. It is to be hoped that clinicians will not use the book as a manual of signs for the deceptively easy identification of syndromes and traits, but will utilize it as a source book of hypotheses for systematic exploration.

[136]

Thematic Apperception Test. Ages 7 and over; 1943; also called TAT; individual; 1 form; no data on reliability; $6 per set of testing materials; cash orders postpaid; nontimed (120) minutes; Henry A. Murray; Harvard University Press. (Oxford University Press, London: 1944; 28s.)

REFERENCES

1–101. See 3:103.
102. DERI, SUSAN K. The Psychological Effects of Electric Shock Treatments on Depressive Patients. Master's thesis, State University of Iowa (Iowa City, Iowa), 1943.
103. SPOERL, DOROTHY TILDEN. "Bilinguality and Emotional Adjustment." J Abn & Social Psychol 38:37–57 Ja '43. * (PA 17:3837)
104. HENRY, WILLIAM EARL. An Exploration of the Validity and Usefulness of the Thematic Apperception Technique in the Study of Culture-Personality Relations. Doctor's thesis, University of Chicago (Chicago, Ill.), 1945. (PA 22:213, title only)
105. RAUTMAN, A. L., AND BROWER, EDNA. "War Themes in Children's Stories." J Psychol 19:191–202 Ap '45. * (PA 19:1603)
106. FRENKEL-BRUNSWIK, ELSE. "Personality and Prejudice in Women." Abstract. Am Psychol 1:239 Jl '46. * (PA 20:3696, title only)
107. HOLT, ROBERT R., Editor. The TAT Newsletter 1:1–5 S '46.
108. ROE, ANNE. "Artists and Their Work." J Personality 15:1–40 S '46. * (PA 21:2330)
109. SHERRIFFS, ALEXANDER CARLTON. A New Projective Technique. Doctor's thesis, Stanford University (Stanford, Calif.), 1946. (Abstracts of Dissertations....1946–47, 1947, pp. 132–5.)
110. CERF, ARTHUR Z. "The Thematic Apperception Test, CE706A," pp. 637–45. In Printed Classification Tests. Edited by J. P. Guilford with the assistance of John I. Lacey. Army Air Forces Aviation Psychology Program Research Reports, Report No. 5. Washington, D.C.: U.S. Government Printing Office, 1947. Pp. xi, 919. * (PA 22:4145)
111. FRENCH, VERA V. "The Structure of Sentiments: III, A Study of Philosophicoreligious Sentiments." J Personality 16:209–44 D '47. * (PA 22:4840)
112. HOLT, ROBERT R., Editor. The TAT Newsletter 1:1–5 Ag '47.
113. LEAVITT, HARRY C.; WITH THE TECHNICAL ASSISTANCE OF MARTIN S. BERGMANN. "A Case of Hypnotically Produced Secondary and Tertiary Personalities." Psychoanalytic R 34:274–95 Jl '47. * (PA 22:4841)
114. MARTINEZ-ARANGO, CARLOS; IN COLLABORATION WITH JOSE LASAGA Y TRAVIESO. "Psychotherapy Based on the Thematic Apperception Test." Q R Psychiatry & Neurol 2:271–87 Jl '47. * (PA 22:723)
115. ROE, ANNE. "Personality and Vocation." Trans N Y Acad Sci 9:257–67 My '47. * (PA 21:4392)
116. SINGH, JAGDISH. "Assessment of Personality by Projection Tests." Indian J Psychol 22:127–37 nos 1–4 '47. * (PA 24:5883)
117. WHEELER, ERMA T. A Study of Certain Aspects of Personality as Related to the Electroencephalogram. Doctor's thesis, University of Pittsburgh (Pittsburgh, Pa.), 1947. (Abstracts of Doctoral Dissertations...., 1948, pp. 183–96.)
118. ARON, BETTY. "A Method For the Analysis of the Thematic Apperception Test." Abstract. Am Psychol 3:341 Ag '48. * (PA 23:742, title only)
119. ATKINSON, JOHN W., AND McCLELLAND, DAVID C. "The Projective Expression of Needs: II, The Effect of Different Intensities of the Hunger Drive on Thematic Apperception." J Exp Psychol 38:643–58 D '48. * (PA 23:1639)
120. BELL, JOHN ELDERKIN. Chap. 8, "The Thematic Apperception Test," pp. 207–38; Chap. 9, "Direct Modifications of the Thematic Apperception Test," pp. 239–52. In his Projective Techniques: A Dynamic Approach to the Study of the Personality. New York: Longmans, Green and Co., Inc., 1948. Pp. xvi, 533. * (London: Longmans, Green & Co. Ltd., 1949.) (PA 23:1284)
121. BROWER, DANIEL. "The Relations of Visuo-Motor Conflict to Personality Traits and Cardio-Vascular Activity." J General Psychol 38:69–99 Ja '48. * (PA 22:3383)
122. BUTLER, OCTAVIA PEARL. Parent Figures in Thematic Apperception Test Stories of Children in Disparate Family Situations. Doctor's thesis, University of Pittsburgh (Pitts-

burgh, Pa.), 1948. (*Abstracts of Doctoral Dissertations....1948, 1949*, pp. 220–6.) (*PA* 23:353, 24:1191; title only)

123. Cox, Beverly F., and Sargent, Helen D. "The Common Responses of Normal Children to Ten Pictures of the Thematic Apperception Test Series." Abstract. *Am Psychol* 3:363 Ag '48. * (*PA* 23:748, title only)

124. Dymond, Rosalind F. "A Preliminary Investigation of the Relation of Insight and Empathy." *J Consult Psychol* 12:228–33 Jl–Ag '48. * (*PA* 23:1159)

125. Eron, Leonard D. "Frequency of Themes and Identifications of Characters in TAT Stories of Schizophrenic Patients and Non-Hospitalized College Students." Abstract. *Am Psychol* 3:363 Ag '48. * (*PA* 23:867, title only)

126. Eron, Leonard D. "Frequencies of Themes and Identifications in the Stories of Schizophrenic Patients and Non-Hospitalized College Students." *J Consult Psychol* 12:387–95 N–D '48. * (*PA* 23:2229)

127. Eron, Leonard D., and Hake, Dorothy T. Chap. 15A, "Psychometric Approach to the Evaluation of the Thematic Apperception Test," 14 pages. In *Manual of Projective and Cognate Techniques.* By Joseph Zubin in collaboration with Kathleen M. Young. Madison, Wis.: College Typing Co., 1948. Pp. 175 (pagination by chapters). Paper, mimeographed. Out of print. *

128. Fine, Reuben. *The Personality of the Asthmatic Child.* Doctor's thesis, University of Southern California (Los Angeles, Calif.), 1948. (*Abstracts of Dissertations....1948*, 1949, pp. 165–9.) (*PA* 23:4855)

129. Frenkel-Brunswik, Else. "Dynamic and Cognitive Categorization of Qualitative Material: I, General Problems and the Thematic Apperception Test." *J Psychol* 25:253–60 Ap '48. * (*PA* 22:4420)

130. Garfield, Sol L., and Eron, Leonard D. "Interpreting Mood and Activity in TAT Stories." *J Abn & Social Psychol* 43:338–45 Jl '48. * (*PA* 23:753)

131. Gough, Harrison G. "The Frame of Reference of the Thematic Apperception Test." *J Clin Psychol* 4:90–2 Ja '48. * (*PA* 22:5426)

132. Holt, Robert R., Editor. *The TAT Newsletter* 1:1–7 My '48.

133. Holt, Robert R. "The Assessment of Psychiatric Aptitude From the TAT." Abstract. *Am Psychol* 3:271 Jl '48. * (*PA* 22:5428, title only)

134. Holt, Robert R., Editor. *The TAT Newsletter* 2:1–7, 1–9, Ag, N '48. *

135. Kannenberg, K. M. *A Comparison of Results Obtained From the Thematic Apperception Test Under Two Conditions of Administration.* Master's thesis, University of Wisconsin (Madison, Wis.), 1948.

136. Kannenberg, Katherine M. "A Comparison of Results Obtained From the Thematic Apperception Test Under Two Conditions of Administration." Abstract. *Am Psychol* 3:363 Ag '48. * (*PA* 23:760, title only)

137. Kasin, Edith Diana. *An Exploratory Comparison of Personality Descriptions Obtained From Nondirective Interviews and the Thematic Apperception Test.* Master's thesis, University of Chicago (Chicago, Ill.), 1948. (*PA* 23:374, title only)

138. Kass, Walter, and Ekstein, Rudolf. "Thematic Apperception Test Diagnosis of a Nazi War Criminal: Anonymous Post-Mortem Evaluation by a Group of Graduate Clinical Psychology Students: Problems of Inter-Judge Consistency." *Trans Kans Acad Sci* 51:344–50 S '48. * (*PA* 23:2055)

139. Lasaga, Jose I., and Martinez-Arango, Carlos. "Four Detailed Examples of How Mental Conflicts of Psychoneurotic and Psychotic Patients May Be Discovered by Means of the TAT." *J Psychol* 26:299–345 O '48. * (*PA* 23:1783)

140. Rosenzweig, Saul. "The Thematic Apperception Technique in Diagnosis and Therapy." *J Personality* 16:437–44 Je '48. * (*PA* 23:2234)

141. Sarason, Seymour B. "The TAT and Subjective Interpretation." *J Consult Psychol* 12:285–99 S–O '48. * (*PA* 23:1776)

142. Schafer, Roy. *The Clinical Application of Psychological Tests: Diagnostic Summaries and Case Studies.* Foreword by David Rapaport. The Menninger Foundation Monograph Series, No. 6. New York: International Universities Press, Inc., 1948. Pp. 236. (London: George Allen & Unwin, Ltd., 1949.) (*PA* 23:778)

143. Schafer, Sarah, and Leitch, Mary. "An Exploratory Study of the Usefulness of a Battery of Psychological Tests With Nursery School Children." *Am J Psychiatry* 104:647–52 Ap '48. * (*PA* 23:813)

144. Sears, Richard. "Castration Anxiety in an Adult as Shown by Projective Tests." Abstract. *Am Psychol* 3:281 Jl '48. * (*PA* 22:5371, title only)

145. Shorr, Joseph Errol. *A Method of Scaled Scoring of the Thematic Apperception Test to Be Used by the Vocational Counselor.* Master's thesis, University of Southern California (Los Angeles, Calif.), 1948.

146. Shorr, Joseph E. "A Proposed System for Scoring the TAT." *J Clin Psychol* 4:189–94 Ap '48. * (*PA* 23:170)

147. Stein, Morris I. *The Thematic Apperception Test: An Introductory Manual for Its Clinical Use With Adult Males.* Foreword by James G. Miller. Cambridge, Mass.: Addison-Wesley Press, Inc., 1948. Pp. viii, 95. Lithotyped. * (London: H. K. Lewis & Co. Ltd.) (*PA* 22:4959)

148. Suesholtz, Z. *Formal Characteristics of Children's Fantasies as Measured by the Thematic Apperception Test.* Master's thesis, College of the City of New York (New York, N.Y.), 1948.

149. Symonds, Percival M. "Survey of Projective Techniques," pp. 3–18. In *Exploring Individual Differences: A Report of the 1947 Invitational Conference on Testing Problems, New York City, November 1, 1947.* Henry Chauncey, Chairman. American Council on Education Studies, Vol. 12, Series 1, No. 32. Washington, D.C.: the Council, October 1948. Pp. vii, 110. Paper. *

150. Thompson, Charles E. "A Revision of the Murray TAT for Use With a Minority Group." Abstract. *Am Psychol* 3:283 Jl '48. * (*PA* 22:5438, title only)

151. Winchester, T. H. *A Study of Differences Between Written and Oral Protocols From the Thematic Apperception Test.* Master's thesis, University of Denver (Denver, Colo.), 1948.

152. Wyatt, Frederick. "Measurement and the Thematic Apperception Test: V, The Problems of Quantification and Objectification in Personality: A Symposium." *J Personality* 17:169–76 D '48. * (*PA* 25:3195)

153. Arnold, Magda B. "A Demonstration Analysis of the TAT in a Clinical Setting." *J Abn & Social Psychol* 44:97–111 Ja '49. * (*PA* 23:3744)

154. Aron, Betty. *A Manual for Analysis of the Thematic Apperception Test: A Method and Technique for Personality Research.* Foreword by R. Nevitt Sanford. Berkeley, Calif.: Willis E. Berg, 1949. Pp. xiii, 163. Lithotyped. * (*PA* 24:644)

155. Bell, John Elderkin. "The Case of Gregor: Psychological Test Data." *Rorsch Res Exch & J Proj Tech* 13:155–205 no 2 '49. * (*PA* 24:2589)

156. Bellak, Leopold; Pasquarelli, Blaise A.; and Braverman, Sydell. "The Use of the Thematic Apperception Test in Psychotherapy." *J Nerv & Mental Dis* 110:51–65 Jl '49. * (*PA* 24:4109)

157. Berk, Norman. *A Personality Study of Suicidal Schizophrenics.* Doctor's thesis, New York University (New York, N.Y.), 1949. Abstract: *Microfilm Abstracts* 10:155–6 no 2 '50. * (*PA* 25:479, title only)

158. Bock, Carson. *The Attitudes of Delinquent and Non-Delinquent Boys to Their Parents as Indicated by the Thematic Apperception Test.* Master's thesis, University of Toronto (Toronto, Canada), 1949. Pp. 44.

159. Burton, Arthur. "The Use of Psychometric and Projective Tests in Clinical Psychology." *J Psychol* 28:451–6 O '49. * (*PA* 24:2595)

160. Fest, Beverly, and Seward, Georgene H. "A Further Analysis of Personality in Spastic Colitis Patients." Abstract. *Am Psychol* 4:387–8 S '49. * (*PA* 24:2021, title only)

161. Hartman, A. A. *An Experimental Examination of the Thematic Apperception Technique in Clinical Diagnosis.* American Psychological Association, Psychological Monographs: General and Applied, Vol. 63, No. 8, Whole No. 303. Washington, D.C.: the Association, Inc., 1949. Pp. v, 48. Paper. * (*PA* 24: 6354)

162. Hartman, A. Arthur. *An Experimental Examination of the Thematic Apperception Technique in the Clinical Diagnosis of Personality.* Doctor's thesis, University of Chicago (Chicago, Ill.), 1949. Pp. 80.

163. Henry, William E., and Gardner, Burleigh B. "Personality Evaluation in the Selection of Executive Personnel." *Pub Personnel R* 10:67–71 Ap '49. * (*PA* 23:6481)

164. Hire, A. William. *Use of the Rorschach and Thematic Apperception Tests in the Counseling and Guidance of College Students.* Doctor's thesis, Harvard University (Cambridge, Mass.), 1949. Abstract: *Harvard Ed R* 21:65–8 w '51. *

165. Holt, Robert R., Editor. *The TAT Newsletter* 2:1–5 and 1–14, 1–5 Mr, Je '49. *

166. Holt, Robert R., Editor. "The TAT Newsletter, Vol. 3, Nos. 1–3." *Rorsch Res Exch & J Proj Tech* 13:225–32, 345–9, 485–92, nos 2, 3, 4 '49. *

167. Iazzeta, Vernie. *An Exploratory Study of Certain Differences Between Delinquent and Non-Delinquent Girls as Indicated by the Group Thematic Apperception Test.* Master's thesis, University of Denver (Denver, Colo.), 1949.

168. Joel, Walther, and Shapiro, David. "A Genotypical Approach to the Analysis of Personal Interaction." *J Psychol* 28:9–17 Jl '49. * (*PA* 24:657)

169. Luborsky, Lester. "The Personality Requisites for Work in Psychiatry as Revealed in the TAT." Abstract. *Am Psychol* 4:258 Jl '49. * (*PA* 23:5908, title only)

170. McClelland, David; Clark, Russell A.; Roby, Thornton B.; and Atkinson, John W. "The Projective Expression of Needs: IV, The Effect of the Need for Achievement on Thematic Apperception." *J Exp Psychol* 39:242–55 Ap '49. * (*PA* 23:4828)

171. Meyer, Mortimer M. "Integration of Test Results With Clinical Observations: A Diagnostic Case Study." *Rorsch Res Exch & J Proj Tech* 13:325–40 S '49. * (*PA* 24:3202)

172. Monroe, Ruth L. "Diagnosis of Learning Disabilities Through a Projective Technique." *J Consult Psychol* 13:390–5 D '49. * (*PA* 24:3226)

173. Roe, Anne. "Psychological Examinations of Eminent Biologists." *J Consult Psychol* 13:225–46 Ag '49. * (*PA* 24:1525)

174. Rosenzweig, Saul. "Apperceptive Norms for the Thematic Apperception Test: I, The Problem of Norms in Projective Methods." *J Personality* 17:475–82 Je '49. * (*PA* 25:3182)

175. Rosenzweig, Saul, and Fleming, Edith E. "Apper-

ceptive Norms for the Thematic Apperception Test: II, An Empirical Investigation." *J Personality* 17:483–503 Je '49. * (*PA* 25:3185)

176. ROSENZWEIG, SAUL; WITH THE COLLABORATION OF KATE LEVINE KOGAN. *Psychodiagnosis: An Introduction to Tests in the Clinical Practice of Psychodynamics,* pp. 139–59. New York: Grune & Stratton, Inc., 1949. Pp. xii, 380. * (*PA* 23: 3761)

177. SARASON, SEYMOUR B. "The Thematic Apperception Test," pp. 252–9. In his *Psychological Problems in Mental Deficiency.* New York: Harper & Brothers, 1949. Pp. xi, 366. * (*PA* 24:2682)

178. SHNEIDMAN, EDWIN S. "Some Comparisons Among the Four Picture Test, Thematic Apperception Test, and Make A Picture Story Test." *Rorsch Res Exch & J Proj Tech* 13:150–4 no 2 '49. * (*PA* 24:2614)

179. STEIN, MORRIS I. "Thematic Apperception Test: The Case of Gregor: Interpretation of Test Data: Symposium Presented at American Psychological Association Meeting, Denver, 1949." *Rorsch Res Exch & J Proj Tech* 13:450–7 D '49. (*PA* 24:3734)

180. SUPER, DONALD E. *Appraising Vocational Fitness By Means of Psychological Tests,* pp. 524–7. New York: Harper & Brothers, 1949. Pp. xxiii, 727. * (*PA* 24:2130)

181. SYMONDS, PERCIVAL M. Chap. 2, "A Review of Literature on the Thematic Apperception Test," pp. 10–51; "Bibliography on the Thematic Apperception Test," pp. 375–84. In his *Adolescent Fantasy: An Investigation of the Picture-Story Method of Personality Study.* New York: Columbia University Press, 1949. Pp. xii, 397. * (London: Oxford University Press.) (*PA* 24:650)

182. THOMPSON, CHARLES E. "The Thompson Modification of the Thematic Apperception Test." *Rorsch Res Exch & J Proj Tech* 13:469–78 D '49. (*PA* 24:3743)

183. THOMPSON, CHARLES EUGENE. *A Modification of the Murray Thematic Apperception Test.* Doctor's thesis, Tulane University (New Orleans, La.), 1949. Pp. 58. (*Abstracts of Theses 1949,* pp. 32–5.)

184. TOMKINS, SILVAN S. "The Present Status of the Thematic Apperception Test." *Am J Orthopsychiatry* 19:358–62 Ap '49. * (*PA* 23:6221)

185. WALCOTT, WILLIAM O. "Reading Thematic Apperception," pp. 148–50. In *Claremont College Reading Conference, Fourteenth Yearbook, 1949: Conference Theme: The Problems and Techniques Involved in Reading Social Relationships.* Claremont, Calif.: Claremont College Curriculum Laboratory, 1949. Pp. viii, 191. Paper. *

186. WILSON, CLAUDE E. *Differences Between Personal Characteristics of Students Who Have Failed in High School and Those Who Have Not Failed.* Doctor's thesis, University of Southern California (Los Angeles, Calif.), 1949. (*Abstracts of Dissertations....1949,* 1950, pp. 195–7.)

187. WITTENBORN, J. R. "Some Thematic Apperception Test Norms and a Note on the Use of the Test Cards in the Guidance of College Students." *J Clin Psychol* 5:157–61 Ap '49. * (*PA* 24:2086)

188. ALEXANDER, THERON, JR. "The Prediction of Teacher-Pupil Interaction With a Projective Test." *J Clin Psychol* 6:273–6 Jl '50. * (*PA* 25:2054)

189. ARON, BETTY. Chap. 14, "The Thematic Apperception Test in the Study of Prejudiced and Unprejudiced Individuals," pp. 489–544. In *The Authoritarian Personality.* By T. W. Adorno, Else Frenkel-Brunswik, Daniel J. Levinson, and R. Nevitt Sanford in collaboration with Betty Aron, Maria Hertz Levinson, and William Morrow. New York: Harper & Brothers, 1950. Pp. xxxiii, 990. * (*PA* 24:5 96)

190. BELLAK, LEOPOLD. "The Effect of Situational Factors on the TAT: A Note on the TAT's of Two Nazi Leaders." *J Proj Tech* 14:309–14 S '50. * (*PA* 25:4557)

191. BELLAK, LEOPOLD. "Thematic Apperception: Failures and the Defenses." *Trans N Y Acad Sci* 12:122–6 F '50. * (*PA* 24:5254)

192. BELLAK, LEOPOLD. "The Thematic Apperception Test in Clinical Use," pp. 185–229. (*PA* 25:2447) In *Projective Psychology: Clinical Approaches to the Total Personality.* Edited by Lawrence Edwin Abt and Leopold Bellak. New York: Alfred A. Knopf, Inc., 1950. Pp. xvii, 485, xiv. *

193. BELLAK, LEOPOLD. "Thematic Apperception Test and Related Apperceptive Techniques," pp. 532–40. In *Progress in Neurology and Psychiatry: An Annual Review, Vol. V.* Edited by E. A. Spiegel. New York: Grune & Stratton, Inc., 1950. Pp. xiv, 621. * (*PA* 24:1286)

194. BELLAK, LEOPOLD; LEVINGER, LEAH; AND LIPSKY, ESTHER. "An Adolescent Problem Reflected in the TAT." *J Clin Psychol* 6:295–7 Jl '50. * (*PA* 25:1783)

195. BILLS, ROBERT E. "Animal Pictures for Obtaining Children's Projections." *J Clin Psychol* 6:291–3 Jl '50. * (*PA* 25: 1784)

196. BILLS, ROBERT E.; LEIMAN, CHARLES J.; AND THOMAS, RICHARD W. "A Study of the Validity of the TAT and a Set of Animal Pictures." *J Clin Psychol* 6:293–5 Jl '50. * (*PA* 25:1785)

197. CALIGOR, LEOPOLD. *The Determination of the Individual's Unconscious Conception of His Own Masculinity-Femininity Identification.* Doctor's thesis, New York University (New York, N.Y.), 1950. Abstract: *Microfilm Abstracts* 10:292–3 no 4 '50. * (*PA* 25:4418, title only)

198. CALVIN, JAMES S., AND WARD, LEO C. "An Attempted Experimental Validation of the Thematic Apperception Test." *J Clin Psychol* 6:377–81 O '50. * (*PA* 25:8074)

199. COHEN, WILLIAM J. *Manifestations of Differences in Ego Development in the Thematic Apperception Test.* Doctor's thesis, Western Reserve University (Cleveland, Ohio), 1950. (*PA* 25:6541, title only)

200. COX, BEVERLY F. *The Common Responses of Normal Children to Ten Pictures of the Thematic Apperception Test.* Doctor's thesis, Northwestern University (Evanston, Ill.), 1950. (*Summaries of Doctoral Dissertations....June–September 1950,* 1951, pp. 590–5.)

201. COX, BEVERLY, AND SARGENT, HELEN. "TAT Responses of Emotionally Disturbed and Emotionally Stable Children: Clinical Judgment Versus Normative Data." *J Proj Tech* 14: 61–74 Mr '50. * (*PA* 25:1091)

202. DAVISON, ARTHUR H. *A Comparison of the Fantasy Productions on the Thematic Apperception Test of Sixty Hospitalized Psychoneurotic and Psychotic Patients.* Doctor's thesis, Purdue University (Lafayette, Ind.), 1950.

203. DREGER, RALPH MASON. *Some Personality Correlates of Religious Attitudes as Determined by Projective Techniques.* Doctor's thesis, University of Southern California (Los Angeles, Calif.), 1950. (*Abstracts of Dissertations:...1950,* 1951, pp. 202–5.) (*PA* 26:170, title only)

204. ERON, LEONARD D. *A Normative Study of the Thematic Apperception Test.* American Psychological Association, Psychological Monographs: General and Applied, Vol. 64, No. 9, Whole No. 315. Washington, D.C.: the Association, Inc., 1950. Pp. v, 48. Paper. * (*PA* 25:6211)

205. ERON, LEONARD D., AND HAKE, DOROTHY T. Chap. 16, "Psychometric Approach to the Evaluation of the Thematic Apperception Test," pp. 1–14. In *Quantitative Techniques and Methods in Abnormal Psychology.* By Joseph Zubin. New York, N.Y.: Columbia University Bookstore, 1950. Pp. 220. Paper, mimeographed. * (*PA* 25:6933)

206. ERON, LEONARD D.; TERRY, DOROTHY; AND CALLAHAN, ROBERT. "The Use of Rating Scales for Emotional Tone of TAT stories." *J Consult Psychol* 14:473–8 D '50. * (*PA* 26: 912)

207. FERGUSON, A. B. *An Investigation Into the Use of the Thematic Apperception Test as an Indicator of Intelligence.* Master's thesis, University of Toronto (Toronto, Canada), 1950. Pp. 2⁻.

208. FISHER, SEYMOUR. *Patterns of Personality Rigidity and Some of Their Determinants.* American Psychological Association, Psychological Monographs: General and Applied, Vol. 64, No. 1, Whole No. 307. Washington, D.C.: the Association, Inc., 1950. Pp. v, 48. Paper. * (*PA* 24:6255)

209. FREEMAN, FRANK S. *The Theory and Practice of Psychological Testing,* pp. 417–28. New York: Henry Holt & Co., 1950. Pp. xxiii, 518. * (London: Sir Isaac Pitman & Sons, Ltd., 1951.) (*PA* 24:4344)

210. GLAD, DONALD D., AND HAMMACK, BARBARA W. "An Interest Validation and Normative Study of the Rorschach and TAT with Schizophrenia." Abstract. *J Colo-Wyo Acad Sci* 4:65–6 O '50. * (*PA* 25:5495, title only)

211. GOUDEY, ELIZABETH. *An Investigation of the Validity of One Aspect of TAT Analysis: Conformity Using a Conformity Rating Scale.* Master's thesis, University of Toronto (Toronto, Canada), 1950. Pp. 34.

212. GROTZ, ROBERT C. *A Comparison of Thematic Apperception Test Stories and Manifest Dream Narratives.* Master's thesis, Western Reserve University (Cleveland, Ohio), 1950. (*PA* 25:6552)

213. HANEY, HAROLD RUSSELL. *Motives Implied by the Act of Stuttering as Revealed by Prolonged Experimental Projection.* Doctor's thesis, University of Southern California (Los Angeles, Calif.), 1950. (*Abstracts of Dissertations....1950,* 1951, pp. 16–9.) (*PA* 25:8183, title only)

214. HARRIS, LESTER LEE. *A Clinical Study of Nine Stuttering Children in Group Psychotherapy.* Doctor's thesis, University of Southern California (Los Angeles, Calif.), 1950. (*PA* 25:8184, title only)

215–6. HOLT, ROBERT R., EDITOR. "The TAT Newsletter, Vol. 3, No. 4, and Vol. 4, Nos. 1–3." *J Proj Tech* 14:80–100, 203–10, 327–33, 471–7 Mr, Je, S, D '50. *

217. KELLY, E. LOWELL, AND FISKE, DONALD W. "The Prediction of Success in the VA Training Program in Clinical Psychology." *Am Psychol* 5:395–406 Ag '50. * (*PA* 25:2183)

218. KIEFER, ROBERTA. *The Thematic Apperception Test Pictures: A Study of Common Stories as Told by Normal Adult Females.* Master's thesis, University of Alberta (Edmonton, Alberta, Canada), 1950. Pp. 183. (*PA* 25:6560, title only)

219. KLEHR, HAROLD. *An Investigation of Some Personality Factors in Women With Rheumatoid Arthritis.* Doctor's thesis, Northwestern University (Evanston, Ill.), 1950. (*Summaries of Doctoral Dissertations....June–September 1950,* 1951, pp. 605–6.)

220. KLIMAN, E. M. *A Method of Evaluating the Productivity of Thematic Apperception Test Cards and the Derivation of a Short Form of the Male Series of the Test.* Master's thesis, University of Toronto (Toronto, Canada), 1950. Pp. 40.

221. KORCHIN, SHELDON J.; MITCHELL, HOWARD E.; AND MELTZOFF, JULIAN. "A Critical Evaluation of the Thompson Thematic Apperception Test." *J Proj Tech* 14:445–52 D '50. * (*PA* 26:3413)

222. KORNER, ANNELIESE FRIEDSAM. "Theoretical Considerations Concerning the Scope and Limitations of Projective Tech-

niques." *J Abn & Social Psychol* 45:619-27 O '50. * *(PA 25:2460)*

223. LASAGA, J. I. "A Non-psychoanalytic Symbolic Interpretation of the Thematic Apperception Test," pp. 83-4. Abstract. In *Proceedings and Papers of the Twelfth International Congress of Psychology Held at the University of Edinburgh, July 23rd to 29th, 1948.* Edinburgh, Scotland: Oliver & Boyd Ltd., 1950. Pp. xxviii, 152. Paper. *

224. LOWELL, E. L. *A Methodological Study of Projectively Measured Achievement Motivation.* Master's thesis, Wesleyan University (Middletown, Conn.), 1950.

225. MERCER, MARGARET, AND WRIGHT, S. C. "Diagnostic Testing in a Case of Latent Schizophrenia." *J Proj Tech* 14: 287-96 S '50. * *(PA 25:4733)*

226. MITCHELL, HOWARD E. "Social Class and Race as Factors Affecting the Role of the Family in Thematic Apperception Test Stories." Abstract. *Am Psychol* 5:299-300 Jl '50. * *(PA 25:1102, title only)*

227. MUSSEN, PAUL H. "Some Personality and Social Factors Related to Changes in Children's Attitudes Toward Negroes." *J Abn & Social Psychol* 45:423-41 Jl '50. * *(PA 25: 312)*

228. OPPENHEIM, SADI, AND GOLDWASSER, MIRIAM L. "Psychological Report of the Cyprus Psychiatric Mission." *J Proj Tech* 14:245-61 S '50. * *(PA 25:4547)*

229. PICKERING, WILLIAM DONALD. *A Comparison of Predominant Verbal Levels on the Thematic Apperception Test With the Rorschach Experience Balance.* Doctor's thesis, University of Pittsburgh (Pittsburgh, Pa.), 1950. *(Abstracts of Doctoral Dissertations....1950, 1951, pp. 309-16.)*

230. PIOTROWSKI, ZYGMUNT A. "A New Evaluation of the Thematic Apperception Test," pp. 13-22. *(PA 25:6877)* In *Projective and Expressive Methods of Personality Investigation ("Diagnosis").* Personality-Symposium No. 2, April 1950. Edited by Werner Wolff. New York: Grune & Stratton, Inc., April 1950. Pp. ii, 76. Paper. *

231. PIOTROWSKI, ZYGMUNT A. "A New Evaluation of the Thematic Apperception Test." *Psychoanalytic R* 37:101-27 Ap '50. * *(PA 25:5875)*

232. RIESS, BERNARD F.; SCHWARTZ, EMANUEL K.; AND COTTINGHAM, ALICE. "An Experimental Critique of Assumptions Underlying the Negro Version of the TAT." *J Abn & Social Psychol* 45:700-9 O '50. * *(PA 25:2466)*

233. SAXE, CARL H. "A Quantitative Comparison of Psychodiagnostic Formulations From the TAT and Therapeutic Contacts." *J Consult Psychol* 14:116-27 Ap '50. * *(PA 24:5880)*

234. SHIELDS, DOROTHY LOUISE. *An Investigation of the Influence of Disparate Home Conditions Upon the Level at Which Children Responded to the Thematic Apperception Test.* Master's thesis, University of Pittsburgh (Pittsburgh, Pa.), 1950. *(PA 24:5564, title only)*

235. SHNEIDMAN, EDWIN S. "Thematic Test Analysis." Abstract. *Am Psychol* 5:472 S '50. * *(PA 25:4593, title only)*

236. SLACK, CHARLES WILLIAM. "Some Intellective Functions in the Thematic Apperception Test and Their Use in Differentiating Endogenous Feeble-Mindedness From Exogenous Feeble-Mindedness." *Train Sch B* 47:156-69 O '50. * *(PA 25:2540)*

237. STONE, GIDEON BARTO, II. *A Study of Parent-Child Relationships in Patients with Peptic Ulcer and Bronchial Asthma, as Revealed by Projective Techniques.* Doctor's thesis, University of Southern California (Los Angeles, Calif.), 1950. *(Abstracts of Dissertations....1950, 1951, pp. 188-91.)*

238. TERRY, DOROTHY J. *An Analysis by the Use of Rating Scales of Thematic Apperception Test Protocols Obtained Under Different Conditions of Test Administration.* Doctor's thesis, University of Wisconsin (Madison, Wis.), 1950. *(Summaries of Doctoral Dissertations....July 1949 to June 1950, 1951, pp. 210-1.)*

239. THOMPSON, CHARLES E. *An Annotated Bibliography of the Thematic Apperception Test.* Microfilm Document 2863. Washington, D.C.: American Documentation Institute, 1950. Pp. 434. Abstract: *J Proj Tech* 14:327 S '50. * *(PA 25:4594, title only)*

240. THOMPSON, CHARLES E., AND HOLT, ROBERT R. "Bibliography for Thematic Apperception Test." *J Proj Tech* 14:80-100 Mr '50. * *(PA 25:1096)*

241. VALENTINE, MAX, AND ROBIN, ASHLEY A. "Aspects of Thematic Apperception Testing: Depression." *J Mental Sci* 96:435-47 Ap '50. * *(PA 25:5523)*

242. VALENTINE, MAX, AND ROBIN, ASHLEY A. "Aspects of Thematic Apperception Testing: Paranoid Schizophrenia." *J Mental Sci* 96:869-88 O '50. * *(PA 25:5524)*

243. WEISSKOPF, EDITH A. "An Experimental Study of the Effect of Brightness and Ambiguity on Projection in the Thematic Apperception Test." *J Psychol* 29:407-16 Ap '50. * *(PA 24:5887)*

244. WEISSKOPF, EDITH A. "A Transcendence Index as a Proposed Measure in the TAT." *J Psychol* 29:379-90 Ap '50. * *(PA 24:5888)*

245. WENTWORTH-ROHR, IVAN. *A Study in the Differential Diagnosis of Idiopathic and Symptomatic Epilepsy Through Psychological Tests.* Doctor's thesis, New York University (New York, N.Y.), 1950. Abstract: *Microfilm Abstracts* 11:180-1 no 1 '51. * *(PA 26:2374, title only)*

246. WHITE, MARY ALICE, AND SCHREIBER, HANNA. "A Note on T.A.T. Administration." *J Clin Psychol* 6:417 O '50. * *(PA 25:8115)*

247. WILSON, DONALD MURRAY, *A Study of the Personalities of Stuttering Children and Their Parents as Revealed Through Projection Tests.* Doctor's thesis, University of Southern California (Los Angeles, Calif.), 1950. *(PA 25:8189, title only)*

248. WITTENBORN, J. R. "The Implications of Certain Assumptions Involved in the Use of the Thematic Apperception Test." *J Consult Psychol* 14:216-25 Je '50. * *(PA 25:373)*

249. BEIER, ERNST G.; GORLOW, LEON; AND STACEY, CHALMERS L. "The Fantasy Life of the Mental Defective." *Am J Mental Def* 55:582-9 Ap '51. * *(PA 25:7525)*

250. BIJOU, SIDNEY W., AND KENNY, DOUGLAS T. "The Ambiguity Values of TAT Cards." *J Consult Psychol* 15:203-9 Je '51. * *(PA 26:6251)*

251. BRACKBILL, GLEN A. "Some Effects of Color on Thematic Fantasy." *J Consult Psychol* 15:412-8 O '51. * *(PA 26:6991)*

252. BRACKBILL, GLEN A., AND BRACKBILL, BETTY J. "Some Effects of Age on TAT Stories." Abstract. *Am Psychol* 6:351 Jl '51. *

253. BROWER, DANIEL, AND OPPENHEIM, SADI. "The Effects of Electroshock Therapy on Mental Functions as Revealed by Psychological Tests." *J General Psychol* 45:171-88 O '51. *

254. CALIGOR, LEOPOLD. "The Determination of the Individual's Unconscious Conception of His Own Masculinity-Femininity Identification." *J Proj Tech* 15:494-509 D '51. * *(PA 26:6228)*

255-6. CARLSON, HILDING B., AND VANDEVER, MARGUERITE G. "The Effectiveness of Directive and Non-Directive Counseling in Vocational Problems as Measured by the T.A.T. Test." *Ed & Psychol Meas* 11:212-23 su '51. * *(PA 26:3013)*

257. COHEN, WILLIAM J. *Application of the Contest-Form Method of Analysis of the Thematic Apperception Test: Manifestations of Differences in Ego Development.* Doctor's thesis, Western Reserve University (Cleveland, Ohio), 1951.

258. CRANDALL, VAUGHN J. "Induced Frustration and Punishment-Reward Expectancy in Thematic Apperception Stories." *J Consult Psychol* 15:400-4 O '51. * *(PA 26:7098)*

259. ERIKSEN, CHARLES W. "Some Implications for TAT Interpretation Arising From Need and Perception Experiments." *J Personality* 19:282-8 Mr '51. * *(PA 26:3404)*

260. ERON, LEONARD D., AND RITTER, ANNE M. "A Comparison of Two Methods of Administration of the Thematic Apperception Test." *J Consult Psychol* 15:55-61 F '51. * *(PA 26:6265)*

261. FITZGERALD, DON C. "Success-Failure and TAT Reactions of Orthopedically Handicapped and Physically Normal Adolescents." *Personality* 1:67-83 Ja '51. * *(PA 25:7054)*

262. FROMM, ERIKA O., AND ELONEN, ANNA S. "The Use of Projective Techniques in the Study of a Case of Female Homosexuality." *J Proj Tech* 15:185-230 Je '51. * *(PA 26:3498)*

263. GOODMAN, MORRIS I. *Validation of a Manual for Thematic Apperception Test Analysis.* Doctor's thesis, Western Reserve University (Cleveland, Ohio), 1951. *(PA 25:6550, title only)*

264. HARLOW, ROBERT G. "Masculine Inadequacy and Compensatory Development of Physique." *J Personality* 19:312-23 Mr '51. * *(PA 26:3673)*

265. HAYS, WILLIAM; GELLERMAN, SAUL; AND SLOAN, WILLIAM. "A Study of the Relationship Between the Verb-Adjective Quotient and the Rorschach Experience Balance." *J Clin Psychol* 7:224-7 Jl '51. * *(PA 26:916)*

266. HENRY, WILLIAM E. Chap. 8, "The Thematic Apperception Technique in the Study of Group and Cultural Problems," pp. 230-78. In *An Introduction to Projective Techniques.* Edited by Harold H. Anderson and Gladys L. Anderson. New York: Prentice-Hall, Inc., 1951. Pp. xxiv, 720. *

267. HEPPELL, H. K., AND RAIMY, V. C. "Projective Pictures as Interview Devices." *J Consult Psychol* 15:405-11 O '51. * *(PA 26:7000)*

268. HOLT, ROBERT R. Chap. 7, "The Thematic Apperception Test," pp. 181-229. In *An Introduction to Projective Techniques.* Edited by Harold H. Anderson and Gladys L. Anderson. New York: Prentice-Hall, Inc., 1951. Pp. xxiv, 720. *

269. HOLT, ROBERT R. "TAT Bibliography: Supplement for 1950." *J Proj Tech* 15:117-23 Mr '51. * *(PA 26:298)*

270. HOLT, ROBERT R., EDITOR. "The TAT Newsletter, Vol. 4, No. 4, and Vol. 5, Nos. 1-4." *J Proj Tech* 15:110-23, 281-7, 410-4, 537-44 Mr, Je, S, D '51. *

271. HOLZBERG, JULES D.; CAHEN, ELEANOR R.; AND WILK, EDWARD K. "Suicide: A Psychological Study of Self-Destruction." *J Proj Tech* 15:339-54 S '51. *

272. HOLZBERG, JULES D., AND POSNER, RITA. "The Relationship of Extrapunitiveness on the Rosenzweig Picture-Frustration Study to Aggression in Overt Behavior and Fantasy." *Am J Orthopsychiatry* 21:767-79 O '51. * *(PA 26:5619)*

273. KATZ, JOSEPH. *The Projection of Assaultive Aggression in the Human Figure Drawings of Adult Male Negro Offenders: A Study of Inmates Convicted of Homicide or Assault by Means of Human Figure Drawings, Rorschach, Thematic Apperception Test, and Szondi.* Doctor's thesis. New York University (New York, N.Y.), 1951. Abstract: *Microfilm Abstracts* 11:1096-8 no 4 '51.

274. KELLY, E. LOWELL, AND FISKE, DONALD W. *The Prediction of Performance in Clinical Psychology.* Ann Arbor, Mich.: University of Michigan, 1951. Pp. xv, 311. Lithotyped. *

275. MCCLELLAND, DAVID C. "Measuring the Motivation in Phantasy: The Achievement Motive," pp. 191-205. In *Groups*

Leadership, and Men: Research in Human Relations. Edited by Harold Guetzkow. New Brunswick, N.J.: Rutgers University Press, 1951. Pp. ix, 293. * *(PA 26:803)*

276. MITCHELL, HOWARD E. *Social Class and Race as Factors Affecting the Role of the Family in Thematic Apperception Test Stories of Males.* Doctor's thesis, University of Pennsylvania (Philadelphia, Pa.), 1951. Abstract: *Microfilm Abstracts* 11:428–9 no 2 '51. *(PA 25:1102, title only)*

277. MURRAY, HENRY A. Sect. 8, "Thematic Apperception Test," pp. 54–71. In *Military Clinical Psychology.* Department of the Army Technical Manual TM 8–242; Department of the Air Force Manual AFM 160–45. Washington, D.C.: U.S. Government Printing Office, 1951. Pp. iv, 197. Paper. *

278. MURRAY, HENRY A. "Uses of the Thematic Apperception Test." *Am J Psychiatry* 107:577–81 F '51. * *(PA 26:309)*

279. NAGGE, WILLIAM W. *A Study of the Behavior of Paranoid Schizophrenics on the Thematic Apperception Test.* Doctor's thesis, University of Kentucky (Lexington, Ky.), 1951.

280. NEEDELMAN, STANLEY DAVID. *Ideational Concepts of Parental Figures in Paranoid Schizophrenia: An Investigation Into the Relationship Between Level of Adjustment and an Area of Interpersonal Relationships, as Measured by Four Techniques.* Doctor's thesis, New York University (New York, N.Y.), 1951. Abstract: *Microfilm Abstracts* 11:1116–7 no 4 '51.

281. RAUTMAN, ARTHUR L., AND BROWER, EDNA. "War Themes in Children's Stories: II, Six Years Later." *J Psychol* 31:263–70 Ap '51. * *(PA 26:773)*

282. REICHARD, SUZANNE. "Some Contributions of Psychological Tests to Therapeutic Planning." Discussion by Anneliese F. Korner. *Am J Orthopsychiatry* 21:532–41, discussion 541–2 Jl '51. * *(PA 26:3445)*

283. ROE, ANNE. "Psychological Tests of Research Scientists." *J Consult Psychol* 15:492–5 D '51. * *(PA 26:7292)*

284. RUBIN, HARRY K. *The Influence of Variation in Structure Upon Projection in the Thematic Apperception Test.* Doctor's thesis, University of Chicago (Chicago, Ill.), 1951.

285. SCHNECK, JEROME M. "Hypnoanalysis, Hypnotherapy, and Card 12M of the Thematic Apperception Test." *J General Psychol* 44:293–301 Ap '51. * *(PA 26:4830)*

286. SCHWARTZ, EMANUEL K.; RIESS, BERNARD F.; AND COTTINGHAM, ALICE. "Further Critical Evaluation of the Negro Version of the TAT." *J Proj Tech* 15:394–400 S '51. * *(PA 26:4018)*

287. SEWARD, GEORGENE H.; MORRISON, LESTER M.; AND FEST, BEVERLY; WITH THE ASSISTANCE OF NELLIE M. YOUNG AND VANCE BOILEAU. *Personality Structure in a Common Form of Colitis.* American Psychological Association, Psychological Monographs: General and Applied, Vol. 65, No. 1, Whole No. 318. Washington, D.C.: the Association, Inc., 1951. Pp. v, 26. Paper. * *(PA 25:7024)*

288–9. SHATIN, LEO. *Relationships Between the Rorschach Test and the Thematic Apperception Test.* Doctor's thesis, Harvard University (Cambridge, Mass.), 1951.

290. SHNEIDMAN, EDWIN S.; WITH THE COLLABORATION OF WALTHER JOEL AND KENNETH B. LITTLE. *Thematic Test Analysis.* Chapters by Magda Arnold, Betty Aron, Leopold Bellak, Leonard Eron, Reuben Fine, A. Arthur Hartman, Robert R. Holt, Walther Joel, David Shapiro, Seymour Klebanoff, Sheldon Korchin, Jose J. Lagasa, Julian B. Rotter, Shirley Jessor, Helen D. Sargent, Percival M. Symonds, and Ralph K. White. Foreword by Henry A. Murray. New York: Grune & Stratton, Inc., 1951. Pp. xi, 320. * *(PA 26:3422)*

291. SMITH, JACKSON A.; BROWN, WARREN T.; AND THROWER, FLORENCE L. "The Use of a Modified Thematic Apperception Test in a Neuropsychiatric Clinic in a General Hospital." *Am J Psychiatry* 107:498–500 Ja '51. * *(PA 25:8110)*

292. SMYKAL, ANTHONY, AND THORNE, FREDERICK C. "Etiological Studies of Psychopathic Personality: II, Asocial Type." Case Study. *J Clin Psychol* 7:299–316 O '51. * *(PA 26:3532)*

293. SUESSMILCH, FREDERICK L. "A Long-Term Maladjustment Culminating in Catatonic Episodes During Adolescence." Case Study. *J Proj Tech* 15:461–79 D '51. *

294. THOMPSON, CHARLES E., AND BACHRACH, ARTHUR J. "The Use of Color in the Thematic Apperception Test." *J Proj Tech* 15:173–84 Je '51. * *(PA 26:3425)*

295. VERNIER, CLAIRE M., AND KENDIG, ISABELLE V. "Analysis of the Relationships Between Various Measures of Creative Productivity in Two Projective Tests." Abstract. *Am Psychol* 6:349–50 Jl '51. *

296. WATSON, ROBERT I. Chap. 16, "The Thematic Apperception Test," pp. 436–523. In his *The Clinical Method in Psychology.* New York: Harper & Bros., 1951. Pp. xii, 770. *

297. WEBSTER, HAROLD D., JR. *The Prediction of Personality Data From Thematic Apperception Test Scores.* Doctor's thesis, University of California (Berkeley, Calif.). 1951.

298. WEISSKOPF, EDITH A., AND DIEPPA, JORGE J. "Experimentally Induced Faking of TAT Responses." *J Consult Psychol* 15:469–74 D '51. * *(PA 26:7017)*

299. WITTENBORN, J. R., AND ERON, L. D. "An Application of Drive Theory to TAT Responses." *J Consult Psychol* 15:45–50 F '51. * *(PA 26:6308)*

ARTHUR L. BENTON, *Professor of Psychology, State University of Iowa, Iowa City, Iowa.*

In the *Third Mental Measurements Yearbook,* appraisals of this instrument were generally favorable. However, at least two of the reviews carried the implication that the clinical utility of the test lay in the opportunity for evaluation both of the specific productions and of general behavior which it afforded the experienced clinician rather than in any distinctive merits it possessed as an objective psychodiagnostic instrument. Thus Rotter concluded that "the TAT cannot be considered as a clinical instrument apart from the person who uses it. The value, significance, nature, and validity of the tests are dependent upon the interpreter, his experience, and his approach to the field of personality." And the present reviewer commented that "the general validity of the test is fairly well established if one means that in the hands of a competent examiner the test data permit true, meaningful inferences. At the present time the greatest hindrance to its usefulness is the lack of normative data on the test productions."

Recent research on the test has been devoted both to the problem of making it a more objective procedure and to communicating clinical experience with it. Shorr (*146*) proposes a new scoring system which apparently possesses a high degree of inter-examiner agreement and which apparently yields data amenable to statistical treatment. Lyon,[1] after reviewing different systems of interpretation (Murray, Wyatt, Henry, and Lasaga), illustrates his own procedure which is more or less a blend of previous systems. Stein (*147*) offers a useful manual for the test's administration and interpretation. Aron (*154*) presents a new, highly developed scoring system which is objective in character and which is supported by preliminary evidence suggesting clinical validity. In an experimental study, Hartman (*161*) demonstrates that many TAT categories are significantly related to clinically important personality variables.

That the *Thematic Apperception Test* enjoys wide use in clinical facilities is undeniable. Yet, one has the impression that for the most part it is extensively utilized only in those setups where the psychologist's functions are restricted to diagnostic testing with evaluative interviewing and psychotherapy being the province of the psychiatrist and the psychiatric social worker. Indeed, even the friendly observer cannot escape the impression that in many instances the utilization of this rather tedious and time-consuming tech-

[1] Lyon, Charles Aldunate. "Étude Critique du Thematic Apperception Test." *Psyché* 3:1108–24 '48 *(PA 23:4827)*

nique serves no purpose that could not be accomplished more efficiently by personal interview. This implies that the TAT has no special merits, i.e., that it does not provide data which are not readily elicitable in other situations and that the data it does provide are no more objective than ordinary interview data. Happily, the indications of the newer investigative work are that both implications are unwarranted. There is real promise that, with the development of useful scoring systems, such as that of Aron, and the establishment of empirically verified principles of interpretation, the test will achieve distinctive value as a psychodiagnostic instrument.

For reviews by Arthur L. Benton, Julian B. Rotter, and J. R. Wittenborn and an excerpt from a review, see 3:103; for related reviews, see 137–41, 3:104, and 3:104a.

[137]

★[*Re* Thematic Apperception Test.] Bellak TAT Blank. Ages 7 and over; 1947; a form for recording and analyzing responses to the *Thematic Apperception Test;* $1.10 per 10; $1.50 per 100 analysis sheets; 35¢ per manual; 60¢ per specimen set; postpaid; Leopold Bellak; Psychological Corporation. *

J Consult Psychol 12:126 Mr–Ap '48. Except for almost blank pages for recording and for final summary, the Bellak TAT blank consists entirely of the analysis page, which provides a check-list differing considerably from the method introduced by Murray. The 14 components of the analysis are: main theme, main hero, attitudes to superior figures and to society, figures introduced, objects introduced, objects omitted, attribution of blame, significant conflicts, punishment for crime, attitude to hero, signs of inhibition, outcome, pattern of need gratification, and structure of plot. The manual gives directions for the administration of the TAT, and describes the scoring categories.

[138]

★Thematic Apperception Test: Thompson Modification. Negroes ages 7 and over; 1949; individual; 1 form; no data on reliability and validity; no norms; $6 per set of testing materials; cash orders postpaid; nontimed (120) minutes; Charles E. Thompson; Harvard University Press. (Oxford University Press, London: 1949; 32s. 6d.)

REFERENCES
1. THOMPSON, CHARLES E. *A Modification of the Murray Thematic Apperception Test.* Doctor's thesis, Tulane University (New Orleans, La.), 1949. Pp. 58. (*Abstracts of Theses 1949,* pp. 32–5.)
2. THOMPSON, CHARLES E. "The Thompson Modification of the Thematic Apperception Test." *Rorsch Res Exch & J Proj Tech* 13:469–78 D '49. (PA 24:3743)
3. KORCHIN, SHELDON J.; MITCHELL, HOWARD E.; AND MELTZOFF, JULIAN. "A Critical Evaluation of the Thompson Thematic Apperception Test." *J Proj Tech* 14:445–52 D '50. *
4. RIESS, BERNARD F.; SCHWARTZ, EMANUEL K.; AND COTTINGHAM, ALICE. "An Experimental Critique of Assumptions

Underlying the Negro Version of the TAT." *J Abn & Social Psychol* 45:700–9 O '50. * (PA 25:2466)
5. SCHWARTZ, EMANUEL K.; RIESS, BERNARD F.; AND COTTINGHAM, ALICE. "Further Critical Evaluation of the Negro Version of the TAT." *J Proj Tech* 15:394–400 S '51. *

Am J Orthopsychiatry 21:208 Ja '51. Eugenia Hanfmann. * the author....concludes that identification is likely to be greatest when the pictorial material reflects the culture of the individual. Regardless of whether this conclusion is justified in this generalized form, it is certainly advantageous to have a parallel series available for further experimentation in this field. In comparing the results of the two series it is essential to keep in mind that the redrawn pictures differ from the original ones not only in regard to the race of the figures, but also in some other detail. In particular the change of color of the figures from light to dark often necessitates the change of background from dark to light, which in some cards modifies considerably the immediate emotional effect produced by the scene. *

Brit J Med Psychol 24:79–80 pt 1 '51. H. Phillipson. * This modification, which is extremely well drawn and produced, sets a pattern for TAT pictures of use in testing minority cultural groups within a white culture. The social situation and the objective environment of the picture limits their usefulness with other "negro" groups. With the T-TAT is published a very brief manual adapted and abridged from the manual accompanying the original TAT. There is no mention in the manual of the effect of the "white" examiner in the test situation, except in general terms of rapport which means friendliness and encouragement, or in the case of difficult children the promise of a present. One feels also that there is too much emphasis on the usefulness of TAT as a method of getting material "in spite of the patient"—which suggests that the author may be making too little use of the "therapeutic situation" in clinical testing to supply the motivation for good co-operation by the subject.

J Consult Psychol 13:311 Ag '49. * The author's clinical impression is that richer records are secured from Negro subjects by the use of the new cards. A further suggestion might be the use of the two sets of cards to explore racial attitudes.

[139]

★[*Re* Thematic Apperception Test.] ARON, BETTY. A Manual for Analysis of the Thematic Apperception Test: A Method and Technique for Personality Research. Foreword by R. Nevitt Sanford. Berkeley, Calif.: Willis E. Berg, 1949. Pp. xiii, 163. Lithotyped. $3.50. * (PA 24:644)

J Clin Psychol 6:106 Ja '50. * an important contribution, both theoretically and in terms of practical clinical applications.

J Consult Psychol 13:381 O '49. Laurance F. Shaffer. Since its first appearance fourteen years ago, the TAT has remained an elusive technique, despite its wide use. Although Murray originally proposed a somewhat quantifiable scoring in terms of needs and presses, many users have preferred a "global" or "intuitive" interpretation. The apparent unsatisfactoriness of the original scoring might be due to either of two defects: that it is faulty in principle, or that it is insufficiently elaborated and developed. Miss Aron's work supports the latter hypothesis. Her manual presents a further development of the Murray-Sanford scoring of content, which may be checked for scoring reliability, and which permits the quantitative comparison of individuals and groups, a first step toward experimental validation. Although complicated and not rapid, the scoring technique is clear enough to be mastered, and is at least practicable for research. As yet, the research procedures do not permit statistical tests of significance, which may lead to unjustified conclusions. For example, in one of Miss Aron's sample research studies, she concludes that "a general decrease in expression is found at the pre-puberty stage," on the basis of a lowered output in three out of four groups of children 11 to 12 years old, numbering 4 or 5 in each group. Any step of true research in the projective field is encouraging, as is Miss Aron's study, but much of the path of progress lies ahead.

TAT Newsletter 4:1–5 su '50. Robert R. Holt. The greatest single obstacle to the wider use of the TAT is the lack of a scoring system comparable to Rorschach's in simplicity, the ease with which it may be learned and applied, and in the significance of the distinctions it makes. It seems unlikely that such a system will ever be worked out, due to differences in the kinds of data yielded by the two tests; in spite of the anchoring effect of the pictures, the TAT story has (so to speak) many more degrees of freedom than the Rorschach response, whence its peculiar combination of richness and impalpability. It is no discredit to Miss Aron, therefore, to say that her book does not succeed in providing the philosopher's stone. Just what ores, precious or base, are locked within the stonily forbidding difficulties of her method it is difficult to say on the basis of merely reading her book. It would be necessary to learn and to apply the system she outlines, and preferably to compare the differentiations it yields to those afforded by other methods of analyzing stories. Judging from its careful, psychologically-based construction and from the suggestive results of the sample studies she reports, it is well worth such a trial by those interested in personality research. As the subtitle explicitly states, this is a method for research and the author is careful to make it clear that she does not expect much immediate clinical application of it. She is careful throughout to avoid sweeping claims, and she does not underestimate the difficulties of the way she is pointing. It is presented as having gone through enough stages of revision to be shared with other workers, while still further revisions will be made. It is as a working document, oriented toward research, that it will be evaluated here. It is too bad that a method of the importance I believe this one will prove to have, had to be presented with such a constant eye to economy. That probably accounts for the book's over-brevity. In about a hundred pages of text, Miss Aron presents in a condensed manner an explanation of the steps through which a scorer must go to use her system; she lists and defines the many variables used and the notations that modify them in ways indicated above as well as a few others; she gives fifteen stories drawn from quite different populations of subjects, with complete scoring; she describes certain technical procedures for recording and summarizing the scores and concludes with detailed citation of four "sample studies" which illustrate the kinds of data provided by the system and the kinds of interpretations that can be made on their basis. It seems to me that 100 pages is too narrow a compass within which to attempt so much, though she wastes little of the space. There are seven steps through which the scorer goes. First, he sets down on a worksheet an abbreviation designating each character or object in the study to which any variable is attributed— including "The Environment," if necessary. Each such notation is put at the head of a column, in which are listed all variables relevant to it. Second, the scorer identifies the hero or heroes. Third, he reads through the story, noting all variables under the appropriate columns. When a striving is the hero's, it is *need;* when it is someone else's, it is recorded as *press.* Fourth, "the source of complementary variables, i.e., the source of the precipitating press or the precipitated need, is recorded in front of the variable in question." Fifth, note is made (by the symbols for kinds of defenses) of the ways scorable trends are described when not freely expressed by the hero. Sixth, the scorer assigns numerical "intensity values" to each variable in the main story content. Finally, he records the outcome of each episode. It is clear, from this description, that the technique has certain limitations, most of which are admitted. It deals only with content, deliberately leaving the question of formal aspects aside, for the most part. It is somewhat atomistic, in that each dynamically meaningful subpart of a story is scored separately, yet with an ingenious system of notations that preserves many of the important aspects of its context. Miss Aron started out to revise the Murray-Sanford method of scoring needs and press to make it more useful, and she found that it could be simplified only by making it more complex. The many clinicians who have dismissed Murray's approach as impracticable will undoubtedly feel the same way about this one when they spy the scores of distinctions that are now required, and will go back to their global, intuitive analyses. For daily clinical use, they are quite justified, but if this attitude is expressed by a researcher, he can only be advised to choose a less complex field of inquiry than is personality. To do justice to the multifariousness of human motives, a handful of concepts simply will not do. Those familiar with the Murray-Sanford system of analyzing TAT stories will recognize only the second, third, sixth and (to some extent) seventh steps as carry-overs. In modifying the older scoring method, the author says that she was guided by both theoretical and empirical considerations: the distinctions made were those suggested by psychoanalysis and by Murray's personology, but when they could not be reliably scored by different raters they were changed until they could be, or were dropped. How is one to evaluate the changes? The ultimate test can only be an empirical one: the demonstration that the new system differentiates better between groups known to be diversely constituted psychologically, or that the new quantitative scores correlate more highly with indices of known validity—in each case, as compared to the earlier system, or as compared to any other scoring schemes (for example, Wyatt's or Henry's). One gets the impression that the failure of the Murray-Sanford scoring to differentiate prejudiced groups in the Berkeley Public Opinion Study was responsible for the changes, and that the revision did provide good differentiation. But in the present book Miss Aron tells us nothing of all this, possibly because she has discussed it in her chapter in the forthcoming report of the total research project on which she was working, *The Authoritarian Personality.* Some citation of results from the studies of anti-semitism would have helped the present book, nevertheless. In the lack of empirical data, then, the modification will have to be evaluated on theoretical bases and by rule of thumb. I think that the first modification—recording the figures and objects to and from which dynamic trends emanate and are directed—is prima facie an excellent one. In totalling the scores for Nurturance in mother-son stories (card 6BM), for example, it is desirable to be able to separate the son's nurturance towards the mother from the mother's towards the son. In large part, this distinction is made by differentiating needs and press, but even so it is often lost. The second major innovation sounds like a valuable one, too: the introduction of special notations to record certain kinds of defenses that operate in relation to the trends expressed: conflict, denial, rejection (i.e., unacceptability), displacement of identification (which includes a special notation, *f*, for fantasy, memory, wish or dream instead of action) and "restriction of ego expression by describing static [i.e., characterological] features rather than behavior" of a figure. The exact psychological significance of all these defenses is not easy to determine, but research on this problem should be well worth the doing. A further contribution of the present manual is that it provides relatively objective and understandable criteria for performing some of the more judgmental aspects of scoring: identifying the hero, and especially quantifying ratings of the intensity of needs and press. Regrettably, it does not do so well in defining and making clear the differences between all of the variables used. Miss Aron's suggestions about procedures to be used in research are knowing and helpfully concrete. A further set of differences from Murray is in the specific variables used. Here my prejudices and preferences do not always agree with the author's. The additions of *p Blamavoidance, p Infavoidance* and *n Blamescape* (the latter from Sanford) sound good to me, and I think little was lost by dropping *n Exposition,* and (for many purposes) *n Excitance.* But why no *n Nutriance* (the taking of food and drink)? Why no *n Passivity?* These are often very significant features of TAT stories. Likewise, I should have retained the distinction of *n Aggression: Destruction* from *n Aggression: Physical:* as it is, the same score is given when the hero fights with somebody and when he smashes his car in an auto accident—events with quite different significance. Combining *n Order, n Achievement* and *n Construction* under the last heading loses frequently useful distinctions. A few other minor criticisms may be levelled at specific variables: in addition to the "endogenous benefit" of Mental Health, there is another called Mental Health-Intelligence, which is scored for any kind of talent. With the present headings, one would get into an absurd fix trying to score the statement: "The boy is bright though rather neurotic." Then, it seems forced, to say the least, to score thinking, planning, and studying as "Mental Sentience" and then to combine it, in summarizing, with other "sensory aspects of behavioral trends"—physical, sexual and esthetic sentience! These are not basic objections, by any means. If they have weight, they can be incorporated into a revision of the Aron scheme which would not change it in principle to the slightest extent. The same is true of other minor criticisms that might be made of the book itself, which contains a rather annoying number of typographical errors. Only one of them is of much consequence: on pp. 79–84 and 136–141, the good old boy-and-violin that has always led off is persistently called Card 7 instead of Card 1. The book could have been further improved by the addition of a sorely-needed glossary for the great number of new abbreviations. To conclude these minor criticisms, I cannot resist the temptation to point out a rather funny "interpretation" of the shortcomings in the pioneering efforts of two practising psychoanalysts, Murray and Sanford, to quantify dynamic content: they, "like many other personality psychologists who have been influenced by research with lower animals, tended to overlook mechanisms, many of which are specific to man, that make for a vast range of personality differences!" Whenever a complex scheme for the analysis of qualitative data is proposed, the interested researcher may well ask about "observer reliability"—how well do different scorers agree? It is not easy to answer such a question when one's system contains so many dimensions of variability. Miss Aron has approached the problem with the intent of finding one or two measures that will demonstrate

the overall reliability of the method. This is an essentially defensive approach, and its results in this case are not very helpful. By a complicated system of rating all differences between raters, she arrives at a set of overall figures which claims from 69% to 85% "complete agreement," on different samples, with from 9% to 12% full errors. But it cannot be concluded that these figures mean that two raters assign identical scores a majority of the time. Many differences are considered to be "no difference," because they have approximately the same interpretative significance—which makes one want to ask, why make such distinctions in the first place, then? Other differences are considered separately as "lack of acuity" on the part of one rater: where one rater scores something that the other simply failed to see. The result of using this method of reporting reliability is to make anyone who has a skeptical turn of mind suspect that there was not actually a very high degree of agreement on many categories, especially considering the fact that the scorers had been trained and closely supervised by the author. It is quite sensible and legitimate to distinguish between differences that are serious and those that are less so, but it would have been much better to have kept separate the actual agreements and the insignificant differences. And, of course, overall reliability doesn't mean much in such a system; the important question about reliability is: *which ones* of the many discriminations called for can be made with a satisfactory degree of agreement, which ones are difficult or impossible to make? Improvement of the method demands the latter approach. As far as validity is concerned, we get a number of encouraging hints in the chapter on Sample Studies, but nothing definite. Of course, the problem of validating such a method as Miss Aron's is a very thorny one. But it would have been more convincing to have enlarged the N on one or two of the four miniature studies so that a few significant differences between groups could have been reported instead of a larger number of interesting, often plausible, but very possibly unreliable trends. What the chapter does show is that the method yields quantitative group results that lend themselves easily to psychodynamic interpretations with a minimum of far-fetched inferences. This fact alone is a weighty endorsement of the Aron method as a promising research instrument. Looking back, I see that I have found more to criticize than to blame. Yet I feel that the criticisms are mostly minor, the good points mostly major, and that in the balance Miss Aron has made a contribution of solid importance to research with the TAT.

[140]

★[Re Thematic Apperception Test.] Stein, Morris I. The Thematic Apperception Test: An Introductory Manual for Its Clinical Use With Adult Males. Foreword by James G. Miller. Cambridge, Mass.: Addison-Wesley Press, Inc., 1948. Pp. viii, 95. Lithotyped. $3.00. * (PA 22:4959)

Am J Psychiatry 106:945 Je '50. Helen Thompson. * a welcome publication * The techniques of administering and analysing the test are succinctly, clearly, yet fully outlined * This compact, concise book should prove valuable to all students of clinical psychology whether in formal course instruction or in self-education. For the psychiatrist who does not have available the services of a psychologist, it might be a helpful guide to the use of the TAT in his own practice for both diagnostic and therapeutic work.

Int J Psycho-Analysis 30:209–10 pt 3 '49. Joseph Sandler. * There is an obvious parallel between the interpretation of the T.A.T. phantasies and the interpretation of dreams. On this account T.A.T. analysis should be of theoretical interest to the psycho-analyst, and indeed Murray's need-theory, on which the test is based, deserves a little more attention from psychoanalysts. On the other hand, precisely because of the closeness between T.A.T. interpretation and dream productions, the psycho-analyst must regard any T.A.T. manual in rather the same light as a manual of dream analysis designed for the use of non-analysed, and perhaps non-analytical, psychologists. The T.A.T. is perhaps the best of the projective tests, in terms of usefulness to the psycho-analyst, and Stein's manual should prove as valuable as the two other books reviewed here.

J Abn & Social Psychol 44:429–31 Jl '49. Roy Schafer. * in the main, a bold and praiseworthy effort to meet the greatly increased demand for training by providing a supervisory conference for mass consumption. The last 41 pages of this 91-page manual are taken up with a detailed, sentence-by-sentence analysis of a complete verbatim TAT record. The presentation of the analytic process is easy, clear reading with an adventurous quality: Expectations (hypotheses) are stimulated, subsequently strengthened, discouraged, qualified, amplified, and integrated, and slowly and surely a living personality takes shape before us. The author's reasoning is never flashy or obscure, but rather is cautious, modest, sensitive, and conscientious. (It may be mentioned here, however, that despite his strong warning to the contrary, the author himself makes historical predictions that often seem far too concrete and specific; this is evident in the summary of his test analysis on pages 87–90.) If Stein could have published 20 such analyses, using a representative variety of clinical cases, he would have given us a true manual for the TAT; his present volume, because it takes up only one case in detail, can be considered only introductory. A further limitation on this level is the restriction of the entire discussion to only the set of 20 pictures administered to adult males. Stein....provides concrete, helpful examples from actual stories to illustrate how each of the press and need variables may be expressed. There follows a brief supplementary chapter on dynamically significant formal—as opposed to content —aspects of the test responses. (This topic should have been treated more fully, since formal aspects of stories are crucial in locating and identifying significant needs, conflicts, and goals; in the lengthy case discussion, Stein makes liberal use of these formal, non-content indications.) Finally, before the case discussion, there is a three-page discussion of "syndrome or cluster analysis." It is here that Stein will be most disappointing to his readers, for syndrome analysis is nothing but the construction of an integrated personality picture from the fragmentary hypotheses suggested by single themes, perceptions, and significant verbalizations; and the construction of an integrated personality picture is the stumbling block that persists longer in the development of skillful handling of the TAT than any other. A discussion of how to establish need-hierarchies is missing; the presentation of the Murray need-press orientation does not help for it unfortunately has a catalog quality and not a hierarchic quality. For example, n Sex and n Aggression are listed as if they had the same depth, breadth, and genetic significance as n Playmirth, and n Change, Travel, and Adventure. Stein thinks hierarchically in his case discussion but does not instruct his reader how to do so, beyond emphasizing frequency, intensity, and duration of expression of need in the stories as keys to the place of the needs in the subject's hierarchy. Actually, however, these aspects of need expression tell us more about the subject's present picture of his need-hierarchy, how he experiences or is able to communicate his needs, and may not be dynamically accurate. Here is where the main outlines of the Freudian psychoanalytic theory or personality dynamics could have been of great help to Stein as a teacher—for they do implicitly help him when, as a clinician, he grapples with concrete case material. Psychoanalytic findings and theory have to a great extent centered on this problem of need-hierarchy or "psychic structure." Particularly clarifying would have been invoking the distinction between deep-lying needs and defenses against these needs, a distinction that Stein treats rather casually. When interpreting a TAT story, or any clinical material for that matter, we must answer the question, "Does this material express a consciously accepted need, a rejected and to some degree unconscious need, or a defense against an unconscious need?" Many subjects tell us much more about their defenses in their TAT stories than about deeper-lying needs which they cannot integrate with their preferred self-image. The intensively discussed case, for example, again and again shows how he continually tries to resist consciously acknowledging to himself and to others his very strong dependent needs. (Stein points this out in his final summary interpretation, but gives no real place to this aspect of personality dynamics in his previous rationale of interpretation.) Often the underlying need does not show itself at all clearly and we can infer its presence and strength only by the rigidity and overemphasis on the defenses commonly associated with it—for example, denial of and reaction formation against hostility. Often we see little more than the defensive structure with little idea about the underlying needs. The play of intra-psychic forces is, then, not only indicated in the stories, as is Stein's chief assertion in this connection, but they also select and shape, and thereby *limit*, the content of the very stories themselves. Limitations of content can be understood in terms of ego-defenses and the scope of interpretations is thereby broadened beyond the limits of the Murray approach. It is not implied here that a manual adequately incorporating psychoanalytic insights can now be written by anyone; this is a task waiting on much more research and conceptual analysis. The crucial role of the ego in the perceptual-associative interplay that goes into the development of stories has yet to be studied. But Stein might have advised the student more fully as to where the answers to the problems of integration of inferences might most hopefully be sought. Never-

theless this little volume is well worth careful study by the beginning TAT worker.

J Consult Psychol 13:147 Ap '49. Laurance F. Shaffer. A brief manual, giving a condensed but well-illustrated account of the Harvard Psychological Clinic's method of administering, analyzing and interpreting the TAT. * The use of the TAT has remained an art rather than a science, depending more on a broad knowledge of personality and on clinical insights than on distinctive methods of scoring. For the student who already has some grasp of dynamic psychology, Stein's manual seems an economical and sufficient introduction to the TAT, to be enriched more by further clinical experience than by additional psychometric complications of the technique itself.

J Mental Sci 96:549–50 Ap '50. Ralph Hetherington. * Stein's introductory manual....is rather disappointing since its data are confined to adult males * As well as analysing the intra-individual material, the author suggests that comparisons between individuals might be of value with the caveat that the former type of comparison has the greater value. He provides a "common story" for each of the 20 pictures for men. These stories are "based on clinical experience" and it would be of great interest to learn the method used to arrive at these common stories. This is of vital importance if they are to be used in any way as norms, but the author does not apparently regard them as such, but simply intends that they should stand as examples of the type of material that may be expected from the use of the test. It seems that an opportunity has been missed. If a thoroughly systematic method of arriving at the common story had been employed, it would have been possible to make more exact comparisons between individuals. In other words, some kind of standardization would have been achieved. This would have enhanced the usefulness of the test. * A sample protocol is analysed and intercepted to illustrate the technique. Clinicians will note that this analysis of a single case covers 40 pages of the book, and the patient's first remarks: "Well, first of all,...." and "as far as I'm concerned,...." take two pages for their interpretation! The author states, however, that this analysis is more detailed than would normally be necessary, since he has endeavoured to include all the possible steps in the procedure in order to illustrate the method. It is interesting that the author suggests a blind analysis of the protocol should be undertaken, that is, that no more of the patient should be known than his age, sex, occupation, marital status, whether he has any siblings and whether his parents are living or dead. This book will not be as useful as the more comprehensive manual the author has promised us.

J Nerv & Mental Dis 110:263 S '49. (Zygmunt A.) Piotrowski. * The author, less restrained than Murray, makes the assumption that "the same set of principles which are utilized in analyzing and interpreting daily behavior may be utilized in working with the TAT material." It seems doubtful that words can be treated as actions. This assumption appears to be an evasion rather than a solution of the problem to what degree the TAT reflects overt behavior and to what extent it gives fantasies that are not acted out.

TAT Newsletter 2:4–7 Ag '48. Robert R. Holt. In a compact little volume, Dr. Stein has given the beginning student of the TAT a very valuable manual which will set his feet properly on the path to effective professional use of the test. He does not pretend to have furnished an exhaustive or complete monograph, but explicitly states that it is limited to the application of twenty cards to the testing of one population, adult males. The author is also careful to state that the book is not for beginners in psychology; "it is designed as a manual for those who have had some training in the analysis of personality and who are adequately oriented towards clinical practise." Taken for what it is, then, the manual is the best book I know of for the clinician who knows something about his trade but who needs an introduction to the TAT. Murray's and Bellak's otherwise excellent pamphlets are too brief for the purpose; Rapaport's chapter in Vol. II of *Diagnostic Psychological Testing* is on a level of technical complexity suited to the more advanced worker, and Tomkins' book, like Aron's forthcoming manual, presents a system primarily oriented towards research rather than clinical practise. Written in a clearly structured way—at times it is almost an outline, stripped of everything but essential points—the book actually contains a good deal more than its short length would suggest. In successive chapters, there are descriptions of the pictures and stories most often told to them, a good summary of the main points to be learned about administration, some general comments on the technique of analysis with a presentation of a list of variables useful in approaching the stories,

two short chapters describing the method and materials of interpretation, and finally a complete protocol with a blow-by-blow account of how it was analyzed and interpreted. A few comments are in order on each chapter. Dr. Stein notes that his accounts of the typical stories yielded by each picture and the kinds of problems that each touches on are based on his own clinical experience. He points out the need for research to determine the "popular" stories for each picture, and the slight discrepancies between his experience and that of others underlines this need. In my experience, for example, it is *not* "usually said that the figure at the window (in card 14) is spending a sleepless night." Fortunately, the attention of researchers is turning to this problem, and after the central file of TAT stories has been set up it will not be a very difficult matter to solve it. Meanwhile, statements of experience such as the one given here, for Set D, and by Rapaport for Set B, are useful. In the chapter on administration, most of the familiar rules and admonitions are repeated in a clear, succinct manner. In addition there is an excellent discussion of the various possible methods of recording, with the pros and cons of each. About inquiry there seem to be two rather distinct schools of thought and practise, to one of which Stein and Tomkins belong, while the other is mainly composed of Rapaport and his students. The former method is one of considerable caution, particularly with respect to what Stein calls "intermittent inquiry." One who has tried both methods may get the impression that this caution is really timidity, or that it is based only on the acknowledged fact that clumsy inquiry while the test is going on can disrupt the situation and invalidate the results just as much in the case of the TAT as with any other test. It is possible, nevertheless, to develop skill in non-directive inquiry so that the usefulness of the total material obtained is considerably enhanced. The example given of pushing a patient too hard is indeed a lesson in how not to inquire, but the same situation could have been handled adequately, without abandoning inquiry until the end of the test, at which time the various chains of thought have been broken. One additional (rather petty) point: I have yet to see anyone bring forward *evidence* that inquiry about sources of stories yields anything of value; likewise for the procedures recommended here of choosing which pictures are liked and disliked, which are remembered, or other flourishes. I know it is hard to produce convincing evidence on such matters and I concede that my criticism is a little unfair, but I still think the reader is entitled to see something more than just the assertion that such procedures "frequently yield valuable data." Students of the test would be better advised to stick to essentials and master straight administration and interpretation; thereafter they can experiment with variations which in the early stages will only confuse things. The author begins his discussion of the technique of analysis by a sensible discussion of diagnosis vs. label-giving, with a warning against trying to predict symptoms. The last point could have been made a little more strongly. It too often happens that clinical psychologists play games with themselves and psychiatrists, particularly when they practise "blind analysis," amazing everyone with their cleverness in deducing from tests which take hours to administer simple information which can be obtained in five minutes' direct questioning. Not only will the psychologist err often when he tries to "predict" the presence of an ulcer, or a particular obsession, or what not, but he will be wasting his time and missing the point of the kind of contribution that he can make to the study of the patient. All of which raises the point of blind diagnosis. Stein presents the main points in favor of it: it gives an independent judgment on the case, the tester will often notice aspects of the case which would have been overlooked if he had approached it with a preconception (I think this is the point being made, though it is not clear); and doing blind analysis sharpens the psychologist's wits and perceptions for the many times when he does have to work in more or less ignorance about the patient. These and similar arguments are valid in support of doing considerable blind testing as training, and doing it under special circumstances, but not for making it regular practise. A psychiatrist who is secure enough in his own methods of studying the patient can get more out of a psychologist's services when he tells the latter what is established about the patient and enables the psychologist to use these data in interaction with his test findings to yield information and hypotheses about areas that are unclear or inaccessible to him. * Another implication of the position taken by Stein seems to be that one should analyze the TAT without reference to other psychological tests, though he does not say so in so many words. Such a procedure is again good training, but not good clinical practise. A TAT is often much more meaningful in light of the Rorschach and Szondi results, which can help a good deal to establish, for example, what is overt and what is repressed, or whether a stimulus-bound stereotypy is organic or depressive in nature. It is clear that the author operates in such a way himself; it is a pity that he does not discuss the use of the TAT in a battery of tests. The assumptions underlying his technique of analysis, the author states next, are that people reveal much about themselves in telling stories ostensibly about others, and that the people, situations, and problems in the stories are the same as those in everyday life. From these he draws the quite acceptable conclusion that the same principles and variables used to analyze real behavior should be used in test interpretation, and the rather surprising one that "the patient telling the story should be regarded as participating in or having participated in the situations described." That this is merely an unclear wording of his meaning is immediately plain when he warns in the next paragraph against the common error of too-literal interpretation. What is lacking in the quoted statement is an addition such as the following: "on some level of generalization: principally, with respect to the emotionally meaningful aspects of these situations." The trickiness of the TAT lies in the very fact that sometimes stories are direct autobiography (the subject really was helped by his parents in a career as violinist, as the story says); sometimes they need to be generalized only in minor aspects (the parents did help him along in his career, though the subject didn't study the violin); sometimes the story represents a wishful fantasy of situations the subject *never* experienced in reality (he was really an orphan and always longed for such helpful parents): or it may be related to a conscious plan (the subject has a son of his own and intends to help *him* along). We are given a list of principles which help in avoiding over-literalism and in finding the appropriate level on which a story holds true of its author. To it however might be added Tomkins' concepts of the *level* of action, and the *remoteness* of the picture or of the setting; also the subject's apparent attitude of acceptance or rejection of the action in question, and its consistency with inferences drawn from other stories and from other tests. The list of factors (variables) involved in clinical analysis, is straight out of the tradition of the mimeographed manuals by Murray, Sanford, White and Bellak. Press, needs, cathexes (including attitudes and sentiments), inner states, "the manner in which the behavior is expressed" (Tomkins' *levels*), and outcomes, all from the standpoint of the hero—these are old friends, dressed here in simple but becoming garb. The specific factors (e.g., p Aggression: Physical, Social) are defined and illustrated by quotations from actual stories. Stein states straightforwardly that these factors are useful chiefly in training, so that one may become sensitized to all of the important aspects in the stories, and that in clinical practice they are used quite informally and unsystematically. A short chapter takes up succinctly additional (non-contentual) factors to be studied: the patient's behavior during the test, the use of time sequence and emphasis on different temporal epochs, aspects of the patient's perceptual response to the picture, and other formal characteristics of the TAT performance. The section on the use of language is good as far as it goes, but it is disappointingly brief. A potentially rich vein of ore has here been little more than scratched. The definitive treatment of formal aspects of the TAT is still that of Rapaport, Schafer and Gill. The section on symbolism, however, is something not found in most other sources, and is quite good. Symbolism here refers to the interpretation of certain stories according to psychoanalytic symbol-translation, not the conscious use of symbolism by the subject in his stories (a matter which is not discussed). A three-page chapter on the technique of interpretation illustrates with examples the basic principles of abstracting similar elements from a number of different stories to reach a conclusion. Most of what the book has to tell us about interpretation is contained in the final chapter; which makes up nearly half of the book. Here in great detail we are shown how the author applies all that he has told us to a concrete case.— something that Tomkins unfortunately never did. All twenty stories, with the examiner's inquiry in full, are printed on one side of the page, while a commentary of analysis and interpretation is on the other. One could wish for more such cases, illustrating a variety of nosological types, but the comments made about this one have a gratifyingly broad range of relevance to other problems. The analysis itself is a thorough and painstaking one, in which almost everything in the stories has been exploited. Every clinician will of course have his own criticisms and additions to make, as always, but they will deal with quite minor matters. The steps in the reasoning are very explicitly set forth and should be very helpful to those who are relatively unfamiliar with the test. The only criticism I would make of this chapter is that the author seems to make even less use of the need-press variables than he had led us to expect. The sceptic who has already looked with a jaundiced eye on the long list of more or less neologistic terms and their definitions that he is supposed to learn, will probably decide to skip it after reading this final chapter. I don't think that Stein has given an adequate picture of how useful the variables can be in everyday application. One closes the book with a certain sense of incompleteness. It is good that there is another manual for the TAT for this one comes closest to being a workable handbook. But it is very short—only 91 pages—and one wonders why it was not much longer. The author's ease and assurance in dealing with subtle interpretative problems in the one case given show that he has actually a great deal more of clinical experience than he has seen fit to share with us here. We are promised further publications dealing with "the application of the technique to the variety of cases that are encountered in clinical practise." Meanwhile, however, the reader is likely to get the impression that the TAT is useful only in affording descriptions of personality and dynamic formulations (important though they are). After he has mastered this practical and sound introduction, he will do well to go on to Rapaport's *Diagnostic Psychological Testing* if he wishes to use the test in clinical diagnostic practise, to Tomkin's *The Thematic Apperception Test* if he is interested more in research and the finer analysis of personality in normal and neurotic subjects.

[141]

[*Re* Thematic Apperception Test.] TOMKINS, SILVAN S.; WITH THE COLLABORATION OF ELIZABETH J. TOMKINS. **The Thematic Apperception Test: The Theory and Technique of Interpretation.** New York: Grune & Stratton, Inc., 1947. Pp. xi, 297. $5.00. * (*PA* 22: 1658)

Am J Med Sci 216:716 D '48. E. B. * a careful, systematic approach * Most clinicians should find the method of TAT analysis found here quite useful. The author begins with an all-too-brief history of the development of the test, mentioning only vaguely its relation to other projective techniques and to the concept of mental testing in general. He then proceeds with a discussion of reliability and validity, largely in terms of statistical coefficients, derivation of which is left entirely to the reader's imagination or to his enterprise in looking up the references given. In a short chapter on administration, general instructions are given. The scoring system suggested by Tomkins is admittedly cumbersome and time-consuming and will probably prove more useful as an instrument for research than as a practical clinical tool. The elements included in the system, however, undoubtedly constitute a helpful guide and should be very useful if kept in mind while working with the test, even though most clinicians will find it inexpedient to use the system formally. * There is a distinct gap in the relationship between the scoring system and the interpretation, which seems not to depend to any great extent on quantitative findings. The bulk of the book is devoted to the problem of interpretation and includes many helpful sample stories. * One of the most valuable chapters is that devoted to "Level Analysis" in which the relation between the story and the story-teller is probed.

Am J Orthopsychiatry 18:369–70 Ap '48. Suzanne Reichard. As the first published text devoted entirely to the Thematic Apperception Test, the present volume constitutes a milestone in the development of this test. After an historical introduction the author presents his own scoring scheme which, however, is still closely wedded to Murray's system of needs and press. This is unfortunate, inasmuch as the Murray scoring has not been widely used by clinical psychologists because of two basic disadvantages; atomization of personality, and the use of a special terminology not meaningful to the other members of the clinical team—psychiatrists and social workers. For this reason the book fails to fulfill the need for an authoritative manual based on a system of interpretation communicable to all clinicians. However, in discussing actual case material, the author discards esoteric language and presents good practical interpretations of personality dynamics that are meaningful alike to the professional worker and to the layman. This is not to say that a somewhat systematized approach to the problem of interpretation lacks value. For instance, the author's application of Mill's deductive methods to the precise determination of the conditions under which a subject is likely to react in a certain manner is quite ingenious. Also his classification of themes into four main areas of life-adjustment; namely, family, love and sexual

relationships, social relationships, and work setting, makes good sense. Another valuable contribution is the use of punishment versus feelings of remorse in the stories to determine whether the superego is externalized or internalized. His concepts of "levels," "qualifiers," and "remoteness" permit subtle shadings of interpretation that might otherwise be missed. The author uses both levels of psychological function, wish versus behavior, and nearness or remoteness of time and place, as means to decide the vexed question of whether an expressed drive is overt or covert. The assumption is that if a drive is expressed as behavior in the stories, rather than as wish or dream, the chances are that the subject actually behaves this way. Unfortunately, in the reviewer's experience the relationship is not always so clear-cut. Thus stories of drunkenness are always expressed as behavior, even when told by people who do not drink to excess. In such cases one has to study the pattern in other tests in order to gain a clue as to whether the oral needs are acted out overtly as alcoholism. Perhaps the weakest aspect of this book is its failure to discuss the question of psychiatric diagnosis. In this connection we disagree with the author's belief that the relationship of the story to the picture is unimportant. It may be relatively so in dealing with a population of normals, but it is of crucial importance in the diagnosis of psychotics. In order to have an objective estimate of the amount of deviation in the subject's thinking, it is necessary to have story-norms for each of the pictures, and it is to be regretted that the author has not provided his readers with some statistically established norms of this kind. Despite certain limitations of approach, all students of TAT will find in this book a number of valuable general principles to help them in their work, and a wealth of interesting and instructive interpretations of case material.

Am J Psychiatry 105:157 Ag '48. T. W. Richards. * The author has elaborated carefully and extensively a psychology of motivation which seems to lend him a frame of reference for analyzing the stories told by subjects given the test. A scoring scheme (explained in some detail in one chapter, but generally ignored in later discussion of protocols) involves concepts of vectors, levels, and other characteristics of the stories somewhat similar to the variables Murray designated as "needs" and "press." * In four extensive chapters, discussion of TAT stories is developed in regard to "regions" of (a) the family, (b) love, sex, and marital relationships, (c) social relationships, and (d) work and vocational setting. This reviewer was impressed particularly with the author's comments regarding the family region, and with the emphasis given to the varying significance of the age of the central figure in the stories. * Throughout, the author's points are well illustrated by original protocols, and the author is to be commended for careful organization of his material according to his theoretical positions. This reviewer feels that some discussion of the TAT as but one of several projective techniques would have been pertinent. The book is well indexed and presents a good bibliography of TAT studies (though these are discussed briefly in the text).

Am J Psychol 61:439–40 Jl '48. R. M. Ogden. [The review excerpted also includes a review of *Personality* by Gardner Murphy.] * The conclusion that the "origins and structure" of personality, as conceived by Murphy, lack a definite scientific meaning, is even more insistent when we consider the contribution of the Tomkins book. This "work of one who turned from psychology to the study of philosophy" when "the theory of value seemed....an inquiry more pertinent to the study of man than did any investigation of either the higher or lower mental processes" (p. viii), is simply bewildering. Although described as "a work-book and not a compilation of established doctrine" (p. vii), the uninitiated reader might expect some concession to his ignorance of what TAT is and tries to do; especially so, when the chief author is a professed philosopher who returned to psychology after the rewarding experiences which he gained in the Harvard Psychological Clinic. One gathers, though he is never precisely told, that TAT has to do with a set of pictures about which subjects are asked to write stories. These pictures, however, are not reproduced, nor even described. Instead; the book is filled with stories by unknown persons, sometimes vaguely called "X, Y and Z." The content of the stories reveals that the same picture suggests different themes to different persons, yet no attempt is made to classify either the subjects or the themes. Instead, we are given a complicated and, to the reviewer, an incomprehensible "Scoring Scheme," followed by an "Introduction to the Technique of Interpretation" and a discussion of "Level Analysis." The four succeeding chapters are on the "Diagnosis of Personality," in which stories are recounted and discussed with reference to "The Region of the Family," "The Region of Love, Sex and Marital Relationships," "The Region of Social Relationships" and "Work and Vocational Setting." Even the final chapter of the book on "Diagnosis and Psychotherapy" fails to do more than give a few cautious suggestions for a possible application and utilization of the. method. As Murphy describes this test, along with other "projective methods," like the Rorschach, one gains an impression that they are all devised for the purpose of securing symptomatic data. When interpreted, these data serve in the same way that the knowledge and insight of a family physician, or a sympathetic parent, friend, or teacher will serve to gain understanding of human desires and motives that are often hidden or incompletely expressed by the person under examination and treatment. Yet, without a guiding philosophy of life, or at least some scheme of logically definable terms of reference, it is hard to see the use to which these data may be put. In a clinical or an educational situation where a patient or pupil is known to have certain difficulties of adjustment and achievement, the analysis of his personality and character is a primary consideration. Both formal and informal means of analysis are then indicated, and the subsequent behavior which the counselor or teacher may direct or induce can be recorded in ways that demonstrate the utility of the diagnosis and method of treatment. What one misses most in all of these books is any statement of concrete problems and their solution. Supplying, though they do, a storehouse of human vagaries, one learns very little of educational or therapeutic outcomes.

B Menninger Clinic 12:109 My '48. Rudolf Ekstein. Dr. Tomkins has done more in this volume than ably describe the test and review conscientiously 15 years of T.A.T. literature. Being one of the main contributors in research on projective techniques he has, for example, introduced a new scoring system and has deepened the meaning of the psychoanalytic concept of repression in order to adapt it to T.A.T. level analysis. His book can be looked at as a projection, a "story" response of the psychological profession, and thus shows the many different uses of the T.A.T. structure in different branches of psychological and sociological inquiry and application, in the framework of different psychological ideologies. A comparatively small part of the volume concerns itself with the use of the T.A.T. in therapy which again is perhaps a reflection of the present situation in clinical psychology. Dr. Tomkins' own efforts seem to indicate a shift in emphasis, a more useful occupation with diagnosis for therapy, with aspects of the psychotherapeutic relationship, and the problem of therapeutic change. This volume is highly recommended as a basic text and as an asset to the expert.

Digest Neurol & Psychiatry 16:580 S '48. As the first manual to be published, devoted exclusively to the Thematic Apperception Test, this book meets a long-felt need in an area of clinical psychology still at a highly experimental and fluid stage—that of statistical analysis and standardization of the qualitative material derived from projective test techniques. * If, from the chapters devoted to principles of scoring and interpretation, the reader gains the impression of a somewhat atomistic approach to the study of personality structure, this impression is agreeably dispelled in subsequent chapters where the theoretical constructs are applied to analysis of illustrative case material in the regions of the Family, of Love, Sex and Marriage, and of Work and Vocational Setting. It is this section which will probably be most rewarding to psychiatrists, for the author shows an appreciation of dynamic relationships that carries his concepts beyond the rather esoteric terms in which they are couched in earlier chapters. The author lists four college groups among the populations he has studied, and upon which, apparently, his methods of scoring and interpretation are based. The impression gained that Tomkin's case material is weighted with subjects functioning on a relatively high intellectual level is supported by the nature of the illustrative protocol reports.

J Abn & Social Psychol 43:403–6 Jl '48. Robert R. Holt. * of all the techniques for diagnosis and personality study used today, the Rorschach and TAT are the most complex, having the most to offer but making the most demands on the interpretative skill of the examiner. Popular though the TAT has become, its wider acceptance has been delayed because of the lack of a definitive book on its interpretation. In the last few years, two books have appeared which, complementing each other, have done much to fill the gap. The first was the second volume of Rapaport, Schafer, and Gill's *Diagnostic Psychological Testing,* in which a long chapter was devoted to the diagnostic use of the TAT with patients, the emphasis being primarily on the formal aspects of the stories. The second is the new volume by Tomkins, in which extended consideration is given to the analysis of the content of stories. The experience on which his book is founded, the author tells us frankly enough, has been mainly with college students. * The book contains a short section on problems of administering the test (in which he has little to add to Murray's suggestions), a proposal for a scoring scheme, and a short final section on the TAT as an adjunct to therapy; there is also an excellent short summary of most of the important literature. By far the bulk (225 pages) of Tomkins' work, however, is devoted to problems of interpretation, or diagnosis of personality. The introductory survey of literature is organized around one of the most lucid and comprehensive analyses of the problems of reliability and validity of a projective test that this reviewer has yet seen. The point is well taken that validity is "a characteristic of inferences based on the TAT rather than a characteristic of the test itself," and that it is dependent upon the maturity of the science of personality. The breadth and catholicity of outlook expressed in this chapter are admirable; unfortunately the rest of the book does not have these particular virtues to so great an extent. The scoring scheme (Chapter III) proposed by Tomkins, like some Rorschach scoring systems, seems to imply that the clinician has only one test, on which all conclusions are to be based. It is a cumbersome and unwieldy mechanism for squeezing every last drop of juice from no matter how small an orange. Each story must be rewritten to bring out the orderly sequence of ideas; each phrase is examined for the *vectors* (patterned after E. H. Erikson's more intelligible list), *levels* (e.g., behavior, wish, memory), *conditions* (e.g., lack, danger, gratuities) and *qualifiers* (e.g., temporal characteristics, intensity, contingency) expressed in it— also the *objects* of the first three classes of variables. The exposition of the method, which is applied to a simple two-sentence story, takes up over six pages, and then it is still not clear just what one does after having dissected each phrase and strung its innards up on a complex two-dimensional frame. The author is aware that no busy clinician will give his system more than a curious glance. He claims, however, that it has great merit as a training device and as a way of extracting meaning from seemingly empty stories. The first of these claims has some justification; surely it would be good practice in sensitivity to easily overlooked aspects of stories to work through a few records by this method, though the reviewer has not yet found this reward tempting enough to make him try the job. And it would be unfortunate to train a neophyte by this method only; he would later have to unlearn the language (for who is going to understand reports in terms of "a high degree of the vector 'on'"?) and readjust his perspective rather drastically. As far as the second claim is concerned, a clinical psychologist would usually be better advised to leave the refractory protocol after an hour or so of poring and turn to a variety of other techniques, some of which would circumvent the subject's resistances and in turn throw light retrospectively on the stories. If one *is* going to be exhaustive in the evaluation of stories taken alone, then there are many other approaches which can be used fruitfully, especially analysis of formal aspects, which unfortunately the book entirely ignores. A good case can be made for training in many approaches, since one of the most important things for the TAT analyst to learn is *flexibility of approach,* so that he may choose his tools to fit the nature of the job set by each unique protocol. It is perhaps the author's very neglect of the formal aspects of TAT productions that is responsible for the absence of any information about the use of the test in the diagnosis of mental disorder in the chapter on diagnosis and psychotherapy. Here the limitations of the book will be most disappointingly apparent to the diagnostic tester who has come to it for help. It is good to look, as the author does in this chapter, at the dynamics underlying an illness rather than be content just to christen it, but a less extreme rejection of current nosologies (inadequate though they are), and a balanced point of view in which dynamics and diagnosis are integrated with personality description, would have been preferable. The discussion of the TAT in therapy contains some interesting suggestions, while omitting reference to the new technique of self-interpretation. Tomkins has used this test to assess attitudes toward therapy, to elicit repressed memories, to ventilate repressed grief, and as what he calls a kind of play therapy with children. He has also used the test in psychotherapy in an experimental, exploratory way, and is com-

mendably frank in discussing and learning from his mistakes. Now for the main issue: interpretation. Tomkins' method is an ingenious and highly rational one, in constructive contrast to the usual *don't-ask-me-how-I-know-this* intuition of many "experts." He shows throughout a psychoanalytic orientation, but does not plunge into deep symbolic waters. By his circumspection in this respect he sets a good example to beginners. In each of four chapters dealing with different "regions" of personality (the family, love and sex, morality, and work) he starts by delineating the most important dimensions of the region, describing with examples the range of variation in each. He then tells us to examine the variability of each dimension —say, the intensity of a love relationship— throughout any particular set of stories, and discover to what it is causally related, according to the principles laid down in two general chapters on interpretation. In numerous case histories, the techniques are exemplified and the TAT findings checked against the clinical history. These concrete cases are among the book's most valuable features; one can only wish there were more of them, and that full protocols had been included. Interpretation is, then, primarily a means of uncovering the cause-and-effect relations that form the structure of the individual's dynamics. Tomkins is not primarily interested in assessing the strength of needs or other motivational variables, nor in discerning the ego-structure or the principal mechanisms of defense. He does not attempt, either, to get at what might be called by analogy with dream interpretation the *latent content* of the stories. Following J. S. Mill's logical rules, he describes the methods of *agreement* (in effect the proposition that if A is always accompanied by B while other things change, there is a causal relationship between them), of *difference* (if two stories are alike in all but one respect and in outcome, the latter is the effect of the former), and the method of *concomitant variation* (in effect the proposition that correlation implies cause). Used separately or in combination, these logical analytic approaches make plain the complex causal relationships that exist consciously or unconsciously in the subject's private world. There is a beautiful simplicity in this approach to interpretation which does much to remove the nimbus of false mystery that too often hovers over TAT analysis. Yet it seems to promise too much, for it is presented without any indication of its limitations. In practice, there are not always enough stories, for example, which deal with the themes one wants to understand better. Conversely, one can do much more by way of sketching a total personality picture with many TAT's than Tomkins' method would allow. In the light of Horn's findings, which Tomkins quotes in his first chapter—that only in interaction with other data, such as Rorschach's results, may the TAT be of greatest help in understanding a case—best of all would have been some cases in which the subtle interplay of reasoning back and forth from one test to another could have been expounded. The chapter on analysis of levels is a solid contribution to TAT interpretation. There is a sophisticated criticism of the assumption that quantified need-ratings from TAT stories are measures of covert strivings: many levels may be represented in the stories, and a sensitive, qualitative analysis is necessary before one can determine whether a fantasy trend is a reflection of overt behavior, conscious wish, unconscious need, or something else. Furthermore, the author gives clear and understandable criteria by which one may approach this most subtle interpretative problem with some success. The most advanced worker with the test can profit from a close reading of this chapter, with its systematic exposition of how much can be gained from careful attention to the level (that is, wish, behavior, daydream, etc.) on which dynamic trends appear. There is still the complaint to be made that it is made to seem a little too simple. Every subject, it appears, really knows and will tell you the conditions of his own happiness, for example, or of success in love or work, and you have only to look carefully in the stories to find them. Alas, the test often disappoints its staunchest adherents (as all tests do), and is silent at the point where we wish it to speak loudest; or the subject is self-deceived unconsciously as well as consciously. A section is devoted to the exposition of a revised theory of repression, and its application to TAT analysis. To oversimplify somewhat: any need may be repressed by almost any other need with which it conflicts. If the energy (called by Tomkins "pressure") of the repressing need is in considerable excess of the repressed, no serious effects will come about unless the combined energy of both makes up a large part of the total energy available to the personality. The most pathogenic conflicts

occur when both needs are strong and evenly matched, comprising between them a large proportion of the total energy. Such a conflict would be found in a prepsychotic condition. In its neglect of the problems of ego structure, of other defense mechanisms and their relations to repression and in its implications for a number of theoretical problems, this theory leaves a good deal to be desired. But as applied here to the study of unconscious conflicts by means of the TAT, it leads to impressive results. They are the more remarkable in that they require a number of highly questionable assumptions (such as that the sum of the forces manifested in 20 stories equals the total "pressure" of the personality). With all of these reservations, one must still admire, in his three illustrative cases, the way reasonably rigorous derivations are made, predictions about the nature of certain stories and the effects of special conditions are recorded and the experiments successfully carried out. Of course, much more work of this sort would be necessary to validate the procedure, but Tomkins has set future workers on the problem of repression a good example of an approach which is at the same time experimental and thoroughly dynamic. When one turns to the application of these general principles of interpretation set forth so well in Chapters IV and V to specific problems in the next four chapters, he suffers a disappointment. There is much unnecessary quoting of stories (many of them over and over, to serve different purposes) to illustrate most of the possible reactions that are so exhaustively catalogued under each "region." One might call this padding; a more serious criticism would be that the casual reader can easily get the impression that the textual remarks which preface each such quoted story are its interpretation, and that they refer to the teller of the story in some direct way. Since the reviewer fell at first into the assumption that some of these comments were deductions about the life histories of the story-tellers, it is perhaps in order to supply other readers with warnings which the author has neglected to provide in enough quantity. Other minor criticisms could be added, but taken as a whole, the book is an important and useful piece of work, and will be required reading for everyone who uses the TAT. He must not mistake it for a complete guide to the use of the test, but if he reads it in conjunction with a judicious selection of the other published TAT material, he will have most of what can be given at present by the printed word. There still is not, however, and there probably can never be, any substitute for extended clinical experience.

J Am Med Assn 137:217 My 8 '48. * clear, concise, well written * an excellent bibliography and an adequate index. The book is recommended to all those who are interested in personality study, particularly to psychologists and sociologists, who could well use this volume as a textbook for study and teaching.

J Nerv & Mental Dis 109:466–7 My '49. (Zygmunt A.) Piotrowski. * Tomkins' book is the first large and important work on the test. The methodological basis of the TAT has been scrutinized by Tomkins and modified by him; the applications and implications of his approach have been made explicit in a very thorough, consistent and lucid manner. * The author describes the precursors and the history of the TAT, the technique of administration in great detail, the scoring scheme and a very accurate procedure of interpretation. The manner of applying the test to problems of personality description, psychiatric diagnosis and therapy is fully illustrated. * Tomkins states that the determination of the relationship between story and storyteller is the keystone of TAT interpretation. He agrees with others that when stories are verbalized in the indicative mood and present tense, they are likely to reflect drives which are not repressed but are realized directly in action; on the other hand, if the stories are presented as mere probabilities, they are said to reflect unrealized or repressed drives. This can hardly be considered a satisfactory solution if for no other reason than that the vast majority of stories sound like reports of actual happenings. Inhibitions are not as rare as expressions of doubt in the TAT. In his thorough application of Mill's principles Tomkins, in many a case, unwittingly treats the stories as if they described the subject's actual behavior. This shift from phantasy production to reality description is facilitated by the author's psychological viewpoint, e.g., he states "there is no reason to doubt that the individual can project himself into the past as easily as he can divulge his present preoccupations." This optimistic belief in the ease and directness with which the attitudes of the past as well as many other tendencies allegedly are expressed in the TAT would lead to handling the TAT as a description of genuine tendencies, hardly disguised or

displaced. In spite of oversimplifications Tomkins' contribution is of great value because it makes the reader face the fundamental problems of the TAT and teaches him a great deal about the test. Even the controversial parts help the reader in clarifying his thinking. The book is a fruit of a great effort and of many years of experience.

J Proj Tech 14:321–6 S '50. Frederick Wyatt. * The first chapter....presents an excellent, well-organized account of the results and of the problems of research in the TAT, up to 1947. It prepares the ground and arraigns all the material necessary for the ideas subsequently expounded. In addition it provides one of the best topical summaries in recent clinical writing. * The fourth chapter, as an introduction to the technique of interpretation, adapts J. S. Mill's Theory of Induction to the needs of diagnostic inference. While a little startling at first, the suggestion as such is original and fruitful and worth a good deal of reflection. There is a real (and much neglected) need for a canon of procedures how to argue from the raw data of testing and clinical observation to the complex pattern of personality. One wonders though, whether Mill's Logic is particularly suited for the purpose at hand. Generally, the problem of individual meaning paramount in everything that concerns fantasy, will render futile any categorical approach. * In order to sharpen the sensitivity of the test for repressed material, Tomkins undertakes a revision and extension of Freud's theory of repression. He assumes personality to be a closed system with a finite quantum of energy. Any wish within this closed system may have any force if it does not exceed a total available energy. "Deeply" repressed wishes, Tomkins points out, contrary to common opinion, are less pathogenic than others held under smaller pressure. Conflict between wishes is pathogenic either if it claims the entire energy of the system or if the forces on either side are near equal. Imagination, as manifested in the TAT, allows the individual to reduce the force of repression by moving at a distance what otherwise would have to be repressed more firmly. Comparing the behavior of figures acting under "normal" conditions, that is, reasonably near the everyday reality of the testee, with those remote from this reality by dint of the setting will give us an idea of the force of repression. Anti-social behavior undertaken by figures and in situations similar to those of the testee's life, indicates that the wishes underlying it are subject to no great repression. Tomkins' theory of repression thus becomes the gauge of the most important question that can be asked of the TAT. While appealing through its clarity, the theory itself, nevertheless, invites a good deal of doubt. The fundamental deficit of his concept is that the ego is missing. Ego-psychology which has become the center of organization in our understanding of man's behavior, suggests that repression is only one of several mechanisms which the ego uses in order to avoid conflict. Conflict, again, will be of different origin at different occasions and consequently will appear differently in fantasy. Nor will it be sufficient to account for fantasy by a simple combination of wish and the force that opposes it. Tomkins' argument for the benign quality of deeply repressed wishes is, I think, based on a semantic misunderstanding. A distinction must be made between *early* repression, that is, at a period when the ego is relatively weak, and *successful* repression which may have taken place earlier or later. It is finally the lack of appreciation of the organismic or field quality of any psychological event, or its projection into fantasy, which seems to vitiate the explanatory value of Tomkins' schema of repression. No wish can be determined as to how much it is repressed or how much harm it will do when it emerges, unless one would consider at the same time under what conditions repression took place, what function it had, and what the psychological meaning of its emergence is. The measure of *remoteness* hence applies conditionally only. * The scoring scheme as described in Chapter 2 and the theory of repression are the focal points and Tomkins' most personal contributions. The scoring scheme itself is probably the most complete and elaborate of its kind. Only Henry's methodology is equal to it in subtlety and in the number of provisions made for grasping what will escape the examiner who is not armed with so precise an instrument. It might be argued that this scoring scheme, although it proceeds on a less minuscule basis than that of the Need-Press analysis inaugurated by Murray, and systematized first by Sanford and White, then by Bellak, still loses sight of the forest for too much logical attention to the trees. Yet, if we want to be accurate, it seems that we have to go into cumbersome detail; and if we want to hold on to the organis-

mic, inseparable unit of mood and thought and desire expressed in a story—a true reflection of the integrative function of the ego—then we have to sacrifice accuracy for perceptiveness. Reliability studies afterwards will have to render objective what could be accomplished only through an act of subjectivity. It is a more specific question whether in Tomkins' scheme the conative aspects of behavior have been focussed at the expense of the feeling tones of subjective experience and subjective reaction. All these arguments, however, seem to me secondary to a purely pragmatical one: the number and variety of categories designed by Tomkins for the analysis of TAT responses, that make it difficult to keep them in mind and to handle them properly. Specific training would be necessary for it—in and by itself a completely justifiable demand. Were this system now used for research purposes, let us say, for the study of a quality peculiar to a certain group of patients, then a very large number of variables would have to be manipulated continually in order to arrive at a few meaningful correlations. If the use of this scheme might be cumbersome for research purposes, the same reason would make it prohibitive for the daily routine of the clinic. Interpretation does not immediately come from analysis, in fact, it begins only after the material has been properly fitted into the analytic scheme. Yet there is no demonstration in the book how this should be done. The second part of the book presents many interesting hints in this direction, but does not yield a procedure. What Tomkins shows, actually, is nothing but that the vast variety of human experience is really reflected in the responses to the TAT, which is as much as to say: fantasy is valid as a source of studying man. As the author pointed out in a spirited polemic, we may well take that for granted by now. There is a pervasive impression, too, that what these stories voice, is essentially taken at face value. Yet it would seem that the display of attitudes and tendencies in TAT stories is sometimes entirely defensive in its meaning. When one attempts finally to evaluate Tomkins' book, one should make it clear that its merits are his own, its shortcomings those of an inchoate field of investigation. This book abounds with interesting illustrative material. It makes a number of stimulating cases available for the careful perusal of the student. It presents a lot of good ideas and if they are open to controversy they are no less worth careful pondering especially as the style of the book is exemplary for its clarity and control. The shortcomings of this book (as has been indicated before) may be seen in the absence of a theory of fantasy upon which all interpretation could be based. What is the function of fantasy? What are its workings? Only from such premises can we hope to derive directives as to the meaning of the individual example. The disavowal of the picture stimulus, explicitly stated by Tomkins, in itself makes for a grave limitation. What should we say about a directed fantasy if we would not compare first the stimulus from which it took off, with the direction in which it went? All this, one would suspect, is related to the basic limitation of this book, the variety of which is dependent upon one kind of material without the benefit of enlargement through psychopathology. With a very few exceptions only, the group from which these records were taken has the features and problems of an above-average college group. It differs significantly from any average population in intelligence, socio-cultural level, and articulateness. All this makes for a fantasy material which will give fascinating insight at the price of distortion. Clinical patients will be less cooperative and more suspicious, less articulate and more inhibited in fantasy and self-observation. If we want to study their fantasies, which, I am convinced, is theoretically and practically as fruitful as it is with the highly selected group from which the first experiences with the TAT were gleaned, then we have to make the necessary adjustments in our methods. When this correction has not taken place, suggestions about diagnostic procedures will remain one-sided and conditional. Thus, with all the author's diagnostic adroitness, the book appears to the retrospective reader sometimes a little remote and a little academic. All these remarks imply standards for the realization of which we can hope and work, but which we cannot expect to be fulfilled in any single book: Tomkins' book is too difficult and too complex, and at the same time too specific and too conditional to be used as a text for the diagnostic beginner. It will be read with pleasure by the experienced worker and will stimulate him to transcend its premises or set him again to reflect critically and productively on the newly developed clinical usefulness of man's most indigenous faculty.

Mental Hyg 33:476–81 Jl '49. Helen Oexle

Pierce. * Tomkins includes a very fine chapter on the analysis of work needs and vocational setting. *

Psychoanalytic Q 17:552–4 O '48. Adolf G. Woltmann. * There exist over one hundred publications on various phases of this test. Dr. Tomkins has assembled the materials available in the first comprehensive textbook about this test, removing some of the major obstacles in the way of a more universal application of this projective technique. Among these are the thorny problems of reliability and validity. Scoring and interpretation were other neglected areas. The rich documentation of various test aspects with clinical case material is a tremendous help to the student of human behavior and to the professional worker. * excellent chapter on Level Analysis * The TAT might be one projective technique which the psychoanalyst may adapt to his own professional needs. He is trained to analyze dream material and free associations, and should not, therefore, encounter difficulties in eliciting and analyzing stories patients create around the TAT pictorial situations; however Rapaport, in his 1943 paper, states that "....an interpretation of the TAT should not be considered a dream interpretation; nor can it, in the majority of cases, be handled as material allowing for symbolic interpretation; nevertheless, the clinical and psychodynamic interrelations of attitudes, strivings, etc., have to be utilized in order to come to a meaningful understanding of how the world of thoughts of the subject is organized, and how the subject himself envisages his world and environment." The book is well written, well organized and richly illustrated with case material which adequately covers all the points raised. A comprehensive up-to-date bibliography is appended. Dr. Tomkins' volume is sincerely recommended as a textbook and instruction manual to the professional worker who deals with human, dynamic behavior, its deviations and curative efforts.

Psychol B 45:461–2 S '48. Helen Sargent. * Tomkins' book is the work of a philosopher and scholar, as well as an able clinician. It contributes an original approach to the problems of scoring, interpretation and research, based upon a rationale which considers the instrument in the larger setting of scientific methodology with special reference to the science of personality. It is presented as "a workbook, rather than as a compilation of established doctrine" and offers a system of interpretation which in many respects is essentially new. Perhaps a peculiarity of the TAT is the fact that no system so far presented has gained general use, and it seems unlikely that this contribution will supplant eclecticism, or replace more flexible approaches of the type set forth by Rapaport. The scoring is based upon a set of variables ("vectors," "levels," "conditioners," and "qualifiers") which, in the hands of anyone but their originator, are likely to prove unduly labored. Of particular interest from the standpoint of methodology are the opening chapters which undertake an analysis of the analytic process engaged in by the interpreter, for the purpose of demonstrating that "The interpretation of TAT stories may employ canons of inference long accepted by other sciences." This examination of the logic of deduction is a valuable corrective to our sometimes myopic research for substantiation of hypotheses in a complex matrix of validating criteria. Nevertheless, some students of personality are likely to find in Tomkins an over-emphasis upon reductionistic, case-effect analysis, impressive in its grammarian thoroughness, but likely to obscure, especially for beginners, less abstract and more illuminating interdependencies in the data. The approach is from microscopic to macroscopic analysis, whereas the reverse is the method of preference for many. The practicing clinician is likely to find greatest satisfaction in the later chapters in which, after the author has described his tools, he demonstrates their use. The sections on personality diagnosis, in which the various regions of family, love and sex, social relationships, work and vocational settings are discussed in significant dimensions, are rich in case material, with interpretation masterfully handled, and new diagnostic insights supplied. In the writer's opinion, a highly important contribution is Tomkins' discussion of repression. Here he takes issue with orthodox psychoanalytic conceptions regarding the pathogenic nature of "deep" repression, enunciating a theory by which the seriousness of conflict is judged not by depth of repression, but by the intensity and extensity of conflicting wishes and the degree of deadlock between them. This concept has import for therapy and for theory of personality, as well as for the prognostic potentialities of the TAT. The book opens with a useful summary of important research in the Thematic Apperception Test and closes with

a discussion of the test as an adjunct to therapy. Although it is unlikely to fill the need for an integrative text in the field, it marks the coming of age of an important psychodiagnostic device, and by reason of its thorough exposition and systematic contribution deserves to become an essential reference in TAT research development.

Q R Biol 23:187 Je '48. Stanley B. Williams. * Most of the pages of this book are taken up with illustrative case material, which is more voluminous, perhaps, than is necessary. The historical introduction is too brief to be satisfactory. Of chief interest are two sections: the first, an application of Mill's principles of logical analysis (methods of agreement, concomitant variation, etc.) to the story material; the second, a novel statement of the theory of repression, cast in quantitative terminology. Neither contribution is sufficiently integrated with the TAT material. However, despite these shortcomings, the book is the best over-all treatment of the TAT and will for that reason alone find a place in the library of the clinician as a useful reference.

[142]

★The Travis-Johnston Projective Test: For the Exploration of Parent-Child Relationships. Ages 4–15; 1949; individual; separate sets of 44 pictures for boys and for girls; no data on reliability and validity with test (for data prepared under the direction of the authors and presented elsewhere, see *1–3*) ; no manual; no normative data; $19 per test, postage extra; (90) minutes; Lee E. Travis and Joseph J. Johnston; Griffin-Patterson Co., 544 W. Colorado Blvd., Glendale 4, Calif. *

REFERENCES
    1. HARRIS, LESTER LEE. *A Clinical Study of Nine Stuttering Children in Group Psychotherapy.* Doctor's thesis, University of Southern California (Los Angeles, Calif.), 1950. (PA 25:8184)
    2. WILSON, DONALD MURRAY. *A Study of the Personalities of Stuttering Children and Their Parents as Revealed Through Projection Tests.* Doctor's thesis, University of Southern California (Los Angeles, Calif.), 1950.
    3. CHRISTENSEN, ARDEN HANS. *A Quantitative Study of Personality Dynamics in Stuttering and Nonstuttering Siblings.* Doctor's thesis, University of Southern California (Los Angeles, Calif.), 1951.

ROBERT R. HOLT, *Director, Psychological Staff, The Menninger Foundation, Topeka, Kansas.*

Here is another of the all too numerous family of prematurely published, unvalidated projective tests, in this case a variation of the *Thematic Apperception Test* for children. The child is asked to tell a story (obviously only a very brief one) about each of 44 pictures, the stories to be interpreted in whatever way the examiner chooses or finds possible.

For a very stiff price, the prospective user gets a handsome box filled with 88 pictures.

printed on heavy paper (*not* on stiff cardboard, like the TAT). That's all. No manual, no norms, no data on reliability, validity, or any other published research is furnished; and only a single, dittoed page is included of off-the-cuff comment about the test's purpose, possible uses, and the method of administration, all of which is so brief as to be nearly useless. It seems to be assumed that the user will be trained in the administration and interpretation of the TAT (which is nowhere mentioned, even to acknowledge any indebtedness of the authors to it). There is a brief note to the effect that "standardization of test results is proceeding on a sampling of approximately 400 children." The least the authors could have done would have been to hold up publication until they could present the results of this preliminary study.

The pictures, then, must stand or fall on their own merits. They are not very attractive, rough black and white sketches of children and adults with a minimum of detail. They do not seem very interest provoking—not nearly as much so as the gay animal pictures of the *Children's Apperception Test*. They are a curious compromise between the contrasting ideals of maximum ambiguity and a high degree of structuredness. On the one hand, their sketchiness and the stolid formlessness of the faces is apparently intended to allow any expression to be projected and to "be interpreted the same for any culture or socio-economic status"—the last a highly dubious, naive, and unproved assertion. On the other hand, situations assumed to be crucial in socialization, involving "sibling rivalry, child-parent rivalry, discipline, eating, sleeping, toilet training, cleanliness and sexual development," are presented in generally unmistakable fashion and usually with all combinations of ages and sexes rather mechanically spelled out. Thus, for boys there are pictures of a little boy going to the toilet alone, with a woman, with a man, and with a girl watching, and of a boy watching a woman, a man, and a girl, respectively,—a total of seven pictures involving flush toilets (which are of course a feature of all cultures and socio-economic levels!). These are paralleled by a similar series of seven for girls. Each situation is treated in this unimaginative, repetitious way.

The result is a large series of pictures, which probably contains a few useful ones not duplicated in the other competing tests, all of which are better established by research: the Murray

TAT (series for children), the *Michigan Picture Test, Symonds' Picture-Story Test,* the *Children's Apperception Test,* and the *Blacky Pictures.* The prospective user who feels the need of pictures not found in these tests, however, would do better to draw his own rather than buy this portfolio; the results would probably be in every way as satisfactory, as well as a lot cheaper and simpler.

Anyone can put together a set of pictures to which stories may be told. Before marketing it as a test, however, he should furnish some evidence that his pictures contribute something new to the study of personality or something more than do the established instruments. There is no indication that the Travis-Johnston test makes any such contribution.

[143]

★Twitchell-Allen Three-Dimensional Apperception Test. Ages 5 and over; 1948–51; 1 form ('48); no data on reliability; no norms; manual ('48), dittoed supplement ('51); $37.50 per complete set of 28 plastic forms, manuals, 10 summary blanks, and 50 recording sheets; $1.10 per 10 summary blanks; $1 per 50 recording sheets; postpaid; (40–120) minutes; Doris Twitchell-Allen; Psychological Corporation. *

REFERENCES
1. TWITCHELL-ALLEN, DORIS. "A 3-Dimensional Apperception Test: A New Projective Technique." Abstract. *Am Psychol* 2:271–2 Ag '47. * (PA 21:4667, title only)

EDWARD JOSEPH SHOBEN, JR., *Associate Professor of Education, Teachers College, Columbia University, New York, New York.*

The purpose of this test, presented as a projective technique, is "to elicit the overt expression of the subject's interests, needs, goals, sentiments, feelings, and emotions, to stimulate him to project his inner self into the external environment."

The approach is through the use of 28 ambiguous plastic figures varying from geometric forms to generalized organic forms to more concrete human or animal forms. Subjects are confronted with two tasks. In the first, they are asked to choose one or more of the forms and "make up a story" about them, using them in any way they see fit to dramatize their tale. This aspect of the procedure is referred to as the Psychodramatic Test. The second task requires the subject to name the various forms and explain the determinants of his labeling. This is called the Naming Test. Recording in both instances is in terms of reaction time and the kinds of gestures and verbalizations the subject employs.

The recommended analysis of the resultant

data shows the relationship of the *Three-Dimensional Apperception Test* to other projective devices. In the Naming Test, the subject's responses are categorized as to content, determinants (movement, color, form, texture, and size), form quality (F+ and F−), and originals. These modalities conform, of course, to those used in analyzing Rorschach responses. In the case of the Psychodramatic Test, the responses are interpreted as dramatized themata, reflecting characteristics of the subject's personality. This corresponds roughly to the type of analysis used with the *Thematic Apperception Test,* psychodrama, and various forms of play interviews with children.

If one considers the *Three-Dimensional Apperception Test* as a diagnostic *test,* the first question that comes to mind is that of validity. There seems to be little helpful data bearing on this crucial question. The only reports are of the I-know-a-case variety, describing the responses of subjects whose pathological characteristics were known in advance. These responses are certainly different, but two queries are relevant: (*a*) Are the differences *between* individuals (or diagnostic groupings) greater than the differences *within* individuals on repeated administrations? and (*b*) Are the various responses of individuals consistent with those of other individuals ordered to the same class, such as aggressive, anxious, neurotic, schizophrenic, or delinquent? Until answers to such questions are provided, it seems unlikely that the test can be used diagnostically as anything other than a kind of informal observational situation from which experienced clinicians may be able to draw significant inferences about the personalities of their subjects. This is not necessarily to suggest that the instrument is devoid of diagnostic utility, but it does raise doubt as to whether it reduces the sources of error implicit in clinical judgment. It should be pointed out that the function of the psychological examination in the differential diagnostic situation has been traditionally to do just this.

On the other hand, if one regards the *Three-Dimensional Apperception Test* as an ingenious stimulus situation, the response correlates of which are yet to be determined, a large number of fruitful research problems emerge. For example, do the individuals who produce large numbers of movement responses on the two-dimensional Rorschach also produce large numbers of movement responses with these three-dimensional stimuli? If they do, it seems much more probable that movement is a consistent mode of perceptual response and that it is likely to be related to other significant characteristics of personality. Likewise, interesting questions can be raised about the ways in which various classes of people respond to the varying degrees of structuredness of the stimulus forms. This could throw much light on the relative contributions of external stimulus conditions and (e.g.) pathological states to the kinds of responses obtained.

Thus, as a research situation and as a condition under which the skilled clinician may possibly make significant observations, the *Three-Dimensional Apperception Test* promises a good deal. As a test which differentiates with statable degrees of accuracy among defined classes of respondents, it hardly exists, although future research and refinement may bring it into being.

[144]

*Visual Motor Gestalt Test. Ages 4 and over; 1938–46; individual; 1 form, '46; complete manual *A Visual Motor Gestalt Test and Its Clinical Use* ('38); instructions for administering ('46); $1 per set of cards and booklet of instructions; $3.50 per complete manual; postpaid; (10) minutes; Lauretta Bender; American Orthopsychiatric Association, Inc. * ($1.80 per pad of 50 scoring forms ('51), $6.50 per manual *The Bender-Gestalt Test* ('51); postage extra; Gerald R. Pascal and Barbara J. Suttell; Grune & Stratton, Inc.)

REFERENCES

1–8. See 3:108.
9. BENDER, LAURETTA. "Principles of Gestalt in Copied Form in Mentally Defective and Schizophrenic Persons." *Arch Neurol & Psychiatry* 27:661–86 Mr '32. * (*Pa* 8:5498)
10. BILLINGSLEA, FRED Y. "The Bender-Gestalt: An Objective Scoring Method and Validating Results." Abstract. *Am Psychol* 1:286 Jl '46. * (*PA* 20:3688, title only)
11. BILLINGSLEA, FRED Y. *Reproduction of Geometric Designs and Their Relation to Personality Salients in Humans.* Doctor's thesis, Ohio State University (Columbus, Ohio), 1946.
12. WISCHNER, GEORGE J.; ROTTER, JULIAN B.; AND GILLMAN, ROBERT D. Chap. 9, "Projective Techniques," pp. 144–57. In *The Psychological Program in AAF Convalescent Hospitals.* Edited by Sidney W. Bijou. Army Air Forces Aviation Psychology Program Research Reports, Report No. 15. Washington, D.C.: U.S. Government Printing Office, 1947. Pp. viii, 256. *
13. BELL, JOHN ELDERKIN. Chap. 16, "Visual-Motor Tests," pp. 341–9. In his *Projective Techniques: A Dynamic Approach to the Study of the Personality.* New York: Longmans, Green & Co., Inc., 1948. Pp. xvi, 533. * (London: Longmans, Green & Co. Ltd., 1949.) (*PA* 23:1284)
14. BILLINGSLEA, FRED Y. *The Bender-Gestalt: An Objective Scoring Method and Validating Data.* Clinical Psychology Monograph No. 1. New Orleans, La.: the Author, Tulane University, 1948. Pp. 27. Paper. (Reprinted from *J Clin Psychol* 4:1–27 Ja '48. *) (*PA* 22:5419)
15. MCDONOUGH, DOROTHEA B. *The Use of the Sentence Completion and Visual Motor Gestalt Tests in the Discrimination of Clinical and Control Groups.* Master's thesis, Fordham University (New York, N.Y.), 1948.
16. PHILLIPS, E. LAKIN; BERMAN, ISABEL R.; AND HANSON, HAROLD B. *Intelligence and Personality Factors Associated With Poliomyelitis Among School Age Children.* Monographs of the Society for Research in Child Development, Vol. 12, No. 2, Serial No. 45. Evanston, Ill.: Child Development Publications, the Society, 1948. Pp. vii, 60. Paper, lithotyped. *
17. SEARS, RICHARD. "Castration Anxiety in an Adult as Shown by Projective Tests." Abstract. *Am Psychol* 3:281 Jl '48. * (*PA* 22:5371, title only)

18. SOLOMON, JOSEPH C. "Adult Character and Behavior Disorders." *J Clin Psychopath* 9:1–55 Ja '48. *
19. BARKLEY, BILL J. "A Note on the Development of the Western Reserve Hapto-Kinesthetic Gestalt Test." *J Clin Psychol* 5:179–80 Ap '49. * (*PA* 24:1878)
20. BELL, JOHN ELDERKIN. "The Case of Gregor: Psychological Test Data." *Rorsch Res Exch & J Proj Tech* 13:155–205 no 2 '49. * (*PA* 24:2589)
21. BENDER, LAURETTA. "Psychological Principles of the Visual Motor Gestalt Test." *Trans N Y Acad Sci* 11:164–70 Mr '49. * (*PA* 23:5515)
22. BURLESON, DERWOOD EDDIE. *A Personality Study of Fourth, Fifth, and Sixth Grade Stutterers and Non-Stutterers Based on the Bender Visual Motor Gestalt Test.* Master's thesis, University of Pittsburgh, (Pittsburgh, Pa.), 1949. (*PA* 24: 4908, title only)
23. HALPERIN, SIDNEY L. "A Study of the Personality Structure of the Prisoner in Hawaii." Abstract. *Rorsch Res Exch & J Proj Tech* 13:243 no 2 '49. * (*PA* 24:2707, title only)
24. HUTT, MAX L. "The Bender-Gestalt Test: The Case of Gregor: Interpretation of Test Data: Symposium Presented at American Psychological Association Meeting, Denver, 1949." *Rorsch Res Exch & J Proj Tech* 13:443–6 D '49. (*PA* 24: 3734)
25. MADDOCK, MARIE E. *The Bender-Gestalt Visual Motor Test as an Instrument in the Discrimination of Institutionalized Boys From Those Noninstitutionalized.* Master's thesis, Fordham University (New York, N.Y.), 1949.
26. STANFORD, MARGARET J. "The Bender Motor Gestalt Test Assists Reading," pp. 156–9. In *Claremont College Reading Conference, Fourteenth Yearbook, 1949: Conference Theme: The Problems and Techniques Involved in Reading Social Relationships.* Claremont, Calif.: Claremont College Curriculum Laboratory, 1949. Pp. viii, 191. Paper. *
27. BALDWIN, MARCELLA VIG. "A Note Regarding the Suggested Use of the Bender Visual Motor Gestalt Test as a Measure of School Readiness." *J Clin Psychol* 6:412–5 O '50. * (*PA* 25:8275)
28. BARNES, T. CUNLIFFE. "Electroencephalographic Validation of the Rorschach, Hunt and Bender Gestalt Tests." Abstract. *Am Psychol* 5:322 Jl '50. * (*PA* 25:1088, title only)
29. HANVIK, LEO J., AND ANDERSEN, A. LLOYD. "The Effect of Focal Brain Lesions on Recall and on the Production of Rotations in the Bender Gestalt Test." *J Consult Psychol* 14:197–8 Je '50. * (*PA* 25:503)
30. HARRIMAN, MILDRED, AND HARRIMAN, PHILIP LAWRENCE. "The Bender Visual Motor Gestalt Test as a Measure of School Readiness." *J Clin Psychol* 6:175–7 Ap '50. * (*PA* 24:6353)
31. KELLY, E. LOWELL, AND FISKE, DONALD W. "The Prediction of Success in the VA Training Program in Clinical Psychology." *Am Psychol* 5:395–406 Ag '50. * (*PA* 25:2183)
32. KITAY, JULIAN I. "The Bender Gestalt Test as a Projective Technique." *J Clin Psychol* 6:170–4 Ap '50. * (*PA* 24:6356)
33. PASCAL, GERALD R. "Quantification of the Bender Gestalt: A Preliminary Report." *Am J Orthopsychiatry* 20:418–23 Ap '50. * (*PA* 25:2465)
34. WILSON, ROBERT G. *A Study of Expressive Movements in Three Groups of Adolescent Boys, Stutterers, Non-Stutterers Maladjusted and Normals, by Means of Three Measures of Personality, Mira's Myokinetic Psychodiagnosis, the Bender-Gestalt, and Figure Drawing.* Doctor's thesis, Western Reserve University (Cleveland, Ohio), 1950. (*PA* 25:6584, title only)
35. WOLTMANN, ADOLF G. "The Bender Visual-Motor Gestalt Test," pp. 322–56. (*PA* 25:2473) In *Projective Psychology: Clinical Approaches to the Total Personality.* Edited by Lawrence Edwin Abt and Leopold Bellak. New York: Alfred A. Knopf, Inc., 1950. Pp. xvii, 485, xiv. *
36. CALDEN, GEORGE, AND CARP, ABRAHAM. "A Comparison of Three Projective Techniques in a Longitudinal Study of a Post-Lobotomized Patient." Abstract. *Am Psychol* 6:343–4 Jl '51. *
37. HALPERN, FLORENCE. Chap. 11, "The Bender Visual Motor Gestalt Test," pp. 324–40. In *An Introduction to Projective Techniques.* Edited by Harold H. Anderson and Gladys L. Anderson. New York: Prentice-Hall, Inc., 1951. Pp. xxiv, 720. *
38. HANVIK, LEO J. "A Note on the Limitations of the Use of the Bender Gestalt Test as a Diagnostic Aid in Patients With a Functional Complaint." *J Clin Psychol* 7:194 Ap '51. * (*PA* 25:8215)
39. HUTT, MAX L. Chap. 2, "Bender-Gestalt Drawings," pp. 227–33. In *Thematic Test Analysis.* By Edwin S. Shneidman with the collaboration of Walther Joel and Kenneth B. Little. Foreword by Henry A. Murray. New York: Grune & Stratton, Inc., 1951. Pp. xi, 320. * (*PA* 26:3422)
40. LUM, VERNON K. *A Modified Use of the Visual Motor Gestalt Test as a Projective Instrument With Neuropsychiatric Subjects.* Doctor's thesis, University of Michigan (Ann Arbor, Mich.), 1951.
41. PASCAL, GERALD R., AND SUTTELL, BARBARA J. *The Bender-Gestalt Test: Its Quantification and Validity for Adults.* Foreword by David G. Wright. New York: Grune & Stratton, Inc., 1951. Pp. xiii, 274. * (*PA* 25:8106)
42. KELLY, E. LOWELL, AND FISKE, DONALD W. *The Prediction of Performance in Clinical Psychology.* Ann Arbor, Mich.: University of Michigan, 1951. Pp. xv, 311. Lithotyped. *

ARTHUR L. BENTON, *Professor of Psychology, State University of Iowa, Iowa City, Iowa.*

The early status of this test is well described by the reviews appearing in *The Third Mental Measurements Yearbook.* Line remarked that the author's "theoretical statements are hard to summarize, and at this stage, to evaluate" and the test's "validity and practical value....as well as its classification, must await further research." He concluded that it nevertheless "represents a very stimulating contribution to a challenging and complex field." Rickers-Ovsiankina pointed out that "the theory expressed is certainly not a theory in the sense that it leads to predictions and conclusions or even factual statements of a specific nature." She too felt that "the study is a stimulating one and the test has considerable promise for clinical purposes."

Now, ten years after these reviews were written, it may be asked how well the promise has been performed. During the war, reports of the wondrous efficacy of this instrument emanated from some military clinical facilities. It was therefore with keen interest that clinical psychologists looked forward to seeing it in action in the postwar period. The outcome was most disappointing. Watching an "expert," trained at one of the military installations, interpret a "Bender" was to witness the crudest sort of crystal gazing. It was particularly dismaying to have to come to terms with the fact that this kind of operation was taking place in many university clinical facilities, those presumed citadels of the new "dynamo-scientific" clinical psychology. Reaction on the part of competent clinical psychologists was swift and also somewhat overgeneralized. The scorn which was justifiably poured on the crystal gazing extended to the instrument itself.

However, this general attitude of rejection on the part of the more competent clinical psychologists has not deterred a few serious attempts at validation, the two major efforts in this regard being the studies of Billingslea (*14*) and Pascal and Suttell (*41*). Billingslea's results were almost completely negative. Most of the scoring categories utilized in the application of the test during the war proved to have insufficient reliability for diagnostic purposes and the factors advanced by Hutt[1] as characteristic of the performances of psychoneurotics failed to be discriminative. The findings of Pascal and Suttell

[1] Hutt, Max L. *A Tentative Guide for the Administration and Interpretation of the Bender-Gestalt Test.* Privately distributed by the Author, 1945.

were more positive in nature but in general not highly impressive. The authors are cautious in their interpretations and in many ways this detailed study is an exploration of possibilities rather than a validation in the strict sense. Minor studies are reported by Glueck [2] and by Hanvik and Andersen (29). Glueck found that test performance failed to discriminate between normal subjects and psychotic patients. Hanvik and Andersen found rotation of figures to be characteristic of brain-injured patients as compared with a control sample. The two groups did not differ significantly in respect to number of figures recalled correctly.

The reviewer's evaluation of the present status of the test is as follows: It belongs to a class of test procedures, that of visuomotor and visual memory tests, which have been demonstrated to possess distinctive clinical merits, particularly in the evaluation of cerebral injury and disease. Where disturbances in visuomotor behavior and visual perception exist, performance on the test should be able to reflect these disabilities. That it possesses any power to identify psychogenic disturbances, as in the psychoneuroses, remains to be demonstrated. The chief deterrent to its sagacious use at the present time is the confusion engendered by the extravagant claims made for it by uncritical enthusiasts.

HOWARD R. WHITE, *Chief Clinical Psychologist, Veterans Administration Hospital, Jefferson Barracks, Missouri.*

The Bender-Gestalt is becoming a frequently used test, but only recently has some of the needed basic experimental data been appearing.

One group of workers is concerned with the problem of maturation. There is general agreement that the significant màturation occurs within the age range of 4–11 years, with fairly stable patterns (5, 35, 41). There is some relation to reading factors, but this is limited by intelligence and emotion (7, 27, 30).

In the records of adults, those with organic brain damage are impressive (5, 35, 41). The Bender-Gestalt can be used for screening and for prognosis for therapy (41). Significant relations to schizophrenia are reported (5, 35, 41), although it is not primarily a test to establish psychiatric diagnosis. There is difficulty in setting a significant scoring pattern for neurotics (14, 38). Significant relations with certain Ror-

schach factors can be found (32). Hutt has failed to publish more data since his army reports, but apparently many workers are applying and expanding his suggestions (without publishing).

The reviewer concludes that the test has merit, but that it still cries for adequate experimental development. On the basis of current literature, it is apparently useful in measuring certain aspects of maturation. It is useful in measuring the presence of organic brain involvement. It is frequently useful in recognizing the schizophrenic, and at present somewhat less useful with the neurotic. It is limited by age and, possibly, by low intelligence. The role of cultural influences has not been explored.

For related reviews see 145, 3:109, and 40: B843.

[145]

★[*Re* Visual Motor Gestalt Test.] PASCAL, GERALD R., AND SUTTELL, BARBARA J. **The Bender-Gestalt Test: Its Quantification and Validity for Adults.** Foreword by David G. Wright. New York: Grune & Stratton, Inc., 1951. Pp. xiii, 274. $6.50. *

J Clin Psychol 7:388 O '51. * This is the most objective research work which has thus far appeared in this field.

J Ed Psychol 42:438–9 N '51. Lee J. Cronbach. * Until the publication of this manual, the test has been inadequately supplied with scoring standards and norms, and validation has been much needed. Pascal and Suttell administered the tests to hundreds of cases and identified features most likely to occur in records of patients as contrasted with normals. These features are embodied in a careful set of scoring guides of a near-objective sort. Unfortunately the report on item validity (Table 1) involves faulty statistical methods, but the total scoring method appears acceptable. Two scorers use it independently, on a sample of very wide range, with a correlation between scorings of .90. For norms and validity studies, the investigators rely on hit-and-miss samples, testing whatever groups could be obtained. Granting that availability is a requisite, it is nonetheless unfortunate that so much effort should be expended on unplanned samples in this and other clinical research. The authors present their findings with due caution and with commendable modesty; they often admit to having no idea what certain findings mean where less restrained clinicians would write several pages of rationalization. Yet they are not constricted: at one point (p. 23) they squeeze a

2 Glueck, G. "Psicopatologia della Percezione della Forma: Principi della Forma nei Disegni Copiati di Malati Mentali." *Archivio de Psicologia, Neurologia e Psichiatria* 1: 603–64 '40. (PA 20:2499)

hypothesis out of data from three cases. The evidence for the Bender-Gestalt test is seemingly solid. Not only does it distinguish patients from community persons with bi-serial validities about .70; much more valuable in practice, it discriminates substantially between patients who improve and those who do not, tested at admission. The authors discuss the qualitative indications that their experience suggests consideration of, illustrate records of children, organics, and psychogenic cases with diagnostic discussion, and provide samples for training scorers. There are one hundred four pages of text, apart from appendices, which will be of great assistance to those who use the test. Both the style and organization of the material are rambling, but the authors' ideas advance the usefulness of the Bender-Gestalt appreciably.

Psychiatric Q Sup 25:144 pt 1 '51. Pascal and Suttell have presented....an objective scoring device for the Bender Visual Motor Gestalt Test. The method proposed is exhaustively illustrated with the scorable deviations in test performance. * It is to the authors' credit that the inherent limitations of any such device are well recognized; and their method is presented in a factual manner with a minimum of speculation and generalization. The book is of value to the clinical psychologist; and, although it is hoped that there will be refinement regarding diagnostic categories, nevertheless, it lends an objective element to a test that has always been surrounded by subjectivity.

[146]

★The Vocational Apperception Test. College; 1949; individual; separate sets of pictures for men ['49] and for women ['49]; no data on reliability in manual (for data presented elsewhere by the authors, see *1* below); mimeographed manual; $7.25 per set of 18 picture cards (8 for men, 10 for women) and manual, postage extra; (60) minutes; Robert B. Ammons, Margaret N. Butler, and Sam A. Herzig; Southern Universities Press, 2122 Confederate Place, Louisville 8, Ky. *
a) [FORM FOR MEN.] Preferences in 8 areas: teacher, executive or office worker, doctor, lawyer, engineer, personnel or social worker, salesman, laboratory technician.
b) [FORM FOR WOMEN.] Preferences in 10 areas: laboratory technician, dietician, buyer, nurse, teacher, artist, secretary, social worker, mother, housewife.

REFERENCES

1. AMMONS, ROBERT B.; BUTLER, MARGARET NEWMAN; AND HERZIG, SAM A. "A Projective Test for Vocational Research and Guidance at the College Level." *J Appl Psychol* 34:198–205 Je '50. * (*PA* 25:3850)

BENJAMIN BALINSKY, *Assistant Professor of Psychology, City College, New York, New York.*

This test was devised to elicit vocational interests in the context of personality characteristics. The standard paper and pencil measures of interest patterns, such as the *Kuder Preference Record* and the Strong *Vocational Interest Blank,* measure the degree of interest in vocational areas or in kinds of work without relating the interests to personality characteristics. Interest patterns can be considered part of the total personality, and measuring them in a test that also allows for personality description may make the interest patterns more meaningful. This is essentially the rationale for the *Vocational Apperception Test.*

In order to measure vocational interests as related to personality characteristics, a projective technique is used resembling that of the *Thematic Apperception Test.* The situations, however, are primarily vocational rather than social.

The test actually consists of 18 line drawings on fairly sturdy cardboard 8½ by 5½ inches in dimensions. Ten of the cards are for females and eight for men. Each card shows an individual (male or female) in a specific occupation: males are shown as teacher, executive or office worker, doctor, lawyer, engineer, personnel or social worker, salesman, and laboratory technician; females as laboratory technician, dietician, buyer, nurse, teacher, artist, secretary, social worker, mother, and housewife. In most cards other people are depicted so that there is opportunity to express social interaction. The most prominently pictured, however, are those in the specific occupations.

The test is individually administered with a verbatim record taken. An inquiry would seem necessary after the test to determine the reasons for the subject's responses. Clinical interviewing skill would be required for this purpose.

The contents of the cards are simple and relatively unambiguous. The cards were purposely drawn that way after "five preliminary plates for five occupations were used to test fifteen college men and women informally" (*1*). This pretesting would by itself be inadequate. A more rigidly controlled experiment or series of experiments should have been undertaken to test the content of the cards. Perhaps the contents should be more complex and more ambiguous. In the current projective tests, for example, the Rorschach, Thematic Apperception, Incomplete Sentences, the content is not too simple or unambiguous. This is so to allow for greater range and depth of expression.

Although it is not mentioned by the authors of the test, I would assume from my own experience that the simplicity and unambiguity were believed necessary to obtain expressions of vocational interest in the occupations depicted. Otherwise the interest patterns might be lost in the larger context of personality.

The manual for the test states that validity was indicated by "the clear relationship observed between stories and personal information already available." This statement is not elaborated nor is any data presented in the manual to substantiate it. In a later report on the test (1) a similar statement is found, but again the evidence is not delineated. We must assume that the evidence exists although it is not specifically reported. A brief story given by a male subject to one card is offered as an illustration of what the test can elicit. This may pass for some evidence on validity. The story shows evidence of personality characteristics such as not wanting too much responsibility, wondering if he is going to succeed, and not being sure of himself. As for vocational interests, the subject would seem not to like the kind of work depicted. The reviewer assumes these characteristics were checked against other information. Much more validity data needs to be cited.

The manual has no case reports. Scoring and interpretation include many definitions of terms in various scoring areas. The areas include general preference for an occupation, reasons for entering, those of concern to the individual, mechanisms used in solution of conflict and outcomes. Interpretation in these terms demands a high level of clinical training with many case reports studied.

The authors of the test require users of the test to be familiar with vocational problems and methods of projective testing. This is rightly so. The consistency of scoring was approximately 86 per cent for experienced scorers rescoring after a week and 69 per cent between experienced and inexperienced scorers. These percentages are indications of the reliability of the test but show the need for caution as well as for experience.

A few more comments need be included. The test was standardized on only 40 female and 35 male subjects, all college students. These are small numbers. Many more subjects need to be tested. The test is for college people but not necessarily for the whole collegiate range. It could be that other occupations might be added to those already in the test. The cards are not numbered. They should be if for no other reason than to make identification of the stories easier.

The *Vocational Apperception Test* seems to rest on a sound rationale. The test itself can be considered to have good potential for eliciting vocational interests related to personality characteristics but is in its early stages of development.

WILLIAM E. HENRY, *Associate Professor of Psychology, The University of Chicago, Chicago, Illinois.*

This test attempts to take cognizance of the fact that specific vocational choices, and individual success or failure in those vocations, are closely related to broader personality attributes. The testmakers here have assumed that the kind of personality data elicited by the TAT can be similarly elicited by a test which portrays a number of specific vocations. It is assumed, however, that the personality data so derived will have direct applicability to vocational attitudes, rather than being of the more general sort derived from pictures which portray a wider range of basic life situations. In so doing, they have placed their reliance upon an area of technical projective technique method which is at best in its early stages of formulation. One may ask to what extent it is possible to determine in advance, by picture specificity, the particular area of personality or constellation of personality related attitudes which will be stimulated. While there is little question but what this can indeed be done to some extent, I would wonder whether the *Vocational Apperception Test* does not assume a specificity of attitude formation which in fact does not exist in the ordinary person and does not rely upon a further untried assumption. This latter assumption is that when a subject talks about a picture showing, let us say, a housewife, she is indeed giving you her attitudes toward the vocational aspects of the housewife role. Or is she telling you about her image of the adult female? Or are these two the same, possibly? If they are not the same, then are you getting specific attitudes towards specific vocations (the housewife) or are you getting deeper personality data? If you are getting deeper personality data, what evidence is there that it is the deeper personality data which structures the response toward vocation? If the latter is the fact, then this test will indeed reveal the relationship between vocational attitude and deeper personality attributes. It is this which the test claims to do.

The real test as to whether the VAT is doing what it proposes to do lies in further research in this complex area—an area of which the test authors are by no means unaware. The system for categorizing answers which the authors provide seems to me not to be the area upon which they should rest their case. It is rather in the very qualitative flexibility which the authors themselves observe. Further work should take the direction of exploring on a broader basis, possibly in established vocational groups rather than the college population previously used, the various relationships between responses to the test, vocational attitudes, and deeper personality attributes. In a sense, I feel that "scores" have been set up prematurely, before the basic nature of the data derived from this very promising test is understood.

J Proj Tech 15:534–6 D '51. *George S. Rhodes.* * the first projective test specifically designed to elicit information regarding the counselee's vocational goals. In my own experience for the past several years, I have felt keenly the same inadequacies in vocational counseling instruments which the authors experienced and which led to the development of this test. First, they recognize that vocational problems are but one facet of the individual's total adjustment, so the important variables of personality and the individual's total social adjustment must be evaluated in relation to the vocational problem; second, they describe the apparent weakness of objective vocational interest tests and the questionnaire personality tests which are the usual measures of these variables in the vocational guidance clinic; finally, they attempt to solve this problem by adapting the TAT technique to the vocational counseling setting. As they state, their purpose is, "to provide a projective test that would measure vocational attitudes and interests, and at the same time, give information concerning related psychological forces operating within the individual's personality." The materials of the test consist of two sets of $5\frac{1}{2} \times 8\frac{1}{2}$ line drawings. For men, the eight cards portray persons engaged in the following occupations: teacher, executive or office worker, doctor, lawyer, engineer, personnel or social worker, salesman

and laboratory technician. For women the ten pictures depict the occupations of laboratory technician, dietitian, buyer, nurse, teacher, artist, secretary, social worker, mother and housewife. The plates were designed to portray specific occupational situations and yet make the stimulus figures as ambiguous as possible in the facial expression, posturing and emotional feeling. Judging by a couple of trial administrations, the authors have accomplished these objectives in plate design. The content of the pictures limits the usefulness of the test, particularly the set of plates for men. If the test is intended to measure vocational attitudes and interests it should sample both the longitudinal hierarchy of occupations and the breadth of the occupational world. For example, without unduly lengthening the test, adding pictures of a typical outdoor occupation, of a skilled craftsman and of a laboring man should provide more adequate information about the client's level of aspiration, his attitude toward people in lower level occupations and his relative interest in the large area of outdoor occupations. The instructions for administering the test are simple and concise. The preface to the specific task assignment in emphasizing "understanding the behavior of others in getting along with them" closely resembles the instructions for Sargent's Insight Test. The specific directions require the client to tell how the person came to be in the situation portrayed, how he feels about it, and what the future holds in store. The type of pictorial material presented and the slanting of the directions, in the vocational counseling setting at least, should eliminate most of the resistance not infrequently encountered in administering the TAT. The administration of the test, the recording of the stories and the inquiries are essentially the same as for the TAT. For each of the two trial cases the total administrative time was about one hour. The scoring system presented by the authors consists of a qualitative scheme for classifying the following information: *Vocational attitude or interest.* A five category scale ranging from "like," to "dislike," with ambivalence added as a final class, is provided for rating the client's interest in each vocation. *Reasons for entering the occupation.* Some 21 different reasons are listed. *Areas of concern.* Eight major areas of conflict with seven subareas under personal conflict provide a basis for classifying the problems expressed in the stories. *Mechanisms used in solution of conflicts.* Ten mechanisms which fairly completely cover the responses of individuals to conflictful situations are provided. *Outcomes.* Seven story endings ranging from success to disaster are given for men and three solutions involving marriage are added for women. Some figures are given on the reliability of these categories: self-agreement for two scorers on five protocols of 86%, and inter-observer agreement between four graduate students and the experienced examiners of 69%. Reliability was best for general attitude toward occupations and for outcomes, worst for areas of conflict. In using this scoring scheme I found it occasionally difficult to classify the story elements into the established categories since the category descriptions are brief and are not uniform in terminology. Experimental use of the test will doubtless lead to more adequate systems of scoring the responses. Standardization data for the test are so limited as to be quite inadequate. The authors report experience with only 40 college women and 35 college men. The characteristic responses of this group in terms of the rough scoring scheme have been tabulated, but the test user is expected to write to the A.D.I. for microfilm copies of the tables, which do not appear in the manual! The A.D.I. reference is given in the authors' article in the *Journal of Applied Psychology,* a reprint of which is furnished as a kind of supplementary manual. Statistical evidence of validity is scanty, being suggested only in a comparison of general attitude toward several occupations and ratings on the Strong which yielded Chi-Squares significant at the 10% level of confidence for women and at the 2% level for men. In its present level of development, then, the test is little more than an interesting experiment. If it is to prove useful enough in the counseling of clients—especially those who are not college students—to justify the time it takes to administer and interpret, a great deal more work needs to be done on it. The scoring categories need to be clarified and their useful-ness to the counselor demonstrated. The evidence presented by the authors suggests that the test has merit for the clinically trained vocational counselor, and my trial experiences with it have been intriguing. I wonder, however, whether the TAT and the standard measures of vocational interest, used along with counseling interviews, might not provide more personality information and at least as valid measures of vocational interest as does the VAT. My analysis of trial tests both according to the authors' scoring scheme and by my abbreviated version of Tomkins' Scoring of the TAT, in the work setting, provided interesting and useful results, but the variety of information about personality obtained does not seem to be as great as the TAT affords, because of the structuring of the pictures.

[147]

★The World Test. Ages 2 and over; 1941–50; a revision of *The World Test: A Measurement of Emotional Disturbance* originally published by Psychological Corporation in 1941; the earlier test was an adaptation of Margaret Lowenfeld's *World Technique;* individual; 1 form, '49; 160- or 300-item sets; manual ('49); record blank ('50); $60 per 160-item box of test materials; $100 per 300-item box of test materials; $3 per 100 record blanks; (20–45) minutes; original edition by Charlotte Buhler and Gayle Kelly; revised edition by Charlotte Buhler; published by Charlotte Buhler, 1127 North Sweetzer Ave., Los Angeles 46, Calif. *

REFERENCES

1. LOWENFIELD, MARGARET. "The World Pictures of Children: A Method of Recording and Studying Them." *Brit J Med Psychol* 18:65–101 pt 1 '39. * (*PA* 13:3897)
2. MICHAEL, JOSEPH C., AND BUHLER, CHARLOTTE. "Experience With Personality Testing in a Neuropsychiatric Department of a Public General Hospital." *Dis Nerv Sys* 6:205–11 Jl '45. * (*PA* 19:3038)
3. BELL, JOHN ELDERKIN. Chap. 23, "The World Test," pp. 468–73. In his *Projective Techniques: A Dynamic Approach to the Study of the Personality.* New York: Longmans, Green & Co., Inc., 1948. Pp. xvi, 533. * (London: Longmans, Green & Co. Ltd., 1949.) (*PA* 23:1284)
4. ROSENZWEIG, SAUL; with the collaboration of Kate Levine Kogan. *Psychodiagnosis: An Introduction to Tests in the Clinical Practice of Psychodynamics,* pp. 159–67. New York: Grune & Stratton, Inc., 1949. Pp. xii, 380. * (*PA* 23:3761)
5. BUHLER, CHARLOTTE; LUMRY, GAYLE KELLY; AND CARROL, HELEN SARA. *World-Test Standardization Studies.* Child Care Monographs No. 4. New York: Child Care Publications, 1951. Pp. 81. Paper. * A reprint from *J Child Psychiatry* 2:1–81 '51. * (*PA* 26:2743)
6. BUHLER, CHARLOTTE; LUMRY, GAYLE KELLY; AND CARROL, HELEN SARA. "World-Test Standardization Studies." *J Child Psychiatry* 2:1–81 '51. * (*PA* 26:2743)

PERSONALITY—FIFTH MMY

REVIEWS BY *C. J. Adcock, Dan L. Adler, Mary D. Ainsworth, Dwight L. Arnold, Andrew R. Baggaley, Benjamin Balinsky, Warren R. Baller, Frank Barron, Robert H. Bauernfeind, Brent Baxter, Kenneth L. Bean, Samuel J. Beck, John E. Bell, George K. Bennett, Åke Bjerstedt, John D. Black, Donald T. Campbell, Cherry Ann Clark, Dorothy M. Clendenen, Charles N. Cofer, Lee J. Cronbach, W. Grant Dahlstrom, Richard H. Dana, D. Russell Davis, Dorothy H. Eichorn, Albert Ellis, Leonard D. Eron, H. J. Eysenck, Donald W. Fiske, John P. Foley, Jr., John W. French, Benno G. Fricke, N. L. Gage, Eugene L. Gaier, Cecil A. Gibb, John W. Gittinger, Harrison G. Gough, Wilson H. Guertin, J. P. Guilford, John W. Gustad, Nelson G. Hanawalt, Philip L. Harriman, Dale B. Harris, J. Thomas Hastings, Alfred B. Heilbrun, Jr., William E. Henry, Wayne H. Holtzman, John E. Horrocks, Arthur R. Jensen, Richard Jessor, Cecil D. Johnson, Walter Kass, E. Lowell Kelly, Douglas T. Kenny, Morris Krugman, Edward Landy, Roy D. Lewis, Maurice Lorr, Raymond J. McCall, Arthur W. Meadows, T. R. Miles, Kenneth R. Newton, Warren T. Norman, Raymond C. Norris, C. Robert Pace, John Pierce-Jones, Albert I. Rabin, John A. Radcliffe, John W. M. Rothney, Bert R. Sappenfield, David R. Saunders, William Schofield, S. B. Sells, Laurance F. Shaffer, Edwin S. Shneidman, Verner M. Sims, William Stephenson, Naomi Stewart, L. Joseph Stone, C. R. Strother, J. P. Sutcliffe, Clifford H. Swensen, Jr., Percival M. Symonds, Florence M. Teagarden, Robert L. Thorndike, Herbert A. Tonne, Neil J. Van Steenberg, Wimburn L. Wallace, Harold Webster, George Westby and C. Gilbert Wrenn.*

NONPROJECTIVE

[28]

A-S Reaction Study: A Scale for Measuring Ascendance-Submission in Personality. College and adults; 1928–39; Form for men ('28), Form for women ('39); manual, second edition ('39); $3.04 per 35 tests; 40¢ per complete specimen set; postage extra; (20) minutes; Gordon W. Allport and Floyd H. Allport; Houghton Mifflin Co. *

REFERENCES

1–19. See 40:1198.
20–30. See 3:23.
31. THOMPSON, CLAUDE EDWARD. "Selecting Executives by Psychological Tests." *Ed & Psychol Meas* 7:773–8 w '47. * (PA 23:321)
32. BROWER, DANIEL. "The Relations of Visuo-Motor Conflict to Personality Traits and Cardio-Vascular Activity." *J General Psychol* 38:69–99 Ja '48. * (PA 22:3383)
33. HARDY, VIRGINIA T. "Relation of Dominance to Non-Directiveness in Counseling." *J Clin Psychol* 4:300–3 Jl '48. * (PA 23:179)
34. BARNETTE, W. LESLIE, JR. *Occupational Aptitude Patterns of Counseled Veterans.* Doctor's thesis, New York University (New York, N.Y.), 1949. *
35. CARTER, LAUNOR, AND NIXON, MARY. "Ability, Perceptual, Personality, and Interest Factors Associated With Different Criteria of Leadership." *J Psychol* 27:377–88 Ap '49. * (PA 23:4183)
36. HORRALL, BERNICE MOODY. "Relationships Between College Aptitude and Discouragement-Buoyancy Among College Freshmen." *J Genetic Psychol* 74:185–243 Je '49. * (PA 24:2090–1)
37. UHRBROCK, RICHARD STEPHEN. "Construction of a Selection Test for College Graduates." *J General Psychol* 41:153–93 O '49. * (PA 24:4874)
38. BENDER, I. E., AND HASTORF, A. H. "The Perception of Persons: Forecasting Another Person's Responses on Three Personality Scales." *J Abn & Social Psychol* 45:556–61 Jl '50. * (PA 25:988)
39. HOLMES, FRANK J. "Validity of Tests for Insurance Office Personnel." *Personnel Psychol* 3:57–69 sp '50. * (PA 24:5490)
40. BARNETTE, W. LESLIE, JR. "Occupational Aptitude Patterns of Selected Groups of Counseled Veterans." *Psychol Monogr* 65(5):1–49 '51. * (PA 26:2794)
41. HOLZBERG, JULES D., AND POSNER, RITA. "The Relationship of Extrapunitiveness on the Rosenzweig Picture-Frustration Study to Aggression in Overt Behavior and Fantasy." *Am J Orthopsychiatry* 21:767–79 O '51. * (PA 26:5619)
42. McKENNA, FRANK S. "An Analysis of Nine Personality Scales." Abstract. *Proc Ind Acad Sci* 62:294 '52. *
43. STARER, EMANUEL. "Aggressive Reactions and Sources

of Frustration in Anxiety Neurotics and Paranoid Schizophrenics." *J Clin Psychol* 8:307–9 Jl '52. * (PA 27:5979)
44. BEAVER, ALMA P. "Dominance in the Personality of the Student Nurse as Measured by the A-S Reaction Study." *J Psychol* 38:73–8 Jl '54. * (PA 29:4842)
45. REINDL, MARY OLIVIA. *The Relationship Between Attitudes Toward Obedience and Personality Characteristics Measured by the A-S Reaction Study and the Gordon Personal Profile.* Master's thesis, Fordham University (New York, N.Y.), 1957.

For a review by William U. Snyder, see 3:23; for a review by Doncaster G. Humm of the 1928 edition, see 40:1198.

[29]

***Activity Vector Analysis.** Adults; 1948–58; title on test is *Placement Analysis;* 5 scores: aggressiveness, sociability, emotional adjustment, social adaptability, activity level; Form A ('54); administrator's manual ('56); technical supplement ('58); profile ('53); distribution restricted to persons who have completed a 3-week course offered by the publisher; course fee, $1500; test materials must be purchased separately; postage extra; (5–10) minutes; [Walter V. Clarke]; Walter V. Clarke Associates, Inc. *

REFERENCES

1. MOSEL, JAMES N. "Response Reliability of the Activity Vector Analysis." *J Appl Psychol* 38:157–8 Je '54. * (PA 29:4076)
2. CLARKE, WALTER V. "The Construction of an Industrial Selection Personality Test." *J Psychol* 41:379–94 Ap '56. * (PA 31:5185)
3. CLARKE, WALTER V. "The Personality Profiles of Life Insurance Agents." *J Psychol* 42:295–302 O '56. *
4. CLARKE, WALTER V. "The Personality Profiles of Loan Office Managers." *J Psychol* 41:405–12 Ap '56. * (PA 31:5186)
5. CLARKE, WALTER V. "Personality Profiles of Self-Made Company Presidents." *J Psychol* 41:413–8 Ap '56. * (PA 31:5172)
6. FITZPATRICK, EUGENE D., AND McCARTY, JOHN J. "Validity Information Exchange, No. 9–47: D.O.T. Code 1–86.45, Salesman, Communication Equipment." *Personnel Psychol* 9:526–7 w '56. *
7. WALLACE, S. RAINS; CLARKE, WALTER V.; AND DRY, RAYMOND J. "The Activity Vector Analysis as a Selector of Life Insurance Salesmen." *Personnel Psychol* 9:337–45 au '56. * (PA 31:8979)
8. HARKER, JOHN B. "A Comparison of Personality and Interest Patterns." Abstract. *Am Psychol* 12:408 Jl '57. *

9. WHISLER, LAURENCE D. "A Study of the Descriptive Validity of Activity Vector Analysis." *J Psychol* 43:205–23 Ap '57. *

10. MERENDA, PETER F., AND CLARKE, WALTER V. "AVA as a Predictor of Occupational Hierarchy." *J Appl Psychol* 42: 289–92 Ag '58. *

11. MUSIKER, HAROLD R., AND CLARKE, WALTER V. "Descriptive Reliability of Activity Vector Analysis." *Psychol Rep* 4:435–8 S '58. *

BRENT BAXTER, *Director of Agencies Research, Prudential Insurance Company, Newark, New Jersey.*

The *Activity Vector Analysis* (AVA) is more than a test; it has become part of a system of personality analysis, part of a theory of personality. The role of the AVA is hard to define since the descriptions of its function have been modified from time to time. Originally it was a comprehensive measure of all significant aspects of personality. Later it was expanded to "become a human relations philosophy based on the understanding obtained from the study of people by the analysis." It has also been described as a tool to be used along with other personality tests (largely projective) and biographical information as an aid in helping the analyst understand the person tested.

Such variation in claimed function makes evaluation difficult. The last description makes the AVA results so interrelated with other data as to make separate evaluation of the AVA practically impossible. Let us turn to the available approaches to validity.

Many data have been provided to show that the test responses of members of one occupation differ from those in other occupations. In other words, presidents describe themselves in ways different from the general population. Your reviewer does not regard this as a useful form of validity if it can be regarded as validity at all. In business and industry it is more important to know whether the test can tell which members of an occupation are successful or, better yet, tell the probable future success of a person about to enter that occupation.

Several studies have been made by the test author and publisher to see if the test can tell which persons on a given job are successful, but these usually fail to have any cross validation to support them. The publisher does not always point out the lack of cross validation and concludes incorrectly that the data show the test is valid. Moreover, the comparison of results between two occupations has been improperly presented as cross validation. A few studies made by independent research men have not shown the test to be effective in sorting out the more and less successful men on a given job.

In the AVA's early history, claims were made that prediction of job success was a simple function of this instrument. The publisher has since pointed out that this type of prediction does not rest alone on a sound measure of personality even if available. For one thing, an understanding of the relationship between personality and job function is necessary. Thus, some early failures to predict job success, it would seem, led the publisher to develop a parallel method of measuring job personality requirements. Research is still needed to determine the value of this job analysis method. Similarly, more evidence is needed to show if the test can contribute to the prediction of job success under any conditions.

The publisher has emphasized from the outset the importance of the function of the test administrator and, especially, of the test analyst to the validity of the instrument. For this reason a special training course is required for those wishing to use the test. The AVA Administrator is authorized only to administer and score the test, a relatively easy job. The interpretation is the responsibility of an AVA Analyst and "cannot be done by anyone other than that person." It is claimed that lay persons can become effective analysts with three weeks of training. While fairly standard interpretations that lay people can learn readily have been developed for some score profiles, there is conflicting evidence as to whether or not people with such training are likely to make the same test interpretations. It seems doubtful that such brief training can produce effective personality analysts.

There is evidence of fairly high consistency of responses made within a given test administration. Test-retest correlations run lower. One cannot tell whether this reflects unreliability of the instrument or sensitiveness to real changes in personality. Concern about reliability should not deter further study of this instrument.

The test publisher has made and is making extensive intratest analyses. Factor analyses and intercorrelation of score patterns have been made at length. While these purport to disclose the organization of personality, it is probably more a contribution to revealing the semantic jungle in which our personality vocabulary is involved.

In summary: Because of claims and counter-claims over the validity of this test, its use has become controversial. After an extensive search for studies which have tried an impartial evaluation of the instrument, your reviewer has seen little evidence on which to recommend its use. The analyses and interpretations derived from this test seem much more extensive than the original self-descriptions of the examinee justify. It must be recognized, however, that many of the criticisms directed toward this test can similarly be directed toward other personality instruments.

GEORGE K. BENNETT, *President, The Psychological Corporation, New York, New York.*

The *Activity Vector Analysis* is not a test which can be purchased but is part of a system which involves a contractual relationship, the training of "analysts," and other complexities. Consequently, this review deals both with the questionnaire and with the system.

The instrument which is central to the system is a single-sided sheet, 8½ by 11 inches in dimension, entitled "Placement Analysis." It contains blanks for identifying data, instructions, and a box for scores, as well as the list of 81 adjectives which constitute the form. Each adjective is preceded by two blank spaces. The instructions preceding the list read: "Place an X in the Columns headed (1) before every word that has *ever* been used by *anyone* in describing you. Draw a line through any word you do not understand. Be honest with yourself—remember no one is perfect." At the foot of the list are these instructions: "Now go back and place an X in the Columns headed (2) before every word which you honestly believe is descriptive of you. When you have finished, turn in your paper."

The 81 descriptive terms deal generally with overt aspects of personality and include such words or phrases as "good-natured," "persistent," "harmonious," "aesthetic," and "argumentative." The author describes them as nonderogatory and in general the term seems appropriate, although one might question it as applied to "scairdy cat," "nervy," and "egotist." An oddity in the list is the word "inducive," categorized as "rare" in Webster's unabridged dictionary.

Responses are counted separately for the columns and then added to obtain a "resultant" or total score. The first, or "activity," score is merely the number of X's. The remaining scores, V-1 to V-5, are obtained from a series of mask keys. With few exceptions, the same words are scored in both columns.

It is perhaps best to let the author define the scores. Quoting Clarke, we learn,

The following postulate, therefore, results: An organism behaves in a positivistic or negativistic manner in terms of the attitudes resulting from its perception of the given situation at that time, resulting in four basic ways of acting:
1. Positivistic, or approach behavior in a favorable or favorably perceived situation.
2. Positivistic, or approach behavior in an unfavorable or unfavorably perceived situation.
3. Negativistic, or avoidant behavior in a favorable or favorably perceived situation.
4. Negativistic, or avoidant behavior in an unfavorable or unfavorably perceived situation.
These four possible ways of acting are described by many different words depending upon *a*) the situation, and *b*) the degree of energy output.
Since these four behavior elements are dynamic—have direction and magnitude—they are designated as vectors and are numbered to eliminate the confusion often resulting from the interpretation of verbalized labels. The four major aspects of behavior are as follows:
Vector 1—Aggressiveness. In a less scientific description, it might be called "Do-ability."
Vector 2—Sociability, or "Social-ability."
Vector 3—Emotional Stability or Emotional Control. A less scientific description is "Sit-ability."
Vector 4—Social Adaptability, or the less scientific label of "Flex-ability."

If the reader feels less than thoroughly informed regarding the significance of the "Activity" and "V-5" scores, the reviewer is equally at sea, in spite of a diligent attempt to discover their meaning.

The V-1 score is based on 16 adjectives in each of the two columns. These include such words as "persistent," "forceful," and "determined." V-2 results from the marking of 19 in each column; representative words are "attractive," "enthusiastic," and "impressive." For V-3 there are 10 words in the first column and 14 in the second. Samples are "mild," "kind," and "complacent." V-4 derives from 30 adjectives in each column; among these are "harmonious," "obliging," and "fatalistic." V-5 has 12 words in the first and 7 in the second column. Words scored in one column are usually scored for the same vector in the other. Except for V-5, there is little overlap among the keys.

The 12 numbers from the scoring and the 6 sums or "resultants" are transferred to a "Record Summary" card. Here the raw scores are plotted in terms of "T" score units so that three profiles emerge, one for each column and one for the total or "resultant." Although the standard units are referred to as T scale scores (which are defined as having a mean of 50 and a standard deviation of 10), the effective range on the summary card is from 28 to about 110 units. The V-1 scale extends from 40 to 105, a most remarkable degree of asymmetry. Furthermore, the profiles for presidents, accountants, salesmen, machine operators, and teachers, as reported by Clarke, have means clustering around 60, with no single point falling so low as the ostensible mean of 50.

Up to this point the AVA Administrator has been permitted to proceed. Quoting from the manual:

> The AVA Administrator is authorized only to administer and score the Activity Vector Analysis. The interpretation of an AVA is the responsibility of a Certified AVA Analyst and cannot be done by anyone other than that person. Any attempt on the part of the Administrator to interpret an AVA will result not only in withdrawal of endorsement of the Administrator concerned but, more important, may result in irreparable harm to the person concerned.

Interpretation of the profiles is the function of the AVA Analyst, a person trained by Walter V. Clarke Associates for a fee of $1,500.00 in an intensive three-week course. In the booklet entitled *Ethical Standards for Activity Vector Analysts* there appears a form of Hippocratic oath:

> I hereby agree, in view of the responsibility placed upon me by my company, and in view of having been accepted by Walter V. Clarke Associates for training in the Activity Vector Analysis Program for Effective Human Relations, to make use of the knowledge and information bestowed upon me for the welfare of my fellow man; to maintain the confidential nature of the information entrusted in me; to act in accord with the highest ethical standards consistent with the professional nature of my work; to maintain the dignity and stability essential to the great responsibility vested in me; and to carry on the established principles of Activity Vector Analysis to the best of my ability.

The process used by the analyst in interpreting the profiles is not described. However, some clues appear in three supplementary publications furnished to analysts. The first of these, the *Manual for Job Activity Rating,* describes a method of job analysis by which a particular job is rated on a 9-point scale for each of 25 factors. Weighted equivalents for each factor scale are given in a series of tables in this manual. In a "Job Activity Rating" form these weights are added and converted into what seems to be an ideal "AVA Pattern Shape." The rationale underlying this protracted exercise in arithmetic is not disclosed. The weights are so arranged that the four values of any pattern shape will add to 20.

The pattern shape is then translated into a "Universe Shape," apparently through arbitrary expansion of the deviations from the pattern mean. In the example shown in the manual, the profile values of 4.8, 3.5, 6.5, and 5.2 became respectively 4, 1, 9, and 6. These latter numbers define the job pattern shape.

The second publication contributing to our knowledge of the process is entitled *Preliminary Atlas of AVA Pattern Universe 258*. The face page describes the content:

> This Preliminary Atlas contains a projected map of the spherical universe of AVA pattern shapes.
> Included are duplicate sheets without the pattern shapes which can be used for three dimensional distributions.
> A complete Atlas including all pattern intercorrelations will be made available at a later date.

The number of the "Universe" seems to derive from the fact that 258 profiles are shown in a sort of Mercator projection. The sum of the four values in each pattern is 20 and each has one or more extreme values.

The third supplementary publication is entitled *Correlation Tables: AVA Pattern Universe*. It consists of over 165 large pages. The prefatory section indicates that the purpose is to substitute a numerical and spatial definition of profile shapes for the "word-pictures" used in the past. The first portion of this volume is devoted to a description of vector theory and its relationship to AVA patterns. The major portion consists of 258 tables, one for each pattern shape, giving the correlation coefficients between that pattern and the remaining 257 patterns of the "Pattern Universe." Finally, there are distribution charts and polar tabulation charts.

Space does not permit, nor does the content warrant, a detailed discussion of the fallacies involved in the erection of this questionable mathematical superstructure. It is of more concern to examine the dependability and utility of the *Activity Vector Analysis*.

There is a series of articles prepared by the staff of Walter V. Clarke Associates dealing with various characteristics of the AVA. There is also a smaller number of reports of studies conducted by persons not so affiliated. Some of Clarke's articles have been published in the *Journal of Psychology,* others are private publications of Walter V. Clarke Associates, Inc.; while only one, under the joint authorship of Wallace, Clarke, and Dry (7) appears in a journal which adheres to conventional professional editorial standards.

With the exception of the latter article, the Clarke publications fail to describe the procedures used or to report the basic data in such manner as to permit independent replication of any of these investigations. This reviewer has been forced to the conclusion that the purpose of these writings is not to inform but to overwhelm and impress the naive or casual reader. All sorts of complex statistical techniques are flashed before the eyes without a report of the basic data or even a reasonably complete description of the circumstances under which the study took place. Cases are dropped for such reasons as, "Examination of the forty-one AVA resultant profiles obtained from the analyses resulted in the elimination of five (5) cases on the basis of the pattern shape deviation standard established for this Study." Such selective elimination of cases is, of course, a notorious way of obtaining spurious indications of validity.

It is customary, when the claims made by the originator of a technique seem extravagant, to look for verification through investigations conducted by competent and unbiased persons. Consequently, the available independent reports deserve careful attention.

Mosel (1) reports estimated reliabilities of .74 and .73 for "other" and "self" choices. These values approximate those reported for test-retest coefficients in the manual but raise questions regarding the dependability of profiles based on these variables.

A General Electric Company report entitled "A Study to Determine How Well the Activity Vector Analysis Measures Personality Characteristics of Draftsmen," prepared by H. H. Meyer in 1954, concludes that the AVA showed little correlation with the ratings of supervisors or associates on some 11 personality traits and that two trained analysts rating some 50 draftsmen on "Over-all Suitability for Drafting Work" agreed with each other to the extent represented by a correlation coefficient of .19.

Another study conducted by D. J. Moffie of North Carolina State College with employees of the Hanes Hosiery Mills Company was concerned with the productivity of 47 hosiery inspectors and 100 hosiery loopers. Two AVA Analysts working independently classified the inspectors into three categories of productivity. No significant relationship with production was found for the ratings of either analyst. With the 100 loopers, three analysts working independently classified the subjects into three categories of productivity. In this instance, none of the three analysts produced results significantly superior to chance. Moffie also investigated the extent of agreement between pairs of analysts and found that one of the three pairs agreed to a slightly greater extent than could be attributed to chance, while the remaining pairs showed less agreement.

A second General Electric Company report entitled "A Research Study of the Use of Tests and the Interview for Evaluating Technical Personnel," conducted at the Fort Wayne Works and reported in 1954, included 164 engineers. A composite ranking procedure was used to divide the group into quarters for criterion purposes. The AVA was scored and interpreted by a representative of Walter V. Clarke Associates. Comparison was made between the top and bottom quarters with respect to the criterion. For each group 55 per cent were given "Average" or "High" AVA ratings. Quoting the report, "This test purports to measure the ability and personality characteristics which contribute to success in engineering work. The ratings made by the test analyst in this study, however, showed no relationship to the job performance ratings made by the supervisors."

The most thorough of the investigations of the validity of the AVA is the one reported by Wallace, Clarke, and Dry (7). The subjects were 899 "financed" life insurance agents employed by any of five insurance companies. Each of these men took the AVA at the time of employment, but the AVA scores were not used in the hiring decision. The AVA forms were sent to the Clarke home office for scoring. Each man also completed the LIAMA *Aptitude Index,* which scores were used in selection. The criterion of success was remaining with the company throughout the period and producing more than the median volume of business for current first year agents of that company. About 24 per cent met these requirements for the first year and 17 per cent for the second. Neither for the first nor for the second year did the AVA ratings show any significant relationship to success.

Over the past forty years a great number of self-descriptive inventories have been constructed and tried out. This reviewer is unable to recall a well established instance of useful validity for this class of questionnaire against a criterion of occupational success. The *Activity Vector Analysis* is simply another such inventory, and, from a technical standpoint, a poorly constructed one. The mumbo jumbo of allegedly sophisticated statistical procedures is no substitute for demonstrated validity. The awarding of titles to those trained in administration and interpretation, the gaudy names given the accessory materials, and the apparent reluctance to disclose basic data are scarcely representative of a conservative scientific approach.

Subsequent to the preparation of the paragraphs above, three additional dittoed reports by Merenda and Clarke were received by *The Mental Measurements Yearbook* office and transmitted to the reviewer. These have been read with care, and in the reviewer's opinion, conform to the pattern of incomplete, statistically pretentious, and misleading accounts previously described.

[30]

The Adjustment Inventory. Grades 9–16, adults; 1934–39; 1 form; 2 levels; 50¢ per specimen set, cash orders postpaid; (20–25) minutes; Hugh M. Bell; [Consulting Psychologists Press, Inc.] *
a) STUDENT FORM. Grades 9–16; 1934–39; 4 scores: home, health, social, emotional; 2 editions; manual ['34]; tentative norms.
1) [*Regular Edition.*] 1934–39; 1 form ('34); $3 per 25 tests; separate answer sheets ('39) may be used; $1.75 per 50 IBM answer sheets; $2.50 per set of hand scoring stencils and manual; $1.75 per set of machine scoring stencils.
2) [*IBM Test-Answer Sheet Edition.*] 1939; $3.75 per 50 tests; $2.50 per set of machine scoring stencils.
b) ADULT FORM. Adults; 1938–39; 5 scores: home, occupational, health, social, emotional; 1 form ('38); manual ['38]; prices same as for Regular Edition of Student Form; separate answer sheets ('39) may be used.

REFERENCES

1–15. See 40:1200.
16–119. See 4:28.
120. AARONS, WILLIAM B. *A Study of Intra-Family Personality Similarities and Differences as Measured by Test Performance on the Bell Adjustment Inventory.* Master's thesis, Temple University (Philadelphia, Pa.), 1942.
121. HAHN, MILTON EDWIN. *An Investigation of Measured Aspects of Social Intelligence in a Distributive Occupation.* Doctor's thesis, University of Minnesota (Minneapolis, Minn.), 1942.
122. SOLOMON, LEWIS E. *Some Relationships Between Reading Ability and Degree of Academic Success in College.* Doctor's thesis, University of Colorado (Boulder, Colo.), 1944.
123. CASNER, DANIEL. *Certain Factors Associated With Success and Failure in Personal-Adjustment Counseling.* Doctor's thesis, New York University (New York, N.Y.), 1950.
124. JOHNSON, RALPH H., AND BOND, GUY L. "Reading Ease of Commonly Used Tests." *J Appl Psychol* 34:319–24 O '50. * (PA 26:299)
125. GOULD, HENRY. *Relation of Certain Personality Components to Achievement in Secondary School Science.* Doctor's thesis, New York University (New York, N.Y.), 1951. (DA 12:160)
126. MARSHALL, MAX L. *A Comparison of the Effects of Two Response Sets on a Structured Personality Test.* Master's thesis, Vanderbilt University (Nashville, Tenn.), 1951.
127. PAULSON, STANLEY F. "Changes in Confidence During a Period of Speech Training: Transfer of Training and Comparison of Improved and Non-Improved Groups on the Bell Adjustment Inventory." *Speech Monogr* 18:260–5 N '51. *
128. NEWMAN, SIDNEY H.; FRENCH, JOHN W.; AND BOBBITT, JOSEPH M. "Analysis of Criteria for the Validation of Selection Measures at the United States Coast Guard Academy." *Ed & Psychol Meas* 12:394–407 au '52. * (PA 27:6159)
129. OSBORNE, R. TRAVIS; GREENE, JAMES E.; AND SANDERS, WILMA B. "Urban-Rural Differences in Personality of College Students as Measured by an Adjustment Inventory." *Rural Sociol* 17:61–2 Mr '52. *
130. PRATT, MARTHA A. *The Predictive Significance of Scores on Bell's School Inventory.* Master's thesis, University of Georgia (Athens, Ga.), 1952.
131. SHAMES, GEORGE HERBERT. *An Investigation of Prognosis and Evaluation in Speech Therapy.* Doctor's thesis, University of Pittsburgh (Pittsburgh, Pa.), 1952.
132. CANTONI, LOUIS J. *A Follow-Up Study of the Personal Adjustment of the Subjects Who Participated in the 1939-1943 Flint, Michigan, Guidance Demonstration.* Doctor's thesis, University of Michigan (Ann Arbor, Mich.), 1953.
133. O'CONNOR, WILLIAM F. *The Relationship Between Emotionality as Measured by a Verbal Discrimination Scale and the Bell Adjustment Inventory.* Master's thesis, Fordham University (New York, N.Y.), 1953.
134. ABERNETHY, ETHEL M. "The Effect of Sorority Pressures on the Results of a Self-Inventory." *J Social Psychol* 40:177–83 Ag '54. * (PA 29:6189)
135. MUNGER, PAUL F. "Factors Related to Persistence in College of Students Who Ranked in the Lower Third of Their High School Class." *J Counsel Psychol* 1:132–6 fall '54. * (PA 29:6258)
136. PIERCE-JONES, JOHN. "The Readability of Certain Standard Tests." *Calif J Ed Res* 5:80–2 Mr '54. * (PA 28:8729)
137. SANDRA, M. ELAINE. *A Comparative Study of the Scores Obtained by Institutional Adolescent Girls on the Bell Adjustment Inventory and the P-F Test.* Master's thesis, Fordham University (New York, N.Y.), 1954.
138. SIMS, VERNER M. "Relations Between the Social-Class Identification and Personality Adjustment of a Group of High School and College Students." *J Social Psychol* 40:323–7 N '54. * (PA 29:7190)
139. CANTONI, LOUIS J. "High School Tests and Measurements as Predictors of Occupational Status." *J Appl Psychol* 39:253–5 Ag '55. * (PA 30:4722)
140. CANTONI, LOUIS J. "A Study in Emotional Adjustment: The Correlation of Student and Adult Forms of the Bell Adjustment Inventory Over a Period of Thirteen Years." *Ed & Psychol Meas* 15:137–43 su '55. * (PA 30:2449)
141. CHANCE, JUNE ELIZABETH. "Prediction of Changes in a Personality Inventory on Retesting." *Psychol Rep* 1:383–7 D '55. * (PA 30:5979)
142. JESSEN, MARGARET S. "Factors in Parents' Prediction of Adolescent Responses to Selected Items on the Bell Adjustment Inventory." Abstract. *Am Psychol* 10:365 Ag '55. *
143. THOMAS, CHARLES W., JR. *An Evaluation of the Bell Adjustment Inventory as a Predictor of Successful Medical School Candidates at John Carroll University.* Master's thesis, John Carroll University (Cleveland, Ohio), 1955.
144. WILLIAMS, JOSEPH L. *An Evaluation of the Bell Adjustment as an Instrument for Predicting Academic Success at Texas Southern University.* Master's thesis, Texas Southern University (Houston, Tex.), 1956.
145. BOYKIN, LEANDER L. "The Adjustment of 2,078 Negro Students." *J Negro Ed* 26:75–9 w '57. * (PA 32:922)

For reviews by Nelson G. Hanawalt and Theodore R. Sarbin, see 4:28; for reviews by Raymond B. Cattell, John G. Darley, C. M. Louttit, and Percival M. Symonds of the Student Form, and reviews by S. J. Beck, J. P. Guilford, and Doncaster G. Humm of the Adult Form, see 40:1200 (1 excerpt); for a review by Austin H. Turney of the Student Form, see 38:912 (although three reviews are listed under 38:912, only the review by Austin H. Turney is a review of Bell's Adjustment Inventory; the other two are reviews of Bell's School Inventory).

[31]

★Adjustment Questionnaire. Ages 12–17; 1951; 11 scores: self-confidence, sense of personal worth, sense of personal freedom, recognition, social relationships, nervous symptoms, moral attitudes, family relationships, school relationships, emotionality, total; IBM;

1 form ['51]; mimeographed manual ['51]; separate answer sheets must be used; 16s. per 100 tests; 5s. per 100 IBM answer sheets; postage extra; specimen set not available; Afrikaans edition available; (25–30) minutes; National Bureau of Educational and Social Research. *

[32]

★Behavior Preference Record: *What Would You Do?* (A Study of Some Home and School Problems). Grades 4–6, 7–9, 9–12; 1953; 6 scores: cooperation, friendliness, integrity, leadership, responsibility, critical thinking; IBM; Forms A, B; 3 levels: Elementary, Intermediate, Advanced; separate answer sheets must be used; $2.80 per 35 tests; 7¢ per Scoreze answer sheet; 4¢ per IBM answer sheet; 60¢ per set of scoring stencils; postage extra; 50¢ per specimen set of any one level, postpaid; (30–45) minutes; Hugh B. Wood; California Test Bureau. *

J. Thomas Hastings, *University Examiner; Director of Unit on Evaluation in Bureau of Educational Research; Professor of Education, University of Illinois, Urbana, Illinois.*

Of the four purposes stated by the author for this instrument—to determine understanding of democratic ideals, to determine stated preferences for various types of behavior, to determine the rationalization (critical thinking) for preferred behaviors, and to stimulate discussion and decisions about desirable social behavior—the fourth is by far the most appropriate. The "record" grew out of a discussion in an eighth grade class of characteristics of democratic behavior and a subsequent search for a means for "measuring" the characteristics. As a teaching device directed at getting students to think systematically about their behavior in daily situations and its meaning for democratic ideals, this type of discussion project should be useful in the hands of a good teacher. It does not follow that the instrument with its scores and norms on behavioral traits is equally useful.

To the contrary, the good teacher who wishes to use the *method* probably would find that the categorization of democratic behavior into five "traits" and an ability is restrictive of meaningful thinking on the part of the students. Certainly the teacher who cannot on his own handle such a discussion project usefully would be apt to err seriously in using the device as a measure of the characteristics. In the latter case, serious harm could come from labeling pupils (or helping them label themselves) according to the score categories—very high, high, average, low, and very low—on the five characteristics: cooperation, friendliness, integrity, leadership, and responsibility. It should be made clearer in the manual that these "characteristics" are labels for constructs which *may* seem to explain or make clearer the expressed choice of action in a given situation. In many cases some other label may be of more use in explaining the choice of action for certain individuals. For example, "aggressiveness" may seem a more useful construct than does "leadership" when a pupil chooses to tell others "to be quiet." Or again, "shyness" may be a more useful label than "integrity" when a student waits to ask a question until a teacher finishes talking to another student.

The manual does suggest what would appear to be some useful activities in a classroom discussion of the answers recorded by pupils in the class. However, the suggestion that regular teachers do individual counseling with students whose test scores show "unusual anti-social tendencies" is very likely to be harmful. The reliability and validity of the scores, the basis for norms, and the concepts themselves warrant individual counseling only by a well trained counselor, and such a counselor would not need the test for this purpose. The caution that the teacher refer cases which he should not handle is meaningless, since untrained people cannot sense referral needs.

The scores on characteristics are computed by giving one point on the characteristic if a student chooses a certain action in a given problem and by subtracting a point on that characteristic for the choice of some other action. The instrument is keyed in such a fashion that a given choice of action may add a point (or subtract a point) on two or three characteristics. Although the manual states that, from a table of intercorrelations, "it may be assumed that fairly discrete characteristics are being measured," it should be noted that some of the traits seem to appear together rather frequently on the key. For example: On one form containing 20 problems there is an aggregate of 70 possible actions. Twenty-eight of these would give a point on cooperation, whereas 18 are keyed to give a point on friendliness. Actually, 10 of the actions are common for the two characteristics, i.e., give a point on each. Therefore, more than half of the "friendliness points" are also "cooperation points." By the same type of count, only three of the choices which take a point away from friendliness do not also take a point away from cooperation. The user should be aware of the fact that there is this type of "built in" relationship, especially when he is using the profile.

Following the set of three to five possible actions among which the examinee may choose for each problem situation, there are a number of "reasons for choosing the action" which he may mark. The form of the test necessarily restricts the student to choosing among those reasons given—he cannot write out his own. Although this fact should be taken into consideration by the test user, he should also recognize that these reasons were pulled from among those most frequently given when the test was first designed. The "critical thinking" score for a student is the percentage representing the number of "keyed" or right reasons which he has marked. Two questions should be kept in mind by the user: (a) Do these reasons for action actually represent the construct I have for "critical thinking"? (b) Is the percentage for a given student based upon many, several, or few marked reasons? A high percentage based upon few attempts certainly suggests a different behavior from the one suggested by the same percentage based upon many attempts.

The author states, "The scores of over eight thousand students were used in developing the norms." According to the table in the manual, the total number of students taking any form at any level of any of the five editions since 1938 is 8,275. A statement to the effect that some 1,700 students were utilized for the norms on the 1953 edition should be noted to mean *all* students taking *all* forms at *all* levels. Actually, the norms for any one form of the current edition are based upon approximately 300 cases.

In summary, the main function of this test should be to serve as an informal teaching device, and the average teacher would run less danger of doing harm if he were to use it for class discussion without scoring it at all. Trained counselors might find it useful for eliciting certain clues or for starting certain kinds of client discussions, but it should certainly not be used by regular teachers as a measure of the traits or ability named in the scores.

EDWARD LANDY, *Director, Division of Counseling Services, Newton Public Schools, Newton, Massachusetts.*

The *Behavior Preference Record* employs the device of briefly describing a situation to which a pupil might respond in a variety of ways. He is then asked to select from several alternatives a course of action and the reasons for his selection. The accompanying manual states that the primary value of the BPR lies in the opportunities which it presents for teaching by providing a tool for informal, but directed, character education. Face examination of the materials would seem to indicate that this is a valid claim.

It is unfortunate that the publishers were not content to stop with this claim, which is a very important one in its own right. Elsewhere in the manual the publishers make these additional claims: "The *Behavior Preference Record* is designed to: (a) provide a systematic analysis of some behavior situations to determine the individual's understanding of democratic ideals, (b) to determine his stated preferences for various types of behavior, (c) to determine his rationalizations (critical thinking) for his preferred behavior, and (d) to stimulate discussions and decisions about desirable social behavior." It is very doubtful to what extent (a) and (c) are achieved, if at all. What stopping or not stopping at a red traffic light, or liking or not liking your mother's cooking (these are samples of situations) have to do with democratic ideals is unclear. Instead of obtaining (c), one might, and probably does in many instances, get the pupil's best guess as to what he thinks teacher would like to have him answer.

The manual seems to make still another claim for which it presents no substantial evidence. It states: "The *Behavior Preference Record* provides analytical evidence on the extent of development of certain behavioral characteristics of the individual. From this evidence it is possible to identify certain shortcomings and recommend remedial measures to correct them." This statement can be interpreted as saying much or saying little. In the hands of the clinically unsophisticated classroom teacher it may lead to harm rather than good.

The possible confusion as to the interpretation of results is illustrated by the sample profile given on page 5 of the manual. The boy's profile ranks are very low in cooperation and critical thinking, low in friendliness, average in responsibility, high in integrity, and very high in leadership. The accompanying interpretation reads as follows: "The boy whose profile appears below shows an unusual potential for Leadership but he has a very low score in Cooperation and Critical Thinking. *This suggests aggressive rather than real leadership* [reviewer's italics]. He should be given special assistance in clarifying the concepts and developing the skills related to Cooperation." One is left wondering just what the labeled characteristics do measure.

An elaborate system of scoring with tables of norms and profiles tends to give an appearance of rigorous quantitative measurement of "certain characteristics of democratic behavior" which is not substantiated, in this review's judgment, by any evidence presented in the manual.

If the BPR were presented simply as a device for stimulating discussion and self-examination, particularly with respect to rationalization tendencies, it could be recommended as a useful teaching tool. It cannot be recommended as an instrument for measuring clearly defined characteristics of democratic behavior upon which remedial measures can be based.

J Consult Psychol 17:401–2 O '53. Laurance F. Shaffer. * While the blank may evoke some useful thinking about the social characteristics of pupils, it suffers from numerous faults. The prestige values of the responses were not controlled. As in all such short questionnaires, radically different interpretations from "average" to "very high" may be drawn from scores which differ by as little as 3 points when the standard error of measurement is as great as 2.8 points.

[33]
★**Bonney-Fessenden Sociograph.** Grades 4–12; 1955; 1 form; 50¢ per set of sociograph, 40 answer slips, and manual; 15¢ per sociograph; 15¢ per 40 answer slips; 25¢ per manual; postage extra; administration time not reported; Merl E. Bonney and Seth A. Fessenden; California Test Bureau. *

ÅKE BJERSTEDT, *Department of Psychology, University of Lund, Lund, Sweden.*

For the recording of interpersonal relations, two groups of devices have been mainly used: sociograms and sociomatrices. The *Bonney-Fessenden Sociograph* might, perhaps, be most quickly described as a folded sociomatrix: the ordinary sociomatrix, in which each pair-relation is described by two cells, may be thought of as folded along the main diagonal so that the two cells common to two people coincide. More concretely, we deal with a tabulation form of triangular shape, where each cell has two compartments, one for outgoing choices and one for incoming choices. By this device, mutual choices between two individuals occur in *one* cell and are consequently much more readily revealed than in the nonfolded type of tabulation. This is, in fact, the unique contribution of the socio-

graph, which could, therefore, be recommended as a timesaving device when we are especially interested in two-way relations.

Having pointed out its valuable contribution, the reviewer now has to criticize the overly enthusiastic claims made for this new technique in the manual. It is stated there that the sociograph not only simplifies the recording of sociometric data, but also "retains all of the advantages of the sociogram and the matrix heretofore required for sociometric appraisal." This is certainly not the truth. For example, the sociograph does not retain the surveyability for several-people relations, which is the unique feature of a good sociogram: one cannot trace chains, triangles, and squares as easily as one can in such a diagram. Neither does the sociograph retain all the advantages of the conventional sociomatrix: for example, one is not so easily able to use the tabulation as a basis for various computational analyses (array totals, matrix multiplication for the determination of several-step relations, and the like). Certain specific sociographic devices such as the target diagram and the chessboard diagram have made it possible to compare in a surveyable manner total status with single choice relations or status at different time points in one diagram. None of these possibilities exists in the sociograph. This criticism is not directed against the sociograph as such, for one instrument cannot have every advantage at the same time. However, it is directed against the "wholesale" statements in the manual about its value and uniqueness, statements which could be very misleading to those who are not familiar with existing techniques.

Besides, it should be pointed out that the simplifying effect of the sociograph is mainly limited to the locating of pair relations. In several other respects it is more confusing than the ordinary sociomatrix. In the conventional matrix, for example, outgoing choices may simply be read from the row of an individual and incoming choices from his column. In the sociograph, on the other hand, outgoing choices have to be read from the left half of the cells in an individual's row *plus* the right half of the cells in his column, and incoming choices from the right half of the cells in his row *plus* the left half of the cells in his column. That this is much more complicated is admitted implicitly when it is recommended that outgoing choices should be tabulated from the answer sheets rather than from the sociograph.

From the tabulation we are often interested in getting individual sums not only for the six basic variables (positive and negative choices given, received, and reciprocated), but also for the corresponding socioperceptual variables (positive and negative choice-guesses), for different preference levels, and for different choice aspects (criteria). In the flexible and informal sociomatrix, which we line up for our specific purpose on squared paper, we may include all these variables without great difficulty. On the present printed form, however, we cannot include more than six variables in all since space is supplied only for six array totals.

As this instrument is primarily a recording device and not a test, ordinary questions as to administration, norms, reliability, and validity are not of immediate concern. The manual, however, does give a helpful discussion of administration, including some original suggestions; the use of answer slips, for example, is not usual in conventional sociometry, but may be an important timesaver among group members sufficiently careful not to introduce unnecessary errors during the number checking procedure. Further, the manual presents a discussion of reliability, validity, and utility as related to the sociometric method in general. This discussion is, of course, very brief, but the authors succeed all the same in outlining some of the most important features in a helpful and judicious manner, although they seem too optimistic in a few instances.

Summing up, the *Bonney-Fessenden Sociograph* is a specific form of sociometric tabulation which, for certain purposes, especially for the quick location of mutual preferences, may be very useful. Its manual, in addition, outlines certain more general methodological questions within the field of sociometry in a helpful way. However, the explicit claims that at the same time it retains all the advantages of other types of sociograms and matrices do *not* seem warranted.

C. ROBERT PACE, *Professor of Psychology and Chairman of the Department, Syracuse University, Syracuse, New York.*

This is not a test; it is a tabulation chart for recording sociometric data. Its virtue is to be judged by the convenience of its format and by the explanations and cautions which its authors give prospective users. On all these matters the device appears to be useful.

The chart may be used for groups up to 40 in number. Students are provided with answer slips on which they record their choices by checking numbers corresponding to the names of the persons chosen. The slips are then laid on the tabulation chart, and the choices recorded. Summary columns provide space for noting the number of choices given and received, the mutual choices, the rejections, and other information typically looked for in the sociometric technique. Directions for using the device are specific and detailed.

The manual contains a general discussion of the reliability and validity of sociometric scores, based on a selective survey of related literature. The suggestions for using and interpreting sociometric data are helpful and well balanced. Classroom teachers should welcome this systematic method and convenient chart for simplifying what, under the best of circumstances, is still a rather complicated task.

[34]

★A Book About Me. Grades kgn-1; 1952; workbook for gathering data about children's background, maturity, interests, and attitudes; 1 form; norms for experimental form only; 10 or more copies, 39¢ each; 60¢ per 20 analysis sheets; 50¢ per specimen set; postage extra; Edith Sherman Jay; Science Research Associates. *

FLORENCE M. TEAGARDEN, *Emeritus Professor of Psychology, University of Pittsburgh, Pittsburgh, Pennsylvania.*

By her choice of materials and her suggestions for their use the author shows intimate knowledge of kindergarten and first grade children as well as a philosophy underlying good curricula for these ages. The material to be used by the children is a workbook consisting of 32 pages of pictures (several hundred in all) of people and things pertinent to the lives of kindergarten and first grade children. The nature and use of this material will be most easily understood if readers will first thumb through all the pictures to see their charm, realism, and practicality, and then read carefully pages 18–30 and 1–17 in the manual.

If this sequence is followed, the reader will see that the pictures may actually be used as a *test* of the contents of the child's mind at the time he enters school. This, of course, should be done before the children are given individual copies of *A Book About Me* to use as a workbook. Directions for so using the book and for scoring the test are given in the teacher's manual. Such a test would require one class period every day for a week. Analysis sheets provide for the recording of pertinent data from this test, the results of which can become a part of each child's cumulative school record.

Innumerable suggestions are given for the use of *A Book About Me* as a workbook in the usual classroom sense. Questions which may be asked about the pictures are given, as are examples of ways in which the pictures may be marked, cut out, and mounted by the children.

In addition to suggestions for the use of *A Book About Me* as a survey testing device and as a classroom workbook, the author gives several interesting accounts of the ways in which individual teachers with particular aims in mind have used the book, e.g., the teacher who wanted to improve her children's oral English; the teacher who wanted a concrete way of acquainting parents with what the child and the school were doing; the teacher of older dull children obliged to do very elementary work; the teacher of ungraded classes, and the like. Examples of the book's use in college classes in child development, in clinic interviews, and even in play therapy sessions are also given.

Because of the various ways in which *A Book About Me* can be and has been used, there is little that can or need be said about matters of reliability and validity. The author does, however, show some interesting age and sex differences on responses to three pages of pictures by 50 boys and 50 girls at each age from 4 through 7—400 responses in all.

The reviewer is quite impressed with the possible uses of this device. She is obliged to say, however, that she would have come to an understanding of the purposes and uses of the material more readily if the suggestions made above as to the order in which the teacher or clinician should read the manual had been come by a little sooner and with less trial and error. As a clinical psychologist working primarily with preschool children, the reviewer hopes that some day the author will use her demonstrated ability to give us more material of this kind that can be used, particularly as a projective device, with little children.

[35]

★Bristol Social-Adjustment Guides. Ages 5–15; 1956–58; 1 form ('56); 3 rating scales; 4s. per 12 diagnostic forms ('56) for each scale; 25s. per manual ('58); 3s. per specimen set; postage extra; (10–20)

minutes; D. H. Stott and E. G. Sykes (*a*, *b*); University of London Press Ltd. *
a) THE CHILD IN SCHOOL. Separate editions for boys and girls; 6s. per 12 scales; 6d. per single copy; 3s. per set of scoring keys.
b) THE CHILD IN RESIDENTIAL CARE. 6s. per 12 scales; 6d. per single copy; 4s. per set of scoring keys.
c) THE CHILD IN THE FAMILY. Life history chart ('56); 9s. per 12 scales; 9d. per single copy; 2s. 6d. per scoring key.

[36]

Brown Personality Inventory for Children. Grades 4–9; 1935–46; 1 form ['35]; manual ['46]; $2.15 per 25 tests; 35¢ per specimen set; postpaid; administration time not reported; Fred Brown; Public School Publishing Co. *

REFERENCES
1–8. See 40:1240.
9. BROWN, FRED. "A Comparative Study of Stability and Maturity of Non-Delinquent, Pre-Delinquent, and Delinquent Boys." Abstract. *Psychol B* 34:779–80 N '37. *
10. MORRIS, CHARLES M. "An Experimental Analysis of Certain Performance Tests." Abstract. *Psychol B* 34:716–7 N '37. *
11. KORAN, S. *A Study of Developmental Age, Brown Personality Inventory Scores, and Certain Traits in Elementary School Boys.* Master's thesis, Pennsylvania State College (State College, Pa.), 1938.
12. BROWN, FRED. "An Experimental Study of Parental Attitudes and Their Effects on Child Adjustment." *Am J Orthopsychiatry* 12:224–30 Ap '42. * (*PA* 16:3336)
13. BROWN, FRED. "An Experimental Study of the Validity and Reliability of the Brown Personality Inventory for Children." *J Psychol* 17:75–89 Ja '44. * (*PA* 18:1449)
14. GOOCH, PAUL H. *A Study of the Responses of Children Nine to Fourteen Years of Age to the Brown Personality Inventory.* Master's thesis, Kansas State Teacher's College (Emporia, Kan.), 1953.
15. NOWELL, ANN. "Peer Status as Related to Measures of Personality." *Calif J Ed Res* 4:37–41 Ja '53. * (*PA* 28:1514)
16. ABRAMS, JULES C. *A Study of Certain Personality Characteristics of Non-Readers and Achieving Readers.* Doctor's thesis, Temple University (Philadelphia, Pa.), 1955. (*DA* 16:377)
17. NEUHAUS, EDMUND C. "A Personality Study of Asthmatic and Cardiac Children." *Psychosom Med* 20:181–6 My–Je '58. *
18. SARASON, SEYMOUR B.; DAVIDSON, KENNETH; LIGHTHALL, FREDERICK; AND WAITE, RICHARD. "Rorschach Behavior and Performance of High and Low Anxious Children." *Child Develop* 29:277–85 Je '58. *

For reviews by S. J. Beck and Carl R. Rogers, see 40:1240.

[37]

★California Psychological Inventory. Ages 13 and over; 1956–57; 18 scores: dominance (Do), capacity for status (Cs), sociability (Sy), social presence (Sp), self-acceptance (Sa), sense of well-being (Wb), responsibility (Re), socialization (So), self-control (Sc), tolerance (To), good impression (Gi), communality (Cm), achievement via conformance (Ac), achievement via independence (Ai), intellectual efficiency (Ie), psychological-mindedness (Py), flexibility (Fx), femininity (Fe); IBM; 1 form ('56); administrator's guide ('57, reprinted from manual); separate answer sheets must be used; $6.25 per 25 tests; $3.75 per 100 profiles ['57] and either hand scored or IBM answer sheets; $3 per set of either hand scoring stencils or IBM scoring stencils; $3 per manual ('57); $1 per specimen set; postage extra; scoring service available; (45–60) minutes; Harrison G. Gough; Consulting Psychologists Press, Inc. *

REFERENCES
1. GOUGH, HARRISON G. "A New Dimension of Status: I, Development of a Personality Scale." *Am Sociol R* 13:401–9 Ag '48. * (*PA* 24:523)
2. GOUGH, HARRISON G. "A New Dimension of Status: II, Relationship of the St Scale to Other Variables." *Am Sociol R* 13:534–7 O '48. * (*PA* 24:524)

3. GOUGH, HARRISON G. "The Construction of a Personality Scale to Predict Academic Achievement in Introductory Psychology Courses." Abstract. *Am Psychol* 7:367–8 Jl '52. *

4. GOUGH, HARRISON G. "Identifying Psychological Femininity." *Ed & Psychol Meas* 12:427–39 au '52. * (*PA* 27:5873)

5. GOUGH, HARRISON G. "On Making a Good Impression." *J Ed Res* 46:33–42 S '52. *

6. GOUGH, HARRISON G. "Predicting Social Participation." *J Social Psychol* 35:227–33 My '52. * (*PA* 27:3455)

7. GOUGH, HARRISON G., AND PETERSON, DONALD R. "The Identification and Measurement of Predispositional Factors in Crime and Delinquency." *J Consult Psychol* 16:207–12 Je '52. * (*PA* 27:5279)

8. GOUGH, HARRISON G.; McCLOSKY, HERBERT; AND MEEHL, PAUL E. "A Personality Scale for Social Responsibility." *J Abn & Social Psychol* 47:73–80 Ja '52. * (*PA* 26:6270)

9. GILMAN, SAMUEL F. *An Experiment in Validation of the Gough and Peterson Delinquency Prediction Scale.* Master's thesis, Boston College (Chestnut Hill, Mass.), 1953.

10. GOUGH, HARRISON G. "The Construction of a Personality Scale to Predict Scholastic Achievement." *J Appl Psychol* 37:361–6 O '53. * (*PA* 29:1565)

11. GOUGH, HARRISON G. "What Determines the Academic Achievement of High School Students." *J Ed Res* 46:321–31 Ja '53. * (*PA* 28:1563)

12. WEBSTER, HAROLD. "Derivation and Use of the Masculinity-Femininity Variable." *J Clin Psychol* 9:33–6 Ja '53. * (*PA* 27:7803)

13. GOUGH, HARRISON G. "Systematic Validation of a Test for Delinquency." Abstract. *Am Psychol* 9:381 Ag '54. *

14. GOWAN, J. C., AND GOWAN, MAY SEAGOE. "The Guilford-Zimmerman and the California Psychological Inventory in the Measurement of Teaching Candidates." *Calif J Ed Res* 6:35–7 Ja '55. * (*PA* 29:7990)

15. KLUGH, HENRY E., AND BENDIG, A. W. "The Manifest Anxiety and ACE Scales and College Achievement." Abstract. *J Consult Psychol* 19:487 D '55. *

16. OETTEL, ARNOLD M. "Leadership: A Psychological Study." Abstract. *Am Psychol* 10:342 Ag '55. *

17. BENDIG, A. W., AND KLUGH, HENRY E. "A Validation of Gough's Hr Scale in Predicting Academic Achievement." *Ed & Psychol Meas* 16:516–23 w '56. * (*PA* 32:934)

18. BROWN, DONALD R., AND BYSTRYN, DENISE. "College Environment, Personality, and Social Ideology of Three Ethnic Groups." *J Social Psychol* 44:279–88 N '56. *

19. DUNNETTE, MARVIN D., AND AYLWARD, MERRIAM S. "Validity Information Exchange, No. 9-21: D.O.T. Code, Design and Development Engineers." *Personnel Psychol* 9:245–7 su '56. *

20. GOUGH, HARRISON G. "Potential Use of Personality Scales in Schools and Colleges," pp. 3–20. In *Fifth Annual Western Regional Conference on Testing Problems, April 13, 1956.* Princeton, N.J.: Educational Testing Service, [1956]. Pp. iii, 78. * (*PA* 31:8486)

21. NIYEKAWA, AGNES M. "A Comparative Analysis of Foreign and American Female College Groups on Three Personality Variables: Anxiety, Level of Aspiration and Femininity." *Psychol Newsl* 7:72–91 My–Je '56. * (*PA* 31:3697)

22. BENDIG, A. W. "The Validity of Two Temperament Scales in Predicting Student Achievement in Introductory Psychology." *J Ed Res* 50:571–80 Ap '57. *

23. BENNETT, LAWRENCE A., AND RUDOFF, ALVIN. "Evaluation of Modified Administration of the California Psychological Inventory." *J Clin Psychol* 13:303–4 Jl '57. *

24. CUADRA, CARLOS A., AND REED, CHARLES F. "Prediction of Psychiatric Aide Performance." *J Appl Psychol* 41:195–7 Je '57. *

25. DINITZ, SIMON; KAY, BARBARA; AND RECKLESS, WALTER C. "Delinquency Proneness and School Achievement." *Ed Res B* 36:131–6 Ap 10 '57. *

26. JACKSON, DOUGLAS N. "Response Acquiescence in the California Psychological Inventory." Abstract. *Am Psychol* 12:412–3 Jl '57. *

27. MORRIS, ROBERT P. "An Exploratory Study of Some Personality Characteristics of Gamblers." *J Clin Psychol* 13:191–3 Ap '57. * (*PA* 32:3294)

28. BENDIG, A. W. "Comparative Validity of Empirical Temperament Test Keys in Predicting Student Achievement in Psychology." *J Ed Res* 51:341–8 Ja '58. *

29. BENDIG, A. W. "Comparison of the Validity of Two Temperament Scales in Predicting College Achievement." *J Ed Res* 51:605–9 Ap '58. *

30. DUNNETTE, MARVIN D., AND KIRCHNER, WAYNE K. "Validation of Psychological Tests in Industry." *Personnel Adm* 21:20–7 My–Je '58. *

31. DUNNETTE, MARVIN D.; KIRCHNER, WAYNE K.; AND DE-GIDEO, JoANNE. "Relations Among Scores on Edwards Personal Preference Schedule, California Psychological Inventory, and Strong Vocational Interest Blank for an Industrial Sample." *J Appl Psychol* 42:178–81 Je '58. *

32. GOWAN, J. C. "Intercorrelations and Factor Analysis of Tests Given to Teaching Candidates." *J Exp Ed* 27:1–22 S '58. *

33. LIDDLE, GORDON. "The California Psychological Inventory and Certain Social and Personal Factors." *J Ed Psychol* 49:144–9 Je '58. *

LEE J. CRONBACH, *Professor of Education and Psychology, University of Illinois, Urbana, Illinois.*

The CPI is designed on the principle that questionnaire items which correlate with socially significant criteria are important, whether or not they fit into available personality theories. In this it resembles the *Minnesota Multiphasic Personality Inventory,* but the psychiatric states which provided the armature for the MMPI are here replaced by such external reference variables as social class membership, grade in introductory psychology, and prominence as a leader. Each criterion locates extreme groups who presumably have some psychological similarity, and a scale is formed from items which discriminate these extremes. The scale is thought of as measuring that underlying psychological complex, not merely as predicting the erstwhile criterion. The psychological nature of the complex is then established by further inquiry. The capacity-for-status (Cs) score, for example, consists of items marked differently in different social strata, and is regarded as a measure of whatever attitudes and attributes "underlie and lead to status," including ambition, communication effectiveness, and versatility.

The instrument has 480 true-false items (12 of which are duplicates), some from MMPI and others written to tap social and personal attitudes and interests. The items range over an exceptional variety of manifest content. Scores on 18 scales offer a descriptive profile of the high school student or adult. Eleven scales were based on external criteria. Four more scales were formed from items judged homogeneous. Finally, there are three control keys: Wb, based on responses given by normals asked to "fake bad"; Gi, based on responses given by normals when "faking good"; and Cm, a count of highly popular responses. Marked deviation on a control score casts doubt on the validity of the individual profile.

The development and technical work on the scale are of a high order. The reliabilities were carefully determined by retesting. Validity of each scale was determined by comparing groups which the scale presumably ought to discriminate; dozens of cross validities on sizeable samples are reported. Norms for males and females are based on several thousand accumulated cases; it might be better to have truly representative samples, but this is no serious weakness. The manual gives plentiful correlations with other tests. With its scientific yet readable style, its illustrative case interpretations, and its extensive data, the manual is in some respects a model for personality inventories. It does not, however, indicate recommended uses and necessary cautions as adequately as does the manual for the *Minnesota Counseling Inventory*.

The manual fails to tell what criteria were used in scale development. Tracing these in the literature, one finds puzzling disparities between the scale designations and the original criteria; e.g., the sociability scale consists of items that correlate with the number of extracurricular activities engaged in.

The presentation of validities, based largely on differences between extreme groups, is seriously misleading. On dominance, for example, the mean for 89 female leaders in high school is 29; for 4,056 nonleaders, 24. The SD within each group is 6, and CR is 8. This result would look less impressive if the substantial overlap were pointed out. For the same scale a CR of 6.42 is reported between girls rated high and girls rated low in dominance; the manual also reports a biserial *r* of .67 and a point biserial *r* of .53. These are illegitimate figures, since they ignore the intermediate group. Assuming that the selected cases are the highest and lowest 3 per cent of the group and estimating the product-moment *r* for all cases, we may conclude that the true validity is only about .22. This validity is representative. The extreme groups chosen to validate other scales also have notable overlap; for example, female jail inmates average at the 30th percentile of all females on the socialization scale. Ratings by qualified assessment teams never correlate above .50 with the corresponding CPI score, and values are often as low as .25.

Some aspects of the validity report are puzzling. In at least one instance a validity coefficient is given, not for the CPI key, but for an earlier scale using more items. For another scale, the manual gives no data but says that low scorers tend to be seen as cautious, confused, and easygoing; the published article on this scale gives data showing that they are seen as cynical, headstrong, and impatient. It would have been wiser to report meticulously a small number of well-substantiated findings than to invite misinterpretation by reporting too much, too casually.

One is inclined to say that personality scores with validities in the .20's are worthless, but Gough makes the possibly valid point that we should not expect any one scale to correlate highly with any datum on observed personality. Interpretation ought to rest on configurations: high Cs plus high responsibility, he says, implies efficiency and poise, but high Cs with low Re implies aggressiveness and opportunism. No data are offered to support this interesting proposal to take advantage of the superior "bandwidth" of this instrument. Ultimately we should be told the precise probability that a description inferred from an entire profile will correspond to the person's actual behavior.

Although actuarial instruments sometimes permit indirect and subtle measurement, the CPI is not appreciably less direct than other questionnaires on adjustment and character. Twelve of the principal scales are much affected by a desire to fake good or bad. Among males, eleven keys correlate .48 or higher with Bernreuter Self-Confidence. Despite the complex manner in which keys were developed, the test must be regarded as no more than a tabulation of overt self-descriptions. The chief difference between CPI and the majority of other inventories for school use is that its profile is much more elaborate. It measures the same seven dimensions as the new *Minnesota Counseling Inventory* (with no worse validities) and adds seven others.

The variables describe character in value loaded terms. Teachers and principals very likely will approve this, but the inventory seems to encourage the idea that there is just one ideal personality. Such scale titles as Responsibility, Tolerance, and Socialization have a pronounced ethical overtone which suggests that low scores reflect faults, rather than symptoms of needs, skills, and cultural pressures. Because of this implicit conflict with modern views of personality, it would be deplorable if CPI profiles were interpreted by principals, teachers, parents, or students without guidance from a psychologically-trained person. For use by the well-qualified counselor, the reviewer regards the *Edwards Personal Preference Schedule* as more suitable, its profile being more descriptive and less evaluative. To identify students needing counseling and to aid in counseling by teachers, the simpler *Mooney Problem Checklist* seems preferable. Further research may prove that the CPI patterns are richly significant. The reviewer's prejudices, however, lead him to prefer profiles describing the individual in psychological terms to profiles defined around complex social resultants such as disciplinary problems, presence in numerous school activities, and high grades. Gough is to be commended for pursuing his own contrary view skillfully, but the usefulness of his instrument is still in question.

ROBERT L. THORNDIKE, *Professor of Education, Teachers College, Columbia University, New York, New York.*

This inventory has been described as the "sane man's MMPI." That is, it is an inventory the development of which proceeded essentially by (*a*) assembling a large stock of items of various types which looked as though they might relate to something of significance about personality, (*b*) identifying criterion groups that differed sharply in some attribute judged to be socially significant and psychologically meaningful, and (*c*) developing a scoring key which included those items that were found empirically to differentiate the criterion groups. The criterion groups were, in this case, groups from the general population which differed in some significant respect.

This procedure has both strength and weakness. The strength lies in the efficiency of the scoring key for discriminating with respect to the *specific* criterion dimension on the basis of which the items were selected. The weakness lies in the possibility that this criterion dimension may not have clear, distinctive, and unequivocal psychological meaning. Furthermore, there is no limit to the number of criterion dimensions with respect to which one may undertake to establish keys (note, for example, the more than 40 keys for the *Strong Vocational Interest Blank*).

In the case of the CPI, the evidence is not clear as to how many of the 18 dimensions for which keys are provided by the author have a unique practical value that would justify them on that basis. However, it *is* clear that the 18 provide a very redundant, inefficient, and (to the reviewer) confused picture of individual personalities. Correlations between many of the scales are high—in some cases apparently approaching the reliabilities of the individual scales. Of the 18 scales, there are only 4 that fail to correlate at least .50 with some other scale, and many have correlations of this size with several others. There is, of course, no limit

to the number of scales that *can* be developed for an inventory such as this except that set by the endurance of the originator. The problem is how many and which ones provide an efficient, parsimonious, and understandable description of an individual. Eighteen highly overlapping scores, many of which appear redundant both in name and in statistics, hardly appear to accomplish this.

Evidence provided on the reliability of the scales is hardly adequate to permit an appraisal of the uniqueness, if any, of the separate scales. Since the items making up a particular scale can be thought of as a sample from a universe of items that might have been used, it seems reasonable to ask for evidence on the split-half reliability, or some other indication of stability over samples of items. No such evidence is provided, data being limited to retest reliability on the same items. Application of Kuder-Richardson formula 21 to some of the data reported in the manual suggests that split-half reliabilities would be likely to be in the .70's.

The author has shown commendable industry in obtaining data for his instrument from many criterion groups. Selections from this material are presented in the manual. Unfortunately, the presentation is marred by faulty statistical analysis. Repeatedly, biserial correlations are reported for extreme groups, leaving out a large middle group. The resulting coefficients are, of course, grossly inflated and provide an unrealistic picture of the accuracy with which the instrument would make discriminations in an intact group.

It is conceivable that there may be a role for a personality inventory developed by the procedures and following the rationale of the CPI. However, this reviewer feels that the role will not be that of providing a clear, efficient, and simple personality description.

J Consult Psychol 21:359 Ag '57. Laurance F. Shaffer. * bears considerable resemblance to the group MMPI, from which about 200 of its 468 items were adapted. But the purpose of the CPI is quite different. It is intended primarily for use with normal subjects, not patients, and strives to assess personality characteristics important for social living. * The manual contains a wealth of information on the validities of scales and on the interpretations of single scales, interactions, and profiles. * By both objective and subjective evaluation, the CPI appears to be a major achievement. It will surely receive wide use for research and for practical applications.

[38]

*California Test of Personality, 1953 Revision.
Grades kgn–3, 4–8, 7–10, 9–16, adults; 1939–53; 15 scores: self-reliance, sense of personal worth, sense of personal freedom, feeling of belonging, withdrawing tendencies, nervous symptoms, total personal adjustment, social standards, social skills, anti-social tendencies, family relations, school relations or occupational relations, community relations, total social adjustment, total adjustment; IBM for grades 4 and over; Forms AA, BB ('53); 5 levels; manual ('53); profile ('53); $3.15 per 35 tests; separate answer sheets may be used; 4¢ per IBM answer sheet; 7¢ per Scoreze answer sheet; 20¢ per hand scoring stencil; 60¢ per machine scoring stencil; postage extra; 50¢ per specimen set of any one level, postpaid; (45–60) minutes; Louis P. Thorpe, Willis W. Clark, and Ernest W. Tiegs; California Test Bureau. *

a) PRIMARY. Grades kgn–3; 1942–53.
b) ELEMENTARY. Grades 4–8; 1939–53.
c) INTERMEDIATE. Grades 7–10; 1939–53.
d) SECONDARY. Grades 9–16; 1942–53.
e) ADULT. Adults; 1942–53.

REFERENCES

1–24. See 3:26.
25. WALKER, ELSIE MEINE. *A Comparative Study of Personalities of Elementary and Secondary Education Majors.* Master's thesis, North Texas State Teachers College (Denton, Tex.), 1941.
26. ADOLPHSON, GUDRUN. *The Relation of General Motor Ability to Personality Adjustment.* Master's thesis, University of Colorado (Boulder, Colo.), 1942.
27. MARY VERA, Sister. "A Critical Study of Certain Personality Factors as Determining Elements in a Remedial Reading Program." *Cath Ed R* 40:145–61 Mr '42. *
28. ANDERSON, WILLIAM E. *A Study of the Personality Characteristics of 153 Negro Pupils, Dunbar High School, Okmulgee, Oklahoma.* Doctor's thesis, Colorado State College of Education (Greeley, Colo.), 1944.
29. YOUNG, LYLE L., AND COOPER, DAN H. "Some Factors Associated With Popularity." *J Ed Psychol* 35:513–35 D '44. * (PA 19:1000)
30. BOWERS, SCOTT T. *Some Aspects of Personality Development of Children in an Institution.* Master's thesis, Ohio University (Athens, Ohio), 1945.
31. ENGLE, T. L. "Personality Adjustments of Children Belonging to Two Minority Groups." *J Ed Psychol* 36:543–60 D '45. * (PA 20:2136)
32. BUTTIMORE, DENNIS J. *Some Aspects of the Personality of Male Juvenile Delinquents.* Doctor's thesis, New York University (New York, N.Y.), 1946.
33. BURKE, HENRY R. *Personality Traits of Successful Minor Seminarians.* Washington, D.C.: Catholic University of America Press, 1947 Pp. viii, 65. * (PA 22:848)
34. EDMISTON, R. W.; HINTON, M. E.; AND RASOR, FLOYD. "Special Emphases to Improve Attendance." *J Ed Res* 41:35–40 S '47. * (PA 22:1856)
35. McFADDEN, JOHN HAROLD. *Emotional and Personality Adjustment of Public School Children.* Master's thesis, University of North Dakota (Grand Forks, N.D.), 1947.
36. PFLIEGER, ELMER F. "Pupil Adjustment Problems and a Study of Relationships Between Scores on the California Test of Personality and the Mooney Problem Check List." *J Ed Res* 41:265–78 D '47. * (PA 22:2746)
37. SEEMAN, MELVIN. *Prejudice and Personality: A Study in the Social Psychology of Attitudes.* Doctor's thesis, Ohio State University (Columbus, Ohio), 1947.
38. ALLEN, CHARLES L. *The Development of a Battery of Psychological Tests for Determining Journalistic Interests and Aptitudes.* Doctor's thesis, Northwestern University (Evanston, Ill.), 1948.
39. CALIFORNIA TEST BUREAU, EDITORIAL STAFF. *California Test of Personality.* Summary of Investigations, No. 1. Los Angeles, Calif.: California Test Bureau, 1948. Pp. 19. *
40. GROSSMAN, BEVERLY, AND WRIGHTER, JOYCE. "The Relationship Between Selection-Rejection and Intelligence, Social Status, and Personality Amongst Sixth Grade Children." *Sociometry* 11:346–55 N '48. * (PA 25:7667)
41. HORGAN, CORNELIUS M. *A Comparative Study of Leaders and Non-Leaders Among Catholic Boy Scouts.* Doctor's thesis, Fordham University (New York, N.Y.), 1948.
42. HUNTER, E. C. "A Summary of Mental Health Survey of Spartanburg County, Spartanburg, South Carolina." *J Exp Ed* 17:294–308 D '48. * (PA 23:4804)

43. PHILLIPS, E. LAKIN; BERMAN, ISABEL R.; AND HANSON, HAROLD B. *Intelligence and Personality Factors Associated With Poliomyelitis Among School Age Children.* Monographs of the Society for Research in Child Development, Vol. 12, No. 2, Serial No. 45. Evanston, Ill.: Child Development Publications, the Society, 1948. Pp. vii, 60. *
44. SEIDENFELD, MORTON A. "The Psychological Sequelae of Poliomyelitis in Children." *Nerv Child* 7:14–28 Ja '48. * (PA 22:4080)
45. SNYDER, WILLIAM U., AND SNYDER, BARBARA JUNE. "Implications for Therapy of Personality Changes Resulting From a Course in Mental Hygiene." Abstract. *Am Psychol* 3:286–7 Jl '48. *
46. BAIRD, FRANCES. *The Adjustment of Orphanage Children.* Master's thesis, Miami University (Oxford, Ohio), 1949.
47. CALIFORNIA TEST BUREAU, EDITORIAL STAFF. *California Test of Personality, Revised Edition.* Summary of Investigations, No. 1 (Revised Edition). Los Angeles, Calif.: California Test Bureau, 1949. Pp. 24. *
48. CHRISTY, WILLIAM J. *A Study of Relationships Between Sociometric Scores and Personality Self-Ratings.* Master's thesis, North Texas State College (Denton, Tex.), 1949.
49. DENT, RALPH W. *Varied Reliability Coefficients for the California Test of Personality, Obtained by Different Methods.* Master's thesis, University of Toronto (Toronto, Ont., Canada), 1949.
50. EAGER, MARY FLOY. *A Comparative Study of the Personality Traits of Handicapped and Normal Children.* Master's thesis, North Texas State College (Denton, Tex.), 1949.
51. EDMISTON, R. W., AND BAIRD, FRANCES. "The Adjustment of Orphanage Children." *J Ed Psychol* 40:482–8 D '49. * (PA 24:3103)
52. GLASER, ROBERT. "A Methodological Analysis of the Inconsistency of Response to Test Items." *Ed & Psychol Meas* 9:727–39 w '49. * (PA 26:2747)
53. JENSEN, GERALD LEROY. *Relationship Between School Achievement and Scholastic Aptitude: Techniques for Ascertaining This Relationship, Their Application to Data From a Group of High School Pupils and Their Use in School Practice.* Doctor's thesis, Stanford University (Stanford, Calif.), 1949.
54. KING, CLYDE D. *Personality Traits of Teachers.* Master's thesis, North Texas State College (Denton, Tex.), 1949.
55. LEHNER, GEORGE F. J. "Some Relationships Between Scores for Self and Projected 'Average' Scores on a Personality Test." Abstract. *Am Psychol* 4:390 S '49. *
56. PURVIS, LEO C. *Relationship Between Intelligence as Determined by California Test of Mental Maturity and Achievement in the Seventh Grade.* Master's thesis, North Texas State College (Denton, Tex.), 1949.
57. RICCIUTI, EDWARD A. *A Study of Listeners and Non-Listeners to Various Types of Radio Programs in Terms of Selected Ability, Attitude and Behavior Measures.* Doctor's thesis, Fordham University (New York, N.Y.), 1949.
58. ROBINSON, CLARE AVIS. *The Relationship of Estimates of Personal and Social Adjustment to Attained Scores of the California Test of Personality.* Master's thesis, Pennsylvania State College (State College, Pa.), 1949.
59. THOMPSON, BILLYE FAYE. *The Relationship of Personality to Accident-Prone and Accident-Free Pupils in the North Dallas High School.* Master's thesis, North Texas State College (Denton, Tex.), 1949.
60. VOLBERDING, ELEANOR. "Characteristics of Successful and Unsuccessful Eleven-Year-Old Pupils." *El Sch J* 49:405–10 Mr '49. * (PA 23:5003)
61. ZAKOLSKI, F. C. "Studies in Delinquency: I, Personality Structure of Delinquent Boys." *J Genetic Psychol* 74:109–17 Mr '49. * (PA 23:4925)
62. BEEBE, EMILY NOYES. *A Study of Personality and Personality Deficiencies Among Intermediate Grade Pupils in Three New Orleans Public Schools.* Master's thesis, Tulane University (New Orleans, La.), 1950.
63. BRYAN, J. R. *A Study of Personality Adjustment Differences of Delinquent and Nondelinquent Groups as Measured by the Bell Adjustment Inventory and the California Test of Personality.* Master's thesis, University of Toronto (Toronto, Canada), 1950.
64. BURNS, L. *A Correlation of Scores on the Wechsler Intelligence Scale for Children and the California Test of Personality Obtained by a Group of 5th Graders.* Master's thesis, Pennsylvania State College (State College, Pa.), 1950.
65. CASSEL, RUSSELL N. *An Experimental Investigation of the "Reality-Strata" of Certain Objectively Defined Groups of Individuals by Use of the Level of Aspiration Technique.* Doctor's thesis, University of Southern California (Los Angeles, Calif.), 1950.
66. CLARK, JERRY H. "Interest Variability on the California Test of Mental Maturity in Relation to the Minnesota Multiphasic Personality Inventory." *J Consult Psychol* 14:32–4 F '50. * (PA 24:4112)
67. CURRY, EDNA MAE. *Relationship of Achievement and Personality in the Fourth, Fifth, and Sixth Grades of the Northwest Elementary School, Justin, Texas.* Master's thesis, North Texas State College (Denton, Tex.), 1950.
68. GIBSON, NORMA LEE BODENHEIMER. *The Influence of the Study of Biographies Upon the Personality Adjustment of the Junior High School Student as Measured by the California Test of Personality.* Master's thesis, University of Southern California (Los Angeles, Calif.), 1950.

69. HAND, WILL M. *A Comparison and Analysis of Scores in Self and Social Adjustment Made on the California Test of Personality and the Bernreuter Personality Inventory.* Master's thesis, University of Florida (Gainesville, Fla.), 1950.

70. KING, F. J. *Item Analysis of the California Test of Personality.* Master's thesis, North Texas State College (Denton, Tex.), 1950.

71. SALYERS, MARTHA HOPKINS. *An Item Analysis of the California Test of Personality as Correlated With Intelligence.* Master's thesis, Illinois State Normal University (Normal, Ill.), 1950.

72. WOODWARD, RICHARD HUGH. *An Examination of the Internal Consistency of the California Test of Personality, Series 1, Form A.* Master's thesis, Miami University (Oxford, Ohio), 1950.

73. CARLIN, LESLIE ORVILLE. *A Comparison of the College Marks by Subject Made by 312 of the June, 1950 Graduating Seniors at Central Michigan College of Education With Their Battery of Guidance Tests and Inventory Percentile Scores.* Doctor's "Field Study No. 2," Colorado State College of Education (Greeley, Colo.), 1951.

74. COWEN, EMORY L., AND THOMPSON, GEORGE G. "Problem Solving Rigidity and Personality Structure." *J Abn & Social Psychol* 46:165-76 Ap '51. * (PA 25:7940)

75. ELIAS, JACK Z. *Non-Intellective Factors in Certain Intelligence and Achievement Tests: An Analysis of Factors in Addition to the Cognitive Entering Into the Intelligence and Achievement Scores of Children at the Sixth Grade Level.* Doctor's thesis, New York University (New York, N.Y.), 1951. (*Microfilm Abstr* 11:558)

76. ELLIOT, JANE. *Personality Traits of 199 School Children With Speech Deviations as Indicated by the California Test of Personality, Primary and Elementary Series, Form A.* Master's thesis, University of Michigan (Ann Arbor, Mich.), 1951.

77. FORLANO, GEORGE, AND WRIGHTSTONE, J. WAYNE. "Sociometric and Self-Descriptive Technics in Appraisal of Pupil Adjustment." *Sociometry* 14:340-50 D '51. * (PA 28:6531)

78. SINGER, ARTHUR. "Certain Aspects of Personality and Their Relation to Certain Group Modes, and Constancy of Friendship Choices." *J Ed Res* 45:33-42 S '51. * (PA 26:2998)

79. SKIDMORE, REX A., AND McPHEE, WILLIAM M. "The Comparative Use of the California Test of Personality and the Burgess-Cottrell-Wallin Schedule in Predicting Marital Adjustment." *Marriage & Family Living* 13:121-6 Ag '51. * (PA 26:2197)

80. WEILAND, ELIZABETH JUNE. *The Use of the California Test of Personality as a Measure of the Personality Adjustment of a Seventh Grade Population in Relation to Achievement in School.* Master's thesis, Pennsylvania State College (State College, Pa.), 1951.

81. BROWN, LILLIAN PENN; GATES, HELEN D.; NOLDER, EVANGFLINE L.; AND VAN FLEET, BARBARA. "Personality Characteristics of Exceptional Children and of Their Mothers." *El Sch J* 52:286-90 Ja '52. * (PA 27:6444)

82. LINDGREN, HENRY CLAY. "The Development of a Scale of Cultural Idealization Based on the California Test of Personality." *J Ed Psychol* 43:81-91 F '52. * (PA 26:7004)

83. MASTEN, FRANK D. *The Personality Development and Occupational Interests of the Sixth, Seventh, and Eighth Grade Pupils at Father Flanagan's Boys' Home, Boys Town, Nebraska.* Doctor's field study, Colorado State College of Education (Greeley, Colo.), 1952.

84. SEWELL, WILLIAM H. "Infant Training and the Personality of the Child." *Am J Sociol* 58:150-9 S '52. * (PA 27:3388)

85. TAYLOR, CHARLES, AND COMBS, ARTHUR W. "Self-Acceptance and Adjustment." *J Consult Psychol* 16:89-91 Ap '52. *

86. BURRALL, LUCILLE. *A Study of Internal or Trait Variability in Achievement of Pupils at the Fifth Grade Level.* Doctor's thesis, Pennsylvania State College (State College, Pa.), 1953.

87. CARILLO, EDITH MARIA. *Relationship of Certain Personality Characteristics to the School-Related Problems of Junior High School Pupils.* Doctor's thesis, University of Michigan (Ann Arbor, Mich.), 1953. (DA 13:331)

88. CARLIN, LESLIE C. "A Longitudinal Comparison of Freshman-Senior Standing." *J Ed Res* 47:285-90 D '53. * (PA 28:6586)

89. FEIVESON, PHILIP. "The Value of a Personality Inventory in a Self-Appraisal Course on the Secondary School Level." *Calif J Ed Res* 4:69-72 Mr '53. * (PA 28:1472)

90. HINKELMAN, EMMET ARTHUR. "A Comparative Investigation of Differences in Personality Adjustment of Delinquents and Non-Delinquents." *J Ed Res* 46:595-601 Ap '53. * (PA 28:2971)

91. LEIBMAN, OSCAR BERNARD. *The Relationship of Personal and Social Adjustment to Academic Achievement in the Elementary School.* Doctor's thesis, Columbia University (New York, N.Y.), 1953. (DA 14:67)

92. NOWELL, ANN. "Peer Status as Related to Measures of Personality." *Calif J Ed Res* 4:37-41 Ja '53. * (PA 28:1514)

93. ROS, PAZ DE MINGO MELITON. *Social Acceptance or Rejection as Related to Personality Adjustment and Participation in Group Task Roles.* Doctor's field study, Colorado State College of Education (Greeley, Colo.), 1953.

94. SCANDRETTE, ONAS C. "Classroom Choice Status Re-

lated to Scores on Components of the California Test of Personality." *J Ed Res* 47:291-6 D '53. * (PA 28:6545)

95. BURRALL, LUCILLE. "Variability in Achievement of Pupils at the Fifth Grade Level." *Calif J Ed Res* 5:68-73 Mr '54. * (PA 28:9038)

96. CURRAN, GRACE THERESE. "The Effect of Immediate Experiences Upon Responses on the California Personality Test." *J Ed Res* 48:289-95 D '54. * (PA 29:7266)

97. HANLON, THOMAS E.; HOFSTAETTER, PETER R.; AND O'CONNOR, JAMES P. "Congruence of Self and Ideal Self in Relation to Personality Adjustment." *J Consult Psychol* 18:215-8 Je '54. * (PA 29:2229)

98. LANGFORD, LOUISE M., AND ALM, O. W. "A Comparison of Parent Judgments and Child Feelings Concerning the Self Adjustment and Social Adjustment of Twelve-Year-Old Children." *J Genetic Psychol* 85:39-46 S '54. * (PA 29:5381)

99. LINDEMANN, SALLY J. *The Effect on Scores of Individual vs. Group Administration of the California Test of Personality.* Master's thesis, Pennsylvania State University (State College, Pa.), 1954.

100. ZELEN, SEYMOUR L. "Acceptance and Acceptability: An Examination of Social Reciprocity." Abstract. *J Consult Psychol* 18:316 O '54. *

101. BAKER, LAURENCE S. *The Relationship of Maternal Understanding of the Child and Attitudes Toward the Child to the Adjustment of the Child.* Doctor's thesis, New York University (New York, N.Y.), 1955. (DA 16:567)

102. CHANNELL, R. R. *Self Inventories, Teacher Ratings and Interviews as a Means of Determining Maladjustment.* Master's thesis, Utah State Agricultural College (Logan, Utah), 1955.

103. COWDEN, RICHARD C. "Empathy or Projection?" *J Clin Psychol* 11:188-90 Ap '55. * (PA 30:905)

104. KELLEY, ELVAN PRESSLOR. *An Investigation Into the Value of Selected Tests and Techniques for Guidance of Prospective Teachers Enrolled in Community Experiences Course.* Doctor's thesis, University of Houston (Houston, Tex.), 1955. (DA 15:1209)

105. PHILLIPS, BEEMAN N., AND DeVAULT, M. VERE. "Relation of Positive and Negative Sociometric Valuations to Social and Personal Adjustment of School Children." *J Appl Psychol* 39:409-12 D '55. * (PA 30:7706)

106. SHUTTLESWORTH, REBA HUDSON. *The Relationship of Socio-Economic Status to the Measured Adjustment of Seventh Grade Students in Johnston Junior High School, Houston, Texas, for the Year of 1951-1952.* Doctor's field study, Colorado State College of Education (Greeley, Colo.), 1955.

107. SMITH, LOUIS MILDE. *A Validity Study of Six Personality and Adjustment Tests for Children.* Doctor's thesis, University of Minnesota (Minneapolis, Minn.), 1955. (DA 16:791)

108. TINDALL, RALPH H. "Relationships Among Indices of Adjustment Status." *Ed & Psychol Meas* 15:152-62 su '55. * (PA 30:2330)

109. DAGER, EDWARD ZICCA. *Social Factors in Personality Change.* Doctor's thesis, Ohio State University (Columbus, Ohio), 1956. (DA 17:1619)

110. KEELER, HAROLD JAY. *Predicting Teacher Effectiveness of Graduates of the State University of New York Teachers Colleges.* Doctor's thesis, Cornell University (Ithaca, N.Y.), 1956. (DA 17:545)

111. LEHNER, GEORGE F. J. "Personal Adjustment Scores and Assigned 'Average' Scores." *J Psychol* 42:227-36 O '56. *

112. MELTON, WILLIAM R., JR. *An Investigation of the Relationship Between Personality and Vocational Interest.* *J Ed Psychol* 47:163-74 Mr '56. * (PA 31:8791)

113. SPILKA, BERNARD, AND STRUENING, E. L. "A Questionnaire Study of Personality and Ethnocentrism." *J Social Psychol* 44:65-71 Ag '56. *

114. GUNNELL, DOROTHY C., AND NUTTING, RUTH E. "Prediction of Achievement in Schools of Nursing." *Calif J Ed Res* 8:184-91 S '57. *

115. MITCHELL, JAMES V., JR. "The Identification of Items in the California Test of Personality That Differentiate Between Subjects of High and Low Socio-Economic Status at the Fifth- and Seventh-Grade Levels." *J Ed Res* 51:241-250 D '57. *

116. CLEVENGER, THEODORE, JR. *An Analysis of Variance of the Relationship of Experienced Stage Fright to Selected Psychometric Inventories.* Doctor's thesis, Florida State University (Tallahassee, Fla.), 1958. (DA 19:598)

117. SMITH, LOUIS M. "The Concurrent Validity of Six Personality and Adjustment Tests for Children." *Psychol Monogr* 72(4):1-30 '58. *

VERNER M. SIMS, *Professor of Psychology, University of Alabama, University, Alabama.*

Rereading reviews of this test in earlier *Yearbooks* has impressed this reviewer with the fact that a review of a personality test reveals at least as much concerning the frame of reference within which the reviewer approaches the task as it does of the test itself. Let us start off, therefore, with a statement of this reviewer's own bias: He feels, first of all, that in spite of the fact that authors often have exaggerated ideas concerning the usefulness of self-inventories and that in the hands of unskilled persons they be harmful, there is a place for them in the scheme of psychological testing; and secondly, he takes the position that the worth of such inventories is to be measured in terms of the extent to which they meet the conventional criteria of good measurement.

Since the earlier edition was evaluated in the *Yearbook* by five competent persons, this review is limited chiefly to a consideration of changes that have been made in the current revision. According to its authors, "Among the reasons which led to the 1953 Revision....were: (1) the development of additional validity data, (2) the extension of suggestions for interpretation, (3) the development of additional data regarding reliability (particularly for the lower scores on the test instrument), (4) the reexamination of the comparability of the two forms for each level so that one set of norms could be utilized, and (5) the reorganization of items for each of the equivalent components so that one SCOREZE answer sheet could be used with either Form AA or BB on each level." Examination of the test and manual leaves one with the feeling that another reason may well have been the attempt to answer criticisms of the test made by previous reviewers. And, as a matter of fact, some of the criticisms of the early test are no longer valid. Other shortcomings pointed out are, however, defended, ignored, or brushed aside as not worthy of comment.

Evidence on the validity of personality inventories will, generally speaking, be indirect. The authors in this edition base their case mainly on the care taken in the construction of the revised test, and the reported usefulness of the first edition as a pre- and in-service training device for teachers, as an aid to counselors, clinical psychologists, and teachers in the study of problem cases, and as a tool useful in personality research. In support of their contention, they marshal a considerable amount of evidence, although one wishes at times that it all were reported with the exactitude contained in the statement that in some 90 publications of research the test has been found useful. Such expressions as "school officials in increasing number" or "many clinical psychologists" are, for example, not too easy to interpret.

In spite of limitations, however, the additional evidence on validity reported or referred to in the manual not only answers some of the earlier criticisms but convinces this reviewer that as a measure of self-concept in the, as of now, vaguely defined area called adjustment, this test is as valid as most such instruments.

An attempt has been made to word the questions so as to reduce to a minimum any suggestion that they should be answered a certain way. In spite of this effort, the "right" answer to many items is probably obvious to all except the very naive. Although this is a limitation of most personality inventories (all that the writer has seen), it means, nevertheless, that the validity of this test will vary with the degree of rapport established with the testee. This fact raises serious doubt concerning its usefulness in the selection and placement of employees, a use which the authors recommend.

Tests of internal consistency are reported for the revision in considerable detail. They indicate a fair degree of reliability for the total and the two main components, social and personal adjustment, particularly for the lower scores. They do not, however, convince this reviewer that use of the six subscores under each of these two components is justified for individual diagnosis. For example, let us look at Withdrawing Tendencies in the primary form. The chances are 1 in 3 that the true score is 1.08 points greater or less than the obtained score. From the table of norms it can be seen that this means that the chances are that the true score of 1 child in 3 with a score of 5 (40th percentile) is above the 60th percentile or below the 30th percentile, and that for 1 child in 20 the true score is below the 20th or above the 80th percentile. Expressed in such terms, it is hard to see that we have any very dependable information on how far he withdraws! And this is not an exaggerated example. Here is another from the secondary form: A student answering 8 of the 15 items correctly on Self-reliance is rated at the 30th percentile. The chances are 1 in 3 that his true score is below the 15th or above the 45th percentile, and 1 in 20 that it is below the 5th or above the 70th percentile. How self-reliant is he? Interestingly enough, subscores on the adult form appear to be the least reliable of all.

In a forced-choice test it is inevitable that some questions will be answered at random, and in a yes-no test it is obvious that their weight will also be at a maximum. In a self-inventory the number of such "guesses" would presumably vary with such things as reading ability, the amount of self-understanding, a willingness to introspect, and the desire to report things as they are. It would, therefore, seem highly desirable, particularly in a test recommended for use with groups relatively unskilled in reading and not too understanding, that chance responses move a person toward a neutral position. This might mean that we miss some cases who are maladjusted but it would prevent us from labeling as maladjusted poor readers, persons without self-understanding, and the like.

Spencer (3:26) called attention to the disproportionate number of "No's" among the correct answers in the first edition. In the current edition this ratio continues to be between 60 and 70 per cent instead of the expected 50 per cent. Add to this the fact that at all levels the median score of the group used to establish norms was well above the median number of questions in the test and it is inevitable that one who answers the questions on a basis of chance will show up as seriously maladjusted. In the primary test, for example, he would be at the 10th percentile in personal, social, and total adjustment; in the secondary test he would be at the 5th, 2nd, and 5th percentiles. The subscores tell an even worse story. The reviewer does not mean to imply that many of those tested will answer all questions on the basis of chance, but rather to point out that in this test any questions so answered increase the apparent maladjustment of the testee. The fact that many other personality inventories are subject to the same criticism is irrelevant.

The test itself is mechanically satisfactory and it and the manual are made up in a manner which makes for ease and accuracy in administering and scoring. The printing is excellent. In many schools, however, poor reading ability of the children will require that the elementary form be read to the children well beyond the recommended fourth grade. The profile which appeared on the front of the test booklet in the earlier editions has been moved to the back of the answer sheet. The manual still contains a section on the uses of test results which undertakes to classify personality problems and suggests ways of dealing with the various types of difficulties. This reviewer, like previous reviewers, is skeptical of the worth of this material. In the hands of untrained users it may actually be harmful, and persons with a minimum of train-

ing in counseling or clinical psychology would have no need for it.

The norms on this edition are considerably better than those for the earlier test. The samples are much larger and, if one can assume that the cases are fairly distributed among the states from which they were drawn, are geographically more representative. All in all, in spite of criticism, as personality inventories go, the California test would appear to be among the better ones available.

For reviews by Laurance F. Shaffer and Douglas Spencer of the original edition, see 3:26 (1 excerpt); for reviews by Raymond B. Cattell, Percival M. Symonds, and P. E. Vernon of the elementary and secondary levels, see 40:1213 (1 excerpt).

[39]
★The Cassel Group Level of Aspiration Test, 1957 Revision. Grades 5–16 and adults; 1952–57; 7 scores: clinical difference, Hausmann, aspiration difference, first goal, psychological response to failure, physiological response to failure, level of aspiration quotient; 1 form ('57); manual ('57); $4 per 25 tests, postpaid; specimen set not available; 247 seconds (40 minutes); Russell N. Cassel; Western Psychological Services. *

REFERENCES
1. CASSEL, RUSSELL N., AND SAUGSTAD, RANDOLF G. "Level of Aspiration and Sociometric Distance." *Sociometry* 15:319–25 Ag–N '52. * (PA 27:7386)
2. CASSEL, RUSSELL N. "The Relationship of Certain Factors to the Level of Aspiration and Social Distance for Forty Four Air Force Prisoners." *J Crim Law & Criminology* 44(5):604–10 Ja–F '54. *
3. CASSEL, RUSSELL N., AND VAN VORST, ROBERT. "Level of Aspiration as a Means for Discerning Between 'In-Prison' and 'Out-of-Prison' Groups of Individuals." *J Social Psychol* 40: 121–35 Ag '54. * (PA 29:5692)
4. CASSEL, RUSSELL N., AND VAN VORST, ROBERT. "Level of Aspiration Comparisons for Varying Stages of Penal Experience." *J Ed Res* 48:597–603 Ap '55. * (PA 30:1295)
5. NIYEKAWA, AGNES M. "A Comparative Analysis of Foreign and American Female College Groups on Three Personality Variables: Anxiety, Level of Aspiration and Femininity." *Psychol Newsl* 7:72–91 My–Je '56. * (PA 31:3697)

W. GRANT DAHLSTROM, *Associate Professor of Psychology, University of North Carolina, Chapel Hill, North Carolina.*

The revised form of this test is based upon eight repetitions of a simple motor task: drawing squares around small circles as rapidly as possible. For each trial the subject estimates the number of squares he will be able to complete in 30 seconds. Group administration requires that the subject record his aspiration in the form of a bid, tally his performance, and correct his score for any discrepancies with his bid. The next to the last trial is stopped three seconds short of the usual time in an effort to introduce failure, the effects of which are evaluated in the bid (psychological response) and in the performance (physiological response) on his last trial.

The test booklet is simple, neat, and well planned. The scoring blanks are labeled so explicitly, however, that some of the features of the test may be given away, e.g., "Psychological Response to Failure." The test instructions are very complicated, including five elaborate rules covering the level of aspiration bids, the performance, and the scoring. Little effort is made in these instructions to convey to the subject just why he should do well or why he should try to make his bids correspond to his subsequent performance. There is no reason why a subject should not pace his performance to fit his prior bid.

The manual contains several errors per page, some seriously interfering with the administration and the scoring of the test. Although in the revision of this test the basic psychomotor task has been changed from making small circles above and below an X to drawing squares around circles, the manual does not indicate this change or the degree of equivalence of the two forms. Most of the normative data in the manual are based upon the original form, precisely the same cutting scores being retained, although this is not indicated anywhere in the tables. In fact, no references to previous research on the test are included in the manual. Although normative data from general, Latin descent, and penal populations are listed, no description is provided of the sampling procedures used in collecting them, the background characteristics of the groups, the nature of any sex differences, or the representativeness of these data.

The directions for administration are poorly organized. The examiner and the subjects begin reading the directions together. Then, in the middle of a paragraph, the examiner has the subjects fill in the test headings and turn to the next page of the test booklet; finally he has them return to the first page for the remainder of the directions. The vocabulary level is uneven and the self-recording provisions are poorly written and confusing.

The scoring instructions are also lacking in organization. The sequence does not correspond to the order on the test profile. The examiner is asked to compute one score based upon another that is yet to be defined. This score (clinical difference score) is a qualitative series of categories but is treated like a 7-interval continuous scale; means, standard deviations, and T score

conversions are provided for it! The instructions for the psychological response to failure score involve the wrong trials. Computation of the level of aspiration quotient (LAQ), which the author considers to be the most valuable score in the test, is based in part on an intelligence quotient that cannot be obtained from this test itself. No specification of the test to be used to furnish the IQ is included in the LAQ instructions; any standard intelligence test is deemed acceptable. Reference to the *California Test of Mental Maturity* is made in some of the tables in the manual, but no recommendation is made to use this instrument. Apparently the assumption is made that IQ's from different tests are completely equivalent in their central tendencies, their dispersions, and in the abilities they sample. The conversion table for IQ's assumes a mean of 100 and a standard deviation of 16 points.

The LAQ is the ratio of two standard scores with means of 5.0 and standard deviations of 1.0, one for the IQ and the other for the Hausmann score which is the average weighted achievement score on trials three through six. Use of this ratio assumes that for subjects who are well adjusted in their level of aspiration the Hausmann score and intelligence are generally proportional. No evidence is submitted for this assumption; only the correlation of .39 between the Hausmann score and IQ (test unspecified) is given in the manual.

Intercorrelations among the component scores are provided based on two different populations, but the columnar headings for one table are so misleading as to make the data uninterpretable.

Correlations of odd and even trials (corrected for attenuation) and test-retest coefficients are reported for each score except the LAQ. The author says the reliabilities for the LAQ will be the same as the Hausmann score on which it is partly based. This latter point is in error since the LAQ is also a function of the IQ derived from some other recent test. The retest interval over which the temporal stability of these scores was determined is not specified for either group studied.

In spite of the numerous errors and limitations already listed, the question of validity is the most important one in evaluating this instrument. The manual mentions briefly and superficially four forms of validity: face, content, construct, and status. It is difficult to assess these validities from the descriptions and data provided by the author. Although he calls his test a measure of level of aspiration, Cassel seems to disclaim any intention to measure this attribute. However, many test users will turn to this device seeking a measure of an individual's general level of aspiration. Except for the trivial face validity of the goal-setting behavior on a simple psychomotor task, there is no evidence of construct validity of this sort implied in the title. There is very little evidence [1] that there is any trait of this sort with enough generality to be useful in describing individuals. The research on this problem has been based on many kinds of tasks from the dart-throwing problem of Hausmann to the pool-cue manipulations of the Rotter board. There seems to be a cavalier disregard for the particular task used to sample goal-setting behavior, as if an individual were equally confident or self-doubting in all situations. Cassel offers no evidence that guesses about one's accomplishments in drawing squares bear any relationship to professional striving or any other aspirations.

Cassel prefers to discuss the test implications in terms of an "irreality dimension" of personality. "The term irreality here refers to the presence of reality, rather than the non-existence of it, but implies a degree of absence of acceptable sensory phenomena for the generation of self-perceptions in relation to previous performance." The manual does not provide sufficient material elaborating this construct or its interpretative implications to judge the suitability of these scores for this personality characteristic. The previous writings of the author [2] help elaborate the concept of reality levels, but they are not definitive enough to be clinically useful.

The manual also implies that predictive validity for delinquent behavior (delinquency proneness) has been established, but the evidence offered applies only to status validity, since Cassel examined delinquent and penal samples after they had developed their propensities and had been apprehended and incarcerated (2, 3, 4).

Cassel implies these scores can evaluate an individual's popularity, as measured by socio-

metric preferences. While there was some tendency for the clinical discrepancy score and the LAQ from the first edition of the test to show a curvilinear relationship to sociometric distance (1), this separation did not stand up on a young prisoner group (2). There is mention made of the test's implications of neurotic tendencies, hypochondriacal and hysterical ailments, vulnerability to culture, or disorientation, but no data are provided on these attributes.

This test is poorly prepared and presented, inadequately standardized, and pretentious in its claims. It is unready for the test market and should be labeled FOR RESEARCH ONLY. A need exists for a simple, objective measure of tendencies either to overrate or underevaluate one's abilities and capacities; this test does not fill this need.

HARRISON G. GOUGH, *Associate Professor of Psychology, University of California, Berkeley, California.*

This test has eight parts, each containing three rows of 20 small circles (60 circles per part). Within the time allotted for each part, the subject is asked to draw squares around as many of these circles as he can. Before beginning each part, he must predict how many squares he will draw. After time has been called, he counts the number actually drawn. His score for each part is based directly on his "bid" or estimate. If he bids 26 squares and draws 26 or more, his score is 26. If he fails to make his bid he is penalized two points for each missing square. This procedure is designed to encourage optimistic, but cautious, forecasts.

Based on various combinations and manipulations of the bids, actual performance figures, and these adjusted scores, five scores which comprise the "level of aspiration profile" are derived. The two additional scores which can be obtained (those for psychological response to failure and physiological response to failure) are computed only when "failure," as defined in the manual, has taken place. Part 7 has, unknown to the subject, a reduced time of 27 seconds. Presumably many subjects, therefore, will fail to make their bids on Part 7. These two scores are concerned with the effect of this failure on the subject's estimates and performance.

The above gives an idea of the mechanics of the test. The manual ties the tasks and the scored variables to a prolix and murky discussion of the "irreality scale of human personali-

[1] ROTTER, JULIAN B. "Level-of-Aspiration Techniques as Measures of Personality," pp. 313–26. In his *Social Learning and Clinical Psychology.* New York: Prentice-Hall, Inc., 1954. Pp. xiv, 466. *
[2] CASSEL, RUSSELL N. "An Experimental Investigation of the 'Reality-Strata' of Certain Objectively Defined Groups of Individuals by Use of the Level of Aspiration Technique." Abstract. *Am Psychol* 5:471–2 Ag '50. *
   CASSEL, RUSSELL N. "Psychological Aspects of Happiness." *Peabody J Ed* 32:73–82 S '54. *
   CASSEL, RUSSELL N. "Motivation as a Synthesis of Contemporary Psychology." *J Ed Psychol* 43:157–66 Mr '52. *

ties," Lewin's "life space" notion, and Tolman's view (alleged) that all behavior is goal-directed. This theorizing, in the reviewer's judgment, is not only poorly done but is more or less gratuitous to the specific tasks assigned in the test and to the scorings made.

The manual, however, has more serious deficiencies. One of these is a distressing series of errors. Seventeen typographical, grammatical, and content errors were found in the text. In one of the tables two columns of correlation coefficients are erroneously identified.

Instructions for scoring the seven defined variables are not given in a clear, succinct fashion; most readers would find it very difficult to decide just what specific steps to take to score certain of the variables, especially the clinical "D" score.

The section of the manual on "validity and standardization" contains misleading and confused discussions of topics like "content validity" and "construct validity," and little evidence pertaining to what one would expect to be the key external criteria for this test: indices of ambition or "level of aspiration" in various life settings and (perhaps) on other "level of aspiration" tests. Most of the data which are presented have to do with school and educational achievement, or with differences between delinquent and nondelinquent populations.

It is with respect to this latter distinction that the test shows its greatest promise. The Hausmann score, for example, yielded mean 28.4 and SD 5.4 in a nondelinquent sample of 1,710 as compared to mean 21.5 and SD 5.3 in a sample of 775 delinquents. The difference is obviously highly significant. However, one is tempted to ascribe it more to the difficulty the delinquents had with the strict time requirements and the record-keeping than to basic differences in the "level of aspiration" aspect of personality.

To summarize, this test does seem to offer certain promises, for example in the study of "under-control" and problems of asocialization. The chief weakness is the manual, which is poorly organized, frequently in error, and written in an awkward, stilted manner. The reduction of the number of scored variables to those having greatest predictive significance for nontest behavior, preparation of clear and precise instructions for scoring, elimination of superfluous theorizing, and a thoroughgoing editorial review for matters of grammar, form, and clarity would do a lot for this device.

J. P. SUTCLIFFE, Senior Lecturer in Psychology, University of Sydney, Sydney, Australia.

The test was devised to measure "irreality" and face validity is claimed for it on the basis that one may consider discrepancies between the "real world" (performance) and the "perceived world" (aspiration). Scores from the test are reported to have medium or low correlations with age, intelligence, school achievement, and certain background and social insight factors of personality. Also reported are some small differences in the scores of "delinquent" and "normal" groups. Reliabilities range from .55 to .93 and vary with type of score and sample. Some norms are reported for "typical" individuals, "delinquent and in-prison" subjects, and "youth of Latin descent." No literature is cited; information in Cassel's other publications is scant.

A group test of "aspiration" could be a useful tool. The author of this test, however, appears not to have consulted the literature on level of aspiration concerning generality and validity. He gives no rationale for his choice of the particular task used, or for the manner of scoring recommended. As a consequence, the test has a major defect which completely invalidates it as a measure of aspiration or irreality.

All of the seven scores derived are functions, directly or indirectly, of performance on the square drawing task. To make the functions explicit, one must consider the relationship of aspiration to performance. Cassel does not report data which would specify this relationship, but, on other grounds,[1] one would expect high dependence of aspiration on performance on this task. This was confirmed by the following results using the CGAT with a sample of 20 subjects (clerical workers and university students, 10 men and 10 women, aged 18–30). Inter- and intra-subject variance and covariance of aspiration and performance was analyzed, and split-half reliabilities of mean aspiration and performance per subject were determined from odd and even trials. When the variance of aspiration was adjusted for regression of aspiration on performance, subject variance dropped to 11 per cent of the original and trial variance dropped to 30 per cent of the original. Part, if not all, of this residual variance would be due to measurement error (unreliability), so that variance of "aspiration," independent of perform-

1 SUTCLIFFE, J. P. Task Variability and the Level of Aspiration. Australian Journal of Psychology Monograph Supplement No. 2. Melbourne, Australia: Melbourne University Press, October 1955. Pp. 86. *

ance and error, is negligible. It is doubtful, then, that a subject's "aspiration" or judgment of performance is anything but another measure of that performance, i.e., a measure of manual dexterity. This result is not surprising when it is seen that the test is a "low variability" task with a stable and predictable performance trend, and that the test instructions demand accurate estimation by the subject.

Taking this argument to the limit, one would substitute performance for aspiration in all of Cassel's scores to find that they are all concerned either with level of performance or with rate of change of performance. Cassel's reported results are explicable in these terms. The relatively high reliability of his scores follows from the high reliability of average performance. Dexterity with a pencil should have some correlation with age and school achievement. The group differences between delinquents, normals, and Latins would need to be reconsidered in terms of the elements involved—viz., average performance on the CGAT, mental age, and chronological age—since selection with respect to any one of these could be responsible for the differences reported.

While the sample upon which these contentions are based is small, the results are so clear cut that the same pattern may confidently be expected to occur with larger samples.

To conclude: Aspiration on the CGAT is primarily, if not wholly, a measure of dexterity with a pencil. If one wishes to measure "aspiration," one must seek a situation in which it is independent of performance. The necessary conditions are described elsewhere,[2] together with the mathematical rationale of level of aspiration scoring. A group level of aspiration test adequate in the latter sense to the measurement of "irreality" has yet to be devised.

B Menninger Clinic 17:115 My '53. Robert R. Holt. (Review of manual.) One of the familiar techniques of the psychological laboratory has been made into a group test, here reported in a brief manual that is exemplary for the confusion, and pretentiousness of the author's thinking and writing. The test's reliability is insufficient for use in counseling individuals, as the author recommends, and its validation is a muddle because of the author's evident misunderstanding of theoretical foundations.

2 *Ibid.*

J Consult Psychol 16:476 D '52. Laurance F. Shaffer. * The author may be commended for standardizing a useful but hitherto unstandardized technique, and for publishing such relatively full data about it. At the present time, however, our knowledge of the level-of-aspiration experiment by no means justifies all of the clinical implications that Cassel seems to draw from some of his scores. The test is a good instrument for further research, not a finished clinical tool.

[40]

★The Cassel Psychotherapy Progress Record. Mental patients; 1953; 3 ratings: emotional development, barrier vulnerability development, overall psychotherapy development; no data on reliability and validity; no norms; $6 per set of 25 record forms and manual, postpaid; specimen set not available; Russell N. Cassel; Western Psychological Services. *

[41]

★Child Personality Scale. Grades kgn–9; 1951; scale for ratings by classmates and teachers, and for self-ratings; 22 ratings: pep, intelligence, sociability, nervous-calmness, popularity, religiousness, punctuality, courtesy, cooperation, generosity, persistence, honesty, neatness, patience, interests, disposition, good sport, quietness, entertaining, thoughtfulness, sense of humor, dependability; 1 form; no data on reliability and validity; $2.50 per 25 scales; 50¢ per specimen set; postpaid; (20–40) minutes for rating 10 classmates; Mary Amatora; C. A. Gregory Co. *

REFERENCES

1. TSCHECHTELIN, M. AMATORA. *An Investigation of Some Elements of Teachers' and Pupils' Personalities.* Purdue University, Studies in Higher Education, No. 48; Further Studies in Attitudes, Series 6. Lafayette, Ind.: the Division, January 1943. Pp. 87. *
2. TSCHECHTELIN, M. AMATORA. "Comparability of Child and Adult Personality Rating Scales." *J Ed Psychol* 35:309–13 My '44. * (PA 18:3780)
3. TSCHECHTELIN, M. AMATORA. "Factor Analysis of Children's Personality Rating Scale." *J Psychol* 18:197–200 O '44. * (PA 19:178)
4. TSCHECHTELIN, M. AMATORA. "A 22-Trait Personality Rating Scale." *J Psychol* 18:3–8 Jl '44. * (PA 19:177)
5. TSCHECHTELIN, M. AMATORA. "Self-Appraisal of Children." *J Ed Res* 39:25–32 S '45. * (PA 20:614)
6. TSCHECHTELIN, M. AMATORA. "Teachers Rate Their Pupils." *Ed Adm & Sup* 31:22–6 Ja '45. * (PA 19:1608)
7. TSCHECHTELIN, M. AMATORA. "Teacher Ratings of Pupil Personality." *Ed Adm & Sup* 34:412–20 N '48. *
8. AMATORA, MARY. "Studies in Personality: The Age Factor." *Cath Ed R* 48:223–30 Ap '50. *
9. TSCHECHTELIN, M. AMATORA. "Norms on a Child Personality Scale." *El Sch J* 51:209–13 D '50. *
10. TSCHECHTELIN, M. AMATORA. "A Study in Teacher Personality." *J Ed Res* 44:709–14 My '51. * (PA 26:1730)
11. AMATORA, MARY. "Boys' Personality Appraisals Differentiate Teacher Groups." *Sch & Soc* 76:184–7 S 20 '52. *
12. TSCHECHTELIN, M. AMATORA. "Reliability of a Personality Scale." *Ed & Psychol Meas* 12:132–6 sp '52. * (PA 27:5912)
13. AMATORA, MARY. "Pupil Evaluation or Teacher Evaluation in Personality?" *Prog Ed* 31:44–5+ N '53. *
14. AMATORA, MARY. "Contrasts in Boys' and Girls' Judgments in Personality." *Child Develop* 25:51–62 Mr '54. * (PA 29:5352)
15. AMATORA, MARY. "Similarity in Teacher and Pupil Personality." *J Psychol* 37:45–50 Ja '54. * (PA 28:8097)
16. AMATORA, MARY. "Comparisons in Personality Self-Evaluation." *J Social Psychol* 42:315–21 N '55. * (PA 31:601)
17. AMATORA, MARY. "Validity in Self Evaluation." *Ed & Psychol Meas* 16:119–26 sp '56. * (PA 31:6054)
18. AMATORA, MARY. "Developmental Trends in Pre-Adolescence and in Early Adolescence in Self-Evaluation." *J Genetic Psychol* 91:89–97 S '57. *

ROBERT H. BAUERNFEIND, *Director, Test Department, Science Research Associates, Chicago, Illinois.*

The *Child Personality Scale* provides a means for having each child rated on 22 traits by himself, by his classmates, and by his teacher. Each trait is rated on a 10-point scale.

In theory, this instrument presents a promising idea for sociometric research, for programs of child study, and for improving teachers' understanding of their own values and those of their pupils. Consensus ratings on the part of 10 children should show a high degree of reliability in most classroom situations. Another promising idea is the profile, which permits comparisons of ratings among the several traits for each child. Use of 10-point scales is another plus-value, such scales permitting and encouraging graded expressions of opinion on the part of each rater.

In its present form, however, this scale presents serious obstacles to the fulfillment of its own purposes. Some of these obstacles are:

a) The manual lacks a statement of rationale. Many readers will feel a need to know something of the history of the instrument and the author's reasons for suggesting ratings of these particular 22 traits.

b) The directions are awkward, wordy, and too rigid for use with all children in grades 3 to 9. The manual offers no encouragement to teachers who would prefer to ad-lib the directions at a level appropriate to their classes.

c) The published forms fail to give children help in interpreting each new item in terms of a 10-point scale. Many third, fourth, and fifth grade pupils will experience difficulty in making ratings appropriately in the absence of specific visual aids.

d) The instrument includes an explicitly religious item:

Does he like to pray and go to church?
not at all .... very much

This item per se, not to mention its interpretation, would cause difficulties in many public schools.

e) The instrument includes at least one ambiguous item:

Is he generally quiet, or loud and rude?
noisy, must be heard .... very quiet

This item covers two traits: "noisy—quiet," *and* "rude—sensitive." While interpretation of all 22 items will require searching value judgments, this item will present special difficulties. The

values of our Western civilization clearly prefer sensitivity to rudeness; however, our cultural values (and certainly the constructs of clinical psychology) do not necessarily prefer quietness to noisiness.

f) The manual suggests, without qualification, that children be shown their self-ratings, teacher ratings, and classmates' ratings for purposes of planning programs of self-improvement. Recalling that some children will have been rated by their teachers and classmates as "very dull," "very boring," or "has no sense of humor," most responsible readers will feel this broad suggestion to be extremely hazardous.

g) The manual includes no résumé of the author's research, although the bibliography shows that nine research studies have been reported in the professional literature.

h) The problem of assessing "growth," always elusive in measurement, would be even more difficult in the case of this instrument. While each child draws on his own background of experience in making ratings, his background for evaluating child behavior is largely drawn from experiences with his own classmates. On this type of rating scale, therefore, significant growth on the part of one or two pupils in a classroom would often result in lower ratings for the other pupils—even though the other pupils' qualities of behavior on the trait in question remained constant, or even improved slightly! There can be no "norms," elusive as they are, and there can be no absolutes to help in interpreting changes in ratings derived from this scale. Thus, the second section of the manual, dealing with improvement of character and personality, is oversimplified. Much research is needed on the problem of how this type of instrument can measure fairly changes in character and personality for all members of a class

In summary, the *Child Personality Scale* in its present form is not recommended for general school use. The instrument may have occasional value as a fact-finding device for study of individual "problem" youngsters. Even in these cases, however, users are cautioned that the manual will be of very little help and that efforts at interpretation will often confront them with unexpected problems in basic personal philosophy as well as in measurement.

DALE B. HARRIS, *Professor of Psychology, and Director, Institute of Child Development and*

Welfare, University of Minnesota, Minneapolis, Minnesota.

The manual recommends that each child rate 10 preassigned children in his school class and himself. A child's "scores" on the several traits consist of the mean of 10 ratings assigned him on each trait. No data are offered in the manual to indicate the reliability of ratings based on such a small sample, or how 10 was selected as an adequate number of judges to rate one case. Although the principle of the graphic rating scale is followed, the form of such a scale is not used. The teacher places a model containing 10 steps on the blackboard. The child rater selects a digit which he enters on his answer sheet as his rating for that trait in the child under consideration. Working trait by trait, each child rates his 10 preassigned "subjects," entering their scores under the names which he has written at the top of 10 adjacent columns.

The author affirms that this method can be successfully used for peer ratings as low as the third grade. This reviewer has not had success with graphic methods with children in the intermediate grades, even when a graphic form is reproduced separately for each quality to be rated. Nor do these children successfully transfer their responses from a stimulus page to an answer sheet. The reviewer would, therefore, question the validity of peer judgments of children 8 or 9 years of age when recorded by this method. He does not question this method, however, for ratings by teachers, although the measurement literature suggests that an odd rather than an even number of ratings has certain advantages, and that 7 points rather than 10 may represent the discriminations which can be made optimally by many raters.

The nomination or "Guess Who" technique, because of the type of judgments required, appeals to this reviewer as having more validity with elementary school children than the rating scale technique. While the former technique is bound to the group wherein judgments are made, and the latter technique is theoretically more related to a general norm or "average," the reviewer questions the elementary school child's ability to conceptualize a range of differences along a trait dimension and to make accurate judgments with respect to particular children. The ability of children to make such judgments could well be a subject for study and experiment. With more adequate research on children's concepts and their judgmental processes concerning personality phenomena, we would be in a better position to formulate scales for use by children.

It is well to point out that the traits do not appear on the rating sheet as named in the entry above. For example, "punctuality" appears as "Is he usually on time?" with the extremes of the characteristic being designated as "usually late" and "never late." The careful grading of the language is a distinct advantage of these scales.

The author is to be commended for her diligent reporting in professional journals of much useful data concerning the scales; it is regrettable that her data on reliability and validity and grade differences do not appear in the manual. The norms that are supplied give means and standard errors of peer ratings and ratings by teachers for several thousand children of mixed ages. Means (but no measures of variance or of standard error) are also given for girls' ratings of peers of each sex, for boys' ratings of peers of each sex, for teachers' ratings of boys and girls, and for self ratings, by sex. The value to the ordinary teacher of such "norms," virtually all of which approximate the theoretical midpoint between 5 and 6 on a 10-point scale, is not at once apparent. If she follows instructions faithfully and relates her judgment to her experience, her mean can scarcely deviate from this theoretical value.

The principal value of these scales, as the manual suggests, is probably in identifying deviates in the classroom group, and in identifying children who consider themselves deviates. One may hold some philosophical reservations about the author's assertions that group and self-ratings of this type should be made the subject of concern and study by young children.

The instructions in the manual are adequate for the few classroom teachers who are thoroughly sophisticated in rating procedures, but hardly so for the many who have only the usual experiences with such evaluations. To use the scales most effectively, one should have knowledge of guidance and counseling theory and procedures as well as of measurement theory and practice.

[42]

★Community Improvement Scale. Adults; 1955; community morale; 1 form; hectographed manual; $3 per 50 tests; $1 per specimen set (must be purchased to obtain manual); postage extra; [5-10] minutes; Inez Fay Smith; Psychometric Affiliates. *

WIMBURN L. WALLACE, *Director, Professional Examinations Division, The Psychological Corporation, New York, New York.*

The 2-page hectographed manual states that the *"Community Improvement Scale* is a device for measuring neighborhood morale while at the same time obtaining a diagnostic analysis of principal areas of neighborhood morale maintenance. * It samples such attitudes as those relating to local business people, recreation, beauty, gossiping, public library facilities, transportation, school convenience, economic status, outlook, community services, friendliness." Only 13 items are used to obtain the single score. The items are multiple choice in form, with each set of alternatives arranged as a 5-point scale rating from bad to good a particular aspect of the respondent's neighborhood. Unfortunately, some of the sets of alternatives do not lie on a true continuum.

The printed questionnaire is bizarre. It comprises a peculiar collection of type faces and is bordered with baroque scrollwork and other symbols. The system of responding to the items calls for the tearing of arrowheads at the edge of the page next to the option; this is an awkward procedure with no apparent advantage over conventional marking with a pen or pencil.

Development of the scale involved tryout of a preliminary form on 100 respondents in the northwest Chicago area, and modification in the light of suggestions received. Since directions for administration prohibit telling the respondents that the purpose of the scale is to measure neighborhood morale, the suggestions of even sophisticated respondents could hardly have been pertinent.

All the data reported in the manual were gathered in the Chicago area. The corrected odd-even coefficient of reliability is given as .86 "for a random sample of 150 Chicago-area homes." One norms table shows percentile equivalents for raw scores for "218 individuals randomly sampled from the Chicago metropolitan area." How the score of an individual is to be interpreted in terms of "neighborhood morale" is not made clear. Along with the norms table, median scores are given for 19 suburban and postal zone areas of Chicago; the number of cases in each area is not shown. It is striking that the medians for 15 of these 19 areas exceed the median shown in the norms table; the undescribed sampling methods appear to yield results which need clarification.

The one validity study mentioned in the manual used postal zone numbers in Chicago as a criterion measure. Unidentified research is supposed to have shown that "residential conditions" are worst near the "business core of the city" and improve in direct proportion to the distance from that center. One has to infer that the magnitude of postal zone numbers in Chicago indicates distance from the center of the city. Cases were drawn from 31 postal zone areas and five suburbs. Number of respondents, sampling technique, mean scores, and standard deviations are not given. The coefficient of correlation between zone numbers and scores on the scale is reported as .67. The extent to which this statistic provides evidence that the scale measures neighborhood morale is patently questionable. Nothing is mentioned concerning the applicability of the scale elsewhere than in Chicago.

In summary, it may be said that the *Community Improvement Scale* is an unsophisticated attempt to measure neighborhood morale. In its present state it meets practically none of the criteria of worthiness for publication for sale. Almost any sociologist could quickly write a questionnaire that would immediately have at least as much value as this one.

[43]

Cornell Index. Adults; 1944–49; revision for civilian use of the *Cornell Selectee Index Form N* and the *Cornell Service Index;* title on test is C.I.—Form N2; psychosomatic and neuropsychiatric symptoms; Form N2 ['45]; revised manual ('49); $2.80 per 50 tests; 35¢ per specimen set; postpaid; (5–15) minutes; Arthur Weider, Harold G. Wolff, Keeve Brodman, Bela Mittelmann, and David Wechsler; Psychological Corporation. *

REFERENCES

1–41. See 4:37.
42. RICHARDS, T. W. "Personality of the Convulsive Patient in Military Service." *Psychol Monogr* 66(14):1–23 '52. * (*PA* 27:7364)
43. TAAFFE, GORDON. *The Discrimination of Alcoholics, Psychopaths, and Psychoneurotics by Means of the Manson Evaluation, the Pd Scale, MMPI, and the Cornell Index.* Master's thesis, University of Southern California (Los Angeles, Calif.), 1952.
44. WILLIAMS, MARIE E. *A Comparison of the Cornell Index, Form N2 With the Psycho-Somatic Experience Blank.* Master's thesis, Fordham University (New York, N.Y.), 1952.
45. LAUFER, LUDWIG G. "Cultural Problems Encountered in Use of the Cornell Index Among Okinawan Natives." *Am J Psychiatry* 109:861–4 My '53. * (*PA* 28:2483)
46. LYON, BLANCHARD; MOLISH, HERMAN B.; AND BRIGGS, DENNIE L. "The Cornell Index: A Comparison of a Matched Sample of Psychiatric 'Suspects' and Nonsuspects." *US Armed Forces Med J* 4:977–85 Jl '53. * (*PA* 29:2454)
47. BARNES, JAMES R. *A Critical Study of the Results of the Mooney Problem Check List and the Cornell Index as a Means of Identifying Possible Cases of Psychosomatic Illness Among 400 North Carolina College Students.* Master's thesis, North Carolina College (Durham, N.C.), 1954.
48. TUCKMAN, JACOB; LORGE, IRVING; AND ZEMAN, FREDERIC D. "Retesting Older People With the Cornell Medical Index and With the Supplementary Health Questionnaire." *J Gerontol* 9:306–8 Jl '54. * (*PA* 29:5436)

For reviews by Hans J. Eysenck, Nelson G. Hanawalt, and Laurance F. Shaffer, see 4:37.

[44]

★**Cornell Word Form 2.** Adults; 1946–55; civilian edition of *Cornell Word Form* designed for use in military psychiatric screening; title on test is *C.W.F.–2;* 1 form ['55]; manual ('55, reprint of *11* below); $5 per 100 tests; specimen set free; postage extra; [5–15] minutes; Arthur Weider, Bela Mittelmann, David Wechsler, and Harold Wolff; Cornell University Medical College (Room F-636, 1300 York Ave., New York, N.Y.). *

REFERENCES

1. MITTELMANN, BELA; WEIDER, ARTHUR; VONACHEN, HAROLD A.; KRONENBERG, MILTON; WEIDER, NORMA; BRODMAN, KEEVE; AND WOLFF, HAROLD G.; WITH THE TECHNICAL ASSISTANCE OF MARGARET D. MEIXNER. "Detection and Management of Personality and Psychosomatic Disorders Among Industrial Personnel." *Psychosom Med* 7:359–67 N '45. * (*PA* 20:1654)
2. MITTELMANN, BELA, AND BRODMAN, KEEVE. "The Cornell Indices and the Cornell Word Form: 1, Construction and Standardization." *Ann NY Acad Sci* 46:573–7, discussion 603–5 Jl 30 '46. * (*PA* 20:4674)
3. WEIDER, ARTHUR, AND WECHSLER, DAVID. "The Cornell Indices and the Cornell Word Form: 2, Results." *Ann NY Acad Sci* 46:579–87, discussion 603–5 Jl 30 '46. * (*PA* 20:4684)
4. WOLFF, HAROLD G. "The Cornell Indices and the Cornell Word Form: 3, Application." *Ann NY Acad Sci* 46:589–91, discussion 603–5 Jl 30 '46. * (*PA* 20:4688)
5. BROWER, DANIEL. "The Relations of Visuo-Motor Conflict to Personality Traits and Cardio-Vascular Activity." *J General Psychol* 38:69–99 Ja '48. * (*PA* 22:3383)
6. STACK, HERBERT J. *Personal Characteristics of Traffic-Accident Repeaters.* Saugatuck, Conn.: Eno Foundation for Highway Traffic Control, 1948. Pp. 64. *
7. SASLOW, GEORGE, AND SHOBE, FRANK O. "Evaluation of a Psychiatric Screening Test: Cornell Word Form–I." *Am J Psychiatry* 106:37–45 Jl '49. * (*PA* 24:1207)
8. DuBOIS, PHILIP H., AND WATSON, ROBERT I. "The Selection of Patrolmen." *J Appl Psychol* 34:90–5 Ap '50. * (*PA* 25:2076)
9. DuBOIS, PHILIP H., AND WATSON, ROBERT I. "Validity Information Exchange, No 7–075: D.O.T. Code 2-66.23, Policeman." *Personnel Psychol* 7:414–7 au '54. *
10. BARRY, JOHN R.; SELLS, SAUL B.; AND TRITES, DAVID K. "Psychiatric Screening of Flying Personnel With the Cornell Word Form." Abstract. *J Consult Psychol* 19:32 F '55. *
11. WEIDER, ARTHUR; MITTELMANN, BELA; WECHSLER, DAVID; AND WOLFF, HAROLD G. "Further Developments of the Cornell Word Form." *Psychiatric Q* 29:588–94 O '55. *

[45]

★**DF Opinion Survey.** Grades 12–16 and adults; 1954–56; IBM; 1 form ('54); 10 scores: need for attention, liking for thinking, adventure vs. security, self-reliance vs. dependence, aesthetic appreciation, cultural conformity, need for freedom, realistic thinking, need for precision, need for diversion; separate answer sheets must be used; $3.75 per 25 tests; 20¢ per single copy; 3¢ per IBM answer sheet; $2 per set of either hand or machine scoring stencils; 3¢ per profile ('55); 25¢ per manual ('56); postage extra; [45] minutes; J. P. Guilford, Paul R. Christensen, and Nicholas A. Bond, Jr.; Sheridan Supply Co. *

ANDREW R. BAGGALEY, *Associate Professor of Psychology, University of Wisconsin—Milwaukee, Milwaukee, Wisconsin.*

This inventory is based on an extensive factor analysis. It attempts to encompass dimensions of "motivation" as well as "vocation-interest." Thus it is a kind of combination of the approaches of the *Kuder Preference Record* and *Edwards Personal Preference Schedule,* although it differs from both in using the "yes-?-no" response form instead of forced choices.

Thirty items are scored for each of 10 scales. Most of the questions are of the form "You would like to...," which seems rather awkward. Also, many testees may wonder whether Parts 1 and 2 are separately timed.

Odd-even reliabilities are given for male and female college students separately and combined. The mean of the latter (by Fisher's *z* transformation) is .86. Also, scale intercorrelations are reported for both sexes. Most of these are below .30. Thus the reliability of intraindividual differences as measured by the scales is quite high. All in all, the construct validity of the survey is rather convincing, although it would be interesting to have correlations with similarly-named scales of inventories already in wide use. The authors claim nothing further about the validity of this inventory and recommend separate predictive validation in each practical application. In fact they call it an "experimental test" in the manual, though not on the test booklet. Nevertheless, if the survey is to be used for vocational guidance, as the authors suggest, it would obviously be useful to have available some predictive validities for *general* types of criterion activities, so that a counselor could judge in advance whether or not administration of the survey would be a complete waste of time for some of his problems. College norms are given for each sex separately on those scales showing significant sex differences. As the authors imply, this inventory should probably be used for guidance rather than selection, since it seems not too difficult for a testee to "fake" a desired impression on the scale scores.

In summary, this is a well designed inventory with certain limitations—limitations which are clearly stated in the manual. It should provide good competition for both temperament and interest inventories already on the market.

JOHN W. FRENCH, *Research Associate, Educational Testing Service, Princeton, New Jersey.*

The *DF Opinion Survey* is a well set up personality questionnaire based on the authors' long research experience. It is intended to fill a need for an "extensive, rational coverage of the many variables that should be included in an adequate assessment of personality." It can be said that nobody is sure yet exactly how best to describe personality, whether it should be in terms of traits, interests, attitudes, motivations, or some combination of things. This instrument concentrates on "dynamic factors" and yields 10 scores as listed in the above entry. The manual explains that these traits were selected as being non-vocational interest or motivational traits found by factor analysis. While this kind of selection seems reasonable, no specific reasons are given for including some traits rather than others. Why, for example, are interests in thinking and in aesthetics included, while interests in athletics and in people are not? Why are self-reliance and conformity included, while emotionality, persistence, and sociability are not? Why are the needs for attention, precision, diversion, and security included, while the need for affection is not? While answers to these questions are not provided, the reviewer has no specific reason for criticizing the selection that was made. Considering that the test requires less than one hour to administer, the areas of the personality domain represented seem to cover very well the important motivational factors.

As one takes the *DF Opinion Survey,* there appears a noticeable repetitiveness associated with certain columns on the answer sheet. This is a consequence of (*a*) simplifying the scoring keys by placing all items for a given scale in the same column, and (*b*) insuring high reliability by including many items of each type. This replication of similar items was done for subcategories within each of the 10 reportable scores rather than for the reportable scores themselves. In some cases the subcategories within a score do not seem, on an introspective basis, likely to be related to each other as well as they should be. For example, adventure vs. security consists of four homogeneous item subcategories: exploration, personal risk-taking, harm avoidance, and monotony. Each one of these is probably highly reliable for the number of items involved. Yet the reportable score would suffer if, for example, people who would like exploring do not usually enjoy taking needless personal risks. Another seemingly odd mixture of subcategories occurs in the cultural conformity score, where conscientious and competitive people are grouped with conventional conformists. Perhaps the manual could be improved by the inclusion of factor-analytic or other evidence justifying the subcategories that are listed for the 10 scores. Similar reliability, less repetitiveness, and greater validity might have been achieved by having the items more evenly cover the full scope of each reportable score rather than having them repetitively define subcategories. On the other hand, the homogenous subcategories of items make available some opportunities for research that would not have been available had the items been set up more ideally for operational measurement of the survey's 10 scores. For example, with a reasonably large population of subjects, a satisfactory validation could be made separately for each of more than 30 groups of items. The manual mentions the possible use of the item subcategories in factor analysis studies.

This inventory, as the authors suggest, should be regarded to some extent as a research instrument, because evidence for its validity is not yet available. Nevertheless, the general findings of the authors and others in the field of personality measurement make it seem likely that the factors being measured here will serve an important function when used as recommended in conjunction with vocational interest inventories for vocational guidance, for predicting happiness in an occupation, and for gathering information about personal adjustment.

ARTHUR W. MEADOWS, *Head, Psychology Department, University of Adelaide, Adelaide, Australia.*

This inventory of dynamic factors of interest is the result of a factor-analytic investigation. Each of the 10 traits it measures is contributed to by a number of categories of interest, e.g., "liking for thinking" is contributed to by items assessing interest in mathematics, logical processes, organising, and puzzle solving; "need for freedom," by items designed to reveal aversion to organising, nonconformity, independence, and disorderliness, and so on. The original variables selected were developed from a large number of human needs including those formulated by Murray in his *Explorations in Personality.* The survey is administered with a separate answer sheet and is hand or machine scored.

The authors selected items by item analysis from a pool and prepared new items after trial. The resulting items were analysed again on the basis of the factor scores. An attempt was made to make the items as unidimensional as possible. Interpretation of the scores is given in terms which generalise from the original items. For example, a high score on "need for attention" is said to imply a craving for recognition, the enjoyment of status, and exhibitionism. These terms are derived from the implications and sense of the items. Careful perusal of the items indicates that, with very slight rephrasing, the inventory could be used in English speaking countries other than America.

Reliabilities of the trait scores were computed separately for men and for women, and for men and women combined. The corrected odd-even coefficients range from .65 to .96. The intercorrelations of the scores on the traits indicate that 70 per cent of the coefficients are below .30. Thus, a fair proportion of the scores are relatively independent.

There are clear sex differences and differences due to educational level (probably due to age), but separate norms in terms of means and standard deviations of scores on each scale are provided for men and women and for high school and college groups.

This test should prove useful in conjunction with vocational interest inventories because certain occupations may sometimes be distinguished more clearly than others as including such interest factors as "liking for thinking," "need for precision," and "need for diversion." In addition, behaviour problems might be predictable on the basis of scores on such factors as, say, "need for freedom" and "cultural conformity."

There are no validity data with practical criteria and the survey must be designated as an experimental test for future use in vocational and counseling fields.

[46]

*Detroit Adjustment Inventory. Ages 5–8, grades 3–6, 7–12; 1942–54; title on test for Gamma and Alpha Forms is *Telling What I Do;* 3 levels; record blanks (no date); no data on reliability; no norms; $3.25 per 25 tests; 55¢ per specimen set; 95¢ per set of remedial leaflets; postage extra; Harry J. Baker; Public School Publishing Co. *

a) DELTA FORM. Ages 5–8; 1954.
b) GAMMA FORM. Grades 3–6; 1950–52; test ('52); manual ('52); (20–50) minutes.
c) ALPHA FORM. Grades 7–12; 1942; (20–40) minutes.

REFERENCE
1. BOUISE, LOUISE METOYER. "Emotional and Personality Problems of a Group of Retarded Readers." *El Engl* 32:544–8 D '55. *

LAURANCE F. SHAFFER, *Professor of Education, Teachers College, Columbia University, New York, New York.*

Although the three levels of the *Detroit Adjustment Inventory* were published from 1942 to 1954, they bear a marked resemblance to the primitive instruments for appraising personality that first appeared in the 1920's. Their characteristics have to be summed by a string of negatives—no evidence about item construction except reference to the author's subjective experience, no sign of item analysis against internal or external criteria, no data on reliability, no norms. The only evidence of validity, for Alpha and Gamma, is the ability of the total score to distinguish extremely maladjusted pupils in special classes from superior or average pupils. There is no evidence at all about Delta.

The items in all three forms of the test are arranged under 24 topics. The Alpha and Gamma forms are pupil-answered questionnaires of 120 five-choice and 128 three-choice items, respectively. Delta, completed by the teacher from observation and parent interviews, has 64 four-choice items.

The complete program for the use of the inventory does not stop with diagnosis, but goes on to treatment. Pupils who have taken Alpha may receive any of 24 remedial leaflets selected according to the areas of their maladjustment. For Gamma there are 16 pupil leaflets, and for Delta, 16 for the use of teachers and parents. These leaflets were not seen by the reviewer, but the manual for Alpha gives four samples. These are not at all impressive.

In spite of its shortcomings, the inventory may have some value when used by teachers or counselors whose skills and attitudes are optimal. The very absence of the trappings of psychometrics may make a wise teacher look beyond the ridiculously numerous "scores," and see the primary communication from the pupil. But even for this purpose, modern conceptions of test construction can surely produce a far sharper instrument.

For a review by Albert Ellis of the Alpha Form, see 3:31.

[47]

★Edwards Personal Preference Schedule. College and adults; 1953–57; 15 scores: achievement, deference, order, exhibition, autonomy, affiliation, intraception, succorance, dominance, abasement, nurturance, change, endurance, heterosexuality, aggression; 2 supplementary scores: test consistency, profile stability; IBM; 1 form ('53); revised manual ('57); college norms only; separate answer sheets must be used; $3 per 25 tests; $2.25 per 50 hand scoring answer sheets; $2.20 per 50 IBM answer sheets; $1.50 per set of either hand or machine scoring stencils; 60¢ per specimen set; postpaid; (40–55) minutes; Allen L. Edwards; Psychological Corporation.

REFERENCES
1. EDWARDS, ALLEN L. "The Relationship Between the Judged Desirability of a Trait and the Probability That the Trait Will Be Endorsed." *J Appl Psychol* 37:90–3 F '53. * (*PA* 28:551)
2. NAVRAN, LESLIE, AND STAUFFACHER, JAMES C. "Social Desirability as a Factor in Edwards' Personality Preference Schedule Performance." Abstract. *J Consult Psychol* 18:442 D '54. *
3. SCHLAG, MADELEINE. *The Relationship Between the Personality Preference Schedule and the Allport, Vernon and Lindzey Study of Values: A Personality Study of a Group of*

Medical Students. Master's thesis, University of Washington (Seattle, Wash.), 1954.

4. MERRILL, REED M. "Relation of the Edwards Personal Preference Schedule to the Clinical and Experimental Scales of the MMPI." Abstract. *Am Psychol* 10:366 Ag '55. *

5. PIROJNIKOFF, L. *The Achievement Motive and Other Personality Traits as Measured by Edwards Personal Preference Schedule and Their Relation to Learning, the Authoritarian Scale, and Speed of Performance.* Master's thesis, University of Washington (Seattle, Wash.), 1955.

6. STROTHER, CHARLES R., AND SCHAIE, K. WARNER. "Age Differences in Personality: A Comparison of Young and Old Groups of Superior Ability." Abstract. *Am Psychol* 10:339 Ag '55. *

7. BENDIG, A. W. "The Personality of Judges and Their Agreement With Experts in Judging Clinical Case Histories." Abstract. *J Consult Psychol* 20:422 D '56. *

8. FUJITA, BEN. *An Investigation of the Applicability of the Edwards Personal Preference Schedule to a Cultural Sub-Group, the Nisei.* Master's thesis, University of Washington (Seattle, Wash.), 1956.

9. HORN, J. B. *A Comparison of Robbers, Burglars, and Forgers on the Edwards PPS.* Master's thesis, University of Washington (Seattle, Wash.), 1956.

10. KLETT, C. J. *A Study of the Edwards Personal Preference Schedule in Relation to Socio-Economic Status.* Doctor's thesis, University of Washington (Seattle, Wash.), 1956.

11. MERRILL, REED M., AND HEATHERS, LOUISE B. "The Relation of the MMPI to the Edwards Personal Preference Schedule on a College Counseling Center Sample." *J Consult Psychol* 20:310-4 Ag '56. * (*PA* 31:7949)

12. SHEPHERD, JOHN R., AND SCHEIDEL, THOMAS M. "A Study of the Personality Configuration of Effective Oral Readers." *Speech Monogr* 23:298-304 N '56. * (*PA* 32:2128)

13. TOBIN, W. W. *Use of the Edwards Personal Preference Schedule in Establishing Personality Profiles for Teachers and Education Students.* Master's thesis, University of Washington (Seattle, Wash.), 1956.

14. ALLEN, ROBERT M. "Edwards Personal Preference Schedule Intercorrelations for Two Groups." *Psychol Rec* 7:87-91 Jl '57. *

15. ALLEN, ROBERT M. "The Relationship Between the Edwards Personal Preference Schedule Variables and the Minnesota Multiphasic Personality Inventory Scales." *J Appl Psychol* 41:307-11 O '57. *

16. ALLEN, ROBERT M., AND DALLEK, JEFFREY I. "A Normative Study of the Edwards' Personal Preference Schedule." *J Psychol* 43:151-4 Ja '57. *

17. ANDREWS, JOHN H. M. "Administrative Significance of Psychological Differences Between Secondary Teachers of Different Subject Matter Fields." *Alberta J Ed Res* 3:199-208 D '57. *

18. BERNARDIN, ALFRED C., AND JESSOR, RICHARD. "A Construct Validation of the Edwards Personal Preference Schedule With Respect to Dependency." *J Consult Psychol* 21:63-7 F '57. * (*PA* 32:485)

19. CROW, W. R. *Relationships Between Edwards PPS and the MMPI.* Master's thesis, University of Washington (Seattle, Wash.), 1957.

20. FISHER, SEYMOUR, AND MORTON, ROBERT B. "An Exploratory Study of Some Relationships Between Hospital Ward Atmospheres and Attitudes of Ward Personnel." *J Psychol* 44:155-64 Jl '57. *

21. FUJITA, BEN. "Applicability of the Edwards Personal Preference Schedule to Nisei." *Psychol Rep* 3:518-9 D '57. *

22. GRAINE, GEORGE N. "Measures of Conformity as Found in the Rosenzweig P-F Study and the Edwards Personal Preference Schedule." Abstract. *J Consult Psychol* 21:300 Ag '57. *

23. GROSSACK, MARTIN M. "Some Personality Characteristics of Southern Negro Students." *J Social Psychol* 46:125-31 Ag '57. *

24. JACKSON, PHILIP W., AND GUBA, EGON G. "The Need Structure of In-Service Teachers: An Occupational Analysis." *Sch R* 65:176-92 Je '57. *

25. KELLEHER, D. *The Social Desirability Factor in Edwards PPS.* Master's thesis, University of Washington (Seattle, Wash.), 1957.

26. KLETT, C. JAMES. "Performance of High School Students on the Edwards Personal Preference Schedule." *J Consult Psychol* 21:68-72 F '57. * (*PA* 32:949)

27. KLETT, C. JAMES. "The Social Desirability Stereotype in a Hospital Population." *J Consult Psychol* 21:419-21 O '57. *

28. KLETT, C. JAMES. "The Stability of the Social Desirability Scale Values in the Edwards Personal Preference Schedule." *J Consult Psychol* 21:183-5 Ap '57. *

29. KLETT, C. JAMES, AND TAMKIN, ARTHUR S. "The Social Desirability Stereotype and Some Measures of Psychopathology." Abstract. *J Consult Psychol* 21:450 D '57. *

30. KLETT, SHIRLEY LOUISE. *The Edwards Personal Preference Schedule and Academic Achievement.* Doctor's thesis, University of Washington (Seattle, Wash.), 1957. (*DA* 18:1490)

31. KOPONEN, ARTHUR. *The Influence of Demographic Factors on Responses to the Edwards Personal Preference Schedule.* Doctor's thesis, Columbia University (New York, N.Y.), 1957. (*DA* 17:2697)

32. SILVERMAN, ROBERT E. "The Edwards Personal Preference Schedule and Social Desirability." *J Consult Psychol* 21:402-4 O '57. *

33. VENING, GEORGE H., AND PEPINSKY, HAROLD B. "Normative Data Information Exchange, No. 10-16." *Personnel Psychol* 10:235 su '57. *

34. ALLEN, ROBERT M. "An Analysis of Edwards Personal Preference Schedule Intercorrelations for a Local College Population." *J Ed Res* 51:591-7 Ap '58. *

35. BENDIG, A. W. "Comparison of the Validity of Two Temperament Scales in Predicting College Achievement." *J Ed Res* 51:605-9 Ap '58. *

36. BORISLOW, BERNARD. "The Edwards Personal Preference Schedule (EPPS) and Fakability." *J Appl Psychol* 42:22-7 F '58. *

37. CORAH, NORMAN L.; FELDMAN, MARVIN J.; COHEN, IRA S.; GRUEN, WALTER; MEADOW, ARNOLD; AND RINGWALL, EGAN A. "Social Desirability as a Variable in the Edwards Personal Preference Schedule." *J Consult Psychol* 22:70-2 F '58. *

38. DUNNETTE, MARVIN D., AND KIRCHNER, WAYNE K. "Validation of Psychological Tests in Industry." *Personnel Adm* 21:20-7 My-Je '58. *

39. DUNNETTE, MARVIN D.; KIRCHNER, WAYNE K.; AND DEGIDIO, JoANNE. "Relations Among Scores on Edwards Personal Preference Schedule, California Psychological Inventory, and Strong Vocational Interest Blank for an Industrial Sample." *J Appl Psychol* 42:178-81 Je '58. *

40. FRENCH, ELIZABETH G. "A Note on the Edwards Personal Preference Schedule for Use With Basic Airmen." *Ed & Psychol Meas* 18:109-15 sp '58. *

41. GEBHART, G. GARY, AND HOYT, DONALD P. "Personality Needs of Under- and Overachieving Freshmen." *J Appl Psychol* 42:125-8 Ap '58. *

42. HEILBRUN, ALFRED B., JR. "Relationships Between the Adjective Check-List, Personal Preference Schedule and Desirability Factors Under Varying Defensiveness Conditions." *J Clin Psychol* 14:283-7 Jl '58. *

43. KELLEHER, DANIEL. "The Social Desirability Factor in Edwards' PPS." Abstract. *J Consult Psychol* 22:100 Ap '58. *

44. LÖVAAS, O. IVAR. "Social Desirability Ratings of Personality Variables by Norwegian and American College Students." *J Abn & Social Psychol* 57:124-5 Jl '58. *

45. MANN, JOHN H. "Self-Ratings and the EPPS." *J Appl Psychol* 42:267-8 Ag '58. *

46. MELIKIAN, LEVON H. "The Relationship Between Edwards' and McClelland's Measures of Achievement Motivation." *J Consult Psychol* 22:296-8 Ag '58. *

47. PETERSON, TED TANGWALL. *Selecting School Administrators: An Evaluation of Six Tests.* Doctor's thesis, Stanford University (Stanford, Calif.), 1958. (*DA* 19:262)

48. STOLTZ, ROBERT E. "Note on Intercorrelations of Edward's Personal Preference Schedule Variables." *Psychol Rep* 4:239-41 Je '58. *

49. SUMNER, EARL DAVID. *On the Relation of Manifest Needs to Personal Values: A Factor Analytic Study Involving R and Q Techniques.* Doctor's thesis, Wayne State University (Detroit, Mich.), 1958. (*DA* 18:2219)

50. ZUCKERMAN, MARVIN. "The Validity of the Edwards Personal Preference Schedule in the Measurement of Dependency-Rebelliousness." *J Clin Psychol* 14:379-82 O '58. *

FRANK BARRON, *Research Psychologist, Institute of Personality Assessment and Research, University of California, Berkeley, California.*

The freewheeling explorations in personality which were carried on in depth and breadth at the Harvard Psychological Clinic under the aegis of Henry A. Murray in the early 1930's have proved in the intervening two decades to be peculiarly resistant to compression into the sort of "objective" psychometric mapping which personality inventories seek to provide. Murray and his co-workers did in fact construct quite subtle and comprehensive inventory type scales (e.g., the *Psychological Insight Test*) to measure the variables in the need system which was the fundament of their research, but as time went on they became increasingly dissatisfied with those scales and finally abandoned them. Oddly enough, they did so in the face of evidence (which Murray reports in the section on questionnaires in *Explorations in Personality*) that the correlations between the scales and staff ratings of the same variables, given in ignorance of the scale scores, were steadily increasing with each study, to the final point of an average correlation of .57, which in that more sanguine climate of psychological truth seeking apparently was interpreted as rather discouraging.

The Murray need system did, of course, continue its psychometric life in a somewhat more complex but less rigorous embodiment, the scoring scheme for the *Thematic Apperception Test*. This or that "need" has also been taken into camp by individual investigators, so that scales bearing such names as "deference," "dominance," "abasement," "orderliness," and "achievement" have appeared in inventory type tests, both of the factor-analytically based sort and the empirically based kind. However, until the development of the *Edwards Personal Preference Schedule* no really thoroughgoing attempt had been made to measure most of the manifest needs in the Murray system by the inventory method.

Fifteen of the variables of the Murray need system were selected for inclusion in the Edwards schedule: achievement, deference, order exhibition, autonomy, affiliation, intraception, succorance, dominance, abasement, nurturance, change, endurance, heterosexuality, and aggression. The schedule consists of 210 pairs of items in a forced-choice format, with items from each of the 15 scales being paired off twice against items from the other 14. In addition, 15 items are repeated in order to obtain an estimate of the respondent's consistency. The pairing of variables against one another thus yields an assessment of the relative strength of competing needs within the person; however, the relative strength of such needs in persons representative of the general population remains the basic point of reference.

The first step in the construction of the schedule was to establish a pool of 140 items, 10 for each of 14 scales, which appeared face valid for measurement of the need variables when a true-false rather than paired comparison format was used. In an early study with the schedule in that form, however, Edwards found (*1*) that the frequency of endorsement of an item was closely related to the judged social desirability of the item. Using the method of successive intervals [1] for the scaling of the items (with 152 judges),

he discovered that social desirability correlated .87 with actual frequency of endorsement in a new sample when the items were responded to as a test.

This rather disconcerting finding led Edwards to adopt a forced paired comparison method, with the items in each pair being matched for scale values on the social desirability scale. However, when he fitted the items into pairs he did not take the further step of ascertaining whether the social desirability of the item changed as a result of the changed context in which it was presented. Nevertheless, he had succeeded in introducing a new wrinkle into personality test construction by his dramatization of the importance of social desirability as a determinant of response. In doing so, he continued to build upon the experience of the Harvard group; speaking of the *Psychological Insight Test*, Murray had commented in *Explorations in Personality*, "As might be expected, however, it was found that there was a general tendency for the subjects to give themselves relatively high marks on the more desirable traits and relatively low marks on the less desirable."

A series of studies by Klett (*26, 27, 28*) and an unpublished master's thesis by Fujita (*8*) have provided supporting evidence for the generality of the social desirability stereotype found in Edwards' original study. In a high school sample, Klett found a correlation of .94 between social desirability scale values (using the 140 items singly) and those obtained by Edwards. He also found high agreement concerning social desirability between normal subjects and individuals hospitalized with mental illness, both psychotic and nonpsychotic. Fujita established equally high agreement (*circa* .90) between the Edwards scale values and social desirability of the items as judged by nisei college students. Klett makes reference to a personal communication from Ivar Lövaas in Norway, who obtained similar results with Norwegian judges.

A fly has appeared in the ointment, however, with the publication of a study by Corah, Feldman, et al. (*37*) which took up the question of whether items in pairs retained the approximately equated social desirability values assigned to them singly. Using 30 item pairs which in the PPS provide comparisons between needs for achievement, order, succorance, abasement, heterosexuality, and aggression, they found highly significant differences in social desirabil-

---

[1] Edwards, Allen L. "The Scaling of Stimuli by the Methods of Successive Intervals." *J Appl Psychol* 36:118–22 Ap '52. * (*PA* 27:21)

ity between paired items which presumably were matched for it. Indeed, they discovered that the correlation between social desirability scale values for the items in pairs and actual choice of alternatives A or B was .88, which wins by a nose over the correlation of .87 reported by Edwards in his disenchanting earlier report. It appears that the *Edwards Personal Preference Schedule* is a promising test, but that something needs to be done about its failure to control for social desirability!

This unusually ironic retaliation points up one of the major failures of work thus far with the PPS. On a number of counts it appears soundly based: (*a*) it is tied to a powerful theoretical formulation concerning motives in psychologically normal human beings; (*b*) by use of the forced-choice method and systematic comparisons of strengths of needs within the person it avoids some of the difficulties inherent in the simple true-false dichotomy employed by earlier inventories; (*c*) it has satisfactory reliability and it offers measures which are relatively independent of one another, although perhaps not so independent as was first thought (*15*). While thus well begun, the PPS nevertheless cannot be said to have demonstrated validity in measurement of the variables. Following the publication of the manual in 1954, which set forth trenchantly the virtues of the test but which had to be content with a promissory note on validity, a number of studies have been reported. However, a good deal of the energy of the interested University of Washington researchers seems to have been expended in tilting at the *Minnesota Multiphasic Personality Inventory* and in beating the drums for inventories which will be free of "social desirability variance," with consequent impoverishment of imagination and effort in the task of assessing the real world validity of the face valid scales incorporated into the schedule.

In their first enthusiasm over the discovery that social desirability of a trait affects the likelihood that an individual will attribute it to himself, such investigators as Klett and Tamkin (*29*) proceeded rapidly to the limit and argued that tests (particularly such a test as the MMPI) which did not control for social desirability could hardly be valid for the diagnostic categories which served as the empirical basis for the construction of scales. This argument ignores two facts: (*a*) that one may candidly ascribe to oneself with high accuracy some traits, particularly symptoms, which even to oneself appear quite undesirable; and (*b*) that among a set of traits of a high degree of social undesirability there may exist substantial communities of variance corresponding to covariances in the real world. In assessing the validity of a measure, one looks for direct evidence pro or con; one does not say that a measure cannot be valid because high scores on it are socially desirable and low scores are socially undesirable. And conversely, nothing may be promised concerning the validity of a test simply because social desirability is controlled.

These remarks should, in the face of the Corah, Feldman et al. results, give some comfort to users of the PPS, since it may yet prove to have validity in spite of the uncontrolled variance in social desirability. To date, however, the evidence for validity is rather scanty. Bernardin and Jessor (*18*) have shown, on the positive side, that "dependent" subjects (those who score at or above the 70th percentile on need: deference and at or below the 50th percentile on need: autonomy) perform less well on a maze learning task when they are subjected to critical comments from the experimenter, and that when confronted with difficult problems, they are more likely to ask for help. These same investigators, however, in a third experiment using the Asch technique of putting subjects under pressure to agree with an apparent group consensus which is false, found no difference in yielding tendencies between dependent and independent subjects (classified on the basis of PPS scores). Graine (*22*) found, contrary to expectations, that need: autonomy had a significant positive correlation with the group conformity rating derived from the *Rosenzweig Picture-Frustration Study*. Gebhart and Hoyt (*41*) studied academic overachievement and underachievement in first year college students, and established that overachievers score significantly higher on such needs as achievement, order, and intraception, and lower on such needs as nurturance, affiliation, and change. Interestingly enough, when ability level is considered independently of overachievement and underachievement, persons of high ability also score higher on need: achievement, which conceivably could reflect either motivation to do well on tests of ability as a result of high need: achievement, or, on the other hand, the development of strong achievement drive as a result of a history of positive reinforcement of good academic performance.

Apart from these few studies which do make some approach to assessing the construct validity of some of the PPS measures, the only validity evidence available in the literature at the time of this review consisted of correlations of PPS scales with scales of the MMPI (*11, 15*), the *California Psychological Inventory* (*39*), and the *Strong Vocational Interest Blank* (*39*). Allen (*15*) found 90 (of a possible 630) correlations between PPS and MMPI scales significant at the .05 level; he also, however, found that one third of the correlations among PPS scales themselves were statistically significant. Dunnette, Kirchner, and De Gidio (*39*) have shown that a number of the PPS scales correlate significantly with CPI variables, although the correlations are generally not over .40 and do not make any consistent sense. For example, need:heterosexuality correlates —.38 with the CPI good impression scale, —.29 with sense of well-being, and —.26 with responsibility; need: achievement correlates positively with sociability, but does not relate to the CPI achievement scales, which were developed by item analysis against the criterion of actual academic performance in high schools and colleges throughout the country. Need:order also produces some unexpected relationships, among them an r of —.37 with capacity for status. All in all, the yield from these tangential sorts of validity studies may be described not only as meagre but as rather spotty at best.

Judging from the literature on the PPS at this date, the verdict of caution would be that the test is not yet ready for use in counseling or personnel selection. A study by Borislow (*36*) indicates that the PPS is readily fakable, and that neither the consistency score nor an index of profile stability (designed to reveal uniformity of response) distinguishes faked profiles from profiles earned under ordinary self-appraisal conditions. This is a particularly fatal defect in the personnel selection situation, where the respondent is not so motivated to be candid as he would be in a counseling center. The crucial point, however, is not the susceptibility to faking, but the fact that there is no warrant in available research for considering the PPS to have met even minimum standards of evidence for validity.

ÅKE BJERSTEDT, *Department of Psychology, University of Lund, Lund, Sweden.*

It has been a definite drawback in many inventories that subjects tend to endorse desirable and reject undesirable items. One outstanding characteristic of the *Edwards Personal Preference Schedule* is the attempt to minimize this disturbing influence by means of a specific kind of forced choice. The subject is forced to choose in each pair of statements the one which is most characteristic of himself. The two statements in each pair represent different personality variables, but—and this is the important point— they have at the same time a comparable degree of social desirability, as operationally determined by a scaling procedure using the method of successive intervals. We may regret that the manual gives too few details about this prequestionnaire scaling research, as well as too little discussion of the possible disadvantages of the forced-choice technique in the case of experienced "equal preference." Nevertheless, it gives us sufficient information about the *effect* of this scaling: low correlations with specific "desirability" scales are evidently obtained for most of the present variables.

Although this equating for social desirability is an interesting and important step forward, it should be pointed out that the desirability values of questionnaire items cannot be stable entities, equally valid in all times and places. On the contrary, we must expect that different social norm groups will have very different value hierarchies. This does not mean, of course, that attempts to minimize the influence of social desirability are unimportant or useless; but it means that test users should be careful when applying the instrument to other groups of subjects. It might well be that the influence of social desirability is much stronger in other samples than in the one in which the primary scaling was carried through. The problem of social desirability as a disturbing factor should, therefore, not be thought to have been solved once and for all (a fact of which the test constructor is, of course, well aware) but should be the subject of continuous interest and research.

The questionnaire furnishes scores for 15 personality variables selected from the lists presented by Murray in his *Explorations in Personality*. The manual gives no information concerning the criteria of selection: we do not know why certain variables were chosen and others rejected. Neither do we know how the specific items, representing these different variables, were selected. Nevertheless, the items chosen in most instances give the impression of adequate face validity, and, what may be more important, internal-consistency coefficients reported are in most cases satisfactory, as is the fact of low intercorrelations between most of the variables.

The manual gives data from a normative sample of 749 college women and 760 college men, in which certain sex differences were found. The men, for instance, scored higher on achievement, autonomy, dominance, heterosexuality, and aggression. There is no discussion of whether these differences may be partly a function of age (the modal age interval among the men being 20–24; among the women, 15–19).

Very little information on validity is reported in the manual. Some correlations with two other questionnaires are given, but, as the variables of these two are only very slightly related to the present instrument, this information is not very helpful. A few studies of ratings are referred to, but no quantitative results are given. The kind of validity investigation which would seem to be the most natural and immediately interesting would be a comparison between TAT measures of the 15 variables and the PPS measures of the same variables. Unfortunately, no such investigation is mentioned. We have the general impression that the test constructor has been somewhat more interested in the technical aspects of his instrument than in its psychological rationale. However, the good work done in the technical phase will certainly give the test sufficient research appeal. This should, at the same time, be a definite guarantee that such problems of construct validity as are still unsolved will not remain unsolved for long.

Summing up, the *Edwards Personal Preference Schedule* is an instrument which has several unique and useful characteristics and which promises to be very helpful in general personality-oriented research. More information as to the variability of social desirability values in different social groups and more studies on validity are desirable, however, if we wish to use this instrument confidently for *other* than research purposes.

DONALD W. FISKE, *Associate Professor of Psychology, University of Chicago, Chicago, Illinois.*

This schedule represents a desirable departure from the classical personality inventory in several respects: intended function, item form and construction, and variables measured. It "was designed primarily as an instrument for research and counseling purposes" with college students. For a self-report procedure, these functions are more suitable than diagnosis or selection.

The items are in forced-choice form, with the alternatives rather closely matched on social desirability. This is a technically optimal practice which is still uncommon in test construction: it minimizes or eliminates several response sets which attenuate or confound much personality measurement.

The forced-choice format makes the resulting scores slightly interdependent. They tend to have small negative intercorrelations because the sum of the 15 scores is a fixed quantity. This is a slight disadvantage for persons wishing to use the several scales separately. However, the resulting profile for each subject is ipsative: the format requires the subject to order the several variables in terms of their applicability to him. In the reviewer's opinion, this is a theoretically desirable approach in self-administered personality assessment.

Another consequence of the forced-choice technique is the narrow range of content involved in the assessment of each variable. It would appear that nine statements are utilized for each variable, most of which are used three times.

The schedule has the advantage of being based on a more sophisticated theoretical formulation than most inventories: it assesses 15 of Murray's variables. In addition, it provides a measure of consistency of response within a single testing session and a measure of profile stability (consistency of relative standing on the 15 variables). The latter is a promising innovation. Unfortunately, the manual reports little data on these stability scores, probably because of the time required to compute a product-moment correlation for each case. Since the essential information is the ordering of the 15 variables, a rank correlation (rho or tau) would seem appropriate and convenient.

The manual reports test-retest coefficients between .74 and .88. The internal consistencies estimated from split-half correlations range from .60 to .87. In view of the intended research applicability of the schedule, it would seem advisable to report, in addition, the estimated homogeneity of each score. No internal consistency is given for the test consistency score and no reliability figure of any kind is reported for the measure of profile stability.

From the published table of consistency scores, the median proportion of consistent responses appears to be about .78. This is lower than that for some other inventories because the responses on this schedule are relatively free from the influence of social desirability, an effect which increases consistency of response.

The validation of scores for variables such as these requires extensive research. The manual reports studies comparing scores with subjects' rankings of the same variables described in essentially the same words, but no descriptive statistic is given. The sex differences in the normative group and the reported correlations with other inventories are supportive but insufficient. The evaluation of the validity of the schedule must be withheld until further studies are reported.

The order of the items was apparently based on convenience for hand scoring. As a result, half of the items for each variable occur in blocks of five, with the alternative for that variable being in the same position within each of the several items. Furthermore, the format of both the IBM and the hand scored answer sheet is determined by these considerations. Thus, position sets might enter, and subjects might detect the basis for the groupings. While these are probably minor weaknesses, it is possible that the unusual sequence of item positions on the answer sheets may produce some confusion or irritation in subjects.

The possibility of inverted factor analyses from the profiles of scores is mentioned, but the reader is not cautioned about the instability of correlations based on 15 pairs of observations. While the manual has an extensive bibliography, the text occasionally fails to indicate relevant citations from it. Only one trivial error was noted in the manual, in a page reference.

In general, the manual is highly satisfactory. It presents in detail the procedures for administration and scoring, and the background of the schedule. It is conservative and professional in tone. The inventory itself represents a distinct step forward in techniques for the measurement of personality. While it is admittedly based on self-report, it is theoretically oriented and technically sound.

J Consult Psychol 19:156 Ap '55. Laurance F. Shaffer. * An ingenious and novel instrument for personality assessment which will surely evoke wide comment, considerable clinical use, and much research. The *Schedule* is designed in terms of 15 of Murray's manifest needs—achievement, deference, order, exhibition, autonomy, etc.—each of which is paired twice with each of the others. The 225 forced-choice items each consist of a pair of alternatives carefully equated for social desirability. As a result of this unusual and valuable matching, only two of the need scores have correlations with social desirability significantly above zero and these two are low (.32). The *PPS* thereby sidesteps that pitfall of many questionnaires, ego involvement. Because the need scales are short, the modest reliabilities are not unexpected: internal consistencies range from .60 to .87, and retest correlations from .74 to .88. The subscore intercorrelations are low. The validity of such a schedule is not easily expressed in simple terms, but the manual contains interesting data on clinical observations, and on relationships with ratings and other questionnaires. It is a long time since this reviewer has seen a questionnaire that seems to possess such potentialities for use and research.

J Consult Psychol 20:322–4 Ag '56. John W. Gustad. * Either Edwards has based his claims for the validity of the PPS on construct validity or on some other kind. Since the manual contains nothing to support claims of any other kind of validity, we must consider his efforts in regard to construct validity. He has correlated his scales with four others, drawn from the Guilford-Martin and the Taylor. The significant correlations are not interpreted to bear on the construct validity of the PPS. That is to say, no reasons are given to support the notion that the PPS does in fact measure the manifest needs proposed by Murray. It would seem, therefore, that the only conclusion to be drawn is that no usable information is presented regarding the validity of the PPS. It is the responsibility of the test author and the test publisher to establish the validity of any instrument made available commercially for use in one or several practical situations. In the case of this instrument, both the author and the publisher seem to have fallen short of meeting their responsibilities in this respect. One single, simple step might have been—and still might be—taken to correct this. Across the front of each test and each manual, there should be stamped, in large, red letters (preferably letters which will glow in the stygian darkness of the personality measurement field) the word EXPERIMENTAL. It is experimental. It is an intriguing, promising, in many ways very carefully conducted experiment, but it is still an experiment. Until its validity has been established, it must remain an experiment, and it should not be released for any other purpose. [See original review for additional critical comments not excerpted.]

[48]

★The Ego Strength Q-Sort Test. Grades 9–16 and adults; 1956–58; 6 scores: ego-status, social status, goal setting and striving, good mental health, physical status, total; 1 form ('56, essentially the same as the form copyrighted in 1956); manual ('58); no data on reliability; $5 per examiner's kit of 25 tests, manual, stencils, sorting board; $3 per 25 tests; postage extra; (50–90) minutes; Russell N. Cassel; Psychometric Affiliates. *

[49]

★Embedded Figures Test. Ages 10 and over; 1950–57; 1 form ['57]; manual ('50, reprint of 1 below); college norms only; $5 per set of test materials, postage extra; (15–40) minutes; Herman A. Witkin; the Author. *

REFERENCES

1. WITKIN, H. A. "Individual Differences in Ease of Perception of Embedded Figures." *J Personality* 19:1–15 S '50. * (*PA* 25:5958)
2. WITKIN, H. A.; LEWIS, H. B.; HERTZMAN, M.; MACHOVER, K.; MEISSNER, P. BRETNALL; AND WAPNER, S. *Personality Through Perception: An Experimental and Clinical Study.* New York: Harper & Brothers, 1954. Pp. xxvi, 571. * (*PA* 28:8566)
3. BELL, ELAINE GRAHAM. *Inner Directed and Other Directed Attitudes.* Doctor's thesis, Yale University (New Haven, Conn.), 1955.
4. FLIEGEL, ZENIA ODWS. *Stability and Change in Perceptual Performance of a Late Adolescent Group in Relation to Personality Variables.* Doctor's thesis, New School for Social Research (New York, N.Y.), 1955.
5. GRUEN, ARNO. "The Relation of Dancing Experience and Personality to Perception." *Psychol Monogr* 69(14):1–16 '55. * (*PA* 31:218)
6. JACKSON, DOUGLAS N. "A Short Form of Witkin's Embedded-Figures Test." *J Abn & Social Psychol* 53:254–5 S '56. * (*PA* 32:2897)
7. LONGENECKER, E. D. *Form Perception as a Function of Anxiety, Motivation, and the Testing Situation.* Doctor's thesis, University of Texas (Austin, Tex.), 1956.
8. TAYLOR, JAMES N. *A Comparison of Delusional and Halluncinatory Individuals Using Field-Dependency as a Measure.* Doctor's thesis, Purdue University (Lafayette, Ind.), 1956.
9. BIERI, JAMES; BRADBURN, WENDY M.; AND GALINSKY, M. DAVID. "Sex Differences in Perceptual Behavior." *J Personality* 26:1–12 Mr '58. *

[50]

*The Empathy Test. Ages 13 and over; 1947–55; Forms A ('47), B ('51), C ('54, adaptation of Form A for Canadian use); manual ('55); $3 per 50 tests; $1 per specimen set (must be purchased to obtain manual); postage extra; (10–15) minutes; Willard A. Kerr and Boris J. Speroff; Psychometric Affiliates. *

REFERENCES

1. TOBOLSKI, FRANCIS P., AND KERR, WILLARD A. "Predictive Value of *The Empathy Test* in Automobile Salesmanship." *J Appl Psychol* 36:310–1 O '52. * (*PA* 27:5479)
2. VAN ZELST, RAYMOND H. "Empathy Test Scores of Union Leaders." *J Appl Psychol* 36:293–5 O '52. * (*PA* 27:5463)
3. HALL, HARRY S., AND BELL, GRAHAM B. "The Relationship Between Two Tests of Empathy: Dymond's and Kerr's." Abstract. *Am Psychol* 8:361–2 Ag '53. *

4. SPEROFF, B. J. "Empathic Ability and Accident Rate Among Steel Workers." *Personnel Psychol* 6:297–300 au '53. * (*PA* 28:5077)
5. VAN ZELST, RAYMOND H. "Validation Evidence on the Empathy Test." *Ed & Psychol Meas* 13:474–7 au '53. * (*PA* 28:4403)
6. ALDEN, PRISCILLA JEAN. *An Exploratory Study of Self-Rated Empathy.* Doctor's thesis, University of Michigan (Ann Arbor, Mich.), 1954.
7. BASS, BERNARD M.; KARSTENDIEK, BARBARA; McCULLOUGH, GERALD; AND PRUITT, RAY C. "Validity Information Exchange, No. 7-024: D.O.T. Code 2-66.01, 2-66.11, 2-66.12, 2-66.23, Policemen and Detectives, Public Service." *Personnel Psychol* 7:159–60 sp '54. *
8. BELL, GRAHAM B., AND HALL, HARRY E., JR. "The Relationship Between Leadership and Empathy." *J Abn & Social Psychol* 49:156–7 Ja '54. * (*PA* 28:7326)
9. KERR, WILLARD A., AND SPEROFF, BORIS J. "Validation and Evaluation of the Empathy Test." *J General Psychol* 50:269–76 Ap '54. * (*PA* 29:4067)
10. SIEGEL, ARTHUR I. "An Experimental Evaluation of the Sensitivity of the Empathy Test." *J Appl Psychol* 38:222–3 Ag '54. * (*PA* 29:5728)
11. SMITH, FRANK JOHN. *The Role of an Empathy Score in Predicting Supervisory Success.* Master's thesis, Illinois Institute of Technology (Chicago, Ill.), 1954.
12. SPEROFF, B. J. "Relationship Between Empathic Ability and Supervisory Knowledge." *J Personnel Adm & Ind Rel* 1:195–7 '54. * (*PA* 29:8103)
13. BELL, GRAHAM B., AND STOLPER, RHODA. "An Attempt at Validation of the Empathy Test." *J Appl Psychol* 39:442–3 D '55. * (*PA* 30:7186)
14. JARRARD, LEONARD E. "Empathy: The Concept and Industrial Applications." *Personnel Psychol* 9:157–67 su '56. * (*PA* 31:8993)
15. ROSE, GRACE; FRANKEL, NORMAN; AND KERR, WILLARD. "Empathic and Sociometric Status Among Young Teen-Agers." *J Genetic Psychol* 89:277–8 D '56. *
16. TOBOLSKI, FRANCIS P.; JULIANO, CHARLES V.; AND KERR, WILLARD A. "Conformity and Success in the Field of Dramatics." *J Social Psychol* 43:269–73 My '56. *
17. McCARTY, JOHN J. "Normative Data Information Exchange, No. 10-11." *Personnel Psychol* 10:227 su '57. *
18. McCARTY, JOHN J. "Normative Data Information Exchange, No. 10-25." *Personnel Psychol* 10:359 au '57. *
19. McCARTY, JOHN J. "Validity Information Exchange, No. 10-14: D.O.T. Code 1-33.01, Secretary." *Personnel Psychol* 10:202–3 su '57. *
20. McCARTY, JOHN J. "Validity Information Exchange, No. 10-15: D.O.T. Code 1-33.01, Secretary." *Personnel Psychol* 10:204–5 su '57. *

ROBERT L. THORNDIKE, *Professor of Education, Teachers College, Columbia University, New York, New York.*

In this so-called *Empathy Test,* the author attempts to measure the ability of examinees to predict the behavior of what we may call the "generalized other." This he does by calling for rankings of (*a*) the popularity of 15 types of music for a defined type of worker, (*b*) the circulation of 15 magazines, and (*c*) the prevalence of 10 types of annoyances. The key is based on certain empirical facts in each case.

The author's use of the term "empathy" is different from the usual usage in which it means ability to react in a differential way to the "specific other." The two abilities may be quite different. The reviewer is not aware of evidence to show that they are related.

There appears to be no inherent validity in the operations called for in this test, and so its validity must be established empirically through its ability to predict socially important criteria, or its relationships to other variables that would make it a meaningful construct. The manual reports several studies presenting evidence on the validity of the test, and certain of these appear quite impressive. However, the relatively few studies by persons not associated with the author have tended to yield predominantly negative results. Unless the positive results reported in the manual are verified in the findings of other workers, this test cannot be recommended as either a useful practical device or a contribution to the description and understanding of an individual.

[51]

★Evaluation Modality Test. Adults; 1956; 3 scores: realism, moralism, individualism; 1 form; no data on reliability; $1.95 per 20 tests; $1 per specimen set (must be purchased to obtain manual) including 10 tests, manual, and scoring key; postage extra; (25–35) minutes; Hugo O. Engelmann; Psychometric Affiliates. *

WILSON H. GUERTIN, *Supervisory Research Psychologist, Veterans Administration Hospital, Knoxville, Iowa.*

This test purports to measure the characteristic way an individual "valuates." "The test is restricted to those modes of valuation which are most significant in contemporary American society, *viz.,* the moralist, realist, and individualist one [sic]." A test item will illustrate the nature of the test:

3. If you were to consider joining an organization would you ask yourself whether:
——a) doing so would be likely to improve your economic opportunities or your standing in the community?
——b) joining this organization would make it easier or harder for you to do the things you want to do?
——c) it is the right thing to do and/or the organization stands for the right things?

The author claims that the first response would be selected by a realist, the second by an individualist, and the third by a moralist.

This very brief test with its minimal statistical buttressing provokes some interesting thought. Psychologists ordinarily do not concern themselves about an individual's mode of valuation; thus, the use of the test is restricted by the limited professional interest in the area evaluated. The author states, "Information on the mode in which an individual valuates most frequently should prove useful in general counseling and particularly in occupational placement."

The test has several apparent shortcomings: (*a*) Social desirability is not controlled. (*b*) No item analysis has been made. (*c*) Reliability is not reported. (*d*) The standardization sample is inadequately described. (*e*) There are no norms for college subjects. (*f*) There is no information about various variables and data that might be related to the test scores.

At present the test would seem to be primarily a research tool. At best, it might prove to be a preliminary form of a test that could be developed eventually into a usable instrument.

[52]

*Examining for Aphasia: A Manual for the Examination of Aphasia and Related Disturbances, Revised Edition. Adolescents and adults; 1946–54; 1 form ('46); no data on reliability and validity; no norms; $6 per set of 25 record booklets and manual; $3.50 per 25 record booklets ('54); $3.50 per manual ('54); postpaid; (30–120) minutes; Jon Eisenson; Psychological Corporation. *

REFERENCES

1. BLATT, BENJAMIN. *The Problem of Language Localization Into Specific Brain Areas: Psychological Tests as a Means of Localizing Brain Lesions in Patients With Aphasia.* Doctor's thesis, New York University (New York, N.Y.), 1949. (*Microfilm Abstr* 10:145)
2. EISENSON, JON. "Examining for Aphasia and Related Disturbances," pp. 766–71. (*PA* 27:7766) In *Contributions Toward Medical Psychology: Theory and Psychodiagnostic Methods, Vol. II.* Edited by Arthur Weider. New York: Ronald Press Co., 1953. Pp. xi, 459–885. *
3. FELDMAN, LOUISE P. *An Investigation and Analysis of Scores Made by First to Sixth Grades on the Eisenson Test for Aphasia and Related Disturbances.* Master's thesis, University of Michigan (Ann Arbor, Mich.), 1953.

T. R. MILES, *Lecturer in Psychology, University College, Bangor, Wales.*

This seems to the reviewer an excellent manual, both on the theoretical and on the practical side. The opening sections contain a discussion of the different types of aphasic disability, and reference is made to earlier work on the subject, in particular that of Goldstein and Scheerer and that of Weisenburg and McBride. This is followed by a series of tests, suitable both for children and adults, based on the author's own theory of how aphasic disorders should be classified—tests of visual, auditory, and tactile recognition, tests of comprehension, naming, calculation, and so on. The problem of classification must inevitably remain for the moment a matter of controversy; broadly, what is required is that we should be able to recognise similarities between apparently different failures at the behavioural level, and at the same time produce a theory of cortical breakdown which accounts for all failures which have been classified as similar. The classification in this manual is at any rate suggestive and helpful, and this is all, in the reviewer's opinion, that the author would wish to claim.

Nowhere does Eisenson make the mistake of oversimplification. He is never content, for instance, with a straightforward summing of test scores in the hope that they will make a meaningful whole. Recognised tests, such as the Kohs block design, the Goddard and Seguin formboards, and the Goldstein-Scheerer battery, receive favourable mention, but the author clearly views with disfavour an overrigid administrative procedure. Nor does he make the mistake of supposing that the test situation involves purely cognitive factors; on the contrary, he recognizes that the patient's motivation is an all-important variable which may be different on different occasions. In effect, throughout the manual the user is encouraged to look for a general clinical picture rather than for a quantitative measure of the degree of aphasic impairment. In the present state of knowledge, this policy seems to the reviewer clearly right. At one point the author even warns that, in the case of paraphasic errors such as substitution of the wrong word, an explanation in psychodynamic terms should not be ruled out. In view of the widespread rivalry between those who offer explanations in terms of unconscious motivation and those who want to explain in terms of cortical failure, such a warning seems to the reviewer commendably broad-minded, though whether the two types of explanation are mutually exclusive, as Eisenson assumes, is perhaps open to question.

A further merit is that the style is always lucid; the more formidable varieties of technical jargon are avoided, and there is no waste of words.

There is a useful bibliography. A minor criticism here is that, of the British writers who have made contributions in this field, only Hughlings Jackson and Head are mentioned. Some reference to the pioneer work of Hinshelwood and the more recent work of Brain, Zangwill, and McMeeken might have been helpful. McMeeken's concept of *developmental aphasia,* introduced as a result of the finding that disabilities resembling standard aphasic ones can occur in children even when there is no independent evidence for brain injury, seems to the reviewer to be of considerable importance. Eisenson's dichotomy into *congenital* and *acquired* aphasia, according to whether the injury occurred before or after the time of speech development, does not allow for a third group of this kind.

In general, this manual seems to the reviewer to be both a useful instrument for practical purposes and a valuable contribution to the psychology of thinking.

Am J Mental Def 60:196–7 Jl '55. Louis M. DiCarlo. * The plates Eisenson presents for testing in the revised manual are more appropriate than his earlier plates, since the selection of these plates is based upon materials which would appear in present-day situations. The variations in the pictures are beneficial and provide important cues for the examiner. Color for testing color agnosia is somewhat sharper and the selection of his reading material would appear judicious. The theoretical and clinical material presented in the first section of the book (Chapters I to IV) may be confusing to an unsophisticated examiner. For one who has a great deal of experience with aphasia, the first few chapters offer an excellent review and also tend to emphasize the importance of not only observing the language disability that the aphasic individual presents, but also indicate the importance of arriving at adequate estimates of his perceptive impairments. Dr. Eisenson's discussion of aphasic children certainly may not bring about agreement since many individuals do not feel that aphasia occurs where language has not already been established. In his desire to sharpen some of the problems, he has introduced several controversial concepts, specifically "dis-inclination to assume and use the abstract attitude" as opposed to the definition of abstract-concrete by Goldstein. One wonders whether this material would be best presented in a text or article rather than in a manual. This revised manual is more than a manual but at the same time, less than a text. For the individual who is skillful in testing the aphasic individual, the book certainly provides him with a very efficient tool. If used judiciously and under supervision, the manual ought to become a very good instrument for the beginning examiner and can help him while he is crystallizing his methodology. Dr. Eisenson's new manual is consistent in terms of testing specific functions and higher order performance. This manual should be part of every psychologist's and hearing and speech therapist's clinical kit.

J Consult Psychol 18:309 Ag '54. Laurance F. Shaffer. * An examination for aphasia is necessarily qualitative, and the tests therefore cannot be judged by the usual standards for reliability and validity. Some approximate quantifications of these tests would be helpful, however, at least to give an examiner clues for judging whether the disability in a given area is "moderate" or "severe." The manual is more extensively revised than the test itself, the first 28 pages comprising a miniature textbook on nature, symptoms, and varieties of aphasia, and the examination of aphasic children. Perhaps because of its condensation, this introductory material tends to be arbitrary and uncritical. Still, it provides a useful check list of definitions and procedures for the use of experienced psychologists.

For a review by D. Russell Davis, see 4:42 (2 excerpts); for a review by C. R. Strother, see 3:39 (1 excerpt).

[53]

★Family Adjustment Test. Ages 12 and over; 1952–54; title on test is *Elias Family Opinion Survey;* 11 scores: attitudes toward mother, attitudes toward father, father-mother attitude quotient, oedipal, struggle for independence, parent-child friction-harmony, interparental friction-harmony, family inferiority-superiority, rejection of child, parental qualities, total; 1 form ('52); manual ('54); $2 per 20 tests; $1 per specimen set (must be purchased to obtain manual); postage extra; (35–45) minutes; Gabriel Elias; Psychometric Affiliates.*

REFERENCES

1. ELIAS, G. *Construction of a Test of Non-Homeyness and Related Variables.* Doctor's thesis, Purdue University (Lafayette, Ind.), 1949.
2. BLACKSHIRE, R. E., AND DILES, D. *Student Cheating.* Master's thesis, University of Arkansas (Fayetteville, Ark.), 1950.
3. RICHMOND, ELISE. *Relationship Between Selected Variables and Homelessness Test Scores, and Suggested Varying Standardizations.* Master's thesis, University of Arkansas (Fayetteville, Ark.), 1950.
4. GARDNER, R. *The Relationship Between Elias Family Opinion Survey Scores and Selected Indices of Undesirable Behavior.* Master's thesis, University of Arkansas (Fayetteville, Ark.), 1951.
5. ELIAS, GABRIEL. "A Measure of 'Homelessness.'" *J Abn & Social Psychol* 47:62–6 Ja '52. * (PA 26:6209)
6. STEVENSON, FRANK. *A Study of Objective Measurement of Family Feelings Among a High School Population.* Master's thesis, Alabama Polytechnic Institute (Auburn, Ala.), 1953.

ALBERT ELLIS, *Consulting Psychologist, 333 West 56th St., New York 19, New York.*

This relatively new instrument is of the "projective" questionnaire type. Its 114 questions are indirectly stated in the form: "Parents are _____ happy when they are together" and "Children _____ have to make excuses for their parents." The subject responds by inserting in the blank whichever one of the words "always, often, sometimes, rarely, never" will make the sentence most correct for him. The assumption is that the respondents will project their own attitudes and feelings into the answering of these questions, rather than give objective responses. The scoring of the subject's "homey" or "homeless" feelings in general, as well as the subtest categories listed at the head of this review, is based on this assumption.

The *Elias Family Opinion Survey* (or *Family Adjustment Test,* as it is called in its non-disguised form) has several advantages when used within a limited area. It measures several aspects of home life and attitudes which few other paper and pencil tests try to assess. When used with a "homey" and a "homeless" group of subjects, the test impressively showed virtually no overlap between the scores of the two groups. Its armchair validity has been checked and attested to by several groups of clinical psychologists.

On the other hand, the survey appears to have several possible shortcomings:

a) Some of the subtest scores, such as oedipal, struggle for independence, and parental qualities, are calculated on the basis of the subject's answers to very few questions.

b) Although group validity, as noted above, is impressively high, the manual contains no validity figures for the subtests.

c) No allowance seems to be made for individual respondents who do not project their own attitudes into the test, but who answer all or most of the questions with reasonable objectivity. Thus, the objective or "true" answer to most of the questions on the test quite obviously is "sometimes." But this answer is invariably given the fairly high or "negative" weight of 3 in the scoring key. If, therefore, any respondent consistently gives this answer to the questions, he will obtain a total score of 352 on the 114-item test. Such a score puts him at about the 99th percentile as far as his being "overtly homeless" is concerned. Quite a negative premium, apparently, for the subject's being objective and "truthful"!

d) The basic assumption of the test, that the average respondent *will* project his own attitudes into these paper and pencil test answers, is one that has never been clearly substantiated. There is much reason to believe that adults or very bright children might easily see through the "projective" aspects of the test; and there is some experimental evidence [1] that while *some* children actually do project themselves into this kind of test in the assumed manner, many definitely do not.

In conclusion: the *Elias Family Opinion Survey* is an interesting and somewhat unique "projective" paper and pencil test which may be useful for experimental purposes, but should be employed for clinical diagnosis only with extreme caution.

[1] ELLIS, ALBERT. "A Comparison of the Use of Direct and Indirect Phrasing in Personality Questionnaires." *Psychol Monogr* 61(3):1–41 '47. *

[54]

★**Fatigue Scales Kit.** Adults; 1944–54; 1 form; 3 scales; mimeographed manual ('54); $5 per set of test materials including 25 copies of each scale; $2 per 50 copies of any one scale; postage extra; specimen set not available; (10) minutes; [Willard A. Kerr]; Psychometric Affiliates. *

a) INDUSTRIAL SUBJECTIVE FATIGUE AND EUPHORIA SCALES. Adults; 1944–54; 1 form ('54, identical with scale published in 1944).

b) RETROSPECTIVE WORK CURVE FEELINGS FOR NATIONAL RESEARCH PROGRAM ON EMPLOYEE FEELINGS AT WORK. Adults; 1954.

c) STUDY OF DAY [MOTHER'S DAY FATIGUE SCALE]. Housewives; 1954; no data on validity.

[55]

★**The Freeman Anxiety Neurosis and Psychosomatic Test.** Mental patients; 1952–55; title on test is *The Freeman AN and PS Test;* 9 scores: anxiety neurosis, psychosomatic syndrome, and 7 subscores; 1 form ('52); no norms for subscores; revised manual ('55); revised profile ('55); $1.75 per 10 tests; $1.25 per manual; postage extra; specimen set not available; administration time not reported; M. J. Freeman; Grune & Stratton, Inc. *

REFERENCES

1. FREEMAN, M. J. "The Standardization of a Psychosomatic Test: Validation of a Psychosomatic Syndrome." *J Personality* 19:229–43 D '50. * (PA 25:6608)
2. FREEMAN, M. J. "The Development of a Test for the Measurement of Anxiety: A Study of Its Reliability and Validity." *Psychol Monogr* 67(3):1–19 '53. * (PA 28:2903)
3. ENDS, EARL J., AND PAGE, CURTIS W. "A Study of Functional Relationships Among Measures of Anxiety, Ego Strength and Adjustment." *J Clin Psychol* 13:148–50 Ap '57. *

[56]

★**Friend-Critic Statement.** Adults; 1948; subject's essays on himself as seen by a good friend and by a strong critic; 1 form ['48]; no manual; no data on reliability and validity; $1.50 per 25 forms; cash orders postpaid; free specimen set; [20–30] minutes; Aptitude Associates. *

[57]

★Goldstein-Scheerer Tests of Abstract and Concrete Thinking. Adults; 1941–51; individual; 1 form; 5 tests; manual ('41, see 9 below); supplementary manual ('47); no data on reliability; no norms; $58 per complete set of test materials; $2.25 per manual; postpaid; [30–60] minutes; Kurt Goldstein, Martin Scheerer, and Louis Rosenberg (*c*, record booklet); Psychological Corporation.

a) GOLDSTEIN-SCHEERER CUBE TEST. 1941–45; $3.40 per 50 record booklets ('45) for designs 1–6; $3.40 per 50 record booklets ('45) for designs 7–12.

b) GELB-GOLDSTEIN COLOR SORTING TEST. 1941–51; $2.70 per 50 record booklets ('51).

c) GOLDSTEIN-SCHEERER OBJECT SORTING TEST. 1941–51; $4.10 per 50 record booklets ('51); supplement sheet ('51) for experiment 3, $1 per 100 copies.

d) WEIGL-GOLDSTEIN-SCHEERER COLOR FORM .SORTING TEST. 1941–45; $2.70 per 50 record booklets ('45).

e) GOLDSTEIN-SCHEERER STICK TEST. 1941–45; $2.70 per 50 record booklets ('45).

REFERENCES

1–28. See 3:41.
29. TOOTH, GEOFFREY. "On the Use of Mental Tests for the Measurement of Disability After Head Injury: With a Comparison Between the Results of These Tests in Patients After Head Injury and Psychoneurotics." *J Neurol Neurosurg & Psychiatry* 10:1–11 F '47. *
30. BOYD, FOSTER. "A Provisional Quantitative Scoring With Preliminary Norms for the Goldstein-Scheerer Cube Test." *J Clin Psychol* 5:148–53 Ap '49. * (PA 24:1880)
31. ROSENBERG, LOUIS M. *A Comparison of Concept Forma-*

tion in Poorly-Educated Normals, Non-Deteriorated Schizophrenics and Brain-Damaged Patients. Doctor's thesis, New York University (New York, N.Y.), 1951. (*Microfilm Abstr* 11:761)
32. SCHEERER, MARTIN. Sect. 11, "Measures of Impairment of Intellectual Function: The Goldstein-Scheerer Tests," pp. 116–50. In *Military Clinical Psychology.* Department of the Army Technical Manual TM 8–242; Department of the Air Force Manual AFM 160–45. Washington, D.C.: U.S. Government Printing Office, 1951. Pp. iv, 197. *
33. WATSON, ROBERT I. *The Clinical Method in Psychology,* pp. 366–89. New York: Harper & Brothers, 1951. Pp. xii, 779. * (PA 26:5577)
34. MCFIE, J., AND PIERCY, M. F. "The Relation of Laterality of Lesion to Performance on Weigl's Sorting Test." *J Mental Sci* 98:299–305 Ap '52. * (PA 27:625)
35. BROWN, IRWIN. *Abstract and Concrete Behavior of Dysphasic Patients and Normal Subjects on the Goldstein-Scheerer Tests.* Doctor's thesis, University of Michigan (Ann Arbor, Mich.), 1953. (DA 13:908)
36. GOLDSTEIN, KURT, AND SCHEERER, MARTIN. "Tests of Abstract and Concrete Behavior," pp. 702–30. (PA 27:7768) In *Contributions Toward Medical Psychology: Theory and Psychodiagnostic Methods, Vol. II.* Edited by Arthur Weider. New York: Ronald Press Co., 1953. Pp. xi, 459–885. *
37. HEALD, JAMES E., AND MARZOLF, STANLEY S. "Abstract Behavior in Elementary School Children as Measured by the Goldstein-Scheerer Stick Test and The Weigl-Goldstein-Scheerer Color Form Sorting Test." *J Clin Psychol* 9:59–62 Ja '53. * (PA 27:7679)
38. RAPPAPORT, SHELDON R. "Intellectual Deficit in Organics and Schizophrenics." *J Consult Psychol* 17:389–95 O '53. * (PA 28:6365)
39. SCHULMAN, IRVING. "Concept Formation in the Schizophrenic Child: A Study of Ego Development." *J Clin Psychol* 9:11–5 Ja '53. * (PA 27:7942)
40. HALPIN, VIRGINIA G., AND PATTERSON, RUTH M. "The Performance of Brain-Injured Children on the Goldstein-Scheerer Tests." *Am J Mental Def* 59:91–9 Jl '54. * (PA 29:4551)
41. KORSTVEDT, ARNE; STACEY, CHALMERS L.; AND REYNOLDS, WILLIAM F. "Concept Formation of Normal and Subnormal Adolescents on a Modification of the Weigl-Goldstein-Scheerer Color Form Sorting Test." *J Clin Psychol* 10:88–90 Ja '54. * (PA 28:7694)
42. SATTER, GEORGE, AND MCGEE, EUGENE. "Retarded Adults Who Have Developed Beyond Expectation: Part II, Non-Intellectual Functions." *Training Sch B* 51:67–81 Je '54. * (PA 29:2663)
43. HALPIN, VIRGINIA G. "Rotation Errors Made by Brain-Injured and Familial Children on Two Visual-Motor Tests." *Am J Mental Def* 59:485–9 Ja 55. * (PA 29:7487)
44. COONS, W. H. "Abstract Ability in Schizoprenia and the Organic Psychoses." *Can J Psychol* 10:43–50 Mr '56. * (PA 31:3452)
45. KRESS, ROY ALFRED, JR. *An Investigation of the Relationship Between Concept Formation and Achievement in Reading.* Doctor's thesis, Temple University (Philadephia, Pa.), 1956. (DA 16:573)
46. THALER, MARGARET. "Relationships Among Wechsler, Weigl, Rorschach, EEG Findings, and Abstract-Concrete Behavior in a Group of Normal Aged Subjects." *J Gerontol* 11:404–9 O '56. * (PA 31:5871)
47. MCGAUGHRAN, LAURENCE S., AND MORAN, LOUIS J. "Differences Between Schizophrenic and Brain-Damaged Groups in Conceptual Aspects of Object Sorting." *J Abn & Social Psychol* 54:44–9 Ja '57. *
48. PARKER, JAMES W. "The Validity of Some Current Tests for Organicity." *J Consult Psychol* 21:425–8 O '57. *
49. SEMEONOFF, BORIS. "Projective Techniques in Selection for Counseling." *Human Relations* 11:113–22 no 2 '58. *

For reviews by Kate Levine Kogan, C. R. Strother (with Ludwig Immergluck), and O. L. Zangwill, see 3:41; for a related review, see 3:42.

[58]

★**Gordon Personal Inventory.** Grades 9–16 and adults; 1956, c1955–56; 4 scores: cautiousness, original thinking, personal relations, vigor; 1 form ('56); revised manual ('56); no adult norms; $2.75 per 35 tests, postage extra; 50¢ per specimen set including the complementary *Gordon Personal Profile* (see 59), postpaid; (15–20) minutes; Leonard V. Gordon; World Book Co. *

REFERENCE

1. BASS, BERNARD M. "Normative Data Information Exchange, No. 11–5." *Personnel Psychol* 11:269–70 su '58. *

BENNO G. FRICKE, *Assistant Chief, Evaluation and Examinations Division, and Assistant Professor of Psychology, University of Michigan, Ann Arbor, Michigan.*

The *Gordon Personal Inventory* has much in common with the *Gordon Personal Profile*. The writer's review of the profile contains additional material applicable to the inventory.

The major difference in the manuals for the two tests is to be found in the validity section. In the manual for the Personal Inventory not one bit of information is presented to support the presumed validity of the test. A footnote indicates, "A number of validation studies are presently under way, the results of which will be presented in a revised manual. The author will welcome reports of the results of any other studies that may be undertaken." Although it is about three years since the test was released for use, the reviewer has been unable to find a single study by the author or anyone else in which the inventory has been reported upon. Certainly it seems fair to conclude that if the test has any validity not many people know about it.

In the section on validity and elsewhere in the manual, the point is made that the forced-choice item used is effective in reducing faking. But a more important point is that if a test has no initial validity, then it is not possible to fake "good" or "poor" scores because there are none; high and low scale scores are no better or worse than average scores on an invalid test. Of course, if two reasonably valid tests have the same initial validity, the one which is least fakable is to be preferred.

Despite the lack of validity data, the manual for the inventory, as did the manual for the profile, presents many suggestions in the section on uses of the test. The author claims, for example, that the inventory "has certain attributes which give it unique potentialities for use in personnel activities, such as the selection of individuals for specific types of work, the placement of individuals in specific jobs, and the counseling or transferring of employees not performing well in their present job."

The inventory was constructed by essentially the same rational-factor analytic method used to construct the profile, but with a little more care in equating the social desirability of the four parts of each item. An inspection of the phrases in the items suggests that their preference value is not likely to be the same for ninth graders, college seniors, and employed adults,

but the inventory is recommended as being suitable for them and, it would appear, for almost anyone able to take a group test. While the potential number to be tested is certainly increased by maintaining that a test is appropriate for a wide age or education range, such a claim should only be made after substantiating research data have been assembled. The entire testing business might profit from having test producers design their tests more specifically for a particular and relatively limited group.

The four scales of the inventory measure reliably (median of 15 coefficients is about .83) and independently (median of the intercorrelations is about .22) something that is not related to ACE aptitude scores (median of 15 intercorrelations is about .10) or profile scores (median of 16 intercorrelations is about .19).

The manual states that the inventory is a companion instrument to the *Gordon Personal Profile* and that "the two instruments may be used together to provide an economical coverage of eight important factors in the personality domain." Even if these instruments do in fact measure eight important dimensions of personality in college students, a user would still have difficulty in comparing accurately the performance of subjects on the two tests since different norm groups have been used. One wonders why Gordon did not attach the 20 items in the inventory at the end of the 18 items in the profile; while this would not solve his major problem (lack of external validity) it would have improved matters considerably for those who might wish to obtain the eight scores.

But frankly, and in summary, the reviewer at this time can see no good reason why a test user should want to obtain the *Gordon Personal Inventory* scores.

JOHN A. RADCLIFFE, *Lecturer in Psychology, University of Sydney, Sydney, Australia.*

This is a companion test to the *Gordon Personal Profile* and is intended to measure four additional "significant" aspects of personality. Test format, administrative instructions, marking procedure, and recommendations concerning score interpretation are almost identical between the two. For the inventory, however, both high school and college norms are provided. Split-half (.77–.89, n = 103, high school; .80–.88, n = 168, college) and Kuder-Richardson (.79–.88, n = 124, college) reliabilities are reported and are comparable with those reported for the profile. No retest coefficients are given, however.

The general development of the inventory has followed lines similar to those of the profile —choice of factors to be measured, construction of a questionnaire, factor analysis of the questionnaire, and construction of forced-choice items testing some of the factors obtained. But, in the case of the inventory, no external criterion was used. For this reason and because the test had been developed too recently for other validity data to be available, the only data on validity reported relate to internal consistency— illustrative factor loadings obtained from the questionnaire analysis, intercorrelations among the scales, and brief descriptions of a number of revisions, "each....improving the balance of preference values within the tetrads and the reliabilities of the scales." With the profile, it is noted that low scores have been found to indicate "poor personality adjustment." This has *not* been verified for the inventory. Again, Gordon has made no attempt to relate his factors to those of other investigators.

The author reports considerable data for the profile to support his contention that the factors are "significant" and "meaningful." No such data are reported for the inventory. The profile is a workmanlike job. The inventory has been rushed into print and spoils the author's record. Except as an exploratory device and a "companion test," there is little to justify its use.

*J Consult Psychol 21:281 Je '57. Laurance F. Shaffer. * Like the earlier questionnaire, the *Inventory* is characterized by brevity, the use of tetrads of statements controlled for social desirability, and the identification of components by factor analysis. The method of construction shows a high degree of technical competence. * The two Gordon questionnaires commend themselves favorably for use when economy of time is essential. Few other instruments obtain as broad a picture of self-reported personality in less than 30 minutes.

*J Counsel Psychol 4:76 sp '57. Laurence Siegel. * An outstanding weakness of the *Personal Inventory* from an operational standpoint, is that predictive validities are not reported in the manual. * Until such validation data become available, however, the *Personal Inventory* must be treated as an experimental instrument. This deficiency is not sufficiently emphasized in the manual. Furthermore a poor choice of wording

on the folder containing specimen sets of both the *Profile* and *Inventory* may lead to the erroneous conclusion that validation is not only accomplished, but that the resultant coefficients are high! A bold-face heading on the folder asserts: "Forced-choice responses make for high validity." While it is theoretically possible for a forced-choice format to improve the validity potential of an instrument, there is no evidence that this format has improved the validity of the *Inventory*. In fact, there is no evidence that the instrument is valid, *period*. A better choice of words for this heading might have been something like: "Forced-choice responses a feature." If, for research purposes, one wants to measure the four traits included in the *Gordon Personal Inventory,* this instrument will yield results with a minimum expenditure of subject testing time. The application of the *Inventory* in the counseling situations suggested by the manual should, however, be undertaken with extreme caution and with the realization that this is still an experimental form pending validation.

[59]

★**Gordon Personal Profile.** Grades 9–16 and adults; 1953–54; c1951–53; 5 scores: ascendancy, responsibility, emotional stability, sociability, total; 1 form ('53); manual ('53); supplementary mimeographed norms ['54]; $2.75 per 35 tests, postage extra; 50¢ per specimen set including the complementary *Gordon Personal Inventory* (see 58), postpaid; (15–20) minutes; Leonard V. Gordon; World Book Co. *

REFERENCES
1. GORDON, LEONARD V. "Validities of the Forced-Choice and Questionnaire Methods of Personality Measurement." *J Appl Psychol* 35:407–12 D '51. * (*PA* 27:424)
2. GORDON, LEONARD V. "The Effect of Position on the Preference Value of Personality Items." *Ed & Psychol Meas* 12:669–76 w '52. * (*PA* 27:6531)
3. GORDON, LEONARD V. "Personal Factors in Leadership." *J Social Psychol* 36:245–8 N '52. * (*PA* 27:7115)
4. GORDON, LEONARD V. "Some Interrelationships Among Personality Item Characteristics." *Ed & Psychol Meas* 13:264–72 su '53. * (*PA* 28:4037)
5. BASS, BERNARD M. "Validity Information Exchange, No. 7-045: ROTC Cadets." *Personnel Psychol* 7:279 su '54. *
6. BASS, BERNARD M.; KARSTENDIEK, BARBARA; McCULLOUGH, GERALD; AND PRUITT, RAY C. "Validity Information Exchange, No. 7-024: D.O.T. Code 2-66.01, 2-66.11, 2-66.12, 2-66.23, Policemen and Dectectives, Public Service." *Personnel Psychol* 7:159–60 sp '54.
7. FICK, DORCAS J. *A Comparison of Personality Traits of a Group of Sunday School Teachers and a Group of Non-Sunday School Teachers as Found on the Heston Personal Adjustment Inventory and the Gordon Personal Profile.* Master's thesis, Boston University (Boston, Mass.), 1955.
8. BRESEE, CLYDE WESLEY. *Affective Factors Associated With Academic Underachievement in High-School Students.* Doctor's thesis, Cornell University (Ithaca, N.Y.), 1956. (*DA* 17:90)
9. GORDON, LEONARD V., AND STAPLETON, ERNEST S. "Fakability of a Forced-Choice Personality Test Under Realistic High School Employment Conditions." *J Appl Psychol* 40:258–62 Ag '56. * (*PA* 31:6084)
10. PHILLIPS, RAYMOND V. *A Study of Attitude and Personality Variables Among In-Service Teachers.* Doctor's thesis, Temple University (Philadelphia, Pa.), 1956. (*DA* 16:2528)
11. RUSMORE, JAY T. "Fakability of the Gordon Personal Profile." *J Appl Psychol* 40:175–7 Je '56. * (*PA* 31:6661)
12. BASS, BERNARD M. "Faking by Sales Applicants of a Forced Choice Personality Inventory." *J Appl Psychol* 41:403–4 D '57. *
13. COOK, JOHN M., AND FARBRO, PATRICK C. "Normative

Data Information Exchange, No. 10–15." *Personnel Psychol* 10:233–4 su '57. *

14. REINDL, MARY OLIVIA. *The Relationship Between Attitudes Toward Obedience and Personality Characteristics Measured by the A-S Reaction Study and the Gordon Personal Profile.* Master's thesis, Fordham University (New York, N.Y.), 1957.

15. BARRETT, RICHARD S. "The Process of Predicting Job Performance." *Personnel Psychol* 11:39–57 sp '58. *

16. WILLINGHAM, WARREN W.; NELSON, PAUL; AND O'CONNOR, WILLIAM. "A Note on the Behavioral Validity of the Gordon Personal Profile." *J Consult Psychol* 22:378 O '58. *

BENNO G. FRICKE, *Assistant Chief, Evaluation and Examination Division, and Assistant Professor of Psychology, University of Michigan, Ann Arbor, Michigan.*

The method used to construct the *Gordon Personal Profile* will probably please those who favor the rationally and factor-analytically constructed personality tests and displease those who prefer the empirically constructed ones. Gordon has succeeded very well in obtaining four reliable and independent measures which he has called Ascendancy (A), Responsibility (R), Emotional Stability (E), and Sociability (S). Whether the test scores indicate aspects in the nontest behavior of subjects or merely aspects in their test behavior (i.e., tendency to mark responses they and the author believe indicate certain behavior) remains to be seen. It is readily apparent from the generally well written manual that the author believes that the four factor scores are "external validity indicators," that they tell something about the test takers nontest-taking behavior. He has shown himself to be much more sensitive than most nonempirical personality test constructors to the importance of relating test scores to real life behavior.

Unfortunately, and this is the major point of the review, while Gordon has given some validity data and makes many references to completed studies, the total impression is that adequate validity has not been demonstrated. Most of the studies involve very small validity-check samples (e.g., "17 applicants for jobs with a state highway patrol," "30 salespeople at a large department store," 27 clients rated by "the senior counselor at the Boston University counseling center," "54 clients at a counseling center to whom the *Personal Profile* had been administered"). In other studies, very little information is provided (e.g., "In one study, the average A score of administrators was found to be significantly higher (at the 1% level) than the average of college men"; "In one study of engineers, the average R score was found to be significantly higher than that of college men (at the 1% level)"; "In one study of external salesmen, the average S score was found to be significantly

higher (at the 1% level) than the average S score of college men"). The reviewer was inclined to wonder whether all pertinent data and studies were included in the manual. For instance, if more than one study of engineers and external salesmen was conducted, the results would be of interest, especially since the test is recommended for personnel purposes.

The reviewer's first but rapid reading of the manual, particularly the first seven pages dealing with general characteristics, directions for administering, directions for scoring, conversion to percentiles, meaning of scales, and interpretation of scores was favorable, but after serious study of the entire manual (particularly the last three pages dealing with validity and the development of the profile), the reviewer began to feel that the manual represents the author and publisher "with best foot forward." Used too rarely are phrases such as "the profile might be of value for such and such"; too frequently, too much is claimed (e.g., "Extensive evidence substantiates the conclusion that the *Profile* does measure these traits, as defined."). If there is extensive and convincing evidence it is not shared with the reader.

On the last page we learn that "From 657 applicants for college admission, the high school records of individuals with T [total] scores below the 5th percentile were examined. Summary statements made by the high school principals showed definite problem or personality maladjustment indications for a very large proportion of this group. No such indications were found in a sampling of cases selected at random." It would be helpful to know precisely the proportion of "personality maladjustment indications" found in the "below the 5th percentile" and "cases selected at random" groups. While sufficient detail is not given on this important aspect, complete information is given on the relationship of the profile scores to scores on two scholastic aptitude tests. Rather than presenting the 20 low intercorrelations it would have been quite satisfactory simply to have indicated the median value, about .10.

At times when an attempt seems to have been made to spell out a validity study the explanation is ambiguous. For example, in discussing research with the "first experimental form" Gordon states that "empirical scoring keys were developed on one group (n = 104) and cross-validated on the other two groups at the second college." If Gordon is familiar with the procedure for developing empirical scoring keys and if he did what he says, then he should have presented validity coefficients (correlations with ratings made by dormitory students) for eight scales (four rational-factor keys, and four empirical keys). But coefficients are given for only four scales. Are they for the rational-factor keys or for the special empirical keys? The coefficients certainly are high (median about .54), higher than most coefficients obtained with empirical keys and much higher than those obtained with rational-factor keys.

A few final comments need to be made concerning validity, the only really important consideration for this or any test. The acid test for any test is validity demonstrated by individuals other than the author or those linked intimately with the test's design and construction. The manual cites validity data from one such study. Although the manual presents the validity coefficients (.21, .50, .25, and .34 for A, R, E, and S respectively), it does not point out that for the 22 cases in the study only the .50 coefficient is statistically significant, and then at only the 5 per cent level. Since the profile became available commercially in 1953, it is perhaps significant that the reviewer was unable to locate one study in the literature bearing on the test's validity; not only have individuals other than the author not reported on its validity, but the author himself has not done so. If the claims the author makes for the test are even partially substantiated by other investigators, it would definitely be a test worth using.

Now for some relatively minor matters. Like almost all standardized tests, the profile has adequate reliability (median of 24 coefficients is about .85); the author is to be congratulated for devoting little space to reliability and for not claiming much for the test because of its adequate reliability. The directions to the test taker are very clear. The test takes little time to complete, "from 7 to 15 minutes." The forced-choice type of item consisting of two complimentary and two uncomplimentary phrases from which the test taker selects the one (of the four) which is "most like" him and the one which is "least like" him, seems like a good one. But no attention appears to have been given to the relative social desirability of the phrases after they were combined in the tetrad item format.

It is not clear whether any of the research results that are presented in the manual were obtained by use of the present form or by use of earlier forms. For example, after the intercorrelations of the scales for the "First Form (N = 118)" and the "Early Revision (N = 200)" are discussed and presented in table 9 (the next to last table on the next to last page of the manual), the following statement is found: "Revisions of the *Personal Profile* ensued, each designed to heighten the validity of the scales." Although the main point here is that it seems that none of the data in the manual pertains to the present form, it is worth noting that the nature and extent of the revisions which ensued are not mentioned.

Probably the inclusion of a scale to assess the extent to which test takers have given the most socially desirable response would be profitable. Similarly, a scale to identify those who give infrequently marked responses (similar to the F scale of the MMPI) would seem to be worthwhile. The existence of other response sets, such as the set to mark as "most like" the first of the four response alternatives, should be investigated and, if found, either controlled or used in arriving at the traits the test purports to measure. In short, if the profile's four scales (A, R, E, S) are shown to be useful in indicating something about the test taker's *nontest-taking* behavior (i.e., to function as external validity indicators), then some additional scales should be developed to indicate something about the test taker's *test-taking* behavior (i.e., to function as internal validity indicators). Internal validity indicators would permit test users to determine, at least better than at present, whether an individual's external validity indicators are correct or distorted. In this connection, the trait scores of a die are of interest. The reviewer obtained the following college norm percentile ranks on the first "take" by marking answers according to the dictates of a die: A 4, R 63, E 29, and S 13. Effective internal validity indicators would disclose to the test user that the owner of this profile of scores had not behaved appropriately in taking the test (i.e., did not read the items but marked a "most like" and a "least like" response for each item at random), and therefore would discourage him from concluding that the subject was about average in responsibility (R 63), very submissive (A 4), etc.

Gordon concludes his 16-page manual by expressing his belief that "the present form of the Personal Profile is sufficiently reliable and valid to warrant meaningful interpretation for the individual case." On the basis of the information available to the reviewer, he does not share Gordon's belief, nor does he recommend the profile for routine use with groups. He does recommend that a few investigators who are interested in researching upon "rational-factor" personality tests conduct satisfactory validity studies to determine how much, if any, validity the profile has, and that the results be communicated to prospective users.

JOHN A. RADCLIFFE, *Lecturer in Psychology, University of Sydney, Sydney, Australia.*

The *Gordon Personal Profile* is intended to measure five aspects [1] of personality considered to be "especially significant in the daily functioning of the normal person." Four of these aspects are said to be "relatively independent, psychologically meaningful factors" and the fifth (total or overall self-evaluation) to have been "found to have value in its own right." The main features of the profile are: (*a*) factorial derivation of the traits being measured; (*b*) use of both internal and external validating procedures; (*c*) frequent cross validations against external criteria; (*d*) use of forced-choice responses; and (*e*) the more-than-average validity data reported in the manual.

The test consists of 18 sets of four descriptive phrases (tetrads), all four factors being represented in each tetrad. This tetrad arrangement is preferable to forced-choice sets composed of only two or three items because the greater sense of freedom of choice is more acceptable to the respondent. The subject responds to each tetrad by choosing the phrase which is least like himself and that which is most like himself. A natural consequence is that a respondent may not score high or low simultaneously on all four factors, but this is believed not to constitute "a practical limitation" and the evidence seems to support this view.

The forced-choice technique is stated to be less subject to faking and more valid than the conventional questionnaire method, particularly for low criterion individuals. The validity data are certainly more impressive than that typical of questionnaires. On fakability, two studies are reported in which changes on some profile scores occurred between guidance and employment conditions, but these changes were smaller than those usually obtained with questionnaires under comparable conditions.

Illustrations of the profile's possible use for educational and personnel purposes are given, accompanied by sample profiles, but, especially for personnel work, the author insists that they are *illustrations only* and that, for the present, the user must establish his own critical scores. He does, however, consider that the data he reports (for example, on differences between occupational groups and on relationship with sales proficiency) indicate that the test is likely to prove useful. Validation data on the meaning of the scales is well reported and quite extensive.

In all, this is a carefully constructed test which is easily administered and scored. For a personality test, reliabilities are encouraging, especially those for the total score. Validity data are above average, yet the author commits no extravagances. The manual is clearly written and well organised and there are no significant omissions.

An improvement in future editions of the manual would be that the author indicate how his factors relate to those found by others, especially the dimensions reported by investigators such as Cattell, Eysenck, and Guilford. This is desirable for three reasons: (*a*) He began by choosing items to measure some of Cattell's and one of Mosier's factors, but does not relate his results to theirs.[2] (*b*) He uses the little known Wherry-Gaylord iterative procedure of factor analysis, a form of cluster analysis which does not require the calculation of a complete intercorrelation matrix. Comparison of his factors with those obtained with more traditional procedures would add to the scant data available on the use of this method. (*c*) Factor analyses have become so numerous that cross identifications among studies, preferably related to a standard list such as the Universal Index which has been proposed by Cattell, are becoming increasingly necessary.

J Consult Psychol 18:154 Ap '54. Laurance F. Shaffer. * Like many other recently developed inventories, and in marked contrast to the subjectivity of earlier ones, this questionnaire is issued with an impressive array of research evidence. * The tentative norms....are based only on college students from one geographical region * As in the case of other short questionnaires, the problem of interpreting score differences with due regard for standard errors is

---

[1] Four additional "significant aspects" are measured by the *Gordon Personal Inventory* (see 58).

[2] Profile factors are closely related to Cattell's E (dominance), G (super-ego strength), C (general emotionality), and A (cyclothymia-schizothymia).

bothersome. The suggestions for interpretation are, however, conservatively stated in terms of probabilities.

[60]

★The Grassi Block Substitution Test: For Measuring Organic Brain Pathology. Mental patients; 1947–53; formerly called *The Fairfield Block Substitution Test;* individual; 1 form ['47]; revised record booklet ('49); $12 per set of blocks; $4.50 per 25 record booklets; $3.50 per manual ('53, see *1* below); postpaid; (20) minutes; Joseph R. Grassi; Western Psychological Services. *

REFERENCES

1. GRASSI, JOSEPH R. "The Fairfield Block Substitution Test for Measuring Intellectual Impairment." *Psychiatric Q* 21:474–89 Jl '47. * (*PA* 22:5203)
2. GRASSI, JOSEPH R. *The Grassi Block Substitution Test for Measuring Organic Brain Pathology.* Springfield, Ill.: Charles C Thomas, 1953. Pp. ix, 75. * (*PA* 28:105)
3. PTACEK, JAMES E., AND YOUNG, FLORENCE M. "Comparison of the Grassi Block Substitution Test With the Wechsler-Bellevue in the Diagnosis of Organic Brain Damage." *J Clin Psychol* 10:375–8 O '54. * (*PA* 29:4082)
4. HARRIS, PEARL. "Validity of the Grassi-Fairfield Block Substitution Test in Differential Diagnosis." Abstract. *J Consult Psychol* 19:330 O '55. *
5. HIRT, MICHAEL. "An Evaluation of the Grassi Test for Organic Involvement." *J Clin Psychol* 14:48–50 Ja '58. *

Can J Psychol 8:240 D '54. J. G. McMurray. * This diagnostic device may prove to be a valuable addition to the growing field of neuropsychology.

J Clin Psychol 9:405 O '53. * The standardization data indicate that this test may be a sensitive indicator of organic brain pathology.

[61]

★The Grayson Perceptualization Test. Detection of cortical impairment; 1950–57; Forms A, B ('56); mimeographed manual ('57); no data on reliability; no norms; $4 per 25 tests, cash orders postpaid; specimen sets not available; 4(15) minutes; Harry M. Grayson; Western Psychological Services. *

D. RUSSELL DAVIS, *Reader in Clinical Psychology, University of Cambridge, Cambridge, England.*

The test involves reading letters in relatively small print and marking off words by vertical lines. The main score is one of speed of performance. The other score, which is based on the quality of performance and which would appea.· to be more useful, has not been standardised. Both scores are said to be affected by age, education, and intelligence. The author claims no more than that the test is a device for the rapid screening of "organics" from normals.

The limitations of the test are severe. It is not suitable for use with poorly educated or elderly patients or with those who suffer from visual or motor defects. Patients in poor health and those who are depressed or retarded are likely to obtain low scores, whether or not they also suffer from organic disease of the brain.

The test does not appear to have any use in the differential diagnosis of organic impairment, functional impairment, and mental deficiency, although it may help to distinguish the impaired, whatever the cause, from the normal.

WILLIAM SCHOFIELD, *Associate Professor of Psychology and Psychiatry, University of Minnesota, Minneapolis, Minnesota.*

This is an ingenious task which was devised in 1947 as part of a psychological test battery for use in screening hospital admissions. It has been used in a variety of settings; experience gained over 10 years has contributed to its present format and content. The rationale for this test is similar to that for the *Sherman Mental Impairment Test,* i.e., it is held that patients with brain pathology of a nonfocal type suffer a "relative inflexibility of mental processes" and that presence of such inflexibility will be reflected in tasks requiring a continual "shifting" in perception and cognition.

Two forms of the GPT are available, each consisting of two simple reading selections of 100 words, with equal spacing between letters of words and between words. The subject's task is to separate the letters with vertical pencil lines so as to create words which are both individually meaningful and fit a context.

Directions to the subject are printed on the test booklet, which also includes a practice exercise and 10 clinical "stop" questions such as, "I once had a serious head injury." The administrator's task is simple and consists primarily of indicating the two-minute time limit for each selection.

Two scores are derived, a speed score and a quality score. The speed score consists of the total number of words marked off, without regard to accuracy, and can be obtained quickly by use of a keyed guide. The quality score is determined by the relative presence of three types of error: omissions of separation marks, concrete errors (marking off words which are real but do not make contextual sense), and bizarre errors (marking off letters which do not form meaningful words).

The amount and nature of the standardization material reported is very inadequate. Both forms were administered to two samples of normals (n = 32, 35) and two samples of "organics" (n = 40, 43). No descriptive data such as age and sex are provided for the normals; the only description of the organics consists of the statement that they cover a "wide range of diagnoses and degrees of impairment" and the listing of the kinds of diagnoses represented. No cross-validational studies are reported. Use of optimal cutting scores on the original groups resulted in correct identification of approximately 82 per cent of organics and 85 per cent of normals. Numerous clinical observations are offered as to the significance of various kinds of performance on the GPT. The author states that it may be "expected" that schizophrenics will yield the same percentage of false positives as normals.

The GPT is an ingenious task and deserves study as one of a battery of measures of intellectual function. One would seriously question the justification for its being formally offered as a *test* of cortical impairment.

[62]

★Group Cohesiveness: A Study of Group Morale. Adults; 1958, c1957–58; title on test is *A Study of Group Morale;* 5 scores: satisfaction of individual motives, satisfaction of interpersonal relations, homogeneity of attitude, satisfaction with leadership, total; 1 form ('57) ; $3 per 30 tests; 50¢ per manual ('58) ; $1 per specimen set; postage extra; (10–15) minutes; Bernard Goldman; Psychometric Affiliates. *

[63]

The Guilford-Martin Inventory of Factors GAMIN, Abridged Edition. Grades 10–16 and adults; 1943–48; 5 scores: general activity, ascendance-submission, masculinity-femininity, inferiority feelings, nervousness; IBM; 1 form ('43) ; mimeographed supplement ('46) ; $2.50 per 25 tests; 10¢ per single copy; separate answer sheets may be used; 3¢ per IBM answer sheet; 25¢ per scoring key; $2.50 per set of either hand or machine scoring stencils; 15¢ per manual ['48] ; postage extra; (30) minutes; [J. P. Guilford and H. G. Martin] ; Sheridan Supply Co. *

REFERENCES

1-7. See 3:43.
8-25. See 4:47.
26. BRUECKEL, JOYCE E. *A Comparison of the Three Guilford-Martin Personality Inventories With Self-Ratings and Student-Ratings.* Master's thesis, University of Colorado (Boulder, Colo.), 1948.
27. GUILFORD, J. S. *The Relative Value of Fourteen Test Variables for Predicting Success in Executive and Supervisory Positions.* Master's thesis, University of Southern California (Los Angeles, Calif.), 1951.
28. MANZANO, ILUMINADO BILLARINIA. *The Relation of Personality Adjustment to Occupational Interests.* Doctor's thesis, University of Southern California (Los Angeles, Calif.), 1951.
29. BAEHR, MELANY E. "A Factorial Study of Temperament." *Psychometrika* 17:107–26 Mr '52. * (PA 27:1834)
30. BORG, WALTER R. "Personality Characteristics of a Group of College Art Students." *J Ed Psychol* 43:149–56 Mr '52. * (PA 27:3764)
31. COCKRUM, LOGAN V. "Personality Traits and Interests of Theological Students." *Relig Ed* 47:28–32 Ja–F '52. * (PA 26:4229)
32. GUILFORD, J. P. "When Not to Factor Analyze." *Psychol B* 49:26–37 Ja '52. * (PA 27:33)
33. GUILFORD, JOAN S. "Temperament Traits of Executives and Supervisors Measured by the Guilford Personality Inventories." *J Appl Psychol* 36:228–33 Ag '52. * (PA 27:3801)
34. MARQUIS, DOROTHY P.; SINNETT, E. ROBERT; AND WINTER, WILLIAM D. "A Psychological Study of Peptic Ulcer Patients." *J Clin Psychol* 8:266–72 Jl '52. * (PA 27:6072)
35. MOORE, JOSEPH E., AND STURM, NORMAN H. "Relation of Hand Strength to Personality Measures." *Am J Psychol* 65:111 Ja '52. * (PA 27:2749)

36. NEILEN, GORDON C. *A Study of the Cattell 16 PF Test by Comparison With the A. C. E. and Guilford-Martin Personality Battery.* Master's thesis, Kent State University (Kent, Ohio), 1952.
37. POE, WESLEY A., AND BERG, IRWIN A. "Psychological Test Performance of Steel Industry Production Supervisors." *J Appl Psychol* 36:234–7 Ag '52. *
38. TOMEDY, FRANCIS JOSEPH. *The Relationship of Personality Characteristics to Measured Interests of Women Teachers of English, Social Science, Mathematics, and Physical Science in Certain Senior High Schools.* Doctor's thesis, New York University (New York, N.Y.), 1952. (Abstracts: DA 12:540, Am Psychol 7:384)
39. KORNREICH, MELVIN. "Variations in the Consistency of the Behavioral Meaning of Personality Test Scores." *Genetic Psychol Monogr* 47:73–138 F '53. * (PA 27:6535)
40. ROSENBERG, NATHAN; IZARD, CARROLL E.; AND HOLLANDER, E. P. "Middle Category ("?") Response: Reliability and Relationship to Personality and Intelligence Variables." Abstract. *Am Psychol* 8:425 Ag '53. *
41. TRUMBELL, RICHARD. "A Study of Relationships Between Factors of Personality and Intelligence." *J Social Psychol* 38:161–73 N '53. * (PA 28:5589)
42. ABERNETHY, ETHEL M., AND WHITE, JAMES CLYDE, JR. "Correlation of a Self-Inventory of Personality Traits With Laboratory Measures of Vigor and Motility." *J Social Psychol* 40:185–8 Ag '54. * (PA 29:5295)
43. GOCHE, L. N. *Relationship of Interests and Temperament Traits to Attrition and Survival of Engineering Students.* Master's thesis, Iowa State College (Ames, Iowa), 1954.
44. GUILFORD, J. P. "The Validation of an 'Indecision' Score for Prediction of Proficiency of Foremen." *J Appl Psychol* 38:224–6 Ag '54. * (PA 29:6369)
45. HUEBER, JOANNE. "Validity Information Exchange, No. 7-089: D.O.T. Code 5-83.641, Maintenance Mechanic II." *Personnel Psychol* 7:565–6 w '54. *
46. NORMAN, RALPH D., AND AINSWORTH, PATRICIA. "The Relationships Among Projection, Empathy, Reality, and Adjustment, Operationally Defined." *J Consult Psychol* 18:53–8 F '54. * (PA 28:8700)
47. BORG, WALTER R. "The Effect of Personality and Contact Upon a Personality Stereotype." *J Ed Res* 49:289–94 D '55. * (PA 30:6911)
48. BROWN, VICTOR H. *Relationship of the Cureton Strength-Weight Index to the Guilford-Martin Inventory of Factors GAMIN.* Master's thesis, Iowa State College (Ames, Iowa), 1955.
49. COOPER, MATTHEW NATHANIEL. *To Determine the Nature and Significance, If Any, of Certain Differences in the Social and Personal Adjustment of Fifty-One Successful and Fifty-One Non-Successful College Students at Texas Southern University.* Doctor's thesis, New York University (New York, N.Y.), 1955. (DA 16:497)
50. JACOBS, ALFRED, AND LEVENTER, SEYMOUR. "Response to Personality Inventories With Situational Stress." *J Abn & Social Psychol* 51:449–51 N '55. * (PA 31:3041)
51. ROSENBERG, NATHAN; IZARD, CARROLL E.; AND HOLLANDER, E. P. "Middle Category Response: Reliability and Relationship to Personality and Intelligence Variables." *Ed & Psychol Meas* 15:281–90 au '55. * (PA 30:4592)
52. THURSTON, DONALD REID. *An Investigation of the Possibilities of Parole Prediction Through the Use of Five Personality Inventories.* Doctor's thesis, Michigan State University (East Lansing, Mich.), 1955. (DA 15:1206)
53. ZIMMERMAN, WAYNE S., AND GUILFORD, J. P. "The Guilford-Martin Inventories Reanalyzed." Abstract. *Am Psychol* 10:330 Ag '55. *
54. GUILFORD, J. P., AND ZIMMERMAN, WAYNE S. "Fourteen Dimensions of Temperament." *Psychol Monogr* 70(10):1–26 '56. * (PA 31:5789)
55. HINES, VYNCE A. "F Scale, GAMIN, and Public School Principal Behavior." *J Ed Psychol* 47:321–8 O '56. *
56. SPROTT, JUANITA. *Personality Correlates of Religious Attitudes.* Master's thesis, Vanderbilt University (Nashville, Tenn.), 1956.
57. COE, ROBERT STANFORD. *The Personality and Adjustment Characteristics of Females in Various Occupational Groups.* Doctor's thesis, University of Houston (Houston, Tex.), 1957. (DA 17:2309–10)
58. FARBRO, PATRICK C., AND COOK, JOHN M. "Normative Data Information Exchange, No. 10-12." *Personnel Psychol* 10:228 su '57. *

For a review by Hubert E. Brogden, see 4:47; for a review by H. J. Eysenck, see 3:43; for a related review, see 3:45.

[64]

The Guilford-Martin Personnel Inventory. Grades 10–16 and adults; 1943–46; 3 scores: objectivity, agreeableness, cooperativeness; IBM; 1 form ('43) ; mimeographed supplement ('46) ; $2.50 per 25 tests; 10¢ per single copy; separate answer sheets may be used; 3¢ per IBM answer sheet; 25¢ per scoring key; $2.50 per set of either hand or machine scoring stencils; 15¢ per manual ['43]; 3¢ per profile ['43]; postage extra; (30) minutes; [J. P. Guilford and H. G. Martin]; Sheridan Supply Co.

REFERENCES

1-7. See 3:44.
8-27. See 4:48.
28. BRUECKEL, JOYCE E. *A Comparison of the Three Guilford-Martin Personality Inventories With Self-Ratings and Student-Ratings.* Master's thesis, University of Colorado (Boulder, Colo.), 1948.
29. GUILFORD, J. S. *The Relative Value of Fourteen Test Variables for Predicting Success in Executive and Supervisory Positions.* Master's thesis, University of Southern California (Los Angeles, Calif.), 1951.
30. MANZANO, ILUMINADO BILLARINIA. *The Relation of Personality Adjustment to Occupational Interests.* Doctor's thesis, University of Southern California (Los Angeles, Calif.), 1951.
31. BAEHR, MELANY E. "A Factorial Study of Temperament." *Psychometrika* 17:107-26 Mr '52. * (*PA* 27:1834)
32. BORG, WALTER R. "Personality Characteristics of a Group of College Art Students." *J Ed Psychol* 43:149-56 Mr '52. * (*PA* 27:3764)
33. GUILFORD, JOAN S. "Temperament Traits of Executives and Supervisors Measured by the Guilford Personality Inventories." *J Appl Psychol* 36:228-33 Ag '52. * (*PA* 27:3801)
34. NEILEN, GORDON C. *A Study of the Cattell 16 PF Test by Comparison With the A. C. E. and Guilford-Martin Personality Battery.* Master's thesis, Kent State University (Kent, Ohio), 1952.
35. POE, WESLEY A., AND BERG, IRWIN A. "Psychological Test Performance of Steel Industry Production Supervisors." *J Appl Psychol* 36:234-7 Ag '52. * (*PA* 27:3794)
36. TOMEDY, FRANCIS JOSEPH. *The Relationship of Personality Characteristics to Measured Interests of Women Teachers of English, Social Science, Mathematics, and Physical Science in Certain Senior High Schools.* Doctor's thesis, New York University (New York, N. Y.), 1952. (Abstracts: *DA* 12:540, *Am Psychol* 7:384)
37. ROSENBERG, NATHAN; IZARD, CARROLL E.; AND HOLLANDER, E. P. "Middle Category ("?") Response: Reliability and Relationship to Personality and Intelligence Variables." Abstract. *Am Psychol* 8:425 Ag '53. *
38. STACEY, CHALMERS L., AND GOLDBERG, HERMAN D. "A Personality Study of Professional and Student Actors." *J Appl Psychol* 37:24-5 F '53. * (*PA* 28:1685)
39. GRANT, DONALD L. "Validity Information Exchange, No. 7-085: D.O.T. Code 1-01.05, Budget Clerk." *Personnel Psychol* 7:557-8 w '54.*
40. GRANT, DONALD L. "Validity Information Exchange, No. 7-086: D.O.T. Code 1-01.05, Budget Clerk." *Personnel Psychol* 7:559-60 w '54. *
41. GUILFORD, J. P. "The Validation of an 'Indecision' Score for Prediction of Proficiency of Foremen." *J Appl Psychol* 38:224-6 Ag '54. * (*PA* 29:6369)
42. MCCARTY, JOHN J. "Validity Information Exchange, No. 7-077: D.O.T. Code 5-92.621, (Foreman II)." *Personnel Psychol* 7:420-1 au '54. *
43. MCCARTY, JOHN J.; WESTBERG, WILLIAM C.; AND FITZPATRICK, EUGENE D. "Validity Information Exchange, No. 7-001: D.O.T. Code 5-92.621, (Foreman II)." *Personnel Psychol* 7:568-9 w '54. *
44. WESTBERG, WILLIAM C.; FITZPATRICK, EUGENE D.; AND MCCARTY, JOHN J. "Validity Information Exchange, No. 7-073: D.O.T. Code 1-37.32, Typist." *Personnel Psychol* 7:411-2 au '54. *
45. WESTBERG, WILLIAM C.; FITZPATRICK, EUGENE D.; AND MCCARTY, JOHN J. "Validity Information Exchange, No. 7-087: D.O.T. Code 1-37.32, Typist." *Personnel Psychol* 7:561-2 w '54. *
46. BORG, WALTER R. "The Effect of Personality and Contact Upon a Personality Stereotype." *J Ed Res* 49:289-94 D '55. * (*PA* 30:6911)
47. COOPER, MATTHEW NATHANIEL. *To Determine the Nature and Significance, If Any, of Certain Differences in the Social and Personal Adjustment of Fifty-One Successful and Fifty-One Non-Successful College Students at Texas Southern University.* Doctor's thesis, New York University (New York, N.Y.), 1955. (*DA* 16:497)
48. KELLEY, ELVAN PRESSLOR. *An Investigation Into the Value of Selected Tests and Techniques for Guidance of Prospective Teachers Enrolled in Community Experiences Course.* Doctor's thesis, University of Houston (Houston, Tex.), 1955. (*DA* 15:1209)
49. ROSENBERG, NATHAN; IZARD, CARROLL E.; AND HOLLANDER, E. P. "Middle Category Response: Reliability and Relationship to Personality and Intelligence Variables." *Ed & Psychol Meas* 15:281-90 au '55. * (*PA* 30:4592)
50. ZIMMERMAN, WAYNE S., AND GUILFORD, J. P. "The Guilford-Martin Inventories Reanalyzed." Abstract. *Am Psychol* 10:330 Ag '55. *
51. GUILFORD, J. P., AND ZIMMERMAN, WAYNE S. "Fourteen Dimensions of Temperament." *Psychol Monogr* 70(10):1-26 '56. * (*PA* 31:5789)
52. MCCARTY, JOHN J., AND FITZPATRICK, EUGENE D. "Validity Information Exchange, No. 9-26: D.O.T. Code 5-92.621, (Foreman II)." *Personnel Psychol* 9:253 su '56. *
53. COE, ROBERT STANFORD. *The Personality and Adjustment Characteristics of Females in Various Occupational Groups.* Doctor's thesis, University of Houston (Houston, Tex.), 1957. (*DA* 17:2309)
54. FARBRO, PATRICK C., AND COOK, JOHN M. "Normative Data Information Exchange, No. 10-1." *Personnel Psychol* 10:93 sp '57. *

For a review by Neil Van Steenberg, see 4:48; for a review by Benjamin Shimberg, see 3:44; for a related review, see 3:45.

[65]
The Guilford-Zimmerman Temperament Survey. Grades 9-16 and adults; 1949-55; revision and condensation of *Inventory of Factors STDCR, Guilford-Martin Inventory of Factors GAMIN,* and *Guilford-Martin Personnel Inventory;* 10 scores: general activity, restraint, ascendance, sociability, emotional stability, objectivity, friendliness, thoughtfulness, personal relations, masculinity; IBM; 1 form ('49); norms ('55); separate answer sheets must be used; $3.75 per 25 tests; 20¢ per single copy; 3¢ per IBM answer sheet; $2 per set of either hand or machine scoring stencils; 2¢ per profile ('55); 25¢ per manual ('49); $3.25 per set of scoring stencils and manual for *Falsification Scales* ('55) by Alfred Jacobs and Allan Schlaff; 2¢ per copy of *G-Z Temperament Map* ('52) by Philip C. Perry; postage extra; (50) minutes; J. P. Guilford and Wayne S. Zimmerman; Sheridan Supply Co.

REFERENCES

1-5. See 4:49.
6. PINKSTON, JOHN RAY. *An Evaluation of Teaching Techniques as Evidenced by the Guilford-Martin Temperament Inventory.* Master's thesis, North Texas State College (Denton, Tex.), 1950.
7. VAUGHAN, GEORGE E., JR. *Interest and Personality Patterns of Experienced Teachers.* Master's thesis, North Texas State College (Denton, Tex.), 1950.
8. OLTMAN, RUTH M. *A Study of the Difference Between Art and Non-Art Students as Measured by the Guilford-Zimmerman Temperament Survey and a Biographical Questionnaire.* Master's thesis, Western Reserve University (Cleveland, Ohio), 1951.
9. BARNES, CHARLES A. "A Statistical Study of the Freudian Theory of Levels of Psychosexual Development." *Genetic Psychol Monogr* 45:105-75 My '52. * (*PA* 27:3112)
10. HOLLEY, JASPER W. *The Isolation of Personality Traits in the Domain of Military Leadership.* Doctor's thesis, University of Southern California (Los Angeles, Calif.), 1952.
11. ISAACSON, LEE E. "Predictors of Success for Cooperative Occupational Education Classes in Kansas City, Missouri, High Schools." Abstract. *Am Psychol* 7:379 Jl '52. *
12. ISAACSON, LEE E., AND COTTLE, WILLIAM C. "The Guilford-Zimmerman Temperament Survey: II, Urban High School Students." *Univ Kans B Ed* 6:46-50 F '52. *
13. JOHNSON, ANN, AND COTTLE, WILLIAM C. "The Guilford-Zimmerman Temperament Survey: III, With Urban Negro High School Students." *Univ Kans B Ed* 6:75-80 My '52. *
14. KRUMM, RICHARD L. *Inter-Relationships of Measured Interests and Personality Traits of Introductory Psychology Instructors and Their Students as Related to Student Achievement.* Doctor's thesis, University of Pittsburgh (Pittsburgh, Pa.), 1952.
15. SCHAPERO, MAX, AND HIRSCH, MONROE J. "The Relationship of Refractive Error and Guilford-Martin Temperament Test Scores." *Am J Optom* 29:32-6 Ja '52. * (*PA* 26:4569)
16. WRENN, C. GILBERT. "The Selection and Education of Student Personnel Workers." *Personnel & Guid J* 31:9-14 O '52. * (*PA* 27:4782)
17. SMITH, FLOYD RAY. *Changes in Some Personal Qualities of Student Teachers at the University of Missouri.* Doctor's thesis, University of Missouri (Columbia, Mo.), 1953.
18. BENDIG, A. W., AND SPRAGUE, J. L. "The Guilford-Zimmerman Temperament Survey as a Predictor of Achievement Level and Achievement Fluctuation in Introductory Psychology." *J Appl Psychol* 38:409-13 D '54. * (*PA* 29:4990)
19. BERNBERG, RAYMOND E. "Personality Correlates of Social Conformity." *J Appl Psychol* 38:148-9 Je '54. * (*PA* 29:3664)
20. COTTLE, W. C., AND LEWIS, W. W., JR. "Personality Characteristics of Counselors: II, Male Counselor Responses to the MMPI and GZTS." *J Counsel Psychol* 1:27-30 F '54. * (*PA* 28:7476)

21. HERZBERG, FREDERICK. "Temperament Measures in Industrial Selection." *J Appl Psychol* 38:81–4 Ap '54. * (*PA* 29:3133)

22. MILLER, ROBERT S. *A Study of the Relationships Between MMPI Scales and GZTS Scales.* Master's thesis, University of Kansas (Lawrence, Kan.), 1954.

23. PIERCE, KYLE KARR. *The Personality Inventory Correlates of the Level of Aspiration.* Doctor's thesis, University of Arizona (Tucson, Ariz.), 1954. (*DA* 14:1102)

24. BEAVER, ALMA P. "Temperament and Nursing." *Psychol Rep* 1:339–44 D '55. * (*PA* 30:6431)

25. BENDIG, A. W. "Ability and Personality Characteristics of Introductory Psychology Instructors Rated Competent and Empathetic by Their Students." *J Ed Res* 48:705–9 My '55. * (*PA* 30:162)

26. FELZER, STANTON B. "A Statistical Study of Sex Differences on the Rorschach." *J Proj Tech* 19:382–6 D '55. * (*PA* 30:7194)

27. FITZPATRICK, EUGENE D., AND McCARTY, JOHN J. "Validity Information Exchange, No. 8-35: D.O.T. Code 9-00.91, Assembler VII (Electrical Equipment)." *Personnel Psychol* 8:501–4 w '55. *

28. GOWAN, J. C., AND GOWAN, MAY SEAGOE. "The Guilford-Zimmerman and the California Psychological Inventory in the Measurement of Teaching Candidates." *Calif J Ed Res* 6:35–7 Ja '55. * (*PA* 29:7990)

29. MILLER, ROBERT S., AND COTTLE, WILLIAM C. "Evidenced Relationships Between MMPI and GZTS Scales: An Adult Male Sample." *Univ Kans B Ed* 9:91–4 My '55. *

30. WOEHR, HARRY JOSEPH. *The Relationship of Masculinity-Femininity Scores to Temperament and Interest Profiles.* Doctor's thesis, Temple University (Philadelphia, Pa.), 1955. (*DA* 16:388)

31. ASHCRAFT, K. B. "Normative Data Information Exchange, No. 14." *Personnel Psychol* 9:389 au '56. *

32. FINKLE, ROBERT B., AND McCABE, FRANK J. "Normative Data Information Exchange, No. 1." *Personnel Psychol* 9:263–4 su '56. *

33. GOODLING, RICHARD A. "Relationship Between the IM Scale of the SVIB and Scales of the Guilford-Zimmerman Temperament Survey." *J Counsel Psychol* 3:146+ su '56. *

34. JONES, MARGARET LOIS. "Analysis of Certain Aspects of Teaching Ability." *J Exp Ed* 25:153–80 D '56. *

35. KIRKPATRICK, JAMES J. "Validation of a Test Battery for the Selection and Placement of Engineers." *Personnel Psychol* 9:211–27 su '56. * (*PA* 31:8964)

36. LEEDS, CARROLL H. "Teacher Attitudes and Temperament as a Measure of Teacher-Pupil Rapport." *J Appl Psychol* 40:333–7 O '56. * (*PA* 31:8873)

37. PORTER, LOUIS G., AND STACEY, CHALMERS L. "A Study of the Relationships Between Self-Ratings and Parent-Ratings for a Group of College Students." *J Clin Psychol* 12:243–8 Jl '56. * (*PA* 31:6628)

38. REISNER, MARTIN. *A Comparative Investigation of Personality Factors Associated With Appropriate and Inappropriate Levels of Vocational Aspiration.* Doctor's thesis, New York University (New York, N.Y.), 1956. (*DA* 17:678)

39. VOAS, ROBERT B. "The Relationship Between Self-Descriptive and Socially Acceptable Responses to Two Personality Inventories." Abstract. *Am Psychol* 11:406 Ag '56. *

40. BRUCE, MARTIN M. "Normative Data Information Exchange, No. 10-36." *Personnel Psychol* 10:525–6 w '57. *

41. COOKE, TERENCE F. *Premature Responses in Simple Reaction Time as Related to Traits of General Activity and Restraint in the Guilford-Zimmerman Temperament Survey.* Master's thesis, Fordham University (New York, N.Y.), 1957.

42. HEDBERG, RAYMOND, AND BAXTER, BRENT. "A Second Look at Personality Test Validation." *Personnel Psychol* 10:157–60 su '57. *

43. KAESS, WALTER A., AND WITRYOL, SAM L. "Positive and Negative Faking on a Forced-Choice Authoritarian Scale." *J Appl Psychol* 41:333–9 O 57. *

44. McCARTY, JOHN J. "Normative Data Information Exchange, No. 10-13." *Personnel Psychol* 10:229–30 su '57. *

45. McCARTY, JOHN J. "Validity Information Exchange, No. 10-14: D.O.T. Code 1-33.01, Secretary." *Personnel Psychol* 10:202–3 su '57. *

46. McCARTY, JOHN J. "Validity Information Exchange, No. 10-15: D.O.T. Code 1-33.01, Secretary." *Personnel Psychol* 10:204–5 su '57. *

47. SHAH, SALEEM ALAM. *An Investigation of Predictive Ability in Hospital Personnel and University Students.* Doctor's thesis, Pennsylvania State University (State College, Pa.), 1957. (*DA* 18:288)

48. VOAS, ROBERT B. "Personality Correlates of Reading Speed and the Time Required to Complete Questionnaires." *Psychol Rep* 3:177–82 Je '57. *

49. VOAS, ROBERT B. "Validity of Personality Scales for the Prediction of Success in Naval Aviation Training." Abstract. *Am Psychol* 12:465 Jl '57. *

50. BARRETT, RICHARD S. "The Process of Predicting Job Performance." *Personnel Psychol* 11:39–57 sp '58. *

51. COROSO, JOAN. *Relationship Between the IPAT Music Preference Test of Personality and E, S, and T Scores on the Guilford-Zimmerman Temperament Survey.* Master's thesis, College of New Rochelle (New Rochelle, N.Y.), 1958.

52. GOWAN, J. C. "Intercorrelations and Factor Analysis of Tests Given to Teaching Candidates." *J Exp Ed* 27:1–22 S '58. *

53. VOAS, ROBERT B. "A Procedure for Reducing the Effects of Slanting Questionnaire Responses Toward Social Acceptability." *Ed & Psychol Meas* 18:337–45 su '58. *

DAVID R. SAUNDERS, *Research Associate, Educational Testing Service, Princeton, New Jersey.*

With the passage of time since the publication of this survey in 1949, it has become possible to apply fresh yardsticks to its evaluation. Because the instrument has appeared to merit relatively widespread use, substantial practical experience has been accumulated and begun to be reported. Thus, rather than reconsider how well the survey satisfies any idealized criteria for a factor-analytic personality inventory, we may examine the degree of its demonstrated utility for two classes of application representative of the interests of most users—in individual evaluation and in personality research.

The bottleneck in the use of any personality instrument for individual evaluation is the step whereby the information contained in the test scores is transmuted into a specific prediction of how an individual will perform. The relevant expectation if one listens to factorial theory is that, with a properly developed inventory, whatever validity exists for a particular criterion will be concentrated into one or just a few of the scales, rather than be present a little bit in most or all of them. In other words, one expects the parsimony that has been achieved for the factorial descriptions of the items to carry over into the realm of their correlations with as yet unstudied variables. The achievement of this result will depend primarily on the skill with which the underlying factor studies have been rotated. Several validity studies employing this survey have been reported, some yielding highly significant correlations and some yielding nothing. It is notable that the only studies in which a major proportion of these scales have been significant have employed relatively nonspecific criteria, i.e., criteria with only indirect significance for test interpretation in an individual case. Given a reasonably defined criterion, there appears to be about a fifty-fifty chance that one or perhaps two or three of the survey scales will be significantly related to it. All this is as it should be.

Now, if the validity of the survey is really effectively confined to just one or two scales in a particular application, this means that no one needs to get tangled up in the difficult and uncertain task of integrating—whether clinically or statistically—the clues from a number of individually almost insignificant sources. But this also puts a premium on the reliability of each of the individual scales in the survey. Reliabilities of the order of .8 are *not* generally considered to be sufficient to bear the burden of this kind of interpretation, at least not unless one is willing to hedge or to regard as uninterpretable a rather broad band of scores near the cutting level. These scales cannot suffice if one must always make a definite recommendation.

On the other hand, one almost never has to make a recommendation about the subjects used in personality research. (Certainly this is the most common application of this instrument if one may judge by the number of master's and doctoral studies in which it has been used.) The principal consideration in such use is the sheer efficiency of information collection, for the experimenter is typically trying to cram as much testing into a few hours as his harried subjects will permit. Three subjects who independently respond to 10 factorially homogeneous items will almost surely provide more information bearing on the basic objectives of such research than could any one of them by marking 30 items all belonging to the same scale. One can easily generate a statistically significant correlation for any relation of practical importance using scales with reliabilities of the order of .5, and one can even investigate nonlinear and interactive effects without much more than this. It is notable that a good many of the results reported using scales from this survey *do* involve these relatively complex forms of relationship.

In short, in the light of present knowledge it seems fair to say that studies using this survey have done much to demonstrate the potential advantages of the factor-analytic approach to personality measurement, but that the instrument itself is neither fish nor fowl so far as practical applications are concerned. Since other instruments which may better serve the researcher's purposes already exist, it would seem advisable to focus attention on changes in the survey that would improve the reliability of the individual scales, even at the expense of some increase in overall length.

For reviews by William Stephenson and Neil Van Steenberg, see 4:49.

[66]

Heston Personal Adjustment Inventory. Grades 9-16 and adults; 1949; 6 scores: analytical thinking, sociability, emotional stability, confidence, personal relations, home satisfaction; IBM; 1 form; no non-college adult norms; $4.25 per 35 tests; separate answer sheets may be used; $1.80 per 35 IBM answer sheets; 40¢ per set of machine scoring stencils; postage extra; 50¢ per specimen set, postpaid; (40-55) minutes; Joseph C. Heston; World Book Co. *

REFERENCES

1-2. See 4:50.
3. FARBER, ROBERT HOLTON. *Guidance Implications of the Freshman Testing Program at DePauw University.* Doctor's thesis, Indiana University (Bloomington, Ind.), 1951.
4. McKENNA, FRANK S. "An Analysis of Nine Personality Scales." Abstract. *Proc Ind Acad Sci* 62:294 '52. *
5. TYLER, FRED T. *The Prediction of Student-Teaching Success From Personality Inventories.* University of California, Publications in Education, Vol. 11, No. 4. Berkeley, Calif.: University of California Press, 1954. Pp. 233-313. * (*PA* 29:4709)
6. FICK, DORCAS J. *A Comparison of Personality Traits of a Group of Sunday School Teachers and a Group of Non-Sunday School Teachers as Found on the Heston Personal Adjustment Inventory and the Gordon Personal Profile.* Master's thesis, Boston University (Boston, Mass.), 1955.
7. HOLMES, JACK A. "Personality and Spelling Ability." Abstract. *Am Psychol* 10:353-4 Ag '55. *
8. LODATO, FRANCIS JOSEPH. *The Relationship Between Interest and Personality as Measured by the Kuder and the Heston and Gordon Inventories.* Doctor's thesis, St. John's University (Brooklyn, N.Y.), 1955.
9. TINDALL, RALPH H. "Relationships Among Indices of Adjustment Status." *Ed & Psychol Meas* 15:152-62 su '55. * (*PA* 30:2330)
10. ARBUCKLE, DUGALD S. "Client Perception of Counselor Personality." *J Counsel Psychol* 3:93-6 su '56. * (*PA* 31:4639)
11. AUBLE, DONAVON. "Validity Indices for the Heston Personal Adjustment Inventory." *J Appl Psychol* 41:79-81 Ap '57. *
12. SCARBOROUGH, BARRON B., AND WRIGHT, JOHN C. "The Assessment of an Educational Guidance Clinic." *J Counsel Psychol* 4:283-6 w '57. *
13. GINGLES, RUBY HEATHER. "Personality Adjustment of College Students." *J Home Econ* 50:194-200 Mr '58. *

For reviews by Albert Ellis, Hans J. Eysenck, and E. Lowell Kelly, see 4:50. (1 excerpt).

[67]

★**Hospital Adjustment Scale.** Mental patients; 1951-53; 4 ratings: communication and interpersonal relations, self-care and social responsibility, work and recreation, total; 1 form ('53); $3 per 25 tests; 25¢ per set of scoring key and manual ('53); 50¢ per specimen set; cash orders postpaid; (10-20) minutes; James T. Ferguson, Paul McReynolds, and Egerton L. Ballachey (test); [Consulting Psychologists Press, Inc.]. *

REFERENCES

1. McREYNOLDS, PAUL; BALLACHEY, EDGERTON; AND FERGUSON, JAMES T. "Development and Evaluation of a Behavioral Scale for Appraising the Adjustment of Hospitalized Patients." Abstract. *Am Psychol* 7:340-1 Jl '52. *
2. DUTTON, CHARLES EDWIN. *An Investigation of the Internal Consistency and Validity of the Hospital Adjustment Scale.* Doctor's thesis, Stanford University (Stanford, Calif.), 1953. (*DA* 13:589)
3. LORR, MAURICE. "Rating Scales and Check Lists for the Evaluation of Psychopathology." *Psychol B* 51:119-27 Mr '54. *
4. GUERTIN, WILSON H. "A Factor Analysis of Schizophrenic Ratings on the Hospital Adjustment Scale." *J Clin Psychol* 11:70-3 Ja '55. * (*PA* 29:7648)
5. STILSON, DONALD W.; MASON, DONALD J.; SYNTHER, MALCOLM D.; AND GERTZ, BORIS. "An Evaluation of the Comparability and Reliabilities of Two Behavior Rating Scales for Mental Patients." *J Consult Psychol* 22:213-6 Je '58. *

MAURICE LORR, *Director, Neuropsychiatric Research Laboratory, Veterans Benefits Office, Washington, D.C.*

The *Hospital Adjustment Scale* (HAS) purports to provide an estimate of hospital adjustment for use with adult patients of either sex hospitalized in any type of psychiatric institution. The scale consists of 90 statements descriptive of the behavior of hospitalized psychiatric patients. Each statement is marked as "True" (T), "Not True" (NT), or, in some cases, "Doesn't Apply" (DA). The scale is designed to be completed by the psychiatric aide, psychiatric technician, or nurse familiar with the day-to-day behavior of the patient. The recommended observation period is from two weeks to three months.

The statements were derived from descriptions made by psychiatric aides and rated by 16 professional judges on a 9-point scale with respect to goodness of hospital adjustment measured. The final set was selected on the basis of percentage of T, NT, and DA, measures of internal consistency, item reliabilities, and weighted scale values. There are two scoring methods, one a rather cumbersome item weight scoring method, and the other a more straightforward system in which items are keyed as indicating "expanding" or "contracting" personality traits. Expansion (E) refers to increased ability in social functioning and work efficiency; contraction (C) refers to decreased ability in social functioning and work efficiency.

Norms are based on the records of 353 men and 165 women drawn from four hospitals and clinics. Each sample is described in terms of age range, types of psychiatric disorder represented, type of treatment extended, length of hospitalization, and minimum period of observation prior to rating.

Four scores, three group scores and a total score, are obtained from the HAS. One group score is based on 42 items relating to communication and interpersonal relations; a second, on 25 items relating to care of self and social responsibility; and a third on 23 items relating to work activities and recreation. The total score is based on all 90 items. A table of percentile values is provided for interpretation of the raw scores. Of the 180 possible T and NT choices, 79 are keyed E, 57 are keyed C, and 44 are not keyed. The correlations among the subscales are sufficiently high (.72, .70, and .71) to render questionable their independent value. Correlations of each of the subscores with the total scores are .93, .89, and .85, respectively.

The validity of the HAS is primarily based on the judgments of the expert experienced raters. Additional evidence is available in the form of a comparison of the scores of two groups of patients, one approaching release

from the hospital and one judged to be extremely disturbed or long term residents. These differed at the .01 level of confidence. Further, the HAS distinguished a group of schizophrenics in remission from a group not in remission. Item reliabilities are presented in the form of phi coefficients between pairs of raters rating the same patients. The reported reliability of the total scores (ratio of expansion score to expansion plus contraction score) is .84 for two different aides.

The HAS is probably the best developed of the commercially available checklists for use in describing hospital adjustment. The manual is clear, the scoring is simple and straightforward, and the norms are well described. However, a few lacks should be noted. The flexible observation period of two weeks to three months is likely to alter the score from a record of current behavior to a statement of history. Information is needed as to the minimum observation period required to note the behaviors listed. The internal consistency appears to be sufficiently high to suggest that a shorter scale could measure the same function with equal reliability. Finally, further evidence is needed that the expansion-contraction scoring is more than a duplicate of the sum of the weighted keyed items.

[68]

★Human Relations Inventory. Grades 9–16 and adults; 1954–55; social conformity; Form A ('54); mimeographed manual ['54]; additional norms ('55); $2 per 20 tests; $1 per specimen set (must be purchased to obtain manual); postage extra; (20) minutes; Raymond E. Bernberg; Psychometric Affiliates. *

REFERENCES

1. BERNBERG, RAYMOND E. "A Measure of Social Conformity." J Psychol 39:89–96 Ja '55. * (PA 29:8529)
2. BERNBERG, RAYMOND E. "Personality Correlates of Social Conformity: II." J Social Psychol 43:309–12 My '56. *

RAYMOND C. NORRIS, Associate Professor of Psychology, George Peabody College for Teachers, Nashville, Tennessee.

The test consists of 37 items aimed at six determinant areas of social conformity: moral values, positive goals, reality testing, ability to give affection, tension level, and impulsivity. Each item is presented as a 5-option multiple choice question concerning the percentage of some group who hold or exercise a certain belief in one of the determinant areas. Since there is presumably no foundation in fact for a choice among the possible answers, "the tendency of the subject to deviate toward one extreme or the other is presumed to express a direction of per-

ception based on his need-value system." It
speaks well for the realism of the test items that,
with some clarification of terms, data could be
obtained on the questions posed by most of the
items. However, it also is apparent that under
any customary definition of terms most of the
responses which contribute toward the nonconformity score are the bizarre, unrealistic responses. Whether this instrument provides a
measure of the direction rather than extent of
social perception is a question on which the
prospective user must satisfy himself before he
accepts the inventory as a measure of social conformity.

The author states that conformity scores are
not significantly influenced by the intelligence,
socioeconomic level, cultural background, age,
sex, or religious affiliation of the respondent.
The studies on which these contentions are
based are not described in sufficient detail to
permit close evaluation. However, in accepting
the author's evaluation of his evidence, the nature of the variable measured by the inventory
is once again called into question. The relationships between conformity to essentially middle
class standards and such variables as cultural
background, age, etc. seem sufficiently well established to warrant general acceptance; failure
to verify them with the inventory suggests the
test may be lacking in either sensitivity or relevance as a measure of conformity. Since the
test scores do successfully differentiate a heterogeneous general population group from such
diverse groups as regular churchgoers, police
officer trainees, male juvenile offenders, and
both male and female prison inmates whose
medians often differ only slightly, lack of sensitivity does not seem to be an issue.

With a format that would make reading the
items, making a response, and obtaining a score
simpler than it now is, the *Human Relations Inventory* would seem quite worthy of further research. However, uncertainty as to the phenomenon being measured, the inadequate norms, and
the absence of predictive validity evidence
would argue against its use as a screening or
diagnostic instrument at this time.

JOHN A. RADCLIFFE, *Lecturer in Psychology,
University of Sydney, Sydney, Australia.*

This is intended to be a measure of social conformity, defined by "the tendencies of members
of a society to manifest communality of attitudes" in six arbitrarily defined "determinant

areas": moral values, positive goals, reality testing, ability to give affection, tension level, and
impulsivity. No bases for the selection of these
determinant areas are given, nor is there any
correlation data to show that they do represent
separable areas. A factor analysis would have
been relevant here. Actually, high scores represent *nonconformity* defined by choice of responses which are atypical of people in general
(high school seniors), especially in so far as
these atypical responses are characteristic of
prison inmates. Item weights for 17 of the 37
items were derived from differences between
the response distributions of high school seniors and prison inmates. It would be useful if
the manual indicated which are these 17 items.

Norms consist of scores corresponding to the
25th, 50th, 75th, and 99th percentiles for seven
samples—two for people in general (high school
seniors and college students); two for "conformists" (churchgoers and police officers);
and three for prison inmate samples. Validity
consists in showing that the scores for these
broad groupings differ in the expected way.
When differences are stated to have p > .001
presumably this is intended to mean p < .001.
Additional norms provide percentile ranks for
14-year-old male high school freshmen (n =
159) and male delinquents (= 124), but differences between these groups are too slight to
suggest that the test can differentiate between
delinquents and nondelinquents at this age level.
Reliability is only fair—split-half, .77 with a
youth prison group (sample size not stated but
presumably 160).

The main feature of the test is its use of what
the author calls the "direction of perception"
technique, an outgrowth of the Hammond er-
ror-choice method to which acknowledgement
might well have been made in the manual. The
items are of the form: "Social studies reveal
what percentage of young men feel women are
inferior and dirty? a) 10% b) 20% c) 30% d)
40% e) 50%." Choice of alternative is presumed to express "direction of perception"
based on the subject's "need-value system."
This is a device similar to that used by Cattell
as a measure of Autism, based upon the rationale that the subject will perceive others to be
like himself. In this sense, the data show that
prison inmates and nonprison inmates have different perceptions. It is interesting that typical
high school responses are not necessarily "desirable" responses, for example: "It has been

found that the following percentage of people who find lost articles return them to their owners: a) 27% b) 40% c) 53% d) 66% e) 79%." The conforming responses to this item are a) and b). Perhaps it may be argued that this shows how "realistic" the technique is, but one is surprised to find that in Item 5 ["According to a well-known report, what percentage of unmarried American males would attempt sexual intercourse if they were sure of not being caught? a) 15% b) 24% c) 33% d) 42% e) 51%"], a) is the *atypical* response of people in general, and presumably the *typical* response of prison inmates! This illustrates the need for an indication of which items were weighted by comparing high school and prison inmate responses and how, in their present form, the scores represent a mixture both of deviation from the conforming norm and similarity with the nonconforming norm.

Some of the items are strangely worded—for example, the item above on inferiority and dirtiness in women. This would seem more appropriate in a "neuroticism" questionnaire, but perhaps neuroticism is a form of social nonconformity. But, in all, the items are a heterogeneous lot and better evidence that they constitute a meaningful pool or set of subpools would be an improvement. All the items are worded to apply to men only, but, in the later stages of validation, the scale was also applied to women. While the author reports absence of sex differences in the test, it is unclear whether this refers to total scores or to item responses. It remains likely that item wording could lead to sex differences in responses to some items. There is no evidence on fakability.

The author suggests the scale be used "(1) as a research tool; (2) as a demonstration tool of a socio-psychological concept and indirect method of attitude measurement; and (3) for screening and diagnostic purposes where social conformity as defined is either desirable or undesirable." There is no evidence on screening or diagnostic value, or on conditions under which "social conformity as defined" might be relevant. In its present unpolished form, the test is unlikely to be useful for (1). This leaves (2) as its most likely area of use, and this is far too limited an area of application to have justified its publication as a psychological test.

[69]

*The Humm-Wadsworth Temperament Scale. Adults; 1935–56; 41 scores: normal (4 subscores),

hysteroid (6 subscores), manic (4 subscores), depressive (5 subscores), autistic (5 subscores), paranoid (3 subscores), epileptoid (4 subscores), response bias, self mastery (component control, integration index); 1 form ('34); revised manual ('54–55); work sheet ('54); nomograph ('54); distribution restricted; license fees for business organizations retaining publisher as consultant: $1,350 for first year, $120 a year thereafter; no license fees for psychologists; test materials are rented to licensees only; $25 for use of a set of test materials for first year, $5 a year thereafter; 25¢ per answer sheet; postage extra; (45–90) minutes; Doncaster G. Humm and Kathryn A. Humm; Humm Personnel Consultants. *

REFERENCES

1–13. See 40:1223.
14–44. See 3:48.
45. HATHAWAY, S. R. "The Personality Inventory as an Aid in the Diagnosis of Psychopathic Inferiors." *J Consult Psychol* 3:112–7 Jl–Ag '39. * (*PA* 13:5704)
46. CERF, ARTHUR Z. "The Humm-Wadsworth Temperament Scale, CE418A," pp. 581–5. In *Printed Classification Tests.* Edited by J. P. Guilford. Army Air Forces Aviation Psychology Program Research Reports, Report No. 5. Washington, D.C.: U.S. Government Printing Office, 1947. Pp. xi, 919. * (*PA* 22:4145)
47. MARSHALL, HELEN. *A Study of the Personality of Alcoholic Males.* Doctor's thesis, Stanford University (Stanford, Calif.), 1947.
48. HUMM, DONCASTER G. "Note Concerning 'The Validity of Standard and Custom-Built Personality Inventories in a Pilot Selection Program' by Donald E. Super." *Ed & Psychol Meas* 8:257–61 su '48. * (*PA* 23:4446)
49. JURGENSEN, C. E. "Note on Personality Questionnaires." Letter. *Mgmt Rec* 10:177 Mr '48. *
50. CAINE, THOMAS MACKENZIE. *An Investigation of the Relationship Between the Performance of Pilot Trainees on the Humm-Wadsworth Temperament Scale and Their Subsequent Success in Flying Training.* Master's thesis, University of Toronto (Toronto, Ont., Canada), 1949.
51. CONRAD, HERBERT S., AND ELLIS, ALBERT. "Reply to the Humms' 'Notes on "The Validity of Personality Inventories in Military Practice."'" *Psychol B* 46:307–8 Jl '49. * (*PA* 24:2598)
52. FORTUNE, DONALD McA. *An Investigation of the Validity of the Humm-Wadsworth Temperament Scale in Predicting Academic Achievement of Second Year Pass Arts University Students.* Master's thesis, University of Toronto (Toronto, Ont., Canada), 1949.
53. HARRELL, THOMAS W. "Humm-Wadsworth Temperament Scale and Ratings of Salesmen." *Personnel Psychol* 2:491–5 w '49. * (*PA* 24:4279)
54. HUMM, DONCASTER G. "Some Considerations Basic to the Interpretation of Measures of Temperament, With Special Reference to the Humm-Wadsworth Temperament Scale." *J Social Psychol* 30:293–304 N '49. * (*PA* 24:4117)
55. HUMM, DONCASTER G., AND HUMM, KATHRYN A. "Notes on 'The Validity of Personality Inventories in Military Practice,' by Ellis and Conrad." *Psychol B* 46:303–6 Jl '49. * (*PA* 24:2604)
56. CANNING, WILLIAM; HARLOW, GEORGE; AND REGELIN, CLINTON. "A Study of Two Personality Questionnaires." *J Consult Psychol* 14:414–5 O '50. * (*PA* 25:4561)
57. HUMM, DONCASTER G., AND HUMM, KATHRYN A. "Humm-Wadsworth Temperament Scale Appraisals Compared With Criteria of Job Success in the Los Angeles Police Department." *J Psychol* 30:63–75 Jl '50. * (*PA* 25:1311)
58. HUMM, DONCASTER G., AND HUMM, KATHRYN A. "Measure of Mental Health From the Humm-Wadsworth Temperament Scale." *Am J Psychiatry* 107:442–9 D '50. * (*PA* 25:6870)
59. GILLILAND, A. R. "The Humm-Wadsworth and the Minnesota Multiphasic." *J Consult Psychol* 15:457–9 D '51. * (*PA* 26:6998)
60. GREENBERG, PAUL, AND GILLILAND, A. R. "The Relationship Between Basal Metabolism and Personality." *J Social Psychol* 35:3–7 F '52. * (*PA* 27:3345)
61. GILLILAND, A. R., AND NEWMAN, S. E. "The Humm-Wadsworth Temperament Scale as an Indicator of the 'Problem' Employee." *J Appl Psychol* 37:176–7 Je '53.* (*PA* 28:3350)
62. HUMM, D. G., AND HUMM, KATHRYN A. "Discussion of Gilliland and Newman's 'The Humm-Wadsworth Temperament Scale as an Indicator of the "Problem" Employee.'" *J Appl Psychol* 38:131–2 Ap '54. * (*PA* 29:3135)
63. SMITH, GUDMUND, AND MARKE, SVEN. "The Influence on the Results of a Conventional Personality Inventory by Changes in the Test Situation: A Study on the Humm-Wadsworth Temperament Scale." *J Appl Psychol* 42:227–33 Ag '58. *
64. SMITH, GUDMUND, AND MARKE, SVEN. "The Internal Consistency of the Humm-Wadsworth Temperament Scale." *J Appl Psychol* 42:234–40 Ag '58. *

For reviews by H. J. Eysenck, H. Meltzer, and Lorenz Misbach of the 1940 edition; see 3:48; for reviews by Forrest A. Kingsbury and P. E. Vernon, see 40:1223; for a review by Daniel A. Prescott of an earlier edition, see 38:920.

[70]

★The IPAT Anxiety Scale. Ages 14 and over; 1957; title on test is *IPAT Self Analysis Form;* 6 scores: self sentiment development, ego strength, protension or paranoid trend, guilt proneness, ergic tension, total anxiety; 1 form; mimeographed manual; $3 per 25 tests; 40¢ per scoring key; $1 per manual; $2 per specimen set including 5 tests, scoring keys, and manual; cash orders postpaid; (5-10) minutes; Raymond B. Cattell; Institute for Personality and Ability Testing. *

REFERENCES

1. CATTELL, RAYMOND B. "The Conceptual and Test Distinction of Neuroticism and Anxiety." *J Clin Psychol* 13:221-33 Jl '57. *
2. RAWN, Moss L. "The Overt-Covert Anxiety Index and Hostility." *J Clin Psychol* 14:279-80 Jl '58. *

J. P. GUILFORD, *Professor of Psychology, University of Southern California, Los Angeles, California.*

The author claims for this 40-item questionnaire that it is "probably the most effective available brief questionnaire instrument for supplementary clinical diagnosis and giving an objective measure for research purposes." The instrument is based upon considerable background research.

The author defines his anxiety syndrome as comprising the qualities of tension, irritability, lack of self-confidence, unwillingness to take risks, tremor, and various psychosomatic signs. This definition suggests to the reviewer that the primary traits of composure-nervousness, confidence-inferiority, and liking for adventure versus security are involved. Examination of the items suggests that the first two of these traits are heavily represented, as are the primary traits of depression and emotional immaturity, but that there are no items on liking for adventure versus security, at least to casual inspection.

In addition to the scores mentioned in the entry preceding this review, two other scores can be obtained. One is said to indicate the "role of personality structures in contributing to anxiety," and the other, "overt, symptomatic anxiety" versus "covert anxiety, not consciously displayed." Little is said in the manual concerning interpretation or use of these scores.

Raw scores are converted to common-scale scores on the "sten" and decile scales. Before making conversions, the user is to apply minor corrections in raw scores for age of the subject.

Separate male and female norms are given, based upon fairly large samples, with no demographic information being supplied concerning the samples.

For the total score, split-half reliabilities of .84 in a normal population and .91 in a mixed normal and pathological population are reported. No estimates of reliability are given for the component trait scores which are based upon only 4 to 12 items each.

Validity studies were made against three kinds of external criteria—ratings of anxiety in pathological subjects given by psychiatrists, physiological and behavioral test scores, and performances of classified groups of normals, neurotics, and anxiety hysterics. A validity coefficient of .92 is mentioned in connection with the first criterion. This is evidently a loading in a factor that the ratings and scores have in common, and not their intercorrelation. Discrimination of anxiety hysterics from normals is reported as highly significant, as is the discrimination of neurotics from normals. It would seem that the anxiety score would correlate very highly with a score for neuroticism. No information of this kind is given.

The author recommends that in using the total score, sten scores of 7 and higher indicate that the person "could be" an anxiety neurotic and that scores of 8 and higher indicate that the person definitely needs help. In the former instance, the highest 31 per cent of the cases would be involved and, in the latter case, the highest 16 per cent.

It would seem that the instrument should have its best use as a quick screening device used with large groups. The use of the five part scores cannot be recommended except for suggestive leads calling for further analytical testing. For the sake of orientation of users, it would have been desirable for the author to report correlations between his score and scores from other recognized measures purported to assess anxiety, even though he could maintain that he has the best information concerning construct validity in terms of factor-analytical results.

A general comment would be that there is a danger that such an instrument indicates too much. The score discriminates neurotics from normals somewhat, which is reasonable, since anxiety cases are also in the general category of neurotic, but it is hinted by the author that the score also discriminates psychotics. Questions on lack of confidence, nervousness, and depression represent item types that any person who does not feel well for any reason is likely to answer similarly, particularly if he knows he is not well and is ready to admit it.

E. LOWELL KELLY, *Professor of Psychology, University of Michigan, Ann Arbor, Michigan.*

This 40-item inventory is a highly promising, brief assessment instrument. Although but recently published, it is a product of the author's very extensive program of research aimed at mapping the "personality sphere" and hence deserves more serious consideration than the typical newly offered inventory.

The inventory consists of a neatly printed 4-page folder. The first page provides a set of instructions sufficiently clear to make the instrument self-administering for most subjects. Page 2 contains 20 items judged by the author to be the more subtle or cryptic items; hence, responses to them are scored separately to provide an estimate of "cryptic anxiety." Page 3 contains the remaining 20 presumably less subtle items; these are scored to provide an estimate of "overt anxiety." The total score based on all 40 items is labeled "total anxiety." The author suggests that the ratio of "overt to cryptic" scores may prove to have clinical significance but provides no norms, reliability estimates, or evidence for the validity of this ratio score.

The author's decision to publish an inventory to assess "general anxiety" was based on a second order factor analysis [1] of the 75 most representative items from his earlier *Sixteen Personality Factor Questionnaire.* Of the four resulting second order factors, the one accounting for the largest amount of variance had loadings ranging from .53 to .66 for five of the 16 PF scores: $Q_3(-)$, "lack of will control"; $O(+)$ "insecurity or free floating anxiety"; $Q_4(+)$ "nervous tensions (somatic anxiety)"; $L(+)$ "paranoid trend"; and $C(-)$ "lack of ego strength." Other studies ([1]) showed that this second order factor correlated highly with other accepted indices of anxiety (e.g., judgments of psychiatrists, scores on the *Taylor Manifest Anxiety Scale,* and the author's Factor U.I. 24, based on objective performance and autonomic measures).

The 40 items included in the scale were se-

lected to represent the above 16 PF dimensions in proportion to the loadings of each of the five on the second order factor: O(guilt proneness), 12 items; Q_4(ergic tension or id pressure), 10 items; Q_3- (lack of will control, relabeled "defective integration or binding by the organized self-sentiment"), 8 items; C— (lack of ego strength), 6 items; and L(protension or paranoid insecurity), 4 items. These items have been grouped in a manner which permits five separate scores thus providing a very crude estimate of the relative contribution of each of these five components to the total anxiety score. However, the manual emphasizes the low reliability of subscores based on so few items per scale and suggests that the user regard even extreme subscores "as evidence of a probable 'problem'....worthy of investigation in conjunction with other evidence" and more extended testing.

The reliability of the total score is reported to be .84 for a sample of 240 normal adults, and .91 for a mixed group of normals and hospitalized neurotics. These reliability estimates compare favorably with those for other available inventories, some containing many more items and hence being more time consuming. The reliabilities for the five component scores are reported as .46 for O, .55 for Q_4, .47 for Q_3, .44 for C, and .26 for L.

What about validity? The term anxiety appears to mean different things to different people; for example, the interjudge agreement of two psychiatrists who interviewed subjects is reported as only .29([1]). Since scores on this instrument correlate higher with the pooled judgment of the two psychiatrists than with the ratings of either, the scale would appear to be measuring whatever was common to each of them when perceiving "anxiety." Furthermore, the relatively high reported correlation of this second order factor with scores on other "anxiety" scales suggests that the present scale is not mislabeled.

The author, however, defends the validity of the scale on two other grounds: the external or construct validity of the items used and its validation against external criteria. With respect to the former, he reminds us that the 40 items finally selected out of 2,000 tried out are the most highly correlated with the five oblique primary factors making up this second order factor of general anxiety, now replicated in six separate studies. As evidence for external valid-

1 CATTELL, RAYMOND B. "Second-Order Personality Factors in the Questionnaire Realm." *J Consult Psychol* 20:411–8 D '56. * (PA 32:1614)

ity, he emphasizes (*a*) the correlation of the scores with psychiatrists' estimates of anxiety level in 85 patients, (*b*) its correlations with behavioral, physiological and other laboratory tests of anxiety, and (*c*) the degree to which the scores differentiate between normals, neurotics, and anxiety hysterics, e.g., roughly three fourths of a sample of anxiety hysterics have a standard score (sten) above 7 and three fourths of a sample of normals score below this point. Separation of diagnosed neurotics and normals is less dramatic but still highly significant, CR = 10.67. This finding is in accord with Cattell's related research (*1*) pointing to a correlation but nonidentity of "anxiety" and "neuroticism."

Standard score and decile norms are provided. These are based on 795 men and women (proportions not specified). Since slight sex and age differences appear, appropriate corrections are suggested.

Judged by the criteria established by the APA Committee on Test Standards, the mimeographed manual is reasonably adequate, especially for a newly published instrument. It suffers somewhat from the author's use of his own specialized vocabulary and parts of it are probably more argumentative than necessary. Unfortunately, as is the case with most test manuals, the reader is not provided with correlations between the particular instrument and other widely used measures of the same variable. A limited amount of such information is provided in the references listed.

This is a highly promising brief scale for assessing a pervasive personality variable. It is likely to be widely used as a research instrument and probably should be in view of the substantial evidence for its construct validity. Clinicians who are willing to give the scale a trial (in spite of its being a by-product of factor analysis!) are likely to find it a useful diagnostic device for initial screening purposes.

J Consult Psychol 21:438 O '57. Laurance F. Shaffer. In view of the widespread current interest in the concept of anxiety, the publication of a new scale for its measurement is a noteworthy event. The *I.P.A.T. Anxiety Scale* is product of its author's extensive studies of the factorial structure of personality. A prominent second-order factor of his *Sixteen Personality Factor Questionnaire* has been identified as anxiety * The present questionnaire consists of 40 items which best represent the five scales

most heavily loaded in the anxiety factor * the *I.P.A.T. Anxiety Scale* has a sounder conceptual base than other current instruments of its type. Many of the functional properties of its scores remain to be established by future research, which will almost surely be forthcoming.

[71]

★IPAT Contact Personality Factor Test. Grades 8-16 and adults; 1954-56; title on test is C.P.F.; 2 scores: extroversion-introversion, distortion; Forms A, B ('54); mimeographed bits serving as manual ['56]; adult norms ('54) only; 20¢ per test (10¢ to educational institutions); $2 per complete specimen set (must be purchased to obtain manual); cash orders postpaid; (10) minutes; Raymond B. Cattell, Joseph E. King, and A. K. Schuettler; Institute for Personality and Ability Testing. * (Form A is also published by Industrial Psychology, Inc.)

REFERENCE
1. CATTELL, RAYMOND B. *Personality and Motivation Structure and Measurement.* Yonkers, N.Y.: World Book Co., 1957. Pp. xxv, 948. *

CECIL D. JOHNSON, *Task Leader, New Classification Techniques, Personnel Research Branch, The Adjutant General's Office, Department of the Army, Washington, D.C.*

The CPF is designed to measure a "contact personality factor," often referred to as extroversion-introversion, which is more or less the centroid of five more basic factors. The test purports to be basically designed for "sales and other contact job areas." However, no basis of item selection is given other than loadings on the particular primary factor each item represents. The basic factors and number of items representing each are as follows: cyclothymia versus schizothymia (10), dominance versus submission (6), surgency versus desurgency (6), adventurousness versus withdrawal (6), and group identification versus self-sufficiency (6). In addition to the keyed items, there are six additional items in each form from which a distortion (exaggeration of CPF tendencies) score can be obtained. Correlation of results on the two forms for 125 cases yielded a coefficient of .86.

The factor loadings of items are provided for one factor only. Loadings range in magnitude from .11 to .57. Mean loadings across the two forms range from .20 for items contributing to group identification versus self-sufficiency to .38 for items contributing to surgency versus desurgency. The table for converting CPF raw scores to 9-point ranks indicates that examinees in the standardization sample selected the nonkeyed alternatives as often as the keyed responses. Such independence between direction of keying and examinee preference for alternatives would usually indicate a relatively low relationship between direction of keying and the social desirability of responses. Thus, the CPF may be relatively uncontaminated with this general factor which permeates most self-description tests used for personnel selection.

Each item is a self-descriptive statement which is either to be completed by the selection of one of two alternatives or an intermediate response, or, where the statement is already complete, to be answered with "yes," "no," or such intermediate responses as "rarely," "uncertain," or "partly." The keyed response is given a weight of 2 and is always at one end of the 3-point response scale; the intermediate and opposite responses are given weights of 1 and 0, respectively.

Approximately 300 companies are said to be cooperating to supply a minimum of 200 cases in each of 24 basic job areas. These studies will be used for converting raw scores to stanine scores, relating scores to merit ratings, and possibly (at some later date) developing job area scoring keys. Pending the completion of these studies, a table has been prepared, based "both on statistical evidence and on clinical judgment," which labels one or more stanine scores on the CPF as identifying, for each of the 24 job areas, the underqualified, minimum qualified, well qualified, and best qualified. Extreme CPF stanine scores (9, 1, and 2) are not credited with identifying the "best qualified" for any job. No one of the 24 basic job areas is recognized by the test authors as yielding less predictive validity than any other.

The optimal score on CPF for performance on each job is recommended, without sufficient indication as to the kind of evidence leading to the recommendation. Neither is the level of validity indicated for any of the jobs.

The present content of this test and the contemplated further development of it, as described in the accompanying literature, constitute a step in the direction of recognizing that pure factors identified in the absence of job performance measures are seldom of interest to personnel departments. It has been a short step, however, and those who value knowing what they are measuring factorwise over predicting job criteria are the most likely to be satisfied with the present test and norms.

S. B. SELLS, *Professor of Psychology, Texas Christian University, Fort Worth, Texas.*

This streamlined, 40-item, three-choice format, factored personality questionnaire is one of several special purpose tests for clinical and industrial application described by Cattell in his latest book summarizing a monumental research program on the structure and measurement of personality and motivation (*1*). The overall program has been summarized and analyzed critically by this reviewer elsewhere.[1]

The term "contact personality factor" is a nontechnical name for Cattell's second order questionnaire factor of extraversion-introversion which is assumed by the test authors to provide a basis for accurate measurement of the needs of people for contact with other people in their work. For example, the authors' confidential manual on interpretation of the CPF describes a person with the highest stanine score of 9 as follows:

This employee needs a job assignment which is completely contact. His duties should stress continuous association with people, and 95 per cent or more of his time should be spent in contact work. He has more contact personality than 19 out of every 20 adults. He is overly enthusiastic, talkative, expressive, participating, assertive, adventurous, uninhibited in emotional response. This employee would be definitely maladjusted in a non-contact job. Due to his very high extraversion, the 9-employee may lack emotional balance.

At the other extreme, the person with the lowest stanine score of 1 is described as showing:

extreme withdrawal and self-sufficiency. He is happy to work things and ideas, with no sense of deprivation if he has no contacts at all. Such an employee would show such characteristics as being inaccessible, hard to understand, and cantankerous. He will tend to be melancholic, cold, stiff, depressed, withdrawing, individualistic. He may be respected by other employees, if he maintains his emotional stability and character.

The confidential manual on the development of this test states that for some time there has been a need for "a shorter measure of personality to differentiate the contact versus the non-contact personality type in business and industry." The specific need for this test is attributed to the recognition, following the release of a personnel testing manual to 6,000 member associations by the United States Savings and Loan League in 1953, that "in savings associations the contact personality factor was of equal importance with aptitude in predicting

1 SELLS, S. B. "Review of *Personality and Motivation Structure and Measurement* by Raymond B. Cattell." *Am J Psychol* 71:620–8 S '58. *
SELLS, S. B. "Structured Measurement of Personality and Motivation: A Review of Contributions of Raymond B. Cattell." *J Clin Psychol* (in press)

job success." No evidence is presented or referenced in support of these sweeping assumptions or of the cookbook interpretations, norms, and job qualification standards presented for the using public. One wonders whether these were regarded as self-evident by the authors.

Each form of the test consists of 34 factored items from Cattell's pool of factor-analyzed personality test items, developed in conjunction with the 16 PF test, plus 6 "distortion" items which in combination provide a score representing the extent of favorable distortion of response by industrial examinees. All items are structured for response to variants of yes, in-between, or no. The 34 factored items represent markers from each of the primary questionnaire factors comprising the second order factor in Cattell's broader taxonomic research. These are: A—cyclothymia versus schizothymia (10 items), and E—dominance versus submission, F—surgency versus desurgency, H—adventurousness versus withdrawal, and Q_2—group identification versus self-sufficiency (6 items each). Each item is scored for only one factor and the total C (contact factor) score is the linear sum of the 34 items; these are uniformly weighted 2, 1, 0 in the positively loaded direction of the primary on the second order factor. The test format is simple and easy to handle. The tests are printed clearly on green, eye-ease paper and a simple overlay stencil is used to score both forms of this and the companion *IPAT Neurotic Personality Factor Test*.

The standardization of this test is yet to be done. The only research data presented are the factor loadings of the personality items on their respective primary factors; these are incorporated in the present test as by-products of the 16 PF research. The factor loadings (for all five factors) range from .14 to .57 with a median of .34 for Form A, and from .11 to .53 with a median of .28 for Form B. The larger representation of Factor A in the test structure reflects its greater loading in the secondary factor. Internal validity is claimed on the basis of these data; however, no quantitative estimate of internal validity for the composite of the two samples of 34 items each is reported. The implication seems to be that since these items are taken from the 16 PF, a test made up from them must have internal validity.

A reliability estimate is given for a sample of 125 otherwise undescribed cases, for whom the correlation between Forms A and B was .86.

No information is available on predictive, external validity and the only statement concerning the basis for the norms presented is that they are based on "the employed adult population." Validity studies are reported in progress in 300 companies in the United States and Canada, with minimum samples of 200 cases in each of 24 job areas. However, although this test was published in 1954, no data in support of its validity have yet emerged, to this writer's knowledge.

No clear-cut statement is presented concerning the reliability and validity of the distortion scale and no attempt has apparently been made to incorporate it quantitatively into the personality measure as a "correction." Neither the small number of items nor the account of their development inspires confidence in the distortion index. Although the importance of test taking attitudes in selection and other employment testing is recognized by the authors, provision for them here appears more as a gesture than as a competent correction scale. The manual needs an adequate demonstration of the validity of the contact personality score, under the various employment conditions for which the test is designed, in which a correction for hypothesized distortion is included.

On the basis of information available it appears that the CPF test is a preliminary draft, implementing an idea about its possible use, which requires the full research treatment of any new test. Unfortunately, it is being made available to the public (personnel administrators and guidance counselors) with norms, interpretation and employment qualification guides, and a pretence of extensive research which cannot be defended. The relation of the second order factor of introversion-extraversion to various job requirements is an important and valid research problem. Whether the present streamlined (possibly too abbreviated) test measures this factor adequately and whether either the factor or this measure of it has any relevance to job success should have been determined before the test was offered for sale to users. Its use by research workers, in industry particularly, is presently of greater importance.

[72]

★IPAT High School Personality Questionnaire. Ages 12-18; 1953-58; formerly called *The Junior Personality Quiz;* title on test is H.S.P.Q.; 14 scores: schizothymia vs. cyclothymia, mental defect vs. general intelligence, general neuroticism vs. ego strength, phlegmatic temperament vs. excitability, submissiveness vs.

dominance, desurgency vs. surgency, lack of rigid internal standards vs. super ego strength, threctia vs. parmia, harria vs. premsia, dynamic simplicity vs. neurasthenic self-critical tendency, confident adequacy vs. guilt proneness, group dependency vs. self-sufficiency, poor self sentiment formation vs. high strength of self sentiment, low ergic tension vs. high ergic tension; Forms A, B ('58); mimeographed supplement ['58]; separate answer sheets must be used; $4 per 25 tests; $1.90 per 50 answer sheets; 60¢ per set of scoring stencils; $2.20 per manual ('58); $3.10 per specimen set; postage extra; (40) minutes; R. B. Cattell, H. Beloff, and R. W. Coan; Institute for Personality and Ability Testing. *

REFERENCES

1. CATTELL, RAYMOND B., AND BELOFF, HALLA. "Research Origin and Construction of the I.P.A.T. Junior Personality Quiz." J Consult Psychol 17:436–42 D '53. * (PA 28:7514)
2. CATTELL, RAYMOND B.; BLEWETT, DUNCAN B.; AND BELOFF, JOHN R. "The Inheritance of Personality: A Multiple Variance Analysis Determination of Approximate Nature-Nurture Ratios for Primary Personality Factors in Q-Data." Am J Human Genetics 7:122–46 Je '55. * (PA 30:2451)
3. CATTELL, RAYMOND B., AND GRUEN, WALTER. "Primary Personality Factors in the Questionnaire Medium for Children Eleven to Fourteen Years Old." Ed & Psychol Meas 14:50–76 sp '54. *
4. CATTELL, RAYMOND B. Personality and Motivation Structure and Measurement. Yonkers, N.Y.: World Book Co., 1957. Pp. xxv, 948. *

[73]

★IPAT Music Preference Test of Personality. Ages 6 and over; 1952–53; 11 scores of which the following 8 are profiled: adjustment vs. frustrated emotionality, hypomanic self-centeredness vs. self-distrust and doubt, tough sociability vs. tenderminded individuality, introspectiveness vs. social contact, anxiety and concern vs. paranoid imperiousness, complex eccentricity vs. stability normality, resilience vs. withdrawn schizothymia, schizothyme tenacity vs. relaxed cyclothymia; Forms A, B (on one record); adult norms only; $13.50 per LP microgroove 12-inch record (33⅓ rpm), 100 answer sheets ('53), scoring stencil, and manual ['52]; $1.80 per 50 answer sheets; $1.60 per specimen set without record; cash orders postpaid; (25–30), (30–35) minutes for Forms A, B; Raymond B. Cattell and Jean C. Anderson; Institute for Personality and Ability Testing. *

REFERENCES

1. CATTELL, RAYMOND B., AND ANDERSON, JEAN C. "The Measurement of Personality and Behavior Disorders by the I.P.A.T. Music Preference Test." J Appl Psychol 37:446–54 D '53. * (PA 29:912)
2. CATTELL, RAYMOND B., AND SAUNDERS, DAVID R. "Musical Preferences and Personality Diagnosis: I, A Factorization of One Hundred and Twenty Themes." J Social Psychol 39:3–24 F '54. * (PA 28:8495)
3. CATTELL, RAYMOND B. Personality and Motivation Structure and Measurement. Yonkers, N.Y.: World Book Co., 1957. Pp. xxv, 948. *
4. COROSO, JOAN. Relationship Between the IPAT Music Preference Test of Personality and E, S, and T Scores on the Guilford-Zimmerman Temperament Survey. Master's thesis, College of New Rochelle (New Rochelle, N.Y.), 1958.

NEIL J. VAN STEENBERG, Research Psychologist, Personnel Research Branch, Personnel Research and Procedures Division, The Adjutant General's Office, Department of the Army, Washington, D.C.

This test is designed to measure various personality traits by the scores obtained from recorded reactions ("like," "indifferent," or "dislike") of subjects to musical selection items presented on a gramophone record. There are, in all, 100 such items, each consisting of a 15- to 20-second piano rendition of a musical composition, with 50 items on each side of the record. The test is suitable for group administration. All necessary instructions for the subjects, including those for marking the answer sheet, are given audibly on the A side of the record. (If the B side is not played directly after the A side, it is necessary to play the instructions and fore-exercise from the A side, then stop and reverse the record). Apart from the 3-minute time of instruction, Form A (i.e., the 50 items on the A side) takes about 24 minutes, Form B about 27 minutes.

Overlay keys are furnished with the test. With the use of these, scores are obtained on 11 factors. Maximum raw scores vary from 12 to 24 (combined score of A and B forms). Some items are negatively weighted and thereby purify the factor measured. The raw scores are changed to standardized ones by the use of tables furnished in the manual. Norms are given for Form A separately and for Forms A and B taken together. Separate norms are given for men and women; minor adjustments are made for age on some factors. These standardized scores are then interpreted in terms of seven or eight of the factors. The three or four additional factors are not considered reliable enough for interpretation.

Beyond the references cited above, no mention has been found in the literature on the use of this instrument; this review must therefore be based entirely on a priori judgment of the available references and the test material itself.

The power of music to influence the mood of listeners has, of course, been recognized for centuries. That certain personality types should prefer a definite type of music is a new hypothesis assumed in this study. It will be necessary here to differentiate between what Thurstone has called temperament, that is, the stable enduring aspects of personality, and the ephemeral aspects such as attitudes, opinion, and moods. If mood, then, is defined as that which is influenced by music, the assumption implies that a certain type of mood is a permanent aspect of a definite personality trait. This assumption may be questioned. The authors (2) suggest that "factors other than enduring personality traits which might be responsible for consistent patterns are: the mood of subjects through events prior to listening; the stimulus situation; a special pattern of musical or general cultural level" (social status, age). There is little evidence for assuming any permanence of such a mood. The authors state that correlation of test-retest data on the 120 (the number of items used in this study) choices ranged from .36 to .75 with a mean of .54 when retesting was done after a lapse of 24 hours, .38 to .58 with a mean of .48 after a lapse of two months, and .33–.39 with a mean of .36 after a lapse of one year. The latter measurement is for two persons! This is indeed scant evidence of any permanence of preference. One might well ask if the same type of music would be preferred by the average individual at the breakfast table and in an easy chair after the day's worries were put aside. The differential degrees of musical sophistication must also be a factor to be considered.

Tetrachoric correlation coefficients were computed between the expressed preferences, and these coefficients in turn were divided into two matrices, one of 62 and the other of 80 items (20 items of the first matrix were included in the second as controls). Both matrices were then factor analyzed and 9 factors were extracted from one, 11 from the other. Next the reference vectors for the configurations were rotated toward simple structure (but not positive manifold). The final positions are almost orthogonal. An examination of the factor loadings on the rotated vectors reveals about as many negative as positive factor loadings and both of about the same magnitude. The factor loadings on the overlapping items show that the two configurations are very close to identical. Factors are then identified by the dual loadings of 19 of the overlapping items. Many of these loadings are less than what is commonly acceptable for these purposes but they do occur in two independently derived matrices. The identification of 9 factors in terms of 19 variables used for this purpose is also somewhat unorthodox. Some items are used in identification of as many as three of four factors. Two additional factors are extracted from the 80-item matrix. It is also worth noting that the numbers of 62 and 80 must be accepted with the understanding that many items contribute little or nothing toward determination of the structure. The 142 communalities vary between .07 and .94 with a median of .44 (seven lie between .10 and .19 and fourteen between .20 and .29). It would therefore appear that either many of the tetrachorics were so small as to make questionable

their suitability for the total superstructure erected, or the factors account for only a relatively small proportion of the covariances.

With reference to the use of this test to discriminate between normal and abnormal subjects, and among various types of abnormalities, the authors seem to have established a valid procedure. This raises a point of whether in such cases the abnormal individuals may be said to suffer from a "frozen" mood enabling interpretation of the factor to be based, at least in part, on these extreme values.

The testing instrument could have been improved considerably by the use of a clean tape. Side A in particular suffers from leakage of incompletely erased sounds. A tape record might also serve better.

If further research in this field is to be undertaken, the following ideas might be suggested for consideration: (a) Some question might be raised about the medium. All selections are recorded from the piano playing of a single individual. It is too much to expect that such an individual will perform equally well on all kinds of music. In the present case, the rendition of classical music is uniformly good, sometimes even superb. The modern music items do not appear up to the same standards. If the music is to be confined to piano renditions (the authors state that this medium is chosen to control other factors), could not several pianists be employed? (b) The point of confining the music to that from a piano in order to control preference for a particular instrument does not appear to be well taken. If the items were played in the instrumentation for which they were originally intended, even more reliable results should be obtained. The music could be dubbed in from existing records. Some compositions do tend to "fall flat" when played on the piano (e.g., "Prelude to Tristan and Isolde"), and the listener, if he knows the original, might be puzzled over how to mark his answer. He might answer "I dislike this," meaning the rendition, or he might remember the strings and answer "I like this," meaning the composition as he remembers it. (c) There is, finally, a question whether the abrupt endings of the various selections lead to better results than would a gradual fade out.

In summary, it might be noted that this test (at least as one of the tests at a session) is of very high interest value to the listeners, that it is exploring a new field, and that it represents a good beginning. The test should serve as a basis for further critical research on personality and its anomalies, but, at its present stage of development, the results obtained from it should be interpreted with the utmost caution.

[74]

★IPAT Neurotic Personality Factor Test. Grades 8–16 and adults; 1955; title on test is N.P.F.; 2 scores: neuroticism, distortion; 1 form ('55); mimeographed manual ['55]; adult norms ['55] only; 20¢ per test (10¢ to educational institutions); $2 per specimen set (must be purchased to get manual); cash orders postpaid; (10–15) minutes; R. B. Cattell, J. E. King, and A. K. Schuettler; published jointly by Institute for Personality and Ability Testing and Industrial Psychology, Inc. *

S. B. SELLS, *Professor of Psychology, Texas Christian University, Fort Worth, Texas.*

This is a companion test to the *Contact Personality Factor Test* in Cattell's series of personality tests for clinical and industrial application. Its purpose is to provide business and industry with "a short, but scientifically sound, test of neurotic versus stable personality in employees." By sampling marked items representing six primary personality factors which Cattell has included in the 16 PF test and which his research has shown to be related to neuroticism, the validity of the present 34-item NPF scale is assumed to be demonstrated. The six factors are: C—mature versus emotional, G—conscientious versus changeable, I—tough-minded versus sensitive, N—realistic versus sentimental, O—confident versus insecure, and Q—steady and relaxed versus tense and overanxious.

The confidential bulletins which make up the manual for this test present even less information than those for the CPF; item factor loadings have been omitted and no reliability correlations are reported. All of the critical comments incorporated for the CPF apply equally to this test. It is brief; but whether this streamlined test is an adequate measure of the neurotic versus stability factor and whether either the factor or this measure of it has any relevance to job success is still a research problem which should have been investigated by the authors before the test was offered for sale to industrial users.

WILLIAM STEPHENSON, *Consulting Psychologist, 20 Brookside Drive, Greenwich, Connecticut.*

This questionnaire is an application of Cattell's factor system of personality evaluation. Its two pages (of a 4-page folder) contain 40

questions with "yes," "no," and middle answers. The language of the questions, we are told, is that of the daily newspaper. The test is given without a time limit, and purportedly takes about 5 minutes to complete—10 or 15 minutes would perhaps be a better guess.

Thirty-four of the 40 questions cover 6 of the 16 factors which Cattell relates to neurotic versus stable personality tendencies. The other six items are an innovation: they are called "distortion" questions, and are a built-in effort to determine whether the subject is distorting his responses to give a favorable impression. Maximum score for distortion suggests that high scores on the NPF should be "definitely questioned."

The questionnaire was designed to spot neurotic and maladjusted employees, as well as to select individuals of high stability and (sense of) responsibility. It is suggested in the confidential notes going with the instructions, that "even when neurotic employees do not actually make trouble, their presence considerably lowers the morale and productivity of the group." Nothing is said about what might be done with such unfortunates, but a number of companies in the United States and Canada are cooperating with Cattell and his associates in validating the questionnaire on samples of not less than 200 each for 24 job areas.

To this reviewer the questionnaire legitimately follows the factorial system of personality appraisal. For some practical purposes, if 10 minutes is about all the time that can be made available for personality assessment, it might be very difficult to find anything better than this, in principle, and granted everything works according to plan. Granted the premises, the questionnaire makes use of the best available knowledge and technology, and the "distortion" probe is particularly interesting.

Unhappily, though, the man who gains the highest score for stability also gains the highest for "distortion." Moreover, though the authors caution against the tentative nature of the "distortion" probe, there are reasons to suppose that it, rather than the NPF, is on the "right line." The reasons are as follows.

It is noted by the authors that a "goodly number of the relations between N.P.F. and job efficiency are curvilinear (middle score is most desirable), rather than linear (high score is most desirable)." This is what we should expect if the highest scorers on the NPF are indeed the biggest self-deceivers; or, at least, if their supposed stability is a pose of defensive conformity.

Again, one should consider the highest scoring person on the NPF, as interpreted by Cattell and his associates, in terms of the answers with which he gains his high score. According to the interpretation, he is "an employee of outstanding emotional stability, responsibility, and resistance to stress." He will "tend to view situations with great objectivity and realism, to be highly dependable, and to show great reserves against nervous exhaustion and stress." His answers to questions show him to be interested in baseball, wrestling, bullfights, and poker (a hard game of cards) rather than in dancing or art galleries. He never gets tense or anxious at train time, and hardly ever gets annoyed at unnecessary waiting for people. He takes the untidiness of people as "all in the day's work," and never gets irritated by rules and regulations which, in calmer moments, he knows are right. He practically never thinks that a lot of work around him is pretty poor; nor does he ever "get worked up" on hearing people say unpleasant things about him. Yet, of course, he insists on getting his way! At least, if he is responsible for a group project, he "insists on having his own way in any dispute in the group, or else he resigns." Mercifully (or else the scoring key is in error) he has several times "come near to fainting at a sudden pain or the sight of blood." It seems to this psychologist that any man acceding to the above list of virtues is either very dull or else of little discernment; and if these qualities add up to stability, then the less of this kind of stability there is in the leadership of men, or in responsible positions, the better for industry.

But facts will tell. The curvilinear relationships restore this reviewer's faith in the essential verities. It is easy enough, of course, for the questionnaire to pick up the grossly timid, the frightened, or the alarmed, at the neurotic end of the NPF scale.

Because of his known prejudices, this reviewer leans heavily backwards to do justice to a questionnaire of this kind. It is hard, however, in face of a contradiction of the above order, to believe that this particular test has achieved what it set out to do. Revision of norms and interpretation may bring about adjustment, but the necessity for this raises some question concerning the soundness of a theory that lends itself so readily to distortions of this order.

[75]

★Institute of Child Study Security Test. Grades 4–8; 1957; title on test is *The Story of Jimmy*; 2 scores: consistency, security; Elementary Form; reliability data for grade 5 only; tentative norms; $3.75 per 25 tests; 90¢ per specimen set; postage extra; (20–25) minutes; Michael F. Grapko; distributed by Guidance Centre. ★

LAURANCE F. SHAFFER, *Professor of Education, Teachers College, Columbia University, New York, New York.*

The *Institute of Child Study Security Test* is a verbal method, based on the assumption of projection, which seeks to disclose a child's degree of security, the levels of behavior by which he maintains it, and his consistency in the use of these levels. The child reads "The Story of Jimmy," which is interrupted 15 times by a need to make a decision. At each of these points, the child ranks five statements which are designed to illustrate "independent security," "mature dependent security," "immature dependent security," "deputy agent" (equivalent to the use of various defense mechanisms), and "insecurity."

The teacher or psychologist interprets the child's performance by means of a conveniently designed scoring form. The security score is a measure, ranging from 0 to 100, of the degree to which the child's ranking of the items agrees with an "ideal" order. The consistency score measures the degree of uniformity the child shows in giving the same rank to the 15 statements for each of the five security categories. The latter is calculated by means of Kendall's coefficient of concordance, W, but the ingenious worksheet removes all terrors of statistics. Any teacher who can enter grades in a classbook can score this test.

How good is the test? Its author tries to tell his readers candidly. Retest reliability after two months is satisfactory for grade 5 (.91 for security and .85 for consistency scores). There are no data for the other grades. Data relevant to validity are not strong, but some are given—a rare and praiseworthy exception among new projective methods. Judges show good agreement with the selection of the items as illustrative of the types of behavior specified. There is some increase in "independent security" and some decrease in inferior choices with increasing age. In grades 4 and 5, both the security and consistency scores show reasonable correlations (.20 to .50) with teacher ratings of pupil adjustment, but the correlations are mainly insignificant for grades 6 to 8. The author reasons that the younger child is more naive, while the older one "resists a spontaneous identification (or 'projection') with the child in the story, or attains a sophistication in understanding the intention of the test items." Probably so.

Percentile norms, properly called tentative, are given for boys and girls and for grades 4–5 and 6–8. Girls in grades 4–5 are more consistent than boys, but not more secure. The sexes differ significantly in both scores in the higher grades.

The data reveal some perplexities and some further problems. The security and consistency scores are logically quite separate, but they correlate .87, as high as the reliability of either. Why? The child in the story is a boy, and the projective hypothesis is thereby made hazardous for girl subjects. But the author does not discuss the validity of the method for boys and for girls separately.

In spite of these shortcomings, the *Institute of Child Study Security Test* clearly demands consideration, at least as an instrument for children 10 to 11 years old. It has more evident merit than many better known tests, and deserves further development.

[76]

Interaction Chronograph. All ages; 1944–57; device for recording interaction between 2 individuals; used in a standardized interview to obtain ratings on 29 personality characteristics; 1 form ['47]; hectographed manual ('56); profile ['57]; no data on reliability; price information and sales arrangements for renting test materials available from publisher; no charge for manual; postage extra; [35–55] minutes; Eliot D. Chapple; E. D. Chapple Co., Inc. *

REFERENCES

1–5. See 3:688.
6. CHAPPLE, ELIOT D. "Quantitative Analysis of the Interaction of Individuals." *Proc Nat Acad Sci* 25:58–67 F '39. * (PA 13:3770)
7. CHAPPLE, ELIOT D. "'Personality' Differences as Described by Invariant Properties of Individuals in Interaction." *Proc Nat Acad Sci* 26:10–6 Ja '40. * (PA 14:2470)
8. CHAPPLE, ELIOT D.; with the collaboration of CONRAD M. ARENSBERG. "Measuring Human Relations: An Introduction to the Study of the Interaction of Individuals." *Genetic Psychol Monogr* 22:3–147 F '40. * (PA 14:3069)
9. CHAPPLE, ELIOT D. "Applied Problems in Industry." *Appl Anthrop* 1:2–9 O–D '41. *
10. CHAPPLE, E. D., AND LINDEMANN, ERICH. "Clinical Implications of Measurements of Interaction Rates in Psychiatric Interviews." *Appl Anthrop* 1:1–11 Ja–Mr '42. * (PA 17:1982)
11. FINESINGER, JACOB E.; LINDEMANN, ERICH; BRAZIER, MARY A. B.; AND CHAPPLE, ELIOT D. "The Effect of Anoxia as Measured by the Electroencephalogram and the Interaction Chronogram on Psychoneurotic Patients." *Am J Psychiatry* 103:738–47 My '47. * (PA 22:1813)
12. "Machine Helps Interview Job Applicants." *Ind Relations* 5:31 Mr '48. *
13. CHAPPLE, ELIOT D. "The Interaction Chronograph: Its Evolution and Present Application." *Personnel* 25:295–307 Ja '49. * (PA 24:177)
14. SHARP, L. HAROLD, AND HOUSTON, THOMAS J. "Relationship Between Check-List and Machine Recordings of the Interaction Chronograph Interview." Abstract. *Am Psychol* 5:332 Jl '50. *
15. GOLDMAN-EISLER, FRIEDA. "The Measurement of Time Sequences in Conversational Behaviour." *Brit J Psychol, Gen Sect* 42:355–62 N '51. * (PA 26:5548)
16. GOLDMAN-EISLER, FRIEDA. "Individual Differences Between Interviewers and Their Effect on Interviewees' Conversational Behavior." *J Mental Sci* 98:660–70 O '52. * (PA 27:5844)
17. CHAPPLE, ELIOT D. "The Standard Experimental (Stress) Interview as Used in Interaction Chronograph Investigations." *Human Org* 12:23–32 su '53. * (PA 29:5503)
18. GOLDMAN-EISLER, F. "A Study of Individual Differences and of Interaction in the Behaviour of Some Aspects of Language in Interviews." *J Mental Sci* 100:177–97 Ja '54. *
19. SASLOW, GEORGE; MATARAZZO, JOSEPH D.; AND GUZE, SAMUEL B. "The Stability of Interaction Chronograph Patterns in Psychiatric Interviews." *J Consult Psychol* 19:417–30 D '55. * (PA 30:7176)
20. MATARAZZO, JOSEPH D.; SASLOW, GEORGE; AND GUZE, SAMUEL B. "Stability of Interaction Patterns During Interviews: A Replication." *J Consult Psychol* 20:267–74 Ag '56. *
21. MATARAZZO, JOSEPH D.; SASLOW, GEORGE; AND MATARAZZO, RUTH G. "The Interaction Chronograph as an Instrument for Objective Measurement of Interaction Patterns During Interviews." *J Psychol* 41:347–67 Ap '56. * (PA 31:4662)
22. SASLOW, GEORGE; GOODRICH, D. W.; AND STEIN, MARVIN. "Study of Therapist Behavior in Diagnostic Interviews by Means of the Interaction Chronograph." *J Clin Psychol* 12:133–9 Ap '56. * (PA 31:4665)
23. PHILLIPS, JEANNE S.; MATARAZZO, JOSEPH D.; MATARAZZO, RUTH G.; AND SASLOW, GEORGE. "Observer Reliability of Interaction Patterns During Interviews." *J Consult Psychol* 21:269–75 Je '57.*
24. SASLOW, GEORGE; MATARAZZO, JOSEPH D.; PHILLIPS, JEANNE S.; AND MATARAZZO, RUTH G. "Test-Retest Stability of Interaction Patterns During Interviews Conducted One Week Apart." *J Abn & Social Psychol* 54:295–302 My '57. *
25. MATARAZZO, RUTH G.; MATARAZZO, JOSEPH D.; SASLOW, GEORGE; AND PHILLIPS, JEANNE S. "Psychological Test and Organismic Correlates of Interview Interaction Patterns." *J Abn & Social Psychol* 56:329–38 My '58. *

CECIL A. GIBB, *Professor of Psychology, Canberra University College, Canberra, Australia.*

Essentially the *Interaction Chronograph* is an ingenious computing device which permits an observer, operating two keys only to record, with 11 different clocks and counters, a great variety of data relating to time sequences in a conversation between two persons. Presumably it could be used for a larger group but operation would undoubtedly become very demanding. One key is depressed whenever individual A is acting, i.e., talking, nodding, gesturing or in other ways communicating with B, and the same is done for the other person.

The direct interaction chronograph variables in a conversation between A and B are: (*a*) A's units, a frequency count of the actions of A; (*b*) B's units, a frequency count of the actions of B; (*c*) Tempo, the duration of each action plus its following interaction; (*d*) Activity, a comparison measure of activity with silence; (*e*) A's adjustment, a count of the duration of A's interruptions of B minus the duration of A's failures to respond to B; (*f*) B's adjustment, a similar measure for B; (*g*) Initiative, a count, recorded only after a period of silence, added when A takes the initiative in breaking the silence and subtracted when B takes the initiative; (*h*) Dominance, a count of the frequency with which A outtalks or outacts B when there has been an interruption; (*i*) A's synchronization, a count of the number of times A interrupts B or fails to respond to B, i.e., fails to synchronize with B; and (j) B's synchronization, a similar count for B.

In a report on the reliability of these variables Saslow, Matarazzo, and Guze (*19*) say: "Some of these variables may seem unusually arbitrary, since they represent algebraic sums of two variables rather than individual measures of each of these variables. Apparently Chapple, in developing his interaction theory of personality, has found these derived variables more useful than the first order variables from which they were obtained." The "apparently" in this last sentence is a significant key to the state of validation data relating to this instrument. The 1956 manual does nothing to correct the deficiency. The manual is equally silent on the question of stability of interaction patterns or reliability. Goldman-Eisler (*15*) however, reports that she has "strong support for the hypothesis that certain relations of time sequences of action and silence in conversation tend to be constant within limits and characteristic of individuals independent of changing partners and topics." Saslow, Matarazzo, and Guze confirm the reliability of the variables, but find a flexibility of pattern in a standard psychiatric interview with different interviewers.

The *Interaction Chronograph,* as described in the 1956 manual, however, is much more than a research recording instrument. It is integrated with a standard stress interview (*17*) of the nondirective type to become a personality test. Under these conditions measures are derived from the record of variables printed out by the machine of nine "personality factors" and some twenty "temperament factors." Space forbids any detailed account of these factors. Since all follow the same pattern of very rash generalization and since none seem to have more than putative validity, a sample or two of the claims of the manual will suffice.

The initiative factor is measured directly by the initiative variable as described above. "This" says the manual, "is the 'drive' aspect of behavior for it is an indicator of the subject's willingness and ability to start action."

"The anxiety factor is determined by the drop in Activity and Tempo from the first period to very low values in the second [silence] period, and by the relative stability of the values of the periods thereafter." And of this factor it is said: "Although the presence of the Anxiety Factor is evidence of psychoneurosis, it occurs in many people who have various so-called neurotic symptoms associated with feelings of anxiety, who may not have overt anxiety attacks during the interview."

Apart from the extraordinary generality of these claims, with no validating evidence at all, sight seems to have been lost of the fact that this is action vis-à-vis an interviewer who is seen in the role of expert. If the action were between equals, the generalizations would be easier to accept, though they still would demand testing. As hypotheses these proposals would be reasonable in most instances, but as dogmatic assertions in a manual they must remain unacceptable. No indication is given even of correlation among the variables, though frequent assertions are made that imply that some might be taken together as cooperating factors.

The *Interaction Chronograph* seems to be a most ingenious device demanding research attention. A few isolated studies confirm the reliability of the measures. Very little is known of their validity for any purpose whatever. Publication of the manual in its present form is presumptuous.

[77]
Interaction Process Analysis. Groups of from 2–20 people (ages 4 and over) ; 1948–50; method of analyzing group character and processes; scoring form ['50] ; manual ('50, see *2*) out of print; the *Interaction Recorder,* an optional instrument which facilitates the recording of observations in sequence, is described in *2*; Robert F. Bales; Addison-Wesley Publishing Co., Inc. *

REFERENCES
1–3. See 4:56.
4. BALES, ROBERT F. "A Set of Categories for the Analysis of Small Group Interaction." *Am Sociol R* 15:257–63 Ap '50. * (*PA* 26:4733)
5. BUTLER, WILLIAM R. *A Study of Interaction Process Analysis in Problem-Solving Situations as Revealed by Ohio University Students in Human Relations Classes.* Master's thesis, Ohio University (Athens, Ohio), 1951.
6. BORGATTA, EDGAR F., AND BALES, ROBERT F. "The Consistency of Subject Behavior and the Reliability of Scoring in Interaction Process Analysis." *Am Sociol R* 18:566–9 O '53. *
7. HEINICKE, CHRISTOPH, AND BALES, ROBERT F. "Developmental Trends in the Structure of Small Groups." *Sociometry* 16:7–38 F '53. * (*PA* 28:692)
8. PARSONS, TALCOTT; BALES, ROBERT F.; AND SHILS, EDWARD A. *Working Papers in the Theory of Action.* Glencoe, Ill.: Free Press, 1953. Pp. 269. *
9. BALES, ROBERT F. "How People Interact in Conferences." *Scientific Am* 192:31–5 Mr '55. *
10. BALES, ROBERT F., AND BORGATTA, EDGAR F. "Size of Group as a Factor in the Interaction Profile," pp. 396–413. In *Small Groups: Studies in Social Interaction.* Edited by A. Paul Hare, Edgar F. Borgatta, and Robert F. Bales. New York: Alfred A. Knopf, Inc., 1955. Pp. xv, 666. *
11. BORGATTA, EDGAR F., AND BALES, ROBERT F. "Sociometric Status Patterns and Characteristics of Interactions." *J Social Psychol* 43:289–97 My '56. *
12. FINE, HAROLD J., AND ZIMET, CARL N. "A Quantitative Method of Scaling Communication and Interaction Process." *J Clin Psychol* 12:268–71 Jl '56. * (*PA* 31:5917)
13. BORGATTA, EDGAR F.; COTTRELL, LEONARD S., JR.; AND MANN, JOHN H. "The Spectrum of Individual Interaction Characteristics: An Inter-Dimensional Analysis." *Psychol Rep* 4:279–319 Je '58. *

CECIL A. GIBB, *Professor of Psychology, Canberra University College, Canberra, Australia.*

The *Interaction Recorder* is a mechanical device to provide a continuously and constantly moving paper tape, some 12 inches wide, on which a sequential record of group behavior may be kept by an observer who indicates the "who-to-whom" action in a small group by categories. These categories are the crucial feature of the Bales instrument.

There are 12 Bales categories, developed over a period of research from a starting list of 89 categories which were "gradually refined by experience and theoretical criticism." [1] Unfortunately, this is probably the least empirical of all Bales' researches. The data relevant to the refinement from 89 to 12 categories have not been made available in published form. What criticism there is of the Bales method is largely centered about this categorization. In *The Fourth Mental Measurements Yearbook,* Carter indicated that he had found these categories to be "not entirely appropriate for groups engaged in work on tasks requiring manipulation of material." This reviewer has had a similar experience, but it must be added that it may well be that the categories could be made appropriate by slight extension of the definitions and by an extended training of observers with this kind of group situation. Another criticism has been directed to the high proportion of all actions which fall in two categories: "gives opinion, evaluation, analysis, expresses feeling, wish"; and "gives orientation, information, repeats, clarifies, confirms." In general, a little more than half of all actions recorded are in these two categories (*10*). On the basis of the very full definitions given by Bales (*2*) and in view of the fact that each of these categories has several subcategories, one wonders if more useful results would be given if these two categories were subdivided. Some of the neat formality of Bales' set might be lost, but formality for its own sake is of little value.

Bales has at all times revealed an acute awareness of the need to demonstrate both between-observer reliability and self-self observer reliability. In the former case, correlations ranging from .75 to .95 depending upon the category are reported by Heinicke and Bales (*7*). It is reasonable to expect that self-self reliability will be at least as high as this, though direct testing of

the latter can be achieved only when complete reproductions of the situation—as in film—can be obtained. Borgatta and Bales (*6*), however, find self-self reliabilities for trained observers working from limited written protocols to range between .65 for Category 8 ("asks for opinion, evaluation, analysis, expression of feeling") and .98 for Category 1 ("shows solidarity, raises others status, gives help, reward"). With respect to reliability, the *Interaction Process Analysis,* used by trained observers, is quite adequate to its purposes.

As Carter pointed out in his earlier review, "the validity of the technique is self-evident since it allows the recording of immediately perceived behavior."

Finally, though this instrument has not been widely used outside the Harvard Laboratory, it has been used there by a number of people; and in judging it, one cannot overlook the valuable findings in group dynamics with which its use has been associated. Among these are Phase Movement in Groups (*8*), the effects of group size on the kind of social interaction among members (*10*), and consistency of subject behavior in groups (*6*).

Interaction Process Analysis presents a technique for recording and analyzing as much as possible of the social interaction among and between members of small groups. The wealth of data now obtained with the technique by Bales and his coworkers must recommend it to research workers in this area. The problems of extending the technique to larger "real life" groups are great and have not yet been faced, but they are by no means clearly insuperable.

For a review by Launor F. Carter, see 4:56; for related reviews, see 4:57.

[78]

An Inventory of Factors STDCR. Grades 9-16 and adults; 1934-46; 5 scores: social introversion-extraversion, thinking introversion-extraversion, depression, cycloid disposition, rhathymia; IBM; 1 form ('40); revised manual ['45]; mimeographed supplement ('46); $2.50 per 25 tests; 10¢ per single copy; separate answer sheets may be used; 3¢ per IBM answer sheet; 25¢ per scoring key; $2.50 per set of either hand or machine scoring stencils; 15¢ per manual; postage extra; (30) minutes; J. P. Guilford; Sheridan Supply Co. *

REFERENCES

1-10. See 3:55.
11-27. See 4:59.
28. BRUECKEL, JOYCE E. *A Comparison of the Three Guilford-Martin Personality Inventories With Self-Ratings and Student-Ratings.* Master's thesis, University of Colorado (Boulder, Colo.), 1948.
29. NEUMANN, THOMAS MICHAEL. *A Study of the Relation of Occupational Interests to Certain Aspects of Personality.*

1 BALES, ROBERT F. *Some Uniformities of Behavior in Small Groups.* Unpublished report, Laboratory of Social Relations, Harvard University (Cambridge, Mass.), 1952.

Master's thesis, Illinois State Normal University (Normal, Ill.), 1950.

30. GUILFORD, J. S. *The Relative Value of Fourteen Test Variables for Predicting Success in Executive and Supervisory Positions.* Master's thesis, University of Southern California (Los Angeles, Calif.), 1951.

31. MANZANO, ILUMINADO BILLARINIA. *The Relation of Personality Adjustment to Occupational Interests.* Doctor's thesis, University of Southern California (Los Angeles, Calif.), 1951.

32. BAEHR, MELANY E. "A Factorial Study of Temperament." *Psychometrika* 17:107–26 Mr '52. * *(PA* 27:1834)

33. BORG, WALTER R. "Personality Characteristics of a Group of College Art Students." *J Ed Psychol* 43:149–56 Mr '52. * *(PA* 27:3764)

34. CARROLL, JOHN B. "Ratings on Traits Measured by a Factored Personality Inventory." *J Abn & Social Psychol* 47:626–32 Jl '52. * *(PA* 27:3340)

35. COCKRUM, LOGAN V. "Personality Traits and Interests of Theological Students." *Relig Ed* 47:28–32 Ja–F '52. * *(PA* 26:4229)

36. GUILFORD, J. P. "When Not to Factor Analyze." *Psychol B* 49:26–37 Ja '52. * *(PA* 27:33)

37. GUILFORD, JOAN S. "Temperament Traits of Executives and Supervisors Measured by the Guilford Personality Inventories." *J Appl Psychol* 36:228–33 Ag '52. * *(PA* 27:3801)

38. MCKENNA, FRANK S. "An Analysis of Nine Personality Scales." Abstract. *Proc Ind Acad Sci* 62:294 '52. *

39. NEILEN, GORDON C. *A Study of the Cattell 16 PF Test by Comparison With the A. C. E. and Guilford-Martin Personality Battery.* Master's thesis, Kent State University (Kent, Ohio), 1952.

40. SHAMES, GEORGE HERBERT. *An Investigation of Prognosis and Evaluation in Speech Therapy.* Doctor's thesis, University of Pittsburgh (Pittsburgh, Pa.), 1952.

41. TOMEDY, FRANCIS JOSEPH. *The Relationship of Personality Characteristics to Measured Interests of Women Teachers of English, Social Science, Mathematics, and Physical Science in Certain Senior High Schools.* Doctor's thesis, New York University (New York, N.Y.), 1952. (Abstracts: *DA* 12:540, *Am Psychol* 7:384)

42. KORNREICH, MELVIN. "Variations in the Consistency of the Behavioral Meaning of Personality Test Scores." *Genetic Psychol Monogr* 47:73–138 F '53. * *(PA* 27:6535)

43. ROSENBERG, NATHAN; IZARD, CARROLL E.; AND HOLLANDER, E. P. "Middle Category ("?") Response: Reliability and Relationship to Personality and Intelligence Variables." Abstract. *Am Psychol* 8:425 Ag '53. *

44. STACEY, CHALMERS L., AND GOLDBERG, HERMAN D. "A Personality Study of Professional and Student Actors." *J Appl Psychol* 37:245 F '53. * *(PA* 28:1685)

45. GOCHE, L. N. *Relationship of Interests and Temperament Traits to Attrition and Survival of Engineering Students.* Master's thesis, Iowa State College (Ames, Iowa), 1954.

46. GUILFORD, J. P. "The Validation of an 'Indecision' Score for Prediction of Proficiency of Foremen." *J Appl Psychol* 38:224–6 Ag '54. * *(PA* 29:6369)

47. BORG, WALTER R. "The Effect of Personality and Contact Upon a Personality Stereotype." *J Ed Res* 49:289–94 D '55. * *(PA* 30:6911)

48. COOPER, MATTHEW NATHANIEL. *To Determine the Nature and Significance, If Any, of Certain Differences in the Social and Personal Adjustment of Fifty-One Successful and Fifty-One Non-Successful College Students at Texas Southern University.* Doctor's thesis, New York University (New York, N.Y.), 1955. *(DA* 16:497).

49. ROSENBERG, NATHAN; IZARD, CARROLL E.; AND HOLLANDER, E. P. "Middle Category Response: Reliability and Relationship to Personality and Intelligence Variables." *Ed & Psychol Meas* 15:281–90 au '55. * *(PA* 30:4592)

50. THURSTON, DONALD REID. *An Investigation of the Possibilities of Parole Prediction Through the Use of Five Personality Inventories.* Doctor's thesis, Michigan State University (East Lansing, Mich.), 1955. *(DA* 15:1206)

51. ZIMMERMAN, WAYNE S., AND GUILFORD, J. P. "The Guilford-Martin Inventories Reanalyzed." Abstract. *Am Psychol* 10:330 Ag '55. *

52. GUILFORD, J. P., AND ZIMMERMAN, WAYNE S. "Fourteen Dimensions of Temperament." *Psychol Monogr* 70(10):1–26 '56. * *(PA* 31:5789)

53. NELSON, MARVEN O., AND SHEA, SALLY. "MMPI Correlates of the Inventory of Factors STDCR." *Psychol Rep* 2:433–5 D '56. * *(PA* 31:4704)

54. SPILKA, BERNARD, AND STRUENING, E. L. "A Questionnaire Study of Personality and Ethnocentrism." *J Social Psychol* 44:65–71 Ag '56. *

55. COE, ROBERT STANFORD. *The Personality and Adjustment Characteristics of Females in Various Occupational Groups.* Doctor's thesis, University of Houston (Houston, Tex.), 1957. *(DA* 17:2309)

For a review by Hubert E. Brogden, see 4:59; for a review by H. J. Eysenck, see 3:55; for a related review, see 3:45.

---

[79]

*KD Proneness Scale and Check List. Grades 7–12, ages 7 and over; 1950–56; 1 form; revised manual ('53); supplement ('56, reprinted from 6 below); $3.70 per set of 35 scales and check lists; 75¢ per supplement; postage extra; 35¢ per specimen set, postpaid; William C. Kvaraceus; World Book Co. *

a) KD PRONENESS SCALE. Grades 7–12; also called *Delinquency Proneness Scale;* 1 form ('50); (15–25) minutes.

b) KD PRONENESS CHECK LIST. Ages 7 and over; ratings made by teachers; 1 form ('53); no data on reliability; norms for grades 5–8 only; [6–25] minutes.

REFERENCES

1. WRIGHT, MILDRED LACEY. *A Study of Juvenile Proneness Groups.* Master's thesis, Alabama Polytechnic Institute (Auburn, Ala.), 1952.
2. PATTERSON, CHARLES C. *The Relationship Between Pupil Citizenship as Rated by Teachers and Delinquent Tendencies as Shown by K.D. Proneness Scale and Check List Scores.* Master's thesis, Boston University (Boston, Mass.), 1953.
3. MCDONELL, ISABELLE. *A Study of the Validity of the K.D. Proneness Scale.* Master's thesis, Catholic University of America (Washington, D.C.), 1954.
4. BALOGH, JOSEPH K., AND RUMAGE, CHARLES J. *Juvenile Delinquency Proneness: A Study of the Kvaraceus Scale.* Washington, D.C.: Public Affairs Press, 1956. Pp. iv, 35. * *(PA* 31:3398)
5. KOVALCHIK, ROBERT J. *A Study of the Use of the K.D. Proneness Scale in a Counseling Program.* Master's thesis, Catholic University of America (Washington, D.C.), 1956.
6. KVARACEUS, WILLIAM C. "Forecasting Juvenile Delinquency: Supplement to the Manual of Directions for KD Proneness Scale and Check List." *J Ed (Boston)* 138:1–43 Ap '56. *

JOHN W. M. ROTHNEY, *Professor of Education, University of Wisconsin, Madison, Wisconsin.*

The author suggests that various studies comparing delinquents and nondelinquents have identified specific traits or environmental features—such as truancy, immaturity, family mobility, school retardation, and family relationships—that tend to characterize boys and girls who are "exposed to the disease of delinquency." The *KD Proneness Scale* is said to use these predictive signs to identify the delinquent as early as possible. The *KD Proneness Check List* is provided as an aid in the process. Both instruments are said to be useful supplements for persons who find it necessary to identify youth who are especially vulnerable to the development of delinquent behavior.

The scale consists of 75 multiple choice items in the form of incomplete statements. Asserting that one can have more fun around midnight than in the morning or afternoon; that watching a prize fight is preferable to watching baseball, basketball and horse racing; and that going to college is a waste of time and money adds to one's plus score (delinquency proneness). A "minus score," reflecting the opposite, is obtained by indicating that failure usually results from lack of hard work; that going to high school is necessary for success; that going to a concert is preferable to going to a dance, movie, or bowling alley; and that most policemen try to help, rather than scare, boss, or get something on you. The total score is the difference between plus and minus scores. Separate keys for boys and girls are offered. A visual check shows that many items are scored similarly for both sexes, although there seem to be more responses by which boys can indicate delinquency proneness or lack of it.

Many studies have compared scores made by students of "high morale" (those who are doing well scholastically and are good citizens in school), "average morale," and "low morale" students, random groups of high school pupils, and institutionalized delinquents. The differences reported between the average scores of the groups are usually significant but there is so much overlap in the distributions that one could not possibly use the scale for individual prognosis. Although a supplement to the manual is entitled "Forecasting Juvenile Delinquency," *no evidence of predictive validity is presented*. The author promises to report on predictive studies now being made. The scores correlate negatively with intelligence test scores and it is said that this finding "is in accordance with the frequently reported observation that delinquents, as a group, tend to have average IQ's of approximately 90." No further interpretation or comment follows the statement.

Stability studies made by administering the scale to 53 institutionalized girls twice within a six-week period and to 37 boys in an industrial school with a two-day interval produced coefficients of .75 and .71. A Spearman rank correlation coefficient obtained from scores of 24 boys in a summer camp obtained on two successive days was .81. The authors states that on the basis of these three coefficients the scale is "sufficiently reliable for use in spot-checking and survey purposes in the process of identifying those children who may be susceptible to the development of delinquent patterns of behavior." Since the subjects used in the studies are insufficiently described and few in number, the generalization is questionable. Certainly the coefficients suggest that use of the scale with individuals cannot be recommended.

The checklist consists of 70 statements such as, " 'runs' with a 'gang,' " "attends movies at least twice a week," "drunkenness in family," and "mother is employed outside the home." These are to be answered by an observer who

checks "yes," "no," or "?". Three studies involving 130 delinquent boys and 434 boys and girls in general school populations indicate that the delinquents are usually given more checks in the yes column. The results might have been anticipated in view of the fact that the delinquents had already been institutionalized. No evidence of use of the checklist with subjects whose delinquency records were not known to the rater is provided.

The author of this scale and checklist has written much and well on the subject of delinquency. The fact that he has produced two instruments which can be described only as crude survey devices of questionable stability and of unknown prognostic value attests to the difficulties involved in the use of instruments in which individuals are invited to indict themselves. The many problems in securing adequate uncontaminated information in the area of delinquency and dependable longitudinal data upon individuals who develop delinquent patterns of behavior have not been solved in the process of developing either the scale or the checklist. Persons who buy these instruments should be warned that there is little evidence that they indicate delinquency proneness of individuals who have not already been caught and sent to correctional institutions.

For reviews by Douglas Courtney and Dale B. Harris, see 4:64.

[80]

Kuder Preference Record—Personal. Grades 9-16 and adults; 1948-54; 6 scores: group activity, stable situations, working with ideas, avoiding conflict, directing others, verification; IBM; 1 form ('48); 2 editions; manual, fourth edition ('53); separate answer pads or answer sheets must be used; $9.80 per 20 tests; 60¢ per 20 profile sheets for adults ('52) or for children ('49); 90¢ per 20 profile leaflets for adults ('54) or for children ('53) for comparing vocational and personal scores; 75¢ per specimen set of either edition; postage extra; (40-45) minutes; G. Frederic Kuder; Science Research Associates. *
a) [HAND SCORING EDITION.] Form AH ('48); $2.35 per 20 answer pads.
b) [MACHINE SCORING EDITION.] IBM; Form AM ('48); $5 per 100 IBM answer sheets; $4 per set of scoring stencils.

REFERENCES

1-4. See 4:65.
5. FJELD, HARRIETT A. "A Comparison of Major Groups of College Women on the Kuder Preference Record—Personal." *Ed & Psychol Meas* 12:664-8 w '52. * (PA 27:6755)
6. WARDLOW, MARY E., AND GREENE, JAMES E. "An Exploratory Sociometric Study of Peer Status Among Adolescent Girls." *Sociometry* 15:311-8 Ag-N '52. * (PA 27:7097)
7. ISCOE, IRA, AND LUCIER, OMER. "A Comparison of the Revised Allport-Vernon Scale of Values (1951) and the Kuder Preference Record (Personal)." *J Appl Psychol* 37:195-6 Je '53. * (PA 28:3352)
8. MURRAY, L. E., AND BRUCE, MARTIN M. "Normative Data

Information Exchange, No. 10-2." *Personnel Psychol* 10:94–6 sp '57. *
9. SMITH, D. D. "Abilities and Interests: I, A Factorial Study." *Can J Psychol* 12:191–201 S '58. *

DWIGHT L. ARNOLD, *Professor of Education, Kent State University, Kent, Ohio.*

The Kuder-Personal deals with the important area between measurement of interests, which has proved valid and useful in vocational guidance, and measurement of personality, which has not yet proved valid in this field. Such an instrument would be useful if distinct differences in scores could be shown between different vocational groups and if the traits measured seemed to represent factors which could be identified and named.

Do the scales of the Kuder-Personal actually measure what the titles and explanations indicate? The method of developing the test is described in the manual. A survey of the literature on factorial analyses of personality and interest tests was made. From this survey a list of factors was assembled. Then seven scales, two of which were later abandoned, were selected, and items judged to be measures of pertinent factors were assembled for each scale. As far, then, as construction of the test is concerned, the validity of this instrument rests largely upon the judgment of the author that these items actually measure the interest patterns as named and explained.

The evidence presented in the manual does not support the belief that these five subtests measure traits or behavior patterns of sufficient stability and clarity to be very useful in individual counseling. Nor do these data support the assumption that the titles to these subtests are accurate and valid. This opinion is supported by the very low correlations reported between parts of the Kuder-Personal and similarly labeled parts of the *Thurstone Temperament Schedule*. The highest correlation, .57, is found between Part A, Preference for Being Active in Groups, and Part 4, Dominance, on the Thurstone schedule. The titles do not suggest a common factor. Likewise, Part E, Preference for Directing Others, correlates only .30 with Part 4 of the Thurstone test, a relationship which should be much higher if the titles really mean what they indicate.

Of 34 traits scored for Part A, 8 have to do with public speaking, 7 with prestige situations such as sitting next to an honored guest rather than with a well known friend, and 2 with enjoying being watched "while you work." It is difficult to figure out what these items actually measure, but it is very doubtful that we can say to the student that his response to these items indicates that he likes "working with people."

On the profile sheet is this statement about Part E: "Preference for directing others. High interest indicates that you like situations in which you can influence the thoughts and activities of other people. You like to be in a position of authority." All this can be found out about an individual by the way he responds to 38 groups of three items each! Of the 38 traits used for Part E, 26 involve terms indicating distinct prestige positions such as being President of the United States, an executive, a manager, or a judge. For a student to mark these may mean that he likes the symbols of prestige, or that he likes to say that he wants to be president; but to say to such a student that he likes "to be in a position of authority" goes entirely too far.

There is real danger with instruments such as the Kuder-Personal that the title of a part will be taken as a defined, accurately measured factor in planning and counseling, when it is not. To the person taking this test the title of a part easily becomes an important characteristic of his personality. Especially is this likely to be true in the early years of high school when students have not yet developed mature patterns of judgment. It is very doubtful whether this instrument should be used at all below the 11th or the 12th grade until more data are secured which relate the scores to actual behavior or choices in the earlier age group.

The greatest value of the Kuder-Personal lies in the fact that for several occupational groups significantly different scores are found on parts of the test. For engineers, lawyers, physicians and surgeons, public school superintendents, administrators, insurance salesmen, and factory foremen, the cases on which the scores are based number more than one hundred. Thus a counselor can say, "You have a score on Part A which is similar to the average score made by a group of over a hundred insurance salesmen." This is helpful. For other occupational groups the number of cases is so small as to make the data of doubtful value in individual counseling.

In summary, because of the weaknesses discussed above, the reviewer is of the opinion that the *Kuder Preference Record—Personal* is of only limited value. Counselors using it should guard carefully against overinterpretation.

[81]

★**Life Experience Inventory.** Ages 13 and over; 1957; 4 scores: childhood, social, emotional, total; 1 form; $3.50 per 25 tests; 50¢ per manual; 65¢ per specimen set; postpaid; (50–60) minutes; Gilbert L. Betts and Russell N. Cassel; distributed by C. A. Gregory Co. *

REFERENCE

1. CASSEL, RUSSELL N., AND BETTS, GILBERT L. "The Development and Validation of a *Life Experience Inventory* for the Identification of 'Delinquency Prone' Youth." Abstract. *Am Psychol* 11:366 Ag '56. *

DAN L. ADLER, *Professor of Psychology, San Francisco State College, San Francisco, California.*

The *Life Experience Inventory* purports to assess the delinquency-proneness of "youth" by sampling life experiences under the categories of Childhood and Early Family Experiences; Social, Recreational and Educational Experiences; and Personal Feelings. Such, at any rate, is the tenor of the concluding remarks and the examples to be found in the manual. Unfortunately, the introduction to this same manual implies that, in addition, the inventory will measure on an individual basis, the *sources* of accident-proneness, alcoholism, narcotic addiction, suicide, and adult untrustworthiness. It will serve, it is claimed, as "either a supplement or as a substitute for the Case History of an individual." It may, finally, "be used to formulate a preventive program—one exactly suited to local needs."

Since achieving the first-stated objective alone would constitute a sufficient *raison d'être,* the reviewer was interested naturally in the validity of the inventory. No less than five kinds of validity are presented: face validity, content validity, status validity, prediction validity, and construct validity. One would expect from this array of "evidence" that the achievement of the objective would be amply and convincingly demonstrated. In truth, there is an indication of suggestive relationship between scores on the inventory and the status of delinquent and "typical" groups. However, there is no evidence (despite a 10-year period of "research and development") that the inventory actually pre-selects delinquency-prone youngsters. There is certainly no evidence presented which links inventory scores to other nonsocial behaviors.

The standardization information also leaves much to be desired. One has difficulty in finding appropriate normative tables amid the welter of criterion groups—each used for different "types" of validation and consisting in different sized or variously combined populations. One

should have misgivings about the (apparent) normative pooling of "in-prison airmen" with "delinquent youths" ranging upward from 13 years of age. One should also look askance at a group referred to only as "typical Latin youth" which contains a mixture (proportions unknown) of males and females, although sex-linked differences are clearly evident from other data and recognized specifically by the authors.

The usefulness of the inventory must surely lie within the frame of reference intended by the authors. Nevertheless, the manual gives no research definition of "delinquency," nor does it supply information about the nature of the delinquent acts represented in the populations used—either of which might give the potential user a referent for linking score values to behavior.

Finally, since the authors acknowledge the dangers of individual prediction from the inventory, it seems particularly inappropriate to emphasize the value of the device for "formulating preventive programs." No such program can be derived from the inventory, and one would not readily alter the environmental situation of an individual who *might* be delinquency-prone unless committed to the assumption that he is. This assumption cannot be justified by reference to the standardization data since, as the authors point out, cutting scores have not been shown to predict delinquency.

It does not appear reasonable, therefore, to put much faith in the inventory as a selector of delinquency-prone youth or untrustworthy adults unless one is interested in group investigations. In such cases, it might be worthwhile restandardizing the material on well defined populations with a view to eventually establishing pragmatic criteria of validity. In no case does it appear likely that the instrument will supplant the social case history.

DOUGLAS T. KENNY, *Associate Professor of Psychology, University of British Columbia, Vancouver, British Columbia, Canada.*

This inventory covers, in 150 four-choice items, what the authors believe to be the three areas of life experience which are causally related to delinquency. It is designed to identify adolescents who will become delinquents, to be used as either a supplement to or a substitute for the case history of an individual, and to be of value in screening out untrustworthy job applicants.

A critical incident study of the life experiences of 500 delinquents, drawn primarily from correctional institutions of three states, formed the basis for both the item content and the division of the scale into three parts. Fifteen hundred critical incidents were obtained and items were written "to incorporate proportionate numbers of items paralleling the number of critical incidents." The authors presume that such a procedure will produce a sampling of questions which are representative of those life experiences "which might conceivably be related to delinquency." Unless it may be assumed that delinquents from three states, supplemented by "smaller numbers" of military prisoners from 25 other states, have had life experiences similar to those of delinquents in other regions of the country and that few nondelinquents have had similar experiences, such a claim would be open to question.

The inventory is self-administering and has brief, clear instructions. However, the weighted scoring and the lack of a separate answer sheet makes it a time-consuming inventory to score. One wonders if the weighted scores could not have been validly replaced by unit weights.

Unfortunately, the four alternatives for every item are arranged so that alternative A is always the least socially desirable answer and D the most socially desirable, with alternative C more desirable than B. While such a sequence facilitates scoring, it probably means that most testees could spot the arrangement.

T scores and quality scores which indicate the degree of normality are provided for the three parts and the total. The T score norms are reported for typical individuals of mixed sex (n = 1,710), delinquent male youth and adults (n = 515), delinquent female youth (n = 260), and typical youth of Latin (sic) descent (150 of mixed sex). It is unfortunate that the manual does not provide descriptive information about these groups, such as geographic spread, age distribution, educational level, socioeconomic status, and nature of delinquencies. The combining of the sexes, the mixing of youths with adults, the failure to provide descriptive information mean that one cannot be sure that it would be meaningful to compare a given case with the normative groups.

The authors are to be commended for providing extensive data on reliability and the standard error of measurement for the part and total scores. While the reliability coefficients,

based on seven different groups, are not strikingly high, they are adequate. The odd-even reliability is of the order .82 for Part 1, .73 for Part 2, and .76 for both Part 3 and total score. In view of the size of the reliability coefficients and the substantial intercorrelations (ranging from .54 to .62) between the part scores, the manual might have cautioned users that most differences between part scores are not likely to be reliable.

Can this inventory pick out youths who will eventually become delinquents? While this would seem to be the crucial validity question for a delinquency scale, no data are presented to enable one to answer this question. Can this inventory discriminate between those in and out of correctional institutions? The manual presents quite a bit of data showing that it might be able to perform this function fairly well, having yielded an accuracy of correct classification of about 80 per cent for all cases. As the reviewer is convinced that the main purpose of a delinquency scale is to predict *who will become delinquent,* he is not overly impressed with data showing correlations between scores and the dichotomous criterion of in-out of prison.

While the manual states that the inventory can be used as a supplement or substitute for the case history and is useful in spotting adults who would be untrustworthy on a job, no data are presented to substantiate such ingenuous assertions. It is doubtful that this inventory would be useful in an employment situation because it is open to serious distortion.

While the inventory has face validity and much work has gone into its construction, it is not known whether it will identify a youth who will become a delinquent. Hence, the authors have not yet achieved what they set out to do, namely, to devise a predictive scale.

[82]

★The MACC Behavioral Adjustment Scale: An Objective Approach to the Evaluation of Behavioral Adjustment of Psychiatric Patients. Mental patients; 1957; 5 ratings: affect, cooperation, communication, total adjustment, motility; 1 form; mimeographed manual; $4 per 25 scales, postpaid; specimen set not available; [5–15] minutes; Robert B. Ellsworth; Western Psychological Services. ∗

MAURICE LORR, *Director, Neuropsychiatric Research Laboratory, Veterans Benefits Office, Washington, D.C.*

This scale purports to be a measure of levels of behavioral adjustment of hospitalized psychiatric patients. It consists of 14 five-point linear scales which yield four cluster scores— motility, affect, cooperation, and communication—and a total adjustment score. The total adjustment score is based on the last three cluster measures.

The scales included were selected by means of a comparison of drug-improved and drug-nonimproved groups. The selected items were submitted to two cluster analyses, which resulted in four relatively independent groups of scales. The number and types of patients compared are not stated in the manual. Only stability (test-retest) coefficients are offered as indices of reliability. The more important and essential inter-rater reliabilities for the clusters are not reported. It is reported that two raters correlate .86 on their total score ratings. Here, however, compensation for differences between raters on individual scales can increase the correlation.

The behavior clusters (except motility) and the total adjustment score are reported as discriminating significantly between closed and open ward patients. The amount of overlap and number of correct identifications are not reported.

The norms provided in the manual are based on all patients from one western hospital and a representative sample drawn from another. Unfortunately, such characteristics of the norms sample of 335 patients as age, sex, length of hospitalization, educational background, or severity of illness are left to the reader's imagination. The length of the observation period and the types of observers used are also left unspecified. The manual does indicate that the age range was wide and that a variety of diagnostic groups was sampled. The user is provided with a profile chart with centile ranks spaced to approximate an equal-interval sigma scale. However, since some of the distributions are positively skewed and others are negatively skewed, interpretation is clouded. Profile reliability is not reported.

The MACC scale is said to be unique in that nearly all personnel working with patients can complete the form. Further, it is contended that most other behavior scales do not measure clearly defined areas of behavior. Both of these assertions seem questionable. Nor is it demonstrated that different types of personnel can in fact apply the scale with equal reliability.

In summary, the MACC scale appears to be a promising device for the evaluation of behavioral adjustment in a limited number of areas. It compares favorably with the *Gardner Behavior Chart,* the Ward Section of the *Multidimensional Scales for Rating Psychiatric Patients,* and the *Northampton Activity Rating Scale.* Routine use of this scale is questionable in view of the limited normative data presented and the restricted validational information.

[83]

★McCleery Scale of Adolescent Development. Grades 9-12; 1955; 11 scores: peer relations, social role, physique acceptance, independence of adults, economic independence, occupational preference, family life, civic competence, social responsibility, ethical system, total maturity; IBM; 1 form ['55]; profile ['55]; separate answer sheets must be used; $3.50 per set of 25 tests; 50¢ per 25 IBM answer sheets; postage extra; specimen set not available; (30) minutes; Robert L. McCleery; University of Nebraska Press. *

REFERENCE

1. NELSON, SUZANNE. *Changes in the Solution of Adolescent Tasks by Eleventh Grade Boys During One Year and in Terms of Socio-Economic Status.* Doctor's thesis, University of Nebraska (Lincoln, Neb.), 1957. (*DA* 17:1952)

EUGENE L. GAIER, *Assistant Professor of Psychology, Louisiana State University, Baton Rouge, Louisiana.*

According to the author, this scale was constructed to enable comparison of the responses of the individual adolescent with those of mature and immature adolescents to items relating to the 10 developmental tasks described by Havighurst. In taking the scale, the subject checks 150 statements dealing with problems which "many young persons face" as being "important," "of little importance," or "of no importance" to him.

The norms supplied, based on responses of 316 high school boys, are limited both in number and meaning, though the manual indicates that "there is reason to believe that the norms.... presented will be representative of the responses of adolescents nationwide." This assumption is based on the fact that the performance of the mature group, drawn from a nationwide sampling of high school boys in attendance at the 1953 National Hi-Y Congress (n = 71), differed significantly from that of a randomly selected group of high school students in Nebraska (n = 235). From the limited discussion presented in the manual, one may conclude that the only thing "normative" about these data is the mean scores reported for each group. In selecting the two samples, the author apparently reasoned that leaders, as defined by election to office, are mature (ergo, have more successfully mastered the developmental tasks presented in the scale), and any other unselected group is immature. What, thus, emerges is that the norms indicate nothing more than the fact that the average leader is more "mature" as defined by the author than a more heterogeneous high school group.

The range of odd-even reliability coefficients for the parts varies from .60 to .99 (.75 to .99 when computed according to the Spearman-Brown formula). The author indicates that the reliability coefficients are "presumed adequate by criteria presently in wide acceptance." The presented coefficients have implied adequacy, and are offered as proof of the extent to which the scale "differentiates between mature....and immature boys." The odd-even and Spearman-Brown coefficients are apparently to be accepted as indicating the reliability of differences in scores. In the 1955 manual, the validity coefficients had not been completed, "since this is done by comparing a test with an established criterion. The lack of such standard is the primary reason for the origination of this scale." At best, one would have to be most skeptical to accept as justification for the lack of attempts at validation the author's implication that no other means exist for differentiating mature and immature adolescents than this scale.

The advantages of this scale are the ease of administration and scoring, but these features do not serve to offset the question of the real meaning of the scores after the profile has been constructed. The items are evidently also intended for use with adolescent girls (e.g., "Knowing what is expected of a husband or wife."), yet no norms have been established for women. Failure to take into account socioeconomic differences as well as area pressures for developmental skills further serves to depress the scale's usefulness.

After studying the scale, one can only ask the question, "So what?" If the subject, in making up his profile for the 10 task areas, falls below the presented standards for maturity, where do we go from there? The present reviewer feels that the test constructor, especially when constructing an instrument geared for an age range in which comparisons with age mates and differences in maturity rate are all-important, is under some obligation to tell how not to use the test and to indicate what implications and responsibilities hold for both the subject and the test administrator. Finally, the title appears misleading for the standardization procedure employed. The term *adolescence* is used in the title for a scale standardized with all levels of high school boys, yet adolescence may commence as early as age 11, which may be long before high school.

JOHN E. HORROCKS, *Professor of Psychology, The Ohio State University, Columbus, Ohio.*

This is a 150-item test yielding a whole score and 10 subscores. Each item requires the examinee to indicate whether, to him, the item represents a problem area of importance, of little importance, or of no importance. The test has been designed to provide a relative picture of a late teen-ager's "maturity" status based on his answers to items related to the "developmental tasks" discussed by Havighurst, Tryon, and others.

Persons who use the McCleery scale must be willing to accept the concept of "developmental tasks" as a useful means of describing a child's developmental status. They must further accept the premise that deviation from the "mature" criterion group selected by McCleery represents some kind of "immaturity." Many who work with adolescents would be unwilling to accept either the concept of "developmental tasks" or the premises provided by McCleery's criterion group of "mature" children. Even if one did accept the statement in the manual that "the person who may be called 'well-adjusted' is one who has attained a harmonious relationship between his own fundamental psychological needs and the cultural restrictions and requirements which impinge on him," it is difficult to see how the test items are able to provide an index to such a large picture. The 8-page manual does not tell how the items were arrived at, and, other than satisfactory subscore reliabilities and norms based on 316 high school boys, does not provide any statistical information. Norms are cited in terms of the mean scores of "mature" and "immature" boys on the whole test and on each of the 10 subscores. The profile sheet provided does not tell what deviation from the mean represents. It may be assumed from the profile that a high score represents deviation toward "immaturity," but it is not stated what deviation in the other direction represents. Such cursory citation of normative information is most unfortunate and represents a real defect of this scale. The normative group of 316 is inadequate and, in the opinion of this reviewer, can only provide a basis for meaningless information. No validity data are cited because, according to the author, of the lack of an established criterion. Criteria do exist and some attempt to provide various kinds of validity information should have been attempted.

Most unfortunate of all is the author's selection of a "mature" group. This consisted of 71 seventeen- and eighteen-year-olds who, as elected officers of a local Hi-Y or other organization, attended a 1953 National Hi-Y Congress. The members of such a group might possess interesting characteristics to distinguish them from other youth, but maturity might not be among those characteristics. It is not clear from the manual whether these youth were selected because they were at the convention or because they did well on the basis of a previously prepared "arm-chair" key to the test. The manual leaves nearly all the pertinent questions unanswered.

A number of the items are ambiguous to the point that a respondent might interpret an answer in either of two ways with a corresponding difference in his answer. Occasionally a loaded item appears, such as "getting *needed* experience" [reviewer's italics]. The test rephrases the same items from time to time and children may tend to grow uninterested in finishing it after they have completed about one third of the items.

The McCleery scale is an interesting attempt and the author might well continue to work on it, but it would appear that its publication was premature. In its present form, it yields information of dubious meaning and significance; a great deal of statistical information as well as adequate norms should be worked up. The title is misleading since the scale is presumably confined to boys. On the whole, the McCleery scale is representative of the too-numerous category of tests that find publication several years before they are ready. Under the circumstances, the unavailability of a sample set for the prospective user's examination before purchasing 25 sets is to be regretted.

[84]

★A Marriage Prediction Schedule. Adults; 1939–58; 1 form ['58]; reprinted from *Predicting Success or Failure in Marriage* (see *1* below); manual ['58]; no data on reliability and validity; $2.50 per 25 tests; 35¢ per specimen set; postage extra; (30–50) minutes; Ernest W. Burgess; Family Life Publications, Inc. *

REFERENCES
1. BURGESS, ERNEST W., AND COTTRELL, LEONARD S., JR. *Predicting Success or Failure in Marriage.* New York: Prentice-Hall, Inc., 1939. Pp. xxiii, 472. *
2. STROUP, ATTLEE L. *A Study of the Burgess-Cottrell System of Predicting Marital Success or Failure.* Doctor's thesis, Ohio State University (Columbus, Ohio), 1950.
3. FRUMKIN, R. M. *A Critical Analysis of the Kirkpatrick Scale of Family Interests as an Instrument for the Indirect Assessment of Marital Adjustment.* Master's thesis, Ohio State University (Columbus, Ohio), 1951.
4. KING, CHARLES E. *Factors Making for Success or Failure in Marriage Among 466 Negro Couples in a Southern City.* Doctor's thesis, University of Chicago (Chicago, Ill.), 1951.
5. SKIDMORE, REX A., AND MCPHEE, WILLIAM M. "The Comparative Use of the California Test of Personality and the Burgess-Cottrell-Wallin Schedule in Predicting Marital Adjustment." *Marriage & Family Living* 13:121–6 Ag '51. * (*PA* 26:2197)
6. KING, CHARLES E. "The Burgess-Cottrell Method of Measuring Marital Adjustment Applied to a Non-White Southern Urban Population." *Marriage & Family Living* 14:280–5 N '52. * (*PA* 27:5820)
7. FRUMKIN, ROBERT M. "The Kirkpatrick Scale of Family Interests as an Instrument for the Indirect Assessment of Marital Adjustment." *Marriage & Family Living* 15:35–7 F '53. * (*PA* 28:725)
8. FRUMKIN, ROBERT M. *Measurement of Marriage Adjustment.* Washington, D.C.: Public Affairs Press, 1954. Pp. ii, 13. Paper. * (*PA* 29:2358)

[85]

★Minnesota Counseling Inventory. High school; 1953–57; 9 scores: family relationships, social relationships, emotional stability, conformity, adjustment to reality, mood, leadership, validity, questions; IBM; 1 form ('53); profile ('57); manual ('57); no data on reliability of question score; separate answer sheets must be used; $3.50 per 25 tests; $3.60 per 50 IBM answer sheets; $1.90 per 50 Hankes answer sheets; 60¢ per set of hand scoring stencils and manual ('57); 90¢ per set of machine scoring stencils and manual; 75¢ per specimen set; postpaid; scoring service available; (50) minutes; Ralph F. Berdie and Wilbur L. Layton; Psychological Corporation. *

J Consult Psychol 22:241 Je '58. Laurance F. Shaffer. * The extensive data given in the Manual reveal both favorable and unfavorable features of the development of the Inventory. Both split-half and retest reliabilities are mainly satisfactory. * Standard score norms....are based on adequate methods and numbers. The manual's suggestions for interpretation are explicit and appropriately modest. One weakness is revealed by the data on validities and intercorrelations. Validities of entire scales are reported in terms of the CRs of differences between the scores of random samples of pupils and of extreme cases nominated by teachers and school administrators. There is no indication of item analysis against a criterion. Some scales, such as *SR,* differentiate well, but others, such as *R* (*Sc*), fail to do so. The tables of intercorrelations show that most *r*'s run from .35 to .60, but that the correlations between *SR* and *L,* and between *ES* and *R,* are as high as the scales' reliabilities. The authors might well have refined the scales further by item analysis, or at least might have warned users that the evidence points to five interpretable scores, not seven.

Even so, the Inventory is a serviceable instrument for counselors whose knowledge of test construction permits them to be aware of its limitations.

[86]

*Minnesota Multiphasic Personality Inventory, Revised Edition. Ages 16 and over; 1943–51; 14 scores: hypochondriasis (Hs, '43), depression (D, '43), hysteria (Hy, '43), psychopathic deviate (Pd, '43), masculinity and femininity (Mf, '43), paranoia (Pa, '43), psychathenia (Pt, '43), schizophrenia (Sc, '43), hypomania (Ma, '43), social (Si, '51), question (?, no key), lie (L, no key), validity (F, '43), test taking attitude (K, '46); IBM; 1 form; 2 editions (individual and group); $1.50 per manual ('51); postpaid; (30–90) minutes; Starke R. Hathaway and J. Charnley McKinley; Psychological Corporation. *

a) INDIVIDUAL FORM ("THE CARD SET"). 1943–51; $24 per set of testing materials ('43) including 50 record blanks ('43); $3 per 50 record blanks; $8.50 per set of manual and scoring stencils.

b) GROUP FORM ("THE BOOKLET FORM"). 1943–51; IBM; separate answer sheets must be used; $5.50 per 25 tests ('43); $3.60 per 50 sets of IBM answer sheet and case summary card ('43); $4.50 per set of manual and either hand or machine scoring stencils; $1.75 per specimen set without scoring stencils.

REFERENCES

1–72. See 3:60.
73–283. See 4:71.
284. BOLANDER, W. G. A Study of the MMPI as an Indicator in the Prediction of College Success. Master's thesis, University of Oregon (Eugene, Ore.), 1947.
285. ALBEE, GEORGE W. "Psychological Concomitants of Pulmonary Tuberculosis." Am R Tuberc 58:650–61 D '48. * (PA 25:492)
286. DALY, JULIETTE M. Relationship of MMPI and Kuder Preference Record Scores. Master's thesis, Catholic University of America (Washington, D.C.), 1948.
287. BENARICK, STANLEY JOHN, JR. An Investigation of the Schizophrenia Scale of the Minnesota Multiphasic Personality Inventory. Master's thesis, Pennsylvania State College (State College, Pa.), 1950.
288. CASNER, DANIEL. Certain Factors Associated With Success and Failure in Personal-Adjustment Counseling. Doctor's thesis, New York University (New York, N.Y.), 1950.
289. DE CILLIS, OLGA E., AND ORBISON, WILLIAM D. "A Comparison of the Terman-Miles M-F Test and the Mf Scale of the MMPI." J Appl Psychol 34:338–42 O '50. * (PA 26:294)
290. FASSETT, KATHERINE K. "Interest and Personality Measures of Veteran and Non-Veteran University Freshman Men." Ed & Psychol Meas 10:338–41 su '50. * (PA 25:6212)
291. HORLICK, REUBEN S. The Relationships of Psychometric Test Scores to Personality Disorders. Doctor's thesis, New York University (New York, N.Y.), 1950.
292. JOHNSON, RALPH H., AND BOND, GUY L. "Reading Ease of Commonly Used Tests." J Appl Psychol 34:319–24 O '50. * (PA 26:299)
293. MCALLISTER, CATHERINE ELIZABETH. A Study of Item Behavior in the Depression Scale of the Minnesota Multiphasic Personality Inventory. Master's thesis, Pennsylvania State College (State College, Pa.), 1950.
294. MITCHELL, WALTER M. An Analysis of the Relationship Between Performance on the MF Scale of the Minnesota Multiphasic Personality Inventory and the Strong Vocational Interest Blank for Men. Master's thesis, Montana State University (Missoula, Mont.), 1950.
295. MORGAN, CARL ELWOOD. Selected Curricular Choices and Personality Tendencies as Measured by the Minnesota Multiphasic Personality Inventory. Master's thesis, Kansas State College (Manhattan, Kan.), 1950.
296. PEMBERTON, W. H. Test Characteristics of Student Teachers Rated at the Extremes of Teaching Ability. Doctor's thesis, University of California (Berkeley, Calif.), 1950. (PA 26:4334)
297. ANDRULONIS, JEROME A. Relation Between Machover's Drawing of the Human Figure Test and Certain Variables on the Minnesota Multiphasic Personality Inventory. Master's thesis, Fordham University (New York, N.Y.), 1951.
298. BLAU, THEODORE H. Effects of High Intensity Sound on Certain Psychological Variables. Doctor's thesis, Pennsylvania State College (State College, Pa.), 1951.
299. BOTWINICK, JACK, AND MACHOVER, SOLOMON. "A Psychometric Examination of Latent Homosexuality in Alcoholism." Q J Studies Alcohol 12:268–72 Je '51. (PA 26:390)
300. CARPENTER, LEWIS G., JR.; FREEDMAN, MERVIN B.; HARRIS, ROBERT E.; AND SOKOLOW, MAURICE. "A Scale for the Measurement of Personality in Patients With Essential Hypertension." Abstract. Am Psychol 6:493 S '51. *
301. FELDMAN, MARVIN J. "A Prognostic Scale for Shock Therapy." Psychol Monogr 65(10):1–27 '51. * (PA 26:7028)
302. GALLAGHER, JAMES J. An Investigation Into Factors Differentiating College Students Who Discontinue Non-Directive Counseling From College Students Who Continue Counseling. Doctor's thesis, Pennsylvania State College (State College, Pa.), 1951.
303. GOINES, VALMORE R. Personality Characteristics of a Certain Ethnic Group. Doctor's thesis, Northwestern University (Evanston, Ill.), 1951.
304. GOULDING, CHARLES W. A Study of the Distribution of MMPI Profiles in a College Population. Master's thesis, University of Minnesota (Minneapolis, Minn.), 1951.
305. GROSSMAN, DONNA J. A Study of the Parents of Stuttering and Nonstuttering Children Using the MMPI and Minnesota Scale of Parents Opinion. Master's thesis, University of Wisconsin (Madison, Wis.), 1951.
306. HANSON, ANNA JEAN. An Analysis of "Drop Out" Students at Montana State University. Master's thesis, Montana State University (Missoula, Mont.), 1951.
307. HOLTZMAN, PAUL DOUGLAS. An Experimental Study of Some Relationships Among Several Indices of Stage Fright and Personality. Doctor's thesis, University of Southern California (Los Angeles, Calif.), 1951.
308. HUFFMAN, WARREN JUSTUS. Personality Variations Among Men Preparing to Teach Physical Education. Doctor's thesis, University of Illinois (Urbana, Ill.), 1951. (DA 12:28–9)
309. HUNT, FOLGER DEFOE. A Study of the Relationship of Personality Scores to Level of Achievement. Master's thesis, Ohio University (Athens, Ohio), 1951.
310. JOHN, WATKINS F. A Study of the Relationship Between the Clinical Variables of the Minnesota Multiphasic Personality Inventory and Major Field of Study of Ohio University Students. Master's thesis, Ohio University (Athens, Ohio), 1951.
311. MANZANO, ILUMINADO BILLARINIA. The Relation of Personality Adjustment to Occupational Interests. Doctor's thesis, University of Southern California (Los Angeles, Calif.), 1951.
312. MORGAN, HENRY HOLLINSHEAD. An Analysis of Certain Structured and Unstructured Test Results of Achieving and Nonachieving High Ability College Students. Doctor's thesis, University of Minnesota (Minneapolis, Minn.), 1951. (DA 12:335)
313. NAVRAN, L. A. A Rationally Derived Minnesota Multiphasic Personality Inventory Scale to Measure Dependence. Doctor's thesis, Stanford University (Stanford, Calif.), 1951.
314. REDLO, MIRIAM. MMPI Personality Patterns for Several Academic Major Groups. Master's thesis, University of New Mexico (Albuquerque, N.M.), 1951.
315. RUBIN, STANLEY B. A Scale of Morale in the Minnesota Multiphasic Personality Inventory. Master's thesis, University of California (Berkeley, Calif.), 1951.
316. TAFEJIAN, THOMAS T. "The E-F Scale, the MMPI and Gough's Pr Scale." Abstract. Am Psychol 6:501 S '51. *
317. WILLIAMS, HAROLD L. Differential Effects of Focal Brain Damage on the Minnesota Multiphasic Personality Inventory. Doctor's thesis, University of Minnesota (Minneapolis, Minn.), 1951. (DA 12:397)
318. WILLIAMS, JANET T. A Study of the Parents of Cerebral Palsied and Noncerebral Palsied Children Using the MMPI. Master's thesis, University of Wisconsin (Madison, Wis.), 1951.
319. ALTUS, WILLIAM D. "Personality Correlates of Q-L Variability on the ACE." J Consult Psychol 16:284–91 Ag '52. * (PA 27:4237)
320. BALIAN, LUCY J. The Performance of 80 Normal Subjects on a German Translation of the MMPI. Master's thesis, University of Minnesota (Minneapolis, Minn.), 1952.
321. BORKO, HAROLD. A Factor-Analytic Study of the Minnesota Multiphasic Personality Inventory Using a Transpose Matrix (Q-Technique). Doctor's thesis, University of Southern California (Los Angeles, Calif.), 1952. (Abstract: Am Psychol 7:342)
322. BROZEK, JOSEF. "Personality of Young and Middle-Aged Normal Men: Item Analysis of a Psychosomatic Inventory." J Gerontol 7:410–8 Jl '52. * (PA 27:3328)
323. BROZEK, JOSEF, AND KEYS, ANCEL. "Personality Differences Between Normal Young and Middle-Aged Men: Item Analysis of A Psychosomatic Inventory." Abstract. Am Psychol 7:402–3 Jl '52. *
324. BUECHLEY, ROBERT, AND BALL, HARRY. "A New Test of 'Validity' for the Group MMPI." J Consult Psychol 16:299–301 Ag '52. * (PA 27:4243)
325. BURSCH, CHARLES W., II. "Certain Relationships Between the Kuder Preference Record and the Minnesota Multiphasic Personality Inventory," Calif J Ed Res 3:224–7+ N '52. * (PA 27:5144)
326. CANTOR, JOEL MALCOLM. Syndromes Found in Psychiatric Population Selected for Certain MMPI Code Endings. Doctor's thesis, University of Minnesota (Minneapolis, Minn.), 1952. (DA 12:394)
327. CLARK, JERRY H. "The Relationship Between MMPI Scores and Psychiatric Classification of Army General Prisoners." J Clin Psychol 8:86–9 Ja '52. * (PA 27:2103)

328. DAHLSTROM, W. GRANT, AND CRAVEN, DOROTHY DRAKE-SMITH. "The Minnesota Multiphasic Personality Inventory and Stuttering Phenomena in Young Adults." Abstract. *Am Psychol* 7:341 Jl '52. *

329. DEVLIN, JOHN P. *A Study of Verbalized Self-Attitudes and Reactions to Social Frustration as Methods of Predicting Success in Brief Psychotherapy.* Doctor's thesis, Pennsylvania State College (State College, Pa.), 1952.

330. DREBUS, RICHARD W. *An Investigation of the Responses of Industrial Supervisors to the Minnesota Multi-Phasic Personality Inventory in Relationship to Their Performance Levels.* Doctor's thesis, University of Wisconsin (Madison, Wis.), 1952.

331. DRUCKER, MELVIN BRUCE. *An Underachiever-Overachiever Scale From the Minnesota Multiphasic Personality Inventory.* Master's thesis, Ohio University (Athens, Ohio), 1952.

332. ESTENSON, LYLE O. *An Investigation of the Relationship Between Personality as Measured by the Minnesota Multiphasic Personality Inventory and Occupational Interests as Measured by Strong's Vocational Interest Blanks.* Doctor's thesis, University of Minnesota (Minneapolis, Minn.), 1952.

333. FELDMAN, MARVIN J. "The Use of the MMPI Profile for Prognosis and Evaluation of Shock Therapy." *J Consult Psychol* 16:376–82 O '52. * (*PA* 27:5922)

334. FOUNTAIN, RALPH WARREN, JR. *Performance of College Students on the Mosaic Test and on the Minnesota Multiphasic Personality Inventory.* Master's thesis, University of Florida (Gainesville, Fla.), 1952.

335. FREEMAN, ROBERT A., AND MASON, HARRY M. "Construction of a Key to Determine Recidivists From Non-Recidivists Using the MMPI." *J Clin Psychol* 8:207–8 Ap '52. * (*PA* 27: 1957)

336. FRY, FRANKLYN D. *A Normative Study of the Reactions Manifested by College Students, and by State Prison Inmates in Response to the Minnesota Multiphasic Personality Inventory, the Rosenzweig Picture Frustration Study, and the Thematic Apperception Test.* Doctor's thesis, Pennsylvania State College (State College, Pa.), 1952.

337. FRY, FRANKLYN D. "A Normative Study of the Reactions Manifested by College Students and by State Prison Inmates in Response to the Minnesota Multiphasic Personality Inventory, the Rosenzweig Picture-Frustration Study, and the Thematic Apperception Test." *J Psychol* 34:27–30 Jl '52. * (*PA* 27:2976)

338. GEIST, HAROLD. "A Comparison of Personality Test Scores and Medical Psychiatric Diagnosis by The Inverted Factor Technique." *J Clin Psychol* 8:184–8 Ap '52. * (*PA* 27:1958)

339. GILBERSTADT, HAROLD. *An Exploratory Investigation of the Hathaway-Meehl Method of Minnesota Multiphasic Personality Inventory Profile Analysis With Psychiatric Clinical Data.* Doctor's thesis, University of Minnesota (Minneapolis, Minn.), 1952. (*DA* 13:256–7)

340. GOUGH, HARRISON G., AND PEMBERTON, WILLIAM H. "Personality Characteristics Related to Success in Practice Teaching." *J Appl Psychol* 36:307–9 O '52. * (*PA* 27:5426)

341. GOUGH, HARRISON G.; McCLOSKY, HERBERT; AND MEEHL, PAUL E. "A Personality Scale for Social Responsibility." *J Abn & Social Psychol* 47:73–80 Ja '52. * (*PA* 26:6270)

342. GREENBERG, PAUL, AND GILLILAND, A. R. "The Relationship Between Basal Metabolism and Personality." *J Social Psychol* 35:3–7 F '52. * (*PA* 27:3345)

343. GUILFORD, J. P. "When Not to Factor Analyze." *Psychol B* 49:26–37 Ja '52. * (*PA* 27:33)

344. GUTHRIE, GEORGE M. "Common Characteristics Associated With Frequent MMPI Profile Types." *J Clin Psychol* 8:141–5 Ap '52. * (*PA* 27:1963)

345. HARMON, LINDSEY RICHARD. *Inter-Relations of Patterns on the Kuder Preference Record and the Minnesota Multiphasic Personality Inventory.* Doctor's thesis, University of Minnesota (Minneapolis, Minn.), 1952. (*DA* 13:257–8)

346. HATHAWAY, STARKE R., AND MONACHESI, ELIO D. "The Minnesota Multiphasic Personality Inventory in the Study of Juvenile Delinquents." *Am Sociol R* 17:704–10 D '52. * (*PA* 28:1290)

347. HERZBERG, FREDERICK I. "A Study of the Psychological Factors in Primary Dysmenorrhea." *J Clin Psychol* 8:174–8 Ap '52. * (*PA* 27:2155)

348. HOLLAND, JOHN LEWIS. *A Study of Measured Personality Variables and Their Behavioral Correlates as Seen in Oil Painting.* Doctor's thesis, University of Minnesota (Minneapolis, Minn.), 1952. (*DA* 12:380)

349. JANDA, EARL JOSEPH. *On the Relationship Between Anxiety and Night Vision.* Doctor's thesis, University of Michigan (Ann Arbor, Mich.), 1952. (*DA* 12:219)

350. JENKINS, WILLIAM LORNE. *The Minnesota Multiphasic Personality Inventory Applied to the Problem of Prognosis in Schizophrenia.* Doctor's thesis, University of Minnesota (Minneapolis, Minn.), 1952. (*DA* 12:381)

351. KIRK, BARBARA. "Test Versus Academic Performance in Malfunctioning Students." *J Consult Psychol* 16:213–6 Je '52. * (*PA* 27:5417)

352. KLETTI, LEROY. *The Agreement in Anxiety Measurement Between the Rorschach Test and the Minnesota Multiphasic Personality Inventory.* Master's thesis, University of North Dakota (Grand Forks, N.D.), 1952.

353. LAYTON, WILBUR L. "The Variability of Individuals' Scores Upon Successive Testings on the Minnesota Multiphasic Personality Inventory." Abstract. *Am Psychol* 7:384 Jl '52. *

354. LEADINGHAM, ROBERT L. *A Validity Study of an Underachiever-Overachiever Scale From the Minnesota Multiphasic Personality Inventory.* Master's thesis, Ohio University (Athens, Ohio), 1952.

355. LINDGREN, HENRY CLAY. "The Development of A Scale of Cultural Idealization Based on The California Test of Personality." *J Ed Psychol* 43:81–91 F '52. * (*PA* 26:7004)

356. MACDONALD, GORDON L. "Effect of Test-Retest Interval and Item Arrangement on the Shortened Forms of the MMPI." *J Clin Psychol* 8:408–10 O '52. * (*PA* 27:5883)

357. MACDONALD, GORDON L. "A Study of the Shortened Group and Individual Forms of the MMPI." *J Clin Psychol* 8:309–11 Jl '52. * (*PA* 27:5884)

358. MACHOVER, SOLOMON, AND SCHWARTZ, ANITA. "A Homeostatic Effect of Mood on Associative Abstractness and Reaction Time." *J Personality* 21:59–67 S '52. * (*PA* 27:5697)

359. McQUARY, JOHN P., AND TRUAX, WILLIAM E., JR. "A Comparison of The Group and Individual Forms of The Minnesota Multiphasic Personality Inventory." *J Ed Res* 45:609–14 Ap '52. * (*PA* 27:2742)

360. MALOS, HERBERT BERNARD. *Some Psychometric Evaluations of Epilepsy.* Doctor's thesis, University of Minnesota (Minneapolis, Minn.), 1952. (*DA* 12:396)

361. MEE, ELIZABETH ANN. *A Psychometric Study of Diffuse and Focal Cerebral Pathology Groups.* Doctor's thesis, University of Minnesota (Minneapolis, Minn.), 1952. (*DA* 12:338)

362. MELEIKA, LOUIS KAMEL. *Intra-Individual Variability in Relation to Achievement, Interest, and Personality.* Doctor's thesis, Stanford University (Stanford, Calif.), 1952.

363. MORGAN, HENRY H. "A Psychometric Comparison of Achieving and Nonachieving College Students of High Ability." *J Consult Psychol* 16:292–8 Ag '52. * (*PA* 27:4570)

364. MORTON, SHELDON IVAN. *Personality Differences in Preprofessional Groups.* Doctor's thesis, Stanford University (Stanford, Calif.), 1952.

365. MYATT, MARY FRANCES. *A Study of the Relationship Between Motivation and Test Performance of Patients in a Rehabilitation Ward.* Doctor's thesis, University of Minnesota (Minneapolis, Minn.), 1952. (*DA* 12:339)

366. NARCISO, JOHN C., JR. "Some Psychological Aspects of Dermatosis." *J Consult Psychol* 16:199–201 Je '52. * (*PA* 27:5335)

367. NAVRAN, LESLIE. "The Dependence Scale Scores of Graduate Students Classified by Major Subjects." Abstract. *Calif J Ed Res* 3:182 S '52. *

368. NAVRAN, LESLIE. *A Rationally Derived Minnesota Multiphasic Personality Inventory Scale to Measure Dependence.* Doctor's thesis, Stanford University (Stanford, Calif.), 1952.

369. NELSON, SHERMAN EDDIE. *The Development of an Indirect, Objective Measure of Social Status and Its Relationship to Certain Psychiatric Syndromes.* Doctor's thesis, University of Minnesota (Minneapolis, Minn.), 1952. (*DA* 12:782)

370. NORMAN, RALPH D., AND REDLO, MIRIAM. "MMPI Personality Patterns for Various College Major Groups." Abstract. *J Colo-Wyo Acad Sci* 4:80 O '52. *

371. NORMAN, RALPH D., AND REDLO, MIRIAM. "MMPI Personality Patterns for Various College Major Groups." *J Appl Psychol* 36:404–9 D '52. * (*PA* 27:6750)

372. PETERSON, DONALD ROBERT. *Predicting Hospitalization of Psychiatric Outpatients.* Doctor's thesis, University of Minnesota (Minneapolis, Minn.), 1952. (*DA* 12:783)

373. PURCELL, CLAIRE KEPLER. "The Relationship Between Altitude—I.Q. Discrepancy and Anxiety." *J Clin Psychol* 8:82–5 Ja '52. * (*PA* 27:1978)

374. RICHARDS, T. W. "Personality of the Convulsive Patient in Military Service." *Psychol Monogr* 66(14):1–23 '52. * (*PA* 27:7364)

375. RITTENHOUSE, CARL H. "Masculinity and Femininity in Relation to Preferences in Music." Abstract. *Am Psychol* 7:333 Jl '52. *

376. RITTENHOUSE, CARL H. *Masculinity and Femininity in Relation to Preferences in Music.* Doctor's thesis, Stanford University (Stanford, Calif.), 1952.

377. ROSEN, ALBERT. *Development of Some New Minnesota Multiphasic Personality Inventory Scales for Differentiation of Psychiatric Syndromes Within an Abnormal Population.* Doctor's thesis, University of Minnesota (Minneapolis, Minn.), 1952. (*DA* 12:785)

378. ROSEN, ALBERT. "Reliability of MMPI Scales." Abstract. *Am Psychol* 7:341 Jl '52. *

379. ROSEN, EPHRAIM. "MMPI and Rorschach Correlates of the Rorschach White Space Response." *J Clin Psychol* 8:283–8 Jl '52. * (*PA* 27:5899)

380. ROSEN, IRWIN C. *Parallel Researches in Sexual Psychopathology: I, A Comparison of a Group of Rapists and Controls on Certain Psychological Variables.* Doctor's thesis, University of Pittsburgh (Pittsburgh, Pa.), 1952.

381. SANDERSON, J. WESLEY. *An Evaluation of a Technique of Profile Classification for the Minnesota Multiphasic Personality Inventory.* Doctor's thesis, University of California (Los Angeles, Calif.), 1952.

382. SEEMAN, WILLIAM. "'Subtlety' in Structured Personality Tests." *J Consult Psychol* 16:278–83 Ag '52. * (*PA* 27:4270)

383. SHNEIDMAN, EDWIN S. "The Case of Jay: Psychological Test and Anamnestic Data." *J Proj Tech* 16:297–345 S '52. * (*PA* 28:2676)

384. SOPCHAK, ANDREW L. "College Student Norms for the

Minnesota Multiphasic Personality Inventory." *J Consult Psychol* 16:445–8 D '52. * (*PA* 28:969)

385. SOPCHAK, ANDREW L. "Parental 'Identification' and 'Tendency Toward Disorders' as Measured by the Minnesota Multiphasic Personality Inventory." *J Abn & Social Psychol* 47:159–65 Ap '52. * (*PA* 27:2825)

386. SULLIVAN, PATRICK L., AND WELSH, GEORGE S. "A Technique for Objective Configural Analysis of MMPI Profiles." *J Consult Psychol* 16:383–88 O '52. * (*PA* 27:5908)

387. SUNDBERG, NORMAN, DALE. *The Relationship of Psychotherapeutic Skill and Experience to Knowledge of Other People.* Doctor's thesis, University of Minnesota (Minneapolis, Minn.), 1952. (*DA* 12:390)

388. SUTTON, MARY LYON. *Profile Patterning and Descriptive Correlates of Patients Having Low Scores on Scale 9 of the MMPI.* Doctor's thesis, University of Minnesota (Minneapolis, Minn.), 1952. (*DA* 12:786)

389. TAAFFE, GORDON. *The Discrimination of Alcoholics, Psychopaths, and Psychoneurotics by Means of the Manson Evaluation, the Pd Scale, MMPI, and the Cornell Index.* Master's thesis, University of Southern California (Los Angeles, Calif.), 1952.

390. TAYLOR, KENNETH E. *Parallel Researches in Sexual Psychopathology: II, A Comparison of a Group of Pedophiliacs and Controls on Certain Psychological Variables.* Doctor's thesis, University of Pittsburgh (Pittsburgh, Pa.), 1952.

391. TREECE, RUSSELL RAY. *A Study of a Group of Imprisoned Homosexuals, Using the Minnesota Multiphasic Personality Inventory.* Master's thesis, University of Pittsburgh (Pittsburgh, Pa.), 1952.

392. WELSH, GEORGE S. "An Anxiety Index and an Internalization Ratio for the MMPI." *J Consult Psychol* 16:65–72 F '52. * (*PA* 27:1985)

393. WELSH, GEORGE S. "A Factor Study of the MMPI Using Scales With Item Overlap Eliminated." Abstract. *Am Psychol* 7:341–2 Jl '52. *

394. WEST, PHILIP M.; BLUMBERG, EUGENE M.; AND ELLIS, FRANK W. "An Observed Correlation Between Psychological Factors and Growth Rate of Cancer in Man." Abstract. *Cancer Res* 12:306–7 Ap '52. *

395. WHOOLEY, JOHN P. *The Application of the Minnesota Multiphasic Personality Inventory to Hospitalized Tuberculous Patients.* Master's thesis, Catholic University of America (Washington, D.C.), 1952.

396. WIENER, DANIEL N. "Personality Characteristics of Selected Disability Groups." *Genetic Psychol Monogr* 45:175–255 My '52. * (*PA* 27:3746)

397. WILLIAMS, HAROLD L. "The Development of a Caudality Scale for the MMPI." *J Clin Psychol* 8:293–7 Jl '52. * (*PA* 27:6088)

398. WILLIAMSON, E. G., AND HOYT, DONALD. "Measured Personality Characteristics of Student Leaders." *Ed & Psychol Meas* 12:65–78 sp '52. * (*PA* 27:6135)

399. WILLMOTT, ELIZABETH H. *An Experimental Study of the Relationship Between the Success of Group Counselors at a Therapeutic Camp and Their Personality Characteristics as Measured by the Minnesota Multiphasic Personality Inventory.* Master's thesis, University of Michigan (Ann Arbor, Mich.), 1952.

400. WINDLE, CHARLES. "Psychological Tests in Psychopathological Prognosis." *Psychol B* 49:451–82 S '52. * (*PA* 27:3567)

401. WINFIELD, DON L. "An Investigation of the Relationship Between Intelligence and the Statistical Reliability of the Minnesota Multiphasic Personality Inventory." *J Clin Psychol* 8:146–8 Ap '52. * (*PA* 27:1987)

402. WRENN, C. GILBERT. "The Selection and Education of Student Personnel Workers." *Personnel & Guid J* 31:9–14 O '52. * (*PA* 27:4782)

403. ALTUS, W. D., AND TAFEJIAN, T. T. "MMPI Correlates of the California EF Scale." *J Social Psychol* 38:145–9 Ag '53. * (*PA* 28:6011)

404. APPLEZWEIG, MORTIMER H. "Educational Levels and Minnesota Multiphasic Profiles." *J Clin Psychol* 9:340–4 O '53. * (*PA* 28:4327)

405. ASHBAUGH, JAMES H. Study 3, "Personality Patterns of Juvenile Delinquents in an Area of Small Population," pp. 54–60. In *Analyzing and Predicting Juvenile Delinquency With the MMPI.* Edited by Starke R. Hathaway and Elio D. Monachesi. Minneapolis, Minn.: University of Minnesota Press, 1953. Pp. viii, 153. * (*PA* 28:2970)

406. AUSUBEL, DAVID P.; SCHIFF, HERBERT M.; AND ZELENY, MARJORIE P. " 'Real-Life' Measures of Level of Academic and Vocational Aspiration in Adolescents: Relation to Laboratory Measures and to Adjustment." *Child Develop* 24:155–68 S–D '53. * (*PA* 29:3700)

407. BARRON, FRANK. "An Ego-Strength Scale Which Predicts Response to Psychotherapy." *J Consult Psychol* 17:327–33 O '53. * (*PA* 28:6072)

408. BARRON, FRANK. "Some Test Correlates of Response to Psychotherapy." *J Consult Psychol* 17:235–41 Ag '53. * (*PA* 28:4410)

409. BEAVER, ALMA PERRY. "Personality Factors in Choice of Nursing." *J Appl Psychol* 37:374–9 O '53. * (*PA* 29:1484)

410. BECHTOLDT, HAROLD P. "Response Defined Anxiety and MMPI Variables." *Proc Iowa Acad Sci* 60:495–9 '53. * (*PA* 29:2429)

411. BEIER, ERNST G., AND RATZEBURG, FRED. "The Parental

Identifications of Male and Female College Students." *J Abn & Social Psychol* 48:569–72 O '53. * (*PA* 28:6529)

412. BERGER, EMANUEL M. "Relationships Among Expressed Acceptance of Self, Expressed Acceptance of Others, and the MMPI." Abstract. *Am Psychol* 8:320–1 Ag '53. *

413. BITTERMAN, M. E., AND KNIFFIN, CALVIN W. "Manifest Anxiety and 'Perceptual Defense.' " *J Abn & Social Psychol* 48:248–52 Ap '53. * (*PA* 28:2266)

414. BLACK, JOHN DAVIES. *The Interpretation of MMPI Profiles of College Women.* Doctor's thesis, University of Minnesota (Minneapolis, Minn.), 1953. (*DA* 13:870)

415. BURGESS, ELVA. *Personality Factors in Over- and Under-Achievers in Engineering.* Doctor's thesis, Pennsylvania State College (State College, Pa.), 1953.

416. CALVIN, A. D., AND HOLTZMAN, WAYNE H. "Adjustment and the Discrepancy Between Self Concept and Inferred Self." *J Consult Psychol* 17:39–44 F '53. * (*PA* 28:932)

417. CALVIN, ALLEN, AND McCONNELL, JAMES. "Ellis on Personality Inventories." *J Consult Psychol* 17:462–4 D '53. * (*PA* 28:7513)

418. CAPWELL, DORA F. Study 1, "Personality Patterns of Adolescent Girls: Delinquents and Nondelinquents," pp. 29–37. In *Analyzing and Predicting Juvenile Delinquency With the MMPI.* Edited by Starke R. Hathaway and Elio D. Monachesi. Minneapolis, Minn.: University of Minnesota Press, 1953. Pp. viii, 153. * (*PA* 28:2970)

419. CLARK, J. H. "Grade Achievement of Female College Students in Relation to Non-Intellective Factors: MMPI Items." *J Social Psychol* 37:275–81 My '53. * (*PA* 28:3187)

420. CLARK, JERRY H. "Additional Applications of the AWOL Recidivist Scale." *J Clin Psychol* 9:62–4 Ja '53. * (*PA* 27:7914)

421. CLARK, JERRY H. "The Interpretation of the MMPI Profiles of College Students: A Comparison by College Major Subject." *J Clin Psychol* 9:382–4 O '53. * (*PA* 28:4915)

422. COHART, MARY S. *The Differential Value of the Group Rorschach and the MMPI in the Evaluation of Teacher Personality.* Doctor's thesis, Yale University (New Haven, Conn.), 1953.

423. COTTLE, WILLIAM C. *The MMPI: A Review.* Kansas Studies in Education, Vol. 3, No. 2. Lawrence, Kan.: University of Kansas Press, March 1953. Pp. vi, 82. *

424. DRAKE, L. E. "Differential Sex Responses to Items of the MMPI." *J Appl Psychol* 37:46 F '53. * (*PA* 28:937)

425. ELLIS, ALBERT. "Recent Research With Personality Inventories." *J Consult Psychol* 17:45–9 F '53. * (*PA* 28:939)

426. FELDMAN, MARVIN J. "The Effects of the Size of Criterion Groups and the Level of Significance in Selecting Test Items on the Validity of Tests." *Ed & Psychol Meas* 13:273–9 su '53. * (*PA* 28:3569)

427. FRICK, J. W. *The Prediction of Academic Achievement in a College Population From a Test of Aptitude and a Standardized Personality Inventory.* Master's thesis, University of Southern California (Los Angeles, Calif.), 1953.

428. GALLAGHER, JAMES J. "Manifest Anxiety Changes Concomitant With Client-Centered Therapy." *J Consult Psychol* 17:443–6 D '53. * (*PA* 28:7589)

429. GALLAGHER, JAMES J. "MMPI Changes Concomitant With Client-Centered Therapy." *J Consult Psychol* 17:334–8 O '53. * (*PA* 28:6100)

430. GANUNG, G. R. *A Study of Scholastic Achievement Related to Personality as Measured by the Minnesota Multiphasic Personality Inventory.* Master's thesis, Utah State Agricultural College (Logan, Utah), 1953.

431. GOUGH, HARRISON G. "Minnesota Multiphasic Personality Inventory," pp. 545–67. (*PA* 27:7769) In *Contributions Toward Medical Psychology: Theory and Psychodiagnostic Methods, Vol. II.* Edited by Arthur Weider. New York: Ronald Press Co., 1953. Pp. xi, 459–885. *

432. GRANICK, SAMUEL, AND SMITH, LEON J. "Sex Sequence in the Draw-a-Person Test and Its Relation to the MMPI Masculinity-Femininity Scale." *J Consult Psychol* 17:71–3 F '53. * (*PA* 28:950)

433. GULLION, MARY E. *An Elementary Teacher Attitude Study: Using an Inventory of Teacher Adjustment to Selected Problem Situations and the Minnesota Multiphasic Personality Inventory.* Master's thesis, University of Oregon (Eugene, Ore.), 1953.

434. HAMPTON, PETER JAN. "The Development of a Personality Questionnaire for Drinkers." *Genetic Psychol Monogr* 48:55–115 Ag '53. * (*PA* 28:4571)

435. HANES, BERNARD. *A Factor Analysis of MMPI, Aptitude Test Data and Personal Information Using a Population of Criminals.* Doctor's thesis, Ohio State University (Columbus, Ohio), 1953.

436. HANES, BERNARD. "Reading Ease and MMPI Results." *J Clin Psychol* 9:83–5 Ja '53. * (*PA* 27:7771)

437. HARDER, DONALD FREDERICK. *A Study of Item Responses on the Minnesota Multiphasic Personality Inventory of Male Senior Students in Business, Education, and Engineering Curricula.* Doctor's thesis, University of Kansas (Lawrence, Kan.), 1953.

438. HATHAWAY, STARKE R., AND MONACHESI, ELIO D., EDITORS. *Analyzing and Predicting Juvenile Delinquency With the MMPI.* Minneapolis, Minn.: University of Minnesota Press, 1953. Pp. viii, 153. * (*PA* 28:2970)

439. HATHAWAY, STARKE R.; HASTINGS, DONALD W.; CAPWELL, DORA F.; AND BELL, DOROTHY M. Study 5, "The Relationship Between MMPI Profiles and Later Careers of Juvenile

Delinquent Girls," pp. 70–86. In *Analyzing and Predicting Juvenile Delinquency With the MMPI.* Edited by Starke R. Hathaway and Elio D. Monachesi. Minneapolis, Minn.: University of Minnesota Press, 1953. Pp. viii, 153. * (*PA* 28:2970)

440. HATTON, ROBERT OLIVER. *Personality Patterns of Agricultural Extension Workers as Related to Selected Aspects of Work Adjustment.* Doctor's thesis, Michigan State College (East Lansing, Mich.), 1953. (*DA* 15:374)

441. HOLMES, W. O. *The Development of an Empirical MMPI Scale for Alcoholism.* Master's thesis, San Jose State College (San Jose, Calif.), 1953.

442. HOVEY, H. BIRNET. "MMPI Profiles and Personality Characteristics." *J Consult Psychol* 17:142–6 Ap '53. * (*PA* 28:2639)

443. HOVEY, H. BIRNET, AND STAUFFACHER, JAMES C. "Intuitive Versus Objective Prediction From a Test." *J Clin Psychol* 9:349–51 O '53. * (*PA* 28:4362)

444. LAUBER, MARGARET, AND DAHLSTROM, W. GRANT. Study 4, "MMPI Findings in the Rehabilitation of Delinquent Girls," pp. 61–9. In *Analyzing and Predicting Juvenile Delinquency With the MMPI.* Edited by Starke R. Hathaway and Elio D. Monachesi. Minneapolis, Minn.: University of Minnesota Press, 1953. Pp. viii, 153. * (*PA* 28:2970)

445. MACHOVER, SOLOMON, AND ANDERSON, HELEN J. "Validity of a Paper-and-Pencil Form of the MMPI Psychopathic Deviate Scale." *J Consult Psychol* 17:459–61 D '53. * (*PA* 28:7537)

446. MACLEAN, ANGUS G.; TAIT, ARTHUR T.; AND CATTERALL, CALVIN D. "The F Minus K Index on the MMPI." *J Appl Psychol* 37:315–6 Ag '53. * (*PA* 28:6044)

447. MILL, CYRIL R. "Personality Patterns of Sociometrically Selected and Sociometrically Rejected Male College Students." *Sociometry* 16:151–67 My '53. * (*PA* 28:4886)

448. REGAL, JACOB. *Pattern Analysis of the Minnesota Multiphasic Personality Inventory.* Doctor's thesis, University of California (Berkeley, Calif.), 1953.

449. RINNE, KONRAD WILLIAM. *A Differential Analysis of Various Group Responses to Characteristics of Personality as Measured by the Minnesota Multiphasic Personality Inventory.* Doctor's thesis, Indiana University (Bloomington, Ind.), 1953. (*DA* 13:1263)

450. RORABAUGH, MILDRED E., AND GUTHRIE, GEORGE. "The Personality Characteristics of Tuberculous Patients Who Leave the Tuberculosis Hospital Against Medical Advice." *Am R Tuberc* 67:432–9 Ap '53. * (*PA* 30:3275) *

451. ROSEN, ALBERT. "Test-Retest Stability of MMPI Scales for a Psychiatric Population." *J Consult Psychol* 17:217–21 Je '53. * (*PA* 27:2669)

452. SANDERSON, JAMES WESLEY. *An Evaluation of a Technique of Profile Classification for the Minnesota Multiphasic Personality Inventory.* Doctor's thesis, University of California (Berkeley, Calif.), 1953.

453. SCHMIDT, RICHARD H. H. *The Value of the Minnesota Multiphasic Personality Inventory in Assessing the Desirability of Dormitory Residences.* Doctor's thesis, Oklahoma Agricultural and Mechanical College (Stillwater, Okla.), 1953.

454. SCHOFIELD, WILLIAM. "A Further Study of the Effects of Therapies on MMPI Responses." *J Abn & Social Psychol* 48:67–77 Ja '53. * (*PA* 28:1075)

455. SCHOFIELD, WILLIAM. "A Study of Medical Students With the *MMPI*: I, Scale Norms and Profile Patterns." *J Psychol* 36:59–65 Jl '53. * (*PA* 28:3445)

456. SCHOFIELD, WILLIAM. "A Study of Medical Students With the *MMPI*: II, Group and Individual Changes After Two Years." *J Psychol* 36:137–41 Jl '53. * (*PA* 28:3446)

457. SCHOFIELD, WILLIAM. "A Study of Medical Students With the *MMPI*: III, Personality and Academic Success." *J Appl Psychol* 37:47–52 F '53. * (*PA* 28:1683)

458. SEEMAN, WILLIAM. "Concept of 'Subtlety' in Structured Psychiatric and Personality Tests: An Experimental Approach." *J Abn & Social Psychol* 48:239–47 Ap '53. * (*PA* 28:2674)

459. SKRINCOSKY, PETER C. *A Comparative Study of the Standard Form of the Minnesota Multiphasic Personality Inventory and a Modified Form of the Same Adapted for a Seminary Group.* Master's thesis, Fordham University (New York, N.Y.), 1953.

460. STERNBERG, CARL. "Differences in Measured Interest, Values, and Personality Among College Students Majoring in Nine Subject Areas." Abstract. *Am Psychol* 8:442–3 Ag '53. *

461. STERNBERG, CARL. *The Relation of Interests, Values and Personality to the Major Field of Study in College.* Doctor's thesis, New York University (New York, N.Y.), 1953. (*DA* 13:1095)

462. SWAN, ROBERT JUNIOR. *The Application of a Couple Analysis Approach to the Minnesota Multiphasic Personality Inventory in Marriage Counseling.* Doctor's thesis, University of Minnesota (Minneapolis, Minn.), 1953. (*DA* 13:1095)

463. SWEETLAND, ANDERS, AND QUAY, HERBERT. "A Note on the K Scale of the Minnesota Multiphasic Personality Inventory." *J Consult Psychol* 17:314–6 Ag '53. * (*PA* 28:4398)

464. SYDOW, DONALD WAYNE. *A Psychometric Differentiation Between Functional Psychotics and Non-Psychotics With Organic Brain Damage.* Doctor's thesis, University of Minnesota (Minneapolis, Minn.), 1953. (*DA* 13:1267)

465. TAYLOR, JANET A. "A Personality Scale of Manifest Anxiety." *J Abn & Social Psychol* 48:285–90 Ap '53. * (*PA* 28:2683)

466. TONNINGSEN, EDWARD L. *The Standardization of the Minnesota Multiphasic Personality Inventory on a Norm Group*

of High School Seniors. Master's thesis, University of California (Berkeley, Calif.), 1953.

467. TRUMBULL, RICHARD. "A Study of Relationships Between Factors of Personality and Intelligence." *J Social Psychol* 38:161–73 N '53. * (*PA* 28:5589)

468. TYDLASKA, MARY, AND MENGEL, ROBERT. "A Scale for Measuring Work Attitude for the MMPI." *J Appl Psychol* 37:474–7 D '53. * (*PA* 29:1662)

469. TYLER, FRED T., AND MICHAELIS, JOHN U. "A Comparison of Manual and College Norms for the MMPI." *J Appl Psychol* 37:273–5 Ag '53. * (*PA* 28:6057)

470. TYLER, FRED T., AND MICHAELIS, JOHN U. "K-Scores Applied to MMPI Scales for College Women." *Ed & Psychol Meas* 13:459–66 au '53. * (*PA* 28:4973)

471. WEST, LOUIS J. "Measurement of Changing Psychopathology With the Minnesota Multiphasic Personality Inventory." Discussion by Burtrum C. Schiele. *Am J Psychiatry* 109:922–8 Je '53. * (*PA* 28:2691)

472. WILLERMAN, BEN. "The Relation of Motivation and Skill to Active and Passive Participation in the Group." *J Appl Psychol* 37:387–90 O '53. * (*PA* 29:715)

473. WINFIELD, DON L. "The Relationship Between IQ Scores and Minnesota Multiphasic Personality Inventory Scores." *J Social Psychol* 38:299–300 N '53. * (*PA* 28:6063)

474. YOUNG, NORMAN, AND GAIER, EUGENE L. "A Preliminary Investigation Into the Prediction of Suggestibility From Selected Personality Variables." *J Social Psychol* 37:53–60 F '53. * (*PA* 28:571)

475. ZWETSCHKE, EARL THEODORE. *The Function of the MMPI in Determining Fitness for Student Teaching at the Nursery School, Kindergarten, and Primary School Level.* Doctor's thesis, University of Minnesota (Minneapolis, Minn.), 1953. (*DA* 14:500)

476. ABDEL-MEGUID, SAAD GALAL MOHAMED. *Delinquency Related to Personality, Intelligence, School Achievement, and Environmental Factors.* Doctor's thesis, Stanford University (Stanford, Calif.), 1954. (*DA* 14:1616)

477. ABRAMSON, HAROLD A., AND TIEGE, ERNA. "Minnesota Test as a Guide to Therapy in Multiple Sclerosis." *Ann NY Acad Sci* 58:648–55 Jl 28 '54. *

478. ARNDT, WILLIAM B. "Minnesota Multiphasic Personality Inventory: A Supplementary Method for Its Clinical Analysis." *Med Tech B* 5:267–8 N–D '54. *

479. AUMACK, LEWIS. "Misconceptions Concerning the Interpretation of Sub-Group Variations Within Normative Data." *J Psychol* 38:79–82 Jl '54. * (*PA* 29:3281)

480. AUSUBEL, DAVID P.; SCHIFF, HERBERT M.; AND ZELENY, MARJORIE P. "Validity of Teachers' Ratings of Adolescents' Adjustment and Aspirations." *J Ed Psychol* 45:394–406 N '54. * (*PA* 29:7981)

481. BRACKBILL, GLEN, AND LITTLE, KENNETH B. "MMPI Correlates of the Taylor Scale of Manifest Anxiety." *J Consult Psychol* 18:433–6 D '54. * (*PA* 29:7260)

482. BROIDA, DANIEL C. "An Investigation of Certain Psychodiagnostic Indications of Suicidal Tendencies and Depression in Mental Hospital Patients." *Psychiatric Q* 28:453–64 Jl '54. * (*PA* 29:6019)

483. BURDOCK, EUGENE I. *A Statistical Technique for the Isolation of Personality Types by Means of the Minnesota Multiphasic Personality Inventory.* Doctor's thesis, University of California (Los Angeles, Calif.), 1954.

484. CHAREN, SOL. "A Note on the Use of a Paper-and-Pencil Form of the MMPI Hs Scale for Hospital Use." Abstract. *J Consult Psychol* 18:344 O '54. *

485. CLARK, JERRY H. "The Interpretation of the *MMPI* Profiles of College Students: Mean Scores for Male and Female Groups." *J Social Psychol* 40:319–21 N '54. * (*PA* 20:7264)

486. CONNER, HAROLD THOMAS. *An Investigation of Certain Factors for the Selection and Guidance of Prospective Students Entering a School of Public Health.* Doctor's thesis, University of North Carolina (Chapel Hill, N.C.), 1954.

487. COOK, WALTER W., AND MEDLEY, DONALD M. "Proposed Hostility and Pharisaic-Virtue Scales for the MMPI." *J Appl Psychol* 38:414–8 D '54. * (*PA* 29:5694)

488. COTTLE, W. C., AND LEWIS, W. W., JR. "Personality Characteristics of Counselors: II, Male Counselor Responses to the MMPI and GZTS." *J Counsel Psychol* 1:27–30 F '54. * (*PA* 28:7476)

489. COTTLE, WILLIAM C. "Interest and Personality Inventories." *Personnel & Guid J* 33:162–7 N '54. * (*PA* 29:5695)

490. DAHLSTROM, W. GRANT. "Prediction of Adjustment After Neurosurgery." Abstract. *Am Psychol* 9:353–4 Ag '54. *

491. DOLEYS, E. J., JR. *The Validity of the Depression Scale of the MMPI.* Master's thesis, De Paul University (Chicago, Ill.), 1954.

492. DRAKE, L. E. "MMPI Profiles and Interview Behavior." *J Counsel Psychol* 1:92–5 su '54. * (*PA* 29:3012)

493. DYMOND, ROSALIND. "Interpersonal Perception and Marital Happiness." *Can J Psychol* 8:164–71 S '54. * (*PA* 29:3901)

494. ERIKSEN, CHARLES W. "Psychological Defenses and 'Ego Strength' in the Recall of Completed and Incompleted Tasks." *J Abn & Social Psychol* 49:45–50 Ja '54. * (*PA* 28:7217)

495. GALLAGHER, JAMES J. "Test Indicators for Therapy Prognosis." *J Consult Psychol* 18:409–13 D '54. * (*PA* 29:7356)

496. GLASSCOCK, EDWIN MOORE. *An Investigation of the Value of the Minnesota Multiphasic Personality Inventory as a*

Prognostic Instrument. Doctor's thesis, Washington University (St. Louis, Mo.), 1954. (*DA* 15:874)

497. GOLDBERG, SHEPHARD; HUNT, RAYMOND G.; COHEN, WALTER; AND MEADOW, ARNOLD. "Some Personality Correlates of Perceptual Distortion in the Direction of Group Conformity." Abstract. *Am Psychol* 9:378 Ag '54. *

498. GOODSTEIN, LEONARD D. "Regional Differences in MMPI Responses Among Male College Students." *J Consult Psychol* 18:437-41 D '54. * (*PA* 29:7279)

499. GOUGH, HARRISON G. "Some Common Misconceptions About Neuroticism." *J Consult Psychol* 18:287-92 Ag '54. * (*PA* 29:4468)

500. GREENE, EDWARD B. "Medical Reports and Selected MMPI Items Among Employed Adults." Abstract. *Am Psychol* 9:384 Ag '54. *

501. HANCOCK, JOHN W., AND CARTER, GERALD C. "Student Personality Traits and Curriculae of Enrollment." *J Ed Res* 48:225-7 N '54. * (*PA* 29:7909)

502. HATHAWAY, STARKE R., AND MONACHESI, ELIO D. "The Occurrence of Juvenile Delinquency With Patterns of Maladjustment as Exemplified in MMPI Profiles." Abstract. *Am Psychol* 9:391-2 Ag '54. *

503. HORGAN, JAMES FRANCIS. *A Comparison of the Relative Effectiveness of Prediction and Postdiction Methods in Assessing Ethnocentrism From Scores on the Minnesota Multiphasic Personality Inventory.* Doctor's thesis, University of Pittsburgh (Pittsburgh, Pa.), 1954. (*DA* 14:873)

504. HOVEY, H. BIRNET. "*MMPI* Aberration Potentials in a Nonclinical Group." *J Social Psychol* 40:299-307 N '54. * (*PA* 29:8156)

505. HOYT, DONALD P., AND NORMAN, WARREN T. "Adjustment and Academic Predictability." *J Counsel Psychol* 1:96-9 su '54. * (*PA* 29:3043)

506. KOSTLAN, ALBERT. "A Method for the Empirical Study of Psychodiagnosis." *J Consult Psychol* 18:83-8 Ap '54. * (*PA* 29:2415)

507. LaFORGE, ROLFE; LEARY, TIMOTHY F.; NABOISEK, HERBERT; COFFEY, HUBERT S.; AND FREEDMAN, MERVIN B. "The Interpersonal Dimension of Personality: II, An Objective Study of Repression." *J Personality* 23:129-53 D '54. * (*PA* 29:5313)

508. LA PLACE, JOHN P. "Personality and Its Relationship to Success in Professional Baseball." *Res Q* 25:313-9 S '54. *

509. LAYTON, WILBUR L. "The Variability of Individuals' Scores Upon Successive Testings on the Minnesota Multiphasic Personality Inventory." *Ed & Psychol Meas* 14:634-40 w '54. * (*PA* 29:7292)

510. LEVITT, EUGENE E. "A Note on the Welsh MMPI Anxiety Index." Abstract. *J Consult Psychol* 18:112 Ap '54. *

511. LITTLE, KENNETH B., AND SHNEIDMAN, EDWIN S. "The Validity of MMPI Interpretations." *J Consult Psychol* 18:425-8 D '54. * (*PA* 29:7295)

512. LOCKMAN, ROBERT F. "Some Relationships Between the MMPI and a Problem Checklist." *J Appl Psychol* 38:264-7 Ag '54. * (*PA* 29:5716)

513. McGEE, SHANNA. "Measurement of Hostility: A Pilot Study." *J Clin Psychol* 10:280-2 Jl '54. * (*PA* 29:2699)

514. MASTEJ, M. MARTINA. *A Study of the Influence of Religious Life on the Personality Adjustment of Religious Women as Measured by a Modified Form of the Minnesota Multiphasic Personality Inventory.* Doctor's thesis, Fordham University (New York, N.Y.), 1954.

515. MILLER, CHRISTINE. "Consistency of Cognitive Behavior as a Function of Personality Characteristics." *J Personality* 23:233-49 D '54. * (*PA* 29:5315)

516. MILLER, ROBERT S. *A Study of the Relationships Between MMPI Scales and GZTS Scales.* Master's thesis, University of Kansas (Lawrence, Kan.), 1954.

517. MILLS, WILLIAM WILLIS. *MMPI Profile Pattern and Scale Stability Throughout Four Years of College Attendance.* Doctor's thesis, University of Minnesota (Minneapolis, Minn.), 1954. (*DA* 14:1259)

518. NAVRAN, LESLIE. "A Rationally Derived MMPI Scale to Measure Dependence." Abstract. *J Consult Psychol* 18:192 Je '54. *

519. OLSON, GORDON W. "The Hastings Short Form of the Group MMPI." *J Clin Psychol* 10:386-8 O '54. * (*PA* 29:4078)

520. PEARSON, JOHN SUMNER. *Psychometric Correlates of Emotional Immaturity.* Doctor's thesis, University of Minnesota (Minneapolis, Minn.), 1954. (*DA* 14:2129)

521. PETERSON, DONALD R. "The Diagnosis of Subclinical Schizophrenia." *J Consult Psychol* 18:198-200 Je '54. * (*PA* 29:2821)

522. PETERSON, DONALD R. "Predicting Hospitalization of Psychiatric Outpatients." *J Abn & Social Psychol* 49:260-5 Ap '54. * (*PA* 29:1094)

523. PIERCE, KYLE KARR. *The Personality Inventory Correlates of the Level of Aspiration.* Doctor's thesis, University of Arizona (Tucson, Ariz.), 1954. (*DA* 14:1102)

524. PIERCE-JONES, JOHN. "The Readability of Certain Standard Tests." *Calif J Ed Res* 5:80-2 Mr '54. * (*PA* 28:8729)

525. QUAY, HERBERT, AND SWEETLAND, ANDERS. "The Relationship of the Rosenzweig PF Study to the MMPI." *J Clin Psychol* 10:296-7 Jl '54. * (*PA* 29:2464)

526. REGAL, JACOB M. *Pattern Analysis of the Minnesota Multiphasic Personality Inventory.* Doctor's thesis, University of California (Berkeley, Calif.), 1954.

527. ROESSEL, FRED PAUL. *Minnesota Multiphasic Personality Inventory Results for High School Drop-Outs and Gradu-*

ates. Doctor's thesis, University of Minnesota (Minneapolis, Minn.), 1954. (*DA* 14:942)

528. ROSEN, ALBERT; HALES, WILLIAM M.; AND SIMON, WERNER. "Classification of 'Suicidal' Patients." *J Consult Psychol* 18:359-62 O '54. * (*PA* 29:6040)

529. RUBIN, HAROLD. "Validity of a Critical-Item Scale for Schizophrenia on the MMPI." *J Consult Psychol* 18:219-20 Je '54. * (*PA* 29:2831)

530. SCHULTZ, STARLING DONALD. *A Differentiation of Several Forms of Hostility by Scales Empirically Constructed From Significant Items on the Minnesota Multiphasic Personality Inventory.* Doctor's thesis, Pennsylvania State University (University Park, Pa.), 1954.

531. SIMON, WERNER, AND GILBERSTADT, HAROLD. "Minnesota Multiphasic Personality Inventory Patterns Before and After Carbon Dioxide Inhalation Therapy." *J Nerv & Mental Dis* 119:523-9 Je '54. * (*PA* 29:4173)

532. SINGER, ARTHUR. "Social Competence and Success in Teaching." *J Exp Ed* 23:99-131 D '54. * (*PA* 29:8009)

533. TURBOVSKY, JOSEPH M. *Developing a Teaching Interest Scale from the Minnesota Multiphasic Personality Inventory.* Master's thesis, Fresno State College (Fresno, Calif.), 1954.

534. TYLER, FRED T. *The Prediction of Student-Teaching Success From Personality Inventories.* University of California, Publications in Education, Vol. 11, No. 4. Berkeley, Calif.: University of California Press, 1954. Pp. 233-313. * (*PA* 29:4709)

535. VAN DYKE, PAUL. *An Investigation of Self-Mutilation at the Texas Prison System in Terms of the Minnesota Multiphasic Personality Inventory and Other Measures.* Master's thesis, University of Texas (Austin, Tex.), 1954.

536. WALNUT, FRANCIS. "A Personality Inventory Item Analysis of Individuals Who Stutter and Individuals Who Have Other Handicaps." *J Speech & Hearing Dis* 19:220-7 Je '54. * (*PA* 29:4346)

537. WEISGERBER, CHARLES A. "Norms for the Minnesota Multiphasic Personality Inventory With Student Nurses." *J Clin Psychol* 10:192-4 Ap '54. * (*PA* 29:967)

538. WEXNER, LOIS B. "Relationship of Intelligence and the Nine Scales of the Minnesota Multiphasic Personality Inventory." *J Social Psychol* 40:173-6 Ag '54. * (*PA* 29:5734)

539. WILLIAMS, HAROLD L., AND LAWRENCE, JAMES F. "Comparison of the Rorschach and MMPI by Means of Factor Analysis." *J Consult Psychol* 18:193-7 Je '54. * (*PA* 29:2484)

540. WORSLEY, ROBERT. *An Investigation of the Minnesota Multiphasic Personality Inventory as a Device for Differentiating Parole Violators, Non-Violators, Burglars and Forgers.* Master's thesis, University of Texas (Austin, Tex.), 1954.

541. WRIGHT, STUART. "Some Personality Characteristics of Academic Underachievers." Abstract. *Am Psychol* 9:496 Ag '54. *

542. BARRON, FRANK, AND LEARY, TIMOTHY F. "Changes in Psychoneurotic Patients With and Without Psychotherapy." *J Consult Psychol* 19:239-45 Ag '55. * (*PA* 30:4616)

543. BARTELME, KENWOOD, AND RILEY, GORDON L. "A Study of Psychiatric Technicians on Selected Measures of Intelligence and Personality." Abstract. *Am Psychol* 10:321 Ag '55. *

544. BERGER, EMANUEL M. "Relationships Among Acceptance of Self, Acceptance of Others, and MMPI Scores." Comment by Victor Raimy. *J Counsel Psychol* 2:279-84 w '55. * (*PA* 31:1020)

545. BLOCK, JACK, AND THOMAS, HOBART. "Is Satisfaction With Self a Measure of Adjustment?" *J Abn & Social Psychol* 51:254-9 S '55. * (*PA* 30:4178)

546. BONK, EDWARD C. *Counseling Implications of the Minnesota Multiphasic Personality Inventory for Blind People in Selected Occupations.* Doctor's thesis, Indiana University (Bloomington, Ind.), 1955. (*DA* 15:2095)

547. BROTMAN, SANFORD. "An Investigation of Psychological and Physiological Factors Related to Rate or Recovery in Pulmonary Tuberculosis." Abstract. *Am Psychol* 10:362 Ag '55. *

548. BROZEK, JOSEF. "Personality Changes With Age: An Item Analysis of the Minnesota Multiphasic Personality Inventory." *J Gerontol* 10:194-206 Ap '55. * (*PA* 30:2587)

549. CALDEN, GEORGE; THURSTON, JOHN R.; STEWART, BARBARA M.; AND VINEBERG, SHALOM E. "The Use of the MMPI in Predicting Irregular Discharge Among Tuberculosis Patients." *J Clin Psychol* 11:374-7 O '55. * (*PA* 30:6203)

550. CANTOR, JOEL M. "A Brief Screening Scale for Psychopathological Patients Developed From MMPI Score-Patterning." *J Clin Psychol* 11:20-4 Ja '55. * (*PA* 29:7262)

551. CLARKE, S. C. T., AND McGREGOR, J. R. "Teachers' Adjustment and Teachers' Achievement in University Courses." *Can J Psychol* 9:55-8 Mr '55. * (*PA* 30:1641)

552. CONWELL, D. V.; KURTH, C. J.; AND MURPHY, PAUL G. "Use of Psychologic Tests in Determining Prognosis and Treatment in Geriatric Mental Illness." *J Am Geriatrics Soc* 3:232-8 Ap '55. *

553. COOK, WALTER W., AND MEDLEY, DONALD M. "The Relationship Between Minnesota Teacher Attitude Inventory Scores and Scores on Certain Scales of the Minnesota Multiphasic Personality Inventory." *J Appl Psychol* 39:123-9 Ap '55. * (*PA* 30:1642)

554. COOMBS, ROBERT WARREN. *The Appraisal of Personal Problems of High School Seniors.* Doctor's thesis, University of Southern California (Los Angeles, Calif.), 1955.

555. COOPER, MATTHEW NATHANIEL. *To Determine the Nature and Significance, If Any, of Certain Differences in the*

Social and Personal Adjustment of Fifty-One Successful and Fifty-One Non-Successful College Students at Texas Southern University. Doctor's thesis, New York University (New York, N.Y.), 1955. (*DA* 16:497)

556. CRADDICK, R. A. *MMPI Scores of Psychopathic and Non-Psychopathic Prisoners of a Provincial Gaol.* Master's thesis, University of Alberta (Edmonton, Alta., Canada), 1955.

557. DAHLSTROM, W. GRANT, AND WAHLER, H. J. "Application of Discriminant Function Techniques to Problems of Psychiatric Classification." Abstract. *Am Psychol* 10:478 Ag '55. *

558. ERIKSEN, CHARLES W., AND DAVIDS, ANTHONY. "The Meaning and Clinical Validity of the Taylor Anxiety Scale and the Hysteria-Psychasthenia Scales From the MMPI." *J Abn & Social Psychol* 50:135-7 Ja '55. * (*PA* 29:7273)

559. FREEDMAN, MERVIN B.; WEBSTER, HAROLD; AND SANFORD, NEVITT. "Some Psychodynamic Correlates of Authoritarianism in Women." Abstract. *Am Psychol* 10:341 Ag '55. *

560. FRICK, J. W. "Improving the Prediction of Academic Achievement by Use of the MMPI." *J Appl Psychol* 39:49-52 F '55. * (*PA* 30:1618)

561. GOWAN, J. C. "Relation of the 'K' Scale of the MMPI to the Teaching Personality." *Calif J Ed Res* 6:208-12 My '55. * (*PA* 30:6349)

562. GOWAN, J. C., AND GOWAN, MAY SEAGOE. "A Teacher Prognosis Scale for the MMPI." *J Ed Res* 49:1-12 S '55. * (*PA* 30:5261)

563. GRAYSON, HARRY M., AND OLINGER, LEONARD B. "Simulation of 'Normalcy' by Psychiatric Patients on Psychological Tests (MMPI)." Abstract. *Am Psychol* 10:332 Ag '55. *

564. HACKETT, HERBERT R. "Use of the MMPI to Predict College Achievement." *J Counsel Psychol* 2:68-9 sp '55. *

565. HALBOWER, CHARLES CARSON. *A Comparison of Actuarial Versus Clinical Prediction to Classes Descriminated by the Minnesota Multiphasic Personality Inventory.* Doctor's thesis, University of Minnesota (Minneapolis, Minn.), 1955. (*DA* 15:1115)

566. HANLEY, CHARLES. "Judged Social Desirability and Probability of Endorsement of Items on the MMPI *Sc* and *D* Scales." Abstract. *Am Psychol* 10:404-5 Ag '55. *

567. HECHT, SHIRLEY, AND KROEBER, THEODORE C. "A Study in Prediction of Attitudes of Patients Toward Brief Psychotherapy." Abstract. *Am Psychol* 10:370 Ag '55. *

568. HOLMES, JACK A. "Personality and Spelling Ability." Abstract. *Am Psychol* 10:353-4 Ag '55. *

569. HORLICK, REUBEN S. "The Discriminant Value of Minnesota Multiphasic Personality Inventory Items in Personality Disorders." *J Clin Psychol* 11:362-5 O '55. * (*PA* 30:5984)

570. JACOBS, ALFRED, AND LEVENTER, SEYMOUR. "Response to Personality Inventories With Situational Stress." *J Abn & Social Psychol* 51:449-51 N '55. * (*PA* 31:3041)

571. JOHNSTON, R. W. *Selection of Candidates for Adult Probation in Saskatchewan by the Use of a Biographical Questionnaire and the Minnesota Multiphasic Personality Inventory.* Master's thesis, University of Saskatchewan (Saskatoon, Sask., Canada), 1955.

572. KAMMAN, GORDON R., AND KRAM, CHARLES. "Value of Psychometric Examinations in Medical Diagnosis and Treatment." *J Am Med Assn* 158:551-60 Je 18 '55. * (*PA* 31:1044)

573. KAUFMAN, MELVIN. *The Formation of Learning Sets With Mentally Retarded Children.* Doctor's thesis, University of Pittsburgh (Pittsburgh, Pa.), 1955. (*DA* 16:156)

574. KOSTLAN, ALBERT. "A Reply to Patterson." *J Consult Psychol* 19:486 D '55 *

575. LABUE, ANTHONY C. "Personality Traits and Persistence of Interest in Teaching as a Vocational Choice." *J Appl Psychol* 39:362-5 O '55. * (*PA* 30:7783)

576. LAVER, A. B. *Item Analysis of the Minnesota Multiphasic Personality Inventory Against an Army Misconduct Criterion.* Master's thesis. Queen's University (Kingston, Ont., Canada), 1955.

577. LITTLE, KENNETH B., AND SHNEIDMAN, EDWIN S. "A Comparison of the Reliability of Interpretations of Four Psychological Tests." Abstract. *Am Psychol* 10:322 Ag '55. *

578. MCQUARY, JOHN P., AND TRUAX, WILLIAM E., JR. "An Under-Achievement Scale." *J Ed Res* 48:393-9 Ja '55. * (*PA* 29:8997)

579. MAHLER, IRWIN. "Use of the MMPI With Student Nurses." *J Appl Psychol* 39:190-3 Je '55. * (*PA* 30:3657)

580. MARSH, JAMES T.; HILLIARD, JESSAMINE; AND LIECHTI, ROBERT. "A Sexual Deviation Scale for the MMPI." *J Consult Psychol* 19:55-9 F '55. * (*PA* 29:8644)

581. MATARAZZO, JOSEPH D. "MMPI Validity Scores as a Function of Increasing Levels of Anxiety." *J Consult Psychol* 19:213-7 Je '55. * (*PA* 30:2900)

582. MERRILL, REED M. "Relation of the Edwards Personal Preference Schedule to the Clinical and Experimental Scales of the MMPI." Abstract. *Am Psychol* 10:366 Ag '55. *

583. MILLER, ROBERT S., AND COTTLE, WILLIAM C. "Evidenced Relationships Between MMPI and GZTS Scales: An Adult Male Sample." *Univ Kans B Ed* 9:91-4 My '55. *

584. PAGE, HORACE; THURSTON, JOHN; NUTHMANN, CONRAD; CALDEN, GEORGE; AND LORENZ, THOMAS. "An Empirical Study of the Relationship of Four Classes of Body Habitus to Responses on the MMPI." *Psychol Rep* 1:159-65 S '55. * (*PA* 30:5770)

585. PATTERSON, C. H. "Diagnostic Accuracy or Diagnostic Stereotypy?" *J Consult Psychol* 19:483-5 D '55. * (*PA* 30:7171)

586. QUAY, HERBERT. "The Performance of Hospitalized Psychiatric Patients on the Ego-Strength Scale of the MMPI." *J Clin Psychol* 11:403-5 O '55. * (*PA* 30:6182)

587. QUAY, HERBERT, AND ROWELL, JOHN T. "The Validity of a Schizophrenic Screening Scale of the MMPI." *J Clin Psychol* 11:92-3 Ja '55. * (*PA* 29:7309)

588. REID, ALICE RUTH. *The Contribution of the Freshman Year of Physical Education in a Liberal Arts College for Women to Certain Personality Variables.* Doctor's thesis, State University of Iowa (Iowa City, Iowa), 1955. (*DA* 15:2091)

589. REITAN, RALPH M. "Affective Disturbances in Brain-Damaged Patients: Measurements With the Minnesota Multiphasic Personality Inventory." *A.M.A. Arch Neurol & Psychiatry* 73:530-2 My '55. * (*PA* 30:1436)

590. REMPEL, PETER. *The Use of Multivariate Statistical Analysis of Minnesota Multiphasic Personality Inventory Scores in the Classification of Delinquent and Nondelinquent High School Boys.* Doctor's thesis, University of Minnesota (Minneapolis, Minn.), 1955. (*DA* 15:1788)

591. ROSS, ALEXANDER T., AND REITAN, RALPH M. "Intellectual and Affective Functions in Multiple Sclerosis." *A.M.A. Arch Neurol & Psychiatry* 73:663-77 Je '55. * (*PA* 30:3319)

592. SHONTZ, FRANKLIN C. "MMPI Responses of Patients With Multiple Sclerosis." Abstract. *J Consult Psychol* 19:74 F '55. *

593. SMITH, ROBERT EDWARD. *Personality Configurations of Adult Male Penal Populations as Revealed by the Minnesota Multiphasic Personality Inventory.* Doctor's thesis, University of Minnesota (Minneapolis, Minn.), 1955. (*DA* 16:160)

594. SNYDER, WILLIAM U. "The Personality of Clinical Students." *J Counsel* 2:47-52 sp '52. * (*PA* 30:182)

595. STANTON, JOHN M. *The Use of the Minnesota Multiphasic Personality Inventory to Determine the Group Personality Profile of State Prison Inmates and the Relation of Selected Aspects of Known Anti-Social Behavior to Profile Components.* Doctor's thesis, Fordham University (New York, N.Y.), 1955.

596. STATON, WESLEY M., AND RUTLEDGE, JOHN A. "Measurable Traits of Personality and Incidence of Somatic Illness Among College Students." *Res Q* 26:197-204 My '55. * (*PA* 30:1571)

597. STERNBERG, CARL. "Personality Trait Patterns of College Students Majoring in Different Fields." *Psychol Monogr* 69(18):1-21 '55. * (*PA* 31:1705)

598. STEWART, BARBARA M., AND VINEBERG, SHALOM E. "MMPI Characteristics of Hospitalized Tuberculosis Patients." Abstract. *Am Psychol* 10:361-2 Ag '55. *

599. THURSTON, DONALD REID. *An Investigation of the Possibilities of Parole Prediction Through the Use of Five Personality Inventories.* Doctor's thesis, Michigan State University (East Lansing, Mich.), 1955. (*DA* 15:1206)

600. WADSWORTH, HELEN MARY MAERTENS. *The Relationship Between Experimentally Induced Stress and the Characteristic Mode of Expression and Level of Anxiety.* Doctor's thesis, University of Michigan (Ann Arbor, Mich.), 1955. (*DA* 15:883)

601. WINDLE, CHARLES. "Further Studies of Test-Retest Effect on Personality Questionnaires." *Ed & Psychol Meas* 15:246-53 au '55. * (*PA* 30:4608)

602. WINDLE, CHARLES. "The Relationships Among Five MMPI 'Anxiety' Indices." *J Consult Psychol* 19:61-3 F '55. * (*PA* 29:8657)

603. WIRT, ROBERT D. "Further Validation of the Ego-Strength Scale." Abstract. *J Consult Psychol* 19:444 D '55. *

604. ANDERSON, WAYNE. "The MMPI: Low Pa Scores." *J Counsel Psychol* 3:226-8 fall '56. * (*PA* 31:7889)

605. ARBUCKLE, DUGALD S. "Client Perception of Counselor Personality." *J Counsel Psychol* 3:93-6 su '56. * (*PA* 31:4639)

606. BARNES, EUGENE H. "Factors, Response Bias, and the MMPI." *J Consult Psychol* 20:419-21 D '56. * (*PA* 32:1608)

607. BARNES, EUGENE H. "Response Bias and the MMPI." *J Consult Psychol* 20:371-4 O '56. * (*PA* 31:7892)

608. BARTHOL, RICHARD P., AND KIRK, BARBARA A. "The Selection of Graduate Students in Public Health Education." *J Appl Psychol* 40:159-63 Je '56. * (*PA* 31:6666)

609. BEALL, HERBERT S., AND PANTON, JAMES H. "Use of the Minnesota Multiphasic Personality Inventory as an Index to 'Escapism.'" *J Clin Psychol* 12:392-4 O '56. *

610. BEAVER, ALMA P. "Psychometric Data and Survival in a College of Nursing." *Psychol Rep* 2:223-6 Je '56. * (*PA* 31:1738)

611. BELLEVILLE, RICHARD E. "MMPI Score Changes Induced by Lysergic Acid Diethylamide (LSD-25)." *J Clin Psychol* 12:279-82 Jl '56. * (*PA* 31:6057)

612. BERNBERG, RAYMOND E. "Personality Correlates of Social Conformity: II." *J Social Psychol* 43:309-12 My '56. *

613. BORGHI, EUGENE. *A Study Comparing the Basic Personalities of the Mothers of Stuttering Sons with Mothers of Non-Stutterers as Measured by the MMPI.* Master's thesis, University of Redlands (Redlands, Calif.), 1956.

614. BURGESS, ELVA. "Personality Factors of Over- and Under-Achievers in Engineering." *J Ed Psychol* 47:89-99 F '56. * (*PA* 31:8811)

615. BUTTON, ALAN D. "A Study of Alcoholics With the Minnesota Multiphasic Personality Inventory." *Q J Studies Alcohol* 17:263-81 Je '56. * (*PA* 31:6307)

616. CLARK, JERRY H., AND DANIELSON, JACK R. "A Shortened Schizophrenic Scale for Use in Rapid Screening." *J Social Psychol* 43:187-90 F '56. * (*PA* 31:3449)

617. COHN, THOMAS S. "The Relation of the F Scale to a Response Set to Answer Positively." J Social Psychol 44:129–33 Ag '56.*

618. COLE, DAVID L. "The Use of the MMPI and Biographical Data in Predicting Practice-Teaching Performance and Subsequent Attitudes Toward Teaching." Abstract. Am Psychol 11:367 Ag '56.*

619. DANSEREAU, RAYMOND A. An Analysis of the Responses of Public and Private High School Students on the Minnesota Multiphasic Personality Inventory. Doctor's thesis, Fordham University (New York, N.Y.), 1956.

620. DIDATO, S. VINCENT, AND KENNEDY, THOMAS M. "Masculinity-Femininity and Personal Values." Psychol Rep 2:231 Je '56.* (PA 31:608)

621. DRAKE, L. E. "Interpretation of MMPI Profiles in Counseling Male Clients." J Counsel Psychol 3:83–8 su '56.* (PA 31:4683)

622. EARLE, J. B. The Development of a Quantitative Method for Differentiating Between Pathological Groups With the MMPI. Doctor's thesis, University of Ottawa (Ottawa, Ont., Canada), 1956.

623. EVERSMEYER, GOLDA JOAN. Personality, Stress, and Temporal Generalization. Doctor's thesis, State University of Iowa (Iowa City, Iowa), 1956. (DA 16:1943)

624. FORDYCE, WILBERT E. "Social Desirability in the MMPI." J Consult Psychol 20:171–5 Je '56.* (PA 31:6076)

625. FREEDMAN, MERVIN; WEBSTER, HAROLD; AND SANFORD, NEVITT. "A Study of Authoritarianism and Psychopathology." J Psychol 41:315–22 Ap '56.* (PA 31:4688)

626. FRACK, J. W., AND KEENER, HELEN E. "A Validation Study of the Prediction of College Achievement." J Appl Psychol 40:251–2 Ag '56.* (PA 31:6674)

627. FRICKE, BENNO G. "Conversion Hysterics and the MMPI." J Clin Psychol 12:322–6 O '56.*

628. FRICKE, BENNO G. "Response Set as a Suppressor Variable in the OAIS and MMPI." J Consult Psychol 20:161–9 Je '56.* (PA 31:6080)

629. GASTON, CHARLES O.; TAULBEE, EARL S.; SEAQUIST, MAURICE R.; AND SELLS, SAUL B. "A Conversion Table for Relating the MMPI Group and Individual Form Items." J Clin Psychol 12:49–52 Ja '56.* (PA 30:4572)

630. GOODSTEIN, LEONARD D. "MMPI Profiles of Stutterers' Parents: A Follow-Up Study." J Speech & Hearing Disorders 21:430–5 D '56.* (PA 31:4903)

631. GOODSTEIN, LEONARD D., AND DAHLSTROM, W. GRANT. "MMPI Differences Between Parents of Stuttering and Nonstuttering Children." J Consult Psychol 20:365–70 O '56.* (PA 31:8387)

632. GOWAN, J. C. "Achievement and Personality Test Scores of Gifted College Students." Calif J Ed Res 7:105–9 My '56.* (PA 31:3783)

633. GREENFIELD, NORMAN S., AND FEY, WILLIAM F. "Factors Influencing Utilization of Psychotherapeutic Services in Male College Students." J Clin Psychol 12:276–9 Jl '56.* (PA 31:6653)

634. HAFNER, JAMES L. Social Leadership as Related to the Minnesota Multiphasic Personality Inventory. Doctor's thesis, Oklahoma Agricultural and Mechanical College (Stillwater, Okla.), 1956.

635. HANLEY, CHARLES. "Social Desirability and Responses to Items From Three MMPI Scales: D, Sc, and K." J Appl Psychol 40:324–8 O '56.* (PA 31:7920)

636. HARTSHORN, ELIZABETH. "A Comparison of Certain Aspects of Student Leadership and Non-Leadership; Significant Differences on Four Psychometric Tests." J Ed Res 49:515–22 Mr '56.* (PA 31:5098)

637. HEWER, VIVIAN H. "A Comparison of Successful and Unsuccessful Students in the Medical School at the University of Minnesota." J Appl Psychol 40:164–8 Je '56. * (PA 31:6675)

638. KANUM, CLARA. Predicting Delinquency From the MMPI Using Items Instead of Clinical Scales. Doctor's thesis, University of Minnesota (Minneapolis, Minn.), 1956. (DA 16:2547)

639. KARSON, SAMUEL, AND FREUD, SHELDON L. "Predicting Psychiatric Diagnoses With the MMPI." J Clin Psychol 12:376–9 O '56.*

640. KORNETSKY, CONAN, AND HUMPHRIES, OGRETTA. "The Relationship Between the Effects of a Number of Centrally Acting Drugs and Four MMPI Scales." Abstract. Am Psychol 11:366 Ag '56.*

641. LAVER, A. B. Item Analysis of the Minnesota Multiphasic Personality Inventory. Master's thesis, Queen's University (Kingston, Ont., Canada), 1956.

642. LEWINSOHN, PETER M. "Personality Correlates of Duodenal Ulcer and Other Psychosomatic Reactions." J Clin Psychol 12:296–8 Jl '56. * (PA 31:6484)

643. MEIER, MANFRED JOHN. Interrelationships Among MMPI Variables, Kinesthetic Figural Aftereffect, and Reminiscence in Motor Learning. Doctor's thesis, University of Wisconsin (Madison, Wis.), 1956. (DA 17:678)

644. MERRILL, REED M., AND HEATHERS, LOUISE B. "The Relation of the MMPI to the Edwards Personal Preference Schedule on a College Counseling Center Sample." J Consult Psychol 20:310–4 Ag '56. * (PA 31:7949)

645. NELSON, MARVEN O., AND SHEA, SALLY. "MMPI Correlates of the Inventory of Factors STDCR." Psychol Rep 2:433–5 D '56. * (PA 31:4704)

646. OLMSTED, DONALD W., AND MONACHESI, ELIO D. "A

Validity Check on MMPI Scales of Responsibility and Dominance." J Abn & Social Psychol 53:140–2 Jl '56. * (PA 32:1638)

647. OSBORNE, R. T.; SANDERS, WILMA B.; AND YOUNG, FLORENE M. "MMPI Patterns of College Disciplinary Cases." J Counsel Psychol 3:52–6 sp '56. * (PA 31:3699)

648. PEEK, ROLAND M., AND STORMS, LOWELL H. "Validity of the Marsh-Hilliard-Liechti MMPI Sexual Deviation Scale in a State Hospital Population." J Consult Psychol 20:133–6 Ap '56. * (PA 31:6115)

649. POTHAST, MILES DALE. A Personality Study of Two Types of Murderers. Doctor's thesis, Michigan State University (East Lansing, Mich.), 1956. (DA 17:898)

650. PRAAG, JULES VAN. A Rorschach and MMPI Study of a Fundamentalist Religious Sect. Doctor's thesis, University of Denver (Denver, Colo.), 1956.

651. RAYMAKER, HENRY, JR. Relationships Between the Self-Concept, Self-Ideal Concept and Maladjustment. Doctor's thesis, Vanderbilt University (Nashville, Tenn.), 1956. (DA 17:409)

652. ROSEN, EPHRAIM. "Self-Appraisal and Perceived Desirability of MMPI Personality Traits." J Counsel Psychol 3:44–51 sp '56. * (PA 31:3070)

653. ROSEN, EPHRAIM. "Self-Appraisal, Personal Desirability, and Perceived Social Desirability of Personality Traits." J Abn & Social Psychol 52:151–8 Mr '56. * (PA 31:2568)

654. SARASON, IRWIN G. "The Relationship of Anxiety and 'Lack of Defensiveness' to Intellectual Performance." J Consult Psychol 20:220–2 Je '56. * (PA 31:5779)

655. SIEGEL, SAUL M. "The Relationship of Hostility to Authoritarianism." J Abn & Social Psychol 52:368–72 My '56. * (PA 31:4494)

656. SMITH, DAVID WAYNE. The Relation Between Certain Physical Characteristics and Selected Scales of the Minnesota Multiphasic Personality Inventory. Doctor's thesis, Indiana University (Bloomington, Ind.), 1956. (DA 16:1953)

657. SMITH, ROBERT E. "Personality Configurations of Adult Male Penal Populations as Revealed by the MMPI." Abstract. Am Psychol 11:382 Ag '56. *

658. SPILKA, BERNARD, AND STRUENING, E. L. "A Questionnaire Study of Personality and Ethnocentrism." J Social Psychol 44:65–71 Ag '56. *

659. STERNBERG, CARL. "Interests and Tendencies Toward Maladjustment in a Normal Population." Personnel & Guid J 35:94–9 O '56. * (PA 31:7975)

660. STONE, DAVID R., AND GANUNG, GEORGE R. "A Study of Scholastic Achievement Related to Personality as Measured by the Minnesota Multiphasic Personality Inventory." J Ed Res 50:155–6 O '56. * (PA 32:959)

661. STONE, DAVID R., AND WEST, LEROY L. " 'First Day' Orientation Testing With the Minnesota Multiphasic Personality Inventory Contrasted With a Re-Test." J Ed Res 49:621–4 Ap '56. * (PA 31:5152)

662. STRAIGHT, GLENN H. Identifiable Personality Characteristics Resulting From Membership in a Conspicuous Religious Minority in Public High Schools. Doctor's thesis, University of Nebraska (Lincoln, Neb.), 1956. (DA 17:810)

663. SUNDBERG, NORMAN D. "The Use of the MMPI for Cross-Cultural Personality Study: A Preliminary Report on the German Translation." J Abn & Social Psychol 52:281–3 Mr '56. * (PA 31:3083)

664. SUNDBERG, NORMAN D., AND BACHELIS, WARREN D. "The Fakability of Two Measures of Prejudice: The California F Scale and Gough's Pr Scale." J Abn & Social Psychol 52: 140–2 Jl '56. * (PA 31:2757)

665. TESSENEER, RALPH, AND TYDLASKA, MARY. "A Cross-Validation of a Work Attitude Scale From the MMPI." J Ed Psychol 47:1–7 Ja '56. * (PA 31:6139)

666. THOMPSON, JORGEN SOGN. A Study of the Relationships Between Certain Measured Psychological Variables and Achievement in the First Year of Theological Seminary Work. Doctor's thesis, University of Minnesota (Minneapolis, Minn.), 1956. (DA 16:1846)

667. VOAS, ROBERT B. "Comparison of the Taylor Anxiety Scale Administered Separately and Within the MMPI." Psychol Rep 2:373–6 D '56. * (PA 31:4720)

668. WEINER, IRA W. "Psychological Factors Related to Results of Subtotal Gastrectomy." Psychosom Med 18:486–91 N–D '56. *

669. WELSH, GEORGE SCHLAGER, AND DAHLSTROM, W. GRANT, EDITORS. Basic Readings on the MMPI in Psychology and Medicine. Minneapolis, Minn.: University of Minnesota Press, 1956. Pp. xvii, 656. * (PA 31:1080)

670. WINTER, WILLIAM D., AND FREDERICKSON, WILBUR K. "The Short-Term Effect of Chlorpromazine on Psychiatric Patients." J Consult Psychol 20:431–4 D '56. * (PA 32:1876)

671. WIRT, ROBERT D. "Actuarial Prediction." J Consult Psychol 20:123–4 '56. * (PA 31:6037)

672. ZEAMAN, JEAN BURGDORF. Some of the Personality Attributes Related to Achievement in College: A Comparison of Men and Women Students. Doctor's thesis, Michigan State University (East Lansing, Mich.), 1956. (DA 18:290)

673. ZIMET, CARL N., AND BRACKBILL, GLEN A. "The Role of Anxiety in Psychodiagnosis." J Clin Psychol 12:173–7 Ap '56. * (PA 31:4722)

674. ADRIAN, ROBERT JOHN. The Relationship of Parental Personality Structures to Child Adjustment and Adoption Selection. Doctor's thesis, University of Minnesota (Minneapolis, Minn.), 1957. (DA 17:1386)

675. ALLEN, ROBERT M. "The Relationship Between the Ed-

wards Personal Preference Schedule Variables and the Minnesota Multiphasic Personality Inventory Scales." *J Appl Psychol* 41:307–11 O '57. *

676. BEIER, ERNST G.; GARFIELD, REED L.; AND ROSSI, ASCONIA M. "Projections of Personality Characteristics on Liked and Disliked Persons." Abstract. *Am Psychol* 12:372 Jl '57. *

677. BRAMS, JEROME MARTIN. *The Relationship Between Personal Characteristics of Counseling Trainees and Effective Communication in Counseling.* Doctor's thesis, University of Missouri (Columbia, Mo.), 1957. (*DA* 17:1510)

678. BRAYFIELD, ARTHUR H., AND MARSH, MARY MARKLEY. "Aptitudes, Interests, and Personality Characteristics of Farmers." *J Appl Psychol* 41:98–103 Ap '57. *

679. BRUCE, MARTIN M. "Normative Data Information Exchange, No. 10-24." *Personnel Psychol* 10:357–8 au '57. *

680. CALVIN, ALLEN D., AND HANLEY, CHARLES. "An Investigation of Dissimulation on the MMPI by Means of the 'Lie Detector.' " *J Appl Psychol* 41:312–6 O '57. *

681. CHANSKY, NORMAN M., AND BREGMAN, MARTIN. "Improvement of Reading in College." *J Ed Res* 51:313–7 D '57. *

682. COMREY, ANDREW L. "A Factor Analysis of Items on the MMPI Depression Scale." *Ed & Psychol Meas* 17:578–85 w '57. *

683. COMREY, ANDREW L. "A Factor Analysis of Items on the MMPI Hypochondriasis Scale." *Ed & Psychol Meas* 17:568–77 w '57. *

684. COMREY, ANDREW L. "A Factor Analysis of Items on the MMPI Hysteria Scale." *Ed & Psychol Meas* 17:586–92 w '57. *

685. COMREY, ANDREW L. "Factors in the Items of the MMPI." Abstract. *Am Psychol* 12:437 Jl '57. *

686. CROW, W. R. *Relationships Between Edwards PPS and the MMPI.* Master's thesis, University of Washington (Seattle, Wash.), 1957.

687. DAHLSTROM, W. G., AND MEEHL, P. E. "Objective Configural Identification of Psychotic MMPI Profiles." Abstract. *Am Psychol* 12:367 Jl '57. *

688. DANA, RICHARD H. "MMPI Performance and Electroshock Treatment." *J Clin Psychol* 13:350–5 O '57. *

689. DEAN, SIDNEY I. "Adjustment Testing and Personality Factors of the Blind." *J Consult Psychol* 21:171–7 Ap '57. *

690. DRAKE, L. E., AND OETTING, EUGENE R. "An MMPI Pattern and a Suppressor Variable Predictive of Academic Achievement." *J Counsel Psychol* 4:245–7 fall '57. *

691. DRASGOW, JAMES, AND BARNETTE, W. LESLIE, JR. "F-K in a Motivated Group." *J Consult Psychol* 21:399–401 O '57. *

692. ENDS, EARL J., AND PAGE, CURTIS W. "A Study of Functional Relationships Among Measures of Anxiety, Ego Strength and Adjustment." *J Clin Psychol* 13:148–50 Ap '57. * (*PA* 32:3074)

693. FRICKE, BENNO G. "A Response Bias (B) Scale for the MMPI." *J Counsel Psychol* 4:149–53 su '57. *

694. FRICKE, BENNO G. "Subtle and Obvious Test Items and Response Set." *J Consult Psychol* 21:250–2 Je '57. *

695. GRAYSON, HARRY M., AND OLINGER, LEONARD B. "Simulation of 'Normalcy' by Psychiatric Patients on the MMPI." *J Consult Psychol* 21:73–7 F '57. * (*PA* 32:491)

696. HANLEY, CHARLES. "Deriving a Measure of Test-Taking Defensiveness." *J Consult Psychol* 21:391–7 O '57. *

697. HATHAWAY, STARKE R., AND BRIGGS, PETER F. "Some Normative Data on New MMPI Scales." *J Clin Psychol* 13:364–8 O '57. *

698. HOLZ, WILLIAM C.; HARDING, GEORGE F.; AND GLASSMAN, SIDNEY M. "A Note on the Clinical Validity of the Marsh-Hilliard-Liechti MMPI Sexual Deviation Scale." *J Consult Psychol* 21:326 Ag '57. *

699. JENSEN, ARTHUR R. "Authoritarian Attitudes and Personality Maladjustment." *J Abn & Social Psychol* 54:303–11 My '57. *

700. KARSON, SAMUEL, AND POOL, KENNETH BRYNER. "The Construct Validity of the Sixteen Personality Factors Test." *J Clin Psychol* 13:245–52 Jl '57. *

701. KIMBER, J. A. MORRIS. "An Alphabetical List of MMPI Items." *J Clin Psychol* 13:197–202 Ap '57. * (*PA* 32:2902)

702. LAIRD, JAMES T. "Emotional Disturbances Among the Physically Handicapped." *Personnel & Guid J* 36:190–1 N '57. *

703. LEARY, TIMOTHY. *Interpersonal Diagnosis of Personality: A Functional Theory and Methodology for Personality Evaluation.* New York: Ronald Press Co., 1957. Pp. xix, 518. (*PA* 31:2556)

704. LINGOES, JAMES C. "Minnesota Multiphasic Personality Inventory Test Correlates of Szondi Picture Preferences." *Szondi Newsl* 6:1–6 S '57. *

705. MAYO, GEORGE DOUGLAS, AND GUTTMAN, ISAIAH. "Faking in a Vocational Classification Situation." Abstract. *Am Psychol* 12:424 Jl '57. *

706. MILLER, ROBERT S., AND COTTLE, WILLIAM C. "Relationships Between MMPI Scales and GZTS Scales: An Adult Female Sample." *Univ Kans B Ed* 11:54–9 F '57. *

707. MOORE, CLARK H., AND COLE, DAVID. "The Relation of MMPI Scores to Practice Teaching Ratings." *J Ed Res* 50:711–6 My '57. *

708. MORRICE, J. K. W. "The Minnesota Multiphasic Personality Inventory in Recidivist Prisoners." *J Mental Sci* 103:632–5 Jl '57. *

709. MURPHY, DONAL GERALD. *Psychological Correlates of*

Alcohol Addictions. Doctor's thesis, Columbia University (New York, N.Y.), 1957. (*DA* 18:1496)

710. NELSON, KENNETH G. "Use of the MMPI as a Predictor of High School Teacher Effectiveness." Abstract. *Am Psychol* 12:390 Jl '57. *

711. O'CONNOR, JAMES P.; STEFIC, EDWARD C.; AND GRESOCK, CLEMENT J. "Some Patterns of Depression." *J Clin Psychol* 13:122–5 Ap '57. * (*PA* 32:2914)

712. QUINN, STANLEY BRITTAIN. *Relationships of Certain Personality Characteristics to College Achievement.* Doctor's thesis, University of Wisconsin (Madison, Wis.), 1957. (*DA* 17:809)

713. REED, MAX R. "The Masculinity-Femininity Dimension in Normal and Psychotic Subjects." *J Abn & Social Psychol* 55:289–94 N '57. *

714. SCOTT, EDWARD M. "Personality and Movie Preference." *Psychol Rep* 3:17–8 Mr '57. *

715. SHELDON, M. STEPHEN. "The Fakability of Four MMPI Scales Used in Teacher Selection." Abstract. *Am Psychol* 12:390 Jl '57. *

716. SMITH, DAVID WAYNE. "The Relation Between Ratio Indices of Physique and Selected Scales of the Minnesota Multi-Phasic Personality Inventory." *J Psychol* 43:325–31 Ap '57. *

717. SOPCHAK, ANDREW L. "Relation Between MMPI Scores and Musical Projective Test Scores." *J Clin Psychol* 13:165–8 Ap '57. * (*PA* 32:2921)

718. SWAN, ROBERT J. "Using the MMPI in Marriage Counseling." *J Counsel Psychol* 4:239–44 fall '57. *

719. SYME, LEONARD. "Personality Characteristics and the Alcoholic: A Critique of Current Studies." *Q J Studies Alcohol* 18:288–302 Je '57. *

720. TAFT, RONALD. "A Cross-Cultural Comparison of the MMPI." *J Consult Psychol* 21:161–4 Ap '57. *

721. TAFT, RONALD. "The Validity of the Barron Ego-Strength Scale and the Welsh Anxiety Index." *J Consult Psychol* 21:247–9 Je '57. *

722. TAMKIN, ARTHUR S. "An Evaluation of the Construct Validity of Barron's Ego-Strength Scale." *J Clin Psychol* 13:156–8 Ap '57. * (*PA* 32:2923)

723. TAMKIN, ARTHUR S., AND SCHERER, ISIDOR W. "What Is Measured by the 'Cannot Say' Scale of the Group MMPI?" Abstract. *J Consult Psychol* 21:370 O '57. *

724. TAULBEE, EARL S., AND SISSON, BOYD D. "Configurational Analysis of MMPI Profiles of Psychiatric Groups." *J Consult Psychol* 21:413–7 O '57. *

725. TOPETZES, NICK JOHN. "A Program for the Selection of Trainees in Physical Medicine." *J Exp Ed* 25:263–311 Je '57. *

726. VOAS, ROBERT B. "Personality Correlates of Reading Speed and the Time Required to Complete Questionnaires." *Psychol Rep* 3:177–82 Je '57. *

727. VOAS, ROBERT B. "Validity of Personality Scales for the Prediction of Success in Naval Aviation Training." Abstract. *Am Psychol* 12:465 Jl '57. *

728. WATSON, GEORGE. "Vitamin Deficiencies in Mental Illness." *J Psychol* 43:47–63 Ja '57. *

729. YEOMANS, WILLIAM N., AND LUNDIN, ROBERT W. "The Relationship Between Personality Adjustment and Scholarship Achievement in Male College Students." *J General Psychol* 57:213–8 O '57. *

730. AARONSON, BERNARD S. "Age and Sex Influences on MMPI Profile Peak Distributions in an Abnormal Population." *J Consult Psychol* 22:203–6 Je '58. *

731. ALTUS, WILLIAM D. "Q-L Variability, MMPI Responses, and College Males." *J Consult Psychol* 22:367–71 O '58. *

732. BINDER, ARNOLD. "Personality Variables and Recognition Response Level." *J Abn & Social Psychol* 57:136–42 S '58. *

733. BOOTH, E. G., JR. "Personality Traits of Athletes as Measured by the MMPI." *Res Q* 29:127–38 My '58. *

734. BRIGGS, PETER F. "Prediction of Rehospitalization Using the MMPI." *J Clin Psychol* 14:83–4 Ja '58. *

735. COMREY, ANDREW L. "A Factor Analysis of Items on the F Scale of the MMPI." *Ed & Psychol Meas* 18:621–32 au '58. *

736. COMREY, ANDREW L. "A Factor Analysis of Items on the K Scale of the MMPI." *Ed & Psychol Meas* 18:633–9 au '58. *

737. COMREY, ANDREW L. "A Factor Analysis of Items on the MMPI Hypomania Scale." *Ed & Psychol Meas* 18:313–23 su '58. *

738. COMREY, ANDREW L. "A Factor Analysis of Items on the MMPI Paranoia Scale." *Ed & Psychol Meas* 18:99–107 sp '58. *

739. COMREY, ANDREW L. "A Factor Analysis of Items on the MMPI Psychasthenia Scale." *Ed & Psychol Meas* 18:293–300 su '58. *

740. COMREY, ANDREW L. "A Factor Analysis of Items on the MMPI Psychopathic Deviate Scale." *Ed & Psychol Meas* 18:91–8 sp '58. *

741. COMREY, ANDREW L., AND MARGGRAFF, WALTRAUD M. "A Factor Analysis of Items on the MMPI Schizophrenia Scale." *Ed & Psychol Meas* 18:301–11 su '58. *

742. DRASGOW, JAMES, AND McKENZIE, JAMES. "College Transcripts, Graduation and the MMPI." *J Counsel Psychol* 5:196–9 fall '58. *

743. ERIKSEN, CHARLES W.; KUETHE, JAMES W.; AND SUL-

livan, Daniel F. "Some Personality Correlates of Learning Without Verbal Awareness." *J Personality* 26:216–28 Je '58. *

744. FELDMAN, MARVIN J. "An Evaluation Scale for Shock Therapy." *J Clin Psychol* 14:41–5 Ja '58. *

745. FINE, BERNARD J. "The Relationship Between Certain Scales of the Minnesota Multiphasic Personality Inventory and Susceptibility to Prestige Suggestion." *Psychol Newsl* 9:200–3 My–Je '58. *

746. GOWAN, J. C. "Intercorrelations and Factor Analysis of Tests Given to Teaching Candidates." *J Exp Ed* 27:1–22 S '58. *

747. GRAHAM, LEO R. "Personality Factors and Epileptic Seizures." *J Clin Psychol* 14:187–8 Ap '58. *

748. GREENFIELD, NORMAN S. "Personality Patterns of Patients Before and After Application for Psychotherapy." Abstract. *J Consult Psychol* 22:280 Ag '58. *

749. GRIFFITH, ALBERT V.; UPSHAW, HARRY S.; AND FOWLER, RAYMOND D. "The Psychasthenic and Hypomanic Scales of the MMPI and Uncertainty in Judgments." *J Clin Psychol* 14:385–6 O '58. *

750. HARDING, GEORGE F.; HOLZ, WILLIAM C.; AND KAWAKAMI, DANIEL. "The Differentiation of Schizophrenic and Superficially Similar Reactions." *J Clin Psychol* 14:147–9 Ap '58. *

751. HOYT, DONALD P., AND SEDLACEK, GORDON M. "Differentiating Alcoholics From Normals and Abnormals With the MMPI." *J Clin Psychol* 14:69–74 Ja '58. *

752. JACKSON, KARMA RAE, AND CLARK, SELBY G. "Thefts Among College Students." *Personnel & Guid J* 36:557–62 Ap '58. *

753. JENSEN, VERN H. "Influence of Personality Traits on Academic Success." *Personnel & Guid J* 36:497–500 Mr '58. *

754. KARSON, SAMUEL. "Second-Order Personality Factors and the MMPI." *J Clin Psychol* 14:313–5 Jl '58. *

755. LINDE, TOM, AND PATTERSON, C. H. "The MMPI in Cerebral Palsy." *J Consult Psychol* 22:210–2 Je '58. *

756. LITTLE, KENNETH B., AND FISHER, JEROME. "Two New Experimental Scales of the MMPI." *J Consult Psychol* 22:305–6 Ag '58. *

757. McCALL, RAYMOND J. "Face Validity in the D Scale of the MMPI." *J Clin Psychol* 14:77–80 Ja '58. *

758. MEHLMAN, BENJAMIN, AND KAPLAN, JANICE E. "A Correction: A Comparison of Some Concepts of Psychological Health." *J Clin Psychol* 14:438 O '58. *

759. MELLO, NANCY K., AND GUTHRIE, GEORGE M. "MMPI Profiles and Behavior in Counseling." *J Counsel Psychol* 5:125–9 su '58. *

760. MOTTO, JOSEPH J. "The MMPI Performance of Veterans With Organic and Psychiatric Disabilities." Abstract. *J Consult Psychol* 22:304 Ag '58. *

761. PANTON, JAMES H. "MMPI Profile Characteristics of Physically Disabled Prison Inmates." *Psychol Rep* 4:529–30 S '58. *

762. PANTON, JAMES H. "MMPI Profile Configurations Among Crime Classification Groups." *J Clin Psychol* 14:305–8 Jl '58. *

763. PANTON, JAMES H. "Predicting Prison Adjustment With the Minnesota Multiphasic Personality Inventory." *J Clin Psychol* 14:308–12 Jl '58. *

764. PINNEAU, SAMUEL R., AND MILTON, ALEXANDER. "The Ecological Veracity of the Self-Report." *J Genetic Psychol* 93:249–76 D '58. *

765. PUMROY, DONALD K., AND KOGAN, WILLIAM S. "A Validation of Measures That Predict the Efficacy of Shock Therapy." *J Clin Psychol* 14:46–7 Ja '58. *

766. PUSTELL, THOMAS E. "A Note on Use of the MMPI in College Counseling." *J Counsel Psychol* 5:69–70 sp '58. *

767. REMPEL, PETER P. "The Use of Multivariate Statistical Analysis of Minnesota Multiphasic Personality Inventory Scores in the Classification of Delinquent and Nondelinquent High School Boys." *J Consult Psychol* 22:17–23 F '58. *

768. ROSEN, ALBERT; HALES, WILLIAM N.; AND PEEK, ROLAND M. "Comparability of MMPI Card and Booklet Forms for Psychiatric Patients." *J Clin Psychol* 14:387–8 O '58. *

769. SLOAN, THOMAS J., AND PIERCE-JONES, JOHN. "The Bordin-Peninsky Diagnostic Categories: Counselor Agreement and MMPI Comparisons." Comments by William A. Hunt. *J Counsel Psychol* 5:189–95 fall '58. *

770. SOPCHAK, ANDREW L. "Spearman Correlations Between MMPI Scores of College Students and Their Parents." *J Consult Psychol* 22:207–9 Je '58. *

771. SPILKA, B., AND KIMBLE, GLORIA. "Personality Correlates of Q-L Differentials on the ACE." Abstract. *J Consult Psychol* 22:142 Ap '58. *

772. SULLIVAN, PATRICK L.; MILLER, CHRISTINE; AND SMELSER, WILLIAM. "Factors in Length of Stay and Progress in Psychotherapy." *J Consult Psychol* 22:1–9 F '58. *

773. TARNAPOL, LESTER. "Personality Differences Between Leaders and Non-Leaders." *Personnel J* 37:57–60 Je '58. *

774. TAULBEE, EARL S. "Relationship Between Certain Personality Variables and Continuation in Psychotherapy." *J Consult Psychol* 22:83–9 Ap '58. *

775. TAULBEE, EARL S. "A Validation of MMPI Scale Pairs in Psychiatric Diagnosis." *J Clin Psychol* 14:316 Jl '58. *

776. VOAS, ROBERT B. "A Procedure for Reducing the Effects of Slanting Questionnaire Responses Toward Social Acceptability." *Ed & Psychol Meas* 18:337–45 su '58. *

777. WATTRON, JOHN B. "Validity of the Marsh-Hilliard-Liechti MMPI Sexual Deviation Scale in a State Prison Population." Abstract. *J Consult Psychol* 22:16 F '58. *

778. WILCOX, GEORGE T. "Note on a Rapid Scoring Procedure for the Card Form MMPI." *J Clin Psychol* 14:85 Ja '58. *

779. WINTER, WILLIAM D., AND SALCINES, RAMON A. "The Validity of the Objective Rorschach and the MMPI." *J Consult Psychol* 22:199–202 Je '58. *

ALBERT ELLIS, *Consulting Psychologist, 333 West 56th St., New York 19, New York.*

Although there have been no significant changes in the format, administration, scoring, or interpretation of the MMPI itself since the revised manual and *Atlas* were issued in 1951, basic research with the instrument has continued apace, culminating in Hathaway and Monachesi's *Analyzing and Predicting Juvenile Delinquency with the MMPI* (438) and Welsh and Dahlstrom's *Basic Readings on the MMPI in Psychology and Medicine* (669). As a result of this continuing research, it can confidently be stated that in the whole history of modern psychology there has been no other personality inventory on which so much theoretical and practical work has been done.

In spite of all this research activity, the question of just how valid a clinical instrument the MMPI is has still not been finally settled. Calvin and McConnell (417), objecting vigorously to some general remarks on personality inventories made by the present reviewer (425), assayed 80 research studies in which the MMPI was used from 1940 to 1950 and reported that significant discriminations between different kinds of groups tested were found in 71 out of 80 studies. Calvin and McConnell's sample of research studies, however, is far from being complete. The reviewer found 160 studies employing the MMPI published between 1946 and 1951. Of these studies, 102 (64 per cent) showed significant discriminations. Of 339 research studies employing other personality inventories published during the same period, 188 (55 per cent) showed significant discriminations. Although it may be concluded, therefore, that the MMPI may be *more* valid for group discrimination than the average inventory, its *absolute* validity remains in doubt.

Assuming that the MMPI has some fair degree of validity for distinguishing one kind of group from another, the efficacy of its use for individual diagnosis still remains to be proved. As the manual attests, "a high score on a scale has been found to predict postively the corresponding final clinical diagnosis or estimate in more than 60 per cent of new psychiatric admissions." But the same manual also makes it clear that "it should be continually kept in mind that the great majority of persons having deviant profiles are not, in the usual sense of the word, mentally ill, nor are they in need of psychological treatment. Having no more information about a person than that he has a deviant profile, one should always start with the assumption that the subject is operating within the normal range." The *Atlas* then, which encourages test users to compare obtained profiles to those of mental hospital patients and contains no profiles of "normal" subjects with deviant scores, seems to add to the confusion regarding whether or not individual diagnosis is to be taken too seriously.

Another relevant question in regard to clinical use of the MMPI is whether the game is worth the candle in terms of time consumed in scoring and interpreting the test. Aside from literally scores of hours which a conscientious MMPI user must now take to acquaint himself with the theory and practice of the test, he must also spend from two to three hours checking, profiling, analyzing, and comparing each protocol in relation to the material in the manual, the *Atlas,* the *Basic Readings,* and various other MMPI researches. It is to be wondered whether the clinical psychologist who cannot, in equal or less time, get more pertinent, incisive, and depth-centered "personality" material from a straightforward interview technique, is worth his salt.

On the whole, one must have considerable respect for the great amount of time and effort that have gone into MMPI research since the first studies on it appeared in 1940. This time and effort has borne sufficient fruit to make it now appear that the instrument is quite useful for many kinds of group discrimination. About its usefulness for individual clinical diagnosis the present reviewer, for one, is still far from enthusiastic.

WARREN T. NORMAN, *Instructor in Psychology, University of Michigan, Ann Arbor, Michigan.*

The current manual, revised in 1951, is intended to serve primarily as a "basic guide to administration and interpretation" rather than as a "general treatise on the MMPI." It provides detailed information on the item content and format, the administration, recording, and scoring of both the card and booklet forms, and procedures and norms for plotting profiles and for coding them, using Hathaway's system. Information on the development and characteristics of the standard validity (in the sense of test-taking attitude) and clinical scales is brief and, in one major aspect to be discussed below, seriously inadequate. The discussion of profile interpretation, while properly cautious, is general and unsystematic and cannot serve as more than a minimal introduction to the usefulness and the problems of multiscale personality assessment with this inventory.

Test-retest stability coefficients reported range from .46 to .93 over periods of from three days to one year and cluster about a median of .76. The manual contains no table of intercorrelations among the scales of the inventory, no correlations with other personality measures, no information on internal consistency among items comprising a given scale, nor any explicit indication of the number or names of general factors of personality tapped by the several empirically derived scales.

The most serious shortcoming of the manual, however, is the absence of detailed predictive and concurrent validity information. Neither data from the original development samples nor data from subsequent studies against psychiatric diagnoses or other behavioral criteria are presented. Considerable information of this sort is now available but mostly in scattered journal articles. In short, the manual is adequate in its coverage of general test description, administration, and scoring details; it is inadequate in its report of the empirical and construct validities of the scales and ought to be revised accordingly.

Fortunately for the clinical or research user of the MMPI, many of the manual's deficiencies are compensated by other available references. The volume (*263*) of case histories compiled by Hathaway and Meehl is valuable both for purposes of training in profile interpretation and as a reference source. Hathaway and Monachesi (*438*) have reported a series of studies in predicting juvenile delinquency. A somewhat earlier monograph by Cottle (*423*) provides some technical material not covered in the test manual. But perhaps the most valuable adjunct is the Welsh and Dahlstrom collection of readings (*669*). This volume contains 66 of the most important articles on the MMPI that appeared from 1940 through 1954, plus information on the development of certain scales not previously available. In addition, it provides a bibliography of 689 titles directly relevant to the MMPI.

Previous reviews (3:60, 4:71) have been critical concerning the predictive validity of the clinical scales for differential psychiatric diagnosis. That issue is not yet fully resolved. However, a tally of the Welsh and Dahlstrom bibliography indicates that some 70 studies were concerned with empirical validity in psychiatric classification or other behavior pathology contexts and an additional 50 or so were related to therapy and guidance.

From 80 to 90 studies have been concerned with relations of the MMPI scales to other personality measures, about 15 each to interest and attitude variables, about 35 to ability and achievement, approximately 50 to occupational, educational, and economic variables, sex, or age status, and about 65 to medical disease, drug effects, and other physical characteristics. In addition, some 17 factor analyses had been done by late 1954 and current work by Comrey (682-4, 735-41) adds further information on the internal structure of several scales. In brief, the amount of data relevant to the construct validities of the inventory's scales is impressive.

The aim of the authors to provide an instrument that will ultimately yield scores on all the important phases of personality (even from the clinician's viewpoint) may be unrealistic. Whatever the case, the aim has not thus far been fulfilled. Over 30 articles published prior to 1955 proposed new scales for the MMPI and no sign of slackening has since appeared. Some 20 studies have been concerned with the problem of response set and test-taking attitude detection.

This instrument is probably the most carefully constructed and thoroughly researched inventory available for personality assessment. It is likely to be an increasingly useful clinical tool.

For a review by Arthur L. Benton, see 4:71; for reviews by Arthur L. Benton, H. J. Eysenck, L. S. Penrose, and Julian B. Rotter, see 3:60 (1 excerpt); for related reviews, see B199, B200, B467, and 4:72.

[87]

Minnesota Personality Scale. Grades 11-16; 1941; 5 scores: morale, social adjustment, family relations, emotionality, economic conservatism; IBM; separate forms for men and women; $3 per 25; separate answer sheets must be used; $2.20 per 50 IBM answer sheets; $1.25 per set of IBM scoring stencils; 50¢ per set of hand scoring stencils; 60¢ per specimen set; postpaid; nontimed (45) minutes; John G. Darley and Walter J. McNamara; Psychological Corporation. *

REFERENCES

1-9. See 3:61.
10. HAHN, MILTON EDWIN. *An Investigation of Measured Aspects of Social Intelligence in a Distributive Occupation.* Doctor's thesis, University of Minnesota (Minneapolis, Minn.), 1942.
11. JACOBSEN, CARLYLE F. "Interest and Attitude as Factors in Achievement in Medical School." *J Assn Am Med Col* 21: 152-9 My '46. *
12. CERF, ARTHUR Z. "Minnesota Personality Scale, CE438A," pp. 601-3. In *Printed Classification Tests.* Edited by J. P. Guilford. Army Air Forces Aviation Psychology Program Research Reports, Report No. 5. Washington, D.C.: U.S. Government Printing Office, 1947. Pp. xi, 919. * (PA 22:4145)
13. LOVELL, GEORGE D.; LAURIE, GLORIA; AND MARVIN, DORIS. "A Comparison of the Minnesota Personality Scale and the Bell Adjustment Inventory for Student Counseling." *Proc Iowa Acad Sci* 54:247-51 '47. * (PA 23:5524)
14. WINBERG, WILMA C. "Some Personality Traits of Collegiate Underachievers." *Proc Iowa Acad Sci* 54:267-70 '47. * (PA 23:5759)
15. KELLEY, RAY R., AND JOHNSON, PAUL E. "Emotional Traits in Pacifists." *J Social Psychol* 28:275-86 N '48. * (PA 23:2646)
16. OWENS, WILLIAM A., AND JOHNSON, WILMA C. "Some Measured Personality Traits of Collegiate Underachievers." *J Ed Psychol* 40:41-6 Ja '49. * (PA 23:5014)
17. STEPAT, DOROTHY L. *A Study of Clothing and Appearance Problems in Relation to Some Aspects of Personality and Some Cultural Patterns in a Group of College Freshman Girls.* Doctor's thesis, New York University (New York, N.Y.), 1949. Pp. 181. (*Microfilm Abstr* 10:64)
18. TYLER, F. T. "Personality Tests and Teaching Ability." *Can J Psychol* 3:30-7 Mr '49. * (PA 23:4443)
19. COCHRAN, SAMUEL W., AND DAVIS, FREDERICK B. "Predicting Freshman Grades at George Peabody College for Teachers." *Peabody J Ed* 27:352-6 My '50. *
20. CROSBY, MARION JOSEPHINE. *Personality Adjustment, Academic Achievement and Job Satisfaction.* Doctor's thesis, Columbia University (New York, N.Y.), 1950. (*Microfilm Abstr* 10:99)
21. DARLEY, JOHN G.; GROSS, NEAL; AND MARTIN, WILLIAM E. "Studies of Group Behavior: Stability, Change, and Interrelations of Psychometric and Sociometric Variables." *J Abn & Social Psychol* 46:565-76 O '51. * (PA 26:3915)
22. GILBERT, HARRY B. *An Evaluation of Certain Procedures in the Selection of Camp Counselors Based on Objective Test Data as Predictive of Practical Performance.* Doctor's thesis, New York University (New York, N.Y.), 1951. (*Microfilm Abstr* 11:953)
23. NOLL, VICTOR H. "Simulation by College Students of a Prescribed Pattern on a Personality Scale." *Ed & Psychol Meas* 11:478-88 au '51. * (PA 27:5893)
24. GILBERT, HARRY B. "The Use of Tests and Other Objective Data in the Selection of Camp Counselors." Abstract. *Am Psychol* 7:369 Jl '52. *
25. PALUBINSKAS, ALICE L. "Personality Changes in College Women During Four Years of College Experience." *Proc Iowa Acad Sci* 59:389-91 '52. * (PA 28:6543)
26. PALUBINSKAS, ALICE L. *Potential Utility of the Minnesota Personality Scale in Counseling Home Economic Students at Iowa State College.* Doctor's thesis, Iowa State College (Ames, Iowa), 1952.
27. BENNETT, THELMA, AND WALTERS, JAMES. "Personal and Social Adjustment of College Home Economics Freshmen." *J Home Econ* 45:29-31 Ja '53. *
28. PALUBINSKAS, ALICE L. "A Four-Year Study of Selected Socioeducational Variables and the Minnesota Personality Scale." Abstract. *Am Psychol* 8:412-3 Ag '53. *
29. BERDIE, RALPH F. "Aptitude, Achievement, Interest, and Personality Tests: A Longitudinal Comparison." *J Appl Psychol* 39:103-14 Ap '55. * (PA 30:1498)
30. JOHNSON, BERNADINE. *Family Relations and Social Adjustment Scores on the Minnesota Personality Scale as Related to Home and School Backgrounds of a Selected Group of Freshman Women.* Doctor's thesis, Florida State University (Tallahassee, Fla.), 1956. (DA 16:1438)
31. STONE, SOLOMON. *The Contribution of Intelligence, Interests, Temperament and Certain Personality Variables to Academic Achievement in a Physical Science and Mathematics Curriculum.* Doctor's thesis, New York University (New York, N.Y.), 1957. (DA 18:669)

For reviews by Philip Eisenberg and John W. French, see 3:61.

[88]

Minnesota Rating Scale for Personal Qualities and Abilities, [Fourth Revision]. College and adults; 1925-38; revision of Part II of *Rating Scale for Teachers of Home Economics;* 1 form ('38); mimeographed manual ('38); no data on reliability; $1.75

per 100 scales; 25¢ per specimen set; postage extra; Clara M. Brown; University of Minnesota Press. *

REFERENCE
1. BROWN, CLARA M. *An Evaluation of the Minnesota Rating Scale for Home Economics Teachers.* Minneapolis, Minn.: University of Minnesota Press, 1931. Pp. 29.

DOROTHY M. CLENDENEN, *Assistant Director, Test Division, The Psychological Corporation, New York, New York.*

Although this rating scale was first published in 1925, and this 1938 edition represents the fourth revision, the mimeographed manual presents no statistical information, and few details are reported of the analysis of 1,400 individual ratings which the manual states was made prior to revision. There is a discussion of the general development of the instrument, suggestions for its use, and instructions for raters.

The scale consists of 20 items regarded by home economics faculty members at Minnesota as representing important personal qualities for home economics students. However, it is recommended for use with other groups. Suggested uses are "in counseling, in determining scholarship awards, and in recommending graduates for positions."

Personal qualities such as poise, voice, personal appearance, management of work, command of English, and professional attitude are included in a graphic scale which has, for each item, descriptive phrases indicating three levels. Check marks are converted to numerical values on a scale of 1 to 10. Values are added and averaged to obtain a "score."

Statements describing the qualities to be rated are in terms of observable behavior and are specific. An attempt has been made to keep all three levels equally attractive to the rater so that neither the extremes nor the average will be generally avoided. Rating all members of the group on one characteristic at a time is recommended. Anecdotal records are encouraged as supplementary information to explain a rating.

No studies of reliability are reported. This seems especially unfortunate in view of the number of ratings available to the author, and the ease with which such studies could have been made. Since rating scales have often been shown to be low in reliability, the reviewer finds absence of such information on this scale to be a serious limitation in its use. Nor is any evidence of the validity of the scale given, and one wonders, for example, to what extent teacher rating of leadership, based on observation in the classroom or department, correlates with other

criteria of leadership. The same question might be asked concerning the qualities judgment, discretion, resourcefulness, and others.

As a convenient method of summarizing the observer's general impression, this scale seems to be well thought out. For use in recommending graduates, it provides a positive record of the teacher's estimate of attributes not evaluated in course grades, in place of nebulous recall at the time when a recommendation is requested. However, no evidence is presented to support acceptance of the score or its component ratings as an accurate and objective summary of the personality and behavior of the one who has been rated. Therefore, its use in counseling or in determining scholarship awards is open to question. Instruments of known reliability and validity would be more appropriate.

[89]

Mooney Problem Check List, 1950 Revision. Grades 7–9, 9–12, 13–16, adults; 1941–50; IBM for Forms JM, HM, and CM; 4 levels; manuals ('50); no norms—authors recommend the use of local norms; separate answer sheets must be used with Forms JM, HM, and CM; $1.75 per 25 tests (Forms J, H, C, A); $2.40 per 25 tests (Forms JM, HM, CM); $1.90 per 50 IBM answer sheets; 35¢ per specimen set of any one level; postpaid; (20–50) minutes; Ross L. Mooney and Leonard V. Gordon (College and Adult Forms); Psychological Corporation. *

a) JUNIOR HIGH SCHOOL FORM. Grades 7–9; 1942–50; 7 scores: health and physical development, school, home and family, money-work-the future, boy and girl relations, relations to people in general, self-centered concerns; Form J or JM ('50).

b) HIGH SCHOOL FORM. 1941–50; 11 scores: health and physical development, finances-living conditions-employment, social and recreational activities, social-psychological relations, personal-psychological relations, courtship-sex-marriage, home and family, morals and religion, adjustment to school work, the future-vocational and educational, curriculum and teaching procedures; Form H or HM ('50).

c) COLLEGE FORM. Grades 13–16; 1941–50; 11 scores: same as for High School Form; Form C or CM ('50).

d) ADULT FORM. Adults; 1950; 9 scores: health, economic security, self-improvement, personality, home and family, courtship, sex, religion, occupation; Form A.

REFERENCES
1–17. See 3:67.
18–30. See 4:73.
31. KOHRT, CARL FRED. *Problems of High-School Seniors in Douglas County, Illinois.* Master's thesis, Illinois State Normal University (Normal, Ill.), 1950.
32. McINTYRE, CHARLES JOHN. *The Validity of the Mooney Problem Check List, High School Form.* Master's thesis, Pennsylvania State College (State College, Pa.), 1950.
33. GALLAGHER, JAMES J. *An Investigation Into Factors Differentiating College Students Who Discontinue Non-Directive Counseling From College Students Who Continue Counseling.* Doctor's thesis, Pennsylvania State College (State College, Pa.), 1951.
34. TUCKER, JOHN E. *Investigation of Criteria for Evaluating Non-Directive Psychotherapy With College Students.* Doctor's thesis, Pennsylvania State College (State College, Pa.), 1951.
35. BENNETT, BRUCE L. "The Use of the Mooney Problem Check List for a College Hygiene Course." *Ed Res B* 31:231–40+ D 10 '52. *
36. BROWN, CURTIS P. *The Mooney Problem Check List and*

the SRA Youth Inventory in Comparison. Master's thesis, University of Southern California (Los Angeles, Calif.), 1952.

37. FICK, REUEL L. "The Problem Check List: A Valuable Approach in Counseling." *Occupations* 30:410–2 Mr '52. * (PA 26:6533)

38. GARRISON, KARL C., AND CUNNINGHAM, BEN W., JR. "Personal Problems of Ninth-Grade Pupils." *Sch R* 60:30–3 Ja '52. *

39. WARDLOW, MARY E., AND GREENE, JAMES E. "An Exploratory Sociometric Study of Peer Status Among Adolescent Girls." *Sociometry* 15:311–8 Ag–N '52. * (PA 27:7097)

40. BATES, LAWRENCE R., AND COTTLE, WILLIAM C. "A Study of Relationships Between Measured Intelligence and Problems of Ninth Grade Pupils." *Univ Kans B Ed* 8:5–6 N '53. *

41. BROWN, WILLIAM H. "The Problems of Probation and Honor Students." *Ed Res B* 32:14–6+ Ja '53. *

42. MCINTYRE, CHARLES J. "The Validity of the Mooney Problem Check List." *J Appl Psychol* 37:270–2 Ag '53. * (PA 28:6577)

43. TAN, HASAN. *A Survey of Student Problems With the Mooney Problem Check List in a Secondary School in Istanbul, Turkey.* Master's thesis, University of Maryland (College Park, Md.), 1953.

44. THREADCRAFT, MATTIE H. *A Comparative Study of Problems of Adolescent Boys and Girls (as Measured by the Mooney Problem Checklist) in the Arlington Vocational High School, Arlington, Georgia.* Master's thesis, Atlanta University (Atlanta, Ga.), 1953.

45. BARNES, JAMES R. *A Critical Study of the Results of the Mooney Problem Check List and the Cornell Index as a Means of Identifying Possible Cases of Psychosomatic Illness Among 400 North Carolina College Students.* Master's thesis, North Carolina College (Durham, N.C.), 1954.

46. GALLAGHER, JAMES J. "Test Indicators for Therapy Prognosis." *J Consult Psychol* 18:409–13 D '54. * (PA 29:7356)

47. CARR, JAMES FRANCIS, JR. *The Problem Areas of a Selected Group of Students at Florida State University as Indicated by the Mooney Problem Check List.* Doctor's thesis, Indiana University (Bloomington, Ind.), 1955. (DA 15:1524)

48. MCCOULLOUGH, CHESTER A. *A Statistical Study of the Relationships Between Scores Obtained by 400 North Carolina College Students on the Mooney Problem Check List and the College Inventory of Academic Adjustment.* Master's thesis, North Carolina College (Durham, N.C.), 1955.

49. SIMPSON, ELIZABETH JANE. *Distinctive Personal Problems of Home Economics Students at the University of Illinois.* Doctor's thesis, University of Illinois (Urbana, Ill.), 1955. (DA 16:287)

50. WELLINGTON, JOHN ADAM. *Factors Related to the Academic Success of Resident Freshman Men at a Midwestern Liberal Arts College During the Academic Year 1952-1953.* Doctor's thesis, Northwestern University (Evanston, Ill.), 1955. (DA 16:69)

51. GROW, MILTON D. *An Analysis of Problems of Students in Selected Junior High Schools.* Doctor's thesis, Northwestern University (Evanston, Ill.), 1956. (DA 17:2498)

52. KOILE, EARL A., AND BIRD, DOROTHY J. "Preferences for Counselor Help on Freshman Problems." *J Counsel Psychol* 3:97–106 su '56. * (PA 31:5132)

53. PAQUIN, LAURENCE GILBERT. *A Plan for the Improvement of a Secondary School Program Based on an Analysis of Certain Problems of Pupils as Revealed by the Mooney Problem Check List.* Doctor's thesis, New York University (New York, N.Y.), 1956. (DA 17:820)

54. WALLER, LYNN T. *Use of the Mooney Problem Checklist in a Comparative Analysis of the Problems of Outstanding Students Versus Unsuccessful Students in the Eighth Grade of the Thomas Hunt Morgan School, Shoreline School District 412, Seattle, Washington.* Master's thesis, University of Washington (Seattle, Wash.), 1956.

55. GRAFF, FRANKLYN ARTHUR. *Occupational Choice Factors in Normally Achieving and Underachieving Intellectually Superior Twelfth Grade Boys.* Doctor's thesis, University of Connecticut (Storrs, Conn.), 1957. (DA 17:2207)

56. SINGER, STANLEY L., AND STEFFLRE, BUFORD. "Concurrent Validity of the Mooney Problem Check List." *Personnel & Guid J* 35:298–301 Ja '57. * (PA 32:1647)

For reviews by Harold E. Jones and Morris Krugman, see 4:73; for reviews by Ralph C. Bedell and Theodore F. Lentz of an earlier edition, see 3:67.

[90]

★**Objective-Analytic Personality Test Batteries.** Ages 11–16, adults; 1955; 18 factors: children and adults-competent assertiveness, (U.I. 16), restraint-timidity, (U.I. 17), hypomanic overcompensation, (U.I. 18), critical-dominant exactness, (U.I. 19), sociable willingness, (U.I. 20), energetic decisiveness, (U.I. 21), nervous-alert reactivity, (U.I. 22), neural

reserves vs. neuroticism, (U.I. 23), anxiety-to-achieve, (U.I. 24), accurate realism vs. psychoticism, (U.I. 25), cultured introspective self-control, (U.I. 26), sociable-emotional evasiveness, (U.I. 28), sympathetic mobilization of energy, (U.I. 29), stolid super ego satisfaction, (U.I. 30), adults only-wary realism, (U.I. 31), schizoid tenacity, (U.I. 32), dourness, (U.I. 33), apathetic temperament, (U.I. 27); 1 form; mimeographed tests; 2 levels; 3 batteries for each level; 2 editions: group, individual; no data on reliability; no norms; $3 per tape recording (7.5 ips); $5 per manual; cash orders postpaid; additional apparatus needed for various subtests; Raymond B. Cattell, A. R. Baggaley, L. Checov, E. A. Cogan, D. Flint, W. Gruen, E. Husek, T. Meeland, D. R. Saunders, and H. Schiff; Institute for Personality and Ability Testing. *

a) THE ADULT 18 O–A BATTERY. Ages 16 and over; 18 factors (U.I. 16–33); $23.20 per set of slides.

1) *Group.* 43 tests; $25 per set of 43 tests; 266(300) minutes in 6 sessions.

2) *Individual.* 54 tests; $29 per set of 54 tests; 276(310) minutes in 7 sessions.

b) THE ADULT 12 O–A BATTERY. Ages 16 and over; 12 factors (U.I. 16–27); $21.60 per set of slides.

1) *Group.* 38 tests; $20 per set of 38 tests; 240(280) minutes in 5 sessions.

2) *Individual.* 46 tests; $25 per set of 46 tests; 299(350) or 305(355) minutes in 6 sessions.

c) ADULT SINGLE FACTOR BATTERIES. Adults; 18 factors (U.I. 16–33); $5 per set of testing materials for any one factor; $23.20 per set of slides.

d) THE CHILDREN 14 O–A BATTERY. Ages 11–16; 14 factors (U.I. 16–26, 28–30); $25 per set of slides.

1) *Group.* 42 tests; $25 per set of 42 tests; 267(300) or 273(310) minutes in 6 sessions.

2) *Individual.* 52 tests; $29 per set of 52 tests; 323(350) minutes in 7 sessions.

e) THE CHILDREN 10 FACTOR O–A BATTERY. Ages 11–16; 10 factors (U.I. 16, 17, 19–23, 26, 28, 29); 2 editions: group, individual; $25 per set of slides.

1) *Group.* 35 tests; $20 per set of 35 tests; 229.25-(290) or 235.75(295) minutes in 5 sessions.

2) *Individual.* 43 tests; $25 per set of 43 tests; 271.25(305) or 284.25(320) minutes in 6 sessions.

f) CHILDREN SINGLE FACTOR BATTERIES. Ages 11–16; 14 factors (U.I. 16–26, 28–30); 2 editions: group, individual; $25 per 4 sets of 47 colored and 17 black and white slides.

REFERENCES

1. CATTELL, RAYMOND B. "The Principal Replicated Factors Discovered in Objective Personality Tests." *J Abn & Social Psychol* 50:291–314 My '55. * (PA 30:2450)

2. CATTELL, RAYMOND B., AND GRUEN, WALTER. "The Primary Personality Factors in 11-Year-Old Children, by Objective Tests." *J Personality* 23:460–78 My '55. * (PA 30:2527)

3. ROSENTHAL, IRENE. *A Factor Analysis of Anxiety Variables.* Doctor's thesis, University of Illinois (Urbana, Ill.), 1955. (DA 16:376)

4. CATTELL, RAYMOND B. "The Conceptual and Test Distinction of Neuroticism and Anxiety." *J Clin Psychol* 13:221–33 Jl '57. *

5. CATTELL, RAYMOND B. *Personality and Motivation Structure and Measurement.* Yonkers, N.Y.: World Book Co., 1957. Pp. xxv, 948. *

6. CATTELL, RAYMOND B.; STICE, GLEN F.; AND KRISTY, NORTON F. "A First Approximation to Nature-Nurture Ratios for Eleven Primary Personality Factors in Objective Tests." *J Abn & Social Psychol* 54:143–59 Mr '57. *

H. J. EYSENCK, *Professor of Psychology, Institute of Psychiatry, University of London, London, England.*

This battery of tests is something almost entirely new in psychological measurement. It constitutes a tremendous achievement. In spite of its many imperfections (of which Cattell himself is only too well aware and to which he draws attention at various points in the handbook which accompanies the test kit), it must be taken to mark the beginning of a new phase, a departure from the customary reliance of psychologists working in the personality field on interviews, questionnaires, and projective techniques. No judgment would be fair which leaves out of account the pioneering nature of this venture which attempts to put personality measurement on a solid, scientific basis.

The battery is based on Cattell's well known factor analytic studies, and attempts to provide measures for 18 of these factors. It is, of course, not necessary to use all the tests provided, or measure all the factors. Several different batteries, giving measures of between 10 and 18 factors, can be made up, both for children and for adults, from the set of tests provided; it is, of course, possible for the research psychologist or the clinical worker to concentrate on just one or two factors judged to be relevant to his problem.

Cattell claims three major achievements for his battery. He claims that the tests measure behaviour in actual situations instead of introspective self examination; that they are scored by keys through which all psychometricians get the same answers; and that they measure functional unities in personality structure which have been established by repeated factor analytic and experimental studies. He warns users that the tests are not as simple to administer as questionnaires; they take more time than many projective tests; and they require considerable skill and psychological knowledge for administration and interpretation.

The nature of the tests is very variable, and many would not ordinarily have been considered as personality tests at all. To name a few at random, the battery includes tests of flicker fusion, body sway suggestibility, colour-form sorting, readiness to act out animal sounds, estimation of passing time, aesthetic sense in colour planning, personal tempo, and so on and so forth. Just looking through the descriptions of the tests given in the test kit handbook will impress the reader with the tremendous range over which Cattell's choice has extended, and his ingenuity and originality in adapting these various measures to personality assessment. A whole year's course on personality measurement could easily be centred on working through this

enormous mass of material with a class of students.

Up to a point the critical evaluation of the test battery depends upon one's estimate of the factorial studies underlying the choice of tests. These studies are unrivalled from the point of view of extensiveness and technical competence. Yet the reviewer cannot wholeheartedly accept Cattell's claim to have discovered 18 independent personality traits in this work. Correlations between tests tend to be quite low on the whole, and Cattell's acceptance of factor matchings from one study to another is based on less stringent criteria than one might wish. Populations are seldom large enough to make one feel very confident about the statistical significance of the last four or five factors extracted, and the choice of populations studied has been somewhat restricted. These remarks are not criticisms so much as statements of fact; when it is realised that practically all the work has been done by Cattell himself and his associates, it will come as no surprise that no finality had been reached. Until this work is duplicated in other departments using the same tests on varying normal and abnormal populations, no final judgment is possible of Cattell's claims. That no such check has been applied can hardly be blamed on Cattell, who, it must be assumed, would like nothing better!

Two important points which the user of this battery must bear in mind are: (a) There are no norms, so that the user will have to build up his own norms as he goes along, basing them on his own group. (b) The meaning of the factors in terms of their relationships to clinical, industrial, and other outside criteria is hardly known at all; and while it would be unfair to say that here we have 18 factors in search of a criterion, it must be realised that this is a research battery of tests rather than one which can be applied directly to practical problems. Of course, Cattell himself draws attention to this restriction and does not pretend that his battery is more advanced than in fact it is. As a research instrument it can hardly be praised too highly; no comparison with existing tests can indeed be made because nothing like it exists at the moment.

Granted then that this battery constitutes a great and important achievement, the reviewer has certain nagging doubts regarding the actual use of the battery and the comparability of data from one user to another. Not all the tests specify in sufficient detail the mode of administration, or lay down methods for excluding external sources of error. As an illustration of the former difficulty, we may mention the body sway test of suggestibility. Cattell leaves it open to the user to have the suggestions made through a record or a tape recorder, or to say the words himself. The reviewer has found great differences in effectiveness of suggestion between people, and between personal and recorded suggestion. Unless this is taken into account, scores on this test will not be comparable and will in fact mean different things in different laboratories. As an example of the second objection, we may take the flicker fusion test. Anyone familiar with the detailed reviews of this phenomenon by Carney Landis will see how insufficient the instructions of this test are to rule out a wide variety of sources of error, quite apart from the fact that the instrument recommended is a very poor one for the measurement of C.F.F.!

One last point should perhaps be made. Users of personality tests are well aware of the fact that many of these techniques require them to become thoroughly acquainted with a particular set of concepts, terms, and theories. The Rorschach mythology and Murray's system of need and press are well known examples. Something of the kind is necessary here, too. No one could use these tests in any sensible way who was not thoroughly familiar with Cattell's writings and the development of the factors measured by his tests. This is probably inevitable, but it does mean a quite lengthy period of initiation to those not already in the know. The promise held out by this test battery would, in the reviewer's opinion, well justify the time and trouble taken.

[91]

★Personal Adaptability Test. Grades 11–13 and adults; 1957; 4 scores: botheredness, mental malfunctioning, physiological malfunctioning, total; 1 form; 4 editions: separate editions for men and for women, separate editions for grades 11–13 and for business; mimeographed manual; $2.60 per 25 tests; 50¢ per manual; $1.45 per specimen set; postpaid; (20–30) minutes; Guy E. Buckingham; Public School Publishing Co. *

REFERENCE

1. BUCKINGHAM, GUY E. "Making a Personal Adaptability Test." Abstract. Am Psychol 5:330–1 Jl '50. *

HAROLD WEBSTER, Research Associate Psychologist, Center for the Study of Higher Education, University of California, Berkeley, California.

The rationale for this test is based on the assumption that "abnormal personal and social behavior is the same as error in any other kind of learning." "Botheredness," as measured by the first scale, refers to irritation, annoyance, and the like, admitted by testees when confronted by shortcomings of others or themselves; botheredness is thought to precede development of the malfunctioning measured by the other two scales.

This test appears to measure a kind of neurotic syndrome well known to psychologists. It would be advantageous, therefore, to have correlations of the scales and of the total scale with other tests for measuring neurotic reactions. The combination of irritability and hypochondriasis which is measured would surely be accompanied by a decrease in ability to get along well with others, especially in certain kinds of jobs, *unless the subject decided beforehand not to reveal his irritability and hypochondriasis*. A person who above all wants acceptance by others should be able to achieve a good score on this test despite his other personality difficulties. The test may therefore be as much a measure of complaisance or obeisance as it is a measure of other kinds of adaptability. Because of this and the other limited evidence of validity, the test cannot be recommended for general use.

[92]

★The Personal and Social Development Program. Grades kgn–9; 1956; form for recording behavior incidents in 8 areas: personal adjustment, responsibility and effort, creativity and initiative, integrity, social adjustment, sensitivity to others, group orientation, adaptability to rules and conventions; 1 form; no data on reliability; $5.10 per 40 record forms; 50¢ per administrator's manual; $1.50 per teacher's guide; $2 per specimen set; postage extra; John C. Flanagan; Science Research Associates. *

EDWARD LANDY, Director, Division of Counseling Services, Newton Public Schools, Newton, Massachusetts.

The authors and publishers are to be commended for pioneering in the use of the "critical incident" technique to help elementary school teachers identify systematically and in proper balance the behavioral strengths and weaknesses in their pupils. This is one of the two majors aims of the *Personal and Social Development Program* and is as well done as can be reasonably expected in the light of current knowledge of personality growth and development and of the present level of sophistication now existing among elementary school teachers. The major instrument for accomplishing this purpose, called the Performance Record, has been carefully constructed to be used with a minimum of time and effort. The teacher's guide is replete with easily understood and carefully selected examples of how to keep the Performance Record. The explanation offered for selecting and recording behavior also contains much that would be considered as soundly based in acceptable mental health knowledge and theory. The manual for school administrators and supervisors may prove to be a useful aid in getting teachers to accept the program and to fill out the Performance Record accurately.

This reviewer is less optimistic than the authors and publishers appear to be as to whether most, or even many, elementary school teachers would be willing to undertake the program at all. For, in spite of all the careful work done to reduce the record keeping to a minimum, it is questionable whether elementary school teachers (not under the stimulus of participating in a special tryout program) will accept the self-discipline and added clerical burden of interrupting their daily schedules to fill in the blanks or to do so after school without administrative pressure which may defeat the purpose for which the record is being kept.

The second major aim of the program is to try to get teachers to use the collected anecdotal information to encourage desirable pupil behavior. Unless this second aim can be accomplished, the first aim simply results in added clerical work. This reviewer was unable to discover any rigorous evidence as to the effectiveness of achieving the second aim by means of the Performance Record. The kind of evidence provided in the teacher's guide, as exemplified by "The Case of Martie," is of the sort which this reviewer has heard from many teachers who have never used the Performance Record or even made any effort to collect anecdotal information in any systematic way.

There are several real dangers in this program. First, it assumes far more sophistication about child growth and development and the causes and treatment of personality difficulties than most school administrators and supervisors have. Thus, teachers may be lulled into believing they are getting more expert advice from their administrators and supervisors than they really are. Second, it tends to oversimplify the problems of parent-child relationships, teacher-parent interviewing, etc. "The Case of Martie,"

as described, is an illustration of this point. Third, some teachers may start to play the roles of amateur clinical psychologists or psychiatrists.

In all fairness, however, it should be remembered that a program of this kind may be better than the alternatives of doing nothing or taking action without any understanding or data. And it should be stated that the teacher's guide does make an honest and skillful effort at developing in teachers desirable understanding and techniques useful for improving pupil behavior. Given the right kind of leadership and without overly optimistic expectations, the program would seem worth trying out.

C. GILBERT WRENN, *Professor of Educational Psychology,* and ROY D. LEWIS, *Teaching Assistant, University of Minnesota, Minneapolis, Minnesota.*

The Personal and Social Development Program consists of a 4-page performance record for each elementary school child, a 63-page teacher's guide, and a 32-page manual for school administrators. The record is a double-page spread. On one page is a chart in blue for recording incidents that are considered "Behaviors to be Encouraged" in four personal adjustment categories and four social adjustment categories. The opposite page consists of a chart in red for recording "Behaviors Needing Improving" in the same eight personal and social adjustment categories.

The total approach is an attempt to make systematic the familiar anecdotal record system by providing a list of suggested "critical incidents" under each of the categories, and to supply manuals that will help a school develop a program of attention to personality development. The manuals are persuasively written—but the concept contains several "critical concepts" with which the reviewers are concerned.

The items in each category were based upon several thousand critical incidents in pupil behavior contributed by teachers. The critical incident technique is one for which Flanagan is famous, but a serious question arises when so much dependence is placed upon the insight of teachers for what is truly "critical" in the lives of growing children. Teachers have grown mightily since the days of the Wickman study but teachers in general are still not as qualified as school psychologists and mental health specialists in the provision of penetrating insights on significant elements in personality development. This distinction is significant, for in this program the 42 critical behaviors provide the necessary and sufficient basis for guiding a child. The incidents were not gathered for research purposes but to build a program for guiding personality development.

This suggests the second concern of the reviewers. Teachers are encouraged to talk to children after enough incidents have accumulated to suggest a "trend." The assistance given to teachers on this task is simply and clearly written, but there is too much suggestion that children must conform to the concept of personality developed in the guide. This represents a dangerous road to viewing personality development as *adjustment* and not as creative and individual patterns of growth. The author did not intend this of course, but the use of the program has this hazard.

One of the problems inherent in this plan is the same difficulty that is inherent in any anecdotal record attempt. Only the interested and cooperative teacher will "remember" to record incidents or to use them as a basis of counseling. The program makes an attack upon this problem by setting up a schoolwide plan and a common record for all to use. Not only does the program depend upon the teacher's interest and cooperation (what doesn't, of course!); it also rests upon the validity of the incidents recorded. The criteria for selecting a critical incident for recording are (*a*) has the child done or failed to do something *noteworthy;* (*b*) is the incident *indicative* of a child's social development, character and citizenship growth, or manners and morals; (*c*) is the behavior to be *encouraged* or does it need correction; (*d*) am I being *completely objective* in picking out the facts of my observations. It seems obvious to the reviewers that inherent in these criteria are questions which raise some doubt about the "facts" that are recorded. The italics in each instruction are the reviewers'—but each suggests a carefulness and accuracy of judgment that is truly critical. For example: What is a noteworthy behavior? What is the criterion for social development or manners and morals? Upon what basis except a personal one does the teacher determine what behaviors need correction or need to be praised? Are most persons capable of determining the extent of their objectivity?

In summary, the record and program are brave and well intentioned. Under appropriate conditions of interest, informed effort, and freedom for individual variation of both teacher and pupil behavior they could be useful adjuncts to teacher performance. The professional consultants to the program apparently think so, and they and the author are distinguished figures. It just happens that the reviewers believe that the hazards involved may outweigh the benefits. These are hazards of encapsulating behavior to be noticed within a framework of 42, or any number of, critical behaviors suggested by teachers, of quantifying and recording "facts" which are teacher opinions and values, of a uniformity of control in the school even under what are the best intentioned of efforts.

[93]

★**The Personal Preference Scale.** Ages 15 and over; 1947–54; 10 scores: active-inactive, sociable-individualistic, permissive-critical, consistent-inconsistent, efficient-inefficient, self-effacing-egocentric, masculine-effeminoid, feminine-masculinoid, emotionally mature-emotionally immature, socially mature-socially immature; 1 form ('51); guide ['53]; manual ('54, see *1* below); no norms below college level; 10¢ per test copy, postage extra; specimen set free; manual must be purchased separately; (20) minutes; Maurice H. Krout and Johanna Krout Tabin; Maurice H. Krout, 1938 Cleveland Ave., Evanston, Ill. *

REFERENCES

1. KROUT, MAURICE H., AND TABIN, JOHANNA KROUT. "Measuring Personality in Developmental Terms: The Personal Preference Scale." *Genetic Psychol Monogr* 50:289–335 N '54. *
2. STAGNER, ROSS; LAWSON, EDWIN D.; AND MOFFITT, J. WELDON. "The Krout Personal Preference Scale: A Factor-Analytic Study." *J Clin Psychol* 11:103–13 Ap '55. *

[94]

★**The Personality Evaluation Form: A Technique for the Organization and Interpretation of Personality Data.** Ages 2 and over; 1955; 1 form; mimeographed manual; $5 per 25 booklets, postpaid; specimen set not available; Charlotte Buhler and Gertrude Howard; Western Psychological Services. *

DOROTHY H. EICHORN, *Assistant Research Psychologist, Institute of Child Welfare, University of California, Berkeley, California.*

This 12-page booklet provides a clear and comprehensive outline for the summarization of case material for one individual. Objections to the form per se are relatively minor. Insufficient space is allotted for medical history. The section for developmental data consists of a list of "important age-characteristic functions and activities," followed by a yes-no column to be checked and a column for remarks. Most of these items are not usefully rated simply as present or absent; at least a 5-point scale is needed. The remarks column remedies this deficiency, but renders the yes-no column superfluous. There is a misprint in the heading of the subsection for adolescence—it should read 12 to 20 years, not 2 to 20. Section 6 carries the confusing notation, "To be filled in by Counselor," leaving one to wonder who should have filled in the previous five.

The form is purported to facilitate "interpretations and inferences based on premises generally accepted by modern clinicians and specialists in the study of personality and psychopathology." The principal device for accomplishing this objective is a section subtitled "Dynamic Data for Interpretation," organized around the concepts of the individual's needs, the environmental demands upon him, his ability to utilize and cope with reality, and his values and goals. Whether this framework will be helpful depends on the clinician's own theoretical orientation.

The manual—largely an elementary treatise on personality theory—states that the PEF is "based on well recognized dynamic concepts" but "designed for use by teachers and counselors who may have had little clinical training and experience." Neither the source of, nor the evidence for, the concepts is given. Alternative constructs are not discussed. Considerable space is devoted to descriptions of various "Need-Demand" patterns of child rearing and the behavioral results to be expected from each. These summaries lend themselves to diagnosis by the inexperienced in quite the same way as tests which may be used in "cookbook" fashion. The sections on recommendations and follow-up are replete with pious and obvious instructions such as "Every effort should be made to carry out the recommendations made" and "All available personnel and facilities in the school should be used to help maladjusted and unhappy children with their problems." A long list of possible recommendations is included. One can imagine a confused, overworked amateur poring over the list and finally choosing Number 14, "Stimulating the use of outside professional resources for the professional growth of the teachers who work with children who have problems." In both the form and the manual a point is made of distinguishing between data and interpretation. The intention is laudable, but the distinction is incomplete and may mislead the unsophisticated. No recognition is given to the fact that such items as "Home Situation: Describe briefly; adequacy for Counselee's needs" and "Record factual data: how counselee's basic needs—care, security, affection—were met" involve interpretation as well as information.

The major objection to the PEF is the encouragement which the manual gives to untrained persons to accumulate and use clinical case material. Ethically, this practice is as questionable as providing laymen with tests which may be misused. It is doubtful that many trained clinicians need the booklet. Most clinics and private practitioners have their own method of summarization, peculiar to their case loads and theoretical orientations. Those in the process of evolving a summary form might find this one helpful, at least as a model. The PEF can probably best serve as a teaching device—in practicum situations for students' appraisals which are to be reviewed by the instructor, and in the classroom as an illustration of the kinds of data which go into a clinical evaluation. The manual could be used as supplementary textual material.

J Consult Psychol 20:160 Ap '56. *Laurance F. Shaffer.* Described by its authors as "a technique for the organization and interpretation of personality data," the *Personality Evaluation Form* is a 12-page booklet consisting mainly of a series of headings with blank spaces for entering data, inferences, and conclusions. As an outline for case study, the form has some merit. Like all such blanks, however, it lacks flexibility. In attempting to meet the requirements of all situations and all clients, it inevitably provides too little space for some topics and too much for other less relevant issues. Somewhat dangerous is the implication that it may be used by teachers with little psychological training. Well-trained clinicians hardly need such a blank; others should not attempt its use.

[95]

The Personality Inventory. Grades 9–16 and adults; 1931–38; 6 scores: neurotic tendency, self-sufficiency, introversion-extroversion, dominance-submission, confidence, sociability; IBM; 1 form ('35); manual ('35); tentative norms ('38); $3.25 per 25; $1.50 per 50 profile sheets (no date); 25¢ per specimen set; separate answer sheets may be used; $1.75 per 50 IBM answer sheets; $1.50 per 100 Hankes answer sheets; $1 per set of hand scoring stencils; $5 per set of IBM scoring stencils; postage extra; (25) minutes; Robert G. Bernreuter; Consulting Psychologists Press, Inc. *

REFERENCES

1–71. See 40:1239.
72–259. See 4:77.
260–1. MAUNEY, JACK E. *Effect of a Social Weekend Upon the Personality of College Students, as Measured by the Bernreuter Personality Inventory.* Master's thesis, University of Florida (Gainesville, Fla.), 1947.
262. BERNARD, JESSIE; HECHT, CAROL ANN; SCHWARTZ, SYLVIA; LEVY, SYLVIA; AND SCHIELE, WILLIAM. "The Relationship Between Scores on the Bernreuter Personality Inventory and Three Indexes of Participation in a College Community." *Rural Sociol* 15:271–3 S '50. *

263. BLAIR, W. R. N. "A Comparative Study of Disciplinary Offenders and Non-Offenders in the Canadian Army, 1948." *Can J Psychol* 4:49-62 Je '50. * (*PA* 24:6428)

264. HAND, WILL MASON. *A Comparison and Analysis of Scores in Self and Social Adjustment Made on the California Test of Personality and the Bernreuter Personality Inventory.* Master's thesis, University of Florida (Gainesville, Fla.), 1950.

265. KLINE, NATHAN S. "Characteristics and Screening of Unsatisfactory Psychiatric Attendants and Attendant-Applicants." *Am J Psychiatry* 106:573-86 F '50. *

266. MOSS, FREDERICK JAMES, JR. *Intelligence and the Bernreuter Personality Inventory.* Master's thesis, Southern Methodist University (Dallas, Tex.), 1950

267. GEHMAN, WINFIELD SCOTT, JR. *Analysis of a Program Involving Required Psychological Counseling and Other Services for a College Population Having Serious Scholastic Difficulties.* Doctor's thesis, Pennsylvania State College (State College, Pa.), 1951.

268. GOULD, HENRY. *Relation of Certain Personality Components to Achievement in Secondary School Science.* Doctor's thesis, New York University (New York, N.Y.), 1951. (*DA* 12:160)

269. HUMPHREY, BETTY M. "Introversion-Extraversion Ratings in Relation to Scores in ESP Tests." *J Parapsychol* 15:252-62 D '51. * (*PA* 27:4109)

270. HUNT, FOLGER DEFOE. *A Study of the Relationship of Personality Scores to Level of Achievement.* Master's thesis, Ohio University (Athens, Ohio), 1951.

271. PAGE, MAUREEN. *Two Proposed Modifications of the Bernreuter Personality Inventory.* Master's thesis, Pennsylvania State College (State College, Pa.), 1951.

272. SIMES, FRANK J. *The Development of a Basis for the Selection of Resident Advisers at the Pennsylvania State College.* Doctor's thesis, Pennsylvania State College (State College, Pa.), 1951.

273. BANKS, CHARLOTTE, AND KEIR, GERTRUDE. "A Factorial Analysis of Items in the Bernreuter Personality Inventory." *Brit J Psychol, Stat Sect* 5:19-30 Mr '52. *

274. BROWN, MANUEL N. "Powell's Study on Ratings of Personality Adjustment: A Note." *Ed & Psychol Meas* 12:126-8 sp '52. * (*PA* 27:5859)

275. GEIST, HAROLD. "A Comparison of Personality Test Scores and Medical Psychiatric Diagnosis by the Inverted Factor Technique." *J Clin Psychol* 8:184-8 Ap '52. * (*PA* 27:10958)

276. GUILFORD, J. P. "When Not to Factor Analyze." *Psychol B* 49:26-37 Ja '52. * (*PA* 27:33)

277. LIEN, ARNOLD JUEL. "A Comparative-Predictive Study of Students in the Four Curricula of a Teacher Education Institution." *J Exp Ed* 21:81-219 D '52. *

278. MASON, ROBERT JOSEPH. *A Comparison of Responses on the Rosenzweig Picture-Frustration Study, the Bernreuter Personality Inventory, and a Self-Rating Form.* Master's thesis, University of Western Ontario (London, Ont., Canada), 1952.

279. MOFFIE, DANNIE J., AND MILTON, CHARLES R. "The Relationship of Certain Psychological Test Scores to Academic Success in Chemical Engineering." Abstract. *Am Psychol* 7:379-80 Jl '52. *

280. POE, WESLEY A., AND BERG, IRWIN A. "Psychological Test Performance of Steel Industry Production Supervisors." *J Appl Psychol* 36:234-7 Ag '52. * (*PA* 27:3794)

281. RICHARDSON, HELEN M., AND HANAWALT, NELSON G. "Leadership as Related to the Bernreuter Personality Measures: V, Leadership Among Adult Women in Social Activities." *J Social Psychol* 36:141-53 N '52. * (*PA* 27:7124)

282. WESMAN, ALEXANDER G. "Faking Personality Test Scores in a Simulated Employment Situation." *J Appl Psychol* 36:112-3 Ap '52. * (*PA* 27:449)

283. BRUCE, MARTIN M. "The Prediction of Effectiveness as a Factory Foreman." *Psychol Monogr* 67(12):1-17 '53. * (*PA* 28:5019)

284. ROSENBERG, NATHAN; IZARD, CARROLL E.; AND HOLLANDER, E. P. "Middle Category ("?") Response: Reliability and Relationship to Personality and Intelligence Variables." Abstract. *Am Psychol* 8:425 Ag '53. *

285. YOUNG, NORMAN, AND GAIER, EUGENE L. "A Preliminary Investigation Into the Prediction of Suggestibility From Selected Personality Variables." *J Social Psychol* 37:53-60 F '53. * (*PA* 28:571)

286. ALBIZU-MIRANDA, CARLOS. *An Experimental Study of Middle Class Bias on the Bernreuter Personality Inventory.* Doctor's thesis, Purdue University (Lafayette, Ind.), 1954.

287. BRUCE, MARTIN M. "Validity Information Exchange, No. 7-004: D.O.T. Code 0-97.61, Manager, Sales." *Personnel Psychol* 7:128-9 sp '54. *

288. BRUCE, MARTIN M. "Validity Information Exchange, No. 7-076: D.O.T. Code 5-91.101, Foreman II." *Personnel Psychol* 7:418-9 au '54. *

289. CASH, WILLIAM LEVI, JR. *Relation of Personality Traits to Scholastic Aptitude and Academic Achievement of Students in a Liberal Protestant Seminary.* Doctor's thesis, University of Michigan (Ann Arbor, Mich.), 1954. (*DA* 14:630)

290. GEHMAN, W. SCOTT. "Problems of College Sophomores With Serious Scholastic Difficulties." *J Counsel Psychol* 2:137-41 su '55. * (*PA* 30:3406)

291. GOWAN, J. C. "Relationship Between Leadership and Personality Measures." *J Ed Res* 48:623-7 Ap '55. * (*PA* 30:1558)

292. HOFFMAN, MARTIN L., AND ALBIZU-MIRANDA, CARLOS. "Middle Class Bias in Personality Testing." *J Abn & Social Psychol* 51:150-2 Jl '55. * (*PA* 30:4573)

293. KELLY, E. LOWELL. "Consistency of the Adult Personality." *Am Psychol* 10:659-81 N '55. * (*PA* 30:6915)

294. BRUCE, MARTIN M. "Normative Data Information Exchange, No. 26." *Personnel Psychol* 9:533-4 w '56. *

295. BURGESS, ELVA. "Personality Factors of Over- and Under-Achievers in Engineering." *J Ed Psychol* 47:89-99 F '56. * (*PA* 31:8811)

296. STRAIGHT, GLENN H. *Identifiable Personality Characteristics Resulting From Membership in a Conspicuous Religious Minority in Public High Schools.* Doctor's thesis, University of Nebraska (Lincoln, Neb.), 1956. (*DA* 17:810)

297. WITKIN, ARTHUR AARON. *The Prediction of Potentials for Effectiveness in Certain Occupations Within the Sales Field.* Doctor's thesis, New York University (New York, N.Y.), 1956. (*DA* 16:1718)

298. BRUCE, MARTIN M. "Validity Information Exchange, No. 10-3: D.O.T. Code 1-86.11, Salesman, Commercial Equipment and Supplies." *Personnel Psychol* 10:77-8 sp '57. *

299. BRUCE, MARTIN M. "Normative Data Information Exchange, No. 11-1." *Personnel Psychol* 11:127-8 sp '58. *

For a review by Leona E. Tyler, see 4:77; for reviews by Charles I. Mosier and Theodore Newcomb, see 40:1239; for related reviews, see 38:B358 and 36:B108.

[96]

★Pictorial Study of Values: Pictorial Allport-Vernon. Ages 14 and over; 1957; title on test is *The Pictorial Study;* 7 scores: aesthetic, economic, political, religious, social, theoretical, strength of liking things in general; 1 form; preliminary norms; separate answer sheets must be used; $1.95 per 20 tests; $1 per 20 answer sheets; $1 per specimen set (must be purchased to obtain manual); postage extra; (20–30) minutes; Charles Shooster; Psychometric Affiliates. *

ANDREW R. BAGGALEY, *Associate Professor of Psychology, University of Wisconsin—Milwaukee, Milwaukee, Wisconsin.*

This test represents an attempt to translate the verbal content of the Allport-Vernon-Lindzey *Study of Values* into pictorial content while continuing to measure the same processes. The six pictorial scales, with names identical to those of the SOV scales, were derived by correlating "like ratings" on a 5-point scale for 60 pictures with scores on the six SOV scales using a sample of "100 subjects." No further description of these subjects is given. By this empirical method pictures were assigned to the scales according to their "significance level" (not further specified). The *same* subjects were then scored on the pictorial scales, and correlations with their scores on the verbal scales were calculated. The author admits that these correlations, with a mean of .58, are spuriously high; however, it would obviously be better to use a cross-validation group and report the resulting correlations in future editions of the manual.

The author suggests that this version of the SOV may be useful for testees with language difficulty, and this supposition seems plausible if it can be assumed that the testees are familiar with the content of the pictures. The pictures are rather small and in some cases indistinct or too crowded with objects. The middle category of the 5-point response scale is "for the ones you have no opinion about," and the next category is "for those you have less-than-average opinion of." These seem illogical as consecutive categories on a scale.

The reported validity of the test is based mostly on correlations with self-ratings. Intercorrelations of the pictorial scales are also given. These are roughly similar to those published on the SOV verbal scales (although the political-economic correlation is significantly *negative* for the pictures). Thus the test seems to have a moderate amount of construct validity; however, further evidence on its concurrent and predictive validity, beyond that reported for a small group of engineers, is needed before the test can be used confidently in guidance situations. No reliability data whatsoever are given! Norms are given for male and female adults and for two small groups of high school boys. Like its parent SOV, this test should probably be used for guidance rather than selection, since it seems rather easy to "fake" extreme scores on its scales.

In summary, this *Pictorial Study of Values* is an intriguing derivation from a well known test, and it holds much theoretical promise. However, continuing research along the lines indicated above is necessary before the test can be recommended for use in practical counseling work.

HARRISON G. GOUGH, *Associate Professor of Psychology, University of California, Berkeley, California.*

The goal of this test is to assess Spranger's six value types (aesthetic, economic, political, religious, social, and theoretical), using a set of 60 pictures. The criterion for assignment of a picture to a values dimension was its correlation with the relevant values score on the Allport-Vernon-Lindzey *Study of Values* in a sample of 100 "subjects" (no other designation in the manual).

The respondent checks a 5-point scale for each picture, ranging from "like best" through "have no opinion about" to "little or no liking for." An additional "genlike" score, taken from E. L. Thorndike's concept of liking for things in general, may be obtained by tallying the total number of "like best" and "like next best" responses.

With six value scales to be scored over 60 items, the number of items per scale must necessarily be small. This problem is heightened in difficulty by the fact that 11 of the pictures are scored, if at all, only for "genlike." Twenty-four items are scored on only one value scale, 17 items on two, 7 on three, and 1 item is scored on four scales.

Eighteen pictures contribute to the aesthetic score, 8 to the economic, 16 to the political, 13 to the religious, 14 to the social, and 14 to the theoretical. It seems unlikely that enough items have been included on any one of these six scales to permit reliable assessment of it. This reviewer's experience has been that, except for items having unusually high factorial homogeneity, scale reliability can seldom be maintained with less than 20 items.

The pictures seem to have been assembled in an *ad hoc,* intuitive, and unspecified way. The manual gives very little attention to the bases for the inclusion or exclusion of pictures, and it does not describe any steps taken to insure an adequate range of variation among pictures. Given the focus on "values," some of the 11 unscored pictures appear to be poor choices, and in some cases even to be incompatible with the testing instructions. For example, the instructions begin by saying: "You are looking at pictures of things that people have done. Look at Picture Number 1 and decide how much you would like to engage in that activity." Picture 15, however, merely presents a somber landscape with a road leading off toward the horizon. In general, the pictures are unattractively grouped and poorly reproduced. The author could well have invested a much greater amount of time and effort in establishing the set of stimulus materials.

This reviewer's greatest dissatisfaction, however, must be reserved for the manual, which is surely one of the most ill-prepared and inadequate manuals he has seen. The writing in it is diffuse, periphrastic, and frequently ungrammatical. Furthermore, it simply fails to provide the essential material required. For instance, no discussion of scale reliability is offered and no figures whatsoever of either test-retest or internal consistency reliability are given. One cannot help wondering what a scale reliability check of either type would have shown for the 8-item "economic" scale.

The manual is equally deficient with respect to the test's validity. The main evidence here is taken from self-ratings of the value dimensions correlated with the subjects' *Pictorial Study of Values* scale scores. The means of the intercorrelation coefficients reported between self-ratings and scores on the six scales are approximately .18, .14, and .39 for cross-validating samples of 41, 57, and 50 cases, respectively. These coefficients are certainly too low to warrant non-research use of the test, even if the legitimacy of the self-ratings as a criterion is granted.

On the question of specific meanings (operational validity) of each scale the manual is again silent. That is, no information is presented about the question many test users consider to be the crucial one, namely, what kind of a person is it, in everyday "protocol" language, who gets a high or a low score on each of these scales? Information about such things as item selection and scale intercorrelations is of little help for inquiries of this sort. What is needed is a study of people who do in fact represent significant deviations on the scales, and a reporting of their psychodynamic and other characteristics. The manual is also weak in its presentation of norms, utilizing only three male samples (n's of 110, 57, and 41) and one female sample (n = 40).

In the reviewer's judgment, the commercial publication of this test was an unfortunate event. The initial idea—the assessment of personological values by means of pictorial stimuli—is a good one and one deserving of full research support. However, the publication of a "test" on which the necessary research study has only been started, which is entirely lacking in reliability and operational validity data, and whose manual has been badly and unclearly written is another matter. As it stands, the test reflects little credit to either publisher or author.

[97]

★The Power of Influence Test. Grades 2–13; 1958; seating preference sociometric test; 1 form; no data on validity; norms for grades 5–11 only; $3.50 per 50 tests; 50¢ per manual; postage extra; specimen set not available; [10–15] minutes; Roy Cochrane and Wesley Roeder; Psychometric Affiliates. *

[98]

★Practical Policy Test. Adults; 1948; also called *Test of Cynicism;* Form C-S; no manual; no data on reliability and validity; typewritten college norms ['48] only; 5¢ per test; free specimen set; postpaid; [10–20] minutes; Martin F. Fritz and Charles O. Neidt; Martin F. Fritz, Student Counseling Service, Iowa State College. *

REFERENCES

1. FRITZ, MARTIN F. "A Test Study of Cynicism and Idealism." *Proc Iowa Acad Sci* 53:269–72 '46. * (PA 23:588)
2. NEIDT, CHARLES O. "Relation of Cynicism to Certain Other Variables." *Proc Iowa Acad Sci* 53:277–83 '46. * (PA 23:591)
3. FRITZ, MARTIN F. "Co-variation of Cynicism and Idealism." *Proc Iowa Acad Sci* 54:231–4 '47. * (PA 23:5279)
4. NEIDT, CHARLES O. *Analysis of College Student Reaction to the Fritz Test of Cynicism.* Master's thesis, Iowa State College (Ames, Iowa), 1947.
5. NEIDT, CHARLES O. "Selection of the Optimal Scoring Plan for the Fritz Test of Cynicism." *Proc Iowa Acad Sci* 54:253–62 '47. * (PA 23:5527)
6. FRITZ, MARTIN F. "A Short-Form Test of Cynicism." *Proc Iowa Acad Sci* 55:319–22 '48. *
7. FRITZ, MARTIN F. "Relation of the Fritz-Neidt Practical Policy Test to Freshman Entrance Tests." *Proc Iowa Acad Sci* 57:379–80 '50. *
8. NEIDT, CHARLES O., AND FRITZ, MARTIN F. "Relation of Cynicism to Certain Student Characteristics." *Ed & Psychol Meas* 10:712–7 w '50. * (PA 25:6425)
9. FRITZ, MARTIN F. "Statements of Cynicism Rated by College Students." *Proc Iowa Acad Sci* 58:345–9 '51. *

[99]

★Primary Empathic Abilities. Grades 9–16 and adults; 1957–58; 7 scores: diplomacy, industrial, with insecure people, with conscientious middle class, with lower middle class, with stable young married people, with upper social levels; Form A ('57); manual ('57), supplement ('58); no college norms; separate answer pads must be used; 29¢ per test; $1.95 per 20 answer pads; $2 per 50 profiles: high school ('57), adults ('57); $1 per specimen set (must be purchased to obtain manual); postage extra; (45) minutes; Willard Kerr; Psychometric Affiliates. *

ROBERT L. THORNDIKE, *Professor of Education, Teachers College, Columbia University, New York, New York.*

The *Primary Empathic Abilities* is an instrument designed to extend the basic idea of the *Empathy Test* by the same author to the measurement of a number of distinct empathy factors. Empathy means to the author ability to predict the actions of the "generalized other"; the distinct empathy factors are identified with specific classes of others, such as insecure people, the lower middle class, and stable young married people. The reviewer found a good deal of difficulty in rationalizing the factor names in some cases on the basis of the items keyed in the particular factor score.

The identification of seven factors was apparently based on the intercorrelations among 86 items for a population of 200 cases. When the number of variables is so large relative to the number of observations, one may expect the results of a factor analysis to be very fragile and unstable. That this was true is suggested by the fact that all but one of the seven factor scores had reliabilities below .55. The reviewer feels that the separate factors have not been demonstrated as meaningful and stable phenomena and very much suspects that they are largely artifacts of the analysis. If this be so, the results from the test seem largely meaningless.

[100]

★Pupil Adjustment Inventory. Grades kgn–12; 1957; ratings in 7 areas: academic, social, emotional, physical, activities and interests, school's influence on pupil, home background; short and long forms (short form is used to identify pupils who should be rated on the long form) ; $2.70 per set of 35 short forms, 5 long forms, and manual; 80¢ per specimen set; postpaid; (5–15) minutes for short form, (2–5) hours for long form; Group B of the Suburban School Study Council, Educational Service Bureau, School of Education, University of Pennsylvania; Houghton Mifflin Co. *

ROBERT H. BAUERNFEIND, *Director, Test Department, Science Research Associates, Chicago, Illinois.*

This inventory is designed to provide a graphic overview of the pupil's experience and growth in seven areas. The Long Form provides 55 specific considerations to be rated. The entire form is printed on a single side of a sheet measuring 12 by 50 inches. The form could be useful in intensive programs of child study, but it is really too long and too complex for general use with all pupils in a school system. The Short Form, suggested for use with all pupils, provides 15 considerations to be rated. This form is printed on a single side of a sheet measuring 12 by 20 inches. In this format teachers and counselors are encouraged to view and interrelate all 15 ratings at the same time. In addition to blanks for the ratings, both forms have a wide margin for noting sources of information on which each rating is based.

The format is a significant plus-value for three reasons: First, it requires raters to think in terms of facts, rather than general impressions, in making their ratings. Second, it provides a much needed opportunity for school personnel to record important pupil information data on one central reference piece. Third, in the wide margin additional facts can be recorded from time to time concerning pupil behavior, interview findings, and results of recent educational tests and medical examinations.

The inventory manual is attractive and readable. Teachers and counselors will appreciate the authors' work in providing a fairly extensive review of important literature in child development and guidance.

The discussions of reliability and validity are, of necessity, somewhat weak. Our conventional concepts of reliability and validity simply do not apply to this type of form, and the authors acknowledge this point in a frank and searching way. There are, however, other points at which additional research data would be welcome. One wonders, for example, whether the scale points on each continuum were developed by any scaling technique. Several of the verbalizations for

scale points appear not to be equidistant when compared with others. If the verbalizations were assigned judgmentally, it would be good to have some discussion of this development. Also, one wonders about the statement that "the *third,* or *middle* description on each scale denotes accomplishment, ability, or adjustment of the average student." Until there are confirming data, users are cautioned that this will not necessarily be the case in individual schools, or, indeed, among national samples.

This reviewer also suggests that the Short Form might better have included the three Long Form entries in the academic area—for reading, language, and mathematics. These three entries presented separately would surely be appreciated by teachers since they would add important information in the realm of the teacher's primary responsibilities.

There are theoretical problems inherent in an instrument of this type. For one thing, 15 ratings can serve only to "scratch the surface" in the appraisal of a personality. For another, there will be problems of comparability of norms or perspectives in comparing the several ratings. Nonetheless, as a central point of departure for interrelating test scores, anecdotal records, medical reports, and teachers' observations, the *Pupil Adjustment Inventory* is an excellent publication. This reviewer recommends it to any school whose pupil information is scattered or unrelated, and whose teachers are sincerely interested in pupil guidance. For such schools, the value of the form will far exceed the modest per pupil cost of the materials.

JOHN PIERCE-JONES, *Associate Professor of Educational Psychology, The University of Texas, Austin, Texas.*

This inventory is intended to identify "maladjusted" pupils needing experts' attention and to enhance teachers' understanding of children. As the manual prudently observes, the inventory is not a test, but a record form. On it a teacher notes information from divers sources (standardized tests, anecdotal records, and interviews) as ratings of a potpourri of pupil characteristics such as "language usage," "attitude toward schoolwork," "types of associates," "emotional stability," and "sexuality." Spaces exist for recording demographic facts and the sources of data used as bases for ratings.

Most routine standards of rating scale development have apparently been ignored in the construction of this device. In some instances, e.g., "chronological age at grade," the traits to be rated seem to represent reasonable single dimensions, but in many cases, e.g., "hobbies and interests," several constructs have been so confounded that single rating scales are inappropriate. The descriptions of points along the scales are often phrased in ambiguous, value-laden terms, not explicitly and behaviorally. For example, the most favorable scale description of the child's attitude toward his family is "creatively active in the family group." Several of the attributes to be rated are briefly defined in a glossary. The manual presents only some 150 words concerning specific rating procedures; more detailed suggestions are given for the Long Form.

No satisfactory rationale, beyond teacher convenience, supports the development of the Short Form, and operations by which the Short Form (15 scales) was generated from the Long Form (55 scales) are not reported. There is no evidence from factorial or other analyses to justify the selection of Long Form scales appearing in the Short Form nor for the coalescences, in the Short Form, of various Long Form scales. The manual suggests that three deviant ratings on the Short Form "makes further study of a pupil by use of the Long Form advisable." Why this would be even presumptively true in the case of positive deviations from midscale ratings is unclear, and one cannot help wondering why three rather than, say, two or four negative deviations should be deemed significant. That the two forms would, generally, point to the same children as "maladjusted" is not demonstrated, although both forms are intended for identifying purposes as well as for systematizing varied data and teachers' impressions.

It seems not to have occurred to the authors of this inventory that the reliability of ratings can be assessed by other than the test-retest model which they reject. Interrater agreement has not been examined. Forty pupils' self-ratings were "significantly" correlated with teachers' ratings, but the relevance of this to reliability is not evident. A textbook definition of validity is presented, but acceptable evidence of validity is entirely absent. It is reported, however, that clinicians found the inventory "most helpful in analyzing each pupil," and it is argued that the methods of constructing the device and the reactions of school people to its use indicate its "construct validity." This reviewer's under-

standing of construct validity leads him to look for more rigorous theory and for better empirical evidence than the informal opinions of teachers and clinicians. It seems likely that many ratings afforded by this inventory may be inadequately anchored in representative objective observations. Indeed, there seems little recognition that the ratings may more accurately reflect teacher personality than child behavior. The possibility that reification of their impressions by naive or insensitive teachers may endow some children with ill-deserved reputations should surely be considered.

More disturbing than the several technical flaws are various signs of superficial and erroneous thinking about the nature of human adjustment. There is, for instance, a failure to distinguish between adjustment and the degree of the child's socialization in a matrix of culturally valued behavior. One would infer from the inventory that best adjustment includes an IQ of 140 or higher, being emulated and admired, invariable acceptance of life as worthwhile, accelerated physical maturity, general acceptance as a leader, "always (having) money to meet legitimate needs," etc. Such values need not be abjured, but to make ideal adjustment from kindergarten through high school coterminous with them is to be an apostle of the cult of conformity. Finally, there is little evidence that psychodynamic formulations influenced the development of this instrument, and it is difficult to see how "adjustment" can be conceptualized satisfactorily outside such formulations.

In the reviewer's opinion, this inventory should be viewed with great scepticism by potential users. It has been developed without elementary attention to psychometric niceties, the complexities of individual diagnosis, or the difficulties attending sophisticated thinking about adjustment. The inventory cannot be recommended for use without such extensive revision as to make it unrecognizable as the creation of the committee who produced it.

J Consult Psychol 21:507 D '57. Laurance F. Shaffer. * The content and form of the items seem sound. The *Rater's Manual* gives adequate instructions for the use of the scales and anecdotes supporting their value; it is deficient in that it provides no statistical data. The best use of the scales will be to increase the involvement of teachers in the thoughtful consideration of their pupils as persons.

[101]

*The Purdue Rating Scale for Administrators and Executives. Administrators and executives; 1950–51; 36 ratings plus factor scores; 1 form ('50); 3 editions; Report Forms A, B, C ('51); 3¢ per rating scale; 5¢ per any one report form; 25¢ per manual ('51); 35¢ per specimen set; postage extra; (15–20) minutes; H. H. Remmers and R. L. Hobson; Personnel Evaluation Research Service, Division of Educational Reference, Purdue University. *

a) REPORT FORM A. College administrators; 3 factor scores: fairness to subordinates, administrative achievement, democratic orientation.

b) REPORT FORM B. Business executives; 2 factor scores: social responsibility for subordinates and society, executive achievement; no norms for part scores.

c) REPORT FORM C. School administrators.

REFERENCES

1–7. See 4:83.
8. REMMERS, H. H., AND ELLIOTT, D. N. "The Indiana College and University Staff-Evaluation Program." *Sch & Soc* 70:168–71 S 10 '49. * (*PA* 26:2440)

JOHN P. FOLEY, JR., *President, J. P. Foley & Co., Inc., New York, New York.*

This scale is intended as an aid to the executive or administrator in discovering his job-related strengths and weaknesses, thereby providing information which can be utilized in his individual growth and development. Specifically, the scale is designed to measure subordinates' opinions of the effectiveness of executives and administrators in business and industry as well as in public schools and higher educational institutions.

The scale consists of 36 items, selected from an extensive literature survey and through personal conferences with executives, administrators, and their subordinates. These items are classified under the following ten major headings, each containing from one to ten items: intellectual balance, emotional balance, administrative leadership, administrative planning, use of funds, capacity for work, accomplishment, relations with subordinates, public relations, and social responsibility. Responses are recorded in terms of a 5-point scale which for most items consists of the terms: always, usually, sometimes, seldom, never. For certain items other, more suitable, terms are substituted. The scale is printed on the two sides of a single 8½ by 11 inch sheet, and is preceded by brief instructions. The rating process ordinarily requires 15–20 minutes.

Since the scale is to be used as a basis for self-improvement, the authors recommend that the administrator's superior not have access to the results. The administrator himself should participate voluntarily and should retain the results for his own use. In this connection, it

should be noted that norms and other research data have been obtained only in situations where cooperation was voluntary on the part of the administrator rated, where all results were confidential, and where anonymity of raters was guaranteed.

In the accompanying manual, scorer reliability for each item is reported. Coefficients are stepped up by the Spearman-Brown formula. In the case of the industrial data, it is stated in a footnote in the manual that "2 vs. 2" raters were utilized, instead of the "10 vs. 10" reported in the table. The latter coefficients are obviously stepped-up estimates, although this is not made clear. In general, however, rater agreement appears to be high. Validity is discussed only in terms of content. It is maintained that no better criterion for the judgment of a subordinate's rating of his superior can be found than the judgment of that subordinate himself. The reliability and validity coefficients for scale items thus become identical.

Scoring is accomplished by plotting the mean score assigned by all raters to each item on the percentile profile chart provided in a separate report form. Three report forms are available: Form A for college and university administrators, Form B for business and industrial executives, and Form C for administrators in elementary and secondary schools. Three types of interpretation are suggested: (*a*) comparative—determination of the percentile rank for each item with reference to the appropriate normative group; (*b*) literal—selection of the descriptive scale term which most closely corresponds to the assigned mean rating for each item; and (*c*) distributive—examination of the range of ratings on each item in order to determine where disagreement exists among subordinates.

Factor analysis was applied to the data from the A and B groups mentioned above. In the business and industrial group, item intercorrelations yielded two factors, described as "social responsibility for subordinates and society" and "executive achievement." These are said to represent the twofold responsibility of an executive to "the people in his immediate and larger society" and to "his job and employers." Three factors were isolated in the college and university administration group, designated as "fairness to subordinates," "administrative achievement," and "democratic orientation." These factors are claimed to represent the tridimensional responsibility of an administrator to his staff, to his job or superiors, and to society. A list of items from which such factors can be found, as well as corresponding percentile norms, is provided. These data, however, are available only for the group of college and university administrators.

Although the *Purdue Rating Scale for Administrators and Executives* represents a sound attempt to secure appraisal information relating to supervisory strengths and weaknesses, it is subject to a number of limitations. In most industrial and educational organizations, evaluative information is desired for administrative purposes as well as for individual development. In fact, most management development programs in business and industry clearly recognize these two major goals. The authors of the Purdue scale specifically state that the instrument should not be used for the first of these two objectives. The reviewer would concur with the statement that "inverse rating" is ordinarily an inappropriate technique for management decisions relating to placement, transfer, promotion, and compensation, but would call attention to the fact that other types of appraisal procedures can often be utilized for *both* individual development and administrative purposes.

The scale is necessarily subject to all of the limitations imposed upon a "canned" rating scale. In the reviewer's opinion, a scale which is specifically tailored to the needs of a particular organization will often prove more meaningful and of greater value. The reviewer also feels that insufficient emphasis is placed upon the training of raters. True, a bow is made in this direction through the suggestion that a "staff-meeting method" may be used in administering the scale. Other methods are also suggested, however, such as the "work-place method," which involves sending the scale to the rater along with a standard letter of instruction. Most professionals in the rating field would probably agree that poor ratings are more likely to result from attitudinal problems, such as faulty mental set or unwillingness to rate accurately, than from sheer inability to make accurate appraisals. For such reasons, the reviewer would have a real question concerning the value of canned rating procedures in most practical situations.

Careful scrutiny of the scale itself will lead to other, more specific criticisms. No attempt is made to integrate the obtained appraisals with such measurable factors as tested abilities. Nor is any provision whatever made for the appraisal of such ability factors. Yet, it is evident that the presence or absence of varying degrees of relevant ability will most certainly influence the performance of an executive or administrator. Moreover, a particular level of a given ability will often influence the significance of an administrator's standing on another trait, as rated by his subordinates. Other criticisms relating to the content of the scale can be illustrated. In the case of Area I, Intellectual Balance, for example, it is difficult to subscribe to this designation for factors relating solely to general and specific knowledge. Area V, which is designated as Use of Funds, contains three items, dealing with employment of personnel, selection of equipment, and effort to obtain funds for subordinate improvement, respectively. What about such factors as equipment operation and maintenance, personnel utilization, and other factors relating to the maintenance of an economical and cost-conscious operation?

Within the limitations of a readymade rating scale, the present instrument can undoubtedly be utilized effectively. For most purposes, however, a carefully tailored instrument, integrated with relevant test information and administered to raters who have been carefully trained, will probably yield better appraisal results.

HERBERT A. TONNE, *Professor of Education, New York University, New York, New York.*

The authors do not assume that this scale measures administrative or executive ability. It is simply an opinion scale against which workers may measure their superiors. The scale serves this use quite well. It is easy to take. The authors have made every effort possible to assure that the scale will be used intelligently in job situations.

The only interpretive data provided are in terms of average ratings. Such measures give no evidence of the degree of rater agreement. However, the manual does encourage the administrator who is analyzed to study the tally sheet to determine to what extent there was agreement among those who rated him.

Quite wisely no attempt is made to determine a reliability coefficient for the scale as a whole. The coefficients for the individual items range from .99 for one item, as marked by collegiate raters, to .43 for another, as marked by public school raters. In general, the reliabilities are sufficiently high to be of some significance.

The reviewer questions the assumption that since the scale is concerned with the rating of a superior by his subordinates and since the subordinates make the judgments, the validity is, therefore, the same as the reliability. As the manual indicates, we can and must question frankness and honesty; we must also question interpretation and understanding of items. However, the scale does seem as valid as is possible for such a device.

The scale should be a useful device for the evaluation of administrative and supervisory personnel if used with much care. Unfortunately, we all have overmuch a tendency to assume that a formal printed instrument is more scientific than the authors themselves claim it to be.

For a review by Kenneth L. Heaton, see 4:83.

[102]

★Rating Scale for Pupil Adjustment. Grades 3–9; 1950–53; 1 form ('53); $1.20 per 20 scales; 10¢ per manual ('53); postage extra; specimen set not available; [10] minutes; [Gwen Andrew, Samuel W. Hartwell, Max L. Hutt, and Ralph E. Walton]; Science Research Associates. *

WILLIAM E. HENRY, *Associate Professor of Human Development and Psychology, University of Chicago, Chicago, Illinois.*

The scale, based upon 11 areas of personality, was developed by the Michigan Department of Mental Health as a part of a research with the *Michigan Picture Test.* The areas—overall emotional adjustment, social maturity, tendency toward depression, tendency toward aggressive behavior, extroversion-introversion, emotional security, motor control, impulsiveness, emotional irritability, school achievement, and school conduct—are each rated on a 5-point scale. A final item lists 12 physical conditions like "unusually tall for age," "physical disfigurement," "special handicap," which may influence adjustment. These do not contribute to the score, but may be noted if they apply.

The instrument is intended for use by teachers. The ratings are made against a hypothetical total population of children of the age in question, rather than against children in the particular classroom.

A weighting system is provided to permit the derivation of a total score—the higher scores reflecting better general adjustment. No cutoff scores are available, but it is suggested that the lower portion of the scores in a class—from 25 to 33 per cent—be referred to the school psychologist for further study. Research upon the validity of the scale is reported as in progress.

One reliability study is reported. It provides a product-moment correlation of .84 between two sets of ratings of 23 children made a month apart by the same teacher.

The usefulness of such an instrument clearly depends upon the training of the rater in its use and will thus differ with teachers and school systems. This one seems a well conceived instrument, provided it is used by skilled persons primarily as a framework for recording observations.

MORRIS KRUGMAN, *Assistant Superintendent in Charge of Guidance, New York Public Schools, New York, New York.*

Originally designed for use as a validity criterion for the *Michigan Picture Test,* this rating scale can be used by classroom teachers in locating poorly adjusted children. It is recommended for schools having diagnostic and treatment services available, and is intended to improve the accuracy of referrals to such services.

Used in the recommended manner, this rating scale has merit. As the manual warns, not all children referred will necessarily be seriously disturbed, and not all disturbed children will be referred. However, even rating scales not so carefully designed as this have proven the value of systematic rating of pupil adjustment by teachers who have observed children over an extended period of time. The danger of such rating scales lies in their use without benefit of subsequent evaluation by psychologists or psychiatrists. It becomes too easy for teachers to label children, and this needs to be guarded against.

The scale consists of 11 areas of adjustment to be assigned ratings of from A (good) through E (poor) and one item dealing with physical handicaps. A system of weighted scoring is used. The authors suggest referral of the lowest quarter or third of the class, depending upon the availability of therapeutic services. A validity study is now being conducted. Results of this study are promised in forthcoming editions of the manual.

If used with appropriate safeguards, this scale can have value for the improvement of child referral procedures. It should not be used alone for personality evaluation.

[103]

★SAQS Chicago Q Sort. College and adults; 1956–57; 1 form (no date); no data on reliability; $2 per set of 10 record sheets ('56), 10 profiles ('57), cards (no date), and manual ('56); $3 per 50 record sheets; $3 per 50 profiles; postage extra; (15–20) minutes; Raymond Corsini; Psychometric Affiliates. *

REFERENCES

1. CORSINI, RAYMOND J. "Multiple Predictors of Marital Happiness." *Marriage & Family Living* 18:240–2 Ag '56. *
2. CORSINI, RAYMOND J. "Understanding and Similarity in Marriage." *J Abn & Social Psychol* 52:327–32 My '56. * (PA 31:4536)

WILLIAM STEPHENSON, *Consulting Psychologist, 20 Brookside Drive, Greenwich, Connecticut.*

This is a set of 50 personal adjectives, such as "original," "high-strung," "sarcastic," and "excitable," to be sorted so as to describe one's self or other people. In this reviewer's opinion, the SAQS provides a straightforward introductory pack. The instructions are clear and constructive. Minor improvements might be made; for example, it scarcely seems necessary to have "sensitive" and "insensitive" together in the same pack.

The author suggests that his set of adjectives should not be expected to have general validity. What, then, is to give the SAQS scientific value? Its author suggests a wide range of uses for the pack: personality study, marital counseling, and job prediction, for example. These are important areas of psychological concern. One may ask, therefore, what is there about these adjectives that gives them scientific value? The author, we suppose, could answer in two or three different ways.

First, he has chosen the adjectives from seven personality areas (life style, intelligence, social sensitivity, emotional stability, dominance, activity, and mood), and, for this reason, the pack presumably has a certain implied general validity. That is, it can generate *explanations* of facts which, at face value, most psychologists might accept. Next, some data are provided in the form of percentile "profiles" for husband-wife Q sort correlations. However, the data are for only a few husband and wife combinations and are not norms in any sense. Third, reference is made to two papers by the author (1, 2) dealing with the use of the adjectives in marital counseling. For psychologists interested in such counseling, the pack, used in conjunction with these published papers, would no doubt be of some interest.

But, aside from these three indications of some validity, what justifies publication of a pack of adjectives such as SAQS? Is general validity at issue? Are norms and "profiles" necessary? Since this instrument is likely to be the forerunner of other standard packs of Q cards, such questions need to be discussed. It would seem to the reviewer that if a psychologist has a good theory, general validity is not what he is looking for, at least not general validity in the form of norms or similar kinds of data. He is more likely to want to test his theory in concrete situations, to explain what is going on, for example, between a particular husband and wife under conditions of marital stress. The focus might be on some fascinating dynamic relationships that the theory, and its operational use by way of the Q pack, had brought to light. Without such a theoretical basis, even a rag and bone merchant could put together 50 adjectives and suggest that by correlating data for husbands and wives, information would be obtained which, suitably percentiled, would—well, what?

It is important, therefore, for the author of a pack of Q cards to offer some account of the instrument's theoretical implications for the purposes for which it is recommended. If the theoretical basis is interesting and suitably exemplified, there would usually be little need to ask questions about general validity, or to give profiles or other norm-implying tables. But, at face value, there is really nothing to suggest that these particular cards will serve cogently in marital counseling, job selection, or personality study. If they will, we would all be very interested to know how they do it and why they work. Of course, any clever psychologist versed in dynamic theory and knowing the person doing the Q sort could suitably interpret it. Even in this case, however, one would like to know what there is in these adjectives that is peculiarly interesting for projective purposes.

Thus, it would seem to be incumbent upon authors of packs of Q cards to elaborate on any theory they involve in their cards, and to suggest how the theory is to be used to help the psychologist find his way about in the facts the technique reveals. The *SAQS Chicago Q Sort* would be acceptable for student training purposes and for illustrating methods of Q sorting and correlation. Wider use would require much more in the way of theoretical involvement to warrant it.

CLIFFORD H. SWENSEN, JR., *Associate Professor of Psychology, University of Tennessee, Knoxville, Tennessee.*

This test has been made available "for general experimental research use" because (according to the author): (*a*) it is a convenient instrument; (*b*) it has unusual item characteristics; and (*c*) what is already known about its characteristics indicates that it is useful. The author's first claim is undoubtedly justified. The test can be given quite easily and quickly, and the correlation of one Q sort with another is accomplished quite rapidly by using the scoring form and correlation chart provided. However, the latter two justifications are not quite so apparent. Presumably the items are unusual in that they consist of words rather than sentences, and in that the words are familiar to most adults, unambiguous, unstereotyped, and representative of "seven major areas or 'factors' of personality." The author does not provide an explicit statement of how the words were selected. Neither does he indicate to what the seven factors of personality according to which he has classified the words are related. The test itself was derived from Stephenson's better known work with Q sorts, and is apparently intended as a shorter, more convenient method of getting at these same factors. The justification concerning what is already known about the test's characteristics is partially supported by evidence.

The manual cites two studies in which high agreement between husbands and wives in the sorts is related to marital happiness. However, no evidence relating the results of the sorts to personality factors is presented. In fairness to the author, it should be pointed out that he states that the test should probably not be thought of as having general validity, but as being valid for particular purposes. By particular purposes he presumably means research rather than diagnostic purposes.

Test-retest reliabilities of .81 for 27 college women and .79 for 31 college men are reported with a one week interval between administrations. Reliability studies with larger and more heterogeneous samples would be preferable.

The author presents 10 tables of norms for the intercorrelations between various kinds of sorts. One of these is the correlation between the individual's sort for Self and for Ideal Self. The remaining nine are various types of correlations between the sorts of husbands and wives. These nine are based upon 20 or more married couples. The norms for the Self-Ideal Self sort are based upon 40 college students. No additional information about the samples is provided. It would be desirable to have norms based upon larger and more heterogeneous samples,

and the manual should present more detailed information concerning the samples upon which the present norms are based. No indication of the significance of high or low intercorrelations is given, with the exception of the previously mentioned studies. Such information would be highly desirable, as would norms and validation data for other kinds of intercorrelations among sorts, and information concerning how the test was constructed.

One other minor criticism should be noted. The words are presented on very small cards that are rather difficult to handle. It would be a little easier to sort and score the cards if they were about twice their present size.

The test appears to be an easily administered research instrument, but of unknown validity for other purposes.

[104]
*SRA Junior Inventory. Grades 4–8; 1951–57; problems checklist; 5 scores: school, home, myself, people, health (Form A), general (Form S); 2 forms; Form S is an extensive revision of Form A rather than a parallel form; postage extra; H. H. Remmers and Robert H. Bauernfeind; Science Research Associates. *
a) FORM A. 1951; separate answer pads must be used; $9.80 per 20 tests; $2.15 per 20 answer pads; $1.20 per 20 pupil profile leaflets ('51); 75¢ per specimen set; (40) minutes.
b) FORM S, REVISED EDITION. 1955–57; test ('57); manual ('57); $2 per 20 tests; $1.05 per 20 profiles ('57); 50¢ per specimen set; (45) minutes.

REFERENCES
1. BAUERNFEIND, ROBERT H. The Development of a Needs and Problems Inventory for Elementary School Children. Doctor's thesis, Purdue University (Lafayette, Ind.), 1951.
2. RABINOVITCH, VIVIAN. The Construction and Validation of a Basic Difficulty Index for the SRA Junior Inventory. Master's thesis, Purdue University (Lafayette, Ind.), 1953.
3. NIXON, WARREN WINTERS. The Science Research Associates Junior Inventory: A Validity Study. Doctor's field study, Colorado State College of Education (Greeley, Colo.), 1954.
4. BAUERNFEIND, ROBERT H. "Measuring Children's Strength of Response to Attitude Items." Ed & Psychol Meas 15:63–70 sp '55. * (PA 30:664)
5. HERNÁNDEZ, CARLOS. The Spanish Revision of the S.R.A. Junior Inventory, Form A. Doctor's thesis, Purdue University (Lafayette, Ind.), 1958. (DA 19:354)

WARREN R. BALLER, Professor of Educational Psychology, The University of Nebraska, Lincoln, Nebraska.

Form S of this needs and problems checklist is a thoroughly revised edition of Form A (1951), and, as such, retains the desirable features of its predecessor while benefiting from changes which experience with the earlier form suggested. The wording of the items appears to be well suited to the aim of presenting children's problems in the form in which they recognize and express them. The words "I want," "I wish," "I need," "I am," "I would like," or their negatives introduce all but a small percentage of the items. The reading level of the statements is consistent with the grade level involved.

A matter which gave the authors some concern in their interpretation of responses to the earlier form was the difficulty of determining differences in strength of feeling. This difficulty has been resolved to a considerable extent in Form S. Three response boxes of different sizes are provided for each item. The checking of the big box means "Big Problem"; the middle sized box is for indicating a "Middle-Sized Problem"; the little box is for a "Little Problem." The Fourth response choice, a circle, is to be checked to indicate no problem. The differentially-sized response box method for determining intensity of feeling is a particularly noteworthy development.

As one approach to interpretation, the authors suggest the identification of the areas in which a child's major interests and problems lie, and the differential comparison of scores in the several areas. For this purpose they suggest that values of 3, 2, and 1, respectively, be given to big-, middle-sized-, and small-box responses. A pupil profile based on national norms for each of the five problem areas is provided for depicting the resulting scores. The use of the profile chart with a problems checklist will be looked upon with some misgivings by numerous counseling psychologists and others who do not consider that interpretation based on a system of norms contributes to the best use of such an instrument. For one thing, the existence of the profile chart is an invitation to *rate* (i.e., score) pupil responses—a dubious practice when it is associated with the search for important pupil problems and interests. The authors' suggestion that each area of responses may prove to be interpretable "as a 'psychological test score'" will meet with resistance from persons who deem the functions of inventories and tests to be basically different.

In addition, in spite of evidence of the statistical reliability of the area classifications of responses, there remains the bothersome question of whether some "unlikes" have not been grouped together in such a way as to cast doubt on the meaning of profile scores. Some items in a given area appear to relate to *problems;* others in the same area seem best to be described as *interests.* The authors use the two terms. As a result, it is difficult to see what the area score for school, for example, means with both these kinds of items contributing to it.

There also seems to be room for serious doubt about whether the same profile score for different pupils will convey reasonably comparable indications of problems in view of the different point-value compositions that are possible. Conceivably, one pupil might rank high on a given area by checking many small boxes, while another pupil could receive the same score by checking a small number of large boxes. The criticism would seem all the more justified in light of the fact that the authors disregard entirely small box checking when they compute frequencies of scores for the invoicing of a class as a whole.

As another aid to interpretation, selected items have been grouped, on the basis of content analysis, into eight categories: Reading Problems, Curriculum Planning and Teaching Methods, Identifying Potential Drop-Outs, Health Problems, Relationships with Older Youngsters, Relationships with Adults, Personal Adjustment, and Objective Interests and Problems. The manual makes it clear that these are suggestive and tentative groupings. As such, they should have real value for the purpose of enlisting the interest of school nurses, attendance officers, curriculum specialists, and others in data that might point the way to desirable changes in school practices and policies.

Among the numerous good features of the inventory are the unusually complete set of directions and the inclusion in the manual of several suggestions as to how the instrument may be used. Professional workers who take the pains to read these suggestions carefully will be likely to plan for important activities which they otherwise would not have thought about. Finally, there is much about the inventory that points to its potential usefulness in important research. The authors are to be commended for suggesting a number of possibilities for further refinement of the instrument and for studies into various phases of curriculum improvement and improvement of pupil personnel services in which the inventory might advantageously be used.

J Consult Psychol 21:282 Je '57. Laurance F. Shaffer. * The revised form is clearly an improvement. It also continues to show the merits which characterized the earlier version—the good scope of technical information provided in the manual, and the modesty of the suggested interpretations.

J Counsel Psychol 4:328–9 w '57. Laurence Siegel. * To the extent that this inventory will be used by teachers and counselors as an evaluational tool for the purpose of stimulating discussions with students, it will serve a very useful purpose. It is doubtful, however, that the *Junior Inventory,* in its present form, deserves the refinements of scoring and profile analysis also suggested by the authors. The statistical rationale underlying the development of this inventory is simply too weak to justify the derivation and interpretation of "scores" for the five subscales. Considered as an evaluational checklist rather than as a measuring instrument, the *Junior Inventory* possesses tremendous potential for application. The items in the inventory are phrased in the youngsters' jargon since most of these items were extracted from "My Problems" essays written by elementary school children. The format of the booklet is ingenious in providing a readily comprehensible system for rating each of the self-descriptive statements as a "big problem," "middle-sized problem," "little problem" or "not a problem." By and large, the manual is well written and will be understandable to persons who might be required to administer the inventory in the absence of any specialized training in testing procedures. * There is little doubt that the perceptive teacher, and counselor, will gain much in the way of useful information about individual pupils by studying their replies to specific items. Analysis of group responses to specific items (i.e., problems) may provide a sound basis for evaluating the school's success in achieving nonacademic objectives and may well stimulate classroom discussions constituting a mental hygiene program at the elementary school level. These are, however, the limits of application of the *Junior Inventory.* Statistical considerations.... prohibit proper interpretations of scores on the five subscales. The starting point for development of clusters or subscales within the *Junior Inventory* rested upon the frequently used procedure whereby provisional clusters are hypothesized and items are grouped into these provisional clusters for the purpose of deriving subscores. The allocations of items is then verified by correlating every item with every provisional subscale. The resultant item-cluster correlations normally dictate the removal of certain items and the reassignment of others. Unfortunately this procedure was aborted in the development of the *Junior Inventory.* The em-

pirical portion of the item analysis was not iterated because the authors somehow established a rationale which prevented the expected mobility of items. This rationale is not clarified in the manual, but it is quite obvious that certain clusters were permitted to retain items which did *not* correlate substantially with the rest of the subscale! The "Myself" cluster, for example, contains at least one item with a 0.00 correlation. How many such items were retained to contaminate the subscales is not discussed in the manual. Furthermore, a usual procedure in this type of analysis is to retain only those items which correlate significantly with one or perhaps two of the subscales. The magnitudes of intercorrelations between the subscales are sufficiently high to indicate that the *Junior Inventory* contains many items which correlate with several subscales. In fact, the authors' contentions that the intercorrelations between the five areas "....are satisfactorily low to justify treating each area as an independent measure" is probably untenable. These intercorrelations range between .39 and .77 with a median value of .52. Although the data were not factor analyzed, it is probable that one general factor would account for a large portion of the total variance. And two factors, combining the "School" and "Home" clusters and the "Myself" and "People" clusters would probably remove virtually all of the variance. Thus, the data now available on the *Junior Inventory* do not justify computation of the five subscores advocated in the manual. Furthermore, since predictive validities have not yet been demonstrated, it is unlikely that one would want to score the inventory anyway. The *Junior Inventory* is a valuable supplement to general evaluational techniques in the area of personality at the elementary school level. When considered in this light, it has excellent potential. It is unlikely, however, that it can be treated as a multiscored measuring instrument at the present time.

For a review by Dwight L. Arnold of Form A, see 4:90.

[105]

*SRA Youth Inventory. Grades 7–12; 1949–56; problems checklist; 9 scores: school, future, myself, people, home, dates and sex, health, general, basic difficulty; IBM; 2 forms; Form S is an extensive revision of Form A rather than a parallel form; 75¢ per specimen set; postage extra; (30–40) minutes; H. H. Remmers, Benjamin Shimberg, and Arthur J. Drucker (manual for Form A) ; Science Research Associates. *

a) FORM A. 1949–53; listed as Forms AH and AM in publisher's catalog; IBM; 1 form ('49); manual, second edition ('53); technical supplement ('53); separate answer sheets or pads must be used; $9.80 per 20 tests; $4.50 per 100 IBM answer sheets; $2.15 per 20 hand scoring answer pads; $2.50 per set of machine scoring stencils; 50¢ per hand scoring basic difficulty key; $1.20 per 20 profile leaflets ('50) for students in grades 7–10; $1.20 per 20 profile leaflets ('49) for students in grades 9–12.

b) FORM S. 1955; only test booklet available.

REFERENCES

1–7. See 4:91.
8. BROWN, CURTIS P. *The Mooney Problem Check List and the SRA Youth Inventory in Comparison.* Master's thesis, University of Southern California (Los Angeles, Calif.), 1952.
9. DRUCKER, A. J., AND REMMERS, H. H. "Environmental Determinants of Basic Difficulty Problems." *J Abn & Social Psychol* 47:379–81 Ap '52. * (PA 27:2975)
10. DRUCKER, A. J., AND REMMERS, H. H. "A Validation of the SRA Youth Inventory." *J Appl Psychol* 36:186–7 Je '52. *
11. FICK, REUEL L. "The Problem Check List: A Valuable Approach in Counseling." *Occupations* 30:410–2 Mr '52. * (PA 26:6533)
12. WARDLOW, MARY E., AND GREENE, JAMES E. "An Exploratory Sociometric Study of Peer Status Among Adolescent Girls." *Sociometry* 15:311–8 Ag–N '52. * (PA 27:7097)
13. KEISLAR, EVAN R. "Peer Group Judgments as Validity Criteria for the SRA Youth Inventory." *Calif J Ed Res* 5:77–9 Mr '54. * (PA 28:9026)
14. WEIMER, LOIS B. *An Experiment Using the SRA Inventory With a Selected Group of Adolescents in a Latin-American Community in a Texas City.* Master's thesis, University of Wyoming (Laramie, Wyo.), 1954.
15. COOMBS, ROBERT WARREN. *The Appraisal of Personal Problems of High School Seniors.* Doctor's thesis, University of Southern California (Los Angeles, Calif.), 1955.
16. PAISIOS, JOHN P., AND REMMERS, H. H. "A Factor Analysis of the SRA Youth Inventory." *J Ed Psychol* 46:25–30 Ja '55. * (PA 29:8998)
17. DE LOPATEGUI, MIGUELINA N. *Needs and Problems of Puerto Rican High School Students Related to N Variables.* Doctor's thesis, Purdue University (Lafayette, Ind.), 1957. (DA 18:2197)
18. SPIVAK, MONROE L. "School Problems Reported by Seventh and Ninth-Grade Children Entering the Same Junior High School." *J Ed Res* 50:631–3 Ap '57. *
19. PAULEY, BERTHOLD. "Relationship Between SRA Youth Inventory Scores and School Citizenship." *Personnel & Guid J* 37:207–11 N '58. *

For reviews by Kenneth E. Clark and Frank S. Freeman of Form A, see 4:91.

[106]

★The Science Research Temperament Scale. Grades 12–16 and adults; 1955; title on test is *The S.R.T. Scale;* Form A; mimeographed manual ['55]; $3 per 50 tests; $1 per specimen set (must be purchased to obtain manual); postage extra; (10–30) minutes; William C. Kosinar; Psychometric Affiliates. *

REFERENCE

1. KOSINAR, WILLIAM C. *Predicting Some Aspects of Research Productivity.* Doctor's thesis, Illinois Institute of Technology (Chicago, Ill.), 1954.

JOHN D. BLACK, *President, Consulting Psychologists Press, Inc., Palo Alto, California; and Director, Counseling and Testing Services, Stanford University, Stanford, California.*

The ludicrous appearance of this test, which among other things is embellished with a hideous border reminiscent of a cheap premium certificate, may lead some subjects to think it must be a gag. A glance at the manual, which does similar violence to the most rudimentary esthetic and reproduction standards, scarcely dispels this impression. Only by reading the manual is one reassured that the SRT Scale is a serious attack on an important psychological problem.

The scale was developed "to aid in the identification of personality traits that are associated with research productivity." It is a 1-page test consisting of 37 different adjectives descriptive of human behavior presented in 42 pairs roughly equated for social desirability. Subjects check which of each pair of adjectives best describes them. The score is based on responses which successfully discriminated between the top and the bottom 10 per cent of a group of 310 research workers objectively ranked for productivity in research. The 4-page mimeographed manual provides an adequate summary of the limited data available. Decile norms are given for four male groups ranging in size from 20 to 310, and, oddly enough, for two subgroups: the most and the least productive of the 310 scientists.

The author quite properly points out that the scale "is more discriminative at its two extremes rather than in its middle range." It is interesting to note that there is almost 100 per cent overlap among the distributions of research workers, college students, and "average" high school students, and that the means of these groups are virtually identical. In other words, the scale does not discriminate between research workers and other people. Its usefulness, therefore, would appear to be confined to evaluations of men engaged in research work or persons seeking to enter it. Unfortunately, from the data presented, it does not appear to contribute materially to such evaluations.

Correlation of the scale with productivity scores of 310 research workers, including the ones on which item selection was based, is given as .28, which "is underestimative (sic) because of some curvilinearity in the scatterplot." Two cross validation studies yielded rank order correlations of .26 and .36—correlations which, because of the small n's involved are significant only when considered jointly. The author candidly acknowledges that SRT scores accounted for only 7 to 13 per cent of the variance in productivity ratings of the scientists, which is certainly disappointing in a test designed for that specific function. If the author could demonstrate that in combination with other predictive measures the SRT appreciably increases multiple correlations, this disappointment might be ameliorated. Test-retest reliability (time interval not reported) is given as .76, which is also discouraging. One wonders if the item pool is too limited or too heavily weighted with a few items. The entire score actually depends on 18 adjectives; the three most frequently scored (imaginative, self-confident, and impulsive) contribute 15 of the possible 42 points on the scale.

As a research tool for investigating the personalities of research scientists, the SRT Scale probably has less to offer than a good adjective checklist with a larger repertory of descriptive words, although the forced choice technique is an interesting contribution. As a tool for selection, the scale's mediocre showing on the validity studies reported makes it of dubious value. In basic conception, the test seems sound and the author's work appears to have been carefully done. Considerably more validation and refinement is required, however, before publication of this test can be justified.

DAVID R. SAUNDERS, *Research Associate, Educational Testing Service, Princeton, New Jersey.*

According to its manual, this instrument was developed "to aid in the identification of personality traits that are associated with research productivity." It yields a single score, based on all of the 42 forced choice items included in the form, and is reported by the author to have a test-retest reliability of .76 for a sample of graduate and undergraduate students. Since such a group is, if anything, more heterogeneous with respect to "research productivity" than the groups to which this instrument would most naturally be applied, this reliability figure must be treated as an upper bound on the reliability that would be attained in a practical application. Thus, from the point of view of reliability, we are forced to be exceedingly cautious in interpreting any but the most extreme scores that may be earned by individuals.

There is evidence for the validity of scores on this scale which is of unquestionable *statistical* significance, but not of much *practical* significance. Statistical significance is readily achieved, as in this case, by carrying out validation and cross validation studies on relatively large samples. However, the manual states that "performance on the scale on cross validation accounted for 7% to 13% of the variance in scientific and technical productivity." This would be an acceptable degree of validity *only if*

there were a tremendous pool of talent from which we could select only the most extreme individuals, *and only if* we were quite unconcerned by the number of truly talented individuals who would not be selected. Such seems hardly to be the case.

In summary, in view of both the scantiness of the available data on the scale and the failure of even the data reported in the manual to justify its application to practical situations, we can only advise that its use be restricted to situations in which the scores earned by individuals genuinely do not count.

[107]
★Security-Insecurity Inventory. Grades 9–16 and adults; 1945–52; title on test is *The S–I Inventory*; 1 form ('52); $3 per 25 tests; 25¢ per scoring stencil and manual ('52); 50¢ per specimen set; cash orders postpaid; (15–25) minutes; A. H. Maslow, E. Birsh, I. Honigmann, F. McGrath, A. Plason, and M. Stein; [Consulting Psychologists Press, Inc.]. *

REFERENCES
1. MASLOW, A. H. "The Dynamics of Psychological Security-Insecurity." *Char & Pers* 10:331–44 Je '42. * (*PA* 17:206)
2. MASLOW, A. H. "Conflict, Frustration, and the Theory of Threat." *J Abn & Social Psychol* 38:81–6 Ja '43. * (*PA* 17:2737)
3. MASLOW, A. H.; HIRSH, ELISA; STEIN, MARCELLA; AND HONIGMANN, IRMA. "A Clinically Derived Test for Measuring Psychological Security-Insecurity." *J General Psychol* 33:21–41 Jl '45. * (*PA* 20:202)
4. GOUGH, HARRISON G. "A Note on the Security-Insecurity Test." *J Social Psychol* 28:257–61 N '48. * (*PA* 23:2706)
5. SMITH, HENRY CLAY. "Psychometric Checks on Hypotheses Derived From Sheldon's Work on Physique and Temperament." *J Personality* 17:310–20 Mr '49. * (*PA* 23:2916)
6. SWEETLAND, ANDERS, AND SHEPLER, BERNARD. "Unweighted Scoring Norms for the Security-Insecurity Test." *J General Psychol* 49:309–10 O '53. * (*PA* 28:7555)
7. BRESEE, CLYDE WESLEY. *Affective Factors Associated With Academic Underachievement in High-School Students.* Doctor's thesis, Cornell University (Ithaca, N.Y.), 1956. (*DA* 17:90)
8. MORRIS, ROBERT P. "An Exploratory Study of Some Personality Characteristics of Gamblers." *J Clin Psychol* 13:191–3 Ap '57. * (*PA* 32:3294)
9. BENNETT, CARSON M., AND JORDAN, THOMAS E. "Security-Insecurity and the Direction of Aggressive Responses to Frustration." *J Clin Psychol* 14:166–7 Ap '58. *
10. MEHLMAN, BENJAMIN, AND KAPLAN, JANICE E. "A Correction: A Comparison of Some Concepts of Psychological Health." *J Clin Psychol* 14:438 O '58. *

NELSON G. HANAWALT, *Professor of Psychology, Douglass College, Rutgers University, New Brunswick, New Jersey.*

The *S–I Inventory* is a product of Maslow's research program which earlier produced the *Social Personality Inventory for College Women;* although the two tests are uncorrelated by design, they are nevertheless related to each other. Specifically, the test arose from Maslow's clinical and theoretical research in emotional security. Security-insecurity is a global concept or, as Maslow expresses it, a syndrome, more precisely defined by 14 subsyndromes which were judged on the basis of clinical experience to be a part of the generic concept. Table 1 in the manual lists these subsyndromes in terms of both security and insecurity. However, there is no delusion on the part of the author that these are pure factors, for he thinks of the generic syndrome and the subsyndromes as fitting into each other like a nest of cubes.[1]

The purpose of the test is to measure feelings of security, judged by Maslow to be one of the most important determinants of mental health, if not synonymous with it, and to discover something about the individual variables which make up the syndrome of security-insecurity. On this basis he recommends its use by institutions as a general survey test to single out cases of neurotic tendencies, maladjustment, conflict, suicidal tendencies, etc. How successful the test would be for such a screening purpose is not known; at least this reviewer has found no published study where it has been evaluated in this respect. Until such studies are available, it would be advisable to use a test of better known limitations such as the *Cornell Index* or Bell's *Adjustment Inventory* for screening purposes.

Maslow makes a number of statements about the relationship of S-I and self-esteem which are interesting if they can be substantiated. In the manual he says that "a person testing low in S-I and also testing low in self-esteem will almost certainly express his neurotic tendencies in a more passive fashion, e.g., schizoid tendencies, withdrawal, fantasy, inhibition. But a person scoring equally low on S-I and scoring high in self-esteem will rather be compensating, over-aggressive, and dominating." Elsewhere [1] he says that "in Jews there is a tendency to be simultaneously high in self-esteem and low in security, while in Catholic women we find often low self-esteem joined with high security." Are these clinical hunches or are they statements based upon a systematic study? Maslow does not say. At any rate, there are some interesting research possibilities suggested in the interaction of these two tests.

Gough (4) demonstrated that a simple counting of the insecure answers was practically as good as Maslow's original weighted scoring. Maslow adopted Gough's system; consequently, scoring is now easy and speedy. This change in scoring system has resulted in a little confusion in the literature because the chief article describing the test (3) is written in terms of the old scoring where a high score indicated security. Gough found the S-I test to be unrelated to

intelligence, academic performance, or socio-economic status in his high school senior group. In comparing S-I with the *Minnesota Multiphasic Personality Inventory,* Gough found the highest correlation to be with the psychasthenic scale, which also correlates with the usual personality inventory. Maslow reports correlations of .68 and .58 with the *Thurstone Personality Schedule* and the neurotic tendency score on Bernreuter's *Personality Inventory,* respectively. Another line of research is suggested in Gough's finding that femininity in the boy is more damaging to security feeling than masculinity in the girl, and that security feeling in the girl is more vulnerable to hypochondriacal complaints than it is in the boy. In an unpublished study, the reviewer found a correlation of only .20 (n = 61, college girls) between S-I and *Pressey Interest-Attitude Test* results. Apparently, emotionally immature as well as mature people can feel secure.

The S-I test was very carefully constructed. In the description of the test (3), 11 attempted controls which follow good test construction principles are listed. Items were eliminated which in actual testing revealed sex, religious, self-esteem, or age differences, and the number of items representing the different subsyndromes was equalized as far as possible. Also, the items indicating security were equally divided between "yes" and "no" answers. An item analysis was made at several stages in the construction of the test to improve differentiation of secure and insecure people. The final 75 items were selected from over 300 used at various stages in construction of the test.

The reliability of the test is satisfactory. The validity, however, is not well established. Maslow depended heavily upon the clinical nature of the construction process as evidence for its validity. Of 177 college students who took the test, 88 per cent said that it was either a fairly accurate or an extremely accurate measure of their feeling of security. Maslow also cites his own experience with tested people, both in and out of the clinic, as evidence for its validity. The reviewer and some of his students have done some unpublished validity studies (1958) which are briefly reported here.

In two independent studies test scores of college girls were correlated with ratings of a house chairman (a senior selected by the college administration as being especially qualified to be in charge of a house containing about 20

1 MASLOW, A. H. "Dynamics of Personality Organization, II." *Psychol R* 50:541–58 N '43. * (*PA* 18:520)

girls). Each house chairman was instructed to rate only those girls she knew well. The rank correlation coefficients (rho) were .63 (n = 25) and .50 (n = 20). The respective median scores were 19 and 15.5. In another study 26 college girls rated themselves on security-insecurity and had two friends rate them. Self-ratings and test scores correlated .51, but average ratings of the two friends and test scores correlated only .24. However, the correlation between the ratings of friend A and friend B was only .50, and that between self-rating and average friend rating, .45. Obviously the friends' ratings on security-insecurity did not mean much. In a small class of six girls which met in the reviewer's office for two semesters, and which became sort of a little club, the girls' average rankings of each other on security-insecurity and test scores showed almost perfect agreement, with only ranks 5 and 6 being reversed. Self-rating and test scores of this group of advanced psychology majors correlated .80. It is quite clear that the better the rater, and the better the rater knows the person rated, the higher the correlation between the rating and the test score. In all of the above ratings, the rater was given a mimeographed sheet with Maslow's 14 subsyndromes fully reproduced. At the bottom of the page was a linear rating scale with seven verbal descriptive categories running from "very secure" to "very insecure." The rater was instructed to indicate with a tic the appropriate place on the scale for the S.

Two other studies were made: one in a correctional home for girls and the other in a school for the deaf. Both of these groups were found to be quite insecure, as was predicted. The median scores were 37 and 36 with standard deviations of 12.7 and 9.1, respectively. Correlations with the teachers' ratings of security were positive but not significant. It is doubtful whether teachers know many of their students well enough to make a meaningful rating of security feeling.

The S-I Inventory is a very carefully constructed test in a very important area of human adjustment. The reliability is satisfactory, and the validity is about as good as can be expected. The means and standard deviations were quite stable in the five samples which were drawn from Douglass College students; they compared favorably with those reported by Maslow for college students. The precautions listed by the author in the manual should be studied

carefully by anyone using the test. Its chief use at present would appear to be as a research tool and as an aid in the understanding of an individual in a counseling situation.

HAROLD WEBSTER, Associate Research Psychologist, Center for the Study of Higher Education, University of California, Berkeley, California.

This instrument was constructed by item selection based on responses of subjects known to be either secure or insecure, according to "the clinical criteria" of the late 1930's. A large number of persons were studied by means of interviews and autobiographies, which enabled the author to identify those who were either secure or insecure. After several years of this study it was possible to construct a preliminary test, composed of 349 items to be responded to by "Yes," "No," or "?" which was administered to 500 college students. The students who, according to their total test scores, were most secure and most insecure were interviewed; further validation work was undertaken; and the best 130 items were retained as a second test. This second test was administered to over 1,000 students, and after further analysis a final test of 75 items was obtained, the split-half reliability of which was .93.

The analysis which preceded the final test included procedures which minimized response bias, eliminated differences due to age, sex, religion, and, to a limited extent, culture, and balanced the test so that the 14 descriptive aspects of "the generalized unitary concept of security" would each be represented by approximately equal numbers of items.

Better than average data concerning reliability and validity are presented in the manual. It is likely that total score reliability shrinks more for new samples than is contended in the authors' interpretation; however, the reliability is likely in most cases to remain in the high .80's, which, considering the brevity of the test and the complexity of what is measured, is high enough for most purposes.

Some limitations, all of which are mentioned in the manual, may be noted. Accuracy of scores depends upon both the honesty of subjects and the adequacy of their self-knowledge. The concept, or construct, of security underlying the test was altered in order to reduce the correlation with another test developed by the same authors for measuring self-esteem in college women. The test measures a trait similar to those measured (probably less well) by numerous other instruments, some of which are mentioned in the manual. Finally, obtained distributions are skewed so that a disproportionate number of subjects receive low (secure) scores; for such a carefully constructed test the implications of this could be important for personality theory, but the authors attempt no explanation.

On the positive side it may be said immediately that it is doubtful that there are other personality tests the authors of which have exercised such great care to insure item validity. The test can be recommended without reservations as a valid measure of security-insecurity, as this trait is described by the authors.

[108]

Self-Analysis Inventory. Adults; 1945; title on test is *"How'm I Doin'?"*; interviewing aid for locating maladjustment in 37 problem areas; 1 form; no data on reliability and validity; $3.40 per 25 tests; 85¢ per specimen set; postpaid; (30–60) minutes; Harry J. Baker; Public School Publishing Co. *

WARREN R. BALLER, *Professor of Educational Psychology, The University of Nebraska, Lincoln, Nebraska.*

The *Self-Analysis Inventory* consists of a 12-page booklet of 148 items, a record blank, a handbook of suggestions for the use of the inventory, and separate leaflets of remedial suggestions applicable, respectively, to each of 37 problem areas into which the inventory items have been divided.

In the handbook the author has strongly emphasized the desirability of using the inventory as an interviewing aid rather than as a method of measurement. Many of the items of the instrument appear to be well suited to such a use: to furnish "leads....which become the basis for personal interview." For the most part, the problem areas covered are those with which a well planned personal interview with a young adult would be expected to deal. They include matters of health, and attitudes related thereto; experiences and attitudes pertaining to home; problems of growing up, marriage, peer relationships, and recreation; numerous aspects of self-appraisal; "serious personality problems" stemming from worry, fear, and the like; and miscellaneous other matters related to citizenship, school, vocations, and social interests.

As an interviewing aid, the inventory would seem not to suffer because of the absence of precise norms and evidence of validity and re-

liability. It is unfortunate, therefore, that the author went to considerable lengths in the handbook to suggest schemes for interpretation which, to be trustworthy, would have to be subjected to more validation than is in evidence. Anyone who uses these schemes now is taking a precarious step in the interpretation of data.

Specifically, the reviewer is skeptical of the 4-point scale under which responses to the inventory are classified: destructive, detrimental, doubtful, desirable. The a priori judgment that the response "being very tall makes me uncomfortable" should be classified as destructive, rather than detrimental or just doubtful, is not convincing in the absence of evidence from item analysis. And the classification of this response under the same heading with "I have a bad reputation for cruelty" begs even more for item analysis. For the user to go through the operation of transferring responses from the inventory booklet to the record blank only to arrive at a product (classification) of dubious validity may be worse than a waste of time; it may be misleading as a step in the interviewing process. To take a further step recommended by the author—totalling the number of responses in each classification to arrive at a sort of diagnostic profile—appears to be additionally risky business. The user of the inventory probably will do well to proceed cautiously with interpretation based on total scores or distributions of scores and to heed the author's suggestion that when normative data are needed the distribution of scores should be studied and "statistical tables developed accordingly." On the basis of these criticisms, the present reviewer would be much inclined to omit entirely the use of the record blank and employ only the booklet of response items, thus avoiding the problems of normative interpretation sans norms.

The claim is made in the handbook that the items of the instrument are presented in an order ranging from less serious to more serious problems, thus facilitating favorable initial attitudes on the part of the respondent—with the attendant likelihood that the favorable attitude will then persist throughout the marking of the inventory. Granting that it may be desirable to provide for this sort of progression from less serious to more serious problems, the reviewer finds it difficult to discern any such arrangement among the items. Equally difficult to accept, without supporting evidence, is the assertion that items 113 to 148 inclusive are less emotionally toned than those preceding and that, since they are the later items, they will permit the respondent to finish "with the feeling he has just been expressing himself on his most recent years with their adult interests." Sample responses from this section of the inventory are: "I have always gotten by with poor ideals" (Item 118), "I get back at people by gossiping" (Item 121), "The foremen and supervisors find too much fault with me" (Item 147).

The inventory has some favorable features. As stated earlier, there is in the booklet a wealth of interviewing items which should furnish valuable "leads" to follow-up procedures. The 4-choice response scheme, which is aimed at getting evidence of intensity of feeling about each of the inventory items, is a commendable feature. Possibly equally good, if not better, results would follow from the use of four unlabeled boxes for checking—with, of course, appropriate rewording of the response items. Indeed it might be a thoroughly worthwhile research project to determine which of the two formats, the existing one or the one suggested, would pay better dividends. The title of the inventory booklet is intriguing. Whether it appeals to every user of the instrument or not, at least it represents a way of avoiding emotionally toned wording on the cover page of an interviewing aid.

JOHN W. GUSTAD, *Professor of Psychology, and Director, University Counseling Center, University of Maryland, College Park, Maryland.*

Strictly speaking, this is *not* a test. Rather, it is what its title suggests: a means for collecting subjects' self descriptions. Its primary purpose, according to the author, is to furnish the psychologist, psychiatrist, or personnel interviewer with information which will help him structure a subsequent interview. In certain respects it is like the *Mooney Problem Check List*.

The inventory consists of 12 pages containing 148 items. The items are assembled under 37 topics ranging from physical health to morals and vocational problems. It was apparently intended to cover the entire range of human problems. No time limit is assigned; 30 to 60 minutes are usually required to complete the form. Four choices are provided as alternatives in each item. This, the author feels, makes the inventory more true to life than the yes-no al-

ternative situation. Alternatives within items are arranged randomly to reduce response bias.

Scoring is done by tallying responses within topics under four headings: desirable, doubtful, deterimental, and destructive. Omitted items are to be noted and (perhaps) discussed with the client during the interview. Baker suggests, without much enthusiasm, that the items may be weighted from one to four and summed. He says, "Obviously well adjusted individuals will make much higher total scores than the poorly-adjusted on the Inventory." The reviewer wonders whether the comma after "obviously" was omitted accidentally or intentionally. In either case, the conclusion is far from obviously correct.

There are no norms presented, and the author seems to feel that, for most users, these are unnecessary. He does suggest that personnel workers may wish to develop norms for special cases. Others, however, will simply locate topics in which the subject has admitted to problems and use these as the basis for interviews.

It is difficult to evaluate this instrument within the framework of tests. It is not a test. At the same time, the claims for its usefulness relate to problems which other test developers have had to face. Baker has not faced these, and this failure makes the utility of the instrument very suspect

He assumes, for instance, that well adjusted individuals will say that they have fewer problems than will badly adjusted ones. Nearly 40 years of research, beginning with the Woodworth inventory, have demonstrated that this assumption simply does not hold. Several studies have shown that normals will often confess to having *more* problems than will neurotics and psychotics. This being so, anyone who uses the *Self-Analysis Inventory* must face two problems: the false positives—normals who admit to many problems, and the false negatives—disturbed individuals who deny that they have problems. The existence of these groups makes the usefulness of the inventory very questionable.

There is literally no information given with respect to either the validity or the reliability of this instrument. Baker talks throughout about his successful experiences with the inventory, but this cannot be accepted as indicating validity. In one place, he says, "The author's experience....has shown that the great majority of individuals rate themselves honestly and sincerely on these types of inventories." This may or may not be true. Even if true, it is *not* the great majority with whom most interviewers are most concerned; it is those with problems who may also be the ones who choose to engage in dissimulation, conscious or unconscious.

This inventory was designed as an instrument to aid the interviewer. Baker suggests that the interviewer look over the "scores" in the various problem areas and then decide whether and how much information should be given to the interviewee. If there are many problem areas, the interviewer must decide where to start. Most present day interviewers would feel uncomfortable about such a procedure, especially if they were worried about problem areas which were not admitted to. In the absence of norms, it is difficult to decide what constitutes a critical score, one which indicates a problem in a given area. This further reduces the usefulness of the inventory for its stated purpose.

In Baker's defense, it must be pointed out that the inventory was developed in 1945. A great deal has been learned since then about assessing personality. That was the year in which Meehl published his classical study of the K factor as a suppressor variable. Nevertheless, since the instrument remains on the market, its author and its publisher have the responsibility for keeping it up to date with respect to what is known about test development. This has not been done.

The reviewer finds it difficult to conceive of a situation in which this instrument would be validly applicable in terms of its stated purposes. At best, it leaves the interviewer with most or all of his original task of finding out what the problems are; at worst, in the hands of an unskilled person, it could be dangerously misleading. Unless the *Self-Analysis Inventory* is brought up to date, it should be withdrawn from circulation and sale immediately.

[109]

★Self-Perception Inventory: An Adjustment Survey With Special Reference to the Speech Situation. High school and college; 1940-54; formerly called *Personal-Social Adjustment Inventory;* 8 scores: self-centered introversion, objective introversion, self-centered extroversion, objective extroversion, self-centeredness, objectivity, introversion, extroversion; IBM; 1 form ('54); revised manual ('55); separate answer sheets must be used; 20¢ per test; 5¢ per IBM answer sheet; 5¢ per hand scoring answer sheet; 10¢ per hand scoring stencil; 20¢ per manual ('55); postpaid; [45-50] minutes; Lawrence W. Miller and Elwood Murray; University of Denver Bookstores. *

C. R. STROTHER, *Professor of Clinical Psychology, University of Washington, Seattle, Washington.*

This 45-item, multiple choice, self-rating inventory is designed to measure the following tendencies: (*a*) self-centered introversion; (*b*) objective introversion; (*c*) self-centered extroversion; and (*d*) objective extroversion. Through combination of these scores, separate ratings may also be computed on self-centeredness, objectivity, introversion, and extroversion. The items relate, principally, to attitude toward, and behavior in, situations involving verbal communication. The inventory is designed primarily for use in improving adjustment to speech situations.

The items were selected on the basis of their capacity to discriminate between the highest and lowest 10 per cent of an unspecified population of college students. Split-half reliabilities for the four basic scales range from .81 to .87 (n = 125). Percentile ranks are given for 423 college students and, separately, for 484 high school students.

Good agreement is reported between test scores of 160 students and ratings by themselves and by teachers and clinicians on the personality variables with which the test purports to deal. No information is provided on the procedure by which these estimates of agreement were arrived at. Introversion and extroversion scores on this test correlate .37 and −.38, respectively, with scores on the introversion-extroversion scale of Bernreuter's *Personality Inventory* (n = 90).

This test is vulnerable to the usual objections to self-rating inventories. The probability of contamination by the social desirability factor is high. However, disregarding the question of the meaningfulness of the scores, self-descriptive statements by the student may be of value to the speech teacher as a basis for instruction or counseling.

[110]

★The Sherman Mental Impairment Test. Adults; 1955-57; 2 scores: letter finding, reaction time; 1 form ['57]; record blank ('57); no data on reliability for reaction time score; young adult norms only; $13.50 per 100 tests; $4 per cards and manual ('56); $7 per set of 25 tests, cards, and manual; postpaid; specimen set not available; (10) minutes; Murray H. Sherman; Western Psychological Services. *

REFERENCE
1. SHERMAN, MURRAY H. "A Brief, Objective Test for the Measurement of Mental Impairment." *J General Psychol* 52: 285-96 Ap '55. * (*PA* 30:4598)

D. RUSSELL DAVIS, *Reader in Clinical Psychology, University of Cambridge, Cambridge, England.*

The test material consists of 10 designs, each composed of a number of letters of the alphabet and random lines mixed together. Two scores are obtained for each design: the number of letters found by the subject, and the time elapsing before the first letter is identified. The standardisation is based on the sum total of all letters given (the letter finding score), and the sum total of "reaction" times (the reaction time score).

The test has been standardised on young adults only. Both scores are claimed to distinguish normal subjects and "general medical patients" from schizophrenics, schizoid personalities, the organically impaired, and the mental defective. The letter finding score does not distinguish between organics and schizophrenics or organics and mental defectives. The reaction time score distinguishes, although not highly reliably, between organics and mental defectives but not between organics and schizophrenics.

The correlation between the letter finding score and intelligence is not significant in normal subjects, but is of the order of .50 in the patient groups. Too few data are given to evaluate these findings. One may suspect that it is partly the result of the method of selecting the samples for the standardisation. The task is an easy one for normal subjects of average intelligence, and it is possible that intelligence level becomes of importance only when it is below average. In any event, it appears difficult to make allowances for the effects of intelligence. The effect of age is not known; it is likely to be relatively large.

The test is likely to have little value in routine clinical work because of the considerations above. At most it can help in deciding between normality and impairment from whatever cause, if the subject is young and of average or above average intelligence.

WILLIAM SCHOFIELD, *Associate Professor of Psychology and Psychiatry, University of Minnesota, Minneapolis, Minnesota.*

The author's rationale for this test is that it is a measure of mental flexibility, that is, "ability to focus on two or more mental contents in an approximately simultaneous manner," and that loss of such flexibility is one index of mental impairment. The test consists of designs reproduced on cards. Each is composed of a number of alphabetic letters and random lines mixed together to constitute a geometric design of varying complexity. One item, for example, is a square. The subject is required to identify as many letters of the alphabet as he can see in each design. The administrator's instructions to the subject are given in the manual explicitly and adequately; unfortunately, the administrator is encouraged to paraphrase these excellent formal instructions as he sees fit. There is no time limit. Two scores are recorded: the total number of letters identified on the 10 test cards, and the sum of the reaction times (time from presentation of each card to identification of first letter) to the 10 cards. The author's claims of easy, simple administration and of quick, objective scoring are satisfied.

The test has been standardized exclusively on a sample of 214 young males, representing seven diagnostic groups (normals, general medical patients, schizophrenics, organics, defectives, schizoids, and emotionally unstable patients). Ranges, medians, means, and standard deviations are reported for the two scores for all seven groups. Percentage overlap statistics for the various samples would better illustrate the limitations of this test as a single differentiating or diagnostic test.

This test has the ever-sought advantages of speed, simplicity, and objectivity. It does show some relation to impairment of mental function. Its simple nature and limited range of difficulty, plus the absence of data on the precise relationship of scores to degree of impairment, make its use as a solitary measure of intellectual inefficiency inadvisable. It has promise for inclusion in a battery of other tests of different aspects of mental function.

[111]

Shipley-Institute of Living Scale for Measuring Intellectual Impairment. Adults; 1939–46; formerly called *Shipley-Hartford Retreat Scale for Measuring Intellectual Impairment;* 4 scores: vocabulary, abstractions, total, conceptual quotient; 1 form ('39); manual ('46, identical with manual copyrighted in 1940 except for title); $2 per 25 tests; 50¢ per specimen set; postpaid; 20(25) minutes; Walter C. Shipley; distributed by William U. Shipley, P.O. Box 39, Yale Station, New Haven, Conn. *

REFERENCES

1–25. See 3:95.
26. SLATER, PATRICK. "Scores of Different Types of Neurotics on Tests of Intelligence." *Brit J Psychol* 35:40–2 Ja '45. * (PA 19:966)
27. BIJOU, SIDNEY W., AND LUCIO, WILLIAM H. Chap. 8, "Measures of Mental Function for Evaluating Severity of Disturbance," pp. 133–43. In *The Psychological Program in AAF Convalescent Hospitals.* Edited by Sidney W. Bijou. Army Air Forces Aviation Psychology Program Research Reports, Report

No. 15. Washington, D.C.: U.S. Government Printing Office, 1947. Pp. viii, 256. *

28. MAGARET, ANN, AND SIMPSON, MARY. "A Comparison of Two Measures of Deterioration in Psychotics." Abstract. *Am Psychol* 2:425 O '47. *

29. WHEELER, ERMA T. *A Study of Certain Aspects of Personality as Related to the Electroencephalogram.* Doctor's thesis, University of Pittsburgh (Pittsburgh, Pa.), 1947.

30. GARFIELD, SOL L., AND FEY, WILLIAM F. "A Comparison of the Wechsler-Bellevue and Shipley-Hartford Scales as Measures of Mental Impairment." *J Consult Psychol* 12:259–64 Jl–Ag '48. * (*PA* 23:1289)

31. MAGARET, ANN, AND SIMPSON, MARY M. "A Comparison of Two Measures of Deterioration in Psychotic Patients." *J Consult Psychol* 12:265–9 Jl–Ag '48. * (*PA* 23:1407)

32. SOLOMON, JOSEPH C. "Adult Character and Behavior Disorders." *J Clin Psychopath* 9:1–55 Ja '48. *

33. BENTON, ARTHUR L., AND WESLEY, ELIZABETH L. "Preliminary Report of the Development of a Test for the Valuation of Intellectual Impairment." Abstract. *Am Psychol* 4:268 Jl '49. *

34. GRAY, CONSTANCE V. *An Investigation of the Shipley Hartford and Wechsler-Bellevue Scales and Measures of Deterioration.* Master's thesis, University of Toronto (Toronto, Ont., Canada), 1949. Pp. 35.

35. SCHERER, ISIDOR W. "The Psychological Scores of Mental Patients in an Individual and Group Testing Situation." *J Clin Psychol* 5:405–8 O '49. * (*PA* 24:3740)

36. HALSTEAD, H. "Abilities of Male Mental Hospital Patients." *J Mental Sci* 96:726–33 Jl '50. *

37. HORLICK, REUBEN S. *The Relationships of Psychometric Test Scores to Personality Disorders.* Doctor's thesis, New York University (New York, N.Y.), 1950.

38. CHODORKOFF, BERNARD, AND MUSSEN, PAUL. "Qualitative Aspects of the Vocabulary Responses of Normals and Schizophrenics." *J Consult Psychol* 16:43–8 F '52. *

39. GARFIELD, SOL L., AND BLEK, LIBBY. "Age, Vocabulary Level, and Mental Impairment." *J Consult Psychol* 16:395–8 O '52. * (*PA* 27:5739)

40. AARONSON, BERNARD S.; NELSON, SHERMAN E.; AND HOLT, SHIRLEY. "On a Relation Between Bender-Gestalt Recall and Shipley-Hartford Scores." *J Clin Psychol* 9:88 Ja '53. (*PA* 27:7748)

41. SHIPLEY, WALTER C. "Shipley-Institute of Living Scale for Measuring Intellectual Impairment," pp. 751–6. (*PA* 27:7794) In *Contributions Toward Medical Psychology: Theory and Psychodiagnostic Methods, Vol. II.* Edited by Arthur Weider. New York: Ronald Press Co., 1953. Pp. xi, 459–885. *

42. SYDOW, DONALD WAYNE. *A Psychometric Differentiation Between Functional Psychotics and Non-Psychotics with Organic Brain Damage.* Doctor's thesis, University of Minnesota (Minneapolis, Minn.), 1953. (*DA* 13:1267)

43. WINFIELD, DON L. "The Shipley-Hartford Vocabulary Test and Pre-Trauma Intelligence." *J Clin Psychol* 9:77–8 Ja '53. * (*PA* 27:7807)

44. HORLICK, REUBEN S., AND MONROE, HAROLD J. "A Study of the Reliability of an Alternate Form for the Shipley-Hartford Abstraction Scale." *J Clin Psychol* 10:381–3 O '54. * (*PA* 29:4062)

45. HARRISON, ROSS; HUNT, WINSLOW; AND JACKSON, THEODORE A. "Profile of the Mechanical Engineer: 1, Ability." *Personnel Psychol* 8:219–34 su '55. * (*PA* 30:5414)

46. BENNETT, HOWARD J. "The Shipley-Hartford Scale and the Porteus Maze Test as Measures of Functioning Intelligence." *J Clin Psychol* 12:190–1 Ap '56. * (*PA* 31:4669)

47. PARKER, JAMES W. "The Validity of Some Current Tests for Organicity." *J Consult Psychol* 21:425–8 O '57. *

48. SINES, LLOYD K. "Intelligence Test Correlates of Shipley-Hartford Performance." *J Clin Psychol* 14:399–404 O '58. *

For reviews by E. J. G. Bradford, William A. Hunt, and Margaret Ives, see 3:95.

[112]

*Sixteen Personality Factor Questionnaire. Ages 16 and over; 1949–57; title on test is *16 P.F.*; also called *The 16 P.F. Test;* 16 or 17 scores: aloof vs. warm-outgoing (A), dull vs. bright (B), emotional vs. mature (C), submissive vs. dominant (E), glum-silent vs. enthusiastic (F), casual vs. conscientious (G), timid vs. adventurous (H), tough vs. sensitive (I), trustful vs. suspecting (L), conventional vs. eccentric (M), simple vs. sophisticated (N), confident vs. insecure (O), conservative vs. experimenting (Q1), dependent vs. self-sufficient (Q2), lax vs. controlled (Q3), stable vs. tense (Q4), motivational distortion scale (optional); IBM; Forms A ('56), B ('57), C ('56); tabular supplement ['57]; mimeographed decile standardization table ['57]; separate answer sheets must be used; $2.25 per 50 answer sheets; $1.80 per 50 profiles ('56); $2.70 per 50

answer-profiles; $1 per scoring key; $6 per complete specimen set; cash orders postpaid; IBM answer sheets available on special order; R. B. Cattell, D. R. Saunders (A, B), and G. Stice (A, B); Institute for Personality and Ability Testing. *

a) FORMS A AND B. $7 per 25 tests; (40–50) minutes.
b) FORM C. $10 per 25 tests; 80¢ per supplementary manual ('56); (20–30) minutes.

REFERENCES

1–8. See 4:87.

9. GOINES, VALMORE R. *Personality Characteristics of a Certain Ethnic Group.* Doctor's thesis, Northwestern University (Evanston, Ill.), 1951.

10. LAMKE, TOM ARTHUR. "Personality and Teaching Success." *J Exp Ed* 20:217–59 D '51. * (*PA* 27:681)

11. CATTELL, R. B., AND HOROWITZ, J. Z. "Objective Personality Tests Investigating the Structure of Altruism in Relation to Source Traits A, H, and L." *J Personality* 21:103–17 S '52. * (*PA* 26:5862)

12. NEILEN, GORDON C. *A Study of the Cattell 16 PF Test by Comparison With the A. C. E. and Guilford-Martin Personality Battery.* Master's thesis, Kent State University (Kent, Ohio), 1952.

13. STICE, GLEN F., AND CATTELL, RAYMOND B. "Personality Differences Found in Small-Group Leaders Selected by Four Independent Criteria of Leadership." Abstract. *Am Psychol* 8:443 Ag '53. *

14. SUHR, VIRTUS W. "The Cattell 16 P.F. Test as a Prognosticator of Accident Susceptibility." *Proc Iowa Acad Sci* 60:558–61 '53. * (*PA* 29:3218)

15. CATTELL, RAYMOND B., AND STICE, GLEN F. "Four Formulae for Selecting Leaders on the Basis of Personality." *Human Relations* 7:493–507 N '54. * (*PA* 29:5450)

16. ERICKSON, HARLEY ELLWOOD. "A Factorial Study of Teaching Ability." *J Exp Ed* 23:1–39 S '54. * (*PA* 29:6927)

17. MONTROSS, HAROLD WESLEY. "Temperament and Teaching Success." *J Exp Ed* 23:73–97 S '54. * (*PA* 29:6302)

18. WRIGHT, STUART. "Some Personality Characteristics of Academic Underachievers." Abstract. *Am Psychol* 9:496 Ag '54. *

19. CATTELL, R. B., AND DREVDAHL, J. E. "A Comparison of the Personality Profile (16 P.F.) of Eminent Researchers With That of Eminent Teachers and Administrators, and of the General Population." *Brit J Psychol* 46:248–61 N '55. * (*PA* 30:7189)

20. ROSENTHAL, IRENE. *A Factor Analysis of Anxiety Variables.* Doctor's thesis, University of Illinois (Urbana, Ill.), 1955. (*DA* 16:376)

21. CATTELL, RAYMOND B. "Second-Order Personality Factors in the Questionnaire Realm." *J Consult Psychol* 20:411–8 D '56. * (*PA* 32:1614)

22. CATTELL, RAYMOND B. "A Shortened 'Basic English' Version (Form C) of the 16 PF Questionnaire." *J Social Psychol* 44:257–78 N '56. *

23. CATTELL, RAYMOND B. "Validation and Intensification of the Sixteen Personality Factor Questionnaire." *J Clin Psychol* 12:205–14 Jl '56. * (*PA* 31:6064)

24. CATTELL, R. B.; DAY, M.; AND MEELAND, T. "Occupational Profiles on the 16 Personality Factor Questionnaire." *Occupational Psychol* 30:10–9 Ja '56. * (*PA* 31:3207)

25. CATTELL, RAYMOND B. *Personality and Motivation Structure and Measurement.* Yonkers, N.Y.: World Book Co., 1957. Pp. xxv, 948. *

26. KARSON, SAMUEL, AND POOL, KENNETH BRYNER. "The Construct Validity of the Sixteen Personality Factors Test." *J Clin Psychol* 13:245–52 Jl '57. *

27. DE PALMA, NICHOLAS, AND CLAYTON, HUGH D. "Scores of Alcoholics on the Sixteen Personality Factor Questionnaire." *J Clin Psychol* 14:390–2 O '58. *

28. DREVDAHL, JOHN E., AND CATTELL, RAYMOND B. "Personality and Creativity in Artists and Writers." *J Clin Psychol* 14:107–11 Ap '58. *

29. KARSON, SAMUEL, AND POOL, KENNETH B. "Second-Order Factors in Personality Measurement." *J Consult Psychol* 22:299–303 Ag '58.

C. J. ADCOCK, *Senior Lecturer in Psychology, Victoria University of Wellington, Wellington, New Zealand.*

This test is undoubtedly a major development in the personality area. Originally based on a comprehensive factor analysis, it has been extended to three forms (plus a special form for children) and the factorisation thrice checked by independent experiment. A prodigious amount of statistical work has gone into it. No other test covers such a wide range of personality dimensions and never before have the dimensions been so meticulously determined. It is little wonder that half a dozen foreign translations have already appeared. Nothing succeeds like success and it can be expected that there will soon be a vast amount of data available with regard to norms and correlation with criteria. The 1957 handbook already contains mean profiles for 28 occupational groups.

THE PERSONALITY FACTORS. Apart from intelligence there are 15 factors which cover a wide field. It might have been of some advantage if they could have been grouped in some way and not simply listed in haphazard order. The reviewer would like to arrange them in three groups: traits largely determined by heredity, traits largely dependent on environmental influences, and traits related to ego formation.

To the first group we might assign three factors according to the evidence of Cattell's own studies: [1]

A—Cyclothymia versus schizothymia. The essential core appears to be good-natured sociability, which this reviewer is tempted to regard as related to parental drive, possibly influenced by hormone control.
H—Parmia versus threctia. In the negative form this is characterized by shyness and timidity. It is probably related to constitutional differences in autonomic thresholds for fear response.
E—Dominance versus submission. This again would appear to be related to autonomic thresholds, this time for anger. Since Cattell found the ratio between heredity and environment for the inter-family variance to be about 10:1, the genetic factor in this trait seems fairly certain.

On the evidence of Eysenck [2] one would like to add to this group factor C, emotional stability, which Cattell considers to be similar to the former's general neuroticism, but Cattell's own evidence is to the contrary.[1] This raises some doubts about the nature of C which are reinforced by a consideration of the two second-order factors. These are designated "anxiety" and "introversion-extraversion" respectively, and appear to correspond rather closely to Eysenck's general neuroticism and "introversion-extraversion." Cattell's emotional stability factor may, therefore, be rather more a matter of learned control.

The second group would consist of eight factors:

1 CATTELL, RAYMOND B.; BLEWETT, DUNCAN B.; AND BELOFF, J. R. "The Inheritance of Personality: A Multiple Variance Analysis Determination of Approximate Nature-Nurture Ratios for Primary Personality Factors in Q-Data." Am J Human Genetics 7:122-46 Je '55. * (PA 30:2451)
2 EYSENCK, H. J. The Structure of Human Personality. London: Methuen & Co. Ltd., 1953. Pp. xix, 348. *

M—Autia versus praxernia. This might correspond to Guilford's introverted thinking or the "inner life" of the Rorschach. (The Form C description of "eccentric versus practical" is open to criticism.)
O—Guilt proneness versus confident adequacy. The description of "anxious insecurity" seems right.
Q4—High ergic tension, or "raw nerves," versus low ergic tension.
L—Protension, or paranoid tendency, versus relaxed security.
Q1—Radicalism versus conservatism of temperament.
Q2—Self-sufficiency versus group dependency. (Is this related to Riesman's "inner-directed" as opposed to "other-directed"?)
I—Premsia versus harria, or sensitivity versus toughness. This is not a constitutional toughness. Cattell associates it with "*protected emotional sensitivity,*" whence the name.
N—Shrewdness versus naïveté, or sophistication.

All these factors are well established. O and Q4 are both appreciably correlated with the timidity factor (.41 and .35 for factor scores) and both are anxiety measures. A question may be raised as to the boundary between personality traits and interest dimensions. Radicalism and sophistication might well qualify as examples of the latter.

The third group of factors relating to ego structure might include:

G—Super-ego strength.
F—Surgency.
Q3—High self-sentiment formation.

Factors G and Q3 are both concerned with ego organization. Since the term "super-ego" is usually associated with the moral aspects of ego organization, it might be applied to both of these factors. G appears to be concerned with the setting of high standards whereas Q3 is concerned with the control of behaviour by the super-ego regardless of what its standards are. The former suggests the person who has taken refuge in the safety of "correct" behaviour, possibly as a means of obtaining parental approval or to resolve guilt. The latter suggests a well integrated personality, but the items involved appear to place little stress on the moral aspects of the super-ego. Perhaps "ego-control" might be a more suitable reference in that it does not emphasise moral aspects. Popular language would probably refer to the factor as "will."

The stress in the manual on energy and persistence as characterizing G seems to be somewhat misplaced if one judges by the items involved. It is possible, however, that we have here an obsessional need for correctness which includes a need to persist until a task is satisfactorily completed. If so, it may be related to the anal character described in Freudian literature. The fact that professional researchers are shown to have a mean sten score of only 3.4 on this factor does not accord well with this factor's being the major source of energy and persistence.

Surgency is tentatively included here because it appears to be in some way related to ego-striving. The surgent person is perhaps less inclined to be ego-involved and so able to adopt a less serious attitude towards life. This might account for the low rating of research workers on this trait. Cattell suggests that surgent people have been influenced by a more optimism creating environment. There appears to be some relation to Sheldon's viscerotonia, but the Cattell studies indicate that it is not a genetically determined trait. It includes aspects which Guilford found in his Rhathymia, but French[3] doubts whether the two can be regarded as equivalent. Cattell is inclined to favour Rhathymia as an independent factor with stress on happy-go-lucky, carefree attitudes, but he has not yet made provision for this in the 16 PF test. Further work on this factor seems desirable.

It is appropriate at this stage to ask what other personality factors have been omitted from the test since, in view of its size, it may be expected to be pretty comprehensive. Others from the Universal Index,[4] all derived from French's survey, are missing. Psychotic tendency is probably not important for the usual case for which the test will be required, and the same may be true of masculinity-femininity and autistic tendency, which should not be confused with the P.M. Autia. Self-confidence is more relevant but we need to be more certain as to how it differs from the insecurity pattern of O.

That the list of important factors is exhausted by this discussion is very unlikely. Many more will need to be added later. Some of these may not be suitable for general measurement, as, for example, sex drive. Some may be difficult to measure. One notable exception should be mentioned. This is the anal character mentioned above. A query may be raised with regard to the intelligence items. Since these consist of 13 questions in each of the A and B forms, and of 8 in the C form, they need to have a very high validity. The situation is complicated by the lack of a time limit. One is surprised that, under these conditions, 144 professional research workers get a near sten score of only 6.8, and wonders whether factors other than intelligence may not play an important part. Examination of the items suggests that some (e.g., A103, A153, B54, B153) provide some room for argument as to the right answer and random choice may lead a testee to accept the poorer alternative. In the case of B54 it is possible that highly intelligent people may be more likely to prefer the noncredited response.

VALIDITY AND RELIABILITY. Split-half reliabilities (n = 450) range from .71 to .93, ten coefficients being above .80. This is quite good; but even more pleasing is the fact that validities (based on factor loadings) range from .73 to .96 with eleven coefficients exceeding .80. For a multi-dimensional test of this kind one could not hope for much more. Evidently, despite the reputation of questionnaire methods as unreliable, this test does succeed. It should be noted, however, that the structure of the test does not require that the questions be taken at their face value. They are considered as stimulus variables, and a variable is assigned to a factor measure not because of its meaning but because of the usual mode of response to it. Of course, any questionnaire is subject to deliberate distortion and some check on this is desirable. Form C provides a motivational distortion score for this purpose. The authors believe that the best protection against such distortion is the selection of items highly loaded for a given factor but not appearing to involve it. They point out that with regard to many of the factors one pole does not appear to be morally or aesthetically more desirable than another. For the remaining factors they claim that no systematic motivational distortion has yet been experimentally found. This may be so when the test is used under circumstances where there is no high incentive to distortion, but only special studies will show whether the test can be appreciably distorted when the subject finds a need for this. No such investigation has yet been reported. In the meantime users might be advised not to use Forms A and B where motivational distortion is thought likely.

ADMINISTRATION AND SCORING. The test is very easy to give and most subjects find it interesting. Scoring can be done by hand or machine and is so simple that hand scoring is claimed to be superior for any number less than a thousand! Scores can be converted into stens

3 FRENCH, JOHN W. The Description of Personality Measurements in Terms of Rotated Factors. Princeton, N.J.: Educational Testing Service, 1953. Pp. 287. * (PA 28:5670)
4 CATTELL, RAYMOND B. "A Universal Index for Psychological Factors." Psychologia 1:74–85 '57. *

or deciles and, for Form C, into stanines. Appropriate information is given about each of these forms. It is to be hoped that more tests will make use of the convenient sten (standard 10-point) scale.

INTERPRETIVE DATA. In assessing the value of a personality test, an important consideration is the amount of data available with regard to the predictive significance of its scores. The tremendous effort made in conjunction with this test assures a wealth of such data. Average profiles for 28 occupation groups and 6 behavior disorders are already available. What are needed now are personality profiles for very *successful* members of various occupational groups as compared with low success members. A large scale investigation with regard to the relevance of the factors for teacher success is already under way in New Zealand and further data of this kind may be expected.

Form C has available weighted score grids for 24 major occupations. Using these, it is possible to predict success in a given occupation by the simple process of reading off the appropriate weights for each factor score, summing and consulting a 5-point table. Presumably these tables are based on typical occupational profiles and have all the weaknesses of this approach. If 80 per cent of workers in occupation X have false teeth, it does not follow that having false teeth will help one to succeed in the occupation, and a similar criticism may apply to some of the factor score requirements based on typical patterns. It is to be hoped that there will soon be profiles available based on more rigorous criteria. In the meantime, however, some guidance other than the intuition of the tester is provided.

SUMMARY. The 16 PF test bids fair to become the standard questionnaire-type personality test of the future. It provides a comprehensive range of trait scores which should be useful for occupational guidance and as a background to clinical examination. Used with due caution, it may be of help for selection purposes, but only with the motivational distortion score included. Although 16 factors may seem a lot (15 without intelligence), they are all independent, although not completely uncorrelated, and are all necessary to span the personality area involved. Indeed, a few more major factors will doubtless have to be added. The test is not, however, unwieldy and testers who are primarily concerned with only a few of the dimensions will find it well worthwhile to know some-

thing of what is happening to the other factors at the same time. Obviously this test does not take the place of a projective test like the TAT, but users of the latter would probably find an assessment of the basic dimensions of the 16 PF a valuable addition to their data.

For reviews by Charles M. Harsh, Ardie Lubin, and J. Richard Wittenborn, see 4:87.

[113]
*Social Participation Scale, 1952 Edition. Adults; 1928–52; 1 form ('52); manual ('52); $1.50 per 50 scales, postage extra; specimen set not available; administration time not reported; F. Stuart Chapin; University of Minnesota Press. *

[114]
Study of Values: A Scale for Measuring the Dominant Interests in Personality, Revised Edition. Grades 13 and over; 1931–51; 6 scores: theoretical, economic, aesthetic, social, political, religious; 1 form ('51); manual ('51); $3.80 per 35 tests; 40¢ per specimen set; postage extra; (20) minutes; Gordon W. Allport, Philip E. Vernon, and Gardner Lindzey; Houghton Mifflin Co. *

REFERENCES

1–61. See 3:99.
62–86. See 4:92.
87. JOHNSON, RALPH H., AND BOND, GUY L. "Reading Ease of Commonly Used Tests." *J Appl Psychol* 34:319–24 O '50. * (*PA* 26:299)
88. DIDATO, SALVATORE. *The Influence of Values, as Measured by the Allport-Vernon Study of Values, on Perceptual Estimations of Size.* Master's thesis, Catholic University of America (Washington, D.C.), 1951.
89. HORGAN, JAMES FRANCIS. *A Validation Study of the Allport-Vernon Study of Values.* Master's thesis, University of Pittsburgh (Pittsburgh, Pa.), 1951.
90. HUFFMAN, WARREN JUSTUS. *Personality Variations Among Men Preparing to Teach Physical Education.* Doctor's thesis, University of Illinois (Urbana, Ill.), 1951. (*DA* 12:28)
91. ANDERSON, MARY ROBERDEAU. *A Descriptive Study of Values and Interests of Four Groups of Graduate Women at the University of Minnesota.* Doctor's thesis, University of Minnesota (Minneapolis, Minn.), 1952. (*DA* 12:851)
92. BERNBERG, RAYMOND E. "Attitudes of Personnel Managers and Student Groups Toward Labor Relations." *J Appl Psychol* 36:291–2 O '52. * (*PA* 27:5456)
93. BROGDEN, HUBERT E. "The Primary Personal Values Measured by the Allport-Vernon Test, 'A Study of Values.'" *Psychol Monogr* 66 (16):1–31 '52. * (*PA* 27:7191)
94. EVANS, RICHARD I. "Personal Values as Factors in Anti-Semitism." *J Abn & Social Psychol* 47:749–56 O '52. * (*PA* 27:5090)
95. HAIGH, GERARD V., AND FISKE, DONALD W. "Corroboration of Personal Values as Selective Factors in Perception." *J Abn & Social Psychol* 47:394–8 Ap '52. * (*PA* 27:2441)
96. KARN, HARRY W. "Differences in Values Among Engineering Students." *Ed & Psychol Meas* 12:701–6 w '52. * (*PA* 27:6757)
97. KLEHR, HAROLD. "An Investigation of Some Personality Factors in Women With Rheumatoid Arthritis." Abstract. *Am Psychol* 7:344–5 Jl '52. *
98. POE, WESLEY A., AND BERG, IRWIN A. "Psychological Test Performance of Steel Industry Production Supervisors." *J Appl Psychol* 36:234–7 Ag '52. * (*PA* 27:3794)
99. SCHMEIDLER, GERTRUDE RAFFEL. "Personal Values and ESP Scores." *J Abn & Social Psychol* 47:757–61 O '52. * (*PA* 27:4909)
100. SPOERL, DOROTHY TILDEN. "The Values of the Post-War College Student." *J Social Psychol* 35:217–25 My '52. * (*PA* 27:3769)
101. STANLEY, JULIAN C., AND WALDROP, ROBERT S. "Intercorrelations of Study of Values and Kuder Preference Record Scores." *Ed & Psychol Meas* 12:707–19 w '52. * (*PA* 27:5906)
102. TOMEDY, FRANCIS JOSEPH. *The Relationship of Personality Characteristics to Measured Interests of Women Teachers of English, Social Science, Mathematics, and Physical Science in Certain Senior High Schools.* Doctor's thesis, New York University (New York, N.Y.), 1952. (*DA* 12:540)
103. WRENN, C. GILBERT. "The Selection and Education of Student Personnel Workers." *Personnel & Guid J* 31:9–14 O '52. * (*PA* 27:4782)

104. ADAMS, JOE, AND BROWN, DONALD R. "Values, Word Frequencies, and Perception." *Psychol R* 60:50–4 Ja '53. * (*PA* 28:3716)
105. BIESHEUVEL, S.; JACOBS, G. F.; AND COWLEY, J. J. "Maladjustments of Military Personnel." *J Nat Inst Personnel Res* 5:138–68 D '53. *
106. ISCOE, IRA, AND LUCIER, OMER. "A Comparison of the Revised Allport-Vernon Scale of Values (1951) and the Kuder Preference Record (Personal)." *J Appl Psychol* 37:195–6 Je '53. * (*PA* 28:3352)
107. SHORR, JOSEPH E. "The Development of a Test to Measure the Intensity of Values." *J Ed Psychol* 44:266–74 My '53. * (*PA* 28:3914)
108. STANLEY, JULIAN C. *"Study of Values* Profiles Adjusted for Sex and Variability Differences." *J Appl Psychol* 37:472–3 D '53. * (*PA* 29:960)
109. STERNBERG, CARL. "Differences in Measured Interest, Values, and Personality Among College Students Majoring in Nine Subject Areas." Abstract. *Am Psychol* 8:442–3 Ag '53. *
110. STERNBERG, CARL. *The Relation of Interests, Values and Personality to the Major Field of Study in College.* Doctor's thesis, New York University (New York, N.Y.), 1953. (*DA* 13:1095)
111. BURDOCK, E. I. "A Case of ESP: Critique of 'Personal Values and ESP Scores' by Gertrude R. Schmeidler." *J Abn & Social Psychol* 49:314–5 Ap '54. * (*PA* 29:216)
112. GUILFORD, J. P.; CHRISTENSEN, PAUL R.; BOND, NICHOLAS A., JR.; AND SUTTON, MARCELLA A. "A Factor Analysis Study of Human Interests." *Psychol Monogr* 68(4):1–38 '54. *
113. MILAM, ALBERT T., AND SUMNER, F. C. "Spread and Intensity of Vocational Interests and Evaluative Attitudes in First-Year Negro Medical Students." *J Psychol* 37:31–8 Ja '54. * (*PA* 28:8027)
114. SCHLAG, MADELEINE. *The Relationship Between the Personality Preference Schedule and the Allport, Vernon and Lindzey Study of Values: A Personality Study of a Group of Medical Students.* Master's thesis, University of Washington (Seattle, Wash.), 1954.
115. STOTT, STERLING S. *A Comparison of the Authoritarian Personality F-Scale With the Allport-Vernon-Lindzey Study of Values.* Master's thesis, University of Utah (Salt Lake City, Utah), 1954.
116. BLEDSOE, JOSEPH C. "A Comparative Study of Values and Critical Thinking Skills of a Group of Educational Workers." *J Ed Psychol* 46:408–17 N '55. * (*PA* 31:3774)
117. BOUSFIELD, W. A., AND SAMBORSKI, GLORIA. "The Relationship Between Strength of Values and the Meaningfulness of Value Words." *J Personality* 23:375–80 My '55. * (*PA* 30:2448)
118. DUKES, WILLIAM F. "Psychological Studies of Values." *Psychol B* 52:24–50 Ja '55. *
119. KELLY, E. LOWELL. "Consistency of the Adult Personality." *Am Psychol* 10:659–81 N '55. * (*PA* 30:6915)
120. MAYZNER, MARK S., JR., AND TRESSELT, M. E. "Concept Span as a Composite Function of Personal Values, Anxiety, and Rigidity." *J Personality* 24:20–33 S '55. * (*PA* 30:5740)
121. ROSENTHAL, DAVID. "Changes in Some Moral Values Following Psychotherapy." *J Consult Psychol* 19:431–6 D '55. * (*PA* 30:7306)
122. STERNBERG, CARL. "Personality Trait Patterns of College Students Majoring in Different Fields." *Psychol Monogr* 69(18):1–21 '55. * (*PA* 31:1705)
123. DIDATO, S. VINCENT, AND KENNEDY, THOMAS M. "Masculinity-Femininity and Personal Values." *Psychol Rep* 2:231 Je '56. * (*PA* 31:608)
124. GOWAN, J. C. "Achievement and Personality Test Scores of Gifted College Students." *Calif J Ed Res* 7:105–9 My '56. * (*PA* 31:3783)
125. GUBA, E. G., AND GETZELS, J. W. "Interest and Value Patterns of Air Force Officers." *Ed & Psychol Meas* 16:465–70 w '56. * (*PA* 32:977)
126. HARTSHORN, ELIZABETH. "A Comparison of Certain Aspects of Student Leadership and Non-Leadership: Significant Differences on Four Psychometric Tests." *J Ed Res* 49:515–22 Mr '56. * (*PA* 31:5098)
127. LEVY, JEROME. *Reducing the Language Complexity of the Study of Values: A Revision.* Doctor's thesis, University of Denver (Denver, Colo.), 1956.
128. SCHROEDER, CLIFFORD E. *Personality Patterns of Advanced Protestant Theology Students and Physical Science Students.* Doctor's thesis, Michigan State University (East Lansing, Mich.), 1956. (*DA* 18:154)
129. SHEPHERD, JOHN R., AND SCHEIDEL, THOMAS M. "A Study of the Personality Configuration of Effective Oral Readers." *Speech Monogr* 23:298–304 N '56. * (*PA* 32:2128)
130. VAN LEEUWEN, EMIL. "Validity Information Exchange, No. 9-36: D.O.T. Code 1-57.10, Salesman, Life Insurance." *Personnel Psychol* 9:381 au '56. *
131. ANDREWS, JOHN H. M. "Administrative Significance of Psychological Differences Between Secondary Teachers of Different Subject Matter Fields." *Alberta J Ed Res* 3:199–208 D '57. *
132. FARBRO, PATRICK C., AND COOK, JOHN M. "Normative Data Information Exchange, No. 10-14." *Personnel Psychol* 10:231–2 su '57.
133. GOWAN, J. C., AND SEAGOE, MAY. "The Relation Between Interest and Aptitude Tests in Art and Music." *Calif J Ed Res* 8:43–5 Ja '57. *

134. HALPERN, HOWARD M. "Predictive Empathy and the Study of Values." Abstract. *J Consult Psychol* 21:104 Ap '57. *
135. KAESS, WALTER A., AND WITRYOL, SAM L. "Positive and Negative Faking on a Forced-Choice Authoritarian Scale." *J Appl Psychol* 41:333–9 O '57. *
136. LEVY, JEROME. *Reducing the Language Complexity of the Study of Values: A Revision.* Doctor's thesis, University of Denver (Denver, Colo.), 1957.
137. SHOOSTER, CHARLES N. *Ability of the Allport-Vernon-Lindzey Scale to Predict Certain Pictorial Perceptions.* Master's thesis, Illinois Institute of Technology (Chicago, Ill.), 1957.
138. BARRETT, RICHARD S. "The Process of Predicting Job Performance." *Personnel Psychol* 11:39–57 sp '58. *
139. GOWAN, J. C. "Intercorrelations and Factor Analysis of Tests Given to Teaching Candidates." *J Exp Ed* 27:1–22 S '58. *
140. LEVY, JEROME. "Readability Level and Differential Test Performance: A Language Revision of the Study of Values." *J Ed Psychol* 49:6–12 F '58. *
141. NICKELS, JAMES B., AND RENZAGLIA, GUY A. "Some Additional Data on the Relationships Between Expressed and Measured Values." *J Appl Psychol* 42:99–104 Ap '58. *
142. PETERSON, TED TANGWALL. *Selecting School Administrators: An Evaluation of Six Tests.* Doctor's thesis, Stanford University (Stanford, Calif.), 1958. (*DA* 19:262)
143. SUMNER, EARL DAVID. *On the Relation of Manifest Needs to Personal Values: A Factor Analytic Study Involving R and Q Techniques.* Doctor's thesis, Wayne State University (Detroit, Mich.), 1958. (*DA* 18:2219)

N. L. GAGE, *Professor of Education, Bureau of Educational Research, University of Illinois, Urbana, Illinois.*

The hybrid vigor of this cross between American empiricism and European rationalism has made it one of the most viable of tests. This review deals mainly with aspects of the 1951 revision and the 1931 original that were not considered in earlier reviews.

According to the manual, the revision "offers certain improvements without in any way changing the basic purpose of the test or limiting its scope of usefulness." These improvements were made by introducing new questions and changing old questions on the basis of three successive item analyses, by simplifying and modernizing the wording of certain items, by making scoring more economical of time and labor, by preparing fresh norms, and by restricting the definition of the "social" value to altruistic love or philanthropy as against conjugal, familial, or religious love.

Correlations between the old and revised forms, taken two weeks apart by 50 male college students, are all, according to the manual, "significantly high." They seem low enough, however, to cause this reviewer to raise questions as to whether the meaning of the scores has not changed. That the social value has indeed been redefined is reflected by the *r* of only .31 between old and revised forms. The other *r*'s are only .48 for the theoretical, .74 for the economic, .55 for the esthetic, .45 for the political, and .75 for the religious values. Certainly these *r*'s (even if corrected for attenuation) are so low as to call for revalidation of the test in the many senses in which the old form was validated.

The split-half reliabilities of the six scores on the revised form are all higher than those on the old form, averaging .82 as against .70. (The manual is unclear as to whether the Spearman-Brown formula was applied, although it is unthinkable that it was not.) Repeat reliabilities for the revised form average .89 over a one-month interval. Whether these are superior to those obtainable with the old form is left in doubt since the authors note that the retesting with the old form took place after a greater length of time and was done with other subjects. It is regrettable that the comparisons of internal consistency and repeat reliabilities were not made with more appropriate data. If reliability is worth taking seriously, it deserves less cavalier treatment.

In discussing the correlations among values, the authors correctly point out that it is not strictly legitimate to state intercorrelations among values scores which are interdependent, in the sense that a high score on one value can be obtained only at the expense of low scores on others. Hence, as the authors recognize, the obtained intercorrelations are artifactually negative in general, and are reported merely to indicate "the *relative* degree to which various pairs of values are associated." This problem could have been circumvented to some extent, however, by scoring each value afresh for each correlation into which it entered. Thus, if value i is to be correlated with value j, the items in Part 1 consisting of forced choices between values i and j can be disregarded when the scores for values i and j are obtained; similarly, in Part 2, where 4-choice sets are to be ranked, those choices can be disregarded (in scoring for i) which represent value j. Obtained in this way, r_{ij} will not be artifactually negative.

Scoring no longer requires transferring scores for individual items to a separate score sheet. Now the subject writes his responses into boxes in the test booklet. These boxes are so arranged that the responses scored for a given value fall into the same column. Although the column for a given value shifts from one page to the next, the reviewer wonders whether this format may not make the test even more transparent than it was. The college student or college educated adult for whom the scale is primarily designed may have little trouble in seeing through this arrangement and discerning which choices represent the same kind of "personal preferences."

If he wants to fake, he gets a helping hand from this arrangement.

Response sets in psychological tests may introduce reliable but irrelevant variance. In Part 1, such a response set may come into play. Here, the subject can respond with two degrees of intensity: (a) with 3 and 0 if he agrees with alternative A and disagrees with B, or (b) with 2 and 1 if he has a slight preference for A over B. The reviewer is willing to predict that reliable individual differences will be found in the degree to which subjects use the 3-0 way of responding as against the 2-1, or less "intense," way. And the 3-0, or more intense, way of responding will probably result in a more jagged profile of values. The question arises as to whether this stylistic variable is psychologically relevant to the subject's values.

Research using the revised form has been reported in a variety of studies. Iscoe and Lucier (*106*) correlated it with the *Kuder Preference Record—Personal*. Bledsoe (*116*) found no differences in values after an intensive course in research methodology. Bousfield and Samborski (*117*) found that the religious and theoretical values correlated significantly with the frequency of associations to religious and theoretical words. Mayzner and Tresselt (*120*) found relationships between concept span and values.

In the meantime, further research with the old form has been reported. In 1952 Brogden reported a factor analysis (*93*) which yielded 10 first-order factors (general aesthetic interest, interest in fine arts, belief in "culture," antireligious evaluative tendency, anti-aggression, humanitarian tendency, interest in science, tendency toward liberalism, theoretic interest, and "rugged individualism"), which were carefully compared with those resulting from a factor analysis reported in 1936 by Lurie (*22*).

The most impressive new findings with the old form are those reported by Kelly in his APA presidential address (*119*). Over a 20-year interval, "only 5 of the possible 12 changes [six values for each sex]....are significant. By all odds, the largest, and in fact the most significant, of all changes to be reported is that for Religious values. Both the men and women score about 5 points higher in their middle years than as young men and women....Since scores derived from the Scale of Values are relative, this shift toward higher religious values was necessarily accompanied by a downward shift on one or more of the other value scales. For the women, most of this downward shift occurred in aesthetic values; for the men, it was about equally divided between aesthetic and theoretical values." Correlationally, the stability of values over 20 years is indicated by r's ranging from .52 (aesthetic) to .32 (social). The values measured by the *Study of Values* proved to be the most stable of the five kinds of variables (vocational interests, self-ratings on personality traits, Bernreuter and Strong personality trait scores, and attitudes) compared by Kelly.

Looking ahead to the next revision, the reviewer hopes that the authors will consider the objections raised against type concepts by Humphreys [1]; at the least, the kind of ipsative or relative scale embodied in the *Study of Values* ought to be supplemented by normative scales. Relative scales reduce everyone's profile to the same mean level, impose negative correlations among scores, and imprison predictive efforts within a possibly inappropriate model. Normative scales do not have these limitations.

At least one attempt to develop a normative test of values, in the form of Thurstone-type (equal-appearing interval) attitude scales for various values, has already been made (*107*). Although this attempt has laudable features, it served mainly to remind the reviewer of an often overlooked virtue of the Allport-Vernon-Lindzey test, namely, the impression it gives of being an intelligent test for intelligent people.

Second, the reviewer hopes that due regard will be given the results of empirical work on the organization of values, as represented by Lurie's and Brogden's factor analyses. If the authors were willing to depart from Spranger's definition of social value in the light of empirical results (low reliability), should they not also be willing to revise other values in the light of results from factor analyses? Have not Spranger's armchair speculations held sway long enough? Brogden's data were collected in 1936 and 1937; one wonders whether, had they been reported in time, his results would have influenced the authors of this 1951 revision away from Spranger's typology. For the future, at least, we have the nice question of whether the factorists should be allowed to rotate the armchair.

Finally, some account should be taken of the criticism leveled by Adams and Brown (*104*): "the Allport-Vernon test confounds to some ex-

tent two psychological dimensions which can be separated, namely *interest* and *value*. An individual can be interested in a given area even though he has a strong disagreement with individuals or institutions operating in that area. For example, a militant atheist may be very interested in religion though harboring little value for religious beliefs or experience. Because of the way in which the Allport-Vernon test is constructed and scored, it seems to us that interest and value are confounded, though no doubt these two variables are correlated to some extent."

For the present, however, the *Study of Values* will continue to serve us well. For classroom demonstration, for counseling and vocational guidance, and for research on a wide variety of psychological questions, the test is already very good. Maybe that is why we cannot help wanting it to be even better.

For reviews by Harrison G. Gough and William Stephenson, see 4:92 (I excerpt); for a review by Paul E. Meehl of the original edition, see 3:99.

[115]

★**Temperament and Character Test.** College and adults; 1952; 11 scores: nervous, sentimental, choleric, passionate, sanguine, phlegmatic, amorphous, apathetic, emotivity, activity, perseveration; 1 form ['52]; no data on reliability and validity; no norms; $1.25 per 25 tests; 25¢ per mimeographed manual ['52]; 35¢ per mimeographed booklet of temperaments and characters ['52]; 15¢ per mimeographed descriptive booklet ['52]; 75¢ per specimen set; postage extra; French edition available; Institut pedagogique Saint-Georges, Mont-de-la-Salle, Montreal, Canada. *

[116]

★**Survey of Attitudes and Beliefs.** Grades 9-12; 1954-55; 3 scores: society, education and work, sex-marriage-family; Form AH ('54); manual ('55); $2.75 per 20 tests; $1.20 per 20 profiles ('55); 75¢ per specimen set; postage extra; (40) minutes; Leslie W. Nelson; Science Research Associates. *

DONALD T. CAMPBELL, *Professor of Psychology, Northwestern University, Evanston, Illinois.*

This test seems designed primarily as an instrument for counseling purposes with high school students rather than as a research instrument. It measures the extent to which the attitudes of students approximate those which responsible adults would like them to have toward society; education and work; and sex, marriage, and family. In several respects, it seems carefully prepared, having gone through several revisions, with both statistical editing against criterion groups and qualitative editing by panels

1 HUMPHREYS, LLOYD G. "Characteristics of Type Concepts With Special Reference to Sheldon's Typology." *Psychol B* 54:218-28 My '57. *

of educators, employers, parents, and children, followed by a standardization on a national sample of classrooms (2,923 students in 13 schools, probably all urban). Reliabilities (Kuder-Richardson formula 21) ranging from .65 to .80 are reported. Norms are provided by sex and by grade for each of the three attitude areas. No validity data are presented. Regional and social class norms are not given. No mention is made of the correlations among the three scores, which are probably as high as the reliabilities. On the other hand, the heterogeneity of content within each area cries out for more analytic subscores, factor analysis among items, or homogeneous keying. Agree and disagree items enter into all scores in about equal numbers, thus avoiding acquiescence response set.

The claim of the test instructions that there are no "right" or "wrong" answers is especially hollow in this test. The profile material for students and the discussion guides for teachers have a heavy moralizing tone, pushing for "acceptance of the expectations our society imposes upon us." Disagreement is equated with "misunderstanding of the reasons for society's expectations." The correct answers are regarded as "desirable and important to happy and productive living." When we look at the correct ("positive") answers, we see that the best citizens and educators of Contra Costa County, California (the correct answers were *not* based upon a national sample) took a *middle* position on many dimensions of attitude in which our mores are ambiguous. Thus a "negative" attitude toward high school sex includes *both* refusing to kiss on a date *and* heavy petting. Thus one should dislike a bookworm and favor compulsory education. The normative orientation thus pools for scoring purposes two opposite deviations from Contra Costa ideals. It would seem diagnostically valuable to have kept these deviations separate in the scoring system although, in general, the greatest opportunity for deviation lies in the direction of lower class customs. Girls score more positively than boys, and an increase in positive attitudes occurs from the 9th to 11th grades, followed by a drop in the 12th grade. In general, the pattern of correct answers provides an interesting sociological document.

For the purpose of discussing the answers with students, it is probably unfortunate that some of the items involve matters of fact, not of personal preference, with the factually incorrect answer scored positively. Thus the adjusted answer is to *deny* that "self consciousness often causes people to avoid being in groups," and to deny that "people usually fear being unpopular with the opposite sex." As with so many attitude tests, this test seems least plausible when examined at the item level.

C. ROBERT PACE, *Professor of Psychology and Chairman of the Department, Syracuse University, Syracuse, New York.*

Survey of Attitudes and Beliefs is designed to identify the attitudes of high school students in three areas. Area 1, Attitude toward Society, deals with responsibilities of good citizenship and positive attitudes toward other people; Area 2, Attitude toward Education and Work, concerns beliefs about the importance of education and the responsibility to develop and use one's talents constructively; and Area 3, Attitude toward Sex, Marriage, and Family, covers understanding of acceptable sexual behavior and the role of the family. The 147 statements in the survey are approximately equally divided among the three areas. Students respond to each item by agreeing, disagreeing, or indicating an undecided attitude. The score in each area consists of the number of statements to which the student's response indicates a desirable attitude. Desirability was determined by judges.

The survey is a good and fairly typical example of a device for educational evaluation. A profile folder is provided in which students can record their scores and compare them with scores made by other students. Simple and helpful comments are given to aid the student in evaluating his score. Teachers are encouraged to find interesting items for class discussion. Guidance counselors can discuss the scores and the item responses with students who wish to talk about them. The survey is, then, a useful evaluation and teaching device; this is its chief value and its recommended use.

The survey was carefully developed, tried out, revised, criticized, and discussed by school teachers, administrators, and interested citizens over a period of several years before the present form was given to a standardization group of 2,923 students in grades 9 through 12 in 13 schools representing 7 states and all 4 geographic regions of the country. Test reliabilities, reported by grade and sex groups, are generally in the .60's and .70's, although coefficients in the .80's and .90's were obtained from a group of 500 seniors in an earlier trial. Quite properly, the manual does not attach too much significance to the test scores, for any score which falls between the 25th and 75th percentiles is described as average, and more extreme scores are merely labeled higher or lower than average. Actually, the typical difference between the 20th and 80th percentiles is only 10 to 11 raw score points. Thus, the use of the survey as a measuring instrument is not emphasized.

Desirable scores on the survey are, ideologically, in the main stream of Riesman's other-directed man, Whyte's organization man, *McCall's* togetherness, and Norman Vincent Peale's positive thinking. These represent solid virtues, having the status of widely held objectives of high school education, although some school teachers, one hopes, may be privately glad that there are a few vigorous dissenters among the adult community.

[117]

Test of Personality Adjustment. Ages 9-13; 1931; 5 scores; personal inferiority, social maladjustment, family maladjustment, daydreaming, total; separate forms for boys and girls; $2.50 per 25 tests; 75¢ per specimen set; postage extra; (40-50) minutes; Carl R. Rogers; Association Press. *

REFERENCES

1. ROGERS, CARL R. *Measuring Personality Adjustment in Children Nine to Thirteen Years of Age.* Columbia University, Teachers College, Contributions to Education, No. 458. New York: Bureau of Publications, the College, 1931. Pp. v, 107. * (PA 6:1978)
2. BABCOCK, MARJORIE E. *A Comparison of Delinquent and Non-Delinquent Boys by Objective Measures of Personality.* Honolulu, H.I.: the Author, 1932. Pp. 74. * (PA 8:438)
3. BOYNTON, PAUL L., AND WALSWORTH, BARRIER M. "Emotionality Test Scores of Delinquent and Nondelinquent Girls." *J Abn & Social Psychol* 38:87-92 Ja '43. * (PA 17:3899)
4. GRUEN, EMILY W. "Level of Aspiration in Relation to Personality Factors in Adolescents." *Child Develop* 16:181-8 D '45. * (PA 20:2393)
5. CLARKE, HELEN JANE. "The Diagnosis of a Patient With Limited Capacity." *J Personality* 15:105-12 D '46. * (PA 21:3001)
6. EPSTEIN, HANS L., AND SCHWARTZ, ARTHUR. "Psychodiagnostic Testing in Group Work: Rorschach and Painting Analysis Technique." *Rorsch Res Exch & J Proj Tech* 11:23-41 no 2-4 '47. * (PA 22:4945)
7. CHRISTY, WILLIAM J. *A Study of Relationships Between Sociometric Scores and Personality Self-Ratings.* Master's thesis, North Texas State College (Denton, Tex.), 1949.
8. GIBSON, ROBERT L. *A Study on the Personality Pattern of Male Defective Delinquents as Indicated by the Rogers Test of Personality Adjustment.* Master's thesis, Pennsylvania State College (State College, Pa.), 1951.
9. MENSH, IVAN N., AND MASON, EVELYN P. "Relationship of School Atmosphere to Reactions in Frustrating Situations." *J Ed Res* 45:275-86 D '51. *
10. SPAETH, C. F., JR. *A Validation of Rogers' Test of Personality Adjustment.* Master's project, University of Southern California (Los Angeles, Calif.), 1952.
11. LEIBMAN, OSCAR BERNARD. *The Relationship of Personal and Social Adjustment to Academic Achievement in the Elementary School.* Doctor's thesis, Columbia University (New York, N.Y.), 1953. (DA 14:67)
12. NOWELL, ANN. "Peer Status as Related to Measures of Personality." *Calif J Ed Res* 4:37-41 Ja '53. * (PA 28:1514)
13. PRICKETT, FRANCES S. *An Analytical Study of Greene's Revision of Rogers' Test of Personality Adjustment.* Master's thesis, University of Georgia (Athens, Ga.), 1954.
14. SATTERLEE, ROBERT LOUIS. "Sociometric Analysis and Personality Adjustment." *Calif J Ed Res* 6:181-4 S '55. * (PA 30:6295)
15. SMITH, LOUIS MILDE. *A Validity Study of Six Personality and Adjustment Tests for Children.* Doctor's thesis, University of Minnesota (Minneapolis, Minn.), 1955. (DA 16:791)
16. BURCHINAL, LEE G.; HAWKES, GLENN R.; AND GARDNER, BRUCE. "The Relationship Between Parental Acceptance and Adjustment of Children." *Child Develop* 28:65-77 Mr '57. *
17. BURCHINAL, LEE; GARDNER, BRUCE; AND HAWKES, GLENN R. "Children's Personality Adjustment and the Socio-Economic Status of Their Families." *J Genetic Psychol* 92:149-59 Je '58. *
18. BURCHINAL, LEE G.; GARDNER, BRUCE; AND HAWKES, GLENN R. "A Suggested Revision of Norms for the Rogers Test of Personality Adjustment." *Child Develop* 29:135-9 Mr '58. *
19. SMITH, LOUIS M. "The Concurrent Validity of Six Personality and Adjustment Tests for Children." *Psychol Monogr* 72(4):1-30 '58. *

DANIEL L. ADLER, *Professor of Psychology, San Francisco State College, San Francisco, California.*

This test appears in two identical editions, one published in the United States and the other in Australia. There is nothing to indicate that either varies from the original edition copyrighted in 1931, although the desiderata of test construction and the concepts of adjustment have both changed considerably since that time. In its present form, the test could, at best, be described as little more than a working tool for a pilot study of certain dimensions of child adjustment. The author's evaluation supports this view. He points out that the diagnostic scores on personal inferiority, social maladjustment, family maladjustment, and daydreaming are "not highly accurate" and that they are potentially "misleading in the case of an individual child." The major value of the test, according to the author, lies in the clinician's careful evaluation of the answers to test items, considered singly and in their relationship to one another.

The following limitations of the instrument, considered in the light of modern test sophistication, contraindicate its use for anything but further validation: (*a*) The subtest scores and the total scores have low coefficients of reliability and are reported from an inadequate sample (n = 43). (*b*) Validity is based upon correlations between subtest scores and the ratings made by "clinicians" (not otherwise identified). These correlations range from .38 to .48. (*c*) The norms, based upon 167 children of whom 52 are said to be "problem" children, constitute an obviously inadequate standardization. (*d*) The interpretations of subtest response syndromes are neither objective nor convincing. (*e*) The scoring system is cumbersome and conducive to unreliability. (*f*) The case histories, cited as examples of diagnoses based on test scores, are not likely to be extrapolated meaningfully by the rank and file test user.

Considering these shortcomings, the author would do a service to test users, students of testing, and himself by withdrawing the *Test of*

Personality Adjustment from circulation, at least in its present form.

HARRISON G. GOUGH, *Associate Professor of Psychology, University of California, Berkeley, California.*

This test seeks to measure the adequacy of the child's adjustment at home, among his peers, and in his daydreams and fantasies. Separate test booklets for boys and girls are provided, each containing skillfully probing questions grouped under six task categories. In one category, the child is asked to choose three wishes he would like to have come true from a listing including things like "to have the boys and girls like me better," "to have a different father and mother,"¹ "to have more money to spend," and "to have my father and mother love me more." In another, he checks what he considers to be the "true" answer in each multiple choice item as:

> 13. Do other children play mean tricks on you? (A) Never. (B) Sometimes. (C) Very often.
> 17. Do you wear good clothes to school? (A) I don't have any nice clothes. (B) My clothes are nice enough. (C) I have very good clothes.
> 21. Do you want people to like you? (A) I just can't stand it, if people don't like me. (B) I always try very hard to make people like me. (C) I don't care very much, but I'm glad when people like me. (D) I don't care a bit whether people like me or not.

Five quantitative scores are obtained for personal inferiority, social maladjustment, family maladjustment, daydreaming, and a total. Instructions for scoring are clear and precise, although the scoring methods themselves are needlessly cumbersome and awkward. The manual recommends, wisely, that the user read through the individual child's booklet in addition to examining his profile of scores.

The manual was copyrighted in 1931, and is apparently unchanged today. One would expect that a manual 28 years old would be in need of some revision, and as a matter of fact the publisher has no business continuing to issue a document as badly in need of modification as this one. Since 1931 this test has undoubtedly been given to thousands of children; systematic data are certainly available in a number of child psychology centers. It would be a relatively easy matter to compile extensive age and sex norms and validity data of both clinical and longitudinal kinds. If the publisher plans to continue selling this test, these things should be done and the manual brought up to date.

Having said this, it is my pleasant duty to re-turn to the manual which, except for the deficiencies just noted, is a low-keyed work of art. The tone of the writing is patient and benevolent and almost necessarily implants a charitable and therapeutic attitude in the reader who is to use the test. The intercalated comments about children and their problems are deeply insightful. The cautions about test usage are in the best tradition of clinical testing. The section on interpretation goes directly to the kind of behavioral implications which the test was designed to elucidate and in which the user is presumably most interested. The manual closes with that rarity of rarities, a series of case analyses in which the author shows how the test results can be utilized in the explication and diagnosis of the individual person.

In summary, the test itself is, in this reviewer's judgment, an exemplary device. The areas covered are important ones, and the questions asked are sagacious and penetrating. The mechanics of answering and scoring could easily be simplified and improved. The test is greatly in need of revision from this standpoint. The manual is woefully lacking in information pertaining to age and sex norms, correlations of scores with other behavioral and test variables, and longitudinal implications of the test's scores. Considering the wide usage this test has had since its publication, its author and publisher have a professional obligation to bring it up to date. One would hope, however, that in doing this the really remarkable personological insight and operational relevance of the present sections on interpretation and case analysis can be retained.

For a review by C. M. Louttit, see 40:1258.

[118]

Thurstone Temperament Schedule. Grades 9–16 and adults; 1949–53; 7 scores: active, vigorous, impulsive, dominant, stable, sociable, reflective; IBM; 1 form ('49); 2 editions; manual, second edition ('53); separate answer sheets or pads must be used; $9.80 per 20 tests; 75¢ per specimen set; postage extra; (15–25) minutes; L. L. Thurstone; Science Research Associates. *
a) [FORM AH FOR HAND SCORING]. $2.15 per 20 answer pads.
b) [FORM AM FOR MACHINE SCORING]. IBM; $5 per 100 IBM answer sheets; $2.50 per set of scoring stencils.

REFERENCES

1. THURSTONE, L. L. "The Dimensions of Temperament." *Psychometrika* 16:11–20 Mr '51. * *(PA* 25:7327)
2. ERICKSON, HARLEY ELLWOOD. "A Factorial Study of Teaching Ability." *J Exp Ed* 23:1–39 S '54. * *(PA* 29:6927)
3. MONTROSS, HAROLD WESLEY. "Temperament and Teaching Success." *J Exp Ed* 23:73–97 S '54. * *(PA* 29:6302)
4. NATHANSON, SHERMAN NOEL. *The Relationship Between the Traits Measured by Thurstone's Temperament Schedule and Convictions for Traffic Violations Among a Group of Junior*

College Students. Master's thesis, University of Southern California (Los Angeles, Calif.), 1954.
5. KEISLAR, EVAN R. "The Validity of the Thurstone Temperament Schedule With High School Students." Abstract. *Am Psychol* 10:389-90 Ag '55. *
6. JONES, LYLE V., AND MORRIS, CHARLES. "Relations of Temperament to the Choice of Values." *J Abn & Social Psychol* 53:345-9 N '56. *
7. KUSHMAN, HOWARD S., AND CANFIELD, ALBERT A. "Validity Information Exchange, No. 9-32: D.O.T. Code 1-18.63, Order Clerk-Clerical 11 (Telephone)." *Personnel Psychol* 9:375-7 au '56. *
8. WORPELL, DONALD FREDERICK. *A Study of Selection Factors and the Development of Objective Criteria for Measuring Success in a Co-operative General Machine Shop Training Program.* Doctor's thesis, University of Michigan (Ann Arbor, Mich.), 1956. (*DA* 17:1270)
9. DUGGAN, JOHN M. *A Factor Analysis of Reading Ability, Personality Traits and Academic Achievement.* Doctor's thesis, Yale University (New Haven, Conn.), 1957.
10. HEATH, EARL DAVIS. *The Relationships Between Driving Records, Selected Personality Characteristics and Biographical Data of Traffic Offenders and Non-Offenders: A Study of Selected Personality Characteristics and Selected Biographical Data of Motor Vehicle Traffic Offenders and Non-Offenders and the Relating of Differences Obtained to Records of Their Driving Performance.* Doctor's thesis, New York University (New York, N.Y.), 1957. (*DA* 17:1949)
11. STONE, SOLOMON. *The Contribution of Intelligence, Interests, Temperament and Certain Personality Variables to Academic Achievement in a Physical Science and Mathematics Curriculum.* Doctor's thesis, New York University (New York, N.Y.), 1957. (*DA* 18:669)
12. BRUCE, MARTIN M. "Normative Data Information Exchange, No. 11-12." *Personnel Psychol* 11:129 sp '58. *

NEIL J. VAN STEENBERG, *Research Psychologist, Personnel Research Branch, Personnel Research and Procedures Division, The Adjutant General's Office, Department of the Army, Washington, D.C.*

The schedule is designed to yield scores along seven aspects of temperament. "Temperament" the author defines as those aspects of personality which are of a relatively stable nature, as contrasted with the more ephemeral qualities, such as attitudes, opinions, and moods, which fluctuate with impact of recent experience. The seven factors are the result of analysis of scores made by normal individuals; hence, they have no intentional connection with any psychotic or neurotic classification. The schedule is self-administering and may be given with or without supervision, individually or by groups.

The schedule contains 140 items, each asking a question which is to be answered by marking "Yes," "?," or "No." The questions are presented in simple language suitable for high school students, and decisions on how to answer them are seemingly more easily reached than on some other personality tests. Items are printed in a 6-page booklet of "step-down" format, permitting the answer sheet to remain in a fixed position, and in exactly the right position for marking the answers as the pages are turned. It is by far the most ingeniously contrived testing booklet the reviewer has seen.

Interpretation of the scores is made in terms of seven traits or continua of temperament, as follows: (A) Active, (V) Vigorous, (I) Impulsive, (D) Dominant, (E) Stable, (S) Sociable, and (R) Reflective. The seven traits are derived from a factor analysis of scores in the 13 personality areas measured by the *Guilford-Martin Inventory of Factors GAMIN,* the *Guilford-Martin Personnel Inventory,* and the *Inventory of Factors STDCR.*

The reliabilities of the seven individual factor scores are relatively low; they vary from .45 to .86 with a median of .64 for four different groups. Such results can be expected where there are only 20 items per score. If seven separate scores are to be obtained, it would seem to be distinctly worthwhile to double the time of administration and the number of items.

The manual, like the schedule, is of a high standard, informative, and objectively written. It presents a number of tables of norms for various groups investigated, and includes a section which deals with the reliabilities of a profile. This section indicates the effect of possible fluctuation of individual scores, and the relative stability of the profile as a whole. By implication, the user is cautioned against too rigid interpretation of separate scores. (Again, it must be observed that the inventory should have been twice or three times as long as it is.)

In the second edition of the manual, the section on validity studies which was promised in the first edition has been added. One study gives information on the correlation of forced choice ratings by supervisors on the seven traits with the score attained by the employees on the seven scales used. Other studies using effectiveness of job performance as a criterion show the use of the schedule for predictive purposes. The subjects for the various studies were teachers, office workers, retail store sales employees, sales supervisors, and managers of small retail stores. For all groups except the office workers, *some* of the scores were valid predictors, though the particular scores which were found useful varied from study to study.

In a recent unpublished thesis, Heath (*10*) reports that Scales I, S, and R differentiated between motor vehicle traffic offenders and non-offenders. In an impressive, but yet unpublished, study made by the Psychological Service Section of Sears, Roebuck and Company,[1] a significant difference was found in scores attained on Scales A, V, I, D, and S by two groups of employees—

1 SEARS, ROEBUCK AND COMPANY, NATIONAL PERSONNEL DEPARTMENT, PSYCHOLOGICAL RESEARCH AND SERVICES. *The Five Year Predictive Validity of the Combined Retail Battery of Psychological Tests.* An unpublished study. Chicago, Ill.: Sears, Roebuck and Co., 1957. Pp. 32.

those who had received promotions in a 5-year period and those who had not. In still another unpublished doctor's thesis, Duggan (9) found considerably higher reliabilities (both test-retest and split-half) than were found in the original study. He also found what is perhaps a secondary factor which is defined by I, D, S, and A, and conjectures that this factor might best be encompassed by the term "extravert."

In conclusion, the schedule should prove useful for employment managers and counselors, though it would be desirable to have a number of additional validity studies published. Until such time as this is accomplished, advice given or action taken in nonvalidated areas must be made with caution. Meanwhile the instrument seems to be well established as an "anchor" for further research on personality and its implications.

For reviews by Hans J. Eysenck, Charles M. Harsh, and David G. Ryans, see 4:93 (1 excerpt).

[119]

★Tulane Factors of Liberalism-Conservatism. Social science students; 1946–55; title on test is *Tulane Factors of L-C: General Attitudinal Values Profile;* 5 scores: political, economic, religious, social, aesthetic; 1 form ('46); manual ('55); college norms only; $3 per 50 tests; $1 per specimen set (must be purchased to obtain manual); postage extra; (25–35) minutes; Willard A. Kerr; Psychometric Affiliates. *

REFERENCES
1. KERR, WILLARD A. "Untangling the Liberalism-Conservatism Continuum." *J Social Psychol* 35:111–25 F '52. * (*PA* 27:3426
2. VOOR, J. J. *The Relationship Between the Religious Attitude and the Conservative-Radical Attitude Among Seminarians Studying for the Catholic Priesthood.* Master's thesis, Catholic University of America (Washington, D.C.), 1953.

DONALD T. CAMPBELL, *Professor of Psychology, Northwestern University, Evanston, Illinois.*

This test, first copyrighted in 1946, seems not to have been used in any published research in spite of the popularity of the problem area. The manual cites only two studies, one by the author himself. "Liberalism" in political, economic, religious, social, and aesthetic matters is measured by from 12 to 25 Likert-type items in each category. All items are worded in the (to Kerr) "liberal" direction, thus making the test vulnerable to acquiescence response set. On the aesthetic, social, and political dimensions, Kerr's concept of "liberal" is so out of line with that of other social psychologists as to make his total scores meaningless. For example, it is aesthetically liberal to like "surrealistic" imaginative

painting, "paintings by the old masters," "colored comic cartoons," "classical music," and "humorous and novelty music." It is socially liberal both to "enjoy talking with citizens of small towns" and to believe that "whites and Negroes [should] be permitted to intermarry." It is politically liberal to believe that "congressmen try to do a good job in representing the people," that "most elected politicians are honest," and that "all races and creeds [should] have the right to vote." This heterogeneity of content calls for undone factorial analyses among the items of each scale to justify their combination into total scores, and makes difficult the interpretation of the correlations reported between total scores. On the more typical economic and religious liberalism scales, the oft-found results are replicated, e.g., Democrats are more liberal than Republicans, Jews more liberal than Catholics. Kerr's tests are in no wise superior to the older ones in demonstrating these facts, however. The lowness of the correlation (.10) between religious and economic liberalism found for 246 Tulane men is perhaps a novel and interpretable finding. Once again one is reminded that in the area of social attitudes the copyrighted tests are of inferior quality to the uncopyrighted ones.

C. ROBERT PACE, *Professor of Psychology and Chairman of the Department, Syracuse University, Syracuse, New York.*

This attitude test battery contains five subtests dealing with political, economic, religious, social, and aesthetic topics. Responses are scored on a liberal-conservative dimension. The subtests are short. The political and social subtests have 12 items each; the economic test has 13, the religious test 14, and the aesthetic test 25. To the first four subtests, responses are made by checking "Yes," "Probably Yes," "Undecided," "Probably No," or "No." To the aesthetic items, the response is made by checking "Like It Much," "Like it Some," "Don't Care," "Dislike it Some," or "Dislike it Much." Five points are given for the most liberal response (Yes) and one point for the most conservative response (No), with score weights of 4, 3, and 2 assigned to the responses in between. Intercorrelations among the five scales range from −.02 to +.40. Split-half reliabilities are adequately high for four of the scales, but low (r = .55) for the political scale.

The author, in the manual of instructions, describes the rationale for each of the subtests. One's reaction to these explanations will determine in large part his judgment as to the general usefulness of the test and its adequacy as a measuring device. The political subtest is described by the author as a composite. This was also the reviewer's reaction, for no clear dimension seemed to be present. On the economic scale liberalism is defined as being favorable to practices and policies commonly associated with the welfare state. The religious scale is again rather eclectic, although, generally, the liberal response is one which minimizes the importance of religion. Liberalism in the social scale is similar to the concept of social distance, with a high score given to responses which indicate that one likes different kinds of people and agrees that different kinds of people can become good citizens. The aesthetic scale simply lists a variety of items—such as Greek sculpture, hillbilly music, flowers, primitive pottery—with liberalism being defined as liking everything.

Test results are reported for 291 men enrolled in Protestant or nondenominational colleges (242 of these at Tulane University) and for 251 seminarians studying for the Roman Catholic priesthood. The test is printed on both sides of a single sheet. The typography is poor and the format is cluttered.

No relationships are reported between the results on this test and any of the hundreds of other tests and researches over the past 30 years which have dealt with similar topics or with the concepts of liberalism-conservatism or the measurement of values. If such relationships had been investigated, the meaning of scores on the test might have been established more adequately, or, as seems more likely to this reviewer, the test might not have been published. In its present state, there is little reason for using the test unless the user is curious about a lot of relationships which the test author has not investigated, or at least has not reported.

[120]

★**Vineland Social Maturity Scale.** Birth to maturity; 1935–53; individual; 1 form ('46); $1.80 per 25 tests; $1.25 per 39-page manual ('47); $7.75 per 682-page manual ('53, see 83 below); postage extra; $1.25 per specimen set, postpaid; (20–30) minutes; Edgar A. Doll; Educational Test Bureau. *

REFERENCES

1–58. See 3:107.
59–79. See 4:94.
80. KELLMER, MIA L. *A Study of Doll's Social Maturity Scale as Applied to a Representative Sample of British Children Between the Ages of 6 and 8 Years.* Master's thesis, University of London (London, England), 1951.
81. HOLLINSHEAD, MERRILL T. "Patterns of Social Competence in Older Mental Retardates." *Am J Mental Def* 56:603–8 Ja '52. * *(PA* 26:4876)
82. CASSEL, MARGARET E., AND RIGGS, MARGARET M. "Comparison of Three Etiological Groups of Mentally Retarded Children on the Vineland Social Maturity Scale." *Am J Mental Def* 58:162–9 Jl '53. * *(PA* 28:2854)
83. DOLL, EDGAR A. *The Measurement of Social Competence: A Manual for the Vineland Social Maturity Scale.* Minneapolis, Minn.: Educational Test Bureau, Educational Publishers, Inc., 1953. Pp. xviii, 664. * *(PA* 28:4347)
84. DOLL, EDGAR A. "Vineland Social Maturity Scale," pp. 495–506. *(PA* 27:7765) In *Contributions Toward Medical Psychology: Theory and Psychodiagnostic Methods, Vol. II.* Edited by Arthur Weider. New York: Ronald Press Co., 1953. Pp. xi, 459–885. *
85. GOLDSTEIN, HERBERT. *An Experiment With the Vineland Social Maturity Scale to Determine Its Utility as a Screening Aid in Vocational Placement of Mentally Retarded.* Master's thesis, San Francisco State College (San Francisco, Calif.), 1953.
86. MAXFIELD, KATHRYN E., AND KENYON, EUNICE L. *A Guide to the Use of the Maxfield-Fjeld Tentative Adaptation of the Vineland Social Maturity Scale for Use With Visually Handicapped Preschool Children.* New York: American Foundation for the Blind, 1953. Pp. ii, 30. * *(PA* 29:1406)
87. REILE, PATRICIA J. *A Honolulu Standardization of the Vineland Social Maturity Scale.* Master's thesis, University of Hawaii (Honolulu, Hawaii), 1953.
88. ROSS, GRACE. "Testing Intelligence and Maturity of Deaf Children." *Excep Child* 20:23–4+ O '53. * *(PA* 28:4794)
89. SATTER, GEORGE, AND MCGEE, EUGENE. "Retarded Adults Who Have Developed Beyond Expectation: Part I. Intellectual Functions." *Training Sch B* 51:43–55 My '54. * *(PA* 29:2662)
90. CROKE, KATHERINE. *A Comparative Study of the Revised Stanford-Binet Intelligence Scale for Children, and the Vineland Maturity Scale.* Master's thesis, Wisconsin State College (Milwaukee, Wis.), 1955.
91. SATTER, GEORGE. "Psychometric Scatter Among Mentally Retarded and Normal Children." *Training Sch B* 52:63–8 Je '55. * *(PA* 30:3078)
92. SATTER, GEORGE. "Retarded Adults Who Have Developed Beyond Expectation: Part III, Further Analysis and Summary." *Training Sch B* 51:237–43 F '55. * *(PA* 29:7498)
93. GOTTSEGEN, MONROE G. "The Use of the Vineland Social Maturity Scale in the Planning of an Educational Program for Non-Institutionalized Low-Grade Mentally Deficient Children." *Genetic Psychol Monogr* 55:85–137 F '57. *
94. ISCOE, IRA. "A Profile for the Vineland Scale and Its Clinical Applications." Abstract. *Am Psychol* 12:381 Jl '57. *

For reviews by William M. Cruickshank and Florence M. Teagarden, see 4:94; for reviews by C. M. Louttit and John W. M. Rothney, see 3:107 (1 excerpt); for reviews by Paul H. Furfey, Elaine F. Kinder, and Anna S. Starr of Experimental Form B, see 38:1143; for related reviews, see B121.

[121]

★**A Weighted-Score Likability Rating Scale.** Ages 6 and over; 1946; 10 ratings: honesty, cooperation, courtesy, responsibility, initiative, industry, attentiveness, enthusiasm, perseverance, willingness; 1 form; no data on reliability and validity; $2.50 per set of 24 scales and 12 profiles ['46], postpaid; [1–2] minutes; A. B. Carlile; the Author, 330 West 44th St., Indianapolis 8, Ind. *

[122]

★**What I Like to Do: An Inventory of Children's Interests.** Grades 4–7; 1954–58; 8 scores: art, music, social studies, active play, quiet play, manual arts, home arts, science; IBM; 1 form ('54); no norms for grade 7; $3 per 20 tests; separate answer sheets may be used; $5 per 100 IBM answer sheets; $1.50 per set of machine scoring stencils; 90¢ per 20 profiles ('54); 25¢ per manual ('54); 35¢ per teacher's handbook ('58); 50¢ per specimen set; postage extra; (60) minutes in 2 sessions for grade 4, (50) minutes for grades 5–7; Louis P. Thorpe, Charles E. Meyers, and Marcella Ryser Sea [Bonsall]; Science Research Associates. *

JOHN W. M. ROTHNEY, *Professor of Education, University of Wisconsin, Madison, Wisconsin.*

This inventory consists of 294 yes-no-? items designed to ascertain what pupils would like to do, would not like to do, or neither like nor dislike.

Any person who is considering the use of a test should examine the manual first for evidence of validity. There is no section on validity in the manual and no direct mention is made of the subject until one comes to the next to the last paragraph in a section entitled "Future Research." In that paragraph it is stated that, because interests are believed to shift rapidly in the intermediate grades, long range predictions from the inventory will *probably* show only limited validity. The authors state their belief that "observations of a child's current activity choices will correlate highly with his interest scores." They plan to explore this belief, based largely on the "content validity" of the items, in future research. This claim for content validity seems questionable, however, in view of the following statement which appears on page 10 of the manual. "It may come as a surprise to many parents to learn that supposed interests, claimed preferences and even activity choices may differ from the measured interests revealed by the inventory." The candor of the authors is commendable. In effect, they have warned the potential purchaser not to buy this instrument until the proposed future research has determined whether it has any kind of validity.

Sixty-four reliability coefficients (Kuder-Richardson) based on sex and age groups ranging in size from 34 to 126 are reported for the area scores. Of these 18 are .90 or greater, 36 between .80 and .89, and 10 between .70 and .79. Seven of the 8 for the art area (30 items) are below .80 and all 8 in the science area (62 items) are above .90. No mention is made of the differences in reliabilities of these area scores in the discussion of the profiles that are to be drawn from the data, and no interpretation of the table of reliability coefficients is offered. There is no evidence of stability of the scores obtained by retests over any periods of time, but there are frequent references to shifting interests of pupils at the elementary and intermediate grade levels. Thus there is no evidence that the profile obtained on one day would be repeated a day, a week, a month, or a year later. In view of this lack of evidence of stability one must

question the lengthy statements of the possible use of the inventory in classroom situations, curriculum planning, individual guidance, and parent conferences.

One hundred twelve intercorrelation coefficients among area scores are reported. Of these 4 are greater than .70, 14 lie between .60 and .69, 48 between .50 and .59, 36 between .40 and .49, and 10 between .30 and .39. The scores are not, then, highly independent but no mention is made of this matter in the discussion of profiling that is to be done with the scores. The dips and tips in a profile may not, then, indicate real differences in the areas of a child's interests.

Although there is much mention of sex differences throughout the manual and separate profiles for boys and girls are offered, an examination of the profiles reveals very few differences in sex scores. The authors report "some significant differences between the interest patterns of boys and girls" but they give no data to back up the statement. The norms used as the basis for the profiles were obtained on 3,803 fourth, fifth, and sixth grade pupils from 51 schools in 33 (unnamed) states and all 9 census geographic areas.

Space does not permit consideration of problems that children may have with particular items, the fact that only "yes" items are scored, the lack of provision for scoring of intensity of interests, the possibility of faking responses, the admitted inclusion of items of questionable readability, and many of the other common limitations of the inventory method. It seems to the reviewer that all the elaborate mechanics of this device have failed to avoid the inherent difficulties in the use of the inventory method. Good teachers will not find such an instrument useful; poor ones seem more likely to be helped by spending more time with their pupils than by manipulating the symbols that this instrument produces.

NAOMI STEWART, *Formerly Staff Associate, Educational Testing Service, Princeton, New Jersey.*

Teachers who want to adapt their classroom work to the particular interests of their pupils will find *What I Like to Do* a helpful tool if they take care to use it with a cautious eye on its limitations.

The most important of these is that the meaning of the various scores has not been established, either rationally or empirically. The score categories were apparently not derived in any way that would support an a priori assumption that they represent genuine functional entities, and no experimental results that might help build up a picture of their meaning and relevance are given.

Another limitation is that the norms were derived from data for a comparatively small number of boys and girls in each grade. For that reason, the interest profiles are plotted in units which have a high degree of unreliability —quite apart from any question of their validity.

In light of these and other causes for concern about the scores, it would be safest for the teacher to utilize the inventory merely as a device for obtaining the pupil's reactions to a large number of activity items. The amount of valuable information to be gained from a perusal of the item responses alone should not be underestimated; in fact, the teacher's handbook describes a number of situations in which *item responses,* rather than *scores,* provided the most helpful cues to the teacher.

Unfortunately, it is not a workable solution to urge teachers to use the inventory solely at the item level. Since it is much easier to assimilate information in score form than in item form, most teachers who use the inventory at all will probably wind up making use of the scores. If they use them only in a relatively informal way as a teaching adjunct—as an aid to understanding and "reaching" difficult pupils or as a guide in selecting projects for different groups of pupils—there is little likelihood that any harm will be done. It would definitely not be advisable, however, to use the scores as the basis for administrative decisions that might in any way affect the pupil's subsequent educational placement and progress. Suggestions in the manual encouraging such use should be carefully ignored.

It would not seem desirable, either, to encourage the pupils themselves to take their scores very seriously, yet they can hardly help doing so if the profile folder is used according to the publisher's directions. These directions call for the pupils to plot their own interest profiles and discuss them with teacher and classmates, not just once but three or four times at yearly intervals, each time looking to see what changes might have occurred in the interim. Not only might this procedure cause the inventory scores to assume wholly unwarranted importance in the pupils' minds; it might also tend to

cause distortion in the scores themselves. Ordinarily, children are not likely to "slant" their answers to an interest questionnaire, but if too much fuss is made over the results the first time the inventory is administered, the responses may not be quite so spontaneously honest the second time. The profile folder is intended by the publisher to expedite longitudinal studies of interests, but its use according to the publisher's directions would seem almost bound to yield distorted results.

What I Like to Do, with its full-scale array of accessory materials, is a much more ambitious and elaborate undertaking than earlier interest inventories (see 3:52, 63) designed for use in the intermediate grades, but as a measuring device it does not seem to afford any improvement over the others. Since the inventories differ considerably in item content, probably the best basis for selecting among them is for the teacher to decide which affords the coverage that best suits her purposes.

J Consult Psychol 19:237 Je '55. Laurance F. Shaffer. * an uninspired but workmanlike job in the construction of an interest inventory for grades 4 to 6 and, by implication but without data, for grade 7 *

[123]

★**Wittenborn Psychiatric Rating Scales.** Mental patients; 1955; 9 ratings: acute anxiety, conversion hysteria, manic, depressed, schizophrenic, paranoid, paranoid schizophrenic, hebephrenic schizophrenic, phobic compulsive; 1 form; $2.75 per 25 scales; 35¢ per specimen set; postpaid; (15–25) minutes; J. Richard Wittenborn; Psychological Corporation. *

REFERENCES

1. WITTENBORN, J. R. "Symptom Patterns in a Group of Mental Hospital Patients." *J Consult Psychol* 15:290–302 Ag '51. * (PA 26:6243)
2. WITTENBORN, J. R., AND HOLZBERG, J. D. "The Generality of Psychiatric Syndromes." *J Consult Psychol* 15:372–80 O '51. *
3. WITTENBORN, J. R., AND HOLZBERG, J. D. "The *Wechsler-Bellevue* and Descriptive Diagnosis." *J Consult Psychol* 15: 325–29 Ag '51. *
4. WITTENBORN, J. R., AND METTLER, FRED A. "Practical Correlates of Psychiatric Symptoms." *J Consult Psychol* 15: 505–10 D '51. *
5. WITTENBORN, J. R. "The Behavioral Symptoms for Certain Organic Psychoses." *J Consult Psychol* 16:104–6 Ap '52. *
6. WITTENBORN, J. R., AND BAILEY, CLARK. "The Symptoms of Involutional Psychosis." *J Consult Psychol* 16:13–7 F '52. *
7. WITTENBORN, J. R., AND WEISS, WALTER. "Patients Diagnosed Manic Depressive Psychosis—Manic State." *J Consult Psychol* 16:193–8 Je '52. * (PA 27:5318)
8. WITTENBORN, J. R.; HERZ, MARVIN I.; KURTZ, KENNETH H.; MANDELL, WALLACE; AND TATZ, SHERMAN. "The Effect of Rater Differences on Symptom Rating Scale Clusters." *J Consult Psychol* 16:107–9 Ap '52. *
9. WITTENBORN, J. R.; HOLZBERG, J. D.; AND SIMON, B.; with the collaboration of E. K. WILK, N. TOLL, P. E. YU, A. SANTICCIOLI, C. E. BOYD, AND D. P. SCAGNELLI. "Symptom Correlates for Descriptive Diagnosis." *Genetic Psychol Monogr* 47:237–301 My '53. (PA 28:2606)
10. LORR, MAURICE. "Rating Scales and Check Lists for the Evaluation of Psychopathology." *Psychol B* 51:119–27 Mr '54. *
11. PUMROY, SHIRLEY S., AND KOGAN, WILLIAM S. "The Reliability of Wittenborn's Scales for Rating Currently Dis-

cernible Psychopathology." *J Clin Psychol* 11:411–2 O '55. *
(*PA* 30:5997)
   12. LORR, MAURICE. "Orthogonal Versus Oblique Rotations."
J Consult Psychol 21:448–9 D '57. *
   13. LORR, MAURICE. "The Wittenborn Psychiatric Syndromes: An Oblique Rotation." *J Consult Psychol* 21:439–44 D '57. *
   14. LORR, MAURICE; O'CONNOR, JAMES P.; AND STAFFORD, JOHN W. "Confirmation of Nine Psychotic Symptom Patterns." *J Clin Psychol* 13:252–7 Jl '57. *
   15. WITTENBORN, J. R. "Rotational Procedures and Descriptive Inferences." *J Consult Psychol* 21:445–7 D '57. *

H. J. EYSENCK, *Professor of Psychology, Institute of Psychiatry, University of London, London, England.*

There are 52 symptom rating scales contained in Wittenborn's set. These are arranged in random order and are intended to measure nine psychiatric clusters ranging from acute anxiety and conversion hysteria to schizophrenic excitement and paranoid condition. Each scale is composed of three or four statements so arranged that successive statements reveal increasingly conspicuous disorder of a particular kind. The clusters into which the scales are grouped resulted from extensive factorial analysis of various abnormal groups. An ingenious method of scoring makes it quite easy to obtain weighted scores for the various clusters; these scores can then be arranged in terms of profiles and compared with standardisation data given in the manual.

The whole attempt is very workmanlike throughout and in the reviewer's opinion constitutes the best available set of rating scales for psychiatric disorders. Wittenborn has made an attempt to deal entirely with directly observable behaviour, and in the reviewer's experience his claim that ratings can be readily made by psychiatrists, psychologists, nurses, or other competent observers is amply justified. The types of behaviour included are well chosen and are indicative of close personal experience. The wording of the scales is simple and straightforward and does not commit the "fallacy of the implied theory" so frequent in psychiatric terminology. The research background for the scale is unusually thorough and shows a high degree of statistical competence, somewhat unusual in this field.

The reliability of the cluster scores is not always very high, being only .67 for Depressed State and .76 for Paranoid Condition. The only one to exceed .90 is for Manic State. An additional five clusters have reliabilities between .8 and .9. Wittenborn somewhat plaintively says that these "odd-item estimates of reliability are likely to be spuriously low because of the hetereogeneity of sets of rating scales." It is curi-

ous that he should have used so old-fashioned a method for the estimation of reliability when more modern methods are readily available. It is also curious that he does not give test-retest reliabilities for the same observer, or interobserver reliabilities for different psychiatrists. Such data would be much more relevant and interesting than odd-even reliabilities; our experience suggests that they would be somewhat lower than the reliabilities actually quoted.

The clusters are by no means independent. The correlation between Schizophrenic Excitement and Hebephrenic Schizophrenia is .88, which is higher than the mean reliability of the scales. It is difficult to see any justification for retaining both clusters under these circumstances. There are four other correlations above .66, most of them involving Manic State. In addition there is a correlation of .79 between Paranoid Condition and Paranoid Schizophrenic; this correlation also is higher than the mean reliability of the two cluster scores. Wittenborn's own evidence, therefore, suggests that instead of nine clusters there are seven clusters at most, and possibly only six. It seems a great pity that no oblique factor analysis was attempted and no second order factors established.

In summary, it may be said that the good points of this work far outweigh the bad ones and that, for anyone wanting to use a psychiatric rating scale, the Wittenborn scales can be recommended as superior, on the whole, to the available alternatives. It is to be hoped, however, that in future editions the supererogatory scales will be dropped, second order factor analyses reported, and inter-rater reliabilities given.

MAURICE LORR, *Director, Neuropsychiatric Research Laboratory, Veterans Benefits Office, Washington, D. C.*

The Wittenborn scales are a procedure designed for recording currently observable behavior and symptoms of mental patients. The 52 rating scales sample patient behavior "ordinarily considered important by psychiatrists." To reduce bias, the scales are presented in a randomized unlabeled order. Each scale consists of three or four statements arranged so that successive statements reveal increasing disorder. Each scale must be checked for every patient.

The form is intended for completion by a psychiatrist, psychologist, nurse, or other "competent observer." Competence is not defined nor are data made available concerning relative reliability of the scales when used by different types of observers. Surprisingly, no instructions are provided in the manual on how observations are to be made or over what period of time. The directions only recommend the recording of currently discernible behavior. Accordingly the user is left to his own devices on such matters as to interview or not to interview the patient and to observe patient ward behavior for a couple of hours or for several weeks or months.

This issue is reflected in the reliability information provided. Odd-even estimates of cluster score reliability for 100 patients range from .67 to .92 with a median of .82. Inter-rater reliability of the cluster scores is not reported. Yet confident use of the scales by single raters demands data on inter-rater agreement levels.

The validity of the scales is not discussed. No information is given the user concerning possible concurrent validation against other psychiatric measures of psychopathology. On the other hand, no claim is made for the usefulness of the scales beyond the recording of what was observed or what changed. The cluster scores which result from factoring the scales imply, of course, a type of construct validity.

The manual presents a table of intercorrelations between the clusters based on 100 newly admitted cases. Of the 36 correlations, one third are .41 or higher. The correlation between Hebephrenic and Schizophrenic Excitement is .88. An examination reveals that all but one of the seven hebephrenic scales are included in the excitement cluster. Paranoid Condition and Paranoid Schizophrenic correlate .79. The high correlations suggest that the clusters could be combined and reduced to a substantially smaller number.

Norms for the scales are based on 1,000 consecutive admissions to a state hospital. The median cluster scores for various functional and organic diagnostic groups are also reported in the manual. There are no accompanying data descriptive of the age, sex, marital status, or educational background of the norm group. Also lacking is information as to where and how observations were made in collecting the ratings. The scoring of the form and the conversion of the raw scores into standard cluster scores is easy and rapid.

The Wittenborn instrument is the product of considerable research. It is undoubtedly one of the best developed rating schedules available to the research worker and the practical clinician in need of a procedure for recording patient behavior and symptoms. However, the manual is in need of modification. An appropriate method and optimum period of observation should be specified. Further details descriptive of the norm group and levels of inter-rater agreement on the clusters should be provided the reader. Some of the available validational data should be included.

J Consult Psychol 19:320 Ag '55. Laurance F. Shaffer. A series of 18 research articles since 1950 has reported the development and application of the Wittenborn scales. Now they are made available for general use in an attractive and convenient format. The scales are an aid to the objective description of psychiatric patients in terms of their observable symptoms. On each of 52 areas of behavior, a patient is rated by selecting the one of four statements which describes him best. The quantified ratings are turned into scores on nine factors identified by factor analytic studies. The corrected split-half reliabilities of the factor scores range from .67 to .92, with only one scale below .76; their intercorrelations are generally low. The new blank greatly simplifies the calculation of the factor scores by reducing it to the addition of digits in conveniently arranged columns and the use of a simple table. With their new convenience and availability, the scales will probably receive wider use in research. They make a valuable contribution to the knottiest problem in studies of psychopathology, the problem of the criterion.

PROJECTIVE

[124]

★**The Auditory Apperception Test.** Grades 9 and over; 1953; 1 form; no data on reliability; $25 per set of five 7-inch records (45 rpm), 25 record booklets, 25 story booklets, and manual; $5.50 per 25 record booklets; $5.50 per 25 story booklets; $3 per manual; postpaid; specimen set not available; 50(80) or (50-80) minutes in 2 sessions; Western Psychological Services. *

REFERENCES

1. STONE, D. R. "A Recorded Auditory Apperception Test as a New Projective Technique." *J Psychol* 29:349–53 Ap '50. * (PA 24:5884)
2. OVERLADE, DAN C. *A Comparison of Responses of Schizophrenics to Sounds and Pictures.* Master's thesis, Utah State Agricultural College (Logan, Utah), 1951.
3. BALL, THOMAS S., AND BERNARDONI, LOUIS C. "The Application of an Auditory Apperception Test to Clinical Diagnosis." *J Clin Psychol* 9:54–8 Ja '53. * (PA 27:7753)

KENNETH L. BEAN, *Professor of Psychology, Baylor University, Waco, Texas.*

This projective technique is similar in many ways to the well established *Thematic Apperception Test,* but with auditory rather than visual stimuli. The test consists of 10 sets of 3 sound situations. After listening to each set, the subject is asked to make up a story, using as many of the sounds as he can, telling what led up to the sounds, what is happening, and how the story ends. The material is designated as appropriate for high school, college, and adult subjects.

A tabulation of the responses of 220 college students to each set is presented in the manual under the following headings: order of sounds in stories, description of sounds, length of stories, characters named, situations, outcomes, and general observations. No real evidence of reliability or validity is furnished in the manual, nor are any sample responses interpreted with detailed description of personality dynamics revealed. The absence of detailed instructions for interpreting stories is disappointing and frustrating.

The 45 rpm discs contain many sounds that are interesting and well done, such as the dialogue in Set 3, the saw cutting in Set 5, and the typewriter in Set 8. Unfortunately, there are others so artificial in quality as to be rather unrealistic to the listener. These probably will result in a poorer quality of content in the stories elicited from subjects. Examples include the severe wind in Set 1, which the examiner probably produced by blowing and whistling simultaneously into his microphone, and the train crash in Set 6, probably similarly "faked" in the laboratory. The reviewer's hi-fi ears may be more discriminating than those of the average listener because of his past experience with music and sound effects, but it is his opinion that the ship's whistle or foghorn and the thunder or explosions could be made much more realistic by obtaining and copying available recorded sound effects now widely used in radio and television work. This viewpoint is supported by the reviewer's own tryout of 60 sound effect sequences on groups of subjects before selecting the most productive of these stimuli for his own *Sound Apperception Test,* not yet published. Realistic high fidelity sounds were found to produce much more meaningful stories than the "faked" ones the reviewer tried. With improvement in quality of the stimuli named

above, the sequences should be adequate to bring out much more interesting content than the present version of the test has produced.

The *Auditory Projective Test* of the American Foundation for the Blind is considerably different in content from the AAT, but its purpose is much the same. On the whole, its quality of recording is better, but it also is insufficiently standardized and validated. The reviewer suggests that the *Auditory Apperception Test,* after revision of the recording, may become a very valuable and interesting tool for further research using neurotics, psychotics, blind persons, and normal subjects for its validation as a diagnostic instrument. Until much further development of norms and guides for interpretation has been completed, however, the user of this test should be cautious in making any speculations regarding the significance of individual protocols on the basis of his general knowledge of projective techniques. The simultaneous construction and standardization of three or more auditory projective devices recently is a wholesome trend provided each is done thoroughly, correlated with the others, and correlated with the better established visual Rorschach and TAT.

CLIFFORD H. SWENSEN, JR., *Associate Professor of Psychology, University of Tennessee, Knoxville, Tennessee.*

The author claims that the AAT "has achieved validity and reliability comparable to those of other projective devices," but presents no data relative to either the reliability or validity of the test. He states further that "the principle claim justifying and encouraging the use of the AAT is in its productivity of useful diagnostic signs." Nowhere does the manual present such diagnostic signs. The manual does present methods for analyzing test results, but these methods are based upon work done with the *Thematic Apperception Test.* No evidence is presented to support the implicit contention that stories produced by the AAT may justifiably be interpreted in the same manner as TAT stories. In fact, evidence is produced that might suggest that the AAT stories are useless. The author refers to Tomkins who refers to Murray as saying that stories on the TAT under 140 words were nearly useless. Yet, the mean of the mean lengths of AAT stories reported in the "apperceptive norms" is 88 words. The author also reports a study of schizophrenics in which no significant difference was found between the subjects' productivity on the AAT and the TAT in terms of mean number of responses per subject.

Norms for characters, themes, etc. referred to in the stories are presented, but these are based upon 220 college students who had no grossly deviant scores on the *Minnesota Multiphasic Personality Inventory*. It is highly questionable that such a population provides useful norms for a test designed for clinical use.

Many of the sounds used as stimuli were apparently produced by the use of sound effects. Their artificiality is quite apparent when they are played over high fidelity equipment. They sound much more authentic when played over a low fidelity reproducer.

The test appears to produce the same type of material as the TAT. Since it is less convenient to administer, depending as it does upon sound producing equipment, it probably would be preferable to use the TAT in most clinical settings. However, the AAT would probably prove useful in group situations and with subjects who have defective vision.

[125]

The Blacky Pictures: A Technique for the Exploration of Personality Dynamics. Ages 5 and over; 1950; psychosexual development; individual; 1 form; no data on reliability and validity; no norms; $11 per set of test materials and 25 record blanks; $3.50 per 25 record blanks; $1 per manual; postpaid; (35-55) minutes; Gerald S. Blum; Psychological Corporation. *

REFERENCES

1-7. See 4:102.
8. HART, ROBERT D. *An Evaluation of the Psychoanalytic Theory of Male Homosexuality by Means of the Blacky Pictures.* Doctor's thesis, Northwestern University (Evanston, Ill.), 1951.
9. HILGEMAN, LOIS M. B. *Developmental and Sex Variations in the Blacky Test.* Doctor's thesis, Ohio State University (Columbus, Ohio), 1951.
10. LINDNER, HAROLD. *An Analysis of the Psychological Characteristics of a Selected Group of Imprisoned Sexual Offenders.* Doctor's thesis, University of Maryland (College Park, Md.), 1951.
11. BLUM, GERALD S., AND HUNT, HOWARD F. "The Validity of the Blacky Pictures." *Psychol B* 49:238-50 My '52. * (PA 27:2707)
12. BLUM, GERALD S., AND KAUFMAN, JEWEL B. "Two Patterns of Personality Dynamics in Male Peptic Ulcer Patients as Suggested by Responses to the Blacky Pictures." *J Clin Psychol* 8:273-8 Jl '52. * (PA 27:6060)
13. BLUM, GERALD S., AND MILLER, DANIEL R. "Exploring the Psychoanalytic Theory of the 'Oral Character.'" *J Personality* 20:287-304 Mr '52. * (PA 27:2353)
14. GOLDSTEIN, STANLEY. "A Projective Study of Psychoanalytic Mechanisms of Defense." Abstract. *Am Psychol* 7:317-8 Jl '52. *
15. KLEHR, HAROLD. "An Investigation of Some Personality Factors in Women With Rheumatoid Arthritis." Abstract. *Am Psychol* 7:344-5 Jl '52. *
16. McNEIL, ELTON B., AND BLUM, GERALD S. "Handwriting and Psychosexual Dimensions of Personality." *J Proj Tech* 16:476-84 D '52. *
17. ROSEN, IRWIN C. *Parallel Researches in Sexual Psychopathology: I, A Comparison of a Group of Rapists and Controls on Certain Psychological Variables.* Doctor's thesis, University of Pittsburgh (Pittsburgh, Pa.), 1952.
18. TAYLOR, KENNETH E. *Parallel Researches in Sexual Psychopathology: II, A Comparison of a Group of Pedophiliacs and Controls on Certain Psychological Variables.* Doctor's thesis, University of Pittsburgh (Pittsburgh, Pa.), 1952.
19. ARONSON, MARVIN L. "A Study of the Freudian Theory of Paranoia by Means of the Blacky Pictures." *J Proj Tech* 17:3-19 Mr '53. * (PA 28:2981)
20. ELLIS, ALBERT. "The Blacky Test Used With a Psychoanalytic Patient." *J Clin Psychol* 9:167-72 Ap '53. * (PA 28:2627)
21. LINDNER, HAROLD. "The Blacky Pictures Test: A Study of Sexual and Non-Sexual Offenders." *J Proj Tech* 17:79-84 Mr '53. * (PA 28:2975)
22. SINNETT, EARLE ROBERT. *An Experimental Investigation of the Defense Preference Inquiry for the Blacky Pictures.* Doctor's thesis, University of Michigan (Ann Arbor, Mich.), 1953. (DA 13:442)
23. TOBER, LAWRENCE H. *An Investigation of the Personality Dynamics and Behavior Patterns of Older People in a Mental Hospital as Measured by the Blacky Pictures and a Q-Rating Scale of Behavior.* Doctor's thesis, Western Reserve University (Cleveland, Ohio), 1953.
24. DICKSON, STANLEY. *An Application of the Blacky Test to a Study of the Psychosexual Development of Stutterers.* Master's thesis, Brooklyn College (Brooklyn, N.Y.), 1954.
25. FIELD, LEWIS WILLIAM. *Personality Correlates of College Achievement and Major Areas of Study.* Doctor's thesis, University of Houston (Houston, Tex.), 1954. (DA 14:1344)
26. HOGAN, VIRGINIA. *The Reliability of the Blacky Pictures With Institutionalized Senile Psychotics.* Doctor's thesis, Western Reserve University (Cleveland, Ohio), 1954.
27. SMOCK, CHARLES D., AND THOMPSON, GEORGE F. "An Inferred Relationship Between Early Childhood Conflicts and Anxiety Responses in Adult Life." *J Personality* 23:88-98 S '54. *
28. TEEVAN, RICHARD C. "Personality Correlates of Undergraduate Field of Specialization." *J Consult Psychol* 18:212-4 Je '54. * (PA 29:3007)
29. WINTER, WILLIAM DAVID. *The Prediction of Life History Data and Personality Characteristics of Ulcer Patients From Responses to the Blacky Pictures.* Doctor's thesis, University of Michigan (Ann Arbor, Mich.), 1954. (DA 14:717)
30. BERNSTEIN, LEWIS, AND CHASE, PHILIP H. "The Discriminative Ability of the Blacky Pictures With Ulcer Patients." *J Consult Psychol* 19:377-80 O '55. * (PA 30:6002)
31. REED, WOODROW WILSON. *Parent-Child Relationships Reflected by "The Blacky Pictures" Test.* Doctor's thesis, University of Nebraska (Lincoln, Neb.), 1955. (DA 15:2298)
32. WINTER, WILLIAM D. "Two Personality Patterns in Peptic Ulcer Patients." *J Proj Tech* 19:332-44 S '55. * (PA 30:5075)
33. BLUM, GERALD S. "Defense Preferences in Four Countries." *J Proj Tech* 20:33-41 Mr '56. * (PA 31:3007)
34. BLUM, GERALD S. "'Reliability of the Blacky Test': A Reply to Charen." *J Consult Psychol* 20:406 O '56. * (PA 31:7899)
35. BLUMBERG, ALBERT IRWIN. *A Methodological Study of Two Approaches to the Validation of the Blacky Pictures.* Doctor's thesis, Western Reserve University (Cleveland, Ohio), 1956.
36. CHAREN, SOL. "Regressive Behavior Changes in the Tuberculous Patient." *J Psychol* 41:273-89 Ja '56. * (PA 31:5000)
37. CHAREN, SOL. "Reliability of the Blacky Test." Abstract. *J Consult Psychol* 20:16 F '56. *
38. CHAREN, SOL. "A Reply to Blum." *J Consult Psychol* 20:407 O '56. * (PA 31:7899)
39. SMITH, WENDELL, AND POWELL, ELIZABETH K. "Responses to Projective Material by Pre- and Post-Menarcheal Subjects." *Percept & Motor Skills* 6:155-8 S '56. * (PA 31:4715)
40. WINTER, LOUISE MORRISON. *Development of a Scoring System for the Children's Form of the Blacky Pictures.* Doctor's thesis, University of Michigan (Ann Arbor, Mich.), 1956. (DA 17:175)
41. WOLFSON, WILLIAM, AND WOLFF, FRANCES. "Sexual Connotation of the Name Blacky." *J Proj Tech* 20:347 S '56. * (PA 31:6150)
42. JACOBS, MILDRED O. *A Validation Study of the Oral Erotic Scale of the Blacky Pictures Test.* Doctor's thesis, University of Oklahoma (Norman, Okla.), 1957. (DA 17:1811)
43. TRENT, RICHARD D., AND AMCHIN, ABRAHAM. "An Exploration of Relationships Between Manifest Anxiety and Selected Psychosexual Areas." *J Proj Tech* 21:318-22 S '57. *
44. GRANICK, SAMUEL, AND SCHEFLEN, NORMA A. "Approaches to Reliability of Projective Tests With Special Reference to the Blacky Pictures Test." *J Consult Psychol* 22:137-41 Ap '58. *
45. RABIN, A. I. "Some Psychosexual Differences Between Kibbutz and Non-Kibbutz Israeli Boys." *J Proj Tech* 22:328-32 S '58. *

KENNETH R. NEWTON, *Associate Professor of Psychology, University of Tennessee, Knoxville, Tennessee.*

The *Blacky Pictures* are a series of 12 cartoon drawings designed to point up the psychosexual development of the individual through analysis of the stories he builds around these drawings. The drawings concern a family of dogs with Blacky being the central character. In addition to Blacky, who can be of either sex, there is the mother, the father, and a sibling figure who can be either a brother or a sister. This technique was initially designed by the author as a means of investigating the psychoanalytic theory of psychosexual development. The activities portrayed in each drawing are supposedly symbolic of one of the psychoanalytic dimensions in the theory of psychosexual development. The technique and instructions are quite similar to the *Thematic Apperception Test* with the exception that as the examiner presents each card he gives a preliminary statement which tends to structure the picture somewhat for the patient. There are individual record blanks provided which contain rather complete directions for administration and space for recording the stories. After each cartoon has been presented and a story elicited, there is an inquiry or series of standardized questions that must be asked.

The author's description of the Blacky test as being a "modified projective technique" is a rather generous view of projective techniques. The cartoons themselves, the instructions involved in presenting them, and the inquiry that follows are somewhat obvious and almost directive in nature. In an attempt to obtain material on the various areas of psychosexual development, the author has structured his pictures and inquiries in such a way as to make the responses fit the theory. The interpretation of the individual's responses would quite likely yield positive findings if the subject did no more than offer affirmative or negative responses to the pictures and to the various questions of the inquiry. It seems that the patient is placed in the position of the well known defendant who has been asked, "When did you stop beating your wife?"

In his original publication, the author admits that the assumption that this test measures psychoanalytic dimensions has not been systematically explored and, therefore, that the validity of the test is still open to question. Since the hypotheses and conclusions that are drawn from the material obtained from this technique are based upon the assumption that the Blacky test is a measure of psychoanalytic dimensions, this seems to be a serious shortcoming. In the man-

ual accompanying the series of cartoons, the author attempts to present some criteria for stories that will illustrate "strong" and "not strong" involvement in the particular psychosexual spheres. He states that the clinician's own experience with the Blacky test will enable him to develop some sort of "concept of normality" for the stories presented. In addition, he offers a sample case work-up which does little in the way of strengthening this technique in the hands of the clinician.

Although the technique was developed on adults, the author states that the *Blacky Pictures* are "well-suited for use with children." There are as yet no norms or even illustrations or examples of good or bad, strong or not strong stories for children. Children do respond readily to such a technique, but the interpretation of their responses needs further investigation.

This "modified projective technique" could be an interesting tool with which one might conceivably explore psychoanalytic concepts. However, pointing toward various concepts and making a direct effort to elicit the subject's reactions to situations involving his feelings toward various areas of psychosexual development perhaps represents a weighting of the evidence toward the theory that one wishes to prove. It seems likely that well developed and well directed questions concerning these various periods of psychosexual development might yield even more reliable results than does this "modified projective technique." That is to say, the author seems to be asking specific questions concerning specific types of situations which might just as well be handled in an interview situation without use of any cartoons or story telling. The specificity of the questions being asked in this technique seems to require a certain degree of specificity of response.

The *Blacky Pictures* attempt to portray the various spheres of psychosexual development hypothesized by the psychoanalytic school of thought. The individual's responses to the drawings and his responses to specific inquiry questions supposedly indicate the degree of his involvement in these various psychosexual spheres. Admittedly, other than the clinician's own knowledge of psychoanalytic theory, there is little in the way of normative data. At this time this technique would appear to be of little value to the practicing clinician. Its value depends upon the psychoanalytic training of the administrator, but even here there is little data available from which one could determine a "good" or "bad" response.

J Consult Psychol 20:487–8 D '56. *Samuel J. Beck.* * Blum has devised a test *ad hoc* for psychoanalytic theory by the ingenious technique which activates certain of the psychoanalytically formulated unconscious traits, at the same time that it provides the defenses enabling the patient to liberate and communicate these forbidden trends—the defenses of identification and displacing. * The test has....a differentiating potency, and without a doubt it has the projective instrument value of opening a window to latent character traits. At the same time results are suspect, as I see it, by reason of a major fallacy in the technique of treating the data. This consists in the method of "scoring" each story and the other criteria as "strong" and the various gradations of "strong." The judgments are made by each examiner, without recourse to any frame of reference. Scorings must, therefore, be a function of each scorer. They can, I will concede, be made reliable as between two investigators who have worked together closely and have learned the same signs and language, in recognizing and naming the psychological traits or "dimensions." Except between two such colleagues, or for some one examiner, results are only spuriously comparable. The degree of error to which the procedure is subject is seen in Blum's own monograph: a denial of a response is construed as a repression, and since a repression involves strong emotion, the response is scored "strong." To construe denial as repression—which is a hypothesis and not a datum—is interpretation. Thus a quantitative profile is developed and is reported as *S*'s production although it is actually the examiner's interpretation of *S*'s production. This criticism touches on what is the Achilles' heel of each projective test. It dictates the need, therefore, of exploiting the objectivity potential in the test. The needed technique is that of patterning out its data into impersonal structure to be described operationally, and so creating some stable frames of reference by which the productions of any *S* can be judged, if not measured. Some of the projective tests do lend themselves more easily to such impersonal structuralization than others. But to the extent that the instrument falls short of such objectivity, it is not a test but a two-person situation, two persons—*S* and examiner, each of whom may influence the results. Schafer

has been especially emphatic concerning the interpersonal relation between examiner and subject, and the possible role of the examiner's personality in fashioning the final test picture. Brunswik writing from another theoretical viewpoint, arrives at a similar conclusion. "Since in any testing procedure the examiner constitutes part of the external stimulus situation, representative design demands that examiners should also be sampled," and he refers to the "double jeopardy of generalization." An important implication follows from these positions of Schafer and of Brunswik: projective test investigations will need to find some method of keeping the examiner factor constant, if reports by two or more persons are to be comparable. The problem becomes at this point the baby of the theorists and logicians of science. This circumstance does not, however, ease the burden of the psychologists searching personality by means of projective tests. The fact is they have so far been arriving at right answers, even if they do not know how. Their answers are bound to be that much more accurate as they are based in sound method, and as they take pains to devise such. This is where I see Blacky and his growing pains at the present. The test has the promise warranting its developing. In spite of the fallacy in the scoring procedure, its agreement with clinical theory is logically sound. It can serve, further, as an example of other *ad hoc* techniques which can be devised to explore psychoanalytic theory.

For a review by Albert Ellis, see 4:102 (3 excerpts).

[126]

*Children's Apperception Test. Ages 3–10; 1949–55; individual; 1 form; 2 editions; no data on reliability and validity; $6 per set of 10 pictures and manual of either edition; $2.50 per 25 short form record booklets ('55); postage extra; [15–50] minutes; Leopold Bellak and Sonya Sorel Bellak; C.P.S. Co. *
a) CHILDREN'S APPERCEPTION TEST. 1949–55; also called CAT; 1 form ('49); [revised] picture 2 ['51]; revised manual ('50).
b) CHILDREN'S APPERCEPTION TEST—SUPPLEMENT. 1952–55; also called CAT-S; 1 form ('52); manual ('52).

REFERENCES

1–2. See 4:103.
3. AINSWORTH, MARY D., AND BOSTON, MARY. "Psychodiagnostic Assessments of a Child After Prolonged Separation in Early Childhood." *Brit J Med Psychol* 25:169–201 pt 4 '52. * (*PA* 27:7845)
4. MILLAR, MARY A. *A Study of Common Stories Told by Nursery School Children on the Children's Apperception Test.* Master's thesis, University of Alberta (Edmonton, Alta., Canada), 1952. Pp. 111.
5. TOPPELSTEIN, SANFORD. *Apperceptive Norms for the Children's Apperception Test.* Master's thesis, Ohio University (Athens, Ohio), 1952.
6. BIERSDORF, KATHRYN R., AND MARCUSE, F. L. "Responses

of Children to Human and to Animal Pictures." *J Proj Tech* 17:455–9 D '53. * (*PA* 28:6019)

7. SHNEIDMAN, EDWIN S. "CAT Issue No. 2: The TAT Newsletter, Vol. 7, No. 4, December 1953." *J Proj Tech* 17:499–502 D '53. *

8. WEISSKOPF-JOELSON, EDITH A., AND LYNN, DAVID B. "The Effect of Variations in Ambiguity on Projection in the Children's Apperception Test." *J Consult Psychol* 17:67–70 F '53. * (*PA* 28:977)

9. BELLAK, LEOPOLD. *The Thematic Apperception Test and the Children's Apperception Test in Clinical Use.* New York: Grune & Stratton, Inc., 1954. Pp. x, 282. * (*PA* 29:4032)

10. BYRD, EUGENE, AND WITHERSPOON, RALPH L. "Responses of Preschool Children to the Children's Apperception Test." *Child Develop* 25:35–44 Mr '54. * (*PA* 29:5691)

11. LIGHT, BERNARD H. "Comparative Study of a Series of TAT and CAT Cards." *J Clin Psychol* 10:179–81 Ap '54. * (*PA* 29:933)

12. MAINORD, FLORENCE R., AND MARCUSE, F. L. "Responses of Disturbed Children to Human and to Animal Pictures." *J Proj Tech* 18:475–7 D '54. * (*PA* 29:7299)

13. KAGAN, MARION G. *A Preliminary Investigation of Some Relationships Between Functional Articulation Disorders and Responses to the Children's Apperception Test.* Master's thesis, Boston University (Boston, Mass.), 1955.

14. HOLDEN, RAYMOND H. "The Children's Apperception Test With Cerebral Palsied and Normal Children." *Child Develop* 27:3–8 Mr '56. * (*PA* 31:3561)

15. WHEELER, W. M. "Psychodiagnostic Assessments of a Child After Prolonged Separation in Early Childhood, II." *Brit J Med Psychol* 29:248–57 pt 3–4 '56. *

16. FURUYA, KENJI. "Responses of School-Children to Human and Animal Pictures." *J Proj Tech* 21:248–52 S '57. *

17. GINSPARG, HAROLD TVI. *A Study of the Children's Apperception Test.* Doctor's thesis, Washington University (St. Louis, Mo.), 1957. (*DA* 17:3082)

DOUGLAS T. KENNY, *Associate Professor of Psychology, University of British Columbia, Vancouver, British Columbia, Canada.*

Since its last review in *The Fourth Mental Measurements Yearbook,* three improvements or additions have occurred in this story-telling projective technique for personality evaluation: (*a*) 10 supplementary pictures, with an accompanying manual, have been added; (*b*) Bellak has published a valuable and instructive book on the interpretation of thematic material, entitled *The TAT and CAT in Clinical Use;* and (*c*) Bell's criticism that "the pictures are printed on a matt finish cardboard that soils easily" (4:103) has been partially removed in the 1952 printing of the original 10 CAT cards by having them lacquered. It is unlikely that the lacquered cards will make any basic differences in story content.

The pictures, intended for use with children between 3 and 10 years of age, contain animal figures because it is assumed that children will more readily identify with animals than humans. While the experimental findings on this assumption are ambiguous, clinical material from psychoanalysis points to its reasonableness. The pictures in the basic set were drawn with the hope that they would elicit dynamic material relating to oral conflicts, sibling rivalry, perceptions of parents, oedipal problems, and general drives and modes of responding to the world. The CAT Supplement, consisting of 10 animal scenes, was designed primarily to elicit themes "not *necessarily pertaining to universal prob-*

lems, but which occur often enough to make it desirable to learn more about them as they exist in a good many children." In general, these pictures are intended to probe fears in play situations, interpersonal problems in the classroom, fantasies about being an adult, oral themes, reactions to physical handicaps or castration fears, competitiveness to others, body image ideas, fears of physical illness, bathroom reactions, and fantasies about pregnancy. A further use of the supplement is as a play technique, particularly recommended as a means of obtaining some clinical data on children who find it hard to tell stories. In the latter use, all the supplementary cards are made available and the child's reactions to them are recorded.

Evaluating the CAT and its supplement is a difficult task because much patient research will be required before its optimal usefulness can be realized. Since little is actually known about the kinds of valid inferences that might be drawn from the thematic material that is elicited by the cards, caution must be shown in any clinical inferences based on this technique. Moreover, without a large body of accumulated research, unequivocal evaluative statements cannot be made.

In terms of the standards applied to measures of intelligence, aptitude, and achievement, the CAT and CAT-S would not be regarded as suitable for operational use. They have many technical deficiencies, some of which are meagre normative data of limited generality, no information on the reliability of clinical inferences, a paucity of validity data, and a relatively unstandardized method of administration. On the other hand, there is little doubt that, given a highly trained clinician, one can make valid and useful inferences about the personality of a child from the thematic material produced by this instrument, despite the forementioned technical weaknesses. This is not to say, of course, that this instrument will be clinically useful for all children. Research has yet to show for whom the technique will be most suitable.

In order to obtain meaningful stories for interpretation, the CAT seems to require more skill than its parent, the *Thematic Apperception Test.* It is not a good technique for the novice in test administration and interpretation. At the moment, the interpretation of CAT stories is on shifting grounds because practically nothing is known about how much of the story content reflects the deep underlying structure of the child and how much of it mirrors the conditions immediately antecedent to the testing, the atmosphere created by the test administration, and the pictures themselves. Until a great deal more is known about how such variables operate, caution must be shown in going from the raw stories to psychological attributes of the child and then inferring from these attributes the behavior of the child. Bellak's book (9) should be of great help to the beginner in learning how to infer from raw content to psychological attributes, but of less help in getting to behavior. Of course, the latter problem is one that beclouds the use of all projective techniques, not just the CAT. As this technique requires extensive knowledge and experience in the fields of child testing, pathology, and development, one would question Bellak's statement that "the C.A.T. may be profitable in the hands of.... the social worker, and the teacher."

In summary, this technique will be of value to the experienced clinician in indicating the psychological dispositions of a child. Its valid usefulness seems to lie in providing hypotheses about a child that require checking by other procedures. The potential usefulness of the instrument could be increased if more were known about which inferences from it are valid and with what kind of children it can be most profitably used.

ALBERT I. RABIN, *Professor of Psychology, and Director, Psychological Clinic, Michigan State University, East Lansing, Michigan.*

The *Children's Apperception Test* (CAT) for children between the ages of 3–10 was designed as a sort of downward extension of the TAT. The 10 CAT cards, bearing pictures of animals in a variety of situations, are expected by the authors to reflect common problem areas and conflicts faced by children in the early developmental stages. Problems of orality, identification with parental and sibling figures, aggression, mastery, primal scene fears, and masturbation are some of the issues expected to be projected in stories told in response to the pictures. In 1952 the authors published a supplement (CAT-S) which consists of 10 additional animal pictures, not designed to elicit stories related to "universal" problems, but to relate to issues which are of a more transitory, but important, nature in the lives of many young children. Such themes as physical injury, pregnancy of the mother, social play and aggressiveness,

and teacher and peer relationships are but a few of the ones which may be projected into these pictures.

The two manuals (for CAT and its supplement) were supplemented in 1954 by a more extensive treatment (9) by the author. The manuals supply the prospective examiner with some suggestions for administration, protocols, and samples of interpretation. A record booklet is also provided to facilitate the recording and analysis of stories. Some excerpts of a larger study by Fear and Stone reporting normative data are included in the manual to the supplement. Detailed proposals for collecting norms are given in the book. However, such norms are not yet available.

As a clinical tool for use with children, the CAT enjoys considerable popularity in the United States as well as abroad. Although a good deal of research with this technique is in progress, little information concerning its reliability and validity is available. The normative data by Byrd and Witherspoon (10) are a good beginning. Also, some of the emerging research on disturbed children by Simon [1] and on cerebral palsied children by Holden (14) attest to the usefulness and vitality of this instrument.

In summary it may be stated that the CAT, like most projective techniques, is a clinical technique rather than a psychometric method. Its use by many clinicians and clinical investigators attests to its potency as a tool for the study of psychodynamics in young children. Its acceptance by the critical worker and its survival will depend upon further normative studies and carefully executed research.

For reviews by John E. Bell and L. Joseph Stone, see 4:103 (5 excerpts); for related reviews, see B63.

[127]
*Controlled Projection for Children, Second Edition. Ages 6–12; 1945–51; individual; 1 form ('51) ; no data on reliability and validity; *20s.* per manual ('51), postage extra; administration time not reported; John C. Raven; H. K. Lewis & Co. Ltd. *

REFERENCES
1. KALDEGG, A. "Responses of German and English Secondary School Boys to a Projection Test." *Brit J Psychol* 39:30–53 S '48. * (*PA* 24:1141)
2. RAVEN, J. C. "Establishing Typical and A-Typical Responses to a Controlled Projection Test." Abstract. *Q B Brit Psychol Soc* 1:186–7 Jl '49. *
3. BAKER, CORINNE F. *An Evaluation of the Raven Controlled Projection Test: A Multi-Technique Study.* Doctor's thesis, Western Reserve University (Cleveland, Ohio), 1950.
4. FOULDS, G. A. "Characteristic Projection Test Responses

1 SIMON, MARIA D. "Der Children's Apperception Test bei gesunden und gestörten Kindern." *Z diagnos Psychol* 2:195–219 '54.

of a Group of Defective Delinquents." *Brit J Psychol, Gen Sect* 40:124–7 Mr '50. * (*PA* 24:5955)
5. RAVEN, J. C. "The Comparative Assessment of Personality." *Brit J Psychol, Gen Sect* 40:115–23 Mr '50. * (*PA* 24:5879)
6. KALDEGG, A. "A Study of German and English Teacher-Training Students by Means of Projective Techniques." *Brit J Psychol, Gen Sect* 42:56–113 Mr & My '51. * (*PA* 26:550)
7. MARTIN, A. W., AND WEIR, A. J. "A Comparative Study of the Drawings Made by Various Clinical Groups." *J Mental Sci* 97:532–44 Jl '51. * (*PA* 26:2189)
8. ANDERSON, J. W. " 'Controlled Projection' Responses of Delinquent Boys." *J Mental Sci* 100:643–56 Jl '54. * (*PA* 29:4349)

Brit J Ed Psychol 22:221 N '52. This is the second edition of the book first published in 1944. Since then the author has continued work on "Controlled Projection," and this edition takes account of that work and of recent investigations by other psychologists. The appendices contain a great mass of details (responses and reactions, etc.) by 150 school children and 80 children visiting Child Guidance Clinics. The author disclaims any pretence to give a comprehensive account of personality or of its measurement, but seeks chiefly to describe the technique and show its uses for genetic, social and clinical psychology.

Brit J Psychol 44:272 Ag '53. R. W. Pickford. * The test forms a useful method of research into the social attitudes, habits and personal relationships of children, and for examination of children for clinical purposes. It has been widely used and a number of interesting papers have been published about its application. The present edition is amplified in useful ways and contains some illustrations of children's drawings, beautifully reproduced, two of them in colour, tabulated responses of 150 children of ages 6½, 9½ and 12½ years, and a great amount of other valuable material obtained by the application of the test. *

Psychoanalytic Q 22:589–90 O '53. Geraldine Pederson-Krag. * Ideally the subject's responses are written down by a stenographer so as to allow the testing psychologist unimpeded opportunity to note the subject's behavior, but in practice it seems that the psychologist usually does his own recording. * All terms used are meticulously defined. The logic of the rules for scoring appears to be impeccable. The method seems to fulfil its goal which is to determine the extent to which each child tested resembles others in its group. It can also be used to show similarities and differences among various groups. It is perhaps irrelevant to criticize this book for its failure to reach objectives it does not seek. It may, however, be observed that the concepts and classifications upon which this technique is based are too loose and superficial to be useful to those

schooled in psychoanalysis. Though the material gathered by the spontaneous drawings and the answers to specific questions on intimate subjects is rich, the interpretation given according to the directions cited here is confused and meager.

For reviews by Arthur L. Benton and Percival M. Symonds of the original edition, see 3:29.

[128]
★**Curtis Completion Form.** Grades 11–16 and adults; 1950–53; emotional maturity and adjustment; Form A ('50); manual ('53); $2 per 20 tests; 25¢ per specimen set; postage extra; (45) minutes; James W. Curtis; Science Research Associates. *

REFERENCE
1. WATSON, WALTER S. "The Validity of the Curtis Completion Form as a Predictor of College Student Personality Deviates." *Yearb Nat Council Meas Used Ed* 12(pt 2):82–5 '55. *

ALFRED B. HEILBRUN, JR., *Assistant Professor of Psychology, State University of Iowa, Iowa City, Iowa.*

This 52-item sentence completion test combines features of both objective and projective personality measures. The first 50 items are in the form characteristic of the usual completion task: set-producing words followed by space for the free response. Items 51 and 52 are more highly structured but still allow the subject to formulate his own answer. Space is provided at the end of the form for remarks which the subject considers important.

Although the item format does not differ much from that of many other published sentence completion tests, the *Curtis Completion Form* retains some individuality in the manner in which the items were developed and the way in which they are scored. Evaluation of the responses is partially objective, making possible the derivation of a cumulative point score which serves as the primary basis for personality inferences. This contrasts with the usual method in which the examiner makes his appraisal of the responder through more intuitive clinical judgments of the free responses. Each item is given a score of 2, 1, or 0, with a higher score indicative of poorer emotional adjustment. Two points are assigned to responses characterized by antagonism, suspicion, jealousy, self-pity or pessimism, insecurity, social inadequacy, environmental deprivation, or severe conflict (Group A factors). Unclear, incomplete, or avoidant sentences (Group B factors) receive a score of 1, as do responses containing erasures, crossed-out content, or emphatic punctuation (Group C factors). The remarks section at the end is evaluated for Group A factors only, and a 4-point weight is assigned if any are judged to be present. Curtis reports rather high agreement when pairs of judges scored independently the same tests; interjudge correlations ranged from .89 to .95.

The only validation data which could be found are those reported in the manual. The following mean scores were obtained for three groups rated as showing substantial differences in adjustment by clinical personnel: normals, 22.6; neurotics, 37.0; and psychotics, 49.5. These results, if replicable, would lend a great deal of confidence to the use of the instrument in making this kind of gross discrimination.

Even though it is designed primarily for educational and industrial use, there is nothing about the test which precludes a wider range of application. The reported low correlation with intelligence, .09, is advantageous in this kind of measure. On the other hand, some caution is suggested by the split-half reliability coefficient of .83 which is not out of line with most personality measures but still leaves something to be desired. There is much in the development and limited validational data to recommend the clinical and research use of the *Curtis Completion Form,* but as with all new psychometric procedures reasonable caution should be maintained until further studies substantiate its effectiveness.

[129]

★Draw-A-Person Quality Scale. Ages 16–25; 1955; level of intellectual functioning; 1 form; $2 per manual, postpaid; [10–20] minutes; Mazie Earle Wagner and Herman J. P. Schubert; Herman J. P. Schubert, 500 Klein Road, Route 2, Buffalo 21, N.Y. *

REFERENCES

1. WAGNER, MAZIE EARLE, AND SCHUBERT, HERMAN J. P. "Figure Drawing Norms, Reliability, and Validity Indices for Normal Late-Adolescents: II, Development of a Pictorial Scale of DAP Quality." Abstract. *Am Psychol* 10:321 Ag '55. *
2. SCHUBERT, HERMAN J. P., AND WAGNER, MAZIE EARLE. "Deviant Perspective of DAP Figures Associated With Other Deviant Behavior." Abstract. *Am Psychol* 12:409–10 Jl '57. *
3. WAGNER, MAZIE EARLE, AND SCHUBERT, HERMAN J. P. "Atypical DAP Page Placement as an Indication of Atypical Behavior." Abstract. *Am Psychol* 12:389 Jl '57. *

PHILIP L. HARRIMAN, *Professor of Psychology, Bucknell University, Lewisburg, Pennsylvania.*

The authors evidently regard the Goodenough draw-a-man scale as meritorious but atomistic. It can be inferred that they also believe that the Machover technique does not fill the need for a "global test"—a drawing test in which the total final impression is rated. The Wagner-Schubert scale requires two drawings, one of each sex, which are rated in terms of a seven-point quality scale. Any production which emphasizes such details as toe nails, genitalia, or other representations indicating mental disturbances is arbitrarily relegated to Quality 8. Attention is concentrated upon qualities ranging from artistic, life-like human figures (Scale Value 1) to figures which are barely recognizable as human beings (Scale Value 7). Additional gradations at 0 and 8 are also described for productions as superior or inferior in quality that they are almost never found in "normal populations."

Guidance in estimating the quality of the productions is given by four series of rated pictorial specimens, front view and side view each for male and female. These typical drawings were chosen from 1,579 specimens collected from normal late adolescents and college students. In fact, this scale purports to deal only with gradations in the quality of drawings done by normal young persons. It also purports to furnish a basis for a quantification of the rater's impressionistic evaluation of each production. The authors imply that the numerical score on this test is a reasonably useful measure of academic aptitude for college work.

Obviously, the test has merit as a measure of aptitude for freehand drawing of the human figure. The authors, however, are most impressed with its use as a predictor of marks in a teachers college. Though they strive to maintain an austere point of view regarding clinical insights, they make one interesting comment of an intuitive nature. High-quality productions, they observe, may indicate conformity behavior, and college teachers—in some places, at least—regard it by assigning high marks. Caricatures of the human figure, as well as drawings of a figure with a glass in hand, are said to presage low marks at the end of the term. Steig and Adams, rated by this scale, would stand little chance for success in the elementary-education curriculum where this test was standardized.

Young adults who are facile in drawing the human figure are not dolts. Consequently, it occasions no surprise to find that many who achieve a high rating on this scale are also successful in a teachers college. This association between freehand-drawing quality and marks at the end of one term in a teachers college is to be expected. The fact, once admitted, does not obviate the need for the College Board or the American Council tests as the appropriate predictors. This initial and exploratory report on some in-

teresting research, however, is a rather important supplement to draw-a-person techniques.
This reviewer wishes that the authors had not
imposed upon themselves a rigid hostility
towards clinical intuitions. It does seem a bit
doubtful whether they have succeeded in "bringing back the drawing-of-a-person into the focus
of attention of those who wish to predict human
behavior."

A considerable amount of study would be required to develop a coherent and tenable theory
for this test. Its publication at this time seems
to be premature. In cases where human welfare
is involved, the *Draw-A-Person Quality Scale*
is contraindicated. The hackneyed phrase of
many other reviewers of novel projective techniques is pertinent here: Much further research
should be done.

[130]

★**The Drawing-Completion Test: A Projective
Technique for the Investigation of Personality.**
Ages 5 and over; 1952; based on *Wartegg Test Blank;*
1 form ['52]; manual (see *1* below); no data on re-
liability; $3 per 100 tests; $3 per 100 profiles ['52];
$7.50 per manual; postage extra; (15–40) minutes; G.
Marian Kinget; Grune & Stratton, Inc. *

REFERENCES

1. KINGET, G. MARIAN. *The Drawing-Completion Test: A
Projective Technique for the Investigation of Personality Based
on the Wartegg Test Blank.* New York: Grune & Stratton,
Inc., 1952. Pp. xv, 238. * (PA 27:430)
2. OLSON, JOHN T. *The Test-Retest Reliability of the Kinget
Drawing-Completion Test.* Master's thesis, Fresno State Col-
lege (Fresno, Calif.), 1956.
3. KINGET, G. MARIAN. Chap. 15, "The Drawing Completion
Test," pp. 344–64. In *The Clinical Application of Projective
Techniques.* Edited by Emanuel F. Hammer. Springfield, Ill.:
Charles C Thomas, 1958. Pp. xxii, 663. *

*Am J Psychol 66:669–70 O '53. John P.
Foley, Jr.* * No objective norms are reported.
In discussing the interpretation of scores,
Kinget reverts to the usual vague and subjective statements which have plagued most projective tests for many years. The validation
sample is described as consisting of 383 adults,
between the ages of 18 and 50; presumably, all
were Europeans. The criterion data were obtained by: (1) a self-report inventory, (2) a
forced-choice test, and (3) a rating scale filled
out by friends and acquaintances of the *S*s. One
searches in vain for an adequate report of the
procedures employed in analyzing these data.
Despite Symonds' statement, in the *Foreword,*
that he is impressed by "the criterion against
which she determined the significance of each
element of the drawings" (p. v), no objective
method is described whereby the criterion status
of each *S* was determined. After pointing out
(p. 21) that there was considerable lack of
agreement among the three criterion measures,

Kinget rejected any attempt to arrive at a
composite criterion in favor of a criterion based
upon "the main trends manifested" in the three
criterion measures. There is no indication of the
degree of consistency necessary to constitute a
"main trend." Here, then, we are confronted
with a highly subjective instrument. Until such
time as more objective scoring procedures are
developed, and until the validity of the test has
been more clearly established, it is virtually
worthless as a measuring instrument. For these
reasons, the unqualified and popularized account
of this test in such a magazine as *Life* (June 9,
1952, p. 65 ff.) would seem to be premature and
misleading.

*B Menninger Clinic 17:114 My '53. Walter
Kass.* Similar to the Horn-Hellersberg method,
this projective drawing completion technique is
briefer (containing only 8 stimulus frames),
easier therefore to administer, and also more
readily interpretable according to the rationale
supplied by the author. It is offered as a means
of analyzing certain structural and functional
aspects of personality. Since psychopathologic
conditions were not included in its validation, it
is not immediately applicable as a clinical test.
But, as with other drawing products, diagnostic
inferences are possible. The ingenuity of its
small graphic stimulus elements, the brevity of
its format, and the richness of the productions it
elicits, presage a popularity for this test as a research instrument applicable to clinical populations.

*J Ed Psychol 44:251–3 Ap '53. Goldine C.
Gleser.* * It is particularly gratifying to note that
the scoring for the Drawing-completion test
was established on the basis of an investigation
of three hundred eighty-three "normal" subjects, divided about equally between the sexes,
and ranging in age from eighteen to fifty years.
A three-fold criterion was used, consisting of a
questionnaire, a forced-choice test, and a rating
scale, all designed expressly to measure the psychological functions represented in the personality schema. However, apparently the author
has employed the questionable expedient of
using the same data both for validation of the
test and for subsequent changes and elaboration
of the scoring system. Thus the diagnostic value
of the final scoring variables as presented in this
book cannot be considered to have been validated. Part two of the book, entitled "The Diagnostic Mechanism," presents the method of administration, the basis for interpretation, and

the scoring procedure for the test. This is the most extensive portion of the book. Each scoring category is defined and discussed in terms of the personality characteristics which it is claimed that it reveals or indicates. In these interpretations, the author appears to have allowed her enthusiasm to carry her far beyond the personality schema previously presented. * The author is to be congratulated for having designed a projective test which can be scored on objective criteria and for having attempted to establish the scoring on the basis of experimental evidence. However, as a test manual, this book leaves much to be desired. At least three major omissions make it impossible to evaluate the usefulness of the test, or to take advantage of the underlying experimental data in utilizing the test. In the first place, almost no statistical data are presented; in fact, the only results presented from the experimental study are the percentages of agreement between the three-fold criterion and the drawing test on three of the four functions measured. It appears from the text that the stated agreement was computed solely on the relative weight of the polar aspects of these functions; i.e., whether the person was more outgoing than seclusive, etc. However, it is impossible to ascertain the exact method by which the results were obtained, or their statistical significance. The only facts which are evident are that there was a greater amount of agreement among the tests for the females than for the males, and for both sexes the validity was lower for Emotion and Activity than for Intellect. Considering the enormous amount of work which has evidently gone into the investigation of relationships between personality and drawing characteristics, it is unfortunate that the author did not deem it practical to present a more complete summary of results in this manual, nor make it available in published form elsewhere. The second omission is that the author has made no attempt to provide any norms for the profile scores. She excuses this omission on the ground that "free drawings, like all products of creative activity, do not permit establishment of rigorous norms." However, in the case studies remarks such as the following are made: "The degree of Emotion and Imagination exhibited here is exceptional for a male, though admissible at the age level of A." It is evident that without some idea of what is "normal" for a given age and sex it would be difficult to draw such conclusions, and hence norms are implied

even though they are not presented. Lastly, no data are presented regarding the reliability of the external criteria used in developing the qualitative interpretations of the various scoring categories. This is particularly important, since these interpretations were derived from study of clusters of items and even differential responses to single items in the criterion tests (page 24). As a preliminary manual to aid in the attainment of standard administration and scoring procedures and some common basis of interpretation this book should be of service to those who may wish to do research on this test. However, it is hoped that other material in the form of norms and validity data will soon be made available to aid the clinician in his interpretation of the drawings and his evaluation of the usefulness of the test.

J Proj Tech 17:367–8 S '53. Fred Brown. * Much work and thought have gone into the construction and validation of this test, but the psychodynamically oriented and sophisticated clinician will be disappointed with a technique which follows an outmoded typology. The author states that it is not her intention to offer a depth exploring instrument, but the critical reader will then wonder why she uses the term "diagnosis" so often. Psychoanalytically trained clinicians, accustomed and attuned to the depth implications of other methods, will look in vain for the dynamic material which gives diagnosis as such its intrinsic significance. They will find, instead, diffuse categorizations, trait-name listings, and philosophically attenuated descriptions which possess only the remotest significance for an integrated diagnostic formulation. One would be inclined to take issue with the typological schema itself as a base of operations, especially when it is noted that the author herself seems to be committed to unconfirmed generalizations and stereotypes (e.g., "The remaining stimuli....have the round and supple character of the organic world which generally appeals more to the predominantly emotional-imaginative character of the feminine mind," p. 125). Such terms as "nature-relatedness," "life-relatedness," and "esthetic-emotional" would seem to have slight value for the clinician who maintains a psychologist-psychiatrist relationship and who is interested in delineating the personality and character structure in terms of psychosexual levels, areas of arrest and/or regression, predominant figures, defenses, conflicts, and diagnostic formulation. Study of the case illustrations makes one doubt whether the results of a very detailed, highly refined, and time-consuming evaluative procedure are sufficiently rewarding. At the very least, the personality profiles impress one as markedly intellectualistic and over-abstract. The author is undoubtedly familiar with other projective methods and the current trend in American psychiatry and clinical psychology. Her orientation in this work does not reflect this knowledge. Apart from these criticisms, the psychologist who works with graphic projective and expressive techniques will find much that is thought-provoking in the author's detailed explanations of her variables. Shrewd insights, based upon the structural aspects of the drawings, may well be utilized in the interpretation of other drawing tests. But while the Drawing-Completion Test has heuristic and research potentialities, its immediate acceptance as a member of the practicing psychologist's test battery is contraindicated by its narrow and obsolete typological foundation.

[131]

★The Eight Card Redrawing Test (8CRT). Ages 7 and over; 1950–57; 1 form ('56); directions for administering ('56); no data on reliability; no norms; $6 per set of test materials; $4.50 per manual ('57, see 5 below); postpaid; (30–60) minutes; Leopold Caligor; 8CRT. *

REFERENCES

1. CALIGOR, LEOPOLD. *The Determination of the Individual's Unconscious Conception of His Own Masculinity-Femininity Identification.* Doctor's thesis, New York University (New York, N.Y.), 1950. (*Microfilm Abstr* 10:292)
2. CALIGOR, LEOPOLD. "The Determination of the Individual's Unconscious Conception of His Own Masculinity-Femininity Identification." *J Proj Tech* 15:494–509 D '51. * (*PA* 26:6228)
3. CALIGOR, LEOPOLD. "The Detection of Paranoid Trends by the Eight Card Redrawing Test." *J Clin Psychol* 8:397–401 O '52. * (*PA* 27:5861)
4. CALIGOR, LEOPOLD. "Quantification on the Eight Card Redrawing Test (8CRT)." *J Clin Psychol* 9:356–61 O '53. * (*PA* 28:4338)
5. CALIGOR, LEOPOLD. *A New Approach to Figure Drawing: Based Upon an Interrelated Series of Drawings.* Springfield, Ill.: Charles C Thomas, 1957. Pp. xii, 149. * (*PA* 31:7902)
6. HAMMER, EMANUEL F., EDITOR. *The Clinical Application of Projective Drawings*, pp. 418–34, 459–70, passim. Springfield, Ill.: Charles C Thomas, 1958. Pp. xxii, 663. *

CHERRY ANN CLARK, *The Meyers Clinic, Los Angeles, California.*

The *Eight Card Redrawing Test* (8 CRT) is another variation on the projective method of figure drawing. The test requires the subject to draw successively eight human figures, using a special drawing pad in which a blank cardboard is interleafed to block from the subject's view all but the immediately preceding drawing. *A New Approach to Figure Drawing* is not a formal test manual, but the author does refer to it as a manual in his development of the scoring rules. Caligor writes that the book is intended "(1) to describe each of the test's scoring di-

mensions in detail; (2) to formulate a tentative definition of each dimension's personality implications, and (3) to demonstrate to the experienced clinician how the integration of the presently delineated structural dimensions and cumulative, interrelated graphic content can yield a personality picture."

Over a period of about 10 years Caligor has evolved a rather complex scoring system to analyze the structural aspects of the series of eight interrelated figure drawings. He asserts that his method of analysis leads to more stable test-retest evaluation than does content analysis of drawings. The assertion seems plausible, but the available evidence is unconvincing.

Caligor attempted to demonstrate the interscorer reliability of three trained judges, using an inspection technique to diagnose paranoid schizophrenic characteristics in drawings done by hospitalized paranoid schizophrenics. Using but one drawing per subject, the judges found 25 per cent of them showing strong paranoid trends; using the 8 CRT, the same judges found 85 per cent showing paranoid trends. With no further support than this single inadequate instance, the author writes, "This study affirmed that the 8 CRT could prove valuable to the clinician, especially within the context of a battery of tests."

As a demonstration that the 8 CRT lends itself to objective quantification, Caligor cites two examples: drawings can be scored for sex of figure and its physical maturity, placing the subject on a 7-point scale ranging from adult identification with one's own sex through infantile undifferentiated sexual identification to adult identification with the opposite sex. On the basis of the evidence, the validity of these claims is unsupported.

Equally unconvincing is the evidence offered for the relevance of the scoring system. Using "clinical experience and pilot studies," the author devised deviation scores "from a statistical norm approximating the mode scores of normal subjects." The scoring system thus devised was found to differentiate satisfactorily college students (with scores ranging from 0 to 6) from hospitalized schizophrenic patients (with scores ranging from 6 to 66).

These three studies which allegedly demonstrate the psychodiagnostic merits of the techniques are unacceptable evidence beyond the level of clinical intuition.

Caligor describes in detail the scoring dimensions. Dimensions are scored in three groups: along a graded scale, by placement within one of a group of categories, and for presence or absence. Among the dimensions scored are part-whole relations, height of figure, page placement, head and body direction, sex, physical maturity, erasures, line quality, symmetry, eyes, and omissions. Four masks for scoring body angle, figure placement and symmetry are included among the test materials.

The scoring system based upon the successive, interrelated sampling of performance on figure drawings is an ingenious one, but the reviewer questions the relevance and practicality of the procedure after repeated failures to maintain patients' cooperation for the complete administration of the test. In an informal study, no better planned than those reported by Caligor, the reviewer failed to gain agreement of even two out of five clinical psychologists in scoring the protocols of 11 willing subjects on two or more dimensions within any set of drawings.

As a diagnostic technique the 8 CRT has scarcely got off the drawing board. In the reviewer's mind it cannot be said to meet even minimal standards of test development for psychodiagnostic techniques. Only three studies of a decidedly clinical and intuitive nature are reported in the book. These studies are interesting as far as they go, but the adequacy of the experimental methodology employed in them is questionable. The clinical inferences Caligor makes from the three case presentations are probably as legitimate as other informal case study evaluations. Far more questions and issues are raised than are met in the book. One may philosophize that there is room for every effort of any kind in a clinician's armamentarium, but clinical procedures must not be confused with the goals of formal assessment and measurement of human behavior.

PHILIP L. HARRIMAN, *Professor of Psychology, Bucknell University, Lewisburg, Pennsylvania.*

The Caligor extension of the draw-a-person technique in psychodiagnostics has two original features.

The first feature is the ingenious method of obtaining an interrelated series of eight drawings of the human figure. The subject is instructed by the examiner to draw a whole person. After the drawing has been completed, the examiner rolls a sheet of thin paper over it, and instructs the subject again to draw a whole person. After the second drawing has been finished, a cardboard insert is placed over the first drawing and the instructions are repeated. The process is continued until eight drawings have been done, in each instance only the immediately preceding figure being exposed under the onionskin sheet added seriatim. Hence, Caligor's technique is appropriately labeled the 8CRT, or the *Eight Card Redrawing Test*.

The second feature is the elaborate attempt to develop an objective scoring plan. Explicit instructions are given for scoring in terms of 23 major dimensions. There being eight drawings, and provision having been made for some trend analysis, the score blank includes more than 200 cells. These symbolic data, properly entered on the blank, make an impressive appearance. A novice in the 8CRT recalls nostalgically the Klopfer-Davidson scoring blank for the Rorschach, which is rather similar in general plan. Though it is most commendable to objectify the scoring of a draw-a-person series, the reviewer is perplexed about Caligor's reasons for a choice of "dimensions." Further publications are to be expected, however, and this issue may be more fully discussed later on.

The interpretations of the dimensions, following Caligor's intuitive understandings and clinical experience, are quite interesting. They are expounded with assurance and made plausible by three sample records analyzed by the author. By this time, most students of psychology are familiar with the glib, winsome styles used by enthusiastic proponents of ingenuous, and ingenious, expressive drawing techniques. Here, through a minor lapse, Caligor interrupts the student's trance by alluding to "lowered critical and corrective faculties." Quite acceptable as a literary term, "faculties" may have been the result here of a purposive accident. The directions for interpreting the interrelated series of drawings may, indeed, be intended, not as an empirical-clinical exposition, but as literature. If so, a Titchener would genially but forcefully exclaim, "Verboten!" were a candidate for a degree to propose to write a term paper incorporating 8CRT results.

Even though the objective scores might lend themselves to impressive charts and tabular arrays of data, and even though the interpretations were couched in the style of a Walter Pater, it is doubtful whether any academic psychologist would regard this test, and other diagnostic draw-a-person techniques, seriously. Challenging, novel, fun to try out in a class, helpful in keeping a pedagogue's intellectual joints supple—yes, such techniques cannot be disregarded as literary psychology. As for tangible evidence to substantiate the admirable enthusiasms of those who make them up, these psychodiagnostic techniques are still in the ovum stage of development. Caligor's technique is not an exception. Yet he toiled valiantly for more than a decade, and a reviewer feels chastened not to be able to recommend this test as the royal road to a valid diagnosis of personality.

Brit J Psychol 48:319–20 N '57. H. C. Gunzburg. * The new technique is intriguing—the subject goes from one drawing to the next whilst the preceding drawing is visible to him through the transparent paper; he may trace it and virtually repeat it, modify it or ignore it completely. His handling of this situation, as well as the various details of the drawing, the placement and line quality are considered valid diagnostic clues. Dr Caligor provides a scoring system based on objectively scorable dimensions and attains a high interscores agreement. The scores are stated "in terms of a deviation from a statistical norm approximately the mode scores of normal subjects." Unfortunately the book contains no statistical material and the only relevant reference given by the author refers to a study of items differentiating between 21 college males and 21 hospitalized paranoid schizophrenics—this could scarcely be called a normative study serving as a basis for a complete test manual to be used in clinical practice. Even more disappointing is the systematic list of suggested interpretations for the various scoring categories which are, no doubt, based on wide clinical experience, but which would be more convincing and valid if supported by some evidence. Though Dr Caligor's technique shares this fault with the systems devised by his predecessors, one feels that nowadays, having demonstrated the wealth of clinical material obtainable from drawings, investigators should approach this field more systematically and not by-pass such important factors as sex, age, intelligence, cultural background, etc. In the meantime, this new publication's main merit is the presentation of a novel and promising projective technique and of a scoring method which may well be used for testing experimentally the validity of drawing interpretations.

[132]

★Family Relations Test: An Objective Technique for Exploring Emotional Attitudes in Children. Ages 3–7, 7–15; 1957; individual; 1 form ['57]; 2 levels; 132s. per set of test materials; 12s. 9d. per manual; postpaid within the United Kingdom; (20–25) minutes; Eva Bene and James Anthony; distributed by National Foundation for Educational Research in England and Wales. *

a) YOUNGER CHILDREN. Ages 3–7; 40 item cards; 3s. 6d. per 10 record booklets ['57].

b) OLDER CHILDREN. Ages 7–15; 86 item cards; 3s. 6d. per 10 record booklets; 2s. 9d. per 10 scoring blanks.

REFERENCE

1. ANTHONY, E. J., AND BENE, EVA. "A Technique for the Objective Assessment of the Child's Family Relationships." *J Mental Sci* 103:541–55 Jl '57. *

JOHN E. BELL, *Acting Chief, Mental Health Services, United States Public Health Service, San Francisco, California.*

The test materials consists of 20 cardboard figures representing people of various ages from babyhood to old age. These are relatively ambiguous and permit a child to select figures to represent each member of his family including himself. In addition, a figure standing for "Nobody" is included in the materials. The figures are attached to cardboard boxes with slots in the top. In the form for children 8 years old and above there are 86 cards containing statements reflecting feelings of like and dislike, stronger feelings of love and hate, and attitudes relating to parental overprotection and overindulgence. In the form for younger children there are 40 similar cards.

After selecting figures to represent his own family, the child places each card in a box behind the figure for which the statement is most appropriate. If the statement applies to none, it is deposited in the box attached to "Nobody." The child's test performance is tallied on a scoring sheet; evaluation of the results and behavior notes are entered on a separate record sheet.

The distinct advantage of the test is its relative objectivity. There are a limited number of standardized responses that can be made in the test situation. This permits a formal analysis to be undertaken and facilitates the establishing of norms and the conducting of statistical studies of the test performance with various subjects under different conditions. Little research with the technique is presently available.

The test is subtitled "An Objective Technique for Exploring Emotional Attitudes in Children." Its objectivity is, however, only partial. The test involves a rather complex set of choices. Each card may apply to one family member other than the self, several family members other than the self, the self alone, the self along with one or more other family members, or nobody. Functionally, the child has to hold in mind all these possibilities and make appropriate choices for each item in terms of them. It may appear that the full range of possible responses is considered each time, but this demands that attention to the instructions has been of a high quality and that memory for them and a set for carrying them out are kept alive. Thus, while the actual manipulation of the cards engenders objectivity, the task itself is sufficiently complex that one may not be sure that the test conditions are comparable from one subject to another, or from one testing to another with the same subject. This has real importance, since the deductions about the performance are based on tallies of the responses without regard to the quality of the subject's attention and memory, his conceptual ability, and the processes by which he makes decisions.

An additional factor confounding the results grows out of the implicit assumption that the task of perceiving the self in the family situation is comparable to the task of perceiving the other. In practice, different processes are involved in evaluating the pertinence of the test items to the self than in assessing their relevance to others. The value of the test figures of other members of the family for symbolizing those individuals differs from the value of the self figure for personifying the self. In the former instances there is a closer parallel between the object nature of the test figure and the family member; in the latter instance there is a subject-object confusion in the approach to the figure and variability in the amount of distance of the self as embodied there. It might be constructive, then, to test the comparability of performances when the self-figure is included and excluded. The test items would not seem to lend themselves especially well to a test of reactions to the self where the simple choice of "applies" or "does not apply" would be required of the child, although this might be examined.

It is apparent that actualizing the family members by the pictures, concretizing the test task by placing items in the slots, and limiting the responses by standardized items represent a new combination of features in attitude testing. The clinical illustrations in the manual

demonstrate that the test has real merit for rapid assessment of latent and overt attitudes to the family. It does not permit discrimination between the felt and the expressed attitudes, but it reduces the range of observations required additionally to produce a realistic picture of family relations.

DALE B. HARRIS, *Professor of Psychology, and Director, Institute of Child Development and Welfare, University of Minnesota, Minneapolis, Minnesota.*

This is an ingenious projective "test" which records the subject's reactions through the sorting of cards on which stimulus items appear. Thus it has the virtue of presenting identical stimulus material to all subjects while preserving some of the flexibility considered essential to projective devices. The emphasis, however, is on the reaction to the items printed on cards. The schematic human figures are primarily vehicles to facilitate the child's reaction to the content of the printed items; they are not designed to elicit elaborate fantasy. The authors believe this technique appeals directly to the child's interest in manipulating materials and his tendencies to respond covertly, and to express emotion through play. The items are presented to the child after he has identified the members of his own family circle from among the role figures.

The items devised for older children are of this type: "This person in the family is sometimes a bit too fussy." Items are grouped into several categories as follows: mild positive (affectionate) feelings coming from the child, strong positive (sexualized) feelings coming the child, mild negative feelings coming from the child (the example above is taken from this category), and strong negative (hostile) feelings coming from the child. Four additional groups of items in the same patterns of affect represent feelings going *towards* the child. An example of the fourth type of feeling toward the child is "This person in the family hits me a lot." Three additional groups of items represent maternal over-protection, paternal overindulgence, and maternal overindulgence.

The items for young children are expressed more simply and represent five classes only: positive and negative feelings coming from the child, positive and negative feelings going toward the child, and dependence. "N....[name of child subject] wants you to tuck him (her) into bed at night. Who should tuck N....in at night?" represents this last category.

In theory the test helps the child express conscious attitudes, including those very private feelings which he would find difficult to state directly. The test admittedly does not investigate unconscious attitudes. The authors believe, however, that it is important to investigate the child's phenomenal world, or as they speak of it, his "psychic reality."

Scoring is accomplished by tallying the items assigned to particular role figures, excluding the items assigned to "Nobody." The balance among proportions of items in the several degrees and directions of affect assigned to the several family roles provides the basis for interpretation. The manual offers profiles for a number of briefly described examples in each of the following personality patterns: idealizing tendency, paranoid tendency, and egocentric states, both auto-aggressive and auto-erotic. Other dynamic mechanisms revealed by the use of items include reaction formation, projection, regression, displacement, idealization and denial. The authors attach considerable significance to the child's selection and treatment of significant figures, to his deviation from a theoretical frequency of items expected to be assigned to the usual family roles, to the balance he achieves between self love and self hate items (which indicates his egocentric state), to the relationship between positive and negative outgoing and positive and negative incoming affect items used by the child (which indicates his ambivalence, or lack of it, toward family figures).

The authors rest the case for the test's validity on the concept of construct validity, on comparison of test results with extensive case history material for several small groups of children (which showed considerable correspondence), on comparisons of results of mutual feelings reported in sets of siblings, where agreement of 64 per cent satisfied the 5 per cent level of confidence, and on the congruence of test findings with predictions made independently from psychiatric diagnoses in several small samples of cases. Some data are quoted to show that results are independent of the sex of the examiner. Split-half reliabilities for combinations of affect categories vary from .68 to .90, number of cases not reported.

As is frequently the case with tests of this type, no norms are given beyond a few illustrative cases and interpretations: The test is ingenious and simple, and the questions are phrased in children's language and represent common personal and family experiences; none are too threatening, on the surface at least. The device of sending "messages" should appeal to many children; the test certainly deserves further study.

Arthur R. Jensen, *USPHS Research Fellow, Institute of Psychiatry, University of London, London, England.*

The *Family Relations Test* (FRT) is a semistandardized play situation which permits the child to express his emotional attitudes toward members of his family and the attitudes he believes that members of his family have toward him.

The test materials consist of 20 cardboard figures "representing people of various ages, shapes, and sizes, sufficiently stereotyped to stand for members of any child's family, yet ambiguous enough to become, under suggestion, a specific family." Each figure is attached to a red cardboard box into which can be inserted small cards which bear various expressions of attitudes: positive feelings, negative feelings, dependence, maternal overprotection, and paternal overindulgence, some expressed as emanating from the child toward family figures and some expressed as emanating from family figures toward the child. There are two sets of cards, 40 for use with younger children and 86 for use with older children.

The subject is asked to select from the 20 figures a figure to represent each member of his family, including himself. Another figure, Nobody, is introduced by the examiner to receive those attitudes which the child will not assign to any member of the family. The statement on each card is then read aloud by the examiner and the card given to the child, who is instructed to deposit it in the box attached to the family figure to whom it best applies. If the statement does not fit anybody, the card is put in Nobody. If the statement fits several people, the examiner makes a note of it. The cards are collected from the boxes and are tabulated on a special scoring form, the scoring consisting of counting the number of items of each kind of feeling assigned by the child to each member of his family. The test takes between 20 and 25 minutes to administer.

The test would seem to have possibilities, considering that there are few, if any, other objective techniques which serve the functions for which it is designed and that projective techniques are of doubtful validity. A good deal of clinical wisdom as well as an accumulation of experience with the FRT would, however, seem to be necessary for making judicious interpretations from the test material. Unfortunately neither the manual nor the one article (1) on the test presents any normative data. Apparently the test has never been given to normal children; at least, only clinical patients are described in the reports of the test's use. The evidence for the test's validity is too meagre and unsystematic to provide an adequate basis for evaluation. From a statistical point of view the reliability evidence is not impressive. Also some of the statistical procedures and computations in the manual and the article are both inappropriate and incorrect. For example, a 2×2 contingency table is presented in the manual (p. 48) as evidence of a significant relationship between an independent rating and the FRT regarding sibling conflicts. The "measure of agreement" is given as 64 per cent. When the appropriate test, chi square, is performed, however, it shows the results to be quite nonsignificant ($\chi^2 = .292$). In another instance (p. 46) the authors have slighted the actual significance of their data. Simply dividing the sum of the diagonal frequencies of the contingency table by the total frequencies, the authors report 64 per cent agreement and state that this result is significant at the 5 per cent level. The 5 per cent significance level was probably based on a chi square test (not given by the authors), but actually the chi square is significant at the 5 per cent level only if it is interpreted as a one-tailed test, a rather unusual procedure in the case of chi square. A more appropriate test of the significance of these data is by means of a test of trend,[1] a more refined and powerful test than chi square. When a test of trend was performed, the results show a relationship significant beyond the o.1 per cent level.

The FRT may be a potentially useful test in the clinic, though this still remains to be demonstrated; at present it must be regarded as being in the trial stage. It can be recommended for use by those who are primarily interested in investigating the test itself. It is not a finished product about which there is sufficient informa-

1 ARMITAGE, P. "Tests for Linear Trends in Proportions and Frequencies." *Biometrics* 11:375–86 S '55. *

tion to warrant its being recommended for routine clinical assessment of child-family relationships.

[133]
★The Five Task Test: A Performance and Projective Test of Emotionality, Motor Skill and Organic Brain Damage. Ages 8 and over; 1955; 1 form; mimeographed manual; no data on reliability; $15 per set of test materials; $3 per manual; postpaid; (15–20) minutes; Charlotte Buhler and Kathryn Mandeville; Western Psychological Services. *

DOROTHY H. EICHORN, *Assistant Research Psychologist, Institute of Child Welfare, University of California, Berkeley, California.*

Adequacy of standardization varies with the subtest, category of scoring, and age group. The first three tasks—cutting out a circle, heart, and star—are scored for "quality" ("edge-cutting," "form-cutting," and "symmetry") and "quantity" (number of scraps). "Quality" scores measure "manual dexterity," "artistic ability," and "level of aspiration." "Quantity" scores indicate "emotionality." These tasks have been administered to 327 Viennese girls aged 8–15 years, 233 parochial school children from one American city, 141 public school children from two cities, and 30 adults. However, the only statistical data reported for the "quality" scores are the means for 134 boys and 145 girls, aged 8–13 years, drawn from the American samples. Validation of the "quantity" scores as an indication of "emotionality" consists of one table listing the per cent of each of three "adjustmental" groups (good, average, and poor) producing 15 or more scraps. Adjustment was rated by teachers. The sample is some portion of the American groups, but the frequencies from which the percentages were derived are not given.

The fourth task, a projective cutout, has not been standardized.

The fifth task, Terman's ball and field problem, is used to assess "emotionality." Solutions are assigned to one of 10 categories (5 positive and 5 negative or "problematic"). Validation is based primarily on 165 solutions by 157 children, aged 7–15 years—65 by neurotic children and 100 by "emotionally stable" children (25 of high intelligence; 39, average; 24, low; and 12, mentally defective). The proportion of positive solutions was significantly lower for the neurotics than for any of the first three "normal" groups. Mystified that the percentage passing a subtest of the Stanford-Binet should be almost identical for these three groups, the reviewer referred to Buhler's original article.[1] This study includes a table of the number of solutions in the various categories by normals, neurotics, and mental defectives at each of nine age levels. The frequencies within the table do not always sum to the marginal totals, and the marginal totals differ slightly between article and manual. Nevertheless, the reviewer computed tests of the goodness of fit of the age distributions of passes for normals and neurotics against the marginal proportions for the two groups combined. Chi square in each case had a probability of about .60. Further tests revealed that the higher total proportion of passes by normals was due to three age groups (9–10, 10–11, and 11–12 years) where the number of normals passing (33 out of 34) was much larger than at subsequent ages for this subgroup (46–80 per cent) or the same ages for the Stanford-Binet standardization sample (27–47 per cent). The difference between normals and neurotics may be attributable to biased sampling rather than "emotionality." Buhler's article describes the total sample as children tested in her clinics in London and the United States.

Diagnosis of organic brain damage apparently rests on the performance of the 12 mental defectives. Four failures among this group were by children under 10 years. Above 10 years, the proportion passing is higher than for the normals.

The subgroups are further differentiated on the basis of the type of negative solution, e.g., neurotics tend to give "Confused, Involved, and Formalistic" solutions. An incomprehensible table entitled "Independent Values with the Contingency Correlation by Groups" constitutes the evidence. After much experimentation the reviewer found these values to be $(o - e)/e$, not even $(o - e)^2/e$, where o is the observed frequency and e is the expected or theoretical frequency. Without Buhler's article, the bewildered reader cannot compute the contingency coefficient for himself. The contingency table of "problematic" solutions for normals versus neurotics, combining "Borderline" and "Gives Up" solutions to avoid small expected frequencies, yields a chi square with a probability between .20 and .10. The chi square for sex differences on the same categories has a probability between .10 and .05, although sex differences are not claimed to be significant.

1 BUHLER, CHARLOTTE. "The Ball and Field Test as a Help in the Diagnosis of Emotional Difficulties." *Char & Pers* 6:257–73 Je '38. *

The fifth task was also validated against ratings of adjustment. Neither the sample nor the raters are identified, but the proportions passing differ significantly among children rated as making a "good," "average," or "poor" adjustment (n's of 33, 74, and 18 respectively).

With no reliability data (test-retest or rater agreement on "quality" subscores or classification of ball and field solutions) and only meager validation data, this test must be regarded as exploratory. Such data as are available for "quantity" scores on the circle, heart, and star tasks and failure patterns on the ball and field problem are suggestive. These subtests may merit more adequate attempts at standardization. It is doubtful that the "quality" score constitutes a satisfactory measure of "motor skill," since intercorrelations among motor tests have almost uniformly been found to be low.

BERT R. SAPPENFIELD, *Professor of Psychology, Montana State University, Missoula, Montana.*

The subtitle of this test, "A Performance and Projective Test of Emotionality, Motor Skill and Organic Brain Damage," is reminiscent of the medicine show nostrum which promised a cure for every ill. As would be expected, the *Five Task Test* is found wanting when measured against the promise of its subtitle. There are better tests of emotionality, better tests of motor skills, and better tests of organic brain damage (if indeed this one may be regarded as a test of brain damage at all).

Many children, and some adults, will probably find the five tasks interesting to perform. It is to be hoped, however, that performance on them will not be the basis of decisions significantly affecting the futures of persons who take the test.

The *Five Task Test* was designed, it would appear, after accidental observations that performance on tests of "manual skill" (freehand scissors cutting of circle, heart, and star) and of "practical judgment" (Terman's ball-and-field test) was affected by non-intellectual variables. Systematic studies subsequently yielded evidence indicating (a) that the number of scraps produced in cutting the circle, heart, and star was related to rated adjustment level in children, but not related to age, sex, or intelligence level; and (b) that quality ratings of the cut-out circle, heart, and star were related to age of children up to 9 years, but not related to either intelligence level or adjustment level. The fifth task (numbered fourth in sequence of administration), which involves asking the subject to cut out anything he wishes, was apparently added without prior experimental justification.

The test is represented to be applicable to both children and adults, although quality scoring of the circle-heart-star tasks shows no age differentiation after age 9. Interpretations involving the quality score are suggested, without restrictions as to age group or otherwise, on the basis of intuitive hypotheses for which no validity evidence is given in the manual.

Although some of the scores obtainable on the *Five Task Test* would lend themselves to reliability studies, the manual does not provide any evidence concerning reliability or objectivity of scores. Perhaps, in any case, such evidence would be of little value, in view of the fact that data relative to the test's validity are at variance with the authors' suggestion that the test be used, however tentatively, for individual diagnosis. While it is true that the tabular data presented in the manual suggest a positive relationship between number of scraps produced and level of adjustment, and between type of solutions to the ball-and-field task and level of adjustment, these data also indicate that, if cutting scores on these tasks were utilized to predict level of adjustment, the percentage of false diagnoses would be extremely high. It is also worth mentioning that, although cutting scores are prescribed in the manual for dividing subjects into three levels of adjustment, these cutting scores have not been cross validated.

Finally, there is not to be found in the manual any reference to data in support of the assumption that the *Five Task Test* may be used for interpretations concerning the possibility of organic brain damage, in spite of the fact that the subtitle of the test makes such a claim.

In summary, it may be concluded that, although the *Five Task Test* is interesting and somewhat ingenious in its conception, there appears to be little justification for its publication or use as a test.

J Consult Psychol 20:159–60 Ap '56. Laurance F. Shaffer. Buhler's "five tasks" are related performance tests, which are reported to have some relationships to emotionality and organic brain damage. The first three tasks are to cut a circle, a heart, and a star from four-inch

squares of paper. The qualities of the products are rated against scaled specimens, and the number of scraps is counted as a measure of "emotionality." The fourth task is cutting "anything you wish" and is given a projective interpretation. The fifth task, the Terman ball-and-field test, is rated as normal, borderline, or problematic with the aid of scoring specimens. Like many other behavior samples, performance on these tasks may give a sensitive and alert psychologist many clues about a child's typical responses to his world. The evidence supporting these particular tasks as clinical instruments is weak. No data on reliability are given; the very moderate reported validities were tested against inadequately defined criteria. Perhaps the test is worthy of further research; perhaps it will remain a subjective instrument of some value to clinicians who depend on observations and hunches rather than on scores.

[134]

★The Forer Structured Sentence Completion Test. Ages 10–18, adults; 1957; 1 form; separate editions for boys, girls, men, and women; mimeographed manual; no data on reliability; no norms; $4 per set of either 25 tests or 25 record booklets; 75¢ per manual; $8.50 per set of 25 tests, 25 record booklets, and manual; specimen set not available; [30–45] minutes; Bertram R. Forer; Western Psychological Services. *

REFERENCES
1. FORER, BERTRAM R. "A Structured Sentence Completion Test." *J Proj Tech* 14:15–30 Mr '50. * (*PA* 25:665)
2. SHNEIDMAN, EDWIN S. "The Case of Jay: Psychological Test and Anamnestic Data." *J Proj Tech* 16:297–345 S '52. * (*PA* 28:2676)
3. CARR, ARTHUR C. "Intra-Individual Consistency in Response to Tests of Varying Degrees of Ambiguity." *J Consult Psychol* 18:251–8 Ag '54. * (*PA* 29:4041)
4. MEYER, MORTIMER M., AND TOLMAN, RUTH S. "Parental Figures in Sentence Completion Test, in TAT, and in Therapeutic Interviews." Abstract. *J Consult Psychol* 19:170 Je '55. * (*PA* 30:2904)
5. CARR, ARTHUR C. "The Relation of Certain Rorschach Variables to Expression of Affect in the TAT and SCT." *J Proj Tech* 20:137–42 Je '56. * (*PA* 31:4674)

CHARLES N. COFER, *Professor of Psychology, University of Maryland, College Park, Maryland.*

This test consists of 100 incomplete sentences designed to yield diagnostic information of value for therapeutic planning. The forms for men and women are virtually identical except for personal pronouns; the forms for boys and girls differ from those for adults in a number of sentences but closely resemble each other. The sentence stems, supposedly, are sufficiently specific so that the kind of situation to which the completion is being made can be identified with some accuracy.

The 100 sentence stems are allocated to a number of categories. On the record form, for example, the several stems are indicated as pertaining to six types of interpersonal figures (mother, males, females,. groups, father, authority); to wishes; to causes of one's own aggression, anxiety (fear), giving up, failure, guilt, and inferiority feelings; and to reactions to aggression, rejection, failure, responsibility, and school. For each sentence a number of spaces are provided so that the particular completion may be evaluated by a check mark under the appropriate category. For causes of one's own aggression, for example, the examiner may check any one of the following categories as descriptive of a particular completion: unclear, denial, aggression (press), aggression (own), authority, criticism, economic, failure, family, father, females, future, health, inadequacy, males, mother, others' welfare, rejection, physical events, sex. A different but overlapping set of categories is provided for each of the other broad areas (interpersonal figures, wishes, reactions). The record form also provides space for summarizing predominant affective attitudes, for evaluating direction and amount of aggression, and for indicating the total number of items in which affective words are used.

The manual indicates the significance of a variety of reactions, such as omissions, denials, unclear responses, and variations in response length more or less along the lines of "complex" indicators in free word association. A number of other comments are made like the suggestion that "schizoids" and "compulsives" will show few affective responses, whereas many will be given by "hysterics" and "hypomanics."

Most of what is said in the manual is plausible, but there is not a shred of evidence that completions to these particular sentences applied to just anybody can or should be validly interpreted in the ways indicated. There are no norms, and neither the word reliability nor the word validity occurs in the manual. This test, if "test" can be appropriately used here, is an open invitation to free clinical speculation. One must take the completions, enter an evaluation in the appropriate space on the record blank, and then compare and contrast, following whatever speculative hunches one may have. We know nothing about what responses are common or unusual or what comparisons and contrasts have validity. Speculation is not objectionable, but it should, in a practical clinical situation, be subject, in the interest of the client, to the constraints provided by norms and the limits of known reliability and validity.

PERCIVAL M. SYMONDS, *Professor of Education, Teachers College, Columbia University, New York, New York.*

For this projective technique there is no evidence as to validity or reliability, and no norms are provided. However, in the judgment of this reviewer these data do not seem to be called for since the test is intended to be used essentially as a clinical or diagnostic instrument.

The author attributes the structured nature of the test to the item arrangement and item form employed. The items, designed to explore a number of predetermined categories, are scattered throughout the test in such a way that the subject is not called upon to respond to items in the same category in sequence; however, the items that furnish evidence for each of the categories are indicated in the checklist and clinical evaluation sheet which accompanies the test. The author uses Item 5 to illustrate how structure is implemented by item form: "When she refused him, he...." The addition of the "he" in this sentence requires that the subject taking the test respond in some way to the refusal of the female in the first part of the sentence. The author calls this an "open-ended attitude test" because of the controls that are used.

There is an excellent manual which describes the test, the categories under which the results may be analyzed, and the uses of the checklist and clinical evaluation folder. Responses are evaluated in terms of interpersonal figures in the subject's life, dominant needs or drives, causes of various personality trends, reactions to interpersonal relationships, predominant emotional attitudes, direction and amount of aggressive tendencies, and total affective level. Special attention is given to those responses which are unclear, which indicate denial, or which have been omitted. The manual also provides a number of general and heuristic hypotheses which may be used as guides in interpreting the sentence completions. As is true with any projective technique, the meaning of the responses cannot be defined unequivocally in a manual; much depends upon the judgment, sagacity, and experience of the test user. The author is quite aware that no response on a projective technique can be interpreted singly, but that it must be looked at in the light of other responses and interpreted in context of other facts known about the subject.

The *Forer Structured Sentence Completion Test* seems to have been constructed with con-

siderable thought and care. It should be serviceable for clinical use within the somewhat narrow limits of any test which yields responses in
terms of isolated sentences.

[135]

★The Forer Vocational Survey. "Young adolescents"; 1957, vocational adjustment; 1 form; separate
editions for men and for women; mimeographed manual; no data on reliability and validity; no norms;
$13.50 per set of either 100 tests or 100 record blanks;
$1.50 per manual; $8 per 25 sets of both editions and
manual; postpaid; specimen set not available; [20–30]
minutes; Bertram R. Forer; Western Psychological
Services. *

BENJAMIN BALINSKY, *Associate Professor of
Psychology, Bernard M. Baruch School of Business and Public Administration, The City College, New York, New York.*

This is a sentence completion test devised to
explore nonintellectual processes related to job
functioning. The forms for men and women
are identical except for the use of she (he) and
her (him). While this practice is apparently
customary for sentence completion tests, there
may be some question as to whether the same
items are equally applicable in vocational situations since differences in attitude between the
sexes toward work and employment conditions
have been found in various studies.

No studies of validity are reported. This is
an oversight that requires remedy as soon as
possible. Authors of other sentence completion
tests, like Rotter (see 156) and Spache (see
142), have attempted studies of validity. The
specific items could have been tested for discriminability if for no other reason than to determine which might be the strongest ones to
include in the test. In a study of the sentence
completion test of the Office of Strategic Services, Stein[1] included measures of an index of
stereotypy and an index of individuality. Those
responses that had high stereotypy, being answered similarly by 50 to 75 per cent of the
sampling, were eliminated. We have no way of
knowing without further research which of
Forer's sentence completion items lend themselves to stereotyped responses.

The test items are structured to a greater extent than is usual in sentence completion tests.
This was done deliberately in order to gain more
specific information about the examinee's reactions to different work conditions and to relationships with others in the work setting. Al-

1 STEIN, MORRIS I. "The Use of a Sentence Completion Test
for the Diagnosis of Personality." *J Clin Psychol* 3:47–56 Ja
'47. * (*PA* 21:2337)

though this may mean a gain in specific information, it may also mean a loss in free expression. However, since the author expects the test
to be used more as an interview aid than as a
test by itself, the answer to any incomplete sentence can be explored more fully in the interview situation.

The selection of items was guided by a rationale that includes three sectors: (*a*) reactions to authorities, co-workers, criticism, failure, taking orders, and responsibility; (*b*)
causes of feelings and actions of aggression,
anxiety, failure, and job change; and (*c*) vocational goals and positive and negative factors
that motivate job satisfaction and vocational
choice. While these three sectors seem to include much that is important in vocational functioning, there are other factors that might have
proved even more significant.

The interpretation of the responses is qualitative, and the proper cautions are advised by the
author. However, he supplies only one sample
protocol and does not give the original responses, only the comments about them. In itself this is not enough. While more detailed interpretational material for this test is given in
the manual for the *Forer Structured Sentence
Completion Test* (see 134), additional samples
are needed in the manual for this test.

As a research instrument or as an aid to the
interview, the *Forer Vocational Survey* will
serve a useful purpose. It does seem to stimulate the expression of clues important to vocational adjustment; however, the counselor must
follow these clues through with other tests and
techniques and not accept them at face value.

CHARLES N. COFER, *Professor of Psychology,
University of Maryland, College Park, Maryland.*

This test consists of 80 incomplete sentences,
designed to get at material relevant to facts concerning "work adjustment, attitudes, interests
and conflicts of use to a vocational counselor or
clinician." Many items explicitly refer to jobs,
such as "Responsibility at work....," "The job
looked impossible, so he (she)...." (the word
"impossible" is misspelled on the form for men
which the reviewer examined). The editions
for men and women differ mainly in the pronouns used in the sentence stems. The sentence
stems themselves are described as highly structured, a feature designed to help the examiner
discover to what the client's completion refers.

The 80 items are allocated to 11 areas of interest, and the record blank provides space for a summary of reactions to each of these areas (in one case the names of the areas do not correspond in the manual and the record blank). Six areas pertain to situations "representative of significant work problems" involving reactions to authorities, to co-workers, to criticism, to failure (or challenge), to taking orders, and to responsibility. Four other areas pertain to the client's beliefs about the causes of his own aggression, anxiety, failure, and job change, and the eleventh area deals with vocational goals.

The manual provides a "sample protocol and FVS record form data." However, the information provided includes what are apparently summaries of sentence completions given to the items which tap the 11 areas listed above; the sentence completions themselves are not given. The summary of impressions for this case is organized around headings such as Stability of Occupational Choice, Realism of Occupational Choice, and Capacity to Use Abilities in Chosen Occupational Setting. There is no discussion of how the summary evaluations on these points were derived from the 11 area summaries of the sentence completions.

The reliability and the validity of this test admittedly have not been determined. It is the counselor, rather than the test, which "is the crucial factor in determining test data validity." Since the counselor receives few guides in terms either of instructions or of data about experience with or use of the test (let alone norms), it will be impossible for him to know, without careful follow-up studies, how well his inferences hold up against criteria. Furthermore, there is no evidence to support the claim of validity for the content of the items as representative of the areas to which they are ordered. How does one know, for example, that "the items dealing with authorities and co-workers reveal habitual emotional attitudes and patterns of relationships which define the nature of the client's interpersonal feelings as manifested in the work situations"? While the author says the FVS is a "research instrument" (underlining in manual), almost everything the manual says suggests that it is to be used by the counselor or clinician in his daily work with clients.

What we have here is a set of 80 incomplete sentences which have unknown validity as indices to 11 areas important to vocational functioning and which are unevaluated so far as the reliability and validity of clients' responses to them are concerned. While the items may be quite useful as a sort of interview aid, it is inappropriate to call them a test, even a projective test, since none of the properties ordinarily associated with a test is indicated here.

J Counsel Psychol 5:74–5 sp '58. *Laurence Siegel.* * One is tempted to wonder....who does the major share of projecting when projective inventories are interpreted. To what extent does the interpretation made by the evaluator reveal his own personality rather than that of the client? As with anything else, some persons are probably much more insightful in extrapolating from the FVS than others. It is appropriate to inquire about the agreement in interpretation of FVS responses using a technique like that of "blind analysis" and several interpreters. This question is not approached in the manual. The matter of validity is also treated much too lightly. The absence of validity data is excused in the manual on the grounds that FVS is a projective instrument. One must agree with the assertion that "responses will most likely be interpreted qualitatively rather than in routine metric fashion." It is possible, however, to validate categories of qualitative interpretation against behavioral criteria. * The user is here cautioned against equating written responses on the record form with a client's behavior in the job setting. The FVS provides the counselor with another set of stimuli generated by his client. The old saw that *anything* a client does reveals something of himself may be invoked to justify the use of the instrument. To this may be added the potential values of FVS as an "icebreaker," source of interview material, and fertile spawning ground for clues about client behavior and hunches regarding the dynamics of a client's personality. There is always the danger, however, of looking to the datum that a client scratches his left ear (rather than his right) to serve the same ends. The manual asserts that interpretation of FVS responses is much dependent upon the experience, ingenuity and insight of the interpreter. This art of interpretation may nonetheless legitimately be subjected to certain logical requirements of verifiability and replicability. These further steps still need to be taken with the FVS, even if its use is to be restricted to research rather than operational applications.

[136]

★**Franck Drawing Completion Test.** Ages 6 and over; 1951–52; masculinity-femininity; 1 form ['51]; mimeographed; preliminary manual ['52]; no data on reliability and validity; 9s. per 10 tests; 3s. per 10 scoring sheets; 2s. 6d. per manual; 6s. 6d. per specimen set; postpaid within Australia; (15–60) minutes; Kate Franck; Australian Council for Educational Research. *

REFERENCES

1. FRANCK, KATE, AND ROSEN, EPHRAIM. "A Projective Test of Masculinity-Femininity." *J Consult Psychol* 13:247–56 Ag '49. * (*PA* 24:874)
2. ARONSON, MARVIN LUCIUS. *A Study of the Freudian Theory of Paranoia by Means of a Group of Psychological Tests.* Doctor's thesis, University of Michigan (Ann Arbor, Mich.), 1951. (*Microfilm Abstr* 11:443)
3. SHEPLER, BERNARD F. "A Comparison of Masculinity-Femininity Measures." *J Consult Psychol* 15:484–6 D '51. * (*PA* 26:7011)
4. KOOSER, EDWIN DeTURCK. *The Relationship of Masculinity-Femininity Orientation to Self-Report of Anxiety.* Master's thesis, University of North Carolina (Chapel Hill, N.C.), 1955.
5. REED, MAX R. "The Masculinity-Femininity Dimension in Normal and Psychotic Subjects." *J Abn & Social Psychol* 55:289–94 N '57. *

ARTHUR W. MEADOWS, *Head, Department of Psychology, University of Adelaide, Adelaide, Australia.*

This masculinity-femininity test requires the subject to complete a number of incomplete drawings. From the application of seven principles to the analysis of the finished drawings, a score is derived which is said to place the person on a masculinity-femininity continuum. The test has been released, to quote, "not as a finished product, but rather as a useful tool in a clinical battery of tests."

The instructions and scoring are simple and the manual is adequate. The test takes anything from 15 minutes to one hour to complete.

Cultural factors are less emphasized in this test than in the Miles-Terman masculinity- femininity test (see 3:24). The present 36 drawings are those of an original 60 which showed statistically significant differences between methods of completion by men and by women (n = 250) in an elementary psychology class. By comparing the performances of eight nationality groups (men and women separately) comprising anything from 10 to 70 subjects, it was shown that there were no significant differences between the mean scores of men of different nationalities and that, among women, only some non-English speaking groups differed significantly. Results from small groups of children, in age groups 6, 10, and 14, showed differences between boys and girls in the hypothesized direction.

After training, scoring differences between scorers is low, the reliability coefficients ranging from .84 to .90. Although reference is made to the reliability of scoring, there is no indica-

tion of the reliability, i.e., the repeatability, of the test.

In support of validity, evidence is presented to show that there is a significant difference between the mean scores of 265 men and 132 women. This difference does not establish the existence of a masculinity-femininity continuum. What is needed is a correlation between the test scores and some admitted criterion of masculinity-femininity characteristic or, say, evidence that certain deviant groups like homoerotics are significantly placed on the scale.

The rationale of the test has some weaknesses. It is said that it is a projective-constructive test in which the subject both projects and represents his body image in the drawings.

This is an ingenious technique and merits consideration for inclusion in experimental batteries in which validation of the existence of the masculinity-femininity continuum could be obtained from criterion groups.

[137]

★**The Graphomotor Projection Technique.** Mental patients; 1948–54; individual; 1 form ['48]; $3.50 per set of test materials; $5.75 per 25 record blanks ('48); $3.75 per manual ('54, see 7 below); postage extra; (20–30) minutes; Samuel B. Kutash and Raymond H. Gehl; C. H. Stoelting Co. *

REFERENCES

1. GEHL, RAYMOND H., AND KUTASH, SAMUEL B. "Psychiatric Aspects of a Graphomotor Projection Technique." *Psychiatric Q* 23:539–47 Jl '49. * (*PA* 24:6351)
2. KUTASH, SAMUEL B., AND GEHL, RAYMOND H. "A Simple Scoring Device for Quantifying Graphic Productions." *J Clin Psychol* 5:424–5 O '49. *
3. GEHL, RAYMOND H., AND KUTASH, SAMUEL B. "A Reply to Elkisch's Critique of the Graphomotor Projection Technique." *J Proj Tech* 15:510–3 D '51. * ELKISCH, PAULA. "Comment to a Reply by Drs. Gehl and Kutash." *J Proj Tech* 15:513–5 D '51. * (*PA* 26:6264, 6269)
4. LEVINE, SOLOMON. *The Relationship Between Personality and Efficiency in Various Hospital Occupations.* Doctor's thesis, New York University (New York, N.Y.), 1951. (*Microfilm Abstr* 11:741)
5. KUTASH, SAMUEL B. "A New Personality Test: The Graphomotor Projection Technique." *Trans N Y Acad Sci,* Series II 15:44–6 D '52. * (*PA* 27:6874)
6. KEYES, EDWARD J., AND LAFFAL, JULIUS. "The Use of a Graphomotor Projective Technique to Discriminate Between Failure and Success Reactions in a Level of Aspiration Situation." *J Clin Psychol* 9:69–71 Ja '53. * (*PA* 27:7779)
7. KUTASH, SAMUEL B., AND GEHL, RAYMOND H. *The Graphomotor Projection Technique: Clinical Use and Standardization.* Springfield, Ill.: Charles C Thomas, 1954. Pp. xi, 133. * (*PA* 29:1768)

PHILIP L. HARRIMAN, *Professor of Psychology, Bucknell University, Lewisburg, Pennsylvania.*

The administration of the Kutash-Gehl technique is simple and inexpensive. S assumes a writing posture, listens to simple instructions, and then, blindfolded, is asked to move the pencil freely on the paper but to try not to make anything. E makes notes during the performance, which requires 5 minutes. Then S is directed to repeat the performance on a second sheet of paper, after which, still blindfolded, he is asked to report what he wrote or drew on the first paper and on the second, and what thoughts ran through his mind while he was working. After the removal of the blindfold, S indicates on superimposed onionskin any meaningful or imaginary representations discernible in the originals. His free associations are carefully recorded. With college students who volunteered to serve as S's, the reviewer found that from 30 to 45 minutes were required for administration.

The scoring methodology is clearly expounded in the manual. The hints for clinical interpretations of the data, however, seem to be an admixture of intuitive opinions and the authors' own experience in the use of the technique on normal and schizophrenic individuals. Some of the interpretive comments are based upon statistical reports; others are based upon broad experience, particularly with psychotics. Rigidly following the vague counsel for interpreting some graphomotor projection records and notes, the reviewer found incipient or grave indices to mental ill health among his volunteer subjects.

Techniques of this pattern are customarily developed in mental hosptials, outpatient clinics, or other centers for diagnosis and rehabilitation of maladjusted persons. Naturally, "all looks yellow to the jaundic'd eye." Symptoms, latent or manifest, distribute the S's on a continuum of psychopathology. The Kutash-Gehl technique is no exception. Clinical write-ups become, willy-nilly, "sicklied o'er with the pale cast" of morbidity. To be sure, Case C described in the manual, is a norm of reference for understanding how to interpret a nonpsychotic's record; and Case A, which deals with a youth just emerging from adolescence, is discussed in some detail. But more reports are needed for normal young adults. It would be interesting, also, to have more data on young women. The single case presented in the manual suggests that these authors have a mild hostility (!) towards women.

The *Graphomotor Projection Technique* does not seem to be well enough standardized for use in cases where human welfare is involved. Recommendations for commitment to, or release from, an institution for treatment of mental disturbance should not be based on performance on this technique. Used by college deans and counselors, with but a layman's acquaintance with psychopathology, it would induce profound

dysphoria. It does, however, seem to be decidedly worthy of further research, particularly by those who are neither recognized nor "volunteer" psychiatrists. For a term paper by a first year graduate student in clinical psychology, the data collected through the use of the Kutash-Gehl technique, on, say, 50 candidates for the doctorate, might rate a "B." Perhaps, however, the time might be better devoted to mastering courses in experimental design, intermediate statistics, and administration of a Binet-type test.

Am J Psychiatry 111:877–8 My '55. Marion Font. * An interesting aspect of the technique is the use of a blindfold, which the authors believe enables a subject to confront himself and be receptive to prompting from within. * It would seem....that a psychodiagnostic tool of real merit has been added to the armamentarium of the clinical psychologist. Only application of the method over an extensive period, to a wide variety of cases, can determine its clinical value.

Brit J Psychol 46:73 F '55. H. Phillipson. * Some claim is made for this projective technique that it is an attempt to realize an aim, which arose out of the Allport and Vernon Studies in Expressive Movement, that it is important to study movements not in isolation nor as single traits but rather in respect to the basic motivation of the individual. Although the authors for the most part adopt a holistic and dynamic approach, this claim is not substantiated. In the reviewer's opinion a projective technique designed for clinical use should be capable of throwing light on the nature of personality dynamics, conflicts and their causation in terms of concepts directly relatable to therapeutic work. The rationale of the test and the results demonstrated are in far too general terms for this purpose. As an aside one would also express doubts as to whether the test, in the way it is given, represents a task which patients can readily and meaningfully accept. The book makes some thoughtful contributions to an interesting area of research; it may well be that it would have been more advisable at this stage to present the work as such, rather than as a clinical technique. As with all books from this publishing company the production is serviceable and pleasing.

[138]

Group Projection Sketches for the Study of Small Groups. Groups of 3-40 people (ages 16 and over); 1949; 1 form; mimeographed manual; no data on reliability and validity; $2.50 per set of 5 pictures and manual, postpaid; (60) minutes; William E. Henry and Harold Guetzkow; Department of Psychology, University of Michigan. *

REFERENCE

1. HENRY, WILLIAM E., AND GUETZKOW, HAROLD. "Group Projection Sketches for the Study of Small Groups." *J Social Psychol* 33:77–102 F '51. (PA 26:917)

CECIL A. GIBB, *Professor of Psychology, Canberra University College, Canberra, Australia.*

It is difficult to decide whether this technique should be treated seriously in 1958. The manual was first published (in mimeograph form) in 1949 and a quick review of the literature since that date reveals only the commission of the mimeo to print in the *Journal of Social Psychology.* Two quite favorable reviews were presented in *The Fourth Mental Measurements Yearbook,* but no research worker seems to have been encouraged to produce the validation data which would, perhaps, recommend the method to investigators of small groups.

The *Group Projection Sketches* were developed by analogy with TAT, and on the assumption (now frequently made) that groups have properties analogous to the personality properties of individuals. There are five pictures, each 21 by 18 inches, attractively presented and quite easily seen by members of groups as large as 20. The group is asked to write a story about each picture, taking about 10 minutes for each story. (In groups as large as 20 this time limit is rather too short, even when one wishes to preserve a time pressure as is recommended.)

Analysis is focused upon the final written stories and, indeed, the procedure was developed to avoid the necessity for observation and recording of the group process itself. Two methods of analysis are suggested: (*a*) a clinical type interpretation, and (*b*) a type of quantitative analysis based on a number of rating scales expressing judgments of the analyst.

In most cases, however, one has the feeling that the clinical interpretation could be made at least as well by a person who observed the group process, while many of the judgments called for by the rating scales could be far better done by an observer of process. It may be cute to make such judgments from group stories, but more reliable data would almost certainly be obtained by the process observer. One of the reasons this technique has not won advocates, as TAT has, would seem to be that, whereas the TAT protocol gives quick access to personality material otherwise available only with depth interviewing, the *Group Projection*

Sketches offer very little, if anything, which is not openly available to the process observer.

Further restrictions upon the use of the technique are almost certainly the absence of reliability and validity data and the failure of the authors to fulfil their promise of producing these at a later date, and the highly tentative way in which the manual presents the analysis.

Criticism has also been leveled at the pictures themselves for their failure to meet the needs of female groups and of non-white-collar, non-urban male groups. These restrictions, however, hardly account for the assiduity with which the *Group Projection Sketches* have been ignored. A far more serious stricture is that this technique overlooks direct information about the relationships of individuals to the group and within the group.

It may still be true, as the authors hopefully observed in 1949, that "the instrument holds promise....in suggesting clues to insightful analysis of the structure and internal dynamics of groups."

For reviews by Robert R. Holt and N. W. Morton, see 4:106.

[139]

*H-T-P: House-Tree-Person Projective Technique. Ages 5 and over; 1946–56; 1 form; manual ('48, see 6 below); no norms for ages 5–14; $2 per 25 drawing forms ['46]; $3.50 per 25 interrogation folders: adult form ('50), children's form ('56); $3.50 per 25 scoring folders ('50); $3 per manual; postpaid; specimen set not available; (60–90) minutes; John N. Buck and Isaac Jolles (children's interrogation folder); Western Psychological Services. *

REFERENCES

1–5. See 3:47.
6–19. See 4:107.
20. DEMMING, J. A. *The H-T-P Test as an Aid in the Diagnosis of Psychopathic Personality.* Master's thesis, Kent State University (Kent, Ohio), 1949.
21. SIEGEL, J. H. *A Preliminary Study of the Validity of the House-Tree-Person Test With Children.* Master's thesis, Southern Methodist University (Dallas, Tex.), 1949.
22. GÜNZBURG, H. C.; LOND, B. A.; AND VIENNA, PHIL. "The Significance of Various Aspects in Drawings by Educationally Subnormal Children." *J Mental Sci* 96:951–75 O '50. * (PA 25:5413)
23. SINGER, R. H. *A Study of Drawings (H-T-P) Produced by a Group of College Students and a Group of Hospitalized Schizophrenics.* Master's thesis, Pennsylvania State College (State College, Pa.), 1950.
24. BROWN, FRED. Chap. 10, "House-Tree-Person and Human Figure Drawings," pp. 173–84. (PA 27:3546) In *Progress in Clinical Psychology, Vol. I, Sect. 1.* Edited by Daniel Brower and Lawrence E. Abt. New York: Grune & Stratton, Inc., 1952. Pp. xi, 328. *
25. JOLLES, ISAAC. *A Catalogue for the Qualitative Interpretation of the H-T-P.* Beverly Hills, Calif.: Western Psychological Services, 1952. Pp. 97. *
26. JOLLES, ISAAC. "A Study of the Validity of Some Hypotheses for the Qualitative Interpretation of the H-T-P for Children of Elementary School Age: I, Sexual Identification." *J Clin Psychol* 8:113–8 Ap '52. * (PA 27:1968)
27. JOLLES, ISAAC. "A Study of the Validity of Some Hypotheses for the Qualitative Interpretation of the H-T-P for Children of Elementary School Age: II, The 'Phallic Tree' as an Indicator of Psycho-Sexual Conflict." *J Clin Psychol* 8:245–55 Jl '52. * (PA 27:5879)

28. Buck, John N. "House-Tree-Person Drawing Technique," pp. 688–701. (PA 27:7758) In *Contributions Toward Medical Psychology: Theory and Psychodiagnostic Methods, Vol. II.* Edited by Arthur Weider. New York: Ronald Press Co., 1953. Pp. xi, 459–885. *

29. Duffy, F. X. *The Development of Form Concepts in the Drawing of a Tree by Children: Kindergarten Through the Ninth Grade.* Master's thesis, Richmond Professional Institute (Richmond, Va.), 1953.

30. Hammer, Emanuel F. "Frustration-Aggression Hypothesis Extended to Socio-Racial Areas: Comparison of Negro and White Children's H-T-P's." *Psychiatric Q* 27:597–607 O '53. * (PA 28:5880)

31. Hammer, Emanuel F. "An Investigation of Sexual Symbolism: A Study of H-T-P's of Eugenically Sterilized Subjects." *J Proj Tech* 17:401–13 D '53. * (PA 28:6029)

32. Hammer, Emanuel F. "Negro and White Children's Personality Adjustment as Revealed by a Comparison of Their Drawings (H-T-P)." *J Clin Psychol* 9:7–10 Ja '53. * (PA 27:7715)

33. Hammer, Emanuel F. "The Role of the H-T-P in the Prognostic Battery." *J Clin Psychol* 9:371–4 O '53. * (PA 28:4437)

34. Hammer, Emanuel F., and Piotrowski, Zygmund A. "Hostility as a Factor in the Clinician's Personality as It Affects His Interpretation of Projective Drawings (H-T-P)." *J Proj Tech* 17:210–6 Je '53. * (PA 28:4359)

35. Jolles, Isaac, and Beck, Harry S. "A Study of the Validity of Some Hypotheses for the Qualitative Interpretation of the H-T-P for Children of Elementary School Age: III, Horizontal Placement." *J Clin Psychol* 9:161–4 Ap '53. * (PA 28:2640)

36. Jolles, Isaac, and Beck, Harry S. "A Study of the Validity of Some Hypotheses for the Qualitative Interpretation of the H-T-P for Children of Elementary School Age: IV, Vertical Placement." *J Clin Psychol* 9:164–7 Ap '53. * (PA 28:2641)

37. Landisberg, Selma. "Relationship of the Rorschach to the H-T-P." *J Clin Psychol* 9:179–83 Ap '53. * (PA 28:2645)

38. Levine, Murray, and Galanter, Eugene H. "A Note on the 'Tree and Trauma' Interpretation in the HTP." *J Consult Psychol* 17:74–5 F '53. * (PA 28:956)

39. Michal-Smith, Harold. "The Identification of Pathological Cerebral Function Through the H-T-P Technique." *J Clin Psychol* 9:293–5 Jl '53. * (PA 28:3136)

40. Rubin, Harold. "A Quantitative Study of the H-T-P and Its Relationship to the Wechsler-Bellevue Scale." Abstract. *Am Psychol* 8:426–7 Ag '53. *

41. Diamond, Solomon. "The House and Tree in Verbal Fantasy: I, Age and Sex Differences in Themes and Content." *J Proj Tech* 18:316–25 S '54. * (PA 29:4046)

42. Diamond, Solomon. "The House and Tree in Verbal Fantasy: II, Their Different Roles." *J Proj Tech* 18:414–7 D '54. * (PA 29:7270)

43. Hammer, Emanuel F. "A Comparison of H-T-P's of Rapists and Pedophiles." *J Proj Tech* 18:346–54 S '54. * (PA 29:4370)

44. Hammer, Emanuel F. "Guide for Qualitative Research With the H-T-P." *J General Psychol* 51:41–60 Jl '54. * (PA 30:2882)

45. Hammer, Emanuel F. "Relationship Between Diagnosis of Psychosexual Pathology and the Sex of the First Drawn Person." *J Clin Psychol* 10:168–70 Ap '54. * (PA 29:920)

46. Johnson, Warren R.; Hutton, Daniel C.; and Johnson, Granville B., Jr. "Personality Traits of Some Champion Athletes as Measured by Two Projective Tests: Rorschach and H-T-P." *Res Q* 25:484–5 D '54. *

47. Markham, Sylvia. "An Item Analysis of Children's Drawings of a House." *J Clin Psychol* 10:185–7 Ap '54. * (PA 29:935)

48. Pennington, L. W., Jr. *Developmental Patterns in Drawings of a Person by Children From the Age 4½ to 15.* Master's thesis, Richmond Professional Institute (Richmond, Va.), 1954.

49. Repucci, L. C. *A Quantitative Scoring System for Children's Drawings of a House in the H-T-P.* Master's thesis, Richmond Professional Institute (Richmond, Va.), 1954.

50. Rubin, Harold. "A Quantitative Study of the HTP and Its Relationship to the Wechsler-Bellevue Scale." *J Clin Psychol* 10:35–8 Ja '54. * (PA 28:7545)

51. Satter, George, and McGee, Eugene. "Retarded Adults Who Have Developed Beyond Expectation: Part II, Non-Intellectual Functions." *Training Sch B* 51:67–81 Je '54. * (PA 29:2663)

52. Sloan, William. "A Critical Review of H-T-P Validation Studies." *J Clin Psychol* 10:143–8 Ap '54. * (PA 29:957)

53. Woods, Walter A., and Cook, William E. "Proficiency in Drawing and Placement of Hands in Drawings of the Human Figure." *J Consult Psychol* 18:119–21 Ap '54. * (PA 29:2485)

54. Beck, Harry S. "A Study of the Applicability of the H-T-P to Children With Respect to the Drawn House." *J Clin Psychol* 11:60–3 Ja '55. * (PA 29:7256)

55. Cowden, Richard C.; Deabler, Herdis L.; and Feamster, J. Harry. "The Prognostic Value of the Bender-Gestalt, H-T-P, TAT, and Sentence Completion Test." *J Clin Psychol* 11:271–5 Jl '55. * (PA 30:2864)

56. Digiammo, J. J. *Relationship Between Performance on*

Visual-Form Perception Measures and Drawings on the H-T-P Technique. Master's thesis, Richmond Professional Institute (Richmond, Va.), 1955.

57. Hammer, Emanuel F. "A Comparison of H-T-P's of Rapists and Pedophiles: III, The 'Dead' Tree as an Index of Psychopathology." *J Clin Psychol* 11:67–9 Ja '55. * (PA 29:7530)

58. Hammer, Emanuel F. *The H-T-P Clinical Research Manual.* Beverly Hills, Calif.: Western Psychological Services, 1955. Pp. iii, 58. *

59. Johnson, Warren R., and Hutton, C. Daniel. "Effects of a Combative Sport Upon Personality Dynamics as Measured by a Projective Test." *Res Q* 26:49–53 Mr '55. * (PA 30:1559)

60. Kline, Milton V. "Hypnodiagnosis With a Visual-Imagery Induction Technique and Modification of the House-Tree-Person and Thematic Apperception Tests." *Psychiatric Q Sup* 29:267–71 pt 2 '55. * (PA 31:1122)

61. Korkes, Lenore, and Lewis, Nolan D. C. "An Analysis of the Relationship Between Psychological Patterns and Outcome in Pulmonary Tuberculosis." *J Nerv & Mental Dis* 122:524–63 D '55. *

62. Lyons, Joseph. "The Scar on the H-T-P Tree." *J Clin Psychol* 11:267–70 Jl '55. * (PA 30:2897)

63. Meyer, Bernard C.; Brown, Fred; and Levine, Abraham. "Observations on the House-Tree-Person Drawing Test Before and After Surgery." *Psychosom Med* 17:428–54 N–D '55. * (PA 30:7215)

64. Quirk, Eve-Lyn. *The Reliability and Validity of the H-T-P as a Measure of Intelligence in Adolescents.* Master's thesis, University of Toronto (Toronto, Ont., Canada), 1955.

65. Vernier, Claire M.; Whiting, J. Frank; and Meltzer, Malcolm L. "Differential Prediction of a Specific Behavior From Three Projective Techniques." *J Consult Psychol* 19:175–82 Je '55. * (PA 30:2932)

66. Waxenberg, Sheldon E. "Psychosomatic Patients and Other Physically Ill Persons: A Comparative Study." *J Consult Psychol* 19:163–9 Je '55. * (PA 30:3281)

67. Bailey, Robert Bain. *A Study of Predicting Academic Success in Elementary School Reading From Projective Tests.* Doctor's thesis, University of Oklahoma (Norman, Okla.), 1956. (DA 16:1397)

68. Bieliauskas, Vytautas J. "Scorer's Reliability in the Quantitative Scoring of the H-T-P Technique." *J Clin Psychol* 12:366–9 O '56. *

69. Bolin, B. J.; Schneps, Ann; and Thorne, W. E. "Further Examination of the Tree-Scar-Trauma Hypothesis." *J Clin Psychol* 12:395–7 O '56. *

70. Kirkham, Sandra L. *The Identification of Organicity Using the House-Tree-Person Test on an Institutionalized Population.* Master's thesis, Richmond Professional Institute (Richmond, Va.), 1956.

71. Nazario-Ortiz, I. *Quantitative Differences Between Puerto-Rican and Resident American College Students on H-T-P Drawings.* Master's thesis, Richmond Professional Institute (Richmond, Va.), 1956.

72. Perkinson, Patricia R. *Shading on the H-T-P Drawings and Its Relationship With Anxiety and Intelligence.* Master's thesis, Richmond Professional Institute (Richmond, Va.), 1956.

73. Bieliauskas, Vytautas J. *The H-T-P Bibliography.* Los Angeles, Calif.: Western Psychological Services, July 1957. Pp. 10. *

74. Heidgerd, Everett. *The Validity of the H-T-P as a Detector of Aggression in Boys 8 to 12.* Doctor's thesis, Columbia University (New York, N.Y.), 1957.

75. Jolles, Isaac. "Some Advances in Interpretation of the Chromatic Phase of the H-T-P." *J Clin Psychol* 13:81–3 Ja '57. *

76. Royal, E. Ann. *A Comparative Study of the Qualitative Aspects of the Achromatic and Chromatic H-T-P Test.* Master's thesis, Richmond Professional Institute (Richmond, Va.), 1957.

77. Bieliauskas, Vytautas J., and Kirkham, Sandra L. "An Evaluation of the 'Organic Signs' in the H-T-P Drawings." *J Clin Psychol* 14:50–4 Ja '58. *

78. Cassel, Robert H.; Johnson, Anna P.; and Burns, William H. "Examiner, Ego Defense, and the H-T-P Test." *J Clin Psychol* 14:157–60 Ap '58. *

79. Hammer, Emanuel F., Editor. *The Clinical Application of Projective Drawings*, pp. 163–308, passim. Contributions by Emanuel F. Hammer, Isaac Jolles, Fred Brown, and John N. Buck. Springfield, Ill.: Charles C Thomas, 1958. Pp. xxii, 663. *

80. Wawrzaszek, Frank; Johnson, Orval G.; and Sciera, John L. "A Comparison of H-T-P Responses of Handicapped and Non-Handicapped Children." *J Clin Psychol* 14:160–2 Ap '58. *

Philip L. Harriman, *Professor of Psychology, Bucknell University, Lewisburg, Pennsylvania.*

Among the freehand drawing techniques in personality appraisal, the *H-T-P* technique cannot be cavalierly dismissed as just one more contribution to projective methods. The literature on this technique already extends to more than 100 titles. Rather complete and explicit manuals are available for those who desire to have a systematic exposition of the technique, its rationale, and its use in clinical studies and research. Interest in Buck's contribution is no evanescent phenomenon. On the contrary, to judge from accelerations in journal articles since 1948, the *H-T-P* cannot be ignored by students of personality theory or by clinical psychologists. It is trite, though germane here, to remark, *pari passu,* that many other projective drawing tests have had a brief heyday, and then passed into well-deserved oblivion. No such fate seems to await the *H-T-P* in the immediate future.

To administer this test is both absurdly easy and unduly arduous. This paradox will be discovered by anyone who makes a serious effort to learn what the ingenious Buck has done. The subject is asked to draw first a house, then a tree, and finally a person. What could be easier for a teacher or a clinical psychologist than to establish rapport and to obtain those three drawings? The arduous task, however, is to make copious notes on sequences of detail, spontaneous comments, tempo, and general behavior. This reviewer, proceeding as a rank amateur on the *H-T-P* periphery, wished that he had learned W. S. Taylor's system of note-taking. It was convincing, however, to attempt to take notes and find out why they are considered indispensable and why Buck insists upon their necessity.

In a second meeting the subject may be asked to use an 8-color assortment of crayons in another set of freehand drawings of a house, a tree, and a person. This extension of the Buck technique, initiated by Payne (*15*), has been adopted by Buck as a very helpful way of obtaining further data for exploring personality dynamics. Both the achromatic and the chromatic drawings may be obtained from groups as well as from individual testing sessions. A group administration, it is evident, precludes any clinical notes, though it may be a convenient screening device. This reviewer believes that the author has a reserved opinion about the *H-T-P* as a group technique. As in the case of the Binet-Simon scale, administration of the *H-T-P* technique requires a face-to-face situation for maximum usefulness. In the reviewer's opinion Buck should have held to his convictions about this matter.

An inquiry follows the administration of the technique. This takes the form of a planned interview, but the examiner is encouraged to ask supplemental questions, especially about deviant aspects of the productions. Again, a user of the *H-T-P* will regret inability to record notes in an efficient manner. The free associations are impeded if one must ask for a repetition. Nevertheless, about six pages of notes were collected by the reviewer on the behavior of each of several congenial students and a few children of faculty members. Thus, a total of more than 120 pages of *H-T-P* data, all from normal individuals, represents this reviewer's momentary enthusiasm for his task. No doubt, a pedagogue's excursion into this phase of *H-T-P* will be incorporated into many a classroom discussion henceforth.

Quantitative scoring might be learned from the manual. A helpful supplement is the mimeographed report (*14*) from the 1950 Veterans Administration seminar on the *H-T-P*. Innumerable questions arise, and the self-taught examiner soon becomes frustrated. Mons, it is well known, became an expert in Rorschach through his self-directed mastery of the literature. Perhaps, with great patience and assiduity, a psychologist could achieve some competence in quantitative scoring of the Buck technique. A skilled textbook writer might clarify the expositions. Meanwhile, the reviewer would strongly advise a residence in one of the *H-T-P* workshops.

Qualitative scoring, presumably an infinitely more recondite problem, is not difficult. A thorough knowledge of neo-Freudian and psychoanalytic concepts, experience in the intuitive judgments of a psychoclinician, and a complete renunciation of all the objective-experimental psychology one had to learn in graduate school would facilitate the interpreter's work. A flair for convincing expression of bold hypotheses, an austere rejection of nomothetic studies of personality, and a will to believe are further assets in *H-T-P* qualitative appraisals. These comments are not intended to be judgmental or captious. The reviewer is second to none in his admiration of the insights of Buck and Jolles, based upon their own clinical use of the *H-T-P* technique. An academic fuddyduddy would be a lively instructor, indeed, if he or she had similar clinical insights and eagerness to impart them.

Three conclusions are ventured. First, the *H-T-P* technique cannot be properly mastered from manuals and journal articles. Secondly, it seems to be one of the most thorough projective techniques of its type, and it must be taken with utmost seriousness. It is not yet beyond its early adolescence; it should be brought to a higher development. Buck and his enthusiastic colleagues should be afforded every encouragement. Thirdly, most of the *H-T-P* publications are from the pens, or the typewriters, of those who have *Sprachgefühl*. No matter what technique they might advocate, it would be plausible and lucid per se. The next morning wish, however, is for more empirical data. Perhaps, while still adhering to Windelband's ideographic method, members of the *H-T-P* group are going to become more self-critical and cautious about their qualitative interpretations.

For reviews by Albert Ellis and Ephraim Rosen, see 4:107 (1 excerpt); for reviews by Morris Krugman and Katherine W. Wilcox, see 3:47; for related reviews, see B234.

[140]
★**The Holtzman Inkblot Test.** Preschool children through adults; 1958; 24 provisional scoring categories: location, space, form definiteness, form appropriateness, color, shading, movement energy level, pathognomic verbalization, integration, human, animal, anatomy, sex, abstract, anxiety, hostility, barrier, penetration, balance, affect arousal, reaction time, card position, popularity-originality, number of rejections; individual; Forms A, B; no norms; present distribution restricted for research use; no charge for test booklets, provisional manual, manual supplements, or sets of the inkblots when used for research purposes during initial standardization and validation phase; (75) minutes; Wayne H. Holtzman; the Author, University of Texas, Austin, Texas. *

REFERENCE

1. HOLTZMAN, WAYNE H. "Development of an Experimental Inkblot Test, a New Departure From the Rorschach." Abstract. *Am Psychol* 11:400 Ag '56. *

[141]
★**The Howard Ink Blot Test.** Adults; 1953; individual; 1 form; no data on reliability; $12.50 per set of 12 cards; $2 per manual (reprint of *I* below); cash orders postpaid; (90–105) minutes; James W. Howard; *Journal of Clinical Psychology.* *

REFERENCES

1. HOWARD, JAMES W. "The Howard Ink Blot Test: A Descriptive Manual." *J Clin Psychol* 9:209–55 Jl '53. * (*PA* 28: 1848)
2. SCOTT, EDWARD M., AND DOUGLAS, FREDERICK. "A Comparison of Rorschach and Howard Tests on a Schizophrenic Population." *J Clin Psychol* 13:79–81 Ja '57. *
3. SCOTT, EDWARD M. "A Comparison of Rorschach and Howard Ink Blot Tests on a Schizophrenic Population From a Content Point of View." *J Clin Psychol* 14:156–7 Ap '58. *

C. R. STROTHER, *Professor of Clinical Psychology, University of Washington, Seattle, Washington.*

This test consists of a series of 12 Rorschach-type plates, 6 of which are chromatic. They are slightly larger than the Rorschach blots and contain more variations in shading. Three principal criteria entered into the selection of blots: a reasonable degree of uniformity of responses, the use of a fair number and range of determinants other than form, and the exclusion of blots which tended to stimulate large numbers of responses.

Administration and scoring follow Beck's system. The manual is clear and explicit. Norms are provided for a population of 229 adult, English-speaking Canadians of average intelligence or above, with at least a high school education, and without "obviously disabling personality difficulties." No information is given as to the methods used in obtaining this sample.

The author maintains that this test produces more white space, shading, color, movement, and human content responses than the Rorschach blots. The limited amount of published data available tends to support this claim, at least with respect to use with a schizophrenic population.

A great deal of time, care, and ability has been invested in the development of this test. Scoring can be easily learned, particularly by an examiner familiar with Beck's system. For anyone seeking an ink blot test other than the Rorschach, the choice lies between the Howard and the Behn blots. Responses obtained with the Howard blots will probably differ from Rorschach protocols to a greater extent than will protocols obtained from the Behn series.

J Proj Tech 18:254–6 Je '54. *Walter G. Klopfer.* The advertising for the Howard Ink Blot Test, which is extensive, makes statements such as, "The test is derived experimentally;" "It has a wider range of stimulating features;" "There are statistical findings from a 'normal' group;" and "It has greater diagnostic sensitivity." Some of these statements will be examined in the review below. In regard to the question of experimental derivation Howard points out in the manual that he had a large number of ink blots from which the present series have been selected. The data presented in the manual are derived from 229 subjects. He makes the statement, "It is believed that some of these differences (from the Rorschach) may indicate that the test is worthy of the research effort by clinicians or other interested psychologists." This is at some variance with the advertising claim that this research has already been done. Later on in the preface to the manual he states that it would not be possible at this time to give a full description of the administration and scoring of the test and that nothing at all would be said about the interpretation of findings since it was assumed that these could be done by anyone familiar with the Rorschach Test. This is stated in spite of the fact that the author continually emphasizes the point that this test is different from the Rorschach Test and that the cards have a considerably different stimulus value. Why he should, therefore, assume that the principles of interpretation empirically derived from the Rorschach Test should be applicable to this different test is difficult to determine. During the rest of this very brief manual the author makes a number of other statements which might be thrown into question by the clinical observer. Discussing the derivation of this test, he makes the statement that the Rorschach (when used as a group test) could not furnish sufficient data for appraising or describing the individual personality. He cites no evidence to support this contention. He makes the point that the Howard Ink Blot Test is a better test because it has more ink blots, more color, more movement, et cetera. These features he describes as greater "sensitivity" of the test. The reader is left at a loss to know why these features should make the test more sensitive to the assessment of personality, and it is not clear just exactly what the author means by "sensitivity." There is some reason to believe that the Rorschach Test has been found to be of some use in the assessment of personality. There is no evidence at all that the Howard Ink Blot Test has been able to be of any use in this regard. At least, if there is some evidence, it has not been presented in the material discussed here. Howard's "statistics" in regard to the "manner of approach" consist of giving the mean and standard deviation of the various location categories for his normal group. This is not very useful to the clinician since it is not expressed in such a way as to be applicable to a record with any number of responses. His subsequent discussion of the various determinants is the

practice of group averaging which the author himself admits distorts the individual patterns. If this is the case, what is the particular point in presenting this kind of data? He points out that there are more color and more human movement responses elicited by his blots. It seems to the present reviewer that if this is the case, an entirely new rationale and new method of interpreting these determinants must be found because the interpretative hypotheses derived from the Rorschach Test are quite closely bound up with the stimulus value of the particular blots used in that test. His "new" symbol IF, standing for interior form, bears a striking resemblance to a symbol, di, which was suggested by Klopfer eleven years ago. His list of plus and minus form responses presumably analogous to the list presented by Beck and Hertz are completely unjustifiable in view of the fact that the author has not done any extensive standardization in comparing normal and pathological groups. In conclusion it is the opinion of the present reviewer that the Howard Ink Blot Test does not appear upon the market place of clinical psychology with sufficient evidence to back up any of the contentions made. No adequate standardization data have been presented. No research concerning validity has been done, and no information has been presented whatsoever about the means that should be used in interpreting the responses to this kind of material. Indeed, under these circumstances, the question might be raised as to the appropriateness of publishing this test at this time for commercial distribution.

[142]

★An Incomplete Sentence Test for Industrial Use. Adults; 1949; Forms M (men), W (women); no data on reliability; no norms; 5¢ per test; 25¢ per manual ['49]; postage extra; (15–25) minutes; George Spache; the Author, Reading Laboratory and Clinic, University of Florida, Gainesville, Fla. ★

BENJAMIN BALINSKY, *Associate Professor of Psychology, Bernard M. Baruch School of Business and Public Administration, The City College, New York, New York.*

The test was devised to obtain more useful information about an employee's personality trends than paper and pencil personality tests might give. It was considered that a more unstructured test would allow for fuller and truer expressions than the usual personality tests. The latter certainly have been shown to be fakable. The more unstructured tests are less obviously fakable, but it has not been demonstrated how well the sentence completion technique forestalls the tendencies of people to try to show their most desirable points in a job situation. Spache is aware of the fact that some people will give evasive or noncommittal responses. It can be presumed that one will have to utilize other techniques to obtain information about personality and not leave it all to the sentence completion test.

Only 27 of the 84 items have been validated. There was a good attempt at standardizing, validating, and devising a scoring key for a larger group of items based upon the personality symptoms and attitudes sampled in an inventory used earlier by the author. However, only 50 people were included in this validation sampling and the scoring key did not function well. The 27 items which were found to have highest validity were used as the core of the present test. The manual does not indicate that the remaining items have been validated. It would have been much better to have tried out the test as it is published; as it stands now, one cannot be certain about its validity. However, incomplete sentence tests have been found to be useful in individual instances where they offered clues about the personality that fitted and bolstered clues obtained from other sources. It is in this respect that the test most likely offers valid information.

The personality categories to which items are assigned resemble those reported by Stein [1] on a sentence completion test developed in the Office of Strategic Services Assessment Program. Whether these are the best categories is not known and only much more understanding of the nature of personality will tell. The number of incomplete sentence items measuring each category varies and no reason is given for this variation. Presumably, some categories require more items than others because of differences in complexity, but this has not been spelled out.

Following the suggestion of Stein, Spache employs the first person as well as the third person in his incomplete sentences. Since there is some evidence from other sources that the third person is more "projective" than the first person, it would have been a good idea to have experimented more upon this point.

Suitable cautions regarding the interpreting of the test are provided, along with an interpretation of one actual case. More criteria than the

manual presents could well have been supplied to aid in the interpretation of the incomplete sentences and of the test as a whole. However, in comparison with some other incomplete sentence tests, this one has had more than the average amount of standardization. It will be useful as an additional aid in the study of personality, but it cannot be relied upon as the sole source of information. It is particularly slanted toward employees and will probably supply worthwhile information about worker problems and attitudes.

[143]

★The Insight Test: A Verbal Projective Test for Personality Study. Adults; 1944–53; title on test is *Test of Insight Into Human Motives;* Forms 1, 2 ('53); separate editions for men and women; manual ('53, see 2 below); tentative norms; $2.50 per pad of 50 tests of either edition; $2.50 per pad of 50 scoring charts ('53); $7.50 per manual; postage extra; (60) minutes; Helen D. Sargent; Grune & Stratton, Inc. *

REFERENCES
1. FASSETT, KATHERINE K. "A Preliminary Investigation of the Sargent Test." *J Clin Psychol* 4:45–56 Ja '48. * *(PA* 22:5424)
2. SARGENT, HELEN D. *The Insight Test: A Verbal Projective Test for Personality Study.* The Menninger Clinic Monograph Series No. 10. New York: Grune & Stratton, Inc., 1953. Pp. xii, 276. * *(PA* 28:2672)
3. FASSETT, KATHERINE K. "Note on an Experimental Scoring System for the Insight Test." *J Clin Psychol* 10:393 O '54. * *(PA* 29:4051)
4. SARGENT, HELEN D. "Insight Test Prognosis in Successful and Unsuccessful Rehabilitation of the Blind." *J Proj Tech* 20:429–41 D '56. * *(PA* 32:1961)
5. DE VOS, GEORGE A. "Japanese Value-Attitudes Assessed by Application of Sargent's Insight Test Method." Abstract. *Am Psychol* 11:410 Ag '56. *
6. DEAN, SIDNEY I. "Adjustment Testing and Personality Factors of the Blind." *J Consult Psychol* 21:171–7 Ap '57. *
7. FISKE, DONALD W. "An Intensive Study of Variability Scores." *Ed & Psychol Meas* 17:453–65 w '57. *
8. ENGEL, MARY. "The Development and Applications of the Children's Insight Test." *J Proj Tech* 22:13–25 Mr '58. *

RICHARD JESSOR, *Associate Professor of Psychology, and Director, Clinical Training Program, University of Colorado, Boulder, Colorado.*

The *Insight Test* is a very interesting verbal projective technique consisting of 15 items, called armatures, in each of which a problem or conflict is described. The task of the subject is to write or state what the leading character in the situation did and why, and how he or she felt. Ambiguity of the stimulus items is sought by minimal description of the situations or the persons involved, and task- rather than self-orientation is emphasized in the instructions. The test, which is not a measure of insight despite its title, is assumed by its author to assess the characteristic affective and cognitive reactions and expressions of the subject across a variety of areas of conflict such as family, opposite sex, and vocation. There are eight forms of the test: two alternate forms for men and

1 STEIN, MORRIS I. "The Use of a Sentence Completion Test for the Diagnosis of Personality." *J Clin Psychol* 3:47–56 Ja '47. * *(PA* 21:2337)

two for women, and short (10-item) forms corresponding to each of these.

The present manual, an elaboration of an earlier monograph, is a model of clarity and comprehensiveness. The author skillfully describes the development of the test, its rationale, and its role in clinical diagnosis and personality appraisal, and judiciously calls attention to deficiencies, gaps, and unanswered questions. The reader is unlikely to be mislead as to the test's assets or liabilities.

As to the former, the *Insight Test* shares the virtues of techniques like story completion, sentence completion, and the TAT. It presents a socially meaningful situation to which the subject must react in a directed way. Unlike the more ambiguous tasks such as those presented by the Rorschach, there is coordination of the subject's behavior to a concrete interpersonal context. Unfortunately, this latter asset is not fully exploited by the author who, following psychoanalytic theory within which the test is interpreted, tends to consider content as relatively superficial and to stress, instead, analysis of formal structural aspects of the protocol. She does point out, however, that *Insight Test* protocols are amenable to analysis by any procedure for scoring or interpreting verbal productions, e.g., the various schemes employed in TAT content analyses. Another virtue of the test is its adaptability to particular problem areas for which specific armatures can be constructed. Sargent (4) reports, for example, on the special use of the test with blind subjects; it should be an interesting instrument also for studies of different culture groups, developmental levels (Engel (8) has developed a children's form), etc.

These latter points stress the potential value of the *Insight Test* protocol when used in much the same way as is the TAT. The author aspires, however, to a different goal—the achievement of a quasi-psychometric scoring scheme which will show the degree of balance between emotion and feeling (impulse) on the one hand, and coping or defense (impulse-control) on the other. The manual presents an elaborate scoring scheme with satisfactory definitions of variables and illustrative protocols from various diagnostic groups. There are three major scores: affect (A), defense (D), and malignancy (M), and various subscores within and in addition to these categories. When the *Insight Test* is considered from this viewpoint, however, it is an extremely dubious instrument.

The reasons for this conclusion are several: (*a*) Foremost is the fact that the standardization research is very limited and inadequate both in the number and variety of subjects tested and in the control of variables which very likely affect performance on the test. Thus, only 20 normal subjects were used in the reference or "control" group, and these were all university students. Further, the normals and the different groups of patients were not matched on such important variables as age, education, and intelligence. Conclusions about differences between groups are, therefore, difficult to ascribe to the particular pathology. For example, in a task where different categories of verbalization are scored, intelligence is very likely a contribution to variance. Yet no thorough attempt has been made to ascertain what relation exists between IQ and the various *Insight Test* scores. The recent study by Engel did show one statistically significant correlation between Stanford-Binet IQ and a subscore on the *Children's Insight Test*. Given a more heterogeneous population, it seems probable that other such correlations might be found. Research, therefore, is needed to show just how much of what the test is measuring is simply verbal fluency. (*b*) Reliability, both test-retest and interscorer, is unimpressive. The former has not been adequately assessed experimentally, and it is simply not clear what degree of consistency of performance can be expected over given time intervals. The main problem with interscorer reliability is getting agreement on what constitutes a scorable unit in a protocol. With further training, however, it should be possible to achieve satisfactory agreement among scorers. (*c*) Validity of the major scoring variables, especially the ratio of affect to defense scores, A/D, on which the author places so much importance, has not been demonstrated. In fact, two recent researches—Sargent's (4) with blind subjects and Engel's with children—showed no relation between A/D and level of psychological adjustment. Part of the validity problem seems to this reviewer to revolve around the theoretical framework within which the test was developed. There is a tendency to speak of entities like *amounts* of affect or *amounts* of cognition, and there is an undue reliance on traditional psychiatric nosology as a validity criterion.

Thus far, then, the value of the *Insight Test* as a psychometric instrument remains dubious or at least unproven. As a clinical instrument, like the TAT or incomplete sentences, it is highly provocative, seems to provide a valuable sample of verbal behavior, and strongly merits further research and development. Such research should involve rigorous experimental tests of the theoretical properties of the concepts employed, as well as adequate standardization and the accumulation of norms. Given such research, the *Insight Test* seems to this reviewer to have promise.

For related reviews, see B370.

[144]

★**Interpersonal Diagnosis of Personality.** Adults; 1955–58; a combination of assessment procedures consisting of the *Minnesota Multiphasic Personality Inventory,* the *Interpersonal Check List,* and the *Thematic Apperception Test* or the *Interpersonal Fantasy Test* (see *e* below); $12.50 per manual ('56); free specimen sets of booklets listed below; cash orders postpaid; Timothy Leary; Rolfe LaForge and Robert Suczek (*a*); Psychological Consultation Service. *
a) INTERPERSONAL CHECK LIST. [1955]; 1 form; $4 per 20 tests; $3 per scoring template, Form 4 ['54]; (15–45) minutes, depending on number of persons rated.
b) RECORD BOOKLET FOR INTERPERSONAL DIAGNOSIS OF PERSONALITY. [1955]; $5 per 20 booklets.
c) RECORD BOOKLET FOR INTERPERSONAL ANALYSIS OF GROUP DYNAMICS. [1956]; $5 per 20 booklets.
d) RECORD BOOKLET FOR INTERPERSONAL DIAGNOSIS OF FAMILY DYNAMICS. [1956]; $5 per 20 booklets.
e) INTERPERSONAL FANTASY TEST. 1957–58; 1 form ('57); no data on reliability and validity; manual ('58), free; $15 per set of 26 cards. *

REFERENCES

1. FREEDMAN, MERVIN B.; LEARY, TIMOTHY F.; OSSORIO, ABEL G.; AND COFFEY, HUBERT S. "The Interpersonal Dimensions of Personality." *J Personality* 20:142–61 D '51. *
2. LAFORGE, ROLFE; LEARY, TIMOTHY F.; NABOISEK, HERBERT; COFFEY, HUBERT S.; AND FREEDMAN, MERVIN B. "The Interpersonal Dimension of Personality: II, An Objective Study of Repression." *J Personality* 23:129–53 S '54. *
3. LEARY, TIMOTHY, AND COFFEY, HUBERT S. "The Prediction of Interpersonal Behavior in Group Psychotherapy." *Group Psychother* 7:7–51 My '54. * (*PA* 29:4144)
4. LAFORGE, ROLFE, AND SUCZEK, ROBERT F. "The Interpersonal Dimension of Personality: III, An Interpersonal Check List." *J Personality* 24:94–112 S '55. * (*PA* 30:5990)
5. LEARY, TIMOTHY. "The Theory and Measurement Methodology of Interpersonal Communication." *Psychiatry* 18:147–61 My '55. * (*PA* 30:2694)
6. LEARY, TIMOTHY, AND COFFEY, HUBERT S. "Interpersonal Diagnosis: Some Problems of Methodology and Validation." *J Abn & Social Psychol* 50:110–24 Ja '55. * (*PA* 29:7241)
7. LEARY, TIMOTHY. "A Theory and Methodology for Measuring Fantasy and Imaginative Expression." *J Personality* 25:159–75 D '56. *
8. LEARY, TIMOTHY, AND HARVEY, JOAN S. "A Methodology for Measuring Personality Changes in Psychotherapy." *J Clin Psychol* 12:123–32 Ap '56. *
9. EDWARDS, ALLEN L. "Social Desirability and Probability of Endorsement of Items in the Interpersonal Check List." *J Abn & Social Psychol* 55:394–6 N '57. * (Abstract: *Am Psychol* 11:378)
10. LEARY, TIMOTHY. *Interpersonal Diagnosis of Personality: A Functional Theory and Methodology for Personality Evaluation.* New York: Ronald Press Co., 1957. Pp. xix, 518. * (*PA* 31:2556)
11. ARMSTRONG, RENATE GERBOTH. "The Leary Interpersonal Check List: A Reliability Study." *J Clin Psychol* 14:393–4 O '58. *

For related reviews, see B261.

[145]

★**Kahn Test of Symbol Arrangement.** Ages 6 and over; 1949–57; 1 form; record blank ('56); worksheet ('56); summary card ['57]; administrative manual ('56, see *11* below); clinical manual ('57, see *14* below); $25 per set of test materials; $7.50 per 50 record blanks; $2 per administrative manual; $3 per clinical manual; postage extra; (15–30) minutes; Theodore C. Kahn; Psychological Test Specialists. *

REFERENCES

1–2. See 4:110.
3. FILS, DAVID H. "Comparative Performance of Schizophrenics and Normals on a New Projective Test of Object-Symbol Arrangement." Abstract. *Am Psychol* 6:501 S '51. *
4. KAHN, THEODORE C. "Comparative Performance of Psychotics With Brain Damage and Non-Psychotics on an Original Test of Symbol Arrangement." Abstract. *Am Psychol* 6:501 S '51. *
5. KAHN, THEODORE CHARLES. *Comparative Performance of Psychotics With Brain Damage and Nonpsychotics on an Original Test of Symbol Arrangement.* Doctor's thesis, University of Southern California (Los Angeles, Calif.), 1951.
6. BRODSLY, WILLIAM J. *Comparison of Epileptic and Non-Epileptic Children on a Projective Symbol Arrangement Test.* Master's thesis, University of Southern California (Los Angeles, Calif.), 1952.
7. ESTERLY, G. R. *Comparison of Chronic Undifferentiated Schizophrenics With Brain Damaged Psychotics Using the Kahn Test of Symbol Arrangement.* Master's thesis, Trinity University (San Antonio, Tex.), 1954.
8. SZENAS, J. J. *Comparative Performance of Paranoid Schizophrenics and Brain Damaged Psychotics on a Projective Symbol Arrangement Test.* Master's thesis, Trinity University (San Antonio, Tex.), 1954.
9. KAHN, THEODORE C. "Cross Validation of the Organic Brain Pathology Scale for a Test of Symbol Arrangement." Abstract. *J Consult Psychol* 19:130 Ap '55. *
10. KAHN, THEODORE C. "Personality Projection on Culturally Structured Symbols." *J Proj Tech* 19:431–42 D '55. * (*PA* 30:7169)
11. KAHN, THEODORE C. "Kahn Test of Symbol Arrangement: Administration and Scoring." *Percept & Motor Skills* 6:299–334 D '56. * (*PA* 31:6092)
12. FINK, HOWARD H., AND KAHN, THEODORE C. "A Comparison Between Normal and Emotionally Ill Children on the Kahn Test of Symbol Arrangement." Abstract. *Am Psychol* 12:373 Jl '57. *
13. GOULDING, A. V. *Overt Acceptance of the Regulations of the Parole Board of Parolees From a Maximum Security Prison as Measured by the Kahn Test of Symbol Arrangement.* Doctor's thesis, New York University (New York, N.Y.), 1957.
14. KAHN, THEODORE C. "Kahn Test of Symbol Arrangement: Clinical Manual." *Percept & Motor Skills* 7:97–168 Je '57. * (*PA* 32:2899)
15. MURPHY, PAUL D.; FERRIMAN, M. RICHARD; AND BOLINGER, RUSSELL W. "The Kahn Test of Symbol Arrangement as an Aid to Psychodiagnosis." *J Consult Psychol* 21:503–5 D '57. *
16. KAHN, THEODORE C. "Performance of Two Types of Depressives on a Test of Symbol Arrangement." *J Clin Psychol* 14:197–9 Ap '58. *
17. KAHN, THEODORE C., AND MURPHY, PAUL D. "A New Symbol Approach to Personality Assessment." *Am J Psychiatry* 114:741–3 F '58. *
18. MURPHY, PAUL D.; BOLINGER, RUSSELL W.; AND FERRIMAN, M. RICHARD. "Screening Neuropsychiatric Patients by Means of the Kahn Test of Symbol Arrangement." *Behavioral Sci* 3:344–6 O '58. *

CHERRY ANN CLARK, *The Meyers Clinic, Los Angeles, California.*

In preparing his 1956–57 test manuals, the author obviously has given serious consideration to the *Technical Recommendations for Psychological Tests and Diagnostic Techniques,* as well as to Shoben's critique of the test in *The Fourth Mental Measurements Yearbook.* Compared with other manuals for projective techniques, Kahn's work appears to be a singularly praiseworthy effort.

The Kahn test has made notable advances in its psychometric development, but it still requires a great deal of work to establish its reliability and validity, with larger, more hetero- geneous samples and nonparametric methods, and more rigorous experimental designs to over- come the possible distorting effects of irregu- larities in the distribution of samples. Investi- gation of specific sources of variance in relation to criterion validation seems to be desirable and feasible. To the reviewer, this would seem to be one projective technique whose underlying as- sumptions, such as the variations in cultural de- termination of symbol meaning, would be rela- tively amenable to experimental investigation. A parallel test would be a very valuable adjunct to the continuing psychometric and construct validation of the test. As a technique useful for theoretical and empirical investigation of rela- tively complex personality functions, the *Kahn Test of Symbol Arrangement* appears to war- rant further carefully planned experimentation. Before the larger theoretical problems can be effectively handled, a concerted effort to collect normative data remains an urgent need if the test is to attain status as a psychometric instru- ment.

RICHARD JESSOR, *Associate Professor of Psy- chology, and Director, Clinical Training Pro- gram, University of Colorado, Boulder, Colo- rado.*

The *Kahn Test of Symbol Arrangement* (KTSA) employs a set of 16 small plastic ob- jects, such as dogs, hearts, stars, butterflies, an anchor, a circle, and a cross, which are arranged by a subject along a narrow felt strip marked off into 15 equal segments numbered consecutively from 1 to 15. Five arrangements are required— the first two are made any way the subject wishes; the third is made exactly like the second (from memory); the fourth is ordered accord- ing to the subject's liking for the objects; and the fifth is again made any way the subject wishes. During the various trials the subject is asked to name the objects, to give reasons for his arrangements and for his likings and dislikings, and to state what each object symbolizes. These verbalizations are categorized as to level of sym- bolization or abstraction and are the basis for the major score—the symbol pattern—provided by the test. When the various arrangements have been concluded, the subject is required to sort the objects into eight categories: Love, Hate, Bad, Good, Living, Dead, Small, Large. The administration and scoring of the test is simple and the manual provides adequate in-

structions for both. Interscorer reliability has been shown to be very high (above .95 in several studies), but test-retest correlations of .95 in two studies and .66 in one study leave this aspect of reliability still in some doubt. The test would seem to be of interest to a wide variety of sub- jects, although the required repetition of ar- rangements and the apparent arbitrariness of certain instructions, e.g., the placing of some of the objects over other objects, may irritate some adults.

No satisfactory rationale is provided for the test either in its construction or its validation. The rationale section of the clinical manual is not well thought out and is sometimes confus- ing, as in its discussion of the problem of be- havior sampling in testing. While the author of the test asserts the need to utilize stimuli which are representative of life situations, there is no demonstration of the representativeness of the plastic objects employed. The most obvious omissions are human objects, and their exclu- sion is difficult to understand. Inclusion of hu- man figures would seem to provide a more di- rect basis for eliciting and inferring interper- sonal reactions and attitudes than any of the present set of objects.

The empiricism of the development of this test is best seen in the attempts at validation. These have been oriented almost exclusively to- ward the prediction of psychiatrists' decisions. Beginning with the original study by the author of the test, several attempts using various em- pirically derived formulas have been made to demonstrate differential diagnosis of normals, psychotics, brain damaged psychotics, charac- ter disorders, neurotics, etc. The research evi- dence does show some success in differential diagnosis based primarily on the symbol pattern score. Nevertheless, this is not sufficient evi- dence to justify adoption of the test for screen- ing purposes. What remains to be shown is that the test improves classification significantly be- yond the efficiency of simple reliance on popu- lation base rates, or that it predicts diagnosis by the psychiatrist more successfully than, say, a 15-minute interview. Claims for the utility of the test in a remarkable array of activities from determining vocational interests to indicating prognosis in psychotherapy are extravagant and unwarranted at this stage of development. While the author is commendably cautious in qualifying his interpretation and conclusions, the overall impression given the reader by the clinical manual and the publisher's descriptive sheet is, unfortunately, an inflated one.

While the KTSA seems to yield a potentially interesting sample of symbolizing behavior, the meaning of such behavior and its relation to other classes of behavior is still unclear. A thoroughgoing construct validation research program oriented toward specifying the conceptual properties of the KTSA variables would seem highly desirable if the test is to be employed in any way beyond differential diagnosis. The latter function, its main claim to fame thus far, seems of little importance to this reviewer, given the well known unreliability of disease-entity language. Where the test is used for personality evaluation rather than clinical diagnosis, its interpretation relies, according to the clinical manual, on a great deal of arbitrary analogy and undemonstrated psychoanalytic symbolism rather than on any systematic theory coordinating the test with behavior prediction. Other tests, such as the *Thematic Apperception Test*, would seem more useful than the Kahn test for such personality or motivational appraisal.

At one point in the clinical manual, the author cautions the reader that "the work presented here represents only the beginning of the long and difficult process of establishing validity." The need for further and more thoughtful research is clear. Considering the variety of already available tests, there is some question in this reviewer's mind as to whether the KTSA, as developed thus far, has shown itself worthy of such additional labor.

J Consult Psychol 21:506–7 D '57. *Laurance F. Shaffer.* * an intriguingly novel method for clinical appraisal which combines some features of an objective test with some of a projective technique * The *General Manual* gives clear and orderly instructions for administering and scoring the test. * The 15 research studies, several of them not previously published, give considerable information about the validity of the KTSA but have a number of shortcomings. Two studies show clear success in differentiating brain damaged cases from normals. In one study, schizophrenics were not satisfactorily separated from either normals or the brain damaged; in another all psychotics including organics were thrown together in unspecified proportions. Studies seem to give conflicting evidence as to whether neurotics are differentiated to a clinically useful degree. In no study

was attention given to the troublesome problem of the base rate. If the base rate for psychosis is 1%, the test probably yields more false positives than true positives. The projective interpretations of the instrument are stated with becoming modesty, e.g., "slanting hearts *may* indicate hostility to the opposite sex." As with many other projective methods, such interpretations spring from clinical sense and may well lead to useful idiographic hypotheses. They are supported by no evidence. Although the KTSA has been under development for about ten years, it shows many signs of still being in a process of evolution. For example, the rules for interpretation given in the manual are not those used in any reported research study. The symbol pattern interpretations stated on a reference card supplied with the set even differ a little from those in the manual. The test is clearly an interesting device for further research, but it is not yet ready for unqualified use.

For a review by Edward Joseph Shoben, Jr., see 4:110.

[146]

★**The Lowenfeld Kaleidoblocs.** Ages 2.5 and over; 1958; individual; 1 form ['58]; 2 mimeographed manuals ['58]; no data on reliability and validity; no norms; 52s. 6d. per set of test materials, postage extra; adults: 46[60] minutes; children: [30–60] minutes; Margaret Lowenfeld; Badger Tests Co., Ltd. *

REFERENCES

1. AMES, LOUISE BATES, AND LEARNED, JANET. "Developmental Trends in Child Kaleidoblock Responses." *J Genetic Psychol* 84:237–70 Je '54. * (*PA* 29:4023)
2. AMES, LOUISE BATES, AND LEARNED, JANET. "Individual Differences in Child Kaleidoblock Responses." *J Genetic Psychol* 85:3–38 S '54. * (*PA* 29:5686)

[147]

***Lowenfeld Mosaic Test.** Ages 2 and over; 1930–58; 1 form ['30]; 2 sets: standard (456 pieces), minor (228 pieces); directions for administering ['58]; no data on reliability; 205s. per standard set; 110s. per minor set; 10s. 6d. per tray; 21s. per 25 record booklets ('51); 50s. per manual ('54, see 25 below); postage extra; directions for administering available in French, German, and Spanish; (20–40) minutes; Margaret Lowenfeld; Badger Tests Co., Ltd. *

REFERENCES

1–13. See 4:115.
14. LOWENFELD, MARGARET. "The Mosaic Test." *Am J Orthopsychiatry* 19:537–50 Jl '49. * (*PA* 24:1891)
15. BLISS, WILLIAM. *The Effect of Set on Performance on the Mosaic Test.* Master's thesis, University of Florida (Gainesville, Fla.), 1950.
16. WRONG, ELIZABETH. *Comparison of the Mosaic Constructions of Children and Adults With Mental Ages Held Constant.* Master's thesis, George Washington University (Washington, D.C.), 1950.
17. BOWEN, BARBARA. *Experimentally Induced Variations in Lowenfeld Mosaic Design Types.* Master's thesis, College of the City of New York (New York, N.Y.), 1951.
18. BOWEN, BARBARA. "An Extension of the Mosaic Test, Designed to Increase Its Prognostic Value." Abstract. *J Proj Tech* 16:388–9 S '52. *
19. DÖRKEN, HERBERT, JR. "The Mosaic Test: Review." *J Proj Tech* 16:287–96 S '52. * (*PA* 28:2626)
20. FOUNTAIN, RALPH WARREN, JR. *Performance of College Students on the Mosaic Test and on the Minnesota Multiphasic*

Personality Inventory. Master's thesis, University of Florida (Gainesville, Fla.), 1952.

21. GELBMANN, FREDERICK. *A Study of Sex Differences in Personality Characteristics of the Deaf as Determined by the Mosaic Test.* Master's thesis, Catholic University of America (Washington, D.C.), 1952.

22. GOLDSTEIN, SEDELL. *An Exploratory Investigation of Mosaic Patterns Made by Dysphasic Clients.* Master's thesis, University of Michigan (Ann Arbor, Mich.), 1952.

23. HEALEY, ROBERT E. *A Study of Personality Differences Between Hearing and Non-Hearing Girls as Determined by the Mosaic Test.* Master's thesis, Catholic University of America (Washington, D.C.), 1952.

24. LOWENFELD, MARGARET. "The Lowenfeld Mosaic Test." *J Proj Tech* 16:200–2 Je '52. * (PA 28:2651)

25. LOWENFELD, MARGARET. *The Lowenfeld Mosaic Test.* New York: Grune & Stratton, Inc., 1952. Pp. 4. *

26. PASCAL, GERALD R. Chap. 11, "Gestalt Functions: The Bender-Gestalt, Mosaic and World Tests," pp. 185–90. (PA 27:3559) In *Progress in Clinical Psychology, Vol. I, Sect. 1.* Edited by Daniel Brower and Lawrence E. Abt. New York: Grune & Stratton, Inc., 1952. Pp. xi, 328. *

27. SCHANBERGER, WILLIAM J. *A Study of the Personality Characteristics of the Deaf and Non-Deaf as Determined by the Mosaic Test.* Master's thesis, Catholic University of America (Washington, D.C.), 1952.

28. SHNEIDMAN, EDWIN S. "The Case of Jay: Psychological Test and Anamnestic Data." *J Proj Tech* 16:297–345 S '52. * (PA 28:2676)

29. STEWART, URSULA G., AND LELAND, LORRAINE A. "American Versus English Mosaics." *J Proj Tech* 16:246–8 Je '52. * (PA 28:2505)

30. BOVA, LOUIS WILLIAM, JR. *The Effect of Restrictions on Pattern Stability in Mosaic Productions.* Master's thesis, University of Florida (Gainesville, Fla.), 1953.

31. FORTIER, ROBERT H. "The Response to Color and Ego Functions." *Psychol B* 50:41–63 Ja '53. * (PA 27:7046)

32. LANE, WILLIAM PERRY. *A Replication of the Mosaic Test at Different Time Intervals.* Master's thesis, University of Florida (Gainesville, Fla.), 1953.

33. PEAK, HORACE M. *A Quantitative Approach to the Lowenfeld Mosaic Test.* Doctor's thesis, University of Southern California (Los Angeles, Calif.), 1953.

34. WIDEMAN, HARLEY R. "The Application of Quantitative Procedures to the Scoring and Validation of the Lowenfeld Mosaic Test." Abstract. *Am Psychol* 8:455 Ag '53. *

35. WIDEMAN, HARLEY R. *Development and Initial Validation of an Objective Scoring Method for the Lowenfeld Mosaic Test.* Doctor's thesis, University of Toronto (Toronto, Ont., Canada), 1953.

36. WOOLF, HENRIETTE, AND GERSON, ELAINE. "Some Approaches to the Problem of Evaluation of Mental Ability With the Mosaic Test." Discussion by M. Gertrude Reiman. *Am J Orthopsychiatry* 23:732–9 O '53. * (PA 28:6665)

37. BOWEN, BARBARA. "An Extension of the Mosaic Test Designed to Increase Its Prognostic Value." *J Proj Tech* 18:5–10 Mr '54. * (PA 29:910)

38. LALONDE, GISELE. *The Use of Twenty Characteristics in the Discrimination of Masculinity and Femininity With the Mosaic Test.* Master's thesis, University of Ottawa (Ottawa, Ont., Canada), 1954.

39. LOWENFELD, MARGARET. *The Lowenfeld Mosaic Test.* London: Newman Neame Ltd., 1954. Pp. 360. *

40 MAHER, BRENDAN A., AND MARTIN, ANTHONY W. "Mosaic Productions in Cerebro-arteriosclerosis." *J Consult Psychol* 18:40–2 F '54. * (PA 28:8039)

41. MARTIN, ANTHONY WILLIAM. *A Correlation of Affective States With the Use of Color on the Mosaic Test.* Doctor's thesis, Purdue University (Lafayette, Ind.), 1954. (DA 14: 2129)

42. MORAN, MAURICE J. *An Experimental Study of Certain Aspects of Paranoid Schizophrenic Mosaic Field Organization and Their Interrelationships.* Washington, D.C.: Catholic University of America Press, 1954. Pp. 55. * (PA 29:2814)

43. RIOCH, MARGARET J. "The Mosaic Test as a Diagnostic Instrument and as a Technique for Illustrating Intellectual Disorganization." *J Proj Tech* 18:89–94 Mr '54. * (PA 29: 948)

44. BRODY, CLAIRE M. H. *A Study of the Personality of Normal and Schizophrenic Adolescents Using Two Projective Tests: A Differentiation on the Basis of Structural and Behavioral Rigidity Using the Lowenfeld Mosaic and Rorschach Tests.* Doctor's thesis, New York University (New York, N.Y.), 1955. (DA 16:381)

45. HORNE, E. PORTER, AND BLISS, WILLIAM. "The Effect of Set on Mosaic Test Performance." *J General Psychol* 53: 329–33 O '55. * (PA 31:7924)

46. STEWART, URSULA G., AND LELAND, LORRAINE A. "Lowenfeld Mosaics Made by First Grade Children." *J Proj Tech* 19:62–6 Mr '55. * (PA 30:1063)

47. WIDEMAN, HARLEY R. "Development and Initial Validation of an Objective Scoring Method for the Lowenfeld Mosaic Test." *J Proj Tech* 19:177–91 Je '55. * (PA 30:2936)

48. WOLFF, FRANCES. *An Exploratory Study of the Relationship of Certain Aspects of the Mosaic Test to Self-Esteem.* Master's thesis, Cornell University (Ithaca, N.Y.), 1955.

49. DÖRKEN, HERBERT, JR. "The Mosaic Test: A Second Review." *J Proj Tech* 20:164–71 Je '56. * (PA 31:4681)

50. LEVIN, MONROE L. "Validation of the Lowenfeld Mosaic Test." *J Consult Psychol* 20:239–48 Ag '56. * (PA 31:7941)

51. MILBURN, BRAXTON. *Performance of the Deaf on the Lowenfeld Mosaic and the Mooney Closure Tests.* Master's thesis, University of Texas (Austin, Tex.), 1956.

52. JOHNSON, THOMAS F. "The Function of the Mosaic Test in Clinical Practice." *J General Psychol* 56:51–8 Ja '57. *

53. ROBERTSON, MALCOLM H. "Scoring Intelligence on the Lowenfeld Mosaic Test." Abstract. *J Consult Psychol* 21:418 O '57. *

54. STEWART, URSULA; LELAND, LORRAINE; AND STRIETER, EDITH. "Mosaic Patterns of Eighth Grade Children." *J Proj Tech* 21:73–9 Mr '57. * (PA 32:2922)

55. WALKER, RICHARD NORRIS. *Children's Mosaic Designs: A Normative and Validating Study of the Lowenfeld Mosaic Test.* Doctor's thesis, University of Minnesota (Minneapolis, Minn.), 1957. (DA 19:367)

56. CARR, GWEN L. "Mosaic Differences in Non-Institutionalized Retarded Children." *Am J Mental Def* 62:908–11 Mr '58. *

C. J. ADCOCK, *Senior Lecturer in Psychology, Victoria Univesrity of Wellington, Wellington, New Zealand.*

This test invites a very ambivalent attitude. On the one hand, one observes a vast range of responses to the invitation to "make anything you want" with the delightful collection of brightly coloured squares, triangles, and diamonds provided. An examination of several such efforts convinces one that it should be possible to discover fundamental principles underlying the variety. On the other hand, when one attempts to interpret the results in the light of the 300-odd pages of text now available, one is impressed by how little in the way of systematic principles is at one's disposal. Patterns can be classified as representational, conceptual, or abstract; as edge, frame, corner, or pendant; as compact, intermediate, or spaced. But when all this has been learned, one has merely acquired a few useful descriptive terms and must wrestle with new subtleties—some very difficult to convey and all very difficult to assess.

Most projective tests depend upon skill rather than any simple set of rules, but this applies with special force to the mosaic test. Long training under an expert and much experience are necessary for the would-be user. The need for such extensive training may be simply a reflection of the fact that this test is responsive to so many influences, cognitive, affective, and environmental, and that there are no simple factors of a psychological nature underlying it. It appears never to be safe to make a blind diagnosis, even with regard to the most obvious matters. Nevertheless, the testee does appear to reveal in his designs important aspects of his way of life. The test invites a useful slice of behaviour and sometimes, e.g., with schizophrenics, obtains this sample when most other methods fail. As a clinical tool it has very important possibilities. Used in conjunction with interview and analytic techniques, it might be very fruitful, but it might be a very dangerous instrument in the hands of the unskilled and without the insight of the trained analyst.

This reviewer cannot help feeling that some of the difficulty in the application of this test arises from the fact that it has been developed largely in a clinical setting with little opportunity or incentive to carry out careful statistical investigations. Systematic experimentation might reveal some useful information with regard to personality variables involved or, at least, throw some light on factors of a nonpersonality type which influence the test and which need to be allowed for interpretation. In the meantime, it is safe to say that the mosaic test is not for the dabbler.

For related reviews, see B274.

[148]

Machover Draw-A-Person Test. Ages 2 and over; 1949; also called *Machover Figure Drawing Test;* individual; $4.25 (30s.) per manual (see 5 below); cash orders postpaid; (5–60) minutes without associations, (20–90) minutes with associations; Karen Machover; Charles C Thomas, Publisher. * (English publisher: Blackwell Scientific Publications, Ltd.)

REFERENCES

1–13. See 4:111.

14. ANDRULONIS, JEROME A. *Relation Between Machover's Drawing of the Human Figure Test and Certain Variables on the Minnesota Multiphasic Personality Inventory.* Master's thesis, Fordham University (New York, N.Y.), 1951.

15. FINNEGAN, SHIRLEY DEWITT. *Comparison of Responses of a Matched Group of Normal and Mentally Retarded Children on the Children's Apperception Test and the Machover Draw-a-Person Test.* Master's thesis, San Francisco State College (San Francisco, Calif.), 1951.

16. MARLENS, HANNA STEINER. *Graphic Syndromes of Reading Disabilities in the Machover Human Figure Drawing Test.* Master's thesis, College of the City of New York (New York, N.Y.), 1951.

17. BROWN, FRED. Chap. 10, "House-Tree-Person and Human Figure Drawings," pp. 173–84. (PA 27:3546) In *Progress in Clinical Psychology, Vol. I, Sect. 1.* Edited by Daniel Brower and Lawrence E. Abt. New York: Grune & Stratton, Inc., 1952. Pp. xi, 328. *

18. HOLTZMAN, WAYNE H. "The Examiner as a Variable in the Draw-A-Person Test." *J Consult Psychol* 16:145–8 Ap '52. *

19. SHNEIDMAN, EDWIN S. "The Case of Jay: Psychological Test and Anamnestic Data." *J Proj Tech* 16:297–345 S '52. * (PA 28:2676)

20. BARKER, ALMAN J.; MATHIS, JERRY K.; AND POWERS, CLAIR A. "Drawing Characteristics of Male Homosexuals." *J Clin Psychol* 9:185–8 Ap '53. * (PA 28:2885)

21. GRANICK, SAMUEL, AND SMITH, LEON J. "Sex Sequence in the Draw-a-Person Test and Its Relation to the MMPI Masculinity-Femininity Scale." *J Consult Psychol* 17:71–3 F '53. * (PA 28:950)

22. MAINORD, FLORENCE R. "A Note on the Use of Figure Drawings in the Diagnosis of Sexual Inversion." *J Clin Psychol* 9:188–9 Ap '53. * (PA 28:2654)

23. MACHOVER, KAREN. "Drawings of the Human Figure." *Monogr Soc Res Child Develop* 16(53):89–137, 214–316 '53. * (PA 28:4077)

24. WHARTON, LYLE HARRISON. *Effect of Stress-Produced Anxiety on Rorschach, Draw-A-Person, and Visual Performance.* Doctor's thesis, State University of Iowa (Iowa City, Iowa), 1953. (DA 13:1268)

25. BLISS, MONTE, AND BERGER, ANDREW. "Measurement of Mental Age as Indicated by the Male Figure Drawings of the Mentally Subnormal Using Goodenough and Machover Instructions." *Am J Mental Def* 59:73–9 Jl '54. * (PA 29:4253)

26. BLUM, RICHARD H. "The Validity of the Machover DAP Technique: A Study in Clinical Agreement." *J Clin Psychol* 10:120–5 Ap '54. * (PA 29:906)

27. GALLESE, ARTHUR J., JR., AND SPOERL, DOROTHY TILDEN. "A Comparison of Machover and Thematic Apperception Test Interpretation." *J Social Psychol* 40:73–7 Ag '54. * (PA 29:5703)

28. MACHOVER, K. Chap. 12, "The Figure-Drawing Test," pp. 235–54, passim. In *Personality Through Perception: An Experimental and Clinical Study.* By H. A. Witkin and others. New York: Harper & Brothers, 1954. Pp. xxvii, 571. * (PA 28:8566)

29. WILLE, WARREN S. "Figure Drawings in Amputees." *Psychiatric Q Sup* 28:192–8 pt 2 '54. * (PA 29:7814)

30. WITKIN, H. A.; LEWIS, H. B.; HERTZMAN, M.; MACHOVER, K.; MEISSNER, P. BRETNALL; AND WAPNER, S. *Personality Through Perception: An Experimental and Clinical Study.* New York: Harper & Brothers, 1954. Pp. xxvi, 571. * (PA 28:8566)

31. FRANK, GEORGE H. "A Test of the Use of a Figure Drawing Test as an Indicator of Sexual Inversion." *Psychol Rep* 1:137–8 S '55. * (PA 30:6111)

32. HAWARD, L. R. C., AND ROLAND, W. A. "Some Inter-Cultural Differences on the Draw-a-Man Test: Part II, Machover Scores." *Man* 55:27–9 F '55. *

33. HAWARD, L. R. C., AND ROLAND, W. A. "Some Inter-Cultural Differences on the Draw-a-Man Test: Part III, Conclusion." *Man* 55:40–2 Mr '55. *

34. SWENSEN, CLIFFORD H., AND NEWTON, KENNETH R. "The Development of Sexual Differentiation on the Draw-A-Person Test." *J Clin Psychol* 11:417–9 O '55. * (PA 30:6006)

35. BAILEY, ROBERT BAIN. *A Study of Predicting Academic Success in Elementary School Reading From Projective Tests.* Doctor's thesis, University of Oklahoma (Norman, Okla.), 1956. (DA 16:1397)

36. CRAMER-AZIMA, FERN J. "Personality Changes and Figure Drawings: A Case Treated with ACTH." *J Proj Tech* 20:143–9 Je '56. * (PA 31:4678)

37. EVERETT, EVALYN G. *A Comparative Study of Paretics, Hebephrenics, and Paranoid Schizophrenics on a Battery of Psychological Tests.* Doctor's thesis, New York University (New York, N.Y.), 1956. (DA 16:1502)

38. LAKIN, MARTIN. "Certain Formal Characteristics of Human Figure Drawings by Institutionalized Aged and by Normal Children." *J Consult Psychol* 20:471–4 D '56. * (PA 32:1629)

39. MACHOVER, KAREN, AND ZADEK, MILDRED. "Human Figure Drawings of Hospitalized Involutionals." *Psychiatric Q Sup* 30:222–40 pt 2 '56. *

40. MARCUS, MURRAY. *Behavioral Differences on the Machover Draw-A-Person Test Between Slow and Fast College Readers.* Doctor's thesis, University of Denver (Denver, Colo.), 1956.

41. REZNIKOFF, MARVIN, AND TOMBLEN, DONALD. "The Use of Human Figure Drawings in the Diagnosis of Organic Pathology." *J Consult Psychol* 20:467–70 D '56. * (PA 32:1642)

42. SIPPRELLE, CARL N., AND SWENSEN, CLIFFORD H. "Relationship of Sexual Adjustment to Certain Sexual Characteristics of Human Figure Drawings." *J Consult Psychol* 20:197–8 Je '56. * (PA 31:6133)

43. SWENSEN, CLIFFORD H., AND SIPPRELLE, CARL N. "Some Relationships Among Sexual Characteristics of Human Figure Drawings." *J Proj Tech* 20:224–6 Je '56. * (PA 31:4717)

44. WANNER, PAUL W. *A Partial Test of Validity of the Machover Drawing-of-a-Human-Figure Technique.* Master's thesis, Sacramento State College (Sacramento, Calif.), 1956.

45. MURPHY, MARY MARTHA. "Sexual Differentiation of Male and Female Job Applicants on the Draw-A-Person Test." *J Clin Psychol* 13:87–8 Ja '57. *

46. REED, MAX R. "The Masculinity-Femininity Dimension in Normal and Psychotic Subjects." *J Abn & Social Psychol* 55:289–94 N '57. *

47. SOHLER, DOROTHY TERRY; HOLZBERG, JULES D.; FLECK, STEPHEN; CORNELISON, ALICE R.; KAY, ELEANOR; AND LIDZ, THEODORE. "The Prediction of Family Interaction From a Battery of Projective Techniques." *J Proj Tech* 21:199–208 Je '57. *

48. FELDMAN, MARVIN J., AND HUNT, RAYMOND G. "The Relation of Difficulty in Drawing to Ratings of Adjustment Based on Human Figure Drawings." *J Consult Psychol* 22:217–9 Je '58. *

49. GRAMS, ARMIN, AND RINDER, LAWRENCE. "Signs of Homosexuality in Human-Figure Drawings." Abstract. *J Consult Psychol* 22:394 O '58. *

50. REZNIKOFF, MARVIN, AND NICHOLAS, ALMA L. "An Evaluation of Human-Figure Drawing Indicators of Paranoid Pathology." *J Consult Psychol* 22:395–7 O '58. *

51. SHERMAN, LEWIS J. "Sexual Differentiation or Artistic Ability?" *J Clin Psychol* 14:170–1 Ap '58. *

52. VILHOTTI, ANTHONY J. "An Investigation of the Use of the D.A.P. in the Diagnosis of Homosexuality in Mentally Deficient Males." *Am J Mental Def* 62:708–11 Ja '58. *

For reviews by Philip L. Harriman and Naomi Stewart, see 4:111; for related reviews, see 4:112.

[149]

*Make A Picture Story. Ages 6 and over; 1947-52; individual; 1 form ('47); manual ('52, see 27 below); no data on reliability and validity; $16 per set of test materials, 25 figure location sheets, and manual; $1.60 per 25 figure location sheets ('48); $2.50 per manual; postpaid; (45-90) minutes; Edwin S. Shneidman; Psychological Corporation. *

REFERENCES

1-19. See 4:113.
20. FRAIMOW, IDA SYLVIA. *The Use of the Make-A-Picture-Story Tests (MAPS) With Mentally Retarded Children and Children of Normal Intellectual Development.* Master's thesis, Pennsylvania State College (State College, Pa.), 1950.
21. CONANT, JAMES C. *A Comparison of Thematic Fantasy Among Normals, Neurotics, and Schizophrenics.* Doctor's thesis, University of Southern California (Los Angeles, Calif.), 1951.
22. SHNEIDMAN, EDWIN S.; JOEL, WALTHER; AND LITTLE, KENNETH B. "An Empirical Categorization of Psychological Test Report Items." Abstract. *Am Psychol* 6:492 S '51. *
23. FINE, REUBEN. "Interpretation of Jay's Make-A-Picture-Story Method: The Case of Jay: Interpretations and Discussion." *J Proj Tech* 16:449-53, discussion 444-5, 462-73 D '52. * (*PA* 28:2678)
24-5. McDONALD, FRANKLIN RANDOLPH. *The Effect of Differential Cultural Pressures on Projective Test Performances of Negroes.* Doctor's thesis, University of Southern California (Los Angeles, Calif.), 1952.
26. SHNEIDMAN, EDWIN S. "The Case of Jay: Psychological Test and Anamnestic Data." *J Proj Tech* 16:297-345 S '52. * (*PA* 28:2676)
27. SHNEIDMAN, EDWIN S. *Manual for the Make A Picture Story Method.* Projective Techniques Monograph No. 2. New York: Society for Projective Techniques and Rorschach Institute, Inc., July 1952. Pp. iv, 92. * (*PA* 27:6542)
28. CHAREN, SOL. "The Interaction of Background and Characters in Picture Test Story Telling." *J Clin Psychol* 10:290-2 Jl '54. * (*PA* 29:2439)
29. VAN KREVELEN, ALICE. "A Study of Examiner Influence on Responses to MAPS Test Materials." *J Clin Psychol* 10:292-3 Jl '54. * (*PA* 29:2482)
30. FINE, REUBEN. "Manual for a Scoring Scheme for Verbal Projective Techniques (TAT, MAPS, Stories and the Like)." *J Proj Tech* 19:310-6 S '55. * (*PA* 30:4570)
31. LITTLE, KENNETH B., AND SHNEIDMAN, EDWIN S. "A Comparison of the Reliability of Interpretations of Four Psychological Tests." Abstract. *Am Psychol* 10:322 Ag '55. *
32. SPIEGELMAN, MARVIN. "Jungian Theory and the Analysis of Thematic Tests." *J Proj Tech* 19:253-63 S '55. * (*PA* 30:4601)
33. PROUD, ANN P. *Response to Picture-Thematic Stimulus Material as a Function of Stimulus Structure.* Doctor's thesis, University of California (Los Angeles, Calif.), 1956.
34. SMITH, JOHN R., AND COLEMAN, JAMES C. "The Relationship Between Manifestations of Hostility in Projective Tests and Overt Behavior." *J Proj Tech* 20:326-34 S '56. * (*PA* 31:6134)
35. SPIEGELMAN, MARVIN. "A Note on the Use of Fine's Scoring System with the MAPS Tests of Children." *J Proj Tech* 20:442-4 D '56. * (*PA* 32:1648)
36. BINDON, D. MARJORIE. "Make-A-Picture Story (MAPS) Test Findings for Rubella Deaf Children." *J Abn & Social Psychol* 55:38-42 Jl '57. *
37. HOOKER, EVELYN. "The Adjustment of the Male Overt Homosexual." *J Proj Tech* 21:18-31 Mr '57. *
38. EDGAR, CLARA LEE, AND SHNEIDMAN, EDWIN S. "Some Relationships Among Thematic Projective Tests of Various Degrees of Structuredness and Behavior in a Group Situation." *J Proj Tech* 22:3-12 Mr '58. *

For reviews by Albert I. Rabin and Charles R. Strother, see 4:113; for related reviews, see 4:114.

[150]

★The Michigan Picture Test. Ages 8-14; 1953; individual; 1 form; $6.50 per set of pictures; $1.80 per 20 record blanks; $2 per manual; $9 per specimen set including the complementary *Rating Scale for Pupil Adjustment* (see 102); postage extra; (60) minutes; Gwen Andrew, Samuel W. Hartwell, Max L. Hutt, and Ralph E. Walton; Science Research Associates. *

REFERENCES

1. ANDREW, GWEN; WALTON, RALPH E.; HARTWELL, SAMUEL W.; AND HUTT, MAX L. "The Michigan Picture Test: The Stimulus Values of the Cards." *J Consult Psychol* 15:51-4 F '51. * (*PA* 26:6247)
2. HARTWELL, SAMUEL W.; HUTT, MAX L.; ANDREW, GWEN; AND WALTON, RALPH E. "The Michigan Picture Test: Diagnostic and Therapeutic Possibilities of a New Projective Test in Child Guidance." *Am J Orthopsychiatry* 21:124-37 Ja '51. * (*PA* 25:8094)
3. RINGWALL, EGAN AUGUST. *Some Picture Story Characteristics as Measures of Personality Traits of Children.* Doctor's thesis, University of Michigan (Ann Arbor, Mich.), 1951. (*Microfilm Abstr* 11:752)
4. WALTON, R. E.; ANDREW, GWEN; HARTWELL, S. W.; AND HUTT, M. L. "A Tension Index of Adjustment Based on Picture Stories Elicited by the Michigan Picture Test." *J Abn & Social Psychol* 46:438-41 Jl '51. * (*PA* 26:2199)
5. GURIN, MAIZIE G. "Differences Between Latents and Adolescents: A Psychoanalytic Study Utilizing the Michigan Picture Test." *Papers Mich Acad Sci Arts & Letters* 38:495-503 '53. *
6. GURIN, MAIZIE G. *Differences in the Psychological Characteristics of Latency and Adolescence.* Doctor's thesis, University of Michigan (Ann Arbor, Mich.), 1953.
7. CLOONAN, THEODORE F. *Objective Identification of Maladjustment in Children by Use of a Modified Projective Technique.* Doctor's thesis, Purdue University (Lafayette, Ind.), 1958. (*DA* 19:360)

WILLIAM E. HENRY, *Associate Professor of Human Development and Psychology, The University of Chicago, Chicago, Illinois.*

This test is the result of a study to evaluate the emotional reactions of children 8 to 14 years of age undertaken by the Michigan Department of Mental Health. The study involved, among other things, the development of a set of 16 TAT-like pictures. Four of the pictures are for use with boys only and four for use with girls only; thus, only 12 pictures are presented to any one child. Four core pictures may be used as a short screening test for general emotional adjustment.

This 16-card set was selected from a much larger series on the basis of the results of a number of preliminary studies. The pictures themselves are moderately realistic but yet ambiguous representations of scenes depicting intrafamilial conflicts, conflicts with authority figures, conflicts involving physical danger, sexual difficulties, school situation conflicts, feelings of personal inadequacy, confusions in self-percept, conflicts involving aggressive drives, and feelings of social inadequacy.

Responses to the test have been analyzed in terms of a number of variables. The "tension index" refers to the frequency of verbalized expressions of unresolved conflict. The score is based on seven psychological needs—love, extrapunitiveness, intropunitiveness, succorance, superiority, submission, and personal adequacy. Four of these needs were found to be useful in discriminating between groups of well and poorly adjusted children—love, extrapunitiveness, submission, and personal adequacy. Critical scores computed for the tension index show the probability that a given score will place a child within the well or poorly adjusted groups. Thus, at grade 3, a child with a tension index of

4 has a 78 per cent probability of belonging to the poorly adjusted group, and a 55 per cent probability of belonging to the well adjusted group; if the tension index is 5, the probability of poor adjustment increases.

Interscorer reliability based on ratings of two judges differs for the various needs, but for all needs at all grade levels averages .98. Similarly high reliabilities are reported for other variables, such as tense of verbs used and direction of forces. This latter variable refers to the expressed actions in the story—whether they emanate from the central figure, are directed upon the central figure, or are neutral in that no direction is indicated. Still other variables, for which trends are reported but for which no statistically significant findings have been determined, are psychosexual level, interpersonal relationships, personal pronouns, and level of interpretation.

The test, analyzed in the terms above, has also shown good results from three other projects briefly summarized. The accompanying manual reports the development of the test and the research that has been done on it. It also describes the technique of administering the pictures and the method of scoring the responses, and presents a sample analyzed case. A scoring form is provided. From the work reported to date, the *Michigan Picture Test* seems to hold considerable promise as a semi-objective test of important personality and adjustment variables for school children.

MORRIS KRUGMAN, *Assistant Superintendent in Charge of Guidance, New York Public Schools, New York, New York.*

As a rule, authors of projective tests do not utilize acceptable objective techniques for the validation of their instruments. In this respect the *Michigan Picture Test* is different; the authors apparently spared no effort in their attempt to avoid the errors of other personality test constructors. The manual appropriately summarizes their rationale and procedures.

In spite of excellent effort, however, the results are disappointing thus far. The authors hold high hopes for the test ultimately, but they are meticulously honest in interpreting their standardization data and making no exaggerated claims for currently available results.

The test consists of 16 pictures to be interpreted, four of which are for boys only and four for girls only. A core of four pictures can be used for screening purposes. The test purports to measure emotional reactions of children 8 to 14 years of age. The pictures were carefully selected to present a minimum of trauma and to contain characters with which children of the particular age group could identify. Although 1,400 children in representative school systems and child guidance clinics in Michigan were experimented with, only 700 were included in the standardization.

An 11-item *Rating Scale for Pupil Adjustment* (see 102), filled in by teachers of regular public school classes, was used to locate children upon whom validity studies could be conducted. The upper and lower thirds of the classes, rated on the basis of "total emotional adjustment," were assumed to be, respectively, the well adjusted and the poorly adjusted children. Without in the least attempting to be facetious, this reviewer would like to ask why it is necessary to attempt to develop a complex clinical instrument that accomplishes much less effectively what a simple rating scale used by classroom teachers is assumed to do much better?

The authors selected eight variables considered by them to have high degrees of discrimination. Five of these they found to be "variables for which trends were indicated, but in which differences were not statistically significant." These were psychosexual level, interpersonal relationships, personal pronouns, popular objects, and level of interpretation. The other three are described as variables that "effectively discriminate between groups of well- and poorly-adjusted children at some, if not all, grade levels." These variables are not nearly so discriminating as this general statement would seem to indicate. Following are some specific limitations, in the authors' words, of the three variables:

Tension Index ("verbalized psychological needs"): "There will be many 'false positives' with critical scores which include about half of the well-adjusted children, but scrutiny of the particular needs a child most often expresses will help to eliminate those who are well-adjusted." In other words, not the critical score, but subjective judgment determines the state of a child's adjustment.

Verb Tense (relative emphasis on past, present, and future): "Specific tests of these hypotheses are not yet available, but we do have evidence of the over-all relationship between tense and adjustment."

Direction of Forces (whether the central figure tends to act or be acted upon): "This procedure was carried out for all grade levels and no significant differences were found." (Direction of forces was found to relate to adjustment but frequency of directional reference was not.) In addition, "note that although one might expect the centrifugal direction to be most commonly used by well-adjusted, and centripetal by poorly-adjusted children, this does not actually prove to be true." Well adjusted children were found to use more of both directions.

The *Michigan Picture Test,* then, has value if used by the skillful clinician as an indicator of trends in designated directions. It is an instrument that has considerable promise, but cannot, as yet, be considered a satisfactorily validated test of "emotional reactions."

J Consult Psychol 18:475–6 D '54. Laurance F. Shaffer. * No other picture-story test has been accompanied by so much data relevant to its standardization and validation. * Scoring reliability is good, but there are no data on subject response reliability. * well-prepared manual * a useful clinical tool for an age group hitherto ignored in the construction of apperception tests.

J Proj Tech 19:192–3 Je '55. Edwin S. Shneidman. * How does this test differ from, or add to, the TAT? In what ways is it an improvement over Symond's Picture Story materials? Or, over the Travis-Johnston Projection Test? Or Bellak's CAT? Further, is it sound psychological practice to prepare a different set of picture-thematic materials for each age group? And, to what extent should psychological test materials be tailor-made for specific age, ethnic, and political groups? * This reviewer feels like Dr. Robert Holt when he wrote: "So the NAT....and the UAT....are joining the CAT...., VAT....and the rest of them. Soon we'll get to the ZAT, and there I hope the new variants will stop, because zat's enough." A more severe criticism lies in the neglect of the Michigan authors to relate their new materials (no matter how good) to previous materials, especially *the* TAT. This error of omission is a conspicuous shortcoming in their project. * The authors have evidently thought about the problem of selection and know the relevant literature. In addition, they have evolved a set of seven criteria which each picture should meet. It seems disappointing, then, after all this effort that one reads in the manual that "the selection

of the areas of conflict to be sampled by the Michigan pictures was an 'armchair' process which we could only hope would be adequate ....we were developing the scoring methods and the test pictures concurrently. We were forced, therefore, to evaluate the scoring in terms of pictures which had been selected on an *a priori* basis....This fact implies the need for future revision of the test." Little is stated as to how the pictures were actually selected. * The manual is, in many ways, the best manual for a projective technique to date. There is much wisdom and many springboards for research ideas within it. It is well organized and clearly expressed. (Only in the first few chapters of the manual was I disturbed by vagueness and generalities where I sought specific information.) In many ways the manual measures up to the "Essential" standards proposed by the Cronbach Committee and in this way, too, sets a new standard for techniques of this sort. One of the "Essential" standards indicated by the Cronbach Committee is that the professional qualifications required to administer and interpret the test should be indicated. The manual under discussion does not clearly indicate these, although the manual does use the words "examiner," "clinician" and "the clinical staff"; the matter is confused, however, by the printed notice that accompanied the review copy which stated that "teachers and counselors will find the SRA *Michigan Picture Test* valuable in the study of child behavior." * In spite of the critical and negative comments above, this reviewer feels that the *Michigan Picture Test* looks interesting, seems useful, deserves a trial, presents a manual which might well be emulated, and leaves one with admiration for the authors' labors.

[151]

★The Object Relations Technique. Ages 11 and over; 1955; 1 form ['55]; manual ('55, see 3 below); no data on reliability; 63s. ($10) per set of 13 cards and manual, postage extra; (90) minutes; Herbert Phillipson; Tavistock Publications Ltd. (United States distributor: Free Press). *

REFERENCES

1. PHILLIPSON, H. "A Modification of Thematic Apperception Technique Based on the Psychoanalytic Theory of Unconscious Object Relations." Abstract. *B Brit Psychol Soc* (19): 28 Ja '53. *
2. O'KELLY, E. "The Object Relations Test: Some Quantitative Findings Relating to Early Separation From the Mother." *Brit Rorsch Forum* (7):23–5 N '55. *
3. PHILLIPSON, HERBERT. *The Object Relations Technique.* London: Tavistock Publications, Ltd., 1955. Pp. x, 224. (PA 30:5441)
4. STAUNTON, G. J. "A Comparative Analysis of Rorschach and T.A.T. Responses With Reference to a Particular Case Study." Abstract. *Brit Rorsch Forum* (6):1–4 Ap '55. *
5. ALCOCK, A. THEODORA, AND PHILLIPSON, H. "The Use of

Rorschach and Object Relations Technique in Vocational Selection Work." Abstract. *Rorsch Newsl* 1:18–9 D '56. *
6. O'KELLY, ELIZABETH. "An Investigation, by Means of the Object Relations Test, Into Some of the Effects of Early Separation From the Mother on the Personal Relationships of Adolescent Delinquent Girls." *J Mental Sci* 103:381–91 Ap '57. *

GEORGE WESTBY, *Head, Department of Psychology, The University of Hull, Hull, England.*

Among the many over-elaborated projective techniques, often of forced "originality," which followed upon the clinical popularity of the Rorschach and the TAT, few show both specificity of theoretical background and novelty of construction. The Phillipson *Object Relations Technique* can undoubtedly claim these distinctions. Moreover, since it has evolved very largely in the theoretical and practical ferment which followed recent experiments in group therapy by a number of workers at the Tavistock Clinic, London, it owes much to the latest developments of the "English" wing of the psychoanalytic school in Britain associated with Klein and Fairbairn (to be distinguished from the viewpoint of Anna Freud and Glover). It is the opinion of this reviewer that the test need not stand or fall with the "object relations" theory. From the test construction viewpoint, it is true that the development of the technique has been based upon an acceptance of the theory and not on empirical experimentation with a view to the prediction of external criteria. In this respect it is matched in the field of personality assessment only by the *Szondi Test,* which is bound even more closely to a theory which must be esoteric to the majority of present-day psychologists.

It is not appropriate in this review to do more than indicate that the underlying theoretical contribution of Fairbairn to the psychology of human motives may yet prove to be a significant step towards a true integration of the Freudian contribution with current "drive-reduction and social learning" theories. Fairbairn certainly stresses "adaptation to the social environment" as the specific subject of enquiry of the psychologist. It is certain, however, that Phillipson would scarcely be satisfied if clinical psychologists attempted to use this test (as many have indeed used the van Lennep *Four-Picture Test* and similar techniques) with eclectic theory or empirical principles taken "off the cuff." If one wishes to understand fully the purpose of the test, a thorough acquaintance is advised not only with the author's discussion in the textbook manual of the theoretical basis of the technique, but also with Fairbairn's *Psycho-Analytic Studies of the Personality* [1] or, at the very least, the summary by Money-Kyrle of object relations theory in the early chapters of *Psychoanalysis and Politics.*[2] Not unexpectedly, Phillipson, like all psychoanalytic workers in this field, lays great stress on the need for "patient accumulation of experience of unconscious dynamics" as a necessary foundation for the profitable use of this (as of all) projective techniques.

The test consists of three series of four pictures on cards of convenient size, and includes the well known TAT blank card item. Each picture of each series is designed to elicit the characteristic modes of response ("the unconscious object relations") of the subject to one of the following situations: (*a*) the one person relationship, (*b*) the two person relationship, (*c*) the three person relationship, and (*d*) a group relationship. Pilot work has also been done on a presentation of the four person relationship to cover the first sibling situation, but experience suggested, says Phillipson, that the attempt to cover this "did not outweigh the disadvantage of extending the whole series." The patience and care with which the five years of preparatory work on this test was carried out is worthy of special comment; this is in sharp contrast to the hasty productions of many self-conscious innovators in this field who have, at all costs, attempted to leap on the bandwagon with their own little drums while the circus was still attracting the crowds.

While not so unstructured as the Stern cloud pictures or the Rorschach blots, the cards have a far higher degree of ambiguity than the TAT or Symonds pictures. They are in some respects —the ambiguous sex of the figures and the "soft" artistic treatment, for instance—reminiscent of the pictures of the Jackson *Test of Family Attitudes,* except that there is, in Series C, an attempt to use subtle pastel color with a little sharp red in a manner obviously much influenced by Rorschach theory. The suggestion is made that "the introduction of colour intensifies the threats and supports in the stimulus in terms of real emotional involvement." In the B series the ambiguous shadowgraph figures are placed in very general but significant everyday environments—in a kitchen, in a bedroom, outside a house, in a public place.

The administration of the test is carefully de-

1 FAIRBAIRN, W. R. D. *Psycho-Analytic Studies of the Personality.* London: Tavistock Publications, Ltd., 1952.
2 MONEY-KYRLE, R. E. *Psychoanalysis and Politics.* London: Gerald Duckworth & Co., Ltd., 1951.

scribed. It has obviously been determined by the classical clinical attitude to individual testing, but there are a few interesting points. "It should be presented with a purpose which the subject can share," warns the author. An introductory conversational enquiry which is intended to act as a lead-in to establish rapport and guarantee productivity of response is outlined; the general nature is indicated by the question: "Will you tell me....the sort of things you really enjoy most and then those you're not so keen on, or that you really dislike?" An after-test enquiry is also recommended which follows conventional lines, except for an attempt to introduce a Rorschach-type "testing of the limits" in cases where no solution has been offered. However, the time taken by the test (an average of one and one-half hours), as Phillipson confesses, leaves little time for such extra enquiry. Indeed, perhaps a major criticism of the whole technique is that if, in addition to administration, four or five hours are spent in scoring and interpretation, the test is too expensive in time for the average clinical psychologist. It is either a luxury research instrument which may eventually lead to a more economical technique, or it is to be considered as a possible routine method of examination for those generously staffed teaching hospitals and clinics which are the overprivileged and the envied of the profession.

The manual includes a remarkably detailed case study with a full clinical background. There are full interpretations of the test protocols which throw much light on the way in which object relations theory may be used. A suggested scheme is added for scoring the themes and the "main dynamics of the tension systems." There are also half a dozen shorter case illustrations. On the other hand, normative data are at present limited to a psychiatric outpatient clinic sample of 50 patients of above average intelligence, and 40 normal adolescent girls from secondary schools. The author sees the need for further data. Unfortunately, the difficulties of research which will satisfy even the most liberal scientific criteria of reliability and validity are particularly intractable with this type of test.

The dust-jacket "blurb" claims that the pictures used in the *Object Relations Technique* have been shown to be *"particularly* suitable for use by experienced psychologists working *outside* the clinical field, in social research and in personnel selection in industry" (reviewer's italics). There are no data on validity in these fields referred to by the author. Since the test is presented in the manual exclusively as a clinical tool, it seems a pity that the publishers have felt it necessary to make such sweeping claims instead of perhaps entertaining a more realistic hope of its use as a research tool for the gathering of data upon which a useful judgment of its value outside the clinical situation could be made.

A test of this theoretically explicit type necessarily has the defect of its special merit. Those who cannot accept the object-relations brand of psychoanalytic theory will refuse to consider the practical usefulness of the instrument. In this particular case, in the reviewer's opinion, this would be regrettable because many of the special features of the test come from a notably reflective consideration of the problems which have emerged in the psychology of perception, and from the practical experience of a variety of psychologists with projective techniques over the past quarter of a century. The test could be used with a minimum of depth-psychological theory.

The summary conclusion is offered that the test has original features which may eventually justify its addition to a practical apparatus for clinical assessment and enquiry, even by those who would wish to reject the object relations theory in its present form.

For related reviews, see B338.

[152]
★The Picture Impressions: A Projective Technique for Investigating the Patient-Therapist Relationship. Adolescents and adults; 1956; individual; Forms F ['56, women], M ['56, men]; supplied free to qualified clinical and research workers; postpaid; (20-35) minutes; Lester M. Libo; Department of Psychiatry, School of Medicine, University of Maryland. *

REFERENCE
1. LIBO, LESTER M. "The Projective Expression of Patient-Therapist Attraction." *J Clin Psychol* 13:33–6 Ja '57. *

J Proj Tech 22:250 Je '58. Steven G. Vandenberg. This new technique is custom made to study the patient's expectations regarding the therapist. Four pictures are presented—a different set for males than for females—and four questions are asked about each story. The therapist in the line drawings which constitute the pictures seems to be wearing the short white jacket commonly worn by younger physicians in hospitals. The fact that the test is thus rather definitely structured toward therapy in such a setting may limit its usefulness in other situations. The 14 page manual recommends a simple coding procedure in which the positive and negative attraction scores for the 4 cards are added to provide a measure of the individual's presumed attractions to his doctor. A story is only scored if it contains references to a therapist, a patient, a diagnostic or therapeutic function, the self. Misperceptions such as "The man in the suit is asking for a job. The other man is thinking of giving him the job" are not scored. There is a brief paragraph about qualitative analysis in the manual. In it perceptual distortions are listed as revealing phenomena, but no effort has been made to relate their occurrence to the patient's attitudes toward therapy. While the limitations indicated above may be regrettable, the definite structuring of the materials should result in more focused protocols. This new technique should prove useful for the purpose for which it is designed.

[153]

★The Picture World Test. Ages 6 and over; 1955–56; 1 form ('56); symbol sheet ('55); no data on reliability; $20 per set of test materials; $4 per 25 record booklets ('56); $3.50 per manual ('56); postpaid; (15–30) minutes; Charlotte Buhler and Morse P. Manson; Western Psychological Services. *

WALTER KASS, *Associate Professor of Psychology, Albert Einstein College of Medicine, Yeshiva University, New York, New York.*

The *Picture World Test* (PWT) is a projective technique purporting to tell about (*a*) motivations specific to goal-setting, conscious and unconscious, internal and external; (*b*) integrating and conflicting aspects of emotions, ambitions, and interests; (*c*) cultural and environmental influences; and (*d*) reactions to life and to the world as a whole. It is said by the authors to complement Rorschach revelations of current personality processes and *Thematic Apperception Test* (TAT) depictions of "genetic or past" forces in a person's life, and, in addition, to indicate "future directional outlook." From the case examples cited in the manual and a limited trial, this reviewer doubts the special claim on the future made by the authors for this picture world method. Future-directed and aspirational material may just as easily be derived from goals and outcomes expressed in TAT and other story telling techniques.

The test is applicable to children, adolescents, and adults, individually or in groups. Subjects write stories about a number of structured scenes which they select from a set of 12 and which they may elaborate with additional figures and objects drawn from a list of 36 diagrammatic representations; the scenes are to be interconnected in thematic sequences, according to the individual's phantasy.

Advantages of the PWT over its prototype, the *Toy World Test,* appear mainly in the group- and self-administering possibilities of a paper and pencil procedure. Like *Make A Picture Story* (MAPS), which replaces the stimulus pictures of the TAT with background sets to be populated by cutout cardboard figures, the PWT substitutes linkable background pictures to be filled with figure drawings in place of the miniature-life toy arrangements of the original *World Test*. Unlike the MAPS innovation, the PWT replaces a three-dimensional with a two-dimensional product. The authors say (but do not show) that with this exchange the PWT "offers greater potentialities for revealing the dynamics underlying adjustments to cultural pressures." But according to MAPS rationale, increased phantasy scope is secured through manipulatable material in preference to a flat graphic medium. The content of the PWT scenes may indeed enhance emergence of cultural dynamics, though it is questionable whether this format is actually superior to the original toy technique, especially with children.

The scenes, simply, clearly, and interestingly drawn, are unambiguous and predominantly reality-oriented. Dream World, the most symbolically nuanced, shows a naked woman running through an open door in a detached wooden wall toward a phallic object and the label "Shame." A preacher in a pulpit on the near side of the wall, flying saucers, an eye in the wall, and a ghoulish figure atop the wall suggest the forces of nature and morality.

Data are provided on 94 adults (53 men and 41 women), aged 18 to 85 years, 27 of whom were adequately adjusted. The remaining 67 were clinically classified as psychoneurotic, character disordered, psychotic, or brain damaged. Data are also given on 22 children (9 boys and 13 girls) 6 to 16 years of age, 10 adequately adjusted, 12 psychoneurotic. There are frequency tables on scenes selected, themes and symbols used, and story categories. The tables are sparse and distinctions between normal and clinical productions are untested and unsubstantiated. Interpretations of the sample cases cited are of the clinical kind common to all thematic techniques. There is no effort to relate test categories diagnostically with personality processes or psychopathology.

As presented, the PWT is an interesting paper and pencil modification of the *World Test* which contributes another original set of stimulus pictures to thematic testing. The innovation is a small one in technique of administration. There is great merit in the basic idea of a projective technique designed to pursue a person's concept of the world as he sees it and would wish it to be. With further development, the PWT may possibly fulfill this pursuit, especially if it helps explain how people go about creating and maintaining the worlds they thematically depict. It is insufficiently developed for valid clinical use, and is at this stage more of a good idea than a test. One wishes the authors had themselves carried out at least some of their 25 research suggestions before publishing a technique as a test. Perhaps it is in the trend of our times thus to give birth to a brain child for others to adopt and raise to maturity.

J Consult Psychol 20:237 Je '56. Laurance F. Shaffer. The *Picture World Test* is essentially a picture version of the well-known *World Test,* designed to explore how a person perceives and structures his world, with emphasis on his goal-setting activities. The examinee is presented with 12 small drawings of structured scenes, a large sheet of blank paper, and a chart of 36 simple symbols by which he can add persons, vehicles, buildings, and animals to the scenes. He is asked to choose any number of the scenes he wishes "to make up a world as it is or as you would like it to be; the world you like or dislike; the world of your dreams...." The examinee gums the scenes to the blank sheet, connects the scenes as he wishes, adds symbols, gives his world a name or title, and tells a story about it. The manual describes methods of interpreting the world scenes and world stories. Some data are given on the frequencies of the main story categories in relation to age and quality of adjustment. Twenty-eight illustrative case studies demonstrate the clinical use and interpretation of the test. All in all, the *Picture World Test* seems to be an interesting and challenging instrument, likely to evoke self-revealing responses of considerable clinical value.

[154]

*Rorschach. Ages 3 and over; 1921–57; variously referred to by such titles as Rorschach Method, Rorschach Test, Rorschach Ink Blot Test, Rorschach Psychodiagnostics; many variations and modifications are in use with no one method of scoring and interpreting generally accepted; unless otherwise indicated, the word

"Rorschach" may be interpreted as referring to the use of Rorschach's Psychodiagnostic Plates listed as *f* below.

a) *BEHN RORSCHACH TEST. 1941–56; a parallel set of ink blots; $10 per set of cards; $3 per set of record blanks ('51); $7.50 per manual ('56); postage extra; Hans Zulliger; Hans Huber. (U.S. distributor: Grune & Stratton, Inc.) *

b) ★THE BUHLER-LEFEVER RORSCHACH DIAGNOSTIC SIGN LIST AND RECORD OF THE RORSCHACH STANDARDIZATION STUDIES FOR THE DETERMINATION AND EVALUATION OF THE BASIC RORSCHACH SCORE. 1954; $3.50 per 25 booklets, postpaid; Charlotte Buhler, Karl Buhler, and D. Welty Lefever; Western Psychological Services. *

c) HARROWER'S GROUP RORSCHACH. Ages 12 and over; 1941–45; $11 per set of the original Rorschach ink blots on Kodaslides for standard projector; $3.75 per set of 25 record blanks; postpaid; (70–90) minutes; M. R. Harrower and M. E. Steiner; distributed by Psychological Corporation.

d) HARROWER'S MULTIPLE CHOICE TEST. Ages 12 and over; 1943–45; for use with either cards or slides; $2.50 per 25 record blanks; postage extra; M. R. Harrower; distributed by Psychological Corporation. *

e) PSYCHODIAGNOSTIC INKBLOTS. 1945; a parallel set of ink blots; $5.50 per set of cards; $2 per manual; postage extra; M. R. Harrower and M. E. Steiner; Grune & Stratton, Inc. *

f) *PSYCHODIAGNOSTIC PLATES, FIFTH EDITION. 1921–54; $12 per set of cards ('54, identical with original edition copyrighted in 1921); $3 per set of 100 record blanks; $6.50 per copy of manual, fifth edition ('51 translation of German edition, '42, with the addition of a bibliography); postage extra; Hermann Rorschach; Hans Huber. (U.S. distributor: Grune & Stratton, Inc.) *

g) ★RORSCHACH COMBINED LOCATION AND RECORD FORM. 1957; 1 form; $2.75 per 25 booklets; 30¢ per specimen set; postpaid; Nicholas De Palma; the Author, Davidson County Hospital, Nashville 8, Tenn. *

h) ★THE RORSCHACH EVALOGRAPH. 1954; 1 form; $2.50 per 10 booklets, postpaid; Morse P. Manson and George A. Ulett; Western Psychological Services. *

i) ★RORSCHACH LOCATION CHARTS (BECK'S SCORING AREAS). 1951–54; 1 form ('54, identical with set copyrighted in 1951); 9.80 *fr.* ($3) per set of 10 cards, postage extra; Julian C. Davis; Hans Huber. * (U.S. distributor: Grune & Stratton, Inc.)

j) RORSCHACH METHOD OF PERSONALITY DIAGNOSIS. 1939–42; $2.95 per 35 record blanks ('42); Bruno Klopfer and Helen H. Davidson; World Book Co. *

k) ★THE RORSCHACH MINIATURE INK BLOTS: A LOCATION CHART. 1955; $2 per examiner's card; $3.50 per pad of 100 record sheets; postpaid; Morse P. Manson; Western Psychological Services. *

REFERENCES

1–147. See 40:1246.
148–598. See 3:73.
599–1219. See 4:117.
1220. KLOPFER, BRUNO. "Pseudopsychotic Reactions in Rorschach Records of Pre-School Children." Abstract. *Psychol B* 38:597 Jl '41. *
1221. IMMERGLUCK, LUDWIG. *A Comparison Between the Personality Characteristics of Adolescents With Behavior Disorders and the Personality Structures of Their Parents.* Doctor's thesis, State University of Iowa (Iowa City, Iowa), 1947.
1222. MARTIN, DOROTHY RANDOLPH. *A Comparative Study of the Rorschach Test With Aspiration Level Tests and the K-Maze.* Doctor's thesis, University of Colorado (Boulder, Colo.), 1947.
1223. ALLEE, RUTH. *Rorschach Responses of Extreme Deviation in an Experimental Stress Condition.* Master's thesis, University of Missouri (Columbia, Mo.), 1948.
1224. GUILFORD, J. P. "Some Lessons From Aviation Psychology." *Am Psychol* 3:3–11 Ja '48. *
1225. LITTELL, SUZANNE DUPUY. *A Study of the Relationship Between the Rorschach Anxiety Signs and Other Measures of Anxiety.* Master's thesis, University of Colorado (Boulder, Colo.), 1948.
1226. SHOEMAKER, H. A., AND ROHRER, J. H. "Relationship Between Success in the Study of Medicine and Certain Psy-

chological and Personal Data." *J Assn Am Med Col* 23:190–201 My '48. * (*PA* 23:951)

1227. DAVIDSON, N. "Some Aspects of the Rorschach Test." *B Nat Inst Personnel Res* 1:19–23 Jl '49. *

1228. DRYZER, E. *The Group Rorschach.* Master's thesis, Wayne University (Detroit, Mich.), 1949.

1229. LINDERFELT, F. MARGARET. *A Comparative Study of the Rorschach Protocols of Japanese and Caucasian College Students.* Master's thesis, University of Hawaii (Honolulu, Hawaii), 1949.

1230. ROOK, LEROY HUBERT. *Evidence of Change in a Group Therapy Situation as Described by the Rorschach Method.* Master's thesis, University of Oklahoma (Norman, Okla.), 1949.

1231. STAIMAN, MARTIN G. *Comparative Study of Psychoneurotic Veterans Who Continue and Discontinue Psychotherapy.* Doctor's thesis, New York University (New York, N.Y.), 1949.

1232. ABBOTT, GRETCHEN VAN CLEVE. *A Comparative Study of Adjustment Ratings of Graduate Students.* Master's thesis, Southern Methodist University (Dallas, Tex.), 1950.

1233. DOWNING, WILLARD O. *A Comparative Study of Two Different Methods of Inquiry on the Rorschach Test.* Master's thesis, University of Denver (Denver, Colo.), 1950.

1234. FINK, MARIANNE A. *Personality Differences of Acculturating Navaho Adolescent Girls as Revealed by the Rorschach Test.* Master's thesis, University of New Mexico (Albuquerque, N.M.), 1950.

1235. HORLICK, REUBEN S. *The Relationships of Psychometric Test Scores to Personality Disorders.* Doctor's thesis, New York University (New York, N.Y.), 1950.

1236. MOLISH, HERMAN B.; MOLISH, ELLEN ELSTE; AND THOMAS, CAROLINE BEDELL. "A Rorschach Study of a Group of Medical Students." *Psychiatric Q* 24:744–74 O '50. * (*PA* 26:3089)

1237. PEMBERTON, W. H. *Test Characteristics of Student Teachers Rated at the Extremes of Teaching Ability.* Doctor's thesis, University of California (Berkeley, Calif.), 1950.

1238. SCHRAM, HARRIET JEAN. *Differences on Rorschach Test Between Accepted and Non-Accepted High School Freshmen.* Master's thesis, Southern Methodist University (Dallas, Tex.), 1950.

1239. SILVERBERG, JACOB. *A Study in Body-Concept.* Doctor's thesis, University of Kentucky (Lexington, Ky.), 1950.

1240. WARE, KENNETH E. *Evaluation of a Group Rorschach Technique as a Predictor of Academic Success of Medical Students.* Master's thesis, Southern Methodist University (Dallas, Tex.), 1950.

1241. WITT, EUGENE LESTER, JR. *A Study of the Relation of Form Perception in Color on the Rorschach Ink Blot Test and Performance on the Wechsler-Bellevue Block Design Subtest.* Master's thesis, Southern Methodist University (Dallas, Tex.), 1950.

1242. ABEL, THEODORA M., AND CALABRESI, RENATA A. Chap. 13, "The People as Seen From Their Rorschach Tests," pp. 306–18, 463–90. (*PA* 26:2685) In *Life in a Mexican Village: Tepoztlán Restudied.* By Oscar Lewis. Urbana, Ill.: University of Illinois Press, 1951. Pp. xxvii, 512. *

1243. ALLISON, HARRY WILLIAM. *The Validation of Two Quantitative Measures of General Adjustments as Assessed by the Rorschach Method of Personality Diagnosis.* Master's thesis, Pennsylvania State College (State College, Pa.), 1951.

1244. ARKOFF, ABE. *An Investigation of Some Rorschach Indices of "Realistic" Behavior.* Doctor's thesis, State University of Iowa (Iowa City, Iowa), 1951.

1245. BOYD, ROBERT W. *The Use of the Multiple Choice Rorschach Test in a Study of School Attendance and School Success.* Master's thesis, Catholic University of America (Washington, D.C.), 1951.

1246. DIVNEY, HERBERT P. *A Comparative Study of the Rorschach Factors of Three Groups of Alcoholics.* Master's thesis, Catholic University of America (Washington, D.C.), 1951.

1247. DÖRKEN, HERBERT, AND KRAL, V. ADALBERT. "Psychological Investigation of Senile Dementia." *Geriatrics* 6:151–63 My–Je '51. * (*PA* 27:567)

1248. FEURFILE, DAVID. *The Validity of the Selected Signs in the Rorschach: Outgoing Adjustment, Dominance and Submissiveness.* Master's thesis, Pennsylvania State College (State College, Pa.), 1951.

1249. FINNEY, BEN C. "Rorschach Test Correlates of Assaultive Behavior." Abstract. *Am Psychol* 6:490 S '51. *

1250. GALLAGHER, JAMES J. *An Investigation Into Factors Differentiating College Students Who Discontinue Non-Directive Counseling From College Students Who Continue Counseling.* Doctor's thesis, Pennsylvania State College (State College, Pa.), 1951.

1251. GOINES, VALMORE R. *Personality Characteristics of a Certain Ethnic Group.* Doctor's thesis, Northwestern University (Evanston, Ill.), 1951.

1252. GROSSMAN, B. L. "Older People Live in Institutions." Abstract. *Int Gerontol Congr* 2:97 '51. *

1253. HARROWER, M. R., AND KRAUS, JANE. "Psychological Studies on Patients With Multiple Sclerosis." *A.M.A. Arch Neurol & Psychiatry* 66:44–57 Jl '51. * (*PA* 26:1643)

1254. HAWKINS, WILLIAM ANDREW. *Rorschach Patterns Related to Leaderless Group Discussion Behavior.* Master's thesis, Louisiana State University (Baton Rouge, La.), 1951.

1255. HERTZ, MARGUERITE R. *Frequency Tables for Scoring Responses to the Rorschach Inkblot Test, Third Edition.* Cleve-

land, Ohio: Press of Western Reserve University, 1951. Pp. iv, 240. * (*PA* 26:7001)

1256. INGRAM, WINIFRED. *Prediction of Aggression From the Rorschach Test.* Doctor's thesis, Northwestern University (Evanston, Ill.), 1951.

1257. JANOFF, IRMA Z. *The Relation Between Rorschach Form Quality Measures and Children's Behavior.* Doctor's thesis, Yale University (New Haven, Conn.), 1951.

1258. JOSEPH, ALICE, AND MURRAY, VERONICA F. *Chamorros and Carolinians of Saipan: Personality Studies*, pp. 143–228, 347–64, passim. Cambridge, Mass.: Harvard University Press, 1951. Pp. xviii, 381. * (*PA* 26:3359)

1259. KELLEY, PAUL. *Rorschach Measures of Affect-Adjustment in Candidates to the Religious Life.* Master's thesis, Catholic University of America (Washington, D.C.), 1951.

1260. KUHLEN, R. G. "Expansion and Constriction of Life Activities During the Adult Life Span as Reflected in Organizational, Civic, and Political Participation." Abstract. *Int Gerontol Congr* 2:115 '51. *

1261. LANGER, LEONARD HAROLD. *A Comparison of Twelve-Year-Old White and Negro Boys on the Rorschach Test.* Master's thesis, University of Southern California (Los Angeles, Calif.), 1951.

1262. LORD, EDITH. "Group-Rorschach Responses of Thirty-Five Leprosarium Patients." Abstract. *Am Psychol* 6:500 S '51. *

1263. LOTTRIDGE, DORIS SWOBODA. *A Comparative Personality Study of Philosophy and Engineering Students by Means of the Rorschach Technique.* Master's thesis, Stanford University (Stanford, Calif.), 1951. *

1264. MACKAY, EDWARD A. *The Brief-Contact Method of Rorschach Administration: A Validation Study.* Master's thesis, University of Alberta (Edmonton, Alb., Canada), 1951.

1265. MEADOWS, A. W. *An Investigation of the Rorschach and Behn Tests.* Doctor's thesis, University of London (London, England), 1951.

1266. MUNGER, MANUS R. *The Differentiation of Overachievers in Engineering School by the Group Rorschach Test.* Master's thesis, Catholic University of America (Washington, D.C.), 1951.

1267. MURNEY, RICHARD G. *The Relationship Between Certain Thematic Apperception Test and Rorschach Test Scores.* Master's thesis, Catholic University of America (Washington, D.C.), 1951.

1268. NICHOLS, E. G. *A Study of Differences on the Rorschach Test Between Individuals Having Dominant Religious Values and Those Having Dominant Economic Values.* Master's thesis, Dalhousie University (Halifax, N.S., Canada), 1951.

1269. OETZEL, JAMES L., AND STERNBERG, THOMAS H. "A Personality Study of Neurodermatitis (Atopic)." Abstract. *Am Psychol* 6:493 S '51. *

1270. PICKARD, PHYLLIS M. *A Study of the More Important Traits—Assessed by the Rorschach Group Test.* Master's thesis, University of London (London, England), 1951.

1271. POMPILO, PETER T. *The Personality of Epileptics as Indicated by the Rorschach Test: A Comparison With Neurotic Subjects.* Master's thesis, Catholic University of America (Washington, D.C.), 1951.

1272. PORTER, HELEN M. *An Investigation of the Validation of Movement Responses in the Rorschach Test.* Master's thesis, University of Toronto (Toronto, Ont., Canada), 1951.

1273. RAKUSIN, JOHN M. *The Role of Rorschach Variability in the Prediction of Client Behavior During Psychotherapy.* Doctor's thesis, Pennsylvania State College (State College, Pa.), 1951.

1274. REES, W. LINFORD, AND JONES, A. M. "An Evaluation of the Rorschach Test as a Prognostic Aid in the Treatment of Schizophrenia by Insulin Coma Therapy, Electronarcosis, Electroconvulsive Therapy and Leucotomy." *J Mental Sci* 97:681–9 O '51. * (*PA* 26:2903)

1275. ROE, ANNE. "A Psychological Study of Eminent Biologists." *Psychol Monogr* 65(14):1–68 '51. * (*PA* 27:1516)

1276. ROULETTE, THOMAS GRIER. *The Validity of Selected Signs in the Rorschach: Anxiety, Compulsion, and Depression.* Master's thesis, Pennsylvania State College (State College, Pa.), 1951.

1277. SALFIELD, D. J. "Psychiatric Differential Diagnosis and Psychological Testing." Abstract. *Q B Brit Psychol Soc* 2:39 Ap '51. *

1278. SCHAEFER, EARL S. *A Comparison of Personality Characteristics of Deaf and Hearing College Students as Revealed by a Group Rorschach Method.* Master's thesis, Catholic University of America (Washington, D.C.), 1951.

1279. SCHLOSSER, JOHN R. *An Investigation of Examiner Influence on Results of Rorschach Examinations.* Doctor's thesis, Stanford University (Stanford, Calif.), 1951.

1280. SHEEHAN, JOSEPH, AND ZUSSMAN, CHARLES. "Rorschachs of Stutterers Compared With a Clinical Control." Abstract. *Am Psychol* 6:500 S '51. *

1281. SMITH, SYDNEY RUSSELL. *The Rorschach Examination and General Intelligence: A Validation Study.* Doctor's thesis, University of California (Berkeley, Calif.), 1951.

1282. SMYKAL, ANTHONY, JR. "The Significance of the Rorschach Pure Color Response." *Proc Okla Acad Sci* 32:116–21 '51. * (*PA* 27:4271)

1283. STEAD, LUCY SASSCER GORE. *A Comparative Study of Schizophrenic Signs on the Rorschach and the Wechsler-Bellevue.* Master's thesis, Stanford University (Stanford, Calif.), 1951.

1284. STEISEL, IRA M. "The Rorschach Test and Suggestibility: An Experimental Study." Abstract. *Am Psychol* 6:490 S '51. *

1285. STOPOL, MURRAY S. *An Experimental Investigation of the Consistency of Stress Tolerance and Related Rorschach Factors.* Doctor's thesis, Columbia University (New York, N.Y.), 1951. (*DA* 12:390)

1286. STORMENT, CHARLYNE TOWNSEND, AND FINNEY, BENJAMIN C. "Prediction of Violent Behavior in Neuropsychiatric Patients." Abstract. *Am Psychol* 6:490 S '51. *

1287. THOMAS, HOBART F. "A Study of Movement Responses on the Rorschach as Related to the Mechanism of Projection." Abstract. *Am Psychol* 6:500 S '51. *

1288. THOMAS, HOBART FULLER. *The Relationship of Movement Responses on the Rorschach Test to the Defense Mechanism of Projection.* Doctor's thesis, Stanford University (Stanford, Calif.), 1951.

1289. THOMPSON, LAURA. "Perception Patterns in Three Indian Tribes." *Psychiatry* 14:255–63 Ag '51. * (*PA* 26:2128)

1290. TUCKER, JOHN E. *Investigation of Criteria for Evaluating Non-Directive Psychotherapy With College Students.* Doctor's thesis, Pennsylvania State College (State College, Pa.), 1951.

1291. WHITMAN, DOROTHY. *Relationship of Certain Rorschach Indicators to a Vocational Interest Group of Male Kansas State Freshmen.* Master's thesis, Kansas State College (Manhattan, Kan.), 1951.

1292. WILEY, JOHN MASON. *The Use of a Modified Form of the Graphic Rorschach Technique With Brain Injured Subjects.* Master's thesis, University of North Carolina (Chapel Hill, N.C.), 1951.

1293. YOUMANS, CHARLES L., JR. *A Study of the Psychogenic Aspects of Ulcerative Colitis Using the Rorschach Technique.* Master's thesis, Tulane University (New Orleans, La.), 1951.

1294. ZIMMERMAN, IRLA LEE; NEWTON, BERNAUR W.; SULLIVAN, ELLEN B.; DORCUS, ROY M.; STERNBERG, THOMAS H.; AND ZIMMERMAN, MURRAY C. "An Evaluation of the Psychological Processes of the Neurosyphilitic: III, A 'Sign' Approach to the Rorschach in Neurosyphilis." Abstract. *Am Psychol* 6:500 S '51. *

1295. AINSWORTH, MARY D., AND BOSTON, MARY. "Psychodiagnostic Assessments of a Child After Prolonged Separation in Early Childhood." *Brit J Med Psychol* 25:169–201 pt 4 '52. * (*PA* 27:7845)

1296. ALEXANDER, LEO, AND AX, ALBERT F. Chap. 12, "Rorschach Studies in Combat Flying Personnel," pp. 219–43. (*PA* 27:591) In *Relation of Psychological Tests to Psychiatry.* Edited by Paul H. Hoch and Joseph Zubin. New York: Grune & Stratton, Inc., 1952. Pp. viii, 301. *

1297. ALLEN, ROBERT M.; MANNE, SIGMUND H.; AND STIFF, MARGARET. "The Influence of Color on the Consistency of Responses in the Rorschach Test." *J Clin Psychol* 8:97–8 Ja '52. * (*PA* 27:1946)

1298. ALLERHAND, MELVIN E. *Evaluation of the Chiaroscuro Determinant of the Rorschach Ink Blot Tests as an Indicator of Manifest Anxiety.* Doctor's thesis, University of Nebraska (Lincoln, Neb.), 1952. (Abstract: *Am Psychol* 7:359)

1299. ALTUS, WILLIAM D., AND ALTUS, GRACE THOMPSON. "Rorschach Movement Variables and Verbal Intelligence." *J Abn & Social Psychol* 47:531–3 Ap '52. * (*PA* 27:2698)

1300. AMES, LOUISE BATES; LEARNED, JANET; METRAUX, RUTH W.; AND WALKER, RICHARD N. *Child Rorschach Responses: Developmental Trends From Two to Ten Years.* New York: Paul B. Hoeber, Inc., 1952. Pp. xv, 310. * (*PA* 27:7066)

1301. ARONSON, MARVIN L. "A Study of the Freudian Theory of Paranoia by Means of the Rorschach Test." *J Proj Tech* 16:397–411 D '52. * (*PA* 28:2981)

1302. AXELROD, JOSEPH. *An Evaluation of the Effect on Progress in Therapy of Similarities and Differences Between the Personalities of Patients and Their Therapists.* Doctor's thesis, New York University (New York, N.Y.), 1952. (*DA* 12:329)

1303. BANDURA, ALBERT. *A Study of Some of the Psychological Processes Associated With the Rorschach White Space Response.* Doctor's thesis, State University of Iowa (Iowa City, Iowa), 1952.

1304. BARRELL, ROBERT P. "The Relationship of Various Types of Movement Responses in the Rorschach Test to Personality Trait Ratings." Abstract. *Am Psychol* 7:358 Jl '52.

1305. BARRY, JOHN R.; BLYTH, DAVID D.; AND ALBRECHT, ROBERT. "Relationships Between Rorschach Scores and Adjustment Level." *J Consult Psychol* 16:30–6 F '52. *

1306. BECK, SAMUEL J. "The Experimental Validation of the Rorschach Test: IV, Discussion and Critical Evaluation." *Am J Orthopsychiatry* 22:771–5 O '52. * (*PA* 27:5854)

1307. BECK, SAMUEL J. *Rorschach's Test: III, Advances in Interpretation.* New York: Grune & Stratton, Inc., 1952. Pp. x, 301. * (*PA* 28:926)

1308. BELL, ALICE; TROSMAN, HARRY; AND ROSS, DONALD. "The Use of Projective Techniques in the Investigation of Emotional Aspects of General Medical Disorders: I, The Rorschach Method." *J Proj Tech* 16:428–43 D '52. * (*PA* 28:2613)

1309. BENNETT, CLAYTON LEON. *An Experimental Study of Relationships Between Human Electroencephalograms and Certain Rorschach Scoring Categories.* Doctor's thesis, University of Southern California (Los Angeles, Calif.), 1952.

1310. BENTON, ARTHUR L. "The Experimental Validation of the Rorschach Test: II, The Significance of Rorschach Color Responses." *Am J Orthopsychiatry* 22:755–63 O 52. * (*PA* 27:5856)

1311. BERNSTEIN, LEONARD. *The Effects of Pre-Operative Stress Upon Rorschach Test Factors Alleged to Be Signs of Anxiety.* Doctor's thesis, Fordham University (New York, N.Y.), 1952.

1312. BLANTON, RICHARD LINN. *The Effect of Induced Anxiety on Flexibility of Set-Shifting in Rigid and Non-Rigid Subjects.* Doctor's thesis, Vanderbilt University (Nashville, Tenn.), 1952. (*DA* 12:777–8)

1313. BLANTON, RICHARD, AND LANDSMAN, TED. "The Retest Reliability of the Group Rorschach and Some Relationships to the MMPI." *J Consult Psychol* 16:265–7 Ag '52. * (*PA* 27:4241)

1314. BLECHNER, JANET ELISCU. *The Influence of Educational Conditioning on Two Scoring Factors of the Group-Administered Rorschach Test.* Doctor's thesis, University of California (Berkeley, Calif.), 1952.

1315. BLUM, GERALD S., AND MILLER, DANIEL R. "Exploring the Psychoanalytic Theory of the 'Oral Character.'" *J Personality* 20:287–304 Mr '52. * (*PA* 27:2353)

1316. BROWN, FRED; LINDNER, ROBERT; SCHAFER, ROY; SCHUMACHER, AUDREY; AND WYATT, FREDERICK. "Symposium: Problems of Content Analysis in the Rorschach." Abstract. *J Proj Tech* 16:389 S '52. *

1317. BUHLER, CHARLOTTE; LEFEVER, D. WELTY; KALLSTEDT, FRANCIS E.; AND PEAK, HORACE M. *Development of the Basic Rorschach Score: Supplementary Monograph.* Los Angeles, Calif.: Rorschach Standardization Study, 1952. Pp. iv, 71. * (*PA* 26:5602)

1318. BUKER, SAMUEL L. *A Study of Personality Variables Associated With Responses to the Achromatic Features of the Rorschach Stimulus Cards.* Doctor's thesis, Northwestern University (Evanston, Ill.), 1952.

1319. BURCHARD, EDWARD M. L. "The Use of Projective Techniques in the Analysis of Creativity." *J Proj Tech* 16:412–27 D '52. * (*PA* 28:2242)

1320. CALDEN, GEORGE. *The Relationship of Varied Test Definitions and Degrees of Ego-Involvement to Rorschach Test Performance.* Doctor's thesis, University of Michigan (Ann Arbor, Mich.), 1952. (*DA* 12:214)

1321. CALDWELL, BETTYE McD.; ULETT, GEORGE A.; MENSH, IVAN N.; AND GRANICK, SAMUEL. "Levels of Data in Rorschach Interpretation." *J Clin Psychol* 8:374–9 O '52. * (*PA* 27:5860)

1322. CAMPBELL, ELIZABETH FLETCHER. *The Effects of Colour in the Wechsler-Bellevue Block Design Subtest and in the Rorschach.* Master's thesis, University of Western Ontario (London, Ont., Canada), 1952.

1323. CARLSON, RAE. "A Normative Study of Rorschach Responses of Eight Year Old Children." *J Proj Tech* 16:56–65 Mr '52. * (*PA* 27:415)

1324. CARLSON, VIRGIL R., AND LAZARUS, RICHARD S. "A Repetition of Williams' Experiment on Stress and Associated Rorschach Factors." Abstract. *Am Psychol* 7:317 Jl '52. *

1325. CHARLES, HARVEY. *The Use of a Selected Projective Technique in the Teacher Selection Process.* Doctor's thesis, Indiana University (Bloomington, Ind.), 1952.

1326. COHEN, LEON B. *The Influence of Two Attitudinal Variables on Group Rorschach Test Performance.* Doctor's thesis, University of Michigan (Ann Arbor, Mich.), 1952. (*DA* 12:215)

1327. CORTER, HAROLD M. "Factor Analysis of Some Reasoning Tests." *Psychol Monogr* 66(8):1–31 '52. * (*PA* 27:4995)

1328. DAVIDSON, HELEN H., AND KRUGLOV, LORRAINE. "Personality Characteristics of the Institutionalized Aged." *J Consult Psychol* 16:5–12 F '52. * (*PA* 27:1875)

1329. DEVOS, GEORGE A. *Acculturation and Personality Structure: A Rorschach Study of Japanese Americans.* Doctor's thesis, University of Chicago (Chicago, Ill.), 1952.

1330. DEVOS, GEORGE. "A Quantitative Approach to Affective Symbolism in Rorschach Responses." *J Proj Tech* 16:133–50 Je '52. * (*PA* 28:2625)

1331. DÖRKEN, HERBERT, JR., AND KRAL, V. ADALBERT. "The Psychological Differentiation of Organic Brain Lesions and Their localization by Means of the Rorschach Test." *Am J Psychiatry* 108:764–70 Ap '52. * (*PA* 26:7182)

1332. DUNN, WESLEY A. "A Comparison Between Certain Rorschach Scoring Signs, College Freshman Orientation Test Scores, and Grade Point Indices." Abstract. *Am Psychol* 7:358–9 Jl '52. *

1333. ERIKSEN, CHARLES W. "Ego Strength and the Recall of Completed Versus Incompleted Tasks." Abstract. *Am Psychol* 7:316 Jl '52. *

1334. ERIKSEN, CHARLES W., AND LAZARUS, RICHARD S. "Perceptual Defense and Projective Tests." *J Abn & Social Psychol* 47:302–8 Ap '52. * (*PA* 27:2716)

1335. ERIKSEN, CHARLES W.; LAZARUS, RICHARD S.; AND STRANGE, JACK R. "Psychological Stress and Its Personality Correlates: Part II, The Rorschach Test and Other Personality Measures." *J Personality* 20:27–86 Mr '52. * (*PA* 27:2551)

1336. FERGUSON, ROBERT A. *An Investigation of the Animal Response With Particular Reference to Its Appearance on the Rorschach Inkblot Test.* Doctor's thesis, University of Kentucky (Lexington, Ky.), 1952.

1337. FILMER-BENNETT, GORDON. "Prognostic Indices in the Rorschach Records of Hospitalized Patients." *J Abn & Social Psychol* 47:502–6 Ap '52. * (*PA* 27:2878)

1338. FORER, B. R.; FARBEROW, N. L.; MEYER, M. M.; AND TOLMAN, R. S. "Consistency and Agreement in the Judgment of Rorschach Signs." *J Proj Tech* 16:346–51 S '52. * (*PA* 28:2631)

1339. FORTIER, R. *A Study of the Relation of the Response to Color and Some Personality Functions: I, The Response to Color and Ego Functions: An Effect-Color Theory; II, An Analysis of Groups of Dream Series Differing in the Frequency of Dreams in Color; III, Some Rorschach Variables Associated With the Frequency of Dreams in Color.* Doctor's thesis, Western Reserve University (Cleveland, Ohio), 1952.

1340. FOSBERG, IRVING ARTHUR. "Nationalization of Rorschach Research: A Plan for a Cooperative Research Project." Abstract. *Am Psychol* 7:359 Jl '52. *

1341. FRANK, IRVING H. *A Genetic Evaluation of Perceptual Structurization in Certain Psychoneurotic Disorders by Means of the Rorschach Technique.* Doctor's thesis, Boston University (Boston, Mass.), 1952.

1342. FRANKLE, ALLAN H. "Validity of Rorschach *M* and *H* Plus *Hd* for Predicting Fieldwork Performance of Student Social Workers." Abstract. *Am Psychol* 7:289 Jl '52. *

1343. FRIEDMAN, HOWARD. "A Comparison of a Group of Hebephrenic and Catatonic Schizophrenics With Two Groups of Normal Adults by Means of Certain Variables of the Rorschach Test." *J Proj Tech* 16:352–60 S '52. * (*PA* 28:2995)

1344. GIBBY, ROBERT G. "Examiner Influence on the Rorschach Inquiry." *J Consult Psychol* 16:449–55 D '52. * (*PA* 28:949)

1345. GIBBY, ROBERT G.; MILLER, DANIEL R.; AND WALKER, EDWARD L. "Examiner Variance in the Rorschach Protocols of Neuropsychiatric Patients." Abstract. *Am Psychol* 7:337–8 Jl '52. *

1346. GILHOOLY, FRANCIS M. *The Validity and Reliability of the Rorschach and the Thematic Apperception Tests When These Tests Are Interpreted by the Method of Blind Analysis.* Doctor's thesis, Fordham University (New York, N.Y.), 1952.

1347. GLADSTONE, ROY. "A Factor in the Degeneration of Discussions." *J Ed Psychol* 43:176–8 Mr '52. * (*PA* 27:3323)

1348. GORLOW, LEON; ZIMET, CARL N.; AND FINE, HAROLD J. "The Validity of Anxiety and Hostility Rorschach Content Scores Among Adolescents." *J Consult Psychol* 16:73–5 F '52. * (*PA* 27:1961)

1349. GRANT, MARGUERITE Q.; IVES, VIRGINIA; AND RANZONI, JANE H. "Reliability and Validity of Judges' Ratings of Adjustment on the Rorschach." *Psychol Monogr* 66(2):1–20 '52. * (*PA* 27:2724)

1350. GRAYSON, HARRY M. "The Grayson-Brentwood Rorschach Series: I, Rorschach Productivity and Card Preferences as Influenced by Experimental Variation of Color and Shading." Abstract. *J Proj Tech* 16:389 S '52. *

1351. GREMBOWICZ, EUGENE T. *Color and Affectivity in the Rorschach Test.* Doctor's thesis, Loyola University (Chicago, Ill.), 1952.

1352. GURVITZ, MILTON S., AND MILLER, JOSEPH S. A. Chap. 11, "Some Theoretical and Practical Aspects of the Diagnosis of Early and Latent Schizophrenia by Means of Psychological Testing," pp. 189–207. (*PA* 27:571) Discussion by Paul H. Hoch, pp. 215–6. In *Relation of Psychological Tests to Psychiatry.* Edited by Paul H. Hoch and Joseph Zubin. New York: Grune & Stratton, 1952. Pp. viii, 301. *

1353. HALES, WILLIAM M. "Profile Patterning and Coding of the Rorschach Test: A Preliminary Report of Research Methods and Materials." *J Consult Psychol* 16:37–42 F '52. * (*PA* 27:1964)

1354. HARROWER, MOLLY. *Appraising Personality: The Use of Psychological Tests in the Practice of Medicine,* pp. 41–80. New York: W. W. Norton & Co., Inc., 1952. Pp. xvii, 197. * (*PA* 27:6532)

1355. HAYS, WILLIAM. "Age and Sex Differences on the Rorschach Experience Balance." *J Abn & Social Psychol* 47:390–3 Ap '52. * (*PA* 27:2726)

1356. HERTZ, MARGUERITE R. Chap. 8, "The Rorschach: Thirty Years After," pp. 108–48. (*PA* 27:3555) In *Progress in Clinical Psychology, Vol. I, Sect. 1.* Edited by Daniel Brower and Lawrence E. Abt. New York: Grune & Stratton, Inc., 1952. Pp. xi, 328. *

1357. HERTZ, MARGUERITE R., AND LOEHRKE, LEAH M. "The Application of the Piotrowski and the Hughes Signs of Organic Defect to a Group of Patients Suffering From Post-traumatic Encephalopathy." Abstract. *J Proj Tech* 16:384–5 S '52. *

1358. HERTZ, MARGUERITE R., AND LOEHRKE, LEAH M. "An Evaluation of the Rorschach Method for the Study of Brain Injury." Abstract. *Am Psychol* 7:349–50 Jl '52. *

1359. HESSEL, MARTHA G., AND TRAVERS, ROBERT M. W. "Relationships Between Rorschach Performance and Student Teaching." Abstract. *Am Psychol* 7:370 Jl '52. *

1360. HOLT, ROBERT R., AND LUBORSKY, LESTER. "Research in the Selection of Psychiatrists: A Second Interim Report." *B Menninger Clinic* 16:125–35 Jl '52. * (*PA* 27:3916)

1361. HOLTZMAN, WAYNE H. "Adjustment and Leadership: A Study of the Rorschach Test." *J Social Psychol* 36:179–89 N '52. * (*PA* 27:7117)

1362. HOLZBERG, JULES D., AND BELMONT, LILLIAN. "The Relationship Between Factors on the Wechsler-Bellevue and Rorschach Having Common Psychological Rationale." *J Consult Psychol* 16:23–9 F '52. * (*PA* 27:1966)

1363. HOLZBERG, JULES D., AND CAHEN, ELEANOR R. "The Relationship Between Psychiatric Improvement and Certain Pathologic Changes in the Rorschach During Electroconvulsive Therapy." *J Clin & Exp Psychopathol* 13:237–46 D '52. * (*PA* 28:3001)

1364. HOLZBERG, JULES D., AND HAHN, FRED. "The Picture-Frustration Technique as a Measure of Hostility and Guilt Reactions in Adolescent Psychopaths." Discussion by Goldie R. Kaback. *Am J Orthopsychiatry* 22:776–97 O '52. * (*PA* 27:5995)

1365. HOROWITZ, MILTON J. *Developmental Changes in Rorschach Test and Thematic Apperception Test Performances of Children, Six Through Nine Years of Age: An Exploratory Study.* Doctor's thesis, University of Kansas (Lawrence, Kan.), 1952.

1366. HOWIE, MARGARET M. "The Rorschach Test Applied to a Group of Scottish Children." Abstract. *Brit J Ed Psychol* 22:214–6 N '52. *

1367. HSÜ, E. H. "Further Comments on the Rorschach Response and Factor Analysis." *J General Psychol* 47:239–41 O '52. * (*PA* 27:5877)

1368. JACOBS, STEVEN M., AND GRAHAM, E. ELLIS. "A Comparison of the Rorschachs of Juvenile Auto Thieves and Juvenile Burglars." Abstract. *J Colo-Wyo Acad Sci* 4:76 O '52. *

1369. JOHNSON, ELIZABETH Z. "The Use of the Rorschach Prognostic Scale With Raven's Progressive Matrices to Predict Playtherapy Progress Among Retarded Children." Abstract. *J Proj Tech* 16:385 S '52. *

1370. KAHN, MARVIN W. *Perceptual Consistency of Rorschach Factors With Therapy Interview Responses, and Generalization Change as a Predictor of Psychotherapeutic Success.* Doctor's thesis, Pennsylvania State College (State College, Pa.), 1952.

1371. KALLSTEDT, FRANCES E. "A Rorschach Study of Sixty-Six Adolescents." *J Clin Psychol* 8:129–32 Ap '52. * (*PA* 27:1861)

1372. KASS, WALTER. *Rorschach Indications for Predicting Proficiency in the Selection of Physicians for Training in Psychiatry in a Residency Program.* Doctor's thesis, New York University (New York, N.Y.), 1952.

1373. KEEHN, J. D. "Rorschach Validation: I, A Rationale." *J Mental Sci* 98:697–706 O '52. * (*PA* 27:5880)

1374. KJENAAS, NANCY K., AND BROZEK, JOSEF. "Personality in Experimental Semistarvation." *Psychosom Med* 14:115–28 Mr–Ap '52. * (*PA* 26:6701)

1375. KLATSKIN, ETHELYN HENRY. "An Analysis of the Effect of the Test Situation Upon the Rorschach Record: Formal Scoring Characteristics." *J Proj Tech* 16:193–9 Je '52. * (*PA* 28:2644)

1376. KLETTI, LEROY. *The Agreement in Anxiety Measurement Between the Rorschach Test and the Minnesota Multiphasic Personality Inventory.* Master's thesis, University of North Dakota (Grand Forks, N.D.), 1952.

1377. KNOPF, IRWIN J. *A Study of the Effects of Recent Perceptual Training and Experience on the Rorschach Performance.* Doctor's thesis, Northwestern University (Evanston, Ill.), 1952.

1378. KOTKOV, BENJAMIN, AND MURAWSKI, BENJAMIN. "A Rorschach Study of the Personality Structure of Obese Women." *J Clin Psychol* 8:391–6 O '52. * (*PA* 27:6069)

1379. KROUT, JOHANNA; KROUT, MAURICE H.; AND DULIN, THEODORE J. "Rorschach Test-Retest as a Gauge of Progress in Psychotherapy." *J Clin Psychol* 8:380–4 O '52. * (*PA* 27:5933)

1380. LAWSON, J. L., JR. *A Rorschach Study of the Epileptic Personality.* Doctor's thesis, University of Kentucky (Lexington, Ky.), 1952.

1381. LEDWITH, NETTIE H. "Rorschach Responses of the Elementary School Child: Progress Report." *J Proj Tech* 16:80–5 Mr '52. * (*PA* 27:433)

1382. LEIMAN, CHARLES J. *An Investigation of the Perception of Movement on the Rorschach Ink-Blots.* Doctor's thesis, University of Kentucky (Lexington, Ky.), 1952.

1383. LEVI, JOSEPH, AND KRAEMER, DORIS. "Significance of a Preponderance of Human Movement Responses on the Rorschach in Children Below Age Ten." *J Proj Tech* 16:361–5 S '52. * (*PA* 28:2649)

1384. LEVY, RUTH J. "The Rorschach Pattern in Neurodermatitis." *Psychosom Med* 14:41–9 Ja–F '52. * (*PA* 26:6476)

1385. LIPTON, EDMOND, AND CERES, MILDRED. "Correlation of Clinical Improvement of Intensively Treated Psychoneurotics With Changes in Consecutive Rorschach Tests." *Psychiatric Q Sup* 26:103–17 pt 1 '52. * (*PA* 27:4489)

1386. LOEHRKE, LEAH M. *An Evaluation of the Rorschach Method for the Study of Brain Injury.* Doctor's thesis, Western Reserve University (Cleveland, Ohio), 1952.

1387. LUKE, WALTER. *The Relationship Between Suggestibility and the Rorschach Test.* Master's thesis, University of Detroit (Detroit, Mich.), 1952.

1388. McDONALD, FRANKLIN RANDOLPH. *The Effect of Differential Cultural Pressures on Projective Test Performances of Negroes.* Doctor's thesis, University of Southern California (Los Angeles, Calif.), 1952.

1389. MAGARET, ANN. "Clinical Methods: Psychodiagnostics," pp. 297–302. (*PA* 26:4799) In *Annual Review of Psychology, Vol. 3.* Edited by Calvin P. Stone and Donald W. Taylor. Stanford, Calif.: Annual Reviews, Inc., 1952. Pp. ix, 462. *

1390. MALCOM, EDWARD V. *A Study of the Validity of Individual Personality Profiles Based on Each of Four Projective Techniques.* Doctor's thesis, University of Michigan (Ann Arbor, Mich.), 1952. (*DA* 12:221)

1391. MARQUIS, DOROTHY P.; SINNETT, E. ROBERT; AND WINTER, WILLIAM D. "A Psychological Study of Peptic Ulcer Patients." *J Clin Psychol* 8:266–72 Jl '52. * (*PA* 27:6072)

1392. MARSH, JAMES T. *An Investigation of Some Examiner Influences on Productivity in the Rorschach Test.* Doctor's thesis, University of California (Los Angeles, Calif.), 1952.

1393. MARTIN, HARRY. *A Rorschach Study of Suicide.* Doctor's thesis, University of Kentucky (Lexington, Ky.), 1952.

1394. MATARAZZO, JOSEPH D., AND MENSH, IVAN N. "Reaction Time Characteristics of the Rorschach Test." *J Consult Psychol* 16:132–9 Ap '52. * (*PA* 27:2744)

1395. MATARAZZO, RUTH G.; WATSON, ROBERT I.; AND ULETT, GEORGE A. "Relationship of Rorschach Scoring Categories to Modes of Perception Induced by Intermittent Photic Stimulation—A Methodological Study of Perception." *J Clin Psychol* 8:368–74 O '52. * (*PA* 27:6117)

1396. MEHR, HELEN MARGULIES. "The Application of Psychological Tests and Methods to Schizophrenia in Children." *Nerv Child* 10:63–93 no 1 '52. * (*PA* 27:6040)

1397. MENSH, IVAN N. "The Experimental Validation of the Rorschach Test: III, Treatment of Data." *Am J Orthopsychiatry* 22:764–70 O '52. * (*PA* 27:5889)

1398. MEYER, GEORGE, AND THOMPSON, JACK. "The Performance of Kindergarten Children on the Rorschach Test: A Normative Study." *J Proj Tech* 16:86–111 Mr '52. * (*PA* 27:436)

1399. MILLER, CARMEN. *A Comparison of Personality Characteristics of High-Accident and Low-Accident Bus and Street Car Operators.* Doctor's thesis, Western Reserve University (Cleveland, Ohio), 1952.

1400. MINDESS, HARVEY. *Predicting Patients' Responses to Psychotherapy; A Preliminary Investigation of the Validity of "The Prognostic Rating Scale for the Rorschach."* Doctor's thesis, University of California (Los Angeles, Calif.), 1952.

1401. MITCHELL, MILDRED B. "Preferences for Rorschach Cards." *J Proj Tech* 16:203–11 Je '52. * (*PA* 28:2659)

1402. MONTALTO, FANNIE D. "Maternal Behavior and Child Personality: A Rorschach Study." *J Proj Tech* 16:151–78 Je '52. * (*PA* 28:2338)

1403. MURPHY, WILLIAM F. "Evaluation of Psychotherapy With Modified Rorschach Techniques." *Am J Psychother* 6:471–83 Jl '52. * (*PA* 27:3589)

1404. MYATT, MARY FRANCES. *A Study of the Relationship Between Motivation and Test Performance of Patients in a Rehabilitation Ward.* Doctor's thesis, University of Minnesota (Minneapolis, Minn.), 1952. (*DA* 12:339)

1405. NEWTON, RICHARD L. *An Investigation of Clinical Judgment: A Comparison of Results Obtained With Judgment Scales Applied to the Rorschach and to Case Material.* Doctor's thesis, University of Pittsburgh (Pittsburgh, Pa.), 1952.

1406. NORMAN, RALPH D.; LIVERANT, SHEPHARD; AND REDLO, MIRIAM. "The Influence of a Superficial Immediately Preceding 'Set' Upon Responses to the Rorschach." *J Consult Psychol* 16:261–4 Ag '52. * (*PA* 27:4266)

1407. OLTEAN, MARY. "Organic Pathology Accompanying Diabetes Mellitus as Indicated by the Rorschach." *J Proj Tech* 16:485–8 D '52. * (*PA* 28:3091)

1408. PAGE, CURTIS W., AND GLAD, DONALD D. "Experimental Use of the Rorschach and Emotional Projection Tests in the Study of Emotional Changes Coincident to Cortisone Therapy." Abstract. *J Colo-Wyo Acad Sci* 4:78–9 O '52. *

1409. PASCAL, GERALD R., AND HERZBERG, FREDERICK I. "The Detection of Deviant Sexual Practice From Performance on the Rorschach Test." *J Proj Tech* 16:366–73 S '52. * (*PA* 28:2927)

1410. PECK, CECIL P. *An Investigation of the Association-Provoking Properties and Meanings Attributed to the Rorschach Inkblots.* Doctor's thesis, University of Kentucky (Lexington, Ky.), 1952.

1411. PEÑA, CESAREO D. *Genetic Parallels of Perceptual Structurization in Cerebral Pathology as Reflected in Rorschach Test Responses.* Doctor's thesis, Boston University (Boston, Mass.), 1952.

1412. PEPINSKY, HAROLD B.; CLYDE, ROBIN J.; OLESEN, BARBARA A.; AND VAN ATTA, ELLIS L. "The Criterion in Counseling: I, Individual Personality and Behavior in a Social Group." *Ed & Psychol Meas* 12:178–93 su '52. * (*PA* 27:5942)

1413. PIOTROWSKI, ZYGMUNT A., AND ABRAHAMSEN, DAVID. "Sexual Crime, Alcohol, and the Rorschach Test." *Psychiatric Q Sup* 26:248–60 pt 2 '52. * (*PA* 27:5259)

1414. PIOTROWSKI, ZYGMUNT A., AND LEWIS, NOLAN D. C. Chap. 4, "An Experimental Criterion for the Prognostication of the Status of Schizophrenics After a Three-Year-Interval Based on Rorschach Data," pp. 51–72. (*PA* 27:586) Discussion by Joseph Zubin (pp. 100–3) and Joseph F. Kubis (pp. 105–7). In *Relation of Psychological Tests to Psychiatry.* Edited by Paul H. Hoch and Joseph Zubin. New York: Grune & Stratton, Inc., 1952. Pp. viii, 301. *

1415. PIOTROWSKI, ZYGMUNT, AND SCHREIBER, MARTIN. "Rorschach Perceptanalytic Measurement of Personality Changes During and After Intensive Psychoanalytically Oriented Psychotherapy," pp. 337–61. In *Specialized Techniques in Psychotherapy.* Edited by Gustav Bychowski and J. Louise Despert. New York: Basic Books, Inc., 1952. Pp. xii, 371. * (*PA* 27:1194)

1416. PRATT, CAROLYN. "A Validation Study of Intropunitive and Extrapunitive Signs on the Rorschach Test, Based Upon Records Given by Suicidal and Homicidal Subjects." Abstract. *Proc Ind Acad Sci* 62:296 '52. *

1417. PRATT, CAROLYN. *Validation Study of the Intropunitive and Extrapunitive Signs in the Rorschach Test.* Doctor's thesis, Purdue University (Lafayette, Ind.), 1952.

1418. RACUSEN, FRANCES RHEA. *An Exploratory Investigation of the Creativity and Productivity Variables on the Rorschach and Thematic Apperception Tests.* Doctor's thesis, State University of Iowa (Iowa City, Iowa), 1952.

1419. RICHARDS, T. W. "Personality of the Convulsive Patient in Military Service." *Psychol Monogr* 66(14):1–23 '52. * (*PA* 27:7364)

1420. ROCHLIN, ISAIAH. "The Investigation, Through the Use of Projective Techniques, of Non-intellectual Factors in the Learning of Mathematics." Abstract. *Am Psychol* 7:368 Jl '52. *

1421. ROE, ANNE. "Analysis of Group Rorschachs of Psychologists and Anthropologists." *J Proj Tech* 16:212–24 Je '52. * (*PA* 28:3443)

1422. ROE, ANNE. "Group Rorschachs of University Faculties." *J Consult Psychol* 16:18–22 F '52. * (*PA* 27:2258)

1423. ROE, ANNE. "Two Rorschach Scoring Techniques: The Inspection Technique and the Basic Rorschach." *J Abn & Social Psychol* 47:263–4 Ap '52. * (*PA* 27:2760)

1424. ROHRER, JOHN H.; BAGBY, JAMES W., JR.; AND WILKINS, WALTER L. "The Reliability of Individual Inquiries and Scorings of the Rorschach." Abstract. *Am Psychol* 7:290–1 Jl '52. *

1425. ROSEN, EPHRAIM. "MMPI and Rorschach Correlates of the Rorschach White Space Response." *J Clin Psychol* 8:283–8 Jl '52. * (*PA* 27:5899)

1426. ROSEN, IRWIN C. *Parallel Researches in Sexual Psychopathology: I, A Comparison of a Group of Rapists and Controls on Certain Psychological Variables.* Doctor's thesis, University of Pittsburgh (Pittsburgh, Pa.), 1952.

1427. ROSENBERG, SELIG. *The Relationship of Certain Personality Factors to Prognosis in Psychotherapy.* Doctor's thesis, New York University (New York, N.Y.), 1952. (*DA* 12:388)

1428. SALTER, MARY D. *The Rorschach Method: Notes Based on the Klopfer Method.* Toronto, Canada: University Bookstore, University of Toronto, [1952]. Pp. i, 77. *

1429. SAMUELS, HENRY. "The Validity of Personality-Trait Ratings Based on Projective Techniques." *Psychol Monogr* 66(5):1–21 '52. * (*PA* 27:5161)

1430. SANDERSON, HERBERT. "Card Titles in Testing the Limits in Rorschach." *J Psychol* 33:27–9 Ja '52. * (*PA* 26:6287)

1431. SARBIN, THEODORE R., AND FARBEROW, NORMAN L. "Contributions to Role-Taking Theory: A Clinical Study of Self and Role." *J Abn & Social Psychol* 47:117–25 Ja '52. * (*PA* 26:6111)

1432. SCHAFER, ROY. "Rorschach Imagery in Aging Psychiatric Patients." Abstract. *J Proj Tech* 16:385–6 S '52. *

1433. SCHWARTZ, EMANUEL K. "Personality Correlates of Paraplegia Indicated in the Rorschach Situation." Abstract. *J Proj Tech* 16:386 S '52. *

1434. SCHWARTZ, MILTON M. "The Relationship Between Projective Test Scoring Categories and Activity Preferences." *Genetic Psychol Monogr* 46:133–81 N '52. * (*PA* 27:4269)

1435. SHAMES, GEORGE HERBERT. *An Investigation of Prognosis and Evaluation in Speech Therapy.* Doctor's thesis, University of Pittsburgh (Pittsburgh, Pa.), 1952.

1436. SHATIN, LEO. "Psychoneurosis and Psychosomatic Reactions: A Rorschach Contrast." *J Consult Psychol* 16:220–3 Je '52. * (*PA* 27:5324)

1437. SHEPHERD, JOHN RALPH. *An Experimental Study of the Responses of Stage-Frightened Students to Certain Scoring Categories of the Group Rorschach Test.* Doctor's thesis, University of Southern California (Los Angeles, Calif.), 1952.

1438. SHERESHEVSKI-SHERE, EUGENIA, AND LASSER, LEONARD M. "An Evaluation of Water Responses in the Rorschachs of Alcoholics." *J Proj Tech* 16:489–95 D '52. * (*PA* 28:2939)

1439. SHERMAN, MURRAY. "A Comparison of Formal and Content Factors in the Diagnostic Testing of Schizophrenia." *Genetic Psychol Monogr* 46:183–234 N '52. * (*PA* 27:4473)

1440. SHNEIDMAN, EDWIN S. "The Case of Jay: Psychological Test and Anamnestic Data." *J Proj Tech* 16:297–345 S '52. * (*PA* 28:2676)

1441. SIIPOLA, ELSA, AND TAYLOR, VIVIAN. "Reactions to Ink Blots Under Free and Pressure Conditions." *J Personality* 21:22–47 S '52. * (*PA* 27:5903)

1442. SINGER, HARRY. *Validity of the Projection of Sexuality in Drawing the Human Figure.* Master's thesis, Western Reserve University (Cleveland, Ohio), 1952.

1443. SINGER, JEROME L. "The Behn-Rorschach Inkblots: A Preliminary Comparison With the Original Rorschach Series." *J Proj Tech* 16:238–45 Je '52. * (*PA* 28:2679)

1444. SINGER, JEROME L.; MELTZOFF, JULIAN; AND GOLDMAN, GEORGE D. "Rorschach Movement Responses Following Motor Inhibition and Hyperactivity." *J Consult Psychol* 16:359–64 O '52. * (*PA* 27:5904)

1445. SPIES, KATHRYN ELAINE. *A Comparison of Dream and Rorschach Content of Psychotics and Non-Psychotics.* Master's thesis, University of Chicago (Chicago, Ill.), 1952.

1446. STARER, EMANUEL. "Aggressive Reactions and Sources of Frustration in Anxiety Neurotics and Paranoid Schizophrenics." *J Clin Psychol* 8:307–9 Jl '52. * (*PA* 27:5979)

1447. STEISEL, IRA M. "The Rorschach Test and Suggestibility." *J Abn & Social Psychol* 47:607–14 Jl '52. * (*PA* 27:3563)

1448. STOTSKY, BERNARD A. "A Comparison of Remitting and

Nonremitting Schizophrenics on Psychological Tests." *J Abn & Social Psychol* 47:489–96 Ap '52. * (PA 27:2898)

1449. TAYLOR, KENNETH E. *Parallel Researches in Sexual Psychopathology: II, A Comparison of a Group of Pedophiliacs and Controls on Certain Psychological Variables.* Doctor's thesis, University of Pittsburgh (Pittsburgh, Pa.), 1952.

1450. THETFORD, WILLIAM N. "Fantasy Perceptions in the Personality Development of Normal and Deviant Children." *Am J Orthopsychiatry* 22:542–50 Jl '52. * (PA 27:5314)

1451. THETFORD, WILLIAM N. "Personality Characteristics of Schizophrenic Children Viewed Through the Rorschach Test." Abstract. *Am Psychol* 7:301–2 Jl '52. *

1452. THIESEN, J. WARREN. "A Pattern Analysis of Structural Characteristics of the Rorschach Test in Schizophrenia." *J Consult Psychol* 16:365–70 O '52. * (PA 27:6045)

1453. THOMAS, HOBART F. *The Relationship of Movement Responses on the Rorschach Test to the Defense Mechanism of Projection.* Doctor's thesis, Stanford University (Stanford, Calif.), 1952.

1454. TOMKINS, SILVAN S. Chap. 6, "Personality and Intelligence: Integration and Psychometric Technics," pp. 87–95. (PA 27:445) Discussion by Joseph Zubin, pp. 103–4. In *Relation of Psychological Tests to Psychiatry.* Edited by Paul H. Hoch and Joseph Zubin. New York: Grune & Stratton, Inc., 1952. Pp. viii, 301. *

1455. UEHLING, HAROLD F. "Rorschach 'Shock' for Two Special Populations." *J Consult Psychol* 16:224–5 Je '52. * (PA 27:5167)

1456. VORHAUS, PAULINE G. "Case Study of an Adolescent Boy With Reading Disability." *J Proj Tech* 16:20–41 Mr '52. * (PA 27:650)

1457. VORHAUS, PAULINE G. "Interpretation of Jay's Rorschach Test: The Case of Jay: Interpretations and Discussion." *J Proj Tech* 16:453–6, discussion 444–5, 462–73 D '52. * (PA 28:2678)

1458. VORHAUS, PAULINE G. "Rorschach Configurations Associated With Reading Disability." *J Proj Tech* 16:3–19 Mr '52. * (PA 27:651)

1459. VORHAUS, PAULINE G. "The Use of the Rorschach in Preventive Mental Hygiene." *J Proj Tech* 16:179–92 Je '52. * (PA 28:2588)

1460. WALLACE, ANTHONY F. C. *The Modal Personality of the Tuscarora Indians as Revealed by the Rorschach Test.* Smithsonian Institution, Bureau of American Ethnology, Bulletin 150. Washington, D.C.: U.S. Government Printing Office, 1952. Pp. viii, 120. * (PA 27:6505)

1461. WATKINS, JOHN G., AND STAUFFACHER, JAMES C. "An Index of Pathological Thinking in the Rorschach." *J Proj Tech* 16:276–86 S '52. * (PA 28:2686)

1462. WENAR, CHARLES. "A Comparison of Rorschach Findings on Aging Subjects With Their Psychiatric and Social Ratings." Abstract. *Am Psychol* 7:403 Jl '52. *

1463. WESTROPE, MARTHA R. *An Investigation of the Relations Among Rorschach Indices, Manifest Anxiety, and Performance Under Stress.* Doctor's thesis, State University of Iowa (Iowa City, Iowa), 1952.

1464. WHITE, MARY ALICE, AND SCHREIBER, HANNA. "Diagnosing 'Suicidal Risks' on the Rorschach." *Psychiatric Q Sup* 26:161–89 pt 2 '52. * (PA 27:5264)

1465. WILLIAMS, MEYER. "The Experimental Validation of the Rorschach Test: I, Experimental Correlations." *Am J Orthopsychiatry* 22:749–54 O '52. * (PA 27:5913)

1466. WILSON, GLEN P., JR. *Intellectual Indicators in the Rorschach Test.* Doctor's thesis, University of Texas (Austin, Tex.), 1952.

1467. WINDLE, CHARLES. "Psychological Tests in Psychopathological Prognosis." *Psychol B* 49:451–82 S '52. * (PA 27:3567)

1468. WIRT, ROBERT DUANE. *Ideational Expression of Hostile Impulses.* Doctor's thesis, Stanford University (Stanford, Calif.), 1952.

1469. WYATT, FREDERICK. "Prediction in the Rorschach Test." *J Proj Tech* 16:252–8 Je '52. * (PA 28:2693)

1470. ABEL, THEODORA M., AND WEISSMANN, SERENA. Chap. 5, "Psychological Aspects," pp. 130–65. In *Facial Deformities and Plastic Surgery: A Psychosocial Study.* By Frances Cooke Macgregor, Theodora M. Abel, Albert Bryt, Edith Lauer, and Serena Weissmann. Springfield, Ill.: Charles C Thomas, 1953. Pp. xv, 230. * (PA 28:6403)

1471. ALCOCK, A. T. "A Study of Mother-Child Relationships, Using the Rorschach Technique, With a Pair of Identical Twins, One Schizophrenic, the Other Healthy." Abstract. *B Brit Psychol Soc* (19):29 Ja '53. *

1472. ALLEN, ROBERT M. *Introduction to the Rorschach Technique: Manual of Administration and Scoring.* New York: International Universities Press, Inc., 1953. Pp. ii, 126. * (PA 28:2607)

1473. ALLEN, ROBERT M. "The M Determinant and Color in Rorschach's Test." *J Clin Psychol* 9:198–9 Ap '53. * (PA 28:2608)

1474. ALLEN, ROBERT M.; RAY, CHARLES D.; AND POOLE, ROBERT C. "The Levy Movement Test: Suggestions for Scoring and Relationship to Rorschach Movement Responses." *J Consult Psychol* 17:195–8 Je '53. * (PA 28:2609)

1475. ALLEN, ROBERT M.; STIFF, MARGARET P.; AND ROSENZWEIG, MILTON. "The Role of Color in Rorschach's Test: A Preliminary Survey of Neurotic and Psychotic Groups." *J Clin Psychol* 9:81–3 Ja '53. * (PA 27:7749)

1476. AMES, LOUISE B.; LEARNED, JANET; METRAUX, RUTH; AND WALKER, RICHARD. "Development of Perception in the

Young Child as Observed in Responses to the Rorschach Test Blots." *J Genetic Psychol* 82:183–204 Je '53. * (PA 28:6012)

1477. ARBITMAN, HERMAN D. "Rorschach Determinants in Mentally Defective and Normal Subjects." *Training Sch B* 50:143–51 N '53. * (PA 28:6205)

1478. ARLUCK, EDWARD W., AND BALINSKY, BENJAMIN. "Possible Shifts in Functioning Through Hypnotic Suggestion." *J Proj Tech* 17:447–54 D '53. * (PA 28:6013)

1479. AULD, FRANK, JR., AND ERON, LEONARD D. "The Use of Rorschach Scores to Predict Whether Patients Will Continue Psychotherapy." *J Consult Psychol* 17:104–9 Ap '53. * (PA 28:2701)

1480. AUSUBEL, DAVID P.; SCHIFF, HERBERT M.; AND GOLDMAN, MORTON. "Qualitative Characteristics in the Learning Process Associated With Anxiety." *J Abn & Social Psychol* 48:537–47 O '53. * (PA 28:6226)

1481. BARKER, G. B. "Four Rorschach Records and Case History of a Male Schizophrenic Patient." Abstract. *B Brit Psychol Soc* (19):28–9 Ja '53. *

1482. BARRELL, ROBERT P. "Subcategories of Rorschach Human Movement Responses: A Classification System and Some Experimental Results." *J Consult Psychol* 17:254–60 Ag '53. * (PA 28:4328)

1483. BARRON, FRANK. "Some Test Correlates of Response to Psychotherapy." *J Consult Psychol* 17:235–41 Ag '53. * (PA 28:4410)

1484. BATT, HAROLD VERNON. *An Investigation of the Significance of the Rorschach Z Score.* Doctor's thesis, University of Nebraska (Lincoln, Neb.), 1953.

1485. BECK, SAMUEL J. "Rorschach Test," pp. 599–610. (PA 27:7754) In *Contributions Toward Medical Psychology: Theory and Psychodiagnostic Methods, Vol. II.* Edited by Arthur Weider. New York: Ronald Press Co., 1953. Pp. xi, 459–885. *

1486. BECK, SAMUEL J., AND NUNNALLY, J. C. "Two Researches in Schizophrenia." Discussion by Helen D. Sargent. *Am J Orthopsychiatry* 23:223–37 Ap '53. * (PA 28:2984)

1487. BEIER, ERNST G. "The Effects of Rorschach Interpretations on Intellectual Functioning of Adjusted, Questionably Adjusted, and Maladjusted Subjects." *J Proj Tech* 17:66–9 Mr '53. * (PA 28:2612)

1488. BERGER, DAVID. "The Rorschach as a Measure of Real-Life Stress." *J Consult Psychol* 17:355–8 O '53. * (PA 28:6018)

1489. BERKOWITZ, MARTIN, AND LEVINE, JACOB. "Rorschach Scoring Categories as Diagnostic 'Signs.'" *J Consult Psychol* 17:110–2 Ap '53. * (PA 28:2616)

1490. BERLOW, NATHAN. *Psychosexual Indicators on the Rorschach Test.* Doctor's thesis, University of Michigan (Ann Arbor, Mich.), 1953. (DA 13:429)

1491. BILLS, ROBERT E. "Rorschach Characteristics of Persons Scoring High and Low in Acceptance of Self." *J Consult Psychol* 17:36–8 F '53. * (PA 28:930)

1492. BLECHNER, JANET E. "Constancy of Rorschach Movement Responses Under Educational Conditioning." *Calif J Ed Res* 4:173–6 S '53. * (PA 28:4332)

1493. BRADWAY, KATHERINE, AND HEISLER, VERDA. "The Relation Between Diagnoses and Certain Types of Extreme Deviations and Content on the Rorschach." *J Proj Tech* 17:70–4 Mr '53. * (PA 28:2620)

1494. BRANSTON, W. T. "A Study of the Rorschach Test Applied to a Group of Thirteen-Year-Old Children." *Brit J Ed Psychol* 23:67–70 F '53. *

1495. BRODY, GERTRUDE GILLENSON. "A Study of the Effects of Color on Rorschach Responses." *Genetic Psychol Monogr* 48:261–311 N '53. * (PA 28:7509)

1496. BROWN, FRED. "An Exploratory Study of Dynamic Factors in the Content of the Rorschach Protocol." *J Proj Tech* 17:251–79 S '53. * (PA 28:4335)

1497. BRUCE, J. MARSHALL, JR., AND THOMAS, CAROLINE BEDELL. "A Method of Rating Certain Personality Factors as Determined by the Rorschach Test for Use in a Study of the Precursors of Hypertension and Coronary Artery Disease." *Psychiatric Q Sup* 27:207–38 pt 2 '53. * (PA 28:4708)

1498. BRUDO, CHARLES S. *The Alpha Index in the Electroencephalogram and Movement Responses on the Rorschach and PMS Tests.* Doctor's thesis, Northwestern University (Evanston, Ill.), 1953. (DA 14:393)

1499. BUHLER, CHARLOTTE; KENDIG, ISABELLE V.; PHILLIPS, LESLIE; AND PIOTROWSKI, ZYGMUNT A. "Contributions of Projective Techniques to the Understanding of Basic Psychopathology." Abstract. *J Proj Tech* 17:381–2 S '53. *

1500. BURGESS, ELVA. *Personality Factors in Over- and Under-Achievers in Engineering.* Doctor's thesis, Pennsylvania State College (State College, Pa.), 1953.

1501. CALDEN, GEORGE. "Psychosurgery in a Set of Schizophrenic Identical Twins—A Psychological Study." *J Proj Tech* 17:200–9 Je '53. * (PA 28:4641)

1502. CALDEN, GEORGE, AND COHEN, LEON B. "The Relationship of Ego-Involvement and Test Definition to Rorschach Test Performance." *J Proj Tech* 17:300–11 S '53. * (PA 28:4337)

1503. CANTER, FRANCIS M. "Personality Factors in Seizure States With Reference to the Rosenzweig Triadic Hypothesis." *J Consult Psychol* 17:429–35 D '53. * (PA 28:7844)

1504. CARLSON, VIRGIL R., AND LAZARUS, RICHARD S. "A Repetition of Meyer Williams' Study of Intellectual Control Under Stress and Associated Rorschach Factors." *J Consult Psychol* 17:247–53 Ag '53. * (PA 28:4340)

1505. CHAPMAN, A. H. "The Rorschach Examination in a

Case of Erotomania." *J Clin Psychol* 9:195-8 Ap '53. * (*PA* 28:2894)

1506. CHAPMAN, A. H., AND REESE, D. G. "Homosexual Signs in Rorschachs of Early Schizophrenics." *J Clin Psychol* 9:30-2 Ja '53. * (*PA* 27:7928)

1507. CHAREN, SOL. "A Critique of 'An Exploratory Study of Dynamic Factors in the Content of the Rorschach Protocol.'" Letter. Reply by Fred Brown. *J Proj Tech* 17:460-4 D '53. * (*PA* 28:6021)

1508. COHART, MARY S. *The Differential Value of the Group Rorschach and the MMPI in the Evaluation of Teacher Personality.* Doctor's thesis, Yale University (New Haven, Conn.), 1953.

1509. COLLET, GRACE MARGARET. *Prediction and Communication Problems Illustrated With the Rorschach.* Doctor's thesis, Ohio State University (Columbus, Ohio), 1953. (*DA* 18:1852)

1510. COOPER, MAX. "An Evaluation of Rorschach Patterns in Headache Patients." Abstract. *Am Psychol* 8:336-7 Ag '53. *

1511. DÖRKEN, HERBERT, JR. "Projective Tests and the Consistency of the Personality Structure: A Pilot Study." *J Abn & Social Psychol* 48:525-31 O '53. * (*PA* 28:6022)

1512. EARLE, JEFFREY B. *The Diagnostic Value of the FLK Scales of the MMPI.* Master's thesis, University of Ottawa (Ottawa, Ont., Canada), 1953.

1513. ERIKSEN, CHARLES W., AND EISENSTEIN, DONALD. "Personality Rigidity and the Rorschach." *J Personality* 21:386-91 Mr '53. * (*PA* 28:2628)

1514. FABRIKANT, BEN. "Perceptual Control on the Rorschach Test." *J Clin Psychol* 9:396-7 O '53. * (*PA* 28:4429)

1515. FABRIKANT, BENJAMIN. *The Effects of an Experimental Set on Rorschach Test Performance.* Doctor's thesis, University of Buffalo (Buffalo, N.Y.), 1953. (*DA* 13:431)

1516. FISKE, DONALD W., AND BAUGHMAN, EMMETT E. "Relationships Between Rorschach Scoring Categories and the Total Number of Responses." *J Abn & Social Psychol* 48:25-32 Ja '53. * (*PA* 27:942)

1517. FORER, BERTRAM. ["An Annotated Bibliography of 28 Foreign Articles on Projective Techniques."] *J Proj Tech* 17: 373-5 S '53. *

1518. FORRER, GORDON R.; DRAPER, CHARLINE; AND GRISELL, JAMES L. "Pharmacotoxic Therapy With Atropine Sulfate: Remission in Two Cases With Rorschach Findings." *J Nerv & Mental Dis* 117:226-33 Mr '53. * (*PA* 29:1232)

1519. FORTIER, ROBERT H. "The Response to Color and Ego Functions." *Psychol B* 50:41-63 Ja '53. * (*PA* 27:7046)

1520. FRAMO, JAMES L., JR. *Structural Aspects of Perceptual Development in Normal Adults: A Tachistoscopic Study With the Rorschach Technique.* Doctor's thesis, University of Texas (Austin, Tex.), 1953.

1521. FRANKLE, ALLAN H. *Rorschach Human Movement and Human Content Responses as Indices of the Adequacy of Interpersonal Relationships of Social Work Students.* Doctor's thesis, University of Chicago (Chicago, Ill.), 1953.

1522. FRIEDMAN, HOWARD. "Perceptual Regression in Schizophrenia: An Hypothesis Suggested by the Use of the Rorschach Test." *J Proj Tech* 17:171-85 Je '53. * (*PA* 28:4650)

1523. GEORGE, C. E. "Some Unforeseen Correlates Between the Studies of Shaw and Wallen." *J Abn & Social Psychol* 48: 150 Ja '53. * (*PA* 28:948)

1524. GIBBY, ROBERT G., AND STOTSKY, BERNARD A. "The Relation of Rorschach Free Association to Inquiry." *J Consult Psychol* 17:359-64 O '53. * (*PA* 28:6027)

1525. GIBBY, ROBERT G.; MILLER, DANIEL R.; AND WALKER, EDWARD L. "The Examiner's Influence on the Rorschach Protocol." *J Consult Psychol* 17:425-8 D '53. * (*PA* 28:7524)

1526. GIBBY, ROBERT G.; STOTSKY, BERNARD A.; MILLER, DANIEL R.; AND HILER, E. WESLEY. "Prediction of Duration of Therapy From the Rorschach Test." *J Consult Psychol* 17: 348-54 O '53. * (*PA* 28:6101)

1527. GLADWIN, THOMAS, AND SARASON, SEYMOUR B. *Truk: Man in Paradise,* pp. 290-527. Viking Fund Publications in Anthropology, No. 20. New York: Wenner-Gren Foundation for Anthropological Research, Inc., 1953. Pp. 774. * (*PA* 28:8668)

1528. GLUCK, MARTIN RICHARD. *A Study of the Relationship Between the Amount of Hostility in the Content of Projective Techniques and the Amount of Hostility Expressed in Behavior.* Doctor's thesis, University of Pittsburgh (Pittsburgh, Pa.), 1953.

1529. GOERTZEL, VICTOR. *Shifts in Personality in the Rorschach Test and in Psychotherapy.* Doctor's thesis, University of Michigan (Ann Arbor, Mich.), 1953. (*DA* 13:433)

1530. GRAUER, DAVID. "Prognosis in Paranoid Schizophrenia on the Basis of the Rorschach." *J Consult Psychol* 17:199-205 Je '53. * (*PA* 28:2998)

1531. GREENBERG, N. *Psychosurgery: The Use of the Rorschach Test for Prognosis in Prefrontal Lobotomy.* Master's thesis, University of Montreal (Montreal, Que., Canada), 1953.

1532. GUERTIN, WILSON H., AND TREMBATH, WILLIAM E. "Card VI Disturbance on the Rorschachs of Sex Offenders." *J General Psychol* 49:221-7 O '53. * (*PA* 28:7787)

1533. GURVITZ, MILTON S. "Personality and Intellectual Correlates of the Aging Process as Measured by the Rorschach Technique." Abstract. *Am Psychol* 8:360 Ag '53. *

1534. HALPERN, FLORENCE. *A Clinical Approach to Children's Rorschachs.* New York: Grune & Stratton, Inc., 1953. Pp. xv, 270. * (*PA* 28:2635)

1535. HARRINGTON, ROBERT WILLARD. *Prediction of Maladap-*

tive Responses Under Conditions of Habit-Interference From Rorschach Color Responses. Doctor's thesis, Michigan State College (East Lansing, Mich.), 1953. (*DA* 14:555)

1536. HARROWER, MOLLY R. "Group Rorschach," pp. 620-4. (*PA* 27:7774) In *Contributions Toward Medical Psychology: Theory and Psychodiagnostic Methods, Vol. II.* Edited by Arthur Weider. New York: Ronald Press Co., 1953. Pp. xi, 459-885. *

1537. HEMMENDINGER, LARRY. "Perceptual Organization and Development as Reflected in the Structure of Rorschach Test Responses." *J Proj Tech* 17:162-70 Je '53. * (*PA* 28:4082)

1538. HENRY, JULES, AND SPIRO, MELFORD E. "Psychological Techniques: Projective Tests in Field Work," pp. 417-29. In *Anthropology Today: An Encyclopedic Inventory.* Edited by A. L. Kroeber. Chicago, Ill.: University of Chicago Press, 1953. Pp. xv, 966. *

1539. HILER, E. WESLEY; STOTSKY, BERNARD A.; MILLER, DANIEL R.; AND GIBBY, ROBERT G. "Rorschach Criteria for Predicting Duration of Therapy." Abstract. *Am Psychol* 8:367-8 Ag '53. *

1540. HOWARD, THOMAS W. *Physiological, Diagnostic, and Rorschach Indices of Anxiety.* Doctor's thesis, Tulane University (New Orleans, La.), 1953.

1541. IVES, VIRGINIA; GRANT, MARGUERITE Q.; AND RANZONI, JANE H. "The 'Neurotic' Rorschachs of Normal Adolescents." *J Genetic Psychol* 83:31-61 S '53. * (*PA* 28:5734)

1542. JACOBS, ROBERT, AND WILKINSON, MARGARET A. "A Brief Study of Response Types on the Multiple-Choice Rorschach as They Relate to Vocational Interests." *Yearb Nat Council Meas Used Ed* 10:25-29 '53. *

1543. JOHNSON, ELIZABETH Z. "Klopfer's Prognostic Scale Used With Raven's Progressive Matrices in Play Therapy Prognosis." *J Proj Tech* 17:320-6 S '53. * (*PA* 28:4363)

1544. JOURARD, SIDNEY MARSHALL. *A Study of Ego Strength by Means of the Rorschach Test and the Interruption of Tasks Experiment.* Doctor's thesis, University of Buffalo (Buffalo, N.Y.), 1953. (*DA* 13:435)

1545. KALDEGG, A. "German and English Personality: A Comparative Study of Individual Groups Using Projective Techniques." Abstract. *B Brit Psychol Soc* (19):29 Ja '53. *

1546. KANTOR, ROBERT E.; WALLNER, JULIUS M.; AND WINDER, C. L. "Process and Reactive Schizophrenia." *J Consult Psychol* 17:157-62 Je '53. * (*PA* 28:3002)

1547. KAUFMAN, LAWRENCE WILLARD. *Rorschach Responses Associated With Experimentally Induced Anxiety.* Doctor's thesis, Columbia University (New York, N.Y.), 1953. (*DA* 14:187)

1548. KEEHN, J. D. "Rorschach Validation: II, The Validity of Colour Shock in the Diagnosis of Neuroticism." *J Mental Sci* 99:224-34 Ap '53. * (*PA* 28:952)

1549. KEEHN, J. D. "Rorschach Validation: III, An Examination of the Role of Colour as a Determinant in the Rorschach Test." *J Mental Sci* 99:410-38 Jl '53. * (*PA* 28:4366)

1550. KELLMAN, SAMUEL. "Multiple Choice Rorschach," pp. 625-35. (*PA* 27:7778) In *Contributions Toward Medical Psychology: Theory and Psychodiagnostic Methods, Vol. II.* Edited by Arthur Weider. New York: Ronald Press Co., 1953. Pp. xi, 459-885. *

1551. KESSLER, JANE W., AND WOLFENSTEIN, CHARLOTTE M. "A Comparison of Rorschach Retests With Behavior Changes in a Group of Emotionally Disturbed Children." Discussion by Elizabeth A. Bremner. *Am J Orthopsychiatry* 23:740-54 O '53. * (*PA* 28:6159)

1552. KIRKNER, FRANK J.; WISHAM, WAYNE W.; AND GIEDT, F. HAROLD. "A Report on the Validity of the Rorschach Prognostic Rating Scale." *J Proj Tech* 17:465-70 D '53. * (*PA* 28:6113)

1553. KLEIN, ABRAHAM, AND ARNHEIM, RUDOLF. "Perceptual Analysis of a Rorschach Card." *J Personality* 22:60-70 S '53. * (*PA* 28:4368)

1554. KOBLER, FRANK J., AND STIEL, AGNES. "The Use of the Rorschach in Involutional Melancholia." *J Consult Psychol* 17:365-70 O '53. * (*PA* 28:6355)

1555. KORNREICH, MELVIN. "Variations in the Consistency of the Behavioral Meaning of Personality Test Scores." *Genetic Psychol Monogr* 47:73-138 F '53. * (*PA* 27:6535)

1556. KOTKOV, BENJAMIN, AND MEADOW, ARNOLD. "Rorschach Criteria for Predicting Continuation in Individual Psychotherapy." *J Consult Psychol* 17:16-20 F '53. * (*PA* 28:1030)

1557. KRATHWOHL, DAVID R. *The Prediction of Objective Test Behavior by Means of the Group Rorschach Test.* Doctor's thesis, University of Chicago (Chicago, Ill.), 1953. (Abstract: *Am Psychol* 8:382)

1558. LANDISBERG, SELMA. "Relationship of the Rorschach to the H-T-P." *J Clin Psychol* 9:179-83 Ap '53. * (*PA* 28:2645)

1559. LEDWITH, NETTIE H. "Rorschach Responses of Elementary School Children: A Normative Study." Abstract. *Am Psychol* 8:385 Ag '53. *

1560. LEIBMAN, OSCAR BERNARD. *The Relationship of Personal and Social Adjustment to Academic Achievement in the Elementary School.* Doctor's thesis, Columbia University (New York, N.Y.), 1953. (*DA* 14:67)

1561. LEVIN, MAX M. "The Two Tests in the Rorschach." Comments by W. G. Klopfer and S. J. Beck. *J Proj Tech* 17: 471-6 D '53. * (*PA* 28:6036)

1562. LEVINE, JUDITH, AND DAVIDSON, HELEN H. "Are Abbreviated Rorschach Records Useful?" Abstract. *Am Psychol* 8:388 Ag '53. *

1563. LODGE, GEORGE T. "A Method for the Dynamic Representation of Personality Data." *J Proj Tech* 17:477–81 D '53. * (*PA* 28:6037)

1564. LODGE, GEORGE T., AND GIBSON, ROBERT L. "A Coaction Map of the Personalities Described by H. Rorschach and S. J. Beck." *J Proj Tech* 17:482–8 D '53. * (*PA* 28:6038)

1565. LODGE, GEORGE T., AND STEENBARGER, CHARLES J. "Charting the Course of the Rorschach Interview." *J General Psychol* 48:67–73 Ja '53. * (*PA* 28:957)

1566. LOTSOF, ERWIN J. "Intelligence, Verbal Fluency, and the Rorschach Test." *J Consult Psychol* 17:21–4 F '53. * (*PA* 28:958)

1567. LUFT, JOSEPH. "Interaction and Projection." *J Proj Tech* 17:489–92 D '53. * (*PA* 28:6040)

1568. LUNDIN, WILLIAM H., AND SCHPOONT, SEYMOUR. "The Application of the Rorschach Prognostic Rating Scale to One Intensively Followed Case." *J Proj Tech* 17:295–9 S '53. * (*PA* 28:4374)

1569. McCALL, RAYMOND J. "Psychometric Evaluation of Rorschach Records in Brain-Operated Patients." Abstract. *Am Psychol* 8:394 Ag '53. *

1570. McFARLAND, ROBERT L.; BECKER, WESLEY; DOCTER, RICHARD; SESSIONS, ALWYN; AND ULLMANN, LEONARD. "Measures of Reality Orientation." Abstract. *Am Psychol* 8:396 Ag '53. *

1571. MANN, LESTER. *The Relation of Rorschach Indices of Extratension and Introversion to a Measure of Responsiveness to the Immediate Environment.* Doctor's thesis, University of North Carolina (Chapel Hill, N.C.), 1953.

1572. MARADIE, LOUIS JOSEPH. "Productivity on the Rorschach as a Function of Order of Presentation." *J Consult Psychol* 17:32–5 F '53. (*PA* 28:959)

1573. MEER, BERNARD. "The Relative Difficulty of the Rorschach Cards." Abstract. *Am Psychol* 8:404 Ag '53. *

1574. MELTZOFF, JULIAN; SINGER, JEROME L.; AND KORCHIN, SHELDON J. "Motor Inhibition and Rorschach Movement Responses: A Test of the Sensory-Tonic Theory." *J Personality* 21:400–10 Mr '53. (*PA* 28:2656)

1575. MEYER, BILL THOMAS. *An Investigation of Developmental Change in the Rorschach Responses of Young Children.* Doctor's thesis, University of Nebraska (Lincoln, Neb.), 1953.

1576. MEYER, GEORGE. "Some Relationships Between Rorschach Scores in Kindergarten and Reading in the Primary Grades." *J Proj Tech* 17:414–25 D '53. * (*PA* 28:6510)

1577. MILL, CYRIL R. "Personality Patterns of Sociometrically Selected and Sociometrically Rejected Male College Students." *Sociometry* 16:151–67 My '53. * (*PA* 28:4886)

1578. MILLER, DANIEL R. "Prediction of Behavior by Means of the Rorschach Test." *J Abn & Social Psychol* 48:367–75 Jl '53. * (*PA* 28:2658)

1579. MINDESS, HARVEY. "Predicting Patients' Responses to Psychotherapy: A Preliminary Study Designed to Investigate the Validity of the 'Rorschach Prognostic Rating Scale.'" *J Proj Tech* 17:327–34 S '53. * (*PA* 28:4377)

1580. MUNROE, RUTH L. "Inspection Rorschach," pp. 611–9. (*PA* 27:7785) In *Contributions Toward Medical Psychology: Theory and Psychodiagnostic Methods, Vol. II.* Edited by Arthur Weider. New York: Ronald Press Co., 1953. Pp. xi, 459–885. *

1581. NASH, HELEN T.; MARGOLIN, JOSEPH B.; AND MACGREGOR, ROBERT. "A Method for Systematizing Rorschach Evaluation." *J General Psychol* 48:195–208 Ap '53. * (*PA* 28:963)

1582. NOWELL, ANN. "Peer Status as Related to Measures of Personality." *Calif J Ed Res* 4:37–41 Ja '53. * (*PA* 28:1514)

1583. ORANGE, ARTHUR J. "Perceptual Consistency as Measured by the Rorschach." *J Proj Tech* 17:224–8 Je '53. * (*PA* 28:4389)

1584. PAGE, MARTHA HESSEL, AND TRAVERS, ROBERT M. W. "Relationships Between Rorschach Performance and Student-Teaching." *J Ed Psychol* 44:31–40 Ja '53. * (*PA* 28:1586)

1585. PATTIE, FRANK A. "The Effect of Hypnotically Induced Hostility on Rorschach Responses." Abstract. *Am Psychol* 8:413 Ag '53. *

1586. PAULSEN, ALMA A. *Personality Development in the Middle Childhood Years, a Ten-Year Longitudinal Study of 30 Public School Children by Means of Rorschach Tests and Social Histories.* Doctor's thesis, New York University (New York, N. Y.), 1953. (*DA* 13:592)

1587. PEÑA, CESAREO D. "A Genetic Evaluation of Perceptual Structurization in Cerebral Pathology: An Investigation by Means of the Rorschach Test." *J Proj Tech* 17:186–99 Je '53. * (*PA* 28:4762)

1588. PHILLIPS, LESLIE, AND SMITH, JOSEPH G. *Rorschach Interpretation: Advanced Technique.* New York: Grune & Stratton, Inc., 1953. Pp. xiii, 385. * (*PA* 28:2666)

1589. PINNEAU, SAMUEL RICHARD. *Differences Between Normals and Various Types of Schizophrenics on a Multiple-Choice Rorschach Test.* Doctor's thesis, University of California (Berkeley, Calif.), 1953.

1590. PRICE, ARTHUR COOPER. *A Rorschach Study of the Development of Personality Structure in White and Negro Children in a Southeastern Community.* Doctor's thesis, University of Florida (Gainesville, Fla.), 1953. (*DA* 15:2578)

1591. PURCELL, CLAIRE KEPLER. *A Rorschach Study of Ad-*

justment Prediction, Developmental Trends and Normative Data With Kindergarten Children. Doctor's thesis, University of Nebraska (Lincoln, Neb.), 1953.

1592. RABINOVITCH, MORTIMER S. *An Experimental Investigation of Anxiety Indicators on the Rorschach Test.* Doctor's thesis, Purdue University (Lafayette, Ind.), 1953.

1593. RACUSEN, FRANCES RHEA. "An Exploratory Investigation of the Creativity and Productivity Variables on the Rorschach and Thematic Apperception Tests." Abstract. *Am Psychol* 8:417 Ag '53. *

1594. REITAN, RALPH M. "Intellectual Functions in Myxedema." *A.M.A. Arch Neurol & Psychiatry* 69:436–49 Ap '53. * (*PA* 28:3094)

1595. REITAN, RALPH M. "Psychological Factors in Essential Hypertension as Indicated by the Rorschach Test." Abstract. *Am Psychol* 8:418–9 Ag '53. *

1596. RICHARDS, T. W. "Personality Development as Reflected in Rorschach Behavior: A Case Study." Abstract. *Am Psychol* 8:420 Ag '53. *

1597. RIEMAN, GLENN W. "The Effectiveness of Rorschach Elements in the Discrimination Between Neurotic and Ambulatory Schizophrenic Subjects." *J Consult Psychol* 17:25–31 F '53. * (*PA* 28:1163)

1598. ROCKBERGER, HARRY. *The Effectiveness of a Rorschach Prognostic Scale for Predicting Results in Psychotherapy: A Study of the Relationship Between a Rorschach Prognostic Rating Scale, and the Improvement Status of Psychoneurotic and Ambulatory Schizophrenic Veterans Undergoing Individual Psychotherapy.* Doctor's thesis, New York University (New York, N.Y.), 1953. (*DA* 14:399)

1599. RODELL, CHARLES. *A Validation Study of the Rorschach Technique for the Differential Diagnosis of Psychopathic Groups.* Doctor's thesis, Pennsylvania State College (State College, Pa.), 1953.

1600. ROE, ANNE. "A Psychological Study of Eminent Psychologists and Anthropologists, and a Comparison With Biological and Physical Scientists." *Psychol Monogr* 67(2):1–55 '53. * (*PA* 28:1956)

1601. ROEHRIG, WILLIAM CRUDEN. *Eysenck's Ranking Rorschach Test Proposed as an Aid in Predicting Academic Performance.* Master's thesis, University of Florida (Gainesville, Fla.), 1953.

1602. ROGERS, LAWRENCE S., AND HAMMOND, KENNETH R. "Prediction of the Results of Therapy by Means of the Rorschach Test." *J Consult Psychol* 17:8–15 F '53. * (*PA* 28:1070)

1603. RUBIN, HAROLD, AND LONSTEIN, MURRAY. "A Cross-Validation of Suggested Rorschach Patterns Associated With Schizophrenia." *J Consult Psychol* 17:371–2 O '53. * (*PA* 28:6051)

1604. RUST, RALPH M., AND RYAN, F. J. "The Relationship of Some Rorschach Variables to Academic Behavior." *J Personality* 21:441–56 Je '53. * (*PA* 28:4858)

1605. SACKMAN, HAROLD. *An Investigation of Certain Aspects of the Validity of the Formal Rorschach Scoring System in Relation to Age, Education, and Vocabulary Score.* Doctor's thesis, Fordham University (New York, N.Y.), 1953.

1606. SANDERS, RICHARD, AND CLEVELAND, SIDNEY E. "The Relationship Between Certain Examiner Personality Variables and Subjects' Rorschach Scores." *J Proj Tech* 17:34–50 Mr '53. * (*PA* 28:2670)

1607. SANDLER, J. "A Comparative Study of Psychopaths, Using the Rorschach Test." Abstract. *B Brit Psychol Soc* (19):28 Ja '53. *

1608. SARASON, SEYMOUR B. "The Rorschach Test," pp. 223–52. In his *Psychological Problems in Mental Deficiency, Second Edition.* New York: Harper & Brothers, 1953. Pp. xi, 402. * (*PA* 28:2876)

1609. SAYONS, K., AND SAYONS, Z. "Weighted Scale and Psychogram for the Rorschach Score." *Can J Psychol* 7:60–8 Je '53. * (*PA* 28:4388)

1610. SCHAFER, ROY. "Content Analysis in the Rorschach Test." *J Proj Tech* 17:335–9 S '53. * (*PA* 28:4389)

1611. SCHNEIDER, STANLEY FRED. *The Prediction of Certain Aspects of the Psychotherapeutic Relationship From Rorschach's Test: An Empirical and Exploratory Study.* Doctor's thesis, University of Michigan (Ann Arbor, Mich.), 1953. (*DA* 13:879)

1612. SCHULMAN, IRVING. *The Relation Between the Perception of Movement on the Rorschach Test and Levels of Conceptualization: An Experimental Study and Theoretical Analysis of Thought Processes Involved in the Perception of Movement on the Rorschach Test.* Doctor's thesis, New York University (New York, N.Y.), 1953. (*DA* 14:303)

1613. SECORD, PAUL F. "An Analysis of Perceptual and Related Processes Occurring in Projective Testing." *J General Psychol* 49:65–85 Jl '53. * (*PA* 28:6053)

1614. SHATIN, LEO. "Rorschach Adjustment and the Thematic Apperception Test." *J Proj Tech* 17:92–101 Mr '53. * (*PA* 28:2675)

1615. SHEEHAN, JOSEPH G. "Rorschach Changes During Psychotherapy in Relation to Personality of the Therapist." Abstract. *Am Psychol* 8:434–5 Ag '53. *

1616. SHEPHERD, JOHN RALPH. *An Experimental Study of the Responses of Stage-Frightened Students to Certain Scoring Categories of the Group Rorschach Test.* Doctor's thesis, University of Southern California (Los Angeles, Calif.), 1953.

1617. SHERESHEVSKI-SHERE, EUGENIA; LASSER, LEONARD M.; AND GOTTESFELD, BENJAMIN H. "An Evaluation of Anatomy

Content and F+ Percentage in the Rorschachs of Alcoholics, Schizophrenics and Normals." *J Proj Tech* 17:229-33 Je '53. * (*PA* 28:4592)

1618. SIEGEL, EDWARD L. "Genetic Parallels of Perceptual Structuralization in Paranoid Schizophrenia: An Analysis by Means of the Rorschach Technique." *J Proj Tech* 17:151-61 Je '53. * (*PA* 28:4675)

1619. SILVA, JOSEPH J. *The Effect of Variation in Instructions Upon Certain Rorschach Variables in Schizophrenic and Psychoneurotic Subjects.* Doctor's thesis, Fordham University (New York, N.Y.), 1953.

1620. SILVERMAN, HERBERT. *The Prediction of Consciousness of Conflict in the Self From the Rorschach.* Doctor's thesis, University of Michigan (Ann Arbor, Mich.), 1953. (*DA* 13: 438)

1621. SOBOL, ALBERT LEO. *The Use of the Rorschach Test in Psychiatric Diagnosis and Treatment Planning.* Doctor's thesis, New York University (New York, N.Y.), 1953. (*DA* 13:1264)

1622. SOLOMON, RUTH H. Chap. 3, "Personality Adjustment to Reading Success and Failure," pp. 64-82. In *Clinical Studies in Reading, II.* Edited by Helen M. Robinson. University of Chicago, Supplementary Educational Monographs, No. 77. Chicago, Ill.: University of Chicago Press, January 1953. Pp. x, 189. *

1623. SPIELBERG, MIMI JOHNSON. *A Study of Intra-Familial Rorschach Patterns in a Rural Community.* Doctor's thesis, University of Nebraska (Lincoln, Neb.), 1953.

1624. SPOERL, DOROTHY TILDEN. "'Category-Scoring' of the Multiple Choice Rorschach." *J Social Psychol* 38:287-91 N '53. * (*PA* 28:6054)

1625. STEINER, META. "The Rorschach Test." *Monogr Soc Res Child Develop* 16(53):34-59, 214-316 '53. * (*PA* 28:4077)

1626. STEPHENSON, WILLIAM. *The Study of Behavior: Q-Technique and Its Methodology*, pp. 293-312. Chicago, Ill.: University of Chicago Press, 1953. Pp. ix, 376. * (*PA* 28:6810)

1627. STONE, HAROLD. *The Relationship of Hostile-Aggressive Behavior to Aggressive Content on the Rorschach and Thematic Apperception Tests.* Doctor's thesis, University of California (Los Angeles, Calif.), 1953.

1628. STORMENT, CHARLYNE TOWNSEND, AND FINNEY, BEN C. "Projection and Behavior: A Rorschach Study of Assaultive Mental Hospital Patients." *J Proj Tech* 17:349-60 S '53. * (*PA* 28:4677)

1629. STOTT, WARREN WALTER. *An Evaluation of the Influence of Learning on Color and Form Responses to Ambiguous Figures.* Doctor's thesis, University of Nebraska (Lincoln, Neb.), 1953.

1630. SWARTZ, MELVIN B. *The Role of Color in Influencing Responses to the Rorschach Test: An Experimental Investigation of the Validity of the Color-Shock Hypothesis as a Sign of Neurotic Disturbance and as a Phenomenon Induced by the Color Stimulus.* Doctor's thesis, New York University (New York, N. Y.), 1953. (*DA* 13:1266)

1631. TAULBEE, EARL SELDON. *The Value of the Rorschach Test for Evaluating the Intellectual Levels of Functioning in Schizophrenics.* Doctor's thesis, University of Nebraska (Lincoln, Neb.), 1953.

1632. THALER, MARGARET. "Three Theories of Personality Applied to the Rorschach." Abstract. *J Colo-Wyo Acad Sci* 4:51 D '53. *

1633. WALKER, ROBERT G. "An Approach to Standardization of Rorschach Form-level." *J Proj Tech* 17:426-36 D '53. * (*PA* 28:6059)

1634. WALTERS, C. A. *A Study of Rorschach and Other Projective Tests as Indicators of Anxiety in Children.* Master's thesis, University of London (London, England), 1953.

1635. WALTERS, RICHARD H. "A Preliminary Analysis of the Rorschach Records of Fifty Prison Inmates." *J Proj Tech* 17:437-46 D '53. * (*PA* 28:6327)

1636. WEBER, LOUIS C. "Ethics in Administering the Rorschach Test." *J Abn & Social Psychol* 48:443 Jl '53. * (*PA* 28:2688)

1637. WERTHEIMER, MICHAEL. "On the Supposed Behavioral Correlates of an 'Eye' Content Response on the Rorschach." *J Consult Psychol* 17:189-94 Je '53. * (*PA* 28:2690)

1638. WERTHEIMER, RITA RAY. *The Relationship Between Sociometric Status, Sex, and Socio-Economic Level and Rorschach Signs of Adjustment With a Group of Adolescent Subjects.* Doctor's thesis, University of Pittsburgh (Pittsburgh, Pa.), 1953.

1639. WESTROPE, MARTHA R. "Relations Among Rorschach Indices, Manifest Anxiety, and Performance Under Stress." *J Abn & Social Psychol* 48:515-24 O '53. * (*PA* 28:6061)

1640. WILLIAMS, HAROLD L., AND LAWRENCE, JAMES F. "Further Investigation of Rorschach Determinants Subjected to Factor Analysis." *J Consult Psychol* 17:261-4 Ag '53. * (*PA* 28:4404)

1641. WIRT, ROBERT D., AND McREYNOLDS, PAUL. "The Reliability of Rorschach Number of Responses." *J Proj Tech* 17:493-4 D '53. * (*PA* 28:6064)

1642. WISHNER, JULIUS. "Neurosis and Tension: An Exploratory Study of the Relationship of Physiological and Rorschach Measures." *J Abn & Social Psychol* 48:253-60 Ap '53. * (*PA* 28:2288)

1643. ZULLIGER, HANS. "The Case of Franz and Lotti." *J Proj Tech* 17:61-5 Mr '53. * (*PA* 28:2696)

1644. ALCOCK, A. THEODORA. "Rorschach Personality Pat-

terns in Asthmatic Children." Abstract. *Brit Rorsch Forum* (4):5-6 Mr '54. *

1645. ALLEE, WAYNE L. *A Comparative Study of Modified Rorschach Techniques as Used in Evaluating the Adjustment Level of College Students.* Doctor's thesis, University of Colorado (Boulder, Colo.), 1954.

1646. ALLEN, ROBERT M. "Continued Longitudinal Rorschach Study of a Child for Years Three to Five." *J Genetic Psychol* 85:135-49 S '54. * (*PA* 29:5685)

1647. ALLEN, ROBERT M. *Elements of Rorschach Interpretation: With an Extended Bibliography.* New York: International Universities Press, Inc., 1954. Pp. 242. * (*PA* 29:2424)

1648. ALLEN, ROBERT M. "Recording the Rorschach Protocol." *J Clin Psychol* 10:195-6 Ap '54. * (*PA* 29:2400)

1649. ALLERHAND, MELVIN E. "Chiaroscuro Determinant of Rorschach Test as Indicator of Manifest Anxiety." *J Proj Tech* 18:407-13 D '54. * (*PA* 29:7253)

1650. ALLISON, HARRY W., AND ALLISON, SARAH G. "Personality Changes Following Transorbital Lobotomy." *J Abn & Social Psychol* 49:219-23 Ap '54. * (*PA* 29:970)

1651. AMES, LOUISE BATES; LEARNED, JANET; METRAUX, RUTH W.; AND WALKER, RICHARD N. *Rorschach Responses in Old Age.* New York: Paul B. Hoeber, Inc., 1954. Pp. xv, 229. * (*PA* 29:637)

1652. ANDERHALTER, O. F. "An Application of Profile Similarity Techniques to Rorschach Data on 2161 Marine Corps Officer Candidates." *Proc Inv Conf Testing Probl* 1953:47-53 '54. * (*PA* 28:6770)

1653. AUSUBEL, DAVID P.; SCHIFF, HERBERT M.; AND ZELENY, MAJORIE P. "Validity of Teachers' Ratings of Adolescents' Adjustment and Aspirations." *J Ed Psychol* 45:394-406 N '54. * (*PA* 29:7981)

1654. BAKER, LAWRENCE M., AND CREAGER, JOHN A. "Rating Scale Technique Applied to Rorschach Responses." *J Clin Psychol* 10:373-5 O '54. * (*PA* 29:4027)

1655. BANDURA, ALBERT. "The Rorschach White Space Response and 'Oppositional' Behavior." *J Consult Psychol* 18:17-21 F '54. * (*PA* 28:8711)

1656. BANDURA, ALBERT. "The Rorschach White Space Response and Perceptual Reversal." *J Exp Psychol* 48:113-8 Ag '54. * (*PA* 29:4028)

1657. BAUGHMAN, E. EARL. "A Comparative Analysis of Rorschach Forms With Altered Stimulus Characteristics." *J Proj Tech* 18:151-64 Je '54. * (*PA* 29:4029)

1658. BAUGHMAN, E. EARL. "Regarding 'The Two Tests in the Rorschach' by Levin." *J Proj Tech* 18:165-8 Je '54. * (*PA* 29:4030)

1659. BECK, SAMUEL J. *The Six Schizophrenias: Reaction Patterns in Children and Adults.* American Orthopsychiatric Association, Research Monographs No. 6. New York: the Association, Inc., 1954. Pp. xi, 238. * (*PA* 29:2760)

1660. BELDEN, ARVORD W., AND BAUGHMAN, E. EARL. "The Effects of Figure-Ground Contrast Upon Perception as Evaluated by a Modified Rorschach Technique." *J Consult Psychol* 18:29-34 F '54. * (*PA* 28:8713)

1661. BERGER, DAVID. "Examiner Influence on the Rorschach." *J Clin Psychol* 10:245-8 Jl '54. * (*PA* 29:2430)

1662. BIALICK, IRVING, AND HAMLIN, ROY M. "The Clinician as Judge: Details of Procedure in Judging Projective Material." *J Consult Psychol* 18:239-42 Ag '54. * (*PA* 29:4033)

1663. BILLS, ROBERT E. "Self Concepts and Rorschach Signs of Depression." *J Consult Psychol* 18:135-7 Ap '54. * (*PA* 29:2432)

1664. BLECHNER, JANET E. "Constancy of Rorschach Color Responses Under Educational Conditioning." *J Exp Ed* 22: 293-5 Mr '54. * (*PA* 29:2433)

1665. BLECHNER, JANET E., AND CARTER, HAROLD D. "Rorschach Personality Factors and College Achievement." Abstract. *Calif J Ed Res* 5:187 S '54. *

1666. BLUM, LUCILLE HOLLANDER; DAVIDSON, HELEN H.; AND FIELDSTEEL, NINA D.; WITH THE ASSISTANCE OF LOUIS GETOFF. *A Rorschach Workbook.* New York: International Universities Press, Inc., 1954. Pp. iv, 169. (*PA* 29:4034)

1667. BOLGAR, HEDDA. "Consistency of Affect and Symbolic Expression: A Comparison Between Dreams and Rorschach Responses." Discussion by Samuel J. Beck. *Am J Orthopsychiatry* 24:538-45 Jl '54. * (*PA* 29:4036)

1668. BOREHAM, J. L. "A Rorschach Record of a Person With Homicidal Tendencies." Abstract. *Brit Rorsch Forum* (4):6-8 Mr '54. *

1669. BROCKWAY, ANN LAWLER; GLESER, GOLDINE C.; AND ULETT, GEORGE A. "Rorschach Concepts of Normality." *J Consult Psychol* 18:259-65 Ag '54. * (*PA* 29:4038)

1670. BROIDA, DANIEL C. "An Investigation of Certain Psychodiagnostic Indications of Suicidal Tendencies and Depression in Mental Hospital Patients." *Psychiatric Q* 28:453-64 Jl '54. * (*PA* 29:6019)

1671. BROIDA, DANIEL C., AND THOMPSON, GEORGE G. "The Relationship Between Certain Rorschach 'Insecurity' Hypotheses and Children's Reactions to Psychological Stress." *J Personality* 23:167-81 D '54. * (*PA* 29:5298)

1672. BUCKLE, D. F. "The Use of the Rorschach Technique in the Diagnosis of Schizophrenia." Abstract. *B Brit Psychol Soc* (22):20 Ja '54. *

1673. CALDWELL, BETTYE McD. "The Use of the Rorschach in Personality Research With the Aged." *J Gerontol* 9:316-23 Jl '54. * (*PA* 29:5419)

1674. CARR, ARTHUR C. "Intra-Individual Consistency in

Response to Tests of Varying Degrees of Ambiguity." *J Consult Psychol* 18:251–8 Ag '54. * (*PA* 29:4041)

1675. CHAMBERS, GUINEVERE S. *An Investigation of the Validity of Judgments Based on "Blind" Rorschach Records.* Doctor's thesis, University of Pittsburgh (Pittsburgh, Pa.), 1954. (*DA* 14:2399)

1676. COHEN, DAVID. "Rorschach Scores, Prognosis, and Course of Illness in Pulmonary Tuberculosis." *J Consult Psychol* 18:405–8 D '54. * (*PA* 29:7721)

1677. CORSINI, RAYMOND J., AND UEHLING, HAROLD F. "A Cross Validation of Davidson's Rorschach Adjustment Scale." *J Consult Psychol* 18:277–9 Ag '54. * (*PA* 29:4042)

1678. COX, FRANCIS N., AND SARASON, SEYMOUR B. "Test Anxiety and Rorschach Performance." *J Abn & Social Psychol* 49:371–7 Jl '54. * (*PA* 29:4043)

1679. COX, RACHEL D. "Personality Dynamics of the Well-Adjusted College Student as Revealed by the Rorschach and Thematic Apperception Tests." Abstract. *Am Psychol* 9:351–2 Ag '54. * (*J Proj Tech* 18:399 S '54. *)

1680. CRASILNECK, HAROLD B. *An Analysis of Differences Between Suicidal and Pseudo-Suicidal Patients Through the Use of Projective Techniques.* Doctor's thesis, University of Houston (Houston, Tex.), 1954. (*DA* 14:1456)

1681. CUMMINGS, S. THOMAS. "The Clinician as Judge: Judgments of Adjustment From Rorschach Single-Card Performance." *J Consult Psychol* 18:243–7 Ag '54. * (*PA* 29:4044)

1682. DANA, RICHARD H. "The Effects of Attitudes Toward Authority on Psychotherapy." *J Clin Psychol* 10:350–3 O '54. * (*PA* 29:4109)

1683. DAVIDSON, KENNETH S. *Accuracy of Self-Appraisal and Clinicians' Interpretations of Rorschach Protocols.* Doctor's thesis, University of Michigan (Ann Arbor, Mich.), 1954. (*DA* 14:1098)

1684. DuBOIS, PHILIP H., AND HILDEN, ARNOLD H. "A P Scale for the Rorschach: A Methodological Study." *J Consult Psychol* 18:333–6 O '54. * (*PA* 29:5700)

1685. DUDEK, STEPHANIE. "An Approach to Fundamental Compatibility in Marital Couples Through the Rorschach." Abstract. *J Proj Tech* 18:400 S '54. *

1686. DUDEK, STEPHANIE, AND GOTTLIEB, SOPHIE. "An Approach to Fundamental Compatibility in Marital Couples Through the Rorschach." Abstract. *Am Psychol* 9:356 Ag '54. *

1687. EICHLER, HERBERT, AND GURVITZ, MILTON S. "Research Possibilities of the Variance in the Stimulus Value of Different Editions of the Rorschach Ink Blots." Abstract. *Am Psychol* 9:359 Ag '54. *

1688. ENDACOTT, JOHN. *Methodology for the Study of Clinical Cases by the Way of Rorschach and Psychoanalytic Theories.* Doctor's thesis, University of Chicago (Chicago, Ill.), 1954.

1689. FABRIKANT, BENJAMIN. "Rigidity and Flexibility on the Rorschach." *J Clin Psychol* 10:255–8 Jl '54. * (*PA* 29:2442)

1690. FAIRCHILD, CHARLES M. *Some Personality Differences Between a Delinquent and a Non-Delinquent Group of Juveniles as Measured by the Rorschach Test.* Doctor's thesis, University of Houston (Houston, Tex.), 1954.

1691. FEINBERG, LEONARD D., AND GURVITZ, MILTON S. "The Normal Adult Rorschach." Abstract. *Am Psychol* 9:363 Ag '54. *

1692. FELDMAN, MARVIN J., AND GRALEY, JAMES. "The Effects of an Experimental Set to Simulate Abnormality on Group Rorschach Performance." *J Proj Tech* 18:326–34 S '54. * (*PA* 29:4052)

1693. FELDMAN, MARVIN J.; GURSSLIN, CAROLYN; KAPLAN, MARVIN L.; AND SHARLOCK, NIDIA. "A Preliminary Study to Develop a More Discriminating F+ Ratio." *J Clin Psychol* 10:47–51 Ja '54. * (*PA* 28:7518)

1694. FELZER, STANTON B. *A Statistical Study of Sex Differences on the Rorschach.* Doctor's thesis, Temple University (Philadelphia, Pa.), 1954. (Abstracts: *DA* 16:569, *Am Psychol* 9:364, *J Proj Tech* 18:398)

1695. FISHER, JEROME, AND GONDA, THOMAS A. "Critique of a Criterion: The Diagnostic Sensitivity of Neurologic Techniques vs. Rorschach Findings in Brain Pathology." Abstract. *Am Psychol* 9:368 Ag '54. *

1696. FLYNN, JAMES J. *Rorschach and Wechsler-Bellevue Changes Following Electric Shock Therapy in the Aged.* Doctor's thesis, Loyola University (Chicago, Ill.), 1954.

1697. FORTIER, ROBERT H. "An Appraisal of Keehn's Critique of 'The Response to Color and Ego Functions.'" *Psychol B* 51:67–9 Ja '54. * (*PA* 28:7521)

1698. GALLAGHER, JAMES J. "Test Indicators for Therapy Prognosis." *J Consult Psychol* 18:409–13 D '54. * (*PA* 29:7356)

1699. GELFAND, LEONARD; QUARRINGTON, BRUCE; WIDEMAN, HARLEY; AND BROWN, JEAN. "Inter-Judge Agreement on Traits Rated From the Rorschach." Abstract. *J Consult Psychol* 18:471 D '54. *

1700. GIBBY, ROBERT G., AND STOTSKY, BERNARD A. "Determinant Shift of Psychoneurotic and Psychotic Patients." *J Consult Psychol* 18:267–70 Ag '54. * (*PA* 29:4055)

1701. GIBBY, ROBERT G.; STOTSKY, BERNARD A.; AND HARRINGTON, ROBERT W. "A Comparison of Normals, Psychoneurotics, and Psychotics or Rorschach Determinant Shift." Abstract. *Proc Ind Acad Sci* 64:239–40 '54. *

1702. GIBBY, ROBERT G.; STOTSKY, BERNARD A.; AND MILLER,

DANIEL R. "Influence of the Preceding Test on the Rorschach Protocol." *J Consult Psychol* 18:463–4 D '54. * (*PA* 29:7278)

1703. GIBBY, ROBERT G.; STOTSKY, BERNARD A.; HILER, E. WESLEY; AND MILLER, DANIEL R. "Validation of Rorschach Criteria for Predicting Duration of Therapy." *J Consult Psychol* 18:185–91 Je '54. * (*PA* 29:2517)

1704. GOLDFARB, ALLAN. *An Experimental Study of Performance Under Stress in Relation to Intellectual Control and Expressed Self-Acceptance.* Doctor's thesis, University of Pittsburgh (Pittsburgh, Pa.), 1954. (*DA* 14:1457)

1705. GOODSTEIN, LEONARD D. "Interrelationships Among Several Measures of Anxiety and Hostility." *J Consult Psychol* 18:35–9 F '54. * (*PA* 28:8722)

1706. GRAHAM, STANLEY ROY. *Histamine Tolerance and Perceived Movement: A Study of Visually Perceived Movement as Related to Performance in the Autokinetic Effect and Rorschach Movement Responses Measured Against Histamine Tolerance.* Doctor's thesis, New York University (New York, N.Y.), 1954. (*DA* 15:1202)

1707. GRAUER, DAVID. "Homosexuality in Paranoid Schizophrenia as Revealed by the Rorschach Test." *J Consult Psychol* 18:459–62 D '54. * (*PA* 29:7645)

1708. GURVITZ, MILTON S., AND FEINBERG, LEONARD D. "Age and Intellectual Dimensions of the Normal Rorschach." Abstract. *Am Psychol* 9:387 Ag '54. * (*J Proj Tech* 18:399 S '54. *)

1709. HAMLIN, ROY M. "The Clinician as Judge: Implications of a Series of Studies." *J Consult Psychol* 18:233–8 Ag '54. * (*PA* 29:4057)

1710. HARRINGTON, ROBERT W. "Maladaptive Responses to Frustration Predicted From Rorschach Color Responses." *J Consult Psychol* 18:455–8 D '54. * (*PA* 29:7532)

1711. HAUCK, PAUL A. *Rorschach Performances of the Ute Indians.* Doctor's thesis, University of Utah (Salt Lake City, Utah), 1954.

1712. HERTZ, MARGUERITE R., AND LOEHRKE, LEAH M. "The Application of the Piotrowski and the Hughes Signs of Organic Defect to a Group of Patients Suffering From Post-Traumatic Encephalopathy." *J Proj Tech* 18:183–96 Je '54. * (*PA* 29:4553)

1713. HERTZMAN, M. Chap. 11, "The Rorschach Test," pp. 205–34, passim. In *Personality Through Perception: An Experimental and Clinical Study.* By H. A. Witkin and others. New York: Harper & Bros., 1954. Pp. xxvii, 571. * (*PA* 28:8566)

1714. HOLSOPPLE, JAMES QUINTER, AND PHELAN, JOSEPH G. "The Skills of Clinicians in Analysis of Projective Tests." *J Clin Psychol* 10:307–20 O '54. * (*PA* 29:4061)

1715. HOLTZMAN, WAYNE H.; ISCOE, IRA; AND CALVIN, A. D. "Rorschach Color Responses and Manifest Anxiety in College Women." *J Consult Psychol* 18:317–24 O '54. * (*PA* 29:5931)

1716. HURWITZ, IRVING. *A Developmental Study of the Relationships Between Motor Activity and Perceptual Processes as Measured by the Rorschach Test.* Doctor's thesis, Clark University (Worcester, Mass.), 1954. (*DA* 14:1805)

1717. INGRAM, WINIFRED. "Prediction of Aggression From the Rorschach." *J Consult Psychol* 18:23–8 F '54. * (*PA* 28:8723)

1718. ISRAËL, MARYSE. "Rorschach Responses of a Group of Adult Asthmatics." *J Mental Sci* 100:753–7 Jl '54. * (*PA* 29:4511)

1719. JAQUES, HOWARD W. *Rorschach's Erlebnistypus and Certain Manifest Behaviors in Children.* Doctor's thesis, University of Tennessee (Knoxville, Tenn.), 1954.

1720. JOHNSON, WARREN R.; HUTTON, DANIEL C.; AND JOHNSON, GRANVILLE B., JR. "Personality Traits of Some Champion Athletes as Measured by Two Projective Tests: Rorschach and H-T-P." *Res Q* 25:484–5 D '54. *

1721. JOURARD, SIDNEY M. "Ego Strength and the Recall of Tasks." *J Abn & Social Psychol* 49:51–8 Ja '54. * (*PA* 28:7222)

1722. KANTER, V. B. "A Validatory Study of a Blind Analysis and an Attempt to Integrate Rorschach Findings With Other Test Material." Abstract. *B Brit Psychol Soc* (22):22 Ja '54. *

1723. KAPLAN, BERT. *A Study of Rorschach Responses in Four Cultures.* Reports of the Ramah Project No. 6. Harvard University, Papers of the Peabody Museum of American Archaeology and Ethnology, Vol. 42, No. 2. Cambridge, Mass.: Peabody Museum, 1954. Pp. ix, 44. *

1724. KEEHN, J. D. "A Re-Interpretation of the Role Played by Colour in the Rorschach Test." *Brit J Med Psychol* 27:89–93 pts 1–2 '54. * (*PA* 28:8726)

1725. KEEHN, J. D. "The Response to Color and Ego Functions': A Critique in the Light of Recent Experimental Evidence." *Psychol B* 51:65–7 Ja '54. * (*PA* 28:7532)

1726. KENDIG, ISABELLE V. "The Basic Rorschach Triad: A Graphic Schema of Presentation." *J Proj Tech* 18:448–52 D '54. * (*PA* 29:7288)

1727. KENNA, J. C. "The Effects of Lysergic Acid on the Rorschach." Abstract. *Brit Rorsch Forum* (5):7–8 Mr '54. *

1728. KEYES, EDWARD J. "An Experimental Investigation of Some Sources of Variance in the Whole Response to the Rorschach Ink Blots." *J Clin Psychol* 10:155–60 Ap '54. * (*PA* 29:930)

1729. KING, GERALD FRANKLIN. *A Theoretical and Experimental Consideration of the Rorschach Movement Response: Its*

Relation to the Neuropsychiatric Patient's Orientation to His Problem. Doctor's thesis, Michigan State College (East Lansing, Mich.), 1954. (*DA* 14:2127)

1730. KLOPFER, BRUNO; AINSWORTH, MARY D.; KLOPFER, WALTER G.; AND HOLT, ROBERT R. *Developments in the Rorschach Technique: Vol. I, Technique and Theory.* Yonkers, N.Y.: World Book Co., 1954. Pp. x, 726. * (*PA* 28:7533)

1731. KNOPF, IRWIN J. "The Effects of Recent Perceptual Training and Experience on Rorschach Performance." *J Clin Psychol* 10:52-6 Ja '54. * (*PA* 28:7534)

1732. KNOPF, IRWIN J., AND SPANGLER, DONALD. "Experimental Evaluation of the Rorschach as a Psychodiagnostic Instrument: I, The Use of Summary Scores." Abstract. *Am Psychol* 9:406-7 Ag '54. *

1733. KORNETSKY, CONAN. "Relationship Between Rorschach Determinants and Psychosis in Barbiturate Withdrawal Syndrome." *A.M.A. Arch Neurol & Psychiatry* 72:452-4 O '54. * (*PA* 29:5937)

1734. KORNETSKY, CONAN, AND GERARD, DONALD L. "Effect of Increasing the Number of Rorschach Responses on *Sum C* and *M*: A Note on Fiske and Baughman's Study." *J Abn & Social Psychol* 49:592-3 O '54. * (*PA* 29:5711)

1735. KOSTLAN, ALBERT. "A Method for the Empirical Study of Psychodiagnosis." *J Consult Psychol* 18:83-8 Ap '54. * (*PA* 29:2415)

1736. KRASNER, LEONARD, AND KORNREICH, MELVIN. "Psychosomatic Illness and Projective Tests: The Rorschach Test." *J Proj Tech* 18:355-67 S '54. * (*PA* 29:4515)

1737. KRUGER, ALICE KASTENBAUM. *Direct and Substitutive Modes of Tension-Reduction in Terms of Developmental Level: An Experimental Analysis by Means of the Rorschach Test.* Doctor's thesis, Clark University (Worcester, Mass.), 1954. (*DA* 14:1806)

1738. KURTZ, JOSEPHINE C., AND RIGGS, MARGARET M. "An Attempt to Influence the Rorschach Test by Means of a Peripheral Set." *J Consult Psychol* 18:465-70 D '54. * (*PA* 29:7291)

1739. KUTASH, SAMUEL B. "Personality Patterns of Old Age and the Rorschach Test." *Geriatrics* 9:367-70 Ag '54. * (*PA* 29:7055)

1740. LA FON, FRED E. *The Relationship Between Behavior on the Rorschach Test and a Measure of Self-Acceptance.* Doctor's thesis, University of Rochester (Rochester, N.Y.), 1954.

1741. LEVENTHAL, HOWARD. *The Influence of Previous Perceptual Experience on the Variance of the Rorschach W and Z Scores.* Master's thesis, University of North Carolina (Chapel Hill, N.C.), 1954.

1742. LEVINE, PHYLLIS R. "Projective Tests in a Vocational Guidance Setting." *J Counsel Psychol* 1:209-14 w '54. * (*PA* 29:7429)

1743. LIBRACH, STEPHANIE J. *Investigation of Differences Between Functioning and Non-Functioning Male Paranoid Schizophrenics by Means of the Rorschach Test.* Doctor's thesis, New School for Social Research (New York, N.Y.), 1954.

1744. LINTON, HARRIET B. "Rorschach Correlates of Response to Suggestion." *J Abn & Social Psychol* 49:75-83 Ja '54. * (*PA* 28:7536)

1745. LORD, EDITH. "Group Rorschach Responses of Thirty-Five Leprosarium Patients." *J Proj Tech* 18:202-7 Je '54. * (*PA* 29:4519)

1746. LORD, EDITH, AND HSU, FRANCIS. "Cultural Variations in Reactions to Color on the Rorschach." Abstract. *Am Psychol* 9:420 Ag '54. *

1747. LOTSOF, ERWIN J., AND CHANCE, JUNE. "Effects of Cortisone on Rorschach Performance." *J Proj Tech* 18:470-4 D '54. * (*PA* 29:7297)

1748. MCARTHUR, CHARLES C., AND KING, STANLEY. "Rorschach Configurations Associated With College Achievement." *J Ed Psychol* 45:492-8 D '54. * (*PA* 29:7867)

1749. MCFARLAND, ROBERT L. "Perceptual Consistency in Rorschach-Like Projective Tests." *J Proj Tech* 18:368-78 S '54. * (*PA* 29:4071)

1750. MCREYNOLDS, PAUL. "The Rorschach Concept Evaluation Technique." *J Proj Tech* 18:60-74 Mr '54. * (*PA* 29:934)

1751. MANDEVILLE, PAUL FREDERICK. *A Study of the Relationship Between Responsiveness to Color on the Rorschach Examination and Impulsive Behavior.* Doctor's thesis, University of Nebraska (Lincoln, Neb.), 1954. (*DA* 14:1251)

1752. MENDOLA, VINCENT S. "The Validity of Indices of Dependency in Clinical Tests." Abstract. *Am Psychol* 9:430 Ag '54. *

1753. MENSH, IVAN N., AND MATARAZZO, JOSEPH D. "Rorschach Card Rejection in Psychodiagnosis." *J Consult Psychol* 18:271-5 Ag '54. * (*PA* 29:4073)

1754. MISCH, ROBERT C. *The Relationship of Motoric Inhibition to Developmental Level and Ideational Functioning: An Analysis by Means of the Rorschach Test.* Doctor's thesis, Clark University (Worcester, Mass.), 1954. (*DA* 14:1810)

1755. MONS, W. E. R. "Normative Study of Children's Rorschachs." Abstract. *Brit Rorsch Forum* (5):5-7 O '54. *

1756. MURRAY, DAVID COWAN. *An Investigation of the Rorschach White Space Response in an Extratensive Experience Balance as a Measure of Outwardly Directed Opposition.* Doctor's thesis, Northwestern University (Evanston, Ill.), 1954. (*DA* 14:1811)

1757. NEFF, WALTER S. "The Use of the Rorschach Test in Differentiating Between Vocationally Rehabilitable and Non-rehabilitable Groups." Abstract. *Am Psychol* 9:438-9 Ag '54. *

1758. NEFF, WALTER S., AND GLASER, NATHAN M. "Norma-tive Data on the Rorschach." *J Psychol* 37:95-104 Ja '54. * (*PA* 28:7540)

1759. NELSON, WILLIAM DONALD. *An Evaluation of the White Space Response on the Rorschach as Figure-Ground Reversal and Intellectual Opposition.* Doctor's thesis, Michigan State College (East Lansing, Mich.), 1954. (*DA* 15:459)

1760. NEWTON, RICHARD L. "The Clinician as Judge: Total Rorschachs and Clinical Case Material." *J Consult Psychol* 18:248-50 Ag '54. * (*PA* 29:4077)

1761. PALM, ROSE, AND ABRAHAMSEN, DAVID. "A Rorschach Study of the Wives of Sex Offenders." *J Nerv & Mental Dis* 119:167-72 F '54. * (*PA* 29:2702)

1762. PATTIE, FRANK A. "The Effect of Hypnotically Induced Hostility on Rorschach Responses." *J Clin Psychol* 10:161-4 Ap '54. * (*PA* 29:940)

1763. PAULSEN, ALMA A. "Personality Development in the Middle Years of Childhood: A Ten-Year Longitudinal Study of Thirty Public School Children by Means of Rorschach Tests and Social Histories." Discussion by Judith I. Krugman. *Am J Orthopsychiatry* 24:336-50 Ap '54. * (*PA* 29:2280)

1764. PETERSON, ARNOLD O. D. "A Comparative Study of Rorschach Scoring Methods in Evaluating Personality Changes Resulting From Psychotherapy." *J Clin Psychol* 10:190-2 Ap '54. * (*PA* 29:1008)

1765. PUGH, DEREK S. "A Note on the Vorhaus Configurations of 'Reading Disability.'" *J Proj Tech* 18:478-80 D '54. * (*PA* 29:7877)

1766. RABIN, ALBERT, AND KEPECS, JOSEPH. "Personality Structure in Atopic Dermatitis: A Rorschach Study." *J General Psychol* 50:171-80 Ap '54. * (*PA* 29:4523)

1767. RABIN, ALBERT; NELSON, WILLIAM; AND CLARK, MARGARET. "Rorschach Content as a Function of Perceptual Experience and Sex of the Examiner." *J Clin Psychol* 10:188-90 Ap '54. * (*PA* 29:945)

1768. RABIN, ALBERT; PAPANIA, NED; AND MCMICHAEL, ALLAN. "Some Effects of Alcohol on Rorschach Performance." *J Clin Psychol* 10:252-5 Jl '54. * (*PA* 29:2465)

1769. RABINOVITCH, M. SAM. "Physiologic Response, Perceptual Threshold, and Rorschach Test Anxiety Indices." *J Proj Tech* 18:379-86 S '54. * (*PA* 29:4083)

1770. RAPPAPORT, SIDNEY M. *An Experimental Investigation of the Effects and Persistence of Set Directed Towards Increasing Responses on the Color Variable in Rorschach.* Doctor's thesis, Temple University (Philadelphia, Pa.), 1954.

1771. REID, MELVIN P. *Emotional Stability in Stress and the Rorschach Personality Test of High School Football Players.* Doctor's thesis, Louisiana State University (Baton Rouge, La.), 1954.

1772. REITAN, RALPH M. "Intellectual and Affective Changes in Essential Hypertension." *Am J Psychiatry* 110:817-24 My '54. * (*PA* 29:1352)

1773. REITAN, RALPH M. "The Performance of Aphasic, Non-Aphasic, and Control Subjects on the Rorschach Test." *J General Psychol* 51:199-212 O '54. * (*PA* 30:3141)

1774. RICKERS-OVSIANKINA, MARIA A. "Longitudinal Approach to Schizophrenia Through the Rorschach Method." *J Clin & Exp Psychopathol* 15:107-18 Je '54. * (*PA* 29:2827)

1775. ROBERTS, LYNN K. "The Failure of Some Rorschach Indices to Predict the Outcome of Psychotherapy." *J Consult Psychol* 18:96-8 Ap '54. * (*PA* 29:2468)

1776. ROCHWARG, HERMAN. *Changes in the Structural Aspects of Perception in the Aged: An Analysis by Means of the Rorschach Test.* Doctor's thesis, Michigan State University (East Lansing, Mich.), 1954. (*DA* 16:1175)

1777. ROCKBERGER, HARRY. *The Effectiveness of a Rorschach Prognostic Scale for Predicting Results in Psychotherapy.* Doctor's thesis, New York University (New York, N.Y.), 1954.

1778. RORSCHACH, HERMANN. "Three Rorschach Interpretations." Translated by Else Sloman and Hanna Liebes. *J Proj Tech* 18:482-95 D '54. * (*PA* 29:7313)

1779. ROSENBLATT, BERNARD, AND SOLOMON, PAUL. "Structural and Genetic Aspects of Rorschach Responses in Mental Deficiency." *J Proj Tech* 18:496-506 D '54. * (*PA* 29:7497)

1780. ROSENTHAL, MELVIN. *Some Behavioral Correlates of the Rorschach Experience-Balance.* Doctor's thesis, Boston University (Boston, Mass.), 1954.

1781. ROSS, HARVEY L. *The Sources and Reliabilities of Interpretations in Rorschach Test Analysis.* Doctor's thesis, University of California (Los Angeles, Calif.), 1954.

1782. ROSVOLD, H. ENGER; ROSS, W. DONALD; AND DÖRKEN, H., JR. "The Rorschach Method as an Experimental Instrument: Review." *J Proj Tech* 18:227-32 Je '54. * (*PA* 29:4084)

1783. RULE, EVELYN T. *The Effect of Experimentally-Produced Sleep Deprivation on Projective Test Data: I, The Rorschach.* Doctor's thesis, University of Tennessee (Knoxville, Tenn.), 1954.

1784. SACKMAN, HAROLD. "An Investigation of Certain Aspects of the Validity of the Formal Rorschach Scoring System in Relation to Age, Education, and Vocabulary Score." Abstract. *Am Psychol* 9:463 Ag '54. *

1785. SAKHEIM, GEORGE A. *Suicidal Responses on the Rorschach Test: A Validation Study. Protocols of Suicidal Mental Hospital Patients Compared With Those of Non-Suicidal Patients.* Doctor's thesis, Florida State University (Tallahassee, Fla.), 1954. (*DA* 14:1253)

1786. SARASON, SEYMOUR B. *The Clinical Interaction: With Special Reference to Rorschach.* New York: Harper & Brothers, 1954. Pp. xi, 425. * (*PA* 29:896)

1787. SCHAFER, ROY. *Psychoanalytic Interpretation in Rorschach Testing: Theory and Application*. Austen Riggs Foundation Monograph Series, No. 3. New York: Grune & Stratton, Inc., 1954. Pp. xiv, 446. * (*PA* 29:2472)

1788. SCHMIDT, HERMANN O., AND FONDA, CHARLES P. "Rorschach Scores in the Manic State." *J Psychol* 38:427–37 O '54. * (*PA* 29:6041)

1789. SCHNEIDER, STANLEY F. "The Prediction of Certain Aspects of the Psychotherapeutic Relationship From Rorschach's Test: An Empirical and Exploratory Study." Abstract. *Am Psychol* 9:466 Ag '54. *

1790. SCHREIBER, HANNA, AND WHITE, MARY ALICE. "Diagnosing Organicity on the Rorschach." *Psychiatric Q Sup* 28: 255–77 pt 2 '54. * (*PA* 29:7316)

1791. SHEEHAN, JOSEPH G. "Rorschach Prognosis in Psychotherapy and Speech Therapy." *J Speech & Hearing Dis* 19: 217–9 Je '54. * (*PA* 29:4345)

1792. SHEEHAN, JOSEPH G.; FREDERICK, CALVIN J.; ROSEVEAR, WILLIAM H.; AND SPIEGELMAN, MARVIN. "A Validity Study of the Rorschach Prognostic Rating Scale." *J Proj Tech* 18:233–9 Je '54. * (*PA* 29:4088)

1793. SHIPMAN, WILLIAM GIBSON. *The Validity of the Interpretation of Scope and Differentiation Response to the Rorschach*. Doctor's thesis, Pennsylvania State University (University Park, Pa.), 1954.

1794. SIMS, NEIL B. *A Study of Perceptual Defense and Defensiveness on the Rorschach as Manifested by Schizophrenic Subjects*. Doctor's thesis, Purdue University (Lafayette, Ind.), 1954.

1795. SINGER, JEROME L., AND HERMAN, JACK. "Motor and Fantasy Correlates of Rorschach Human Movement Responses." *J Consult Psychol* 18:325–31 O '54. * (*PA* 29:5798)

1796. SINGER, JEROME L., AND SPOHN, HERBERT E. "Some Behavioral Correlates of Rorschach's Experience-Type." *J Consult Psychol* 18:1–9 F '54. * (*PA* 28:8898)

1797. SMITH, SYDNEY, AND GEORGE, C. E. "The Harrower Multiple Choice Rorschach: A Critique." *J Proj Tech* 18:507–9 D '54. * (*PA* 29:7320)

1798. SOLOMON, PAUL, AND ROSENBLATT, BERNARD. "A Developmental Rorschach Study of 80 Adult Mental Defectives." Abstract. *Am Psychol* 9:475 Ag '54. *

1799. SOSKIN, WILLIAM F. "Bias in Postdiction From Projective Tests." *J Abn & Social Psychol* 49:69–74 Ja '54. * (*PA* 28:7551)

1800. STEPHENSON, WILLIAM. Chap. 8, "Q-Technique and the Rorschach Test," pp. 147–56. In *The Six Schizophrenias: Reaction Patterns in Children and Adults*. By Samuel J. Beck. American Orthopsychiatric Association, Research Monographs No. 6. New York: the Association, Inc., 1954. Pp. xi, 238. * (*PA* 29:2760)

1801. STEVENS, PHYLLIS WOLFE. *The Rorschach Experience Balance as an Index of Emotional Responsiveness*. Doctor's thesis, University of North Carolina (Chapel Hill, N.C.), 1954.

1802. STEWART, G. KINSEY. *Children's Rorschachs: A Validation Study*. Master's thesis, Tulane University (New Orleans, La.), 1954.

1803. STOPOL, MURRAY S. "Rorschach Performance in Relation to Two Types of Stress." *J Consult Psychol* 18:11–5 F '54. * (*PA* 28:8734)

1804. TAULBEE, EARL S. "The Use of the Rorschach Test for Evaluating the Intellectual Levels of Functioning in Schizophrenics." Abstract. *Am Psychol* 9:481 Ag '54. *

1805. TAULBEE, EARL S., AND SISSON, BOYD D. "Rorschach Pattern Analysis in Schizophrenia: A Cross-Validation Study." *J Clin Psychol* 10:80–2 Ja '54. * (*PA* 28:7556)

1806. THOMAS, ROSS REGINALD. *Instructional Effects on Rorschach Variables in Relation to Subject Characteristics*. Doctor's thesis, Northwestern University (Evanston, Ill.), 1954. (*DA* 14:1816)

1807. VANEK, ZDENEK. *The Role of Color in Learning: An Investigation of the Role of Color in Learning and Its Relationship to the Color Rationale of the Rorschach Psychodiagnostic Test*. Doctor's thesis, New York University (New York, N.Y.), 1954. (*DA* 14:2299)

1808. VAN METRE, DOROTHY ACKERMAN. *An Investigation of the Relationship Between Inkblot Color and Certain Personality Traits*. Doctor's thesis, State University of Iowa (Iowa City, Iowa), 1954. (*DA* 14:2406)

1809. VERNON, P. E. "Problems Relating to the Validation of Rorschach and an Evaluation of Some Methods of Approach." Abstract. *Brit Rorsch Forum* (5):8–9 O '54. *

1810. VORHAUS, PAULINE G. "A Reply to Pugh's 'Note on the Vorhaus Configurations of Reading Disability.'" *J Proj Tech* 18:480–1 D '54. * (*PA* 29:7897)

1811. WALLEN, RICHARD W. "Emotional Labels and Projective Test Theory." *J Proj Tech* 18:240–7 Je '54. * (*PA* 29:4327)

1812. WARSHAW, LEON; LEISER, RUDOLF; IZNER, SANFORD M.; AND STERNE, SPENCER B. "The Clinical Significance and Theory of Sodium Amytal Rorschach Testing." *J Proj Tech* 18:248–51 Je '54. * (*PA* 29:4093)

1813. WEDEMEYER, BARBARA. "Rorschach Statistics on a Group of 136 Normal Men." *J Psychol* 37:51–8 Ja '54. * (*PA* 28:7562)

1814. WELLISCH, E. "The Rorschach Personality Index Study in Measuring Personality." Abstract. *B Brit Psychol Soc* (22):21 Ja '54. *

1815. WERTHEIMER, RITA R. "Rorschach Signs of Adjust-

ment and Their Relationship to Adolescent Sociometric Status, Socioeconomic Level, and Sex." Abstract. *Am Psychol* 9:492 Ag '54. *

1816. WHEELER, W. M. "The Psychoanalytic Theory of Object Relations and the Rorschach Technique." Abstract. *Brit Rorsch Forum* (5):4–5 O '54. *

1817. WHITMAN, ROY M. "The Use of the Rorschach Test in Schizophrenia." *Psychiatric Q Sup* 28:26–37 pt 1 '54. * (*PA* 29:2846)

1818. WILKINSON, MARGARET A., AND JACOBS, ROBERT. "A Brief Study of the Relationships Between Personality Adjustment and Vocational Interests as Measured by the Multiple-Choice Rorschach and the Strong Vocational Interest Blank." *J Ed Res* 48:269–78 D '54. * (*PA* 29:7335)

1819. WILLIAMS, HAROLD L., AND LAWRENCE, JAMES F. "Comparison of the Rorschach and MMPI by Means of Factor Analysis." *J Consult Psychol* 18:193–7 Je '54. * (*PA* 29:2484)

1820. WILLIAMS, MILTON HUGH, JR. *The Influence of Variations in Instructions on Rorschach Reaction Time*. Doctor's thesis, University of Nebraska (Lincoln, Neb.), 1954. (*DA* 14:2131)

1821. WILSON, MARY TEWKSBURY. *Regression in Perceptual Organization: A Study of Adolescent Performance on the Rorschach Test*. Doctor's thesis, Clark University (Worcester, Mass.), 1954. (*DA* 14:1819)

1822. WITKIN, H. A.; LEWIS, H. B.; HERTZMAN, M.; MACHOVER, K.; MEISSNER, P. BRETNALL; AND WAPNER, S. *Personality Through Perception: An Experimental and Clinical Study*. New York: Harper & Brothers, 1954. Pp. xxvi, 571. * (*PA* 28:8566)

1823. WRIGHT, STUART. "Some Personality Characteristics of Academic Underachievers." Abstract. *Am Psychol* 9:496 Ag '54. *

1824. WYSOCKI, B. A. *Analysis of Rorschach Responses by Objective Methods*. Doctor's thesis, University of London (London, England), 1954.

1825. ZELEN, SEYMOUR L. "Behavioral Criteria and Rorschach Measures of Level of Aspiration and Rigidity." *J Personality* 23:207–14 D '54. * (*PA* 29:5333)

1826. ZUBIN, JOSEPH. "Failures of the Rorschach Technique." *J Proj Tech* 18:303–15 S '54. * (*PA* 29:4096)

1827. ZUBIN, JOSEPH. "The Measurement of Personality." Comment by E. Lowell Kelly. *J Counsel Psychol* 1:159–64, 172–3 S '54. *

1828. *Dr. Hermann Rorschach Psychodiagnostics Bibliography: The Most Important Publications About the Rorschach Test (Until 1954)*. New York: Grune & Stratton, Inc., 1955. Pp. 64. *

1829. ABRAMS, ELIAS N. "Prediction of Intelligence From Certain Rorschach Factors." *J Clin Psychol* 11:81–3 Ja '55. * (*PA* 29:7251)

1830. ABRAMS, JULES C. *A Study of Certain Personality Characteristics of Non-Readers and Achieving Readers*. Doctor's thesis, Temple University (Philadelphia, Pa.), 1955. (*DA* 16: 377)

1831. ALCOCK, A. THEODORA. "The Rationale and Scoring of Movement Responses." Abstract. *Brit Rorsch Forum* (6):4–9 Ap '55. *

1832. ALCOCK, THEODORA. "The Use of the Rorschach Technique in Clinical Practice and Research—Data: Valid and Non-Valid." Abstract. *B Brit Psychol Soc* (26):13 inset My '55. *

1833. ALLEN, ROBERT M. "An Analysis of Twelve Longitudinal Rorschach Records of One Child." *J Proj Tech* 19:111–6 Je '55. * (*PA* 30:2513)

1834. ALLEN, ROBERT M. "Nine Quarterly Rorschach Records of a Young Girl." *Child Develop* 26:63–9 Mr '55. * (*PA* 30: 2514)

1835. ARMITAGE, STEWART G.; GREENBERG, PAUL D.; PEARL, DAVID; BERGER, DAVID G.; AND DASTON, PAUL G. "Predicting Intelligence From the Rorschach." *J Consult Psychol* 19:321–9 O '55. * (*PA* 30:5971)

1836. ARSUAGA, ROSA AURORA. *A Comparison of Religious Attitudes of American and Latin American Catholic College Students*. Master's thesis, Fordham University (New York, N.Y.), 1955.

1837. BARD, MORTON. "The Use of Dependence for Predicting Psychogenic Invalidism Following Radical Mastectomy." *J Nerv & Mental Dis* 122:152–160 Ag '55. * (*PA* 31:1583)

1838. BARKER, G. B. "John, a Rorschach Study of a Schizophrenic at Four Stages of His Illness." *J Proj Tech* 19:271–91 S '55. * (*PA* 30:4938)

1839. BARKER, G. B. "A Study of a Child Showing Manic Depressive Mood Swings, Using Rorschach and Paintings." Abstract. *Brit Rorsch Forum* (7):14–23 N '55. *

1840. BARKER, G. B. "The Usefulness of the Rorschach Technique in Clinical Practice." Abstract. *B Brit Psychol Soc* (26): 12–3 inset My '55. *

1841. BARRON, FRANK. "Threshold for the Perception of Human Movement in Inkblots." *J Consult Psychol* 19:33–8 F '55. * (*PA* 29:8629)

1842. BASH, K. W. "Einstellungstypus and Erlebnistypus: C. G. Jung and Hermann Rorschach." *J Proj Tech* 19:236–42 S '55. * (*PA* 30:4175)

1843. BAUGHMAN, E. EARL. "A Reply to Stein's 'Note on a Comparative Analysis of Rorschach Forms With Altered Stimulus Characteristics.'" *J Proj Tech* 19:466–7 D '55. * (*PA* 30:7185)

1844. BECK, S. J. "Personality Research and Theories of Personality Structure: Some Convergences." *J Proj Tech* 19:361–71 D '55. * (PA 30:6910)

1845. BEHN-ESCHENBURG, GERTRUD. "Working With Dr. Hermann Rorschach." *J Proj Tech* 19:3–5 Mr '55. * (PA 30:1010)

1846. BENDIG, A. W., AND HAMLIN, ROY M. "The Psychiatric Validity of an Inverted Factor Analysis of Rorschach Scoring Categories." *J Consult Psychol* 19:183–8 Je '55. * (PA 30:2857)

1847. BENNETT, CLAYTON L. "An Experimental Study of Relationships Between Human Electroencephalograms and Certain Rorschach Scoring Categories." Abstract. *Am Psychol* 10:391–2 Ag '55. *

1848. BENT, RUSSELL J. *The Relationship of the Movement Determinant of the Rorschach Test to Autokinetic Movement.* Master's thesis, Fordham University (New York, N.Y.), 1955.

1849. BILMES, MURRAY. *Resistance to Group Influence of Various Personality Factors—as Measured by the Modification of Individual Rorschach Responses Resulting From an Intervening Group Rorschach Experience.* Doctor's thesis, New York University (New York, N.Y.), 1955. (DA 15:2572)

1850. BLECHNER, JANET E. "Further Explorations Into the Relationship of Personality to College Achievement." Abstract. *Calif J Ed Res* 6:135 My '55. *

1851. BLOOM, BERNARD L. "Prognostic Significance of the Underproductive Rorschach." Abstract. *Am Psychol* 10:325 Ag '55. *

1852. BORGATTA, EDGAR F., AND ESCHENBACH, ARTHUR E. "Factor Analysis of Rorschach Variables and Behavioral Observation." *Psychol Rep* 1:129–36 S '55. * (PA 30:5976)

1853. BOURGUIGNON, ERIKA E., AND NETT, EMILY WESTERKAMM. "Rorschach Populars in a Sample of Haitian Protocols." *J Proj Tech* 19:117–24 Je '55. * (PA 30:2706)

1854. BRECHER, SYLVIA. *The Mother-Son Relationship and Schizophrenic Reactions: An Evaluation of the Rorschach Reaction Patterns of Overprotected and Rejected Schizophrenic Patients.* Doctor's thesis, New York University (New York, N.Y.), 1955. (DA 15:1895)

1855. BRODY, CLAIRE M. H. *A Study of the Personality of Normal and Schizophrenic Adolescents Using Two Projective Tests: A Differentiation on the Basis of Structural and Behavioral Rigidity Using the Lowenfeld Mosaic and Rorschach Tests.* Doctor's thesis, New York University (New York, N.Y.), 1955. (DA 16:381)

1856. CLARKE, JOSEPH I. C., AND LODGE, GEORGE T. "Coaction Compass Positions of Normal, Neurotic, and Psychotic Individuals as Defined by Rorschach Determinant Scores: A Cross-Validation." Abstract. *Am Psychol* 10:325–6 Ag '55. *

1857. COOPER, JAMES G. "The Inspection Rorschach in the Prediction of College Success." *J Ed Res* 49:275–82 D '55. * (PA 30:7508)

1858. CORSINI, RAYMOND J.; SEVERSON, WINFIELD E.; TUNNEY, THOMAS E.; AND UEHLING, HAROLD F. "The Separation Capacity of the Rorschach." *J Consult Psychol* 19:194–6 Je '55. * (PA 30:2863)

1859. CORTNER, ROBERT H. *The Relationship of Diagnostic Criteria of the Rorschach and Szondi Tests and Psychiatric Diagnosis in a Military Population.* Master's thesis, St. Louis University (St. Louis, Mo.), 1955.

1860. CRUMPTON, EVELYN. *The Influence of Color on the Rorschach Test.* Doctor's thesis, University of California (Los Angeles, Calif.), 1955. (Abstract: *Am Psychol* 10:324)

1861. DANA, RICHARD H. "Rorschach Scorer Reliability." *J Clin Psychol* 11:401–3 O '55. * (PA 30:5981)

1862. DATEL, WILLIAM E. *Reliability of Interpretations and Consistency of Determinant Scoring in the Rorschach.* Doctor's thesis, University of California (Los Angeles, Calif.), 1955.

1863. DATEL, WILLIAM E., AND GENGERELLI, J. A. "Reliability of Rorschach Interpretations." *J Proj Tech* 19:372–81 D '55. * (PA 30:7190)

1864. DAVIDSON, HELEN H., AND GOTTLIEB, LUCILLE S. "The Emotional Maturity of Pre- and Post-Menarcheal Girls." *J Genetic Psychol* 86:261–6 Je '55. * (PA 30:6951)

1865. DeVos, GEORGE. "A Quantitative Rorschach Assessment of Maladjustment and Rigidity in Acculturating Japanese Americans." *Genetic Psychol Monogr* 52:51–87 Ag '55. * (PA 30:7192)

1866. DUNCAN, BERTHA K. "The Ego Functions and Response to Color on the Rorschach: (1) Disturbed Children and (2) Institutionalized Children." *Trans Kans Acad Sci* 58:252–8 '55. *

1867. ECKHARDT, WILLIAM. "An Experimental and Theoretical Analysis of Movement and Vista Responses." *J Proj Tech* 19:301–5 S '55. * (PA 30:4565)

1868. ESCHENBACH, ARTHUR E. *The Relationship of Basic Rorschach Scoring Categories to Observed Three-Man-Group Interaction Behavior.* Doctor's thesis, University of Florida (Gainesville, Fla.), 1955. (DA 15:1651)

1869. ESCHENBACH, ARTHUR E., AND BORGATTA, EDGAR F. "Testing Behavior Hypotheses With the Rorschach: An Exploration in Validation." *J Consult Psychol* 19:267–73 Ag '55. * (PA 30:4567)

1870. FABRIKANT, BENJAMIN. "Suggestibility and the Rorschach." *J Clin Psychol* 11:309–10 Jl '55. * (PA 30:2873)

1871. FELZER, STANTON B. "A Statistical Study of Sex Differences on the Rorschach." *J Proj Tech* 19:382–6 D '55. * (PA 30:7194)

1872. FILMER-BENNETT, GORDON. "The Rorschach as a Means

of Predicting Treatment Outcome." *J Consult Psychol* 19:331–4 O '55. * (PA 30:6024)

1873. FINNEY, BEN C. "The Diagnostic Discrimination of the 'Basic Rorschach Score.'" Abstract. *J Consult Psychol* 19:96 Ap '55. *

1874. FINNEY, BEN C. "Rorschach Test Correlates of Assaultive Behavior." *J Proj Tech* 19:6–16 Mr '55. * (PA 30:1338)

1875. FISHER, JEROME, AND GONDA, THOMAS A. "Neurologic Techniques and Rorschach Test in Detecting Brain Pathology: A Study of Comparative Validities." *A.M.A. Arch Neurol & Psychiatry* 74:117–24 Ag '55. * (PA 30:5091)

1876. FISHER, JEROME; GONDA, THOMAS A.; AND LITTLE, KENNETH B. "The Rorschach and Central Nervous System Pathology: A Cross-Validation Study." *Am J Psychiatry* 111:487–92 Ja '55. * (PA 29:5702)

1877. FISHER, SEYMOUR. "Some Observations Suggested by the Rorschach Test Concerning the 'Ambulatory Schizophrenic.'" *Psychiatric Q Sup* 29:81–9 pt 1 '55. * (PA 30:7514)

1878. GEORGE, C. E. "Stimulus Value of the Rorschach Cards: A Composite Study." *J Proj Tech* 19:17–20 Mr '55. * (PA 30:1024)

1879. GIBBY, ROBERT G.; STOTSKY, BERNARD A.; HARRINGTON, ROBERT L.; AND THOMAS, RICHARD W. "Rorschach Determinant Shift Among Hallucinatory and Delusional Patients." *J Consult Psychol* 19:44–6 F '55. * (PA 29:8638)

1880. GLEASON, WALTER JAMES. "Direction of Perceived Movement in Males and Females." Abstract. *J Consult Psychol* 19:8 F '55. *

1881. GLUCK, MARTIN R. "Rorschach Content and Hostile Behavior." *J Consult Psychol* 19:475–8 D '55. * (PA 30:7196)

1882. GOLDMAN, ROSALINE. *Changes in Rorschach Performance and Clinical Improvement in Schizophrenia.* Doctor's thesis, Boston University (Boston, Mass.), 1955.

1883. GOODSTEIN, LEONARD D., AND GOLDBERGER, LEO. "Manifest Anxiety and Rorschach Performance in a Chronic Patient Population." *J Consult Psychol* 19:339–44 O '55. * (PA 30:6065)

1884. GRAHAM, STANLEY R. "Relation Between Histamine Tolerance, Visual Autokinesis, Rorschach Human Movement, and Figure Drawing." *J Clin Psychol* 11:370–3 O '55. * (PA 30:6066)

1885. GRAINER, HANS MARTIN. *Situational Influences on Rorschach Anatomical Responses.* Master's thesis, University of North Carolina (Chapel Hill, N.C.), 1955.

1886. GREENBERG, PAUL D.; ARMITAGE, STEWART G.; AND PEARL, DAVID. "Predicting Intelligence From the Rorschach." Abstract. *Am Psychol* 10:321–2 Ag '55. *

1887. GUTTMAN, LOUIS. "Approximate Circumplex Structures of MMPI Scores." Abstract. *Am Psychol* 10:423 Ag '55. *

1888. HAFNER, ADOLF JACK. *An Investigation of the Relationship Between Specific Setting Factors and Behavior on the Rorschach.* Doctor's thesis, Indiana University (Bloomington, Ind.), 1955. (DA 15:2575)

1889. HAGLUND, CARL A. *An Attempt to Differentiate Between Certain Groups of Schizophrenic and Neurotic Patients by the Use of Rorschach Composite Scores.* Doctor's thesis, New York University (New York, N.Y.), 1955. (DA 15:1785)

1890. HAMLIN, ROY M.; STONE, JOHN T.; AND MOSKOWITZ, MERLE J. "Rorschach Color Theories as Reflected in Simple Card Sorting Tasks." *J Proj Tech* 19:410–5 D '55. * (PA 30:6820)

1891. HAMMER, EMANUEL F., AND JACKS, IRVING. "A Study of Rorschach Flexor and Extensor Human Movement Responses." *J Clin Psychol* 11:63–7 Ja '55. * (PA 29:7281)

1892. HAND, MARY E. *The Rorschach as a Measure of Behavioral Change in Children in a Residential School for Mentally Handicapped.* Doctor's thesis, Michigan State University (East Lansing, Mich.), 1955. (DA 17:1585)

1893. HAUCK, PAUL A. *Ute Rorschach Performances and Some Notes on Field Problems and Methods.* Utah University, Department of Anthropology, Anthropological Papers, No. 23. Salt Lake City, Utah: University of Utah Press, July 1955. Pp. ii, 18. *

1894. HAWARD, L. R. C. "Colour Associations as a Contributing Factor to Neurotic Colour Shock." *Brit J Med Psychol* 28:183–7 Je '55. * (PA 30:2883)

1895. HENRY, JULES; NADEL, S. F.; CAUDILL, WILLIAM; HONIGMANN, JOHN J.; SPIRO, MELFORD E.; FISKE, DONALD W.; SPINDLER, GEORGE; AND HALLOWELL, A. IRVING. "Symposium on Projective Testing in Ethnography." *Am Anthrop* 57:245–70 Ap '55. * (PA 30:4397)

1896. HERTZ, MARGUERITE R., AND LOEHRKE, LEAH M. "An Evaluation of the Rorschach Method for the Study of Brain Injury." *J Proj Tech* 19:416–30 D '55. * (PA 30:7606)

1897. HINSON, RICHARD G. *Failure and Subject-Examiner Interaction Effects Upon Organization of Rorschach Ink-Blots.* Doctor's thesis, University of Denver (Denver, Colo.), 1955.

1898. HIRSCHSTEIN, RALPH, AND RABIN, ALBERT I. "Reactions to Rorschach Cards IV and VII as a Function of Parental Availability in Childhood." *J Consult Psychol* 19:473–4 D '55. * (PA 30:7199)

1899. HOHNE, H. H. *Success and Failure in Scientific Faculties of the University of Melbourne.* Melbourne, Australia: Australian Council for Educational Research, 1955. Pp. vii, 129. * (PA 31:3787)

1900. HOLZBERG, JULES D., AND SCHLEIFER, MAXWELL J. "An Experimental Test of the Rorschach Assumption of the

Impact of Color on the Perceptual and Associative Processes." *J Proj Tech* 19:130–7 Je '55. * (*PA* 30:2886)

1901. JENKIN, NOEL. "Some Relationships Between Projective Test Behavior and Perception." *J Clin Psychol* 11:278–81 Jl '55. * (*PA* 30:2888)

1902. JOHANNSEN, DOROTHEA E., AND BENNETT, EDWARD M. "The Personality of Diabetic Children." *J Genetic Psychol* 87:175–85 D '55. * (*PA* 31:1514)

1903. JOHNSON, GRANVILLE B., JR. "An Evaluation Instrument for the Analysis of Teacher Effectiveness." *J Exp Ed* 23:331–44 Je '55. * (*PA* 30:3484)

1904. JOHNSON, LAVERNE C., AND STERN, JOHN A. "Rigidity on the Rorschach and Response to Intermittent Photic Stimulation." *J Consult Psychol* 19:311–7 Ag '55. * (*PA* 30:3960)

1905. KAMMAN, GORDON R., AND KRAM, CHARLES. "Value of Psychometric Examinations in Medical Diagnosis and Treatment." *J Am Med Assn* 158:555–60 Je 18 '55. * (*PA* 31:1044)

1906. KANTER, V. B. "The Use of Projective Tests in an Investigation of Patients Suffering From Duodenal Ulcers." Abstract. *Brit Rorsch Forum* (7):5–9 N '55. *

1907. KAPLAN, BERT. "Reflections of the Acculturation Process in the Rorschach Test." *J Proj Tech* 19:30–5 Mr '55. * (*PA* 30:870)

1908. KAUFMAN, MELVIN. *The Formation of Learning Sets With Mentally Retarded Children.* Doctor's thesis, University of Pittsburgh (Pittsburgh, Pa.), 1955. (*DA* 16:156)

1909. KING, GERALD F. "Rorschach and Levy Movement Responses: A Research Note." *J Clin Psychol* 11:193–5 Ap '55. * (*PA* 30:1033)

1910. KLEIN, ABRAHAM. "A Preliminary Comparative Study of Some Szondi and Rorschach Test Variables." Abstract. *J Personality* 23:499 Je '55. *

1911. KOSTLAN, ALBERT. "A Reply to Patterson." *J Consult Psychol* 19:486 D '55. *

1912. KORKES, LENORE, AND LEWIS, NOLAN D. C. "An Analysis of the Relationship Between Psychological Patterns and Outcome in Pulmonary Tuberculosis." *J Nerv & Mental Dis* 122:524–63 D '55. *

1913. KORNER, IJA N., AND WESTWOOD, DALE. "Inter-Rater Agreement in Judging Student Adjustment From Projective Tests." *J Clin Psychol* 11:167–70 Ap '55. * (*PA* 30:986)

1914. KRAEMER, DORIS R. *Some Perceptual Aspects of the Movement Responses on the Rorschach in Children.* Doctor's thesis, Yeshiva University (New York, N.Y.), 1955.

1915. KRAMER, GEORGE HARVEY, JR. *The Influence of Training and Personality Characteristics of the Examiner on Rorschach Scores.* Doctor's thesis, University of Houston (Houston, Tex.), 1955. (*DA* 16:572)

1916. KROPP, RUSSELL P. "The Rorschach 'Z' Score." *J Proj Tech* 19:443–52 D '55. * (*PA* 30:7205)

1917. LAZARUS, RICHARD S., AND OLDFIELD, MARGARET. "Rorschach Responses and the Influence of Color." *J Personality* 23:356–72 Mr '55. * (*PA* 30:1036)

1918. LEVINE, A.; ABRAMSON, H. A.; KAUFMAN, M. R.; MARKHAM, S.; AND KORNETSKY, C. "Lysergic Acid Diethylamide (LSD-25): XIV. Effect on Personality as Observed in Psychological Tests." *J Psychol* 40:351–66 O '55. * (*PA* 30:7206)

1919. LEVY, LEON H. "Movement as a 'Rhetorical Embellishment' of Human Percepts." *J Consult Psychol* 19:469–71 D '55. *

1920. LINDZEY, GARDNER, AND HERMAN, PETER S. "Thematic Apperception Test: A Note on Reliability and Situational Validity." *J Proj Tech* 19:36–42 Mr '55. * (*PA* 30:1037)

1921. LITTLE, KENNETH B., AND SHNEIDMAN, EDWIN S. "A Comparison of the Reliability of Interpretations of Four Psychological Tests." Abstract. *Am Psychol* 10:322 Ag '55. *

1922. LOFCHIE, STANLEY H. "The Performance of Adults Under Distraction Stress: A Developmental Approach." *J Psychol* 39:109–16 Ja '55. * (*PA* 29:8334)

1923. LUCAS, WINAFRED B. *The Effect of Experimentally Induced Frustration on the Rorschach Responses of Nine-Year-Old Children: A Contribution to the Study of the Effect of Set on Rorschach Responses.* Doctor's thesis, University of California (Los Angeles, Calif.), 1955. (Abstract: *Am Psychol* 10:324)

1924. McCALL, RAYMOND J., AND DOLEYS, ERNEST J., JR. "Popular Responses on the Rorschach Test in Relation to the Number of Responses." *J. Clin Psychol* 11:300–2 Jl '55. * (*PA* 30:2898)

1925. McNEELY, HAROLD ELLIS. *The Influence of Varied Instructions on the Response Adequacy of Certain Rorschach Intelligence Indicators.* Doctor's thesis, University of Nebraska (Lincoln, Neb.), 1955. (*DA* 15:628)

1926. MANN, LESTER. "The Relation of Rorschach Indices of Extraversion-Introversion to Certain Dream Dimensions." *J Clin Psychol* 11:80–1 Ja '55. * (*PA* 29:7301)

1927. MEER, BERNARD. "The Relative Difficulty of the Rorschach Cards." *J Proj Tech* 19:43–53 Mr '55. * (*PA* 30:1044)

1928. MILLER, CARMEN. "A Comparison of High-Accident and Low-Accident Bus and Street Car Operators." *J Proj Tech* 19:146–51 Je '55. * (*PA* 30:1047)

1929. MILLS, EUGENE S. "Abnormal Psychology as a Selective Factor in the College Curriculum." *J Ed Psychol* 46:101–11 F '55. * (*PA* 30:172)

1930. MINDESS, HARVEY. "Analytical Psychology and the Rorschach Test." *J Proj Tech* 19:243–52 S '55. * (*PA* 30:4584)

1931. MINSKI, LOUIS, AND DESAI, MAHESH M. "Aspects of

Personality in Peptic Ulcer Patients: A Comparison With Hysterics." *Brit J Med Psychol* 28:113–34 Je '55. * (*PA* 30:3268)

1932. MIRIN, BERNARD. "The Rorschach Human Movement Response and Role Taking Behavior." *J Nerv & Mental Dis* 122:270–5 S '55. * (*PA* 31:1455)

1933. MONS, W. E. R. "The Scoring and Rationale of Colour Responses." Abstract. *Brit Rorsch Forum* (6):16–9 Ap '55. *

1934. MURATI, JOHN DENIS. *Differences in Test Behavior Between Paranoid and Non-Paranoid Schizophrenic Groups.* Doctor's thesis, University of Wisconsin (Madison, Wis.), 1955. (*DA* 16:386)

1935. NEFF, WALTER S. "The Use of the Rorschach in Distinguishing Vocationally Rehabilitable Groups." *J Counsel Psychol* 2:207–11 f '55. * (*PA* 30:5143)

1936. NORTH, GEORGE E. *The Rorschach Intellectual Indices: An Investigation of Relationships Between Rorschach and the Wechsler-Bellevue Tests.* Master's thesis, University of Utah (Salt Lake City, Utah), 1955.

1937. ODERBERG, PHILLIP. *A Limited Test of Rorschach Reliability by Means of the Introduction of Experimental Color Stimuli.* Doctor's thesis, University of California (Los Angeles, Calif.), 1955.

1938. OGDON, DONALD POTTER. *Rorschach Relationships With Intelligence Among Familial Mental Defectives.* Doctor's thesis, University of Missouri (Columbia, Mo.), 1955. (*DA* 16:578)

1939. OLSEN, LeROY C. *Rorschach Patterns of Successful College Students.* Doctor's thesis, University of North Dakota (Grand Forks, N.D.), 1955.

1940. ORME, J. E. "Intellectual and Rorschach Test Performances of a Group of Senile Dementia Patients and of a Group of Elderly Depressives." *J Mental Sci* 101:863–70 O '55. * (*PA* 30:7532)

1941. PALMER, JAMES O. "Rorschach's Experience Balance: The Concept, General Population Characteristics, and Intellectual Correlates." *J Proj Tech* 19:138–45 Je '55. * (*PA* 30:2912)

1942. PATTERSON, C. H. "Diagnostic Accuracy or Diagnostic Stereotypy?" *J Consult Psychol* 19:483–5 D '55. * (*PA* 30:7171)

1943. PAYNE, R. W. "The Validity of the Rorschach for Psychiatric Diagnosis." Abstract. *B Brit Psychol Soc* (26):12 inset My '55. *

1944. PAYNE, R. W., AND PHILLIPSON, H. "The Clinical Usefulness of the Rorschach: A Symposium." Abstract. *Brit Rorsch Forum* (6):9–16 Ap '55. *

1945. PIOTROWSKI, ZYGMUNT A. "A Defense Attitude Associated With Improvement in Schizophrenia and Measurable With a Modified Rorschach Test." *J Nerv & Mental Dis* 122:36–41 Jl '55. * (*PA* 30:7534)

1946. PIOTROWSKI, ZYGMUNT A., AND BERG, DOROTHY A. "Verification of the Rorschach Alpha Diagnostic Formula for Underactive Schizophrenics." *Am J Psychiatry* 112:443–50 D '55. * (*PA* 30:7220)

1947. POPPLESTONE, JOHN A. "Scoring Colored Responses in Paintings." *J Clin Psychol* 11:191–3 Ap '55. * (*PA* 30:1050)

1948. POWERS, WILLIAM T., AND HAMLIN, ROY M. "Relationship Between Diagnostic Category and Deviant Verbalizations on the Rorschach." *J Consult Psychol* 19:120–4 Ap '55. * (*PA* 30:1053)

1949. PRUYSER, PAUL W., AND FOLSOM, ANGELA T. "The Rorschach Experience Balance in Epileptics." *J Consult Psychol* 19:112–6 Ap '55. * (*PA* 30:1435)

1950. QUIRK, D. *Construct Validation of Rorschach: Protocol Factors Related to Inter-Rater Disagreement.* Master's thesis, University of Toronto (Toronto, Ont., Canada), 1955.

1951. RABINOVITCH, M. SAM; KENNARD, MARGARET A.; AND FISTER, W. P. "Personality Correlates of Electroencephalographic Patterns: Rorschach Findings." *Can J Psychol* 9:29–41 Mr '55. * (*PA* 30:621)

1952. RAINIO, KULLERVO. *Leadership Qualities: A Theoretical Inquiry and an Experimental Study on Foremen.* Suomalaisen Tiedeakatemian Toimituksia, Annales Academiae Scientiarum Fennicae, Sarja-Ser. B, Nide-Tom. 95.1. Helsinki, Finland: Academiae Scientiarum Fennicae, 1955. Pp. 211. * (*PA* 31:1872)

1953. RANSOM, DOROTHY. "The Experimental Use of Electron Micrographs as a Supplement to the Rorschach Ink Blot Technique." *Psychol Rep* 1:203–20 sup 3 '55. * (*PA* 30:5998)

1954. RAY, JOSEPH BLAND. *The Meaning of Rorschach White Space Responses.* Doctor's thesis, University of Oklahoma (Norman, Okla.), 1955. (*DA* 16:580)

1955. REITAN, RALPH M. "Evaluation of the Postconcussion Syndrome With the Rorschach Test." *J Nerv & Mental Dis* 121:463–7 My '55. * (*PA* 30:5119)

1956. REITAN, RALPH M. "The Relation of Rorschach Test Ratios to Brain Injury." *J General Psychol* 53:97–107 Jl '55. * (*PA* 31:8607)

1957. REITAN, RALPH M. "Validity of Rorschach Test as Measure of Psychological Effects of Brain Damage." *A.M.A. Arch Neurol & Psychiatry* 73:445–51 Ap '55. * (*PA* 30:1438)

1958. RICHARDS, T. W. "Personality Development as Reflected in Rorschach Behavior: A Case Study." *J Proj Tech* 19:54–61 Mr '55. * (*PA* 30:733)

1959. RIGBY, MARILYN K.; WILKINS, WALTER L.; AND ANDERHALTER, O. F. "Comparisons of Profile Analyses of Rorschach Data." Abstract. *Am Psychol* 10:414 Ag '55. *

1960. ROBBERTSE, P. M. "Personality Structure of Socially Adjusted and Socially Maladjusted Children, According to the Rorschach Test." *Psychol Monogr* 69(19):1–20 '55. * (*PA* 30:6983)

1961. ROHRER, J. H.; HOFFMAN, E. L.; BAGBY, J. W., JR.; HERRMANN, ROBERT S.; AND WILKINS, W. L. "The Group-Administered Rorschach as a Research Instrument: Reliability and Norms." *Psychol Monogr* 69(8):1–13 '55. * (*PA* 30:1056)

1962. ROSS, ALEXANDER T., AND REITAN, RALPH M. "Intellectual and Affective Functions in Multiple Sclerosis." *A.M.A. Arch Neurol & Psychiatry* 73:663–77 Je '55. * (*PA* 30:3319)

1963. SAKHEIM, GEORGE A. "Suicidal Responses on the Rorschach Test: A Validation Study." *J Nerv & Mental Dis* 122: 332–44 O '55. *

1964. SALK, LEE. *The Relationship of Elaboration on the Rorschach Inquiry to Continuance in Psychotherapy.* Doctor's thesis, University of Michigan (Ann Arbor, Mich.), 1955. (*DA* 15:630)

1965. SANDLER, JOSEPH. "A Simple and Effective Test of Significance for Use With Rorschach Data." *Brit Rorsch Forum* (6):19–21 Ap '55. *

1966. SCALES, MARGARET BERON. *A Study of Intellectual Functioning in Terms of Rorschach Location Scores and Free Verbal Expression.* Doctor's thesis, Columbia University (New York, N.Y.), 1955. (*DA* 15:879)

1967. SCHMIDT, HERMANN O.; FONDA, CHARLES P.; AND LESTER, JOHN R. "Rorschach Behavior as an Index of Color Anaesthesia." *J Psychol* 40:95–102 Jl '55. * (*PA* 30:2918)

1968. SCHNEIDER, BERTRAM H. *The Effect of Varying Time Intervals on the Reproduction and Recall of Rorschach Responses on Retest.* Doctor's thesis, Michigan State University (East Lansing, Mich.), 1955. (*DA* 15:1653)

1969. SHAH, S. A. *A Study of Missionary Success and Failure Using the Inspection Rorschach Technique.* Master's thesis, Pennsylvania State University (State College, Pa.), 1955.

1970. SHATIN, LEO. "Relationships Between the Rorschach Test and the Thematic Apperception Test." *J Proj Tech* 19: 317–31 S '55. * (*PA* 30:4595)

1971. SHERMAN, MURRAY H. "The Diagnostic Significance of Constriction-Dilation on the Rorschach." *J General Psychol* 53: 11–9 Jl '55. * (*PA* 31:7970)

1972. SINGER, JEROME L., AND SUGARMAN, DANIEL A. "A Note on Some Projected Familial Attitudes Associated With Rorschach Movement Responses." *J Consult Psychol* 19:117–9 Ap '55. * (*PA* 30:1368)

1973. SISSON, BOYD D., AND TAULBEE, EARL S. "Organizational Activity on the Rorschach Test." *J Consult Psychol* 19: 29–31 F '55. * (*PA* 29:8652)

1974. SJOSTEDT, ELSIE MARIE. *A Study of the Personality Variables Related to Assaultive and Acquisitive Crimes.* Doctor's thesis, Purdue University (Lafayette, Ind.), 1955. (*DA* 15:881)

1975. SOLOMON, PAUL. "Differential Rorschach Scores of Successfully and Unsuccessfully Placed Mental Defectives." *J Clin Psychol* 11:294–7 Jl '55. * (*PA* 30:3079)

1976. SPIEGELMAN, MARVIN. "Effect of Personality on the Perception of a Motion Picture." *J Proj Tech* 19:461–4 D '55. * (*PA* 30:6831)

1977. SPITAL, CHARLES. *Prediction of Emotional Control in Children With the Rorschach Test.* Doctor's thesis, Vanderbilt University (Nashville, Tenn.), 1955. (*DA* 16:581)

1978. SPITZ, HERMAN H. *A Clinical Investigation of Certain Personality Characteristics of Twenty Adult Male Exhibitionists.* Doctor's thesis, New York University (New York, N.Y.), 1955. (*DA* 16:387)

1979. STAUNTON, G. J. "A Comparative Analysis of Rorschach and T.A.T. Responses With Reference to a Particular Case Study." Abstract. *Brit Rorsch Forum* (6):1–4 Ap '55. *

1980. STEIN, HARRY. "A Note on 'A Comparative Analysis of Rorschach Forms With Altered Stimulus Characteristics' by E. E. Baughman." *J Proj Tech* 19:465–6 D '55. * (*PA* 30:7228)

1981. STOTSKY, BERNARD A. "Differential Responses of Normals, Psychoneurotics, and Psychotics on Rorschach Determinant Shift." *J Consult Psychol* 19:335–8 O '55. * (*PA* 30:6005)

1982. STOTSKY, BERNARD A., AND LAWRENCE, JAMES F. "Various Rorschach Indices as Discriminators of Marked and Little Conceptual Disorganization Among Schizophrenics." *J Consult Psychol* 19:189–93 Je '55. * (*PA* 30:2928)

1983. SYMONDS, PERCIVAL M. "A Contribution to Our Knowledge of the Validity of the Rorschach." *J Proj Tech* 19: 152–62 Je '55. * (*PA* 30:2929)

1984. TAULBEE, EARL S. "The Use of the Rorschach Test in Evaluating the Intellectual Levels of Functioning in Schizophrenics." *J Proj Tech* 19:163–9 Je '55. * (*PA* 30:3237)

1985. THOMAS, HOBART F. "The Relationship of Movement Responses on the Rorschach Test to the Defense Mechanism of Projection." *J Abn & Social Psychol* 50:41–4 Ja '55. * (*PA* 29:7238)

1986. THOMAS, WILLIAM E. *Perceptual Structurization as a Function of Ego Strength: An Experimental Application of the Rorschach Technique.* Doctor's thesis, Michigan State College (East Lansing, Mich.), 1955.

1987. TINDALL, RALPH H. "Relationships Among Indices of Adjustment Status." *Ed & Psychol Meas* 15:152–62 su '55. * (*PA* 30:2330)

1988. TOWBIN, ALAN P. *Hostility in Rorschach Content and*

Overt Aggressive Behavior. Doctor's thesis, Yale University (New Haven, Conn.), 1955.

1989. ULETT, GEORGE. *Rorschach Introductory Manual: A Primer for the Clinical Psychiatric Worker: With Interpretive Diagram to Permit Clinical Use While Learning the Ink-Blot Technique, Second Edition.* Beverly Hills, Calif.: Western Psychological Services, 1955. Pp. 49. *

1990. VERNIER, CLAIRE M.; WHITING, J. FRANK; AND MELTZER, MALCOLM L. "Differential Prediction of a Specific Behavior From Three Projective Techniques." *J Consult Psychol* 19:175–82 Je '55. * (*PA* 30:2932)

1991. VETTER, HAROLD JOHN, JR. *The Prediction of Rorschach Content From the Psychoanalytic Theory of Obsessive-Compulsive Neurosis.* Doctor's thesis, University of Buffalo (Buffalo, N.Y.), 1955. (*DA* 15:1437)

1992. WALTON, D. "On the Validity of the Rorschach Test in the Diagnosis of Intracranial Damage and Pathology." *J Mental Sci* 101:370–82 Ap '55. * (*PA* 30:2933)

1993. WAXENBERG, SHELDON E. "Psychosomatic Patients and Other Physically Ill Persons: A Comparative Study." *J Consult Psychol* 19:163–9 Je '55. * (*PA* 30:3281)

1994. WHEELER, MARY D. "A Follow-up Study of the Case of Roddy, Reported by Dr. M. Ainsworth in March, 1952." Abstract. *Brit Rorsch Forum* (7):10–3 N '55. *

1995. WINTER, WILLIAM D. "Two Personality Patterns in Peptic Ulcer Patients." *J Proj Tech* 19:332–44 S '55. * (*PA* 30:5075)

1996. ZEICHNER, ABRAHAM M. "Psychosexual Identification in Paranoid Schizophrenia." *J Proj Tech* 19:67–77 Mr '55. * (*PA* 30:1378)

1997. ZIMMERMAN, IRLA LEE, AND OETZEL, JAMES L. "A Comparison of Infectious and Traumatic Brain Damage Utilizing Rorschach 'Signs' of Adjustment and Mental Deterioration." Abstract. *Am Psychol* 10:338 Ag '55. *

1998. ABEL, THEODORA M.; OPPENHEIM, SADI; AND SAGER, CLIFFORD J. "Screening Applicants for Training in Psychoanalytically Oriented Psychotherapy." *Am J Psychother* 10:24–39 Ja '56. * (*PA* 31:126)

1999. ABER, WALTER E. *Rorschach Patterns as Related to Sociometric Status.* Master's thesis, North Texas State College (Denton, Tex.), 1956.

2000. ALCOCK, A. THEODORA, AND PHILLIPSON, H. "The Use of Rorschach and Object Relations Technique in Vocational Selection Work." Abstract. *Rorsch Newsl* 1:18–9 D '56. *

2001. ANSBACHER, H. L. "Social Interest, an Adlerian Rationale for the Rorschach Human Movement Response." *J Proj Tech* 20:363–5 D '56. * (*PA* 32:1605)

2002. APPLEBY, LAWRENCE. *The Relationship of a Rorschach Barrier Typology to Other Behavioral Measures.* Doctor's thesis, University of Houston (Houston, Tex.), 1956. (*DA* 16: 2519)

2003. AYAD, JOSEPH MAGDY. *An Experimental Investigation of the Visual Perceptual Properties of the Rorschach Cards.* Doctor's thesis, University of Denver (Denver, Colo.), 1956.

2004. BECK, S. J.; MOLISH, HERMAN B.; AND SINCLAIR, JEAN. "Concerning Researchers' Thinking in Schizophrenia Research." *Am J Orthopsychiatry* 26:792–800 O '56. * (*PA* 32:1835)

2005. BECKER, WESLEY C. "A Genetic Approach to the Interpretation and Evaluation of the Process-Reactive Distinction in Schizophrenia." *J Abn & Social Psychol* 53:229–36 S '56. *

2006. BELL, FREDERICK B. *Some Relationships Between Rorschach Responses and Form or Color Choices.* Doctor's thesis, Purdue University (Lafayette, Ind.), 1956. (*DA* 16:2512)

2007. BENTON, ARTHUR L. "The Rorschach Test and the Diagnosis of Cerebral Pathology in Children." *Am J Orthopsychiatry* 26:783–91 O '56. * (*PA* 32:1917)

2008. BENTON, ARTHUR L. "The Rorschach Test in Epilepsy." *Am J Orthopsychiatry* 26:420–6 Ap '56. *

2009. BENVENISTE, SAMUEL J. *A Study of Shading Responses on the Rorschach Ink-Blot Test.* Doctor's thesis, University of Pittsburgh (Pittsburgh, Pa.), 1956. (*DA* 16:1171)

2010. BERCEL, NICHOLAS A.; TRAVIS, LEE E.; OLINGER, LEONARD B.; AND DREIKURS, ERIC. "Model Psychoses Induced by LSD-25 in Normals: II, Rorschach Test Findings." *Arch Neurol & Psychiatry* 75:612–8 Je '56. * (*PA* 31:6401)

2011. BERG, JACOB, AND POLYOT, C. J. "The Influence of Color on Reactions to Incomplete Figures." *J Consult Psychol* 20:9–15 F '56. * (*PA* 31:3004)

2012. BIERI, JAMES, AND BLACKER, EDWARD. "External and Internal Stimulus Factors in Rorschach Performance." *J Consult Psychol* 20:1–7 F '56. * (*PA* 31:3005)

2013. BIERI, JAMES, AND BLACKER, EDWARD. "The Generality of Cognitive Complexity in the Perception of People and Ink-blots." *J Abn & Social Psychol* 53:112–7 Jl '56. * (*PA* 32:1610)

2014. BIRJANDI, PARVIN FARZAD. *A Rorschach Study of Psychoanalytic Proposals on Cigarette Smoking.* Doctor's thesis, University of Denver (Denver, Colo.), 1956.

2015. BLECHNER, JANET E., AND CARTER, HAROLD D. "Rorschach Personality Factors and College Achievement." *Calif J Ed Res* 7:72–5 Mr '56. * (*PA* 31:3773)

2016. BLOOM, BERNARD L. "Prognostic Significance of the Underproductive Rorschach." *J Proj Tech* 20:367–71 D '56. * (*PA* 32:1611)

2017. BOSQUET, KENNISON T., AND STANLEY, WALTER C. "Discriminative Powers of Rorschach Determinants in Children"

Referred to a Child Guidance Clinic." *J Consult Psychol* 20: 17–21 F '56. * (*PA* 31:3009)

2018. BRACKBILL, GLEN A., AND FINE, HAROLD J. "Schizophrenia and Central Nervous System Pathology." *J Abn & Social Psychol* 52:310–3 My '56. * (*PA* 31:4943)

2019. BRECHER, SYLVIA. "The Rorschach Reaction Patterns of Maternally Overprotected and Maternally Rejected Schizophrenic Patients." *J Nerv & Mental Dis* 123:41–52 Ja '56. * (*PA* 31:6406)

2020. BROWN, BENJAMIN H. *The Utility of a Rorschach Derived Maturity-Immaturity Dimension in Differentiating Non-Problem From Problem Youths.* Doctor's thesis, New York University (New York, N.Y.), 1956. (*DA* 16:2521)

2021. BROWN, L. B. "English Migrants to New Zealand: A Pilot Rorschach Study." *Austral J Psychol* 8:106–10 D '56. * (*PA* 32:383)

2022. BURGESS, ELVA. "Personality Factors of Over- and Under-Achievers in Engineering." *J Ed Psychol* 47:89–99 F '56. * (*PA* 31:8811)

2023. BUTTON, ALAN D. "A Rorschach Study of 67 Alcoholics." *Q J Studies Alcohol* 17:35–52 Mr '56. * (*PA* 31:3326)

2024. CARR, ARTHUR C. "The Relation of Certain Rorschach Variables to Expression of Affect in the TAT and SCT." *J Proj Tech* 20:137–42 Je '56. * (*PA* 31:4674)

2025. CHAREN, SOL. "Regressive Behavior Changes in the Tuberculous Patient." *J Psychol* 41:273–89 Ja '56. * (*PA* 31: 5000)

2026. CLEVELAND, SIDNEY E., AND FISHER, SEYMOUR. "Psychological Factors in the Neurodermatoses." *Psychosom Med* 18:209–20 My–Je '56. * (*PA* 31:5001)

2027. CLYDE, ROBIN JAMES. *An Investigation of the Construct Validity of Some Rorschach Variables.* Doctor's thesis, Ohio State University (Columbus, Ohio), 1956. (*DA* 16:1501)

2028. COAN, RICHARD. "A Factor Analysis of Rorschach Determinants." *J Proj Tech* 20:280–7 S '56. * (*PA* 31:6666)

2029. COHEN, BERTRAM D.; SENF, RITA; AND HUSTON, PAUL E. "Perceptual Accuracy in Schizophrenia, Depression, and Neurosis, and Effects of Amytal." *J Abn & Social Psychol* 52: 363–7 My '56. * (*PA* 31:4814)

2030. CONSALVI, CONRAD. *Rorschach Determinants and Intelligence: A Factor Analytic Study.* Master's thesis, Vanderbilt University (Nashville, Tenn.), 1956.

2031. COX, RACHEL DUNAWAY. "The Normal Personality: An Analysis of Rorschach and Thematic Apperception Test Responses of a Group of College Students." *J Proj Tech* 20: 70–7 Mr '56. * (*PA* 31:3016)

2032. CRUMPTON, EVELYN. "The Influence of Color on the Rorschach Test." *J Proj Tech* 20:150–8 Je '56. (*PA* 31:4679)

2033. DAVIDS, ANTHONY; JOELSON, MARK; AND McARTHUR, CHARLES. "Rorschach and TAT Indices of Homosexuality in Overt Homosexuals, Neurotics, and Normal Males." *J Abn & Social Psychol* 53:161–72 S '56. * (*PA* 32:2891)

2034. DÖRKEN, HERBERT, JR. "Psychological Structure as the Governing Principle of Projective Technique: Rorschach Theory." *Can J Psychol* 10:101–6 Je '56. * (*PA* 31:4682)

2035. DUNCAN, BERTHA K. "Personality Changes as Reflected in Rorschach Records Concomitant With Psychotherapy." *Trans Kans Acad Sci* 59:87–93 sp '56. *

2036. EVERETT, EVALYN B. *A Comparative Study of Paretics, Hebephrenics, and Paranoid Schizophrenics on a Battery of Psychological Tests.* Doctor's thesis, New York University (New York, N.Y.), 1956. (*DA* 16:1502)

2037. FIEDLER, MIRIAM FORSTER, AND STONE, L. JOSEPH. "The Rorschachs of Selected Groups of Children in Comparison With Published Norms." *J Proj Tech* 20:273–9 S '56. * (*PA* 31:6075)

2038. FIELDING, BENJAMIN, AND BROWN, FRED. "Prediction of Intelligence from Certain Rorschach Factors." *J Clin Psychol* 12:196–7 Ap '56. * (*PA* 31:4687)

2039. FISHER, SEYMOUR, AND CLEVELAND, SIDNEY E. "Relationship of Body Image to Site of Cancer." *Psychosom Med* 18:304–9 Jl–Ag '56. * (*PA* 31:6475)

2040. FISHER, SEYMOUR, AND MENDELL, DAVID. "The Communication of Neurotic Patterns Over Two and Three Generations." *Psychiatry* 19:41–6 F '56. (*PA* 31:3503)

2041. FRANGLEN, SHEILA; WILLIAMS, CELIA; AND BENE, EVA M. "Symposium on the Use of the Rorschach in Various Settings." Abstract. *Rorsch Newsl* 1:1–7 My '56. *

2042. GIBSON, JAMES J. "The Non-Projective Aspects of the Rorschach Experiment: IV, The Rorschach Blots Considered as Pictures." *J Social Psychol* 44:203–6 N '56. *

2043. GOLD, DONALD LEE. *The Effect of Negative Instructions on Rorschach Symbolization.* Doctor's thesis, Columbia University (New York, N.Y.), 1956. (*DA* 16:1281)

2044. GOLDBERG, PHILIP L. *A Study of the Effect of Dependency and Other Personality Characteristics on Airmen in a Familiar Crisis Situation.* Doctor's thesis, New York University (New York, N.Y.), 1956. (*DA* 17:894)

2045. GRAYSON, HARRY M. "Rorschach Productivity and Card Preferences as Influenced by Experimental Variation of Color and Shading." *J Proj Tech* 20:288–96 S '56. * (*PA* 31: 6085)

2046. HAASE, WILLIAM. *Rorschach Diagnosis, Socio-Economic Class, and Examiner Bias.* Doctor's thesis, New York University (New York, N.Y.), 1956. (*DA* 16:1283)

2047. HANFMANN, EUGENIA. "The Non-Projective Aspects of the Rorschach Experiment: III, The Point of View of the Research Clinician." *J Social Psychol* 44:199–202 N '56. *

2048. HARTOCH, ANNA. Chap. 6, "The Child's Reaction to the Rorschach Situation," pp. 153–80. In *Personality in Young Children: Vol. I, Methods for the Study of Personality in Young Children.* By Lois B. Murphy and others. New York: Basic Books, Inc., 1956. Pp. xx, 424. * (*PA* 31:2656)

2049. HENRY, EDITH M. *Situational Influences on Rorschach Response.* Master's thesis, Ohio State University (Columbus, Ohio), 1956.

2050. HENRY, EDITH M., AND ROTTER, JULIAN B. "Situational Influences on Rorschach Responses." *J Consult Psychol* 20:457–62 D '56. * (*PA* 32:1625)

2051. HOLT, ROBERT R. "Gauging Primary and Secondary Processes in Rorschach Responses." *J Proj Tech* 20:14–25 Mr '56. * (*PA* 31:3039)

2052. JOST, HUDSON, AND EPSTEIN, LEON J. "The Rorschach as a Physiological Stress." *J Clin Psychol* 12:259–63 Jl '56. * (*PA* 31:6091)

2053. KAGAN, JEROME. "Psychological Study of a School Phobia in One of a Pair of Identical Twins." *J Proj Tech* 20:78–87 Mr '56. * (*PA* 31:3346)

2054. KAHLER, CAROL. *An Exploratory Study of the Use of Action Research in Student Teaching: A Description and Analysis of the Use of Action Research in Twenty-One Off-Campus Student Teaching Situations.* Doctor's thesis, New York University (New York, N.Y.), 1956. (*DA* 16:1850)

2055. KAHN, ROBERT L.; LINN, LOUIS; AND WEINSTEIN, EDWIN A. "Personality Factors Influencing Rorschach Responses in Organic Brain Disease." Abstract. Discussion by Fred Brown. *A.M.A. Arch Neurol & Psychiatry* 76:266–7 S '56. *

2056. KAHN, SAMUEL. *Rorschach Resume: Rorschach Ink Blot Personality Testing.* Ossining, N.Y.: Dynamic Psychological Society Press, 1956. Pp. vii, 63. * (*PA* 30:5988)

2057. KALDEGG, A. "Psychological Observations in a Group of Alcoholic Patients With Analysis of Rorschach, Wechsler-Bellevue and Bender Gestalt Test Results." *Q J Studies Alcohol* 17:608–28 D '56. * (*PA* 32:648)

2058. KALDEGG, A. "Testing Alcoholics." Abstract. *Rorsch Newsl* 1:14–5 D '56. *

2059. KAPLAN, BERT, AND BERGER, STANLEY. "Increments and Consistency of Performance in Four Repeated Rorschach Administrations." *J Proj Tech* 20:304–9 S '56. * (*PA* 31:6093)

2060. KAPLAN, BERT; RICKERS-OVSIANKINA, MARIA A.; AND JOSEPH, ALICE. "An Attempt to Sort Rorschach Records From Four Cultures." *J Proj Tech* 20:172–80 Je '56. * (*PA* 31:4695)

2061. KASS, WALTER. "Projective Techniques as Research Tools in Studies of Normal Personality Development." *J Proj Tech* 20:269–72 S '56. * (*PA* 31:6096)

2062. KLINGENSMITH, STANLEY W. *A Study of the Effects of Different Methods of Structuring the Rorschach Inquiry on Determinant Scores.* Doctor's thesis, University of Pittsburgh (Pittsburgh, Pa.), 1956. (*DA* 16:2524)

2063. KLOPFER, BRUNO; with contributions by Mary D. Ainsworth, Dorothy V. Anderson, Gertrude Baker, Hedda Bolgar, Jack Fox, A. Irving Hallowell, Eileen Higham, Samuel Kellman, Walter G. Klopfer, Gertrude Meili-Dworetzki, Edwin S. Shneidman, Robert F. Snowden, Marvin Spiegelman, Marie D. Stein, Evelyn Troup, and Gertha Williams. *Developments in Rorschach Technique: Vol. II, Fields of Applications.* Yonkers, N.Y.: World Book Co., 1956. Pp. xx, 828. * (*PA* 30:7202)

2064. KNOPF, IRWIN J. "Rorschach Summary Scores in Differential Diagnosis." *J Consult Psychol* 20:99–104 Ap '56. * (*PA* 31:6099)

2065. KNOPF, IRWIN J. "The Rorschach Test and Psychotherapy." *Am J Orthopsychiatry* 26:801–6 O '56. * (*PA* 32: 1628)

2066. KRAUS, ANTHONY R. "An Experiment With Blurred Exposure of Zulliger's Inkblot Slides." Abstract. *Am Psychol* 11:401 Ag '56. *

2067. KRAUS, ANTHONY R. "Shifts in the Levels of Operating Defenses Induced by Blurring of Inkblot Slides." *J Clin Psychol* 12:337–41 O '56. *

2068. LAL, RAM SURAT. "Rorschach Test and Assessment of Intelligence Under Indian Conditions." *Brit J Ed Psychol* 26: 112–6 Je '56. * (*PA* 31:6101)

2069. LAWTON, M. POWELL. "Stimulus Structure as a Determinant of the Perceptual Response." *J Consult Psychol* 20:351–5 O '56. * (*PA* 31:7938)

2070. LEVENTHAL, HOWARD. "The Effects of Perceptual Training on the Rorschach W and Z Scores." *J Consult Psychol* 20:93–8 Ap '56. * (*PA* 31:6102)

2071. LEVINE, MURRAY, AND MELTZOFF, JULIAN. "Cognitive Inhibition and Rorschach Human Movement Responses." *J Consult Psychol* 20:119–22 Ap '56. * (*PA* 31:6103)

2072. LEVY, LEON H.; BRODY, JANICE R.; AND WINDMAN, GEORGIA O. "The Relationship Between the Inferential Potential of Rorschach and TAT Protocols." *J Consult Psychol* 20: 27–8 F '56. * (*PA* 31:3049)

2073. LIGHT, BERNARD H., AND AMICK, JEAN HOLLANDSWORTH. "Rorschach Responses of Normal Aged." *J Proj Tech* 20:185–95 Je '56. * (*PA* 31:4701)

2074. LISANSKY, EDITH S. "The Inter-Examiner Reliability of the Rorschach Test." *J Proj Tech* 20:310–7 S '56. * (*PA* 31: 6106)

2075. LIT, JACK. *Formal and Content Factors of Projective Tests in Relation to Academic Achievement.* Doctor's thesis, Temple University (Philadelphia, Pa.), 1956. (*DA* 16:1505)

2076. LIUTKUS, STANLEY. *Rorschach Indicators of Maturity:*

A Statistical Study of 200 Males. Doctor's thesis, Temple University (Philadelphia, Pa.), 1956. (*DA* 16:2525)

2077. LUNDIN, WILLIAM H., AND BREIGER, BORIS. "Comparison of Productivity and Fantasy on the Rorschach and Projective Movement Sequences." Abstract. *J Consult Psychol* 20:342 O '56. *

2078. LYLE, J. G. "Obsessive-Compulsive Behaviour: Problems of Rorschach Diagnosis and Classification." *Brit J Med Psychol* 29:280–6 pt 3–4 '56. *

2079. McARTHUR, CHARLES, AND HEINEMAN, ROBERT. "The Use of the Rorschach for Planning Teacher Strategy." *Yearb Nat Council Meas Used Ed* 13:156–60 '56. *

2080. McFARLAND, ROBERT L. "Two Dimensions of Test Structure in Rorschach-Like Projective Tests." *J Proj Tech* 20:398–404 D '56. * (*PA* 32:1630)

2081. MANN, LESTER. "The Relation of Rorschach Indices of Extratension and Introversion to a Measure of Responsiveness to the Immediate Environment." *J Consult Psychol* 20:114–8 Ap '56. * (*PA* 31:6110)

2082. MARADIE, LOUIS J. "The Goal-Spurt Hypothesis and the Rorschach Test." *J Consult Psychol* 20:205–10 Je '56. * (*PA* 31:6111)

2083. MARIANI, EUGENE L. *An Analysis of Relationships Between Test Behavior and Types of Defense.* Doctor's thesis, University of Houston (Houston, Tex.), 1956. (*DA* 16:1506)

2084. MARIANI, ROSE RAMSAY. *A Comparison of a Projective Test Battery With Its Component Tests.* Doctor's thesis, University of Houston (Houston, Tex.), 1956. (*DA* 16:1506)

2085. MELTZOFF, JULIAN, AND LITWIN, DOROTHY. "Affective Control and Rorschach Human Movement Responses." *J Consult Psychol* 20:463–5 D '56. * (*PA* 32:1632)

2086. MINTZ, ELIZABETH E.; SCHMEIDLER, GERTRUDE R.; AND BRISTOL, MARJORIE. "Rorschach Changes During Psychoanalysis." *J Proj Tech* 20:414–7 D '56. * (*PA* 32:1634)

2087. MOLISH, HERMAN B. "The Rorschach Test in Military Psychology and Psychiatry." *Am J Orthopsychiatry* 26:807–17 O '56. * (*PA* 32:1635)

2088. MOLISH, HERMAN B. *Schizophrenic Reaction Types as Evaluated From the Rorschach Test.* Doctor's thesis, University of Chicago (Chicago, Ill.), 1956.

2089. MORRISON, R. L. "Use of the Rorschach Test in Wormwood Scrubs." Abstract. *Rorsch Newsl* 1:5–10 D '56. *

2090. MUELLER, ALFRED D., AND LEFKOVITS, AARON M. "Personality Structure and Dynamics of Patients With Rheumatoid Arthritis." *J Clin Psychol* 12:143–7 Ap '56. * (*PA* 31:5010)

2091. MURSTEIN, BERNARD I. "The Projection of Hostility on the Rorschach and as a Result of Ego-Threat." *J Proj Tech* 20:418–28 D '56. * (*PA* 32:1636) (Abstract: *Am Psychol* 11:384)

2092. MURSTEIN, BERNARD I. *A Study of Projection of Hostility on the Rorschach and in a Stress Condition.* Doctor's thesis, University of Texas (Austin, Tex.), 1956.

2093. NITSCHE, CARL J.; ROBINSON, J. FRANKLIN; AND PARSONS, EDWARD T. "Homosexuality and the Rorschach." Abstract. *J Consult Psychol* 20:196 Je '56. *

2094. NIYEKAWA, AGNES M. "A Comparative Analysis of Foreign and American Female College Groups on Three Personality Variables: Anxiety, Level of Aspiration and Femininity." *Psychol Newsl* 7:72–91 My–Je '56. * (*PA* 31:3697)

2095. OKARSKI, JOSEPH FRANK. *Consistency of Projective Movement Responses.* Doctor's thesis, Columbia University (New York, N.Y.), 1956. (*DA* 16:1508)

2096. O'REILLY, P. O. "The Objective Rorschach: A Suggested Modification of Rorschach Technique." *J Clin Psychol* 12:27–31 Ja '56. * (*PA* 30:4585)

209⁻. ORME, J. E. "A Complementary Method of Assessing Rorschach Responses Applied to Groups of Senile Dementia and Elderly Depressed Patients." *Rorsch Newsl* 1:18–28 My '56. *

2098. PALM, ROSE. "Comparative Study of Symbol Formation in Rorschach Test and Dream." *Psychoanalytic R* 43:246–51 Ap '56. * (*PA* 31:5774)

2099. PALMER, JAMES O. "Attitudinal Correlates of Rorschach's Experience Balance." *J Proj Tech* 20:207–11 Je '56. * (*PA* 31:4706)

2100. PASTO, TARMO A., AND KIVISTO, PAUL. "Group Differences in Color Choice and Rejection." *J Clin Psychol* 12:379–81 O '56. *

2101. PEARLMAN, SAMUEL. "A Tentative Rorschach Frame of Reference for Superior Young Adults." Abstract. *Am Psychol* 11:400 Ag '56. *

2102. PICK, THOMAS. "A Critique of Current Methods of Rorschach Scoring." *J Proj Tech* 20:318–25 S '56. * (*PA* 31:6117).

2103. PIOTROWSKI, ZYGMUNT A. Chap. 2, "Rorschach Method in Review," pp. 16–31 (*PA* 30:7219). In *Progress in Clinical Psychology, Vol. II.* Edited by Daniel Brower and Lawrence E. Abt. New York and London: Grune & Stratton, Inc., 1956. Pp. viii, 364. *

2104. POPE, BENJAMIN, AND JENSEN, ARTHUR R. "The Rorschach as an Index of Pathological Thinking." Abstract. *Am Psychol* 11:363 Ag '56. *

2105. POTHAST, MILES DALE. *A Personality Study of Two Types of Murderers.* Doctor's thesis, Michigan State University (East Lansing, Mich.), 1956. (*DA* 17:898)

2106. PRAAG, JULES VAN. *A Rorschach and MMPI Study of a Fundamentalist Religious Sect.* Doctor's thesis, University of Denver (Denver, Colo.), 1956.

2107. RADFORD, E. "Use of the Rorschach in Industry." *Rorsch Newsl* 1:12–3 D '56. *

2108. RAVEN, J. C. "Projection as a Psychological Concept and Method of Enquiry." *Rorsch Newsl* 1:15–8 D '56. *

2109. REICHARD, SUZANNE. "Discussion: Projective Techniques as Research Tools in Studies of Normal Personality Development." *J Proj Tech* 20:265–8 S '56. * (*PA* 31:6120)

2110. RICCIUTI, HENRY N. "Use of the Rorschach Test in Longitudinal Studies of Personality Development." *J Proj Tech* 20:256–60 S '56. * (*PA* 31:6122)

2111. ROHRER, J. H., AND EDMONSON, BARBARA W. "An Experimental Study of the Effects of Individual and Group Presentation of the Rorschach Plates." *J Clin Psychol* 12:249–54 Jl '56. * (*PA* 31:6124)

2112. RYAN, WILLIAM; BOLING, LENORE; AND GREENBLATT, MILTON. "The Rorschach Test in the Evaluation of Psychiatric Treatment." Abstract. *Am Psychol* 11:361 Ag '56. *

2113. SACKS, JOSEPH M., AND COHEN, MURRAY L. "Contributions of the Rorschach to the Understanding of 'Acting-Out' Behavior." Abstract. *Am Psychol* 11:363 Ag '56. *

2114. SARBIN, ANNE. *An Analysis of the Buhler School Maturity Test as It Relates to Intelligence and Projective Test Data.* Doctor's thesis, University of Southern California (Los Angeles, Calif.), 1956.

2115. SCHAFER, ROY. "Transference in the Patient's Reaction to the Tester." *J Proj Tech* 20:26–32 Mr '56. * (*PA* 31:3073)

2116. SCHROEDER, CLIFFORD E. *Personality Patterns of Advanced Protestant Theology Students and Physical Science Students.* Doctor's thesis, Michigan State University (East Lansing, Mich.), 1956. (*DA* 18:154)

2117. SCOTT, EDWARD M. "Regression or Disintegration in Schizophrenia?" *J Clin Psychol* 12:298–300 Jl '56. * (*PA* 31:6444)

2118. SHAPIRO, DAVID. "Color-Response and Perceptual Passivity." *J Proj Tech* 20:52–69 Mr '56. * (*PA* 31:3076)

2119. SINGER, JEROME L. "The Non-Projective Aspects of the Rorschach Experiment: V, Discussion of the Clinical Implications of the Non-Projective Aspects of the Rorschach." *J Social Psychol* 44:207–14 N '56. *

2120. SINGER, JEROME L., AND OPLER, MARVIN K. "Contrasting Patterns of Fantasy and Motility in Irish and Italian Schizophrenics." *J Abn & Social Psychol* 53:42–7 Jl '56. * (*PA* 32:1868)

2121. SINGER, JEROME L.; WILENSKY, HAROLD; AND McCRAVEN, VIVIAN G. "Delaying Capacity, Fantasy, and Planning Ability: A Factorial Study of Some Basic Ego Functions." *J Consult Psychol* 20:375–83 O '56. * (*PA* 31:8506)

2122. SINNETT, E. ROBERT, AND ROBERTS, RUTH. "Rorschach Approach Type and the Organization of Cognitive Material." *J Consult Psychol* 20:109–13 Ap '56. * (*PA* 31:6132)

2123. SISSON, BOYD D.; TAULBEE, EARL S.; AND GASTON, CHARLES O. "Rorschach Card Rejection in Normal and Psychiatric Groups." *J Clin Psychol* 12:85–8 Ja '56. * (*PA* 30:4599)

2124. SMALL, LEONARD. *Rorschach Location and Scoring Manual.* New York and London: Grune & Stratton, Inc., 1956. Pp. ix, 214. * (*PA* 30:7226)

2125. SMITH, JOHN R., AND COLEMAN, JAMES C. "The Relationship Between Manifestations of Hostility in Projective Tests and Overt Behavior." *J Proj Tech* 20:326–34 S '56. * (*PA* 31:6134)

2126. SPIEGELMAN, MARVIN. "Rorschach Form-Level, Intellectual Functioning and Potential." *J Proj Tech* 20:335–43 S '56. * (*PA* 31:6136)

2127. STARER, EMANUEL. "The Use of the Kaleidoscope as an Adjunct to the Rorschach." Abstract. *J Consult Psychol* 20:466 D '56. *

2128. STAUNTON, G. J. "The Recognition and Interpretation of Perceptual Transfer in the Content Analysis of Rorschach Test Responses." Abstract. *Rorsch Newsl* 1:13–7 My '56. *

2129. STEIN, HARRY. "Developmental Changes in Content of Movement Responses." *J Proj Tech* 20:216–23 Je '56. * (*PA* 31:4716)

2130. SUTCLIFFE, J. P. "On the Methodology of Projective Testing." *Austral J Psychol* 8:180–5 D '56. *

2131. SYMONDS, PERCIVAL M., AND DUDEK, STEPHANIE. "Use of the Rorschach in the Diagnosis of Teacher Effectiveness." *J Proj Tech* 20:227–34 Je '56. * (*PA* 31:4718)

2132. TAULBEE, EARL S.; SISSON, BOYD D.; AND GASTON, CHARLES O. "Affective Ratio and 8-9-10 Per Cent on the Rorschach Test for Normals and Psychiatric Groups." *J Consult Psychol* 20:105–8 Ap '56. * (*PA* 31:6138)

2133. TAYLOR, R. S. "Use of the Rorschach Test in Wandsworth Prison." *Rorsch Newsl* 1:10–1 D '56. *

2134. THALER, MARGARET. "Notes on Three Theories of Personality Applied to the Rorschach Test." *Samiksā* 10:121–54 no 3 '56. *

2135. THALER, MARGARET. "Relationships Among Wechsler, Weigl, Rorschach, EEG Findings, and Abstract-Concrete Behavior in a Group of Normal Aged Subjects." *J Gerontol* 11:404–9 O '56. * (*PA* 31:5871)

2136. THALER, MARGARET, AND SCHEIN, EDGAR H. "Rorschach Responses of American Prisoners of War at the Time of Release From Internment." Abstract. *Am Psychol* 11:401 Ag '56. *

2137. TOLMAN, RUTH S., AND MEYER, MORTIMER M. "A Study of Patients' Identifications From Rorschach Records and

Therapists' Judgments." *J Proj Tech* 20:48–51 Mr '56. * (*PA* 31:3084)

2138. TYCKO, MILICENT. *Rorschach Responses as a Function of Exposure Time.* Doctor's thesis, New York University (New York, N.Y.), 1956. (*DA* 17:899)

2139. VAYHINGER, JOHN MONROE. *Prediction From the Rorschach of Behavior in a Group Situation.* Doctor's thesis, Columbia University (New York, N.Y.), 1956. (*DA* 16:1286)

2140. WALLEN, RICHARD W. Chap. 8, "The Rorschach Method," pp. 191–220; 266–70. In his *Clinical Psychology: The Study of Persons.* New York: McGraw-Hill Book Co., Inc., 1956. Pp. xiii, 388. * (*PA* 30:7155)

2141. WEINER, LEONARD; BROWN, EARL; AND KAPLAN, BERT. "A Comparison of the Ability of Normal and Brain Injured Subjects to Produce Additional Responses on a Second Administration of the Rorschach Test." *J Clin Psychol* 12:89–91 Ja '56. * (*PA* 30:5127)

2142. WERNER, HEINZ, AND WAPNER, SEYMOUR. "The Non-Projective Aspects of the Rorschach Experiment: II, Organismic Theory and Perceptual Response." *J Social Psychol* 44:193–8 N '56. *

2143. WETHERHORN, MITCHELL. "Flexor-Extensor Movement on the Rorschach." Abstract. *J Consult Psychol* 20:204 Je '56. *

2144. WHEELER, W. M. "Psychodiagnostic Assessments of a Child After Prolonged Separation in Early Childhood, II." *Brit J Med Psychol* 29:248–57 pt 3–4 '56. *

2145. WICKES, THOMAS A., JR. "Examiner Influence in a Testing Situation." *J Consult Psychol* 20:23–6 F '56. *

2146. WIENER, GERALD. "Neurotic Depressives' and Alcoholics' Oral Rorschach Percepts." *J Proj Tech* 20:453–5 D '56. * (*PA* 32:1655)

2147. WILLNER, ALLEN EUGENE. *The Interpretation of the Rorschach Test as a Function of Interpreter, Degree of Information, and the Subject's Personality.* Doctor's thesis, Michigan State University (East Lansing, Mich.), 1956. (*DA* 17:1385)

2148. WILSON, MARY D., AND COATES, S. "Symposium on the Use of the Rorschach in a Child Guidance Clinic and a General Hospital." Abstract. *Rorsch Newsl* 1:7–12 My '56. *

2149. WIRT, ROBERT D. "Pattern Analysis of the Rorschach." *J Clin Psychol* 12:382–4 O '56. * (*PA* 32:4211)

2150. WOLTMANN, ADOLF G. "Recent Rorschach Literature." *Am J Orthopsychiatry* 26:193–203 Ja '56. *

2151. ZEICHNER, ABRAHAM M. "Conception of Masculine and Feminine Roles in Paranoid Schizophrenia." *J Proj Tech* 20:348–54 S '56. * (*PA* 31:6458)

2152. ZIMET, CARL N., AND BRACKBILL, GLEN A. "The Role of Anxiety in Psychodiagnosis." *J Clin Psychol* 12:173–7 Ap '56. * (*PA* 31:4722)

2153. ZUBIN, JOSEPH. "The Non-Projective Aspects of the Rorschach Experiment: I, Introduction." *J Social Psychol* 44:179–92 N '56. *

2154. ZUBIN, JOSEPH. "Objective Evaluation of Personality Tests." *Am J Psychiatry* 107:590–76 F '56. *

2155. ZUBIN, JOSEPH; ERON, LEONARD D.; AND SULTAN, FLORENCE. "A Psychometric Evaluation of the Rorschach Experiment." *Am J Orthopsychiatry* 26:773–82 O '56. * (*PA* 32:1658)

2156. ZULLIGER, HANS. *Behn-Rorschach Test: Text.* Bern, Switzerland: Hans Huber, 1956. Pp. 200. (New York: Grune & Stratton, Inc., 1956.) *

2157. ADCOCK, C. J.; MCCREARY, J. R.; RITCHIE, J. E.; AND SOMERSET, H. C. A. "Personality and Physique: A Rorschach Study With Maori and European Subjects." *Austral J Psychol* 9:158–89 D '57. *

2158. ALLEN, ROBERT M. "A Note on Persistent Responses in Longitudinal Rorschach Protocols." *J Proj Tech* 21:362–5 D '57. *

2159. ALLEN, ROBERT M. "The Rorschach Records of a Superior Child." *J Genetic Psychol* 91:115–8 S '57. *

2160. AMES, LOUISE BATES; WALKER, RICHARD N.; AND GOODENOUGH, EVELYN. "Old Age Rorschach Follow-Up Study." *Percept & Motor Skills* 7:68 Je '57. * (*PA* 32:2736)

2161. ARMITAGE, STEWART G., AND PEARL, DAVID. "Unsuccessful Differential Diagnosis From the Rorschach." *J Consult Psychol* 21:479–84 D '57. *

2162. AULD, FRANK, JR. "Is Beck's Sample of Rorschach Testees Representative?" *J General Psychol* 56:135–6 Ja '57. *

2163. BARKER, G. B. "Clinical Study and Rorschach Test." Abstract. *Rorsch Newsl* 2:3–8 Jl '57. *

2164. BIERI, JAMES, AND MESSERLEY, SUSAN. "Differences in Perceptual and Cognitive Behavior as a Function of Experience Type." *J Consult Psychol* 21:217–21 Je '57. *

2165. BINDON, D. MARJORIE. "Rubella Deaf Children: A Rorschach Study Employing Munroe Inspection Technique." *Brit J Psychol* 48:249–58 N '57. *

2166. BROOKS, MARJORIE, AND PHILLIPS, LESLIE. "The Cognitive Significance of Rorschach Developmental Scores." Abstract. *Am Psychol* 12:362–3 Jl '57. *

2167. BROWN, FRED. "The Present Status of Rorschach Interpretation." *J Am Psychoanalytic Assn* 5:164–82 Ja '57. *

2168. CANTER, ARTHUR. "Rorschach Response Characteristics as a Function of Color and Degree of Emotional Constriction." Abstract. *J Consult Psychol* 21:46 F '57. *

2169. CHAMBERS, GUINEVERE S., AND HAMLIN, ROY M. "Rorschach 'Inner Life' Capacity of Imbeciles Under Varied Conditions." *Am J Mental Def* 62:88–95 Jl '57. *

2170. CHAMBERS, GUINEVERE S., AND HAMLIN, ROY M. "The

Validity of Judgments Based on 'Blind' Rorschach Records." *J Consult Psychol* 21:105–9 Ap '57. *

2171. CHAREN, SOL. "Pitfalls in Interpretation of Parental Symbolism in Rorschach Cards IV and VII." *J Consult Psychol* 21:52–6 F '57. * (*PA* 32:488)

2172. CONSALVI, CONRAD, AND CANTER, ARTHUR. "Rorschach Scores as a Function of Four Factors." *J Consult Psychol* 21:47–51 F '57. * (*PA* 32:489)

2173. CROOKES, T. G. "Size Constancy and Literalness in the Rorschach Test." *Brit J Med Psychol* 30:99–106 pt 2 '57. *

2174. CUTTER, FRED. "Rorschach Sex Responses and Overt Deviations." *J Clin Psychol* 13:83–6 Ja '57. *

2175. DESAI, M. "The Rorschach in Depersonalization." Abstract. *Rorsch Newsl* 2:21–2 Jl '57. *

2176. ECKHARDT, WILLIAM. "Stimulus-Determinants of 'Shading' Responses." *J Clin Psychol* 13:172–3 Ap '57. * (*PA* 32:2892)

2177. EISNER, BETTY GROVER. *Some Psychological Differences on the Rorschach Between Infertility Patients and Women With Children.* Doctor's thesis, University of California (Los Angeles, Calif.), 1957.

2178. EPSTEIN, SEYMOUR, AND SMITH, RICHARD. "Thematic Apperception, Rorschach Content, and Judgment of Sexual Attractiveness of Women as Related to the Sex Drive in Males." Abstract. *Am Psychol* 12:383 Jl '57. *

2179. EPSTEIN, SEYMOUR; NELSON, JANE V.; AND TANOFSKY, ROBERT. "Responses to Inkblots as Measures of Individual Differences." *J Consult Psychol* 21:211–5 Je '57. *

2180. FLEISCHER, MURRAY S. *Differential Rorschach Configurations of Suicidal Psychiatric Patients: A Psychological Study of Threatened, Attempted, and Successful Suicides.* Doctor's thesis, Yeshiva University (New York, N.Y.), 1957. (*DA* 19:568)

2181. FOWLER, RAYMOND D., JR. *Psychopathology and Social Adequacy: A Rorschach Developmental Study.* Doctor's thesis, Pennsylvania State University (University Park, Pa.), 1957. (*DA* 17:1117)

2182. GRIFFIN, DOROTHY PARK. "Psychometric Scales for the Rorschach Popular Response." *J Clin Psychol* 13:283–7 Jl '57. *

2183. GRUEN, ARNO. "Rorschach: Some Comments on Predicting Structured Behavior From Reactions to Unstructured Stimuli." *J Proj Tech* 21:253–7 S '57. *

2184. HALPERN, HOWARD M. "A Rorschach Interview Technique: Clinical Validation of the Examiner's Hypotheses." *J Proj Tech* 21:10–7 Mr '57. * (*PA* 32:2896)

2185. HAYWARD, LIONEL R. C. "Some Physiological Concomitants of the Rorschach Test." Abstract. *Rorsch Newsl* 2:18–20 Jl '57. *

2186. HERSCH, CHARLES. *The Cognitive Functioning of the Creative Person: A Developmental Analysis by Means of the Rorschach Test.* Doctor's thesis, Clark University (Worcester, Mass.), 1957. (*DA* 18:296)

2187. HOOKER, EVELYN. "The Adjustment of the Male Overt Homosexual." *J Proj Tech* 21:18–31 Mr '57. * (*PA* 32:3083)

2188. JOHNSON, GRANVILLE B., JR. "An Experimental Technique for the Prediction of Teacher Effectiveness." *J Ed Res* 50:679–89 My '57. *

2189. KARSON, SAMUEL, AND POOL, KENNETH BRYNER. "The Abstract Thinking Abilities of Mental Patients." *J Clin Psychol* 13:126–32 Ap '57. * (*PA* 32:3023)

2190. KATAGUCHI, YASUFUMI. "The Development of the Rorschach Test in Japan." *J Proj Tech* 21:258–60 S '57. *

2191. KLINGENSMITH, STANLEY W. "Effects of Different Methods of Structuring the Rorschach Inquiry Upon Determinant Scores." *J Clin Psychol* 13:279–82 Jl '57. *

2192. KLOPFER, BRUNO. "Psychological Variables in Human Cancer." *J Proj Tech* 21:331–40 D '57. *

2193. KORET, SYDNEY, AND RUBIN, ELI Z. "Utilization of Projective Tests as a Prediction of Casework Movement." Discussion by Emily C. Faucett. *Am J Orthopsychiatry* 27:365–76 Ap '57. *

2194. LACY, O. W., AND NASH, DENNISON J. "The American Composer: Implications of Selected Rorschach Responses for Rôle Adjustment." Abstract. *Am Psychol* 12:407 Jl '57. *

2195. LAX, RUTH F. "An Experimental Investigation of the Influence of Color on the Perception of Movement in Ink Blots." *Psychol Newsl* 8:61–75 Ja–F '57. * (*PA* 32:2904)

2196. LEVINE, MURRAY; GLASS, HARVEY; AND MELTZOFF, JULIAN. "The Inhibition Process, Rorschach Human Movement Responses, and Intelligence." *J Consult Psychol* 21:41–5 F '57. * (*PA* 32:496)

2197. LEVITT, EUGENE E. "Alleged Rorschach Anxiety Indices in Children." *J Proj Tech* 21:261–4 S '57. *

2198. LEVY, LEON H., AND KURZ, RONALD B. "The Connotative Impact of Color on the Rorschach and Its Relation to Manifest Anxiety." *J Personality* 25:617–25 S '57. *

2199. MACHOVER, SOLOMON. "Rorschach Study on the Nature and Origin of Common Factors in the Personalities of Parkinsonians." *Psychosom Med* 19:332–8 Jl–Ag '57. *

2200. MALAN, D. H., AND PHILLIPSON, H. "The Psychodynamics of Diagnostic Procedures: A Case Study Reporting the Effects on the Patient of Psychiatric Interview and Rorschach Investigation." *Brit J Med Psychol* 30:92–8 pt 2 '57. *

2201. MARIANI, EUGENE L., AND SHEER, DANIEL E. "Relationships Between Rorschach Test Behavior and Types of Defense." Abstract. *Am Psychol* 12:383–4 Jl '57. *

2202. METRAUX, RHODA, AND ABEL, THEODORA M. "Normal and Deviant Behavior in a Peasant Community: Montserrat,

B.W.I." *Am J Orthopsychiatry* 27:167–84 Ja '57. * (*PA* 32: 1510)

2203. MINDESS, HARVEY. "Psychological Indices in the Selection of Student Nurses." *J Proj Tech* 21:37–9 Mr '57. * (*PA* 32:2908)

2204. MONROE, HAROLD JAY. *A Comparative Rorschach Investigation of Functional and Non-Functional Hearing Impairment.* Doctor's thesis, University of Denver (Denver, Colo.), 1957.

2205. Moss, C. SCOTT. "A Note on the Use of the Schizophrenic in Rorschach Content Analysis." *J Proj Tech* 21:384–90 D '57. *

2206. MURRAY, DAVID C. "An Investigation of the Rorschach White Space Response in an Extratensive Experience Balance as a Measure of Outwardly Directed Opposition." *J Proj Tech* 21:40–6 Mr '57. * (*PA* 32:2910)

2207. MURRAY, DAVID C. "White Space on the Rorschach: Interpretation and Validity." *J Proj Tech* 21:47–53 Mr '57. * (*PA* 32:2911)

2208. PAGE, HORACE A. "Studies in Fantasy—Daydreaming Frequency and Rorschach Scoring Categories." *J Consult Psychol* 21:111–4 Ap '57. *

2209. PALMER, JAMES O. "Some Relationships Between Rorschach's Experience Balance and Rosenzweig's Frustration-Aggression Patterns." *J Proj Tech* 21:137–41 Je '57. *

2210. PATTERSON, C. H. "The Use of Projective Tests in Vocational Counseling." *Ed & Psychol Meas* 17:533–55 W '57. *

2211. PIOTROWSKI, ZYGMUNT A. *Perceptanalysis: A Fundamentally Reworked, Expanded, and Systematized Rorschach Method.* New York: Macmillan Co., 1957. Pp. xix, 505. * (*PA* 32:501)

2212. POPE, BENJAMIN, AND JENSEN, ARTHUR R. "The Rorschach as an Index of Pathological Thinking." *J Proj Tech* 21: 54–62 Mr '57. * (*PA* 32:2915)

2213. RABIN, A. I. "Personality Maturity of Kibbutz (Israeli Collective Settlement) and Non-Kibbutz Children as Reflected in Rorschach Findings." *J Proj Tech* 21:148–53 Je '57. *

2214. RADER, GORDON E. "The Prediction of Overt Aggressive Verbal Behavior From Rorschach Content." *J Proj Tech* 21:294–306 S '57. *

2215. RAIFMAN, IRVING. "Rorschach Findings in a Group of Peptic Ulcer Patients and Two Control Groups." *J Proj Tech* 21:307–12 S '57. *

2216. RIESS, ANNELIESE. *A Study of Some Genetic Behavioral Correlates of Human Movement Responses in Children's Rorschach Protocols.* Doctor's thesis, New York University (New York, N.Y.), 1957. (*DA* 18:668)

2217. RIESSMAN, FRANK. "Social Class and Projective Techniques." Abstract. *Am Psychol* 12:412 Jl '57. *

2218. RODGERS, DAVID A. "Sources of Variance in Students' Rorschach Interpretations." *J Proj Tech* 21:63–8 Mr '57. * (*PA* 32:2919)

2219. SACKS, JOSEPH M., AND COHEN, MURRAY L. "Contributions of the Rorschach Test to the Understanding of 'Acting-Out' Behavior." *J Nerv & Mental Dis* 125:133–6 Ja–Mr '57. *

2220. SASLOW, HARRY L., AND SHIPMAN, WILLIAM G. "The Tendency of the Dörken and Kral Brain Damage Measure to Score False Positives." Abstract. *J Consult Psychol* 21:434 O '57. *

2221. SCHWARTZ, FRED, AND KATES, SOLIS L. "Behn-Rorschach and Rorschach Under Standard and Stress Conditions." *J Consult Psychol* 21:335–8 Ag '57. *

2222. SCHWARTZ, FRED, AND KATES, SOLIS L. "Rorschach Performance, Anxiety Level, and Stress." *J Proj Tech* 21:154–60 Je '57. *

2223. SCOTT, EDWARD M., AND DOUGLAS, FREDERICK. "A Comparison of Rorschach and Howard Tests on a Schizophrenic Population." *J Clin Psychol* 13:79–81 Ja '57. *

2224. SETZE, LEONARD A.; SETZE, KATUSHA DIDENKO; BALDWIN, JOAN C.; DOYLE, CHARLES I.; AND KOBLER, FRANK J. "A Rorschach Experiment With Six, Seven, and Eight Year Old Children." *J Proj Tech* 21:166–71 Je '57. *

2225. SHAH, SALEEM ALAN. "Use of the Inspection Rorschach Technique in Analyzing Missionary Success and Failure." *J Proj Tech* 21:69–72 Mr '57. * (*PA* 32:2920)

2226. SHAW, MERVILLE C., AND CRUICKSHANK, WILLIAM M. "The Rorschach Performance of Epileptic Children." *J Consult Psychol* 21:422–4 O '57. *

2227. SHIPMAN, WILLIAM G. "The Generality of Scope and Differentiation Responses to the Rorschach." *J Proj Tech* 21:185–8 Je '57. *

2228. SILVER, IRVING HERMAN. *Attitudes Toward the Self and Others of a Group of Psychoanalysands: A Determination of the Relationship Between Attitudes Toward Self and Toward Others and Human and Human-Like Responses on the Rorschach.* Doctor's thesis, New York University (New York, N.Y.), 1957. (*DA* 17:1815)

2229. SINGER, ROLAND H. *Various Aspects of Human Figure Drawings as a Personality Measure With Hospitalized Psychiatric Patients.* Doctor's thesis, Pennsylvania State University (University Park, Pa.), 1957. (*DA* 18:290)

2230. SOHLER, DOROTHY TERRY; HOLZBERG, JULES D.; FLECK, STEPHEN; CORNELISON, ALICE R.; KAY, ELEANOR; AND LIDZ, THEODORE. "The Prediction of Family Interaction From a Battery of Projective Techniques." *J Proj Tech* 21:199–208 Je '57. *

2231. SOMMER, ROBERT. "Rorschach Animal Responses and Intelligence." *J Consult Psychol* 21:358 Ag '57. *

2232. STANFORD, MARGARET J. *A Rorschach Study of the Personality Structure of a Group of Eight Year Old Children.* Doctor's thesis, Claremont College (Claremont, Calif.), 1957.

2233. STOTSKY, BERNARD A. "Factor Analysis of Rorschach Scores of Schizophrenics." *J Clin Psychol* 13:275–8 Jl '57. *

2234. SWARTZ, MELVIN B. "The Role of Color in Influencing Responses to the Rorschach Test." Abstract. *Am Psychol* 12:383 Jl '57. *

2235. SYME, LEONARD. "Personality Characteristics and the Alcoholic: A Critique of Current Studies." *Q J Studies Alcohol* 18:288–302 Je '57. *

2236. THALER, MARGARET; WEINER, HERBERT; AND REISER, MORTON F. "Exploration of the Doctor-Patient Relationship Through Projective Techniques: Their Use in Psychosomatic Illness." *Psychosom Med* 14:228–30 My–Je '57. *

2237. TOLOR, ALEXANDER. "The Stability of Tree Drawings as Related to Several Rorschach Signs of Rigidity." *J Clin Psychol* 13:162–4 Ap '57. * (*PA* 32:2924)

2238. WATKINS, CHARLES, AND DEABLER, HERDIS L. "Responses of Chronic Schizophrenic Patients to Tachistoscopic Presentation of Rorschach Figures." *J Proj Tech* 21:404–9 D '57. *

2239. WELLS, STEPHEN. *The Relationships Between Real and Apparent Movement and Rorschach Form Perception.* Doctor's thesis, Syracuse University (Syracuse, N.Y.), 1957. (*DA* 17:1817)

2240. WERTHEIMER, MICHAEL. "Perception and the Rorschach." *J Proj Tech* 21:209–16 Je '57. *

2241. WERTHEIMER, RITA R. "Relationships Between Specific Rorschach Variables and Sociometric Data." *J Proj Tech* 21:94–7 Mr '57. * (*PA* 32:2932)

2242. WILLIAMS, CECELIA. "Differential Diagnosis in Elderly Patients Showing Depressive and Other Symptoms." Abstract. *Rorsch Newsl* 2:14–7 Jl '57. *

2243. WILLIAMS, ROBERT J., AND MACHI, VINCENT S. "An Analysis of Interperson Correlations Among Thirty Psychotics." *J Abn & Social Psychol* 55:50–7 Jl '57. *

2244. WISE, FRED. *Effects of Chronic and Stress-Induced Anxiety on Rorschach Determinants.* Doctor's thesis, Columbia University (New York, N.Y.), 1957. (*DA* 17:1603)

2245. WOHL, JULIAN. "A Note on the Generality of Constriction." *J Proj Tech* 21:410–3 D '57. *

2246. WOLF, IRVING. "Hostile Acting Out and Rorschach Test Content." *J Proj Tech* 21:414–9 D '57. *

2247. WYSOCKI, BOLESLAW A. "Assessment of Intelligence Level by the Rorschach Test as Compared With Objective Tests." *J Ed Psychol* 48:113–7 F '57. *

2248. WYSOCKI, BOLESLAW A. "Differentiation Between Introvert-Extravert Types by Rorschach Method as Compared with Other Methods." *J Psychol* 43:41–6 Ja '57. *

2249. ALTMAN, CHARLOTTE H. "Relationships Between Maternal Attitudes and Child Personality Structure." *Am J Orthopsychiatry* 28:160–9 Ja '58. *

2250. ALTUS, WILLIAM D. "Group Rorschach and Q-L Discrepancies on the ACE." *Psychol Rep* 4:469 S '58. *

2251. BAUGHMAN, E. EARL. "The Role of the Stimulus in Rorschach Responses." *Psychol B* 55:121–47 My '58. *

2252. BAUGHMAN, E. EARL, AND GUSKIN, SAMUEL. "Sex Differences on the Rorschach." *J Consult Psychol* 22:400–1 O '58. *

2253. BIERI, JAMES; BRADBURN, WENDY M.; AND GALINSKY, M. DAVID. "Sex Differences in Perceptual Behavior." *J Personality* 26:1–12 Mr '58. *

2254. BLANK, LEONARD. "Suggestions for Research With Projective Techniques." *J Proj Tech* 22:263–6 S '58. *

2255. BROOKS, MARJORIE O., AND PHILLIPS, LESLIE. "The Cognitive Significance of Rorschach Developmental Scores." *J Personality* 26:268–90 Je '58. *

2256. CARTWRIGHT, ROSALIND DYMOND. "Predicting Response to Client-Centered Therapy With the Rorschach PR Scale." Comment by W. U. Snyder. *J Counsel Psychol* 5:11–7 sp '58. *

2257. CLARK, SELBY G. "The Rorschach and Academic Achievement." *Personnel & Guid J* 36:339–41 Ja '58. *

2258. COSTELLO, C. G. "The Rorschach Records of Suicidal Patients: An Application of a Comparative Matching Technique." *J Proj Tech* 22:272–5 S '58. *

2259. DOOB, LEONARD W. "The Use of Different Test Items in Nonliterate Societies." *Public Opinion Q* 21:499–504 W 57–58 ['58].

2260. ELKINS, ELISE. "The Diagnostic Validity of the Ames 'Danger Signals.'" *J Consult Psychol* 22:281–7 Ag '58. *

2261. FRIEDMAN, IRA. "A Critique of Shneidman and Farberow's 'TAT Heroes of Suicidal and Non-Suicidal Subjects.'" *J Proj Tech* 22:281–3 S '58. *

2262. FRIES, MARGARET E. "Psychoanalytic Concepts and Principles Discernible in Projective Personality Tests: Workshop, 1956: 4, Application of Psychoanalytic Principles to the Rorschach Perceptanalysis in a Longitudinal Study." *Am J Orthopsychiatry* 28:61–6 Ja '58. *

2263. GRIFFIN, DOROTHY PARK. "Movement Responses and Creativity." *J Consult Psychol* 22:134–6 Ap '58. *

2264. HAFNER, A. JACK. "Response Time and Rorschach Behavior." *J Clin Psychol* 14:154–5 Ap '58. *

2265. HAMLIN, ROY M., AND POWERS, WILLIAM T. "Judging Rorschach Responses: An Illustrative Protocol." *J Clin Psychol* 14:240–2 Jl '58. *

2266. HOOKER, EVELYN. "Male Homosexuality in the Rorschach." *J Proj Tech* 22:33–54 Mr '58. *

2267. HOWARD, L. R. C., AND MARSZALEK, K. "The Munroe Check List: A Note on Its Validity in Clinical Research." *J Mental Sci* 104:483–4 Ap '58. *

2268. JOHNSON, LAVERNE C. "Rorschach Concept Evaluation Test as a Diagnostic Tool." *J Consult Psychol* 22:129–33 Ap '58. *

2269. KAGAN, JEROME; SONTAG, LESTER W.; BAKER, CHARLES T.; AND NELSON, VIRGINIA L. "Personality and IQ Change." *J Abn & Social Psychol* 56:261–6 Mr '58. *

2270. KATES, SOLIS L., AND SCHWARTZ, FRED. "Stress, Anxiety and Response Complexity on the Rorschach Test." *J Proj Tech* 22:64–9 Mr '58. *

2271. LAIR, CHARLES V. "Empathy and Its Relation to Stimulus Meaning." *J Clin Psychol* 14:175–7 Ap '58. *

2272. LANDISBERG, SELMA. "Relationship of the Rorschach to Projective Drawings," pp. 613–9. In *The Clinical Application of Projective Techniques.* Edited by Emanuel F. Hammer. Springfield, Ill.: Charles C Thomas, 1958. Pp. xxii, 663. *

2273. LEVY, EDWIN. "Stimulus-Values of Rorschach Cards for Children." *J Proj Tech* 22:293–6 S '58. *

2274. LIPTON, HERBERT; KADEN, STANLEY; AND PHILLIPS, LESLIE. "Rorschach Scores and Decontextualization: A Developmental View." *J Personality* 26:291–302 Je '58. *

2275. LOTSOF, ERWIN J.; COMREY, ANDREW; BOGARTZ, W.; AND ARNSFIELD, P. "A Factor Analysis of the WISC and Rorschach." *J Proj Tech* 22:297–301 S '58. *

2276. MATARAZZO, RUTH G.; MATARAZZO, JOSEPH D.; SASLOW, GEORGE; AND PHILLIPS, JEANNE S. "Psychological Test and Organismic Correlates of Interview Interaction Patterns." *J Abn & Social Psychol* 56:329–38 My '58. *

2277. MOLISH, HERMAN B., AND BECK, SAMUEL J. "Psychoanalytic Concepts and Principles Discernible in Projective Personality Tests: Workshop, 1956: 3, Mechanisms of Defense in Schizophrenic Reaction Types as Evaluated by the Rorschach Test." *Am J Orthopsychiatry* 28:47–60 Ja '58. *

2278. MURPHY, MARY MARTHA. "Utilization of O'Reilly's Objective Rorschach as a Screening Test for State Colony Job Applicants." *J Clin Psychol* 14:65–7 Ja '58. *

2279. MYERS, ROBERT L. *An Analysis of Sex Differences in Verbalizations and Content of Responses to the Rorschach and to the Thematic Apperception Test.* Doctor's thesis, Temple University (Philadelphia, Pa.), 1958. (*DA* 19:365)

2280. NEUHAUS, EDMUND C. "A Personality Study of Asthmatic and Cardiac Children." *Psychosom Med* 20:181–6 My–Je '58. *

2281. OKARSKI, JOSEPH F. "Consistency of Projective Movement Responses." *Psychol Monogr* 72(6):1–26 '58. *

2282. PIOTROWSKI, ZYGMUNT A. "Psychoanalytic Concepts and Principles Discernible in Projective Personality Tests: Workshop, 1956: 1, Freud's Psychoanalysis and Rorschach's Perceptanalysis." *Am J Orthopsychiatry* 28:36–41 Ja '58. *

2283. POWERS, WILLIAM T., AND HAMLIN, ROY M. "A Comparative Analysis of Deviant Rorschach Response Characteristics." *J Consult Psychol* 22:123–8 Ap '58. *

2284. PURCELL, KENNETH. "Some Shortcomings in Projective Test Validation." *J Abn & Social Psychol* 57:115–8 Jl '58. *

2285. RICHARDS, T. W. "Personal Significance of Rorschach Figures." *J Proj Tech* 22:97–101 Mr '58. *

2286. RICHARDS, T. W., AND MURRAY, DAVID C. "Global Evaluation of Rorschach Performance Versus Scores: Sex Differences in Rorschach Performance." *J Clin Psychol* 14:61–4 Ja '58. *

2287. RUESS, AUBREY L. "Some Cultural and Personality Aspects of Mental Retardation." *Am J Mental Def* 63:50–9 Jl '58. *

2288. SARASON, SEYMOUR B.; DAVIDSON, KENNETH; LIGHTHALL, FREDERICK; AND WAITE, RICHARD. "Rorschach Behavior and Performance of High and Low Anxious Children." *Child Develop* 29:277–85 Je '58. *

2289. SCOTT, EDWARD M. "A Comparison of Rorschach and Howard Ink Blot Tests on a Schizophrenic Population From a Content Point of View." *J Clin Psychol* 14:156–7 Ap '58. *

2290. SHATIN, LEO. "The Constriction-Dilation Dimension in Rorschach and TAT." *J Clin Psychol* 14:150–4 Ap '58. *

2291. SOMMER, ROBERT. "Rorschach M Responses and Intelligence." *J Clin Psychol* 14:58–61 Ja '58. *

2292. SOMMER, ROBERT, AND SOMMER, DOROTHY TWENTE. "Assaultiveness and Two Types of Rorschach Color Responses." *J Consult Psychol* 22:57–62 F '58. *

2293. SOPCHAK, ANDREW L. "Prediction of College Performance by Commonly Used Tests." *J Clin Psychol* 14:194–7 Ap '58. *

2294. TAULBEE, EARL S. "Relationship Between Certain Personality Variables and Continuation in Psychotherapy." *J Consult Psychol* 22:83–9 Ap '58. *

2295. TRIER, THOMAS R. "Vocabulary as a Basis for Estimating Intelligence From the Rorschach." *J Consult Psychol* 22:289–91 Ag '58. *

2296. WEISS, A. A. "Alternating Two-Day Cyclic Behavior Changes." *J Clin Psychol* 14:433–7 O '58. *

2297. WINTER, WILLIAM D., AND SALCINES, RAMON A. "The Validity of the Objective Rorschach and the MMPI." *J Consult Psychol* 22:199–202 Je '58. *

SAMUEL J. BECK, *Professorial Lecturer in Psychology and Psychiatry, University of Chicago and Michael Reese Hospital, Chicago, Illinois.*

To Rorschach? or not to Rorschach? The newcomer to this much debated instrument finds himself before a many-portaled quandary. Not one but several tests confront him and all bear the name Rorschach. Avid for solution of that complex riddle, the human personality, by which door shall the neophyte enter? Let us first consider the test as published by Rorschach.

His intent and his effort were empiric, experimental, and with a regard for statistics. He explicitly so states in his monograph (*285*), and in its subtitle he uses the term "experiment in perception." To test out some of his concepts, he actually did some experimenting. As a control, e.g., on the strong role played by color in the responses of epileptics, he prepared three pictures, as follows: a cat in the colors of a tree-frog; a squirrel in those of a cock; and a frog in those of a chaffinch. He describes another experiment by which he tested out his movement determinant.

Rorschach's closest co-worker and the man who took the leadership in establishing the test's clinical worth following Rorschach's untimely death—at age 37—was Oberholzer. He adhered to Rorschach's method, without deviation. Beck studied the test with Oberholzer in Zürich from March through October 1934, and has adhered to the Rorschach-Oberholzer orientation—with deviations. They are few. He has stayed, in the main, within the Rorschach-Oberholzer orientation. Closely working with Beck for many years, Molish has been utilizing his procedures and has been among the keenest exponents in solidifying the foundations for purpose of clinical interpretation. The literature has come to refer to these procedures as the "Beck system." This is a misnomer on two counts. It is not Beck's, and it is not a system. It is the Rorschach-Oberholzer nuclear test. And it has not the closed finality of a system. The procedure constantly watches for new evidence, as clinically validated, that throws light on the associations and that dictates changes in the norms and other spheres of reference whereby it guides itself. It is thus a living tool, altering in accordance with empiric evidence.

Striking out in radical independence from Rorschach's course, Klopfer has developed his "Rorschach technique." Klopfer's orientation is phenomenalist (*2063*) and as such departs from a behavioral-empiricist approach. It is explicitly nonstatistical. The details selected by an examiner are "the result of the phenomenological analysis of the blot properties....and are, therefore, conceptually defined dimensions rather than statistically defined categories." As the reviewer sees the technique, it frees each examiner to use his own subjective judgment in processing the associations. His critique of its method, its logic, and the errors inherent therein are stated more fully elsewhere.[1] Except for the use of Rorschach's inkblot figures and some of his letter symbols, the technique has now so little in common with Rorschach's test, either in method or in some important basic presuppositions, that it represents a quite different approach. Critics of the test, however, make no distinction in their sharp, sometimes phobic, reactions to anything with the name "Rorschach" in its title. It would go far towards clearing up the present state of confusion if Klopfer and his associates ceased to identify their method by the term "Rorschach." Their technique is widely used and gives satisfying results to many clinicians. Some implications from Rorschach's thinking are no doubt comfortable in a phenomenalist bed. But it is a basic error to treat phenomenalist data as though they were behavioristic, an issue which Snygg clearly states.[2] And American psychologists, being behaviorists by training, too frequently commit just that error with their Rorschach data. What a resolution it would be of the present perplexity and confusion, both for users of the test and its critics, if the test and the technique were unmistakably distinguished not only in fact but also in name.

Before the unresolved problems of validation are considered, comment is in order concerning other schools of thought in the Rorschach test field. Hertz keeps close to structure and follows the rationale published by Rorschach, with modifications incident to her own slants. Statistics has always been a right hand to her, but she leans heavily on nomothetic method. Any research in objects of organized complexity, such as we humans are, must, after the nomothetic parameters have been set up, take the next step, to idiography. On the subject of statistics in a datum of organized complexity, see Weaver;[3] and on its application to the Rorschach test, a paper by the reviewer (1844).

For ideas that are most original and intriguing, the newcomer should seek out Piotrowski (2211). His orientation rests soundly on the clinical observation with which he tests out his results, and the foundation stones of Rorschach's thinking on which he has built. He appears to believe in signs, however. He undertakes to depart from the "master's footsteps," but with filial loyalty he expects that his effort will really redound to the good of Rorschach's experiment. But he goes to the extreme of seeing the test as a "new science," a proposal which the reviewer fears is producing restless stirrings in its inventor's bones. Nothing in the *Psychodiagnostik*—and Piotrowski is well acquainted with it—warrants the suggestion that Rorschach had any intent other than to work within the canons of established science, experimental and psychonanalytic. Nor is it necessary to tread beyond these confines in order to use the test and its logic. Then, too, Piotrowski indulges in a bit of romanticizing when he interprets some responses within the framework of the laws of motion as in physics. All of which is too bad, since Piotrowski is one of our most reliable workers with the test. The seduction of the imagination is here carrying him to ethereal heights. For a thorough and just evaluation of Piotrowski and his "Perceptanalysis," the designation under which he subsumes his thinking, see Molish.[4]

Investigators well grounded in psychoanalytic theory will find themselves at home in Schafer's approach (1787). He emphasizes the thematic content in the associations and its significance when interpreted in accordance with psychoanalytic knowledge. He does not disregard structure, but it carries less weight in his exposition. Phillips and Smith (1588) also lean heavily on content, also as seen within the psychoanalytic frame of reference. Their interpretations appear to be, in instances, extravagant, too far removed from the evidence in their texts. They do, however, stay close to Rorschach's fundamental principles of structure with keen, fresh suggestions for exploiting the potential in them for objectivity. Sarason (1786) makes a salutary contribution in accenting the interaction between examiner and patient as affecting a test production and the ob-

1 BECK, SAMUEL J. "Statistics and the Rorschach." Book review. *Cont Psychol* 2:253-4 O '57. *
2 SNYGG, DONALD. "The Need for a Phenomenological System of Psychology." *Psychol R* 48:404-24 '41.
3 WEAVER, WARREN. "Science and Complexity." *Am Scientist* 36:536-44 O '48. *

4 MOLISH, HERMAN B. "Can a Science Emerge From Rorschach's Test?" Book review. *Cont Psychol* 3:189-92 Jl '58. *

tained results (a topic also preoccupying Schafer). This arrests the examiner's attention on his own role in the total testing process and on the need for sifting out the subjective factors which can weight heavily against validity of findings.

In the problem of validation, the confusions generated by the incompatible orientations have been long compounded by the drag on statistical thinking in psychology. This has attempted to statisticize what is probably the most complex datum in nature—the human personality—by techniques devised for what are problems of simplicity and of "disorganized complexity" (Weaver). All sorts of results have come out that have made no sense, either to the strict experimentalist or to the Rorschach test investigator. Let it be said at once and unequivocally that validation such as is sought in a laboratory experiment is not at present to be expected for whole personality findings, whether by the Rorschach test or by any other. We do not know what variables may be complicating the person's behavior and are not being reached by our available tests. Then there are the interactions of forces within the personality, interactions which play a major role in shaping the man or woman as known by others. Experimental psychology must first devise a non-Rorschach technique appropriate to test out the test's concepts, derived as these are from clinical concepts.

But how soundly based in established clinical knowledge concerning human beings are these Rorschach test principles? This is the area proper for validation of the Rorschach test. The measure of validity must be limited to indicating a *direction*. It cannot be a number such as a correlation or other coefficient. It must be a statement of a direction of the psychologic trend or process, a direction away from some one known personality group as point of reference. The patient before us is more (or less) intelligent than, more (or less) excitable than, more (or less) depressed than, more (or less) imaginative than, more (or less) self-controlled than a representative sample of our normative group. The frame of reference which the reviewer uses is the normal (*sic*) adult. One can choose any other—the feebleminded, the schizophrenic, or the depressed. Let him only find, by statistical means, his norms for these, and use them as points of departure. The norms referred to are those for the Rorschach test variables. Rorschach arrived at

certain conclusions concerning the general psychologic significances (e.g., the color determinant as evidence of lively feeling; F+, accurate perception; and others). These conclusions require unremitting testing out. But they are problems of general psychology, and hence this validating job goes to the experimentalist. The validation of the whole characterological picture, whether described in clinical or other terms, must be done by extra-Rorschach data. After the person has been described strictly from the Rorschach test, i.e., "blind" findings, his description is compared with one obtained by another method of observation. The amount of agreement, i.e., the validity of the test, can thus be judged.

One of the abuses of the test originates in the use of cues from nontest sources to produce some of the "amazing" diagnoses which have been excitedly reported. Thus, in its earlier years, the test was uncritically applied and interpreted by methods that were little more than a speaking with tongues. The test was set to do a task for which it was not intended—that of being the final if not the sole diagnostic approach to a mental ill. As an aid towards diagnosis it can greatly facilitate the observer's task, more quickly uncover the likely major reaction patterns, eliminate false scents, and suggest hypotheses as to the depth of and the dynamics in the patient's illness. But it is always an aid to, not a substitute for, clinical diagnosis.

Another pitfall has been that of using it practically before the necessary research has been carried on for the problem presented by the personality group in question. Thus the general principles concerning the test, known from its use in, say, the neuroses, will be applied in attempting to diagnose for brain damage or for the dynamics in stuttering; or perhaps to etch some personality structure in which an industrial plant is interested, such as that of a foreman or of an executive. The empiric research must always first establish the personality pattern, in whatever group. Another principal abuse has been the aura of infallibility which some examiners generate around the test, together with the complementary readiness of their working colleagues to accept the findings. Actually, any conclusions arrived at from the test, whether in regard to separate traits in the person or the whole picture, must be looked on not as facts but as hypotheses, questions which the test asks about that person and which the subsequent investigation is still to verify. What-ever the length and variety of one's experience, he will still make errors. Some 20 years ago this writer stated the criteria which he then consid-ered essential to a soundly trained user of the test (*110*). These criteria still hold. They are: (*a*) broad general experience in psychopathol-ogy; (*b*) understanding of psychoanalytic the-ory; (*c*) use of the test in many clinical groups; (*d*) orientation in the Rorschach-Oberholzer tradition; and (*e*) a foundation in experimental psychology.

But where is the newcomer in the field to ob-tain this equipment? One looks first, and natu-rally, to the universities. The reaction to this look is a mixed one. Such information as is available indicates an extremely wide variation in the numbers of courses and hours of teaching which they provide, and in the competence of the instructors, the especial deficit being their lack of clinical sophistication. More disturbing, the reviewer detects in the universities what he can look on only as unresolved ambivalence to-wards the test. They seem uncertain of whether to teach it and afraid not to teach it. Behind their uncertainty are the difficulties, above noted, involved in immersing it into the labora-tory's crucible. Behind their fear is its increas-ingly wide use throughout the United States and Europe, and their recognition of the aid that it can be as a tool in personality study. The spread is much broader than in the clinical fields of psychiatry and psychology. It includes an-thropology, sociology with especial reference to delinquency, education, business, and industry, and the military services, with a scattering of interest in remoter fields e.g., forensic psychia-try and art. While the more significant clinical research must of necessity be carried on in hos-pitals, the basic researches are properly the tasks of the universities. Centers which can combine the two teaching resources, the clinic and the academic experimental laboratory, must provide the setups most likely to train the young student in a sound use of the test.

H. J. EYSENCK, *Professor of Psychology, In-stitute of Psychiatry, University of London, London, England.*

There are several difficulties in reviewing this test. The number of investigations using it must be in the thousands, and the reviewer cannot claim to have read more than a reasonably large fraction of these. Different investigators use the test in different ways and interpret it according to widely differing principles; this makes com-parison of findings difficult, particularly as these principles are not always stated in detail. Statis-tical treatment of the data is not only frequently, but almost invariably faulty to an extent which makes interpretation impossible. Usually the statistical details given are not sufficient to re-calculate the appropriate significance values. As Cronbach has pointed out in a detailed and competent analysis of the issues involved: "Per-haps ninety per cent of the conclusions so far published as a result of statistical Rorschach studies are unsubstantiated—not necessarily false, but based on unsound analysis" (*795*).

The greatest difficulty of all, however, is a lack of agreement among psychologists on a frame of reference and on the appropriate cri-teria for judging a test such as the Rorschach. Clinical psychologists claim that personal ex-perience, favourable comments by users of test reports such as psychiatrists, and a general feel-ing of clinical usefulness are sufficient to out-weigh any negative results achieved along more experimental lines, and suffice to establish the validity of the Rorschach. Experimental psy-chologists and psychometricians argue that, on the contrary, subjective considerations of the kind mentioned are irrelevant and only serve to establish the claims of the test to be worthy of experimental validation. They point out that many fallacious procedures have in the past re-ceived such "clinical" support—phrenology is one obvious example—and maintain that the same experimental and statistical rigour re-quired in the verification of deductions in learn-ing theory is necessary in the validation of Rorschach postulates also. The present review is written on the basis of this latter point of view.

The writer has recently reviewed [1] the litera-ture of the last five years with respect to the validity of the Rorschach in its various applica-tions and has summarised his results in a set of 10 conclusions which run as follows:

1. There is no consistent meaningful and testable theory underlying modern projective devices.
2. The actual practice of projective experts fre-quently contradicts the putative hypotheses on which their tests are built.
3. On the empirical level, there is no indisputable evidence showing any kind of marked relationship be-

[1] EYSENCK, H. J. "Personality Tests: 1950–55," pp. 118–59. In *Recent Progress in Psychology, Vol. 3.* Edited by G. W. T. H. Fleming. London: J. & A. Churchill, Ltd., 1959. Pp. 397.

tween global projective test interpretation by experts, and psychiatric diagnosis.

4. There is no evidence of any marked relationship between Rorschach scoring categories combined in any approved statistical fashion into a scale, and diagnostic category, when the association between the two is tested on a population other than that from which the scale was derived.

5. There is no evidence of any marked relationship between global or statistically derived projective test scores and outcome of psychotherapy.

6. There is no evidence for the great majority of the postulated relationships between projective test indicators and personality traits.

7. There is no evidence for any marked relationship between projective test indicators of any kind and intellectual qualities and abilities as measured, estimated, or rated independently.

8. There is no evidence for the predictive power of projective techniques with respect to success or failure in a wide variety of fields where personality qualities play an important part.

9. There is no evidence that conscious or unconscious conflicts, attitudes, fears, or fantasies in patients can be diagnosed by means of projective techniques in such a way as to give congruent results with assessments made by psychiatrists independently.

10. There is ample evidence to show that the great majority of studies in the field of projective techniques are inadequately designed, have serious statistical errors in the analysis of the data, and/or are subject to damaging criticisms on the grounds of contamination between test and criterion.

These conclusions are not in principle different from those obtained by other reviewers; thus Cronbach [1] has stated, "The test has repeatedly failed as a predictor of practical criteria. * There is nothing in the literature to encourage reliance on Rorschach interpretations." Similarly, Payne [2] came to the conclusions that "there is no evidence that the test is of any practical use at the moment, either for describing personality or for predicting behaviour" and "there is no evidence that the Rorschach can be used to assess whether or not individuals are well or poorly adjusted." In addition to the damning evidence regarding the validity of the Rorschach, it should perhaps also be pointed out that studies of the reliabilities of different Rorschach scores have shown these to be very low indeed. On all the usual criteria, therefore, it must be concluded that the Rorschach has failed to establish its scientific or practical value. This is becoming more widely recognised, largely as a consequence of the improved standard of Rorschach research in recent years, which has given rise to many well controlled and well analysed studies, the results of which

1 Cronbach, Lee J. "Assessment of Individual Differences," pp. 173–96. In *Annual Review of Psychology, Vol. 7.* Stanford, Calif.: Annual Reviews, 1956. Pp. x, 448. *
2 Payne, R. W. "L'utilité du test de Rorschach en psychologie clinique." *Revue de Psychologie Appliquée* 5:255–64 '55. (*PA* 31:1062)

have been uniformly negative. As a consequence many of the best known training institutions have dropped the Rorschach, while others are keeping it on only because of continued psychiatric demand.

How can the unfavourable judgment given above be reconciled with the many positive findings reported in the literature? The answer is very simply that positive findings are usually achieved in investigations which do not control adequately certain well known sources of error. Some of these errors arise through contamination; Rorschach report and diagnosis or other criterion are not derived separately but are allowed to influence each other directly or indirectly. Other methodological errors involve a failure to test findings from one population on another; this failure of cross validation leads to many positive findings which are later on negatived by other investigators using different populations or subjects. Statistical errors, as already pointed out, are frequent and give an appearance of validity and significance to data which are quite insignificant. Some investigators will compare two or more populations with respect to anything up to several hundred Rorschach scores and claim significance for a few of these which exceed the usual 5 per cent level. Such a procedure ignores the fact that out of so many comparisons you would expect a few to appear statistically significant by chance alone. In the review mentioned above, the writer has shown that quite a high correlation exists between the methodological and statistical excellence of validation studies and their negative outcome, thus supporting the belief that most of the alleged verifications of Rorschach hypotheses are achieved only through the admission of uncontrolled sources of error.

We may add to the empirical demonstration of the uselessness of the Rorschach theoretical consideration. It is claimed in favour of the Rorschach that it measures the whole personality rather than any particular aspect of it. This differentiates it sharply from scientific measuring instruments which are constructed specifically to measure one clearly identifiable attribute of reality at a time. No physicist would entertain for one minute the claims of a device said to measure the whole universe in all its salient aspects; in line with scientific tradition he relies on measuring instruments which are more restricted in their function. It may be surmised that several such restricted measuring instruments could be constructed to test theories embodied in the Rorschach, and it is not impossible that these theories might in fact be verified. By putting all his eggs in one basket as it were, the Rorschach expert makes certain that none of his hypotheses can in fact be verified because none can be tested along the orthodox lines of scientific practice.

RAYMOND J. McCALL, *Professor of Psychology and Chairman of the Department, Marquette University, Milwaukee, Wisconsin.*[1]

PRESENT STATUS OF THE RORSCHACH. Despite several recent faith-shaking reports, the Rorschach remains the most widely used clinical test for the assessment of personality. It is also probably the method on which the opinions of clinicians and psychometricians are most sharply divided. Its partisans have claimed for it an almost clairvoyant power of revealing the inner structure of motive and emotion, while its more determined critics have regarded it as a fragment of clinical liturgy, having low reliability and little validity, that is worthless as a research instrument. Still, the vast majority of those who have used the test clinically are convinced that it has some objective value, particularly in the assessment of abnormality, although the metrically sophisticated among them acknowledge that careful studies have generally failed to support the claims of Rorschach enthusiasts. What controlled research has indicated at best, they say, is a qualified and limited validity which provides small basis for clinical punditry.

DESCRIPTION AND HISTORY. The material of the test is 10 symmetrical inkblots—5 in gray-black against a white ground, 2 adding a brilliant scarlet, and 3 substituting a variety of pastel shades for the gray-black. Its originator was Hermann Rorschach, a German-Swiss psychiatrist of great enterprise and invention. After several years (mostly in the period 1916–1919) of experimenting with inkblots as a diagnostic aid to the classification of patients in a public mental hospital, Rorschach became convinced that the method could be extended to the exploration of normal personality. Though he referred to his work as an "experiment" and maintained that all of its results were predominantly empirical and without theoretical foundation, he did not mean "experiment" in the

sense of controlled observation; his mode of reasoning was actually more analytico-intuitive than inductive, and, despite the disclaimer, appears to have involved many theoretical assumptions derived from Bleulerian associationism, constitutionally oriented psychiatry, and the like. Moreover, while pointing to the need for further work with "standardized parallel series of plates and appropriate control experiments," Rorschach did not hesitate at times to make generalizations that sound anything but tentative, and to treat his limited sample as though representative of mental patients and normals generally. He felt quite sure apparently that the method laid bare the individual's "affective dynamics" and the balance of introversive and "extratensive" tendencies, and provided an intelligence test almost completely independent of previous knowledge, practice, and education. Less than a year after the publication of the *Psychodiagnostik* (1921) in which his "experiment" was described and these views set forth, Rorschach's brilliant career was cut short by his death at 37 years of age.

Though Rorschach was by no means the first to look upon responses to inkblots as revelatory of individual differences, his emphasis upon the sensitivity of the individual to certain perceptual qualities in the blots themselves (the "determinants") as the key to understanding the personality structure was indeed unique. Da Vinci and Botticelli in the 15th century had regarded ink splotches as appropriate stimuli to the painter's imagination, and Binet in the 19th century had included responses to inkblots on his intelligence scales as measures of imaginativeness. Somewhat similar uses were advocated and furthered by Dearborn and Whipple before 1910. Rorschach was probably unaware of these studies, but he pointedly cites the work of Szymon Hens (published in 1917) on similar blots as having influenced his own efforts. He adds, however, that Hens' work was "incomplete," because it was concerned only with the *content* of the interpretations and did not go beyond imagination as the source of differences. His own distinctive contribution, Rorschach felt, was in stressing the *perceptual* features of the task and in his insistence that the *formal determinants* of perception (such as color, shape, and portion of the blot responded to) revealed more of the deeper personality than did the associative content of the responses.

The appreciation of Rorschach's work was

1 The reviewer is indebted to Dolores Janecky of the Milwaukee County Guidance Clinic for bibliographic assistance and to the Research Committee of Marquette University for a supporting grant.

greatly furthered by his friend, the psycho-
analyst Emil Oberholzer, who edited for post-
humous publication Rorschach's last paper, in
which the important categories of shading and
popularity were introduced. Nevertheless, the
Rorschach technique was not widely accepted in
European university circles in the 1920's and
received only minor attention in the German-
speaking world outside Switzerland. With the
introduction of the test into this country and
the arrival here in the 1930's of a group of ex-
patriate psychologists from Germany, the situation was radically changed. Psychiatrist David
Levy played an important role in this new birth
of interest largely by way of his influence on
Samuel J. Beck, who wrote the first doctoral
dissertation on the Rorschach in this country
(Columbia, 1932) and journeyed to Switzerland to study under Oberholzer. Most influential of the refugee scholars was Bruno Klopfer,
who inaugurated the *Rorschach Research Exchange* (later the *Journal of Projective Techniques*) in 1936. By the mid-1930's such well
known clinical specialists as Hertz and Piotrowski, in addition to Klopfer and Beck, were
publishing regularly on the Rorschach. The interest of the measurement-minded was not slow
to follow. In the mid-30's P. E. Vernon wrote
a number of psychometrically oriented articles
on the Rorschach, and prior to World War II
Zubin had devised his psychometric scales for
rating Rorschach responses.

It was the emergence of clinical psychology
as a profession during and after the war, however, that gave the Rorschach its greatest impetus. To many clinicians, bored and irritated
with the conception of the psychologist as an
intelligence tester, competence in the Rorschach
became a symbol of expertise in clinical diagnosis. Here was promised a means by which the
psychologist could supplement, confirm, and
even correct the assessment arising out of the
psychiatric examination. Many psychiatrists,
moreover, came to respect and depend upon this
supplementation, if few sought themselves to
become expert in the method.

Among psychologists, it is the clinicians,
rather than the psychometricians, who are responsible for the widespread popularity of the
method and who have chiefly determined the direction which its development in this country
has taken. Psychometrically oriented researchers like Vernon and Burt in England and Guilford and Thurstone here have deplored the

"cult" of Rorschach, while Zubin and Cronbach
have written friendly but critical suggestions
for making the Rorschach methodologically respectable. There is no doubt that this psychometric approach has had some influence on the
enormous bulk of Rorschach research literature. In particular, it can be discerned in the
studies of Sen and Sandler in England, and of
Wittenborn, Adcock, Coan, Hsü, Williams, and
Lawrence in this country, who have explored
the factorial structure of Rorschach scores, and
in the work of Allen, Baughman, Holtzman,
and Siipola, who have studied most ingeniously
the influence of experimental variations in test
procedures on Rorschach performance. Nevertheless, in the standard Rorschach manuals
statistical and experimental considerations are
pretty much laid aside, and virtually all "explanation" of the psychological meaning of
Rorschach test behavior is clinically, rather than
empirically, derived. The original interpretive
suggestions of Rorschach were based on his
analysis—which was, as we have pointed out,
largely intuitive rather than controlled—of the
records of some 288 Swiss mental patients and
117 normals. Though tens of thousands of
Rorschach tests have been administered by
hundreds of trained professionals since that
time, and while many relationships to personality dynamics and behavior have been hypothesized, the vast majority of these interpretive relationships *have never been validated empirically,* despite the appearance of more than
2,000 publications on the test. This holds not
only for the claims made by Rorschach himself,
but equally for the extensions and modifications
of these advanced by Klopfer, Beck, Piotrowski, Rapaport, Loosli-Usteri, Schafer, and others. Insightful and plausible though they may
be, the evidence in their favor is almost entirely
subjective and impressionistic. As Wittenborn
indicated in *The Third Mental Measurements
Yearbook:* "What passes for research in this
field is usually naively conceived, inadequately
controlled, and only rarely subjected to usual
standards of experimental rigor."

SCORING. In the customary method of administering the Rorschach, the examiner, after noting for each card the time of the initial response
and recording verbatim the subject's description
of what each of the 10 blots looks like to him,
goes over his responses with the subject, endeavoring by discreet inquiry to find out just
where in each blot the reported impression was

localized, and *what* about this area suggested this response to him. From the subject's replies to these inquiries, each response is scored for *location, determinants,* and *content.*

a) *Location* is scored as whole (W), common detail (D), or unusual detail (Dd—often subdivided in various ways). Tendency to use white space (S) as figure is also noted.

b) *Determinants* include form (F); form and color with form primary (FC), or with color primary (CF), or with form absent and color only influencing the response (C); shading or chiaroscuro similarly construed (variously abbreviated Ch, c, K, Sh, and scored Fc, cF, FK, KF, c, etc.). Form is also usually designated as good (F+) or poor (F−). Curiously, human movement (M) is scored as a determinant, even though it is obviously not present in the blots as color and form are. This reflects Rorschach's associationist leanings and his belief that we could not truly perceive movement without a kinesthetic sensation which "determined" the perception. Why those who have distinguished animal movement (FM) and inanimate movement (m) from Rorschach's M (which is confined to human or human-like movement) continue to view these as "determinants" rather than projected content remains a mystery.

c) *Content.* What the subject "sees" in the blots is classified under certain general categories, such as entire humans (H) or animals (A) or parts thereof (Hd and Ad), inanimate objects (Obj), plants (Pl), anatomy (At), sexual objects (Sex), blood (Bl), clouds (Cl), X-rays, symbols (Sym), and maps. In addition, content is usually scored for popularity (P) and sometimes, as with Rorschach himself, for originality (O).

INTERPRETATION. Though Rorschach theorists insist that no one feature of the scored responses can be interpreted by itself, and that the total configuration must be visualized holistically and dynamically, they take, both in principle and practice, certain scoring categories to reflect faithfully, if not linearly, certain tendencies or dispositions of the personality. These dispositions interact, as do their Rorschach equivalents, so that it is possible, according to the manuals, to identify from the Rorschach isolable qualities (like impulsiveness, sensitivity, intelligence) and, with even greater accuracy, the general personality constellation or global

adjustment of the individual. Let us consider certain of these identifications.

Location. W is taken as an indicator of intelligence though no research evidence supports this connection, and studies by Wittenborn (*894*), Wilson (*1466*), and E. K. Sarason (*1024*) report no relation between W and intelligence in the superior, and negative relationship between W and MA in the inferior. The hypothesized connection between D and concern for the practical and concrete is also unevidenced by research. Prevalence of Dd is supposed to be positively related to obsessive-compulsive trends, and for this there is some slight support. One cannot take this support too seriously, however, since in no case was the number of responses (R) partialed out or held constant for different subjects, and the number of Dd is known to correlate highly with R.

White space responses (S) are supposed to indicate negativistic tendencies. The evidence for this is very slight indeed, and from the few published studies one could probably make out a better case for S as a sign of indecisiveness rather than of negativism (*1655*).

Determinants. Among the "determinants," bright color was reported by Rorschach as the most sensitive indicator of affect or emotionality. Primary C responses, i.e., those in which there is no consideration of form or shape, are the "representatives of impulsiveness." CF responses are analogous to pure C but are less pathognomonic. To Rorschach they represented the urge to live outside oneself, and connoted emotional instability, irritability, sensitivity, suggestibility, and egocentricity. These characteristics of "extratension" (which is, by the way, very different from Jung's "extraversion") are found more frequently, he blandly said, in women than in men! FC responses are most common in normals and indicate the kind of emotional lability necessary to achieve environmental rapport. FC thus represents adaptive rather than egocentric affectivity, and this is said to be especially true when the form is clearly visualized (FC+).

Rorschach also described the phenomenon of "color shock," "an emotional and associative stupor" that occurs when the colored Card 8 is shown after the preceding black and white card. This, he concluded, was always a sign of neurotic repression of affect. Among signs of color shock Beck lists delay in giving response to the card, failure to respond (rejection of card), reduction in number of responses, lowering of form quality, and lack of popular responses.

It is difficult to deny that the chromatic cards tend to produce an affective reaction in many subjects. Several studies have shown that colored cards are significantly less likely to be adjudged neutral and more likely to contribute to expression of unpleasant emotion than equivalent cards photographically reproduced in black and white. That this tendency generalizes to other affective stimuli, or is a measure of habitual affectivity in interpersonal relations, however, is by no means self-evident. Combinations of musical tones, for example, qualify also as emotionally charged stimuli which tend to produce judgments of pleasantness—unpleasantness and other affective reactions. We do not conclude on this account that the individual's entire repertory of affectivity is implicit in his response to certain vague tonal sequences. Perhaps it is, but empirical establishment of particular connections is required before we regard this kind of proposition as more relevant to science than to poetry.

The experimental researches of Allen (*1297*), Baughman (*1657*), Crumpton (*2032*), Keehn (*1548–9*), Lazarus (*828*), Siipola (*1032*), and many others make it doubtful that color per se has very much influence on the responses of subjects to inkblots. Virtually all the signs of "color shock," for example, are elicited as frequently by equivalent achromatic cards as by the originals, and are found as often in the records of normals as neurotics.

The "lack of perceptual control" connoted by the CF and C responses seems to be an empirically identifiable factor (*895, 1215, 2172*), but it, too, applies equally to the achromatic and the chromatic cards. The studies of Wittenborn would tend to indicate further that the three kinds of color responses (FC, CF, and C) do not all pertain to the same factor or dimension of scoring. It would follow, then, that to assign a numerical value of .5 to FC, 1.0 to CF, and 1.5 to C, as is done in traditional Rorschach scoring, in order to calculate the *sum C* or "affective balance" of the individual, is not only arbitrary and supposititious but in all probability quite meaningless. There is some support for the assumed connection between CF and C scores on the one hand and ratings of impulsiveness on the other, but color responses alone distinguish the impulsive from the nonimpulsive

less clearly than they do in combination with achromatic responses (*963, 2292*).

Turning from chromatic to achromatic features of the blots, we may note that the interpretation of chiaroscuro or shading responses was suggested only tentatively by Rorschach in the paper with Oberholzer as bearing on "affective adaptability," but indicating "a timid, cautious, and hampered sort of adaptability.... and a tendency toward a fundamentally depressive disposition."

The most complicated detailing of responses to chiaroscuro is advocated by Klopfer, who distinguishes nine aspects of shading responses for purposes of scoring. Reaction to shading in general he reports as related to the way a person "handles his primary security need and derived needs for affection and belongingness." Shading taken as a sign of diffusion or undifferentiated depth (K, KF), e.g., "smoke" or "clouds," indicates "anxiety of a diffuse and free-floating nature." Shading used to produce three-dimensional vista responses (FK, or FV in Beck's system) represents an attempt to "handle his affective anxiety by introspective efforts, by an attempt to objectify his problem by 'gaining perspective' on it, by 'putting it at some distance.'" The juxtaposing of terms like "diffusion" with "diffuse anxiety," of "three-dimensional vista" with "gaining perspective" and "putting it at some distance" suggests a primitive isomorphism between Rorschach response and mental state the like of which has not been seriously advanced by anyone since Empedocles in the 5th century B.C. ("For earth is known by earth in us; water by water.") Not all interpretation of vista and diffusion is as naively metaphorical as this.

The perception of shading as *texture* is scored in the Klopfer system as c, cF, or Fc, analogous to color. The c responses indicate "an infantile, undifferentiated, crude need for affection." The "cF responses represent a relatively crude continuation of an early need for closeness....an infantile sort of dependence on others"; while Fc responses indicate "an awareness of and acceptance of affectional needs experienced in terms of desire for approval, belongingness, and response from others." All of these interpretations are, of course, pure suppositions, unencumbered by empirical considerations. When we turn to reports of research investigations, we are likely to find one study which indicates that undifferentiated shading responses are commoner among maladjusted than adjusted college students, which would dovetail with the "lack of perceptual control" factor identified by Wittenborn (*1215*), but which is not so evidently consistent with the finding of Cox and Sarason (*1678*) that total of c responses (c + cF + Fc) is *lower* among test-anxious subjects than among the nontest-anxious.

Such more or less conflicting results in empirical studies of the Rorschach have been noted as typical by Levy [1] who suggests that a partial explanation is to be found in the extreme variability and unreliability of the validating criteria employed, a situation also remarked on by Sargent in *The Fourth Mental Measurements Yearbook*. Thus test anxiety in students is not the same as general maladjustment, nor is either concept clearly denoted empirically. How, therefore, compare Rorschach findings for the two? If the Rorschach signs fail to accord with such constructs as "maladjustment," or with psychiatric diagnosis, ratings of social adequacy, or stated improvement under psychotherapy, this may reflect only the dubious nature of these criteria. At the same time, agreement between the Rorschach and such poorly defined criterion variables, especially where tester and "validator" share theoretical convictions and accept a common universe of clinical discourse, is likely to indicate only indeliberate collusion or, in a very special sense, correlation between persons. Herein is the weakness of "validation" by matching or by blind analysis.

Extreme emotional reaction to the achromatic cards (especially Cards 4 and 6 and to some extent Cards 5 and 7) is designated "gray black shock" (Beck) or "shading shock" (Klopfer) or "dark shock" (Piotrowski). It is said to indicate "fear of fear," "frustration of affectional needs," or an "anergic state." Neither the existence of the phenomenon nor its interpretive significance is attested to by any controlled investigation.

The F responses, or those determined by the blot contours alone, are viewed ambivalently by the Rorschach authorities. On the one hand, F is taken as the prime indicator of intellectual or rational activity, and its quality as good (F+) or poor (F−) as the chief sign of ego-strength and self-control or ego-weakness and regression. On the other hand, a preponderance of exclu-

sively form-determined responses (to the neglect of color, shading, and dynamic qualities) is generally regarded as evidence of "neurotic constriction," and this is in no way mitigated by the fact that the "form level" (F+ factor) is high. In fact, the picture of "constriction" or "coartation" is made sharper by a high proportion of F+ responses.

Certain conceptual difficulties present themselves here. In the first place, the concept of good form or F+ is a highly variable one. Beck and Klopfer, for example, use very different criteria of good form, while those of Hertz and Piotrowski are somewhat different from either and from each other. In a review published in 1950 Kimball (*974*) has nicely pointed up the problem. Comparing the lists of Beck and Hertz, Kimball found disagreement as to whether a given response was F+ or F− ranging from 11 per cent on Card 7 to 62 per cent on Card 6, and averaging 32 per cent. When Kimball had judges of varying experience rate on a 6-point scale 100 whole responses taken from these lists, there was *disagreement* in rating on 63 per cent of the responses. It would appear that the interjudge reliability of form-level estimates is disquietingly low. As much may be said for the scoring of determinants generally. (*853, 1079, 1099*)

In the second place, the distinction between form-determined (F) and dynamic responses (M) is truly an ambiguous one, since form per se is not necessarily static. In fact, Baughman showed that the silhouette equivalents of the Rorschach blots (in which peripheral form is not altered but shading variations and chromatic color are removed) elicited *more M* responses than the standard series. The relevant contrast is actually between static and dynamic *content*, and not between determinants in the sense of qualities present in the blot which are logically antecedent to perception. The so-called pure F response, then, is a shape-determined identification of a *nonmoving or static object*, and is not just the shape-determined response in itself.

Within the limits of reliability mentioned above, it does appear that form quality, as reflected in the percentage or proportion of good form and of poor form responses, bears a moderate relation to such characteristics as impulse control, reality contact, and critical judgment, though the alleged connection between F+% and intelligence has not on the whole been borne out by research (*596, 775, 1257*).

1 LEVY, LEON H. "Varieties of Rorschach Research." Unpublished paper presented at the 1958 meeting of the Midwestern Psychological Association, Detroit, Michigan.

The human movement response (M) has been endowed with an almost hieratic significance by some Rorschach theorists. To Beck, Rorschach's penetration to the essence of the movement response is his greatest achievement; to Piotrowski, it is his "most original contribution to the experimental study of personality"; Klopfer regards "M's of good form level" as "signs of high intellectual capacity," of one's freedom "to use his imaginal processes to enrich his perception of the world," of "creative potential," of "inner resources upon which the person can fall back in periods of stress," and of "an inner system of conscious values."

Rorschach himself appears to have held, following J. Mourly Vold, that "fantasy" or "inner living" depended upon the actual inhibition of movement and that residues of the motor impulse would remain in the form of kinesthetic sensations or images. Though few today would take seriously the associationistic rationale which Rorschach offered for his views on M, the disposition to regard human movement responses as revealing the "creative inner life" and the deepest reaches of the personality continues. To Beck, "Producing M is, generically, the creative act"; for Piotrowski, "The M stands for the most individual and integrated strivings which dominate the individual's life."

Controlled research has failed to reveal any connection between M responses and independent ratings of creative ability, intellectual productivity and originality, or any other signs of election for salvation, psychologically speaking (1600). With brain-operated patients, Zubin (2154) showed that increase in movement responses, whether of humans or non-humans, is positively correlated with psychiatric judgments of increased anxiety, while Cox and Sarason (1678) found significantly more M among test-anxious than among nontest-anxious students. These results were not predictable from classical Rorschach theory and had little conceivable connection with intraversiveness in Rorschach's sense.

The ratio of human movement to color responses (M:ΣC) is supposed to reflect the balance of introversion-extratension, and to this "experience balance" Rorschach devoted many pages of speculation (285). Another widely used ratio is that of whole to human movement responses (W:M), indicating the relation of drive or aspiration to creative potential. Proportions greater than 2/1 in either direction for either M:ΣC or W:M are said to reflect excessive fantasy, flight into reality, too high level of aspiration, or failure to live up to capacity. Empirical studies of these ratios are few, partly because their significance is difficult to determine quantitatively, since small absolute differences (e.g., 2 versus 1 M) may cause rather large ratio differences (e.g., in W to M 4/1 versus 4/2) (795). A further impediment to research studies of these and many other suggested ratios follows from the condition noted by Sarason (1786): "When the significance attributed to each of the scores is determined by fiat and has little or no foundation in controlled research, whatever significance is attributed to their inter-relationship will probably be of very dubious validity."

The identification of animal movement, for some obscure reason designated by Klopfer "FM," with felt "impulses to immediate gratification" which "stem from the most primitive or archaic layers of the personality," represents a strenuous effort to find a place in the Rorschach for the Freudian id. Klopfer does not explain why "animal movement" should be regarded as a determinant, since such a response does not, like M, imply empathy. The suggestion that perception of animal movement is determined by "animal impulses" in us is indeed fetching, if a little preposterous.

Inanimate movement (m), beyond a maximum of one or two responses, supposedly reflects "awareness of forces outside the control of the subject, which threaten the integrity of his personality organization." These forces are naturally productive of "tension and conflict." Piotrowski thinks of m as revealing "unattainable roles," "the habit of daydreaming," and "superior intelligence." The basis on which these theories are advanced remains quite obscure.

Content. As previously noted, Rorschach himself attached relatively little significance to the content of the responses. "The problems of the experiment," he says in the Summary to the *Psychodiagnostik,* "deal primarily with the formal principles (pattern) of the perceptive process. The actual content of the interpretations comes into consideration only secondarily." The percentage of animal responses he took to be an indicator of stereotyped thinking, and repetition of content as reflecting perseverative or complex-determined thinking. Parts of humans (Hd) are seen more frequently than entire humans (H), he noted, by the anxious, the depressed, and the unintelligent; and conceptually confused ("contaminated") content is symptomatic of psychotic deterioration. The only other aspect of content in which he showed great interest was originality or popularity. Original responses (those occurring only once in a hundred records) of good form quality (O+) were regarded by Rorschach as indicators of creativity and superior intelligence, those of poor form quality as indicators of schizophrenia, feeble-mindedness, and other psychopathological conditions. At the other extreme is the popular response (P) which Rorschach dealt with very briefly but on which Beck (*780*) and Hertz (*260*) have gathered extensive, if not clearly representative, data. Zubin and his students have constructed scales for the rating of all responses along a popularity-originality continuum, and these scales have shown some utility in predicting outcome of treatment in psychosis (*1152*). The number of popular responses is limited, and shows high positive correlation with number of responses (R), while per cent of P is negatively correlated with R. It is desirable, therefore, to evaluate P only in relation to R, and this is seldom done (*1924*).

Many clinicians make far greater use of the content of responses in evaluating a record than Rorschach himself would have countenanced. Thus, Schafer's clinical analyses (*749, 1787*), whether diagnostically or psychoanalytically oriented, unravel every thread of symbolic or thematic significance from the content of the associations, while Klopfer indulges his penchant for extravagant isomorphism with respect to content also (*1730, 2063*). Burt and his student Sen (*874*) claim that their psychometric scaling of content yields average correlations in the .60's with pooled independent ratings of various personality traits, though Burt has never published his scales for general use. Elizur, in a model doctoral thesis (*799*), showed that non-experts could validly detect anxiety and hostility in subjects from the evaluation of anxious and hostile content of Rorschach responses. Sandler and Ackner (*1184*) in England found that certain aspects of response content related significantly to case histories of neuropsychiatric patients, while Watkins and Stauffacher (*1461*) in this country successfully used the content category of "deviant verbalization" to distinguish among normals, neurotics, and psychotics. Though comparatively few studies have been concerned primarily with the content of re-

sponses, the proportion of these which have shown some predictive efficacy is encouragingly high. This has moved Zubin (*1827*) to suggest the abandonment of the Rorschach as a weakly reliable and doubtfully valid *test* and its installation as a standardized interview, the content of which can be readily quantified and analyzed.

It is certainly doubtful that the so-called formal or perceptual scoring categories are really as independent of content as alleged by Rorschach. Movement of any type, as already noted, is content rather than form. The distinction between good and poor form is also a matter of content, specifically of how well the object "seen" fits the contour of the area responded to. Similarly, such "formal" categories as KF, FK or FV, Fk, Fc, cf are scored almost entirely from the content of the percept, e.g., "smoke," "a mountain view," "an X-ray" or "map," "a fur piece." The notion that the subject's introspections form the best basis for deciding what determines his responses is a naive one to begin with, and presently quite untenable in view of Baughman's work with altered blot stimuli (*1080, 1657*). Thus, few report dark color or shading as essential to the popular response "bat" on Card I, but when these qualities are removed from the stimulus, the response "bat" is seldom given. Even the distinction between C and CF or between CF and FC is made in nearly all cases on the basis of content, e.g., "blood" or "blue of the sky" is C, "spattered blood" or "ice cream" is CF, while "red butterfly" or "green caterpillar" is FC. It may be because so many allegedly formal categories pertain really to content that the factor analysis of formal categories, as in Sen's study, yields results strikingly similar to the factor analysis of content. Very possibly the rotation of extracted formal factors brings out their content values. Rorschach's faith in the determinants as a kind of Kantian perceptual form, transcending content, remains unsupported.

Holistic or global assessments derived from the Rorschach may be clinically satisfying, but they too have not stood up well in research. Certain examiners, like Hertz (*709, 810*) and Schachtel (*1185*), using qualitative and not easily replicated methods, have had good success in identifying delinquents, neurotics, depressives, and schizophrenics from the total Rorschach, evaluated clinically. But one gathers here that the Rorschach is a simple adjunct to the extraordinary clinical acumen of some few examiners rather than a technique in which all clinicians can share. Thus in the Michigan study of trainees in clinical psychology, Rorschach personality assessment correlated less than .30 with pooled ratings based on all sources of assessment, though two of six clinicians did well with the Rorschach (*1429*). Its failure to predict adjustment in the Armed Services has been repeatedly noted, and its utility as a general instrument for differential diagnosis is apparently very slight (*1214, 1224, 2161*).

Munroe's inspection technique (*387*) and the Davidson check list of adjustment signs (*928*) are rapid methods of evaluation which represent a compromise between the molecular and molar approaches. They have shown some value as screening devices.

FUTURE DEVELOPMENTS. In any case, the future of the traditional Rorschach will probably see greater emphasis on the content of responses —the appropriateness of content (F+ or F−), its popularity, originality, and dynamic characteristics, its expression of anxious or hostile feeling, its rich variety and conceptual clarity, or its stereotyped poverty. It should also see increasing emphasis on locating better criteria of validity for Rorschach predictions and on experimental designs which insure some cross validation of results. Lastly, if the Rorschach is viewed increasingly as an interview to be interpreted rather than a test to be scored, there should be greater emphasis on the interactional or interpersonal aspects of Rorschach administration: the effects of examiner differences, of the subject's task-set, of varying instructions, or of other aspects of the clinical interaction. Sarason and Baughman and Schafer have in their very different fashions shown the relevancy of these interpersonal considerations, but much more in the way of basic research is called for here.

Baughman's proposal (*2251*) to revise radically the procedure of inquiry may serve to objectify scoring of the standard Rorschach, especially with regard to "determinants." In view of the low reliability of determinant scores as noted to date, this might prove to be an important development.

The Harrower-Erickson and similar forms of the group Rorschach have shown reasonably good reliability but little validity either as research or screening instruments. The Harrower multiple choice Rorschach and the objective Rorschach of O'Reilly have been quite disappointing despite early favorable reports (*1797, 1961, 2096, 2297*).

Holtzman has attempted to overcome one of the great difficulties in obtaining reliable scoring of responses, viz., the variability in number of responses from one card to another, by constructing two new series of parallel blots, each consisting of 45 cards. Only one response is permitted for each card, so that the number of responses is, barring refusals, held constant. This greatly simplifies scoring and has contributed to high reliability coefficients for the determinant scores, averaging +.70 for the two alternate forms, +.84 split-half, and about +.98 for interscorer consistency. With the development of content analyses of comparable reliability, the *Holtzman Inkblot Test* may prove to be a research instrument of great value.

SUMMARY. The inkblot test devised by Rorschach has shown a high degree of clinical viability despite the general failure of empirical studies to support the sweeping claims of the Rorschach enthusiasts. The scoring systems devised for the Rorschach are various and often imperfectly conceptualized, and the interpretive significance of the categories employed is at best doubtful. Rorschach's original notion of the primary importance of the perceptual aspects of the test has not stood up at all well under research investigations, while the analysis of content (which he disparaged) has shown some promise both clinically and experimentally. Recent developments in experimental variations of the blot stimuli may eventually provide an objective and quantifiable basis for this kind of projective technique.

As the cult of the Rorschach declines, the integration of clinical methods with a critical and research orientation should advance. Among clinical psychologists few have done more than Sarason to further the appreciation of research studies. His words may serve to summarize this review. "The clinician who is not guided in his clinical work by these studies operates outside the realm of science, thereby performing a disservice to his patients as well as his profession" (*1786*).

LAURANCE F. SHAFFER, *Professor of Education, Teachers College, Columbia University, New York, New York.*

For how long does a diagnostic method stay "promising"? More than two decades ago, the present reviewer concluded one of the earliest descriptions of the Rorschach to appear in an American psychology textbook with these words: "With further development, this method promises to be a useful one." [1] The Rorschach seemed "promising" in 1936, and many other commentators have since echoed the sentiment. Perhaps it is now time to judge the extent to which the promise has been fulfilled.

As with any other method for the appraisal of persons, the central issue about the Rorschach is its validity. Does it work? How do clinicians use it? For what purposes? To what degree are the conclusions they draw confirmed by other evidence? In spite of the protests of some Rorschachists, the validity is researchable. The user makes certain practical decisions or predictions—and he may make them objectively from scores or intuitively from global interpretations. In either case, the user has only to count his hits and misses, and he obtains evidence relevant to validity.

CLINICAL VALIDITY. Among the broad criteria of interest to psychology and psychiatry, two stand out clearly. Of any patient, we want to know two things—what's the matter with him, and will he get well? The criterion of diagnosis is therefore of great importance, as is also the criterion of improvement through treatment. These decisions are practical and realistic ones. Every day, psychologists in clinics and hospitals make inferences from the Rorschach about the diagnosis of patients and about the likelihood of their recovery.

Only in recent years have soundly designed research studies probed the validity of the Rorschach for these applications, by both score counting and global judgment methods. To review all of the research comprehensively would require a book, but it is helpful to examine a few representative studies.

In a study of the relationship of Rorschach scores to diagnosis, Knopf (2064) gathered the Rorschach records of 339 unambiguously diagnosed patients: 131 psychoneurotics, 106 psychopaths, and 100 schizophrenics. Appropriate nonparametric statistics were used to test whether 34 Rorschach summary scores differentiated the groups. Only four scores—rare details, populars, sex, and anatomy—significantly discriminated at the .05 level, and these separated only the psychopaths from the neurotics and schizophrenics. Not a single score made the

much sought distinction between the psychoneurotics and schizophrenics. Other studies have found little more. Typically, one study may find a few signs or patterns that are weakly significant, but a replication fails to confirm them (1301, 1452, 1603, 1707).

Many Rorschach workers are not surprised when scores fail to give valid diagnoses. But the method of global judgment has also been investigated. In one very competent study, Chambers and Hamlin (2169) sent a set of 5 scored Rorschach protocols to each of 20 well qualified judges, many of them eminent authorities. Each set was different, but each contained the same assortment of uncontroversially diagnosed cases—one involutional depression, one anxiety neurosis, one paranoid schizophrenia, one brain damage from neurosyphilis, and one adult imbecile. The judges were informed of the groups represented, and had the apparently simple task of assigning one protocol of the five to each diagnosis. The results exceeded chance, but did not confirm the supposition that this simplified task can be done perfectly by all competent psychologists. Mental deficiency was the easiest to judge, and was correctly identified by 18 of the 20 judges. The other four diagnoses were correctly judged in 51 per cent of the instances. To cite one typical example, involutional depression was correctly designated by 10 of the 20 judges, but was called neurosis by 4, schizophrenia by 1, brain damage by 4, and mental deficiency by 1. Global diagnosis from the Rorschach had nonchance validity, but not very much validity—far too little for the dependence that clinicians often place on it.

Other soundly designed studies have found no more global validity, and often less. Scores, profiles, and global judgments have failed to distinguish diagnostic classifications better than chance (2161). The Rorschach has shown nonchance but low agreement with criteria from psychiatric interviews (1321) and from biographical data (1714). Only about half of a group of judges matched Rorschach interpretations with Rorschach protocols better than chance (1863). Global judgments, then, fail to show either validity or reliability sufficient to the task of personality description or diagnosis.

The prediction of the outcome of treatment has fared even less well than the identification of diagnosis. In this area, also, some studies have seemed to find a little validity, only to fail in cross validation (1479, 1556). Two extensive

[1] SHAFFER, LAURANCE F. *The Psychology of Adjustment*, p. 303. Boston, Mass.: Houghton Mifflin Co., 1936. Pp. xxii, 600. * (PA 10:2550)

studies (*1602, 1775*) of Rorschach scores and signs did not find any that were associated with therapeutic improvement. Global judgments of Rorschachs are no more valid than scores in predicting the results of treatment (*1483, 1872*). Of all the most widely employed applications of the Rorschach, the prediction of whether a patient will improve receives the least support from well designed research.

In response to the growing evidence that conventional interpretations of the Rorschach have low validity, some workers have turned to the analysis of Rorschach content. Content, of course, can be so varied that many years would be required to evaluate the merit of all such proposals. So far, the results have not been encouraging. Hostile content (*1881*) and the "eye" response supposed to indicate paranoid suspicion (*1637*) are little related to appropriate criteria. The common practice of identifying a "father" card and a "mother" card is most dubious (*2171*). In sum, there is little hope that the interpretation of Rorschach content will be a means for valid clinical appraisal.

VALIDITY AGAINST EXPERIMENTAL CRITERIA. Clinical users of the Rorschach have generally belittled attempts to relate single Rorschach scores to specific behavioral criteria. Such studies are dismissed as "atomistic," with the observation that they do not use the Rorschach in the same way as do the practical workers in hospitals and clinics. Still, it must be recognized that Rorschach himself gave specific meanings to certain scores and other authorities have followed his example. And surprisingly enough, many studies which have assessed scores against objective behavioral criteria have found results more favorable to the Rorschach than have studies which compared global judgments to clinical criteria.

Let us take the S, or white space, response as an example. Some examinees reverse figure and ground, so that "the white spaces are interpreted rather than the black or colored parts of the figure" (*285*). Rorschach wrote that such perceptions mark "stubborn, eccentric" persons who are given to "tendency to opposition" (*285*). Bandura (*1655*) had 59 high school students each rated by five teachers on personality variables such as negativism and assertiveness. The ratings were sufficiently in agreement, with reliabilities of about .80; the split-half reliability of the S scores was .84. The hypothesis was confirmed. The S scores were correlated

.34 with the ratings of negativism, an *r* significantly different from zero at the .01 level. This brief synopsis does scant justice to Bandura's study. He also investigated the hypothesis that S scores have different meaning for introversive and extratensive subjects, but his data gave no support to such a difference. In a similar but independent study, Ingram (*1717*) frustrated 22 college students by challenging, in an interview, their competence for their chosen vocations. The subgroup high in S differed from the low-S subjects in their initiative, resistance, and hostility in response to this attack on their self-regard. The high-S subjects, again, were more "oppositional."

Somewhat more subtle in their rationale are the studies which have dealt with the meaning of the human movement response, M, perhaps Rorschach's most novel and interesting invention. Seeing human movement in the inkblots, Rorschach hypothesized, gives evidence of kinaesthetic imagery and is therefore related to "more individualized intelligence, more creative ability, more 'inner' life....and measured, stable motility" (*285*). Some features of this remarkable intuitive hunch have been confirmed by research; others have not. The studies of Singer and Spohn (*1796*) and Singer and Herman (*1795*) offer illustrations of well conceived research on the correlates of M. The subjects of Singer and Spohn were 50 male veterans diagnosed as schizophrenic. Two tests were made. In the first test patients were rated on degree of activity during a 15-minute period in a waiting room well supplied with casual distractions. Protocols of detailed observations of waiting room behavior were rated on a scale ranging from no gross motor activity to considerable restlessness, noticing and manipulating many objects. The second test was also a motor inhibition task—writing a phrase as slowly as possible. The 50 subjects had been chosen so that 25 had high M on the Rorschach and 25 had low M. The high-M patients, as predicted, had significantly lower activity ratings and higher motor inhibition scores. The correlations, while significantly different from zero, were low; M correlated $-.23$ with activity and .29 with motor inhibition. A replication by Singer and Herman found a higher correlation, .54, between M and motor inhibition, and one of $-.27$ with waiting room activity. Further confirmation came from the finding of Levine and Meltzoff (*2071*) that cognitive inhibition is related to M, and from that of Meltzoff and Litwin (*2085*) that M correlates .42 with the ability to inhibit laughter.

In addition to his hypotheses about M alone, Rorschach made others about the relation of movement responses to those determined by color. His M to Sum C ratio determined the experience type. A person is said to be introversive if M predominates, or extratensive if he shows more color-determined responses. The extratensive man has more "outward" life, is more immediately responsive to his environment. Mann (*2081*) has reported an ingenious experiment to study "responsiveness to the immediate environment." In a small room which contained a variety of furnishings and accessories, he administered Binet's old word naming test: "Write twenty-five words, any twenty-five words as they come to mind. Write no sentences." The task was repeated three times. An inquiry then disclosed the basis for the subject's choice of each word. A score of responsiveness to the immediate environment was the number of words determined by immediately present sights and sounds. The tetrachoric correlation between the score and the introversive-extratensive classification was − .43; the extratensives were more environment-oriented, the introversives sought their words in revery or fantasy. Mann's study was a neat validation of one of Rorschach's most subtle hypotheses, but how good was the validity? A tetrachoric *r* of − .43 sounds fairly substantial but, in simpler percentage figures, Mann noted that the M to Sum C ratio correctly classified the subjects 64 per cent of the time when chance would be 50 per cent. The troublesome issue here occurs again. There is validity—but not very much validity.

SOME CONCLUSIONS. The Rorschach has *some* empirical validities. Assessments based on it can exceed those made by chance, at least with respect to such variables of personality as activity level, motor inhibition, capacity for fantasy, oppositional tendency, and responsiveness to the environment. But the Rorschach is also a most imperfect instrument, not qualified to perform the tasks that many psychologists demand of it. The predictive or concurrent validity of the Rorschach is, in the areas of its best competence, perhaps of the order of .20 to .40. Its interpretation needs to be accompanied by a visual image of a correlation chart showing the relationship between two variables when *r* equals .2 to .4, and when from about 4 per cent to about 16 per cent of the variance is identified. The fault of

many clinicians is that they use the Rorschach as if its validity were 1.00. And, contrary to the opinions of many, the use of the Rorschach by global judgment shows poorer, not better, validity than the psychometric application of some of its scores.

In view of the relatively unfavorable evidence, why is the Rorschach held in such high esteem? Without attempting to be comprehensive, three reasons may be suggested. First, we have an intense need for a subtle and comprehensive instrument to assess personality. As recent research in social psychology shows, motivation and belief are highly related. When one has a strong need, evidence of little objective merit may be perceived as conclusive. Second, the Rorschach is projective for the examiner as well as for the examinee. One readily "reads into" the vague verbalizations of the Rorschach protocol all that one already knows and believes about the examinee. For each individual examiner, therefore, the Rorschach seems to confirm his other knowledge and he has an intuitive and personal sense of the validity of the instrument. Third, the Rorschach is not wholly without validity—it is sometimes "right." And evidence from the psychology of learning shows that a schedule of intermittent reinforcements may form as strong a habit, and one as resistant to extinction, as reinforcement on every occasion. To overcome these hazards, clinical psychologists need to be more aware of their own frailties as persons, and more aware of the fact that the scientific method of inquiry provides a means for guarding against such errors.

Still another reason for complacency about the Rorschach is that textbooks continue to cite older "research studies" which seem to affirm its validity. One widely used book, for example, contains a chapter on "validating and experimental studies with the Rorschach method" (*1171*). Many of the studies which it cites (*115, 272, 293, 753*) are notable for faulty experimental designs, poor controls, absence of appropriate tests of significance, and conclusions which transcend the data. It is instructive for any psychologist who is concerned with the Rorschach to reread such studies with a newly critical eye, and thereby to reexamine the bases of his earlier beliefs.

Within limits, the Rorschach can be improved to overcome some of its present shortcomings. Rorschach's most ingenious invention, the human movement response, provides one example.

It has an appealing and sound rationale, and the empirical evidence is relatively favorable. Why does M not have a higher validity than .2 to .4? One evident reason is that M is a distressingly poor variable when judged by standards of psychometrics. Its distribution has small variance and is badly skewed. In typical samples of persons, whether normal or disturbed, half of the M scores are 0 or 1. It is indeed a wonder that so faulty a variable correlates with anything. We can learn to make better measures of M. Barron's M-threshold scale (*1841*) is probably not the final answer, but it may point the way. Another feature that can be improved is the process of making judgments or inferences from Rorschach protocols. Hamlin (*1709*) and various collaborators have pointed out that scores provide units too simple for analysis, and that global judgments are so complex that confusion results. Intermediate units, such as responses to single cards, seem to yield better results. In many other respects, projective methods can be improved by invention and research.

In conclusion, it seems clear that the research of the past decade gives poor support to the uncritical use of *the* Rorschach. It is time that psychologists abandon this beguiling but dubious orthodoxy, and strike out in new directions which will retain some of the demonstrated values, but avoid the numerous pitfalls, of unstructured projective methods.

For a review by Helen Sargent, see 4:117; for reviews by Morris Krugman and J. R. Wittenboru, see 3:73; for related reviews, see B32, B34, B40–1, B60, B73, B79, B190, B247–8, B337, B369, B372, B402, 4:118–28 and 3:74–91.

[155]

Rosenzweig Picture-Frustration Study. Ages 4–13, 14 and over; 1944–49; also called *Rosenzweig P-F Study;* 1 form ('48); 2 levels; no data on reliability and validity; $5 per 25 tests; $1.25 per 25 record blanks ('48); postage extra; specimen set not available; Saul Rosenzweig; the Author, 8029 Washington St., St. Louis 14, Mo. *

a) FORM FOR CHILDREN. Ages 4–13; 1948; $1.25 per manual ('48, reprinted from *21*); [20] minutes.

b) REVISED FORM FOR ADULTS. Ages 14 and over; 1944–49; revised norms ('49); norms for ages 20–29 only; $1.25 per manual ('47, reprinted from *15*); [15] minutes.

REFERENCES

1–77. See 4:129.
78. LANGE, CARL J. *The Effect of Sleep Deprivation on the Rosenzweig Picture-Frustration Study.* Master's thesis, University of Pittsburgh (Pittsburgh, Pa.), 1948.
79. COWEN, JUDITH. *An Analysis of the Types of Responses Given by Negro Students at the College of the City of New York to Negro and White Aggressors as Revealed by a Modified Form of the Picture-Frustration Projective Technique.* Mas-

ter's thesis, College of the City of New York (New York, N.Y.), 1949.
80. LORD, L. *A Comparison of the Tendencies Revealed by the Rosenzweig Picture-Frustration Study Between a Selected Population of Simple and Paranoid Schizophrenics.* Master's thesis, Southern Illinois University (Carbondale, Ill.), 1949.
81. EILBERT, LEO, AND SCHMEIDLER, GERTRUDE R. "A Study of Certain Psychological Factors in Relation to ESP Performance." *J Parapsychol* 14:53–74 Mr '50. *
82. McDOWELL, GLORIA MAE. *A Study of the Relationship of the Rosenzweig Picture-Frustration Response to the Scholastic Achievement of Two Hundred High School Juniors and Seniors.* Master's thesis, Pennsylvania State College (State College, Pa.), 1950.
83. TOWNER, W. C. *A Comparison of the Frustration Reactions of Delinquent and Non-Delinquent Adolescent Boys as Measured by the Rosenzweig Picture-Frustration Study.* Master's thesis, University of Washington (Seattle, Wash.), 1950.
84. BORNSTEIN, HARRY. *An Analysis of Frustration Behavior in a Puzzle-Solving Situation in Relation to Scores on the Rosenzweig Picture-Frustration Study.* Master's thesis, Fordham University (New York, N.Y.), 1951.
85. CONNERS, GEORGE ALBERT. *A Method for Investigating Frustration Reactions in Social Situations Involving Negro-White Interpersonal Relations.* Master's thesis, Tulane University (New Orleans, La.), 1951.
86. FRASCADORE, EDMUND R. *A Comparison of the Reaction to Frustration in Negro and White Children as Measured by the Rosenzweig P-F Study.* Master's thesis, Fordham University (New York, N.Y.), 1951.
87. KATES, SOLIS L. "Suggestibility, Submission to Parents and Peers, and Extrapunitiveness, Intropunitiveness, and Impunitiveness in Children." *J Psychol* 31:233–41 Ap '51. * (PA 26:769)
88. MENSH, IVAN N., AND MASON, EVELYN P. "Relationship of School Atmosphere to Reactions in Frustrating Situations." *J Ed Res* 45:275–86 D '51. *
89. MOORE, JACQUELINE A. *The Use of the Rosenzweig Picture-Frustration Test in Differentiating Delinquents From Non-Delinquents.* Master's thesis, Fordham University (New York, N.Y.), 1951.
90. MORRISON, EDWARD J. *An Experimental Study of Certain Factors Affecting the Validity and Reliability of the Rosenzweig P-F Study.* Master's thesis, Tulane University (New Orleans, La.), 1951.
91. PERSONS, EDWARD THOMAS. *A Study of the Relationship Between the Rosenzweig Picture-Frustration Study and Test Duration, Sims Socio-Economic Status Score, and Religion of High School Seniors.* Master's thesis, Pennsylvania State College (State College, Pa.), 1951.
92. SAWYER, GEORGE WILLIAM, JR. *A Study of the Relation Between the Allport A-S Study and the Rosenzweig P-F Study.* Master's thesis, University of Florida (Gainesville, Fla.), 1951.
93. SCOTT, JAMES STUART. *A Comparison of the Effects of Projective and Questionnaire Instructions Upon Responses to Pictures of the Rosenzweig PF Study Type.* Master's thesis, University of British Columbia (Vancouver, B.C., Canada), 1951.
94. SIEGEL, NORMA FRANCES. *An Investigation of the Interchangeable Use of the Adult Form and the Children's Form of the Rosenzweig P-F Study on Three Levels of Development.* Master's thesis, Pennsylvania State College (State College, Pa.), 1951.
95. TRONZO, RAYMOND GASPER. *The Rosenzweig Picture-Frustration Study as a Device in the Selection of Department Store Salespersons.* Master's thesis, Pennsylvania State College (State College, Pa.), 1951.
96. URBAN, HUGH BAYARD. *An Analysis of the Behavior Level of Responses by College Students to the Rosenzweig Picture-Frustration Study.* Master's thesis, Pennsylvania State College (State College, Pa.), 1951.
97. VACCARO, JOSEPH J. *A Study of Psychological Factors That Contrast the Most and Least Efficient Psychiatric Aids in a Mental Hospital.* Doctor's thesis, Fordham University (New York, N.Y.), 1951.
98. WALKER, ROBERT G. "A Comparison of Clinical Manifestations of Hostility With Rorschach and MAPS Test Performances." *J Proj Tech* 15:444–60 D '51. *
99. WALLACE, DOROTHY. *An Application of Cronbach's "Pattern Tabulation" Method to Rosenzweig's Picture-Frustration Study.* Master's thesis, University of Pittsburgh (Pittsburgh, Pa.), 1951.
100. ANGELINO, HENRY, AND SHEDD, CHARLES L. "A Comparison of Scores on the Rosenzweig Picture-Frustration Study Between Selected and Unselected School Populations." *Proc Okla Acad Sci* 33:288–92 '52. * (PA 29:7254)
101. DEVLIN, JOHN P. *A Study of Verbalized Self-Attitudes and Reactions to Social Frustration as Methods of Predicting Success in Brief Psychotherapy.* Doctor's thesis, Pennsylvania State College (State College, Pa.), 1952.
102. FRY, FRANKLYN D. *A Normative Study of the Reactions Manifested by College Students, and by State Prison Inmates in Response to the Minnesota Multiphasic Personality Inventory, the Rosenzweig Picture Frustration Study, and the Thematic Apperception Test.* Doctor's thesis, Pennsylvania State College (State College, Pa.), 1952. (*J Psychol* 34:27–30 Jl '52. *) (PA 27:2976)

103. HYBL, A. R., AND STAGNER, ROSS. "Frustration Tolerance in Relation to Diagnosis and Therapy." *J Consult Psychol* 16:163–70 Je '52. * (*PA* 27:5220)

104. KATES, SOLIS L. "Subjects' Evaluation of Annoying Situations After Being Described as Being Well Adjusted and Poorly Adjusted." *J Consult Psychol* 16:429–34 D '52. *

105. MADISON, LE ROI, AND NORMAN, RALPH D. "A Comparison of the Performance of Stutterers and Non-Stutterers on the Rosenzweig Picture-Frustration Test." *J Clin Psychol* 8: 179–83 Ap '52. * (*PA* 27:2096)

106. MASON, ROBERT JOSEPH. *A Comparison of Responses on the Rosenzweig Picture-Frustration Study, the Bernreuter Personality Inventory, and a Self-Rating Form.* Master's thesis, University of Western Ontario (London, Ont., Canada), 1952.

107. MIRMOW, ESTHER L. *The Method of Successive Clinical Predictions in the Validation of Projective Techniques With Special Reference to the Rosenzweig Picture-Frustration Study.* Doctor's thesis, Washington University (St. Louis, Mo.), 1952.

108. MIRMOW, ESTHER LEE. Chap. 13, "The Rosenzweig Picture-Frustration Study," pp. 209–21. (*PA* 27:3558) In *Progress in Clinical Psychology, Vol. I, Sect. 1.* Edited by Daniel Brower and Lawrence E. Abt, New York: Grune & Stratton, Inc., 1952. Pp. xi, 328. *

109. PARKER, DONALD HENRY. *Relationship Between Reading Retardation and the Rosenzweig P-F Study.* Master's thesis, University of Florida (Gainesville, Fla.), 1952.

110. ROSENZWEIG, SAUL, AND ROSENZWEIG, LOUISE. "Aggression in Problem Children and Normals as Evaluated by the Rosenzweig P-F Study." *J Abn & Social Psychol* 47:683–7 Jl '52. * (*PA* 27:3562)

111. SCHWARTZ, MILTON M. "The Relationship Between Projective Test Scoring Categories and Activity Preferences." *Genetic Psychol Monogr* 46:133–81 N '52. * (*PA* 27:4269)

112. SMOCK, CHARLES, AND CRUICKSHANK, WILLIAM M. "Responses of Handicapped and Normal Children to the Rosenzweig P-F Study." *Q J Child Behavior* 4:156–64 Ap '52. *

113. STARER, GEORGE. "Personality Characteristics of Retarded Readers as Measured by the Picture-Frustration Study." Abstract. *Am Psychol* 7:376 Jl '52. *

114. STARER, EMANUEL. "Aggressive Reactions and Sources of Frustration in Anxiety Neurotics and Paranoid Schizophrenics." *J Clin Psychol* 8:307–9 Jl '52. * (*PA* 27:5979)

115. TAYLOR, MAHLON V., JR. "Internal Consistency of the Scoring Categories of the Rosenzweig Picture-Frustration Study." *J Consult Psychol* 16:149–53 Ap '52. *

116. WEINBERG, WILLIAM L. *A Study of the Relationship of the Extrapunitive Category of the Rosenzweig P-F Study to Overt Behavioral Aggression in Prisoners.* Master's thesis, University of Oregon (Eugene, Ore.), 1952.

117. ABRAMS, ELIAS N. "A Comparison of Normals and Neuropsychiatric Veterans on the Rosenzweig Picture-Frustration Study." *J Clin Psychol* 9:24–6 Ja '53. * (*PA* 27:7946)

118. BANGAS, MARY V. *Aggressive Tendencies in the Psychopathic Deviate as Measured by the Rosenzweig Picture-Frustration Study.* Master's thesis, Kent State University (Kent, Ohio), 1953.

119. BURGESS, ELVA. *Personality Factors in Over- and Under-Achievers in Engineering.* Doctor's thesis, Pennsylvania State College (State College, Pa.), 1953.

120. CANTER, FRANCIS M. "Personality Factors in Seizure States With Reference to the Rosenzweig Triadic Hypothesis." *J Consult Psychol* 17:429–35 D '53. * (*PA* 28:7844)

121. KARLIN, LAWRENCE, AND SCHWARTZ, MILTON M. "Social and General Intelligence and Performance on the Rosenzweig Picture-Frustration Study." *J Consult Psychol* 17:293–6 Ag '53. * (*PA* 28:4364)

122. KORNREICH, MELVIN. "Variations in the Consistency of the Behavioral Meaning of Personality Test Scores." *Genetic Psychol Monogr* 47:73–138 F '53. * (*PA* 27:6535)

123. MARKENSON, DAVID. *Diagnostic Effectiveness of Interpretive Tests.* Doctor's thesis, Washington University (St. Louis, Mo.), 1953. (*DA* 14:1100)

124. QUARRINGTON, BRUCE. "The Performance of Stutterers on the Rosenzweig Picture-Frustration Test." *J Clin Psychol* 9:189–92 Ap '53. * (*PA* 28:2957)

125. ROSENZWEIG, SAUL. "Rosenzweig Picture-Frustration Study," pp. 650–9. (*PA* 27:7790) In *Contributions Toward Medical Psychology: Theory and Psychodiagnostic Methods, Vol. II.* Edited by Arthur Weider. New York: Ronald Press Co., 1953. Pp. xi, 459–885. *

126. SHAPIRO, A. EUGENE. *A Comparative Evaluation of the Reactions to Frustration of Delinquent and Non-Delinquent Male Adolescents.* Doctor's thesis, New York University (New York, N.Y.), 1953. (*DA* 14:400)

127. WEISS, GEORGE. *A Study of Mothers' Responses and Mothers' Expectations of Children's Responses as Possible Factors Affecting the Actual Responses of Children on the Rosenzweig Picture Frustration Test.* Master's thesis, Kent State University (Kent, Ohio), 1953.

128. WINFIELD, DON L., AND SPARER, P. J. "Preliminary Report of the Rosenzweig P-F Study in Attempted Suicides." *J Clin Psychol* 9:379–81 O '53. * (*PA* 28:4602)

129. BROWN, ROBERT L., AND LACEY, OLIVER L. "The Diagnostic Value of the Rosenzweig P-F Study." *J Clin Psychol* 10:72–5 Ja '54. * (*PA* 28:7511)

130. CATTELL, RAYMOND B., AND SHOTWELL, ANNA M. "Personality Profiles of More Successful and Less Successful Psychiatric Technicians." *Am J Mental Def* 58:496–9 Ja '54. * (*PA* 28:6861)

131. GOODRICH, DAVID C. "Aggression in the Projective Tests and Group Behavior of Authoritarian and Equalitarian Subjects." Abstract. *Am Psychol* 9:380 Ag '54. *

132. HUSMAN, BURRIS FREDERICK. *An Analysis of Aggression in Boxers, Wrestlers, and Cross Country Runners as Measured by the Rosenzweig P-F Study, Selected TAT Pictures, and a Sentence Completion Test.* Doctor's thesis, University of Maryland (College Park, Md.), 1954. (*DA* 15:759)

133. LINDZEY, GARDNER, AND GOLDWYN, ROBERT M. "Validity of the Rosenzweig Picture-Frustration Study." *J Personality* 22:519–47 Je '54. * (*PA* 29:2452)

134. MEEK, CLINTON R. *The Effect of Knowledge of Aptitude Upon Interest Scores.* Doctor's thesis, George Peabody College for Teachers (Nashville, Tenn.), 1954.

135. PORTNOY, BERNARD, AND STACEY, CHALMERS L. "A Comparative Study of Negro and White Subnormals on the Children's Form of the Rosenzweig P-F Test." *Am J Mental Def* 59:272–8 O '54. * (*PA* 29:5895)

136. QUAY, HERBERT, AND SWEETLAND, ANDERS. "The Relationship of the Rosenzweig PF Study to the MMPI." *J Clin Psychol* 10:296–7 Jl '54. * (*PA* 29:2464)

137. SANDRA, M. ELAINE. *A Comparative Study of the Scores Obtained by Institutional Adolescent Girls on the Bell Adjustment Inventory and the P-F Test.* Master's thesis, Fordham University (New York, N.Y.), 1954.

138. SCHWARTZ, MILTON M., AND KARLIN, LAWRENCE. "A New Technique for Studying the Meaning of Performance on the Rosenzweig Picture-Frustration Study." *J Consult Psychol* 18:131–4 Ap '54. * (*PA* 29:2474)

139. SINAIKO, H. WALLACE. "Validity Information Exchange, No. 7-071: D.O.T. Code 0-75.10, Manager, Floor." *Personnel Psychol* 7:407–8 au '54. *

140. SOMMER, ROBERT. "On the Brown Adaptation of the Rosenzweig P-F for Assessing Social Attitudes." *J Abn & Social Psychol* 49:125–8 Ja '54. * (*PA* 28:7382)

141. SPACHE, GEORGE D. "Personality Characteristics of Retarded Readers as Measured by the Picture-Frustration Study." *Ed & Psychol Meas* 14:186–92 sp '54. * (*PA* 28:8001)

142. VANE, JULIA R. "Implications of the Performance of Delinquent Girls on the Rosenzweig Picture-Frustration Study." Abstract. *J Consult Psychol* 18:414 D '54. *

143. WENDLAND, LEONARD V. "A Preliminary Study of Frustration Reactions of the Post-Poliomyelitic." *J Clin Psychol* 10:236–40 Jl '54. * (*PA* 29:2911)

144. WRIGHT, STUART. "Some Personality Characteristics of Academic Underachievers." Abstract. *Am Psychol* 9:496 Ag '54. *

145. ANGELINO, HENRY, AND SHEDD, CHARLES L. "Reactions to Frustration Among Normal and Superior Children." *Except Child* 21:215–8+ Mr '55. * (*PA* 29:8452)

146. HUSMAN, BURRIS F. "Aggression in Boxers and Wrestlers as Measured by Projective Techniques." *Res Q* 26:421–5 D '55. *

147. JENKIN, NOEL. "Some Relationships Between Projective Test Behavior and Perception." *J Clin Psychol* 11:278–81 Jl '55. * (*PA* 30:2888)

148. JOHANNSEN, DOROTHEA E., AND BENNETT, EDWARD M. "The Personality of Diabetic Children." *J Genetic Psychol* 87: 175–85 D '55. * (*PA* 31:1514)

149. KORKES, LENORE, AND LEWIS, NOLAN D. C. "An Analysis of the Relationship Between Psychological Patterns and Outcome in Pulmonary Tuberculosis." *J Nerv & Mental Dis* 122:524–63 D '55. *

150. LEVITT, EUGENE E., AND LYLE, WILLIAM H., JR. "Evidence for the Validity of the Children's Form of the Picture-Frustration Study." *J Consult Psychol* 19:381–6 O '55. * (*PA* 30:5991)

151. LYON, WILLIAM, AND VINACKE, W. EDGAR. "Picture-Frustration Study Responses of Institutionalized and Non-Institutionalized Boys in Hawaii." *J Social Psychol* 41:71–83 F '55.* (*PA* 30:1039)

152. MEHLMAN, BENJAMIN, AND WHITEMAN, STEPHEN LEE. "The Relationship Between Certain Pictures of the Rosenzweig Picture-Frustration Study and Corresponding Behavioral Situations." *J Clin Psychol* 11:15–9 Ja '55. * (*PA* 29:7303)

153. MINSKI, LOUIS, AND DESAI, MAHESH M. "Aspects of Personality in Peptic Ulcer Patients: A Comparison With Hysterics." *Brit J Med Psychol* 28:113–34 Je '55. * (*PA* 30:3268)

154. PARSONS, EDWARD T. "Relationships Between the Rosenzweig P-F Study and Test Duration, Socioeconomic Status, and Religion." Abstract. *J Consult Psychol* 19:28 F '55. *

155. SMITH, LOUIS MILDE. *A Validity Study of Six Personality and Adjustment Tests for Children.* Doctor's thesis, University of Minnesota (Minneapolis, Minn.), 1955. (*DA* 16:791)

156. SUTCLIFFE, J. P. "An Appraisal of the Rosenzweig Picture-Frustration Study." *Austral J Psychol* 7:97–107 D '55. * (*PA* 31:1070)

157. ZUCKERMAN, MARVIN. "The Effect of Frustration on the Perception of Neutral and Aggressive Words." *J Personality* 23:407–22 Je '55. *

158. ANGELINO, HENRY, AND SHEDD, CHARLES L. "A Study of the Reactions to 'Frustration' of a Group of Mentally Retarded Children as Measured by the Rosenzweig Picture-Frustration Study." *Psychol Newsl* 8:49–54 N–D '56. * (*PA* 31:3290)

159. BORNSTON, FRIEDA L., AND COLEMAN, JAMES C. "The Relationship Between Certain Parents' Attitudes Toward Child

Rearing and the Direction of Aggression of Their Young Adult Offspring." *J Clin Psychol* 12:41–4 Ja '56. * (*PA* 30:5183)

160. BRESEE, CLYDE WESLEY. *Affective Factors Associated With Academic Underachievement in High-School Students.* Doctor's thesis, Cornell University (Ithaca, N.Y.), 1956. (*DA* 17:90)

161. BURGESS, ELVA. "Personality Factors of Over- and Under-Achievers in Engineering." *J Ed Psychol* 47:89–99 F '56. * (*PA* 31:8811)

162. GREY, OREVA. *An Analysis of the Frustration Pattern of a Defective-Hearing Group as Revealed by Rosenzweig's Picture-Frustration Study.* Master's thesis, Fordham University (New York, N.Y.), 1956.

163. KAMENETZKY, JOSEPH; BURGESS, GEORGE G.; AND ROWAN, THOMAS. "The Relative Effectiveness of Four Attitude Assessment Techniques in Predicting a Criterion." *Ed & Psychol Meas* 16:187–94 su '56. * (*PA* 31:5101)

164. LEWINSOHN, PETER M. "Personality Correlates of Duodenal Ulcer and Other Psychosomatic Reactions." *J Clin Psychol* 12:296–8 Jl '56. * (*PA* 31:6484)

165. McCARY, J. L. "Picture-Frustration Study Normative Data for Some Cultural and Racial Groups." *J Clin Psychol* 12:194–5 Ap '56. * (*PA* 31:4702)

166. McGUIRE, FREDERICK L. "Rosenzweig Picture Frustration Study for Selecting Safe Drivers." *US Armed Forces Med J* 7:200–7 F '56. * (*PA* 31:1054)

167. MUELLER, ALFRED D., AND LEFKOVITS, AARON M. "Personality Structure and Dynamics of Patients With Rheumatoid Arthritis." *J Clin Psychol* 12:143–7 Ap '56. * (*PA* 31:5010)

168. MURPHY, MARY MARTHA. "Social Class Differences in Frustration Patterns of Alcoholics." *Q J Studies Alcohol* 17:255:62 Je '56. * (*PA* 31:6329)

169. ROSENZWEIG, SAUL. "Projective Methods and Psychometric Criteria: A Note of Reply to J. P. Sutcliffe." *Austral J Psychol* 8:152–5 D '56. *

170. SIEGMAN, ARON W. "A 'Culture and Personality' Study Based on a Comparison of Rorschach Performance." *J Social Psychol* 44:173–8 N '56. *

171. COX, F. N. "The Rosenzweig Picture-Frustration Study (Child Form)." *Austral J Psychol* 9:141–8 D '57. *

172. GRAINE, GEORGE N. "Measures of Conformity as Found in the Rosenzweig P-F Study and the Edwards Personal Preference Schedule." Abstract. *J Consult Psychol* 21:300 Ag '57. *

173. HEDBERG, RAYMOND. "The Rosenzweig Picture-Frustration Study in Relation to Life Insurance Salesmen." Abstract. *Am Psychol* 12:408 Jl '57. *

174. KAHN, HARRIS. "Responses of Hard of Hearing and Normal Hearing Children to Frustration." *Excep Child* 24:155–9 D '57. *

175. McCARY, J. L., AND TRACKTIR, JACK. "Relationship Between Intelligence and Frustration-Aggression Patterns as Shown by Two Racial Groups." *J Clin Psychol* 13:202–4 Ap '57. * (*PA* 32:2799)

176. PALMER, JAMES O. "Some Relationships Between Rorschach's Experience Balance and Rosenzweig's Frustration-Aggression Patterns." *J Proj Tech* 21:137–41 Je '57. *

177. SCHWARTZ, MILTON M. "Galvanic Skin Responses Accompanying the Picture-Frustration Study." *J Clin Psychol* 13:382–7 O '57. *

178. SCHWARTZ, MILTON M. "The Importance of the Pictorial Aspect in Determining Performance on the Picture-Frustration Study." *J Clin Psychol* 13:399–402 O '57. *

179. SILVERSTEIN, A. B. "Faking on the Rosenzweig Picture-Frustration Study." *J Appl Psychol* 41:192–4 Je '57. *

180. SPACHE, GEORGE. "Personality Patterns of Retarded Readers." *J Ed Res* 50:461–9 F '57. *

181. SUTCLIFFE, J. P. "A Rejoinder to Rosenzweig on 'Projective Methods and Psychometric Criteria.'" *Austral J Psychol* 9:91–2 Je '57. *

182. WALLON, EDWARD J., AND WEBB, WILSE B. "The Effect of Varying Degrees of Projection on Test Scores." *J Consult Psychol* 21:465–72 D '57. *

183. BENNETT, CARSON M., AND JORDAN, THOMAS E. "Security-Insecurity and the Direction of Aggressive Responses to Frustration." *J Clin Psychol* 14:166–7 Ap '58. *

184. FOSTER, ARTHUR LEE. "The Relationship Between EEG Abnormality, Some Psychological Factors and Delinquent Behavior." *J Proj Tech* 22:276–80 S '58. *

185. FRIEDMAN, BERT. *A Study of the Szondi Assumptions of Identification Utilizing Modified Versions of the Rosenzweig P-F Study on Criminal Groups.* Master's thesis, Fordham University (New York, N.Y.), 1958.

186. SMITH, LOUIS M. "The Concurrent Validity of Six Personality and Adjustment Tests for Children." *Psychol Monogr* 72(4):1–30 '58. *

RICHARD H. DANA, *Assistant Professor of Psychology, University of Nevada, Reno, Nevada.*

FORM FOR ADULTS. Psychological testing is one expression of our culturally conceived empiricism. The *Rosenzweig Picture-Frustration Study* exemplifies those few projective instruments with rational origins. This test thus constitutes an attempted statement of Rosenzweig's frustration theory in operational terms. Elaboration of the theory by means of scoring dimensions is available in a previous review (4:129). Assessment of the adequacy of this statement of theory is the focus for this review.

The P-F test consists of 24 semi-structured, cartoon-like, two or more person stimulus situations with two caption boxes, one containing descriptive or frustrating words, the other blank for the subject's response. Test stimuli were selected to represent ego-blocking (16 items) and superego blocking (8 items). Exact selection procedures and item analyses are not reported in 20 articles dealing with description and theory. Items 2, 3, and 14 are frequently misunderstood by subjects. It is unknown whether item ambiguity is a function of uncontrolled item selection procedures. Unless the correlates of misperception are determined, the item selection procedures remain suspect.

Eight studies have examined reliability. Internal consistency coefficients have been uniformly low. To beg this question by contending the desirability of item heterogeneity is no substitute for an experimental approach to item selection. Subjects do not obtain scores which are particularly consistent over time. While it may be unrealistic to demand test-retest figures of a given magnitude, it is mandatory that such figures be available for varying periods of time and on subjects comparable to norm groups.

Administration and instructions have been systematically varied in unpublished studies to the confirmation of current practice. The scoring system may be applied with moderate agreement between independent scorers. The reported figure of 70 per cent initial agreement which augments to 85 per cent with practice compares favorably with 75 per cent for the Rorschach. That nearly one half of the discrepancies between scorers occur on only seven stimulus items (with Item 8 contributing one fourth of total scorer disagreement) again argues the need for item analysis.

Norms are reported in 26 studies for a variety of special groups. The order of normative studies has been unfortunate here. Representative, national norms predicated on adequate standardization should antedate local norms for clearly defined populations. That these national norms can now be obtained should encourage test authors to restandardize their instruments following the examples afforded by the *Tomkins-Horn Picture Arrangement Test* and the *Wechsler Adult Intelligence Scale*. Relevant variables such as intelligence, social class, and occupation are not controlled in current norms. Separate norms have been compiled for African, Finnish, French, German, Italian, and Japanese translations (35 studies).

One score, the group conformity rating, or capacity for conformity with conventional behavior under stress, has been fixated by six studies as a particular *bête noir*. The GCR has been cited as unreliable, but nonetheless the same components are consistently identified in separate studies. Relationships are found with *Edwards Personal Preference Schedule* autonomy and *Minnesota Multiphasic Personality Inventory* dominance and achievement. This accentuates the problems of validity. Of 25 extant validity studies in English, 19 were classified as to type of validity and the studies tallied as supportive, nonsupportive, or equivocal. The results of this exercise indicate that seven predictive and congruent studies are consistently supportive; eight concurrent studies are nonsupportive or equivocal; and, of four content studies, two experimental studies are supportive and two correlation studies are nonsupportive. This leaves open the salient issue of what level of behavior is being measured, but does suggest that "validity for what?" is an appropriate question. In addition, the practice of using the P-F alone for individual prediction would not be justified on the basis of current validation.

The P-F has been a potent generator of research with 25 published studies and as many more dissertations. In approximately 25 years the P-F has demonstrated that responses to frustrating situations are measurable and have meaning consistent with other pilgrimages into the unconscious, both rational and empirical. The major shortcomings of the P-F pertain to reliability. Reliability is a function of test construction procedures employed. Systematic sampling of potential test stimuli does not really violate assumptions for projective techniques. While it is patently too late for such test construction nostrums, restandardization with a national, representative sample would seem imperative. Only with a solid nomothetic basis can idiographic techniques be maximally useful in clinical and research situations. The publication of a revised manual including all relevant reliability and validity data as well as scoring procedures is advisable. The P-F test lacks the breadth and sensitivity of the TAT or Rorschach. However, for the stated limited measurement purposes it is perhaps as close to a model instrument as any projective technique currently in use.

FORM FOR CHILDREN. The children's P-F has stimulated approximately 30 studies in 20 years. It was designed to parallel the adult P-F (16 similar items) with 14 ego-blocking stimulus situations and 8 superego blocking situations. Apparently there was an earlier form with more than 24 items, which the manual indicates was shortened because "it proved to add relatively little." As in the manual for the adult level, the test user must infer the criteria for item selection. The test is presented in the guise of a "game," with either examiner or subject filling in blanks for each pictured situation.

Scoring follows the format for the adult P-F, with 11 scores derived from combinations of direction of aggression (extra-, intro-, impunitive) and reaction type (obstacle-dominance, ego-defense, need-persistive). Use is made of the group conformity rating and 15 possible trend scores which indicate change during the course of the test.

Norms are presented for 256 children, aged 4–13, in two-year levels. Children aged 4–7 were tested individually in a private school; children aged 8–13 were tested in groups in public schools. No controls for intelligence, social class, father's occupation, and the like, were employed. The test user can never know the comparability of his own subjects to the standardization group on variables other than age, sex, and kind of school situation. Limited normative data have been reported for such groups as 7- to 9-year old diabetics (*148*), 10- to 14-year old institutionalized Hawaiian boys (*151*), and retarded readers (*141, 180*). Translations have been made into French, German, Italian, and Japanese.

Test reliability and scorer reliability figures are not reported and the unwarranted assumption is made that the figures for the children's form will resemble those for the adult form. Evidence for validity has been inferred from progressive age changes in P-F responses. Extrapunitive responses decrease with age; GCR, indirect expressions of hostility, and superego patterns increase with age (*110*). Trends are usable as a gross index of instability and low frustration tolerance (57). Direction of aggression scores are related to differential submission to parents and peers (87). Need-persistence is positively associated with peer ratings for persistence, i.e., best "sticker";[1] extrapunitiveness has some congruent validity with a problems situations test (150). The single study with less uniformly favorable results (133) has been criticized for design and statistics (150). Although these indications for validity are meager, their consistency should stimulate further study.

When the children's P-F is considered for clinical or research use, the tentative status of test and scorer reliability, norms, and validation must be recognized. The manual, although a distinct improvement over the manual for the adult level, should be revised to include much more of the available data. The major potential contribution of the P-F is to our knowledge of child behavior. Longitudinal studies of the P-F developmental process of specified groups of children are needed. These data could become a concrete substitute for inferences from present group norms. The most outrageous example of such inferences stems from the lumping together of private and public school children of different ages and making a continuous interpretation of changes in scoring variables as a function of age.

Rosenzweig has often stated his concern with that critical research area which attempts to determine the projective level of given responses. The problem of ambiguous level is cited to account for the results of controversial validity studies. It is known that different degrees of control can be exercised over the content of projections, especially as stimulus dimensions conform closely to everyday experience. This does not necessarily imply that such control is a function of age as the manual suggests. While assumptions concerning projective level as a function of age may legitimately be made, it should be explicitly stated that these are indeed assumptions and not facts.

Comparisons of the children's P-F with such tests as *Blacky Pictures, Children's Apperception Test,* and *Michigan Picture Test* are difficult because of extreme differences in stimulus structure. The P-F test is highly structured, limited in purpose, with a relatively objective scoring system. This makes for efficiency in measurement of subjective reactions to frustra-

tion with a necessary loss of sensitivity in other areas. It is unquestionably one of the most useful projective techniques in use with children today.

BERT R. SAPPENFIELD, *Professor of Psychology, Montana State University, Missoula, Montana.*

The P-F Study differs from many other projective tests in that its stimulus material was chosen and its scoring rationale formulated in terms of guiding hypotheses. One of these is the familiar hypothesis concerning the relation between frustration and aggression; another is Rosenzweig's hypothesis concerning the possibility of categorizing all reactions to frustration in terms of "type of reaction" and "direction of aggression."

The manual for each form describes the scoring system in sufficient detail and provides scoring samples based on responses of approximately 500 subjects to each of the 24 situations that serve as items.

There are few indications in the manuals to imply that the authors were concerned about problems of reliability or validity. The main exceptions to this statement include one mention (in the manual for the children's form) of retest reliability findings for the Adult form, and a brief discussion (also in the children's manual) relative to the "projective level from which the responses made by the subject issue." There is no mention in either manual of internal consistency, of the degree of interscorer agreement, or of the findings from validation studies.

Norms for the various categories, as reported for the children's form, are based on responses of 256 school children, aged 4 to 13. Even if this should be regarded as an adequate sample on which to base norms (provided that representativeness were also demonstrated), it is questionable whether the resulting samples are sufficiently large when the total group is subdivided into two-year age groupings. Norms for the adult form are based on responses of 236 males and 224 females, aged 20 to 29. No additional data are given concerning the composition of the adult sample.

Sixteen situations in the adult form and 14 in the children's form are intended to involve "ego-blocking," while 8 situations in each form are intended to involve "superego-blocking." The authors state that not all subjects perceive the situations as they are intended to be per-

1 MACARTHUR, R. S. "An Experimental Investigation of Persistence in Secondary School Boys." *Can J Psychol* 9:42–54 '55. (*PA* 30:1562)

ceived, so that an inquiry is often desirable in order to determine the appropriate basis for scoring. Better tests might have resulted if the authors had designed separate forms for ego-blocking and for superego-blocking situations, and if they had performed item analyses to insure high internal consistency among stimulus values for items retained in each of the forms.

A group conformity ratio can be computed for responses to the P-F Study; this ratio can reasonably be interpreted to indicate the degree to which a subject's reactions resemble those of the standardization group. No frequency data are provided, however, for deriving an opposite kind of interpretation (namely, the occurrence of relatively rare or idiosyncratic responses) except in the case of responses that occurred with zero frequency.

The zero-frequency information alluded to in the preceding paragraph reveals that only two cartoons (Items 4 and 6) of the adult form and only one cartoon (Item 9) of the children's form actually yielded responses scorable in all of the nine theoretically possible categories. The mean number of scoring categories not used for each of the remaining cartoons amounted to 3.0 (range 1–6) on the adult form and 3.4 (range 1–5) on the children's form. The fact that the pattern of nonused categories also varies from cartoon to cartoon on each of the forms is consistent with the findings of Taylor (*115*), which indicated low inter-item consistency.

Aside from the fact of inadequate inter-item consistency, the zero-frequency information points to another deficiency in the items. High ambiguity (maximum interindividual variation in response yield) is a desideratum for all projective tests; nearly all of the items fail to meet this ambiguity criterion, since they do not elicit all of the theoretically possible types of responses. Other projective tests may, of course, also be deficient in this regard; for example, the achromatic Rorschach blots do not yield FC, CF, or C responses.

In summary, the P-F Study can, in principle, be regarded as a highly promising projective technique, since its general design and scoring rationale are based on sound psychodynamic hypotheses. However, it appears that the test could be improved in important respects if more attention were given to the problem of item selection and to the development of internally consistent forms which assess single variables. Until such basic revisions have been made, the P-F Study will have limited usefulness either as a test or as a research instrument.

For reviews by Robert C. Challman and Percival M. Symonds, see 4:129.

[156]

The Rotter Incomplete Sentences Blank. Grades 9–12, 13–16, adults; 1950; 3 levels, 1 form; manual and standardization data based on college level only; $1.25 per 25 tests; $1.90 per manual; postpaid; specimen set not available; (20–40) minutes; Julian B. Rotter and Janet E. Rafferty (manual); Psychological Corporation. *

REFERENCES

1–6. See 4:130.
7. BERG, WILBERT ARTHUR. *Determining Validity of the Incomplete Sentences Blank Through Appraisal of Qualitative Interpretations.* Doctor's thesis, University of Missouri (Columbia, Mo.), 1952. (*DA* 12:504)
8. SMITH, WALTER E. *A Comparison of the Responses of Stutterers and Non-Stutterers in a College Population on the Rotter Incomplete Sentences Blank.* Master's thesis, Bowling Green State University (Bowling Green, Ohio), 1952.
9. WALTER, VERNE A. *A Comparison of the Adjustment Scores Obtained by College Freshmen Women on Two Forms of an Incomplete Sentences Blank.* Master's thesis, Bowling Green State University (Bowling Green, Ohio), 1952.
10. CLARKE, S. C. T. "The Effect of Teachers' Adjustment on Teachers' Attitudes." *Can J Psychol* 7:49–59 Je '53. * (*PA* 28:4958)
11. ROTTER, JULIAN B., AND RAFFERTY, JANET E. "Rotter Incomplete Sentences Blank," pp. 590–8. (*PA* 27:7792) In *Contributions Toward Medical Psychology: Theory and Psychodiagnostic Methods, Vol. II.* Edited by Arthur Weider. New York: Ronald Press Co., 1953. Pp. xi, 459–885. *
12. BASS, BERNARD M.; KARSTENDIEK, BARBARA; McCULLOUGH, GERALD; AND PRUITT, RAY C. "Validity Information Exchange, No. 7-024: D.O.T. Code 2-66.01, 2-66.11, 2-66.12, 2-66.23, Policemen and Detectives, Public Service." *Personnel Psychol* 7:159–60 sp '54. *
13. ROTTER, JULIAN B.; RAFFERTY, JANET E.; AND LOTSOF, ANTOINETTE B. "The Validity of the Rotter Incomplete Sentences Blank: High School Form." *J Consult Psychol* 18:105–11 Ap '54. * (*PA* 29:2470)
14. SECHREST, LEE B., AND HEMPHILL, JOHN K. "Motivational Variables in the Assuming of Combat Obligation." *J Consult Psychol* 18:113–8 Ap '54. * (*PA* 29:3144)
15. BIERI, JAMES; BLACHARSKY, EDWARD; AND REID, J. WILLIAM. "Predictive Behavior and Personal Adjustment." *J Consult Psychol* 19:351–6 O '55. * (*PA* 30:5974)
16. CHURCHILL, RUTH, AND CRANDALL, VAUGHN J. "The Reliability and Validity of the Rotter Incomplete Sentences Test." *J Consult Psychol* 19:345–50 O '55. * (*PA* 30:5980)
17. CLARKE, S. C. T., AND McGREGOR, J. R. "Teachers' Adjustment and Teachers' Achievement in University Courses." *Can J Psychol* 9:55–8 Mr '55. * (*PA* 30:1641)
18. TINDALL, RALPH H. "Relationships Among Indices of Adjustment Status." *Ed & Psychol Meas* 15:152–62 su '55. * (*PA* 30:2330)
19. BERGER, IRVING L., AND SUTKER, ALVIN R. "The Relationship of Emotional Adjustment and Intellectual Capacity to Academic Achievement of College Students." *Mental Hyg* 40:65–77 Ja '56. * (*PA* 31:3770)
20. LIT, JACK. *Formal and Content Factors of Projective Tests in Relation to Academic Achievement.* Doctor's thesis, Temple University (Philadelphia, Pa.), 1956. (*DA* 16:1505)
21. ARNOLD, FRANK C., AND WALTER, VERNE A. "The Relationship Between a Self- and Other-Reference Sentence Completion Test." *J Counsel Psychol* 4:65–70 sp '57. * (*PA* 32:484)
22. DEAN, SIDNEY I. "Adjustment Testing and Personality Factors of the Blind." *J Consult Psychol* 21:171–7 Ap '57. *
23. SOHLER, DOROTHY TERRY; HOLZBERG, JULES D.; FLECK, STEPHEN; CORNELISON, ALICE R.; KAY, ELEANOR; AND LIDZ, THEODORE. "The Prediction of Family Interaction From a Battery of Projective Techniques." *J Proj Tech* 21:199–208 Je '57. *
24. FITZGERALD, BERNARD J. "Some Relationships Among Projective Test, Interview, and Sociometric Measures of Dependent Behavior." *J Abn & Social Psychol* 56:199–203 Mr '58. *

For reviews by Charles N. Cofer and William Schofield, see 4:130.

[157]

★Self Valuation Test. Ages 7–15, adults; 1957; verbal and non-verbal projective test employing several stimuli simultaneously; title on test is S.V.T.; individual; 1 form ['57]; 2 levels: children, adults (separate forms for men and women); manual ['57]; 84s. per set of test materials, 100 comparison sheets, and 50 record booklets, postpaid; 20s. per 100 record booklets; 8s. 4d. per 100 comparison sheets; postage extra; specimen set not available; (5–25) minutes; John Liggett; J. & P. Bealls Ltd. *

REFERENCES

1. LIGGETT, JOHN. "A Non-Verbal Approach to the Phenomenal Self." *J Psychol* 43:225–37 Ap '57. *
2. LIGGETT, J. "The Simultaneous Use of Several Unstructured Stimuli in the Study of Attitudes." Abstract. *B Brit Psychol Soc* (35):20 My '58. *

[158]

*Sentence Completions Test. Ages 12 and over; 1940–57; revision of *Payne Sentence Completion Blank* ('29); 1 form ('53); record booklet ('47); manual ('57, see 4 below); reliability and validity data for 1940 form only; $15 per set of 25 tests, 25 record booklets, and manual; $4 per 25 tests; $4 per 25 record booklets; $7.75 per manual; postpaid; (30–60) minutes; Amanda R. Rohde; distributed by Western Psychological Services. *

REFERENCES

1–3. See 4:131.
4. ROHDE, AMANDA R. *Sentence Completion Method: Its Diagnostic and Clinical Application to Mental Disorders.* New York: Ronald Press Co., 1957. Pp. xii, 301. *

For reviews by Charles N. Cofer and Charles R. Strother of an earlier edition, see 4:131; for related reviews, see B358.

[159]

★Structured-Objective Rorschach Test: Preliminary Edition. Adults; 1958; also called *S-O Rorschach Test;* 15 scores (for deriving 26 traits); wholeblot (W), major details (D), minor details (Dd), white space (S), form resemblance (F), poor form resemblance (F−), human movement (M), animal movement (FM), color and form resemblance (FC), color and poor form resemblance (CF), shading (Fch), animal figure (A), human figure (H), modal responses (P), rare responses (O); IBM; 1 form; 2 editions; separate answer sheets must be used; $1.50 per set of hand scoring stencils; postage extra; scoring service available; Joics B. Stone; California Test Bureau. *
a) ILLUSTRATED EDITION. $7.50 per test; 20(30) minutes.
b) NON-ILLUSTRATED EDITION. To be used with slides or cards; $5 per 10 tests; 10¢ per IBM answer sheet; $12 per set of ink-blot cards; $11 per set of kodaslides; $1 per specimen set, postpaid; 20(30) minutes.

[160]

★Symbol Elaboration Test. Ages 6 and over; 1950–53; title on test is S.E.T.; 1 form ('53); manual ('50, see 1 below); $12 per set of 50 tests and manual; $10 per 50 tests; $2 per manual; postage extra; administration time not reported; Johanna Krout; C. H. Stoelting Co. *

REFERENCE

1. KROUT, JOHANNA. "Symbol Elaboration Test (S.E.T.): The Reliability and Validity of a New Projective Technique." *Psychol Monogr* 64(4):1–67 '50. * (PA 25:3167)

RICHARD H. DANA, *Assistant Professor of Psychology, University of Nevada, Reno, Nevada.*

Eight years have elapsed since the publication of the SET. Users of projective techniques have not responded with enthusiasm to these 11 stimulus patterns to be elaborated by drawing. This unpopularity may be due to three unstated assumptions: (*a*) symbols for basic life experiences have universal meanings, (*b*) eleven universal symbols are represented by the *particular* stimulus patterns employed, and (*c*) a drawing response to each stimulus pattern is associated with the subject's attitude toward the symbolic meaning of the stimulus.

While one may assume that symbols have fixed meanings, it is an empirical problem whether or not particular stimulus patterns actually have the meaning ascribed to them. No such experimental scrutiny of possible stimulus patterns was attempted. Similarly, relatively small differences in stimulus line placements are given important meanings, e.g., maleness versus male society, or intimate heterosexuality versus competitive heterosexuality. Item analysis would have suggested what magnitude of difference in line placements is empirically relevant. Suitable criteria could have been found in consensus of clinical judgment on other projective data.

The validation material is a curious compound of misplaced conviction and statistical miscellany. The standardization sample contained 169 subjects from five groups identified vaguely as to age, sex, and source of group. These groups included "volunteers," "normal" adults from other studies, psychiatric patients, Indian children, etc. The groups are neither comparable, representative, nor adequately described.

Blind clinical interpretations were made of each drawing. Validation data consisting of other projective and clinical material had been independently gathered in connection with other studies. Case conferences were held (whether the SET analyst contributed to these conferences is not stated) and the results compared with the blind SET interpretations. A 7-category rating scale ("complete corroboration" to "no evidence") was used. Thus, there were two sets of abstractions, each one fairly distant from the raw data. The high agreement obtained may be a function of method. This further suggests that if the pool of possible validation statements is very large and sufficiently generalized, the possibility of any single judge making unverifiable interpretations is minimized.

Two individual cases are presented as additional samples of validity. However, this process is one of "validation by suggestion." The interpretation for each drawing is made; then the subject is asked, in effect, whether or not the interpretation is correct. Social desirability, attempts to please the examiner, and generality of statements contaminate the process and substantial agreement is obtained.

Scorer reliability was approached in several ways. (*a*) One scorer was used and questions devised from interpretations of 15 cases. These questions were given to an independent scorer who searched the validation data for "answers." Agreement was 84 per cent. This is presented as evidence for reliable *selection* from response data. It appears merely that reliability and validity procedures are analogous, i.e., "reliability by suggestion," since data the independent scorer is to look for are at least partially indicated. (*b*) Reliability of the *ratings* themselves was investigated by giving paired statements (test interpretation and corresponding validation statement) to an independent scorer and asking for a judgment in one of the seven categories. Agreement was 94 per cent. (*c*) Reliability of the *criterion* was approached by having scorers rerate representative cases after two months. Agreement was from 82 to 98 per cent. (*d*) One fundamental reliability problem with projective data is agreement between two independent scorers in their specific interpretations, or reliability of the *method* of analysis. Two independent and trained scorers interpreted 10 records with 96 per cent agreement. This remarkably high figure evokes necessity for identification of scorer characteristics, complete specification of the scoring procedure, and an extension of the sample of scorers. No other projective technique has substantiated a comparable reliability claim for interpretive statements.

When the SET is evaluated as an example of test construction and clear communication of procedural detail, the results are disappointing. The most salient criticisms are: (*a*) Dogma was evidenced in uncritical acceptance of potentially testable hypotheses as assumptions. (*b*) Test stimuli were selected by fiat as opposed to experimentation. (*c*) The validation sample was gathered by "opportunity sampling" with no consideration for generality of results.

(*d*) The validation procedure itself is suspect and follows the axiom that agreement between test data and criterion is a function of the level of abstraction employed, (*e*) Scorer reliability procedures attempt at completeness, but results may be artificially inflated by structured scorer tasks and by inadequate identification of scorers.

However, the SET does represent increased concern with *stimulus properties* of a projective technique. The assumption of a specific symbolic meaning for each stimulus figure provides the possibility for reopening this important theoretical issue. The SET is usable only as an exploratory instrument at the same level of hypothesis testing within the single case as the DAP, the H-T-P, or the Franck test. The validation data should be disregarded. The potential usefulness for controlled research on symbols and their specific representation that may be afforded by the SET must not be overlooked.

[161]

Symonds Picture-Story Test. Grades 7–12; 1948; individual; 1 form; 2 parts (Sets A and B); Set B may be administered alone or Sets A and B together; no data on reliability; $5.25 per set of test materials, cash orders postpaid; (60–70) minutes per set; Percival M. Symonds; Bureau of Publication, Teachers College, Columbia University. *

REFERENCES

1–2. See 4:132.
3. GORLOW, LEON; ZIMET, CARL N.; AND FINE, HAROLD J. "The Validity of Anxiety and Hostility Rorschach Content Scores Among Adolescents." *J Consult Psychol* 16:73–5 F '52. * (*PA* 27:1961)
4. SYMONDS, PERCIVAL M., AND JENSEN, ARTHUR R. "Psychoanalytic Concepts and Principles Discernible in Projective Personality Tests: Workshop, 1956: 6, The Predictive Significance of Fantasy." *Am J Orthopsychiatry* 28:73–84 Ja '58. *

WALTER KASS, *Associate Professor of Psychology, Albert Einstein College of Medicine, Yeshiva University, New York, New York.*

The *Symonds Picture-Story Test* is a set of 20 pictures designed for administration to adolescents as a projective technique like the *Thematic Apperception Test.* Subjects are asked to make up a story for each of the pictures; the thematic content is then interpreted for personality implications. In devising the pictures and presenting quantitative and qualitative methods of analyzing story material, Symonds makes a diligent effort to forge a projective technique into a standard test. However, the mixed marriage of a psychometric approach with a polymorphous projective medium unhappily does not hold up well. The result is two parallel methods of analysis, each with its rules of rigor, which sometime supplement one another but which combine only in the author's respect for the merits of both.

In the quantitative treatment of the data, Symonds and his assistants identified and tabulated all the overtly expressed themes they could find (without regard to latent meanings or motives) in 1,680 stories told by 20 school boys and 20 school girls, 12 to 18 years of age, to 42 stimulus pictures. From a total of 10,797 themes, 1,850 occurring three or more times were culled for statistical treatment. Twenty of the 42 trial pictures were then selected for publication in the final test version.

Inventoried themes are classified as "psychological" ("eroticism," "altruism," "success," "craziness," "fatigue"); "environmental" ("punishment," "gossip," "food," "work," "appearance"); and "stylistic" ("style," "ending"). Here, for the sake of categorization, some rather arbitrary assumptions were made: "What you do to another person is psychological; what another person does to you is environmental," depending on the "character in the story taken as the point of reference." Ambivalence in the activity-passivity continuum, dynamic concepts of drive, aim, and object, and multiple aspects of the identification process are bypassed in this schema where aggression is classed as psychological and punishment as environmental, according to the rule that "what a person does is more important, in general, than what is done to him."

Frequency norms are given in terms of medians and upper and lower quartiles "for interpretation of the significance....of fantasy material." "Normal" is defined as the interquartile range. "Themes occurring with a greater frequency than the upper quartile should have special significance"; "those occurring less frequently than the lower quartile should play an exceptionally insignificant role." This, of course, tells something about popularity of thematic categories, but nothing about motivating forces at play in their production. Such quantification negates the clinical observation that it is the rare theme or rare variation of a frequent theme that often provides the clue to unique aspects of personality (e.g., as in pathognomonic responses). But this is covered in the assumption that "the only themes that are significantly found in picture-story fantasy material" are the tabulated 30 main themes and their subcategories. Absence is significant only in the case of six main themes (Family, Aggression, Economics, Punishment, Separation, Eroticism) and four subsidiary themes (Mother, Father, Death, Money)—but no others. Only themes other than those listed, in *any* frequency, are considered both rare and signficant.

The author contests the belief that thematic analysis alone can "directly enable one to interpret trends in the overt personality and behavior" as a "gratuitous assumption" that "has not passed the usual tests of validity." Comparative studies of fantasy material and personality descriptions are required. Theme counts, behavior ratings by teachers, estimates of adjustment by the author and his associates, and Sheviakov-Friedberg questionnaire self-ratings by the students were intercorrelated. The usefulness of the kind of theme counting conducted in this study is thrown into question by the author's conclusion that able clinicians often differ on meanings of designated themes, and that themes with apparently different meanings may correlate more highly than ones with the same name or similar meaning.

From a clinical viewpoint, another major weakness of Symonds' theme counting emphasis is that it not only confines significance to thematic prominence or paucity, but it also relegates interpretation to correlation with "overt personality and behavior." The projective hypothesis in clinical use is hampered by preclusion of inferences about existing personality trends imperceptible to observation. The concern shown for verifiability is certainly commendable, but it fails to recognize possibilities of verification through what is now known about thought processes in dream-work, various lapses, and ideational symptom formation. The function of fantasy in the continuum of conscious and subconscious productions is not discussed. The PST in its quantitative application is a limited tally-type or "Geiger counter" kind of instrument for detection of thematic concentrations.

The qualitative applications are actually far more extensive than the normative part of the study indicates, for Symonds also emphasizes that the essence of a projective technique is lost in a psychometric scoring approach, its value being in the "dynamically integrated picture of the inidividual" that the interpreter is able to build from the stories. He also notes that interpreter "subjectivity may consist more of incompleteness rather than inaccuracy." A chapter in *Adolescent Fantasy* (2) on "Comparison of Fantasy and Character" deals with dimensions of personality, including psychoanalytic concepts useful in interpretation (e.g., super-ego, oedipus complex, castration, masochism). A basic principle of interpretation put forth is that conflicts worked out in reality or in symptoms are usually manifested "in behavior and character, but not in fantasy"; another is that the personality may take on a character exactly opposite to the trend expressed in fantasy. Conflict kept from expression in performance will find its way into fantasy. But distinctions of the form of conflict, its origin, level of manifestation in character, symptoms, or behavior, are not differentiated for the test user. However, "principal correspondences" are noted "between the character of the stories and the character of the individuals telling them." A few contrasts are also drawn between "normal, happy," and "less well-adjusted" students.

The test pictures parallel the TAT scenes but contain more youthful figures. It is held that identifications cross age and sex lines, and the same pictures are to be given to both sexes. The possibility of homosexual identification is provided in several pictures with ambivalent attributes (A2, A4, B3) and one shadowy figure without distinctive features (B9).

Those seeking to learn about the nature of adolescence and the fantasy characteristics of this important stage of maturation will be disappointed in the slim chapter (8 pages) on "Characteristics of Adolescent Fantasy." Those who interpret fantasy material according to dynamic concepts of drives, their modifications in expression, and the ebb and flow of conscious and subconscious processes, as well as those needing norms of expressive behavior, will welcome this study as a major contribution to the field of thematic testing.

KENNETH R. NEWTON, *Associate Professor of Psychology, University of Tennessee, Knoxville, Tennessee.*

This test consists of a set of 20 drawings designed to elicit stories from adolescents that will be reflections of their fantasy life. The author has stated quite thoroughly in his manual the procedure to be followed in administering the test. The instructions, which are rather involved and time consuming, do not seem to have any advantage over a more simplified set of instructions.

All pictures involved in this technique were designed and drawn by the same artist. The author does little to defend this procedure other than to state that the stories given might to some extent be influenced by the fantasy life of the artist; he believes, however, that this is not a very important factor. In addition, the author states that he presented the artist with a list of 42 specifications for the various pictures. Then he admits that it is not possible to define how these specifications were developed. Thus, it seems the initial error of having all pictures designed by one artist is further compounded by having the list of specifications for each picture derived by one individual. Another rather consistent error in this technique is the admission that on the whole the pictures are gloomy, severe, morose, and mournful and that there is a certain similarity of expression in all faces utilized. It would seem that these consistent and influential errors would lead to considerable similarity in stories and much transfer from one picture to another.

In the author's initial attempts to standardize this technique, 42 stories were collected from each of 40 normal adolescent boys and girls of junior and senior high school ages. These 1,680 stories were analyzed for their thematic content and an attempt was made to determine norms for various types of themes and interpretations. The statement is made that these stories most successfully revealed the personality when they were interpreted dynamically. This statement is supported with the remark that the stories and their themes are those which would be expected from the findings obtained through dynamic psychology and psychoanalytic theory. This seems somewhat circuitous since any material presented by patients or subjects, when interpreted dynamically, would most likely be in keeping with the findings expected from dynamic psychology.

This is a very long-drawn projective technique which, again admittedly, is operating at its peak of efficiency only after some 20 stories have been presented by the subject. This picture-storytelling technique is apparently an extension of history taking. With this particular test and other similar ones the statement has been made that the more that is known about the individual the greater is the significance of the stories that the individual gives. Thus it seems a thorough history from the patient may very well serve in the place of such a technique. If the individual is verbal enough to give 20 or more stories in response to the pictures, it is likely that he has the verbal facility to give a thorough history which may be of greater value and which may negate the requirement of administering this test. The *Symonds Picture-Story Test* has been designed as an extension of the *Thematic Apperception Test*. It does not, however, appear to be any more adequate a tool than the TAT, except, possibly, for psychologists working exclusively with adolescents.

The manual of directions is quite thorough; however, one should not attempt to administer or interpret from this test without first referring to the author's book *Adolescent Fantasy* (2). While there has been an attempt made to set up norms for the various findings, the clinical psychologist's experience continues to be the major validation for such a technique.

For a review by E. J. G. Bradford, see 4:132 (1 excerpt); for related reviews, see 4:133.

[162]

*Szondi Test. Ages 4 and over; 1937–52; 8 factors, 4 vectors (each vector is a total of 2 factors): homosexual, sadistic, sexual vector; epileptic, hysteric, paroxysmal vector, catatonic, paranoic, schizophrenic vector; depressive, manic, contact vector; individual or group; IBM; 1 form ('47); $5.50 per Deri manual ('49, see 11 below); $13.50 per Szondi manual ('52, see 87 below); $11 per set of 48 pictures ('47); separate answer sheets may be used; $1.80 per 50 IBM answer sheets ('51, labeled Form D); $3 per 100 profile sheets ('49, labeled Form B); $3 per 50 folders of profile sheet and table of tendency tension ('49, labeled Form A); postage extra; test must be administered "at least six, preferably ten, times with at least one day intervals between administrations"; (10–15) minutes per administration; Lipot Szondi; Hans Huber. * (U.S. distributor: Grune & Stratton, Inc.)

REFERENCES

1-64. See 4:134.
65. GEERS, JOHN BYRON. *Szondi Test Patterns in a Criminal Population.* Master's thesis, Southern Methodist University (Dallas, Tex.), 1950.
66. KELTNER, DONALD. *Comparison of Two Criminal Groups on the Szondi Test.* Master's thesis, Southern Methodist University (Dallas, Tex.), 1950.
67. SAUNDERS, ROGER. *The Effect of an Experimentally Established Frame of Reference on the Consistency of Responses on the Szondi Test.* Master's thesis, Southern Methodist University (Dallas, Tex.), 1950.
68. BALL, MAY TOWNSON. *The Relationship of Szondi Profiles of 100 Drug Addicts and the Psychoanalytic Theory of Drug Addiction.* Master's thesis, Southern Methodist University (Dallas, Tex.), 1951.
69. NEWELL, JOHN MICHAEL. *Reliability Study of the Stimulus Material of the Szondi Test.* Master's thesis, Southern Methodist University (Dallas, Tex.), 1951.
70. PATTERSON, HARRY OSCAR. *A Study of Matching Behavioral Descriptions With Szondi Pictures.* Master's thesis, University of Nebraska (Lincoln, Neb.), 1951.
71. BARRACLOUGH, PATRICIA; COLE, DAVID; AND REEB, MILDRED. "The Influence of Test Instructions on Szondi Results." *J Clin Psychol* 8:165-7 Ap '52. * (PA 27:1948)
72. CHANEY, JOHN W., JR. *A Validity Study of the Szondi Test: Comparison of Normal and Alcoholic Subjects in Their Preferences of Eight Szondi Portraits as Presented in Triads.* Master's thesis, Catholic University of America (Washington, D.C.), 1952.
73. DAVID, HENRY P., AND RABINOWITZ, WILLIAM. "Szondi Patterns in Epileptic and Homosexual Males." *J Consult Psychol* 16:247-50 Ag '52. * (PA 27:4285)
74. DAVIS, N. ELAINE, AND RAIMY, VICTOR C. "Stimulus Functions of the Szondi Cards." *J Clin Psychol* 8:155-60 Ap '52. * (PA 27:1954)
75. DERI, SUSAN K. Chap. 14, "The Szondi Test," pp. 222-33. (PA 27:3549) In *Progress in Clinical Psychology, Vol. I,* Sect. 1. Edited by Daniel Brower and Lawrence E. Abt. New York: Grune & Stratton, Inc., 1952. Pp. xi, 328. *
76. DUDEK, FRANK J. "Determining 'Chance Success' When a Specific Number of Items Are Sorted Into Discrete Categories." *J Consult Psychol* 16:251-6 Ag '52. * (PA 27:3880)
77. DUDEK, FRANK J., AND PATTERSON, HARRY O. "Relationships Among the Szondi Test Items." *J Consult Psychol* 16:389-94 O '52. * (PA 27:5866)
78. GOLDMAN, GEORGE D. "The Validation of the Paroxysmal Vector of the Szondi Test." *J Abn & Social Psychol* 47:475-7 Ap '52. * (PA 27:2723)
79. GUERTIN, WILSON H., AND RABIN, ALBERT I. "The Szondi Test as a Forced-Choice Technique." *J Clin Psychol* 8:161-4 Ap '52. * (PA 27:1962)
80. HARROWER, MOLLY. *Appraising Personality: The Use of Psychological Tests in the Practice of Medicine,* pp. 115-38. New York: W. W. Norton & Co., Inc., 1952. Pp. xvii, 197. * (PA 27:6532)
81. JACKSON, VICTOR A. *Factors in Preferences for Szondi Test Pictures.* Doctor's thesis, University of Chicago (Chicago, Ill.), 1952. (Abstract: *Am Psychol* 7:347)
82. KOBLER, ARTHUR L. *An Experimental Examination of the Szondi Test as a Clinical Tool.* Doctor's thesis, University of Kansas (Lawrence, Kan.), 1952.
83. MUSSEN, PAUL H., AND KRAUSS, SHIRLEY R. "An Investigation of the Diagnostic Validity of the Szondi Test." *J Abn & Social Psychol* 47:399-405 Ap '52. * (PA 27:2750)
84. RABIN, ALBERT I. "Genetic Factors in the Selection and Rejection of Szondi's Pictures: A Study of Twins." *Am J Orthopsychiatry* 22:551-6 Jl '52. * (PA 27:5159)
85. RICHARDSON, HELEN M. "The Discriminability of the 'Drive Factors' Represented in the Szondi Pictures." *J Clin Psychol* 8:384-90 O '52. * (PA 27:5896)
86. SCHERER, I. W.; WINNE, J. F.; PAGE, H. A.; AND LIPTON, H. "An Analysis of Patient-Examiner Interaction With the Szondi Pictures." *J Proj Tech* 16:225-37 Je '52. * (PA 28:2673)
87. SZONDI, L. *Experimental Diagnostics of Drives.* New York: Grune & Stratton, Inc., 1952. Pp. x, 254. * (PA 27:5910)
88. WARNER, F. L. *A Szondi of Some Schizophrenic Patients Before and After Shock.* Master's thesis, Pacific University (Forest Grove, Ore.), 1952.
89. BEST, HAROLD L., AND SZOLLOSI, ETIENNE. "Recognition as a Criterion in the Szondi Test." *J Clin Psychol* 9:75-6 Ja '53. * (PA 27:7755)
90. BORSTELMANN, L. J., AND KLOPFER, W. G. "The Szondi Test: A Review and Critical Evaluation." *Psychol B* 50:112-32 Mr '53. * (PA 28:931)
91. DAVID, HENRY P.; ORNE, MARTIN; AND RABINOWITZ, WILLIAM. "Qualitative and Quantitative Szondi Diagnosis." *J Proj Tech* 17:75-8 Mr '53. * (PA 28:2623)
92. FLEISHMAN, MARTIN. *An Experimental Investigation of the Validity of the Szondi Test.* Doctor's thesis, University of California (Los Angeles, Calif.), 1953.
93. GORDON, LEONARD V. "A Factor Analysis of the 48 Szondi Pictures." *J Psychol* 36:387-92 O '53. * (PA 28:4356)
94. RAY, J. B., AND HILL, VIRGIL T. "Szondi and Matching Probabilities." *Szondi Newsl* 4:16-22 O '53. *
95. SAUNDERS, WILLIAM WINSTON. "A Methodology for the Testing of Two Assumptions Basic to Szondi Test Theory." *Szondi Newsl* 4:22-4 O '53. *
96. SIMPSON, WILLIAM H., AND HILL, VIRGIL T. "The Effects of Verbal Reward and Punishment Upon Picture Selection on the Szondi Test." *Szondi Newsl* 4:2-15 O '53. *
97. STEINBERG, ARTHUR. "Szondi's Pictures: Discrimination of Diagnoses as a Function of Psychiatric Experience and of Internal Consistency." *J Proj Tech* 17:340-8 S '53. * (PA 28:4397)
98. CASTON, WILLIAM FRANK. *The Szondi Test and Criminality.* Doctor's thesis, Vanderbilt University (Nashville, Tenn.), 1954. (DA 14:1096)
99. COHEN, JACOB, AND FEIGENBAUM, LOUIS. "The Assumption of Additivity on the Szondi Test." *J Proj Tech* 18:11-6 Mr '54. * (PA 29:913)
100. DAVID, HENRY P. "A Szondi Test Bibliography, 1939-1953." *J Proj Tech* 18:17-32 Mr '54. * (PA 29:914)
101. DERI, SUSAN K. "Introduction to This Issue." *J Proj Tech* 18:3-4 Mr '54. *
102. DERI, SUSAN K. "Differential Diagnosis of Delinquents With the Szondi Test." *J Proj Tech* 18:33-41 Mr '54. * (PA 29:1197)
103. FLEISHMAN, MARTIN. "The Discriminative Power of Szondi's Quotient of Tendency Tension." *J Proj Tech* 18:42-6 Mr '54. * (PA 29:916)
104. FLEISHMAN, MARTIN. "The Discriminative Power of Szondi's Syndromes." *J Consult Psychol* 18:89-95 Ap '54. * (PA 29:2443)
105. GORDON, LEONARD V., AND LAMBERT, EDWARD J. "The Internal Consistency of the Szondi 'Factors.'" *J Social Psychol* 40:67-71 Ag '54. * (PA 29:5705)
106. HILL, VIRGIL T. *The Szondi Test With Children: A Critical Evaluation of Theory and Practice.* Doctor's thesis, University of Oklahoma (Norman, Okla.), 1954.
107. KRIMSKY, MARTIN L. "The Szondi Test in a Psychological Battery: Two Case Studies." *J Proj Tech* 18:47-59 Mr '54. * (PA 29:932)

108. LEFFORD, ARTHUR. *An Experimental Study of the Szondi Test Stimuli.* Doctor's thesis, New York University (New York, N.Y.), 1954. (*DA* 15:1111)

109. MOSER, ULRICH. "The Determination of the Relative Strength of Masculine-Feminine Drives by Means of the Szondi Procedure." *J Proj Tech* 18:75–88 Mr '54. * (*PA* 29:938)

110. SAUNDERS, WILLIAM W. *A Methodology for the Testing of Two Assumptions Basic to Szondi Test Theory.* Doctor's thesis, University of Oklahoma (Norman, Okla.), 1954.

111. SCHUBERT, JOSEF. "The Stimulus Value of the Szondi Pictures: A Theoretical and Empirical Study." *J Proj Tech* 18: 95–106 Mr '54. * (*PA* 29:953)

112. SHORT, PHILIP L. "Experiments on the Rationale of the Szondi Test." *J Mental Sci* 100:384–92 Ap '54. * (*PA* 29:2477)

113. VAN KREVELEN, ALICE. "Some Effects of Subject-Examiner Interaction on Projective Test Performance." *J Proj Tech* 18:107–9 Mr '54. * (*PA* 29:963)

114. CORTNER, ROBERT H. *The Relationship of Diagnostic Criteria of the Rorschach and Szondi Tests and Psychiatric Diagnosis in a Military Population.* Master's thesis, St. Louis University (St. Louis, Mo.), 1955.

115. KLEIN, ABRAHAM. "A Preliminary Comparative Study of Some Szondi and Rorschach Test Variables." Abstract. *J Personality* 23:499 Je '55. *

116. KORKES, LENORE, AND LEWIS, NOLAN D. C. "An Analysis of the Relationship Between Psychological Patterns and Outcome in Pulmonary Tuberculosis." *J Nerv & Mental Dis* 122:524–63 D '55. *

117. PEARL, DAVID, AND JACOBS, DURAND. "Sociometric Choice and the Szondi Test." *J Clin Psychol* 11:385–8 O '55. * (*PA* 30:5996)

118. SAUNDERS, ROGER E., AND NORTH, ALVIN J. "The Effect of an Experimentally Established Frame of Reference on the Consistency of Responses on the Szondi Test." Abstract. *J Personality* 23:500 Je '55. *

119. SCOTT, EDWARD M. "An Investigation of Juvenile Profiles on the Szondi Test." *J Clin Psychol* 11:46–50 Ja '55. * (*PA* 29:7317)

120. FANCHER, EDWIN C. "A Comparative Study of Adolescents With the Szondi Test." *J Genetic Psychol* 88:89–93 Mr '56. * (*PA* 31:4685)

121. FANCHER, EDWIN C., AND WEINSTEIN, MORRIS. "A Szondi Study of Developmental and Cultural Factors in Personality: The Seven-Year-Old." *J Genetic Psychol* 88:81–8 Mr '56. * (*PA* 31:4686)

122. GRANT, RICHARD A. "Institutional Adjustment of Prison Inmates and the Szondi Paroxysmal Vector." *Szondi Newsl* 5: 8–11 Ap '56. * (*PA* 31:1393)

123. KRIMSKY, MARTIN. "The Application of the 'Shadow Method' in Szondi Test Interpretation." *Szondi Newsl* 5:3–7 F '56. * (*PA* 31:1047)

124. KRIMSKY, MARTIN. "A Szondi Profile Followed by an Epileptic Seizure." *Szondi Newsl* 5:12 Ap '56. * (*PA* 31:1569)

125. LASZLO, CARL. "On the Modification of the Szondi Test (L-Test)." *Szondi Newsl* 5:2–7 Ap '56. * (*PA* 31:1049)

126. MAHONEY, STANLEY C. "Szondi Bibliography: 1954–1955." *Szondi Newsl* 5:13–5 Ap '56. * (*PA* 31:1055)

127. RAINWATER, LEE. "A Study of Personality Differences Between Middle and Lower Class Adolescents: The Szondi Test in Culture-Personality Research." *Genetic Psychol Monogr* 54: 3–86 Ag '56. *

128. AUMACK, LEWIS. "The Szondi: Internal or External Validation?" *Percept & Motor Skills* 7:7–15 Mr '57. * (*PA* 32:4162)

129. HURLEY, JOHN R. "Psychodiagnostic Limitations of Szondi Interseries Changes." *J Clin Psychol* 13:396–9 O '57. *

130. LASSOFF, SAUL. *The Ability of the Szondi Test to Differentiate Between Law Students and Theology Students.* Doctor's thesis, University of Denver (Denver, Colo.), 1957.

131. LINGOES, JAMES C. "Minnesota Multiphasic Personality Inventory Test Correlates of Szondi Picture Preferences." *Szondi Newsl* 6:1–6 S '57. *

132. MAHONEY, STANLEY, AND KRIMSKY, MARTIN. "Validity, Interpretation, and the Szondi Test." *Szondi Newsl* 6:7–12 S '57. *

133. MORRIS, JOHN R., JR. "A Szondi Study of an Atypical Child." *Szondi Newsl* 6:6–8 D '57. *

134. PASEWARK, RICHARD ARTHUR. *The Use of Finger Paintings in Differentiating Epileptics and Paranoid Schizophrenics: An Evaluation of the Identification Hypotheses Underlying the Szondi Test.* Doctor's thesis, New York University (New York, N.Y.), 1957. (*DA* 17:1814)

135. RAY, THOMAS S., AND OLDROYD, CARL R. "Skin Resistance Changes and Individual Personality Factors as Reflected in the Szondi Test: A Pilot Study." *Szondi Newsl* 6:1–5 D '57. *

136. SILVERSTEIN, A. B. "'Diagnosing' Szondi's Pictures." *J Proj Tech* 21:396–8 D '57. *

137. FRIEDMAN, BERT. *A Study of the Szondi Assumptions of Identification Utilizing Modified Versions of the Rosenzweig P-F Study on Criminal Groups.* Master's thesis, Fordham University (New York, N.Y.), 1958.

138. HARROWER, MOLLY. "The First Offender: A Study of Juvenile Delinquents by the Szondi Test." *Szondi Newsl* 6:1–16 Je '58. *

For reviews by Ardie Lubin and Albert I. Rabin, see 4:134; for a review by Susan K. Deri, see 3:100; for related reviews, see B418 and 4:135.

[163]

★**A Test of Family Attitudes.** Ages 6–12; 1952; pictorial projection; individual; no data on reliability; no norms; 12s. 6d. per manual, postage extra; (30–60) minutes; Lydia Jackson; Methuen & Co. Ltd. *

REFERENCES

1. JACKSON, LYDIA. "Emotional Attitudes Towards the Family of Normal, Neurotic and Delinquent Children." *Brit J Psychol* 41:35–51 S '50. * (*PA* 25:3740)
2. JACKSON, LYDIA. "Emotional Attitudes Towards the Family of Normal, Neurotic and Delinquent Children, Part II." *Brit J Psychol* 41:173–85 D '50. * (*PA* 25:7975)

JOHN E. BELL, *Acting Chief, Mental Health Services, United States Public Health Service, San Francisco, California.*

The *Test of Family Attitudes* is a picture-story test based on a set of seven specially designed pictures portraying situations between children and adults. The drawings represent relations likely to arouse emotion in the child. They convey impressions of maternal protection and child dependence, the child's exclusion from intimacy between the parents, adaptation to a sibling in the presence of the parents (two forms of this picture are available, one for each sex), isolation as punishment, the possibility of aggression from a father figure, the attraction of forbidden fruit, and a clash between the parents in the child's presence. The pictures are published in a convenient, small manual (5 by 7 inches), along with a description of the test, a report of an initial evaluation of its use with normal (n = 40), neurotic (n = 40), and delinquent (n = 30) boys and girls, simple instructions, and a set of standard questions to ask about each picture.

The test appears to offer little advantage over other picture-story methods, such as the TAT, CAT, and pictures used by Mallet, LeShan and LeShan, and others. Whether an examiner would find the pictures of this test more suitable than others for exploring children's experiences with their parents and consequent attitudes towards them would be a matter of taste or experience. It is evident from the pictures that the parent-child dimension of the family is more adequately represented than the sibling bond. The pictures tend to depict the parents together rather than singly.

Through a method such as this test uses, one is exploring the characteristics of an individual's memories, fantasies, feelings, and concepts about families, including his own. Action and communication vectors that actually exist in his family may be reflected, but the test offers no opportunity for verifying the authenticity of these forms of behavior. Thus, interpretations of the family life must be cautiously advanced and tested against reality through observation of other members of the family, especially as they interact. Because the test carries a title that might imply that it is a potential source of information about families, it might be well to recognize that it is essentially a test of a child's attitudes toward his parents and sibs. It does not tap attitudes of all members of a family, and thus does not yield data on habits of mind in all the various interrelationships, e.g., between parents, between parents and children. More precisely, it might be called a test of attitudes toward family rather than a test of family attitudes.

[164]

Thematic Apperception Test. Ages 4 and over; 1936–43; commonly known as TAT; individual; 1 form ('43); no data on reliability; $6 per set of test materials; 50¢ per manual ('43); cash orders postpaid; 100(120) minutes in 2 sessions 1 day apart; Henry A. Murray; Harvard University Press. * (*TAT Summary Record Blank*. 1952; $1.55 per set of 35 record blanks and manual, postage extra; 20¢ per specimen set, postpaid; Pauline G. Vorhaus; World Book Co. *)

REFERENCES

1–101. See 3:103.
102–299. See 4:136.
300. SAXE, CARL HERMAN. *A Comparison of Personality Description Obtained From the Thematic Apperception Test and From Therapeutic Contacts.* Doctor of education report, Teachers College, Columbia University (New York, N.Y.), 1947.
301. GARDNER, BURLEIGH B. "What Makes Successful and Unsuccessful Executives?" *Adv Mgmt* 13:116–25 S '48. * (PA 23:967)
302. McCLELLAND, DAVID C., AND ATKINSON, JOHN W. "The Projective Expression of Needs: I, The Effect of Different Intensities of the Hunger Drive on Perception." *J Psychol* 25:205–22 Ja '48. *
303. MITCHELL, DOROTHY PAULA. *The Validity of the Thematic Apperception Test and Its Implications for Group Therapy.* Master's thesis, University of Oklahoma (Norman, Okla.), 1949.
304. BRICE, BARBARA C. *A Pilot Study of the Relationship of Selected Voice Quality Deviations and Anxiety Level as Determined by the Thematic Apperception Test.* Master's thesis, Florida State University (Tallahassee, Fla.), 1950.
305. PITTLUCK, P. *The Relation Between Aggressive Fantasy and Overt Behavior.* Doctor's thesis, Yale University (New Haven, Conn.), 1950.
306. BIALICK, IRVING. *The Relationship Between Reactions to Authority Figures on the T.A.T. and Overt Behavior in an Authority Situation by Hospital Patients.* Doctor's thesis, University of Pittsburgh (Pittsburgh, Pa.), 1951.
307. BRADT, KENNETH HAROLD. *Effect of Personal Interview Upon College Grade Performance.* Doctor's thesis, Northwestern University (Evanston, Ill.), 1951.
308. CARLILE, J. ST H. *A Comparison of a Thematic Apperception Test as Applied to Neurotic and Non-Neurotic Children.* Master's thesis, University of London (London, England), 1951.
309. CHRISTENSEN, ARDEN HANS. *A Quantitative Study of Personality Dynamics in Stuttering and Nonstuttering Siblings.* Doctor's thesis, University of Southern California (Los Angeles, Calif.), 1951.
310. FIELD, WILLIAM FRANKLIN. *The Effects on Thematic Apperception of Certain Experimentally Aroused Needs.* Doctor's thesis, University of Maryland (College Park, Md.), 1951.
311. LUCE, GEORGE C. *A Study of Emotional Tone in the Thematic Apperception Test Stories of Paranoid Schizophrenics and Anxiety State Neurotics.* Master's thesis, University of Western Ontario (London, Ont., Canada), 1951.
312. MORGAN, HENRY HOLLINSHEAD. *An Analysis of Certain Structured and Unstructured Test Results of Achieving and Nonachieving High Ability College Students.* Doctor's thesis, University of Minnesota (Minneapolis, Minn.), 1951. (DA 12:335)
313. MURNEY, RICHARD G. *The Relationship Between Certain Thematic Apperception Test and Rorschach Test Scores.* Master's thesis, Catholic University of America (Washington, D.C.), 1951.
314. OSTERBERG, MARY N. *A Comparison of Aggression in Dreams and TAT Stories.* Master's thesis, Western Reserve University (Cleveland, Ohio), 1951.
315. ROE, ANNE. "A Psychological Study of Eminent Biologists." *Psychol Monogr* 65(14):1–68 '51. * (PA 27:1516)
316. SHNEIDMAN, EDWIN S.; JOEL, WALTHER; AND LITTLE, KENNETH B. "An Empirical Categorization of Psychological Test Report Items." Abstract. *Am Psychol* 6:492 S '51. *
317. SRIVASTAVA, SITAWAR SARAN. "Curative Use of T.A.T. Pictures in a Case of Mental Disorder." *Samiksa* 5:189–95 no 3 '51. * (PA 27:1187)
318. THURSTON, JOHN R., AND MUSSEN, PAUL H. "Infant Feeding Gratification and Adult Personality." *J Personality* 19:449–58 Je '51. * (PA 26:3335)
319. BEIGEL, HUGO G. "The Influence of Body Position on Mental Processes." *J Clin Psychol* 8:193–99 Ap '52. * (PA 27:1768)
320. BELLAK, LEOPOLD, AND ORT, EILEEN. Chap. 9, "Thematic Apperception Test and Other Apperceptive Methods," pp. 149–72. (PA 27:3542) In *Progress in Clinical Psychology, Vol. I, Sect. 1.* Edited by Daniel Brower and Lawrence E. Abt. New York: Grune & Stratton, Inc., 1952. Pp. xi, 328. *
321. BLUM, GERALD S., AND MILLER, DANIEL R. "Exploring the Psychoanalytic Theory of the 'Oral Character.'" *J Personality* 20:287–304 Mr '52. * (PA 27:2353)
322. CARLILE, JUNE ST H. "The Thematic Apperception Test Applied to Neurotic and Normal Adolescent Girls." *Brit J Med Psychol* 25:244–8 pt 4 '52. * (PA 27:7947)
323. CARLSEN, NORAH. *The Relationship Between Empathy and Adjustment as Shown in the Thematic Apperception Test.* Master's thesis, University of Toronto (Toronto, Ont., Canada), 1952.
324. CATTELL, R. B., AND WENIG, P. W. "Dynamic and Cognitive Factors Controlling Misperception." *J Abn & Social Psychol* 47:797–809 O '52. * (PA 27:5000)
325. CAUDILL, WILLIAM. "Japanese-American Personality and Acculturation." *Genetic Psychol Monogr* 45:61–102 F '52. * (PA 27:3466)
326. CLARK, RUSSELL A. "The Projective Measurement of Experimentally Induced Levels of Sexual Motivation." *J Exp Psychol* 44:391–9 D '52. *
327. COOK, RICHARD A. "Identification and Ego Defensiveness in Thematic Apperception." Abstract. *J Colo-Wyo Acad Sci* 4:83 O '52. *
328. DAVENPORT, BEVERLY FEST. *The Ambiguity, Universality, and Reliable-Discrimination of TAT Interpretations.* Doctor's thesis, University of Southern California (Los Angeles, Calif.), 1952.
329. DAVENPORT, BEVERLY FEST. "The Semantic Validity of TAT Interpretations." *J Consult Psychol* 16:171–5 Je '52. * (PA 27:5146)
330. FRY, FRANKLYN D. *A Normative Study of the Reactions Manifested by College Students, and by State Prison Inmates in Response to the Minnesota Multiphasic Personality Inventory, the Rosenzweig Picture Frustration Study, and the Thematic Apperception Test.* Doctor's thesis, Pennsylvania State College (State College, Pa.), 1952. (J Psychol 34:27–30 Jl '52. *) (PA 27:2976)
331. GARFIELD, SOL L.; BLEK, L.; AND MELKER, F. "The Influence of Method of Administration and Sex Differences on Selected Aspects of TAT Stories." *J Consult Psychol* 16:140–4 Ap '52. * (PA 27:2718)
332. GILHOOLY, FRANCIS M. *The Validity and Reliability of the Rorschach and the Thematic Apperception Tests When These Tests Are Interpreted by the Method of Blind Analysis.* Doctor's thesis, Fordham University (New York, N.Y.), 1952.
333. GOODMAN, MORRIS. "An Indirect Validation of a Thematic Apperception Test Scoring Manual." *J Clin Psychol* 8:149–54 Ap '52. * (PA 27:1960)
334. GORDON, HIRAM L. *A Comparative Study of Dream Analysis and the Thematic Apperception Test as Projective Techniques.* Doctor's thesis, Duke University (Durham, N. C.), 1952.
335. HASSOL, LEONARD; CAMERON, NORMAN; AND MAGARET, ANN. "The Production of Scattered Speech via Personalized Distraction: An Investigation of Continuity in Normal and Schizophrenic Language." Abstract. *Am Psychol* 7:351–2 Jl '52. *
336. HERMAN, GLORIA N. *A Comparison of the Thematic Apperception Test Stories of Pre-Adolescent School Children Differing in Social Acceptance.* Master's thesis, University of Toronto (Toronto, Ont., Canada), 1952.
337. HOLT, ROBERT R. "Interpretation of Jay's Thematic Apperception Test: The Case of Jay: Interpretations and Discussion." *J Proj Tech* 16:457–61, discussion 444–5, 462–73 D '52. * (PA 28:2678)
338. HOLT, ROBERT R. "TAT Bibliography: Supplement for 1951." *J Proj Tech* 16:114–23 Mr '52. * (PA 27:428)
339. HOLT, ROBERT R., AND LUBORSKY, LESTER. "Research in the Selection of Psychiatrists: A Second Interim Report." *B Menninger Clinic* 16:125–35 Jl '52. * (PA 27:3916)

340. HOWARD, KENNETH GILBERT. *Certain Variables in the Thematic Apperception Test.* Master's thesis, University of Western Ontario (London, Ont., Canada), 1952.

341. IVERSON, NORMAN E. *A Descriptive Study of Some Personality Relationships Underlying a Range of Speaker Confidence, as Determined by the Thematic Apperception Test.* Doctor's thesis, University of Denver (Denver, Colo.), 1952.

342. KAPLAN, HAROLD; HAUCK, HERBERT; AND KLEINMAN, MILTON L. "An Unusual Response to the Thematic Apperception Test." *Am J Psychiatry* 108:918–20 Je '52. * (*PA* 27: 1969)

343. KEELY, H. W., AND GLAD, DONALD D. "The Schizophrenic Thematic Apperception Test Responses and Behavior in Acutely Psychotic and Social Remission Stages." Abstract. *J Colo-Wyo Acad Sci* 4:82 O '52. *

344. KIEFER, R. *TAT Normative Data From Common Stories Told by Normal Adult Females.* Master's thesis, University of Alberta (Edmonton, Alta., Canada), 1952.

345. KLEHR, HAROLD. "An Investigation of Some Personality Factors in Women With Rheumatoid Arthritis." Abstract. *Am Psychol* 7:344–5 Jl '52. *

346. LEVINSON, DANIEL J. "Criminality From a Sense of Guilt: A Case Study and Some Research Hypotheses." *J Personality* 20:402–29 Je '52. * (*PA* 27:3679)

347. LINDZEY, GARDNER. "Thematic Apperception Test: Interpretive Assumptions and Related Empirical Evidence." *Psychol B* 49:1–25 Ja '52. * (*PA* 27:435)

348. LOWE, WILLIAM F. "Effect of Controlling the Immediate Environment of Responses to the Thematic Apperception Test." Abstract. *Percept & Motor Skills Res Exch* 4:98 '52. *

349. McDONALD, FRANKLIN RANDOLPH. *The Effect of Differential Cultural Pressures on Projective Test Performances of Negroes.* Doctor's thesis, University of Southern California (Los Angeles, Calif.), 1952.

350. McDOWELL, JAMES V. *Developmental Aspects of Phantasy Production on the Thematic Apperception Test.* Doctor's thesis, Ohio State University (Columbus, Ohio), 1952.

351. MALCOM, EDWARD VARTAN. *A Study of the Validity of Individual Personality Profiles Based on Each of Four Projective Techniques.* Doctor's thesis, University of Michigan (Ann Arbor, Mich.), 1952. (*DA* 12:221)

352. MARQUIS, DOROTHY P.; SINNETT, E. ROBERT; AND WINTER, WILLIAM D. "A Psychological Study of Peptic Ulcer Patients." *J Clin Psychol* 8:266–72 Jl '52. * (*PA* 27:6072)

353. MASON, BETH. "Social Class and the TAT." Abstract. *Percept & Motor Skills Res Exch* 4:41 '52. *

354. MASON, BETH B. "An Experimental Investigation of the Effect of Repetition and Variation in Administration Upon the Thematic Apperception Test." Abstract. *Percept & Motor Skills Res Exch* 4:98 '52. *

355. MORGAN, HENRY H. "A Psychometric Comparison of Achieving and Nonachieving College Students of High Ability." *J Consult Psychol* 16:292–8 Ag '52. * (*PA* 27:4570)

356. PALMER, JAMES O. "A Note on the Intercard Reliability of the Thematic Apperception Test." *J Consult Psychol* 16: 473–4 D '52. * (*PA* 28:964)

357. PARK, PAUL DAVID. *The Performance of Normal and Schizophrenic Adult Males on the Thematic Apperception Test in Terms of: Transcendent Reactions; Categorized Affectivity; and Verbal Enumeration.* Doctor's thesis, Yeshiva University (New York, N.Y.), 1952. (*DA* 13:1262)

358. PIOTROWSKI, ZYGMUNT A. "The Thematic Apperception Test of a Schizophrenic Interpreted According to New Rules." *Psychoanalytic R* 39:230–51 Jl '52. * (*PA* 27:5308)

359. PITTS, M. HENRY. *An Experimental Study of the Influence of Social Psychological Factors Upon Production in the Thematic Apperception Test.* Doctor's thesis, University of Chicago (Chicago, Ill.), 1952. *

360. RACUSEN, FRANCES R. *An Exploratory Investigation of the Creativity and Productivity Variables on the Rorschach and Thematic Apperception Tests.* Doctor's thesis, State University of Iowa (Iowa City, Iowa), 1952. (Abstract: *Am Psychol* 8: 417)

361. RICHARDS, T. W. "Personality of the Convulsive Patient in Military Service." *Psychol Monogr* 66(14):1–23 '52. * (*PA* 27:7364)

362. RITTER, ANNE M., AND ERON, LEONARD D. "The Use of the Thematic Apperception Test to Differentiate Normal From Abnormal Groups." *J Abn & Social Psychol* 47:147–58 Ap '52. * (*PA* 27:2758)

363. SAMUELS, HENRY. "The Validity of Personality-Trait Ratings Based on Projective Techniques." *Psychol Monogr* 66(5):1–21 '52. * (*PA* 27:5161)

364. SHIPLEY, THOMAS E., JR., AND VEROFF, JOSEPH. "A Projective Measure of Need for Affiliation." *J Exp Psychol* 43:349–56 My '52. * (*PA* 27:5163)

365. SHNEIDMAN, EDWIN S. "The Case of Jay: Psychological Test and Anamnestic Data." *J Proj Tech* 16:297–345 S '52. * (*PA* 28:2676)

366. SHNEIDMAN, EDWIN S., EDITOR. "The TAT Newsletter, Vol. 6, Nos. 1–4." *J Proj Tech* 16:260–5, 378–82, 510–4 Je, S, D '52. *

367. SONTAG, L. W.; CRANDALL, VAUGHN; AND LACEY, JOHN I. "Dynamics of Personality: Resolution of Infantile Dependent Need." Discussion by Harold H. Anderson. *Am J Orthopsychiatry* 22:534–41 Jl '52. * (*PA* 27:5010)

368. SUTTER, EVERETT L. *Some Audio-Mirror Effects of The-*

matic Apperception Test Stories Upon Self Awareness. Doctor's thesis, University of Texas (Austin, Tex.), 1952.

369. TERRY, DOROTHY. "The Use of a Rating Scale of Level of Response in TAT Stories." *J Abn & Social Psychol* 47:507–11 Ap '52. * (*PA* 27:2766)

370. TUMEN, ETHEL. *A Comparison of TAT Personality Readings With Psychoanalytic Findings.* Master's thesis, City College of New York (New York, N.Y.), 1952.

371. VORHAUS, PAULINE G. "Case Study of an Adolescent Boy With Reading Disability." *J Proj Tech* 16:20–41 Mr '52. *

372. WEBSTER, HAROLD. "Rao's Multiple Discriminant Technique Applied to Three TAT Variables." *J Abn & Social Psychol* 47:641–8 Jl '52. * (*PA* 27:3566)

373. WEISSKOPF, EDITH A., AND DUNLEVY, GEORGE P., JR. "Bodily Similarity Between Subject and Central Figure in the TAT as an Influence on Projection." *J Abn & Social Psychol* 47:441–5 Ap '52. * (*PA* 27:2770)

374. WILSON, CLAUDE E. "Differences Between Personal Characteristics of Students Who Have Failed in High School and Those Who Have Not Failed." *Yearb Nat Council Meas Used Ed* 9:42–50 '52. *

375. WRIGHT, CARL S. *Age and Associated Characteristics Affecting Cross-Identification of Sex on the Thematic Apperception Test.* Doctor's thesis, Western Reserve University (Cleveland, Ohio), 1952.

376. BELL, ALICE; TROSMAN, HARRY; AND ROSS, DONALD. "The Use of Projective Techniques in the Investigation of Emotional Aspects of General Medical Disorders: Part II, Other Projective Techniques and Suggestions for Experimental Design." *J Proj Tech* 17:51–60 Mr '53. * (*PA* 28:2614)

377. BERGMAN, MURRAY, AND FISHER, LOUISE A. "The Value of the Thematic Apperception Test in Mental Deficiency." *Psychiatric Q Sup* 27:22–42 pt 1 '53. * (*PA* 28:1176)

378. BERNTSON, R. K. *A Study of Adolescent Development as Reflected by the Thematic Apperception Test.* Master's thesis, Utah State Agricultural College (Logan, Utah), 1953.

379. BILLS, NORMAN. *The Personality Structure of Alcoholics, Homosexuals, and Paranoids as Revealed by Their Responses to the Thematic Apperception Test.* Doctor's thesis, Western Reserve University (Cleveland, Ohio), 1953

380. BRAMLETTE, CARL A., JR. *Some Relationships Between the Self-Concept, the Thematic Apperception Test, and Personality Adjustment.* Doctor's thesis, Duke University (Durham, N.C.), 1953.

381. BUCHER, S. *A Study of the Thematic Apperception Test Applied to a Group of Girls Aged 11 to 13 Years.* Master's thesis, University of London (London, England), 1953.

382. BURGESS, ELVA. *Personality Factors in Over- and Under-Achievers in Engineering.* Doctor's thesis, Pennsylvania State College (State College, Pa.), 1953.

383. CANTER, FRANCIS M. "Personality Factors in Seizure States With Reference to the Rosenzweig Triadic Hypothesis." *J Consult Psychol* 17:429–35 D '53. * (*PA* 28:7844)

384. CHAPIN, NED. "A Dynamic Approach to the TAT." *Psychiatric Q Sup* 27:62–89 pt 1 '53. * (*PA* 28:935)

385. COOK, RICHARD A. "Identification and Ego Defensiveness in Thematic Apperception." *J Proj Tech* 17:312–9 S '53. * (*PA* 28:4343)

386. DAVISON, ARTHUR H. "A Comparison of the Fantasy Productions on the Thematic Apperception Test of Sixty Hospitalized Psychoneurotic and Psychotic Patients." *J Proj Tech* 17:20–33 Mr '53. * (*PA* 28:2810)

387. DUNLEVY, GEORGE P., JR. *Intentional Modification of Thematic Apperception Test Stories as a Function of Adjustment.* Doctor's thesis, Purdue University (Lafayette, Ind.), 1953.

388. ERON, LEONARD D. "Responses of Women to the Thematic Apperception Test." *J Consult Psychol* 17:269–82 Ag '53. * (*PA* 28:4350)

389. FOULDS, GRAHAM. "A Method of Scoring the T.A.T. Applied to Psychoneurotics." *J Mental Sci* 99:235–46 Ap '53. * (*PA* 28:943)

390. FRY, FRANKLYN D. "Manual for Scoring the Thematic Apperception Test." *J Psychol* 35:181–95 Ap '53. * (*PA* 28: 945)

391. FRY, FRANKLYN D. "TAT Scoring Blank." *J Psychol* 35:197–200 Ap '53. * (*PA* 28:946)

392. GLADWIN, THOMAS, AND SARASON, SEYMOUR B. *Truk: Man in Paradise*, pp. 209–46, 290–462, 573–651. Viking Fund Publications in Anthropology, No. 20. New York: Wenner-Gren Foundation for Anthropological Research, Inc., 1953. Pp. 774. *

393. GLUCK, MARTIN RICHARD. *A Study of the Relationship Between the Amount of Hostility in the Content of Projective Techniques and the Amount of Hostility Expressed in Behavior.* Doctor's thesis, University of Pittsburgh (Pittsburgh, Pa.), 1953.

394. GORDON, HIRAM L. "A Comparative Study of Dreams and Responses to the Thematic Apperception Test: I, A Need-Press Analysis." *J Personality* 22:234–53 D '53. * (*PA* 28: 6006)

395. GREENBAUM, MARVIN; QUALTERE, THOMAS; CARRUTH, BRUCE; AND CRUICKSHANK, WILLIAM. "Evaluation of a Modification of the Thematic Apperception Test for Use With Physically Handicapped Children." *J Clin Psychol* 9:40–4 Ja '53. * (*PA* 27:7770)

396. HARRISON, ROSS. "The Thematic Apperception Test."

Monogr Soc Res Child Develop 16(53):60–88, 214–316 '53. * (*PA* 28:4077)

397. KADIS, ASYA L.; GREENE, JANET S.; AND FREEDMAN, NORBERT. "Early Childhood Recollections—An Integrative Technique of Personality Test Data." *Am J Indiv Psychol* 10:31–42 nos 1–2 '52–53 ['53]. * (*PA* 28:910)

398. KENNY, DOUGLAS T., AND BIJOU, SIDNEY W. "Ambiguity of Pictures and Extent of Personality Factors in Fantasy Responses." *J Consult Psychol* 17:283–8 Ag '53. * (*PA* 28:4367)

399. KLINE, MILTON V. "An Hypnotic Experimental Approach to the Genesis of Occupational Interests and Choice: II, The Thematic Apperception Test (A Case Report)." *J General Psychol* 48:79–82 Ja '53. * (*PA* 28:1114)

400. KLINE, MILTON V., AND HAGGERTY, ARTHUR D. "An Hypnotic Experimental Approach to the Genesis of Occupational Interests and Choice: III, Hypnotic Age Regression and the Thematic Apperception Test—A Clinical Case Study in Occupational Identification." *J Clin & Exp Hypnosis* 1:18–31 Jl '53. * (*PA* 28:2802)

401. KNEHR, C. A.; VICKERY, A.; AND GUY, M. "Problem-Action Responses and Emotions in Thematic Apperception Test Stories Recounted by Alcoholic Patients." *J Psychol* 35:201–26 Ap '53. * (*PA* 28:1232)

402. LEVIN, BERNARD MYRON. *Predicting Progress in Psychotherapy: A Comparison of Thematic Apperception Test Results and Psychiatric Judgments.* Doctor's thesis, University of Pittsburgh (Pittsburgh, Pa.), 1953.

403. LINDZEY, GARDNER, AND GOLDBERG, MORTON. "Motivational Differences Between Male and Female as Measured by the Thematic Apperception Test." *J Personality* 22:101–17 S '53. * (*PA* 28:4372)

404. LUBORSKY, LESTER. "Self-Interpretation of the TAT as a Clinical Technique." *J Proj Tech* 17:217–23 Je '53. * (*PA* 28:4373)

405. McARTHUR, CHARLES. "The Effects of Need Achievement on the Content of TAT Stories: A Re-Examination." *J Abn & Social Psychol* 48:532–6 O '53. * (*PA* 28:6041)

406. McCLELLAND, DAVID C.; ATKINSON, JOHN W.; CLARK, RUSSELL A.; AND LOWELL, EDGAR L. *The Achievement Motive.* New York: Appleton-Century-Crofts, Inc., 1953. Pp. xxiii, 384. *

407. MARKENSON, DAVID. *Diagnostic Effectiveness of Interpretive Tests.* Doctor's thesis, Washington University (St. Louis, Mo.), 1953. (*DA* 14:1100)

408. MILL, CYRIL R. "Personality Patterns of Sociometrically Selected and Sociometrically Rejected Male College Students." *Sociometry* 16:151–67 My '53. * (*PA* 28:4886)

409. MUNSTERBERG, ELIZABETH, AND MUSSEN, PAUL H. "The Personality Structures of Art Students." *J Personality* 21:457–66 Je '53. * (*PA* 28:4064)

410. MURRAY, HENRY A. "Thematic Apperception Test," pp. 636–49. (*PA* 27:7786) In *Contributions Toward Medical Psychology: Theory and Psychodiagnostic Methods, Vol. II.* Edited by Arthur Weider. New York: Ronald Press Co., 1953. Pp. xi, 459–885. *

411. MUSSEN, PAUL H. "Differences Between the TAT Responses of Negro and White Boys." *J Consult Psychol* 17:373–6 O '53. * (*PA* 28:5888)

412. NOWELL, ANN. "Peer Status as Related to Measures of Personality." *Calif J Ed Res* 4:37–41 Ja '53. * (*PA* 28:1514)

413. ROBBINS, ARTHUR. *An Experimental Study of the Relationship Between Needs as Manifested on the Thematic Apperception Test and Kuder Preference Record Scales of Adolescent Boys.* Doctor's thesis, Columbia University (New York, N.Y.), 1953.

414. ROCK, M. L., AND HAY, E. N. "Investigation of the Use of Tests as a Predictor of Leadership and Group Effectiveness in a Job Evaluation Situation." *J Social Psychol* 38:109–19 Ag '53. * (*PA* 28:5831)

415. SARASON, SEYMOUR B. "The Thematic Apperception Test," pp. 252–9. In his *Psychological Problems in Mental Deficiency, Second Edition.* New York: Harper & Brothers, 1953. Pp. xi, 402. * (*PA* 28:2876)

416. SEN, AMYA. "A Preliminary Study of the Thematic Apperception Test." *Brit J Stat Psychol* 6:91–100 N '53. *

417. SHATIN, LEO. "Rorschach Adjustment and the Thematic Apperception Test." *J Proj Tech* 17:92–101 Mr '53. * (*PA* 28:2675)

418. SHNEIDMAN, EDWIN S. "TAT Bibliography: Supplement for 1952." *J Proj Tech* 17:109–15 Mr '53. * (*PA* 28:2677)

419. SHNEIDMAN, EDWIN S., Editor. "The TAT Newsletter, Vol. 7, Nos. 2–4." *J Proj Tech* 17:242–3, 376–9, 499–502 Je, S, D '53. *

420. STONE, HAROLD. *The Relationship of Hostile-Aggressive Behavior to Aggressive Content on the Rorschach and Thematic Apperception Tests.* Doctor's thesis, University of California (Los Angeles, Calif.), 1953.

421. SUTTER, EVERETT L.; KELL, BILL L.; AND McGUIRE, CARSON. "Some Audio-Mirror Effects of TAT Stories Upon Self-Awareness." Abstract. *Am Psychol* 8:444 Ag '53. *

422. WEBB, WILSE B., AND HILDEN, ARNOLD H. "Verbal and Intellectual Ability as Factors in Projective Test Results." *J Proj Tech* 17:102–3 Mr '53. * (*PA* 28:2687)

423. WEBSTER, HAROLD. "Derivation and Use of the Masculinity-Femininity." *J Clin Psychol* 9:33–6 Ja '53. * (*PA* 27:7803)

424. WEISSKOPF-JOELSON, EDITH, AND MONEY, LESTER, JR.

425. YOUNG, RAYMOND J., JR. *The Effect of the Interpreter's Personality on the Interpretation of Thematic Apperception Test Protocols.* Doctor's thesis, University of Texas (Austin, Tex.), 1953.

426. ARMSTRONG, MARY ANN SMITH. "Children's Responses to Animal and Human Figures in Thematic Pictures." *J Consult Psychol* 18:67–70 F '54. * (*PA* 28:8710)

427. ATKINSON, JOHN W.; HEYNS, ROGER W.; AND VEROFF, JOSEPH. "The Effect of Experimental Arousal of the Affiliation Motive on Thematic Apperception." *J Abn & Social Psychol* 49:405–10 Jl '54. * (*PA* 29:4025)

428. AULD, FRANK, JR., AND ERON, LEONARD D. "Application of Guttman's Scaling Method to the TAT." Abstract. *Am Psychol* 9:323–4 Ag '54. *

429. BELLAK, LEOPOLD. "A Study of Limitations and 'Failures': Toward an Ego Psychology of Projective Techniques." *J Proj Tech* 18:279–93 S '54. * (*PA* 29:4031)

430. BELLAK, LEOPOLD. *The Thematic Apperception Test and the Children's Apperception Test in Clinical Use.* New York: Grune & Stratton, Inc., 1954. Pp. x, 282. * (*PA* 29:4032)

431. BRIGGS, DENNIE L. "A Modification of the Thematic Apperception Test for Naval Enlisted Personnel (*N-TAT*)." *J Psychol* 37:233–41 Ap '54. * (*PA* 28:8716)

432. BROIDA, DANIEL C. "An Investigation of Certain Psychodiagnostic Indications of Suicidal Tendencies and Depression in Mental Hospital Patients." *Psychiatric Q* 28:453–64 Jl '54. * (*PA* 29:6019)

433. CARR, ARTHUR C. "Intra-Individual Consistency in Response to Tests of Varying Degrees of Ambiguity." *J Consult Psychol* 18:251–8 Ag '54. * (*PA* 29:4041)

434. COX, RACHEL D. "Personality Dynamics of the Well-Adjusted College Student as Revealed by the Rorschach and Thematic Apperception Tests." Abstract. *Am Psychol* 9:351–2 Ag '54. * (*J Proj Tech* 18:399 S '54. *)

435. CRASILNECK, HAROLD BERNARD. *An Analysis of Differences Between Suicidal and Pseudo-Suicidal Patients Through the Use of Projective Techniques.* Doctor's thesis, University of Houston (Houston, Tex.), 1954. (*DA* 14:1456)

436. DANA, RICHARD H. *The Diagnostic Efficacy of a Theoretically Derived Objective Scoring System for the Thematic Apperception Test.* Doctor's thesis, University of Illinois (Urbana, Ill.), 1954.

437. DYMOND, ROSALIND F. Chap. 8, "Adjustment Changes Over Therapy From Thematic Apperception Test Ratings," pp. 109–20. (*PA* 29:4113) In *Psychotherapy and Personality Change.* Edited by Carl R. Rogers and Rosalind F. Dymond. Chicago, Ill.: University of Chicago Press, 1954. Pp. x, 447. *

438. ERON, LEONARD D., AND AULD, FRANK, JR. *A Study of TAT Stories and Sentence Completions of Subjects in Operation Hideout.* Medical Research Laboratory Report No. 243. Washington, D.C.: Bureau of Medicine and Surgery, Department of the Navy, 1954. Pp. iii, 64. *

439. GALLESE, ARTHUR J., JR., AND SPOERL, DOROTHY TILDEN. "A Comparison of Machover and Thematic Apperception Test Interpretation." *J Social Psychol* 40:73–7 Ag '54. * (*PA* 29:5703)

440. GOODRICH, DAVID C. "Aggression in the Projective Tests and Group Behavior of Authoritarian and Equalitarian Subjects." Abstract. *Am Psychol* 9:380 Ag '54. *

441. GRUMMON, DONALD L., AND JOHN, EVE S. Chap. 9, "Changes Over Client-Centered Therapy Evaluated on Psychoanalytically Based Thematic Apperception Scales," pp. 121–44. (*PA* 29:4124) In *Psychotherapy and Personality Change.* Edited by Carl R. Rogers and Rosalind F. Dymond. Chicago, Ill.: University of Chicago Press, 1954. Pp. x, 447. *

442. HAGGERTY, ARTHUR D. "A Note on the Use of an Audio-Visual Technique With the *TAT* in Psychotherapy." *J General Psychol* 51:173–4 Jl '54. * (*PA* 30:2954)

443. HERTZKA, M. Chap. 13, "The Thematic Apperception Test," pp. 255–80, passim. In *Personality Through Perception: An Experimental and Clinical Study.* By H. A. Witkin and others. New York: Harper & Bros., 1954. Pp. xxvii, 571. * (*PA* 28:8566)

444. HOLSOPPLE, JAMES QUINTER, AND PHELAN, JOSEPH G. "The Skills of Clinicians in Analysis of Projective Tests." *J Clin Psychol* 10:307–20 O '54. * (*PA* 29:4061)

445. HUSMAN, BURRIS FREDERICK. *An Analysis of Aggression in Boxers, Wrestlers, and Cross Country Runners as Measured by the Rosenzweig P-F Study, Selected TAT Pictures, and a Sentence Completion Test.* Doctor's thesis, University of Maryland (College Park, Md.), 1954. (*DA* 15:759)

446. KENNY, DOUGLAS T. "Transcendence Indices, Extent of Personality Factors in Fantasy Responses, and the Ambiguity of TAT Cards." *J Consult Psychol* 18:345–8 O '54. * (*PA* 29:5710)

447. LaFORGE, ROLFE; LEARY, TIMOTHY F.; NABOISEK, HERBERT; COFFEY, HUBERT S.; AND FREEDMAN, MERVIN B. "The Interpersonal Dimension of Personality: II, An Objective Study of Repression." *J Personality* 23:129–53 D '54. * (*PA* 29:5313)

448. LESSA, WILLIAM A., AND SPIEGELMAN, MARVIN. *Ulithian Personality as Seen Through Ethnological Materials and Thematic Test Analysis.* University of California Publications in Culture and Society, Vol. 2, No. 5. Berkeley, Calif.: University of California Press, 1954. Pp. iii, 243–301. * (*PA* 29:757)

449. LEVINE, PHYLLIS R. "Projective Tests in a Vocational

Guidance Setting." *J Counsel Psychol* 1:209–14 w '54. * (*PA* 29:7429)

450. LIGHT, BERNARD H. "Comparative Study of a Series of TAT and CAT Cards." *J Clin Psychol* 10:179–81 Ap '54. * (*PA* 29:933)

451. LINDZEY, GARDNER, AND NEWBURG, ARTHUR S. "Thematic Apperception Test: A Tentative Appraisal of Some 'Signs' of Anxiety." *J Consult Psychol* 18:389–95 D '54. * (*PA* 29:7294)

452. McINTYRE, CHARLES J. "Sex, Age, and Iconicity as Factors in Projective Film Tests." *J Consult Psychol* 18:337–43 O '54. * (*PA* 29:5718)

453. MILAM, JAMES R. "Examiner Influences on Thematic Apperception Test Stories." *J Proj Tech* 18:221–6 Je '54. * (*PA* 29:4074)

454. MILLER, JEROME S. *The Predictive Significance of Usualness and Unusualness of Thematic Apperception Test Stories.* Master's thesis, Ohio State University (Columbus, Ohio), 1954.

455. MUSSEN, PAUL H., AND NAYLOR, H. KELLY. "The Relationships Between Overt and Fantasy Aggression." *J Abn & Social Psychol* 49:235–40 Ap '54. * (*PA* 29:1148)

456. PHILLIPSON, H. *The Development of a Rationale for the Thematic Apperception Test: A Proposed Modification of the Test Based on the Psycho-Analytic Theory of Unconscious Object Relations.* Master's thesis, University of London (London, England), 1954.

457. REEVES, MARGARET PEGRAM. *An Application of the Semantic Differential to Thematic Apperception Test Material.* Doctor's thesis, University of Illinois (Urbana, Ill.), 1954. (*DA* 14:2121)

458. RICHARDSON, STEPHEN ALEXANDER. *A Study of Selected Personality Characteristics of Social Science Field Workers.* Doctor's thesis, Cornell University (Ithaca, N.Y.), 1954. (*DA* 14:2403)

459. SHANK, KENNON. *An Analysis of the Degree of Relationship Between the Thematic Apperception Test and an Original Projective in Measuring Symptoms of Personality Dynamics of Speech Handicapped Children.* Doctor's thesis, University of Denver (Denver, Colo.), 1954.

460. SHNEIDMAN, EDWIN S. "TAT Bibliography: Supplement for 1953." *J Proj Tech* 18:111–9 Mr '54. * (*PA* 29:956)

461. SHNEIDMAN, EDWIN S., Editor. "The TAT Newsletter, Vol. 8, Nos. 1 and 2, March, June 1954." *J Proj Tech* 18:111–9, 267–8 Mr '54. *

462. SINGER, JEROME L. "Projected Familial Attitudes as a Function of Socioeconomic Status and Psychopathology." *J Consult Psychol* 18:99–104 Ap '54. * (*PA* 29:2478)

463. SOSKIN, WILLIAM F. "Bias in Postdiction From Projective Tests." *J Abn & Social Psychol* 49:69–74 Ja '54. * (*PA* 28:7551)

464. STEPHENSON, WILLIAM. *The Study of Behavior: Q-Technique and Its Methodology,* pp. 313–25. Chicago, Ill.: University of Chicago Press, 1953. Pp. ix, 376. * (*PA* 28:6810)

465. STRAUSS, F. H. "Interpretation of Thematic Test Material: A Jungian Approach." Abstract. *B Brit Psychol Soc* (23):12–3 My '54. *

466. WHITMAN, EVELYN BUSCH. "Personality of Fourth Grade Children as Measured by Modified T.A.T. and Improvisation Techniques." *Group Psychother* 7:255–61 D '54. * (*PA* 31:1081)

467. WITKIN, H. A.; LEWIS, H. B.; HERTZMAN, M.; MACHOVER, K.; MEISSNER, P. BRETNALL; AND WAPNER, S. *Personality Through Perception: An Experimental and Clinical Study.* New York: Harper & Brothers, 1954. Pp. xxvi, 571. * (*PA* 28:8566)

468. AULD, FRANK, JR.; ERON, LEONARD D.; AND LAFFAL, JULIUS. "Application of Guttman's Scaling Method to the T.A.T." *Ed & Psychol Meas* 15:422–35 w '55. * (*PA* 30:7183)

469. BARD, MORTON. "The Use of Dependence for Predicting Psychogenic Invalidism Following Radical Mastectomy." *J Nerv & Mental Dis* 122:152–160 Ag '55. * (*PA* 31:1583)

470. BORENSTEIN, BETTY A. *A Study of the Relationship Between Thematic Apperception Test Fantasy and Overt Behavior.* Doctor's thesis, University of California (Berkeley, Calif.), 1955.

471. CLARK, RUSSELL A., AND SENSIBAR, MINDA RAE. "The Relationship Between Symbolic and Manifest Projections of Sexuality With Some Incidental Correlates." *J Abn & Social Psychol* 50:327–34 My '55. * (*PA* 30:2861)

472. COWDEN, RICHARD C.; DEABLER, HERDIS L.; AND FEAMSTER, J. HARRY. "The Prognostic Value of the Bender-Gestalt, H-T-P, TAT, and Sentence Completion Test." *J Clin Psychol* 11:271–5 Jl '55. * (*PA* 30:2864)

473. DANA, RICHARD H. "Clinical Diagnosis and Objective TAT Scoring." *J Abn & Social Psychol* 50:19–24 Ja '55. * (*PA* 29:7267)

474. DANA, RICHARD H. "The Objectification of Projective Techniques: Rationale." *Psychol Rep* 1:93–102 Je '55. *

475. DAVIDS, ANTHONY; HENRY, ANDREW F.; McARTHUR, CHARLES C.; AND McNAMARA, LEO F. "Projection, Self Evaluation, and Clinical Evaluation of Aggression." *J Consult Psychol* 19:437–40 D '55. * (*PA* 30:7191)

476. ERON, LEONARD D. "Some Problems in the Research Application of the Thematic Apperception Test." *J Proj Tech* 19:125–9 Je '55. * (*PA* 30:2871)

477. ERON, LEONARD D.; SULTAN, FLORENCE; AND AULD, FRANK, JR. "The Application of a Psychometric Scoring Procedure to a Group Modification of the Thematic Apperception

Test (N-TAT)." *J Consult Psychol* 19:83–9 Ap '55. * (*PA* 30:1019)

478. ERVIN, SUSAN M. "The Verbal Behavior of Bilinguals: The Effects of Language of Response Upon the TAT Stories of Adult French Bilinguals." Abstract. *Am Psychol* 10:391 Ag '55. *

479. FESHBACH, SEYMOUR. "The Drive-Reducing Function of Fantasy Behavior." *J Abn & Social Psychol* 50:3–11 Ja '55. *

480. FINE, REUBEN. "Manual for a Scoring Scheme for Verbal Projective Techniques (TAT, MAPS, Stories and the Like)." *J Proj Tech* 19:310–6 S '55. * (*PA* 30:4570)

481. FINE, REUBEN. "A Scoring Scheme for the TAT and Other Verbal Projective Techniques." *J Proj Tech* 19:306–9 S '55. * (*PA* 30:4571)

482. GLUCK, MARTIN R. "The Relationship Between Hostility in the TAT and Behavioral Hostility." *J Proj Tech* 19:21–6 Mr '55. * (*PA* 30:1025)

483. GOLDMAN, ROSALINE, AND GREENBLATT, MILTON. "Changes in Thematic Apperception Test Stories Paralleling Changes in Clinical Status of Schizophrenic Patients." *J Nerv & Mental Dis* 121:243–9 Mr '55. * (*PA* 30:3206)

484. GOODSTEIN, LEONARD D.; MARTIRE, JOHN G.; AND SPIELBERGER, CHARLES D. "The Relationship Between 'Achievement Imagery' and Stuttering Behavior in College Males." *Proc Iowa Acad Sci* 62:399–404 '55. *

485. HARRISON, ROSS; TOMBLEN, DON T.; AND JACKSON, THEODORE A. "Profile of the Mechanical Engineer: III, Personality." *Personnel Psychol* 8:469–90 w '55. * (*PA* 31:1941)

486. HEYMANN, GARY M. *Some Relationships Among Hostility, Fantasy Aggression, and Aggressive Behavior.* Doctor's thesis, Michigan State University (East Lansing, Mich.), 1955. (*DA* 16:793)

487. HURLEY, JOHN R. "The Iowa Picture Interpretation Test: A Multiple-Choice Variation of the TAT." *J Consult Psychol* 19:372–6 O '55. * (*PA* 30:5985)

488. HUSMAN, BURRIS F. "Aggression in Boxers and Wrestlers as Measured by Projective Techniques." *Res Q* 26:421–5 D '55. *

489. JOHNSON, GRANVILLE B., JR. "An Evaluation Instrument for the Analysis of Teacher Effectiveness." *J Exp Ed* 23:331–44 Je '55. * (*PA* 30:3484)

490. KAMMAN, GORDON R., AND KRAM, CHARLES. "Value of Psychometric Examinations in Medical Diagnosis and Treatment." *J Am Med Assn* 158:555–60 Je 18 '55. * (*PA* 31:1044)

491. KANDIL, B. A. *A Study of the Thematic Apperception Test as Applied to a Group of Institutional Children.* Master's thesis, University of London (London, England), 1955.

492. KLINE, MILTON V. "Hypnodiagnosis With a Visual-Imagery Induction Technique and Modification of the House-Tree-Person and Thematic Apperception Tests." *Psychiatric Q Sup* 29:267–71 pt 2 '55. * (*PA* 31:1122)

493. LEBO, DELL. "Immediate Affective Reaction to TAT Cards." *J Clin Psychol* 11:297–9 Jl '55. * (*PA* 30:2893)

494. LICCIONE, JOHN V. "The Changing Family Relationships of Adolescent Girls." *J Abn & Social Psychol* 51:421–6 N '55. * (*PA* 30:4581)

495. LIGHT, BERNARD H. "A Further Test of the Thompson TAT Rationale." *J Abn & Social Psychol* 51:148–50 Jl '55. * (*PA* 30:4581)

496. LINDZEY, GARDNER, AND HEINEMANN, SHIRLEY H. "Thematic Apperception Test: Individual and Group Administration." *J Personality* 24:34–55 S '55. * (*PA* 30:5992)

497. LINDZEY, GARDNER, AND HERMAN, PETER S. "Thematic Apperception Test: A Note on Reliability and Situational Validity." *J Proj Tech* 19:36–42 Mr '55. *

498. LITTLE, KENNETH B., AND SHNEIDMAN, EDWIN S. "A Comparison of the Reliability of Interpretations of Four Psychological Tests." Abstract. *Am Psychol* 10:322 Ag '55. *

499. LITTLE, KENNETH B., AND SHNEIDMAN, EDWIN S. "The Validity of Thematic Projective Technique Interpretations." *J Personality* 23:285–94 Mr '55. * (*PA* 30:1038)

500. LUBIN, NATHAN M. "The Effect of Color in the TAT on Productions of Mentally Retarded Subjects." *Am J Mental Def* 60:366–70 O '55. * (*PA* 30:6093)

501. McARTHUR, CHARLES. "Personality Differences Between Middle and Upper Classes." *J Abn & Social Psychol* 50:247–54 Mr '55. * (*PA* 30:873)

502. MEYER, MORTIMER M., AND TOLMAN, RUTH S. "Correspondence Between Attitudes and Images of Parental Figures in TAT Stories and in Therapeutic Interviews." *J Consult Psychol* 19:79–82 Ap '55. * (*PA* 30:989)

503. MEYER, MORTIMER M., AND TOLMAN, RUTH S. "Parental Figures in Sentence Completion Test, in TAT, and in Therapeutic Interviews." Abstract. *J Consult Psychol* 19:170 Je '55. * (*PA* 30:2904)

504. MILLER, JEROME S., AND SCODEL, ALVIN. "The Diagnostic Significance of Usual and Unusual TAT Stories." *J Consult Psychol* 19:91–5 Ap '55. * (*PA* 30:1045)

505. MUSSEN, PAUL H., AND SCODEL, ALVIN. "The Effects of Sexual Stimulation Under Varying Conditions on TAT Sexual Responsiveness." Abstract. *J Consult Psychol* 19:90 Ap '55. *

506. NEWBIGGING, P. LYNN. "Influence of a Stimulus Variable on Stories Told to Certain TAT Pictures." *Can J Psychol* 9:195–206 D '55. * (*PA* 30:7217)

507. OHLSEN, MERLE M., AND SCHULZ, RAYMOND E. "Projective Test Response Patterns for Best and Poorest Student Teachers." *Ed & Psychol Meas* 15:18–27 sp '55. * (*PA* 30:1659)

508. SHATIN, LEO. "Relationships Between the Rorschach Test and the Thematic Apperception Test." J Proj Tech 19: 317-31 S '55. * (PA 30:4595)

509. SHULMAN, HAROLD S. Congruences of Personality Expression in Self-Conceptions, the Thematic Apperception Test, and Dreams. Doctor's thesis, Western Reserve University (Cleveland, Ohio), 1955.

510. SPIEGELMAN, MARVIN. "Jungian Theory and the Analysis of Thematic Tests." J Proj Tech 19:253-63 S '55. * (PA 30:4601)

511. STAUNTON, G. J. "A Comparative Analysis of Rorschach and T.A.T. Responses With Reference to a Particular Case Study." Abstract. Brit Rorsch Forum (6):1-4 Ap '55. *

512. STEIN, MORRIS I. Thematic Apperception Test: An Introductory Manual for Its Clinical Use With Adults, Second Edition. Cambridge, Mass.: Addison-Wesley Publishing Co., Inc., 1955. Pp. xviii, 365. * (PA 29:7324)

513. ULLMANN, LEONARD PAUL. The Definition of Stimuli in the Evaluation of Test Behavior. Doctor's thesis, Stanford University (Stanford, Calif.), 1955. (DA 15:1910)

514. VERNIER, CLAIRE M.; WHITING, J. FRANK; AND MELTZER, MALCOLM L. "Differential Prediction of a Specific Behavior From Three Projective Techniques." J Consult Psychol 19:175-82 Je '55. * (PA 30:2932)

515. VINEYARD, EDWIN EARLE. A Longitudinal Study of the Relationship of Differential Aptitude Test Scores With College Success. Doctor's thesis, Oklahoma Agricultural and Mechanical College (Stillwater, Okla.), 1955.

516. WAXENBERG, SHELDON E. "Psychosomatic Patients and Other Physically Ill Persons: A Comparative Study." J Consult Psychol 19:163-9 Je '55. * (PA 30:3281)

517. ZEICHNER, ABRAHAM M. "Psychosexual Identification in Paranoid Schizophrenia." J Proj Tech 19:67-77 Mr '55. * (PA 30:1378)

518. APPLEZWEIG, MORTIMER H.; MOELLER, GEORGE; AND BURDICK, HARVEY. "Multi-Motive Prediction of Academic Success." Psychol Rep 2:489-96 D '56. * (PA 31:5139)

519. BELLAK, LEOPOLD. "Freud and Projective Techniques." J Proj Tech 20:5-13 Mr '56. * (PA 31:1963)

520. BENTSEN, IVAR BEN. Effect of Sodium Amytal on Conventionality, Commonality of Response to the Word Association Test, and Thematic Apperception Test. Doctor's thesis, University of California (Los Angeles, Calif.), 1956.

521. BERNSTEIN, LEWIS. "The Examiner as an Inhibiting Factor in Clinical Testing." J Consult Psychol 20:287-90 Ag '56. * (PA 31:7898)

522. BURGESS, ELVA. "Personality Factors of Over- and Under-Achievers in Engineering." J Ed Psychol 47:89-99 F '56. * (PA 31:8811)

523. CARR, ARTHUR C. "The Relation of Certain Rorschach Variables to Expression of Affect in the TAT and SCT." J Proj Tech 20:137-42 Je '56. * (PA 31:4674)

524. CHILD, IRVIN L.; FRANK, KITTY F.; AND STORM, THOMAS. "Self-Ratings and TAT: Their Relations to Each Other and to Childhood Background." J Personality 25:96-114 S '56. * (PA 31:7905)

525. CLARK, RUSSELL A., AND McCLELLAND, DAVID C. "A Factor Analytic Integration of Imaginative and Performance Measures of the Need for Achievement." J General Psychol 55: 73-83 Jl '56. *

526. CLARK, RUSSELL A.; TEEVAN, RICHARD; AND RICCIUTI, HENRY N. "Hope of Success and Fear of Failure as Aspects of Need for Achievement." J Abn & Social Psychol 53:182-6 S '56. *

527. CLEVELAND, SIDNEY E., AND FISHER, SEYMOUR. "Psychological Factors in the Neurodermatoses." Psychosom Med 18:209-20 My-Je '56. * (PA 31:5001)

528. COX, RACHEL DUNAWAY. "The Normal Personality: An Analysis of Rorschach and Thematic Apperception Test Responses of a Group of College Students." J Proj Tech 20:70-7 Mr '56. * (PA 31:3016)

529. DANA, RICHARD H. "An Application of Objective TAT Scoring." J Proj Tech 20:159-63 Je '56. * (PA 31:4680)

530. DANA, RICHARD H. "Cross Validation of Objective TAT Scoring." J Consult Psychol 20:33-6 F '56. * (PA 31:3019)

531. DANA, RICHARD H. "Selection of Abbreviated TAT Sets." J Clin Psychol 12:36-40 Ja '56. * (PA 30:4560)

532. DAVIDS, ANTHONY; JOELSON, MARK; AND McARTHUR, CHARLES. "Rorschach and TAT Indices of Homosexuality in Overt Homosexuals, Neurotics, and Normal Males." J Abn & Social Psychol 53:161-72 S '56. * (PA 32:2891)

533. EDELSTEIN, RUTH R. The Evaluation of Intelligence From TAT Protocols. Master's thesis, City College of New York (New York, N.Y.), 1956.

534. EPSTEIN, SEYMOUR, AND SMITH, RICHARD. "Thematic Apperception as a Measure of the Hunger Drive." J Proj Tech 20:372-84 D '56. * (PA 32:1619)

535. FISHER, SEYMOUR, AND MENDELL, DAVID. "The Communication of Neurotic Patterns Over Two and Three Generations." Psychiatry 19:41-6 F '56. * (PA 31:3503)

536. GROH, LESLIE S. "A Study of Ego Integration by Means of an Index of Identification Derived from Six TAT Cards." J Proj Tech 20:387-97 D '56. * (PA 32:1358)

537. GUREL, LEE. "Quantitative Differences in Responses to Twenty Stimulus Cards of the Thematic Apperception Test." Abstract. Am Psychol 11:364 Ag '56. *

538. HENRY, WILLIAM E. The Analysis of Fantasy: The Thematic Apperception Technique in the Study of Personality.

New York: John Wiley & Sons, Inc., 1956. Pp. xiii, 305. * (PA 30:8292)

539. HEYMANN, GARY M. "Some Relationships Among Hostility, Fantasy Aggression, and Aggressive Behavior." Abstract. Am Psychol 11:391 Ag '56. *

540. JENSEN, ARTHUR ROBERT. Aggression in Fantasy and Overt Behavior. Doctor's thesis, Columbia University (New York, N.Y.), 1956. (DA 16:794)

541. JONES, RICHARD M. "The Negation TAT: A Projective Method for Eliciting Repressed Thought Content." J Proj Tech 20:297-303 S '56. * (PA 31:6090)

542. KAGAN, JEROME, AND MUSSEN, PAUL H. "Dependency Themes on the TAT and Group Conformity." J Consult Psychol 20:29-32 F '56. * (PA 31:3042)

543. KERNER, OLIVER J. B. "Stress, Fantasy, and Schizophrenia: A Study of the Adaptive Processes." Genetic Psychol Monogr 53:189-281 My '56. *

544. KLEIN, ARMIN, JR. The Influence of Stimulus Material and Geographical Region on Responses to a Thematic Test. Doctor's thesis, Columbia University (New York, N.Y.), 1956. (DA 16:1284)

545. LEBLANC, H. J. The Thematic Apperception Test Applied to Army Officer Selection. Master's thesis, University of Western Ontario (London, Ont., Canada), 1956.

546. LEVY, LEON H.; BRODY, JANICE R.; AND WINDMAN, GEORGIA O. "The Relationship Between the Inferential Potential of Rorschach and TAT Protocols." J Consult Psychol 20: 27-8 F '56. * (PA 31:3049)

547. LINDZEY, GARDNER, AND TEJESSY, CHARLOTTE. "Thematic Apperception Test: Indices of Aggression in Relation to Measures of Overt and Covert Behavior." Am J Orthopsychiatry 26:567-76 Jl '56. * (PA 31:7943)

548. McPHERSON, MARION WHITE. "Speech Behavior and Egocentricity." J Clin Psychol 12:229-35 Jl '56. * (PA 31: 6014)

549. MASON, BETH, AND AMMONS, R. B. "Note on Social Class and the Thematic Apperception Test." Percept & Motor Skills 6:88 Je '56. *

550. MINER, JOHN B. "Motion Perception, Time Perspective, and Creativity." J Proj Tech 20:405-13 D '56. *

551. MORAN, LOUIS J.; FAIRWEATHER, GEORGE W.; FISHER, SEYMOUR; AND MORTON, ROBERT B. "Psychological Concomitants to Rate of Recovery From Tuberculosis." J Consult Psychol 20:199-203 Je '56. * (PA 31:6487)

552. PAGE, HORACE A. "Studies in Fantasy: Daydreaming and the TAT." Abstract. Am Psychol 11:392 Ag '56. *

553. PURCELL, KENNETH. "The TAT and Antisocial Behavior." J Consult Psychol 20:449-56 D '56. * (PA 32:1641)

554. ROBBINS, ARTHUR. "Emotional Status of the U.S. Soldier and Length of Tour in Korea." US Armed Forces Med J 7:888-94 Je '56. *

555. SARBIN, ANNE. An Analysis of the Buhler School Maturity Test as It Relates to Intelligence and Projective Test Data. Doctor's thesis, University of Southern California (Los Angeles, Calif.), 1956.

556. SCHAW, LOUIS C., AND HENRY, WILLIAM E. "A Method for the Comparison of Groups: A Study in Thematic Apperception." Genetic Psychol Monogr 54:207-53 N '56. *

557. SEMEONOFF, BORIS. "The Use of Projective Techniques in Selection for Counselling." Abstract. B Brit Psychol Soc (29):45-6 My '56. *

558. SILVERSTEIN, ARTHUR B. The Expression of Acceptable and Unacceptable Needs in Thematic Apperception. Doctor's thesis, New York University (New York, N.Y.), 1956. (DA 17:410)

559. SINGER, JEROME L., AND OPLER, MARVIN K. "Contrasting Patterns of Fantasy and Motility in Irish and Italian Schizophrenics." J Abn & Social Psychol 53:42-7 Jl '56. * (PA 32:1868)

560. STONE, HAROLD. "The TAT Aggressive Content Scale." J Proj Tech 20:445-52 D '56. * (PA 32:1650)

561. WALLEN, RICHARD W. Chap. 9, "The Thematic Apperception Test," pp. 221-55. In his Clinical Psychology: The Study of Persons. New York: McGraw-Hill Book Co., Inc., 1956. Pp. xiii, 388. * (PA 30:7155)

562. WINCH, ROBERT F., AND MORE, DOUGLAS M. "Does TAT Add Information to Interviews? Statistical Analysis of the Increment." J Clin Psychol 12:316-21 O '56. * (PA 32:4210)

563. WYATT, FREDERICK, AND VEROFF, JOANNE B. Chap. 3, "Thematic Apperception and Fantasy Tests," pp. 32-57. (PA 30:7238) In Progress in Clinical Psychology, Vol. II. Edited by Daniel Brower and Lawrence E. Abt. New York and London: Grune & Stratton, Inc., 1956. Pp. viii, 364. *

564. YOUNG, FLORENE M. "Responses of Juvenile Delinquents to the Thematic Apperception Test." J Genetic Psychol 88:251-9 Je '56. *

565. ZEICHNER, ABRAHAM M. "Conception of Masculine and Feminine Roles in Paranoid Schizophrenia." J Proj Tech 20: 348-54 S '56. * (PA 32:6458)

566. BRADLEY, MARY O. The Test-Retest Reliability of the Thematic Apperception Test. Master's thesis, Fordham University (New York, N.Y.), 1957.

567. CALOGERAS, ROY CUNO. Some Relationships Between Fantasy and Self-Report Behavior. Doctor's thesis, Columbia University (New York, N.Y.), 1957. (DA 17:1591)

568. CLINE, VICTOR B.; EGBERT, ROBERT; FORGY, EDWARD; AND MEELAND, TOR. "Reactions of Men Under Stress to a

Picture Projective Test." *J Clin Psychol* 13:141-4 Ap '57. *
(*PA* 32:2889)

569. DANA, RICHARD H. "Norms for Three Aspects of TAT
Behavior." *J General Psychol* 57:83-9 Jl '57. *

570. EPSTEIN, SEYMOUR, AND SMITH, RICHARD. "Thematic
Apperception, Rorschach Content, and Ratings of Sexual Attractiveness of Women as Measures of the Sex Drive." *J Consult Psychol* 21:473-8 D '57. * (Abstract: *Am Psychol* 12:
383)

571. FISHER, SEYMOUR, AND MORTON, ROBERT B. "An Exploratory Study of Some Relationships Between Hospital Ward
Atmospheres and Attitudes of Ward Personnel." *J Psychol*
44:155-64 Jl '57. *

572. FISHER, SEYMOUR, AND MORTON, ROBERT B. "Levels of
Prediction From the TAT." *J Consult Psychol* 21:115-20 Ap
'57. *

573. FRIEDMAN, IRA. "Objectifying the Subjective: A Methodological Approach to the TAT." *J Proj Tech* 21:243-7 S
'57. *

574. HOOKER, EVELYN. "The Adjustment of the Male Overt
Homosexual." *J Proj Tech* 21:18-31 Mr '57. * (*PA* 32:3083)

575. JENSEN, ARTHUR R. "Aggression in Fantasy and Overt
Behavior." *Psychol Monogr* 71(16):1-13 '57. *

576. LAKIN, MARTIN. "Assessment of Significant Role Attitudes in Primiparous Mothers by Means of a Modification of
the TAT." *Psychosom Med* 19:50-60 Ja-F '57. * (*PA* 32:
1407)

577. LEARY, TIMOTHY. *Interpersonal Diagnosis of Personal-
ity: A Functional Theory and Methodology for Personality
Evaluation.* New York: Ronald Press Co., 1957. Pp. xix, 518. *
(*PA* 31:2556)

578. LEBO, DELL, AND HARRIGAN, MARGARET. "Visual and
Verbal Presentation of TAT Stimuli." *J Consult Psychol* 21:
339-42 Ag '57. *

579. LYLE, J. G., AND GILCHRIST, A. A. "Problems of Thematic Apperception Test Interpretation and the Diagnosis of
Delinquent Trends." Abstract. *B Brit Psychol Soc* (32):21
inset My '57. *

580. MANDLER, GEORGE; LINDZEY, GARDNER; AND CROUCH,
ROBERT G. "Thematic Apperception Test: Indices of Anxiety
in Relation to Test Anxiety." *Ed & Psychol Meas* 17:466-74
w '57. *

581. SCODEL, ALVIN. "Heterosexual Somatic Preference and
Fantasy Dependency." *J Consult Psychol* 21:371-4 O '57. *

582. SCODEL, ALVIN, AND LIPETZ, MILTON E. "TAT Hostility and Psychopathology." *J Proj Tech* 21:161-5 Je '57. *

583. SHERWOOD, EDWARD T. "On the Designing of TAT
Pictures, With Special Reference to a Set for an African People
Assimilating Western Culture." *J Social Psychol* 45:161-90
My '57. *

584. SOHLER, DOROTHY TERRY; HOLZBERG, JULES D.; FLECK,
STEPHEN; CORNELISON, ALICE R.; KAY, ELEANOR; AND LIDZ,
THEODORE. "The Prediction of Family Interaction From a Battery of Projective Techniques." *J Proj Tech* 21:199-208 Je
'57. *

585. ULLMANN, LEONARD P., AND MCFARLAND, ROBERT L.
"Productivity as a Variable in TAT Protocols: A Methodological Study." *J Proj Tech* 21:80-7 Mr '57. * (*PA* 32:2928)

586. WEISSKOPF-JOELSON, EDITH; ASHER, E. J.; ALBRECHT,
KENNETH J.; AND HOFFMAN, MARTIN L. "An Experimental Investigation of 'Label-Avoidance' as a Manifestation of Repression." *J Proj Tech* 21:88-93 Mr '57. * (*PA* 32:2931)

587. DAVIDS, ANTHONY, AND ROSENBLATT, DANIEL. "Use of
the TAT in Assessment of the Personality Syndrome of Alienation." *J Proj Tech* 22:145-52 Je '58. *

588. FITZGERALD, BERNARD J. "Some Relationships Among
Projective Test, Interview, and Sociometric Measures of Dependent Behavior." *J Abn & Social Psychol* 56:199-203 Mr
'58. *

589. HENRY, WILLIAM E., AND SHLIEN, JOHN M. "Affective
Complexity and Psychotherapy: Some Comparisons of Time-
Limited and Unlimited Treatment." *J Proj Tech* 22:153-62 Je
'58. *

590. HOLT, ROBERT R. "Formal Aspects of the TAT: A
Neglected Resource." *J Proj Tech* 22:163-72 Je '58. *

591. KAGAN, JEROME; SONTAG, LESTER W.; BAKER, CHARLES
T.; AND NELSON, VIRGINIA L. "Personality and IQ Change."
J Abn & Social Psychol 56:261-6 Mr '58. *

592. LINDZEY, GARDNER. "Thematic Apperception Test: The
Strategy of Research." *J Proj Tech* 22:173-80 Je '58. *

593. LINDZEY, GARDNER, AND KALNIUS, DAGNY. "Thematic
Apperception Test: Some Evidence Bearing on the 'Hero Assumption.'" *J Abn & Social Psychol* 57:76-83 Jl '58. *

594. LINDZEY, GARDNER; TEJESSY, CHARLOTTE; AND ZA-
MANSKY, HAROLD S. "Thematic Apperception Test: An Em-
pirical Examination of Some Indices of Homosexuality." *J Abn
& Social Psychol* 57:67-75 Jl '58. *

595. LYLE, J.; GILCHRIST, A.; AND GROH, L. "Three Blind
Interpretations of a TAT Record." *J Proj Tech* 22:82-96 Mr
'58. *

596. MELIKIAN, LEVON H. "The Relationship Between Edwards' and McClelland's Measures of Achievement Motivation."
J Consult Psychol 22:296-8 Ag '58. *

597. MURSTEIN, BERNARD I. "Nonprojective Determinants of
Perception on the TAT." *J Consult Psychol* 22:195-8 Je '58. *
(Abstract: *Am Psychol* 12:412)

598. MURSTEIN, BERNARD I. "The Relationship of Stimulus

Ambiguity on the TAT to the Productivity of Themes." Abstract. *J Consult Psychol* 22:348 O '58. *

599. MYERS, ROBERT L. *An Analysis of Sex Differences in
Verbalizations and Content of Responses to the Rorschach and
to the Thematic Apperception Test.* Doctor's thesis, Temple
University (Philadelphia, Pa.), 1958. (*DA* 19:365)

600. PURCELL, KENNETH. "Some Shortcomings in Projective
Test Validation." *J Abn & Social Psychol* 57:115-8 Jl '58. *

601. RUESS, AUBREY L. "Some Cultural and Personality Aspects of Mental Retardation." *Am J Mental Def* 63:50-9 Jl
'58. *

602. SARASON, BARBARA R., AND SARASON, IRWIN G. "The
Effect of Type of Administration and Sex of Subject on Emo-
tional Tone and Outcome Ratings of TAT Stories." *J Proj
Tech* 22:333-7 S '58. *

603. SCHAFER, ROY. "How Was This Story Told?" *J Proj
Tech* 22:181-210 Je '58. *

604. SEMEONOFF, BORIS. "Projective Techniques in Selection
for Counseling." *Human Relations* 11:113-22 no 2 '58. *

605. SHATIN, LEO. "The Constriction-Dilation Dimension in
Rorschach and TAT." *J Clin Psychol* 14:150-4 Ap '58. *

606. SHNEIDMAN, EDWIN S. "Some Relationships Between
Thematic and Drawing Materials," pp. 620-7. In *The Clinical
Application of Projective Techniques.* Edited by Emanuel F.
Hammer. Springfield, Ill.: Charles C Thomas, 1958. Pp. xxii,
663. *

607. SHNEIDMAN, EDWIN S., AND FARBEROW, NORMAN L.
"TAT Heroes of Suicidal and Non-Suicidal Subjects." *J Proj
Tech* 22:211-28 Je '58. *

608. SUMERWELL, HARRIET C.; CAMPBELL, MARY M.; AND
SARASON, IRWIN G. "The Effect of Differential Motivating In-
structions on the Emotional Tone and Outcome of TAT Stories."
J Consult Psychol 22:385-8 O '58. *

609. ULLMANN, LEONARD P. "Clinical Correlates of Facilitation and Inhibition of Response to Emotional Stimuli." *J Proj
Tech* 22:341-7 S '58. *

610. WYATT, FREDERICK. "A Principle for the Interpretation
of Fantasy." *J Proj Tech* 22:229-45 Je '58. *

LEONARD D. ERON, *Director of Research, Rip
Van Winkle Foundation, Hudson, New York.*

It was the impression of the reviewer in *The
Fourth Mental Measurements Yearbook* that
in the busy clinic the use of the TAT was largely
a luxury, since the material obtained by use of
this rather "tedious and time-consuming technique" could be more efficiently obtained in a
personal interview. He saw the possibility, however, that "with the development of useful scoring systems, such as that of Aron (*154*), and
the establishment of empirically verified principles of interpretation, the test will achieve distinctive value as a psychodiagnostic instrument."

Over the last five years much research with
the TAT has been published, but it is still doubtful that its utility as an efficient clinical tool has
been established and it is uncertain whether the
amount of time necessary to evaluate all the
nuances of the TAT protocol could not better
be spent in other pursuits in behalf of the patient. Aron's scoring system, which is an elaboration and development of the Murray scheme
described in the test manual, has proved no boon
to the clinician. She reports that a minimum of
10 minutes is required for scoring each story,
making it hardly likely that her system can be
used economically in the clinic. One complication is that needs and press are scored for everybody in the story, not just the hero. Although
this may eliminate the arbitrary judgment sometimes needed in selecting a hero, it makes the

whole procedure that much more unwieldy. The lack of normative and validational data, except for a few hints in studies with very small numbers which did not permit statistical differentiation of groups, as well as the questionable method used in establishing reliability of scoring categories, also makes one hesitate to recommend the Aron scoring procedure for clinical use. It is unlikely that a busy clinician could make more than an impressionistic analysis of the patient's TAT protocol, especially when it is just one of a battery of tests used in psychodiagnosis. As a timesaving device, group administration of the TAT has been attempted and it has been found that the stories yielded in group administration do not differ significantly in very many ways from stories obtained in routine individual administration (260, 497). Multiple choice answers and objective scoring have been tried (40, 477, 487), but not with too much success, at least for clinical use. In the clinic where patients usually are seen individually and where the clinician is interested in analyzing more than just one or two needs or traits which are being manipulated experimentally or otherwise, it is doubtful that the group method can be adapted in such a way that it would serve as an efficient, timesaving method and, at the same time, give sufficient information about the subject to be of value.

Benton's second condition has not been fulfilled either. Unfortunately, research has not yielded verification of principles of interpretation which have been reported as successful in the clinic. For example, the traditional "signs" of anxiety in TAT stories have been shown to have little or no relationship to independent "clinical" observation of anxiety in the subjects (451, 580). The same can be said of many other "signs" which have been reported to be clinically useful but which, on independent empirical testing, fall short of validation (204, 503).

Although the usefulness of the TAT as a routine clinical tool has not yet been demonstrated, as a research technique it has had wide and successful application. A number of scoring schemes of good reliability have been introduced (204, 473, 481) and rating scales have been developed which make TAT productions amenable to sound statistical handling without sacrificing too much in the way of clinical judgment (206, 369, 372, 468, 573). These scales have been used in a variety of investigations, both into personality processes, and into the nature of the psychological act of telling stories in response to pictures (299, 362, 438, 494, 516, 521, 529).

It cannot be assumed that, because the subject is presented with an ambiguous picture about which he is instructed to make up a story, the content of his productions will be determined solely, or even chiefly, by his own needs and attitudes. In fact, a number of studies have shown either an inverse or, at best, a curvilinear relationship between degree of ambiguity of stimulus picture and extent of personality factors involved in the response (204, 398, 446). It has been amply demonstrated that each of the pictures has its own "pull" in terms of the thematic content and emotional tone of stories told in response to it. Most of the pictures routinely elicit sad stories, and there are reliable differences among the pictures as to the degree of dysphoric affect, productivity of material, themes, level of response, need systems, etc., which they evoke (204, 206, 251, 369, 585). The outcome of the stories, however, is one variable which seems to be based more on interpersonal dynamics (204, 299). Stereotyped responses for each of the cards have been described and a fair amount of normative data is now available (147, 175, 204, 388, 538).

Aside from the stimulus properties of the cards themselves, a number of other variables extraneous to the personality content of the individual subject contribute to a determination of both the formal and the content aspects of the productions. The interaction between the examiner and the subject is important. Although it is assumed that the results are a representation of an individual's private fantasy, it has been shown that the mere presence of an examiner, whether the stories are orally administered or written down by the subject himself, is an inhibiting factor in the production of strongly emotional material on the TAT (521). However, the more the subject is made to feel that he is in a permissive, accepting, noncritical, nonevaluative situation, the more likely is he to contribute fantasies which approximate his unshared ideation and imagery. The examiner can no doubt control some of this atmosphere by the instructions he gives and the manner in which he gives them, by the extra-test comments he makes, and by his general demeanor. There are other factors, however, which are immutable and cannot be changed by the examiner, e.g., sex, age, race, social status, and intelligence. All of these variables have been shown to affect TAT productions, especially when there are differences in them between the subject and the experimenter (*331, 403, 411, 462, 501, 549*).

Quite apart from the kinds of stories elicited by different examiners is the effect of the examiner on the interpretation of the stories which are made. No systematic study of this kind of confounding has been reported, although many authors have warned of the danger of the experimenter's injecting his own theoretical bias, personality shortcomings, and predilections into the interpretations. Davenport (*329*) found little agreement among six clinical psychologists in their application of 207 statements previously rated for ambiguity, etc., to each of six records from heterogeneous subjects. The judges tended to apply statements rated as universal and loaded with psychoanalytic terminology to any subject, while avoiding use of more specific statements; and they rarely selected statements about positive assets or traits of personality, even though some of the TAT records were from normal individuals.

As in any psychological test, the cooperativeness of the subject is important, and it cannot be assumed that the "cover story" given by the examiner, e.g., "This is a test of intelligence," takes care of the attitudes, set, and preconceived notions of the subject. TAT productions have been shown to be susceptible to distortion when the subject makes a conscious effort to give a specific kind of picture of himself. Individuals can influence the diagnosis of their personalities made by experienced TAT examiners and, to some extent, can manipulate their answers in accordance with their purpose in taking the test (*298*). However, the subject need not be consciously aware of any effort to distort his stories; he may be set in such a way that it is inevitable that stories will fit in with his predominant attitudes. Differences in TAT stories have been related to physiologically controlled needs such as hunger (*302, 534*), sex (*326, 471, 505*), and sleep deprivation,[1] hypnotically produced attitudes such as sadness and criticalness,[2] and psychologically induced motivations such as need for achievement (*170*) and need for affiliation (*427*). Similarly, a number

of experiments have shown that conditions directly antecedent to the test administration will affect the productions (*496*). Although most of these studies have dealt with the effect of specific frustration (*21, 29, 258, 479, 482*), there is evidence that the immediate surroundings in general have their influence, too (*204, 281*).

Despite all these seemingly extraneous influences, there still remains a large portion of the individual's idiosyncratic, deep seated motivation that seems to be reflected in his TAT productions. However, the exact nature of this relationship between overt behavior and fantasy as represented by the TAT has yet to be delineated (*476*). Much of the research concerned with this correlation has centered around the variable of aggression and, indeed, the relationship is not uncomplicated. There is no one-to-one relationship between amount of aggressive need depicted on the TAT and the overt, or even covert, behavior of the subject. The "sign" approach advocated by a number of writers, by which one can supposedly translate what the subject says or fails to say or the way he says it to how he will act (e.g., avoidance of the gun in pictures 3 and 8 means that the subject has to inhibit strong aggressive tendencies, or the use of forceful language or the fantasying of death or failure in nonheroes signifies the tendency to act out aggression), has been demonstrated to be a failure (*547, 582*). However, when a theory of behavior is used to posit the relationship between TAT fantasy and overt behavior, results are more successful. For example, Pittluck (*305*) reasoned that both the aggressive drive and the anxiety opposing expression of this drive must be taken into account when predicting the likelihood of overt aggressive behavior in any individual. The indications of anxiety which she obtained from TAT stories included rejection or denial of aggression, excusing of the aggression by placing it in a socially acceptable context, noncompletion of aggressions planned by a fantasy character, and displacement of the aggression to nonhuman objects. These mechanisms are considered to be defensive in purpose; by their use the aggressive response becomes a compromise between aggressive impulses and the anxiety opposing their expression. It was found that the tendency to use these mechanisms in TAT stories was negatively related to the tendency to act out. The subjects who used more defense mechanisms in proportion to their out-

---

[1] MURRAY, E. J. "Thematic Apperception During Sleep Deprivation." Paper read at Eastern Psychological Association, Philadelphia, 1958.

[2] LEUBA, CLARENCE, AND LUCAS, CHARLES. "The Effects of Attitudes on Descriptions of Pictures." *J Exp Psychol* 35:517-24 D '45.

going, aggressive fantasies tended to act out less than the subjects who used proportionally fewer such mechanisms. In addition, the subjects who used proportionally more unmodified, primitive responses in fantasy tended to act out more than patients with proportionally fewer fantasies of this nature. Therefore, Pittluck concluded that measures of aggressive fantasy can provide direct clues to overt aggressive behavior if these measures stress not the absolute frequency of aggressive responses but the extent to which such responses are free from modifications which are the result of anxiety.

According to behavior theory, anxiety about a given behavior usually results from the association of punishment with that behavior sometime in the past. Mussen and Naylor (455) found that subjects who anticipated punishment for aggression in their TAT stories demonstrated less overt aggression than subjects who did not anticipate such punishment. A further refinement of this relationship, which makes for more efficient prediction from TAT to behavior, is found in a study by Purcell (553) who showed that anticipated internal punishment must be distinguished from retaliatory punishment since the latter variable did not differentiate antisocial from non-antisocial subjects while the former did.

This relationship between aggressive fantasy and overt behavior was more efficiently related to actual learning conditions by Lesser [3] who compared the relationship between these two variables among boys whose mothers encouraged expression of aggression as contrasted with boys whose mothers discouraged such behavior. Where aggressive behavior had maternal encouragement, there was significant positive relationship between aggression scores obtained from stories and behavioral ratings obtained from peers; but where mothers were relatively discouraging of aggression, there was a negative relationship of about the same magnitude. If both groups had been pooled, the correlation would have been no better than zero.

The foregoing studies, which have placed analysis of TAT behavior solidly in the main line of current psychological theory, seem to support a positive or representational type of relationship between fantasy and behavior. However, they have dealt only with outwardly directed aggression. An investigation by Davids,

Henry, McArthur, and McNamara (475) on inwardly directed aggression invokes cultural pressures to explain the negative relationship found between TAT stories and such behavior. The investigators reason that overt expression of this type of need (intra-aggression) is made difficult in western culture while its expression in fantasy is facilitated. Therefore, there would not necessarily be a relationship between the two methods of expression of this need; indeed, if the need were strong enough and it were difficult to find expression for it in overt behavior, it might very likely then be expressed in fantasy, here represented by TAT stories. This type of validation study, in which one variable at a time is rigorously defined and systematically manipulated or observed in carefully selected subjects who form clearly defined criterion groups to whom the TAT is then administered, seems to yield positive results. Other types, which depend on retrospective accounts (318, 524) or concurrent clinical evaluation (201, 204, 503), are less successful.

In summary, it seems the TAT cannot be used in the clinic as a standardized procedure in the same sense as an intelligence test, although, as one more impressionistic tool in the armamentarium of the clinician, it may have some practical utility. However, the research possibilities of the TAT are manifold. Much of what occurs in the psychological act of telling stories in response to pictures has been clearly delineated. The effect of order of presentation, picture content, presence or absence of color; the influence of the age, sex, race, intelligence, social status, etc., of both the subject and the experimenter; the immediately preceding experience, the set of the subject, the setting in which the experiment is conducted, the method of administration—all have been investigated and their effect assessed. The crucial question of just how TAT fantasy is related to overt behavior has not been so clearly demonstrated. Most of the work has been done in the area of aggression; and the consensus here is that there is a representative relationship between TAT fantasy and behavior, at least for outwardly directed aggression, if a number of modifying mechanisms such as anxiety, and other variables such as learning conditions, are taken into account. For aggression directed inward, the evidence from one study is that the relationship is compensational, and this has been tentatively related to cultural pressures pro-

---

[3] LESSER, GERALD S. "The Relationship Between Overt and Fantasy Aggression as a Function of Maternal Response to Aggression." *J Abn & Social Psychol* 55:218–21 S '57. *

hibiting overt expression. It should be clearly understood, however, that in none of the studies relating TAT behavior to overt behavior is the obtained relationship ever high enough to permit prediction in individual cases with any degree of confidence. In clinical situations such predictions should not be made without corroboration from additional sources including other test data, interview material, and behavioral cues.

ARTHUR R. JENSEN, *USPHS Research Fellow, National Institute of Mental Health, Institute of Psychiatry, University of London, London, England.*

The TAT has now been with us for 23 years and has become one of the three or four best known and most widely used clinical psychological tests. Anyone entering the field had better begin with general reviews of the TAT literature (*181, 320, 563*), for there are now close to a thousand references on the TAT. Henry (*538*) gives a very extensive and up-to-date bibliography.

The TAT is not a test that anyone can use after merely studying the manual or a few books on interpretation. In untrained and inexperienced hands it can do more harm than good. It is a test for trained clinical psychologists. Its technique is best learned through practice in a clinical setting under the supervision of a seasoned clinician who is skilled in projective techniques. While it is possible to be a good clinician without knowing the TAT, it is not possible to use the TAT judiciously without being a good clinician. Experience with the TAT is usually gained as a part of the psychologist's clinical training, and expertness with the test seems to be associated with training along "dynamic" or psychoanalytic lines as well as experience in psychotherapy.

ADMINISTRATION. The TAT is perhaps the least standardized of all psychological tests as regards administration, scoring, and interpretation. The instructions to the subject given in Murray's original manual are roughly followed, but few clinicians ever use all 20 cards on one subject. From their own experience clinicians come to have favorite pictures and they sometimes add a few others they think relevant for the subject they are examining. Seldom are more than 10 pictures used. Clinicians have various methods for eliciting fantasy material. Some even ask the subject, "What is the one thing that could *not* be happening in this picture?" This is claimed to get at repressed psychic content better than the usual method of administration (*541*). It apparently makes little difference if the stories are obtained orally or are written by the subject, either alone or in a group (*260, 497*). The thematically "richest" TAT stories the reviewer has seen were written by subjects in a group situation (*575*).

SCORING. In addition to Murray's original schema and its later variations for scoring "needs" and "presses," there are a number of other scoring schemes (*389, 430, 473, 481*). In actual practice, however, formal scoring is little used. It is usually thought to be too time-consuming and often seems to miss the individual essence of the subject's production as well as the holistic impression the clinician wishes to obtain. In addition to the themas, attitudes, motivations, and defenses revealed in the stories, the clinician's analysis is based also on the so-called "formal" aspects, such as style, structure, the subject's complaisance with instructions, language characteristics, logical coherence, realism, bizarreness, emotional tone, productivity, and fluency. Perhaps the chief value of the schemes of scoring or tabulating various aspects of TAT productions is for students learning the TAT. Since the several scoring methods analyze the material from somewhat different angles, practice with them is a means of developing sensitivity to the many facets of TAT material that enter into interpretation.

INTERPRETATION. Rather meagre normative data on content and formal characteristics have been published (*204, 388*), but TAT interpretation is not based on the comparison of "scores" with standard norms. In practice the only "norms" are those held subjectively by the clinician from his own experience with the test. Analysis of as many as 50 to 100 TAT records may be required before one begins to have subjective "norms" for the TAT. It is largely for this reason that clinicians are reluctant to change to new sets of pictures, such as the *Symonds Picture-Story Test* or Bellak's *Children's Apperception Test,* for which subjective "norms" have not been accumulated. Murray, the inventor of the TAT, has restated and elaborated some of his ideas on interpretation (*278*), and there are now a number of good manuals on the art of TAT interpretation (*430, 512, 538*). There is no best or one authentic method of TAT interpretation. This fact is demonstrated in Shneidman's book (*290*) in which each of 15 TAT experts analyzes the same protocol and explains his own method of interpretation. The clinician brings to the task of interpretation all his psychological knowledge, clinical experience, sensitivity, and intuition. The more actual experience the examiner has had with patients, especially if gained through psychotherapy, the more knowledge he has of dynamic psychology, psychoanalysis, and other projective techniques, the more meaning will he derive from the TAT. It is generally agreed that the TAT should not be interpreted "blind," for then it is too apt to miss the mark by far and have no value in "elucidating" the case history material. TAT interpretations tend more to ring true when they are made in conjunction with the case history and with impressions gained from interviews and other tests.

RELIABILITY. The question of reliability has been quite neglected in the TAT literature.[1] Reliability of scoring, of internal consistency, of test-retest, and of interpretation must be evaluated separately.

In searching the TAT literature, the writer has found only 15 estimates of scoring reliability based on sound statistical methods and presented in the form of the product-moment correlation coefficient so as to be strictly comparable to the usual measures of test reliability. These reliability coefficients range from .54 to .91, with an average of .77. For reliability of *scoring* (i.e., interscorer agreement), these figures must be considered quite low. Scoring reliability below .80 is generally considered unacceptable in scoring essay examinations, for example.

There is a widely held misconception that split-half or internal consistency reliability is meaningless in the TAT. Actually it is no less meaningful in the case of the TAT than for any other test comprised of a number of elements which are combined into some kind of "score." A proper coefficient of internal consistency for any TAT variable may be obtained by the Kuder-Richardson formula or by a rank correlation method. When the proper technique was applied (*524*) to 10 of the major Murray TAT variables (Achievement, Aggression, Autonomy, etc.) the internal consistency reliability of the various themes ranged from −.07

1 JENSEN, ARTHUR R. "The Reliability of Projective Techniques." *Acta Psychologica*, in press.

to +.34, with a mean of .13. These reliabilities are typical of most internal consistency measures on the TAT (*497*). What they mean in practice is that any scoring system based on the addition of themes elicited by various pictures is fallacious. A theme on one card is not sufficiently correlated with the same theme on another card to justify an additive treatment of TAT variables. It would be like adding together pounds, gallons, and inches. Each card seems to be a unique test in itself and is correlated little, if at all, with other cards (*248*). This fact casts serious doubt on the validity of many methods of TAT interpretation.

Test-retest reliability estimates are rare and are usually more a measure of the subject's memory for his first productions. When subjects were required to make up *different* stories on retest, the reliability coefficients of only 3 out of 17 scored variables were significantly greater than zero (*497*). McClelland (*406*) reports a retest reliability (1 week interval) of *.22* for his quantitatively scored *n* Achievement.

Reliability of interpretation is a more important consideration. Friedman (*573*) found the correlations (from a Q-sort) between different interpreters' ideas about the characteristics of the TAT "hero" to average .74, with a range from .37 to .88 for various protocols. This study unfortunately tells us nothing about the discriminating power of the TAT with respect to subjects, but indicates only the fact that there is some agreement between interpreters about the manifest characteristics of the central figure in the stories. Davenport (*329*) had six clinicians rate six TAT records on 207 typical interpretive statements as they applied to each record. The major finding was the lack of reliable discrimination. There was little agreement among the judges in the differential use of the statements for the six TAT records. The judges tended to apply statements rated as universal to almost any patient while avoiding the use of more specific statements. They rarely made statements about positive aspects of personality even though normal subjects were used.

VALIDITY. With such low reliability it is not surprising to find that the validity of the TAT is practically nil. But in discussing validity, one must distinguish two main classes of variables derived from the TAT protocol: thematic material and formal characteristics (style, language, fluency, etc.). On the criterion side one must distinguish between (*a*) temporary or situationally induced affects, drives, etc., and (*b*) relatively stable personality characteristics, traits, etc. In experimental studies there have been found significant but low correlations between certain thematic content (e.g., *n* Achievement, *n* Aggression, *n* Sex) and experimentally induced affects or drives (*406, 497, 597*). These relationships, however, have been so low and are so dependent upon particular experimental conditions as to be of no practical value in the individual clinical application of the TAT. Thematic content has not shown significant relationships to relatively stable behavioral tendencies, personality traits, or psychiatric diagnosis (*204, 482, 575*).

Formal aspects of the TAT show a low but significant relationship to personality characteristics and diagnostic categories (*389, 473, 575*). TAT material when analyzed not for its fantasy content but as a "behavior sample" (the subject's complaisance, attitude toward the examiner, degree of social inhibition, etc.) may have some predictive power. For example, adolescent boys who habitually acted out aggressively in ways regarded as taboo in school responded also to the TAT with socially tabooed content and language (*575*). But these relationships are tenuous; they depend upon a large number of cases for their statistical significance and are of little value in clinical prediction.

Various studies indicate that the TAT has little if any validity as a clinical test. It is generally agreed that the TAT is invalid for nosological diagnosis (*181, 204, 320*), although certain formal characteristics have been shown to have some relationship to certain broad diagnostic categories (*389, 473*). Brief, easily scored objective questionnaires, however, can do this sort of thing much more effectively than the TAT. While an objective questionnaire—the *Psychosomatic Inventory*—correlated .69 with pooled clinical ratings of anxiety, only 3 out of 18 commonly accepted TAT signs of anxiety correlated significantly with the clinical ratings. The highest of these correlations was .40 (*451*). In another study Child, Frank, and Storm (*524*) summarize their findings: "We have explored 10 forms of social behavior, and anxiety about each, through two techniques of data gathering. A questionnaire in which subjects rated themselves on 10 items believed relevant to each variable yielded meas-

ures of very satisfactory reliability and, for three variables for which a pertinent criterion was available, substantial validity. A group TAT using eight standard pictures relevant to our variables yielded measures of generally very low reliability, of no validity (by the same criterion applied to the questionnaire), and of no apparent relation to the corresponding measures obtained from the questionnaire." Hartman (*161*) made comparisons between a clinician's ratings based on the TAT and two other clinicians' ratings based on case history material. The degree of correspondence between interpretations based on the TAT and those based on the case history was barely above the chance level. The median correlations between two raters using case history material and the TAT interpreter were .19 and .28. Most of the significant correlations were based on formal characteristics of the TAT material. In terms of predictive power, Winch and More (*562*) found that the TAT adds nothing significant to information gained in an interview.

Murray (*278*) and others have argued that the real proof of the TAT would be the correspondence between TAT material and the deeper layers of personality which are revealed only in the process of psychotherapy. Murray has mentioned one case in which the TAT "adumbrated all the chief trends which five months of analysis were able to reveal." Studies based on larger samples have not found much correspondence between TAT and therapy material. Meyer and Tolman (*502*) sought a correspondence between attitudes concerning parents expressed in psychotherapeutic interviews and in TAT protocols. There was "no predictability from TAT to therapy as to whether or not parents were discussed, and when they were discussed, no similarity was found between those attitudes and images given in TAT stories and in psychotherapy." Saxe (*233*) had a TAT clinician rate a personality questionnaire tapping typical TAT variables on 20 patients. After the patients had undergone four months of psychotherapy, the therapist rated the patients on the same questionnaire. There was greater than chance (5 per cent level) agreement in only half of the cases.

If the TAT is short on actual validity, it certainly is not lacking in what might be called "subjective validity" (akin to "faith validity"). This is a feeling gained by the clinician using the TAT that it contributes something to his understanding of the case. Some psychologists have a greater capacity than others for experiencing subjective validity. This capacity seems to be associated with training and experience in psychoanalysis, psychotherapy, and projective techniques in general. The TAT also provides the clinical psychologist with the kind of dynamically interpretable material that can be appreciated by the psychoanalytically oriented psychiatrist to whom the clinician addresses his report. Thus clinicians are heard to speak of the TAT as being "useful" rather than as having validity. It is probably for these reasons that the TAT survives in clinical practice.

SUMMARY. The TAT is a nonstandardized assessment technique which is best left to clinical psychologists who have had special training in its use. While research has shown the TAT to have low reliability and negligible validity, many clinical psychologists continue to use it, apparently with some satisfaction.

For a review by Arthur L. Benton, see 4:136; for reviews by Arthur L. Benton, Julian B. Rotter, and J. R. Wittenborn, see 3:103 (1 excerpt); for related reviews, see B63, B204, B395, 4:137–41, 3:104, and 3:104a.

[165]

★Thematic Apperception Test for African Subjects. Ages 10 and over; 1953; 1 form ['53]; no data on reliability; 12s. 6d. per set of test materials, postage extra; [60–120] minutes; S. G. Lee; University of Natal Press. *

REFERENCE

1. LEE, S. G. *A Preliminary Investigation of the Personality of the Educated African by Means of a Projective Technique.* Master's thesis, University of Natal (Natal, Union of South Africa), 1949.

MARY D. AINSWORTH, *Associate Professor of Psychology, The Johns Hopkins University, Baltimore, Maryland.*

Impressed with the fruitfulness of the thematic apperception approach, Lee attempted to use the standard TAT materials for the investigation of the personality of Zulu subjects, but found that they were not adequately stimulated to imaginative production. He therefore devised his own set of pictures for use with African subjects. In order to "cross the cultural gap" and to arrive at pictorial materials that would be stimulating, he based his pictures on fantasy productions collected from Bantu inmates of a mental hospital.

His version of the TAT consists of 22 cards, 8 for males, 8 for females, and 6 (including a blank card) for both males and females. In some respects the cards impress this reviewer as being more ambiguous than the cards of the standard TAT. The faces of the figures are either highly ambiguous in expression or hidden from view. The backgrounds include little detail. The line of the drawings is more sketchy and hence less structured than that of the standard TAT drawings. On the other hand, many of the figures are portrayed in vigorous action or exaggerated posture that seems less ambiguous than that of the figures of the standard TAT and might be expected to be highly provocative of kinaesthetic empathy.

There seems to have been no attempt systematically to vary the number, sex, and apparent age of the figures in order to sample various types of relationships. Two cards, both in the female series, seem designed to elicit stories of parent-child relations, presumably from the mother's viewpoint. One card portrays a heterosexual situation. However, most of the pictures present single figures, and only six show two or more figures together.

Although the pictures were originally designed for the Zulu and contain some characteristically Zulu features, Lee reports that they have been used effectively among other African peoples (he specifies the tribes) and among both educated and uneducated subjects. Nevertheless, it may not be assumed that his *Thematic Apperception Test for African Subjects* is therefore applicable to all African peoples. The fact that 12 of the cards depict near-naked figures would undoubtedly be a disadvantage with tribes such as the Ganda of East Africa who traditionally clothe themselves from top to toe and consider it immodest to display the feet when sitting.

The 42-page manual provides in concise form an excellent guide for the administration and interpretation of a TAT-type test. The initial instructions contain all the essential points included in Murray's original instructions, but are worded more simply and might well be adapted to good effect in administering the standard TAT. Lee recommends that a recall phase be included at the conclusion of the storytelling phase, in which the subject is asked to recall as many of the pictures as he can in as much detail as possible. He further recommends a follow-up interview when the subject is asked to explain the sources of his plots.

Lee's suggestions for analysis and interpretation emphasize the form as well as the content of the story. In his suggestions for analysis, he has been influenced obviously by publications of other authors and he acknowledges his sources in his bibliography. His selection of points to be observed in analysis is commendable. Although his examples are selected from the records of the 140 African subjects to whom he has given his modification of the TAT, the manual might well serve as a useful guide to the beginner using any version of the TAT. He provides no normative material in statistical form, but lists the common responses he has obtained for each card. The manual concludes with a specimen analysis.

In short, Lee's TAT for African subjects recommends itself for the personality evaluation of individual subjects and for the investigation of culture-personality interaction among African peoples who may be presumed to be able to identify with near-naked African figures, although for some tribes either the Thompson modification of the TAT or some other special modification may be more appropriate.

[166]

Thematic Apperception Test: Thompson Modification. Negroes ages 4 and over; 1949, c1943-49; individual; 1 form ['49]; manual ('49); no data on reliability and validity; no norms; $6 per set of test materials, cash orders postpaid; (120) minutes in 2 sessions 1 day apart; Charles E. Thompson; Harvard University Press. *

REFERENCES

1-5. See 4:138.
6. WEBER, GEORGE HENRY. *A Social-Psychological Schema for the Analysis of the Thompson Thematic Apperception Tests.* Doctor's thesis, University of Kansas (Lawrence, Kan.), 1949.
7. COOK, RICHARD A. "Identification and Ego Defensiveness in Thematic Apperception." *J Proj Tech* 17:312-9 S '53. * (*PA* 28:4343)
8. LIGHT, BERNARD H. "A Further Test of the Thompson TAT Rationale." *J Abn & Social Psychol* 51:148-50 Jl '55. * (*PA* 30:4581)
9. KLEIN, ARMIN, JR. *The Influence of Stimulus Material and Geographical Region on Responses to a Thematic Test.* Doctor's thesis, Columbia University (New York, N.Y.), 1956. (*DA* 16:1284)

MARY D. AINSWORTH, *Associate Professor of Psychology, The Johns Hopkins University, Baltimore, Maryland.*

Thompson's purpose in modifying the TAT was to provide an instrument to facilitate a more valid clinical evaluation of Negro subjects by increasing the extent to which they can identify with the figures portrayed. His intention was to construct a series of pictures similar to those of the TAT in every respect except for changing the figures to have dark skin color and negroid features. Twenty-one of the 31 original pictures were redrawn or rephotographed (Card 13B). In the redrawing, the stimulus value of

the cards may well have been changed in respects other than the racial characteristics of the figures, for the dark backgrounds were lightened in order to provide a contrast with the dark faces, and the quality of the line was changed markedly in some of the pictures, especially in those originally reproduced from paintings, for example, Cards 2 and 7GF. Two additional and unexplained changes were made: the blank card was changed from white to gray, and Card 10 was dropped so that the complete series consists of 19 instead of 20 cards. The remaining cards (11, 12BG, 14, 15, 17GF, 19 and 20) are unchanged. The manual for the Thompson modification follows Murray's manual very closely, except for the omission of the section on analysis and interpretation of the stories.

The T-TAT differs significantly from other modifications designed for studies of culture-personality interaction,[1] in which the pictures are constructed to be appropriate to the group under investigation, not only in terms of racial characteristics of the figures portrayed, but also in features characteristic of the culture, including clothing, activities, distinctive objects, style of buildings, and so on. Henry[1] has demonstrated that such materials yield records permitting exploration of the "idiosyncratic component" of personality as well as providing data on the communal and role components.

The consensus in the literature is that the T-TAT may be useful in exploring racial attitudes and stereotypes in both Negro and white subjects. However, Thompson's contention that the T-TAT is better than the standard TAT for the clinical evaluation of individual Negroes has been challenged by other authors.

Thompson bases his claim for the superiority of the T-TAT upon a study (2) undertaken with 26 southern male Negro college students, who produced significantly longer protocols to 10 modified cards than they did to the equivalent cards of the standard version. From this and from qualitative data he concludes that the modified TAT facilitates identification and empathy in Negro subjects. Other studies with northern Negroes (4), predominantly southern Negroes (7) and white subjects (4, 7, 8) failed to demonstrate significant differences between the T-TAT and standard TAT with respect to

1 HENRY, WILLIAM E. Chap. 8, "The Thematic Apperception Technique in the Study of Group and Cultural Problems," pp. 230-78. In *An Introduction to Projective Techniques.* Edited by Harold H. Anderson and Gladys L. Anderson. New York: Prentice-Hall, Inc., 1951. Pp. xxiv, 720. *

length of stories. No significant differences were found for "idea count" (5) or for 12 measures of ego defensiveness (7). Subjective reports (7) indicated that Negroes could identify with TAT and T-TAT figures whereas white subjects thought of the T-TAT figures as Negroes rather than "people in general."

Qualitative differences between the stories evoked by the T-TAT and standard TAT cards were noted by several authors (3, 5, 8) but these were not considered to indicate increased empathy for figures with racial characteristics similar to those of the subject. Riess, Schwartz, and Cottingham (4) claim that Negroes in our culture, unaccustomed to seeing Negroes portrayed in pictures, become self-conscious about their racial status, and that this tends to defeat the basic purpose of the projective method, and highlights social distance and racial stereotypes. Korchin, Mitchell, and Meltzoff (3) view the changed figures of the T-TAT as representing an undesirable reduction in ambiguity, which evokes attitudes toward Negro problems rather than eliciting idiosyncratic material.

Length of story seems obviously inadequate as the major criterion of the adequacy of a protocol for clinical evaluation. Qualitative differences between T-TAT and TAT productions have not been systematically studied. In the absence of studies comparing the relative thematic yield of the two versions of the test for Negro groups, similar to Mussen's study [2] using the standard TAT to compare white and Negro groups, it seems premature to conclude either that the Thompson modification is superior to the standard TAT for all Negroes or that it is a "bastardization of the projective techniques" (4).

When deciding whether to use the T-TAT or the standard version, the clinician may wish to judge whether the Negro subject in question has so little sense of social distance that the standard version may be preferable or whether he is sufficiently removed from white groups that the T-TAT seems more promising. The clinician may also be influenced by the extent to which he believes that a reflection of the subject's racial attitudes will enrich the personality evaluation to be derived from the total battery of tests or possibly impoverish the evaluation by crowding out the information about needs

2 MUSSEN, PAUL H. "Differences Between the TAT Responses of Negro and White Boys." *J Consult Psychol* 17:373–6 O '53. * (PA 28:5888)

and press that he relies upon the TAT to provide.

See 4:138 (3 excerpts).

[167]

★**The Tomkins-Horn Picture Arrangement Test.** Ages 10 and over; 1942–57; IBM; 1 form ('44); $15 per 50 tests; $25 per set of scoring materials ['57]; $4.50 per 100 scoring sheets ('57); $10 per manual ('57, see 5 below); postage extra; (30–60) minutes; Silvan S. Tomkins, Daniel Horn, and John B. Miner (manual); Springer Publishing Co., Inc. *

REFERENCES

1. TOMKINS, SILVAN S. "The Tomkins-Horn Picture-Arrangement Test." *Trans N Y Acad Sci, Series II* 15:46–50 D '52. * (PA 27:7208)
2. SJOSTEDT, ELSIE MARIE. *A Study of the Personality Variables Related to Assaultive and Acquisitive Crimes.* Doctor's thesis, Purdue University (Lafayette, Ind.), 1955. (DA 15: 881)
3. TOMKINS, SILVAN S. "The Role of Tests in the United States With Particular Reference to the Tomkins-Horn Picture Arrangement Test." *Inter-Am Congr Psychol* 1:218–23 '55. *
4. TOMKINS, SILVAN S., AND MINER, JOHN B. "Contributions to the Standardization of the Tomkins-Horn Picture Arrangement Test: Plate Norms." *J Psychol* 39:199–214 Ja '55. * (PA 29:8654)
5. TOMKINS, SILVAN S., AND MINER, JOHN B. *The Tomkins-Horn Picture Arrangement Test.* New York: Springer Publishing Co., Inc., 1957. Pp. xvi, 383. * (PA 32:2926)
6. KARON, BERTRAM P. *The Negro Personality: A Rigorous Investigation of the Effects of Culture.* New York: Springer Publishing Co., Inc., 1958. Pp. viii, 184. *

DONALD W. FISKE, *Associate Professor of Psychology, University of Chicago, Chicago, Illinois.*

This "abbreviated projective test" was designed to yield material with some of the richness of the *Thematic Apperception Test* but with greater ease of administration and scoring. Each of the 25 items consists of three sketches. The subject is instructed to indicate the order for the three pictures "which makes the best sense" and to write one sentence for each picture to tell the story.

The intended function of the technique is not made explicit. There is a passing comment that it was "originally designed for purposes of selection and guidance of industrial personnel," but later "redesigned for more general use." However, the emphasis in the book implies that the authors are concerned with clinical diagnosis, with case studies. The content of the pictures reflects the development of the procedure —14 of the 25 items portray a shop setting. The odd distribution over content areas does not clarify the problem of the appropriate utilization of the instrument. The authors indicate that they attempted to sample three areas: social orientation, optimism-pessimism, and level of functioning.

The highly commendable and unique feature of this test's development was its administration to a representative "normal" sample (n =

1,500) of the United States population. A vocabulary test administered at the same time made it possible to publish norms for various groups identified by intelligence as well as by age, education, and other demographic characteristics. Hundreds of abnormals were also tested, but less representatively.

Although the administration is simple, the scoring is exceedingly complex. It is based on a clinical rationale that diagnosis must be based on responses which are rare for the subject's group, as determined by his age, IQ, and education. Thus, the authors practically throw away all information contained in "common" responses or patterns (occurring with frequencies greater than 5 per cent). They do, however, have conformity keys indicating popular tendencies, but these are "intended primarily for research purposes." They also note that cross-cultural comparisons should be based on modal tendencies for groups.

Hand scoring and interpretation are said to take only an hour, but scoring on an IBM accounting machine requires 20 minutes per subject. At the time the normative study was conducted, the scoring of individual records was so cumbersome that group statistics are reported rather than frequency distributions of scores for individuals.

Once the scoring of a single protocol has identified the pertinent keys from the 655 specified patterns, the trained psychologist can proceed with an essentially clinical interpretation. If he wishes, he may use the subject's qualitative sentences in this step.

In spite of the enormous amount of work expended on the PAT, adequate psychometric analyses have not been reported in the book which serves as manual. No alternate form is available and the authors dismiss as inappropriate the investigation of internal consistency, although at one point they imply that the correlation between items is very low.

Two studies of stability are reported, with three weeks and three years between administrations: 33 and 45 per cent, respectively, of the responses changed on retest. The authors make the dubious interpretation that the test is sensitive to personality changes over a three-year period but fail to grasp the serious weakness implied by the large change over three weeks. (No data on changes in pattern are reported.)

The authors note that over plates or items the smaller the modal response, the more frequently

such modal responses changed. Although they do not report data on this point, there is reason to expect that the more atypical a subject's response, the more likely it is to be changed.[1] Thus, the rare responses and the rare patterns are probably the least stable. But it is just these on which the authors base their scoring and interpretation! They are well aware of changes in a subject from day to day, but they make no provision for distinguishing momentary tendencies from enduring dispositions.

The manual is especially deficient on the problem of validity. A few sentences are devoted to one study which found correlations with independently assessed personality characteristics that were in the expected directions but low and "too weak to be diagnostically useful." Pertinent but not definitive evidence is presented in the patterns associated with each of the several abnormal groups.

The exposition in the book is not concise and clear. No sample protocols are presented.

This procedure is one of several recent innovations which attempt to apply current knowledge and technical developments to personality assessment. While the work on norms is commendable, the technique has not been investigated sufficiently to justify its use for any purpose except methodological research. The use of ordered and objectively scored responses to approach thematic material is a step in the right direction, but this study indicates the high cost of this method.

JOHN W. GITTINGER, *Field Representative, Society for the Investigation of Human Ecology, Forest Hills, New York.*

The *Tomkins-Horn Picture Arrangement Test* is an ingenious group projective personality test, adapted for machine scoring, utilizing simple social and work situations. The test consists of 25 plates, each containing three sketches which can be combined into a variety of sequences or "a story that makes sense" by the subject. The subject is asked to arrange the three pictures and to write three sentences explaining the selected sequence. It is the subject's selection of one of a variety of possible sequences that makes it possible to measure the projective nature of the test. Theoretically, the test is concerned with the personality or dynamic meaning revealed by the selection of sequence

[1] FISKE, DONALD W. "The Constraints on Intra-Individual Variability in Test Responses." *Ed & Psychol Meas* 17:317-37 au '57. *

rather than with the best, most common, or most conventional sorting. In fact, the emphasis in the development of the keys has been on the rare response.

Although the authors indicate that their inspiration was the *Thematic Apperception Test,* their model was the Picture Arrangement subtest of the Wechsler-Bellevue. Based on their observations that personality factors seemed to influence Picture Arrangement scores on the Wechsler-Bellevue, they developed their series of highly structured interpersonal relationships mainly in work situations. Though the authors state that the test was originally designed for use with industrial personnel, it is not clear why, with the broadening of its use, the concentration on work situations rather than the relatively more versatile interpersonal situations used by the Wechsler-Bellevue has been retained. The book-manual presents a highly systematic and orderly description of how the test was developed and how the 655 scoring patterns were derived.

In evaluating the test as published, there only can be admiration for the care with which the standardization population was selected, the methods by which the keys were constructed, and the detail in which the mechanical results are reported. Some exception will undoubtedly be taken to the discussion of reliability because it is somewhat unique and certainly unconventional. The authors argue that some of the change noted in a test-retest situation must be attributable to personality changes over time, and that, if the test is sensitive to changes in personality, less stability would be expected over longer retest intervals. They have, however, stated their case convincingly and, while the argument may be controversial, it certainly is not unscientific.

The rationale for the test is presented in but 21 pages of the 383-page book. These pages are filled with provocative but tantalizing and at times highly elusive comments. To a very large extent, the average reader will finish the presentation somewhat confused about what the test purports to measure. In spite of the fact that the test is claimed to be uncommitted to "any contemporary theory of personality," the composition and interpretation of the keys depends upon some type of conceptual framework which is nowhere clearly explained. The presentation of the descriptive terms for the keys, their definitions, and their relationship to one another does not show the same care and precision that characterizes the material on the construction of the test.

To a large extent the PAT is a well constructed projective device whose meaning and purpose is obscure. Its immediate clinical application is limited, but as a research tool it has much implied promise. It is hoped that future research can contribute to transforming the test from a clever measuring device to a well rounded clinical instrument.

WAYNE H. HOLTZMAN, *Associate Professor of Psychology, and Associate Director, The Hogg Foundation for Mental Health, The University of Texas, Austin, Texas.*

Inspired by the *Thematic Apperception Test,* the *Picture Arrangement Test* (PAT) was constructed as an extension of the well known picture arrangement method in the testing of intelligence. The test is comprised of 25 plates, each containing three simple, cartoon-like drawings. The subject is instructed to indicate the order in which the three situations make the best sense and to write three brief sentences, one for each drawing, explaining the situation. The same central figure is depicted in every drawing, making it possible for the subject to project some of his own personality into the short story he formulates. The three drawings are shown at angles of 120 degrees to minimize spurious effects due to position and order of presentation. Use of standard test booklets and simple instructions makes it possible to administer the PAT to any number of subjects at one time.

The majority of the plates emphasize the work situation of a laborer in an industrial setting. Other drawings were chosen to obtain information about social orientation, optimism-pessimism, and level of functioning with respect to the "relative strength of thinking, phantasy, affect, and behavior in the economy of the individual." Time for test administration is typically one hour but may take as long as 10 hours in several sessions for some psychotic patients.

One highly significant aspect of the PAT from a methodological point of view is the extent to which its authors have developed an empirical system for scoring complex patterns of response. Numerous individuals have sung the praises of configural scoring, pattern analysis, or clinical-global treatment of information as opposed to the use of single isolated scores. But few, if any, have achieved the degree of success in the actual employment of such pattern scoring as Tomkins and Miner. Of the almost infinite number of permutations that are possible when all 25 plates are considered simultaneously, only those combinations which seemed plausible for interpretive purposes on a priori grounds were examined empirically for frequency of occurrence in the normative sample. Wisely focusing upon the rare response patterns rather than hoping to find meaningful data in every response of every subject, Tomkins and his colleagues have painstakingly developed 96 conformity keys, 559 content keys, and 12 keys designed to detect undue effects of position or order. Special techniques have been developed for efficient pattern scoring so that a given protocol can be hand scored by a clerk in about 45 minutes.

A second highly commendable feature of the PAT is the use of a representative nationwide sample of 1,500 subjects for the establishment of norms. Tomkins was fortunate in having the resources of the Gallup Poll for standardization of his test. His extensive norms for different ages, educational levels, and degrees of intelligence as measured by a short vocabulary test are probably the best that can be reasonably obtained and surpass by far the usual standard for projective techniques. In addition to the primary normative sample, data were obtained from 755 abnormal subjects in 84 different clinics and mental hospitals.

In spite of an elaborate, complex scoring system based on a well developed rationale and an adequate normative sample, the interpretation of an individual test record leaves much to be desired. Test-retest reliability is not high, nor are any studies cited that demonstrate the validity of the PAT.

Basic to the interpretation of the pattern norms is the assumption that the situation depicted by the drawing placed last in sequence on any given plate is the significant one with respect to the respondent's personality. For example, if the subject invariably ends his arrangement with the hero working when other endings might have been just as plausible, it is inferred that the subject has high general interest in work. While the content keys may seem reasonable enough on an a priori basis to merit serious consideration, interpretation of the PAT will remain largely speculative until further research is undertaken dealing with their validity

with respect to the subject's personality. It is one thing to classify patterns of response according to the subject's preferences and quite another matter to draw valid inferences about his personality.

Personnel & Guid J 36:289-90 D '57. Leonard D. Goodstein. This is a fascinating but frustrating book presenting a new *standardized* projective test of personality * contains a brief theoretical paper dealing with the rationale of projective personality tests in general and the PAT in particular, a long and extremely confusing description of the development and standardization of the PAT, a discussion of the techniques of administering and scoring the PAT, together with a presentation of the interpretative significance of the several PAT scores. * Norms are not only available for single plates but also for *patterns* or *keys* which are scored over several plates by means of special answer sheets and scoring templates. These patterns or keys are based upon the authors' *a priori* interpretations of certain consistencies in theme from plate to plate; for example, the High General Work Interest Key (Pattern 217) showing "a preference for physical work" is scored over 14 plates, involving 34 different arrangements. Depending upon the subject's education, intelligence, and age (the three breakdowns for the pattern norms), a score of 9 or 10 on the High General Work Key would be regarded as *interpretable,* that is given by less than five per cent of the normal standardization group. There is no data, unfortunately, on the responses of the pathological groups on these keys. This is an extremely frustrating book to read especially for the first time. The organization is very weak and quite confusing; there is detailed discussion of the significance of certain scores (pp. 83-93) before the techniques for obtaining the scores are explained. Nowhere is there a simple, straight-forward, organized description of the procedures and steps involved in administering, scoring, and interpreting an individual PAT protocol. The tables are poorly labeled (especially those for the pattern norms), difficult to follow without a careful prior reading of the text, and inconsistent in the type of data presented (the plate norms are in percentages while the pattern norms are in actual frequencies). Many of these problems could have been eliminated by careful editing. There is no discussion of the problem of the *validity,* that is, the non-test behavioral correlates, of the PAT nor is any evidence on this point presented except for the data on the differences between the normal and patient response frequencies on each plate. Whether or not high or low scores on the High General Work Interest Key are related to occupational success or any other behavior index still remains a problem for empirical solution. It is the reviewer's hope that the difficulties and obscurities of the text will not limit its use or that of the PAT. Here is a new and quite different approach to projective personality assessment and one that may live up to the publisher's enthusiastic statement that this is the beginning of "a new era of projective testing."

[168]

*The Toy World Test. Ages 2 and over; 1941–55; formerly called *The World Test;* individual; 1 form ('49); 4 sets of test materials differing in number of pieces, materials used, and country where manufactured; $75 per American set; $90 per American-French set; $90 per German set; $130 per French set; $2 per 25 record blanks ('55); $1.50 per manual ('49); postage extra; (20–45) minutes; Charlotte Buhler; distributed by Joyce B. Baisden, 4570 Mont Eagle Place, Los Angeles 41, Calif. *

REFERENCES

1–6. See 4:147.
7. BOLGAR, HEDDA, AND FISCHER, LISELOTTE K. "Personality Projection in the World Test." *Am J Orthopsychiatry* 17:117–28 Ja '47. * *(PA* 21:2317)
8. FISCHER, LISELOTTE K. "A New Psychological Tool in Function: Preliminary Clinical Experience With the Bolgar-Fischer World Test." *Am J Orthopsychiatry* 20:281–92 Ap '50. * *(PA* 25:2453)
9. FISCHER, LISELOTTE K. "The World 'Test,'" pp. 62–76. *(PA* 25:6869) In *Projective and Expressive Methods of Personality Investigation ("Diagnosis").* Edited by Werner Wolff. New York: Grune & Stratton, Inc., April 1950. Pp. ii, 76. *
10. BUHLER, CHARLOTTE. "The World Test." *J Child Psychiatry* 2:2–3 sect 1 '51. * *(PA* 26:2743)
11. BUHLER, CHARLOTTE. "The World Test: A Projective Technique." *J Child Psychiatry* 2:4–23 sect 1 '51. * *(PA* 26:2741)
12. BUHLER, CHARLOTTE. "The World Test: Manual of Directions." *J Child Psychiatry* 2:69–81 sect 1 '51. * *(PA* 26:2743)
13. BUHLER, CHARLOTTE, AND CARROL, HELEN SARA. "A Comparison of the Results of the World Test With the Teacher's Judgment Concerning Children's Personality Adjustment." *J Child Psychiatry* 2:36–68 sect 1 '51. * *(PA* 26:2742)
14. LUMRY, GAYLE KELLY. "Study of World Test Characteristics as a Basis for Discrimination Between Various Clinical Categories." *J Child Psychiatry* 2:24–35 sect 1 '51. * *(PA* 26:2751)
15. BUHLER, CHARLOTTE. "National Differences in 'World Test' Projection Patterns." *J Proj Tech* 16:42–55 Mr '52. * *(PA* 27:352)
16. PASCAL, GERALD R. Chap. 11, "Gestalt Functions: The Bender-Gestalt, Mosaic and World Tests," pp. 185–90. *(PA* 27:3559) In *Progress in Clinical Psychology, Vol. I, Sect. 1.* Edited by Daniel Brower and Lawrence E. Abt. New York: Grune & Stratton, Inc., 1952. Pp. xi, 328. *
17. WENAR, CHARLES. "The Effects of a Motor Handicap on Personality: III, The Effects on Certain Fantasies and Adjustive Techniques." *Child Develop* 27:9–15 Mr '56. * *(PA* 31:3594)

L. JOSEPH STONE, *Professor of Child Study, Vassar College, Poughkeepsie, New York.*

The *Toy World Test,* like most other projective devices, can be considered a "test" only in a special sense. To the extent to which it per-

mits or invites free expressive use of the materials, i.e., invites projection, it defies standardization in the usual understanding of that term; to the extent that fixed classification and quasi-standardization is carried out, the special qualities of idiosyncratic personality portrayal inherent in projective methods may be sacrified. Investigators have stationed themselves at different points on the imaginary line that can be drawn between the horns of this dilemma. In the test itself the alternative emphases are evident in the ways in which it has been handled by its originator, Lowenfeld, who does not call it a test, and by Buhler, whose approach is the subject of this review. A use of the same materials that is comparable in many ways to Buhler's but follows a different approach to standardization and scoring is that of Bolgar and Fischer *(7–9).*

The earliest version of the miniature toys used in the test is lost in antiquity. However, the first organized approach to a "world on the floor" is found in H. G. Wells' *Floor Games* [1] in which there are descriptions and photographs of the elaborate miniature constructions like stage sets which he designed for (and with?) his children.

Klein and other child analysts first used miniature toys for the purpose of eliciting fantasy as a substitute for the free associations which children could not be instructed to supply. This approach was first systematized by Lowenfeld, who, like Klein, considers Lowenfeld's *World Technique* [2] to be primarily a psychotherapeutic instrument. Lowenfeld has published her findings with the procedure and her instructions for its systematic use; she has also circulated an unpublished revision for the use of American investigators in adapting the approach and materials to the American scene in a cooperative investigation now under way. Somewhat different versions of the use of miniature toys have been worked out by Erikson [3] in his *Dramatic Productions Test,* Murphy [4] in her *Miniature Life Toys,* and others.

Buhler observed the "world play" material in 1935 at Lowenfeld's Institute of Child Psychology in London and proposed a standardiza-

1 WELLS, H. G. *Floor Games.* London: F. Palmer, 1911.
2 LOWENFELD, MARGARET. "The World Pictures of Children: A Method of Recording and Studying Them." *Brit J Med Psychol* 18:65–101 pt 1 '39. * *(PA* 13:3897)
3 HOMBURGER [ERIKSON], ERIK. "Configurations in Play: Clinical Notes." *Psychoanalytic Q* 6:139–214 '37. *(PA* 11:4564)
4 MURPHY, LOIS BARCLAY. *Personality in Young Children: Vol. I, Methods for the Study of Personality in Young Children.* New York: Basic Books, Inc., 1956. Pp. xx, 424. *

tion. The first effort along these lines was represented by the Van Wylick dissertation [5] published in 1937 in Vienna under the direction of K. Wolff. In recent years Buhler has instigated or supervised a series of standardization studies. Her current prescribed set of materials, renamed the *Toy World Test* to distinguish it from her newly developed *Picture World Test,* consists of 160 or 300 wooden items, less elaborate, colorful, and varied than the Lowenfeld materials; she has departed from the use of sand and water which Lowenfeld considers essential. In Buhler's approach the children use the toys on the floor or table.

Buhler's standardization, which has gone through several stages, now includes a fixed, reproducible form of the materials (produced by the Los Angeles Crippled Children's Society) not subject to whims of toy manufacturers, standardized instructions and recording procedures, and, most important of all, the interpretation of the results in terms of "signs." In such an approach the projective requirements are met by permitting the child (or adult) to use the materials with considerable freedom ("Now you may play"), while the requirements of standardization are met by "scoring"—which is to say, more accurately, sorting or classifying—various aspects of the completed productions under the heading of several signs. First, the number of "elements" used (i.e., kinds of toys, such as men, women, trees, and animals) are recorded; next, the presence of A-Signs (aggressions), CDR-Signs (distortions, including closed-in areas, disarrangements, and rigid arrangements), and S-Signs (symbolic arrangements in which important qualitative material is revealed), is judged and recorded. In addition, although the manual, oddly enough, does not include the definition of E-Signs, it is apparent from the score sheet and from various published articles that this sign (empty, or relatively sparse and unpopulated worlds) is also intended as an important indicator.

Briefly, A-Signs alone are said to indicate superficial and perhaps temporary problems; E-Signs may indicate retardation or various kinds of emotional disturbance; CDR-Signs are held to be "more significant symptoms of deep emotional disturbances....present in all psychoneurosis and psychosis cases in children and adults." Of the latter, R-Signs are considered

5 VAN WYLICK, M. *Die Welt des Kindes in seiner Darstellung.* Vienna: Gerold, 1937.

the gravest: except with the very young and the mentally deficient, their use indicates obsessive compulsive trends, with deep anxiety. Beyond the use of these standardized signs as descriptive entities, interpretation includes qualitative consideration of the subject's remarks and elaboration in his play.

In summarizing a series of studies carried out under her supervision, Buhler (6) compared 30 normal (N) children, 117 problem (P) children, and 27 retarded (R) children in 174 American and European cases. In comparing their productions, using the criterion of no symptoms (subvarieties of Signs) as against "symptoms," she found critical ratios of differences among the groups as follows: N and P, 3.58; N and R, 3.50; P and R, .70. A criterion of two or more symptoms increased the critical ratio for P and R to 1.99 but somewhat lowered the others.

Lumry (6) examined four different groups of children of 25 each: normal, stuttering, withdrawing, and retarded. The mean numbers of symptoms in these four groups were .32, 2.32, 2.52, and 2.52, respectively, leading to the conclusion that "the frequency of appearance of symptoms is of clinical importance in differentiating the well adjusted child and the one who has certain psychological difficulties, but does not provide a quantitative basis for differential diagnosis." Certain symptoms were found to be particularly significant. For example, no normal child showed the symptom "no men and women," while this was found among 50 per cent of the children with psychological problems.

These and related studies suggest that while the sign approach as used by Buhler and her coworkers is approaching the stage where considerable reliance may be placed on the quantitative "scoring," it has not yet reached that point of statistical validation generally required of tests primarily quantitative in nature. It seems to the reviewer that one essential stage has been omitted in the attempt to make this projective material quantitatively manipulable. In none of the studies is there any evidence of the reliability of the scoring or of the clinical skill or training required to make these classificatory judgments. Since the presence of even two "symptoms" may be important, the criteria for assigning a symptom score should be much more precise if critical quantitative use is to be made of them. Their usefulness as clinical indicators or signposts in the understanding of the individual child is, of course, another matter.

[169]

*The Travis Projective Pictures. Ages 4 and over; 1949–57; revision of *The Travis-Johnston Projective Test: For the Exploration of Parent-Child Relationships;* 1 form ['57]; directions sheet ['57]; no data on reliability and validity; no norms; $8.50 per set of 29 pictures, postage extra; administration time not reported; [Lee E. Travis]; Griffin-Patterson Co. Inc. *

REFERENCES

1–3. See 4:142.
4. TRAVIS, LEE EDWARD, AND SUTHERLAND, LAVERNE DEEL. Chap. 25, "Suggestions for Psychotherapy in Public School Speech Correction," pp. 805–31. In *Handbook of Speech Pathology.* Edited by Lee Edward Travis. New York: Appleton-Century-Crofts, Inc., 1957. Pp. vii, 1088. *

EDWIN S. SHNEIDMAN, *Co-Principal Investigator, Central Research Unit, V.A. Center, Los Angeles, California.*

If a psychological test can be defined as consisting of a set of stimuli and, *in addition,* having accrued to it some normative data, reliability data, and conceptual notions (all subsumed under the purview of some general personality theory), then the *Travis Projective Pictures* is not a test, nor does Travis make any attempt to indicate otherwise. The reviewer telephoned the author and asked him about his materials. He said that the pictures were simply a set of stimulus materials; that there had never been a manual; that he had made no effort at norms or standards. He did indicate that the pictures had been given to around 150 school children and that the examiners "got some very fine responses." He stated that a number of speech correctionists—a field in which Travis has an international reputation—had "picked up" the materials and that the materials were being used mainly as an adjunct to speech therapeutic processes.

An interesting feature of the set of materials —which consist of freehand drawings of either one or two children and one or two adults "in various situations and relationships centering in some important and potentially troublesome areas of the socializing process of the child"— is that the pictures are focused around specific parent-child problem areas, such as punishment, hostility, parent-child rivalry, and toilet training. This is consistent with current thinking in some thematic test circles about the special advantages of using stimulus materials which focus on specific psychodynamic areas. The only reference to these materials appears in Travis' recent text on speech pathology *(4).*

The suggestions for administration are quite flexible. Travis indicates:

As a rule children respond well verbally to the pictures. They are instructed simply to tell a story about a picture. The speech therapist can make the situation a group or an individual one as time and circumstances warrant. Also, she can use a picture only, or she can present a picture while the child is doing something else, such as working with clay, playing with puppets, or playing a role in sociodrama. Although the cards are numbered, they need not necessarily be used in numerical order. The experienced therapist will choose the picture that fits best into the forward flowing process of therapy.

Travis does well in calling his materials *Travis Projective Pictures* rather than a test. One can hardly argue with an author who presents a set of stimulus materials and makes no special claims for them. *Caveat emptor.*

For a review by Robert R. Holt of the original edition, see 4:142.

[170]

★The Tree Test. Ages 9 and over; 1949–52; 1 form ('52); manual ('52, see 1 below); no data on reliability and validity; 15.95 *Sw. fr.* ($4.50) per manual, postage extra; [5–10] minutes; Charles Koch; Hans Huber. * (U.S. distributor: Grune & Stratton, Inc.)

REFERENCES

1. KOCH, CHARLES. *The Tree Test: The Tree-Drawing Test as an Aid in Psychodiagnosis.* Berne, Switzerland: Hans Huber, 1952. Pp. 87. * *(PA* 27:3137)
2. TOLOR, ALEXANDER. "The Stability of Tree Drawings as Related to Several Rorschach Signs of Rigidity." *J Clin Psychol* 13:162–4 Ap '57. * *(PA* 32:2924)

For related reviews, see B251.

[171]

*Twitchell-Allen Three-Dimensional Personality Test. Ages 3 and over (sighted and sightless); 1948–58; formerly called *Twitchell-Allen Three-Dimensional Apperception Test;* 1 form ('48); revised manual ('58); revised record blank ('58); $62 per set of testing materials, 50 recording blanks, and manual; $2 per manual; postage extra; (60) minutes; Doris Twitchell-Allen; C. H. Stoelting Co. *

REFERENCES

1. TWITCHELL-ALLEN, DORIS. "A 3-Dimensional Apperception Test: A New Projective Technique." Abstract. *Am Psychol* 2:271–2 Ag '47. *
2. STARER, EMANUEL. "An Examination of the Responses of a Group of Young Normal Female and a Group of Female Psychotic Patients on the Three-Dimensional Apperception Test." *J Clin Psychol* 9:47–50 Ja '53. * *(PA* 27:7944)
3. FEIN, LEAH GOLD, AND ALLEN, DORIS TWITCHELL. "Parts of Speech Ratio: A Maturational and Diagnostic Index to Personality Function." *Psychol News* 9:162–6 '58. *

For a review by Edward Joseph Shoben, Jr., see 4:143.

[172]

Visual Motor Gestalt Test. Ages 4 and over; 1938–46; commonly called *Bender Gestalt Test;* individual; 1 form ('46); manual ('38, see 5 below); no data on reliability; $1.10 per set of cards and directions for administering ('46); $3.80 per manual; postpaid; [10] minutes; Lauretta Bender; American Orthopsychiatric Association, Inc. * ($2 per pad of 50 scoring sheets

['51]; $7.25 per manual, *The Bender-Gestalt Test*
('51); postage extra; Gerald R. Pascal and Barbara
J. Suttell; Grune & Stratton, Inc.)

REFERENCES

1–8. See 3:108.
9–42. See 4:144.
43. BENDER, LAURETTA. Chap. 6, "The Bender Gestalt Test
and Analysis," pp. 136–42, passim. In *Chamorros and Carolinians of Saipan: Personality Studies.* By Alice Joseph and
Veronica F. Murray. Cambridge, Mass.: Harvard University
Press, 1951. Pp. xviii, 381. *
44. DINWIDDIE, FRANK W. *A Comparative Study of the
Bender-Gestalt Records of Two Groups of Alcoholics.* Master's
thesis, Catholic University of America (Washington, D.C.),
1951.
45. HALPERIN, SIDNEY L. "A Study of the Personality Structure of the Prisoner in Hawaii." *J Clin & Exp Psychopathol*
12:213–21 S '51. * (*PA* 27:1331)
46. PEEK, ROLAND M., AND QUAST, WENTWORTH. *A Scoring
System for the Bender-Gestalt Test.* Hastings, Minn.: Roland
M. Peek (Box 292) or Minneapolis, Minn.: Wentworth Quast
(2810 42nd St.), 1951. Pp. iii, 72. * (*PA* 27:1183)
47. SUTTELL, BARBARA JANE. *The Development of Visual-
Motor Performance in Children as Estimated by the Bender-
Gestalt Test.* Master's thesis, University of Pittsburgh (Pittsburgh, Pa.), 1951.
48. ADDINGTON, MILTON C. "A Note on the Pascal and Suttell Scoring System of the Bender-Gestalt Test." *J Clin Psychol*
8:312–3 Jl '52. * (*PA* 27:5851)
49. ADDINGTON, MILTON C. *Some Aspects of the Reliability
and Validity of the Bender-Gestalt Test.* Doctor's thesis, University of Tennessee (Knoxville, Tenn.), 1952.
50. BARKLEY, BILL J. *A Study Comparing the Performance
of Brain Damage Cases on the Bender Visual Motor Gestalt
Test and a Tactual-Kinesthetic Version of the Same.* Doctor's
thesis, Western Reserve University (Cleveland, Ohio), 1952.
51. BENDER, LAURETTA. *Child Psychiatric Techniques: Diagnostic and Therapeutic Approach to Normal and Abnormal Development Through Patterned, Expressive, and Group Behavior,*
pp. 50–103. Springfield, Ill.: Charles C Thomas, 1952. Pp. xi,
335. *
52. BENSBERG, GERARD J. "Performance of Brain-Injured and
Familial Mental Defectives on the Bender Gestalt Test." *J
Consult Psychol* 16:61–4 F '52. *
53. BORKO, HAROLD. *A Factor-Analytic Study of the Minnesota Multiphasic Personality Inventory Using a Transpose
Matrix (Q-Technique).* Doctor's thesis, University of Southern California (Los Angeles, Calif.), 1952.
54. DEMING, BURTON. *A Study of the Emotional Adjustment
of Functional Articulation Cases as Indicated by the Bender-
Gestalt Test.* Master's thesis, University of Oklahoma (Norman, Okla.), 1952.
55. DOSIER, CHARLOTTE H. *The Bender-Gestalt Test as an
Instrument for the Differentiation of Subcategories of Schizophrenia.* Doctor's thesis, University of Colorado (Boulder,
Colo.), 1952.
56. FELDMAN, IRVING S. *Psychological Differences Among
Moron and Borderline Mental Defectives as a Function of
Etiology: I, Visual-Motor Functioning.* Doctor's thesis, University of Pittsburgh (Pittsburgh, Pa.), 1952.
57. GOBETZ, WALLACE. *A Quantification, Standardization, and
Validation of the Bender-Gestalt Test on an Adult Population
in Terms of Its Ability to Differentiate Normal and Psychoneurotic Levels of Adjustment.* Doctor's thesis, New York University (New York, N.Y.), 1952.
58. GUERTIN, WILSON H. "A Factor Analysis of the Bender-
Gestalt Tests of Mental Patients." *J Clin Psychol* 8:362–7 O
'52. * (*PA* 27:5874)
59. HOLLON, THOMAS HARRY. *The Relationship of the Visual-
Motor Gestalt Function to Mental Age.* Master's thesis, Catholic
University of America (Washington, D.C.), 1952.
60. MYATT, MARY FRANCES. *A Study of the Relationship Between Motivation and Test Performance of Patients in a Rehabilitation Ward.* Doctor's thesis, University of Minnesota
(Minneapolis, Minn.), 1952. (*DA* 12:339)
61. PASCAL, GERALD R. Chap. 11, "Gestalt Functions: The
Bender-Gestalt, Mosaic and World Tests," pp. 185–90. (*PA*
27:3559) In *Progress in Clinical Psychology, Vol I, Sect. 1.*
Edited by Daniel Brower and Lawrence E. Abt. New York:
Grune & Stratton, Inc., 1952. Pp. xi, 328. *
62. SACKS, JAMES. *A Study of Normal and Paranoid Schizophrenic Responses to the Tachistoscopic Presentation of the
Bender Gestalt Test.* Master's thesis, University of Chicago
(Chicago, Ill.), 1952.
63. SAMUELS, HENRY. "The Validity of Personality-Trait
Ratings Based on Projective Techniques." *Psychol Monogr*
66(5):1–21 '52. * (*PA* 27:5161)
64. SUCZEK, ROBERT F. *Reliability, Generality, and Some
Personality Correlates of Bender Gestalt Responses.* Doctor's
thesis, University of California (Berkeley, Calif.), 1952.
65. SUCZEK, ROBERT F., AND KLOPFER, WALTER G. "Interpretation of the Bender Gestalt Test: The Associative Value of
the Figures." *Am J Orthopsychiatry* 22:62–75 Ja '52. *
66. SUTTELL, BARBARA J., AND PASCAL, GERALD R. " 'Regression' in Schizophrenia as Determined by Performance on the

Bender-Gestalt Test." *J Abn & Social Psychol* 47:653–7 Jl
'52. * (*PA* 27:3707)
67. ZOLIK, E. *The Reproduction of Visuo-Motor Gestalten by
Delinquent and Nondelinquent Children.* Master's thesis, Catholic University of America (Washington, D.C.), 1952.
68. AARONSON, BERNARD S.; NELSON, SHERMAN E.; AND
HOLT, SHIRLEY. "On a Relation Between Bender-Gestalt Recall and Shipley-Hartford Scores." *J Clin Psychol* 9:88 Ja '53. *
(*PA* 27:7748)
69. BLUM, RICHARD H., AND NIMS, JERRY. "Two Clinical
Uses of the Bender Visual-Motor Gestalt Test." *U S Armed
Forces Med J* 4:1592–9 N '53. * (*PA* 29:4035)
70. BOSSOM, J. *The Effect of Certain Variables Upon Recall:
A Study of the Bender-Gestalt Test.* Master's thesis, New York
University (New York, N.Y.), 1953.
71. CALDEN, GEORGE. "Psychosurgery in a Set of Schizophrenic Identical Twins: A Psychological Study." *J Proj Tech*
17:200–9 Je '53. * (*PA* 28:4641)
72. CURNUTT, ROBERT H. "The Use of the Bender Gestalt
With an Alcoholic and Non-Alcoholic Population." *J Clin Psychol* 9:287–90 Jl '53. * (*PA* 28:2896)
73. GOBETZ, WALLACE. "A Quantification, Standardization,
and Validation of the Bender-Gestalt Test on the Normal and
Neurotic Adults." *Psychol Monogr* 67(6):1–28 '53. * (*PA* 28:
4354)
74. HANVIK, LEO J. "A Note on Rotations in the Bender
Gestalt Test as Predictors of EEG Abnormalities in Children."
J Clin Psychol 9:399 O '53. * (*PA* 28:4361)
75. HUTT, MAX L. "Revised Bender Visual-Motor Gestalt
Test," pp. 660–87. (*PA* 27:7776) In *Contributions Toward
Medical Psychology: Theory and Psychodiagnostic Methods,
Vol. II.* Edited by Arthur Weider. New York: Ronald Press
Co., 1953. Pp. xi, 459–885. *
76. KATES, SOLIS L., AND SCHMOLKE, MERTON F. "Self-Related and Parent-Related Verbalizations and Bender-Gestalt
Performance of Alcoholics." *Q J Studies Alcohol* 14:38–48 Mr
'53. * (*PA* 28:1231)
77. PEEK, ROLAND M. "Directionality of Lines in the Bender-
Gestalt Test." *J Consult Psychol* 17:213–6 Je '53. * (*PA* 28:
2665)
78. ROBINSON, NANCY MAYER. "Bender-Gestalt Performances
of Schizophrenics and Paretics." *J Clin Psychol* 9:291–3 Jl
'53. * (*PA* 28:3024)
79. SWENSEN, C. H., AND PASCAL, G. R. "A Note on the
Bender-Gestalt Test as a Prognostic Indicater in Mental Illness." *J Clin Psychol* 9:398 O '53. * (*PA* 28:4678)
80. TAYLOR, GERRY M. *A Study of the Validity of the Pascal
and Suttell Scoring System for the Bender-Gestalt Test.* Master's thesis, Baylor University (Waco, Tex.), 1953.
81. THORNTON, SAM M. *A Clinical Evaluation of the Bender-
Gestalt Test.* Master's thesis, Ohio University (Athens, Ohio),
1953.
82. CURNUTT, ROBERT H., AND LEWIS, WILLIAM B. "The
Relationship Between Z Scores on the Bender Gestalt and F+%
on the Rorschach." *J Clin Psychol* 10:96–7 Ja '54. * (*PA* 28:
7515)
83. GUERTIN, WILSON H. "A Factor Analysis of Curvilinear
Distortions on the Bender-Gestalt." *J Clin Psychol* 10:12–7 Ja
'54. * (*PA* 28:7525)
84. GUERTIN, WILSON H. "A Transposed Analysis of the
Bender Gestalts of Brain Disease Cases." *J Clin Psychol* 10:
366–9 O '54. * (*PA* 29:4550)
85. GUERTIN, WILSON H. "A Transposed Factor Analysis of
Schizophrenic Performance on the Bender-Gestalt." *J Clin
Psychol* 10:225–8 Jl '54. * (*PA* 29:2789)
86. HAMMER, EMANUEL F. "An Experimental Study of Symbolism on the Bender Gestalt." *J Proj Tech* 18:335–45 S '54. *
(*PA* 29:4058)
87. KORCHIN, SHELDON J., AND BASOWITZ, HAROLD. "The
Tachistoscopic Bender-Gestalt Test." Abstract. *Am Psychol*
9:408 Ag '54. *
88. LINDSAY, JOHN. "The Bender-Gestalt Test and Psychoneurotics." *J Mental Sci* 100:980–2 O '54. * (*PA* 29:7708)
89. LONSTEIN, MURRAY. "A Validation of a Bender-Gestalt
Scoring System." *J Consult Psychol* 18:377–9 O '54. * (*PA*
29:5717)
90. PARKER, JAMES W. "Tactual-Kinesthetic Perception as a
Technique for Diagnosing Brain Damage." *J Consult Psychol*
18:415–20 D '54. * (*PA* 29:7778)
91. PEIXOTTO, H. E. "The Bender Gestalt Visual Motor Test
as a Culture Free Test of Personality." *J Clin Psychol* 10:369–
72 O '54. * (*PA* 29:4081)
92. SATTER, GEORGE, AND McGEE, EUGENE. "Retarded Adults
Who Have Developed Beyond Expectation: Part II, Non-Intellectual Functions." *Training Sch B* 51:67–81 Je '54. * (*PA*
29:2663)
93. SLOCOMBE, EDNA ELIZABETH. *The Relation of Certain
Aspects of Anxiety to Performance on the Bender Visual-Motor
Gestalt Test.* Doctor's thesis, University of Michigan (Ann
Arbor, Mich.), 1954. (*DA* 14:1260)
94. TERRY, JAMES H. *A Study of the Diagnostic Validity of
a Five-Second Presentation of the Bender Gestalt Test.* Doctor's thesis, University of Denver (Denver, Colo.), 1954.
95. ABRAMSON, H. A.; WAXENBERG, S. E.; LEVINE, A.;
KAUFMAN, M. R.; AND KORNETSKY, C. "Lysergic Acid Diethylamide (LSD-25): XIII, Effect on Bender-Gestalt Test Performance." *J Psychol* 40:341–9 O '55. * (*PA* 30:7182)
96. BYRD, EUGENE. *The Clinical Validity of the Bender Ges-

talt Test With Children: A Developmental Comparison of Children in Need of Psychotherapy and Children Judged Well-Adjusted. Doctor's thesis, Florida State University (Tallahassee, Fla.), 1955. (*DA* 15:1254)

97. COWDEN, RICHARD C.; DEABLER, HERDIS L.; AND FEAMSTER, J. HARRY. "The Prognostic Value of the Bender-Gestalt, H-T-P, TAT, and Sentence Completion Test." *J Clin Psychol* 11:271–5 Jl '55. * (*PA* 30:2864)

98. GOODSTEIN, LEONARD D.; SPIELBERGER, CHARLES D.; WILLIAMS, JOHN E.; AND DAHLSTROM, W. GRANT. "The Effects of Serial Position and Design Difficulty on Recall of the Bender-Gestalt Test Designs." *J Consult Psychol* 19:230–4 Je '55. * (*PA* 30:2880)

99. GREENBAUM, RICHARD S. "A Note on the Use of the Word Association Test as an Aid to Interpreting the Bender-Gestalt." *J Proj Tech* 19:27–9 Mr '55. * (*PA* 30:1027)

100. GUERTIN, WILSON H. "A Transposed Analysis of the Bender-Gestalts of Paranoid Schizophrenics." *J Clin Psychol* 11:73–6 Ja '55. * (*PA* 29:7649)

101. HALPIN, VIRGINIA G. "Rotation Errors Made by Brain-Injured and Familial Children on Two Visual-Motor Tests." *Am J Mental Def* 59:485–9 Ja '55. * (*PA* 29:7487)

102. KAMMAN, GORDON R., AND KRAM, CHARLES. "Value of Psychometric Examinations in Medical Diagnosis and Treatment." *J Am Med Assn* 158:555–60 Je 18 '55. * (*PA* 31:1044)

103. KELLER, JAMES E. "The Use of a Bender Gestalt Maturation Level Scoring System With Mentally Handicapped Children." Discussion by Winifred Ingram. *Am J Orthopsychiatry* 25:563–73 Jl '55. * (*PA* 30:4791)

104. KLEINMAN, BERNARD. *A Study of Factors Involved in the Reproduction of Bender Designs in Normal and Schizophrenic Subjects.* Doctor's thesis, University of Oklahoma (Norman, Okla.), 1955. (*DA* 15:2569)

105. LACHMANN, FRANK MICHAEL. *Perceptual-Motor Development in Children Retarded in Reading Ability.* Doctor's thesis, Northwestern University (Evanston, Ill.), 1955. (*DA* 15:1900)

106. McPHERSON, MARION WHITE, AND PEPIN, LORETTA A. "Consistency of Reproductions of Bender-Gestalt Designs." *J Clin Psychol* 11:163–6 Ap '55. * (*PA* 30:1040)

107. MARK, JOSEPH C., AND MORROW, ROBERT S. "The Use of the Bender-Gestalt Test in the Study of Brain Damage." Abstract. *Am Psychol* 10:323 Ag '55. *

108. PEEK, ROLAND M., AND OLSON, GORDON W. "The Bender-Gestalt Recall as an Index of Intellectual Functioning." *J Clin Psychol* 11:185–8 Ap '55. * (*PA* 30:1048)

109. ROSENTHAL, DAVID, AND IMBER, STANLEY D. "The Effects of Mephenesin and Practice on the Bender-Gestalt Performance of Psychiatric Outpatients." *J Clin Psychol* 11:90–2 Ja '55. * (*PA* 29:7314)

110. RUSSELL, IVAN LEE. *The Visual Motor Function as Related to Child Growth and Reading Development.* Doctor's thesis, University of Michigan (Ann Arbor, Mich.), 1955. (*DA* 15:532)

111. SONDER, SYLVIA L. "Perceptual Tests and Acute and Chronic Status as Predictors of Improvement in Psychotic Patients." *J Consult Psychol* 19:387–92 O '55. * (*PA* 30:6187)

112. TAYLOR, JAMES R., AND SCHENKE, LOWELL W. "The Bender Visual-Motor Gestalt Test as a Measure of Aggression in Children." *Proc Iowa Acad Sci* 62:426–32 '55. *

113. VATOVEC, EDWARD A. *A Validation Study of the Bender-Gestalt Test.* Master's thesis, Kent State University (Kent, Ohio), 1955.

114. WAXENBERG, SHELDON E. "Psychosomatic Patients and Other Physically Ill Persons: A Comparative Study." *J Consult Psychol* 19:163–9 Je '55. * (*PA* 30:3281)

115. WISSNER, FRED. *The Improvement of a Clinic Population Undergoing Psychotherapeutic Treatment: Pascal and Suttell's Quantification of the Bender-Visual Motor Gestalt Test as a Predictive Instrument in Psychotherapy.* Doctor's thesis, New York University (New York, N.Y.), 1955. (*DA* 15:1910)

116. BOWLAND, JOHN A., AND DEABLER, HERDIS L. "A Bender-Gestalt Diagnostic Validity Study." *J Clin Psychol* 12:82–4 Ja '56. * (*PA* 30:4554)

117. BYRD, EUGENE. "The Clinical Validity of the Bender Gestalt Test With Children: A Developmental Comparison of Children in Need of Psychotherapy and Children Judged Well-Adjusted." *J Proj Tech* 20:127–36 Je '56. * (*PA* 31:4673)

118. CRASILNECK, H. B., AND MILLER, CARMEN. "Performance on the Bender Under Hypnotic Age Regression." Abstract. *Am Psychol* 11:364 Ag '56. *

119. EVERETT, EVALYN G. *A Comparative Study of Paretics, Hebephrenics, and Paranoid Schizophrenics on a Battery of Psychological Tests.* Doctor's thesis, New York University (New York, N.Y.), 1956. (*DA* 16:1502)

120. INGLIS, J.; SHAPIRO, M. B.; AND POST, F. " 'Memory Function' in Psychiatric Patients Over Sixty, the Role of Memory in Tests Discriminating Between 'Functional' and 'Organic' Groups." *J Mental Sci* 102:589–98 Jl '56. * (*PA* 31:7926)

121. JACOBS, BEVERLY BLOM. *Study of Performances on the Bender-Gestalt for Possible Differentiation Between Brain-Damaged, Deaf, and Normal Children.* Master's thesis, Emory University (Emory University, Ga.), 1956.

122. KALDEGG, A. "Psychological Observations in a Group of Alcoholic Patients With Analysis of Rorschach, Wechsler-Bellevue and Bender Gestalt Test Results." *Q J Studies Alcohol* 17:608–28 D '56. * (*PA* 32:648)

123. MEHLMAN, BENJAMIN, AND VATOVEC, EDWARD. "A Validation Study of the Bender-Gestalt." *J Consult Psychol* 20:71–4 F '56. * (*PA* 31:3056)

124. MORTENSON, RODNEY H. *An Investigation of the Use of the Bender Gestalt Test as a Device for Screening Mentally Retarded Children.* Master's thesis, Claremont College (Claremont, Calif.), 1956.

125. MURRAY, EDWARD J., AND ROBERTS, FRANCIS J. "The Bender-Gestalt Test: In a Patient Passing Through a Brief Manic-Depressive Cycle." *US Armed Forces Med J* 7:1206–8 Ag '56. * (*PA* 31:3058)

126. POPPLESTONE, JOHN A. "Variability of the Bender Gestalt Designs." *Percept & Motor Skills* 6:269–71 D '56. * (*PA* 31:6118)

127. SCOTT, EDWARD M. "Regression or Disintegration in Schizophrenia?" *J Clin Psychol* 12:298–300 Jl '56. * (*PA* 31:6444)

128. SHAW, MERVILLE C., AND CRUICKSHANK, WILLIAM M. "The Use of the Bender-Gestalt Test With Epileptic Children." *J Clin Psychol* 12:192–3 Ap '56. * (*PA* 31:5037)

129. TOLOR, ALEXANDER. "A Comparison of the Bender-Gestalt Test and the Digit-Span Test as Measures of Recall." *J Consult Psychol* 20:305–9 Ag '56. * (*PA* 31:7979)

130. WINTER, WILLIAM D., AND FREDERICKSON, WILBUR K. "The Short-Term Effect of Chlorpromazine on Psychiatric Patients." *J Consult Psychol* 20:431–4 D '56. * (*PA* 32:1876)

131. AARONSON, BERNARD S. "The Porteus Mazes and Bender Gestalt Recall." *J Clin Psychol* 13:186–7 Ap '57. * (*PA* 32:2882)

132. BAROFF, GEORGE S. "Bender-Gestalt Visuo-Motor Function in Mental Deficiency." *Am J Mental Def* 61:753–60 Ap '57. * (*PA* 32:3038)

133. CLAWSON, AILEEN. *The Bender Visual Motor Gestalt Test as an Index of Emotional Disturbance in Children.* Doctor's thesis, University of Houston (Houston, Tex.), 1957.

134. CRASILNECK, HAROLD B., AND MICHAEL, CARMEN MILLER. "Performance on the Bender Under Hypnotic Age Regression." *J Abn & Social Psychol* 54:319–22 My '57. *

135. GOLDBERG, FRANKLIN H. "The Performance of Schizophrenic, Retarded, and Normal Children on the Bender-Gestalt Test." *Am J Mental Def* 61:548–55 Ja '57. * (*PA* 32:2894)

136. KEEHN, J. D. "Repeated Testing of Four Chronic Schizophrenics on the Bender-Gestalt and Wechsler Block Design Tests." *J Clin Psychol* 13:179–82 Ap '57. * (*PA* 32:3167)

137. NADLER, EUGENE B. "Prediction of the Sheltered Shop Work Performance of Individuals With Severe Physical Disability." *Personnel & Guid J* 36:95–8 O '57. *

138. OLIN, TOM D., AND REZNIKOFF, MARVIN. "Quantification of the Bender-Gestalt Recall: A Pilot Study." *J Proj Tech* 21:265–77 S '57. *

139. PARKER, JAMES W. "The Validity of Some Current Tests for Organicity." *J Consult Psychol* 21:425–8 O '57. *

140. QUAST, WENTWORTH. *Visual-Motor Performance in the Reproduction of Geometric Figures as a Developmental Phenomenon in Children.* Doctor's thesis, University of Minnesota (Minneapolis, Minn.), 1957.

141. REZNIKOFF, MARVIN, AND OLIN, TOM D. "Recall of the Bender-Gestalt Designs by Organic and Schizophrenic Patients: A Comparative Study." *J Clin Psychol* 13:183–6 Ap '57. * (*PA* 32:3189)

142. SHAPIRO, M. B.; FIELD, JACK; AND POST, F. "An Enquiry Into the Determinants of a Differentiation Between Elderly 'Organic' and 'Non-Organic' Psychiatric Patients on the Bender Gestalt Test." *J Mental Sci* 103:364–74 Ap '57. *

143. STEWART, HORACE F., JR. "A Note on Recall Patterns Using the Bender-Gestalt With Psychotic and Non-Psychotic Patients." *J Clin Psychol* 13:95–7 Ja '57. *

144. TAMKIN, ARTHUR S. "The Effectiveness of the Bender-Gestalt in Differential Diagnosis." *J Consult Psychol* 21:355–7 Ag '57. *

145. TOLOR, ALEXANDER. "Structural Properties of Bender-Gestalt Test Associations." *J Clin Psychol* 13:176–8 Ap '57. * (*PA* 32:2925)

146. TRIPP, CLARENCE A. *Some Graphomotor Features of the Bender Visual-Motor Gestalt Test in Relation to Delinquent and Non-Delinquent White Adolescent Males.* Doctor's thesis, New York University (New York, N.Y.), 1957. (*DA* 18:671)

147. VITANZA, ANGELO A. *A Comparative Study of Selected Psychological and Physiological Measures to Evaluate Psychiatric Conditions.* Doctor's thesis, New York University (New York, N.Y.), 1957. (*DA* 18:671–2)

148. WOHL, JULIAN. "A Note on the Generality of Constriction." *J Proj Tech* 21:410–3 D '57. *

149. EBER, MILTON. *A Bender Gestalt Validity Study: The Performance of Mentally Retarded Children.* Doctor's thesis, Florida State University (Tallahassee, Fla.), 1958. (*DA* 18:296)

150. HANNAH, LEWIS D. "Causative Factors in the Production of Rotations on the Bender-Gestalt Designs." *J Consult Psychol* 22:398–9 O '58. *

151. KOPPITZ, ELIZABETH MUNSTERBERG. "The Bender Gestalt Test and Learning Disturbances in Young Children." *J Clin Psychol* 14:292–5 Jl '58. *

152. KOPPITZ, ELIZABETH MUNSTERBERG. "Relationships Between the Bender Gestalt Test and the Wechsler Intelligence Test for Children." *J Clin Psychol* 14:413–6 O '58. *

153. OLIN, TOM D., AND REZNIKOFF, MARVIN. "A Compari-

son of Copied and Recalled Reproductions of the Bender-Gestalt Designs." *J Proj Tech* 22:320-7 S '58. *

154. PEEK, ROLAND M., AND STORMS, LOWELL H. "Judging Intellectual Status From the Bender-Gestalt Test." *J Clin Psychol* 14:296-9 Jl '58. *

155. SCHON, MARTHA, AND WAXENBERG, SHELDON E. "Effect of Hypophysectomy on Bender-Gestalt Test Performance." *J Clin Psychol* 14:299-302 Jl '58. *

156. STENNETT, R. G., AND UFFELMANN, RUTH. "The Bender Gestalt Test: Manner of Approach." *Can J Psychol* 12:184-6 S '58. *

157. STEWART, HORACE, AND CUNNINGHAM, SAM. "A Note on Scoring Recalled Figures of the Bender Gestalt Test Using Psychotics, Non-Psychotics and Controls." *J Clin Psychol* 14:207-8 Ap '58. *

158. TOLOR, ALEXANDER. "Further Studies on the Bender-Gestalt Test and the Digit-Span Test as Measures of Recall." *J Clin Psychol* 14:14-8 Ja '58. *

159. TUCKER, JOHN E., AND SPIELBERG, MIMI J. "Bender-Gestalt Test Correlates of Emotional Depression." Abstract. *J Consult Psychol* 22:56 F '58. *

160. ZOLIK, EDWIN S. "A Comparison of the Bender Gestalt Reproductions of Delinquents and Non-Delinquents." *J Clin Psychol* 14:24-6 Ja '58. *

For reviews by Arthur L. Benton and Howard R. White, see 4:144; for related reviews, see B330, 4:145, 3:109, and 40:B843.

PERSONALITY—SIXTH MMY

REVIEWS BY *C. J. Adcock, Lewis E. Albright, Anne Anastasi, Alexander W. Astin, Andrew R. Baggaley, Richard S. Barrett, Kenneth L. Bean, Wesley C. Becker, H. R. Beech, John Elderkin Bell, P. M. Bentler, Åke Bjerstedt, John D. Black, C. B. Blakemore, Harold Borko, Arthur H. Brayfield, Thomas C. Burgess, Alvin G. Burstein, Donald T. Campbell, Dugal Campbell, Joel T. Campbell, Dorothy M. Clendenen, Richard W. Coan, Bertram D. Cohen, Jacob Cohen, John O. Crites, Lee J. Cronbach, Douglas P. Crowne, W. Grant Dahlstrom, Richard H. Dana, Charles F. Dicken, Marvin D. Dunnette, Ralph D. Dutch, Allen L. Edwards, William J. Eichman, Leonard D. Eron, H. J. Eysenck, Paul R. Farnsworth, Seymour Fisher, Bertram R. Forer, Norman Frederiksen, Robert L. French, Eric F. Gardner, Cecil A. Gibb, James R. Glennon, Goldine C. Gleser, Leonard D. Goldstein, Harrison G. Gough, Wilson H. Guertin, Wallace B. Hall, Philip L. Harriman, Dale B. Harris, Jesse G. Harris, Jr., J. Thomas Hastings, Richard S. Hatch, Mary R. Haworth, Alfred B. Heilbrun, Jr., William H. Helme, John K. Hemphill, Marshall S. Hiskey, John D. Hundleby, Arthur R. Jensen, Walter Katkovsky, E. Lowell Kelly, Philip M. Kitay, Paul M. Kjeldergaard, Benjamin Kleinmuntz, Milton V. Kline, Wilbur L. Layton, S. G. Lee, Eugene E. Levitt, John Liggett, James C. Lingoes, Maurice Lorr, David T. Lykken, Boyd R. McCandless, Winton H. Manning, Gerald A. Mendelsohn, T. R. Miles, Terence Moore, G. A. V. Morgan, C. Scott Moss, Allyn Miles Munger, Bernard I. Murstein, Theodor F. Naumann, Robert C. Nichols, Warren F. Norman, David B. Orr, Jerome D. Pauker, R. W. Payne, Donald R. Peterson, John Pierce-Jones, M. L. Kellmer Pringle, John A. Radcliffe, Ralph M. Reitan, Alan O. Ross, John W. M. Rothney, Floyd L. Ruch, H. Bradley Sagen, Bert R. Sappenfield, Irwin G. Sarason, Johann M. Schepers, William Schofield, Stanley J. Segal, S. B. Sells, Boris Semeonoff, Laurance F. Shaffer, Otfried Spreen, William Stephenson, Lawrence J. Stricker, Norman D. Sundberg, William N. Thetford, Robert L. Thorndike, Leona E. Tyler, Forrest L. Vance, Donald J. Veldman, Philip E. Vernon, Norman E. Wallen, John G. Watkins, Harold Webster, Henry Weitz, George Westby, Jerry S. Wiggins, J. Robert Williams, and Robert D. Wirt.*

NONPROJECTIVE

[57]

A-S Reaction Study: A Scale for Measuring Ascendance-Submission in Personality. College and adults; 1928–39; separate forms (8 pages) for men ('28), women ('39); manual, second edition ('39, 16 pages); $3.40 per 35 tests; 60¢ per complete specimen set; postage extra; (20) minutes; Gordon W. Allport and Floyd H. Allport; Houghton Mifflin Co. *

REFERENCES

1–19. See 40:1198.
20–30. See 3:23.
31–45. See 5:28.
46. READER, NATALIE, AND ENGLISH, HORACE B. "Personality Factors in Adolescent Female Friendships." *J Consult Psychol* 11:212–20 Jl–Ag '47. * (*PA* 22:261)
47. SKIFF, STANLEY CUBE. *A Study of Some Relationships Between Personality Traits and Learning Ability.* Doctor's thesis, University of Kentucky (Lexington, Ky.), 1950. (*DA* 20:3861)
48. RAY-CHOWDHURY, K., AND GANDHI, J. S. "Allport's Ascendance-Submission Reaction Study in Indian Situation: II, Ascendance-Submission Trait Difference Among Three Groups of Women Chosen on the Basis of Three Different Provinces They Belong To." *Indian Psychol B* 3:22–3 Ja '58. * (*PA* 33:9983)
49. RAY-CHOWDHURY, K., AND HUNDAL, PIARA SINGH. "Allport's Ascendance-Submission Reaction Study of Indian Situation: I, Ascendance-Submission Trait Difference Among Three Groups of Men Chosen on the Basis of Three Different Provinces They Belong To." *Indian Psychol B* 3:11–22 Ja '58. * (*PA* 33:9984)
50. FLANAGAN, J. J., JR., AND HERR, V. V. "Ascendance-Submission and the Psychogalvanic Response to Mild Stress." *Psychol Rep* 5:289–92 Je '59. * (*PA* 34:2760)
51. MANN, RICHARD D. "A Review of the Relationships Between Personality and Performance in Small Groups." *Psychol B* 56:241–70 Jl '59. * (*PA* 34:4194)
52. BRONZAFT, A.; HAYES, R.; WELCH, L.; AND KOLTUV, M. "Relationships Between Extraversion, Neuroticism, and Ascendance." *J Psychol* 50:279–85 O '60. * (*PA* 35:6475)
53. BRONZAFT, ARLINE; HAYES, ROSLYN; WELCH, LIVINGSTON; AND KOLTUV, MYRON. "Relationship Between PGR and Measures of Extraversion, Ascendance, and Neuroticism." *J Psychol* 50:193–5 O '60. * (*PA* 35:6522)
54. PARAMESWARAN, E. G., AND OLIVER, A. G. "An Ascendance-Submission Inventory for Use With Adolescents (A Preliminary Investigation)." *Indian J Psychol* 36:149–54 D '61. * (*PA* 37:6684)
55. BROWER, JULIAN LEWIS. *Patient-Personnel Interpersonal Choice on a State Mental Hospital Ward.* Doctor's thesis, University of Buffalo (Buffalo, N.Y.), 1962. (*DA* 23:2982)
56. PARAMESWARAN, E. G., AND SUNDARAM, K. "Item Validity of the A. S. Reaction Test for Use With Adolescent." *Indian J Psychol* 37:107–14 S '62. * (*PA* 38:8430)

WARREN T. NORMAN, *Associate Professor of Psychology, The University of Michigan, Ann Arbor, Michigan.*

The principal criticism one can make of this device is that no effort has been made by the authors and publisher in the past 25 years to bring the item content and psychometric characteristics of the test up to date. With regard to item content, the situations are biased, as they always have been, toward college environs and some are described in what would be considered today rather stilted language even by persons with college experience.

But more crucial to the user is the second matter which includes the absence of current data on such things as norms based on pertinent subpopulations, validities against independent external criteria, relationships to other closely related, as well as presumably unrelated, dimensions, and the ability of respondents to fake or "slant" responses in one or another direction. The test has been used extensively in the last two decades and much of the information required to modernize the manual and the test is readily available in scattered published sources. A carefully executed normative study employing an appropriately stratified sampling scheme would go a long way to augment these numerous but more limited and diverse research findings.

On the positive side, the test has done yeoman service in research investigations of personality functioning and development. Strangely enough, however, it seems to have been particularly unsuccessful in certain social psychological applications where it would seem to be most relevant. For example, in the identification of leaders in small groups both the Ascendance scale of the *Guilford-Zimmerman Temperament Survey* and the Dominance scale of Cattell's *Sixteen Personality Factor Questionnaire* have yielded positive results whereas the *A-S Reaction Study* has not (*51*). Nor has the general concept of dominance or ascendance, however measured, been found to relate as one might expect to other aspects of performance in small groups, except possibly to conforming behavior and to task activity.

In a more positive vein, scores on the test have been found (*a*) to distinguish between grossly dissimilar occupational groups that one would expect to differ on ascendance-submission, (*b*) to be unrelated to measured intelligence, and (*c*) to be slightly to moderately correlated with educational achievement and neuroticism (both negatively) and with extroversion and persistence (both positively). Reliabilities between .85 and .96 have been reported for the two forms of this test. But, as noted earlier, all of these results are based on research done over 25 years ago and the operating characteristics of this device may well have changed in the interim.

In brief, as a short, crude device for assessing a major dimension (or related cluster of traits), the *A-S Reaction Study* has filled an important need in personality and social psychological research during the last three and one half decades, though with limited success. But it is time at least to recalibrate this instrument or preferably to completely rebuild it if it is to be of continued service. Alternatively,

it might be better simply to withdraw it from the market in deference to other devices more recently standardized—especially some of the multivariate instruments that provide, simultaneously, comparable standard scores on several relatively independent attributes of each respondent. The day when much can be learned from measures on only one or a few attributes of a person has passed. In the more sophisticated and complex research being done today in the areas of personality and social phenomena, multivariate instruments, standardized on a single (though carefully stratified) normative sample, are to be preferred to patchwork batteries of simpler devices with their separate and idiosyncratic bases of interpretation.

For a review by William U. Snyder, see 3:23; for a review by Doncaster G. Humm of the 1928 edition, see 40:1198; for a review by Doncaster G. Humm of an out of print revision for business use, see 40:1199.

[58]

*Activity Vector Analysis. Ages 16 and over; 1948-63; test booklet title is *Placement Analysis;* personality characteristics related to job success; 6 scores: aggressiveness, sociability, emotional adjustment, social adaptability, intelligent behavior, activity level; Forms A ('62, c1945-62), B ('62), C ('62), (3 pages); general information ('62, 15 pages); manual ('63, 43 looseleaf pages); directions for administering ['62, 1 page]; directions for scoring ['62, 1 page]; manual of correlation tables ('58, 161 looseleaf pages); profile ('62, 1 page) for each form; looseleaf Manual for Job Activity Rating includes separately copyrighted sections on job analysis ('56, 26 pages) and Jarsort procedure of job profile determination ('62, 9 pages), illustrative job analysis form ['56, 7 pages], 10 blank Jarsort profiles ('60, 2 pages), and 10 Jarsort correlation forms ('60, 2 pages); Jarsort cards ('60, 60 cards); distribution restricted to persons who have completed a training course offered by the publisher; quotations on course fee available on request; test materials must be purchased separately; postage extra; French and Spanish editions available; (5-10) minutes; Walter V. Clarke Associates, Inc.; AVA Publications, Inc. *

REFERENCES

1-11. See 5:29.
12. FARRINGTON, ALLEN D. "Validity Information Exchange, No. 11-29: D.O.T. Code 8-19.01, Laborer, Process (Textile)." *Personnel Psychol* 11:586 w '58. *
13. HAMMER, CHARLES HOWARD. *A Validation Study of the Activity Vector Analysis.* Doctor's thesis, Purdue University (Lafayette, Ind.), 1958. (*DA* 19:1108)
14. MERENDA, PETER F., AND CLARKE, WALTER V. "AVA Validity for Textile Workers." *J Appl Psychol* 43:162-5 Je '59. * (*PA* 34:6653)
15. MERENDA, PETER F., AND CLARKE, WALTER V. "Activity Vector Analysis Validity for Life Insurance Salesmen." *Eng & Ind Psychol* 1:1-11 sp '59. * (*PA* 34:4884)
16. MERENDA, PETER F., AND CLARKE, WALTER V. "Factor Analysis of a Measure of 'Social Self.'" *Psychol Rep* 5:597-605 D '59. * (*PA* 34:5021)
17. MERENDA, PETER F., AND CLARKE, WALTER V. "A Further Note on Self-Perceptions of Management Personnel and Line Workers." *Eng & Ind Psychol* 1:49-54 su '59. * (*PA* 35:5398)

18. MERENDA, PETER F., AND CLARKE, WALTER V. "Personality Profiles of Self-Made Company Presidents—A Second Look." *Eng & Ind Psychol* 1:95-101 au '59. * *(PA* 35:1353)

19. MERENDA, PETER F., AND CLARKE, WALTER V. "The Predictive Efficiency of Temperament Characteristics and Personal History Variables in Determining Success of Life Insurance Agents." *J Appl Psychol* 43:360-6 D '59. * *(PA* 34:8503)

20. MERENDA, PETER F., AND CLARKE, WALTER V. "Test-Retest Reliability of Activity Vector Analysis." *Psychol Rep* 5:27-30 Mr '59. * *(PA* 34:150)

21. MERENDA, PETER F.; FARRINGTON, ALLEN D.; AND CLARKE, WALTER V. "Prediction of Performance of Textile Workers." *Eng & Ind Psychol* 1:120-7 w '59. * *(PA* 35: 4064)

22. MERENDA, PETER F., AND CLARKE, WALTER V. "Multiple Inferential Selves of Male and Female College Students." *J Psychol Studies* 11:206-12 My-Je '60. * *(PA* 34:7408)

23. MERENDA, PETER F.; CLARKE, WALTER V.; AND KESSLER, SYDNEY. "AVA and the Kessler PD Scale as Measures of Passive-Dependency." *J Clin Psychol* 16:338-41 Jl '60. * *(PA* 36:2HF38M)

24. MERENDA, PETER F.; MUSIKER, HAROLD R.; AND CLARKE, WALTER V. "Relation of the Self-Concept to Success in Sales Management." *Eng & Ind Psychol* 2:69-77 su '60. * *(PA* 37:2052)

25. MERENDA, PETER F., AND CLARKE, WALTER V. "Influence of College Experience on the Self-Concepts of Young Male Job Applicants." *J Psychol Studies* 12:49-60 Mr '61. *

26. MERENDA, PETER F.; CLARKE, WALTER V.; AND HALL, CHARLES E. "Cross-Validity of Procedures for Selecting Life Insurance Salesmen." *J Appl Psychol* 45:376-80 D '61. * *(PA* 37:2053)

27. MERENDA, PETER F.; CLARKE, WALTER V.; MUSIKER, HAROLD R.; AND KESSLER, SYDNEY. "AVA and KPDS as Construct Validity Coordinates." *J Psychol Studies* 13:35-42 Ja '61. *

28. DUNNETTE, MARVIN D., AND KIRCHNER, WAYNE K. "Validities, Vectors, and Verities." *J Appl Psychol* 46:296-9 Ag '62. * *(PA* 37:3088, title only)

29. LOCKE, EDWIN A., AND HULIN, CHARLES L. "A Review and Evaluation of the Validity Studies of Activity Vector Analysis." *Personnel Psychol* 15:25-42 sp '62. * *(PA* 37:3114)

30. MERENDA, PETER F., AND CLARKE, WALTER V. "Rejoinder to 'Validities, Vectors, and Verities' by Marvin D. Dunnette and Wayne K. Kirchner." *J Appl Psychol* 46:300-2 Ag '62. * *(PA* 37:3092)

31. MERENDA, PETER F., AND CLARKE, WALTER V. "Comparison of Concepts of Multiple Inferential Selves Between Clinical Psychologists and School Guidance Counselors." *J Clin Psychol* 19:355-9 Jl '63. *

32. MERENDA, PETER F., AND CLARKE, WALTER V. "Forced-Choice vs. Free-Response in Personality Assessment." *Psychol Rep* 13:159-69 Ag '63. * *(PA* 38:6089)

LEWIS E. ALBRIGHT, *Assistant Director, Employee Relations Research, Standard Oil Company (Indiana), Chicago, Illinois.*

The *Activity Vector Analysis* (AVA) is a self-report adjective checklist used to measure several aspects of personality. The test was designed for use in business and industry. The subject first checks those adjectives which he believes anyone has ever used in describing him, then marks the list again to indicate the words which he feels are truly descriptive of himself. There is no time limit. Three forms of the test now exist. Revised Form A has 81 items; new Forms B and C each have 84 items.

The rationale on which the AVA is based is that all behavior can be described in terms of Aggressiveness, Sociability, Emotional Adjustment, and Social Adaptability. The test is scored on these four scales (vectors) plus "Activity Level" (total number of words checked). These dimensions were isolated initially by means of a cluster analysis of the 81 words and later verified by factor analysis. De-

spite these statistical niceties, can anyone seriously believe that only four factors (or vectors) are sufficient to account for *all* human behavior? Apparently even the test author is dubious since he has identified a fifth vector, named "social intelligence," which consists of words found to discriminate high and low scorers on an Otis test of mental ability. It is not clear, however, to what extent this vector is used in the interpretation of the test profile.

The manual states that in constructing the original 81-word AVA form, all derogatory words were eliminated. Remaining, however, are terms such as "scaridy cat," "argumentative," and "conformist" which can hardly be considered flattering and are certainly less desirable than other words in the same list such as "pleasant," "decisive," and "admirable." In short, there could still be great differences in social desirability of the words which could be contaminating whatever is being measured.

Reliability of the AVA is given in three ways for each vector: split-half, test-retest, and parallel forms. The split-half coefficients have been stepped up by the Spearman-Brown formula and are all in the 90's. The test-retest reliabilities range from .62 for Vector 3 to .75 for Activity Level (mean retest interval was one year). These coefficients suggest that the test has only a fair degree of stability over time. The parallel forms coefficients (given only for the new Forms B and C) look satisfactory until one realizes that these are, in fact, not parallel forms, but variations of the same form because many of the same words are used on both. This reviewer counted at least 30 words common to *all three forms*. The overlap of each pair of forms is even greater; therefore, if the parallel forms coefficients were computed without removal of the common elements (as appears to be the case), these values are spurious and misleading.

The manual includes no norms whatever—a gross omission in view of the fact that the test has been given to hundreds of thousands of people in industry. (It should be mentioned, however, that standard scores are provided on profile cards for each form, but their usefulness is limited due to the fact that only Certified AVA Analysts may interpret the instrument.) Similarly, nothing is said about the possible fakability of this instrument. The entire validity issue is handled by referring the reader to an annotated bibliography of both published and unpublished investigations, mostly conducted by Walter V. Clarke, the author and publisher, and his associates. After a thorough examination of the published articles, this reviewer agrees with Locke and Hulin (*29*), who concluded in their critique of these same studies that "AVA has failed to demonstrate any practical utility as a *selection device* in industry. Nearly all the studies involved incorrect validation procedures....or erroneous interpretation of the actual data. In the only study in which there was both correct procedure and a sufficiently large N, the authors reported inconclusive results." It should be noted that Locke and Hulin were concerned primarily with the ability of the AVA, given at the time of hiring, to predict subsequent job performance (predictive validity). The instrument has, on occasion, shown some degree of concurrent validity (discrimination of presently employed workers—either in different occupational groups or more and less effective workers in the same occupational group). This feature might make the AVA useful as a counseling or placement tool rather than a selection device. Clarke and associates could make a contribution here by using their vast store of data to show us with which groups and under what circumstances the AVA can discriminate.

Accompanying the AVA is a card sorting method, called the JARsort procedure, for analyzing jobs in terms of AVA test profiles. Apparently, the user is to find the AVA pattern required by the *job,* then search for candidates whose AVA test scores match this pattern. An instruction manual, 60 cards, and a box for sorting the cards constitute the materials necessary for the JARsort analysis. The manual, called Manual for Job Activity Rating, describes the Job Activity Analysis method of job description based on observation and the SKILLsort card sort procedure (related to the publisher's *Measurement of Skill* battery) in addition to the JARsort procedure. Each JARsort card contains a statement describing a job element, for example, "Requires answering the telephone." The cards are to be sorted into a forced normal distribution of seven piles according to the importance of each element to the job in question. By some method not described, an AVA pattern shape has been determined for each card. The analyst computes an overall Universe Pattern Shape using the 20 most important job elements resulting from the

sorting process. No data are presented to support the implied relationship of pattern shape to job success. It is claimed that with the JAR approach "one may rate and directly compare all jobs in both shop and office, from sweeper to president." Again no evidence is given to justify this claim; in this reviewer's opinion, many of the statements are so vague and general that they might indeed apply to all jobs and therefore be of no value for differentiating one job from another.

To summarize, the questionable reliability and validity data for the AVA make it unsuitable at present as a selection device in industry. It may have some use as a counseling or placement aid, but even here more evidence is needed before it could be recommended. With perhaps half a million or more AVA's given in industry to date, the authors must be in possession of all the information necessary to provide a conclusive test of the instrument if they would do so. If not, they may soon be able to construct a fourth test form—composed of derogatory terms used by reviewers in describing the AVA!

ALEXANDER W. ASTIN, *Director of Research, American Council on Education, Washington, D.C.*

Because of the unusual terminology associated with the *Activity Vector Analysis,* one needs to keep in mind just what the test is: a checklist of 81 adjectives (e.g., "persuasive," "timid," "tactful") which can be scored on four personality scales ("Vectors" 1–4). The scoring keys for the four scales were developed by internal consistency procedures: factor analyses and cluster analyses of item intercorrelations. These four scores provide the main basis for interpretation of the AVA profile, although two other scores are also available: V-5 (initially obtained by an item analysis against an Otis mental ability test) and the total number of adjectives checked ("Activity Level"). The subject is first asked to check those adjectives which have "ever been used by anyone in describing you." Using an identical list, he then checks each adjective "which you honestly believe is descriptive of you." The six AVA scores (Vectors 1–5 and Activity Level) can be obtained separately for the first list ("Column 1"), for the second list ("Column 2"), and for the sum of the two ("Resultant"). According to the manual, the AVA is a "measuring device for determining the probable behavior of a normal individual in a given job situation." In a brochure distributed by the publisher, it is stated that the AVA enables the executive to make more accurate predictions about the consequences of hiring, placing, or promoting a given employee, and also gives him "valuable insight into the best methods of supervising his workers."

AVA, however, is not merely a personality inventory to be purchased and used by the trained industrial psychologist or personnel manager. The publisher states that any person who desires to interpret the AVA must first take a course (length varies but the cost of a two-week course may be as much as $975) in order to qualify as a "Certified Analyst." Interpretation of AVA profiles by anyone other than a Certified Analyst may result in "irreparable harm to the person concerned." In addition to training in interpretation of AVA profiles, this course includes training in a method of job analysis called the Job Activity Rating (JAR). The publisher provides a deck of Q-sort cards describing different job requirements, and a cardboard device containing seven bins labeled "least important" to "most important." The cards are to be sorted into a forced normal distribution in terms of their relative importance to the job in question. These "JARsorts" yield a profile of personality traits for the job which are to be compared with the worker's AVA test profile. A basic assumption in AVA analysis appears to be that the probability of job success is a direct function of the degree of congruence between the person's AVA profile and the JAR profile for the job.

The publisher also provides a supplementary booklet of AVA Correlation Tables which show correlations between every possible AVA and JAR profile. The analyst can also obtain a visual comparison between a given JAR profile and several AVA profiles at one time by using the "distribution" chart or one of the "polar tabulation" charts from the "AVA Pattern Universe." In the introductory section of this booklet the author presents his view that the pattern of AVA scores indicates the probable "directions" of a person's behavior. No supporting evidence for this assumption is actually presented.

The plastic hand scoring stencil included in the test materials is cleverly designed and appears to be convenient for scoring a few tests at a time. The likelihood of scoring error might be greatly increased, though, if a large number of tests are scored at one sitting, since the stencil's differently colored markings for the different scales require a continuous change of set on the part of the scorer.

The AVA manual appears to be deficient in several respects. For example, practically no information is presented on the meanings of the four scores (Vectors 1–4) except for the statement that the adjective clusters in an early version of the test "were suggestive of aggressive, sociable, stable, and avoidant behavior." The meanings of the Vector 5 and Activity Level scores are even more obscure. Corrected split-half reliabilities of an earlier form of the test are high, ranging from .92 to .97; retest coefficients over a one-year interval range from .62 to .75. No retest reliability data are given for current forms of the test.

It is difficult to determine from the manual just how the alternate forms (A, B, and C) of the AVA were derived. There is a considerable amount of item overlap among all three forms. One puzzling feature is that the same adjectives are often keyed differently in the different forms. A comparison of the hand scoring stencils revealed at least 15 discrepancies between Forms A and C in the scoring of identical items, 11 discrepancies in scoring between Forms A and B, and 3 discrepancies in scoring between Forms B and C.

These facts make it difficult to interpret the correlations between alternate Forms B and C given in Tables 4–6 of the manual. The high degree of item overlap would tend to inflate the correlations, but the discrepancies in scoring would serve to attenuate them. Some of the correlations between parallel scales in Forms B and C are, in fact, not significantly higher than correlations between certain nonparallel scales. Correlations of Forms B and C with Form A (which was involved in most of the scoring inconsistencies) are not given in the manual.

The last section of the AVA manual contains an annotated bibliography of studies, apparently as a substitute for a section on validity. Abstracts of the studies are vague and give the reader little information about either the construct validity of the scales or the potential usefulness of the AVA in practice. Quantitative results are often omitted and replaced by phrases such as "positive evidence of predictive validity," "statistically significant discriminant functions," or "substantially correct classifications."

This published research actually provides very little evidence on the validity of the AVA when used in the manner proposed by the publisher, i.e., when clinical predictions of job success are made by trained AVA analysts. In one study (*14, 21*), a single trained analyst was able to predict job performance of textile workers significantly better than chance. However, in a large scale selection study of life insurance salesmen (*7*), clinical predictions of job success made by AVA analysts were of no value. Interestingly enough, the AVA appears to have some validity for selecting life insurance salesmen when used actuarially (*19, 26*), although this finding does not seem to have persuaded the publisher to begin training his Analysts in the procedures of empirical test validation.

The author's attempt to develop objective methods for comparing worker traits (AVA) with job requirements (JAR) is commendable. What he has yet failed to do is to show that the two types of profiles are in fact comparable and useful in practice. It seems likely that the four factored AVA scales are not too different in meaning from some of the scales on other personality instruments which have been developed by internal analyses of item responses (e.g., the *Sixteen Personality Factor Questionnaire, Edwards Personal Preference Schedule,* and the *Guilford-Zimmerman Temperament Survey*). The AVA differs from these instruments, however, in that its publisher has made more extravagant claims for its validity in practical situations and has set down a rigid and costly set of conditions for its use. Under these circumstances, the potential user would seem justified in expecting much more evidence on validity than is presently available.

WINTON H. MANNING, *Associate Professor of Psychology, Texas Christian University, Fort Worth, Texas.*

The AVA is a controversial test which has, especially in the last two or three years, provoked considerable discussion among psychologists and others concerned with research in personnel selection and industrial psychology. Part of the controversy centers about the test itself, but the principal focus of criticism has been on the claims for validity made by the test developer and the relationship of these claims to alleged defects in experimental designs, and to the manner in which results have been statistically treated and discussed.

In previous reviews in *The Fifth Yearbook* and in critiques by others (*28, 29*) a number of characteristics of the research on the AVA reported by the test publisher and his associates have been identified. These include such criticisms as: (*a*) failure to distinguish between predictive and concurrent validity, (*b*) absence of concern about or failure to report when and under what conditions the AVA had been administered to subjects, (*c*) failure to provide cross validation before entering claims of predictive validity, (*d*) erroneous interpretations of data, (*e*) emphasis upon statistical significance when overlap between distributions is large, (*f*) tendency to equate statistical significance *per se* with practical validity, (*g*) failure to report procedures in sufficient detail to permit replication by other disinterested experimenters, (*h*) presentation of research in a style of reporting evidently designed less to inform than to overwhelm the naïve reader, and (*i*) the adoption of such trappings as titles for test administrators and gaudy names for accessory materials entirely inconsistent with conservative scientific practice.

After studying over two dozen articles concerned with the AVA this reviewer concluded that, sadly, these criticisms were in every instance amply supported.

A review of all the studies published on the AVA since 1959 is not warranted because the latter studies conform rather highly to the unfortunate pattern described above. Of particular interest, however, has been the question of cross validation, and hence, some discussion should be directed to two recent articles by Merenda and Clarke (*19*) and Merenda, Clarke, and Hall (*26*). It should be noted at the outset that only one adequately designed study involving cross validation of *predictive* validity of the AVA has been performed. This study (*7*) found that for selection of life insurance salesmen the AVA had no validity.

In the first of the above mentioned articles Merenda and Clarke report the results of a study of the efficacy of four AVA variables and five personal history variables in discriminating between 108 successful and 414 unsuccessful life insurance salesmen. It should be pointed out that this involved a follow-up of 522 subjects who had at least three years earlier been tested at the time of hiring, and that at that time the general agents, who evaluated the applicants, made use of the AVA in deciding whether to hire or not to hire the applicant. Further, the authors state that the general agents placed greater reliance on the AVA profiles than upon the personal history variables for the reason that "an integrated personality profile determined to be 'best' for life insurance salesmen was being used by the company....whereas no such profile was determined for the personal history variables." The authors note that this condition would serve to restrict the range of their AVA variables more than the personal history variables. They fail to consider the possibility that the decision to *fire or terminate* an "unsuccessful" employee might also be influenced by the AVA profile which evidently counted so heavily in the general agents' decisions as to whether or not to hire. An unsuccessful agent is defined as one who fails to reach production goals, has his contract terminated, or leaves the company within a three year period. Thus, it would seem that we are in the dark as to the extent to which the criterion of success or failure may or may not be contaminated. Nevertheless, a conclusion is ultimately reached by the authors that the AVA has validity, for the discriminant function is significant at the .001 level. This is accomplished despite the fact that, as reported by Dunnette and Kirchner (*28*), the multiple correlation is only .21, and that, at a minimum, 85 per cent of scores of successful salesmen are duplicated by unsuccessful salesmen. It would seem justified to point out the well known fact that a "significant" result may not always be a "salient" result.

Following this first study Merenda, Clarke, and Hall (*26*) report a cross validation of the discriminant function developed earlier. Although it is not mentioned, we assume that in this study of 535 agents the same conditions regarding administration of tests, comparison with a determined *"best"* profile, and the consequent influence of these factors on the general agents' decisions to hire (and perhaps to fire!) prevailed. The results showed, of course, some shrinkage. Using a phi coefficient as an indicator of predictive efficiency, the reviewer calculates a correlation in the validation sample of

.11 between the dichotomized linear composite and the success-failure criterion. An analogous correlation of .09 would obtain in the cross validation sample. Of course, these are somewhat lower than would be found if the linear composite were treated continuously. It seems, in sum, however, that with the possibility of criterion contamination present and the low correlations which exist, there is little ground for concluding on the basis of this study that the AVA is a valid predictor of success as a life insurance agent.

Exhaustive discussion of the other studies seems pointless to the reviewer. It would be a dreary task to set it down on paper, and an even drearier one to read it. Also, no amplification is needed concerning Bennett's cogent remarks (see 5:29) on the precarious superstructure of mathematical hocus-pocus which surrounds the calculation of vector scores and profile indices. Unfortunately, the AVA is not alone guilty in this respect, for personality assessment instruments have many times exhibited a functional independence between scoring procedures and adequacy of observational foundations. In reflecting upon the evident enthusiastic adoption of the AVA by some naive test givers, the story of St. Denis comes irresistibly to mind. As I recall, the martyred saint was observed to be stalking the streets of Paris carrying his severed head in his hands. When implored by an astonished passerby how he was able to do such a bewildering thing, the good saint is said to have replied, "It is only the first step which is difficult." To a dispassionate reader of the AVA literature, the meaning is obvious.

For reviews by Brent Baxter and George K. Bennett, see 5:29.

[59]

*The Adjustment Inventory. Grades 9–16, adults; 1934–63; IBM; 1 form; 2 levels; postage extra; specimen set not available; (20–30) minutes; Hugh M. Bell; Consulting Psychologists Press, Inc. *
a) REVISED STUDENT FORM, RESEARCH EDITION (1962). Grades 9–16; 1934–63; 6 scores: home, health, submissiveness, emotionality, hostility, masculinity; 1 form ('62, 4 pages); manual ('63, c1962, 27 pages); profile ('62, 2 pages); separate answer sheets must be used; $3.25 per 50 tests; $3.75 per 50 IBM answer sheets; $2 per set of hand or machine scoring stencils; $1.25 per manual.
b) ADULT FORM. Adults; 1938–39; 6 scores: home, occupational, health, social, emotional, total; 1 form ('38, 4 pages); manual ['38, 4 pages]; $3 per 25 tests; separate answer sheets may be used; $2.20 per 50

IBM answer sheets; 50¢ per set of hand scoring stencil and manual; $1.75 per machine scoring stencil.
c) [ORIGINAL] STUDENT FORM. Grades 9–16; 1934–39; 5 scores: home, health, social, emotional, total; 2 editions; manual ['34, 4 pages]; tentative norms.

1) [*Regular Edition.*] 1934–39; 1 form ('34, 4 pages); $3 per 25 tests; separate answer sheets may be used; $2.20 per 50 IBM answer sheets; 50¢ per set of hand scoring stencil and manual; $1.75 per set of machine scoring stencils.

2) [*IBM Test-Answer Sheet Edition.*] 1939; $3.75 per 50 tests; $2.50 per set of machine scoring stencils.

REFERENCES

1–15. See 40:1200.
16–119. See 4:28.
120–145. See 5:30.
146. SCHOLL, GERALDINE. "Some Notes on the Use of Two Personality Tests With Visually Handicapped Students." *New Outlook Blind* 47:287–95 D '53. *
147. HOLMES, JACK A. "Factors Underlying Major Reading Disabilities at the College Level." *Genetic Psychol Monogr* 49:3–95 F '54. * (*PA* 28:8982)
148. RISHER, CHARITY CONRAD. *Some Characteristics Which Differentiate Between Academically Successful and Unsuccessful College Business Students.* Doctor's thesis, University of Missouri (Columbia, Mo.), 1958. (*DA* 19:2006)
149. MATHUR, KRISHNA. "Relationship of Socio-Economic Status to Personality Adjustment Among the High School Boys and Girls at Aligarh." *Indian Psychol B* 4:30–1 Ja '59. *
150. STRUNK, ORLO, JR. "Interest and Personality Patterns of Preministerial Students." *Psychol Rep* 5:740 D '59. * (*PA* 34:5635)
151. WINTHROP, HENRY. "Self-Images of Personal Adjustment vs. the Estimates of Friends." *J Social Psychol* 50:87–99 Ag '59. * (*PA* 35:3516)
152. DANA, RICHARD H., AND BAKER, DAVID H. "High School Achievement and the Bell Adjustment Inventory." *Psychol Rep* 8:353–6 Ap '61. * (*PA* 36:1KL53D)
153. DAS, RHEA S. "Validity Information Exchange, No. 14-05: D.O.T. Code 2–66.01, Police Lieutenant." *Personnel Psychol* 14:459–61 w '61. *
154. DEAN, DWIGHT G. "Romanticism and Emotional Maturity: A Preliminary Study." *Marriage & Family Living* 23:44–5 F '61. * (*PA* 36:3HF44D)
155. LOCKWOOD, DORIS H., AND GUERNEY, BERNARD, JR. "Identification and Empathy in Relation to Self-Dissatisfaction and Adjustment." *J Abn & Social Psychol* 65:343–7 N '62. *
156. VORREYER, WARREN J. "Relationship of Selected Adjustment Factors, College Ability, and Achievement to Dropouts and Nondrop-Outs of College Freshmen." *J Ed Res* 56:362–5 Mr '63. *

FORREST L. VANCE, *Administrative Officer, American Psychological Association, Washington, D.C.* [Review of Revised Student Form.]

This revision of the Bell *Adjustment Inventory* provides a total face lifting for this venerable member of the first generation of objectively scored personality questionnaires. The manual provides extensive theoretical discussion and devotes considerable space to interpretive guidelines, features that are in happy contrast to the perfunctory, sink-or-swim introductory materials provided with many devices.

The inventory proper consists of 200 questions to be answered by a "yes," "no," or "?," as on earlier forms. New items have been added, however, and scores are now obtained on scales labeled "hostility" and "masculinity-femininity" as well as the four variables pres-

ent in the original (1934) edition. In the construction of these new scales, Bell's strategy continues to be a three stage sequence: (*a*) writing items that seem appropriate; (*b*) eliminating items that fail to correlate with the scale as a whole; and (*c*) validating the surviving scale against external criteria (expert ratings, similar scales, life history data). This results in an instrument that yields scores that reflect an individual's subjective impression of his own adjustment in areas determined by the author, *plus* an element of predictive information concerning the probable nature of independent evaluations of his adjustment in these same areas.

Data in the manual indicate that the Bell differentiates very well between groups judgmentally identified as high and low on the dimensions named in the individual scales. No information is given concerning amount of overlap between the high and low distributions, but values of *t* for six validation studies (one for each of the six scales) have a median of approximately 6.0, with a range of 2.7 to 32.6, the latter for 316 men versus 347 women on masculinity-femininity. Aside from the masculinity-femininity study, the degrees of freedom associated with these *t* values range from 39 to 100, making it evident that very wide differences are involved.

Concurrent validity is demonstrated by correlations between the Bell and other inventories. Except for masculinity-femininity, the relationships presented in the manual are astonishingly high. For some reason, Bell masculinity-femininity scores correlate only .13 for men and .38 for women with MF scores on the *Minnesota Multiphasic Personality Inventory.* The remaining relationships range from .72, between Bell submissiveness and Allport ascendance-submission, to an astronomical .93 between Bell emotionality and the related score on Thurstone's *Personality Schedule.* As would be expected from this validity information, the reported reliabilities of the Bell scales are high. Yet, the odd-even reliabilities, corrected upward by the Spearman-Brown prophecy formula, are all in the .80's. One can only conclude that the very high correlations reported with some other scales are probably maximal estimates and not likely to be replicated frequently.

The normative sampling for this instrument

is rather scanty. Percentile norms are given for 295 high school boys and 372 girls. College norms are based on 316 men and 347 women. None of the high school sample comes from any community east of Ashtabula, Ohio, and the college group is from Rochester, Minnesota, and points west. Furthermore, the high school norms combine students in grades 10, 11, and 12, and the college norms are based on a composite of freshmen, sophomores, and juniors.

In general, the Revised Student Form of the Bell *Adjustment Inventory* is supported by sufficient validity data to justify trial use as a screening device. It should go without saying that such use requires that evidence of specific validity must be obtained for the purpose involved. Such local validity is possibly less crucial where the instrument is used only as a source of counseling hypotheses, which will be checked by other information. Still, even in this situation, one would be professionally remiss to continue the use of any instrument unless it leads to correct hunches with some determinable and significant frequency.

J Counsel Psychol 11:98–9 sp '64. Laurence Siegel. * The current revision has been newly normed for high school and college students. However, the normative groups are quite small (approximately 300 for each sex) and far from representative. * On the whole, the revision of this inventory is not likely either to encourage or discourage more widespread use of the instrument.

For reviews by Nelson G. Hanawalt and Theodore R. Sarbin, see 4:28; for reviews by Raymond B. Cattell, John G. Darley, C. M. Louttit, and Percival M. Symonds of the original Student Form, and reviews by S. J. Beck, J. P. Guilford, and Doncaster G. Humm of the Adult Form, see 40:1200 (1 excerpt); for a review by Austin H. Turney of the Student Form, see 38:912.

[60]

The Alcadd Test. Adults; 1949; identification of alcoholic addicts and individuals with alcoholic problems; 6 scores: regularity of drinking, preference for drinking over other activities, lack of controlled drinking, rationalization of drinking, excessive emotionality, total; 1 form (4 pages); manual (2 pages); no data on reliability of subscores; $6.50 per 25 tests, postpaid; specimen set not available; (5–15) minutes; Morse P. Manson; Western Psychological Services. *

REFERENCES
1. MANSON, MORSE P. "A Psychometric Determination of Alcoholic Addiction." *Am J Psychiatry* 106:199–205 S '49. * (*PA* 24:3271)
2. BARILLAS, MARIO G. *A Study of the Validity and Reliability of the Alcadd Test as a Psychometric Instrument for the Identification of Male Alcoholics.* Master's thesis, Fordham University (New York, N.Y.), 1952.
3. MURPHY, DONAL G. *The Validity and Reliability of the Manson Evaluation and the Alcadd Test in the Identification of Female Alcoholics.* Master's thesis, Fordham University (New York, N.Y.), 1955.
4. MURPHY, DONAL G. "The Revalidation of Diagnostic Tests for Alcohol Addiction." *J Consult Psychol* 20:301–4 Ag '56. * (*PA* 31:8340)
5. CLARK, JAMES WARD. *Personality Syndromes in Chronic Alcoholism: A Factorial Study.* Doctor's thesis, Queen's University (Kingston, Ont., Canada), 1958. (Abstract: *Can Psychologist* 1:116–7)
6. SMART, REGINALD G. "A Critical Evaluation of the Alcadd Test." *O.P.A. Q* 14:70–5 D '61. *

DUGAL CAMPBELL, *Assistant Professor of Psychology, Queen's University, Kingston, Ontario, Canada.*

The Alcadd Test consists of a set of 65 questions on drinking behaviour (for example, "I get drunk about every pay-day"). The score on these questions, each answered either Yes or No, is intended to measure the extent to which a patient is controlled by his alcoholism. The questions are designed to measure five traits: regularity of drinking, preference for drinking over other activities, lack of controlled drinking, rationalization of drinking, and excessive emotionality.

Murphy (4) gave the test to four groups: active alcoholics, members of Alcoholics Anonymous, social drinkers, and abstainers. Critical ratios between all four groups were significant and from 80 to 100 per cent of the four groups were correctly identified using Manson's cut-off scores.

No systematic work has been reported for this test. Consequently the criticisms made in the original *Mental Measurements Yearbook* reviews (the five traits are subjective conceptions and have no objective analysis to warrant them, and it is not known how well the test will work with subjects who do not admit to alcoholism) remain unanswered. Until data relevant to these criticisms are obtained, the test appears to be of little practical value.

For reviews by Charles Honzik and Albert L. Hunsicker, see 4:30.

[61]

Attitude-Interest Analysis Test. Early adolescents and adults; 1936–38; also called *M-F Test;* masculinity-femininity; Form A ('36, 14 pages); manual ('38, 21 pages, out of print); $4.50 per 25 tests, postage extra; specimen set not available; (40–50) minutes; Lewis M. Terman and Catherine Cox Miles; McGraw-Hill Book Co., Inc. *

REFERENCES

1-20. See 3:24.
21. CERF, ARTHUR Z. "General Information, CE505GX3," pp. 676-7. In *Printed Classification Tests*. Edited by J. P. Guilford. Army Air Forces Aviation Psychology Program Research Reports, Report No. 5. Washington, D.C.: United States Government Printing Office, 1947. Pp. xi, 919. * (*PA* 22:4145)
22. HARDY, VIRGINIA T. "Relation of Dominance to Non-Directiveness in Counseling." *J Clin Psychol* 4:300-3 Jl '48. * (*PA* 23:179)
23. CARTER, LAUNOR, AND NIXON, MARY. "Ability, Perceptual, Personality, and Interest Factors Associated With Different Criteria of Leadership." *J Psychol* 27:377-88 Ap '49. * (*PA* 23:4183)
24. DE CILLIS, OLGA E., AND ORBISON, WILLIAM D. "A Comparison of the Terman-Miles M-F Test and the Mf Scale of the MMPI." *J Appl Psychol* 34:338-42 O '50. * (*PA* 26:294)
25. LEE, MARILYN C. *Relationship of Masculinity-Femininity to Tests of Mechanical and Clerical Abilities*. Master's thesis, University of Minnesota (Minneapolis, Minn.), 1950.
26. ROSS, ROBERT T. "Some Characteristics of the M-F Score." Abstract. *Am Psychol* 5:471 S '50. *
27. ARONSON, MARVIN LUCIUS. *A Study of the Freudian Theory of Paranoia by Means of a Group of Psychological Tests*. Doctor's thesis, University of Michigan (Ann Arbor, Mich.), 1951. (*Microfilm Abstr* 11:443)
28. BOTWINICK, JACK, AND MACHOVER, SOLOMON. "A Psychometric Examination of Latent Homosexuality in Alcoholism." *Q J Studies Alcohol* 12:268-72 Je '51. * (*PA* 26:390)
29. FISHER, SEYMOUR, AND HINDS, EDITH. "The Organization of Hostility Controls in Various Personality Structures." *Genetic Psychol Monogr* 44:3-68 Ag '51. * (*PA* 26:2889)
30. SHEPLER, BERNARD F. "A Comparison of Masculinity-Femininity Measures." *J Consult Psychol* 15:484-6 D '51. * (*PA* 26:7011)
31. VACCARO, JOSEPH J. *A Study of Psychological Factors That Contrast the Most and Least Efficient Psychiatric Aids in a Mental Hospital*. Doctor's thesis, Fordham University (New York, N.Y.), 1951.
32. FORD, C. FENTON, JR., AND TYLER, LEONA E. "A Factor Analysis of Terman and Miles' M-F Test." *J Appl Psychol* 36:251-3 Ag '52. * (*PA* 27:3551)
33. LEE, MARILYN C. "Relationship of Masculinity-Femininity to Tests of Mechanical and Clerical Abilities." *J Appl Psychol* 36:377-80 D '52. * (*PA* 27:6431)
34. PARKER, FREDERICK B. "A Comparison of the Sex Temperament of Alcoholic and Moderate Drinkers." *Am Sociol R* 24:366-74 Je '59. * (*PA* 34:4618)
35. STANEK, RICHARD J. "A Note on the Presumed Measures of Masculinity-Femininity." *Personnel & Guid J* 37:439-40 F '59. *
36. ENGEL, ILONA MARIA. *A Factor Analytic Study of Items From Five Masculinity-Femininity Tests*. Doctor's thesis, University of Michigan (Ann Arbor, Mich.), 1962. (*DA* 23:307)

For a review by Starke R. Hathaway, see 3:24; for excerpts from related book reviews, see 40:B1094, 38:B498, and 36:B256.

[62]

★**Attitudes Toward Industrialization.** Adults; 1959; community attitude toward industrial expansion; 1 form (1 page); manual (4 pages); $3 per 50 tests; $1 per specimen set (must be purchased to obtain manual); cash orders postpaid; (10) minutes; Donald E. Kaldenberg; Psychometric Affiliates. *

MARVIN D. DUNNETTE, *Professor of Psychology, University of Minnesota, Minneapolis, Minnesota.*

This is a short 18-item attitude scale designed to assess the attitudes of community groups toward industrial expansion. As the author states, "Rather intense interest and some controversy in Iowa on the issue [of industrial expansion] precipitated the present research. Controversy was expressed in speeches by state political leaders, newspaper editorials,

and 'letters to the editor' from ordinary citizens."

The brief 4-page manual is unusually explicit in describing the development of the scale. An original pool of 97 statements was gleaned from the content of nine hours of tape recorded interviews. Twenty eight of the 97 items were discarded because of ambiguity after ratings on a 5-point scale by five psychologists. The remaining items were then administered to 110 Iowa State University students who responded to the items using the usual 5-step Likert response format. Both internal and external criteria were used to obtain internal consistency and validity coefficients for each of the statements. The external criterion consisted of each subject's status on eight background variables, such as father's occupation and population of home community, which enabled an *a priori* assignment of subjects into groups presumably favorably and unfavorably disposed toward industrialization. The final 18 items of the scale are those which possessed phi coefficients above .25 on both the internal and external criteria.

Unfortunately, the author computed reliability and validity estimates for the 18-item scale on the same group of subjects used for the item analyses, obtaining a corrected odd-even coefficient of .80 and a validity coefficient of .55 against the 8-item background criterion. It is evident, of course, that these fold-back coefficients cannot be relied on to be accurate estimates of the scale's reliability and validity when applied to an independently selected group of subjects; the scale should not have been released for publication until it had been tried out on such a group. Both the author and particularly the publisher should be chastised for not demanding this final and simple test of the scale's merit prior to its release for distribution and sale to the public.

Norms are provided for 100 Northwestern University and Illinois Institute of Technology students as well as for the original group of 110 Iowa State University students, but apparently reliability and validity data were *not* computed for the Northwestern and Illinois students.

In summary, *Attitudes Toward Industrialization* appears to be a well conceived and carefully developed scale directed toward measuring attitudes toward industrial expansion. It still needs to be cross validated, but even in its present form it constitutes a worthy research instrument which may well be tried out by investigators concerned with the general questions raised by the issue of industrialization.

[63]

★The Ayres Space Test. Ages 3 and over; 1962; brain damage; 3 scores: accuracy, time, accuracy less adjustment for time; individual; 1 form; record booklet (4 pages); mimeographed manual (27 pages); no norms for ages 11 and over; $30 per set of test materials including two formboards, blocks, pegs, 25 record booklets, and manual; $4.50 per manual; postpaid; specimen set not available; (20–30) minutes; A. Jean Ayres; Western Psychological Services. *

REFERENCES
1. AYRES, A. JEAN. *Space Perception and Visualization in Cerebral Dysfunction.* Doctor's thesis, University of Southern California (Los Angeles, Calif.), 1961. (*DA* 22:1708)
2. SLEEPER, MILDRED L. *Correlation of Body Balance and Space Perception in Cerebral Palsied Individuals.* Master's thesis, University of Southern California (Los Angeles, Calif.), 1962.

ALVIN G. BURSTEIN, *Associate Professor of Psychology, Neuropsychiatric Institute, University of Illinois College of Medicine, Chicago, Illinois.*

This test, the author of which has had extensive experience as an occupational therapist, is intended "to measure space relations: namely, the speed of perception of stimuli composed largely of spatial elements, position in space or directionality, and space visualization"; the test "is designed particularly for use with subjects age three through adulthood who have or are suspected of having perceptual difficulty." The test manual clearly recommends the use of the test as part of a battery for the diagnosis of brain damage.

The testing materials consist of two formboards (one for diamond shaped, one for egg shaped blocks), eight blocks (four of each shape), and four wooden pegs. The four similarly shaped blocks differ in that each has a hole drilled in one of four different positions; thus, each formboard, with a change in the position of a peg, can become uniquely appropriate for a single block. The test consists of a series of 40 items in each of which the patient is presented with the formboard and two blocks. Difficulty is varied, increasing through the test, by increasing the similarity between the blocks to be discriminated and by varying the angles at which the constituent pieces are presented.

The item pool is, then, highly homogeneous.

The scoring involves noting the accuracy and time involved in each choice.

Overall, the test is clearly in the tradition of well known formboard performance tests such as those in the Pintner-Paterson battery, and the Arthur, the Ferguson and Kent-Shakow formboards.

The apparent difference is in the simplicity of the required response, and the effort given to grading item difficulty without involving more than minimal motor skill. A further contribution is the recognition that the formboard task, familiar in developmental studies, might be of additional relevance to the study of the brain damaged.

In the absence of published research on the test, it is necessary to rely heavily on the manual for an assessment of the test's worth and, unfortunately, the manual appears inadequate for a device offered for applied clinical use.

Carelessness can be identified on several levels in the manual. The first example, excusable but by no means desirable, involves the sort of lapse that merely inconveniences the reader, e.g., mistaken references to page and table numbers, and careless writing of crucial definitions. An example displaying imprecision of definition has already been quoted in the first paragraph of this review; a second is the statement that, "Space is a quality an individual attributes to sensation." Whether the intent is to characterize the phenomenology or the ontogeny of spatial perception is not clear and is never clarified.

A second, and much more critical, level of carelessness is involved in the presenting of inadequate standardization data. For example, although the test is described as appropriate for patients "through adulthood," reported standardization data relevant to adults is limited to 26 cases with cerebral palsy, aged "17–44." Further, the standardization data for children appears somewhat questionable. Misleading reference is first made to a study in which the test was administered to 100 brain-damaged subjects and 100 subjects without brain damage. The age range is said to be 3 to 77 years, with a division into five age groups. It is further stated that "subjects were matched by mean age." It is unclear whether this means that the groups at each age division were so matched or whether the total groups were so matched. Even more important, the disposition of subjects across this very wide age range on a highly age-dependent performance task is not mentioned. Nor is there any attempt to specify degree, site, or variety of cerebral damage, despite the obvious importance of such factors. Also omitted is control of variables such as educational status and cultural background.

Initial reference to these data as misleading is based on the fact that though the data are presented in a section entitled "Population Used," they are based *not* on the use of the clinical form of the test, but on an earlier, much longer, experimental version of the test.

Basic normative data are apparently based on the scores of 15 male and 15 female children "at each year of age from 3–10 years." While the sample here would seem more nearly adequate in terms of numbers at each age level, lack of clarity persists in several places. For example, performance is to be evaluated in terms of standardized rather than raw scores. For one age group, the standard deviation of that group was used to achieve the desired conversion; mysteriously, for the remaining seven groups the standard deviation specific to the group was replaced by the geometric mean of the seven standard deviations, with no explanation for this peculiar computational divergence. Further, clinical comparisons are to be based on an "adjusted score" which is derived by reducing the accuracy score by differential amounts based on the time used by the S. Such an adjustment may, in fact, be quite reasonable, but no discussion of how the degree of adjustment was determined is presented.

Further carelessness exists at the level of specifying how the test is to be given. For example, with respect to timing, it seems quite unclear as to just where in a series of implicit or explicit trials and errors the examiner may decide that S has made a mistake "for keeps" and hence to interrupt the crucial timing. Reliable time scores correct to the second, required for scoring the adjusted scores, would seem most difficult to achieve.

The above listing of errors and ambiguities is not exhaustive, but is, in the reviewer's opinion, sufficient indication that this test, interesting as it may be, cannot in good faith be recommended for general clinical use. It is difficult to understand why the publisher and author have collaborated in producing the test so prematurely.

ALFRED B. HEILBRUN, JR., *Associate Professor of Psychology, State University of Iowa, Iowa City, Iowa.*

The *Ayres Space Test* includes 60 form-board items requiring relatively simple spatial discriminations. It is intended primarily as a diagnostic tool for detection of brain damage, although the manual suggests that its properties make it useful in a variety of other situations—in research, as an adjunct in therapy, and for training and retraining purposes. However, since there is no evidence presented to substantiate these rather extensive claims, they must be considered premature at best.

Items were selected by determining which spatial perception problems best discriminated between heterogeneous groups of brain damaged individuals and normals at five different age levels extending from 3 to 77 years. Despite the wide age span used for item derivation and the manual's contention that the test is intended for persons from 3 through adulthood, norms are provided only for ages 3 through 10. Apparently one reason for this is a ceiling effect which is reached by age 14. The norms are not only curtailed in range of years but also are minimally constituted with respect to numbers; there were but 30 children sampled at each year.

An even more glaring deficit in the manual is the almost total lack of validating evidence for the test as a predictor of brain pathology. Four studies are considered in the validation section. Two have no relevance to the detection of brain damage, and a third reports the performance of 7- to 10-year old cerebral palsied groups with n's ranging between 3 and 6. The fourth study of 50 brain damaged children is open to serious criticism if the test constructor used the same children for item derivation and for this validation study, since discrimination would be spuriously high. The failure of the manual to be explicit allows for such a conclusion.

Reliability is reported in terms of internal consistency coefficients, and these run high at each age level. A test-retest stability measure would have been preferable, especially since the similarity in task performance from item to item makes internal consistency almost a foregone conclusion. Stability of children's performance over a length of time is another matter.

As mentioned above, mean scores on the

test increase rapidly with age until a ceiling is reached, presumably around 14 years. A point which is completely neglected by the manual is the likelihood that test performance is substantially correlated with mental age and with IQ. If so and the Ayres test is to be seriously proposed as a diagnostic indicant of brain damage, then the relationship between intelligence and spatial perception should be considered somewhere in the normative procedures.

There certainly is room in the clinician's diagnostic battery for a simple, reliable, and valid test which will enhance his ability to detect brain pathology in children. This test may someday qualify in this regard, but the best that can be said now is that a great deal more work is necessary before a judgment can be rendered. The manual both claims too much and provides too little; it is obscure in some spots and redundant in others. In the opinion of this reviewer, much of the criticism of the test could have been averted if publication had been postponed until the rudimentary attributes of the test were more thoroughly investigated. Although the manual in no place mentions the preliminary status of this test, the test user would do well to employ the AST with considerable caution until its merits are more clearly established.

[64]

*Babcock Test of Mental Efficiency. Ages 7 and over; 1930-62; formerly called *Babcock Test of Mental Deterioration;* record booklet title is *The Revised Examination for the Measurement of Efficiency of Mental Functioning;* individual; 10 scores: easy tests, repetition, initial learning, recall and recognition, motor A, motor B, perception time, easy continuous work, total efficiency (based on 8 previous scores), efficiency deviation; 1 form ('40); mimeographed manual ('62, 68 pages); record booklet ('42, 8 pages); reliability data the same as reported in 1940; $20 per set of testing materials, 25 record booklets, and manual; $10 per 25 record booklets; $6.50 per manual; postpaid; (70) minutes; Harriet Babcock and Lydia Levy (test); Western Psychological Services. *

REFERENCES

1-14. See 40:1248.
15-35. See 3:71.
36-45. See 4:31.
46. BABCOCK, HARRIET. "Measuring the Efficiency Variable," pp. 741-50. (*PA* 27:7752) In *Contributions Toward Medical Psychology: Theory and Psychodiagnostic Methods, Vol. II.* Edited by Arthur Weider. New York: Ronald Press Co., 1953. Pp. xi, 459-885. *
47. HOOK, MARION EMERSON. *A Factorial Analysis of Some Tests of Mental Efficiency.* Doctor's thesis, Ohio State University (Columbus, Ohio), 1954. (*DA* 20:2375)
48. SHAPIRO, M. B., AND NELSON, E. H. "An Investigation of the Nature of Cognitive Impairment in Co-operative Psychiatric Patients." *Brit J Med Psychol* 28:239-56 pt 4 '55. * (*PA* 30:6185)
49. PAYNE, R. W.; MATTUSSEK, P.; AND GEORGE, E. I. "An Experimental Study of Schizophrenic Thought Disorder." *J Mental Sci* 105:627-52 Jl '59. * (*PA* 34:6384)

50. PAYNE, R. W., AND HEWLETT, J. H. G. Chap. 1, "Thought Disorder in Psychotic Patients," pp. 3-104. In *Experiments in Personality: Vol. 2, Psychodiagnostics and Psychodynamics.* Edited by H. J. Eysenck. London: Routledge & Kegan Paul Ltd., 1960. Pp. viii, 333. *
51. PAYNE, R. W. Chap. 6, "Cognitive Abnormalities," pp. 193-261. In *Handbook of Abnormal Psychology: An Experimental Approach.* Edited by H. J. Eysenck. New York: Basic Books, Inc., 1961. Pp. xvi, 816. * (*PA* 35:6719)

For reviews by D. Russell Davis and Seymour G. Klebanoff, see 4:31; for excerpts from related book reviews, see 3:72.

[65]

*Behavior Cards: A Test-Interview for Delinquent Children. Delinquents having a reading grade score 4.5 or higher; 1941-50; individual; 1 form ('41, 150 cards); mimeographed manual, third edition ('50, c1941, 20 pages); record sheet ('41, 2 pages); $5.35 per set of cards, 25 record sheets, and manual; $1 per 25 record sheets; postage extra; (15-30) minutes; Ralph M. Stogdill; distributed by C. H. Stoelting Co. *

REFERENCES

1-3. See 3:25.
4. ZAKOLSKI, F. C. "Studies in Delinquency: I, Personality Structure of Delinquent Boys." *J Genetic Psychol* 74:109-17 Mr '49. * (*PA* 23:4925)

For reviews by W. C. Kvaraceus and Simon H. Tulchin, see 3:25.

[66]

★Billett-Starr Youth Problems Inventory. Grades 7-9, 10-12; 1961, c1953-61; problems checklist; 12 scores: physical health and safety, getting along with others, boy-girl relationships, home and family life, personal finance, interests and activities, school life, personal potentialities, planning for the future, mental-emotional health, morality and religion, total; 1 form ('61, c1953-58, 12 pages); 2 levels; manual ('61, 24 pages); no data on reliability; $4.70 per 35 tests; 40¢ per specimen set of both levels; postage extra; (70-80) minutes; Roy O. Billett and Irving S. Starr; Harcourt, Brace & World, Inc. *

REFERENCES

1. TRIFARI, THERESA ELEANOR. *The Identification of the Problems of Junior High School Youths and the Determination of the Relative Stability of These Problems.* Doctor's thesis, Boston University (Boston, Mass.), 1959. (*DA* 20:3638)

THOMAS C. BURGESS, *Associate Professor, Counseling Center, Portland State College, Portland, Oregon.*

The Billett-Starr inventory is a relatively long checklist consisting of 432 problems for the junior high school level and 441 problems for the senior high school level. Problems are arranged into the 11 areas listed above, with the number of problems per area ranging from 9 in the area of Personal Finance to 87 (or 88) in the area of School Life. Neither the rationale nor the procedure used to assign problems to these groups is mentioned. Problems within areas are arranged in an order designed to give continuity among related items.

Time required for completing the inventory is said to range from 26 to 120 minutes, though recommended time allowances (including time for directions) are 80 minutes for junior high school and 70 minutes for senior high school students. It is suggested that these somewhat excessive time requirements could be avoided in guidance classes by administering only one area at a time. While this procedure might be useful if the results are to be used only as a stimulus for class discussions, any reliance on the results for other purposes would be limited by the question of possible differences from what one might expect to obtain in a single session and reduced comparability with norms and the results reported by others. No data are presented to show that such results would be comparable, nor is the possibility of different results mentioned.

In responding to the inventory the student is asked to consider each item and to indicate whether it is no problem for him (NP), somewhat of a problem for him (S), or much of a problem for him (M) by crossing out one of these symbols. His score is simply a count of the number of problems marked M or S, the differences in the felt intensity of the problem being ignored. Total scores may be evaluated by reference to percentile norms for each sex at each level based on what appear to be reasonably appropriate groups. The authors take the reasonable position that the S and M responses should be considered by the counselor in making a study of an individual, but that to consider these different responses in routine scoring would unnecessarily complicate the tabulation and interpretation of the results.

Quartile norms based on the same groups are presented for each of the area scores. This seems a good idea, but examination of the norms reveals that for some areas the checking of as few as two problems will move the student from the bottom quarter to the top quarter of the distribution. Areas with so little differentiation between the top and bottom of the distribution would seem to be subject to considerable error, and should either be expanded by the addition of more popular problems in the area or should be combined with other related areas in the inventory.

The manual also gives useful frequency data on each item separately for boys and girls at each of the two levels.

An interesting feature of the inventory is the attempt to label certain items as indicators of "Very Serious" or "Urgent" problems. Items so labeled were those identified by the "consensus" of a jury of 20 specialists ("school counselors, school psychologists, directors of guidance, college professors of psychology, and the like"). Problems designated "Urgent" were judged to demand immediate attention. No indication is given of what was considered to constitute "consensus," a question which may be raised since consensus seems to have been reached on every item. And while judgments of a group of specialists provide a good starting point, further studies should be made to provide follow-up information on students who mark these items. To what extent do they tend to have serious problems? According to the item frequencies some of these items are checked by as many as 15 per cent in some of the groups of students sampled (no frequencies are reported for 7 of the 12 items rated "Urgent") suggesting a fairly high rate of false positive identifications may result.

The authors argue that the validity of the inventory "is to be determined largely by inspection of the instrument itself in light of the method used to obtain its content." Items were collected from students who were asked to write statements of their problems. These items were then sorted to eliminate overlapping and edited to eliminate ambiguity. The inventory "is a valid list of the problems of youth because it was derived from what young people themselves report as being their problems." This argument is supported by the normative data, by both the frequencies for items and the distributions of scores, which indicate that students do respond to the items. While this indicates that the items have been drawn from the domain of student problems it says nothing about how thoroughly this domain has been covered or how adequately it has been sampled. Furthermore, no external evidence of validity is given. There are no data on the relationship between responses to the inventory and any non-inventory behavior, problem diagnoses from case studies, or performance on any other standardized instrument. Such data should be gathered, both for the total score and for the 11 area scores.

No data are given on reliability. It is argued appropriately that the split-half estimate of reliability would be inappropriate because the content is not homogeneous. The retest method is rejected by the authors because the inventory is so long it would be too time consuming, because of the influence of memory over a short interval of time, and because of the probability of real changes in problems over any period long enough to eliminate the influence of memory. While there is merit in these arguments it would be preferable to have the estimates made and the data presented, and then to consider the shortcomings of the procedures in the light of obtained data—not in the darkness of absent data.

In summary, it would appear that this is a potentially useful checklist, but one on which more information is needed. It lacks, at this time, the completeness of information contained in the manual of the *SRA Youth Inventory* and the more voluminous validity data contained in the published research on the *Mooney Problem Check List*.

J. THOMAS HASTINGS, *Director, Office of Educational Testing; University Examiner; and Professor of Educational Psychology; University of Illinois, Urbana, Illinois.*

The areas of adjustment suggested by the 11 parts of this inventory are certainly of real concern to student and to educator alike. Perhaps a major contribution of the instrument is to focus the attention (however briefly) of teachers, counselors, administrators, and parents on these critical domains of problems. An instrument which looks like a test might do it when a pamphlet which looks like a sermon might not; "scores" on real youngsters may be more apt to motivate adults to attend to real problems than will generalized statements about such problems. The main difficulty, however, with considering this motivational-focusing effect as a contribution of the *Billett-Starr Youth Problems Inventory* is that there already were, at the time of its publication, three other similar instruments available: The *Mooney Problem Check List,* the *SRA Junior Inventory,* and the *SRA Youth Inventory.* It is true that the parts do not have exactly the same titles (problem areas) in all four instruments, but almost any topic in one can be found in the other two.

The task set the student in the Billett-Starr inventory is that of marking *each* of a series of statements (Junior Level, 432; Senior Level, 441) as either "NP," not a problem

to him, or as a problem to him. If he believes the statement represents a problem, he is to designate whether it is a problem which worries him "some" or a problem which worries him "very much." This further discrimination may give some advantage over the Mooney and the SRA inventories—but certainly no data are presented to show that it does. Furthermore, the manual (page 7) recommends that no distinction be made between "problems marked S [some] and those marked M [much]" in scoring the test. Just following this suggestion is the statement that "neither of the two types of norms furnished....is broken down into the Some and Much classifications." Later on, Table 4 presents for each of the 11 parts the percentage (in "a representative sample of 6390 cases") of items marked "much" on a base of items marked as problems. The authors support having the respondents make the distinction—S and M—on the basis that it improves "the student's general attitude and the validity of his responses." No data are given to support this generalization, and yet such data could be acquired rather easily.

Validity is pinned to the validity of the statements as problems, i.e., all of the statements represent "real problems." This claim is supported by the assertion that all items are "based on the freely written statements of large numbers of students in junior and senior high schools." This basis is a necessary condition but certainly not sufficient—nor does it add anything new to the available instruments. A further statement is made to the effect that counselors report good agreement between the results from this instrument and information gained in personal interviews. The possible user should beware of basing a decision on such a claim unless he can find out more about the extent of agreement and the conditions of comparison.

No data are given in the manual concerning the reliability of the instrument. After explaining at great length why "the traditional approach to reliability is not applicable," the authors dismiss a need for test-retest data (after all, the user should be interested in the stability over time of the problems) with the statement that "this procedure would be unduly time-consuming." The user might be justified in replying that administering and "scoring" the inventory is certainly unduly time-consuming if no picture of stability of the problems is presented.

The one thing added to this inventory that does not appear in the earlier ones is a coding of items (in the inventory and in the norms) in terms of judged seriousness of each problem. The authors had 20 specialists—an unspecified mixture of counselors, school psychologists, professors of psychology, "and the like"—rate each statement on a 3-point scale: minor, in-between, and very serious problem. These same judges also marked a number of items at each level as "urgent." The very serious and the urgent problems are coded for the user. Since the ratings were made apart from application to any individual or context, it is probably preferable for the user to make his own judgments regarding these dimensions at the time of use. If he is incapable of making better judgments concerning seriousness for a particular student than were the judges who didn't know the student, he probably should not be using the instrument.

In summary, there is no evidence to indicate that the Billett-Starr inventory is better than the earlier published instruments of the same type; and since it has not been as widely used as the Mooney or the SRA inventories, it lacks some of the data available on them in the journals. It can be hoped that through controlled use of the instrument the authors will collect and publish the kinds of data which will make the inventory more useful to the general test buyer.

HENRY WEITZ, *Associate Professor of Education, and Director, Bureau of Testing and Guidance, Duke University, Durham, North Carolina.*

Billett and Starr have compiled a list of questions related to the concerns of youth, grouped them into 11 "problem areas," furnished a response system which is only occasionally unnecessarily confusing, applied a scoring system which requires only the ability to count, presented a set of "norms" which contribute little to the use of the instrument, and made the claim that the inventory "provides (1) information that contributes to the counselor's fuller understanding of each *individual* student, and (2) facts about the prevalence of certain problems within school or other community *groups.*"

As in the case of other inventories of this sort, the present document drew its items from "the freely written statements of large numbers of students in junior and senior high schools." This appears to be the instrument's principal claim to validity.

No evidence of reliability is provided because, the authors insist, scores obtained on this kind of instrument may not be legitimately treated by the usual correlation analysis. They may well have a point here, yet other procedures could have been used to examine response consistency. The argument that "if the attitudes and feelings of any individual are subject to great variation over relatively short periods of time this is a very important fact to know about him even though it would mitigate against the conventional notion of reliability for the instrument," makes one wonder about the general utility of an instrument which is so subject to momentary fluctuations of mood. The counselor is urged to use the student's responses to gain some insight into the student's problems. If the authors' arguments about reliability hold, the counselor may be gaining insight into problems which have no lasting significance in the child's adjustment.

The manual provides abundant information on the mechanics of administering, scoring, and tallying responses for various uses, but it provides inadequate information on effective ways in which the instrument can be used and no evidence to support the recommended uses.

One device introduced in this test may have some promise. It involves identification by single and double dots printed in the booklet of those problems considered "very serious" and "urgent" by a jury of 20 specialists. Thirty six of the 432 items at the junior level and 41 of the 441 items at the senior level are identified as very serious or urgent. No evidence is given that these items can identify students with behavioral problems or that they can tell very much about the nature of the child's problem.

The student taking the test is asked to differentiate between problems which bother him somewhat and those which bother him a great deal. Little use is made of these differentiated responses since the scoring involves simply counting both kinds of responses together. The suggestion is made that the counselor may use the indicated severity of the problem as a guide to his counseling.

The *Billet-Starr Youth Problems Inventory* appears to do no more and, perhaps, very little less than, for example, the *Mooney Problem Check List* or the *SRA Youth Inventory*. It is to the credit of the authors of the present instrument that they have made no excessive claims for their inventory. Yet instruments of this sort suffer from a common ailment: they represent an elaborate and expensive procedure for securing unreliable answers to simple questions. The effective counselor does not require this sort of a crutch to gain understanding of his clients. The unskilled, inexperienced, or inept counselor should not be allowed to use such an instrument, for it is likely to retard his professional growth. The only possible use that might legitimately be made of instruments of this kind would be for preliminary large scale group surveys of student problems where individual interviews are impractical.

[67]

★Biographical Inventory for Students. Grades 12–13; 1955–62; for research use only; 10 scores: action, social activities, heterosexual activities, religious activities, literature-music-art, political activities, socioeconomic status, economic independence, dependence on home, social conformity; IBM; Form KDRD1 ('58, c1955–58, 14 pages); mimeographed manual ('62, c1955–58, 38 pages); separate answer sheets must be used; $2.50 per 25 tests; 25¢ per single copy; $1 per 25 IBM scorable answer sheets; scoring stencils must be prepared locally; $1 per manual; postage extra; (55–60) minutes; Laurence Siegel; distributed by Educational Testing Service. *

REFERENCES

1. SIEGEL, LAURENCE. "Note on a Biographical Inventory for Students." *J Counsel Psychol* 1:116–8 su '54. * (PA 29:3022)
2. SIEGEL, LAURENCE. "A Biographical Inventory for Students: I, Construction and Standardization of the Instrument." *J Appl Psychol* 40:5–10 F '56. * (PA 31:3079)
3. SIEGEL, LAURENCE. "A Biographical Inventory for Students: II, Validation of the Instrument." *J Appl Psychol* 40:122–6 Ap '56. * (PA 31:6128)
4. KAUSLER, DONALD H., AND LITTLE, NEAL D. "The BIS Dependency Scale and Grades in Psychology Courses." *J Counsel Psychol* 4:322–3 w '57. * (PA 33:6919)
5. KAUSLER, DONALD H., AND TRAPP, E. PHILIP. "Anxiety Level and Score on a Biographical Inventory." *J Appl Psychol* 42:305–7 O '58. * (PA 33:9755)
6. DUFF, O. LEE, AND SIEGEL, LAURENCE. "Biographical Factors Associated With Academic Over- and Underachievement." *J Ed Psychol* 51:43–6 F '60. * (PA 34:8398, 35:2261)

[68]

★Bristol Social-Adjustment Guides. Ages 5–15; 1956–63; ratings by teachers or other adults; 3 scales and 1 supplementary key; 1 form ('56, 4 pages) of each scale; diagnostic form ('56, 1 page) for each scale; manual, second edition ('63, 63 pages); 8s. per 25 diagnostic forms; 25s. per manual; 3s. per specimen set of a–c (without manual); postage and purchase tax extra; (10–20) minutes per scale; D. H. Stott and E. G. Sykes (a, b); University of London Press Ltd. *
a) THE CHILD IN SCHOOL. 1956–63; separate editions for boys and girls; 12s. per 25 scales; 6d. per single copy; 3s. per set of scoring keys.
b) THE CHILD IN RESIDENTIAL CARE. 1956–63; 12s. per 25 scales; 6d. per single copy; 4s. per set of scoring keys.

c) THE CHILD IN THE FAMILY. 1956–63; life history chart ('56, 1 page); 17s. 6d. per set of 25 scales and 25 charts; 9d. per single copy of each; 2s. 6d. per scoring key.
d) DELINQUENCY PREDICTION INSTRUMENT. Boys ages 5–15; 1961–63; consists of a delinquency prediction key to be used with the diagnostic form for *The Child in School* scale and a teacher's questionnaire ('61, 1 page) for preliminary identification of pupils to be rated on the scale; manual ('61, 4 pages, also available as part of the manual for a–c above); no data on reliability; 2s. 6d. per 12 questionnaires; 3d. per single copy; 1s. per key; 9d. per separate manual; (10–15) minutes.

REFERENCES

1. STOTT, D. H. *Unsettled Children and Their Families.* London: University of London Press Ltd., 1956. Pp. 240. * (PA 32:3012)
2. STOTT, D. H. "Boys on Probation: Maladjusted or Normal." Abstract. *Adm Sci Q* 15:498–502 Je '59. *
3. LUNZER, E. A. "Aggressive and Withdrawing Children in the Normal School: 1, Patterns of Behaviour." *Brit J Ed Psychol* 30:1–10 F '60. *
4. STOTT, D. H. "Delinquency, Maladjustment and Unfavourable Ecology." *Brit J Psychol* 51:157–70 My '60. * (PA 35:1114)
5. STOTT, D. H. "A New Delinquency Prediction Instrument Using Behavioural Indications." *Int J Social Psychiatry* 6:195–205 au '60. * (PA 36:4JO95S)
6. STOTT, D. H. "The Prediction of Delinquency From Non-Delinquent Behaviour." *Brit J Delinq* 10:195–210 Ja '60. *
7. STOTT, D. H. "Relationship Between Delinquency, Non-Delinquent Social Maladjustment and Neighbourhood Factors." Abstract. *Acta Psychologica* 19:425 '61. *
8. CRAFT, MICHAEL; FABISCH, WALTER; STEPHENSON, GEOFFRY; BURNAND, GORDON; AND KERRIDGE, DAVID. "100 Admissions to a Psychopathic Unit." *J Mental Sci* 108:564–83 S '62. * (PA 38:2138)
9. PETRIE, I. R. J. "Residential Treatment of Maladjusted Children: A Study of Some Factors Related to Progress in Adjustment." *Brit J Ed Psychol* 32:29–37 F '62. * (PA 37:893)
10. STOTT, D. H. "The Bristol Guides." *Child Care* 16:76–8 Jl '62. *
11. STOTT, D. H. "Evidence for a Congenital Factor in Maladjustment and Delinquency." *Am J Psychiatry* 118:781–94 Mr '62. *
12. STOTT, D. H. "Delinquency Proneness and Court Disposal of Young Offenders." *Brit J Criminol* 4:37–42 Jl '63. *
13. STOTT, DENIS. "Truancy and Crime." *Scottish Ed J* 46:189–90 Mr 8 '63. *

G. A. V. MORGAN, *Former Principal Psychologist, North Wales Child Guidance Service, Denbighshire, Wales.*

BRISTOL SOCIAL-ADJUSTMENT GUIDES. The Guides are basically checklists of statements describing items of behaviour significantly related to the emotional adjustment of children from 5 to 15 years of age. The three forms of the Guides cover the areas of school, residential care, and home background.

It is envisaged that the Child in School and the Child in Residential Care will be completed by persons best acquainted with the child, usually the teacher in charge of the child. The observer is given freedom to select from scrambled items in paragraphs statements which describe the child. Completion of each Guide for one child takes 10–20 minutes, depending on the skill of the observer. Items checked are scored by means of a transparent key and scores are transferred to a diagnostic form. This procedure is estimated to take some seven minutes.

The Child in the Family clearly requires knowledge of both family and child, and the implication is that this Guide will need to be used by a social worker or other professionally qualified person. Interpretation of the checklist on the child is made in terms of similar evidence on parents and the relationship within the family. The observations are reduced to patterns and measured finally in terms of two components, the number and severity of adverse factors in the child's situation and the degree to which he is affected by these.

The Guides were empirically based on collections of statements, describing the various forms of maladjusted behaviour in children, made by workers with children in residential care. This led to the development of the Child in Residential Care and this in turn to similar work with teachers on the Child in School. The items in the Guides are concerned with behaviour *symptomatic of maladjustment,* not with *personality traits* (e.g., "maladjustment," rather than "neuroticism" or "introversion"). Although the statements in the Guides were collected and sifted quite empirically with respect to their ability to distinguish maladjusted children from "normal" controls, the authors made use of their "clinical" knowledge of the significance of various kinds of behaviour and their observed associations to identify and score various subgroups of items relating to "syndromes" of maladjusted response, e.g., the "withdrawn," "hostile," and "anxious for affection." To this extent, Stott's own theories and generalizations are built into the Guides. The manual describes mainly the development and evaluation of the Child in School, which appears to be the Guide at present in most use. Careful and skilful revisions of the sample items for all Guides are described, passing through five versions for the Child in School and four for the Child in Residential Care. Items were analysed statistically and revised or discarded. Of 195 items, 133 finally achieved high significance in discriminating between maladjusted and normal groups.

The author rejects the total score on maladjustment based on counting disturbed responses as meaningless, in view of the variations in forms of maladjusted response; the diagnostic form provides for "syndrome" scores. It seems a pity that an attitude scaling technique should not have been used to confirm the groupings of items and suggest optional weighting. It would have been profitable, too, to cross validate the items within the experimental group to avoid well known sampling fluctuation effects.

The question of the reliability of the Guides is a complex one. Consistency of assessment between observers, or by the same observer over a period of time, appears analogous to "reader reliability" in assessing written work. Yet the various aspects of reliability do not appear to have been systematically explored. Evidence on the reliability of the Guides is sparse. One would estimate that the retest reliability coefficient of the two forms of the Guide is about .80. On present evidence, they are useful for comparison of groups but will need to be interpreted with liberal limits of score in classifying and comparing individuals.

Since the Guides were developed from empirical "common sense" observations, the validity and generality of their definitions of maladjustment depend on the degree to which items are representative of varieties of maladjustment and the extent to which the criterion groups were representative. The author points out that the original categories of maladjustment on the Guides were influenced by his delinquency studies and there is evidence, from the distribution of items, that the associated groups of aggressive-anxious behaviour bulk larger than withdrawn or unforthcoming (timid and introverted) behaviour. Some forms of disturbed behaviour commonly found in referrals to child guidance clinics are probably less adequately sampled than aggressive and delinquent behaviour. The manual does not specify the way in which the criterion "maladjusted" group was chosen. A later reference showed that the first groups used for developing the Child in School were composed of groups of three children (normal, unsettled, and maladjusted) each chosen by 20 teachers from among their class. This seems to be a very small and subjective criterion group. It is not reported that children referred to child guidance clinics or other psychiatric help, likely to be among the most extreme of the maladjusted population, were used. At the final revision of the Child in School, 234 of 613 children were maladjusted, but no criterion for the choice for the maladjusted group is given. The maladjusted group was larger than the control group. This was necessary to allow for identification of subgroups, with respect to syndrome associations between items. Since, however, maladjusted children are in a minority in the general population, the degree of efficiency of discrimination in terms of the percentage of maladjusted children identified by any given range of score cannot be established, even though items discriminated between maladjusted and controls at a high level of significance. This is a criticism brought up by Stott himself (5) in discussing the need to adjust percentages to approximately correct numbers of those at risk, in deciding the efficacy of a predictive scale.

The validity of the Guides rests on their agreement with the usual criteria of what constitutes maladjustment. The available evidence in the manual shows consistent success in this in a wide variety of settings. For example, the reliability and validity of the Child in School and the Child in Residential Care were "moderately good" in showing agreement with ratings by the warden on children's behaviour and improvement over 18 months in a special school for maladjusted children, whereas various projective tests were by contrast poor (9). In a study by the National Foundation for Educational Research, poor readers were found to be significantly more withdrawn than matched good readers at the ages of 9–10 and significant improvement over a year could be measured pari-passu with reading.

In view of the lack of knowledge of exactly what "maladjustment" means and its limits and sampling variations, "standardization" of instruments such as the Guides presents some complications, as pointed out by the author. Data on the distribution of scores are available on a random sample of children of 7–8 years in Liverpool, on delinquent and nondelinquent boys of 9–14 years in Glasgow, and on "delicate" children of 8, 10, and 14 in London. These tables printed in the manual should have percentiles for various scores to be useful and, as far as possible, some indication should be given of limits indicating the normal range and severity of maladjustment. There is a need for a comprehensive standardization on adequately randomized samples.

The manual contains a considerable amount of useful information on the development, evaluation, and purpose of the Guides, but requires careful reading. It would be more convenient if one section were devoted to direct and specific instructions for completing and scoring each of the Guides.

When using the Child in the Family careful diagnostic work needs to be done. The family patterns described tend to reflect the more extreme forms of parental tension, rejection, and neglect likely to be related to the author's particular interests. It is not so clear whether some subtler, latent patterns of emotional involvement found in many disturbed children referred to child guidance clinics are adequately represented by this Guide. This seems to be a matter for experiment and development. One would be interested to know the degree to which the Child in the Family is known to or accepted by the professional workers who might profitably use it, and how it would be considered by them to supplement or replace the usual full case history.

In summary, The Bristol Guides are based on a pragmatic approach to maladjustment. Clinical workers will be sceptical of the descriptive and "symptomatic" approach, but the Guides to the Child in School and the Child in Residential Care appear to have a great deal to offer in helping the everyday observer sharpen his observations of children. The Guides have already played a valuable part in research and, unlike self-scored personality questionnaires, seem to work as effectively in the practical setting as in research. Despite their limitations, they have a useful contribution to make, and are capable of further development. They are probably used more widely in Britain than any other single assessment of personality outside those solely in professional use.

DELINQUENCY PREDICTION INSTRUMENT. This instrument was developed by Stott from observations that delinquents (boys of 9–14 on probation in Glasgow) showed significantly higher scores than "normal" controls on the Bristol Guides in such areas as hostility to adults and children, anxiety for affection, and lack of normal emotional involvement. Fifty four items from the Child in School Guide which occurred four times more frequently among delinquents were chosen to form the instrument, the items being roughly weighted in proportion to the differences in response.

The effectiveness of the instrument is expressed in terms of two ratios. One is the predictive range of the instrument in a "normal" mixed population of boys containing an average expected number of delinquents. The range, for any given score, specifies the number of delinquents who will be included, with normals, in the sample defined. A low criterion score will ensure that a majority of delinquents is brought into the sample, but at the cost of including a fairly large number of nondelinquents, and, conversely, a high criterion score will eliminate nondelinquents but also a significant number of delinquents. This is the usual dilemma of any selection procedure.

The second measure, the selectivity ratio, describes the efficiency of the instrument in isolating a group which has a high probability of being delinquent, that is, the proportion of the group defined by each score level who are likely to be delinquent.

The two criteria have curves which are in opposite directions. When a low score is used as a criterion the number of delinquents caught up along with normals will be large, but the actual proportion of delinquents in the group (or selectivity) will be low. Conversely, when a high score is used, a large number of actual or potential delinquents will be eliminated, but those in the group defined will have a high probability of being delinquent. The author discusses this issue rather more lucidly and at greater length in another reference (5) than in the manual to the Bristol Guides. He suggests as the best compromise the 50 per cent level of selectivity; this would detect 70 per cent of all delinquents.

A table is given in the manual representing range and selectivity ratios for given scores on the Delinquency Prediction Instrument. In addition, a table is given of prediction scores for individuals, in terms of the probability that an individual will be or become delinquent. To lighten work in screening delinquents, the author offers a list of six questions on delinquent and aggressive attitudes observed in schools; these are to be used by teachers in selecting children for full assessment on this instrument. This useful procedure is parallel to that proposed by Stott in his six questions for screening the children in a class likely to be sufficiently maladjusted to warrant fuller investigation with the Child in School Guide.

The author points out that, since the instrument provides an objective rating procedure and takes only 10–15 minutes per child, it is a simple and effective procedure for classifying children likely to be or become delinquents, particularly by contrast with the case histories and prediction tables based on a variety of weighted factors which are described by the Gluecks.[1] Stott criticizes the proportional effectiveness of such prediction tables in isolating delinquents from a natural mixed population. There is evidence that the Delinquency Prediction Instrument is sensitive to degrees of maladjustment or delinquency within the delinquent group as related to the number of further offences committed during probation, or recidivism. It is claimed that it isolates the psychological factors of delinquency even within areas varying widely in sociological factors related to delinquency.

The instrument has not been extended for routine use with girls or for use with boys outside the age range described. No reliability studies have been reported: it is clear that wide limits of score are needed to classify individuals with a high degree of accuracy. As far as the emotional aspects of predelinquent behaviour which can be described in school are concerned, the Delinquency Prediction Instrument appears to form a most useful addition to measures for the assessment and prediction of delinquency.

M. L. KELLMER PRINGLE, *Director, National Bureau for Co-operation in Child Care, London, England.*

The purpose of the *Bristol Social-Adjustment Guides* is, in the author's words, to "offer a method for detecting and diagnosing maladjustment, unsettledness or other emotional handicap in children of school age. They constitute a clinical instrument by which a comprehensive report of how the child behaves and reacts in real life can be furnished to the psychologist or psychiatrist, and a system for the interpretation of the behaviour. Educationally they are a means of judging whether a child is suffering from emotional difficulties, such as might be the cause of failure in school-work, or which might act as a warning sign of the possibility of delinquent-breakdown."

Adults familiar with the child are presented with a list of statements and are required to underline those which describe his habitual mode of response. No expert knowledge or

1 GLUECK, SHELDON, AND GLUECK, ELEANOR. *Unraveling Juvenile Delinquency,* pp. 257–62. New York: Commonwealth Fund, 1950. Pp. xv, 399. * (PA 25:2578)

insight is needed by the teacher or residential staff who are completing the Guides since the interpretations will be made by clinicians of one kind or another. It would seem, however, that the Guide relating to the Child in the Family is to be filled in by a trained social worker who also evaluates the results. All the Guides are couched in everyday, jargon-free language, describing readily observable behaviour; the completion of the schedules takes only 10 to 20 minutes. The method aims at providing a general statement about the social adjustment of a child which is as free as possible from the unreliability of subjective, personal judgment. Since only contemporary adjustment is being assessed, change and improvement, whether spontaneous or as a result of treatment, can be measured by obtaining another record after a period of time. Stott has deliberately refrained from expressing the diagnosis in terms of a quotient or score. This he considers "would be artificial because there are different ways of being maladjusted which are hardly comparable to one another." Rather, children are classified into three main groups—stable, unsettled, or maladjusted—or, according to the predominant behaviour pattern which they show, aggressive, withdrawn, etc. For research purposes, however, there is, in Stott's view, no objection to using a score derived either by simple counting or by some kind of weighting.

The manual falls between several stools. Teachers and house parents looking for a simple explanation of the aims of the Guides and for some suggestions to help with their completion (for example, on how to avoid a halo effect) are likely to be disappointed; even the first chapter, entitled "Explanations and Directions" is not only too technical but too detailed and long for this purpose. The staff of psychological services will wish for much greater clinical detail, for example, some case studies and profiles to illustrate patterns shown by unsettled and maladjusted children, respectively, or some explanation of how Stott arrived at his 12 "Patterns of Family-Situation." Research workers will regret that the discussion of "Methodology and Compilation" has been compressed into a mere 13 pages, 4 of which are devoted to a general consideration of current controversies regarding the nature of personality and its scientific measurement. Moreover, a curious method has been chosen for presenting this chapter. It begins with a list of 37 headings, such as "The conflict between Objectivists and the Understanders," "The Concept of 'proof,'" and "Weakness of sectional hypotheses." Only subsequently does it become apparent that each of them is being discussed in turn. Since they are not repeated at the beginning of the relevant section, one has to keep on going back to the beginning of the chapter to check on the topic under discussion. All readers will hope that the third edition will be revised so as to serve the conventional purposes of a manual more adequately; that the contents page will also contain page numbers and a list of the tables; and that certain obscure statements will be clarified (for example, "Experience with the Guide itself tends to even out discrepancies" on p. 8 or "In a few groups two 'normal' items are given, but this is to drain off a variety of normality which may otherwise be included in an 'unsettled' item"). It would also be useful to have all the various guides, diagnostic forms, and templates included in the manual.

As yet no comprehensive standardisation of the Guides on a randomized sample has been carried out. The results of a number of pilot studies are quoted which show significant differences between boys and girls in the incidence of maladjustment, as well as differences between delinquent and nondelinquent groups. Arguing that it is difficult to find some external validation for tests of social adjustment, Stott suggests that "some element of validation is achieved if the results tally with the assessments of teachers or others who know the children well in a day-to-day working relationship." This was found in a number of studies. Similarly, an adequate survey has not yet been made of the extent to which teachers' or house parents' recordings differ either among themselves or between each other. Again, there is some evidence from a number of experimental studies. In a project carried out by the National Foundation for Educational Research in England and Wales, pairs of teachers completed Guides independently for some 88 children; correlations between "maladjusted" scores were .76 and, between "unsettled" scores, .78. The Residential Guide was completed three times independently by nurses, rating 45 young adults who were patients in a hospital unit for psychopaths; the intercorrelations were .49, .58, and .55, respectively.

The Delinquency Prediction Instrument aims at diagnosing "delinquency-proneness." The author recommends that in the first place the teacher complete for every pupil the "preliminary sorting procedure"; this consists of six questions about the child which are answered by either "yes" or "no." "These questions are framed so as to cover the maladjusted attitudes which the prediction instrument show to be most conducive to delinquency." Then the full Bristol Guide is filled in for every child who receives one or more "yes" answers in the "preliminary sorting procedure." After this is scored, a delinquency prediction score is obtained by means of a transparent delinquency prediction key. Caution is urged in interpreting and in using this score since it has been derived from one study of Glasgow boys. At present no other data are available, either from boys in the same city or from other areas, nor have these predictive procedures been applied to girls.

In summary, the *Bristol Social-Adjustment Guides* are useful instruments for obtaining judgments of children's behaviour from teachers and house staff which will aid clinicians both in selecting children for individual examination and in diagnosing the nature of their difficulties. However, for the time being their greatest value lies in their being new research tools. Until adequate standardisation data become available, it would be unwise to recommend their widespread adoption as reliable instruments for the detection of maladjustment or for the prediction of delinquency. The present manual would benefit from being divided into two parts: a simple, concise manual giving directions for the use and scoring of the Guides and a much enlarged volume describing and giving data for all the pilot studies which preceded the present schedules, the theoretical and practical considerations which underlie them, and case studies of individual children and their families.

A.M.A. Arch Gen Psychiatry 1:556 N '59. Mary Engel. * On first blush, the "Bristol Social Adjustment Guides" seem to offer a quick, easy, and rather accurate technique, if not for understanding the dynamics of a child's disturbance, at least for selecting a potential patient from a large group of children. However, the various discussions, expositions, and arguments in the "Manual" give cause for concern over a number of issues conscientiously raised but too lightly dismissed. The authors pride themselves on their empirical approach, yet cannot resist making theoretical statements which not only are poorly integrated with the empirical attitude but also are mere restatements of rather well-known theoretical positions. For example, their discussion of "normal responses to unfavorable situations which ....get into a state of overreadiness" (p. 11) is simply a naïve expression of the concept of overuse of the defense mechanism. While the authors urge the reader to be "free of conceptual models" and accept the "empirical discipline [as] a counsel of perfection" (p. 15), they do not follow their own advice. Conceptual models are present in the "Manual"; only they are hidden and unrecognized. The "Bristol Social Adjustment Guides" have limitations for the American user in that the language of the items is often unfamiliar. It would be a difficult matter to rate a child on such items as "feckless," "seems to play daft," "spivvish dress," or "has stupid moods,"—the last being perhaps as good an example of linguistic difficulty as of the clearly judgmental nature of "objective" ratings in general.

Brit J Ed Psychol 30:187–8 Je '60. P. E. Vernon. * The Manual, though somewhat difficult to follow, is worthy of close attention from child psychologists and others interested in personality. Dr. Stott criticises both the rigidity of the "objectivist," with his fixed traits or types of personality, and the subjectivity of the clinician. All that he claims to supply is a series of records of behaviour in particular contexts, grouped under a number of syndromes or "attitudes" (Anxiety, Hostility to Adults, Restlessness, etc.) and graded for their seriousness in respect of unsettledness or maladjustment. Clearly, these can be of considerable value to the psychologist in the educational clinic, the teacher, or others concerned with maladjusted or delinquent children, in giving a codified, all-round picture of a child's personality. They represent a genuine attempt to get away from the artificiality of the objective, projective or questionnaire test, and the bias of the ordinary personality rating. Nevertheless, a number of doubts arise. First, how far can any observer, who has sufficient acquaintance with the child to answer the questions, avoid halo and subjectivity even in underlining such apparently concrete "bits of behaviour"? Dr. Stott provides some evidence of reliability (inter-observer agreement), but other studies of the problem reported in the literature are unpromising. Secondly, it is not easy to follow just why these particular categories were chosen, nor how the items were assigned to one rather than another. Quite legitimately, the author eschews any overall score or quotient for maladjustment, but one would like to know much more about the internal consistency of the categories and their overlapping. Thirdly, while frequency tables for the "School" symptoms are provided, it would be valuable to have something in the nature of norms for each category, and for different age groups. It seems unlikely that the same patterns of normality and abnormality occur in children all the way from 5 to 15 years. However, this type of information can well be collected by the author and others who use the Guides, and we will look forward to future reports. It is unfortunate that the cost, particularly of the Manual, is so high. *

J Child Psychol & Psychiatry 1:249 O '60. R. G. Andry. * In an age when we have become accustomed to tests which are usually easy to administer, to score and to interpret, Dr. Stott's new scales come as a mild shock. At first sight they appear complicated to the layman and over-simplified to the psychometrician, but they are easy to score and deserve to be considered, because they reveal at once the skilful touch of the clinician. * The author ....challenges bravely all those who, in the study of personality theory, demand rigorous quantification, "objectivity" and "proof," pointing out that it is high time that researchers returned sensibly to making factual statements about a person (e.g., whether he reverts to hostility when his need for attention is not met, etc.). The author seems to imply that before we can leap to describing personality in terms of a few "higher order factors," we should first concentrate on isolating many "lower-order" attitudinal trait-factors with more microscopic clinical care than is usual with psychometricians, who often reveal a lack of clinical knowledge. He does not recognize, however, that the function of a psychometrician is different from that of a clinician and that he often considers it his task to advance the behavioural sciences, by enabling people to perceive the uniformities underlying the rich variety of concrete life-situations. The author's

sympathy with Tinbergen's theory of instinct is undisguised. At the same time he is far from decrying the need for a quantified or experimental approach. With propriety and insight Dr. Stott merely urges caution at this stage *vis-à-vis* the development of the still-growing plant of psychology. He concludes by advancing a concept of his own which he calls "situation attitude," as contrasted with the constancy of traits in various situations, which is often assumed. Rightly he does not pursue this further in this manual, whose function is to give the background to these interesting and rather skilfully devised inventories. One great lesson seems to emerge from this work: the need for clinician and psychometrician to team up as equal partners in tackling the thorny problem of evolving a theory of personality.

J Consult Psychol 24:99 F '60. Read D. Tuddenham. * a careful attempt to render more objective and precise the observations of teachers, social workers, and foster parents, with respect to children's social adjustment. The *Guides* are intended to save time for the psychologist by providing accounts of behavior more standardized and compact than anecdotal protocols, and more specific than impressionistic ratings. Since the *Guides* encourage accuracy in observing children and provide a system for classifying symptomatic behavior, they have a place also as aids in clinical training. Each *Guide* consists of numerous adjectives and phrases grouped by topic and scrambled as to desirability, though with negative indications in the majority. The observer simply underlines those terms which apply to the child concerned. * Their reliability (interrater agreement) in a preliminary study is given as around .76. More data are needed, but reliability is likely to depend as much upon the raters' skills and opportunities as upon the content of these forms. The validity of each item in differentiating between the stable and the maladjusted is presented, but without cross-validation. Normative data for the interpretation of total scores on each attitude are lacking. This is not a serious omission for American users who will need to develop their own norms anyway. Differences between the English and American languages constitute a more fundamental problem. The author's success in finding meaningful descriptive phrases drawn from the colloquial speech of nurses, teachers, etc., e.g., "spivvish dress," or "feckless," will occasionally create problems of understanding for Americans. Even clinical vocabulary has its differences—e.g., "unforthcomingness" for "shy," or "unsettled" for "mildly maladjusted." Those of us used to the euphemistic polysyllables of "psychopathic deviate" may feel decidedly self-conscious characterizing a child as a "knave." The *Guides,* in summary, will probably not achieve their potential value in this country until someone undertakes to translate them from the authors' English into ours.

Q J Exp Psychol 12:126 My '60. A. W. Heim. * Reliability is remarkably high for this field, correlations between pairs of teachers, for instance, being 0.78 for "unsettled scores" and 0.76 for "maladjusted scores." * Inevitably, a number of criticisms suggest themselves. There is, for instance, too much philosophizing and self-interested history in the Section called "Methodology and Compilation"; there is, also, an infuriating tendency to assume familiarity on the part of the reader with the particular jargon chosen; and certain sections of the Manual suggest that, despite six years' work, publication in this form may be slightly premature. In general, however, the Guides are impressive. Stott and Sykes have tackled a perplexing problem without underestimating its difficulties and without oversimplifying method or interpretation. It is one of the most hopeful attempts yet made in this important field.

[69]

★**Cain-Levine Social Competency Scale.** Mentally retarded children ages 5–13; 1963; rating scale based upon information obtained from parents; 5 scores: self-help, initiative, social skills, communication, total; 1 form (7 pages); manual (19 pages); mimeographed supplementary data (24 pages); $3.85 per 25 tests; $1 per specimen set; postage extra; supplementary data free on request; Leo F. Cain, Samuel Levine, and Freeman F. Elzey; Consulting Psychologists Press, Inc. *

Marshall S. Hiskey, *Professor of Educational Psychology, and Director, Educational Psychological Clinic, University of Nebraska, Lincoln, Nebraska.*

This scale is designed primarily for use with moderately retarded children or those who are frequently referred to as "trainable." Educational goals for such children are usually defined in terms of social competency behaviors. In the past there have been few, if any, specifically designed instruments of evalu-

ation for assessing the development of retarded children. This scale is concerned with evaluation of the extent of development of learned skills which ultimately permit the child to achieve self-sufficiency and socially contributing behaviors. As such it will be welcomed by many who work closely with retarded children.

This scale is based on the assumption that the "child's development of social competency is reflected by" (*a*) "an increase of his manipulative abilities"; (*b*) his "moving from other-directed to self-initiated behavior"; (*c*) his changing "from self-oriented to other-oriented behavior"; and (*d*) an "increased ability to make himself understood." It utilizes four subtests: Self-Help, Initiative, Social Skills, and Communication.

"The Self-Help subscale (SH) is designed to estimate the child's manipulative ability, or motor skills." It is concerned "with motor performance *per se*" on the assumption that "the greater the....manipulative ability, the greater his independence."

The Initiative subscale (I) attempts "to measure the degree to which the child's behavior is self-directed." It assumes that "the child who must be directed to an activity is more dependent than the child who initiates that activity."

"The Social Skills subscale (SS) seeks to assess the degree to which the child engages in interpersonal relationships with other children and adults." It is hypothesized that "the more able a child is in relating to others and participating in group situations, the greater his independence."

"The Communication subscale (C) is designed to measure the degree to which a child makes himself understood." It is utilized on the assumption that "the child who makes his wants known is more independent than the child who does not."

Each of the 44 activities listed in the scale is followed by four or five descriptive statements which represent varying degrees of independence. They are printed in an expendable booklet with the items grouped by content rather than by subscale. Percentile ratings are available for each subtest and for the total social competency score.

The standardizing group consisted of 716 trainable mentally retarded children (414 males and 302 females) in the state of California. The subjects had intelligence quotients ranging from 25 through 59 with mental ages 2 through 7 and chronological ages 5 through 13. Tables for chronological ages 5 through 13 permit the user to determine a child's percentile rank relative to his age group. With the exception of the five year level, norms are listed at two year intervals, since mentally retarded children change and progress so slowly.

It should be emphasized that this is a *rating* device and not a scale that is administered directly to the child. The social competency rating is obtained by conducting an interview to determine the habitual or typical performance of the child in regard to each of the items. Since the items are social competency behaviors which are explicitly observable in the home it is suggested that the best respondent is usually the mother or the house parent. However, most of the behaviors are observable in the special class or school and may be rated by the teacher(s) for school evaluation purposes.

Validity of this instrument is based on the criteria of expert judges and an item analysis after tryout. Test-retest reliability coefficients were obtained by re-rating a random sample of 35 subjects after an interval of three weeks. The coefficients vary from .88 to .97 for the subscales, with the "total" listed as .98. Whereas these approaches to validity and reliability are appropriate under the circumstances, it must be recognized that they can be affected by the inconsistencies within the respondent or among respondents. Thus validity and reliability quotations should be accepted tentatively until more rigorous approaches can be utilized.

The manual is rather complete and the material is well presented. Part 2 gives a good word description of the derivation of the scale and the tables summarize the most important statistical information; further statistical data on individual items are available without charge from the publisher. Part 1 of the manual is concerned with the utilization of the scale and lists some very important considerations and cautions concerning respondents and the interviewing procedure. Since the interviewer does *not* read the description statements to the respondent the manual would be of even greater value to the user had it included some further examples of the general questions which could be utilized with each item.

It is unfortunate that the title of the scale does not make known that the scale is to be used with retarded children, or, even better yet, with the moderately retarded (trainable). Whereas the scale can show the status of any child in relation to the skills sampled, the percentile norms are established on children in the 25–59 IQ range. If utilized with a child with an intelligence quotient of 75 or 80, the percentile ratings could present a very distorted evaluation of the individual. One cannot assume that a scale such as this one will be employed only by individuals who are sufficiently sophisticated to avoid such pitfalls.

Perhaps the greatest value of this scale rests in the evaluation or recognition of the progress of the individual, rather than the possibility of comparing him with others. Likewise, it provides a limited method for identifying more specifically a child's tendency to improve somewhat rapidly in one area while showing little or no gain in another. Since these children progress so slowly, teachers and parents often become discouraged if positive changes are not identified.

The percentile ranks have specific advantages also. One can compare the child with other trainable children of his age in terms of overall social competence and also his relative status on each subscale. Such information can be helpful in grouping children and in planning future training for the individual. From a research standpoint the scale can be quite useful.

In summary, this scale is a much needed and useful instrument in the area of mental retardation. It is one of a very few attempts at a "standardization" on a group that is intellectually deficient. In the hands of a specially trained (professional) individual, it can provide pertinent and worthwhile information to parents, teachers, and researchers. As a new instrument and one which uses respondents to obtain the resulting ratings, it is in need of well designed follow-up studies relative to respondent variables.

[70]

★The California Medical Survey (CMS). Medical patients ages 10–18, adults; 1962; checklist of medical and psychological information; 18–23 scores: chronicity of illness, emotional conditions, familial background, basic medical information, psychiatric symptoms, specific disorder, medical background, genito-urinary, neuro-mus-skeletal, cardio-vas-blood, sensory, digestive, respiratory, 5 gynecologic scores

(Form W only), anxiety-stress, psychiatric, habits-traits, sexual-social, energy level; 2 levels; summary sheet (1 page); mimeographed manual (9 pages); no data on reliability and validity; no norms; $3 per 10 tests; $5 per 30 summary sheets; $2 per manual; postpaid; specimen set not available; (10–20) minutes; Harold L. Snow and Morse P. Manson; Western Psychological Services. *

a) CHILDREN'S FORM. Ages 10–18; Form C (4 pages).
b) ADULT FORMS. Adults; Forms M (for men), W (for women), (6 pages).

[71]

California Psychological Inventory. Ages 13 and over; 1956–60; 18 scores: dominance (Do), capacity for status (Ca), sociability (Sy), social presence (Sp), self-acceptance (Sa), sense of well-being (Wb), responsibility (Re), socialization (So), self-control (Sc), tolerance (To), good impression (Gi), communality (Cm), achievement via conformance (Ac), achievement via independence (Ai), intellectual efficiency (Ie), psychological-mindedness (Py), flexibility (Fx), femininity (Fe); IBM and NCS; 1 form ('56, 12 pages); manual ("re-issued 1960," c1957, 39 pages, same as earlier 1957 manual except for some omissions and additions of validity data); administrator's guide ('57, 15 pages, reprinted from manual); profiles ['57, 2 pages]; separate answer sheets must be used; $9.75 per counselor's kit of 5 tests, 25 hand scored answer sheets, 25 profiles, set of stencils, and manual; $6.25 per 25 tests; $3.75 per 50 sets of profiles and either hand scored or IBM answer sheets; $4.50 per set of hand scoring stencils; $6 per set of IBM scoring stencils; $3.25 per 50 NCS answer sheets (scored by National Computer Systems only, see 671); 75¢ per administrator's guide; $3 per manual; $1 per specimen set (includes abstract of manual); postage extra; scoring service available; Italian, French, and German editions available; (45–60) minutes; Harrison G. Gough; Consulting Psychologists Press, Inc. *

REFERENCES

1-33. See 5:37.
34. BARRON, FRANK. "The Disposition Toward Originality." J Abn & Social Psychol 51:478–85 N '55. * (PA 31:2533)
34a. HOLMEN, MILTON G.; KATTER, ROBERT V.; JONES, ANNE M.; AND RICHARDSON, IRVING F. "An Assessment Program for OCS Applicants." HumRRO Tech Rep 26:1–50 F '56. * (PA 31:8957)
35. GOWAN, J. C. "A Summary of the Intensive Study of Twenty Highly Selected Elementary Women Teachers." J Exp Ed 26:115–24 D '57. * (PA 33:4731)
36. HEUSINKVELD, EDWIN D. A Study of the Relationship of Certain Scores on the California Psychological Inventory to Student Adjustment in a College Dormitory. Master's thesis, State University of Iowa (Iowa City, Iowa), 1957.
37. JOHNSTON, ROY PAUL. The Isolation of Social Personality Dimensions Through a Factor Analysis of the California Psychological Inventory. Doctor's thesis, University of North Carolina (Chapel Hill, N.C.), 1957.
38. SANFORD, NEVITT; WEBSTER, HAROLD; AND FREEDMAN, MERVIN. "Impulse Expression as a Variable of Personality." Psychol Monogr 71(11):1–21 '57. * (PA 33:3336)
39. COULSON, ROGER WAYNE. Relationships Among Personality Traits, Ability and Academic Efficiency of College Seniors. Doctor's thesis, State University of Iowa (Iowa City, Iowa), 1958. (DA 19:1647)
40. DINITZ, SIMON; RECKLESS, WALTER C.; AND KAY, BARBARA. "A Self Gradient Among Potential Delinquents." J Crim Law & Criminol 49:230–3 S-O '58. * (PA 33:10646)
41. KELLY, E. LOWELL; MILLER, JAMES G.; MARQUIS, DONALD G.; GERARD, R. W.; AND UHR, LEONARD. "Personality Differences and Continued Meprobamate and Proclorperazine Administration." A.M.A. Arch Neurol & Psychiatry 80:241–6 Ag '58. * (PA 33:10420)
42. BENDIG, A. W. "Personality Variables Related to Individual Performance on a Cognitive Task." J General Psychol 60:265–8 Ap '59. * (PA 36:2HJ65B)
43. BRENGELMANN, J. C. "Differences in Questionnaire Responses Between English and German Nationals." Acta Psychologica 16(5):339–55 '59. * (PA 34:5788)
44. COHEN, LEONARD MARLIN. The Relationship Between Certain Personality Variables and Prior Occupational Stabil-

ity of Prison Inmates. Doctor's thesis, Temple University (Philadelphia, Pa.), 1959. (DA 20:3375)
45. HOLLAND, JOHN L. "The Prediction of College Grades From the California Psychological Inventory and the Scholastic Aptitude Test." J Ed Psychol 50:135–42 Ag '59. * (PA 35:2796)
46. KEOGH, JACK. "Relationship of Motor Ability and Athletic Participation in Certain Standardized Personality Measures." Res Q 30:438–45 D '59. * (PA 35:4989)
47. KOENIG, KATHRYN, AND McKEACHIE, W. J. "Personality and Independent Study." J Ed Psychol 50:132–4 Je '59. * (PA 35:1201)
48. MERRIMAN, J. BURTON. The Relationship of Personality Traits to Motor Ability. Doctor's thesis, State University of Iowa (Iowa City, Iowa), 1959. (DA 20:950)
49. OBST, FRANCES. "A Study of Selected Psychometric Characteristics of Home Economics and Non-Home Economics Women at the University of California, Los Angeles." Calif J Ed Res 10:180–4+ S '59. * (PA 34:7957)
50. TUDDENHAM, READ D. "Correlates of Yielding to a Distorted Group Norm." J Personality 27:272–84 Je '59. * (PA 34:4096)
51. WHITLOCK, GLENN EVERETT. The Relationship Between Passivity of Personality and Personal Factors Related to the Choice of the Ministry as a Vocation. Doctor's thesis, University of Southern California (Los Angeles, Calif.), 1959. (DA 20:2392)
52. ZEDEK, MEIRA E. "The Conditioning of Verbal Behavior With Negative Cultural Connotations." J Personality 27:477–86 D '59. *
53. BARNES, TED JOHN. An Investigation of the Relationships Between Certain Personality Traits and Elements of Speaking Effectiveness. Doctor's thesis, State University of Iowa (Iowa City, Iowa), 1960. (DA 20:4750)
54. BAY, JUNG HONG. The Validity of Two Objective Measures of Academic Motivation. Doctor's thesis, State University of Iowa (Iowa City, Iowa), 1960. (DA 20:4585)
55. BLOCK, JACK. "Commonality in Word Association and Personality." Psychol Rep 7:332 O '60. * (PA 35:2202)
56. BOGARD, HOWARD M. "Union and Management Trainees —A Comparative Study of Personality and Occupational Choice." J Appl Psychol 44:56–63 F '60. * (PA 34:7496)
57. DICKEN, CHARLES F. "Simulated Patterns on the California Psychological Inventory." J Counsel Psychol 7:24–31 sp '60. * (PA 35:2218)
58. GOUGH, HARRISON G. "Theory and Measurement of Socialization." J Consult Psychol 24:23–30 F '60. * (PA 34:7554)
59. GOWAN, JOHN C. "Intercorrelations of the California Psychological Inventory and the Guilford-Zimmerman Temperament Survey With Intelligence as Measured by the ACE." Calif J Ed Res 11:213–5 N '60. * (PA 35:4856)
60. HILL, ROBERT E., JR. "Dichotomous Prediction of Student Teaching Excellence Employing Selected CPI Scales." J Ed Res 53:349–51 My '60. *
61. HILLS, DAVID ALLEN. The California Personality Inventory Flexibility Scale, Motivation Instructions, and Some Measures of Behavioral Rigidity. Doctor's thesis, State University of Iowa (Iowa City, Iowa), 1960. (DA 21:2003)
62. JACKSON, DOUGLAS N. "Stylistic Response Determinants in the California Psychological Inventory." Ed & Psychol Meas 20:339–46 su '60. * (PA 35:6420)
63. KEIMOWITZ, ROBERT I., AND ANSBACHER, HEINZ L. "Personality and Achievement in Mathematics." J Indiv Psychol 16:84–7 My '60. * (PA 34:7392)
64. MAXWELL, MARTHA JANE. An Analysis of the California Psychological Inventory and the American Council on Education Psychological Test as Predictors of Success in Different College Curricula. Doctor's thesis, University of Maryland (College Park, Md.), 1960. (DA 21:549)
65. MERRIMAN, J. BURTON. "Relationship of Personality Traits to Motor Ability." Res Q 31:163–73 My '60. * (PA 36:1HA63M)
66. MITCHELL, JAMES V., JR., AND PIERCE-JONES, JOHN. "A Factor Analysis of Gough's California Psychological Inventory." J Consult Psychol 24:453–6 O '60. * (PA 35:4893)
67. SIMPSON, JON E.; DINITZ, SIMON; KAY, BARBARA; AND RECKLESS, WALTER C. "Delinquency Potential of Pre-Adolescents in High-Delinquency Areas." Brit J Delinq 10:211–5 Ja '60. *
68. VINCENT, CLARK E. "Unwed Mothers and the Adoption Market: Psychological and Familial Factors." Marriage & Family Living 22:112–8 My '60. *
69. BARNETTE, W. LESLIE, JR. "A Structured and a Semi-Structured Achievement Measure Applied to a College Sample." Ed & Psychol Meas 21:647–56 au '61. * (PA 36:4KL47B)
70. CRITES, JOHN O.; BECHTOLDT, HAROLD P.; GOODSTEIN, LEONARD D.; AND HEILBRUN, ALFRED B., JR. "A Factor Analysis of the California Psychological Inventory." J Appl Psychol 45:408–14 D '61. * (PA 37:1192)
71. DICKEN, CHARLES F. "Note on Biserial Correlation and the Validity of the California Personality Inventory." J Counsel Psychol 8:185–6 su '61. * (PA 36:3HC85D)
72. GOODSTEIN, LEONARD D.; CRITES, JOHN O.; HEILBRUN, ALFRED B., JR.; AND REMPEL, PETER P. "The Use of the California Psychological Inventory in a University Counseling

Service." *J Counsel Psychol* 8:147–53 su '61. * (*PA* 36: 3KI47G)

73. HEILBRUN, ALFRED B., JR. "Male and Female Personality Correlates of Early Termination in Counseling." *J Counsel Psychol* 8:31–6 sp '61. * (*PA* 36:3KI31H)

74. HILL, ROBERT E., JR. "An Investigation of the California Psychological Inventory Empirically Keyed for Dichotomous Prediction of Student Teacher Excellence." *Yearb Nat Council Meas Ed* 18:107–9 '61. *

75. HUNT, JAMES G. *A Study of Nonintellectual Factors Related to Academic Achievement Among College Seniors at Ball State Teachers College.* Doctor's thesis, Purdue University (Lafayette, Ind.), 1961. (*DA* 22:157)

76. JACKSON, DOUGLAS N., AND PACINE, LEONARD. "Response Styles and Academic Achievement." *Ed & Psychol Meas* 21:1015–28 w '61. *

77. LESSINGER, LEON M., AND MARTINSON, RUTH A. "The Use of the California Psychological Inventory With Gifted Pupils." *Personnel & Guid J* 39:572–5 Mr '61. * (*PA* 35:7201)

78. McKEE, JOHN P., AND TURNER, WALTER S. "The Relationship of 'Drive' Ratings in Adolescence to CPI and EPPS Scores in Adulthood." *Vita Hum* 4(1–2):1–14 '61. * (*PA* 36:1HF01M)

79. MAHONEY, THOMAS A.; JERDEE, THOMAS H.; AND NASH, ALLAN N. *The Identification of Management Potential: A Research Approach to Management Development.* Dubuque, Iowa: Wm. C. Brown Co., 1961. Pp. xiii, 79. *

80. MERRITT, MYRTLE AGNES. *The Relationship of Selected Physical, Mental, Emotional and Social Factors to the Recreational Preferences of College Women.* Doctor's thesis, State University of Iowa (Iowa City, Iowa), 1961. (*DA* 22:2675)

81. MUSSEN, PAUL. "Some Antecedents and Consequents of Masculine Sex-Typing in Adolescent Boys." *Psychol Monogr* 75(2):1–24 '61. * (*PA* 36:3FH24M)

82. NUGENT, FRANK A. "The Relationship of Discrepancies Between Interest and Aptitude Scores to Other Selected Personality Variables." *Personnel & Guid J* 39:388–95 Ja '61. * (*PA* 35:6212)

83. PIERCE, JAMES V. "Personality and Achievement Among Able High School Boys." *J Indiv Psychol* 17:102–7 My '61. * (*PA* 36:1KL02P)

84. RIGNEY, FRANCIS J., AND SMITH, L. DOUGLAS. *The Real Bohemia: A Sociological and Psychological Study of the "Beats."* New York: Basic Books, Inc., 1961. Pp. xxi, 250. * (*PA* 36:1GB50R)

85. SIEGMAN, ARON WOLFE. "A Cross-Cultural Investigation of the Relationship Between Ethnic Prejudice, Authoritarian Ideology, and Personality." *J Abn & Social Psychol* 63:654–5 N '61. * (*PA* 37:1085)

86. WEINBERG, NORRIS; MENDELSON, MYER; AND STUNKARD, ALBERT. "A Failure to Find Distinctive Personality Features in a Group of Obese Men." *Am J Psychiatry* 117:1035–7 My '61. *

87. CERBUS, GEORGE, AND NICHOLS, ROBERT C. "Personality Correlates of Picture Preferences." *J Abn & Social Psychol* 64:75–8 Ja '62. * (*PA* 37:3139)

88. CLARK, HOWARD GATES. *Prediction of Teacher and Peer Group Concepts of Ninth Grade High School Students With the California Psychological Inventory.* Doctor's research study No. 1, Colorado State College (Greeley, Colo.), 1962. (*DA* 23:3769)

88a. COBB, BART B. "Problems in Air Traffic Management: 2, Prediction of Success in Air Traffic Controller School." *Aerospace Med* 33:702–13 Je '62. *

88b. DATEL, WILLIAM E. "Socialization Scale Norms on Military Samples." *Mil Med* 127:740–4 S '62. *

89. DINITZ, SIMON; SCARPITTI, FRANK R.; AND RECKLESS, WALTER C. "Delinquency Vulnerability: A Cross Group and Longitudinal Analysis." *Am Sociol R* 27:515–7 Ag '62. * (*PA* 37:5447)

90. ENGEL, ILONA MARIA. *A Factor Analytic Study of Items From Five Masculinity-Femininity Tests.* Doctor's thesis, University of Michigan (Ann Arbor, Mich.), 1962. (*DA* 23:307)

91. FINK, MARTIN B. "Objectification of Data Used in Underachievement-Self Concept Study." *Calif J Ed Res* 13:105–12 My '62. * (*PA* 37:3883)

92. FOX, RONALD ERNEST. *Personality Patterns of Resident Psychotherapists.* Doctor's thesis, University of North Carolina (Chapel Hill, N.C.), 1962. (*DA* 23:4743)

93. GILMORE, SUSAN KAY. *A Study of Differences in Personality Patterns Between Pentecostal Groups of Differential Religious Emphases.* Master's thesis, University of Oregon (Eugene, Ore.), 1962. (*MA* 1:57)

94. HEILBRUN, ALFRED B., JR. "Psychological Factors Related to Counseling Readiness and Implications for Counselor Behavior." *J Counsel Psychol* 9:353–8 w '62. * (*PA* 39:2298)

95. HEILBRUN, ALFRED B., JR.; DANIEL, JOHN L.; GOODSTEIN, LEONARD D.; STEPHENSON, RICHARD R.; AND CRITES, JOHN O. "The Validity of Two-Scale Pattern Interpretation on the California Psychological Inventory." *J Appl Psychol* 46:409–16 D '62. * (*PA* 37:5637)

96. HILGARD, ERNEST R., AND LAUER, LILLIAN W. "Lack of Correlation Between the California Psychological Inventory and Hypnotic Susceptibility." *J Consult Psychol* 26:331–5 Ag '62. * (*PA* 38:4432)

97. HIRT, MICHAEL L., AND COOK, RICHARD A. "Effectiveness of the California Psychological Inventory to Predict Psychiatric Determinations of Socialization." *J Clin Psychol* 18:176–7 Ap '62. * (*PA* 38:8519)

98. HOLLAND, JOHN L., AND ASTIN, ALEXANDER W. "The Prediction of the Academic, Artistic, Scientific, and Social Achievement of Undergraduates of Superior Scholastic Aptitude." *J Ed Psychol* 53:132–43 Je '62. * (*PA* 37:2010)

99. JOHNSON, RICHARD T., AND FRANDSEN, ARDEN N. "The California Psychological Inventory Profile of Student Leaders." *Personnel & Guid J* 41:343–5 D '62. * (*PA* 37:6624)

99a. KALIS, BETTY L.; TOCCHINI, JOHN J.; AND THOMASSEN, PAUL R. "Correlation Study Between Personality Tests and Dental Student Performance." *J Am Dental Assn* 64:656–70 My '62. *

100. KORMAN, MAURICE. "A Factorial Study of Judgmental Space." *Psychol Rep* 10:739–46 Je '62. * (*PA* 37:5651)

101. KORN, HAROLD A. "Differences Between Majors in Engineering and Physical Sciences on CPI and SVIB Scores." *J Counsel Psychol* 9:306–12 w '62. * (*PA* 39:2870)

102. LANIER, WILLIAM JETT. *The Predictive Value of Selected Personality and College Adjustment Instruments Used With the American College Testing Program.* Doctor's thesis, Purdue University (Lafayette, Ind.), 1962. (*DA* 23:2424)

103. LETON, DONALD A. "Personality Ratings of High School Students." *J Ed Res* 56:160–3 N '62. *

104. LETON, DONALD A., AND WALTER, SIDNEY. "A Factor Analysis of the California Psychological Inventory and Minnesota Counseling Inventory." *Calif J Ed Res* 13:126–33 My '62. * (*PA* 37:3446)

105. MACKINNON, DONALD W. "The Personality Correlates of Creativity: A Study of American Architects," pp. 11–39. (*PA* 37:4958) In *Personality Research.* Proceedings of the XIV International Congress of Applied Psychology, Vol. 2. Copenhagen, Denmark: Munksgaard, Ltd., 1962. Pp. 229. *

106. MILBRATH, LESTER W., AND KLEIN, WALTER W. "Personality Correlates of Political Participation." *Acta Sociologica* 6(1–2):53–66 '62. *

107. NELSON, JOHN ANDREWS, JR. *The California Psychological Inventory as a Predictor of the Behavior of the Secondary Student Teacher While Teaching.* Doctor's thesis, University of California (Berkeley, Calif.), 1962.

108. NICHOLS, ROBERT C. "Subtle, Obvious and Stereotype Measures of Masculinity-Femininity." *Ed & Psychol Meas* 22:449–61 au '62. * (*PA* 37:5014)

109. PIERCE-JONES, JOHN; MITCHELL, JAMES V., JR.; AND KING, F. J. "Configurational Invariance in the California Psychological Inventory." *J Exp Ed* 31:65–71 S '62. * (*PA* 37:8012)

110. PUMROY, DONALD K. "Relationship Between the Social Desirability Scale and the California Psychological Inventory." *Psychol Rep* 10:795–6 Je '62. * (*PA* 37:5015)

111. ROSENBERG, LEON A. "Idealization of Self and Social Adjustment." Abstract. *J Consult Psychol* 26:487 O '62. *

112. ROSENBERG, LEON A.; McHENRY, THOMAS B.; ROSENBERG, ANNA MARIA; AND NICHOLS, ROBERT C. "The Prediction of Academic Achievement With the California Psychological Inventory." *J Appl Psychol* 46:385–8 D '62. * (*PA* 37:5670)

113. ROSENHAN, DAVID. "Naysaying and the California Psychological Inventory." *J Consult Psychol* 26:382–3 Ag '62. * (*PA* 38:4314)

114. SIEGMAN, ARON WOLFE. "Personality Variables Associated With Admitted Criminal Behavior." Abstract. *J Consult Psychol* 26:199 Ap '62. * (*PA* 37:5459)

115. STEWART, LOUIS H. "Social and Emotional Adjustment During Adolescence as Related to the Development of Psychosomatic Illness in Adulthood." *Genetic Psychol Monogr* 65:175–215 F '62. *

116. STRUMPFER, DEODANDUS J. W., AND NICHOLS, ROBERT C. "A Study of Some Communicable Measures for the Evaluation of Human Figure Drawings." *J Proj Tech* 26:342–53 S '62. * (*PA* 37:3240)

117. WINKELMAN, SIDRA LEVI. *California Psychological Inventory Profile Patterns of Underachievers, Average Achievers, and Overachievers.* Doctor's thesis, University of Maryland (College Park, Md.), 1962. (*DA* 23:2988)

118. YOUNG, CHARLES RAY. *Factors Associated With Achievement and Underachievement Among Intellectually Superior Boys.* Doctor's thesis, University of Missouri (Columbia, Mo.), 1962. (*DA* 23:2406)

119. AIKEN, LEWIS R., JR. "The Relationships of Dress to Selected Measures of Personality in Undergraduate Women." *J Social Psychol* 59:119–28 F '63. * (*PA* 38:910)

120. ALLER, FLORENCE D. "Some Factors in Marital Adjustment and Academic Achievement of Married Students." *Personnel & Guid J* 41:609–16 Mr '63. *

121. APPLEY, MORTIMER H., AND MOELLER, GEORGE. "Conforming Behavior and Personality Variables in College Women." *J Abn & Social Psychol* 66:284–90 Mr '63. * (*PA* 37:8237)

122. CANTER, FRANCIS M. "Simulation on the California Psychological Inventory and the Adjustment of the Simulator." *J Consult Psychol* 27:253–6 Je '63. * (*PA* 38:992)

123. CAPLAN, STANLEY W.; RUBLE, RONALD A.; AND SEGEL, DAVID. "A Theory of Educational and Vocational Choice in Junior High School." *Personnel & Guid J* 42:129–35 O '63. *

124. CAPRETTA, PATRICK J.; JONES, REGINALD L.; SIEGEL, LAURENCE; AND SIEGEL, LILA C. "Some Noncognitive Characteristics of Honors Program Candidates." *J Ed Psychol* 54:268–76 O '63. * (*PA* 38:4674)

124a. CARNEY, RICHARD E., AND McKEACHIE, WILBERT J. "Religion, Sex, Social Class, Probability of Success, and Student Personality." *J Sci Study Relig* 3:32–42 f '63. *

125. COROTTO, LOREN V. "An Exploratory Study of the Personality Characteristics of Alcohol Patients Who Volunteer for Continued Treatment." *Q J Studies Alcohol* 24:432–42 S '63. *

126. DAHLKE, ARNOLD E., AND DANA, RICHARD H. "Intra-individual Verbal-Numerical Discrepancies and Personality." Abstract. *J Consult Psychol* 27:182 Ap '63. *

127. DICKEN, CHARLES. "Good Impression, Social Desirability, and Acquiescence as Suppressor Variables." *Ed & Psychol Meas* 23:699–720 w '63. * (*PA* 38:8516)

128. DICKEN, CHARLES F. "Convergent and Discriminant Validity of the California Psychological Inventory." *Ed & Psychol Meas* 23:449–59 au '63. * (*PA* 38:6090)

129. DURFLINGER, GLENN W. "Academic and Personality Differences Between Women Students Who Do Complete the Elementary Teaching Credential Program and Those Who Do Not." *Ed & Psychol Meas* 23:775–83 w '63. *

130. DURFLINGER, GLENN W. "Personality Correlates of Success in Student-Teaching." *Ed & Psychol Meas* 23:383–90 su '63. * (*PA* 38:1427)

131. FINK, MARTIN. "Cross Validation of an Underachievement Scale." *Calif J Ed Res* 14:147–52 S '63. * (*PA* 38:6642)

132. GOODSTEIN, LEONARD D., AND SCHRADER, WILLIAM J. "An Empirically-Derived Managerial Key for the California Psychological Inventory." *J Appl Psychol* 47:42–5 F '63. * (*PA* 37:8352)

133. KIRK, BARBARA A.; CUMMINGS, ROGER W.; AND HACKETT, HERBERT R. "Personal and Vocational Characteristics of Dental Students." *Personnel & Guid J* 41:522–7 F '63. *

134. KNAPP, ROBERT R. "Personality Correlates of Delinquency Rate in a Navy Sample." *J Appl Psychol* 47:68–71 F '63. * (*PA* 37:8179)

135. MITCHELL, JAMES V., JR. "A Comparison of the First and Second Order Dimensions of the 16 PF and CPI Inventories." *J Social Psychol* 61:151–66 O '63. * (*PA* 38:8499)

136. NICHOLS, ROBERT C., AND SCHNELL, RICHARD R. "Factor Scales for the California Psychological Inventory." *J Consult Psychol* 27:228–35 Je '63. * (*PA* 38:961)

137. PODELL, HARRIETT A. "Note on Successive Dimensional Analysis Applied to Affective, Cognitive, and Personality Traits." *Psychol Rep* 13:813–4 D '63. * (*PA* 38:8503)

138. SHURE, GERALD H., AND ROGERS, MILES S. "Personality Factor Stability for Three Ability Levels." *J Psychol* 55:445–56 Ap '63. * (*PA* 38:1001)

139. SILVERMAN, PAUL L. "Some Personality Correlates of Attributive Projection." *Percept & Motor Skills* 17:947–53 D '63. * (*PA* 38:6131)

140. SPRINGOB, H. KARL. "Relationship of Interests as Measured by the Kuder Preference Record to Personality as Measured by the California Psychological Inventory Scales." *Personnel & Guid J* 41:624–8 Mr '63. * (*PA* 39:1760)

141. STEWART, CHARLES ALLEN, JR. *Prediction of Academic Success in Selected United States Army Medical Field Service School Courses.* Doctor's thesis, University of Texas (Austin, Tex.), 1963. (*DA* 24:597)

142. TONRA, MARY FIDELIS. *Differentiation Between a Female Delinquent and a Female Non-Delinquent Group on the Socialization Scale of the California Psychological Inventory.* Master's thesis, Fordham University (New York, N.Y.), 1963.

143. WEBB, ALLEN P. "Sex-Role Preferences and Adjustment in Early Adolescents." *Child Develop* 34:609–18 S '63. *

144. WHITLOCK, GLENN E. "Role and Self Concepts in the Choice of the Ministry as a Vocation." *J Pastoral Care* 17:208–12 w '63. * (*PA* 38:9350)

E. LOWELL KELLY, *Professor of Psychology, The University of Michigan, Ann Arbor, Michigan.*

The CPI, as it is now widely known, was developed to make possible the comprehensive, multidimensional assessment of normal persons in a variety of settings. The resulting inventory, composed of 480 statements, is essentially self-administering for literate subjects who are instructed to respond to each item on a separate answer sheet, "True" or "False" according to whether they agree or disagree with a statement or feel that "it is" or "is not" true about them. Three types of answer sheets are available: one for hand scoring and two for machine scoring.

The inventory yields 18 raw scores; transferring them to a profile form provides for graphic conversion to standard scores with mean 50 and SD 10. The norms on one side of the profile sheet are based on over 6,000 males and those on the reverse side on over 7,000 female cases. While the author does not claim that these normative groups represent a random sample of the general population, he states that they include a wide range of ages, socioeconomic groups, and geographical areas.

In addition to these separate norms for males and females, the manual presents separate mean profiles for college and high school subjects of each sex. The manual also includes totals showing the raw score means and standard deviations of 30 special groups (19 male and 11 female) for each of the 18 scores.

As noted above, the inventory yields 18 scores: 11 of these are based on empirically derived scoring weights assigned to responses found to differentiate defined criterion groups; four of the scores are based on weights originally judged by the author as indicating the presence of a designated variable and refined by internal consistency analysis. The remaining three scores were also derived empirically to detect tendencies of subjects to fake (good or bad) or to respond in a manner which makes the other scores of doubtful validity.

The number of items contributing to the 18 scores varies from 22 to 56 (median = 37). Test-retest reliabilities based on 200 male prisoners retested after one to three weeks range from .49 to .87 with a median of .80. For high school subjects tested after one year, the median test-retest correlation is .65 for males and .68 for females. The manual does not report any reliability estimates based on a single administration, but presumably these would be higher than the test-retest consistency coefficients noted above, and hence sufficiently high for both group and individual use.

How many and what psychological variables are assessed by the CPI? According to the manual, there are 18 different characteristics, each with a name, and for each the author presents some evidence for some validity. For example, the first scale is called Dominance, abbreviated Do. Scoring weights for this scale were empirically determined on the basis of differential responses of high school students nominated as "most" and "least" dominant by their principals. In cross-validational samples, students nominated "most dominant" tend to score about one standard deviation higher than those nominated as "least dominant." The difference is significant at the .01 level for both boys and girls. Furthermore, Do scores were found to correlate .48 and .40 with staff ratings of dominance in two different assessment studies.

Similar evidence is presented for each of the 11 scales based on empirically derived response weights of contrasting groups. While the discrimination of extreme groups is less sharp than one might expect, and while one may not always agree with the author in his choice of name for the psychological continuum underlying certain of these scales, there is convincing evidence that each of the scales has some validity when judged against life performance criteria. This is true even for the scales developed on the basis of *a priori* weights and then refined through item analysis (internal consistency). Thus, Self-Acceptance (Sa) scores significantly differentiate between high school students rated as high and low on self-acceptance, and correlate positively (.32) with assessment staff ratings of "self-acceptance," negatively (−.57) with staff Q-sorting of the phrase, "Has a readiness to feel guilty."

Additional evidence of the functional validity of each of the scales is provided by a list of the adjectives indicating the way in which persons scoring high and low on each of the scales are seen by assessment staff members or peers in an assessment program. Thus even for Communality (Cm), based on the modal response to only 28 items and one of the least reliable of the 18 scales, high scoring persons are seen as "Dependable, moderate, tactful, reliable, sincere, patient, steady, and realistic; as being honest, conscientious; and as having common sense and good judgment." Low scorers, on the other hand, are seen as: "Impatient, changeable, complicated, imaginative, disorderly, nervous, restless, and confused; as being guileful and deceitful; inattentive and forgetful; and as having internal conflicts and problems."

Similarly, extensive lists of adjectives are provided to characterize the high and low ends of each of the 18 scales. These lists combined with the critical ratios showing the ability of

each set of scores to differentiate between extreme groups gives the impression that the CPI measures a very large number of important personality variables. A crucial question, of course, is how many? The author does not imply that the 18 dimensions are independent but groups them into four categories as follows: (*a*) "Measures of Poise, Ascendancy, and Self-Assurance" (Do, Cs, Sy, Sp, Sa, and Wb); (*b*) "Measures of Socialization, Maturity, and Responsibility" (Re, So, Sc, To, Gi, and Cm); (*c*) "Measures of Achievement Potential and Intellectual Efficiency" (Ac, Ai, and Ie); and (*d*) "Measures of Intellectual and Interest Modes" (Py, Fx, and Fe).

Two factor analytic studies (66, 70) both indicate that most of the information contained in the 18 scores could be reflected in 4 or 5 scores. More important, both for users of the instrument and as indication of the hazards of not paying enough attention to the intercorrelations of the scales as reported in the manual, these studies both point to probably incorrect locations of certain of the scales in the author's classification. For example, for reasons which are not clear, Gough groups Wb (Sense of Well-being) in class (*a*) above and Ac (Achievement via Conformance) in class (*c*) even though his own data show that these two scales are intercorrelated to the extent of .58 for men and .66 for women and that both are more highly correlated with class (*b*) scales than with class (*a*) or (*c*) scales. The author was apparently more confident of his theorizing than of his empirical data!

Like most test authors, Gough tends to be somewhat more enthusiastic about and confident of the validity of his instrument than is justified by the evidence available. For example, the manual suggests that in interpretation, considerable weight be given to "interactions among scales," to patterns of profiles, and to "internal variability of the profile." While a logical case can be made for the probable validity of such interpretational inferences, the only evidence presented is a series of profile analyses of individual cases.

All in all, however, the CPI in this reviewer's opinion is one of the best, if not the best, available instruments of its kind. It was developed on the basis of a series of empirical studies and the evidence for the validity of its several scales is extensive. The manual is one of the most complete of any available and "wonders of wonders" reports intercorrelations of CPI scores with those of several other widely used tests of personality. Unfortunately, these data suggest that the CPI does not yield nearly as much information nor such unique information as the CPI scale names would imply. For example, about half of the 18 CPI scales correlate .50 or higher with scores on Bernreuter's *Personality Inventory* first published in 1931. By contrast, however, the intercorrelations of CPI and MMPI scales tend to be quite low in spite of the fact that the two inventories have some 200 items in common. Perhaps it is too much to ask of any test author or publisher, but this reviewer regrets that the manual does not indicate the correlation of the CPI scores with those derived from the most similar (and competitive!) inventories which also purport to yield a multidimensional profile of the normal personality albeit utilizing markedly different trait or factor labels.

The degree of professional acceptance of the CPI and its impact on personality research is reflected in the large number of references which have appeared since the last edition of the MMY.

For reviews by Lee J. Cronbach and Robert L. Thorndike, see 5:37 (1 excerpt).

[72]

★**The California Q-Set: A Q-Sort for Personality Assessment and Psychiatric Research.** Adults; 1961; observer ratings; Form 3 (110 cards); manual (166 pages, see *1* below); record sheet (1 page); $8.75 per set of cards and manual; $2.25 per set of cards; $1.75 per 25 record sheets; $6.75 per manual; postage extra; administration time not reported; Jack Block; distributed by Consulting Psychologists Press, Inc. *

REFERENCES

1. BLOCK, JACK. *The Q-Sort Method in Personality Assessment and Psychiatric Research.* Springfield, Ill.: Charles C Thomas, Publisher, 1961. Pp. ix, 161. * (PA 36:5HE61B)
2. MACKINNON, DONALD W. "The Personality Correlates of Creativity: A Study of American Architects," pp. 11–39. (PA 37:4958) In *Personality Research.* Proceedings of the XIV International Congress of Applied Psychology, Vol. 2. Copenhagen, Denmark: Munksgaard, Ltd., 1962. Pp. 229. *

ALLEN L. EDWARDS, *Professor of Psychology, University of Washington, Seattle, Washington.*

The *California Q-Set* consists of 100 carefully selected statements which are intended to provide "a comprehensive description, in contemporary psychodynamic terms, of an individual's personality." The statements are supposedly of sufficiently broad coverage that "ideally—and the set is not yet ideal—the items should permit the portrayal of any kind of psychopathology and of any kind of normality."

Personality descriptions are obtained by having an observer describe another person, using whatever information he has about the person, with the CQ-Set. The statements are sorted into nine categories, from most to least salient, with a fixed number of statements being assigned to each category. Satisfactory reliability of the personality descriptions can be obtained by having several observers describe the same person and then averaging their independently made Q-sorts to obtain a composite Q-sort.

The CQ-Set is not a test or scale which purports to measure any specific personality variable. Instead, it is a pool of items which, like those in the MMPI, can conceivably be used in the development of many different scales. Suppose, for example, that each of a number of psychiatrists describes his conception of a male paranoid with the CQ-Set. Their ratings can be combined to obtain a composite. The composite is called a criterion or defining Q-sort. If a given individual is described in terms of the CQ-Set, his Q-sort can be correlated with the criterion sort and the resulting correlation coefficient is regarded by Block as a score. A convenient table for converting the sum of squared discrepancies between the ratings of two Q-sorts into the correlation coefficient is given in Block's monograph. It is obvious that, by means of defining Q-sorts, as many different scales can be developed as there are concepts or variables about which professionally competent judges can show some degree of agreement in their Q-sorts of the concepts.

Three defining Q-sorts, based upon the judgments of nine clinical psychologists, are presented in the monograph: the optimally adjusted individual, the male paranoid, and the female hysteric. Presumably, if the Q-sort for a given individual has a high positive correlation with the optimally adjusted composite, he would be regarded as having a higher adjustment score than an individual whose Q-sort correlates only moderately with the composite—as adjustment is conceived by the nine clinical psychologists. It should be obvious that the defining Q-sort does *not* solve the problem of construct validity. If correlations with a defining Q-sort are to be interpreted as scores, then further research on construct validity is necessary.

Block implies that social desirability considerations are not involved when observer evaluations are obtained from professionally competent people, the use emphasized in the monograph. That this is not necessarily the case is indicated by a study by Kogan, Quinn, Ax, and Ripley,[1] a reference not cited by Block.

The reviewer had nine judges Q-sort the CQ-Set for social desirability. The composite social desirability sort was then correlated with the optimally adjusted sort. The resulting correlation coefficient was .88. Is "optimal adjustment," as conceived by clinical psychologists, more or less equivalent to "social desirability"?

In general, Block's monograph is a sound and complete treatment of Q-sorts as a means of obtaining observer evaluations. Various potential research applications of Q-sorts are described in sufficient detail that they may be tried by others. The monograph should be read by anyone interested in personality assessment. If one proposes to use a Q-sort to obtain personality descriptions, the CQ-Set is probably as good as, if not better than, any other available on the commercial market. The items are neatly printed on 2¼ by 3½ inch cards. The cards are sturdy and after nine Q-sorts showed little wear.

DAVID T. LYKKEN, *Associate Professor of Psychiatry and Psychology, University of Minnesota, Minneapolis, Minnesota.*

Many clinicians would agree, although admittedly in some cases not without a fight, that most current personality testing—as actually, clinically used—is not measurement at all. It is true that many of the available tests have, either in the course of their construction or through subsequent research, been shown to be able to differentiate among various diagnostic (or otherwise specifiable) groups, or able to estimate certain characterological or behavioral dimensions identified by, e.g., factor analysis, or to be correlated with some other criterion of interest. The practical reality, however, is that the predictions or estimates which these tests have been empirically proved to be able to make are not usually a

sufficient basis for the important decisions which the clinician is required to make. Therefore, one finds the clinician making inferences from the test data for which there is no existing empirical support, inferences which are a necessary guide for the decisions which are required of him and the validity of which depends upon, among other things, his experience and skill.

Thus, in effect, the clinician commonly uses the test protocol as a surrogate for the subject; the test, so to speak, has interviewed the subject, has elicited from him a more-or-less standardized behavior sample which hopefully is rich in information relevant to a wide variety of questions. And an important advantage of the test, thus used, over other opportunities for sampling the behavior of the subject (in interviews, on the ward, in work or play situations, etc.) is that the observations of the test are provided in a codified, reasonably standardized form. Unlike the human observer, the test always remembers what it has seen and formulates its observations in the same clear, simple standard vocabulary every time. By way of contrast, the clinician, after he has interviewed his subject, must in a real sense score himself; he must consider what he has seen in the subject, decide what descriptive generalizations are warranted, and determine the relative degrees of confidence he is willing to place on each such facet. Whether this task is approached deliberately and systematically or not, it logically must be done somehow before the clinician can hope to bring to bear his knowledge and previous experience in formulating inferences based upon his observations or before he can communicate his impression of the subject to others.

Of the various devices which have been developed to assist the clinician in this difficult task of "self-scoring"—devices such as the structured interview, the standardized rating schedule, the adjective checklist, etc.—perhaps the most promising is the Q-sort. And the most skillfully designed and carefully developed standard set of Q-sort items now available in published form is the *California Q-Set,* the result of some 10 years of thoughtful planning on the part of Jack Block and his associates of the University of California at Berkeley. The CQ-Set consists of 100 items printed on 2¼ by 3½ inch cards for convenience of sorting. Some of the items describe the immediate

1 Kogan, William S.; Quinn, Robert; Ax, Albert F.; and Ripley, Herbert S. "Some Methodological Problems in the Quantification of Clinical Assessment by Q Array." *J Consult Psychol* 21:57–62 F '57. *

social persona of the subject: "Is an interesting, arresting person," "Is cheerful," "Is verbally fluent; can express ideas well." Others require an assessment of long term behavior trends or dispositions: "Expresses hostile feelings directly," "Is self-indulgent," "Is a genuinely dependable and responsible person." Many transcend sheer behavioral description and demand varying degrees of clinical insight: "Has a readiness to feel guilty," "Tends to project his own feelings and motivations onto others," "Handles anxiety and conflicts by, in effect, refusing to recognize their presence; repressive or dissociative tendencies." Overall, the items make little reference to psychiatric symptoms or abnormal phenomena; the CQ-Set is aimed at delineating general personality organization, whereas other instruments, such as the *Wittenborn Psychiatric Rating Scales,* might be more suited to differentiating syndromes of severe psychiatric illness.

The clinician describes his subject by sorting these 100 items along a nine point scale according to a forced quasi-normal distribution; that is, 5 items are to be placed in each of the extreme categories One and Nine, 8 items in Two and in Eight, 12 items in both Three and Seven, and so on. A complete sort requires in the neighborhood of 30 minutes. The placement of the items is to depend on the judge's estimate of the salience of the trait in question in relation to understanding the subject being described. That is, a trait is rated in terms of its importance in specifying the unique and essential characteristics of the subject, rather than according to how strong the trait is in him in relation to other people. Thus, for example, in Q-sorting an acute schizophrenic patient, an item such as "Appears to have a high degree of intellectual capacity" might well be rated in the middle range even though the subject was known to have an IQ of 160, since intellectual capacity is a relatively less important facet of the essential portrait of this particular subject.

This codified, standard-language distillation of the observer-subject interaction should have many uses in both research and clinical settings. Agreement between two or more judges rating the same subject can be easily measured by intercorrelating their Q-sorts to determine, for example, whether enough discrepancy exists to indicate that the subject in question

should be studied further before decisions are reached about him. Item by item comparisons will help identify areas of disagreement. Two or more subjects may be compared either globally by intercorrelation or item by item. One promising technique is to combine the wisdom and varying perspectives of the members of a clinical or research team by averaging their Q-sorts of the same subject, thus hopefully producing a more valid assessment by the summation of veridical insights and the cancellation of "noisy" error. The Q-sort is a convenient datum for longitudinal or "P-type" studies of, e.g., developmental changes and progress of treatment, or it might be applied in reverse as a means of assessing clinical skill. Finally, of course, the Q-sort can be used as raw material for the development of specialized actuarial prediction tables or formulas. Imagine, for example, a diagnostic center where juvenile offenders are observed for a period of weeks by a team of psychologists, social workers, and attendants and whose function is to determine whether individual boys should best be sent home, to a work camp, to a psychiatric hospital, or to a high security prison. Within a reasonable time, a large file of consensus Q-sorts averaged over the members of the diagnostic team, together with follow-up data on the results of the disposition made, could be accumulated. From such a file, one could readily develop "criterion Q-sorts," e.g., by averaging across groups of individuals for whom the follow-up indicates that prison assignment would have been appropriate and against which subsequent cases could be compared; or, one could employ ordinary item analysis to construct recidivism scales and the like.

The "manual" designed to accompany the *California Q-Set* is in fact a hard-cover treatise which not only describes at length the development of the CQ-Set but which also contains a thorough and thoughtful appraisal of the Q-sort method generally by an authority in the field. The book is recommended reading for all clinicians and essential study for prospective users of the method.

As the foregoing will attest, this reviewer considers the Q-sort method to hold great promise for both clinical and research applications and has high regard for the contributions of Block and his associates in this area. This is not to say, however, that one cannot argue with certain of Block's views, nor would Block himself pretend that the present CQ-Set is unimprovable. While there is no room here for an extended critique, it seems appropriate to alert readers new to this field to at least some possible areas of controversy, beginning with perhaps the most basic issue of all: Is it possible with *any* standard set of items of manageable length to satisfactorily describe the essence of the individual personality? This is, of course, the old nomothetic-ideographic issue, which, in the reviewer's opinion, has yet to be adequately resolved. One line of argument can be adumbrated by noting that if individuality is in part a result of (learned) *structural* uniqueness, as evidenced by idiosyncratic behavior patterning (i.e., unique traits) or idiosyncratic systems of S-R relationships, then —to the extent that the behaviors one wants to predict are mediated by such unique aspects of structure—to that extent will *any* nomothetic assessment be found wanting. One means of answering this essentially empirical question is, of course, by exploring the limits of the nomothetic approach with the most sophisticated techniques available, among which the Q-sort method has to be included.

Block treats at length in the manual with the reasons which led him (*a*) to require sorters to allocate specific numbers of items to each of the nine scale categories and (*b*) to identify the sorting dimension as "salience" rather than asking, "Which of these items most accurately describe the subject?" or "How does the subject compare on these traits with people in general?" Block's arguments on these two closely related issues have considerable weight and rest in part upon specific research findings. Thus, against the complaint that "salience" is a subtle concept and especially difficult to rationalize in relation to many items of the CQ-Set, Block can point to repeated findings of retest reliabilities of .8 and .9; although judges may complain that they cannot sort some items for "salience," they do in fact sort all the items with remarkable consistency. On the matter of "forcing" the Q-distribution, Block refers to a study in which unforced sorting distributions were found to reflect peculiarities of the judges and contained no information about the subjects not available in forced sortings that were collected later. However, this one finding, based on a rather atypical sorting situation, needs considerable extension before it can be generalized to all sets of items, all judges, all subjects, and other sorting criteria than "salience." Nor, of course, does a high retest reliability guarantee validity—that the items being consistently sorted are also accurately reflecting the judge's clinical impression of the subject.

Finally, of course, one must consider the quality of the items themselves; does sorting the particular 100 items of the CQ-Set allow one to encapsulate the essence of the individual under study, to record all of the impressions and insights one feels he has in hand about the subject? When one first attempts to sort the CQ-Set, the selection of items almost inevitably seems arbitrary, and it is easy to be critical of their content and to think of additional or alternative items which "should obviously be included." In fact, the choice of these 100 items was not at all capricious but the result of careful editing, selection, and testing; the present set incorporates suggestions from over 50 clinicians who had experience with earlier versions. An important point to keep in mind here is that a descriptive dimension, property, or trait need not be the explicit subject of a specific Q-item in order for it to be expressable via the Q-sort as a whole; many attributes can be communicated by means of the configuration of pairs or groups of item placements so that, in principle at least, many times 100 descriptive properties can be captured in the Q-sorting of 100 well chosen (and perhaps relatively atomistic) items. Perhaps one should continue the analogy drawn earlier between the global, nomothetic personality description attempted by the Q-sort and the similarly global representation commonly read into protocols of personality tests like the MMPI. Modern psychometric practice considers responses to questionnaire items to be bits of behavior, the meaning of which devolves from the empirical item correlations. It is considered naïve to criticize (or to interpret) an MMPI item on the basis of its content. It may be that a similar attitude should govern one's evaluation of a Q-Set. Clearly, in both cases, every resource of logic, theory, prior experience, and clinical intuition should be utilized in generating the original item pool and formulating the rules of procedure in the "context of discovery" phase of test or Q-Set construction. But the ultimate evaluation of the end product must hang upon an empirical assessment of the instrument's properties and capacities.

The Q-sort method deserves the active and enlightened attention of all practicing clinicians and those whose research involves personality assessment. In the 10 years since Stephenson introduced the method, only a comparative handful of psychologists have been exploring its problems and possibilities and much remains to be learned. It seems likely that many workers will eventually find it most useful to develop their own set of items and a sorting procedure tailored to their particular application. One can expect many changes in technique and in theory as experience accumulates. In the meanwhile, Block's manual provides an excellent and provocative introduction to the method and his *California Q-Set* is the appropriate starting point at least for any potential user.

Arch Gen Psychiatry 7:230–1 S '62. Samuel J. Beck. [Review of the manual.] * should prove of much value to researchers employing the technique and to other investigators who are interested in results of researchers using the method but who are not experienced in using it. The book is at once both a primer of instruction for applying the basic procedures and an elucidation of the orienting statistical theory. Appendices supply supporting information, results, and tables. An extensive list of reading references will be helpful to the interested students.

Cont Psychol 8:389–90 O '63. John E. Exner, Jr. [Review of the manual.] The materials presented in this monograph provide a substantial argument supporting the usefulness in research of the general scaling procedure known as the Q-sort technique. The author, well grounded in his knowledge and experience with the technique, is admittedly interested in presenting this argument so as to discuss in turn the relative merits of a specific Q-sort, the California Q-set (CQ). Thus, the material becomes narrowed considerably in its total scope but nevertheless continues throughout to be thought provoking. Several of the frequently voiced criticisms of the Q-sort technique are dealt with in adequate depth and sufficient clarity to leave even the most negativistic reader somewhat impressed. * there are points in the text where the reader almost has the impression that if publication of the monograph had been delayed another year or two

and subsequent data had been included, the entire impact of the material would have been significantly greater. The over-all description of the development and uses of the CQ set is quite good. The enormity of work devoted to its construction is very impressive and the care given to the rationale of the set is admirable indeed and could well serve as a model for the construction of other such sets. Even the decision to construct the CQ set as a forced-choice type, which ordinarily could open the door to much criticism, is based on solid reasoning to which most researchers would be agreeable. It seems realistic to suggest that if many of the earlier articles pertaining to the Q-sort technique contained the theoretical and practical thoroughness as is demonstrated in the construction of the CQ set, the entire status of the technique as a research tool could be much greater than is currently apparent. The arguments favoring the usefulness of the technique in general, and the CQ set in particular, in individual personality assessment are considerably less attractive and realistic than are the statements favoring its use as a research tool. * Possibly the most unfortunate aspect of the monograph is that it is too short. After struggling through arguments, and bits of data, all of which lend themselves quite well to the notion that the Q-sort technique is really worthwhile, the reader is left with little information concerning some of the most practical applications of the technique. For example, any teacher of clinical students could not help but be impressed by suggestions of how the technique can be helpful in evaluation of the degree to which personality appraisals agree. But alas, little elaboration is provided here. Also mentioned far too briefly is the applicability of the technique to the study of highly specific personality characteristics such as need achievement, reality testing, etc. A more thorough approach concerning the various applications of the technique would not only make the book more palatable, but could have easily made it useful as a good seminar text. In its present form it provides useful information to the reader but much of this information only serves to raise questions rather than answer them. Its full clarity is probably derived only if the reader has some previous familiarity with Q-sort. The author has done a very good job in light of his apparent objectives. But I wish the book were longer.

Ed & Psychol Meas 23:208–10 sp '63. Harold Borko. [Review of the manual.] * In this slim volume Block lucidly presents the details of the Q-sort procedure and the advantages of applying this method to the study of personality types and psychiatric classifications. * primarily concerned with a description and discussion of the special Q-sort procedure designated as the California Q-set * By describing the methods and rationale of these procedures Block has increased and updated our knowledge of the technique. By pointing out the kinds of research applications in which the Q-sort is appropriate, he has extended the range of its usefulness. Through having developed a comprehensive set of 100 items, he has made the California Q-set readily available for personality research. He has accomplished a great deal, and the monograph is recommended to those researchers who are interested in exploring the applicability of the Q-sort method for personality assessment.

[73]

California Test of Personality, 1953 Revision. Grades kgn–3, 4–8, 7–10, 9–16, adults; 1939–53; 16 scores: self-reliance, sense of personal worth, sense of personal freedom, feeling of belonging, withdrawing tendencies, nervous symptoms, total personal worth, social standards, social skills, anti-social tendencies, family relations, school relations, occupation relations, community relations, total social adjustment, total adjustment; IBM for grades 4 and over; Forms AA, BB, ('53, 8 pages); 5 levels; manual ('53, 32 pages); profile ('53, 1 page); $3.50 per 35 tests; separate answer sheets may be used; 5¢ per IBM answer sheet; 9¢ per Scoreze answer sheet; 20¢ per hand scoring stencil; 75¢ per machine scoring stencil; postage extra; 50¢ per specimen set of any one level, postpaid; (45–60) minutes; Louis P. Thorpe, Willis W. Clark, and Ernest W. Tiegs; California Test Bureau. *

a) PRIMARY. Grades kgn–3; 1940–53.
b) ELEMENTARY. Grades 4–8; 1939–53.
c) INTERMEDIATE. Grades 7–10; 1939–53.
d) SECONDARY. Grades 9–16; 1942–53.
e) ADULT. Adults; 1942–53.

REFERENCES

1–24. See 3:26.
25–117. See 5:38.
118. SERPENTO, SANTINO T. "The Personality Adjustment of a Seventh Grade Population in Relation to Reading Ability." *W Va Univ B* 24:137–43 Je '53. *
119. HOLMES, JACK A. "Factors Underlying Major Reading Disabilities at the College Level." *Genetic Psychol Monogr* 49:3–95 F '54. * (*PA* 28:8982)
120. ABRAMS, DOROTHY FRANCES. *A Comparative Study of the Dominant Personality Tendencies, as Shown by the California Test of Personality, of Selected Cerebral Palsied and Selected Physically Normal Children.* Doctor's thesis, New York University (New York, N.Y.), 1956. (*DA* 19:167)
121. SEWELL, WILLIAM H., AND HALLER, ARCHIE O. "Social Status and the Personality Adjustment of the Child." *Sociometry* 19:114–25 Mr '56. * (*PA* 31:5849)
122. RATLIFF, JOHN ALLEN. *A Comparison of Mothers' Estimates With the Measured Adjustments of Their Junior High School Children.* Doctor's thesis, University of Houston (Houston, Tex.), 1957. (*DA* 19:3218)
123. SEMLER, IRA JACKSON. *Relationship Among Various Measures of Pupil Adjustment.* Doctor's thesis, State University of Iowa (Iowa City, Iowa), 1957. (*DA* 17:2923)

124. BURCHINAL, LEE G. "Parents' Attitudes and Adjustment of Children." *J Genetic Psychol* 92:69–79 Mr '58. * (*PA* 36:1FG69B)
125. CALDWELL, EDWARD. *A Study of the Stability of Scores on a Personality Inventory Administered During College Orientation Week.* Doctor's thesis, Florida State University (Tallahassee, Fla.), 1958. (*DA* 19:1998)
126. CARTER, CLEO DORRIS. *The Relationship Between Personality and Academic Achievement (Reading and Arithmetic) of Seven Year-Olds.* Doctor's thesis, Indiana University (Bloomington, Ind.), 1958. (*DA* 19:1027)
127. KOLLMEYER, LOUIS ADOLPH. *The Relationship Between Children's Drawings and Reading Achievement, Personal-Social Adjustment, and Intelligence.* Doctor's thesis, University of Oregon (Eugene, Ore.), 1958. (*DA* 19:2269)
128. OXFORD, LAKE C. *A Study of Personal and Social Adjustment of Seventh Grade Boys and Girls as Influenced by Physical Size, Athletic Ability, Acceptance by Peers, and Acceptance of Peers.* Doctor's thesis, University of Maryland (College Park, Md.), 1958. (*DA* 20:3634)
129. REINBOLD, EMMA J. *A Study of the Relationship Between Emotional Adjustment and School Citizenship.* Doctor's thesis, Temple University (Philadelphia, Pa.), 1958. (*DA* 19:1956)
130. SMITH, PAUL MILTON. *Personality Characteristics of Rural and Urban Southern Negro Children.* Doctor's thesis, Indiana University (Bloomington, Ind.), 1958. (*DA* 19:1019)
131. TERRELL, GLENN, JR., AND SHREFFLER, JOY. "A Developmental Study of Leadership." *J Ed Res* 52:69–72 O '58. * (*PA* 34:1063)
132. WILSON, JOHN A. R. "Differences in Achievement Attributable to Different Educational Environments." *J Ed Res* 52:83–93 N '58. * (*PA* 33:10949)
133. CALDWELL, EDWARD. "Stability of Scores on a Personality Inventory Administered During College Orientation Week." *Personnel & Guid J* 38:305–8 D '59. * (*PA* 35:1259)
134. EASTON, JUDITH C. "Some Personality Traits of Underachieving and Achieving High School Students of Superior Ability." *B Maritime Psychol Assn* 8:34–9 Ap '59. * (*PA* 34:4786)
135. JACKSON, PHILIP W., AND GETZELS, JACOB W. "Psychological Health and Classroom Functioning: A Study of Dissatisfaction With School Among Adolescents." *J Ed Psychol* 50:295–300 D '59. * (*PA* 34:8368, 36:1FH95J)
136. MATHIS, CLAUDE. "Note on the Susceptibility of the California Test of Personality to Faking." *Psychol Rep* 5:527 S '59. * (*PA* 38:4279)
137. MONTGOMERY, GRACE I. *The Use of the California Test of Personality in Identifying Children's Personality Problems.* Master's thesis, Central Washington College of Education (Ellensburg, Wash.), 1959.
138. MOORE, PHELMA NEWTON. *A Survey of the Orientation Problems Common to Entering Freshmen in Pan American College for the First Semester of the 1958–1959 School Year.* Doctor's thesis, University of Houston (Houston, Tex.), 1959. (*DA* 20:2103)
139. MUNSON, BYRON E. "Personality Differentials Among Urban, Suburban, Town, and Rural Children." *Rural Sociol* 24:257–64 S '59. * (*PA* 35:725)
140. NORMAN, RALPH D., AND DALEY, MARVIN F. "The Comparative Personality Adjustment of Superior and Inferior Readers." *J Ed Psychol* 50:31–6 F '59. * (*PA* 35:2003)
141. ROFFEE, DOROTHY T. *A Study of Personality Traits of Elementary School Stutterers as Revealed by the California Test of Personality.* Master's thesis, Boston University (Boston, Mass.), 1959.
142. SEWELL, WILLIAM H., AND HALLER, A. O. "Factors in the Relationship Between Social Status and the Personality Adjustment of the Child." *Am Sociol R* 24:511–20 Ag '59. *
143. WILSON, J. A. R. "Achievement, Intelligence, Age and Promotion Characteristics of the Students Scoring at or Below the Tenth Percentile on the California Test of Personality." *J Ed Res* 52:283–92 Ap '59. * (*PA* 34:4101)
144. CONDIT, ELROY J. *How High School Students Interpret Items of the California Test of Personality.* Master's thesis, Drake University (Des Moines, Iowa), 1960.
145. HORLICK, REUBEN S., AND MILLER, MAURICE H. "A Comparative Personality Study of a Group of Stutterers and Hard of Hearing Patients." *J General Psychol* 63:259–66 O '60. * (*PA* 35:3756)
146. ISCOE, IRA, AND COCHRAN, IRENE. "Some Correlates of Manifest Anxiety in Children." Abstract. *J Consult Psychol* 24:197 F '60. * (*PA* 34:8047)
147. LEHNER, GEORGE F. J. "Some Relationships Among Personal Adjustment Self-Ratings, Self-Scores, and Assigned 'Average' Scores." *J Psychol* 50:333–7 O '60. * (*PA* 35:6488)
148. LOWE, MARJORIE A. *An Analysis of the California Test of Personality Results and Other Data Contained From 22 Juvenile Delinquents.* Master's thesis, East Tennessee State College (Johnson City, Tenn.), 1960.
149. SEMLER, IRA J. "Relationships Among Several Measures of Pupil Adjustment." *J Ed Psychol* 51:60–4 Ap '60. * (*PA* 35:2741)
150. SNELLGROVE, JOHN LOUIS. *A Study of Relationships Between Certain Personal and Socio-Economic Factors and Underachievement.* Doctor's thesis, University of Alabama (University, Ala.), 1960. (*DA* 21:1859)

151. CLEVELAND, GERALD ARTHUR. *A Study of Certain Psychological and Sociological Characteristics as Related to Arithmetic Achievement.* Doctor's thesis, Syracuse University (Syracuse, N.Y.), 1961. (*DA* 22:2681)
152. DUNKLEBERGER, CLARENCE J., AND TYLER, LEONA E. "Interest Stability and Personality Traits." *J Counsel Psychol* 8:70–4 sp '61. * (*PA* 36:3FF70D)
153. HARRISON, MAHALAH J. *The Correlation Between the Children's Form of the Manifest Anxiety Scale and the California Test of Personality.* Master's thesis, University of Tennessee (Knoxville, Tenn.), 1961.
154. HILLS, JOHN R. "The Influence of Instructions on Personality Inventory Scores." *J Counsel Psychol* 8:43–8 sp '61. * (*PA* 36:3HF43H)
155. ROTH, ROBERT M. "The Adjustment of Negro College Students at Hampton Institute." *J Negro Ed* 30:72–4 w '61. *
156. SEROT, NAOMI M., AND TEEVAN, RICHARD C. "Perception of the Parent-Child Relationship and Its Relation to Child Adjustment." *Child Develop* 32:373–8 Je '61. * (*PA* 36:3FG73S)
157. SMITH, PAUL M., JR. "Personal and Social Adjustment of Negro Children in Rural and Urban Areas of the South." *Rural Sociol* 26:73–7 Mr '61. * (*PA* 36:1FF73S)
158. CLARK, EDWARD T., AND MURRAY, JOHN B. "Student Perceptions of Adjustment of Priest and Lay Professors." *Cath Ed R* 60:386–91 S '62. *
159. HALLER, A. O., AND WOLFF, CAROLE ELLIS. "Personality Orientations of Farm, Village, and Urban Boys." *Rural Sociol* 27:275–93 S '62. * (*PA* 37:2989)
160. HALLER, ARCHIBALD O., AND THOMAS, SHAILER. "Personality Correlates of the Socioeconomic Status of Adolescent Males." *Sociometry* 25:398–404 D '62. * (*PA* 38:4094)
161. KERN, WILLIAM H., AND PFAEFFLE, HEINZ. "A Comparison of Social Adjustment of Mentally Retarded Children in Various Educational Settings." *Am J Mental Def* 67:407–13 N '62. * (*PA* 37:5412)
162. MELLENBRUCH, P. L. "The Validity of a Personality Inventory Tested by Hypnosis." *Am J Clin Hypnosis* 5:111–4 O '62. * (*PA* 37:5234)
163. BUTTS, HUGH F. "Skin Color Perception and Self-Esteem." *J Negro Ed* 32:122–8 sp '63. *
164. GOFF, REGINA M. "Trait Identification as a Means of Predicting Academic Goal Attainment." *J Exp Ed* 31:297–302 Mr '63. *
165. PEAK, BOYD D. *The California Test of Personality: A Study of Validation.* Doctor's thesis, Florida State University (Tallahassee, Fla.), 1963. (*DA* 24:1281)
166. ROTH, ROBERT M. "A Method for Identifying Prospective Counselees in College." *J Ed Res* 56:275–6 Ja '63. *

For a review by Verner M. Sims, see 5:38; for reviews by Laurance F. Shaffer and Douglas Spencer of the original edition, see 3:26 (1 excerpt); for reviews by Raymond B. Cattell, Percival M. Symonds, and P. E. Vernon of the elementary and secondary levels, see 40:1213 (1 excerpt).

[74]
The Cassel Psychotherapy Progress Record. Mental patients; 1953; 3 ratings: emotional development, barrier vulnerability development, overall psychotherapy development; 1 form (8 pages); manual (41 pages); no data on reliability and validity; no norms; $10 per set of 25 forms and manual; postpaid; specimen set not available; Russell N. Cassel; Western Psychological Services. *

WILLIAM SCHOFIELD, *Professor of Psychology, University of Minnesota, Minneapolis, Minnesota.*

The *Cassel Psychotherapy Progress Record* (CPPR) "was designed to provide a standardized and objective means for recording and evaluating the progress of psychotherapy for individuals." Although the title and general format suggest that the CPPR is intended for general use by therapists of varying theoretical persuasion, it appears from the manual and

the consistent reference to "clients" (rather than patients) that the author's orientation is to client-centered therapy. The CPPR consists of three scales on each of which the client is to be rated following each therapy contact. The "Overall Psychotherapy Development Scale" is described as the "basic record"; this 14-step scale bears a close resemblance to the 15-step scale of the same author's *Client-Centered Counseling Progress Record* (see 76).

The other two scales (each with 14 steps) are labeled: "The Emotional Development Scale" and "The Barrier Vulnerability Development Scale." With respect to the former, the manual states: "The emotional development of the client appears to progress from the stage of destructive feelings through stages of negative, neutral, positive feelings to feelings of client independence tempered by an interdependence type of vulnerability." The 14 steps of this scale are described in accordance with this theoretical progression. There is no reference to research findings substantiating that this is in fact the generalized sequence of expression of client feeling in psychotherapy.

The rationale of the Barrier Vulnerability Development Scale involves the notion of deliberate use of barriers by the therapist in order to provide "problem situations for client adaptation" and "an evaluation basis for determining progress and growth status" within therapy. Four kinds of barriers used in therapy are listed as: responsibility, time, hostility, and affection.

The manual includes 10 pages of discourse on the "nature of psychotherapy" and extended descriptions and definitions of the intended meanings of each of the 14 positions of each of the 3 scales. It is unfortunate that there are no concrete examples of client behavior that would be relevant to particular ratings. Certain of the ratings involve an appreciation of concepts (for example, "nucleus genetic emotional experience") that receive extremely abstract and ambiguous definition in the text; it is unlikely that these variables could be comfortably assimilated or reliably noted by a therapist not steeped in the author's approach to therapy. Overlap of the three scales is illustrated in the respective specification of step 14 for the emotional, barrier, and overall development scales: "Considerable independence of the client emerges"; "Self-acceptance and assumption of full responsibility"; and "Client-independence, self-reliance, and self-activity." No data are offered from any studies of the reliability with which these scales are applicable to a specified sample.

The provision of a simple graphic rating form on which to record the session-to-session progress of the psychotherapy patient would meet an important need of both the clinician and researcher. The development of a form of sufficient objectivity and generality to permit of reliable application by therapists of different schools would require more research than appears to have gone into the CPPR. Nevertheless, the CPPR could be useful, especially in supervision of neophyte therapists who were simultaneously being trained in Cassel's version of client-centered psychotherapy.

[74a]

★The Child Behavior Rating Scale. Grades kgn-3; 1960–62; ratings by teachers or parents; 6 adjustment scores: self, home, social, school, physical, total; 1 form ('62, 4 pages); manual ('62, 17 mimeographed pages); no data on reliability of subscores; $6 per 25 tests and manual; $1.50 per manual; postpaid; specimen set not available; [5–10] minutes; Russell N. Cassel; Western Psychological Services. *

[74b]

★Children's Embedded Figures Test. Ages 5–12; 1963; revision of the Goodenough-Eagle modification (see 2 below) of the *Embedded Figures Test;* for research use only; 1 form (25 cards plus demonstration and practice materials); manual (15 pages); single sets of test materials and manual free to persons planning research with the test; [10–20] minutes plus practice session; Stephen A. Karp and Norma L. Konstadt; Cognitive Tests. *

REFERENCES

1. GOODENOUGH, DONALD R., AND KARP, STEPHEN A. "Field Dependence and Intellectual Functioning." *J Abn & Social Psychol* 63:241–6 S '61. * (*PA* 37:1214)
2. GOODENOUGH, DONALD R., AND EAGLE, CAROL JOHNSON. "A Modification of the Embedded-Figures Test for Use With Young Children." *J Genetic Psychol* 103:67–74 S '63. *

[75]

★The Children's Hypnotic Susceptibility Scale. Ages 5–12, 13–16; 1963, c1962; downward extension of *Stanford Hypnotic Susceptibility Scale,* on which its content is based; individual; 2 levels: younger form, older form; manual ('63, c1962, 62 pages, including both forms and sample scoring and observation form); scoring and observation form (4 pages); no data on reliability; no norms; $5.50 per examiner's kit of manual and 25 scoring and observation forms; $6.50 per 50 scoring and observation forms; $2.25 per manual; postage extra; (50–60) minutes; Perry London; Consulting Psychologists Press, Inc. *

REFERENCES

1. LONDON, PERRY. "Hypnosis in Children: An Experimental Approach." *Int J Clin & Exp Hypnosis* 10:79–91 Ap '62. * (*PA* 37:3385)
2. MOORE, ROSEMARIE K., AND LAUER, LILLIAN W. "Hypnotic Susceptibility in Middle Childhood." *Int J Clin & Exp Hypnosis* 11:167–74 Jl '63. * (*PA* 38:6278)

C. SCOTT MOSS, *Mental Health Consultant, National Institute of Mental Health, United States Public Health Service, San Francisco, California.*

Based on the *Stanford Hypnotic Susceptibility Scale, The Children's Hypnotic Susceptibility Scale* is a standardized induction procedure for children 5 to 16 years. Part 1 of the Children's Scale parallels Forms A and B of the original scale. Nine of the 10 items of Part 2 are selected from among the items of the unpublished *Stanford Depth Scales*. In all cases items were rewritten to make them suitable for use with children. In addition, there are younger and older forms of the Children's Scale for ages 5–12 and 13–16 respectively, which differ only with respect to the level of wording of some of the instructions.

The purpose of the Children's Scale is "to discover the extent to which a child will respond to hypnotic suggestions which are made in a standard way and which permit a standard means for evaluating responses." At the same time it is recognized that effective use of the scale depends more on the ability of the investigator to establish effective relationships with children than upon experience in the use of hypnosis. "It is as nearly impossible to overstate the importance of getting and keeping good rapport in testing children as it is to overstate the importance of adhering to standard test procedures. Serious or persistent violation of either rule will invalidate the test results." The point to be emphasized is that, as with many psychological tests, the administration appears deceptively simple, and valid results require a high degree of psychological sophistication; for instance, in determination of when and how to deviate from the standardized instructions and what has been the precise effect of that departure.

A virtue of the Children's Scale is that it may be scored in terms of a single dichotomy of pass or fail, as is the *Stanford Hypnotic Susceptibility Scale,* or along a four-point continuum which provides a more refined index of the child's responses. A limitation is that little information is available in the manual on normative data, other than the statement that the scale had been administered to over 250 children. Who were these children and how were they obtained? It is suspected that a problem of volunteer bias would be manifest in that a uniqueness obtains in families where parents volunteer their children for hypnosis experiments.

In a later article London (*1*) reports that interscorer reliability ranged from .90 to .96, and retest reliability was found to be .92. London also reports on the simultaneous use of two scoring systems, one measuring *overt behavior,* the other measuring *subjective involvement,* an approach referred to in a footnote in the manual and reflective of concern over the genuineness of the behavior elicited by the hypnotic suggestions.

A fundamental question indeed is the nature of so-called hypnotic phenomena. As London recognizes, children are likely to respond with docility to the wishes of adult authority, and they may produce responses to the explicit demands and even implicit expectations of the examiner without, in fact, being hypnotized. A control group of well motivated young simulators might help clarify this question. In the later article referred to above, London found a linear relationship between age and role-playing ability ($r = .67$). He speculates that, to the extent a suspected curvilinear relationship of age and susceptibility actually exists, it may be a function of the confounding of simulation ability and motivation with hypnotic behavior.

In terms of the amount of normative data provided, publication of this scale may be viewed as premature. However, if the author's stated intent of encouraging other investigators to employ and report on standard procedures of hypnosis in children is fulfilled, the effort will have been worthwhile in view of the dearth of empirical studies of hypnotizability with children. A basic value of this scale is that it provides the possibility of a developmental perspective to studies of hypnotic susceptibility.

JOHN G. WATKINS, *Chief Clinical Psychologist, Veterans Administration Hospital, Portland, Oregon.*

This scale represents an extension of the approach used by Weitzenhoffer and Hilgard in the *Stanford Hypnotic Susceptibility Scales.* The London scale presents a "Younger Form" covering the age range 5–12, and an "Older Form" advised for ages 13–16. Each form is composed of 12 simpler items in Part 1 followed by 10 more difficult items in Part 2. The Part 1 items include postural sway, eye closure, hand lowering, arm immobilization, finger lock, arm rigidity, hands together, verbal inhibition,

auditory hallucination, eye catalepsy, post-hypnotic suggestion, and amnesia. In Part 2 are found items of post-hypnotic suggestion (reinduction), visual and auditory hallucination, cold hallucination, anesthesia, taste hallucination, small hallucination, visual hallucination, age regression, dream, awakening, and post-hypnotic suggestion.

These represent essentially the same items found in the Stanford scale but reworded to be more appealing and understandable to children. It should be noted that many of these items have been historically considered as tests of suggestibility and have been reported by various earlier writers.[1] The Stanford scale, which was the original standardized instrument for measuring hypnotic susceptibility, was the product of considerable study and research by well known investigators in the field and is certainly the best validated test of this type currently available. Accordingly, the children's scale inherits both the assets which accrued to the carefully prepared Stanford work and the liabilities which may inhere in this kind of an approach aimed at objectifying hypnotic responses.

Perhaps the most credit should be given to the author's explicit and detailed instructions for administration. Clearly written, they cover not only all the physical conditions, equipment, props, etc., needed for giving the scale, but especially praiseworthy is the care given to alteration of wordings in order to adapt the items to the intellectual level and interests of children. In themselves they constitute a good verbatim presentation of techniques for inducing trance in young people. Since eye closure is initiated in the second item, and since all subsequent items are administered with the subject's eyes closed, the more inexperienced administrator can read the suggestions and thus present a standardized wording. The author wisely makes provision for individual differences and advises appropriate modifications as needed. A separate Scoring and Observation Form is available on which individual scoring can be noted.

An attempt at greater precision of scoring is proposed in that four levels of response for

[1] DAVIS, LAWRENCE W., AND HUSBAND, RICHARD W. "A Study of Hypnotic Susceptibility in Relation to Personality Traits." *J Abn & Social Psychol* 26:175–82 Jl–S '31. * (*PA* 6:648)
FRIEDLANDER, J. W., AND SARBIN, T. R. "The Depth of Hypnosis." *J Abn & Social Psychol* 33:453–75 O '38. * (*PA* 13:1412)

each item, scored 3, 2, 1, and 0 are listed, each being specifically defined. Some of the items are timed and the Scoring and Observation Form provides space for timing the responses. In the original Stanford scale only the fact of response (scored plus or minus), not the degree of response, is required. The London scale permits either plus-minus or numerical scoring.

The greatest current deficiency in this scale is its lack of published standardization and normative data. In regards to this matter the author states: "At this writing, the present form....has been administered in standard fashion to over two hundred and fifty children of both sexes within the age range for which the test was developed. * Information from pilot studies clearly indicates that the scale is sufficiently reliable to warrant publication. Norms will be published at the earliest possible date."

In summary, the scale is a carefully prepared extension of the earlier well-designed Stanford scale adapted to the needs of children. As such it is a welcome addition to the few instruments of evaluation currently available in this area. However, the entire approach is based on a concept of the nature of hypnosis, which, although widely held, is not universally accepted. This is the view that hypnosis is a relatively stable state, and hypnotizability a behavior characteristic that remains fairly constant within any given individual. The Stanford studies [2] seem to bear out this contention. According to such a concept a given subject achieves his normal level of hypnosis under any standard approach, regardless of who administers the induction.

There are a number of workers in the field who maintain that hypnosis is more than a state, but a complex interpersonal relationship process, and that it is subject to such influences as transference and countertransference reactions.[3] According to this view the hypnotizability of a given subject would vary widely depending on the exact nature of the hypnotic relationship, the technique of induction used,

the unconscious psychodynamic needs within the subject, and the personality and motivation of the hypnotist. From such a viewpoint a "standardized" approach to hypnotic induction leaves much to be desired. This second school of thought is closer to psychoanalytic theory and is espoused more by clinicians and "subjectivists." Final determination of the most appropriate form for hypnotic susceptibility scales must await more precise theoretical formulations as to the exact nature of hypnosis.

Am J Clin Hypnosis 5:336–7 Ap '63. André Weitzenhoffer. * According to the author: "The purpose of the *Children's Scale*....is to discover the extent to which a child will respond to hypnotic suggestions which are made in an entirely standard way and which permit a standard means for evaluating responses. The Children's Scale is thus a test of *typical* performance rather than one of *maximum* performance. Used properly, it should give reliable information about how susceptible a child is to attempts at hypnotic induction under certain typical conditions, *not* how susceptible he is to the application of a maximum effort at induction." * At first look the physical arrangement of the scale gives one the impression of a somewhat complicated device. However, this may not be as serious as it sounds upon actual application of the scale. This writer, admittedly, has not had an opportunity to use it. The author of the scale also emphasizes the fact that the ability to establish an effective relationship with children is of primary importance in the successful use of the scale. He considers previous experience with such tests as the *Stanford Binet* and the *Wechsler Intelligence Scale for Children* to be a considerable aid. This is clearly an inherent weakness in the scale which will probably limit its use by investigators, but it must be recognized that this probably is not so much a reflection upon the test instrument itself as a function of the nature of the population to be tested. The scale is the result of careful, thoughtful work by a well trained and serious investigator and has been shown to be both practical and useful. It has the virtue of not only being standardized, but of giving scores which can be related to scores obtained on adult populations by means of other standardized scales which are being increasingly used in research on hypnosis. It also demonstrates that it is fully possible to do hypnotic

2 HILGARD, ERNEST R.; WEITZENHOFFER, ANDRE M.; LANDES, JUDAH; AND MOORE, ROSEMARIE K. "The Distribution of Susceptibility to Hypnosis in a Student Population: A Study Using the Stanford Hypnotic Susceptibility Scale." *Psychol Monogr* 75(8):1–22 '61. *
HILGARD, ERNEST R.; WEITZENHOFFER, ANDRE M.; AND GOUGH, PHILIP. "Individual Differences in Susceptibility to Hypnosis." *Proc Nat Acad Sci* 44:1255–9 D '58. *
3 KLINE, MILTON V. *Freud and Hypnosis: The Interaction of Psychodynamics and Hypnosis.* New York: The Julian Press, Inc., 1958. Pp. xii, 210. *
WATKINS, JOHN G. Chap. 1, "Transference Aspects of the Hypnotic Relationship," pp. 5–24. In *Clinical Correlations of Experimental Hypnosis.* Edited by Milton V. Kline. Springfield, Ill.: Charles C Thomas, Publisher, 1963. Pp. xv, 524. *

research on children, and opens the door to further work of this kind. The Children's Scale, even more than the Stanford Scale will probably not have much appeal to medical practitioners for whom it probably would be of limited usefulness anyway; but it should prove a valuable instrument in academic research and must be considered a definite contribution to scientific hypnotism.

[76]
*Client-Centered Counseling Progress Record. Adults and children undergoing psychotherapeutic counseling; 1950–60; form for rating progress in up to 40 counseling visits; 1 form ('59, 4 pages); manual ('60, 8 pages); no norms; $2 per 25 records, postage extra; $1 per specimen set, postpaid; [3–5] minutes; Russell N. Cassel; Associated Publishers. *

WILLIAM SCHOFIELD, *Professor of Psychology, University of Minnesota, Minneapolis, Minnesota.*

This is a simple, four-page pamphlet that affords the client-centered counselor a convenient grid on which to plot his estimate of the general clinical status of a client as revealed in each counseling session. A total of 40 sessions may be rated on a single form. The cover page provides for recording general identifying information and the back page is lined for the recording of "significant changes."

The status of the patient at a given interview is recorded on a single 15-step chart based largely on Rogers' theories of personality and the counseling process. The 15 steps are divided into 4 sections of the scale, each presumably reflecting a different major focus of the counseling process. These are labeled: "Developing Counseling Readiness," "Deeper Personality Layer—Negative Reflections," "Middle Personality Layer—Positive Reflections," and "Outer Personality Layer—Educational Process." Stages that exemplify each of these "layers," respectively, are: "Client decides on clinic or therapist for obtaining assistance, and makes the necessary arrangements"; "Client accepts own individuality, and is able to perceive differences in own various self worlds"; "Significant changes in various client self worlds, and with the 'perceived' self approaching the 'would be' self"; and "Re-education directed at an effective client goal-setting and goal-striving process."

The manual refers to the chart as a rating scale and the process of assigning the client's position for a particular interview is clearly a rating procedure; the format of the record suggests a rating continuum from early, and presumably poorer or "lower" (note the numeration), to "higher" and presumably better stages. The manual provides no information as to precisely how each of the stages was derived or, more important, as to how the sequence of stages was derived. Such ordering could well have been based on the rich research literature on nondirective, client-centered counseling, but there is no discussion of any specific research on which the rating continuum is based. While there is moderately extended discussion of the meaning and observations pertinent to each of the 15 stages, no data are offered as to the reliability with which this form can be applied in appraisal of a series of counseling sessions by independent evaluators. The statement that the record "is far superior to the traditional technique of using descriptive narrative summaries" suggests that it might be completely substituted for the latter. While such a quantified summary rating of therapy progress is a highly desirable addition to the usual clinical notes, the latter are not dispensable with respect to adequate professional records or for purposes of teaching or research.

For client-centered counselors, and especially for counselors in training, the use of such a standardized record form has distinct value in sensitizing the counselor to the need to appraise progress and clinical status of the counselee, in providing a graphic record which is useful for cross-case comparisons, and in enhancing awareness of the accumulation of sessions.

For a more elaborate version of a comparable recording instrument, see the *Cassel Psychotherapy Progress Record.*

[77]
The College Inventory of Academic Adjustment. College; 1949; 7 scores: curricular adjustment, maturity of goals and level of aspiration, personal efficiency-planning and use of time, study skills and practices, mental health, personal relations, total; 1 form (4 pages); manual (10 pages); $3 per 25 tests; 25¢ per set of manual and scoring stencils; 50¢ per specimen set; cash orders postpaid; (15–25) minutes; Henry Borow; [Consulting Psychologists Press, Inc.]. *

REFERENCES

1–3. See 4:34.
4. BURGESS, ELVA. *Personality Factors in Over- and Under-Achievers in Engineering.* Doctor's thesis, Pennsylvania State College (State College, Pa.), 1953.
5. McCOULLOUGH, CHESTER A. *A Statistical Study of the Relationships Between Scores Obtained by 400 North Carolina College Students on the Mooney Problem Check List and the Borow College Inventory of Academic Adjustment.* Master's thesis, North Carolina College (Durham, N.C.), 1954.
6. SPENCER, GEORGE MINARD. *An Investigation of Some Non-*

Intellectual Factors Presumably Affecting the Academic Adjustment of College Students at Florida State University. Doctor's thesis, Florida State University (Tallahassee, Fla.), 1955. (*DA* 15:1436)

7. BURGESS, ELVA. "Personality Factors of Over- and Under-Achievers in Engineering." *J Ed Psychol* 47:89–99 F '56. * (*PA* 31:8811)

8. CHRISTENSEN, CLIFFORD M. "A Note on Borow's College Inventory of Academic Adjustment." *J Ed Res* 50:55–8 S '56. * (*PA* 31:6669)

9. MOORE, MARY ROWENA. *The Effects of Two Interview Techniques on Academic Achievement and Certain Non-Intellectual Factors Affecting Academic Success.* Doctor's thesis, Indiana University (Bloomington, Ind.), 1958. (*DA* 19:2853)

10. CURRAN, ANN MARIE. *Non-Intellective Characteristics of Freshman Underachievers, Normal Achievers, and Overachievers at the College Level.* Doctor's thesis, University of Connecticut (Storrs, Conn.), 1960. (*DA* 21:2584)

11. POPHAM, W. JAMES, AND MOORE, MARY R. "A Note on the Validity of Borow's College Inventory of Academic Adjustment." *J Ed Res* 54:115–7 N '60. *

12. POPHAM, W. JAMES, AND MOORE, MARY R. "A Validity Check on the Brown-Holtzman Survey of Study Habits and Attitudes and the Borow College Inventory of Academic Adjustment." *Personnel & Guid J* 38:552–4 Mr '60. * (*PA* 35:7094)

13. ALLEN, ROSCOE JACKSON. *An Analysis of the Relationship Between Selected Prognostic Measures and Achievement in the Freshman Program for Secretarial Majors at the Woman's College of the University of North Carolina.* Doctor's thesis, Pennsylvania State University (University Park, Pa.), 1961. (*DA* 23:122)

14. CENTI, PAUL. "Personality Factors Related to College Success." *J Ed Res* 55:187–8 D–Ja '62. *

15. LANIER, WILLIAM JETT. *The Predictive Value of Selected Personality and College Adjustment Instruments Used With the American College Testing Program.* Doctor's thesis, Purdue University (Lafayette, Ind.), 1962. (*DA* 23:2424)

LEONARD D. GOODSTEIN, *Professor of Psychology, and Director, University Counseling Service, University of Iowa, Iowa City, Iowa.*

The College Inventory of Academic Adjustment is a 90-item, self-administering questionnaire which presumably taps 6 areas of college adjustment: curricular adjustment (12 items), maturity of goals and level of aspiration (14 items), personal efficiency (16 items), study skills and practices (21 items), mental health (14 items), and personal relations (13 items). These items, which are quite obvious in content and hence easily faked, are answered directly in the test booklet, using the alternative responses of yes, no, or undecided, and are scored by means of a convenient, but time consuming, transparent overlay stencil. Scores are obtained for each of the six areas and are combined into a single unweighted total score. Percentile equivalents are available, separately for the sexes, for the total scores, and quartile norms are provided, again, by sex, for the six area scores.

The split-half reliability coefficients of the total score are .92 for males ($n = 155$) and .90 for females ($n = 130$), both coefficients corrected by the Spearman-Brown formula. The test-retest reliability coefficient of the total score is .92, while the test-retest reliability coefficients for the six area scores range from .81 to .89 ($n = 130$ females).

Five types of information are presented as validity data: (*a*) item selection procedures (items included in the inventory are those that statistically differentiated between groups of male and female overachievers and underachievers at Pennsylvania State College); (*b*) high interjudge agreement about which of the six areas the specific items tapped; (*c*) significant correlations between inventory scores and college grade point average (for 155 males these range from .16 for the personal relations score to .41 for the personal efficiency score); (*d*) mean differences between the inventory scores of 81 female overachievers and 67 female underachievers (these differences are statistically significant with the overachievers higher on the total and each of the area scores, except for the personal relations area); and (*e*) correlations between the several inventory scores and scores on Wrenn's *Study Habits Inventory,* Bell's *Adjustment Inventory,* and Bernreuter's *Personality Inventory,* most of which are said to be "in accord with logical expectation."

None of these validity data, however, bears directly upon the question of whether or not this inventory can serve as "a diagnostic aid in counseling," a major use professed for the test by its author. Clues as to sources of difficulty are presumably given by the six area scores but these rationally derived indices share considerable common variance as indicated by the table of intercorrelations presented in the manual (the r's range from .23 to .56 with median r .44). The theoretical implications of such intercorrelated area scores either for a theory of academic adjustment or for the practical problems of identifying the sources of a student's difficulties are largely ignored. While the author was not unaware of these problems, the 14 years since the publication of the manual have not seen any attempt to relieve the situation, either in the research literature or in a revision of the manual.

Even more serious is the failure to extend and update the norms. These norms appear to be based upon data collected between 1945 and 1948, approximately, and only involve the scores of 237 male students from two institutions and 454 female students from one institution. Considering the changes in the nature of the student body which have taken place over the past 15 or more years and what is now known about the diversity of student characteristics from institution to institution, these norms are grossly inadequate for any practical purpose.

Some of the inventory items, approximately 15 per cent by this reviewer's estimate, have a slightly archaic or moralistic flavor, for example, "Do you have a keen desire for success?" or "Are you guilty of not taking things seriously enough?" that limit the suggested usefulness of the individual item responses for providing "valuable diagnostic clues." The failure of the test publishers to provide machine scorable answer sheets in these days of high speed electronic test scoring machines is still another instance of how outdated this test has become. Under these circumstances, one must not only question the standards of the publisher in continuing to market the test but also those of users who might purchase it.

In summary, there is very little to recommend this inventory for use in any applied situation. There has been no attempt to cross-validate the findings of the original validation work (a criticism previously noted some ten years ago in the *Fourth Mental Measurements Yearbook,* see 4:34), both the test booklet and the manual are obviously dated, and there is very little recently reported evidence that would suggest this inventory is a useful one. College counselors and others seeking techniques for assessing the nonintellectual factors in collegiate achievement should look elsewhere.

For reviews by Lysle W. Croft and Harrison G. Gough, see 4:34.

[78]

Concept Formation Test. Normal and schizophrenic adults; 1940; individual; 1 form (a set of blocks); mimeographed instructions ['40, 4 pages]; no data on reliability and validity; no norms; $13.75 per set of testing materials, postage extra; (10–60) minutes; Jacob Kasanin and Eugenia Hanfmann; C. H. Stoelting Co. *

REFERENCES

1–19. See 3:27.
20–27. See 4:35.
28. PENNY, RONALD. "The Vigotsky Block Test: A Form of Administration." *Austral J Psychol* 3:65–83 D '51. * (PA 27:1184)
29. CORTER, HAROLD M. "Factor Analysis of Some Reasoning Tests." *Psychol Monogr* 66(8):1–31 '52. * (PA 27:4995)
30. SEMEONOFF, B., AND LAIRD, A. J. "The Vigotsky Test as a Measure of Intelligence." *Brit J Psychol, Gen Sect* 43:94–102 My '52. * (PA 27:1982)
31. HANFMANN, EUGENIA. "Concept Formation Test," pp. 731–40. (PA 27:7772) In *Contributions Toward Medical Psychology: Theory and Psychodiagnostic Methods, Vol. II.* Edited by Arthur Weider. New York: Ronald Press Co., 1953. Pp. xi, 459–885. *
32. LOVIBOND, S. H. "The Object Sorting Test and Conceptual Thinking in Schizophrenia." *Austral J Psychol* 6:52–70 Je '54. * (PA 29:6035)
33. BRESSLER, MILDRED BLOOM. *A Study of an Aspect of Concept Formation in Brain-Damaged Adults With Aphasia.* Doctor's thesis, New York University (New York, N.Y.), 1955. (DA 16:568)

34. EDRINGTON, THOMAS CRAIGHEAD. *A Revised Test of Concept Formation as Related to Intelligence and Interests.* Doctor's thesis, Tulane University (New Orleans, La.), 1955.
35. MILLER, ELEANOR O. "New Use for the Vigotsky Blocks." *J Clin Psychol* 11:87–9 Ja '55. * (PA 29:7304)
36. KRESS, ROY ALFRED, JR. *An Investigation of the Relationship Between Concept Formation and Achievement in Reading.* Doctor's thesis, Temple University (Philadelphia, Pa.), 1956. (DA 16:573)
37. O'NEILL, JOHN J., AND DAVIDSON, JOANN L. "Relationship Between Lipreading Ability and Five Psychological Factors." *J Speech & Hearing Disorders* 21:478–81 D '56. * (PA 31:4907)
38. VON HOLT, HENRY W., JR.; SENGSTAKE, CORD B.; SONODA, BEVERLY C.; AND DRAPER, WILLIAM A. "Orality, Image Fusions and Concept-Formation." *J Proj Tech* 24:194–8 Je '60. * (PA 35:4943)

For a review by Kate Levine Kogan (with William S. Kogan), see 4:35; for a review by O. L. Zangwill, see 3:27; for excerpts from related book reviews, see 3:28.

[79]

★**Constant-Choice Perceptual Maze Attitude of Responsibility Test.** Ages 4 and over; 1938–63; formerly called the *Line Centering Test;* "liking or disliking of required behavior"; 3 scores: intensity of quality (self-initiative), persistency of quality (self-importance), reaction tendencies (self-confidence); 1 form ('53, 4 pages); trial test ('53, 2 pages); administrative and scoring manual ('53, 16 pages); interpretive norms manual ('54, 118 pages); "personal testing" manual ['63, 56 unnumbered pages, including materials copyrighted 1958–63]; $25 per 50 sets of test and trial test; $1 per administration and scoring manual; $5 per interpretive norms manual; $5 per "personal testing" manual; $1.25 per 25 sets of various record and report forms; $2 per specimen set of test, trial test, and administration and scoring manual; postage extra; 3(15) minutes; John C. Park; the Author. *

[80]

Cornell Word Form 2. Adults; 1946–55; civilian edition of *Cornell Word Form* designed for use in military psychiatric screening; title on test is *C.W.F.-2;* psychosomatic and neuropsychiatric symptoms; 1 form ['55, 2 pages]; manual ('55, 8 pages, reprint of 11 below); $5 per 100 tests; specimen set free; postage extra; [5–15] minutes; Arthur Weider, Bela Mittelmann, David Wechsler, and Harold Wolff; Cornell University Medical College. *

REFERENCES

1–11. See 5:44.
12. *Personal Characteristics of Traffic-Accident Repeaters,* pp. 27–9. Saugatuck, Conn.: Eno Foundation for Highway Traffic Control, 1948. Pp. 64. *

S. B. SELLS, *Professor of Psychology, and Director, Institute of Behavioral Research, Texas Christian University, Fort Worth, Texas.*

This test is a revision of an earlier form developed by a Cornell Medical School research group (Weider, Mittelmann, Brodman, Wechsler, and Wolff) for military use in World War II. Its original purpose was for screening of psychologically unfit recruits at induction stations. It has subsequently been used productively in clinical, occupational, and military (including aviation) situations and in discriminating accident-free civilians from accident repeaters.

The form consists of 80 items, containing 80 stimulus words and 160 response words, 20 of the former and 24 of the latter from the Kent-Rosanoff list. Each item contains a stimulus word and two response choices, one of which is selected by the subject on the basis of "reminding" him most of the stimulus word. Some of the choices are fairly obvious. For example, to the stimulus word "sleep," the response words "comfort" and "restless" are given. In other cases, the implication is less apparent. For example, to the stimulus word "brother" the response words "man" and "my brother" are given. A number of neutral, filler items are dispersed among those that are intended to discriminate.

Although high validities have never been reported, published results with this instrument have been both consistent enough and discriminating enough to warrant consideration as a screening instrument. The items are highly sensitive to varying population characteristics, however, such as intelligence, education, occupation, and to the purposes of screening, in relation to test taking attitudes. It is therefore necessary to carry out thorough validation research and to standardize keys for any formal screening program in which it may be used. For this reason, inclusion in any informal clinical testing batteries may prove to be worthless, while at the same time, this pool of items may produce a valuable adjunct to a screening battery in competent psychometric hands.

[81]

★Cotswold Personality Assessment P.A. 1. Ages 11–16; 1960; manual subtitle is *A Study of Preferences and Values for Use in Schools and Clubs;* 6 scores: 3 preference scores (things, people, ideas) and 3 attitude scores (using one's hands, being with other people, talking about school) ; 1 form ['60, 8 pages] ; manual ['60, 6 pages] ; no norms for attitude scores; 9d. per test; 1s. per manual; postage extra; (40) minutes; C. M. Fleming; Robert Gibson & Sons (Glasgow), Ltd. *

REFERENCES

1. FLEMING, C. M. "A New Personality Test." *Indian Psychol B* 4:59–66 S '59. *

RALPH D. DUTCH, *Principal Lecturer in Educational Psychology, Aberdeen College of Education, Aberdeen, Scotland.*

This test is described as "an aid to the assessment of the personal characteristics of boys and girls as these are represented by predominating interests and prevailing values." The adolescent testee is asked to identify himself more or less strongly with various opinions and statements expressed by members of an imaginary youth club, and his total scores show the relative strength of his preferences and attitudes. The information thus obtained is described as having shown itself useful (*a*) in educational guidance, (*b*) in vocational guidance and selection, (*c*) in sociometric grouping in youth clubs. The test can be given to a group, with verbal explanations, or can be used as a self-administered individual test.

The first page of the test is used for recording a summary of the results and also for giving instructions to the subject. The wording of these instructions is important: "give 4 votes to the statements with which you agree very strongly, 3 to the next most sensible ones, 2 to the next, 1 to the ones with which you agree least, and 0 to those with which you do not agree at all." The use of the word "sensible" here seems unfortunate and may puzzle a testee with sufficient self knowledge to appreciate that the point of view with which he agrees very strongly is not necessarily the most "sensible," either for himself or for the imaginary character who is supposed to be putting it forward. Also, where does agreement stop and disagreement begin on a scale thus worded? In fact, these instructions can be read in so many different ways that one becomes immediately doubtful of the value of any averages or norms produced by the test.

The test divides into 9 subtests, arranged in 3 sections. In the first section the places for recording the answers to the 5 subtests are so arranged that the relative strength of the subject's preferences for "Things," "People," "Ideas" can easily be seen by adding the scores on three columns. Similarly, the results of the 3 subtests in the attitudes section appear in two columns—favourable and unfavourable. In the final subtest, a list of 45 common adolescent activities is presented and the subject is asked to record which of these he has engaged in, or would like to have engaged in, during the last fortnight.

The amount and type of standardisation varies between the three sections. The reliability of the test is good, with a split-half reliability coefficient of .88 for the whole test, and test-retest figures for the subtests varying between .81 and .93. As each testee could consistently follow his own interpretation, the reliability coefficient would not, of course, necessarily be impaired by any ambiguity in the instructions. The items on the "Preference" tests were carefully selected to give content validity, but no coefficients are quoted and we are merely told that "the validity of the whole was later confirmed by case studies." If the test is being used for guidance and selection, however, as is confirmed by the test author in a personal letter, this will not do, and some predictive validities, or at least a concurrent validity, will have to be provided. The testee's "preference" results can be expressed as a profile, which can then be compared with the scores (averages and standard deviations) of various groups of adolescents. These scores, however, are not presented in any systematic order and it is difficult to see the value of such a comparison, specially when the standard deviations are so large. The author herself, in the same letter, indicates belief that the main finding of the test is the extent of the overlap between groups. The results of the "attitudes" tests, the items on which were again "validated" by the opinion of judges, express the attitudes of the testee on a simple + or − scale, but in the absence of any norms whatsoever it is impossible to interpret an individual score. The items on the final subtest, which is linked to the "Preferences" section, were chosen from an item analysis of 700 pupils' interests. Nothing is claimed for this last test other than that its results are "often corroborative of the information given by the other tests."

Some general points about the whole test are: (a) The instructions seem ambiguous and the wording of many of the items is peculiar; e.g., one is asked to record an attitude towards "Managing people (like a bus conductor, a hospital sister, a lawyer, a doctor)"—hardly a homogeneous collection! (b) The tentative norms in the "preference" section show great overlapping between groups so the implication that a kind of tri-partite division can be made is unfortunate. (c) The danger of contamination by self delusion or the social desirability factor appears great, as in most self-rating inventories. The manual stresses the need for good "rapport" between examiner and subject, but this cuts down the area of the test's use drastically, and where this good relationship already exists it is doubtful if the test would be necessary. (d) If one is led by the numerical system of scoring, with a profile and tentative norms, to expect some kind of fairly rigorous quantitative assessment, then the test is disappointing.

In this reviewer's opinion the test, as it stands, is best suited not to provide numerical results but to elicit certain clues about personality or to start off a discussion. Used thus, the tester may find it useful as a basis for guidance and advice without scoring the results at all.

G. A. V. MORGAN, *Former Principal Psychologist, North Wales Child Guidance Service, Denbighshire, Wales.*

This test falls into three parts: the measurement of interests and values based on preferences for dealing with things, people, and ideas; three attitude scales partly related to the above; and a checklist of leisure activities classified under the three preference headings. The latter was suggested by an item analysis of the activities reported by 700 pupils whose interests were known from their responses to the remainder of the test.

The assumption underlying the test is, as in the Allport-Vernon *Study of Values,* that consistent and permanent personal interests and values are reflected in preferences for particular activities and situations. As in the *Kuder Preference Record—Vocational* this indirect use of preferences is claimed to be useful in vocational guidance.

Items are arranged in five subtests such as "Talking About Wishes" and "Spending Money." There are 66 questions, with 22 items referring to each preference category. Responses are expressed, in a hypothetical "club" discussion, as a "vote" of from 0 to 4 for each item. This procedure is claimed to be attractive to adolescents. It seems doubtful whether rating over this range is natural or easy for unsophisticated subjects, as compared with a simple three-point scale. In fact, the average scores may conceal individual variation in range of response.

The test originated from the work of the author on the psychology of adolescents, backed by a considerable amount of unpublished research on their interests and attitudes done by students in the University of London from 1947 to 1958. Validation of the preference test by comparison of item scores with teachers' estimates of pupils' interests and case studies is satisfactory. Although the author suggests that the test might with modifications be given to "duller" adolescents or younger children, the test probably has a lower age and ability limit in terms of the reading level and the type of response required. All data given describe selected groups of secondary school children, that is, the upper 20 to 33 per cent in ability of age groups 11 to 16 years.

"Norms" are given only for the preference tests for ages 11 to 16, but mainly for 13-year-old groups. These norms consist of 15 school raw score means and standard deviations, which are useful only as a rough guide. No effective standards are available for age, sex, or type of school in terms of percentiles or standard scores. Variation among individual schools and types of school is quite marked. No data are given on the relative ability level or sociocultural background of the groups.

The manual could with effect have been more simply written. In its present form it is a manual for a research instrument, but not convenient for general use. The reviewer initially found difficulty in following the test from the manual: a minor irritation is the dual description of subtests by page letters and roman figures whereas the test form uses arabic figures. The section on interpretation of the test is brief and vague, leaving the interpretation in effect up to the test user. Despite apparent detail on the test's characteristics, insufficient data are given on the groups on which reliability and validity studies were carried out. "Personal communication" is quoted for important issues such as reliability, and background references are mainly to unpublished theses, many known to the reviewer, but not in general accessible.

The reliability data seem satisfactory for this kind of material and length of test. A split-half reliability coefficient for the whole test was .88, and test-retest coefficients (one month interval) ranged from .81 to .90 for preference and attitude subtests, based on small groups only in each instance. Since a profile of the three preference scores is proposed, the standard error of score differences should be available. A difference of seven between scores is suggested as "definitive," but this is a vague formulation.

The attitude scales, developed by means of a modified Thurstone-Chave technique, with neutral items omitted, are given scores from 4 to 0 to indicate degree of agreement with positive or negative statements. Total scores are based on the difference between positive and negative totals. Two of the scales corroborate to some extent the preference scores, but it is not clear how "attitude to school" is interpreted. The absence of norms makes interpretation of this part of the test difficult.

The main differentiation appears to be between interest in things and interest in people or ideas. This is more marked with age and among more intelligent pupils. The things-people dichotomy also probably, in the reviewer's opinion, reflects a social class variation in Britain. Girls tend to prefer activities related to people; boys to things. In general, the school means show a tendency for technical school boys to score higher on things and grammar school boys (academically superior) on people or ideas. This is also reflected by the small but useful correlations reported between preference for things and later success in technical and commercial secondary courses.

In summary, this test appears to be an interesting and useful research instrument; there is in Britain a scarcity of published tests of personal preferences and attitudes with the background of development of this one. It seems unlikely that it is, in its present form, suitable for routine individual guidance, as suggested in the manual. At the present stage of educational practice, it appears improbable too that it will be widely used in youth clubs or grammar schools where it might prove most useful.

[82]

★Cowell Personal Distance Scale. Grades 7–9; 1958–63; title on scale is *Confidential Personal Distance Ballot;* social distance ratings of classmates; 1 form ['58, 1 page]; directions ['63, 1 page]; norms ['58, 1 page] for boys only; $2 per pad of 50 scales, postpaid; specimen set free; (30) minutes; Charles C. Cowell; [Tri-State Offset Co.]. *

REFERENCES
1. COWELL, C. C., AND ISMAIL, A. H. "Validity of a Football Rating Scale and Its Relationship to Social Integration and Academic Ability." *Res Q* 32:461–7 D '61. *
2. COWELL, CHARLES C., AND ISMAIL, A. H. "Relationships Between Selected Social and Physical Factors." *Res Q* 33: 40–3 Mr '62. * (*PA* 37:1917)
3. CLARKE, H. HARRISON, AND GREENE, WALTER H. "Relationships Between Personal-Social Measures Applied to 10-Year-Old Boys." *Res Q* 34:288–98 O '63. *

[83]

★Cowell Social Behavior Trend Index. Grades 7–9; 1958–61; social adjustment ratings by 3 teachers; 2 parts ['58, 1 page] completed 1 week apart: Form A (positive behavior), Form B (negative behavior); directions ['61, 1 page]; norms ['58, 1 page] for boys only; supplementary data ('58, 12 pages, reprint of *1* below); $2 per set of pads containing 100 copies of each part, postpaid; specimen set free; (30) minutes per part for rating 30 students; Charles C. Cowell; [Tri-State Offset Co.]. *

REFERENCES

1. COWELL, CHARLES C. "Validating an Index of Social Adjustment for High School Use." *Res Q* 29:7–18 Mr '58. * (*PA* 33:5979)
2. COWELL, CHARLES C., AND ISMAIL, A. H. "Relationships Between Selected Social and Physical Factors." *Res Q* 33: 40–3 Mr '62. * (*PA* 37:1917)

[84]

★Cree Questionnaire. Industrial employees; 1957–59; creativity and inventiveness; 1 form ('57, 8 pages); manual ('59, 17 pages); no data on reliability; norms for males only; $6 per 20 tests, postage extra; $1 per specimen set, postpaid; (15–20) minutes; Thelma Gwinn Thurstone (test), John Mellinger (test), and Measurement Research Division, Industrial Relations Center, University of Chicago (manual); Education-Industry Service. *

ALLYN MILES MUNGER, *Associate Director, Personnel and Marketing Research Division, The Psychological Corporation, New York, New York.*

"The *Cree Questionnaire* is a semi-disguised test of creativity and inventiveness." It has been used with engineers, engineer supervisors, research development personnel, salesmen, craftsmen, and others. This test is a product of research initiated by the A C Spark Plug Division of General Motors and was carried out under the direction of L. L. Thurstone in the Psychometric Laboratory at the University of North Carolina.

Besides items written specifically for this test, items were also drawn from the *Thurstone Temperament Schedule.* The original validation was done on 283 men selected by the chief engineers at 18 General Motors divisions. Essentially, the chief engineers were asked to select, one by one, engineers whom they knew to be creative and at the same time to choose another group in the same department or type of work whom they definitely knew were not creative. This method of choosing a criterion group would maximize the differences to be expected in response to the items in the questionnaire.

There is no evidence in either the test manual or in the references secured from the authors that any attempt was made to study a hold-out group or cross validation group. This means that we have a study of concurrent validity performed on two extreme groups without any hypothesis of what should discriminate. This would tend to maximize the differences to be found in favor of the researcher. In all other data supplied on this test, the scores were combined with other parts of a test battery so that it was impossible to evaluate the questionnaire as a separate instrument.

In evaluating the entire battery, one must go along with the original authors in their statement that it must be used with extreme caution in any other but the original environment. It is to be appreciated that General Motors has seen fit to release this study. However, the potential user should not regard this as a test ready to select creative individuals, but rather as an experimental set of items with certain research findings which need to be studied in each new environment. The questionnaire is a good example of a well-designed experimental test and should be labeled as such.

THEODOR F. NAUMANN, *Associate Professor of Psychology, Central Washington State College, Ellensburg, Washington.*

The manual describes this instrument as a "semi-disguised test of creativity and inventiveness." The eight-page test booklet contains 145 items; for each item a Y, ?, or N is to be circled in the booklet. The questionnaire is untimed and can be completed in about 20 minutes. Raw scores are obtained by matching each part of the scoring sheet with the answer sections on the margins of the respective test booklet pages.

The norms and the section of the manual dealing with them are somewhat confusing. The 1959 manual lists separate standard scores for four groups of employees and for the combined total ($n = 496$). The "new norms" which have more recently been attached to the manual are nothing but the old "combined total." This makes most of the manual's paragraph on norms irrelevant. Reliability data are not given. The validity discussion deals only with a group of engineers dichotomized into inventors and noninventors.

This is a rather conventionally prepared questionnaire. The more recent methods of test development have apparently not been utilized. There is also no indication that the results of modern research on creativity have been seriously taken into account. The instrument should be considered as a research device usable for rough screening and only applicable to a limited population.

[84a]

★Developmental Potential of Preschool Children. Handicapped children ages 2–6; 1958–62; title on record form is *Educational Evaluation of Preschool Children;* subtitle on report form is *Inventory of Developmental Levels;* level and pattern of intellectual, sensory, and emotional functioning and "readiness to profit from an educational program"; individual; 1

form (a series of objects, toys, and test cards) ; manual ('58, 297 pages, see B230) ; directions for assembling and constructing test kit ('62, 8 pages) ; recording form ('62, 7 pages, reprinted from manual) ; report form ('62, 4 pages) ; test cards ('62, 6 cards) ; no data on reliability ; $5 per set of 20 recording forms and 20 report forms ; $5.50 per set of test cards ; $2.25 per manual for assembling test kit ; $8.75 per manual ; postage extra ; test materials, except for cards, must be assembled locally ; (45–120) minutes in 1 or 2 sessions ; Else Haeussermann ; Grune & Stratton. *

REFERENCES

1. HAEUSSERMANN, ELSE. *Developmental Potential of Pre-school Children: An Evaluation of Intellectual, Sensory, and Emotional Functioning.* New York: Grune & Stratton, Inc., 1958. Pp. xvii, 285. * (PA 34:2998)

For an excerpt from a review of the manual, see B230.

[85]

*Diplomacy Test of Empathy. Business and industry ; 1957–60 ; revision of *Primary Empathic Abilities* ('57) ; title on test is *Diplomacy Test of Empathic Ability;* 1 form ('60, 4 pages) ; manual ('60, 4 pages) ; separate answer sheets must be used ; $9 per 50 tests ; $2 per 50 answer sheets ; $1 per specimen set (must be purchased to obtain manual and key) ; postage extra ; (20–25) minutes ; Willard A. Kerr ; Psychometric Affiliates. *

REFERENCES

1. SMOUSE, ALBERT D.; ADERMAN, MORRIS; AND VAN BUSKIRK, CHARLES. "Three Empathy Measures as Correlates of Test and Rating Criteria." *Psychol Rep* 12:803–9 Je '63. * (PA 38:6035)

ARTHUR H. BRAYFIELD, *Executive Officer, American Psychological Association, Washington, D.C.*

This test is representative of an interesting idea inadequately developed. Apparently the definition of empathy is the "ability to put yourself in the other person's position, establish rapport, and anticipate his reactions, feelings and behaviors."

The measurement approach is to use as items bits of miscellaneous factual information including verbal reactions of people to a variety of stimuli. Many of the items are based on findings from attitude surveys dealing with work factors, annoyances, and worries. Agreement with the actual results is assumed to index empathy. A sample item from the most and least answer format is: "Most and Least copies printed per issue: (*a*) Popular Mechanics, (*b*) McCalls, (*c*) Forbes." An example of the one answer format is: "Men aged 35 are most likely to worry about: (*a*) Work associates, (*b*) Work efficiency, (*c*) Health, (*d*) Morality of self."

The single odd-even reliability coefficient reported on 114 adults is .56. Norms for six groups, mainly from management, sales, and

business generally, are presented. The groups are described only by broad job classification ; no means and standard deviations are given.

Undoubtedly something is being measured here ; it is difficult to say what. There are insufficient and inadequate data to believe that the construct "empathy" has been isolated. The publisher's catalog says that this test "measures ability to sell, to be persuasive, tactful, and diplomatic." There is only the most indirect and peripheral evidence for any such statement. The salary increase criterion is too hedged with technical issues to be relied upon. The group difference findings are incompletely reported and descriptive data are lacking ; age, experience, socio-economic, and education variables are uncontrolled. The cleanest finding, in my view, is the correlation of .40 between scores and numbers of elective offices held, although again uncontrolled variables may be operative.

In short, here is a basically interesting notion. It merits careful, technically competent, and systematic follow-up. The present instrument should be labeled "For Research Only." The word diplomacy in the test title is meaningless and the personality theory outlined in the manual is naïve. These trappings should not distract the serious investigator, nor should they impress the prospective purchaser.

RICHARD S. HATCH, *Vice President, Dunnette, Kirchner and Associates, Inc., Minneapolis, Minnesota.*

The *Diplomacy Test of Empathy* purports to measure "profundity of understanding of others' feelings and tastes" through predictions by the examinee of the self-descriptions of a large variety of generalized "others," such as persons aged 25–29, the average man, employees, married men, men, women, people, fired people, old people, etc. In addition to this prediction type item, the examinee is asked to estimate such things as the ages at which children are likely to have front teeth missing, academic disciplines in which women receive most and fewest degrees, and the number of farm families owning their own homes in 1950. Scoring is presumably based on a comparison of examinees' predictions with actual self-descriptions by the "others" for whom the predictions were directed—although the test manual does not provide specific references to such test development research.

Most significant are the severe methodological errors and statistical artifacts associated with the measurement approach employed. It has been pointed out by Gage and Cronbach [1] that empathic measurement approaches of the type employed in this test present artifactually "linked" components. These are Assumed Similarity, Real Similarity, and Accuracy. The degree to which the examinee possesses attitudes similar to the "others" for whom he is predicting (Real Similarity) and the degree to which the examinee assumes that the "others" possess attitudes like his own (Assumed Similarity) dictate Accuracy. Research has repeatedly demonstrated that individuals tend to assume a high degree of similarity between their own self-descriptions and the self-descriptions of "others" toward whom they are predicting; consequently, the Real Similarity between the examinee's own attitudes and those possessed by the "others," a factor unrelated to any empathic sensitivity possessed by the examinee, will determine Accuracy. In this test the degree of Real Similarity between the examinee and the "others" is uncontrolled, as well as the degree to which examinees "assume similarity" with the generalized "others." No control of examinees' response sets has been attempted. Without statistical or procedural controls either in the scoring or in the design of the test itself, the responses to exercises of the type presented in this test are uninterpretable. Most probably, the test simply provides scores which closely reflect the degree with which examinees possess attitudes similar to those of the generalized "others" for whom they are predicting, and if so, it is unwarranted to characterize examinees scoring high on the test as "empathic" or differentially sensitive in their interpersonal perceptions of others' attitudes and preferences.

The test manual only provides information on validation studies by the author, and these are not referenced. The reviewer strongly recommends that potential users interested in personnel selection and placement carry out specific validation research within their own prediction environments before basing decisions of any consequence on the test. Interpretation of scores as provided by the manual is definitely not recommended.

Investigators of interpersonal perception may desire, for research purposes, the scores

generated by the test, although the reliability of the test is somewhat unsatisfactory—the odd-even reliability being .56. This reviewer considers use of the test in experimental studies to be a waste of time in view of the test's reliance upon a methodologically inadequate approach to empathic measurement. Researchers in the area would do better to pursue more sophisticated measurement techniques and design new measures of this elusive "trait" than to perpetuate the measurement fallacies inherent in the approach incorporated in this test.

In summary, research on the measurement of interpersonal perception processes has not, as yet, yielded an acceptable approach to the construction of an "off-the-shelf" test of empathic sensitivity. Consequently, the reviewer is unaware of any valid standardized empathy test which might be recommended in lieu of the *Diplomacy Test of Empathy*. It is encouraging to note, however, that empathy has been successfully measured in the "laboratory." It is not unreasonable, then, considering the potential usefulness of this social skill, to expect early applications of methodologically acceptable empathic measurement approaches to the practical problems of personnel selection.

For a review by Robert L. Thorndike of the earlier test, see 5:99.

[86]

★**Dynamic Personality Inventory.** Ages 15 or 17 and over with IQ's of 80 and over; 1956–61; for research and experimental use only (not so labeled in distributor's catalog); 33 scores: hypocrisy, passivity, seclusion-introspection, orality, oral aggression, oral dependence, emotional independence, verbal aggression, impulsiveness, unconventionality, hoarding behavior, attention to details, conservatism, submissiveness, anal sadism, insularity, phallic symbol interest, narcissism, exhibitionism, active Icarus complex, passive Icarus complex, sensuality, Icarian exploits, sexuality, tactile impression enjoyment, creative interests, masculine sexual identification, feminine sexual identification, social role seeking, social activity interest, need to give affection, ego defense persistence, initiative; 1 form ('56, 7 pages); also available, in abbreviated form and without scores for orality, phallic symbol interest, and sexuality, under the title *Likes and Interests Test* ('56, 6 pages) for use with apprentices and employee applicants ages 15 and over; mimeographed temporary manual ('61, 8 pages); the interpretive manual which the temporary manual says will be available "shortly" is not yet available as of summer 1963; DPI score-norms sheets ('56, 6 sheets, separate sheets for male students, female students, general population males, general population females, male neurotics, female neurotics); LIT score-norms sheets ('56, 2 sheets, separate sheets for male apprentices, female technical college students); separate answer sheets must be used; 15s. per 25 tests of either

1 GAGE, N. L., and CRONBACH, LEE J. "Conceptual and Methodological Problems in Interpersonal Perception." *Psychol R* 62:411–22 S '55. *

title; 13s. per 100 answer sheets; 42s. 6d. per set of DPI scoring keys; 41s. per set of LIT scoring keys; 25s. per 100 score-norms sheets for any one population; 4s. per manual; 8s. per specimen set; prices include purchase tax; postpaid within U.K.; (40) minutes; T. G. Grygier; distributed by National Foundation for Educational Research in England and Wales. *

REFERENCES

1. BARRON, FRANK. "The Disposition Toward Originality." *J Abn & Social Psychol* 51:478–85 N '55. * (*PA* 31:2533)
2. GRYGIER, PATRICIA. "The Personality of Student Nurses: A Pilot Study Using the Dynamic Personality Inventory." *Int J Social Psychiatry* 2:105–12 au '56. * (*PA* 32:2238)
3. GRYGIER, T. G. "The Dynamic Personality Inventory: A Preliminary Notice." *B Nat Found Ed Res Engl & Wales* (9):39–42 Mr '57. *
4. GRYGIER, T. G. "Psychometric Aspects of Homosexuality." *J Mental Sci* 103:514–26 Jl '57. * (*PA* 32:5664)
5. GRYGIER, TADEUSZ. "Homosexuality, Neurosis and 'Normality': A Pilot Study in Psychological Measurement." *Brit J Deling* 9:59–61 Jl '58. * (*PA* 33:10330)
6. GRYGIER, TADEUSZ. "Statistical and Psychoanalytical Criteria in the Development of the Dynamic Personality Inventory." *Rorsch Newsl* 3:5–7 Je '58. *
7. BEACH, LEE. "Rorschach Variables and Vocational Choice." *B Maritime Psychol Assn* 8:28–33 Ap '59. *

S. B. SELLS, *Professor of Psychology, and Director, Institute of Behavioral Research, Texas Christian University, Fort Worth, Texas.*

Although offered for sale for clinical, industrial selection, and other practical uses, this test, published in 1956, has available only a temporary manual, copyrighted in 1961. It has apparently enjoyed some considerable use in research, as indicated by a typewritten list of references, plus a list of 19 papers in preparation, submitted by the author. The 1961 manual cites no references.

The DPI is designed to provide a "general picture of personality organisation in developmental terms." It is psychoanalytic in conception and the author acknowledges the influence of M. H. Krout and J. Krout Tabin regarding theoretical principles of measurement. The inventory, which was originally a modification of the Krout-Tabin *Personal Preference Scale* (5:93) but has since been extensively modified, consists of 325 items, arranged nonsystematically, which are responded to in terms of like or dislike. Manual scoring by overlay stencils yields 33 scales (of from 8 to 24 items per scale, with a median of 12) that purport to measure "tendencies, sublimations, reaction-formations, and defence mechanisms associated with the various patterns of psychosexual development, with masculine and feminine identifications, with some patterns of mature interests, and with two aspects of ego-strength." The items consist of objects (hot milk, strong drinks, torrential rain), activities (diving, prolonged kissing, watching explosions), and concepts (keeping all foreigners out

of the civil service, staying in familiar surroundings, a Negro family settling in a house opposite) that are associated with one or more of the "traits" measured. They are designed to stimulate imagination and subjects are instructed to give free rein to their imagination, assessing each item according to first reaction.

Psychometrically, this test is difficult to evaluate. While a careful reading of the items against the key suggests a considerable degree of face validity in terms of psychoanalytic rationale, this is insufficient except to give insight into the author's approach. Unfortunately, the temporary manual is not only of no help to the sophisticated critic, but rather quite frustrating. Under "Principles of Scale Construction," the author states that, over a dozen experimental editions were constructed, and "succeeding editions of the test were factorized, examined for internal consistency and repeat reliability, validated and cross-validated." No statements are included concerning factor structure. But the claims for the excellence of the test are extreme. Indeed, *most* of the scales now in use (many of the original ones were abandoned or empirically modified) are claimed to have satisfied the criteria of (*a*) adequate split-half reliability, (*b*) adequate retest reliability, (*c*) content validity in relation to theoretical formulation (the reviewer has termed this face validity), (*d*) concurrent validity with other personality measures, and (*e*) construct validity in factor-analytic studies. Five scales are acknowledged to be "experimental." The items are claimed to be (*a*) neither universally liked nor disliked, (*b*) highly and significantly correlated with their own scales and appropriately correlated with other scales, (*c*) not unduly highly correlated with conceptually unrelated scales, (*d*) relatively unaffected by social desirability, (*e*) stable in patterns of relationship on cross validation, (*f*) productive of emotional reactions and free associations in accordance with the test design, and (*g*) the mental processes interpretations have been analyzed.

Unfortunately no data are presented in support of most of these claims which would be considered extravagant in relation to any other personality test known to the reviewer. Some data are mentioned on reliability, which is said to average .75 for split-half and .80 for retest, but reliability data are not reported by scale. Since the scales range from 8 to 24 items, this is rather important. The validity discussion merely mentions correlations with "several hundred independent measures." Although industrial uses are recommended, no data are presented, and not even any claims of validity for such application.

The reviewer has sampled the references supplied by the author and there are a number of interesting results which lend partial support to the validity of various individual scales. For example, Barron (*1*) obtained borderline significance on the relation of measures of *anality* and originality. However, this is more than a giant step away from proof of the sweeping statements of the author. If data are available to substantiate his claims, he may have a magnificent test and he should make all haste to publish them. But it is doubtful that this is the case. The very nature of the psychoanalytic constructs that the test purports to measure raises questions of a more fundamental, theoretical nature, as well as measurement problems of definition, testability, and behavioral correlates that appear to be overwhelming.

At the same time, this test booklet may provide a fruitful research instrument for quantitative investigation of a more conventional (nonpsychoanalytic) nature. The pool of items is both interesting and novel and research with them may lead to new formulations of personality and motivational traits of considerable value.

[87]

*Edwards Personal Preference Schedule.** College and adults; 1953–59; 15 scores: achievement, deference, order, exhibition, autonomy, affiliation, intraception, succorance, dominance, abasement, nurturance, change, endurance, heterosexuality, aggression; IBM and NCS; 1 form ('54, 8 pages); revised manual ('59, 25 pages); answer sheet-profile ('59, c1952-59, 2 pages); separate answer sheets must be used; $3.50 per 25 tests; $2.50 per 50 hand scoring answer sheets; $2.40 per 50 IBM answer sheets; $3.25 per 50 NCS answer sheets (scored by National Computer Systems only, see 671); set of manual and keys: 60¢ with hand scoring template, $1.50 with set of hand scoring stencils for IBM answer sheets, $1.65 with set of machine scoring stencils; 75¢ per specimen set; postpaid; (40–55) minutes; Allen L. Edwards; Psychological Corporation. *

REFERENCES

1–50. See 5:47.
51. BENDIG, A. W. "Manifest Anxiety and Projective and Objective Measures of Need Achievement." Abstract. *J Consult Psychol* 21:354 Ag '57. * (*PA* 33:1671, title only)
52. BENNIS, WARREN; BURKE, RICHARD; CUTTER, HENRY; HARRINGTON, HERBERT; AND HOFFMAN, JOYCE. "A Note on Some Problems of Measurement and Prediction in a Training Group." *Group Psychother* 10:328–41 D '57. * (*PA* 33:5971)
53. EDWARDS, ALLEN L. *The Social Desirability Variable in Personality Assessment and Research.* New York: Dryden Press, Inc., 1957. Pp. xv, 108. * (*PA* 32:464)
54. NAVRAN, LESLIE, AND STAUFFACHER, JAMES C. "The Personality Structure of Psychiatric Nurses." *Nursing Res* 5:109–14 F '57. * (*PA* 34:2283)
55. STARR, HAROLD. *Personality Correlates of Time Estimation.* Doctor's thesis, Purdue University (Lafayette, Ind.), 1957. (*DA* 18:2217)
56. WRIGHT, CALVIN E. *Relations Between Normative and Ipsative Measures of Personality.* Doctor's thesis, University of Washington (Seattle, Wash.), 1957. (*DA* 18:1487)
57. ABE, STEVEN KIYOSHI. *Nisei Personality Characteristics as Measured by the Edwards Personal Preference Schedule and Minnesota Multiphasic Personality Inventory.* Doctor's thesis, University of Utah (Salt Lake City, Utah), 1958. (*DA* 19:2648)
58. ANDERSON, DARRELL EDWARD. *Personality Variables and Verbal Conditioning.* Doctor's thesis, University of Nebraska (Lincoln, Neb.), 1958. (*DA* 19:1811)
59. BENDIG, A. W. "Objective Measures of Needs and Course Achievement in Introductory Psychology." *J General Psychol* 59:51–7 Jl '58. * (*PA* 36:2KJ51B)
60. BOSDELL, BETTY JANE. *Perceptions of Guidance Services as Related to Personality Needs and Job Title.* Doctor's thesis, University of Illinois (Urbana, Ill.), 1958. (*DA* 19:1010)
61. CABRER, SEBASTIAN M. *Exploration of Behavioral Correlates of Perseveration.* Doctor's thesis, Purdue University (Lafayette, Ind.), 1958. (*DA* 19:1444)
62. DILWORTH, TOM, IV. "A Comparison of the Edwards PPS Variables With Some Aspects of the TAT." Abstract. *J Consult Psychol* 22:486 D '58. * (*PA* 33:10321)
63. DILWORTH, TOM, IV. *A Comparison of the Edwards Personal Preference Schedule Variables With Some Aspects of the Thematic Apperception Test.* Master's thesis, Southern Methodist University (Dallas, Tex.), 1958.
64. GISVOLD, DARRELL. "A Validity Study of the Autonomy and Deference Subscales of the EPPS." *J Consult Psychol* 22:445–7 D '58. * (*PA* 33:10092)
65. HIMELSTEIN, PHILIP; ESCHENBACH, ARTHUR E.; AND CARP, A. "Interrelationships Among Three Measures of Need Achievement." *J Consult Psychol* 22:451–2 D '58. * (*PA* 33:9953)
66. KARR, CHADWICK. *A Comparison of EPPS Scores Obtained From the Standard Forced-Choice Procedure and a Rating-Scale Procedure.* Doctor's thesis, University of Washington (Seattle, Wash.), 1958. (*DA* 19:3382)
67. KELLY, E. LOWELL; MILLER, JAMES G.; MARQUIS, DONALD G.; GERARD, R. W.; AND UHR, LEONARD. "Personality Differences and Continued Meprobamate and Prochlorperazine Administration." *A.M.A. Arch Neurol & Psychiatry* 80:241–6 Ag '58. * (*PA* 33:10420)
68. LEVY, LEO. *A Study of Some Personality Attributes of Independents and Conformers.* Doctor's thesis, University of Washington (Seattle, Wash.), 1958. (*DA* 19:1823)
69. MARLOWE, DAVID. "Some Psychological Correlates of Field Independence." Abstract. *J Consult Psychol* 22:334 O '58. * (*PA* 34:1044)
70. MICHEL, JOHN. *Non-Intellectual Dimensions of Performance in Reading.* Doctor's thesis, University of Texas (Austin, Tex.), 1958. (*DA* 19:2285)
71. MITCHELL, PETER MICHAEL. *Perceptual Correlates of Anxiety.* Doctor's thesis, Purdue University (Lafayette, Ind.), 1958. (*DA* 18:2213)
72. MORONEY, FRANCES MARY. *Methods of Studying Self-Concepts of Teachers.* Doctor's thesis, Pennsylvania State University (University Park, Pa.), 1958. (*DA* 19:90)
73. NAVRAN, LESLIE, AND STAUFFACHER, JAMES C. "A Comparative Analysis of the Personality Structure of Psychiatric and Nonpsychiatric Nurses." *Nursing Res* 7:64–7 Je '58. *
74. NIMNICHT, GLENDON PERRIN. *A Study of Successful Superintendents and Their Leadership Ability.* Doctor's thesis, Stanford University (Stanford, Calif.), 1958. (*DA* 19:720)
75. NUNNERY, MICHAEL Y. *A Study in the Use of Psychological Tests in Determining Effectiveness and Ineffectiveness Among Practicing School Administrators.* Doctor's thesis, University of Tennessee (Knoxville, Tenn.), 1958. (*DA* 19:1276)
76. PARKER, SEYMOUR. "Personality Factors Among Medical Students as Related to Their Predisposition to View the Patient as a 'Whole Man.'" *J Med Ed* 33:736–44 O '58. * (*PA* 34:3539)
77. PEPPER, ROGER S. *The Relationship Between Certain Dimensions of Psychological Need and the Achievement of First-Semester College Freshmen.* Doctor's thesis, University of Michigan (Ann Arbor, Mich.), 1958. (*DA* 19:732)
78. SANDERS, ELLA MOYE. *The Relationship Between Verbal-Quantitative Ability and Certain Personality and Metabolic Characteristics.* Doctor's thesis, University of Texas (Austin, Tex.), 1958. (*DA* 19:2540)
79. SCHEIDEL, THOMAS M.; CROWELL, LAURA; AND SHEPHERD, JOHN R. "Personality and Discussion Behavior: A Study of Possible Relationships." *Speech Monogr* 25:261–7 N '58. * (*PA* 33:9990)
80. THORPE, JO ANNE. "Study of Personality Variables Among Successful Women Students and Teachers of Physical Education." *Res Q* 29:83–92 Mr '58. * (*PA* 33:5974)
81. VERRILL, BERNARD VICTOR. *An Investigation of the Concept of Impulsivity.* Doctor's thesis, University of Houston (Houston, Tex.), 1958. (*DA* 19:183)
82. VOGEL, BERTRAM. *Humor and Personality: A Study of the Relationship Between Certain Selected Aspects of Person-*

ality and the Preference for Aggressive or Non-Aggressive Written Humor. Doctor's thesis, New York University (New York, N.Y.), 1958. (DA 19:2157)

83. YADOFF, BERNARD. An Attempt to Change Word Meaning and a Personality Test Score Through Semantic Generalization. Doctor's thesis, University of Pittsburgh (Pittsburgh, Pa.), 1958. (DA 19:2161)

84. ZUCKERMAN, MARVIN, AND GROSZ, HANUS J. "Suggestibility and Dependency." Abstract. J Consult Psychol 22:328 O '58. * (PA 34:1435)

85. ANDREWS, JOHN H. M., AND BROWN, ALAN F. "Can Principals Exclude Their Own Personality Characteristics When They Rate Their Teachers?" Ed Adm & Sup 45:234–42 Jl '59. * (PA 34:6579)

86. ARKOFF, ABE. "Need Patterns in Two Generations of Japanese Americans in Hawaii." J Social Psychol 50:75–9 Ag '59. * (PA 35:3319)

87. BADAL, ALDEN WESLEY. The Relationship of Selected Test Measures to Administrator Success in the Elementary School. Doctor's thesis, Stanford University (Stanford, Calif.), 1959. (DA 20:1263)

88. BENDIG, A. W. "Comparative Validity of Objective and Projective Measures of Need Achievement in Predicting Students' Achievement in Introductory Psychology." J General Psychol 60:237–43 Ap '59. * (PA 36:2KL37B)

89. BENDIG, A. W. "Personality Variables Related to Individual Performance on a Cognitive Task." J General Psychol 60:265–8 Ap '59. * (PA 36:2HJ65B)

90. BURCHINAL, LEE G. "Adolescent Role Deprivation and High School Age Marriage." Marriage & Family Living 21:378–84 N '59. * (PA 36:2IQ78B)

91. CARON, ALBERT J., AND WALLACH, MICHAEL A. "Personality Determinants of Repressive and Obsessive Reactions to Failure-Stress." J Abn & Social Psychol 59:236–45 S '59. * (PA 34:3310)

92. COLEMAN, WILLIAM, AND COLLETT, DOROTHY MANLEY. "Development and Applications of Structured Tests of Personality." R Ed Res 29:57–72 F '59. * (PA 34:5604)

93. DICKEN, CHARLES F. "Simulated Patterns on the Edwards Personal Preference Schedule." J Appl Psychol 43:372–8 D '59. * (PA 34:7379)

94. EDWARDS, ALLEN L.; WRIGHT, CALVIN E.; AND LUNNEBORG, CLIFFORD E. "A Note on 'Social Desirability as a Variable in the Edwards Personal Preference Schedule.'" J Consult Psychol 23:558 D '59. * (PA 34:5607)

95. FRYE, ROLAND L., AND ADAMS, HENRY E. "Effect of the Volunteer Variable on Leaderless Group Discussion Experiments." Psychol Rep 5:184 Je '59. * (PA 34:2762)

96. GOODSTEIN, LEONARD D., AND HEILBRUN, ALFRED B., JR. "The Relationship Between Personal and Social Desirability Scale Values of the Edwards Personal Preference Schedule." Abstract. J Consult Psychol 23:183 Ap '59. * (PA 34:1365, title only)

97. HARDISON, JAMES, AND PURCELL, KENNETH. "The Effects of Psychological Stress as a Function of Need and Cognitive Control." J Personality 27:250–8 Je '59. * (PA 34:4071)

98. HEILBRUN, ALFRED B., JR., AND GOODSTEIN, LEONARD D. "Relationships Between Personal and Social Desirability Sets and Performance on the Edwards Personal Preference Schedule." J Appl Psychol 43:302–5 O '59. * (PA 34:5719)

99. HOOKER, WILLIAM DOUGLAS. A Study of Certain Personal Characteristics and Attitudes of Full-Time and Part-Time Student Teachers and Certified Beginning Teachers. Doctor's thesis, University of Texas (Austin, Tex.), 1959. (DA 20:2677)

100. HORST, PAUL, AND WRIGHT, CALVIN E. "The Comparative Reliability of Two Techniques of Personality Appraisal." J Clin Psychol 15:388–91 O '59. * (PA 36:1HC88H)

101. KAHN, SAMUEL. The Relationship of Needs to Friendship Choices in Adolescence. Doctor's thesis, Columbia University (New York, N.Y.), 1959. (DA 20:756)

102. KARR, CHADWICK. "Two Methods for Scoring Self-Rating Scales to Approximate Forced Choice Results." Psychol Rep 5:773–9 D '59. * (PA 34:4962)

103. KENNEY, RAYMOND CARROLL. An Analysis of Self Perceptions in Counselor Trainees. Doctor's thesis, University of Texas (Austin, Tex.), 1959. (DA 20:2677)

104. KLETT, C. JAMES, AND YAUKEY, DAVID W. "A Cross-Cultural Comparison of Judgments of Social Desirability." J Social Psychol 49:19–26 F '59. * (PA 35:4763)

105. KRUG, ROBERT E. "Over- and Underachievement and the Edwards Personal Preference Schedule." J Appl Psychol 43:133–6 Ap '59. * (PA 34:3439)

106. LEVONIAN, EDWARD; COMREY, ANDREW; LEVY, WILLIAM; AND PROCTER, DONALD. "A Statistical Evaluation of Edwards Personal Preference Schedule." J Appl Psychol 43:355–9 D '59. * (PA 34:7401)

107. LEWIS, WILLIAM A. "Emotional Adjustment and Need Satisfaction of Hospital Patients." J Counsel Psychol 6:127–31 su '59. * (PA 34:4315)

108. MARLOWE, DAVID. "Relationships Among Direct and Indirect Measures of the Achievement Motive and Overt Behavior." J Consult Psychol 23:329–32 Ag '59. * (PA 34:4394)

109. MERRILL, REED M., AND MURPHY, DANIEL T. "Personality Factors and Academic Achievement in College." J Counsel Psychol 6:207–10 f '59. * (PA 35:3935)

110. MILAM, JAMES ROBERT. An Application of the Edwards Personal Preference Schedule to Problems in Psychopathology. Doctor's thesis, University of Washington (Seattle, Wash.), 1959. (DA 20:1075)

111. MORTON, JOHN. "An Investigation Into the Effects of an Adult Reading Efficiency Course." Occupational Psychol 33:222–37 O '59. * (PA 34:6523)

112. NUNNERY, MICHAEL Y. "How Useful Are Standardized Psychological Tests in the Selection of School Administrators." Ed Adm & Sup 45:349–56 N '59. * (PA 35:7092)

113. PENA, CESAREO D. "Influence of Social Desirability Upon Rorschach Content." J Clin Psychol 15:313–6 Jl '59. * (PA 35:3436)

114. RITCHEY, RONALD E. The Relationship Between Academic Achievement and the Personality Variables Measured by the Edwards Personal Preference Schedule. Master's thesis, University of Nebraska (Lincoln, Neb.), 1959.

115. RODGERS, FRANK P. A Psychometric Study of Certain Interest and Personality Variables Associated With Academic Achievement in a College Level Printing Curriculum. Doctor's thesis, University of Buffalo (Buffalo, N.Y.), 1959. (DA 19:3219)

116. SCHUMACHER, CHARLES FREDRICK. A Comparison of Three Methods for Keying Interest and Personality Inventories. Doctor's thesis, University of Minnesota (Minneapolis, Minn.), 1959. (DA 20:370)

117. SHELDON, M. STEPHEN; COALE, JACK M.; AND COPPLE, ROCKNE. "Concurrent Validity of the 'Warm Teacher Scale.'" J Ed Psychol 50:37–40 F '59. * (PA 35:2810)

118. TREHUB, ARNOLD. "Ego Disjunction and Psychopathology." J Abn & Social Psychol 58:191–4 Mr '59. * (PA 34:1064)

119. TUCKER, WOODIE L. The Relationship Between Personality Traits and Basic Skill in Typewriting. Doctor's thesis, University of Pittsburgh (Pittsburgh, Pa.), 1959. (DA 20:1694)

120. TUDDENHAM, READ D. "Correlates of Yielding to a Distorted Group Norm." J Personality 27:272–84 Je '59. * (PA 34:4096)

121. WAGGONER, GLEN HASTINGS. Administrator's Scores on Selected Standardized Tests and His Administrative Performance as Reported by Classroom Teachers. Doctor's thesis, Stanford University (Stanford, Calif.), 1959. (DA 20:3169)

122. WALSH, RICHARD P. "The Effect of Needs on Responses to Job Duties." J Counsel Psychol 6:194–8 f '59. * (PA 35:3514)

123. WARD, PAUL LEWIS. A Study of the Relationship of Evaluative Attitudes to Scholastic Ability and Academic Achievement. Doctor's thesis, Ohio State University (Columbus, Ohio), 1959. (DA 20:3639)

124. WEISS, PETER; WERTHEIMER, MICHAEL; AND GROESBECK, BYRON. "Achievement Motivation, Academic Aptitude, and College Grades." Ed & Psychol Meas 19:663–6 w '59. * (PA 34:6575)

124a. WEYBREW, BENJAMIN B., AND MOLISH, H. B. "Approaches to the Study of Motivation of Officer Candidates for the Submarine Service." U S Naval Med Res Lab Rep 18:1–47 O '59. * (PA 34:8530)

125. ZUCKERMAN, MARVIN, AND OLTEAN, MARY. "Some Relationships Between Maternal Attitude Factors and Authoritarianism, Personality Needs, Psychopathology, and Self-Acceptance." Child Develop 30:27–36 Mr '59. * (PA 34:3176)

126. ATKINSON, JOHN W., AND LITWIN, GEORGE H. "Achievement Motive and Test Anxiety Conceived as Motive to Approach Success and Motive to Avoid Failure." J Abn & Social Psychol 60:52–63 Ja '60. * (PA 34:7132)

127. BAY, JUNG HONG. The Validity of Two Objective Measures of Academic Motivation. Doctor's thesis, State University of Iowa (Iowa City, Iowa), 1960. (DA 20:4585)

128. BERNBERG, RAYMOND E. "An Analysis of the Responses of a Male Prison Population to the Edwards Personal Preference Schedule." J General Psychol 62:319–24 Ap '60. * (PA 34:8097)

129. BERNHARDT, HAROLD E., JR. "'Intraception' Test Score and Psychiatry Grade as a Freshman and as a Sophomore Medical Student: A Validational Study of a Subscale of the Edwards Personal Preference Schedule." Ed & Psychol Meas 20:365–79 su '60. * (PA 35:6426)

130. BOYCE, RICHARD DUDLEY. An Empirical Evaluation of Five Tests for Administrator Selection: The Composite Study. Doctor's thesis, Stanford University (Stanford, Calif.), 1960. (DA 21:2546)

131. BROWN, DONALD JAMES. An Investigation of the Relationships Between Certain Personal Characteristics of Guidance Counselors and Performance in Supervised Counseling Interviews. Doctor's thesis, Ohio State University (Columbus, Ohio), 1960. (DA 21:810)

132. BUNIN, SANFORD MELVIN. Non-Intellectual Dimensions of Some Academic Performance. Doctor's thesis, University of Texas (Austin, Tex.), 1960. (DA 20:4586)

133. CHANCE, JUNE ELIZABETH, AND MEADERS, WILSON. "Needs and Interpersonal Perception." J Personality 28:200–9 Je '60. * (PA 35:2260)

134. CLARK, CHARLES MARVIN. Changes in Response Patterns of Counseling Institute Trainees. Doctor's thesis, Ohio State University (Columbus, Ohio), 1960. (DA 21:811)

135. DICKEN, CHARLES F. "Simulated Patterns on the

California Psychological Inventory." *J Counsel Psychol* 7:24–31 sp '60. * (*PA* 35:2218)

136. DIENER, CHARLES L. "Similarities and Differences Between Over-Achieving and Under-Achieving Students." *Personnel & Guid J* 38:396–400 Ja '60. *

137. DIVESTA, FRANCIS J., AND COX, LANDON. "Some Dispositional Correlates of Conformity Behavior." *J Social Psychol* 52:259–68 N '60. * (*PA* 35:4813)

138. DUNNETTE, MARVIN D., AND KIRCHNER, WAYNE K. "Psychological Test Differences Between Industrial Salesmen and Retail Salesmen." *J Appl Psychol* 44:121–5 Ap '60. * (*PA* 35:4029)

139. EBERT, FRANCIS JOHN. *An Empirical Evaluation of Five Tests for the Selection of Elementary School Principals.* Doctor's thesis, Stanford University (Stanford, Calif.), 1960. (*DA* 21:2548)

140. EDWARDS, ALLEN L.; HEATHERS, LOUISE B.; AND FORDYCE, WILBERT E. "Correlations of New MMPI Scales With Edwards SD Scale." *J Clin Psychol* 16:26–9 Ja '60. * (*PA* 36:1HF26E)

141. FELDMAN, MARVIN J., AND CORAH, NORMAN L. "Social Desirability and the Forced Choice Method." *J Consult Psychol* 24:480–2 D '60. * (*PA* 36:1HF80F)

142. FISKE, DONALD W. "Variability Among Peer Ratings in Different Situations." *Ed & Psychol Meas* 20:283–92 su '60. * (*PA* 35:6337)

143. FISKE, DONALD W.; HOWARD, KENNETH; AND RECHENBERG, WILLIAM. "The EPPS Profile Stability Coefficient." Abstract. *J Consult Psychol* 24:370 Ag '60. *

144. FORDYCE, WILBERT E., AND CROW, WILLIAM R. "Ego Disjunction: A Failure to Replicate Trehub's Results." *J Abn & Social Psychol* 60:446–8 My '60. * (*PA* 35:4954)

145. GARDNER, MARGARET SEYMOUR. *Factors Associated With Success in First Grade Teaching.* Doctor's thesis, Northwestern University (Evanston, Ill.), 1960. (*DA* 21:2609)

145a. GARDNER, RILEY W.; JACKSON, DOUGLAS N.; AND MESSICK, SAMUEL J. "Personality Organization in Cognitive Controls and Intellectual Abilities." *Psychol Issues* 2(8):1–149 '60. * (*PA* 36:2HA49G)

146. GUSTAFSON, MONTANE C. *Relationship Between Manifest Needs and Differential Achievement of High School Students.* Doctor's thesis, University of Nebraska (Lincoln, Neb.), 1960. (*DA* 20:4335)

147. GUSTAV, ALICE. "Use of Two Tests in Brief Counseling." *J Counsel Psychol* 7:228–9 f '60. *

148. HAINES, LEWIS EDGAR. *An Evaluation of the FIRO-B and the EPPS for Predicting College Roommate Compatibility.* Doctor's thesis, Washington State University (Pullman, Wash.), 1960. (*DA* 21:2173)

149. HEIST, PAUL. "Personality Characteristics of Dental Students." *Ed Rec* 41:240–52 Jl '60. * (*PA* 35:7081)

150. IZARD, CARROLL E. "Personality Characteristics Associated With Resistance to Change." *J Consult Psychol* 24:437–40 O '60. * (*PA* 35:4985)

151. IZARD, CARROLL E. "Personality Characteristics of Engineers as Measured by the Edwards Personal Preference Schedule." *J Appl Psychol* 44:332–5 O '60. * (*PA* 35:4016)

152. IZARD, CARROLL E. "Personality Similarity and Friendship." *J Abn & Social Psychol* 61:47–51 Jl '60. * (*PA* 35:2117)

153. IZARD, CARROLL E. "Personality Similarity, Positive Affect, and Interpersonal Attraction." *J Abn & Social Psychol* 61:484–5 N '60. * (*PA* 36:2GE84I)

154. JAMES, KENNETH RAYMOND. *An Empirical Evaluation of Five Tests for Administrator Selection in a Metropolitan School District.* Doctor's thesis, Stanford University (Stanford, Calif.), 1960. (*DA* 21:2556)

155. JOHNSON, RONALD ENGLE. *A Quantification and Measurement of Three Qualitative Changes in the Recall of Complex Verbal Materials.* Doctor's thesis, Ohio State University (Columbus, Ohio), 1960. (*DA* 21:2358)

156. KATZ, IRWIN; GLUCKSBERG, SAM; AND KRAUSS, ROBERT. "Need Satisfaction and Edwards PPS Scores in Married Couples." *J Consult Psychol* 24:205–8 Je '60. * (*PA* 35:6685)

157. KAZMIER, LEONARD JOHN. *Validation of a Technique for Predicting Over- and Under-Achievement Through Objective Testing.* Doctor's thesis, Ohio State University (Columbus, Ohio), 1960. (*DA* 21:2359)

158. KIRCHNER, WAYNE K.; DUNNETTE, MARVIN D.; AND MOUSLEY, NANCY. "Use of the Edwards Personal Preference Schedule in the Selection of Salesmen." *Personnel Psychol* 13:421–4 w '60. * (*PA* 36:1LD21K)

159. LUDEGREN, HERBERTA MARIE. *Personality Traits of Successful and Unsuccessful Women Counselors in Girls' Private and Agency Camps.* Doctor's thesis, State University of Iowa (Iowa City, Iowa), 1960. (*DA* 20:4579)

160. MARSHALL, SIMONE. "Personality Correlates of Peptic Ulcer Patients." *J Consult Psychol* 24:218–23 Je '60. * (*PA* 35:6970)

161. MERRILL, REED M. "Comparison of Education Students, Successful Science Teachers and Educational Administrators on the Edwards PPS." *J Ed Res* 54:38–40 S '60. *

162. MESSICK, SAMUEL. "Dimensions of Social Desirability." *J Consult Psychol* 24:279–87 Ag '60. * (*PA* 35:2211)

163. MILLER, SUTHERLAND, JR. *The Relationship of Personality to Occupation, Setting and Function.* Doctor's thesis, Columbia University (New York, N.Y.), 1960. (*DA* 21:3518)

164. MOGAR, ROBERT EDWARD. *Personality Correlates of Differential Performance in a Competitive Situation.* Doctor's thesis, State University of Iowa (Iowa City, Iowa), 1960. (*DA* 21:1631)

165. NEWMAN, JOSEPH, AND WISCHNER, GEORGE J. "The Performance of a Hospitalized Neuropsychiatric Sample on the Edwards Personal Preference Schedule." *J Clin Psychol* 16:99–100 Ja '60. * (*PA* 36:1HF99N)

166. NORRELL, GWEN, AND GRATER, HARRY. "Interest Awareness as an Aspect of Self-Awareness." *J Counsel Psychol* 7:289–92 w '60. * (*PA* 36:1HF89N)

167. RALEY, COLEMAN LAVAN. *Personality Traits of High-Academic Achievers at Oklahoma Baptist University, 1958–1959.* Doctor's thesis, University of Oklahoma (Norman, Okla.), 1960. (*DA* 20:2680)

168. REILLY, MARY ST. ANNE; COMMINS, WILLIAM D.; AND STEFIC, EDWARD C. "The Complementarity of Personality Needs in Friendship Choice." *J Abn & Social Psychol* 61:292–4 S '60. * (*PA* 35:4822)

169. RICHTER, PAUL D. *The Relationship of Personality Traits Measured by the Edwards Personal Preference Schedule to Ratings of Supervisory Success.* Master's thesis, Pennsylvania State University (University Park, Pa.), 1960.

170. SANDERS, ELLA M.; MEFFERD, ROY B., JR.; AND BOWN, OLIVER H. "Verbal-Quantitative Ability and Certain Personality and Metabolic Characteristics of Male College Students." *Ed & Psychol Meas* 20:491–503 au '60. * (*PA* 35:3550)

171. UHLINGER, CAROLYN A., AND STEPHENS, MARK W. "Relation of Achievement Motivation to Academic Achievement in Students of Superior Ability." *J Ed Psychol* 51:259–66 O '60. * (*PA* 36:1KL59U)

172. VAN DE CASTLE, R. L. "Perceptual Defense in a Binocular Rivalry Situation." *J Personality* 28:448–62 D '60. * (*PA* 35:5010)

173. WILSON, GORDON GILBERT. *Relationships Among Three Measured Levels of Personality Functioning: Self-Assessment, Fantasy, Coping Activity and Their Relationships to Ratings of Real-Life Behavior.* Doctor's thesis, University of Denver (Denver, Colo.), 1960. (*DA* 22:921)

174. WORELL, LEONARD. "EPPS N Achievement and Verbal Paired-Associates Learning." *J Abn & Social Psychol* 60:147–50 Ja '60. * (*PA* 34:7187)

175. ANDERSON, THELMA HILL. *Dimensions of the Characteristics Related to the High- and Low-Achievement of a Selected Group of Negro College Students.* Doctor's thesis, University of Oklahoma (Norman, Okla.), 1961. (*DA* 22:1082)

176. ARKOFF, ABE; MEREDITH, GERALD; AND JONES, RONALD. "Urban-Rural Differences in Need Patterns of Third Generation Japanese-Americans in Hawaii." *J Social Psychol* 53:21–3 F '61. * (*PA* 35:6260)

177. BAZNIK, CHARLES ARTHUR. *An Attempt by College Students to Assume the Need System of Veteran Teachers on the Edwards Personal Preference Schedule.* Doctor's thesis, University of Kansas (Lawrence, Kan.), 1961. (*DA* 22:2303)

178. BELL, TERREL HOWARD. *The Characteristics of Weber School District Teachers Who Had Negative and Positive Attitudes Toward a Major Change in the District's Instructional Program.* Doctor's thesis, University of Utah (Salt Lake City, Utah), 1961. (*DA* 22:1475)

179. BLUM, STUART H. "The Desire for Security: An Element in the Vocational Choice of College Men." *J Ed Psychol* 52:317–21 D '61. * (*PA* 38:3175)

180. BORGATTA, EDGAR F. "Mood, Personality, and Interaction." *J General Psychol* 64:105–37 Ja '61. * (*PA* 35:6415)

181. BORGATTA, EDGAR F., AND GLASS, DAVID C. "Personality Concomitants of Extreme Response Set (ERS)." *J Social Psychol* 55:213–21 D '61. * (*PA* 36:3HE13B)

182. BORGATTA, EDGAR F.; IN COLLABORATION WITH HENRY J. MEYER. "Make a Sentence Test: An Approach to Objective Scoring of Sentence Completions." *Genetic Psychol Monogr* 63:3–65 F '61. * (*PA* 35:6435)

183. CARLSON, EARL R. "Motivation and Set in Acquiring Information About Persons." *J Personality* 29:285–93 S '61. * (*PA* 37:3137)

184. CHRISTENSEN, C. M. "Use of Design, Texture, and Color Preferences in Assessment of Personality Characteristics." *Percept & Motor Skills* 12:143–50 Ap '61. * (*PA* 36:1HB43C)

185. COOK, DESMOND L.; LINDEN, JAMES D.; AND McKAY, HARRISON E. "A Factor Analysis of Teacher Trainee Responses to Selected Personality Inventories." *Ed & Psychol Meas* 21:865–72 w '61. * (*PA* 36:5HF65C)

186. COPEMAN, JAMES; PASCOE, ROBERT; AND WARD, GEORGE, II. "The Edwards Personal Preference Schedule and Revised Cooperative English Test as Predictors of Academic Achievement." *Proc W Va Acad Sci* 33:124–6 '61. * (*PA* 36:5KL24C)

187. CORAH, NORMAN L. "A Factor Analytic Study of Edwards' Personal Preference Schedule." *Psychol Rep* 9:147–50 Ag '61. *

188. CRANDALL, VAUGHN J., AND PRESTON, ANNE. "Verbally Expressed Needs and Overt Maternal Behaviors." *Child Develop* 32:261–70 Je '61. * (*PA* 36:3FG61C)

189. DAY, BARBARA R. "A Comparison of Personality Needs of Courtship Couples and Same Sex Friendships." *Sociol & Social Res* 45:435–40 Jl '61. * (*PA* 36:3HJ35D)

190. DEMOS, GEORGE D., AND SPOLYAR, LUDWIG J. "Aca

demic Achievement of College Freshmen in Relation to the Edwards Personal Preference Schedule." *Ed & Psychol Meas* 21:473–9 su '61. * (*PA* 36:2KL73D)

191. DUNKLEBERGER, CLARENCE J., AND TYLER, LEONA E. "Interest Stability and Personality Traits." *J Counsel Psychol* 8:70–4 sp '61. * (*PA* 36:3FF70D)

192. ENDLER, NORMAN S. "Conformity Analyzed and Related to Personality." *J Social Psychol* 53:271–83 Ap '61. * (*PA* 36:1GE71E)

193. GARRISON, KARL C., AND SCOTT, MARY HUGHIE. "A Comparison of the Personal Needs of College Students Preparing to Teach in Different Teaching Areas." *Ed & Psychol Meas* 21:955–64 w '61. * (*PA* 36:5KM55G)

194. GOCKA, EDWARD F., AND ROZYNKO, VITALI. "Some Comments on the EPPS Disjunction Score." *J Abn & Social Psychol* 62:458–60 Mr '61. * (*PA* 36:4HF58G)

195. HEILBRUN, ALFRED B., JR., AND GOODSTEIN, LEONARD D. "Consistency Between Social Desirability Ratings and Item Endorsement as a Function of Psychopathology." *Psychol Rep* 8:69–70 F '61. * (*PA* 36:1H69H)

196. HEILBRUN, ALFRED B., JR., AND GOODSTEIN, LEONARD D. "The Relationships Between Individually Defined and Group Defined Social Desirability and Performance on the Edwards Personal Preference Schedule." *J Consult Psychol* 25:200–4 Je '61. *

197. HEILBRUN, ALFRED B., JR., AND GOODSTEIN, LEONARD D. "Social Desirability Response Set: Error or Predictor Variable." *J Psychol* 51:321–9 Ap '61. * (*PA* 35:6430)

198. HEILIZER, FRED. "A Scale of Compatibility and Incompatibility of Pairs of Needs." *Psychol Rep* 9:565–72 D '61. *

199. HETLINGER, DUANE F., AND HILDRETH, RICHARD A. "Personality Characteristics of Debaters." *Q J Speech* 47:398–401 D '61. *

200. HOWARD, MAURICE LLOYD. *A Study of Under-Achieving College Students With High Academic Ability From the Phenomenological Frame of Reference.* Doctor's thesis, University of Colorado (Boulder, Colo.), 1961. (*DA* 22:3040)

201. JERRY, DONALD H. *References and Problems of Thirty High School Football Players and Thirty Non-Football Players.* Master's thesis, Ohio State University (Columbus, Ohio), 1961.

202. KAZMIER, LEONARD J. "Cross-Validation Groups, Extreme Groups, and the Prediction of Academic Achievement." *J Ed Psychol* 52:195–8 Ap '61. * (*PA* 38:3204)

203. KRUG, ROBERT E., AND MOYER, K. E. "An Analysis of the F Scale: II, Relationship to Standardized Personality Inventories." *J Social Psychol* 53:293–301 Ap '61. * (*PA* 36:1HC93K)

204. LIPETZ, MILTON E. "Reliability of EPPS Autonomy for Males and Females." *Psychol Rep* 8:456 Je '61. * (*PA* 36:2HF56L)

205. MCKEE, JOHN P., AND TURNER, WALTER S. "The Relationship of 'Drive' Ratings in Adolescence to CPI and EPPS Scores in Adulthood." *Vita Hum* 4(1–2):1–14 '61. * (*PA* 36:1HF01M)

206. MEDLEY, DONALD M. "Teacher Personality and Teacher-Pupil Rapport." *J Teach Ed* 12:152–6 Je '61. *

207. MILTON, G. A., AND LIPETZ, MILTON E. "EPPS Consistency Score: Inconsistency or Equality of Need?" *Psychol Rep* 8:310 Ap '61. * (*PA* 36:1HE10M)

208. MOORE, ROBERT BURKLAND. *A Comparison of Test Performance and Current Status of Administrative Candidates in Twenty-Four School Districts.* Doctor's thesis, Stanford University (Stanford, Calif.), 1961. (*DA* 22:476)

209. MORGAN, J. B. *Personality Variables of Industrial Arts Teachers.* Doctor's research study No. 1, Colorado State College (Greeley, Colo.), 1961. (*DA* 22:4225)

209a. MUSSEN, PAUL. "Some Antecedents and Consequents of Masculine Sex-Typing in Adolescent Boys." *Psychol Monogr* 75(2):1–24 '61. * (*PA* 38:2479)

210. NEVIS, EDWIN C., AND PARKER, JAMES W. "The Use of Published Norms in the Industrial Setting." *Personnel Psychol* 14:59–65 sp '61. * (*PA* 36:4LD59N)

211. PARKER, AILEEN WEBBER. *A Comparative Study of Selected Factors in the Vocational Development of College Women.* Doctor's thesis, Indiana University (Bloomington, Ind.), 1961. (*DA* 22:1087)

212. PECK, JOAN H. *The Appropriateness of the Edwards Personal Preference Schedule for Use With Junior High School Students.* Master's thesis, University of Maryland (College Park, Md.), 1961.

213. PHARES, E. JERRY, AND ADAMS, CALVIN K. "The Construct Validity of the Edwards PPS Heterosexuality Scale." *J Consult Psychol* 25:341–4 Ag '61. * (*PA* 37:1262)

213a. REDDEN, JAMES W., AND SCALES, ELDRIDGE E. "Nursing Education and Personality Characteristics." *Nursing Res* 10:215–8 f '61. *

213b. REECE, MICHAEL M. "Personality Characteristics and Success in Nursing." *Nursing Res* 10:172–6 su '61. *

214. SATZ, PAUL, AND ALLEN, ROBERT M. "A Study of the Edwards Personal Preference Schedule: Regional Normative Approach." *J Social Psychol* 53:195–8 Ap '61. * (*PA* 36:1HF95S)

215. SHANKER, PREM. *The Contribution of EPPS Scores to Differential and Multiple Absolute Academic Prediction.*

Doctor's thesis, University of Washington (Seattle, Wash.), 1961. (*DA* 22:2065)

216. SHAW, MERVILLE C. "Need Achievement Scales as Predictors of Academic Success." *J Ed Psychol* 52:282–5 D '61. * (*PA* 38:3209)

217. SPILKA, BERNARD. "Social Desirability: A Problem of Operational Definition." *Psychol Rep* 8:149–50 F '61. * (*PA* 36:1HE49S)

218. TOLOR, ALEXANDER. "The Relationship Between Insight and Intraception." *J Clin Psychol* 17:188–9 Ap '61. * (*PA* 38:988)

219. VAN WAGENEN, DONALD RICHARD. *The Relation of Selected Non-Intellectual Factors to Academic Achievement in Several College Groups.* Doctor's thesis, Syracuse University (Syracuse, N.Y.), 1961. (*DA* 23:539)

220. WEGNER, KENNETH WALTER. *An Analysis of Interest Patterns and Psychological Need Structures Related to L-I-D Response Patterns on the Strong Vocational Interest Blank for Women.* Doctor's thesis, University of Kansas (Lawrence, Kan.), 1961. (*DA* 22:3931)

221. WRIGHT, CALVIN E. "A Factor Dimension Comparison of Normative and Ipsative Measurements." *Ed & Psychol Meas* 21:433–44 su '61. * (*PA* 36:2HE33W)

222. ZUCKERMAN, MARVIN; LEVITT, EUGENE E.; AND LUBIN, BERNARD. "Concurrent and Construct Validity of Direct and Indirect Measures of Dependency." *J Consult Psychol* 25:316–23 Ag '61. *

223. ABRAHAM, HENRY H. L. "The Suggestibility Personality: A Psychological Investigation of Susceptibility to Persuasion." *Acta Psychologica* 20(2):167–84 '62. * (*PA* 37:6862)

224. ARMATAS, JAMES P., AND COLLISTER, E. GORDON. "Personality Correlates of SVIB Patterns." *J Counsel Psychol* 9:149–54 su '62. * (*PA* 37:6710)

225. BENDIG, A. W., AND MARTIN, ANN M. "The Factor Structure and Stability of Fifteen Human Needs." *J General Psychol* 67:229–35 O '62. * (*PA* 37:8001)

226. BORGATTA, EDGAR F. "The Coincidence of Subtests in Four Personality Inventories." *J Social Psychol* 56:227–44 Ap '62. * (*PA* 37:1247)

227. BRADY, JOHN PAUL; THORNTON, DOUGLAS R.; PAPPAS, NICHOLAS; AND TAUSIG, THEODORE N. "Edwards Personal Preference Schedule Correlates of Operant Behavior." *J Clin Psychol* 18:224–6 Ap '62. * (*PA* 38:8476)

228. BROMER, JOHN A.; JOHNSON, J. MYRON; AND SEVRANSKY, PAUL. "Validity Information Exchange, No. 15-02: D.O.T. Code 4-97.010, 4-75.120, 4-85.040, Craft Foremen Correspond to Foreman I; 5-91.875, 5-91.088, 5-91.091, 5-91.831, 5-91.812, Process, Production, and Warehouse Foremen Correspond to Foremen II." *Personnel Psychol* 15:107–9 sp '62. *

229. BROWER, JULIAN LEWIS. *Patient-Personnel Interpersonal Choice on a State Mental Hospital Ward.* Doctor's thesis, University of Buffalo (Buffalo, N.Y.), 1962. (*DA* 23:2982)

230. CAIRNS, ROBERT B., AND LEWIS, MICHAEL. "Dependency and the Reinforcement Value of a Verbal Stimulus." *J Consult Psychol* 26:1–8 F '62. * (*PA* 37:4976)

231. CAMPBELL, JOEL T.; OTIS, JAY L.; LISKE, RALPH E.; AND PRIEN, ERICH P. "Assessments of Higher-Level Personnel: II, Validity of the Over-All Assessment Process." *Personnel Psychol* 15:63–74 sp '62. * (*PA* 37:3908)

231a. CRANE, WILLIAM J. "Screening Devices for Occupational Therapy Majors." *Am J Occup Ther* 16:131–2 My–Je '62. * (*PA* 37:4078)

232. EDWARDS, ALLEN L., AND DIERS, CAROL JEAN. "Social Desirability and Conflict." *J Social Psychol* 58:349–56 D '62. * (*PA* 37:6731)

233. EDWARDS, ALLEN L., AND WALKER, JERALD N. "Relationship Between Probability of Item Endorsement and Social Desirability Scale Value for High and Low Groups on Edwards' SD Scale." *J Abn & Social Psychol* 64:458–60 Je '62. * (*PA* 38:979)

234. FENZ, WALTER D., AND ARKOFF, ABE. "Comparative Need Patterns of Five Ancestry Groups in Hawaii." *J Social Psychol* 58:67–89 O '62. * (*PA* 37:6539)

235. FORD, LEROY H., JR., AND SEMPERT, EDITH L. "Relations Among Some Objective Measures of Hostility, Need Aggression, and Anxiety." Abstract. *J Consult Psychol* 26:486 O '62. *

236. FORREST, D. W., AND LEE, S. G. "Mechanisms of Defense and Readiness in Perception and Recall." *Psychol Monogr* 76(4):1–28 '62. * (*PA* 37:1339)

237. FRANCESCO, E. "A Pervasive Value: Conventional Religiosity." *J Social Psychol* 57:467–70 Ag '62. * (*PA* 37:4855)

238. FUSTER, JOACHIM M. "A Study of the Edwards Personal Preference Schedule on Indian College Students." *J Social Psychol* 57:309–14 Ag '62. * (*PA* 37:4814)

239. GARRISON, KARL C., AND SCOTT, MARY HUGHIE. "The Relationship of Selected Personal Characteristics to the Needs of College Students Preparing to Teach." *Ed & Psychol Meas* 22:753–8 w '62. * (*PA* 37:6732)

240. GOODMAN, MARVIN. *A Pilot Study of the Relationship Between Degree of Expressed Self-Acceptance and Interspousal Need Structure in the Mate Selection Process.* Doctor's thesis, Michigan State University (East Lansing, Mich.), 1962. (*DA* 24:867)

241. GOODSTEIN, LEONARD D., AND HEILBRUN, ALFRED B., JR. "Prediction of College Achievement From the Edwards Personal Preference Schedule at Three Levels of Intellectual Ability." *J Appl Psychol* 46:317–20 O '62. * (*PA* 37:5661)

242. GRAT, EDWIN CASIMER. *A Study of Personality Preferences of Student Speech Therapists on the Basis of the Edwards Personal Preference Schedule.* Master's thesis, University of Oregon (Eugene, Ore.), 1962. (*MA* 1:63)

243. GRAY, JAMES TERRY. *Manifest Needs in Secondary Teachers, Accountants, and Mechanical Engineers: An Exploratory Study.* Doctor's thesis, University of Houston (Houston, Tex.), 1962. (*DA* 23:1413)

244. GYNTHER, MALCOLM D., AND GERTZ, BORIS. "Personality Characteristics of Student Nurses in South Carolina." *J Social Psychol* 56:277–84 Ap '62. * (*PA* 37:1256)

245. GYNTHER, MALCOLM D.; MILLER, FRANCIS T.; AND DAVIS, HUGH T. "Relations Between Needs and Behavior as Measured by the Edwards PPS and Inter-Personal Check List." *J Social Psychol* 57:445–51 Ag '62. * (*PA* 37:5063)

246. HARTLEY, RAYMOND E., AND ALLEN, ROBERT M. "The Minnesota Multiphasic Personality Inventory (MMPI) and the Edwards Personal Preference Schedule (EPPS): A Factor Analytic Study." *J Social Psychol* 58:153–62 O '62. * (*PA* 37:6733)

247. HEILBRUN, ALFRED B., JR. "Social Desirability and the Relative Validities of Achievement Scales." *J Consult Psychol* 26:383–6 Ag '62. * (*PA* 38:4310)

248. HEILIZER, FRED, AND TREHUB, ARNOLD. "Relationships of the EPPS Need Profile Among Eight Samples." *J Clin Psychol* 18:461–4 O '62. * (*PA* 39:5178)

249. HOGUE, J. PIERRE; OTIS, JAY L.; AND PRIEN, ERICH P. "Assessments of Higher-Level Personnel: VI, Validity of Predictions Based on Projective Techniques." *Personnel Psychol* 15:335–44 au '62. * (*PA* 37:7249)

250. HULL, J., AND ZUBEK, JOHN P. "Personality Characteristics of Successful and Unsuccessful Sensory Isolation Subjects." *Percept & Motor Skills* 14:231–40 Ap '62. *

251. HUTCHINS, EDWIN B. "The Student and His Environment." *J Med Ed* 37:67–82 D '62. *

252. IZARD, CARROLL E. "Personality Change During College Years." Abstract. *J Consult Psychol* 26:482 O '62. *

253. IZARD, CARROLL E. "Personality Characteristics (EPPS), Level of Expectation, and Performance." Abstract. *J Consult Psychol* 26:394 Ag '62. * (*PA* 38:4311)

254. KARR, CHADWICK. "Note on the Edwards Personal Preference Schedule and Between-Subjects Variance." *Psychol Rep* 10:55–8. F '62. * (*PA* 37:1258)

255. KATZELL, RAYMOND A., AND KATZELL, MILDRED E. "Development and Application of Structured Tests of Personality." *R Ed Res* 32:51–63 F '62. * (*PA* 37:1197)

256. KEMP, C. GRATTON. "Counseling Responses and Need Structures of High School Principals and of Counselors." *J Counsel Psychol* 9:326–8 w '62. * (*PA* 39:1805)

257. KIRCHNER, WAYNE K. "'Real-Life' Faking on the Edwards Personal Preference Schedule by Sales Applicants." *J Appl Psychol* 46:128–30 Ap '62. *

258. KORMAN, MAURICE, AND COLTHARP, FRANCES. "Transparency in the Edwards Personal Preference Schedule." *J Consult Psychol* 26:379–82 Ag '62. * (*PA* 38:4313)

259. LANG, GERHARD; SFERRA, AMEDEO; AND SEYMOUR, MARJORIE. "Psychological Needs of College Freshmen and Their Academic Achievement." *Personnel & Guid J* 41:359–60 D '62. * (*PA* 37:7193)

260. LANG, PETER J., AND LAZOVIK, A. DAVID. "Personality and Hypnotic Susceptibility." *J Consult Psychol* 26:317–22 Ag '62. * (*PA* 38:4433)

261. LEVY, LEON H. "Age and Personal Need Correlates of Expectancy for Change." *Percept & Motor Skills* 15:351–6 O '62. * (*PA* 37:8033)

262. LIPETZ, MILTON E., AND MILTON, G. A. "Prediction of Autonomy Behavior From Situational Modifications of the EPPS n Autonomy Scale." *Psychol Rep* 11:487–93 O '62. * (*PA* 37:7984)

263. LOCKE, LAWRENCE F. "Performance of Administration Oriented Male Physical Educators on Selected Psychological Tests." *Res Q* 33:418–29 O '62. *

264. LONGENECKER, E. D. "Perceptual Recognition as a Function of Anxiety, Motivation, and the Testing Situation." *J Abn & Social Psychol* 64:215–21 Mr '62. * (*PA* 38:1723)

265. LUBIN, BERNARD; LEVITT, EUGENE E.; AND ZUCKERMAN, MARVIN. "Some Personality Differences Between Responders and Non-Responders to a Survey Questionnaire." *J Consult Psychol* 26:192 Ap '62. * (*PA* 37:5013)

266. MEHLMAN, BENJAMIN. "Similarity in Friendships." *J Social Psychol* 57:195–202 Je '62. * (*PA* 37:3839)

267. MOGAR, ROBERT E. "Competition, Achievement, and Personality." Abstract of doctor's thesis. *J Counsel Psychol* 9:168–72 su '62. * (*PA* 37:7197)

268. MOTT, CAROL COWLES. *A Study of Personality Variables Among Counselor Education Majors, Counselors, and Graduate Students in Administration, Curriculum, and Supervision as Shown by the Edwards Personal Preference Schedule.* Doctor's thesis, Florida State University (Tallahassee, Fla.), 1962. (*DA* 23:3779)

269. PATTERSON, C. H. "A Note on the Construct Validity of the Concept of Empathy." *Personnel & Guid J* 40:803–6 My '62. * (*PA* 37:3448)

270. PATTERSON, C. H. "Test Characteristics of Rehabilitation Counselor Trainees." *J Rehabil* 28:15–6 S–O '62. * (*PA* 37:6953)

271. PECKENS, RUSSELL GEORGE. *A Factor-Analytic Study of Edwards Personal Preference Schedule Need Scores as a Function of Age and Sex.* Doctor's thesis, University of Tennessee (Knoxville, Tenn.), 1962. (*DA* 23:3781)

272. PULOS, LEE; NICHOLS, ROBERT C.; LEWINSOHN, PETER M.; AND KOLDJESKI, THEODORE. "Selection of Psychiatric Aides and Prediction of Performance Through Psychological Testing and Interviews." *Psychol Rep* 10:519–20 Ap '62. * (*PA* 37:3401)

273. RENZAGLIA, GUY A.; HENRY, DONALD R.; AND RYBOLT, GAYLORD A., JR. "Estimation and Measurement of Personality Characteristics and Correlates of Their Congruence." *J Counsel Psychol* 9:71–8 sp '62. * (*PA* 38:2704)

274. SALTZ, ELI; REECE, MICHAEL; AND AGER, JOEL. "Studies of Forced-Choice Methodology: Individual Differences in Social Desirability." *Ed & Psychol Meas* 22:365–70 su '62. * (*PA* 37:3180)

275. SCANDRETTE, ONAS. "Differential Need Patterns of Women Elementary and Secondary Level Student Teachers." *J Ed Res* 55:376–9 My '62. * (*PA* 37:5685)

276. SINGH, PARAS NATH; HUANG, SOPHIA CHANG; AND THOMPSON, GEORGE G. "A Comparative Study of Selected Attitudes, Values, and Personality Characteristics of American, Chinese, and Indian Students." *J Social Psychol* 57:123–32 Je '62. * (*PA* 37:3847)

277. SMITH, RONALD E. *Parents, Children, Preferences, and Achievement.* Master's thesis, Ohio State University (Columbus, Ohio), 1962.

278. SOUTHWORTH, HORTON COE. *A Study of Certain Personality and Value Differences in Teacher Education Majors Preferring Early and Later Elementary Teaching Levels.* Doctor's thesis, Michigan State University (East Lansing, Mich.), 1962. (*DA* 23:1284)

279. SPANGLER, DONALD P., AND THOMAS, CHARLES W. "The Effects of Age, Sex, and Physical Disability Upon Manifest Needs." *J Counsel Psychol* 9:313–9 w '62. *

280. STEFFLRE, BUFORD; KING, PAUL; AND LEAFGREN, FRED. "Characteristics of Counselors Judged Effective by Their Peers." *J Counsel Psychol* 9:335–40 w '62. * (*PA* 39:2312)

281. STUCKEY, JUNE ELIZABETH. *The Relationship of Academic Achievement to Selected Personality Needs.* Doctor's thesis, Ohio State University (Columbus, Ohio), 1962. (*DA* 24:185)

282. SUPER, DONALD E., AND CRITES, JOHN O. *Appraising Vocational Fitness by Means of Psychological Tests, Revised Edition,* pp. 537–55. New York: Harper & Row, Publishers, Inc., 1962. Pp. xv, 688. * (*PA* 37:2038)

283. TOLOR, ALEXANDER. "The Personality Need Structure of Psychiatric Attendants." *Mental Hyg* 46:218–22 Ap '62. *

284. TUTKO, THOMAS A., AND SECHREST, LEE. "Conceptual Performance and Personality Variables." *J Consult Psychol* 26:481 O '62. * (*PA* 39:1766)

285. UHLIR, GLADYS ANN. *The Prediction of Success in the Professional Preparation of Health and Physical Education Teachers.* Doctor's thesis, Columbia University (New York, N.Y.), 1962. (*DA* 24:646)

286. VACEK, WILLIAM LEE. *Personality Variables of Freshmen College Majors With Emphasis on Industrial Arts.* Doctor's research study No. 1, Colorado State College (Greeley, Colo.), 1962. (*DA* 23:1285)

287. VESTRE, NORRIS D. "The Relationship Between Verbal Conditionability and the Edwards Personal Preference Schedule." *J Clin Psychol* 18:513–5 O '62. * (*PA* 39:5186)

288. VINEYARD, EDWIN E.; DRINKWATER, RUBY; AND DICKISON, WALTER L. "Teacher Education and Pharmacy Students: A Comparison of Their Need Structures." *J Teach Ed* 13:409–13 D '62. *

289. WIEMANN, CARL BARGE, JR. *Social Desirability and the Edwards Personal Preference Schedule.* Doctor's research study No. 1, Colorado State College (Greeley, Colo.), 1962. (*DA* 23:3789)

290. *Normative Information: Manager and Executive Testing.* New York: Richardson, Bellows, Henry & Co., Inc., May 1963. Pp. 45. *

291. APPLEY, MORTIMER H., AND MOELLER, GEORGE. "Conforming Behavior and Personality Variables in College Women." *J Abn & Social Psychol* 66:284–90 Mr '63. * (*PA* 37:8237)

292. BANTA, THOMAS J., AND HETHERINGTON, MAVIS. "Relations Between Needs of Friends and Fiancés." *J Abn & Social Psychol* 66:401–4 Ap '63. * (*PA* 37:7941)

293. BENDIG, A. W., AND MARTIN, ANN M. "The Factor Structure of Temperament Traits and Needs." *J General Psychol* 69:27–36 Jl '63. * (*PA* 38:4297)

294. BREWINGTON, WILLIAM IVEN. *A Statistical Analysis of Low Achieving and High Achieving Freshman Chemistry Students at the University of Arkansas.* Doctor's thesis, University of Arkansas (Fayetteville, Ark.), 1963. (*DA* 24:570)

295. CARRIER, NEIL A. "Need Correlates of 'Gullibility.'" *J Abn & Social Psychol* 66:84–6 Ja '63. * (*PA* 37:5056)

296. COOK, DESMOND L.; LEBOLD, WILLIAM; AND LINDEN, JAMES D. "A Comparison of Factor Analyses of Education and Engineering Responses to Selected Personality Inventories." *J Teach Ed* 14:137–41 Je '63. *

297. GHEI, S. N. "The Reliability and Validity of Edwards Personal Preference Schedule: A Cross-Cultural Study." *J Social Psychol* 61:241–6 D '63. * (PA 38:8414)

298. GORDON, IRA J. "Personality Patterns of Volunteers for an Experimental Professional Education Program." *J Exp Ed* 32:115–21 f '63. *

299. GRAY, JAMES T. "Needs and Values in Three Occupations." *Personnel & Guid J* 42:238–44 N '63. *

300. HAAS, KURT. "Personality Needs of Academically Superior Students and Their Parents." *J Ed Res* 56:389–90 Mr '63. *

301. HARRIS, DOROTHY V. "Comparison of Physical Performance and Psychological Traits of College Women With High and Low Fitness Indices." *Percept & Motor Skills* 17:293–4 Ag '63. * (PA 38:8356)

302. HEILBRUN, A. B. "Evidence Regarding the Equivalence of Ipsative and Normative Personality Scales." *J Consult Psychol* 27:152–6 Ap '63. * (PA 37:7982)

303. HEILBRUN, ALFRED B., JR. "Configural Interpretation of the Edwards Personal Preference Schedule and the Prediction of Academic Performance." *Personnel & Guid J* 42:264–8 N '63. *

304. HEILBRUN, ALFRED B., JR. "Social Value–Social Behavior Inconsistency and Early Signs of Psychopathology in Adolescence." *Child Develop* 34:187–94 Mr '63. * (PA 38:5808)

305. HEILIZER, FRED. "An Ipsative Factor Analysis of the Ipsative EPPS." *Psychol Rep* 12:285–6 F '63. * (PA 38:2669)

306. IZARD, CARROLL E. "Personality Profile Similarity as a Function of Group Membership." *J Abn & Social Psychol* 67:404–8 O '63. * (PA 38:4193)

307. IZARD, CARROLL E. "Personality Similarity and Friendship: A Follow-Up Study." *J Abn & Social Psychol* 66:598–600 Je '63. * (PA 38:920)

308. KAMANO, DENNIS K. "Relationship of Ego Disjunction and Manifest Anxiety to Conflict Resolution." *J Abn & Social Psychol* 66:281–4 Mr '63. * (PA 37:8035)

309. KOLE, DELBERT M., AND MATARAZZO, J. D. "Intellectual and Personality Characteristics of Medical Students." Abstract. *J Med Ed* 38:138–9 F '63. *

310. KUHLEN, RAYMOND G. "Needs, Perceived Need Satisfaction Opportunities, and Satisfaction With Occupation." *J Appl Psychol* 47:56–64 F '63. * (PA 37:8347)

311. LEVITT, EUGENE E.; BRADY, JOHN PAUL; AND LUBIN, BERNARD. "Correlates of Hypnotizability in Young Women: Anxiety and Dependency." *J Personality* 31:52–7 Mr '63. *

312. LIND, AMY. "Measured Personality Characteristics of Occupational Therapy Graduates and Undergraduates at the University of North Dakota." *Univ N Dak Col Ed Rec* 48:69–73 F '63. *

313. McDONALD, ROBERT L., AND GYNTHER, MALCOLM D. "Nonintellectual Factors Associated With Performance in Medical School." *J Genetic Psychol* 103:185–94 S '63. *

313a. MANHOLD, J. H.; SHATIN, LEO; AND MANHOLD, BEVERLY S. "Comparison of Interests, Needs, and Selected Personality Factors of Dental and Medical Students." *J Am Dental Assn* 67:601–5 O '63. *

314. MEHLMAN, MARY R., AND FLEMING, JAMES E. "Social Stratification and Some Personality Variables." *J General Psychol* 69:3–10 Jl '63. * (PA 38:4169)

315. MOLDOVAN, STANLEY. "Some Familial Antecedents of Personality Needs." *B Maritime Psychol Assn* 12:28–40 sp '63. * (PA 38:4244)

316. MORRIS, KENNETH TURNER. *A Comparative Study of Selected Needs, Values, and Motives of Science and Non-Science Teachers.* Doctor's thesis, University of Georgia (Athens, Ga.), 1963. (DA 24:2325)

317. NUNNALLY, JUM C., AND FLAUGHER, RONALD L. "Correlates of Semantic Habits." *J Personality* 31:192–202 Je '63. *

317a. PEMBERTON, W. A. *Ability, Values, and College Achievement.* University of Delaware Studies in Higher Education, No. 1. Newark, Del.: the University, 1963. Pp. xii, 77. * (PA 38:6573)

318. POOL, DONALD ALFRED. *The Relation of Personality Needs to Vocational Counseling Outcome.* Doctor's thesis, University of Texas (Austin, Tex.), 1963. (DA 24:1922)

319. RADCLIFFE, J. A. "Some Properties of Ipsative Score Matrices and Their Relevance for Some Current Interest Tests." *Austral J Psychol* 15:1–11 Ap '63. *

320. RYCHLAK, JOSEPH F. "Personality Correlates of Leadership Among First Level Managers." *Psychol Rep* 12:43–52 F '63. * (PA 38:2600)

321. SCHUMACHER, CHARLES F. "Interest and Personality Factors as Related to Choice of Medical Career." *J Med Ed* 38:932–42 N '63. *

322. SCHWARTZ, MILTON M.; JENUSAITIS, EDMUND; AND STARK, HARRY. "Motivational Factors Among Supervisors in the Utility Industry." *Personnel Psychol* 16:45–53 sp '63. * (PA 38:3327)

323. SCOTT, WILLIAM A. "Social Desirability and Individual Conceptions of the Desirable." *J Abn & Social Psychol* 67:574–85 D '63. * (PA 38:5953)

324. SUZIEDELIS, ANTANAS, AND STEIMEL, RAYMOND J. "The Relationship of Need Heirarchies to Inventoried Interests." *Personnel & Guid J* 42:393–6 D '63. * (PA 39:1761)

325. VAN EVRA, JUDY PAGE, AND ROSENBERG, B. G. "Ego Strength and Ego Disjunction in Primary and Secondary Psychopaths." *J Clin Psychol* 19:61–3 Ja '63. * (PA 39:2409)

326. WRIGHT, MORGAN W.; SISLER, GEORGE C.; AND CHYLINSKI, JOANNE. "Personality Factors in the Selection of Civilians for Isolated Northern Stations." *J Appl Psychol* 47:24–9 F '63. * (PA 37:8319)

JOHN A. RADCLIFFE, *Senior Lecturer in Psychology, University of Sydney, Sydney, Australia.*

This test is designed to assess the relative strengths of 15 manifest needs selected from Murray's need system. Each need is represented by nine statements. A statement from each need is paired twice with one from every other need (210 items). Additionally, to allow an indication of the consistency of a subject's responses, for each need one of these pairs is repeated (15 items). Another indication of the consistency of responses (the profile stability coefficient) is available by correlating the scores obtained on the first and second set of item pairings, but this assumes that the nine statements for each need have equivalent need content. Scale values for social desirability have been assigned to the 135 statements and within each item the two statements have approximately equal social desirability scale values. This design was introduced to attempt to control social desirability as a source of variance and is usually regarded as one of the particular merits of the test. The forced choice paired-comparison format of the EPPS requires that the total scores for each subject are constant so that the scores are ipsative. To allow interindividual comparisons and to allow for sex differences, centile rank norms (college and general adult) and T score norms (college only) based on large samples are presented for males and females separately. Internal consistency ($n = 1,509$; range .60 to .87; median .78) and one-week retest ($n = 89$; range .74 to .87; median .83) reliability coefficients are quoted, and Mann (45) has reported three-week retest coefficients ($n = 96$; range .55 to .87; median .73). Validity data in the manual are meagre.

The procedure here will be to review the evidence on the control of social desirability; to consider some technical features of the test, especially the equivalence of the statements within each need and the effects of ipsative scoring; to outline some of the conditions known to affect test scores; and to review the evidence on predictive, concurrent, and construct validity.

SOCIAL DESIRABILITY. Research on social desirability has been directed mainly towards investigating (*a*) the generality of the social desirability scale values originally obtained by Edwards (*21, 26–8, 44, 104*); (*b*) the degree of control of the influence of the social desirability stereotype on test scores by matching for social desirability the two statements in each item (*2, 28, 32, 36, 42–3, 45, 106*), especially considering the possibility that this pairing may introduce a new context that destroys the matching based upon judgments made singly (*37, 94, 141*); (*c*) whether personal desirability may be an additional source of influence on test scores (*36, 96, 98*); and (*d*) whether social desirability may involve idiosyncratic interpretations whose effects have been masked by attention to group averages only (*196–7*).

In relation to (*b*), it is now clear that judgments of social desirability are influenced by context (*141*), with the result that the statements in pairs do not retain the approximately equal social desirability scale values assigned to them singly (*37*). Edwards and others (*94*) have attempted to refute this latter finding by arguing that it was obtained with a sample of items removed from their original context in the test, and by demonstrating that, with the entire test, the correlation between the proportions choosing alternative A under normal and social desirability instructions is much lower (.69) than that obtained by Corah and others (.88). But it remains that the correlation is still substantial and that the argument about the relevance of context could apply equally to the difference in context between judgments of the statements singly and the judgment in pairs. Thus there now seems little doubt that the test design does not control the social desirability stereotype as much as was indicated by earlier studies that took no account of the effects of context (*2, 28, 32, 36, 42–3, 45*).

Regarding the role of personal desirability, investigators have concluded both that personal and social desirability are the same (*36*), and that they are different (*98*). That the personal and social desirability scale values of the 135 statements correlate .90 implies identity (*96*), but in a subsequent study (*98*) the same authors concluded that, although personal desirability makes a contribution to variance additional to that made by social desirability, it is insufficient "to represent a crucial flaw in Edwards' attempt to minimise desirability of verbal statements as an important source of performance variance." That a subject's profile correlation between normal versus personal desirability instructions does not differ from that between normal versus social desirability instructions also implies identity (*36*), but the inappropriate use of *T* scores for the profile correlations may well have obscured results here. The non-occurrence of similar profiles among the subjects under social desirability instructions in this latter study suggests that the social desirability ratings of statements may have idiosyncratic features, perhaps generated even by their grammatical form (*129*). This possibility is supported by the finding (*196*) that the item alternative rated as the more *individually* socially desirable was chosen (on the average) 67 per cent of the time, as compared with 56 per cent endorsement of the *group* defined more socially desirable alternative. From this and other evidence (*197*), Heilbrun and Goodstein concluded that social desirability is not a "response set" but a "content" variable and that both individually defined and group defined social desirability may affect scores on the EPPS.

Even aside from the need to recognise that the earlier generality ascribed to Edwards' social desirability scale values (*21, 26, 27, 28, 44*) may in fact be restricted to the United States (*104*), from the foregoing it is apparent that the design of the EPPS does not control the desirability of verbal statements as much as was originally believed. This does not necessarily constitute an intrinsic weakness of the test. The control of desirability alone, even if sufficient to allow test usage under a wide variety of conditions, would not guarantee any validity. Nor would the ineffectual control of desirability necessarily imply invalidity. Validity remains an empirical question in specified circumstances. However, it will be seen that the forced choice character of the items and the resultant ipsative scores introduce particular problems in the way of answering validity questions with the EPPS.

TECHNICAL FEATURES. In using nine statements for each need, Edwards assumes that each of the statements has equivalent need content, but he does not justify this assumption by presenting evidence on how the statements were selected. The only investigation of the equivalence of need statements that seems to have been made is that by Levonian et al. (*106*).

They believed that the assumption implies that for each need separately factor analysis of the item intercorrelations would produce, *inter alia*, a general factor, and they showed that their expectations were not confirmed. However, their expectations and analyses were misconceived. For each need, there are three types of pairs of items that may occur and yield item intercorrelations: (*a*) an "identical" pair, represented by the two "consistency" items and involving the same needs and the same statements; (*b*) a "fraternal" pair, represented by the items that produce the two separate row and column scores on the answer sheet (e.g., items 2 and 6, for Achievement), these items involving the same needs but, in general, different statements; and (*c*) an "unrelated" pair, which involves different needs and different statements. For each need, there will be one correlation between "identical" items, 14 between "fraternal" items, and, since there are 29 items for each need, 15 between "unrelated" items. Only the "identical" and "fraternal" item correlations can be expected to be non-zero. A meaningful general factor could not occur from such a peculiar correlation matrix, and factor analysis would seem a quite inappropriate technique. Consequently, as reported, the study by Levonian and others contributes no evidence on the equivalence of the statements because the 15 correlations that would be expected to be non-zero for each scale are not given.

So far there appear to be only two lines of evidence relevant to the equivalence of the statements; viz. the internal consistency coefficients and the profile stability coefficients given by Edwards in the manual. "Uncorrected" values of the former are more appropriate than "corrected" values. From Edwards' "corrected" values, the "uncorrected" values would range .43 to .71, with median .64, and would give a rough indication of what the correlation between "fraternal" items could be. Either some statements have little "equivalence" or the responses to them include considerable "error." Perhaps idiosyncratic conceptions of desirability are relevant here. Edwards reports subjects' profile stability coefficients ranging from zero to unity, with mean .74 and median approximately the same. Fiske and others (*143*) have reported similar values. Do low profile stability coefficients indicate non-equivalence of the statements for those subjects, or do they derive from inconsistency of responses? Edwards

might have reported the correlation between consistency scores and profile stability coefficients. There is, then, need for more evidence on the equivalence of the statements.

The scores derived from the EPPS are ordinal ipsative scores, but surprisingly little attention has been paid to their implications (*48, 254, 319*). That Edwards makes no mention of ipsatization and lack of independence in the manual is particularly striking, because Clemans,[1] at Edwards' own university, made a detailed analysis of some of the features of deviational ipsative scores. Karr's (*102*) attempts to predict ipsative from normative scores are based on a dependence between the two that occurs only with deviational ipsative and not with ordinal ipsative scores (*319*), but in any case have no practical value. Stoltz (*48*) emphasizes the need for caution in the correlational use of ipsative scores, but in his suggested regression usage of the MMPI K-score for indirect ipsatization he seems to believe that the major aim of ipsatization with the EPPS is to remove social desirability variance. Rather the major aim seems to be to serve as a substitute for the lack of more direct measures of need strength. Heilbrun's conclusion (*302*) that ipsative and normative scores are substantially equivalent for making normative predictions does not seem justified by the correlations he obtained. Radcliffe (*319*) has considered some consequences of ordinal and deviational ipsative scoring. Those for ordinal ipsative scores of most relevance here are that the average intercorrelation among the EPPS scales will tend to $-1/(n-1) = -.071$ (which is the average of those reported by Edwards), and that the average correlation of the scales with any other variable will tend to zero. These consequences of lack of independence among the scores emphasize the necessity for cross validation (c.f. the higher absolute values of the scale intercorrelations reported by Allen, *14, 15, 34*). Additionally, Edwards fails to emphasize the need for care in the use of normative centile ranks and T scores based on EPPS ipsative scores. These centile ranks and T scores may be used meaningfully to compare an individual's relative strength on a need with that of others, but their use in a profile as he recommends seems inadvisable for the general

1 CLEMANS, W. V. *An Analytical and Empirical Examination of Some Properties of Ipsative Measures.* Doctor's thesis, University of Washington (Seattle, Wash.), 1956.

test user. To take his sample profile as an example, Endurance does not have the lowest relative strength in the original profile, and yet it is markedly the lowest in the centile rank profile. Another example would be that the person with an average centile rank profile (50th centile rank on all needs) would not be a person in whom all needs had the same relative strength. In short, the rank orders of the needs may change considerably when the scores are expressed normatively, and it is questionable if this latter rank order is that which is of interest.

DEMOGRAPHIC DIFFERENCES. Scores are known to be affected by test taking attitudes and by cultural and other demographic factors. Singh and others (276) report that Koponen (31) found age, sex, educational level, income level, and geographic differences among his large sample of adults. Since Edwards' adult norms are taken from this sample, it would have been preferable had he at least reported the age and educational level. As it is, the interested user is required to order a microfilm from the test publisher.

High school norms are also available from the publisher. Reliabilities are lower and scale intercorrelations are higher with high school than with college subjects (26), and social desirability scale values in the items are less adequately matched (28). Occupational differences also occur and will be considered later. All cultural comparisons have used college students: Chinese and Indian (276), Southern Negroes (23), Japanese American (21, 86). Some of the obtained differences are inconsistent (21, 86), but some make good sense and possibly attest to the Schedule's research potential. For example, compared with white college norms, both male and female Southern Negroes are higher on Deference, Order, Abasement, and Endurance, and lower on Exhibition, Autonomy, Affiliation, Dominance, and Heterosexuality. But when instructed to simulate a "good impression," college students increased their scores on Deference, Order, Endurance, and Achievement, and decreased them on Autonomy, Heterosexuality, Aggression, Change, Succorance, and Exhibition (93), giving a pattern something like that of the Southern Negro! High needs for Order, Dominance, and Change can also be successfully simulated, and the nature of the simulated patterns clearly reflects the non-independence of

the scales, the correlations between the rank order of the changes and that of the scale intercorrelations for the relevant scales being .85, .55, and .03, respectively (93). Equivalent correlations calculated by this reviewer and based on the scale intercorrelations reported by Allen (15) are .81, .58, and .79. This evidence on "fakability" augurs ill for the test's use in any selection situation.

VALIDITY. In considering validity data, account needs to be taken that the average correlation of the scales with another variable must tend to zero. This requires that "significant" correlations that are "predicted" be given more credence than those "discovered," and that even the former should be replicated. On predictive validity nothing of any merit has been obtained. Two studies (59, 111) have reported approximately .40 correlation of Achievement with course results, but one study (186) reported zero correlation. Bernhardt (129) did not obtain an expected correlation between Intraception and psychiatry course grades. It may be, as Heathers suggests in the manual, that the EPPS contributes to "understanding the client" and to "stimulating discussions....[that] are frequently very fruitful," but there is nothing to indicate that the Schedule has any other counseling use.

Data on concurrent validity fall under two main heads: (a) correlations with other "motivational" or "interest" measures; and (b) correlations with inventory and self-rating measures of personality traits. The limited available evidence (39) shows little meaningful relation between any EPPS scale and an "interest area" on the *Strong Vocational Interest Blank*. When EPPS scores are treated normatively there seems no doubt that they are not related to "projective" motivational measures derived from the TAT or the French Insight Test (46, 51, 65, 69, 108, 117, 222), and it seems unlikely that this is due to scorer unreliability with the projective tests (65). Nor do EPPS variables seem likely to have any relations with scores derived from the *Rosenzweig Picture-Frustration Study* (22). Only one study has followed what seems to be the more correct procedure, the rank order correlation for each subject between the relative strengths of the need measures on the two tests (62). But again there was no relationship. Melikian (46) suggests that the EPPS and the TAT measure at different levels, while Marlowe (108) believes that "social learning theory" would require the obtained zero relationship. Interpretations of these findings will be left to the reader's predilections.

Expectations concerning correlations of EPPS scales with rating or inventory measures of personality traits present a problem. In the manual Edwards does not make clear what he expects himself. He says that correlations with the Taylor MAS and the *Guilford-Martin Personnel Inventory* are in the expected direction, but he does not comment on their low magnitude, seeming in fact to imply that smallness is desirable because otherwise the correlations would indicate contamination of the EPPS by social desirability. Ignoring for the moment complications introduced by ipsative scoring, the optimal expectation would seem to be "moderate" correlation of an EPPS scale with a similarly named personality trait. Since both motives and traits typically are inferred from the same data—what the individual does, says he does, or says he would do—some correlation would be expected. But too high correlation would negate the virtues of the EPPS variables as "motivational" measures. If .50 is accepted as a "moderate" correlation, then moderate correlations have been obtained between Aggression and Guilford-Martin Agreeableness scores (manual) ; between combined measures of "dependency" derived from the EPPS and the MMPI, respectively (*222*) ; and, within "mothers" but not within "non-mothers," between some EPPS scales and the Hostility-Rejection scale of the Parental Attitude Research Inventory (*125*). With these exceptions, studies involving the *Guilford-Martin Personnel Inventory* (manual), *Guilford-Zimmerman Temperament Survey* (*185, 203*), *California Test of Personality* (*39*), MMPI (*15*), Gough's Hr scale (*89*), hostility scales (*235*), and self ratings (*45*) have not produced moderate correlations. Two factor analyses (*185, 203*) agree rather well on the factors extracted, primarily intra-inventory and intra-EPPS factors in both cases. EPPS scales and personality inventories, then, do not share the expected common variance. But the effects of ipsatization may have intruded here. When normatively used, deviational ipsative scoring typically will reduce positive and increase negative correlation with another variable (*319*). Since it removes overall between-subjects variance (*254*) and at least partially removes general

factor covariance in the deviational case (*319*), it might be expected to have similar effects with ordinal scores. It is likely, then, that intra-subject profile correlations of the EPPS variables with measures of similarly named traits would be a more appropriate procedure. This has been used only between EPPS variables and self rankings on the same variables. There were substantial individual differences in the correlations. Edwards comments that these differences were probably due largely to difficulties in interpreting the statements. A similar procedure with inventory measures might hold more promise.

Most of the evidence on the use of the EPPS scales relates to their construct validity, and any assistance that it offers to their interpretation depends on opinions on the source of the hypotheses tested or on the plausibility of any differences observed. This review merely will indicate the kinds of research that have been carried out and will make little attempt at evaluation. Achievement is related to paired-associates verbal learning (*174*) but not to the solution of crossword puzzles (*89*). Heterosexuality affects preference for pictures involving "sexual elements," but not selective memory for sexual material (*213*). Areas of investigation that have produced conflicting results have been the use of EPPS scales to classify conforming and dependent subjects in the study of conforming and dependent behaviour (*18, 64, 192, 291*) ; the similarity of need patterns of friends and courtship couples (*152, 189, 266, 292, 307*) ; and the relationship between EPPS defined ego-disjunction and degree of psychopathology (*118, 144*). Demographic factors probably need to be controlled in the use of this ego-disjunction measure (*194*). Since ego-disjunction and manifest anxiety interact to prolong conflict resolution (*308*), the fact that ego-disjunction was not found to be related to conflict intensity (*118*) may have been due in part to the use of T scores and the failure to allow for demographic factors. Some EPPS scales, notably Intraception, are related to "gullibility" (*295*) and there are some unimpressive relationships with some of the "semantic habit" scales (*317*). Hypnotisable women are emotionally unstable, anxious, and dependent, when "dependency" is derived from Autonomy, Dominance, and Aggression, but not when it is derived from Deference, Succorance, and Abasement (*311*).

Physiological and other data suggest that persons with a high verbal and low quantitative ability pattern have introverted characteristics, and their high Autonomy would not be inconsistent with this (*170*). EPPS scores are unrelated to success at withstanding sensory isolation (*250*), seeking rhinoplasty,[2] volunteering for participation in leaderless group discussions (*95*), to "field independence" (*69*), and to being a member of the personnel of a hospital ward having a "satisfied" atmosphere (*20*). Differences between second and third generation Japanese Americans tend to be consistent with an acculturation interpretation (*86*). The score patterns of prison inmates (*128*) and differences between high school and college students are plausible (*26*), but those between "accurate" and "inaccurate" judges of personality are not markedly so (*133*). Likes and dislikes of "job duties" (*122*), being a "warm teacher" (*117*), and electing to teach in different educational fields (*193*) have been reported to be related to EPPS scores. Achievement is one of the major sources of motivation of dental students (*149*); psychiatry students have high Intraception (*129*); basic airmen (*40*) have some plausible score patterns; and engineers and engineering students differ from liberal arts and science students (*41, 151*). The most studied occupational group has been nurses (*50, 54, 222, 244*), but the only characteristic that has withstood replication has been low Dominance. With some of these reported differences the possible role of stereotype simulation cannot be overlooked. Perhaps the most consistent evidence comes from studies of overachievers (*41, 105*). Though there are some differences that were not replicated in the two studies, both report that overachievers have higher Achievement and Order and lower Affiliation than underachievers, and that high aptitude students have high Dominance and low Abasement, Deference, and Order.

SUMMARY. In all, the evidence on the use of the EPPS remains "spotty." Some of the most convincing evidence lies in occupational and other demographic differences, but failure to achieve the desired control of social desirability and evidence on simulation of responses raise doubts that these differences reflect actual characteristics of the persons. On correlational evidence, the EPPS measures relatively unique aspects of the person (whatever they may be) but interpretation here is obscured by the effects of ipsative scoring. There is nothing to suggest that the counselor will find the *Edwards Personal Preference Schedule* particularly useful, except possibly to "stimulate discussion." Its record so far in the testing of psychological hypotheses is unimpressive, though the fault here may of course be with the "hypotheses" themselves. It may be that future research that takes better account of the role of ipsative scoring will permit the EPPS to become a useful addition to the psychologist's test repertoire, but this remains to be seen, and for the time being it must be regarded primarily as a research tool.

LAWRENCE J. STRICKER, *Research Psychologist, Educational Testing Service, Princeton, New Jersey.*[1]

Since its appearance a decade ago, the *Edwards Personal Preference Schedule* (EPPS) has been very widely used and has generated a tremendous amount of research. This popularity stems from the theoretical relevance and potential usefulness of the personality variables that it is intended to measure—15 of Murray's needs—and its attempt to minimize the effects of social desirability response style, in the light of Edwards' (*1*) well known finding that the rated social desirability of a set of personality items correlated .87 with their frequency of endorsement.

CONSTRUCTION. The paired comparison method was used in constructing the EPPS. Each need was represented by nine items. The items for each need were paired with items from the other needs that had similar average social desirability ratings. Each pair of needs is compared twice in this way, and 210 pairs of items are needed for this purpose. The EPPS provides three kinds of scores: scores for each need (the number of times that the need was chosen as being more descriptive than the other needs); a consistency score (agreement in responses on 15 pairs of items that are identical); and a profile stability score (the correlation between the score profiles for the two halves of the inventory).

2 MEYER, EUGENE; JACOBSEN, WAYNE E.; EDGERTON, MILTON T.; AND CANTER, ARTHUR. "Motivational Patterns in Patients Seeking Elective Plastic Surgery: 1, Women Who Seek Rhinoplasty." *Psychosom Med* 22:193–201 My–Je '60. * (PA 35:4998)

1 Only those studies of the EPPS that are published and are based on the administration of the standard form of the inventory are cited in this review. Unless otherwise indicated, the .05 level of significance is employed.

Some of the procedures used in constructing the EPPS may have limited or altered its meaning in unforeseen ways:

a) The paired comparison method produces ipsative scores, reflecting intraindividual differences, rather than the normative scores, reflecting interindividual differences, which are usually encountered in personality inventories. The current (third) edition of the manual surprisingly does not mention this feature of the EPPS scores, even though the psychological meaning of variables is so radically affected by being placed in an ipsative format (depending, in large part, on the particular nature and sheer number of the other ipsative scales in that format) that ipsative variables and their normative counterparts may have very little in common.

A normative score reflects the absolute level of the variable; an ipsative score reflects the level of the variable relative to the other variables in the ipsative format. Hence, two people with the same normative score on a variable may differ markedly in their ipsative scores on that same variable because of differences on one or more of the other variables that are included in the ipsative format.

The relative, within-individual, meaning of ipsative scores complicates interpretations of relationships between an ipsative variable and a normative variable because such relationships, in effect, take a form such as "those who are high on a particular variable relative to all the other variables are also higher (or lower) on a particular normative variable."

More importantly, the precise extent of the relationships between ipsative and normative variables is affected by statistical properties of ipsative scales. Hence, although the typical statistical indexes reported, such as correlation coefficients, accurately describe these relationships, these indexes may not describe the corresponding relationships between the same normative variables and the normative counterparts of the ipsative variables. The two relevant statistical properties of ipsative scales are as follows: when a set of ipsative scales has equal variances, the correlations of the set with any normative variable sum to zero; and these positive correlations tend to be lower and the negative correlations tend to be higher than the corresponding correlations for normative scales. As an illustration of this effect, the mean of the correlations reported in the manual between

the EPPS scales and the Cooperativeness, Agreeableness, and Objectivity scales of the *Guilford-Martin Personnel Inventory* are $-.06$, $.00$, and $-.16$, respectively (*319*).

A related property of ipsative scales affects their interrelationships: the mean intercorrelation of a set of ipsative scales is $-1/(n-1)$, n being the number of scales. This value for the EPPS (*319*) is $-.071$, precisely the mean of the intercorrelations reported in the manual.

b) The use of the nine items in each scale in 28 comparisons with the other need items—eight are used three times each and the ninth is used four times—produced item overlap between and within scales.

An item overlaps between its own scale and the other scale with which it is compared because the endorsement of this item increases the score on its own scale and decreases the score on the other scale; the rejection of this item has the opposite effect. This artifact is not inherent in the paired comparison method, for the item could be used in a comparison with another item but not contribute to the score on its own scale if it is endorsed. The between-scale overlap precludes an accurate assessment of the interrelationships among the scales (*106*).

Similarly, there is item overlap within a scale because the nine items on a scale enter into a total of 28 comparisons, all of which contribute to the score for that scale. This overlap inflates internal-consistency reliability estimates.[2]

c) It is uncertain that the sets of nine items reflect the needs that they are intended to measure or, even if they do, that each set represents the same level of its need. These items appear to have been selected entirely on two bases: that their content manifestly reflected the needs, and that their social desirability ratings were appropriate. No data exist concerning the validity of the sets of items, but it is known that their internal-consistency reliability is low; the lower-bound Kuder-Richardson formula 21 estimates for the scales range from .13 to .75, with a median of .52 (*225*). Moreover, there are no data about the extent to which the sets of items represent equal levels of their needs, which is a prerequisite if the strength of needs within a person is to be ordered accurately. The ordering of two needs, for example, would obviously be inaccurate if one was represented

2 MESSICK, SAMUEL. "Review of *The Social Desirability Variable in Personality Assessment and Research* by Allen L. Edwards." *Ed & Psychol Meas* 19:451–4 au '59. *

by an item (or set of items) reflecting a high level of the need, but the other need was represented by an item (or set of items) reflecting a much lower level of the need.

d) Matching the items on the basis of average social desirability ratings of *unpaired* items may reduce social desirability as a response determinant, even though such matching is not as precise as matching on the basis of average social desirability ratings of *paired* items, but it cannot eliminate this tendency entirely in view of the multidimensionality of social desirability judgments (*162*).

INTERCORRELATIONS. The intercorrelations of the scales reported in the manual and obtained in other studies (*14, 26, 128, 145a, 185, 221*) are generally low. However, these results do not necessarily support the manual's conclusion that "the variables being measured by the EPPS are relatively independent" in view of the distortion produced by the ipsative nature of the scores (*48, 319*), as indicated previously. This ipsatization also makes it difficult to interpret factor and cluster analyses of the EPPS (*145a, 185, 203, 221, 226, 246*).

RELIABILITY. The reliability of most of the EPPS scales is roughly comparable to that of other personality inventories, but the reliability of some of the scales may be so low as to vitiate their usefulness. Test-retest reliability estimates, based on a three-week interval, ranged from .55 to .87, with a median of .73 (*45*). The other available reliability estimates are not as readily interpretable. The test-retest reliability estimates, based on a one-week interval, that are reported in the manual (the median is .79) and by Horst and Wright (*100;* the median is .80) may be affected by memory factors because of the short length of time involved. Moreover, the split-half reliability coefficients reported in the manual (the median is .78) and elsewhere (*26, 204*) are inflated by the previously described duplication of items within each scale.

NORMS. The norms in the current edition of the manual are excellent. Norms are presented for college students (based on a total of 760 males and 749 females drawn from a number of colleges throughout the country) and adults (based on 4,031 males and 4,932 females who participated in a nationwide survey of heads of households). These adult norms reflect one of the few instances in which norms for any personality inventory are based on a truly representative national sample of adults. In addition, norms based on 799 male and 760 female high school students exist (*26*), but are not reported in the manual.

VALIDITY. The validity data reported in the manual are scanty and inadequate. Only five studies—all unpublished—are described, and not always in sufficient detail, despite the vast number of relevant published studies (some of which are cited in the manual's bibliography). While the sheer number of these studies precludes a review of them all, the results bearing on some of the more important issues concerning the validity of the EPPS will be considered. The bulk of these studies involve the relationship of the EPPS with one or more normative variables, and, hence, are affected by the previously described limitations that are imposed on such relationships by the statistical properties of ipsative scores.

SELF-REPORT MEASURES. The relationships of the EPPS with self-report measures of the same needs—self-ratings or scores on projective tests and personality inventories—have been investigated in several studies.

The studies of self-ratings generally find moderate relationships between the EPPS and self-ratings. In Q-type analyses, the means of the EPPS scores and the means of the corresponding self-ratings correlated −.03 (*2*) and .56 (*258*). Moreover, the correlation between the EPPS scores and corresponding self-ratings, when computed on an individual basis, ranged from −.59 to .90, with a median of .39 (*273*). In R-type analyses, EPPS scores and real-self ratings were significantly related for 10 to 14 scales, and the median correlations ranged from .26 to .35 (*45, 258, 273*). EPPS scores and ideal-self ratings were significantly related for one scale (*45*).

The most relevant of the studies that compare the EPPS with projective tests and other personality inventories concern instruments which yield scores for the same needs found on the EPPS. These instruments include the *Thematic Apperception Test* (TAT), and various modifications of it, as well as the *Adjective Check List*. Most of these studies concern the relationship of the Achievement scale of the EPPS with two need achievement measures modeled after the TAT—McClelland's and the French Test of Insight. Almost without exception, these studies find that the EPPS Achievement scale is not significantly related to the other measures. The EPPS scale was significantly related ($r = .26$) to the McClelland measure in one study (*124*), but not in five others[3] (*46, 51, 65, 216*). It was significantly related ($r = .51$) to the French Test of Insight in one of four groups in one study (*216*), but not related at all in two other studies (*65, 126*). Less is known about the correspondence between the other need scales of the EPPS and the need scores on the TAT. In a Q-type analysis, the average rho was .15 between the score profiles on the two instruments, when the correlations were computed separately for each individual (*62*). And, in an R-type analysis, a dependency measure—a composite of Abasement, Autonomy, Deference, Dominance, and Succorance scores—on the two instruments was not significantly related (*222*). In the one study of the *Adjective Check List,* the means of the EPPS scores and the means of the *Adjective Check List* scores correlated .60 when the real self was described, and .57 and .64 when the ideal self was described (*42*).

NONTEST MEASURES OF UNDERLYING CONSTRUCTS. The relationships of the EPPS with a variety of non-test variables which reflect one or more of the constructs that the EPPS is intended to measure have been investigated in a great many studies.

Two studies bear directly on the need for achievement variable and support the finding that the EPPS Achievement scale was unrelated to standard measures of need for achievement. In one study (*126*), high scorers on the EPPS Achievement scale *avoided* intermediate risks in a ring toss game more than low scorers, and the two groups did not differ significantly in the time that they spent on a final course examination. In contrast, need for achievement theory predicts that those with high need for achievement should *prefer* such risks and spend more time on the examination, and these predictions were confirmed by the French Test of Insight. In a second study (*253*), level of expectation—the subjects' predictions of their scores on a course examination—was significantly related to only one scale—Endurance—and only for men and not women.

Studies of interpersonal influence—conformity, suggestibility, and hypnotizability—bear di-

rectly on the construct validity of the Autonomy and Deference scales.

The results of studies of one form of interpersonal influence—conformity in an Asch-type situation—are generally negative, and the few positive findings are not replicable. One scale was significantly related to conformity in two of the studies that reported the results for all EPPS scales (*137, 291*); none of the EPPS scales were so related in the third study (*192*); and in a fourth study (*120*), which used the .10 level of significance, one scale was significantly related to conformity for males and three for females. In a fifth study (*64*), which just reported the results for the Autonomy and Deference scales, the first scale was significantly (and negatively) related to conformity. Finally, a sixth study (*18*) found no significant difference in conformity between those classified as high on dependency (high on the Deference scale and low on the Autonomy scale) and those classified as low on dependency (low on the Deference scale and high on the Autonomy scale). Moreover, only the Achievement scale was significantly (and negatively) related to conformity in more than one (*120, 137*) of the first five studies.

The results of studies of other forms of interpersonal influence—suggestibility and hypnotizability—are contradictory. Postural sway was significantly (and positively) related to Deference and Affiliation in a study (*260*) that reported the results for all scales, but it was significantly (and negatively) related to only the Autonomy scale in a study (*84*) that reported the results for three scales—Autonomy, Deference, and Succorance. A related phenomenon, hypnotic susceptibility, was not significantly related to any of the EPPS scales in the Lang and Lazovik study (*260*), but another study (*311*) found that hypnotizable subjects were significantly lower than refractory subjects on one dependency measure—a composite of the Aggression, Autonomy, and Dominance scales—although the two groups did not differ significantly on another dependency measure—a composite of the Abasement, Deference, and Succorance scales.

Studies of dependency also bear on the construct validity of the Deference and Autonomy scales, as well as others. There is almost no agreement in the results of these studies, which employ behavioral variables—verbal condition-

3 MCCLELLAND, DAVID C. Chap. 1, "Methods of Measuring Human Motivation," pp. 7–42. In *Motives in Fantasy, Action, and Society: A Method of Assessment and Study.* Edited by John W. Atkinson. Princeton, N.J.: D. Van Nostrand Co., Inc., 1958. Pp. xv, 873. *

ing, performance decrement following stress, and seeking help—as well as peer ratings.

In one study of verbal conditioning (*230*), those classified as high in dependency (on the basis of the Deference and Autonomy scales) were more conditionable when aggressive words were reinforced, but the two dependency groups did not differ significantly in conditionability when dependency words were reinforced. And in a second study (*287*), which reinforced pronouns, the more conditionable subjects were significantly higher on the Deference scale and significantly lower on the Autonomy scale, as well as being significantly higher on the Affiliation, Abasement, and Order scales and significantly lower on the Achievement and Dominance scales.

In studies of decrement in performance as a result of stress, those classified as high in dependency (on the basis of the Deference and Autonomy scales) had a significantly greater decrement than those classified as low in dependency in one study (*18*), but did not differ significantly in a second study (*97*).

In studies of the tendency to ask the experimenter for help on a hard task after being instructed that such help would be provided on request, those classified as high in dependency (on the basis of the Deference and Autonomy scales) asked for more help than those classified as low in dependency in one study (*18*), but the two groups did not differ significantly in this tendency in a second study (*230*).

In a study of peer ratings, those rated as either dependent, submissive, or conforming were significantly higher than those rated as rebellious on the Abasement, Deference, and Succorance scales and significantly lower on the Aggression, Autonomy, and Dominance scales (*50*).

Relatively little evidence exists about the construct validity of the other EPPS scales, but some relevant studies do concern four scales—Dominance, Change, Abasement, and Aggression.

The validity of the Dominance scale is supported by a study in which management personnel were rated for leadership by observers and peers on the basis of the subjects' performance in a simulated business situation and group discussion; the observers' ratings correlated positively with the Dominance and Intraception scales and negatively with the Abasement and Nurturance scales, and the peers'

ratings correlated positively with the Dominance and Aggression scales and negatively with the Abasement and Nurturance scales (*320*).

Support for the validity of the Change scale comes from the finding that expectation of change correlated positively with the Change and Intraception scales, and correlated negatively with the Deference and Dominance scales (*261*).

On the other hand, the validity of the Abasement scale is questioned by the finding that those male students who predicted, on the first day of a course, that their final course grade would be *lower* and those who predicted that it would be *higher* than their grade-point average for the previous semester differed significantly in the scores on the Abasement scale, but the difference was in the wrong direction (those predicting higher course grades had higher Abasement scores); and the two female groups did not differ significantly in their Abasement scores (*197*).

Similarly, the meaning of the Aggression scale is challenged by the finding that those scoring high and those scoring low on that scale did not differ significantly in their perception of aggressive words in a binocular rivalry situation or in their acceptance of aggressive Rorschach percepts (*172*).

ACADEMIC ACHIEVEMENT AND OCCUPATIONAL PERFORMANCE. Relatively little is known about the ability of the EPPS to predict socially important variables. Most of the available data concern the relationship of the EPPS to academic performance—academic achievement (e.g., grade-point average) and "over-under achievement" (e.g., grade-point average with ability held constant)—or occupational performance. The academic performance findings, in addition to their bearing on the predictive validity of the EPPS, are relevant to the construct validity of the Achievement scale, and probably the Endurance scale as well.

Academic achievement was significantly (and positively) related to the Achievement scale in seven samples (*59, 111, 124, 239, 253*), but not in three others (*126, 253, 264*)—the median of the reported correlations was .35. In the studies that report the results for other scales (*59, 111, 129, 239, 253*), only the Abasement and Change scales were significantly (and negatively) related to achievement in more than one of the samples (*59, 239, 253*).

The results concerning over-under achievement are less consistent. This variable was significantly related to the Achievement scale in five samples (*41, 105, 197, 241, 267*), but not in nine others (*109, 190, 197, 216, 241, 247, 267*). In those studies which also report the results for the other scales, five scales were significantly related to over-under achievement in two or three of the eight samples—positively related scales were Dominance (*109, 267*), Order (*41, 105*), and Endurance (*105, 109*); negatively related ones were Affiliation (*41, 105, 109*) and Change (*41, 109*).

Studies of occupational performance have found some scattered relationships with the EPPS scales. Three of these studies concern nurses or hospital aides. Compared with those student nurses who were classified by their supervisors as "poor" in terms of their overall desirability as a nurse, those who were classified as "good" were significantly lower on the Order scale and significantly higher on the Dominance scale (*244*); nurses and aides in satisfied and dissatisfied wards did not differ significantly on any of 12 EPPS scales (all but the Change, Endurance, and Heterosexuality scales) that were investigated (*20*); and the efficiency ratings of psychiatric employees only correlated significantly (and positively) with one scale—Autonomy (*272*). The other studies concern performance in industrial settings. Four of the EPPS scales' correlations with managers' ratings of selling effectiveness were significant for either retail salesmen or industrial salesmen—the Dominance scale was significantly correlated (*r* = .29 and .32) for both groups (*138*); overall performance ratings of foremen correlated significantly with three EPPS scales—positively with Endurance (*r* = .27), and negatively with Nurturance (*r* = −.32) and Succorance (*r* = −.32) (*228*); and, in a study of telephone employees who had worked at isolated Arctic stations, those who received the highest ratings by their supervisors on work and social adjustment were significantly higher on the Deference and Order scales, and significantly lower on the Aggression scale (*326*).

SOCIAL DESIRABILITY RESPONSE STYLE AND FAKING. In view of the importance of social desirability as a response determinant and the special precautions taken in constructing the EPPS to minimize the effects of this response style, how much does it affect the EPPS?

Studies of this issue have been carried out at the item level and the score level.

At the item level, a substantial tendency exists to endorse the more socially desirable item in each pair of EPPS items, but it is not as great as that endorsement tendency on unpaired items. The obtained correlations, ranging from .37 to .69, in studies reported in the manual and elsewhere (*28, 53, 94, 196*) of the relationship between the difference in social desirability ratings of the items in each pair and their frequency of endorsement are in contrast with the correlation of .87 between social desirability ratings and frequency of endorsement of unpaired items originally obtained by Edwards (*1*). In addition to a tendency to endorse the more socially desirable item in each pair, there is a related tendency to endorse the more personally desirable (the desirability of a trait in oneself rather than its desirability in others) item (*98*).

In contrast to the trend of these other studies, the correlations, computed separately for each item pair, between choice of item within the pair and a social desirability response style (SD) scale clustered around zero; and the number of times that the more socially desirable item in each pair was chosen was not significantly correlated with the score on the SD scale (*43*).

At the score level, the average EPPS score for each scale correlated −.01 (*2*) and .46 (*258*) with the average social desirability rating of the need and .63 and .56 with the average personal desirability rating of the need (*42*). More to the point, none of the correlations between EPPS score profiles and social desirability ratings of the needs, when computed separately for each individual, were significant (*2*).

Also at the score level, an independent measure of social desirability response style was significantly related to several of the EPPS scales in three studies, but these relationships were generally lower than corresponding relationships of this response style with personality inventories that use a true-false or a yes-no format, such as the MMPI (cf., *11*). The difference in magnitude of these relationships, however, may be due, at least in part, to the statistical properties of ipsative scores described earlier. A study reported in the manual found that the Edwards SD scale significantly correlated with two scales—Endurance (*r* = .32)

and Succorance $(r = -.32)$; another study
(11), using the same SD scale, found that it
correlated significantly with four scales—Dominance $(r = .51)$, Exhibitionism $(r = .28)$,
Abasement $(r = -.46)$, and Aggression $(r = -.26)$; and a third study (32) found that
another measure of this response style—the
difference between performance on the standard Manifest Anxiety Scale and a forced choice
version of it—correlated significantly with five
scales—Achievement $(r = -.24)$, Autonomy
$(r = -.29)$, Abasement $(r = .29)$, Endurance
$(r = .32)$, and Aggression $(r = -.25)$.

Also relevant to the issue of social desirability response style, as well as the general issue
of faking, are studies that compare normal
performance on the EPPS with performance
under conditions where the subjects attempt to
make a desirable impression, either as a result
of explicit instructions or situational pressures.

In studies where subjects were instructed to
choose socially desirable or personally desirable
responses, there was only slight inter-subject
agreement in score profiles—the average rho
was .25 (36) and .14 (274)—but in a study in
which subjects were instructed to make a "good
impression" there was substantial inter-subject
agreement—the average rho was .58 (93).
While the first two studies, though not the
third, indicate that *group* standards of social
desirability have been eliminated from the
EPPS, other findings in these two studies indicate that *individual* standards of social desirability remain. In the Borislow study (36), the
mean of the correlations, computed separately
for each individual, between the score profile
when the EPPS was taken originally with
standard instructions and the score profile when
it was taken again with social desirability or
personal desirability instructions was significantly lower than the mean of the correlations
between the score profiles for a control group
that took the EPPS both times with standard
instructions. And in the Saltz study (274),
there was high intra-subject agreement between
the score profiles for the two halves of the
EPPS—the median was .70 of the rhos computed separately for each individual.

Other evidence points to the existence of
group standards on the EPPS. Instructions to
make a good impression produced significant
mean changes on 11 scales, and separate instructions to simulate high Change, high Order,
and high Dominance produced significant

changes on 10, 11, and 12 scales, respectively
(93); Air Force trainees who were told that
instructors would see their test results differed
significantly on eight scales from trainees who
responded anonymously (40); and applicants
for retail sales jobs differed significantly on
four scales from those already employed on
such jobs, but applicants for industrial sales
jobs did not significantly differ on any scale
from those already employed on such jobs
(257).

The consistency and profile stability scores
generally do not detect such explicit attempts
to make a good impression. In the Borislow
study (36) neither measure differed significantly between the standard condition and
either the social desirability or personal desirability conditions; and in the Dicken study (93)
the consistency score did not differ between the
standard condition and either the Good Impression or Order conditions, although it did
differ between the standard condition and both
the Dominance and Change conditions. Furthermore, the consistency and profile stability
scores were not significantly correlated in the
standard condition of the Borislow study.

SUMMARY. The EPPS set out to measure an
interesting set of variables and its construction
represented an important attempt to minimize
the effects of social desirability response style.
Its reliance on a paired comparison format,
however, has complicated interpretations of the
resulting ipsative scores and appraisals of their
statistical relationships. Moreover, its development apparently concentrated on the control
of the response style to the neglect of other
validity considerations. As a result, although
the influence of the response style was reduced
—the EPPS is affected by it, but less so
than most other personality inventories—a
decade of research into the validity of the
EPPS offers little justification for assuming
that its scales measure the constructs that they
are intended to reflect, or that, with the important exception of the link between the
Achievement scale and academic achievement,
the scales are useful in predicting socially important variables. Consequently, the likelihood
of obtaining meaningful measures of personality variables within the normal range would
seem to be greater if, instead of the EPPS,
any of several personality inventories whose
construction focused particularly on the validity
of their scales was employed. Such inventories

include the *Guilford-Zimmerman Temperament Survey* and the 16 PF, both of which use the traditional true-false or yes-no format. If an inventory of this kind is employed, it would be wise to administer the inventory with a standard measure of social desirability response style so as to be able to gauge its effects on the results obtained.

J Consult Psychol 23:471 O '59. Edward S. Bordin. [Review of 1959 revision of manual.] This revision of the 1954 manual....differs in only minor respects from the original. The directions for administration now include a section on machine scoring; a general adult sample now provides an additional norm group; the bibliography has been expanded from 9 to 82 references, most of the new references representing studies in which the EPPS figured. The general adult sample is less than adequate for normative purposes because it consists of a nationwide sample of male and female household heads who are members of a consumer purchase panel used for market surveys. It is not clear what this means with regard to its possible biases with respect to age, education, and class status. The mean scores of this sample vary from those in the other norm group, college students. But there is no effort to analyze the significance of these differences for the validity of the test. In fact, it is astonishing that no effort was made to summarize the relevance of the large body of studies in the bibliography to the test's validity and reliability. The reviews of the first manual pointed to its deficiencies with regard to validating evidence. One wonders why the author and publisher bothered to offer a revision which revises so little and is so unresponsive to criticism.

For reviews by Frank Barron, Åke Bjerstedt, and Donald W. Fiske, see 5:47 (2 excerpts.)

[88]

The Ego Strength Q-Sort Test. Grades 9-16 and adults; 1956-58; 6 scores: ego-status, social status, goal setting and striving, good mental health, physical status, total; 1 form ('58, 4 pages, essentially the same as form copyrighted in 1956) ; manual ('58, 53 pages) ; no data on reliability; $9 per examiner's kit of 25 tests, 2 item sheets (from which sort slips for 2 examinees may be prepared), manual, stencils, and sorting board; $3 per 25 tests; cash orders postpaid; (50-90) minutes; Russell N. Cassel; Psychometric Affiliates. *

REFERENCES
1. CASSEL, RUSSELL N. "Comparing the Effectiveness of the Ego-Strength Q-Sort Test by Use of R- and Q-Methodologies." *J Genetic Psychol* 94:161-8 Je '59. *
2. CASSEL, RUSSELL N., AND HARRIMAN, B. LYNN. "A Comparative Analysis of Personality and Ego Strength Test Scores for In-Prison, Neuro-Psychiatric and Typical Individuals." *J Ed Res* 53:43-52 O '59. * (*PA* 35:810)
3. BAILEY, MATTOX A.; WARSHAW, LEON; AND COHEN, JACOB. "An Obverse Factor Analytic Study of Values in Psychologists, Psychiatrists, Social Workers and Nurses." *J Clin Psychol* 19:120-4 Ja '63. * (*PA* 39:1650)

ALLEN L. EDWARDS, *Professor of Psychology, University of Washington, Seattle, Washington.*

The total score on the ESQT is based upon the correlation between the ratings assigned to the 60 items by a subject and a standard set of ratings. The standard ratings are based upon the judgments of six different groups. Since a simple averaging of the mean ratings assigned by each group was used in establishing the standard ratings, the chaplains ($n = 31$) and psychologists ($n = 25$) contribute to the standard ratings to the same degree as delinquent and wayward girls ($n = 100$) and typical secondary male youth ($n = 200$).

Evidence is presented, in the form of point-biserial coefficients ranging from .22 to .60, that differences occur between the mean correlations (total scores) when various groups are compared. No information is provided concerning the test-retest stability of the total score nor is any information given concerning the stability of the five part scores. One of the part scores, Physical Status, is based upon the ratings assigned to only two items. Low correlations, between −.28 and .16 are reported between total score and three other proposed measures of ego strength. The part scores have similarly low correlations with the other ego strength measures, the highest in absolute value being −.36 between Social Status and the Es scale of the MMPI.

Scoring keys are provided for each of the six original groups of judges in addition to the standard set of ratings for the combined groups. However, at least one of these keys, that for ordained ministers, contains irregularities in the number of items assigned to each of the rating categories. For example, 7 items are supposed to be assigned to category 4, but the manual shows 10 items in this category for ordained ministers.

The items in the ESQT were typed on an 8½ by 11 inch page and then photographed. The original typing was bad and the reproduction is worse. Furthermore, the items are on thin paper and the cards or items are so small, approximately ¾ by 2 inches, that they are awkward to handle.

The scoring stencil for the total score is not in alignment with the test booklet in which the Q-sort is recorded. In addition, the standard ratings on the scoring stencil opposite a given item number are not always the same as the ratings given in the manual. For example, the manual assigns a rating of 11 to item 55, whereas this rating appears opposite item 56 on the scoring stencil. This occurs because the rating assigned item 47 is misplaced.

The manual contains no references to any published research with the ESQT. This reviewer can find nothing in the manual which would lead to his recommendation of the test's use as a measure of ego strength.

HARRISON G. GOUGH, *Professor of Psychology, University of California, Berkeley, California.*

This test consists of 60 statements (e.g., "continued recognized progress towards personal goals," "adjusts to progressive change readily," "knows how to relax and practices it," and "gets a fair share of the luxuries of life relative to group") which the subject is asked to Q-sort into 11 categories of specified frequency (1, 3, 5, 7, etc.). The continuum of judgment underlying the sorting is the presumed relevance of each statement to "happiness." The 60 items were selected from an original library of 4,275 and maintain the same relative balance among five themes (ego status, social status, goal setting, mental health, and physical health) as observed among the full set of items.

The principal score on the test is the correlation of an individual's sorting of the items with the modal sorting derived from an unweighted average of the mean placements of each item by six samples; these original samples are described in the manual as "federal reformatory prisoners" ($n = 200$); "delinquent and wayward girls" ($n = 100$); "typical secondary male youth" ($n = 200$); "typical secondary female youth" ($n = 100$); "chaplains (all religious faiths)" ($n = 31$); and "research psychologists" ($n = 25$).

The operations defining the scoring key, it is clear, are similar to those used to define such indices as Rorschach P, Rosenzweig's Group Conformity Ratio, the F scale on the MMPI (except that F is scored for uncommon responses), and the Cm or communality scale of the *California Psychological Inventory*. The basic presumption concerning the total score on the ESQT, therefore, is that it is a measure of conventionality, conformance to modal standards, and the internalization of manifest norms.

Unfortunately, the manual carries no hint of these theoretical implications and, in fact, in its continual emphasis on total score as a measure of "ego strength," does violence to them. This review's first conclusion, therefore, is that the ESQT is flawed by an inherent confusion between ego strength and conformity.

This basic deficiency is augmented by other errors and misconceptions almost too numerous to list, and by a manual which is so inadequate and badly written that one wonders why either publisher or author would permit it to be released. As illustrations of the latter point, consider the following passages:

> It is presumed that an individual can live only his or her own life, and that only he or she, in the final analysis, can forge for their own happiness.
> It [happiness] falls on a continuum scale which ranges in scope from that of an individual with a "passive and vegetable" like existence of a feeble-minded and apathetic type, through that of the truly happy person, to that of a person with a hyper-mania, non-satiable, effervescing, and additive type of manifestations....
> The diversity of human beings with respect to what constitutes happiness is rather unique from one person to the other, and, therefore, is infinite in scope.

Singular subjects with plural verbs, plural subjects with singular verbs, misspellings, incorrect uses of prepositions, solecisms, and barbarisms abound in the text of the manual. These are not technical errors, to be sure, but it is nonetheless embarrassing to think of psychological testing being represented by a manual as poorly written as this one.

With respect to technical errors, there is a very unsatisfactory handling of the validity problem. The Cronbach-Meehl convention of defining four types of validity is dutifully followed, but is misunderstood. Construct validity is seen merely as "the relationship between scores on the ESQT and scores....for other tests" (p. 15), and "prediction validity" (*sic*) is allegedly demonstrated by showing discriminations between (*a*) hospitalized and non-hospitalized airmen; and (*b*) schizophrenic patients and unselected adults.

The data presented do nothing to allay the

anxieties aroused by these conceptual misunderstandings. In a sample of 200 adults, the total score on the ESQT correlated −.19 with Barron's ego strength scale, −.03 with Taylor's scale for manifest anxiety, +.25 with the *Army General Classification Test,* and +.04 with last school grade completed. Other correlations ranging from −.44 to +.16 are also cited, but are either with relatively unknown instruments (e.g., the "Ego Strength Rating Scale by B. Hartman," *r* = −.28), or with instruments whose validity is not unequivocally established (*Cassel Group Level of Aspiration Test,* first goal, *r* = −.12).

In addition to the total score (the correlation of an individual sorting with the modal sorting), separate scores may also be obtained for the five clusters of items (Ego Status, Social Status, Goal Setting and Striving, Mental Health, and Physical Status), and standard score conversions are provided. No evidence on the reliability of these part scores is offered, and one must doubt whether two of these scores (Ego Status with 10 items, and Physical Status with 2 items) could meet minimum standards. Evidence on the reliability of the total score is also lacking, although the reviewer's expectation is that a sort-resort correlation for a 60-item deck would be adequate.

Perhaps the most fundamental deficiency in the manual, considering that the test is a Q-sort deck, is the absence of a table giving intercorrelations among the 60 items and mean placements of each one (although these latter can be to some extent inferred from the scoring key). In an optimum Q-deck, one which maximizes differences among people and in which all items are functional, the intercorrelations among items should be at a minimum and the mean placement of items in a large and heterogeneous sample should converge on the middle step of the Q-distribution. If the mean placement of an item is near either extreme of the continuum, the item is by definition weak as a differentiator; if two items are highly correlated there is redundancy of response. There is no evidence in the manual that these two basic technical points were considered in the selection and evaluation of items.

More problems could be raised, but enough has been said to lead to an overall summary. The reviewer wishes to apologize for the harshness of his judgment, but can see no way of avoiding the conclusion that this test is clearly below minimal publication standards. Its basic variable is misunderstood and misidentified, evidence on validity is unconvincing and inadequate, and reliability is totally neglected. Even the Q-sort method, on which the test is based, appears to be misconceived, as essential technical information pertaining to this deck is neither discussed nor presented. A Q-sort test of ego strength might indeed be developed, and the work already done on this test could constitute a first step toward such a goal, but as it stands, this instrument is not ready for publication and commercial release.

[89]

***Embedded Figures Test.** Ages 10 and over; 1950–62; individual; 1 form ['57, 32 cards, may also be administered as a short form using only 12 cards]; manual ('50, 15 pages, reprint of *1* below); supplementary instructions and data ['62, 6 hectographed sheets]; college norms only; $3 per set of testing materials, postpaid; (15–25) minutes; Herman A. Witkin; the Author. *

REFERENCES

1–9. See 5:49.
10. BAUMAN, GERALD. *The Stability of the Individual's Mode of Perception, and of Perception-Personality Relationships.* Doctor's thesis, New York University (New York, N.Y.), 1951.
11. LINTON, HARRIET B. *Relations Between Mode of Perception and Tendency to Conform.* Doctor's thesis, Yale University (New Haven, Conn.), 1952.
12. ROSENFELD, IRWIN JOSEPH. *Mathematical Ability as a Function of Perceptual Field-Dependency and Certain Personality Variables.* Doctor's thesis, University of Oklahoma (Norman, Okla.), 1958. (*DA* 19:880)
13. DANA, RICHARD H., AND GOOCHER, BUELL. "Embedded-Figures and Personality." *Percept & Motor Skills* 9:99–102 Je '59. * (*PA* 38:4299)
14. GARDNER, RILEY W.; HOLZMAN, PHILIP S.; KLEIN, GEORGE S.; LINTON, HARRIET B.; AND SPENCE, DONALD P. "Cognitive Control: A Study of Individual Consistencies in Cognitive Behavior." *Psychol Issues* 1(4):1–186 '59. * (*PA* 35:2266)
15. BIERI, JAMES. "Parental Identification, Acceptance of Authority, and Within-Sex Differences in Cognitive Behavior." *J Abn & Social Psychol* 60:76–9 Ja '60. * (*PA* 34:7526)
16. DANA, RICHARD H., AND GOOCHER, BUELL. "Pessimism Reaffirmed: A Reply to Witkin." *Percept & Motor Skills* 11:243–4 D '60. * (*PA* 35:2206)
17. GARDNER, RILEY W.; JACKSON, DOUGLAS N.; AND MESSICK, SAMUEL J. "Personality Organization in Cognitive Controls and Intellectual Abilities." *Psychol Issues* 2(8):1–149 '60. * (*PA* 36:2HA49G)
18. MEUX, MILTON OTTO. *The Role of Reasoning and Spatial Abilities in Performance at Three Difficulty Levels of the Embedded Figures Task.* Doctor's thesis, University of Illinois (Urbana, Ill.), 1960. (*DA* 21:1625)
19. WITKIN, HERMAN A. "'Embedded Figures and Personality': A Reply." *Percept & Motor Skills* 11:15–20 Ag '60. * (*PA* 35:3447)
20. GOODENOUGH, DONALD R., AND KARP, STEPHEN A. "Field Dependence and Intellectual Functioning." *J Abn & Social Psychol* 63:241–6 S '61. * (*PA* 37:1214)
21. ISCOE, IRA AND CARDEN, JOYCE ANN. "Field Dependence, Manifest Anxiety, and Sociometric Status in Children." Abstract. *J Consult Psychol* 25:184 Ap '61. * (*PA* 36:4FF84I)
22. LEAGUE, BETTY JO, AND JACKSON, DOUGLAS N. "Activity and Passivity as Correlates of Field-Independence." *Percept & Motor Skills* 12:291–8 Je '61. * (*PA* 36:2HJ91L)
23. LOEFF, RICHARD. *Embedding and Distracting Field Contexts as Related to the Field Dependence Dimension.* Master's thesis, Brooklyn College (New York, N.Y.), 1961.
24. WITKIN, HERMAN A. "Cognitive Development and the Growth of Personality." *Acta Psychologica* 18(4):245–57 '61. * (*PA* 36:5HJ45W)
25. KARP, STEPHEN A. *A Factorial Study of Overcoming Embeddedness in Perceptual and Intellectual Functioning.* Doctor's thesis, New York University (New York, N.Y.), 1962.
26. LONGENECKER, E. D. "Perceptual Recognition as a Function of Anxiety, Motivation, and the Testing Situation." *J Abn & Social Psychol* 64:215–21 Mr '62. * (*PA* 38:1723)

27. STEWART, HORACE F., JR. *A Study of the Relationship Between Certain Personality Measures and Hallucinoidal Visual Imagery.* Doctor's thesis, University of Florida (Gainesville, Fla.), 1962. (*DA* 24:827)
28. WITKIN, H. A.; DYK, R. B.; FATERSON, H. F.; GOODENOUGH, D. R.; AND KARP, S. A. *Psychological Differentiation: Studies of Development.* New York: John Wiley & Sons, Inc., 1962. Pp. xii, 418. * (*PA* 37:819)
29. COPPINGER, NEIL W.; BORTNER, RAYMAN W.; AND SAUCER, RAYFORD T. "A Factor Analysis of Psychological Deficit." *J Genetic Psychol* 103:23–43 S '63. * (*PA* 39:174)
30. ELKIND, DAVID; KOEGLER, RONALD R.; AND GO, ELSIE. "Field Independence and Concept Formation." *Percept & Motor Skills* 17:383–6 O '63. * (*PA* 38:5349)
31. FISHBEIN, GERALD M. "Perceptual Modes and Asthmatic Symptoms: An Application of Witkin's Hypothesis." *J Consult Psychol* 27:54–8 F '63. * (*PA* 37:8205)
32. GOODENOUGH, DONALD R., AND EAGLE, CAROL JOHNSON. "A Modification of the Embedded-Figures Test for Use With Young Children." *J Genetic Psychol* 103:67–74 S '63. *
33. KARP, STEPHEN A.; POSTER, DOROTHY C.; AND GOODMAN, ALAN. "Differentiation in Alcoholic Women." *J Personality* 31:386–93 S '63. *

HARRISON G. GOUGH, *Professor of Psychology, University of California, Berkeley, California.*

This test consists of 24 complex colored figures, derivations of those used by Gottschaldt in the 1920's in his work on the influence of experience on perception. Each complex figure contains one of eight simple figures. In administering the test, a card on which a complex figure appears is shown to the subject for 15 seconds, and he is asked to describe it. Then a card containing the simple figure embedded in that complex figure is shown for 10 seconds. Following this, the complex figure is again presented and the subject's task is to find the simple figure and to trace it with a blunt stylus.

The score on each item is the time taken to find the embedded figure. A maximum of five minutes per card is allowed, after which a failure is recorded and the next card is presented. Reexamination of the simple figure is permitted when requested, for 10-second periods; the time record is held in abeyance during any such interval.

The items differ considerably in difficulty, ranging from mean times of 10 seconds to over two minutes for college males, and for failure rates from 0 to 27 per cent for college females. For the full test, mean time scores are reported of 16 minutes 39 seconds and 23 minutes 4 seconds for adult males and females, and 58 minutes 4 seconds and 62 minutes 16 seconds for 10-year-old boys and girls. Reliability coefficients, whether by the odd-even, test-retest, or analysis of variance method, are excellent, the median coefficient in 10 studies being .905.

Although the test is viewed by its author as related to such well known devices as the Kohs blocks, Guilford's tests of adaptive flexi-

bility, and Wechsler's subtests for block design, picture completion, and object assembly, it is not interpreted as an index of general ability. Its diagnostic implications, on the contrary, are seen as related to (*a*) field independence, (*b*) cognitive clarity, (*c*) an analytic versus global perceptual mode, and (*d*) a general disposition to articulate and structure experience. These notions, it should be observed, are not just ad hoc comments on the apparent nature of the test, but are basic theoretical principles arising from a vast amount of careful and convincing experimentation by Witkin and his associates. Indeed, one of the most attractive features of this test is its firm anchoring in a systematic context of theory and empirical evidence.

There is no question concerning the importance of the approach to cognitive testing represented by this device. From Gottschaldt in the 1920's, through Thurstone in the 1940's, to 1950 when Witkin's first paper on the embedded figures test appeared, one can discern the gradual crystallizing of a concept of measurement of truly fundamental significance. This reviewer has no doubt but that within 15 to 20 years the embedded figure kind of content will be as basic in cognitive test batteries as analogies, progressions, spatial manipulations, and quantitative analyses are today. There are also the exciting potentialities of a test of this type for cross-cultural usage.

The importance of the innovative trend exemplified by Witkin's test, therefore, cannot be overemphasized; but this does not mean that the test as it stands is free from flaws and imperfections. One major difficulty is the lack of a manual. Witkin's paper "Individual Differences in Ease of Perception of Embedded Figures" (*1*) is distributed with the test materials, and a later paper, "Cognitive Development and the Growth of Personality" (*24*) is also available. The former is an excellent research report and the latter a stimulating exposition of theory, but neither is a test manual. Information which a manual would contain—e.g., intercorrelations among items, correlations of the EFT with other well established cognitive measures, norms for various groups, correlations with utilitarian criteria such as school grades and job success, and the meaning and dependability of scores obtained in retesting—is lacking.

A second area of difficulty concerns the unwieldiness of the test in its present form.

Experimentation with group forms is needed, as there seems to be no reason in principle for insisting on individual testing. Group testing would probably require a shift from time to error scores, but again there seems to be no compelling theoretical rationale for use of time scores. A shorter maximum time per item (e.g., two minutes) would do away with the hour-long and frustrating sessions which occur with some frequency among children and which are not unknown even with adults. A conventional item versus total score internal consistency analysis might also permit a reduction in length by elimination of undifferentiating items. All of these modifications—toward a shorter test with briefer time allotments and in a group test format—would make for a more service-able, wieldy, and convenient device. They should all be attainable without loss of any intrinsic validity.

A third need is for a parallel form of this test. Learning during the test itself must be appreciable, and it is doubtful whether the test could be given more than once to adults. Yet the function being measured is almost by definition a growth function calling for longi-tudinal assessment. At least two equivalent forms are therefore necessitated.

A fourth issue concerns Witkin's present opinion that this test assesses a cognitive mode (analytical structuring) while being more or less independent of the general level of intel-lectual ability. On the basis of extensive work with R. S. Crutchfield's adaptation of Gott-schaldt's figures (Crutchfield's test is some-what comparable to Witkin's), this reviewer is of the opinion that the embedded figures pro-cedure does assess intellectual ability and that, were studies conducted, Witkin's EFT would in fact reveal significant correlations with such tests as the Henmon-Nelson, Raven's matrices, Cattell's culture-fair test, and similar instru-ments in widespread usage. At the same time, and here in agreement with Witkin, the re-viewer sees the EFT as not merely synonymous with these other indices, but as an instrument which assesses a new and important facet of the cognitive domain.

The intention of these comments is entirely constructive. Witkin's use of the hidden figures technique to test cognitive and perceptual modes is a development of fundamental sig-nificance. Although in its current form the instrument is crude and unwieldy, there is every reason to believe that it can be improved and simplified and that parallel forms can be developed. With such technical improvement, the test will provide a worthy and auspicious addition to psychology's list of valid devices of measurement.

LEONA E. TYLER, *Professor of Psychology, University of Oregon, Eugene, Oregon.*

Since World War II various researchers have been studying individual differences in perception, cognitive style, or cognitive control principles. (The same domain has been vari-ously labeled by different workers at different times.) This research effort has had a theo-retical rather than a practical orientation, and none of the tests have been placed on the market for general use. It is unlikely that procedures such as Witkin's Tilting Room-Tilting Chair will ever be employed very widely as practical testing procedures because of the elaborate equipment they require. But the *Em-bedded Figures Test* (EFT), Witkin's adap-tation of the Gottschaldt figures, is a con-venient and usable instrument. It consists of 24 complex geometrical figures, some in black and white and some in color, presented to the subject on separate cards. His task is to locate in the complex figure a simple figure he has previously been shown. His score for each item is the time it takes him to do this. The test can be used with children as well as with adults.

The trait or characteristic measured by this test was labeled field dependence in the first major report by Witkin and associates (*2*), field articulation in factor analytic studies car-ried on by Gardner and others (*14*), psycho-logical differentiation by Witkin and his co-workers in their more recent study of children (*28*). The fact that EFT showed significant and generally high correlations with most of the scores based on tests of bodily orientation (the Tilting Room-Tilting Chair, Rotating Room, and Rod and Frame test) indicated that all of these procedures must make some similar demand upon subjects. What subjects who did well with them seemed to have was the ability to analyze a complex configuration and then to respond to some parts of it, ignoring others. Subsequent studies showed that this ability was related to temperament or personality charac-teristics as well as to the spatial aspects of intelligence. Field-dependent persons, those having great difficulty with EFT as well as with the body orientation tests, showed up as more passive and anxious about control of body impulses, with lower self esteem and less well differentiated body images than those who did well. Females scored significantly more field dependent than males.

The reliability coefficients reported in the studies in which the EFT has been used indicate that, whatever this trait is, individuals manifest it consistently on different parts of the test and at different times. Test-retest coefficients for men and women, even with a three year interval between administrations, were .89. Stability coefficients over shorter intervals and split-half coefficients have tended to run even higher.

Since there has been no attempt to publish the EFT and make it available to regular consumers of tests, no manual has been issued. If one wishes to use EFT in a research undertaking, Witkin sends a reprint of his 1950 paper (*1*), which contains instructions and essential information, along with some dittoed material based on other studies. But in order to use the test intelligently a researcher really needs to read in their entirety the books and monographs to which reference has been made earlier in this review.

Until or unless more extensive norms and more readily available technical information are developed, EFT is not a practical instrument for diagnosis or selection purposes. Perhaps the time has now come for special studies in which its utility in clinics, counseling offices, and personnel departments is assessed. The characteristics to which it points would seem to be important enough to justify this effort.

[90]

*Emo Questionnaire. Adults; 1958–60; 14 scores: rationalization, inferiority feelings, fear and anxiety, N vector (total of preceding 3 scores), depression, projection, unreality, withdrawal, Z vector (total of preceding 4 scores), hostility, sex, organic response, total diagnostic, buffer score; 1 form ('58, 8 pages); manual ('59, 37 pages); report form ('60, 4 pages); no data on reliability of current form; $7.50 per 20 tests; postage extra; $1 per specimen set, postpaid; (20–30) minutes; George O. Baehr (test), Melany E. Baehr (test), and Measurement Research Division, Industrial Relations Center, University of Chicago (manual); Education-Industry Service. *

REFERENCES

1. PISHKIN, VLADIMIR; OLSON, LOIS O.; AND JACOBS, DURAND F. "An Objective Attempt to Analyze Emotional Interactions Between Psychiatric Patients and Nursing Staff." *J Clin Psychol* 17:383–9 O '61. * (*PA* 38:8804)

BERTRAM D. COHEN, *Professor of Psychology, and Director of Clinical Training, Rutgers, The State University, New Brunswick, New Jersey.*

This paper-and-pencil questionnaire was devised for both industrial placement and clinical diagnostic purposes. Group or individual administration techniques are feasible. The scores may be used as an adjunctive device in the selection of industrial personnel (i.e., to screen potentially effective workers) or as a basis for individualized personality description. The items are grouped into a series of specific "diagnostic" categories such as "hostility," "fear and anxiety," and "depression." These categories, in turn, are grouped into three composite scores: total diagnostics, neurotic vector, and psychotic vector. Finally, the system includes three kinds of scores for each diagnostic category or composite vector: frequency of response, intensity of response, and conformity of response.

Although the authors offer industrial selection and placement as important purposes of the test, the major attempts at validity determination concern comparison of the scores of presumably normal industrial workers with those of hospitalized psychiatric patients, mostly schizophrenic. The results show that the test (particularly the conformity of response scores) can discriminate reliably between these groups, and holds up on cross-validation. Also, in an independent study (*1*), scores on the test successfully differentiated nursing personnel from a hospitalized patient group. The major shortcoming of this work is the lack of validity criteria that are genuinely relevant to the industrial situations within which the test is intended to apply. It is hardly sufficient to know that industrial workers score differently most of the time from hospitalized psychotic patients, even if all other variables (e.g., age, sex, etc.) had been adequately controlled.

For certain clinical purposes, there are some indications that the test and its special scoring methods may be of some specific value. The authors report studies indicating that scores differentiate between psychiatric patients who showed "steady progress" and those who "suffered a temporary relapse during the course of treatment." The test has also been used to determine the relative effectiveness of individual psychotherapy, group therapy, and combined individual and group therapy.

As for individual personality description, there are as yet no grounds for evaluating the usefulness of the test. The apparent content validity of the diagnostic category items is all one would have to go on.

In summary, the main feature of this test that might prove intriguing to test users is the use of "intensity" and "conformity" measures along with the more traditional frequency counts employed in most personality inventories. Further work with more practical and relevant criterion groups and situations is clearly necessary before the test can be considered a viable competitor among personality inventories.

W. Grant Dahlstrom, *Professor of Psychology, The University of North Carolina, Chapel Hill, North Carolina.*

This instrument is advanced for use in industry, hospitals, and private clinical practice for two applications: screening of emotional health problems and individual personality diagnosis. Different scoring procedures are utilized for these two purposes but the manual provides the interpretive guidelines for screening use only. For individual personality appraisal the manual recommends that the protocol and score sheet from the subject be sent to the test author for interpretation (fee unspecified).

The test booklet contains 140 items out of 230 originally developed (and presumably scaled for the 14 component scores) in a previous test by G. O. Baehr, the Baehr Discontentment Scale (1951). The items surviving in this test were pruned for hospital related experiences. The test is represented to the subject as a measure of how well he understands himself. The format of the present instrument calls for a judgment about each item first as having happened to the subject within the last month or not, and then requests an additional four-step rating of the subject's reactions to the items that are relevant. These ratings range from "pleased" to "troubled very much" to describe each particular experience. Thus the test subject is able to describe his current range of experiences and his recent reactions to these experiences without being trapped into continuing to respond to some previously true test item as currently characteristic of him merely because of an arbitrary tense of some verb. The range of content among the items is wide

but some subjects may be forced to deny a number of items if they have been confined in a hospital, prison, or some other special environment during the preceding month. The authors indicate that nine or more items must be admitted and rated to provide a valid basis for screening, but nearly a fourth of one hospitalized group of 87 patients and over 10 per cent of an industrial employee sample failed to meet this minimum completion standard. If these trends are typical, this could be a serious source of invalidity in practical application.

Two additional checks are provided for guardedness in test response: first, the number of items rated "not affected" (earning a scale value of 2) in intensity; second, the total number of answers given to the 30 buffer items scattered throughout the booklet. No data are provided on how well these measures rule out undesirable test response sets in screening or diagnosis.

Three different scoring systems are employed: frequency of item endorsements, intensity of item ratings of endorsed items, and deviations from typical patterns of item intensity judgments for the various content areas. These scoring steps are not handled by separate scoring stencils (as in the SVIB) but the authors attempt to provide all of these data reduction procedures on a single score sheet. The result is utterly chaotic, making it next to impossible to get a record free of clerical errors and computational blunders. Since the manual does not provide the interpreter with any basis for drawing inferences from these various scores once they have been derived, the scoring procedure is a masterful study in frustration. One would certainly be tempted to send the protocol to the author before scoring rather than after.

Reliability data on this test form are not available. The stability of one score from the original test (intensity score) over a day's time for 86 neurotic patients is reported as .84 prior to treatment. No information is provided to judge the effect of removal of 90 items upon even this score. No validation data are provided for the separate component scales or even on how they were derived. In the manual, validation but not cross validation data are given for screening hospitalized and nonhospitalized male adults. Eleven "Emotional Disturbance Indicators" are reported. For the groups on which the indices were established, the best separation occurs using intensity response patterns as Emotional Disturbance Indicators. The criterion of presence of one or more such indicators identified 77.3 per cent of 66 hospitalized cases as unhealthy and falsely called 22.4 per cent of 107 industrial workers emotionally disturbed. Even without the inevitable shrinkage were these separations to be applied to a sample of 1,000 adults with, at the outside, about 200 of them having some emotional illness, the results would not be very favorable. Using the criterion of presence of one or more Emotional Disturbance Indicators based on intensity responses, the *Emo Questionnaire* would screen out as disturbed 155 of the 200 sick ones (missing 45); of the 800 normals, 179 would be called sick. So, more of the cases labeled "sick" would be normal than sick (179:155).

On the available evidence, this instrument, with its current scoring format, cannot be recommended for the uses proposed. As a screening device it is lengthy to administer, laborious to score, and too sensitive to defensiveness and false positive errors. As an individual diagnostic device it carries the same burdens of scoring problems but these are magnified at least threefold and, in addition, it is devoid of all evidence of validity and all interpretive material for diagnostic use. In its present format, it is hard to see how the *Emo Questionnaire* could be utilized even for research purposes.

[91]

*The Empathy Test. Ages 13 and over; 1947-61; Forms A ('47), B Revised ('61, c1951), C ('54, adaptation of Form A for Canadian use), (1 page); manual ('55, 4 pages); $3 per 50 tests; $1 per specimen set (must be purchased to obtain manual); cash orders postpaid; (10–15) minutes; Willard A. Kerr and Boris J. Speroff; Psychometric Affiliates. *

REFERENCES

1–20. See 5:50.
21. WOLFSON, BEATRICE NATALIE. *A Study of Personality Variables, as Measured by Certain Instruments, That May Differentiate School Guidance Counselors From Classroom Teachers.* Doctor's thesis, University of Connecticut (Storrs, Conn.), 1958. (*DA* 19:2816)
22. GLENNON, J. R.; ALBRIGHT, LEWIS E.; AND SMITH, WALLACE J. "Normative Data Information Exchange, Nos. 12-1, 12-2." *Personnel Psychol* 12:143–4 sp '59. *
23. RICH, JOSEPH McELROY. *Individual Empathy in Relation to Certain Aspects of Group Functioning.* Doctor's thesis, Temple University (Philadelphia, Pa.), 1959. (*DA* 20:742)
24. GIBLETTE, JOHN FRANKLIN. *Differences Among Above Average, Average, and Below Average Secondary School Counselors.* Doctor's thesis, University of Pennsylvania (Philadelphia, Pa.), 1960. (*DA* 21:812)
25. STRUNK, ORLO, JR., AND REED, KENNETH E. "The Learning of Empathy: A Pilot Study." *J Pastoral Care* 14:44–8 sp '60. *
26. SMITH, WILLIAM REED. "Empathy and Writing Ability." *Percept & Motor Skills* 13:315–8 D '61. *
27. DIGHTMAN, CAMERON R., AND FAHRION, STEVEN L. "An Experimental Approach to the Study of Empathy." *Proc Mont Acad Sci* 21:124–31 '62. * (*PA* 37:3144)
28. PATTERSON, C. H. "A Note on the Construct Validity of the Concept of Empathy." *Personnel & Guid J* 40:803–6 My '62. * (*PA* 37:3448)
29. PATTERSON, C. H. "Test Characteristics of Rehabilitation Counselor Trainees." *J Rehabil* 28:15–6 S–O '62. * (*PA* 37:6953)

WALLACE B. HALL, *Assistant Research Psychologist, Institute of Personality Assessment and Research, University of California, Berkeley, California.*

Each form of this test contains three sections: (*a*) a list of 14 common types of music to be ranked in order of popularity; (*b*) 15 names of magazines to be ranked according to paid circulation; and (*c*) 10 common annoying experiences to be ranked from most to least annoying. One total score is obtained, the sum of the differences in ranks assigned by the subject from those in the normative group used in making up the scoring key.

There is generally some disagreement on just what defines empathy. The test measures, according to the manual, "the subject's ability to 'anticipate' certain typical reactions of defined normative persons." English and English [1] define empathy as an "apprehension of the state of mind of another person without feeling (as in sympathy) what the other feels," and the "attitude in empathy is one of acceptance and understanding, of an implicit 'I see how you feel.'" In this test, the defined normative groups which the examinee is asked to "place yourself in the position of" range from "non-office factory workers of the United States" to "persons over age 40"; in the case of the magazine circulation section the implication is that he must isolate subscribers as a group from the entire American population. Such an extension would seem rather distant from the usual person-to-person interaction which is of presumed interest in this test.

Although Form A was copyrighted in 1947, the key indicates that a substitution was made in part 2 for one of the magazines which has ceased publication. Form B was revised in 1961, the revision consisting of the substitution of four magazine names from the 1957 list. No references since 1954 are cited, and more recent and critical studies such as that of Patterson (*28*) are ignored. The printing of the test, manual, and scoring key is carelessly done, and errors in the copy are uncor-

1 ENGLISH, HORACE B., AND ENGLISH, AVA CHAMPNEY. *A Comprehensive Dictionary of Psychological and Psychoanalytical Terms.* New York: Longmans, Green & Co., 1958. Pp. xiv, 594. *

rected or poorly made, so that the entire work presents a rather unprofessional appearance.

The normative data for music preferences were obtained "in a national survey program." The 1962 scoring key shows no change in ranking of preferences from the earlier 1954 scoring key. Normative data for the annoying experiences "are the extensive findings of Hulsey Cason." These findings are neither described nor their source indicated. Some checking of the current appropriateness of all norms would seem to be in order, particularly in the domain of musical taste.

In view of these negative features and the implication that the test is more a measure of general information and prediction of opinions than of interpersonal empathy, there appears little to recommend this test for the purposes stated by its authors.

For a review by Robert L. Thorndike, see 5:50.

[92]

★[**Environment Indexes.**] Grades 9–13, 13–16, adults, employees; 1957–63; environmental press (see 180 for a related test of personal needs covering the same areas); 41 scores for each index: 30 press scores (abasement-assurance, achievement, adaptability-defensiveness, affiliation-rejection, aggression-blame avoidance, change-sameness, conjunctivity-disjunctivity, counteraction-inferiority avoidance, deference-restiveness, dominance-tolerance, ego achievement, emotionality-placidity, energy-passivity, exhibitionism-inferiority avoidance, fantasied achievement, harm avoidance-risk taking, humanities and social science, impulsiveness-deliberation, narcissism, nurturance-rejection, objectivity-projectivity, order-disorder, play-work, practicalness-impracticalness, reflectiveness, science, sensuality-puritanism, sexuality-prudishness, supplication-autonomy, understanding) and 11 factor scores based on combinations of the press scores (aspiration level, intellectual climate, student dignity, academic climate, academic achievement, self-expression, group life, academic organization, social form, play-work, vocational climate); NCS; 4 levels; combined scoring and college norms manual ('63, 30 pages plus sample copies of each of these indexes and the *Stern Activities Index*) for *b* below and the *Stern Activities Index;* no data on reliability and validity; no norms for *a* or *c–d;* separate answer sheets must be used; 25¢ per test; $3.25 per 50 NCS answer sheets; $6 per set of hand scoring stencils (machine scoring by the distributor only); $3.50 per scoring and norms manual; postpaid; scoring and profiling fees: 75¢ to 95¢ per answer sheet, depending on quantity; (20–90) minutes; distributed by National Computer Systems. *
a) HIGH SCHOOL CHARACTERISTICS INDEX. Grades 9–13; 1960; experimental form; no norms; Form 960 ('60, 7 pages); George G. Stern.
b) COLLEGE CHARACTERISTICS INDEX. Grades 13–16; 1957–63; Form 1158 ('58, 7 pages); press score profile ('63, 1 page); factor score profile ('63, 1 page); George G. Stern and C. Robert Pace.
c) EVENING COLLEGE CHARACTERISTICS INDEX. Adults; 1961; experimental form; no norms; Form 161 ('61,

7 pages); George G. Stern, Clifford L. Winters, Jr., N. Sidney Archer, and Donald L. Meyer.
d) ORGANIZATIONAL CLIMATE INDEX. Employees; 1958–63; experimental forms; no norms; Form 1163 ('63, c1958–63, 7 pages); George G. Stern and Carl R. Steinhoff.

REFERENCES
1. PACE, C. ROBERT, AND STERN, GEORGE G. "An Approach to the Measurement of Psychological Characteristics of College Environments." *J Ed Psychol* 49:269–77 O '58. * (*PA* 36:2KA69P)
2. McFEE, ANNE. *The Relation of Selected Factors to Students' Perception of a College Environment.* Master's thesis, Syracuse University (Syracuse, N.Y.), 1959.
3. THISTLETHWAITE, DONALD L. "College Press and Student Achievement." *J Ed Psychol* 50:183–91 O '59. * (*PA* 35:3964)
4. PACE, C. ROBERT. "Five College Environments." *Col Board R* 41:24–8 sp '60. * (*PA* 35:7056)
5. STERN, GEORGE G. "Congruence and Dissonance in the Ecology of College Students." *Student Med* 8:304–39 Ap '60. *
6. STERN, GEORGE G. "Student Values and Their Relationship to the College Environment," pp. 67–104. In *Research on College Students: Institute Lectures Considering Recent Research on College Student's Motivation, Values and Attitudes, and Campus Cultures.* Edited by Hall T. Sprague. Boulder, Colo.: Western Interstate Commission for Higher Education, 1960. Pp. iv, 188. *
7. HUTCHINS, EDWIN B. "The 1960 Medical School Graduate: His Perception of His Faculty, Peers, and Environment." *J Med Ed* 36:322–9 Ap '61. *
8. McFEE, ANNE. "The Relation of Students' Needs to Their Perceptions of a College Environment." *J Ed Psychol* 52:25–9 F '61. * (*PA* 36:2KD25M)
9. PACE, WALTER THOMAS. *Profiles of Personal Needs and College Press of Negro Teacher Trainees.* Doctor's thesis, Wayne State University (Detroit, Mich.), 1961. (*DA* 22:3748)
10. STERN, GEORGE G. "Recent Research on Institutional Climates: 1, Continuity and Contrast in the Transition From High School to College," pp. 33–58. In *Orientation to College Learning—A Reappraisal: Report of a Conference on Introduction of Entering Students to the Intellectual Life of the College.* Edited by Nicholas C. Brown. Washington, D.C.: American Council on Education, 1961. Pp. xi, 143. *
11. BEST, SHEILA ANNE. *The Relationship Between the College Characteristics Index and Other Measures of College Environment.* Master's thesis, Syracuse University (Syracuse, N.Y.), 1962.
12. PACE, C. ROBERT. "Implications of Differences in Campus Atmosphere for Evaluation and Planning of College Programs," pp. 43–61. (*PA* 37:5613) In *Personality Factors on the College Campus: Review of a Symposium.* Edited by Robert L. Sutherland, Wayne H. Holtzman, Earl A. Koile, and Bert Kruger Smith. Austin, Tex.: Hogg Foundation for Mental Health, 1962. Pp. xii, 242. * (*PA* 37:5621)
13. SAGEN, HARRY BRADLEY. *The Relationship of Certain Personality and Environmental Variables to the Satisfaction With Present Position of Faculty in Selected Liberal Arts Colleges.* Doctor's thesis, University of Minnesota (Minneapolis, Minn.), 1962. (*DA* 23:3241)
14. STERN, GEORGE G. Chap. 3, "The Measurement of Psychological Characteristics of Students and Learning Environments," pp. 27–68. In *Measurement in Personality and Cognition.* Edited by Samuel Messick and John Ross. New York: John Wiley & Sons, Inc., 1962. Pp. xi, 334. * (*PA* 38:2638)
15. STERN, GEORGE G. Chap. 21, "Environments for Learning," pp. 690–730. In *The American College: A Psychological and Social Interpretation of the Higher Learning.* Edited by Nevitt Sanford. New York: John Wiley & Sons, Inc., 1962. Pp. xvi, 1084. * (*PA* 36:5KA84S)
16. NUNNALLY, JUM C.; THISTLETHWAITE, DONALD L.; AND WOLFE, SHARON. "Factored Scales for Measuring Characteristics of College Environments." *Ed & Psychol Meas* 23:239–48 su '63. * (*PA* 38:1370)
17. RAAB, WILLIAM EDWIN. *Congruence and Dissonance Between Need and Press in Determining Satisfaction or Dissatisfaction in the University Environment.* Doctor's research study No. 1, Colorado State University (Fort Collins, Colo.), 1963. (*DA* 24:1923)
18. STERN, GEORGE G. "Characteristics of the Intellectual Climate in College Environments." *Harvard Ed R* 33:5–41 w '63. *
19. THISTLETHWAITE, DONALD L. Chap. 21, "The College Environment as a Determinant of Research Potentiality," pp. 265–77. In *Scientific Creativity: Its Recognition and Development.* Edited by Calvin W. Taylor and Frank Barron. New York: John Wiley & Sons, Inc., 1963. Pp. xxiv, 419. * (*PA* 38:2689)

[93]

★**Eysenck Personality Inventory.** High school and college and adults; 1963; revision of *Maudsley Personality Inventory;* 3 scores: extraversion, neuroticism, lie; Forms A, B (2 pages); preliminary manual (16 pages); no data on reliability of the lie scale; British norms only; no norms for the lie scale; $3 per 25 tests; $1.50 per set of scoring stencils; 50¢ per manual; $1.75 per specimen set; postage extra; [15–20] minutes; H. J. Eysenck and Sybil B. G. Eysenck; Educational and Industrial Testing Service. (British edition: University of London Press Ltd.) *

REFERENCES

1. EYSENCK, SYBIL B. G., AND EYSENCK, HANS J. "An Experimental Investigation of 'Desirability' Response Set in a Personality Questionnaire." *Life Sci* 5:343-55 My '63. * (*PA* 38:2712)

JAMES C. LINGOES, *Associate Professor of Psychology, The University of Michigan, Ann Arbor, Michigan.*

The *Eysenck Personality Inventory* (EPI), like the *Maudsley Personality Inventory* (MPI), is an instrument intended to measure the two most important sources of personality questionnaire variance found by Eysenck in a large number of factor analytic studies, i.e., extraversion-introversion (E) and neuroticism-stability (N). Although the EPI and MPI are differently named, they are the same tests in respect to principal authorship, theoretical motivation, traits measured, and methodological derivation. Indeed some items in the two tests are but rewordings of each other, e.g., "Do other people regard you as a lively individual?" (item 44, MPI); "Do other people think of you as being very lively?" (item 27, Form A, EPI); and, "Are you rather lively?" (item 17, Form B, EPI).

Despite the above similarities, nowhere is it stated in the EPI manual that the EPI is a *revision* of the MPI. Nevertheless, the authors explicitly invoke the similarity in respect to content and the high, but regrettably omitted, correlations between the EPI and MPI to buttress their claims for the theoretical and experimental validity of the newer test. In addition, the authors put forth the EPI manual as a preliminary supplement to the MPI manual, further confirming the relatedness of these two tests. Without belaboring the point much more, it is unfortunate, for whatever reasons, that this particular aspect of the status of the EPI was left unclear.

It is this reviewer's opinion that the EPI is in fact a revision of the MPI and has a number of advantages over the latter, the most important of which are: (*a*) the presence of two parallel forms, thus permitting retesting for experimental purposes or increasing the reliability of the instrument; (*b*) the addition in each form of nine different items adapted from the Lie scale of the MMPI to tap one kind of test taking attitude, i.e., to put oneself in a socially favorable light; and (*c*) a better selection of items to minimize the correlation between the two measures, E and N (although further replication with larger and more diverse samples of psychotics than the reported one of size 90 will be needed to substantiate this particular improvement). For non-psychotic samples orthogonality seems adequate.

In regard to the inclusion of a Lie scale (L), although this is a commendable addition in principle, it is strongly suspected that such a scale will prove neither more nor less effective in this test than it has been in the MMPI, the clinical consensus being that the more sophisticated and intelligent examinee can easily avoid this obvious form of deception and that the L scale is probably more useful as a personality measure than a validity scale. One might have hoped for a better set of items or an improved psychometric approach to this important problem with our present knowledge of test taking attitudes. Having adopted the Lie scale, however, the authors could have at least provided norms for L and indicated the equivalent forms reliability coefficient, as well as the correlations between L and E and N for both forms.

Although many of the criticisms leveled against the MPI apply equally to the EPI— e.g., the lack of interpretative richness in a two-dimensional approach to personality for clinical purposes—an additional point can be made about the two forms of the EPI relative to the MPI in the form of the following argument.

If the EPI and MPI, in respect to both E and N, correlate as high or higher than both forms within the EPI, then to that extent the MPI can be considered yet another form of the EPI. If one or both forms of the EPI correlate significantly higher with the MPI than is indicated by the equivalent forms coefficient of around .75 for E and .86 for N of the EPI, then if there are to be only two forms, the MPI should be one of them. On the other hand, if the MPI correlates much less with either form than the forms do with one another, then it is difficult to see how anyone could entertain the hypothesis, especially in reference to E, that univocal scales for these two important dimensions have been constructed. Furthermore, the authors' appeal to the large amount of experimental findings based upon the MPI could not suffice to carry or support EPI validity.

Until the relationships between the MPI and the EPI have been clarified or EPI's superiority has been established, administration of both tests is recommended, or, if only one is practicable, the MPI is to be preferred, since more is known about it. If the EPI is used, however, it will be necessary to establish norms other than the British norms provided in the manual.

[94]

★FIRO-B: [Fundamental Interpersonal Relations Orientation—Behavior]. High school and adults; 1957–61; 6 scores: expressed inclusion, wanted inclusion, expressed control, wanted control, expressed affection, wanted affection; 1 form ('57, 2 pages); no specific manual (technical data are presented in Chapter 4 of 2 below); hectographed norms ['61, 1 page]; no high school norms; 8¢ per test; $1 per scoring template; $6.50 per text ('58, 275 pages, published by Holt, Rinehart & Winston, Inc.); postage extra; (8–15) minutes; William C. Schutz; the Author. *

REFERENCES

1. BENNIS, WARREN; BURKE, RICHARD; CUTTER, HENRY; HARRINGTON, HERBERT; AND HOFFMAN, JOYCE. "A Note on Some Problems of Measurement and Prediction in a Training Group." Group Psychother 10:328–41 D '57. * (PA 33:5971)
2. SCHUTZ, WILLIAM C. FIRO: A Three-Dimensional Theory of Interpersonal Behavior. New York: Holt, Rinehart & Winston, Inc., 1958. Pp. xiii, 267. * (PA 33:2479)
3. GROSS, RICHARD LOUIE. Therapy Group Composition: Personal-Interpersonal Variable. Doctor's thesis, University of Utah (Salt Lake City, Utah), 1959. (DA 20:3377)
4. SCHUTZ, WILLIAM C., AND GROSS, EUGENE F. "The FIRO Theory of Interpersonal Behavior: Empirical Tests and Applications to Business Administration," pp. 161–72. In Contributions to Scientific Research in Management. The Proceedings of the Scientific Program Following the Dedication of the Western Data Processing Center, Graduate School of Business Administration, January 29–30, 1959. [Los Angeles, Calif.: the Center, 1959.] Pp. xi, 172. *
5. BORG, WALTER R. "Prediction of Small Group Role Behavior From Personality Variables." J Abn & Social Psychol 60:112–6 Ja '60. * (PA 34:7528)
6. FISKE, DONALD W. "Variability Among Peer Ratings in Different Situations." Ed & Psychol Meas 20:283–92 su '60. * (PA 35:6337)
7. HAINES, LEWIS EDGAR. An Evaluation of the FIRO-B and the EPPS for Predicting College Roommate Compatibility. Doctor's thesis, Washington State University (Pullman, Wash.), 1960. (DA 21:2173)
8. GARD, JOHN GRIFFIN. Fundamental Interpersonal Relations Orientations in Clinical Groups. Doctor's thesis, University of Pittsburgh (Pittsburgh, Pa.), 1961. (DA 22:4080)
9. SCHUTZ, WILLIAM C. Chap. 4, "The Ego, FIRO Theory and the Leader as Completer," pp. 48–65. In Leadership and Interpersonal Behavior. Edited by Luigi Petrullo and Bernard M. Bass. New York: Holt, Rinehart & Winston, Inc., 1961. Pp. xxxiv, 382. * (PA 36:1GF82P)
10. SCHUTZ, WILLIAM C. "On Group Composition." J Abn & Social Psychol 62:275–81 Mr '61. * (PA 36:4GE75S)
11. VODACEK, JOHN, JR. A Study of the Relationship of FIRO-B Measures of Compatibility to Teacher Satisfaction and Congruence of Role Expectations for the Principal. Doctor's thesis, University of Wisconsin (Madison, Wis.), 1961. (DA 22:1895)
12. CONNERS, C. KEITH. "Birth Order and Needs for Affiliation." J Personality 31:408–16 S '63. *
13. LORR, MAURICE, AND McNAIR, DOUGLAS M. "An Interpersonal Behavior Circle." J Abn & Social Psychol 67:68–75 Jl '63. * (PA 38:765)
14. SCHUTZ, WILLIAM C. Chap. 10, "The FIRO Theory of Interpersonal Behavior," pp. 141–63. In Educational Research: New Perspectives. Edited by Jack A. Culbertson and Stephen P. Hensley. Danville, Ill.: Interstate Printers & Publishers, Inc., 1963. Pp. ix, 374. *
15. SMITH, PETER B. "Differentiation Between Sociometric Rankings: A Test of Four Theories." Human Relations 16:335–50 N '63. * (PA 38:5901)

For excerpts from related reviews, see B432.

[95]

Family Adjustment Test. Ages 12 and over; 1952–54; title on test is Elias Family Opinion Survey; 11 scores: attitudes toward mother, attitudes toward father, father-mother attitude quotient, oedipal, struggle for independence, parent-child friction-harmony, interparental friction-harmony, family inferiority-superiority, rejection of child, parental qualities, total; 1 form ('52, 6 pages); manual ('54, 4 pages); $4 per 25 tests; $1 per specimen set (must be purchased to obtain manual and key); cash orders postpaid; (35–45) minutes; Gabriel Elias; Psychometric Affiliates. *

REFERENCES

1–6. See 5:53.

JOHN ELDERKIN BELL, Program Director, National Institute of Mental Health, United States Public Health Service, San Francisco, California.

The critical issue with this well developed test is to identify precisely what it measures. The instructions ask the subject to respond to 114 statements through giving "opinions only about the general family life that existed in your neighborhood when you were a child." It is assumed that this leads to an expression of feelings directly related to the current adjustment of the subject and his family. More particularly, the test is "designed to measure feelings of intrafamily homeyness—homelessness."

Efforts to determine validity have shown the test to differentiate sharply (almost no overlap) between institutionalized juvenile delinquents and matched youths identified by club leaders as from families "as homey as the most homey quarter of New York State families." The homelessness scores are related to age, increasing from ages 10 to 19, then tapering off to a constant level; to sex, male scores being higher than female at all ages; and to extreme poverty as found in city slum or rural shanty economic levels. In contrast, when age, sex, and extreme poverty were held constant, no significant differences were found among racial groups (white, colored, Indian, and yellow); religious groups (Catholic, Hebrew, Mohammedan, and Protestant, as well as among various Protestant subgroups); residents of New York City and towns, cities, and farms of Arkansas. Nor were homelessness scores found to be related to size of family, birth order, mother's occupation, regularity of testee's church attendance, his birthplace or that of his parents, and his nationality descent. Thus, the author claims that the test "appears to be largely culture-free; and differences in race, religion, residence, nationality, and intelligence can be disregarded in its interpretation."

But can they be? Are these factors operative but masked because of the test items and instructions? The family is an open system very much influenced by the community and culture of which it is a part. Family solidarity is only one of the characteristics of the family responsive to these broad influences. A test of "homeyness" that does not reflect cultural variation may not be a test of this variable at all, but of some other which would be worth measuring only if we knew what it is that we are measuring.

Does the test measure feelings of family solidarity? How are we to know? And, if so, are we measuring a generalization based on years of family living or feelings associated with a single or relatively few concrete instances remembered from the distant past or the present moment?

Do we perhaps measure a different approach to the test as we give it to children of varying ages, and thus gain information less about feelings towards the family than about age-level responses to test instructions?

Or does the test measure a prevailing mood, called into expression by the emotionally toned words and phrases of the test items? Are we collecting data on a general positive or negative orientation to the immediate life circumstances in which the subject's mood is being engendered, rather than to his family?

Or does his test performance represent a sincere aim to subsume the community experiences at a historical period when he was a child? Obviously, history is modified by the personal characteristics of the historian, and by his own family experiences, but it may have more rather than less relationship to community data than to his own family.

These are only a few possible hypotheses about what the test measures; until such suggestions and others that might be even more pertinent are tested out, we shall need extreme caution in attributing the results to "homeyness."

For a review by Albert Ellis, see 5:53.

[96]

★**Famous Sayings.** Grades 9-16 and business and industry; 1958, c1957-58; 4 scores: conventional mores, hostility, fear of failure, social acquiescence; Form 1 ('58, c1957-58, 4 pages); manual ('58, 19 pages, reprint of 6 below); $4.50 per set of test materials; $4 per 50 tests; $1.50 per manual; cash orders postpaid; specimen set not available; (15-30) minutes; Bernard M. Bass; Psychological Test Specialists. *

REFERENCES
1. BASS, BERNARD M. "Development and Evaluation of a Scale for Measuring Social Acquiescence." *J Abn & Social Psychol* 53:296-9 N '56. * (*PA* 32:4058)
2. BASS, BERNARD M. "Development of a Structured Disguised Personality Test." *J Appl Psychol* 40:393-7 D '56. * (*PA* 32:1350)
3. KIM, K. S. *The Use of the ACE and the Revised Famous Sayings Test in the Prediction of Academic Achievement.* Master's thesis, Louisiana State University (Baton Rouge, La.), 1956.
4. PALMER, GEORGE J., JR. *Discrimination of Psychopaths, Normal Prisoners and Non-Prisoners With a Disguised Structured Technique.* Master's thesis, Louisiana State University (Baton Rouge, La.), 1956.
5. BASS, BERNARD. "Validity Studies of a Proverbs Personality Test." *J Appl Psychol* 41:158-60 Je '57. * (*PA* 33:2352)
6. BASS, BERNARD M. "Famous Sayings Test: General Manual." *Psychol Rep* 4:479-97 S '58. * (*PA* 33:5073)
7. GAIER, EUGENE L., AND BASS, BERNARD M. "Regional Differences in Interrelations Among Authoritarianism, Acquiescence, and Ethnocentrism." *J Social Psychol* 49:47-51 F '59. * (*PA* 35:4782)
8. COUCH, ARTHUR, AND KENISTON, KENNETH. "Yeasayers and Naysayers: Agreeing Response Set as a Personality Variable." *J Abn & Social Psychol* 60:151-74 Mr '60. * (*PA* 34:7376)
9. VIDULICH, ROBERT N., AND BASS, BERNARD M. "Relation of Selected Personality and Attitude Scales to the Famous Sayings Test." *Psychol Rep* 7:259-60 O '60. * (*PA* 35:2215)
10. HUSEK, T. R. "Acquiescence as a Response Set and as a Personality Characteristic." *Ed & Psychol Meas* 21:295-307 su '61. * (*PA* 36:2HE95H)
11. MURSTEIN, BERNARD I. "The Relation of the Famous Sayings Test to Self- and Ideal-Self-Adjustment." Abstract. *J Consult Psychol* 25:368 Ag '61. * (*PA* 37:1312)
12. SHAW, MARVIN E. "Some Correlates of Social Acquiescence." *J Social Psychol* 55:133-41 O '61. * (*PA* 36:4HE33S)
13. SHUMSKY, WALTER; KONICK, ANDREW; AND WARD, GEORGE, II. "A Note Concerning Extreme Position Response Sets and the California F Scale." *Proc W Va Acad Sci* 34:194-5 N '62. *
14. *Normative Information: Manager and Executive Testing.* New York: Richardson, Bellows, Henry & Co., Inc., May 1963. Pp. 45. *
15. BRAUN, JOHN R., AND DUBE, C. S., II. "Note on a Faking Study With the Famous Sayings Test." *Psychol Rep* 13:878 D '63. * (*PA* 38:8403)
16. COPPINGER, NEIL W.; BORTNER, RAYMAN W.; AND SAUCER, RAYFORD T. "A Factor Analysis of Psychological Deficit." *J Genetic Psychol* 103:23-43 S '63. * (*PA* 39:174)
17. FRYE, ROLAND L., AND BASS, BERNARD M. "Behavior in a Group Related to Tested Social Acquiescence." *J Social Psychol* 61:263-6 D '63. *

WESLEY C. BECKER, *Professor of Psychology, University of Illinois, Urbana, Illinois.*

Famous Sayings is a relatively new personality test devised with the hope of providing measures which are less transparent to the test taker than those found in the typical personality inventory. The test consists of 130 sayings or proverbs with which the testee is to indicate his agreement or disagreement. The initial item pool for the test was formed by selecting, *a priori,* 20 sayings which might be relevant to each of 13 needs from Murray's system of classification. Factor analysis of the 13 preliminary scales revealed 3 content factors which were labeled Conventional Mores (CM),

Hostility (HO), and Fear of Failure (FF). An item analysis on a new sample was carried out to determine the scoring system. After examining reliabilities, 10 new items were written for the FF scale. For college sophomores, the corrected split-half reliabilities for the 30-item scales are: CM, .73; HO, .69; and FF, .75. These reliabilities are too low to consider using the test for making decisions in individual cases. Intercorrelations among the scales approach an average of .50 for a heterogeneous sample. Homogeneous samples (prisoners and college students) yield lower and conflicting intercorrelations.

A fourth scale, Social Acquiescence (SA), was developed to measure the tendency to accept "a wide variety of generalizations concerning how persons behave or should behave." SA was assumed to be the factor which accounted for the moderate correlations among the first three scales when a heterogeneous population was used. The SA scale consists of 56 items which differentiated persons who agreed with many proverbs from those who agreed with few. Fifteen items in the SA scale overlap with CM, HO, or FF. The author correctly suggests that it may be desirable to remove the overlap for some research purposes. With a sample of West Coast residents and southern college students the corrected split-half reliability of the full SA scale (including the overlapping items) was .92. For 1,491 Louisiana college freshmen the reliability was .81 (KR 21).

Bass has undertaken a number of validity studies and is to be commended for presenting the findings in a straightforward manner. CM, HO, and FF differentiate salesmen from non-salesmen, prison inmates from non-inmates, college students from high school students, and Southerners from non-Southerners in ways consistent with the construct implications of the scales. The magnitude of the differences for salesmen is not sufficient to warrant the test's use as a sole selection device in personnel work, but it might contribute some additional variance as part of a selection battery. The scales have not been found useful in predicting scholastic success, the success of factory supervisors, or the success of grocery products salesmen or sales supervisors. Two studies have related scores from *Famous Sayings* to other self-report measures using college samples (5, 9). A number of correla-

tions, usually on the order of .25 to .30, were found with CM and HO. Conventional Mores shows positive correlations with self-report measures of traits labeled sociability, cooperativeness, conservatism, nurturance, affiliation, and conscientiousness, and negative correlations with ethnocentrism and autonomy. Hostility correlates positively with other measures labeled aggression and suspicious-jealous, and negatively with emotional stability, responsibility, and maturity. Fear of Failure to date has failed to relate to other questionnaire trait measures. Social Acquiescence correlates in the .40's with peer nominations of "likes to help" and "thinks well of most," and in the high .20's and low .30's with questionnaire measures of sociability.

The author suggests that the test might best be used as an "industrial and professional screening and classification technique." While the author clearly indicates the test's shortcomings and advises the industrial user to develop his own validity data, the indications from presently available reliability and validity evidence are that *Famous Sayings* is not likely to contribute much to decision making in industry. The Social Acquiescence scale may turn out to have some value in prediction situations, but the reviewer believes it is the responsibility of the test developer to demonstrate this before recommending usage in applied settings. One critical point in judging the potential value of the test over other self-report devices has not yet been examined, namely, the degree to which the test can be faked to make a good impression. The reviewer is not convinced that the test is as unstructured for the subject as the author assumes. Empirical examination of this question is needed.

For the most part, the reviewer's critical reservations about the usefulness of this test reflect the excellent job its author has done in exploring and reporting on the limitations of its construct, concurrent, and predictive validity.

ROBERT L. THORNDIKE, *Professor of Education, and Head, Department of Psychological Foundations, Teachers College, Columbia University, New York, New York.*

In this instrument the author has attempted to devise a structured and objectively scorable, but indirect, measure of three dimensions of personality content which he designates Conventional Mores, Hostility, and Fear of Failure, and one dimension of response style, Social Acquiescence. Unfortunately, though in his discussion the author recognizes the significance of acquiescence as a response set influencing inventory responses, in his instrument he makes no provision for controlling it. In all instances, scoring is based on the "Yes" and "?" responses. Thus, his first three scores are contaminated to an unknown degree by the stylistic factor that his fourth score undertakes to measure. The potential user is left even more in the dark because the manual does not report any correlations between Social Acquiescence and the other three scores. One would like to know what the reliability of the other dimensions would be if the acquiescence factor were balanced out with items keyed both "Yes" and "No," and what would happen to the scale intercorrelations under these circumstances. The reviewer suspects that Hostility would then show fairly substantial negative correlations with Conventional Mores and Fear of Failure.

At least one of the content scores may be a reflection of another stylistic factor. It may be that rather than "hostility" we should speak of "readiness to endorse negatively toned statements." Maybe this is the essence of hostility. The point, however, is that what produces this reaction may be a relatively superficial response set rather than something deep-seated in the personality dynamics of the individual.

The author also seems to be going rather beyond his data in applying the designation "fear of failure" to a group of items that seem to center around the achievement motif. Possibly this *is* the underlying dynamic, but the author presents little to document this conclusion.

As is common with most personality appraisal devices, the evidence on validity is rather unsatisfying. It consists of an assortment of differences in group means, a few modest correlations with scores or ratings on ability and personality tests, and a group of largely non-significant correlations with sales success.

Though the reviewer would be willing to accord *Famous Sayings* the status of an instrument suitable for research and exploratory studies, he questions whether in its present form it would repay time spent upon it.

[97]

Fatigue Scales Kit. Adults; 1944–54; 3 scales; hectographed manual ('54, 4 pages); $5 per set of 25 sets of the 3 scales and manual; $3 per 50 copies of any one scale; cash orders postpaid; specimen set not available; [10] minutes; [Willard A. Kerr]; Psychometric Affiliates. *

a) INDUSTRIAL SUBJECTIVE FATIGUE AND EUPHORIA SCALES. Adults; 1944–54; 2 scores: fatigue, unpleasantness; 1 form ('54, 1 page, identical with scale published in 1944).

b) RETROSPECTIVE WORK CURVE FEELINGS FOR NATIONAL RESEARCH PROGRAM ON EMPLOYEE FEELINGS AT WORK. Adults; 1 form ('54, 1 page).

c) STUDY OF DAY [MOTHER'S DAY FATIGUE SCALE]. Housewives; 1 form ('54, 1 page); no data on validity.

REFERENCES

1. GRIFFITH, JOHN W.; KERR, WILLARD A.; MAYO, THOMAS B., JR.; AND TOPAL, JOHN R. "Changes in Subjective Fatigue and Readiness for Work During the Eight-Hour Shift." *J Appl Psychol* 34:163–6 Je '50. * (PA 25:4014)

RICHARD S. BARRETT, *Associate Professor of Management Engineering and Psychology, New York University, New York, New York.*

The three Fatigue Scales are each printed on a single sheet of paper, to be used as a tear ballot, that is, the subject is instructed to "answer each of these questions by *TEARING THE PAPER WITH YOUR FINGERS* at the points where you would check your answers if you were using a pencil." Such a format limits the number of questions which can be asked since the scales must be printed on the edge of the paper. In addition to age and sex, the respondents can report the hours when they are most tired, how tired they are at the moment, what kind of activity they find most tiring, etc.

The manual omits essential information such as the name of the author, the conditions under which normative and other data were collected, and the justification behind statements such as the following, quoted in its entirety, regarding the reliability of one Fatigue Scale: "Various sub-samples yield similar subjective fatigue curves. This implies a substantial level of reliability."

Anyone who wishes to obtain ratings of fatigue can develop as valuable a scale in a few minutes.

[98]

★**The Forty-Eight Item Counseling Evaluation Test.** Adolescents and adults; 1963; 7 problem area scores: anxiety-tension-stress, compulsive-obsessive-rigid behavior, depressive-defeatist thoughts and feelings, friendship-socialization, religious-philosophical goals, inadequacy feelings and behavior, total; 1 form (4 pages); manual (15 pages plus copy of test); no data on reliability of subscores; $8 per examiner's kit of 25 tests, key, and manual; $6.50 per 25 tests; 50¢

per key; $2 per manual; postpaid; (10–20) minutes; Frank B. McMahon; Western Psychological Services. *

[99]

The Freeman Anxiety Neurosis and Psychosomatic Test. Mental patients; 1952–55; title on test is *The Freeman AN and PS Test;* 9 scores: anxiety neurosis, psychosomatic syndrome, and 7 subscores; 1 form ('52, 10 pages); revised manual ('55, 11 pages); revised profile ('55, 1 page); no norms for subscores; $1.75 per 10 tests; $1.25 per manual; postage extra; specimen set not available; administration time not reported; M. J. Freeman; Grune & Stratton, Inc. *

REFERENCES

1–3. See 5:55.
4. ALPERT, RICHARD, AND HABER, RALPH NORMAN. "Anxiety in Academic Achievement Situations." *J Abn & Social Psychol* 61:207–15 S '60. * (*PA* 35:5357)
5. MEYERS, WILLIAM J., AND HOHLE, RAYMOND H. "Questionnaire-Anxiety and Social Conformity." *Psychol Rep* 11:436 O '62. *
6. ACKER, CHARLES W. "Personality Concomitants of Autonomic Balance: 2, Inventory Measures." *J Proj Tech* 27:20–2 Mr '63. *
7. GOLDSTEIN, IRIS BALSHAN. "A Comparison Between Taylor's and Freeman's Manifest Anxiety Scales." Abstract. *J Consult Psychol* 27:466 O '63. *

GERALD A. MENDELSOHN, *Assistant Professor of Psychology, University of California, Berkeley, California.*

This instrument purports to provide a measure of "the nuclear anxiety structure underlying the symptom complex of anxiety neurosis, psychosomatic involvements and the particular neurosis trends of this emotional disorder." It consists of two major parts, the Anxiety Neurosis (or Manifest Anxiety) Test and the Psychosomatic Syndrome Test. In all, nine variables are mentioned in the manual—six diagnostic categories: anxiety neurosis, psychosomatic syndrome, neurasthenia, psychasthenia, conversion hysteria, and hypochondriasis; and three structural types: overconscientious (perfectionistic), comfort (conflict-avoidance), and composite (bi-polar: overconscientious and comfort). In fact, however, the validity data available for the test are relevant only to the anxiety neurosis and psychosomatic syndrome variables.

The items of the test are of two kinds, judgments about the way people in general behave, e.g., "One who often loses his temper feels sorry afterwards. Yes ( ) No ( )," and a checklist of symptoms of both a physical and psychological nature, such as "Headcolds" and "Frequent discouragement." It is claimed that this format and the instructions for the test disguise its intent and "immeasurably" reduce or eliminate faking. Unfortunately, no data whatever are offered to support these assertions, nor is there any provision for assessing

the presence of faking in an individual protocol. Thus, two of the "advancements in personality testing" claimed for this instrument are only assumptions.

Kuder-Richardson reliability coefficients for Anxiety Neurosis and Psychosomatic Syndrome are, respectively, .73 and .81, but they are based only on the responses of normal, non-hospitalized male subjects ($n = 100$). While the coefficients indicate a level of internal consistency adequate by present day standards, there is reason to question their generality. Further, there is no information about the stability of scores, since test-retest data are lacking. A considerable amount of additional work would be necessary to obtain an adequate assessment of the reliability of the test.

The criterion group used in validating the Anxiety Neurosis score consisted of hospitalized patients, not necessarily from neuropsychiatric wards, judged by physicians and psychiatrists to display severe manifest anxiety, i.e., "through the behavior of fear and apprehension to an abnormal degree." Their responses to an initial item pool (whose origin is not indicated) were compared to those of hospitalized and non-hospitalized normals and those items which differentiated significantly were combined to produce a total score which was cross validated on new samples. The criterion group seems to have been reasonably well selected, but since the variable of hospitalization makes some difference, it would have been useful to include an unhospitalized manifest anxiety group in developing the test. The means of the criterion and control groups in the cross validation study are significantly different, but using the cutoff score for a diagnosis of manifest anxiety suggested in the manual produces a false positive rate of 30 per cent and a false negative rate of about 40 per cent, both rather high. No data relating the anxiety measure to other test scores are provided in the manual, but an independent study by Ends and Page (*3*) reports pre- and post-therapy correlations of the Freeman and Taylor Manifest Anxiety scores as .06 and .24 and of the Freeman and Pt scale as .14 and .35. These are disappointingly low.

The criterion group used in the validation of the Psychosomatic Syndrome section consisted of hospitalized patients with illnesses for which no organic basis could be found by an examining physician during a (minimum) 30-day observation period. While the criterion group consists of males and females, only males were used for the normal control group. The test author, in an independent paper (*1*), considers this a limitation of the test, but the manual makes no mention of this, nor of the failure to match the criterion and control groups for age. The differentiation of the groups is better for the Psychosomatic Syndrome than for the Anxiety Neurosis part of the test, false positives constituting 30 per cent and false negatives 20 per cent of the cross validation sample. However, in light of the author's statement in the 1950 paper that the test should be administered only after "a medical examination which discloses no organic basis for the physical complaint," it becomes difficult to perceive the utility of the instrument. If the assessment of a psychosomatic syndrome is to be made only after the same assessment has already been made more directly, what purpose does the test serve?

As noted before, validation data are available only for the two basic scores. Scoring of the other diagnostic categories is based on the symptoms checked, but the rationale or evidence for categorizing items as pertaining to one syndrome as opposed to another is not included. Likewise, the system for determining the structural type is based upon a content system which is not explicitly described. The expected test performance of only the comfort type is discussed in the manual, once again with no supporting data. The utility of these additional scores is thus impossible to assess.

The manual supplied with the test is inadequate from a number of standpoints. There is a minimum of validation data, the limitations of the instrument noted elsewhere by the author are omitted, and there is much jargon and unclear writing. Basically, the manual does not provide the test user with the information necessary to apply the instrument sensibly.

In summary, this reviewer finds little utility for the *Freeman Anxiety Neurosis and Psychosomatic Test*. Given the inadequate quantity and quality of the validation and standardization data, other means of assessing anxiety (e.g., MMPI scales, and medical observation and examination) seem preferable.

ROBERT C. NICHOLS, *Program Director, National Merit Scholarship Corporation, Evanston, Illinois.*

This test, constructed for Freeman's doctoral dissertation at Claremont Graduate School, consists of two major groups of items: 141 "anxiety" items in which the subject gives his opinion about the thoughts, feelings, and behavior of "most people" or the "average person," and 98 "psychosomatic" items in which the subject indicates the physical and emotional symptoms or diseases he suffers frequently or constantly. Fifty-six of the "anxiety" items are scored as an "Anxiety Neurosis" (AN) scale and 78 of the "psychosomatic" items are scored as a "Psychosomatic Syndrome" (PS) scale. The remaining items are not used. Forty-two items of the PS scale are categorized, by an unstated method, into four subscales: Neurasthenia, Psychasthenia, Conversion Hysteria, and Hypochondriasis. On the basis of the relationship of the AN and PS scales the profile is classified as one of three structural types: Overconscientious Type (high AN with high PS), Comfort Type (low AN with high PS), and Composite Type (AN and PS about equal).

The subject marks his responses in the 10-page test booklet, and the test is scored by comparing the responses with a key in the manual. The test could be adapted to an answer sheet, however.

The 11-page manual (the cover is counted as one page) is inadequate and misleading so that it is necessary to refer to the two papers by Freeman (*1, 2*) to discover how the test was constructed. Although the manual implies that the scored items survived several item analyses of samples totaling 310 hospitalized patients and 461 "normals," only one item analysis was used actually to select items. Any item which differentiated 150 hospitalized patients diagnosed as showing manifest anxiety from 116 nonhospitalized students was used regardless of its showing on preliminary item analyses. Only 40 of the AN items significantly differentiated these groups, but since this 40 item scale had a reliability (KR 21) of only .49, 16 nonsignificant items were added, raising the reliability to .73. Seventy-one of the PS items significantly differentiated the groups and this scale had a reliability of .81. The last seven items of the PS scale were not included in the item analysis and are stated by the manual to be of "clinical value" only; yet they are included in the scoring key for the scale. The normative data presented in Table 4, however, seem to be based on the 71 item scale.

The recommended cutting scores in the manual are the intersections of percentage frequency distributions of 30 hospitalized anxiety patients and 100 heterogeneous normals. It should be pointed out, in addition to the obvious instability of cutting scores based on such small n's, that these cutting scores are optimal only in groups with equal numbers in the two categories. Even with this ideal base rate the errors of classification would be high.

The manual is almost completely lacking in statistical information about the scales. No correlations with other variables (not even the correlation between AN and PS) are presented. The only validity data is a table which shows that both AN and PS significantly discriminate cross validation groups of normals and hospitalized anxiety patients. The manual reports the sample size for both normal and hospitalized groups as 100, but elsewhere Freeman (1) reports the same comparison for the PS scale with identical means, standard deviations, and t-ratio, but with the n for the hospitalized group indicated as 30.

Other indications that the manual was hastily or carelessly put together are the reporting of the same normative data for the MA scale in both Tables 2 and 4 with the range given as 20 in the former and 29 in the latter; and in the bibliography there are errors in the titles of both of Freeman's articles and in the page reference of the first.

In view of these deficiencies the test cannot be recommended for use. Even the usual recommendation that more research be done does not seem to be called for in regard to this test. Additional tests which differentiate hospitalized mental patients from non-hospitalized normals are not needed and are essentially useless in practice. For the researcher interested in constructing scales to discriminate other groups, much better item pools are available than that represented by this test.

[100]

★G. C. Personality Development Record. High school; 1959; ratings by teachers on 9 traits; adapted from a form used in the schools of Newark, N.J.; 1 form ['59, 1 page]; no manual or other accessories; no data on reliability and validity; no norms; 38¢ per pad of 50 records, postage extra; [5] minutes; Guidance Centre. *

[101]

Goldstein-Scheerer Tests of Abstract and Concrete Thinking. Adults; 1941–51; individual; 1 form; 5 tests; manual ('41, 156 pages, see 9 below); supplementary manual ('47, 4 pages) for a and e; no data on reliability; no norms; $64 per complete set of test materials; $2.25 per manual; postpaid; [30–60] minutes; Kurt Goldstein, Martin Scheerer, and Louis Rosenberg (c, record booklet); Psychological Corporation. *

a) GOLDSTEIN-SCHEERER CUBE TEST. 1941–45; separate record booklets ('45, 6 pages) for designs 1–6, 7–12; $5.75 per set of 2 design booklets and supplementary manual; $4.50 per set of Kohs' blocks; $3.50 per 50 copies of either record booklet.

b) GLEB-GOLDSTEIN COLOR SORTING TEST. 1941–51; record booklet ('51, 4 pages); $14.50 per set of wool skeins; $2.80 per 50 record booklets.

c) GOLDSTEIN-SCHEERER OBJECT SORTING TEST. 1941–51; record booklet ('51, 8 pages); supplementary sheet ('51, 1 page) for experiment 3; $16 per set of objects; $4.20 per 50 record booklets; $1 per 50 supplementary sheets.

d) WEIGL-GOLDSTEIN-SCHEERER COLOR FORM SORTING TEST. 1941–45; record booklet ('45, 4 pages); $7.25 per set of blocks; $2.80 per 50 record booklets.

e) GOLDSTEIN-SCHEERER STICK TEST. 1941–45; record booklet ('45, 4 pages); $4.25 per set of sticks and supplementary manual; $2.80 per 50 record booklets.

REFERENCES

1–28. See 3:41.
29–49. See 5:57.
50. LIDZ, THEODORE; GAY, JAMES R.; AND TIETZE, CHRISTOPHER. "Intelligence in Cerebral Deficit States and Schizophrenia Measured by Kohs Block Test." Arch Neurol & Psychiatry 48:568–82 O '42. * (PA 17:862)
51. SHAPIRO, M. B. "Experimental Studies of a Perceptual Anomaly: 1, Initial Experiments." J Mental Sci 97:90–110 Ja '51. * (PA 25:6220)
52. McFIE, J., AND PIERCY, M. F. "Intellectual Impairment With Localized Cerebral Lesions." Brain 75:292–311 S '52. * (PA 27:7649)
53. LOVIBOND, S. H. "The Object Sorting Test and Conceptual Thinking in Schizophrenia." Austral J Psychol 6:52–70 Je '54. * (PA 29:6035)
54. YATES, AUBREY J. "The Validity of Some Psychological Tests of Brain Damage." Psychol B 51:359–79 Jl '54. *
55. BROWN, IRWIN. "Abstract and Concrete Behavior of Dysphasic Patients and Normal Subjects." J Speech & Hearing Disorders 20:35–42 Mr '55. * (PA 30:5083)
56. McGAUGHRAN, LAURENCE S., AND MORAN, LOUIS J. "'Conceptual Level' vs. 'Conceptual Area' Analysis of Object-Sorting Behaviour of Schizophrenic and Nonpsychiatric Groups." J Abn & Social Psychol 52:43–50 Ja '56. * (PA 31:3473)
57. HALPIN, VIRGINIA GOULD. "The Performance of Mentally Retarded Children on the Weigl-Goldstein-Scheerer Color Form Sorting Test." Am J Mental Def 62:916–9 Mr '58. * (PA 33:6537)
58. PAYNE, R. W.; MATTUSSEK, P.; AND GEORGE, E. I. "An Experimental Study of Schizophrenic Thought Disorder." J Mental Sci 105:627–52 Jl '59. * (PA 34:6384)
59. SEMEONOFF, BORIS. "An Analysis of the Counsellor Personality." Rorsch Newsl 4:13–20 Je '59. *
60. WECKOWICZ, T. E., AND BLEWETT, D. B. "Size Constancy and Abstract Thinking in Schizophrenic Patients." J Mental Sci 105:909–34 O '59. * (PA 34:6402)
61. PAYNE, R. W., AND HEWLETT, J. H. G. Chap. 1, "Thought Disorder in Psychotic Patients," pp. 3–104. In Experiments in Personality: Vol. 2, Psychodiagnostics and Psychodynamics. Edited by H. J. Eysenck. London: Routledge & Kegan Paul Ltd., 1960. Pp. viii, 294. *
62. SILVERSTEIN, A. B. "A Cluster Analysis of Object Sorting Behaviour." J Consult Psychol 24:98 F '60. * (PA 34:7864)
63. SILVERSTEIN, A. B. "Relations Between Intelligence and Conceptual Levels in Active and Passive Concept Formation." Psychol Rep 7:202 O '60. * (PA 35:1736)
64. KATES, SOLIS L.; KATES, WILLIAM W.; MICHAEL, JAMES; AND WALSH, TERRENCE M. "Categorization and Related Verbalizations in Deaf and Hearing Adolescents." J Ed Psychol 52:188–94 Ag '61. * (PA 38:2951)
65. NIELSEN, HELLE H. "Visual-Motor Functioning of Cerebral Palsied and Normal Children." Nordisk Psykologi 14(2):41–103 '62. * (PA 37:3551)
66. PAYNE, R. W., AND FRIEDLANDER, D. "A Short Battery

of Simple Tests for Measuring Overinclusive Thinking."
J Mental Sci 108:362–7 My '62. * (*PA* 37:3228)
    67. SILVERMAN, LLOYD H., AND SILVERMAN, DORIS K. "Ego
Impairment in Schizophrenia as Reflected in the Object Sorting Test." *J Abn & Social Psychol* 64:381–5 My '62. * (*PA*
38:1332)
    68. SILVERSTEIN, A. B., AND MOHAN, PHILIP J. "Perform-
ance of Mentally Retarded Adults on the Color Form Sorting
Test." *Am J Mental Def* 67:458–62 N '62. * (*PA* 37:5419)
    69. TUTKO, THOMAS A., AND SECHREST, LEE. "Conceptual
Performance and Personality Variables." *J Consult Psychol*
26:481 O '62. * (*PA* 39:1766)
    70. GOLDMAN, ALFRED E., AND LEVINE, MURRAY. "A De-
velopmental Study of Object Sorting." *Child Develop* 34:649–
66 S '63. * (*PA* 38:7924)
    71. PAYNE, R. W.; FRIEDLANDER, D.; LAVERTY, S. G.; AND
HADEN, P. "Overinclusive Thought Disorder in Chronic Schizophrenics and Its Response to 'Proketazine.' " *Brit J Psychiatry*
109:523–30 Jl '63. *
    72. SILVERSTEIN, A. B., AND MOHAN, PHILIP J. "Concep-
tual Area Analysis of the Test Performance of Mentally Retarded Adults." *J Abn & Social Psychol* 66:255–60 Mr '63. *
(*PA* 37:8165)

R. W. PAYNE, *Associate Professor of Psychology, Queen's University, Kingston, Ontario,
Canada.*

The authors developed the five tests of
abstract thinking which comprise this battery
after having had a great deal of experience
with brain damaged patients during and following the first world war. They believe that the
main effect of brain damage is "concreteness,"
an impairment of the "abstract attitude," which
they define in terms of the following eight
characteristics: (*a*) "To detach our ego from
the outerworld or from inner experiences."
(*b*) "To assume a mental set." (*c*) "To account for acts to oneself; to verbalize the
account." (*d*) "To shift reflectively from one
aspect of the situation to another." (*e*) "To
hold in mind simultaneously various aspects."
(*f*) "To grasp the essential of a given whole;
to break up a given whole into parts, to isolate
and to synthesize them." (*g*) "To abstract
common properties reflectively; to form hierarchic concepts." (*h*) "To plan ahead ideationally; to assume an attitude towards the
'mere possible' and to think or perform symbolically."

It is difficult, after reading this extensive
definition, to say precisely how the ability to
adopt the abstract attitude differs from general intelligence. If the operational definition
in terms of the five Goldstein tests is accepted,
the distinction becomes even more difficult,
because variations of these five tests have
nearly all been used in the past as measures of
general intelligence.

At least one study suggests that it may not
be possible to distinguish between "g" and
abstract ability as defined by Goldstein's tests.
Payne and Hewlett (*61*) assembled a large
battery of tests thought to measure "psychoti-

cism," general intelligence, psychomotor retardation, overinclusive thinking, and concreteness.
These were given to carefully matched groups
of 20 normals, 20 neurotics, 20 depressives,
and 20 schizophrenics. The tests were intercorrelated for all 80 subjects, and a factor
analysis carried out. Two relatively independent
factors of thought disorder, "retardation," and
"over-inclusive thinking" could be defined according to several criteria. A third independent
factor of "general intelligence" was obtained,
defined by such standard tests as the *Mill Hill
Vocabulary Scale*, the *Nufferno Level Test*,
and the *Wechsler-Bellevue Intelligence Scale*.
Ratings of concreteness were obtained from
the Goldstein-Scheerer color form and object
sorting tests, by objectifying and quantifying
the main levels of performance set out in some
detail in Goldstein and Scheerer's monograph
(*9*). The Goldstein-Scheerer test ratings
proved to be just as good measures of this
intelligence factor as any of the other measures,
and, like the other intelligence measures, were
unrelated to the two specific factors of thought
disorder obtained.

These findings do not, of course, invalidate
the proposition that brain damaged subjects
tend to do poorly on the Goldstein-Scheerer
tests. There is some evidence that tests of general intelligence *can* be used to differentiate
between brain damaged subjects and a matched
control group (*28*). Intelligence tests seem to
differentiate best if they are as little as possible
influenced by old learning.[1] Thus, for instance,
vocabulary tests differentiate poorly.

Unfortunately, as intelligence tests (or as
tests of the abstract attitude) the Goldstein-
Scheerer tests have several serious disadvantages. First of all, while a relatively standard
method of administration is described in the
monograph (and even here, there are serious
ambiguities), no standard system of scoring is
suggested for any of the tests. The psychologist
is left to assess the patient's performance subjectively. For these reasons, Goldstein and
Scheerer are unable to give objective standardization data of any sort for their battery,
nor are measures of reliability available.
Indeed, they seem to make the naive assumption that all normal people will be able to
perform all the tests perfectly. In view of the

[1] MEYER, V. Chap. 14, "Psychological Effects of Brain
Damage," pp. 529–65. In *Handbook of Abnormal Psychology:
An Experimental Approach.* Edited by H. J. Eysenck. New
York: Basic Books, Inc., 1961. Pp. xvi, 816. * (*PA* 35:6719)

considerable amount of precise verbal explanation expected in some of the tests, this assumption seems to be completely unwarranted. This objection alone would be sufficient for most clinical psychologists to prefer a test battery with a scoring system which has been standardized on the various groups (normals, functionals, and brain damaged) which they are likely to encounter in their practical experience.

The Goldstein-Scheerer tests have been used fairly widely in measuring "concreteness" in both brain damaged and schizophrenic patients. The fact that both groups are thought by some investigators to show this deficit, further emphasizes the need for accurate norms, if the tests are ever to be useful in differential diagnosis.

In addition to the general criteria for various levels of abstract performance on these tests, Goldstein and Scheerer describe in detail a large number of specific anomalies of test performance. There seems to be little doubt that these detailed descriptions are the result of years of careful clinical observation. However, it has never been demonstrated that these anomalies are related in any way, nor that they are all, in fact, associated with concreteness, as the authors assume. Indeed, it has never been demonstrated that the overall ratings of concreteness for each test are significantly correlated.

WEIGL-GOLDSTEIN-SCHEERER COLOR FORM SORTING TEST. This test consists of four small plastic squares, four triangles, and four circles, each reproduced in one of four colors. The subject is asked to sort them into groups (form a concept, e.g., color) and then to resort them in a different way (form a second concept, e.g., form). For those who fail, various relatively standard prompting procedures are adopted.

Bolles and Goldstein (3) studying 18 schizophrenic patients, and Hanfmann (7) studying a single case, report that schizophrenics are "concrete" on this test. However these studies can be dismissed, as no control group of any sort was tested. Payne, Matussek, and George (58) and Payne and Hewlett (61), developing their own standard scoring system, failed to find significant differences between schizophrenics, normals, and neurotics on this test.

McFie and Piercy (52), merely scoring the test "pass" or "fail," found that a sizeable proportion of brain damaged patients "passed"

the test, and Tooth (29) found the test able to differentiate significantly between brain damaged and normal cases, but not between brain damaged and neurotic patients. This literature seems to suggest that the range of brain damaged performance is so variable on this simple test that it is probably not useful diagnostically because a substantial proportion of all types of cases can complete the test perfectly.

GOLDSTEIN-SCHEERER OBJECT SORTING TEST. The object sorting test consists of a number of everyday objects which must be sorted into groups according to as many different principles as possible.

Some writers, on the basis of earlier studies (3, 7, 20), report schizophrenics to be concrete on this test. However these studies cannot be assessed, as no standard scoring system or control group was used. McGaughran [2] (47) and McGaughran and Moran (56) have developed a scoring system in which behaviour is assessed along two separate dimensions, "open-closed" (conceptual freedom or concreteness) assessed by the number of objects the concept covers, and an unrelated "public-private" dimension, which is the extent to which the concept is usual, or generally accepted. When scored in this way, there is no evidence,[3] (27, 53, 58, 61) that schizophrenic patients are abnormally concrete. However, they do tend to produce significantly more "private" sortings. Payne[4] has suggested that this is the result of overinclusive thinking. Lovibond (53), who formulated a similar hypothesis, has developed a standard method of rating overinclusive thinking from this test. Payne and others (61, 66, 71) have also suggested that a simple measure of overinclusive thinking can be derived from the "handing over" section of this test, which is merely the average number of objects selected as belonging together (a high score indicates overinclusion). Payne and Hewlett (61) and Payne and Friedlander (66) have published norms for normals, neurotics, depressives, and schizophrenics (but not brain damaged patients) for this score and have provided evidence, both factorial and in terms of its ability

2 McGAUGHRAN, LAURENCE S. "Predicting Language Behaviour From Object Sorting." *J Abn & Social Psychol* 49: 183–95 Ap '54. *
3 McCONAGHY, N. "The Use of an Object Sorting Test in Elucidating the Hereditary Factor in Schizophrenia." *J Neurol Neurosurg & Psychiatry* 22:243–6 Ag '59. *
4 PAYNE, R. W. Chap. 6, "Cognitive Abnormalities," pp. 193–261. In *Handbook of Abnormal Psychology: An Experimental Approach.* Edited by H. J. Eysenck. New York: Basic Books, Inc., 1961. Pp. xvi, 816. * (PA 35:6719)

to differentiate groups, of its validity. Over-inclusive thinking as assessed by this measure seems to be confined to schizophrenic patients.

There is some evidence that, unlike schizophrenics, brain damaged patients, as Goldstein initially suggested, are concrete on this test. McGaughran (47) found that, using his scoring system, brain damaged patients produced more "closed" (concrete) sortings. Other research,[5] using a very similar test, suggests that frontal lobe damage in particular may produce inability to perform this test. Unfortunately, there are still far too few norms using some such standard scoring system as McGaughran's for different groups of normals and functional patients, to make this test of practical value in detecting brain damage. At present it would seem therefore to be more useful in detecting overinclusive thinking, using either Payne's or Lovibond's techniques.

GELB-GOLDSTEIN COLOR SORTING TEST. The third sorting test in the Goldstein-Scheerer battery consists of a large number of skeins of wool of varying hue, brightness, and saturation. The subjects are required to sort the skeins into groups according to two different principles, "hue" and "brightness" (although the manual suggests that the authors themselves may not be clear about the difference between brightness and saturation; they do not seem to expect subjects ever to produce this third category). No objective scoring system has ever been devised, and this test appears neither to have been used or modified by other workers. This is perhaps because of the extreme difficulty in getting any subjects, normal or abnormal, to behave in the "abstract" ways specified in this rather obscure section of the manual.

GOLDSTEIN-SCHEERER CUBE TEST. The fourth test is quite unlike the three sorting tests so far. discussed. It is merely a modified version of the Kohs *Block Design Test*. The modification consists of a standard set of aids, given to subjects who cannot complete the design (e.g., copying from a life-size picture, from a picture divided up, from a model, etc.). It is amazing in view of the objective nature of this test that no standard scoring system

was suggested by the authors, although other workers (28, 30) have devised their own systems.

The studies which have been done using this test (28, 29, 30, 50) suggest that, like other nonverbal intelligence tests, the *Block Design Test* tends to differentiate between brain damaged subjects and other groups. However the overlap is extremely large, and the range of brain damaged performance is very wide, since it probably is largely a function of pre-illness intellectual level. This makes the test of very little practical value at the moment, as nearly all scores must be ambiguous. However, it does suggest that, if very extensive normative data were collected using, for instance, Boyd's (30) scoring system, for individuals of differing pre-illness IQ levels (as measured perhaps by vocabulary), a useful test for brain damage might ultimately emerge.

It is worth pointing out that one particular anomaly described by Goldstein and Scheerer, the "rotation" of constructed block patterns out of their proper orientation, has been subjected to a model of careful experimental analysis by Shapiro and has resulted in a new objective test which appears to be capable of detecting brain damage of a relatively specific type (associated with visual field and "oculomotor" defects).[6]

GOLDSTEIN-SCHEERER STICK TEST. This test requires the subject to copy patterns with small plastic sticks, and to reproduce them from memory. Again, no scoring system is suggested. so that no norms can be given. A number of characteristic anomalies shown by brain damaged patients are described, but no evidence is offered to support the author's contention that

6 SHAPIRO, M. B. "Experimental Studies of a Perceptual Anomaly: 1, Initial Experiments." *J Mental Sci* 97:90–110 Ja '51. *

SHAPIRO, M. B. "Experimental Studies of a Perceptual Anomaly: 2, Confirmatory and Explanatory Experiments." *J Mental Sci* 98:605–17 O '52. *

SHAPIRO, M. B. "Experimental Studies of a Perceptual Anomaly: 3, The Testing of an Explanatory Theory." *J Mental Sci* 99:394–409 Jl '53. *

SHAPIRO, M. B., AND TIZARD, BARBARA. "Experimental Studies of a Perceptual Anomaly: 6, The Application of the 'Peephole' Analogy to the Perception of 'Organic' Psychiatric Patients." *J Mental Sci* 104:792–800 Jl '58. *

SHAPIRO, M. B.; BRIERLEY, J.; SLATER, P.; AND BEECH, H. R. "Experimental Studies of a Perceptual Anomaly: 7, A New Explanation." *J Mental Sci* 108:655–68 S '62. * (PA 38:2989)

WILLIAMS, HAROLD L.; LUBIN, ARDIE; GIESEKING, CHARLES; AND RUBENSTEIN, IRVIN. "The Relation of Brain Injury and Visual Perception to Block Design Rotation." *J Consult Psychol* 20:275–80 Ag '56. * (PA 31:7983)

YATES, A. J. "Experimental Studies of a Perceptual Anomaly: 4, The Effect of Monocular Vision on Rotation." *J Mental Sci* 100:975–9 O '54. *

YATES, AUBREY J. "Experimental Studies of a Perceptual Anomaly: 5, Some Factors Influencing the Appearance of the Block Design Rotation Effect in Normal Subjects." *J Mental Sci* 102:761–71 O '56. *

5 RYLANDER, GÖSTA. *Personality Changes After Operations on the Frontal Lobes: A Clinical Study of 32 Cases.* Acta Psychiatrica et Neurologica Supplementum 20. Copenhagen: Ejnar Munksgaard, 1939. Pp. 327. *

HALSTEAD, WARD C. "Preliminary Analysis of Grouping Behaviour in Patients With Cerebral Injury by the Method of Equivalent and Non-equivalent Stimuli." *Am J Psychiatry* 96:1263–94 My '40. *

these are also due to concreteness. It may be the case that, like block design rotation, these abnormalities are perceptual in nature, and they may be related to very specific cortical or sub-cortical lesions. However, until the necessary research has been done, this test material cannot be put to any practical use. Unlike the other Goldstein tests, the stick test so far seems to have inspired little research to date.

The Goldstein-Scheerer test battery is at present of very limited practical value. Although it was intended to assess brain damage, it cannot be used for this purpose because of the lack of a standardized scoring system and the lack of any norms. However, one of the subtests in this battery, the Object Sorting Test, has been standardized by Lovibond (53) and by Payne and Hewlett (61) as a test of overinclusive thought disorder, which has been found to characterize only schizophrenic patients. Payne and Hewlett have published norms for small groups of normals, neurotics, depressives, and schizophrenics. There are at present, however, no data on the reliability of this test as a measure of schizophrenic thought disorder.

For reviews by Kate Levine Kogan, C. R. Strother (with Ludwig Immergluck), and O. L. Zangwill, see 3:41; for an excerpt from a related book review, see 3:42.

[102]

*Gordon Personal Inventory. Grades 8–16 and adults; 1956–63, c1955–63; 4 scores: cautiousness, original thinking, personal relations, vigor; 1 form ('63, c1955–56, identical with 1956 form except for format and wording changes in directions); 2 editions: hand scored (3 pages), machine scorable (2 pages); revised manual ('63, c1956–63, 20 pages); mimeographed notes on the scoring system ['63, 5 pages] available upon request; tentative norms for high school students; $3.15 per 35 tests of hand scored edition; $2.90 per 35 IBM test-answer sheets for machine scorable edition; 80¢ per set of scoring stencils for machine scorable edition; 60¢ per specimen set including the complementary *Gordon Personal Profile;* postage extra; (15–20) minutes; Leonard V. Gordon; Harcourt, Brace & World, Inc. *

REFERENCES

1. BASS, BERNARD M. "Normative Data Information Exchange, No. 11-5." *Personnel Psychol* 11:269–70 su '58. *
2. MCKINNEY, EVA DORIS. *The Relationships Between Certain Factors of Personality and Selected Components of Physical Fitness of College Freshmen Women.* Doctor's thesis, Boston University (Boston, Mass.), 1958. (*DA* 19:1287)
3. COCHRAN, WILLIAM MORGAN, JR. "A Correlation Comparison Between the Minnesota Multiphasic Personality Inventory and the Combined Gordon Personal Profile and Personal Inventory (Abstract)." *Proc W Va Acad Sci* 30:189 My '59. * (*PA* 34:2359, title only)
4. MAGAW, DAVID CURLEE. *Criminal Antisocial and Inadequate Personalities—A Clinical and Psychometric Comparison.* Doctor's thesis, Wayne State University (Detroit, Mich.), 1959. (*DA* 20:2144)
5. BRAUN, JOHN R. "Correlates of Ghiselli Self-Description Inventory Scores." *Psychol Rep* 9:727–8 D '61. *
6. BRAUN, JOHN R.; ALEXANDER, SUNYA; AND WEISS, RICHARD. "Relationship Between the Gordon Personal Inventory and Consensus of Peer Ratings." *Psychol Rep* 9:455 O '61. *
7. DUGAN, ROBERT D. "Validity Information Exchange, No. 14-01: D.O.T. Code 0-98.07, Manager, Insurance Office." *Personnel Psychol* 14:213–6 su '61. *
8. KRIEDT, PHILIP H., AND DAWSON, ROBERT I. "Response Set and the Prediction of Clerical Job Performance." *J Appl Psychol* 45:175–8 Je '61. * (*PA* 36:4HF75K)
9. RIED, BLANCHE ROSE. *The Development of a Prognostic Device for Job Success of the Medical Assistant Through the Correlation of In-School Evaluations With Employer Evaluation.* Doctor's thesis, New York University (New York, N.Y.), 1961. (*DA* 23:557)
10. BRAUN, JOHN R. "Effects of a Top Management Faking Set on the Gordon Personal Inventory." *Psychol Rep* 10:611–4 Je '62. * (*PA* 37:5006)
11. BRAUN, JOHN R. "Stereotypes of the Scientist as Seen With the Gordon Personal Profile and Gordon Personal Inventory." *J Psychol* 53:453–5 Ap '62. * (*PA* 37:107)
12. BRAUN, JOHN R. "Fakability of the Gordon Personal Inventory: Replication and Extension." *J Psychol* 55:441–4 Ap '63. * (*PA* 38:991)
13. WILLINGHAM, WARREN W., AND AMBLER, ROSALIE K. "The Relation of the Gordon Personal Inventory to Several External Criteria." Abstract. *J Consult Psychol* 27:460 O '63. *

CHARLES F. DICKEN, *Assistant Professor of Psychology, San Diego State College, San Diego, California.*

This inventory follows a rationale and format similar to those of the *Gordon Personal Profile.* The four traits measured, based on factor studies, and typical items are: cautiousness (C), "doesn't care much for excitement," "does not act on the spur of the moment"; original thinking (O), "a very original thinker," "likes to work primarily with ideas"; personal relations (P), "speaks nothing but the best about other people," "believes that all people are basically honest"; and vigor (V), "a very energetic worker," "full of vigor and vitality." As the items indicate, trait P is a matter of trustingness and patience with others rather than of outgoing sociability.

The items are arranged in tetrads of two favorable and two unfavorable items as in the Profile. The time required is 10 to 15 minutes. The scoring scheme of the latest revision is altered to eliminate negative scores but there is no change in the content or structure of the test.

Factor analysis of items, internal consistency analysis, and judgments of item social desirability were used in building the test. Empirical item selection was apparently not used. Intercorrelations among the scales are generally lower than for the Profile, though there is a moderate correlation ($r = .37$) between C and P in student samples. Correlations of the inventory with the Profile are low to moderate. None of the correlations exceeds .47.

The manual is conscientiously prepared. The

reliabilities of the scales are satisfactory, ranging from .77 to .84. There are a variety of norms. Validity studies in several different settings are cited. Validity data are not quite as extensive as for the Profile, and the external validity of the inventory does not seem as well established by the data available. Omission of empirical item selection in constructing the test may have limited its external validity. Most of the validity correlations do not rise above the .30's. There are some high negative correlations with external criteria. Sales criteria were correlated substantially and negatively with C in one sample, and with P in another.

No illustrative individual cases are provided for the inventory. The question of distortion is dealt with in the same manner as for the Profile, and there are data indicating only small changes under differing motivational conditions, although not as much data as for the Profile. Item transparency seems somewhat more of a problem than with the Profile, and again the reviewer would suggest use of a validity scale.

In summary, the *Gordon Personal Inventory* measures four normal personality traits by a method very similar to that devised for the *Gordon Personal Profile*. There is considerable evidence of validity, although it is somewhat less satisfactory than for the Profile. Empirical item selection was apparently not used in the inventory. The manual is of high quality. The inventory seems generally as satisfactory a measure of traits of this type as other self-report devices which are available, although the external validities reported are frequently quite modest.

ALFRED B. HEILBRUN, JR., *Associate Professor of Psychology, State University of Iowa, Iowa City, Iowa.*

The *Gordon Personal Inventory* (GPI) is a brief, largely self-administered questionnaire which provides measures of four personality traits, namely, cautiousness-impulsivity (C), original thinking-noninquisitiveness (O), personal relations (trust in and tolerance of people versus lack of trust in, and criticality of others) (P), and vigor (high versus low vitality) (V). The GPI is a replica of the *Gordon Personal Profile* in its derivation and format, and the manual recommends that the two tests be used in combination when there is interest in extending the breadth of personality assessment.

Gordon considers the GPI to have two principle attributes: (*a*) it was developed via a factor analytic approach, and (*b*) it presents its 20 items in a modified forced-choice format which requires the person to select one of four statements "most" like him and one "least" like him. Each of the four personality scales receives a score for each item with a weight of two assigned for a pair of responses which includes the most socially desirable response for the scale, a zero for a pair of responses which includes the least socially desirable response, and otherwise a one. Gordon suggests that this item format is less susceptible to faking for those individuals motivated to make a good impression. Evidence presented in the manual to support this contention is less cogent than that provided for the companion *Gordon Personal Profile*. In both cases it is assumed that job applicants are more likely to portray themselves favorably whereas counseling clients are more likely to be frank. However, the *Gordon Personal Profile* scores of job applicants were directly compared with employees, whereas GPI comparisons were made only between job applicants and counseling clients (real and simulated). Accordingly, the effects of possible motivation to make a good impression were not separated from group differences in level of adjustment for the GPI.

The percentile norms provided for the inventory are stable and fairly representative, separate norms being provided for males and females at the high school and college level and several occupational groups. Although Gordon recommends the development of local norms for specific testing populations, it would be useful if a "general population" type norm had been provided in the manual for those who wish to use the GPI with samples who are not young, highly educated, or selected from specific industrial work levels.

Reliability is reported in terms of split-half or internal consistency coefficients and is reasonably good (around .80) for all scales. Test-retest stability is not reported, but if the stability of the Profile scales can be assumed, the GPI should also be reasonably reliable over time.

Correlations among the GPI scales tend to be low (.45 or less) and, with the exception of scale O, correlations with measures of intelligence are negligible. Scale O shows a low positive relationship (.26 or less) to both verbal and quantitative tests of ability and a correlation of 31 with total ACE score.

Based upon the validity evidence presented in the manual, the GPI is open to the same criticism as the Profile, probably more so. Not only is there less evidence presented for the validity of the GPI (e.g., no correlations with peer and counselor ratings of the test variables), but the rather dubious procedure was repeated of assuming *any* significant relationship with a performance criterion represents scale validation. For example, the manual gives as validity evidence the finding that scales O and P correlate negatively with rated success as a salesman, whereas in another reported study validity was assumed because the same scales correlate positively with success in an underwater demolition training program. Unless there is some independent evidence or theory which would predict these relationships, the term validity must be treated skeptically. At least, however, the evidence presented in the manual suggests that the GPI scales do allow for group discriminations on certain industrial and training performance criteria.

Summarily, the GPI falls somewhat short of the Profile with respect to what has been accomplished in its development. In many respects a solid beginning has been made in establishing its usefulness as a brief personality measure, but in other respects (commented upon in this review) questions remain which demand further empirical investigation before the test user should employ the instrument without more than the usual caution.

For reviews by Benno G. Fricke and John A. Radcliffe, see 5:58 (2 excerpts).

[103]

Gordon Personal Profie. Grades 9–16 and adults; 1953–63, c1951–63; 4 scores: ascendancy, responsibility, emotional stability, sociability; 1 form ('63, c1951–53, identical with 1953 form except for format and wording changes in directions); 2 editions: hand scored (3 pages), machine scorable (2 pages); revised manual ('63, c1953–63, 27 pages); mimeographed notes on the scoring system ['63, 5 pages] available upon request; $3.15 per 35 tests of hand scored edition; $2.90 per 35 IBM test-answer sheets for machine scorable edition; 80¢ per set of scoring stencils for machine scorable edition; 60¢ per specimen set including the complementary *Gordon Personal Inventory;* postage extra; (15–20) minutes; Leonard V. Gordon; Harcourt, Brace & World, Inc. *

REFERENCES

1–16. See 5:59.
17. MUDGE, BERTRAM R. *A Study of the Relationship Between the Gordon Personal Profile and Academic Achievement in College.* Master's thesis, Boston University (Boston, Mass.), 1956.
18. DUFFICY, EDWARD C. *The Relationship Between Scores on the Otis Gamma Quick Scoring Mental Ability Test, the Gordon Personal Profile, and Success in Latin in a Minor Seminary.* Master's thesis, De Paul University (Chicago, Ill.), 1957.
19. WARNE, EARL KEITH. *A Study to Determine Whether the Gordon Personal Profile Will Tend to Measure the Success of Cadet Teachers.* Doctor's research study No. 1, Colorado State College (Greeley, Colo.), 1957.
20. ARBUCKLE, DUGALD S. "Self-Ratings and Test Scores on Two Standardized Personality Inventories." *Personnel & Guid J* 37:292–3 D '58. * (*PA* 34:2359, title only)
21. MCKINNEY, EVA DORIS. *The Relationships Between Certain Factors of Personality and Selected Components of Physical Fitness of College Freshmen Women.* Doctor's thesis, Boston University (Boston, Mass.), 1958. (*DA* 19:1287)
22. VAN BUSKIRK, WILLIAM L. "Normative Data Information Exchange, No. 11-16." *Personnel Psychol* 11:445–6 au '58. *
23. COCHRAN, WILLIAM MORGAN, JR. "A Correlation Comparison Between the Minnesota Multiphasic Personality Inventory and the Combined Gordon Personal Profile and Personal Inventory (Abstract)." *Proc W Va Acad Sci* 30:189 My '59. * (*PA* 34:2359, title only)
24. LOHMANN, KAJ; ZENGER, JOHN H.; AND WESCHLER, IRVING R. "Some Perceptual Changes During Sensitivity Training." *J Ed Res* 53:28–31 S '59. * (*PA* 34:5628)
25. MCCONAGHY, N. "The Use of an Object Sorting Test in Elucidating the Hereditary Factor in Schizophrenia." *J Neurol Neurosurg & Psychiatry* 22:243–6 Ag '59. * (*PA* 34:8166)
26. OAKES, FREDERICK, JR. *The Contribution of Certain Variables to the Academic Achievement of Gifted Seventh Grade Students in an Accelerated General Science Curriculum.* Doctor's thesis, New York University (New York, N.Y.), 1959. (*DA* 20:4002)
27. SMITH, D. D. "Traits and College Achievement." *Can J Psychol* 13:93–101 Je '59. * (*PA* 34:4780)
28. United States Naval Personnel Research Field Activity. "Normative Data Information Exchange, No. 12-4." *Personnel Psychol* 12:146–7 sp '59. *
29. ASH, PHILIP. "Validity Information Exchange, No. 13-05: D.O.T. Code 1-86.12, Salesman, Typewriters." *Personnel Psychol* 13:454 w '60. *
30. BROWN, ALAN W., AND LANDSBERGER, HENRY A. "The Sense of Responsibility Among Young Workers: Part 1, Definition and Measurement." *Occup Psychol* 34:1–14 Ja '60. * (*PA* 35:7236)
31. CAMPBELL, JOEL T.; PRIEN, ERICH P.; AND BRAILEY, LESTER B. "Predicting Performance Evaluations." *Personnel Psychol* 13:435–40 w '60. * (*PA* 36:1LD35C)
32. COSGROVE, AZARIAS MICHAEL. *A Comparison of Personality Patterns as Measured by the Gordon Personal Profile and the Figure Drawing Test.* Master's thesis, Manhattan College (New York, N.Y.), 1960.
33. HUGHES, J. L. "Comparison of the Validities of Trait and Profile Methods of Scoring a Personality Test for Salesmen." *Eng & Ind Psychol* 2:1–7 sp '60. *
34. BRAUN, JOHN R. "Correlates of Ghiselli Self-Description Inventory Scores." *Psychol Rep* 9:727–8 D '61. *
35. HUGHES, J. L., AND DODD, W. E. "Validity Versus Stereotype: Predicting Sales Performance by Ipsative Scoring of a Personality Test." *Personnel Psychol* 14:343–55 w '61. * (*PA* 37:5910)
36. RIED, BLANCHE ROSE. *The Development of a Prognostic Device for Job Success of the Medical Assistant Through the Correlation of In-School Evaluations With Employer Evaluation.* Doctor's thesis, New York University (New York, N.Y.), 1961. (*DA* 23:557)
37. TUCKER, W. T., AND PAINTER, JOHN J. "Personality and Product Use." *J Appl Psychol* 45:325–9 O '61. * (*PA* 36:5LO25T)
38. BRAUN, JOHN R. "Stereotypes of the Scientist as Seen With the Gordon Personal Profile and Gordon Personal Inventory." *J Psychol* 53:453–5 Ap '62. * (*PA* 37:107)
39. APPLEY, MORTIMER H., AND MOELLER, GEORGE. "Conforming Behavior and Personality Variables in College Women." *J Abn & Social Psychol* 66:284–90 Mr '63. * (*PA* 37:8237)
40. GREENBERG, HERBERT; GUERINO, ROSEMARIE; LASHEN, MARILYN; MAYER, DAVID; AND PISKOWSKI, DOROTHY. "Order of Birth as a Determinant of Personality and Attitudinal Characteristics." *J Social Psychol* 60:221–30 Ag '63. * (*PA* 38:4337)
41. MAHER, HOWARD. "Validity Information Exchange, No. 16-01: D.O.T. Code 0-06.71, Feature Writer; 0-06.73, Columnist; 0-06.92, Copyreader (Rewrite Man)." *Personnel Psychol* 16:71–3 sp '63. *

CHARLES F. DICKEN, *Assistant Professor of Psychology, San Diego State College, San Diego, California.*

The Profile was designed to measure four

personality traits, shown with typical high-loading items: ascendancy (A), "takes the lead in group discussions," "able to make important decisions without help"; responsibility (R), "sees a job through despite difficulties," "thorough in any work undertaken"; emotional stability (E), "calm and easygoing in manner," "free from worry or care"; and sociability (S), "enjoys having lots of people around," "a good mixer socially."

The items are arranged in tetrads of two favorably worded and two unfavorably worded items. The examinee selects one most descriptive and one least descriptive item from each tetrad. The reviewer found the format somewhat annoying since identical items occur repeatedly; however the time required to complete the test is refreshingly brief, less than 15 minutes.

The Profile was constructed on the basis of an extensive series of investigations. Traits were initially selected on the basis of personality factors obtained by Cattell and Mosier. Items devised for the traits were factored to derive scales. Item social desirability values were established by ratings in a large subject pool and used to determine the pairings in the tetrads. Peer rating criteria were used to further refine the items, as was internal consistency analysis. There were five revisions in all. The scoring system in the 1963 version has been revised to eliminate negative scores, but there is no change in the content or structure of the Profile itself or in the item weights. As in the earlier edition, no item response is keyed for more than one trait, although the mechanics of arranging the revised stencils give the initial impression that all items are scored on all keys.

Although the four traits were selected as theoretically independent dimensions, scales A and S and scales E and R intercorrelate fairly substantially in most samples. Peer ratings show the same correspondencies, however, suggesting that the overlap may be in the traits themselves rather than the result of an avoidable problem of measurement method.

The manual maintains a high standard. Pertinent data are presented in detail. The discussion of interpretation is conservative, limitations and cautions being specifically pointed out. There are percentile norms for a good variety of groups, including students, low and middle level employees, managers, salesmen,

and foremen. Means and sigmas are furnished for 27 different groups.

Reliability estimates based on several populations and computed by several standard methods are satisfactorily high. The validity of the scores in predicting external criteria in more than 20 studies is cited, and low or zero correlations are included as well as higher ones. These data are extensive enough to give the potential user a fair approximation of what he might expect in his own population. Validity correlations with peer ratings of college students are especially impressive, ranging from .47 to .73, but these subjects appear to be the same on which the item analyses were based. Three of the four scores correlate more than .50, however, with counselors' trait ratings in an independent study. How much of the validity in these studies is due to common "halo" or overall-merit variance and how much is due to specific validity of the separate scales for separate ratings is not determinable.

Validities obtained in various employment and military settings are typically lower, but the criteria (mostly supervisory ratings or administrative decisions) are probably not as good as peer nominations. The validities suggest that the A and R scores are probably most valuable in employment applications. Except for the peer data, external validities rarely exceed .30 or .35, although there are some outstanding exceptions. This level of validity is probably typical of the better inventories of normal personality traits, with the criteria available.

Illustrative individual cases are provided which give profile scores and independently obtained personality data. A wider variety of these cases would enhance the value of the manual as an aid in interpretation.

The problem of distortion or "faking" is discussed in a sophisticated manner. The author's basic argument is that the forced-choice format compels the examinee to choose between two favorable (or unfavorable) items and that he will tend to choose the item he feels is most complimentary, which will turn out to be the item actually like him. The author also states that the utility of the test must rest on its validity in operational situations, not on its resistance to distortion.

The evidence presented seems mainly to support this reasoning. Gordon found forced-choice versions of his items more valid than true-false items in constructing the Profile. Several comparisons of scores obtained under differing motivational conditions, including application, guidance, post-employment, and simulated employment-seeking, show only small increases in the scores of subjects presumably motivated to make a favorable impression.

There is, however, some degree of face validity apparent in the items keyed for the various traits. The data do not resolve the problem of role-playing by subjects who are informed or sophisticated as to the traits desired in a given context. The test lacks an explicit control for the total number of favorable items checked, a factor which tends to penalize the candid subject, since endorsement of favorable items increases scores on all scales. It seems possible that at least some items which are valid for the traits, although socially less favorable, could have been found, although this is admittedly difficult. The earlier published version included norms for a total (T) score and a suggestion that extreme values be interpreted as questioning the validity of the record. This is now omitted, unfortunately in the opinion of the reviewer, although a percentile value based on the earlier norms can be obtained through a short series of calculations. The reviewer raised his own A score 58 centile units on the male executive norm by adopting a "leadership" set after first responding with a "candid" set. His T score rose above the 99th percentile, however, which would easily have unmasked the deception.

In summary, the Profile is a brief, forced-choice inventory for four normal personality traits. The inventory was carefully constructed and standardized, and a variety of norms are furnished. Validity data are thoroughly and conscientiously presented. The problem of distortion is considered in detail, and evidence is presented which indicates it is minimal in typical operational settings. However, a validity scale could and probably should be used as a check for distortion. Generally, the validity of the *Gordon Personal Profile* seems as good as usually found in the better inventories of this type.

ALFRED B. HEILBRUN, JR., *Associate Professor of Psychology, State University of Iowa, Iowa City, Iowa.*

The *Gordon Personal Profile* (GPP) is a brief 18-item questionnaire, essentially self-administering, and applicable to individuals ranging in age from about 15 years through adulthood. It is proposed as a measure of four significant personality dimensions: (*a*) ascendancy-passivity (A), (*b*) responsibility-irresponsibility (R), (*c*) emotional stability-instability (E), and (*d*) sociability-social introversiveness (S). The statements included in each scale were selected by factor analytic means and underwent a series of revisions which were aimed at sharpening scale prediction and determining which combination elicited an acceptable number of endorsements for each statement of the four in a given item.

The GPP provides a modified forced-choice format which the manual proposes as a control for favorability in self-description. In each of the 18 items, four statements representing the four personality dimensions are grouped so that two are high preference and two are low preference. The individual is asked to select the statement "most" and "least" like himself from each item tetrad. Gordon presents evidence which suggests that faking on the test does not markedly influence group scale score means if it is assumed that application for employment systematically elicits more favorable self-descriptions from job candidates.

Generally speaking, the 1963 revised manual is a commendable product. The empirical groundwork necessary to satisfy the basic requirements of a published test has been satisfactorily completed and presented in the manual in a clear, orderly fashion. Stable and fairly representative college and high school percentile norms are provided as well as several sets of specific norms which might be of interest to those working within a business setting. No "general population" type norm is provided which may limit the effectiveness of the test's use with samples which are not young, highly educated, or selected from one of a few industrial levels. Reliability figures suggest that the GPP scales are both internally consistent and stable over time.

Although the scales are only slightly correlated with measures of intelligence, there are some surprisingly high intercorrelations between some of the scales considering that the traits were derived from a factor analysis. Scales showing the greatest intercorrelation are A and S ($r = .64$ to $.71$) and R and E ($r = .51$ to $.61$). The fact that the GPP measures but four traits and a moderate correlation exists between some of these would indicate a rather restricted range of inferences which the test user can make from the test. This restriction can be alleviated to some extent by presenting the *Gordon Personal Inventory* in tandem with the GPP, thereby adding four more personality dimensions and increasing testing time by only somewhere between 15 and 30 minutes. In fact, one is led to wonder why the two tests are not published as a single test instrument since their formats are identical.

The validity data bear testimony to the usefulness of the GPP scales. Moderate correlations between them and both counselor and peer ratings of behavior have been demonstrated. The manual also presents numerous correlations between the GPP and indices of performance adequacy in industrial and training situations. These tend to be low but significant, highlighting the fact that the GPP has little power for individual prediction of nontest behavior, which is not surprising since no other objective personality instrument has either. The one feature of the validity findings which leaves the reviewer uneasy is that *any* significant relationship between a scale and a performance rating is regarded as an indicant of validity. For example, it is not specified why ascendancy should relate to one criterion and emotional stability to another.

In summary, if there is interest in a short, convenient measure of a limited number of salient personality traits, the GPP is about as good as you can do. It is carefully conceived, reliable, adequately normed, and has received at least suggestive validation.

For reviews by Benno G. Fricke and John A. Radcliffe, see 5:59 (1 excerpt).

[104]

Group Cohesiveness: A Study of Group Morale. Adults; 1958, c1957–58; title on test is *A Study of Group Morale;* 5 scores: satisfaction of individual motives, satisfaction of interpersonal relations, homogeneity of attitude, satisfaction with leadership, total; 1 form ('57, 1 page); manual ('58, 4 pages); no data on reliability of subscores; $3 per 30 tests; $1 per specimen set; cash orders postpaid; (10–15) minutes; Bernard Goldman; Psychometric Affiliates. *

REFERENCES
1. GOLDMAN, BERNARD. *A Scale for the Measurement of Group Cohesiveness.* Doctor's thesis, University of Buffalo (Buffalo, N.Y.), 1952. (*DA* 12:554)

ERIC F. GARDNER, *Professor of Education and Psychology, and Chairman, Department of Psychology, Syracuse University, Syracuse, New York.*

Group morale is considered by the author to be comparable to group cohesiveness as described by T. R. Newcomb. Four criteria posited as indicators of group cohesiveness and adapted by the author as his definition of morale were used as the basis for item construction. Items, each of which was related to one of the four criteria of morale, were constructed as measures of the four subtest scores presented. The 20 best items, selected by editing and by use of phi coefficients to differentiate between high and low scoring groups, were retained for the test. Each item is scored using a Likert type scale (strongly agree to strongly disagree) and the score of each subtest is obtained by summing the responses where "4" represents the highest degree of cohesiveness.

Although the general procedure is reasonable, the reviewer has serious doubts about certain aspects of its implementation. The selection of the most appropriate items was dependent upon the adequacy of the two criterion groups used. As a criterion, the total responses of the top and bottom 50 scores among 184 nurses leaves much to be desired. An inspection of the final items does nothing to allay one's concern about their adequacy. Many of the statements appear to be rather extreme and not especially adaptable for indicating variability among respondents. For example, the inclusion of the word "all" in the item "I believe that all my associates in this group hold beliefs that are unreasonable" causes the respondent some difficulty in deciding upon the degree of his agreement.

A reliability coefficient of .94 is reported for the total test. The score on the first 10 items was correlated with scores on the second 10 items for a sample of 209 subjects and the result corrected by the Spearman-Brown prophecy formula. Such an index is not very meaningful without more information about the group utilized, especially its variability. No reliability coefficients are reported for the four subtest scores. Since these scores contain from 4 to 7 items each, the reliability coefficients are probably low for use in measuring individual differences.

A table of norms based upon the mean performance of 14 groups for each subtest and the total score is presented. Since there are 20 categories of percentile rank and only 14 observations, the reviewer is unable to understand what operation the author has performed or what he has in mind.

Attempts at the establishment of validity were made by comparing the responses of various groups where cohesiveness or noncohesiveness was presumed to be known. Mean differences which are shown to be statistically significant are presented between (a) Great Book study groups ranging from a beginner's group to a leader's group, (b) organized dramatic groups compared with informal groups, and (c) classrooms using seminar methods contrasted with a group who had been taught by the lecture method. Small mean differences in the direction hypothesized were obtained. These small differences are not too surprising, especially since there is little evidence that the groups labeled high morale groups really had better morale than did the groups labeled low in morale.

The topic is important and a beginning has been made to develop useful measures. It seems to the reviewer that the test is being presented prematurely. Much work needs to be done, including additional item analysis, reliability studies for appropriate specific groups, and validation studies.

CECIL A. GIBB, *Professor of Psychology, The Australian National University, Canberra City, Australia.*

Much as the psychologist concerned with work groups and groups in other settings would welcome an instrument to measure cohesiveness, the approach to this scale will be very cautious indeed. The very equation of "morale" and "cohesiveness," in which Goldman has followed Newcomb, leads to difficulties; for example, rejection of the statement "I believe that the work I do now keeps me in a rut" contributes positively to the "cohesiveness" score and also, in some peculiar way, to a score called "homogeneity of attitude."

Nor will the data given by Goldman dispel many doubts. Development procedures seem to have been standard and a corrected split-half reliability of .94 is claimed, certainly "adequate" for a 20-item scale. Some validity also is demonstrated in terms of scale differentiation between selected criterion groups. However, detailed presentation of means and standard deviations for these groups indicates a rather less happy situation than that suggested by the analysis of variance data offered in the "Validity" discussion.

Goldman claims, "The four criteria of cohesiveness adopted for the purpose of constructing the scale are probably valid measures, in part, of group cohesiveness." This conclusion was arrived at on the sole evidence of part-whole correlation coefficients ranging from .67 to .47—not a very impressive array of data when any part constitutes at least 20 per cent of the whole and in one case as much as 35 per cent. Confidence is further strained when in the next paragraph it is claimed: "The four criteria of cohesiveness are relatively independent of one another as shown by the low intercorrelations among them," and this on the basis of correlations ranging between .49 and .28 with no overlap of items. Other difficulties will certainly face users of this scale, which is presented as being intended for use with groups in general although many of the questions relate only to work and work situations. Much more seriously, the instructions never call for the respondent to identify a group. He is asked to respond, anonymously, to statements about "this group," "my associates," and "the leader of this group" without any attempt at establishing which of the many groups he belongs to is intended, what nature of relationship defines an "associate," and which of many possible "leaders" is to be kept in mind.

It is difficult to see that *Group Cohesiveness: A Study of Group Morale* can make any positive contribution to any of the objectives claimed for it.

[105]

★Group Dimensions Descriptions Questionnaire. College and adult groups; 1956; for research use only; 13 group dimensions scores: autonomy, control, flexibility, hedonic tone, homogeneity, intimacy, participation, permeability, polarization, potency, stability, stratification, viscidity; IBM; Form ERG (8 pages); manual (75 pages, see 4 below); tentative norms; separate answer-profile sheets must be used; $3.50 per 25 tests; 30¢ per single copy; $2 per 25 IBM answer sheets; scoring stencils must be prepared locally; $2.50 per manual; postage extra; [45–60] minutes; John K. Hemphill and Charles M. Westie; distributed by Educational Testing Service. *

REFERENCES
1. HEMPHILL, JOHN K., AND WESTIE, CHARLES M. "The Measurement of Group Dimensions." *J Psychol* 29:325–42 Ap '50. * (PA 24:5789)
2. HEMPHILL, JOHN K. "Description of Group Characteristics." *Proc Inv Conf Testing Probl* 1954:85–90; discussion, 91–5 '55. * (PA 30:826)
3. BORGATTA, EDGAR F.; COTTRELL, LEONARD S., JR.; AND MEYER, HENRY J. "On the Dimensions of Group Behavior." *Sociometry* 19:223–40 Mr '56. * (PA 32:1440)
4. HEMPHILL, JOHN K. *Group Dimensions: A Manual for Their Measurement.* Ohio State University Bureau of Business

Research, Research Monograph No. 87. Columbus, Ohio: the Bureau, 1956. Pp. xi, 66. * (*PA* 31:7657)

5. HILL, THOMAS BARLOW, JR. *The Relationships Between Teacher Morale and the Ability to Establish Rapport With Pupils and Other Selected Variables.* Doctor's thesis, North Texas State College (Denton, Tex.), 1961. (*DA* 22:789)

For an excerpt from a review of the manual, see 5:B203.

[106]

★**Guidance Inventory.** High school; 1960; identification of problems related to underachievement and need for counseling; 1 form (2 pages); manual (21 pages); no data on reliability; $20 per 200 tests and manual; $1.75 per manual purchased separately; 50¢ per specimen set; postpaid; (50) minutes; Ralph Gallagher; the Author. *

JOHN W. M. ROTHNEY, *Professor of Education, University of Wisconsin, Madison, Wisconsin.*

The 130 items which constitute this inventory are printed on both sides of a cardboard sheet. The student answers by circling a NO or YES for each question. The questions vary from the usual "Do you feel 'low' much of the time?" type of question to such specifics as "Do your teeth need dental attention?" Ninety New Jersey high school principals and superintendents helped the author to decide upon the items that are in the final form. In order to overcome the tendency of students to give favorable answers and cover up difficulties, the author says that the inventory has "carefully inter-related responses, and emotionally charged items have been kept at a minimum."

It is difficult to assess this inventory because the data and the methods of reporting do not follow the usual patterns. There are no reliability coefficients and no evidence of validity of the usual kind. It is said that identification of elements, other than the usual intellectual or academic factors, that are different for pupils doing good and poor work in school is based on "nearly 5,000,000 responses by equal numbers of pupils doing good and poor work in nearly 300 american [spelled with a small a] high schools in 1960." No further identification of populations is given.

A report is given about each of the 130 items. On the fifth item, for example, "Do you often lose your temper?," it is reported that "frequent loss of tempers were reported by over ⅓ of good students. They were reported 1½ times as often by poor students." This is followed by two queries that the counselor might make as to why the pupils lose their tempers and whether or not the pupil is acquainted

with the loss of efficiency that accompanies temper outbursts. The counselor is then referred to answers to other items on the inventory such as item 14, "Are you as popular as you would like to be?" Supporting data offered indicates that 43 per cent of all pupils answered YES to item 5 and that from 24 to 60 per cent of pupils in different schools did so. Percentages of girls and boys doing good and poor work who answered YES to the item are given. On the front cover of the manual it is indicated that the percentages are based on 18,668 pupils doing good work and 18,298 pupils doing poor work. No definition of good and poor work is given and there is no further description of the populations or the schools from which they came.

All of the usual objections to such devices can be raised against this one. When one adds lack of evidence of reliability, validity, norms, lack of adequate editing of the manual, and general vagueness one must conclude that counselors could get along without this instrument.

[107]

★**Guilford-Holley L Inventory.** Adults; 1953–63; leadership behavior; 5 scores: benevolence, ambition, meticulousness, discipline, aggressiveness; IBM; 1 form ('53, 4 pages); manual ('63, 6 pages); separate answer sheets must be used; $3.50 per 25 tests; 4¢ per IBM answer sheet; $1.25 per scoring stencil; 4¢ per profile; 35¢ per manual; 65¢ per specimen set; postage extra; (25) minutes; J. P. Guilford and J. W. Holley; Sheridan Supply Co. *

[108]

The Guilford-Martin Inventory of Factors GAMIN, Abridged Edition. Grades 12–16 and adults; 1943–48; 5 scores: general activity, ascendance-submission, masculinity-femininity, inferiority feelings, nervousness; IBM; 1 form ('43, 4 pages); revised manual ['48, 3 pages]; college norms only; $3.50 per 25 tests; 20¢ per single copy; $1 per scoring key; separate answer sheets may be used; 4¢ per IBM answer sheet; $2.50 per set of either hand or machine scoring stencils; 25¢ per manual; postage extra; (30) minutes; [J. P. Guilford and H. G. Martin]; Sheridan Supply Co. *

REFERENCES

1–7. See 3:43.
8–25. See 4:47.
26–58. See 5:63.
59. TSUJIOKA, BIEN; SONOHARA, TARO; AND YATABE, TATSURO. "A Factorial Study of the Temperament of Japanese College Male Students by the Yatabe-Guilford Personality Inventory." *Psychologia* 1:110–9 D '57. * (*PA* 35:4899)
60. BUDD, WILLIAM C., AND BLAKELY, LYNDA S. "The Relationship Between Ascendancy and Response Choice on the Minnesota Teacher Attitude Inventory." *J Ed Res* 52:73–4 O '58. * (*PA* 34:2027)
61. RISS, ERIC. *Originality and Personality: An Exploratory Investigation to Study the Relationship of Originality to Certain Personality Variables in Art Students.* Doctor's thesis, New York University (New York, N.Y.), 1958. (*DA* 20:743)
62. THOMAS, EDWIN RUSSELL. *The Relationship Between the Strong Vocational Interest Blank and the Guilford-Martin Personality Inventory Among Salesmen.* Doctor's thesis, Syracuse University (Syracuse, N.Y.), 1958. (*DA* 19:2139)

63. GUILFORD, J. P. *Personality.* New York: McGraw-Hill Book Co., Inc., 1959. Pp. xiii, 562. *
64. KELLY, E. LOWELL, AND GOLDBERG, LEWIS R. "Correlates of Later Performance and Specialization in Psychology: A Follow-Up Study of the Trainees Assessed in the VA Selection Research Project." *Psychol Monogr* 73(12):1-32 '59. * *(PA* 34:7952)
65. CARRIGAN, PATRICIA M. "Extraversion-Introversion as a Dimension of Personality: A Reappraisal." *Psychol B* 57: 329-60 S '60. * *(PA* 35:4976)
66. CURRAN, ANN MARIE. *Non-Intellectual Characteristics of Freshman Underachievers, Normal Achievers, and Over-achievers at the College Level.* Doctor's thesis, University of Connecticut (Storrs, Conn.), 1960. *(DA* 21:2584)
67. MITCHELL, LONNIE E., AND ZAX, MELVIN. "Psychological Response to Chlorpromazine in a Group of Psychiatric Patients." *J Clin Psychol* 16:440-2 O '60. * *(PA* 37:3341)
68. BESSENT, EDGAR WAILAND. *The Predictability of Selected Elementary School Principals' Administrative Behavior.* Doctor's thesis, University of Texas (Austin, Tex.), 1961. *(DA* 22:3479)
69. NICHOLS, ROBERT C. "Subtle, Obvious and Stereotype Measures of Masculinity-Femininity." *Ed & Psychol Meas* 22:449-61 au '62. * *(PA* 37:5014)

For a review by Hubert E. Brogden, see 4:47; for a review by H. J. Eysenck, see 3:43; for a related review, see 3:45.

[109]

The Guilford-Martin Personnel Inventory. Adults; 1943-46; 3 scores: objectivity, agreeableness, cooperativeness; IBM; 1 form ('43, 4 pages); manual ['43, 2 pages]; mimeographed supplement ('46, 5 pages); $3.50 per 25 tests; 20¢ per single copy; $1 per scoring key; separate answer sheets may be used; 4¢ per IBM answer sheet; $2.50 per set of either hand or machine scoring stencils; 25¢ per manual; postage extra; (30) minutes; [J. P. Guilford and H. G. Martin]; Sheridan Supply Co. *

REFERENCES

1-7. See 3:44.
8-27. See 4:48.
28-54. See 5:64.
55. TSUJIOKA, BIEN; SONOHARA, TARO; AND YATABE, TATSURO. "A Factorial Study of the Temperament of Japanese College Male Students by the Yatabe-Guilford Personality Inventory." *Psychologia* 1:110-9 D '57. * *(PA* 35:4899)
56. THOMAS, EDWIN RUSSELL. *The Relationship Between the Strong Vocational Interest Blank and the Guilford-Martin Personality Inventory Among Salesmen.* Doctor's thesis, Syracuse University (Syracuse, N.Y.), 1958. *(DA* 19:2139)
57. GUILFORD, J. P. *Personality.* New York: McGraw-Hill Book Co., Inc., 1959. Pp. xiii, 562. *
58. KELLY, E. LOWELL, AND GOLDBERG, LEWIS R. "Correlates of Later Performance and Specialization in Psychology: A Follow-Up Study of the Trainees Assessed in the VA Selection Research Project." *Psychol Monogr* 73(12):1-32 '59. * *(PA* 34:7952)
59. United States Naval Personnel Research Field Activity. "Normative Data Information Exchange, No. 12-3." *Personnel Psychol* 12:145 sp '59. *
60. CARRIGAN, PATRICIA M. "Extraversion-Introversion as a Dimension of Personality: A Reappraisal." *Psychol B* 57: 329-60 S '60. * *(PA* 35:4976)
61. MACKINNEY, ARTHUR C., AND WOLINS, LEROY. "Validity Information Exchange, No. 13-01, Foreman II, Home Appliance Manufacturing." *Personnel Psychol* 13:443-7 w '60. *
62. BESSENT, EDGAR WAILAND. *The Predictability of Selected Elementary School Principals' Administrative Behavior.* Doctor's thesis, University of Texas (Austin, Tex.), 1961. *(DA* 22:3479)
63. BUEL, WILLIAM D., AND BACHNER, VIRGINIA M. "The Assessment of Creativity in a Research Setting." *J Appl Psychol* 45:353-8 D '61. * *(PA* 37:1211)

For a review by Neil Van Steenberg, see 4:48; for a review by Benjamin Shimberg, see 3:44; for a related review, see 3:45.

[110]

The Guilford-Zimmerman Temperament Survey. Grades 12-16 and adults; 1949-55; revision and con-

densation of *Inventory of Factors STDCR, Guilford-Martin Inventory of Factors GAMIN,* and *Guilford-Martin Personnel Inventory;* 10 scores: general activity, restraint, ascendance, sociability, emotional stability, objectivity, friendliness, thoughtfulness, personal relations, masculinity; IBM; 1 form ('49, 8 pages); manual ('49, 12 pages); norms ('55); profile ('55, 1 page); 3 *Falsification Scales* (gross-falsification, subtle falsification, carelessness-deviancy) and manual ('55, 3 pages) by Alfred Jacobs and Allan Schlaff; *G-Z Temperament Map* ('52, 2 pages) by Philip C. Perry; separate answer sheets must be used; $4 per 25 tests; 25¢ per single copy; 5¢ per IBM answer sheet; $2.50 per set of either hand or machine scoring stencils; 4¢ per profile; 35¢ per manual; $4.25 per set of scoring stencils and manual for falsification scales; 4¢ per copy of temperament map; postage extra; (50) minutes; J. P. Guilford and Wayne S. Zimmerman; Sheridan Supply Co. *

REFERENCES

1-5. See 4:49.
6-53. See 5:65.
54. FERGUSON, JOHN L., JR. *A Factorial Study of the Minnesota Teacher Attitude Inventory.* Doctor's thesis, University of Missouri (Columbia, Mo.), 1953. *(DA* 13:1087)
55. BARBER, THEODORE XENOPHON. "A Note on 'Hypnotizability' and Personality Traits." *J Clin & Exp Hypnosis* 4:109-14 Jl '56. * *(PA* 32:3288)
56. BERKOWITZ, LEONARD. "Personality and Group Position." *Sociometry* 19:210-22 Mr '56. * *(PA* 32:1435)
57. HOLMEN, MILTON G.; KATTER, ROBERT V.; JONES, ANNE M.; AND RICHARDSON, IRVING F. "An Assessment Program for OCS Applicants." *HumRRO Tech Rep* 26:1-50 F '56. * *(PA* 31:8957)
58. KEMPE, JAMES EDWIN. *An Experimental Investigation of the Relationship Between Certain Personality Characteristics and Physiological Responses to Stress in a Normal Population.* Doctor's thesis, Michigan State University (East Lansing, Mich.), 1956. *(DA* 19:3383)
59. CRIST, ROBERT L. *A Study of Mean Differences in the R, S, and T Traits of the Guilford-Zimmerman Temperament Survey for Upper and Lower Quarter Students on the Minnesota Teacher Attitude Inventory.* Master's thesis, Purdue University (Lafayette, Ind.), 1957.
60. GOWAN, J. C. "A Summary of the Intensive Study of Twenty Highly Selected Elementary Women Teachers." *J Exp Ed* 26:115-24 D '57. * *(PA* 33:4731)
61. MURRAY, JOHN B. *Training for the Priesthood and Personality Interest Test Manifestations.* Doctor's thesis, Fordham University (New York, N.Y.), 1957.
62. SCHOLL, CHARLES ELMER, JR. *The Development and Evaluation of Methods for Isolating Factors That Differentiate Between Successful and Unsuccessful Executive Trainees in a Large, Multibranch Bank.* Doctor's thesis, University of Michigan (Ann Arbor, Mich.), 1957. *(DA* 18:2034)
63. STARR, HAROLD. *Personality Correlates of Time Estimation.* Doctor's thesis, Purdue University (Lafayette, Ind.), 1957. *(DA* 18:2217)
64. COULSON, ROGER WAYNE. *Relationships Among Personality Traits, Ability and Academic Efficiency of College Seniors.* Doctor's thesis, State University of Iowa (Iowa City, Iowa), 1958. *(DA* 19:1647)
65. HALL, OLIVE A. "Factors Related to Achievement of Home Economics Majors in Chemistry." *J Home Econ* 50: 767-8 D '58. *
66. LINDEN, JAMES D. *The Development and Comparative Analysis of Two Forced-Choice Forms of the Guilford-Zimmerman Temperament Survey.* Doctor's thesis, Purdue University (Lafayette, Ind.), 1958. *(DA* 18:2199)
67. McKINNEY, EVA DORIS. *The Relationships Between Certain Factors of Personality and Selected Components of Physical Fitness of College Freshmen Women.* Doctor's thesis, Boston University (Boston, Mass.), 1958. *(DA* 19:1287)
68. SHAW, MERVILLE C., AND GRUBB, JAMES. "Hostility and Able High School Underachievers." *J Counsel Psychol* 5:263-6 w '58. * *(PA* 34:3413)
69. SINGER, STANLEY L.; STEFFLRE, BUFORD; AND THOMPSON, FRED W. "Temperament Scores and Socio-economic Status." *J Counsel Psychol* 5:281-4 w '58. * *(PA* 34:2791)
70. WEBB, SAM C., AND GOODLING, RICHARD A. "Test Validity in a Methodist Theology School." *Ed & Psychol Meas* 18:859-66 w '58. * *(PA* 34:2123)
71. WEITZENHOFFER, ANDRÉ M., AND WEITZENHOFFER, GENEVA B. "Personality and Hypnotic Susceptibility." *Am J Clin Hypnosis* 1:79-82 O '58. * *(PA* 34:4414)
72. BENDIG, A. W. "The Relationship of Scales of Extraversion-Introversion and Emotionality to Guilford's O, F, and P Scales." *J Psychol Studies* 11:49-51 N-D '59. * *(PA* 34:5597)
73. GAY, JAMES D. "A Comparison of Certain Aspects of

Personality of College Fraternity and Nonfraternity Men."
Proc W Va Acad Sci 29:87–90 My '59. * (*PA* 34:2764)
74. GRUBER, JOSEPH JOHN, JR. *A Comparative Study of Employed Male Physical Education Graduates and Physical Education Undergraduate Students on Selected Instruments.* Doctor's thesis, Purdue University (Lafayette, Ind.), 1959. (*DA* 20:2676)
75. GUILFORD, J. P. *Personality*, pp. 184–7. New York: McGraw-Hill Book Co., Inc., 1959. Pp. xiii, 562. *
76. JACOBS, ALFRED, AND SCHLAFF, ALLAN. "Falsification on the Guilford-Zimmerman Temperament Survey." *Psychol Newsl* 10:138–45 Ja-F '59. * (*PA* 34:1024)
77. KENNEY, RAYMOND CARROLL. *An Analysis of Self Perceptions in Counselor Trainees.* Doctor's thesis, University of Texas (Austin, Tex.), 1959. (*DA* 20:2677)
78. KHAN, LILIAN. *Factor Analysis of Certain Aptitude and Personality Variables.* Doctor's thesis, University of Southern California (Los Angeles, Calif.), 1959. (*DA* 20:2889)
79. KLUGH, HENRY E., AND BENDIG, A. W. "The Guilford-Zimmerman Temperament Survey and Intelligence." *Psychol Newsl* 10:96–7 Ja-F '59. * (*PA* 34:1033)
80. LINDEN, JAMES D., AND OLSON, KAY W. "A Comparative Analysis of Selected Guilford-Zimmerman Temperament Survey Scales With the Taylor Manifest Anxiety Scale." *J Clin Psychol* 15:295–8 Jl '59. * (*PA* 35:3457)
81. MANHEIM, HENRY L. "Personality Differences of Members of Two Political Parties." *J Social Psychol* 50:261–8 N '59. * (*PA* 35:4833)
82. MANN, RICHARD D. "A Review of the Relationships Between Personality and Performance in Small Groups." *Psychol B* 56:241–70 Jl '59. * (*PA* 34:4194)
83. PALACIOS, JOHN RAYMOND. *A Validation Study of Selected Tests for Possible Use in Admission to Professional Education Sequences at Purdue University.* Doctor's thesis, Purdue University (Lafayette, Ind.), 1959. (*DA* 20:2679)
84. PATTERSON, HOWARD ROSCOE. *The Relationship Between Personality Traits and Preferences for Instructional Methods.* Doctor's thesis, North Texas State College (Denton, Tex.), 1959. (*DA* 20:2906)
85. ROBINSON, TED R. *Guilford-Zimmerman Temperament Profiles of Iowa Vocational Agriculture Instructors.* Master's thesis, Iowa State University (Ames, Iowa), 1959.
86. THRASH, PATRICIA ANN. *Women Student Leaders at Northwestern University: Their Characteristics, Self-Concepts, and Attitudes Toward the University.* Doctor's thesis, Northwestern University (Evanston, Ill.), 1959. (*DA* 20:3638)
87. TUCKER, WOODIE L. *The Relationship Between Personality Traits and Basic Skill in Typewriting.* Doctor's thesis, University of Pittsburgh (Pittsburgh, Pa.), 1959. (*DA* 20:1694)
88. VINEYARD, EDWIN E. "A Study of the Independence of Choice of Science or Non-Science Major and Measures of Personality Traits." *Sci Ed* 43:130–3 Mr '59. *
89. WAGNER, EDWIN ERIC. *Predicting Success for Young Executives From Objective Test Scores and Personal Data.* Doctor's thesis, Temple University (Philadelphia, Pa.), 1959. (*DA* 20:3371)
90. WILSON, JOHN E. "Evaluating a Four Year Sales Selection Program." *Personnel Psychol* 12:97–104 sp '59. * (*PA* 34:3533)
91. WITHERSPOON, PAUL, AND MELBERG, M. E. "Relationship Between Grade-Point Averages and Sectional Scores of the Guilford-Zimmerman Temperament Survey." *Ed & Psychol Meas* 19:673–4 w '59. * (*PA* 34:6577)
92. BALDWIN, THOMAS SANDERSON. *The Relationships Among Personality, Cognitive, and Job Performance Variables.* Doctor's thesis, Ohio State University (Columbus, Ohio), 1960. (*DA* 21:3171)
93. BARROWS, GORDON A., AND ZUCKERMAN, MARVIN. "Construct Validity of Three Masculinity-Femininity Tests." *J Consult Psychol* 24:441–5 O '60. * (*PA* 35:4891)
94. BENDIG, A. W. "Age Differences in the Interscale Factor Structure of the Guilford-Zimmerman Temperament Survey." *J Consult Psychol* 24:134–8 Ap '60. * (*PA* 34:7365)
95. BENDIG, A. W. "Item Analyses of Guilford's GZTS Objectivity, Friendliness, and Personal Relations Scales." *J Psychol Studies* 11:215–20 My-Je '60. *
96. BROWN, DONALD JAMES. *An Investigation of the Relationships Between Certain Personal Characteristics of Guidance Counselors and Performance in Supervised Counseling Interviews.* Doctor's thesis, Ohio State University (Columbus, Ohio), 1960. (*DA* 21:810)
97. CARRIGAN, PATRICIA M. "Extraversion-Introversion as a Dimension of Personality: A Reappraisal." *Psychol B* 57:329–60 S '60. * (*PA* 35:4976)
98. CLARK, CHARLES MARVIN. *Changes in Response Patterns of Counseling Institute Trainees.* Doctor's thesis, Ohio State University (Columbus, Ohio), 1960. (*DA* 21:811)
99. EVANS, GLORIA CAREY. "Validity of Ascendance Measurements in Group Interaction." *Psychol Rep* 7:114 Ag '60. * (*PA* 35:3374)
100. GOWAN, J. C. "A Teaching Prognosis Scale for the Guilford-Zimmerman Temperament Survey." *J Ed Res* 53: 345–8 My '60. *
101. GOWAN, JOHN C. "Intercorrelations of the California Psychological Inventory and the Guilford-Zimmerman Tem-

perament Survey With Intelligence as Measured by the ACE." *Calif J Ed Res* 11:213–5 N '60. * (*PA* 35:4856)
102. GRUBER, JOSEPH JOHN. "Personality Traits and Teaching Attitudes." *Res Q* 31:434–9 O '60. *
103. JAMES, ALICE M. *A Study of the Relationship Between the Guilford-Zimmerman Temperament Traits and the Clinical Practice Grade for Physical Therapy Students.* Master's thesis, Boston University (Boston, Mass.), 1960.
104. KIMBELL, FONTELLA THOMPSON. *The Use of Selected Standardized Tests as Predictors of Academic Success at Oklahoma College for Women.* Doctor's thesis, University of Oklahoma (Norman, Okla.), 1960. (*DA* 20:4335)
105. MACKINNEY, ARTHUR C., AND WOLINS, LEROY. "Validity Information Exchange, No. 13-01, Foreman II, Home Appliance Manufacturing." *Personnel Psychol* 13:443–7 w '60. *
106. MARMORALE, ANN M. *The Interrelationships of Measures of Sensory Variability, Scores on Selected Performance Tests, and the Guilford-Zimmerman Temperament Survey.* Doctor's thesis, Fordham University (New York, N. Y.), 1960.
107. PEARSON, WAYNE ORLANDO. *The Relationship Between Item Difficulty and Interitem Correlation in the Minnesota Multiphasic Personality Inventory and the Guilford-Zimmerman Temperament Survey.* Doctor's thesis, Cornell University (Ithaca, N.Y.), 1960. (*DA* 20:4177)
108. SHIRLEY, JACK HAROLD. *A Comparative Study of the Academic Achievements, Interests, and Personality Traits of Athletes and Non-Athletes.* Doctor's thesis, University of Oklahoma (Norman, Okla.), 1960. (*DA* 20:4005)
109. WAGNER, EDWIN E. "Differences Between Old and Young Executives on Objective Psychological Test Variables." *J Gerontol* 15:296–9 Jl '60. * (*PA* 35:1328)
110. BAKER, ROBERT L., AND SCHUTZ, RICHARD E. "A Criterion Factor Analysis of the Case of Mickey Murphy." *Personnel & Guid J* 40:282–5 N '61. * (*PA* 36:4KD82B)
111. BENDIG, A. W. "Improving the Factorial Purity of Guilford's Restraint and Thoughtfulness Scales." Abstract. *J Consult Psychol* 25:462 O '61. * (*PA* 37:3136)
112. BENDIG, A. W., AND EIGENBRODE, CHARLES R. "A Factor Analytic Investigation of Personality Variables and Reminiscence in Motor Learning." *J Abn & Social Psychol* 62:698–700 My '61. * (*PA* 36:4CF98B)
113. BORGATTA, EDGAR F. "Mood, Personality, and Interaction." *J General Psychol* 64:105–37 Ja '61. * (*PA* 35:6415)
114. BORGATTA, EDGAR F.; IN COLLABORATION WITH HENRY J. MEYER. "Make A Sentence Test: An Approach to Objective Scoring of Sentence Completions." *Genetic Psychol Monogr* 63:3–65 F '61. * (*PA* 35:6435)
115. COOK, DESMOND L.; LINDEN, JAMES D.; AND McKAY, HARRISON E. "A Factor Analysis of Teacher Trainee Responses to Selected Personality Inventories." *Ed & Psychol Meas* 21:865–72 w '61. * (*PA* 36:5HF65C)
116. FOX, AUGUSTA MEREDITH. *Relationships Between Personality and Leader Behavior of Elementary School Principals.* Doctor's thesis, North Texas State College (Denton, Tex.), 1961. (*DA* 22:2263)
117. HAND, JACK, AND REYNOLDS, HERBERT H. "Suppressing Distortion in Temperament Inventories." *J Consult Psychol* 25:180–1 Ap '61. * (*PA* 36:4HF80H)
118. HOWARD, MAURICE LLOYD. *A Study of Under-Achieving College Students With High Academic Ability From the Phenomenological Frame of Reference.* Doctor's thesis, University of Colorado (Boulder, Colo.), 1961. (*DA* 22:3040)
119. HUBERT, WILLIS JONES. *Personality Differences and Similarities Between Offender and Non-Offender Air Force Motor Vehicle Operators.* Doctor's thesis, New York University (New York, N.Y.), 1961. (*DA* 22:156)
120. JACKSON, JAY M. "The Stability of Guilford-Zimmerman Personality Measures." *J Appl Psychol* 45:431–4 D '61. * (*PA* 37:1257)
121. KAESS, WALTER A.; WITRYOL, SAM L.; AND NOLAN, RICHARD E. "Reliability, Sex Differences, and Validity in the Leaderless Group Discussion Technique." *J Appl Psychol* 45:345–50 O '61. * (*PA* 36:5GF45K)
122. KRUG, ROBERT E., AND MOYER, K. E. "An Analysis of the F Scale: 2, Relationship to Standardized Personality Inventories." *J Social Psychol* 53:293–301 Ap '61. * (*PA* 36:1HC93K)
123. McKENNA, HELEN VERONICA. "Religious Attitudes and Personality Traits." *J Social Psychol* 54:379–88 Ag '61. * (*PA* 36:3GD79M)
124. MARKS, ALVIN; MICHAEL, WILLIAM B.; AND KAISER, HENRY F. "Dimensions of Creativity and Temperament in Officer Evaluation." *Psychol Rep* 9:635–8 D '61. *
125. MARKS, ALVIN; MICHAEL, WILLIAM B.; AND KAISER, HENRY F. "Sources of Noncognitive Variance in 21 Measures of Creativity." *Psychol Rep* 9:287–90 O '61. *
126. REES, MARJORIE E., AND GOLDMAN, MORTON. "Some Relationships Between Creativity and Personality." *J General Psychol* 65:145–61 Jl '61. * (*PA* 36:2HD45R)
127. SUTTER, CYRIL ROBERT. *A Comparative Study of the Interest and Personality Patterns of Major Seminarians.* Doctor's thesis, Fordham University (New York, N.Y.), 1961. (*DA* 22:328)
128. VAN WAGENEN, DONALD RICHARD. *The Relation of Selected Non-Intellectual Factors to Academic Achievement in*

Several College Groups. Doctor's thesis, Syracuse University (Syracuse, N.Y.), 1961. (*DA* 23:539)

129. WATLEY, DONIVAN JASON. *Prediction of Academic Success in a College of Business Administration.* Doctor's thesis, University of Denver (Denver, Colo.), 1961. (*DA* 22:3527)

130. WITHERSPOON, ROBERT PAUL. *A Comparison of the Temperament Trait, Interest, Achievement, and Scholastic Aptitude Test Score Patterns of College Seniors Majoring in Different Fields at the Arkansas State Teachers College.* Doctor's thesis, University of Arkansas (Fayetteville, Ark.), 1961. (*DA* 22:1091)

131. BALSHAN, IRIS D. "Muscle Tension and Personality in Women." *Arch Gen Psychiatry* 7:436–48 D '62. * (*PA* 38:2771)

132. BENDIG, A. W. "Factor Analyses of the Guilford Zimmerman Temperament Survey and the Maudsley Personality Inventory." *J General Psychol* 67:21–6 Jl '62. * (*PA* 37:3169)

133. BENDIG, A. W. "The Factorial Validity of the Guilford Zimmerman Temperament Survey." *J General Psychol* 67:309–17 O '62. * (*PA* 37:8008)

134. BORGATTA, EDGAR F. "The Coincidence of Subtests in Four Personality Inventories." *J Social Psychol* 56:227–44 Ap '62. * (*PA* 37:1247)

135. BORGATTA, EDGAR F. "A Systematic Study of Interaction Process Scores, Peer and Self-Assessments, Personality and Other Variables." *Genetic Psychol Monogr* 65:219–91 My '62. * (*PA* 37:3030)

136. CAMPBELL, JOEL T.; OTIS, JAY L.; LISKE, RALPH E.; AND PRIEN, ERICH P. "Assessments of Higher-Level Personnel: II, Validity of the Over-All Assessment Process." *Personnel Psychol* 15:63–74 sp '62. * (*PA* 37:3908)

137. CAMPBELL, ROBERT E. "Counselor Personality and Background and His Interview Subrole Behavior." *J Counsel Psychol* 9:329–34 w '62. * (*PA* 39:2294)

138. COOK, DESMOND L. "A Note on the Relationships Between MTAI and GZTS Scores for Three Levels of Teacher Experience." *J Ed Res* 55:363–7 My '62. * (*PA* 37:5678)

139. GUPTA, G. C. "Guilford-Zimmerman Temperament Survey and Nursing Profession: A Validational Study." *Manas* 9:51–4 '62. * (*PA* 38:4309)

140. HICKS, JOHN A., AND STONE, JOICS B. "The Identification of Traits Related to Managerial Success." *J Appl Psychol* 46:428–32 D '62. * (*PA* 37:5714)

141. HOGUE, J. PIERRE; OTIS, JAY L.; AND PRIEN, ERICH P. "Assessments of Higher-Level Personnel: VI, Validity of Predictions Based on Projective Techniques." *Personnel Psychol* 15:335–44 au '62. * (*PA* 37:7249)

142. KHAN, LILIAN. "Factor Analysis of Certain Aptitude and Personality Variables." *Indian J Psychol* 37:27–38 Mr '62. * (*PA* 37:6716)

143. LANNA, MATTHEW GEORGE. *Vocational Interests in Relation to Some Aspects of Personality and Adjustment.* Doctor's thesis, Columbia University (New York, N.Y.), 1962. (*DA* 23:4421)

144. MILES, JAMES B. "Aesthetic Learning Through Experiences in a Correlated Program of Instruction in Art, Music and Modern Dance." *Studies Art Ed* 4:34–45 f '62. *

145. ROBINSON, WILLIS. *A Validity Study of the Testing Program for the Selection of Students for Teacher Education.* Doctor's thesis, Purdue University (Lafayette, Ind.), 1962. (*DA* 23:2812)

146. RUPIPER, OMER JOHN. "A Psychometric Evaluation of Experienced Teachers." *J Ed Res* 55:368–71 My '62. *

147. SKLAR, MAURICE, AND EDWARDS, ALLAN E. "Presbycusis: A Factor Analysis of Hearing and Psychological Characteristics of Men Over 65 Years Old." *J Auditory Res* 2:194–207 Jl '62. *

148. STAATS, A. W.; STAATS, C. K.; HEARD, W. G.; AND FINLEY, J. R. "Operant Conditioning of Factor Analytic Personality Traits." *J General Psychol* 66:101–14 Ja '62. * (*PA* 36:3CJo1S)

149. STAGNER, ROSS. "Personality Variables in Union-Management Relations." *J Appl Psychol* 46:350–7 O '62. * (*PA* 37:5811)

150. THOM, WILLIAM T., 3RD. *A Validation of Children's Behavioral Categories Based on Fear, Against the Guilford-Zimmerman Temperament Survey.* Doctor's thesis, Pennsylvania State University (University Park, Pa.), 1962. (*DA* 23:1090)

151. WATLEY, DONIVAN J., AND MARTIN, H. T. "Prediction of Academic Success in a College of Business Administration." *Personnel & Guid J* 41:147–54 O '62. * (*PA* 37:5656)

152. WILLIAMS, DONALD EARL. *The Interrelatedness of Student Teachers' Temperament Traits, Their Attitudes Toward Youth, and Their Teacher-Pupil Interpersonal Problems.* Doctor's thesis, North Texas State University (Denton, Tex.), 1962. (*DA* 23:3255)

153. *Normative Information: Manager and Executive Testing.* New York: Richardson, Bellows, Henry & Co., Inc., May 1963. Pp. 45. *

154. BAGGALEY, ANDREW R. "Comparison of Temperament Scores of Jewish and Gentile Male Students." *Psychol Rep* 13:598 O '63. * (*PA* 38:8232)

155. BENDIG, A. W., AND MARTIN, ANN M. "The Factor

Structure of Temperament Traits and Needs." *J General Psychol* 69:27–36 Jl '63. * (*PA* 38:4297)

156. BENDIG, A. W., AND MEYER, WILLIAM J. "The Factorial Structure of the Scales of the Primary Mental Abilities, Guilford Zimmerman Temperament Survey, and Kuder Preference Record." *J General Psychol* 68:195–201 Ap '63. * (*PA* 38:53)

157. BRITTON, JOSEPH H. "Dimensions of Adjustment of Older Adults." *J Gerontol* 18:60–5 Ja '63. * (*PA* 38:4098)

158. COOK, DESMOND L.; LEBOLD, WILLIAM; AND LINDEN, JAMES D. "A Comparison of Factor Analyses of Education and Engineering Responses to Selected Personality Inventories." *J Teach Ed* 14:137–41 Je '63. *

159. COOLEY, WILLIAM W. "Predicting Choice of a Career in Scientific Research." *Personnel & Guid J* 42:21–8 S '63. *

160. DASS, S. L. "Selection of Situations for a Personality Test Based on Movie Pictures." *J Psychol Res* 7:10–5 Ja '63. * (*PA* 38:2691)

161. GOLDSTEIN, IRIS BALSHAN. "A Comparison Between Taylor's and Freeman's Manifest Anxiety Scales." Abstract. *J Consult Psychol* 27:466 O '63. *

162. HUGHES, BILLIE EDWARD. *Predicting Achievement in a Graduate School of Education.* Doctor's thesis, North Texas State University (Denton, Tex.), 1963. (*DA* 24:1448)

163. KASSARJIAN, HAROLD H. "Success, Failure, and Personality." *Psychol Rep* 13:567–74 O '63. * (*PA* 38:8591)

164. KJELDERGAARD, PAUL M., AND CARROLL, JOHN B. "Two Measures of Free Association Response and Their Relations to Scores on Selected Personality and Verbal Ability Tests." *Psychol Rep* 12:667–70 Je '63. * (*PA* 38:6021)

165. LEE, EUGENE C. "Career Development of Science Teachers." *J Res Sci Teach* 1:54–63 Mr '63. *

166. LEVITT, EUGENE E.; BRADY, JOHN PAUL; AND LUBIN, BERNARD. "Correlates of Hypnotizability in Young Women: Anxiety and Dependency." *J Personality* 31:52–7 Mr '63. *

167. MARWELL, GERALD. "Visibility in Small Groups." *J Social Psychol* 61:311–25 D '63. * (*PA* 38:8309)

168. MURRAY, JOHN B., AND GALVIN, JOSEPH. "Correlational Study of the MMPI and GZTS." *J General Psychol* 69:267–73 O '63. * (*PA* 39:1751)

169. SINGER, JEROME L., AND ANTROBUS, JOHN S. "A Factor-Analytic Study of Daydreaming and Conceptually-Related Cognitive and Personality Variables." *Percept & Motor Skills* 17:187–209 Ag '63. * (*PA* 38:7418)

170. WANSER, BYRON ROTHWELL. *The Effect of Loss of Father Upon the Development of Certain Personality Traits.* Doctor's thesis, University of Denver (Denver, Colo.), 1963. (*DA* 24:1484)

171. WIMSATT, WILLIAM R., AND VESTRE, NORRIS D. "Extra-experimental Effects in Verbal Conditioning." *J Consult Psychol* 27:400–4 O '63. * (*PA* 38:4429)

172. WINFREE, PAGE, AND MEYER, MERLE. "Sociability and the Conditioning of Pronouns 'I' and 'We.'" *Psychol Rep* 13:781–2 D '63. * (*PA* 38:8325)

173. ZACHAREWICZ, MARY MISAELA. *Relations Between Teaching Attitudes of Prospective Teachers and Their Self Descriptions.* Doctor's thesis, Fordham University (New York, N.Y.), 1963. (*DA* 24:876)

For a review by David R. Saunders, see 5:65; for reviews by William Stephenson and Neil Van Steenberg, see 4:49 (1 excerpt).

[111]

★**The Handicap Problems Inventory.** Ages 16 and over with physical disabilities; 1960; 4 scores: personal, family, social, vocational; 1 form (4 pages); manual (14 pages); $3 per 25 tests, postage extra; $1 per specimen set, postpaid; (30–35) minutes; George N. Wright and H. H. Remmers; [University Book Store]. *

DOROTHY M. CLENDENEN, *Assistant Director, Test Division, The Psychological Corporation, New York, New York.*

This checklist of 280 items was developed for use with the physically handicapped, and is designed to provide "an estimate of the impact of disability as the client sees it and is able to verbalize it." The manual notes that, for the present at least, the HPI should not be used for screening purposes, since correlational studies using outside criteria have not been made.

Statements obtained from 2,870 responses to 70 sentence completion items which had been administered to a random sample of 100 disabled persons were edited to eliminate duplicate problems and problems applicable only to a specific impairment. Editorial changes were kept to a minimum, except to insure that all words used are at or easier than the fifth grade level. Illustrative items include "Try to forget about being handicapped," "Worry because handicap works a hardship on family," "Lack a well-rounded social life," "Find it hard to make a living."

Those items selected were randomized and submitted to 27 psychologists for assignment to one of four "context" categories, resulting in the following classification: 96 personal items, 68 family items, 54 social items, 62 vocational items. A tryout with another sample of 100 disabled individuals, including interviews with 35, provided evidence of clarity of instructions and items, and of comprehensiveness of the list. The normative sample of 1,027 was randomly selected from those eligible for services of a state department of vocational rehabilitation. Other kinds of agencies are urged to study the composition of the sample prior to assuming that their client group is comparable. Percentile norms are presented for each subtest; although "total test" norms are reported, their use is not recommended.

All administrations of the inventory, including that of the final form for which normative and reliability data were obtained, were by mail. The per cent of return exceeded 86, and "this, and statistically derived information of a technical nature, leads to the conclusion that no important bias resulted from the nonparticipating group." This statistical information should have been clearly presented in the manual.

The inventory is well designed for ease of both administration and hand scoring. A single template for each of the four areas is used on all four pages of the test. Although the manual states that the inventory is machine scorable, such scoring keys must be prepared locally (or by the publisher, at additional cost). The answer sheet has been designed for the IBM 805 test scoring machine, but it was not printed by IBM and inspection indicates the probability that the registration may not be sufficiently

exact for accurate and trouble-free machine scoring.

Reliability estimates, computed by Kuder-Richardson formula 20, range from .91 to .95 for the subtests, which suggests sufficiently high internal consistency for use in individual counseling. Means and sigmas are not given. No test-retest coefficients are reported, although these would provide useful evidence of stability, a fact which is noted in the manual under needed research. One also wonders why inter-correlation among the subtests has not been reported, since such information would be of value both from a statistical and from a psychological point of view.

Instructions to the examinee include the sentence "Skip over, do not mark, those problems which you do not have or which you feel have nothing to do with being handicapped." This may mean that some of the problems felt by a disabled person but not, in his thinking, related to his disability will not be checked; these will have to be sought by other instruments or through the interview. The manual, in discussing interpretation, points out that "Area scores indicate which life situations bear the brunt of the greatest impact of the disablement." It cautions the counselor to note that low scores may mean a tendency to minimize one's handicap, or to cover up serious problems. Commendably, it is stated that "Avoidance of known problems....suggests the possibility of intense emotional feelings which must be handled with great caution. Only counselors well trained in clinical psychology should attempt to probe into such defenses."

Frequency of choice for each item by various disability groups is reported; also comparison of means for each subtest by such personal background variables as age, education, years disabled. These data are useful in enabling the counselor to compare an individual's scores with the average of appropriate subgroups. Since statistically significant differences are found on several of these demographic variables, and since the n's are sizable, one wonders why norms are presented only for the total sample.

So far as this reviewer is aware, the manual is accurate in stating that the HPI is "the only instrument of its kind especially constructed for the disabled population." The developmental work has been carefully done, and the manual is modest in its claims. The publisher's interest in cooperative research is made explicit and a list of 12 areas for further research is given, including studies of the relationship of area scores to the individual's actual personality adjustment; studies of predictive validity in reference to outcome of rehabilitation counseling; test-retest studies not only over a short term (for stability), but for comparison of retest scores after application of various rehabilitation services. Despite the reviewer's belief that such research is imperative if the inventory is to achieve maximum usefulness, and a belief that at least some of the above mentioned research should have been done prior to general publication, the HPI may well be used as an aid to the interview and to assist the counselor in understanding the problems of a disabled client.

[112]

★Harvard Group Scale of Hypnotic Susceptibility. College and adults; 1959–62; adaptation of Form A of the *Stanford Hypnotic Susceptibility Scale* for group administration; Form A ('62, 8 pages); manual ('62, 22 pages); no data on reliability; $6.50 per 25 tests; $1.25 per manual; $1.50 per specimen set; postage extra; (50–70) minutes; Ronald E. Shor and Emily Carota Orne; Consulting Psychologists Press, Inc. *

REFERENCES

1. BENTLER, P. M., AND HILGARD, ERNEST R. "A Comparison of Group and Individual Induction of Hypnosis With Self-Scoring and Observer-Scoring." *Int J Clin & Exp Hypnosis* 11:49–54 Ja '63. * (PA 37:8085)
1a. BENTLER, P. M., AND ROBERTS, MARY R. "Hypnotic Susceptibility Assessed in Large Groups." *Int J Clin & Exp Hypnosis* 11:93–7 Ap '63. * (PA 38:4430)
2. ROSENHAN, DAVID, AND LONDON, PERRY. "Hypnosis: Expectation, Susceptibility, and Performance." *J Abn & Social Psychol* 66:77–81 Ja '63. * (PA 37:5238)
3. SHOR, RONALD E., AND ORNE, EMILY CAROTA. "Norms on the Harvard Group Scale of Hypnotic Susceptibility, Form A." *Int J Clin & Exp Hypnosis* 11:39–47 Ja '63. * (PA 37:8102)

SEYMOUR FISHER, *Research Professor of Psychology, and Director, Psychopharmacology Laboratory, Boston University School of Medicine, Boston, Massachusetts.*

The *Harvard Group Scale of Hypnotic Susceptibility* provides a quantitative approach to the selection of subjects for participation in hypnotic studies. It is thus particularly aimed at the researcher who requires relatively large numbers of a certain kind of hypnotic subject (e.g., very poor, or excellent) but is seeking some way to avoid individual evaluations of hypnotic susceptibility. Although group induction of hypnosis has long been utilized by researchers for preliminary screening and selection, the Harvard Group Scale permits a more systematic approach than heretofore available.

This approach is based upon self-report scoring by each subject at the termination of a standardized induction procedure. Available data indicate good concordance between a subject's self-report and observer ratings, suggesting that (under these conditions) "*S*s who have been relieved of amnesia following hypnotic induction are able, retrospectively, to report their performance under hypnotic suggestion with a high degree of accuracy" (*1*).

The Group Scale itself is modeled after Form A of the *Stanford Hypnotic Susceptibility Scale,* and yields a single score (from 0 to 12) of susceptibility. The score obtained in a group session correlates .74 with an observer's score in a subsequent individual session (*1*). Individual scores can be predicted from the group score with a standard error of estimate of 1.8.

Availability of the Group Scale should be of immense practical value to the hypnotic researcher as a rapid assessment, screening, and selection device. Other uses of the Group Scale will undoubtedly be suggested with continued use. For certain kinds of studies (e.g., attempts to modify susceptibility), where retesting on an individual basis would seem desirable, it is likely that additional precision may be obtained by including an individual pretest—that is, use the Group Scale as a preliminary means of excluding subjects, and then utilize individual evaluations for those subjects who will participate in the research.

[113]

Heston Personal Adjustment Inventory. Grades 9–16 and adults; 1949; 6 scores: analytical thinking, sociability, emotional stability, confidence, personal relations, home satisfaction; IBM; 1 form (16 pages); manual (39 pages); no non-college adult norms; $5 per 35 tests; separate answer sheets may be used; $1.85 per 35 IBM answer sheets; 40¢ per set of machine scoring stencils; 45¢ per manual; 60¢ per specimen set; postage extra; (40–55) minutes; Joseph C. Heston; [Harcourt, Brace & World, Inc.]. *

REFERENCES

1–2. See 4:50.
3–13. See 5:66.
14. DOTSON, ELSIE JENOISE. *A Study of the Agreement of Introversion-Extroversion Factors as Defined by Various Factor Analysts.* Doctor's thesis, University of Kentucky (Lexington, Ky.), 1951. (DA 18:1095)
15. ARBUCKLE, DUGALD S. "Self-Ratings and Test Scores on Two Standardized Personality Inventories." *Personnel & Guid J* 37:292–3 D '58. * (PA 36:2HE92A)
16. HOLMES, JACK A. *Personality and Spelling Ability.* University of California Publications in Education, Vol. 12, No. 4. Berkeley, Calif.: University of California Press, 1959. Pp. vii, 213–91. *
17. WRIGHT, JOHN C. "Personal Adjustment and Its Relationship to Religious Attitudes and Certainty." *Relig Ed* 54:521–3 N–D '59. *
18. McDANIEL, ERNEST D., AND STEPHENSON, HOWARD W. "Prediction of Scholastic Achievement in Pharmacy at the University of Kentucky." *Am J Pharm Ed* 24:162–9 sp '60. *
19. MAGNUSSEN, M. H., AND MAGNUSSEN, M. G. "The Relationship Between University Dispensary Visits, Academic Ability, and Personality Factors." *J Psychol Studies* 11:221–3 My–Je '60. *
20. WELNA, CECILIA THERESA. *A Study of Reasons for Success or Failure in College Mathematics Courses.* Doctor's

thesis, University of Connecticut (Storrs, Conn.), 1960. (*DA* 21:1811)
    21. HOSFORD, PRENTISS MCINTYRE. *Characteristics of Science-Talented and Language-Talented Secondary School Students.* Doctor's thesis, University of Georgia (Athens, Ga.), 1961. (*DA* 22:2687)
    22. KIESSLING, RALPH J., AND KALISH, RICHARD A. "Correlates of Success in Leaderless Group Discussion." *J Social Psychol* 54:359–65 Ag '61. * (*PA* 36:3GE59K)
    23. KINGSTON, ALBERT J. "The Relationship of Heston Personal Adjustment Inventory Scores to Other Measures Commonly Employed in Counseling." *J Ed Res* 55:83–6 O '61. *
    24. CRANE, WILLIAM J. "Screening Devices for Occupational Therapy Majors." *Am J Occup Ther* 16:131–2 My–Je '62. * (*PA* 37:4078)
    25. NICHOLS, ROBERT C. "Subtle, Obvious and Stereotype Measures of Masculinity-Femininity." *Ed & Psychol Meas* 22:449–61 au '62. * (*PA* 37:5014)
    26. DURFLINGER, GLENN W. "Academic and Personality Differences Between Women Students Who Do Complete the Elementary Teaching Credential Program and Those Who Do Not." *Ed & Psychol Meas* 23:775–83 w '63. *
    27. DURFLINGER, GLENN W. "Personality Correlates of Success in Student-Teaching." *Ed & Psychol Meas* 23:383–90 su '63. * (*PA* 38:1427)

For reviews by Albert Ellis, Hans J. Eysenck, and E. Lowell Kelly, see 4:50 (1 excerpt).

[114]

★**The Hoffer-Osmond Diagnostic Test (HOD).** Mental patients; 1961; also called *H.O.D. Test;* card sorting test for the diagnosis of schizophrenia; 3 scores: paranoid, perceptual, total; individual; 1 form ['61, 145 cards]; instructions-norms ['61, 6 cards]; record sheet ['61, 1 page]; $22.50 per set of cards, instructions, 100 record sheets, and copy of journal containing reference 2 below; postpaid; [15–20 minutes]; A. Hoffer and H. Osmond; Gilbert & Co. *

REFERENCES

    1. HOFFER, A., AND MAHON, M. "The Presence of Unidentified Substances in the Urine of Psychiatric Patients." *J Neuropsychiatry* 2:331–62 Jl–Ag '61. *
    2. HOFFER, A., AND OSMOND, H. "A Card Sorting Test Helpful in Making Psychiatric Diagnosis." *J Neuropsychiatry* 2:306–30 Jl–Ag '61. *
    3. HOFFER, A., AND OSMOND, H. "The Relationship Between an Unknown Factor ('US') in Urine of Subjects and HOD Test Results." *J Neuropsychiatry* 2:363–70 Jl–Ag '61. *
    3a. HOFFER, A., AND OSMOND, H. "The Association Between Schizophrenia and Two Objective Tests." *Can Med Assn J* 87:641–6 S 22 '62. *
    4. HOFFER, A., AND OSMOND, H. "A Card Sorting Test Helpful in Establishing Prognosis." *Am J Psychiatry* 118:840–1 Mr '62. *
    5. STEWART, CHARLES N., AND MAHOOD, MARGARET C. "A Multiple Group Comparison of Scores on the Hoffer-Osmond Diagnostic Test." *Can Psychiatric Assn J* 8:133–7 Ap '63. *

MAURICE LORR, *Chief, Outpatient Psychiatric Research Laboratory, Veterans Benefits Office; and Lecturer in Psychology, Catholic University of America; Washington, D.C.*

The HOD is a card sorting test designed to differentiate schizophrenics from other diagnostic groups and normal people. The test consists of 145 statements printed on 3 by 5 cards which are to be sorted by the examinee, after shuffling, into two boxes marked True and False. Card responses may be recorded on a separate answer sheet.

The HOD items are concerned with aberrations in perception, thought, and feeling. One group of items resembling WAIS similarity problems measures the way the subject classifies objects; that is, it tests whether he uses a visual or functional classification. The total score is defined as the number of statements sorted True. A paranoid score is based on 15 statements while the perceptual score derives from responses to 53 statements.

The norm sample consisted of patients and normals tested by psychiatric nurses in two Saskatchewan hospitals, one a provincial and the other a university hospital. Patients in the university hospital were tested soon after admission and before active treatment. The chronic schizophrenics from the provincial hospital consisted of patients already hospitalized. Included in the norm sample were 121 non-schizophrenic patients, 100 normals, 158 schizophrenics, and 13 patients with organic psychoses. The non-schizophrenics are grouped by diagnosis, but the schizophrenics are separated only on the basis of duration of illness.

Conventional estimates of reliability are not given nor is it possible to compute these as no measures of score dispersion are provided. Reliability is defined as the experimental ratio of different to similar responses divided by the ratio expected by chance. Since the retest data are confined to repetitions just before patient discharge, their value is questionable.

What evidence is there in support of the validity of HOD? The tables indicate (*a*) scores increase with duration of hospitalization for schizophrenia; (*b*) schizophrenic subjects score significantly higher than neurotics; (*c*) after treatment, clinically improved schizophrenics have lowered scores. Only a few tests of significance are reported, and basic data such as standard deviations are not provided. However, from the frequency distributions of the perceptual and the total scores, it is possible to determine that if a total score of 30 or less is used as a cutting point, 71 per cent of hospitalized schizophrenics may be identified. The perceptual score does better since a cutting score of three or less identifies correctly 79 per cent of schizophrenics and 72 per cent of the non-schizophrenics. However, as no base rates for the various diagnostic groupings are given, the advantage of test identification over base rate prediction cannot be assessed. Structural aspects of the test items and of the subtests, such as their popularity or intercorrelations, are not reported. Only the correlation between paranoid and total scores is given.

The HOD test must thus be viewed as an interesting, partly validated research device in an early stage of development and in need of further statistical analysis. Especially lacking are data characterizing the norm sample and base rates on diagnostic groups. Since intelligence and education may well play an important role in response, evidence concerning these variables should be supplied.

WILLIAM SCHOFIELD, *Professor of Psychology, University of Minnesota, Minneapolis, Minnesota.*

This is an objectively scored card sorting test designed primarily to differentiate schizophrenic from other psychiatric conditions. Format of both the test materials and scoring sheets is attractive and convenient. The 145 items appear singly in large, black type on 8.7 × 6.1 cm. plastic cards. Instructions for administration, recording, and scoring, and norms are reproduced on similar cards, and all are enclosed in a small telescoping box which separates into cover and box proper, labeled, respectively, in large print, "FALSE" and "TRUE"; these provide convenient containers into which the subject sorts the test items to indicate his response. The test can be easily administered by nonprofessional hospital or clinic personnel and is claimed to be applicable to "over 90%" of patients. Scoring is simple, objective, and should be completely reliable within the limits of clerical error.

The 145 symptomatic items represent perceptual distortion in the areas of vision, audition, touch, taste, smell, and time perception; thought disturbances and feelings are also tapped. A check on consistency of response, and presumably on the care with which all items are answered, is afforded by a subset of 20 items adapted from the Similarities subtest of the Wechsler scales. These items permit a response indicative of either a visual or functional classification; by repeating the same content with reverse format, consistency of response is tapped (e.g., "An axe is like a saw because they have handles, rather than because they are tools" and "An axe is like a saw because they are tools, rather than because they have handles").

Items are scored only when answered "True." Weighted scores (either 1, 2, or 5 points) for each card are based solely upon the frequency of a "True" response in a sample of "about

150 normal and non-schizophrenic subjects." Cards seldom (never or once) sorted as "True" by this sample are given 5 points; examples: "There are some people trying to do me harm" and "People look as if they were dead now." Examples of 1-point cards are: "People are often envious of me" and "My body odor is much more unpleasant now." Three scores are obtained: total score, paranoid score, and perceptual score. In a sample of 162 schizophrenics, the paranoid scores and total score correlate .82, while the comparable statistic is .69 for a sample of 125 nonschizophrenic patients.

Test-retest reliability as computed by any of the standard methods is not reported for either psychiatric or normal samples. Cumbersome and ambiguous ratios of the number of true responses constant from test to retest are reported for samples of normals and patients as evidence of reliability. It is probable that orthodox reliability coefficients would be satisfactory.

Failure to use customary analytic techniques in item selection coupled with the grossness of item content results in an instrument of limited diagnostic utility. There is sizeable overlap in the score distributions for schizophrenic and nonschizophrenic patients. Applied in an outpatient setting where borderline pathology and subtlety of symptoms make diagnosis difficult, this test would yield a high rate of false negatives. The authors report that one third of the lowest scores (least pathology) they have observed were obtained by diagnosed schizophrenics.

In a psychiatric hospital population of severely ill patients, the test would probably prove less useful for differentiation of schizophrenia than for measurement of levels of perceptual pathology and especially, by retest, for checking on the effectiveness of therapeutic programs.

[115]

★**Holland Vocational Preference Inventory, Research Edition, Third Revision.** College and adults; 1953–59; 12 or 13 scores: omitted items, infrequency, acquiescence, physical activity (males only), intellectuality, social responsibility, conformity, verbal activity, emotionality, control, aggressiveness, masculinity-femininity, status; separate forms ('53, 2 pages) for men and women; mimeographed preliminary manual ('59, 36 pages); profile [no date, 2 pages] of temporary norms for college students; no data on reliability for omitted items; tentative norms; $2.25 per 25 tests; $1 per set of keys; $1 per 25 profiles; $1 per manual; $1.50 per specimen set; postage extra; (30–

45) minutes; John L. Holland; Consulting Psychologists Press, Inc. *

REFERENCES
1. WALSH, R. P. *Vocational Interest, Their Stability and Personality Correlates in Hospitalized Tuberculosis Patients.* Master's thesis, University of Maryland (College Park, Md.), 1956.
2. HOLLAND, JOHN L. "A Personality Inventory Employing Occupational Titles." *J Appl Psychol* 42:336–42 O '58. * (*PA* 33:9955)
3. HOLLAND, JOHN L. "Some Limitations of Teacher Ratings as Predictors of Creativity." *J Ed Psychol* 50:219–23 O '59. * (*PA* 36:1KH19H)
4. HOLLAND, JOHN L. "The Prediction of College Grades From Personality and Aptitude Variables." *J Ed Psychol* 51:245–54 O '60. * (*PA* 36:1KL45H)
5. HOLLAND, JOHN L. "The Relation of the Vocational Preference Inventory to the Sixteen Personality Factor Questionnaire." *J Appl Psychol* 44:291–6 Ag '60. * (*PA* 35:4015)
6. FORSYTH, RALPH P., AND FAIRWEATHER, GEORGE W. "Psychotherapeutic and Other Hospital Treatment Criteria: The Dilemma." *J Abn & Social Psychol* 62:598–604 My '61. * (*PA* 36:4IE98F)
7. HOLLAND, JOHN L. "Creative and Academic Performance Among Talented Adolescents." *J Ed Psychol* 52:136–47 Je '61. * (*PA* 38:3201)
8. HOLLAND, JOHN L. "Some Explorations With Occupational Titles." Comment by Henry Borow. *J Counsel Psychol* 8:82–7 sp '61. * (*PA* 36:3LB82H)
9. HOLLAND, JOHN L. "Some Explorations of Theory of Vocational Choice: 1, One- and Two-Year Longitudinal Studies." *Psychol Monogr* 76(26):1–49 '62. * (*PA* 38:9340)
10. HOLLAND, JOHN L., AND ASTIN, ALEXANDER W. "The Prediction of the Academic, Artistic, Scientific, and Social Achievement of Undergraduates of Superior Scholastic Aptitude." *J Ed Psychol* 53:132–43 Je '62. * (*PA* 37:2010)
11. HOLLAND, JOHN L. "Explorations of a Theory of Vocational Choice: Part 1, Vocational Images and Choice." *Voc Guid Q* 11:232–9 su '63. * (*PA* 38:4746)
12. HOLLAND, JOHN L. "Explorations of a Theory of Vocational Choice: Part 2, Self-Descriptions and Vocational Preferences; Part 3, Coping Behavior, Competencies, and Vocational Preferences." *Voc Guid Q* 12:17–24 au '63. * (*PA* 38:6694)
13. HOLLAND, JOHN L. "Explorations of a Theory of Vocational Choice: Part 4, Vocational Daydreams." *Voc Guid Q* 12:93–7 w '63–64. * (*PA* 38:9339)

ROBERT L. FRENCH, *Vice President for Research and Testing, Science Research Associates, Inc., Chicago, Illinois.*

This is a "Research Edition" of a personality instrument designed for use with people of college age or beyond. In form it is a vocational interest checklist involving 300 occupational titles, to each of which a subject responds by indicating interest or lack of interest in the occupation, or, by leaving it unmarked, indecision. The instrument rests on the reasonable assumption that such preferences reflect the operation of significant personality variables. At the same time a unique advantage of the approach appears to be that subjects can provide this information without feeling that it is particularly self-revelatory.

A score can be obtained on each of 13 scales (12 in the case of the woman's form). These reflect an essentially pragmatic rather than a systematic, theoretical orientation. Potentially fruitful scoring dimensions were defined in the first instance after a review of the literature on personality factors in interest and vocational choice. Eight of the scales were then established by assigning items (occupational titles)

which appeared intuitively to epitomize a scale definition. These were subsequently revised several times on the basis of analysis of internal consistency data and scale intercorrelations. Of the other five scales, three—Omitted Items, Infrequency, and Acquiescence—are response set scales. The Status scale items are derived from previous studies of occupational status rankings; Masculinity-Femininity items, from analysis of actual sex differences in item response.

Although some of the original scales were eliminated as a result of a cluster analysis and a useful degree of independence was achieved among those remaining, some of the reported intercorrelations are high enough to suggest that further reduction might be possible and desirable. Thus, of the 66 intercorrelations obtained for 12 scales on a sample of 100 male college freshmen, 38 are significant at the .05 level of confidence ($r = .30$) and 8 exceed a value of .65. It should be noted that there is some item overlap between scales; for example, a count of overlaps by pairs of scales for men reveals approximately 60 items in which the same response is scored in a pair of scales, and approximately 40 items in which opposite responses contribute to two scales. This condition does not necessarily reduce the value of the scales, but for simplicity of interpretation it would be desirable either to eliminate all item overlap or to provide in the manual a picture of the extent to which intercorrelations among scales are affected by this factor.

Most of the scales have acceptable levels of reliability. Corrected split-half reliabilities based on 100 male college freshmen range from .72 to .95 on various scales, with a median of .85. For 100 females, they range from .68 to .90, with a median of .79. Test-retest data for 38 tuberculosis patients yielded correlations over a period of about four months which ranged from .58 to .87, with a median of .74.

Various studies, mostly on a fairly small scale, have been reported bearing on the validity of the instrument. Statistically significant and meaningful differences are found, for example, between psychiatric patients and normal controls, and between these groups and samples of tuberculosis patients and criminal psychopaths. Likewise, meaningful differences in profiles have been reported for freshman students in the different colleges of a large university.

It is worth noting that certain scales contribute to the prediction of college achievement among students of superior academic aptitude. Significant correlations have also been obtained between certain scales and selected scales from the MMPI, *Gordon Personal Profile, Strong Vocational Interest Blank, Kuder Preference Record,* and Cattell's 16 PF test. Correlations with intelligence are negligible. Some significant correlations are found with age, most of these, interestingly, being negative.

The manual contains an interesting, useful, and conservatively stated section on interpretation, which summarizes for each scale the empirical correlates thus far established, outlines .a clinical interpretation of the scale variable, and offers an heuristic, conceptual definition of the variable. Several actual cases are presented in conclusion, a development which hopefully might be expanded in a future edition of the manual. Tentative normative data are available from the studies of the various populations already noted. These are most extensive for the college student samples, which provide the basis for a profile chart furnished with the test.

In format the test blank, manual, profiles, and scoring keys are appropriate—possibly too appropriate—to a "Research Edition." Administration presents no particular problems, though it would seem that necessary time could be reduced by elimination of the last 40 items, only a few of which are used, and these in the "Infrequency" scale. The test is awkward to score, and it may be hoped that further development will produce a more convenient mechanical scoring procedure.

In summary, the Holland inventory is an ingenious empirical approach to personality measurement which is in a relatively early stage of development. At this stage the author recommends it only for experimental use by students of adult personality, a recommendation which this reviewer can endorse with warmth. Further work with the instrument should help to improve its efficiency and to identify more clearly important areas of application.

H. BRADLEY SAGEN, *Assistant Professor of Education, University of Iowa, Iowa City, Iowa.*

The HVPI is essentially a personality inventory based upon attitudes toward various occupations. The inventory consists of 300 occupational titles to which the respondent replies like or dislike. The items are grouped into 13 scales, including 10 personality scales and 3 response set scales which also serve as check scores. There is virtually no information about the female HVPI and all references will be to the male form.

Although the development of the HVPI is of a generally high order, several points can be raised regarding the resultant characteristics of the scales. The personality scales are not at all independent of the response sets. Six of the 10 scales correlate .54 or above with Acquiescence and 4 correlate .54 or above with Infrequency; i.e., "unpopular" responses. The reason for the high correlations with Acquiescence is obvious, since 7 of the 10 scales are composed entirely of "like" responses. Because an instrument may still be valid or invalid regardless, of the extent to which response sets are controlled, the foregoing remarks do not necessarily constitute a major criticism of the HVPI. Nevertheless, the failure to control these additional sources of variance must be considered in any interpretation of the scales.

The relationships of the scale intercorrelations to the respective scale descriptions, although generally consistent, do indicate a few contradictions. The term "passive" is applied to high scores on the Responsibility scale and to low scores on the Aggressive scale, yet the relationship between the two scales is positive ($r = .41$). Similarly, persons with low Infrequency scores and those with high Conformity scores are described as culturally conforming, even though the correlation is again positive ($r = .25$). The most striking example is that in the suggestions for profile interpretation, Holland states: "For example, a subject who has the Responsibility scale as one of the high points would be expected to have the Mf scale low." The actual correlation between the two scales, however, is positive ($r = .41$).

Several of the scale distributions are quite positively skewed and thus are less than satisfactory for assessing differences among individuals at the lower end of the group. For example, on three of the scales 30 per cent of the respondents have raw scores of less than 3. Other examples of susceptibility to chance variation are also found; e.g., a person at the 50th percentile on the Mf scale may shift 20 percentile ranks up or down by the addition or deletion of two responses. (It should be pointed out, however, that the actual scale reliabilities are generally adequate. Only two have a split-half reliability of less than .80.)

The validity data are, for the most part, unimpressive. The majority of the HVPI scales significantly differentiate "normal adults" from psychiatric patients, but the difference is seldom more than one half a standard deviation, and hence the inventory would be of little use for screening purposes. Correlations with several other inventories are also reported, but few of these are substantial enough to be regarded as evidence of construct validity.

Several aspects of the validity data raise questions as to scale interpretation. Persons scoring high on Intellectuality are described as having literary and aesthetic interests, yet there is no empirical evidence to substantiate this point and, on the contrary, the scale fails to correlate significantly with either the Artistic or Literary scales of the Kuder. Secondly, the correlation between the Welsh A scale and Emotionality is nonsignificant, even though both scales are described as indicators of anxiety. Finally, the Intellectuality scale would be expected to differentiate the norm groups of college freshmen and normal adults, described as having the intelligence of semiskilled factory workers. The difference, although not tested by Holland, is obviously nonsignificant.

It is somewhat early to draw any definitive conclusions about the HVPI. Due to the almost total absence of adequate validity data, the inventory is not recommended for individual assessment or for routine use with groups. Furthermore, to this reviewer the failure to control for response sets, the inconsistencies in the intercorrelations, and the sometimes skewed or restricted scale distributions suggest the need for further revision. On the other hand, the attention given to the HVPI's initial development entitles the inventory to serious investigation before any final statement is made regarding its worth.

[116]

★The Hooper Visual Organization Test. Ages 14 and over; 1957–58; organic brain pathology; 1 form ('57, 4 pages); manual ('58, 13 pages); $18 per set of testing materials including manual, 25 tests for group administration, card material for individual administration, and 25 scoring forms; postpaid; specimen set not available; (15–20) minutes; H. Elston Hooper; Western Psychological Services. *

REFERENCES

1. HOOPER, H. ELSTON. A Study in the Construction and Preliminary Standardization of a Visual Organization Test for Use in the Measurement of Organic Deterioration. Master's thesis, University of Southern California (Los Angeles, Calif.), 1948.
2. HOOPER, H. ELSTON. "Use of the Hooper Visual Organization Test in the Differentiation of Organic Brain Pathology From Normal, Psychoneurotic, and Schizophrenic Reactions." Abstract. Am Psychologist 7:350 Jl '52. *
3. WALKER, ROBERT G. "The Revised Hooper Visual Organization Test as a Measure of Brain Damage." J Clin Psychol 12:387–8 O '56. * (PA 32:4482)
4. WALKER, ROBERT G. "Schizophrenia and Cortical Involvement." J Nerv & Mental Dis 125:226–8 Ap–Je '57. * (PA 33:4404)

RALPH M. REITAN, Professor of Psychology (Neurology), and Director, Section of Neuropsychology, Indiana University Medical Center, Indianapolis, Indiana.

The Hooper Visual Organization Test consists of 30 drawings of common objects, each of which is cut into two or more parts. The subject's task is to name the object. No time limit is set for the subject's response, but he is encouraged to guess after one minute. The score is the number of correct responses, half credit being given on certain responses to 11 of the items.

The manual describes the purpose of the test as being to differentiate subjects with and without brain damage. Some data are presented regarding validity, reliability, and the effects of age, education, and intelligence, but the references are to unpublished studies. While the manual summarizes these studies in some detail, desirable points of information are sometimes omitted. For example, in the only study referred to in which diagnoses were carefully established (normal, psychoneurotic, schizophrenic reactions, and brain damage), no direct comparisons of the groups were made with respect to age, education, or socioeconomic status. The brain damaged group performed significantly more poorly than the other groups and the distributions of scores formed the basis for a recommended cutoff score. However, it is difficult to assess the value and specificity of this finding without specific information regarding the extent to which the groups may or may not have been comparable on other variables. A second unpublished study, cited to indicate the validity of the test as a screening instrument for brain damage, used groups in which the diagnoses were admittedly insecure. Again, the subjects with presumed brain damage performed more poorly than groups with personality disturbances. However, they were also 6.2 to 8.8 years older than the other groups and had

1.2 to 3.3 years less education than the other groups (probability levels not given). Even though additional unpublished data showed a low correlation ($r = .27$) between education and Hooper VOT score and similar findings occurred in studying age, the possible influence of these variables deserves specific assessment in each study. Reliability data was based upon scores of college students and psychoneurotics rather than brain damaged samples, yielding coefficients of .82 and .78, respectively. Two published studies using the Hooper VOT have appeared. In one of these (4), evidence was derived to indicate that the scores were related to prognosis in chronic schizophrenia. The other study (3) compared "control" patients with patients suspected of having cerebral cortical involvement. The groups did not differ significantly in terms of the usual scoring procedures, but when a special scoring procedure was applied, the intergroup differences were significant.

In summary, there is not yet sufficient evidence to recommend the Hooper VOT as an instrument with special promise for detecting the psychological effects of brain lesions. Some of the preliminary results are of promise and suggest the need for further research. The effects of brain disease or damage are sufficiently diversified and complex that it would be naive to expect a single test to provide a very complete answer. It seems entirely possible that the Hooper VOT might eventually be shown to provide valuable information in the assessment of brain lesions if used as part of a psychological test battery.

OTFRIED SPREEN, *Assistant Research Professor of Neurology, State University of Iowa, Iowa City, Iowa.*

Thirty objects, cut into several parts and arranged randomly on the stimulus cards, have to be named in this test. It utilizes the deficit of visual organization or "Gestalt function" in a similar manner as Rybakoff's geometric designs, Gottschaldt's imbedded figures, fragmented figures, and similar tests which have been used for the detection of brain damage. Since these tests are not available in standardized form, Hooper's test supplements effectively the available tests of drawing, object arrangement, immediate memory, and other tests of organicity by a predominantly perceptual task excluding motor and memory functions.

The manual is rather slim and poorly organized; there is no reason why the two available validation studies should be reported in journal style rather than integrated into the rest of the manual. From the first of these studies it can be inferred that a surprisingly high number of 79 per cent of the brain damaged patients were correctly classified with no misclassification in the normal group. In the second study, this percentage dropped to a more reasonable, but still respectable 64 per cent. The validative value of such percentages depends, of course, on the type and severity of impairment in the brain damaged groups and can successfully be compared with those of other tests only when all tests are given to the same patients. Furthermore, interpretation of the sample differences reported in the manual is difficult because no matching of brain damaged and control groups is reported. Misclassification for other than brain damaged diagnostic groups is described as very low for neurotics and relatively low for two chronic schizophrenic groups (22 and 33 per cent) in the manual, whereas another study (4) used the test expressly and successfully for the differentiation and prognosis of chronic and reactive schizophrenia with the chronic schizophrenia group achieving "brain-damaged" scores on the test. This obvious contradiction of Hooper's findings warrants further investigation.

The manual reports split-half reliability coefficients of .82 and .78.

No adjustment of test scores for intelligence and age has been made. From the data presented a moderate to low correlation between test scores and educational level and intelligence in normals and a fairly high correlation with intelligence in retarded subjects can be expected. The age correlation is reported to be insignificant in several normal and clinical groups up to the age of 60, but relatively high in aged subjects. In a second study with five younger adult clinical groups, the manual states that "the absence of significant correlations between the VOT and age and education as well as intelligence....imply that the differences are not due to such factors." It appears that an adjustment for age in older subjects is necessary and that the contradictory results in regard to intelligence need clarification; the results with other tests of this type suggest that adjusted scores for different intelligence levels may be necessary.

Qualitative features have been mentioned as significant aspects for interpretation. For example, neologistic, bizarre, perseverative, or "isolate" responses may be noted in a patient's response. No data are reported as to frequency of occurrence, significance, etc. It appears doubtful whether this aspect of a test with a small number of items, only a few of which are failed by most subjects, will be amenable to systematic use, scoring, and standardization.

The manual claims that "language functions are not important in the test." This statement is rather challenging in view of the fact that the test requires naming or writing of names and is designed for the detection of brain damage. A look at the brain damaged groups, divided into right and left hemisphere lesions might have been sufficient to convince the author that the influence of language functions cannot be avoided in the present form of the test although the vocabulary level of the items is low. The whole question of locus of lesion in relation to test scores remains untouched in this first edition.

The test appears to be a promising addition to the neuropsychological laboratory. For use as a single indicator of brain damage in a screening battery, other more established tests might be preferred until comparative studies with such tests have been made. The test might be more useful if supplemented with alternate administrations avoiding the use of language (e.g., picture multiple choice). It would seem necessary to investigate further the role of locus of lesion in test performance and to adjust the scoring for the influence of intelligence and age.

[117]

Hospital Adjustment Scale. Mental patients; 1951–53; 4 ratings: communication and interpersonal relations, self-care and social responsibility, work and recreation, total; 1 form ('53, 4 pages); manual ('53, 12 pages); $3 per 25 tests; 25¢ per set of scoring key and manual; 50¢ per specimen set; postage extra; (10–20) minutes; James T. Ferguson, Paul McReynolds, and Egerton L. Ballachey (test); [Consulting Psychologists Press, Inc.]. *

REFERENCES

1–5. See 5:67.
6. GERTZ, BORIS; STILSON, DONALD W.; AND GYNTHER, MALCOLM D. "Reliability of the HAS as a Function of Length of Observation and Level of Adjustment." *J Clin Psychol* 15:36–9 Ja '59. * (PA 34:3267)
7. McREYNOLDS, PAUL, AND WEIDE, MARIAN. "Psychological Measures as Used to Predict Psychiatric Improvement and to Assess Behavioural Changes Following Prefrontal Lobotomy." *J Mental Sci* 106:256–73 Ja '60. * (PA 35:6530)
8. URMER, ALBERT H.; MALEK, ZENA; AND WENDLAND, LEONARD V. "A Hospital Adjustment Scale for Chronic Disease Patients." *J Clin Psychol* 16:397–8 O '60. * (PA 37:3425)

WILSON H. GUERTIN, *Associate Professor of Education and Psychology, University of Florida, Gainesville, Florida.*

The *Hospital Adjustment Scale* (HAS) is an instrument for rating the behavior of psychiatric patients. It has been adequately described in Lorr's review in the previous *Mental Measurements Yearbook.*

The scale's 90 items are marked as "True," "Not True," or "Doesn't Apply" by a psychiatric attendant or nurse familiar with the patient's everyday behavior. Three subscores are computed: (*a*) Communication and interpersonal relations; (*b*) Care of self and social responsibility; and (*c*) Work, activities, and recreation. Total score is derived by combining the subscale scores.

The chief criticism of the HAS relates to its weakness in reflecting multiple aspects of a psychiatric patient's adjustment. The subscales correlate with one another in the .70's. Subscale (*a*) items appear to sample in a rather haphazard fashion, but subscales (*b*) and (*c*) seem to sample important realms of behavior (*4*).

The HAS was the first published scale for rating hospitalized psychotics on the basis of behavior only. This worthy pioneer effort served to demonstrate the feasibility of constructing such a scale but it in turn has been made obsolete by the appearance of the *MACC Behavioral Adjustment Scale* and the even more recent *Psychotic Reaction Profile.* Lorr's *Psychotic Reaction Profile* seems superior to the other two in most respects.

For a review by Maurice Lorr, see 5:67.

[118]

★**How Well Do You Know Yourself?** High school, college, office and factory workers; 1959–61; 19 scores: irritability, practicality, punctuality, novelty-loving, vocational assurance, cooperativeness, ambitiousness, hypercriticalness, dejection, general morale, persistence, nervousness, seriousness, submissiveness, impulsiveness, dynamism, emotional control, consistency, test objectivity; Form NE-21 ('61, 6 pages, identical with test copyrighted in 1959 except for two interchanges of items); 3 editions (identical except for profiles): secondary school, college, personnel; manual ('59, 28 pages); supplement ('61, 2 pages); $7.50 per 30 tests; $2.50 per specimen set; postage extra; (20) minutes; Thomas N. Jenkins, John H. Coleman (manual), and Harold T. Fagin (manual); Executive Analysis Corporation. *

REFERENCES
1. JENKINS, THOMAS N. "The Problem of Individual Appraisal of Personality With Large Test Batteries." *J Psychol Studies* 12:261–71 N '61 [issued Ap '63]. *
2. JENKINS, THOMAS N. "The Second Order Components of Human Personality." *J Psychol Studies* 12:237–60 N '61 [issued Ap '63]. *

LEE J. CRONBACH, *Professor of Education and Psychology, Stanford University, Stanford, California.*

HWDYKY is an anachronism, harking back to that innocent prewar period when every psychologist interested in measurement had his own list of trait names and a companion "personality test." Unlike those instruments, however, it grows out of a long program of research. The late Professor T. N. Jenkins embarked on a mapping of the domain of self-description about 1940, and for some twenty years elaborated his factor analysis until he had identified no less than 139 "primary traits" ranging from the old standbys "General Morale" and "Conscientiousness" to such oddities as "Naso-Buccal Epicureanism," "Auditory Orexis for Non-Musical Sounds," and (!) "Sexorexia." His interest was principally in basic investigation and secondarily in the development of a "global" instrument of 720 items, selected from a 7,000-item pool, which he proposed to score on all 139 dimensions. Though the outcome of this most solemn of all attempts to factor-analyze personality is a reductio ad absurdum, the work was scholarly and informed. Unfortunately, Professor Jenkins' caution led him to postpone publication until shortly before his death, and his findings are now available only in a few rather incomplete papers and manuscripts.

The present short test, which extracts a mere 17 factorial scores from 120 items, is no more than a casual by-product of the research. The traits included were selected from the list of 139, but they are not in any significant way derived from the factor analysis. Traits with much the same names and meanings were present in the pre-1940 instruments of Guilford and others. The 17 traits appear to have been selected in the interest of practical appeal, because common-sense interpretations of them are available and because counselors and industrial personnel men are likely to consider them important. HWDYKY has been placed on the market essentially without validation, except as one can extrapolate from fragmentary observations reported incidental to Jenkins' other research.

Items are transparent, and items within a scale are often redundant. The "Irritability" scale consists of six items in which the subject confesses that he is cross or loses his temper when people criticize him, or when he is ill, or when things go wrong. Items were allegedly chosen to have high stability on retest and to have high loadings on the factors for which they are scored. Jenkins calls for responses on a six-point scale ranging from "Always" to "Never." This is likely to be less ambiguous than the response scales of other instruments, though not all the items lend themselves to this type of response. Since the scoring system allows from 0 to 5 points per response and each trait is based upon six items, trait scores range from 0 to 30. The person's score is markedly affected by any response set to use, or not use, extreme response positions; saying "Almost always" in preference to "Always" can have a substantial effect on his percentile standing. There are two control scores. One examines consistency on certain repeated items. The other, measuring "Test Objectivity," was constructed empirically and its significance is far from apparent; one way to earn a high score is to stick with the noncommittal responses "Sometimes" and "Often."

One criticism of score reporting in HWDYKY applies to almost every personality inventory. Testers ought to abandon the practice of plotting a profile along a percentile scale. In this instrument, a student falls at the 80th percentile for Irritability, and at the 15th percentile for Punctuality, if he earns 15 points out of a possible 30 on each scale. Even granting that a profile of raw scores is much affected by the wording of items, it is probably more nearly accurate to say that this boy is about as punctual as he is irritable, than to say that he is exceedingly irritable and exceedingly unpunctual. A profile plotted in raw score (or percentage) form, would emphasize the person's salient traits rather than his salient differences from other persons. Percentiles could be superimposed as supplementary information. In measuring personality and interests and attitudes, describing the individual is a more basic concern than comparing him with others.

Although the manual presents its information honestly, it is distinctly unsatisfactory. There are rambling discussions of certain points such as the implications of a low "Objectivity" score. There are unnecessarily technical remarks on factor analysis that the typical consumer cannot possibly follow. A multiple correlation of each score with the "factor score" it represents is given; this value of .90 or above is grossly misleading, being inflated by the fact that the items used in the multiple correlation also contribute to the factor score. A similar inflation vitiates interpretation of the factor loadings for items on which the claim for validity rests. (The manual provides a prime exhibit of the reasons for never using the phrase "factorial validity.") The vitally necessary score intercorrelations are not reported. While retest reliabilities are given, there are no internal-consistency analyses from which we can decide how well the items in a score represent the larger collection of behaviors implied by the trait designation. The description of the norm groups (e.g., "100 twelfth-grade boys") is damnably inadequate, and no doubt the selection of the groups is equally indefensible. Professor Jenkins' research program was extensive, but this test was so far from his center of interest that almost none of the calculations required to make it useful were carried out.

What can we say about the usefulness of the test? A median stability over several weeks of .75 and an estimated standard error of 2 points are not bad for a 20-minute test yielding 17 trait scores. A well trained interpreter will know that the instrument offers no more than a sketchy self-description. Unfortunately, the test is reportedly being sold to counselors and personnel men who have had just one graduate course in tests and measurements; HWDYKY is not at all suited for interpretation by such persons. Even if the manual were ideally clear, few users are able to make the intuitive corrections for differences in "Objectivity" that the authors call for.

HWDYKY is a reasonably well-edited and well-grouped collection of items. It is completely unvalidated with respect to practical decisions. Any subject who wants to falsify his report will have no difficulty in doing so. Its use should be restricted to well qualified counselors who employ a multiscore profile from a brief test as a starting point for an interview.

Harrison G. Gough, *Professor of Psychology, University of California, Berkeley, California.*

The current (1961) version of this questionnaire contains 120 items and yields 19 scores. Seventeen of the scales were factorially derived, and two (consistency and objectivity) were developed by nonfactorial methods. The 17 factorial variables were selected by Jenkins from the full set of 131 identified in his studies of personality structure.

The reasons for choosing the particular set of 17 traits are summarized in the manual (p. 1) in this way:

The seventeen trait scores provided by this inventory are primary factors. They represent trait estimates of personality characteristics which have been found, from general experience in guidance and personnel functions, to be important for a wide range of the work, career, and interpersonal activities in which normal individuals are commonly involved.

The appeal, that is to say, is to the practical utility of the variables scaled in personnel and guidance work with normal individuals. These objectives are legitimate, but evidence, of course, is necessary to demonstrate that the variables in this test do have this practical relevance.

Unfortunately, very little such evidence is offered in the manual. Only three validational studies are mentioned, and these refer to differentiations between specialists and nonspecialists in the Air Force, between students who sought and who avoided counseling, and to correlations between the scales and the degree of disruption of speech under varying intensities of audiogenic stress. Perhaps a later edition of the manual will bring together a larger number of studies, and studies of more relevance to the uses for which the inventory is recommended.

In light of this lack of evidence, it is rather disturbing to find the section on case interpretations making many statements for which no validational bases have been established. For example, in the case of "Rhoda," a high school girl of modest ability who recently decided to seek a career in nursing, low scores on the scales for practicality and seriousness are said to cast doubt on the authenticity of her decision, and a high score on impulsiveness is seen as strengthening this doubt. Would a dependable research study of the stability of vocational choices among high school girls show the practicality, seriousness, and impulsiveness scales to have such diagnostic value? At least some evidence should be obtained before test users are encouraged to make inferences of this type.

In the case of "Dorothea," a stenographer being considered for assignment as a secretary to a major officer, a high score on the scale titled submissiveness is seen as a favorable quality. Should not scores on the scale for submissiveness be studied as predictors of job performance *before* such interpretation is recommended? An occasional "clinical interpretation" of this type would pose no problem, and indeed would serve to raise some interesting hypotheses. The difficulty in the manual is that gratuitous interpretations of this kind are made repeatedly, with no apparent recognition of the need for evidence and research documentation.

Another problem in the manual is its unsatisfactory handling of reliability. The 17 factorial scales contain only six items each; the attainment of an adequate level of reliability with scales as short as this would be extremely difficult. The manual offers test-retest coefficients (which range from .32 to .96, median of .76), mean item loadings on the factor represented by each scale, and the estimated multiple correlations between each set of six items and its factor. However, no measures of internal consistency for the 19 scales, as they are presented and scored in this inventory, are offered.

The manual attempts to justify this omission by saying, "current methods of measuring reliability can be highly misleading when applied to short tests." This disclaimer does not seem acceptable in a test developed factorially and whose principal appeal is to the unidimensionality and homogeneity of the items in its scales. Internal consistency data on reliability should be given along with the test-retest figures.

A third problem, and as surprising to encounter as the absence of internal consistency reliability data in a factorially-developed instrument, is the lack of any information on intercorrelations among the scales. The manual asserts in several places that the scales are independent and that they do not "influence" each other; yet no data are offered in support of this claim. An intercorrelation matrix among the 19 measures contained in this test is a necessity. Claims concerning absence of correlation between and among scales should be supported by empirical data.

A fourth problem is the contention in the manual that "almost all presently available personality questionnaires....view the subject's personality in terms of the presence or absence of behavior pathology," and that the present test is therefore an "important departure from ....tradition" which offers a "new and hitherto unavailable type of personality assessment." These assertions are highly dubious, as users of questionnaires such as the *Study of Values,* the *Sixteen Personality Factor Questionnaire,* the *Edwards Personal Preference Schedule,* and many others could testify. *How Well Do You Know Yourself?* is not unique in its concern with the normal individual functioning in a normal context. It might also be observed, parenthetically, that four of its scales (dejection, general morale, nervousness, and emotional control) would be hard to distinguish from the psychiatrically oriented devices with which it is contrasted.

A fifth problem is that the psychological implications of the scales are derived almost entirely from a study of the items each one contains. The danger in this procedure is that it provides no check on the common circumstance in which people who talk one way behave another. Are people who say that they (*a*) "always" or "almost always" find that others like to work with them, (*b*) like teamwork, and (*c*) see to it that others do their share of the work, properly described as "cooperative"? The way to find out is to study these people directly in their social behavior, to see if their behavior can properly be characterized as cooperative. The acceptance of inventory responses at face value can lead to rather serious errors in the forecasting of interpersonal and other non-test behavior.

This leads to a final criticism, which is that no data on dissimulation are presented. The test is recommended for practical use, and in some settings, clearly, respondents will be seeking to "fake" certain kinds of desirable outcomes. What would happen to scores on this test if an applicant for a job as a bank clerk, e.g., would try to describe himself as highly honest, punctual, and constructively ambitious, free from any rebellious or self-assertive tendencies? Could such dissembling alter the pattern of scores, and if so, could the fact that simulation had occurred be detected? A manual for a test proposed for use in personnel and industrial settings should consider such topics and offer specific evidence.

In summary, this test offers an interesting set of variables for measurement; its manual is well organized and clearly written, and the case studies point the way toward the kind of individualized interpretation which should be the aim of every test. However, these commendable features are opposed by a number of negative factors. Essential information on reliability, validity, and scale intercorrelations is lacking, unwarranted claims to uniqueness are prominently advanced, and personological data pertaining to the implications of high and low scores on the scales are entirely absent. Interpretations of an arm-chair, speculative nature are the rule rather than the exception, and no attention is paid to problems of dissimulation and self-deception or to the general issue of incongruity between manifest self-description and social behavior. At the present time, therefore, this test should be used only by skilled psychologists, whose personal insight and experience can compensate for the deficiencies of the manual.

J Consult Psychol 23:564 D '59. Edward S. Bordin. This 120-item inventory yields 17 trait scores, e.g., Irritability, Novelty Loving, Vocational Assurance, Submissiveness, Impulsiveness, and two scores regarding test taking attitudes, Consistency and Objectivity. The trait scores are founded on factor analyses. Consistency is simply the tendency to give the same answer to the same item at two different times. The test objectivity items are a refinement of a set empirically derived by differentiating two groups of subjects who, on the basis of interviews, were judged to differ in the realism of their conceptions of themselves. The general format of the test and manual leave something to be desired. The test booklet incorporates a profile and answer sheet and, thus, is expendable, which naturally increases the cost of using this instrument. The manual is written in a pedantic, sometimes opaque style. This test may prove equal or superior to other personality inventories, but the case is not proved by the data summarized in the manual. Although satisfactorily high multiple correlations are reported for the six items of each factor with that factor, the test-retest correlations, not unexpectedly, are low in too many instances. Norms for secondary school, college undergraduate, and office and factory populations of both sexes are based on small inadequately de-

fined samples. While there is evidence of considerable internal analysis of the test, external validation is limited to three studies, all doctoral theses, only one of which has been reported in the general literature. Much more needs to be done.

J Counsel Psychol 6:248–9 f '59. Laurence Siegel. * The test-retest correlational values leave something to be desired, particularly in view of the paucity of validity data presently available for this inventory. The least reliable subscale is the one purporting to measure Consistency. The Consistency measure is so inconsistent as to lead to test-retest coefficients ranging only between .32 and .46. The authors maintain, "This, however, does not decrease the importance of the *Consistency* score as an individual index of consistency in answering test items." This statement is predicated upon the questionable assumption that it is better to measure unreliably with a brief (nine-item) factorially complex scale than not to measure at all. * the validity....is assumed from three validation studies performed upon the global battery which served as an intermediate criterion in the development of this instrument * This is slim evidence indeed for the validity of an inventory for which the authors make some extravagant claims. * The percentile norms.... are exceedingly weak. * These norms are deficient on two counts. First, the norms groups are pitifully small, ranging in size from 100 cases for secondary school males to 276 cases for female office and factory workers. Secondly, the constituency of the norms groups with respect to representativeness of the samples is not discussed in the manual. * authors ....have published an inventory with an item format that may prove irritating to the respondent, a set of scales that are not particularly reliable (from a test-retest standpoint), claims for utility which are predicated upon intuition rather than upon demonstrated validity and percentile conversion tables based upon inadequate samples. It is unfortunate that what seems like a good idea is so poorly implemented.

[119]

*Human Relations Inventory.** Grades 9–16 and adults; 1954–59; social conformity; Form A ('54, 4 pages); manual ('59, 4 pages, identical with manual published in 1954 except for format and supplementary validity data and references); no data on reliability; $2 per 20 tests; $1 per specimen set (must be purchased to obtain manual); cash orders postpaid; (20)

minutes; Raymond E. Bernberg; Psychometric Affiliates. *

REFERENCES

1. BERNBERG, RAYMOND E. "The Direction of Perception Technique of Attitude Measurement." *Int J Opin & Attitude Res* 5:397–406 f '51. * (*PA* 27:336)
2. BERNBERG, RAYMOND E. "Personality Correlates of Social Conformity." *J Appl Psychol* 38:148–9 Je '54. * (*PA* 29:3664)
3. BERNBERG, RAYMOND E. "A Measure of Social Conformity." *J Psychol* 39:89–96 Ja '55. * (*PA* 29:8529)
4. BERNBERG, RAYMOND E. "Personality Correlates of Social Conformity: II." *J Social Psychol* 43:309–12 My '56. * (*PA* 33:3492)
5. ADAMS, ANDREW A. "Identifying Socially Maladjusted School Children." *Genetic Psychol Monogr* 61:3–36 F '60. * (*PA* 34:7515)
6. GORFEIN, DAVID S., AND ANDERSON, LARRY M. "A Note on the Validity of the Bernberg Human Relations Inventory." *J Psychol* 54:65–8 Jl '62. * (*PA* 37:3008)

For reviews by Raymond C. Norris and John A. Radcliffe, see 5:68.

[120]
*The Humm-Wadsworth Temperament Scale.
Adults; 1934–60; 47 scores: normal (4 subscores), hysteroid (6 subscores), manic (4 subscores), depressive (5 subscores), autistic (5 subscores), paranoid (3 subscores), epileptoid (4 subscores), response bias (2 subscores), self mastery (6 component control subscores plus integration index); 1 form ('34, 8 pages); mimeographed manual, 1954–55 revision ('55, 126 pages, with addendum copyrighted in 1960); profile-work sheet ('54, 1 page); qualitative analysis tables ('56, 8 pages); nomogram ('54), with response-bias corrector ('50) overleaf; distribution restricted; service fees for business organizations retaining publisher as consultant: $1,350 for first year (includes 3-week training course for 1–5 persons and consultation service), $10 per month thereafter; no service fees for psychologists; test materials rented to licensees only; $25 for the use of 25 tests and accessories for first year, $5 per year thereafter; separate answer sheets must be used; $2.50 per 25 additional tests; 25¢ per answer sheet; specimen set not available; postage extra; (45–90) minutes; Doncaster G. Humm and Kathryn A. Humm; Humm Personnel Consultants. *

REFERENCES

1–13. See 40:1223.
14–44. See 3:48.
45–64. See 5:69.
65. ELLIS, ALBERT, AND CONRAD, HERBERT S. "The Validity of Personality Inventories in Military Practice." *Psychol B* 45:385–426 S '48. * (*PA* 23:1287)
66. SMITH, GUDMUND, AND MARKE, SVEN. "An Economical Design for the Control of Commercial Screening Tests." *Acta Psychologica* 14(2):144–51 '58. * (*PA* 33:9102)
67. GUILFORD, J. P. *Personality*, pp. 175–8. New York: McGraw-Hill Book Co., Inc., 1959. Pp. xiii, 562. *

JAMES R. GLENNON, *Director, Employee Relations Research, Standard Oil Company (Indiana), Chicago, Illinois.*

Those experienced in selection for industrial jobs should be convinced that temperament or personality is an important determinant of subsequent job performance. Those so experienced, whether as industrial psychologists or as practitioners with other background, would further recognize, in this reviewer's opinion, that the first difficulty would be in defining components of temperament and degrees of

personality integration and determining which of these has vital meaning in the performance of most jobs. Assuming resolution of problems of definition, difficulties of measurement would surely constitute the next series of obstacles. Underlying the foregoing challenges would be the knowledge, contended by the Humm-Wadsworth authors, that temperament alone won't guarantee successful job performance even though inadequacies in this area can be highly correlated with failure.

The Humm-Wadsworth scale was designed for use in industry principally for application with job candidates. It has also had clinical applications and has been included in vocational counseling batteries.

The scale asks 318 yes-no questions designed, to quote the manual, "to elicit the patterns of attitudes, social reactions, and emotional tone of the respondent by comparing his answers with the answers of subjects of known temperamental characteristics." Slightly more than one half of the questions, 164 of 318, were found to be significant three decades ago in distinguishing differences in temperament among validation groups consisting of a large number of employed persons and a smaller number of institutional cases. The scored answers produce a primary profile of 7 temperamental components and a further breakdown into 31 subcomponents. Plotted on a two-chart worksheet, these provide the administrator or interpreter with a compact visual summary. Profiles can be interpreted by comparison with patterns presented by the authors (in the extensive manual or, more importantly, under the authors' personal instruction during the training course), or by those combinations based on the test user's experience with the instrument. Industrial norms are provided for interpretation and guidance with both component and subcomponent profiles.

The scale also yields measures of response bias (the number of "no" answers indicating defensiveness or suggestibility) and self mastery. The latter development came from the authors' research on a population of 1,000 permanent employees.

Original definitions of the temperament components came largely from the psychiatric theory of Aaron Rosanoff. Thirty years of industrial use and literally millions of applications have been distilled into observations of temperamental behavior, these descriptions being offered through the manual and through the authors' consulting services.

The seven temperament components measured by the scale are these: normal, hysteriod, manic, depressive, autistic, paranoid, and epileptoid. While these terms carry psychopathological connotations the scoring and interpretation yields plus, minus, or borderline measurements of the characteristics. The operational theory is that these components will be encountered in the general population and are, when in certain balance and control, effective constituents of normal, productive behavior. The user would recognize measures of self mastery and control as of obvious relevance in industrial positions. The weight given to control of these temperamental factors makes this scale, in many respects, a much more realistic approach to such measurement than is true of personality measurement instruments which give unique readings of temperamental qualities without any integral weighting of the dynamic interrelationships.

Early literature claims validity correlations in the .90's between inventory scores and case history assessments. A later report (57) correlated scale appraisals with success or failure as a member of the Los Angeles Police Force (the success criterion was attainment of staff membership and dismissal was the failure criterion) and had validities averaging .72.

This reviewer finds such validity claims beyond anything in his own experience. But this is of little matter, since he would advise all potential users (of any selection instrument or technique) to assure themselves of the contribution that would be added to their own present selection practices, rather than make the risky assumption that validity experienced elsewhere is anything more than suggestive.

Reliability of the scale, or, better still, consistency of the components, has been seriously questioned, in this reviewer's mind, by the work of Smith and Marke (64). These researchers claim that only three of the components (manic, autistic, and depressive) "tend to hang together." Reliability is not mentioned in the H-W manual. A personal check with a major user of the scale did reveal that reliability and "fakability" had been studied in their organization and found to be acceptable. Again, this reviewer would caution that the potential user plan local studies to be sure of these points.

The authors contend the scale should be used in conjunction with other tests, interviews, and other evidence of candidate qualities rather than being used as the only selection instrument. This contention is consistent with reasonable belief that job success or failure cannot be determined by temperamental or other factors acting alone, but rather behavior will be determined by many causations acting in concert.

The H-W scale is not a "shelf" item that can be purchased by mail order as can most psychological tests. The industrial user must, at considerable expense, receive personal training from the authors and enter a contractual agreement governing conditions of continuing use. Furthermore, the user must submit samples of his applications, from time to time, for the authors' review. While less restrictive agreements are possible for clinicians or professional psychological consultants, the authors contend this initial training and periodic follow-up are essential to successful use of the scale.

The scale can be administered to a large group at one time with individuals completing the test in from 45 to 90 minutes. The authors' accumulated experience shows 70 per cent finishing in one hour or less. Scoring by someone well trained can be accomplished in less than 10 minutes.

The manual gives detailed explanation of the history of the instrument and of the rather involved scoring and interpretation procedures incumbent in its use.

This reviewer would not recommend H-W for use in industrial selection where the number of candidates totals fewer than several hundred a year. This is so because the reviewer would insist on local validation and, secondarily, because the expense of using the scale could be justified only in large-scale application. These conditions being met, the scale deserves consideration for inclusion in a selection battery where it is expected a temperament or personality test could make a contribution to improved selection.

Floyd L. Ruch, *President, Psychological Services, Inc., Los Angeles, California.*

In the 15 years that have elapsed since the *Humm-Wadsworth Temperament Scale* was reviewed in generally favorable terms by H. J. Eysenck, H. Meltzer, and Lorenz Misbach in the *Third Mental Measurements Yearbook,* some 20 articles concerning it have appeared in the literature available to this reviewer.

Only seven authors report attempts to measure the test's concurrent or predictive validity. In only two of these studies is it clear that all possibility of criterion contamination (advance knowledge of the predictor scores and/or profiles by the judges who rated performance) was ruled out (46, 61). In these two studies also there was no predictor contamination. That is to say, each Humm-Wadsworth variable was treated separately and not with knowledge of aptitude or other predictor scores.

Cerf's report (46) covers five separate studies, each study based on approximately 200 pilots in primary training. In three of these studies biserial validity coefficients on a pass-fail criterion ranged from 0 to .22. In one of the studies all of the validity coefficients were nonsignificant, ranging from .01 to .16. In each of the two other studies statistically significant validity coefficients were found for both the hysteroid and the epileptoid scales. In each instance, however, the maximum coefficient compared very unfavorably to aptitude test scores and added so little predictive power to aptitude scores that the Humm-Wadsworth was not included in the operational battery.

In one study reported by Cerf, case summaries made by Humm from the cadets' responses to the inventory were compared with training course success or failure. Nonsignificant chi-squares of 1.05 and 4.82 for 4 degrees of freedom were obtained. According to Cerf: "More than 90 per cent of chance deviations would have been as great." In another study based on 195 Air Force pilots, case summaries of temperamental integration made by Humm from the responses to the inventory were compared with the pass-fail criterion. In this study nonsignificant chi-squares of .11 and .34 for 2 degrees of freedom led the author to conclude: "More than 60 per cent of chance deviations would have been as great." This worker concluded that pilot success could not be predicted to an operationally useful degree from Humm's analysis of temperamental integration nor from his case summaries.

A study by Caine (50) of aviation cadets (n = 400) reports failure to obtain a useful degree of predictive validity. This reviewer found a tetrachoric correlation of .25 between the normal component and success, using the data presented by Caine. The other components

were less related, as shown by the chi-square tests reported by Caine. These two studies agree that the various components do not have practical validity when analyzed by conventional statistical techniques.

A study (57) of 506 police officers appointed during the war emergency and 115 civil service appointed police officers in Los Angeles is subject to a number of statistical and design flaws which render it uninterpretable. A Humm-trained technician rated each officer into one of seven categories, from very good to very poor. The criterion was whether the officer was retained or dismissed on the basis of his job performance. Predictor contamination was present from knowledge on the part of the technician of intelligence test and other scores, but its influence was discounted by the authors, who state:

The predictions were based upon test results; but, inasmuch as all officers already had been subjected to selection procedures which would narrow their range of aptitudes and abilities, and inasmuch as temperamental qualifications are among the most difficult to appraise by civil service procedures, it is the consensus of those participating in the collection and analysis of these data that the predictions were influenced powerfully by the findings of the Humm-Wadsworth Temperament Scale. They are, therefore, treated in this paper as predictions based on the Temperament Scale alone. It is probable that, if partial correlation had been used to rule out the effect of intelligence, aptitude, educational preparation, interest, and physical fitness, the effectiveness of the predictions would appear higher than it does here.

For some reason not clear to this reviewer, such partial correlations were not reported. The degree to which an officer's superiors were influenced by their knowledge of the predictor rating in their decision to retain or discharge is not known. If the Humm-Wadsworth ratings were routinely kept in each officer's personnel file and the file was available to each officer's superiors, it is probable that contamination was present.

Glaring as the flaws in the design of the study may be, they are overshadowed by the almost inconceivable misapplication of statistical techniques in the analysis of results. Rather than reporting validity in terms of the correlation between predictor and criterion, the authors divide one sample of 506 police officers into three criterion groups—discharged, resigned, and remaining—and then somewhat mysteriously report a validity coefficient (Sheppard's method of unlike signs) for the discharged group considered alone. This coefficient of .96 is reported as describing the relationship between predictions and this *single* criterion group, without regard to the rest of the sample! Similarly computed correlations on other samples range as low as .54, which is purported to describe the validity of the predictions for a sample of 48 staff members upon which no criterion was available, other than the fact that they were all "successful police workers."

A study of the predictive validity of the Humm-Wadsworth in the selection of salesmen was reported by Harrell (*53*). From the writeup of this study it is not clear whether or not there was predictor contamination. If the practice of the Humm-trained technician was to evaluate the profile and make his prediction with prior knowledge of intelligence test scores as was the case in the Los Angeles police study, there could have been an unknown amount of predictor contamination. If the Humm-Wadsworth ratings went into the employee's file and were available to his superiors, there could have been criterion contamination.

In the Harrell study salesmen ($n = 168$) were rated independently by three supervisors. All three supervisors agreed that 97 of the salesmen were successful and that 39 were unsuccessful. The remainder of 32 were thought to be successful by one supervisor and unsuccessful by another and were omitted from comparison with the test results. Eighty-five of the 136 salesmen who were unanimously rated as either successful or unsuccessful were also evaluated by the Humm-Wadsworth technician as being definitely a good prospect or definitely a poor prospect. Among the 60 prospects recommended on the basis of the Humm-Wadsworth 50, or 83 per cent, proved successful on the job. The corresponding figure for all 85 salesmen was 62, or 73 per cent successful. Because of the lack of knowledge as to the degree of predictor or criterion contamination, it is impossible to determine whether or not the indicated relationship is of practical value.

It is interesting to note that when the mean component scores of the successful and the unsuccessful groups were compared, no statistically or practically significant differences were found. This discrepancy can be explained on the basis that the global profile interpretations advocated by Humm (*54*) can get predictive power out of elements which, taken by themselves, are valueless. Such an interpreta-

tion could be accepted only on the assumption that criterion contamination, as well as predictor contamination, has been ruled out.

A follow-up study by Gilliland and Newman (*61*) of 405 "white collar" employees was made 10 years after they had been tested with the Humm-Wadsworth. Of these, 191 were still employed and were performing satisfactorily at the time of the study, another 139 had terminated but without any unfavorable service record, while another 75 had been dismissed or had resigned while still on probation. Of the still-employed group 9.4 per cent had very good profile ratings. Of the 139 no longer employed but with no evidence of success while employed, the corresponding figure was 12.2 per cent. Of the 75 who were dismissed for cause or withdrew during probation, 12.0 per cent were given very good ratings. This study has been criticized by Humm and Humm (*62*) on the basis that Gilliland and Newman did not understand how to rate profiles.

Several studies have reported relationships between Humm-Wadsworth scores and profiles and criteria other than success or failure in training or job performance. In a study of 30 academic underachievers and 31 overachievers, no significant differences were found by Fortune (*52*). A study (*47*) of 106 hospitalized alcoholics compared with a control group of 179 showed the controls to be significantly higher (1 per cent level) on the normal component, and the alcoholics to be significantly higher (9 per cent level) on the hysteroid component. The control group had nearly two more years of schooling. In a study of 56 college students, Greenberg and Gilliland (*60*) found the Humm-Wadsworth component correlating highest with basal metabolic rate was autistic ($r = -.27$, significant at the 5 per cent level). Two studies (*56, 59*) agree in finding that essentially zero correlation exists between the similarly named components of the Humm-Wadsworth and the MMPI. A recent study by Smith and Marke (*64*) sheds light on the lack of correlation between the similarly defined components of the Humm-Wadsworth and MMPI "scales." These workers, using a method of scale analysis developed by Likert, discovered that the Humm-Wadsworth components are so lacking in internal consistency as to fail to meet quite lenient demands for one-dimensionality.

CONCLUSION. Taken as a whole, the reported evidence suggests that the *Humm-Wadsworth Temperament Scale,* despite its some thirty years of age, be regarded as an experimental device and not a promising one at that.

For reviews by H. J. Eysenck, H. Meltzer, and Lorenz Misbach of the 1940 edition, see 3:48; for reviews by Forrest A. Kingsbury and P. E. Vernon, see 40:1223; for a review by Daniel A. Prescott of an earlier edition, see 38:920.

[121]

*The IPAT Anxiety Scale Questionnaire. Ages 14 and over; 1957–63; also called *IPAT Anxiety Scale;* title on test is *IPAT Self Analysis Form;* 6 scores: self sentiment development, ego strength, protension of paranoid trend, guilt proneness, ergic tension, total anxiety; 1 form ('57, 4 pages); manual, second edition ('63, 16 pages); $3 per 25 tests; 50¢ per scoring key; $1.80 per manual; $2.40 per specimen set; cash orders postpaid; (5–10) minutes; Raymond B. Cattell and I. H. Scheier (manual); Institute for Personality and Ability Testing. *

REFERENCES

1. CATTELL, RAYMOND B. "The Conceptual and Test Distinction of Neuroticism and Anxiety." *J Clin Psychol* 13: 221–33 Jl '57. * (*PA* 32:5484)
2. CATTELL, RAYMOND B., AND SCHEIER, IVAN H. "Clinical Validities by Analyzing the Psychiatrist Exemplified in Relation to Anxiety Diagnoses." *Am J Orthopsychiatry* 28:699–713 O '58. * (*PA* 33:10313)
3. RAWN, Moss L. "The Overt-Covert Anxiety Index and Hostility." *J Clin Psychol* 14:279–80 Jl '58. * (*PA* 33:8387)
4. BENDIG, A. W. "College Norms for Anxiety and Concurrent Validity of Cattell's IPAT Anxiety Scale." *Psychol Newsl* 10:263–7 My–Je '59. * (*PA* 34:1338)
5. BENDIG, A. W. "'Social Desirability' and 'Anxiety' Variables in the IPAT Anxiety Scale." Abstract. *J Consult Psychol* 23:377 Ag '59. * (*PA* 34:4369)
6. CATTELL, RAYMOND B., AND SCHEIER, IVAN H. "Extension of Meaning of Objective Test Personality Factors: Especially Into Anxiety, Neuroticism, Questionnaire, and Physical Factors." *J General Psychol* 61:287–315 O '59. * (*PA* 35:785)
7. WOHL, JULIAN, AND HYMAN, MARVIN. "Relationship Between Measures of Anxiety and Constriction." *J Clin Psychol* 15:54–5 Ja '59. * (*PA* 34:2797)
8. BENDIG, A. W. "Age Related Changes in Covert and Overt Anxiety." *J General Psychol* 62:159–63 Ap '60. * (*PA* 34:8022)
9. BENDIG, A. W. "Factor Analyses of 'Anxiety' and 'Neuroticism' Inventories." *J Consult Psychol* 24:161–8 Ap '60. * (*PA* 34:8195)
10. BENDIG, A. W. "The Factorial Validity of Items on the IPAT Anxiety Scale." Abstract. *J Consult Psychol* 24:374 Ag '60. *
11. Moss, C. SCOTT, AND WATERS, THOMAS J. "Intensive Longitudinal Investigation of Anxiety in Hospitalized Juvenile Patients." *Psychol Rep* 7:379–80 O '60. * (*PA* 35:2278)
12. BENDIG, A. W. "A Factor Analysis of Scales of Emotionality and Hostility." *J Clin Psychol* 17:189–92 Ap '61. * (*PA* 38:1034)
13. CATTELL, RAYMOND B., AND SCHEIER, IVAN H. *The Meaning and Measurement of Neuroticism and Anxiety.* New York: Ronald Press Co., 1961. Pp. ix, 535. * (*PA* 36:1HK27C)
14. WAGNER, EDWIN E. "The Interaction of Aggressive Movement Responses and Anatomy Responses on the Rorschach in Producing Anxiety." *J Proj Tech* 25:212–5 Je '61. * (*PA* 36:2HG12W)
15. BENDIG, A. W. "The Reliability and Factorial Validity of the IPAT Anxiety Scale." *J General Psychol* 67:27–33 Jl '62. * (*PA* 37:3276)
16. CATTELL, RAYMOND B. "Psychological Measurement of Anxiety and Depression: A Quantitative Approach." Discussion, pp. S24–8. *Can Psychiatric Assn J* 7(sup):S11–28 '62. *
17. LEVITT, EUGENE E., AND PERSKY, HAROLD. "Experimental Evidence for the Validity of the IPAT Anxiety Scale." *J Clin Psychol* 18:458–61 O '62. * (*PA* 39:5076)
18. PHILIPPUS, MARION JOHN, AND FLEIGLER, LOUIS. "A Study of Personality, Value and Interest Patterns of Student Teachers in the Areas of Elementary, Secondary, and Special Education." *Sci Ed* 46:247–52 Ap '62. *
19. SINGER, JEROME L., AND ROWE, RICHARD. "An Experimental Study of Some Relationships Between Daydreaming and Anxiety." *J Consult Psychol* 26:446–54 O '62. * *
20. BENDIG, A. W. "Comparative Reliability of Cattell's 'Covert' and 'Overt' Items as Measures of the Anxiety Factor." *J General Psychol* 69:175–9 O '63. * (*PA* 39:1910)
21. FISHER, GARY M., AND KRAMER, RICHARD A. "The Relation of the Marlow-Crowne Social Desirability Scale to the Cattell Anxiety Scale." *J Clin Psychol* 19:204–5 Ap '63. *
22. LEVITT, EUGENE E.; BRADY, JOHN PAUL; AND LUBIN, BERNARD. "Correlates of Hypnotizability in Young Women: Anxiety and Dependency." *J Personality* 31:52–7 Mr '63. *
23. MANHOLD, J. H.; SHATIN, LEO; AND MANHOLD, BEVERLY S. "Comparison of Interests, Needs, and Selected Personality Factors of Dental and Medical Students." *J Am Dental Assn* 67:601–5 O '63. *

JACOB COHEN, *Professor of Psychology, New York University, New York, New York.*

This is a brief, rapidly stencil-scored, objective, self-administrable questionnaire for the assessment of general free anxiety level as distinct from general neurosis or psychosis. It is offered both for mass screening and individual clinical use with functionally literate adolescents and adults.

It is not difficult to write a respectable anxiety (or "neuroticism," or "adjustment") questionnaire which has some validity. Indeed, it may be difficult *not* to. What is notable about this test is that it is a mature fruit of a third of a century of both methodologically and clinically sophisticated large scale factor-analytic research. This point is made not merely as testimony to the quality of the product, but to advise the test user that the manual, although adequate by the standards of the Technical Recommendations, can provide only an overview of, and entry into, the research and theoretical background on which the test and its interpretation are based.

Raw scores are converted by table into sten and percentile scores. Separate and combined sex norms are provided for adults ($n = 935$), college students ($n = 1,392$), and teenagers ($n = 525$). Apart from age, no demographic data are given for the norm samples, a deficiency for some purposes particularly in the case of general adult norms.

The test is an immediate outgrowth of a series of 14 replicated researches with the longer IPAT 16 PF test. The largest of four second-order factors of the correlations of these 16 primaries is interpreted as general or free anxiety and contains loadings for five of the primaries ranging from .45 to .67. The 40 items of the present anxiety scale were selected from these five scales of the 16 PF so as to provide approximate optimal weighting in the total score of the five components.

In addition, the 40 items are also divided so as to yield separate "covert" and "overt" anxiety scores, whose ratio or difference is offered for interpretation. Unlike the five component subscores, the overt-covert distinction receives no warrant from the extensive factor-analytic studies.

Reliability coefficients for the total anxiety score, depending on type and the nature of the group, range from .80 to .93, an adequate level for most purposes. The same cannot be said for the homogeneity reliabilities of the five component scores (based on 4–12 items), which range from .26 to .60. No reliabilities are given in the manual for combinations of overt and covert anxiety scores, but a reference (7) gives .24 for the reliability of their difference. The authors warn about the low reliabilities of the various part scores yet suggest that they might be used as "suggestive 'leads.'" However, what is suggested by a score whose reliability is in the twenties will mislead almost as often as it leads. Adequate measurement of these components demands the use of combined Forms A and B of the parent 16 PF scales.

Evidence for the test's validity is varied and impressive. It rests first on the foundation of replicated factor-analytic researches involving not only questionnaire items but objective test and physiological measures, which established and cross-matched the anxiety factor. From these, "construct" validity coefficients in the range .85 to .90 are claimed. These are multiple correlation functions of factor loadings and are therefore probably somewhat overstated. Nevertheless, they are high enough. As for external validity, many lines of evidence converge: (a) Correlation with a relatively unreliable psychiatric consensus is .30 to .40 (.60 to .70 when the criterion is attenuation-corrected). (b) The mean of 174 anxiety neurotics differs sharply from the population average (by 1.3 standard deviations), which, expressed as a point-biserial r, yields .65 (reviewer's computation, assuming equal numbers of anxiety neurotics and general population adults are being discriminated so as to give a maximum correlation). (c) The means of 23 groups of clinical interest order them in a clinically compelling way. (d) Other data (on occupations, nations, volunteers for experiment, drug effects, etc.) presented or referred to further enrich the background for interpretation and thereby enhance validity.

The test correlates (about −.60) with the Edwards Social Desirability scale (4), but SD-like variables have been shown to load importantly in objective-test measured anxiety; thus, SD is conceptually part of the anxiety construct, rather than a response set which must be partialled out.

The *IPAT Anxiety Scale's* impressive systematic research background commends it for use as an overall measure. No competing test can compete in this crucial regard. For a quick measure of anxiety level in literate adolescents and adults for screening purposes, it has no peer. For individual clinical use, where accurate measurement of the five constituent components is likely to be more important than speed, the parent instrument, the IPAT 16 PF, would be clearly preferable.

For reviews by J. P. Guilford and E. Lowell Kelly, see 5:70 (1 excerpt).

[122]

★IPAT Children's Personality Questionnaire. Ages 8–12; 1959–63; title on test is *What You Do and What You Think;* 14 scores: reserved vs. outgoing (A), less intelligent vs. more intelligent (B), affected by feelings vs. emotionally stable (C), phlegmatic vs. excitable (D), obedient vs. assertive (E), sober vs. happy-go-lucky (F), disregards rules vs. conscientious (G), shy vs. venturesome (H), toughminded vs. tender-minded (I), vigorous vs. doubting (J), forthright vs. shrewd (N), self-assured vs. apprehensive (O), casual vs. controlled (Q3), relaxed vs. tense (Q4); 2 editions; profile ('63, 1 page); $1.90 per pad of 50 profiles; cash orders postpaid; R. B. Porter and R. B. Cattell; Institute for Personality and Ability Testing. *
a) [1959 EDITION.] Forms A, B, ('59, 4 pages); manual ('60, 54 pages); norms for Forms A and B combined also presented; $2.20 per 25 tests; 75¢ per set of keys; $1.80 per manual; $2.70 per specimen set; (50–60) minutes.
b) 1963 EDITION. Forms A, B, ('63, c1959–63, 8 pages); no manual (1959 edition manual used as an interim manual); no data on reliability; no norms; $4 per 25 tests; separate answer sheets may be used; $2.20 per pad of 50 answer sheets; $1.80 per set of scoring stencils; $2.80 per specimen set; (60–120) minutes.

REFERENCES

1. PURCELL, KENNETH; TURNBULL, JOHN W.; AND BERNSTEIN, LEWIS. "Distinctions Between Subgroups of Asthmatic Children: Psychological Test and Behavior Rating Comparisons." *J Psychosom Res* 6:283–91 O–D '62. * (*PA* 37:8210)
2. CATTELL, RAYMOND B. "Teachers' Personality Description of Six-Year-Olds: A Check on Structure." *Brit J Ed Psychol* 33:219–35 N '63. * (*PA* 38:8071)

ANNE ANASTASI, *Professor of Psychology, Fordham University, New York, New York.*

As one of a series of coordinated personality inventories extending from the preschool to the adult level, the *IPAT Children's Personality Questionnaire* (CPQ) should be considered within the framework of the other inventories constructed by Cattell and his associates and of the factorial research on personality traits that led to their development. To facilitate continuity of interpretation, the 14 traits covered by this questionnaire are designated by the same letters and names as the corresponding traits in the earlier *Sixteen Personality Factor Questionnaire* and *IPAT High School Personality Questionnaire*. Each of the two forms of the CPQ consists of 70 two- or three-option items, including five items for each of the 14 traits. As in the case of the earlier inventories in the series, users are urged to administer both forms and obtain a single score based on 10 items for each trait. A 1963 edition, just published at the time of this review, contains twice as many items (140 in Form A_1-A_2 and 140 in Form B_1-B_2). Since the currently available manual covers only the shorter 1959 edition, however, this review will necessarily be limited to that edition.

The CPQ is designed for group administration, answers being marked on the test booklet. The problem of reading difficulty is handled by instructing subjects to ask the examiner for help with words they do not understand. In special cases, entire items or even the whole test may be read to the subject. The manual reports that each factor was balanced for "response sets" by having the same number of "Yes" and "No" answers contributing positively to each trait. This procedure controls only the acquiescence set, not the social desirability set; and there is evidence that the latter materially affects scores, at least in some of the CPQ traits.

Scoring is facilitated by well-designed cardboard stencils. Raw scores are converted to "staves," or 5-point standard scores with a mean of 3 and an SD of 1. Norms are reported for each sex separately, but age differences (which are only significant in three traits) are handled by the use of correction terms. The normative samples comprise 735 boys and 741 girls aged 8 to 12, not otherwise described.

Several types of reliability are reported, of which the most meaningful are probably parallel form correlations and an 18-day retest. When Forms A and B are combined to yield single trait scores, parallel form reliabilities for the 14 traits range from .32 to .67, and retest reliabilities range from .52 to .83. These coefficients were obtained in a group of 260 nine-year-old boys and girls in elementary schools. It is anticipated, of course, that reliabilities will be higher for the longer 1963 forms.

Intercorrelations of the 14 scores indicate little overlap among them. About half of these correlations fall below .20 and none reaches .50. Validity is discussed largely in terms of factorial analysis of items, based primarily on a group of 200 boys and girls not otherwise described. The manual contains detailed interpretations of the 14 traits, much of this discussion apparently drawing upon earlier research with older groups. Utilization of data external to the test is meager and the original studies to which reference is made are not readily accessible to test users. For instance, there are repeated references to unpublished dissertations and to an ONR research report. Many references are to Cattell's *Personality and Motivation Structure and Measurement* (see B119) in which studies pertaining to the age level 8 to 14 receive only brief and general mention because they were still in progress when that book was published. The test authors recommend the computation of an index of profile similarity between an individual's profile and the mean profile of various groups (e.g., delinquents, creative artists), as well as specification equations for predicting criterion performance (e.g., academic achievement); but the data required for these purposes are still largely unavailable.

In summary, it is difficult to evaluate the contribution that the CPQ can make because of inadequacy and vague reporting of validation data and insufficient description of normative samples. Comparative studies of the performance of this instrument in relation to other available instruments would also be desirable, as would direct studies of the longer 1963 forms.

WILBUR L. LAYTON, *Professor of Psychology and Head of the Department, Iowa State University, Ames, Iowa.*

This was this reviewer's first excursion to the wonderful world of perspicacious Professor R. B. Cattell. This man is creative and a prodigious producer of things psychometric. He has a great talent for neologizing and has generated some fascinating labels for the personality factors he has defined. Consider such factor labels as Harria, Parmia, Premsia, and

Zeppia. I can visualize a counselor saying to a student, "Threctia will get you if you don't watch out." After reading the handbook for the *IPAT Children's Personality Questionnaire* (CPQ) and many of Cattell's writings, I was driven to coin the label "Statisticophrenetic" to describe Professor Cattell's professional activities. He has done a tremendous amount of psychologizing about personality traits. Unfortunately, to date, most of his psychologizing has been supported only by factor analysis of items and tests and he has accumulated little evidence (in the nomological net sense) to support the definition of his personality traits. No doubt, further nomological evidence will accumulate.

It is perhaps not worthwhile to review the 1959 edition of the CPQ because it is being lengthened and renormed. However, the revision does not represent a change in the scales and according to Cattell (personal communication) it is aimed primarily at increasing the reliability of the scales. Therefore this review shall discuss information from the handbook (manual for the 1959 edition) and from Cattell, with emphasis on the present edition but with reference to the 1963 edition whenever possible.

The CPQ was planned for use with children in the age range 8 to 12 years. It overlaps by one year both with the as yet unpublished Elementary School Personality Questionnaire (ages 6 to 8) and the *IPAT High School Personality Questionnaire* (ages 12 to high school level). Vocabulary level, according to the test authors, is somewhat difficult for below average third graders and retarded readers. It is permissible to help children with words they don't know. The 1959 edition has two forms, A and B. In each form are 70 items presumably measuring the 14 factors (5 items per factor) considered by Cattell to be the same as those defined at the high school and adult levels. The test authors advocate using both A and B forms so there are a total of 10 items for each factor scale. Administration time for each booklet is approximately 50 minutes. The 1963 edition has two booklets, each containing two 70-item forms, A_1 and A_2 and B_1 and B_2. The authors recommend using all four forms so that one will have 20 items per factor. Separate answer sheets are available for the revised edition.

In the 1959 edition scores are converted to staves (5-point standard score scales with mean 3 and standard deviation 1). In the 1963 edition stens will be used (standard scales of 10-point units, mean 5.5) to align the CPQ with the HSPQ immediately above it and 16 PF for adults.

NORMS. The norms for the 1959 edition are based on 1,476 cases, 735 boys and 741 girls in age range from 8 years through 12 years but centering on 10 years. There is no information given in the handbook to indicate how this sample of children was obtained. There is no further information about the normative sample in the handbook. Profile sheets are available.

RELIABILITY. The handbook presents four types of reliability coefficients (stability, dependability, consistency, and equivalence) for each of the 14 factors for Forms A and B (1959 edition) combined and three types (all but consistency) for the separate forms. The reliability coefficients are based on "260 boys and girls of nine years of age in U.S. elementary schools." Stability coefficients are based on a two-week interval. The coefficients of stability for Forms A and B combined range from .52 to .83 with a median of approximately .70. The dependability coefficients represent test-retest (same form) coefficients without a time interval. These coefficients range from .63 to .87 for the two forms combined, with a median of approximately .75. The coefficients of equivalence estimated for the combination of A and B forms range from .32 to .67 with a median of approximately .55. The coefficients of homogeneity (split-half coefficients based on a mean of three splits) range from .30 to .64 with a median of .54. These reliabilities are reasonably good considering they are based on only 10 items but are not high enough to permit use of factor scores with individuals. The authors, of course, are now lengthening the scales so a total of 20 items can enter each factor score. This is in line with the recommendation of Cattell:[1] "it can be shown statistically that a scale meeting reasonable practical demands for validity and reliability requires, over this range, 0.3 to 0.5 loading per item in any required factor ten to thirty items as a minimum."

VALIDITY. "The essential *validity* of a factor scale is determined by the extent to which the

1 CATTELL, RAYMOND B. *Personality and Motivation Structure and Measurement*, p. 171. Yonkers, N.Y.: World Book Co., 1957. Pp. xxv, 948. *

scale score correlates with the pure factor which it claims to measure. This value is its 'construct'—or, as we prefer—its *concept* validity" (handbook, p. 12). Cattell calculates concept validity in three ways: (*a*) By the multiple correlation of the 10 items .in each factor with the pure factor; (*b*) from the equivalence reliability coefficient "assuming that, by reason of suppressor action, the two halves of the test have nothing in common except the common factor they set out to measure"; and (*c*) a circumstantial or indirect validity which is the pattern of relationships between the factor of interest and the other personality and general ability factors defined by the questionnaire.

Theoretically, the use of suppressor action by items is a good one. Thus, Cattell advocates combining in a scale pairs of items, scored in opposite directions, which measure both a wanted factor and an unwanted factor to enable the items to suppress the unwanted factor in each other and to produce on the final scale only variance attributable to the wanted factor. However, the well known unreliability of item responses and instability of coefficients of correlation between pairs of items combine to make the suppressor approach empirically difficult. It is unlikely, even with item suppressor action, that a scale's communality is as great as its reliability. Thus the reliability coefficient is not an adequate estimate of the proportion of common factor variance in the items.

In deriving the coefficient of validity from the coefficient of equivalence Cattell takes the square root. The resulting coefficient is the index of reliability, in Guilford's terms the index of intrinsic validity. This coefficient, of course, is also what Tryon has labeled behavior domain validity. It may be considered to be the correlation between a sample of a trait and its perfect criterion measure. If this index is very high, one knows that the examinees are ranked by observed scores close to their ranking in a perfectly reliable measure of the trait as operationally defined by the items. Cattell might better use the square root of the communality as an index of what Guilford calls relevant validity, the upper limit of the test's validity coefficients.

The range of the indices of validity computed from the coefficients of equivalence range from .56 to .82 for Forms A and B combined, with a median value of approximately .74. The lowest value is for Zeppia vs. Coasthenia (vigorous vs. internally restrained) and the largest for Harria vs. Premsia (tough-minded vs. tender-minded). The data are based on relatively small samples and have not been cross validated. The coefficients of validity presented are based on the first edition (evidently a pre-1959 edition) of the test. They must be regarded as tentative and cross validation is a must before the CPQ can be used in making inferences about individuals.

Since Cattell believes he has discovered 14 or more pure factors in the personality domain, he feels free to discuss the behavioral meaning of these factors at all age levels from 8 to 80. He states:

Finally, it should be noted that throughout these discussions, *young adult and adult* associations (occupation, adjustment, group behavior) are brought in to enrich the meaning of most of the factor-dimensions. These additional associations are a permissible part of the discussion because it has been established that each of the CPQ personality dimensions continues in essentially similar form as applicable to all later ages. Moreover, adult associations of a dimension are *useful* as well as merely permissible, since they point up the adult occupational, mental health, and other expectations for a child in terms of his present profile on the factors.

This statement is not documented in the handbook by longitudinal evidence, factor analytic or other, and if we look at the coefficients of stability given in the manual, the quoted statement is nonsensical.

If one assumes that the factors defined by Cattell through his measurement procedures are well defined operationally, one still must question whether or not he has established meaning for these factors separate from his factor analytic procedures. He has accumulated very little evidence that the factors identified in the CPQ bear a relationship to behavior outside of the test situation. Consequently, the bulk of the material discussed in the section under "Psychological Interpretation of the Fourteen Primary Personality Traits" is pure speculation. Now, all is not lost. Cattell has demonstrated he is a generator of good hypotheses so the handbook is a gold mine of hypotheses which can be tested by him and his colleagues and by interested researchers. However, the evidence for practical validity is inadequate.

CONCLUSION. It is this reviewer's opinion that the 1959 edition of the *IPAT Children's Personality Questionnaire,* because of its low

reliability and insufficient evidence for validity, must be considered a research tool which
should *not* be used in counseling or otherwise
dealing with individual children. It may be
possible for the revised questionnaire to be
used to make inferences if it is more reliable
than the 1959 edition and if there is substantial
evidence that the factor scores allow inferences
to be made about children's behavior. Lacking
such evidence, the new instrument also should
be used solely for research purposes.

ROBERT D. WIRT, *Professor of Psychology,
Child Development, and Psychiatry, University of Minnesota, Minneapolis, Minnesota.*

The *IPAT Children's Personality Questionnaire* (CPQ) is an extension downward, to
the age range from 8 to 12 years, of the
IPAT High School Personality Questionnaire
(HSPQ) and the *Sixteen Personality Factor
Questionnaire* (16 PF). A further extension
to years 6 through 8, the Early School Personality Questionnaire (ESPQ), is promised
for early publication. The series of tests, with
one year overlap between tests, will give continuity from early childhood through adulthood
along what are purported to be the same
dimensions of personality.

The test consists of two forms, A and B.
The authors advise using both forms which
gives for a single administration a scale of
10 items for each scale. Most test users will
appreciate having alternate forms of the test
but will be somewhat dubious of the stability
of even a 10-item scale based upon the use of
both forms.

The format of the booklets is practical for
use by children. The questions are clearly
stated and most questions require an either-or
response which is to be indicated directly on
the test booklet. The scoring is quite straightforward and easily accomplished in a few
minutes; the test yields raw scores which can
be plotted on a profile in staves (normalized
scores ranging from 1 to 5). The handbook
gives tables for converting raw scores to staves
for boys and for girls separately, for conversion of staves to stens (normalized scores
ranging from 0 to 10) and for the properties
of staves as standard scores. Significant sex
and age differences exist on a large number
of the 14 scales.

The language used in defining the dimensions of the CPQ will be bothersome to those
not familiar with the 16 PF. However, test
users well acquainted with the now considerable literature on factored scales will be pleased
that this new addition to the series, as the
authors point out, makes possible some kinds
of longitudinal studies of personality not before available. It is certainly true, as the authors
state in the opening sentence of their handbook,
that there is "a great need for trustworthy
personality measures of children." That the
CPQ is such a trustworthy measure is not
established by the data now available.

The publication of the test was premature.
There are repeated cautions in the handbook
which warn the reader and potential test user
that numerous additional research investigations are underway to clarify one point or
another, to establish the meaning of certain
factors, to improve upon the reliability of
scales, and so forth. It is true, of course, that
continuing research and refinement are desirable in the upgrading of all aspects of mental
measurement and that an author need not wait
upon perfection before publishing his work;
but still he probably should not publish work
designated as a useful practical measuring device and at the same time indicate that much
study is yet required before the instrument can
be safely used. Perhaps the authors of this
instrument should be commended, however,
for the care they have taken in indicating the
areas of weakness which do exist in the CPQ.

The handbook is unusually well written in
parts and quite worth reading for its clear
explication of several important problems of
test construction. There are sections on various
meanings of reliability and validity and on the
clinical use of test data that are elegant examples of careful reasoning and statistical sophistication. But when it comes to the specifics of
the particular standardization of the CPQ one
looks in vain for equal clarity. The numbers
given tell the reader that certain correlations
are based on "260 boys and girls of nine years
of age in U.S. elementary schools" or that
some other figures are derived from a study
of 200 subjects, and still other data are reported to be based on 1,476 children. Nowhere
are there data which *describe* the norm groups.
For this reason it is, of course, impossible to
know with what standard a test user is to
compare results of his subjects.

The writing style of the handbook is often
in poor taste, in that the virtues of the approach

to testing used by these authors and the validity of the CPQ are over-sold. The reader is urged to believe that *all* of the fundamental dimensions of personality of children are reflected in the CPQ. The authors quite blandly assure the test user that the test is equally valid given individually or in groups, whether the items are read by the subjects or read aloud by the examiner, but they do not give data to support these contentions. Perhaps most distressing is the section on reliability and validity. The discussion of these issues relative to general considerations of test purpose is brilliant, but the relationship of these concepts to the CPQ is absent. The reader is given skimpy secondary data on validity and is referred to other sources for further detail. The references cited for this purpose relate almost exclusively to general texts on the subject of test construction and the measurement and theories of personality having nothing whatever to do with the particular standardization of the CPQ.

In summary, it may be said that the CPQ is a hopeful beginning for careful assessment of personality in children, but until further study is made this instrument should be used for research only.

[123]

IPAT Contact Personality Factor Test. High school and adults; 1954–56; title on test is C.P.F.; 2 scores: extroversion-introversion, distortion; Forms A, B, ('54, 3 pages); mimeographed bits ['54–56, 21 pages] serving as manual; adult norms only; 20¢ per test; $2 per complete specimen set (must be purchased to obtain manual and key); cash orders postpaid; Form A also published, under the title *Employee Attitude Series: C.P.F.*, by Industrial Psychology, Inc.; (10) minutes; Raymond B. Cattell, Joseph E. King, and A. K. Schuettler; Institute for Personality and Ability Testing. *

REFERENCES

1. CATTELL, RAYMOND B. *Personality and Motivation Structure and Measurement.* Yonkers, N.Y.: World Book Co., 1957. Pp. xxv, 948. * (*PA* 32:3918)
2. CLARIDGE, GORDON. Chap. 2, "The Excitation-Inhibition Balance in Neurotics," pp. 107–54. In *Experiments in Personality: Vol. 2, Psychodiagnostics and Psychodynamics.* Edited by H. J. Eysenck. London: Routledge & Kegan Paul Ltd., 1960. Pp. viii, 333. *
3. EYSENCK, H. J. Chap. 5, "A Factor Analysis of Selected Tests," pp. 234–44. In his *Experiments in Personality: Vol. 2, Psychodiagnostics and Psychodynamics.* London: Routledge & Kegan Paul Ltd., 1960. Pp. viii, 333. *
4. HOLLAND, H. C. Chap. 4, "Measures of Perceptual Functions," pp. 193–233. In *Experiments in Personality: Vol. 2, Psychodiagnostics and Psychodynamics.* Edited by H. J. Eysenck. London: Routledge & Kegan Paul Ltd., 1960. Pp. viii, 333. *
5. WILLETT, R. A. Chap. 3, "Measures of Learning and Conditioning," pp. 157–92. In *Experiments in Personality: Vol. 2, Psychodiagnostics and Psychodynamics.* Edited by H. J. Eysenck. London: Routledge & Kegan Paul Ltd., 1960. Pp. viii, 333. *
6. FIELD, J. G., AND BRENGELMANN, J. C. "Eyelid Conditioning and Three Personality Parameters." *J Abn & Social Psychol* 63:517–23 N '61. * (*PA* 37:369)

For reviews by Cecil D. Johnson and S. B. Sells, see 5:71.

[124]

★IPAT 8-Parallel-Form Anxiety Battery. Ages 14 or 15 and over; 1960–62; tests and answer sheets labeled *8-Form* and *8-Parallel-Form Battery*, respectively; Forms A, B, C, D, E, F, G, H, ('60, 7 subtests, each on a separate sheet); manual ('60, 6 pages); supplement ('62, 4 pages); $1.75 per 25 copies of any one subtest of any one form; $8.40 per 25 sets of all subtests of any one form; separate answer sheets may be used; $2.20 per pad of 50 answer sheets; 35¢ per set of manual and supplement; $8 per test kit consisting of single-booklet combination of manual and keyed copies of all subtests of all forms (must be purchased to obtain keys for certain subtests); price of test kit includes permission to reproduce up to 500 copies of each subtest; cash orders postpaid; (10–15) minutes; Ivan H. Scheier and Raymond B. Cattell; Institute for Personality and Ability Testing. *

REFERENCES

1. CATTELL, RAYMOND B., AND SCHEIER, IVAN H. *The Meaning and Measurement of Neuroticism and Anxiety.* New York: Ronald Press Co., 1961. Pp. ix, 535. * (*PA* 36:1HK27C)
2. BENDIG, A. W., AND BRUDER, GAIL. "The Effect of Repeated Testing on Anxiety Scale Scores." Abstract. *J Consult Psychol* 26:392 Ag '62. *
3. CATTELL, RAYMOND B. "Advances in the Measurement of Neuroticism and Anxiety in a Conceptual Framework of Unitary-Trait Theory." *Ann N Y Acad Sci* 93:815–39 O 10 '62. * (*PA* 37:6779)
4. SCHEIER, IVAN H. "Experimental Results to Date From the Viewpoint of the Clinician." *Ann N Y Acad Sci* 93:840–50 O 10 '62. * (*PA* 37:6782)

JACOB COHEN, *Professor of Psychology, New York University, New York, New York.*

Like the other tests coming from Cattell's laboratory, the *IPAT 8-Parallel-Form Anxiety Battery* is not the product of a single ad hoc test construction effort, but is based on a long range research program involving hundreds of variables of diverse kinds applied to thousands of subjects of varying age, clinical status, and background. This program is the consequence of, and feeds back into, a detailed theory of the origins, development, and structure of personality and motivation. The factor-analytically derived IPAT tests are simultaneously the products of this research program and its tools. A consequence of this is that truly effective use of these tests requires considerable familiarity with the Cattellian system such as is provided by the two most recent books: Cattell's 1957 *Personality and Motivation Structure and Measurement* (see B119), which describes the system as a whole, and Cattell and Scheier's 1961 *The Meaning and Measurement of Neuroticism and Anxiety* (*1*), which updates the system and applies it to the segment of the clinical area thus far explored.

The immediate background of the test under review is a series of replicated researches which

(a) established anxiety as a second-order factor in questionnaire items, (b) established anxiety as a first-order factor in objective tests, and (c) matched these factors as being the same and found them related to the consensus of clinical ratings of anxiety. From the thousands of items studied, it was then possible to select enough to make up eight equivalent forms, each of 50 items, with inconsequential overlap. The items in each form are divided into seven subtests of from 4–10 items each, selected to tap the following: questionnaire anxiety, susceptibility to annoyance, lack of confidence in untried skills, readiness to confess common faults, the emotionality of chosen reaction to "newspaper items," anxiety-tension symptom self-checklist, and susceptibility to embarrassment. Scoring is objective, and requires the computation of means of attempted items. The term "battery" is somewhat misleading, since the separate subtests in each form are necessarily highly unreliable, and are not recommended by the authors for separate interpretation.

The manual (1960) is headed "For Research and Experimental Purposes Only," and although Supplement #1 (1962) is not so labeled, it should be. Although the impressive research background of the test suggests that it will prove valuable for a variety of uses, the sketchiness of the norms and the ambiguity and incompleteness of the available reliability information permit its use in clinical situations in only the most tentative way.

Preliminary sten and percentile norms are provided for the eight forms for n's varying from 142 to 235 cases. This norm group is not well described, and includes a large (but unspecified) proportion of "abnormal" cases, whose influence was mitigated by a procedure whose details are not given. Furthermore, for any given form about one sixth of the cases represent second administrations for the subject. Finally, the time intervals between forms range from a half day to a week. Given the sophistication of the test's authors, the resultant norms are probably not far from the mark, but confident use of the test requires a tidier norming, which is undoubtedly forthcoming.

The general construct validity provided by the background of the test is supplemented by correlations of each form with a 600-item anxiety estimate for 94 college undergraduates ranging from .50 to .68. Where fewer than eight forms are needed, these values can be raised by the combination of forms.

Some ambiguity attaches to the reliability of the separate forms. The manual gives for the 94 undergraduates, who took all eight forms in a single sitting, interform correlations ranging from .36 to .67, with means per form ranging from .41 to .57. These values are rather low. The supplement provides new determinations ranging from .60 to .85 for subjects taking the forms at two- and seven-day intervals. The authors speculate that this discrepancy may be due to curtailed variance in the single-sitting situation. This is not very convincing, and the easily computed variances are not presented. One would expect the reverse of these findings: equivalence reliabilities on a single occasion should be larger than over an interval of time. The anomaly most likely lies in the difference in composition of the groups or the circumstances of the testing.

The test is offered for the obvious purpose of studying changes in anxiety level over time. For such use, high correlation between forms given on *different* occasions is *not* desirable. What is wanted is that such correlations be low relative to correlations between forms on the *same* occasion, i.e., true equivalence reliabilities. No evidence along these lines (both kinds of correlations on a single defined group, or reliabilities of change scores) is presented, and it must be if the test is to realize its purpose.

In summary, this test comes with a most impressive heritage, although not enough normative and reliability data are yet available to make possible a confident recommendation for routine clinical use. It can, indeed *should*, be used in research which would contribute not only to the understanding of anxiety but to the illumination of its own properties. It is the only available means for objectively studying anxiety fluctuation, and there is probably nothing wrong with it which more data (which are constantly being gathered) will not cure.

PAUL M. KJELDERGAARD, *Assistant Professor of Education, Harvard University, Cambridge, Massachusetts.*

This test, as its name implies, consists of eight equivalent forms of a paper and pencil, multiple choice, anxiety questionnaire developed from a large factor analytic study. Each form consists of seven subtests: (a) questionnaire items (10 items)—the usual personality inventory type item with trichotomous choices, e.g. true, false, or in between; (b) susceptibility to annoyance (7 items)—a list of events to be rated on a three-point scale as to how irritating the respondent would find them; (c) lack of confidence in untried skills (7 items)—the respondent first rates the frequency with which he has had certain types of experiences and then judges his competence to handle such situations, only those situations with which he has had little experience being scored; (d) readiness to confess common faults (7 items)—dichotomous responses to a list of "human frailties"; (e) emotionality of comment (4 items)—trichotomous choice responses to "news items"; (f) anxiety-tension symptom self-checklist (8 items)—respondents utilize a three-point scale to rate themselves in comparison to others as to the degree to which they possess certain behavioral characteristics, e.g., conceit, or the frequency of certain somatic symptoms, e.g. rapid pulse; and (g) susceptibility to embarrassment (7 items)—respondents rate situations on a three-point scale as to the degree of embarrassment the situation would arouse. A total of 350 items were selected from 900 anxiety measure items (60 tests) included in a large factor analytic study. These items were then allocated to the eight forms randomly. Since each form contains 50 items, some item overlap was necessary, although this is minimal.

RELIABILITY. Only equivalent form reliabilities are reported, and then, only the average correlation of each form with all other forms is given.[1] The authors do cite the range of coefficients (.36 to .67) but insofar as the forms involved are not identified this provides minimal information. Subsequent research by another investigator reported somewhat higher interform coefficients (.60 to .85). These discrepancies are explained by differences in procedure and intervals between administrations; the latter results are thought to be more appropriate for the usual application of these instruments.

VALIDITY. The validity coefficients, based upon the correlation of the test with an anxiety factor (a pool of 600 anxiety measure items) range from .50 to .68 with a median coefficient of .54. Although technically these are part-whole correlations, the proportion of test items

included in the criterion measure was so small that this is not a serious limitation.

NORMS. Norms, in terms of stens (standard tens) and percentiles based upon 142 to 235 cases, both normal and abnormal, per form are available for each of the eight forms. A complex and undescribed weighting procedure was used for combining the scores of the normals and abnormals into the normative tables. A high (unspecified) proportion of abnormals were tested and their scores were adjusted and weighted such that they contributed proportionately less to the norms than the normals. In addition, for any given form, all observations are not independent; approximately 15 per cent of the observations represent repeated measurement based upon the same individual.

SUMMARY. On the one hand, this test appears to be the product of careful research by competent investigators who have utilized the digital computer to develop an instrument that two decades ago would not have been possible. It is a unique contribution opening new vistas of research opportunities in the field of anxiety related behavior. On the other hand, one cannot help being negatively impressed by the penurious manner in which the manual and norms supplement were written. Although basic information is presented, in many cases it is minimal or inadequate. One instance of this is the reporting of the interform reliabilities discussed above. Other examples are the use of the term "average correlation" with no indication as to whether this is the median coefficient, the mean coefficient after appropriate transformation, or some other possible measure, and an inadequate description of the normative samples and the statistical procedures used in "weighting" the scores used in the norm table.

The above criticisms are relevant where the test is to be used to make judgments about an individual on a specific occasion. These factors would be of relatively little concern to the researcher making group predictions or in correlational studies where raw scores would suffice. The basic development of the instrument appears sound and was based upon a sufficient number of observations to justify confidence in it as a potentially fruitful research instrument.

[125]

*IPAT Music Preference Test of Personality. "Adults and young adults"; 1952–63; 11 scores of which the following 8 are profiled: adjustment vs. frustrated

1 An 8 x 8 matrix requires so little space that one finds it difficult to comprehend why all coefficients are not reported.

emotionality, hypomanic self-centeredness vs. self-distrust and doubt, tough sociability vs. tenderminded individuality, introspectiveness vs. social contact, anxiety and concern vs. paranoid imperiousness, complex eccentricity vs. stability-normality, resilience vs. withdrawn schizothymia, schizothyme tenacity vs. relaxed cyclothymia; Forms A, B, ['60, on one 12-inch, 33⅓ rpm record]; mimeographed manual ('60, c1954-60, 24 pages, identical with manual published in 1952 except for cover page); mimeographed supplement ('63, 4 pages); answer sheet-profile ('59, 1 page); separate answer sheets must be used; $13.50 per set of record, 100 answer sheets, scoring stencil, and manual; $2.25 per 50 answer sheets; $1.80 per specimen set without record; cash orders postpaid; (25-30) minutes; Raymond B. Cattell and Herbert W. Eber; Institute for Personality and Ability Testing. *

REFERENCES

1-4. See 5:73.
5. WILLIAMS, RAYMOND EDMUND. The Measurement and Prediction of Cooperating Teacher Effectiveness in Music Teacher Education. Doctor's thesis, University of Illinois (Urbana, Ill.), 1958. (DA 19:1023)
6. CHARLES, LOUIS. A Study of the Power of the IPAT Music Preference Test of Personality to Discriminate Between Normal and Abnormal Groups. Master's thesis, Kent State University (Kent, Ohio), 1959.
7. CATTELL, RAYMOND B., AND McMICHAEL, ROBERT E. "Clinical Diagnosis by the IPAT Music Preference Test." J Consult Psychol 24:333-41 Ag '60. * (PA 35:2237)
8. DUDA, WALTER BOLESLAV. The Prediction of Three Major Dimensions of Teacher Behavior for Student Teachers in Music Education. Doctor's thesis, University of Illinois (Urbana, Ill.), 1961. (DA 22:1518)
9. MAYESKE, GEORGE W. Some Associations of Musical Preference Dimensions of Personality. Doctor's thesis, University of Illinois (Urbana, Ill.), 1962. (DA 23:3468)
10. SCHULTZ, CAROL. The Reliability of Music Preference Under Varying Mood Conditions. Master's thesis, Fairleigh Dickinson University (Rutherford, N.J.), 1962.
11. SCHULTZ, CAROL, AND LANG, GERHARD. "The Reliability of Music Preferences Under Varying Mood Conditions." J Clin Psychol 19:506 O '63. *

KENNETH L. BEAN, Clinical Psychologist, Veterans Administration Hospital, Knoxville, Iowa.

This unique approach to a number of aspects of personality has 50 items (brief musical excerpts) in each form. The style of music varies all the way from Bach to boogie-woogie. Some of the phrases are simple in melodic and harmonic structure, with very pronounced rhythm. Others are quite harmonically sophisticated with less definite rhythm and a rather conspicuous absence of any definite melody. Still others have several simultaneous melodic lines. Length of phrases played is held rather constant. The subject is asked to mark his reaction to each selection as "L" (like), "I" (indifferent), or "D" (dislike), and is persuaded to aim at an approximately equal number of responses in each of these three categories, though he is not held rigidly to conformity on this point. Indecision is discouraged, and a rather quick, immediate judgment is requested.

Likes and dislikes have been treated statistically by means of factor analysis, though not all of the 11 factors which emerged were regarded as important. Thorough statistical work has been done with the preferences of an adequate number of adult subjects. A convenient profile quantifies the results in a manner facilitating interpretation, and correlations with personality tests consisting of a different sort of items appear to support validity. Likes and dislikes for the different styles of music included are said to be rather consistent for any one individual, and a preference for each style is said to be associated with a different tendency in personality.

A distortion in the true feelings of some listeners might result from the instructions to approach equal numbers of L, I, and D responses—a suggestion made at the beginning of the recording but immediately partially withdrawn by cautioning the subject not to give too much consideration to this matter. Clearly, it is often demonstrated that one individual may habitually experience slight annoyance in response to nearly all music, while another may be predominantly indifferent, and still another typically favorable toward most kinds of music. Any instruction which would be likely to obscure most such individual differences could result in failure to observe such phenomena as irritability or slight flattening of affect.

Furthermore, the affective response to music is far from free of cultural influences. Chinese music, to give an example not in this test, contains intervals strange and frustrating to American ears. The dissonant harmonic structure of some test items may be disliked by those lacking experience with modern idioms. To a listener hunting for a single melodic line accompanied by chords, the polyphonic structure of Bach can hardly fail to sound confused and impossible to follow as a total pattern. Overworked idioms of simple structure in music can hardly be expected to arouse interest or enthusiasm in the musically sophisticated who would regard them as uninteresting or too simple. To the naive, however, the same selections could prove to be satisfyingly within their capacity to comprehend.

With the wide individual variation known to exist in the listening and performing experiences of people, musical phrases could hardly be expected to be even as appropriate as verbal expressions for stimuli supposed to serve as a means of making a rather pure evaluation of personality. Doubt as to the appropriateness of stimuli selected for this test is further strengthened by the obvious familiarity of many of the selections to most listeners. The inclusion of the hymn "Joy to the World," "Blue Danube Waltz," the violin concerto of Mendelssohn, second movement, and a few popular tunes of the day would seem to invite to enter the evaluation a number of unknown variables which would best be omitted by selecting similar styles and structures totally unfamiliar to most or all subjects. The influence of familiarity, sophistication, and deviations in listening experience has been insufficiently investigated so far by the authors. They should probably clarify the importance of such matters further before assuming that for most people a measure of personality variables can be largely independent of these factors.

Finally, quality of reproduction leaves much to be desired, even if the vast majority of subjects are less aware of distortions and distractions on the disc than is the reviewer. An experienced editor of music tapes could have erased many unwanted sounds from between the desired notes of the music before the disc was cut. Tone quality varies from good to very poor, doubtless affecting some preferences. Critical attitudes regarding what may have been intended as "sloppy" performance of some of the popular selections might be responsible for dislikes by analytical listeners, but no question is raised by the authors regarding the influence of this approach, which is habitual with some individuals. Probably many listeners could disregard performance and tone quality variations and judge only the music itself if instructions were expanded to clarify this point.

As a whole the test is interesting and impressive regarding the thoroughness of quantitative treatment of data, yet the reviewer questions validity for habitual concert goers or musical performers. Refinement by perfection of the recording, choice of unfamiliar examples, and more thorough tryout on populations of musically sophisticated persons might well make the test a more valuable contribution to personality measurement, a contribution whose validity could be more adequately defended.

PAUL R. FARNSWORTH, *Professor of Psychology, Stanford University, Stanford, California.*

The Van Steenberg review of this test in *The Fifth Mental Measurements Yearbook* could well be reprinted almost verbatim in the current volume, for the situation regarding this

measure has changed little since 1959. The test items are still piano-rendered snatches of music which often end awkwardly and appear on a double disc recording which would win no prizes for pianistic or engineering excellence. In fact, many of the items, particularly those taken from contemporary music, are so poorly played and recorded that the more musically sophisticated listeners often rebel at continuing with the test. And, if they are persuaded to listen further, they may complain that they cannot follow the test's suggestion to give "indifference" votes to approximately a third of the items. Their tendency is either to like or dislike an item. They react to the item's musical structure, the manner in which it is played, and the way in which it is recorded—sometimes to one and sometimes to another of these variables. However, one worries about the musical aspects of the test items only when the test is regarded as a measure of musical preferences. Whenever the test is to be used solely to distinguish between normal and the several abnormal groups, one frets less about the exact nature of the items. Other musical, art, or quite different sorts of items could most probably have served the same ends almost as well. This reviewer would like the test much better if it made no attempt to uncover the musical preferences of either normals or abnormals. It has a sufficiently worthwhile task within the area of personality testing.

For a review by Neil J. Van Steenberg, see 5:73.

[126]

★Inpatient Multidimensional Psychiatric Scale (IMPS). Hospitalized mental patients; 1953–62; revision of *Multidimensional Scale for Rating Psychiatric Patients, Hospital Form* ('53–54) by Maurice Lorr, R. L. Jenkins, and J. Q. Holsopple, which was a revision of the *Northport Record* by Maurice Lorr, M. Singer, and H. Zobel; 10 scores based on ratings following an interview: excitement, hostile belligerence, paranoid projection, grandiose expansiveness, perceptual distortion, anxious intropunitiveness, retardation and apathy, disorientation, motor disturbance, conceptual disorganization; question booklet ['62, 8 pages]; answer-profile sheet ['62, 4 pages]; manual ('62, 45 pages, including copy of question booklet and answer-profile sheet) ; separate answer-profile sheets must be used; $5 per 25 question booklets; $3 per 25 answer-profile sheets; $2 per manual; $2 per specimen set; postage extra; (10–15) minutes; Maurice Lorr, James Klett, Douglas M. McNair, and Julian J. Lasky; Consulting Psychologists Press, Inc. *

REFERENCES
1. LORR, MAURICE. *Multidimensional Scale for Rating Psychiatric Patients, Hospital Form.* Veterans Administration

Technical Bulletin, TB 10-507. Washington, D.C.: Veterans Administration, November 16, 1953. Pp. 44. *

2. LORR, MAURICE; RUBINSTEIN, ELI A.; AND REIDY, MARY E. "A Factor Analysis of a Scale for Rating Psychiatric Outpatients." Abstract. *Am Psychol* 8:391–2 Ag '53. *

3. LORR, MAURICE; SCHAEFER, EARL; RUBINSTEIN, ELI A.; AND JENKINS, RICHARD L. "An Analysis of an Outpatient Rating Scale." *J Clin Psychol* 9:296–9 Jl '53. * (*PA* 28:2741)

4. LORR, MAURICE; HOLSOPPLE, JAMES Q.; AND TURK, ELIZABETH. "Development of a Measure of Severity of Mental Illness." Abstract. *Am Psychol* 9:421 Ag '54. *

5. LORR, MAURICE; JENKINS, RICHARD L.; AND HOLSOPPLE, JAMES Q. "Factors Descriptive of Chronic Schizophrenics Selected for the Operation of Prefrontal Lobotomy." *J Consult Psychol* 18:293–6 Ag '54. * (*PA* 29:4429)

6. SCHAEFER, EARL S. "Personality Structure of Alcoholics in Outpatient Psychotherapy." *Q J Studies Alcohol* 15:304–19 Je '54. * (*PA* 29:2709)

7. LORR, MAURICE, AND RUBINSTEIN, ELI A. "Personality Patterns of Neurotic Adults in Psychotherapy." *J Consult Psychol* 20:257–63 Ag '56. * (*PA* 31:8534)

8. LORR, MAURICE; HOLSOPPLE, JAMES Q.; AND TURK, ELIZABETH. "A Measure of Severity of Illness." *J Clin Psychol* 12:384–6 O '56. *

9. LORR, MAURICE; O'CONNOR, JAMES P.; AND STAFFORD, JOHN W. "Confirmation of Nine Psychotic Symptom Patterns." *J Clin Psychol* 13:252–7 Jl '57. *

10. STILSON, DONALD W.; MASON, DONALD J.; GYNTHER, MALCOLM D.; AND GERTZ, BORIS. "An Evaluation of the Comparability and Reliabilities of Two Behavior Rating Scales for Mental Patients." *J Consult Psychol* 22:213–6 Je '58. * (*PA* 35:4887)

11. ELLSWORTH, ROBERT B., AND CLAYTON, WILLIAM H. "Measurement of Improvement in 'Mental Illness.'" *J Consult Psychol* 23:15–20 F '59. * (*PA* 34:1353)

12. KLETT, C. JAMES, AND LASKY, JULIAN J. "Agreement Among Raters on the Multidimensional Scale for Rating Psychiatric Patients." Abstract. *J Consult Psychol* 23:281 Je '59. * (*PA* 34:4387)

13. CASEY, JESSE F.; HOLLISTER, LEO E.; KLETT, C. JAMES; LASKY, JULIAN J.; AND CAFFEY, EUGENE M. "Combined Drug Therapy of Chronic Schizophrenics." *Am J Psychiatry* 117: 997–1003 My '61. *

14. JENKINS, RICHARD L. "Quantitative Aspects of Sentence Completion in the Study of the Improvement of Schizophrenic Patients." *J Proj Tech* 25:303–11 S '61. * (*PA* 36:3HI03J)

15. PASAMANICK, BENJAMIN, AND RISTINE, LEONARD. "Differential Assessment of Posthospital Psychological Functioning: Evaluation by Psychiatrists and Relatives." *Am J Psychiatry* 118:40–6 Jl '61. *

16. CERBUS, GEORGE, AND NICHOLS, ROBERT C. "Personality Correlates of Picture Preferences." *J Abn & Social Psychol* 64:75–8 Ja '62. * (*PA* 37:3139)

17. LASKY, JULIAN J.; KLETT, C. JAMES; CAFFEY, EUGENE M., JR.; BENNETT, J. LAMAR; ROSENBLUM, MARCUS P.; AND HOLLISTER, LEO E. "Drug Treatment of Schizophrenic Patients: A Comparative Evaluation of Chlorpromazine, Chlorprothixene, Fluphenazine, Reserpine, Thioridazine and Triflupromazine." *Dis Nerv System* 23:698–706 D '62. *

18. LORR, MAURICE. "Measurement of the Major Psychotic Syndromes." *Ann N Y Acad Sci* 93:851–6 O 10 '62. * (*PA* 37:6761)

19. LORR, MAURICE; McNAIR, DOUGLAS M.; KLETT, C. JAMES; AND LASKY, JULIAN J. "Evidence of Ten Psychotic Syndromes." *J Consult Psychol* 26:185–9 Ap '62. * (*PA* 37:5468)

20. DURELL, J., AND POLLIN, W. "A Trial on Chronic Schizophrenic Patients of Oxypertine, a Psychotropic Drug With an Indole Ring." *Brit J Psychiatry* 109:687–91 S '63. *

21. EYSENCK, H. J. "Psychoticism or Ten Psychotic Syndromes?" *J Consult Psychol* 27:179–80 Ap '63. * Criticism of 19.

22. LEWINSOHN, PETER M.; NICHOLS, ROBERT C.; PULOS, LEE; LOMONT, JAMES F.; NICKEL, HERBERT J.; AND SISKIND, GEORGE. "The Reliability and Validity of Quantified Judgments From Psychological Tests." *J Clin Psychol* 19:64–73 Ja '63. * (*PA* 39:1893)

23. LORR, MAURICE; McNAIR, DOUGLAS M.; KLETT, C. JAMES; AND LASKY, JULIAN J. "Canonical Variates and Second-Order Factors: A Reply." *J Consult Psychol* 27:180–1 Ap '63. * A reply to 21.

24. MICHAUX, MARY HELEN; OTA, KAY Y.; HANLON, THOMAS E.; AND KURLAND, ALBERT A. "Rater Perseveration in Measurement of Patient Change." *Ed & Psychol Meas* 23: 171–84 sp '63. * (*PA* 38:2731)

25. MOSELEY, EDWARD C.; DUFFEY, ROBERT F.; AND SHERMAN, LEWIS J. "An Extension of the Construct Validity of the Holtzman Inkblot Technique." *J Clin Psychol* 19:186–92 Ap '63. * (*PA* 39:5083)

26. RASKIN, ALLEN, AND CLYDE, DEAN J. "Factors of Psychopathology in the Ward Behavior of Acute Schizophrenics." *J Consult Psychol* 27:420–5 O '63. * (*PA* 38:4616)

[127]

Interpersonal Check List. Adults; 1955–56; part of the *Interpersonal Diagnosis of Personality;* 1 form

['55, 3 pages]; battery manual ('56, 114 pages, see *2* below); $4 per 20 tests; $2 per scoring template; (15–45) minutes depending on number of persons rated; Timothy Leary, Rolfe LaForge (test), Robert Suczek (test), and others (manual); Psychological Consultation Service. *

REFERENCES

1. LAFORGE, ROLFE, AND SUCZEK, ROBERT F. "The Interpersonal Dimension of Personality: 3, An Interpersonal Check List." *J Personality* 24:94–112 S '55. * (*PA* 30:5990)

2. LEARY, TIMOTHY; WITH THE COLLABORATION OF HELEN LANE, ANNE APFELBAUM, MARY DELLA CIOPPA, AND CHARLOTTE KAUFMANN. *Multilevel Measurement of Interpersonal Behavior: A Manual for the Use of the Interpersonal System of Personality.* Berkeley, Calif.: Psychological Consultation Service, 1956. Pp. vii, 110. *

3. ARMSTRONG, RENATE GERBOTH. *Personality Structure in Alcoholism.* Doctor's thesis, University of Colorado (Boulder, Colo.), 1957. (*DA* 18:1851)

4. EDWARDS, ALLEN L. "Social Desirability and Probability of Endorsement of Items in the Interpersonal Check List." *J Abn & Social Psychol* 55:394–6 N '57. * (Abstract: *Am Psychol* 11:378)

5. LEARY, TIMOTHY. *Interpersonal Diagnosis of Personality: A Functional Theory and Methodology for Personality Evaluation.* New York: Ronald Press Co., 1957. Pp. xix, 518. * (*PA* 31:2556)

6. ARMSTRONG, RENATE GERBOTH. "The Leary Impersonal Check List: A Reliability Study." *J Clin Psychol* 14:393–4 O '58. * (*PA* 34:2983)

7. ARMSTRONG, RENATE GERBOTH, AND WERTHEIMER, MICHAEL. "Personality Structure in Alcoholism." *Psychol Newsl* 10:341–9 Jl–Ag '59. * (*PA* 34:3189)

8. DINITZ, SIMON; MANGUS, A. R.; AND PASAMANICK, BENJAMIN. "Integration and Conflict in Self-Other Conceptions as Factors in Mental Illness." *Sociometry* 22:44–55 Mr '59. * (*PA* 34:1623)

9. KRONENBERGER, E. J. *An Investigation of Interpersonal Aspects of Industrial Accident and Non-Accident Men.* Doctor's thesis, University of Ottawa (Ottawa, Ont., Canada), 1959. (Abstract: *Can Psychologist* 1:115)

10. ALTROCCHI, JOHN; PARSONS, OSCAR A.; AND DICKOFF, HILDA. "Changes in Self-Ideal Discrepancy in Repressors and Sensitizers." *J Abn & Social Psychol* 61:67–72 Jl '60. * (*PA* 35:2253)

11. KRONENBERGER, EARL J. "Interpersonal Aspects of Industrial Accident and Non-Accident Employees." *Eng & Ind Psychol* 2:57–62 su '60. * (*PA* 37:2168)

12. LUCKEY, ELEANORE B. "Implications for Marriage Counseling of Self Perceptions and Spouse Perceptions." *J Counsel Psychol* 7:3–9 sp '60. * (*PA* 35:2440)

13. LUCKEY, ELEANORE BRAUN. "Marital Satisfaction and Congruent Self-Spouse Concepts." Abstract. *Social Forces* 39:153–7 D '60. * (*PA* 35:3680)

14. LUCKEY, ELEANORE BRAUN. "Marital Satisfaction and Its Association With Congruence of Perception." *Marriage & Family Living* 22:49–54 F '60. * (*PA* 36:2IQ49L)

15. LUCKEY, ELEANORE BRAUN. "Marital Satisfaction and Parent Concepts." *J Consult Psychol* 24:195–204 Je '60. * (*PA* 35:6686)

16. ALTROCCHI, JOHN. "Interpersonal Perceptions of Repressors and Sensitizers and Component Analysis of Assumed Dissimilarity Scores." *J Abn & Social Psychol* 62:528–34 My '61. * (*PA* 36:4HL28A)

17. BIERI, JAMES, AND LOBECK, ROBIN. "Self-Concept Differences in Relation to Identification, Religion, and Social Class." *J Abn & Social Psychol* 62:94–8 Ja '61. * (*PA* 36:3GC94B)

18. FOA, URIEL G. "Convergences in the Analysis of the Structure of Interpersonal Behavior." *Psychol R* 68:341–53 S '61. *

19. KLOPFER, WALTER G. "A Cross-Validation of Leary's 'Public' Communication Level." *J Clin Psychol* 17:321–2 Jl '61. * (*PA* 38:8426)

20. TERRILL, JAMES McGUFFIN. *The Relationships Between Level II and Level III in the Interpersonal System of Personality Diagnosis.* Doctor's thesis, Stanford University (Stanford, Calif.), 1961. (*DA* 21:3529)

21. WEINBERG, NORRIS; MENDELSON, MYER; AND STUNKARD, ALBERT. "A Failure to Find Distinctive Personality Features in a Group of Obese Men." *Am J Psychiatry* 117: 1035–7 My '61. *

22. WIGGINS, NANCY A. *Structural Aspects of the Interpersonal System of Personality Diagnosis, Level II.* Master's thesis, Stanford University (Stanford, Calif.), 1961.

23. ZUCKERMAN, MARVIN; LEVITT, EUGENE E.; AND LUBIN, BERNARD. "Concurrent and Construct Validity of Direct and Indirect Measures of Dependency." *J Consult Psychol* 25: 316–23 Ag '61. * (*PA* 37:1326)

24. CAIRNS, ROBERT B., AND LEWIS, MICHAEL. "Dependency and the Reinforcement Value of a Verbal Stimulus." *J Consult Psychol* 26:1–8 F '62. * (*PA* 37:4976)

25. DAVIS, J.; MORRILL, R.; FAWCETT, J.; UPTON, V.; BONDY, P. K.; AND SPIRO, H. M. "Apprehension and Elevated

Serum Cortisol Levels." *J Psychosom Res* 6:83–6 Ap–Je '62. * (*PA* 37:5108)

26. GYNTHER, MALCOLM D. "Degree of Agreement Among Three 'Interpersonal System' Measures." Abstract. *J Consult Psychol* 26:107 F '62. * (*PA* 37:4982)

27. GYNTHER, MALCOLM D., AND KEMPSON, J. OBERT. "Seminarians and Clinical Pastoral Training: A Follow-Up Study." *J Social Psychol* 56:9–14 F '62. * (*PA* 36:5GD09G)

28. GYNTHER, MALCOLM D.; MILLER, FRANCIS T.; AND DAVIS, HUGH T. "Relations Between Needs and Behavior as Measured by the Edwards PPS and Inter-Personal Check List." *J Social Psychol* 57:445–51 Ag '62. * (*PA* 37:5063)

29. LOCKWOOD, DORIS H., AND GUERNEY, BERNARD, JR. "Identification and Empathy in Relation to Self-Dissatisfaction and Adjustment." *J Abn & Social Psychol* 65:343–7 N '62. *

30. MCDONALD, ROBERT L. "Intrafamilial Conflict and Emotional Disturbance." *J Genetic Psychol* 101:201–8 D '62. * (*PA* 37:6492)

31. MCDONALD, ROBERT L. "Personality Characteristics of Freshman Medical Students as Depicted by the Leary System." *J Genetic Psychol* 100:313–23 Je '62. * (*PA* 37:3838)

32. SMITH, DONALD C. *Personal and Social Adjustment of Gifted Adolescents.* CEC Research Monograph, Series A, No. 4. Washington, D.C.: Council for Exceptional Children, 1962. Pp. iv, 65. *

33. SPERBER, ZANWIL, AND SPANNER, MARVIN. "Social Desirability, Psychopathology, and Item Endorsement." *J General Psychol* 67:105–12 Jl '62. * (*PA* 37:3238)

34. BENTLER, P. M. "Interpersonal Orientation in Relation to Hypnotic Susceptibility." *J Consult Psychol* 27:426–31 O '63. * (*PA* 38:4226)

35. BRIAR, SCOTT, AND BIERI, JAMES. "A Factor Analytic and Trait Inference Study of the Leary Interpersonal Checklist." *J Clin Psychol* 19:193–8 Ap '63. * (*PA* 37:5040)

36. FROST, BARRY P. "Some Personality Characteristics of Education Students." *Alberta J Ed Res* 9:132–9 S '63. *

37. GUERNEY, BERNARD, JR., AND BURTON, JEAN L. "Relationships Among Anxiety and Self, Typical Peer, and Ideal Percepts in College Women." *J Social Psychol* 61:335–44 D '63. * (*PA* 38:8601)

38. KOGAN, KATE L., AND JACKSON, JOAN K. "Conventional Sex Role Stereotypes and Actual Perceptions." *Psychol Rep* 13:27–30 Ag '63. * (*PA* 38:5865)

39. MCDONALD, ROBERT L., AND GYNTHER, MALCOLM D. "Nonintellectual Factors Associated With Performance in Medical School." *J Genetic Psychol* 103:185–94 S '63. * *See also references for test 233.*

P. M. BENTLER, *United States Public Health Service Fellow, Department of Psychology, Stanford University, Stanford, California.*

The *Interpersonal Check List* (ICL) is a self-rating adjective check list specially devised by LaForge and Suczek to measure personality variables of the *Interpersonal Diagnosis of Personality* (see 223). The ICL was subjected to several revisions before the final version, Form 4, was published in 1955. By agreement of the authors and collaborators, the ICL was not copyrighted. It is seen mainly as a research instrument, and although copies of the ICL are available the authors indicate the ICL may be used for any legitimate social science application by merely duplicating the list of items as found in (*1*) or (*5*) in roughly alphabetical order.[1]

The ICL can be used to measure persons' conscious descriptions of themselves or others; frequently, mother, father, spouse, or ideal self are the objects of description. The descriptions of various persons or objects can be compared in terms of resulting profiles or summary scores

1 LAFORGE, R. "Research Use of the ICL." Unpublished manuscript, Oregon Research Institute, 1963.

(explained below). The format of the ICL requires the examinee to check all phrases applying to one person before proceeding on to descriptions of others. Eight interpersonal traits are represented in the 128 items of the ICL: (*a*) Managerial-Autocratic, (*b*) Competitive-Narcissistic, (*c*) Aggressive-Sadistic, (*d*) Rebellious-Distrustful, (*e*) Self-effacing-Masochistic, (*f*) Docile-Dependent, (*g*) Cooperative-Overconventional, and (*h*) Responsible-Hypernormal. These eight interpersonal traits are considered to be present in each person to some extent; however, extreme amounts of any of the traits are considered to be undesirable. While each of the eight variables was subdivided into two components as indicated by the hyphenated phrases above, the eight trait system has been most accepted.

Potential words or phrases entering into the ICL had to meet the criteria of the trait theory outlined above. For each item, psychologists had to agree on the trait to which a phrase belonged, the "intensity" of the phrase, and its expected, hypothesized value in the patient culture for whom the ICL was originally devised. The intensity of an item referred to the amount of the trait; low intensity items referred to trait manifestations in necessary and moderate amounts, while high intensity items referred to trait manifestations in inappropriate and extreme amounts. Intensity referred, in addition, to endorsement frequency of the items: the final four rated intensity levels corresponded approximately to 90, 67, 33, and 10 per cent of examinees agreeing with the phrases as being self-descriptive. Item selection continued on the basis of the following sources of data in addition to the ratings mentioned above: frequencies with which the intensity levels were checked, average test scores, tallies of words not understood by patients, summaries of verbal complaints obtained from interviews, trait intercorrelations, and item intercorrelations.

In addition to the phrase and interpersonal trait measurement levels of the ICL, a higher-order unity is hypothesized to be represented by the variables. The eight personality traits are circularly arranged along the circumference of a circle which is marked with the two bipolar dimensions Dominance-submission (Dom) and Love-hate (Lov). A scoring scheme utilizing several variables allows one to plot a person's Dom and Lov scores within this circle.

The importance of the ICL is seen in its

measurement of replicable dimensions of interpersonal behavior (*18*). It can be administered quickly. The ability to assess the examinee's evaluation of persons other than himself on the same dimensions used for describing the self, thus allowing the ICL to be used sociometrically (*26*), is a great achievement in view of evidence indicating the lack of agreement between a variety of tests and scales presumably measuring the same constructs.[2] Although scoring systems have not yet been devised for projective tests which are succesfully related to ICL dimensions (*20*), this possibility still exists and warrants further investigation (see *223*, Wiggins' review of the *Interpersonal Diagnosis of Personality*). The ICL has been used in a variety of situations (e.g., *5, 17, 24, 28, 35*), and these situations provide some validation for the hypothesized dimensions of the ICL.

The Dom and Lov dimensions of the ICL have recently been confirmed by factor analysis by Foa (*18*) and Wiggins and the reviewer (in press). However, this dimensionality exists only when persons' differential tendency to agree with adjectives irrespective of content is taken into account. Thus, it is imperative for the test user to compute the average intensity of the items checked if he uses the ICL within an interpersonal framework.[3] Fortunately, the Dom and Lov summary scores take this checking tendency into account. These scores have a very low intercorrelation (e.g., *17*).

While this reviewer clearly recommends the use of the ICL in practical situations, he urges focus on further test development research. Average endorsement frequencies are unequal for the traits[4] (*1, 22*); average social desirability values for the traits are unequal,[5] being 5.3, 4.7, 4.4, 3.2, 4.1, 4.7, 5.9, and 5.7 on a nine-point scale for college students and neuropsychiatric patients combined (the ratings were similar for both groups); further, correlations between a social desirability criterion score and endorsement frequency varies with the trait (*20*). These problems are particularly important since the ICL construction aimed at

equating these characteristics. This reviewer recommends that an interested researcher take charge of compiling standardization data and making it publicly available.[6] Since so many of the ICL manuscripts are now difficult to obtain, such a procedure would be highly desirable. At the very least such data could be filed with the American Documentation Institute. This reviewer urges gathering of certain fundamental data on the ICL which is currently unavailable: the stability of summary scores and the stability of Dom-Lov difference scores and a variety of related difference scores so that these may be evaluated.

For excerpts from related book reviews, see 5:B261.

[128]

An Inventory of Factors STDCR. Grades 9–16 and adults; 1934–45; 5 scores: social introversion-extraversion, thinking introversion-extraversion, depression, cycloid disposition, rhathymia; IBM; 1 form ('40, 4 pages); revised manual ['45, 2 pages]: $3.50 per 25 tests; 20¢ per single copy; $1 per scoring key; separate answer sheets may be used; 4¢ per IBM answer sheet; $2.50 per set of either hand or machine scoring stencils; 25¢ per manual; postage extra; (30) minutes; J. P. Guilford; Sheridan Supply Co. *

REFERENCES

1–10. See 3:55.
11–27. See 4:59.
28–55. See 5:78.
56. DOTSON, ELSIE JENOISE. *A Study of the Agreement of Introversion-Extroversion Factors as Defined by Various Factor Analysts.* Doctor's thesis, University of Kentucky (Lexington, Ky.), 1951. (*DA* 18:1095)
57. BOOTH, MARY D. "A Study of the Relationship Between Certain Personality Factors and Success in Clinical Training of Occupational Therapy Students." *Am J Occup Ther* 11:93–6+ Mr–Ap '57. * (*PA* 32:4585)
58. TSUJIOKA, BIEN; SONOHARA, TARO; AND YATABE, TATSURO. "A Factorial Study of the Temperament of Japanese College Male Students by the Yatabe-Guilford Personality Inventory." *Psychologia* 1:110–9 D '57. * (*PA* 35:4899)
59. DUNN, SANDRA; BLISS, JOAN; AND SIIPOLA, ELSA. "Effects of Impulsivity, Introversion, and Individual Values Upon Association Under Free Conditions." *J Personality* 26:61–76 Mr '58. * (*PA* 33:5742)
60. JENKIN, NOËL. "Size Constancy as a Function of Personal Adjustment and Disposition." *J Abn & Social Psychol* 57:334–8 N '58. * (*PA* 33:10816)
61. THOMAS, EDWIN RUSSELL. *The Relationship Between the Strong Vocational Interest Blank and the Guilford-Martin Personality Inventory Among Salesmen.* Doctor's thesis, Syracuse University (Syracuse, N.Y.), 1958. (*DA* 19:2139)
62. CARON, ALBERT J., AND WALLACH, MICHAEL A. "Personality Determinants of Repressive and Obsessive Reactions to Failure-Stress." *J Abn & Social Psychol* 59:236–45 S '59. * (*PA* 34:3310)
63. GUILFORD, J. P. *Personality.* New York: McGraw-Hill Book Co., Inc., 1959. Pp. xiii, 562. *
64. KELLY, E. LOWELL, AND GOLDBERG, LEWIS R. "Correlates of Later Performance and Specialization in Psychology: A Follow-Up Study of the Trainees Assessed in the VA Selection Research Project." *Psychol Monogr* 73(12):1–32 '59. * (*PA* 34:7952)
65. KELTY, EDWARD JOHN. *Normal Electrocortical Activity in Relation to Personality Factors.* Doctor's thesis, Duke University (Durham, N.C.), 1959. (*DA* 20:756)
66. BEACH, LESLIE R. "Sociability and Academic Achievement in Various Types of Learning Situations." *J Ed Psychol* 51:208–12 Ag '60. * (*PA* 35:3977)
67. BORG, WALTER R. "Prediction of Small Group Role

2 For example: CARTWRIGHT, DESMOND S.; KIRTNER, WILLIAM L.; AND FISKE, DONALD W. "Method Factors in Changes Associated With Psychotherapy." *J Abn & Social Psychol* 66:164–75 F '63. *
3 LAFORGE, *op. cit.*
4 LAFORGE, R., AND SUCZEK, R. F. "Supplementary Information on the Research Use of the Interpersonal Checklist." Unpublished manuscript, University of Illinois Library, 1958.
5 Allen L. Edwards and William S. Kogan kindly made data available. The data were scaled as described by Edwards (*4*).
6 Rolfe LaForge of the Oregon Research Institute is carrying out basic ICL research; his ideas greatly aided the preparation of this review.

Behavior From Personality Variables." *J Abn & Social Psychol* 60:112–6 Ja '60. * (*PA* 34:7528)

68. CARRIGAN, PATRICIA M. "Extraversion-Introversion as a Dimension of Personality: A Reappraisal." *Psychol B* 57: 329–60 S '60. * (*PA* 35:4976)

69. FRANKS, C. M.; SOUIEFF, M. I.; AND MAXWELL, A. E. "A Factorial Study of Certain Scales From the MMPI and the STDCR." *Acta Psychologica* 17(5):407–16 '60. * (*PA* 35:3428)

70. BESSENT, EDGAR WAILAND. *The Predictability of Selected Elementary School Principals' Administrative Behavior.* Doctor's thesis, University of Texas (Austin, Tex.), 1961. (*DA* 22:3479)

71. KREITMAN, NORMAN. "Psychiatric Orientation: A Study of Attitudes Among Psychiatrists." *J Mental Sci* 108:317–28 My '62. * (*PA* 37:3400)

72. PANEK, RICHARD E., AND HANNUM, THOMAS E. "Relation Between Autokinesis and Introversion-Extraversion." Abstract. *J Consult Psychol* 26:477 O '62. *

For a review by Hubert E. Brogden, see 4:59; for a review by H. J. Eysenck, see 3:55; for a related review, see 3:45.

[129]

★**It Scale for Children.** Ages 5–6; 1956; for research use only; sex role preference; 1 form (37 cards); manual (20 pages, see 2 below); $15 per set of cards and manual, cash orders postpaid; (7–8) minutes; Daniel G. Brown; Psychological Test Specialists. *

REFERENCES

1. BROWN, DANIEL G. "Masculinity-Femininity Development in Children." Abstract. *Am Psychol* 11:415 Ag '56. *
2. BROWN, DANIEL G. "Sex-Role Preference in Young Children." *Psychol Monogr* 70(14):1–19 '56. * (*PA* 31:5815)
3. BROWN, DANIEL G. "The Development of Sex-Role Inversion and Homosexuality." *J Pediatrics* 50:613–9 My '57. * (*PA* 33:4196)
4. BROWN, DANIEL G. "Masculinity-Femininity Development in Children." *J Consult Psychol* 21:197–202 Je '57. *
5. BROWN, DANIEL G. "Sex-Role Development in a Changing Culture." *Psychol B* 55:232–42 Jl '58. * (*PA* 33:8147)
6. KOBASIGAWA, AKIRA. "Sex-Role Preference in Okinawan Pre-school Children." *Psychologia* 2:124–7 Je '59. * (*PA* 35:3236)
7. MUSSEN, PAUL, AND DISTLER, LUTHER. "Masculinity, Identification, and Father-Son Relationships." *J Abn & Social Psychol* 59:350–6 N '59. * (*PA* 34:5673)
8. RICHARDSON, D. H. "Sex-Role Preference in Children." *Ont Hosp Psychol B* 5:10–5 Ap '59. *
9. HARTUP, WILLARD W., AND ZOOK, ELSIE A. "Sex-Role Preferences in Three- and Four-Year-Old Children." *J Consult Psychol* 24:420–6 O '60. * (*PA* 35:4719)
10. BORSTELMANN, L. J. "Sex of Experimenter and Sex-Typed Behavior of Young Children." *Child Develop* 32:519–24 S '61. * (*PA* 36:4FF19B)
11. BROWN, DANIEL G. "Sex-Role Preference in Children: Methodological Problems." *Psychol Rep* 11:477–8 O '62. * (*PA* 37:7881)
12. HARTUP, WILLARD W. "Some Correlates of Parental Imitation in Young Children." *Child Develop* 33:85–96 Mr '62. * (*PA* 37:917)
13. CLARK, EDWARD T. "Sex Role Preference in Mentally Retarded Children." *Am J Mental Def* 67:606–10 Ja '63. * (*PA* 37:7009)
14. CLARK, EDWARD T. "Sex-Role Preference in Mentally Retarded Females." *Am J Mental Def* 68:433–9 N '63. * (*PA* 38:8956)
15. EPSTEIN, RALPH, AND LIVERANT, SHEPHARD. "Verbal Conditioning and Sex-Role Identification in Children." *Child Develop* 34:99–106 Mr '63. * (*PA* 38:5765)
16. HARTUP, WILLARD W.; MOORE, SHIRLEY G.; AND SAGER, GLEN. "Avoidance of Inappropriate Sex-Typing by Young Children." *J Consult Psychol* 27:467–73 D '63. *
17. MUSSEN, PAUL, AND RUTHERFORD, ELDRED. "Parent-Child Relations and Parental Personality in Relation to Young Children's Sex-Role Preferences." *Child Develop* 34:589–607 S '63. * (*PA* 38:800⁻)
18. NICKERSON, RAYMOND S., AND BROWN, CHARLES R. "A Stimulus Ordering Technique for Controlled Lag Recognition Memory Experiments." *Psychol Rep* 13:319–22 O '63. * (*PA* 38:8006)

PHILIP L. HARRIMAN, *Professor of Psychology, Bucknell University, Lewisburg, Pennsylvania.*

In their monumental inquiry into the masculinity-femininity continuum, Terman and Miles [1] pointed out the need for an adequate measure of sex-role preferences of young children. Except for their research reported in 1936 and their measure of the M-F interest pattern (see 61), objective tests, with scores expressed in statistics of variables, have been lacking. Expository and argumentative discussions, illuminated oftentimes by case histories, attested to the *Sprachgefühl* of their proponents but added little to empirical knowledge.

The ITSC ranks among the first empirical measures of sex-role preferences of middle class, urban American children who are about 5 or 6 years of age. In fact, the children used in standardizing this measure ranged from 5-4 to 6-4, with a median age of 5-10. Whereas in the Terman-Miles M-F measure there are more than 400 items in each form of the test and a wide variety of test patterns, the ITSC includes only 36 picture cards, 3 by 4 inches. Word associations (which for small children might be given orally), inkblots, or items dealing with opinions, ethical attitudes, and emotional situations (which would lend themselves to pictorial adaptation), do not appear in the ITSC. Perhaps one reason why the Terman-Miles precedent was not adapted for small children is that Brown wished to make a simple measure which would not strain the attention span of children, which would be given in just one testing session, and which would not necessitate the laborious statistical analyses used in the Terman-Miles to validate each single item.

ITSC may be illustrated by one example. "It" is a figure drawing of indeterminate sex. Then (Set 2, Group 1) the child chooses the toys that "It" would like to play with, each toy being a stereotype of a masculine or a feminine object. Choice of a toy locomotive, obviously, is taken to indicate a masculine sex-role preference, whereas a doll represents a feminine choice. The scale yields a quantified rating of sex-role preference, with a range from 0 (F) through 84 (M). Marked deviations, plus or minus, from 42 are interpreted as indicative of M or F, respectively.

This reviewer tried out the ITSC with 12 small children in the kindergarten class of a daily vacation church school. After a half day

1 TERMAN, LEWIS M., AND MILES, CATHERINE COX. *Sex and Personality: Studies in Masculinity and Femininity.* New York: McGraw-Hill Book Co., Inc., 1936. Pp. xii, 600. * (*PA* 10:5879)

of testing this reviewer concluded that (*a*) small children seem to enjoy the test, (*b*) administration is easy and pleasant, (*c*) the scale might profitably be extended, (*d*) a more thorough inquiry into sex-role preferences may be desirable using two or three sessions, and (*e*) the present scale points the way to many rewarding pieces of very minor research by students in an undergraduate class in child psychology.

The disquieting issue, however, is the vagueness of definition regarding the M-F continuum. Social class structures involve different types of social learning, even in early childhood. Sex roles, apart from the subculture in America, are subtle, elusive, and intangible to define. Whether it is possible to avoid turgid arguments about the M-F continuum is doubtful. Brown has resolved the difficulty by taking a benignly dogmatic position in this scale. Choices of some of the cards as preferred by "It" indicate M; of other cards, F. *Ipse dixit.* At least, the ITSC merits commendation as a pioneer quantification of a facet of personality. Whether it actually exists as anything more than a hypostatization of an omnibus abstruse concept is still an unanswered question.

Boyd R. McCandless, *Professor of Education and Psychology; Director, University School Clinic Complex; and Chairman, Department of Special Education; Indiana University, Bloomington, Indiana.*

The basic rationale of the It Scale is based on theories of sex-typing and sex-role identification. The roots of Brown's thinking are, of course, Freudian, but his approach to measurement has been substantially modified by such neo-analytic-learning theorists as Mowrer and such sociologists as Parsons. In other words, one can think of him as an "eclectic yet dynamic" theorist, with a certain flair for translating theory (and cloudy much of the theory in this area is!) into a surprisingly clear and sensible complex of operations which results in a masculinity-femininity score. Furthermore, this score has been shown to improve certain of our predictions, particularly about behavior and reputed environment of kindergarten and first grade males from a Western culture.

THE MANUAL. Brown (*2*) describes his test in a noncommercial, American Psychological Association monograph which serves as the manual, and gave It its maiden airing at pro-fessional psychological meetings. Instructions for administering and scoring are adequate and simple, although the rather small sample (for a normative study) is not fully described: we learn only that there are 78 male and 68 female kindergartners from Denver, aged 5-4 to 6-4 years, who came predominantly from the middle class. He reports more extensive data later (*4*). Reliability (test-retest, interval approximately one month) is reasonably satisfactory: $r = .71$ for boys, .84 for girls.

The "hero" or "protagonist" of the test is "It," a presumably sexless stick figure drawing. Hypothetically, the testee identifies with It, and it is It rather than the child who "takes the test." In other words, the test is a "structured projective."

The most feminine possible score It can earn is zero, the most masculine 84. This score is based on three subtests: (*a*) 8 points for choosing all masculine toys from 16 pictured toys, 8 of which are masculine and 8 feminine (zero is scored for 8 feminine toy choices); (*b*) 64 points for totally masculine choices for 8 pairs of pictures: which would It rather be (for example), a male or a female Indian?; and (*c*) 12 points (completely masculine) if It's preference is for the picture of a boyish boy over the pictures of a girlish boy, a boyish girl, and a girlish girl (again, zero is scored if the choice is for a girlish girl and intermediate weights are assigned to the other two possible choices).

Brown's manual gives some report on item validity, but neglects statistical workup on the power and attractiveness (aside from their differential sex pull) of items or subsections, and does not report the adequacy of the assignment of subtest and subsection weights. The latter is probably a serious flaw in view of the recent and repeated demonstrations of the effectiveness of toy choices in discriminating between the sexes. This flaw, of course, would not be difficult to correct.

THE TEST. The test is conveniently put together in a small plastic box; envelopes containing the items are clearly labeled; administration is simple; and the drawings are generally adequate, although not all are as clear as one would like. The reviewer and a former colleague (Iqbal Dar) found in an unpublished study that, with a little redrawing, the test appears to be as suitable for an Eastern (West Pakistan) culture as for a Western one.

RELATED LITERATURE. The space allotted for this review permits only a selection of findings. Findings suggest that progression with age is clear for boys, "full masculinity" apparently having been "gained" by early school ages. This conclusion is based on several United States populations and one Pakistani population ranging in age from two well on into elementary school. Findings are less clear for United States girls, the theory adduced being that in our culture the feminine role is both less desirable and less clearly modeled, and thus later and more reluctantly assumed. The logical flaw here is that there seems to be a tendency for United States girls, even at very early ages, to identify It as a boy and thus, presumably, to respond in terms of cultural expectations rather than projectively. This is a serious drawback in using the test with girls, although this difficulty was not found with a four- to seven-year-old sample of 50 Pakistani girls where, it should be added, the feminine role is exaggeratedly clear.

Other research suggests that children will change It's choices according to logical dynamic predictions when It is labeled as a boy or a girl or is actually assigned the subject's name, and that high masculine boys condition more effectively than low masculine boys for a male than a female examiner. A combination of paternal warmth and power in child rearing practices (judged from projectives and interviews) seems more characteristic of high than low masculine scoring boys, with tentative results following a similar sex-appropriate pattern for girls. Social class differences have not been adequately investigated, although Brown, in a subanalysis within his rather homogeneous original sample, found no such differences. Hartup and Zook (9), studying preschool youngsters, also failed to reveal social class differences. However, they worked with a rather special set of nursery school attending lower class youngsters, most of whom were from mother-only homes. Hartup, Moore, and Sager (16) did not find approach-avoidance tendencies toward sex-appropriate toys, which were otherwise age-progressive and sex-differential, to be related to It scores for either sex.

EVALUATIVE SUMMARY. This is an ingenious, simple test, related rather sensibly to theory. At present, the It Scale can be recommended as a potentially profitable research tool, particularly for boys; and, with further careful

research, it may develop into something useful for clinical practice.

[130]

Johnson Temperament Analysis. Grades 12–16 and adults; 1941–45; 9 scores: nervous-composed, depressive-gay-hearted, active-quiet, cordial-cold, sympathetic–hard-boiled, subjective-objective, aggressive-submissive, critical-appreciative, self-mastery–impulsive; IBM; Form A ('41, 7 pages); manual ('44, 16 pages); revised profile ('45, 1 page); separate answer sheets must be used; $3.50 per 35 tests; 5¢ per IBM answer sheet; $1.05 per set of hand and machine scoring stencils for unweighted scoring; $1.75 per set of hand scoring stencils for weighted scoring; 2¢ per profile; postage extra; 50¢ per specimen set, postpaid; (40–60) minutes; Roswell H. Johnson; California Test Bureau. *

REFERENCES

1–6. See 4:62.
7. HINKELMAN, EMMET ARTHUR. "Relation of Certain Personality Variables to High-School Achievement." *Sch R* 60: 532–4 D '52. *
8. TOMEDY, FRANCIS J. "The Relationship of Personality Characteristics to Measured Vocational Interests in High School Women Teachers of English, Social Science, Mathematics, and Physical Science." Abstract. *Am Psychol* 7:384 Jl '52. *
9. TOMEDY, FRANCIS JOSEPH. *The Relationship of Personality Characteristics to Measured Interests of Women Teachers of English, Social Science, Mathematics, and Physical Science in Certain Senior High Schools.* Doctor's thesis, New York University (New York, N.Y.), 1952. (*DA* 12:540)
10. WARD, WILLIAM DAVID. *An Investigation of the Predictability of Academic Success of the A.C.E. and Certain Factors Measured by the Johnson Temperament Analysis.* Doctor's thesis, Bradley University (Peoria, Ill.), 1953. (*DA* 13:518)
11. HOLMES, JACK A. "Factors Underlying Major Reading Disabilities at the College Level." *Genetic Psychol Monogr* 49:3–95 F '54. * (*PA* 28:8982)
12. TYLER, FRED T. *The Prediction of Student-Teaching Success From Personality Inventories.* University of California, Publications in Education, Vol. 11, No. 4. Berkeley, Calif.: University of California Press, 1954. Pp. 233–313. * (*PA* 29:4709)
13. HOLMES, JACK A. "Personality and Spelling Ability." Abstract. *Am Psychol* 10:353–4 Ag '55. *
14. THURSTON, DONALD REID. *An Investigation of the Possibilities of Parole Prediction Through the Use of Five Personality Inventories.* Doctor's thesis, Michigan State University (East Lansing, Mich.), 1955. (*DA* 15:1206)
15. HOLMES, JACK A. *Personality and Spelling Ability.* University of California Publications in Education, Vol. 12, No. 4. Berkeley, Calif.: University of California Press, 1959. Pp. vii, 213–91. *
16. ROZEHNAL, BOHUSLAV JAN. *A Study of the Relationship of Certain Temperament Scale Scores to Persistence in College.* Doctor's thesis, University of Minnesota (Minneapolis, Minn.), 1960. (*DA* 21:814)

For a review by Albert Ellis, see 4:62; for a review by H. Meltzer, see 3:57.

[131]

Jr.-Sr. High School Personality Questionnaire. Ages 12–18; 1953–64; 14 scores: reserved vs. outgoing (A), less intelligent vs. more intelligent (B), affected by feelings vs. emotionally stable (C), phlegmatic vs. excitable (D), obedient vs. assertive (E), sober vs. happy-go-lucky (F), disregards rules vs. conscientious (G), shy vs. venturesome (H), tough-minded vs. tender-minded (I), vigorous vs. doubting (J), self-assured vs. apprehensive (O), group dependent vs. self-sufficient (Q2), casual vs. controlled (Q3), relaxed vs. tense (Q4); 3 editions; separate answer sheets must be used; (40–50) minutes; Raymond B. Cattell and Halla Beloff.
a) [IPAT EDITIONS.] 1953–64; 2 editions; manual, second edition ('62, 26 pages) used with both editions; profile ('63, 1 page) for both editions; $4 per 25 tests;

$2.25 per pad of 50 answer sheets; $1.90 per scoring key; $1.90 per pad of 50 profiles; $2.20 per manual; $4 per specimen set; cash orders postpaid; Institute for Personality and Ability Testing. *

1) *IPAT High School Personality Questionnaire,* [*1958 Edition*]. Formerly called *The Junior Personality Quiz;* title on test is H.S.P.Q.; revised edition listed below; Forms A, B, ('58, 8 pages); norms supplement ('60, 4 pages); norms for combination of Forms A and B also presented.

2) *Jr.-Sr. High School Personality Questionnaire, 1963 Edition.* A 3-alternative response adaptation of the 1958 edition; title on test is Jr.-Sr. H.S.P.Q.; Forms A, B, second edition ('63, c1958–63, 8 pages); mimeographed norms supplement ('64, 4 pages); no data on reliability.

b) JR.-SR. HIGH SCHOOL PERSONALITY QUESTIONNAIRE, [BOBBS-MERRILL EDITION]. 1958–60; title on test is Jr.-Sr. H.S.P.Q.; Forms A, B, ('60, 8 pages, identical with 1958 IPAT edition except for format, title, and directions); manual ('60, c1958–60, 24 pages); norms supplement ('60, c1958–60, 4 pages, identical with IPAT edition except for format and title); profile ('60, 1 page); $4.95 per 35 tests; $1.50 per 35 answer sheets; 40¢ per scoring key; $1.50 per 35 profiles; 75¢ per manual and norms supplement; $1 per specimen set (includes norms supplement but not manual); Bobbs-Merrill Co., Inc. *

REFERENCES

1–4. See 5:72.
5. CATTELL, RAYMOND B.; COAN, RICHARD W.; AND BELOFF, HALLA. "A Re-examination of Personality Structure in Late Childhood, and Development of the High School Personality Questionnaire." *J Exp Ed* 27:73–88 D '58. * (*PA* 34:2819)
6. CATTELL, RAYMOND B. "Anxiety, Extraversion, and Other Second-Order Personality Factors in Children." *J Personality* 27:464–76 D '59. *
7. REID, JACKSON B.; KING, F. J.; AND WICKWIRE, PAT. "Cognitive and Other Personality Characteristics of Creative Children." *Psychol Rep* 5:729–37 D '59. * (*PA* 34:5632)
8. CLEMENTS, SAM D. *The Predictive Utility of Three Delinquency Proneness Measures.* Doctor's thesis, University of Houston (Houston, Tex.), 1960. (*DA* 20:3827)
9. GIBB, CECIL A. "A Note on the I.P.A.T. High School Personality Questionnaire." *Austral J Psychol* 13:77–86 Je '61. *
10. GUINOUARD, DONALD EDGAR. *Personality Traits and Mental Health Habits of Sociometrically Popular and Unpopular Sixth and Eighth Grade Students.* Doctor's thesis, Washington State University (Pullman, Wash.), 1961. (*DA* 22:1085)
11. KOCHNOWER, WILLIAM. "Personality Factors and Success in Mathematics." *High Points* 43:65–72 Ap '61. *
12. McGUIRE, CARSON. "The Prediction of Talented Behavior in the Junior High School." *Proc Inv Conf Testing Probl* 1960:46–67 '61. *
13. GOTTESMAN, IRVING I. "Differential Inheritance of the Psychoneuroses." *Eug Q* 9:223–7 D '62. * (*PA* 37:7729)
14. GUINOUARD, DONALD E., AND RYCHLAK, JOSEPH F. "Personality Correlates of Sociometric Popularity in Elementary School Children." *Personnel & Guid J* 40:438–42 Ja '62. * (*PA* 36:5KD38G)
15. PURCELL, KENNETH; TURNBULL, JOHN W.; AND BERNSTEIN, LEWIS. "Distinctions Between Subgroups of Asthmatic Children: Psychological Test and Behavior Rating Comparisons." *J Psychosom Res* 6:283–91 O–D '62. * (*PA* 37:8210)
16. BUTCHER, H. J.; AINSWORTH, M.; AND NESBITT, J. E. "Personality Factors and School Achievement: A Comparison of British and American Children." *Brit J Ed Psychol* 33:276–85 N '63. * (*PA* 38:7961)
17. CATTELL, RAYMOND B. "Theory of Fluid and Crystallized Intelligence: A Critical Experiment." *J Ed Psychol* 54:1–22 F '63. * (*PA* 37:7991)
18. GOTTESMAN, IRVING I. "Heritability of Personality: A Demonstration." *Psychol Monogr* 77(9):1–21 '63. * (*PA* 38:423)
19. PIERSON, GEORGE R., AND KELLY, ROBERT F. "Anxiety, Extraversion, and Personality Idiosyncrasy in Delinquency." *J Psychol* 56:441–5 O '63. * (*PA* 38:4582)
20. PIERSON, GEORGE R., AND KELLY, ROBERT F. "HSPQ Norms on a State-Wide Delinquent Population." *J Psychol* 56:185–92 Jl '63. * (*PA* 38:4584)
21. SCHAIE, K. WARNER. "Scaling the Scales: Use of Expert Judgment in Improving the Validity of Questionnaire Scales." *J Consult Psychol* 27:350–7 Ag '63. * (*PA* 38:2713)

C. J. ADCOCK, *Associate Professor of Psychology, Victoria University of Wellington, Wellington, New Zealand.* [Review of the 1958 IPAT and 1960 Bobbs-Merrill Editions.]

This is a junior version of the *Sixteen Personality Factor Questionnaire* but is based upon separate research with adolescents. The number of factors is reduced from 16 to 14 but of these, 2 (D and J) are newcomers. The four missing factors are L, M, N, and Q1. It is quite understandable that paranoid tendencies (L) and sophistication (N) should not have had time to develop as consistent behavioural patterns in children and that radicalism (Q1) would be difficult to measure anyway, but the absence of M (autism) is more surprising. Two new factors appear: D (phlegmatic, stodgy versus excitable, unrestrained) and J (vigorous, group acting versus doubting, individualistic).

Subject to these changes the factor schema has all the strengths and weaknesses of the 16 PF. It is based on careful factor studies, covers a wide range of traits, and is constructed according to the best statistical requirements. Correspondingly it shares some of the weaknesses of the 16 PF. The reviewer has already discussed the meaning of the factors involved in the 16 PF in *The Fifth Mental Measurements Yearbook* (see 5:112) and will not repeat that here. He would like to draw attention, however, to a distinction he would make between what he would call *ego-system components* and what he would describe as simple *traits*. The latter are broad behavioural tendencies resulting from the conditioning of basic drives but the former are functional units in a system which determines choice behaviour. H (shy versus adventurous) and O (confident adequacy versus guilt proneness) are examples of simple traits while G (ego strength) and Q3 (self-sentiment strength) would be examples of ego-system components. Both C and D would be included with the latter but herein is one of the problems with regard to the test. In the 16 PF, Factor C is regarded as a factor of emotional stability and has much in common with Q3 (including a high correlation) and in the HSPQ the actual designation "ego strength" is applied to both C and G while Q3 is again described in terms which have much in common. To complicate the position, D is also presented as an aspect of control (stodgy versus unrestrained, or phlegmatic versus excitable). It seems evident that the control aspects of behaviour have not been well differentiated.

It might be suggested that manifest emotional control involves two major aspects: the degree of braking function manifested and the degree of emotion to be controlled. Unstable behaviour can result from either high emotional charge which accentuates the motivation or poor capacity to inhibit. It is one thing to control emotion and quite another to lack emotion which needs control. Q3 seems to have a definite claim to be regarded as a form of positive control ("will power") while G is concerned with degree of acceptance of moral standards and so another dimension of positive control. C on the other hand, in its negative aspect, involves emotional instability which could just as well come from undue emotion as from poor control. The truth seems to be that the concept of emotionality has never been properly recognised in the preparation of the test items. An inspection of the items scored for Q3 (Form A) shows that they uniformly involve positive control aspects while the C items involve both emotionality, as in the question about being able to take a big meal before an examination, and control, as in making an effort to speak to a new teacher. The D factor also involves many items which indicate emotional sensitivity and it becomes difficult to decide whether C or D might best be regarded as a measure of emotionality. It would appear that D presents a definite problem. It was not included in the 16 PF, although some adult analyses indicated it, but it is included in the junior version. There seems room to doubt whether the actual difference between age groups is sufficient to justify this procedure.

At first sight Factor J seems to be very like Q2 since their low-score aspects are described as "goes readily with group" and "a 'joiner' and sound follower," respectively. The actual correlation between the factor scores, however, is only .12. The distinction probably lies in the fact that the person with high Q2 goes his own way because of strength of character (inner-directed?) while the person with high J avoids the group rather because of weakness. He is a Hamlet rather than a Caesar. But again the problem arises: why is this factor in children but not in adults?

It is gratifying to find that provision has been made for the scoring of two second-order

factors. These are the well established anxiety and introversion-extraversion. Two such factors have now turned up in a number of investigations but the naming of the first one is not universally accepted; some would prefer the term "emotionality." The second factor is well agreed upon but there is a complication with regard to the test. According to the matrix of intercorrelations presented, the items which define this extraversion factor do not constitute a consistent cluster. Of the six intercorrelations involved, only one exceeds .07 and one has a negative sign ($-.14$). An analysis of these data indicates a second factor rather different from the usual introversion-extraversion factor.

Considerable space has been devoted to the question of the nature of the factors because there seems to be no point in considering the validity of measurements unless one knows what they are and whether they are what one wants.

The validity of the factor scores from the full test (Forms A and B combined) ranges from .73 (J and Q3) to .88 (O) on the basis of multiple correlation and from .65 (Q3) to .83 (C and H) when derived from equivalence coefficients. The policy of incorporating "suppressor" items in the test to neutralize effects not required means that the usual consistency coefficients are no longer suitable measures of reliability but one is rather disturbed by the low equivalence correlations (A and B forms) as compared with the validity figures. One cannot help wondering whether the latter do not exaggerate the practical value. The fact that the intercorrelations of the factor scores are appreciably lower than with the 16 PF may be further indication of the lower reliability of the junior version.

The general impression with which one is left is that the HSPQ has rather lower reliability and validity than the 16 PF. This is no reflection on the test construction. The section in the manual dealing with "Construction of the Test" is admirable. The truth seems to be that questionnaire tests are not so satisfactory with children and need to be used with caution. It seems desirable that some further work should be done on the factorial basis of the test but for adequate measurement of child personality hope seems to lie rather in the work being done by Cattell's laboratory on objective forms of test. The ego system components, however, may not all prove amenable to objective measurement. In that case an improved form of the present test may have a very important role to play. To this reviewer it seems the most hopeful of this type yet offered.

PHILIP E. VERNON, *Professor of Educational Psychology, Institute of Education, University of London, London, England.* [Review of the 1958 IPAT and 1960 Bobbs-Merrill Editions.]

Cattell's *Sixteen Personality Factor Questionnaire* and its derivation are too well known to require description. The *Jr.-Sr. High School Questionnaire* aims to measure 12 of the same factors (plus 2 new factors) by items more suitable for adolescents. It also overlaps with the *IPAT Children's Personality Questionnaire* (CPQ) at the bottom end of its intended age range so as to allow repeated assessment from ages 7 or 8 to mature adulthood.

Each of the two forms contains 10 two-choice items referring to each factor, and takes about 40 minutes to answer. The answer sheet is ingeniously arranged so that a single hand scoring stencil yields all 14 scores in one or two minutes. Raw scores are converted to a 10-point scale of stens (mean 5.5, SD 1), or to deciles. The stens may be plotted on a profile sheet labeled with simplified descriptions of the factors. The manual provides ample material on the presumed significance of the factors to aid the school counselor in interpretation. Sex differences are allowed for in the norms; age differences, except perhaps on Factors B and Q3, are negligible.

Cattell's aim is to cover all the major dimensions or source traits of personality as fully as can be done in a short time. One wonders, however, whether counselors will not find it difficult to handle so many rather indistinct and unfamiliar traits simultaneously, and might not prefer a smaller number of more conventional variables. Some grouping of traits is possible; second order factor scores for extraversion-introversion and anxiety may be obtained. Also, a simple regression equation for predicting academic achievement is provided which is claimed to add considerably to predictions from ability measures only. (It might have been better to exclude Factor B, intelligence, from this equation, so as to avoid giving the highest weight to a 10-item intelligence test.) The user could, of course, work out further such equations against other important criteria.

Some will query how far any personality inventory can be said to measure source traits —for Cattell would not agree to accept the scores as merely delineating the subject's self-concepts. He admits the possibility of faking, but states that no systematic changes have been found when the test is answered anonymously, and he hopes to eliminate acquiescence response sets by arranging for roughly equal numbers of "Yes" and "No" responses for each factor. That the social desirability effect is not large is suggested by the rather low intercorrelations between factor scores, despite some intentional obliquity of the factors. The mean of the absolute values of r is .13, though this figure might well be considerably larger if the separate scores were more reliable.

The generally low reliabilities constitute a serious drawback. Even when, as the author suggests, both forms are given, the coefficients fall below conventional standards for individual diagnosis. For one form, the mean retest coefficient after two weeks is .59, the mean split-half coefficient is .32, and the correlation of Form A with Form B is .38. This is to be expected when each response to a single item normally brings about a change of one half a standard deviation in the sten score. Cattell suggests that only sten scores of 7 or higher and 4 or lower (out of 10) be regarded as "definitely departing from the average." Though he agrees, eventually, that adolescent responses are inherently somewhat less reliable than those of adults, especially when the test is not given under the most favourable possible conditions, he argues that reliability is less important than good factorial validity; indeed high reliability is apt to show that the items are too narrowly specific instead of giving a broad sampling of the content of a factor. He is able to show that the factorial validities are satisfactory, but these, of course, refer to a purely internal criterion. Users would be more interested to receive fuller evidence of correlations with external criteria. Cattell claims good agreement with ratings, with other questionnaires such as the 16 PF, and with various real life criteria. But the only evidence presented in the manual consists of profiles for several pairs of contrasted groups, which are not very impressive. For example, the largest differences between delinquents and boy scouts are 2.2 stens on Factor B (intelligence) and 1.0 on G (super ego strength), though a few other smaller differences also appear meaningful.

One fears that there might be considerable danger of over-interpretation if the HSPQ were applied by such persons as teachers and psychology students. Fortunately, sales are restricted; and trained counselors and educational and clinical psychologists should be well aware of the limitations of personality questionnaires in general and they should often find this workmanlike and ambitious instrument suggestive of personality trends in their clients.

[132]

*Kuder Preference Record—Personal. Grades 9–16 and adults; 1948–60; 6 scores: group activity, stable situations, working with ideas, avoiding conflict, directing others, verification; IBM; 1 form ('48); 2 editions: profile sheets: children ('49), adults ('52), (2 pages); profile leaflets for comparing vocational (see 1063) and personal scores: children ('53), adults ('54), (4 pages); manual, fifth edition ('60, 16 pages, identical with 1953 manual except for bibliography); separate answer pads or answer sheets must be used; $11 per 20 tests; 70¢ per 20 profile sheets; 90¢ per 20 profile leaflets; 75¢ per specimen set of either edition; postage extra; (40–45) minutes; G. Frederic Kuder; Science Research Associates, Inc. *

a) [HAND SCORING EDITION.] Form AH ('48, 16 pages); $2.60 per 20 answer pads.
b) [MACHINE SCORING EDITION.] IBM; Form AM ('48, 19 pages); $5 per 100 IBM answer sheets; $4 per set of scoring stencils.

REFERENCES

1–4. See 4:65.
5–9. See 5:80.
10. FLOWERS, J. F. Some Aspects of the Kuder Preference Record—Personal as an Instrument for Prediction and Guidance in Ontario Secondary Schools. Master's thesis, University of Toronto (Toronto, Ont., Canada), 1957.
11. SCHOLL, CHARLES ELMER, JR. The Development and Evaluation of Methods for Isolating Factors That Differentiate Between Successful and Unsuccessful Executive Trainees in a Large, Multibranch Bank. Doctor's thesis, University of Michigan (Ann Arbor, Mich.), 1957. (DA 18:2034)
12. SMITH, D. D. "Abilities and Interests: 2, Validation of Factors." Can J Psychol 12:253–8 D '58. * (PA 33:9347)
13. WARD, PAUL LEWIS. A Study of the Relationship of Evaluative Attitudes to Scholastic Ability and Academic Achievement. Doctor's thesis, Ohio State University (Columbus, Ohio), 1959. (DA 20:3639)
14. ASH, PHILIP. "Validity Information Exchange, No. 13-05: D.O.T. Code 1-86.12, Salesman, Typewriters." Personnel Psychol 13:454 w '60. *
15. COSTELLO, CHARLES G., AND ANDERSON, MARIAN E. "The Vocational and Personal Preferences of Psychiatric and General Nurses." Nursing Res 9:155–6 su '60. *
16. WAGNER, EDWIN E. "Differences Between Old and Young Executives on Objective Psychological Test Variables." J Gerontol 15:296–9 Jl '60. * (PA 35:1328)
17. FLOWERS, JOHN F. An Evaluation of the Kuder Preference Record—Personal for Use in Ontario. Atkinson Study of Utilization of Student Resources, Supplementary Report No. 4. Toronto, Canada: Department of Educational Research, Ontario College of Education, 1961. Pp. viii, 31. *
18. MCGUIRE, FREDERICK L. "The Kuder Preference Record—Personal as a Measure of Personal Adjustment." J Clin Psychol 17:41–2 Ja '61. * (PA 37:3262)
19. SUPER, DONALD E., AND CRITES, JOHN O. Appraising Vocational Fitness by Means of Psychological Tests, Revised Edition, pp. 555–60. New York: Harper & Brothers, 1962. Pp. xv. 688. * (PA 37:2038)
20. BLOCHER, DONALD H. "A Multiple Regression Approach to Predicting Success in a Counselor Education Program." Counselor Ed & Sup 3:19–22 f '63. *

DOROTHY M. CLENDENEN, Assistant Director, Test Division, The Psychological Corporation, New York, New York.

The Kuder Preference Record—Personal was published in 1948, and since then it has had wide use. The 1953 (fourth) edition of the manual stated that since publication scores had been obtained for over 14,000 adults and high school students. This manual also reported (a) validity based on relation between preference scores and job satisfaction, and between preference scores and behavior ratings of dominance, (b) mean profiles of more than three thousand men and women who like their work, and (c) profiles of satisfied and dissatisfied adults in eight occupations. Norms have been published based on samples of 3,650 boys, 3,924 girls, 1,000 men, and 532 women. New data have not been added in the 1960 (fifth) edition of the manual, which differs from the 1953 edition only in its list of references.

The test has 168 items of the forced choice, triad type in which the examinee selects the activity most liked and the one least liked. Personal or social activities are described in terms of behavior by such items [1] as "Be the editor of a magazine," "Change the subject if you find a person doesn't agree with you," and "Get what you want with no effort." With the publication of the 1953 manual, the earlier one-word scale titles were changed to be more descriptive: preference for being active in groups (A), preference for familiar and stable situations (B), preference for working with ideas (C), preference for avoiding conflict (D), and preference for directing or influencing others (E). There is also a sixth scale, verification, developed to check on the "value" of an individual's responses. A scale to identify the "faker" is reported as still in an experimental stage.

Since it was found that two scales (B and D) are positively correlated with age, correction tables have, since 1952, been included on the adult profile sheet to make scores comparable from one age to another.

Items for the Kuder Personal were selected after several tryouts and revisions designed to form relatively independent, homogeneous scales. Two scales appearing in the experimental form were dropped when they did not meet these requirements. Intercorrelations among

1 Examples are not from the same triad.

the remaining scales (shown for the 1,000 men in the norms group and for samples of college men and college women) support the claim of independence, the highest reported coefficient being .384 between Scales A and E. Reliability estimates, computed by the Kuder-Richardson formula 21, range from .76 to .89. These reliability coefficients are based on the adult norms groups, and on samples of the student groups; the latter are not, however, the same groups as those used for the intercorrelations. No test-retest coefficients are reported, although these would give useful indications of stability. Results from retesting after a considerable lapse of time would be especially useful in a test of this kind.

Means and standard deviations are not given either with the table of intercorrelations or with the reliability data. In another portion of the manual one finds this information for the adult norm groups for each scale. Since a later section on the use of Fisher's discriminant function seems to assume that users of the manual are relatively sophisticated in statistical methodology, it is difficult to understand why such basic supporting statistics as means and standard deviations have not been included throughout.

According to the manual, adult norms represent a 20 per cent response from "a mailing to telephone subscribers....chosen at random from a representative set of telephone directories." One can object that such a group does not constitute a representative sample of adults, recalling that a number of years ago a national magazine which subsequently ceased publication predicted the outcome of a national election quite erroneously, using a similar selection procedure. Occupational composition of the norms groups is shown; professional and managerial workers make up 44 per cent of the men and 51 per cent of the women, an excessive proportion to be representative of the population as a whole. Means and standard deviations on the scales are not given by occupation.

Validity for the Kuder Personal is presented for one criterion: expressed job satisfaction. Three tables showing means for "satisfied workers" in various groups (39 occupations for men and 12 for women) are presented. Although in these tables significant differences from the base group are indicated, the standard deviations for the subgroups are not given

so one does not know how homogeneous the individuals in the group were. Of the 51 occupational groups, 28 have 35 or fewer cases, probably not enough to ensure representativeness and stability.

It should be noted that a high score on a scale indicates greater *preference* than most people express for a specific kind of activity; degree of *participation* in that activity is not measured by the scale, nor is skill. The manual calls attention to the fact that "low scores on some scales predict job satisfaction in certain occupations." Table 1, in which jobs are classified according to the interest areas of the *Kuder Preference Record—Vocational,* indicates the Kuder Personal scales on which people in various occupational groups score high or low. The manual states, "For many occupations listed there are *empirical* data that reveal how the people in that occupation tend to score on the *Personal.* These data are indicated by heavy type. * *Personal* scales that appear in light type refer to probable scores. Although empirical data have not yet been obtained from these groups, evidence from related occupations suggests that they *would probably* score in the manner indicated in the table." This reviewer found it difficult, because of the typeface used in printing this table, to distinguish readily the boldface denoting empirical evidence. Actually, only about 40 out of 292 entries (counting combinations as 1 entry) are in boldface; in other words, over 85 per cent of the list is based on armchair speculation, not on data. The reviewer's primary objection here is not that suggestive estimates are offered, but that typefaces were chosen which would minimize rather than emphasize the difference between empirical and speculative entries.

A table showing correlation with other measures has been included in the manual, but since an early experimental form with seven scales was used for the statistics reported, application of the data to the present edition is moot. In the bibliography of the manual, one study is cited which indicates little relationship between Kuder Personal scales and scales of the *Study of Values* having comparable "titles." It would be useful to a counselor interpreting scores to have further evidence to show how similarly named scales on various instruments relate to one another.

In summary, it is the feeling of this reviewer that the Kuder Personal has been carefully developed and could fulfill a need for an instrument which is neither a vocational interest inventory nor a personality inventory, but which is related to both. However, in spite of 15 years of use the test still has limited validity data reported. And although a great deal of statistical work has obviously been done, some essential data have been omitted from the manual. The amount of emphasis on various topics and the assumptions regarding the kinds of knowledge had by the user seem to indicate confusion or ambivalence on the part of the manual writer concerning his audience, so that the user is not given effective aid in understanding the test.

WILBUR L. LAYTON, *Professor of Psychology and Head of the Department, Iowa State University, Ames, Iowa.*

The *Kuder Preference Record—Personal* (KPR-P) was developed to define (measure) interest and personality factors not already covered by the *Kuder Preference Record— Vocational* (KPR-V). Items presented in forced-choice preference triads to adults and high school pupils were selected to yield five scales having high internal consistency and low intercorrelations with each other and with the KPR-V scales.

The five scales were designed to yield information helpful to a person in deciding the interpersonal relationships situation in which he prefers to work. The five scales are titled: (*a*) preference for being active in groups; (*b*) preference for familiar and stable situations; (*c*) preference for working with ideas; (*d*) preference for avoiding conflict; (*e*) preference for directing or influencing others. In addition to these five preference scales there is a verification scale.

The verification (V) score reflects the degree to which the examinee expresses conforming or "popular" responses. Atypical V-scores cast doubt on the meaning of preference scores and may indicate carelessness or ignorance of the examinee in completing the Record. They may also indicate truly unusual preferences which cannot be adequately evaluated by the KPR-P. The acceptable range of scores on the scale was established empirically.

The five preference scales of KPR-P represent an attempt to define constructs useful in counseling. One might have argued with Kuder about the need in counseling for the five constructs he chose to define. However, if we accept his choices, we can only examine critically the measurement operations used by Kuder to determine if they satisfactorily define the chosen constructs.

There is meager evidence supporting the statistical definition of constructs *a* through *e*. Reliability was estimated by Kuder-Richardson formula 21. The resulting internal consistency coefficients range from .76 to .89 over the five scales for six groups: adult men, and women; college men, and women; high school boys, and girls. Considering the item selection procedure employed, there is still considerably more error variance in the scales than one might expect. Furthermore, no evidence of stability of scores or profiles is available. The scale intercorrelations are quite low and are about equally distributed among positive and negative values as one expects from a forced-choice incomplete ipsative procedure. Thus, the constructs defined by the scales have some internal consistency and are relatively well differentiated from each other.

Unfortunately, Kuder has attempted to combine an incomplete ipsative procedure with the normative approach to measurement. Katz[1] and Bauernfeind[2] have criticized the *Kuder Preference Record—Vocational* on this basis. In a complete forced-choice format the scores are experimentally dependent. The scales have the same number of items and every scale is compared equally with every other scale. For every examinee the total number of responses is identical and these responses are divided among the several scales as a closed system. If raw scores on some scales are high, others must be low and one can infer with confidence the examinee's relative preferences. But in the Kuder approach raw score comparisons are not meaningful because the scales vary in total number of items and the frequency with which the items (scales) are combined in triads. Because of this incomplete ipsativity one cannot make meaningful statements about the relative preferences of an examinee such as "your greatest preference is for being active in groups and your lowest preference is for working with ideas." Since many users of KPR-P will make or want to make statements exactly like

1 KATZ, MARTIN. "Interpreting Kuder Preference Record Scores: Ipsative or Normative." *Voc Guid Q* 10:96–100 w '62. * (*PA* 37:1972)
2 BAUERNFEIND, ROBERT H. *Building a School Testing Program*, pp. 213–31. Boston: Houghton-Mifflin Co., 1963. Pp. xvii, 343. *

this anyway, this is a severe defect in the instrument.

Assuming ipsative scores result from KPR-P, one could and should investigate the meaning of *profiles* rather than the meaning of scores on a particular scale. This is equivalent to investigating personality types as defined by the KPR-P. One could determine the frequency of personality types in various groups and investigate important behavior differences among the types. Kuder, on the other hand, assumes normative scores and has established norms and made limited validity studies of scales considered independently.

It is meaningless to use norms with the KPR-P. If it were meaningful, Kuder must be criticized for the norms produced. The adult norms presented in the manual resulted from about a 20 per cent response to mailing to telephone subscribers whose names were drawn from a "representative set of telephone directories for cities, towns, and villages spread out over the United States." The norms for high school pupils are based on 3,650 boys and 3,924 girls from high schools distributed over the country. No data are given in the manual to show the extent to which the norms represent the preferences of adults and high school pupils. However, the occupational distribution of persons in the adult norm groups clearly indicates an over-representation of professional, managerial, sales, and clerical occupations when compared to U.S. census data. Sixty seven per cent of the male norm group and 92 per cent of the female norm group were classified in these upper-level occupational groups!

Even so, in an attempt to give meaning to the preference scores Kuder used the norm groups as reference groups against which to compare scores of men and women in various professional and managerial groups. Consequently, he should be gratified he found some significant differentiation.

Tables 3 and 4 in the manual present means of various occupational groups of men and women compared with the means of the adult norm groups. These data are interesting but for the user of the KPR-P represent the data from the standpoint of the wrong regression line. The user needs to predict occupational placement from test profiles not the reverse.

The manual also reports a study of the relationship of KPR-P scores to job satisfaction. The basic data were taken from the responses of the adult norm groups to the KPR-P and to a question which asked the subject to indicate whether, if given free choice, he would prefer: (*a*) the job he has now; (*b*) the same kind of work but some changes in working conditions or fellow employees; or (*c*) a different kind of work entirely. Those who checked (*c*) were considered dissatisfied and the remainder satisfied workers. Response to a single question of this sort is obviously an unreliable measure of job satisfaction. Mean scores of "satisfied" and "dissatisfied" workers on the five KPR-P scales were compared, and these data are interesting to someone concerned with studying job satisfaction. However, the data yield little information about the predictive validity of the KPR-P scales.

Thus, the KPR-P manual presents only meager evidence supporting the definition of five preference constructs. But the great deficiency of the Kuder procedure is the ill-considered attempt to combine ipsative and normative approaches to psychological measurement. Consequently, the KPR-P in its present form cannot be recommended for use even on an experimental basis.

For a review by Dwight L. Arnold, see 5:80; see also 4:65 (1 excerpt).

[133]

★**The Leadership Ability Evaluation.** Grades 9–16 and adults; 1961; social climate created in influencing others; 5 scores: laissez faire, democratic-cooperative, autocratic-submissive, autocratic-aggressive, decision pattern; 1 form (8 pages); manual (18 pages); $10 per set of 25 tests and manual; $3 per manual; postpaid; specimen set not available; [30] minutes; Russell N. Cassel and Edward J. Stancik (test); Western Psychological Services. *

REFERENCES

1. CASSEL, RUSSELL N., AND HADDOX, GENEVIEVE. "Comparative Study of Leadership Test Scores for Gifted and Typical High School Students." *Psychol Rep* 5:713–7 D '59. * (*PA* 34:5701)
2. CASSEL, RUSSELL N. "A Construct Validity Study on a Leadership and a Social Insight Tests for 200 College Freshmen Students." *J Genetic Psychol* 99:165–70 S '61. * (*PA* 36:3GF65C)
3. CASSEL, RUSSELL N., AND SANDERS, RICHARD A. "A Comparative Analysis of Scores From Two Leadership Tests for Apache Indian and Anglo American Youth." *J Ed Res* 55:19–23 S '61. * (*PA* 36:4GB19C)
4. CASSEL, RUSSELL, AND CHILDERS, RICHARD. "A Study of Certain Attributes of 45 High-School Varsity Football Team Members by Use of Psychological Test Scores." *J Ed Res* 57:64–7 O '63. *

JOHN D. BLACK, *Director, Counseling and Testing Center, and Consulting Associate Professor of Psychology, Stanford University, Stanford; and President, Consulting Psychologists Press, Inc.; Palo Alto, California.*

This test, printed in an attractive eight-page

expendable booklet containing a profile, confronts the subject with four alternative choices for handling each of fifty "leadership situations." Each alternative is scored on one of the four subscales, three of which are then differentially weighted and combined into a total score called the "Decision Pattern."

Study of item content immediately raises the question of whether the authors' definition of leadership situations may be too broad. Typical questions ask what to do if "your mother shows favoritism to your brother or sister," if your wife opens a charge account against your wishes, if you're a pilot whose plane develops engine trouble, if you see a classmate cheating on an examination. Indeed, the items are very similar—in several cases almost identical—to those in the senior author's *Test of Social Insight*, but the scales have different names.

No information on methods of item selection is given nor is it clear how the subscales were built. The manual asserts that "six research psychologists evaluated the social climate structures used in the four part scores of the LAE; *without exception* there was agreement that the leadership patterns were incorporated in the structure of the LAE" (italics added). Despite such unanimity, the reviewer was puzzled by some of the scaling. For example, on an item about what a teacher should do with a girl who "comes to school in an extremely low-cut dress," the alternative "Send her home" is scored Autocratic-Submissive (AS); "Do nothing" is scored Autocratic-Aggressive (AA); and "Discuss this with the dean of girls" is scored Laissez Faire (LF). The pilot with engine trouble receives a point for LF if he decides to make an emergency landing and a point for AA if he decides to abandon ship.

Corrected split-half reliabilities for the five scores are rather variable, ranging from .91 to .29 in different groups. The total score is most reliable with a median r of .82, the AS least reliable with a median of .46. No test-retest reliability is reported, nor are any validity data given for the subscales. Intercorrelations range from .05 to −.72 and are generally low enough to justify use of all scales.

Whatever their limitations, the subscales do represent meaningful ways of conceptualizing leadership behavior and it seems unfortunate that the authors have not made more use of them. Instead, most attention is given to the total score which is computed from the sub-

scales. The authors assert: *"The characteristic decision making pattern* is provided by the *total score* of an individual" (italics theirs). How a single score compounded of three entirely different approaches to leadership situations can constitute a *pattern* is difficult to comprehend.

The total score is obtained by adding 7 times LF and 4 times AS to DC (Democratic-Cooperative), then dividing the sum by 10. Low scores indicate greater leadership ability. AA is excluded from the formula, and the confounding effect of this omission is that one will decrease (i.e., improve) his total score the more Autocratic-Aggressive alternatives he selects. The formula was developed by maximizing discrimination between a group of 100 "leaders" and 200 "typical subjects" (neither group described further). From a study of the table containing the regression weights, it is not entirely clear to the reviewer why AA was omitted and it appears that DC is utilized as a suppressor variable, a confusing situation at best.

One reported cross validation study shows that by using a cutoff score of 10, the LAE total score correctly identifies 60 per cent of a group of 500 "outstanding leaders" of both sexes at the expense of classifying 23 per cent of 500 ninth graders as effective leaders. No doubt the separation would be even less impressive if ordinary adults were substituted for the students. Nevertheless, the manual flatly states that "Total scores of 10 and lower are indicative of effective leaders, while total scores above 10 are indicative of ineffective leaders."

The test authors seem to feel that construct validity of a test is established by reporting a number of miscellaneous correlations with other tests. In this case the data reveal that leadership ability as measured by the LAE is negatively correlated with IQ, reading ability, and a number of other intellectual aptitudes.

Norms provided in the profile for easy conversion of raw to T-scores are based on 2,000 "typical individuals" and 400 "outstanding leaders" (neither identified further). For LF, DC, and total score, the means are reported for a peculiar assortment of groups, many of which have little relevance for a test purporting to measure leadership ability (e.g., "below average typical youth," "delinquent youth," "guidance counselors," "USAF chaplains").

There is a need for a good test of leadership ability; unfortunately, tests of the calibre of this one can only serve to disillusion prospective users. The LAE suffers these principal defects: The item content does not deal primarily with relevant leadership situations. Many of the alternatives representing the four modes of leadership need refinement. Validity has been inadequately studied among groups whose primary function is leadership. The cumbersome formula for total score is inadequately based on a single study and its use as a rigid cutoff score for leadership ability, as recommended by the authors, is entirely unjustified and professionally reprehensible. Finally, the total score, derived as it is, is absolutely devoid of any psychological meaning. It seems likely that the search for a single score to measure leadership ability is futile, and that attention might better be focused on studying patterns of leadership skills required in different situations. In its present form the LAE will not further such useful research.

CECIL A. GIBB, *Professor of Psychology, The Australian National University, Canberra City, Australia.*

General leadership literature suggests that there are many who would be attracted by a test offering assessment of four patterns of leadership described as Laissez Faire, Democratic-Cooperative, Autocratic-Submissive, and Autocratic-Aggressive, though why this should be so is not at all certain.

Even such persons will, however, have misgivings about Cassel's LAE because—if for no other reason—the test form itself rather signals the interpretation to the subject unless he be extraordinarily naive. Four-choice answers are so arranged that the choice letters A, B, C, D are "randomised" to give a particular pattern response always in the same position, and the positions carry the headings AA, AS, DC, and LF in the same order on all six pages of the test. Cassel claims that "face validity" of the test is evident to those taking the LAE and to specialists in test construction. Perhaps this should disqualify the present reviewer.

The 50 items of the LAE are said to "encompass the life activities of an individual in western culture," under the headings of home and family life, work and vocational pursuits, play and avocational pursuits, school and educational pursuits, and community life. There can be little argument but that some of the

items are quite inappropriate to any given individual. Cassel apparently believes in a "lowest common denominator" approach to patterns of leader behavior and evidence of situational determinants of such behavior has not impressed him at all.

Instructions for administration and scoring are adequate and reliability and validity statistics given in the manual seem numerous but often defy interpretation, e.g., on the Democratic-Cooperative dimension Cassel says, "Scores above 35 suggest excessive cooperation by the leader; scores below 20 suggest too little cooperation"; but about one third of the group he designates "outstanding leaders" present scores outside these limits. It is also difficult to understand what a total score on this test can mean, yet it is claimed to be "the most important single indicator of acceptable or unacceptable leadership pattern."

[134]

★The Leadership Q-Sort Test (A Test of Leadership Values). Adults; 1958; 7 scores: personal integrity, consideration of others, mental health, technical information, decision making, teaching and communication, total; 1 form (4 pages); manual (56 pages); no data on reliability of subscores; $9 per examiner's kit of 25 tests, 25 item sheets (must be cut up into sorting slips), set of keys, sorting board, and manual; $3 per 25 tests; $1 per set of keys; $2 per 25 item sheets; $1 per sorting board; $3 per manual; cash orders postpaid; (40–50) minutes; Russell N. Cassel; Psychometric Affiliates. *

REFERENCES

1. CARP, ABRAHAM, AND CASSEL, RUSSELL. "Development and Preliminary Analysis of a New Q Sort Type of Leadership Test." Abstract. *Am Psychologist* 12:464 Jl '57. *
2. CASSEL, RUSSELL N., AND CARP, ABRAHAM. "Combining Criterion Measures From R and Q Methodologies for Purpose of Validating Tests Related to Leadership." Abstract. *Am Psychologist* 12:408–9 Jl '57. *
3. CASSEL, RUSSELL N., AND HARRIMAN, B. LYNN. "Comparing Pre- and Post-Training Leadership Test Scores for Colonels and Federal Prisoners and With Other Test Scores." Abstract. *Am Psychologist* 13:370 Jl '58. *
4. CASSEL, RUSSELL N., AND HADDOX, GENEVIEVE. "Comparative Study of Leadership Test Scores for Gifted and Typical High School Students." *Psychol Rep* 5:713–7 D '59. * (PA 34:5701)
5. CASSEL, RUSSELL N., AND HADDOX, GENEVIEVE. "Leadership Testing." *Voc Guid Q* 7:189–92 sp '59. *
6. CASSEL, RUSSELL N., AND SANDERS, RICHARD A. "A Comparative Analysis of Scores From Two Leadership Tests for Apache Indian and Anglo American Youth." *J Ed Res* 55:19–23 S '61. * (PA 36:4GB19C)

JOEL T. CAMPBELL, *Research Psychologist, Educational Testing Service, Princeton, New Jersey.*

This test is, to quote the author, "concerned with assessing an individual's values with respect to the leadership role. The 60 items which are contained in the test have all been identified by well qualified leaders as being important to the leadership function. Multiple groups of outstanding leaders (and others) have provided ratings on these items which are used as the test norms. By comparing an individual's ratings on the test items with the appropriate test norms a meaningful evaluation is obtained of his leadership values and notions."

The person taking the test is required to sort the 60 items into 11 steps on a scale. The high end of the scale has the description, "Statements most important to good or effective leadership" and the low end, "Statements least important to good or effective leadership." The number of items permitted in each step is controlled so that a normal distribution is forced.

The scoring appears to the reviewer to be a little cumbersome. A two-page form is provided. First, the item numbers are recorded in blocks along the rating scale, so that a check can be made that the proper number of items has been assigned to each step. Then, for each item, the score or step value given by the rater is recorded. (Up to this point, the operations can be performed by the person taking the test.) At this point, a cutout scoring key is applied and, for each item, the *difference* between the score recorded and the keyed value is recorded. These differences are squared, summed, divided by 620, and the quotient subtracted from 1 to obtain a correlation between the Q-sort ratings assigned by the subject and those contained in the norms. By means of a separate table, this is converted to a Fisher's *z* for comparison with various norm groups. Quite likely this is easier to do after one or two trials than it is to describe, but nonetheless it appears quite a cumbersome procedure.

In addition to an overall or total "Leadership Values" score, keys are provided for six subscores. These are labeled Personal Integrity, Consideration, Mental Health, Technical Information, Decision Making, and Teaching and Communication. The 60 items were distributed into these six subtests by the consensual judgment of seven psychologists. The reviewer's experience in comparing factor analysis results with judgment results leads him to question the adequacy of this method of developing subtests.

Normative data are reported for total and part scores for 540 typical youth (mixed sex), 150 USAF colonels, 31 USAF chaplains, and 200 federal reformatory prisoners. Also given are the mean values for each item for these same groups and for 31 research psychologists.

These norms probably will not be relevant for an industrial concern, for example, and the reviewer doubts that they are adequate for use in most educational or counseling situations. A potential user would need to provide his own local norms.

Split-half reliabilities are reported as .83 and .84 for the total score. Measurement of reliability was also approached by correlating three pairs of items which were highly similar in content for six groups of individuals. The resulting 18 correlation coefficients range from .008 to .673, with 12 coefficients significant at the .01 level. No other information is given on the reliability of the test, either for total scores or the part scores. Since two of the subtests have only five items each, an estimate of reliability would seem to be particularly important here. Test-retest coefficients should be obtained and reported.

The author has provided several kinds of validity estimates. One study compared Q-sort total scores with other measures for a sample of 100 preflight cadets. The other measures included leadership instructor ratings, mean academic grades, peer status ratings, and peer affiliate ratings. Peer status ratings were defined as "Cadet peer status ratings as to leadership competency given by all Cadets in group" and peer affiliate ratings were defined as "Cadet peer affiliate ratings, or evaluations given by each Cadet to other members of his group as to their leadership competency." Total Q-sort scores correlated .23 with peer status ratings and .39 with leadership instructor ratings. The correlation with peer affiliate rating was zero and with academic grades .04. No explanation is given of the lack of correlation with peer affiliate rating, nor of the −.22 correlation reported between peer status rating and peer affiliate rating.

Another table gives correlations based on a sample of 200, apparently also preflight cadets, for these variables plus several other test scores. Here the correlation of total Q-sort scores with peer status rating was .15 and with peer affiliate rating, −.12. The author summarizes results from this table as, "there is significant relationship with peer and instructor ratings relative to leadership competency, social insight, personality tension and needs, class standing, other leadership test scores, and the like. There is little or no relationship with academic grades, chronological age, ego strength, and the like." Since several of the significant relationships are negative, the reviewer feels that some further explanation is in order.

A second estimate of validity was comparison of total and part scores before and after a leadership training course for 200 preflight cadets. The total score changed in the direction of greater agreement with the norm group of USAF full colonels, "who are presumed to have greater leadership competency than the Cadets." The part scores changed in the direction of assigning greater importance to Personal Integrity, Technical Information, and Teaching and Communication, and less importance to Consideration of Others, Mental Health, and Decision Making.

A third approach to validity estimation was the comparison of mean total scores for various groups. Full colonels had the highest mean score, followed by research psychologists, preflight cadets after leadership training, USAF chaplains, and so on down to basic airmen. It is interesting that federal prisoners have approximately the same mean score as USAF NCO's!

An additional study reported is an inverse factor analysis of four individuals from each of five groups—chaplains, preflight cadets, colonels, research psychologists, and federal prisoners. Five factors were identified: chaplain leadership pattern, military leadership pattern, in-prison leadership pattern, psychologists' leadership pattern, and general leadership pattern. The reviewer would question the naming of at least the first factor, since two of the four psychologists had higher loadings than any of the chaplains, and two of the chaplains have negative loadings!

Before this test is used in business or education, its validity in such situations should be established. It is at least conceivable that the aspects of leadership considered most important in an institutional setting, such as the Air Force or a federal reformatory, will not be so considered in a less rigidly structured environment, such as a small business, a large business, a college, or a political organization.

The language level of the test directions is quite difficult, and the manual is particularly difficult to read. There are a number of minor irritations, such as a grammatical error in item 1 of the test, and the use in the manual of E rather than the conventional capital sigma to indicate summation.

The basic idea of this test seems well worthwhile—namely, that what a person considers to be important to leadership will be reflected in his competency as a leader. The author deserves credit for doing more research on this test than is done on many tests before they are marketed. The research does have the limitation of having been done almost exclusively in institutional settings, rather than with the kind of population with which most users will need to deal.

CECIL A. GIBB, *Professor of Psychology, The Australian National University, Canberra City, Australia.*

On the face of it the *Leadership Q-Sort Test* (LQT) looks promising. The materials are neatly and satisfactorily designed and the compact manual has such section headings as Theory Underlying the LQT, Ipsative Scores, Q-Methodology, Test Development and Validation, Instructions for Administering, Instructions for Scoring, Interpretation of Scores. It also contains many norm tables. Unfortunately, however, this impeccable framework is clothed in a good deal of unsatisfactory discussion and inadequate quantitative detail.

Probably the most disconcerting feature of the LQT manual is Cassel's insistence upon using popular terms, but using them in his own way. For example, in the introduction he uses the heading Theory Underlying the LQT but offers no theory. He claims to "define" leadership but cannot decide whether he wishes to do this as role or behavior. He offers "dimensions" of leadership which are quite unlike those of any empirical research and yet when he offers categories of related characteristics of an effective leader, he approaches much more nearly known dimensions of leader behavior. Similar difficulties exist with description of ipsative scores, Q-methodology, and the forced-choice technique of which Cassel says: "Since the subject is unable to speculate what ratings will prove of vantage for the various items, the test is said to employ a 'forced choice' technique."

Even the critical characteristics technique employed probably suffers a little from the choice of preflight cadets as respondents rather than men with greater and broader experience of leadership in a variety of situations. However, this technique does give results which accord well with other research. Four hundred cadets produced 3,667 statements which, after being edited for redundancy, were subjectively grouped in seven categories labeled: Personal Integrity, Consideration for Others, Mental Health, Technical Information, Decision Making, Teaching and Communication, and Positive and Favorable Attitude. From this wealth of statements 60 items were then selected (again subjectively) in such a way as to keep the number of items in the 60 roughly proportional to the number within the category; thus Personal Integrity has 17 items while Decision Making has 5. Seven research psychologists then assigned one category label to each of the 60 chosen items. The positive attitude category proved to be infrequently used and most of the items belonging to it were assigned to the mental health category; accordingly all items of these two categories were combined under the heading of mental health.

Validity is approached in a number of ways. Internal validity is alleged on the basis of three pairs of items having somewhat similar meanings. Correlations between pair members for a number of groups vary between .008 and .673. Face validity is claimed because unidentified items given to graduate students in psychology classes were judged to be related to management, supervision, or leadership functions. Status validity is assessed by correlating LQT scores (based upon USAF colonels as models) with peer status ratings, leadership competency ratings, academic grades, and peer affiliate ratings of preflight cadets. LQT scores are found to be significantly correlated with peer status ratings (.23) and leadership competency ratings (.39) but to have zero correlations with the other two criteria. It is shown, however, that as a result of a 44 hour leadership training course, the scores of cadets do show a significant shift in the direction of the colonel model. Many other "validation" data are offered but these seem to do nothing to increase confidence in, or understanding of, the test.

To achieve a general purpose scoring key for the LQT, the mean ranking of items for four groups is used. These were 540 typical youths of mixed sex, 150 USAF colonels, 31 USAF chaplains, and some research psychologists. For a reason, not quite clear, data from 200 federal reformatory prisoners were ex-

cluded. Separate norms are also given for each of these groups, except the psychologists.

Instructions for administration and scoring are adequate. Seven scores are available, a total score and one for each part corresponding to each of the original six categories. The total score takes the form of a rank correlation coefficient calculated between the ranking made and that of the scoring key. This Cassel calls a Pearson r which is then converted to a Fisher z which, in turn, may be referred to norm tables for interpretation. Part scores are obtained directly. Cutout keys identify the items for each scale and ratings assigned are simply summed and the norm tables entered directly with these sums to obtain T scores.

Just what interpretation of such scores may be obtained is a matter of considerable conjecture. Cassel says, "where the total score on the LQT in terms of a Fisher z' score is .400 or above, the individual has values in the area of leadership which are in significant agreement with similar values by demonstrated effective leaders." But, if he has been understood correctly, this is not so, for the scoring key is derived from a very mixed group and certainly not from "demonstrated effective leaders," unless all psychologists, all chaplains, and all youths fall into this category. Interpretation of the part scores would perhaps be more meaningful if one were not continually aware of the unsatisfactory item selection and validation procedures which give rise to them.

For the research worker in this area of measuring leadership potential there will be food for thought in the *Leadership Q-Sort Test,* but one could not confidently recommend it for routine application in any setting.

WILLIAM STEPHENSON, *Professor of Psychology, University of Missouri, Columbia, Missouri.*

This is an ingenious use of Q-technique, but not of Q-methodology. Statements validated for leadership attributes in R-methodology are provided as a Q-sample with which subjects perform a Q-sort to express how important each is for effective leadership of a person. The Q-sort array is then scored in relation to R-methodological norms. No validation of the Q-scores so provided is reported. One need have no objection to the technique as such, so used, provided it can indicate valid measurements.

But the method is not Q-methodological. This is at once clear when one observes that the measurements provided by the technique are dimensions of so called leadership, its values, insight, ego strength, and anxiety. Q-method does not provide measures of such attributes, but, instead, gives evidence for different *types* of persons. Thus, one might have as an outcome of Q a *cautious* type of leader, a *romantic* type, an *impulsive* type, or whatever. Such are the end products of Q-methodology: not even a semblance of the kind issues from this test.

It should not be necessary, as the manual does, to define Q as concerned with "many tests....administered to few persons," whereas R is "few tests....administered to many persons." The statements of a Q-sample are not tests in the sense of the word in R-method. They are, instead, merely synthetic statements, involving "excess meanings," which can be ego-involving (self-referent) for the person. Nor, in any properly constructed Q-sample, can any person "often desire to give all of [the statements] a top rating": on the contrary, the Q-sample is hinged about a *neutral* point (at the mean score) where statements are not ego-involving (i.e., they do not matter to the person providing the Q-sort) and then disperse in positive and negative directions. That is, there are always, in a Q-sample, some statements which the person cannot agree with or which he *dis*likes and some which he agrees with or likes. It is never possible for him to like them all; it is always the case, in a well constructed Q-sample, that the individual will find that most of the statements don't matter to him.

There ought, therefore, to be a rider in any republication of the leadership test to the effect that it involves Q-technique, not Q-methodology in the proper sense of the word. Having said this, the ingenuity of the Cassel procedure deserves comment. It is difficult to provide norms for a genuine use of Q-methodology since type descriptions are at issue. Each person's Q-sort would have to be correlated with the Q-arrays defining the types, and this requires sophistication for the necessary calculations. Cassel's method, whilst it doesn't touch on genuine Q-factors, does suggest that *scoring for type* might be sufficiently indicated if a few statements of the Q-sample, strongly indicative of a factor, were scored accordingly.

The normative data would then be somewhat as follows: "if statements *x, y, z*....gain scores +5 or +4 (on an 11-point scale from +5 to −5), the individual is likely to be of type A"; similarly, a few high-scoring statements could be used to define each type of item.

Again, however, what *use* one could make of such typifications is another matter. This is ordinarily what one means by validity data, and this would be as necessary for proper normative use of Q as it is of Cassel's so called ipsative methodology.

[135]
*The MACC Behavioral Adjustment Scale: An Objective Approach to the Evaluation of Behavioral Adjustments of Psychiatric Patients. Psychotic mental patients; 1957–62; Forms 1, 2, (4 pages); Form 2 is a revision of Form 1 rather than a parallel form; $4 per 25 copies of the *Behavior Charting Record* ('59, 2 pages, cumulative record for use with Form 1) by F. Harold Giedt; $8.50 per 25 scales, postpaid; specimen set not available; [5–15] minutes; Robert B. Ellsworth; Western Psychological Services. *
a) FORM 1. 1957; 5 ratings: affect, cooperation, communication, total adjustment, motility; mimeographed manual (10 pages).
b) FORM 2. 1962; 5 ratings: mood, cooperation, communication, social contact, total adjustment; mimeographed manual (17 pages).

REFERENCES
1. ELLSWORTH, ROBERT B., AND CLAYTON, WILLIAM H. "Measurement of Improvement in 'Mental Illness.'" *J Consult Psychol* 23:15–20 F '59. * (*PA* 34:1353)
2. MARKS, JOHN; STAUFFACHER, JAMES C.; AND LYLE, CURTIS. "Predicting Outcome in Schizophrenia." *J Abn & Social Psychol* 66:117–27 F '63. * (*PA* 37:7076)

WILSON H. GUERTIN, *Associate Professor of Education and Psychology, University of Florida, Gainesville, Florida.*

The MACC is named for the four subscales of Form 1: Motility, Affect, Cooperation, and Communication. It is unique among scales for rating behavior of psychotic patients because instead of an omnibus sampling of behavior, Ellsworth preselected items which differentiated between drug-improved and drug-nonimproved patients.

Form 1 employs 14, and Form 2, 16 scales with descriptive statements of behavior to correspond to each of the five scale points. Items were selected and assigned to subscales on the basis of cluster analyses. When the instrument was revised in 1962, the Motility subscale was dropped; a new item was added to the Affect subscale, the name of which was changed to Mood; and a new four-item subscale, Social Contact, was added.

Form 2 modifications do not reflect criticisms set forth in the previous *Mental Meas-*

urements Yearbook review by Lorr (see 5:82). All norms for Form 2 are from male veterans at one hospital. Such norms are worse than none because they may be misleading. The author should merely state that no norms are required for studies evaluating change after treatment.

The revised manual reports only two validity studies employing Form 2. One found that all subscales significantly differentiated between closed and open ward patients, and another that length of subsequent hospitalization was related to MACC total scores obtained shortly after admission.

Although the reasonable criticisms made by Lorr are not obviated by the revised form, we must applaud any effort to improve existing instruments. But it is difficult to see how Form 2 constitutes an improvement. Whereas Form 1 items were preselected to discriminate between improved and nonimproved patients, Form 2 adds four items seemingly not selected on this basis. Moreover, how much of a change has really been effected when the author reports a correlation of .93 between total scores of Form 1 and 2?

The newer *Psychotic Reaction Profile* (see 167) by Lorr can and should replace the MACC for rating behavior of psychotic patients.

For a review by Maurice Lorr of a, *see 5:82.*

[136]

★M-B History Record. Psychiatric patients; 1957–61; interview questionnaire for use with family informants; separate forms ('57) for men (17 pages), women (18 pages); manual ['60, 7 pages]; mimeographed norms ['61] for form for men; no data on reliability; no norms for form for women; 20 or more records, 15¢ each; $1 per specimen set of both forms (must be purchased to obtain manual and norms); postpaid; [60–90] minutes; Peter F. Briggs; the Author. *

REFERENCES

1. BRIGGS, PETER FARKASCH. *Preliminary Validation of a Standard Personal History for Psychiatric Diagnosis.* Doctor's thesis, University of Minnesota (Minneapolis, Minn.), 1955. (*DA* 15:1113)
2. BRIGGS, PETER F. "Eight Item Clusters for Use With the M-B History Record." *J Clin Psychol* 15:22–8 Ja '59. * (*PA* 34:3262)

[137]

The Manson Evaluation. Adults; 1948; identification of alcoholics, potential alcoholics, and severely maladjusted adults; 8 scores: anxiety, depressive fluctuations, emotional sensitivity, resentfulness, incompleteness, aloneness, interpersonal relations, total; 1 form (4 pages); manual (2 pages); no data on reliability of subscores; $6.50 per 25 tests, postpaid; specimen set not available; (5–15) minutes; Morse P. Manson; Western Psychological Services. *

REFERENCES

1–4. See 4:68.
5. MURPHY, DONAL G. *The Validity and Reliability of the Manson Evaluation and the Alcadd Test in the Identification of Female Alcoholics.* Master's thesis, Fordham University (New York, N.Y.), 1955.
6. MURPHY, DONAL G. "The Revalidation of Diagnostic Tests for Alcohol Addiction." *J Consult Psychol* 20:301–4 Ag '56. * (*PA* 31:8340)
7. CLARK, JAMES WARD. *Personality Syndromes in Chronic Alcoholism: A Factorial Study.* Doctor's thesis, Queen's University (Kingston, Ont., Canada), 1958. (Abstract: *Can Psychologist* 1:116–7.)
8. GIBBINS, ROBERT J.; SMART, REGINALD G.; AND SEELEY, JOHN R. "A Critique of the Manson Evaluation Test." *Q J Studies Alcohol* 20:357–61 Je '59. * (*PA* 34:6018)
9. STOTSKY, BERNARD A. "Accuracy of Configurational and Item Analytic Techniques Based on the Manson Evaluation in Diagnostic Classifications." *J Psychol Studies* 12:68–74 Mr '61. *

DUGAL CAMPBELL, *Assistant Professor of Psychology, Queen's University, Kingston, Ontario, Canada.*

The Manson Evaluation is intended for use as a screening device (*a*) to detect individuals who were formerly alcoholics, (*b*) to detect nonalcoholics who have personality characteristics similar to alcoholics, and (*c*) to obtain information about psychological processes involved in alcoholic or potential alcoholic personalities. The rationale is that alcoholics have distinctive personality characteristics which can be measured, so that an individual's likelihood of becoming an alcoholic under stress (or his likelihood of being an alcoholic at the moment) can be predicted. Questions designed to measure seven traits (three concerning psychoneuroticism and four concerning psychopathy) are used. In the original investigation, misclassification of alcoholics and nonalcoholics, and vice versa, was in the range 16–21 per cent. Murphy (5, 6) tried the test on groups of active alcoholics, Alcoholics Anonymous members, social drinkers, and abstainers. All the critical ratios between the groups were significant.

The test has been severely criticised by Gibbins, Smart, and Seeley (8), who point out that the groups used in the standardisation were not comparable and that the critical score used by Manson is based on an estimate of the prevalence of alcoholism which is very much higher than that actually found in the general population. They conclude: "This seems to eliminate most of the situations in which the use of the test for diagnostic purposes would make any sense."

The questions raised by the original reviewers remain unanswered: (*a*) What will happen when genuine job seekers are motivated to fake their answers? (*b*) Do the results vary when the test is used in different circumstances? (For example, when neither group of subjects consists of admitted alcoholics under treatment.) (c) Will the arrangement of the questions into seven groups stand up to an objective analysis? (d) Will the arrangement be repeated with other subjects? More generally the notion that alcoholics have distinctive personality patterns which are markedly different from those of other groups (both normal and abnormal) has come under fire. Reviews of work based on the idea that alcoholism is associated with particular personality patterns [1] suggest that nothing of this sort has so far been sufficiently clearly demonstrated to provide a practical basis for test construction. Consequently one cannot readily see how the test may be used in either clinical practice or research.

For reviews by Charles H. Honzik and Albert L. Hunsicker, see 4:68.

[138]

★Maudsley Personality Inventory. College and adults; 1959-62; 2 scores: neuroticism, extraversion; H. J. Eysenck. *

a) BRITISH EDITION. 1959; 1 form (2 pages); manual (8 pages); may be administered as a short scale; 6s. 9d. per 25 tests; 4d. per single copy; 2s. per set of keys; 2s. 6d. per manual; postage and purchase tax extra; [5] minutes for short scale, [15] minutes for full scale; University of London Press Ltd.

b) UNITED STATES EDITION. 1962; 1 form ('62, c1959-62, 2 pages, items identical with British edition); manual (21 pages); $3 per 25 tests; $1 per set of test booklet hand scoring stencils; separate answer cards may be used; $5 per 100 IBM port-a-punch cards; $1.25 per manual; $1.75 per specimen set; postage extra; (10-15) minutes; manual by Robert R. Knapp; Educational & Industrial Testing Service.

REFERENCES

1. BENDIG, A. W. "Extraversion, Neuroticism, and Manifest Anxiety." Abstract. *J Consult Psychol* 21:398 O '57. *
2. BENDIG, A. W. "Extraversion, Neuroticism, and Verbal Ability Measures." *J Consult Psychol* 22:464 D '58. * (PA 33:9928)
3. BENDIG, A. W. "Identification of Item Factor Patterns Within the Manifest Anxiety Scale." Abstract. *J Consult Psychol* 22:158 Ap '58. * (PA 35:3448)
4. EYSENCK, H. J. "Hysterics and Dysthymics as Criterion Groups in the Study of Introversion-Extraversion: A Reply." *J Abn & Social Psychol* 57:250-4 S '58. * (PA 33:10806)
5. EYSENCK, H. J. "A Short Questionnaire for the Measurement of Two Dimensions of Personality." *J Appl Psychol* 42:14-7 F '58. *
6. JENSEN, ARTHUR R. "The Maudsley Personality Inventory." *Acta Psychologica* 14(4):314-25 '58. * (PA 33:9958)
7. SIGAL, JOHN J.; STAR, KOLMAN H.; AND FRANKS, CYRIL M. "Hysterics and Dysthymics as Criterion Groups in the Measure of Introversion-Extraversion: A Rejoinder to Eysenck's Reply." *J Abn & Social Psychol* 57:381-2 N '58. * (PA 33:10825)
8. SIGAL, JOHN J.; STAR, KOLMAN H.; AND FRANKS, CYRIL M. "Hysterics and Dysthymics as Criterion Groups in the Study of Introversion-Extraversion." *J Abn & Social Psychol* 57:143-8 S '58. * (PA 33:10826)
9. STORMS, LOWELL H., AND SIGAL, JOHN J. "Eysenck's Personality Theory With Special Reference to 'The Dynamics of Anxiety and Hysteria.'" *Brit J Med Psychol* 31:228-46 pts 3 & 4 '58. *
10. BARTHOLOMEW, ALLEN A. "Extraversion-Introversion

1 SYME, LEONARD. "Personality Characteristics and the Alcoholic: A Critique of Current Studies." *Q J Stud Alcohol* 18:288-302 Je '57. *

and Neuroticism in First Offenders and Recidivists." *Brit J Delinq* 10:120-9 O '59. *
11. BARTHOLOMEW, ALLEN A., AND MARLEY, EDWARD. "Susceptibility to Methylpentynol: Personality and Other Variables." *J Mental Sci* 105:957-70 O '59. *
12. BARTHOLOMEW, ALLEN A., AND MARLEY, EDWARD. "The Temporal Reliability of the Maudsley Personality Inventory." *J Mental Sci* 105:238-40 Ja '59. * (PA 34:1000)
13. BENDIG, A. W. "College Norms for and Concurrent Validity of the Pittsburgh Revisions of the Maudsley Personality Inventory." *J Psychol Studies* 11:12-7 S-O '59. * (PA 34:4053)
14. BENDIG, A. W. "The Relationship of Scales of Extraversion-Introversion and Emotionality to Guilford's O, F, and P Scales." *J Psychol Studies* 11:49-51 N-D '59. * (PA 34:5597)
15. BENDIG, A. W. "Score Reliability of Dichotomous and Trichotomous Item Responses on the Maudsley Personality Inventory." Abstract. *J Consult Psychol* 23:181 Ap '59. * (PA 34:1339, title only)
16. BENDIG, A. W., AND VAUGHAN, CHARLES J. "Extraversion, Neuroticism, and Motor Learning." *J Abn & Social Psychol* 59:399-403 N '59. * (PA 34:6003)
17. BRENGELMANN, J. C. "Differences in Questionnaire Responses Between English and German Nationals." *Acta Psychologica* 16(5):339-55 '59. * (PA 34:5788)
18. EYSENCK, H. J. "The Differentiation Between Normal and Various Neurotic Groups on the Maudsley Personality Inventory." *Brit J Psychol* 50:176-7 My '59. * (PA 34:2991)
19. EYSENCK, H. J. "Personality and the Estimation of Time." *Percept & Motor Skills* 9:405-6 D '59. * (PA 34:5610)
20. FRANKS, C. M., AND LEIGH, D. "The Theoretical and Experimental Application of a Conditioning Model to a Consideration of Bronchial Asthma in Man." *J Psychosom Res* 4:88-98 D '59. * (PA 34:8218)
21. KELTY, EDWARD JOHN. *Normal Electrocortical Activity in Relation to Personality Factors.* Doctor's thesis, Duke University (Durham, N.C.), 1959. (DA 20:756)
22. LYNN, R. "Two Personality Characteristics Related to Academic Achievement." *Brit J Ed Psychol* 29:213-6 N '59. *
23. RAY, OAKLEY S. "Personality Factors in Motor Learning and Reminiscence." *J Abn & Social Psychol* 59:199-203 S '59. * (PA 34:2691)
24. SMITH, C. M., AND HAMILTON, J. "Psychological Factors in the Narcolepsy-Cataplexy Syndrome." *Psychosom Med* 21:40-9 Ja-F '59. * (PA 34:1858)
25. VALENTINE, MAX. "Psychometric Testing in Iran." *J Mental Sci* 105:93-107 Ja '59. * (PA 34:1065)
26. BENDIG, A. W. "Extraversion, Neuroticism, and Student Achievement in Introductory Psychology." *J Ed Res* 53:263-7 Mr '60. *
27. BENDIG, A. W. "Factor Analyses of 'Anxiety' and 'Neuroticism' Inventories." *J Consult Psychol* 24:161-8 Ap '60. * (PA 34:8195)
28. BENDIG, A. W. "Item Factor Analyses of the Scales of the Maudsley Personality Inventory." *J Psychol Studies* 11:104-7 Ja-F '60. * (PA 34:7366)
29. BRENGELMANN, J. C.; HAHN, H.; PEDLEY, J. C.; AND AMATO, J. G. "Learning and Personality: 1, A Pilot Experiment." *Acta Psychologica* 17(2):113-8 '60. * (PA 35:784)
30. BRONZAFT, A.; HAYES, R.; WELCH, L.; AND KOLTUV, M. "Relationships Between Extraversion, Neuroticism, and Ascendance." *J Psychol* 50:279-85 O '60. * (PA 35:6475)
31. BRONZAFT, ARLINE; HAYES, ROSLYN; WELCH, LIVINGSTON; AND KOLTUV, MYRON. "Relationship Between PGR and Measures of Extraversion, Ascendance, and Neuroticism." *J Psychol* 50:193-5 O '60. * (PA 35:6522)
32. CARRIGAN, PATRICIA M. "Extraversion-Introversion as a Dimension of Personality: A Reappraisal." *Psychol B* 57:329-60 S '60. * (PA 35:4976)
33. CLARIDGE, GORDON. Chap. 2, "The Excitation-Inhibition Balance in Neurotics," pp. 107-54. In *Experiments in Personality: Vol. 2, Psychodiagnostics and Psychodynamics.* Edited by H. J. Eysenck. London: Routledge & Kegan Paul Ltd., 1960. Pp. viii, 333. *
34. EYSENCK, H. J. Chap. 5, "A Factor Analysis of Selected Tests," pp. 234-44. In his *Experiments in Personality: Vol. 2, Psychodiagnostics and Psychodynamics.* London: Routledge & Kegan Paul Ltd., 1960. Pp. viii, 333. *
35. EYSENCK, H. J. "Reminiscence, Extraversion and Neuroticism." *Percept & Motor Skills* 11:21-2 Ag '60. * (PA 35:3499)
36. EYSENCK, H. J. *The Structure of Human Personality,* Second Edition. London: Methuen & Co. Ltd., 1960. Pp. xix, 448. *
37. EYSENCK, H. J.; TARRANT, MOLLIE; WOOLF, MYRA; AND ENGLAND, L. "Smoking and Personality." *Brit Med J* (5184): 1456-60 My 14 '60. *
38. EYSENCK, S. B. G. "Social Class, Sex, and Response to a Five-Part Personality Inventory." *Ed & Psychol Meas* 20:47-54 sp '60. * (PA 34:7381)
39. HOLLAND, H. C. Chap. 4, "Measures of Perceptual Functions," pp. 193-233. In *Experiments in Personality: Vol. 2, Psychodiagnostics and Psychodynamics.* Edited by H. J. Eysenck. London: Routledge & Kegan Paul Ltd., 1960. Pp. viii, 333. *
40. KNOWLES, JOHN. "Maudsley Personality Inventory." *Psychometric Res B* (6):[22-5] su '60. *

41. KNOWLES, JOHN B. "The Temporal Stability of MPI Scores in Normal and Psychiatric Populations." Abstract. *J Consult Psychol* 24:278 Je '60. *

42. SAINSBURY, P. "Psychosomatic Disorders and Neurosis in Out-Patients Attending a General Hospital." *J Psychosom Res* 4:261-73 Jl '60. * (*PA* 36:1JU61S)

43. VINSON, D. B., AND ROBBINS, L. R. "Objectivity in the Assessment of the Thyrotoxic Patient." *J Psychosom Res* 4:236-43 Mr '60. * (*PA* 36:1IB36V)

44. VOGEL, MURIEL D. "The Relation of Personality Factors to GSR Conditioning of Alcoholics: An Exploratory Study." *Can J Psychol* 14:275-80 D '60. * (*PA* 35:5200)

45. WILLETT, R. A. Chap. 3, "Measures of Learning and Conditioning," pp. 157-92. In *Experiments in Personality: Vol. 2, Psychodiagnostics and Psychodynamics*. Edited by H. J. Eysenck. London: Routledge & Kegan Paul Ltd., 1960. Pp. viii, 333. *

46. BENDIG, A. W. "A Factor Analysis of Scales of Emotionality and Hostility." *J Clin Psychol* 17:189-92 Ap '61. * (*PA* 38:1034)

46a. COWIE, VALERIE. "The Incidence of Neurosis in the Children of Psychotics." *Acta Psychiatrica Scandinavica* 37(1):37-71 '61. * (*PA* 36:4JV37C)

47. DAS, GITA. "Standardisation of Maudsley Personality Inventory (M.P.I.) on an Indian Population." *J Psychol Res* 5:7-9 Ja '61. * (*PA* 35:5540)

48. FIELD, J. G. "An Interpersonal Validation of the MPI." *Acta Psychologica* 18(5):351-3 '61. * (*PA* 37:1202)

49. FIELD, J. G., AND BRENGELMANN, J. C. "Eyelid Conditioning and Three Personality Parameters." *J Abn & Social Psychol* 63:517-23 N '61. * (*PA* 37:369)

50. FOULDS, G. A. "The Logical Impossibility of Using Hysterics and Dysthymics as Criterion Groups in the Study of Introversion and Extraversion." *Brit J Psychol* 52:385-7 N '61. * (*PA* 36:4H185F) Comments by H. J. Eysenck and J. R. Ingham and reply by G. A. Foulds. *Brit J Psychol* 53:455-9 N '62. *

51. FRANKS, C. M.; HOLDEN, E. A.; AND PHILLIPS, M. "Eysenck's 'Stratification' Theory and the Questionnaire Method of Measuring Personality." *J Clin Psychol* 17:248-53 Jl '61. * (*PA* 38:8489)

52. FURNEAUX, W. D. "Neuroticism, Extraversion, Drive, and Suggestibility." *J Clin & Exp Hypnosis* 9:195-214 O '61. * (*PA* 36:4I195F)

53. FURNEAUX, W. D., AND GIBSON, H. B. "The Maudsley Personality Inventory as a Predictor of Susceptibility to Hypnosis." *J Clin & Exp Hypnosis* 9:167-77 Jl '61. * (*PA* 36:3II67F)

54. KEEHN, J. D. "Response Sets and the Maudsley Personality Inventory." *J Social Psychol* 54:141-6 Je '61. * (*PA* 36:2HF41K)

55. LIPMAN, RONALD S., AND SPITZ, HERMAN H. "Cortical Conductivity and Vocabulary." *J Abn & Social Psychol* 63:459-60 S '61. * (*PA* 37:200)

56. LUCAS, C. J. "Personality of Students With Acne Vulgaris." *Brit Med J* 2(5248):354-6 Ag 5 '61. *

57. LYNN, R., AND GORDON, I. E. "The Relation of Neuroticism and Extraversion to Intelligence and Educational Attainment." *Brit J Ed Psychol* 31:194-203 Je '61. * (*PA* 36:3HD94L)

58. RIM, Y. "Dimensions of Job Incentives and Personality." *Acta Psychologica* 18(5):332-6 '61. * (*PA* 37:2113)

59. SHANMUGAM, T. E. "Voluntary Inhibition and Disinhibition in Relation to Personality Traits." *Psychol Studies* 6:36-40 Ja '61. * (*PA* 37:1319)

60. SINGH, S. D.; SHARMA, N. R.; AND VIMAL, KUMARI. "Personality Differences in Fluctuation of Attention." *Psychol Studies* 6:55-60 Ja '61. * (*PA* 37:1320)

61. VOGEL, MURIEL D. "GSR Conditioning and Personality Factors in Alcoholics and Normals." *J Abn & Social Psychol* 63:417-21 S '61. * (*PA* 37:1725)

62. BENDIG, A. W. "Factor Analyses of the Guilford Zimmerman Temperament Survey and the Maudsley Personality Inventory." *J General Psychol* 67:21-6 Jl '62. * (*PA* 37:3169)

63. BENDIG, A. W. "A Factor Analysis of Personality Scales Including the Buss-Durkee Hostility Inventory." *J General Psychol* 66:179-83 Ap '62. * (*PA* 37:1246)

64. BIGGS, J. B. "The Relation of Neuroticism and Extraversion to Intelligence and Educational Attainment." *Brit J Ed Psychol* 32:188-95 Je '62. * (*PA* 37:3123)

65. BONIER, RICHARD JOSEPH. *Relationships of Psychosomatic States to Emotional Disturbance and Diffuse Autonomic Activity.* Doctor's thesis, Michigan State University (East Lansing, Mich.), 1962. (*DA* 23:1417)

66. EYSENCK, H. J. "Response Set, Authoritarianism and Personality Questionnaires." *Brit J Social & Clin Psychol* 1:20-4 F '62. * (*PA* 37:1252)

67. EYSENCK, H. J., AND CLARIDGE, G. "The Position of Hysterics and Dysthymics in a Two-Dimensional Framework of Personality Description." *J Abn & Social Psychol* 64:46-55 Ja '62. * (*PA* 37:1281)

68. EYSENCK, S. B. G. "The Validity of a Personality Questionnaire as Determined by the Method of Nominated Groups." *Life Sci* 1:13-8 Ja '62. * (*PA* 37:1253)

69. EYSENCK, S. B. G., AND EYSENCK, H. J. "Rigidity as a Function of Introversion and Neuroticism: A Study of Un-

married Mothers." *Int J Social Psychiatry* 8:180-4 su '62. * (*PA* 37:6932)

70. FITCH, J. H. "Two Personality Variables and Their Distribution in a Criminal Population: An Empirical Study." *Brit J Social & Clin Psychol* 1:161-7 O '62. * (*PA* 37:5449)

71. GIBSON, H. B. "The Lie Scale of the Maudsley Personality Inventory." *Acta Psychologica* 20(1):18-23 '62. * (*PA* 37:3173)

72. HOLLAND, H. C. "A Note on Differences in the Duration of the Spiral After-Effect Following Continuous and Intermittant Stimulation." *Acta Psychologica* 20(4):304-7 '62. * (*PA* 38:3539)

73. HOLLAND, H. C. "The Spiral After-Effect and Extraversion." *Acta Psychologica* 20(1):29-35 '62. * (*PA* 37:2296)

74. JENSEN, ARTHUR R. "Extraversion, Neuroticism, and Serial Learning." *Acta Psychologica* 20(2):69-77 '62. * (*PA* 37:6773)

75. KEEHN, J. D. "Neurotic Questionnaire Responses as Simulated by Normal Individuals." *Austral J Psychol* 14:65-8 Ap '62. * (*PA* 38:6086)

76. KISSEN, DAVID M., AND EYSENCK, H. J. "Personality in Male Lung Cancer Patients." *J Psychosom Res* 6:123-7 Ap-Je '62. * (*PA* 37:5531)

77. LANG, PETER J., AND LAZOVIK, A. DAVID. "Personality and Hypnotic Susceptibility." *J Consult Psychol* 26:317-22 Ag '62. * (*PA* 38:4433)

78. McGUIRE, RALPH J. "A Study of the M.P.I. Used With Psychiatric In-Patients." Abstract. *B Brit Psychol Soc* 47:56-7 Ap '62. *

79. PAPALOIZOS, ANTOINE. "Personality and Success of Training in Human Relations." *Personnel Psychol* 15:423-8 w '62. * (*PA* 38:1462)

80. SAVAGE, R. D. "Three Experiments Using the Junior Maudsley Personality Inventory: 2, Personality Factors and Academic Performance." *Brit J Ed Psychol* 32:251-3 N '62. * (*PA* 37:8275)

81. STAR, KOLMAN H. "Ideal-Self Response Set and Maudsley Personality Inventory Scores." *Psychol Rep* 11:708 D '62. * (*PA* 38:1003)

82. WALTON, D., AND MATHER, M. D. "Differential Response to Questionnaire Items of Neuroticism by 'Defensive' and 'Non-Defensive' Subjects." *J Mental Sci* 108:501-4 Jl '62. * (*PA* 37:3243)

83. BARTHOLOMEW, A. A. "Some Comparative Australian Data for the Maudsley Personality Inventory." *Austral J Psychol* 15:46-51 Ap '63. *

84. BEECH, H. R., AND ADLER, F. "Some Aspects of Verbal Conditioning in Psychiatric Patients." *Behav Res Ther* 1:273-82 D '63. *

85. BENDIG, A. W. "A Note on Cattell's Radicalism (Q_1) Scale." *J Social Psychol* 60:107-13 Je '63. * (*PA* 38:4173)

86. BENDIG, A. W. "The Relation of Temperament Traits of Social Extraversion and Emotionality to Vocational Interests." *J General Psychol* 69:311-8 O '63. * (*PA* 39:1800)

87. BENDIG, A. W., AND MARTIN, ANN M. "The Factor Structure of Temperament Traits and Needs." *J General Psychol* 69:27-36 Jl '63. * (*PA* 38:4297)

88. BERG, PAUL SAUL DAVID. *Neurotic and Psychopathic Criminals: Some Measures of Ego Syntonicity, Impulse Socialization and Perceptual Consistency.* Doctor's thesis, Michigan State University (East Lansing, Mich.), 1963. (*DA* 24:2559)

89. CHOPPY, MARYSE, AND EYSENCK, H. J. "Brain Damage and Depressant Drugs: An Experimental Study of Interaction," pp. 313-23. In *Experiments With Drugs: Studies in the Relation Between Personality, Learning Theory and Drug Action.* Edited by H. J. Eysenck. New York: Macmillan Co., 1963. Pp. xii, 421. * (*PA* 38:5527)

90. CLARIDGE, G. S., AND HERRINGTON, R. N. Chap. 5, "Excitation-Inhibition and the Theory of Neurosis: A Study of the Sedation Threshold," pp. 131-68. In *Experiments With Drugs: Studies in the Relation Between Personality, Learning Theory and Drug Action.* Edited by H. J. Eysenck. New York: Macmillan Co., 1963. Pp. xii, 421. * (*PA* 38:5527)

91. CLARIDGE, G. S., AND HERRINGTON, R. N. "An EEG Correlate of the Archimedes Spiral After-Effect and Its Relationship With Personality." *Behav Res Ther* 1:217-29 D '63. *

92. COPPEN, ALEC, AND KESSEL, NEIL. "Menstruation and Personality." *Brit J Psychiatry* 109:711-21 N '63. * (*PA* 38:8347)

93. COSTELLO, C. G., AND SMITH, C. M. "The Relationships Between Personality, Sleep and the Effects of Sedatives." *Brit J Psychiatry* 109:568-71 Jl '63. * (*PA* 38:4487)

94. CROOKES, T. G., AND HUTT, S. J. "Scores of Psychotic Patients on the Maudsley Personality Inventory." *J Consult Psychol* 27:243-7 Je '63. * (*PA* 38:994)

95. DAVIES, M. H.; CLARIDGE, G. S.; AND WAWMAN, R. J. "Sedation Threshold, Autonomic Lability and the Excitation-Inhibition Theory of Personality: 3, The Blood Pressure Response to an Adrenaline Antagonist as a Measure of Autonomic Lability." *Brit J Psychiatry* 109:558-67 Jl '63. * (*PA* 38:3795)

95a. EVANS, FREDERICK J. "The Maudsley Personality Inventory, Suggestibility, and Hypnosis." *Int J Clin & Exp Hypnosis* 11:187-200 Jl '63. * (*PA* 38:6273)

96. EYSENCK, S. B. G., AND EYSENCK, H. J. "Acquiescent Response Set in Personality Questionnaires." *Life Sci* 2:144-7 F '63. * (*PA* 38:995)

97. EYSENCK, S. B. G., AND EYSENCK, H. J. "On the Dual Nature of Extraversion." *Brit J Social & Clin Psychol* 2:46–55 F '63. * (*PA* 38:916)

98. EYSENCK, SYBIL B. G., AND EYSENCK, H. J. "The Validity of Questionnaire and Rating Assessments of Extraversion and Neuroticism, and Their Factorial Stability." *Brit J Psychol* 54:51–62 F '63. * (*PA* 37:8009)

99. FORREST, D. W. "Relationship Between Sharpening and Extraversion." *Psychol Rep* 13:564 O '63. * (*PA* 38:8488)

99a. FURNEAUX, W. D. "Neuroticism, Extraversion, and Suggestibility: A Comment." *Int J Clin & Exp Hypnosis* 11:201–2 Jl '63. *

100. FURNEAUX, W. D., AND LINDAHL, L. E. H. "How Valid Are Questionnaire Validity Studies?" Abstract. *B Brit Psychol Soc* 16:19A Ap '63. *

101. HESELTINE, G. F. "The Site of Onset of Eczema and Personality Trait Differences: An Exploratory Study." *J Psychosom Res* 7:241–6 D '63. * (*PA* 38:8360)

102. HILGARD, ERNEST R., AND BENTLER, P. M. "Predicting Hypnotizability From the Maudsley Personality Inventory." *Brit J Psychol* 54:63–9 F '63. * (*PA* 37:8091)

103. HOWARTH, E. "Some Laboratory Measures of Extraversion-Introversion." *Percept & Motor Skills* 17:55–60 Ag '63. * (*PA* 38:7242)

104. KISSEN, DAVID M. "Personality Characteristics in Males Conducive to Lung Cancer." *Brit J Med Psychol* 36(1):27–36 '63. * (*PA* 38:921)

105. LITTLE, ALAN. "Professor Eysenck's Theory of Crime: An Empirical Test on Adolescent Offenders." Comments by H. J. Eysenck. *Brit J Criminol* 4:152–63 O '03. * (*PA* 38: 6477)

106. LOVIBOND, S. H. "Conceptual Thinking, Personality and Conditioning." *Brit J Social & Clin Psychol* 2:100–11 Je '63. * (*PA* 38:3654)

107. MCGUIRE, R. J.; MOWBRAY, R. M.; AND VALLANCE, R. C. "The Maudsley Personality Inventory Used With Psychiatric Inpatients." *Brit J Psychol* 54:157–66 My '63. * (*PA* 38:1032)

108. MANNE, SIGMUND H.; KANDEL, ARTHUR; AND ROSENTHAL, DAVID. "The Relationship Between Performance Minus Verbal Scores and Extraversion in a Severely Sociopathic Population." *J Clin Psychol* 19:96–7 Ja '63. * (*PA* 39:1676)

109. MEZEY, A. G.; COHEN, SAMUEL I.; AND KNIGHT, E. J. "Personality Assessment Under Varying Physiological and Psychological Conditions." *J Psychosom Res* 7:237–40 D '63. * (*PA* 38:8527)

110. RATH, R., AND MISRA, S. K. "Change of Attitudes as a Function of Some Personality Factors." *J Social Psychol* 60:311–7 Ag '63. * (*PA* 38:4182)

111. ROBINSON, J. O. "A Study of Neuroticism and Casual Arterial Blood Pressure." *Brit J Social & Clin Psychol* 2:56–64 F '63. * (*PA* 38:1347)

112. RUTTIGER, KATHERINE FORD. "Individual Differences in Reaction to Meprobamate: A Study in Visual Perception." *J Abn & Social Psychol* 67:37–43 Jl '63. * (*PA* 38:419)

113. SINGER, JEROME L., AND ANTROBUS, JOHN S. "A Factor-Analytic Study of Daydreaming and Conceptually-Related Cognitive and Personality Variables." *Percept & Motor Skills* 17:187–209 Ag '63. * (*PA* 38:7418)

114. SINGH, S. D. "Extraversion, Neuroticism, and Conformity Behaviour." *J Psychol Res* 7:66–71 My '63. * (*PA* 38:4253)

115. STANLEY, GORDON. "Personality and Attitude Characteristics of Fundamentalist Theological Students." *Austral J Psychol* 15:121–3 Ag '63. * (*PA* 38:6037)

116. TAUSS, W. "A Note on Stability and Equivalence of Long and Short Forms of the M.P.I." *Austral J Psychol* 15:118–20 Ag '63. *

117. VENABLES, ETHEL. "Personality Scores and Achievement Among Technical College Students." Abstract. *B Brit Psychol Soc* 16:58–9 Jl '63. *

ARTHUR R. JENSEN, *Associate Professor of Educational Psychology, and Associate Research Psychologist, Institute of Human Learning, University of California, Berkeley, California.*

By all criteria of excellence in test development the MPI is an impressive achievement. It has grown out of years of intensive research on the dimensional analysis of personality. A great amount of evidence (*36*) has shown that two relatively independent superfactors, identified by Eysenck as neuroticism and extraversion-introversion, represent most of the variance in the personality domain.

While it is possible to slice the variance in this domain into many different ways of making up "scales" consisting of various combinations of many kinds of personality inventory items, these scales are almost always highly intercorrelated, despite their widely differing labels. When they are factor analyzed, either at the scale level or at the item level, the first two or three independent factors almost invariably account for all the appreciable common factor variance in the lot. The MPI has been developed to measure two of the most comprehensive factors, Neuroticism (N) and Extraversion (E). Neuroticism refers to general emotional instability, emotional overresponsiveness, and predisposition to neurotic breakdown under stress. Extraversion refers to outgoing, uninhibited, impulsive, and sociable inclinations. The method of developing the inventory was factor analytic and is adequately described in both the British and American editions of the manual.

The MPI consists of 48 items, of which 24 are keyed to N and 24 to E. Unlike some personality inventories (e.g., the MMPI), none of the items could be construed as socially objectionable; thus the inventory can be used with adolescents or adults in almost any setting. Though the MPI takes only about 10 or 15 minutes, there is also a short form—described in the British manual and by Jensen (*6*)—consisting of six items from each scale. The short form has satisfactory reliability and high correlations with the total scales and can be useful when time is very limited.

The MPI derives much of its importance from its theoretical underpinnings. Probably no other psychological test—certainly no other personality inventory—rivals it in psychological rationale. This is particularly true of the E. dimension, which has been the subject of intensive experimental research in Eysenck's laboratory for more than a decade. A review of this research is, of course, impossible here. The manual prepared by Robert Knapp for the American edition has a bibliography of 112 items of the most relevant literature, and the manual itself summarizes much of the published findings. Factor-analytically sophisticated readers are also referred to Carrigan's (*32*) critical appraisal of E as a dimension of personality.

NORMS. A great deal of normative data are presented, both for English and American subjects. The American manual presents American college norms (percentiles and stanines based on 1,064 university undergraduates). Means and standard deviations are presented for 32 different groups, including various psychiatric, prison, and industrial populations, totaling over 7,000 subjects (including the American norms group of 1,064 and the English norms group of 1,800). Bartholomew (83) has published some Australian norms, which differ little from the English, except that the Australians seem to be slightly more extraverted, as are the Americans.

There are slight sex and social class differences on both the N and E scales; these are fully discussed in the manual. The scales are not correlated with intelligence.

RELIABILITY AND VALIDITY. Split-half and Kuder-Richardson estimates of item intercorrelations for each scale are between .75 and .90 in various samples. N consistently has slightly higher internal consistency than E. Test-retest reliabilities range from .70 to .90. In short, the reliability of the MPI is among the highest to be found for personality inventories. The MPI has also been studied for effects of various types of "response set." These seem to be negligible.

Assessment of the validity of the MPI is a complex matter. There can be little question of its factorial validity. That is to say, the N and E scales invariably have high loadings on factors that are also heavily represented in other measures considered to be indicative of neuroticism or extraversion, and there is little factorial overlap between the scales. Though they were intended to be completely independent measures, it has been found that they are correlated about —.15—slightly more or less depending upon the population sampled. The negative correlation is somewhat higher (usually about —.30) in psychiatric and college populations. Data on correlations with other personality inventories are presented in the manuals. Note, for example, that the N scale correlates almost as highly (.76) with the Taylor Manifest Anxiety Scale as reliability would allow. There is, however, a slightly greater negative correlation between the Taylor scale and the E scale than between the N and E scales.

Descriptive validity of the MPI has been adequately established by the method of nominated groups. Judges rated people on the basis of observable characteristics in terms of neuroticism and extraversion. These ratings show highly significant correlations with the relevant dimensions measured by the MPI.

Most important, but also the most difficult to evaluate, is the "construct validity" of the MPI, that is, the elaborate network of theory, predictions, and experimental findings concerning the N and E dimensions. Adequate discussion of this topic must presuppose the reader's knowledge of Eysenck's theory of personality which relates neuroticism to autonomic lability and extraversion to cortical inhibition.[1] Since an exposition of the theory and the related research is beyond the scope of this review, the reviewer can only give his overall impression of this vast body of work as it relates to the MPI. First, there is no doubt that both N and E scales have shown significant and replicable correlations with experimental phenomena in the fields of perception, motor learning, verbal learning, pain tolerance, and attitudes. Some of these relationships are predictable from Eysenck's and others' theories. All of the research, of course, has not unequivocally supported Eysenck's theoretical deductions and there is a large fringe of ambiguity on the growing edge of the theory which is perhaps somewhat underemphasized in the MPI manuals. It is this area of far reaching, but as yet inadequately substantiated, implications of the theory that has provided Eysenck's critics with an easy target for their often premature unfavorable evaluations. But if one reviews the research of the Maudsley group over the years, it is clear that the theory of personality associated with the MPI is sensitive to experimental findings and is constantly undergoing careful modification and development. It seems to be Eysenck's personal style, more than the facts of the matter, which stimulates criticism and a counsel of caution, since Eysenck tends to stride each step of the way with a rather bold assurance. All in all, it seems safe to say that no other personality test is based upon a body of psychological theory so far reaching and so diligently and ably researched as is the MPI. The chief reason for this is that the MPI is one of the few personality measures that has grown out of a theory concerned with basic psychological

1 EYSENCK, H. J. The Dynamics of Anxiety and Hysteria: An Experimental Application of Modern Learning Theory to Psychiatry. London: Routledge & Kegan Paul Ltd., 1957. Pp. xiv, 311. *

processes rather than out of purely empirical attempts to predict certain currently practical criteria.

USES OF THE MPI. The MPI has been little used in clinical diagnosis. It is not listed in Sundberg's [2] survey of the 62 most widely used tests in clinical practice in the United States. The reasons are not hard to find: Clinicians generally want more detailed information than is provided by a subject's scores on two broad dimensions of personality; the MPI dimensions do not correspond at all well to the presently used diagnostic categories (nor are they intended to), and the psychological theory associated with N and E has not been generally incorporated in diagnostic or therapeutic practice. Those who wish to see how the theory underlying the MPI is related to psychiatric diagnosis and therapy are referred to a discussion by Eysenck.[3] As yet this reviewer has not seen evidence of the practical use of the MPI in clinical settings. Certainly it is not of any value for conventional psychiatric diagnosis. McGuire and others (107) gave the MPI to an unselected group of psychiatric patients and found that the N scale differentiated all diagnostic groups from the nonpsychiatric controls, but neither the N nor the E scale differentiated significantly among the diagnostic groups. Other studies have shown significant differences among various diagnostic categories, but these differences have not been sufficiently reliable to support the use of the MPI for individual diagnosis. Since in the McGuire study all psychiatric groups averaged 10–15 points higher on the N scale than the normal controls, it is suggested that the MPI might be valuable as a psychiatric screening device.

Also, for screening and group prediction in educational and industrial settings, the MPI shows promise based on research. College examination failure rate and academic achievement, for example, have been shown to be related to N and E in ways predictable from Eysenck's theory. Persistence in menial and monotonous tasks also is related to the MPI dimensions.

The present reviewer has had most experience with the MPI as an adjunct to laboratory research in the field of human learning. The MPI can be used by experimentalists who believe personality factors may play a part in the psychological phenomena under investigation and who wish to account for more of the "between subjects" variance as a means of increasing the precision of experiments. The relevance of anxiety in learning and conditioning experiments, for example, has been amply demonstrated with research using Taylor's Manifest Anxiety Scale. The N scale of the MPI can serve the same purpose as the MAS, with the added advantage that it is shorter, more reliable, and has a greater body of psychological research behind it. It has been found that the importance of the neuroticism factor increases as task complexity becomes greater (74). We have also found in our own work that subjects with high N scores are less apt to stand up well throughout an arduous laboratory experiment and are less able to follow complex directions in an experiment, even though they may have high intelligence. The relevance of E to experimental variables, though called for by Eysenck's theory, is not so clearly established at present and must await further investigation. But it is in the realm of experimental psychology, as a covariate in studies of perception, conditioning, learning, persistence, attention, concept attainment, and the like, that this reviewer sees the most immediate potential usefulness of the MPI. The American manual also discusses the uses of the MPI in market research and in vocational selection and counseling.

A word about the British and American editions of the manuals. Both cover the essentials expected of any test manual, but the American edition is more up-to-date and therefore more complete in its coverage of relevant research. Indeed, it is an exemplary model of what a test manual should be.

In summary, the MPI is a brief and highly reliable measure of two relatively independent broad factors of personality—neuroticism and extraversion-introversion. Much sophisticated research has gone into its construction, and the large body of normative data, plus the psychological theory and experimentation associated with the MPI, make it one of the most important of all personality inventories, and certainly the preferred measures of neuroticism (or anxiety) and extraversion.

2 SUNDBERG, NORMAN D. "The Practice of Psychological Testing in Clinical Services in the United States." Am Psychol 16:79–83 F '61. *
3 EYSENCK, H. J. Chap. 3, "A Rational System of Diagnosis and Therapy in Mental Illness." In Progress in Clinical Psychology, Vol. 4. Edited by Lawrence E. Abt and Bernard F. Riess. New York: Grune & Stratton, Inc., 1960. Pp. ix, 181. *

The American edition of a new version of the MPI, called the *Eysenck Personality Inventory* (EPI), has been published by the American publisher of the MPI. The EPI is described in a preliminary edition of the manual (August, 1963) as an attempt to make the MPI scales more useful for certain purposes. The EPI measures the same two factors as the MPI, but the slight correlation that exists between N and E in the MPI scales has been removed entirely, by adding, subtracting, and rewriting items and subjecting them to repeated factor analyses. Also, many of the items have been reworded in such a way as to increase their reliability when used with subjects of low intelligence or little education. There are two equivalent forms of the EPI. The EPI also contains a "lie" scale (borrowed from the MMPI), a worthwhile addition if the inventory is to be used for screening or selection purposes where subjects might be inclined to "fake good." For experimental work the "lie" scale is usually superfluous, however. The reliability of the EPI scales is slightly higher than for the MPI and the normative data for the English population are quite adequate. American users will have to develop their own norms until such data become available. For experimental use with college subjects the EPI does not seem to offer many substantial advantages over the MPI (unless one insists on eliminating the slight correlation between N and E or wishes to do a retest on an equivalent form) and it has the slight disadvantage of being more time consuming, since it contains 9 more items than the MPI. Further research should make possible more valid and detailed comparisons between the MPI and EPI. Potential users should, of course, examine specimen sets of both the MPI and the EPI to decide which inventory might best suit their purposes in terms of the available norms, etc.

James C. Lingoes, *Associate Professor of Psychology, The University of Michigan, Ann Arbor, Michigan.*

The *Maudsley Personality Inventory* (MPI) is a theoretically based instrument designed to measure the two rather pervasive and relatively independent personality dimensions of extraversion-introversion (E) and neuroticism-stability (N) found by Eysenck and others in

a large number of factor analytic studies. The 24 items for each trait were selected on the basis of both item and factor analyses as being the purest questionnaire measures to date of Eysenck's factors.

The MPI is an easily administered, quick, reliable, and fairly simply scored test. With the following exceptions, the manual to the United States edition is commendably successful in meeting the various criteria of technical excellence stipulated in the APA Technical Recommendations. Some minor criticisms of the manual are: (*a*) that the professional qualifications necessary to administer and interpret the test are omitted, and (*b*) that false-positive and false-negative rates are missing in the discussion of validity by nominated groups. Significant mean differences are insufficient to assess properly the value of such studies. More serious deficiencies in the manual are: (*a*) the omission of tables of item intercorrelations and factor loadings as well as other item statistics, essential ingredients for factor based scales; and (*b*) the very inadequate delineation of the N factor as a descriptive or clinical concept to aid the user interpretatively in the individual case, one of the important recommended uses of this test. The user should satisfy himself on the above points by referring to the relevant literature listed in the 112-item bibliography of the manual.

Of more crucial concern to the prospective user are the following observations regarding the test itself and its relationships with other tests purporting to measure the same traits or factors.

First, the MPI is not a general personality test, even though the traits it assesses account for most of the variance in personality inventories. One should not confuse statistical significance with clinical importance, as Eysenck himself would acknowledge. Consequently, if one is looking for a more complete personality profile on a subject, other tests would be more pertinent, e.g., the *Guilford-Zimmerman Temperament Survey* or Cattell's 16PF, being logical choices among factor based tests, or the MMPI, being the best among clinical personality instruments. As a clinical tool the MPI would serve best in an ancillary role, supplementing data from other tests. A two-dimensional approach to personality is insufficient to encompass all the functions and purposes typical of the average clinical setting, no matter how pervasive or important the factors may be.

Second, it has not been established that even for the traits that the MPI measures, it measures them better than comparable instruments. It should be noted that E is only one of several kinds of extraversion, i.e., social, and a number of studies reported in the manual indicate that this trait is measured at least as well by other tests as it is by the MPI if one takes the internal consistency data as a yardstick. Thus, E correlates to the extent of .81 with social extraversion from the *Minnesota T-S-E Inventory* and −.80 with Heron's introversion scale. These validity coefficients lie within the range of Kuder-Richardson and split-half reliability coefficients for E, i.e., between .75 and .85 with the majority above .80, and they are certainly higher than the equivalent forms coefficients (.75) reported for the *Eysenck Personality Inventory*. Furthermore, based upon the original sample of 400 cases used in the item analysis of the MPI, E correlated .79 with the rhathymia scale of the *Inventory of Factors STDCR* and N correlated .92 with the cycloid disposition scale, the latter coefficient being *higher* than the split-half or K-R reliability coefficients reported for N.

Admittedly, other factors must be considered in a consumer's decision to use one test as opposed to others, e.g., cost, ease of administration, ease of distortion or deception, professional time spent in interpretation, the purposes to be served by testing, readability of the items, appeal to the examinees, etc., and while some of the foregoing would favor the MPI, comprehensiveness may well determine the choice in the final analysis given equally good data on reliability and validity.

In conclusion, the present evidence on the MPI would suggest that there was little reason to omit in the American manual the caution expressed in the original British manual, i.e., "In all its applications, the M.P.I. should primarily be regarded as a *research instrument.*" Within Eysenck's theoretical system, the MPI and its revision, the *Eysenck Personality Inventory,* may well indeed be the tests of choice, but more evidence is needed on superior reliability and validity to warrant their supplanting other comparable and better established tests.

WILLIAM STEPHENSON, *Professor of Psychology, University of Missouri, Columbia, Missouri.*

The MPI is excellently produced. The American manual is especially informative and comprehensive, listing 112 references up to the end of 1962. The American norms are for 1,064 university and college students. Validation is with respect to *mean differences* for groups of subjects (sample sizes range from as few as 8 to as many as 1,800 and total some 7,200) variously described as Australian prisoners, psychopaths, industrial apprentices, psychosomatics, hysterics, English normals, recidivist prisoners, neurotics, dysthymics, etc., mostly in Britain.

It would not be difficult, in the present reviewer's judgment, to find other compilations of personality statements which, when subjected to such gross validation procedures, would fare no better or no worse than the set of 48 put together for the MPI. It is possible that they may be useful in experimental studies using samples of the order 100 to 1,000 persons. What is not so certain is the credibility of the data the test provides. The public is warned in this respect. But there is an issue which, it seems to the reviewer, requires consideration as psychology grows professionally After a very careful review of Eysenck's major work,[1] Storms and Sigal (9) have to conclude that the attributes of extraverts and introverts listed by Eysenck in certain studies have not, in fact, been unequivocally demonstrated. Doubt was raised about the validation of the E continuum.

The reviewer would raise again the improbability that a scale based on R-methodological grounds can ever really indicate dynamic conditions such as Eysenck has persistently proposed to examine. Davis,[2] for example, reminded us, and Eysenck in particular, that following a traumatic situation immediate reactions to the situation were apt to be ones of overactivity, or of psychological withdrawal; subsequently, recovery from the shock was attended by preoccupation and fixation of memories, with the establishment of defenses, with the abandonment of defenses, and with a phase of working through the memories.

1 EYSENCK, H. J. *The Dynamics of Anxiety and Hysteria: An Experimental Application of Modern Learning Theory to Psychiatry.* London: Routledge & Kegan Paul Ltd., 1957. Pp. xiv, 311. *
2 DAVIS, D. RUSSELL. "Clinical Problems and Experimental Researches." *Brit J Med Psychol* 31:74–82 pt 2 '58. *

These, it seems to the reviewer, are typical of human reactions: to imagine for a moment that either E or N in general have anything to contribute to such a flow of phenomena seems to the reviewer to be clutching at feathers in the wind. Moreover, there is a simple way to show that dynamic factors can in fact be brought to light, using Eysenck's 48 statements but in the form of a Q-sample so that each person can use the statements relative to one another to display fixations, defenses, etc. The E and N scales never do anything of the kind because they are by definition measurements of behavior *in a general context*. The proof of the matter, that at least one factor common to Q couldn't possibly appear in data derived from R (and vice versa), is there for Eysenck to note. It is astonishing that so diligent a worker has not looked to see what that one factor, at least, could mean for his studies.

PHILIP E. VERNON, *Professor of Educational Psychology, Institute of Education, University of London, London, England.*

Despite the enormous number of available personality inventories, Eysenck's test could well meet a need for a short, simple instrument for use in mental hospitals, in student counseling, and in a variety of experimental researches where it is desired to control major personality differences among the subjects. Only 48 items are included, selected on a factorial basis to give highly saturated measures of extraversion-introversion and neuroticism-stability or anxiety. Reasonable Kuder-Richardson and repeat reliability coefficients ranging from .75 to .85 for Extraversion and from .85 to .90 for Neuroticism are obtained in 10–15 minutes' testing time, and the two scores are virtually uncorrelated except in certain selected groups. The scoring of the American edition can be done by punched card or, in less than a minute per blank, by stencils; the British edition is scored by transparent stencil.

Since his first book in 1947, Eysenck has stressed the pervasiveness of these two personality factors, and in *The Structure of Human Personality* (*36*) he makes a strong case for reducing most of the manifold factors that have been claimed in questionnaire data, ratings, and objective personality tests, to these same dimensions. Much as Spearman, Burt, and the present writer prefer to cover as much variance as possible in abilities by means of *g*

and major group factors, and to regard Thurstone's, Guilford's, and other multiple factors as minor subdivisions—so Eysenck considers personality as hierarchically organized, with these two factors as the most inclusive. Moreover, during the ensuing 16 years, he has linked these with a nomological network based on Hullian learning theory, and collected a considerable amount of experimental evidence to support his theoretical deductions covering extraversion and neuroticism, albeit many of these theories and experimental results are open to dispute. He can reasonably claim, therefore, that scores on this inventory possess a good deal of construct validity derived from positive experimental findings in the field of conditioning and the effects of drugs, from factor loadings, from differentiation between such pathological groups as psychopaths and dysthymic neurotics on the one hand and neurotics and normals on the other, and from correlations with other well known tests of related constructs.

Some comment is called for on the extraversion measure. In many of his writings Eysenck has criticized the American conception of extraversion as consisting largely of sociability, and the consequent tendency for extraversion tests to give rather high negative correlations with neuroticism or emotional instability. He favours, rather, Guilford's notion of rhathymia, or uninhibited carefreeness, as being orthogonal to neuroticism and closer to Jung's original description. However, the definition in the manuals of the present test, together with many of the test items, clearly involves the social aspect of extraversion; the highest correlation of the extraversion scale with another test is .81 with the social introversion–extraversion scale of the *Minnesota T-S-E Inventory*. Indeed the fairly good reliability for so short a scale may be largely due to the reiteration of questions about social mixing. The content of the neuroticism items is, however, more varied.

In the American manual, percentile norms for American college students (one college only) and tables of group means and standard deviations are given. The latter reveal interesting differences. Thus on Extraversion, psychopaths average 31 (out of a possible 48), American women students 29, English students and normal adults around 25, hysterics 24, and dysthymics and neurotics 19. On Neuroticism, the means of psychopaths and neurotics mostly fall in the 32–38 range, English students 23–27, American students 20–21, and English normal population 18–20. Negligible relations are reported with sex, social class, and intelligence, except that men are slightly more extraverted than women and women are slightly more neurotic than men. Among English college students both introversion and neuroticism correlate appreciably with academic achievement. One would have thought that this could be more simply explained in terms of the weaker gregarious interests and greater introspectiveness of the serious student than by means of learning theory constructs.

Responses indicative of extraversion may be either Yes or No, but all neurotic responses are Yes. The author of the American manual draws attention to the possibility of acquiescent response set affecting the latter, but dismisses it. No mention is made of the effects of social desirability. The American manual is well designed, with due attention to the APA Committee's suggestions. But the manual to the original British edition, published in 1959, is much more brief and should be brought up to date.

In general the test should be of some use in educational guidance and personality counseling as a quickly obtained index of two important personality trends. It could be given in mental hospitals by nurses as a preliminary aid in psychological assessment, or included in a battery of tests for surveying a population, for example, in market research or, as already indicated, in experimental researches with normal adult subjects.

Brit J Psychol 51:185–6 My '60. A. Bursill. [Review of the British manual.] This Manual reports up-to-date information available on this Yes, No, ?-type questionnaire (*MPI*) comprising two scales of 24 items each, one purporting to measure neuroticism (*N*), the other introversion-extraversion (*I-E*). * The scales can be conveniently adapted to form an even shorter questionnaire (*SMPI*) comprising six items each for *N* and *I-E,* simply by utilizing the first page of the printed form only. * The two scales *N* and *I-E* intended to be orthogonal, have a low correlation (−0.15 for the *MPI,* and −0.05 for the *SMPI*) for normal samples —the correlation increases to the rather unsatisfactory dimension of −0.3 to −0.4 in neurotic groups. Eysenck assigns these anomalies

to the non-linearity of the regression lines. The argument is supplemented by a graph of regression lines for 1,200 normal subjects which does not show a serious state of affairs except *I*-scores below about 10. But the explanation as it stands is hardly sufficient to give rise to such large negative correlations between *N* and *I-E* in neurotic groups, whose mean scores lie well within the distributions given for the whole range of the population. This needs investigating in more detail. Meanwhile, when attempting to assess the effects of varying degrees of extraversion in any experiment, Eysenck suggests matching criterion groups of *I* and *E* for *N.* A table containing the size of samples, mean scores and S.D.'s for the different standardization groups is given—but the reader is left to work out the significance of the differences. Unfortunately, the original sources of much of the data are omitted, or are still not available, so that the procedures whereby subjects were selected cannot be ascertained in detail. Two methods of validation are presented: (i) comparison of the standardization groups on *N* and *I-E;* (ii) construct validity—i.e. a set of interlocking predictions forming a theory confirmed by experiment. In a strict sense, neither method can yet be said to have reached satisfactory standards in empirical confirmation. * unusual answers to some two to three items are sufficient to place an individual amongst the most extreme group of dysthymics on *I,* whereas some ten unusual answers are required to place an individual amongst dysthymics on *N.* At the very least there is some reason for attempting—in subsequent versions of the test—to stretch the *I-E* dimension somewhat. But the reviewer is not certain whether the data cannot be taken as undermining one of Eysenck's basic tenets, which is not merely that hysterics are more extraverted than dysthymics but that they are also more extraverted than normals. In view of Hildebrand's similar findings with objective tests (*Brit. J. Psychol.* 1958, 49, 1–11), there is an increasing likelihood that the position of these various abnormal groups is a true feature of this *I-E* dimension, and not some distortion in its scale units—particularly at the *E* end. In fact, Eysenck hints at this situation in the Manual and elsewhere, without explicitly recognizing that it contravenes his and Jung's theoretical position. A factor to be taken into consideration, however, is that presumably this scale measures sociability rather than the other facets of extraversion emphasized by Jung— since *I-E* correlates highly with the "social" scale and lowly with the "thinking" and "emotional" scale of the Minnesota *TSE*. Another feature worth noting is the limited range of items, many of which closely overlap in content. There might here be a tendency to sacrifice validity for reliability. Possibly a source of distortion on the *N*-scale, on the other hand, resides in the fact that in all items neurotic responses are scored in the affirmative (yes). Space does not permit an appraisal of Eysenck's attempt to demonstrate "construct validity" in his *Dynamics of Anxiety and Hysteria,* as claimed in the Manual. However worthy this attempt was, there has been a growing tide of criticism (e.g. by Storms and Sigal, Vernon Hamilton, D. E. Broadbent, R. L. Reid, Taylor and Rechtsscaffer, Spivac and Levine) of the evidence presented for the various components of the theory in this monograph. Eysenck's adroit defences do not altogether dispel these criticisms. Consequently, the reader may have to exercise caution in accepting the construct validity as indeed valid. Generally, Prof. Eysenck is to be congratulated on obtaining such an unusual amount of data on one personality test. It is to be hoped that a more detailed Manual will soon make its appearance; some of the original work is published in rather inaccessible foreign journals. * There is the danger that subjects selected on an *N* and *I-E* basis alone will unduly bias and filter the human material and cause much of importance to the clinician to be omitted. *

J Consult Psychol 23:563 D '59. Edward S. Bordin. [Review of the British Edition.] This brief questionnaire of 48 items and its even briefer short form (12 items) have played an integral part in the author's well known research on personality. Many instruments have been launched for full scale use with much less behind them. The manual represents the height of English diffidence. Only the briefest summary is given of a few of the salient results of research and the reader is referred to the relevant publications. He is told that "the M.P.I. should be regarded as a *research instrument.* Different firms, organizations, hospitals, universities, and other bodies have different problems, deal with different samples of the population, and aim at different solutions of their problems. Only applied research

can determine whether instruments such as the M.P.I. can be successfully used by them, and just what form such use can best take." No high powered American merchandising here!

J Psychosom Res 5:66 S '60. G. A. Foulds. [Review of the British Edition.] * The standardization data call for some comment. Neurotics were diagnosed by experienced psychiatrists, or else had their case-papers carefully scrutinized by three experienced clinical psychologists, who arrived at a unanimous diagnosis independently. In his reply (*J. abnorm. soc. Psychol.* 1958, 57, 2) to the paper by Sigal, Starr and Franks (*ibid*) Eysenck rather deplores the latter method. It is unfortunate that their somewhat conflicting results were not available for the Manual, since the claim that "successive samples from different hospitals showed great stability in means and variances" might have required some modification. Eysenck believes that the results obtained on the M.P.I. "in a sense....serve as validation of the scales." This, unfortunately, can only be in an illogical sense. It is not possible to validate the theory and the inventory at the same time. It would be palpably absurd to claim—and certainly Jung did not— that Hysteria and Extraversion are one and the same thing. What Jung said, in effect, was most neurotic extraverts have the characteristics of Hysteria; most neurotic introverts have the characteristics of Dysthymia. A demonstration of differences between Hysteria and Dysthymia does not necessarily tell us anything at all about extraversion:introversion. The differences in the particular instance may be due to quite other characteristics. The M.P.I. has, of course, considerable face-validity for at least some aspects, particularly social, of that elusive concept extraversion. It is doubtful whether reliance on "construct validity" is of any value when there is a large logical hole in the nomological network. In respect of the extraversion:introversion continuum, the position of the recidivist prisoners and the psychosomatic cases is close to the hysterics, a finding which to Eysenck is not unexpected. The reviewer would have expected recidivist prisoners to be closer to hospital psychopaths than to hysterics. With regard to the psychosomatic group, at least one large sub-group consists of people whose intense affective disturbance has resulted in physiological changes such as are rare in hysteria. If Stanley Cobb's two broad categories are correct, one might expect to find the psycho-somatics somewhere between hysterics and dysthymics with a standard deviation larger than either. The Neuroticism scale seems to be of much more certain value.

[139]

★Maxfield-Buchholz Scale of Social Maturity for Use With Preschool Blind Children. Infancy–6 years; 1958; revision of *Maxfield-Fjeld Adaptation of the Vineland Social Maturity Scale;* manual title is *A Social Maturity Scale for Blind Preschool Children;* individual; 1 form ['58]; manual ['58, 46 pages]; record form ['58, 7 pages]; no data on reliability; 75¢ per manual; 10¢ per record form; postpaid; Kathryn E. Maxfield and Sandra Buchholz; American Foundation for the Blind, Inc. *

REFERENCES

1. NORRIS, MIRIAM; SPAULDING, PATRICIA J.; AND BRODIE, FERN H. *Blindness in Children.* Chicago, Ill.: University of Chicago Press, 1957. Pp. xv, 173. * (*PA* 32:824)
2. MAXFIELD, KATHRYN E., AND BUCHHOLZ, SANDRA. *A Social Maturity Scale for Blind Children: A Guide to Its Use.* New York: American Foundation for the Blind, Inc., [1958]. Pp. iv, 43. *

[140]

*Memory-For-Designs Test. Ages 8.5 and over; 1946–60; brain damage; individual; 1 form ('60, 15 cards, identical with cards distributed by the authors in 1946); revised manual ('60, 43 pages, reprinted from *12* below); norms-scoring examples booklet (12 pages, reprinted from manual); $8.50 per set of test materials including manual; $2.50 per manual; cash orders postpaid; (5–10) minutes; Frances K. Graham and Barbara S. Kendall; Psychological Test Specialists. *

REFERENCES

1–5. See 4:69.
6. ARMSTRONG, RENATE GERBOTH. "The Consistency of Longitudinal Performance on the Graham-Kendall Memory-for-Designs Test." *J Clin Psychol* 8:411–2 O '52. * (*PA* 27:6017)
7. HUNT, HOWARD F. Chap. 7, "Testing for Psychological Deficit," pp. 91–107. In *Progress in Clinical Psychology,* Vol. 1. Edited by Daniel Brower and Lawrence E. Abt. New York: Grune & Stratton, Inc., 1952. Pp. xi, 328. * (*PA* 27:3529)
8. RAPPAPORT, SHELDON R. "Intellectual Deficit in Organics and Schizophrenics." *J Consult Psychol* 17:389–95 O '53. * (*PA* 28:6365)
9. HOWARD, ALVIN R., AND SHOEMAKER, DONALD J. "An Evaluation of the Memory-for-Designs Test." Abstract. *J Consult Psychol* 18:266 Ag '54. * (*PA* 29:4063, title only)
10. GARRETT, EPHRAIM S.; PRICE, A. COOPER; AND DEABLER, HERDIS L. "Diagnostic Testing for Cortical Brain Impairment." *A.M.A. Arch Neurol & Psychiatry* 77:223–5 F '57. * (*PA* 32:1926)
11. BURDUS, J. A., AND GILLILAND, J. "Memory for Designs Test." *Psychometric Res B* (4):[21–3] Ag '59. *
12. GRAHAM, FRANCES K., AND KENDALL, BARBARA S. "Memory-for-Designs Test: Revised General Manual." *Percept & Motor Skills* 11:147–88 O '60. * (*PA* 35:2185)
13. HOVEY, H. BIRNET. "An Analysis of Figure Rotations." *J Consult Psychol* 25:21–3 F '61. * (*PA* 36:3HI21H)
14. WALTERS, C. ETTA. "Reading Ability and Visual-Motor Function in Second Grade Children." *Percept & Motor Skills* 13:370 D '61. *
15. FLYNN, PAUL SPENCER. Correlation of Form Memory and Academic Achievement at the Fifth Grade Level. Doctor's thesis, University of Virginia (Charlottesville, Va.), 1962. (*DA* 23:4222)
16. KENDALL, BARBARA S. "Memory-for-Designs Performance in the Seventh and Eighth Decades of Life." *Percept & Motor Skills* 14:399–405 Je '62. * (*PA* 37:2954)
17. LETON, DONALD A. "Visual-Motor Capacities and Ocular Efficiency in Reading." *Percept & Motor Skills* 15:407–32 O '62. * (*PA* 37:8253)
18. TAYLOR, FREDERICK RICHARD. Two New Psychological Tests for Diagnosing Organic Brain Damage. Doctor's thesis, University of Utah (Salt Lake City, Utah), 1962. (*DA* 22:4414)
19. BRILLIANT, PATRICIA J., AND GYNTHER, MALCOLM D. "Relationships Between Performance on Three Tests for Organicity and Selected Patient Variables." *J Consult Psychol* 27:474–9 D '63. * (*PA* 38:8404)
20. CRADDICK, RAY A., AND STERN, MICHAEL R. "Effect of Pre- and Post-Stress Upon Height of Drawings in a Perceptual-Motor Task." *Percept & Motor Skills* 17:283–5 Ag '63. * (*PA* 38:7219)
21. FRIEDMAN, ELLEN C., AND BARCLAY, ALLAN. "The Discriminative Validity of Certain Psychological Tests as Indices of Brain Damage in the Mentally Retarded." *Mental Retardation* 1:291–3 O '63. * (*PA* 38:8935)
22. KORMAN, MAURICE, AND BLUMBERG, STANLEY. "Comparative Efficiency of Some Tests of Cerebral Damage." *J Consult Psychol* 27:303–9 Ag '63. * (*PA* 38:2985)
23. TORTORELLA, WILLIAM M. A Study of the Performance of Normal Children and Feebleminded Adults of Similar Mental Ages on the Graham-Kendall Memory-for-Designs Test. Master's thesis, Fordham University (New York, N.Y.), 1963.

OTFRIED SPREEN, *Assistant Research Professor of Neurology, State University of Iowa, Iowa City, Iowa.*

In this immediate memory test the subject is required to draw each of 15 geometric designs after it has been shown for five seconds. The test is comparable to other visual memory tests, such as the drawing of figures in the *Wechsler Memory Scale* and the *Benton Visual Retention Test,* and supplements such nonvisual memory tests as the digit span, sentence repetition, and similar techniques, all of which have been shown to be sensitive to brain pathology.

Since its first publication in 1946, the MFD has been considerably refined in scoring technique and a sizable amount of data has been published. The correlation with age and intelligence to be expected in a test of this kind has been accounted for by the presentation of expected score tables for adults and children (age range 8-6 to 60 years) although one subsequent study (*22*) claimed that such a correction was unnecessary for their groups, and another (*19*) found a significant age correlation even after their data had been adjusted on the basis of the expected score tables. Adequate scoring samples are provided in the new manual. An attempt has been made to add a copying of designs administration to the test, but the difficulty level of the test items was found too low for such a procedure.

The original validation was supplemented by two cross validation samples of brain damaged patients and controls (including neurotics and psychotics). With a cutoff point set at a level which would give 4 per cent false positives in the control groups, the correct identification of brain damaged patients varied between 42 and 50 per cent. It should be noted that in these validation studies diagnostic criteria were relatively strict so that a higher proportion of severely brain damaged patients was likely to be included in the brain damaged group. Five other studies (7, 9, 10, 19, 22) report correct classifications of 63, 67.5, 43, 57.1, and 90 per cent of their brain damaged patients, respectively. It appears that the validity demonstrated in these studies varies widely with the type of sample used and the group discrimination which was attempted. It should be noted, that in two studies reporting high true-positives (7, 10) the brain damaged group included subjects who were considerably older (age ranging up to 84 years) than their normal controls. Whereas all other studies used the "conservative" cutoff point suggested by the test authors, Korman and Blumberg (22) use an "optimal" cutting score for their groups with 10 per cent misclassification of non-organics; with Graham and Kendall's cutoff point their hit-rate would have dropped to 32.5 per cent.

Immediate retest reliabilities are reported in the range of .72 to .90. Retesting after 10-day intervals indicated that patients with cortical damage show a higher practice effect than schizophrenics (6).

Several special problems have been investigated. Psychotics and neurotics without evidence of mental deterioration achieve scores in the normal range as reported by the test authors. It appears that some independence of test performance from acute motivational and emotional disorders has been established although such independence could not be demonstrated for "chronic psychotic" and "chronic organic psychotic" groups (6, 9). Ideopathic epileptics with psychosis and without evidence of brain damage were found to have scores which did not differ significantly from normal groups. Attempts to relate test performance to locus of lesion have so far been unsuccessful. Korman and Blumberg (22) report that patients with bilateral brain lesions tend to have higher scores than patients with either right or left hemisphere damage.

An investigation of old subjects (16) showed that the mild linear increase of test scores with age turns into a more geometric increase after the age of 60; adjusted scoring tables have not been published so far. Whereas an older study (3) did not find a relation between MFD scores and reading ability, more recently (14) reading retardation in second grade children was shown to be strongly related. Hovey (13) found a highly significant incidence of rotations in a group of brain damaged subjects with evidence

of episodic EEG disturbances as compared to those with general EEG abnormalities only. In addition to rotations, several other qualitative features of performance are reported in the manual to be significantly higher in brain damaged as compared to controls; the presented figures are, however, hard to interpret since no adjustment has been made for the overall difference in error score between the two groups. In the general scoring of the test, qualitative features are not routinely evaluated.

The present scoring system as a rule allows two errors in the reproduction of a design without penalty, although rotations are somewhat more heavily penalized. It would seem that this lenient scoring unduly lowers the ceiling of the test and makes it too easy for a considerable proportion of subjects. Considering the results of the validation studies, the information contained in the first two errors on a given design could be utilized to improve the validity of the test as well as to gain information on particular types of errors, some of which have been shown to have considerable diagnostic validity.

Three comparative studies of the MFD and other tests for organicity are available. One study (19) found the predictive validity of all three tests investigated (Bender-Gestalt Test, Benton Visual Retention Test, MFD) significant at the .001 level in a comparison of severely brain damaged subjects with psychotic, psychopathic, and neurotic groups. A second study (22) found the discriminative power of the MFD to rank before the Spiral Aftereffect Test, the Trail Making Test, and the Bender-Gestalt Test in a comparison of matched groups of severely brain damaged and psychotic, neurotic, psychopathic, and normal subjects. The third study [1] compared the Bender-Gestalt, the Visual Retention Test, the Wechsler Block Design, and the MFD in matched groups of mildly brain damaged and normal hospitalized patients and found the MFD to have the poorest discriminative power with a contribution of the MFD in a multiple validity formula not significantly different from zero. It appears from these studies that the value of the MFD in the diagnosis of severely brain damaged cases is more clearly established than in the mildly im-

[1] KEREKJARTO, M. V. "Untersuchung über die Diskriminierungskraft dreier Tests zur Erfassung zerebraler Schäden," pp. 186–7. In Bericht ueber den 23 Kongress der Deutschen Gesellschaft fuer Psychologie. Edited by G. Lienert. Göttingen: Hogrefe, 1962.

paired patient. The suggested improvement in scoring may recover the predictive value of the MFD for this diagnostically important group. A reevaluation of the necessity for age corrections and the possible refinement of the scoring of qualitative errors in relation to locus of lesion may further increase the usefulness of this valuable instrument.

[141]

*Mental Health Analysis, 1959 Revision. Grades 4–8, 7–9, 9–16, adults; 1946–59; 13 scores: close personal relationships, inter-personal skills, social participation, satisfying work and recreation, adequate outlook and goals, total assets, behavioral immaturity, emotional instability, feelings of inadequacy, physical defects, nervous manifestations, total liabilities, total; IBM; 1 form ('59, 11 pages, identical with 1946 form except for format and wording changes); 4 levels; manual ('59, 24 pages); $3.15 per 35 tests; separate answer sheets may be used; 5¢ per IBM answer sheet; 40¢ per set of either hand or machine scoring stencils; postage extra; 50¢ per specimen set of any one level, postpaid; (45–50) minutes; Louis P. Thorpe and Willis W. Clark; California Test Bureau. *

REFERENCES

1. BLEDSOE, JOSEPH C. "Sex Differences in Mental Health Analysis Scores of Elementary Pupils." J Consult Psychol 25:364–5 Ag '61. * (PA 37:876)
2. CLARKE, H. HARRISON, AND CLARKE, DAVID H. "Social Status and Mental Health of Boys as Related to Their Maturity, Structural, and Strength Characteristics." Res Q 32: 326–34 O '61. *
3. GUINOUARD, DONALD EDGAR. Personality Traits and Mental Health Habits of Sociometrically Popular and Unpopular Sixth and Eighth Grade Students. Doctor's thesis, Washington State University (Pullman, Wash.), 1961. (DA 22:1085)
4. BUCKALEW, ROBERT J. An Investigation of the Interrelationships Among Measures of Interests, Intelligence, and Personality for a Sample of One Hundred Sixty-Two Eighth Grade Boys. Doctor's thesis, Temple University (Philadelphia, Pa.), 1962. (DA 23:3232)
5. McGREEVEY, JAMES C. "Interlevel Disparity and Predictive Efficiency." J Proj Tech 26:80–7 Mr '62. * (PA 37: 3152)
6. WARNER, BERNARD E. "Relationships Between Health and Socio-Moral Behavior Pertinent to Health Guidance." J Sch Health 32:368–71 N '62. *
7. BLEDSOE, JOSEPH C. "The Relation of Mental Health Analysis Scores to Teacher Ratings of Mental Health Status of Elementary Pupils." J Ed Res 56:488–91 My–Je '63. *
8. NICKOLS, JOHN E., JR. "Changes in Self-Awareness During the High School Years: A Study of Mental Health Using Paper-and-Pencil Tests." J Ed Res 56:403–9 Ap '63. * (PA 38:9222)

J. ROBERT WILLIAMS, Director, Child Study Clinic, and School Psychologist, Public Schools, Kankakee, Illinois.

This revision of the Mental Health Analysis (MHA) involves no basic change in purpose or procedure. The instrument is again offered as a means of providing a picture of mental health status, analyzed broadly in terms of the categories of "assets" and "liabilities" and further defined by 5 "components" within each category. As before, 200 questions make up the MHA, with 20 questions keyed to each component and "designed to sample the individual's adjustment" in the areas designated. By use of percentile norms the 10 component, 2 subtotal,

and total scores can be translated into a profile. In the 1959 revision the categories have been transposed to promote a more positive approach to the use of the results. As a consequence, mental health is conceived to be "a combination of freedom from liabilities and the possession of assets."

The authors appear to have been only partially successful in eliminating the main shortcomings listed in the reviews of the 1946 version. Reliability results are now provided for each component score as well as for the assets, liabilities, and total scores. However, the two sets of results are not altogether comparable. Both standard errors of measurement and reliability coefficients are given for the assets, liabilities, and total scores, the coefficients having been computed by Kuder-Richardson formula 21. Only coefficients of reliability are given for component scores and are "expressed as the estimated correlation between a subject's 'obtained score' and his 'true score'....where the component scores are reported in the five percentile intervals drawn on the profile." The coefficients listed for the categories range from .87 to .93 and those for the components from .79 to .87.

The reviews of the former version reported a lack of validity, some being especially critical of the way fundamental problems of validity had been lightly regarded. In the manual of the revision the authors have at least approached these issues with more system and thoroughness, even though the reported results are not yet convincing. The new manual treats both content and concurrent validity. Under content validity the relevance, discriminatory capacity, and disguised nature of the items are discussed. As to relevance, the reader is given little specific information about procedures used to determine the item pool. Generally complete and accurate information is presented to show the discriminating power of items, but the prospective user likely would have welcomed a simpler explanation in addition to the "phi coefficient" value which was used. In spite of the reported attempts to "minimize the inaccuracy of self-judgments" by framing questions in "indirect" form, an examination of the items reveals several questions not so framed.

Five studies are given lengthy treatment as the main basis for evaluating concurrent validity. None of these are recent, although all have occurred since the first publication. Generally, they have to do with comparison of the MHA scores of two oppositely characterized groups—"normal" and "delinquent," "accepted" and "rejected," "successful" and "unsuccessful"—determined in advance by conventional criteria. The reported results of these studies are highly favorable on test-of-significance grounds. However, the adequacy of the criterion in each case remains in doubt, since no data on its reliability are given. Even if reliability is assumed, the nature of validity furnished by such studies is "retrospective" rather than "predictive." The case for validity would be greatly strengthened if individual classifications, predicted on the basis of MHA scores, could then be shown to be significantly related to reliable, independent criteria of such groups.

The question of relationships among categories, components, and total scores has been answered, but only for 100 cases at the adult level. The data show all intercorrelations among the scores to be positive. The r's between components within each category are somewhat larger than those between components of different categories, as one would expect.

Despite some limitations of a fundamental nature, the reviewer is of the opinion that the revised MHA is a definite improvement over the original. The practical considerations related to the everyday use of the analysis appear to have been raised considerably by the refinements. The new manual (combining all 4 levels) simplifies administration, scoring, and some aspects of interpretation. The "completely re-designed" profile sheet facilitates both the determination and location of individual strengths and weaknesses. There is at least a fair amount of logical and consistent material to serve as a guide in interpretation. Claims for the test's diagnostic power are modest, since the manual clearly states that it is "offered as an aid" and that it "does not provide a diagnosis-in-depth of adjustment problems." Justifiable caution has been given for the inexperienced or unwary user.

Confined to the role of a *screening* device or used as a means of getting a *first approximation* to an individual's adjustment in the areas covered, the MHA would seem to be of some usefulness. The specific nature of the questions should aid in giving clues to the direction of further diagnostic work and to a suitable starting point for counseling interviews.

If there were two forms and less overlap of meanings among components, its worth would be considerably enhanced. In this respect it is inferior to the factor-based questionnaires of Cattell and associates (CPQ, HSPQ, and 16 PF) covering somewhat the same age levels.

For reviews by William E. Coffman, Henry E. Garrett, C. M. Louttit, James Maxwell, and Douglas Spencer of the original edition, see 3:59 (1 excerpt).

[142]

Minnesota Counseling Inventory. High school; 1953–57; based on *Minnesota Multiphasic Personality Inventory* and *Minnesota Personality Scale;* 9 scores: family relationships, social relationships, emotional stability, conformity, adjustment to reality, mood, leadership, validity, question; IBM; 1 form ('53, 10 pages); profile ('57, 2 pages); manual ('57, 27 pages); no data on reliability of question score; separate answer sheets must be used; $3.50 per 25 tests; $3.75 per 50 IBM answer sheets; 60¢ per set of hand scoring stencils and manual; 90¢ per set of machine scoring stencils and manual; 75¢ per specimen set; postpaid; (50) minutes; Ralph F. Berdie and Wilbur L. Layton; Psychological Corporation. *

REFERENCES

1. DIMMICK, KENNETH D. *An Exploratory Study of the Minnesota Counseling Inventory as an Index of Oral Communication Ability.* Master's thesis, Ohio University (Athens, Ohio), 1957.
2. BROWN, FREDERICK GRAMM. *Measured Personality Characteristics of Liberal Arts College Freshmen.* Doctor's thesis, University of Minnesota (Minneapolis, Minn.), 1958. (*DA* 19:3009)
3. WHITE, ROBERT MARSHALL. *The Predictive Relationship of Selected Variables to the Vocational Interest Stability of High School Students.* Doctor's thesis, University of Minnesota (Minneapolis, Minn.), 1958. (*DA* 19:2141)
4. BERDIE, RALPH F., AND LAYTON, WILBUR L. "Research on the Minnesota Counseling Inventory." *J Counsel Psychol* 7:218–24 f '60. * (*PA* 36:1HC18B)
5. BROWN, FREDERICK G. "Identifying College Dropouts With the Minnesota Counseling Inventory." *Personnel & Guid J* 39:280–2 D '60. * (*PA* 35:3923)
6. BROWN, FREDERICK G. "The Validity of the Minnesota Counseling Inventory in a College Population." *J Appl Psychol* 44:132–6 Ap '60. * (*PA* 35:3449)
7. CANTY, JAMES J., JR. *Use of the Minnesota Counseling Inventory in Identifying Male Adolescent "Nonconformists."* Master's thesis, Fordham University (New York, N.Y.), 1962.
8. FALLON, JUSTIN M. *An Adaptation of the Minnesota Counseling Inventory for Use With Religious Counseling.* Master's thesis, De Paul University (Chicago, Ill.), 1962.
9. LETON, DONALD A., AND WALTER, SIDNEY. "A Factor Analysis of the California Psychological Inventory and Minnesota Counseling Inventory." *Calif J Ed Res* 13:126–33 My '62. * (*PA* 37:3446)
10. KJELDERGAARD, PAUL M., AND CARROLL, JOHN B. "Two Measures of Free Association Response and Their Relations to Scores on Selected Personality and Verbal Ability Tests." *Psychol Rep* 12:667–70 Je '63. * (*PA* 38:6021)

NORMAN FREDERIKSEN, *Director of Research, Educational Testing Service, Princeton, New Jersey.*

The *Minnesota Counseling Inventory* is intended for use in counseling high school students. It consists of 355 statements that are to be answered true or false and was constructed by selecting scales and revising items from two earlier inventories, the *Minnesota Personality Scale* and the *Minnesota Multiphasic Person-*

ality Inventory. The editing was intended to make the items more readable by high school students and acceptable to teachers and parents.

The inventory yields nine scores, one of which is merely the number of items omitted (the Question score). Three scales, Social Relationships, Family Relationships, and Emotional Stability, were derived from the *Minnesota Personality Scale* and are supposed to identify "areas in which students may be adjusting particularly well or poorly." Four scales from the MMPI, Conformity, Adjustment to Reality, Mood, and Leadership, are said to provide information about "methods students employ in making adjustments." The MMPI scales from which they were derived are, respectively, Psychopathic Deviate, Schizophrenia, Depression, and Social Introversion. A fifth MMPI-derived scale is the Validity scale, which comes from the Lie scale.

The number of items contributing to each score varies from 14 for the Validity scale to 61 for Social Relationships. Next to the Validity scale, the smallest number of items is 35. There is a small amount of item overlap, the greatest involving six items common to the Mood and Adjustment to Reality scales. Interestingly enough, two Validity (Lie scale) items contribute to scores on other scales.

The most reliable scales are Family Relationships, Social Relationships, Emotional Stability, and Adjustment to Reality, with odd-even coefficients all above .80 and ranging as high as .95. But the Conformity and Mood reliabilities are rather low for use in a counseling situation; the median of the reported reliability coefficients, is about .63. The "average" test-retest reliability of the Validity scale is said to be about .65, but no details are given.

The correlation between Social Relationships (an "area" of adjustment) and Leadership (a "method") is more than .80, higher than the reliability of the Leadership scale. Such relationships indicate the desirability of reducing the number of scores. The correlations of the Validity scale with other scales are not reported.

Evidence for validity was obtained by asking teachers to nominate students who best conformed to personality descriptions that correspond to extremes of the scales. Each nominated group was compared with its contrasting group when possible and with a random sample of students, with respect to mean score on the relevant scale. Differences and critical ra-

tios are reported. The poorest validities, as judged by the critical ratios, are for Emotional Stability, Adjustment to Reality, and Mood. These are the scales that purport to measure traits that are most private in nature and hence least apparent to an observer. For other scales the critical ratios predominantly show significance. The evidence for validity, however, is based only on a comparison of means, and there is considerable overlapping of score distributions, even for contrasting groups. The authors suggest that the scales may be more valid than the criteria, and they may be right, since the criterion problem is especially difficult in the case of personality measures. Although the authors' conclusion that the scales have "reasonably acceptable" validity is fairly cautious, even this statement is too strong in the light of the evidence presented for one or two of the scales.

Recent studies have shown that a good deal of the variance in MMPI scores can be attributed to response sets, particularly sets toward acquiescence and toward giving socially desirable responses. Since the *Minnesota Counseling Inventory* is a direct descendant of the MMPI, the possibility of response bias in the new inventory must be considered. The effects of acquiescence can be controlled by balancing the items with respect to the proportion keyed true and false for each scale. None of the MCI scales is perfectly balanced, and for some the imbalance is extreme. All 14 items of the Validity scale are keyed false, and all 43 items of the Emotional Stability scale are keyed true. Thus a high score on Emotional Stability might be due in part to acquiescence, a tendency to agree to propositions presented. The number of items keyed true and false, respectively, for the remaining scales is as follows: Family Relations, 26-10; Social Relations, 33-28; Conformity, 21-14; Adjustment to Reality, 47-8; Mood, 18-28; and Leadership, 19-16.

Bias toward giving socially desirable responses is less easily controlled. The solution in this case was to include the Validity scale, which is interpreted as revealing an attempt on the part of the examinee to "look good." A raw score of 8 or higher on this scale is said to invalidate the other scores; this cutting score would eliminate about two per cent of the answer sheets. The basis for selecting this criterion is not stated, and no evidence is presented on the effectiveness of the Validity scale. A more reliable validity scale that is less susceptible to acquiescence would certainly be desirable.

Counselors may find the *Minnesota Counseling Inventory* to be useful. But from a technical point of view there seems little reason to prefer it to some of the older inventories. It does not constitute a significant advance in the development of questionnaires for personality assessment.

JOHN W. M. ROTHNEY, *Professor of Education, University of Wisconsin, Madison, Wisconsin.*

The inventory consists of 355 statements to which students with not less than eighth grade reading levels respond by marking a T if they think the statement is true or mostly true, and an F if it is not usually true as applied to them. The statements such as "I get excited easily," "I like to flirt," "I usually feel that life is worthwhile," "No one seems to understand me" are the kind that commonly appear on the many instruments that are labeled as personality tests.

If a student omits 26 to 50 items, which means that his question score is 25 or above, it is suggested that it is best to discuss the situation with him and to "retest" at a later date. Fourteen items are used to arrive at a validity score. If he makes a score of 6 one suspects the validity of the profile, and scores of 8 or higher invalidate the meaning of the other scales because, it is suggested, "It is more likely that such a score reflects a naïve attempt on the part of the student to 'look good' on the inventory." The scores on the question and validity scales are quite different from the other 7 scores named in the description above. The latter are said to provide "means whereby teachers, counselors, and others working with high school age youth can acquire information about the personality dynamics, personality structure, and personality problems of young people." A large order for any instrument!

The authors offer a word of caution in their very candid statement that no evidence is available concerning the validity of combinations of scores on the inventory. In view of this statement and the varying degrees of reliability of the scales one wonders why profile sheets are offered and their use encouraged.

Twenty-eight odd-even reliability coefficients are reported for the 7 scales. Of these, 6 range

from .90 to .95, 11 from .80 to .89, 4 from .70 to .79, 5 lie between .60 and .69, and 2 are less than .60. Twenty-eight test-retest coefficients (1 to 3 month intervals) are reported. Of these only one is above .90, 12 are in the .80 to .89 range, 14 are in the .70's, and one was as low as .56. These coefficients do not suggest high enough stability for use in certain situations as in counseling when one is concerned with one subject at a time. Reliability coefficients for the Mood scale are consistently low. The authors were wise in making the statement that "students' attitudes toward taking the inventory may vary considerably from time to time." Can it then be *really* useful in counseling?

The authors attempted to validate the scales by securing behavior descriptions of students who exhibited unusual negative or positive behavior and comparing their inventory scores with those of samples of subjects for whom no such descriptions were offered by teachers, principals, and other school personnel. There is some evidence of mean differentiation of scores (but "extensive overlapping is found among groups when the distributions themselves are compared") which suggests that the inventory scores sometimes elaborate what was already obvious to teachers and principals. It is suggested that the inventory scores *may* be more valid than the criteria but no evidence is offered. Appropriately enough there is a statement in the validity section about the need for refinement and measurement of suitable criteria for personality scales. In any case the authors suggest that the scales have "reasonably acceptable validity."

Much is made of the point that scores have been obtained from students in 9 or 10 states. The composition of the norm groups that are offered for use is, however, local. Of the 19 schools in Iowa which provided normative data, 13 are in Des Moines, and of the 6 in Minnesota, 5 are in the Minneapolis-St. Paul area. Some earlier studies had indicated that the differences between the data for the norm groups and the data based on samples which included students from other states were very small. Much use is made of data obtained from giving the inventory to the entire population of Phoenix, Arizona, high schools.

No attempt has been made to show how the inventory may be used in counseling. It appears that if counselors *in cities* want to spot those students whose teachers and principals have already recognized as unusual, the inventory may *sometimes* help in that process. In view of the authors' highly commendable critique of their own product, however, one must question seriously whether the test will provide dependable evidence of the "personality dynamics, personality structure, and personality problems of young people."

For an excerpt from a review, see 5:85.

[143]
Minnesota Multiphasic Personality Inventory, Revised Edition. Ages 16 and over; 1942-51; 14 scores: hypochondriasis (Hs, '43), depression (D, '43), hysteria (Hy, '43), psychopathic deviate (Pd, '43), masculinity and femininity (Mf, '43), paranoia (Pa, '43), psychasthenia (Pt, '43), schizophrenia (Sc, '43), hypomania (Ma, '43), social (Si, '51), question (?), lie (L), validity (F, '43), test taking attitude (K, '46); IBM, NCS, and Hankes; 1 form ('43); 2 editions (individual and group); manual ('51, 30 pages); $1.50 per manual; postpaid; (30-90) minutes; Starke R. Hathaway and J. Charnley McKinley; Psychological Corporation. *
a) INDIVIDUAL FORM ("THE CARD SET"). 1942-51; 550 cards plus sorting guides ('43); record blank ('48, 2 pages); $25.50 per set of testing materials including 50 record blanks; $3.75 per 50 record blanks; $8.50 per set of manual and scoring stencils.
b) GROUP FORM ("THE BOOKLET FORM"). 1943-51; IBM, NCS, and Hankes; test ('43, 15 pages); profile ('48, 2 pages); separate answer sheets must be used; $5.50 per 25 tests; $4 per 50 sets of IBM answer sheets and profiles; $2 per 50 Hankes answer sheets (scored by Testscor only, see 667); $3.25 per 50 NCS answer sheets (scored by National Computer Systems only, see 671); $4.50 per set of manual and hand scoring stencils; $4.65 per set of manual and machine scoring stencils; $1.75 per specimen set without scoring stencils.

REFERENCES

1-72. See 3:60.
73-283. See 4:71.
284-779. See 5:86.
780. MONACHESI, ELIO D. "Some Personality Characteristics of Delinquents and Non-Delinquents." *J Crim Law & Criminol* 38:487-500 Ja-F '48. * (*PA* 22:3459)
781. THOMAS, RICHARD WALLACE. *An Investigation of the Psychoanalytic Theory of Homosexuality.* Doctor's thesis, University of Kentucky (Lexington, Ky.), 1951. (*DA* 20:3847)
782. REID, L. LEON. "Comparison of Staff Diagnosis and M.M.P.I. Diagnosis." *Proc W Va Acad Sci* 24:152-3 Je '53. *
783. BLUMBERG, EUGENE M. "Results of Psychological Testing of Cancer Patients," pp. 30-61; discussion by Bruno Klopfer and J. F. T. Bugental, pp. 62-71. In *The Psychological Variables in Human Cancer.* Edited by Joseph A. Gengerelli and Frank J. Kirkner. Berkeley, Calif.: University of California Press, 1954. Pp. vi, 135. *
784. ELLIS, F. W., AND BLUMBERG, E. M. "Comparative Case Summaries With Psychological Profiles in Representative Rapidly and Slowly Progressive Neoplastic Diseases," pp. 72-83; discussion by Eugene Ziskind, Solon D. Samuels, Philip M. West, and Bruno Klopfer, pp. 84-94. In *The Psychological Variables in Human Cancer.* Edited by Joseph A. Gengerelli and Frank J. Kirkner. Berkeley, Calif.: University of California Press, 1954. Pp. vi, 135. *
785. HUNT, J. McV.; EWING, THOMAS N.; LaFORGE, ROLFE; AND GILBERT, WILLIAM M. "An Integrated Approach to Research on Therapeutic Counseling With Samples of Results." *J Counsel Psychol* 6:46-54 sp '54. * (*PA* 34:5955)
786. WEBSTER, A. STANLEY. "Personality and Intelligence of Convicts in West Virginia." *J Crim Law & Criminol* 45:176-9 Jl-Ag '54. * (*PA* 29:6017)
787. BARRON, FRANK. "The Disposition Toward Originality." *J Abn & Social Psychol* 51:478-85 N '55. * (*PA* 31:2533)
788. CORRIGAN, SHIRLEY M. *Psychological Correlates of the*

Physiological Response to Mecholyl in Psychiatric Outpatients. Doctor's thesis, University of Minnesota (Minneapolis, Minn.), 1955. (*DA* 15:1650)
789. IMIG, CHARLES. *Personality Differences in Curriculum as Measured by the Minnesota Multiphasic Personality Inventory.* Master's thesis, Illinois Normal University (Normal, Ill.), 1955.
790. FURST, EDWARD J., AND FRICKE, BENNO G. "Development and Applications of Structured Tests of Personality." *R Ed Res* 26:26-55 F '56. * (*PA* 31:6081)
790a. KENDIG, ISABELLE V.; CHAREN, SOL; AND LEPINE, LOUIS T. "Psychological Side Effects Induced by Cycloserine in the Treatment of Pulmonary Tuberculosis." *Am R Tuberc* 73:438-41 Mr '56. *
791. LEARY, TIMOTHY; WITH THE COLLABORATION OF HELEN LANE, ANNE APFELBAUM, MARY DELLA CIOPPA, AND CHARLOTTE KAUFMANN. *Multilevel Measurement of Interpersonal Behavior: A Manual for the Use of the Interpersonal System of Personality.* Berkeley, Calif.: Psychological Consultation Service, 1956. Pp. vii, 110. *
792. SHNEIDMAN, EDWIN S. Chap. 17, "Some Relationships Between the Rorschach Technique and Other Psychodiagnostic Tests," pp. 595-642. In *Developments in the Rorschach Technique: Volume 2, Fields of Application.* By Bruno Klopfer and others. Yonkers, N.Y.: World Book Co., 1956. Pp. xx, 828. * (*PA* 30:7202)
793. STANTON, JOHN M. "Group Personality Profile Related to Aspects of Antisocial Behavior." *J Crim Law & Criminol* 47:340-9 S-O '56. * (*PA* 31:8441)
794. TRUMM, OLIVE. *A Critical Investigation of the Personality Scores of the Tuberculosis Patient by the Use of the Minnesota Multiphasic Inventory.* Master's thesis, Marquette University (Milwaukee, Wis.), 1956.
795. WAUCK, LE ROY. *An Investigation of the Usefulness of Psychological Tests in the Selection of Candidates for the Diocesan Priesthood.* Doctor's thesis, Loyola University (Chicago, Ill.), 1956.
796. WEBSTER, HAROLD. "Some Quantitative Results." *J Social Issues* 12(4):29-41 '56. *
797. BOOTH, E. G., JR. *Personality Traits of Athletes.* Doctor's thesis, State University of Iowa (Iowa City, Iowa), 1957. (*DA* 18:925)
798. BRISKIN, GERALD J., AND STENNIS, JAMES W. "Improving Predictability of Minnesota Multiphasic Personality Inventory." *U S Armed Forces Med J* 8:539-43 Ap '57. * (*PA* 33:3819)
799. CONGER, JOHN J.; GASKILL, HERBERT S.; GLAD, DONALD D.; RAINEY, ROBERT V.; SAWREY, WILLIAM L.; AND TURRELL, EUGENE S. "Personal and Interpersonal Factors in Motor Vehicle Accidents." *Am J Psychiatry* 113:1069-74 Je '57. * (*PA* 32:6071)
800. EDWARDS, ALLEN L. *The Social Desirability Variable in Personality Assessment and Research.* New York: Dryden Press, Inc., 1957. Pp. xv, 108. * (*PA* 32:464)
801. GEIST, HAROLD. "Emotional Aspects of Dermatitis." *J Clin & Exp Psychopathol* 18:87-93 Mr '57. * (*PA* 32:4433)
802. HATHAWAY, STARKE R., AND MONACHESI, ELIO D. "The Personalities of Predelinquent Boys." *J Crim Law & Criminol* 48:149-63 Jl-Ag '57. * (*PA* 33:1764)
803. KILDAHL, JOHN P. *Personality Correlates of Sudden Religious Converts Contrasted With Persons of Gradual Religious Development.* Doctor's thesis, New York University (New York, N.Y.), 1957. (*DA* 18:2210)
804. LEWIS, ROY D. *Some Factors Associated With Perseverence in the Field of Education as Measured by the Minnesota Multiphasic Personality Inventory.* Master's thesis, University of Utah (Salt Lake City, Utah), 1957.
805. LINDE, THOMAS FRANK. *Personality Elements of Thirty-Three Adults With Cerebral Palsy as Measured on the Minnesota Multiphasic Personality Inventory.* Master's thesis, University of Illinois (Urbana, Ill.), 1957.
806. McNEIL, ELTON B., AND COHLER, J. ROBERT, JR. "The Effect of Personal Needs on Counselors' Perception and Behavior." *Papers Mich Acad Sci Arts & Letters* 42:281-8 pt 2 '57. * (*PA* 37:6924)
807. MURRAY, JOHN B. *Training for the Priesthood and Personality Interest Test Manifestations.* Doctor's thesis, Fordham University (New York, N.Y.), 1957.
808. POLLOCK, EDMUND. *An Investigation Into Certain Personality Characteristics of Unmarried Mothers.* Doctor's thesis, New York University (New York, N.Y.), 1957. (*DA* 18:2215)
809. SANFORD, NEVITT; WEBSTER, HAROLD; AND FREEDMAN, MERVIN. "Impulse Expression as a Variable of Personality." *Psychol Monogr* 71(11):1-21 '57. * (*PA* 33:3336)
810. SMATHERS, SANDRA. *An Analysis of the Responses of Mild and Severe Stutters to Items on the Minnesota Multiphasic Personality Inventory.* Master's thesis, Pennsylvania State University (University Park, Pa.), 1957.
811. STEININGER, EDWARD HENRY. *Changes in the MMPI Profiles of First Prison Offenders During Their First Year of Imprisonment.* Doctor's thesis, Michigan State University (East Lansing, Mich.), 1957. (*DA* 19:3394)
812. TAKALA, MARTTI; PIHKANEN, TOIVO A.; AND MARKKANEN, TOUKO. *The Effects of Distilled and Brewed Beverages: A Physiological, Neurological, and Psychological Study.* The Finnish Foundation for Alcoholic Studies, No. 4. Stock-

holm, Sweden: Almqvist & Wiksell, 1957. Pp. 195. * (PA 31:4890)

813. ABE, STEVEN KIYOSHI. Nisei Personality Characteristics as Measured by the Edwards Personal Preference Schedule and Minnesota Multiphasic Personality Inventory. Doctor's thesis, University of Utah (Salt Lake City, Utah), 1958. (DA 19:2648)

814. ALTUS, WILLIAM D. "The Broken Home and Factors of Adjustment." Psychol Rep 4:477 S '58. * (PA 33:6053)

815. BUER, CARL FREDERICK. An MMPI Configural Index for Determination of Somatization. Doctor's thesis, University of Minnesota (Minneapolis, Minn.), 1958. (DA 19:1443)

816. CABANSKI, STANLEY J. A Comparison of Psychogalvanic Responses With Certain Categories of the MMPI. Master's thesis, Loyola University (Chicago, Ill.), 1958.

817. CHANCE, JUNE ELIZABETH. "Adjustment and Prediction of Others' Behavior." J Consult Psychol 22:191-4 Je '58. * (PA 35:4977)

818. CLARK, JAMES WARD. Personality Syndromes in Chronic Alcoholism: A Factorial Study. Doctor's thesis, Queen's University (Kingston, Ont., Canada), 1958. (Abstract: Can Psychologist 1:116-7)

819. COMREY, ANDREW L., AND LEVONIAN, EDWARD. "A Comparison of Three Point Coefficients in Factor Analyses of MMPI Items." Ed & Psychol Meas 18:739-55 w '58. * (PA 34:107)

820. COULSON, ROGER WAYNE. Relationships Among Personality Traits,, Ability and Academic Efficiency of College Seniors. Doctor's thesis, State University of Iowa (Iowa City, Iowa), 1958. (DA 19:1647)

821. DONAT, GERTRUDE McADAM. Factors Related to Measured Masculinity Among Students Majoring in Secondary Education. Doctor's thesis, University of Minnesota (Minneapolis, Minn.), 1958. (DA 19:1834)

822. DRASGOW, JAMES, AND RACE, RALPH. "The College Success of Psychologically Disturbed and Normal Personalities." J Higher Ed 29:444-9 N '58. *

823. DUKER, JAN. The Utility of the MMPI Atlas in the Derivation of Personality Descriptions. Doctor's thesis, University of Minnesota (Minneapolis, Minn.), 1958. (DA 19:3021)

824. FAW, VOLNEY, AND WILCOX, WARREN W. "Personality Characteristics of Susceptible and Unsusceptible Hypnotic Subjects." J Clin & Exp Hypnosis 6:83-94 Ap '58. *

825. FIELDS, SIDNEY J. "Personality Inventory Profiles During and After Real Life Stress." J Med Ed 33:221-4 Mr '58. * (PA 34:2264)

826. GALLESE, ARTHUR JAMES, JR. Personality Characteristics and Academic Achievement in School of Engineering Students. Doctor's thesis, University of Minnesota (Minneapolis, Minn.), 1958. (DA 19:3022)

827. GULLION, MARY ELIZABETH, AND PIERCE-JONES, JOHN. "MMPI in Relation to Elementary Teachers' Adjustments to Teaching." Psychol Rep 4:619-22 D '58. * (PA 34:2133)

828. HOGAN, JOE. Configural Analysis of MMPI Scores With Special Reference to Student Teachers in Nursing Education. Doctor's thesis, University of Minnesota (Minneapolis, Minn.), 1958. (DA 19:2851)

829. IRONSIDE, W. "Medical Students and the M.M.P.I." Abstract. J Am Med Assn 168:433 S 27 '58. *

830. JORGENSEN, C. "A Short Form of the MMPI." Austral J Psychol 10:341-50 D '58. * (PA 34:2769)

831. KELLY, E. LOWELL; MILLER, JAMES G.; MARQUIS, DONALD G.; GERARD, R. W.; AND UHR, LEONARD. "Personality Differences and Continued Meprobamate and Proclorperazine Administration." A.M.A. Arch Neurol & Psychiatry 80:241-6 Ag '58. * (PA 33:10420)

832. KLEINMUNTZ, BENJAMIN. An Investigation of the Verbal Behavior of Paranoid Psychotic Patients and Normals. Doctor's thesis, University of Minnesota (Minneapolis, Minn.), 1958. (DA 19:1444)

833. KNOWLES, REX HANNA. Differential Characteristics of Successful and Unsuccessful Seminary Students. Doctor's thesis, University of Nebraska (Lincoln, Neb.), 1958. (DA 19:1655)

834. KORN, HAROLD ALLEN. Guessing Behavior Modified by Schedules of Reinforcement of Individuals With Selected MMPI Profiles. Doctor's thesis, University of Minnesota (Minneapolis, Minn.), 1958. (DA 19:1445)

835. MARTIN, JAMES WINSTON. The Development and Validation of a Scale for the Minnesota Multiphasic Personality Inventory to Differentiate Presidents from Non-Presidents of College Student Organizations. Doctor's thesis, University of Missouri (Columbia, Mo.), 1958. (DA 19:2003)

836. MATHEWS, ANNE, AND WERTHEIMER, MICHAEL. "A 'Pure' Measure of Perceptual Defense Uncontaminated by Response Suppression." J Abn & Social Psychol 57:373-6 N '58. * (PA 33:9974)

837. PURDOM, GLEN A., JR. Comparison of Performance of Competent and Incompetent Readers in a State Training School for Delinquent Boys on the WAIS and the Rosenzweig P-F Study. Doctor's thesis, University of Oregon (Eugene, Ore.), 1958. (DA 19:1016)

838. RAND, MARTIN E. Face Validity of the Minnesota Multiphasic Personality Inventory. Master's thesis, Kent State University (Kent, Ohio), 1958.

839. RAPAPORT, GERALD M. " 'Ideal Self' Instructions,

MMPI Profile Changes, and the Prediction of Clinical Improvement." J Consult Psychol 22:459-63 D '58. * (PA 33:10761)

840. RHEINSTROM, DIANA. The Minnesota Multiphasic Personality Inventory as Predictor of Subsequent Emotional Problems. Master's thesis, University of Utah (Salt Lake City, Utah), 1958.

841. RICE, PATRICK J. An MMPI Study of Religious Seminarians. Master's thesis, Loyola University (Chicago, Ill.), 1958.

842. ROMMEL, ROBERT CHARLES SHERWOOD. Personality Characteristics, Attitudes, and Peer Group Relationships of Accident-Free Youths and Accident-Repeating Youths. Doctor's thesis, Pennsylvania State University (University Park, Pa.), 1958. (DA 19:3046)

843. ROSEN, ALBERT. "Differentiation of Diagnostic Groups by Individual MMPI Scales." J Consult Psychol 22:453-7 D '58. * (PA 33:10358)

844. SHAW, MERVILLE C., AND GRUBB, JAMES. "Hostility and Able High School Underachievers." J Counsel Psychol 5:263-6 w '58. * (PA 34:3413)

845. SIMON, WERNER, AND GILBERSTADT, HAROLD. "Analysis of the Personality Structure of 26 Actual Suicides." J Nerv & Mental Dis 127:555-7 D '58. *

846. SINGER, MARGARET THALER, AND SCHEIN, EDGAR H. "Projective Test Responses of Prisoners of War Following Repatriation." Psychiatry 21:375-85 N '58. * (PA 33:10113)

847. STEIMEL, RAYMOND J. A Study of the Relationship of Recalled Childhood Identification and Association to Masculinity-Femininity of Interest Scores on the MMPI and SVIB Among Scholarship Finalists. Doctor's thesis, University of Kansas (Lawrence, Kan.), 1958.

848. SWENSON, W. M., AND GRIMES, B. P. "Characteristics of Sex Offenders Admitted to a Minnesota State Hospital for Pre-Sentence Psychiatric Investigation." Psychiatric Q Sup 32(1):110-23 '58. * (PA 34:3250)

849. TRUELOVE, JAMES WILSON. A Study of Patterns in Motivation Among Entering College Freshmen and of the Relationships Between Motivation and Certain Personality Factors. Doctor's thesis, University of Alabama (University, Ala.), 1958. (DA 19:2857)

850. VOLDSETH, EDWARD VICTOR. The Development of an Empirically Constructed Scale From the Minnesota Multiphasic Personality Inventory for Identifying Students Likely to Be Elected to Positions of Leadership in College Extra-Curricular Activities. Doctor's thesis, State University of Iowa (Iowa City, Iowa), 1958. (DA 19:2858)

851. WALTER, PAUL BROWNING. A Study of Anxiety Among Elementary and Secondary Education Majors in the School of Education of the University of North Carolina. Doctor's thesis, University of North Carolina (Chapel Hill, N.C.), 1958. (DA 19:2542)

852. WEBB, SAM C., AND GOODLING, RICHARD A. "Test Validity in a Methodist Theology School." Ed & Psychol Meas 18:859-66 w '58. * (PA 34:2123)

853. AALTO, ENSIO EMIL. Psychological Factors Associated With Appropriateness and Inappropriateness of Vocational Choices. Doctor's thesis, University of Minnesota (Minneapolis, Minn.), 1959. (DA 20:1262)

854. AARONSON, BERNARD S. "A Comparison of Two MMPI Measures of Masculinity-Femininity." J Clin Psychol 15:48-50 Ja '59. * (PA 34:2744)

855. AARONSON, BERNARD S. "Hypochondriasis and Somatic Seizure Auras." J Clin Psychol 15:450-1 O '59. * (PA 36:1JU50A)

856. ANASTASIO, MARY M. The Relationship of Selected Personality Characteristics to the Chronology of the Menstrual Cycle in Women. Doctor's thesis, New York University (New York, N.Y.), 1959. (DA 20:3823)

857. ASTIN, ALEXANDER W. "A Factor Study of the MMPI Psychopathic Deviate Scale." J Consult Psychol 23:550-4 D '59. * (PA 34:6224)

858. BAIRDAIN, ERNEST FREDERICK. Psychological Characteristics of Adolescents Who Have Had Imaginary Companions. Doctor's thesis, Columbia University (New York, N.Y.), 1959. (DA 20:747)

859. BALLARD, ROBERT G. "The Interaction Between Marital Conflict and Alcoholism as Seen Through MMPI's of Marriage Partners: The Interrelatedness of Alcoholism and Marital Conflict: Symposium 1958." Am J Orthopsychiatry 29:528-46 Jl '59. * (PA 34:4600)

860. BENDIG, A. W. "An Inter-Item Factor Analysis of Two 'Lie' Scales." Psychol Newsl 10:299-303 My-Je '59. * (PA 34:94)

861. BRUCE, MARTIN M. "Normative Data Information Exchange, Nos. 12-13, 12-14." Personnel Psychol 12:329-30 su '59. *

862. CADITZ, SYLVAN B. "Effect of a Training School Experience on the Personality of Delinquent Boys." J Consult Psychol 23:501-9 D '59. * (PA 34:6312)

863. CALDEN, GEORGE, AND HOKANSON, JACK E. "The Influence of Age on MMPI Responses." J Clin Psychol 15:194-5 Ap '59. * (PA 35:4739)

864. CALDWELL, MORRIS G. "Personality Trends in the Youthful Male Offender." J Crim Law & Criminol 49:405-16 Ja-F '59. * (PA 33:10641)

865. CASSIUS, JOSEPH. The Effects of Self-Defense Training

on Morale, Social Adjustment and Emotionality in Male High School Students: An Evaluation and Analysis of Personality Changes Due to Training in Methods of Self-Defense Known as Judo. Doctor's thesis, Yeshiva University (New York, N.Y.), 1959.

866. COCHRAN, WILLIAM MORGAN, JR. "A Correlation Comparison Between the Minnesota Multiphasic Personality Inventory and the Combined Gordon Personal Profile and Personal Inventory (Abstract)." Proc W Va Acad Sci 30:189 My '59. * (PA 34:2359, title only)

867. COLEMAN, WILLIAM, AND COLLETT, DOROTHY MANLEY. "Development and Applications of Structured Tests of Personality." R Ed Res 29:57–72 F '59. * (PA 34:5604)

868. COMREY, ANDREW L. "Comparison of Two Analytic Rotation Procedures." Psychol Rep 5:201–9 Je '59. * (PA 34:2467)

869. CURTIS, QUIN F.; BENDALL, JOHN W.; AND WILFONG, HARRY D., JR. "Some Problems in the Prediction of Supervisory Success." Proc W Va Acad Sci 30:186–8 My '59. * (PA 34:3495)

870. CUTTER, FRED. "Psychological Changes in Sexual Psychopaths." Psychol Newsl 10:322–9 My-Je '59. * (PA 34:1699)

871. DANA, RICHARD H., AND CHRISTIANSEN, KENNETH. "Repression and Psychopathology." J Proj Tech 23:412–6 D '59. * (PA 35:4981)

872. DESOTO, CLINTON B., AND KUETHE, JAMES L. "The Set to Claim Undesirable Symptoms in Personality Inventories." J Consult Psychol 23:496–500 D '59. * (PA 34:5605)

873. DRAKE, L. E., AND OETTING, E. R. An MMPI Codebook for Counselors. Minneapolis, Minn.: University of Minnesota Press, 1959. Pp. vii, 140. * (PA 34:6013)

874. EICHMAN, WILLIAM J. "Discrimination of Female Schizophrenics With Configural Analysis of the MMPI Profile." J Consult Psychol 23:442–7 O '59. * (PA 34:6351)

875. ENRIGHT, JOHN BURKE. Profile Types and Prediction From the Minnesota Multiphasic Personality Inventory. Doctor's thesis, University of California (Berkeley, Calif.), 1959.

876. ESCHENBACH, ARTHUR E., AND DUPREE, LOUIS. "The Influence of Stress on MMPI Scale Scores." J Clin Psychol 15:42–5 Ja '59. * (PA 34:2757)

877. FILLENBAUM, SAMUEL. "Some Stylistic Aspects of Categorizing Behavior." J Personality 27:187–95 Je '59. * (PA 34:4063)

878. FINE, BERNARD J., AND GAYDOS, HENRY F. "Relationship Between Individual Personality Variables and Body Temperature Response Patterns in the Cold." Psychol Rep 5:71–8 Mr '59. * (PA 34:424)

879. FITZELLE, GEORGE T. "Personality Factors and Certain Attitudes Toward Child Rearing Among Parents of Asthmatic Children." Psychosom Med 21:208–17 My-Je '59. * (PA 34:4731)

880. FOULDS, G. A. "The Relative Stability of Personality Measures Compared with Diagnostic Measures." J Mental Sci 105:783–7 Jl '59. * (PA 34:6016)

881. FOULDS, G. A., AND CAINE, T. M. "The Assessment of Some Symptoms and Signs of Depression in Women." J Mental Sci 105:182–9 Ja '59. * (PA 34:1359)

882. FOULDS, G. A., AND CAINE, T. M. "Symptom Clusters and Personality Types Among Psychoneurotic Men Compared With Women." J Mental Sci 105:469–75 Ap '59. * (PA 34:4715)

883. FULKERSON, SAMUEL C. "Individual Differences in Response Validity." J Clin Psychol 15:169–73 Ap '59. * (PA 35:4876)

884. GARFIELD, SOL L., AND SINEPS, JON. "An Appraisal of Taulbee and Sisson's 'Configurational Analysis of MMPI Profiles of Psychiatric Groups.'" J Consult Psychol 23:333–5 Ag '59. * (PA 34:4381)

885. GROSS, LEONARD R. "MMPI L-F-K Relationships With Criteria of Behavioral Disturbance and Social Adjustment in a Schizophrenic Population." J Consult Psychol 23:319–23 Ag '59. * (PA 34:4678)

886. GUILFORD, J. P. Personality, pp. 178–83. New York: McGraw-Hill Book Co., Inc., 1959. Pp. xiii, 562. *

887. HAERTZEN, CHARLES A., AND HILL, HARRIS E. "Effects of Morphine and Pentobarbital on Differential MMPI Profiles." J Clin Psychol 15:434–7 O '59. * (PA 36:1C34H)

888. HANVIK, LEO J., AND BYRUM, MILDRED. "MMPI Profiles of Parents of Child Psychiatric Patients." J Clin Psychol 15:427–31 O '59. * (PA 36:1HF27H)

889. HARDER, DONALD F. "Differentiation of Curricular Groups Based Upon Responses to Unique Items of the MMPI." J Counsel Psychol 6:28–34 sp '59. * (PA 34:6554)

890. HATHAWAY, STARKE R.; MONACHESI, ELIO D.; AND YOUNG, LAWRENCE A. "Rural-Urban Adolescent Personality." Rural Sociol 24:331–46 D '59. * (PA 34:7639)

891. HOLMES, JACK A. Personality and Spelling Ability. University of California Publications in Education, Vol. 12, No. 4. Berkeley, Calif.: University of California Press, 1959. Pp. vii, 213–91. *

892. HOVEY, H. BIRNET; KOOI, KENNETH A.; AND THOMAS, MADISON H. "MMPI Profiles of Epileptics." J Consult Psychol 23:155–9 Ap '59. * (PA 34:1849)

893. KASSEBAUM, GENE G.; COUCH, ARTHUR S.; AND SLATER, PHILIP E. "The Factorial Dimensions of the MMPI." J Consult Psychol 23:226–36 Je '59. * (PA 34:4074)

894. KELLY, E. LOWELL, AND GOLDBERG, LEWIS R. "Correlates of Later Performance and Specialization in Psychology: A Follow-Up Study of the Trainees Assessed in the VA Selection Research Project." Psychol Monogr 73(12):1–32 '59. * (PA 34:7952)

895. KELTY, EDWARD JOHN. Normal Electrocortical Activity in Relation to Personality Factors. Doctor's thesis, Duke University (Durham, N.C.), 1959. (DA 20:756)

896. KING, GERALD F., AND SCHILLER, MARVIN. "A Research Note on the K Scale of the MMPI and 'Defensiveness.'" J Clin Psychol 15:305–6 Jl '59. * (PA 35:3455)

897. KING, PAUL; NORRELL, GWEN; AND ERLANDSON, F. L. "The Prediction of Academic Success in a Police Administration Curriculum." Ed & Psychol Meas 19:649–51 w '59. * (PA 34:6166)

897a. KLERMAN, GERALD L.; DIMASCIO, ALBERTO; GREENBLATT, MILTON; AND RINKEL, MAX. Chap. 18, "The Influence of Specific Personality Patterns on the Reactions to Phrenotropic Agents," pp. 224–38; discussion by Anthony Sainz and G. J. Sarwer-Foner, pp. 239–42. In Biological Psychiatry. Proceedings of the Scientific Sessions of the Society of Biological Psychiatry, San Francisco, May 1958. Edited by Jules H. Masserman. New York: Grune & Stratton, Inc., 1959. Pp. xv, 338. * (PA 35:2326)

898. KNEHR, CHARLES A., AND KOHL, RICHARD N. "MMPI Screening of Entering Medical Students." J Psychol 47:297–304 Ap '59. * (PA 34:5907)

899. KRASNOFF, ALAN. "Psychological Variables and Human Cancer: A Cross-Validation Study." Psychosom Med 21:291–5 Jl-Ag '59. * (PA 34:4736)

900. LEARMONTH, GEORGE J.; ACKERLY, WILLIAM; AND KAPLAN, MIKE. "Relationships Between Palmar Skin Potential During Stress and Personality Variables." Psychosom Med 21:150–7 Mr-Ap '59. * (PA 34:1384)

901. LEVITAN, SEYMOUR; GOLDFARB, JACK H.; AND JACOBS, ALFRED. "The Relationship Between an Actuarial and a Clinical Analysis of MMPI Profiles." Psychol Newsl 10:295–8 My-Je '59. * (PA 34:142)

902. LITTLE, KENNETH B., AND SHNEIDMAN, EDWIN S. "Congruencies Among Interpretations of Psychological Test and Anamnestic Data." Psychol Monogr 73(6):1–42 '59. * (PA 34:3010)

903. LIVERANT, SHEPHARD. "MMPI Differences Between Parents of Disturbed and Nondisturbed Children." J Consult Psychol 23:256–60 Je '59. * (PA 34:4393)

904. LOY, DONALD L. "The Validity of the Taulbee-Sisson MMPI Scale Pairs in Female Psychiatric Groups." J Clin Psychol 15:306–7 Jl '59. * (PA 35:3458)

905. MACHOVER, SOLOMON; PUZZO, FRANK S.; MACHOVER, KAREN; AND PLUMEAU, FRANCIS. "Clinical and Objective Studies of Personality Variables in Alcoholism: III, An Objective Study of Homosexuality in Alcoholism." Q J Studies Alcohol 20:528–42 S '59. * (PA 34:6254)

906. MAGAW, DAVID CURLEE. Criminal Antisocial and Inadequate Personalities—A Clinical and Psychometric Comparison. Doctor's thesis, Wayne State University (Detroit, Mich.), 1959. (DA 20:2144)

907. MARKS, PHILIP ANDRE. The Validity of the Diagnostic Process in a Child Guidance Setting: A Multidisciplinary Approach. Doctor's thesis, University of Minnesota (Minneapolis, Minn.), 1959. (DA 20:2387)

908. MAYO, GEORGE DOUGLAS, AND GUTTMAN, ISAIAH. "Faking in a Vocational Classification Situation." J Appl Psychol 43:117–21 Ap '59. * (PA 34:2776)

909. MEEHL, PAUL E. "A Comparison of Clinicians With Five Statistical Methods of Identifying Psychotic MMPI Profiles." J Counsel Psychol 6:102–9 su '59. * (PA 34:4396)

910. MEES, HAYDEN LEROY. Preliminary Steps in the Construction of Factor Scales for the MMPI. Doctor's thesis, University of Washington (Seattle, Wash.), 1959. (DA 20:2905)

911. MICHAEL, WILLIAM B.; JONES, ROBERT A.; AND HANEY, RUSSELL. "The Development and Validation of a Test Battery for Selection of Student Nurses." Ed & Psychol Meas 19:641–3 w '59. * (PA 34:6171)

912. NIELSON, LESTER J., JR. Minnesota Multiphasic Personality Inventory Profiles of Persons Applying for Licenses to Operate Nursing and Convalescent Homes. Master's thesis, University of Utah (Salt Lake City, Utah), 1959.

913. O'CONNOR, JAMES P., AND STEFIC, EDWARD C. "Some Patterns of Hypochondriasis." Ed & Psychol Meas 19:363–71 au '59. * (PA 34:6040)

914. PANTON, JAMES H. "The Response of Prison Inmates to MMPI Subscales." J Social Ther 5(3):233–7 '59. * (PA 34:6195)

915. PANTON, JAMES H. "The Response of Prison Inmates to Seven New MMPI Scales." J Clin Psychol 15:196–7 Ap '59. * (PA 35:5216)

916. PEEK, ROLAND M., AND OLSON, GORDON W. Organization and Internal Structure of the MMPI, Second Edition. St. Paul, Minn.: Department of Public Welfare, State of Minnesota, 1959. Pp. vi, 66. * (PA 35:793)

917. PETERSON, MARTHA ELIZABETH. An Evaluation of Relationships Between Test Data and Success as a Residence Hall Counselor. Doctor's thesis, University of Kansas (Lawrence, Kan.), 1959. (DA 21:3364)

918. RIECK, ELMER CHRISTIAN. A Comparison of Teachers'

Response Patterns on the Minnesota Multiphasic Personality Inventory With Response Patterns of Selected Non-Teacher Groups. Doctor's thesis, University of Wisconsin (Madison, Wis.), 1959. (*DA* 20:594)

919. ROGERS, ARTHUR H., AND WALSH, TERRENCE M. "Defensiveness and Unwitting Self-Evaluation." *J Cl.n Psychol* 15:302–4 Jl '59. * (*PA* 35:3510)

920. ROGGE, HAROLD JOHN. *A Study of the Relationships of Reading Achievement to Certain Other Factors in a Population of Delinquent Boys.* Doctor's thesis, University of Minnesota (Minneapolis, Minn.), 1959. (*DA* 20:4037)

921. ROSEN, ALBERT. "Punched-Card Methods for Item Analysis in the Development of Structured Personality Scales." *J General Psychol* 61:127–35 Jl '59. * (*PA* 35:3441)

922. SAUTÉ, GEORGE DEWITT. *Accuracy of Psychomotor Performance as a Function of Instructions, Expression-Repression, and Anxiety.* Doctor's thesis, University of North Carolina (Chapel Hill, N.C.), 1959. (*DA* 20:2908)

923. SCHUBERT, DANIEL S. P. "Personality Implications of Cigarette Smoking Among College Students." Abstract. *J Consult Psychol* 23:376 Ag '59. * (*PA* 34:4088)

924. SHELDON, M. STEPHEN. "Conditions Affecting the Fakability of Teacher-Selection Inventories." *Ed & Psychol Meas* 19:207–19 su '59. * (*PA* 34:4093)

925. SHELDON, M. STEPHEN; COALE, JACK M.; AND COPPLE, ROCKNE. "Concurrent Validity of the 'Warm Teacher Scale.'" *J Ed Psychol* 50:37–40 F '59. * (*PA* 35:2810)

926. SINES, LLOYD K. "The Relative Contribution of Four Kinds of Data to Accuracy in Personality Assessment." *J Consult Psychol* 23:483–92 D '59. * (*PA* 34:6046)

927. SMITH, C. M., AND HAMILTON, J. "Psychological Factors in the Narcolepsy-Cataplexy Syndrome." *Psychosom Med* 21:40–9 Ja–F '59. * (*PA* 34:1858)

928. SMITH, EWART E. "Defensiveness, Insight, and the K Scale." *J Consult Psychol* 23:275–7 Je '59. * (*PA* 34:4411)

929. STANEK, RICHARD J. "A Note on the Presumed Measures of Masculinity-Femininity." *Personnel & Guid J* 37:439–40 F '59. *

930. SULZER, EDWARD STANTON. *The Psychological Effects of Promazine on Chronic Psychiatric Patients.* Doctor's thesis, Columbia University (New York, N.Y.), 1959. (*DA* 20:1075)

931. TAMKIN, ARTHUR S. "An MMPI Scale Measuring Severity of Psychopathology." *J Clin Psychol* 15:56 Ja '59. * (*PA* 34:3223)

932. TAYLOR, JAMES BENTLEY. "Social Desirability and MMPI Performance: The Individual Case." *J Consult Psychol* 23:514–7 D '59. * (*PA* 34:6398)

933. TOOBERT, SAUL; BARTELME, KENWOOD F.; AND JONES, EUGENE S. "Some Factors Related to Pedophilia." *Int J Social Psychiatry* 4:272–9 sp '59. * (*PA* 34:6281)

934. WALTON, DONALD; MATHER, MARICA; AND BLACK, D. A. "The Validity of the Meehl M.M.P.I. Psychotic Scale in the Diagnosis of Schizophrenia." *J Mental Sci* 105:869–71 Jl '59. * (*PA* 34:6056)

935. WARD, JOHN. *An Investigation of the Minnesota Multiphasic Personality Inventory in Selecting for the Advanced Air Force Reserve Officer Corps at Purdue University.* Doctor's thesis, Purdue University (Lafayette, Ind.), 1959. (*DA* 20:1647)

936. WIGGINS, JERRY S. "Interrelationships Among MMPI Measures of Dissimulation Under Standard and Social Desirability Instructions." *J Consult Psychol* 23:419–27 O '59. * (*PA* 34:5643)

937. WIGGINS, JERRY S., AND RUMRILL, CLARK. "Social Desirability in the MMPI and Welsh's Factor Scales *A* and *R*." *J Consult Psychol* 23:100–6 Ap '59. * (*PA* 34:1434)

938. WIGGINS, JERRY S., AND VOLLMAR, JUDITH. "The Content of the MMPI." *J Clin Psychol* 15:45–7 Ja '59. * (*PA* 34:2795)

939. WIRT, ROBERT D., AND BRIGGS, PETER F. "Personality and Environmental Factors in the Development of Delinquency." *Psychol Monogr* 73(15):1–47 '59. * (*PA* 35:5219)

940. WIRT, ROBERT D., AND SIMON, WERNER. *Differential Treatment and Prognosis in Schizophrenia.* Springfield, Ill.: Charles C Thomas, Publisher, 1959. Pp. xii, 198. *

941. WOHL, JULIAN, AND HYMAN, MARVIN. "Relationship Between Measures of Anxiety and Constriction." *J Clin Psychol* 15:54–5 Ja '59. * (*PA* 34:2797)

942. ZUCKERMAN, MARVIN, AND OLTEAN, MARY. "Some Relationships Between Maternal Attitude Factors and Authoritarianism, Personality Needs, Psychopathology, and Self-Acceptance." *Child Develop* 30:27–36 Mr '59. * (*PA* 34:3176)

943. AARONSON, BERNARD S. "A Dimension of Personality Change With Aging." *J Clin Psychol* 16:63–5 Ja '60. * (*PA* 36:1HE63A)

944. AFFLECK, D. C., AND GARFIELD, SOL L. "The Prediction of Psychosis With the MMPI." *J Clin Psychol* 16:24–6 Ja '60. * (*PA* 36:1HI24A)

945. ALTROCCHI, JOHN; PARSONS, OSCAR A.; AND DICKOFF, HILDA. "Changes in Self-Ideal Discrepancy in Repressors and Sensitizers." *J Abn & Social Psychol* 61:67–72 Jl '60. * (*PA* 35:2253)

946. BALDWIN, THOMAS SANDERSON. *The Relationships Among Personality, Cognitive, and Job Performance Variables.* Doctor's thesis, Ohio State University (Columbus, Ohio), 1960. (*DA* 21:3171)

947. BALL, JOHN C. "Comparison of MMPI Profile Differences Among Negro-White Adolescents." *J Clin Psychol* 16:304–7 Jl '60. * (*PA* 36:2HF04B)

948. BALL, JOHN C., AND CARROLL, DONNA. "Analysis of MMPI Cannot Say Scores in an Adolescent Population." *J Clin Psychol* 16:30–1 Ja '60. * (*PA* 36:1HF30B)

949. BARROWS, GORDON A., AND ZUCKERMAN, MARVIN. "Construct Validity of Three Masculinity-Femininity Tests." *J Consult Psychol* 24:441–5 O '60. * (*PA* 35:4891)

950. BENDIG, A. W. "Factor Analyses of 'Anxiety' and 'Neuroticism' Inventories." *J Consult Psychol* 24:161–8 Ap '60. * (*PA* 34:8195)

951. BROWN, DONALD JAMES. *An Investigation of the Relationships Between Certain Personal Characteristics of Guidance Counselors and Performance in Supervised Counseling Interviews.* Doctor's thesis, Ohio State University (Columbus, Ohio), 1960. (*DA* 21:810)

952. BROWN, PAUL L., AND BERDIE, RALPH F. "Driver Behavior and Scores on the MMPI." *J Appl Psychol* 44:18–21 F '60. * (*PA* 34:8467)

953. CAINE, T. M. "The Expression of Hostility and Guilt in Melancholic and Paranoid Women." *J Consult Psychol* 24:18–22 F '60. * (*PA* 34:7967)

954. CALDEN, GEORGE; DUPERTUIS, C. WESLEY; HOKANSON, JACK E.; AND LEWIS, WILLIAM C. "Psychosomatic Factors in the Rate of Recovery From Tuberculosis." *Psychosom Med* 22:345–55 S–O '60. * (*PA* 35:5280)

955. CANTER, ARTHUR. "The Efficacy of a Short Form of the MMPI to Evaluate Depression and Morale Loss." *J Consult Psychol* 24:14–7 F '60. * (*PA* 34:7837)

956. CARRIGAN, PATRICIA M. "Extraversion-Introversion as a Dimension of Personality: A Reappraisal." *Psychol B* 57:329–60 S '60. * (*PA* 35:4976)

957. CHANCE, JUNE ELIZABETH. "Personality Differences and Level of Aspiration." *J Consult Psychol* 24:111–5 Ap '60. * (*PA* 34:7138)

958. CHRISTENSEN, CLIFFORD M., AND MACDONALD, JOHN. "Directed Cognition and Personality Change." *Alberta J Ed Res* 6:211–7 D '60. * (*PA* 36:2HJ11C)

959. CLARIDGE, GORDON. Chap. 2, "The Excitation-Inhibition Balance in Neurotics," pp. 107–54. In *Experiments in Personality: Vol. 2, Psychodiagnostics and Psychodynamics.* Edited by H. J. Eysenck. London: Routledge & Kegan Paul Ltd., 1960. Pp. viii, 333. *

960. CLARK, CHARLES MARVIN. *Changes in Response Patterns of Counseling Institute Trainees.* Doctor's thesis, Ohio State University (Columbus, Ohio), 1960. (*DA* 21:811)

961. COMREY, ANDREW L. "Comparison of Certain Personality Variables in American and Italian Groups." *Ed & Psychol Meas* 20:541–50 su '60. * (*PA* 35:3450)

962. COMREY, ANDREW L., AND SOUFI, ALLADIN. "Further Investigation of Some Factors Found in MMPI Items." *Ed & Psychol Meas* 20:777–86 w '60. * (*PA* 35:3390)

963. CORLIS, RAHE BASSETT. *Personality Factors Related to Underachievement in College Freshmen of High Intellectual Ability.* Doctor's thesis, University of Florida (Gainesville, Fla.), 1960. (*DA* 24:832)

964. COUCH, ARTHUR, AND KENISTON, KENNETH. "Yeasayers and Naysayers: Agreeing Response Set as a Personality Variable." *J Abn & Social Psychol* 60:151–74 Mr '60. * (*PA* 34:7376)

965. CRITES, JOHN O. "Ego-Strength in Relation to Vocational Interest Development." *J Counsel Psychol* 7:137–43 su '60. * (*PA* 35:4012)

966. CROWNE, DOUGLAS P., AND MARLOWE, DAVID. "A New Scale of Social Desirability Independent of Psychopathology." *J Consult Psychol* 24:349–54 Ag '60. * (*PA* 35:2183)

967. CRUMPTON, EVELYN; CANTOR, JOEL M.; AND BATISTE, CURT. "A Factor Analytic Study of Barron's Ego Strength Scale." *J Clin Psychol* 16:283–91 Jl '60. * (*PA* 36:2HF83C)

968. DAHLSTROM, W. GRANT, AND PRANGE, ARTHUR J., JR. "Characteristics of Depressive and Paranoid Schizophrenic Reactions on the Minnesota Multiphasic Personality Inventory." *J Nerv & Mental Dis* 131:513–22 D '60. * (*PA* 35:5225)

969. DAHLSTROM, W. GRANT, AND WELSH, GEORGE SCHLAGER. *An MMPI Handbook: A Guide to Use in Clinical Practice and Research.* Minneapolis, Minn.: University of Minnesota Press, 1960. Pp. xx, 559. * (*PA* 35:2217)

970. DOEHRING, DONALD G., AND REITAN, RALPH M. "MMPI Performance of Aphasic and Nonaphasic Brain-Damaged Patients." *J Clin Psychol* 16:307–9 Jl '60. * (*PA* 36:2HI07D)

971. DOIDGE, WILLIAM T., AND HOLTZMAN, WAYNE H. "Implications of Homosexuality Among Air Force Trainees." *J Consult Psychol* 24:9–13 F '60. * (*PA* 34:8034)

972. EDWARDS, ALLEN L.; HEATHERS, LOUISE B.; AND FORDYCE, WILBERT E. "Correlations of New MMPI Scales With Edwards SD Scale." *J Clin Psychol* 16:26–9 Ja '60. * (*PA* 36:1HF26E)

973. EYSENCK, H. J. Chap. 5, "A Factor Analysis of Selected Tests," pp. 234–44. In his *Experiments in Personality: Vol. 2, Psychodiagnostics and Psychodynamics.* London: Routledge & Kegan Paul Ltd., 1960. Pp. viii, 333. *

974. FLANAGAN, CARROLL EDWARD. *A Study of the Relationship of Scores on the Minnesota Multiphasic Personality Inventory to Success in Teaching as Indicated by Supervisory*

Ratings. Doctor's thesis, University of Wisconsin (Madison, Wis.), 1960. (*DA* 21:546)

975. FORSYTH, RALPH PATTERSON, JR. *MMPI and Demographic Correlates of Post-Hospital Adjustment in Neuropsychiatric Patients.* Doctor's thesis, University of North Carolina (Chapel Hill, N.C.), 1960. (*DA* 21:2783)

976. FOULDS, G. A.; CAINE, T. M.; AND CREASY, M. A. "Aspects of Extra- and Intro-Punitive Expression in Mental Illness." *J Mental Sci* 106:599–610 Ap '60. * (*PA* 35:6429)

977. FRANKS, C. M.; SOUIEFF, M. I.; AND MAXWELL, A. E. "A Factorial Study of Certain Scales From the MMPI and the STDCR." *Acta Psychologica* 17(5):407–16 '60. * (*PA* 35:3428)

978. FULKERSON, SAMUEL C. "Individual Differences in Reaction to Failure-Induced Stress." *J Abn & Social Psychol* 60:136–9 Ja '60. * (*PA* 34:7385)

979. GILBERSTADT, HAROLD, AND DUKER, JAN. "Case History Correlates of Three MMPI Profile Types." *J Consult Psychol* 24:361–7 Ag '60. * (*PA* 35:2219)

980. GOCKA, EDWARD F. "The Introversion-Extraversion Factor and Social Desirability." *J Clin Psychol* 16:380–3 O '60. * (*PA* 37:3174)

981. GOCKA, EDWARD F., AND MEES, HAYDEN L. "The Representation of MMPI Scales by MMPI Factor Scales." *J Clin Psychol* 16:291–5 Jl '60. * (*PA* 36:2HF91G)

982. GOODSTEIN, LEONARD D. "MMPI Differences Between Parents of Children With Cleft Palates and Parents of Physically Normal Children." *J Speech & Hearing Res* 3:31–8 Mr '60. * (*PA* 35:6785)

983. GOODSTEIN, LEONARD D. "Personality Test Differences in Parents of Children With Cleft Palates." *J Speech & Hearing Res* 3:39–43 Mr '60. * (*PA* 35:6786)

984. GOTTESMAN, IRVING ISADORE. *The Psychogenetics of Personality.* Doctor's thesis, University of Minnesota (Minneapolis, Minn.), 1960. (*DA* 21:957)

985. GRAVES, BERNICE COURTNEY. *Interrelationships Between Some Personality and Decision-Making Variables.* Doctor's thesis, University of Texas (Austin, Tex.), 1960. (*DA* 20:4729)

986. GRIFFITH, ALBERT V., AND FOWLER, RAYMOND D. "Psychasthenic and Hypomanic Scales of the MMPI and Reaction to Authority." *J Counsel Psychol* 7:146–7 su '60. * (*PA* 35:3429)

987. HACKETT, HERBERT R. "Use of M.M.P.I. Items to Predict College Achievement." *Personnel & Guid J* 39:215–7 N '60. * (*PA* 35:3955)

988. HANEY, RUSSELL; MICHAEL, WILLIAM B.; JONES, ROBERT A.; AND GADDIS, L. WESLEY. "Cognitive and Non-Cognitive Predictors of Achievement in Student Nursing." *Ed & Psychol Meas* 20:387–9 su '60. * (*PA* 35:7120)

989. HATHAWAY, STARKE R.; MONACHESI, ELIO D.; AND ERICKSON, MARY LEE. "Relationship of College Attendance to Personality Characteristics and Early Delinquent Behavior." *Sociol Q* 1:97–106 Ap '60. * (*PA* 36:3JO97H)

990. HATHAWAY, STARKE R.; MONACHESI, ELIO D.; AND YOUNG, LAWRENCE A. "Delinquency Rates and Personality." *J Crim Law & Criminol* 50:433–40 Ja–F '60. *

991. HILL, HARRIS E.; HAERTZEN, CHARLES A.; AND GLASER, ROBERT. "Personality Characteristics of Narcotic Addicts as Indicated by the *MMPI.*" *J General Psychol* 62:127–39 Ja '60. * (*PA* 34:8044)

992. HOKANSON, JACK E., AND CALDEN, GEORGE. "Negro-White Differences on the MMPI." *J Clin Psychol* 16:32–3 Ja '60. * (*PA* 36:1HF32H)

993. HOLLAND, H. C. Chap. 4, "Measures of Perceptual Functions," pp. 193–233. In *Experiments in Personality: Vol. 2, Psychodiagnostics and Psychodynamics.* Edited by H. J. Eysenck. London: Routledge & Kegan Paul Ltd., 1960. Pp. viii, 333. *

994. JUDSON, ABE J., AND MACCASLAND, BARBARA W. "The Effects of Chlorpromazine on Psychological Test Scores." Abstract. *J Consult Psychol* 24:192 Ap '60. * (*PA* 34:7888)

995. KANUN, CLARA, AND MONACHESI, ELIO D. "Delinquency and the Validating Scales of the Minnesota Multiphasic Personality Inventory." *J Crim Law & Criminol* 50:525–34 Mr–Ap '60. * (*PA* 35:6897)

996. KELSEY, CLYDE EASTMAN, JR. *A Factor Analysis of the MMPI and the Mirror-Tracing Task.* Doctor's thesis, University of Denver (Denver, Colo.), 1960.

997. KENNEDY, WALLACE A.; NELSON, WILLARD; LINDNER, RON; TURNER, JACK; AND MOON, HAROLD. "Psychological Measurements of Future Scientists." *Psychol Rep* 7:515–7 D '60. * (*PA* 35:1522)

998. KEOGH, JACK. "Comments on the Selection of Data for Presentation." Letter. *Res Q* 31:240 My '60. * (Criticism of 733)

999. KINGSLEY, LEONARD. "MMPI Profiles of Psychopaths and Prisoners." *J Clin Psychol* 16:302–4 Jl '60. * (*PA* 36:2HF02K)

1000. KLEINMUNTZ, BENJAMIN. "An Extension of the Construct Validity of the Ego Strength Scale." *J Consult Psychol* 24:463–4 O '60. * (*PA* 35:4892)

1001. KLEINMUNTZ, BENJAMIN. "Identification of Maladjusted College Students." *J Counsel Psychol* 7:209–11 f '60. * (*PA* 36:1KD09K) Comment by Clyde A. Parker: 8:88–9 sp '61. * Reply by Benjamin Kleinmuntz: 8:279–80 f '61. *

1002. KLEINMUNTZ, BENJAMIN. "Two Types of Paranoid Schizophrenia." *J Clin Psychol* 16:310–2 Jl '60. * (*PA* 36:2JQ10K)

1003. KNAPP, ROBERT H., AND GREEN, SAMUEL. "Preferences for Styles of Abstract Art and Their Personality Correlates." *J Proj Tech* 24:396–402 D '60. * (*PA* 35:4841)

1004. KNAPP, ROBERT R. "A Reevaluation of the Validity of MMPI Scales of Dominance and Social Responsibility." *Ed & Psychol Meas* 20:381–6 su '60. * (*PA* 35:6431)

1005. KODMAN, FRANK, JR., AND McDANIEL, ERNEST. "Further Investigation of the Reliability of an MMPI Scale for Auditory Malingerers." *J Clin Psychol* 16:451 O '60. * (*PA* 37:3110)

1006. KODMAN, FRANK J.; SEDLACEK, GORDON; AND McDANIEL, ERNEST. "Performance of Suspected Auditory Malingerers on the Subtle-Obvious Keys of the MMPI." *J Clin Psychol* 16:293–5 Ap '60. * (*PA* 36:2HF93K)

1007. KORMAN, MAURICE. "Ego Strength and Conflict Discrimination: An Experimental Construct Validation of the Ego Strength Scale." *J Consult Psychol* 24:294–8 Ag '60. * (*PA* 35:2220)

1008. KORMAN, MAURICE. "Two MMPI Scales for Alcoholism: What Do They Measure?" *J Clin Psychol* 16:296–8 Jl '60. * (*PA* 36:2HC96K)

1009. KUETHE, JAMES L., AND HULSE, STEWART H. "Pessimism as a Determinant of the Tendency to Claim Undesirable Symptoms on Personality Inventories." *Psychol Rep* 7:435–8 D '60. * (*PA* 35:2221)

1010. L'ABATE, LUCIANO. "The Effect of Paternal Failure to Participate During the Referral of Child Psychiatric Patients." *J Clin Psychol* 16:407–8 O '60. * (*PA* 37:3259)

1011. LAVER, A. B. "Testing in Canada: Report No. 2." *Can Psychologist* 1:31–3 Ja '60. *

1012. LEBOVITS, BINYAMIN Z.; VISOTSKY, HAROLD M.; AND OSTFELD, ADRIAN M. "LSD and JB 318: A Comparison of Two Hallucinogens." *A.M.A. Arch Gen Psychiatry* 2:390–407 Ap '60. * (*PA* 35:5948)

1013. LEVENTHAL, ALLEN M. "Character Disorders, Disciplinary Offenders, and the MMPI." *U S Armed Forces Med J* 11:660–4 Je '60. *

1014. LINGOES, JAMES C. "MMPI Factors of the Harris and the Wiener Subscales." *J Consult Psychol* 24:74–83 F '60. * (*PA* 34:7402)

1015. LUNDIN, ROBERT W., AND KUHN, JERALD P. "The Relationship Between Scholarship Achievement and Changes in Personality Adjustment in Men After Four Years of College Attendance." *J General Psychol* 63:35–42 Jl '60. * (*PA* 35:6432)

1016. MARKWARDT, FREDERICK CHARLES, JR. *Pattern Analysis Techniques in the Prediction of College Success.* Doctor's thesis, University of Minnesota (Minneapolis, Minn.), 1960. (*DA* 21:2990)

1017. MEEHL, PAUL E., AND DAHLSTROM, W. GRANT. "Objective Configural Rules for Discriminating Psychotic From Neurotic MMPI Profiles." *J Consult Psychol* 24:375–87 O '60. * (*PA* 35:4962)

1018. MEHLMAN, BENJAMIN, AND RAND, MARTIN E. "Face Validity of the *MMPI.*" *J General Psychol* 63:171–8 O '60. * (*PA* 35:3459)

1019. MILLER, SUTHERLAND, JR. *The Relationship of Personality to Occupation, Setting and Function.* Doctor's thesis, Columbia University (New York, N.Y.), 1960. (*DA* 21:3518)

1020. MOSS, C. SCOTT, AND WATERS, THOMAS J. "Intensive Longitudinal Investigation of Anxiety in Hospitalized Juvenile Patients." *Psychol Rep* 7:379–80 O '60. * (*PA* 35:2278)

1021. NAKAMURA, CHARLES Y. "Validity of K Scale (MMPI) in College Counseling." *J Counsel Psychol* 7:108–15 su '60. * (*PA* 35:3435)

1022. OAKES, WILLIAM F., AND DROGE, ARNOLD E. "Operant Conditioning of Responses to Social Introversion Scale Items on the MMPI." *Psychol Rep* 6:223–5 Ap '60. * (*PA* 35:6433)

1023. PANTON, JAMES H. "MMPI Code Configurations as Related to Measures of Intelligence Among a State Prison Population." *J Social Psychol* 51:403–7 My '60. * (*PA* 34:8116)

1024. PANTON, JAMES H. "A New MMPI Scale for the Identification of Homosexuality." *J Clin Psychol* 16:17–21 Ja '60. * (*PA* 36:1HF17P)

1025. PEARSON, WAYNE ORLANDO. *The Relationship Between Item Difficulty and Interitem Correlation in the Minnesota Multiphasic Personality Inventory and the Guilford-Zimmerman Temperament Survey.* Doctor's thesis, Cornell University (Ithaca, N.Y.), 1960. (*DA* 20:4177)

1026. PURCELL, KENNETH; MODRICK, JOHN A.; AND YAMAHIRO, ROY. "Item vs. Trait Accuracy in Interpersonal Perception." *J General Psychol* 62:285–92 Ap '60. * (*PA* 34:7596)

1027. RASCH, PHILIP J.; HUNT, M. BRIGGS; AND ROBERTSON, PORT C. "The Booth Scale as a Predictor of Competitive Behavior of College Wrestlers." *Res Q* 31:117–8 Mr '60. *

1028. REMPEL, PETER P. "Analysis of MMPI Data for Classification Purposes by Multivariate Statistical Techniques." *J Exp Ed* 28:219–28 Mr '60. *

1029. RIPPY, MARK LEO, JR. *Certain Relationships Between Classroom Behavior and Attitude and Personality Characteristics of Selected Elementary Teachers.* Doctor's thesis, George Peabody College for Teachers (Nashville, Tenn.), 1960. (*DA* 21:814)

1030. ROBINOWITZ, RALPH. "A Shortened Schizophrenic Scale: Application to Confined Groups." *J Clin Psychol* 16: 301–2 Jl '60. * (*PA* 36:2HI01R)

1031. ROSEN, ALEXANDER C. "A Comparative Study of Alcoholic and Psychiatric Patients With the MMPI." *Q J Studies Alcohol* 21:253–66 Je '60. * (*PA* 35:1087)

1032. SARASON, SEYMOUR B.; DAVIDSON, KENNETH S.; LIGHTHALL, FREDERICK K.; WAITE, RICHARD R.; AND RUEBUSH, BRITTON K. *Anxiety in Elementary School Children: A Report of Research,* pp. 102–8. New York: John Wiley & Sons, Inc., 1960. Pp. viii, 351. * (*PA* 34:7494)

1033. SHIRLEY, JACK HAROLD. *A Comparative Study of the Academic Achievements, Interests, and Personality Traits of Athletes and Non-Athletes.* Doctor's thesis, University of Oklahoma (Norman, Okla.), 1960. (*DA* 20:4005)

1034. SHULTZ, LYLE BRITTON. "Personality and Physical Variables as Related to Refractive Errors." *Am J Optom* 37: 551–71 N '60. * (*PA* 36:3HN51S)

1035. SILVER, REUBEN J., AND SINES, LLOYD K. "MMPI High Point Code Frequencies in a State Hospital Population." *J Clin Psychol* 16:298–300 Jl '60. * (*PA* 36:2HF98S)

1036. SINES, LLOYD K., AND SILVER, REUBEN J. "MMPI Correlates of Ward Placement Among State Hospital Patients." *J Clin Psychol* 16:404–6 O '60. * (*PA* 37:3423)

1037. SIVANICH, GEORGE. *Test-Retest Changes During the Course of Hospitalization Among Some Frequently Occurring MMPI Profiles.* Doctor's thesis, University of Minnesota (Minneapolis, Minn.), 1960. (*DA* 21:2787)

1038. STEIMEL, RAYMOND J. "Childhood Experiences and Masculinity-Femininity Scores." *J Counsel Psychol* 7:212–7 f '60. * (*PA* 36:1HF12S)

1039. STEINER, IVAN D. "Sex Differences in the Resolution of A-B-X Conflicts." *J Personality* 28:118–28 Mr '60. * (*PA* 36:3GE18S)

1040. URMER, ALBERT H.; BLACK, HORACE O.; AND WENDLAND, LEONARD V. "A Comparison of Taped and Booklet Forms of the Minnesota Multiphasic Personality Inventory." *J Clin Psychol* 16:33–4 Ja '60. * (*PA* 36:1HF33U)

1041. WALLACH, MICHAEL A., AND GAHM, RUTHELLEN C. "Effects of Anxiety Level and Extraversion-Introversion on Probability Learning." *Psychol Rep* 7:387–98 D '60. * (*PA* 35:1682)

1042. WHITMORE, ELVERN LYLE. *The Use of the Minnesota Multiphasic Personality Inventory for Identifying College Freshmen Men With Potential Personal and Social Adjustment Difficulties.* Doctor's research study No. 1, Colorado State College (Greeley, Colo.), 1960.

1043. WIENER, DANIEL N. "Personality Correlates of Type of Outpatient Psychotherapy Chosen." *Am J Orthopsychiatry* 30:819–26 O '60. * (*PA* 35:6470)

1044. WILLETT, R. A. Chap. 3, "Measures of Learning and Conditioning," pp. 157–92. In *Experiments in Personality: Vol. 2, Psychodiagnostics and Psychodynamics.* Edited by H. J. Eysenck. London: Routledge & Kegan Paul Ltd., 1960. Pp. viii, 333. *

1045. YAMAHIRO, ROY S., AND GRIFFITH, RICHARD M. "Validity of Two Indices of Sexual Deviancy." *J Clin Psychol* 16:21–4 Ja '60. * (*PA* 36:1HE21Y)

1046. ZILLER, ROBERT C., AND BRANCA, ALBERT A. "Personality Correlates of Preferred Reality Testing Schedule." *Psychol Rep* 7:251–2 O '60. * (*PA* 35:2784)

1047. ZIMET, CARL N., AND BERGER, ALLAN S. "Emotional Factors in Primary Glaucoma: An Evaluation of Psychological Test Data." *Psychosom Med* 22:391–9 S–O '60. * (*PA* 35: 5300)

1048. ZUCKERMAN, MARVIN, AND BUSS, ARNOLD. "Perceptual Defense and 'Prerecognition Responsivity' in Relation to Hostility, Anxiety and Impulsivity." *J Clin Psychol* 16:45–50 Ja '60. * (*PA* 36:1HL45Z)

1049. AARONSON, BERNARD S., AND GRUMPELT, HOWARD R. "Homosexuality and Some MMPI Measures of Masculinity-Femininity." *J Clin Psychol* 17:245–7 Jl '61. * (*PA* 38:8473)

1050. ALTROCCHI, JOHN. "Interpersonal Perceptions of Repressors and Sensitizers and Component Analysis of Assumed Dissimilarity Scores." *J Abn & Social Psychol* 62:528–34 My '61. * (*PA* 36:4HL28A)

1051. ANASTASI, ANNE. *Psychological Testing, Second Edition,* pp. 498–507. New York: Macmillan Co., 1961. Pp. xiii, 657. * (*PA* 36:1HA57A)

1052. ANDERSON, THELMA HILL. *Dimensions of the Characteristics Related to the High- and Low-Achievement of a Selected Group of Negro College Students.* Doctor's thesis, University of Oklahoma (Norman, Okla.), 1961. (*DA* 22: 1082)

1053. ANKER, JAMES M. "Chronicity of Neuropsychiatric Hospitalization: A Predictive Scale." *J Consult Psychol* 25: 425–32 O '61. * (*PA* 37:3210)

1054. ARCHIBALD, HERBERT C.; BELL, DOROTHY; MILLER, CHRISTINE; AND THOMPSON, CLARE W. "Psychosomatic V." *J Psychol* 52:281–5 O '61. * (*PA* 36:3JU81A)

1055. ASTIN, ALEXANDER W. "A Note on the MMPI Psychopathic Deviate Scale." *Ed & Psychol Meas* 21:895–7 w '61. * (*PA* 36:5HF95A)

1056. BANNISTER, D., AND BEECH, H. R. "An Evaluation of the Feldman Prognosis Scale for Shock Therapy." *J Mental Sci* 107:503–8 My '61. * (*PA* 36:3ID03B)

1057. BARGER, PATRICIA M., AND SECHREST, LEE. "Con-

vergent and Discriminant Validity of Four Holtzman Inkblot Test Variables." *J Psychol Studies* 12:227–36 N '61 [issued Ap '63]. *

1058. BECKER, WESLEY C. "A Comparison of the Factor Structure and Other Properties of the 16 PF and the Guilford-Martin Personality Inventories." *Ed & Psychol Meas* 21:393–404 su '61. * (*PA* 36:2HF93B)

1059. BEIER, ERNST G.; ROSSI, ASCANIO M.; AND GARFIELD, REED L. "Similarity Plus Dissimilarity of Personality: Basis for Friendship?" *Psychol Rep* 8:3–8 F '61. * (*PA* 36:1GE08B)

1060. BENDIG, A. W. "A Factor Analysis of Scales of Emotionality and Hostility." *J Clin Psychol* 17:189–92 Ap '61. * (*PA* 38:1034)

1061. BINDER, ARNOLD, AND SALOP, PHYLLIS. "Reinforcement and Personality Factors in Verbal Conditioning." *J Psychol* 52:379–402 O '61. * (*PA* 36:3CI79B)

1062. BLOOM, BERNARD L., AND ARKOFF, ABE. "Role Playing in Acute and Chronic Schizophrenia." *J Consult Psychol* 25: 24–8 F '61. * (*PA* 36:3JQ24B)

1063. BOOTH, E. G., JR. "Personality Traits of Athletes as Measured by the MMPI: A Rebuttal." *Res Q* 32:421–3 O '61. * (*PA* 36:4HF21B)

1064. BRANCA, ALBERT A., AND PODOLNICK, EDWARD E. "Normal, Hypnotically Induced, and Feigned Anxiety as Reflected in and Detected by the MMPI." *J Consult Psychol* 25:165–70 Ap '61. * (*PA* 36:4II65B)

1065. BRIGGS, PETER F.; WIRT, ROBERT D.; AND JOHNSON, ROCHELLE. "An Application of Prediction Tables to the Study of Delinquency." *J Consult Psychol* 25:46–50 F '61. * (*PA* 36:3JQ46B)

1066. BROTHERS, WILBUR L. "Some Correlates With the Minnesota Multiphasic Personality Inventory." *J Ed Res* 55:36–8 S '61. *

1067. BYRNE, DONN. "The Repression-Sensitization Scale: Rationale, Reliability, and Validity." *J Personality* 29:334–49 S '61. * (*PA* 37:3290)

1068. CABEEN, CHARLES W., AND COLEMAN, JAMES C. "Group Therapy With Sex Offenders: Description and Evaluation of Group Therapy Program in an Institutional Setting." *J Clin Psychol* 17:122–9 Ap '61. * (*PA* 38:1107)

1069. CADITZ, SYLVAN B. "Effects of a Forestry Camp Experience on the Personality of Delinquent Boys." *J Clin Psychol* 17:78–81 Ja '61. * (*PA* 37:3630)

1070. CARKHUFF, ROBERT R. *The MMPI: An Outline for General Clinical and Counseling Use.* Lexington, Ky.: the Author, University of Kentucky, 1961. Pp. vi, 60. * (*PA* 37:6811)

1071. CHRISTENSEN, C. M. "Use of Design, Texture, and Color Preferences in Assessment of Personality Characteristics." *Percept & Motor Skills* 12:143–50 Ap '61. * (*PA* 36:1HB43C)

1072. CHYATTE, CONRAD, AND GOLDMAN, IRWIN J. "The Willingness of Actors to Admit to Socially Undesirable Behavior on the MMPI." *J Clin Psychol* 17:44 Ja '61. * (*PA* 37:3170)

1073. CLAGETT, ARTHUR F. "Hathaway vs. Welsh on Coding the MMPI and a Method Proposed to Reconcile Differences of Viewpoint." *J Clin Psychol* 17:154–6 Ap '61. * (*PA* 38:993)

1074. COATS, J. E.; WITH THE ASSISTANCE OF R. G. GARNER. *A Study of the Nature of the Chemical Operator's Occupation and the Personal Qualities That Contribute to Successful Operator Performance.* Midland, Mich.: Dow Chemical Co., March 1961. Pp. iv, 112. *

1075. COLE, DAVID L. "The Prediction of Teaching Performance." *J Ed Res* 54:345–8 My '61. * (*PA* 36:3KM45C)

1076. COMREY, ANDREW L., AND NENCINI, RODOLFO. "Factors in MMPI Responses of Italian Students." *Ed & Psychol Meas* 21:657–62 au '61. * (*PA* 36:4HF57C)

1077. COOK, DESMOND L.; LINDEN, JAMES D.; AND McKAY, HARRISON E. "A Factor Analysis of Teacher Trainee Responses to Selected Personality Inventories." *Ed & Psychol Meas* 21:865–72 w '61. * (*PA* 36:5HF65C)

1078. COUCH, ARTHUR, AND KENISTON, KENNETH. "Agreeing Response Set and Social Desirability." *J Abn & Social Psychol* 62:175–9 Ja '61. * (*PA* 36:3HF75C)

1079. DENBERG, M. L.; PHILLIPS, R. L.; AND SPERRAZZO, G. "The Relationship Between M.M.P.I. and Prison Disciplinary Reports." *Proc 91st Annual Congr Am Corr Assn* 1961:233–6 '61. *

1080. DUDA, WALTER BOLESLAV. *The Prediction of Three Major Dimensions of Teacher Behavior for Student Teachers in Music Education.* Doctor's thesis, University of Illinois (Urbana, Ill.), 1961. (*DA* 22:1518)

1081. DYER, DOROTHY TUNELL, AND LUCKEY, ELEANORE BRAUN. "Religious Affiliation and Selected Personality Scores as They Relate to Marital Happiness of a Minnesota College Sample." *Marriage & Family Living* 23:46–7 F '61. * (*PA* 36:3JQ46D)

1082. EDWARDS, ALLEN L. "Social Desirability of Acquiescence in the MMPI? A Case Study With the SD Scale." *J Abn & Social Psychol* 63:351–9 S '61. * (*PA* 37:1249)

1083. EDWARDS, ALLEN L., AND WALKER, JERALD N. "A Note on the Couch and Keniston Measure of Agreement Response Set." *J Abn & Social Psychol* 62:173–4 Ja '61. * (*PA* 36: 3HF73E)

1084. EDWARDS, ALLEN L., AND WALKER, JERALD N. "A

Short Form of the MMPI: The SD Scale." *Psychol Rep* 8:485-6 Je '61. * (*PA* 36:2HF85E)

1085. EDWARDS, ALLEN L., AND WALKER, JERALD N. "Social Desirability and Agreement Response Set." *J Abn & Social Psychol* 62:180-3 Ja '61. * (*PA* 36:3HF80E)

1086. EICHMAN, WILLIAM J. "Replicated Factors on the MMPI With Female NP Patients." *J Consult Psychol* 25:55-60 F '61. * (*PA* 36:3HF55E)

1087. FIELD, J. G., AND BRENGELMANN, J. C. "Eyelid Conditioning and Three Personality Parameters." *J Abn & Social Psychol* 63:517-23 N '61. * (*PA* 37:369)

1088. FILLENBAUM, SAMUEL, AND JACKMAN, ARNOLD. "Dogmatism and Anxiety in Relation to Problem Solving: An Extension of Rokeach's Results." *J Abn & Social Psychol* 63:212-4 Jl '61. * (*PA* 36:4HK12F)

1089. FINE, BERNARD J. "Welsh's Internalization Ratio as a Behavioral Index." *J Appl Psychol* 45:117-9 Ap '61. * (*PA* 36:3LD17F)

1090. FINNEY, JOSEPH C. "The MMPI as a Measure of Character Structure as Revealed by Factor Analysis." *J Consult Psychol* 25:327-36 Ag '61. * (*PA* 37:1254)

1091. FLANAGAN, CARROLL EDWARD. "A Study of the Relationship of Scores on the MMPI to Success in Teaching as Indicated by Supervisory Ratings." *J Exp Ed* 29:330-54 Je '61. *

1092. FLORIDO, HERMINIA A. *Personality Patterns of 141 Unmarried Mothers on the MMPI.* Master's thesis, Immaculate Heart College (Los Angeles, Calif.), 1961.

1093. FORSYTH, RALPH P., AND FAIRWEATHER, GEORGE W. "Psychotherapeutic and Other Hospital Treatment Criteria: The Dilemma." *J Abn & Social Psychol* 62:598-604 My '61. * (*PA* 36:4IE98F)

1094. FORT, GERALD MARSHALL. *An Actuarial Identification of Characteristics Which Discriminate Among Certain Specified Student Subgroups Enrolled in a Midwestern Land Grant College During a Recent Six Year Period.* Doctor's thesis, University of Minnesota (Minneapolis, Minn.), 1961. (*DA* 22:2683)

1095. GIEDT, F. HAROLD, AND DOWNING, LES. "An Extraversion Scale for the MMPI." *J Clin Psychol* 17:156-9 Ap '61. * (*PA* 38:996)

1096. GILBERSTADT, HAROLD, AND FARKAS, EDWIN. "Another Look at MMPI Profile Types in Multiple Sclerosis." *J Consult Psychol* 25:440-4 O '61. * (*PA* 37:3218)

1097. GOCKA, EDWARD F., AND MARKS, JOHN B. "Second-Order Factors in the 16 PF Test and MMPI Inventory." *J Clin Psychol* 17:32-5 Ja '61. * (*PA* 37:3175)

1098. GOOD, PATRICIA KING-ELLISON, AND BRANTNER, JOHN P. *The Physician's Guide to the MMPI.* Minneapolis, Minn.: University of Minnesota Press, 1961. Pp. 69. *

1099. GOODSTEIN, LEONARD D., AND KIRK, BARBARA A. "A Six-Year Follow-Up Study of Graduate Students in Public Health Education." *J Appl Psychol* 45:240-3 Ag '61. * (*PA* 36:4LB40B)

1100. GOODSTEIN, LEONARD D., AND ROWLEY, VINTON N. "A Further Study of MMPI Differences Between Parents of Disturbed and Nondisturbed Children." Abstract. *J Consult Psychol* 25:460 O '61. * (*PA* 37:2919)

1101. GORMAN, JOHN R. *A Study of Adjustment and Interests for Fourth Year Minor Seminarians Studying for the Diocesan Priesthood.* Master's thesis, Loyola University (Chicago, Ill.), 1961.

1102. GOUWS, DAVID J. "Prediction of Relapse for Psychiatric Patients." *J Consult Psychol* 25:142-5 Ap '61. * (*PA* 36:4IB42G)

1103. GYNTHER, MALCOLM D. "The Clinical Utility of 'Invalid' MMPI F Scores." *J Consult Psychol* 25:540-2 D '61. * (*PA* 37:5039)

1104. GYNTHER, MALCOLM D., AND MCDONALD, ROBERT L. "Personality Characteristics of Prisoners, Psychiatric Patients, and Student Nurses as Depicted by the Leary System." *J General Psychol* 64:387-95 Ap '61. * (*PA* 36:1HF87G)

1105. HANLEY, CHARLES. "Social Desirability and Response Bias in the MMPI." *J Consult Psychol* 25:13-20 F '61. * (*PA* 36:3HF13H)

1106. HATHAWAY, STARKE R., AND MONACHESI, ELIO D. *An Atlas of Juvenile MMPI Profiles.* Minneapolis, Minn.: University of Minnesota Press, 1961. Pp. xviii, 402. * (*PA* 36:2HF02H)

1107. HEILBRUN, ALFRED B., JR. "The Psychological Significance of the MMPI K Scale in a Normal Population." *J Consult Psychol* 25:486-91 D '61. * (*PA* 37:5010)

1108. HENRY, PHYLLIS MELLOR. *The Relationship Between Empathic Behavior and Personality Variables Among Teachers.* Doctor's thesis, University of Buffalo (Buffalo, N.Y.), 1961. (*DA* 22:2705)

1109. JACKSON, DOUGLAS N., AND MESSICK, SAMUEL. "Acquiescence and Desirability as Response Determinants on the MMPI." *Ed & Psychol Meas* 21:771-90 w '61. * (*PA* 36:5HF71M)

1110. KARMEL, LOUIS JOSEPH. *An Analysis of the Personality Patterns, and Academic and Social Backgrounds of Persons Employed as Full-Time Counselors in Selected Secondary Schools in the State of North Carolina.* Doctor's thesis, University of North Carolina (Chapel Hill, N.C.), 1961. (*DA* 23:531)

1111. KIESLER, CHARLES A., AND KING, GERALD F. "Individual Differences in Making Perceptual Inferences." *Percept & Motor Skills* 13:3-6 Ag '61. *

1112. KIRESUK, THOMAS JACK. *The Effect of Test Sophistication on the Diagnostic Validity of the Minnesota Multiphasic Personality Inventory and the Rorschach With Paranoid Schizophrenics.* Doctor's thesis, University of Minnesota (Minneapolis, Minn.), 1961. (*DA* 22:2875)

1113. KLEINMUNTZ, BENJAMIN. "The College Maladjustment Scale (MT): Norms and Predictive Validity." *Ed & Psychol Meas* 21:1029-33 w '61. *

1114. KLOPFER, WALTER G. "A Cross-Validation of Leary's 'Public' Communication Level." *J Clin Psychol* 17:321-2 Jl '61. * (*PA* 38:8426)

1115. KUETHE, JAMES L. "The Interaction of Personality and Muscle Tension in Producing Agreement on Commonality of Verbal Associations." *J Abn & Social Psychol* 62:696-7 My '61. * (*PA* 36:4HJ96K)

1116. LAFORGE, ROLFE. "Objective Estimates of Clinical Judgments." *J Consult Psychol* 25:360-1 Ag '61. * (*PA* 37:1288)

1117. LAUTERBACH, CARL; LONDON, PERRY; AND BRYAN, JAMES. "MMPI's of Parents of Child Guidance Cases." *J Clin Psychol* 17:151-4 Ap '61. * (*PA* 38:700)

1118. LEWIS, JOHN W., AND CALDWELL, WILLARD E. "A Psycholinguistic Investigation of Verbal Psychological Tests." *J General Psychol* 65:137-44 Jl '61. * (*PA* 36:2HF31L)

1119. LICHTENSTEIN, EDWARD; QUINN, ROBERT P.; AND HOVER, GERALD L. "Dogmatism and Acquiescent Response Set." *J Abn & Social Psychol* 63:636-8 N '61. * (*PA* 37:1231)

1120. LOWE, JAMES DOUGLAS. *The MMPI and Prognosis in Alcoholism.* Master's thesis, University of Alabama (University, Ala.), 1961.

1121. LUTZKER, DANIEL R. "A Validity Study of Tamkin's 'MMPI Scale Measuring Severity of Psychopathology.'" *J Clin Psychol* 17:289-90 Jl '61. * (*PA* 38:8525)

1121a. MCCALL, CLARENCE M.; SZMYD, LUCIAN; AND RITTER, RICHARD M. "Personality Characteristics in Patients With Temporomandibular Joint Symptoms." *J Am Dental Assn* 62:694-8 Je '61. *

1122. MCDONAGH, ANDREW J. *A Study of Adjustments and Interests of First-Year College Seminarians for the Diocesan Priesthood.* Master's thesis, Loyola University (Chicago, Ill.), 1961.

1123. MCKENZIE, JAMES DONALD, JR. *An Attempt to Develop Minnesota Multiphasic Personality Inventory Scales Predictive of Academic Over- and Underachievement.* Doctor's thesis, University of Buffalo (Buffalo, N.Y.), 1961. (*DA* 22:632)

1124. MACKINNON, DONALD W. "Fostering Creativity in Students of Engineering." *J Eng Ed* 52:129-42 D '61. * (*PA* 36:4HD29M)

1125. MADDEN, JAMES E. "Semantic Differential Rating of Self and of Self-Reported Personal Characteristics." Abstract. *J Consult Psychol* 25:183 Ap '61. * (*PA* 36:4HF83M)

1126. MARKS, PHILIP A. "An Assessment of the Diagnostic Process in a Child Guidance Setting." *Psychol Monogr* 75(3):1-41 '61. * (*PA* 36:3IQ41M)

1127. MEIER, MANFRED J. "Interrelationships Among Personality Variables, Kinesthetic Figural Aftereffect, and Reminiscence in Motor Learning." *J Abn & Social Psychol* 63:87-94 Jl '61. * (*PA* 36:4HJ87M)

1128. MESSICK, SAMUEL, AND JACKSON, DOUGLAS N. "Acquiescence and the Factorial Interpretation of the MMPI." *Psychol B* 58:299-304 Jl '61. * (*PA* 36:3HF99M)

1129. MESSICK, SAMUEL, AND JACKSON, DOUGLAS N. "Desirability Scale Values and Dispersions for MMPI Items." *Psychol Rep* 8:409-14 Je '61. * (*PA* 36:2HF09M)

1130. MILLER, CHRISTINE; WERTZ, CLARA; AND COUNTS, SARAH. "Racial Differences on the MMPI." *J Clin Psychol* 17:159-61 Ap '61. * (*PA* 38:998)

1131. OLSON, GORDON W. "The Influence of Context on the Depression Scale of the MMPI in a Psychotic Population." *J Consult Psychol* 25:178-9 Ap '61. * (*PA* 36:4HF78O)

1132. OSKAMP, STUART WILLARD. *The Relationship of Clinical Experience and Training Methods to Several Criteria of Clinical Prediction.* Doctor's thesis, Stanford University (Stanford, Calif.), 1961. (*DA* 21:3527)

1133. PALOLA, ERNEST G.; JACKSON, JOAN K.; AND KELLEHER, DANIEL. "Defensiveness in Alcoholics: Measures Based on the Minnesota Multiphasic Personality Inventory." *J Health & Human Behav* 2:185-9 f '61. * (*PA* 37:1724)

1134. PARKER, CLYDE A. "The Predictive Use of the MMPI in a College Counseling Center." *J Counsel Psychol* 8:154-8 su '61. * (*PA* 36:3KI54P)

1135. PEARSON, DEAN N. *An MMPI Syndrome of Scales Pd, Mf, and Pa, With Counseled University Women.* Master's thesis, Brigham Young University (Provo, Utah), 1961.

1136. PHILIPPUS, MARION JOHN. *A Study of Personality, Value and Interest Patterns of Student Teachers in the Areas of Elementary, Secondary and Special Education.* Doctor's thesis, University of Denver (Denver, Colo.), 1961. (*DA* 22:3926)

1137. RANDOLPH, MARY H.; RICHARDSON, HAROLD; AND JOHNSON, RONALD C. "A Comparison of Social and Solitary Male Delinquents." *J Consult Psychol* 25:293-5 Ag '61. * (*PA* 37:1752)

1138. REES, MARJORIE E., AND GOLDMAN, MORTON. "Some Relationships Between Creativity and Personality." *J General Psychol* 65:145–61 Jl '61. * (*PA* 36:2HD45R)

1139. RHUDICK, PAUL J., AND DIBNER, ANDREW S. "Age, Personality, and Health Correlates of Death Concerns in Normal Aged Individuals." *J Gerontol* 16:44–9 Ja '61. * (*PA* 35:6241)

1140. RICHARDSON, CHARLES E. "Health Education or Hypochondriasis." *Am J Pub Health* 51:1561–71 O '61. *

1141. RIECK, ELMER CHRISTIAN. "A Comparison of Teachers' Response Patterns on the MMPI With Response Patterns of Selected Non-Teacher Groups." *J Exp Ed* 29:355–72 Je '61. *

1142. RIGNEY, FRANCIS J., AND SMITH, L. DOUGLAS. *The Real Bohemia: A Sociological and Psychological Study of the "Beats."* New York: Basic Books, Inc., 1961. Pp. xxi, 250. * (*PA* 36:1GB50R)

1143. ROSEN, EPHRAIM, AND MINK, SHIRLEY HOLT. "Desirability of Personality Traits as Perceived by Prisoners." *J Clin Psychol* 17:147–51 Ap '61. * (*PA* 38:1000)

1144. ROSEN, EPHRAIM, AND RIZZO, GIOVANNI B. "Preliminary Standardization of the MMPI for Use in Italy: A Case Study in Inter-Cultural and Intra-Cultural Differences." *Ed & Psychol Meas* 21:629–36 au '61. * (*PA* 36:4HF29R)

1145. SECHREST, LEE. "Social Intelligence and Accuracy of Interpersonal Predictions." *J Personality* 29:167–82 Je '61. * (*PA* 36:4HA67S)

1146. SECTER, IRVING I. "Personality Factors of the MMPI and Hypnotizability." *Am J Clin Hypnosis* 3:185–8 Ja '61. * (*PA* 36:1I185S)

1146a. SECTER, IRVING I., AND TREMAINE, DONAHUE L. "Hypnosis and the Personality of the Operator." *J Am Dental Assn* 63:106–8 Jl '61. *

1147. SILVER, REUBEN J., AND SINES, LLOYD K. "MMPI Characteristics of a State Hospital Population." *J Clin Psychol* 17:142–6 Ap '61. * (*PA* 38:1002)

1148. SINGER, JEROME L., AND SCHONBAR, ROSALEA A. "Correlates of Daydreaming: A Dimension of Self-Awareness." *J Consult Psychol* 25:1–6 F '61. *

1149. SINNETT, E. ROBERT. "The Prediction of Irregular Discharge Among Alcoholic Patients." *J Social Psychol* 55:231–5 D '61. * (*PA* 36:3JK31S)

1150. SPRUNGER, JAMES A. "The Ability of the Individual to Contribute to His Group." *Personnel Psychol* 14:317–30 au '61. * (*PA* 37:5729)

1151. STIAVELLI, RICHARD E. *A Minnesota Multiphasic Personality Inventory Study of College Freshmen.* Master's thesis, Fresno State College (Fresno, Calif.), 1961.

1152. STRICKER, GEORGE. "A Comparison of Two MMPI Prejudice Scales." *J Clin Psychol* 17:43 Ja '61. * (*PA* 37:3181)

1153. STROMMEN, ELLEN, AND AMMONS, ROBERT BRUCE. "Relationship of Value Placed on Intellectual Activity to Social Desirability of Attitude, Theoretical Orientation, and Interest in Problem-Solving." *Proc Mont Acad Sci* 20:78–84 '61. * (*PA* 36:1GD78S)

1153a. SULZER, EDWARD S. "The Effects of Promazine on MMPI: Performance in the Chronic Psychiatric Patient." *Psychopharmacologia* 2(2):137–40 '61. *

1154. SWENSON, WENDELL M. "Structured Personality Testing in the Aged: An MMPI Study of the Gerontic Population." *J Clin Psychol* 17:302–4 Jl '61. * (*PA* 38:8534)

1155. SWICKARD, DON L., AND SPILKA, BERNARD. "Hostility Expression Among Delinquents of Minority and Majority Groups." *J Consult Psychol* 25:216–20 Je '61. *

1156. TAFT, RONALD. "A Psychological Assessment of Professional Actors and Related Professions." *Genetic Psychol Monogr* 64:309–83 N '61. * (*PA* 36:3LC09T)

1157. TAMKIN, ARTHUR S. "Effect of Psychopathology Upon Mirror Drawing Performance." *Percept & Motor Skills* 13:82 Ag '61. *

1158. TAULBEE, EARL S. "The Relationship Between Rorschach Flexor and Extensor M Responses and the MMPI and Psychotherapy." *J Proj Tech* 25:477–9 D '61. *

1159. THURSTON, JOHN R.; BRUNCLIK, HELEN L.; AND FINN, PATRICIA A. "The Relationship of MMPI Scores to Personality and Achievement Levels of Student Nurses." *J Psychol Studies* 12:75–86 Mr '61. *

1160. TOMS, ESTHER C. "A Comparative Study of Selected Tranquilizers in the Treatment of Psychiatric Patients." *J Nerv & Mental Dis* 132:425–31 My '61. *

1161. VERTEIN, LESTER DALE. "A Study of the Personal-Social and Intellectual Characteristics of a Group of State College Students Preparing to Teach." *J Exp Ed* 30:159–92 D '61. *

1162. WAGNER, RUDOLPH F., AND WILLIAMS, JOHN E. "An Analysis of Speech Behavior in Groups Differing in Achievement Imagery and Defensiveness." *J Personality* 29:1–9 Mr '61. * (*PA* 36:1HE01W)

1163. WAHLER, H. J. "Response Styles in Clinical and Non-clinical Groups." *J Consult Psychol* 25:533–9 D '61. * (*PA* 37:5020)

1164. WALKER, JERALD NEIL. *An Examination of the Role of the Experimentally Determined Response Set in Evaluating Edwards' Social Desirability Scale.* Doctor's thesis, University of Washington (Seattle, Wash.), 1961. (*DA* 22:1712)

1165. WEITZENHOFFER, ANDRE M., AND SJOBERG, BERNARD M. "Suggestibility With and Without 'Induction of Hypnosis.' " *J Nerv & Mental Dis* 132:204–20 Mr '61. * (*PA* 36:1I104W)

1166. WIENER, DANIEL N. "Evaluation of Selection Procedures for a Management Development Program." *J Counsel Psychol* 8:121–8 su '61. * (*PA* 36:3LD21W)

1167. ZUCKERMAN, MARVIN; LEVITT, EUGENE E.; AND LUBIN, BERNARD. "Concurrent and Construct Validity of Direct and Indirect Measures of Dependency." *J Consult Psychol* 25:316–23 Ag '61. * (*PA* 37:1326)

1168. ACKER, CHARLES W., AND NAKAMURA, CHARLES Y. "Performance of Chronic Schizophrenics on Inventory Measures of Over-Controlled and Under-Controlled Behavior." *J Clin Psychol* 18:488–90 O '62. * (*PA* 39:5739)

1169. ADAMS, HENRY B., AND COOPER, G. DAVID. "Three Measures of Ego Strength and Prognosis for Psychotherapy." *J Clin Psychol* 18:490–4 O '62. * (*PA* 39:5142)

1170. BALL, JOHN C. *Social Deviancy and Adolescent Personality: An Analytical Study With the MMPI.* Lexington, Ky.: University of Kentucky Press, 1962. Pp. xv, 119. * (*PA* 37:8176)

1171. BENDIG, A. W. "A Factor Analysis of 'Social Desirability,' 'Defensiveness,' 'Lie,' and 'Acquiescence' Scales." *J General Psychol* 66:129–36 Ja '62. * (*PA* 36:3HF29B)

1172. BERNARD, JOHN L. "Manipulation of Verbal Behavior Without Reinforcement." *Psychol Rep* 11:390 O '62. * (*PA* 37:7960)

1173. BRADY, JOHN PAUL; PAPPAS, NICHOLAS; TAUSIG, THEODORE N.; AND THORNTON, DOUGLAS R. "MMPI Correlates of Operant Behavior." *J Clin Psychol* 18:67–70 Ja '62. * (*PA* 38:8512)

1174. BRECHER, HAROLD. *An Investigation of the Relationship Between Repression-Sensitization and Perception.* Doctor's thesis, Temple University (Philadelphia, Pa.), 1962. (*DA* 23:699)

1175. BRIGGS, PETER F.; JOHNSON, ROCHELLE; AND WIRT, ROBERT D. "Achievement Among Delinquency-Prone Adolescents." *J Clin Psychol* 18:305–9 Jl '62. * (*PA* 39:1886)

1176. BROWN, ROBERT A., AND GOODSTEIN, LEONARD D. "Adjective Check List Correlates of Extreme Scores on the MMPI Depression Scale." *J Clin Psychol* 18:477–81 O '62. *

1177. BUTTERFIELD, EARL C., AND WARREN, SUE ALLEN. "The Use of the MMPI in the Selection of Hospital Aides." *J Appl Psychol* 46:34–40 F '62. * (*PA* 36:5LD34B)

1178. CANTER, ARTHUR; DAY, CHARLES W.; IMBODEN, JOHN B.; AND CLUFF, LEIGHTON E. "The Influence of Age and Health Status on the MMPI Scores of a Normal Population." *J Clin Psychol* 18:71–3 Ja '62. * (*PA* 38:8514)

1179. CENTI, PAUL. "Personality Factors Related to College Success." *J Ed Res* 55:187–8 D–Ja '62. *

1180. CERBUS, GEORGE, AND NICHOLS, ROBERT C. "Personality Correlates of Picture Preferences." *J Abn & Social Psychol* 64:75–8 Ja '62. * (*PA* 37:3139)

1181. CHRISTENSEN, C. M. "Dimensions and Correlates of Texture Preferences." *J Consult Psychol* 26:498–504 D '62. *

1182. CLEGG, HERMAN D., AND DECKER, ROBERT L. "The Evaluation of a Psychological Test Battery as a Selective Device for Foremen in the Mining Industry." *Proc W Va Acad Sci* 34:178–82 N '62. *

1183. COROTTO, LOREN V., AND CURNUTT, ROBERT H. "Ego Strength: A Function of the Measuring Instrument." *J Proj Tech* 26:228–30 Je '62. *

1184. CRAFT, MICHAEL; FABISCH, WALTER; STEPHENSON, GEOFFRY; BURNAND, GORDON; AND KERRIDGE, DAVID. "100 Admissions to a Psychopathic Unit." *J Mental Sci* 108:564–83 S '62. * (*PA* 38:2138)

1185. DAHLSTROM, W. GRANT. Chap. 9, "Commentary: The Roles of Social Desirability and Acquiescence in Responses to the MMPI," pp. 157–68. In *Measurement in Personality and Cognition.* Edited by Samuel Messick and John Ross. New York: John Wiley & Sons, Inc., 1962. Pp. xi, 334. * (*PA* 38:2638)

1186. DONOGHUE, JOHN R. "A Consideration of Taulbee and Sisson's 'Configurational Analysis of MMPI Profiles of Psychiatric Groups.' " *J Clin Psychol* 18:309–12 Jl '62. *

1187. DRAKE, L. E. "MMPI Patterns Predictive of Underachievement." *J Counsel Psychol* 9:164–7 su '62. * (*PA* 37:7186)

1188. EADDY, MORRIS LEE. *An Investigation of the Cannot Say Scale of the Group Minnesota Multiphasic Personality Inventory.* Doctor's thesis, University of Florida (Gainesville, Fla.), 1962. (*DA* 23:1070)

1189. EDWARDS, ALLEN L. Chap. 6, "The Social Desirability Hypothesis: Theoretical Implications for Personality Measurement," pp. 91–108. In *Measurement in Personality and Cognition.* Edited by Samuel Messick and John Ross. New York: John Wiley & Sons, Inc., 1962. Pp. xi, 334. * (*PA* 38:2638)

1190. EDWARDS, ALLEN L. "Social Desirability and Expected Means on MMPI Scales." *Ed & Psychol Meas* 22:71–6 sp '62. * (*PA* 37:1250)

1191. EDWARDS, ALLEN L., AND DIERS, CAROL J. "Social Desirability and the Factorial Interpretation of the MMPI." *Ed & Psychol Meas* 22:501–9 au '62. * (*PA* 37:5008)

1192. EDWARDS, ALLEN L., AND HEATHERS, LOUISE B. "The First Factor of the MMPI: Social Desirability or Ego Strength?" *J Consult Psychol* 26:99–100 F '62. * (*PA* 37:5007)

1193. EDWARDS, ALLEN L.; DIERS, CAROL J.; AND WALKER, JERALD N. "Response Sets and Factor Loadings on Sixty-One Personality Scales." *J Appl Psychol* 46:220–5 Je '62. * (*PA* 37:1226)

1194. EICHMAN, WILLIAM J. "Factored Scales for the MMPI: A Clinical and Statistical Manual." *J Clin Psychol* 18:363–95 O '62. * (*PA* 39:5173)

1195. ENGEL, ILONA MARIA. *A Factor Analytic Study of Items From Five Masculinity-Femininity Tests.* Doctor's thesis, University of Michigan (Ann Arbor, Mich.), 1962. (*DA* 23:307)

1196. EYSENCK, H. J. "Response Set, Authoritarianism and Personality Questionnaires." *Brit J Social & Clin Psychol* 1:20–4 F '62. * (*PA* 37:1252)

1197. FEINGOLD, BEN F.; GORMAN, FRANK J.; SINGER, MARGARET THALER; AND SCHLESINGER, KURT. "Psychological Studies of Allergic Women: The Relation Between Skin Reactivity and Personality." *Psychosom Med* 24:195–202 Mr–Ap '62. * (*PA* 37:3757)

1198. FIGURA, C. JOHN. *Validity of the Beall-Panton MMPI Index of "Escapism" in a State Training School Population.* Master's thesis, Loyola University (Chicago, Ill.), 1962.

1199. FISHER, GARY M., AND PARSONS, THOMAS H. "The Performance of Male Prisoners on the Marlowe-Crowne Social Desirability Scale." *J Clin Psychol* 18:140–1 Ap '62. * (*PA* 38:8487)

1199a. GARETZ, FLOYD K., AND TIERNEY, ROBERT W. "Personality Variables in Army Officer Candidates." *Mil Med* 127:669–72 Ag '62. *

1200. GAURON, EUGENE; SEVERSON, ROGER; AND ENGELHART, ROLAND. "MMPI F Scores and Psychiatric Diagnosis." Abstract. *J Consult Psychol* 26:488 O '62. *

1201. GILBERSTADT, HAROLD. "A Modal MMPI Profile Type in Neurodermatitis." *Psychosom Med* 24:471–6 S–O '62. * (*PA* 37:5525)

1201a. GILLER, DONALD W. "Some Psychological Correlates of Recovery From Surgery." *Tex Rep Biol & Med* 20:366–73 f '62. *

1202. GOCKA, EDWARD F. "Scoring Direction and Social Desirability Effects." *J Psychol Studies* 13:31–4 Mr '62 [issued N '63]. *

1203. GOCKA, EDWARD F., AND HOLLOWAY, HILDEGUND. "A Composite MMPI Introversion-Extraversion Scale." *J Clin Psychol* 18:474–7 O '62. * (*PA* 39:5176)

1204. GOLDEN, JULES; MANDEL, NATHAN; GLUECK, BERNARD C., JR.; AND FEDER, ZETTA. "A Summary Description of Fifty 'Normal' White Males." *Am J Psychiatry* 119:48–56 Jl '62. * (*PA* 37:5009)

1205. GOLDFRIED, MARVIN R. "Rorschach Developmental Level and the MMPI as Measures of Severity of Psychological Disturbance." *J Proj Tech* 26:187–92 Je '62. * (*PA* 37:3219)

1206. GOLDMAN, IRWIN J. "Social Desirability, Manifest Anxiety, and Schizophrenic Response." *Psychol Rep* 11:637–8 D '62. * (*PA* 38:2694)

1207. GOLDMAN, IRWIN J. *The Willingness of Music and Visual Art Students to Admit to Socially Undesirable and Psychopathological Characteristics.* Doctor's thesis, Columbia University (New York, N.Y.), 1962. (*DA* 23:732)

1208. GOLDSTEIN, ROBERT H., AND SALZMAN, LEONARD F. "Correlates of Clinical Judgment in Psychiatry." *J Med Ed* 37:1101–4 O '62. *

1209. GOTTESMAN, IRVING I. "Differential Inheritance of the Psychoneuroses." *Eug Q* 9:223–7 D '62. * (*PA* 37:7729)

1210. GYNTHER, MALCOLM D. "Crime and Psychopathology." *J Abn & Social Psychol* 64:378–80 My '62. * (*PA* 38:1295)

1211. GYNTHER, MALCOLM D. "Degree of Agreement Among Three 'Interpersonal System' Measures." Abstract. *J Consult Psychol* 26:107 F '62. * (*PA* 37:4982)

1212. HANEY, RUSSELL; MICHAEL, WILLIAM B.; AND GERSHON, ARTHUR. "Achievement, Aptitude, and Personality Measures as Predictors of Success in Nursing Training." *Ed & Psychol Meas* 22:389–92 su '62. * (*PA* 37:3869)

1213. HANLEY, CHARLES. "The 'Difficulty' of a Personality Inventory Item." *Ed & Psychol Meas* 22:577–84 au '62. * (*PA* 37:4934)

1214. HARTLEY, RAYMOND E., AND ALLEN, ROBERT M. "The Minnesota Multiphasic Personality Inventory (MMPI) and the Edwards Personal Preference Schedule (EPPS): A Factor Analytic Study." *J Social Psychol* 58:153–62 O '62. * (*PA* 37:6733)

1215. HATHAWAY, STARKE R. "Problems of Personality Assessment," pp. 144–60. (*PA* 37:5040) In *Personality Research.* Proceedings of the XIV International Congress of Applied Psychology, Vol. 2. Copenhagen, Denmark: Munksgaard, Ltd., 1962. Pp. 229. *

1216. HETRICK, W. ROBERT, AND HAAS, KURT. "Some Personality Correlates of Verbal Conditioning." *J Psychol* 53:409–15 Ap '62. * (*PA* 37:371)

1217. HEWITT, JOHN H., AND ROSENBERG, LEON A. "The MMPI as a Screening Device in an Academic Setting." *Ed & Psychol Meas* 22:129–37 sp '62. * (*PA* 37:1991)

1218. HILL, HARRIS E.; HAERTZEN, CHARLES A.; AND DAVIS, HOWARD. "An MMPI Factor Analytic Study of Alcoholics, Narcotic Addicts, and Criminals." *Q J Studies Alcohol* 23:411–31 S '62. *

1219. HISPANICUS, PETREOLUS. "Selecting Seminarians," pp. 65–105. In *Screening Candidates for the Priesthood and Religious Life.* By Magda B. Arnold and others. Chicago, Ill.: Loyola University Press, 1962. Pp. x, 205. *

1220. HOENE, EDWARD. *PGR Ratio and the MMPI: An Experimental Approach as to How a Person Handles Emotions.* Master's thesis, Loyola University (Chicago, Ill.), 1962.

1221. HOOKE, JAMES F., AND MARKS, PHILIP A. "MMPI Characteristics of Pregnancy." *J Clin Psychol* 18:316–7 Jl '62. * (*PA* 39:1836)

1222. HULL, J., AND ZUBEK, JOHN P. "Personality Characteristics of Successful and Unsuccessful Sensory Isolation Subjects." *Percept & Motor Skills* 14:231–40 Ap '62. * (*PA* 37:312)

1223. JACKSON, DOUGLAS N., AND MESSICK, SAMUEL. Chap. 8, "Response Styles and the Assessment of Psychopathology," pp. 129–55. In *Measurement in Personality and Cognition.* Edited by Samuel Messick and John Ross. New York: John Wiley & Sons, Inc., 1962. Pp. xi, 334. * (*PA* 38:2638)

1224. JACKSON, DOUGLAS N., AND MESSICK, SAMUEL. "Response Styles on the MMPI: Comparison of Clinical and Normal Samples." *J Abn & Social Psychol* 65:285–99 N '62. *

1225. JENKINS, THOMAS N. "Efficiency of the Jenkins Global Personality Inventory." *J Psychol Studies* 13:11–20 Mr '62 [issued N '63]. *

1226. JOHANNSEN, WALTER J.; FRIEDMAN, SAMUEL H.; FELDMAN, EDWARD I.; AND NEGRETE, ABELARDO. "A Re-examination of the Hippuric Acid-Anxiety Relationship." *Psychosom Med* 24:569–78 N–D '62. * (*PA* 37:8046)

1226a. KALIS, BETTY L.; TOCCHINI, JOHN J.; AND THOMASSEN, PAUL R. "Correlation Study Between Personality Tests and Dental Student Performance." *J Am Dental Assn* 64:656–70 My '62. *

1227. KANFER, FREDERICK H., AND MARSTON, ALBERT R. "The Relationship Between Personality Variables and Verbal Response Characteristics." *J Clin Psychol* 18:426–8 O '62. *

1228. KATZELL, RAYMOND A., AND KATZELL, MILDRED E. "Development and Application of Structured Tests of Personality." *R Ed Res* 32:51–63 F '62. * (*PA* 37:1197)

1229. KENNEDY, WALLACE A. "MMPI Profiles of Gifted Adolescents." *J Clin Psychol* 18:148–9 Ap '62. * (*PA* 38:9248)

1230. KENNEDY, WALLACE A., AND SMITH, ALVIN H. "A High Performance MMPI Scale for Adolescents." *Psychol Rep* 11:494 O '62. * (*PA* 37:8257)

1231. KERR, MARILYN; MAKI, BOBBIN; AND AMMONS, R. B. "Personality, Values, and 'Intellectualism.'" *Proc Mont Acad Sci* 21:132–6 '62. * (*PA* 37:3149)

1232. KIRK, BARBARA A.; CUMMINGS, ROGER W.; AND GOODSTEIN, LEONARD D. "Predicting Student Success in Graduate Business Courses." *Calif Mgmt R* 5:63–6 f '62. *

1233. KLEINMUNTZ, BENJAMIN. "Annotated Bibliography of MMPI Research Among College Populations." *J Counsel Psychol* 9:373–96 w '62. *

1234. KLEINMUNTZ, BENJAMIN, AND ALEXANDER, L. BARTON. "Computer Program for the Meehl-Dahlstrom MMPI Profile Rules." *Ed & Psychol Meas* 22:193–9 sp '62. * (*PA* 37:72)

1235. KLØVE, HALLGRIM, AND DOEHRING, DONALD G. "MMPI in Epileptic Groups With Differential Etiology." *J Clin Psychol* 18:149–53 Ap '62. * (*PA* 38:8521)

1236. KNAPP, ROBERT H.; GEWIRTZ, HERBERT; AND HOLZBERG, JULES D. "Some Personality Correlates of Styles of Interpersonal Thought." *J Proj Tech* 26:398–403 D '62. * (*PA* 37:6717)

1237. KODMAN, FRANK, JR., AND SEDLACEK, GORDON. "MMPI Changes Following a Course in Mental Hygiene." *Mental Hyg* 46:95–7 Ja '62. *

1238. KREITMAN, NORMAN. "Psychiatric Orientation: A Study of Attitudes Among Psychiatrists." *J Mental Sci* 108:317–28 My '62. * (*PA* 37:3400)

1239. L'ABATE, LUCIANO. "MMPI Scatter as a Single Index of Maladjustment." *J Clin Psychol* 18:142–3 Ap '62. * (*PA* 38:8523)

1240. L'ABATE, LUCIANO. "The Relationship Between WAIS-Derived Indices of Maladjustment and MMPI in Deviant Groups." *J Consult Psychol* 26:441–5 O '62. *

1241. LaDOU, JOSEPH; ELLMAN, GEORGE L.; CALLAWAY, ENOCH, III; EDMINSTER, IVAN F.; AND CHRISTENSEN, ROBERT L. "Correlates of Manifest Anxiety." *J Psychosom Res* 6:41–7 Ja–Mr '62. * (*PA* 37:3323)

1242. LaFORGE, ROLFE. "A Correlational Study of Two Personality Tests: The MMPI and Cattell 16 PF." *J Consult Psychol* 26:402–11 O '62. * (*PA* 39:1743)

1243. LAIR, CHARLES V., AND TRAPP, E. PHILIP. "The Differential Diagnostic Value of MMPI With Somatically Disturbed Patients." *J Clin Psychol* 18:146–7 Ap '62. * (*PA* 38:8524)

1244. LANG, PETER J., AND LAZOVIK, A. DAVID. "Personality and Hypnotic Susceptibility." *J Consult Psychol* 26:317–22 Ag '62. * (*PA* 38:4433)

1245. LAUTERBACH, CARL G.; VOGEL, WILLIAM; AND HART, JOHN. "Comparison of the MMPI's of Male Problem Adolescents and Their Parents." *J Clin Psychol* 18:485–7 O '62. *

1246. LEVINE, DAVID, AND COHEN, JACOB. "Symptoms and Ego Strength Measures as Predictors of the Outcome of Hospitalization in Functional Psychoses." *J Consult Psychol* 26:246–50 Je '62. * (*PA* 38:1304)

1247. LEVINSON, BORIS M. "The MMPI in a Jewish Traditional Setting." *J Genetic Psychol* 101:25–42 S '62. * (*PA* 38:4278)

1248. LIPSHER, DAVID HAROLD. *Consistency of Clinicians' Judgments Based on MMPI, Rorschach and TAT Protocols.* Doctor's thesis, Stanford University (Stanford, Calif.), 1962. (*DA* 22:4409)

1249. McDONALD, ROBERT L. "Personality Characteristics of Freshman Medical Students as Depicted by the Leary System." *J Genetic Psychol* 100:313–23 Je '62. * (*PA* 37:3838)

1250. McDONALD, ROBERT L., AND GYNTHER, MALCOLM D. "MMPI Norms for Southern Adolescent Negroes." *J Social Psychol* 58:277–82 D '62. * (*PA* 37:6692)

1251. MACKINNON, DONALD W. "The Personality Correlates of Creativity: A Study of American Architects," pp. 11–39. (*PA* 37:4958) In *Personality Research.* Proceedings of the XIV International Congress of Applied Psychology, Vol. 2. Copenhagen, Denmark: Munksgaard, Ltd., 1962. Pp. 229. *

1252. MARKS, PHILIP A., AND SEEMAN, WILLIAM. "Addendum to 'An Assessment of the Diagnostic Process in a Child Guidance Setting.' " Abstract. *J Consult Psychol* 26:485 O '62. *

1253. MARKWELL, EARL D., JR. "Autonomic Nervous System Measures and Factor Correlates With Personality Indices in a Tuberculous Population." Abstract. *J Consult Psychol* 26:194 Ap '62. * (*PA* 37:5533)

1254. MARTIN, CAROL, AND NICHOLS, ROBERT C. "Personality and Religious Belief." *J Social Psychol* 56:3–8 F '62. * (*PA* 36:5GD03M)

1255. MEGARGEE, EDWIN I., AND MENDELSOHN, GERALD A. "A Cross-Validation of Twelve MMPI Indices of Hostility and Control." *J Abn & Social Psychol* 65:431–8 D '62. *

1256. MOOS, RUDOLF H. "Effects of Training on Students' Test Interpretations." *J Proj Tech* 26:310–7 S '62. * (*PA* 37:3201)

1257. MORSE, PAUL KENNETH. *The Strong Vocational Interest Blank and Minnesota Multiphasic Personality Inventory as Measures of Persistence Toward the Ministry as a Vocational Goal.* Doctor's thesis, University of Michigan (Ann Arbor, Mich.), 1962. (*DA* 23:3239)

1258. MURPHREE, HENRY B.; KARABELAS, MICHAEL J.; AND BRYAN, LAURENCE L. "Scores of Inmates of a Federal Penitentiary on Two Scales of the MMPI." *J Clin Psychol* 18:137–9 Ap '62. * (*PA* 38:8528)

1259. MURPHY, LEONARD. *Changes in the MMPI Scores of Three Groups of Seminarians Retested After One, Two, and Three Years.* Master's thesis, Fordham University (New York, N.Y.), 1962.

1260. NICHOLS, ROBERT C. "Subtle, Obvious and Stereotype Measures of Masculinity-Femininity." *Ed & Psychol Meas* 22:449–61 au '62. * (*PA* 37:5014)

1261. OSKAMP, STUART. "The Relationship of Clinical Experience and Training Methods to Several Criteria of Clinical Prediction." *Psychol Monogr* 76(28):1–27 '62. * (*PA* 38:8654)

1262. PANTON, JAMES H. "The Identification of Habitual Criminalism With the MMPI." *J Clin Psychol* 18:133–6 Ap '62. * (*PA* 38:8529)

1263. PANTON, JAMES H. "The Identification of Predispositional Factors in Self-Mutilation Within a State Prison Population." *J Clin Psychol* 18:63–7 Ja '62. * (*PA* 38:8502)

1264. PANTON, JAMES H. "Use of the MMPI as an Index to Successful Parole." *J Crim Law & Criminol* 53:484–8 D '62. * (*PA* 37:8181)

1265. PATTERSON, C. H. "A Note on the Construct Validity of the Concept of Empathy." *Personnel & Guid J* 40:803–6 My '62. * (*PA* 37:3448)

1266. PATTERSON, C. H. "Test Characteristics of Rehabilitation Counselor Trainees." *J Rehabil* 28:15–6 S–O '62. * (*PA* 37:6953)

1267. PERKINS, JULIA ELLEN. *Contextual Effects on the MMPI.* Doctor's thesis, University of Oregon (Eugene, Ore.), 1962. (*DA* 23:3981)

1268. PRUITT, WALTER A., AND VAN DE CASTLE, R. L. "Dependency Measures and Welfare Chronicity." *J Consult Psychol* 26:559–60 D '62. * (*PA* 39:1896)

1269. RAPAPORT, GERALD M., AND MARSHALL, ROBERT J. "The Prediction of Rehabilitative Potential of Stockade Prisoners Using Clinical Psychological Tests." *J Clin Psychol* 18:444–6 O '62. * (*PA* 39:5087)

1270. ROSEN, ALBERT. "Development of the MMPI Scales Based on a Reference Group of Psychiatric Patients." *Psychol Monogr* 76(8):1–25 '62. * (*PA* 37:3098)

1271. ROWLEY, VINTON N., AND STONE, F. BETH. "MMPI Differences Between Emotionally Disturbed and Delinquent Adolescents." *J Clin Psychol* 18:481–4 O '62. * (*PA* 39:5181)

1272. SECHREST, LEE, AND JACKSON, DOUGLAS N. "The Generality of Deviant Response Tendencies." *J Consult Psychol* 26:395–401 O '62. * (*PA* 39:1822)

1273. SHIPE, DOROTHY; DINGMAN, HARVEY F.; WINDLE, CHARLES; AND MOTICHA, KATHERINE. "Validity of a Measure of Escape Proneness." *Am J Mental Def* 66:872–7 My '62. * (*PA* 37:1708)

1274. SILVER, REUBEN J., AND SINES, LLOYD K. "Diagnostic Efficiency of the MMPI With and Without the K Correction." *J Clin Psychol* 18:312–4 Jl '62. * (*PA* 39:1846)

1275. SINNETT, E. ROBERT. "The Relationship Between the Ego Strength Scale and Rated In-Hospital Improvement." *J Clin Psychol* 18:46–7 Ja '62. * (*PA* 38:8702)

1276. SLATER, PHILIP E. "Parental Behavior and the Personality of the Child." *J Genetic Psychol* 101:53–68 S '62. * (*PA* 38:4090)

1276a. SMALL, JOYCE G.; MILSTEIN, VICTOR; AND STEVENS, JANICE R. "Are Psychomotor Epileptics Different? A Controlled Study." *Arch Neurol* 7:187–94 S '62. * (*PA* 37:3521)

1277. SMITH, RONALD E. "A Minnesota Multiphasic Personality Inventory Profile of Allergy." *Psychosom Med* 24:203–9 Mr–Ap '62. * (*PA* 37:3770)

1278. SMITH, RONALD E. "A Minnesota Multiphasic Personality Inventory Profile of Allergy: II, Conscious Conflict." *Psychosom Med* 24:543–53 N–D '62. * (*PA* 37:8211)

1279. SMITH, THOMAS E., AND BOYCE, ERNEST M. "The Relationship of the Trail Making Test to Psychiatric Symptomatology." *J Clin Psychol* 18:450–4 O '62. * (*PA* 39:5096)

1280. SPIELBERGER, CHARLES D.; WEITZ, HENRY; AND DENNY, J. PETER. "Group Counseling and the Academic Performance of Anxious College Freshmen." *J Counsel Psychol* 9:195–204 f '62. * (*PA* 38:3184)

1281. STEWART, HORACE F., JR. *A Study of the Relationship Between Certain Personality Measures and Hallucinoidal Visual Imagery.* Doctor's thesis, University of Florida (Gainesville, Fla.), 1962. (*DA* 24:827)

1282. SULZER, EDWARD S., AND SCHIELE, BURTRUM C. "The Prediction of Response to Tranylcypromine Plus Trifluoperazine by the MMPI." *Am J Psychiatry* 119:69–70 Jl '62. *

1283. SUPER, DONALD E., AND CRITES, JOHN O. *Appraising Vocational Fitness by Means of Psychological Tests, Revised Edition,* pp. 520–37. New York: Harper & Brothers, 1962. Pp. xv, 688. * (*PA* 37:2038)

1284. TART, CHARLES T. "Frequency of Dream Recall and Some Personality Measures." *J Consult Psychol* 26:467–70 O '62. * (*PA* 39:2213)

1285. ULLMANN, LEONARD P. "An Empirically Derived MMPI Scale Which Measures Facilitation-Inhibition of Recognition of Threatening Stimuli." *J Clin Psychol* 18:127–32 Ap '62. * (*PA* 38:8535)

1286. VOGEL, WILLIAM. "Some Effects of Brain Lesions on MMPI Profiles." *J Consult Psychol* 26:412–5 O '62. *

1287. WALKER, JERALD N. "An Examination of the Role of the Experimentally Determined Response Set in Evaluating Edwards' Social Desirability Scale." *J Consult Psychol* 26:162–6 Ap '62. * (*PA* 37:5021)

1288. WEISGERBER, CHARLES A. "Survey of a Psychological Screening Program in a Clerical Order," pp. 107–48. In *Screening Candidates for the Priesthood and Religious Life.* By Magda B. Arnold and others. Chicago, Ill.: Loyola University Press, 1962. Pp. x, 205. *

1289. WIGGINS, JERRY S. Chap. 7, "Definitions of Social Desirability and Acquiescence in Personality Inventories," pp. 109–27. In *Measurement in Personality and Cognition.* Edited by Samuel Messick and John Ross. New York: John Wiley & Sons, Inc., 1962. Pp. xi, 334. * (*PA* 38:2638)

1290. WIGGINS, JERRY S. "Strategic, Method, and Stylistic Variance in the MMPI." *Psychol B* 59:224–42 My '62. * (*PA* 37:3183)

1290a. WITTON, KURT, AND ELLSWORTH, ROBERT B. "Social and Psychological (MMPI) Changes 5–10 Years After Lobotomy." *Dis Nerv System* 23:440–4 Ag '62. *

1291. ADAMS, HENRY B.; COOPER, G. DAVID; AND CARRERA, RICHARD N. "The Rorschach and the MMPI: A Concurrent Validity Study." *J Proj Tech* 27:23–34 Mr '63. * (*PA* 38:976)

1292. ANDERSEN, L. BRYCE, AND SPENCER, PATRICIA A. "Personal Adjustment and Academic Predictability Among College Freshmen." *J Appl Psychol* 47:97–100 Ap '63. * (*PA* 37:8281)

1293. ANKER, JAMES M.; TOWNSEND, JOHN C.; AND O'CONNOR, JAMES P. "A Multivariate Analysis of Decision Making and Related Measures." *J Psychol* 55:211–21 Ja '63. * (*PA* 37:6186)

1294. BECKER, ANTHONY J. "A Study of the Personality Traits of Successful Religious Women of Teaching Orders." *Yearb Nat Council Meas Ed* 20:124–5 '63. * (*PA* 38:9287)

1295. BENDIG, A. W., AND MARTIN, ANN M. "The Factor Structure of Temperament Traits and Needs." *J General Psychol* 69:27–36 Jl '63. * (*PA* 38:4297)

1296. BUTTERFIELD, EARL C., AND WARREN, SUE A. "Prediction of Attendant Tenure." *J Appl Psychol* 47:101–3 Ap '63. * (*PA* 37:8112)

1297. BYRNE, DONN; BARRY, JAMES; AND NELSON, DON. "Relation of the Revised Repression-Sensitization Scale to Measures of Self-Description." *Psychol Rep* 13:323–34 O '63. * (*PA* 38:8478)

1298. CARTWRIGHT, DESMOND S.; KIRTNER, WILLIAM L.; AND FISKE, DONALD W. "Method Factors in Changes Associated With Psychotherapy." *J Abn & Social Psychol* 66:164–75 F '63. * (*PA* 37:6833)

1299. COPPINGER, NEIL W.; BORTNER, RAYMAN W.; AND SAUCER, RAYFORD T. "A Factor Analysis of Psychological Deficit." *J Genetic Psychol* 103:23–43 S '63. * (*PA* 39:174)

1300. COSTA, LOUIS D.; LONDON, PERRY; AND LEVITA, ERIC.

"A Modification of the F Scale of the MMPI." *Psychol Rep* 12:427–33 Ap '63. * (*PA* 38:4308)

1301. CRADDICK, RAY A. "MMPI Scatter of Psychopathic and Non-Psychopathic Prisoners." *Psychol Rep* 12:238 F '63. * (*PA* 38:2708)

1302. CRADDICK, RAY A., AND STERN, MICHAEL R. "Note on the Reliability of the MMPI Scatter Index." *Psychol Rep* 13:380 O '63. * (*PA* 38:8407)

1303. DANA, RICHARD H., AND CONDRY, JOHN C., JR. "MMPI Retest Results: Context, Order, Practice, and Test-Taking Anxiety." *Psychol Rep* 12:147–52 F '63. * (*PA* 38:2709)

1304. DANIELS, ROBERT S.; MARGOLIS, PHILIP M.; AND CARSON, ROBERT C. "Hospital Discharges Against Medical Advice." *Arch Gen Psychiatry* 8:120–30 F '63. * (*PA* 38:2881)

1305. DEMPSEY, PAUL. "The Dimensionality of the MMPI Clinical Scales Among Normal Subjects." *J Consult Psychol* 27:492–7 D '63. * (*PA* 38:8515)

1306. DRAGUNS, JURIS G. "Response Sets on the MMPI and in Structuring Ambiguous Stimuli." *Psychol Rep* 13:823–8 D '63. * (*PA* 38:8484)

1307. EDWARDS, ALLEN L., AND WALSH, JAMES A. "The Relationship Between the Intensity of the Social Desirability Keying of a Scale and the Correlation of the Scale With Edwards' SD Scale and the First Factor Loading of the Scale." *J Clin Psychol* 19:200–3 Ap '63. * (*PA* 39:5054)

1308. EDWARDS, ALLEN L.; WALSH, JAMES A.; AND DIERS, CAROL J. "The Relationship Between Social Desirability and Internal Consistency of Personality Scales." *J Appl Psychol* 47:255–9 Ag '63. * (*PA* 38:2693)

1309. ELVEKROG, MAURICE O., AND VESTRE, NORRIS D. "The Edwards Social Desirability Scale as a Short Form of the MMPI." *J Consult Psychol* 27:503–7 D '63. * (*PA* 38:8518)

1310. ENDICOTT, NOBLE A., AND ENDICOTT, JEAN. "'Improvement' in Untreated Psychiatric Patients." *Arch Gen Psychiatry* 9:575–85 D '63. * (*PA* 38:8643)

1311. ENDICOTT, NOBLE A., AND ENDICOTT, JEAN. "Objective Measures of Somatic Preoccupation." *J Nerv & Mental Dis* 137:427–37 N '63. * (*PA* 38:6356)

1312. EXNER, JOHN E., JR.; McDOWELL, EUGENE; PABST, JOAN; STACKMAN, WILLIAM; AND KIRK, LYNN. "On the Detection of Willful Falsifications in the MMPI." *J Consult Psychol* 27:91–4 F '63. *

1313. GETZELS, J. W., AND JACKSON, P. W. "Minnesota Multiphasic Personality Inventory," pp. 534–45. In *Handbook of Research on Teaching*. Edited by N. L. Gage. Chicago, Ill.: Rand McNally Co., 1963. Pp. xiii, 1218. * (*PA* 38:9132)

1314. GOCKA, EDWARD F., AND BURK, HAROLD W. "MMPI Test Taking Time and Social Desirability." *J Clin Psychol* 19:111–3 Ja '63. * (*PA* 39:1833)

1314a. GONIK, URI, AND BLUMBERG, STANLEY. "Psychophysical Correlates of Personality Test Variables and Some Properties of Auditory Stimuli." *Tex Rep Biol & Med* 21:198–206 su '63. * (*PA* 38:8636)

1315. GOODSTEIN, LEONARD D.; CRITES, JOHN O.; AND HEILBRUN, ALFRED B., JR. "Personality Correlates of Academic Adjustment." *Psychol Rep* 12:175–96 F '63. * (*PA* 38:3150)

1316. GOTTESMAN, IRVING I. "Heritability of Personality: A Demonstration." *Psychol Monogr* 77(9):1–21 '63. * (*PA* 38:423)

1317. GUTHRIE, GEORGE M., AND McKENDRY, MARGARET S. "Interest Patterns of Peace Corps Volunteers in a Teaching Project." *J Ed Psychol* 54:261–7 O '63. * (*PA* 38:4126)

1318. GYNTHER, MALCOLM D. "A Note on the Meehl-Dahlstrom Rules for Discriminating Psychotic From Neurotic MMPI Profiles." *J Clin Psychol* 19:226 Ap '63. *

1319. HAERTZEN, CHARLES A., AND HILL, HARRIS E. "Assessing Subjective Effects of Drugs: An Index of Carelessness and Confusion for Use With the Addiction Research Center Inventory (ARCI)." *J Clin Psychol* 19:407–12 O '63. *

1320. HAMERLYNCK, LEO AUGUST. *Personality, Academic Aptitude, and Attitudes of Inexperienced Teachers of Retarded Children.* Doctor's thesis, University of Oregon (Eugene, Ore.), 1963. (*DA* 24:624)

1321. HATHAWAY, STARKE R., AND MONACHESI, ELIO D. *Adolescent Personality and Behavior: MMPI Patterns of Normal, Delinquent, Dropout, and Other Outcomes.* Minneapolis, Minn.: University of Minnesota Press, 1963. Pp. xiii, 193. * (*PA* 38:8110)

1322. HEILBRUN, ALFRED B., JR. "Revision of the MMPI K Correction Procedure for Improved Detection of Maladjustment in a Normal College Population." *J Consult Psychol* 27:161–5 Ap '63. * (*PA* 37:7976)

1323. HEILBRUN, ALFRED B., JR. "Social Value-Social Behavior Inconsistency and Early Signs of Psychopathology in Adolescence." *Child Develop* 34:187–94 Mr '63. * (*PA* 38:5808)

1324. HENRICHS, THEODORE. "The Effects of Brief Sensory Reduction on Objective Test Scores." *J Clin Psychol* 19:172–6 Ap '63. * (*PA* 39:5151)

1325. HOOD, ALBERT B. "A Study of the Relationship Between Physique and Personality Variables Measured by the MMPI." *J Personality* 31:97–107 Mr '63. *

1326. JENKINS, THOMAS N. "The Primary Trait Anatomy of the MMPI." *J Psychol* 55:49–61 Ja '63. * (*PA* 37:6739)

1327. JORDAN, EDWARD J., JR. "MMPI Profiles of Epileptics: A Further Evaluation." *J Consult Psychol* 27:267–9 Je '63. * (*PA* 38:1233)

1328. JURJEVICH, R. M. "Interrelationships of Anxiety Indices of Wechsler Intelligence Scales and MMPI Scales." *J General Psychol* 69:135–42 Jl '63. * (*PA* 38:4305)

1329. JURJEVICH, R. M. "Normative Data for the Clinical and Additional MMPI Scales for a Population of Delinquent Girls." *J General Psychol* 69:143–6 Jl '63. * (*PA* 38:4312)

1330. JURJEVICH, R. M. "Relationships Among the MMPI and HGI Hostility Scales." *J General Psychol* 69:131–3 Jl '63. * (*PA* 38:4304)

1331. KLEINMUNTZ, BENJAMIN. "MMPI Decision Rules for the Identification of College Maladjustment: A Digital Computer Approach." *Psychol Monogr* 77(14):1–22 '63. * (*PA* 38:8520)

1332. KLEINMUNTZ, BENJAMIN. "Personality Test Interpretation by Digital Computer." *Sci* 139:416–8 F 1 '63. * (*PA* 38:2696)

1333. KLEINMUNTZ, BENJAMIN. "Profile Analysis Revisited: A Heuristic Approach." Comment by Allen Newell. *J Counsel Psychol* 10:315–24 w '63. * (*PA* 38:8648)

1334. KNOWLES, J. B. "Acquiescence Response Set and the Questionnaire Measurement of Personality." *Brit J Social & Clin Psychol* 2:131–7 Je '63. * (*PA* 38:4306)

1335. KOGAN, KATE L.; FORDYCE, WILBERT E.; AND JACKSON, JOAN K. "Personality Disturbance in Wives of Alcoholics." *Q J Studies Alcohol* 24:227–38 Je '63. *

1336. LAKIN, FRANK PIERCE. *Factors Relative to a Grade Point Average Increase for a Select Group of Students After Matriculation to Oregon State University.* Doctor's thesis, Oregon State University (Corvallis, Ore.), 1963. (*DA* 24:627)

1337. LAVER, A. B. "Testing in Canada." *Can Psychologist* 4:22–3 Ja '63. *

1338. LAWTON, M. POWELL. "Deliberate Faking on the Psychopathic Deviate Scale of the MMPI." *J Clin Psychol* 19:327–30 Jl '63. *

1339. LEVEE, JOHN RICHARD. *A Pilot Investigation Into the Effects of an Interpersonal Therapy Approach Upon Mental Patients in a General Hospital Short-Term Psychiatric Setting.* Doctor's thesis, Michigan State University (East Lansing, Mich.), 1963. (*DA* 24:1245)

1340. LUNDIN, ROBERT W., AND LATHROP, WILLIAM. "The Relationship Between Field of Major Concentration and Personality Adjustment in College Males." *J General Psychol* 69:193–6 O '63. * (*PA* 39:2871)

1341. LYTLE, MILFORD BURTON, JR. *A Recidivism Scale for Adult Male Probationers From the Minnesota Multiphasic Personality Inventory.* Doctor's thesis, University of Minnesota (Minneapolis, Minn.), 1963. (*DA* 24:1077)

1342. MacANDREW, CRAIG, AND GEERTSMA, ROBERT H. "An Analysis of Responses of Alcoholics to Scale 4 of the MMPI." *Q J Studies Alcohol* 24:23–38 Mr '63. *

1343. McDONALD, ROBERT L., AND GYNTHER, MALCOLM D. "MMPI Differences Associated With Sex, Race, and Class in Two Adolescent Samples." *J Consult Psychol* 27:112–6 Ap '63. * (*PA* 37:8011)

1344. McHUGH, RICHARD B., AND SIVANICH, GEORGE. "Assessing the Temporal Stability of Profile Groups in a Comparative Experiment or Survey." *Psychol Rep* 13:145–6 Ag '63. * (*PA* 38:4859)

1345. MARKS, JOHN; STAUFFACHER, JAMES C.; AND LYLE, CURTIS. "Predicting Outcome in Schizophrenia." *J Abn & Social Psychol* 66:117–27 F '63. * (*PA* 37:7076)

1346. MARKS, PHILIP A., AND SEEMAN, WILLIAM. *The Actuarial Description of Personality: An Atlas for Use With the MMPI.* Baltimore, Md.: Williams & Wilkins Co., 1963. Pp. xxv, 331. *

1347. MARTIN, D. V., AND CAINE, T. M. "Personality Change in the Treatment of Chronic Neurosis in a Therapeutic Community." *Brit J Psychiatry* 109:267–72 Mr '63. * (*PA* 38:2812)

1348. MICHAEL, WILLIAM B.; HANEY, RUSSELL; AND GERSHON, ARTHUR. "Intellective and Non-Intellective Predictors of Success in Nursing Training." *Ed & Psychol Meas* 23:817–21 w '63. *

1349. MILLER, WILLIAM G., AND HANNUM, THOMAS E. "Characteristics of Homosexually Involved Incarcerated Females." Abstract. *J Consult Psychol* 27:277 Je '63. * (*PA* 38:1288, title only)

1350. MOSELEY, EDWARD C.; DUFFEY, ROBERT F.; AND SHERMAN, LEWIS J. "An Extension of the Construct Validity of the Holtzman Inkblot Technique." *J Clin Psychol* 19:186–92 Ap '63. * (*PA* 39:5083)

1351. MURRAY, JOHN B. "The MF Scale of the MMPI for College Students." *J Clin Psychol* 19:113–5 Ja '63. *

1352. MURRAY, JOHN B., AND GALVIN, JOSEPH. "Correlational Study of the MMPI and GZTS." *J General Psychol* 69:267–73 O '63. * (*PA* 39:1751)

1353. NEALE, CHARLES RUSSELL, JR. *An Investigation of Perception of Visual Space Among Alcoholics.* Doctor's thesis, University of Utah (Salt Lake City, Utah), 1963. (*DA* 24:1702)

1354. NELSON, THOMAS D. *Judgmental Diagnoses Versus*

Actuarial Diagnoses. Doctor's thesis, University of Denver (Denver, Colo.), 1963. (*DA* 24:2126)

1355. NUNNALLY, JUM C., AND FLAUGHER, RONALD L. "Correlates of Semantic Habits." *J Personality* 31:192–202 Je '63. *

1356. PODELL, HARRIETT A. "Note on Successive Dimensional Analysis Applied to Affective, Cognitive, and Personality Traits." *Psychol Rep* 13:813–4 D '63. * (*PA* 38:8503)

1357. POMERANZ, DAVID M. *The Repression-Sensitization Dimension and Reactions to Stress.* Doctor's thesis, University of Rochester (Rochester, N.Y.), 1963. (*DA* 24:2605)

1358. POPPLESTONE, JOHN A. "A Scale to Assess Hyperchondriasis: The Converse of Hypochondriasis." *Psychol Rec* 13:32–8 Ja '63. * (*PA* 38:1050)

1359. REGAL, LOUIS HARVEY. *Personality Patterns in Narcotic Addiction.* Doctor's thesis, University of California (Los Angeles, Calif.), 1963. (*DA* 23:3982)

1360. RORER, LEONARD GEORGE. *The Function of Item Content in MMPI Responses.* Doctor's thesis, University of Minnesota (Minneapolis, Minn.), 1963. (*DA* 24:2566)

1361. ROSEN, ALBERT. "Diagnostic Differentiation as a Construct Validity Indicator for the MMPI Ego-Strength Scale." *J General Psychol* 69:293–7 O '63. * (*PA* 39:1845)

1362. ROSEN, EPHRAIM; SIEGELMAN, ELLEN; AND TEETER, BARBARA. "A Dimension of Cognitive Motivation: Need to Know the Known vs the Unknown." *Psychol Rep* 13:703–6 D '63. * (*PA* 38:7236)

1363. SCHULMAN, ROBERT E., AND LONDON, PERRY. "Hypnotic Susceptibility and MMPI Profiles." *J Consult Psychol* 27:157–60 Ap '63. * (*PA* 37:8101)

1364. SHAFFER, JOHN W. "A New Acquiescence Scale for the MMPI." *J Clin Psychol* 19:412–5 O '63. *

1365. SHARPE, D. TRUDY. *A Study of Response Set as a Personality Variable.* Doctor's thesis, New York University (New York, N.Y.), 1963. (*DA* 24:1077)

1366. SHIPMAN, WILLIAM G., AND MARQUETTE, CARL H. "The Manifest Hostility Scale: A Validation Study." *J Clin Psychol* 19:104–6 Ja '63. * (*PA* 39:1823)

1367. SHUPE, DONALD R., AND BRAMWELL, PAUL F. "Prediction of Escape From MMPI Data." *J Clin Psychol* 19:223–6 Ap '63. * (*PA* 39:5091)

1368. SILLER, JEROME, AND CHIPMAN, ABRAM. "Response Set Paralysis: Implications for Measurement and Control." *J Consult Psychol* 27:432–8 O '63. * (*PA* 38:4284)

1369. SILVER, ALBERT W. "TAT and MMPI Psychopath Deviant Scale Differences Between Delinquent and Nondelinquent Adolescents." Abstract. *J Consult Psychol* 27:370 Ag '63. * (*PA* 38:3032)

1370. SILVERMAN, JEROME. "The Validity of the Barron Ego Strength Scale in an Individual Form." *J Consult Psychol* 27:532–3 D '63. * (*PA* 38:8531)

1371. SILVERMAN, PAUL L. "Some Personality Correlates of Attributive Projection." *Percept & Motor Skills* 17:947–53 D '63. * (*PA* 38:6131)

1372. SINES, L. K., AND SILVER, R. J. "An Index of Psychopathology (Ip) Derived From Clinicians' Judgments of MMPI Profiles." *J Clin Psychol* 19:324–6 Jl '63. *

1373. SMITH, EWART E., AND GOODCHILDS, JACQUELINE D. "Some Personality and Behavioral Factors Related to Birth Order." *J Appl Psychol* 47:300–3 O '63. * (*PA* 38:4254)

1374. SMITH, JAMES REX. *Personality and Interpersonal Factors Associated With the Duration of Marriage Counseling.* Doctor's thesis, University of Southern California (Los Angeles, Calif.), 1963. (*DA* 24:886)

1375. SPREEN, OTFRIED, AND SPREEN, GEORGIA. "The MMPI in a German Speaking Population: Standardization Report and Methodological Problems of Cross-Cultural Interpretations." *Acta Psychologica* 21(3):265–73 '63. * (*PA* 38:8532)

1376. STIEPER, DONALD R., AND LOPER, RODNEY G. "Some Personality Correlates of Blood Protein Bound Iodine." *J Clin Psychol* 19:45–8 Ja '63. * (*PA* 39:2013)

1377. STONE, F. BETH, AND ROWLEY, VINTON N. "MMPI Differences Between Emotionally Disturbed and Delinquent Adolescent Girls." *J Clin Psychol* 19:227–30 Ap '63. *

1378. STRAITS, BRUCE C., AND SECHREST, LEE. "Further Support of Some Findings About the Characteristics of Smokers and Nonsmokers." *J Consult Psychol* 27:282 Je '63. * (*PA* 38:935, title only)

1379. TAYLOR, A. J. W., AND MCLACHLAN, D. G. "MMPI Profiles of Six Transvestites." *J Clin Psychol* 19:330–2 Jl '63. *

1380. ULLMANN, LEONARD P.; KRASNER, LEONARD; AND GELFAND, DONNA M. "Changed Content Within a Reinforced Response Class." *Psychol Rep* 12:819–29 Je '63. * (*PA* 38:5263)

1381. VAN EVRA, JUDY PAGE, AND ROSENBERG, B. G. "Ego Strength and Ego Disjunction in Primary and Secondary Psychopaths." *J Clin Psychol* 19:61–3 Ja '63. * (*PA* 39:2409)

1382. VAUGHAN, JAMES A., JR., AND KNAPP, ROBERT H. "A Study in Pessimism." *J Social Psychol* 59:77–92 F '63. * (*PA* 38:859)

1383. VAUGHAN, RICHARD P. "The Effect of Stress on the MMPI Scales K and D." *J Clin Psychol* 19:432 O '63. *

1384. VAUGHAN, RICHARD P. "A Psychological Assessment Program for Candidates to the Religious Life: Validation Study." *Cath Psychol Rec* 1:65–70 sp '63. * (*PA* 38:6715)

1385. VOGEL, JOHN L. "Failure to Validate the *Cr* and *Sm* Scales of the MMPI." *J Consult Psychol* 27:367 Ag '63. * (*PA* 38:2714)

1386. VOGEL, WILLIAM, AND LAUTERBACH, CARL G. "Relationships Between Normal and Disturbed Sons' Percepts of Their Parents' Behavior, and Personality Attributes of the Parents and Sons." *J Clin Psychol* 19:52–6 Ja '63. *

1387. WALLACH, MARTIN S. "Dream Report and Some Psychological Concomitants." Abstract. *J Consult Psychol* 27:549 D '63. *

1388. WATTRON, JOHN B. "A Prison Maladjustment Scale for the MMPI." *J Clin Psychol* 19:109–10 Ja '63. *

1389. WIGGINS, JERRY S. "Social Desirability Under Role Playing Instructions: A Reply to Walker." *J Consult Psychol* 27:107–11 Ap '63. * (*PA* 37:8014)

1390. WIMSATT, WILLIAM R., AND VESTRE, NORRIS D. "Extraexperimental Effects in Verbal Conditioning." *J Consult Psychol* 27:400–4 O '63. * (*PA* 38:4429)

1391. WINTER, WILLIAM D., AND STORTROEN, MARCUS. "A Comparison of Several MMPI Indices to Differentiate Psychotics From Normals." *J Clin Psychol* 19:220–3 Ap '63. *

1392. WITTENBORN, J. R., AND PLANTE, MARC. "Patterns of Response to Placebo, Iproniazid and Electroconvulsive Therapy Among Young Depressed Females." *J Nerv & Mental Dis* 137:155–61 Ag '63. *

1393. WRIGHT, MORGAN W.; SISLER, GEORGE C.; AND CHYLINSKI, JOANNE. "Personality Factors in the Selection of Civilians for Isolated Northern Stations." *J Appl Psychol* 47:24–9 F '63. * (*PA* 37:8319)

1394. YOUNG, RHODES CHARLES. *Some Parameters of Personality Description With the MMPI in a State Hospital Population.* Doctor's thesis, University of Minnesota (Minneapolis, Minn.), 1963. (*DA* 24:2129)

C. J. ADCOCK, *Associate Professor of Psychology, Victoria University of Wellington, Wellington, New Zealand.*

The major criterion for any test is its validity but this is not the simple concept that it was. Validity is always relative to some end and we have to ask what the test measures before we concern ourselves with how well it measures. In the personality area this question of what dimensions are involved is especially important. There is as yet no agreed schema of fundamental personality dimensions so for any given test it is highly important to consider what the test aims at measuring.

With regard to what they try to measure, personality tests fall into two broad categories: those which make an attempt to span the whole personality area in a systematic way and those which are concerned with some *ad hoc* objective. The former type are usually based upon factorial studies and cannot be validated by any simple correlation procedure. The latter type may be restricted to a single measure, which further simplifies the problem of validity, but the essential point is that there is an available criterion to control the choice of test items and to measure the validity of the test.

The MMPI falls into the second group. It does not pretend to provide basic personality dimensions but to predict the currently accepted psychiatric categories. These may be basic in their own right but this is beside the point. They have empirical validity in that they are the basis of actual treatment. At the present stage of psychiatry these are the categories which are most meaningful from a diagnostic point of view and the problem of measurement is simplified by the possibility of definite, if not perfectly reliable, criteria. The problem of what is to be measured is therefore a simple one for the MMPI.

The implications of this for the user, however, have not always been understood. Because the test is one of the few multidimensional tests, some people have thought of it as a useful test for a general survey of personality. For this it was not designed. It may draw attention to possibly disabling degrees of mental disorder and indicate the form of such disorder, but whether the pattern of disorder tendencies has any significance when none of the scores falls outside the normal range is another matter altogether. Despite the extensive literature which has developed around this test, there is a paucity of evidence on this point.

It is this fact which has probably inspired the development of a variety of new scales. Only one of these is currently described in the manual although reference is made to others. This social introversion scale (Si), although not strictly a clinical scale, is probably of more clinical significance than most other new scales. It is also one of the two major general personality dimensions and the interest shown in it inclines one to the opinion that, if scores on a set of basic personality dimensions were available from the test, it would both add to the value of the test and combat the tendency to make use of the psychiatric scales outside the psychiatric area. The vast number of items in the test makes it likely that they would yield a fairly wide range of such general measures but, by the same token, the appropriate procedures for deriving such measures become more difficult to apply. The obvious requirement is a factorial analysis of the items, but, although numerous analyses have been made, these have been of individual scales or of the scale scores.

Analysis of the scale scores indicates that they involve the usual second-order factors found in personality material. Kassebaum, Couch, and Slater (893) who analysed 32 scales derived from the MMPI found three factors of which the first two appeared to be very obviously ego strength and introversion-extroversion, corresponding to the major factors found by Eysenck [1] and the second-order

factors of Cattell.[2] There is general agreement about the existence of these two factors but not about the nature of the first of them. Eysenck calls it emotionality, Cattell talks of anxiety, and Kassebaum, Couch, and Slater speak of ego strength. In treating a patient a correct choice among these interpretations might be of some consequence. It may be that each interpretation is quite correct for the test material used but one strongly suspects that the real difficulty is a failure to properly appreciate the complex interrelationships of emotional response. When one test battery provides us with an appropriate differentiation of ego strength, emotionality, and anxiety we shall have more ground for confidence.

In view of the lack of adequate agreement as to the nature of basic personality dimensions it may be argued that it is safer to stick to the strictly empirical approach of the MMPI without playing around with new fangled scales. But this could be no justification for using the psychiatric scales as substitutes for the required basic personality scales and moreover one can raise some awkward questions as to the adequacy of the original scales themselves. Psychasthenia and schizophrenia are regarded as distinct entities but the two scales turn out to be highly correlated. No figures are given in the manual but Kassebaum and others (893) find a correlation of .83. Inspection of the reliability figures suggests that the specific variance in these two scales might well be negligible. The high correlation of the F (validity) and K (correction) scales with Pt and Sc raises some further queries and makes one long for some statistical data to throw light on the psychiatric concepts involved. Do the scales present the best survey of clinical symptoms?

An important event in this respect is Rosen's (1270) report on an attempt to develop five new psychiatric scales. The choice of items is based upon the efficiency in differentiating the particular category of abnormals from a normal population rather than from other abnormals. This is an important point if the test is to be used for screening purposes with a random population sample. A comparison of the new with the old scales is most interesting.

The conversion reaction scale (Cr) replaces

1 EYSENCK, H. J. *The Structure of Human Personality.* London: Methuen & Co. Ltd., 1953. Pp. xix, 348. *

2 CATTELL, RAYMOND B. *Personality: A Systematic Theoretical and Factual Study.* New York: McGraw-Hill Book Co., Inc., 1950. Pp. xii, 689. * (PA 25:4420)

the old Hy scale but has a correlation of $-.24$ with it! This is explained by the common factor of abnormality, it is argued, but the research does not involve any factor analysis which might make these relationships a little clearer. At this stage we can only take warning that items which differentiate hysterics from other abnormals in the old scale may have to be reversed in sign if one wishes to distinguish hysterics from normals. This is another indication of the danger which may be involved in using the test for any purpose other than that for which it was strictly designed.

Rosen's somatization scale (Sm) correlates highly with the Cr scale (slightly higher than either reliability coefficient!) and also has a negative, though insignificant, correlation with Hy. Paranoid schizophrenia (Pz) correlates slightly better with the old Sc (.81) than it does with itself (.79) but the depressive reaction (Dr) scale has no significant correlation with the old D scale. For the anxiety reaction (Ar) scale there is no equivalent among the old scales.

It is perhaps unfortunate that Rosen should have chosen new psychiatric categories at the same time that he used a normal group as a measure of differentiation efficiency. One would very much like to know what would happen if the original psychiatric groups were retained but the scales validated along Rosen lines. It seems rather as though we may have two problems: the choice of scales and the method of item validation.

VALIDITY. The question of validity for a test of this kind (like the manual we omit reference to the new scales at the moment) is relatively simple. It can be expressed simply as a set of correlation coefficients. Somewhat strangely the authors choose not to do this but instead to provide figures as to the success of the scales in predicting the diagnosis of new psychiatric admissions where 60 per cent success is claimed. This reviewer is disturbed by two points in this connection. In the first place one is uncertain as to the degree to which the psychiatric diagnosis has been influenced by the test results. If two psychiatric categories are closely related (for example, Pt and Sc), the test classification could play a major role and give the appearance of success far beyond what might occur with independent assessment.

In the second place it has to be noted that the population to whom the test is applied is already selected as in need of psychiatric treatment and the test is merely called upon to classify. It is quite in order to report the success of the test in doing this but unfortunately it is only too easy for people who quote the validity figures to lose sight of the qualifying circumstances. The authors warn that in an average population more of the deviant profiles may relate to normal persons than to persons requiring treatment, but this is not always remembered by the casual test user who has in mind a 60 per cent hit evaluation. It would be most interesting to know just how many correct hits would be made in application of the test to a random sample of the general population. This information is vitally necessary if the test is to be used for general screening purposes as it often, in fact, is used. The manual might well provide this information. Rosen's work, reported above, emphasises the need for studies in this area.

Another point raised by the authors justifies comment. It is the fact that persons classified under a certain category may not necessarily have the highest scores for the category; for example, a schizophrenic may show a higher score for depression than for schizophrenia. This is quite understandable but provides another trap for the unskilled user of the test. Furthermore, it raises some further queries about the principles of psychiatric classification and specifically raises the question as to whether the MMPI does not make the mistake of lumping together a number of psychiatric terms without adequate consideration of their logical status. One suspects that masculinity-femininity or depression has rather a different status than that of schizophrenia.

There is a special sense in which validity has to be considered in connection with this test. There are internal measures of testee validity built into it. A recent study of these by Exner and others (1312) showed that a group of subjects who were asked to deliberately fake abnormal, but not sufficiently abnormal for institutionalization, raised all their scores significantly *except the lie score!* Attempts to fake good were less successful, the major differences (statistically significant) being in the L, F, K, and Pd scales, in that order. The range of scores for these categories, however, showed too much overlap between honest and fake efforts for any useful individual discrimination. Further doubt about the use of the validity scales is aroused by considering some of the intercorrelations from Rosen's study. In that study F had a correlation of .82 with Pz, and K a correlation of .72 with Cr. In view of the probable reliabilities of these measures one has grave doubts about the amount of their variance related to the correction function.

There is still a steady stream of research reports relating to this test but most of these assume rather than indicate the validity of the test. Some of the comparisons with other tests are of interest. In particular it is worth noting that the MMPI, Guilford-Zimmerman, and Strong measures of masculinity-femininity do not correlate (949) and possibly represent different concepts. Incidentally it is probable that class differences may operate strongly in this connection. Taylor and McLachlan (1379) found that the MMPI Mf scale successfully differentiated in a group of transvestites between those who were practising homosexuals and those not, and may therefore be psychiatrically significant but they have no data on the applicability of other M-F measures to this group.

All this points up the fact that, while the MMPI is an excellent tool for the skilled psychiatrist who has mastered its intricacies and has a due appreciation of the relevant statistical concepts, it can be highly dangerous in the hands of the casual user who has seized upon it as one of the most reputable of personality tests and one free of the problem of subjective scoring.

JAMES C. LINGOES, *Associate Professor of Psychology, The University of Michigan, Ann Arbor, Michigan.*

Since the appearance of *The Fifth Mental Measurements Yearbook* additional valuable material has been published on the widely used MMPI. Expanding the range of cases covered in the Atlas (263) there are now similar books devoted to juvenile MMPI profiles (1106) and to college students seen in a counseling service (873). Most noteworthy, however, is the publication of Dahlstrom and Welsh's *An MMPI Handbook* (969), which complements their earlier publication (669) and serves along with it as an indispensable reference work for both the clinician and researcher. The Handbook provides adequate documentation and an objective appraisal of the uses and limitations of the MMPI, more than compensating for the

deficiencies of the manual. Nevertheless, a revision of the manual is long overdue. In such a revision one should expect to find an up-to-date summarization of the relevant literature on the topics of reliability and validity, for example, as well as suitable references to the basic texts and pertinent journal articles to guide the prospective user in the proper uses of the inventory. In addition, cognizance should be given to methods of interpretation consonant with the recommendations contained in both the Atlas and the Handbook.

To date there are over 1,000 references on the MMPI, a formidable amount of material covering almost every conceivable aspect of test construction, reliability, validity, and use. The proliferation of scales (over 200 in the last two decades) purportedly measuring or differentiating important classes of behavior, has, if nothing else, fulfilled the wildest dreams of the authors of the MMPI when they chose to qualify the inventory as "multiphasic." The validities of many of these scales remain in doubt, but those that have held up in cross validation (for example, Barron's ego strength scale, Feldman's prognosis for electroshock treatment scale, Welsh's factor scales A and R) have added considerably to the power of this test and, if not entirely fulfilling the aim of the authors in yielding scores on *all* important phases of personality, at least have gone some small way toward it.

If one had to summarize the research on the perennial question of the diagnostic validity of this test the summary would be somewhat as follows. The MMPI can differentiate quite well between those who do and do not have emotional and adjustmental problems in a wide variety of settings and can thus serve as an excellent screening device. The use of this instrument for such purposes, however, requires many complex decisions regarding such things as costs, strategies, base rates, and utilities, and, as a consequence, the potential user should become familiar with these vital issues as they relate to his problem in his agency. It may well be that for highly specific problems simpler devices may suffice, such as the *Cornell Index*. While there is no gainsaying the value of the MMPI in differentiating among individuals coming from normal and abnormal populations, there is much conflicting evidence as to the test's sensitivity in discriminating within the abnormal group itself.

Neurotics, character disorders, psychotics, and possibly some psychosomatic conditions, as broad diagnostic groupings, can be reliably separated, if not among each and all of the several categories at least among selected subsets. Finer distinctions within any one of these nosological groups, however, have been in the main unproductive. Typical of the better studies in the area of differential diagnosis is that of Meehl and Dahlstrom (*1017*) using a multistage sequential decision rule for classifying profiles as neurotic, psychotic, or indeterminate. In a cross validation study of 988 cases selected from eight settings, an overall hit rate of 76 per cent was achieved among the 70 per cent considered determinate.

Although there is no other instrument of its kind that has been so thoroughly researched, as a general test of personality the MMPI has a number of weaknesses, not the least of which is its saturation with pathological items to the exclusion or deemphasis of some variables considered important in present day personality theories. Unfortunately, other tests that might be considered competitive have equal or more serious shortcomings. As a clinical instrument used in conjunction with other tests and media of inference, the MMPI has a definite contribution to make and is unequaled. For assessing personality within the normal range of adjustment, however, it will be found wanting.

For reviews by Albert Ellis and Warren T. Norman, see 5:86; for a review by Arthur L. Benton, see 4:71; for reviews by Arthur L. Benton, H. J. Eysenck, L. S. Penrose, and Julian B. Rotter, see 3:60 (1 excerpt); for excerpts from related book reviews, see B64, B113, B146, B159, B206, B241, B414, see 5:B199, 5:B200, 5:B467, and 4:72.

[144]

*Minnesota T-S-E Inventory. Grades 13–16 and adults; 1942–57; for research use only; 3 introversion-extroversion scores: thinking, social, emotional; IBM; Experimental Form FETX ('42, 7 pages); revised manual ('57, 24 pages); separate answer sheets must be used; $3.50 per 25 tests; 30¢ per single copy; $1 per 25 IBM scorable answer sheets; $1.50 per set of scoring stencils; $1 per manual; cash orders postpaid; (25–35) minutes; Catharine Evans and T. R. McConnell; distributed by Educational Testing Service. *

REFERENCES

1–6. See 3:62.
7. CHALMERS, J. W. "Intelligence and Personality Characteristics of Correspondence Teachers." *Can J Psychol* 2:28–34 Mr '48. * (*PA* 22:4633)
8. EVANS, M. CATHARINE. "Differentiation of Home Economics Students According to Major Emphasis." *Occupations* 27:120–5 N '48. * (*PA* 23:4410)

9. TYLER, F. T. "Personality Tests and Teaching Ability." *Can J Psychol* 3:30–7 Mr '49. * (*PA* 23:4443)
10. HARTSHORN, ELIZABETH. "A Comparison of Certain Aspects of Student Leadership and Non-Leadership: Significant Differences on Four Psychometric Tests." *J Ed Res* 49:515–22 Mr '56. * (*PA* 31:5098)
11. STRAIGHT, GLENN H. *Identifiable Personality Characteristics Resulting From Membership in a Conspicuous Religious Minority in Public High Schools.* Doctor's thesis, University of Nebraska (Lincoln, Neb.), 1956. (*DA* 17:810)

For reviews by Philip Eisenberg and John W. French, see 3:62.

[145]

Mooney Problem Check List, 1950 Revision. Grades 7–9, 9–12, 13–16, adults; 1941–50; IBM for grades 7–16; 4 levels; separate manuals ('50) for grades 7–16 (15 pages), adults (4 pages); no data on reliability for scores of individuals; no norms (authors recommend use of local norms); separate answer sheets must be used with machine scorable forms; $1.90 per 25 tests of hand scored forms; $2.40 per 25 tests of machine scorable forms; $2 per 50 IBM answer sheets; 90¢ per specimen set of hand scored forms, $1 per specimen set of machine scorable forms, 50¢ per specimen set of hand scored form of any one level; postpaid; (20–50) minutes; Ross L. Mooney and Leonard V. Gordon (*c* and *d*); Psychological Corporation. *

a) JUNIOR HIGH SCHOOL FORM. Grades 7–9; 1942–50; 7 scores: health and physical development, school, home and family, money-work-the future, boy and girl relations, relations to people in general, self-centered concerns; 2 editions ('50): hand scored Form J (6 pages), machine scorable Form JM (4 pages).

b) HIGH SCHOOL FORM. Grades 9–12; 1941–50; 11 scores: health and physical development, finances-living conditions-employment, social and recreational activities, social-psychological relations, personal-psychological relations, courtship-sex-marriage, home and family, morals and religion, adjustment to school work, the future—vocational and educational, curriculum and teaching procedures; 2 editions ('50): hand scored Form H (6 pages), machine scorable Form HM (4 pages).

c) COLLEGE FORM. Grades 13–16; 1941–50; 11 scores: same as for High School Form; 2 editions ('50): hand scored Form C (6 pages), machine scorable Form CM (4 pages).

d) ADULT FORM. Adults; 1950; 9 scores: health, economic security, self-improvement, personality, home and family, courtship, sex, religion, occupation; Form A (6 pages).

REFERENCES

1–17. See 3:67.
18–30. See 4:73.
31–56. See 5:89.
57. BENNETT, BRUCE L. "Improving College Health Teaching." *J Health Phys Ed & Rec* 23:24–6 D '52. *
58. HASSLER, WILLIAM H. *Use of the Mooney Problem Check List to Determine Potential Drop Outs in the First Two Years of College.* Master's thesis, Pennsylvania State University (University Park, Pa.), 1957.
59. FORMICA, LOUIS ANTHONY. *A Comparative Study of Selected Factors in the Vocational Development of Intellectually Superior College Girls From the Working and Upper-Class Levels.* Doctor's thesis, University of Connecticut (Storrs, Conn.), 1958. (*DA* 19:1012)
60. JONES, WORTH R. "Affective Tolerance and Typical Problems of Married and Unmarried College Students." *Personnel & Guid J* 37:126–8 O '58. * (*PA* 36:2KD26J)
61. SMITH, PAUL MILTON. *Personality Characteristics of Rural and Urban Southern Negro Children.* Doctor's thesis, Indiana University (Bloomington, Ind.), 1958. (*DA* 19:1019)
62. BARNETT, CHARLES D., AND TARVER, WILLIAM N. "Self-Rated Problems of Institutionalized Delinquent vs. Non-Delinquent Girls." *Psychol Rep* 5:333–6 Je '59. * (*PA* 34:3235)
63. HAMMES, JOHN A. "Relation of Manifest Anxiety to

Specific Problem Areas." *J Clin Psychol* 15:298–300 Jl '59. * (PA 35:3453)

64. MOORE, PHELMA NEWTON. *A Survey of the Orientation Problems Common to Entering Freshmen in Pan American College for the First Semester of the 1958–1959 School Year.* Doctor's thesis, University of Houston (Houston, Tex.), 1959. (DA 20:2103)

65. STEFFLRE, BUFORD. "Concurrent Validity of the Vocational Values Inventory." *J Ed Res* 52:339–41 My '59. * (PA 34:4211)

66. AMOS, ROBERT T., AND WASHINGTON, REGINALD M. "A Comparison of Pupil and Teacher Perceptions of Pupil Problems." *J Ed Psychol* 51:255–8 O '60. * (PA 36:1KM55A)

67. BULLOCH, SARAH I. *A Study of the Impact of Guidance Services on Twelfth Grade Students as Measured by the Mooney Problem Check List.* Master's thesis, University of Tennessee (Knoxville, Tenn.), 1960.

68. RICH, RUTH. "Health Education Needs of High School Students in a Large Diversified Metropolitan Area." *Res Q* 31:631–7 D '60. *

69. WITHERSPOON, PAUL. "A Comparison of the Problems of Certain Anglo- and Latin-American Junior High School Students." *J Ed Res* 53:295–9 Ap '60. *

70. GORMAN, JOHN R. *A Study of Adjustment and Interests for Fourth Year Minor Seminarians Studying for the Diocesan Priesthood.* Master's thesis, Loyola University (Chicago, Ill.), 1961.

71. JERRY, DONALD H. *References and Problems of Thirty High School Football Players and Thirty Non-Football Players.* Master's thesis, Ohio State University (Columbus, Ohio), 1961.

72. McDONAGH, ANDREW J. *A Study of Adjustments and Interests of First-Year College Seminarians for the Diocesan Priesthood.* Master's thesis, Loyola University (Chicago, Ill.), 1961.

73. MILLER, ROBERT CARL. *The Relationship Between Academic Success and Stated Problems of Selected High School Pupils.* Doctor's thesis, University of Pittsburgh (Pittsburgh, Pa.), 1961. (DA 22:3895)

74. SMITH, PAUL M., JR. "Problems of Rural and Urban Southern Negro Children." *Personnel & Guid J* 39:599–600 Mr '61. * (PA 35:6309)

75. CRUMBAUGH, JAMES C.; SHAPIRO, DAVID S.; MAHOLICK, LEONARD T.; AND OAKEY, RUTH C. "The Bradley Center Mental Health Assessment Kit: An Analysis of Use in Group Testing." *J Clin Psychol* 18:431–6 O '62. * (PA 39:5047)

76. ESPER, GEORGE H. *A Study of Certain Characteristic Differences in Junior High School Students Who May or May Not Seek Counseling.* Doctor's research study No. 1, Colorado State College (Greeley, Colo.), 1962. (DA 23:3773)

77. ZUNICH, MICHAEL. "The Relation Between Junior High-School Students' Problems and Parental Attitudes Toward Child Rearing and Family Life." *J Ed Res* 56:134–8 N '62. *

78. BERNOFSKY, SHIRLEY. *Problems of Junior High School Students as Expressed Through the Mooney Problem Check List.* Master's thesis, University of Kansas (Lawrence, Kan.), 1963.

79. CHENEY, TRUMAN M., AND VAN LYDEGRAF, MARY ELLEN. "Establishing Counseling Priorities." *Voc Guid Q* 11:297–300 su '63. * (PA 38:4676)

80. DENTON, L. R. "A Survey of Personal Problems of Young People in Public School and University." *B Maritime Psychol Assn* 12:1–27 sp '63. * (PA 38:4678)

81. WILLNER, ERIC. *The Adjustment of Jewish All-Day School Pupils Compared to That of Public School Pupils Attending Afternoon Hebrew Schools: as Determined by the Mooney Problem Check List, a Check List of "Problems Related to Religion," and an Adaptation of the Maslow S-I Inventory.* Doctor's thesis, New York University (New York, N.Y.), 1963. (DA 24:2794)

THOMAS C. BURGESS, *Associate Professor, Counseling Center, Portland State College, Portland, Oregon.*

The *Mooney Problem Check List* does not pretend to be a measuring device. "Rather, the *Problem Check List* is a form of simple communication between the counselee and counselor designed to accelerate the process of understanding the student and his real problems." The forms are composed simply of lists of common problems, and the student is asked to mark those he has, to indicate those which are of most concern to him, and to write a statement about his problems in his own words. On the junior high school, high school, and college forms he is also asked if he would like to discuss his problems with someone, and, on the high school and college forms, to indicate, if he wishes, with whom he would like to talk. There is no mystery here, only a straightforward list of problems and an obvious approach which leaves the counselee free to communicate to the extent of his readiness to do so.

The lists have been compiled carefully by referring to student statements of their problems, case studies, published literature on student problems, and the counseling experience of the authors. Published research reports indicate that students check an average of 20 to 30 problems which suggests that the lists contain a fairly good coverage of problems that students are willing to acknowledge.

Reliability assessment is a problem with this kind of procedure and no reliability figures are given. The manual points out that internal consistency methods are clearly inappropriate, and that retest estimates are subject to error due to rapid changes in the nature of the individual's problems and in the way he perceives them. It is also pointed out in the manual that the way a student perceives his problems may be changed by the process of going through the checklist (which should caution all users to have a control group when using the checklist as recommended by the authors to show the effect of remedial programs on the number of student problems). In spite of the merit in these arguments the reliability should be assessed and reported. The authors do report data indicating considerable stability of pooled results for groups.

To show the validity of the checklist would seem to require the demonstration that actual problems correspond to the problems reported. The obvious, but expensive, method of comparing reported problems with problems established through intensive case studies has apparently not been used. The manual reports the results of one study which contrasted the responses of two groups, a remedial study skills class and a mental hygiene class, and found differences appropriate to the two classes. A number of other studies have been reported in the research literature which also show that problem frequencies differ in appropriate ways when the responses of different groups are compared. For example, intelligent students and honor students check fewer problems than do less intelligent or probation students in the area "Adjustment to (College) School Work." Veterans who check more problems in the area "Occupation" less frequently achieved success in selecting a vocational objective. Results such as these appear to indicate considerable concurrent validity. It would be helpful to have a revised manual incorporating more of this kind of information.

It seems likely, as indicated also by the testimony of students who have taken it, that filling out the checklist gives the student a review of his problems which helps to place them in perspective. It may thus be useful to the students as well as to the counselor, teacher, or researcher who uses it to obtain information about student problems. The authors also recommend its use by school counselors to facilitate the development of the counselor's understanding of the individual case. The suggestions given for its use in counseling seem reasonable but there has been no experimental demonstration of how its use would actually affect the process or results of counseling, or of what circumstances would be most appropriate for the use of such counselor aids.

No norms are given; the authors suggest that local norms would be most appropriate, and that significance does not depend on the number of problems reported. Although this argument is probably correct it would be helpful to have additional information on the relative frequency of the different problems in various groups.

In summary, the information available from all sources suggests that the popularity of the *Mooney Problem Check List* is well deserved, and that it may be used appropriately in the ways suggested by the authors. The authors should be commended for their professionally responsible presentation in the manual, and especially for their repeated warnings about the various ways in which the information from the checklist could be misinterpreted. The user should observe these cautions carefully.

For reviews by Harold E. Jones and Morris Krugman, see 4:73; for reviews by Ralph C. Bedell and Theodore F. Lentz, see 3:67.

[146]

★The Mother-Child Relationship Evaluation. Mothers; 1961; experimental form; 5 scores: 4 di-

rect scores (acceptance, overprotection, overindulgence, rejection) and 1 derived score (confusion-dominance); 1 form (4 pages); mimeographed manual (12 pages); $7 per set of 25 tests and manual; $6.50 per 25 tests; $2.50 per manual; postpaid; specimen set not available; (15–30) minutes; Robert M. Roth; Western Psychological Services. *

JOHN ELDERKIN BELL, *Program Director, National Institute of Mental Health, United States Public Health Service, San Francisco, California.*

Using the definitions of rejection, overindulgence, overprotection, and acceptance developed by Symonds,[1] the author of the test has prepared and selected a series of 48 assertions assumed to reflect these respective attitudes (12 per attitude). By indicating extent of agreement or disagreement with the statements on a five-point scale, the subject provides data for "an objective estimate of a mother's relationship to her child." In addition, a fifth scale seeks to measure the extent to which the relationship between a mother and her child is dominated by an attitude, a combination of attitudes, or confusion. This score is derived from the number of scores on the first four scales that reach the 75th percentile and higher.

The research on which the evaluation of the instrument is based appears modest and the details of the study provided in the manual leave major information gaps. For example, the scores used for developing split-half reliability measures, scale intercorrelations, and percentile norms were secured from 80 middle class mothers, 25 to 35 years of age, living in the same community. No data are supplied regarding marital history, number and ages of children, personality characteristics of the children, and means by which access to the population was secured.

While the instructions and scoring are simple, making for ease in administration, no advice regarding method of interpretation is offered except by indirection through three case illustrations. If the clinical interpretations offered for these cases are meant to suggest uses to which investigators might put the test, only the most radical limitations on the statements generated will protect mothers and children from libel or slander. To state that the test is "primarily an exploratory and experimental one, rather than a refined clinical measurement"

1 SYMONDS, PERCIVAL M. *The Dynamics of Parent-Child Relationships.* New York: Bureau of Publications, Teachers College, Columbia University, 1949. Pp. xvii, 197. *

perhaps means that the author himself is aware of the dangers of its use with individuals.

By far the most dangerous feature of the test is the lack of precision in the definitions of the abstract attitude categories it proposes to measure. Without precise operational definition of the categories or studies to specify behavioral correlates of the test scores, we shall promote unvalidated conclusions from test scores which are assumed but not shown to have a relationship to vaguely-defined global attitudes lacking identified application to a mother's behavior towards her child.

DALE B. HARRIS, *Professor of Psychology and Head of the Department, The Pennsylvania State University, University Park, Pennsylvania.*

Most "tests" of parental attitudes have been designed for specific research projects. In this one, the directions to the parent who responds to the items state: "Keep in mind the child for whom you are seeking help." Thus, despite the disclaimer in the manual, refined clinical measurement is ultimately intended, and the instrument must be judged on this basis.

This scale is global, evaluating the broad dimension of the mother-child relationship identified as acceptance—nonacceptance in the work of P. M. Symonds and his student, Marian Fitz-Simons. The items are general attitude-type, valuative affirmations about "a child," "children," "mothers," "a mother." There are a few items that specifically refer to "my child" or "I." Some of the items obviously tap attitudes rather deeply rooted in middle class folklore and practices of child rearing; others are "iffy," subject to situational contingencies which came to mind at once, and thus are probably not so embedded in strongly held values. The items are Likert-type, permitting five degrees of agreement-disagreement.

The author prepared a pool of 100 items having apparent relevance to one of four dimensions—acceptance, overprotection, overindulgence, and rejection, the latter three being specific expressions of a broader nonacceptance dimension. The 48 items selected for the final scale (12 for each dimension) yielded phi values from .30 to .67, based on the top and bottom 26 per cent of scores made by a homogeneous sample of 80 middle class women on the scales contained in the original pool (unpublished phi values obtained from communication with au-

thor). These 80 cases were then rescored to furnish all the standardization data, including percentile norms, supplied in the manual. Pearson product-moment correlations applied to first-half versus second-half scale scores (12-item scales) yielded results from .41 to .57. Intercorrelations of the scales were of about the same order of magnitude. The acceptance scale correlated negatively ($-.45$ to $-.68$) with each of the other three, which intercorrelated positively (.28 to .56) among themselves.

The derived score, confusion-dominance, takes a value from one to four and is based on the number of the four scale scores which fall into the highest quarter of the norms, a score of "one" presumably indicating high dominance and a score of "four" indicating high confusion.

Thus far in his work the author rests his case entirely on construct validity as set forth only briefly in the manual. In unpublished studies (personal communication) Roth found zero-order correspondence between mothers' responses to the instrument, and their college-age children's perceptions of how the mothers would respond to the instrument. On the acceptance scale (but not the others) 25 mothers who had been to college scored higher than 25 mothers who had not been to college. These two studies do not greatly strengthen the case for empirical validity.

Unlike Schaefer and Bell's Parental Attitude Research Instrument, this test has the merit of using nonthreatening items, none of which morally condemn the respondent whether he agrees or disagrees. Obviously it needs much more careful and complete standardization if it is to be used clinically. Clinical prediction requires highly stable measurement; such is scarcely possible with 12-item opinion scales subject to the known vicissitudes of semantics, momentary "set," situational and other sources of qualification.

[146a]

★**Motivation Analysis Test.** Ages 17 and over; 1959–64; test booklet title is MAT; 45 scores: 4 motivation scores (integrated, unintegrated, total, conflict) for each of 5 drives (mating, assertiveness, fear, narcism-comfort, pugnacity-sadism) and each of 5 sentiment structures (superego, self-sentiment, career, home-parental, sweetheart-spouse), plus 5 optional scores (total integration, total personal interest, total conflict, autism-optimism, information-intelligence); Form A ('64, c1961–64, 17 pages); manual ('64, c1959–64, 53 pages); profile ('64, c1961–64, 1 page);

reliability data for total motivation scores only; separate answer sheets must be used; $15 per 25 tests; $6 per 50 answer sheets; $3 per set of scoring stencils; $4 per pad of 50 profiles; $2 per manual; $4 per specimen set; cash orders postpaid; (55–65) minutes; Raymond B. Cattell and John L. Horn with the assistance of Arthur B. Sweney and John A. Radcliffe; Institute for Personality and Ability Testing. *

[147]

*Myers-Briggs Type Indicator. Grades 9–16 and adults; 1943–62; 4 scores: extraversion vs. introversion, sensation vs. intuition, thinking vs. feeling, judgment vs. perception; IBM; 2 editions (identical except for directions): Forms F ('57, c1943–57, 12 pages, scored locally), Fs ('62, c1943–62, 12 pages, scored by the publisher); manual ('62, 157 pages); separate answer sheets must be used; $6 per 20 tests; $1 per 25 IBM scorable answer sheets for Form F; $7.50 per set of scoring stencils for Form F; 60¢ per Scribe answer sheet and scoring service for Form Fs; postage extra; $3 per specimen set, postpaid (must be purchased to obtain manual); (50–55) minutes; Katharine C. Briggs (test) and Isabel Briggs Myers; Educational Testing Service. *

REFERENCES

1. MACKINNON, DONALD W. "Fostering Creativity in Students of Engineering." J Eng Ed 52:129–42 D '61. * (PA 36:4HD29M)
2. KNAPP, ROBERT H.; GEWIRTZ, HERBERT; AND HOLZBERG, JULES D. "Some Personality Correlates of Styles of Interpersonal Thought." J Proj Tech 26:398–403 D '62. * (PA 37:6717)
3. MACKINNON, DONALD W. "The Personality Correlates of Creativity: A Study of American Architects," pp. 11–39. (PA 37:4958) In Personality Research. Proceedings of the XIV International Congress of Applied Psychology, Vol. 2. Copenhagen, Denmark: Munksgaard, Ltd., 1962. Pp. 229. *
4. MENDELSOHN, GERALD A., AND KIRK, BARBARA A. "Personality Differences Between Students Who Do and Do Not Use a Counseling Facility." J Counsel Psychol 9:341–6 w '62. * (PA 39:1812)
5. ROSS, JOHN. Chap. 4, "Factor Analysis and Levels of Measurement in Psychology," pp. 69–81. In Measurement in Personality and Cognition. Edited by Samuel Messick and John Ross. New York: John Wiley & Sons, Inc., 1962. Pp. xi, 334. * (PA 38:2638)
6. MENDELSOHN, GERALD A., AND GELLER, MARVIN H. "Effects of Counselor-Client Similarity on the Outcome of Counseling." J Counsel Psychol 10:71–7 sp '63. *
7. STRICKER, LAWRENCE J., AND ROSS, JOHN. "Intercorrelations and Reliability of the Myers-Briggs Type Indicator Scales." Psychol Rep 12:287–93 F '63. * (PA 38:2677)
8. VAUGHAN, JAMES A., JR., AND KNAPP, ROBERT H. "A Study in Pessimism." J Social Psychol 59:77–92 F '63. * (PA 38:859)
9. STRICKER, LAWRENCE J., AND ROSS, JOHN. "An Assessment of Some Structural Properties of the Jungian Personality Typology." J Abn & Social Psychol 68:62–71 Ja '64. *
10. STRICKER, LAWRENCE J., AND ROSS, JOHN. "Some Correlates of a Jungian Personality Inventory." Psychol Rep 14:623–43 Ap '64. * (PA 39:1848)

GERALD A. MENDELSOHN, Assistant Professor of Psychology, University of California, Berkeley, California.

The Myers-Briggs Type Indicator (MBTI), a forced choice, self-report inventory designed for use with normal subjects, is based upon a modification of the Jungian theory of type. Since it was originally developed more than 20 years ago and has undergone several revisions, an unusually large body of reliability and validity data is available for the instrument. A substantial part of these data and a detailed presentation of the underlying theory are included in the test manual.

The four dimensions of the test purport to measure the following dichotomous preferences: Judgment-Perception (JP), coming to a conclusion about something or becoming aware of something; Thinking-Feeling (TF), arriving at judgments by impersonal and logical or by subjective processes; Sensation-Intuition (SN), perceiving directly through the five senses or indirectly by way of the unconscious; and Extraversion-Introversion (EI), orienting toward the outer world of people and things or the inner world of concepts and ideas. The TF, SN, and EI scales are independent, but JP is consistently correlated with SN and less consistently with TF. Internal consistency reliabilities for the scales range in general from .75 to .85, with a low coefficient of .44 appearing for TF. There are little data on the stability of the scores; in the one reported study addressed to this point, 14-month, test-retest correlations of approximately .70 were obtained for EI, SN, and JP, and .48 for TF (10). In general, the reliabilities of the test are like those of similar self-report inventories, TF appearing least stable.

Since the construction and successive revisions of the MBTI were guided by an explicit theoretical system, it is necessary to assess the extent to which it embodies the assumptions of that system. Specifically, the following properties are claimed: (a) the scales are bipolar and discontinuous, the zero point representing a true dividing point of psychological significance, i.e., the dimensions are dichotomous; and (b) the four scales interact in a complex manner in relating to behavior. The evidence for both assertions is not convincing. With respect to the former, there is no evidence of bimodality in the score distributions. Moreover, given the reliabilities of the scales, it seems risky to infer basic personality differences when the omission or change of a single item could alter a subject's classification. The primary evidence offered in support of the claimed dichotomous character of the scales, however, is based on the nature of the regression of independent variables on Indicator scores. The regressions shown in the manual change slope or are discontinuous in the area of the zero point. There are weaknesses in this method of demonstrating a dichotomy though. No statistics are offered to indicate that these are other than chance effects, the decision as to whether the regression line changes at the zero point is highly subjective and easily influenced by the form of data presentation (*10*), and, most important, there is no *a priori* rationale given for selecting the particular independent variables included. Thus while there is some evidence for a change in the regression line for some variables and some scales in the zero region, this does not seem sufficient to support the claimed bipolarity and dichotomy.

There is little data bearing on the assumption of interaction of the scales. Considerable theoretical point is made of this, however, involving the idea of the dominant and auxiliary functions and the effect of the EI setting on the interaction of score patterns. Results of studies in which all four dimensions were used to classify subjects seem most simply explained as additive effects. In an analysis of variance undertaken to investigate this question directly, no interactions of any order were significant (*10*). While more data on this point are needed, at present interpretations involving interaction seem unjustified.

In attempting to assess what these scales measure, it is informative to consider their item content as well as their patterns of relationship to independent variables. The EI scale seems to measure extraversion-introversion in the popular senses rather than in the Jungian sense. The items have to do primarily with ease in and liking for interpersonal contact, the factor of interest in the inner world of ideas being unrepresented. This interpretation is supported by a pattern of correlations with such variables as social introversion, gregariousness, and talkativeness, and the lack of correlation with variables related to thinking introversion and theoretical orientation. The items of the SN scale seem to refer to a practical, conventional, realistic attitude as opposed to one more idea and theory oriented, stressing originality, autonomy, and complexity. This interpretation gains strength from loadings on intellectualism factors and strong correlations with groups 1 and 8 on the Strong.[1] It is consistent also with the finding that highly creative individuals are overwhelmingly intuition types. TF items seem to reflect a legalistic, rationalistic versus humanistic, sympathetic approach. Correlations with independent measures are less clear for this scale but it is related to the theoretical and social values of *Study of Values* and nurturance and affiliation on the *Edwards Personal Preference Schedule*. Finally, JP items refer to a preference for order and planning as opposed to spontaneity and novelty. Correlations resemble those of SN but include also a high correlation with order on the EPPS and it is consistently related to behavior ratings of reliability and dependability. In general, then, it appears that the scales measure only limited aspects of their underlying constructs and that the data support the argument that interpretations based on item content are more accurate and parsimonious.

While the weight of the evidence does not support several basic assertions about the MBTI, the reviewer nevertheless considers the instrument of considerable potential utility. This conclusion is based on the findings which indicate that type scores relate meaningfully to a wide range of variables including personality, ability, interest, value, aptitude and performance measures, academic choice, and behavior ratings. (Some of these relationships are indicated in the previous paragraph.) Although there are better predictors available for particular tasks, few instruments appear to provide as much information as can be derived efficiently from the MBTI. It would seem useful, then, for personality research and, given its relationships to measures of interest, value, aptitude, and achievement, for academic counseling.

In summary, a consideration of the available data suggests that the MBTI does not represent a successful operationalization of Jungian concepts. Nevertheless, it does appear to have potential utility for research and counseling if scores are interpreted in the light of their empirical relationships rather than their assumed theoretical significance.

NORMAN D. SUNDBERG, *Professor of Psychology, University of Oregon, Eugene, Oregon.*

The *Myers-Briggs Type Indicator* will undoubtedly arouse much interest among psychologists for the following reasons: (*a*) it is easy to administer and score; (*b*) it provides scores on variables which are important according to both theory and common sense; (*c*) there is evidence of its relationship to some matters of great practical concern in the 1960's, e.g., creativity, achievement, and success at certain jobs. The Indicator consists of 166 forced

---

1 STRICKER, LAWRENCE J., AND ROSS, JOHN. "A Description and Evaluation of the Myers-Briggs Type Indicator." Unpublished research bulletin, Educational Testing Service, Princeton, N.J., Mr '62. Pp. 180. *

PERSONALITY TESTS AND REVIEWS

choice items which can easily be answered within 50 minutes. Item content would usually not be seen as threatening. An example in the instructions is the following: "Are your interests (A) few and lasting, (B) varied." The middle part is somewhat different, rather ambiguously requiring the subject to choose which of two words is more appealing, e.g., "(A) literal," or "(B) figurative." The forced choice format sometimes presents a challenge to the test administrator in establishing test taking motivation as will be discussed later. Scoring of the special answer sheets can be done either by hand or machine and scores are conveniently recorded directly on the answer sheet.

The resulting scores are taken to indicate the subject's preference for four different modes of thinking postulated by Carl Jung's theory of personality types: extraversion-introversion (EI), whether the person prefers to direct his mental activities toward the external world of people and things or toward the inner world of concepts and ideas; sensing-intuition (SN), whether the subject prefers to perceive his world in a factual, realistic way or to perceive inherent, imaginative possibilities; thinking-feeling (TF), whether the person prefers to arrive at decisions by logical analysis or by appreciating personal and interpersonal subjective values; and judgment-perception (JP), whether the subject prefers to take a judgmental attitude or an understanding, perceptive attitude toward his environment. Jungian theory and the exposition in Myers' manual prefer to treat these indexes as alternative choices showing the person's dominant type rather than as scores on a trait continuum. However, it is possible to convert the indexes into continuous scores. The direction of the subject's four preferences are recorded by letter so that he can conveniently be called, for example, an ESTJ type, an INFP type, or an ENFJ type.

Myers' unusually long manual (157 pages) provides an extensive introduction to the theory and interpretation of the results and to related research. She also outlines the history of the inventory starting in 1942 when she and Katharine Briggs tried out items on acquaintances who seemed to represent clear type preferences. The development in recent years turned to extensive norming and revising by internal consistency methods under the aegis of the Educational Testing Service, which published the test in 1962. There is a great deal of appeal to a theoretically developed instrument like this with its logical clarity and scope and its language which fits easily into a personality system. A test interpreter must have an organized system for simplifying results and for grouping individuals. The Jungian types, though not in common usage, could be very helpful in this regard. Unlike the authors of many theoretically derived tests, the workers on MBTI have also endeavored to develop a thorough empirical base.

The Indicator has been answered by several thousands of high school and college students and by certain professional and industrial groups. Reliability studies, which in the manual are limited surprisingly to only internal consistency (split-half) measures, show correlations mostly in the .70 and .80 range for continuous scores. These figures are comparable to those of leading personality inventories. Younger and less capable groups (e.g., underachieving eighth grade boys) tend to obtain somewhat lower reliabilities, and the TF index is less reliable than the others. Since type categories are employed for much of the interpretive theory, it is important to ascertain the reliability of the types as well as continuous scores. Here there is some problem over the appropriate statistic. Stricker and Ross (7) using Guttman's lower bound reliability estimate find correlation figures mostly in the .40's and .50's. However, Myers points out that this statistic is appropriate only where scores were originally dichotomous. Using tetrachoric r's and applying the Spearman-Brown prophecy formula, she reports median r's of .83, a figure almost identical with that obtained from continuous scores. Stricker and Ross (9) report 14-month retest reliability figures on continuous scores for 41 college students: .48 for TF, .69 for SN and JP, and .73 for EI.

Intercorrelations between scales are low except for JP's relation to SN which ranges from .26 to .47. Obviously, more studies for different subjects and periods of time are needed, and a parallel form of the MBTI would be helpful. For individual counseling it would seem advisable to be cautious about interpreting scores near the border between types.

At this point it would be well to note that in the area of test taking attitude the Indicator leaves much to be desired. I asked a class of 39 graduate students in psychology and education to write their reactions after taking the MBTI and to guess at the purposes of the test. Over half of them found fault with the forced choice format. Some went so far as to say that they felt less motivated to be careful because of the unrealistic choices they were asked to make. They also frequently mentioned that the test seemed obvious and easy to manipulate and questioned the correspondence between preferences and personality. When guessing at the test's purposes, over a fourth specified introversion and extraversion and another fourth thought it had something to do with how organized and flexible a person is. The purposes were partially but not wholly transparent to these students, it would seem. The MBTI does not have any direct indicators of test taking attitude, such as the MMPI validity scales. (There has been some experimentation with an unpublished scale of uncommon responses.) Although there is special weighting to take care of differences in popularity between the choices on items, a direct test of social desirability needs to be done. There is also one very interesting item which test interpreters might use to get at an individual's attitude; the last item asks the testee, "Would you have liked to argue the meaning of (A) a lot of these questions, (B) only a few." In my class three fourths said they would have liked to argue a lot of the questions. In this contentious class there were also positive feelings about the test but these were outweighted by the complaints of difficulty and dislike. This experience certainly suggests the importance of carefully establishing a positive involvement with the test. Certainly more empirical work also needs to be done to improve detection of unusual test taking attitudes, particularly for group usage. The distribution between subtle and obvious items needs to be explored. As it stands, I believe the test would be of dubious value for selection, where conscious faking would be a problem. As the author admits, the Indicator, like any self-report, is subject to dissimulation.

The manual's reports on validity rest mainly on concurrent studies—expected relationship to other tests and to ratings and differences between groups. Relationships to a large number of scales on tests of interest, values, and personality are mostly in the expected directions. For example, *Strong Vocational Interest Blank* interest in sales correlates significantly

with extraversion; interest in psychology with intuition; and *Edwards Personal Preference Scale* scores for need for nurturance correlate with a feeling preference. In industrial studies there are scattered reports of useful findings, such as excessive turnover in sales jobs among thinking types and the eventual predominance of extraverted feeling types in such jobs. Creative groups, such as leading architects and writers studied by MacKinnon and others at the Institute of Personality Assessment and Research, have shown distinct preferences for intuition over the sensory approach, which is much more commonly preferred in the general population and less creative groups. Peavy [1] extended the evidence for greater creative activity among intuitive than sensing types to high school seniors. (So far, however, I know of no study doing an item analysis separating the obvious self-report items showing preference for creative and imaginative pursuits from the subtle items; perhaps creative people just say they are interested in being creative and there are no deeper implications regarding personality.) On several samples preferences for the intuitive mode, and to some extent introversion, have low but significant relations to measures of intelligence and school achievement. Also within given aptitude levels judging types achieved higher grades in a large study of Pennsylvania college preparatory schools. Anyone interested in the research should study the extensive material in the manual and in the Educational Testing Service reports.

The question of construct validity is always a complex one: Do these indexes really measure the underlying personality types postulated by Jung's theory? Stricker and Ross (*10*) conclude on the basis of analysis of content of the scales and their correlations with a wide variety of tests that the SN and TF scales may reflect the dimensions they were theorized to represent but that EI and JP are more questionable. A theory attempting to separate people into types requires evidence of separate categories and a cutting point on the measuring scales. Myers recognizes that simple bimodality of distributions does not exist. This finding is in line with the less sophisticated studies of a few decades back showing that instead of being introverts or extraverts most people

1 PEAVY, R. VANCE. *A Study of C. G. Jung's Concept of Intuitive Perception and the Intuitive Type.* Doctor's thesis, University of Oregon (Eugene, Ore.), 1963.

were "ambiverts." The search for answers to the question of dichotomous types has turned to the study of differences in regression lines of the two opposite scales plotted against dependent variables such as grade averages or IQ's. The manual shows that the two regression lines often show a discontinuity or a difference in slope. In contrast Stricker and Ross conclude there is little support for any of the structural properties attributed to the typology, finding with students only a few U-shaped regression lines or discontinuities; TF shows the most likelihood. Apparently we have a controversy here in which methodology and interpretation of type theory are still to be clarified. It may be that sharper distinctions between types could be found with older people than the adolescents mostly studied so far. In any case notions about personality types seem to be enjoying a resurgence in psychology these days, and methodologies are being developed for determining them. Even if one does not accept the structural implications of Jungian theory or even the theory itself, the empirical relations of the inventory's scales can be studied. Purely as a potential research procedure for getting at individual differences in cognitive preferences, it would seem the Indicator would merit a great deal of attention from cognitive theorists.

In regard to application of the MBTI, the manual speaks mostly about vocational counseling in schools and industrial placement. Although there is considerable discussion relating to type requirements of various jobs, there are unfortunately only a few case examples. Little mention is made of clinical applications, although one report in press points to relationships with certain scales on the MMPI, particularly the validity scales. The Jungian hypothesis that lack of clear type preferences is associated with ineffectiveness and maladjustment was not confirmed by Stricker and Ross (9). Mendelsohn and Kirk (4) have shown that students seeking counseling as compared with nonapplicants have greater preferences for intuitive and perceptive modes of thinking. In my beginning counseling use of the MBTI I have found it very easy and interesting to explain to clients; the person is able to see and understand his own preferences. Counseling usage is aided by the manual's pervasive spirit of respect for the different preferences and types; these are seen as positive

choices and not lacks. The suggested interpretations of various types are easy to use but strongly need evidence that they are valid—and not "universally valid"—that is, they need evidence that the descriptions differentiate and individualize persons. An intriguing possibility for use of the Indicator is with groups such as married couples, families, or work groups. Mendelsohn and Geller (6) have shown that similarity of type between counselor and client is related to continuation in counseling and probably to greater ability to communicate with each other. It would seem that similarity of types would be related to compatibility, but for certain tasks to be accomplished it would be necessary to have different types represented.

The course and development of the MBTI will be intriguing to watch. There is much about it that suggests great possibilities, but its limits and its areas of need for supportive combination with other tests are not yet clear. The inventory needs to be tried, in many different contexts, maintaining, as Myers puts it, "a constant search for separate verification and new meanings."

J Counsel Psychol 10:307–8 f '63. Laurence Siegel. * The Indicator may be viewed from three perspectives. First, it contains four scales yielding continuous scores which the user can empirically validate. This treatment of the Indicator is contrary to the theory underlying its development. Nevertheless it is precisely this treatment that was used to estimate the reliabilities and certain of the validities offered in support of the instrument. However, normative data for the four scales continuously scored are not presented. An alternative is to treat the Indicator as yielding eight continuous scores—one for each aspect of the dichotomy embodied within each index. Although limited percentile norms are provided for these eight scores, reliability data are not presented for them. Since these scales are only half as long as those for which reliability *was* estimated, there is some serious question about the utility of these percentile conversions for individual guidance. Finally, the importance of Indicator scores can be minimized in favor of giving primary consideration to the type designations derived from these scores. The Manual states that this interpretation is the most legitimate one. The promise of the Indicator so interpreted would seem to depend more heavily upon clinical or intuitive validation than upon the more usual kind of psychometric validation.

[148]

*The Neuroticism Scale Questionnaire. Ages 16 and over; 1961; title on test is *NSQ;* the *IPAT Neurotic Personality Factor Test* (see 5:74), which is still available, is "an earlier version" of this test; 5 scores: depressiveness, submissiveness, overprotection, anxiety, total; 1 form (4 pages); manual (31 pages); $3.10 per 25 tests; 50¢ per key; $1.70 per manual; $2.30 per specimen set; cash orders postpaid; (10–15) minutes; Ivan H. Scheier and Raymond B. Cattell; Institute for Personality and Ability Testing. *

REFERENCES
1. CATTELL, RAYMOND B., AND SCHEIER, IVAN H. *The Meaning and Measurement of Neuroticism and Anxiety.* New York: Ronald Press Co., 1961. Pp. ix, 535. * (PA 36: 1HK27C)

E. LOWELL KELLY, *Professor of Psychology, The University of Michigan, Ann Arbor, Michigan.*

This is a brief inventory designed to assess "the degree of neurosis in a wide range of situations." According to a footnote in the manual, it is a new "version" of the earlier *IPAT Neurotic Personality Factor Test.* The NSQ is another short inventory derived from the 16 PF but unlike the *IPAT Anxiety Scale* published separately to assess those dimensions constituting a second order personality factor, the NSQ is designed to measure the admittedly impure real life criterion "degree of neuroticism" or "neurotic trend."

Research by the authors (*1*) showed that six of the 16 PF scores differentiate normal persons and those diagnosed neurotic in several different clinical settings. However, since three of the six differentiating scores turned out to be three of the five 16 PF scores constituting the second order anxiety factor, the decision was made to group these three into a single component labeled Anxiety. The other three components are "primary factors" of the 16 PF: I, overprotection, tendermindedness, or sensitivity at the positive pole; F, depressiveness, overseriousness; and E, submissiveness, dependence. Each of the four scales consists of 10 three-response items, scored 0, 1, or 2, with a possible score range of 0 to 20. The neuroticism score is simply the sum of the four part scores. Norm tables (sten values) based on nonclinical subjects (675 men and 393 women) are provided for both component and total scores.

Reliabilities (corrected split-half) based on 300 normal subjects are reported as .55, .57, .47, and .70 for the four component scales and .67 for the total score. The four component scales are relatively independent, the intercorrelations ranging from .08 to .28 for a group of 113 normals.

Two types of validity claims are made in the manual: concept (or construct) and concrete (or concurrent). After making the dubious assumption that the component scores are each pure measures of a single factor, it is argued that the concept validity of each is equal to the square root of its reliability, i.e., the extent to which the score would correlate with a perfect measure of the factor. This logic and method results in reporting highly respectable validity coefficients ranging from .69 to .84 for the four component scores, but precludes a comparable estimate of concept validity for the total score, since it is admittedly not a unitary factor.

Concrete validity is defined in the manual as "the correlation of the test with life performances and categories." Unfortunately, however, the manual does not report any kind of correlation of either total or component scores with any performance or category! The total score of 102 clinically judged neurotics is reported to be significantly higher (at the .0005 level) than the scores of 1,068 normals, but regretfully there is no indication of the amount of overlap of the two distributions. However, the manual reports a mean sten total score of 7.1 for another group of 315 neurotics and, since a sten score of 7 corresponds to a percentile range of 69 to 84 for the norm group, it would appear that nearly 30 per cent of normals score as more neurotic than does the average clinically diagnosed neurotic! Perhaps neuroticism is as widespread in the normal population as these results seem to indicate; alternatively, it is equally possible that the NSQ is such a crude measure of neuroticism that it fails to yield more differentiated distributions of scores for criterion groups. Unfortunately, the evidence for concurrent validity provided in the manual does not enable the reader to decide between these two conclusions. The authors base their argument for concurrent validity largely on the fact that the corresponding 16 PF scores yield statistically significant differences not only between normals and neurotics but also between normals and other clinical groups, e.g., alcoholics, narcotics users, and male homosexuals. Are these groups also to some degree "neurotic" or is the NSQ measuring something other than neuroticism?

Frankly, this reviewer finds it difficult to understand the authors' decision to publish these items as a separate test. If one wishes only to identify persons who will be labeled as neurotic by clinicians, it would appear that the anxiety component score alone would yield higher concurrent validities than the total score. At least the manual shows the 315 neurotics received a sten score of 8.1 on the anxiety component as contrasted with a score of only 7.1 on total neurotic level! One is forced to conclude that the authors hope to find a better or different market for an instrument purporting to assess "Neuroticism" than for the 16 PF or for the Anxiety Scale, either of which would appear to be more useful in simply identifying neurotics. While it is of interest that their research shows clinically diagnosed neurotics to differ from normals on dimensions other than anxiety, the value of constructing a test which combines these several components into a single mixed score is not obvious. Doing so may, in fact, tend to perpetuate the tendency to lump together under a single diagnostic label, individuals who might better be perceived and treated differently.

The manual includes a number of very dubious statements. For example: "Measurement is now recognized as a precondition for dealing with neurosis socially or individually. * The [NSQ] is designed to implement this fundamental measurement precondition." After insisting that the NSQ is designed to give a properly weighted score on neuroticism (p. 4) we read, "Research....shows that about half the differences between neurotics and normals can be accounted for as differences in anxiety level." Yet, a few sentences later, we are told, "the anxiety contribution in the NSQ is weighted at only approximately a fourth of the total neuroticism score." The reason for this weighting is that "anxiety can be measured separately in the IPAT Anxiety Scale." The result of this logic and maneuvering is that the NSQ and Anxiety Scale scores correlate only .36! Using the reported reliabilities of .67 and .84 for these two scales, this value corrected for attenuation becomes .48. Just how does this fit with the earlier claim of "a properly weighted" score?

While admitting that because of the low reliabilities of the several scores the NSQ should be "used cautiously" in diagnosing the individual case, this caution tends to be forgotten in that part of the manual dealing with interpretations where it is suggested that the profile of component scores for an individual can appropriately serve as a basis for deciding on the type of therapy to be used! This and similar expressions of excessive confidence on the part of the authors is almost frightening. For example: "The NSQ can be re-administered to the same persons at intervals of as little as two weeks, e.g., to determine fluctuations in neuroticism level over time and/or in response to therapy or other conditions." Certainly it can be readministered but how much of a change in an individual's score might be expected solely on the basis of errors of measurement?

Whereas this reviewer welcomed the issuance of the separate *IPAT Anxiety Scale* for the assessment of anxiety as a second order personality factor (see 5:70) he feels that there is little if any value to be derived from the use of this particular set of the 16 PF scales which have been found to differentiate persons broadly labeled neurotic by clinicians. Clearly if one wishes to screen for neurotic tendency, the Anxiety Scale is as good and perhaps better than this new scale. If he wishes to use an objective personality measure for individual diagnosis, then surely the testing time required for the total 16 PF or for the MMPI is justified. Incidentally, the manual does not report the relationship between NSQ scores and any other previously published and widely used device for assessing neuroticism. This reviewer finds unconscionable such omissions on the part of those who would sell a new and presumably better instrument for the same purpose.

JEROME D. PAUKER, *Assistant Professor of Clinical Psychology, Medical School, University of Minnesota, Minneapolis, Minnesota.*

The handbook for the NSQ describes the test as being a "brief, accurate, valid, and nonstressful measurement of neurotic trends in the normal or abnormal adult or young adult." In form it is neat, clear, and easily handled by both examiner and subject. There is some question, however, about how well it measures what it sets out to measure.

The NSQ is a more recent version of the *IPAT Neurotic Personality Factor Test* (NPF). It is comprised of 40 questionnaire items, selected from a pool of 200 neuroticism-associated items, which relate to six statistically derived personality dimensions which, according to the research of Cattell and his associates, are the factors that define neuroticism. The term "neuroticism" as used by the authors "is essentially synonymous with 'neurosis' but is intended to convey the recognition that neurosis can vary in degree among normals as well as abnormals."

The test is administered in the form of a four-page booklet, the center two pages containing the 40 questionnaire items in large, dark, easily read letters on an eye-relaxing, light green background. The front page gives instructions and examples, and the back page serves as a record sheet for charting scores and making notes.

The handbook is about as excellent a manual as can be found, with descriptions, administration, scoring, reliability and validity data, tables of norms, interpretations, and so forth all presented in clearly separated and readable form. Scoring is quickly and easily done with the aid of a scoring template, and the results are recorded in the form of standard scores on a ten-unit scale. An explanation of this "sten" system, along with percentile equivalents, is presented in the handbook.

The first three test factors, which are given separate scores, are said to relate, respectively, to overprotected, tenderminded sensitivity, depressive overseriousness, and submissiveness. The final three factors are combined to form one score for anxiety. Fuller descriptions of these factors and how they were derived are given in the handbook and also in Cattell and Scheier's *The Meaning and Measurement of Neuroticism and Anxiety* (*1*). The four component scores are described as being "statistically virtually independent of one another," and are intended to provide a more detailed delineation of the general neuroticism present. Although the handbook lists "profiles" of the four scores for a variety of diagnostic categories, the authors emphasize the greater stability of a fifth score which consists of the sum of the other four scores and they point to the determination of this "total" neuroticism level as being the primary purpose of the test.

Internal consistency is indicated in the form of split-half correlations. Coefficients for the four components are .55, .57, .47, and .70. The coefficient for the total score is .67. These are not of a very encouraging order. There is no measure of stability in the form of test-retest.

The validity section is the weakest in the manual. In the first place, while mention is made of the "very high level of statistical confidence (beyond the .0005 level)" with which the total score differentiates 102 clinically-judged neurotics from 1,068 normals, there is no presentation of cutoff scores for making the differentiation nor is there any discussion of the results in terms of the number of the neurotic group who received "normal" scores and the number of normals who scored as high as the neurotic group did (false negatives and false positives). This information is of particular importance if the test is to be used for individual evaluation. Secondly, data are not presented to support the contention that the test "discriminates sharply, not only between normals and neurotics (or other abnormals), but also, continuously between degrees of neurotic trend running throughout the 'normal' population" (issue No. 16 of the "IPAT News"). A third weakness comes out of the fact that some of the validity data "are less direct in the sense that they did not arise directly from the present NSQ, but rather from that portion of the more comprehensive 16 PF TEST to which the NSQ corresponds." This use of indirect data is justified by the authors on the basis that the same components are being measured in both instances. This logic falters in view of the fact that the indirect data are based on a larger number of items than that in the NSQ, and so are likely to be more reliable. The authors promise that more direct and more extensive validity data will soon become available.

A section on "Interpreting the Test Scores" provides descriptions of behavior presumed to be associated with each of the NSQ components and with the total score. These descriptions run to about a page in length for each part, and this despite the fact that the "minimally acceptable reliability" of each component is stressed. Much of this descriptive section, too, is based on indirect data.

In summary, despite the background of extensive factor analytic work out of which this test was derived, and despite the presence of adequate normative data, there does not as yet seem to be sufficient direct evidence to recommend this test for use in individual evaluation. The total score may be of value for discriminating groups, but even here it should be used cautiously and not as a sole criterion.

This is not a test to be dismissed out-of-hand. It holds promise of being a useful screening device, but until further direct demonstration of its usefulness is forthcoming the promise should be regarded as unfulfilled.

J Counsel Psychol 8:373–4 w '61. John O. Crites. * A brief (5 to 10 minutes) 40 item inventory developed from an analysis of over 4,000 items, the *NSQ* yields part scores on Tender-Mindedness, Depression, Submissiveness, and Anxiety as well as a total Neuroticism score. The sub-scales, which were derived from factor analyses of item intercorrelations, are largely independent of each other, the highest *r* being .28 for Tender-Mindedness and Depression. The rationale for these sub-scales is that "neurotics do not differ from normals on one dimension only, as some have supposed, but on many personality dimensions at once" (Manual, p. 4). The total *NSQ* score is computed because it reflects the over-all neurotic trend of "the statistically relatively rare person who happens to be high on all components at once" (Manual, p. 4). The logic here seems strained, however, since the concept of neuroticism is either multi-dimensional or it is not. If it is the former, then there is no justification for adding the part scores, which represent different *kinds* of behavior, to obtain a composite score, which expresses different *degrees* of behavior. If it is the latter, then one scale is sufficient to measure neuroticism, not four scales. Actually, the validity data reported in the Manual on the four sub-scales of the *NSQ* suggest that "neuroticism" as measured by this inventory is essentially uni-dimensional. The only scale which consistently differentiates the clinically diagnosed groups of neurotics, psychotics, homosexuals, alcoholics, drug addicts, and psychopaths used in the initial standardization of the *NSQ* is the Anxiety scale. The other scales produce some group differences, but they appear practically insignificant and fit no discernible pattern. Unfortunately, the test authors cite no data on the standard deviations of the groups, correlations between scale scores and group membership, percentages of overlap between groups, misclassification rates (false positives and negatives), etc. Furthermore, they fail to substantiate their assertion that "NSQ scores discriminate not only between neurotics and normals, but also between varying degrees

of slighter neurotic trend in persons usually classed as normal" (Manual, p. 4). Finally, they make inferences about the validity of the *NSQ* from data on scales with similar names in the *16 Personality Factor* test which have *different* items! One reason for the low validity of the Tender-Mindedness, Depression, and Submissiveness scales as compared with the Anxiety scale is that they have extremely low reliabilities, even for personality measures. Their respective split-half coefficients, corrected by Spearman-Brown, are .55, .57, and .47, whereas the estimate for Anxiety is .70. The internal consistency coefficient for the total score, based upon the correlation between composites of halves of the sub-scales, is .67. The test authors remark that "Any attempt to augment this reliability by making items in the scale more homogeneous with each other and with the total scale (less different, as between components) would fly in the face of reality— the reality that neuroticism is *not* a single homogeneous thing" (Manual, p. 11). Again, their reasoning reveals the inconsistency between their assumption that "neuroticism" is a multi-dimensional concept and research evidence which indicates the contrary. There are other shortcomings of the *NSQ,* such as its complex scoring key, poorly described norm groups, and unfamiliar trait names, but its major drawbacks are conceptual and empirical. The Manual makes an unconvincing case for the multi-dimensional nature of neuroticism and presents only minimal data on the reliability and validity of the *NSQ.* For the counselor's use in the evaluation of a client's adjustment, the *NSQ* appears to have little demonstrated value. The Anxiety scale may give a rough index of adjustment level, but what the other scales measure with respect to modes of adjustment is unknown, and normative data on adjustment in different areas of life activity are not reported.

J Counsel Psychol 9:280–1 f '62. Ivan H. Scheier. "A Reply to Crites' Review of the Neuroticism Scale Questionnaire (The NSQ)." * Logic aside,….[Crites] claims a failure to demonstrate empirically that neuroticism is multidimensional, since the Anxiety Scale component of the test is (Crites, 1961) "The only scale which consistently differentiates the clinically diagnosed groups of neurotics, psychotics, homosexuals, alcoholics, drug addicts, and psychopaths." Now, the

NSQ *Manual* (top, p. 12) states clearly and unequivocally the (rather obvious, anyhow) point that, primarily, a neurosis test must give different scores for *neurotics* vs. normals; *not* psychotics, homosexuals, etc. vs. normals. If the reviewer had grasped that this neurosis test is validated on neurotics, he would have seen immediately that, not just anxiety, but all four NSQ components tend to deviate significantly from normal over the neurotic groups (*Manual,* Table 5); hence all four are needed to describe the typical neurotic. Neurosis is thereby presented as multidimensional. These are major, emphasized points in the Manual and background literature (Cattell & Scheier, 1961). Homogeneity reliability is +.67 for total NSQ score. The reviewer criticizes this as low, then cites one of the *Manual's* answers to this criticism: that neuroticism is a *heterogeneous* thing (four distinct components), hence, cannot realistically be measured by completely homogeneous items. Here the reviewer argues that neuroticism is homogeneous, but the above two paragraphs just considered have refuted this argument, so the heterogeneity-reducing-reliability point remains. The reviewer might have noted that the *Manual* (p. 11) describes a straightforward way to raise reliability of each NSQ component: add items from comparable scales in the longer 16 PF Test (Cattell & Stice, 1957). The reviewer is actually challenging this well known and accepted comparability principle when he deplores "inferences about the validity of the NSQ from data on scales with similar names in the *16 Personality Factor* test which have different items!" Why so shocked? In an internally consistent set of items measuring, say, anxiety, physical separation of the first and last 50 items doesn't suddenly make them *different* from anxiety and from each other! Just so, certain groups of "different" 16 PF items (Cattell & Stice, 1957) compose "scales with similar names," not coincidentally, but because they actually are comparable forms to the NSQ subscales. Moving now from the test authors' concepts to the reviewer's, 25 per cent of the review considers the concepts of "mode," "area," and "general level" of adjustment. I'm thinking of offering a reward to anyone finding these concepts in the NSQ Manual or background references (Cattell & Scheier, 1961). I can't. "Conceptual coexistence," perhaps, but "conceptual aggression" (attempts to *evaluate and criticize* the NSQ in terms of the reviewer's concepts), no! Example: the NSQ "focuses more upon level than mode or area" and what some of its components "measure with respect to modes of adjustment is unknown." It is "unknown," mainly because the test authors exercised the right to conceptualize their data in their own way. True, an author can't insist on being judged entirely within his own conceptual framework, but whoever imposes a radically different one should identify it as different, even attempt some "translation." The reviewer does neither. * The NSQ key is very simple, requiring only the ability to count and add 1's and 2's for marks showing up through a punched-hole key. Average, or nongenious scoring clerks—I've watched and timed them—need perhaps 2 or 3 minutes to understand instructions, and a minute or so per case after that, for total score. * In all tables and textual references, the NSQ *Manual* uses the basic trait names: "Tender-Mindedness," "Depression," "Submissiveness," "Anxiety," "Neuroticism" or "neurosis," or well-known synonyms for these (e.g., "dependence" for "Submissiveness"). * I am astonished that any psychologist considers terms like "anxiety" and "depression" unfamiliar. I am even more astonished that by the time the reviewer gets around to calling them "unfamiliar," he has already used them himself several times in the review without explaining them to anyone. *

[149]

★**Objective-Analytic (O-A) Anxiety Battery.** Ages 14 and over; 1955-62; revision of anxiety-to-achieve battery (U.I. 24) of *Objective-Analytic Personality Test Batteries* (see 5:90); individual in part (tests 246-I and 2410-I); 1 form ('60); 10 tests from which user may select those appropriate to his needs: 241-G (susceptibility to annoyance, 4 pages), 242-G (honesty in admitting common frailties, 2 pages), 243-G (modesty in assuming skill in untried performance, 7 pages), 244-G (critical severity vs. indulgent standards, 3 pages), 245-G (number of friends recalled, 2 pages), 246-I (increase or recovery of pulse rate), 247-G (emotionality of comment, 4 pages), 248-G (acceptance of good aphorisms, 1 page), 249-G (susceptibility to embarrassment, 5 pages), 2410-I (systolic blood pressure); manual ('60, 15 pages); norms supplement ('62, 4 pages); no data on reliability of 246-I and 2410-I; norms for college students only; no norms for 246-I, 247-G, 248-G, and 2410-I; prices per 25 tests (up to 500 copies of each may be reproduced locally from the test kit): $4 for 241-G and 247-G, $2.40 for 242-G and 245-G, $5.60 for 243-G, $3.30 for 244-G, $1.25 for 248-G, $4.60 for 249-G; separate answer sheets may be used; $2.70 per pad of 50 answer sheets; no scoring stencils for answer sheets; $6 per test kit consisting of one copy of each test and administration and scoring instructions for each; $1.25 per manual; $7 per specimen set consisting of test kit and manual; cash orders postpaid; additional apparatus necessary for tests 246-I and 2410-I; (25–50) minutes for the complete battery; Raymond B. Cattell and Ivan H. Scheier; Institute for Personality and Ability Testing. *

REFERENCES

1. CATTELL, RAYMOND B., AND SCHEIER, IVAN H. "The Nature of Anxiety: A Review of Thirteen Multivariate Analyses Comprising 814 Variables." *Psychol Rep* 4:351–88 Je '58. * (PA 33:5738)
2. CATTELL, RAYMOND B., AND SCHEIER, IVAN H. "The Objective Test Measurement of Neuroticism, U.I. 23 (—)." *Indian J Psychol* 33:217–36 pt 4 '58. *
3. SCHEIER, IVAN H., AND CATTELL, RAYMOND B. "Confirmation of Objective Test Factors and Assessment of Their Relation to Questionnaire Factors: A Factor Analysis of 113 Rating, Questionnaire, and Objective Test Measurements of Personality." *J Mental Sci* 104:608–24 Jl '58. * (PA 33:9345)
4. MOSHIN, S. M. "Plea for a Scientific Aptitude Test and a Preliminary Report of the Development of Such Test." *Indian J Psychol* 34:36–42 pt 1 '59. *
5. CATTELL, RAYMOND B., AND SCHEIER, IVAN H. *The Meaning and Measurement of Neuroticism and Anxiety.* New York: Ronald Press Co., 1961. Pp. ix, 535. * (PA 36:1HK27C)

HAROLD BORKO, *Human Factors Scientist, Advanced Technology and Research Directorate, System Development Corporation, Santa Monica, California.*

In Cattell's factor indexing system, anxiety is labeled U.I. 24, and it has been the subject of over 20 research studies involving literally thousands of subjects and hundreds of tests. From these earlier researches, the 10 best tests were selected for inclusion in the *Objective-Analytic (O-A) Anxiety Battery.*

The battery is designed to measure the clinical concept of "free anxiety" as characterized by "tension and emotionality, guilt and self-depreciation, irritability, susceptibility to embarrassment, loneliness and 'separation,' high expressed sex drive, and some suspicion and hostility." Ten separate tests are combined to make up the battery. Of these 10, 8 are paper and pencil tests which can be administered to a group, while two tests—246 and 2410—are physiological measurements and require individual administration. Test 246 deals with the increase and recovery of pulse rate following the firing of a .22 blank starting gun three feet behind the subject's head or the immersing of the subject's hand in ice water for exactly 30 seconds. This is a rather awkward test to administer and, while Cattell claims that the test has a loading of .65 with the anxiety factor, no figures are available on the reliability of the test and so one can only wonder whether it is worth administering at all. The other individual test, 2410, is entitled Systolic Blood Pressure. Although the manual states that, "in general, it seems clear that high systolic blood

pressure reflects the sheer tension aspects of anxiety," the correlation with the anxiety factor is only .36 and again reliability figures are not available.

The remaining eight tests are paper and pencil, require no special apparatus, and are designed for group administration. The split-half corrected reliability of these eight tests ranges from .56 to .90. The factor validity, which is the multiple correlation of all 10 tests with the factor dimension "is estimated conservatively as .80–.85." The clinical validity of the battery which is its correlation with a "consensus of clinical judgment" of anxiety level is estimated as .35 to .50 with a maximum attainable value, due to the unreliability of clinical judgments, estimated as .70. In essence, these figures indicate that the test battery is reasonably reliable and valid.

One serious difficulty in using this test battery is that norms are available on only 6 of the 10 tests. Furthermore, the standardizing population consists of from 94 to 280 college undergraduates, mostly males. For only three tests were approximately 50 college undergraduate females used and their scores were combined in the norm tables with those of the males. The complete lack of clinical or general population norms, and the inadequacy of the existing norms, necessitates that the prospective user of the battery be very cautious in interpreting any obtained scores. As presently constituted, the *Objective-Analytic (O-A) Anxiety Battery* will be more useful in a research than in a clinical setting.

J Counsel Psychol 7:311 w '60. Gordon V. Anderson. * In contrast to the IPAT Anxiety Scale, which arrives at an anxiety score directly by questionnaire responses indicating the subject's degree of discomfort, apprehensions and related feelings, the new measure assesses the level of anxiety by inferences from a battery of attitude measures. * These objective tests are considered superior because they are not easily "faked." This is a doubtful advantage for counselors, however, to whom clients come for help, not for adulation. The research advantages may justify this approach, however, since such questions as the degree to which anxiety reduces the efficiency of performance, differences in anxiety level among various occupational groups, and effective measures for reducing anxiety, cannot be answered without some attention to this aspect of test taking attitude. * Although this battery is presented for operational use by the publishers, and a lucid, well written manual describes the materials, explains the concepts, and makes suggestions for its application, it is not now possible to give it any meaning in the counselor-client situation. To quote the manual, "Standardization tables will be published and distributed to battery users within about a year." This battery clearly needs much more research. In addition to standardization work, studies need to be made of the stability of O-A Anxiety over time; of its relation to other personality and behavior characteristics. It looks promising, however, and it might help us in problems of motivation and those of translating potential and aspiration into achievement.

[150]

★Omnibus Personality Inventory. College; 1959–63; test booklet title is *Attitude Inventory;* more than four fifths of the items are drawn from other published or unpublished tests, over two thirds of them from *Minnesota Multiphasic Personality Inventory, VC Attitude Inventory, Minnesota T-S-E Inventory,* and *California Psychological Inventory;* for research use only; 16 (Form C) or 12 (Form D) scores: thinking introversion (TI), theoretical orientation (TO), estheticism (Es), complexity (Co), autonomy (Au), developmental status (DS, Form C only), impulse expression (IE), schizoid functioning (SF), social introversion (SI), religious liberalism (RL), social maturity (SM, Form C only), masculinity-femininity (MF), repression and suppression (RS, Form C only), nonauthoritarianism (NA, Form C only, not profiled), lack of anxiety (LA, not profiled for Form C), response set (CK, Form C only, not profiled), response bias (RB, Form D only); IBM and NCS; Forms C ('59, 15 pages), D ('63, 9 pages); Form D is a short form rather than a parallel form; research manual ('62, 81 pages); mimeographed supplement ('63, 4 pages) for Form D; profile ('62, 2 pages) for Form C; separate answer sheets must be used; $3.75 per 25 tests; 20¢ per single copy; $10 per set of stencils for hand scoring IBM answer sheets for Form C; $6.50 per set of stencils for hand scoring NCS answer sheets for Form D; 2¢ per profile for Form C (Form D profiles available only from National Computer Systems); $1.50 per set of manual and supplement; postpaid; specimen set (without manual) free; IBM answer sheets must be purchased elsewhere; see 671 for NCS scoring service accessories and prices; (90–120) minutes for Form C, [50–70] minutes for Form D; OPI Research Program, Center for the Study of Higher Education. *

REFERENCES

1. HEIST, PAUL, AND WEBSTER, HAROLD. "A Research Orientation to Selection, Admission and Differential Education," pp. 21–40. In *Research on College Students: Institute Lectures Considering Recent Research on College Student's Motivation, Values and Attitudes, and Campus Cultures.* Edited by Hall T. Sprague. Boulder, Colo.: Western Interstate Commission for Higher Education, 1960. Pp. iv, 188. *
2. WARREN, JONATHAN R., AND HEIST, PAUL A. "Personality Attributes of Gifted College Students." *Sci* 132:330–7 Ag 5 '60. * (*PA* 35:2214)
3. HEIST, PAUL; McCONNELL, T. R.; MATZLER, FRANK; AND WILLIAMS, PHOEBE. "Personality and Scholarship." *Sci* 133:362–7 F 10 '61. * (*PA* 36:2KD62H)
4. HEIST, PAUL A., AND WILLIAMS, PHOEBE A. "Variation in Achievement Within a Select and Homogeneous Student Body." *J Col Student Personnel* 3:50–9 D '61. *
5. FARWELL, ELWIN D.; WARREN, JONATHAN R.; AND McCONNELL, T. R. "Student Personality Characteristics Associated With Groups of Colleges and Fields of Study." *Col & Univ* 37:229–41 sp '62. *
6. HOLLAND, JOHN L., AND ASTIN, ALEXANDER W. "The Prediction of the Academic, Artistic, Scientific, and Social Achievement of Undergraduates of Superior Scholastic Aptitude." *J Ed Psychol* 53:132–43 Je '62. * (*PA* 37:2010)
7. LAKIE, WILLIAM L. "Personality Characteristics of Certain Groups of Intercollegiate Athletes." *Res Q* 33:566–73 D '62. * (*PA* 38:3155)
8. CANON, HARRY JAMES. *The Counseling Relationship as a Function of Certain Personality Variables.* Doctor's thesis, University of Nebraska (Lincoln, Neb.), 1963. (*DA* 24:3414)
9. CAPRETTA, PATRICK J.; JONES, REGINALD L.; SIEGEL, LAURENCE; AND SIEGEL, LILA C. "Some Noncognitive Characteristics of Honors Program Candidates." *J Ed Psychol* 54: 268–76 O '63. * (*PA* 38:4674)
10. McCONNELL, T. R. "Approaches to the Measurement of Intellectual Disposition." *Proc Inv Conf Testing Probl* 1962: 74–88 '63. * (*PA* 38:2637)
11. SHERRY, NANCY MARIE. *Inconsistency Between Measured Interest and Choice of College Major.* Doctor's thesis, University of California (Berkeley, Calif.), 1963. (*DA* 24: 2368)

PAUL M. KJELDERGAARD, *Assistant Professor of Education, Harvard University, Cambridge, Massachusetts.*

The OPI, a multiscale, true-false, self-administering personality inventory, was developed to assess the personality characteristics of normal, especially the intellectually superior, college students. Utilizing the techniques of item analysis and criterion keying, appropriate scales from previous inventories, or attitude measures, were refined, or new scales were generated from the available item pool. The original 733 items and 18 scales of the experimental versions, Forms A and B, were pared to 585 items yielding 16 scales (Form C).

The scales can perhaps be best described in terms of the factor analysis (principle components) presented in the manual. Most, though not all, scales appear, after rotation, to be relatively pure so that they may be described as measuring one of the five emergent factors. The five factors (the names presented differ somewhat from those proposed by the test authors) and the relevant scales (in parentheses) follow: (*a*) autonomy-independence (Autonomy, Developmental Status, Nonauthoritarianism, and Religious Liberalism); (*b*) adjustment-maladjustment (Impulse Expression, Lack of Anxiety, Repression and Suppression, and Response Set); (*c*) intellectualism (Complexity, Estheticism, Masculinity-Femininity, Theoretical Orientation, and Thinking Introversion); (*d*) masculinity-femininity (Masculinity-Femininity; Estheticism also has a relatively high negative loading on this factor); and (e) social introversion (Social Introversion).

RELIABILITY. The reliability coefficients of the various scales, Kuder-Richardson 21 estimates, vary from .71 (Complexity) to .93 (Regression-Suppression), with a medium coefficient of .84. Inasmuch as these calculations are based upon responses by more than 2,000 subjects, these reliability estimates must be viewed as extremely stable.

The stability of the scales has been measured only by comparing the scores of a small sample (n = 33), all females, who took the test on two occasions separated by four weeks. The correlation coefficients for the scales ranged from .68 (Autonomy) to .94 (Thinking Introversion), with a median coefficient of .83. Although other sample characteristics are not described, it is apparent that at least some of the correlations would be based upon a restricted range of scores (e.g., MF) and thus would be spuriously low. Although more evidence is needed, it would appear that most scales are sufficiently stable to permit their use where one is interested in intraindividual comparisons over time.

There are several sources of validity evidence for most of the scales. The manual is well documented with respect to each of the scales, presenting the relevant data. Although space does not permit a detailed consideration of each of the scales separately, some general comments about the types of validity evidence would be in order.

CONTENT VALIDITY. Any scale which has been adopted, more or less intact, from a previous inventory or aptitude scale must be considered to have content validity to the extent that the previous measure has been shown to measure a given trait for some other population in some other context. Such a statement must be qualified, however, insofar as virtually every adopted scale was modified in terms of item content or item format. Further, it is possible that a new context may significantly alter the item response pattern and thus change the measured behavior. Over and above these considerations, the items for the SF scale were first screened such that they were considered by psychiatrists to be descriptive of the ideation or behavior of schizophrenics and they were responded to in the appropriate direction by a high proportion of schizophrenic patients.

All the new scales were criterion keyed, i.e., items were included only if they were differentially responded to by pre-specified groups. Although it is unclear whether any attempt was made to cross validate these scales, this would be important only if no other evidence of validity were offered; this is not the case.

CONCURRENT VALIDITY. Much, though not all, of the external validity evidence is in the form of correlations with appropriate scales from other personality and attitude measures. In particular, OPI scales are correlated with appropriate scales from the *Study of Values, California Psychological Inventory, Myers-Briggs Type Indicator, Stern Activities Index,* and *Strong Vocational Interest Blank.* Since all correlations are based upon samples of 50 or more, they may be considered to have reasonable stability. The emergent correlation pattern is generally what would be predicted on the basis of the scale description, thus offering positive validity evidence.

CONSTRUCT VALIDITY. Several studies utilizing the preliminary form of the instrument have shown that certain scales, particularly Thinking Introversion, Complexity, Originality (an earlier scale), and Nonauthoritarianism would differentiate various subsets of college students in terms of their chosen major or type of institution attended. The magnitude of the differences was generally small and the relative variability large; the instrument would therefore be of little value as a selection device.

NORMS. The norms, reported in terms of raw to standard score conversions, are based upon 2,390 incoming freshmen at the University of California and San Francisco State College. A reported comparison with separate norms generated at UCLA produced only minor differences.

OPI FORM D. Recently (August 1963) a revised, shorter form of the OPI—consisting of 385 items, 10 unmodified Form C scales, and one new and one modified scale—was released. The new scale, Response Bias (28 items), was empirically keyed from a faking experiment where Ss were told to fake their scores to make a favorable impression. As additional validity evidence, it has been shown that the test would differentiate between already selected school interns and Peace Corps applicants who presumably would be trying to make a favorable impression. It should be pointed out that the K-R reliability coefficient for this scale is rather low, .55 for the original norm group.

In addition to the new scale, the MF scale of Form C has been modified and considerably abridged. The Form D MF scale compares favorably with the earlier version in terms of its reliability and its ability to discriminate between sexes, but correlations with the earlier scale are low and indicate that this scale may be measuring somewhat different aspects of masculinity. The profile sheet for Form D includes the LA scale, which is not on the Form C profile. The scale itself, however, remains unchanged from the earlier form.

SUMMARY. Through cross validation and item analyses, certain of the OPI scales, particularly those dealing with intellectual functions, are unquestionably superior to their predecessors. The clinical scales, though constructed with equal care, appear to be more sensitive to contextual factors and thus may not be measuring the same traits as the instruments from which they were drawn. Witness, for example, the apparent changes that accompanied the truncating of the MF scale from Form C to Form D.

This instrument would be most useful in research on group differences involving relatively normal subjects. As indicated earlier, studies of group differences with various scales have uniformly indicated a degree of distribution overlap that suggests the scales would be of little value for selection or classification in most situations.

NORMAN E. WALLEN, *Associate Professor of Educational Psychology, University of Utah, Salt Lake City, Utah.*

The *Omnibus Personality Inventory* is appropriately named. It is a true-false questionnaire which has neither the alleged theoretical basis of the *Edwards Personal Preference Schedule* nor the avowedly empirical approach of the *California Psychological Inventory*. Rather, it is a collection of items scored for 13 scales plus an additional 3 which are optional. These scales have been gleaned from various sources. The major contributor was the MMPI, though scales and items have also been taken from several other sources. The stated purpose of the inventory is to pull together and refine a number of scales assessing important psychological dimensions appropriate to college students.

Norms for the scales are based on a total of 2,390 entering freshmen at the University of California and San Francisco State College. The manual states that the distribution of scores subsequently obtained at UCLA is essentially the same. No attempt appears to have been made to provide separate norms for males and females, an omission which, in the light of demonstrated sex differences on similar scales in the past, seems rather serious.

With respect to reliability, the Kuder-Richardson 21 coefficients range from .71 to .93 ($n = 2,390$). Test-retest reliabilities across a four-week period provide correlations of about the same magnitude; unfortunately the sample size is only 33.

In the various stages of development of this test the authors have struggled with the problem of developing reliable but independent scales. They discovered, as would be expected, that adding items increased reliability but also increased correlations among scales, a result due at least in part to scoring the same item for several scales. Subsequent shortening increased the independence of the scales at the expense of lower reliability. At present 23 per cent of the intercorrelations are .50 or larger. An attempt to construct new items scored for only one scale would seem to be in order.

One of the more unusual features of Form C of this inventory (upon which this review is based) is the great discrepancy in number of items in various scales. The Estheticism scale, for example, contains only 24 items, whereas the Social Maturity scale contains 144 items. A more recent form (D) is available which omits the DS, SM, RS, NA, and CK scales, has a shortened MF scale and a new Response Bias scale, and profiles the LA scale. The recommended testing time of two hours is presumably reduced by about one third.

The scales have been subjected to factor analysis. With unrotated factors a very impressive general factor emerges which accounts for 31 per cent of the total variance. One is tempted to describe this as a social desirability factor, except for the finding that the two scales which are intended to get at social desirability and which correlate with the Edwards social desirability measure do not load particularly high on this factor. The remaining three factors are described as inhibition, femininity, and introversion. Rotated factors are described as tolerance and autonomy, suppression and repression, scholarly orientation, masculine role, and social introversion. In total, the factor analyses suggest that the principal variables measured are a general intellectual attitude, masculinity-femininity, and social introversion. These factors account for about 75 per cent of the variance on each scale.

A point of possible criticism of the scales pertains to some of the labels used for the measures. Although most of the names utilized appear to be fairly objective descriptions of psychological variables, several are not. In particular, the scales entitled Developmental Status and Social Maturity appear to involve the value judgment that nonauthoritarianism, skepticism, and rebellion are characteristic of greater maturity or higher status.

Validity data consist primarily of correlations with other tests and with ratings and comparison of academic groups. There is fair correspondence between the scales of the OPI and the scales on other instruments bearing similar names, but with exceptions. As an example, the Estheticism scale correlates significantly with Kuder scores in literary and music areas but not artistic. One of the difficulties in evaluating validities of personality inventories is nicely illustrated in a study in which the scales are related to dichotomous judgments made by instructors of 40 graduate students where, among others, judgments were made on the trait described as "originality, self-reliance, freedom of thought." The first question we may ask is what OPI scales would be expected to correlate significantly with such a judgment. Description of the scale traits leads this reviewer to expect significant correlations with Thinking Introversion, Theoretical Orientation, Estheticism, Complexity, Autonomy, Developmental Status, Impulse Expression, Religious Liberalism, Social Maturity, and Repression and Suppression, the latter in a negative direction. Thus, based on the descriptions, one would expect significant correlations between the judgments and almost all of the scales. In fact, only the correlation with Complexity is significant.

To summarize, although the authors do not advocate the clinical use of this instrument, the reliability and validity data are about as impressive (or unimpressive) as for any existing inventories. For the purpose of describing and comparing college groups, the norms based on a defined college group are an attractive feature. Since there is little basis in construct validity for choosing among such question-

naires, workers will probably continue to choose the one containing scales whose names attract them. The OPI certainly deserves further study. Whether it will prove more valuable than other inventories for particular purposes remains to be seen.

J Counsel Psychol 10:99–100 sp '63. Laurence Siegel. * Two features of the OPI are abundantly clear. *First, it was intended and is distributed for research purposes only.* The underlying rationale is not one of aiding selection, placement or counseling procedures. This orientation made it possible to focus scale development upon variables potentially significant for hypothesis verification, and away from vocationally-linked objectives. Second, in spite of its multi-scale nature, OPI is most appropriately to be regarded as *an arsenal of research weapons each of which can be independently fired.* Some researchers may be tempted to fire them all simultaneously to "see what happens." This would be unfortunate since in salvos even poorly aimed or inappropriate weapons sometimes chance to strike the target.

[151]

★Opinion, Attitude and Interest Survey. College-bound high school seniors and entering college freshmen; 1962–64, c1955–64; also called OAIS; tests administered at any time at individual high schools (national program only) and colleges (national or institutional program); factors related to academic interest and success; 14 scores: 3 response bias scores (set for true, infrequent response, social undesirability), 6 personality scores (achiever personality, intellectual quality, creative personality, social adjustment, emotional adjustment, masculine orientation), and 5 interest scores (business, humanities, social science, physical science, biological science); 1 form; 2 editions (identical except for format): MRC-scored edition ('64, 15 pages), NCS-scored edition ('63, c1955–63, 19 pages); a third edition, previously scored by Educational Testing Service and also identical except for format, is no longer available; handbook, preliminary edition ('63, 288 pages); separate answer sheets must be used; $5 per 25 tests of either edition; $4 per handbook; $5 per specimen set of either edition; postage extra; (40–60) minutes; Benno G. Fricke; OAIS Testing Program. *

a) INSTITUTIONAL PROGRAM. College freshmen; MRC and NCS; colleges purchase test materials and pay scoring service fees; scores reported to the student's college only (with an extra copy of the report for the student); $2.50 per 50 answer sheets of either type, postage extra; scoring service fees: 50¢ per student, postage extra, for MRC (fee includes punched card report of percentile ranks and raw scores), 75¢ per student, postpaid, for NCS (fee includes punched card and profile report of percentile ranks and standard scores).

b) NATIONAL PROGRAM. High school seniors and college freshmen; MRC; test materials supplied free; scoring service fee (paid by student): $1.50 per student, postpaid; fee includes report of percentile ranks and raw scores to the student's high school and 1–3 colleges designated at time of testing; scoring by Measurement Research Center only (on 17 specified dates between October and April).

REFERENCES

1. FRICKE, BENNO G. *The Development of an Empirically Validated Personality Test Employing Configural Analysis for the Prediction of Academic Achievement.* Doctor's thesis, University of Minnesota (Minneapolis, Minn.), 1954. (*DA* 14:2118)
2. FRICKE, BENNO G. "A Configural-Content-Intensity Item for Personality Measurement." *Ed & Psychol Meas* 16:54–62 sp '56. * (*PA* 31:5787)
3. FRICKE, BENNO G. "Response Set as a Suppressor Variable in the OAIS and MMPI." *J Consult Psychol* 20:161–9 Je '56. * (*PA* 31:6080)
4. FRICKE, BENNO G. "Student Reactions to a Personality Inventory." Comments by Jane Loevinger. *Personnel & Guid J* 35:171–4 N '56. *

JOHN O. CRITES, *Associate Professor of Psychology, University of Iowa, Iowa City, Iowa.*

The *Opinion, Attitude and Interest Survey* (OAIS) represents an attempt to provide empirically derived measures of fairly comprehensive aspects of the normal personality. Designed to be used primarily with college-bound high school seniors and college freshmen, the OAIS is a multidimensional inventory which yields a total of 14 scores from true-false responses to 396 self-descriptive and general attitudinal items, examples of which are: "I prefer dark to light woodwork in a house" and "Men have a better life than women." No explicit theoretical frame of reference, such as Murray's definitions of needs which were followed by Edwards in the construction of the *Edwards Personal Preference Schedule,* was used in writing items for the OAIS. Rather, an initial pool of 700 items was formed from behavioral observations made by the test's author; statements found in the literature on response sets, academic achievement, social and emotional adjustment, and vocational-educational interests; and experience with the behavior of relatively normal adolescents. The items are well written, being brief in length and reasonably clear in meaning, but they have little or no theoretical relevance. They are "subtle" or phenotypic items which bear no apparent relationships to the variables or genotypic factors they supposedly measure. As a result, the OAIS has restricted heuristic value for the study of the normal personality through research and also limited usefulness for its appraisal and evaluation through counseling and selection activities.

The theoretical barrenness of the OAIS is accentuated by the empirical approach which was taken in constructing its various scales and scoring keys. For each of the 14 scales, criterion groups were constituted for the selection of items much as in the development of the MMPI and SVIB, the critical difference being that it is not clear theoretically why most of the groups for the OAIS were chosen. The Intellectual Quality (Int Q) scale, for example, was constructed from items which differentiated between the top and bottom 30 per cent of freshmen at Michigan and Minnesota who had taken the ACE and the OSUPT or *Cooperative Vocabulary Test.* In other words, this scale amounts to a nonintellective measure of scholastic aptitude, which, according to the validity data reported on it, predicts GPA ($r = .23$ for men, .24 for women at Michigan) less well than the tests used in its initial standardization. Why was the scale constructed in the first place, and what is its unique utility in the measurement of academic promise? Similar questions can be asked about several of the other OAIS scales. The Masculine Orientation scale is simply another in a long line of masculinity-femininity measures derived from the differential responses of males and females which correlates with few variables except sex; the Emotional Adjustment scale provides an index of general adjustment status based upon combined clinical judgments and MMPI scores but has unknown nontest behavioral correlates; and, the interest scales for the five areas of Business, Humanities, Social Science, Physical Science, and Biological Science need further study before their validity is established, since they correlate as expected with some variables but not with others.

Probably the most promising scales of the OAIS from a theoretical standpoint, and the ones for which the empirical evidence is least equivocal, are the Achiever Personality (Ach P) and Creative Personality (Cre P) scales. The Ach P key was developed by comparing the responses of students who were classified as "achievers" or "nonachievers" on the basis of discrepancies between their tested scholastic aptitude and actual academic performance (GPA). In other words, the objective was to construct a scale which would measure the factors in scholastic success not assessed by ability tests, and at least tentatively, it can be concluded that the desired goal was reached. In the Michigan sample, Ach P correlated negligibly with the ACE and Cooperative tests but moderate positively ($r = .39$ for men, .36 for women) with GPA, and it increased the multiple correlations with GPA when combined with the ability tests. The manual states that "for most groups Ach P improves predictive efficiency not only significantly (in the statistical sense) but appreciably, averaging about 17 per cent improvement in percentage of variance accounted for." The Cre P scale was constructed from the items which were answered differently by students who had been nominated as "creative" by their instructors and those who had not been nominated, with ability and achievement controlled as much as possible. Correlations of the scale with the ACE and GPA indicate that it is essentially unrelated to these variables, and other data reveal that it is related to creative behavior as rated by teachers, as recognized in awards for original pieces of writing, and as evaluated by the citation indexes of psychologists.

Other features of the OAIS scales which should be noted are the following:

a) Considerable effort was expended to purify the scales so that they would be statistically independent and would be free of response biases. The results may or may not be advantageous, however, since it may be that the purification of the scales has distorted what their interrelationships to other variables actually are. Several of the scales, for example, correlated with the Social Undesirability (Soc U) scale, which was constructed to detect the tendency to give a good impression in taking the OAIS. Revisions in these scales were made, so that their correlations with Soc U were appreciably reduced. Some behaviors, however, particularly those in making good social adjustments, necessitate creating a good impression, and if they are "purified" out of a social adjustment scale, the scale necessarily loses some of its validity. Similarly, the use of "suppressor variables" to eliminate the correlations between scales which are otherwise related may result in an artifactual representation of the relationships which actually exist among the nontest criterion variables for the scales. Only if scale purifications produce interscale correlations which are isomorphic to the intercriteria relationships are they justified, and there is no evidence in the OAIS manual that such is the case.

b) Two types of reliability data, internal consistency and stability estimates, are reported in the manual, and it is clear from the results that neither is really satisfactory. The internal consistency coefficients range from a high of .64 for Emotional Adjustment to a low of .41 for Infrequent Response, with a majority of the r's in the high 40's and low 50's, and the test-retest ($n = 69$, 2 year interval) coefficients range from a high of .76 for Masculine Orientation to a low of .46 for Social Adjustment, with most of the r's in the 50's and 60's. The author argues that the reliability of the OAIS is not an important consideration, if the inventory can be shown to be valid. He recognizes the ceiling which reliability places upon the validity of a test but ignores the effects of the relatively inadequate reliability of the OAIS upon its validity. Unless it can be shown that the low test-retest reliabilities of the OAIS scales are attributable to developmental changes in the variables which it supposedly measures, and which can be accounted for by introducing an age factor into the regression equations for the inventory, it is doubtful that the scales will have much predictive efficiency. Also, unless the internal consistency of the scales can be increased to an acceptable level, the OAIS will be like an unwieldly shotgun which hits all around a target but seldom on it. To illustrate, consider the best of the OAIS scales, Ach P, which has an internal consistency of .45 and a validity of .39 for GPA: its standard error of measurement is 4.88, its standard error of estimate is 6.07, and its coefficient of alienation is .917, the latter indicating only an 8 per cent improvement in prediction over chance.

c) Most of the data on the OAIS are reported in its lengthy, and frequently discursive, manual which should be carefully and critically read by any user of the inventory. The manual is replete with tables of findings on the OAIS, which are interpreted in the accompanying text, but not one statistical test is reported or significance level cited which allows the reader to evaluate the validity and reliability results according to accepted standards. Rationalizations of contradictory findings can be found throughout the manual, as can unsubstantiated criticisms of other tests in the same area of measurement, in particular the SVIB. Inaccurate interpretations of psychometric concepts are presented, such as the confusion of construct with predictive validity, and the literature on interest and personality measurement is used selectively to support the test author's arguments, the logic of which is often untenable as in his discussions of the unimportance of reliability and the assumed inadequacy of the SVIB. At best the manual can be considered to be a vehicle for the presentation of the test author's biases and opinions; at worst it must be judged as a frequently erroneous and misleading treatment of the data on the OAIS.

Despite the many years of research which have gone into the construction and development of the OAIS, it must be concluded that, with the possible exceptions of the Ach P and Cre P scales, the inventory does not fulfill the claims which are made for it, and it is not ready for use in either vocational-educational counseling or academic selection. It has scant theoretical significance; it has only minimal reliability; and it measures neither variables nor constructs with acceptable validity.

HAROLD WEBSTER, *Associate Research Psychologist, Center for the Study of Higher Education, University of California, Berkeley, California.*

The OAIS handbook contains both the author's philosophy of measurement and some results of a research project of rather heroic proportions. The attitude toward mental measurement is pragmatic and empirical. The presentation in Chapter 2 is oriented toward answering some objections to personality tests. The empirical data, although extensive, are not adequate for answering still other questions often raised by other investigators about the usefulness of tests such as the OAIS. Some case material is presented, but the report lacks a general theory of student functioning that might be supported by these data. Although this last criticism applies to many a published mental test, it seems especially serious when the test focuses upon immediate empirical objectives such as the prediction of school grades or adjustment ratings.

The presentation of the means and standard deviations of untransformed raw scores is inadequate. The manual contains some means and standard deviations for a few small or atypical samples (e.g., pp. 114, 178, 210). The best sample for norms seems to be the one referred to in Table 11, where the means and standard deviations are intended for comparison with random response data. In this sample

of 1,101 freshmen the K-R 21 reliabilities are .54 for Achiever Personality, .54 for Intellectual Quality and .51 for Creative Personality. Although the author thinks reliability is not important, these results show that a random replication of a testing session would very likely reorder the persons quite differently on any scale, that is, with too little precision to warrant use of the scales at the individual level. The attributes measured may indeed be significant, but the measurement is not precise, and the comparison of any two persons on a given scale is therefore hazardous unless their scores happen to be widely separated.

Having dismissed reliability except as it accrues directly from validity, the author presents a large number of validity coefficients. These must of course be interpreted according to the aims of the test development, and with the idea that each coefficient would be inflated by some amount if it could actually be corrected for attenuation.

Apparently the author has isolated some variance shared with freshman grades that is not accounted for by conventional predictors; the uncorrected validity coefficients of .39 for men and .36 for women for the Ach P scale may seem more impressive when we find that this scale has also been adjusted in order to reduce its correlations with several other scales, including response bias scales. Similarly, the second scale, Intellectual Quality, "predicts scores on ability tests about as well as the ability tests predict each other." The latter correlations include .24 with ACE quantitative aptitude, .55 with ACE linguistic aptitude, .48 with English achievement, and .26 with mathematics achievement. With the exception of the masculinity-femininity scale, the Int Q scale appears to have the most satisfactory validity. The strongest correlation for the third scale, Creative Personality, is .31, the correlation for 124 students with their instructors' creativity ratings. The other scales, including two that measure social and emotional adjustment, also have low validity coefficients.

There seems to be a tendency among psychologists generally to assume that correlations around .70 or .80 are unconscionably large, although for many purposes a correlation of .90 is clearly not large enough (for example, in comparing linear composites). For example, the author of this test notes that "three ability tests correlate very highly with each other, about .67." This reviewer would insist that .67 is not a *very* high correlation, even when encountered in the field of mental testing. The author does not hesitate to interpret correlations in the range ±.30 with considerable confidence. It is true that many influences can be envisioned (including unreliability) that might have reduced a validity coefficient from .85 to .35. One problem of mental testing is, however, to mitigate such influences so that scores become more useful and interpretable. It may happen that the validity coefficients near .35 reported in the OAIS handbook will fluctuate somewhat in new samples of students attending other institutions, which is a central problem for future research.

The author presents several factor analyses of OAIS scores, together with other variables. His fear of redundancy does not lie at the factor level, however, but at the scale level; the effort to avoid "contaminating" scales with items that might also measure something else has resulted in weaker scales than might otherwise have been obtained. The OAIS seems to be another test where the desire to measure many subtleties well was not initially supported by enough appropriate experimental items, with the result that some failure of scale independence would normally be expected, due to item overlap, if individual scales were built up to full strength.

Perhaps the most serious criticism is that the scale scoring is not available in the manual. This makes it impossible to study scale content in order to formulate hypotheses about why the scales work as well as they do. At this stage in our understanding of college students, some knowledge of their attitudes, as expressed at the item level, could be valuable.

In brief, the OAIS represents a good beginning in the study of the expressed attitudes of college students, but will require considerably more work before it does more than contribute a small increment of predictability to a few criteria that are presently not well understood.

[152]

★**Organic Integrity Test.** Mental patients; 1960; brain damage or dysfunction shown as chromaphilia (loss of form-perception with increased color-perception); individual; 1 form (15 cards); manual (reprint of *1* below); directions for administering (2 pages); diagnostic chart (1 page); $21.50 per set of cards and directions for administering, postpaid; [4–5] minutes; H. C. Tien; the Author. *

REFERENCES

1. TIEN, H. C. "Organic Integrity Test (O.I.T.): A Quick Diagnostic Aid to Rule in Organic Brain Diseases." *Arch Gen Psychiatry* 3:43–52 Jl '60. *

[153]

★**The Orientation Inventory.** College and industry; 1962; kinds of satisfactions and rewards sought in jobs; 3 scores: self-orientation, interaction-orientation, task-orientation; 1 form (4 pages); mimeographed manual, research edition (21 pages); preliminary norms; $3 per 25 tests; $1 per set of manual and key; $1 per specimen set; postage extra; (20–25) minutes; Bernard M. Bass; Consulting Psychologists Press, Inc. *

REFERENCES

1. BASS, BERNARD M.; DUNTEMAN, GEORGE; FRYE, ROLAND; VIDULICH, ROBERT; AND WAMBACH, HELEN. "Self, Interaction, and Task Orientation Inventory Scores Associated With Overt Behavior and Personal Factors." *Ed & Psychol Meas* 23:101–16 sp '63. * (PA 38:2706)
2. DUNTEMAN, GEORGE, AND BASS, BERNARD M. "Supervisory and Engineering Success Associated With Self, Interaction, and Task Orientation Scores." *Personnel Psychol* 16:13–21 sp '63. * (PA 38:3318)

RICHARD S. BARRETT, *Associate Professor of Management Engineering and Psychology, New York University, New York, New York.*

The *Orientation Inventory* is conceived by the author as a broadly useful instrument which may contribute to such diverse objectives as counseling of students, predicting success on work requiring persistence, and studying self-actualization, social interrelationships, and marital compatibility. It consists of 27 statements of opinions and attitudes. For each statement the subject indicates which of three alternatives is most true or most preferred or most important, and also which alternative is least true or preferred. The set of alternatives for each item contains one alternative of each of the three orientations tapped by the inventory, self-, interaction-, and task-orientation, defined in the manual as follows:

self-orientation: reflects the extent a person describes himself as expecting direct rewards to himself regardless of the job he is doing or the effects of what he does upon others working with him * A person with a high score in self-orientation is more likely to be rejected by others, to be introspective, to be dominating and to be unresponsive to the needs of the others around him. He is concerned mainly with himself, not co-workers' needs or the job to be done.

interaction-orientation: reflects the extent of concern with maintaining happy, harmonious relationships in a superficial sort of way, often making it difficult to contribute to the task at hand or to be of real help to others. Interest in group activities is high, but not ordinarily conducive to the progress of the group in completing tasks.

task-orientation: reflects the extent to which a person is concerned about completing a job, solving problems, working persistently and doing the best job possible. In groups, despite his concern with the task, the task-oriented member tends to work hard within the group to make it productive as possible. If he is interested in what the group is doing, he will fight hard for what he regards as right.

Compared with what would be expected of a commercial test manual, the manual (a research edition) contains more research results, and less normative data (although preliminary norms on 908 college students are presented). Test-retest reliability ranges between .73 and .76 for the three scales. Concurrent validity studies among supervisors show the more successful people to be task-oriented, and the less successful to be self-oriented. The inventory has shown differences between groups based on their training, line of work, and status. The differences, even where significant, are generally small.

The basic lack in the manual is a clear statement of the degree of overlap among the scales. Using the standard that to be classified in one of the orientations a subject's score had to be in the top 25 per cent on that orientation and in the bottom 50 per cent on each of the others, 84 college students were classified into the three orientations, or if they failed to meet these standards, they were placed in a residual category. On reclassification a week later, from 66.6 to 70.6 per cent of those originally classified in one of the three orientations were classified again into the same category. There were many shifts into and out of the residual category. Unfortunately, the data are not clear because they are presented in percentages. When the probable frequencies are reconstructed from the percentages, the residual category is seen to be the largest.

One study reported in the manual seems to confirm the suspicion that the scales are not independent. An unspecified number of salaried management personnel of a large oil refinery participating in a discussion group rated every other participant after a total of 10 two-hour meetings. They used 27 (or 28, the manual is inconsistent) items of behavior to indicate how much the person rated exhibited each of the behaviors. The manual reports the highest correlations between the scale scores of the Ori (as the authors abbreviate it) and the ratings, presumably using .20 in absolute value as the cutoff score. The seven correlations between the behavior ratings and the Self-Orientation scores are independent of the other two, but the Interaction- and Task-Orientations show a pattern which suggests that they are not independent.

Sixteen correlations involving Interaction-Orientation, and 20 involving Task-Orientation are listed; of these, 15 appear in both lists, always with a reversal of signs. The average difference between the 15 pairs of correlations is .91, indicating that the patterns of correlation of the two scales are virtually mirror images of each other. It follows that there must be a high and negative correlation between interaction- and task-orientation as measured by the Ori. The manual would be more useful if data on intercorrelations among the Ori scales were made available.

The Ori is presented primarily as a research instrument with potential in any field where a person's orientation toward himself, his co-workers, or his work is important. Like most self-reports, its usefulness as a selection instrument is limited by its fakability. The usual kind of research on this problem, in which college students are asked first to be honest and then to "fake good" showed that they could manipulate their scores toward Task- and Interaction-Orientation and consequently away from Self-Orientation. Although its usefulness in selection may be limited for this reason, the Ori has promise, some of which has already been fulfilled, as a means of deepening our understanding of how people work. However, it appears that the Ori does not measure three independent orientations as the manual implies, but only two, a self-orientation and a bipolar task-interaction orientation.

H. Bradley Sagen, *Assistant Professor of Education, University of Iowa, Iowa City, Iowa.*

The *Orientation Inventory* (Ori) is a brief forced-choice instrument designed to assess the kinds of rewards and satisfactions sought from interpersonal situations, particularly those situations organized around the solution of problems or the completion of tasks. Possible uses suggested by the author include research in social interrelationships, vocational and educational counseling, and selection in business and industry.

The author's description of the scale format and development raises at least three important issues. (*a*) Although the content of the scales seems generally consistent with the underlying dimensions outlined in the manual, the lack of information about scale development and internal consistency somewhat precludes a clear interpretation of what the Ori is actually measuring. (*b*) There is no evidence that the alternative responses in each triad were equated for social desirability. (*c*) The manual neglects to point out that the three scales are ipsative; i.e., a person's score on one scale is dependent upon his scores on the other scales. Among their other properties, ipsative scales impose negative correlations among the scores and force all subjects' profiles to the same mean. These properties do not necessarily detract from the utility of the Ori, but their relationship to the specific assessment problem should be determined before seriously considering the inventory.

As the author quite rightly notes, test-retest reliabilities of .73, .76, and .75 for the three scales respectively (college students over a one-week period) are somewhat inadequate for purposes of individual diagnosis.

The validity data can best be described as inconclusive. Several of the studies, particularly the correlations with peer ratings and some imaginative demonstrations of the relationship of Ori scores to behavior in prestructured situations, yield results which are consistent with the scale descriptions. On the other hand, the correlations with ratings of experts and with other personality instruments (unfortunately based upon an earlier version of the Ori), are usually barely significant or are nonsignificant. For example, 36 of the 40 "significant" correlations with other instruments are less than .30 and the other 4 are less than .35.

The primary defect in the validity data, however, is that many of the studies are either so lacking in quality or are reported in such haphazard fashion that little can be gained from examining them. A number of the studies reported are based upon small and ill-defined samples. For example, tentative conclusions regarding the effects of maturity are drawn from an analysis of cross-sectional samples consisting of as few as 25 subjects. In other studies the criterion is vague, e.g., "best" versus "less than best" supervisors. In a few cases, the level of significance is not specified and in still others inferences are drawn from nonsignificant results. Finally, a description of the variances is lacking in many of the comparisons so that although the differences may be significant, it is impossible to calculate the amount of overlap between the groups.

An additional point related to validity is that resistance to faking is highly important if the Ori is to be utilized for selection. However, when the mean score changes of college students asked to "fake good" were compared with the mean differences between high and low rated groups in the two studies of job performance, the changes due to faking were greater in all but one comparison.

At present, the greatest potential for the Ori would seem to be as a research instrument. Concepts such as "task orientation," "achievement orientation," etc., abound in the psychological and sociological literature, but little has been accomplished by way of scaling these dimensions. Although the evidence for the Ori is inconclusive, the importance of the dimensions to behavioral research would perhaps justify the time and effort involved in additional validity studies by interested investigators. If such studies are undertaken, the reviewer would suggest the possibility of utilizing the scales normatively as well as in the present ipsative arrangement.

The conclusions are equally uncertain regarding the utility of the Ori for purposes of selection in business and industry. Given adequate validation procedures with respect to specific criteria, and a favorable selection ratio, many of the present criticisms would be reduced in importance. On the other hand, lack of adequate evidence of resistance to faking makes the Ori somewhat suspect as a selection device and in the absence of such evidence this reviewer does not recommend its use where faking is likely to be a possibility.

In view of the somewhat low reliability coefficients and the scarcity of adequate validity data, the Ori is definitely not recommended for individual assessment.

[154]

*Personal Adjustment Inventory. Ages 9–13; 1931–61; formerly called *Test of Personality Adjustment;* title on test booklet is *P.A. Inventory;* 5 scores: personal inferiority, social maladjustment, family maladjustment, daydreaming, total; separate forms ('61, 8 pages, identical with tests copyrighted in 1931 except for four wording changes) for boys and girls; manual ('61, 17 pages, identical with 1931 manual except for introduction and minor revisions) ; $2.50 per 25 tests; 75¢ per specimen set; postage extra; (40–50) minutes; Carl R. Rogers; Association Press. *

REFERENCES

1–19. See 5:117.
20. BURCHINAL, LEE G. "Parents' Attitudes and Adjustment of Children." *J Genetic Psychol* 92:69–79 Mr '58. * (*PA* 36:1FG69B)
21. DORFMAN, ELAINE. "Personality Outcomes of Client-

Centered Child Therapy." *Psychol Monogr* 72(3):1–22 '58. *
(PA 33:8602)

22. OXFORD, LAKE C. *A Study of Personal and Social Adjustment of Seventh Grade Boys and Girls as Influenced by Physical Size, Athletic Ability, Acceptance by Peers, and Acceptance of Peers.* Doctor's thesis, University of Maryland (College Park, Md.), 1958. (DA 20:3634)

23. CLEMENTS, SAM D. *The Predictive Utility of Three Delinquency Proneness Measures.* Doctor's thesis, University of Houston (Houston, Tex.), 1960. (DA 20:3827)

24. L'ABATE, LUCIANO. "The Effect of Paternal Failure to Participate During the Referral of Child Psychiatric Patients." *J Clin Psychol* 16:407–8 O '60. * (PA 37:3259)

25. L'ABATE, LUCIANO. "Personality Correlates of Manifest Anxiety in Children." *J Consult Psychol* 24:342–8 Ag '60. *
(PA 35:1997)

NORMAN D. SUNDBERG, *Professor of Psychology, University of Oregon, Eugene, Oregon.*

If psychologists and educators have a need to assess the personalities of children, as they undoubtedly do, it is most unfortunate that they do not show the interest and persistence needed for the careful research and development of assessment devices. Carl Rogers' inventory is a curious and sad example of how some seminal ideas frozen into a published test have failed to receive the nurturance needed for growth. First published in 1931, under the title *Test of Personality Adjustment,* the same inadequate norms, scoring methods, and validity and reliability data are still being promulgated in the test and manual only slightly revised and reissued in 1961. What a rueful commentary on the influence of earlier *Mental Measurements Yearbook* reviews!

Undoubtedly there is a need for such an instrument as this. The publishers are still selling copies, but they seem unwilling to take on the responsibilities a real revision would demand. The author's interests have swung away from clinical work with children to adult psychotherapy and personality theory. The work of at least collecting simple normative and reliability data would not have been extremely onerous. How one wishes that Rogers or one of his students could have found the time and interest to apply Rogers' great theoretical insights and clinical wisdom to this important task.

Unfortunately the 1961 manual does not even make use of what research has already been done on the inventory, and somehow no one took the trouble to append a bibliography to the manual. Anyone who uses the test should be directed at least to two pieces of research. One study by Burchinal, Gardner and Hawkes (*18*) suggests a revision of the norms for the four subtests (Personal Inferiority, Social Maladjustment, Family Maladjustment, and Daydreaming) on the basis of results with 256 normal fifth graders in rural areas of the Midwest. Rather surprisingly, the investigators found no need to revise the classifications based on the total score—surprising since the original norms came many years earlier from a mixture of 136 normal and problem children in New York City.

The second major reference is Louis Smith's excellent monograph (*19*) on the concurrent validity of six personality tests for children. The six include Rogers' *Personal Adjustment Inventory, California Test of Personality, Rosenzweig Picture-Frustration Study* and three unpublished tests. Using approximately 245 sixth grade boys separated into poorly adjusted, average adjusted, and well adjusted on the basis of a dual criterion of teacher's and peer's nominations, Smith demonstrated significant validity for differentiating the means of these groups using any of the three published children's tests. These leading group tests showed low degrees of correlation with each other. Interestingly, the subtests of the Rogers' inventory showed very low intercorrelations, suggesting that they are really measuring different aspects of personality. At the present stage, Smith wisely warns that the overlap of the distributions of the three adjustment groups was large and that none of the tests would be good for screening of groups when base rates of maladjustment are low.

Summarizing the psychometric characteristics, one can politely say they leave much to be desired. Norms are for small, unusual samples. They do not cover developmental differences within the 9 to 13 age group for which the test is intended. Reliability figures are scanty. Rogers reports one-month retest correlations for subtests ranging from .65 to .72 and for the total, .72. Though these are not far from reliability figures of most personality inventories, there is obvious need for studies with other subjects and different periods of time and for studies of internal consistency and subtest characteristics. An equivalent form would be helpful. Validity figures are far too limited to generate much confidence, although the few reported suggest some promise. The manual in an inadequately reported study states subtest scores' correlations with clinicians' ratings range from .38 for Family Maladjustment to .48 for Daydreaming. These results point to much caution with individual cases and need for further corroboration of findings.

Many questions arise, such as relation to intelligence, influence of test taking attitudes, and effects of psychotherapy. Certainly the cumbersome scoring could be improved. An examination of the scoring on items reveals two interesting facets: (a) sophisticated patterning concepts, e.g., if the child has siblings and answers this way, then give him so many points; and (b) hypotheses about the nature of maladjustment that are suggestive of further research. The inventory is not satisfactory as a psychometric instrument now, but as a potential stimulator of research and as a model for incorporating clinical hypotheses, it is worthy of attention by psychologists.

Evaluating the Rogers inventory from a clinical, as distinguished from a psychometric, standpoint, one finds some appealing features. As Louttit and Gough have noted in previous *Yearbook* reviews, the items are clinically insightful, appropriate, and naturally interesting to children—items asking the child his wishes, interests, comparisons with other children, feelings about his family. The items have some variety, including open-ended ways of answering—such as naming the three people the child would take to a desert island with him. The inventory could readily be used as a structured supplement to an interview with a child. The modern clinician would also want to provide himself with other summarizing language more related to personality theory and to clinical decisions than the terms the four subtests suggest. The manual, unlike too many test manuals, pays attention to the needs of the clinician using the test for individual assessment; four well done case illustrations are presented. It is the clinical use of the inventory which Rogers emphasizes, saying, "the numerical scores, taken by themselves, are not highly accurate, and might be misleading in the case of an individual child." He urges the user to examine individual responses to get at the inner world of the child.

As Rogers' inventory stands, psychologists cannot put much confidence in it as a psychometric device. It can profitably be employed (a) for research purposes and (b) as part of a clinical exploration of adjustment supplemented by other approaches. It is to be hoped that future reviewers will find this inventory supplanted by forms much more carefully cultivated.

ROBERT D. WIRT, *Professor of Psychology, Child Development, and Psychiatry, University of Minnesota, Minneapolis, Minnesota.*

History, it has been said, is a great teacher. There is much to learn from a study of this instrument and its manual. There was a time when psychologists and educators were willing to place considerable confidence in the generality of conclusions based upon the careful study of a single case or a few cases. Nowadays we tend to disparage such research and insist upon large sample statistics and experimental control or matching of many variables. The writing in this instrument represents some of the best available published documentation of sophisticated, sensitive, and clinically useful methods of examiner behavior and interpretation of subject response; it also represents some of the most flagrant disregard for scientific rigor and contemporary test construction methodology in print.

The test was first published in 1931 under the title *Test of Personality Adjustment*. It was reissued, but *not* revised under the new title in 1961. Both Adler and Gough emphasized the need for revision of the test in their reviews in *The Fifth Yearbook*. The failure to meet the need for revision is unsatisfactorily explained in an introduction to the 1961 edition: "The author regrets that no empirical re-study of the instrument has been made. His own interests have moved into other areas and no one else has taken on the task." It would seem to this reviewer that if the publishers could not find someone else to take on the task, the instrument should have been withdrawn, as Adler recommended (5:117), rather than reissued quite unchanged except for a new title. The publisher does not explain the reason for altering the title. It may, of course, mislead some test users into supposing that the well-known author has standardized a new test. In view of Rogers' widely quoted viewpoint regarding the inadvisability of engaging in diagnostic assessment in clinical practice, that would be a remarkable event indeed.

There is much practical material in both the manual and the separate inventories for girls and for boys. The items range over a number of important areas of a child's attitudes toward himself, his family, and his peers. They are worded in clear language and are sensitively geared to the developmental level for which they are designed. The manual is well written where it deals with instructions for giving the test and with interpretation of results. If the instrument were issued as a guide for interviewing children, it could be highly recommended. It is not a useful *test*, however, despite the claim to that status given in the series title, "Series of Character and Personality Tests."

The instrument was developed on a very small sample: 52 "problem" children and 84 "normal" children. Although the author says "no apology is offered for these small numbers," this reviewer wonders why the publishers failed to take Gough's advice (5:117) to use the very extensive data which must in the past 30 years have been collected in child guidance clinics throughout the country. The reliability and validity of the instrument are both unsatisfactory and even the author cautions against using test scores in making predictions. The scoring system is needlessly complicated.

In summary, it may be said that the *Personal Adjustment Inventory* contains material which still has clinical utility and certainly has historical interest and which may be useful as an interview guide with young children. It is not properly a test and it should not be scored and used as a test. It is a great disappointment that in reissuing this instrument neither the author nor the publisher has taken any advantage of the advances in test construction which have occurred in the past thirty years or of the substantial data which would have been readily available.

For reviews by Dan L. Adler and Harrison G. Gough, see 5:117; for a review by C. M. Louttit, see 40:1258.

[155]

★**Personal Qualities Inventory.** Business and industry; 1956-63; 1 form ('56, 3 pages); manual ['63, 6 unnumbered pages]; directions for administering and scoring (no date, 2 pages); norms for males only; $3 per 25 tests; 10¢ per key; $1 per manual; postage extra; $1 per specimen set, postpaid; (15-20) minutes; Richardson, Bellows, Henry & Co., Inc. *

REFERENCES

1. KIRKPATRICK, JAMES J. "Validation of a Test Battery for the Selection and Placement of Engineers." *Personnel Psychol* 9:211-27 su '56. * (PA 31:8964)

[156]

*Personality and Interest Inventory: Elementary Form, Revised. Grades 4-8; 1935-59; 1 form ('59, 2 pages); directions ('36, 1 page); no data on reliability; no norms; $1.50 per 35 tests; 50¢ per specimen set; postpaid; (30-35) minutes; Gertrude Hildreth; Bureau of Publications. *

REFERENCES

1-3. See 40:1238.

For a review by Stephen M. Corey, see 40:1238; for a review by Jack W. Dunlap, see 38:924.

[157]

The Personality Inventory. Grades 9-16 and adults; 1931-38; 6 scores: neurotic tendency, self-sufficiency, introversion-extroversion, dominance-submission, confidence, sociability; IBM; 1 form ('35, 4 pages); manual ('35, 7 pages); profile (no date, 1 page); tentative norms ('38, 2 pages); $3.25 per 25 tests; $1.25 per 50 profiles; 25¢ per manual; separate answer sheets may be used; $2.20 per 50 IBM answer sheets; $1.50 per 50 Hankes answer sheets (scored by Testscor only, see 667); $1 per set of hand scoring stencils; $5 per set of IBM scoring stencils; 50¢ per specimen set; postage extra; (25) minutes; Robert G. Bernreuter; [Consulting Psychologists Press, Inc.]. *

REFERENCES

1-71. See 40:1239.
72-259. See 4:77.
260-299. See 5:95.
300. FOX, VERNON. "The Influence of Personality on Social Non-Conformity." *J Crim Law & Criminol* 42:746-54 Mr-Ap '52. * (PA 28:6298)
301. SCHOLL, GERALDINE. "Some Notes on the Use of Two Personality Tests With Visually Handicapped Students." *New Outlook Blind* 47:287-95 D '53. *
302. GREENBERG, HERBERT M.; ALLISON, LOUISE; FEWELL, MILDRED; AND RICH, CHARLES. "The Personality of Junior High and High School Students Attending a Residential School for the Blind." *J Ed Psychol* 48:406-10 N '57. * (PA 33:817)
303. KNOWLES, REX HANNA. *Differential Characteristics of Successful and Unsuccessful Seminary Students.* Doctor's thesis, University of Nebraska (Lincoln, Neb.), 1958. (DA 19:1655)
304. TAFT, RONALD. "Is the Tolerant Personality Type the Opposite of the Intolerants?" *J Social Psychol* 47:397-405 My '58. * (PA 33:8186)
305. BALL, LEE. *Personality Traits of Varsity Gymnasts as Measured by the Bernreuter Personality Invoice.* Master's thesis, Mankato State College (Mankato, Minn.), 1959.
306. GUILFORD, J. P. *Personality,* pp. 173-5. New York: McGraw-Hill Book Co., Inc., 1959. Pp. xiii, 562. *
307. BOYKIN, LEANDER L. "The Adjustment of 729 Negro College Students as Revealed by the Bernreuter Personality Inventory." *Negro Ed R* 11:43-7 Ja '60. *
308. GAYEN, A. K.; SAHA, R. P.; AND MATHUR, R. K. "Factors in the Study of Personality: Part 2, A Scoring Key for a Short Personality Test." *Indian J Psychol* 35:1-8 pt 1 '60. * (PA 36:4HF01G)
309. HARRELL, THOMAS W. "The Relation of Test Scores to Sales Criteria." *Personnel Psychol* 13:65-9 sp '60. * (PA 35:7192)
310. MACKINNEY, ARTHUR C., AND WOLINS, LEROY. "Validity Information Exchange, No. 13-01, Foreman II, Home Appliance Manufacturing." *Personnel Psychol* 13:443-7 w '60. *
311. SAHA, GOPI BALLAV. "An Investigation Into the School Maturity of High School Students." *Indian J Psychol* 35:47-54 pt 2 '60. * (PA 36:4KD47S)
312. BURGART, HERBERT J. "Art in Higher Education: The Relationship of Art Experience to Personality, General Creativity, and Aesthetic Performance." *Studies Art Ed* 2:14-35 sp '61. *
313. COOLEY, JOHN C. "A Study of the Relation Between Certain Mental and Personality Traits and Ratings of Musical Abilities." *J Res Music Ed* 9:108-17 f '61. *
314. INGENOHL, INGO. "The Significance of the No-Count on the Bernreuter Personality Inventory." *J Social Psychol* 54:17-40 Je '61. * (PA 36:2HF27I)
315. MIDDLETON, RUSSELL, AND PUTNEY, SNELL. "A Note on the Validity of the Bernreuter Personality Inventory Measure of Dominance-Submission." *J Social Psychol* 53:325-30 Ap '61. * (PA 36:1HF25M)
316. ROBBINS, JAMES E., AND KING, DONALD C. "Validity Information Exchange, No. 14-02: D.O.T. Code 0-97.61, Manager, Sales." *Personnel Psychol* 14:217-9 su '61. *
317. CASH, W. L., JR. "Relationship of Personality Traits and Scholastic Aptitude to Academic Achievement in Theological Studies." *J Psychol Studies* 13:105-10 Je '62 [issued F '64]. *
318. LAUDANO, FRANK S. *A Comparative Study of Various Personality Traits of Teachers and Non-Teachers as Measured by the Bernreuter Personality Inventory.* Master's thesis, Southern Connecticut State College (New Haven, Conn.), 1962.

319. Shaw, Marvin E. "The Effectiveness of Whyte's Rules: 'How to Cheat on Personality Tests.'" *J Appl Psychol* 46:21–5 F '62. * (PA 36:5HF21S)

320. De Sena, Paul Ambrose. *Identification of Non-Intellectual Characteristics of Consistent Over-, Under-, and Normal-Achievers Enrolled in Science Curriculums at the Pennsylvania State University.* Doctor's thesis, Pennsylvania State University (University Park, Pa.), 1963. (DA 24:3144)

321. Herbert, N., and Turnbull, G. H. "Personality Factors and Effective Progress in Teaching." *Ed R* 16:24–31 N '63. *

Wesley C. Becker, *Professor of Psychology, University of Illinois, Urbana, Illinois.*

Since this test was last reviewed in *The Fourth Yearbook* there have been no changes in its structure, format, manual, or in the implications of the research evidence. Previous reviewers have been quite skeptical about the value of the *Personality Inventory.* The best that Mosier could say for it was that it offered a checklist of symptoms which might be useful in the hands of a trained clinical psychologist. Mosier also suggested that it might be a useful device for screening some kinds of emotional problems, especially the confidence scale (emotional stability), but that "good" scores on the confidence scale did not necessarily imply good adjustment. Newcomb was willing in 1940 to wait and see if Flanagan's two independent factors might not yet correlate with significant human behaviors, but otherwise could find nothing in the 71 studies completed at that time which would lead him to recommend its use. In her 1953 review, Tyler had available more than 250 research papers on this test. She indicated that it was used fairly successfully as a screening technique in the armed forces programs, probably because men in service were more willing to admit their maladjustments in order to avoid unpleasant duties. Tyler also noted that the Bernreuter has had some success in showing group differences between salesmen and nonsalesmen, campus leaders and nonleaders, etc., but that in no case were validity indicators strong enough to support decisions in individual cases. But most important in Tyler's review was the conclusion that the Bernreuter is of doubtful value in selection programs, since it is quite easy to fake desirable scores. This conclusion obviously covers most industrial applications of the Bernreuter. The research conducted since Tyler's review serves only to reinforce this conclusion. The test is easily faked to give an emotionally stable, somewhat outgoing profile (*282, 319*), and while successful and unsuccessful employees of various sorts are occasionally differentiated (*280, 283*), the differences are so small as to preclude their usefulness in making decisions about individuals.

In view of all this, it is indeed surprising to find the following statement in the publisher's catalog: "One of the most famous of all personality inventories, the test of Dr. Bernreuter is very widely used, particularly in business and industry." We have no reason to question the veracity of this statement. Whyte [1] indicates that in 1953, Stanford University Press sold over 1,000,000 copies of the test. Our surprise arises from the apparent failure of research evidence to have an impact on test usage. Whyte's somewhat high-handed critique of psychological testing in industry and the Bernreuter in particular, is not entirely undeserved.

The Bernreuter can also be criticised on other grounds besides its failure to do any job well enough to justify its existence. The publishers and author have made no attempt to improve the test throughout the 32 years of its existence. Its cumbersome scoring system remains, its six scores are still retained when two would do, and its current manual contains no information which was not available in 1935, although over 300 studies have been undertaken using the test. The consumer seeking a personality inventory would be well advised to look elsewhere.

Donald J. Veldman, *Associate Professor of Educational Psychology, University of Texas, Austin, Texas.*

The first sentence of the manual for this instrument indicates the extent to which it is representative of another era in test construction: "*The Personality Inventory* represents a new departure in the measurement of personality in that it measures several different aspects at one time." Considering that the normative data provided with the manual are dated 1938 and that the most recent attempt at scale revision included in the manual is a 1935 factor analysis of the original four scales, this inventory might be expected to be no more now than a landmark in the development of personality assessment techniques. Consulting Psychologists Press, however, claims that it is "very widely used, particularly in business and industry," and even as recently as 1953 a million copies of the test were reported sold. It is

[1] Whyte, William H., Jr. *The Organization Man*, p. 209. New York: Doubleday & Co., Inc., 1956. Pp. vi, 471. *

difficult to imagine why, when so many more carefully constructed, more adequately standardized, and more thoroughly validated personality inventories are currently available.

SCALE CONSTRUCTION. To determine item weights for the instrument's first four scales (neurotic tendency, self-sufficiency, introversion-extroversion, and dominance-submission), four tests were used to isolate high and low scoring subjects: (a) Thurstone's *Personality Schedule,* (b) Bernreuter's Self-Sufficiency Test, (c) Laird's C2 Introversion Test, and (d) the Allports' *A-S Reaction Study.* The latter also served as the source for the items of the dominance scale. The last two scales (confidence, sociability) are the result of a factor analysis of the original four scales. Intercorrelations of the first four scales are reported in the manual, but the fact that all items are weighted for all of the scales makes the interpretation of this table, and hence the factor analysis results, rather difficult. Nevertheless, the .95 correlation between the first and third scales, and the −.80 correlation between scales one and four strongly suggest that little more than a single construct is actually being measured. The fact that 78 per cent of the total extracted variance of the original scales is accounted for by the first factor confirms this conclusion. To what extent these variables might be "untied" through separation of item sets remains an unanswered question. Although attempts have been made to factor items from the instrument (273), and various authors have advocated simplified weighting systems (51, 175), no extensive attempts to reorganize the scoring of the item pool have appeared in the last ten years. In view of the wealth of multitrait personality inventories now available, such as Cattell's *Sixteen Personality Factor Questionnaire,* there would indeed seem to be little justification for such an investment of research resources.

RELIABILITY. Split-half coefficients ranging from .85 to .92 based on samples of college students are reported in the manual, and coefficients of .86 and .78 obtained from a sample of high school boys are given for the two factor scales. Reports of test-retest reliability, not included in the manual, have been considerably lower, between .52 and .69 (201).

NORMATIVE DATA. Percentile equivalents dated 1938 are provided for high school boys and girls, college men and women, and adult men and women. The extent to which cultural changes have made these norms inappropriate is unknown. From another point of view, Hoffman and Abbizu-Miranda (292), after demonstrating higher neurotic tendency scale scores for lower class subjects, claimed to find "middle-class bias" in the third of the items which accounted for the differences between lower class subjects' scores and the norms.

VALIDITY. Although the scale structure of the instrument is open to serious criticism, the ultimate criterion for any instrument is its predictive validity. The only "validity" evidence included in the manual is a table of correlations between the four original tests and the marker scales from which the weighting system was derived. The literature all the way back to Super's 1942 review (156) of the research has been heavily laden with essentially negative findings. A review of recent investigations, although subject to the bias resulting from editorial policies which inhibit reports of negative findings, still reveals a disquieting number of failures of the instrument to accomplish its intended purposes. Middleton and Putney (315), for instance, attempted to predict dominance-submission in husband-wife dyads from the dominance scale and failed; in fact, the predictions were *less* accurate when only extremely dissimilar couples were compared. Bruce found correlations ranging from −.07 to .20 with ratings of the effectiveness of 107 foremen (283), and from −.08 to .15 with ratings of 73 salesmen (298). With 17 sales managers, however, his coefficients ranged upward to .54 (287). Burgess (295) failed to find relationships with over- and under-achievement in engineering students. Poe and Berg (280) found borderline significance in predicting performance of steel industry production supervisors, and Gowan (291) found no correlations exceeding .11 with leadership ratings. Young and Gaier (285) could not demonstrate significant correlations with measures of suggestibility.

Many critics have attacked the apparent ease with which the scale scores may be shifted by intentional bias on the part of the respondent (282), although some writers defend the use of the instrument in business settings by claiming greater present-day sophistication for personnel specialists (319). Perhaps with unconscious cynicism, Powell (228) treated the scale scores from the instrument as "self-ratings," and was rather sharply criticized by Brown (*274*). In view of the repeated demonstrations of the ability of subjects to consciously manipulate their scores, this would not appear to be an unreasonable way of interpreting the test results.

Although the implications for the validity of the scales of the *Personality Inventory* are far from clear, Taft (*304*) found that subjects in the center of a distribution of "tolerance" scores were *less* emotionally stable than subjects at the extremes, as measured by the scales of the Bernreuter.

RESCALING OF THE ITEMS. Richardson and Hanawalt (*281*) were able to differentiate adult women who held offices in social organizations from those who did not, using the dominance and confidence scales, but found that a specially constructed scale for "office-holding" was more successful in a cross validation sample. Gehman (*290*) selected 32 items which most effectively differentiated scholastic probationers and obtained a correlation of .29 (*n* = 65) on cross validation.

SUMMARY. The research evidence and the opinions of various reviewers seem to weigh most heavily *against* the use of the *Personality Inventory* in precisely those applications for which it is now most extensively employed— namely, in determining the behavior tendencies of individuals in testing situations which might be expected to arouse defensive improvement of self-characterization. Considering the wide range of more adequate devices of this type now available, there appears to be little rational justification for its continued use in business and industrial settings. Because of the lack of recent normative data and the dearth of successful validity studies, there would seem to be little reason for the choice of this instrument even in settings where biased self-characterization would not be expected.

For a review by Leona E. Tyler, see 4:77; for reviews by Charles I. Mosier and Theodore Newcomb, see 40:1239; for excerpts from related book reviews, see 38:B358 and 36:B108.

[158]

Personality Rating Scale. Grades 4–12; 1944–62; test identical with *Child Personality Scale* ('51) except for format; originally called *22-Trait Personality Rating Scale;* modification for use with children of E. Lowell Kelly's *36-Trait Personality Rating Scale* (see *19* below); ratings by classmates and teachers or self-ratings; 22 ratings: pep, intelligence, sociability,

nervousness-calmness, popularity, religiousness, punctuality, courtesy, cooperation, generosity, persistence, honesty, neatness, patience, interests, disposition, good sport, boisterous-quiet, entertaining, thoughtfulness, sense of humor, dependability; 1 form ('62, 7 pages); manual ('62, 25 pages); profile ['62, 1 page]; separate answer sheets must be used; $3.50 per 35 tests; 50¢ per specimen set; postpaid; (30–40) minutes for rating 10–15 classmates; S. Mary Amatora; Educators'-Employers' Tests & Services Associates. *

REFERENCES

1–18. See 5:41.
19. KELLY, E. LOWELL. "A 36-Trait Personality Rating Scale." *J Psychol* 9:97–102 Ja '40. * (*PA* 14:3598)
20. TSCHECHTELIN, M. AMATORA. "Children's Ratings of Associates." *J Exp Ed* 13:20–2 S '44. * (*PA* 19:1608)
21. AMATORA, MARY. "The Education Factor in Personality Appraisal." *J Exp Ed* 21:271–5 Mr '53. * (*PA* 28:1583)
22. TSCHECHTELIN, M. AMATORA. "As Teacher Sees Teacher: A Study in Personality." *J Social Psychol* 38:121–5 Ag '53. * (*PA* 28:6610)

LAURANCE F. SHAFFER, *Professor of Psychology and Education, Teachers College, Columbia University, New York, New York.*

Phenomenology and sociometry, while not always congenial bedfellows, are both currently popular constructs for the study of personality. An effective measure of how a person sees himself, comparable to a measure of how others see him, would be a boon to many worthwhile investigations. The *Personality Rating Scale,* which is a little-altered version of the previously reviewed *Child Personality Scale* (1951, see 5:41), attempts to be such an instrument, and its author deserves credit for ingenious inventiveness.

The examinee's booklet contains 22 separate 10-point scales, each worded so as to be within the comprehension of children above the middle of the elementary school. For example, the scale designated as "co-operation" asks, "How well does he work with others?" and the 10 points range from "never joins in" to "always helps the group." In the use of the instrument, each respondent rates five or more designated boys in his class, five or more designated girls, and himself by entering scale numbers on a separate answer sheet. All are rated on one question before proceeding to the next. Scores for the 22 scales are entered on a profile sheet which displays how an examinee is perceived by boys, by girls, by himself, and, optionally, by his teacher or teachers.

Although interesting in conception, the rating scale does not achieve its best potentialities. Some shortcomings are merely mechanical and could be overcome easily. One trivial vexation arises from the scoring instructions to separate the answer sheet elaborately along "perforations," when there are in fact no perforations but only printed broken lines which successfully resist tearing. A little more fundamental is the author's nonchalance about transferring numbers from the scale booklet to the answer sheet, probably a difficult clerical feat for the lower grades. There should be data, too, on the accuracy of the primitive scoring method of adding and averaging; clerks will not always do such a task without error, much less the upper-grade pupils for whom self-scoring is recommended.

More seriously, the instrument suffers from a lack of sophistication in psychometric concepts that is exceptional even in the rarified field of personality measurement. The issue of reliability is presented only in terms of inter-rater agreement, obtained by correlating one child's ratings with those by one other child and then correcting by the Spearman-Brown formula for four raters. Such data are presented for two independent samples each of 100 boys and 100 girls. But one sample is of unspecified composition, and the other was randomly drawn from children in grades 4–8, permitting a possible inflation due to the presumably greater range of scores. While inter-rater reliability is of real interest (and is not too bad, with a median correlation of .80 for the mean ratings of four judges) other reliabilities are needed, too. The vast accumulation of 797,396 ratings to which the author refers might also have provided information on retest stabilities over varying intervals of time.

The norms are as frustrating as the reliabilities. They consist only of mean ratings, on very large numbers of cases, by boys, by girls, by both sexes, and by teachers, and of self-ratings by boys and by girls. All of these means lie close to the rational scale midpoint of 5.5 and are uninformative. There are no variabilities, no tables showing the ratings by ages or grades, and no attention is paid to discrepancy scores between self-ratings and ratings by others. These omissions are seen as serious in view of the use of raw scores in the profiles. Is a raw score of 7 on one scale always higher than one of 5 on another? Not if the variability of the former is half that of the latter, a likelihood hinted by some of the otherwise not too useful standard errors of means.

The reviewer must express sympathy for the author's struggles with the knotty problem of validity. Conventional concurrent or predictive validities probably have limited applicability to these 22 separate and essentially descriptive scales. The median correlations between self-ratings and others' ratings are reported as about .20 for boys and .38 for girls. These are interesting, but they are not "validities." A factor analysis was performed routinely, reported perfunctorily, and put to no use. As descriptive statistics, the matrix of intercorrelations given in a paper by the author would have been more informative than the rotated factor loadings. Perhaps some construct validities based on group comparisons would be revealing. Many interesting and unanswered questions propose themselves: Do the children rated as punctual, cooperative, persistent, neat, and dependable receive higher marks? Are the nervous, angry, or sad ones referred to guidance agencies? Are the sociable, popular, and "good sport" children elected to office by their peers? In such questions lie more useful concepts of construct validities.

As it now stands, the *Personality Rating Scale* is a good base upon which to build a rewarding instrument for research and perhaps for some limited applications. But it needs quite a bit of building.

For reviews by Robert H. Bauernfeind and Dale B. Harris, see 5:41.

[159]

Personality Schedule, 1929 Edition. Grades 13–16 and adults; 1928–30; neurotic tendencies; 1 form ('29, 4 pages); manual ('30, 4 pages); norms for college freshmen only; $2 per 25 tests; 5¢ per manual; 25¢ per specimen set; postpaid; (30–40) minutes; L. L. Thurstone and Thelma Gwinn Thurstone; University of Chicago Press. *

REFERENCES

1–28. See 40:1243.
29. THURSTONE, L. L., AND THURSTONE, THELMA GWINN. "A Neurotic Inventory." *J Social Psychol* 1:3–30 F '30. * (*PA* 4:1430)
30. WILLOUGHBY, RAYMOND R. "The Personal Equation in Ethical Judgment." *J Social Psychol* 1:424–9 Ag '30. * (*PA* 5:629)
31. DAVIS, LAWRENCE W., AND HUSBAND, RICHARD W. "A Study of Hypnotic Susceptibility in Relation to Personality Traits." *J Abn & Social Psychol* 26:175–82 Jl–S '31. * (*PA* 6:648)
32. PINTNER, R. "Neurotic Tendency and Its Relation to Some Other Mental Traits." *Sch & Soc* 36:765–7 D 10 '32. * (*PA* 7:1375)
33. WILLOUGHBY, RAYMOND R. "Some Properties of the Thurstone Personality Schedule and a Suggested Revision." *J Social Psychol* 3:401–24 N '32. * (*PA* 7:1645)
34. HABBE, STEPHEN. "The Selection of Student Nurses." *J Appl Psychol* 17:564–80 O '33. * (*PA* 8:2727)
35. STAGNER, ROSS. "Improved Norms for Four Personality Tests." *Am J Psychol* 45:303–7 Ap '33. * (*PA* 9:2344)
36. STAGNER, ROSS. "The Relation of Personality to Academic Aptitude and Achievement." *J Ed Res* 26:648–60 My '33. * (*PA* 7:4857)
37. LYON, VERNE WESLEY. "The Use of Vocational and Personality Tests With Deaf." *J Appl Psychol* 18:224–30 Ap '34. * (*PA* 8:5094)
38. WILLOUGHBY, RAYMOND ROYCE. "Norms for the Clark-Thurstone Inventory." *J Social Psychol* 5:91–7 F '34. * (*PA* 8:4167)

39. HESLER, ALICE RACHEL. *An Examination of Items in the Thurstone Personality Schedule for Diagnostic Patterns of Response.* Master's thesis, University of Oregon (Eugene, Ore.), 1935.

40. KUZNETS, G., AND TRYON, R. C. "A Study of the Incidence in Six Populations of Neurotic Responses to Items of the Thurstone Personality Schedule." Abstract. *Psychol B* 32:539-40 O '35. * (PA 10:473, title only)

41. MALLETT, DONALD ROGER. *A Study of the Validity at the College Level of Certain Measures of Personality Adjustment.* Doctor's thesis, University of Iowa (Iowa City, Iowa), 1936.

42. PECK, LEIGH. "A Study of the Adjustment Difficulties of a Group of Women Teachers." *J Ed Psychol* 27:401-16 S '36. * (PA 11:475)

43. ROOT, A. R. "College Achievement." *J Higher Ed* 7:387-8 O '36. * (PA 11:477)

44. BROOKS, ESTHER. "The Value of Psychological Testing." *Am J Nursing* 37:885-90 Ag '37. *

45. CHOU, SIEGEN K., AND MI, CHING-YUAN. "Relative Neurotic Tendency of Chinese and American Students." *J Social Psychol* 8:155-84 My '37. * (PA 11:5174)

46. McKINNEY, FRED. "Concomitants of Adjustment and Maladjustment in College Students." *J Abn & Social Psychol* 31:435-57 Ja-Mr '37. * (PA 11:3784)

47. ROSENBAUM, BETTY B. "Neurotic Tendencies in Crippled Girls." *J Abn & Social Psychol* 31:423-9 Ja-Mr '37. * (PA 11:3785)

48. CROOK, MASON N. "A Further Note on Self-Judgments of Constancy in Neuroticism Scores." *J Social Psychol* 9: 485-7 N '38. * (PA 11:518)

49. ENGLE, T. L. "The Use of a Short Personality Schedule in High School Personnel Work." *J Appl Psychol* 22: 534-8 O '38. * (PA 13:2699)

50. BROWN, PAUL A. "Responses of Blind and Seeing Adolescents to a Neurotic Inventory." *J Psychol* 7:211-21 Ap '39. * (PA 13:4726)

51. PINTNER, R., AND FORLANO, G. "Dominant Interests and Personality Characteristics." *J General Psychol* 21:251-60 O '39. * (PA 14:384)

52. CHILD, IRVIN L. "The Relation Between Measures of Infantile Amnesia and Neuroticism." *J Abn & Social Psychol* 35:453-6 Jl '40. * (PA 14:5517)

53. PAYNE, BRYAN. "Personality Patterns in Reformatory Inmates." *J Genetic Psychol* 56:13-9 Mr '40. * (PA 14:4216)

54. CROOK, MASON N. "Retest Correlations in Neuroticism." *J General Psychol* 24:173-82 Ja '41. * (PA 15:2260)

55. EISENBERG, PHILIP. "Individual Interpretation of Psychoneurotic Inventory Items." *J General Psychol* 25:19-40 Jl '41. * (PA 15:5205)

56. EISENBERG, PHILIP, AND WESMAN, ALEXANDER G. "Consistency in Response and Logical Interpretation of Psychoneurotic Inventory Items." *J Ed Psychol* 32:321-38 My '41. * (PA 16:1041)

57. BRUNING, HERBERT. *A Study of Personality Compared With Personal, Family, and Education Factors.* Master's thesis, Kansas State Teachers College (Emporia, Kan.), 1942.

58. SPERLING, ABRAHAM. "A Comparison of the Human Behavior Inventory With Two Other Personality Measures." *Ed & Psychol Meas* 2:291-7 Jl '42. * (PA 16:4885)

59. CROOK, MASON N. "A Retest With the Thurstone Personality Schedule After Six and One-Half Years." *J General Psychol* 28:111-20 Ja '43. * (PA 17:1236)

60. PINTNER, R., AND FORLANO, G. "Consistency of Response to Personality Tests at Different Age Levels." *J Genetic Psychol* 62:77-83 Mr '43. * (PA 17:2393)

61. ZIMMERMAN, MARY A. *A Study of the Changes in Personality During One Year in College as Shown by the Thurstone Personality Schedule.* Master's thesis, Kansas State Teachers College (Emporia, Kan.), 1943.

62. BURGESS, ERNEST W., AND WALLIN, PAUL. "Homogamy in Personality Characteristics." *J Abn & Social Psychol* 39: 475-81 O '44. * (PA 19:442)

63. SEAGOE, MAY V. "Prognostic Tests and Teaching Success." *J Ed Res* 38:685-90 My '45. * (PA 19:3184)

64. BLACK, WINFRED. *A Study of the Thurstone Personality Schedule Given to Entering Freshmen at Alabama College Between the Years 1931-32 and 1938-39.* Master's thesis, University of North Carolina (Chapel Hill, N.C.), 1949.

65. ZAKOLSKI, F. C. "Studies in Delinquency: I, Personality Structure of Delinquent Boys." *J Genetic Psychol* 74: 109-17 Mr '49. * (PA 23:4925)

66. HSU, E. H. "The Neurotic Score as a Function of Culture." *J Social Psychol* 34:3-30 Ag '51. * (PA 27:222)

For a review by J. P. Guilford, see 40:1243.

[160]

★**Polyfactorial Study of Personality.** Adults; 1959; 11 scores: hypochondriasis, sexual identification, anxiety, social distance, sociopathy, depression, compulsivity, repression, paranoia, schizophrenia, hyperaffectivity; IBM; 1 form (7 pages); manual (12 pages); separate answer sheets must be used; $6.25 per 25 tests; $2.75 per 25 IBM answer sheets; $2 per set of scoring stencils; $2.75 per 25 profiles; $1.75 per manual; $2.50 per specimen set; cash orders postpaid; (45-50) minutes; Ronald H. Stark; Martin M. Bruce. *

BERTRAM D. COHEN, *Professor of Psychology, and Director of Clinical Training, Rutgers, The State University, New Brunswick, New Jersey.*

The development of the PFSP was prompted by the author's dissatisfaction with existing paper and pencil personality tests. The MMPI is explicitly cited in the manual as being too lengthy, poorly worded, insufficient for personality assessment within the normal range, and based on a rationale that is "purely statistical and empirical, but disregards clinical considerations." In addition to the goal of correcting these alleged faults in other tests, the author states that the purpose of the PFSP is to "offer diagnostic profiles approximating those which would be obtained with projective instruments."

Inspection of the PFSP questionnaire indicates that it is indeed less lengthy than the MMPI (containing 300 items rather than 550), and that the items are worded simply and clearly. Beyond this it is not possible to conclude that the instrument represents as yet any substantive improvement over existing tests of its general type.

Initial criteria for selecting items were their correlations with measures from other established objective and projective personality tests, and from clinical interviews. Included were "the Rorschach, the House-Tree-Person Test, the standard clinical scales of the MMPI, and diagnoses based on interviewing." Items were finally chosen on the basis of (a) "purity of factor-analytic relationship with other items in the same nosological category," and (b) "degree of correlation with the criteria and absence of correlation with items in the same category." Subjects used in all phases of the work included over 200 hospitalized psychotic patients, over 550 prison inmates, over 300 psychiatric outpatients, and over 2,500 normal "white collar and mid-management employees" and applicants.

The author cites as evidence for the "content [?] validity" of the test the presence of significant intercorrelations between Anxiety, for example, and such other scales as Compulsivity, Hypochondriasis, and Repression.

While these relationships may be psychodynamically reasonable, the contribution of simple *item overlap* between the correlated scales should have been taken into account or at least noted.

It is unclear from the manual just what relationships obtain between the PFSP items or scales and the various projective test and diagnostic criteria. According to the manual, separate publication of portions of the basic factor analytic data is planned. Correlations between MMPI scales and those of the PFSP are reported in tabular form in the manual. The two tests "show a 41% variance communality." That some communality would be found is to be expected, of course, since the MMPI was used as one of the criteria for item selection in the first place.

A set of correlations is reported between PFSP scales and *Wechsler Adult Intelligence Scale* subtest scores. According to the author "these correlations strongly suggest that the more severe the disturbance, the lower the I.Q." This conclusion is based on data from a portion of the prison population ($n = 217$). It is possible that the negative correlations found are mediated by the effects of a defensiveness or social desirability variable that relates positively to intelligence and negatively to many of the nosological scales of the PFSP. No provision is made to assess or correct for test taking attitudes, e.g., defensiveness, acquiescence set. In this respect the PFSP does not compare favorably with either the MMPI or other more recent personality inventories.

A test-retest study, using a one-week intertest interval, indicates acceptable reliability coefficients for the various scales. These range from .699 for Anxiety to .927 for Schizophrenia. The prison population was used for this study ($n = 400$ male inmates).

In summary, the PFSP is an attempt to refine and to enrich the meaning of previous personality inventories used for clinical diagnostic purposes. While items are more simply and clearly written than those of the MMPI, for example, their usefulness remains in doubt. It is difficult, at this stage of its development, to see how the PFSP represents an effective improvement over its major competitor. Also, even if a minor point, the number of spelling errors in the manual may irritate readers and make them less secure about essential tabular

information. More careful editorial attention in the preparation of the manual should correct this.

DONALD R. PETERSON, *Professor of Psychology, and Director, Psychological Clinic, University of Illinois, Urbana, Illinois.*

This review was written without benefit of detailed information about test development which the author promises to provide in a forthcoming monograph. Material in the manual, however, gives ample substance for a number of comments about the *Polyfactorial Study of Personality* (PFSP).

The test is reasonably brief, the items are straightforwardly and inoffensively stated, scoring is objective, an 11-phase profile, with a "clinical" name for each dimension, is easily derived, and reliabilities are adequate. For these reasons, the test will probably appeal to personnel officers, and find considerable use as an aid in employee selection. But therein lie most of the dangers. Before the test can be recommended for general use, a number of questions about its construction will have to be answered.

Work began with the assembly of 700 truefalse inventory statements. Items were selected, according to the manual, by reference to (*a*) "purity of factor-analytic relationship with other items in the same nosological category," and (*b*) "degree of correlation with the criteria and absence of correlation with items in the same category." Populations employed in the pre-selection are unspecified, and the exact method by which one can choose items which display both pure factor analytic relationships and an absence of correlation with other items in the same category is unclear to the reviewer.

Criteria were then defined. To accompany clinical diagnoses and MMPI scores, over 200 Rorschach scores were reduced to 86 "validated" indices in the analysis, and 24 "validated" H-T-P indices were likewise selected from 100-plus indices. Cross validation is vital in work of this kind. The author does not state whether additional tests of the projective indices were conducted or not. If not, it is questionable practice to call them "validated." If so, if indeed 86 indices from the Rorschach and 24 from the H-T-P have been found to relate dependably to clinical diagnosis, the author of the PFSP has in his possession the most dramatically positive evidence for the validity of the Rorschach and the H-T-P in the entire literature on projective techniques.

The test was given to 1,081 subjects in 15 clinical groups and to 2,576 "normal" white collar employees and job applicants. But just how many of the subjects were used, in what combinations, to develop which scales, is not clear. Presumably none of the 2,000 normals had been given clinical diagnoses. How many of those, and how many of the others had Rorschachs, H-T-P's, and MMPI's cannot be determined from the manual. Even if all S's took all tests, which is unlikely, there is a troublesome lack of information about the particular scores used to represent the criteria. The PFSP yields a measure of "social distance," for example, and another of "repression," but there are no "socially distant" nor "repressed" groups among the clinical samples. If the pertinent scores were developed from the Rorschach, it would be interesting to know how they were "validated."

Statistical procedures are described by listing the various kinds of correlational indices which were used, noting that Rorschach criteria were given double weight, stating that multiple r's were computed between items and each criterion, and asserting that "the correlations of these matrices were employed in the factor analytic procedures to determine purity of items for each nosological category." There is no comment on the techniques of factor extraction and the decisional processes involved in retaining factors for rotation, and no note on how or whether rotations were performed. Variations in some of these procedures can turn the results of a factor analysis upside down. The author was dealing with upwards of 120 criterion variables and an unidentified subset of 700 questionnaire items. Having struggled for years to make sense of much smaller data masses than this, the reviewer is puzzled about the data reduction techniques employed in developing the PFSP. It is difficult to see how factor analysis could have been used in any conventional way. And if unconventional techniques were employed they should be described in the manual. The author appropriately omits "voluminous tables" which "would defeat the purpose of a manual." But further description of procedure would be most desirable.

Claims of validity are supported mainly by reference to the method of derivation, and by tabular citation of intercorrelations with MMPI scales and the *Association Adjustment Inventory* (AAI). The MMPI scales were apparently among the criteria used in original item selection, so the presence of some fairly high and appropriately patterned correlations is not surprising. The AAI, another "adjustment" questionnaire sold by the same publisher, requires only 10 minutes to give, but yields 13 scores in the areas of "deviant thinking," juvenile ideas, and so forth. It was constructed and standardized on the same population used in developing the PFSP. The author says this in the manual, and properly adds that the correlations are probably maximal values. He then goes on to say that the reasonably high and consistent correlations between PFSP and AAI scores "strongly suggest that the 'factor' underlying these high correlations is indeed the ideational disturbances which they both purport to measure." At best, this statement is stronger than the data warrant. At worst, it is untrue. The most accurate statement to make about these data is that two self-report measures standardized on the same population are almost bound to show some high intercorrelations, and that the measures may or may not have anything to do with ideational disturbances as assessed by different means in other settings.

The comments on interpretation tend to be presumptuous and misleading. Consider, for example, the following *non sequitur:* "Because the Rorschach was the major criterion in deriving these scales, it is expected that PFSP profiles will most closely resemble Rorschach profiles." In fact, PFSP profiles do not look like Rorschach profiles at all. Scale descriptions read very much like those for the MMPI, though they are given in a less guarded way, e.g., "When a high SID [Sexual Identification] and HAF [Hyperaffectivity] score appear in the same record, there is strong indication of the acting out of....homoerotic desires." Anyone who considers using the PFSP in personnel selection should be aware that the adequacy of the test in predicting job success is completely unknown.

Indeed it is difficult to see what purpose the test can serve that is not already served better by an existing instrument. If one wants a questionnaire to reflect clinical diagnostic judgment, the MMPI is already available, complete with validity keys and a large body of research. If one is dissatisfied with the particular dimensions involved in the MMPI, the *California Psychological Inventory* is for sale, with another large body of research behind it. If one wants a test developed by rigorous factor analytic techniques, Guilford's *Inventory of Factors STDCR*, the *Guilford-Martin Inventory of Factors GAMIN*, and Cattell's *Sixteen Personality Factor Questionnaire* represent some highly creditable work. If one really wants the kind of profile he might get from the Rorschach, he had better give a Rorschach.

Like other questionnaires, the PFSP will probably be related to a variety of extra-test variables that matter. It may therefore be of use as a research tool. But this is not the way it is presented in the manual. And this is not the way it is billed in the catalog.

J Consult Psychol 24:100 F '60. Edward S. Bordin. A 300-item inventory reportedly selected on the basis of factor analysis and correlations with unspecified criteria. The general impression is that the major criteria may have been other tests, e.g., Rorschach, MMPI, and the H-T-P test. * Test-retest reliability for a prison population suggests that the scores are reasonably stable. No other validation data are offered, even though reference is made to various possible criterion populations. There are no references to published reports. Why was this test issued after so little developmental analysis?

[161]

★Position Response Form and Response Form. Industry; 1958–59; manual ('58, 9 pages including both forms); no norms; scoring and interpretation by the author only; distribution restricted to clients; test prices included in consulting fee; William F. Reiterman, Jr.; the Author. *
a) POSITION RESPONSE FORM. Management personnel; for recording personality requirements of a job; 1 form ('58, 1 page); no data on reliability and validity; (5–10) minutes.
b) RESPONSE FORM. Job applicants; for self-rating of on-the-job personality characteristics; 4 scores: forward action, people action, staying action, dependent action; 1 form ('59, 2 pages, identical with form copyrighted in 1958 except for minor changes); (10–15) minutes.

[162]

The Power of Influence Test. Grades 2–13; 1958; seating preference sociometric test; 1 form (1 page); manual (4 pages); no data on validity; norms for grades 5–11 only; $4 per examiner's kit of 50 tests, scoring sheets, and manual; 50¢ per manual; cash orders postpaid; specimen set not available; [10–15] minutes; Roy Cochrane and Wesley Roeder; Psychometric Affiliates. *

REFERENCES
1. COCHRANE, ROY. "Testing the Sociometric Test." *Univ Wash Col Ed Rec* 16:49–52 F '50. *

ÅKE BJERSTEDT, *Professor of Education, University of Lund, Lund, Sweden.*

The present device is an extremely simplified version of a sociometric technique. The "test" form is nothing more than a half-page sheet with seven spaces (too narrow for many children's large handwriting) for giving seating preferences (the subject and six other pupils he would like to sit near). The only score considered in the manual is the sum of choices received.

Percentile data are given for seven grade levels, and some retest results are briefly referred to. No clear information as to the number and kind of pupils involved at different grade levels is given, nor are we informed of such important factors as class size and sex distribution within the norm groups used. The score yielded is variously referred to as a measure of "power of influence," "friendship capacity," "leadership capacity," and "future ability in salesmanship." Apparently, in the opinions of the authors, these labels are to some extent synonymous, but no data are given to validate these claims or to show any relationships between this particular sociometric score and any other psychological or educational variable. In a report of a study presented by one of the authors in 1950 (*1*), the lack of validation data is admitted, with the statement that such data "would only be obtained by a ten-year follow-up." No explanation is given of why this would be the only way to validate the measure. Now in the sixties, there is still no indication that the authors have tried their own particular kind of ten-year validation; instead, the same general excuse is repeated in the present manual. It is stated that the *Power of Influence Test* has been used "successfully" by "more than" 250 teachers and counselors, but there is no indication of what kind of success is referred to or how it was measured. No references to the large body of sociometric research literature are presented to the reader.

Of course, sociometric techniques similar to the present simple device *can* be extremely helpful instruments to teachers and psychologists for a study of preferential relations as one aspect of group structure. Meaningful correlations with other psychological variables have often been found and give sociometric data additional importance for specific purposes. Teachers interested in such measures (including many other meaningful scores than choices received) are strongly recommended to read the simple guides published by Jennings,[1] Northway and Weld,[2] or the more detailed book by Gronlund,[3] which would be much more helpful guides to a judicious use of sociometric methods than the present manual.

In sum, the reviewer considers the manual oversimplified in its description of sociometric procedures, quasi-exact in presenting norm data of doubtful value, and vague in its general interpretational suggestions. As for the specific "test form," the teacher could probably just as well use a slip of blank paper.

ERIC F. GARDNER, *Professor of Education and Psychology, and Chairman, Department of Psychology, Syracuse University, Syracuse, New York.*

The *Power of Influence Test* is a rather presumptuous title for a diagrammatic format on which a student is asked to write the names of the six fellow students he "would *like* to have sitting near" him. The score, representing the number of times a pupil has been chosen by his classmates, is converted to a "Social Percentile" which is described as "a standard score showing the Friendship Capacity of the individual, his aptitude for making others like him, and his future ability in salesmanship." Since the only data provided are percentile ranks within grades 5 through 11 for the responses of an unspecified number of students, the reader immediately asks himself a series of questions a few of which are: (*a*) What is friendship capacity? (*b*) How do we know the number of choices a student obtains represents his aptitude for *making* others like him? and (*c*) What evidence do we have that a person's score is related to present ability in salesmanship, not to consider the issue of future sales prowess?

After raising serious qualms, the four-page manual stresses the value of the teacher having sociometric data (a point with which the reviewer would concur) but, unfortunately, continues with the same kind of unsupported

1 JENNINGS, HELEN HALL. *Sociometry in Group Relations: A Manual for Teachers, Second Edition.* Washington, D.C.: American Council on Education, 1959. Pp. xi, 105. *
2 NORTHWAY, MARY L., AND WELD, LINDSAY. *Sociometric Testing: A Guide for Teachers.* Toronto, Canada: University of Toronto Press, 1957. Pp. vii, 72. *
3 GRONLUND, NORMAN E. *Sociometry in the Classroom.* New York: Harper & Row, Publishers, Inc., 1959. Pp. xix, 340. *

claims and recommendations to the teacher implied by the title. For example, it reads, "The high ranking pupils on this test can be assumed to be class leaders....The views and opinions expressed by these leaders are the views and opinions of the class. When a teacher disciplines a leader, he is disciplining the whole class." How can one arrive at these and other similar conclusions which are presented? Obviously, one needs help from a greater Power than the *Power of Influence Test*.

The reviewer is favorable to the desires of the authors to promote the use of sociometric data, but he believes they have done a disservice with their extravagant claims and kinds of recommendations for the interpretation of a score from a simple, sociometric, single-choice situation.

[163]
★The Press Test. Industrial employees; 1961; ability to work under stress; 5 scores: reading speed, color-naming speed, color-naming speed with distraction, difference between color-naming speed with and without distraction, difference between reading speed and color-naming speed; 1 form (10 pages); manual (25 pages); reliability and validity data based on shorter time limits; norms for males only; $5 per 20 tests, postage extra; $1 per specimen set, postpaid; 4.5(15) minutes; Melany E. Baehr, Raymond J. Corsini, Richard Renck, and Measurement Research Division, Industrial Relations Center, University of Chicago (manual); Education-Industry Service. *

WILLIAM H. HELME, *Supervisory Research Psychologist, United States Army Personnel Research Office, Washington, D.C.*

The *Press Test* is a brief pencil and paper group test designed to measure ability to work under stress. The stress resides in the task itself. The subject has to respond quickly to one aspect of the stimulus without being distracted by a conflicting aspect. According to the manual, the purpose of the test is to measure the person's ability in "coping with more or less unique situations and emergencies as they arise," as contrasted with ability for jobs which "call for a systematized and routinized day." While there is mention of more dangerous emergencies, the validation attempted so far deals with differences among executives, foremen, salesmen, and others, rather than with emergency situations *per se*.

Research on the test is rather modest to date. Reliability of the three basic scores appears adequate, though based on only 58 "industrial personnel"—.72 for reading speed, and .82 and .80 for color-naming speed (simple) and color-naming speed with distraction, respectively. The derived difference scores, however, are of low reliability, as would be expected from differences between highly correlated (.81, .86) reliable scores. Retest scores after a one-week interval show substantial practice effects.

The major question is, of course, the evidence for validity. Does the test really measure ability to cope with unique situations and emergencies? Two kinds of validation are offered. The one of more direct interest to industrial users is a study of five groups of men in different industrial occupations, with samples ranging from 33 to 92. Mean scores for each group on each of the five measures are compared. The results show that, on the three basic scores, the samples of engineers and chemists, executives and middle management, and white collar and junior executives score significantly higher than a sample of foremen. The other occupational group, salesmen, score significantly lower than the first three groups in the distraction situation, but higher than the foremen on all three basic scores. Thus the major finding is that the first three groups do not only better than the foremen on the "stress" measure, but equally better on the simple perception-speed measures. (Although two "significant" differences between salesmen and the engineer and executive groups are reported on the first derived score above, the appropriate variance statistical tests of the whole set of samples made by the reviewer shows these to be questionable.)

The second kind of validation consists of correlations with factor scores from the *Temperament Comparator.* Statistically significant, but still very modest, relationships (.13 to .22) are found between the three basic scores and tendency toward sociability and excitability, as well as away from cautious-seriousness and stability. These findings are in the direction that would be expected if the *Press Test* scores measure a ready responsiveness to varying stimuli, with distraction. But it is a long jump from the data to assume that these same characteristics are found in coping with important unique situations and emergencies.

Norms on a new time limit for the test are given, based on 170 industrial personnel. The mean on the difference score between color-naming with and without distraction appears

to be a typographical error, but the norm table itself seems correct.

In summary, the statement in the manual that "the test warrants further study and investigation" appears justified. The "evidence for validity of the *Press Test* scores in the selection of higher level personnel, especially upper and middle management, professional, and sales personnel" is very modest, however. The test is not yet sufficiently validated for the industrial user. For users who are prepared to conduct research in their own organizations and who feel that the measurement of such characteristics is worth the effort, the test might be a promising component of a battery of techniques for experimentation. It has simple instructions, and actual testing time after instruction is less than five minutes.

ALLYN MILES MUNGER, *Associate Director, Personnel and Marketing Research Division, The Psychological Corporation, New York, New York.*

The *Press Test,* according to the manual, is expected to differentiate between those individuals who can work in a stress situation and those who cannot. The stress in the test is that part in which the individual is given, in writing, the name of a color, such as green, printed in an ink of a different color, such as yellow. His task is to identify the color of the ink. The validity of the test rests primarily on two approaches.

The first is validation against another test called the *Temperament Comparator.* On securing the information on that test, readily supplied by the authors, it was found that the *Temperament Comparator* was validated on three bases: a factor analytic study of the test itself, correlations with other tests unidentified except for an earlier version of the same test, and differential profiles for industrial personnel. It can only be assumed that the industrial personnel described are the same groups as those used in a second approach for validating the *Press Test* on five groups of industrial personnel. Therefore, a validity approach comparing it to another test can be assumed to be an interesting but not significant measure for industrial use.

In the second approach to validity, the test's ability to discriminate between various industrial groups, there are significant differences between the means for the different groups.

However, the overlap between the distributions would make any use of the test as a selection device extremely tenuous, except for the foreman group. The means rounded off are 72 for engineers and chemists, 73 for executives and middle management, 72 for white collar workers and junior executives, 66 for salesmen, and 55 for foremen. These results would seem to modify the authors' contention that encouraging results have been obtained in discriminating between various industrial groups, but would certainly support the statement that the test warrants further study and investigation.

It is rather common in industrial groups to find differences between the means for any diverse groups on almost any standard test. This is why norms are provided. The need in industry is for a test that will discriminate between good and poor performance within groups. All other tests mentioned in studies in the references were given to an additional group of labor or blue collar personnel, but no mention is made of the administration of this test except the implication given by the statement "these results present some evidence for the validity of the *Press Test* scores in the selection of higher level personnel, especially upper and middle management, professional and sales personnel."

In the manual and in correspondence, the authors are concerned with the low test-retest reliability for the combined scores derived from the test parts. It would seem quite possible that in three 90-second tests of this type, test-retest is not the best method of measuring reliability, as it is quite possible some individuals may learn ways of taking the test which will increase their scores between tests while others may explore another approach which will, in fact, lower their performance. Various forms of this test have been around for several years and, while creating interest, they have failed to show significant validity against rankings and ratings on performance. In its present state, this is an experimental test and should be labeled as such.

[164]

★**A Process for In-School Screening of Children With Emotional Handicaps.** Grades kgn–3, 3–6, 7–12; 1961–62; for research use only; 3 ratings: teacher, peer, and self; manual ('61, 49 pages); technical report ('61, 66 pages); pupil record folder ('62, 3 pages); no norms; 10¢ per screening summary form; 15¢ per pupil record folder; $2 per manual; $2.50 per technical report; postage extra; $10 per complete specimen set, postpaid; to be administered "over a period of two or three months"; Nadine M. Lambert and Eli M. Bower; distributor in California: Bureau of Special Education, State Department of Education; distributor in all other states: Educational Testing Service. *

a) BEHAVIOR RATINGS OF PUPILS. Grades kgn–12; ratings by teachers; 1 form ('62, 11 pages); no data on reliability; $1 per form; administration time not reported.

b) [PEER RATINGS.] Grades kgn–3, 3–7, 7–12; 3 levels; teacher's scoring instructions and worksheet ('62, 6 pages) for all 3 levels; 2) and 3) also include self-ratings; $1 per teacher's worksheet.

  1) *The Class Pictures.* Grades kgn–3; individual; 1 form ('62, 12 cards); record form (1 page); no data on reliability of current edition; $1 per set of pictures; 35¢ per pad of 30 record forms; (15–20) minutes.

  2) *A Class Play.* Grades 3–7; 1 form ('62, 8 pages); 20¢ per test; (35–45) minutes.

  3) *Student Survey.* Grades 7–12; 1 form ('62, 8 pages); no data on reliability; 20¢ per test; administration time not reported.

c) [SELF-RATINGS.] Grades kgn–3, 3–7, 7–12; 3 levels.

  1) *A Picture Game.* Grades kgn–3; separate forms ('62, 66 cards) for boys and girls; $1.75 per set of cards; 15¢ per class record; (30) minutes.

  2) *Thinking About Yourself.* Grades 3–7; Forms A (for boys), B (for girls), ('62, 6 pages); score sheet ('62, 1 page); 20¢ per test; 7¢ per score sheet; 15¢ per class record; administration time not reported.

  3) *A Self Test.* Grades 7–12; 1 form ('62, 6 pages); score sheet ('62, 1 page); no data on reliability; 20¢ per test; 7¢ per score sheet; 15¢ per class record; administration time not reported.

REFERENCES

1. BOWER, ELI M. "A Process for Identifying Disturbed Children." *Children* 4:143–7 Jl '57. *

2. WEISBROD, KENNETH CONRAD. *The Identification of Potentially Maladjusted Children in the Middle Elementary Grades.* Doctor's thesis, University of Maryland (College Park, Md.), 1958. (*DA* 20:3640)

3. BOWER, ELI M. *Early Identification of Emotionally Handicapped Children in School.* Springfield, Ill.: Charles C Thomas, Publisher, 1960. Pp. xiii, 120. * (*PA* 35:809)

ALAN O. ROSS, *Chief Psychologist, Pittsburgh Child Guidance Center, Pittsburgh, Pennsylvania.*

Most workers in the field of mental health share the belief that psychological disturbances can be prevented if emotional vulnerability is identified and prophylactic steps are taken in the early years of life. If the assumption is valid, this approach would be most effective if identification could take place in the preschool years but it is not until the child goes to school that we have a social institution within which routine screening for emotional vulnerability could take place. Screening for a variety of sensory and physical handicaps has become an accepted part of the school's responsibility but when it comes to screening for emotional handicaps we lack both the public acceptance of such an approach and the necessary instruments to carry it out. The authors of the material here under discussion address themselves to this twin problem by presenting an approach which keeps the need for public acceptance and the demand for valid screening devices clearly in view. They are, however, the first to admit that neither of these goals has yet been reached and the Technical Report accompanying the material is careful to stress the preliminary nature of the work.

The authors must have had a great many misgivings and reservations when they decided to publish their material in order to make it available to other research workers. They stress, and it is worth repeating, that these materials are published as experimental instruments, "available only to those professional researchers conducting projects in which the identification of emotionally handicapped children is an integral function and who are willing to share their data with the authors." It would be most unfortunate if this restriction were not heeded for both the public acceptance of large-scale psychological screening and the progress of this device would be jeopardized by premature practical application.

The screening process involves a combination of three techniques: behavior rating by the teacher, peer ratings by classmates, and self-ratings. Identification of the "emotionally handicapped child" is based on his scores on these instruments relative to those of the other children in his class. If his are among the highest scores on two of the three instruments, the child is considered "likely to have emotional problems" and "should be referred to a specialist in mental health for diagnosis and prescription."

In the school population used for the initial development of the process, 10 to 15 per cent of the children were identified as possibly handicapped. Since the approach is one of ranking the children in a classroom it involves the assumption that emotionally handicapped children are uniformly distributed among the school population. In a class with a high percentage of emotionally disturbed children the screening device would identify only the most severely disturbed, while in a class with few or no emotionally disturbed children three or four "false positives" would be selected. The authors are aware of the need for a more sophisticated method of scoring and also warn against viewing a child whom their device identifies as "different" as a child who will necessarily have an emotional problem. Screening,

they say repeatedly, is not the same as diagnosis or classification, but in the final analysis the use or misuse to which these instruments are put will depend largely on the sophistication of school administrators and teachers.

Much work remains to be done before the process can be considered valid for the identification of emotionally handicapped children. But even once this work is completed the question of the practical value of a screening technique of this nature will remain to plague us. What happens to children who are identified as potentially emotionally handicapped? The authors of these instruments hope that their use will encourage teachers to develop "action commitments on behalf of some of the more vulnerable children." They speak of referrals, consultations, and curriculum adjustments and ideally this would indeed be desirable. But how many school systems and teachers are equipped to engage in such efforts and how many parents are willing to accept the recommendations based on even the most careful clinical evaluation which they themselves did not initiate? The Technical Report states, "The fact that school programs are not available to assist emotionally handicapped pupils make a better adjustment to school should not be a deterrent to identifying them." This reviewer cannot help wonder whether, under presently existing conditions, such identification cannot do more harm than good. One can only hope that public sophistication, the enlightenment of school administrators, the sensitivity and understanding of teachers, and the knowledge of what to do for an emotionally handicapped child will keep pace with the development of valid screening procedures toward which the material here discussed has made a major contribution.

J. ROBERT WILLIAMS, *Director, Child Study Clinic, and School Psychologist, Public Schools, Kankakee, Illinois.*

This instrument was developed as a possible aid to schools who are forced to wrestle with the problem of meeting adequately the needs of increasing numbers of children with varied emotional disabilities. It is still strictly a research device as the authors frequently and emphatically state in both manual and previous publications. Teachers and other professional workers in the schools who use it become active participants in an ongoing research program designed to further test the instrument for its ability to serve such purposes as: (*a*) to identify children with emotional handicaps so that they can receive more careful, individual study; (*b*) to help teachers become aware of and better able to cope with these problems from an educational standpoint; and (*c*) to assist schools in setting up plans to work with groups of children having emotional handicaps.

To these ends, those who use the instrument are given, in the Manual for School Administrators and Teachers, a brief but pointed orientation on the nature of emotional handicap, the meaning of "screening" in the present context, and the purpose and use of each of the screening procedures.

In this frame of reference, emotional handicap is conceived by the authors as an internal state which can be inferred from the degree of limited or restricted functioning an individual shows "in choosing from among alternative kinds of behavior." Five types of such limitations as commonly exhibited in the classroom (thus offering cues for identification of emotional handicap) are described in the manual: (*a*) inability to learn, (*b*) inability to build satisfactory interpersonal relationships, (*c*) inappropriate behavior or feelings under normal conditions, (*d*) pervasive mood of unhappiness, and (*e*) tendency to develop physical symptoms associated with personal or school problems.

Three approaches are used in the measurement of (screening for) susceptibility to emotional handicap as above conceived. These include teacher ratings, peer ratings, and self-ratings. The teacher rating of behavior of pupils is done by means of a 7-step scale in a manner simulating the equal-appearing interval procedure. Given a one-sentence description of pupil behavior, the rater is asked to place each pupil on a scale that extends from " 'most like' the pupil described to 'least like' him." This procedure is continued until all pupils are rated on each of eight descriptive behaviors. Scale values of the ratings run from 1 through 7, the higher values being indicative of greater susceptibility to emotional handicap.

Peer ratings are obtained by one of three methods, depending on the grade and reading level as well as the level of interest or maturity of the child. Each method is sociometric in nature, the idea being that each pupil judges

every other pupil (in some cases, himself) in terms of the degree to which he is like a child in a pictured or imagined role or the degree to which his behavior matches that of a verbal, descriptive sample. Both "negative" (maladjusted), "positive," and "neutral" situations are included, and the general rationale is that the greater the tendency for a child to be perceived negatively by his peers (or himself) the greater is the degree of his susceptibility to emotional handicap.

Similarly, self-ratings are obtained by somewhat different methods according to grade- and maturity-level of pupils. At lower levels, the children are asked to sort pictures into piles labeled "happy" and "sad," with greater use of the latter category being indicative of more likelihood of emotional handicap. At the intermediate and upper grade levels, what is sought in self-rating is a measure of the difference between a pupil's perception of self "as he *is*" and "as he would like to be." The pupils read items descriptive of different types of children and are to select on a 4-step scale the degree to which they would (or would not) like to be like the hypothetical examples. On a second section of the exercise or test, they are to judge, in like manner, the degree to which they *are* (or are not) like the same hypothetical examples. Greater degree of emotional handicap is thought to be associated with increased difference between self and ideal.

The actual screening for susceptibility to emotional handicap is done by combining the results of the three types of ratings. By listing those pupils receiving highest susceptibility (negative) ratings on each method, it becomes possible to locate those with "two or more" negative ratings, which is considered a mark of significance in the present procedure.

One cannot properly use standard techniques to evaluate *A Process for In-School Screening of Children With Emotional Handicaps.* It is not offered to schools as a finished product; rather, schools are given the opportunity of using it under the condition that they will become partners in a research program designed to improve it and in the belief that they will, through such participation, become better informed as to the nature of emotional handicap and better able to deal with the complex and trying educational problems it presents.

In addition to the manual, a Technical Report is provided which presents a quite detailed account of the developmental history and present status of each screening instrument. In each case the device now in use is the result of one or more revisions. Reliability studies of most of the peer- and self-rating instruments are given and suggested procedures for more inclusive reliability investigations are made. There is a very thorough account of the research done to date on validity. The results on both reliability and validity are promising. However, the authors would not mislead anyone as the following cautious statement shows: "The authors, far from feeling that the data ....are proof of any virtues in the instruments, hope the little evidence that is offered will be useful to other researchers in ascertaining those things which should be studied next in the procedure."

In summary, the writer is of the opinion that the screening process described here stems from a logically sound, theoretical base and that the experimental procedures used in revising it up to now reflect a high caliber of scientific endeavor. Use of the instrument so far has given encouraging, though admittedly limited, results. More accurate appraisal must await the outcome of further experimentation, by now a byword with the authors.

For excerpts from related book reviews, see B93.

[165]
★**Progress Assessment Chart (P-A-C).** Mentally retarded children, mentally retarded adults; 1962–63; behavior checklist for assessing progress in 4 areas: self-help, communication, socialization, occupation; 2 levels; no data on reliability; 12s. 6d. per 25 charts, postpaid; H. C. Gunzburg; [National Association for Mental Health]. *
a) PROGRESS ASSESSMENT CHART FOR CHILDREN UNSUITABLE FOR EDUCATION AT SCHOOL. Form 1 ['62, 3 pages]; mimeographed notes for users ('62, 1 page). *b*) PROGRESS ASSESSMENT CHART FOR THE MENTALLY HANDICAPPED, AGED 16+. Form 2 ['63, 3 pages]; mimeographed notes for users ('63, 2 pages).

[166]
★**Psychometric Behavior Checklist.** Adults; 1960; also called *Maryland Test Behavior Checklist;* for recording unusual test taking behavior; CC Form 19 ['60, 1 page, mimeographed]; instructions (4 pages, reprint of *I* below); specimen set free (checklist may be reproduced locally), postpaid; administration time varies with task rated; Bernard G. Berenson, Kathryn C. Biersdorf, Thomas M. Magoon, Martha J. Maxwell, Donald K. Pumroy, and Marjorie H. Richey; University Counseling Center. *

REFERENCES
1. BERENSON, BERNARD G.; BIERSDORF, KATHRYN C.; MAGOON, THOMAS M.; MAXWELL, MARTHA J.; PUMROY, DONALD K.; AND RICHEY, MARJORIE H. "A Check-List for

Recording Test Taking Behavior." *J Counsel Psychol* 7:116–9 su '60. * (PA 35:3659)

[167]
★**The Psychotic Reaction Profile (PRP): An Inventory of Patient Behavior for Use by Hospital Personnel.** Mental patients; 1961; ratings by nurses or psychiatric aides; 4 scores: withdrawal, thinking disorganization, paranoid belligerence, agitated depression; 1 form (4 pages); mimeographed manual (9 pages); $7 per 25 tests, postpaid; specimen set not available; (10–15) minutes; Maurice Lorr, James P. O'Connor (test), and John W. Stafford (test); Western Psychological Services. *

REFERENCES
1. LORR, MAURICE; O'CONNOR, JAMES P.; AND STAFFORD, JOHN W. "The Psychotic Reaction Profile." *J Clin Psychol* 16:241–5 Jl '60. * (PA 36:2JP41L)
2. CASEY, JESSE F.; HOLLISTER, LEO E.; KLETT, C. JAMES; LASKY, JULIAN J.; AND CAFFEY, EUGENE M. "Combined Drug Therapy of Chronic Schizophrenics." *Am J Psychiatry* 117: 997–1003 My '61. *
3. LASKY, JULIAN J.; KLETT, C. JAMES; CAFFEY, EUGENE M., JR.; BENNETT, J. LAMAR; ROSENBLUM, MARCUS P.; AND HOLLISTER, LEO E. "Drug Treatment of Schizophrenic Patients: A Comparative Evaluation of Chlorpromazine, Chlorprothixene, Fluphenazine, Reserpine, Thioridazine and Triflupromazine." *Dis Nerv System* 23:698–706 D '62. *
4. LORR, MAURICE, AND O'CONNOR, JAMES P. "Psychotic Symptom Patterns in a Behavior Inventory." *Ed & Psychol Meas* 22:139–46 sp '62. * (PA 37:1260)

WILSON H. GUERTIN, *Associate Professor of Education and Psychology, University of Florida, Gainesville, Florida.*

The *Psychotic Reaction Profile* (PRP) is the most recent of published scales for rating the behavior of psychotic patients. It is clearly superior to the *Hospital Adjustment Scale* and probably will replace the *MACC Behavioral Adjustment Scale* also. Many years of experience developing multidimensional scales for rating psychiatric patients and intensive application of them as criteria in drug studies lie behind this published scale.

The 85 items are marked as "T" (true) or "NT" (not true) by a psychiatric attendant or nurse, who has observed the patient over a three day period. The manual states that these brief, simple items can be completed in 10 to 15 minutes, and, further, that the items are "particularly useful in rating patients who are relatively inaccessible, withdrawn, or disturbed."

Scores on four relatively independent dimensions are: Withdrawal, Thinking Disorganization, Paranoid Belligerence, and Agitated Depression. The authors point out that the last of these is least reliable because only five items relate to it. While other scales of this kind yield a total score, the authors, quite creditably, reject the unidimensional concept of adjustment.

Percentile norms for each sex are based upon data from 500 males and 250 females in

47 hospitals. Little description of the norming sample is given but the norms are of little importance since most users will be working with change scores after treatment.

Reliability of the scales is .90 or better (Kuder-Richardson formula 20) for the first three scales and only .74 for Agitated Depression. Intraclass correlation reliability for the mean ratings of two raters were estimated to range from .58 for Agitated Depression to .92 for Withdrawal.

Validity is supported by the ability of three of the four scales to differentiate between open and closed ward patients. While claims for the scale are very modest, the statement that the manual or the instrument or both are to be regarded as preliminary forms might have been made explicit.

The final 85 items were selected from a pool of 172 items on the basis of their correlations with several predetermined clusters. Only four clusters survived to identify the final scales. Personal correspondence with Lorr discloses his belief that the four final dimensions correspond to second-order factors and that he is continuing his efforts to develop a scale that will evaluate first-order factors.

The PRP may be regarded as a good interim scale for rating the behavior of psychotic patients. It is clearly superior to the much older *Hospital Adjustment Scale* and probably will be preferred over the MACC by most users. Like these other scales, its chief shortcoming seems to be the somewhat limited sampling of the dimensions of behavioral adjustment.

[168]

*The Purdue Master Attitude Scales. Grades 7-16; 1934-60; series title for the first 8 scales was formerly listed as *Generalized Attitude Scales; a–h* have space for insertion of any 5 attitude variables; Forms A, B, ('60, 1 page, the 17 items of each scale were selected from the 37- to 50-item Forms A and B copyrighted in 1934-36); 9 scales; manual ('60, 7 pages); no data on reliability of current forms; $1 per 25 copies of any one scale, postage extra; 50¢ per specimen set of any one scale; $1 per complete specimen set; postpaid; (5-10) minutes per attitude variable; H. H. Remmers (editor and manual author) and others; University Book Store. *
a) A SCALE TO MEASURE ATTITUDE TOWARD ANY SCHOOL SUBJECT. 1934-60; original forms by Ella B. Silance.
b) A SCALE FOR MEASURING ATTITUDES TOWARD ANY VOCATION. 1934-60; original forms by Harold E. Miller.
c) A SCALE FOR MEASURING ATTITUDE TOWARD ANY INSTITUTION. 1934-60; original forms by Ida B. Kelly.
d) A SCALE FOR MEASURING ATTITUDE TOWARD ANY DEFINED GROUP. 1934-60; revision of *A Scale for*

Measuring Attitude Toward Races and Nationalities; original forms by H. H. Grice.
e) A SCALE FOR MEASURING ATTITUDES TOWARD ANY PROPOSED SOCIAL ACTION. 1935-60; original forms by Dorothy M. Thomas.
f) A SCALE FOR MEASURING ATTITUDES TOWARD ANY PRACTICE. 1934-60; original forms by H. W. Bues.
g) A SCALE FOR MEASURING ATTITUDE TOWARD ANY HOME-MAKING ACTIVITY. 1934-60; original forms by Beatrix Kellar.
h) A SCALE FOR MEASURING INDIVIDUAL AND GROUP "MORALE." 1936-60; original forms by Laurence Whisler.
i) HIGH SCHOOL ATTITUDE SCALE. 1935-60; original forms by F. H. Gillespie.

REFERENCES

1–9. See 40:1202.
10–46. See 4:46.

DONALD T. CAMPBELL, *Professor of Psychology, Northwestern University, Evanston, Illinois.*

The revision from forms earlier reviewed consists of shortening all forms to 17 items. All criticisms made in previous reviews still hold. The manual gives no criterion for selecting the retained items. No correlations between original and short forms are provided. No data on reliability or reproducibility or factorial structure of the new scales are provided. All evidence on validity comes from the older forms of the scales, with most references from 1934–1938, the latest from 1947. The one study cited to justify the shortening is actually irrelevant, and is misleadingly presented in the manual. As an example of the disregard of research on attitude measurement, in the abbreviation of the scales, neutral items are still retained (e.g., "I have no particular love or hatred for this group"). The revision has provided no basis whatsoever for changing the negative evaluations reported in the previous reviews, nor any basis for recommending the use of these tests.

For reviews by Donald T. Campbell and Kenneth E. Clark of the earlier forms of a–h, see 4:46; for reviews by W. D. Commins and Theodore Newcomb, see 40:1202; for a review by Stephen M. Corey, see 38:897. For a review by Lee J. Cronbach of the earlier forms of i, see 3:46. For excerpts from related book reviews, see 40:B1050, 36:B215, and 36:B216.

[169]

★Rutgers Social Attribute Inventory. Adults; 1959; perception of others (either real persons or generalized classes); 24 trait ratings: good natured-stubborn, intelligent-unintelligent, tense-relaxed, strong-weak, childish-mature, old fashioned-modern, dominating-submissive, thin-fat, adventurous-cautious, lazy-ambitious, optimistic-pessimistic, masculine-feminine, young-old, responsible-irresponsible, crude-refined, tall-short, suspicious-trusting, talkative-quiet, thrifty-wasteful, dependent-self reliant, unsympathetic-sympathetic, good looking-plain, conventional-unconventional, rich-poor; 1 form (1 page); manual (4 pages); no data on reliability; no norms; $2 per 25 tests, postage extra; specimen set not available; (30–60) minutes; William D. Wells; Psychometric Affiliates. *

DAVID B. ORR, *Senior Research Scientist, American Institute for Research; and Director of School and Survey Research, University of Pittsburgh Project Talent Office; Washington, D.C.*

The author states his purpose as "to help raters record their impressions of persons." This is the key to the *Rutgers Social Attribute Inventory*—it is a convenient form for recording impressions, *not* a test in the sense of providing demonstrably accurate measurement. Contrary to the author's statement, however, it is not a standard form, since no standard instructions are provided either on the blank itself or in the manual. Instead the author states that instructions will vary "depending upon details of the study design." Although his discussion of the merits of alternate rating procedures is appropriate, he does not point out the loss of comparability engendered by such nonstandard conditions.

The inventory consists of a one-page set of 24 eight-step trait scales presented "in the general format of the semantic differential (Osgood, Suci, and Tannenbaum, 1957)."[1] Scales are defined by adjectives at the opposing poles and, unlike Osgood's scales, have adverbs of degree printed beneath a line connecting the two pole adjectives. The author has made an appropriate choice of eight categories to increase discrimination, the even number being intended to eliminate the catch-all, middle-of-the-road choice. The adverbial descriptions of the categories (extremely, very, fairly, slightly, slightly, fairly, very, extremely; in that order) leave something to be desired in terms of providing the equal step intervals which would be most desirable. In this respect, however, the inventory does not differ greatly from many other similar rating scales.

In a commendable effort to give his scales more meaning, the author has based them upon the theoretical and factor analytic work of other researchers. Unfortunately, some of the value of this desirable theoretical undergirding appears to have been lost through alterations. The author states, "For the most part, the scales are simplified translations of the basic personality dimensions found in factor analyses of personality ratings and personality inventories (Cattell, 1957; Guilford, 1959)."[2,3] However, other scales have been added and "in many cases, it proved necessary to sacrifice exacting definition [of scales] for simplicity of vocabulary." How much has been lost in such simplification, translation, and addition is not clear.

The blank itself is crowded in appearance. The scales range from traditional traits such as "bossy and dominating"—"submissive; tends to give in easily" through more complex, and hardly undimensional, traits ("responsible & determined"—"irresponsible & quitting") to more observable physical traits such as "thin—fat." Many of these traits are not likely to be truly scalable psychometric dimensions. Though comprehensiveness was an aim, the author admits that field experience limited the inventory to 24 scales. No evidence is presented, however, to show that these 24 scales are the most important or even among the most important social attributes.

Although a brief discussion of possible analyses of the data collected through the use of the inventory is presented, no treatment of reliability and validity is included. Indeed, these essential topics are not even mentioned. No norms of any kind are presented, though several studies are mentioned as having been done.

More than half of the manual is taken up with a discussion of potential uses and applications of the inventory. Categories of uses suggested in the manual include studies of (*a*) "perception of real [specific] persons," such as family members, foremen, labor leaders; (*b*) "perceptions of classes of persons," such as lawyers, Texans, mothers-in-law; (*c*) "the expressive value of specific [personal] characteristics," such as smoking, wearing a beard, having red hair; (*d*) "the expressive value of brands" wherein respondents are asked to rate the typical users of various brand products; (*e*) "the impressions created by advertise-

1 OSGOOD, CHARLES E.; SUCI, GEORGE J.; AND TANNENBAUM, PERCY H. *The Measurement of Meaning.* Urbana, Ill.: University of Illinois Press, 1957. Pp. vii, 342. *

2 CATTELL, RAYMOND B. *Personality and Motivation Structure and Measurement.* Yonkers, N.Y.: World Book Co., 1957. Pp. xxv, 948. *
3 GUILFORD, J. P. *Personality.* New York: McGraw-Hill Book Co., Inc., 1959. Pp. xiii, 562. *

ments" (on prior impressions of brands and brand-users) ; and (f) "the impressions created by other forms of mass communication."

Finally, the manual presents an unbelievably poor appearance. It is crowded, messy, has extremely small type, and is shot through with typographical errors. If the more than a dozen actual misspellings in the manual are indicative of the care with which this inventory was developed then extreme caution in its use is certainly advisable.

In summary, the author shows commendable candor in emphasizing the exploratory nature of his instrument, in calling attention to the probable unequal nature of the scale intervals, and in describing its function in terms of "impressions" rather than "measurements." However, it is this reviewer's impression that a great deal of additional work will be necessary before this inventory takes a place among our more useful psychometric instruments.

JOHN PIERCE-JONES, *Professor of Educational Psychology, The University of Texas, Austin, Texas.*

The *Rutgers Social Attribute Inventory* (RSAI), published in a single form on a single sheet, presents a rater with two dozen 8-point bipolar rating scales (implicitly 9-point scales, zero points having been omitted to force judgments toward one extreme or the other) upon which descriptions of persons, either individually or in classes, may be rendered. The rating form is clearly printed, apparently by multilith; it should be convenient for raters to use and for clerks to handle. Regrettably, the RSAI provides no spaces for recording any of the following important items : (a) the identity of the subject rated; (b) the identity of the rater; (c) the date of making the ratings; (d) the purpose of the ratings; (e) the degree of the rater's acquaintance with the subject; (f) statements of inability to rate a subject on a trait because of insufficient knowledge; (g) numerical values to be recorded for various data processing purposes. The manual accompanying the RSAI appears to have been printed by a photo-offset and reduction process ; its contents have been so reduced that the booklet may be quite discomfiting to read. The manual deals with such matters as: (a) general uses of the RSAI; (b) illustrations of the utility of the device in relatively specific researches including studies of person percep-

tion, brand images, and the "impressions created by advertisements"; and (c) procedures for obtaining, analyzing, and presenting the ratings.

It is extremely unfortunate that the reliability to be expected of RSAI ratings has not been dealt with in the manual. The construct validity of RSAI ratings, which should have been dealt with in detail, appears, from the manual's content, not to have been considered by the instrument's originator and publisher in any serious way. Evidence concerning the predictive validity, broadly conceived, of this device is very scarce, consisting of illustrative profiles from previously unpublished studies (of which no adequate descriptions were found) suggesting that (a) "the ideal professor" was rated differently from "the average professor" in four RSAI attributes by 50 Rutgers undergraduates; (b) "the average nurse" (and nursing aide) tends to be judged more submissive (less dominating) than "the average doctor" by raters consisting of unspecified numbers of physicians, nurses, and patients of both sexes. The extent to which response set variance affects the validity and reliability of RSAI ratings apparently has not been assayed; it should have been, for it has been shown repeatedly that this influence is usually strong when judgments or self-reports must be registered on the sorts of scales provided by the RSAI.

There now exists among social psychologists and students of personality a substantial, well-founded concern for the development of instruments adequate to assess dimensions of personality and person perception which may be related to "in the world" social behavior. Gough's *California Psychological Inventory,* designed to measure traits such as responsibility and tolerance or factors [1] such as "adjustment by social conformity" and "extraversion," represents one important effort to satisfy this concern with an inventory whose scales are associated with relevant social behavior criteria. Of course, such devices as the CPI are not adapted for obtaining records of the constructions placed by judges on persons individually or in classes. In this connection, the important thing to consider in relation to the RSAI is that structured personality inven-

1 PIERCE-JONES, JOHN; MITCHELL, JAMES V.; AND KING, F. J. "Configurational Invariance in the California Psychological Inventory." *J Exp Ed* 31:65-71 S '62. * (*PA* 37:8012)

tories have generally been examined as pre-dictors of external criteria of the traits pur-portedly measured, whereas there is little evidence that the RSAI has been so studied. It is surely as important that the validity of rating scales be assessed in relation to inde-pendent criteria as it is that more usual scales be so appraised. Moreover, neither the origina-tor nor the publisher of the RSAI should be relieved of clear responsibility for showing (a) that ratings elicited by their device are stable, dependable, and reliable, and (b) that different, but comparably sophisticated raters (with re-spect to the attributes rated), can produce relatively comparable ratings of subjects. These responsibilities do not appear to have been met satisfactorily.

There is some merit in Wells' intention to produce scales, similar to the semantic differ-ential, aimed at being coterminous, in the fac-tor analytic sense, with "the basic personality dimensions found in factor analyses of per-sonality ratings and personality inventories" by such workers as Guilford and Cattell. How-ever, this worthy aim is surely not realized simply by setting up two dozen scales with adjectivally labeled poles (e.g., childish-mature, responsible-irresponsible) and the usual ad-verbial designations of the several degrees of each attribute. We should expect the developer of the RSAI to show by experiment, and we should have expected his publisher to have in-sisted upon, evidence that data obtained with the instrument do, indeed, bear factorial and construct relevance to the dimensions in which they are presumed to reflect differences. With-out the necessary technical information having been made available, the present RSAI is worth little more, in the reviewer's judgment, than the many "home-made" scales investigators often produce for their own purposes.

[170]

*SRA Youth Inventory. Grades 7–12, 9–12; 1949–60; problems checklist; 9 scores: school, future, my-self, people, home, dates and sex, health, general, basic difficulty; IBM; 2 forms; Form S is an extensive re-vision of Form A rather than a parallel form; (30–45) minutes; H. H. Remmers, Benjamin Shimberg, and Arthur J. Drucker (manual for Form A); Science Research Associates, Inc. *
a) FORM A. Grades 7–12; 1949–53; IBM; 1 form ('49, 14 pages, listed as Forms AH and AM in publisher's catalog); manual, second edition ('53, 22 pages); tech-nical supplement ('53, 23 pages); junior high school profile leaflet ('50, 4 pages); senior high school pro-file leaflet ('49, 4 pages); separate answer sheets or pads must be used; $10.80 per 20 tests; $5 per 100

IBM answer sheets (scored by the publisher only; fee: 25¢ per student); $2.40 per 20 self-marking answer pads; 50¢ per hand scoring basic difficulty key; $1.20 per 20 profile leaflets; 75¢ per specimen set.
b) FORM S. Grades 9–12; 1955–60; 1 form ('56, 12 pages); manual ('60, 35 pages); profile ('60, 1 page); $2.40 per 20 tests; $1.05 per 20 profiles; 60¢ per man-ual; 50¢ per specimen set; Spanish edition available.

REFERENCES

1–7. See 4:91.
8–19. See 5:105.
20. NIXON, WARREN WINTERS. A Comparison of Person-ality Adjustment Before and After a Series of Discussions Based on Problems Marked on the Science Research Associ-ates Junior Inventory. Doctor's research study No. 2, Colo-rado State College (Greeley, Colo.), 1956.
21. BARRAGAN, M. FIDELIS. A Study of the Problems of a Selected Number of High School Students as Measured by the SRA Youth Inventory. Master's thesis, Catholic University of America (Washington, D.C.), 1957.
22. BECKWITH, A. VANCE. A Comparison of Responses of Adjusted and Maladjusted Students to the SRA Youth Inven-tory. Master's thesis, Claremont College (Claremont, Calif.), 1957.
23. MUSSELMAN, DAYTON L. Patterns of Circumstances Related to Problems Expressed by Seventh and Eighth Grade Pupils. Doctor's thesis, University of Colorado (Boulder, Colo.), 1958. (DA 19:2537)
24. RICE, DAVID LEE. A Comparative Study of the Personal Adjustment of High School Students Attending a Reorganized Rural School With High School Students Attending Selected Rural Township Schools. Doctor's thesis, Purdue University (Lafayette, Ind.), 1958. (DA 19:2005)
25. SMITH, LOUIS M., AND HUDGINS, BRYCE B. "The SRA Youth Inventory and Mental Health." Personnel & Guid J 37: 303–4 D '58. * (PA 36:2JO03S)
26. TALIANA, LAWRENCE EDWIN. Youth's Problems as They See Them: A Statistical Analysis and Restandardization of the SRA Youth Inventory. Doctor's thesis, Purdue University (Lafayette, Ind.), 1958. (DA 19:167)
27. WEISBRODT, JEROME ALAN. The Effects of Response Set on the SRA Youth Inventory. Master's thesis, Purdue Uni-versity (Lafayette, Ind.), 1959.
28. KULKARNI, S. S. A Marathi Revision of the SRA Youth Inventory. Doctor's thesis, Purdue University (La-fayette, Ind.), 1961. (DA 22:3261)
29. MILBURN, DONNA J. "Defining Units With a Problem-Detecting Inventory." Marriage & Family Living 23:52–3 F '61. *
30. REMMERS, H. H. "Cross-Cultural Studies of Teenagers Problems." J Ed Psychol 53:254–61 D '62. * (PA 37:4767)
31. CLARKE, H. HARRISON, AND GREENE, WALTER H. "Rela-tionships Between Personal-Social Measures Applied to 10-Year-Old Boys." Res Q 34:288–98 O '63. *

FORREST L. VANCE, Administrative Officer, American Psychological Association, Washing-ton, D.C.

The examiner's manual for Form A of this inventory indicates that the instrument's value lies in helping school people identify quickly the self-acknowledged problems of students in grades 7 through 12. This is achieved for a particular student by having him respond to 298 problem statements drawn from autobio-graphical essays obtained from some 15,000 teenagers throughout the United States. In this form of the inventory, the subject checks each item that applies to himself and makes no re-sponse to the remaining problem statements. The results are scored in terms of the eight content headings under which the items are printed in the test booklet. These categories include labels such as, "My School," "About Myself," "Getting Along With Others," and so on. These eight judgmentally determined content areas are then treated as scales, and extensive normative data are provided to translate raw scores for each area into percentile ranks.

The stated mission of the instrument is nicely accomplished. One might quibble about the use of content categories as scales, but there is no question that the inventory provides a rapid survey of a wide variety of possible problems to which a cooperative student can respond, indicating his own concerns. Also, the method of item selection and the normative data (derived from a carefully stratified sample of 2,500 students) are commendable in both concept and execution.

However, the generally good impression up to this point is seriously marred by a gratuitous attempt to use the inventory to diagnose psychopathology. This effort has produced an unfortunate clinical and psychometric concoction called the Basic Difficulty Scale. This scale was derived by asking seven judges to classify each of the inventory items as either indicative of simple recognition of a problem or as more likely to indicate a basic personality disturbance. These seven judges, described as "experts in the fields of guidance, clinical psychology, and education," agreed unanimously that 47 items represented basic difficulty and identified 54 others by a 6 to 1 majority. By the same criteria, 97 items were classified as indicators of non-basic problem recognition.

This procedure is justified initially by the extraordinary statement, "It appears that the ability of experts in the field of mental hygiene to agree on the possible significance of 198 items is probably a good indication of the validity of the *Inventory*." At a later point evidence is introduced that shows that the Basic Difficulty Scale does significantly differentiate students independently rated by school counselors as well-adjusted from students rated poorly-adjusted. However, two of the eight content scales differentiate these groups better than the Basic Difficulty Scale, and four of the remaining scales also distinguish these groups reliably.

The plain fact is that all of the scales on this instrument are positively intercorrelated. Data for the eight content scales show correlation coefficients ranging between .20 and .67 with a median of .46. No correlational data are provided for the Basic Difficulty Scale in the manual, but this scale has substantial item overlap with each of the content scales except for "Looking Ahead," which deals almost exclusively with vocational development. The remaining seven content scales share 12 per cent (Boy Meets Girl) to 80 per cent (About Myself) of their items with the Basic Difficulty Scale, leaving little doubt that this scale will be substantially correlated with the others.

Aside from the high probability that the Basic Difficulty Scale adds no information to what is given by the rest of the inventory, one may question the wisdom of introducing clinical concepts into an instrument intended for broad use by persons without special training in any of the mental health professions. It is this reviewer's opinion that the Basic Difficulty key is not appropriate for general use by nonspecialists, and that its present stage of development cautions against applications, other than experimental, by anyone.

A new form of this instrument, Form S, was published in 1956, with its accompanying manual issued in 1960. Form S is a thorough revision which includes some item changes and a new format in which responses are made to 296 problem statements on a four-point scale indicating intensity of that problem for the individual subject. Seventh and eighth grade norms are eliminated and a self interpreting report form is provided for the content area scores. A new Basic Difficulty Scale of 100 items was developed for Form S, using eleven clinical psychologists as judges.

As in the case of Form A, the scales of Form S are highly reliable and highly intercorrelated. The pattern of item overlap between content scales and Basic Difficulty is also similar to Form A, and validity data for this construct are provided only for the earlier scale, although the two forms are not identical.

In general, this is a well-constructed inventory with appropriate content and format for secondary school use as a counseling tool. The scales, based on content areas, are carefully constructed and reliable, and excellent normative information is given for them. As earlier reviews have pointed out, these scales are designed to indicate what the subject *thinks* are his problems, and as such are not susceptible to evaluation against objective criteria. An attempt is also made to develop a psychodiagnostic indicator, but the resulting Basic Difficulty Scale, which *is* open to empirical study, needs extensive validating research before it can be considered anything other than an experimental device.

J Counsel Psychol 7:226–7 f '60. Laurence Siegel. * A rather unusual and highly desirable feature of the Manual is its inclusion of a summary of responses to individual items by the standardization sample. These data show the percentages of respondents, by sex and by grade, marking each response alternative. This tabular presentation contains a gold mine of interesting information for use in undergraduate teacher-training classes and for in-service training programs. The primary value of the Youth Inventory....will be derived from examining individual item responses rather than profiles of subscale scores. The use of the Basic Difficulty Scale scores for screening purposes may be justified in a very large school system wherein teachers and counselors are unable otherwise to identify pupils who are rather seriously disturbed.

For reviews by Kenneth E. Clark and Frank S. Freeman of Form A, see 4:91.

[171]

★A Scale to Measure Attitudes Toward Disabled Persons. Disabled and nondisabled adults; 1957–60; title on test is *ATDP Scale;* 1 form ('57, 1 page); manual ('60, 16 pages); $2 per 25 scales; $1 per manual; $1.10 per specimen set; postage extra; (10) minutes; Harold E. Yuker, J. R. Block, and William J. Campbell; Human Resources Foundation. *

[172]

★Self-Interview Inventory. Adult males; 1958; 10 scores: current complaints, emotional insecurity, guilt feelings, composite neurotic (based on first 3 scores), prepsychotic or psychotic, behavior problems, childhood illness, composite maladjustment (based on previous 3 scores), validation (lack of carefulness, lack of truthfulness); IBM; 1 form (4 pages); manual (4 pages); profile ['58, 1 page]; no data on reliability; separate answer sheets must be used; $3 per 25 tests; $2 per 25 IBM scorable answer sheets; machine scoring stencil must be constructed locally; $2 per 50 profiles; $1 per specimen set (must be purchased to obtain manual and key); cash orders postpaid; administration time not reported; H. Birnet Hovey; Psychometric Affiliates. *

REFERENCES

1. Hovey, H. Birnet. "A Self-Interview Inventory." *J Clin Psychol* 3:191–3 Ap '47. * (*PA* 21:3121)

Andrew R. Baggaley, *Professor of Psychology, Temple University, Philadelphia, Pennsylvania.*

This inventory attempts "to measure maladjustment potentials in terms of what men declare about their past histories and experiences." One hundred thirty-two of its items were included because they significantly differentiated 50 male neuropsychiatric patients from 50 male Veterans Administration workers in two samples. In addition there are 27 items that differentiated particular subsamples of patients, 10 items constituting a carefulness scale, 10 items constituting a truthfulness scale, and 6 unscored, neutral, introductory items. The fact that 137 of the items are keyed so that an answer of "true" is scored in the direction of "sick" means that a low score can indicate illness, "acquiescence," or some combination of these.

All of the items except the 26 validating and introductory items are scored on a "Composite Maladjustment" scale. By cluster analysis these 159 items (except for 24 "current complaint" items) were grouped into these subscales: Emotional Insecurity, Guilt Feelings, Prepsychotic or Psychotic, Behavior Problems, and Childhood Illness. Additionally, a "Composite Neurotic" scale combines the emotional insecurity, guilt feelings, and current complaint items. A graphic device is provided for transforming scores to standardized scores. The manual also contains a rather long list of suggestions for clinical interpretation.

Since the items within the subscales are listed consecutively in the question booklet, only one scoring template is needed. However, the probable development of response sets tends to offset this advantage; e.g., an examinee who answers "yes" to questions 127 through 154 receives a score of only two on the behavior problems scale. In any case, the publisher should have supplied at least one scoring template made of cardboard rather than soft paper. For all but four items, failure to respond is scored in the direction of "sickness"; the stated rationale is that the patients made somewhat more omissions than the controls. Intercorrelations between the subscales are reported. However, no reliability data whatsoever are given, so the test user has no statistical basis for evaluating the reliability of the profile differences on which the suggested clinical interpretations are based.

The publisher's reproduction of the test materials is abominable. The information was typed and then reproduced by the offset process. There is no double spacing, even between paragraphs. The brightness is uneven, and there are misspellings, poor erasures, and even strikeovers.

In summary, the original research on which this inventory is based provides a good foundation, but there are several technical improvements that should be made in future editions before the inventory can be recommended for general use. Furthermore, the publisher should be urged to do a decent job of reproduction. At present, the inventory can be recommended only as a rough screening device to suggest that some sort of maladjustment (or response set) is present in an adult male.

DAVID T. LYKKEN, *Associate Professor of Psychiatry and Psychology, University of Minnesota, Minneapolis, Minnesota.*

This questionnaire contains 185 MMPI-type true-false items and yields a profile of 10 scale scores. The latter include: a 24 item current complaint scale; 2 putative validity scales of 10 items each; 5 scales based on a rough cluster analysis and labeled Emotional Insecurity (21 items), Guilt Feelings (21 items), Prepsychotic or Psychotic (54 items), Behavior Problems (28 items), and Childhood Illness (11 items); a score obtained by adding the Current Complaints, Emotional Insecurity, and Guilt Feelings scores and labeled Composite Neurotic; and a Composite Maladjustment score based on the sum of all but the two validity scales. One hundred eight of the items are said to have differentiated an unspecified mixture of male VA psychiatric patients from non-patient males at the 5 per cent level in two separate samples of 100 subjects each. The cluster analysis was based upon the data from these same 200 subjects and led to the inclusion of an additional 27 items which appeared to differentiate significantly among clusters. Norms are provided, based on the same 100 control subjects, for converting the 10 scale scores to *T* score equivalents. No additional normative, reliability, or validity data are given.

About one page of the four page manual is devoted to "interpretations." Here the author explains which profile characteristics indicate "an essentially neurotic picture" or "present or impending disintegration of control in a psychopathic personality" or "character disorder with pseudo-psychosis," etc. No empirical justification whatever is provided for any of these interpretations which appear to be based entirely upon simpleminded inference from the item content and the names previously

given by the author to the several clusters. Additional insight into the level of psychometric sophistication embodied in this instrument can be had by noting that the items are presented to the subject (i.e., listed in the test booklet) serially by scale; for example, the 10 items on which a truthful respondent is supposed to admit to "common human 'weaknesses'" (and which comprise the Lack of Truthfulness scale) are all listed together as items 176 through 185!

This is an inane and incompetent imitation of the MMPI and one finds it difficult to understand the motivation of either its author or publisher. Such a product is an embarrassment to psychology in general and to the field of mental measurement in particular.

[173]
Shipley-Institute of Living Scale for Measuring Intellectual Impairment. Adults; 1939–46; formerly called *Shipley-Hartford Retreat Scale for Measuring Intellectual Impairment;* 4 scores: vocabulary, abstractions, total, conceptual quotient; 1 form ('39, 2 pages); manual ('46, c1940–46, 4 pages, identical with manual copyrighted in 1940 except for title); $2 per 25 tests; 50¢ per specimen set; postpaid; 20(25) minutes; Walter C. Shipley; distributed by Mrs. Walter C. Shipley. *

REFERENCES

1–25. See 3:95.
26–48. See 5:111.
49. YATES, AUBREY J. "The Validity of Some Psychological Tests of Brain Damage." *Psychol B* 51:359–79 Jl '54. *
50. BARTELME, KENWOOD, AND RILEY, GORDON L. "A Study of Psychiatric Technicians on Selected Measures of Intelligence and Personality." Abstract. *Am Psychol* 10:321 Ag '55. *
51. SINES, LLOYD K., AND SIMMONS, HELEN. "The Shipley-Hartford Scale and the Doppelt Short Form as Estimators of WAIS IQ in a State Hospital Population." *J Clin Psychol* 15:452–3 O '59. * (PA 36:1HD52S)
52. GARRETT, WILEY S. "Prediction of Academic Success in a School of Nursing." *Personnel & Guid J* 38:500–3 F '60. * (PA 35:3954)
53. SUINN, RICHARD M. "The Shipley-Hartford Retreat Scale as a Screening Test of Intelligence." *J Clin Psychol* 16:419 O '60. * (PA 37:3241)
54. WIENS, ARTHUR N., AND BANAKA, WILLIAM H. "Estimating WAIS IQ From Shipley-Hartford Scores: A Cross-Validation." *J Clin Psychol* 16:452 O '60. * (PA 37:3119)
55. WIENER, DANIEL N. "Evaluation of Selection Procedures for a Management Development Program." *J Counsel Psychol* 8:121–8 su '61. * (PA 36:3LD21W)
56. PULOS, LEE; NICHOLS, ROBERT C.; LEWINSOHN, PETER M.; AND KOLDJESKI, THEODORE. "Selection of Psychiatric Aides and Prediction of Performance Through Psychological Testing and Interviews." *Psychol Rep* 10:519–20 Ap '62. * (PA 37:3401)
57. SKLAR, MAURICE, AND EDWARDS, ALLAN E. "Presbycusis: A Factor Analysis of Hearing and Psychological Characteristics of Men Over 65 Years Old." *J Auditory Res* 2:194–207 Jl '62. *
58. WAHLER, H. J., AND WATSON, LUKE S. "A Comparison of the Shipley-Hartford as a Power Test With the WAIS Verbal Scale." Abstract. *J Consult Psychol* 26:105 F '62. * (PA 37:5001)
59. ELKIND, DAVID; KOEGLER, RONALD R.; AND GO, ELSIE. "Field Independence and Concept Formation." *Percept & Motor Skills* 17:383–6 O '63. * (PA 38:5349)
60. HAERTZEN, CHARLES A., AND HILL, HARRIS E. "Assessing Subjective Effects of Drugs: An Index of Carelessness and Confusion for Use With the Addiction Research Center Inventory (ARCI)." *J Clin Psychol* 19:407–12 O '63. *
61. LEWINSOHN, PETER M. "Use of the Shipley-Hartford Conceptual Quotient as a Measure of Intellectual Impairment." *J Consult Psychol* 27:444–7 O '63. * (PA 38:4291)

For reviews by E. J. G. Bradford, William A. Hunt, and Margaret Ives, see 3:95.

[174]

*Sixteen Personality Factor Questionnaire. Ages 15 or 16 and over; 1949–63; 16 or 17 scores: reserved vs. outgoing (A), less intelligent vs. more intelligent (B), affected by feelings vs. emotionally stable (C), humble vs. assertive (E), sober vs. happy-go-lucky (F), expedient vs. conscientious (G), shy vs. venturesome (H), tough-minded vs. tender-minded (I), trusting vs. suspicious (L), practical vs. imaginative (M), forthright vs. shrewd (N), placid vs. apprehensive (O), conservative vs. experimenting (Q1), group-dependent vs. self-sufficient (Q2), casual vs. controlled (Q3), relaxed vs. tense (Q4), motivational distortion scale (Form C only); NCS for Forms A and B; Forms A ('62, c1956–62, 10 pages), B ('61, c1957–61, 10 pages), C ('56, c1954–56, 8 pages), X ('63, 11 pages); Form C is a short form and is also available, in combination with the *IPAT Culture Fair Intelligence Test*, with tape recorded directions; Form X is a special edition, presented either in booklet form with tape recorded directions for use with semiliterates or entirely on tape for use with illiterates, available either separately or in combination with the *IPAT Culture Fair Intelligence Test*; manual ('57, 56 pages) for Forms A, B, and C; mimeographed norms supplement ('63, 4 pages) for 1961–62 editions of Forms A and B; supplementary manual, second edition ('62, 25 pages) for Form C; manual ('63, 8 pages) for tape administration of Forms C or X; mimeographed supplement ['63, 6 pages] for Form X; profile ('63, 1 page); reliability data for Forms A and B based upon the 1956–57 editions; norms for combination of Forms A and B also presented; no data on reliability for Form X; separate answer sheets must be used; $12.50 per 25 tests of Forms A or B; $10 per 25 tests of Form C (regular booklet edition); $4.50 per pad of 50 hand scoring answer sheets; $5.40 per pad of 50 combined answer sheet-profiles; $2 per set of keys for Forms A or B; $1 per key for Form C; $3.80 per pad of 50 separate profiles; $3.25 per 50 NCS answer sheets for Forms A and B combined (see 671 for scoring service); $2.90 per manual; $1.20 per supplementary manual for Form C; $5 per specimen set of Forms A and B; $4 per specimen set of Form C; $2.40 per abbreviated specimen set of Form C (includes supplementary manual but not manual); $38–$58 per examiner's kit of tape edition of Forms C or X (includes 2 tests, 50 answer sheets, 3¾ ips tape, and manuals); cash orders postpaid; 1956 edition of Form C also published under the title *Employee Attitude Series: 16 P.F.*, by Industrial Psychology, Inc.; (50–60) minutes for Forms A or B, (30–40) minutes for Form C, (50–70) minutes for Form X; Raymond B. Cattell and Herbert W. Eber; Institute for Personality and Ability Testing. *

REFERENCES

1–8. See 4:87.
9–29. See 5:112.
30. DOTSON, ELSIE JENOISE. *A Study of the Agreement of Introversion-Extroversion Factors as Defined by Various Factor Analysts.* Doctor's thesis, University of Kentucky (Lexington, Ky.), 1951. (*DA* 18:1095)
31. McCARTHY, THOMAS N. *The Relationship of Vocational Interests to Personality Traits.* Master's thesis, Catholic University of America (Washington, D.C.), 1952.
32. HOLMEN, MILTON G.; KATTER, ROBERT V.; JONES, ANNE M.; AND RICHARDSON, IRVING F. "An Assessment Program for OCS Applicants." *HumRRO Tech Rep* 26:1–50 F '56. * (*PA* 31:8957)
33. KEMPE, JAMES EDWIN. *An Experimental Investigation of the Relationship Between Certain Personality Characteristics and Physiological Responses to Stress in a Normal Population.* Doctor's thesis, Michigan State University (East Lansing, Mich.), 1956. (*DA* 19:3383)

34. BENNIS, WARREN; BURKE, RICHARD; CUTTER, HENRY; HARRINGTON, HERBERT; AND HOFFMAN, JOYCE. "A Note on Some Problems of Measurement and Prediction in a Training Group." *Group Psychother* 10:328–41 D '57. * (*PA* 33:5971)
35. CATTELL, R. B., AND BAGGALEY, A. R. "A Confirmation of Ergic and Engram Structures in Attitudes Objectively Measured." *Austral J Psychol* 10:287–318 D '58. * (*PA* 34:2748)
36. KELLY, E. LOWELL; MILLER, JAMES G.; MARQUIS, DONALD G.; GERARD, R. W.; AND UHR, LEONARD. "Personality Differences and Continued Meprobamate and Prochlorperazine Administration." *A.M.A. Arch Neurol & Psychiatry* 80:241–6 Ag '58. * (*PA* 33:10420)
37. MELVIN, GEORGIA-LEE VIRGINIA. *Personality and Group Status in Adolescents.* Doctor's thesis, University of Illinois, (Urbana, Ill.), 1958. (*DA* 19:1134)
38. WEITZENHOFFER, ANDRÉ M., AND WEITZENHOFFER, GENEVA B. "Personality and Hypnotic Susceptibility." *Am J Clin Hypnosis* 1:79–82 O '58. * (*PA* 34:4414)
39. WELLS, HAROLD PARK. *Relationships Between Physical Fitness and Psychological Variables.* Doctor's thesis, University of Illinois (Urbana, Ill.), 1958. (*DA* 19:2531)
40. BYRD, EUGENE. "Measured Anxiety in Old Age." *Psychol Rep* 5:439–40 S '59. *
41. CATTELL, RAYMOND B., AND SCHEIER, IVAN H. "Extension of Meaning of Objective Test Personality Factors: Especially Into Anxiety, Neuroticism, Questionnaire, and Physical Factors." *J General Psychol* 61:287–315 O '59. * (*PA* 35:785)
42. COPPEDGE, ROBERT J. *Personality, as Determined by the Sixteen Personality Factor Test, and Its Relationship to Musical Tastes.* Master's thesis, Indiana State Teachers College (Terre Haute, Ind.), 1959. (Abstract: *Teach Col J* 31:34)
43. HOLLAND, JOHN L. "Some Limitations of Teacher Ratings as Predictors of Creativity." *J Ed Psychol* 50:219–23 O '59. * (*PA* 36:KH19H)
44. HUNT, J. McV.; EWING, THOMAS N.; LaFORGE, ROLFE; AND GILBERT, WILLIAM M. "An Integrated Approach to Research on Therapeutic Counseling With Samples of Results." *J Counsel Psychol* 6:46–54 sp '59. * (*PA* 34:5955)
45. KARRAS, EDWARD J. *A Study of the Personality Variables, as Measured by the Cattell 16 Personality Factor Test, Associated With Musical Aptitude, as Measured by the Drake Musical Aptitude Tests.* Master's thesis, Kent State University (Kent, Ohio), 1959.
46. KARSON, SAMUEL. "The Sixteen Personality Factor Test in Clinical Practice." *J Clin Psychol* 15:174–6 Ap '59. * (*PA* 35:4959)
47. MANN, RICHARD D. "A Review of the Relationships Between Personality and Performance in Small Groups." *Psychol B* 56:241–70 Jl '59. * (*PA* (34:4194)
48. RAYGOR, ALTON L. "College Reading Improvement and Personality Change." *J Counsel Psychol* 6:211–7 f '59. * (*PA* 35:3909)
49. ANDERSON, A. W. "Personality Scores of Western Australian University Students Entering From State and Private Schools." *Austral J Ed* 4:123–5 Jl '60. *
50. ANDERSON, A. W. "Personality Traits of Western Australian University Entrants." *Austral J Psychol* 12:4–9 Je '60. * (*PA* 35:3916)
51. ANDERSON, A. W. "Personality Traits of Western Australian University Freshmen." *J Social Psychol* 51:87–91 F '60. * (*PA* 34:7624)
52. CARRIGAN, PATRICIA M. "Extraversion-Introversion as a Dimension of Personality: A Reappraisal." *Psychol B* 57:329–60 S '60. * (*PA* 35:4976)
53. COUCH, ARTHUR, AND KENISTON, KENNETH. "Yeasayers and Naysayers: Agreeing Response Set as a Personality Variable." *J Abn & Social Psychol* 60:151–74 Mr '60. * (*PA* 34:7376)
54. HOLLAND, JOHN L. "The Prediction of College Grades From Personality and Aptitude Variables." *J Ed Psychol* 51:245–54 O '60. * (*PA* 36:1KL45H)
55. HOLLAND, JOHN L. "The Relation of the Vocational Preference Inventory to the Sixteen Personality Factor Questionnaire." *J Appl Psychol* 44:291–6 Ag '60. * (*PA* 35:4015)
56. KARSON, SAMUEL. "Validating Clinical Judgments With the 16 P.F. Test." *J Clin Psychol* 16:394–7 O '60. * (*PA* 37:3221)
57. SCOFIELD, ROBERT W., AND SUN, CHIN-WAN. "A Comparative Study of the Differential Effect Upon Personality of Chinese and American Child Training Practices." *J Social Psychol* 52:221–4 N '60. * (*PA* 35:5008)
58. THOMAS, SHAILER. *Socio-Economic Status and Personality Factors as Measured by Cattell's Sixteen Personality Factor Test.* Master's thesis, Michigan State University (East Lansing, Mich.), 1960.
59. ANDERSON, A. W. "Personality Traits in Reading Ability of Western Australian University Freshmen." *J Ed Res* 54:234–7 F '61. *
60. BECKER, WESLEY C. "A Comparison of the Factor Structure and Other Properties of the 16 PF and the Guilford-Martin Personality Inventories." *Ed & Psychol Meas* 21:393–404 su '61. * (*PA* 36:2HF93B)
61. BORGATTA, EDGAR F. "Mood, Personality, and Interaction." *J General Psychol* 64:105–37 Ja '61. * (*PA* 35:6415)

62. BORGATTA, EDGAR F., AND GLASS, DAVID C. "Personality Concomitants of Extreme Response Set (ERS)." *J Social Psychol* 55:213–21 D '61. * (*PA* 36:3HE13B)

63. BORGATTA, EDGAR F.; IN COLLABORATION WITH HENRY J. MEYER. "Make a Sentence Test: An Approach to Objective Scoring of Sentence Completions." *Genetic Psychol Monogr* 63:3–65 F '61. * (*PA* 35:6435)

64. CADY, LEE D., JR.; GERTLER, MENARD M.; GOTTSCH, LIDA G.; AND WOODBURY, MAX A. "The Factor Structure of Variables Concerned With Coronary Artery Disease." *Behav Sci* 6:37–41 Ja '61. * (*PA* 36:1JU37C)

65. CATTELL, RAYMOND B., AND GREENE, RONALD R. "Rationale of Norms on an Adult Personality Test, the 16 P.F.—For American Women." *J Ed Res* 54:285–90 Ap '61. *

66. CATTELL, RAYMOND B., AND SCHEIER, IVAN H. *The Meaning and Measurement of Neuroticism and Anxiety.* New York: Ronald Press Co., 1961. Pp. ix, 535. * (*PA* 36: 1HK27C)

67. CATTELL, RAYMOND B., AND WARBURTON, FRANK W. "A Cross-Cultural Comparison of Patterns of Extraversion and Anxiety." *Brit J Psychol* 52:3–15 F '61. * (*PA* 36: 1GB03C)

68. DAS, RHEA S. "Validity Information Exchange, No. 14-05: D.O.T. Code 2-66.01, Police Lieutenant." *Personnel Psychol* 14:459–61 w '61. *

69. DAVIES, LILLIAN SCHOLLJEGERDES. *Some Relationships Between Attitudes, Personality Characteristics, and Verbal Behavior of Selected Teachers.* Doctor's thesis, University of Minnesota (Minneapolis, Minn.), 1961. (*DA* 22:3943)

70. GOCKA, EDWARD F., AND MARKS, JOHN B. "Second-Order Factors in the 16 PF Test and MMPI Inventory." *J Clin Psychol* 17:32–5 Ja '61. * (*PA* 37:3175)

71. KARSON, SAMUEL. "Second-Order Personality Factors in Positive Mental Health." *J Clin Psychol* 17:14–9 Ja '61. * (*PA* 37:3176)

72. LEVONIAN, EDWARD. "Personality Measurement With Items Selected From the 16 P.F. Questionnaire." *Ed & Psychol Meas* 21:937–46 w '61. * (*PA* 36:5HB37L)

73. LEVONIAN, EDWARD. "A Statistical Analysis of the 16 Personality Factor Questionnaire." *Ed & Psychol Meas* 21: 589–96 au '61. * (*PA* 36:4HF89L)

74. McLEOD, H. N. "My Two-Hour Psychological Test Battery." *O.P.A. Q* 14:85–7 D '61. *

75. MEYER, M. L., AND PARTIPILO, MICHAEL A. "Examiner Personality as an Influence on the Rorschach Test." *Psychol Rep* 9:221–2 O '61. *

76. MICHAEL, WILLIAM B.; BARTH, GEORGE; AND KAISER, HENRY F. "Dimensions of Temperament in Three Groups of Music Teachers." *Psychol Rep* 9:701–4 D '61. *

77. RAO, M. S. SHARADAMBA. "The Schizophrenic Profile on the 16 P.F. Questionnaire." *Indian J Psychol* 36:93–102 Je '61. *

78. SHIPMAN, W. G.; DANOWSKI, T. S.; AND MOSES, D. C., JR. "The Relation of Some Morphological, Physiological, and Genetic Dimensions to the Cattell 16PF and T.A.T. Scales." Abstract. *Acta Psychologica* 19:208–10 '61. *

79. SUHR, VIRTUS W. "Personality and Driving Efficiency." *Percept & Motor Skills* 12:34 F '61. * (*PA* 35:5720)

80. VERNIER, CLAIRE M.; BARRELL, ROBERT P.; CUMMINGS, JONATHAN W.; DICKERSON, JOSEPH H.; AND HOOPER, H. ELSTON. "Psychosocial Study of the Patient With Pulmonary Tuberculosis: A Cooperative Research Approach." *Psychol Monogr* 75(6):1–32 '61. * (*PA* 36:3JU32V)

81. ARMATAS, JAMES P., AND COLLISTER, E. GORDON. "Personality Correlates of SVIB Patterns." *J Counsel Psychol* 9:149–54 su '62. * (*PA* 37:6710)

82. BORGATTA, EDGAR F. "The Coincidence of Subtests in Four Personality Inventories." *J Social Psychol* 56:227–44 Ap '62. * (*PA* 37:1247)

83. BORTNER, RAYMAN W. "Superego Functioning and Institutional Adjustment." *Percept & Motor Skills* 14:375–9 Je '62. * (*PA* 37:3408)

84. BORTNER, RAYMAN W. "Test Differences Attributable to Age, Selection Processes, and Institutional Effects." *J Gerontol* 17:58–60 Ja '62. * (*PA* 36:5FI58B)

85. BURK, KENNETH WINFIELD. *Biographic, Interest, and Personality Characteristics of Purdue Speech and Hearing Graduates.* Doctor's thesis, Purdue University (Lafayette, Ind.), 1962. (*DA* 23:3021)

86. CATTELL, RAYMOND B. "Personality Assessment Based Upon Functionally Unitary Personality Traits, Factor Analytically Demonstrated," pp. 198–219. (*PA* 37:4977) In *Personality Research.* Proceedings of the XIV International Congress of Applied Psychology, Vol. 2. Copenhagen, Denmark: Munksgaard, Ltd., 1962. Pp. 229. *

87. CATTELL, RAYMOND B. "Psychological Measurement of Anxiety and Depression: A Quantitative Approach." Discussion, pp. S24–8. *Can Psychiatric Assn J* 7(sup):S11–28 '62. *

88. CATTELL, RAYMOND B., AND MORONY, JOHN H. "The Use of the 16 PF in Distinguishing Homosexuals, Normals, and General Criminals." *J Consult Psychol* 26:531–40 D '62. *

89. FRANCESCO, E. "A Pervasive Value: Conventional Religiosity." *J Social Psychol* 57:467–70 Ag '62. * (*PA* 37: 4855)

90. HALLER, A. O., AND WOLFF, CAROLE ELLIS. "Personality Orientations of Farm, Village, and Urban Boys." *Rural Sociol* 27:275–93 S '62. * (*PA* 37:2989)

91. HALLER, ARCHIBALD O., AND THOMAS, SHAILER. "Personality Correlates of the Socioeconomic Status of Adolescent Males." *Sociometry* 25:398–404 D '62. * (*PA* 38:4094)

92. HEMPHILL, JOHN K.; GRIFFITHS, DANIEL E.; AND FREDERIKSEN, NORMAN; WITH THE ASSISTANCE OF GLEN STICE, LAURENCE IANNACCONE, WILLIAM COFFIELD, AND SYDELL CARLTON. *Administrative Performance and Personality: A Study of the Principal in a Simulated Elementary School.* New York: Bureau of Publications, Teachers College, Columbia University, 1962. Pp. xix, 432. *

93. HENDRICKSON, DONNA. "Personality Variables: Significant Departures of Occupational Therapists From Population Norms." *Am J Occup Ther* 16:127–30 My–Je '62. * (*PA* 37:5203)

94. HOLLAND, JOHN L., AND ASTIN, ALEXANDER W. "The Prediction of the Academic, Artistic, Scientific, and Social Achievement of Undergraduates of Superior Scholastic Aptitude." *J Ed Psychol* 53:132–43 Je '62. * (*PA* 37:2010)

95. LaFORGE, ROLFE. "A Correlational Study of Two Personality Tests: The MMPI and Cattell 16 PF." *J Consult Psychol* 26:402–11 O '62. * (*PA* 39:1743)

96. RUBY, WALTER McCLINTOCK, JR. *An Investigation of Differentiating Personality Factors Between Achieving and Low Achieving College Students.* Doctor's thesis, University of Tennessee (Knoxville, Tenn.), 1962. (*DA* 23:3785)

97. STEWART, HORACE F., JR. *A Study of the Relationship Between Certain Personality Measures and Hallucinoid Visual Imagery.* Doctor's thesis, University of Florida (Gainesville, Fla.), 1962. (*DA* 24:827)

98. AIKEN, LEWIS R., JR. "The Relationships of Dress to Selected Measures of Personality in Undergraduate Women." *J Social Psychol* 59:119–28 F '63. * (*PA* 38:910)

99. BENDIG, A. W. "A Note on Cattell's Radicalism (Q_1) Scale." *J Social Psychol* 60:107–13 Je '63. * (*PA* 38:4173)

99a. BURDICK, LOIS A. "Analysis of the Sixteen Personality Factor Questionnaire and Elementary Student Teachers at Indiana State College." *Teach Col J* 35:57–9+ N '63. *

100. CATTELL, RAYMOND B. Chap. 9, "The Personality and Motivation of the Researcher From Measurements of Contemporaries and From Biography," pp. 119–31. In *Scientific Creativity: Its Recognition and Development.* Edited by Calvin W. Taylor and Frank Barron. New York: John Wiley & Sons, Inc., 1963. Pp. xxiv, 419. * (*PA* 38:2689)

101. HORN, JOHN. "Second-Order Factors in Questionnaire Data." *Ed & Psychol Meas* 23:117–34 sp '63. * (*PA* 38:2695)

102. ISAACSON, ROBERT L.; McKEACHIE, WILBERT J.; AND MILHOLLAND, JOHN E. "Correlation of Teacher Personality Variables and Student Ratings." *J Ed Psychol* 54:110–7 Ap '63. * (*PA* 38:3288)

103. KAPOOR, S. D. "A Comparative Study of the Personality Questionnaire Items Presented in the 1st and 2nd Person." *Manas* 10(1):34–41 '63. * (*PA* 38:8496)

104. KELLY, CHARLES M. "Mental Ability and Personality Factors in Listening." *Q J Speech* 49:152–6 Ap '63. *

105. MARKS, JOHN; STAUFFACHER, JAMES C.; AND LYLE, CURTIS. "Predicting Outcome in Schizophrenia." *J Abn & Social Psychol* 66:117–27 F '63. * (*PA* 37:7076)

106. MITCHELL, JAMES V., JR. "A Comparison of the First and Second Order Dimensions of the 16 PF and CPI Inventories." *J Social Psychol* 61:151–66 O '63. * (*PA* 38:8449)

107. NELSON, THOMAS D. *Judgmental Diagnoses Versus Actuarial Diagnoses.* Doctor's thesis, University of Denver (Denver, Colo.), 1963. (*DA* 24:2126)

107a. OSMON, WILLIAM R. "The Personality Patterns of Failing Freshmen, Indiana State College, 1961–62." *Teach Col J* 35:61–5 N '63. *

108. WARBURTON, F. W.; BUTCHER, H. J.; AND FORREST, G. M. "Predicting Student Performance in a University Department of Education." *Brit J Ed Psychol* 33:68–79 F '63. * (*PA* 38:1416)

MAURICE LORR, *Chief, Outpatient Psychiatric Research Laboratory, Veterans Benefits Office; and Lecturer in Psychology, Catholic University of America; Washington, D.C.*

The 16 PF purports to measure all the main dimensions of personality revealed by factor analysis. Forms A and B each consist of 187 items and include 10 to 13 items for each factor. The simplified short Form C consists of 105 items. The majority of statements concern interests and preferences. The remaining statements represent the customary self-reports of behavior. All items are in trichotomous form.

The inventory yields 16 primary factor scores and 2 second order factor scores.

The Handbook has been carefully prepared and offers an unusually wide range of information. Norms for the 1961–62 editions of Forms A and B are given, in the form of stens, in a norms supplement. There are separate norm tables for each form and for Forms A and B combined, for American college students by sex. The Handbook Supplement for Form C presents general population and college student norms (both by sex) for this form. Except for age, characteristics of the norm samples such as occupation, social class, and source are not delineated. This is certainly an elementary requirement.

The corrected split-half reliabilities for the 1956–57 editions of Forms A and B combined range from .93 to .71 and thus from .87 to .54 for single forms. These values suggest that many single form scale internal consistencies are satisfactory for group prediction only. Only a few two-week interval stability indices are offered although such coefficients are of importance for understanding a trait and for prediction. As of January 1964 no reliability data had been published for the 1961–62 editions of Forms A and B. It would also be highly desirable to have intraclass coefficients to represent factor internal consistency. In this connection Levonian (73) studied the 16 PF with regard to its intrafactor interitem phi correlations. He reported that of the 1,612 significant interitem correlations (a) only 183 were intrafactor correlations; (b) of the 183, 10 were in a direction opposite from that intended by test designers; (c) nearly 25 per cent of all intrafactor correlations were in a direction opposite that intended by the test designers; (d) 30 per cent of the items had no significant intrafactor correlations. Such evidence of substantial within-factor heterogeneity calls for a critical reappraisal of scale homogeneity. A reading of the items defining the factors is supportive of this conclusion. Many of the statements making up a factor are introspectively quite diverse.

The claim is made that each of the questionnaire factors corresponds to a primary factor in behavior situations or in the *Objective-Analytic Personality Test Batteries*. Evidence of such correspondence is not explicitly offered although it should be. A report by Becker (60) raises doubts concerning the independence of

the 16 factor scales. His factor analysis of all Form A and B 16 PF scores and scores from Guilford-Martin personality inventories showed at best 8 distinguishable factors within the 16 PF and 5 within the 13 Guilford-Martin factors. This does not imply that there may not be more than eight 16 PF factors but rather that, if such exist, they do not emerge as independent sources of variance as revealed by the tests as presently scored.

Data are provided for predictive use in industry, college, and clinic in the form of possible profile matching and criterion estimation. Tables in the Handbook offer a set of 28 representative occupational profiles. A supplement (IPAT Information Bulletin No. 1, 1959) provides factor sten profiles for 9 clinical syndrome groupings. Other Information Bulletins present additional occupational and clinical data. On the other hand, no statistical data are given as to how well the 16 PF scores discriminate among the clinical or the occupational groups. The Handbook suggests the use of the "pattern similarity coefficient" and offers a nomograph for its rapid calculation. Specification or regression equations are given for a variety of criteria such as accident proneness, scholastic performance, and occupational success of salesmen. However, such essential facts as multiple correlation coefficients and number of misclassifications are not given.

The development of the 16 PF represents and, indeed, reflects a high order of technical skill. Although at present it appears to be the best factor-based personality inventory available, it is the reviewer's view that the 16 PF is still primarily a research instrument. Its major shortcomings are those reported by Levonian and by Becker. These investigations suggest that further critical examination of scale structure and the number of factors measurable by 16 PF is needed. It is recognized that the process of construct validation is lengthy, laborious, and never ended. At the same time more specific facts concerning the construct validity of individual factor scales is needed.

For a review by C. J. Adcock, see 5:112; for reviews by Charles M. Harsh, Ardie Lubin, and J. Richard Wittenborn, see 4:87.

[175]

★A Social Competence Inventory for Adults. Adults; 1960; behavior checklist for use with mentally retarded and senile persons; 1 form (4 pages);

manual (8 pages) ; no data on reliability; $1.25 per 10 tests; 35¢ per specimen set; postage extra; [30] minutes; Katharine M. Banham; Family Life Publications, Inc. *

WILLIAM J. EICHMAN, *Chief, Psychology Service, Veterans Administration Hospital, Salem, Virginia.*

The *Social Competence Inventory for Adults* is described by the author as a checklist and as a standardized interview. It is similar to the *Vineland Social Maturity Scale* in purpose and approach. The trained interviewer must obtain information from a reliable and competent person who is well acquainted with the person involved. The development of the inventory was stimulated by the federal law providing for grants-in-aid to the permanently and totally disabled adult. The author points out that intelligence test results have relatively little relationship to the social adjustment in the moron group with IQ's between 50 and 75. Use of the Vineland scale was considered as an instrument to assess social competency but many of the items appeared to be unsuitable for adults. Many of the items of the present scale "were selected from case records of persons who had proved incapable of taking care of themselves." They are arranged in four groups with relatively homogeneous content. These are (*a*) bodily control, (*b*) sensory or memory deficit, (*c*) care of self, and (*d*) emotional control. The scoring system is a simple point scale with a total of 55 items. Correlations between social competence scores and IQ's on the Stanford-Binet and Wechsler-Bellevue are presented for six groups, ranging in size from 9 to 27, with a median correlation of .51. General interpretive statements are offered for different levels of total score. Validation of the classifications of total score is based upon an analysis of "case histories of more than twenty adults who had a long record of incompetence" but no data are given.

There is a distinct need for an instrument of this type. The inventory has potentiality for meeting this need, but the data provided in the manual do not adequately demonstrate this. The individual items have face validity to a high degree within each category and with regard to "social competence" in general. Nevertheless, studies of item relationship to part score and to total score should be done. Ideally, the item pool should be factor analyzed to support or change the a priori categories which

are currently used. Normative studies should be conducted separately for the various levels of intelligence where the social competence inventory has potential utility. In addition, thorough validity studies should be undertaken.

The *Social Competence Inventory* has current utility as a guided interview when there is question of "social competence." It certainly has the validity of the unstandardized interview and subjective judgment which are currently used. It further guarantees that certain crucial areas of daily living will not be overlooked by the interviewer. It should not interfere with interviewing in other potentially crucial areas; it seems quite possible that the items are not all inclusive.

"Social competency" is not a simple criterion, and it seems unlikely that any psychometric approach based on traditional principles can be adequate to the task of measurement. We can expect various configural effects in general terms, and we can expect considerable variability from one social context to another. In addition, the criterion is not a psychological one which is intrinsic to the behavior of the subject. Instead, social competence can be basically defined as the tolerance of the environment toward the subject.

In general, the inventory appears to be a useful first step toward meeting the social need of evaluating "competency." However, it is a primitive beginning and no evidence for validity or reliability is available. At the present time utility seems confined to the area of a guided interview; total and part scores have not been sufficiently studied to be useful.

JEROME D. PAUKER, *Assistant Professor of Clinical Psychology, Medical School, University of Minnesota, Minneapolis, Minnesota.*

This inventory was devised, the author says, "in the absence....of a suitable rating scale of social competence for adults of limited mental ability." She says that the *Vineland Social Maturity Scale,* for example, has many items which are not appropriate for adults. The *Social Competence Inventory for Adults* is not by any means a standardized technique, nor does its author represent it as such. She states in her Examiner's Manual: "A rating scale of this kind could never be considered an exact measuring device. It is merely a means of general classification." It is essentially an aid in interviewing, containing 55 items divided into sections entitled Motor Skills and Control, Perception and Memory, Self-Care and Self-Help, and Social Relationships and Emotional Control. Those items which apply to a person in question are given a score of 1, and the total score is the sum of the applicable items.

The manual presents some guidelines for interpretation of total scores, e.g.: "An individual who scores between 15 and 30 has inadequate social competence for independent living." These are based on the author's experience with the inventory. She provides no research data to back up such conclusions, although she does write, "This scoring system is tentative, pending standardization on a sample cross-section of the population." She presents some very sketchy and inadequate comparisons with Stanford-Binet and Wechsler-Bellevue IQ's; these might better have been omitted from the manual.

This inventory, then, provides a guide for inquiry into a wide range of appropriate, practical aspects of adult social and independent living. Beyond this, the scoring system which the test author presents remains in need of evaluation.

[176]

*Social Intelligence Test: George Washington University Series, Revised Form. Grades 9–16 and adults; 1930–55; 3 editions; manual ('55, 5 pages); reliability data and norms for total scores only; $3.75 per 25 tests of a or b; $3.25 per 25 tests of c; 75¢ per specimen set of all 3 editions; postage extra; F. A. Moss, Thelma Hunt, K. T. Omwake, and L. G. Woodward (a and manual); Center for Psychological Service. *

a) SECOND EDITION. 1930–55; 6 scores: judgment in social situations, recognition of the mental state of the speaker, memory for names and faces, observation of human behavior, sense of humor, total; 1 form ('49, 11 pages); names and faces sheet ('48, 1 page); 49(55) minutes.

b) SHORT EDITION. 1944–55; 5 scores: same as for Second Edition except for omission of memory for names and faces; 1 form ('44, 6 pages); 40(45) minutes.

c) SP (SPECIAL) EDITION. 1947–55; 3 scores: judgment in social situations, observation of human behavior, total; 1 form ('47, 4 pages); 30(35) minutes.

REFERENCES

1–20. See 40:1253.
21–29. See 3:96.
30–36. See 4:89.
37. BRUCE, MARTIN M. "The Prediction of Effectiveness as a Factory Foreman." Psychol Monogr 67(12):1–17 '53. * (PA 28:5019)
38. BASS, BERNARD M.; KARSTENDIEK, BARBARA; McCULLOUGH, GERALD; AND PRUITT, RAY C. "Validity Information Exchange, No. 7-024: D.O.T. Code 2-66.01, 2-66.11, 2-66.12, 2-66.23, Policemen and Detectives, Public Service." Personnel Psychol 7:159–60 sp '54. *
39. BRUCE, MARTIN M. "Validity Information Exchange, No. 7-004: D.O.T. Code 0-97.61, Manager, Sales." Personnel Psychol 7:128–9 sp '54. *
40. BRUCE, MARTIN M. "Validity Information Exchange, No. 7-076: D.O.T. Code 5-91.101, Foreman II." Personnel Psychol 7:418–9 au '54. *

41. KAESS, WALTER A., AND WITRYOL, SAM L. "Memory for Names and Faces: A Characteristic of Social Intelligence?" J Appl Psychol 39:457–62 D '55. * (PA 30:6866)
42. BRUCE, MARTIN M. "Normative Data Information Exchange, No. 26." Personnel Psychol 9:533–4 w '56. *
43. BRUCE, MARTIN M. "Normative Data Information Exchange, No. 27." Personnel Psychol 9:535–6 w '56. *
44. BRUCE, MARTIN M. "Validity Information Exchange, No. 10-3: D.O.T. Code 1-86.11, Salesmen, Commercial Equipment and Supplies." Personnel Psychol 10:77–8 sp '57. *
45. HECHT, ROBERT, AND BRUCE, MARTIN M. "Normative Data Information Exchange, No. 10-38." Personnel Psychol 10:529 w '57. *
46. JUERGENSON, ELWOOD M. The Relationship Between Success in Teaching Vocational Agriculture and Ability to Make Sound Judgments as Measured by Selected Instruments. Doctor's thesis, Pennsylvania State University (University Park, Pa.), 1958. (DA 19:96)
47. ARON, JOEL, AND HECHT, ROBERT. "Normative Data Information Exchange, No. 12-15." Personnel Psychol 12:331 su '59. *
48. CRANE, WILLIAM J. "Screening Devices for Occupational Therapy Majors." Am J Occup Ther 16:131–2 My-Je '62. * (PA 37:4078)
49. Normative Information: Manager and Executive Testing. New York: Richardson, Bellows, Henry & Co., Inc., May 1963. Pp. 45. *
50. HERBERT, N., AND TURNBULL, G. H. "Personality Factors and Effective Progress in Teaching." Ed R 16:24–31 N '63. *

For reviews by Glen U. Cleeton and Howard R. Taylor, see 3:96; for a review by Robert L. Thorndike, see 40:1253.

[177]

★Spiral Aftereffect Test. Ages 5 and over; 1958; brain damage; individual; 1 form (1 Archimedes spiral); manual (5 pages); supplementary data (8 pages, reprint of 23 below); record form (1 page); $75 per set of spiral, battery operated testing apparatus, record form, manual, and supplementary data; $1.25 per spiral; 75¢ per 50 record forms; $1 per manual and supplementary data; postage extra; [3–10] minutes; Psychological Research & Development Corporation. * [Many variations of the spiral aftereffect procedure are in use. The references and reviews below relate to the procedure in general as well as to the specific test apparatus and accessories described in this entry.]

REFERENCES

1. FREEMAN, ELLIS, AND JOSEY, WILLIAM E. "Quantitative Visual Index to Memory Impairment: A Preliminary Report." Arch Neurol & Psychiatry 62:794–7 D '49. * (PA 25:4377)
2. STANDLEE, LLOYD S. "The Archimedes Negative Aftereffect as an Indication of Memory Impairment." J Consult Psychol 17:317 Ag '53. * (PA 28:4325)
3. PRICE, A. COOPER, AND DEABLER, H. L. "Diagnosis of Organicity by Means of Spiral Aftereffects." J Consult Psychol 19:299–302 Ag '55. * (PA 30:5118)
4. GALLESE, ARTHUR J., JR. "Spiral Aftereffect as a Test of Organic Brain Damage." J Clin Psychol 12:254–8 Jl '56. * (PA 31:6511)
5. SAUCER, RAYFORD T., AND DEABLER, HERDIS L. "Perception of Apparent Motion in Organics and Schizophrenics." J Consult Psychol 20:385–9 O '56. * (PA 31:8243)
6. DAVIDS, ANTHONY; GOLDENBERG, LOUIS; AND LAUFER, MAURICE W. "The Relation of the Archimedes Spiral Aftereffect and the Trail Making Test to Brain Damage in Children." J Consult Psychol 21:429–33 O '57. * (PA 33:1256)
7. EYSENCK, H. J.; HOLLAND, H.; AND TROUTON, D. S. "Drugs and Personality: 3, The Effect of Stimulant and Depressant Drugs on Visual After-Effects." J Mental Sci 103:650–5 Jl '57. * (PA 32:4940)
8. GARRETT, EPHRAIM S.; PRICE, A. COOPER; AND DEABLER, HERDIS L. "Diagnostic Testing for Cortical Brain Impairment." A.M.A. Arch Neurol & Psychiatry 77:223–5 F '57. * (PA 32:1926)
9. HARDING, GEORGE F.; GLASSMAN, SIDNEY; AND HELZ, WILLIAM C. "Maturation and the Spiral Aftereffect." J Abn & Social Psychol 54:276–7 Mr '57. * (PA 33:5281)
10. PAGE, H. A.; RAKITA, G.; KAPLAN, H. K.; AND SMITH, N. B. "Another Application of the Spiral Aftereffect in the Determination of Brain Damage." J Consult Psychol 21:89–91 F '57. * (PA 32:809)
11. SPIVACK, GEORGE, AND LEVINE, MURRAY. "The Spiral Aftereffect and Reversible Figures as Measures of Brain

Damage and Memory." *J Personality* 25:767–78 D '57. *
(*PA* 33:2791)

12. STILSON, DONALD W.; GYNTHER, MALCOLM D.; AND
GERTZ, BORIS. "Base Rate and the Archimedes Spiral Illusion." *J Consult Psychol* 21:435–7 O '57. * (*PA* 33:1323)

13. AARONSON, BERNARD S. "Age, Intelligence, Aphasia and
the Spiral After-Effect in an Epileptic Population." *J Clin
Psychol* 14:18–21 Ja '58. *

14. BERGER, DAVID; EVERSON, RICHARD; RUTLEDGE, LOUIS;
AND KASKOFF, YALE DAVID. "The Spiral Aftereffect in a
Neurological Setting." *J Consult Psychol* 22:249–55 Ag '58. *
(*PA* 34:1867)

15. GILBERSTADT, HAROLD; SCHEIN, JEROME; AND ROSEN,
ALBERT. "Further Evaluation of the Archimedes Spiral Aftereffect." *J Consult Psychol* 22:243–8 Ag '58. * (*PA* 34:1870)

16. GOLDBERG, LEWIS R., AND SMITH, PHILIP A. "The
Clinical Usefulness of the Archimedes Spiral in the Diagnosis
of Organic Brain Damage." *J Consult Psychol* 22:153–7 Ap
'58. * (*PA* 35:3484)

17. HOLLAND, H. C., AND BEECH, H. R. "The Spiral Aftereffect as a Test of Brain Damage." *J Mental Sci* 104:466–71
Ap '58. * (*PA* 33:8353)

18. LONDON, PERRY, AND BRYAN, JAMES H. "The Influence
of Instructions on Spiral Aftereffect Reports." Abstract. *Am
Psychologist* 13:335 Jl '58. *

19. SCHEIN, JEROME DANIEL. *An Experimental Investigation of Some Psychological Functions in Detection of Brain
Damage.* Doctor's thesis, University of Minnesota (Minneapolis, Minn.), 1958. (*DA* 19:2151)

20. PHILBRICK, EMILY B. "The Validity of the Spiral
Aftereffect as a Clinical Tool for Diagnosis of Organic Brain
Pathology." *J Consult Psychol* 23:39–43 F '59. * (*PA* 34:1410)

21. SPIVACK, GEORGE, AND LEVINE, MURRAY. "Spiral Aftereffect and Measures of Satiation in the Brain-Injured and
Normal Subjects." *J Personality* 27:211–27 Je '59. * (*PA*
34:3899)

22. TRUSS, CARROLL V., AND ALLEN, ROBERT M. "Duration
of the Spiral Aftereffect in Cerebral Palsy: An Exploratory
Study." *Percept & Motor Skills* 9:216–8 S '59. * (*PA* 34:
6488)

23. BLAU, THEODORE H., AND SCHAFFER, ROBERT E. "The
Spiral Aftereffect Test (SAET) as a Predictor of Normal and
Abnormal Electroencephalographic Records in Children." *J
Consult Psychol* 24:35–42 F '60. * (*PA* 34:8232)

24. DAY, R. H. "The Aftereffect of Seen Movement and
Brain Damage." *J Consult Psychol* 24:311–5 Ag '60. * (*PA*
35:2508)

25. EYSENCK, H. J., AND EYSENCK, S. B. G. "Reminiscence
on the Spiral Aftereffect as a Function of Length of Rest and
Number of Prerest Trials." *Percept & Motor Skills* 10:93–4
Ap '60. * (*PA* 35:5569)

26. EYSENCK, H. J., AND HOLLAND, H. "Length of Spiral
Aftereffect as a Function of Drive." *Percept & Motor Skills*
11:129–30 O '60. * (*PA* 35:1559)

27. LONDON, PERRY, AND BRYAN, JAMES H. "Theory and
Research on the Clinical Use of the Archimedes Spiral."
J General Psychol 62:113–25 Ja '60. * (*PA* 34:8258)

28. McDONOUGH, JOSEPH M. "Critical Flicker Frequency
and the Spiral Aftereffect With Process and Reactive Schizophrenics." *J Consult Psychol* 24:150–5 Ap '60. * (*PA* 34:
8167)

29. MAYER, EMANUELA, AND COONS, W. H. "Motivation and
the Spiral Aftereffect With Schizophrenics and Brain-Damaged
Patients." *Can J Psychol* 14:269–74 D '60. * (*PA* 35:4961)

30. SCHEIN, JEROME D. "The Duration of the Archimedes
Spiral Afterimage in the Diagnosis of Brain Damage." *J
Consult Psychol* 24:209–306 Ag '60. * (*PA* 35:2247)

31. SAPPENFIELD, BERT R., AND RIPKE, ROBERT J. "Validities of Three Visual Tests for Differentiating Organics From
Schizophrenics and Normals." *J Clin Psychol* 17:276–8 Jl
'61. * (*PA* 38:8892)

32. SINDBERG, RONALD M. "Some Effects of Stimulus Variation on Spiral Aftereffect in Organic and Nonorganic Subjects." *J Consult Psychol* 25:129–36 Ap '61. * (*PA* 36:4JG20S)

33. SOUEIF, M. I., AND METWALLY, A. "Testing for Organicity in Egyptian Psychiatric Patients." *Acta Psychologica*
18(4):285–96 '61. * (*PA* 36:5JG85S)

34. BRYAN, JAMES H., AND LODER, EDWARD. "Anxiety and
the Spiral Aftereffect Test." *J Consult Psychol* 26:351–4 Ag
'62. * (*PA* 38:3535)

35. FREUD, SHELDON L. *A Study of Physiological Mechanisms Underlying the Spiral After Effect.* Doctor's thesis,
University of Connecticut (Storrs, Conn.), 1962. (*PA* 23:1781)

36. LEVINE, MURRAY, AND SPIVACK, GEORGE. "Adaptation
to Repeated Exposure to the Spiral Visual Aftereffect in
Brain Damaged, Emotionally Disturbed, and Normal Individuals." *Percept & Motor Skills* 14:425–6 Je '62. * (*PA*
37:3539)

37. SCOTT, THOMAS R., AND MEDLIN, RUFUS E. "Psychophysical Measurement of the Spiral Aftereffect: The MMG."
Am J Psychol 75:319–21 Je '62. * (*PA* 37:4166)

38. WHITMYRE, JOHN W., AND KURTZKE, JOHN F. "The
Archimedes Spiral Aftereffect and Impaired Mentation." *J
Clin Psychol* 18:118–21 Ap '62. * (*PA* 38:8930)

39. CLARIDGE, G. S., AND HERRINGTON, R. N. "An EEG
Correlate of the Archimedes Spiral After-Effect and Its Relationship With Personality." *Behav Res Ther* 1:217–29 D '63. *

40. FREUD, SHELDON L. "Duration as a Measure of the
Spiral Aftereffect." *Percept & Motor Skills* 17:643–6 O '63. *
(*PA* 38:5073)

41. KORMAN, MAURICE, AND BLUMBERG, STANLEY. "Comparative Efficiency of Some Tests of Cerebral Damage." *J
Consult Psychol* 27:303–9 Ag '63. * (*PA* 38:2985)

42. MANN, LESTER; ALVORD, AGNES; AND PRICE, HARRY.
"The Spiral Aftereffect Test (SAET) as a Predictor of
School Adjustment and Achievement in First Grade Children."
J Clin Psychol 19:206–8 Ap '63. * (*PA* 39:5078)

43. SCOTT, THOMAS R.; BRAGG, ROBERT A.; AND SMARR,
ROY G. "Brain Damage Diagnosis With the MMG." *J Consult
Psychol* 27:45–53 F '63. * (*PA* 37:8146)

WILLIAM J. EICHMAN, *Chief, Psychology
Service, Veterans Administration Hospital,
Salem, Virginia.*

The spiral aftereffect equipment supplied by
this company does not represent a test in the
accepted sense of the term. Although considerable work has been done with this perceptual
phenomenon, techniques and equipment have
varied widely from one investigation to another and cannot be considered entirely comparable. Precise norms on large representative
samples have not been obtained with any single
procedure. This disadvantage is ameliorated by
the fact that perception of the after image
tends to be an all or none phenomenon; but
nevertheless, it remains a problem. The *Spiral
Aftereffect Test* equipment is accompanied by
a manual, scoring sheets, and a reprint by Blau
and Schaffer (*23*). The manual is not at all
satisfactory, but the reprint does contain useful data. These will be discussed separately.
In addition, there is considerable accumulated
literature on the spiral aftereffect task which
deserves additional comment.

The equipment is battery-operated and appears to be well constructed. It has clockwise
and counterclockwise rotations at a speed of
approximately 82 rpm. An Archimedes spiral
of 920° is used. The test procedure is simple
and objective and should not take over 15
minutes for administration. Only a single page
is devoted to interpretation of results, but no
data are presented in regard to reliability, validity, or norms. No references to research are
given. The phrasing contained in the manual
obviously refers to use of the test in a neuropsychiatric setting with adults. Eight trials are
given with a score of 1 for each aftereffect
which is perceived. The normal or psychiatric
patient is expected to achieve the perfect score
of 8; performance at the other end of the
range is indicative of "intra-cranial pathology."
Aside from a few cautionary remarks regarding false positives, this is all that the manual
provides. Thus, it is completely inadequate for
clinical or experimental use.

The reprint which is included with the equipment must be considered as a supplemental manual, although this is not stated in any explicit manner. The instructions for administration differ slightly from the manual to the reprint. Blau and Schaffer present a brief, but adequate, review of the literature up to 1958. Thirteen of these studies used adults as subjects and dealt with the detection of organic pathology; three dealt with children, but one of these was a normative study exclusively. Blau and Schaffer studied 420 children who were examined at an outpatient psychological clinic. A U-shaped distribution of scores was found for this sample. The majority of children achieved perfect scores, and the second peak in the distribution is at 0. None of these children were thought to have organic pathology. Other tests utilized included the Bender-Gestalt, Draw-A-Person, and selected tests from the WISC. The criterion was EEG records. Thus, these investigators set for themselves the most difficult task of discriminating borderline "organic" children (those with low scores) from a normal group (those with high scores). They report extremely significant results for the SAET and less conspicuous but significant prediction for most of the other tests. They report 100 per cent correct prediction for normal EEG records and 86 per cent prediction for the abnormal records.

This very significant prediction is extremely unusual for studies in the area of organic brain damage. The basic criticism of most tests for organic brain damage is that the criteria are very complex, whereas the test is usually quite a simple and limited sampling of the subject's behavior. Most studies use an "organic" group and compare it with one or more control groups. Although the number and types of brain damage are usually reported, the organic group is still dealt with as a homogeneous category. Inconsistent results from one study to another are usually a result of failures to take into account the nature of the brain damage, the location, the severity, and the chronicity. In addition, most studies, whether validation or cross validation, employ an organic group where diagnosis is clearcut. With such groups, it is seldom necessary for psychological tests to be administered. When the test is later applied to more difficult cases in a clinical setting, the results are often quite disappointing. The Blau and Schaffer study avoids this last criticism since their organic subjects do not show symptomatic signs of organic dysfunction. Their experimental task, however, is extremely simple and limited; and it seems too optimistic to expect such positive results in further replications.

The literature on the spiral aftereffects task has expanded considerably since 1958. Blau and Schaffer's hope that other investigators would use their procedures has not been fulfilled except for a few studies. In terms of discriminating adult organics from adult controls, 15 out of 16 studies reviewed report significant results. Thus, this simple task seems to have considerable potentiality for diagnostic screening.

The expanding literature deals with a number of basic psychological or physiological variables which influence the perception of the spiral aftereffect. Several studies indicate that it is only those organics who have memory deficit or impaired mentation who show poor performance. McDonough (28) investigated the process and reactive dimension in schizophrenia and found that these groups do not differ from each other while both can be discriminated from organic subjects. Several studies with normal subjects report that high drive state or anxiety interfere with perception of the after image. Congruent with this, a study by London and Bryan (18) and another study by Mayer and Coons (29) report that organic subjects are able to report the aftereffect when reassuring instructions are used. It seems quite possible that anxiety is an intervening variable in the failure of organic subjects to perceive the aftereffect. Schein's results (30) seem to indicate that the brain damaged patient is more easily confused than the NP patient, that he sees the phenomenon as often as other subjects but fails to report it. Sindberg (32) systematically varied exposure time and speed of rotation with normals, NP patients, and organics. He reports extremely good discrimination of groups (92 per cent of controls and 88 per cent of organics) but also reports that the most successful discrimination is with conditions of medium difficulty. These are at slower rotation speeds than possible with the equipment supplied by this test concern. Optimum exposure time is also greater than that which is used in the Blau and Schaffer study. Several studies report that there is no relationship between task performance and age, sex, intelligence, or length of hospitalization. Reliability appears to be adequate.

Recent literature with children is sparse. Mann and others (*42*) find significant prediction of first grade achievement and adjustment. Bryan and Loder (*34*), using normal children, report that anxious subjects report significantly fewer aftereffects.

In summary, it can be concluded that the spiral aftereffect procedure has considerable potential for the detection of organic brain damage in adults. There are fewer studies with children and greater caution is indicated. The administration of the task is simple, objective, and consumes little time. A fact that seems worthy of note is the successful discrimination of organics from schizophrenic patients; most previous tests for the detection of brain damage appear to have less success in this area. Maximal discrimination appears to be related to a number of variables including instructions, motivational state, exposure time, and rotation speed. The most effective procedure remains to be discovered. Before this task can be standardized, more basic research needs to be done; standardization at this time seems premature. At present, it seems best that the clinician or researcher obtain spiral aftereffect equipment which has adjustable rotation speed rather than the fixed speed provided by this apparatus.

RALPH M. REITAN, *Professor of Psychology (Neurology), and Director, Section of Neuropsychology, Indiana University Medical Center, Indianapolis, Indiana.*

The spiral aftereffect has been investigated rather extensively as a behavioral response subserved by underlying physiological mechanisms of vision (*35*), as an indicator of memory impairment (*1, 2*), and as a test of the organic integrity of the brain. The emphasis in this report will be upon findings related to the last of these areas.

The *Spiral Aftereffect Test* utilizes an Archimedes spiral of 920°, mounted usually on a 6 to 8 inch circular disc. The disc is usually rotated at 78 rpm, but various investigators have employed rotation speeds varying from 18 to 100 rpm. The subject views the spiral at distances that have varied from 6 to 8 feet. Varying exposure times have also been used, but a 30-second exposure was characteristic of

the original studies. Instructions to the subject require him to fixate his vision on the rotating spiral. Following the determined exposure time, the subject is asked to report his observation of what the spiral is doing. Four to 10 trials have usually been used.

The apparatus described in the test entry above permits a clockwise and counterclockwise rotation of a standard Archimedes spiral (920°) which is imprinted on a heavy cardboard disc 7¼ inches in diameter. The manual indicates that rotation speed is approximately 82 rpm. The apparatus is compact and works well and easily. However, on a series of four forward and four reverse trials, as called for by the test, a range of 77 to 85 rpm was obtained. On additional trials, totaling 10 forward and 10 reverse, the speed of rotation deteriorated to a low of 69 rpm. A one-year guarantee is provided the purchaser with respect to mechanical difficulty due to faulty manufacture. The instructions for administration and scoring of the test are perfectly straightforward and clear. Scores of 3, 2, or 1 are equated with the following interpretation: "Highly Indicative of the Presence of Intra-Cranial Pathology. Refer for Neurologic and Electroencephalographic Evaluation." This kind of advice regarding interpretation of the results does not appear to be properly qualified in consideration of the diversity of research findings described below.

Price and Deabler (*3*) reported nearly perfect differentiation of 120 patients with central nervous system disease or damage from 40 psychiatric patients and 40 hospital employees, the brain damaged subjects nearly always failing to report the aftereffect in contrast to the regular reports of the aftereffect by the other subjects. Garrett and others (*8*) obtained very similar results in a validational study. Another instance of outstanding agreement of SAET with criterion information is represented in the study of Blau and Schaffer (*23*) in which the apparatus described in the above entry was used. In a sample of 420 referrals to an outpatient psychological clinic, 50 children were identified who failed to perceive the aftereffect on 8 trials. Twenty control children were selected, matching the experimental group in age, who had obtained maximal scores in perceiving the aftereffect. An independent review of EEG tracings was made for these 70 children, with classifications of normal and abnormal assigned. The normal children were identically classified by the two procedures; the SAET was 86 per cent accurate in predicting abnormal EEG records. Other standard psychological tests used in this study were significant but less accurate in their correlation with EEG classifications. Blau and Schaffer conclude that the SAET "probably in combination with one or more standard psychological instruments, would seem to be the best available technique" for determining which patients should be referred for neurological study. This conclusion, however, is not justified by the design of the study since the groups were selected to maximize SAET differences rather than differences in performances on the other tests used.

A considerable number of studies, using various aftereffect procedures, have reported less striking findings than those cited above. Gallese (4) found that 3 per cent of persons without brain damage were misclassified whereas 66 per cent of persons with cerebral damage (excluding subjects with idiopathic convulsions and brain damage associated with alcoholism) were correctly identified. Page and others (10) found that less than half as many brain damaged subjects reported the aftereffect as did a group with personality disturbances. Davids and others (6) reported that normal children performed better than either children with psychiatric disturbances or brain lesions, but that the group with brain damage was significantly poorer than either other group. Schein (30) found that 37.7 per cent of a brain damaged group failed to report as compared with 8.7 per cent of psychiatric patients and 12.5 per cent of hospitalized normals. Certain of his results suggested, however, that the brain damaged subjects may perceive the aftereffect but are more readily confused than other subjects and fail to report it. Aaronson's results (13) indicated that 44 per cent of 65 epileptic patients made two or more errors, and poor performances were associated with lower Wechsler scores, difficulty in naming common objects, and sensory perceptual impairment especially toward the right side of the body. His findings raise a question of the influence on SAET results of inability to verbalize reactions to an ambiguous stimulus situation. The questions raised by Schein and Aaronson are offered support by the results of a study by Whitmyre and Kurtzke (38). They composed

two groups with brain damage, one having defective mentation as judged from physical neurological examination and the other showing no such apparent defect. The group without mentation defect was comparable to a group with schizophrenic reactions whereas the group with impaired mentation failed to report the aftereffect significantly more frequently than did the other two groups. Spivack and Levine (21) found that the presence of aftereffect was statistically less frequent in a brain damaged group than in controls, but that absence of aftereffect was practically inefficient as a diagnostic sign. The duration of aftereffect, however, was greater for brain damaged subjects. In a later study (36), these investigators confirmed the finding regarding duration of aftereffect and also found that normals and emotionally disturbed subjects demonstrated an increased failure, as compared to the brain damaged group, to report aftereffect in the later trials of a series. Holland and Beech (17), however, found that the duration of aftereffect was reduced in brain damaged subjects as compared to controls, but that both groups were generally able to see the aftereffect. Gilberstadt and others (15) obtained results with regard to reported perception of aftereffect that were within the range of studies reported above. However, when base-rate data were applied, there was no improvement in diagnostic efficiency provided by the test scores. Goldberg and Smith (16) found that normals reported aftereffect in every instance, but that psychiatric, post-EST, and brain damaged subjects, in respective order, performed with decreasing efficiency. When scores were adjusted for age these latter groups became statistically indistinguishable. Generally, however, insignificant relationships between age and perception of aftereffect have been reported. Berger and others (14) found that 28 per cent of patients admitted to a neurological ward were unable to perform satisfactorily on the spiral task. While performances were unrelated to a number of neurological variables, they were significantly related to spinal fluid findings, visual field studies, and global neurological judgments of brain damage. London and Bryan (27) and Bryan and Loder (34) have reported results suggesting that anxiety provoked by the test requirements or by specially structured situations may inhibit reports or possibly perception of aftereffect. In a detailed study, Sindberg (*32*) found that only 6 of 50 brain damaged subjects reported aftereffect 6 or more times in 10 trials, but that 46 of 50 neuropsychiatric subjects reported aftereffect. College students gave results almost identical to the neuropsychiatric group. He found that exposure time, rotation speed, and direction of rotation had certain significant effects on reporting aftereffect and felt that multiple factors are of influence. Among the studies reviewed, Philbrick (*20*) was the only investigator who failed to find results of any significance.

The above findings certainly substantiate a conclusion that perception of spiral aftereffect has something to do with the condition of the cerebrum. The efficiency of the test as an indicator of brain damage, however, varies greatly from one study to another. This same statement would be true of almost any test in which identical apparatus has not been used, conditions of testing have varied, and especially a great variety of groups with and without cerebral damage have been employed. The range and variety of conditions subsumed under the category of brain damage is so diverse and variable that uniform, consistent, or even completely compatible results for a single test could hardly be expected. Although the *Spiral Aftereffect Test* is of potential importance, its usefulness still remains to be determined by the individual clinician through experience regarding its contribution to his own data in his specific setting.

[178]

★**Stanford Hypnotic Susceptibility Scale.** College and adults; 1959-62; Forms A ('59), B ('59), C ('62); Form C, which is for research use only, contains more varied items and is not considered a parallel form; manual for Forms A and B ('59, 56 pages, including both forms and sample interrogatory and scoring blanks); manual for Form C ('62, 52 pages, including test and sample scoring booklet); separate scoring blanks ('59, 1 page) for Forms A, B; interrogatory blank ('59, 1 page) for Forms A and B; scoring booklet ('62, 6 pages) for Form C; norms for college students only; 50¢ per pad of 25 scoring blanks; 75¢ per pad of 50 interrogatory blanks; $2.65 per 25 scoring booklets; $3.25 per manual for Forms A and B; $1.50 per manual for Form C; $4.75 per specimen set of all 3 forms; postage extra; (40) minutes; André M. Weitzenhoffer and Ernest R. Hilgard; Consulting Psychologists Press, Inc. *

REFERENCES

1. HILGARD, ERNEST R.; WEITZENHOFFER, ANDRÉ M.; AND GOUGH, PHILIP. "Individual Differences in Susceptibility to Hypnosis." *Proc Nat Acad Sci* 44:1255-9 D 15 '58. *
2. HILGARD, ERNEST R.; WEITZENHOFFER, ANDRÉ M.; LANDES, JUDAH; AND MOORE, ROSEMARIE K. "The Distribution of Susceptibility to Hypnosis in a Student Population: A Study Using the Stanford Hypnotic Susceptibility Scale." *Psychol Monogr* 75(8):1-22 '61. * (*PA* 36:3II22H)
3. LONDON, PERRY, AND FUHRER, MARCUS. "Hypnosis, Motivation, and Performance." *J Personality* 29:321-33 S '61. * (*PA* 37:3386)
4. WEITZENHOFFER, ANDRÉ M., AND SJOBERG, BERNARD M. "Suggestibility With and Without 'Induction of Hypnosis.'" *J Nerv & Mental Dis* 132:204-20 Mr '61. * (*PA* 36:1II04W)
5. HILGARD, ERNEST R. "Lawfulness Within Hypnotic Phenomena," pp. 1-29. In *Hypnosis: Current Problems*. Edited by George H. Estabrooks. New York: Harper & Row, Publishers, Inc., 1962. Pp. ix, 285. *
6. HILGARD, ERNEST R., AND LAUER, LILLIAN W. "Lack of Correlation Between the California Psychological Inventory and Hypnotic Susceptibility." *J Consult Psychol* 26:331-5 Ag '62. * (*PA* 38:4432)
7. LANG, PETER J., AND LAZOVIK, A. DAVID. "Personality and Hypnotic Susceptibility." *J Consult Psychol* 26:317-22 Ag '62. * (*PA* 38:4433)
8. LONDON, PERRY. "Hypnosis in Children: An Experimental Approach." *Int J Clin & Exp Hypnosis* 10:79-91 Ap '62. * (*PA* 37:3385)
9. LONDON, PERRY; COOPER, LESLIE M.; AND JOHNSON, HAROLD J. "Subject Characteristics in Hypnosis Research: 2, Attitudes Towards Hypnosis, Volunteer Status, and Personality Measures; 3, Some Correlates of Hypnotic Susceptibility." *Int J Clin & Exp Hypnosis* 10:13-21 Ja '62. * (*PA* 37:1455)
10. WEITZENHOFFER, ANDRÉ M. "Estimation of Hypnotic Susceptibility in a Group Situation." *Am J Clin Hypnosis* 5:115-26 O '62. * (*PA* 37:5246)
11. BENTLER, P. M. "Interpersonal Orientation in Relation to Hypnotic Susceptibility." *J Consult Psychol* 27:426-31 O '63. * (*PA* 38:4226)
12. BENTLER, P. M., AND HILGARD, ERNEST R. "A Comparison of Group and Individual Induction of Hypnosis With Self-Scoring and Observer-Scoring." *Int J Clin & Exp Hypnosis* 11:49-54 Ja '63. * (*PA* 37:8085)
13. BENTLER, P. M., AND ROBERTS, MARY R. "Hypnotic Susceptibility Assessed in Large Groups." *Int J Clin & Exp Hypnosis* 11:93-7 Ap '63. * (*PA* 38:4430)
14. HILGARD, ERNEST R., AND BENTLER, P. M. "Predicting Hypnotizability From the Maudsley Personality Inventory." *Brit J Psychol* 54:63-9 F '63. * (*PA* 37:8091)
15. SCHULMAN, ROBERT E., AND LONDON, PERRY. "Hypnotic Susceptibility and MMPI Profiles." *J Consult Psychol* 27: 157-60 Ap '63. * (*PA* 37:8101)
16. SHOR, RONALD E., AND ORNE, EMILY CAROTA. "Norms on the Harvard Group Scale of Hypnotic Susceptibility, Form A." *Int J Clin & Exp Hypnosis* 11:39-47 Ja '63. * (*PA* 37:8102)
17. WEITZENHOFFER, ANDRÉ M. "The Nature of Hypnosis: Part 1." *Am J Clin Hypnosis* 5:295-321 Ap '63. * (*PA* 37:8104, title only)

MILTON V. KLINE, *Consulting Psychologist, 345 West 58th Street, New York, New York.*

The Stanford scales, not tests in the usual sense employed by psychologists, were designed to evaluate the general level of susceptibility to hypnosis. Forms A and B are alternate forms of the same scale. Form C, which includes items not found in Forms A and B, provides for the evaluation of more complex hypnotic phenomena such as age regression, hallucinatory experiences, and sensory alterations.

A standardized induction procedure is outlined and a quantitative system for measuring response to this induction approach is well scaled. The scales are well designed for the objective measuring of an experimental subject's response to the verbal induction of hypnosis and his range of hypnotic responses. As such the procedure provides a basis for some comparative evaluations of a group of subjects who may be employed in research studies.

Scoring is very objective and simple. The

Stanford scales are better constructed (standardized) than previously existing clinical scales, but probably more difficult to utilize in a clinical setting than some of the older techniques like the Davis-Husband scale.

While the authors point out the need for careful inquiry after the hypnotic experience and emphasize the significance of subjective reactions with hypnosis, the Stanford scales themselves do not serve as an effective instrument for diagnostic investigation of the meaningfulness or the psychodynamic basis of the subject's reaction to and management of the hypnotic relationship and process.

In the hands of experimental hypnotists, the Stanford scales are useful, well developed instruments for quantifying some aspects of hypnotic response in experimental settings. They would appear to have little value in a clinical setting and the investigator untrained in hypnosis should not attempt to use the scales as a means of learning how to induce hypnosis.

The *Stanford Hypnotic Susceptibility Scale* represents the most recent attempts at measuring responsiveness to the verbal induction of hypnosis. More specifically this scale quantitatively evaluates reactions of a basically college population group to a standardized means of measuring aspects of susceptibility and hypnotizability, the two not necessarily always being the same. In the hands of experienced research investigators, it can be a useful instrument in attempting to compare experimental groups with respect to certain aspects of hypnotic response.

C. Scott Moss, *Mental Health Consultant, National Institute of Mental Health, United States Public Health Service, San Francisco, California.*

This scale is a modification of one developed by Friedlander and Sarbin in 1938,[1] and is an outgrowth of a long term study of individual differences to hypnosis. The authors operationally define "susceptibility" as the number of times the subject acts like a hypnotized person when hypnosis is induced by a standard procedure and measured by standard test items.

Form A tests the susceptibility of those experiencing hypnosis for the first time, and consists of a complete set of instructions for

hypnotic induction and for measuring susceptibility to the induction on 12 specific tasks. Form B is an alternate form for follow-up use and differs in minor detail from Form A. The equivalence of the two forms is demonstrated by standardization data on 124 Stanford students. Retest reliability after a one or two day interval resulted in a correlation of .83. Validity is attested to by the demonstration that some of the higher and lower scoring subjects made respectively better and worse hypnotic subjects on a later date, though there were inconsistencies.

A noteworthy limitation is that norms are based on undergraduate college students, hardly a sample representative of the general population. A related criticism is that these were "coerced volunteers," that is, students in an introductory psychology course who chose the hypnotic experiment in preference to other less palatable experiments. Because of volunteer bias, as well as other factors in subject selection, norms based on various populations, carefully selected in defined ways, are needed. It is to the credit of the authors that they have anticipated many of the objections enumerated here and are currently engaged in the effort to provide more satisfactory normative data.

Another important uncontrolled factor is the so called *social demand* characteristics of the experimental situation. This study was conducted in a college setting by psychology professors, a situation which may predispose students to a high proportion of positive responses with or without hypnosis. The unanswered question is how much of a subject's score is attributable to the demand qualities of the situation and how much to hypnosis, or to put it another way, what would have been the response of these same subjects in a different setting and with hypnosis induced by someone other than an important authority figure?

This last question raises an important theoretical issue, namely, the seeming assumption of the authors that hypnotic susceptibility is a relatively stable personality characteristic. A large number of studies have attempted to establish a relationship between personality traits and hypnotic susceptibility with contradictory and negative results. It is possible that situational factors play a much greater role than has been generally recognized. There is also the confounding probability that once in-

1 FRIEDLANDER, J. W., AND SARBIN, T. R. "The Depth of Hypnosis." *J Abn & Social Psychol* 33:453-75 O '38. *

duced, there is a spontaneous fluctuation in "depth" on an almost moment-to-moment basis.

The authors express the hope that professional as well as research persons will find the scale useful. The likelihood is that practitioners will reject the standardized induction technique as mechanical and inadequate and the test items as injurious to the therapeutic relationship. Most hypnotherapists avoid the use of challenges altogether these days, and the fact that the authors have interspersed easy and difficult items only compounds the problem. Rightly or wrongly, many experienced hypnotherapists also believe there is little or no relationship between trance depth and therapeutic success (the authors apparently differentiate between "susceptibility" and "depth" though this distinction is not made clear in the discussion of their scale).

Form C is also recommended for the second or later testing, when alternate forms of induction are used (the induction procedure is optional), when it is desired to have test items in ascending order of difficulty (making possible an abbreviated administration), or when subjects are being selected for their capacity to experience more varied hypnotic phenomena (the content is richer). Because Form C will often be substituted for Form B, six of the 12 items from Form A are retained unchanged. Despite the differences in test content, the score distributions for Forms A, B, and C are very similar, and according to the authors intercorrelations between test items indicate that all forms are highly saturated with a common factor.

Attention is called to the *Harvard Group Scale of Hypnotic Susceptibility,* Form A (see 112), an adaptation for group administration with self-report scoring of Form A of the Stanford scale. Norms based on data secured from 132 volunteer college students (*16*) indicate that the group-administered version yields results congruent with the individually-administered original. Experience with 79 additional subjects led Bentler and Hilgard (*12*) to the conclusion that self-scores are very similar to observer ratings and that the hypnotic susceptibility manifested in the group is very comparable to that obtained in the individual administration of hypnotic susceptibility tests.

In summary, the Stanford scale represents the latest in a rather extended series of efforts to devise an objective measure of hypnotic susceptibility. While its predecessors have not met with general acceptance by authorities in the field, the present investigators promise a serious and concerted effort to develop objective criteria which will aid the experimentalist in developing both measures of susceptibility and the identification of experiential and personality correlates. The authors' obvious conviction that hypnotic behavior must follow the same laws as other psychological phenomena and therefore can be subjected to laboratory study is most laudatory. It is to be hoped that the apparent feasibility of a group form will encourage the widespread reporting of the use of this scale by a variety of competent research investigators working with diverse subject populations in a multiplicity of settings.

[179]

★Stanford Profile Scales of Hypnotic Susceptibility. College and adults; 1963; 25 scores: agnosia and cognitive distortion (4 item scores plus total), positive hallucinations (4 item scores plus total), negative hallucinations (4 item scores plus total), dreams and regressions (4 item scores plus total), amnesia and post-hypnotic compulsions (3 item scores plus total), total susceptibility; one of the item scores for amnesia and post-hypnotic compulsions is derived from Form A of the *Stanford Hypnotic Susceptibility Scale* and provision is also made for profiling 3 additional scores (loss of motor coordination and 2 subscores) from this scale; Forms 1, 2, (49 pages, both forms presented in a single booklet); forms may be used separately but administration of both is recommended and profile is based upon administration of both; manual (83 pages, includes sample copy of scoring booklet for each form and stimulus cards for 2 subtests); scoring booklet (12–15 pages) for each form; $1.50 per booklet of both forms; $7.75 per 25 sets of scoring booklets for both forms; $2.50 per manual; $4.25 per specimen set; postage extra; administration time not reported; various equipment necessary for administration; Ernest R. Hilgard, André M. Weitzenhoffer (test), Lillian W. Lauer (manual), and Arlene H. Morgan (manual); Consulting Psychologists Press, Inc. *

SEYMOUR FISHER, *Research Professor of Psychology, and Director, Psychopharmacology Laboratory, Boston University School of Medicine, Boston, Massachusetts.*

The *Stanford Profile Scales of Hypnotic Susceptibility* are specially constructed instruments which, at present, have no "validity" in the conventional sense, and consequently are primarily of immediate interest only to researchers. In the foreword to the published test, three general uses are proposed: subject selection, correlation with personality variables, and a change measure of hypnotic susceptibility. However, the test manual itself does not contain any section on "validity," although

Hilgard argues for its "construct validity" (personal communication) and for its overall utility (cf. page 34 of manual which discusses the interpretation of subscale profiles).

The development of these scales represents a reasonable step in Hilgard's (and his Stanford team's) systematic approach to the study of hypnotic behavior. The first step resulted in the publication of the *Stanford Hypnotic Susceptibility Scale;* subsequently, it was felt that, despite the presence of a strong common factor of general susceptibility, sufficient unexplained variance existed to justify moving on to the second step—i.e., a "kind of scale was needed, appropriate to higher scoring subjects, that would be diagnostic of the special areas of susceptibility and insusceptibility."

The Profile Scales yield standard scores on six subscales, each of which can be plotted to provide a profile for the individual subject. Items were clustered on the basis of "intended function," thus representing "intuitive" factors. Judging from the table of intercorrelations, considerable overlap exists among the six subscales; although the authors indicate their awareness of this problem, the disturbing thought still persists: is there really adequate evidence to warrant the use of these Profile Scales rather than a single susceptibility score? Close to 40 per cent of subjects have flat profiles, and almost 75 per cent "can be accounted for as either nondeviating or deviating as much as 1 S.D. in only one subscale." However, the notion that two moderately susceptible hypnotic subjects with equal total scores can be meaningfully differentiated on the basis of patterns of *particular* items which were passed and failed is an intriguing one, and will certainly appeal to the clinically-oriented investigator who seeks reliable psychodynamic correlates of hypnotic performance.

The clinician may be less happy at the realization that much of the variation being measured here becomes manifest following a somewhat superficial (albeit standardized) induction of hypnosis. Is it possible that the perceived need for profile scales might be obviated by intensive efforts to deepen the "trance" maximally prior to a full-dress testing for susceptibility? Available evidence does indeed suggest that for the subjects at both extremes of susceptibility, the nature and sequence of suggestions are probably unimportant; it could well be, however, that for the very group of intermediate subjects for whom these scales are designed, such factors might prove extremely relevant.

One additional characteristic of these Profile Scales merits comment. It is obvious that, in common with all factor-analytic approaches, if other kinds of items or scoring dimensions had been included in the scale contents, other "factors" could be constructed intuitively and empirically; e.g., suggestions of anxiety or increased heart rate might result in an "Autonomic Lability" subscale; or an appropriate scoring modification of existing items could yield a subscale of "Activity-Passivity," first suggested by White[1] many years ago. I am not implying that these other "factors" would necessarily be either more or less useful than the specific ones put forward by the Stanford team; I am, however, emphasizing the fact that these subscales are selective, and only empirical attempts to relate them (and similar subscales) to personality characteristics and other variables can tell us about their ultimate utility and validity. One should always bear in mind the sobering thought that certain "profiles" can be so unique that there are as many different profiles as there are individuals—fingerprint classification, for instance.

Use of the Profile Scales requires additional materials and equipment which do not come with the scales. The materials are generally minor in nature and easily obtainable, but the recommended electrical stimulator and a metal box with light (used for analgesia and hallucinatory tests, respectively) call for some instrumentation of questionable necessity. At the risk of being labeled "antiscientific," this reviewer with clear conscience recommends substituting "mild," "moderate," and "strong" jabs (the experimenter's judgment will provide adequate definition) with a sterile needle for testing analgesia, and two simple flashlights (one on, the other off) for testing positive hallucinations. Should it be objected that these alterations might destroy the standardization norms, I can only question whether the basic stability of these particular phenomena is worthy of writing home about.

In summary, the Profile Scales are available for researchers interested in hypnotic phenomena. Basically, the meaning of these scales is presently unknown, but they offer the investigator a multivariate criterion of hypnotic susceptibility. The Profile Scales should not be confused with the *Stanford Hypnotic Susceptibility Scale,* the latter providing a single index of overall susceptibility or "depth" of hypnosis. The Profile Scales do not replace or compete with the *Stanford Hypnotic Susceptibility Scale* (total scores from the two measures only correlate about .50). Whether the subscale differences in the Profile Scales are more apparent than real remains to be determined; in the meantime, if one is studying the effects of some treatment (e.g., drugs, social influence) on hypnotic susceptibility, profile scores might be more sensitive to treatment effects than a single total score. Similarly, personality correlates and other organismic variables might be more reliably related to particular profiles than to an overall index of susceptibility. Undoubtedly, these Profile Scales deserve—and will receive—close empirical scrutiny by researchers in coming years. Their clinical application must impatiently await further validity findings.

EUGENE E. LEVITT, *Professor of Clinical Psychology, Indiana University School of Medicine, Indianapolis, Indiana.*

The *Stanford Profile Scales of Hypnotic Susceptibility* are essentially an extension of the *Stanford Hypnotic Susceptibility Scale,* of which there are three forms. Forms A and B, which appeared in 1959, are heavily weighted with motor tasks. While these scales have probably been more widely used in a short time than any of their several predecessors, their ability to predict the subject's performance on more complex tasks frequently leaves something to be desired. Form C, which was published in 1962, was an attempt to augment the variety of behaviors which might be tapped in determining hypnotic susceptibility. The Profile Scales represent a further extension of hypnotic tasks in the direction of complexity.

Each of the two forms of the Profile Scales is composed of nine sensory, perceptual, or cognitive phenomena. There are no motor behaviors in either form, but hypnosis is induced via a simple motor task in both, so that at least a sample of such behavior is available. Items on Form 1 are not duplicated on Form 2, but most are parallel either categorically (positive versus negative hallucination) or in terms of

the sense modality involved (analgesia versus heat hallucination). Performance on each of the items in the Profile Scales is assessed on a 4-point scale, with scores ranging from o to 3. The assignment of numerical values to behaviors is on a logical, rather than an empirical, basis, and will require much clinical judgment at times, but it at least permits the scorer to make a stab at taking into account the consensual belief among experienced hypnotists that hypnotic behavior is often not of the all-or-none variety. The standardization data indicate that distributions of scores of a number of items will tend to be bimodal with modes at o and 3. Further investigation is needed to assess the empirical utility of the 4-point scoring system.

Both of the scales require equipment which is not furnished with the test itself. However, the materials needed for the administration of Form 2 are easily obtainable, and it is therefore likely that it will be employed more frequently than Form 1.

The standardization sample consisted of 112 students at Stanford University, whose scores on Form A of the *Stanford Hypnotic Susceptibility Scale* were at least 4. The test constructors point out that the sample thus is not random or unselected, not even from among their own volunteer group. However, this does not undermine the purpose of the Profile Scales, which is to have an objective basis for selecting subjects for hypnosis experiments in which various kinds of behaviors will be required. They are also intended to investigate the hypnotic behavior of the individual who is "moderately susceptible" to hypnosis, i.e., the individual who performs well enough to be used in hypnosis research. There would be little point in establishing a profile or in finding out more about the behavior of an individual who is such a poor hypnotic subject that he could not be used experimentally. Thus, the deliberate discarding of low scorers on the Susceptibility Scale from the standardization sample for the Profile Scales is warranted. The test constructors have carefully avoided generalizations from their restricted samples to broader populations and make no claims about hypnotic behavior in general.

The matter of validity is not taken up in the manual, but this is a calculated omission. There is no need to demonstrate empirical validity for an instrument like the Profile Scales, if their use is limited to the experimental applications suggested by the test constructors. They function like an aptitude test which is composed of items which are themselves instances of the behaviors which the test seeks to measure. Face validity suffices. A degree of empirical validity is implied by the correlations between the Profile Scales and Form A of the Susceptibility Scale (.53 for Form 1 and .47 for Form 2). These correlations are doubtlessly attenuated by the elimination of low scorers on Form A and by the limited range of possible scores on the Profile Scales.

The correlation between scores on Forms 1 and 2 is .75, which may be considered as a reliability estimate since the forms are parallel in terms of items. If the forms are used together as a single instrument, the reliability estimate attained by the Spearman-Brown formula is .86. Correlations between parallel items on the two forms range from .29 to .51. It should be remembered that "poor" hypnotic subjects were eliminated from the standardization sample, which undoubtedly attenuates all these coefficients.

The Profile Scales are not unique in the sense that they are structurally similar to earlier scales for the assessment of hypnotic susceptibility. However, currently they stand alone as the only reasonably objective instrument for the selection of subjects for hypnosis experiments requiring complex behaviors. It is clear that they are intended for experimental use rather than for clinical application, and they appear to have many intriguing potential uses in hypnosis research.

[180]

★Stern Activities Index. Grades 7–16 and adults; 1950–63; also called *Activities Index;* personal needs (see 92 for related tests of environmental press covering the same areas); 42 scores: 30 need scores (abasement-assurance, achievement, adaptability-defensiveness, affiliation-rejection, aggression-blame avoidance, change-sameness, conjunctivity-disjunctivity, counteraction-inferiority avoidance, deference-restiveness, dominance-tolerance, ego achievement, emotionality-placidity, energy-passivity, exhibitionism-inferiority avoidance, fantasied achievement, harm avoidance-risk taking, humanities and social science, impulsiveness-deliberation, narcissism, nurturance-rejection, objectivity-projectivity, order-disorder, play-work, practicalness-impracticalness, reflectiveness, science, sensuality-puritanism, sexuality-prudishness, supplication-autonomy, understanding) and 12 factor scores based on combinations of the need scores (self-assertion, audacity-timidity, intellectual interests, motivation, applied interests, orderliness, submissiveness, closeness, sensuousness, friendliness, expressiveness-constraint, egoism-diffidence); NCS; Form 1158 ('58,

7 pages); combined scoring and college norms manual ('63, 30 pages plus sample copies of this index and each of the *Environment Indexes*) for this test and the *College Characteristics Index* (see 92); need score profile ('63, 1 page); factor score profile ('63, 1 page); no data on reliability and validity; manual contains college norms only (profile reports based on high school students and adults available on request when scoring service is used); separate answer sheets must be used; 25¢ per test; $3.25 per 50 NCS answer sheets; $6 per set of hand scoring stencils (machine scoring by the distributor only); $3.50 per scoring and norms manual; postpaid; scoring and profiling fees: 75¢ to 95¢ per answer sheet, depending on quantity; see 671 for prices of other services; (20–90) minutes; George G. Stern; distributed by National Computer Systems. *

REFERENCES

1. NAUGLE, FRED W.; STERN, GEORGE G.; AND ESCHENFELDER, WILLIAM. "The Derivation of Quantitative Personality Models for the Assessment and Prediction of Performance." Abstract. *Am Psychologist* 11:356 Ag '56. *
2. STERN, GEORGE G.; STERN, MORRIS I.; AND BLOOM, BENJAMIN S. *Methods in Personality Assessment: Human Behavior in Complex Social Situations.* Glencoe, Ill.: Free Press, 1956. Pp. 271. * (PA 30:6922)
3. BRIGGS, DANIEL A. "A Study of the Use and Application of the Stern Activities Index as a Means of Predicting Acceptable and Nonacceptable Students at the Syracuse University Sagamore Reading Camp." Abstract. *Am Psychologist* 12:373 Jl '57. *
4. NAUGLE, FRED; AGER, JOEL; HARVEY, DORIS; AND STERN, GEORGE G. "Relationships Between Student Self-Descriptions and Faculty-Student Stereotypes of the Ideal Student." Abstract. *Am Psychologist* 12:391 Jl '57. *
5. SIEGELMAN, MARVIN; PECK, ROBERT F.; AND McGUIRE, CARSON. "Distinctive Personality Patterns in Three Vocational Groups as Measured by the Stern Activity Index." Abstract. *Am Psychologist* 12:467 Jl '57. *
6. STERN, GEORGE G.; SCHULTZ, DUANE; AND NAUGLE, FRED. "Resistance to Faking on the Activities Index." Abstract. *Am Psychologist* 12:430 Jl '57. *
7. TATHAM, DAVID F.; STELLWAGEN, WALTER; AND STERN, GEORGE G. "The Stern Activities Index as a Measure of Differences Among Vocational and Academic Groups." Abstract. *Am Psychologist* 12:457 Jl '57. *
8. BRIGGS, DANIEL A. *The Stern Activities Index as a Means of Predicting Social Acceptability and Improvement in Reading Skills.* Doctor's thesis, Syracuse University (Syracuse, N.Y.), 1958. (DA 19:1947)
9. SCANLON, JOHN CIMEON. *The Activities Index: An Inquiry Into Validity.* Doctor's thesis, Syracuse University (Syracuse, N.Y.), 1958. (DA 19:2151)
10. STERN, GEORGE G.. AND SCANLON, JOHN C. "Pediatric Lions and Gynecological Lambs." *J Med Ed* 33:12–8 O '58. *
11. McFEE, ANNE. *The Relation of Selected Factors to Students' Perception of a College Environment.* Master's thesis, Syracuse University (Syracuse, N.Y.), 1959.
12. CRIST, ROBERT LaFOLLETTE. *A Study of the Discrimination Effectiveness of the Stern Activities Index With Achievement Groups in Purdue's Freshmen Engineering Program.* Doctor's thesis, Purdue University (Lafayette, Ind.), 1960. (DA 21:1843)
13. DiVESTA, FRANCIS J., AND COX, LANDON. "Some Dispositional Correlates of Conformity Behavior." *J Social Psychol* 52:259–68 N '60. * (PA 35:4813)
14. SIEGELMAN, MARVIN, AND PECK, ROBERT F. "Personality Patterns Related to Occupational Roles." *Genetic Psychol Monogr* 61:291–349 My '60. * (PA 35:7174)
15. STERN, GEORGE G. "Congruence and Dissonance in the Ecology of College Students." *Student Med* 8:304–30 Ap '60. *
16. STERN, GEORGE G. "Student Values and Their Relationship to the College Environment," pp. 67–104. In *Research on College Students: Institute Lectures Considering Recent Research on College Student's Motivation, Values and Attitudes, and Campus Cultures.* Edited by Hall T. Sprague. Boulder, Colo.: Western Interstate Commission for Higher Education, 1960. Pp. iv, 188. *
17. PACE, WALTER THOMAS. *Profiles of Personal Needs and College Press of Negro Teacher Trainees.* Doctor's thesis, Wayne State University (Detroit, Mich.), 1961. (DA 22:3748)
18. STERN, GEORGE G. "Recent Research on Institutional Climates: 1, Continuity and Contrast in the Transition From High School to College," pp. 33–58. In *Orientation to College Learning—A Reappraisal: Report of a Conference on Introduction of Entering Students to the Intellectual Life of the College.* Edited by Nicholas C. Brown. Washington, D. C.: American Council on Education, 1961. Pp. xi, 143. *
19. COSBY, BETTY WALLACE. *An Investigation of Homogeneity on Selected Personality Variables in Formal Social Groups,*

and the Effect of Such Homogeneity on the Personality of Group Members. Doctor's thesis, Syracuse University (Syracuse, N.Y.), 1962. (*DA* 23:4767)
20. SAGEN, HARRY BRADLEY. *The Relationship of Certain Personality and Environmental Variables to the Satisfaction With Present Position of Faculty in Selected Liberal Arts Colleges.* Doctor's thesis, University of Minnesota (Minneapolis, Minn.), 1962. (*DA* 23:3241)
21. STERN, GEORGE G. Chap. 3, "The Measurement of Psychological Characteristics of Students and Learning Environments," pp. 27–68. In *Measurement in Personality and Cognition.* Edited by Samuel Messick and John Ross. New York: John Wiley & Sons, Inc., 1962. Pp. xi, 334. * (*PA* 38:2638)
22. STERN, GEORGE G. Chap. 21, "Environments for Learning," pp. 690–730. In *The American College: A Psychological and Social Interpretation of the Higher Learning.* Edited by Nevitt Sanford. New York: John Wiley & Sons, Inc., 1962. Pp. xvi, 1,084. * (*PA* 36:5KA84S)
23. LORR, MAURICE, AND MCNAIR, DOUGLAS M. "An Interpersonal Behavior Circle." *J Abn & Social Psychol* 67:68–75 Jl '63. * (*PA* 38:765)
24. MUELLER, WILLIAM J. "The Prediction of Personality Inventory Responses From Tape Analysis." *Personnel & Guid J* 42:368–72 D '63. * (*PA* 39:1815)
25. RAAB, WILLIAM EDWIN. *Congruence and Dissonance Between Need and Press in Determining Satisfaction or Dissatisfaction in the University Environment.* Doctor's research study No. 1, Colorado State University (Fort Collins, Colo.), 1963. (*DA* 24:1923)
26. STERN, GEORGE G. "Characteristics of the Intellectual Climate in College Environments." *Harvard Ed R* 33:5–41 w '63. *
27. STONE, LEROY A. "Masculinity-Femininity as Reflected by the Stern Activities Index—A Brief." *J Counsel Psychol* 10:87 sp '63. *

[181]

★**Straus Rural Attitudes Profile.** Adults; 1956–59; 5 scores: innovation proneness, rural life preference, primary group preference, economic motivation, total; separate forms (Forms M2, F2, '56, 1 page) for men and women; manual ('59, 36 pages, see *1* below); supplementary norms ['59, 1 page, hectographed]; tests must be reproduced locally; single copy, manual, norms, and set of keys free to users agreeing to make results available to the author; (12) minutes; Murray A. Straus; Washington State University. *

REFERENCES

1. STRAUS, MURRAY A. *A Technique for Measuring Values in Rural Life.* State College of Washington, Washington Agricultural Experiment Stations, Institute of Agricultural Sciences, Technical Bulletin 29. Pullman, Wash.: the Institute, August 1959. Pp. ii, 34. *

Sociol & Social Res 44:297 Mr–Ap '60. Emory S. Bogardus. In the "forced-choice techniques" described in this document [the manual], the respondent is asked to choose the one phrase out of four descriptive statements "which is most like himself and the one phrase which is least like himself." The answers to twelve sets of "tetrads" are used to form a profile. This technique is somewhat like the paired comparisons technique, although superior in at least one way. The resultant Rural Attitudes Profile as designed shows certain variables, namely, innovation proneness, rural life preference, primary group preference, and economic motivation. As far as the experiments have thus far been conducted, this technique promises well for use in making rural sociological studies.

[182]

*****Study of Values: A Scale for Measuring the Dominant Interests in Personality, Third Edi-** tion. Grades 13 and over; 1931–60; 6 scores: theoretical, economic, aesthetic, social, political, religious; 1 form ('60, 12 pages, identical with test copyrighted in 1951); revised manual ('60, 19 pages); $4 per 35 tests; 60¢ per specimen set; postage extra; (20) minutes; Gordon W. Allport, Philip E. Vernon, and Gardner Lindzey; Houghton Mifflin Co. *

REFERENCES

1–61. See 3:99.
62–86. See 4:92.
87–143. See 5:114.
144. RICHARDSON, HELEN M. "Community of Values as a Factor in Friendships of College and Adult Women." *J Social Psychol* 11:303–12 My '40. * (*PA* 14:5132)
145. NEWCOMB, THEODORE M. *Personality and Social Change: Attitude Formation in a Student Community,* pp. 41–4. New York: Dryden Press, 1943. Pp. x, 225. *
146. Coffin, Thomas E. "A Three-Component Theory of Leadership." *J Abn & Social Psychol* 39:63–83 Ja '44. * (*PA* 18:2167)
147. GRAY, SUSAN W. "A Note on the Values of Southern College Women: White and Negro." *J Social Psychol* 25:239–41 My '47. * (*PA* 22:1606)
148. FISHER, SARAH CAROLYN. *Relationships in Attitudes, Opinions, and Values Among Family Members.* University of California Publications in Culture and Society, Vol. 2, No. 2. Berkeley, Calif.: University of California Press, 1948. Pp. iii, 29–99. * (*PA* 23:4628)
149. VANDERPLAS, JAMES M., AND BLAKE, ROBERT R. "Selective Sensitization in Auditory Perception." *J Personality* 18:252–66 D '49. * (*PA* 25:2862)
150. MOHSIN, S. H. "A Study of the Relationship of Evaluative Attitudes to Sex Difference, Intellectual Level, Expressed Occupational Interest and Hobbies." *Indian J Psychol* 25:59–70 pts 1–4 '50. * (*PA* 27:7051)
151. POSTMAN, LEO, AND SCHNEIDER, BERTRAM H. "Personal Values, Visual Recognition, and Recall." *Psychol R* 58:271–84 Jl '51. * (*PA* 26:3258)
152. MAWARDI, BETTY HOSMER. *The Allport-Vernon Study of Values as a Tool in Vocational Guidance With Liberal Arts College Women.* Master's thesis, Wellesley College (Wellesley, Mass.), 1952.
153. BROWN, DONALD R., AND ADAMS, JOE. "Word Frequency and the Measurement of Value Areas." *J Abn & Social Psychol* 49:427–30 Jl '54. * (*PA* 29:3783)
154. MOFFETT, CHARLES R. *Operational Characteristics of Beginning Master's Students in Educational Administration and Supervision.* Doctor's thesis, University of Tennessee (Knoxville, Tenn.), 1954.
155. LUTON, JAMES N. *A Study of the Use of Standardized Tests in the Selection of Potential Educational Administrators.* Doctor's thesis, University of Tennessee (Knoxville, Tenn.), 1955.
156. CRAWFORD, C. DELISLE. *Critical Thinking and Personal Values in a Listening Situation: An Exploratory Investigation Into the Relationships of Three Theoretical Variables in Human Communication, as Indicated by the Relation Between Measurements on the Allport-Vernon-Lindzey Study of Values and the Watson-Glaser Critical Thinking Appraisal, and Similar Measurements of Responses to a Recorded Radio News Commentary.* Doctor's thesis, New York University (New York, N.Y.), 1956. (*DA* 19:1845)
157. GRAY, SUSAN W., AND KLAUS, RUPERT. "The Assessment of Parental Identification." *Genetic Psychol Monogr* 54:87–114 Ag '56. * (*PA* 33:3404)
158. CONGER, JOHN J.; GASKILL, HERBERT S.; GLAD, DONALD D.; RAINEY, ROBERT V.; SAWREY, WILLIAM L.; AND TURRELL, EUGENE S. "Personal and Interpersonal Factors in Motor Vehicle Accidents." *Am J Psychiatry* 113:1069–74 Je '57. * (*PA* 32:6071)
159. GOWAN, J. C. "A Summary of the Intensive Study of Twenty Highly Selected Elementary Women Teachers." *J Exp Ed* 26:115–24 D '57. * (*PA* 33:4731)
160. JACOB, PHILIP E. *Changing Values in College: An Exploratory Study of the Impact of College Teaching.* New York: Harper & Brothers, 1957. Pp. xvii, 174. *
161. NOBECHI, MASAYUKI, AND KIMURA, TEIJI. "'Study of Values' Applied to Japanese Students." *Psychologia* 1:120–2 D '57. * (*PA* 35:5331)
162. SMITH, ANTHONY J. "Similarity of Values and Its Relation to Acceptance and the Projection of Similarity." *J Psychol* 43:251–60 Ap '57. * (*PA* 33:5307)
163. BENDER, IRVING E. "Changes in Religious Interest: A Retest After Fifteen Years." *J Abn & Social Psychol* 57:41–6 Jl '58. * (*PA* 33:8194)
164. BENDER, IRVING E. "Changing Patterns of Religious Interest." *Humanist* 18:139–44 My–Je '58. *
165. DEIGNAN, FRANK J. "Note on the Values of Art Students." *Psychol Rep* 4:566 D '58. * (*PA* 34:2031)
166. DUNN, SANDRA; BLISS, JOAN; AND SIIPOLA, ELSA. "Effects of Impulsivity, Introversion, and Individual Values Upon Association Under Free Conditions." *J Personality* 26:61–76 Mr '58. * (*PA* 33:5742)

167. NIMKOFF, M. F., AND GRIGG, C. M. "Values and Marital Adjustment of Nurses." *Social Forces* 37:67–70 O '58. * (*PA* 33:11235)

168. NIMNICHT, GLENDON PERRIN. *A Study of Successful Superintendents and Their Leadership Ability*. Doctor's thesis, Stanford University (Stanford, Calif.), 1958. (*DA* 19:720)

169. NUNNERY, MICHAEL Y. *A Study in the Use of Psychological Tests in Determining Effectiveness and Ineffectiveness Among Practicing School Administrators*. Doctor's thesis, University of Tennessee (Knoxville, Tenn.), 1958. (*DA* 19:1276)

170. RAY-CHOWDHURY, K. "Allport-Vernon Study of Values (Old Form) in Indian Situation: 1, Religious Group Differences in Values." *Indian Psychol B* 3:55–67 My–S '58. * (*PA* 37:4826)

171. RAY-CHOWDHURY, K. "Comparative Study of American and Indian Weight Scores on Allport's Ascendance-Submission Reaction Study." *Indian Psychol B* 3:45–7 My–Je '58. * (*PA* 37:4991)

172. SCHEIDEL, THOMAS M.; CROWELL, LAURA; AND SHEPHERD, JOHN R. "Personality and Discussion Behavior: A Study of Possible Relationships." *Speech Monogr* 25:261–7 N '58. * (*PA* 33:9990)

173. SMITH, ANTHONY J. "Perceived Similarity and the Projection of Similarity: The Influence of Valence." *J Abn & Social Psychol* 57:376–9 N '58. * (*PA* 33:9992)

174. STRUNK, ORLO. "Empathy: Need for Cognition and Value Schemata." *Psychol Newsl* 9:160–1 Mr–Ap '58. * (*PA* 33:3075)

175. ANDREWS, JOHN H. M., AND BROWN, ALAN F. "Can Principals Exclude Their Own Personality Characteristics When They Rate Their Teachers?" *Ed Adm & Sup* 45:234–42 Jl '59. * (*PA* 34:6579)

176. BADAL, ALDEN WESLEY. *The Relationship of Selected Test Measures to Administrator Success in the Elementary School*. Doctor's thesis, Stanford University (Stanford, Calif.), 1959. (*DA* 20:1263)

177. BELENKY, ROBERT LOUIS. *The Relationship Between Accuracy in Self Perception and the Perception of Others: A Study of Estimates of Performance on a Test of Values and a Test of Aspiration Level*. Doctor's thesis, Columbia University (New York, N.Y.), 1959. (*DA* 20:3825)

178. ENGSTROM, WARREN C., AND POWERS, MARY E. "A Revision of the Study of Values for Use in Magazine Readership Research." *J Appl Psychol* 43:74–8 F '59. * (*PA* 34:4859)

179. FRUEHLING, ROYAL T. *An Experimental Study to Determine the Degree to Which the 1951 Revision of the Study of Values Is Reliable for Use With High School Seniors*. Master's thesis, Northwestern University (Evanston, Ill.), 1959.

180. JONES, EDWARD E., AND DAUGHERTY, BOICE N. "Political Orientation and the Perceptual Effects of an Anticipated Interaction." *J Abn & Social Psychol* 59:340–9 N '59. * (*PA* 34:5623)

181. KELLY, E. LOWELL, AND GOLDBERG, LEWIS R. "Correlates of Later Performance and Specialization in Psychology: A Follow-Up Study of the Trainees Assessed in the VA Selection Research Project." *Psychol Monogr* 73(12):1–32 '59. * (*PA* 34:7952)

182. LUNDY, RICHARD M. "The Relationship of Changes in Assimilative Projection to Accepting and Rejecting Interpersonal Groups and to the Order of the Groups." *J Social Psychol* 50:327–33 N '59. * (*PA* 34:4993)

183. MILLER, ELEANOR O. "Nonacademic Changes in College Students." *Ed Rec* 40:118–22 Ap '59. * (*PA* 34:2047)

184. MUNSON, HOWARD ROGER. *Comparison of Interest and Attitude Patterns of Three Selected Groups of Teacher Candidates*. Doctor's thesis, State College of Washington (Pullman, Wash.), 1959. (*DA* 19:3237)

185. NOLAN, EDWARD GILLIGAN. *Uniqueness in Monozygotic Twins*. Doctor's thesis, Princeton University (Princeton, N.J.), 1959. (*DA* 21:247)

186. NUNNERY, MICHAEL Y. "How Useful Are Standardized Psychological Tests in the Selection of School Administrators." *Ed Adm & Sup* 45:349–56 N '59. * (*PA* 35:7092)

187. RAY-CHOWDHURY, K. "Allport-Vernon Study of Values (1958 Modification) in Indian Situation." *Indian Psychol B* 4:67–74 My–Je '59. * (*PA* 37:1263)

188. RAY-CHOWDHURY, K. "Allport-Vernon Study of Values (Old and New Forms) and Sex Difference in Indian Situation." *Indian Psychol B* 4:52–7 My–S '59. * (*PA* 37:1264)

189. RAY-CHOWDHURY, K. "Allport-Vernon-Lindzey Study of Values (Old Form) in Indian Situation: 2, Reliability and Item-Analysis." *Indian Psychol B* 4:7–15 Ja '59. * (*PA* 37:4947)

190. RAY-CHOWDHURY, K. "Allport-Vernon-Lindzey Study of Values (Old Form) in Indian Situation: 3, Occupational Group Differences and Norms in Values at the College Level." *Indian Psychol B* 4:20–9 Ja '59. * (*PA* 37:4948)

191. RICCIO, ANTHONY CARMINE. *The Relationship of Selected Variables to Attitudes Toward Teaching*. Doctor's thesis, Ohio State University (Columbus, Ohio), 1959. (*DA* 20:2159)

192. RODD, WILLIAM G. "Cross-Cultural Use of 'The Study of Values.'" *Psychologia* 2:157–64 S '59. * (*PA* 35:3440)

193. SCODEL, ALVIN; RATOOSH, PHILBURN; AND MINAS, J. SAYER. "Some Personality Correlates of Decision Making Under Conditions of Risk." *Behav Sci* 4:19–28 Ja '59. * (*PA* 34:1057)

194. SHELDON, M. STEPHEN; COALE, JACK M.; AND COPPLE, ROCKNE. "Concurrent Validity of the 'Warm Teacher Scale.'" *J Ed Psychol* 50:37–40 F '59. * (*PA* 35:2810)

195. THRASH, PATRICIA ANN. *Women Student Leaders at Northwestern University: Their Characteristics, Self-Concepts, and Attitudes Toward the University*. Doctor's thesis, Northwestern University (Evanston, Ill.), 1959. (*DA* 20:3638)

196. TRAXLER, ARTHUR E., AND VECCHIONE, NICHOLAS. "Scores of Seniors in Six Secondary Schools on the Allport-Vernon-Lindzey *Study of Values*." *Ed Rec B* 74:75–86 Jl '59. * (*PA* 35:1227)

197. WAGGONER, GLEN HASTINGS. *Administrator's Scores on Selected Standardized Tests and His Administrative Performance as Reported by Classroom Teachers*. Doctor's thesis, Stanford University (Stanford, Calif.), 1959. (*DA* 20:3169)

198. WARD, PAUL LEWIS. *A Study of the Relationship of Evaluative Attitudes to Scholastic Ability and Academic Achievement*. Doctor's thesis, Ohio State University (Columbus, Ohio), 1959. (*DA* 20:3639)

199. WEYBREW, BENJAMIN B., AND MOLISH, H. B. "Approaches to the Study of Motivation of Officer Candidates for the Submarine Service." *U S Naval Med Res Lab Rep* 18:1–47 O '59. * (*PA* 34:8530)

200. BALDWIN, THOMAS SANDERSON. *The Relationships Among Personality, Cognitive, and Job Performance Variables*. Doctor's thesis, Ohio State University (Columbus, Ohio), 1960. (*DA* 21:3171)

201. BOGARD, HOWARD M. "Union and Management Trainees—A Comparative Study of Personality and Occupational Choice." *J Appl Psychol* 44:56–63 F '60. * (*PA* 34:7496)

202. BOYCE, RICHARD DUDLEY. *An Empirical Evaluation of Five Tests for Administrator Selection: The Composite Study*. Doctor's thesis, Stanford University (Stanford, Calif.), 1960. (*DA* 21:2546)

203. BURDOCK, E. I.; CHEEK, FRANCES; AND ZUBIN, JOSEPH. "Predicting Success in Psychoanalytic Training," pp. 176–91. In *Current Approaches to Psychoanalysis*. Proceedings of the 48th Annual Meeting of the American Psychopathological Association Held in New York City, February 1958. Edited by Paul H. Hoch and Joseph Zubin. New York: Grune & Stratton, Inc., 1960. Pp. 207. * (*PA* 36:4IE07H)

204. EBERT, FRANCIS JOHN. *An Empirical Evaluation of Five Tests for the Selection of Elementary School Principals*. Doctor's thesis, Stanford University (Stanford, Calif.), 1960. (*DA* 21:2548)

205. HEIST, PAUL. "Personality Characteristics of Dental Students." *Ed Rec* 41:240–52 Jl '60. * (*PA* 35:7081)

206. JAMES, KENNETH RAYMOND. *An Empirical Evaluation of Five Tests for Administrator Selection in a Metropolitan School District*. Doctor's thesis, Stanford University (Stanford, Calif.), 1960. (*DA* 21:2556)

207. JOHNSON, RONALD ENGLE. *A Quantification and Measurement of Three Qualitative Changes in the Recall of Complex Verbal Materials*. Doctor's thesis, Ohio State University (Columbus, Ohio), 1960. (*DA* 21:2358)

208. KNAPP, ROBERT H., AND GREEN, SAMUEL. "Preferences for Styles of Abstract Art and Their Personality Correlates." *J Proj Tech* 24:396–402 D '60. * (*PA* 35:4841)

209. NEWBIGGING, P. L. "Personal Values and Response Strength of Value-Related Words as Measured in a Pseudo-Perceptual Task." *Can J Psychol* 14:38–44 Mr '60. * (*PA* 35:2280)

210. RALEY, COLEMAN LAVAN. *Personality Traits of High-Academic Achievers at Oklahoma Baptist University, 1958–1959*. Doctor's thesis, University of Oklahoma (Norman, Okla.), 1960. (*DA* 20:2680)

211. RAY-CHOWDHURY, K. "The 1958 Indian Modification of Allport-Vernon-Lindzey Study of Values (1951 Edition): 2, Occupational Group Differences and Norms, in Values at the College Level." *Indian Psychol B* 5:51–60 My '60. *

212. RAY-CHOWDHURY, K. "The 1958 Indian Modification of Allport-Vernon-Lindzey Study of Values (1951 Edition): 3, Variation of 'Values' With Age, Birth-Order, Locality and Region, Socio-Economic Status, and Religion." *Indian Psychol B* 5:61–70 S '60. *

213. RICCIO, ANTHONY C., AND PETERS, HERMAN J. "The Study of Values and the Minnesota Teacher Attitude Inventory." *Ed Res B* 39:101–3 Ap '60. *

214. SCODEL, ALVIN; RATOOSH, PHILBURN; AND MINAS, J. SAYER. "Some Personality Correlates of Decision Making Under Conditions of Risk," pp. 37–49. In *Decisions, Values and Groups: Reports From the First Interdisciplinary Conference in the Behavioral Science Division Held at the University of New Mexico, Vol. I*. Edited by Dorothy Willner. Sponsored by the Air Force Office of Scientific Research. New York: Pergamon Press, 1960. Pp. xxiv, 348. * (*PA* 36:5CP48W)

215. SHIRLEY, JACK HAROLD. *A Comparative Study of the Academic Achievements, Interests, and Personality Traits of Athletes and Non-Athletes*. Doctor's thesis, University of Oklahoma (Norman, Okla.), 1960. (*DA* 20:4005)

216. SMITH, ANTHONY J. "The Attribution of Similarity: The Influence of Success and Failure." *J Abn & Social Psychol* 61:419–23 N '60. * (*PA* 36:2GE19S)

217. WARREN, JONATHAN R., AND HEIST, PAUL A. "Personality Attributes of Gifted College Students." *Sci* 132:330–7 Ag 5 '60. * (*PA* 35:2214)

218. BILLINGSLY, LEON COMMODORE. *Characteristics of Teacher Effectiveness.* Doctor's thesis, University of Arkansas (Fayetteville, Ark.), 1961. (*DA* 22:1082)

219. BUEL, WILLIAM D., AND BACHNER, VIRGINIA M. "The Assessment of Creativity in a Research Setting." *J Appl Psychol* 45:353–8 D '61. * (*PA* 37:1211)

220. DYER, DOROTHY TUNELL, AND LUCKEY, ELEANORE BRAUN. "Religious Affiliation and Selected Personality Scores as They Relate to Marital Happiness of a Minnesota College Sample." *Marriage & Family Living* 23:46–7 F '61. * (*PA* 36:3IQ46D)

221. HEIST, PAUL; McCONNELL, T. R.; MATZLER, FRANK; AND WILLIAMS, PHOEBE. "Personality and Scholarship." *Sci* 133:362–7 F 10 '61. * (*PA* 36:2KD62H)

222. HOWARD, MAURICE LLOYD. *A Study of Under-Achieving College Students With High Academic Ability From the Phenomenological Frame of Reference.* Doctor's thesis, University of Colorado (Boulder, Colo.), 1961. (*DA* 22:3040)

223. MACKINNON, DONALD W. "Fostering Creativity in Students of Engineering." *J Eng Ed* 52:129–42 D '61. * (*PA* 36:4HD29M)

224. PHILIPPUS, MARION JOHN. *A Study of Personality, Value and Interest Patterns of Student Teachers in the Areas of Elementary, Secondary and Special Education.* Doctor's thesis, University of Denver (Denver, Colo.), 1961. (*DA* 22:3926)

225. PYRON, BERNARD. "Belief Q-Sort, Allport-Vernon Study of Values and Religion." *Psychol Rep* 8:399–400 Je '61. * (*PA* 36:2GD99P)

226. SCODEL, ALVIN. "Value Orientations and Preference for a Minimax Strategy." *J Psychol* 52:55–61 Jl '61. * (*PA* 36:2CN55S)

227. SPOERL, DOROTHY TILDEN. "The Values of Unitarian-Universalist Youth." *J Psychol* 51:421–37 Ap '61. * (*PA* 35:6310)

228. STROMMEN, ELLEN, AND AMMONS, ROBERT BRUCE. "Relationship of Value Placed on Intellectual Activity to Social Desirability of Attitude, Theoretical Orientation, and Interest in Problem-Solving." *Proc Mont Acad Sci* 20:78–84 '61. * (*PA* 36:1GD78S)

229. UDRY, J. RICHARD; NELSON, HAROLD A.; AND NELSON, RUTH. "An Empirical Investigation of Some Widely Held Beliefs About Marital Interaction." *Marriage & Family Living* 23:388–90 N '61. *

230. WATLEY, DONIVAN JASON. *Prediction of Academic Success in a College of Business Administration.* Doctor's thesis, University of Denver (Denver, Colo.), 1961. (*DA* 22:3527)

231. YOUMANS, RAYMOND ELTON. *A Further Validation of the Modified Study of Values for High School Students.* Doctor's thesis, University of Denver (Denver, Colo.), 1961. (*DA* 22:3529)

232. BOWIF, B. LUCILE, AND MORGAN, G. GERTHON. "Personal Values and Verbal Behavior of Teachers." *J Exp Ed* 30:337–45 Je '62. *

233. COUTTS, ROBERT LAROY. *Selected Characteristics of Counselor-Candidates in Relation to Levels and Types of Competency in the Counseling Practicum.* Doctor's thesis, Florida State University (Tallahassee, Fla.), 1962. (*DA* 23:1601)

234. CRANE, WILLIAM J. "Screening Devices for Occupational Therapy Majors." *Am J Occup Ther* 16:131–2 My-Je '62. * (*PA* 37:4078)

235. DENNY, TERRY. "Achievement of Catholic Students in Public High Schools—II." *Cath Ed* 60:442–69 O '62. *

236. HUTCHINS, EDWIN B. "The Student and His Environment." *J Med Ed* 37:67–82 D '62. *

237. INOUE, ATSUSHI; AGARI, ICHIRO; MURASHIMA, FUSAKO; YAMASHITA, ISAO; AND USUI, KIMIAKI. "A Factorial Study of Psychological Values." *Psychologia* 5:112–4 Je '62. *

238. KERR, MARILYN; MAKI, BOBBIN; AND AMMONS, R. B. "Personality, Values, and 'Intellectualism.'" *Proc Mont Acad Sci* 21:132–6 '62. * (*PA* 37:3149)

239. KNAPP, ROBERT H.; GEWIRTZ, HERBERT; AND HOLZBERG, JULES D. "Some Personality Correlates of Styles of Interpersonal Thought." *J Proj Tech* 26:398–403 D '62. * (*PA* 37:6717)

240. MACKINNON, DONALD W. "The Personality Correlates of Creativity: A Study of American Architects," pp. 11–39. (*PA* 37:4958) In *Personality Research.* Proceedings of the XIV International Congress of Applied Psychology, Vol. 2. Copenhagen, Denmark: Munksgaard, Ltd., 1962. Pp. 229. *

241. MAEHR, MARTIN L., AND STAKE, ROBERT E. "The Value Patterns of Men Who Voluntarily Quit Seminary Training." *Personnel & Guid J* 40:537–40 F '62. * (*PA* 36:5KI37M)

242. PHILIPPUS, MARION JOHN, AND FLEIGLER, LOUIS. "A Study of Personality, Value and Interest Patterns of Student Teachers in the Areas of Elementary, Secondary, and Special Education." *Sci Ed* 46:247–52 Ap '62. *

243. RAULERSON, LEWIS ALBERT. *A Study of the Values of Doctoral Students in Selected Major Subject Fields.* Doctor's thesis, Florida State University (Tallahassee, Fla.), 1962. (*DA* 23:535)

244. RUPIPER, OMER JOHN. "A Psychometric Evaluation of Experienced Teachers." *J Ed Res* 55:368–71 My '62. *

245. SINGH, PARAS NATH; HUANG, SOPHIA CHANG; AND THOMPSON, GEORGE G. "A Comparative Study of Selected Attitudes, Values, and Personality Characteristics of American, Chinese, and Indian Students." *J Social Psychol* 57:123–32 Je '62. * (*PA* 37:3847)

246. SLIFE, WAYNE GORDON. *The Measurement of Identification and Its Relationship to Behavioral Indices of Personality Organization.* Doctor's thesis, University of Houston (Houston, Tex.), 1962. (*DA* 23:3505)

247. SMITH, MADORAH E. "The Values Most Highly Esteemed by Men and Women in Who's Who Suggested as One Reason for the Great Difference in Representation of the Two Sexes in Those Books." *J Social Psychol* 58:339–44 D '62. * (*PA* 37:6726)

248. SOUTHWORTH, HORTON COE. *A Study of Certain Personality and Value Differences in Teacher Education Majors Preferring Early and Later Elementary Teaching Levels.* Doctor's thesis, Michigan State University (East Lansing, Mich.), 1962. (*DA* 23:1284)

249. SUPER, DONALD E., AND CRITES, JOHN O. *Appraising Vocational Fitness by Means of Psychological Tests, Revised Edition,* pp. 492–9. New York: Harper & Brothers, 1962. Pp. xv, 688. * (*PA* 37:2038)

250. TWOMEY, ALFRED EUGENE. *A Study of Values of a Select Group of Undergraduate Students.* Doctor's research study No. 1, Colorado State College (Greeley, Colo.), 1962. (*DA* 23:3700)

251. WATLEY, DONIVAN J., AND MARTIN, H. T. "Prediction of Academic Success in a College of Business Administration." *Personnel & Guid J* 41:147–54 O '62. * (*PA* 37:5656)

252. *Normative Information: Manager and Executive Testing.* New York: Richardson, Bellows, Henry & Co., Inc., May 1963. Pp. 45. *

253. AIKEN, LEWIS R., JR. "The Relationships of Dress to Selected Measures of Personality in Undergraduate Women." *J Social Psychol* 59:119–28 F '63. * (*PA* 38:910)

254. BAUERNFEIND, ROBERT H. *Building a School Testing Program,* pp. 212–31. Boston, Mass.: Houghton Mifflin Co., 1963. Pp. xvii, 343. *

255. CAPRETTA, PATRICK J.; JONES, REGINALD L.; SIEGEL, LAURENCE; AND SIEGEL, LILA C. "Some Noncognitive Characteristics of Honors Program Candidates." *J Ed Psychol* 54:268–76 O '63. * (*PA* 38:4674)

256. COOLFY, WILLIAM W. "Predicting Choice of a Career in Scientific Research." *Personnel & Guid J* 42:21–8 S '63. * (*PA* 38:4337)

257. DE SENA, PAUL AMBROSE. *Identification of Non-Intellectual Characteristics of Consistent Over-, Under-, and Normal-Achievers Enrolled in Science Curriculums at the Pennsylvania State University.* Doctor's thesis, Pennsylvania State University (University Park, Pa.), 1963. (*DA* 24:3144)

258. DUA, PREM SAKHI. *Identification of Personality Characteristics Differentiating Elected Women Leaders From Non-Leaders in a University Setting.* Doctor's thesis, Pennsylvania State University (University Park, Pa.), 1963. (*DA* 24:3145)

259. GILBERT, JOSEPH. "Vocational Archetypes: A Proposal for Clinical Integration of Interests and Values in Vocational Counseling and Selection." *Psychol Rep* 13:351–6 O '63. *

260. GREENBERG, HERBERT; GUERINO, ROSEMARIE; LASHEN, MARILYN; MAYER, DAVID; AND PISKOWSKI, DOROTHY. "Order of Birth as a Determinant of Personality and Attitudinal Characteristics." *J Social Psychol* 60:221–30 Ag '63. * (*PA* 38:4337)

261. GUTHRIE, GEORGE M., AND McKENDRY, MARGARET S. "Interest Patterns of Peace Corps Volunteers in a Teaching Project." *J Ed Psychol* 54:261–7 O '63. * (*PA* 38:4126)

262. KELSEY, IAN BRUCE. *A Comparative Study of Values of Students Attending the University of British Columbia in 1963 as Measured by the Allport-Vernon Test for Personal Values.* Doctor's thesis, University of Washington (Seattle, Wash.), 1963. (*DA* 24:2813)

263. KINNANE, JOHN F., AND GAUBINGER, JOSEPH R. "Life Values and Work Values." Comment by Harry Beilin. *J Counsel Psychol* 10:362–7 w '63. * (*PA* 38:8278)

264. LEE, EUGENE C. "Career Development of Science Teachers." *J Res Sci Teach* 1:54–63 Mr '63. *

265. LIND, AMY. "Measured Personality Characteristics of Occupational Therapy Graduates and Undergraduates at the University of North Dakota." *Univ N Dak Col Ed Rec* 48:69–73 F '63. *

266. McCUE, KEMPER W.; ROTHENBERG, DAVID; ALLEN, ROBERT M.; AND JENNINGS, THEODORE W. "Rorschach Variables in Two 'Study of Values' Types." *J General Psychol* 68:169–72 Ja '63. * (*PA* 38:2742)

267. MAHER, HOWARD. "Validity Information Exchange, No. 16-01: D.O.T. Code o-06.71, Feature Writer; o-06.73, Columnist; o-06.92, Copyreader (Rewrite Man)." *Personnel Psychol* 16:71–3 sp '63. *

268. MAHER, HOWARD. "Validity Information Exchange, No. 16-02: D.O.T. Code 1-87.26, Advertising Space Salesman." *Personnel Psychol* 16:74–7 sp '63. *

269. MANHOLD, J. H.; SHATIN, LEO; AND MANHOLD, BEVERLY S. "Comparison of Interests, Needs, and Selected Personality Factors of Dental and Medical Students." *J Am Dental Assn* 67:601–5 O '63. *

270. NEWSOME, GEORGE L., JR., AND GENTRY, HAROLD W. "Logical Consistency, Values, and Authoritarianism in a Sample of Public School Superintendents." *J Teach Ed* 14:411–6 D '63. *

271. NOLAN, EDWARD G.; BRAM, PAULA; AND TILLMAN, KENNETH. "Attitude Formation in High-School Seniors: A Study of Values and Attitudes." *J Ed Res* 57:185–8 D '63. *

272. NOLL, VICTOR H., AND NOLL, RACHEL P. "The Social Background and Values of Prospective Teachers." *Yearb Nat Council Meas Ed* 20:108–14 '63. * (*PA* 38:9297)

273. PAIVIO, ALLAN, AND STEEVES, RAY. "Personal Values and Selective Perception of Speech." *Percept & Motor Skills* 17:459–64 O '63. * (*PA* 38:5037)

274. RADCLIFFE, J. A. "Some Properties of Ipsative Score Matrices and Their Relevance for Some Current Interest Tests." *Austral J Psychol* 15:1–11 Ap '63. *

275. RAMSAY, RONALD; JENSEN, SVEN; AND SOMMER, ROBERT. "Values in Alcoholics After LSD-25." *Q J Studies Alcohol* 24:443–8 S '63. *

276. SCHUMACHER, CHARLES F. "Interest and Personality Factors as Related to Choice of Medical Career." *J Med Ed* 38:932–42 N '63. *

277. TERWILLIGER, JAMES S. "Dimensions of Occupational Preference." *Ed & Psychol Meas* 23:525–42 au '63. * (*PA* 38:6698)

278. VAUGHAN, G. M., AND MANGAN, G. L. "Conformity to Group Pressure in Relation to the Value of the Task Material." *J Abn & Social Psychol* 66:179–83 F '63. * (*PA* 37:6621)

279. VAUGHAN, JAMES A., JR., AND KNAPP, ROBERT H. "A Study in Pessimism." *J Social Psychol* 59:77–92 F '63. * (*PA* 38:859)

280. WARBURTON, F. W.; BUTCHER, H. J.; AND FORREST, G. M. "Predicting Student Performance in a University Department of Education." *Brit J Ed Psychol* 33:68–79 F '63. * (*PA* 38:1416)

JOHN D. HUNDLEBY, *Research Assistant Professor of Psychology, University of Illinois, Urbana, Illinois.*

The *Study of Values* has been for many years a test of interest to those concerned with the quantitative assessment of values and interests, and, in particular, those who wish to see standard tests more closely tied to psychological theory. The original, 1931, version of the test contained measures of six values based on Spranger's formulations: theoretical, economic, aesthetic, social, political, and religious. The second edition, published in 1951, included more discriminating items, increased reliability, and reflected a redefining of the social value. The third edition, 1960, with which this review is concerned, shows no change in items from the second. The main difference between these last two editions is the provision of additional normative data. Stability of the test over the past decade necessarily means that many of the problems of earlier versions (considered in earlier reviews) remain, and indeed some have become intensified.

Modifications to the manual of the third edition are slight and are concerned with the presentation of more recent norms and changes in scoring. The norms are presented for total populations (e.g., male students) and also for specific colleges or narrow occupational groups. The means, and usually standard deviations, of each population or subgroup are given for each value. Unfortunately, no further information

on the shape of the distribution is presented. It is also to be regretted that revised reliability estimates were not reported, for the present coefficients are based upon groups of only 100 (split-half) and 34 and 53 subjects (retest).

Of theoretical rather than practical importance is the continued lack of compelling evidence that Spranger's system, and these six measures associated with it, have much more to offer than can be obtained from other standard measures of interests. This is not to say that the *Study of Values* lacks validity in the realm of values and interests, for there is considerable supportive evidence on the usefulness of the test in a variety of settings—particularly counseling and selection. What *is* in question, however, is the psychological theory upon which the test is based, and here direct evidence remains very scanty. The majority of researchers appears to be far more concerned with such problems as obtaining specific value scores (usually for different occupational or educational groups) or changes in such scores, than with the theoretical problems of Spranger's system of values in the context of contemporary theory and research findings.

Definitive statistical information still appears to be lacking on whether or not the six measures are unidimensional and relatively distinct. Factor analytic results are not yet conclusive and are made more difficult in interpretation by the ipsative nature of the scales. Item-total scale correlations, unless they are very high, are not sufficient evidence, since it is possible for scale items to have a similar factorial structure and the final scale be a composite of several dimensions. Certain item-total scale correlations may indeed be quite low for, though no figures are reported in the manual, every item enjoys a significant ($P < .01$) correlation with the total scale, but with an n of 780 this need only be .09.

This reviewer remains puzzled as to why the ipsative form has persisted with the *Study of Values*. Admittedly, to measure each value separately would involve more time of testing, but ipsative items can also be time consuming, if for no other reason than the often difficult choices that are presented to the subject. The test authors do not comment at length on the implications of ipsative measures for the test user, and perhaps further emphasis on this point would be desirable.

The *Study of Values* continues to be a measure closely associated with the college-going or college graduate population. This is readily evident from the norms, for apart from 8,369 college students, almost all of the information on occupational differences (Southern business men, teachers, school administrators, Air Force officers, personnel workers, scoutmasters, and clergymen) concerns persons likely to have had *some* college experience. For purposes associated with higher education this is, of course, no problem, but it does impose a severe limitation on the generality of findings from the test and, indeed, further suggests that the values concerned may be appropriate only for a limited segment of the population. Attempts have been made, however, to extend measurement to populations of lower educational level and systematic developments along these lines are to be hoped for.

In summary, with college or college graduate populations where concern is with dimensions of interest and value broader than those of, say, the *Strong Vocational Interest Blank* or *Kuder Preference Record,* the *Study of Values* is quite likely to prove a helpful tool. Lack of conclusive evidence as to unidimensionality of the scales, the problems of interpretation imposed by ipsative scoring, and lack of any real generality beyond the college population, remain as unresolved research issues.

JOHN A. RADCLIFFE, *Senior Lecturer in Psychology, University of Sydney, Sydney, Australia.*

Designed to measure Spranger's six "value types," the *Study of Values* first appeared in 1931. The second edition made changes in the test itself. In the third edition, changes occur only in the score sheet and in parts of the manual.

The test has two parts. In Part 1 (30 items), each value is paired twice (but with different statements) with every other value, and in Part 2 (15 items), each value is compared (again with different statements) with all combinations of three other values. Now consider Part 1, which has the majority of items. Internal consistency reliability of a subject's score on a value will depend on the equivalence of the item statements and the consistency of his judgments. Retest reliability will depend on the consistency of his judgments over time, and this in turn will depend on the stability of

his relative values. If retest reliability is higher than internal consistency reliability, then the instability of relative values is less than the nonequivalence of the item statements. That is, greater retest than internal consistency reliability will indicate that internal consistency reliability could be improved by better equivalence of the item statements.

This is the case with the *Study of Values.* The average total test reliabilities for the different subscales are .89 and .88 (one and two month retest) and .82 (split-half). While these correlations are based on small samples only and probably do not differ significantly statistically, it seems likely, at least with Part 1, that they represent a genuine difference deriving from the item selection procedure. Greater attention to and possible improvement of statement equivalence would have been achieved if item selection had been based on item intercorrelations rather than item-total (corresponding value) score correlations.

To illustrate: consider items 1 and 15, which both contrast theoretical and economic values, and items 12 and 21, which both contrast theoretical and political. Equivalence of value statements and consistency of the subjects' judgments would require that item 1 correlate highly with item 15, and that item 12 correlate highly with item 21. But, unless the sample were "biased" to consist predominantly of subjects whose theoretical, economic, and political values were in the same order of relative strength, the expected correlations of items 1 and 15 with items 12 and 21 would be *zero.* Thus the expected pattern of item intercorrelations would be high correlations between items contrasting the same pair of values and near zero correlations otherwise. Item selection via item intercorrelation would enable better detection of the weaker equivalents than would item selection via item-total correlations.

Of course, item-total correlations depend on item intercorrelations. Maximising one will maximise the other. But the aim here would be to maximise some item intercorrelations and to minimise others. Moreover, it is common practice to obtain such low item-total correlations that selection consists of omitting those items with the lowest correlations rather than retaining those with the highest. The test authors merely report that they retained only those items whose item-total correlations were "significant at the .01 level of confidence."

With their large sample ($n = 780$) these could have been so low that not even those between equivalent items were maximised.

However, these are minor points of criticism and pertain only to show how the test might have been made better than it is. As it is, it has satisfactory reliability, both internal consistency and split-half, for group use, as attested by the results it has produced. Moreover, even if it were improved by greater attention to item equivalence, the interest areas measured are so broad that probably it never would have any greater individual use than that suggested by the authors, namely, "to secure an initial impression....and as a basis for subsequent interviews."

Since every subject obtains the same total score over the six values, the scores are ipsative and the interests of a subject are interpreted intraindividually. Interindividual comparisons are facilitated by scaling the scores so that the "average" individual has a constant score (40) on each value. Variation of his values around this base shows how his relative values compare with those of the "average" individual. If further normative comparisons are desired, the manual provides, for males and females separately, the means and standard deviations for the total standardisation group and its university subsamples, and the means for specialist educational and occupational groups. It is worth noting that the authors specifically recognise the ipsative character of the scores and do not recommend their expression in a percentile profile as do the authors of some other ipsatively scored tests (e.g., *Edwards Personal Preference Schedule*). Also, possibly because the authors emphasise the lack of independence involved with ipsative scores, there has been less correlational use of the *Study of Values* than with other ipsatively scored tests (*274*).

The test is self-scoring, but, as Gage (5:114) has suggested, the way in which this is achieved probably increases its "transparency." Designed as it is for use "with college students, or with adults who have had some college (or equivalent) education," the test's vocabulary level is twelfth grade by a Flesch count (*140*). Two less verbally complex versions have been produced (*140, 178*). In Levy's revision, equivalence of the item statements for the theoretical and social scales could be improved.

Validity data in the manual consist mainly of showing that educational and occupational groups have value patterns as might be expected. Some additional data of this character will be summarised here, but more attention will be given to data different from that given in the manual.

The overall Japanese pattern is high aesthetic and low religious, and includes more scatter than the American, but the educational specialities have high and low scores much as with American students; e.g., high aesthetic for letters, political for law, and economic for economics (*161*). Compared with the standardisation group, "gifted" students have higher theoretical and aesthetic values, and their pattern has greater scatter (*124, 217*). National Merit Scholarship holders at educational institutions with "high academic productivity" differ from those at "low productivity" institutions by having higher theoretical and aesthetic and lower religious interests (*221*). Measured values do not appear to be related to the study of dentistry (*205*), nor to being a "warm teacher" (*194*).

"Feminine" males have a value pattern like that of "normal" females, including high aesthetic, social, and religious scores (*123*). Both male and female "leaders" of organisations differ from members and nonmembers by having the "masculine" pattern of high theoretical, economic, and political values, but the fact that the "leaders" consisted only of volunteers for the study may have some relevance here (*126*). The value patterns of submarine officer candidates and Air Force officers have also been studied (*125, 199*).

If "low belief in change" is regarded as synonymous with "conservatism," then conservative Protestants and Catholics have high religious and low aesthetic values, nonconservative Protestants have high theoretical and low economic, while nonconservative Jews have high aesthetic and low religious values (*225*). The "masculine" high theoretical-economic-political pattern and the "feminine" high aesthetic-social-religious pattern have been suggested to be related to "extratensive" and "intratensive" personality characteristics, respectively, and the "extratensive" were found to be faster and more "stimulus bound" in their associative reactions (*166*). This is difficult to reconcile with the two factors involving the *Study of Values* obtained by Gowan from its correlations with a number of ability and personality tests (*139*), and with his finding that the "gifted," who do not have the "extra-tensive" pattern, are low on "introversion" and high on "dominance" (*124*).

As well as those cited in the manual, some other studies pertaining to the "construct valid-ity" of the *Study of Values* have included changes in values from freshman to senior year (*183*); the role of values in resistance to pres-sure to conform (*278*); the role of personality similarity and difference in the study of inter-personal relations (*162, 173, 216*); and condi-tions relevant to pseudoperception (*209*).

There are wide individual differences in the degree of association between expressed and measured values and the degree of association does not appear to be related to age (*141*). The values of Air Force officers are consistent with some of their high interest areas on the *Kuder Preference Record* (*125*), but those of "gifted" students are not obviously so (*124*). The values of students at "high" and "low productive" institutions are consistent with their *Strong Vocational Interest Blank* theo-retical-nontechnical and applied-technical inter-est patterns, respectively (*221*).

Attendance at church correlated .79 with religious values in a group of Dartmouth grad-uates (*163*). Magazine reading preferences were consistent with results obtained with a less verbally complex version of the test (*178*). Although the actual results are not given, it appears to have been useful in the study of recruitment in the banking industry.[1] That nurses with high "empathy" have high social and low aesthetic interests is consistent with the description of these values given in the manual (*134*).

Although Spranger's value types have an "armchair" rather than an "empirical" basis, and although it may in some instances fail to distinguish between *value* and *interest* (5:114), the *Study of Values* has remained a useful research instrument. As such, and as a "basis for subsequent interviewing" in individual ap-plication, it should continue to be widely used, but it is hoped that any future revision might include attention to the points raised above concerning item analysis procedures.

For a review by N. L. Gage of the second edition, see 5:114; for reviews by Harrison G. Gough and William Stephenson, see 4:92 (1

---

[1] McMurry, Robert N. "Recruitment, Dependency and Morale in the Banking Industry." *Admin Sci Q* 3:87–117 Je '58. * (PA 33:9096)

excerpt); for a review by Paul E. Meehl of the original edition, see 3:99.

[183]

★**Style of Mind Inventory: Trait, Value and Be-lief Patterns in Greek, Roman and Judeo-Chris-tian Perspectives.** College and adults; 1958–61, c1957–61; formerly called *The Fetler Self-Rating Test;* 3 scores (Greek, Roman, Judeo-Christian) in each of 3 areas (traits, values, beliefs); 1 form ('61, 1 page); explanation sheet ['61, 1 page]; no data on reliability and validity; no norms; 1¢ per test; 1¢ per explana-tion sheet; postage extra; [60] minutes; Daniel Fet-ler; the Author. *

[184]

★**Survey of Interpersonal Values.** Grades 9–16 and adults; 1960–63; 6 scores: support, conformity, recog-nition, independence, benevolence, leadership; 1 form ('60, 3 pages); preliminary manual ('60, 11 pages); mimeographed supplement, revised ('63, 28 pages); $2.40 per 20 tests; 50¢ per key; 50¢ per manual; $1 per specimen set; postage extra; (15) minutes; Leon-ard V. Gordon; Science Research Associates, Inc. *

REFERENCES

1. Gordon, Leonard V. "Conformity Among the Non-Con-formists." *Psychol Rep* 8:383 Je '61. * (PA 36:2JO83G)
2. Wyatt, Thomas C. *A Validation Study of the Gordon Survey of Interpersonal Values.* Master's thesis, Drake Uni-versity (Des Moines, Iowa), 1961.
3. Fleishman, Edwin A., and Peters, David R. "Inter-personal Values, Leadership Attitudes, and Managerial 'Suc-cess.'" *Personnel Psychol* 15:127–43 su '62. * (PA 37:7321)
4. Gordon, Leonard V., and Mensh, Ivan N. "Values of Medical School Students at Different Levels of Training." *J Ed Psychol* 53:48–51 F '62. * (PA 37:1921)
5. Hedberg, Raymond. "More on Forced-Choice Test Faka-bility." *J Appl Psychol* 46:125–7 Ap '62. *
6. Woodard, Barbara. *An Investigation of Some Inter-personal Values of Freshman and Senior Nursing Students at the Texas Woman's University.* Master's thesis, Texas Woman's University (Denton, Tex.), 1962.
7. Blume, Dorothy M. *Interpersonal Values of Nursing Students in One University Program.* Master's thesis, Uni-versity of Texas (Austin, Tex.), 1963.
8. Braun, John R. "Effects of Positive and Negative Faking Sets on the Survey of Interpersonal Values." *Psychol Rep* 13:171–3 Ag '63. * (PA 38:6082)
9. Garrison, W. A.; Wilson, H. E.; and Warne, E. K. "Interpersonal Values Related to College Achievement." *Proc Mont Acad Sci* 22:127–31 '63. *
10. Knapp, Robert R. "Personality Correlates of Delin-quency Rate in a Navy Sample." *J Appl Psychol* 47:68–71 F '63. * (PA 37:8179)
11. Morris, Kenneth Turner. *A Comparative Study of Selected Needs, Values, and Motives of Science and Non-Science Teachers.* Doctor's thesis, University of Georgia (Athens, Ga.), 1963. (DA 24:2325)
12. Wilson, Helen; Garrison, W.; and Warne, E. "Analysis of the F Scale Through Use of the Survey of Inter-Personal Values Scales." *Proc Mont Acad Sci* 22:124–6 '63. *

Lee J. Cronbach, *Professor of Education and Psychology, Stanford University, Stanford, California.*

This is an unpretentious instrument, com-petently presented. About 15 items for each of six scales are arranged into 30 triads. In each triad, the person checks the statement most important to him, and that least important to him. A typical item compares "To be selected for a leadership position," "To be treated as a person of some importance," and "To have things pretty much my own way." The direc-tions are so brief that there is some possibility that subjects will interpret the task in rather different ways. Particularly, it is not clear whether the person is to describe what he wants in a job or what he wants in his life as a whole.

The test construction follows appropriate procedures, though the author perhaps tells too little about four hypothesized dimensions that disappeared in the course of factor analysis, discussing only the six that survived. The reliability information is inadequately analyzed and somewhat misleading. With retest reliabilities in the .80's and internal consistencies in the range .71 to .86, it seems most likely that when one generalizes over *both* items and occasions—as would be required in guidance or theoretically-oriented research—the coefficient would be in the low .70's. The standard errors of scores and of differences within the profile are substantial.

Since the items are quite transparent, the survey is open to faking whenever the subject knows what traits will be considered good in a particular job. The research of Longstaff [1] and French [2] shows quite clearly that forced choice scales are not resistant to faking of patterns, and the test manual promises too much in this respect. The survey is of dubious value for industrial selection, though no more so than other typical questionnaires. The author is on safe ground when he says (in a supplement to the manual), "The SIV is to be treated as a research instrument, and for industrial and other applied purposes should be validated in the situation in which it is intended to be used."

One wonders what an inventory with transparent items will contribute in guidance, beyond what is learned from one simple question or self-rating on each trait. Unlike most manuals, the manual for this test provides a correlational study of just this question, finding contingency coefficients of .47 to .73. The manual points to these as evidence of validity. That they are—but placed alongside the reliability data they indicate that the test has very little *incremental* validity. A conceivable argument for using the inventory in guidance is that converting scores to percentiles (which cannot be done satisfactorily with self-ratings) may enhance their meaning. But the norms, either in-

adequately collected or inadequately presented, are essentially valueless. There are norms based on, for example, 1,075 college males from colleges representing "all major regions of the country." The colleges are listed, but we are told nothing about whether a given college tested all its freshmen, or perhaps only the juniors enrolled in personnel psychology.

The author, in the manual and a supplement, presents a welcome array of correlations of this test with other tests, and abstracts over a dozen diverse studies relating the test to group differences or external criteria. The claims and interpretations made are reasonable, though the author squeezes too much out of some small-sample studies. One dare not conclude, for example, that lack of Sociability is more characteristic of the person high on Independence (sample $r = -.30$ for 144 cases) than is lack of Responsibility (sample $r = -.16$).

The user who for some reason wants scores on six aspects of self-report that can be given a common sense interpretation, in a format that eliminates the social desirability and acquiescence sets from the score, will find the survey suitable. Whether it has any use in personnel selection, future validity studies will show; the studies reported furnish little basis for optimism. As a counseling aid, the survey seems less likely to give the subject or counselor fresh insights than the *Edwards Personal Preference Schedule* with its 15 scores, the *Kuder Preference Record—Personal,* or Gordon's own Personal Profile.

LEONARD D. GOODSTEIN, *Professor of Psychology, and Director, University Counseling Service, University of Iowa, Iowa City, Iowa.*

The *Survey of Interpersonal Values* (SIV) is a 30 item ipsative instrument; each item consists of a triad of statements, each of which presumably reflects some underlying value or motivational pattern affecting the respondent's interpersonal relationships. The respondent is required to select one of the statements or foils within each triad as "most important" and one as "least important," thus rank ordering the three foils. The manual indicates that an effort was made to equate the three foils in each item for social desirability of response but these social desirability values are not actually reported.

The items are answered directly in the question booklet and are hand scored by means of

1 LONGSTAFF, HOWARD P. "Fakability of the Strong Interest Blank and the Kuder Preference Record." *J Appl Psychol* 32:360–9 Ag '48. *
2 FRENCH, ELIZABETH G. "A Note on the Edwards Personal Preference Schedule for Use With Basic Airmen." *Ed & Psychol Meas* 18:109–15 sp '58. *

a punched, overlay stencil. While such hand scoring would inevitably be laborious, the scoring stencil in the specimen set received for review was rather crudely punched making accurate scoring virtually impossible. It is surprising that the publisher did not extend to the SIV the far more convenient pin-punch booklet developed for the *Kuder Preference Record*.

The SIV yields six scores or measures of interpersonal values: (*a*) Support, which involves being treated with understanding, encouragement, and kindness (15 foils); (*b*) Conformity, or doing what is socially correct or acceptable to others (15 foils); (*c*) Recognition, involving being respected or considered important (13 foils); (*d*) Independence, or being free from external controls and regulations (13 foils); (*e*) Benevolence, or helping others less fortunate (15 foils); and (*f*) Leadership, which involves being in charge of others or controlling them (16 foils). Each foil is scored for one of these values (scored 2 if rated as most important, zero if rated least important, and 1 if left unmarked) and no foil is scored for more than a single value.

The basis upon which these particular six values were included in the published version of the SIV is not clearly indicated in the manual. The author started with items tapping 10 such values, presumably rather arbitrarily selected from the literature, which he then subjected to a factor analysis. This analysis yielded eight factors, six of which are included in the SIV. The details of this factor analysis are not presented, nor is any indication given of why two of the factors were eliminated. While the manual presents a table of intercorrelations, it is difficult to decide how independent these six value scores are since the ipsative nature of the test responses produces an indeterminate negative correlation among the scores.

The test-retest reliability coefficients for the six value scores range from .78 to .89 with median *r* .84. The Kuder-Richardson reliability estimates range from .71 to .86 with median *r* .82. Both sets of reliability data suggest adequate reliability, comparable to that reported for other forced choice personality inventories, e.g., *Edwards Personal Preference Schedule*.

Two sets of percentile equivalents for each of the six scores are presented separately by sex: one for college students, based upon 746 females and 1,075 males, and one for high school students, based upon 782 males and 666

females. The collegiate norms were collected at a variety of institutions "selected so as to represent all major regions of the country," while the high school data were all collected in California. The extension of these high school norms to include a more representative sample as well as the development of some nonacademic normative materials would be highly desirable.

The SIV is offered primarily as a research instrument, although the 1963 manual supplement is far more explicit on this point than is the original 1960 manual where there is the suggestion that the SIV can be used directly for vocational guidance and personality counseling. The more recent supplement specifically cautions the potential user to validate the instrument in the specific situation for which use is contemplated and presents illustratively the results of over two dozen studies using the SIV. These include investigations of the SIV as a predictor of job success with such varied samples and criteria as executives in a manufacturing firm and retail sales personnel in a department store and studies of the SIV as a predictor of success in several different military cadet programs. Several studies report upon the changes in SIV scores as a function of educational and other experiences, and there are also a number of highly interesting cross-cultural comparisons of SIV scores. These studies do strongly suggest that the SIV is indeed a useful research tool but the author's caution not to apply these findings directly to new situations without cross validation is very well taken. It is somewhat unfortunate that the supplement rather uncritically includes the reports of a number of studies that were methodologically weak, for example, a study reporting product-moment correlation coefficients based upon small samples of 19 or 25. While the supplement does disclaim any operational usefulness of such findings, reporting of such data does appear to legitimize some questionable procedures.

In summary, the *Survey of Interpersonal Values* appears to be a useful addition to the growing collection of paper and pencil personality tests which attempt to reduce the influence of social desirability response set by a multiple choice format. The major usefulness of the SIV at this time would be for classroom demonstrations and further research. As the body of research evidence grows, however, the usefulness of the SIV for personnel selection, appraisal, and counseling, the other major uses advocated by the author, will certainly increase.

JOHN K. HEMPHILL, *Director, Developmental Research Division, Educational Testing Service, Princeton, New Jersey.*

The *Survey of Interpersonal Values* is the third sibling in the growing family of personality tests issued by Leonard V. Gordon. Like its predecessors, the *Gordon Personal Profile* and the *Gordon Personal Inventory,* it uses a forced choice format and is based upon the results of a factor analysis. The survey consists of 30 groups of 3 statements each. The examinee first responds by selecting the one of the three "which represents what you consider to be most important to you"; he then selects the one he considers to be least important to him, leaving the third statement unmarked. The test yields scores for six values: Support, Conformity, Recognition, Independence, Benevolence, and Leadership.

Norms are available separately for college males ($n = 1,075$), college females ($n = 746$), high school boys ($n = 782$), and high school girls ($n = 666$). College norms were developed on a sample of students from 12 colleges or universities, well distributed geographically over the country. The high school norms, however, are based on four schools, all within the state of California.

The test manual is filled with pertinent information. Clearly written directions for administration and interpretation of scores are followed by a good account of the development of the scales and by comprehensive descriptive statistics. Estimates of reliability are provided both as test-retest coefficients ranging from .78 to .89, and Kuder-Richardson estimates ranging from .71 to .86. Intercorrelations among the six scale scores and correlations of the scores with measures of intelligence, other tests of personality, and with scores from the *Study of Values* are shown. None of the scores correlates substantially (the highest in absolute value is $-.22$) with scores from the *College Qualification Test.* Relationships with scores from the *Gordon Personal Inventory* and the *Gordon Personal Profile* are moderate and range from $-.30$ between "Support" and "Vigor," to .39 between "Leadership" and "Ascendancy." The relationships are regarded as logical and ones to be expected. Relation-

ships between six scores from the *Study of Values* and the six scale scores likewise appear, for the most part, to be logical and consistent. For example, the correlation between "Benevolence" and "Religious" is .52; between "Leadership" and "Political," .30; and between "Conformity" and "Theoretical," $-.36$. Correlations of .42 between "Leadership" and "Theoretical" or of .46 between "Independence" and "Aesthetic," are less obviously reasonable, but might be rationalized.

A virtue of the manual and the supplement (called "Research Briefs") is the emphasis that Gordon places upon reporting about the validity of his scales. Many major and minor studies using the survey are summarized. The total evidence from these studies lends support to Gordon's moderate claims for application of the *Survey of Interpersonal Values* in selection, vocational guidance, counseling, and research. This instrument promises to become a respectable member of its family, and a useful companion to the well known but perhaps overworked *Study of Values.*

J Counsel Psychol 9:92–3 sp '62. Laurence Siegel. * The forced-choice format of SIV was designed to reduce the susceptibility of the inventory to deliberate attempts at falsification. All statements in the Manual about the effectiveness of forced-choice in this regard are appropriately cautious. * Triads were constructed by grouping items representing different factors but similar in social desirability. Unfortunately, the Manual is not as clear as it should be in discussing the way in which social desirability indices were obtained and the subsequent selection of items on the basis of these indices. * Retest reliability coefficients....and Kuder-Richardson estimates....for college students are presented * For the six scales, the former range between .78 and .89 and the latter between .71 and .86. The Manual states in summarizing these coefficients that they "....are sufficiently high to permit interpretation of SIV scores for individual use." This is a strong statement when applied to scales with the relatively narrow score ranges characteristic of SIV and without supporting evidence in the form of standard errors of measurement. Reliability coefficients for noncollege samples are not presented. Potential industrial users of this inventory are cautioned in the Manual to develop their own norms to compensate for possible response distortion in the industrial setting. This caution could well have been extended to all users of SIV on the grounds not only of possible distortion but of the inadequacy of the samples upon which currently published norms are based. Percentile norms for college students are presented in the Manual. These norms tables are based upon relatively small samples (1,075 males and 746 females) and their designation as "National Norms" is misleading. Although the samples were drawn from schools in various parts of the country, the implication of representativeness characteristic of truly national norms is unsupported. * In spite of the fact that the number and variety of reported validity studies exceeds those accompanying many other published instruments, a certain amount of ambivalence is unavoidable in assessing this inventory. This reviewer, at least, remains unconvinced about the necessity for a test measuring what SIV measures. This highly subjective reservation aside, it would have been desirable for the Manual to contain a more comprehensive description of the development of SIV and a more cautious statement about the interpretation of raw scores. Although the Manual's cover is labeled "Preliminary Edition," this small cautionary note can be too easily overlooked by persons who weight heavily the professional qualifications of the test author and the reputation of the publisher. The Supplement to the Manual contains the following important statement: "The SIV is to be treated as an experimental instrument and should be validated or evaluated in the situation in which it is intended to be used." This excellent statement should have been placed also on the face sheet of the Manual itself. Failing this, it should at least have appeared *somewhere* in the Manual.

[185]

★Survey of Personal Attitude "SPA" (With Pictures): Individual Placement Series (Area III). Adults; 1960; subtest of *Individual Placement Series;* 3 scores: social attitude, personal frankness, aggressiveness; Form A (14 pages); no manual; no data on reliability and validity; no description of normative population; separate answer sheets must be used; $32.50 per 25 tests; $1.10 per 25 answer sheets; $1 per key; $3.50 per specimen set; postpaid; [20–25] minutes; J. H. Norman; the Author. *

[186]

★Syracuse Scales of Social Relations. Grades 5–6, 7–9, 10–12; 1958–59; pupil ratings of need interactions with classmates and others; 1 form ('58, 8 pages); 3

levels; manual ('59, 24 pages) for each level; $5.40 per 35 tests; 40¢ per specimen set of any one level; postage extra; (50–65) minutes in 2 sessions; Eric F. Gardner and George Thompson; [Harcourt, Brace & World, Inc.]. *

a) ELEMENTARY LEVEL. Grades 5–6; 4 scores: ratings made, received for succorrance, achievement-recognition.

b) JUNIOR HIGH LEVEL. Grades 7–9; 4 scores: ratings made, received for succorance, deference.

c) SENIOR HIGH LEVEL. Grades 10–12; 4 scores: ratings made, received for succorance, playmirth.

REFERENCES

1. GARDNER, ERIC F., AND THOMPSON, GEORGE G. *Social Relations and Morale in Small Groups.* New York: Appleton-Century-Crofts, Inc., 1956. Pp. xi, 312. * (*PA* 30:8184)
2. deJUNG, JOHN E. *The Measurement of Accuracy of Self-Role Perception.* Doctor's thesis, Syracuse University (Syracuse, N.Y.), 1957. (*DA* 20:776)
3. MEYER, WILLIAM J. *Relationships Between Social Need Strivings and the Development of Heterosexual Affiliations.* Doctor's thesis, Syracuse University (Syracuse, N.Y.), 1957. (*DA* 19:2667)
4. ABEL, HAROLD. *The Relationship of Social Class and Sex to Social Need Satisfaction.* Doctor's thesis, Syracuse University (Syracuse, N.Y.), 1958. (*DA* 19:85)
5. DAVOL, STEPHEN H. *Some Determinants of Sociometric Relationships and Group Structure in a Veterans Administration Domiciliary.* Doctor's thesis, University of Rochester (Rochester, N.Y.), 1958.
6. KUNTZ, ALLEN H. *Some Factors of Learning and Their Relationships to Social Stability.* Doctor's thesis, Syracuse University (Syracuse, N.Y.), 1958. (*DA* 19:3214)
7. SCALEA, CARMEN J. *A Study of Relationships Between the Achievement Need Level of Individuals in a Group and Ratings Given to the Members of the Group for the Potential Satisfaction of This Need.* Doctor's thesis, Syracuse University (Syracuse, N.Y.), 1958. (*DA* 19:91)
8. deJUNG, JOHN E. "Measurement of Accuracy of Self-Role Perception." *Yearb Nat Council Meas Used Ed* 16: 111–6 '59. * (*PA* 34:7378)
9. KUNTZ, ALLEN H. "An Index of Social Stability." *Yearb Nat Council Meas Used Ed* 16:105–10 '59. *
10. MEYER, WILLIAM J. "Relationships Between Social Need Strivings and the Development of Heterosexual Affiliations." *Yearb Nat Council Meas Used Ed* 16:95–104 '59. * (*PA* 34:7488)
11. PAUSLEY, BARBARA HEARNE. *Changes in Need Structure as Measured by the Syracuse Scales of Adolescent Girls in an Organized Camp.* Master's thesis, Syracuse University (Syracuse, N.Y.), 1961.
12. REYNOLDS, JAMES H., AND BRAEN, BERNARD B. "Reliability of a Sociometric Technique Adapted for Use With Disturbed Children." *Psychol Rep* 9:591–7 D '61. *
13. deJUNG, JOHN E., AND GARDNER, ERIC F. "The Accuracy of Self-Role Perception: A Developmental Study." *J Exp Ed* 31:27–41 S '62. * (*PA* 37:8241)
14. deJUNG, JOHN E., AND KUNTZ, ALLEN H. "Peer Status Indices From Nominational and Rating Procedures in Regular and Homogeneous Ability Grouped Sixth Grade Classes." *Psychol Rep* 11:693–707 D '62. * (*PA* 38:1395)
15. KUNTZ, ALLEN H., AND deJUNG, JOHN E. "A Comparison of Achievement Status Indices Obtained in Regular 6th Grade Classes Using Peer Nominational and Rating Procedures." *Yearb Nat Council Meas Used Ed* 19:97–103 '62. *
16. deJUNG, JOHN E., AND MEYER, WILLIAM J. "Expected Reciprocity: Grade Trends and Correlates." *Child Develop* 34:127–39 Mr '63. * (*PA* 38:5729)

ÅKE BJERSTEDT, *Professor of Education, University of Lund, Lund, Sweden.*

The present instrument has grown out of a comprehensive and ambitious research effort, partly described in the book *Social Relations and Morale in Small Groups* (1). It represents a particular kind of sociometric device with several characteristic features, claimed to have these specific advantages: (*a*) *A psychological need definition of the choice situations.* The social choice situations used by most sociometrists are considered to be extremely gross in definition, resulting in individual choices for

quite varying reasons and spuriously heightened correlations between various choice situations. A psychological need definition is aimed
to increase precision and invariance, and the
present scales claim explicitly to deal with
"needs of particular importance at the respective stages of development." (*b*) *A personal
reference population for each subject.* Most
sociometric methods utilize as the only frame
of reference the group within which the choices
are made. This closed system approach makes
certain comparisons between persons and
groups difficult. In the present procedure each
subject first chooses five persons out of "all
persons ever known" to represent dividing
points on each need satisfying continuum
(from the person being best suited to satisfy
the particular need to the person being least
suited). The subsequent rating of the group
members is done with these five persons as reference points. This procedure is claimed to insure "comparability....from pupil to pupil,
group to group, and need to need." (*c*) *All-
to-all reactions.* The typical sociometric nomination process, involving only a limited number
of preferred or non-preferred companions, is
considered to result in a loss of important information. The present scales therefore force
each subject to rate *every* other member of the
group in terms of each choice situation used.

While the reviewer finds these basic arguments interesting and well worth continued
research effort, he considers the authors slightly
overconfident about the value and efficiency of
these specific characteristics in their present
form.

There is no indication in the manual that the
specific needs chosen actually are *the* most important ones at the respective stages of development, nor that *two* needs only (as used in
these scales) sufficiently cover the important
interaction tendencies in these ages, nor that
individual differences in terms of need strength
are small enough to insure comparable stimulus situations between raters. Further, in order
to demonstrate that need-defined ratings actually *are* more precise than more conventionally phrased social choice situations, it would
be necessary to show that intercorrelations between need-defined choice situations are consistently lower than intercorrelations between
other specific choice situations, *and* that such
increased rating specificity is not a verbal arte-
fact, that is, that it leads to better prediction

of person-to-person behavior during actual
group processes. No such demonstration is reported in the manual.

The comparability reached by using the individual's inclusive frame of reference (all
persons ever known) may easily be overestimated. We obtain a certain kind of *intra*-
personal comparability: we increase our possibilities to compare a single individual's judgments about persons from different groups.
But the most basic problem—that of *inter*personal comparability—seems to be still far from
a final solution. The fact that two raters consider a third subject to be at the midpoint of
their respective personal range of experience
as need satisfiers does not seem to insure any
more basic identity of attitude strength between these two raters, as long as the need
strength and experience range may be considerably different. In other words, there may be
some kind of cognitive identity (an isomorphic position within two individuals' cognitive
space) without identity as to *attitudinal-prefer-
ential* strength (as judged from other kinds of
behavior). These are admittedly difficult problems, and the reviewer does not criticize the
authors for not having found *the* final solution,
but only for sometimes acting as if this were
the case.

The final specific characteristic mentioned
above—the all-to-all reactions—is not as unique
within sociometric research as the authors seem
to think: complete rank orders, rating, and
paired comparisons have often been used
(complete rank orders were especially frequent
in early European sociometry). However, the
general feeling among sociometrists having
tried these methods is that the more detailed
information obtained should be considered
against the disadvantages of (*a*) a more time
consuming procedure, (*b*) a less natural and
motivating situation for the subjects, and (*c*)
a forced reaction situation which forces the
group members to statements about phenomena
with no psychological salience in their life-
space. A conventional sociometric choice situation is described in a few sentences, and the
choices are usually made in 5–10 minutes. The
instructions for the present elementary level
form take up *six columns* of text in the manual
for *one* of the need situations only, and it is
easy to imagine that some pupils will have
difficulty in following the instructions or in
finishing the one-need rating within the 30 min-

utes estimated. It is usually a simple and natural affair to select a number of companions for a concrete social situation, but it may seem quite strange and artificial for a child to compare to a person like Uncle Joe all his classmates—boys as well as girls—as satisfiers of his need for achievement-recognition in a hypothetical situation.

These doubts as to the finality of the specific solutions characteristic of this particular sociometric device do not mean that it should be without value. On the contrary, among the few commercially available instruments for assessment of social relations that the reviewer knows of, this should be considered outstanding in several respects. The test forms are well constructed; administration and scoring is clearly described; the manual's handling of interpretational and validational aspects is judicious; and information on data from representative classrooms, including reliability information, is presented in a helpful way. It is also obvious that the novel techniques have opened up stimulating new research possibilities. (The only technical aspects that the reviewer should have liked to see handled in another way are the recommendations on how to score ratings received and mutual ratings. Would it not be a simpler and quicker procedure to compute all scores directly from the tally sheet—without the extra clerical work involved in going back to the individual sheets a second time? But this is a minor matter of differing opinion.)

In sum, the present reviewer doubts that the specific characteristics of this device, which distinguish it from other sociometric techniques, represent final solutions to the difficult problems of (a) comparability, (b) maximal meaningfulness of choice situations, and (c) optimal balance between information received and information "cost." For many situations, the more traditional sociometric choice situations (as described in handbooks by Gronlund,[1] Jennings,[2] Northway,[3] and others) should be just as well or better able to handle the mapping of social relations—especially where simplicity and flexibility are important. On the other hand, for the person wanting a

tailor-made sociometric procedure, commercially available and with potential usefulness both in general research and diagnostic charting, the present instrument may be the best available today.

DONALD T. CAMPBELL, *Professor of Psychology, Northwestern University, Evanston, Illinois.*

The test booklet at each level is an elaborately prepared rating scale for only two topics (psychological needs). Succorance (ratings as a person you'd like to talk over your troubles with) is used at all three age levels. The reasons for varying the second topic are not given. "Achievement-recognition" refers to whom you would choose to help you make something for public exhibition. "Deference" refers to ratings of others on degree admired. "Playmirth" refers to ratings of others as persons with whom one could feel sure one would have a good time and lots of fun. The required setting is one in which members of a group such as a classroom can rate each other. The elaborateness comes in through the careful induction of personal externally-anchored rating scale points prior to the rating of classmates. With the help of a normal curve graph and a detailed example, each rater records, for the particular relation described, the names of persons selected from "everyone you have ever known in your whole life," assigning each name to one of five positions ranging from "least" to "most." Then the classmates are rated in direct comparison with these five reference persons. Because of the elaborateness of this procedure, the booklets are not self administering but require detailed oral instructions which are provided in the manual. Detailed scoring instructions are provided for ratings given and ratings received, and for clique analysis. Norms based upon over 1,000 students per class level are provided. Test-retest reliabilities on scores for midrating made range from .56 to .75. Reliabilities on midrating received range from .61 to .88. The validity data given are indirect and misleadingly emphasize an only partially similar college level study.

The methodological innovation differentiating this from the numerous "guess-who," "sociometric," and other reputational rating devices is the selection of the personal, external reference persons. No evidence is cited

1 GRONLUND, NORMAN E. *Sociometry in the Classroom.* New York: Harper & Row, Publishers, Inc., 1959. Pp. xix, 340. *
2 JENNINGS, HELEN HALL. *Sociometry in Group Relations: A Manual for Teachers, Second Edition.* Washington, D.C.: American Council on Education, 1959. Pp. xi, 105. *
3 NORTHWAY, MARY L., AND WELD, LINDSAY. *Sociometric Testing: A Guide for Teachers.* Toronto, Canada: University of Toronto Press, 1957. Pp. vii, 72. *

showing the superiority of this method over simpler procedures. In regard to the recurrent problems of halo effects or social desirability factors, the methodological precautions would at best affect mean ratings given, and not at all the spuriously high intercorrelation usually found among favorable traits. The intercorrelations between the two ratings are not presented but are probably high. Nor is any other evidence of discriminant validity presented for these measures.

In summary, while these booklets are probably as useful as any two-topic reputational rating device for classroom use, there is no evidence that they are superior to older and simpler procedures.

J Consult Psychol 24:466 O '60. Edward S. Bordin. This sociometric device makes use of two hypothetical situations as a basis for ratings by each student of his classmates. * One of the situations, at all three levels, involves rating others' ability to offer support, comfort, and sympathy, and is intended to reflect need for succorance; the other is specific to the level. At the elementary level achievement-recognition is tapped; at Junior high, deference, at Senior high, playmirth. * Since every pupil is evaluated by every other one, information becomes available on: (*a*) how each pupil views his classmates as being able to satisfy two of his important psychological needs; (*b*) how each pupil is evaluated by his classmates as being able to satisfy their needs. Large samples, unspecified with regard to such relevant factors as intelligence and socio-economic status, provide a not fully satisfactory normative basis for interpreting the average ratings given and received for each need. An instrument like this one departs from the pattern of the simpler pencil and paper tests. Evaluation of its usefulness becomes an extremely complex process. The authors rely on five years of research, mostly with college students. Test-retest measures of stability over a one-to-two-week period suggest that these measures have only moderate stability (from .62 to .94). The manual is deficient in not warning potential users that such factors as the passage of time or the period in the school year might have considerable effect on a given score. This uncertainty would tend to impair its usefulness for routine diagnostic use. It will not be possible to involve a whole class in the

time consuming procedures required every time the need to understand and help a particular pupil is discerned. Its validity is, of course, not susceptible to simple summary. Brief reference is made to studies whose results are suggestive, and the reader is referred to the author's 1956 book and to a number of unpublished doctoral dissertations. There is lacking any comprehensive or coherent framework for interpreting the results. True, it might be argued that providing such a framework requires more space than a manual can provide. Then the potential user ought to be warned that such a gap exists and referred to the proper sources. This reviewer is more impressed with possible usefulness of these scales for research than for everyday clinical or educational work.

[187]

★**Temperament Comparator.** Adults; 1958–61; identical with *Paired Comparison Temperament Schedule* ('58) except for format of presentation; 24 scores: 18 trait scores (calm, cautious, decisive, demonstrative, emotionally stable, energetic, enthusiastic, even-tempered, lively, persevering, prompt starter, quick worker, seeks company, self-confident, serious, socially at ease, steady worker, talkative), 5 factor scores (controlled vs. outgoing, stable vs. unstable, self-reliant vs. dependent, excitable vs. placid, sociable vs. solitary), and consistency; 1 form ('61, 2 pages); manual ('61, 51 pages); profile ('61, 1 page); administered with snap-on trait-pairing disc ('61); reliability data, validity data, and norms based on test in format of the earlier edition; $3 per 20 tests; $1.50 per set of reusable backing folder and disc; $3 per manual; postage extra; $5 per specimen set, postpaid; (15–20) minutes; Melany E. Baehr and R. W. Pranis; Education-Industry Service. *

REFERENCES
1. BAEHR, MELANY E. "A Factorial Study of Temperament." *Psychometrika* 17:107–26 Mr '52. * (PA 27:1834)

LAWRENCE J. STRICKER, *Research Psychologist, Educational Testing Service, Princeton, New Jersey.*

The *Temperament Comparator* is one of a number of forced choice personality inventories which have appeared in the last few years, largely as a reaction to the thorny problems produced by faking and response styles on the traditional true-false personality scales.

This inventory, like the others, is designed to measure variables within the normal range of behavior and is intended for use in applied settings. It consists of 18 descriptive words or phrases, which the manual calls "traits" (e.g., "impulsive," "cheerful," and "socially at ease"), presented in a paired comparison format, the subject choosing the one trait in each of the 153 pairs of traits that best describes him. Each of these 18 traits loaded one of five oblique factors extracted from judges' ratings of others on 22 such traits (*1*). This original pool of 22 traits had been selected to represent an emotionality dimension conceptualized by Heymans and Wiersma and four second-order factors extracted by Baehr from Thurstone's [1] factor analysis of the Guilford personality scales.

Scores are provided for each of the 18 traits, 5 factor scales corresponding to the oblique factors (obtained by summing the appropriate trait scores), and a measure of consistency [2]—the tendency to make responses which do *not* form circular triads, such as choosing A rather than B, B rather than C, but C rather than A.

The meaning of the scores for the traits and the factor scales is open to question. The use of separate trait scores is questionable because the traits were selected, not because they were of intrinsic interest, but simply because they were expected to generate the five dimensions that were at issue. Insofar as the traits successfully produced the five factors, the information they provide is embodied in the factor scales which they form. Even if these particular traits were of interest per se, their meanings would be ambiguous because they are, in reality, one-item scales, whose generality cannot be determined. People may stably discriminate between any one trait and all the others because they are responding to an idiosyncratic quality, clang association, or some other characteristic of the word or phrase that has nothing to do with the psychological variable presumed to underlie the word or phrase. This kind of problem is avoided by most other forced choice scales in which each trait is represented by a homogeneous set of items.

The factor scales are questionable because they were based on factors extracted from ratings of others and, hence, may not be applicable to the self-descriptive responses elicited in the present form of the inventory. The factor structure for the self-description data may be quite different, particularly in view of the massive effect of social desirability response style on self-descriptive responses but not on ratings of others.

The manual fails to mention that the trait

scores are ipsative, a property shared by most other forced choice scales and one which may be troublesome if score interpretations and multivariate computational procedures customarily used with normative scales are not appropriately modified. Some of the ways in which ipsative properties of scores complicate score interpretations and appraisals of statistical relationships are described at length in the present author's review of the *Edwards Personal Preference Schedule* (see 87).

Since the intercorrelations of the 18 traits and the intercorrelations of the 5 factor scales are unknown, the usefulness of interpreting the scores separately cannot be gauged. (The manual does report the intercorrelations of four factor scales on an early version of the *Paired Comparison Temperament Schedule,* which evidently is appreciably different from the *Temperament Comparator,* although the final version of the Schedule differs from the *Temperament Comparator* only in the way that the pairs of traits are presented, the latter using a disc arrangement which will be described later.)

The only available information on reliability is the data reported in the manual on retest-reliability, after a one-week interval, for an industrial sample—the median reliability was .79 for the traits and .90 for the factor scales, and the reliability of the consistency score was .80. These data, however, were obtained with the final form of the Schedule and are based on raw scores, not the normalized standard scores recommended in the manual. Consequently, these reliability estimates are not entirely appropriate for use with the current form of the inventory. The absence of data about the internal-consistency reliability of the factor scales precludes an assessment of their homogeneity, which is particularly crucial in view of the strong possibility that the factor structure for the rating data is not applicable to self-description data.

Very little is known about the validity of this inventory. No published studies could be located, and the manual, despite assertions that the Schedule "has been effectively used in the selection and placement of personnel," reports only two validity studies. One study, which is based on a master's thesis [3] and used an early form of the Schedule, consists of the correla-

1 THURSTONE, L. L. "The Dimensions of Temperament." *Psychometrika* 16:11–20 Mr '51. *

2 KENDALL, MAURICE G. *Rank Correlation Methods, Second Edition.* London: Charles Griffin & Co. Ltd., 1955. Pp. vii, 196. *

3 NOTY, C. *Intercorrelation Design for Determining Executive Placement and Effectiveness.* Master's thesis, Illinois Institute of Technology (Chicago, Ill.), 1960.

tions of four of the five factor scales with the scales of the 16 PF test. The results are more or less consistent with the descriptions of the four factors. The other study consists of comparisons of mean scores on the trait and factor scales, and the consistency measure from the final form of the Schedule for six occupational groups—labor, engineering, executive, white collar, foreman, and sales. The results lend some support to the validity of the inventory, though a statistical analysis which indicated the *extent* to which the scores differentiated between the occupational groups would have been more appropriate.

Despite the advantages claimed by the manual for this approach to personality measurement, including greater reliability of the trait scores and reduction of the effects of social desirability response style, no data on any of these issues are available. Even if the manual did not suggest that this inventory would minimize social desirability response style, data on this issue would be essential in view of its importance. In fact, it seems highly unlikely that the *Temperament Comparator* has succeeded in appreciably minimizing this response style because the traits were not explicitly matched on social desirability; the test authors just selected traits that seemed socially desirable to them and later eliminated a few traits whose scores, when obtained with a paired comparison format, had low means and skewed distributions. Research with the *Edwards Personal Preference Schedule* suggests that even a careful attempt to match items closely on social desirability values does not substantially eliminate social desirability response style, for there is still a tendency to choose the more socially desirable item in each pair [4] and its scales are moderately but significantly correlated with Edwards' [5] social desirability response style scale.[6] This unexpected state of affairs evidently stems from the multidimensionality of social desirability judgments [7] and interaction or context effects which may occur when items are paired.

4 KLETT, C. JAMES. "The Stability of the Social Desirability Scale Values in the Edwards Personal Preference Schedule." *J Consult Psychol* 21:183–5 Ap '57. * *(PA* 33:974)
5 EDWARDS, ALLEN L. *The Social Desirability Variable in Personality Assessment and Research.* New York: Dryden Press, Inc., 1957. Pp. xv, 108. * *(PA* 32:464)
6 MERRILL, REED M., AND HEATHERS, LOUISE B. "The Relation of the MMPI to the Edwards Personal Preference Schedule on a College Counseling Center Sample." *J Consult Psychol* 20:310–4 Ag '56. * *(PA* 31:7949)
7 MESSICK, SAMUEL. "Dimensions of Social Desirability." *J Consult Psychol* 24:279–87 Ag '60. * *(PA* 35:2211)

Although this inventory is intended for general use, the norms that are provided are based on the 478 people from the six occupational groups used in the validity study. Note that these data are based on the final form of the Schedule rather than on the *Temperament Comparator*. The aggregation produced by this indiscriminate pooling of the six groups is a long way from the reasonably representative samples from clearly defined populations required for adequate norms.

Finally, the procedure used to obtain the subjects' choices between each pair of traits—rotating a disc which has each of the 18 traits printed on its circumference and then recording the choice by making a pencil mark through a hole in the disc—may facilitate scoring and may even have some novelty value for the subjects, as the manual suggests, but these marginal advantages are outweighed by the errors that are apt to arise when the subject tries to erase and change his response, loses his place in rotating the disc, or fails to position the disc exactly after each rotation.

In view of the casual way that the *Temperament Comparator* was developed, the uncertain meaning of its scores, and the dearth of relevant data available about it, anyone who intends to measure the kinds of variables found in this inventory would be more likely to obtain useful results if he chose any of several other inventories which are better constructed and better understood, such as the *Guilford-Zimmerman Temperament Survey* or the *Sixteen Personality Factor Questionnaire*. If such inventories, which use a traditional true-false or yes-no format, are chosen, it would be desirable to use them in conjunction with a social desirability response style scale so as to be able to measure the effects of the response style on the inventory results.

ROBERT L. THORNDIKE, *Professor of Education, and Head, Department of Psychological Foundations and Services, Teachers College, Columbia University, New York, New York.*

This device consists of a list of 18 adjectives or adjectival phrases and a gadget. The gadget is a cardboard disc and a record sheet which can be thought to facilitate the paired comparison judgment of each adjective with respect to the other 17. Thus, the individual describes himself (or could be described by others) by the number of times he selects a particular trait name as he compares it with each of the others.

What virtue the instrument has stems from the selection of the trait names. These grew out of previous factor analytic studies, first of personality inventories and then of trait names themselves, and the 18 are considered by the authors to represent the principal dimensions of temperament. The results may be expressed in a profile for the 18 traits, or condensed into a profile of 5 factor scores. All of the traits are designated by rather positive and acceptable labels.

Evidence is reported to indicate that individuals are moderately consistent in their self-descriptions. When the time interval is one week, test-retest reliabilities for single trait names range from .65 to .87, and for factor scores from .78 to .90.

As usual, the validity problem is less happily dealt with. Reference is made to the underlying factor analyses. An assortment of modest correlations are reported with scales of the *Sixteen Personality Factor Questionnaire*. Finally, differences in mean profile scores are reported for sales, labor, and various supervisory and managerial categories.

This device provides a quick technique, possibly appealing to the respondent, for generating an ipsative personality profile based on a set of trait names. Whether the rather abstract and generalized trait names serve as well for this purpose as more specific and concrete behavior descriptions is nowhere made clear to the potential user.

[188]

★**Test of Basic Assumptions.** Adults; 1959, c1957–59; for experimental and research use only; 12 scores: 3 attitude scores (realist, idealist, pragmatist) for each of 4 "life areas" (organization of effort and problem solving, human abilities and the individual, general philosophy of life, economics and business); Form X ('59, 4 pages); manual ('59, 4 pages); score sheet (1 page); reliability data for total attitude scores only; no norms; $3.50 per 25 tests; 75¢ per specimen set; postpaid; (60) minutes; James H. Morrison and Martin Levit (test); James H. Morrison. *

[189]

★**Test of Behavioral Rigidity, Research Edition.** Ages 21 and over; 1960, c1956–60; test booklet title is *TBR;* 4 scores: motor-cognitive rigidity, personality-perceptual rigidity, psychomotor speed, total; items of one component scale of personality-perceptual rigidity score selected from *California Psychological Inventory;* 1 form ('60, c1956, 8 pages); mimeographed preliminary manual ('60, 24 pages); no data on reliability; $4.75 per 25 tests; $1 per manual; $1.50 per specimen set; postage extra; (30) minutes; K. Warner Schaie; Consulting Psychologists Press, Inc. *

REFERENCES

1. SCHAIE, K. W. *Measuring Behavioral Rigidity: A Factorial Investigation of Some Tests of Rigid Behavior.* Master's thesis, University of Washington (Seattle, Wash.), 1953.
2. SCHAIE, K. WARNER. "A Test of Behavioral Rigidity." *J Abn & Social Psychol* 51:604–10 N '55. * (*PA* 31:3074)
3. SCHAIE, K. WARNER. *Some Developmental Concomitants of Rigid Behavior.* Doctor's thesis, University of Washington (Seattle, Wash.), 1956. (*DA* 16:2215)
4. STROTHER, CHARLES R.; SCHAIE, K. WARNER; AND HORST, PAUL. "The Relationship Between Advanced Age and Mental Abilities." *J Abn & Social Psychol* 55:166–70 S '57. * (*PA* 33:3294)
5. SCHAIE, K. WARNER. "Differences in Some Personal Characteristics of 'Rigid' and 'Flexible' Individuals." *J Clin Psychol* 14:11–4 Ja '58. * (*PA* 33:5782)
6. SCHAIE, K. WARNER. "Rigidity-Flexibility and Intelligence: A Cross-Sectional Study of the Adult Life Span From 20 to 70 Years." *Psychol Monogr* 72(9):1–26 '58. * (*PA* 33:9923)
7. KONIETZKO, K. *An Investigation of the Concept of "Behavioral Rigidity" as Applied to a Penal Population.* Doctor's thesis, Temple University (Philadelphia, Pa.), 1959. (*DA* 20:757)
8. SCHAIE, K. WARNER. "The Effect of Age on a Scale of Social Responsibility." *J Social Psychol* 50:221–4 N '59. * (*PA* 35:4895)
9. SHOCKLEY, JAMES T. "Behavioral Rigidity in Relation to Student Success in College Physical Science." *Sci Ed* 46:67–70 F '62. *

DOUGLAS P. CROWNE, *Associate Professor of Psychology, University of Connecticut, Storrs, Connecticut.*

This test is designed to measure rigidity, which the author defines as, "a tendency to perseverate and resist conceptual change, to resist the acquisition of new patterns of behavior, and to refuse to relinquish old and established patterns." The *Test of Behavioral Rigidity* (TBR) consists of three tests: the Capitals Test (copying a paragraph written half in capital and half in small letters); the Opposites Test (giving opposites to a series of words); and the Questionnaire, a true-false personality inventory. The capitals and opposites tests are repeated with the tasks somewhat altered; this gives a measure of ability to shift or change set. Several scores are derived from these tests.

A replicated factor analysis of these and other rigidity measures resulted in three factors. The motor-cognitive rigidity factor, defined by factor loadings of the capitals and opposites tests, is interpreted as an ability to shift activities from one to another. The questionnaire is the chief component of the second factor, personality-perceptual rigidity; this factor is defined as an ability to perceive and adapt to new situations. Psychomotor speed is defined by loadings of the capitals and opposites tests (essentially speed scores) and is interpreted as a speed of response or efficiency factor. Scores on the TBR are factor scores, and the total or composite rigidity score is simply an additive linear combination of the three factor scores.

TBR norms reported in the manual are based on a sample of 500 subjects drawn by stratified random sampling from the membership of a group medical plan. The normative sample is grouped by 5-year intervals, each group containing 25 males and 25 females, from ages 20 to 70. In both educational level and occupational status, the normative sample is significantly above the general population.

No data on reliability are reported; the manual avers that this is a major lack in the test. Reliability can be crudely estimated from the replication of the factor analysis in that the factor structure of rigidity tests was almost exactly duplicated. This establishes only the fact of a minimum level of consistency, and test-retest reliability data are urgently required.

The appropriate validation for the TBR is construct validity given the range of behavioral predictions which may be deduced. The author's concept of rigidity stresses developmental changes from early maturity to old age: rigidity should increase with age. In a cross-sectional study of adults from 20 to 70 years, Schaie (6) found rigidity increasing with age. These changes paralleled intellectual decline, and substantial correlations with the Thurstone PMA were found at every age level. In another study (5), highly rigid individuals were found to be significantly lower than "flexible" persons on each of the following: years of education, income, occupational status, self-rated happiness and success, and social responsibility. Prison inmates have a "rigidity quotient" significantly below that of the normative sample (7). No evidence on differential predictions from the three factors is reported, and the composite rigidity score appears to discriminate best (6). The meaning and usefulness of the three factors is yet to be demonstrated.

While evidence for the validity of the TBR is very limited, there are two other problems of great importance. First, the TBR correlates highly with intelligence, and the predictions so far made with the test could, perhaps, be made equally well with an intelligence measure. Thus, discriminant validity is lacking; there is the very real possibility that the TBR might be reducible to an intelligence test. Second, the definition of rigidity overlaps and fails to discriminate between *defensive rigidity* of the kind seen in compulsive behavior and the perseveration and inability to change associated with aging and other conditions impairing efficiency. These may even be confounded within the test: The questionnaire seems to be face valid as a measure of the former, while the capitals and opposites tests appear to be more like measures of the latter. A more precise definition of the construct of rigidity is needed. If defensive rigidity is included, then validity studies are required.

Summing up, the TBR is currently limited to research use in investigations of rigid behavior; in this regard the manual is commendably labeled "Research Edition." No individual predictions are warranted from this test in the absence of reliability data and further evidence on validity. The definition of rigidity and the interpretation of the three factors must be regarded as heuristic; they await research confirmation. For the time being, this test should be limited to research establishing its validity as a measure of rigidity. On the positive side, it is an interesting approach to behavioral rigidity and probably a more fruitful one than the Water Jar Test. The TBR is comprehensible to subjects, the directions clear, and the scoring straightforward if tedious for a large number of subjects.

BENJAMIN KLEINMUNTZ, *Associate Professor of Psychology, Carnegie Institute of Technology, Pittsburgh, Pennsylvania.*

The TBR is a group test, currently being published in its "research edition," which according to its manual is "designed to measure the ability of the individual to adjust to the stress imposed upon him by constant environmental change." The test is an outgrowth of its author's studies on the interrelationships between rigidity, age, and intelligence; and most of its components have been appropriated from the early literature on rigidity and perseveration. It consists of three parts:

Part 1, the Capitals Test, was adopted from a study by Bernstein on quickness and intelligence and is a performance task which consists of two 150-second writing exercises. The subject is required to copy in writing a 91 word passage. The second part of the Capitals Test requires that the examinee copy the same passage, but this time he is to write a capital letter wherever a small letter appears in the original, and write a small letter wherever a capital letter appears in the original. Part 2, the Opposites Test, suggested by Scheier and

Ferguson's factorial studies of tests of rigidity, consists of three series of writing exercises. In the first series the subject is required to furnish opposites for a list of 40 words. The second and third series of the Opposites Test each require *synonyms* for a list of 40 words, although the third series requires synonyms only when the stimulus word is printed in capital letters and calls for opposites when the stimulus word is printed in small letters. Each of the three parts of the Opposites Test is timed for two minutes. The last section of the TBR, Part 3, called the Questionnaire, consists of 75 true-false items. The R scale, which is comprised of 22 items, was obtained from Gough's *California Psychological Inventory;* 44 "masking" items were borrowed from the CPI Social Responsibility scale, and a 9-item P scale was patterned after some early work done on perseveration by W. Lankes.

The directions for the administration and the scoring procedures for each of the TBR's three parts are reasonably simple and straightforward and are clearly set forth in the accompanying manual. This reviewer did have some difficulty, however, in the scoring of the Opposites Test. The manual instructs the scorer to treat ratio scores as whole numbers; but it does not clarify whether the decimal point is to be dropped before or after performing subsequent arithmetic operations. In this regard the scoring format that is given for the opposites series on page 6 of the test booklet is definitely in error because it punctiliously leads the scorer through the steps of score computation, but omits completely the step where the individual is to multiply by 100. Since the scores resulting from either omission or inclusion of the multiplication process are plausible, the format is misleading and inaccurate.

In addition to a seven category classification scheme, which in the best tradition of early intelligence testing proposes Rigidity Quotients (RQ) ranging from scores of 69 or below ("very rigid") to 130 or above ("very flexible"), an interpretation for each of the three factors is offered. These factors and their interpretations, arrived at by "logical analysis of the experimental operations" are: (*a*) motor cognitive rigidity, which "indicates the individual's ability to shift without difficulty from one activity to another," (*b*) personality-

perceptual rigidity, which "seeks to indicate the individual's ability to adjust readily to new surroundings and change in cognitive and environmental patterns," and (*c*) psychomotor speed, which "indicates the individual's rate of emission of familiar cognitive responses."

There are several features, according to the Technical Recommendations, that must be present in a good psychological test, and the TBR has certain essential ones. It is accompanied by a preliminary manual which summarizes the essential information about the test and which appropriately offers cautious interpretations about the meaning of its several scores. The TBR's standardization procedures assure uniformity of administration and scoring, and the test has been administered to a large representative sample of the type of subjects for whom it is presumably designed. Many hours of careful preparation are reflected in the presentation of this material.

There are two elements missing, however, which are undoubtedly the most important characteristics of a psychometric device. Data on the reliability of the various factors and on the complete test are nonexistent, and validity support is flimsy indeed. The test author acknowledges the lack of the former, but he is a bit disingenuous about the validity of his instrument. Instead of the presentation of validity data and the clear specification of what type of validity is being reported, the author fills the validity and reliability section of his manual with a report of two studies which bear questionable relevance to validity. One of the studies is the TBR author's own in which he compared the personal characteristics of "the 10 most flexible and 10 most rigid members of each age group in the normative sample." As may be expected whenever extremes of two groups are compared, statistically significant differences in the predicted directions were found. However, as should not be expected in a test manual, nor in the literature cited in support of a test being described in a manual, data on the extent of the overlap between the extremes of the groups in question were not presented and if the overlap between the groups was considerable, then even a critical ratio significant at the .0001 level is meaningless.

The second study reported in the validity and reliability section is an unpublished doctoral dissertation done at Temple University, in which the investigator studied a sample of 150 prison inmates "and found their average RQ to be significantly below that of the norm population." To extend this intellectual legerdemain one step further, the test author dazzles the reader with evidence of the above doctoral candidate's "correlation analysis" which "showed the TBR factors to be virtually independent with a maximum correlation of .22 between the motor-cognitive rigidity and psychomotor speed factors." In other words, no validating studies have been made, and here as well as in the case of the evidence for reliability, this reviewer would like to emphasize the test author's plea: "Further data are urgently required."

To summarize, this research edition of the TBR is an outgrowth of its author's studies on the relationships between rigidity and such variables as intelligence and age. It is a potpourri of measures, most of which have been borrowed from the literature on rigidity and perseveration, and which the author has painstakingly rearranged into a psychometric device. In many respects, the TBR qualifies as a psychological test, but in view of the lack of evidence for its validity or reliability, its claim to be a measure of anything is premature.

[190]

★Test of Social Insight. Grades 6–12, 13–16 and adults; 1959–63; 6 scores: withdrawal, passivity, cooperation, competition, aggression, total; IBM; 1 form ('59, 8 pages); 2 levels (essentially the same except for wording changes): youth edition, adult edition; manual ('63, 19 pages); separate answer sheets must be used; $6.25 per 25 tests; $2.75 per 25 IBM answer sheets; $1 per set of scoring stencils; $2.75 per 25 profiles; $1.75 per manual; $2.50 per specimen set of either level; cash orders postpaid; French edition available; [20–25] minutes; Russell N. Cassel; Martin M. Bruce. *

REFERENCES

1. CASSEL, RUSSELL N. "A Construct Validity Study on a Leadership and a Social Insight Tests for 200 College Freshmen Students." J Genetic Psychol 99:165–70 S '61. * (PA 36:3GF65C)
2. CASSEL, RUSSELL N., AND HADDOX, GENEVIEVE. "Comparing Reading Competency With Personality and Social Insight Test Scores." Calif J Ed Res 12:27–30 Ja '61. * (PA 36:1KJ27C)
3. LANGE, MERLE LEROY. A Comparative Analysis of Achieving and Under-Achieving Twelfth Grade Students of Phoenix Central High School on the Non-Intellectual Factors of the Group Personality Projective Test and the Test of Social Insight. Doctor's research study No. 1, Colorado State College (Greeley, Colo.), 1962. (DA 23:3778)
4. CASSEL, RUSSELL, AND CHILDERS, RICHARD. "A Study of Certain Attributes of 45 High-School Varsity Football Team Members by Use of Psychological Test Scores." J Ed Res 57:64–7 O '63. *

JOHN D. BLACK, Director, Counseling and Testing Center, and Consulting Associate Professor of Psychology, Stanford University,

Stanford; and President, Consulting Psychologists Press, Inc., Palo Alto; California.

At first glance this test looks promising. It consists of 60 rather well written and ingenious items, confronting the subject with a choice among 5 alternative responses to difficult interpersonal situations. It reminds the reviewer of a verbal multiple choice version of the Rosenzweig Picture-Frustration Study, using a different theoretical framework. The five subscales seem to represent appropriate categorizations of response tendencies in human interaction and the items cover a suitable range of home, family, work, and social situations. All the test materials are well designed and the attractive 1963 manual contains 10 pages of tables and an extensive treatment of validity. Obviously an enormous amount of work has preceded publication of this test.

It is, therefore, disappointing and a little saddening to be reminded so forcefully upon closer examination that conscientious work is not enough to produce a good test in the absence of clear thinking and methodological sophistication.

The author does not define social insight, but if one takes it to refer to empathic, intuitive, or perceptive capacities for understanding or responding effectively in social situations, then this test has little or nothing to do with it. The Social Insight score is obtained by adding one tenth of the Cooperativeness score and twice the Competitiveness score to the Aggression score, with lower scores indicating greater social insight. (Scores on Withdrawal and Passivity are ignored.) How this computation could add up to social insight, or any meaningful psychological construct for that matter, is difficult to fathom.

This peculiar system of weights was derived from a discriminant function analysis of the 5 subscale scores of 300 high school students and 300 institutionalized delinquents (sex unspecified). Apparently, the reasoning was this: delinquents have less social insight than normals. Therefore, any combination of scores which tends to separate delinquents from normals will constitute a measure of social insight. This fallacious logic is repeated throughout the validity section. For example, since females (including female guidance counselors) obtain better scores than their male counterparts, validity is supported, because everyone knows that women are more socially insightful than men. The same argument is made with respect to age.

A few of the findings give the author difficulty. In one study, it was discovered that pupils with better (i.e., lower) social insight scores had poorer reading ability ($r = .21$), lower academic achievement scores ($r = .26$), more tension and anxiety ($r = .26$), and lower grade averages ($r = .19$). The manual's only comment on these findings is that they "suggest that certain school competence problems should embrace consideration of social and personality phenomenon." To this reviewer they also suggest what was obvious from the methodology; i.e., that the total score on this test is a predictor of delinquency (and not a very powerful one at that—point biserial = .24). To name it a Test of Social Insight is misleading in the extreme: the total score might have been called a delinquency index, or a socialization or rebelliousness score and been closer to the truth.

The discriminant function method is very appropriately applied to selection problems, but it is ridiculous to take a system of weights developed for a specific problem in a particular population (e.g., delinquent versus normal youth) and try to use it to predict another outcome (e.g., the presence of social insight in other populations). Indeed, the manual includes two other regression analyses which reveal that the test would require different weights to separate ninth from twelfth graders depending upon their sex.

The Social Insight score on this test, then, should not be used at all, except as a possible measure of delinquency-proneness among adolescents. There is no occasion which would justify its use in the adult form of the test. Furthermore, published evidence demonstrates that the Pd scale of the *Minnesota Multiphasic Personality Inventory* or the So scale of the *California Psychological Inventory* are much more successful predictors of asocial tendencies.

The five subscales of the TSI probably warrant some study to see whether they might not function as useful measures of various modes of responding to social situations. Unfortunately, the manual provides no information whatever on the criteria for item selection or any comment on the correlations of item alternatives with their respective scale scores. The author acknowledges that reliabilities of the subscales are not impressive. Indeed, of 80 corrected odd-even coefficients reported, only 7 equal or exceed .80, and 31 fall below .50. No test-retest r's are reported, except for total score ($r = .84$).

For the subscales, the author feels that T scores between 40 and 60 are preferable, and low scores on several scales are said to indicate general "social or psycho-social immaturity," but the evidence for these interpretations is not given. One mildly irritating aspect of TSI interpretation is that *low* total scores are supposedly indicative of *greater* social insight, while *high* scores on the subscales indicate more tendency to respond in the indicated fashion. Norm groups are of adequate size for a new test but poorly described (e.g., "adults," "junior high students").

In this reviewer's opinion, the very considerable time, effort, and money that have been invested in this test should have been devoted to perfecting the subscales. It is not a test author's responsibility to develop regression equations for the many possible prediction problems for which his test might be used, and to make one such set of weights a permanent and integral part of a personality measure intended for wide application is not appropriate. Above all, to call this test a measure of social insight is completely misleading and very unfortunate. The thought of an unsuspecting personnel man using the TSI to select socially-insightful employees fills one with horror.

JOHN PIERCE-JONES, *Professor of Educational Psychology, The University of Texas, Austin, Texas.*

The *Test of Social Insight* (TSI), viewed in the terms in which it is presented in the manual, appears to be an interesting and potentially useful personality inventory. Construction of the device apparently occurred as a result of an interest on the part of the test's author in the construct of "social intelligence" as employed by Edward Lee Thorndike in his familiar tripartite analysis of intelligence. Cassel holds that "social insight" is functionally linked to intelligence, and to personality in both its cognitive and affective aspects, by way of the functioning of the ego. Hence, "social insight" may be appraised through sampling the individual's preferences among various possible modes of coping with "social problems" in several realms. This kind of thinking seems relatively straightforward and will have considerable appeal to potential test users who share the relatively widespread contemporary preference among students of personality for ego-centered theories of social-psychological human functioning.

Cassel's TSI, in both its Youth Edition and Adult Edition, is intended to sample an individual's preferences among five modes of resolving problems he encounters in social relationships. These modes—Withdrawal, Passivity, Cooperation, Competition, and Aggression—are adequately defined and are represented in the TSI by the five response alternatives from which an examinee chooses in answering 60 items which cut across four major areas of social intercourse: (*a*) family relations; (*b*) relations with social agencies and authority; (*c*) play and avocations; (*d*) work. The inventory yields subtest scores—one for each of the five modes of social coping—and a total score (using weighted part scores) presumably representing one's level of "social insight." The reusable test booklets are nicely printed, the separate IBM answer sheets are easily scored by means of scoring stencils, a brief but relatively well conceived Examiner's Manual reporting reliability and validity data has been made available recently (1963), and profile sheets with norms are attractive and convenient.

The reliability coefficients reported for both youth and adult forms are generally Spearman-Brown corrected split-halves equivalence correlations, although two stability coefficients, each based on test and retest scores for 100 cases, have also been presented. By and large the stability and equivalence coefficients for the adult form total score ("social insight") range through the middle .70's and .80's, but for the Youth Edition the total score reliabilities tend to be somewhat lower—too low for individual prediction, certainly, but generally satisfactory for distinguishing between groups of examinees. Coefficients of equivalence for the separate subtests tend to be disappointingly low, and subtest intercorrelations are frequently fairly high, albeit their signs suggest sensible relationships. The reliabilities of the subtests and of the test as a whole might well benefit from lengthening, and the norms might be more discriminating. To some extent, however, the relatively low equivalence reliability of the Youth Edition may reflect the consequences of what appear to be only very minor

modifications of wording in taking adult form items over into the youth form. It is this reviewer's impression that many of the items which appear well suited to tapping adults' social coping behavior preferences deal with aspects of social relationships which simply lack relevance for upper elementary school and junior high school youngsters even in sophisticated suburbia. It might have been better to develop children's and adolescents' forms independently than to derive them from the Adult Edition as seems to have been done. And, if it should be that social insight is differently organized in childhood than in adulthood (perhaps around different norms and sanctions which serve to define the modes of social coping), then it may be signally important to try to measure "social insight" in the terms of childhood social intercourse.

Evidence concerning the validities of the TSI appears to be accumulating, although it is not yet highly impressive in amount, and even though some of it—that concerning face validity for example—tends to seem specious. Empirically, TSI "social insight" appears to be associated significantly if modestly with (*a*) being female rather than male; (*b*) chronological age; (*c*) status with one's peers within a single school grade; (*d*) being socio-legally "normal" rather than "delinquent"; and various other test and extra-test criteria including IQ (*California Test of Mental Maturity*), tested scholastic achievement, childhood and family impoverishment, and scores from the *Leadership Ability Evaluation*.

In summary, it is this reviewer's opinion that Cassel's TSI is a promising effort to measure variables of obvious interest and importance to research psychologists, personnel workers, counselors, and educators; that the Youth Edition should not be used with individuals below the ninth grade; that a more relevant form should be devised for children and younger adolescents; that interpretations should be confined to differences between groups; and that individual predictions and diagnoses should not be undertaken until the reliability of the present TSI has been improved.

J Consult Psychol 24:100 F '60. Edward S. Bordin. * The odd-even reliabilities, even after Spearman-Brown corrections, are unsatisfactory, none above .88 and, in some populations, as low as .51. Validities based on inadequately reported unpublished data are more reassuring. Caveat Emptor!

[191]

★**Test of Work Competency and Stability.** Ages 21 and over; 1960–61, c1959–60; for predicting work capacity and identifying persons psychologically incapable of work; individual; 1 form consisting of an interview questionnaire (5 pages, mimeographed, 1 or 2 scores: ego strength and, optionally, occupational stability) and 4 or 6 tests: 2 perceptual tests of intelligence (digits backward, picture arrangement), 2 psychomotor tests (tapping, steadiness), and (optionally) stress test (mirror drawing), digit symbol; manual ('61, c1959, 58 pages, English edition translated from the 1960 French edition which is also available); record booklet ('60, 4 pages); no data on reliability for interview questionnaire, digits backwards, picture arrangement, or digit symbol; $110 per set of test materials including apparatus for tapping, steadiness, and mirror drawing tests, 25 record booklets, 25 questionnaires, 25 mirror tracing records, 25 tapping records, and manual; $3 per 25 questionnaires; $2 per 25 record booklets; $2.50 per manual; prices include purchase tax; postage extra; stopwatch necessary for administration; (30–40) minutes; A. Gaston Leblanc; Institut de Recherches Psychologiques. *

REFERENCES

1. LEBLANC, GASTON A. *Work Adjustment and Its Measurement.* Doctor's thesis, University of Montreal (Montreal, Que., Canada), 1958.
2. WEIL, PAUL G., AND LEBLANC, G. A. "The Assessment and Rehabilitation of the Psychologically Handicapped." *Med Services J Can* 16:765–72 O '60. *

[192]

Thurstone Temperament Schedule. Grades 9–16 and adults; 1949–53; 7 scores: active, vigorous, impulsive, dominant, stable, sociable, reflective; IBM; 2 editions; manual, second edition ('53, 14 pages); separate answer sheets or pads must be used; $10.80 per 20 tests; $1.15 per specimen set; postage extra; (15–25) minutes; L. L. Thurstone; Science Research Associates, Inc. *
a) [HAND SCORED EDITION.] Form AH ('49, 7 pages); $2.40 per 20 answer pads.
b) [MACHINE SCORABLE EDITION.] IBM; Form AM ('49, 7 pages); $5 per 100 IBM answer sheets; $2.50 per set of scoring stencils.

REFERENCES

1–12. See 5:118.
13. CONGER, JOHN J.; GASKILL, HERBERT S.; GLAD, DONALD D.; RAINEY, ROBERT V.; SAWREY, WILLIAM L.; AND TURRELL, EUGENE S. "Personal and Interpersonal Factors in Motor Vehicle Accidents." *Am J Psychiatry* 113:1069–74 Je '57. * (*PA* 32:6071)
14. NUNNERY, MICHAEL Y. *A Study in the Use of Psychological Tests in Determining Effectiveness and Ineffectiveness Among Practicing School Administrators.* Doctor's thesis, University of Tennessee (Knoxville, Tenn.), 1958. (*DA* 19:1276)
15. TALMADGE, MAX. "Expressive Graphic Movements and Their Relationship to Temperament Factors." *Psychol Monogr* 72(16):1–30 '58. * (*PA* 33:9733)
15a. KEISLAR, EVAN R. "The Validity of the Thurstone Temperament Schedule With Adolescents." *Personnel & Guid J* 38:226–8 N '59. * (*PA* 35:3758)
16. KING, PAUL; NORRELL, GWEN; AND ERLANDSON, F. L. "The Prediction of Academic Success in a Police Administration Curriculum." *Ed & Psychol Meas* 19:649–51 w '59. * (*PA* 34:6166)
17. NUNNERY, MICHAEL Y. "How Useful Are Standardized Psychological Tests in the Selection of School Administrators." *Ed Adm & Sup* 45:349–56 N '59. * (*PA* 35:7092)
18. COUCH, ARTHUR, AND KENISTON, KENNETH. "Yeasayers and Naysayers: Agreeing Response Set as a Personality Variable." *J Abn & Social Psychol* 60:151–74 Mr '60. * (*PA* 34:7376)
19. FISKE, DONALD W. "Variability Among Peer Ratings in Different Situations." *Ed & Psychol Meas* 20:283–92 su '60. * (*PA* 35:6337)

20. GIBLETTE, JOHN FRANKLIN. *Differences Among Above Average, Average, and Below Average Secondary School Counselors.* Doctor's thesis, University of Pennsylvania (Philadelphia, Pa.), 1960. (*DA* 21:812)
21. BORGATTA, EDGAR F. "Mood, Personality, and Interaction." *J General Psychol* 64:105–37 Ja '61. * (*PA* 35:6415)
22. BORGATTA, EDGAR F.; IN COLLABORATION WITH HENRY J. MEYER. "Make a Sentence Test: An Approach to Objective Scoring of Sentence Completions." *Genetic Psychol Monogr* 63:3–65 F '61. * (*PA* 35:6435)
23. BUEL, WILLIAM D., AND BAEHNER, VIRGINIA M. "The Assessment of Creativity in a Research Setting." *J Appl Psychol* 45:353–8 D '61. * (*PA* 37:1211)
24. MICHAEL, WILLIAM B.; BARTH, GEORGE; AND KAISER, HENRY F. "Dimensions of Temperament in Three Groups of Music Teachers." *Psychol Rep* 9:701–4 D '61. *
25. BORGATTA, EDGAR F. "The Coincidence of Subtests in Four Personality Inventories." *J Social Psychol* 56:227–44 Ap '62. * (*PA* 37:1247)
26. HULL, J., AND ZUBEK, JOHN P. "Personality Characteristics of Successful and Unsuccessful Sensory Isolation Subjects." *Percept & Motor Skills* 14:231–40 Ap '62. * (*PA* 37:312)
27. BECKER, ANTHONY J. "A Study of the Personality Traits of Successful Religious Women of Teaching Orders." *Yearb Nat Council Meas Ed* 20:124–5 '63. * (*PA* 38:9287)
28. GORDON, IRA J. "Personality Patterns of Volunteers for an Experimental Professional Education Program." *J Exp Ed* 32:115–21 f '63. *

For a review by Neil J. Van Steenberg, see 5:118; for reviews by Hans J. Eysenck, Charles M. Harsh, and David G. Ryans, see 4:93 (1 excerpt).

[193]

★**Triadal Equated Personality Inventory.** Adult males; 1960–63; 22 scores: dominance, self confidence, decisiveness, independence, toughness, suspiciousness, conscientiousness, introversion, restlessness, solemnity, foresight, industriousness, warmth, enthusiasm, conformity, inventiveness, persistence, sex drive, recognition drive, cooperativeness, humility-tolerance, self-control; 1 form ('61, 4 pages); administration and technical manual ('63, 4 pages); norms manual ('61, 4 pages); profile ('61, 1 page); separate answer sheets must be used; $10 per 25 tests; $2 per 25 answer sheets; $20 per set of keys; $2 per 25 profiles; $2 per specimen set (must be purchased to obtain manuals); cash orders postpaid; (60–80) minutes; Research Staff, United Consultants; Psychometric Affiliates. *

[194]

Vineland Social Maturity Scale. Birth to maturity; 1935–53; individual; 1 form ('36, 4 pages); condensed manual ('47, 44 pages); manual ('53, see *83*); $1.80 per 25 record blanks; $1.25 per condensed manual; $7.75 per manual; $1.30 per specimen set; postage extra; Edgar A. Doll; Educational Test Bureau. * (Australian edition: Australian Council for Educational Research.)

REFERENCES

1–58. See 3:107.
59–79. See 4:94.
80–94. See 5:120.
95. DOLL, EDGAR A. "Evaluating Social Maturity." *Ed* 77:409–13 Mr '57. *
96. NORRIS, MIRIAM; SPAULDING, PATRICIA J.; AND BRODIE, FERN H. *Blindness in Children.* Chicago, Ill.: University of Chicago Press, 1957. Pp. xv, 173. * (*PA* 32:824)
97. WERNER, EMMY. "Milieu Differences in Social Competence." *J Genetic Psychol* 91:239–49 D '57. * (*PA* 36:1FC39W)
98. ALLEN, ROBERT M. "Suggestions for the Adaptive Administration of Intelligence Tests for Those With Cerebral Palsy: Part 2, Administration of the Vineland Social Maturity Scale, the Gesell Preliminary Behavior Inventory, and the Cattell Infant Intelligence Scales." *Cerebral Palsy R* 19:6–7 Mr–Ap '58. * (*PA* 33:8853)
99. SMITH, LAURENCE C., JR., AND PHILLIPS, LESLIE. "Social Effectiveness and Developmental Level in Adolescence." *J Personality* 27:239–49 Je '59. * (*PA* 34:3898)
100. ZUK, G. H. "Autistic Distortions in Parents of Re-

tarded Children." *J Consult Psychol* 23:171–6 Ap '59. *
(*PA* 34:1687)
101. DUNSDON, M. I.; CARTER, C. O.; AND HUNTLEY, R.
M. C. "Upper End of Range of Intelligence in Mongolism."
Lancet 7124:565–8 Mr 12 '60. *
102. FRANCEY, RUTH E. "Psychological Test Changes in
Mentally Retarded Children During Training." *Can J Pub
Health* 51:69–74 F '60. *
103. ISCOE, IRA. "A Profile for the Vineland Scale and
Some Clinical Applications." *J Clin Psychol* 16:14–6 Ja
'60. * (*PA* 36:1HC14I)
104. JOHNSON, G. ORVILLE; CAPOBIANCO, RUDOLPH J.; AND
BLAKE, KATHRYN A. "An Evaluation of Behavioral Changes
in Trainable Mentally Deficient Children." *Am J Mental Def*
64:881–93 Mr '60. *
105. KADELL, MARY BELLE. *A Factor Analysis of the Vineland Social Maturity Scale and the Stanford-Binet Intelligence
Scale.* Master's thesis, University of Minnesota (Minneapolis,
Minn.), 1960.
106. PRINGLE, M. L. KELLMER. "Social Learning and Its
Measurement." *Ed Res* 2:194–206 Je '60. * (*PA* 35:4694)
107. SAHA, GOPI BALLAV. "An Investigation Into the School
Maturity of High School Students." *Indian J Psychol* 35:47–
54 pt 2 '60. * (*PA* 36:4KD47S)
108. STEER, M. D., AND DREXLER, HAZEL G. "Predicting
Later Articulation Ability From Kindergarten Tests." *J Speech
& Hearing Disorders* 25:391–7 N '60. * (*PA* 35:3911)
109. LEVINSON, BORIS M. "Parental Achievement Drives for
Preschool Children, the Vineland Social Maturity Scale, and
the Social Deviation Quotient." *J Genetic Psychol* 99:113–28
S '61. * (*PA* 36:3FF13L) (Abstract: *Acta Psychologica* 19:
420–1)
110. SCHERER, ISIDOR W. "The Prediction of Academic
Achievement in Brain Injured Children." *Excep Child* 28:
103–6 O '61. *
111. HURST, JOHN G. "The Meaning and Use of Difference
Scores Obtained Between the Performance on the Stanford-
Binet Intelligence Scale and Vineland Social Maturity Scale."
J Clin Psychol 18:153–60 Ap '62. * (*PA* 38:8422)
112. WOLFENSBERGER, WOLF. "Age Variations in Vineland
SQ Scores for the Four Levels of Adaptive Behavior of the
1959 AAMD Behavioral Classification." *Am J Mental Def*
67:452–4 N '62. * (*PA* 37:5424)
113. BARCLAY, A., AND GOULET, L. R. "An Interpretative
Profile Technique for Use With the Vineland Social Maturity
Scale." *J Clin Psychol* 19:303–4 Jl '63. *
114. GOULET, L. R., AND BARCLAY, A. "The Vineland Social
Maturity Scale: Utility in Assessment of Binet MA." *Am J
Mental Def* 67:916–21 My '63. * (*PA* 38:1273)

*For reviews by William M. Cruickshank and
Florence M. Teagarden, see 4:94; for reviews
by C. M. Louttit and John W. M. Rothney, see
3:107 (1 excerpt); for reviews by Paul H.
Furfey, Elaine F. Kinder, and Anna S. Starr
of Experimental Form B, see 38:1143; for
excerpts from related book reviews, see 5:B121.*

[195]

★The Visual-Verbal Test: A Measure of Conceptual Thinking. Schizophrenic patients; 1959–60;
individual; 1 form ['59, 46 cards]; mimeographed manual ('59, 11 pages); record booklet ('60, 4 pages);
$15 per set of picture cards, 25 record booklets, and
manual; $6.50 per 25 record booklets; $2.50 per manual; postpaid; specimen set not available; (30–130)
minutes; Marvin J. Feldman and James Drasgow;
Western Psychological Services. *

REFERENCES

1. BECKER, P. H. *A Visio-Verbal Test for Differentiating
Organic Brain Damaged Patients From Schizophrenics.* Master's thesis, University of Buffalo (Buffalo, N.Y.), 1950.
2. FELDMAN, MARVIN J., AND DRASGOW, JAMES. "A Visual-
Verbal Test for Schizophrenia." *Psychiatric Q Sup* 25:55–64
'51. * (*PA* 26:5748)
3. DRASGOW, JAMES. *Visio-Verbal Test for Schizophrenia.*
Doctor's thesis, University of Buffalo (Buffalo, N.Y.), 1952.
(*DA* 12:394)
4. SIEGEL, SAUL MARVIN. *A Study of the Visio-Verbal Test
in the Discrimination of Mental Defectives From Other
Clinical Groups.* Master's thesis, University of Buffalo (Buffalo, N.Y.), 1952.
5. JACOBS, ELEANOR A. *An Investigation of Some Relationships Between Personality Disturbance and Perceptual Reorganization.* Doctor's thesis, University of Buffalo (Buffalo,
N.Y.), 1954. (*DA* 15:1118)

6. DRASGOW, JAMES, AND FELDMAN, MARVIN. "Conceptual
Processes in Schizophrenia Revealed by the Visual-Verbal
Test." *Percept & Motor Skills* 7:251–64 D '57. * (*PA* 33:2828)
7. SIEGEL, SAUL M. "Discrimination Among Mental Defec-
tive, Normal, Schizophrenic and Brain Damaged Subjects on
the Visual-Verbal, Concept Formation Test." *Am J Mental
Def* 62:338–43 S '57. * (*PA* 33:1654)
8. PAYNE, R. W.; MATTUSSEK, P.; AND GEORGE, E. I. "An
Experimental Study of Schizophrenic Thought Disorder." *J
Mental Sci* 105:627–52 Jl '59. * (*PA* 34:6384)

R. W. PAYNE, *Associate Professor of Psychology, Queen's University, Kingston, Ontario,
Canada.*

The Feldman-Drasgow test of concept formation consists of a set of cards, each of which
depicts four objects in a row. For example, the
first card pictures four lines. Three are horizontal, and one vertical, and one of the horizontal lines is colored red. The subjects are
asked to indicate for each card three objects
which are alike in one way (e.g., three horizontal lines) and then to indicate three objects
which are alike in some other way (e.g., three
black lines). Subjects are given a time limit of
three minutes per card, and must explain each
concept adequately.

The test is designed to assess the ability to
form concepts. A "single miss" is defined as
missing one of the two concepts on a card, a
"double miss" is defined as missing both. The
reliability of the scores ranges from .70 to .86
(corrected split-half). Schizophrenic and brain
damaged subjects were expected to perform
poorly, and the results given in the manual
suggest that neurotics do slightly worse than
normals, acute schizophrenics significantly
worse than neurotics, chronic schizophrenics
worse still, and brain damaged patients and
mental defectives worst of all. Results for the
affective disorders are not given, an omission
which would limit the use of the test for some
cases of differential diagnosis.

Several carefully controlled studies [1] using
other techniques have reported results which
are inconsistent with these, in that acute schizophrenics were not found to be significantly concrete. In fact, Payne, Mattussek, and George
(8) used a test modeled on the Feldman-
Drasgow test, and did not find acute schizophrenics to be significantly more concrete than
a neurotic control group. Presumably the explanation for such contradictions must lie in
the particular samples tested, and here the main
inadequacies of the present manual become
apparent. The reader is told virtually nothing

1 PAYNE, R. W. Chap. 6, "Cognitive Abnormalities," pp.
193–261. In *Handbook of Abnormal Psychology: An Experimental Approach.* Edited by H. J. Eysenck. New York: Basic
Books, Inc., 1961. Pp. xvi, 816. * (*PA* 35:6719)

about the groups tested. The age, the level of intelligence, the socioeconomic level, the sex, the length of hospitalization, and the major symptomatology are all details which are needed if these norms are to be applied to other populations. Unfortunately none of these data are given. The reader is told that "age and education seem unrelated to error scores on the VVT" but no figures are quoted. Even the mean ages of the groups are not reported. Indeed, the *Visual-Verbal Test* scores themselves are inadequately reported. While the mean and standard deviations of the scores are given, the ranges are not. For such data to be of most use to the practising clinician, the entire histogram should be reproduced.

These deficiencies make the test as presently published of limited value.

DONALD R. PETERSON, *Professor of Psychology, and Director, Psychological Clinic, University of Illinois, Urbana, Illinois.*

Theories relating to schizophrenic thought have been inspiring tests of cognitive deficit for many years. The *Visual-Verbal Test* (VVT) is one of the more recent products, and it appears to be one of the most promising. The theoretical propositions on which the test is based are elementary and familiar: schizophrenics have difficulty (*a*) in forming categorical concepts, and (*b*) in changing to new concepts once primary ideas have been formed. Test materials are innocuous and easy to manipulate. After appropriate demonstrations, 42 cards, each containing 4 printed figures, are displayed. The task is readily comprehensible; subjects are asked to identify three stimulus items which are alike in some way, and then to identify three which are alike in some other way. Scoring is simple and objective. Three error scores are derived, a "double miss" score representing the number of cards on which the subject formed no accurate concepts at all, a "single miss" score representative of failure to develop more than one concept per card, and a "total miss" score obtained by weighting and adding the other two. Interpretation is relatively straightforward, and evidence on discriminatory power is about as convincing as one can expect at this stage in development of the test.

As to reliability, only odd-even consistency indices are reported. These are adequate but unimpressive. The reviewer computed uncor-rected *r*'s ranging from .45 for the double miss score with neurotics to .70 for the single miss score with mental defectives. The manual, of course, reports corrected (Spearman-Brown) values, and these only for the total miss score on three groups. Since much of the useful information from the test is derived from separate single miss and double miss scores, reliabilities of these should also be given. No information is provided on the stability of test performance, and the authors neglect to make proper apologies for the omission.

The test has been given to a variety of clinical groups and to five groups of "normal" adults. Selection of the latter always poses a problem in test development, but the authors of this test have met the problem with greater concern, ingenuity, and effort than is typically shown by the inventors of clinical diagnostic techniques. The original sample was composed of 37 volunteers whose cooperation was solicited while they were sitting around in a bus terminal. Of 40 approached, only 3 refused, and the remaining 37 did not differ reliably from schizophrenics in regard to age, IQ, and reported education. Data have also been obtained from non-psychiatric hospital patients, vocational counselees, and applicants for industrial jobs, as well as the usual group of college students.

The most striking evidence for concurrent validity arises from comparison of schizophrenic patients with the normal groups examined. Single miss scores have differentiated schizophrenics from normals with no overlap whatever. Results like these immediately mobilize some critical suspicions. Considering the limited reliability of psychiatric diagnosis, one begins to wonder whether test performance is not determined by the peculiarities of hospitalization, examiner bias, or some other equally irrelevant influence, rather than the conceptual abilities of subjects. In the knowledge of psychometric history, where one promising device after another has collapsed under careful and continued empirical scrutiny, one grows wary of strong enthusiasm. But Feldman and Drasgow have used no tricky weighting schemes to capitalize on chance; they have examined several groups in most of the classes of subjects, and several different examiners have given the tests. While the need for extensive cross validation remains, the authors appear to have met conventional obligations in a rather commendable way.

Differentiation between clinical groups is less clear, though some interesting patterns of findings have emerged. Acute schizophrenics have differed grossly from normals in single miss scores, and by inference in whatever abilities and dispositions are involved in generating two different concepts per card. On the average, however, acute schizophrenics did not exhibit the massive deficit required to accumulate high double miss scores. Chronic schizophrenics tended to score high in double as well as single errors. In fact the pattern of means for chronic schizophrenics bears close resemblance to that for mental defectives and is not vastly different from that for patients with known organic brain damage. This is consistent with the usual theories of cognitive deficit, but it limits the utility of the test in differential diagnosis and raises some questions about describing the device as a test of conceptual ability *in schizophrenia.* One of the neurotic samples, for instance, obtained a single miss mean nearly as high as that for one of the acute schizophrenic groups. Data on other clinical groups, e.g., affective psychotics, are not given. So the specificity of poor test performance to schizophrenia is in some respects unknown, and in other respects demonstrably limited.

Because of the ease with which the test can be given, and because of the encouraging trend of findings so far, the VVT is rather likely to be used by large numbers of spottily trained examiners, some of whom may test, score, and label patients in an indiscriminate way. The manual contains appropriate warnings about the need for caution in interpreting results, but misuse might be reduced more effectively if the manual offered actual score distributions rather than the "legal" but somewhat misleading schematic distributions which appear, if it contained stronger comment about overlap between clinical groups, and if it deemphasized the notion that conceptual failures are unique to schizophrenia.

Construct validity and predictive utility of the test are essentially unestablished. Minor claims which appear in the manual involve very elastic use of the term "construct validity." Relationships with traditional tests of concept formation, with other tests of psychological function, with behavior observations, treatment outcomes and the like, badly need determination.

But all this can be accomplished through further research. Right now, as it stands, the VVT is a brief, easily administered, fairly homogeneous instrument, yielding objective scores which have so far distinguished clearly between schizophrenic and normal subjects, and which have displayed some patterns, among schizophrenic and mentally retarded subjects particularly, of strong theoretical interest. The test should be given wide use as a research tool. Use as a clinical diagnostic instrument is questionable, but it is fair to say that the test is no less valuable in this regard than most other available instruments.

[196]

★WLW Personal Attitude Inventory. Business and industry; 1954–60; 6 scores: emotional stability, friendliness, aggressiveness, humility and insight, reliability, leadership; 2 editions: third edition ('55, 3 pages), fifth edition ('60, 4 pages); distribution of fifth edition restricted to clients; mimeographed manual ['56, 13 pages] for third edition; mimeographed supplement ('56, 2 pages); profile ('56, 1 page); norms for men only; $7.50 per 25 tests, postpaid; [20] minutes; R. W. Henderson, W. E. Brown, T. L. Chappell, L. D. Edmonson, W. H. E. Geiger, R. L. Kaiser, L. C. Steckle, and L. E. Saddler; William, Lynde & Williams. *

[197]

★Welsh Figure Preference Test, Research Edition. Ages 6 and over; 1959, c1949–59; 27 scores: don't like total, repeat, conformance, *Barron-Welsh Art Scale,* revised art scale, male-female, neuropsychiatric, children, movement, 5 sex symbol scores, and 13 figure-structure preference scores; 1 form ('59, c1949, 53 pages); mimeographed preliminary manual ('59, 35 pages); reliability data, based on earlier forms, for revised art scale and shortened versions of movement and don't like total only; norms below adult level for ages 6–8 only; separate answer sheets must be used; $8.50 per 25 tests; $2.50 per 50 answer sheets; scoring stencils must be constructed locally; $1 per manual; $1.50 per specimen set; postage extra; (50) minutes; George S. Welsh; Consulting Psychologists Press, Inc. *

REFERENCES
1. WELSH, GEORGE S. *A Projective Figure-Preference Test for Diagnosis of Psychopathology: 1, A Preliminary Investigation.* Doctor's thesis, University of Minnesota (Minneapolis, Minn.), 1949.
2. BARRON, FRANK, AND WELSH, GEORGE S. "Artistic Perception as a Possible Factor in Personality Style: Its Measurement by a Figure Preference Test." *J Psychol* 33:199–203 Ap '52. * (PA 26:6844)
3. MACKINNON, DONALD W. "The Development of Useful Tests for the Measurement of Non-Intellectual Functions," pp. 73–88. "Discussion of Professor MacKinnon's Paper," pp. 89–96, by John Dollard. General discussion, pp. 108–13. In *Proceedings of the 1951 Invitational Conference on Testing Problems, November 3, 1951.* Princeton, N. J.: Educational Testing Service, 1952. Pp. 119. *
4. BARRON, FRANK. "The Disposition Toward Originality." *J Abn & Social Psychol* 51:478–85 N '55. * (PA 31:2533)
5. ROSEN, JOHN C. "The Barron-Welsh Art Scale as a Predictor of Originality and Level of Ability Among Artists." *J Appl Psychol* 39:366–7 O '55. * (PA 30:6932)
6. PEPPER, LENNARD JAY. *The Relationship Between Welsh Figure Preference Test Responses and Indices of Anxiety and*

Repression. Master's thesis, University of North Carolina (Chapel Hill, N.C.), 1957.

7. SCHULTZ, K. V., AND KNAPP, W. E. "Perceptual Preferences and Self Descriptions." *Personnel & Guid J* 37:581–4 Ap '59. *

8. EDWARDS, ELISABETH STETSON. *Comparison of Responses of Children, Normal Adults and Schizophrenics on the Perceptual Maturity Scale.* Doctor's thesis, University of Denver (Denver, Colo.), 1961. *(DA* 23:700)

9. GOLANN, STUART EUGENE. *The Creativity Motive.* Doctor's thesis, University of North Carolina (Chapel Hill, N.C.), 1961. *(DA* 23:701)

10. HARRIS, THOMAS LEWIS. *An Analysis of the Responses Made by Adolescents to the Welsh Figure Preference Test and Its Implications for Guidance Purposes.* Doctor's thesis, University of North Carolina (Chapel Hill, N.C.), 1961. *(DA* 22:2687)

11. MACKINNON, DONALD W. "Fostering Creativity in Students of Engineering." *J Eng Ed* 52:129–42 D '61. * *(PA* 36:4HD29M)

12. CARACENA, PHILIP F., AND KING, GERALD F. "Generality of Individual Differences in Complexity." *J Clin Psychol* 18:234–6 Ap '62. * *(PA* 38:8480)

13. GOLANN, STUART E. "The Creativity Motive." *J Personality* 30:588–600 D '62. * *(PA* 39:1777)

14. L'ABATE, LUCIANO; BOELLING, GARY M.; HUTTON, ROBERT D.; AND MATHEWS, DEWEY L., JR. "The Diagnostic Usefulness of Four Potential Tests of Brain Damage." Abstract. *J Consult Psychol* 26:479 O '62. *

15. MACKINNON, DONALD W. "The Personality Correlates of Creativity: A Study of American Architects," pp. 11–39. *(PA* 37:4958) In *Personality Research.* Proceedings of the XIV International Congress of Applied Psychology, Vol. 2. Copenhagen, Denmark: Munksgaard, Ltd., 1962. Pp. 229. *

16. PINE, FRED. "Creativity and Primary Process: Sample Variations." *J Nerv & Mental Dis* 134:506–11 Je '62. * *(PA* 37:3205)

17. SECHREST, LEE, AND JACKSON, DOUGLAS N. "The Generality of Deviant Response Tendencies." *J Consult Psychol* 26:395–401 O '62. * *(PA* 39:1822)

18. VAN DE CASTLE, R. L. "Perceptual Immaturity and Acquiescence Among Various Developmental Levels." *J Consult Psychol* 26:167–71 Ap '62. * *(PA* 37:5019)

19. BARRON, FRANK. "Discovering the Creative Personality," pp. 79–85. In *The Behavioral Sciences and Education.* New York: College Entrance Examination Board, 1963. Pp. vi, 99. *

20. NORMAN, WARREN T. "Relative Importance of Test Item Content." *J Consult Psychol* 27:166–74 Ap '63. * *(PA* 37:7980)

HAROLD BORKO, *Human Factors Scientist, Advanced Technology and Research Directorate, System Development Corporation, Santa Monica, California.*

The *Welsh Figure Preference Test* (WFPT) was designed "to afford non-language stimulus material suitable for a wide range of subjects who could not be tested readily with conventional personality inventories and projective methods." The design of the WFPT was influenced by the *Minnesota Multiphasic Personality Inventory.* This is understandable for Welsh studied at the University of Minnesota, was influenced by the MMPI, and through his own research influenced the development of the MMPI. It will be recalled that a basic tenet of the MMPI is that if the response to an item differentiates between two groups of people, then it is a "good" item. No assumption need be made as to whether the subject has insight into the meaning of the item or into his own dynamics in answering the item. If one adheres to this philosophy, it is a short but significant step to say that the test item can be meaningless, i.e., it can be a picture, as long as it differentiates

between two groups. In essence the WFPT is an abstract form, or picture version, of an MMPI-type test. It consists of a booklet (Welsh also experimented with a card form) containing 400 black and white line drawings. The instructions are simple; the subject is asked "to decide whether you like or don't like each of the drawings on the following pages" and to record the answers on a separate sheet. The test takes 50 to 60 minutes to complete, and the results can be scored objectively.

The reliability of the WFPT has not been satisfactorily demonstrated. In the one reported study, a group of 29 undergraduate students in psychology were given the card form of the test and one week later were given the booklet form containing only 144 items. Another group of 35 students were given the same two tests in reversed order. The protocols were scored for only the Revised Art Scale (RA), a portion of the Movement Scale (MV), and a portion of the Don't Like Scale (DL). The reliability of the RA Scale is high (test-retest correlations of .94 and .90) and, in the words of the author, reflects "remarkable consistency." The reliability of the partial MV Scale is lower (.64 and .74) but still consistent, and the reliability coefficients for the DL Scale are, if anything, remarkably inconsistent (.88 and .51 for the total scale and .92 and .51 for the partial scale). Welsh suggests that, "The markedly lower correlations for the second group were due to two extreme individuals." Perhaps so, but this is all the more reason to use a reasonable sample when obtaining reliability figures. The lack of adequate reliability statistics based upon a representative sample of both normal and patient populations and covering all of the test scales is a most serious deficiency in the test as it now stands. Even the standardizing population is relatively small consisting of (*a*) 100 male patients in a Veterans Administration neuropsychiatric hospital, (*b*) 150 normal adults (75 males and 75 females), and (*c*) 82 children ages 6 to 8 (42 boys and 40 girls).

Putting aside the question of reliability, let us examine the validity of the instrument. The manual states that the WFPT can be used when conventional personality inventories are not appropriate. Since the items are pictorial rather than verbal, the subject need not be literate. This is a distinct advantage, for it does make the test usable when other instruments such as the MMPI would not be appropriate. But what aspects of personality does the test measure? Welsh never really answers this question. He stresses the fact that the test is a research instrument and that the scales are to be considered provisional in nature. He claims that, "One of the scales, the Barron-Welsh Art Scale, has been rather extensively used and can be considered to be in final form." This 65-item scale can separate artists from non-artists. The Revised Art Scale correlates highly with the Barron-Welsh scale, but is apparently not yet in final form. Of the other empirical scales, the Male-Female Scale (MF) has not held up in cross validation. The Children's Scale (CN) which purports to differentiate 6- and 8-year-olds from adults has not yet been validated. On the positive side, the Neuropsychiatric Scale (NP) of 40 items designed to distinguish VA patients from people in general has been cross validated, and the author suggests that it may be used in its present form. There are other scales, both empirical and *a priori* in nature, but they are only suggestive and the scores cannot now be interpreted with any degree of confidence. It appears that the test does not measure many of the personality directions and even these are not measured with much confidence.

As a research instrument the WFPT has potential. The 400 items can be administered to various groups—neurotics and psychotics, gifted and normal, overachievers and underachievers, orientals and Caucasians, etc.—with the objective of finding sets of items that distinguish between these groups. Then the research must be continued and the scales shown to be reliable and valid. Until a set of scales have been validated for the *Welsh Figure Preference Test,* the test has little practical value.

J Counsel Psychol 7:310–11 w '60. Gordon V. Anderson. [Review of the earlier card form.] This psychological instrument is a completely nonverbal measure, the ultimate intent of which is to provide an index of emotional adjustment and to identify and quantify personality characteristics. The format of the test and the instructions for response, however, lead to the inference that it is a measure of aesthetic discrimination or judgment. Indeed, the Barron-Welsh Art Scale is incorporated into the test, yielding a score on aesthetic judgment, which has been accepted by many as one component of artistic ability, although there are better tests of this ability already available. * is made up of 400 "cards" presented to the subject, on each of which is a drawing or design, and the simple instruction is to respond as "Like" or "Don't Like" * The simplicity of the test approach makes it usable with almost any age, and there are no language barriers. * There are two empirically derived scales, the B-W Art scale and a Neuro-psychiatric scale which separates disturbed from normal subjects. Besides these empirical scales, the test yields three other scores: a "Repeat" (RP) score, based on the consistency with which the subject responds to twenty items which have been repeated; a "Don't Like" (DL) score which is a simple count of the total number of items the subject has placed in that category, and a "Conformance" (CF) score, based on a series of items upon which there was high agreement among a general population and artist sample. These scores presently have no known clinical significance, except that the RP score may indicate the possibility of scoring errors or failure of the subject's cooperation. The manual, which is still in preliminary form, doesn't give much information about reliability * The standardization samples for this test are quite small, and should be accepted as only tentative. * The principal purpose in calling this test to the attention of counselors is not in its practical value now. This is quite limited. The test represents, however, a novel line of development which has been spurred during the past few years by psychologists interested in trying to bring together the projective and the psychometric approaches. It would be difficult to guess what lies behind a response on this test. But as careful empirical studies are made, it may be that we can make progress toward discovering what the responses mean for future behavior. In practice, this test may give a useful lead on level of adjustment in cases where a verbal test is not feasible; it may also be useful in working with students interested in the field of art. It is, however, *a research test* and before any reliance can be placed on its scores, further validation work is essential. Most of the scales on the test have been related for one group or another to such leading verbal personality instruments as the Adjective Checklist, the MMPI, the California Psychological Inventory, and the Edwards Personal Preference Schedule. The resulting correlation co-efficients are not high enough to permit generalizing from one to another, but are large enough to give us the basis for believing that here is another lead in the direction of structured personality measurement. Clients who seek counseling seem to enjoy taking tests. This one is less likely than most to bias the counseling relationship, and some good research leads might be developed. It would also be a gain if similar tests with more appealing items could be developed. The Welsh figures in the main seem so neutral that this reviewer finds it hard to understand how a meaningful affective response can be made to most of them.

[198]

*The Western Personality Inventory. Adults; 1948–63; a combination in one booklet of *The Alcadd Test* ('49) and *The Manson Evaluation* ('48); identification of alcoholics and potential alcoholics; 1 form ('63, 6 pages); manual ('63, 4 pages, a combination, including identical norms and technical data, of the 1948 and 1949 manuals for the previously cited tests); $8 per 25 tests and manual; $1 per manual; postpaid; specimen set not available; (20–40) minutes; Morse P. Manson; Western Psychological Services. *

For a review by Dugal Campbell of The Alcadd Test, see 60; for reviews by Charles H. Honzik and Albert L. Hunsicker, see 4:30. For a review by Dugal Campbell of The Manson Evaluation, see 137; for reviews by Charles H. Honzik and Albert L. Hunsicker, see 4:68.

[199]

★William, Lynde & Williams Analysis of Personal Values, Second Edition. Business and industry; 1958–62; 6 scores: theoretical, practical, social, personal power, aesthetic, religious; 1 form ('60, 4 pages); mimeographed combined manual ('62, 8 pages) for this test and test 1074; no data on reliability and validity; $4 per 25 tests, postpaid; [15] minutes; R. W. Henderson; William, Lynde & Williams. *

[Other Tests]

For tests not listed above, see the following entries in *Tests in Print:* 102, 104, 111–2, 114, 116, 119–20, 122, 125, 127, 132, 135, 140–1, 146, 148–9, 151–2, 156, 158, 162, 166–7, 173, 192, 194–6, 198–200, 202, 205–8, 211–4, 225, 233, 235, 235a, 235b, 236, 238–9, 241–2, 244, 247–9, 251–3, 257–8, 260–2, 266, 268, 271, 273, 278–83, 286–7, 292, 295, 298, 303, 310–2, 317–8, 320, and 323–4; out of print: 100, 107, 115, 150, 177, 186, 232, 237, 240, 263, 269–70, 274, 285, 303b, and 322; status unknown: 105, 160, 197, and 245.

PROJECTIVE

[200]

★The African T.A.T. Urban Africans; 1960–61; individual; 1 form ['60, 9 cards]; no manual; interpretive data presented in *1* below; no data on reliability; 60s. per set of cards, postage extra; [180] minutes; J. C. de Ridder; [Industrial Psychological Services.] *

REFERENCES

1. DE RIDDER, J. C. *The Personality of the Urban African in South Africa: A Thematic Apperception Test Study.* London: Routledge & Kegan Paul Ltd., 1961. Pp. xvi, 180. * (PA 37:4811)

For excerpts from related book reviews, see B153.

[201]

★Association Adjustment Inventory. Normal and institutionalized adults; 1959; adaptation of *Kent-Rosanoff Free Association Test;* 13 scores: juvenility, psychotic responses, depressed-optimistic, hysteric-nonhysteric, withdrawal-sociable, paranoid-naive, rigid-flexible, schizophrenic-objective, impulsive-restrained, sociopathic-empathetic, psychosomapathic-physical contentment, anxious-relaxed; total; IBM; 1 form (4 pages); 2 editions: consumable, reusable; manual (15 pages); $5 per 25 tests; $4.50 per set of keys; separate answer sheets must be used with reusable edition; $2.75 per 25 IBM answer sheets; $4.50 per set of scoring stencils; $2.75 per 25 profiles; $1.75 per manual; $5 per specimen set; cash orders postpaid; (10–15) minutes; Martin M. Bruce; the Author. *

W. Grant Dahlstrom, *Professor of Psychology, University of North Carolina, Chapel Hill, North Carolina.*

The AAI is offered "for use as a screening instrument for maladjustment....and immaturity....and as an aid in diagnosing deviate ideation." The method of derivation of this instrument parallels that of many group tests of intellective ability, namely, the reliance upon pre-existing tests and scales to provide criteria of different personality characteristics. Whereas the 1916 Stanford-Binet proved to be sufficiently dependable to provide criterion information for the group tests being scaled against it, there are no scales with sufficient precision or established validity available for new test construction efforts in the area of personality and maladjustment. Thus, this promising method of scale development appears to be prematurely applied in this instance.

The limitation in test construction described above would not, of course, be necessarily a fatal one were the test constructor to proceed with the rest of the job of test validation and try to match his test findings with nontest data. Even four or five years after the appearance of this instrument, the potential user of the AAI has at his disposal no dependable validational data or other guides as to the test's accuracy, efficiency, or utility in serving its avowed purposes. The Examiner's Manual includes sets of intercorrelations of the component scales, correlations of these scales with the basic scales of the MMPI (against which they were in part derived), and correlations with the scales of the *Polyfactorial Study of Personality,* a companion test developed by Bruce and Stark on the same population of subjects. While many of these values of inter-scale relationship are suggestive of useful variance, no meaningful assessment of the utility of the AAI can be drawn from sets of correlational values alone. Detailed tabulations of the degree of clinically relevant separations of selected patients and normals must be made available to determine these performances in practical problems.

The rationale for the AAI is in itself a reasonable one and is advanced as an approach based upon long-standing experimental research. Each of the stimulus words in the Kent-Rosanoff (1910) word list for free association study is provided with four response alternatives in a multiple choice format. The subject is to choose the one alternative that he "associates" with the stimulus word and either circle it (booklet form) or mark the number corresponding to it on the answer sheet (in the reusable form). The alternatives were chosen from words reported in free association studies of adult subjects by Kent and Rosanoff and by Woodrow and Lowell[1] in their study of children's associations. The alternatives for each stimulus word consist of one word that is the most frequent adult association, one that appears rarely (two to six times in a thousand), one that appears only once, and finally one that does not appear in the adult tabulations but is present in the juvenile list of associations. Not all stimulus words could be provided with all four kinds of association alternates, and additional departures from this *a priori* construction of the items were dictated by preliminary studies of the discriminations between normals and disturbed subjects. Since the scoring of four of the scales in the AAI is based upon these item-alternate sources, greater effort could have been extended to get more contemporary sets of responses and frequencies of appearance. Thus, the scale for immaturity, Juvenility (J), is apparently a tally of the number of item alternates marked that came from the children's

free association list. Jenkins and Russell[2] report data suggesting that systematic shifts have occurred over the last three or four decades, at least in adult frequencies. Even more importantly, there is little concern shown in this *a priori* scoring of four of the AAI scales for the change in psychological processes reflected in the modification of the material from free association to multiple choice formats. Here many different response sets seem to be called forth in a situation provided with maximum opportunity for editing and dissimulation. This seems particularly the case when the test author labels the test blank with the highly charged term "adjustment" and provides no other guide or instruction to the test subject.

The empirically derived scales were constructed against some (unspecified) score composites of Rorschach variables, House-Tree-Person scores, and MMPI scales, together with psychiatric diagnosis. The basic data came from hospitalized psychiatric patients, prison inmates, outpatients in psychiatric therapy, and a mixed group of normals including college and school students, job applicants for white collar positions, and employees already in those positions. These scale derivations may have been sound but it is impossible to tell from the data provided in the manual. Norms are presented in z score form ($+5.00$ to -5.00) on all scales for both a population of normals and a population of institutionalized subjects. The scoring materials and profiles are well made, legible, and internally consistent, except that the profile only runs the z scores to ± 4.00.

This reviewer looked in vain for the designation on this test, "For Research Use Only." It must be so designated. Several publications are promised in the body of the manual and when they appear, the worth of this original test may prove to be as good as the author now claims. Until that time, it should not be employed in contexts in which important decisions must rest upon the data it provides.

BERTRAM R. FORER, *Consulting Psychologist, and Executive Editor, Journal of Projective Techniques and Personality Assessment, Suite 307, 8833 Sunset Boulevard, Los Angeles, California.*

The inventory represents one of the feasible kinds of modification of the word association

1 WOODROW, HERBERT, AND LOWELL, FRANCES. "Children's Association Frequency Tables." *Psychol Monogr* 22(5):1–110 '16. *

2 JENKINS, JAMES J., AND RUSSELL, WALLACE A. "Systematic Changes in Word Association Norms: 1910–52." *J Abn & Social Psychol* 60:293–304 My '60. * (*PA* 35:4958)

method for the more sophisticated requirements of contemporary psychological assessment. One line of adaptation is the sentence completion method which, by amplifying the content and structure of test stimuli, elicits a broader spectrum of responses with rich possibilities for individual clinical diagnostic use. But there is a corresponding lowering of the likelihood of obtaining objective scores and measures of reliability and validity.

The *Association Adjustment Inventory,* by providing multiple choice responses to single-word stimuli, restricts freedom of response, insures greater reliability of item scoring, and increases the likelihood of developing scales that can be standardized. The test, then, is minimally projective and individuality is represented exclusively in the quantitative scales and the overall profile of scale scores.

The test's development and the manual seem better psychometrically than clinically. The author's rationale in terms of personality theory is rather thin. The response choices might have made better psychological sense if they had been based on clinical acumen rather than the apparently unsystematic method that was used. But it is clear that the author has taken seriously APA recommendations for test standards.

He has achieved moderately good coverage of varied deviant groups; this coverage is probably more satisfactory than his sampling of normal adults and children. The sample of adult normals lacks cases in lower occupational levels and the professions. The children's group is not specified as to age and it is dubious that preadolescent children would understand the test instructions. Hence the reported lack of differentiation of children and psychotics (based on the total score on the original form of the test) is not clearly understandable.

To this reviewer it seems that insufficient information is presented about the method of validating the scales. It is not clear both how and why the Rorschach was employed as one of the major criteria in item analysis. The author and a colleague refer to subsequent publications on this and other points. Eventually they ought to be incorporated in a revised manual.

The author has done a good deal of empirical work in attempts to pursue tests of validity. The evidence of high scale reliability is reassuring. The separate norms for general and institutionalized populations provide some basis for large scale screening but require implementation with considerably more evidence of successful discrimination of other samples of deviant populations.

In no way does this inventory seem to provide the kind of data obtained from projective methods for individual assessment. It is impossible to predict whether it will be as useful as the MMPI with an equal amount of research behind it. It appears to be a reliable instrument and is worthy of experimental use and a chance to prove itself.

J Consult Psychol 24:100 F '60. Edward S. Bordin. * Test-retest correlations for one week and one month intervals are satisfactory, but the base for claiming validity is very unsatisfactory. There is evidence of some general relationships with MMPI scales and with a largely unvalidated inventory. Reference is made to unreported results of diagnostic validity studies that are unpublished. It should have been marked "For Experimental Use."

[202]
*The Behavioral Complexity Test: A Test for Use in Research.** Ages 5 and over; 1955–61; revision of *The Adult-Child Interaction Test;* 9 scores: continuum (weighted total of scores for 5 complexity of response categories), symbolization (5 scores), emotional perceptional (positive, negative, total); individual; 1 form ('61, 8 cards, same as cards used with 1956 test); manual ('61, 14 pages plus test cards); record blank ['61, 3 pages]; no norms; *out of print;* [20–25] minutes; Theron Alexander; distributed by Campus Stores. *

REFERENCES
1. ALEXANDER, THERON. *The Prediction of Teacher-Pupil Interactions With a Projective Test.* Doctor's thesis, University of Chicago (Chicago, Ill.), 1949.
2. ALEXANDER, THERON. *The Adult-Child Interaction Test: A Projective Test for Use in Research.* Monographs of the Society for Research in Child Development, Inc., Vol. 27, Serial No. 55, No. 2. Champaign, Ill.: Child Development Publications, the Society, 1955. Pp. v, 40, plus 8 cards. * (PA 29:7252)
3. OHLSEN, MERLE M., AND SCHULTZ, RAYMOND E. "Projective Test Response Patterns for Best and Poorest Student Teachers." *Ed & Psychol Meas* 15:18–27 sp '55. *
4. OELKE, MERRITT C. "A Study of Student Teachers' Attitudes Toward Children." *J Ed Psychol* 47:193–8 Ap '56. * (PA 32:2154)

JOHN ELDERKIN BELL, *Program Director, National Institute of Mental Health, United States Public Health Service, San Francisco, California.*

The eight basic stimulus cards appear well designed to provide thematic content around which a subject may invent stories. We have many such cards available, however, and the advantage of these over others as stimuli for narratives should not absorb our time. The distinctive feature of this TAT type instrument is the system developed for categorizing various features of the stories and the blank for recording them. If the user chooses, he may also analyze the stories as projections.

Three overall groups of scores may be developed: (a) the occurrence and organization of a series of defined story elements such as the events in the story, their causation, and the outcome—the Behavioral Continuum; (b) the stimulus elements used or concrete objects added—Symbolization; and (c) the positive and negative feelings and actions attributed to the figures in the cards—the Emotional Perception.

The record blank is well designed for its functions of tabulating for each story the scores in the above three categories and arriving at appropriate overall totals.

Unfortunately, the amount of research based on this test remains limited so that measures of scorer and test-retest reliability and validity recorded in the manual can only suggest that, in respect to these properties, the evidence merits continuing use and evaluation of the test. Because of the objective features of the scoring, the test would seem a particularly valuable complement to the increasing range of instruments for studying the development of perception, imagination, language, and conception in children. It helps to bridge the gap between the perceptual-motor tests and the free story-telling techniques—and in this respect compares with the infrequently used but valuable *Four Picture Test* for adults.

[203]

*[Bender-Gestalt Test.] Ages 4 and over; 1938-64; individual; the original Bender-Gestalt is listed as a below; the modifications listed as b–e consist primarily of alterations in administration procedure, new scoring systems, or expanded interpretive procedures, rather than changes in the test materials; b–e use essentially the same administration procedure as the basic testing procedure; c and d provide, in addition, for use of the materials as projective stimuli for associations. a) VISUAL MOTOR GESTALT TEST. Ages 4 and over; 1938-46; 1 form ('46, 9 cards); directions for administering ('46, 8 pages); manual ('38, see 5 below); no data on reliability; $1.25 per set of cards and directions; $5.35 per manual; postpaid; [10] minutes; Lauretta Bender; American Orthopsychiatric Association, Inc. *
b) THE BENDER GESTALT TEST. Ages 4 and over; 1951; utilizes same test cards as a; scoring sheet ['51, 1 page]; manual ('51, see 41 below); $2.25 per pad of 50 scoring sheets; $7.75 per manual; postage extra; (10) minutes; Gerald R. Pascal and Barbara J. Suttell; Grune & Stratton, Inc. *

c)*REVISED BENDER-GESTALT TEST. Ages 7 and over; 1944-60; also called *Hutt Adaptation of the Bender-Gestalt Test;* 1 form ('60, 9 cards, same as cards of a except for modification in 1 design and in drawing method throughout); record form ('60, 4 pages); manual ('60, see 192 below); no data on reliability of scored factors; $1.25 per set of cards; $2.50 per 25 record forms; $5 per manual; postage extra; [45-60] minutes; Max L. Hutt and Gerald J. Briskin; Grune & Stratton, Inc. *
d)★THE BENDER VISUAL MOTOR GESTALT TEST FOR CHILDREN. Ages 7-11; 1962; utilizes same test cards as a; manual (72 pages); record form (4 pages); no data on reliability and validity; $2.50 per set of cards; $5.50 per 25 record forms; $6 per manual; postpaid; (10) minutes without associations; Aileen Clawson; Western Psychological Services. *
e)★THE BENDER GESTALT TEST FOR YOUNG CHILDREN. Ages 5-10; 1964; a developmental scoring system; utilizes same test cards as a; manual (204 pages, reprint of 259 below); $6.75 per manual, postage extra; administration time not reported; Elizabeth Munsterberg Koppitz; Grune & Stratton, Inc. *
f)★THE VISUAL MOTOR GESTALT TEST TWO-COPY DRAWING FORM. 1964; 1 form (1 page plus backing sheet); $6.50 per 25 forms; Western Psychological Services. *

REFERENCES

1-8. See 3:108.
9-42. See 4:144.
43-160. See 5:172.
161. SILVER, ARCHIE A. "Diagnostic Value of Three Drawing Tests for Children." *J Pediatrics* 37:129-43 Jl '50. * (PA 25:3191)
162. LAKIN, MARTIN. "Clinical Use of the Bender Visual Motor Test in Psychological Assessment of the Aged." *J Am Geriatrics Soc* 4:909-19 S '56. *
163. BATEMAN, WILLIAM J. *The Validity of the Bender-Gestalt Test in Making a Diagnostic Conclusion.* Master's thesis, North Texas State College (Denton, Tex.), 1957.
164. RIBLER, RONALD IRWIN. *The Detection of Brain Damage Through Measurement of Deficit in Behavioral Functions.* Doctor's thesis, Michigan State University (East Lansing, Mich.), 1957. (DA 19:1810)
165. SEAGRAVES, MILTON D. *The Bender-Gestalt Test as a Means of Determining School Readiness.* Master's thesis, University of Tennessee (Knoxville, Tenn.), 1957.
166. CHANG, SIAO-CHANG, AND TANG, KUAN-YING. "A Study of Mental Disturbance Among the Retired Servicemen in the Nuan-Nuan Center." *Acta Psychologica Taiwanica* (1):64-84 N '58. * (PA 34:3157)
167. LOTHROP, WILLIAM W. "Relationship Between Bender-Gestalt Test Scores and Medical Success With Duodenal Ulcer Patients." *Psychosom Med* 20:30-2 Ja-F '58. * (PA 33:6260)
168. SAFIAN, MURRAY Z. *A Study of Certain Psychological Factors in the Rehabilitation of Potentially Employable Homebound Adults.* Doctor's thesis, New York University (New York, N.Y.), 1958. (DA 19:3372)
169. SIMPSON, WILLIAM HAROLD. *A Study of Some Factors in the Bender Gestalt Reproductions of Normal and Disturbed Children.* Doctor's thesis, University of Oklahoma (Norman, Okla.), 1958. (DA 19:1120)
170. VERNIER, CLAIRE M.; STAFFORD, JOHN W.; AND KRUGMAN, ARNOLD D. "A Factor Analysis of Indices From Four Projective Techniques Associated With Four Different Types of Physical Pathology." *J Consult Psychol* 22:433-7 D '58. * (PA 33:9360)
171. VITANZA, A. A.; GRAHAM, STANLEY R.; RAWN, M. L.; AND BRINITZER, WALTER. "Psychological Judgment of the Bender Gestalt Test Compared With Three Physiological Vectors and Psychiatric Judgment." *Psychol Rep* 4:729-30 D '58. * (PA 34:1432)
172. CHOROST, SHERWOOD B.; SPIVACK, GEORGE; AND LEVINE, MURRAY. "Bender-Gestalt Rotations and EEG Abnormalities in Children." Abstract. *J Consult Psychol* 23:559 D '59. * (PA 34:6010)
173. CLAWSON, AILEEN. "The Bender Visual Motor Gestalt Test as an Index of Emotional Disturbance in Children." *J Proj Tech* 23:198-206 Je '59. * (PA 35:4717)
174. GOLDBERG, LEWIS R. "The Effectiveness of Clinicians' Judgments: The Diagnosis of Organic Brain Damage From the Bender-Gestalt Test." *J Consult Psychol* 23:25-33 F '59. * (PA 34:1364)
175. KOPPITZ, ELIZABETH M.; SULLIVAN, JOHN; BLYTH, DAVID D.; AND SHELTON, JOEL. "Prediction of First Grade School Achievement With the Bender Gestalt Test and Human Figure Drawings." *J Clin Psychol* 15:164-8 Ap '59. * (PA 35:5372)

176. LIPSCOMB, DAVID M. *A Study of the Response of Children Enrolled in a School for the Deaf to the Bender Visual Gestalt Test.* Master's thesis, University of Redlands (Redlands, Calif.), 1959.

177. MCDANIEL, JAMES W., JR. *Stimulus Values of the Bender Visual Motor Gestalt Test Designs.* Master's thesis, North Texas State College (Denton, Tex.), 1959.

178. NADLER, EUGENE B.; FINK, STEVEN L.; SHONTZ, FRANKLIN C.; AND BRINK, ROBERT W. "Objective Scoring vs. Clinical Evaluation of the Bender-Gestalt." *J Clin Psychol* 15:39–41 Ja '59. * (*PA* 34:2976)

179. PRICE, JOSEPH W. *Signs of Paranoid Schizophrenic Behavior on the Bender-Gestalt Test.* Master's thesis, North Texas State College (Denton, Tex.), 1959.

180. ARMSTRONG, RENATE G., AND HAUCK, PAUL A. "Correlates of the Bender-Gestalt Scores in Children." *J Psychol Studies* 11:153–8 Mr–Ap '60. * (*PA* 34:7830)

181. AZIMA, FERN CRAMER, AND KRAL, V. A. "Effects of Blindfolding on Persons During Psychological Testing: A Psychometric Study of Various Age Groups." *Geriatrics* 15:780–92 N '60. *

182. COROTTO, LOREN V., AND CURNUTT, ROBERT H. "The Effectiveness of the Bender-Gestalt in Differentiating a Flight Group From an Aggressive Group of Adolescents." *J Consult Psychol* 24:368–9 Ag '60. * (*PA* 35:2204)

183. CROSSON, JAMES E. *Relative Discriminative Efficiency of the Bender-Gestalt and the Modified Vigotsky Tests When Used With Organics, Normals, and Schizophrenics.* Master's thesis, Kansas State College of Pittsburg (Pittsburg, Kan.), 1960.

184. CURNUTT, ROBERT H., AND COROTTO, LOREN V. "The Use of Bender Gestalt Cut-Off Scores in Identifying Juvenile Delinquents." *J Proj Tech* 24:353–4 D '60. * (*PA* 35:5208)

185. FULLER, JERRY B. *Factors Influencing Rotation in the Bender-Gestalt Performance of Children.* Doctor's thesis, University of Ottawa (Ottawa, Ont., Canada), 1960.

186. GARVEY, MARGARET J., AND POPPLESTONE, JOHN A. "Influence of Age and Sex on Bender Gestalt Associations." *Percept & Motor Skills* 11:258 D '60. * (*PA* 35:1975)

187. GAVALES, DANIEL, AND MILLON, THEODORE. "Comparison of Reproduction and Recall Size Deviations in the Bender-Gestalt as Measures of Anxiety." *J Clin Psychol* 16:278–80 Jl '60. * (*PA* 36:2HK78G)

188. GRIFFITH, RICHARD M. AND TAYLOR, VIVIAN H. "Incidence of Bender-Gestalt Figure Rotations." *J Consult Psychol* 24:189–90 Ap '60. * (*PA* 34:7845)

189. HIGBEE, DALE S.; CLARKE, JOHN R.; AND HENDERSON, WAYNE E. "The Bender-Gestalt Test as a Predictor of Length of Hospitalization With Mental Patients." *J Clin Psychol* 16:265–6 Jl '60. * (*PA* 36:2HI65H)

190. HIRSCHENFANG, SAMUEL. "A Comparison of Bender Gestalt Reproductions of Right and Left Hemiplegic Patients." *J Clin Psychol* 16:439 O '60. * (*PA* 37:3534)

191. HUTT, MAX L. "The Revised Bender-Gestalt Visual Motor Test," pp. 30–55, 150–65. In *The Prediction of Overt Behavior Through the Use of Projective Techniques.* Edited by Arthur C. Carr. Springfield, Ill.: Charles C Thomas, Publisher, 1960. Pp. xiii, 177. * (*PA* 36:2HG77C)

192. HUTT, MAX L., AND BRISKIN, GERALD J. *The Clinical Use of the Revised Bender-Gestalt Test.* New York: Grune & Stratton, Inc., 1960. Pp. viii, 168. * (*PA* 35:3384)

193. JUDSON, ABE J., AND MACCASLAND, BARBARA W. "The Effects of Chlorpromazine on Psychological Test Scores." Abstract. *J Consult Psychol* 24:192 Ap '60. * (*PA* 34:7888)

194. KIM, IK CHANG. *The Bender-Gestalt Test: An Analysis of Certain Clinical Groups.* Doctor's thesis, University of Arizona (Tucson, Ariz.), 1960. (*DA* 21:959)

195. KOPPITZ, ELIZABETH MUNSTERBERG. "The Bender Gestalt Test for Children: A Normative Study." *J Clin Psychol* 16:432–5 O '60. * (*PA* 37:3111)

196. KOPPITZ, ELIZABETH MUNSTERBERG. "Teacher's Attitude and Children's Performance on the Bender Gestalt Test and Human Figure Drawings." *J Clin Psychol* 16:204–8 Ap '60. * (*PA* 36:2HE04K)

197. LACHMANN, FRANK M. "Perceptual-Motor Development in Children Retarded in Reading Ability." *J Consult Psychol* 24:427–31 O '60. * (*PA* 35:5339)

198. MCGUIRE, FREDERICK L. "A Comparison of the Bender-Gestalt and Flicker Fusion as Indicators of Central Nervous System Involvement." *J Clin Psychol* 16:276–8 Jl '60. * (*PA* 36:2HI76M)

199. MAGNUSSON, DAVID. "Some Personality Tests Applied on Identical Twins." *Scandinavian J Psychol* 1(2):55–61 '60. * (*PA* 35:6424)

200. MATUNAS, MARIAN ISABEL. *Test Performance of Psychotic Children With Organic Brain Pathology: A Study to Determine Whether the Bender-Gestalt Test, the Benton Visual Retention Test, and the Marble Board Test Can Detect the Presence of Organic Brain Pathology in Psychotic Children.* Doctor's thesis, New York University (New York, N.Y.), 1960. (*DA* 21:1257)

201. PRADO, WILLIAM M.; PEYMAN, DOUGLAS A. R.; AND LACEY, OLIVER L. "A Validation Study of Measures of Flattened Affect on the Bender-Gestalt Test." *J Clin Psychol* 16:435–8 O '60. * (*PA* 37:3231)

202. STORY, R. IAN. "The Revised Bender-Gestalt and Male Alcoholics." *J Proj Tech* 24:186–93 Je '60. * (*PA* 35:1088)

203. TOLOR, ALEXANDER. "The 'Meaning' of the Bender-Gestalt Test Designs: A Study in the Use of the Semantic Differential." *J Proj Tech* 24:433–8 D '60. * (*PA* 35:4845)

204. WIENER, GERALD; CRAWFORD, EDWARD E.; AND SNYDER, ROBERT T. "Some Correlates of Overt Anxiety in Mildly Retarded Patients." *Am J Mental Def* 64:735–9 Ja '60. * (*PA* 35:1055)

205. ASCOUGH, J. C. *The Mosaic Test: Validation and Cross-Validation of Objective Scores, Comparison With Clinical Judgment and the Bender Gestalt Test.* Master's thesis, West Virginia University (Morgantown, W. Va.), 1961.

206. GRIFFITH, RICHARD M., AND TAYLOR, VIVIAN H. "Bender-Gestalt Figure Rotations: A Stimulus Factor." *J Consult Psychol* 25:89–90 F '61. * (*PA* 36:3HC89G)

207. HARRISON, DONNA M. *The Effect of Verbal Reward on Schizophrenic Patients' Performance of the Bender-Gestalt Test.* Master's thesis, University of British Columbia (Vancouver, B.C., Canada), 1961.

208. KEOGH, BARBARA K., AND SMITH, CAROL E. "Group Techniques and Proposed Scoring System for the Bender-Gestalt Test With Children." *J Clin Psychol* 17:172–5 Ap '61. * (*PA* 38:957)

209. KO, YUNG-HO. "A Study of Figure Rotation in the Bender-Gestalt Test." *Acta Psychologica Taiwanica* (3):94–105 Mr '61. * (*PA* 38:8000)

210. KOPPITZ, ELIZABETH M.; MARDIS, VERDENA; AND STEPHENS, THOMAS. "A Note on Screening School Beginners With the Bender Gestalt Test." *J Ed Psychol* 52:80–1 Ap '61. * (*PA* 38:3205)

211. LACHMANN, F. M.; BAILEY, M. A.; AND BERRICK, M. E. "The Relationship Between Manifest Anxiety and Clinicians' Evaluations of Projective Test Responses." *J Clin Psychol* 17:11–3 Ja '61. * (*PA* 37:3113)

212. QUAST, WENTWORTH. "The Bender Gestalt: A Clinical Study of Children's Records." *J Consult Psychol* 25:405–8 O '61. * (*PA* 37:3232)

213. REGER, ROGER, AND DAWSON, ANTOINETTE. "The Use of Psychological Tests to Predict Manual Abilities in Mentally Retarded Boys." *Am J Occup Ther* 15:204+ S–O '61. * (*PA* 36:5JI04R)

214. RIKLAN, MANUEL, AND DILLER, LEONARD. "Visual Motor Performance Before and After Chemosurgery of the Basal Ganglia in Parkinsonism." *J Nerv & Mental Dis* 132:307–14 Ap '61. * (*PA* 36:2JF07R)

215. ROSENBERG, B. G., AND LAUBER, JAMES. "Selected Success and Failure Experiences as Factors in Bender Gestalt Performances." *J General Psychol* 64:31–6 Ja '61. * (*PA* 35:6425)

216. SCHULBERG, HERBERT C., AND TOLOR, ALEXANDER. "The Use of the Bender-Gestalt in Clinical Practice." *J Proj Tech* 25:347–51 S '61. * (*PA* 36:3HI47S)

217. SINGH, BALWANT. "Development of Visuo-motor Capacities in Children from 6–11 Years." Abstract of master's thesis. *Brit J Ed Psychol* 31:299–302 N '61. *

218. SOUEIF, M. I., AND METWALLY, A. "Testing for Organicity in Egyptian Psychiatric Patients." *Acta Psychologica* 18(4):285–96 '61. * (*PA* 36:5JG85S)

219. ASCOUGH, JAMES C., AND DANA, RICHARD H. "Concurrent Validities of the Mosaic and Bender Gestalt Tests." *J Consult Psychol* 26:430–4 O '62. * (*PA* 39:1713)

220. AYLAIAN, ARSEN, AND MELTZER, MALCOLM L. "The Bender Gestalt Test and Intelligence." Abstract. *J Consult Psychol* 26:483 O '62. *

221. BRUCK, MORRIS. "A Note on Modified Instructions for Bender-Gestalt Elaborations and Associations." *J Proj Tech* 26:227 Je '62. *

222. CLAWSON, AILEEN. *The Bender Visual Motor Gestalt Test for Children: A Manual.* Beverly Hills, Calif.: Western Psychological Services, 1962. Pp. ii, 29, 43. *

223. CLAWSON, AILEEN. "Relationship of Psychological Tests to Cerebral Disorders in Children: A Pilot Study." *Psychol Rep* 10:187–90 F '62. * (*PA* 37:1655)

224. COROTTO, LOREN V., AND CURNUTT, ROBERT H. "Ego Strength: A Function of the Measuring Instrument." *J Proj Tech* 26:228–30 Je '62. *

225. FULLER, JERRY B., AND CHAGNON, GILLES. "Factors Influencing Rotation in the Bender-Gestalt Performance of Children." *J Proj Tech* 26:36–46 Mr '62. * (*PA* 37:2833)

226. KO, YUNG-HO. "The Discrepancy Between the B-G Score and the Sum of the Object-Assembly and the Block-Design Test Scores as an Indicator of Organicity." *Acta Psychologica Taiwanica* (4):72–7 Mr '62. * (*PA* 38:6367)

227. KOPPITZ, ELIZABETH MUNSTERBERG. "Diagnosing Brain Damage in Young Children With the Bender Gestalt Test." *J Consult Psychol* 26:541–6 D '62. * (*PA* 39:2476)

228. LETON, DONALD A. "Visual-Motor Capacities and Ocular Efficiency in Reading." *Percept & Motor Skills* 15:407–32 O '62. * (*PA* 37:8253)

229. MCLEAN, MARJORIE J. *A Study of the Bender Visual-Motor Gestalt Test in Relation to Reading Difficulties.* Master's thesis, University of Manitoba (Winnipeg, Man., Canada), 1962.

230. MASTEN, IRVING. *Bender Gestalt Responses of Normal and Deaf Children.* Master's thesis, Brooklyn College (Brooklyn, N.Y.), 1962.

231. NIELSEN, HELLE H. *Visual-Motor Functioning of Cerebral Palsied and Normal Children.* Nordisk Psykologi's

Monografiserie Nr. 14. Copenhagen, Denmark: Ejnar Munks-gaards Forlag, 1962. Pp. 41–103. * Same: *Nordisk Psykologi* 14(2):41–103 '62. * (*PA* 37:3551)

232. ORME, J. E. "Bender Design Recall and Brain Damage." *Dis Nerv System* 23:329–30 Je '62. *

233. PACELLA, MICHAEL J. "Inter-Examiner Effects on the Bender-Gestalt." *J Clin Psychol* 18:23–6 Ja '62. * (*PA* 38:8501)

234. PARRISH, ROBERT EDWIN. *A Study of Some Factors in the Bender-Gestalt Reproductions of Reader and Non-Reader Children.* Doctor's thesis, University of Oklahoma (Norman, Okla.), 1962. (*DA* 23:928)

235. PEOPLES, CROCKER, AND MOLL, RICHARD P. "Bender-Gestalt Performance as a Function of Drawing Ability, School Performance and Intelligence." *J Clin Psychol* 18:106–7 Ja '62. * (*PA* 38:9274)

236. ROOS, PHILIP. "Performance of Psychiatric Patients on Two Measures of Ego Strength." *J Clin Psychol* 18:48–50 Ja '62. * (*PA* 38:8505)

237. SCHELLENBERG, ERNEST DAVID. *A Study of the Relationship Between Visual-Motor Perception and Reading Disabilities of Third Grade Pupils.* Doctor's thesis, University of Southern Calitornia (Los Angeles, Calif.), 1962. (*DA* 23:3785)

238. SCHULBERG, HERBERT C., AND TOLOR, ALEXANDER. "The 'Meaning' of the Bender-Gestalt Test Designs to Psychiatric Patients." *J Proj Tech* 26:455–61 D '62. * (*PA* 37:6725)

239. SEEMAN, WILLIAM, AND MARKS, PHILIP A. "A Study of Some 'Test Dimensions' Conceptions." *J Proj Tech* 26:469–73 D '62. * (*PA* 37:6678)

240. SILVERSTEIN, A. B., AND MOHAN, PHILIP J. "Bender-Gestalt Figure Rotations in the Mentally Retarded." *J Consult Psychol* 26:386–8 Ag '62. * (*PA* 38:4570)

241. SMITH, CAROL E., AND KEOGH, BARBARA K. "The Group Bender-Gestalt as a Reading Readiness Screening Instrument." *Percept & Motor Skills* 15:639–45 D '62. * (*PA* 38:2447)

242. TOLOR, ALEXANDER, AND SCHULBERG, HERBERT C. *An Evaluation of the Bender-Gestalt Test.* Foreword by Lauretta Bender. Springfield, Ill.: Charles C Thomas, Publisher, 1963. Pp. xxiii, 229. * (*PA* 38:967)

243. VIITAMAKI, R. OLAVI. *Psychoses in Children: A Psychological Follow-Up Study.* Annals of the Finnish Academy of Science and Letters, Series B, Vol. 125, Part 2. Helsinki, Finland: Suomalainen Tiedeakatemia, Academia Scientiarum Fennica, 1962. Pp. 52. * (*PA* 38:2650)

244. ALLEN, ROBERT M., AND FRANK, GEORGE H. "Experimental Variation of the Mode of Reproduction of the Bender Gestalt Stimuli." *J Clin Psychol* 19:212–4 Ap '63. *

245. ARMSTRONG, RENATE GERBOTH. "Recall Patterns on the Bender Gestalt: A Re-evaluation." *J Proj Tech & Pers Assess* 27:418–22 D '63. * (*PA* 38:8397)

246. BENDER, LAURETTA. Chap. 5, "The Origin and Evolution of the Gestalt Function, the Body Image, and Delusional Thoughts in Schizophrenia," pp. 38–62. In *Recent Advances in Psychiatry, Vol. 5.* The Proceedings of the Seventeenth Annual Convention and Scientific Program of the Society of Biological Psychiatry, Toronto, Ontario, May 4–6, 1962. Edited by Joseph Wortis. New York: Plenum Press, 1963. Pp. xiii, 380. *

247. BERNSTEIN, IRA H. "A Comparison of Schizophrenics and Nonschizophrenics on Two Methods of Administration of the Bender-Gestalt Test." *Percept & Motor Skills* 16:757–63 Je '63. * (*PA* 38:6105)

248. BILLINGSLEA, FRED Y. "The Bender Gestalt: A Review and a Perspective." *Psychol B* 60:233–51 My '63. *

249. BRILLIANT, PATRICIA J., AND GYNTHER, MALCOLM D. "Relationships Between Performanec on Three Tests for Organicity and Selected Patient Variables." *J Consult Psychol* 27:474–9 D '63. * (*PA* 38:8404)

250. CONDELL, JAMES F. "The Bender Gestalt Test With Mentally Retarded Children Using the Koppitz Revised Scoring System." *J Clin Psychol* 19:430–1 O '63. *

251. EVANS, RAY B., AND MARMORSTON, JESSIE. "Psychological Test Signs of Brain Damage in Cerebral Thrombosis." *Psychol Rep* 12:915–30 Je '63. * (*PA* 38:6413)

252. FULLER, G. B. "A Further Study on Rotation: Cross-Validation." *J Clin Psychol* 19:127–8 Ja '63. * (*PA* 39:1728)

253. GUERTIN, WILSON H., AND DAVIS, HUGH C. "Similarities in Meaning of Elements and Figures of the Bender-Gestalt." *J Proj Tech* 27:68–72 Mr '63. * (*PA* 38:983)

254. KEOGH, BARBARA KOLTS. *The Bender Gestalt as a Predictive and Dianostic Test of Reading Performance.* Doctor's thesis, Claremont Graduate School (Claremont, Calif.), 1963. (*DA* 24:2360)

255. KO, YUNG-HO, AND HUNG, TSU-PEI. "The Localization of Brain Lesions and the Bender-Gestalt Test Figure-Rotation." *Acta Psychologica Taiwanica* (5):31–6 Mr '63. *

256. KORMAN, MAURICE, AND BLUMBERG, STANLEY. "Comparative Efficiency of Some Tests of Cerebral Damage." *J Consult Psychol* 27:303–9 Ag '63. * (*PA* 38:2985)

257. SMITH, CAROL E., AND KEOGH, BARBARA K. "Developmental Changes on the Bender Gestalt Test." *Percept & Motor Skills* 17:465–6 O '63. * (*PA* 38:6070)

258. THWEATT, ROGER C. "Prediction of School Learning Disabilities Through the Use of the Bender Gestalt Test: A

Validation Study of Koppitz's Scoring Technique." *J Clin Psychol* 19:216–7 Ap '63. * (*PA* 39:5104)

259. KOPPITZ, ELIZABETH MUNSTERBERG. *The Bender Gestalt Test for Young Children.* New York: Grune & Stratton, Inc., 1964. Pp. xi, 195. * (*PA* 39:1740)

C. B. BLAKEMORE, *Lecturer in Psychology, Institute of Psychiatry, Maudsley Hospital, University of London, London, England.*

According to a recent survey [1] the Bender-Gestalt remains a very popular test with clinical psychologists. This popularity is understandable in view of its simplicity of materials, ease and speed of administration, and the many claims which have been put forward on its behalf as a diagnostic instrument. It is not surprising, therefore, to find that during the past few years it has joined the ranks of other test giants, such as the Wechsler scales, the Rorschach, and TAT, in having whole books devoted to its administration and scoring (*41, 192*) and evaluations of the literature published on its value in a clinical setting (*242*). In the opinion of this reviewer such popularity and respect for the test cannot be justified on the basis of evidence available in its literature.

It is now some fifteen years since Line was quoted in *The Third Mental Measurements Yearbook* (see 3:109) as having said in the *American Journal of Psychiatry* that the test's "validity and practical value.....must await further research." Since then research has been carried out, but from it has emerged little in favour of the test as a valid and useful clinical tool. It is true, of course, that much of this work has concentrated on the development of systems for scoring test performance. These vary in their objectivity and reliability, but a system such as that developed by Pascal and Suttell (*41*), involving analysis of 105 details of performance over the various designs, has many features to commend it. With such a system moderately respectable correlations of around .70 are reported for test-retest performances, while the reliability of scoring between trained examiners can be in the order of .90. It has also been suggested by Pacella (*233*) that differences between examiners, in terms of their "stress" characteristics, may have little effect on the patient's performance when analysed by this method. In view of its apparent reliability it is understandable that the Pascal and Suttell system, together with the more recent modifications for use with

[1] SUNDBERG, NORMAN D. "The Practice of Psychological Testing in Clinical Services in the United States." *Am Psychologist* 16:79–83 F '61. *

children introduced by Koppitz (*195, 259*), should have proved to be the most popular. However, the development of more objective and reliable scoring criteria has not improved upon the test's validity and usefulness as a diagnostic instrument, for it has enabled us to appreciate the correlation of performance with such variables as intelligence, educational level, and age—variables all too frequently ignored in validation studies of "diagnostic" tests. When these variables are controlled in studies of the Bender-Gestalt, the differences between patient groups, and between patients and non-patient controls, dwindle and the ranges of scores show considerable overlap. Many of these validation studies have found statistically significant mean differences in copying performance on this test between, for example, psychotics versus nonpsychotics or brain damaged versus non-brain damaged patients. From the standpoint of clinical usefulness, however, the overlap of scores is usually so great that the correct prediction of an individual's group membership is little better than chance.

This apparent lack of clinical value as a diagnostic test is not altogether surprising. We have in the Bender-Gestalt what would appear to be a simple copying task, with, in some cases, the added information derived from asking for a recall of the test material after initial performance. The assumption underlying most of the validation studies is that patients suffering from different neurological or psychiatric conditions will perform this task differently. We might ask if one or several performance variables are to be held responsible for these group differences. As yet there is no answer to such a question, but the factor analytic studies of the performance of psychiatric patients carried out by Guertin (*58, 83-5*) suggest that the answer may not be a simple one. Before we can accept the assumption that the apparent group differences on the test are related to neurological or psychiatric diagnosis, we must satisfy ourselves that stimulus variables and the conditions of testing are not responsible for the observed differences. It is in the investigation of such problems that research on the Bender-Gestalt has been particularly weak, and where research has been carried out the findings have usually been revealing. Let us examine, as an example, the claim that rotation of the drawings during copying performance is indicative of brain pathology. A number of studies have investigated such rotations and have reliably demonstrated that they may be due largely to stimulus variables (*150, 206*). Indeed, Fuller and Laird,[2] using two of the Wertheimer designs also used by Bender, have made use of this information in their attempts to develop a more valid test of brain damage. We might find eventually that stimulus variables, such as the orientation to the patient of the design to be copied, have particular relevance only for patients suffering from certain conditions, just as Shapiro and others[3] have demonstrated that rotation of Kohs' blocks is dependent to some extent on the presence of visual field defects. But before we can begin to investigate such relationships we must know what are the appropriate stimulus variables, and this is very relevant when one remembers that there is no standard set of Bender-Gestalt figures—a fact which has been stressed by both Billingslea (*14, 248*) and Popplestone (*126*).

In summary, then, it would seem that although reliable scoring methods can be developed for this test, the mean differences in performance between diagnostic groups so far revealed are of little practical value to the clinical psychologist. In addition, we are still short of information regarding the many variables which might determine performance. We *still* await the research which will demonstrate the test's validity and usefulness.

Psychol B 60:233–51 My '63. Fred Y. Billingslea. "The Bender Gestalt: A Review and a Perspective." * Although there are surprisingly few generalizations that can be made about the BG Test as a result of reviewing the published experiences with it over the past decade, the following seem justified in the light of the preceding discussion: (1) The test continues to be popular with clinicians and deserves to remain as an additional tool in his repertoire. (2) It is in great need of universally accepted standard set of designs. (3) The P&S scoring system has proven useful on adult protocols as has Koppitz' modification of it on children's protocols. (4) Reasonably valid MAs can be obtained with it for chil-

2 FULLER, GERALD B., AND LAIRD, JAMES T. "The Minnesota Percepto-Diagnostic Test." *J Clin Psychol* 19:3–34 Ja '63. * (Also published as a separate Monograph Supplement No. 16.)
3 SHAPIRO, M. B.; BRIERLEY, J.; SLATER, P.; AND BEECH, H. R. "Experimental Studies of a Perceptual Anomaly: 7, A New Explanation." *J Mental Sci* 108:655–68 S '62. * (*PA* 38:2989)

dren 4–12 years and adults with equivalent MAs, but not adolescents and adults with higher MAs. (5) It can be employed as an additional tool in a battery of tests administered to an individual when clues for the possible presence of organic brain pathology are sought. (6) Whether evaluated with objective scores or with some systematic inspection procedure the results tend to discriminate the psychotic from the nonpsychotic and nonpsychiatric subject provided their MAs are 13 or above. It does not detect effectively nonpsychotic emotionally disturbed children, however. (7) When the protocols are interpreted symbolically, the clinician must rely almost completely on the validity of his own subjective professional knowledge. (8) The test has not been standardized sufficiently to permit its use as a norm against which to judge other variables. (9) More research is needed on the perceptual contributions of each design and the effects on such perceptions of their sequential appearance in the protocol.

For reviews by Arthur L. Benton and Howard R. White of a, see 4:144; for excerpts from related book reviews, see B268, B297, B487, 5:B330, 4:145, 3:109, and 40:B843.

[204]

*The Blacky Pictures: A Technique for the Exploration of Personality Dynamics. Ages 5 and over; 1950–62; psychosexual development; individual; 1 form ('50, 12 cards); manual ('50, 24 pages); research guide ('62, 27 pages, reprint of 74 below); inquiry cards ('50, 42 cards, separate sets for boys and girls); record blank ('50, 12 pages); no data on reliability and validity; no norms; $12 per set of test materials and 25 record blanks; $1.25 per research guide; $3.50 per 25 record blanks; postpaid; (35–55) minutes; Gerald S. Blum; Psychological Corporation. *

REFERENCES

1–7. See 4:102.
8–45. See 5:125.
46. SWANSON, G. E. "Some Effects of Member Object-Relationships on Small Groups." *Human Relations* 4(4):355–80 '51. * (PA 26:5486)
47. THOMAS, RICHARD WALLACE. *An Investigation of the Psychoanalytic Theory of Homosexuality.* Doctor's thesis, University of Kentucky (Lexington, Ky.), 1951. (DA 20:3847)
48. MARQUIS, DOROTHY P.; SINNETT, E. ROBERT; AND WINTER, WILLIAM D. "A Psychological Study of Peptic Ulcer Patients." *J Clin Psychol* 8:266–72 Jl '52. * (PA 27:6072)
49. MOLISH, HERMAN B.; LYON, BLANCHARD; AND BRIGGS, DENNIE L. "Character Structure of Adjusted and Maladjusted Naval Recruits as Measured by the Blacky Pictures." *Am J Orthopsychiatry* 24:164–74 Ja '54. * (PA 29:3141)
50. STREITFIELD, HAL S. "Specificity of Peptic Ulcer to Intense Oral Conflicts." *Psychosom Med* 16:315–26 Jl–Ag '54. * (PA 29:4533)
51. BURNHAM, RHODA K. *The Relationship of Personality to Oral Conditions in Children: An Evaluation by Means of the Rorschach and the Blacky Test.* Doctor's thesis, New York University (New York, N.Y.), 1957. (DA 18:1488)
52. ADELSON, JOSEPH, AND REDMOND, JOAN. "Personality Differences in the Capacity for Verbal Recall." *J Abn & Social Psychol* 57:244–8 S '58. * (PA 33:9771)
53. LEICHTY, MARY M. *The Absence of the Father During Early Childhood and Its Effect Upon the Oedipal Situation as Reflected in Young Adults.* Doctor's thesis, Michigan State University (East Lansing, Mich.), 1958. (DA 19:1821)
54. MARTIN, JAMES O. *A Psychological Investigation of Convicted Incest Offenders by Means of Two Projective Techniques.* Doctor's thesis, Michigan State University (East Lansing, Mich.), 1958. (DA 21:241)
55. NEUMAN, GERARD G., AND SALVATORE, JOSEPH C. "The Blacky Test and Psychoanalytic Theory: A Factor-Analytic Approach to Validity." *J Proj Tech* 22:427–31 D '58. * (PA 34:1405)
56. ANSBACHER, H. L. "Can Backy Blacken Testing?" Letter. *Am Psychologist* 14:654 O '59. *
57. BERGER, LESLIE. "Crossvalidation of 'Primary' and 'Reactive' Personality Patterns With Non-Ulcer Surgical Patients." *J Proj Tech* 23:8–11 Mr '59. * (PA 34:6004)
58. CHRISTIANSEN, BJØRN. *Attitudes Towards Foreign Affairs as a Function of Personality,* pp. 148–87. Oslo, Norway: Oslo University Press, 1959. Pp. 283. * (PA 35:3340)
59. DEAN, SIDNEY I. "A Note on Female Blacky Protocols." *J Proj Tech* 23:417 D '59. * (PA 35:4907)
60. LASKY, JULIAN J., AND BERGER, LESLIE. "Blacky Test Scores Before and After Genito-Urinary Surgery." *J Proj Tech* 23:57–8 Mr '59. *
61. MACHOVER, SOLOMON, AND PUZZO, FRANK S. "Clinical and Objective Studies of Personality Variabes in Alcoholism: 1, Clinical Investigation of the 'Alcoholic Personality.'" *Q J Studies Alcohol* 20:505–19 S '59. * (PA 34:6253)
62. MACHOVER, SOLOMON, AND PUZZO, FRANK S. "Clinical and Objective Studies of Personality Variables in Alcoholism: 2, Clinical Study of Personality Correlates of Remission From Active Alcoholism." *Q J Studies Alcohol* 20:520–7 S '59. * (PA 34:6253)
63. MAGNUSSEN, MAX G. "The Blacky Pictures as Personality Measures for Undergraduate Areas of Specialization." *J Proj Tech* 23:351–3 S '59. * (PA 35:4931)
64. MARGOLIS, MARVIN O. *A Psychological Study of Mothers of Asthmatic Children.* Doctor's thesis, Michigan State University (East Lansing, Mich.), 1959. (DA 23:311)
65. BLUM, GERALD S. Chap. 5, "The Blacky Pictures With Children," pp. 95–104. In *Projective Techniques With Children.* Edited by Albert I. Rabin and Mary R. Haworth. New York: Grune & Stratton, Inc., 1960. Pp. xiii, 392. * (PA 35:2229)
66. EASTMAN, DONALD FRANCIS. *An Exploratory Investigation of the Psychoanalytic Theory of Stuttering by Means of the Blacky Pictures Test.* Doctor's thesis, University of Nebraska (Lincoln, Neb.), 1960. (DA 21:1629)
67. PERLOE, SIDNEY I. "Inhibition as a Determinant of Perceptual Defense." *Percept & Motor Skills* 11:59–66 Ag '60. * (PA 35:3509)
68. VROOM, ANN LOUISE WORKMAN. *A Validation Study of the Blacky Analogies Test.* Doctor's thesis, University of Michigan (Ann Arbor, Mich.), 1960. (DA 21:364)
69. BLUM, GERALD S.; IN COLLABORATION WITH JUSTIN L. WEISS, ABRAM MINKOWICH, ANN L. VROOM, GERALD A. MENDELSOHN, SIDNEY I. PERLOE, IRVING W. WOLF, AND ROBERT H. GOLDSTEIN. *A Model of the Mind: Explored by Hypnotically Controlled Experiments and Examined for Its Psychodynamic Implications.* New York: John Wiley & Sons, Inc., 1961. Pp. xi, 229. * (PA 36:5II29B)
70. COHEN, SANFORD L.; SILVERMAN, ALBERT J.; WADDELL, WILLIAM; AND ZUIDEMA, GEORGE D. "Urinary Catechol Amine Levels, Gastric Secretion and Specific Psychological Factors in Ulcer and Non-Ulcer Patients." *J Psychosom Res* 5:90–115 F '61. * (PA 36:3JH90C)
71. DAVIDS, ANTHONY, AND LAWTON, MARCIA J. "Self-Concept, Mother Concept, and Food Aversions in Emotionally Disturbed and Normal Children." *J Abn & Social Psychol* 62:309–14 Mr '61. * (PA 36:4FF09D)
72. ROSSI, ASCANIO M., AND SOLOMON, PHILIP. "A Further Note on Female Blacky Protocols." *J Proj Tech* 25:339–40 S '61. *
73. BERGER, LESLIE, AND EVERSTINE, LOUIS. "Test-Retest Reliability of the Blacky Pictures Test." *J Proj Tech* 26:225–6 Je '62. * (PA 37:3185)
74. BLUM, GERALD S. "A Guide for Research Use of the Blacky Pictures." *J Proj Tech* 26:3–29 Mr '62. * (PA 37:3188)
75. CARP, FRANCES M. "Psychosexual Development of Stutterers." *J Proj Tech* 26:388–91 D '62. * (PA 37:6079)
76. GEIST, HAROLD. *The Etiology of Idiopathic Epilepsy,* pp. 192–201, 278–86. New York: Exposition Press, 1962. Pp. 297. *
77. IRWIN, THOMAS C. *A Contribution to the Construct Validation of the Oral Scales of the Blacky Pictures Test.* Doctor's thesis, University of Rochester (Rochester, N.Y.), 1963. (DA 24:2123)
78. STRICKER, GEORGE. "Stimulus Properties of the Blacky Pictures Test." *J Proj Tech & Pers Assess* 27:244–7 Je '63. * (PA 38:2727)
79. TIMMONS, EDWIN O., AND NOBLIN, CHARLES D. "The Differential Performance of Orals and Anals in a Verbal Conditioning Paradigm." *J Consult Psychol* 27:383–6 O '63. *

BERT R. SAPPENFIELD, *Professor of Psychology, Montana State University, Missoula, Montana.*

The *Blacky Pictures* were designed as stimuli for "a modified projective technique" to be used in a research study of the psychoanalytic theory of psychosexual development (*2*). They were subsequently published in 1950 as stimuli for "a technique for the exploration of personality dynamics." Since their publication, the *Blacky Pictures* have been widely utilized in research investigations and in clinical practice.

THE TEST STIMULI. The *Blacky Pictures* represent events in the life of a family of dogs. Each of the pictures, or "cartoons," depicts an ungainly dog, named "Blacky," who is expected to be perceived as the hero or the character with whom the subject identifies. Male subjects are told that Blacky is the son, and females that Blacky is the daughter. The other members of Blacky's family are named "Papa," "Mama," and "Tippy." In addition to the first picture, which is used merely to introduce the characters, there is a sequence of 11 pictures, each of which is "designed to depict either a stage of psychosexual development or a type of object relationship." Each picture is presented to the subject with an introductory statement calling attention to Blacky and pointing out, with varying degrees of structuredness, what he is doing or experiencing.

The cartoons, and their introductory comments, may be described as follows: (1) Oral Eroticism: "Here is Blacky with Mama." Blacky appears to be taking nourishment from Mama's udders. (2) Oral Sadism: "Here is Blacky with Mama's collar." Blacky appears to be biting a collar with "Mama" inscribed on it. (3) Anal Sadism: "Here Blacky is relieving himself (herself)." Blacky appears to be digging between dog houses marked "Papa" and "Mama," in a row of houses including smaller ones marked "Tippy" and "Blacky." (4) Oedipal Intensity: "Here Blacky is watching Mama and Papa." Blacky covertly observes Mama and Papa, who are showing affection for each other. (5) Masturbation Guilt: "Here Blacky is discovering sex." Blacky is shown in the act of licking his genital-anal zone. (6) Castration Anxiety, for males, or Penis Envy, for females: "Here Blacky is watching Tippy." Blacky observes blindfolded Tippy, whose tail is on a block, apparently about to be chopped off by a descending knife. (7) Positive Iden-

tification: "Here is Blacky with a toy dog." Blacky appears to be instructing, ordering, or dominating a miniature dog on wheels. (8) Sibling Rivalry: "Here Blacky is watching the rest of the family." Blacky is off to one side, observing Papa and Mama, who are showing affection for Tippy. (9) Guilt Feelings: "Here Blacky is very upset." Blacky appears to be cringing before a dog-like "angel" or "conscience" figure, who appears to be expressing hostility toward Blacky. (10) Positive Ego Ideal, for males, or Love-Object, for females: "Here Blacky is having a dream." Blacky, asleep, is having a dream-image of a big black male dog. (11) Positive Ego Ideal, for females, or Love-Object, for males: "Here Blacky is having another dream." Blacky is having a dream-image of a big black female dog.

TEST PROCEDURE. Standard procedure for administering the *Blacky Pictures* requires the subject (*a*) to tell a spontaneous story similar to that required by the TAT and other story-telling projective tests, (*b*) to answer a series of inquiry questions, mostly of the multiple choice type, and (*c*) to sort the pictures into liked and disliked categories, and then to choose the one picture liked most and the one picture disliked most. When used with children, the Blacky instructions are presented in a simplified version and the inquiry questions are, for the most part, asked in open-ended form.

The manual recommends scoring a protocol in terms of four "sources" (spontaneous stories, answers to inquiry questions, cartoon preferences, and related comments on other cartoons), on 13 separate dimensions: (*a*) oral eroticism, (*b*) oral sadism, (*c*) anal expulsiveness, (*d*) anal retentiveness, (*e*) oedipal intensity, (*f*) masturbation guilt, (*g*) castration anxiety (males) or penis envy (females), (*h*) positive identification, (*i*) sibling rivalry, (*j*) guilt feelings, (*k*) positive ego ideal, (*l*) narcissistic love-object, and (*m*) anaclitic love-object.

Two scoring manuals are available for research use of the Blacky technique. The first of these [1] has been utilized for scoring the standard Blacky dimensions in most of the research studies reported to date. The second

1 BLUM, GERALD S. *Revised Scoring System for Research Use of the Blacky Pictures.* Unpublished mimeographed reports, 1951. Male form, 20 pages; female form, 6 pages.

of these (*74*) is based on results of a factor analysis of Blacky variables and various criterion variables, and permits scoring on 30 separate factors; this 1962 research scoring manual is represented by the author as rendering "obsolete" much of the research previously done with the Blacky technique.

RELIABILITY FINDINGS. Reliability investigations have, for the most part, demonstrated that, although the Blacky dimension scores have statistically significant reliabilities, these reliabilities are not usually high enough to commend the dimension scores for use in diagnosing individual personalities.

Charen (*37*) reported test-retest reliabilities, based on inquiry items only, to be "low or negative," except for the castration anxiety score (Cartoon 4), whose fourfold point correlation was .519. Blum (*34*) criticized Charen's findings because they were based on inquiry items alone, and because test-retest reliability involves "an unknown mixture of changes in set, familiarity with items, and....personality changes."

Granick and Scheflen (*44*) investigated several different aspects of the Blacky's reliability; they reported (*a*) that when 10 judges scored 40 sets of spontaneous stories, scoring each story as "strong" or "weak" on a given dimension, the percentages of agreement varied from 68 to 95 on all but the two dimensions (oral sadism and guilt feelings) on which the agreement was not statistically significant at or beyond the .05 level; (*b*) that 5 of 8 judges were able to match the test and retest protocols, when presented in sets produced by 6 or 7 subjects, with from 72 to 100 per cent accuracy; (*c*) that two judges rating thematic content as similar or dissimilar on 20 sets of three stories to each cartoon (two stories from test and retest of the same subjects and one story from a matched subject), agreed in 68 to 88 per cent of their judgments for each of 8 cartoons (excepting 4, 7, and 9); (*d*) that, however, even though thematic content was judged to be similar on test and retest protocols of the same subjects with significantly greater frequency than on matched but different subjects' protocols, "the amount of consistency in thematic productions by the individual S is not very high"; (*e*) that test and retest cartoon preferences were significantly consistent (70 to 95 per cent) for each cartoon for a group of 20 subjects; (*f*) that odd-even

reliability was .92 for verbal fluency (words per story); and (*g*) that odd-even reliability of "structured" versus "unstructured" story responses (utilizing or not utilizing the central theme of the cartoon) was .67, based on scoring by two judges, who showed 100 per cent agreement in their judgments. Except for the last two findings, the study of Granick and Scheflen dealt either with some aspect of interscorer agreement (objectivity rather than reliability) or with some aspect of test-retest reliability (the relevance of which Blum himself has criticized); only the last-mentioned finding, concerning "structured" versus "unstructured" story content, dealt with the internal consistency of one of the Blacky "sources" of scoring (related comments on other cartoons).

A study by Berger and Everstine (*73*) also dealt with test-retest reliability rather than with internal consistency; reliability coefficients varying from .20 to .54 on the separate dimension scores were reported for a group of 50 male college students who had been retested after four weeks.

Although Ellis (*20*) reported high interrater agreements (objectivity) on a single patient's Blacky protocol, no research appears to have been done concerning the split-test or test-retest reliabilities of clinical inferences based primarily on spontaneous stories and related comments, which are likely to be the main sources of interpretation in clinical practice. This research void is, of course, not unique to the Blacky technique, but is shared by many other projective devices.

VALIDITY FINDINGS. As a research instrument, the Blacky technique has been put to many and varied uses. The original revised scoring system is a model of explicit definition and has provided an unusually adequate basis for objective scoring. It is laudable for its built-in provision that each of the sources (spontaneous story, inquiry, related comments, and cartoon preferences) is given approximately equal relative weight in determining the score for each dimension. This scoring system, however, provides only for trichotomous scores (very strong, fairly strong, and weak or absent), and many of the research studies have made use of dichotomous scoring (very strong, and fairly strong, weak, or absent).

A large number of studies which bear, directly or indirectly, on the question of the

Blacky technique's validity have been reported. The research study for which the *Blacky Pictures* were devised (*2*) has been criticized, on methodological grounds, by Seward (*5*). Even though Blum did not originally consider that study to be a validation of the Blacky technique itself, Blum and Hunt (*11*) later reported data from Blum's 1949 report as supporting the test's validity. Subsequent studies have, with few exceptions, been based on the assumption of the Blacky technique's validity for purposes of testing hypotheses derivable from psychoanalytic theory. It is the reviewer's position that studies reported to confirm, in some degree, hypotheses based on the assumption of validity, are themselves to some extent interpretable as validation studies. Brief abstracts of several such studies will be given below.

Michal-Smith, Hammer, and Spitz (*7*) reported a single case in which oral sadism against the mother was expressed in five stories following the one in response to the "mama's collar" cartoon, and in which oedipal content was expressed in four stories subsequent to the "oedipal intensity" cartoon. They reported these "related comments to other cartoons" to be consistent with the clinical findings concerning the subject's adjustment problems.

Blum and Miller (*13*), using a group of 18 third grade boys and girls, investigated, among other problems, the relationship between rankings on oral passivity based on Blacky protocols and several criterion variables thought to be diagnostic of orality. Several significant, though generally low, validity coefficients were found.

Ellis (*20*), after giving the Blacky to a patient who had been in psychoanalysis with him for about 200 hours, submitted the protocol to 22 clinical psychologists and psychological interns, to Blum, to himself, and to the patient, for evaluation in terms of ratings on 38 questions more or less related to the Blacky dimensions, and in terms of a clinical summary. Results showed about 60 per cent agreement by Blum and the psychologists and interns with the criterion (patient and therapist) on the 38 ratings, and 90 agreements as compared with 117 disagreements on statements in the clinical summaries.

Neuman and Salvatore (*55*) factor analyzed the intercorrelations, for males and females separately, which had been reported to occur among the Blacky dimension scores in Blum's investigation (*2*). With data for the male group, six factors interpreted to be consistent with psychoanalytic theory emerged. But, since contradictory and inconsistent findings occurred with the female group data, the question was raised whether the Blacky technique should be used with females.

Several studies have been concerned with testing hypotheses (particularly those of Alexander) relating to the dynamics of peptic ulcer. Blum and Kaufman (*12*) compared a group of 14 male adult ulcer patients with three non-ulcer control groups (paranoid schizophrenics, non-paranoid schizophrenics, and normals), on stories to Cartoon I (oral eroticism), and found that all scorable stories of the ulcer patients (11 subjects) showed strong disturbance on this dimension, while only half of the control group did so. This finding was consistent with prediction from theory. Further exploration of the data seemed to indicate that the ulcer group could be divided, on the basis of inquiry responses, into "primary" and "reactive" subgroups, the "primary" subgroup accepting oral implications and the "reactive" subgroup evading or rejecting such implications. Marquis, Sinnett, and Winter (*48*) used the Blacky technique with another small group of ulcer patients and found it possible, again, to distinguish between "primary" and "reactive" subgroups. The results were interpreted as being consistent with Alexander's theory that ulcer patients fall into two groups, one of which accepts and acts upon oral needs and the other of which denies and represses these needs. Bernstein and Chase (*30*) applied the Blacky in a study of 20 ulcer patients, 20 psychosomatic non-ulcer patients, and 20 nonpsychiatric patients. Although significant differences occurred on some dimensions for each of the intergroup comparisons, there was no significant difference on the oral eroticism dimension; but the ulcer patients, whether high or low on the oral eroticism dimension, did split into "primary" and "reactive" subgroups. Winter (*32*) devised objectively scorable "primary" and "reactive" scales, based on responses to the Blacky as a whole, and applied these in a study of 68 duodenal ulcer patients; he concluded that "two different patterns are found in people with ulcers, and these can be validly measured by the Blacky scales developed in this investigation." Berger (*57*), however, in a study of 30 non-ulcer patients, as a control for Winter's ulcer group, failed to find positive cross validating evidence for Winter's revised scales since neither differentiated significantly between the ulcer and non-ulcer samples. Despite some contradictory findings, the body of evidence seems to indicate that the Blacky technique can be a useful instrument for further studies of peptic ulcer dynamics.

Smith and Powell (*39*), using Cartoons I, 4, 10, and 11, without asking for spontaneous stories, found that 6 of 19 inquiry items differentiated significantly between pre-menarcheal and post-menarcheal girls, although cartoon preferences failed to discriminate. Lasky and Berger (*60*), who compared responses of male urological patients before and after genito-urinary surgery, concluded that "seven of 13 individual Blacky dimensions were considerably affected" by the surgery. Lindner (*21*) compared male sexual deviates with a control group individually matched on 9 variables, and found that 9 Blacky dimensions "showed a significant difference between the sexually deviant group and the non-sexually-deviant controls." The three preceding studies have in common the fact that they indicate sensitivity of the Blacky test to peculiarities of sexual experience.

McNeil and Blum (*16*) found a number of significant relationships between handwriting variables and Blacky scores; anal retentiveness was the one dimension that was related to the greatest number of handwriting variables, and which, according to psychoanalytic theory, should most clearly be expected to show such relationships.

Aronson (*19*) tested predictions from the psychoanalytic theory of paranoia by comparing paranoids, non-paranoid psychotics, and normals on a large number of Blacky variables; an impressively large number of findings (chiefly, but not wholly, involving responses to inquiry items) conformed to theoretical predictions.

Molish, Lyon, and Briggs (*49*), using only the multiple choice inquiry items of the Blacky, compared the responses of 1,847 "normal" naval recruits with responses of 390 recruits discharged as "unsuitable" and found only 5 items on which the modal responses of "normals" did not conform to "neutral" expectations, but found 11 items on which a significant difference occurred between the "normal" and

"unsuitable" groups. This strictly empirical study is, of course, in need of cross validation.

Teevan (*28*) reported that five Blacky dimensions discriminated significantly between undergraduate groups majoring in humanities, social sciences, and natural sciences, respectively. The humanities group showed highest disturbance on oral eroticism; the social science group showed highest disturbance on oral sadism, oedipal intensity, guilt feelings, and anaclitic love-object; the natural science group showed lowest disturbance on all of these dimensions, except oral eroticism. Magnussen (*63*) attempted to replicate Teevan's study and found essentially similar results, except that two of the dimensions (oedipal intensity and anaclitic love-object) showed no significant intergroup differences.

Swanson (*46*) predicted Blacky dimension relationships with variables having to do with participation in a small problem solving group, and found the predictions to be confirmed with respect to five of eight participation variables. Rabin (*45*), using only the multiple choice inquiry items of the Blacky, in a comparison of Kibbutz with non-Kibbutz Israeli boys, found some significant differences in the predicted direction and no significant differences opposite to his predictions. These studies indicate that the Blacky technique shows promise as a research instrument for dealing with problems in social psychology.

About the only reported investigation which has failed to yield some evidence in favor of the validity of the Blacky technique was that of Charen (*36*), in which recovered tubercular patients showed changes in a regressive direction as compared with their pre-recovery responses; however, in this study several other tests were used and none of these yielded significant differences between active tubercular patients and the control groups with which they were compared.

Almost all of the research studies having some bearing on validity have provided some indications in favor of the Blacky technique's validity; typically, in each study some of the predictions from theory have been confirmed and some have failed to be confirmed by statistically significant findings, but only occasionally have statistically significant findings contradicted predictions. In general, then, there appears to be far more evidence for the Blacky's validity than for its lack of validity. Several studies, however, have made use only of responses to the multiple choice inquiry questions, and several other studies have shown responses to the inquiry questions (when "sources" were treated separately) to have relatively great weight in yielding results confirmatory of hypotheses. This relative emphasis on the validity of inquiry responses may imply either that investigators have not been able to score the other "sources" with sufficient objectivity or that, even with adequately objective scoring, the range of individual differences occurring with respect to the other "sources" has not been sufficiently great to yield either significant differences between groups or significant relationships with other variables. Unfortunately, too little data have been reported on the actual distributions of different "source" scores to make it possible to evaluate these possibilities. The fact, however, that responses to these multiple choice questions have yielded impressive validity findings suggests that wider use might be made of combining projective stimuli with multiple choice questions, so as to provide the self-inventory with a distancing device which would make the subject less self-consciously defensive than in the usual case when he must answer questions that are frankly about himself.

Blum's latest "Guide for Research Use of the Blacky Pictures" (74) provides scoring instructions for 30 separate factors. On all but five of these factors (those for which "related comments" could conceivably contribute several points to the score) the responses to inquiry items make disproportionately high contributions to total scores. It would appear that Blum is prepared to think of the Blacky technique, when used as a research instrument, as no longer having the function of a deeply probing projective test, since he has conceived of the inquiry as evoking responses "at or close to the conscious level." No normative information is given for the 30 factor scores, although it should have been possible to publish distributions of these scores for the research sample (210 male undergraduates). Nevertheless, the practicing clinical psychologist should be able to glean from the Guide many useful insights to enrich his interpretations of Blacky protocols. For this reason, it might be well for the author to incorporate some of this new material in the manual, either as a supplement to, or as a substitute for, the interpretative material presently included.

THE BLACKY TECHNIQUE AS A CLINICAL INSTRUMENT. Possibly because of the fact that research scoring has typically given much weight to inquiry items and cartoon preferences, there is very little published evidence concerning the value of the Blacky technique as a clinical procedure. The reviewer suspects (without evidence) that many other clinicians are like himself in preferring to use the *Blacky Pictures* mainly for obtaining spontaneous stories, to be followed up by a minimum of non-suggestive questions to induce the subject to make his stories complete. Interpretation, in such a case, would utilize what is understood about principles of interpreting stories obtained with other picture-stimulated story-telling tests, such as the TAT or the CAT.

A number of problems arise in connection with the adequacy of the *Blacky Pictures* (or cartoons) as stimuli for a story-telling projective technique. Some of these problems have been the subject of research, but others have not been mentioned in the growing research literature.

Blacky, a dog, is assumed to take the role of "hero" in every picture and, consequently, in every spontaneous story. Although the dog is, among all animals, traditionally supposed to be "man's best friend," and although dogs have been cast in "human" form in Disney cartoons, it is still an unknown to us to what extent human subjects are able to identify with dogs, as compared with their ability to identify with other animals. It is reasonable to assume, in the absence of research evidence to the contrary, that ability to identify with any given animal should be amenable to extensive individual differences. If this should be true, then requiring subjects to respond to the same animal character throughout the sequence of pictures may result in limited projective yield for those subjects who fail to identify strongly with dogs. Some subjects may tell "good" stories merely because they have knowledge of canine behavior rather than because of strong identification with Blacky. Moreover, research evidence is not yet available to resolve the issue whether a story-telling test is more productive when the same character is used throughout or when many different characters are available for identification in the test stimuli. The Bellak CAT, which uses different animals in different pictures, might rewardingly be compared with the *Blacky Pictures* in an investigation to aid in resolving this issue.

A second problem relates to the use of the name "Blacky" for the hero of the sequence. Blum (*2*), on the basis of an informal study of the problem, concluded that males tend to think of "Blacky" as a male and that females tend to think of "Blacky" as a female. However, more recent studies (*41, 72*) have demonstrated that "Blacky" tends to be perceived by both males and females as a male, and other reports (*55, 59*) have suggested that the *Blacky Pictures* may be more successful in inducing male subjects than in inducing female subjects to identify with "Blacky." Neuman and Salvatore (*55*) have recommended that a "cat family" sequence of pictures be devised for use with females. Another possible implication of the name "Blacky" relates to racial issues (*7*); dark-skinned subjects may find it relatively easy to identify with Blacky, while light-skinned subjects may avoid identification on the basis of prejudice. Finally, the name "Blacky" may have symbolic values for some subjects, so that he (she) is perceived as a representative of darkness or evil and therefore difficult to identify with, except in terms of the subject's less acceptable impulses. In such cases "Tippy" may be perceived, not as a sibling, but as a representative of the subject's more socialized and acceptable personality components. It would be reasonable, then, at times, to regard stories as expressions of intrapersonal conflicts rather than as expressions of interpersonal attitudes.

The structured content of the Blacky cartoons, such that each is intended to represent a given stage of psychosexual development or a given object relationship, brings into focus the importance of norms (which are not to be found in the manual of instructions or in any other published source). It is generally accepted that the more ambiguous or unstructured the stimulus material is, the more confidence can be felt in interpreting a response as stemming from "inner determinants." Responses to the blank card of the TAT, or dreams, or waking hallucinations, are regarded as highly diagnostic of personality, since they are minimally determined by external stimuli; identification of a simple geometrical figure, on the other hand, would have little diagnostic value, since this response is maximally determined by the exter-

nal stimulus. The Blacky cartoons lie somewhere between these two extremes of structuredness, and, in the absence of norms, it is difficult to determine to what extent responses represent interpretable individual differences in disturbance, conflict, attitudes, object relationships, and the like. The manual, of course, recommends that interpretation be based on latent rather than manifest content of stories; this recommendation is based on the assumption that subjects "know" what the pictures represent and that their denial of this "knowledge" has an interpretable meaning. If this is a fact, then norms should be available to support it. The manual itself, however, contradicts to some extent the principle that interpretation should emphasize latent content, for many examples of "strong" and "not strong" stories appear to emphasize manifest content rather than latent content. Users of the test need to know how to interpret responses, but they are provided with insufficient normative information for this purpose. This criticism is applicable to other story-telling projective techniques, of course, and it can be said of the Blacky, as well as of the others, that clinical experience will provide some normative information, and that any sort of over-emphasis in stories, occurring in response to pictures not demanding such an emphasis, gains significance for interpretation of individual differences. For this reason, the "related comments" source of scoring on the Blacky test should perhaps be given more interpretive importance than it has been given in the manual, since it represents the operation of strong personal trends that overreach the stimulus demands of a given picture.

Still another issue which has remained untouched by the research literature is that related to the sequence of situations as presented to a given subject. The recommended sequence corresponds roughly to the developmental sequence as conceived by Freud's theory of psychosexual development. Apparently no research has been focused on the problem whether the opposite sequence, a gradually regressive sequence, would be more suitable than one which requires a sudden regression by the subject to the infantile attitude of oral erotism. It is true, of course, that using the terms "Papa" and "Mama" to refer to the parents may indeed facilitate the expected regressive attitude; but, on the other hand, continued reference to "Papa" and "Mama" (particularly in the inquiry questions) may function to fixate this regressive attitude in the subject, so that his responses will be unlikely to "mature" along with the developmental sequence of pictured situations.

SUMMARY EVALUATION. In spite of the many questions arising in connection with the Blacky technique as a clinical instrument, it is fair to say that the manual in its present form is one of the most complete and most explicit to be found for projective tests of the picture-story variety, and that the reviewer, and reportedly many other users, have found the Blacky test to provide a rich source of material for clinical evaluation. When used with children, especially boys, having mental ages of about 5 to 10 years, the *Blacky Pictures* often provide adequate material for interpretations concerning problem areas, attitudes toward siblings and parents, characteristic defensive reactions, self-perceptions, and the like. Yet it is the reviewer's impression that, with children of both sexes, aged from about 8 to about 12 years, Bellak's CAT is likely to have a higher interpretive yield than the Blacky. With subjects beyond early adolescence, the reviewer, in most cases, would consider the TAT, rather than the Blacky, to be the instrument of choice. These preferences are based on the various points mentioned above concerning the relative structuredness of the Blacky, the single hero figure available for identification, and various possible objections to the name "Blacky" itself.

It is also the reviewer's judgment that, after 13 years of use, the manual should be thoroughly revised as a guide to clinical interpretation. It appears that dimensional scoring, even though it may have value for research use, should no longer be emphasized for clinical application of the Blacky technique. Although the author has argued against "seeking....to adorn patients with diagnostic labels of an outmoded nosology," the use of dimensional scoring substitutes another nosology, emphasis on which may lead to neglect of significant nuances of personality dynamics. For clinical interpretation, it should be more useful to determine specifically how a subject responds to each of the situations, what defensive maneuvers he characteristically employs, and with what degree of regularity he expresses particular attitudes toward himself, toward his problems, and toward significant others, than to determine in which of the psychosexual areas he manifests greatest "disturbance."

Revision of the manual should also involve, as mentioned above, the inclusion of normative information concerning typical and atypical ways of perceiving the individual cartoons, concerning the relative frequencies of various story plots in response to each of the cartoons, and concerning any other characteristics of responses to the Blacky which would aid in determining whether, and in what ways, an individual protocol deviates from the typical.

For a review by Kenneth R. Newton, see 5:125 (1 excerpt); for a review by Albert Ellis, see 4:102 (3 excerpts).

[205]

★**Buttons: A Projective Test for Pre-Adolescent and Adolescent Boys and Girls.** Grades 7–9; maladjustment; 1963; 1 form (7 pages); manual (36 pages plus sample copy of test and scoring booklet); scoring booklet (4 pages); no data on reliability of scores; $18 per examiner's kit of 25 tests, 25 scoring booklets, and manual; $4 per manual; postpaid; (45) minutes; Esther P. Rothman and Pearl H. Berkowitz; Western Psychological Services. *

[206]

*****Children's Apperception Test.** Ages 3–10; 1949–61; individual; 1 form; 2 editions; short form record booklet ('55, 5 pages) for this test and test 245; no data on reliability and validity; $7.50 per set of cards and manual of either edition; $3 per 25 record booklets; postage extra; [15–50] minutes; Leopold Bellak and Sonya Sorel Bellak; C.P.S. Inc. *
a) CHILDREN'S APPERCEPTION TEST. 1949–61; 1 form ('59, c1949, 10 cards, same as cards published in 1949 and 1951 except for finish); revised manual, fourth edition ('61, c1949, 16 pages, identical with 1959 third edition except for expanded bibliography).
b) CHILDREN'S APPERCEPTION TEST—SUPPLEMENT. 1952–55; 1 form ('52, 10 cards); manual ('52, 8 pages).

REFERENCES

1–2. See 4:103.
3–17. See 5:126.
18. ARMSTRONG, MARY ANN SMITH. "Children's Responses to Animal and Human Figures in Thematic Pictures." *J Consult Psychol* 18:67–70 F '54. * (PA 28:8710)
19. LYLES, WILLIAM KARYLE. *The Effects of Examiner Attitudes on the Projective Test Responses of Children: A Study of the Significance of the Interpersonal Relationship in the Projective Testing of Children.* Doctor's thesis, New York University (New York, N.Y.), 1958. (DA 19:3024)
20. ROSENBLATT, MARVIN S. *The Development of Norms for the Children's Apperception Test.* Doctor's thesis, Florida State University (Tallahassee, Fla.), 1958. (DA 19:2150)
21. LEHMANN, IRVIN J. "Responses of Kindergarten Children to the Children's Apperception Test." *J Clin Psychol* 15:60–3 Ja '59. * (PA 34:2828)
22. NOLAN, ROBERT DALE. *A Longitudinal Comparison of Motives in Children's Fantasy Stories as Revealed by the Children's Apperception Test.* Doctor's thesis, Florida State University (Tallahassee, Fla.), 1959. (DA 20:3387)
23. WALTON, D. "A Children's Apperception Test—An Investigation of Its Validity as a Test of Neuroticism." *J Mental Sci* 105:359–70 Ap '59. * (PA 34:4412)
24. BELLAK, LEOPOLD, AND ADELMAN, CRUSA. Chap. 4, "The Children's Apperception Test (CAT)," pp. 62–94. In *Projective Techniques With Children.* Edited by Albert I. Rabin and Mary R. Haworth. New York: Grune & Stratton, Inc., 1960. Pp. xiii, 392. * (PA 35:2229)
25. BUDOFF, MILTON. "The Relative Utility of Animal and Human Figures in a Picture-Story Test for Young Children." *J Proj Tech* 24:347–52 D '60. * (PA 35:4716)

26. GOLIAS, GEORGE A. *The C.A.T. as a Measure of Therapeutic Change in Children, Age 6–12.* Master's thesis, Kent State University (Kent, Ohio), 1960.

27. MAGNUSSON, DAVID. "Some Personality Tests Applied on Identical Twins." *Scandinavian J Psychol* 1(2):55–61 '60. * (*PA* 35:6424)

28. REDDY, P. V. *A Study of the Reliability and Validity of the Children's Apperception Test.* Doctor's thesis, University of London (London, England), 1960. (Abstract: *Brit J Ed Psychol* 30:182–4)

29. BUTLER, R. L. "Responses of Institutionalized Mentally Retarded Children to Human and to Animal Pictures." *Am J Mental Def* 65:620–2 Mr '61. * (*PA* 36:1JI20B)

30. CAIN, ALBERT C. "A Supplementary Dream Technique With the Children's Apperception Test." *J Clin Psychol* 17: 181–3 Ap '61. * (*PA* 38:1006)

31. WILLIAMS, JESSIE M. "Children Who Break Down in Foster Homes: A Psychological Study of Patterns of Personality Growth in Grossly Deprived Children." *J Child Psychol & Psychiatry* 2:5–20 Je '61. * (*PA* 36:2FF05W)

32. HAWORTH, MARY R. "Responses of Children to a Group Projective Film and to the Rorschach, CAT, Despert Fables and D-A-P." *J Proj Tech* 26:47–60 Mr '62. * (*PA* 37:2893)

33. WEISSKOPF-JOELSON, EDITH, AND FOSTER, HELEN C. "An Experimental Study of the Effect of Stimulus Variation Upon Projection." *J Proj Tech* 26:366–70 S '62. * (*PA* 37:3208)

34. BUDOFF, MILTON. "Animal vs. Human Figures in a Picture Story Test for Young, Mentally Backward Children." *Am J Mental Def* 68:245–50 S '63. * (*PA* 38:5726)

35. GROSS, SEYMOUR Z. "Critique: Children Who Break Down in Foster Homes: A Psychological Study of Patterns of Personality Growth in Grossly Deprived Children." *J Child Psychol & Psychiatry* 4:61–6 Ap '63. *

36. HAWORTH, MARY R. "A Schedule for the Analysis of CAT Responses." *J Proj Tech & Pers Assess* 27:181–4 Je '63. * (*PA* 38:2716)

BERNARD I. MURSTEIN, *Associate Professor of Psychology, Connecticut College, New London, Connecticut.*

The genesis of the CAT stemmed from a discussion between Leopold Bellak and Ernst Kris in which the latter "pointed out how we could expect children to identify themselves much more readily with animals than with persons, a *fact* we have known ever since Freud wrote his story of little Hans in 'The Phobia of a Five Year Old'" (italics mine). Certainly the widespread use of animals with human characteristics in movie cartoons, comic strips, and television would seem to support this "fact." The only contrary note is that a considerable amount of research has been done comparing both the TAT (which contains clearly discernible humans for the most part) and specially created human analogues of the CAT (which were like the CAT cards in every way except for the use of humans rather than animals) with the CAT. Not a single study clearly supports the alleged supremacy of the CAT over pictures with humans. The results of some studies are indecisive or ambiguous [1,2,3]

1 BILLS, ROBERT E. "Animal Pictures for Obtaining Children's Projections." *J Clin Psychol* 6:291–3 Jl '50. * (*PA* 25:1784)

2 BILLS, ROBERT E.; LEIMAN, CHARLES J.; AND THOMAS, RICHARD W. "A Study of the Validity of the TAT and a Set of Animal Pictures." *J Clin Psychol* 6:293–5 Jl '50. * (*PA* 25:1785)

3 BOYD, NANCY A., AND MANDLER, GEORGE. "Children's Responses to Human and Animal Stories and Pictures." *J Consult Psychol* 19:367–71 '55. *

(6), but the majority show a clear superiority for figures employing humans [4] (*11–2, 16, 18, 25*). Among the findings supporting the supremacy of pictures with humans were clinicians' ratings of clinical usefulness (*12*); percentage of stories containing expressions of feeling, containing significant conflict, having definite outcome (*16*); more feelings, different kinds of feelings, conflicts, number and kinds of outcomes, number and kinds of themes, and number of figures (*11*); significantly higher Transcendence Index (more nondescriptive statements) (*18*); more involvement in human cards; [5] longer stories, more rapid verbalization, quicker reaction time, more themes; [6] higher word count, story level, Transcendence Index (*25*).

Evidence in favor of the CAT stems from the finding of Boyd and Mandler that most of their subjects preferred the animal stories and gave more emotional material to them, although more involved in the human series.

The other studies either found no difference or are equivocal because of confounded designs. The data have been discussed by the reviewer in greater detail elsewhere.[7]

Bellak and Adelman in a recent review (*24*) have objected to a few of these studies on the grounds that the human analogues were more structured than the CAT and, further, that the age of the children tested was in the upper half of the 3 to 10 year range suitable for the CAT. The first objection seems unjustified on two counts. First, the humanized analogues are essentially equivalent in many of the studies. It is extremely doubtful that this factor *per se* could account for the overwhelming superiority of the human pictures. Second, Bellak believes that the use of structured stimuli violates the basic principles of projective testing. Elsewhere,[8] this reviewer has tried to show that many of these principles do not agree with the findings of most projective studies. To give but one example, ambiguity and projection are not linearly related but rather show a curvilinear relationship. It is possible to weaken the ability of a card to elicit projection by making it too ambiguous and not allow-

4 SIMSON, EDUARD. Vergleich von CAT und einer inhaltsanslogen Mensch-Bilderserie. *Diagnostica* 5:54–66 '59. (*PA* 36:1FF54S)

5 BOYD AND MANDLER, *op. cit.*

6 SIMSON, *op. cit.*

7 MURSTEIN, BERNARD I. *Theory and Research in Projective Techniques (Emphasizing the TAT).* New York: John Wiley & Sons, Inc., 1963. Pp. xiii, 385. *

8 *Ibid.*

ing the subject to identify with any of the characters.

Bellak's objection to the lack of studies with young children does not seem to take cognizance of the difficulties experienced by very young children in verbalizing. Budoff (*25*) working with four-year-olds whose minimum IQ was greater than 120 concluded that the stories were not too meaningful because of the immaturity of the children, though the few significant differences reported favored the human analogue of the CAT.

It is also noteworthy that the current manual, published in 1961 and containing 46 references, does not contain a single one reporting any of the negative results cited above. Why?

It is possible but still untested that the CAT is better than the TAT or TAT-type cards for such specific problems, for example, as sibling rivalry, oral fixation, and the Oedipal theme. Also, only one study has used disturbed children (*12*). It is possible (though there is no particular reason to believe so) that the CAT may be more successful here. Last, this reviewer would like to see more meaningful variables tackled than word count, length of stories, and quickness of reaction time.

In sum, the research strongly contradicts the belief that children project more readily to pictures of animals than of humans. Accordingly, as a broad-band instrument, the CAT cannot be recommended at this time as being likely to provide as much clinical utility as the TAT or other pictures with human figures. With regard to specific psychoanalytic hypotheses for which the test was primarily designed, there is no evidence favoring or contradicting the use of the instrument.

ROBERT D. WIRT, *Professor of Psychology, Child Development, and Psychiatry, University of Minnesota, Minneapolis, Minnesota.*

The *Children's Apperception Test* (CAT) continues to be difficult to evaluate. As with other projective techniques, the kind of data one gets using the CAT is not easily translated into statistical, measurement language. While Bellak's book (*9*) is certainly a useful guide for interpretation, the categories are variable and quite dependent upon both the user's theoretical orientation and the nature of his clinical experience. Over the years there have been indications that norms were in process of being established, but to date satisfactory data of this

sort do not exist. There is also some question, based on the reviewer's experience, that children actually construe the stimulus material as was hoped by the authors. There was reason to suppose that children might more readily respond to pictures of animals in various situations than to material depicting people. However, it is not at all clear that the CAT succeeds in eliciting stories of such varied thematic properties as, for example, do the children's cards of the TAT. Perhaps this is because the situations shown in the CAT cards are more structured, leading to "popular" responses, and also because the CAT does not really have characters represented (such as young children) with whom a child can immediately identify and upon whom he can project his own self concept. With very young children (under age six) the CAT may be useful in getting at some stereotypy of interpersonal perception in individual cases. But such material is generally fairly evident from other sources, such as the history or free play observation. Perhaps the most useful cards of the CAT are those of the Supplement (the CAT-S) which are designed for assessment of particular problem areas, especially when used as a play technique, as Bellak suggests.

Bellak's book (*9*) is an instructive and necessary companion for the less experienced clinician interested in using the CAT. It is even more useful as an introduction to the TAT. For the CAT it gives an approach to interpretation by employing case material which gives perspective and structure for students in the analysis of children's stories.

The story telling technique has much appeal to children and has been popular with psychologists and psychiatrists for a long time. Nearly all clinical child psychologists would believe that the method has considerable value, but its value comes more from the sensitivity and experience of the clinician than from the particular stimulus material used. Thus far the CAT cannot be said to be any better than any number of other techniques which require a child to tell a story. In fact, the reviewer believes that it is less helpful than using structured doll situations. Until reliable scoring techniques and criteria of interpretation can be standardized the CAT and similar techniques will continue to be of value proportionate to the skill of the interpreter.

For reviews by Douglas T. Kenny and Albert I. Rabin, see 5:126; for reviews by John E. Bell and L. Joseph Stone, see 4:103 (5 excerpts); for excerpts from related book reviews, see 5:B63.

[207]

Controlled Projection for Children, Second Edition. Ages 6–13; 1945–51; individual; 1 form ('51); manual ('51, 178 pages); no data on reliability and validity; 25*s.* per manual, postage and purchase tax extra within U.K.; [20] minutes; John C. Raven; H. K. Lewis & Co. Ltd. * (United States distributor: Psychological Corporation.)

REFERENCES

1–8. See 5:127.

JOHN LIGGETT, *Senior Lecturer in Psychology, University College of South Wales and Monmouthshire, University of Wales, Cardiff, Wales.*

The author's declared aim in the 1944 foreword to the first edition was "to present, not a technique of testing ready for applied psychology, but simply a method of enquiry suitable for experimental work." A good deal of such work has since been undertaken and *Controlled Projection for Children* can now be regarded both as a useful tool and as a model for such enquiries for the future. In refreshing contrast to many megalomanic clinical panaceas the objective here is a carefully limited one: the uncovering—in a reasonably brief testing time, usually about a quarter hour—of some specific aspects of the fantasies and domestic preoccupations of children between the ages of 6 and 13.

The test materials required are of the greatest simplicity: coloured pencils, paper, and a list of 11 questions. The child is asked to draw "anything that comes into your head" and simultaneously to relate a simple story about an imaginary boy or girl. The framework of the story is provided by the psychologist, the detail by the child in response to 11 standard questions about the likes and dislikes, preferred playmates, fears, dreams, parental attitudes and interactions, and other feelings of the imaginary child.

In the manual the author clearly tabulates typical responses made by 150 normal children and 80 clinic cases subdivided into three age groups (6½, 9½, and 12½ years). He gives individual response frequencies and sufficient information to allow the calculation of a "coefficient of conformity" which expresses the extent to which a child's verbal responses are characteristic of his age group. Several children's records are presented in detail with appropriate computations and clinical inferences explicitly presented.

Conclusions derived from the drawings are much more tentative but a useful analytical scheme is presented. The manual is well produced and contains some excellent colour reproductions of children's drawings. The author's arguments are modest and persuasive and, as a record of empirical work in a difficult field, his manual is praiseworthy. There is more than a touch, however, of tedious pedantry in some of his introductory discussion. We should not need to be told (at least in this context) what is meant by "a critical judgement," nor should we need half a page to explain the word "analogy."

Over 12 years of more or less regular use this reviewer has found *Controlled Projection for Children* a powerful yet sensitive clinical aid, a fruitful source of hypotheses about individual cases, and a valuable vehicle for case discussions with psychiatric colleagues. Often, too, with difficult, disturbed cases resistant to interview, it has provided the *only* available route to the inner world of the child.

See 5:127 (3 excerpts); for reviews by Arthur L. Benton and Percival M. Symonds of the original edition, see 3:29 (5 excerpts).

[208]

Curtis Completion Form. Grades 11–16 and adults; 1950–53; emotional maturity and adjustment; Form A ('50, 4 pages); manual ('53, 7 pages); $2 per 20 tests; 25¢ per manual; 25¢ per specimen set; postage extra; (30–35) minutes; James W. Curtis; Science Research Associates, Inc. *

REFERENCES

1. WATSON, WALTER S. "The Validity of the Curtis Completion Form as a Predictor of College Student Personality Deviates." *Yearb Nat Council Meas Used Ed* 12:82–5 pt 2 '55. *
2. FITZSIMMONS, S. J., AND MARCUSE, F. L. "Adjustment in Leaders and Non-Leaders as Measured by the Sentence Completion Projective Technique." *J Clin Psychol* 17:380–1 O '61. * (*PA* 38:8549)

IRWIN G. SARASON, *Associate Professor of Psychology, University of Washington, Seattle, Washington.*

This is a sentence completion test which consists of 52 items. It may be scored objectively by means of a content analysis scoring system described in the manual. The scores may be interpreted by means of a chart which indicates the probabilities with which normal, neurotic, and psychotic behavior would be expected from subjects with varying adjustment scores. The manual describes the test as being of value in any situation in which an evaluation of emotional adjustment is required.

The test appears to be an interesting approach to the sentence completion method and might prove useful in personality research. However, in terms of practical clinical, industrial, and educational work, it is inadequate in several respects. The development of the test was far from thorough. No set of standardized instructions are provided. The sample on which data are provided in the manual involved only 335 subjects, and the description of the subject types is sketchy. The 335 subjects included 199 vocational rehabilitation clients, 87 psychiatric patients who had been referred to one clinical psychologist for testing, and 49 employed adults seeking vocational or personal counseling. Out of this assortment of people, normal, neurotic, and psychotic are differentiated in the manual. This categorization was based on the judgments of clinical workers.

The test's scoring system seems to possess adequate interscorer reliability. However, only four scorers were used in the reliability study reported. The only validity data cited are in terms of the sentence completion adjustment scores obtained by subjects who had been judged by raters to be normal, neurotic, or psychotic. While this finding, if replicated, could be of value, it seems clear that, on the basis of the data presented, the claims for the test are extravagant. For the test to be useful further studies would be required involving better sampling procedures and more validity evidence. If this test is valid, and it may be, it is difficult, with the data available, to say precisely in what way.

LAURANCE F. SHAFFER, *Professor of Psychology and Education, Teachers College, Columbia University, New York, New York.*

This sentence completion test is apparently unchanged, in test form or manual, since it was published in 1950 to 1953, and since it was last reviewed in this series. It consists of 52 completion stems, 50 of the usual sort and 2 partly structured, with a space for the examinee's further remarks. The manual states that it is a measure of "emotional maturity and adjustment"—rather vague concepts whose definition is not elaborated.

In its clarity and objectivity, the scoring method has considerable merit. Each response

showing a "Group A factor"—antagonism, suspicion, jealousy, self-pity and pessimism, insecurity, social inadequacy, environmental deprivation, or severe conflict—receives two points. "Group B factors" of avoidance responses and ambiguous and incomplete responses, and "Group C factors" of erasures, cross-outs, or emphatic punctuation each receive one point. Each type of scorable response is well defined and is illustrated by brief but adequate examples. The reported interscorer correlations of from .89 to .95 seem consistent with the clarity of the scoring method.

At first glance, the manual seems a model of adherence to good professional standards in spite of its six-page brevity. Odd-even reliabilities are reported, and the form's validity receives multiple presentation in terms of means and standard deviations, biserial correlations, and an expectancy table which show the discrimination between groups described as normal, neurotic, and psychotic. The reported validity seems good. In fact, on further cogitation, it seems quite too good to be true. It may be doubted that any assessment method whatsoever has a biserial validity of .97 for the discrimination between normal and neurotic, of .98 between normal and all non-normal, and of .73 between neurotic and psychotic. If these coefficients were sound, the *Curtis Completion Form* would have received international acclaim as the ultimate solution of a hitherto elusive diagnostic problem.

What's the trouble? The application of only a little psychometric sophistication reveals three serious sources of error. First, the biserial correlation coefficient was misused. The validation was based on 335 cases, of which 175 are described as normal, 60 as neurotic, and 100 as psychotic. Thus 48 per cent of the cases were non-normal, in comparison to an incidence that probably does not exceed 10 per cent in an unselected sample. Because biserial correlations are affected by the base rate, the reported coefficients are surely somewhat inflated statistically.

Second, all of the 335 subjects used to establish the validities were clients or patients who were seeking help of some kind, drawn from clients of a rehabilitation service, employed adults seeking vocational or personal counseling, and "psychiatric patients referred to one clinical psychologist for testing." Such persons, as much experience and some data show, tend to label themselves. The well-integrated clients are normally matter-of-fact or defensive; the disturbed ones pour out their woes to document their pleas for help. Therefore the validation data are relevant only if the test were to be used solely for voluntary clients, and show no evidence justifying its use for industrial selection or educational counseling as the manual recommends.

Third, and most seriously, the manual gives no evidence that the criterion classifications and the test scores were independent. The distinction between normal, neurotic, and psychotic examinees was based on "ratings....made by skilled professional personnel—clinical psychologists or psychiatrists," who could have had access to the Completion Form as well as to other evidence. The human nature, even of psychologists, being what it is, it is likely that few subjects showing disturbance on the sentence completions were called "normal." In the absence of clear evidence to the contrary, there must be at least a suspicion that the test performances contaminated the criteria.

In summary, the *Curtis Completion Form* remains an attractive blank with a nicely developed scoring method. Whether it is an effective instrument depends on more carefully gathered evidence, still unavailable ten years after its publication.

For a review by Alfred B. Heilbrun, Jr., see 5:128.

[209]

★**The Draw-A-Person.** Ages 5 and over; 1963; 1 form (1 page plus backing sheet to be interleafed with carbon to make a 2-copy drawing form); manual (33 pages plus sample copies of protocol and interpretive booklets); protocol booklet (4 pages); interpretive booklet (4 pages); $20 per examiner's kit of 25 tests, 25 protocol booklets, 25 interpretive booklets, and manual; $6.50 per 25 copies of either test, protocol booklet, or interpretive booklet; $6 per manual; postpaid; [5–10] minutes; William H. Urban; Western Psychological Services. *

[210]

★**The Driscoll Play Kit.** Ages 2–10; 1952; personality development and adjustment; individual; 1 form (5 dolls and 27 pieces of furniture); manual (6 pages); no scoring or interpretive procedure; $59 per set of materials, postpaid; manual free; administration time not reported; Gertrude P. Driscoll; Psychological Corporation. *

REFERENCES

1. BOOKBINDER, KATHRYN F. *The Relation of Social Status and Punishment as Observed in Stories Obtained With the Driscoll Play-Kit.* Doctor's thesis, Columbia University (New York, N.Y.), 1955. (*DA* 15:1252)
2. McELVANEY, MURIEL BAKER. *Four Types of Fantasy Aggression in the Response of "Rebellious" and "Submissive" Children to the Driscoll Playkit, Structured by Parental-*

Demand and Neutral Stimulus Stories. Doctor's thesis, Columbia University (New York, N.Y.), 1958. (*DA* 19:364)

[211]

The Eight Card Redrawing Test (8CRT). Ages 7 and over; 1950–57; 1 form ('56, 9 pages); manual ('57, see 5 below); directions for administering ('56, 1 page); score sheet ('56, 1 page); no data on reliability; no norms; $6 per set of test materials for 35 administrations; $4 per manual; postpaid; (30–60) minutes; Leopold Caligor; 8CRT. *

REFERENCES

1–6. See 5:131.

Am J Orthopsychiatry 30:213–4 Ja '60. *Alfred B. Heilbrun, Jr.* * The potential merits of this new projective device have already been mentioned—increased reliability, scoring objectivity, and clinical data—and for these Caligor deserves considerable credit. However, the term "potential" was used to emphasize that none of these innovations can be considered a diagnostic contribution until it is more clearly demonstrated empirically that the human figure drawings obtained on the 8 CRT are related to the behavior of the artist in specifiable ways. It is here that the 8 CRT remains most vulnerable since many suggested test interpretations do not as yet have the solid backing of research validation. It is hoped that the publication of the 8 CRT, with its increased objectivity and reliability, will stimulate such research and more clearly establish the diagnostic utility of the figure drawing technique.

Int J Social Psychiatry 4:73 su '58. * Caligor has invented a scoring system as complicated and meticulous as that of the Rorschach Test. Scoring is expressed in terms of number and constancy of deviations from a statistical norm, the accuracy of which we must take on trust since, although we are told that a population of 7 years to 70 years has been tested to obtain normative data, statistical tables have not yet been provided in the book. Interpretation of this data is admitted by the author to be based upon "extensive clinical experience," not accounted for within the context by any attempt at correlative proof. * Within each measurable dimension lies a complex scale of scoring. It should be emphasized that their value as a reliable measurement of personality depends entirely upon the accuracy of Dr. Caligor's interpretations of each deviation within a category. This is the weakness of a test aiming at objectivity. It is important that we should not be mesmerized by a complexity of figures into believing that a test is therefore necessarily reliable in interpretation. All that is ensured is agreement between the scorers and a measurement of deviation. It is by the accuracy of the original premises that such a test should be judged. Learning how to draw a man, when a child, is so often a matter of copying and of being taught, and carry-over of the learnt pattern so frequent in adult life; that this, with many other cultural and environmental factors, powerful in influencing such a design, is probably all too readily ignored. It is in Dr. Caligor's case illustrations that the extreme subjectivity of this test is revealed. Although there is much with which common sense would agree within them, some will feel that the author strains credulity to breaking-point in his interpretations of minute data.

J Consult Psychol 23:470-1 O '59. Seymour Fisher. * Caligor does refer to three studies which were undertaken for validation purposes, but his descriptions of these studies are extremely brief and it is clear that he did not attempt to test directly the validity of the meanings assigned to the various scoring categories. One can see that his formulations regarding the significance of given variables are based almost entirely on his clinical experiences and that one must accept them on faith. The 8 CRT is presently a collection of hunches that have been formalized by Caligor into a scoring system. Some of his hunches are novel and interesting and may prove eventually to have an enriching effect upon figure drawing analysis. Thus one is particularly impressed with the novelty and potential importance of his emphasis on such factors as spatial directionality (e.g., up vs. down and right vs. left), symmetry, and mode of maintaining continuity from one drawing to another. Overall, though, it must be said that his scoring categories are not bound together by a unifying concept or viewpoint. They seem, on the contrary, to consist of heterogenous "signs" which were assembled in an arbitrary fashion. One must also question the value of Caligor's mode of defining many of the scoring categories. His definitions are often very vague and hazy. Illustratively, he refers to various signs as indicating "anxiety," "conflict," "immaturity," "lowered ability to orient oneself in the environment," "ability to use inner resources," "awareness of objects or other persons in the environment." How much more would one know about a given subject for having acquired such vague bits of information about him? The 8 CRT does indeed present some new ideas about figure drawing analysis, but it lacks the rationale or validation to be considered a formal test.

J Proj Tech 23:472-3 D '59. Emanuel F. Hammer. * a closely-reasoned, soundly-balanced presentation of the newest offspring of the projective drawing family * All in all, if the Eight-Card-Redrawing Test is reserved for subjects who appear to enjoy drawing, a rich yield of data may be expected to be the rule rather than the exception. In my experience, I have not found it often worth the time and effort with subjects who do not like to draw. A task which asks such a subject to draw eight figures, in addition to whatever other drawing techniques have been administered, serves only to irritate and place an undue strain upon rapport. When used with subjects who take to drawing, however, it often proves to be one of the most rewarding diagnostic techniques in the projective drawing battery. Caligor's book does not appear to do full justice to his own technique. The book treats only expressive aspects of drawing (although content is touched upon in the three case studies presented at the end of the book). Thus, what for the reviewer is the real drama of the Eight-Card-Redrawing Technique, the one that lies in the shifts in content as one goes from one drawing to the next, is not given the focus it deserves. The writing style is somewhat academically-toned, and sprinkled with terms like "lowered environmental cognizance" and sentences like: "Long strokes reflect impulsivity-lability in response to anxiety and stimulability-impulsivity to tactile-sensuous needs." In passing, the reviewer might mention that he has been curious, since first learning of the Eight-Card-Redrawing Test procedure, as to why Caligor has formed his technique around eight, rather than five, ten, or some other number of drawings. The answer is not given in the book. An overall impression is that for those who employ drawings in a quantitative way, there is here a ready-made tool for doing research on, or with, drawings—a handy book and kit to have.

For reviews by Cherry Ann Clark and Philip L. Harriman, see 5:131 (1 excerpt).

[212]

★**The Family Relations Indicator: A Projective Technique for Investigating Intra-Family Relationships.** Emotionally disturbed children ages 3-16;

1962; 1 form (33 cards; 13 each for boys and for girls plus 4 for both boys and girls and 3 introductory cards); manual (36 pages); behavior item sheets (2 pages); no data on reliability; 85s. per set of cards, 20 behavior item sheets, and manual; 6s. per 20 behavior item sheets; 17s. per manual; prices include purchase tax; postpaid within U.K.; (20-30) minutes; J. G. Howells and John R. Lickorish; distributed by National Foundation for Educational Research in England and Wales. *

REFERENCES

1. HOWELLS, JOHN G., AND LICKORISH, JOHN R. "The Family Relations Indicator: A Projective Technique for Investigating Intra-Family Relationships Designed for Use With Emotionally Disturbed Children." *Brit J Ed Psychol* 33:286–96 N '63. * (PA 38:8552)

C. B. BLAKEMORE, *Lecturer in Psychology, Institute of Psychiatry, Maudsley Hospital, University of London, London, England.*

The authors of this new projective technique, a psychiatrist and a psychologist working in a child psychiatry unit in England, justify their development of yet another test on the grounds that, unlike the majority of alternative tests of this type, it is free from any marked theoretical or psychoanalytic bias. Their aim is to investigate intrafamily relationships that may be involved in the difficulties experienced by an emotionally disturbed child. The theoretical position they adopt is that the child "will ascribe to the figures in the given pictures such actions, attitudes and sayings as are drawn from his own immediate experience."

The test itself consists of a set of cards on each of which is a drawing showing a simple family scene. Each child is shown 20 of the 33 cards making up the set, the selection depending on the child's sex, and is asked to describe in each case what is happening in the scene. The first 3 cards are "warm-up" presentations and are not scored; the remaining 17 cards depict the following six family situations: child and father, child and mother, child alone, child and baby, siblings together, and parents both alone and in the company of children. The stories produced by the child are scored according to their content of expressed attitudes and actions within the family setting. The scoring sheet enables the examiner to evaluate each of the six basic family relationships in terms of such categories as attitudes, verbalisations, actions, deprivations, delinquency, and guilt feelings.

There are no data available on the reliability of either the child's performance or the examiner's analysis and scoring of the stories. The only validation study so far reported is on 50 emotionally disturbed children between the ages of 6 and 17 years, ranging in IQ from 67 to 136. The findings from this study claim a high degree of agreement between a psychologist's assessment of intrafamily relationships on the basis of the test, and a psychiatrist's assessment of these relationships on the basis of clinical interviews. There is, however, the possibility of criterion contamination here, for the psychiatrist had some knowledge of the test findings before he completed his assessment.

It would seem reasonable to conclude that before we can regard the *Family Relations Indicator* as being of any greater value than other projective techniques of a similar type, more work needs to be done on the collection of normative and standardization data, on the assessment of reliability, and on further validation studies. It would be surprising if the test proved to be any more successful than its predecessors when such information is available.

WALTER KATKOVSKY, *Associate Professor of Psychology, Fordham University, New York, New York.*

Several distinctive features of the FRI are noted by the authors in their manual. These are as follows: (*a*) the pictures were designed specifically to depict a series of family situations familiar to children of school age with typical family members represented; (*b*) they differ from many other popular projective tests, such as the *Symonds Picture-Story Test* and the *Object Relations Technique,* in that they are suitable for young children; (*c*) they are less structured than the pictures of Jackson's *Test of Family Attitudes* and the *Michigan Picture Test;* and (*d*) they are not based on a single personality theory as is the case with the *Blacky Pictures.* Associated with the last point is the fact that the information sought by the FRI consists of "behavioral units" or descriptive categories of behavior which the child attributes to the characters in the pictures. These "information units" are relatively concrete, specific dimensions, and they may prove useful for clinical purposes as well as for investigating hypotheses derived from diverse personality theories. In addition, the specificity of the information sought by the FRI constitutes a less ambitious aim than that of tests which use more abstract dimensions and purport to measure the overall personality of the child. This specificity promises greater hope of obtaining validity data than is true for many projective tests.

Apart from the above positive features, the test's present stage of development leaves much to be desired. The manual indicates the authors' awareness of the importance of specifying the purpose of the test, presenting standardized instructions, describing scoring methods, and providing data on the test's utility. Yet each of these matters goes begging for clarification and more specific information.

The purpose of the test cited by the authors is "to provide a description of the relations between the various members of the patient's family" and "to provide factual information about the family." At the same time, the authors note that information provided by the test reflects the patient's own attitude toward the family, i.e., the family situation as the patient sees it. There is no attempt to deal with the question of differentiating between the "factual" and the attitudinal. The authors pay only cursory attention to the point that use of a projective approach to gain factual material is inconsistent with the typical assumption that projective tests measure phantasy rather than real life experiences, and to the possibility that there may be better methods of obtaining factual data than by asking children to describe pictures. The assumption that the test responses "are drawn from his [the child's] own immediate experience" avoids the question of whether the responses depict actual experiences or reflect the child's wishes, needs, fears, or misperceptions, and promotes the possibility that responses will be interpreted erroneously as actual characteristics of the family situation. The meaning of the responses to the pictures needs clarification in line with empirical data.

While standardized instructions for administration are presented, several suggested practices may introduce variations in the responses obtained by different administrators. The authors state that cards relevant to a figure who is not part of the child's family constellation should be omitted. This practice provides one subject with less opportunity to respond than another subject. Several of the responses in the manual indicate that the child referred to a family figure not depicted in the picture he was shown. Consequently, it seems likely that cards showing figures who are not a part of the child's family may elicit material about actual family members. Would it not be more sys-

tematic to present the same number of cards to all subjects and merely ignore responses inapplicable to the subject's family situation than to vary the number of pictures used? Another inconsistency is introduced when a figure depicted in the picture is misperceived. Two instances of this are present in the responses in the manual: a mother was perceived as a "little girl" and a girl was referred to as a boy. Such misperceptions, which are apt to be frequent with young children, subtract from the standardization of the test stimuli. Perhaps they could be minimized if the administrator briefly described the figures as he presented each picture. Still another possible administrative variation may occur in connection with encouraging elaboration of responses. The authors prefer spontaneous responses, but the use of such questions as "What do you think he is saying?" and "Can you tell me any more?" are left to the judgment of the administrator. Lack of systematic questioning, even with such general leads, may result in different administrators obtaining different responses.

No data are presented on interscorer reliability and two points seem likely to operate against agreement. Only one set of responses is presented as scoring examples and these are insufficient to serve as operational definitions of the many scoring categories, most of which are not defined. Such scoring categories as "suspicious," "apathetic," "deceitful" need elaboration. The second criticism pertains to a summary scoring approach in which severity of a reaction of parents to the child is distinguished from the mere presence of that reaction, but no criterion is given for making this distinction.

A final criticism is with the lack of objective data on the FRI. The authors state the unwarranted belief that split-half and test-retest reliability are inapplicable or impractical with respect to the test and that a reliability check must await development of a parallel set of pictures. They report that the test has been given to over 500 children, but data on the responses of this group are not presented. One validity study is cited in which 80 to 90 per cent of the descriptions of parent-child relationships suggested by the tests on 50 children were consistent with a psychiatrist's judgments concerning the parent-child relationships based on his extensive knowledge of the family situation. The significance of these data is weakened, however, because the psychiatrist had knowledge of the test results prior to the time he made his judgments.

In summary, it should be noted that the FRI consists of two things, a new set of pictures and a scoring system. Depending on the examiner's purpose and preference, the pictures may prove to be useful stimuli in assessing a child's attitudes, feelings, phantasies, and experiences relative to his family members. In the absence of norms and reliability and validity data, however, the pictures should be considered adjunctive stimuli to a clinical interview rather than a test. The scoring system proposed by the authors needs elaboration and evidence of interscorer reliability. Nevertheless, categorizing responses into units of behavior is a practice which allows for both specificity and flexibility and has promise for the clinician and researcher using projective stimuli with children.

[213]

*Four Picture Test (1930), Second Edition. Ages 10 and over; 1948–58; 1 form ('58, 4 cards); manual ('58, 15 pages); no data on reliability and validity; no norms; gld. 38 ($10) per set of cards and manual, postpaid; (30–45) minutes; D. J. van Lennep and R. Houwink (manual); publisher and distributor in Holland and Belgium: Netherlands Institute of Industrial Psychology; distributor in all other countries: Martinus Nijhoff. *

REFERENCES

1–3. See 4:105.
4. SHNEIDMAN, EDWIN S. "The Case of Jay: Psychological Test and Anamnestic Data." J Proj Tech 16:297–345 S '52. * (PA 28:2676)
5. SHNEIDMAN, EDWIN S., EDITOR. "The TAT Newsletter, Vol. 6, No. 1, Summer 1952." J Proj Tech 16:260–5 Je '52. *
6. SPIEGELMAN, MARVIN. "Jungian Theory and the Analysis of Thematic Tests." J Proj Tech 19:253–63 S '55. * (PA 30:4601)

S. G. LEE, *Professor of Psychology, University of Leicester, Leicester, England.*

The four pictures comprising this test are executed in a fairly subtle wash, browns and greens predominating. They represent *"four fundamental existential situations"*: (a) being with one other person (two men in a room, a table between them); (b) being personally alone (a bedroom with the possible outline of a head on the pillow); (c) being socially alone (a man standing under a street lamp in the rain); and (d) being with many others in a group (spectators and players at a tennis court). The subject is required to write a single story incorporating all four situations.

Certain advantages accrue from this "four-in-one" technique. (a) The story tends to cover a greater time span in its content than would, say, a TAT protocol. This can be revealing in

terms of, e.g., long term solutions of conflict situations envisaged by the subject. (b) More measurable formal characteristics are found in the structuring of the one story from the four stimuli and this increases the possibilities of the test as a diagnostic or taxonomic device. (c) Story material connecting the pictures is likely to be projective material that is less stimulus bound—"concept-dominated" rather than "picture-dominated." (d) Time taken in administration and scoring is relatively short.

The pictures are unaltered in this second edition of the test, but the accompanying manual is greatly changed. Twenty-two pages of illustrative protocols and analyses have been omitted, together with nearly all the theoretical discussion. The emphasis on order of the pictures in the story is missing. All normative data have been left out and the user is left to apply his own methods of analysis or personality theory to whatever results he may obtain. The acquisition of group norms on which to base any theory is recommended and there is, in contrast to the first edition, no special demand for clinical intuition. Compare the 1958 manual's statement, "Only if comparable (matched) group samples are available, significant differences can be studied," with the following from the 1948 manual: "The understanding is effected in a 'hermeneutical circle,' i.e., each separate expression can only be understood from the composite expressions, and the composite only by way of each separate expression. One has to enter the circle somewhere and must continually confront part and whole with each other in order to arrive at a feeling of evidence. Only a trained psychologist with intuition and experience can have good results."

In brief, this is a manual very slight in content, much more conservative and limited than its predecessor. As an example, one of the most valuable emphases in the test, stressed in the first edition, is on the analysis of formal variables. In the 1958 edition the discussion of these is limited to some three hundred words, anything but exhaustive, and no indication is given of the kind of conclusions to be drawn under such headings as "Style variables proper" or "The writer's attitude towards his own story." In many ways this change would seem to be a pity, for, though the original manual was more controversial in many of its statements, it was fertile in ideas and hypotheses.

The cost of cards and manual has been reduced from $16.90 in 1953 to $10 in 1963. This is an improvement, though your reviewer would regard the first edition as the "better buy." But the second edition is still, for the materials and size of the manual, a very expensive test. In a review excerpted in *The Fourth Mental Measurements Yearbook* (see 4:105) from the *TAT Newsletter,* Robert R. Holt states that he had been assured by the author that "the unusual cost of producing exact duplicates of the original watercolor pictures makes it impossible to market the test [the first edition] for less." This does not carry conviction in the light of recent advances in colour reproduction and the statement in the present manual that the test can be used for groups "if a good colored slide is available." Slight colour changes would not appear likely to alter responses significantly.

Your reviewer has used the test for some years and has found that significant intraperson correlations (in terms of rank orders of need scores) can often be obtained between scores on the FPT and on a complete TAT. The test is a useful one for "main needs" in a personality and will often throw considerable light on environmental pressures on the subject. But two disadvantages should be mentioned. In the description of the pictures above I have used the words "men" and "man" for pictures (a) and (c). While the figures are blurred it has been my experience that practically all subjects see them as male and here doubts may arise as to the comparability of results from male and female subjects. With the latter, "hero" identification is often very awkward. Again, to many adult subjects the pictures carry a definite atmosphere of the 1920's (e.g., in the "tennis" picture the men are wearing long white flannel trousers), and this can on occasion lead to very flippant stories. While this is doubtless of significance it makes the evaluation of some results very difficult.

However, probably the most cheering paragraph in the whole manual is: "For a period of ten years, a great deal of research has been done on the various variables which can be isolated in FPT protocols. In a study of over 4,000 protocols of normal and abnormal subjects, it has been found possible to isolate over 150 different variables, which lend themselves

to more or less objective scoring and which were found to have certain diagnostic importance. The results and statistics of this research cannot be given within the framework of this manual but are to be published at a later date in a book on the Four Picture Test."

Such a book may well prove to be a landmark in the history of projective tests. It should, especially when it is available in English, add incalculably to the value of the *Four Picture Test.*

JOHANN M. SCHEPERS, *Senior Research Officer, National Institute for Personnel Research, Johannesburg, Republic of South Africa.*

The *Four Picture Test* (FPT) belongs to the general class of projective techniques known as "picture-thematic" tests. It consists of four colored plates, representative of the following four "existential situations": (a) being with one other person (two people of ambiguous sex conversing in a room); (b) being personally alone (a bedroom scene with no human form visible); (c) being socially alone (a lone figure standing against a lamppost in the rain); (d) being with many others in a group (a tennis match in progress with four spectators in the foreground).

It is doubtful whether anything has been gained by having the plates produced in color. Color might well constitute a handicap for the colorblind, or else exert a differential influence on their responses. Reproduction in color is also much more costly. It is unlikely that the smudgy use of watercolor has contributed much to the claimed polyvalence of the pictures.

The four plates are presented to the testee simultaneously and in some prearranged serial order. After a lapse of one minute the plates are removed and the testee is requested to *write* a single story, incorporating all four plates. The testee is urged to decide on his own serial order and to write a unified story using all four plates if possible. The authors claim that by requesting a single story, the testee is forced to "historialize" the hero over a longer period of time and so give richer projective material. This constitutes a definite advantage. The test is inherently limited, however, by virtue of the fact that it comprises one item only. Other rival themes might be prevented from showing up under this condition of administration. The solution, of course, is to have more pictures.

The test is untimed, but on the average takes from half an hour to three quarters of an hour to administer. Group administration of the test is also possible, but it is not advisable to have more than about 30 subjects in a group.

It is possible to introduce variations in the instructions of the FPT in order to elicit further projective material. For instance, after the subject has written his ordinary story, he can be asked to write another story in which one of the female figures at the tennis court plays the leading role. It is also possible to fix the serial order of the plates and have the subject relate a story which fits that particular order of the plates. The standardized instruction given in the manual might prove too difficult for subjects of low educational achievement and might well be rewritten in basic English. The authors claim that written protocols are richer in content than ones produced orally, but it is doubtful whether this is true of subjects of borderline intelligence or, for that matter, of psychotics.

In a study of more than 4,000 protocols of both normal and abnormal subjects, the authors have isolated more than 150 different variables which "lend themselves to more or less objective scoring." No attempt, however, is made to introduce the test user to the objective scoring system. There is a promise of a book on the FPT to be published at a later date, but this is no justification for omitting the scoring system from the manual. Some information about the interscorer reliability of the test ought to be given.

The variables isolated can be divided into content variables and formal variables. No information regarding the diagnostic value of these variables is given and, except for a few examples, no interpretive hints are given. The 20 pages on interpretation given in the first edition of the manual have been omitted from the second edition. No illustrative protocols are given and no mention is made of the time or space quality of the stories. In short, the present edition is less satisfactory than the first.

It can be reasonably expected of a test author to give the following information in a test manual: a brief rationale of the test, a standard instruction, a scoring system, an interpretive technique, and normative data. Test-retest reliability, and validity coefficients are

minimal requirements on the statistical side. To be really useful, norms ought to be stratified in terms of age, level of education, and intelligence. Pathological indications ought to be given at a certain level of confidence. Judged in the light of the above criteria, the FPT falls far short of the ideal. The FPT is a one-item test and can at most serve as a rough screening device. By contrast, the *Tomkins-Horn Picture Arrangement Test* meets most of the above mentioned criteria and is favored by the present reviewer.

For reviews by John E. Bell, E. J. G. Bradford, and Ephraim Rosen of the original edition, see 4:105 (1 excerpt).

[214]

★**The Group Personality Projective Test.** Ages 12 and over; 1956–61; formerly called *Kahn Stick Figure Personality Test*; 7 scores: tension reduction quotient, nurturance, withdrawal, neuroticism, affiliation, succorance, total; IBM; 1 form ('58, 17 pages); manual ('61, 20 pages, reprint of 4 below); directions for interpretation ('60, 2 pages); separate answer sheets must be used; $13.50 per examiner's kit of 12 tests, 100 IBM answer-profile sheets, set of scoring stencils, and manual; $2 per manual; cash orders postpaid; specimen set not available; (40–45) minutes; Russell N. Cassel and Theodore C. Kahn; Psychological Test Specialists. *

REFERENCES

1. KAHN, THEODORE C., AND CASSEL, RUSSELL N. "Development and Validation of the Group Personality Projective Test." Abstract. *Am Psychologist* 12:389 Jl '57. *
2. CASSEL, RUSSELL N., AND BRAUCHLE, ROBERT P. "An Assessment of the Fakability of Scores on the Group Personality Projective Test." *J Genetic Psychol* 95:239–44 D '59. *
3. CASSEL, RUSSELL N., AND HARRIMAN, B. LYNN. "A Comparative Analysis of Personality and Ego Strength Test Scores for In-Prison, Neuro-Psychiatric and Typical Individuals." *J Ed Res* 53:43–52 O '59. * (*PA* 35:810)
4. CASSEL, R. N., AND KAHN, T. C. "The Group Personality Projective Test (GPPT)." *Psychol Rep* 8:23–41 F '61. * (*PA* 36:1HB23C)
5. CASSEL, RUSSELL N., AND HADDOX, GENEVIEVE. "Comparing Reading Competency With Personality and Social Insight Test Scores." *Calif J Ed Res* 12:27–30 Ja '61. * (*PA* 36:1KJ27C)
6. LANGE, MERLE LEROY. *A Comparative Analysis of Achieving and Under-Achieving Twelfth Grade Students of Phoenix Central High School on the Non-Intellectual Factors of the Group Personality Projective Test and the Test of Social Insight.* Doctor's research study No. 1, Colorado State College (Greeley, Colo.), 1962. (*DA* 23:3778)
7. CASSEL, RUSSELL, AND CHILDERS, RICHARD. "A Study of Certain Attributes of 45 High-School Varsity Football Team Members by Use of Psychological Test Scores." *J Ed Res* 57:64–7 O '63. *

[215]

*****H-T-P: House-Tree-Person Projective Technique.** Ages 3 and over; 1946–64; 1 form ['46, 4 pages]; manual ('48, see 6); supplement ('64, 119 pages, including copies of drawing form, interrogation folders, and scoring folder); interrogation folder: adult form ('50), children's form ('56), (4 pages); scoring folder ('50, 4 pages); two-copy drawing form ('64); adult norms only; $4 per 25 drawing forms; $6.50 per 25 interrogation folders; $6.50 per 25 scoring folders; $6.50 per 25 two-copy drawing forms; $4 per manual; $5 per supplement; postage extra; specimen set not available; (60–90) minutes; John N. Buck and

Isaac Jolles (children's interrogation folder) ; Western Psychological Services. *

REFERENCES

1–5. See 3:47.
6–19. See 4:107.
20–80. See 5:139.
81. KLINE, MILTON V., AND GUZE, HENRY. "The Use of a Drawing Technique in the Investigation of Hypnotic Age Regression and Progression." *Brit J Med Hypnosis* 3:10–21 w '51. *
82. SCHNECK, JEROME, AND KLINE, MILTON V. "A Control Study Relating to H-T-P Testing and Hypnosis." *Brit J Med Hypnosis* 3:3–11 au '51. *
83. SCHNECK, JEROME, AND KLINE, MILTON V. "The H-T-P and TAT Hypnodiagnostic Studies." *Brit J Med Hypnosis* 5:3–15 au '53. *
84. BERRYMAN, EILEEN. "The Self-Portrait: A Suggested Extension of the HTP." *Percept & Motor Skills* 9:411–4 D '59. * (*PA* 34:5599)
85. BIELIAUSKAS, VYTAUTAS J., AND BRISTOW, ROBIN B. "The Effect of Formal Art Training Upon the Quantitative Scores of the H-T-P." *J Clin Psychol* 15:57–9 Ja '59. * (*PA* 34:2985)
86. HOYT, THOMAS E., AND BARON, MARTIN R. "Anxiety Indices in Same-Sex Drawings of Psychiatric Patients With High and Low MAS Scores." *J Consult Psychol* 23:448–52 O '59. * (*PA* 34:5622)
87. ORGEL, RITA G. "The Relationship of the H-T-P to a Sociometric Evaluation of a Group of Primary Grade School Children in Determining the Degree of Social Acceptance." *J Clin Psychol* 15:222–3 Ap '59. * (*PA* 35:4691)
88. SILVERMAN, LLOYD H. "A Q-Sort Study of the Validity of Evaluations Made From Projective Techniques." *Psychol Monogr* 73(7):1–28 '59. * (*PA* 34:3030)
89. STRUMPFER, DEODANDUS JOHANN WILLHELM. *A Study of Some Communicable Measures for the Evaluation of Human Figure Drawings.* Doctor's thesis, Purdue University (Lafayette, Ind.), 1959. (*DA* 20:2910)
90. BIELIAUSKAS, VYTAUTAS J. "Sexual Identification in Children's Drawings of Human Figure." *J Clin Psychol* 16:42–4 Ja '60. * (*PA* 36:1HE42B)
91. BIELIAUSKAS, VYTAUTAS J., AND HEFFRON, ANN R. "Differences in Performance on the Chromatic vs. Achromatic H-T-P Drawings." *J Clin Psychol* 16:334–5 Jl '60. * (*PA* 36:2HC34B)
92. HAMMER, EMANUEL F. "An Exploratory Investigation of the Personalities of Creative Adolescent Students." Discussion by Margaret Naumberg. *Studies Art Ed* 1:42–72 sp '60. *
93. HAMMER, EMANUEL F. "The House-Tree-Person (H-T-P) Drawings as a Projective Technique With Children," pp. 258–72. In *Projective Techniques With Children.* Edited by Albert I. Rabin and Mary R. Haworth. New York: Grune & Stratton, Inc., 1960. Pp. xiii, 392. * (*PA* 35:2229)
94. JUDSON, ABE J., AND MACCASLAND, BARBARA W. "A Note on the Influence of the Season on Tree Drawings." *J Clin Psychol* 16:171–3 Ap '60. * (*PA* 36:2HE71J)
95. LAIR, CHARLES V., AND TRAPP, E. PHILIP. "Performance Decrement on the H-T-P Test as a Function of Adjustment Level." *J Clin Psychol* 16:431 O '60. * (*PA* 37:3260)
96. P'SIMER, CHRISTINE. "The House-Tree-Person Test: A Case Study." *Personnel & Guid J* 38:574–6 Mr '60. *
97. SANTORUM, ALDO. "A Cross-Validation of the House-Tree-Person Drawing Indices Predicting Hospital Discharge of Tuberculosis Patients." *J Consult Psychol* 24:400–2 O '60. * (*PA* 35:4966)
98. BIELIAUSKAS, VYTAUTAS J., AND MOENS, JOSÉE F. "An Investigation of the Validity of the H-T-P as an Intelligence Test for Children." *J Clin Psychol* 17:178–80 Ap '61. * (*PA* 38:951)
99. DIGIAMMO, JOHN J., AND EBINGER, RONALD D. "The New-Weighted H-T-P Score as a Measure of Abstraction." *J Clin Psychol* 17:55 Ja '61. * (*PA* 37:3125)
100. JOHNSON, ORVAL G., AND WAWRZASZEK, FRANK. "Psychologists' Judgments of Physical Handicap From H-T-P Drawings." *J Consult Psychol* 25:284–7 Ag '61. * (*PA* 37:1598)
101. MEYER, BERNARD C.; BLACHER, RICHARD S.; AND BROWN, FRED. "A Clinical Study of Psychiatric and Psychological Aspects of Mitral Surgery." *Psychosom Med* 23:194–218 My–Je '61. *
102. SAUNDERS, MAUDERIE HANCOCK. *An Analysis of Cultural Differences on Certain Projective Techniques.* Doctor's thesis, University of Oklahoma (Norman, Okla.), 1961. (*DA* 22:490)
103. CASSEL, ROBERT H.; JOHNSON, ANNA P.; AND BURNS, WILLIAM H. "The Order of Tests in the Battery." *J Clin Psychol* 18:464–5 O '62. * (*PA* 39:5042)
104. MOLL, RICHARD P. "Further Evidence of Seasonal Influences on Tree Drawings." *J Clin Psychol* 18:109 Ja '62. * (*PA* 38:8393)
105. WEBSTER, RAYMOND B. "The Effects of Hypnosis on Performance on the H-T-P and MPS." *Int J Clin & Exp Hypnosis* 10:151–3 Jl '62. * (*PA* 37:5245)
106. BARNOUW, VICTOR. Chap. 17, "Drawing Analysis,"
pp. 276–98. In his *Culture and Personality.* Homewood, Ill.: Dorsey Press, Inc., 1963. Pp. xi, 410. *
107. BIELIAUSKAS, VYTAUTAS J. *The House-Tree-Person (H-T-P) Research Review.* Beverly Hills, Calif.: Western Psychological Services, 1963. Pp. 50. *
108. CALLAN, SHEILA, AND DERRICK, NOEL. "An Investigation of the Effect of Seasonal Changes in the Environment on the Tree Drawings of Hospitalized and Non-Hospitalized Groups." *Ont Hosp Psychol B* 8:1–6 Ag '63. *
109. COPPINGER, NEIL W.; BORTNER, RAYMAN W.; AND SAUCER, RAYFORD T. "A Factor Analysis of Psychological Deficit." *J Genetic Psychol* 103:23–43 S '63. * (*PA* 39:174)
110. McHUGH, ANN F. "H-T-P Proportion and Perspective in Negro, Puerto Rican, and White Children." *J Clin Psychol* 19:312–3 Jl '63. *
111. STRUMPFER, D. J. W. "The Relation of Draw-A-Person Test Variables to Age and Chronicity in Psychotic Groups." *J Clin Psychol* 19:208–11 Ap '63. * (*DA* 39:5102)
112. WILDMAN, ROBERT W. "The Relationship Between Knee and Arm Joints on Human Figure Drawings and Paranoid Trends." *J Clin Psychol* 19:460–1 O '63. *

MARY R. HAWORTH, *Associate Professor of Medical Psychology, University of Nebraska College of Medicine, Omaha, Nebraska.*

In essence, this projective technique involves asking the subject to draw first a house, then a tree, and finally a person. The drawings are subsequently evaluated and analyzed for dynamic information relative to personality variables and interactions of the subject with his environment. When this procedure was first formalized in 1948 its purpose was two-fold: a measure of intelligence and a projective tool. Through the years the use of this test for estimating intellectual level has probably diminished to the vanishing point. The nine pages of minute scoring criteria (descriptive and diagrammatic) are so detailed, qualified, and ambiguous that the reliability of scoring is questionable, and no data are offered on this aspect. The time spent in such scoring would be better spent in administering a standard intelligence test.

The H-T-P technique undoubtedly finds its greatest use as a projective instrument with the qualitative interpretations derived therefrom being largely dependent on the clinical acumen, experience, and orientation of the examiner. Buck's original manual (6) and publications by Hammer (58) and Jolles (25) offer numerous interpretive hypotheses for the various drawn details and such overall aspects as proportion, perspective, page placement, and line quality. While very little experimental data can be marshaled in support of such interpretations, nevertheless these publications do serve to make explicit many inferences frequently made by clinicians in interpreting the meaning of drawings. The authors do caution against placing undue significance on individual, isolated items or details without consideration of the total constellation of all three drawings.

According to those who have done the most work with this technique, not only should achromatic drawings be obtained but also a second chromatic set. A structured inquiry should also be conducted. Again, it is questionable whether these procedures have found general clinical adoption. The standard inquiry questions (both the adult and child forms) are highly redundant and repetitive, and many of them do not appear to yield really useful clinical data. Others seem to be "loaded" in a definite direction by their very wording, e.g., "Is the tree alive?" which is soon followed by "Is any part of the tree dead?"; or "Is there a wind blowing?" In giving this test to children, this reviewer has found that most of their responses to the inquiry questions have been rather colorless and lacking in meaningful material, although occasionally a child will use one or several questions as a springboard into a world of dynamic fantasy.

The most recent research studies designed to test various hypotheses connected with the H-T-P's rationale have generally reported nonsignificant findings. This may not so much reflect on any defects in this particular technique but, rather, the usual methodological difficulties encountered when trying to evaluate the reliability and validity of projective instruments. In spite of such unrewarding findings, "clinical" clinicians will continue to use those projective devices which they have found to be most helpful in making personality appraisals.

Variations in the H-T-P are often employed and the test can be blended with the *Machover Draw-A-Person Test* by the additional request to draw a person of the opposite sex after the first human figure. Also there is no reason why one could not, after the usual Machover drawing test, ask for drawings of a house and a tree, if it becomes evident that rich and meaningful material is being elicited in the drawing medium. Certainly drawing techniques generally have been found to serve as a good introduction to testing sessions, reducing anxiety (usually) and facilitating a transition to more verbal tasks. They are also extremely useful for non-verbal subjects, those with speech defects, and the deaf (so long as the instructions can be communicated to the patient). Obviously in such special cases the inquiry must be dispensed with.

Most clinicians would agree that drawings should not be the only projective tool in the test battery, which view is concurred in by those most closely identified with the H-T-P.

In summary, the H-T-P is now, and no doubt will continue to be, used as a rewarding clinical technique in work with both adults and children. The amount of meaningful projective data to be derived from the drawings (and the inquiry, if used) will depend on the experience and orientation of the clinician. The test can serve as a non-threatening "opener" before more formal testing and has usefulness with speech handicapped patients. Too literal interpretation of specific details is to be avoided. Rather, as Buck himself states in the manual, the H-T-P "is intended to be used as a procedure to facilitate the clinician's acquisition of diagnostically significant data."

For a review by Philip L. Harriman, see 5:139; for reviews by Albert Ellis and Ephraim Rosen, see 4:107 (1 excerpt); for reviews by Morris Krugman and Katherine W. Wilcox, see 3:47; for excerpts from related book reviews, see 5:B234.

[216]

★The Hand Test. Ages 6 and over; 1959-62; 10 normed scores: interpersonal, environmental, maladjustive, withdrawal, affection-dependence-communication, direction-aggression, total responses, average initial response time, highest minus lowest response time, pathological; 1 form ('59, 10 cards); scoring sheet ['62, 2 pages]; manual ('62, 65 pages); reliability data for pathological score only; $3 per set of cards; $1 per pad of scoring sheets; $3.50 per manual; postage extra; (10) minutes; Edwin E. Wagner; Mark James Co., Publishers. *

REFERENCES

1. WAGNER, EDWIN E. "The Use of Drawings of Hands as a Projective Medium for Differentiating Normals and Schizophrenics." *J Clin Psychol* 17:279-80 Jl '61. * (PA 38:8572)
2. BRICKLIN, BARRY; PIOTROWSKI, ZYGMUNT A.; AND WAGNER, EDWIN E. *The Hand Test: A New Projective Test With Special Reference to the Prediction of Overt Behavior.* Springfield, Ill.: Charles C Thomas, Publisher, 1962. Pp. x, 100. * (PA 37:1191)
3. WAGNER, EDWIN E. "The Use of Drawings of Hands as a Projective Medium for Differentiating Neurotics and Schizophrenics." *J Clin Psychol* 18:208-9 Ap '62. *
4. WAGNER, EDWIN E. "Hand Test Content Indicators of Overt Psychosexual Maladjustment in Neurotic Males." *J Proj Tech & Pers Assess* 27:357-8 S '63. * (PA 38:4333)
5. WAGNER, EDWIN E., AND COPPER, JOHN. "Differentiation of Satisfactory and Unsatisfactory Employees at Goodwill Industries With the Hand Test." *J Proj Tech & Pers Assess* 27:354-6 S '63. * (PA 38:4334)
6. WAGNER, EDWIN E., AND MEDVEDEFF, EUGENE. "Differentiation of Aggressive Behavior of Institutionalized Schizophrenics With the Hand Test." *J Proj Tech* 27:111-3 Mr '63. * (PA 38:1336)

GOLDINE C. GLESER, *Professor of Psychology, University of Cincinnati Medical School, Cincinnati, Ohio.*

The *Hand Test* is a projective technique in which the subject is shown a series of drawings of a hand in various ambiguous poses and asked what the hand might be doing. The last card is blank, requiring the subject to imagine a hand and describe what it is doing. The test is considered to reveal "significant perceptual-motor tendencies" presently available to the person and readily expressed in his interaction with others and with the environment.

The test has many features similar to the Rorschach in that time to initial response, card turning, and verbatim responses are recorded and the subject is allowed, and to some extent encouraged, to give more than one response to a card. However, it differs from the Rorschach in that each response is categorized into one of 15 categories according to content; the frequency of occurrence of varying combinations of these categories provides the summary quantitative scores. Additional qualitative aspects of the response may also be scored and used in clinical interpretation.

Differences in the categorization of responses and in the treatment of scores may be noted between the monograph (2) and the manual. These are to be expected since the test is still in the process of development. However, the description of categories and the scoring examples given in the manual are sufficiently clear and detailed to enable other investigators to use them with reasonable expectation of comparable results. Only one study of scorer agreement is reported in which three persons scored 100 protocols. Perfect agreement between two scorers was obtained on between 78 and 83 per cent of all responses. Correlations between scorers are reported for the pathological score only and range from .86 to .96.

The normative data on 1,020 cases are presented in a form which has little merit for interpretative purposes. Medians and interquartile ranges are given on the major scoring categories for 17 so-called populations, including normal adults, college students, children, neurotics, psychotics, mental retardates, and antisocial personalities. The groups differ in age, education, socio-economic background, and race-sex composition. No attempt has been made to determine the variance associated with these factors, other than to note that children and teenagers tend to produce higher "acting-out ratios" than do adults. A much broader stratified sample of normal children and adults is needed to assess these factors and to provide a basis for determining the normal range of response. At present, the only clue as to what constitutes an abnormal number of responses in any particular category is an occasional remark in the text of the manual or the monograph.

No studies of the stability of response patterns have been reported, although interpretations imply that responses are characteristic of the person's action tendencies over some interval of time in the absence of radical changes in the subject's environment. Only the pathological score has been examined from the standpoint of generalizability over stimuli (split-half reliability).

Validity studies to date consist of comparison of samples from populations hypothesized to differ with respect to aggressive acting-out or psychopathology. The pathological score differentiated custodial and ambulatory schizophrenics from all other groups, but the median score of first admission schizophrenics was approximately the same as that for neurotics, depressives, mental retardates, and prison inmates. The acting-out score differentiated prison inmates and "acting-out" hospitalized psychiatric patients from normal adults, indigents, and non-acting-out psychiatric patients. No systematic validation of individual differences within a population has been reported, nor have the scores been compared with scores on other tests purporting to measure similar constructs.

The *Hand Test* appears to have possibilities for development as a quantitative multidimensional clinical test relevant to the overt behavior of individuals. However, its psychometric characteristics are essentially unknown so that a great deal more developmental work is needed in order to shape the technique into a measuring instrument rather than a springboard for metaphorical interpretations. Several aspects of the format and administration should be examined for possible improvement. First of all, one wonders to what extent certain maladjustive responses are due to the inadequacies of the original sketches, many of which are so poorly inked as to appear distorted or grotesque. Secondly, additional stimuli should be used in order to obtain a reliable sample of an individual's response tendencies with respect to the 15 categories. Permitting more than one response to a card is not an adequate solution to this problem since additional responses tend to depend more on extraneous factors than on the "total stock of psychic tendencies" of the subject. Furthermore, any advantages which may accrue from allowing number of responses to vary are far outweighed by the disadvantages of handling and interpreting scores, as has been amply demonstrated with the Rorschach. The test at present is of use primarily to those who are interested in further research and development of this technique.

J Proj Tech 26:490–1 D '62. *Irving R. Stone.* * Wagner's test consists of a series of ten cards on nine of which a hand has been drawn. The last card is blank, very much like that of card 16 on the TAT. The cards are presented one at a time and the subject is asked to tell what the hands are doing. For the last card, the subject is asked to imagine a hand and tell what it is doing. Responses are recorded verbatim along with initial response times per card. The responses are then scored and interpreted in accordance with a somewhat formal and a bit involved procedure. The test, to some extent, represents a cross between the Rorschach in its scoring, timing, observation of card turning, and interpretation and the TAT in the form of its responses and the possibility of analysis and interpretation without some of the need for formal scoring. Too, the scoring resembles some factors of those of Murray and Tomkins in that we find scoring compartmentalization into affection, dependence, communication, exhibition, direction, aggression, acquisition, active, passive, tension, crippled, fear, description, bizarre, and failure. The author states that the test can be administered in about ten minutes, scored in about five, that it is completely nonthreatening and can be easily administered to depressed, deteriorated and hostile subjects. Norms, based upon more than 1,000 protocols, from six years of age and up are included. Reliability was based on the independent scoring of three graduate student scorers of 100 protocols and ranged from .86 to .96. The author recognizes that in the development of the protocols for the total 1,020 cases the subjects mostly resided in Ohio at the time of testing, that the N's are low in some categories, and that the seventeen groups of scoring categories are only the major but not the

total of those possible. The drawings are fairly clear but some may lend themselves to misinterpretation (possibly pictures of hands would have been clearer), the manual is clear and complete, and the one sheet scoring blank which has on one side space for recording the initial response time, the responses, and the scoring for each card, and on the reverse side the summary sheet containing the name, address, and other identifying information as well as the ratios, qualitative and administrative observations, case history and diagnostic data, and diagnosis appears to be well-developed. Even though administrative and scoring time would have been extended, it might have been useful to have included some additional cards in which two hands were in some form of relationship. It is hoped that the author will experiment with this to determine whether further development of affectional relationships could be elicited. *

For an excerpt from a related book review, see B95.

[217]

*The Holtzman Inkblot Technique. Ages 5 and over; 1958–61; individual; 22 scores: reaction time, rejections, location, space, form definiteness, form appropriateness, color, shading, movement, pathognomic verbalization, integration, content (human, animal, anatomy, sex, abstract), anxiety, hostility, barrier, penetration, balance, populars; Forms A, B, ('58, 47 cards); manual ('61, 423 pages, see 7 below); administration and scoring guide ('61, c1958–61, 171 pages, reprinted in part from manual); record form ('58, 8 pages) for each form; summary sheet ('58, 2 pages); $26 per set of cards for either form, 25 record forms, and administration and scoring guide; $46 per set of cards and accessories for both forms; $2.75 per 25 record forms and scoring sheets; $3 per administration and scoring guide; $8 per manual; postpaid; (75) minutes; Wayne H. Holtzman, Joseph S. Thorpe (manual), Jon D. Swartz (manual), and E. Wayne Herron (manual); Psychological Corporation. *

REFERENCES

1. HOLTZMAN, WAYNE H. "Development of an Experimental Inkblot Test, a New Departure From the Rorschach." Abstract. *Am Psychologist* 11:400 Ag '56. *
2. SANDERS, ELLA MOYE. *The Relationship Between Verbal-Quantitative Ability and Certain Personality and Metabolic Characteristics.* Doctor's thesis, University of Texas (Austin, Tex.), 1958. (*DA* 19:2540)
3. YOUNG, HARL H. "Relationships Between and Reliability Estimates of New (Holtzman) Ink Blot Variables and Conventional Rorschach Scoring Categories." *Proc Okla Acad Sci* 38: 111–5 D '58. *
4. SANDERS, ELLA M.; MEFFERD, ROY B., JR.; AND BOWN, OLIVER H. "Verbal-Quantitative Ability and Certain Personality and Metabolic Characteristics of Male College Students." *Ed & Psychol Meas* 20:491–503 au '60. * (*PA* 35:3550)
5. SIMKINS, LAWRENCE. "Examiner Reinforcement and Situational Variables in a Projective Testing Situation." *J Consult Psychol* 24:541–7 D '60. * (*PA* 36:1HG41S)
6. BARGER, PATRICIA M., AND SECHREST, LEE. "Convergent and Discriminant Validity of Four Holtzman Inkblot Test Variables." *J Psychol Studies* 12:227–36 N '61 [issued Ap '63]. *
7. HOLTZMAN, WAYNE H.; THORPE, JOSEPH S.; SWARTZ, JON D.; AND HERRON, E. WAYNE. *Inkblot Perception and*

Personality: Holtzman Inkblot Technique. Published for the Hogg Foundation for Mental Health. Austin, Tex.: University of Texas Press, 1961. Pp. xi, 417. * *(PA* 36:5HB17H)

8. STEFFY, RICHARD A., AND BECKER, WESLEY C. "Measurement of the Severity of Disorder in Schizophrenia by Means of the Holtzman Inkblot Test." Abstract. *J Consult Psychol* 25:555 D '61. * *(PA* 37:5505)

9. BIENEN, SANFORD MORTON. *Verbal Conditioning of Inkblot Responses as a Function of Instructions, Social Desirability, and Awareness.* Doctor's thesis, University of Maryland (College Park, Md.), 1962. *(DA* 24:379)

10. BURKE, MARY. *The Control of Response Choice on Projective Techniques.* Doctor's thesis, University of Denver (Denver, Colo.), 1962. *(DA* 24:2119)

11. HERRON, ELMER WAYNE. *Intellectual Achievement-Motivation: A Study in Construct Clarification.* Doctor's thesis, University of Texas (Austin, Tex.), 1962. *(DA* 23:298)

12. MOSELEY, EDWARD CARLETON. *Psychodiagnosis Based on Multivariate Analysis of the Holtzman Inkblot Technique.* Doctor's thesis, University of Texas (Austin, Tex.), 1962. *(DA* 23:313)

13. HERRON, E. WAYNE. "Psychometric Characteristics of a Thirty-Item Version of the Group Method of the Holtzman Inkblot Technique." *J Clin Psychol* 19:450–3 O '63. *

14. HOLTZMAN, WAYNE H. "Inkblot Perception and Personality: The Meaning of Inkblot Variables." *B Menninger Clinic* 27:84–95 Mr '63. *

15. HOLTZMAN, WAYNE H.; MOSELEY, EDWARD C.; REINEHR, ROBERT C.; AND ABBOTT, ELAINE. "Comparison of the Group Method and the Standard Individual Version of the Holtzman Inkblot Technique." *J Clin Psychol* 19:441–9 O '63. *

16. MOSELEY, E. C.; GORHAM, D. R.; AND HILL, EVELYN. "Computer Scoring of Inkblot Perceptions." Abstract. *Percept & Motor Skills* 17:498 O '63. * *(PA* 38:6097)

17. MOSELEY, EDWARD C. "Psychodiagnosis on the Basis of the Holtzman Inkblot Technique." *J Proj Tech* 27:86–91 Mr '63. * *(PA* 38:1020)

18. MOSELEY, EDWARD C.; DUFFEY, ROBERT F.; AND SHERMAN, LEWIS J. "An Extension of the Construct Validity of the Holtzman Inkblot Technique." *J Clin Psychol* 19:186–92 Ap '63. * *(PA* 39:5083)

19. OTTEN, MARK W., AND VAN DE CASTLE, R. L. "A Comparison of Set 'A' of the Holtzman Inkblots With the Rorschach by Means of the Semantic Differential." *J Proj Tech & Pers Assess* 27:452–60 D '63. * *(PA* 38:8562)

20. PALMER, JAMES O. "Alterations in Rorschach's Experience Balance Under Conditions of Food and Sleep Deprivation: A Construct Validation Study." *J Proj Tech & Pers Assess* 27:208–13 Je '63. * *(PA* 38:2723)

21. SWARTZ, JON D., AND HOLTZMAN, WAYNE H. "Group Method of Administration for the Holtzman Inkblot Technique." *J Clin Psychol* 19:433–41 O '63. *

22. THORPE, JOSEPH S., AND SWARTZ, JON D. "The Roles of Intelligence and Social Status in Rejections on the Holtzman Inkblot Technique." *J Proj Tech & Pers Assess* 27:248–51 Je '63. * *(PA* 38:2728)

RICHARD W. COAN, *Professor of Psychology, University of Arizona, Tucson, Arizona.*

Since the *Holtzman Inkblot Technique* is an application of the Rorschach method to a new set of materials, the judgment of any prospective test user must rest first on his evaluation of this method. Projective tests are often constructed in the hope that a broad range of information can be secured through painstaking analysis of a circumscribed kind of behavior. If our ultimate aim is a procedure for comprehensive personality assessment, it is doubtful that this is the best possible strategy. If we are going to invest much time in examining conceptual responses to inkblots, we must assume that Rorschach's choice of a behavioral bit was an unusually fortunate one.

With respect to the mass of theory which has accrued from its use, the Rorschach technique is unique. The applicability of this theory to a different set of inkblots is open to ques-

tion. Current Rorschach theory is a complex mixture of logical extrapolations from a body of perceptual and personality theories and *ad hoc* explanations of concomitances noted with varying regularity by Rorschach workers. To the extent that Rorschach theory rests on generally valid principles of perceptual dynamics, it should be applicable to responses elicited by a wide variety of stimulus materials. To the extent that it capitalizes on accidental and unrecognized peculiarities of the Rorschach blots, it will not apply to responses obtained with any other stimuli. And one might add, to the extent that it capitalizes on accidents of observation and case sampling, it may not apply even to the Rorschach blots.

Despite the great number of studies that have been done, research evidence for the validity of Rorschach interpretations is notoriously meager. On the other hand, much of the intended evidence is of doubtful relevance to standard interpretive theory. In deciding whether it is worthwhile to pursue the Rorschach technique further, we must decide whether to give greater heed to the research evidence or to the widespread conviction of clinicians that the technique taps subtle aspects of the personality not subject to a more direct kind of measurement.

If we decide in favor of the technique, we still cannot deny the fact that Rorschach's own work combined theoretical brilliance with methodological naïveté. The test which has evolved from his labors displays an alarming variety of psychometric deficiencies. From the responses to ten blots, one derives a complex set of unreliable and highly interdependent scores, displaying predominantly skewed distributions. All the basic scoring categories display a systematic dependence on overall productivity, even when they are expressed in percentage form.

By far the most satisfactory way of eliminating, or at least minimizing, the psychometric shortcomings, while preserving the basic virtues of the method, is to employ a larger number of blots and secure only one response per blot. This is the solution that Holtzman and his colleagues have adopted. They have produced a richly varied series of blots that yields a wide range of scores with respect to many important aspects of inkblot performance.

The one major Rorschach score category

that is lost in the Holtzman test is productivity. The test provides more satisfactory scaling for all other basic categories. Some of the specific variables of conventional scoring systems have been eliminated from the Holtzman scoring system. There are no "interaction" categories combining determinants with content or form definiteness. Furthermore, no distinction is made between color and achromatic color, among different types of shading responses, or between usual and unusual details. These losses are not irretrievable since any user of the test can add his own score categories and collect fresh standardization data. And as the manual suggests, the interaction categories can be recaptured to an extent by configural scoring of the Holtzman summary sheet.

Some of the departures from convention can be justified in terms of a need for separate quantification of logically independent variables. Some, such as the independent scaling of form definiteness, can be supported in terms of previous statistical findings for the Rorschach. It should also be noted that certain rare features of inkblot response, which do not lend themselves conveniently to quantitative treatment, can best be handled through a detailed analysis of the protocol without formal scoring. Thus, a clinician may secure useful information by noting a particular subject's use of achromatic color. The mere number of achromatic color responses is a relatively trivial datum.

To the conventional scoring categories that are retained, some additional variables of demonstrated value have been added. Some interdependence of scores has been introduced deliberately, but this does not constitute the serious problem seen in Rorschach scoring systems. There are a few minor disturbing peculiarities: card rejection contributes to the location score in the same way as the whole response, with the result that the location score expresses perceptual differentiation to a greater extent than it otherwise would.

On the whole, it is probably reasonable to conclude that the Holtzman scores constitute an improvement over the Rorschach scores. There is satisfactory evidence of interscorer reliability for most of the Holtzman scores, and the evidence on group score differences and developmental trends looks promising. It would be difficult to demonstrate a similar value with respect to information not for-

mally scored. The clinician accustomed to subjective analysis may feel that something vital has been lost if he cannot observe a sequence of responses to a single stimulus.

It is debatable whether the Rorschach approach to personality evaluation has proven its worth. With respect to most demonstrated differences, the *Holtzman Inkblot Technique* appears to be superior to other tests employing this approach. With respect to undemonstrated differences, it may or may not be as good. It deserves extensive research and exploratory application as a prospective replacement for the Rorschach test.

H. J. EYSENCK, *Institute of Psychiatry, The Maudsley Hospital, London, England.*

The *Holtzman Inkblot Technique* presents an interesting paradox. The authors have set out to use the fundamental conceptions underlying the Rorschach test in the production of a technique which would be capable of standing up to the usual psychometric tests applicable in this field. In this they brilliantly succeeded. There are two sets of 45 newly designed inkblots, carefully prepared and excellently printed, to each of which only one response is required; responses are then scored according to well defined instructions in categories very closely resembling the orthodox ones. Intra- and interscorer consistency are both high and must be accepted as representing probably the best that can be obtained from projective techniques. Split-half reliabilities for the different scoring categories differ widely, of course, being very high for such categories as rejection, location, and form definiteness, and rather low for space, hostility, and balance. However, on the whole, these reliabilities are most encouraging, ranging as they tend to do between .8 and .9 for the majority of categories and groups. Test-retest reliabilities are very much lower even when periods of only a week are in question; after one year they tend to range around .5.

Much information is given on the intercorrelations between categories and it is disturbing to note that "the magnitude of correlation between any two inkblot variables is likely to vary from one sample to the next, even reversing the sign in some instances." However, numerous factor analyses tend to agree in producing three main factors which had also been found previously in similar analyses of orthodox Rorschach scores, to wit, neuroticism, extraversion-introversion, and psychoticism. Several further factors proved difficult to identify. Proponents of the orthodox Rorschach who might look with disfavour upon these changes in the nature and format of their test will be reassured to note that there is considerable agreement between the old and the new; comparisons between the two methods "indicate quite conclusively that the Rorschach and Holtzman systems have a great deal in common as far as the underlying meaning of their respective variables are concerned."

So far so good. Clearly Holtzman and his team have done a first rate job in translating the Rorschach into acceptable psychometric terms without losing the essence of this rather intangible test. Why must their production be considered paradoxical? The answer lies in the disproportionate amount of space devoted to the details of what are essentially reliability studies and the very small amount of space given over to the much more important question of validity. Out of a book of 417 pages, less than 10 deal with validity, and what the results disclose is the usual complete failure of the Rorschach to link up with any form of outside criterion other than gross psychiatric deviation. Here is Holtzman's summing up:

> Clearly, there is little relationship between personality traits measured by the usual paper-and-pencil approaches and inkblot scores. Nor is it likely that peer-ratings of socially observable traits such as manifest anxiety, hostility, shyness, or dominance will have much in common with inkblot scores except in unusual circumstances.

This, one would imagine, would make it unlikely for anyone to wish to master a complicated and time consuming technique, the results of which could not be expected to correlate with observable personality traits. Holtzman defends himself by saying:

> While such results are useful in pointing out certain kinds of inferences about the more superficial aspects of personality that it is unwise to make from inkblot scores, they are largely irrelevant to the broader issues of validity—developmental, cognitive and perceptual aspects of personality—as well as the psychodiagnostic evaluation of individuals with mental or emotional disturbances.

Holtzman does not indicate why these issues are "broader" or why personality traits are dismissed so glibly as being "superficial," nor does he give any evidence to show that, psy-

chodiagnostically, his test would be anything like as good as a simple 10-minute questionnaire. If only the validity studies had come up to the same level of excellence or success as the reliability studies, how welcome would this test have been! As it is it demonstrates pretty conclusively that the underlying notion of the Rorschach test is at fault. No one is likely to do a better job than Holtzman in making the test psychometrically acceptable; if even he did not succeed in making it valid it seems unlikely that anyone ever will.

BERTRAM R. FORER, *Consulting Psychologist, and Executive Editor, Journal of Projective Techniques and Personality Assessment, Suite 307, 8833 Sunset Boulevard, Los Angeles, California.*

Psychometric techniques and clinical sophistication have come a long way since Hermann Rorschach carved new dimensions of perception and personality out of responses to his ten inkblots. Psychometric experts and specialists in projective psychology have been at odds as to whether Rorschach's method was of any value either in diagnosis or in research. There have been extremists on both sides of the argument. Research evidence over the years has pointed to positive value in the method and serious limitations as well. A change was called for. What has been needed is an instrument which elicits basic information about persons that they themselves are unaware of and unable to communicate directly and which at the same time provides objective, mathematically manipulable and psychologically meaningful scales for both clinical and research purposes.

Holtzman and his associates have created a happy liaison between the richness of clinical information available from the Rorschach and modern statistical techniques for describing, defining, and utilizing the information. Starting with two new sets of 45 inkblots designed to maximize differences in perception between mature and disturbed persons, they have developed a group of 22 scales that encompass most of the information commonly obtained from the Rorschach. And they include new dimensions that have grown out of recent Rorschach and personality research, e.g., penetration, barrier, anxiety, hostility, and pathognomic verbalization scores.

To be sure, something may be lost by including different color responses or shading responses in single scores which may conceal differences in the relative role of color and form or shading and form. But the loss is more imagined than real, for three reasons. First, those who wish to utilize conventional Rorschach scores can still do so. Second, the scores that have been developed have demonstrated meaningfulness in terms of both basic Rorschach concepts and detailed validational and intratest correlational research. And third, the item responses and total scales yield repeat and split-half and alternate form reliabilities and interrater agreements greater than those obtained by the Rorschach.

The scores generated by this new method are reproducible and comparable. Systematic control in the design of the blots has insured adequate individual differences in response. Restricting responses to one per card insures comparability of protocols by removing the contaminant of productivity which has been the bugaboo of so much Rorschach research. For every subject this test contains 45 items. The data are in a numerical form that is easily handled statistically and that permits more rigorous tests of validity than the Rorschach does. Hence the research possibilities are enormously enhanced. Scoring samples are abundant and clear and the test manual and record blanks are well set up and complete.

Use of the scales does not preclude conventional (or idiosyncratic) clinical inference. But there is a danger in carrying over Rorschach lore and norms. These are different blots with stimulus properties that differ from those of the Rorschach. Many who wish to use the method will be inclined to take the easy way of avoiding the new scales and scoring criteria and to disregard the book, *Inkblot Perception and Personality,* which describes in great detail the theory, methods, philosophy, and research findings. It is a fat book and full. To avoid it would be a mistake and a loss. The many tables, norms, and intercorrelations are fascinating in themselves and provide a wealth of background material about psychological development and psychopathology.

One limitation of the Rorschach that is most apparent during the formulation of a diagnostic decision is the absence of a dependable supply of normative or reference group data and the consequent reliance of clinicians upon vaguely remembered group data or subjective appraisal of responses. The Holtzman technique provides distributions of all scores for eight adult, child, and diagnostic groups. The latter are too few at present. Eventually a variety of diagnostic groups will be needed and, no doubt, will be forthcoming. The data and some methods are given for demonstrating the degree of similarity of any score or test profile to each reference group, and techniques are suggested for making statistical decisions about diagnosis.

This technique does not and should not replace the contributions of those who deal with the Rorschach as a clinical projective tool; they complement each other. The present set of blots may or may not provide the same amount of clinical content as the Rorschach. That remains to be seen. In any case the clinical lore developed particularly in connection with the Rorschach still has its place in the diagnostic report. The Holtzman method in addition to its superior research possibilities, adds to the clinical Rorschach approach a new kind of profile which can be used clinically. A case study in the book demonstrates the process of making clinical inferences from a systematic study of the 22 scores in connection with normative data.

This reviewer's overall appraisal is that the Holtzman technique is a significant contribution to the field of personality assessment which provides the first real integration of current standards of test construction, past research findings, and clinical projective techniques. Those who like the Rorschach owe it to themselves to try the Holtzman technique, test it, and improve it.

WILLIAM N. THETFORD, *Associate Professor of Medical Psychology, College of Physicians and Surgeons of Columbia University, New York, New York.*

The aim of the Holtzman technique is to develop a new inkblot approach with demonstrated psychometric value, without sacrificing the rich qualitative data yielded by the Rorschach test. The approach represents a serious attempt to overcome many of the Rorschach weaknesses noted by Zubin and others. Holtzman and his co-workers maintain that the numerous psychometric problems encountered in Rorschach evaluation result from the fundamental confusion arising from the "failure to distinguish between the Rorschach as a projective technique in the hands of skilled clinicians, and the Rorschach as a psychometric device." Holtzman believes that by using more than ten inkblots, limiting the number of responses, and avoiding the highly variable inquiry procedure of the Rorschach, most of its psychometric weaknesses can be overcome.

The Holtzman test has two alternate forms, each containing 45 inkblots and two practice cards. The subject is permitted only one response to each inkblot. To compensate for the usual tendency to give whole responses initially, an attempt has been made to choose cards with high "pulling power" by emphasizing details, space, color, and shading. A brief, nonsuggestive, and relatively simple inquiry is administered after each response. Six of the 22 scoring categories—namely, location, color, shading, movement, form definiteness, and form appropriateness—are regarded as primary. A very carefully developed scoring system, in the form of rating scales, has been worked out for these variables.

Six factors, sufficient to account for the correlations obtained between the variables, have been identified by factor analysis, the first three being quite well defined. The first, defined by movement, integration, human, barrier, and popular, was found to account for more of the obtained variance than any of the others. High scores here are thought to be related to well organized ideational activity, good imaginative capacity, well differentiated ego boundaries, and awareness of conventional concepts. The second is a bipolar factor, primarily defined by color and shading. The positive pole is thought to indicate over-reactivity to color, shading, or symmetrical balance, and the negative to be associated with primary concern for form alone. The third factor is defined primarily by pathognomic verbalizations. High scores here are regarded as indicating disordered thought processes and an active but disturbed fantasy life.

Percentile norms have been constructed for eight reference groups, including college students, average adults, seventh graders, elementary school children, five-year-olds, chronic schizophrenics, mental retardates, and depressed patients. In evaluating a particular subject, comparisons can be made with any of the appropriate reference groups. However, since this procedure is limited to one inkblot score at a time, the authors suggest the use of multivariate analytic procedures which can take

into account all of the scores simultaneously. Holtzman gives an example of this kind of approach, along with compelling evidence on behalf of multivariate statistic procedures for classification problems. At present, however, we can only look to the future for the availability of large scale data and high powered computers which such procedures necessarily entail.

Several reliability studies for the different groups are reported. In the main, the obtained coefficients are acceptably high and some are even remarkably so, although on some of the variables they are too low to warrant confidence. Validity studies have dealt primarily with group differences and relationships with other techniques. In the developmental, cognitive, and perceptual aspects of personality functioning, concurrent validity seems reasonably satisfactory. For the identification of psychopathology, the variables of rejection, form appropriateness, movement, pathognomic verbalization, integration, human, and popular are especially powerful.

There are strong indications that the approach has much in common with the Rorschach, particularly in connection with the underlying meanings of their respective categories. Although only one study is reported in which both the Rorschach and Holtzman inkblots were given to the same individuals, a group of eleventh grade students, the correlations between the Beck and Holtzman systems for eight selected scores all reached statistical significance, ranging from .30 to .79.

An enormous amount of excellent statistical work has already been done, and much psychometric data is available. There is, however, much still to be done before it can be said that Holtzman's objective has been met. The eight reference groups require considerable supplementation, and validity studies are far from complete. The Holtzman-Rorschach comparisons are essentially limited, and comparisons based on many more groups would be essential for more conclusive evidence regarding the relationships between the two techniques. Also, while Holtzman believes that the loss of the Rorschach productivity score (R) is well compensated for by the expected gains, the test's empirical value is lessened thereby, and the potential for sequential analysis is lost. Further loss may also be entailed in the Holtzman procedure of using color and shading together, thus losing some of the more traditional Rorschach distinctions.

The Holtzman test is comparatively easy to learn and relatively simple to administer and score. It also has the major advantage of providing parallel forms. However, some of the vagueness of the Rorschach inquiry does remain. The Holtzman technique may also contain another Rorschach weakness in that there are 22 scoring categories which are derived from only 45 responses, which may be asking too much from too little. However, the potentialities for the further development of this test are enormous, and a serious attempt, such as this, to overcome some of the vagueness and the subjective interpretation which frequently characterizes projective test procedures without seriously sacrificing their essential richness, is urgently needed.

For excerpts from reviews of the manual, see B264.

[218]

*Horn-Hellersberg Test. Ages 3 and over; 1945–62; based on drawings adapted from *Horn Art Aptitude Inventory* (see 5:242); "capacity to function or to adapt to a given surrounding"; 1 form ('45, 4 pages); mimeographed manual, third edition ('61, 16 pages, including 1962 instructions for interpreting part of the test as a "scale for determining developmental stages" for ages 3–11); no data on reliability; no data on validity in manual; no description of normative population; $2 per 25 tests; 25¢ per manual; 35¢ per specimen set; postage extra; (30–90) minutes; Elizabeth F. Hellersberg; the Author. *

REFERENCES

1–5. See 4:108.
6. HELLERSBERG, E. F. "The Horn-Hellersberg Test." *Monogr Soc Res Child Develop* 16(53):138–70, 214–316 '53. * (PA 28:4077)

For reviews by Philip L. Harriman and T. W. Richards, see 4:108; for excerpts from related book reviews, see 4:109.

[219]

*The Howard Ink Blot Test. Adults; 1953–60; individual; 1 form ('53, 12 cards); 1953 manual ('53, 47 pages, reprint of *1* below); 1960 manual ('60, 207 pages, see *4* below); no data on reliability; $12.50 per set of cards; $2 per 1953 manual; $5 per 1960 manual; cash orders postpaid; (90–105) minutes; James W. Howard; Journal of Clinical Psychology. *

REFERENCES

1–3. See 5:141.
4. HOWARD, JAMES W. *The Howard Ink Blot Test.* Brandon, Vt.: Journal of Clinical Psychology, 1960. Pp. v, 202. * (PA 35:6381)

JESSE G. HARRIS, JR., *Professor of Psychology and Chairman of the Department, University of Kentucky, Lexington, Kentucky.*

The 12-card *Howard Ink Blot Test* was developed in 1953 from an earlier set of 21 blots devised to elicit a broad range of determinants by the method of group administration. It consists of an irregular sequence of 6 achromatic cards, 3 chromatic cards, and 3 cards which are a mixture of achromatic and chromatic inks. Both cards and blots are larger and colors are more saturated than those of the Rorschach. Individual administration, including notation of reaction and response times, rotation of cards, and inquiry, is similar to that of the conventional Rorschach procedure. The author of the *Howard Ink Blot Test* has engaged in the collection of normative data for approximately 21 years, resulting finally in the publication, in 1960, of a book which is an elaboration of the 1953 manual. The book is distinguished primarily by an enlargement of the earlier sample of 229 normal adults of at least high average, Wechsler-tested intelligence, to 510; the addition of what the author calls a "pseudo-normal" group of 173 subjects having problems in school, work, domestic or social life; and the inclusion of eight clinical groups, ranging in size from 31 to 69 hospitalized adult subjects. The seven additional years of thought and accumulation of data have produced some interesting syntheses and variations of hypotheses, but little of a conceptual nature that is fundamentally new, and with the exception of tabulations of number of responses by the Beck scoring system, virtually nothing of a statistical nature. Tables of comparative data on the responses of normal subjects to the Howard and Rorschach blots are not available in either the manual or the book. There is no clear indication in the author's written contributions that the responses of the Howard normative sample have been compared in unpublished studies with responses of a Rorschach sample of subjects of equally high intelligence, or, as an alternative, that responses to both tests have been obtained from a single group of subjects. If such experimental controls have not been exercised, the advertised "heightened sensitivity" of the *Howard Ink Blot Test* may be a function of differences between the two samples in intelligence alone. A similar restriction on interpretation would be imposed on the analysis of differences reported between the eight clinical groups and the normal sample, particularly since the levels of intelligence and education are reported to be lower for the clinical groups. Many of these differences may even be a function of differences in total number of responses. To the reviewer's knowledge, only two empirical researches (*2-3*) have appeared in American journals, and the results of these studies are highly questionable because they involve an improper application of chi-square technique rather than a more suitable utilization of a matched-pairs nonparametric technique. Even in their inappropriate use of the chi-square method, the authors of the articles have made the elementary error of comparing the Rorschach and Howard tests with respect to total number of responses produced by a single group of schizophrenic subjects to whom the two tests had been administered in counterbalanced order, rather than utilizing the *frequency* of subjects producing a given number of responses in a particular category. Although a lone article [1] in an Italian journal has reported data on the two tests which may appear to be mildly favorable to the Howard test as a possible alternate form of the Rorschach for retesting, the size of the sample (*n* = 20) is too small to provide reliable normative data. There is, at present, no empirically determined evidence for personality correlates of test behavior and no indication that such research is being conducted or planned. Although the traditional Rorschach test has itself been under criticism for many years for lack of conclusive evidence on reliability and on empirical and construct validity, one might expect that a newly advertised marketable test instrument would offer some unique feature which conceivably could elevate it, in some respect, above the controversial status of the Rorschach. With the possible, and doubtful, exception of the article in Italian, there is no empirical research literature to support the use of this instrument in preference to the Rorschach test. The reviewer has suggested in one of his own publications on the Rorschach test the desirability of an open-minded approach to new types of inkblot tests; but there is very little, if any, published evidence that this particular test has contributed anything of a conceptual or statistical nature after two decades of research, beyond what has become the usable

1 FERRACUTI, FRANCO A., AND RIZZO, GIOVANNI B. "Esame Comparativo dei Fattori di Siglatura al Rorschach ed al Test di Howard." ("A Comparison Between Rorschach and Howard Ink Blot Tests.") *Bollettino di Psicologia e Sociologia Applicate* (13–16):135–41 '56. (*PA* 31:7911)

lore of Rorschach interpretation. Although it seems appropriate, in this instance, to acknowledge the investigator's contribution of an intuitive interpretative nature, and his long years of devotion to a new form of inkblot test, it is more difficult to commend him, also, for having made a presently demonstrable contribution to scientific knowledge.

If one chooses to employ this test in preference to the Rorschach, he should do so with an awareness that the *Howard Ink Blot Test*, as a device for measurement, is subject to all of the limitations of the Rorschach. The user of either instrument in the clinical setting will find it necessary to develop an individual frame of reference based on his cumulative experience; the researcher who wishes to establish on a comparative basis the assets and liabilities of each, will probably conclude that the element of novelty in the Howard inkblots can scarcely outweigh the advantage of a large body of empirical knowledge developed after more than 40 years of intensive research of wide range of quality on the Rorschach blots. The investigator who is interested in a fundamentally different approach to inkblot testing might examine the *Structured-Objective Rorschach Test* or the *Holtzman Inkblot Technique*.

BERNARD I. MURSTEIN, *Associate Professor of Psychology, Connecticut College, New London, Connecticut.*

This inkblot test consists of 12 cards slightly larger than the Rorschach and in the opinion of this reviewer somewhat more dynamic, offering greater possibilities for shading and texture responses than the Rorschach, notwithstanding the fact that many of the cards somewhat resemble Rorschach cards. The administration and scoring are closely related to Beck's system though several minor revisions have occurred. In *The Fifth Yearbook,* the excerpt from Walter Klopfer's withering review essentially concluded that Howard offered no research supporting any of the claims that his test was more sensitive to personality measurement than the Rorschach.

What has happened since then? As far as this reviewer can determine no new research has appeared to supplement the two articles by Scott (*2-3*) showing that the Howard evinced more shading, movement, and color than the Rorschach. The original sample of 229 normals has been extended to 510. Other groups include 173 pseudo-normals, 69 paranoid schizophrenics, 48 "other" schizophrenics, 37 psychopaths, 31 manic-depressives, 62 border-line schizophrenics, 32 obsession compulsives, 39 depressive reaction patients, and 43 anxiety reaction cases. Means, standard deviations, and *t* tests are given for various scores between these groups.

In addition the scoring of *F* is no longer wholly subjective. By some intricate but not statistically meaningful manipulations, $F+$ and $F-$ scores are obtained by comparing the normal group with the others. About 12 per cent of scores are still scored subjectively for form accuracy. Last, the 1960 manual has been considerably expanded from 46 to 202 pages with many more scoring examples included.

These changes meet some of Klopfer's criticisms, but unfortunately only the minor ones. Chief among the unmet criticisms is the fact that there is essentially no research to tell us the behavioral or personological correlates of the responses to this test. It would be dangerous simply to transcribe to the Howard test the findings with the Rorschach, whose stimulus structure is considerably different from the Howard set.

The new norms are not very meaningful. No reliability coefficients appear. Further, the ages, sex, education, and other vital statistics of the groups are not given, so that one is by no means sure that the differences reported in the various determinant scores are attributable to behavior influencing the psychiatric classification rather than to more extraneous causes.

Finally, two new inkblot tests have appeared which offer much more to the clinician "ready for a change" than the Howard. The *Holtzman Inkblot Technique* is undoubtedly a great improvement over the Rorschach from a psychometric point of view. The use of 45 cards and limiting the subjects to one response per card greatly improves reliability and allows the examiner to consider the meaning of the various determinants independently of the number of responses given. The method however is still dependent on the standard inquiry method of the Rorschach. This is disadvantageous because one has no confidence that the subject is truly describing the determinants of his perception, either because he does not want to or because he is simply unaware of what

they are. The Baughman method[1] largely overcomes this problem by presenting the orthodox card and one of several modifications emphasizing contour, color, etc. If it is desired to inquire about the role of shading in the percept "bat," a silhouette modification is presented and the subject asked if he still sees a bat.

Where then does this leave the *Howard Ink Blot Test?* It has all of the limitations of the Rorschach with few of its virtues. If one wants to stay with a tested inkblot technique, the Rorschach, with more than 3,000 research articles written about it, cannot be surpassed. If he wants a psychometrically more sound instrument or one more likely to educe the true determinants of perception of an inkblot response, there is more justification for turning to the Baughman or Holtzman innovations, respectively, than to the *Howard Ink Blot Test*.

Can Psychologist 1:140 O '60. H. R. Wideman. [Review of the 1960 manual.] * The book and the test material will be welcomed by those who employ ink blot techniques and wish to experiment in the hope of securing richer protocols. Even those who stick to the *Rorschach* will find many intriguing interpretative hypotheses for their consideration. The reader of this volume will miss clear, logical exposition. In part this is a result of the mixture of theoretical viewpoints and dependence upon discrete clinical hunches; most other texts on projectives have the same failing. However, the writing could have been tightened and more effort put into obtaining a readable style.

For a review by C. R. Strother, see 5:141 (1 excerpt).

[220]

★**The IES Test.** Ages 10 and over and latency period girls; 1956–58; 14 scores: 3 scores each for *a–c* (impulses, ego, superego) plus 5 scores listed in *d* below; individual; 4 tests; manual ('58, 44 pages, reprint of 3 below); instructions ('58, 1 card) for each test; record form ('58, 1 page); norms for females based on fifth and sixth graders only; $28.50 per set of test materials including manual; $3 per manual; cash orders postpaid; (30) minutes; Lawrence A. Dombrose and Morton S. Slobin; Psychological Test Specialists. *
a) ARROW-DOT TEST. 1957–58; reaction to goal barriers; 1 form ('57, .5 pages).
b) PICTURE STORY COMPLETION TEST. 1956–58; conception of outside world; 1 form ('56, 71 cards).

1 BAUGHMAN, E. EARL. "A New Method of Rorschach Inquiry." *J Proj Tech* 22:381–9 D '58. * (PA 34:1333)

c) PHOTO-ANALYSIS TEST. 1956–58; desired self-gratifications; 1 form ('56, 9 cards).

d) PICTURE TITLE TEST. 1956–58; recognition and acceptance of ego pressures; 5 scores: impulse, ego, superego, defense, superego plus defense; 1 form ('56, 12 cards).

REFERENCES

1. DOMBROSE, LAWRENCE A., AND SLOBIN, MORTON S. *An Approach to the Measurement of Relative Strengths of Impulses, Ego, and Superego, and the Determination of the Effects of Impulses and Superego Upon Ego Functions.* Joint doctor's thesis, Western Reserve University (Cleveland, Ohio), 1951.
2. ALEXANDER, WILLIAM AUSTIN, JR. *A Study of Normal and Psychotic Subjects Who Deviate in Their Performance on the IES Tests.* Doctor's thesis, Western Reserve University (Cleveland, Ohio), 1954.
3. DOMBROSE, LAWRENCE A., AND SLOBIN, MORTON S. "The IES Test." *Percept & Motor Skills* 8:347–89 D '58. * (*PA* 34:80)
4. BORTNER, RAYMAN W. "Superego Functioning and Institutional Adjustment." *Percept & Motor Skills* 14:375–9 Je '62. * (*PA* 37:3408)
5. HERRON, WILLIAM G. "IES Test Patterns of Accepted and Rejected Adolescents." *Percept & Motor Skills* 15:435–8 O '62. * (*PA* 37:8031)
6. NICKOLS, JOHN E., JR. "Intelligence, Insight, and the Arrow-Dot Test." *J Clin Psychol* 18:164–6 Ap '62. *
7. RANKIN, RICHARD J., AND JOHNSTON, JAMES O. "Influences of Age and Sex on the IES Test." *Percept & Motor Skills* 15:775–8 D '62. * (*PA* 38:2703)
8. VERRILL, BERNARD V., AND COSTANZA, VICTOR. "The IES Test and Ward Behavior." *J Clin Psychol* 18:295–7 Jl '62. *
9. ARMSTRONG, RENATE G., AND HOYT, DAVID B. "Personality Structure of Male Alcoholics as Reflected in the IES Test." *Q J Studies Alcohol* 24:239–48 Je '63. *
10. BORTNER, RAYMAN W. "The Relationship Between Age and Measures of Id, Ego and Superego Functioning." *J Gerontol* 18:286–9 Jl '63. * (*PA* 38:4097)
11. BORTNER, RAYMAN W. "Research Cooperation in Older Institutionalized Males." *Percept & Motor Skills* 16:611–2 Ap '63. * (*PA* 38:2921)
12. GILBERT, JEANNE G., AND LEVEE, RAYMOND F. "A Comparison of the Personality Structures of a Group of Young, Married and a Group of Middle Aged, Married Women." *Percept & Motor Skills* 16:773–7 Je '63. * (*PA* 38:6117)
13. PINCKNEY, GEORGE A. "Relative Strengths of Impulse, Ego and Superego in Female College Students." *Percept & Motor Skills* 17:340 O '63. * (*PA* 38:6063)
14. REMPEL, HENRY, AND SIGNORI, EDRO I. "Further Research on the IES Photo-Analysis Subtest With Special Reference to Sex Differences." *Percept & Motor Skills* 17:295–8 Ag '63. * (*PA* 38:8394)
15. REMPEL, HENRY; SIGNORI, EDRO I.; AND SAMPSON, DONALD L. G. "Differences in Attribution of Impulse (Id), Ego and Superego Functions to Male and Female Photographs." *Percept & Motor Skills* 17:663–5 D '63. * (*PA* 38:6066)

DOUGLAS P. CROWNE, *Associate Professor of Psychology, University of Connecticut, Storrs, Connecticut.*

The aim of the *IES Test* is to measure "the relative strengths of impulses, ego and superego" and the complex interrelations of these functions. As a psychoanalytic instrument it is intended for both clinical use in diagnosis and for research to validate psychoanalytic concepts. The test is presumably disguised so that the examinee is unaware of the purpose of testing and the meaning to be given to his test responses. The several subtests which make up the *IES Test* include a behavioral task (Arrow-Dot Test), two multiple choice measures (the Photo-Analysis Test, a questionnaire in which the examinee attributes motives and behavior to photographs; and the Picture Story Completion Test), and a semi-projective test (Picture Title Test). These standardized test tasks provide controlled stimulus situations in which it is assumed that impulses, ego, and superego will be shown in behavior in distinctive and measurable ways. The test indications of these personality forces are as follows. The I (impulses) score is given for responses which reflect sexuality, hostility, freedom from control, and externalization, and for violation of prohibitions. The E (ego) score is awarded for test responses which reflect a reality testing and problem solving orientation and control of presumably unacceptable impulses. The expression of guilt and rigid, moralistic, self-depriving, and overcautious behavior are scored S (superego).

RELIABILITY. Both test-retest and internal consistency coefficients are reported in the manual. Over the four tests the median test-retest reliability coefficient is .60. This was computed on a sample of 30 male psychotherapy outpatients over an interval of 30 to 60 days. The median internal consistency coefficient is .55. The latter is a generous estimate, since correlations below .20 are not reported. Obviously, little confidence can be placed in an individual's score with reliability values as low as these.

VALIDITY. The test authors recognize the requirement of construct validity of the test. They present two sets of validity studies essentially using the method of contrasted groups. Normals, neurotics, and psychotics (paranoid schizophrenics) were contrasted in their scores on the various tests, and the mean differences between the groups were interpreted as confirming theoretical expectations. Ten-year-old boys (theoretically in the latent stage) were contrasted with adolescents and normal adults in an attempt to test predicted differences in psychosexual development. In another study, 11-year-old boys and girls rated by teachers as impulsive, constricted, and well adjusted were compared. Geriatric groups have also been investigated. Essentially, the validity criteria in these investigations were psychiatric diagnosis, age, and sex. In the studies of children, psychosexual status was not really predicted by the test since no psychosexual criteria other than age were employed.

No evidence of discriminant validity is offered. Careful test validation requires evidence that the test is unrelated to constructs with which it is presumed to differ. At the very least, correlations with intelligence and social desirability should be reported. In the latter case, many of the test tasks appear to be highly transparent and susceptible to response distortion; thus, the score is more likely to reflect the examinee's need to appear in a favorable light than the way in which he copes with his impulses. The following examples from the Photo-Analysis Test illustrate this problem.

1. When this man doesn't get enough change from a
   clerk, does he
   A. ask for the right amount
      or
   B. call the clerk a crook
      or
   C. forget about it
2. Does he look as if he would
   A. commit suicide
      or
   B. commit murder
      or
   C. live a normal life

The literature on response distortion strongly suggests that disguises such as having the subject attribute characteristics to people depicted in pictures do not succeed in disabusing him of the idea that he is himself being evaluated.

NORMS. Norms in the form of mean scores are presented for 10-year-old boys and girls, adolescents, normal adults, neurotics, paranoid schizophrenics, and the aged. Norms for the clinical groups are based on very small samples, and stratified sampling procedures to control for socioeconomic variables of potential influence on the test scores were not used in sample selection. To take one example, differences in sexual and aggressive behavior (methods of impulse control) associated with social class are well known; since the class characteristics of the normative samples are undetermined we have no way of knowing the effect of this variable on the test. The tables presenting the norms do not report standard deviations nor are cutting scores given. Standard deviations are available from tables elsewhere in the manual, but to look them up is cumbersome and should not be demanded of the test user.

The *IES Test* reflects a rather naïve approach to psychoanalytic test construction. Interpretation of the various test scores appears to be based on the assumption of a direct relationship between behavior and the mediating processes of impulses and impulse control. On the Arrow-Dot Test, for example, crossing forbidden barriers is interpreted as an indica-

tion of uncontrolled impulsivity, and circuitous cautiousness is assumed to reflect the oversevere demands of the superego. The assumption of such a 1:1 theoretical correspondence is superficial. The role of defensive processes (e.g., the effects of repression) is essential to the psychoanalytic understanding of behavior control. Also, the meaning of the test tasks to the examinee needs more careful consideration, and a check on defensive or socially desirable response bias should be incorporated in the test.

SUMMARY. *The IES Test cannot be recommended for individual diagnosis* in view of grossly inadequate reliability and limited evidence of validity. Further, the diagnostic rules by which personality interpretations are to be constructed from the relative values of test scores are not specified, although a sample diagnostic interpretation is offered. For the prediction of psychiatric diagnosis or expected psychiatric classification, the MMPI is infinitely preferable. For the prediction of age and sex there are obviously simpler and more reliable variables. In the prediction of psychosexual conflicts and problems, one might as well use the Blacky test. The use of the *IES Test* is limited to research investigations of its validity as a measure of psychoanalytic constructs, and in this its utility is limited by its superficiality.

WALTER KATKOVSKY, *Associate Professor of Psychology, Fordham University, New York, New York.*

The four tests of the IES utilize testing procedures familiar to diagnosticians; viz., selecting pathways to a target, choosing a picture to complete a story sequence, describing faces, and giving titles to pictures. The test materials and tasks are likely to arouse the interest and motivation of most persons within a broad age range.

More distinctive and significant than the test materials and procedures is the purpose of the test. The authors are interested in working within a psychoanalytic framework and they have constructed the tests to measure three variables in this theory, the strengths of impulses, ego, and superego. They have clearly presented the rationale of each test, indicating the ways in which they believe responses will reflect the variables they wish to measure, and they have worked out a clear scoring system based on their *a priori* ideas as to how impulse, ego, and superego forces will be expressed on the tests. Their ideas generally appear to have face validity and consistency with psychoanalytic theory. Clear instructions for standardized administration and scoring are presented in the manual. Scoring agreement of 91 per cent is reported between two independent scorers.

Despite the authors' deliberate efforts to construct an instrument which measures strength of impulses, ego, and superego, three issues which must be considered raise doubts as to whether they have in fact accomplished their aim. These issues are the validity of the tests, their reliability, and the ease of making interpretations of individual scores and records. The topics of validity and interpretation are particularly complex because of the claim that each test measures a different aspect of impulse, ego, and superego strength. For example, the E scores on the various tests are thought to measure the degree of reality-oriented functioning (Arrow-Dot Test), the objectivity of perceptions of the external world (Picture Story Completion Test), the realism and conventionality of wishes and fantasies (Photo-Analysis Test), and the recognition and acceptance of objective judgment as a determinant of functioning (Picture Title Test). The complexity of the interpretations is increased by the fact that very high E scores on the Arrow-Dot and Picture Title Tests are in some cases described as indicative of a strong superego and denial of conflict and pain rather than as realistic ego functioning.

In discussing the validity of their instrument, the authors refer to several studies which have tested theoretical hypotheses contrasting different groups of subjects. They report that more predictions were supported with the IES than would be expected by chance, and while they cite the need for further research, they state that the tests "have a degree of validity to justify their use." Unfortunately, the authors do not make explicit the hypotheses that were and were not supported and refer the reader to original sources, all of which are relatively difficult to obtain since they are unpublished doctoral dissertations. Since publication of the IES in 1958, several additional studies using the tests have been published. Some of these studies obtained results which support the utility of the instrument and some did not. Herron (5) found that rejected ado-

lescents placed in a residence for neglected children obtained higher I and lower E scores on the Picture Story Completion Test, and lower E scores on the Picture Title Test, than children never separated from their families. This finding is consistent with an explanation of ego deficiency and externalization of impulses in the rejected group. Rankin and Johnston (7) reported several age and sex differences in the scores of college students, and Bortner (11) noted differences between the scores of hospitalized patients who showed up for a research appointment and "no shows." Bortner (4) also found significant F ratios on three of five superego measures obtained from the IES using groups of non-institutionalized men and groups of men well adjusted and poorly adjusted to institutionalized life. His data are difficult to interpret because of lack of controls, but one possible finding is that his subjects with poor institutional adjustment, in comparison with other groups, overinterpreted environmental restrictions placed on them. Two studies using the IES failed to confirm predictions. Verrill and Costanza (8) found no significant correlations between ratings of patients by a psychiatric nurse on impulse, ego, and superego characteristics and corresponding scores on the IES. Gilbert and Levee (12), predicting weaker egos and greater superego-id conflict in women in the menopausal age range than in young women, failed to find any differences between young and middle-aged married women.

It is this reviewer's belief that the reported research on the IES is too limited in scope and significance to warrant use of this instrument for purposes other than research. Controlled investigations of the predictive and construct validity of the individual tests are badly needed. The specific interpretations proposed for test scores should be examined by predicting from the scores to criterion measures, where possible, or to behavior consistent with the interpretations.

Even if the validity of the tests is assumed, problems exist with the interpretation of scores. The test manual presents mean scores for various age and pathological groups, but these are based on small samples and the differences between mean scores are small. Consequently, they provide little guidance in the interpretation of an individual record lacking extreme scores. A sample interpretation of a record can be found in the manual as an example of how scoring interpretations are integrated for the individual case. Interpretation of this record, however, is relatively easy because of extreme scores on two of the tests. Interpreting a record with less deviant scores is likely to be a more difficult and subjective task. A second point pertaining to test interpretation is the question of what variables other than impulse, ego, and superego strength may be related to test performance? For example, intelligence may be significantly correlated with E scores on the Arrow-Dot and Picture Story Completion Tests inasmuch as similar procedures are used to measure intelligence on other tests (e.g., Mazes and Picture Arrangement on the *Wechsler Intelligence Scale for Children*). Interpretations of ego strength may well be confounded with intellectual functioning. Research determining relations between IES scores and other variables would aid interpretation of scores.

The stability of the IES is better than the internal consistency of the tests. Test-retest reliabilities after 30 to 60 days on 30 males receiving outpatient psychotherapy range from .35 to .83. The internal consistency of each of the tests, determined by the Kuder-Richardson formula 20 and reported in the test manual and by Rankin and Johnston (7), tends to be low, particularly on the Picture Title and Photo-Analysis Tests. The Arrow-Dot Test, on the other hand, has satisfactory internal consistency.

The advertisement recommending use of this instrument for individual clinical evaluation "in such areas as ego strength, superego rigidity, and 'acting out' behavior" seems unwarranted. Despite the attractiveness of the materials and the ease of administration, sufficient problems exist in the reliability and validity of scores to discourage their use in making interpretations and decisions about individuals in clinical situations. Some of the tests and interpretations of them do appear to warrant further research.

J Counsel Psychol 9:369–72 w '62. John O. Crites. * The four tests of the IES are well-conceived, following an explicit test rationale, and some are ingenious, in particular the PhA and AD tests. In administering the tests to both children and adults, the reviewer found a high level of interest and involvement in their content, which to the test expert has obvious face validity but which to examinees is not obvious, since they typically inquire about what the tests measure after having taken them. Furthermore, the tests are comprehensive, in that they assess a variety of processes from perception and imagination to problem-solving and social conformity, and they can be scored to yield measures not only of id, ego, and superego functioning but of other constructs which are defined by the interrelationships of these variables. * About the only drawback to the administration of the IES is that it can be given to just one person at a time. * Estimates of the homogeneity of the tests, as determined by Kuder-Richardson Formula 20, were generally low, ranging from .20 to .72 in groups of normals, neurotics, and paranoids for all tests except AD, which had considerably higher coefficients * the reliabilities of the tests are disappointingly low, perhaps not so much because they are intrinsically inaccurate measures but more because the test authors did not fairly evaluate their reliability. Not only is a sample as small as 30 inadequate for the computation of reliability estimates, but the Ss were tested over varying periods of time, instead of at the same time, and they were in psychotherapy, the effects of which, if there were any, are inextricably confounded with the passage of time between test and retest. It is surprising, therefore, not that the data showed the tests to be reliable at all but that they were as reliable as the coefficients indicated. With more adequate data from larger samples, it would seem reasonable to expect that the reliabilities of the IES tests would be considerably higher and within the range generally required for individual appraisal and prediction. * The construct validity studies of the IES are generally favorable and support the promise of the test, but they should be interpreted cautiously for two reasons. First, in the group comparisons it is possible that the differences were due to variables other than those measured by the tests. Only if the groups were comparable on variables which are related to IES performance would it be justifiable to conclude that the test constructs had been validated. * It might be reasonable to expect....that intelligence would be related to the IES ego scores and consequently to the differences between groups on them. Second,....some of the IES tests may be more valid than others and consequently the over-all correct prediction rate should not be generalized to all of the tests without evidence on each one. * it would be extremely helpful to perform a factor analysis on their intercorrelations. It may be that some tests are measuring the same functions or that the id, ego, and superego scores are highly related and define one general factor rather than three relatively independent ones. The IES test has many possibilities for both counseling procedures and research endeavors. Conceptually, it is one of the soundest personality tests which has appeared in some time, dealing as it does with constructs from an explicit theoretical system which has direct relevance for the explanation of counseling and vocational phenomena. Structurally, it is well-designed, conveniently administered, and easily scored, and it captures the interest and motivation of examinees. Empirically, it is based upon some research findings which are encouraging, but a considerable amount of further work is needed before confidence can be had in its reliability and validity. In particular, there should be studies of its factorial structure and its relationships to other test and nontest variables. Until appropriate data are available, the IES should be used with caution and qualification, but it *should* be used. Its potential as a meaningful and useful instrument outweighs its present limitations and commends it to counselors and researchers who are interested in the analysis of cognitive processes and their relationships to adjustment and decision-making.

[221]
*An Incomplete Sentence Test. Employees, college; 1949–53; Forms M (for men), W (for women), (4 pages); 2 editions; no data on reliability; no norms; 15¢ per test; 25¢ per manual for a; 50¢ per specimen set; postpaid; (15–25) minutes; George Spache; [Reading Laboratory and Clinic]. *
a) AN INCOMPLETE SENTENCE TEST FOR INDUSTRIAL USE. Employees; 1949; 2 forms ('49); manual ['49, 8 pages].
b) AN INCOMPLETE SENTENCE TEST [COLLEGE EDITION]. College; 1953; 2 mimeographed forms ['53]; no manual; no data on validity.

For a review by Benjamin Balinsky of a, see 5:142.

[222]
★The Industrial Sentence Completion Form. Employee applicants; 1963; experimental form; 1 form (4 pages); no manual; no data on reliability and validity; no norms; [20–30] minutes; $5 per 25 tests, postage extra; specimen set not available; Martin M. Bruce; the Author. *

[223]
Interpersonal Diagnosis of Personality. Adults; 1955–58; a combination of assessment procedures consisting of the *Minnesota Multiphasic Personality Inventory*, the *Interpersonal Check List*, and the *Thematic Apperception Test* or the *Interpersonal Fantasy Test* (see *e* below); manual ('56, 114 pages, see 12 below); $5.50 per manual; specimen set (without manual) of *a–d* free; cash orders postpaid; Timothy Leary, Rolfe LaForge (a), Robert Suczek (a), and others (manual); Psychological Consultation Service. *
a) INTERPERSONAL CHECK LIST. 1 form ['55, 3 pages]; $4 per 20 tests; $2 per scoring template; (15–45) minutes depending on number of persons rated.
b) RECORD BOOKLET FOR INTERPERSONAL DIAGNOSIS OF PERSONALITY. 1 form ('57, 4 pages); $5 per 20 booklets.
c) RECORD BOOKLET FOR INTERPERSONAL ANALYSIS OF GROUP DYNAMICS. 1 form ['56, 4 pages]; $5 per 20 booklets.
d) RECORD BOOKLET FOR INTERPERSONAL DIAGNOSIS OF FAMILY DYNAMICS. 1 form ['56, 6 pages]; $5 per 20 booklets.
e) INTERPERSONAL FANTASY TEST. 1957–58; 1 form ['57, 26 cards]; no data on reliability or validity; typewritten manual ('58); $15 per set of cards.

REFERENCES
1–11. See 5:144.
12. LEARY, TIMOTHY; WITH THE COLLABORATION OF HELEN LANE, ANNE APFELBAUM, MARY DELLA CIOPPA, AND CHARLOTTE KAUFMANN. *Multilevel Measurement of Interpersonal Behavior: A Manual for the Use of the Interpersonal System of Personality.* Berkeley, Calif.: Psychological Consultation Service, 1956. Pp. vii, 110. *
13. GYNTHER, MALCOLM D.; PRESHER, CHARLES H.; AND McDONALD, ROBERT L. "Personal and Interpersonal Factors Associated With Alcoholism." *Q J Studies Alcohol* 20:321–33 Je '59. * (PA 34:6241)
14. BAUMRIND, DIANA. "An Analysis of Some Aspects of the 'Interpersonal System.'" *Psychiatry* 23:395–402 N '60. * (PA 36:5IF95B)
15. ROMANO, ROBERT L. "The Use of the Interpersonal System of Diagnosis in Marital Counseling." Comment by T. Leary. *J Counsel Psychol* 7:10–9 sp '60. * (PA 35:2441)
16. GYNTHER, MALCOLM D., AND McDONALD, ROBERT L. "Personality Characteristics of Prisoners, Psychiatric Patients, and Student Nurses as Depicted by the Leary System." *J General Psychol* 64:387–95 Ap '61. * (PA 36:1HF87G)
17. CHENAULT, JOANN, AND SEEGARS, JAMES E., JR. "The Interpersonal Diagnosis of Principals and Counselors." *Personnel & Guid J* 41:118–22 O '62. * (PA 37:5285)
18. DAVID, CHARLOTTE. "Interpersonal Measurement of Two Occupational Interest Groups." *J Proj Tech* 26:276–82 S '62. * (PA 37:3895)
19. GAZA, CAESAR THOMAS. *The Prediction of Success in Nursing Training: The Use of the Interpersonal System of Multilevel Personality Diagnosis as an Adjunct to the Selection Program of a Hospital School of Nursing.* Doctor's thesis, New York University (New York, N.Y.), 1963. (DA 24:1684)
20. LORR, MAURICE, AND McNAIR, DOUGLAS M. "An Interpersonal Behavior Circle." *J Abn & Social Psychol* 67:68–75 Jl '63. * (PA 38:765)
21. MITCHELL, HOWARD E. "Application of the Kaiser Method to Marital Pairs." *Family Process* 2:265–79 S '63. *
See also references for 127.

JERRY S. WIGGINS, *Associate Professor of Psychology, University of Illinois, Urbana, Illinois.*

The *Interpersonal Diagnosis of Personality* provides an intricate theoretical framework for viewing an individual's behavior with respect to himself and significant others at several levels of personality functioning. The Interpersonal battery employs three tests which together are presumed to tap four levels of interpersonal behavior in terms of a common system of 16 variables whose intercorrelations form a circular pattern which has recently been dubbed a "circumplex."[1] The manual provides detailed instructions for scoring each test in terms of a reduced set of interpersonal variables (eight octants) by two basic procedures. (a) Graphic scoring involves the pictorial representation of raw (or in one instance standard) scores on the eight variables on a circular profile which serves a supplementary diagnostic function. (b) The primary interpersonal diagnosis is made for each of the four levels by a linear combination of raw scores which yield "vector means" on the two principal coordinates of the system, dominance (Dom) and affiliation (Lov). Dom and Lov vector means are converted to standard scores and plotted as a single point in two dimensional space represented by a circular diagnostic grid. The grid is sectioned into eight equal pie-shaped octants which correspond to the eight interpersonal variables. The octant in which an individual's score falls determines his interpersonal diagnosis and his distance from the center of the circle determines the appropriateness of his behavior. Dom and Lov scores of 800 psychiatric outpatients serve as "norms" for diagnoses made at each of the four levels. Test scores which fall close to the mean of this group are classified as "adaptive" while more extreme scores (one sigma above) are considered "maladaptive." False negative diagnostic decisions would seem likely to occur when an individual is judged to be "well off" by reference to a norm based on psychiatric patients. Such a frame of reference also fails to provide an appropriate baseline for the evaluation of improvement which is one of the avowed purposes of the system (14).

LEVEL I, PUBLIC INTERPERSONAL BEHAVIOR (MMPI). In principle, the social stimulus value of a patient could be assessed by pooling ratings made by significant others. In practice, a highly questionable use is made of selected MMPI clinical and special scales which are presumed to be "predictive" of such sociometric ratings. Eight MMPI scales were selected to represent the eight interpersonal octants on the basis of the correlations of these scales with sociometric ratings (3). The quite meager and often inconsistent nature of these original correlations would not lead one to expect much success in forecasting one set

of measurements from the other. Subsequent studies of the relation between MMPI predictive indices of Dom and Lov and sociometric ratings of the corresponding dimensions[2] fail to provide any additional justification for this procedure. Although the view of an MMPI profile as a communication between the patient and significant others has much to recommend it, there is little evidence that the Interpersonal System scoring procedures represent an improvement upon more conventional diagnostic applications of the MMPI.[3]

LEVEL II, VIEW OF SELF AND OTHERS (ICL). The *Interpersonal Check List* (ICL) was carefully and imaginatively designed as a "flexible observational device for personality research" (4) which reflects the structural properties of the 16 variable circumplex system. Since the ICL is the subject of a separate review (see 127) it will not be described here. It should be noted that the ICL is the only instrument under discussion that was specifically developed for use in the system and it is therefore not surprising that its psychometric properties are vastly superior to those of the other instruments that were later adapted to the requirements of the system.

LEVEL III, FANTASY (TAT). "Preconscious" aspects of the eight interpersonal variables are assessed by application of an objective and apparently reliable method of content analysis to TAT protocols. Although clinicians are encouraged to attend to more qualitative aspects of TAT protocols, the recommended instructions to the subject (write 3 or 4 sentences) are unlikely to yield protocols of sufficient richness for the more traditional kinds of interpretations.[4] Although no rationale is given for the choice of the 10 TAT cards employed, it seems unlikely that these particular cards will generate distributions of interpersonal themes which have the circular ordering required by the system. Available evidence on the intercorrelations among Level III variables[5] suggests that their intercorrelations are predominantly

1 SCHAEFER, EARL S. "A Circumplex Model for Maternal Behavior." *J Abn & Social Psychol* 59:226–35 S '59. *
FOA, U. G. "Convergences in the Analysis of the Structure of Interpersonal Behavior." *Psychol R* 68:341–53 S '61. *

2 GYNTHER, MALCOLM D. "Degree of Agreement Among Three 'Interpersonal System' Measures." Abstract. *J Consult Psychol* 26:107 F '62. * (PA 37:4982)
3 MARKS, PHILIP A., AND SEEMAN, WILLIAM. *The Actuarial Description of Personality: An Atlas for Use With the MMPI.* Baltimore, Md.: Williams & Wilkins Co., 1963. Pp. xxv, 331. *
4 STEIN, MORRIS I. *The Thematic Apperception Test: An Introductory Manual for Its Clinical Use With Adult Males.* Foreword by James G. Miller. Cambridge, Mass.: Addison-Wesley Press, Inc., 1948. Pp. vii, 95. * (PA 22:4959)
5 TERRILL, JAMES McGUFFIN. *The Relationships Between Level II and Level III in the Interpersonal System of Personality Diagnosis.* Doctor's thesis, Stanford University (Stanford, Calif.), 1961. (DA 21:3529)

zero which mitigates against further analysis of their dimensionality. The mapping of the TAT variables on the circular grid seems therefore to be an act of faith.

In the "basic validation study" which provides the rationale for use of the TAT (*10*), hypothesized trends occurred primarily in the control group rather than in the therapy group. This study would thus seem to serve equally well as an argument for abandoning this use of the TAT. Unfortunately, the inappropriate application of the chi-square statistic in this study is not untypical of other studies presenting validating evidence (*14*). As an alternative to the TAT, the *Interpersonal Fantasy Test* (IFT) was designed to give broader coverage of the variables required by the system. There is, as yet, nô published information available on the characteristics of this instrument.

LEVEL V, CONSCIOUS IDEAL (ICL). At the same time that the subject fills out the ICL for self and others, he is asked to rate his ideal self. Distributions of such ideal ratings tend to cluster in the high dominance-high affiliation octants. Although the vector scoring method compensates for this, graphic profiles of Level V variables will tend to be stereotyped. The ICL self-ideal discrepancy measures have had interesting personality research applications [6] but the diagnostic utility of self-ideal and self-other discrepancies in a hospital population has been seriously questioned.[7]

INTERLEVEL DISCREPANCIES. Since scoring procedures at all levels yield separate diagnoses based on what are presumed to be the same eight interpersonal variables, interlevel discrepancy scores may be calculated and interpreted as defense mechanisms reflecting the structure of personality organization. The standards whereby one would evaluate the extent to which the *same* variables are involved at *different* levels are not specified so that one is uncertain as to whether convergent or discriminant validation [8] would be assessed in cross-level correlations. A system of weighted discrepancy scores is proposed which preserves the circular properties of the system, but this seems arbitrary in light of the non-circular properties of the variables on levels other than Level II.[9] LaForge [10] has proposed that the various tests be viewed as sampling behavioral domains rather than levels and has suggested more realistic methods of multivariate analysis.

Despite the attractiveness of the theoretical framework of the Interpersonal System and the considerable ingenuity exercised in the construction and adaptation of instruments, the battery described in the manual is not considered sufficiently validated to recommend its routine application to problems of clinical diagnosis. With the notable exception of the *Interpersonal Check List,* the recommended modifications of the tests do not seem to represent improvements over more conventional diagnostic applications of the same instruments. Considerable additional test development is required before the Interpersonal System can realize its aim of becoming a functional diagnostic system. Because of the complexities of the psychometric shortcomings of the current system, it would be folly for the practicing clinician to attempt to "compensate" intuitively for them in his test interpretations.

For excerpts from related book reviews, see 5:B261. For a review of the Interpersonal Check List, *see 127.*

[224]

*Kahn Test of Symbol Arrangement. Ages 6 and over; 1949–60; individual; 1 form (16 plastic objects); record blank ('56, c1949–56, 4 pages); administrative manual ('56, 37 pages, reprint of *11*); clinical manual ('57, 75 pages, reprint of *14*); auxiliary evaluation guide ('60, 10 pages); $25 per complete set of test materials; $7.50 per 50 record blanks; $2 per administrative manual; $3 per clinical manual; cash orders postpaid; (15–30) minutes; Theodore C. Kahn. *

REFERENCES

1–2. See 4:110.
3–18. See 5:145.
19. FINK, HOWARD H., AND KAHN, THEODORE C. "A Comparison of Normal and Emotionally Ill Children on the Kahn Test of Symbol Arrangement." *J Ed Res* 53:35–6 S '59. * (*PA* 34:5615)
20. BATES, JULIA B. *Use of the Kahn Test of Symbol Arrangement With Adolescents.* Master's thesis, Illinois State Normal University (Normal, Ill.), 1960.
21. GIFFEN, MARTIN B.; KENNY, JAMES A.; AND KAHN, THEODORE C. "Psychic Ingredients of Various Personality Types." *Am J Psychiatry* 117:211–4 S '60. * (*PA* 35:2241)
22. MCLEOD, H. N. "My Two-Hour Psychological Test Battery." *O.P.A. Q* 14:85–7 D '61. *
23. MCLEOD, HUGH N. "The Use of the Kahn Test of Symbol Arrangement as an Aid to Diagnosis With Psychiatric Patients." *Ont Hosp Psychol B* 7:10–20 D '61. *
24. L'ABATE, LUCIANO; BOELLING, GARY M.; HUTTON, ROBERT D.; AND MATHEWS, DEWEY L., JR. "The Diagnostic Usefulness of Four Potential Tests of Brain Damage." Abstract. *J Consult Psychol* 26:479 O '62. *

6 ALTROCCHI, JOHN; PARSONS, OSCAR A.; AND DICKOFF, HILDA. "Changes in Self-Ideal Discrepancy in Repressors and Sensitizers." *J Abn & Social Psychol* 61:67–72 Jl '60. * (*PA* 35:2253)
7 DINITZ, SIMON; MANGUS, A. R.; AND PASAMANICK, BENJAMIN. "Integration and Conflict in Self-Other Conceptions as Factors in Mental Illness." *Sociometry* 22:44–55 Mr '59. * (*PA* 34:1623)
8 CAMPBELL, DONALD T., AND FISKE, DONALD W. "Convergent and Discriminant Validation by the Multitrait-Multimethod Matrix." *Psychol B* 56:81–105 Mr '59. *

9 TERRILL, *op. cit.*
10 LAFORGE, ROLFE. *Research Use of the ICL.* ORI Technical Report, Vol. 3, No. 4. Eugene, Ore.: Oregon Research Institute, October 1963. Pp. i, 49. *

25. THEINER, ERIC C.; HILL, LARRY K.; LATHAM, WILLIAM R.; AND McCARTY, WILBUR D. "Validation Study of the Kahn Test of Symbol Arrangement." *J Clin Psychol* 18:454-7 O '62. * (*PA* 39:5103)

26. CRADDICK, RAY A., AND STERN, MICHAEL R. "Relation Between the WAIS and the Kahn Test of Symbol Arrangement." *Percept & Motor Skills* 17:583-5 O '63. * (*PA* 38: 6052)

27. HILL, LARRY K.; LATHAM, WILLIAM R.; AND THEINER, ERIC C. "Diagnostic Agreement of Variously Trained Psychologists Using the KTSA." *J Clin Psychol* 19:74-7 Ja '63. *

28. L'ABATE, LUCIANO; FRIEDMAN, WILLIAM H.; VOGLER, ROGER E.; AND CHUSED, THOMAS M. "The Diagnostic Usefulness of Two Tests of Brain-Damage." *J Clin Psychol* 19: 87-91 Ja '63. * (*PA* 39:2477)

For reviews by Cherry Ann Clark and Richard Jessor, see 5:145 (1 excerpt); for a review by Edward Joseph Shoben, Jr., see 4:110.

[225]

★The Kell-Hoeflin Incomplete Sentence Blank: Youth-Parent Relations. College, adults; 1959; 2 editions (1 page, identical except for wording changes in 7 items): youth form, parent form; manual (63 pages, see *1* below, includes copies of both editions); no data on reliability of scores for parent form; $2.25 per manual, postpaid; [20] minutes; Ruth Hoeflin and Leone Kell; Child Development Publications, Society for Research in Child Development, Inc. * (Test blanks, available from Leone Kell, $1.25 per 100, postpaid.)

REFERENCES

1. HOEFLIN, RUTH, AND KELL, LEONE. *The Kell-Hoeflin Incomplete Sentence Blank: Youth-Parent Relations.* Monographs of the Society for Research in Child Development, Vol. 24, No. 3, Serial No. 72. Lafayette, Ind.: Child Development Publications, Purdue University, 1959. Pp. 64. * (*PA* 35:767)

2. KENNEDY, WALLACE A., AND WILLCUTT, HERMAN. "Youth-Parent Relations of Mathematically-Gifted Adolescents." *J Clin Psychol* 19:400-2 O '63. *

[226]

Kent-Rosanoff Free Association Test. Ages 4 and over; 1910; for an adaptation, see 201; 1 form ['10, 2 pages]; hectographed manual ['10, 5 pages, reprinted from *Manual of Psychiatry*—seventh edition '38, original edition '05—formerly published by John Wiley & Sons, Inc. and now out of print]; no data on reliability; $3.75 per 50 tests, postage extra; specimen set not available; administration time not reported; G. H. Kent and A. J. Rosanoff; C. H. Stoelting Co. *

REFERENCES

1. KENT, GRACE HELEN, AND ROSANOFF, A. J. "A Study of Association in Insanity." *Am J Insanity* 67:37-96, 317-90 Jl, O '10. *

2. WELLS, FREDERIC LYMAN. "A Preliminary Note on the Categories of Association Reactions." *Psychol R* 18:229-33 Jl '11. *

3. WOODWORTH, R. S., AND WELLS, FREDERIC LYMAN. "Association Tests." *Psychol Monogr* 13(6):73-9 D '11. *

4. EASTMAN, FREDERIC C., AND ROSANOFF, A. J. "Association in Feeble-Minded and Delinquent Children." *Am J Insanity* 69:125-41 Jl '12. *

5. WELLS, FREDERIC LYMAN. "The Question of Association Types." *Psychol R* 19:253-70 Jl '12. *

6. ROSANOFF, ISABEL R., AND ROSANOFF, A. J. "A Study of Association in Children." *Psychol R* 24:43-89 Ja '13. *

7. STRONG, EDWARD K., JR. "A Comparison Between Experimental Data and Clinical Results in Manic-Depressive Insanity." *Am J Psychol* 24:66-98 Ja '13. *

8. OTIS, MARGARET. "A Study of Association in Defectives." *J Ed Psychol* 6:271-88 My '15. *

9. WHIPPLE, GUY MONTROSE. *Manual of Mental and Physical Tests: Part 2, Complex Processes, Second Edition,* pp. 53-71. Baltimore, Md.: Warwick & York, Inc., 1915. Pp. v, 336. *

10. WOODROW, HERBERT, AND LOWELL, FRANCES. "Children's Association Frequency Tables." *Psychol Monogr* 22(5):1-97 '16. *

11. HORN, JOHN LEWIS. "A Case of Pathological Day Dreaming." *Psychol Clinic* 12:89-101 My '18. *

12. OSCHRIN, ELSIE. "Vocational Tests for Retail Saleswomen." *J Appl Psychol* 2:148-55 Je '18. *

13. MITCHELL, IDA; ROSANOFF, ISABEL R.; AND ROSANOFF, A. J. "A Study of Association in Negro Children." *Psychol R* 26:354-9 S '19. *

14. MATEER, FLORENCE. "The Future of Clinical Psychology." *J Delinq* 6:283-93 Ja '21. *

15. MURPHY, GARDNER M. "A Comparison of Manic-Depressive and Dementia Praecox Cases by the Free-Association Method." *Am J Insanity* 77:545-58 Ap '21. *

16. MURPHY, GARDNER M. "Types of Word-Association in Dementia Praecox, Manic-Depressives and Normal Persons." *Am J Psychiatry* 2:539-71 Ap '23. *

17. HUBBARD, LUCILLE M. "Complex Signs in Diagnostic Free Association." *J Exp Psychol* 7:342-57 O '24. *

18. CASON, HULSEY, AND CASON, ELOISE BOEKER. "Association Tendencies and Learning Ability." *J Exp Psychol* 8:167-89 Je '25. *

19. ROSANOFF, AARON J. Chap. 7, "Free Association Test (Kent-Rosanoff)," pp. 546-620. In his *Manual of Psychiatry, Sixth Edition.* New York: John Wiley & Sons, Inc., 1927. Pp. xvii, 697. *

20. WELLS, F. L. Chap. 9, "The Free Association Experiment," pp. 192-231. In his *Mental Tests in Clinical Practice.* Yonkers, N.Y.: World Book Co., 1927. Pp. x, 315. *

21. ELONEN, ANNA S., AND WOODROW, HERBERT. "Group Tests of Psychopathic Tendencies in Children." *J Abn & Social Psychol* 23:315-27 O-D '28. * (*PA* 3:1942)

22. O'CONNOR, JOHNSON. Chap. 2, "Personality," pp. 37-47; and Appendix C, "Responses Given by Two Thousand People in the Free Association Experiment," pp. 225-310. In his *Born That Way.* Baltimore, Md.: Williams & Wilkins Co., 1928. Pp. 323. *

23. McFADDEN, JOHN HOLMAN. *Differential Responses of Normal and Feebleminded Subjects of Equal Mental Age, on the Kent-Rosanoff Free Association Test and the Stanford Revision of the Binet-Simon Intelligence Test.* Doctor's thesis, University of North Carolina (Chapel Hill, N.C.), 1930.

24. SCHELLENBERG, PETER E. *A Group Free-Association Test for College Students.* Doctor's thesis, University of Minnesota (Minneapolis, Minn.), 1930.

25. McFADDEN, JOHN HOLMAN. *Differential Responses of Normal and Feebleminded Subjects of Equal Mental Age, on the Kent-Rosanoff Free Association Test and the Stanford Revision of the Binet-Simon Intelligence Test.* Mental Measurement Monographs No. 7. Baltimore, Md.: Williams & Wilkins Co., 1931. Pp. 85. * (*PA* 5:2589)

26. SYMONDS, PERCIVAL M. Chap. 10, "The Free Association Method," pp. 361-99. In his *Diagnosing Personality and Conduct.* New York: Century Co., 1931. Pp. xvi, 602. *

27. THORNDIKE, EDWARD L. "The Significance of Responses in the Free Association Test." *J Appl Psychol* 16:247-53 Je '32. * (*PA* 7:4323)

28. TENDLER, A. D. "Associative Tendencies in Psychoneurotics." *Psychol Clinic* 22:108-16 Je-Ag '33. *

29. LASLETT, H. R., AND BENNETT, ELIZABETH. "A Comparison of Scores on Two Measures of Personality." *J Abn & Social Psychol* 28:459-61 Ja-Mr '34. * (*PA* 8:4158)

30. SHLAUDEMAN, KARL WHITMAN. *A Correlational Analysis of Idiosyncrasy of Response to Tests of Association, Interest, and Personality.* Doctor's thesis, Stanford University (Stanford, Calif.), 1936.

31. KEPHART, NEWELL C., AND HOUTCHENS, H. MAX. "The Effect of the Stimulus Word Used Upon Scores in the Association-Motor Test." *Am J Psychiatry* 94:393-9 S '37. * (*PA* 12:1222)

32. WHITE, RALPH KIRBY. *A Factor Analysis of Tests Designed to Measure Fluency, Atypicality, and Intellectual Curiosity.* Doctor's thesis, Stanford University (Stanford, Calif.), 1937.

33. MEYERS, RUSSELL, AND BRECHER, SYLVIA. "The So-Called Epileptic Personality as Investigated by the Kent-Rosanoff Test." *J Abn & Social Psychol* 36:413-22 Jl '41. * (*PA* 15:5165)

34. KORCHIN, SHELDON JEROME. *A Comparative Study of Three Projective Techniques in the Measurement of Frustration-Reaction Types.* Master's thesis, Clark University (Worcester, Mass.), 1943.

35. SPOERL, DOROTHY TILDEN. "Bilinguality and Emotional Adjustment." *J Abn & Social Psychol* 38:37-57 Ja '43. * (*PA* 17:3837)

36. ROSEN, HJALMAR. *Correlations Between the Schellenberg Free Association Test and the Minnesota Multiphasic Personality Inventory.* Master's thesis, University of Minnesota (Minneapolis, Minn.), 1944.

37. SCHNACK, GEORGE F.; SHAKOW, DAVID; AND LIVELY, MARY L. "Studies in Insulin and Metrazol Therapy: 1, The Differential Prognostic Value of Some Psychological Tests." *J Personality* 14:106-24 D '45. * (*PA* 20:3669)

38. SCHNACK, GEORGE F.; SHAKOW, DAVID; AND LIVELY, MARY L. "Studies in Insulin and Metrazol Therapy: 2, Differential Effects on Some Psychological Functions." *J Personality* 14:125-49 D '45. * (*PA* 20:3669)

39. TENDLER, ALEXANDER D. "Significant Features of Disturbance in Free Association." *J Psychol* 20:65-89 Jl '45. * (*PA* 19:3392)

40. FRENCH, VERA V. "The Structure of Sentiments: 2, A Preliminary Study of Sentiments." *J Personality* 16:78-108 S '47. * (*PA* 22:2512)

41. MUENCH, GEORGE A. *An Evaluation of Non-Directive*

Psychotherapy by Means of the Rorschach and Other Indices. Applied Psychology Monographs of the American Psychological Association, No. 13. Stanford University, Calif.: Stanford University Press, 1947. Pp. 163. * (*PA* 22:320)

42. LEVI, MARIO. *An Analysis of the Influence of Two Different Cultures on Responses to the Rosanoff Free Association Test.* Master's thesis, University of Chicago (Chicago, Ill.), 1949.

43. SMITH, HENRY CLAY. "Psychometric Checks on Hypotheses Derived From Sheldon's Work on Physique and Temperament." *J Personality* 17:310–20 Mr '49. * (*PA* 25:2916)

44. KEENE, CHARLES M. *Commonality of Response on a Word-Association Test: A Study of Standardization Procedures and an Attempt to Forecast Moderate Emotional Maladjustment.* Doctor's thesis, Stanford University (Stanford, Calif.), 1951.

45. TRESSELT, M. E., AND LEEDS, D. S. "The Frequencies of Responses by 124 Males and Females (Ages 22–25) for Each of the 100 Kent-Rosanoff Stimulus Words." *Psychol Newsl* 5:39–74 D '53. *

46. TRESSELT, M. E., AND LEEDS, DON S. "The Responses and Frequencies of Responses for Males and Females (18–21) to the Kent-Rosanoff Word List." *Psychol Newsl* 5:1–36 S–O '53. * (*PA* 28:7557)

47. RUSSELL, WALLACE A., AND JENKINS, JAMES J. *The Complete Minnesota Norms for Responses to 100 Words From the Kent-Rosanoff Word Association Test.* Studies on the Role of Language in Behavior, Technical Report No. 11. Contract No. N8-ONR-66216, University of Minnesota (Minneapolis, Minn.), August 1954. Pp. 42. *

48. TRESSELT, M. E., AND LEEDS, DONALD S. "The Responses and Frequencies of Responses for Males and Females (26–29) to the Kent-Rosanoff Word List." *Psychol Newsl* 5:144–77 Jl–Ag '54. *

49. TRESSELT, M. E., AND LEEDS, DONALD S. "The Kent-Rosanoff Word Association: 1, New Frequencies for Ages 18–21 and a Comparison With Kent-Rosanoff Frequencies." *J Genetic Psychol* 87:145–8 S '55. * (*PA* 30:7230)

50. TRESSELT, M. E., AND LEEDS, DONALD S. "The Responses and Frequencies of Responses for Males and Females (Ages 30–33 Years) to the Kent-Rosanoff Word List." *Psychol Newsl* 6:95–127 My–Je '55. * (*PA* 30:4606)

51. TRESSELT, M. E.; LEEDS, DONALD S.; AND MAYZNER, MARK S., JR. "The Kent-Rosanoff Word Association: 2, A Comparison of Sex Differences in Response Frequencies." *J Genetic Psychol* 87:149–53 S '55. * (*PA* 30:7231)

52. BECHER, BARBARA ANN. *The Effect of Education and Intelligence on Community of Responses in the Kent-Rosanoff Free Association Test.* Master's thesis, Fordham University (New York, N.Y.), 1956.

53. HERR, VINCENT V. "The Loyola Language Study." *J Clin Psychol* 13:258–62 Jl '57. * (*PA* 32:5501)

54. PETERSON, MARJORIE SCHAEFER, AND JENKINS, JAMES J. *Word Association Phenomena at the Individual Level: A Pair of Case Studies.* Studies on the Role of Language in Behavior, Technical Report No. 16. Contract No. N8-ONR-66216, University of Minnesota (Minneapolis, Minn.), April 1957. Pp. 49.

55. BOYER, ROSCOE A., AND ELTON, CHARLES F. "Effect of Instructions on Free Association." *J Ed Psychol* 49:304–8 D '58. * (*PA* 36:2CIo4B)

56. COFER, CHARLES N. "Comparison of Word Associations Obtained by the Methods of Discrete Single Word and Continued Association." *Psychol Rep* 4:507–10 S '58. * (*PA* 33:5564)

57. TRESSELT, M. E. "The Kent-Rosanoff Word Association List and Geographical Location." *Psychol Newsl* 10:22–6 S–O '58. * (*PA* 33:3597)

58. JENKINS, JAMES J. "Effects on Word-Association of the Set to Give Popular Responses." *Psychol Rep* 5:94 Mr '59. * (*PA* 34:917)

59. SARASON, IRWIN G. "Relationships of Measures of Anxiety and Experimental Instructions to Word Association Test Performance." *J Abn & Social Psychol* 59:37–42 Jl '59. * (*PA* 34:4621)

60. TRESSELT, M. E. "The Responses and Frequencies of Responses for 108 Subjects (Ages 34–41 Years) to the Kent-Rosanoff Word List." *Psychol Newsl* 10:176–212 Mr–Ap '59. * (*PA* 34:1431)

61. BECHER, BARBARA ANN. "A Cross-Sectional and Longitudinal Study of the Effect of Education on Free Association Responses." *J Genetic Psychol* 97:23–8 S '60. * (*PA* 35:6979)

62. BLOCK, JACK. "Commonality in Word Association and Personality." *Psychol Rep* 7:332 O '60. * (*PA* 35:2202)

63. JENKINS, JAMES J. "Commonality of Association as an Indicator of More General Patterns of Verbal Behavior," pp. 307–29. In *Style in Language.* Edited by Thomas A. Sebeok. New York: John Wiley & Sons, Inc., 1960. Pp. xvii, 470. * (*PA* 35:288)

64. JENKINS, JAMES J., AND RUSSELL, WALLACE A. "Systematic Changes in Word Association Norms: 1910–1952." *J Abn & Social Psychol* 60:293–304 My '60. * (*PA* 35:4958)

65. KANFER, FREDERICK H. "Word Association and the Drive Hypothesis of Anxiety." *J Clin Psychol* 16:200–4 Ap '60. * (*PA* 36:2HKooK)

66. SOMMER, ROBERT, AND OSMOND, HUMPHRY. "Association Methods in Anthropology." *Am Anthrop* 62:1051–3 D '60. *

67. SOMMER, ROBERT; DEWAR, ROBERT; AND OSMOND, HUMPHRY. "Is There a Schizophrenic Language?" *Arch Gen Psychiatry* 3:665–73 D '60. * (*PA* 35:3846)

68. TRESSELT, M. E. "The Responses and Frequencies of Responses for 122 Subjects (Ages 42–54 Years) to the Kent-Rosanoff Word List." *J Psychol Studies* 11:118–46 Ja–F '60. * (*PA* 34:7613)

69. ROSENZWEIG, MARK R. "Comparisons Among Word-Association Responses in English, French, German, and Italian." *Am J Psychol* 74:347–60 S '61. * (*PA* 36:3HI47R)

70. ROTHKOPF, ERNST Z., AND COKE, ESTHER U. "Intralist Association Data for 99 Words of the Kent-Rosanoff Word List." *Psychol Rep* 8:463–74 Je '61. * (*PA* 36:2HC63R)

71. ROTHKOPF, ERNST Z., AND COKE, ESTHER U. "The Prediction of Free Recall From Word Association Measures." *J Exp Psychol* 62:433–8 N '61. * (*PA* 37:450)

72. CARROLL, JOHN B.; KJELDERGAARD, PAUL M.; AND CARTON, AARON S. "Number of Opposites Versus Number of Primaries as a Response Measure in Free-Association Tests." *J Verbal Learning & Verbal Behav* 1:22–30 Jl '62. * (*PA* 37:6107)

73. KJELDERGAARD, PAUL M. "Commonality Scores Under Instructions to Give Opposites." Reply by Ray A. Craddick. *Psychol Rep* 11:219–20, reply 238 Ag '62. * (*PA* 37:4983, 4953)

74. PALERMO, DAVID S., AND JENKINS, JAMES J. "Superordinates, 'Maturity' and Logical Analyses of Language." *Psychol Rep* 10:437–8 Ap '62. * (*PA* 37:2843)

75. EICHLER, HERBERT. *Word Association: Commonality and Popularity.* Doctor's thesis, University of Rochester (Rochester, N.Y.), 1963. (*DA* 24:2556)

76. HORTON, DAVID L.; MARLOWE, DAVID; AND CROWNE, DOUGLAS P. "The Effect of Instructional Set and Need for Social Approval on Commonality of Word Association Responses." *J Abn & Social Psychol* 66:67–72 Ja '63. * (*PA* 37:4905)

77. HORVATH, WILLIAM J. "A Stochastic Model for Word Association Tests." *Psychol R* 70:361–4 Jl '63. * (*PA* 38:2626)

78. KJELDERGAARD, PAUL M., AND CARROLL, JOHN B. "Two Measures of Free Association Response and Their Relations to Scores on Selected Personality and Verbal Ability Tests." *Psychol Rep* 12:667–70 Je '63. * (*PA* 38:6021)

79. PALERMO, DAVID S. "Word Associations and Children's Verbal Behavior," pp. 31–68. In *Advances in Child Development and Behavior, Vol. 1.* Edited by Lewis P. Lipsitt and Charles C. Spiker. New York: Academic Press, Inc., 1963. Pp. xiii, 387. *

80. PALERMO, DAVID S., AND JENKINS, JAMES J. "Frequency of Superordinate Responses to a Word Association Test as a Function of Age." *J Verbal Learning & Verbal Behav* 1:378–83 F '63. *

81. TRESSELT, M. E., AND MAYZNER, M. S. "The Kent-Rosanoff Word Association: Word Association Norms as a Function of Age." *Psychon Sci* 1:65–6 Ap '64. *

82. WYNNE, RONALD D. "Are Normal Word Association Norms Suitable for Schizophrenics?" *Psychol Rep* 14:121–2 F '64. * (*PA* 39:2734)

JERRY S. WIGGINS, *Associate Professor of Psychology, University of Illinois, Urbana, Illinois.*

The *Kent-Rosanoff Free Association Test* is the oldest of tests to be reviewed in this issue of the MMY. The test itself is more than a half-century old at this writing, and the technique is as old as scientific psychology. In 1879 Francis Galton [1] wrote a variety of single words on separate pieces of paper and tucked them under a book for future reference. At monthly intervals, he presented the words to himself singly and timed the interval between stimulus presentation and the occurrence of two different ideas. Following the occurrence of ideas, Galton attempted to determine their origin in his own experience by introspection.

[1] GALTON, FRANCIS. "Psychometric Experiments." *Brain* 2:149–62 Jl '79. *
GALTON, FRANCIS. "Psychometric Facts." *Nineteenth Century* 5:425–33 Mr '79.*

He felt that collection of normative data on associations would be of interest and clearly anticipated the possibilities of the technique for individual diagnosis: "They lay bare the foundations of a man's thoughts with a curious distinctness, and exhibit his mental anatomy with more vividness and truth than he would probably care to publish to the world."

Galton's technique was modified in Wundt's laboratory by Trautscholdt [2] who presented words to observers and recorded their reaction time. More precise measures of reaction time were obtained by Cattell [3] by use of lip and voice keys. Cattell and Bryant [4] seem to have been the first to employ a list of stimulus words which were presented visually to the subject. Wundt's student Emil Kraepelin [5] was among the first to recognize the application of the technique to the study of psychopathological conditions. In addition to practice effects, his students studied the effects of drugs, fatigue and hunger on free associations. Both Jung [6] and Wertheimer [7] claimed to have originated the method of individual diagnosis of pathological states on the basis of association records.

Interest in the association experiment was so widespread at the turn of the century that a full account would be almost indistinguishable from a general treatise on the psychology of that era. Several historical reviews of the association technique are available.[8] The approach of Kent and Rosanoff was based on the work of Sommer,[9] who felt that types of mental disorder were reflected in specific forms of word association and that the test could be employed in differential diagnosis. The principal contribution of Kent and Rosanoff was their attempted *standardization* of associations to 100 stimulus words (66 of which were from Sommer's list) by reference to frequency tables based on 1,000 normal adults. That this, in itself, was considered no minor achievement for that day is indicated by the report of the APA Committee on Standardizing Procedure in Experimental Tests: "None of the 'mental tests' possesses this quality [standardization] to a degree comparable with the free association experiment, within the limits of the English language. This is mainly due to the work of Kent and Rosanoff which established a definite standard of normality for a specific association material" (*3*, p. *73*).

In his pioneering investigations of the diagnostic possibilities of free association, Jung had all but abandoned logical and grammatical analysis of the relations between stimuli and associations in psychiatric groups in favor of such measures as reaction time (under speed instructions) and recall of original associations ("reproduction") as indices of individual complexes. Kent and Rosanoff (*1, 19*) chose to ignore both the reaction time and reproduction aspects of the procedure because of their interest in logical and grammatical analysis and the statistical differentiation of diagnostic groups. The different emphases of Jung and Kent-Rosanoff procedures parallel the differences between the dynamic (Freud) and descriptive (Kraepelin) psychiatries of that day.[10] Whipple (*9*) suggested that the K-R associations be timed and it has now become fairly standard procedure to obtain measures of both reaction time and reproduction with the K-R list.

NORMS. The original normative material for the K-R test was based on the associations of 1,000 "mixed adults" who varied widely in age, occupation, mental capacity, education and regional location (*1*). Later normative studies were based on 1,000 adult male factory workers (*22*), 925 entering students at the University of Minnesota (*24*), 500 Stanford stu-

2 TRAUTSCHOLDT, MARTIN. "Experimentelle Untersuchungen über die Association der Vorstellungen." *Philosophische Studien* 1:213–50 '83. *

3 CATTELL, JAMES McKEEN. "Experiments on the Association of Ideas." *Mind* 12:68–74 Ja '87. *

4 CATTELL, J. McK., AND BRYANT, SOPHIE. "Mental Association Investigated by Experiment." Comments by G. F. Stout, F. Y. Edgeworth, E. P. Hughes, C. E. Collet, and S. Bryant. *Mind* 14:230–50 Ap '89. *

5 KRAEPELIN, EMIL. "Der Psychologische Versuch in der Psychiatrie." *Psychologische Arbeiten* 1:1–91 '96. *
KRAEPELIN, EMIL. *Uber die Beeinflussung Einfacher Psychischer Vorgange Durch Einige Arzneimittel.* Jena, Germany: Gustave Fisher Verlag, 1892. Pp. viii, 258.

6 JUNG, C. G., AND OTHERS. *Studies in Word Association: Experiments in the Diagnosis of Psychopathological Conditions Carried Out at the Psychiatric Clinic of the University of Zurich.* Translated by M. D. Eder. London: William Heinemann (Medical Books) Ltd., 1918. Pp. ix, 575. *

7 WERTHEIMER, MAX. "Experimentelle Untersuchungen zur Tatbestandsdiagnostik." *Archiv für die Gesamte Psychologie* 6:59–131 Ag '05. *
WERTHEIMER, MAX, AND KLEIN, J. "Psychologische Tatbestandsdiagnostik." *Archiv für Kriminal-Anthropologie* 15:72–113 '04. *

8 CLAPAREDE, EDOUARD. *L'Association des Idées.* Paris: Octave Doin, Editeur, 1903. Pp. 427. *
JUNG et al., op. cit.
KOHS, SAMUEL C. "The Association Method in Its Relation to the Complex and Complex Indicators." *Am J Psychol* 25:544–94 O '14. *
RAPAPORT, DAVID. *Emotions and Memory.* Menninger Clinic Monograph Series, No. 2. Baltimore, Md.: Williams & Wilkins Co., 1942. Pp. ix, 282. *
WARREN, HOWARD C. *A History of the Association Psychology.* New York: Charles Scribner's Sons, 1921. Pp. ix, 328. *
WOODWORTH, ROBERT S. Chap. 15, "Association," pp. 340–67. In *Experimental Psychology.* New York: Henry Holt & Co., Inc., 1938. Pp. xi, 889. *

9 SOMMER, ROBERT. *Lehrbuch der Psychopathologischen Untersuchungsmethoden.* Berlin, Germany: Urban & Schwarzenberg, 1899. Pp. vi, 399.
10 RAPAPORT, op. cit.

dents (*44*), and 1,008 students of introductory psychology at the University of Minnesota (*47*). In recent years the latter norms of Russell and Jenkins (*47*) seem to have become the most widely used. A comparison of these several normative studies and especially the 1930 and 1954 norms for Minnesota students has been made by Jenkins and Russell (*64*). Although the normative groups are not directly comparable in terms of sampling characteristics, method of administration and method of recording response, some secular trends were noted (*64*). The most popular associations to stimuli ("primaries") appear to be highly stable and to be increasing in their popularity over time. A decrease in the popularity of superordinate responses was also detected.

Norms have been collected for the associations of normal children (*6, 10, 13*) and for mentally defective children (*4, 8*). Normative data from subjects representing a variety of ages, occupations and geographical locations have been collected by Tresselt and Leeds (*45–6, 48–51, 57, 60, 68*). German,[11] French,[12] and Italian (*42*) translations have also appeared and have been studied in their native groups. As one would expect, differences have been reported in the association patterns of these diverse groups, although the uniformities are perhaps more impressive. In directly comparing associations given to English, French, German and Italian versions of the K-R list, Rosenzweig (*69*) found considerable agreement in the meaning of primaries given in each language. Opposite responses and adjective-adjective responses likewise were in agreement among the different forms.

SCORING PROCEDURES. Kent and Rosanoff classified associations as *common* (appearing in the normative tables), *doubtful* (grammatical variants of common words) and *individual*. The latter category was in turn divided into *normal* (on the basis of a set of rules) and *pathological* reactions. Pathological reactions are further classified into categories reflecting perseverative, neologistic, vague and peculiar linguistic habits. Variants of the K-R scoring procedure (of which there are many) tend to

emphasize *grammatical* (noun-adjective), *logical* (contrast), *disturbance* (long reaction time), or *content* categories although the last is employed sparingly even by psychoanalytic writers.[13] Classification systems have been, for the most part, derivatives of the highly elaborate scheme of Jung. Wells (*2*) introduced a modified version of Jung's system which was later further reduced (*20*). Woodworth [14] reviews early classification systems and offers one of his own. Aside from their general unwieldiness, elaborate classification systems suffer from intrinsic unreliability due to arbitrary decisions and frequent category overlap. The number of categories employed in recent years has tended to be smaller and more reliable [15] (*39*).

COMMONALITY. By reference to the K-R tables it is possible to obtain for a subject a commonality score which summarizes that subject's normalcy or typicality with reference to the standardization group. A crude index of commonality may be obtained by tabulating the number of associations per 100 words which appear (irrespective of frequency) in the K-R tables. A more precise index is obtained by calculating the median value of associations based on the actual percentage of occurrence of the associations in the K-R tables.[16] An index which has recently come back into favor (*63*) is provided by counting the number of "primary" (highest frequency) associations given per 100 words.

Commonality of response appears to be related to scores on the Taylor Manifest Anxiety Scale,[17] especially under ego-involving instructions (*59*), but this relationship cannot always be expected to obtain (*65*). Although the *California Psychological Inventory* has a "communality scale," there is a surprising lack of relationship between K-R commonality and all the items of this inventory (*62*). The most systematic investigation of the commonality dimension is found in the work of Jenkins and his associates (*63*). The basic strategy here is

11 RUSSELL, WALLACE A., AND MESECK, OSKAR R. "Der Einfluss der Assoziation auf das Erinnern von Worten in der Deutschen, Französischen und Englischen Sprache." *Zeitschrift für Experimentelle und Angewandte Psychologie* 6(2): 191–211 '59. * (PA 34:3982)
12 ROSENZWEIG, MARK R. "Études sur L'Association des Mots." *L'Année Psychologique* 57(1):23–32 '57. * (PA 33:1163)

13 RAPAPORT, DAVID; GILL, MERTON; AND SCHAFER, ROY. Chap. 2, "The Word Association Test," pp. 13–84. In *Diagnostic Psychological Testing: Vol. 2, The Theory, Statistical Evaluation, and Diagnostic Application of a Battery of Tests.* Chicago: Year Book Publishers, Inc., 1946. Pp. xi, 516. *
14 WOODWORTH, *op. cit.*
15 SIIPOLA, ELSA; WALKER, NANNETTE W.; AND KOLB, DOROTHY. "Task Attitudes in Word Association, Projective and Nonprojective." *J Personality* 23:441–59 Je '55. * (PA 30:2922)
16 WOODWORTH, *op. cit.*
17 BUCHWALD, ALEXANDER M. "Manifest Anxiety-Level, Verbal Response-Strength and Paired-Associate Learning." *Am J Psychol* 72:89–93 Mr '59. * (PA 34:763)

to separate subjects into high and low commonality groups on the basis of associations to
the K-R and contrast the performance of such
groups in biographical reports, personality and
value inventory responses, learning tasks and a
variety of verbal and nonverbal situations. In
accord with previous suggestive evidence (54)
commonality emerged as an important variable
in situations involving a wide variety of intraverbal connections. High commonality generalizes to other word association tasks, is associated with a tendency to make "substitution" responses and is a definite asset in learning high (but not low) strength stimulus-
response pairs.

Aside from the evidence presented for the
centrality of commonality as an intraverbal
stylistic index, Jenkins' (63) findings with respect to personological correlates are not encouraging. Biographical information, reported
social activities, desire for social participation
and conformity were essentially unrelated to
high and low commonality status. Scores on
the *Study of Values* were likewise unrelated
to commonality status. In accord with other
investigators (36, 78), *low* negative correlations were obtained between adjustment scores
(in this case MMPI) and commonality.
MMPI profiles of low commonality subjects
were also found to be somewhat less stable over
time. Jenkins' excellent formulation of the measurement model underlying the construct of
commonality should provide ample discouragement for those who seek simple linear relations
between commonality and personality traits
(63). Elsewhere, the unitary nature of the commonality score itself has been challenged (78).

DIFFERENTIAL DIAGNOSIS. The classic and
frequently cited main result of Kent and
Rosanoff's work may be summarized as follows: when *all* of the associations of a heterogeneous group of psychiatric patients are
pooled, 27 per cent of these associations are not
to be found in the tables for normal adults.
This manner of presenting data, which was
characteristic of early workers, does not allow
for an evaluation of the discriminatory efficiency of the test. It is not clear whether we
should expect the *average* patient to give 27
per cent individual reactions or 27 per cent of
patients to give exclusively individual reactions
and the remaining patients all common reactions. Some indication of overlap may be gained

from a table (*1*, p. 330) comparing a group of
53 normals, who gave more than 15 individual reactions, with several unselected clinical
groups. This group of untypical normals gave
a *higher* proportion of individual reactions than
were found in paranoids, manic-depressives and
general paretics. Subsequent research, based
primarily on schizophrenics, has suggested that
although psychiatric patients tend to give fewer
primary responses, their basic patterns of response hierarchies are the same as normals
(82) and there appear to be no *uniquely* schizophrenic associations (67).

Early and comprehensive investigations by
Murphy (*15-6*) evaluated the diagnostic efficiency of some thirteen logical classifications of
association in discriminating among normals,
schizophrenics, and manic-depressives. His
carefully conducted study "shows in every case
overlapping of the groups, and in most cases
no significant differences in central tendencies"
(16). Overlapping and reversals in signs among
normal, manic and depressed subjects had been
noted earlier by Strong (7). A critical review
of the diagnostic research of the first two
decades of the K-R list led Symonds to conclude: "The method, therefore, is presumptive
or indicative only and cannot in its present
stage safely be used alone in the diagnosis of
insanity" (26). As representative of more recently published negative findings, we may cite
a failure to distinguish epileptics from non-
epileptics (33) and a failure to distinguish
brain-damaged patients from normals.[18]

On the basis of the literature to date and his
own work with neurotics, Tendler (28, 39)
concluded that individual reactions, recall disturbances, slow reaction time and adjective-
noun reactions were of the greatest value for
differential diagnosis. Accordingly, the percentage of each of these categories was tabulated
for all K-R stimuli in 60 adult clinic cases. The
mean percentage of these four categories
served as an index of "stimulus potency,"
which was used to select a subset of 25 K-R
stimuli with the greatest potential for eliciting
such categories. This revised list was administered to a sample of 120 psychiatric in- and
out-patients and the four categories, plus contrast, scored. Corrected odd-even reliabilities

18 APPELBAUM, STEPHEN A. "Automatic and Selective Processes in the Word Associations of Brain-Damaged and Normal Subjects." *J Personality* 28:64–72 Mr '60. * (PA
36:3JF64A)

of the five categories ranged from .80 to .95. On the basis of category intercorrelations, partial correlations, and enthusiastic extrapolations, Tendler (*39*) concluded that contrast responses are characteristic of normals, adjective-noun responses of neurotics and individual responses of psychotics. Percentile scores were determined from a psychiatric population and median splits on contrast, adjective-noun and individual responses employed for a type of profile analysis (e.g., high C, low A-N, high I). The frequency of various profile types in a hospital and a clinic sample offers partial support for this approach, as do the 12 individual cases presented. Aside from minor technical considerations such as the comparability of some of the samples contrasted, the data presented by Tendler do not allow for adequate estimates of the amount of overlap involved when categories are compared among normal, neurotic, and psychotic groups. Although the trends are clear, their utility for diagnostic work is difficult to assess.

INDIVIDUAL COMPLEXES. In addition to demonstrating the applicability of the association method to the detection of individual conflicts, Jung and his associates [19] performed pioneering work in experimental psychopathology by demonstrating the modifiability of associations under distraction conditions and establishing the relation of physiological indices, such as GSR and respiration, to other indices of associative disturbance. Since an individual "complex" is more of a construct than a criterion, early American investigations emphasized the consistency of such indices rather than their diagnostic efficiency. Wells (*5*) reports consistencies in reaction times on two occasions, as well as a "definite fidelity to type" with respect to logical categories of association. The intercorrelations among nine complex signs were studied by Hull and Lugoff [20] under the reasoning that signs which exhibit the greatest covariation with other signs are the most "reliable" diagnostic indices. Repetition and misunderstanding of the stimulus were the most reliable by this criterion, while long reaction time and defective reproduction shared somewhat less common variance with the other signs than was expected. Hull and Lugoff found later

repetition of an association to be of doubtful significance and Hubbard (*17*) likewise failed to find evidence of a perseverative tendency in subsequent reaction times.

Pathological associations are only slightly correlated with neuroticism on the Woodworth Inventory (*21*) and not at all with neuroticism on the Bernreuter (*29*). However, pathological associations are related ($r = .57$) to the rated adjustment of children (*21*). Individual associations are correlated with sales success (*12*) and may be slightly related to psychiatric prognosis (*37–8*), but they are unrelated to body type (*43*). Associative reaction time does not appear to be related to psychometric introversion-extraversion,[21] although such a relationship might be anticipated (*22*). Under relaxed instructions, reaction time and contrast responses appear related to impulsivity and Allport-Vernon-Lindzey values.[22] Reaction time, contrast, and adjective-noun responses are correlated with the Depression Scale of the MMPI.[23]

Aside from their possible reflection of underlying complexes, the Jungian diagnostic signs are highly sensitive to procedural modification or situational pressures. Conditions of distraction,[24] satiation,[25] ego-involvement (*59*), time pressure [26] (*76*), practice,[27] or instructional sets [28] will produce differences in such indices. Alternative (although not incompatible) interpretations of the significance of such complex indicators as long reaction time and reproduction disturbances have been made [29] by appeal to the well established principles that associative reaction time is inversely related to the frequency with which the stimulus ap-

19 JUNG *et al., op. cit.*
20 HULL, CLARK L., AND LUGOFF, L. S. "Complex Signs in Diagnostic Free Association." *J Exp Psychol* 4:111–36 Ap '21. *

21 DUNN, SANDRA; BLISS, JOAN; AND SIIPOLA, ELSA. "Effects of Impulsivity, Introversion, and Individual Values Upon Association Under Free Conditions." *J Personality* 26:61–76 Mr '58. * (*PA* 33:5742)
22 DUNN *et al., op. cit.*
23 MACHOVER, SOLOMON, AND SCHWARTZ, ANITA. "A Homeostatic Effect of Mood on Associative Abstractness and Reaction Time." *J Personality* 21:59–67 S '52. * (*PA* 27:5697)
24 JUNG *et al., op. cit.*
25 SMITH, DONALD E. P., AND RAYGOR, ALTON L. "Verbal Satiation and Personality." *J Abn & Social Psychol* 52:323–6 My '56. * (*PA* 31:4368)
26 FLAVELL, JOHN H.; DRAGUNS, JURIS; FEINBERG, LEONARD D.; AND BUDIN, WILLIAM. "A Microgenetic Approach to Word Association." *J Abn & Social Psychol* 57:1–7 Jl '58. * (*PA* 33:8338)
SIIPOLA *et al., op. cit.*
27 WELLS, FREDERIC LYMAN. "Practice Effects in Free Association." *Am J Psychol* 22:1–13 Ja '11. *
28 HULL AND LUGOFF, *op. cit.*
MARSTON, WILLIAM M. "Reaction-Time Symptoms of Deception." *J Exp Psychol* 3:72–87 F '20. *
MILGRAM, NORMAN, AND GOODGLASS, HAROLD. "Role Style Versus Cognitive Maturation in Word Associations of Adults and Children." *J Personality* 29:81–93 Mr '61. *
29 LAFFAL, JULIUS. "Response Faults in Word Association as a Function of Response Entropy." *J Abn & Social Psychol* 50:265–70 Mr '55. * (*PA* 30:486)

pears in the language [30] (*18*) and positively related to the number of alternative associations which exist for the stimulus.[31]

The modifiability of complex indicators under experimental manipulations and the interpretation of such effects within the broad context of verbal learning (*27*) have, no doubt, contributed to the central position which the word association task occupies in contemporary experimental personality. A considerable literature exists which attests to the fruitfulness of the association test as a laboratory technique for the study of defense mechanisms, emphasizing particularly the modern concepts of "sensitization" and "repression." [32]

SUMMARY. The *Kent-Rosanoff Free Association Test* has enjoyed widespread use in both laboratory and clinic for more than half a century. Unlike many other "mental tests" it has retained its position as a standard laboratory technique because of its lawful relations to other kinds of verbal behavior of interest to verbal learning specialists and because of its utility in the laboratory as an objective measure of certain "defense mechanisms." For these reasons the K-R test occupies a singular position among current psychological tests in that we seem to know more about the mechanisms which underlie responses to this test than we do about the correlates of these responses. This is not to deny that many isolated studies of the personological and adjustmental correlates of response to this test have yielded "promising" or "suggestive" results. Rather, it is to emphasize the fact that no systematic large scale efforts have been made to develop the instrument as a "personality test," in the current usage of these words, since its inception in 1910. Since the test was judged by the critics of 20 and 30 years ago to be unacceptable as a routine device for individual or differential diagnosis, it is not surprising that, in its present unchanged

30 SCHLOSBERG, HAROLD, AND HEINEMAN, CHARLES. "The Relationship Between Two Measures of Response Strength." *J Exp Psychol* 40:235-47 Ap '50. * (*PA* 24:6245)
THUMB, ALBERT, AND MARBE, KARL. *Experimentelle Untersuchungen uber die Psychologischen Grundlagen der Sprachlichen Analogiebildung.* Leipzig, Germany: Englemann, 1901. Pp. 87.
31 LAFFAL, *op. cit.*
WIGGINS, JERRY S. "Two Determinants of Associative Reaction Time." *J Exp Psychol* 54:144-7 Ag '57. * (*PA* 33:755)
32 CARLSON, V. R. "Individual Differences in Recall of Word-Association-Test Words." *J Personality* 23:77-87 S '54. * (*PA* 28:6717)
LEVINGER, GEORGE, AND CLARK, JAMES. "Emotional Factors in the Forgetting of Word Associations." *J Abn & Social Psychol* 62:99-105 Ja '61. * (*PA* 36:3CL99L)
MERRILL, REED M "The Effect of Pre-Experimental and Experimental Anxie on Recall Efficiency." *J Exp Psychol* 48:167-72 S '54. * (*PA* 29:5250)

form, it fails to meet our current standards as an acceptable instrument for these purposes.

[227]

The Lowenfeld Kaleidoblocs. Ages 2.5 and over; 1958; individual; 1 form ['58]; 2 mimeographed manuals ['58]: adults (12 pages), children (9 pages); no data on reliability and validity; no norms; 52s. 6d. ($11) per set of testing materials, postage extra; specimen set not available; (60) minutes; Margaret Lowenfeld; Badger Tests Co., Ltd. *

REFERENCES
1. AMES, LOUISE BATES, AND LEARNED, JANET. "Developmental Trends in Child Kaleidoblock Responses." *J Genetic Psychol* 84:237-70 Je '54. * (*PA* 29:4023)
2. AMES, LOUISE BATES, AND LEARNED, JANET. "Individual Differences in Child Kaleidoblock Responses." *J Genetic Psychol* 85:3-38 S '54. * (*PA* 29:5686)
3. LOWENFELD, MARGARET. "Concerning Unrealized Factors in International Attitudes and Their Bearing on International Health." *Int Mental Health Res Newsl* 4(3-4):5-7 f-w '62. *

T. R. MILES, *Professor of Psychology, University College of North Wales, Bangor, Wales.*

The material for this test comprises 26 painted pieces of wood—cubes, half cubes, triangular and rectangular blocks, and three special shapes with flat bases and curved tops. The adult test has four sections. In the first, the subject is invited to use the blocks to construct whatever he pleases; sections 2-4 consist of problems of varying kinds, e.g., building the blocks into familiar objects, reconstructing a particular arrangement, etc. The children's test has a similar first section, together with a second section of somewhat easier problems.

Work on this test is still only in the initial stages and there has so far been no systematic standardisation and follow-up. Its great merits, however, in the opinion of the reviewer, are first that, within the framework of certain standardised conditions, it allows for the study of *spontaneous* behaviour, and secondly that it includes a genuine attempt to study *imaginative* ability. Psychometrics has given us plenty of statistics, but all too often these statistics relate to performance at fatuous and uninspired test items in highly artificial conditions. No doubt much in the present test depends on the clinical skill of the tester, and, for the first section in particular, worthwhile standardisation may turn out to be difficult, as in the Rorschach test; but Lowenfeld has at least offered a clear challenge to the more orthodox proponents of so-called "intelligence" and "personality" tests.

Plenty of questions remain on the theoretical side. In the introductory section of the instructions we are told: "The task of psychology, in the detailed study of human personality, is to invent methods of estimating the component elements and their structure in any given individual." Lowenfeld is not the first thinker who has wanted to explain the characteristics of big things in terms of the behaviour of smaller or more "elemental" ones. If she is right in trying to do so, then the breakthrough will come when the appropriate smaller things have been *named* (as, for instance, in the case of oxygen). However, in view of the variety of responses which human nervous systems make possible, one wonders whether this approach (which, incidentally, is not very different from that of the factor analysts) is feasible for psychologists studying personality. Indeed, it is not clear that Lowenfeld is doing more than paying lip-service to it, since there is no obvious logical connexion between her reference to "elements" and the actual test items which follow. One wonders if a link-up with the theories of Melanie Klein might in fact turn out to be more promising; if this is right, more could possibly have been done to study the subjects' responses to *people,* e.g., by the introduction of shapes having a greater resemblance to parts of the human body. This, however, is perhaps to ask for a different kind of test.

In the reviewer's opinion the *Lowenfeld Kaleidoblocs* have considerable potentialities. Those who use them, however, will need both flexibility and imagination—and perhaps a mentality similar to that of Lowenfeld herself.

GEORGE WESTBY, *Professor of Psychology, University College of South Wales and Monmouthshire, University of Wales, Cardiff, Wales.*

This is a fascinating test though manifestly still in an experimental stage of development. The *Lowenfeld Kaleidoblocs* are clearly inspired by a commendable respect for the child's right not only to play his way to the development of his personality but to learn his cognitive alphabets as far as possible by spontaneous experiment and with accompanying fun. It is clear that, in the hands of an enthusiast, such a set of brightly coloured wooden blocks embodying basic mathematical relationships will be an aid to exploring the natural resources of ability in the perception and manipulation of forms in space and will be a help in developing insight into basic mathematical relationships. It is not easy to see much use for the blocks in, as the author claims, "professional guidance" and "personnel management" where

prediction is involved. No evidence of such value is presented in the present cyclostyled manuals. There is also a footnote to the effect that no standardization data are as yet available and a further warning that "all the statements made about it [the test]....are tentative and based upon preliminary findings" (presumably at the Institute of Child Psychology Ltd. and at the Gesell Institute of Child Development where the test has been used).

There is no published evidence known to the reviewer of the test's use in the form recommended for adults, which is in four separate sections. The task in the first is similar to mosaic building, the instruction being simply, "Make whatever you like with these blocks." The second section consists of nine "problems" of a type similar to many which have been used to test perceptual and spatial ability. They have differing time limits. The following is typical of a five-minute task. Four large triangular blocks are presented and put together as a single solid block as a demonstration. The instruction is as follows. "This you see is a symmetrical solid block with smooth edges. It can be placed with the broader or narrower side downwards. I want you to see in how many different symmetrical smooth-edged blocks you can arrange these four triangles." There are 21 possible arrangements. The third section consists of a variety of tasks again of varied time limits. They include the making of a person and a common object such as a table or chair from the blocks. In section four all the blocks have to be used as in a jigsaw to make a solid rectangular block.

The children's form uses the same blocks but is in two sections only. The first consists of free building and the second of much simpler problems than in the adult form including, as in Kohs' blocks, the copying of geometrical and colour arrangements.

This group of tasks may well be considered as tools for research in the field of spatial, mathematical attainment, but little criticism can usefully be offered until, by properly designed experimental investigation, they have been compared with alternative methods of achieving similar ends.

[228]

Lowenfeld Mosaic Test. Ages 2 and over; 1930–58; individual; 1 form ['30]; 2 sets: standard (456 pieces), minor (228 pieces); directions for administering ['58, 9 pages, directions printed in English,

French, German, and Spanish in same booklet]; manual ('54, see *39*); revised record booklet ['54, c1951, 4 pages]; no data on reliability; 205s. ($55) per standard set; 110s. ($35) per minor set; 21s. ($3) per tray; 52s. 6d. ($3.25) per 25 record booklets; 50s. ($8.50) per manual; postage extra; (20–40) minutes; Margaret Lowenfeld; Badger Tests Co., Ltd. *

REFERENCES

1–13. See 4:115.
14–56. See 5:147.
57. WERTHAM, FREDERIC. "A New Sign of Organic Brain Disease." Abstract. *Trans Am Neurol Assn* 65:197 '39. *
58. LISTER, ROBERT CARL. *The Use of the Lowenfeld Mosaic Test and the Mooney Closure Test With Seventy-Two Cerebral Palsied Children.* Master's thesis, University of Texas (Austin, Tex.), 1956.
59. McCORMICK, ANNE, AND LIGHT, BERNARD H. "The Lowenfeld Mosaic Test: A Critique." *Proc W Va Acad Sci* 27:108–11 Je '56. *
60. CHASE, J. A. *A Developmental Study of the Lowenfeld Mosaic Test: Ages 6, 7, 8.* Master's thesis, University of Maine (Orono, Me.), 1957.
61. COLMAN, JAMES A. *Projective Test for Children (Modified Mosaic).* Master's thesis, Claremont College (Claremont, Calif.), 1957.
62. ZUCKER, LUISE J. *Ego Structure in Paranoid Schizophrenia.* Springfield, Ill.: Charles C Thomas, Publisher, 1958. Pp. x, 186. * (*PA* 33:1916)
63. ROBINSON, MARY EVANS. *An Investigation of the Performance of Brain-Injured Children on Certain Perceptual Tasks.* Doctor's thesis, Purdue University (Lafayette, Ind.), 1959. (*DA* 20:1870)
64. ABEL, THEODORA M. "Differential Responses to Projective Testing in a Negro Peasant Community: Montserrat, B.W.I." *Int J Social Psychiatry* 6:218–24 au '60. *
65. GLADSTON, ELAINE R., AND AMADO-HAGUENAUER, GINETTE. "Fluidity in the Limits of the Self." *Int J Social Psychiatry* 6:260–8 au '60. *
66. HORNE, E. P., AND BOVA, L. W., JR. "The Effect of Color on Pattern Stability in Mosaic Productions." *J General Psychol* 63:229–32 O '60. * (*PA* 35:3469)
67. HORNE, E. P., AND LANE, W. P. "Constancy or Creativity in Patterning Mosaic Test Performance." *J General Psychol* 63:165–70 O '60. * (*PA* 35:3408)
68. ASCOUGH, J. C. *The Mosaic Test: Validation and Cross-Validation of Objective Scores, Comparison With Clinical Judgment and the Bender Gestalt Test.* Master's thesis, West Virginia University (Morgantown, W. Va.), 1961.
69. METZ, J. RICHARD. "A Method for Measuring Aspects of Ego Strength." *J Proj Tech* 25:457–70 D '61. *
70. PELZ, KURT S.; AMES, LOUISE B.; AND PIKE, FRANCES. "Measurement of Psychologic Function in Geriatric Patients." *J Am Geriatrics Soc* 9:740–54 S '61. *
71. AMES, LOUISE BATES, AND ILG, FRANCES L. *Mosaic Patterns of American Children.* New York: Hoeber Medical Division, Harper & Row, Publishers, Inc., 1962. Pp. xii, 297. *
72. ASCOUGH, JAMES C., AND DANA, RICHARD H. "Concurrent Validities of the Mosaic and Bender Gestalt Tests." *J Consult Psychol* 26:430–4 O '62. * (*PA* 39:1713)
73. LOWENFELD, MARGARET. "Concerning Unrealized Factors in International Attitudes and Their Bearing on International Health." *Int Mental Health Res Newsl* 4(3–4):5–7 f–w '62. *
74. PELZ, KURT; PIKE, FRANCES; AND AMES, LOUISE B. "A Proposed Battery of Childhood Tests for Discriminating Between Different Levels of Intactness of Function in Elderly Subjects." *J Genetic Psychol* 100:23–40 Mr '62. * (*PA* 37:975)
75. ZUCKER, LUISE J. "Evaluating Psychopathology of the Self." *Ann N Y Acad Sci* 96:844–52 Ja 27 '62. * (*PA* 37:6769)
76. AMES, LOUISE BATES. "Usefulness of the Lowenfeld Mosaic Test in Predicting School Readiness in Kindergarten and Primary School Pupils." *J Genetic Psychol* 103:75–91 S '63. * (*PA* 39:1711)

T. R. MILES, *Professor of Psychology, University College of North Wales, Bangor, Wales.*

The material for the LMT comprises 456 small coloured pieces—squares, half squares, diamonds, and equilateral and scalene triangles. Six different colours are used (red, green, blue, yellow, white, and black) and each shape is available in all six colours. The subject is instructed simply to "do something" with this material, with no restriction as to the choice of pieces. The test has been used *inter alia* for assessment of neurotic and psychotic patients of all ages, for detection of brain damage, for industrial selection, for marriage guidance, in the anthropological field, for developmental studies in children, and indeed for much else. The relevant literature is now extensive, though attempts at statistical validation have yielded somewhat inconclusive results (*4*).

The LMT, in the reviewer's opinion, is comparable in stature to the Rorschach test. Moreover by its very nature it is liable to give rise to the same sort of controversy. Confusion exists in the case of tests of this kind as to the criteria by means of which one assesses their value. On the one hand it might be argued that if the test provides its users with relevant information in clinical and other contexts no further justification is needed. On the other hand it could be said that unless one takes seriously the possibility of statistical check one is simply being unscientific and obscurantist. In the reviewer's opinion the concept of "scientific validation" raises more problems than is commonly realised. Grounds for believing something may have all degrees of adequacy. Thus if on the basis of the LMT a user recommends an industrial firm to appoint X rather than Y, then ideally from the point of view of validation one ought to place X in the job for a given length of time, then "put the clock back" and place Y in identical conditions, and compare the results. (One subject in the experimental group and one subject in the control group are in theory all that is needed.) Now it need not be irrational to believe the hypothetical proposition that if per impossible this were done X would receive greater commendation from his employers than Y; and even a casual report from the firm to the effect that X is "doing all right," with no evidence at all about Y, gives some justification, albeit of a flimsy kind, for believing this hypothetical proposition to be true. The choice is not between cast-iron statistical validation on the one hand and sheer irrationality on the other; there is such a thing as a "good bet" and even such a thing as a "bad bet."

The LMT, in the reviewer's opinion, comes into the "good bet" category. It is clear from her book that the author has the flair for breaking new ground. Thus she tells us that it was her observations of different types of embroidery at festivals of peasants in central Europe which first gave her the idea of this kind of test. Again, one's confidence in the test is increased by the variety of different situations in which it can be given. So long as users of the test appreciate that they are exploring, not just following out a routine procedure such as taking someone's temperature, their investigations should certainly be encouraged.

GEORGE WESTBY, *Professor of Psychology, University College of South Wales and Monmouthshire, University of Wales, Cardiff, Wales.*

To the experienced clinical psychologist, the well made and attractively presented Mosaic Test of Margaret Lowenfeld needs little introduction, especially in circles where a holistic or "psychodynamic" approach to personality is paramount. Perhaps the newest recommendation to the more experimentally minded psychologist of this now more widely used technique of personality study is the conclusion of that well known Keeper of the Ark of the Scientific Convenant, Professor Eysenck, namely, that there is a statistically significant correlation between the personality descriptions made by experienced users of the test from subjects' mosaic designs, on the one hand, and the reports of psychiatrists on the other.

The present reviewer, having used the test experimentally without the benefit of norms or data on reliability, well remembers looking forward to reading the full account of the author and her collaborators at the Institute of Child Psychology, London, which she published in 1954 in the form of a definitive manual-text (*39*). One hoped to be able to decide whether the test offered advantages over other projective techniques of enquiry into personality structure, most of which are time consuming and uncertain to the point of frustration in the busy clinic context. The data given in the manual, however, lead one to wonder whether the problems of objectivity of scoring, communicability of results, validation, adequate norms, and reliability yield any more easily to satisfactory solution in the case of the LMT than in the Rorschach, the TAT, or other projective techniques such as free painting.

The claim made by the author is a large one. With these highly structured materials studied "in an exceptionally wide range of subjects" for 25 years, "the response made by the subject," it is stated, "though entirely spontaneous, nevertheless inescapably registers facts, not only

about the subject's personality, but also about his power to perceive and manipulate accurately objects of defined shape. The test is capable, therefore, of providing exact information as to the stage of development or the degree of disturbance of perceptual powers in cases of amentia, severe neurosis or cerebral disease." The data so far available do suggest that some of these claims are true, but no less a claim is made for other well known techniques and with their more extensive published evidence they will naturally appeal more to the worker in the applied field. The LMT is attractive to children and as one would expect elicits an immediate and natural "play" response, a principle central to Lowenfeld's approach. But others offer this appeal also and it is doubtful if the LMT is more economical of time.

The crucial comparative judgments, however, must be made in respect of the "problem" criteria enumerated above.

The *Lowenfeld Mosaic Test* has certainly achieved a high degree of success in respect of the first of the desiderata of a good test—exact description and analysis of test products. The author's highly developed score sheet of four quarto pages requires entries under 23 main divisions of up to 220 defining characteristics, some of which are esoteric (e.g., "Kite reaction," "Fox reaction," "Rhinoceros reaction"), but most of which are in useful terms of commonly accepted and easily agreed geometrical and colour criteria and Gestalt configurative qualities. A careful reference to the 144 coloured plates of designs (which come with the manual in a special box) in the reading of the chapters on classification gives a considerable confidence in the thoroughness of this analysis and of the fitness of the scheme and its reliability for the recording and effectual communication of the common qualities and individuality of the designs produced. But, like many other promising research instruments in the field of personality, these descriptive categories have few, if any, equally impressive behavioural "dimensions" of the abiding personality with which to assess the predictive power of the test in respect of any general "erlebnistyp" (to use Rorschach's term). It is, however, a merit of the test as a research tool that it has not been constructed (like *The Blacky Pictures* for instance) on prematurely dogmatic theoretical foundations. Were it not that the few main syndromes of psychopathology are very firmly based on pre-theoretical empirical observation, the subsequent explanatory underpinning of these by often contradictory but "elastic" (though dogmatic!) theories would have no plausibility whatever. With an empirical (though *not* anti-theoretical) approach in clinical psychology and psychiatry, Lowenfeld's test seems to come to practical agreement. The test data are reality-anchored in observables and describables. Her recent statement of theories she is developing on the basis of her experience with the test is highly cautious. She explicitly states in the manual that she has deliberately eschewed in her description of the test and its uses, "the question of the relation between the forms of pattern produced, and possible psycho-analytic interpretations of such elements of design." She stresses the obvious dangers with such a flexible instrument of "falling into the trap of subjective intuitive interpretation." In the absence of exact analysis, she notes, "it is a dangerous instrument that can easily lead into the bog of superficial analogies that have no real basis." Explicitly in her "Theory of E" she refuses to dogmatize the test descriptions, e.g., in respect of aggressive behaviour as being necessarily due to an aggressive "instinct." "Explanations put forward by different schools," she says, "do not necessarily exclude one another"—a refreshingly scientific sentiment for a projective theorist. Nor does Lowenfeld belong to the cookbook school of colour interpretation. Red must not, she warns, lead one to an interpretation of hidden anger or destructiveness, for only in conversation with the subject can we be certain that the colour has not been used simply because it pleases him. Exclusive use of black and white may, likewise, "be expressive of aesthetic values or of retreat from emotional experience or expression." "Colours," she rightly says, "mean so many different things to different people" that a list of colour associations common in the "area" of the tester should be drawn up before attempting interpretation! And then presumably, even assuming a proper sampling, allowance must be made for individual differences of cultural conditionability and only very tentative suggestions in this field are possible. One cannot be surprised that interpretation is a difficult art.

The author's caution, however, is not so much in evidence outside her own clinical field. In the chapter, "The Use of the L.M.T. in the Study of Cultural Problems," the generalising of cultural attitudes into "Am-type" and "Eu-type," corresponding to the American and European civilisation, seems quite unsupported by any adequate sampling. The hypothesis indeed seems jejune in itself, possibly conceivable in an earlier climate of thought in social anthropology and sociology, but surely greatly weakened by the careful empirical studies of recent decades which have unveiled a bewildering variety of cultures and sub-cultures with complicating internal inconsistencies which render far more doubtful any generalisations about personality differences between "the" American and "the" European.

What of the test's claim to provide a communicable psychogram or diagnostic category? Sadly we must conclude that only insofar as a clinical group-language is shared will this be possible in theoretical terms. Among clinical workers generally, precious few validated and theoretically-anchored "dimensions" of personality continue to exist across the frontiers of the different research groups and analytical schools. As to the diagnostic and prognostic value of the test, insufficient evidence has emerged as yet of a scientifically acceptable kind. Larger groups fully statistically analysed are required and perhaps such research may be forthcoming with the increasing interest of American research workers in the test. Indeed, many of its less promising rivals, earlier and better known by the accident of history, have had much greater efforts lavished upon them. Scientifically precise instruments based on a sufficiency of varied experimental evidence no doubt will eventually be forged for the study of personality and for decision making in the applied fields. To this end the enthusiastic work of Lowenfeld is wholly admirable. But the clinical psychologist hoping to find such an instrument already available must be disappointed. Nevertheless, it is no small thing to be able to say that the LMT has the legitimate character and practical value of a clinical craftsman's "knack" as opposed to a clinical "gimmick." It is as a tool for continuing research, however, that the immediate future of the test, so far unjustifiably neglected, probably most properly lies.

For a review by C. J. Adcock, see 5:147; for excerpts from related book reviews, see B51 and 5:B274.

[229]

Machover Draw-A-Person Test. Ages 2 and over; 1949; also called *Machover Figure Drawing Test;* manual (192 pages, see 5 below) ; no accessories ; $5.50 per manual, cash orders postpaid; (5-60) minutes without associations, (20-90) minutes with associations; Karen Machover; Charles C Thomas, Publisher. *

REFERENCES

1–13. See 4:111

14–52. See 5:148.

53. FATERSON, HANNA. "The Figure Drawing Test as an Adjunct in the Selection of Medical Students." *J Med Ed* 31:323–7 My '56. * (PA 31:1749)

54. BROWN, DANIEL G., AND TOLOR, ALEXANDER. "Human Figure Drawings as Indicators of Sexual Identification and Inversion." *Percept & Motor Skills* 7:199–211 S '57. * (PA 32:4167)

55. GEIST, HAROLD. "Emotional Aspects of Dermatitis." *J Clin & Exp Psychopathol* 18:87–93 Mr '57. * (PA 32:4433)

56. HENRICHS, THEODORE F. *Somatic Preoccupation and the Draw-A-Person Test: A Validation Study.* Master's thesis, Ohio University (Athens, Ohio), 1957.

57. HICKS, DAVID J. *Personality Factors Found in Institutionalized Deaf Adolescents as Compared to Non-Deafened Adolescents as Measured by the Draw-A-Person Test.* Master's thesis, University of Redlands (Redlands, Calif.), 1957.

58. HONIGMANN, JOHN J., AND CARRERA, RICHARD N. "Cross-Cultural Use of Machover's Figure Drawing Test." *Am Anthrop* 59:650–4 Ag '57. * (PA 33:3621)

59. SWENSEN, CLIFFORD H., JR. "Empirical Evaluations of Human Figure Drawings." *Psychol B* 54:431–66 N '57. * (PA 33:3807)

60. WIGGENHORN, ALLAN HAROLD. "An Investigation of Changes in Human Figure Drawings as a Function of Changes in the 'Self-Concept.'" *Provo Papers* 1:15–41 O '57. * (PA 35:2301)

61. COPELAND, LYNN P. "Draw A Person." *Psychometric Res B* (1):[6–8] My '58. *

62. DIAMOND, FLORENCE. *Style and Content in Personality Rigidity.* Doctor's thesis, Claremont Graduate School (Claremont, Calif.), 1958. (DA 20:2901)

63. DWINELL, ALICE J. *An Investigation of the Machover Personality Projection Test as an Approach to Locating Personality Problems at the First Grade Level.* Master's thesis, Boston University (Boston, Mass.), 1958.

64. FISHER, RHODA LEE. "The Effect of a Disturbing Situation Upon the Stability of Various Projective Tests." *Psychol Monogr* 72:1–23 '58. * (PA 34:1357)

65. ROSENFELD, IRWIN JOSEPH. *Mathematical Ability as a Function of Perceptual Field-Dependency and Certain Personality Variables.* Doctor's thesis, University of Oklahoma (Norman, Okla.), 1958. (DA 19:880)

66. VERNIER, CLAIRE M.; STAFFORD, JOHN W.; AND KRUGMAN, ARNOLD D. "A Factor Analysis of Indices From Four Projective Techniques Associated With Four Different Types of Physical Pathology." *J Consult Psychol* 22:433–7 D '58. * (PA 33:9360)

67. ARBIT, JACK; LAKIN, MARTIN; AND MATHIS, ANDREW G. "Clinical Psychologists' Diagnostic Utilization of Human Figure Drawings." *J Clin Psychol* 15:325–7 Jl '59. * (PA 35:3479)

68. BOLOTIN, MAX. *The Use of Human Figure Drawings in Evaluating Children and Adolescents of Special Educational and Cultural Background: An Examination of the Effectiveness of Current Diagnostic Criteria With the Draw-A-Person Test as Applied to Puerto Rican Children and Adolescents.* Doctor's thesis, New York University (New York, N.Y.), 1959. (DA 20:4030)

69. BUTLER, R. L., AND MARCUSE, F. L. "Sex Identification at Different Ages Using the Draw-A-Person Test." *J Proj Tech* 23:299–302 S '59. * (PA 35:4871)

70. CLEVELAND, SIDNEY E. "Personality Dynamics in Torticollis." *J Nerv & Mental Dis* 129:150–61 Ag '59. * (PA 34:6407)

71. COLTHARP, FRANCES C. *A Validation Study of the Draw-A-Person Test.* Master's thesis, Southern Methodist University (Dallas, Tex.), 1959.

72. EPSTEIN, LAWRENCE, AND HARTFORD, HUNTINGTON. "Some Relationships of Beginning Strokes in Handwriting to the Human Figure Drawing Test." *Percept & Motor Skills* 9:55–62 Mr '59. * (PA 34:1354)

73. FISHER, GARY M. "Comment on Starr and Marcuse's 'Reliability in the Draw A Person Test.'" *Percept & Motor Skills* 9:302 S '59. * (PA 34:7842)

74. FISHER, GARY M. "Relationship Between Diagnosis of Neuropsychiatric Disorder, Sexual Deviation, and the Sex of the First-Drawn Figure." *Percept & Motor Skills* 9:47–50 Mr '59. * (PA 34:1356)

75. GRIFFITH, ALBERT V., AND PEYMAN, D. A. R. "Eye-Ear Emphasis in the DAP as Indicating Ideas of Reference." Abstract. *J Consult Psychol* 23:560 D '59. * (PA 34:6020)

76. HOYT, THOMAS E., AND BARON, MARTIN R. "Anxiety Indices in Same-Sex Drawings of Psychiatric Patients With High and Low MAS Scores." *J Consult Psychol* 23:448–52 O '59. * (PA 34:5622)

77. LEPPEL, LEON. *The Stability of Performance of Schizophrenics on the Draw-A-Person Test.* Doctor's thesis, Temple University (Philadelphia, Pa.), 1959. (DA 20:375)

78. LEVITT, EUGENE E., AND GROSZ, HANUS J. "A Note on Sex Sequence in the Draw-A-Person Test." *Psychol Newsl* 10:213–4 Mr–Ap '59. * (PA 34:1387)

79. LUBIN, BERNARD. "Differentiation of Overtly Stable and Unstable Psychiatric Aides by Means of the DAP Test." *Psychol Rep* 5:26 Mr '59. * (PA 34:1388)

80. MACHOVER, SOLOMON, AND PUZZO, FRANK S. "Clinical and Objective Studies of Personality Variables in Alcoholism: 1, Clinical Investigation of the 'Alcoholic Personality.'" *Q J Studies Alcohol* 20:505–19 S '59. * (PA 34:6253)

81. MACHOVER, SOLOMON, AND PUZZO, FRANK S. "Clinical and Objective Studies of Personality Variables in Alcoholism: 2, Clinical Study of Personality Correlates of Remission From Active Alcoholism." *Q J Studies Alcohol* 20:520–7 S '59. * (PA 34:6253)

82. MACHOVER, SOLOMON; PUZZO, FRANK S.; MACHOVER, KAREN; AND PLUMEAU, FRANCIS. "Clinical and Objective Studies of Personality Variables in Alcoholism: 3, An Objective Study of Homosexuality in Alcoholism." *Q J Studies Alcohol* 20:528–42 S '59. * (PA 34:6254)

83. ORME, J. E. "Human Figure Drawings of Schizophrenic and Depressed Patients." *Psychiatria et Neurologia* 138:364–8 '59. *

84. RABIN, A. I., AND LIMUACO, JOSEFINA A. "Sexual Differentiation of American and Filipino Children as Reflected in the Draw-A-Person Test." *J Social Psychol* 50:207–11 N '59. * (PA 35:4765)

85. SCHMIDT, LYLE D., AND McGOWAN, JOHN F. "The Differentiation of Human Figure Drawings." *J Consult Psychol* 23:129–33 Ap '59. * (PA 34:1418)

86. SPOCK, ANNE INGERSOLL. *An Investigation of the Relationship Between Confusion in Sex-Role Identification and Social Maladjustment in Childhood.* Doctor's thesis, American University (Washington, D.C.), 1959. (DA 20:2893)

87. STARR, S., AND MARCUSE, F. L. "Reliability in the 'Draw-A-Person' Test." *J Proj Tech* 23:83–6 Mr '59. *

88. BICKLEY, BENJAMIN R. *A Validity Study of Machover's Homosexual Signs in the Draw-A-Person Test.* Master's thesis, Fresno State College (Fresno, Calif.), 1960.

89. BLIZZARD, B. THEODORE. *Projective Limitations in the Use of the Draw-A-Person With Mentally Retarded Adolescents.* Master's thesis, Kansas State College of Pittsburg (Pittsburg, Kan.), 1960.

90. BODWIN, RAYMOND F., AND BRUCK, MAX. "The Adaptation and Validation of the Draw-A-Person Test as a Measure of Self Concept." *J Clin Psychol* 16:427–9 O '60. * (PA 37:3104)

91. DAVIDS, ANTHONY, AND DeVAULT, SPENCER. "Use of the TAT and Human Figure Drawings in Research on Personality, Pregnancy, and Perception." *J Proj Tech* 24:362–5 D '60. * (PA 35:4872)

92. FISHER, SEYMOUR. "Right-Left Gradients in Body Image, Body Reactivity, and Perception." *Genetic Psychol Monogr* 61:197–228 My '60. * (PA 35:6478)

93. HAGGERTY, ARTHUR D. "Cautions Required in the Interpretation of Projective Tests With Applicants to a School of Professional Nursing." *J General Psychol* 63:57–62 Jl '60. * (PA 35:7080)

94. HUNT, RAYMOND G., AND FELDMAN, MARVIN J. "Body Image and Ratings of Adjustment on Human Figure Drawings." *J Clin Psychol* 16:35–8 Ja '60. * (PA 36:1HE35H)

95. MACHOVER, KAREN. Chap. 13, "Sex Differences in the Developmental Pattern of Children as Seen in Human Figure Drawings," pp. 238–57. In *Projective Techniques With Children.* Edited by Albert I. Rabin and Mary R. Haworth. New York: Grune & Stratton, Inc., 1960. Pp. xiii, 392. * (PA 35:2229)

96. MACHOVER, KAREN, AND LIEBERT, ROBERT. "Human Figure Drawings of Schizophrenic and Normal Adults: Changes Following Administration of Lysergic Acid." *Arch Gen Psychiatry* 3:139–52 Ag '60. *

97. SPOTTS, JAMES V., JR. *A Test of Machover's Hypothesis Regarding the Social Significance of the Head and Face in Children's Human Figure Drawings.* Master's thesis, University of Kansas (Lawrence, Kan.), 1960.

98. ARMSTRONG, RENATE G., AND HAUCK, PAUL A. "Sexual Identification and the First Figure Drawn." *J Consult Psychol* 25:51–4 F '61. * (PA 36:3HE51A)

99. COHEN, SANFORD L.; SILVERMAN, ALBERT J.; WADDELL, WILLIAM; AND ZUIDEMA, GEORGE D. "Urinary Catechol Amine Levels, Gastric Secretion and Specific Psychological Factors in Ulcer and Non-Ulcer Patients." *J Psychosom Res* 5:90–115 F '61. * (PA 36:3JH90C)

100. FISHER, GARY M. "Nudity in Human Figure Drawings." *J Clin Psychol* 17:307–8 Jl '61. * (PA 38:8548)

101. HAWORTH, MARY R., AND NORMINGTON, CHERYL J. "A Sexual Differentiation Scale for the D-A-P Test (for Use With Children)." *J Proj Tech* 25:441–50 D '61. *

102. JONES, LEONA W., AND THOMAS, CAROLINE B. "Studies on Figure Drawings." *Psychiatric Q Sup* 35:212–61 pt 2 '61. * (PA 37:5041)

103. LACHMANN, F. M.; BAILEY, M. A.; AND BERRICK, M. E. "The Relationship Between Manifest Anxiety and Clinicians' Evaluations of Projective Test Responses." *J Clin Psychol* 17:11–3 Ja '61. * (*PA* 37:3113)

104. McGUIRL, DONALD. *Communication in Drawings: An Indirect Validation Study of the "Draw-A-Person" Test Through the Cartoons of William Steig.* Master's thesis, University of Kansas (Lawrence, Kan.), 1961.

105. NIELSEN, HELLE H. "Human Figure Drawings by Normal and Physically Handicapped Children: Draw-A-Person Test." *Scandinavian J Psychol* 2(3):129–38 '61. *

106. SAUNDERS, MAUDERIE HANCOCK. *An Analysis of Cultural Differences on Certain Projective Techniques.* Doctor's thesis, University of Oklahoma (Norman, Okla.), 1961. (*DA* 22:490)

107. STOLTZ, ROBERT E., AND COLTHARP, FRANCES C. "Clinical Judgments and the Draw-A-Person Test." *J Consult Psychol* 25:43–5 F '61. * (*PA* 36:3H43S)

108. WHITAKER, LEIGHTON, JR. "The Use of an Extended Draw-A-Person Test to Identify Homosexual and Effeminate Men." *J Consult Psychol* 25:482–5 D '61. * (*PA* 37:5051)

109. BAUGH, VERNER S., AND CARPENTER, B. L. "A Comparison of Delinquents and Nondelinquents." *J Social Psychol* 56:73–8 F '62. * (*PA* 36:5JO73B)

110. BRUCK, MAX, AND BODWIN, RAYMOND F. "The Relationship Between Self-Concept and the Presence and Absence of Scholastic Underachievement." *J Clin Psychol* 18:181–2 Ap '62. * (*PA* 38:9278)

111. CRADDICK, RAY A. "Draw-A-Person Characteristics of Psychopathic Prisoners and College Students." *Percept & Motor Skills* 15:11–3 Ag '62. * (*PA* 37:5446)

112. CRADDICK, RAY A.; LEIPOLD, WILLIAM D.; AND CACAVAS, PETER D. "The Relationship of Shading on the Draw-A-Person Test to Manifest Anxiety Scores." *J Consult Psychol* 26:193 Ap '62. * (*PA* 37:5080)

113. CROVITZ, HERBERT F. "On Direction in Drawing A Person." Abstract. *J Consult Psychol* 26:196 Ap '62. * (*PA* 37:4978)

114. DALY, WILLIAM, AND HUBER, WILLIAM. "A Note on 'Sexual Identification in Mentally Subnormal Females' by Fisher." *Am J Mental Def* 66:782–3 Mr '62. * (*PA* 37:1683, title only)

115. EXNER, JOHN E., JR. "A Comparison of the Human Figure Drawings of Psychoneurotics, Character Disturbances, Normals, and Subjects Experiencing Experimentally-Induced Fear." *J Proj Tech* 26:392–7 D '62. * (*PA* 37:6754)

116. FISHER, GARY M. "A Note on 'Sexual Identification in Mentally Subnormal Females' by Fisher: Reply to Daly and Huber." *Am J Mental Def* 66:784 Mr '62. * (*PA* 37:1689, title only)

117. HAWORTH, MARY R. "Responses of Children to a Group Projective Film and to the Rorschach, CAT, Despert Fables and D-A-P." *J Proj Tech* 26:47–60 Mr '62. * (*PA* 37:2893)

118. LAIRD, JAMES T. "A Comparison of Male Normals, Psychiatric Patients and Alcoholics for Sex Drawn First." *J Clin Psychol* 18:302 Jl '62. * (*PA* 39:1861)

119. McGUIRL, DONALD, AND MOSS, C. SCOTT. "An Indirect Validation Study of the Draw-A-Person Test Through the Cartoons of William Steig." *J Proj Tech* 26:88–95 Mr '62. * (*PA* 37:3115)

120. MOGAR, ROBERT E. "Anxiety Indices in Human Figure Drawings: A Replication and Extension." Abstract. *J Consult Psychol* 26:108 F '62. * (*PA* 37:4989)

121. NICHOLS, ROBERT C., AND STRÜMPFER, DEODANDUS J. W. "A Factor Analysis of Draw-A-Person Test Scores." *J Consult Psychol* 26:156–61 Ap '62. * (*PA* 37:4990)

122. NICKOLS, JOHN. "Size Judgment and the Draw-A-Person Test." *J Psychol Studies* 13:117–9 Je '62 [issued F '64]. *

123. PEDRINI, DUILIO T., AND PEDRINI, LURA NANCY. "Hearing Efficiency–Inefficiency and Personal-Social Ease–Dis-ease, 2." *Psychiatric Q* 36:428–54 Ja '62. *

124. SHANAN, JOEL. "Intraindividual Response Variability in Figure Drawing Tasks." *J Proj Tech* 26:105–11 Mr '62. * (*PA* 37:3161)

125. STRÜMPFER, DEODANDUS J. W., AND NICHOLS, ROBERT C. "A Study of Some Communicable Measures for the Evaluation of Human Figure Drawings." *J Proj Tech* 26:342–53 S '62. * (*PA* 37:3240)

126. ZUK, G. H. "Relation of Mental Age to Size of Figure on the Draw-A-Person Test." *Percept & Motor Skills* 14:410 Je '62. * (*PA* 37:3325)

127. BARNOUW, VICTOR. Chap. 17, "Drawing Analysis," pp. 276–98. In his *Culture and Personality.* Homewood, Ill.: Dorsey Press, Inc., 1963. Pp. xi, 410. *

128. BRUCK, MAX, AND BODWIN, RAYMOND F. "Age Differences Between SCS-DAP Test Results and GPA." *J Clin Psychol* 19:315–6 Jl '63. *

129. CRADDICK, RAY A. "The Self-Image in the Draw-A-Person Test and Self-Portrait Drawings." *J Proj Tech & Pers Assess* 27:288–91 S '63. * (*PA* 38:4298)

130. ENDICOTT, NOBLE A., AND ENDICOTT, JEAN. " 'Improvement' in Untreated Psychiatric Patients." *Arch Gen Psychiatry* 9:575–85 D '63. * (*PA* 38:8643)

131. EVANS, RAY B., AND MARMORSTON, JESSIE. "Psychological Test Signs of Brain Damage in Cerebral Thrombosis." *Psychol Rep* 12:915–30 Je '63. * (*PA* 38:6413)

132. HEBERLEIN, MARJORIE, AND MARCUSE, F. L. "Personality Variables in the DAP." Abstract. *J Consult Psychol* 27:461 O '63. *

133. KARP, STEPHEN A.; POSTER, DOROTHY C.; AND GOODMAN, ALAN. "Differentiation in Alcoholic Women." *J Personality* 31:386–93 S '63. *.

134. McHUGH, ANN F. "Sexual Identification, Size, and Associations in Children's Figure Drawings." *J Clin Psychol* 19:381–2 Jl '63. *

135. WEST, J. V.; BAUGH, V. S.; AND BAUGH, ANNIE P. "Rorschach and Draw-A-Person Responses of Hypnotized and Nonhypnotized Subjects." *Psychiatric Q* 37:123–7 Ja '63. *

136. WOLFSON, WILLIAM. "Profile Drawings and Procrastination." *Percept & Motor Skills* 17:570 O '63. * (*PA* 38:6112)

PHILIP M. KITAY, *Professor of Psychology, Adelphi University, Garden City, New York.*

This projective technique, second only to the Rorschach in popularity according to Sundberg,[1] has gained a large following probably because it appears to be easy to administer and interpret, economical of time, and interesting. Herein lies a danger. Machover (*12*) admits that the test is vulnerable to misuse because there are no special materials needed, no complicated directions, scoring, and coding to be mastered. She wisely advises that it is best used in combination with other techniques, both in diagnosis and research.

As is typical for projective techniques, the value of the yield from human figure drawings depends upon the clinical skills of the examiner, his knowledge of psychodynamics, and experience with the technique. It is important for the examiner to be well versed on body symbolism, interpretation of expressive movements, and graphomotor functioning.

More skill is required of the examiner in administering the test than is implied in Machover's (*12*) statement that it may be administered to groups of any size since actual administration requires only partial attention of the examiner. In the case of group administration, interpretation based on sequence in drawing body parts, time spent on each, questions asked of the examiner, spontaneous comments, and number of repeated erasures is not possible. The value of the optional associations or post-drawing inquiry depends upon the examiner's skill in handling it. More research is needed upon this aspect of the test.

Insufficient consideration has been given to the possible influences upon the drawings of such variables as the setting and the examinee's perception of the purpose of the examination. Effort and seriousness of approach may be different for individuals participating in a re-

---

1 SUNDBERG, NORMAN D. "The Practice of Psychological Testing in Clinical Services in the United States." *Am Psychologist* 16:79–83 F '61. *

search group administration of the test and for those being privately examined for clinical diagnosis. One would like to know whether the perception of the test as a measurement of creative ability, of intelligence, of artistic aptitude, or of emotional stability has an influence upon the kind of drawing produced. Research studies fail to emphasize sufficiently whether group or individual administration was employed, with the unwarranted implication that it is an unimportant variable.

The Machover manual (5) is most inadequate in its coverage of theoretical bases and procedures for interpretation, reliability, and validity. It is deficient in regard to number of illustrative drawings, exactness of description of drawing items to be interpreted, and rationale and empirical evidence for interpretations offered. Statistical normative data are not presented. A similar omission of statistical data is found in a recent large scale empirical study by Machover (95) of sex differences in drawings of children. There is need for a comprehensive manual providing detailed consideration of administration, description and interpretation of items along a scale, large number of illustrative plates for item and global interpretation, normative data by age, sex, and other population variables, and summary of research studies on reliability and validity.

The examiner may find helpful in overcoming some of the above shortcomings: (a) Vernier's [2] large collection of drawings grouped by psychiatric diagnosis of testees and Gurvitz's appendix (10) of drawings by seventeen patients and (b) "Short Scale of Figure Drawing Items" in Appendix A of *Personality Through Perception* by Witkin and others (30) for exact description of some drawing items. For evaluation of voluminous research on human figure drawing, the review by Swensen (59) of an eight year period and one by Jones and Thomas (102) of a decade are most useful. Swensen concludes that more research evidence contradicts Machover's hypotheses on interpretation than supports them. He urges more research on reliability and validity of patterns of signs rather than of individual signs. Jones and Thomas recommend further research on validity and reliability due to the present unclear picture in regard to them. They

find encouraging the reliability of scoring and satisfactory correlations with other personality assessments demonstrated in the study by Witkin and others (30). In both reviews (59, 102) the sound advice is given that for clinical diagnosis the test be used as part of a battery and that by itself it be used only as a screening device. The reviewer agrees with this position.

Zimmer's [3] complaint that research on validity has employed criteria of adjustment-maladjustment instead of indicators of personality dynamics seems worthy of consideration by researchers. Brown's (17) opinion that many sets of successive drawings, as in the Caligor [4] modification of human figure drawing technique, may be more revealing than a single set should spur more investigation into this approach. An important warning is given by both Brown (17) and Buck [5] that the Draw-A-Person technique is very sensitive to psychopathology. There is danger that the diagnostician may therefore overestimate the degree of pathology present in the personality evaluated.

This reviewer believes that a most promising approach to an increased understanding of the meaning of drawings is to be found in studies of the effects of experimental manipulation of subjects upon their drawings. For example, clinical improvement in patients after regressive electric shock treatment was paralleled in improvement in successive drawings; [6] lowered self-concept resulting from artificially created stress was reflected in before-after drawings (60); and increased use of shading, an anxiety indicator, appeared following experimentally induced fear (115).

In spite of Machover's (5, 28, 95) repeated observations on the differences between males and females in their drawings of the human figure, she fails to provide systematized and separate guides for the interpretation of drawings by males and females. She reported (28)

2 VERNIER, CLAIRE MYERS. *Projective Test Productions: I, Projective Drawings.* New York: Grune and Stratton, Inc., 1952. Pp. vii, 168. *

3 ZIMMER, HERBERT. Chap. 4, "Validity of Sentence Completion Tests and Human Figure Drawings," pp. 58–75. (*PA* 30:7239) In *Progress in Clinical Psychology, Volume II.* Edited by Daniel Brower and Lawrence E. Abt. New York: Grune and Stratton, Inc., 1956. Pp. viii, 364. *

4 CALIGOR, LEOPOLD. "The Determination of the Individual's Unconscious Conception of His Own Masculinity-Femininity Identification." *J Proj Tech* 15:494–509 D '51. *

5 BUCK, JOHN N., EDITOR. *Administration and Interpretation of the H-T-P Test: Proceedings of the H-T-P Workshop Held at Veterans Administration Hospital, Richmond 19, Virginia, March 31, April 1, 2, 1950.* [Beverly Hills, Calif.: Western Psychological Services, 1950.] Pp. 67. Paper, mimeographed. *

6 GLUECK, BERNARD C., JR.; KRASNER, JACK D.; AND PARRES, RAMON. Chap. 13, "The Use of Serial Testing in Regressive Electroshock Treatment," pp. 244–57. In *Relation of Psychological Tests to Psychiatry.* Edited by Paul H. Hoch and Joseph Zubin. New York: Grune & Stratton, Inc., 1952. Pp. viii, 301. *

that body projection as reflected in the D-A-P was more closely related to personality in men than in women. With self-portraits drawn from the mirror by adolescents, Stewart [7] found that girls' portraits were more stereotyped than those done by boys and that the same stylistic graphic variables had very different relationships to personality traits in boys and girls. He noted that the opposite poles on some drawing items were indicators of a similar personality makeup and that the distributions of stylistic variables in the population were of unusual types for which most of the popular tests of statistical significance might be inappropriate. Do these findings on self-portrait apply to the Machover technique? If it is found to be so, approaches to its validation will need modification. There is an urgency for published data on distributions of population samples on graphic variables on the D-A-P.

Since the D-A-P technique is so frequently included in diagnostic test batteries in spite of uncertainty about its reliability and validity, clinicians appear to be impressed by the extent and congruency of its contribution to the evaluation of personality. In the hands of experienced clinicians with their checking on internal consistency and weighting of evidence from various tests in the battery, there is little danger of naïve reliance upon the D-A-P. The many negative findings in the literature should make clinicians more concerned about avoiding a mechanical or reflex type of application of Machover's hypotheses to the interpretation of drawings. The user of the D-A-P test may gain greater exactness and precision in approach by following some of the recommendations made by Buck [8] in his rather overlaborious and highly quantitative approach for his House-Tree-Person test. Inexactness in the description of graphic signs, looseness in exposition of principles of interpretation, and absence of published normative data are the most formidable obstacles to placing the D-A-P technique on the firm foundation that it deserves.

For reviews by Philip L. Harriman and Naomi Stewart, see 4:111; for excerpts from related book reviews, see 4:112.

7 STEWART, LOUIS H. "The Expression of Personality in Drawings and Paintings." *Genet Psychol Monogr* 51:45–103 F '55. (PA 30:628)
8 BUCK, *op. cit.*

[230]

Make A Picture Story. Ages 6 and over; 1947–52; individual; 1 form ('47, 22 background pictures and 67 figure cutouts); figure location sheet ('48, 4 pages); manual ('52, 96 pages, see 27 below); no data on reliability and validity; $17 per set of test materials, 25 figure location sheets, and manual; $2 per 25 figure location sheets; $2.50 per manual; $16.50 per theater (optional); postpaid; (45–90) minutes; Edwin S. Shneidman; Psychological Corporation. *

REFERENCES

1–19. See 4:113.
20–38. See 5:149.
39. SHNEIDMAN, EDWIN S. Chap. 17, "Some Relationships Between the Rorschach Technique and Other Psychodiagnostic Tests," pp. 595–642. In *Developments in the Rorschach Technique: Volume 2, Fields of Application.* By Bruno Klopfer and others. Yonkers, N.Y.: World Book Co., 1956. Pp. xx, 828. * (PA 30:7202)
40. FEFFER, MELVIN H. "The Cognitive Implications of Role Taking Behavior." *J Personality* 27:152–68 Je '59. * (PA 34:4380)
41. LITTLE, KENNETH B., AND SHNEIDMAN, EDWIN S. "Congruencies Among Interpretations of Psychological Test and Anamnestic Data." *Psychol Monogr* 73(6):1–42 '59. * (PA 34:3010)
42. HESS, D. WILSON. *The Evaluation of Personality and Adjustment in Deaf and Hearing Children Using Nonverbal Modification of the Make A Picture Story (MAPS) Test.* Doctor's thesis, University of Rochester (Rochester, N.Y.), 1960.
43. SHNEIDMAN, EDWIN S. Chap. 7, "The MAPS Test With Children," pp. 130–48. In *Projective Techniques With Children.* Edited by Albert I. Rabin and Mary R. Haworth. New York: Grune & Stratton, Inc., 1960. Pp. xiii, 392. * (PA 35:2229)
44. FINE, REUBEN. "The Case of El: The MAPS Test." *J Proj Tech* 25:383–9 D '61. *
45. FORER, BERTRAM R. "The Case of El: Vocational Choice." *J Proj Tech* 25:371–4 D '61. *
46. MURRAY, HENRY A. "Commentary on the Case of El." *J Proj Tech* 25:404–11 D '61. *
47. RASHAP, BERNARD LEONARD. *An Exploratory Study of Mediational Processes in Verbal Behavior: An Investigation of Verbal Mediator Interaction Reflected by Changes in a Form of the Semantic Differential as Applied to a Thematic Projective Technique.* Doctor's thesis, New York University (New York, N.Y.), 1961. (DA 22:653)
48. SHNEIDMAN, EDWIN S. "The Logic of El: A Psychological Approach to the Analysis of Test Data." *J Proj Tech* 25:390–403 D '61. *

ARTHUR R. JENSEN, *Associate Professor of Educational Psychology, and Associate Research Psychologist, Institute of Human Learning, University of California, Berkeley, California.*

The MAPS test is a thematic apperception test—a kind of do-it-yourself TAT—in which the subject makes up his own pictures and then tells stories about the pictures. The test materials consist of 22 pictorial backgrounds, including a blank card, of varying degrees of structure (a living room, a bedroom, a bathroom, a cave, a schoolroom, etc.). These pictures (8½ by 11 inches in size) are held upright in a wooden frame. The dramatis personae are 67 cutout cardboard figures—male and female adults, nudes, children, minority figures such as Negroes, Mexicans, and Orientals, animal figures, legendary and fictitious characters (e.g., Santa Claus), silhouettes, and figures with blank faces. The figures are held upright by insertion into a wooden base. The examiner places a background picture before the subject and asks him to select any figures he wishes to put into the scene and to make up a story about it in much the same manner as subjects are instructed to do for the TAT. Usually not more than 10 of the scenes are used. Even then, the test is very time consuming, usually requiring from 45 to 90 minutes. A study (35) of the clinical use of the test with 64 children from ages 3½ to 16 indicates that 12 clinicians used on the average 8 scenes, with a range from 2 to 12. The average number of figures used by the subjects was 3.9 per card.

The MAPS protocol can be subjected to various elaborate formal scoring schemes (18, 27, 35)[1] which require a great deal of the examiner's time. In clinical practice, however, the protocol is most often interpreted in a holistic, impressionistic manner in much the same way as the TAT is approached. Detailed examples of how the test is interpreted by experts may be found in the book edited by Shneidman (18), the inventor of the MAPS.

Because the MAPS is much more cumbersome to use than the TAT and does not seem to yield anything substantially different from the kinds of psychological insights gained through the TAT, it has not gained widespread popularity as a clinical instrument. Clinicians who have acquired subjective "norms" through extensive use of the TAT are reluctant to take the time required to develop a "feel" for the MAPS. A nationwide survey[2] on the use of psychological tests in clinical practice showed that among 62 tests the MAPS ranks 26th in frequency of usage.

The MAPS has inspired comparatively little research. There are no satisfactory normative data (35), and, indeed, norms would be extremely difficult to establish because of the tremendous variability in the stimulus situation for every subject. Even if norms did exist, it is doubtful that they would serve any practical purpose. Normative data on the TAT, for example, are rarely referred to in clinical practice. The aim of these unstructured tests is to yield protocols that can act as projective materials for the play of the clinician's own intuitions. The clinician's written report of the

interpretation, in turn, might be regarded as projective material for the psychiatrist to whom it is addressed. The question is, how much does it really add to anyone's knowledge of the patient?

RELIABILITY AND VALIDITY. The best study of the reliability and validity of MAPS interpretation is provided by Little and Shneidman (41), who had 12 experts in the use of the MAPS perform a number of interpretive tasks on the protocols of 12 patients equally divided among the categories of psychiatrically normal, psychotic, neurotic, and psychosomatic. (Experts of the Rorschach, TAT, and MMPI performed the same tasks for comparative purposes.) The same interpretive tasks were carried out by 23 psychiatrists and one clinical psychologist on the basis of very thorough anamnestic data.

The reliability was assessed in terms of the agreement among the MAPS judges and the agreement of each judge with himself when performing the same interpretive tasks on the same protocols 10 days later. In the assignment of diagnostic labels there was no greater than chance agreement among the judges. (This was true also for the TAT.) On a set of 117 true-false personality items typical of the statements in psychological reports, the correlations between the MAPS judges and the anamnestic judges ranged from −.19 to .67, with a mean of .33. The same interpretive task performed 10 days later by the MAPS judges produced correlations with their original interpretations ranging from .48 to .94, with a mean of .77. On a set of 100 true-false factual items from the patients' case histories, the MAPS judges produced correlations ranging from −.22 to .50, with a mean of .16. Correlations between interpretations performed 10 days apart ranged from .38 to .91, with a mean of .77. The judges also performed Q-sorts of 76 items typical of interpretive statements found in psychological reports. The correlations among the Q-sorts of the MAPS judges ranged from .07 to .71, with a mean of .35. The correlations of each judge with himself 10 days later ranged from .19 to .94, with a mean of .60. Correlations between Q-sorts of the MAPS judges and of the anamnestic judges ranged from −.39 to .53, with a mean of .13. There was an average correlation of .22 among the Q-sorts of different patients rated by the same judge, indicating that the judges tend to make their in-

[1] FINE, REUBEN. "A Scoring Scheme for the TAT and Other Projective Techniques." *J Proj Tech* 19:306–9 S '55. * (*PA* 30:4571)
[2] SUNDBERG, NORMAN D. "The Practice of Psychological Testing in Clinical Services in the United States." *Am Psychologist* 16:79–83 F '61. *

terpretations in a stereotyped manner more or less independent of the subject.

SUMMARY. The MAPS is a highly unstructured projective technique similar in purpose and product to the TAT. The inter-judge reliability of interpretations based on the MAPS is in the region of .30 to .40 for experts. The validity of interpretation is represented by correlations in the range of .10 to .20 for experts. Validity such as this, of course, is useless for individual assessment. At present there is no basis for recommending the MAPS for any practical use.

For reviews by Albert I. Rabin and Charles R. Strother, see 4:113; for excerpts from related book reviews, see 4:114.

[230a]

★Miner Sentence Completion Scale. Adults, particularly managers and management trainees; 1961–64; 1 form ('61, 4 pages); scoring guide ('64, 64 pages); scoring sheet ('61, 1 page); no data on reliability and validity; $8.50 per set of 50 scales and 50 scoring sheets; $2.75 per scoring guide; postpaid; specimen set not available; [30] minutes; John B. Miner; Springer Publishing Co., Inc. *

REFERENCES

1. MINER, JOHN B. "The Effect of a Course in Psychology on the Attitudes of Research and Development Supervisors." *J Appl Psychol* 44:224–32 Je '60. * (*PA* 35:4094)
2. MINER, JOHN B. "Occupational Differences in the Desire to Exercise Power." *Psychol Rep* 13:18 Ag '63. *

[231]

★Minnesota Percepto-Diagnostic Test. Ages 8–15, 18–65; 1962–63; brain damage and emotional disturbances; individual; 1 form ('62, 6 cards and protractor); manual ('63, 33 pages, reprint of *1* below); separate profiles ('62, 1 page) for children, adults; $3.50 per set of testing materials; $2.50 per 50 profiles; $2.50 per manual; postpaid; administration time not reported; G. B. Fuller and J. T. Laird; Journal of Clinical Psychology. *

REFERENCES

1. FULLER, GERALD B., AND LAIRD, JAMES T. "The Minnesota Percepto-Diagnostic Test." *J Clin Psychol* 19:3–34 Ja '63. * (Also published as a separate Monograph Supplement No. 16.) (*PA* 39:1696)
2. UYENO, ENSLEY. "Differentiating Psychotics From Organics on the Minnesota Percepto-Diagnostic Test." Abstract. *J Consult Psychol* 27:462 O '63. *

RICHARD W. COAN, *Professor of Psychology, University of Arizona, Tucson, Arizona.*

The *Minnesota Percepto-Diagnostic Test* (MPD) utilizes two of Wertheimer's well known designs. Since each of these appears in three different orientations, the test contains a total of six stimulus figures. The subject is asked to copy the figures, as in Bender's *Visual Motor Gestalt Test,* and his reproductions are scored for amount of rotation.

The test rests on a theoretical rationale like that underlying Bender's test, but its aim is the more limited one of differentiating such broad diagnostic classes as organic brain damage, functional disturbance, and clinical normality. To further this aim, the authors have focused on the score variable which offers greatest promise and, in the course of systematic research, have selected the figures yielding best discrimination in terms of this variable. Obvious virtues of the test are a well standardized procedure, simplicity and brevity of administration, and an objective scoring system.

The manual does not purport to provide research findings in detail, but the details it does provide are sometimes misleading. In places, impressive significance levels are cited without the information on statistical procedures, specific comparisons made, and subgroup sample sizes that the reader would need to attach a clear meaning to the probabilities. In the summaries of two preliminary studies, critical scores devised for differential prediction are presented, without proper designation, in lieu of the data from which they are derived. The reader is thereby given the false impression that, without exception, "organics rotated 60 degrees or more, those with a personality disturbance both psychotic and neurotic, rotated from 21 to 59 degrees, and normals rotated under 21 degrees." The critical scores themselves may be appropriate, depending on what errors of diagnostic classification one seeks to minimize, but the manual would have been strengthened by a separate section dealing with the rationale and procedures employed in their derivation. A questionable bit of statistical logic appears in the discussion of a table presumably consisting of correlations (the statistic itself not being explicitly identified). Here the authors suggest that a high and significant relationship between rotation and IQ may be an artifact attributable to the narrow range of intelligence in the sample.

The usefulness of the manual as a whole could have been increased by more careful editing. Here and there, communication is hampered by oddities of grammar and expression. ("Correlations in terms of one score being compared to a retest score lowers the statistical relationship" and "The protractor placed on the base line would have the line extend through degree 90.") Both in the body of the text and in a table, a *positive* value of .40 is reported for the correlation between rotation and IQ in a normal sample. Yet it is stated that "the higher the IQ in a normal group, the less the rotation evidenced." In the scoring example for card 2, an unrotated figure is shown; the line allegedly representing the central axis of the figure is drawn in an incorrect position, and a rotation of 6° is recorded.

Despite these deficiencies, it must be granted that Fuller and Laird have succeeded in devising an instrument that discriminates well between normals and functionally disturbed individuals and between the latter and the organically brain damaged. At least in comparison with other instruments that serve this purpose, the MPD displays quite satisfactory validity. In practical applications, of course, it is not likely to display the same level of efficiency found in research. For one thing, expectancies for different types of disorders in any clinical setting will differ from those in a research employing predetermined numbers of brain damage cases, schizophrenics, etc. The likelihood of correctly diagnosing a case that is actually organic may not be affected by this difference, but the likelihood of interpreting a given score correctly will be affected. In a clinical population with very few organic cases, for example, most cases diagnosed by the test as organic will be false positives. Furthermore, the clinician must often evaluate patients whose symptoms are less clear-cut than those of research cases, and it is questionable whether mild brain damage can be reliably distinguished from, say, schizophrenia on the basis of a single index of rotation. For both of these reasons, it could be argued that the sort of differential diagnosis sought with the MPD can be accomplished best through the use of score patterns (not necessarily those now in use), rather than single indices. It should be noted that Fuller and Laird themselves stress the need for caution in interpreting MPD scores, in view of the fact that the amount of rotation may be affected by intelligence, personality variables (such as perfectionism), and the type and location of brain pathology.

In the present stage of test development, the MPD has much to recommend it. It is a convenient and economical clinical instrument whose most appropriate application is the diagnosis of organic brain damage. In comparison with comparable tests, it displays substantial validity for this purpose. While it may not provide the ultimate solution to a difficult psychodiagnostic problem, it merits inclusion in batteries designed for cases of suspected organicity. It should provide a useful supplement to the information yielded by other kinds of tests.

EUGENE E. LEVITT, *Professor of Clinical Psychology, Indiana University School of Medicine, Indianapolis, Indiana.*

This instrument is based on the view that Bender-Gestalt reproductions of psychiatric patients tend to be rotated from the axis of presentation, the tendency being greater among organics than among those with functional disturbances. In various experimental studies, rotation has been arbitrarily defined as a deviation of at least 30°, or 45°, etc. The MPD is one of the first attempts to derive a continuous, quantitative rotation score.

The test consists of six test figures, Figures A and 3 of the Bender-Gestalt, each presented in three ways: conventionally; on a diamond-shaped card with the figure rotated 90° from the usual presentation; and conventionally on a diamond-shaped card. The subject is not allowed to move the stimulus or the response sheet, and is then required to draw each of the figures. The measure derived is the amount of rotation in degrees from the vertical or horizontal axis, measured with a protractor and ruler. Scores of more than 25° are scored as 25°, so that there is an imposed ceiling of 150° on the subject's test score.

Distributions of scores for fairly large samples show little overlap between normals (mean of 16), those with various emotional disturbances (mean of 38), and a sample with chronic brain syndromes (mean of 77). Using cutoff points based on distributions, more than 80 per cent of the standardization samples were correctly categorized. Within the standardization groups, there are no correlations between test scores and IQ, age, and educational level, except for a correlation of .40 for IQ in the normal sample. However, descriptive sample characteristics suggest the possibility of inter-sample correlations which may have confounded results. Mean intelligence, age, and educational level are clearly related to diagnostic category. The normals are 15 IQ points higher than the emotionally disturbed group, which is 14 points higher than the organics; the normals are youngest and best educated, and so forth. Similar trends are found for IQ and educational level in the standardization sample for children. It cannot be stated definitely that actual confounding has occurred, but it certainly appears that one might predict the diagnostic category as well from IQ, age, and educational level as from test scores.

Discounting for the moment the possibility of confounding in the standardization data, the test does at least as well in discriminating organics as other instruments for this purpose which are easily administered and scored. Using the provided cutoff points, there would be 11 per cent false positives among the normals and 18 per cent false negatives among the organics. This compares favorably with the Trail Making Test, for example, which yields about 15 per cent incorrect identifications in each group.

The MPD has the advantage of not being a speed test and hence is likely to be less affected by functional overlays such as depression. There is a problem in scoring distorted reproductions. Of course, these are likely to be themselves manifestations of organicity to such an extent that the scoring of rotation is gratuitous. In the standardization sample, it appears that a maximum score of 25 was assigned to such figures. One wonders about the possible effect on the standardization group means.

Again ignoring the possibility of confounding factors, the test appears clinically useful in the diagnosis of organicity. That is, it has demonstrated considerable ability to discriminate between persons without brain damage and those who have all sorts of "manifest symptomatology" indicative of brain damage, i.e., severe cases. However, the hospital psychologist is rarely called upon to apply his clinical tests to cases in which the diagnosis of a brain syndrome is so evident. The standardization data do not permit the inference that the test would be clinically successful in diagnosing cases with minimal or even moderate organicity, the sort of questionable case which is often referred to the psychologist for differential diagnosis.

The ability of the test to discriminate between normals and those with emotional disturbances suggests some intriguing possibilities for research, but it does not indicate any important clinical use. Unfortunately, psychotics, neurotics, and character disturbances are lumped together in the standardization data, and there is no way of determining whether the test could discriminate among them, a feat which would, of course, render it clinically useful.

The MPD is new and all the available work with it thus far has been done by the senior test constructor and his collaborators. It is invariably prudent to await additional research findings by disinterested individuals before attempting to make a definite statement about the instrument's utility. Certainly the possibility of confounding of the standardization data by personal factors of the subjects requires further investigation.

[232]

★Myokinetic Psychodiagnosis (MKP). Ages 10 and over; 1951–58; expressive movement technique; individual; 1 form ('58, c1951–58, 8 pages); manual ('58, c1951–58, see 8 below); norms based upon South American subjects; $5 per 25 tests; $6.75 per manual; cash orders postpaid; table of prescribed dimensions, stopwatch, and other accessories required for administration; [20–30] minutes in 2 sessions 1 week apart; English edition ('58, translated from the French edition, '51, by Mrs. Jacques Dubois); Emilio Mira y Lopez; Hoeber Medical Division, Harper & Row, Publishers, Inc. *

REFERENCES

1. MIRA, EMILIO. "Myokinetic Psychodiagnosis: A New Technique of Exploring the Conative Trends of Personality." Proc Royal Soc Med 33:173–94 F '40. * (PA 14:4645)
2. MIRA, EMILIO. Appendix, "Technique and Interpretation of the Myokinetic Psychodiagnosis (M.P.D.)," pp. 159–96, passim. In his Psychiatry in War. New York: W. W. Norton & Co., Inc., 1943. Pp. 206. *
3. BELL, JOHN ELDERKIN. Chap. 15, "Mira Myokinetic Psychodiagnosis," pp. 328–40. In his Projective Techniques: A Dynamic Approach to the Study of Personality. New York: Longmans, Green & Co., Inc., 1948. Pp. xvi, 533. * (PA 23:1284)
4. BELL, JOHN ELDERKIN. "The Case of Gregor: Psychological Test Data." Rorsch Res Exch & J Proj Tech 13(2): 155–205 '49. * (PA 24:2589)
5. LOPEZ, E. M. "Recent Development of the Myokinetic Psychodiagnosis," p. 88. Abstract. In Proceedings and Papers of the Twelfth International Congress of Psychology Held at the University of Edinburgh, July 23rd to 29th, 1948. Edinburgh, Scotland: Oliver and Boyd Ltd., 1950. Pp. xxviii, 152. *
6. WILSON, ROBERT G. A Study of Expressive Movements in Three Groups of Adolescent Boys, Stutterers, Non-Stutterers Maladjusted and Normals, by Means of Three Measures of Personality, Mira's Myokinetic Psychodiagnosis, the Bender-Gestalt, and Figure Drawing. Doctor's thesis, Western Reserve University (Cleveland, Ohio), 1950.
7. TAKALA, MARTTI. "Analysis of the Mira Test," pp. 67–112, passim. In his Studies of Psychomotor Personality Tests I. Annals of the Finnish Academy of Science and Letters, Series B, No. 81, Part 2. Helsinki, Finland: Suomalainen Tiedeakatemia, Academia Scientiarum Fennica, 1953. Pp. 130. * (PA 28:6055)
8. MIRA Y LOPEZ, EMILIO. M.K.P.: Myokinetic Psychodiagnosis. Translated by Mrs. Jacques Dubois from the 1951 French Edition. New York: [Hoeber Medical Division, Harper & Row, Publishers, Inc.], 1958. Pp. xx, 186. * (PA 33:7261)
9. TALMADGE, MAX. "Expressive Graphic Movements and Their Relationship to Temperament Factors. Psychol Monogr 72(16):1–30 '58. * (PA 33:9733)
10. HAKKINEN, SAULI, AND TOIVAINEN, YRJO. "Psychological Factors Causing Labour Turnover Among Underground Workers." Occup Psychol 34:15–30 Ja '60. * (PA 35:7162)

PHILIP L. HARRIMAN, Professor of Psychology, Bucknell University, Lewisburg, Pennsylvania.

A small weight attached to the end of a

string held in the outstretched hand of a blind-folded person moves in an interesting fashion as the holder imagines a particular type of movement. The direction of the swingings, commented upon by Chevreuil as long ago as 1828, was interpreted as one more bit of evidence that motor activities result from ideas. In 1874, William B. Carpenter, the English physiologist, coined the term *ideomotor action* to describe the elicitation of motor response by the presence of strong ideas. Conversely, many informed persons once accepted without question the view that certain patterns of motor activity furnish evidence regarding the ideas unexpressed in writing, speech, or other forms of intentional behavior. To one accepting the interactionist solution of the body-mind problem, what could be more obvious?

The possibilities in analyses of expressive activities, therefore, are said to be well nigh limitless, particularly if the person under scrutiny be unaware of what he is doing, be "caught off guard," or be distracted by some projective technique. Expressive drawings or finger paintings, manipulations of objects, or unimpeded outflows of words may be construed either as "royal roads" to the unconscious or as types of ideomotor actions, depending upon the modernity of their advocate. If Margaret F. Washburn be correct, consciousness itself is, indeed, motor activity—a likelihood that William James almost postulated. Hence, to explore a person's motor activities is to acquire valid knowledge of his innermost mind.

The *Myokinetic Psychodiagnosis* (MKP) is an expressive technique requiring the person merely to draw lines of various types. Administration is simple; materials consist of nothing but pencils, a low table, a chair, a screen to be interposed between the subject's eyes, the paper upon which the lines are drawn, and a manual giving simple, easily comprehended directions. Two sessions are necessary to complete the drawings. The observer takes notes on comments made, alterations in posture, special difficulties encountered, and other types of behavior of the subject. Thus, at the end of the second testing period, preferably a week after the first, there is a booklet filled with the prescribed drawings—half drawn with the right and half with the left hand—and some notes recorded during the sessions. The procedure is simple to administer and easy to carry out by the subject, although some arm fatigue is often reported, a requirement being that the elbow must at all times be raised above the table.

The MKP technique was first popularly known back in 1943, when Emilio Mira y Lopez, at one time professor of psychiatry at Barcelona and then of the faculty at Buenos Aires, published in English his challenging book entitled *Psychiatry in War*. The appendix (*2*) is devoted to an exposition of his novel diagnostic technique, its method of administration, and the types of subjects upon whom he standardized it. A year before—in the Salmon Lecture before the New York Academy of Medicine—he interested a very small group in the diagnostic possibilities of his technique. Mira y Lopez may now gain a wide hearing among psychoclinicians, for a new translation (*8*), this time from French into English, appeared in 1958. Previously, Harold H. Anderson [1] and J. E. Bell (*3*) had devoted some space to the MKP in their well-known expositions of projective techniques. Obviously, therefore, a serious student of psychological tests and measures and of diagnostic techniques ought to be familiar with Mira's contribution. For even though more than 95 per cent of the articles discussing it heretofore have appeared only in Spanish or Portuguese, it may be predicted that research articles will begin appearing in scientific journals in English-speaking countries.

This reviewer believes that quantitative evaluations, following the explicit instructions given by Mira, are relatively easy to make. Further use of the MKP will clear up ambiguities in objective ways of measuring the shiftings of the lines, particularly those which are relative. The temporal aspects of subtests must be examined closely. Objective scorings for disparities between right and left hand drawings await investigation. Qualitative evaluations of MKP test booklets are still in the realm of impressionistic conjectures and intuitive opinions. All that may be safely inferred at this time is that the line drawings of depressed individuals are markedly different from those of hypomanics. The possibilities for research seem to be great. If the promised book by Michael Finn does not give the last

1 ANDERSON, HAROLD H., AND ANDERSON, GLADYS L. *An Introduction to Projective Techniques and Other Devices for Understanding the Dynamics of Human Behavior.* New York: Prentice-Hall, Inc., 1951. Pp. xxv, 720. *

word on the Mira technique, MKP will serve the needs of many a candidate for the master's or the doctor's degree in clinical psychology. As for using the technique to influence judgments in cases involving human welfare, a psychoclinician must be advised to wait at least a decade for nomothetic and idiographic research pertaining to its validity. The reviewer, in a temerarious mood, predicts that the MKP will soon be forgotten.

IRWIN G. SARASON, *Associate Professor of Psychology, University of Washington, Seattle, Washington.*

Mira's book contains a manual for administration of the MKP test, together with normative data and his rationale for construction of the test. The rationale, stated most generally, is that the analysis of expressive movements can provide valuable data relevant to personality diagnosis. On the basis of quantitative and qualitative analysis of expressive movements, Mira believes that valid statements can be made concerning aggressiveness, conflict, degree of psychopathology, emotionality, and other characteristics. In addition, the author believes that inferences concerning intelligence can also be made.

The manual provides a careful description of the materials and procedures required for administration. The MKP test consists of a series of simple motor tasks. The task for the subject is to draw with each hand (and, for one task, with both hands simultaneously) simple geometric figures such as straight and zigzag lines. These drawings are made by the subject under conditions in which the stimulus to be reproduced is in full view and also under conditions in which the subject cannot see the stimulus. The manual states that the test should be administered twice to each subject with a one week time interval. It is further recommended that another pair of protocols be obtained one month following initial testing.

The manual adequately describes the procedure for quantitative scoring of the test. The scoring is in terms of deviations of lines and figures drawn by subjects from the standard stimuli contained in the test booklet. In all, the manual describes 79 measurements of aspects of subjects' drawings which are required for test interpretation. The complexities presented by so many scoring categories, together with the readministration of the test recommended

in the manual, make it an impractical tool. It seems likely that shorter versions of the test could be constructed after appropriate factor analytic and other psychometric studies have been carried out. Test-retest reliabilities for the various drawing tasks are reported as ranging from .53 to .71 with a one week interval and .20 to .76 with a one year interval. Tables of norms (means and standard deviations for a variety of measures of expressive behavior) are provided for normal adults, children and adolescents, primitive people, and criminals. While some quantitative comparisons are reported among these groups, many of Mira's interpretations appear to be based on clinical inference rather than statistical findings. However, the data provided could be used to make such comparisons.

The test is highly original in conception. The manual represents the culmination of over 20 years of work with MKP. Unfortunately, little besides the manual is available in English. Since the test does not call for verbal behavior, cultural factors are probably less pronounced than would be the case for most personality tests. Nonetheless, use in countries other than the South American ones where most of the work on MKP was conducted clearly requires independent normative studies. For this reason MKP, at the present time, must be regarded as a research instrument rather than a well established clinical one. While one might have great sympathy with Mira's emphasis on expressive behavior as a path to understanding personality, it is still necessary to evaluate empirically the various interpretations of expressive behavior contained in the manual.

In conclusion, then, MKP is a test which seems to tap a dimension—that of expressive behavior in the form of subjects' drawings—which has not received much attention by American students of personality. MKP provides a research tool with which this aspect of expressive behavior might profitably be studied. However, the test is neither a very practical nor economical (in terms of time) test for wide clinical usage.

For excerpts from reviews of the manual, see B343.

[233]

The Object Relations Technique. Ages 11 and over; 1955; individual; 1 form ['55, 13 cards]; manual ('55, 232 pages, see 3); no data on reliability; 63s. per set of cards and manual; postage extra; (90) minutes; Herbert Phillipson; Tavistock Publications. *

REFERENCES

1–6. See 5:151.
7. O'Kelly, E. "The Object Relations Test—Some Quantitative Findings Relating to Early Separation From the Mother." B Brit Psychol Soc 29:24 My '56. *
8. Phillipson, H. "The Use of Cognitive and Projective Tests as an Approach to the Therapy of a Student Teacher Who Has Serious Spelling Difficulties." Rorsch Newsl 3:24–31 D '58. *
9. Orme, J. E. "O.R.T. Performance in Schizophrenia." J Mental Sci 105:1119–22 O '59. * (PA 34:6381)
10. Gladston, Elaine R., and Amado-Haguenauer, Ginette. "Fluidity in the Limits of the Self." Int J Social Psychiatry 6:260–8 au '60. *
11. Haskell, Royal J., Jr. "Relationship Between Aggressive Behavior and Psychological Tests." J Proj Tech 25:431–40 D '61. *
12. Vernon, M. D. "The Relation of Perception to Personality Factors." Brit J Psychol 52:205–17 Ag '61. * (PA 36:3HG05V)
13. Viitamaki, R. Olavi. Psychoses in Children: A Psychological Follow-Up Study. Annals of the Finnish Academy of Science and Letters, Series B, Vol. 125, Part 2. Helsinki, Finland: Suomalainen Tiedeakatemia, Academia Scientiarum Fennica, 1962. Pp. 52. * (PA 39:2650)

H. R. Beech, *Lecturer in Psychology, The Institute of Psychiatry, Maudsley Hospital, London, England.*

Information concerning the application and usefulness of this technique has been slow in accumulating. To some extent this may be attributed to satisfaction with better established projective techniques, and those potential users who have considered this test may well feel that Phillipson has not made out a convincing case for a change to be made to the ORT. The technique purports to offer some of the advantages of both the *Thematic Apperception Test* and the Rorschach, this being largely accomplished by having the pictorial representations somewhat more ambiguous than in the TAT, but less so than in the Rorschach. In other particulars the test appears to have some degree of uniqueness, but it is not clear what advantages actually do accrue to, for example, subtle differences in administration and instruction over and above those used in other projective tests.

It seems likely from the published records of patients' responses to the ORT that, thus far, only persons with a specialized knowledge of psychoanalytic theory and a particular kind of experience would be in a position to duplicate the interpretations offered, in which case one might argue that the usefulness of the ORT depends upon the limitations both of the examiner and of psychoanalytic theory.

Whether one accepts or rejects the theoretical orientation common to projective techniques, and the special theoretical position underlying the ORT, appears to be a matter of personal preference, opinion, and training rather than of fact. This is not to say that certain facts are not available, for evidence concerning the reliability and validity of projective tests has accumulated to the point where one can say that, in these respects, such techniques leave much to be desired. In the case of the ORT the course of the development of the technique is not entirely clear, although it appears that the test has been used fairly extensively (presumably by Phillipson and his colleagues) both in the clinic and in a commercial application, and there is no doubt that some individuals have acquired a great deal of personal experience in the use of this test. However, the ORT will prove something of a disappointment for those looking for some evidence concerning the reliability and validity of the tests and techniques they use.

The reliability of the technique is still unknown and, it should be said, would be difficult to establish in view of the kind of material dealt with. No satisfactory evidence is yet available respecting validity which rests almost entirely upon the author's report that he and his colleagues have found the technique suitable and useful for subjects of 14 years and upward, and that comparisons between ORT findings and psychiatric interview reports have been made. This information concerning validity must be taken on trust and no information is provided which would enable one to evaluate these claims and implications. The sparse evidence of the kind which is usually found more acceptable (e.g., 9, 11) does not inspire a great deal of confidence in the technique.

Phillipson seems to be susceptible to two kinds of pressure: that which stems from a psychodynamic theoretical orientation and traditional emphasis upon qualitative global analysis, and that from "scientific" considerations which urge piecemeal assessment and quantification. He has responded, not hopefully, to the latter pressure by providing data respecting the frequency of certain classes of response to ORT cards. These data, obtained from 50 young psychiatric outpatients (almost all with IQ's of 120 or above) and 40 normal adolescent girls, are clearly limited in scope and are not significantly enhanced in this respect by the addition of O'Kelly's (6) quantification of the ORT responses of two groups of delinquent adolescent girls.

It is apparent that the ORT does not differ in any fundamental from currently available projective techniques and that it may even be at some disadvantage in view of its comparatively brief history. Fortunately the gaps created by the exclusion of projective devices show signs of being bridged by techniques characterized by greater emphasis upon the basic attributes of tests which are most usually thought desirable. The most promising of these seems to be the Repertory Grid technique [1] which is extremely flexible and has considerable potential for clinical use both in revealing unique characteristics and relationships of the individual construing system [2] and in its adaptation for diagnostic purposes, on a group basis.[3] To a lesser extent and with some qualifications, the Osgood Semantic Differential,[4] the Q-sort,[5] and the Personal Questionnaire [6] could be adapted to serve some of those functions most often reserved for projective techniques. These techniques could contribute a precision and objectivity characteristically absent in projective tests, and it is a point to be appreciated that they are not wedded to any particular theoretical standpoint.

In summary it might be said that the ORT is a projective technique with a largely unknown development, without information respecting its reliability, and not having any very acceptable evidence concerning its validity. The claims made for the technique have yet to be substantiated and users of projective techniques may well feel that the ORT has no obvious advantages over the available alternatives.

Int J Group Psychother 8:481-2 O '58. *Leopold Bellak.* * The test pictures are well chosen and nicely executed. There are a number of case studies, one done in detail, which demonstrates that the test elicits very useful material (some indications of exhibitionism-

voyeurism seem to have been overlooked in the test material of the first case). The normative data—based on fifty patients of an outpatient clinic and forty adolescent girls—are not better or worse than those of most projective tests and not of primary importance as far as the content is concerned. Such normative data are of more relevance with regard to the effect of the shading nuances, which seem altogether not systematically enough investigated. There is, in fact, ground for reasonable doubt that the special features of the test, in form of object content *or* shading, add significant dimensions of responses. * this is an interesting test, originated and described by a competent psychoanalytic psychologist. It will take a great deal of future empirical evidence, however, to establish whether the Object Relations Test adds anything basically new or better to our armamentarium for diagnosing object relations.

For a review by George Westby, see 5:151; for excerpts from reviews of the manual, see 5:B338.

[234]

★Pickford Projective Pictures. Ages 5–15; 1963; 1 form (120 cards); manual (130 pages, see 5 below); no data on reliability; 25s. ($5) per set of cards; 30s. ($4) per manual; 50s. per set of cards and manual; postage extra; to be administered about 6 pictures at a time over about 20 therapy sessions; R. W. Pickford with the assistance of Ruth Bowyer and John Struthers; Tavistock Publications Ltd. (United States publisher: Springer Publishing Co., Inc.) *

REFERENCES
1. PICKFORD, R. W. "Personality and the Interpretation of Pictures: A New Projection Technique." *J Personality* 17:210–20 D '48. * (*PA* 25:3177)
2. PICKFORD, R. W. "New Projection Material for Child Therapy." *B Brit Psychol Soc* 1:358–63 Jl '50. * (*PA* 27:5202)
3. PICKFORD, R. W. "Pictures for Child Psychotherapy." *Scottish Med J* 5:530–6 D '60. *
4. PICKFORD, R. W. "Picture Projection Material for Child Psychotherapy." Abstract. *Acta Psychologica* 19:860–1 '61. *
5. PICKFORD, R. W.; WITH THE ASSISTANCE OF RUTH BOWYER AND JOHN STRUTHERS. *Pickford Projective Pictures.* London: Tavistock Publications Ltd., 1963. Pp. xi, 122. *

STANLEY J. SEGAL, *Associate Professor of Psychology, and Director, Student Counseling Center, State University of New York at Buffalo, Buffalo, New York.*

The suggested use of these pictures is as a basis for therapeutic interaction with children from 5–15. It is recommended that the 120 ambiguous line drawings of people in a variety of situations be presented over a series of interviews and form the basis for the therapeutic interaction. The manual suggests five approaches that have been followed, from using

1 KELLY, GEORGE A. *The Psychology of Personal Constructs: Vol. 1, A Theory of Personality; Vol. 2, Clinical Diagnosis and Psychotherapy.* New York: W. W. Norton & Co., Inc., 1955. Pp. xviii, 1–556; x, 559–1218. *
2 BEECH, H. R. "Some Practical and Technical Difficulties in the Application of Behaviour Therapy." *B Brit Psychol Soc* 16:25–33 Jl '63. *
3 BANNISTER, D. "Conceptual Structure in Thought Disordered Schizophrenics." *J Mental Sci* 106:1230–49 O '60. *
4 OSGOOD, CHARLES E.; SUCI, GEORGE J.; AND TANNENBAUM, PERCY H. *The Measurement of Meaning.* Urbana, Ill.: University of Illinois Press, 1957. Pp. vii, 342. *
5 STEPHENSON, WILLIAM. *The Study of Behavior: Q-Technique and Its Methodology.* Chicago, Ill.: University of Chicago Press, 1953. Pp. ix, 376. * (With reservations set out by Lee J. Cronbach and Goldine C. Gleser in their review in *Psychometrika* 19:327–30 D '54. See 5:B408 for an excerpt from this review.)
6 SHAPIRO, M. B. "A Method of Measuring Psychological Changes Specific to the Individual Psychiatric Patient." *Brit J Med Psychol* 34:151–5 pt 2 '61. *

the pictures as a cathartic experience for the child to using the responses as a basis for psychoanalytic therapy.

Although there are statements that the pictures have diagnostic value, there is little clear indication of this use of the pictures outside of the context of psychotherapy.

The manual clearly indicates the authors' concern for the need for the accumulation of additional data and the firmer establishment of diagnostic and therapeutic validity for the pictures. The data presented are based on the experiences with 129 children seen in a number of child guidance clinics in and around Glasgow, Scotland. Not all children were given the entire series.

The authors correctly point out that one unique advantage of this instrument is the large number of items available, widening its use. They offer tabulation of responses for each of the pictures typically indicating, separately for boys and girls, frequency of sex identification of the pictured figures, identification of other objects presented, and actions, interactions, or outcomes. There is also a listing of each picture with the most frequent story themes, a descriptive list of the pictures, and a categorization according to the pictured themes using such categories as "relationship of one child to both parent figures," "sexual curiosity," "situations involving tensions over food." These listings can be helpful to users if they plan to use only part of the series for some specific purpose.

The statistical analysis of 129 records uses as a validity criterion clinician's estimate of value, diagnostically, therapeutically, or both. This is a tabulation of clinicians' statements broken down in terms of presenting symptoms, but is not dealt with to produce the usual validity coefficient. The test may be used over the IQ range from 80 and upward with its estimated value being equal for low and high intelligence quotients. As expected, children with high IQ's tend to give longer and more elaborate stories. The data reported suggest that the pictures are equally valuable for boys and girls and for younger and older children, with some comment that older children tend to be more comfortable with this task than with play materials.

This test differs markedly in approach from most others in that the emphasis is on the direct utilization of the materials in therapeutic

work with children, and in this respect it is similar to Lowenfeld's World Material. The length of the series, the authors' attempts to get as many complete records as possible, and the use of the stories as a vehicle of change suggests that the problem of reliability is a difficult one and this may be attested by the lack of such data in the manual. The illustrative cases, which are carefully presented, complete with many stories on each child, gave this reviewer the impression that the themes from story to story were similar enough for different pictures that some attempt at a split-half reliability based on the authors' categorization of pictures might be usefully carried out and presented.

A strength of Pickford's presentation is his insistence that the protocols need not be used within a single theoretical framework. He gives illustrations in a chapter by L. R. Bowyer of a Rogerian approach, while his own illustrative examples are quite clearly within a psychoanalytic framework.

All data are on a British sample, but from the stories presented it would be surprising if American children reacted in a markedly different manner. Only three or four of the pictures present figures that are so typically British that American children would sense the cultural difference.

I would feel that this set of pictures can be a valuable aid to the clinician working with children. Its adequacy as a diagnostic tool is unclear from the data available, and one can only second the authors' comments that a great deal of additional work is needed. There does seem great utility in the series as a focus of therapeutic interaction with a child. The brief comments about its use in helping children with school learning problems are intriguing and exciting. This is an area where great value may well emerge if the few cases discussed prove to be fairly typical of the kind of progress one can expect.

I would encourage child guidance workers and school psychologists to evaluate the manual and the pictures in order to judge whether the *Pickford Projective Pictures* may not represent a valuable addition to the approaches they presently use in working with children.

Brit J Ed Psychol 33:335 N '63. R. Hetherington. Those who have tried the various available forms of picture projective tests with young children, will have noticed the gap that exists between the T.A.T. or Symond's Picture Story Test for older children, and the rather childish and off-putting C.A.T. Professor Pickford's new set of pictures may help to fill this gap. The unwillingness of young children to tell lengthy stories, makes it desirable to have a large number of pictures yielding many short stories in which recurrent themes may be discerned. The Pickford Projective Pictures consist of 120 simple line-drawings which "cover a very wide range of stimulus content" varying from relationships with father figures and authority, and relationships with mother figures including sibling jealousy; to play and conflict between children, and death and ghosts. There are some twenty distinctive themes represented. Professor Pickford suggests that the pictures should be used about six at a time, so that the material will last for about twenty therapeutic sessions. However, for diagnostic use, a larger number of pictures each yielding a short story might well reveal highly significant recurrent themes reflecting some of the child's pre-occupations and worries. The book accompanying the test material contains some very useful data for responses given to the pictures by fairly large groups of children in Glasgow child guidance clinics. Data of this sort are too rarely available for projective tests. The book also contains a chapter on the use of the pictures in analytic treatment which must not be allowed to antagonise people who are allergic to Freudian interpretations of innocent comments by children. For example, the comment, "This little boy stole apples from a rough farmer's orchard" is interpreted as a wish to rob the father of his sexuality. This interpretation goes on, for good measure, to interpret the tummy-ache the boy is said to have after eating the apples as a phantasy of incestuous pregnancy, on the part of the girl telling the story! With or without interpretations of this kind, the pictures seem to have been used successfully in clinics in Glasgow, and should help to fill a gap in our techniques for persuading children to talk in a revealing way about themselves.

Percept & Motor Skills 17:647 O '63. * While standardization of the test does not even approach the official APA standards for test construction, the stimuli and preliminary data indicate that further work is reasonable and likely to be profitable.

Scottish Ed J 46:711 S 20 '63. * The first advantage of this material lies in the number and variety of cards available. The next advantage lies in the fact that freedom of presentation is allowed to the person administering it to the child. Anyone using this material would probably be psychoanalytically inclined, yet it is not essential to subscribe to this school. * Psychologists will find this a useful addition to their equipment but it is doubtful if it could be used by teachers in school who had not a solid background of training in psychology.

[235]

★**Psychiatric Attitudes Battery.** Adults; 1955–61; attitudes toward mental hospitals, psychiatrists, and psychiatric treatment; 5 parts; directions for administration and scoring presented in *2* below; no data on reliability of scores; no data on validity; no norms; $2 per set of cards for *a*; $1 per manual for *b*; postpaid; reprint of *2* below free; test forms may be reproduced locally; Marvin Reznikoff, John Paul Brady, William W. Zeller, and Omneya Souelem (*d*); Institute of Living. *

a) PICTURE ATTITUDES TEST. I form ['59, 3 cards, separate cards for men and women and a general card]; [15] minutes.
b) SENTENCE COMPLETION ATTITUDES TEST. 4 attitude scores: psychiatrists, hospitals, treatment, outcome; I form ['59, 1 hectographed page]; revised scoring manual ('61, 17 hectographed pages); [10] minutes.
c) MULTIPLE CHOICE ATTITUDES QUESTIONNAIRE. I form ['59, 2 hectographed pages]; [5] minutes.
d) SOUELEM ATTITUDES SCALE. Forms A, B, ['55, 2 hectographed pages]; [10] minutes.
e) DEGREE OF IMPROVEMENT RATING SCALE. Ratings by psychiatrists; I form ['59, 1 hectographed page]; "a minute or two."

REFERENCES

1. BRADY, JOHN PAUL; ZELLER, WILLIAM W.; AND REZNIKOFF, MARVIN. "Attitudinal Factors Influencing Outcome of Treatment of Hospitalized Psychiatric Patients." *J Clin & Exp Psychopathol* 20:326–34 D '59. * (*PA* 34:6073)
2. REZNIKOFF, MARVIN; BRADY, JOHN PAUL; AND ZELLER, WILLIAM W. "The Psychiatric Attitudes Battery: A Procedure for Assessing Attitudes Toward Psychiatric Treatment and Hospitals." *J Clin Psychol* 15:260–6 Jl '59. * (*PA* 35:3644)
3. BRADY, JOHN PAUL; REZNIKOFF, MARVIN; AND ZELLER, WILLIAM W. "The Relationship of Expectation of Improvement to Actual Improvement of Hospitalized Psychiatric Patients." *J Nerv & Mental Dis* 130:41–4 Ja '60. * (*PA* 35:6649)
4. REZNIKOFF, MARVIN; BRADY, JOHN PAUL; ZELLER, WILLIAM W.; AND TOOMEY, LAURA C. "Attitudinal Change in Hospitalized Psychiatric Patients." *J Clin & Exp Psychopathol* 21:309–14 D '60. * (*PA* 35:5118)
5. TOOMEY, LAURA C.; REZNIKOFF, MARVIN; BRADY, JOHN PAUL; AND SCHUMANN, DWIGHT W. "Attitudes of Nursing Students Toward Psychiatric Treatment and Hospitals." *Mental Hyg* 45:589–602 O '61. *
6. TOOMEY, LAURA C.; REZNIKOFF, MARVIN; BRADY, JOHN PAUL; AND SCHUMANN, W. DWIGHT. "Some Relationships Between the Attitudes of Nursing Students Toward Psychiatry and Success in Psychiatric Affiliation." *Nursing Res* 10:165–9 su '61. *
7. IMRE, PAUL D. "Attitudes of Volunteers Toward Mental Hospitals Compared to Patients and Personnel." *J Clin Psychol* 18:516 O '62. * (*PA* 39:4807)
8. IMRE, PAUL, AND WOLF, SIDNEY. "Attitudes of Patients and Personnel Toward Mental Hospitals." *J Clin Psychol* 18:232–4 Ap '62. * (*PA* 38:8795)
9. GYNTHER, MALCOLM D.; REZNIKOFF, MARVIN; AND FISHMAN, MELBA. "Attitudes of Psychiatric Patients Toward Treatment, Psychiatrists and Mental Hospitals." *J Nerv & Mental Dis* 136:68–71 Ja '63. *

10. REZNIKOFF, MARVIN. "Attitudes of Psychiatric Nurses and Aides Toward Psychiatric Treatment and Hospitals." *Mental Hyg* 47:360–4 Jl '63. *

[236]

★Rock-A-Bye, Baby: A Group Projective Test for Children. Groups of 9–16 aged 5–10; 1959, c1951–56; sibling rivalry; 6 scores: self concept, jealousy index, aggression to parents, guilt index, anxiety index, index of obsessive trends; stimulus material presented by 35-minute 16 mm. sound film ('56, script previously published in 1951); 1 form ['59]; mimeographed manual ['59, 33 pages, containing record form and analysis sheet which must be reproduced locally]; no data on reliability of scores; no norms for self concept and aggression to parents; film may be rented ($10 per week) or purchased ($157); $1 per manual; monograph (see *1* below) free with manual; postage extra; (60) minutes; Mary R. Haworth and Adolf G. Woltmann; distributed by Psychological Cinema Register. *

REFERENCES

1. HAWORTH, MARY ROBBINS. "The Use of a Filmed Puppet Show as a Group Projective Technique for Children." *Genetic Psychol Monogr* 56:257–96 N '57. * (*PA* 33:10332)
2. HAWORTH, MARY R. Chap. 9, "Films as a Group Technique," pp. 177–90. In *Projective Techniques With Children.* Edited by Albert I. Rabin and Mary R. Haworth. New York: Grune & Stratton, Inc., 1960. Pp. xiii, 392. * (*PA* 35:2229)
3. HAWORTH, MARY R. "Repeat Study With a Projective Film for Children." *J Consult Psychol* 25:78–83 F '61. * (*PA* 36:3HG78H)
4. HAWORTH, MARY R. "Responses of Children to a Group Projective Film and to the Rorschach, CAT, Despert Fables and D-A-P." *J Proj Tech* 26:47–60 Mr '62. * (*PA* 37:2893)

[237]

*Rorschach. Ages 3 and over; 1921–60; variously referred to by such titles as Rorschach Method, Rorschach Test, Rorschach Ink Blot Test, Rorschach Psychodiagnostics; many variations and modifications are in use with no one method of scoring and interpreting generally accepted; unless otherwise indicated, the word Rorschach may be interpreted as referring to the use of the Psychodiagnostic Plates listed as *f* below.

a) BEHN-RORSCHACH TEST. 1941–56; a parallel set of inkblots; also called *The Bero-Test*; 1 form ('41, 10 cards); manual ('56, 198 pages, see *2156* below, translation of the German edition published in 1941); record blank ('51, 1 page); Fr. 19 ($11) per set of cards; Fr. 9 ($3) per pad of 100 record blanks; Fr. 25 ($8) per manual; postage extra; Hans Zulliger; Hans Huber. (United States distributor: Grune & Stratton, Inc.) *

b) THE BUHLER-LEFEVER RORSCHACH DIAGNOSTIC SIGN LIST AND RECORD OF THE RORSCHACH STANDARDIZATION STUDIES FOR THE DETERMINATION AND EVALUATION OF THE BASIC RORSCHACH SCORE. 1954; 1 form (4 pages); $6.50 per 25 booklets, postpaid; Charlotte Buhler, Karl Buhler, and D. Welty Lefever; Western Psychological Services. *

c) HARROWER'S GROUP RORSCHACH. Ages 12 and over; 1941–45; $12.50 per set of the original Rorschach inkblots on slides for standard projector; $4.70 per set of 25 record blanks; postpaid; (70–90) minutes; distributed by Psychological Corporation.

d) HARROWER'S MULTIPLE CHOICE TEST. Ages 12 and over; 1943–45; for use with either cards or slides; $3 per 25 record blanks, postage extra; M. R. Harrower; distributed by Psychological Corporation. *

e) *PSYCHODIAGNOSTIC INKBLOTS. 1945–60; a parallel set of inkblots; manual uses the title *Harrower Inkblots*; 1 form ('45, 10 cards); revised manual ('60, 70 pages); $6.50 per set of cards; $3.50 per manual; postage extra; M. R. Harrower and M. E. Steiner; distributed by Grune & Stratton, Inc. * (Administra-

tion instructions are written in terms of an expendable set of the inkblots, which is available at $2 per set from the author, M. R. Harrower.)

f) PSYCHODIAGNOSTIC PLATES, FIFTH EDITION. 1921–54; 1 form ('54, 10 cards, identical with original edition copyrighted in 1921); manual, fifth edition ('51, 263 pages, translation of the 1942 German edition with the addition of a bibliography); record blank ('47, 1 page); Fr. 27 ($12.50) per set of cards; Fr. 8.50 ($3.50) per pad of 100 record blanks; Fr. 23 ($7) per manual; postage extra; Hermann Rorschach; Hans Huber. (United States distributor: Grune & Stratton, Inc.) *

g) RORSCHACH COMBINED LOCATION AND RECORD FORM. 1957; 1 form (12 pages); $2.75 per 25 booklets; 30¢ per specimen set; postpaid; Nicholas De Palma; the Author. *

h) THE RORSCHACH EVALOGRAPH. 1954; 1 form (28 pages); $5 per 10 booklets, postpaid; Morse P. Manson and George A. Ulett; Western Psychological Services. *

i) RORSCHACH LOCATION CHARTS (BECK'S SCORING AREAS). 1951–54; 1 form ('54, 12 cards, identical with set copyrighted in 1951); Fr. 9.50 ($3.25) per set of cards, postage extra; Julian C. Davis; Hans Huber. (United States distributor: Grune & Stratton, Inc.) *

j)*RORSCHACH METHOD OF PERSONALITY DIAGNOSIS, REVISED EDITION. 1939–60; 1 form ('60, 4 pages); directions ('60, 4 pages); $3.10 per 35 blanks, postage extra; Bruno Klopfer and Helen H. Davidson; [Harcourt, Brace & World, Inc.]. *

k) THE RORSCHACH MINIATURE INKBLOTS: A LOCATION CHART. 1955; $5.50 per pad of 100 sheets, postpaid; Morse P. Manson; Western Psychological Services. *

l) STRUCTURED-OBJECTIVE RORSCHACH TEST: PRELIMINARY EDITION. See 242.

REFERENCES

1–147. See 40:1246.
148–598. See 3:73.
599–1219. See 4:117.
1220–2297. See 5:154.
2298. COFFIN, THOMAS E. "Some Conditions of Suggestions and Suggestibility: A Study of Certain Attitudinal and Situational Factors Influencing the Process of Suggestion," pp. 47–64. *Psychol Monogr* 53(4):1–125 '41. * (*PA* 16:2662)
2299. SHAW, BARRIE. *Sex Populars in the Rorschach.* Doctor's thesis, University of Kentucky (Lexington, Ky.), 1949. (*DA* 20:4178)
2300. ZUBIN, JOSEPH. Chap. 21, "Rorschach Test," pp. 283–95. In *Selective Partial Ablations of the Frontal Cortex: A Correlative Study of Its Effects on Human Psychotic Subjects, Vol. 1.* Edited by Fred A. Mettler. New York: Paul B. Hoeber, Inc., 1949. Pp. xiv, 517. *
2301. "Brief Report on the First International Rorschach Meeting." *Rorschachiana* (3):110–3 '50. *
2302. SKIFF, STANLEY CUBE. *A Study of Some Relationships Between Personality Traits and Learning Ability.* Doctor's thesis, University of Kentucky (Lexington, Ky.), 1950. (*DA* 20:3861)
2303. FISHER, SEYMOUR, AND HINDS, EDITH. "The Organization of Hostility Controls in Various Personality Structures." *Genetic Psychol Monogr* 44:3–68 Ag '51. * (*PA* 26:2889)
2304. JERNIGAN, AUSTIN JACK. *A Rorschach Study of Normal and Psychotic Subjects in a Situation of Stress.* Doctor's thesis, University of Kentucky (Lexington, Ky.), 1951. (*DA* 20:3833)
2305. MARTIN, HARRY. *A Rorschach Study of Suicide.* Doctor's thesis, University of Kentucky (Lexington, Ky.), 1951. (*DA* 20:3837)
2306. PECK, CECIL P. *An Investigation of Association-Provoking Properties and Meanings Attributed to the Rorschach Inkblots.* Doctor's thesis, University of Kentucky (Lexington, Ky.), 1951. (*DA* 20:3841)
2307. HAIMOWITZ, NATALIE READER, AND HAIMOWITZ, MORRIS L. Chap. 3, "Personality Changes in Client-Centered Therapy," pp. 63–93. (*PA* 27:7822) In *Success in Psychotherapy.* Edited by Werner Wolff and Joseph A. Precker. New York: Grune & Stratton, Inc., 1952. Pp. viii, 196. *
2308. HAMLIN, ROY M.; BERGER, BENJAMIN; AND CUMMINGS, S. THOMAS. Chap. 4, "Changes in Adjustment Following Psychotherapy as Reflected in Rorschach Signs," pp. 94–111. (*PA* 27:7823) In *Success in Psychotherapy.* Edited by Werner Wolff and Joseph A. Precker. New York: Grune & Stratton, Inc., 1952. Pp. viii, 196. *

2309. RIZZO, CARLO. "The Rorschach Method in Italy." *Rorschachiana* 1(4):306–20 '53. * (*PA* 28:7543)

2310. THALER, MARGARET B. *An Application of Three Theories of Personality to the Rorschach Records of Seventy-Five Aged Subjects.* Doctor's thesis, University of Denver (Denver, Colo.), 1953.

2311. ALLEN, ROBERT M., AND DORSEY, ROBERT N. "The Effect of Suggestion on Human Movement Productivity in Rorschach's Test." *Zeitschrift für Diagnostische Psychologie und Persönlichkeitsforschung* 2(2):137–42 '54. * (*PA* 29:4021)

2312. BLUMBERG, EUGENE M. "Results of Psychological Testing of Cancer Patients," pp. 30–61; discussion by Bruno Klopfer and J. F. T. Bugental, pp. 62–71. In *The Psychological Variables in Human Cancer.* Edited by Joseph A. Gengerelli and Frank J. Kirkner. Berkeley, Calif.: University of California Press, 1954. Pp. vi, 135. *

2313. ERON, LEONARD D. "Use of the Rorschach Method in Medical Student Selection." *J Med Ed* 29:35–9 My '54. * (*PA* 29:4686)

2314. GARDEBRING, OLOV G. "High P% in the Rorschach Test." *Zeitschrift für Diagnostische Psychologie und Persönlichkeitsforschung* 2(2):142–3 '54. * (*PA* 29:4054)

2315. KELLY, JOSEPH. "The Influence of Mescaline on Rorschach Responses." *Psychologische Forschung* 24(6):542–56 '54. *

2316. KLOPFER, B., AND DAVIDSON, HELEN H. "Explanation of Rorschach-Scoring Symbols." *Zeitschrift für Diagnostische Psychologie und Persönlichkeitsforschung* 2(4):371–5 '54. *

2317. MOFFETT, CHARLES R. *Operational Characteristics of Beginning Master's Students in Educational Administration and Supervision.* Doctor's thesis, University of Tennessee (Knoxville, Tenn.), 1954.

2318. MORGENTHALER, W. "The Battle for Publication of the 'Psychodiagnostics': For Hermann Rorschach's 70th Birthday (November 8, 1954)." *Zeitschrift für Diagnostische Psychologie und Persönlichkeitsforschung* 2(4):355–62 '54. * (*PA* 29:5783)

2319. RICHARDS, T. W. Chap. 4, "The Chinese in Hawaii: A Rorschach Report," pp. 67–89. Discussion by Richard P. Wang. In *Aspects of Culture and Personality: A Symposium.* Edited by Francis L. K. Hsu. New York: Abelard-Schuman, Inc., 1954. Pp. xiii, 305. *

2320. SIEGEL, MAX. "The Personality Structure of Children With Reading Disabilities as Compared With Children Presenting Other Clinical Problems." *Nerv Child* 10(3–4):409–14 '54. * (*PA* 29:2983)

2321. STREITFIELD, HAL S. "Specificity of Peptic Ulcer to Intense Oral Conflicts." *Psychosom Med* 16:315–26 Jl–Ag '54. * (*PA* 29:4533)

2322. YATES, AUBREY J. "The Validity of Some Psychological Tests of Brain Damage." *Psychol B* 51:359–79 Jl '54. *

2323. BAGH, D. "Use of Rorschach's Ink Blot Test Among School Adolescents." *Indian J Psychol* 30:61–4 Jl–D '55. * (*PA* 31:1606)

2324. BARRON, FRANK. "The Disposition Toward Originality." *J Abn & Social Psychol* 51:478–85 N '55. * (*PA* 31:2533)

2325. EWING, RUSSELL M., AND VINCENT, MARGARET STEVENSON. "Study of Patients' Choices of 'Father Card' and 'Mother Card' on the Rorschach Test." *B Maritime Psychol Assn* 4:16–20 D '55. * (*PA* 30:8288)

2326. KENNA, J. C. "The Effects of Lysergic Acid on the Rorschach." Abstract. *B Brit Psychol Soc* 25:27 Ja '55. *

2327. LUTON, JAMES N. *A Study of the Use of Standardized Tests in the Selection of Potential Educational Administrators.* Doctor's thesis, University of Tennessee (Knoxville, Tenn.), 1955.

2328. MONS, W. R. "Normative Study of Children's Rorschachs." Abstract. *B Brit Psychol Soc* 25:26 Ja '55. *

2329. NEWMAN, R. E. "The Application of the Rorschach Technique to a Primitive Group." *Zeitschrift für Diagnostische Psychologie und Persönlichkeitsforschung* 3(3):187–222 '55. * (*PA* 30:5897)

2330. NORGARB, BRIAN N. "Psychodiagnostic Testing and Hypnosis." *J Clin & Exp Hypnosis* 3:44–8 Ja '55. * (*PA* 29:8624)

2331. POWERS, WILLIAM THOMAS. *A Comparative Analysis of Deviant Rorschach Response Characteristics.* Doctor's thesis, University of Pittsburgh (Pittsburgh, Pa.), 1955. (*DA* 16:159)

2332. RAY, P. C. "The Tensional Feelings Among the Abors and Gallongs as Indicated by the Rorschach Technique." *Indian J Psychol* 30:95–103 Mr–Je '55. * (*PA* 31:2788)

2333. RICKERS-OVSIANKINA, MARIA A. "Prognostic Rorschach Indices in Schizophrenia." *Zeitschrift für Diagnostische Psychologie und Persönlichkeitsforschung* 3(3):246–54 '55. * (*PA* 30:6184)

2334. SPINDLER, GEORGE D. *Sociocultural and Psychological Processes in Menomini Acculturation.* University of California Publications in Culture and Society, Vol. 5. Berkeley, Calif.: University of California Press, 1955. Pp. viii, 271. * (*PA* 29:8556)

2335. WHEELER, W. M. "The Psychoanalytic Theory of Object Relations and the Rorschach Technique." Abstract. *B Brit Psychol Soc* 25:25–6 Ja '55. *

2336. WILKENS, WALTER L., AND ADAMS, AUSTIN J. "The Use of the Rorschach Test Under Hypnosis and Under Sodium Amytal in Military Psychiatry." *Brit J Med Hypnosis* 6:22–8 sp '55. *

2337. "The Rorschach Record of a Case of Aphasia." *Rorsch Newsl* 1:29–35 My '56. *

2338. ANDERSON, DOROTHY V., AND HIGHAM, EILEEN. Chap. 6, "The Use of the Rorschach Technique in Child Guidance Clinics," pp. 177–94. In *Developments in the Rorschach Technique: Volume 2, Fields of Application.* By Bruno Klopfer and others. Yonkers, N.Y.: World Book Co., 1956. Pp. xx, 828. * (*PA* 30:7202)

2339. BAKER, GERTRUDE. Chap. 11, "Diagnosis of Organic Brain Damage in the Adult," pp. 318–75. In *Developments in the Rorschach Technique: Volume 2, Fields of Application.* By Bruno Klopfer and others. Yonkers, N.Y.: World Book Co., 1956. Pp. xx, 828. * (*PA* 30:7202)

2340. BAKER, GERTRUDE. Chap. 12. "Diagnostic Case Studies of Male Adults Having Organic Brain Damage," pp. 376–428. In *Developments in the Rorschach Technique: Volume 2, Fields of Application.* By Bruno Klopfer and others. Yonkers, N.Y.: World Book Co., 1956. Pp. xx, 828. * (*PA* 30:7202)

2341. BOLGAR, HEDDA. Chap. 18, "A Re-evaluation of Projective Theory," pp. 643–57. In *Developments in the Rorschach Technique: Volume 2, Fields of Application.* By Bruno Klopfer and others. Yonkers, N.Y.: World Book Co., 1956. Pp. xx, 828. * (*PA* 30:7202)

2342. CAUDILL, WILLIAM, AND DE VOS, GEORGE. "Achievement, Culture and Personality: The Case of the Japanese Americans." *Am Anthrop* 58:1102–26 D '56. *

2343. FOX, JACK. Chap. 4. "The Psychological Significance of Age Patterns in the Rorschach Records of Children," pp. 88–103. In *Developments in the Rorschach Technique: Volume 2, Fields of Application.* By Bruno Klopfer and others. Yonkers, N.Y.: World Book Co., 1956. Pp. xx, 828. * (*PA* 30:7202)

2344. FRIEDEMANN, A. "Inequalities in the Reproduction of the Plates for the Rorschach Form Interpretation Experiment." *Zeitschrift für Diagnostische Psychologie und Persönlichkeitsforschung* 4(1):104–7 '56. *

2345. GEORGE, CLAY E., AND BONNEY, WARREN C. "Rorschach's Affect-Color Hypothesis and Adaptation-Level Theory." *Psychol R* 63:294–8 S '56. * (*PA* 31:6819)

2346. HALLOWELL, A. IRVING. Chap. 14, "The Rorschach Technique in Personality and Culture Studies," pp. 458–544. In *Developments in the Rorschach Technique: Volume 2, Fields of Application.* By Bruno Klopfer and others. Yonkers, N.Y.: World Book Co., 1956. Pp. xx, 828. * (*PA* 30:7202)

2347. HARRIS, RILDA. *A Comparative Study of Two Groups of Boys, Delinquent and Non-Delinquent, on the Basis of Their Wechsler and Rorschach Test Performances.* Master's thesis, Dalhousie University (Halifax, N.S., Canada), 1956.

2348. KENDIG, ISABELLE V.; CHAREN, SOL; AND LEPINE, LOUIS T. "Psychological Side Effects Induced by Cycloserine in the Treatment of Pulmonary Tuberculosis." *Am R Tuberc* 73:438–41 Mr '56. *

2349. KLOPFER, BRUNO. Chap. 8, "The Clinical Situation," pp. 215–66. In *Developments in the Rorschach Technique: Volume 2, Fields of Application.* By Bruno Klopfer and others. Yonkers, N.Y.: World Book Co., 1956. Pp. xx, 828. * (*PA* 30:7202)

2350. KLOPFER, BRUNO, AND SPIEGELMAN, MARVIN. Chap. 9, "Methodological Research Problems," pp. 267–80. In *Developments in the Rorschach Technique: Volume 2, Fields of Application.* By Bruno Klopfer and others. Yonkers, N.Y.: World Book Co., 1956. Pp. xx, 828. * (*PA* 30:7202)

2351. KLOPFER, BRUNO, AND SPIEGELMAN, MARVIN. Chap. 10, "Differential Diagnosis," pp. 281–317. In *Developments in the Rorschach Technique: Volume 2, Fields of Application.* By Bruno Klopfer and others. Yonkers, N.Y.: World Book Co., 1956. Pp. xx, 828. * (*PA* 30:7202)

2352. KLOPFER, BRUNO; FOX, JACK; AND TROUP, EVELYN. Chap. 1, "Problems in the Use of the Rorschach Technique With Children," pp. 3–21. In *Developments in the Rorschach Technique: Volume 2, Fields of Application.* By Bruno Klopfer and others. Yonkers, N.Y.: World Book Co., 1956. Pp. xx, 828. * (*PA* 30:7202)

2353. KLOPFER, BRUNO; SPIEGELMAN, MARVIN; AND FOX, JACK. Chap. 2, "The Interpretation of Children's Records," pp. 22–44. In *Developments in the Rorschach Technique: Volume 2, Fields of Application.* By Bruno Klopfer and others. Yonkers, N.Y.: World Book Co., 1956. Pp. xx, 828. * (*PA* 30:7202)

2354. KLOPFER, WALTER G. Chap. 7, "The Application of the Rorschach Technique to Geriatrics," pp. 195–212. In *Developments in the Rorschach Technique: Volume 2, Fields of Application.* By Bruno Klopfer and others. Yonkers, N.Y.: World Book Co., 1956. Pp. xx, 828. * (*PA* 30:7202)

2355. KUMAR, MYRA. "Rorschach Patterns of a Group of Normal Adults." *Indian J Psychol* 31:153–8 Jl–D '56. *

2356. MEILI-DWORFTZKI, GERTRUDE. Chap. 5, "The Development of Perception in the Rorschach," pp. 104–76. In *Developments in the Rorschach Technique: Volume 2, Fields of Application.* By Bruno Klopfer and others. Yonkers, N.Y.: World Book Co., 1956. Pp. xx, 828. * (*PA* 30:7202)

2357. MONS, W. E. R., AND BARKER, G. B. "Scoring Problems." *Rorsch Newsl* 1:20–2 D '56. *

2358. MOYLAN, JOSEPH J. *The Role of Stimulus Generalization in Projective Test (Rorschach) Behavior.* Doctor's thesis, University of Massachusetts (Amherst, Mass.), 1956.

2359. ROTHNEY, JOHN W. M., AND HEIMANN, ROBERT A. "Development and Applications of Projective Technics." *R Ed Res* 26:56–71 F '56. * (PA 31:6127)

2360. SHANKER, UDAY. "Rorschach Responses of a Group of Juvenile Thieves." *Indian J Psychol* 31:125–30 Jl–D '56. * (PA 35:3823)

2361. SHNEIDMAN, EDWIN S. Chap. 17, "Some Relationships Between the Rorschach Technique and Other Psychodiagnostic Tests," pp. 595–642. In *Developments in the Rorschach Technique: Volume 2, Fields of Application.* By Bruno Klopfer and others. Yonkers, N.Y.: World Book Co., 1956. Pp. xx, 828. * (PA 30:7202)

2362. SIEGEL, SAUL M. "The Relationship of Hostility to Authoritarianism." *J Abn & Social Psychol* 52:368–72 My '56. * (PA 31:4494)

2363. SNOWDEN, ROBERT F. Chap. 16, "Top Management and the Rorschach Technique," pp. 582–92. In *Developments in the Rorschach Technique: Volume 2, Fields of Application.* By Bruno Klopfer and others. Yonkers, N.Y.: World Book Co., 1956. Pp. xx, 828. * (PA 30:7202)

2364. SPIEGELMAN, MARVIN. Chap. 13, "The Rorschach Technique in Social Psychology," pp. 431–57. In *Developments in the Rorschach Technique: Volume 2, Fields of Application.* By Bruno Klopfer and others. Yonkers, N.Y.: World Book Co., 1956. Pp. xx, 828. * (PA 30:7202)

2365. SPIEGELMAN, MARVIN, AND KLOPFER, BRUNO. Chap. 3, "Rorschach Reactions and Child Therapy: A Case Study," pp. 45–87. In *Developments in the Rorschach Technique: Volume 2, Fields of Application.* By Bruno Klopfer and others. Yonkers, N.Y.: World Book Co., 1956. Pp. xx, 828. * (PA 30:7202)

2366. WAUCK, LE ROY. *An Investigation of the Usefulness of Psychological Tests in the Selection of Candidates for the Diocesan Priesthood.* Doctor's thesis, Loyola University (Chicago, Ill.), 1956.

2367. WEBB, EUGENE J. *Statistical Selection of Individuals Forming Groups Using Rorschach Test Scores.* Doctor's thesis, University of Chicago (Chicago, Ill.), 1956.

2368. WHITE, J. M.; JONES, A. M.; AND INGHAM, J. G. "A Rorschach Study of the Neurodermatoses." *J Psychosom Res* 1:84–93 F '56. *

2369. WHITEMAN, DORIT B. *An Experimental Study of the Rorschach Apperceptive Type.* Doctor's thesis, New York University (New York, N.Y.), 1956. (DA 19:3376)

2370. WILLIAMS, GERTHA, AND KELLMAN, SAMUEL. Chap. 15, "The Rorschach Technique in Industrial Psychology," pp. 545–81. In *Developments in the Rorschach Technique: Volume 2, Fields of Application.* By Bruno Klopfer and others. Yonkers, N.Y.: World Book Co., 1956. Pp. xx, 828. * (PA 30:7202)

2371. WYSOCKI, BOLESLAW A. "Rorschach Card Preferences as a Diagnostic Aid." *Psychol Monogr* 70(6):1–16 '56. * (PA 31:6151)

2372. ZUK, GERALD H. "The Influence of Social Context on Impulse and Control Tendencies in Preadolescence." *Genetic Psychol Monogr* 54:117–66 N '56. * (PA 33:3464)

2373. ALLEN, ROBERT M. "A Longitudinal Rorschach Analysis." *Tohoku Psychologica Folia* 15(3–4):23–9 '57. * (PA 32:5475)

2374. BECK, S. J. "Rorschach Scoring Symbols." *Zeitschrift für Diagnostische Psychologie und Persönlichkeitsforschung* 5(1):62–3 '57. *

2375. BECK, SAMUEL J. "The Light-Dark Determinant: A Survey of the Problems," pp. 179–93. In *Rorschachiana V: Proceedings of the III International Rorschach Congress, Rome, September 13–16, 1956.* Beiheft zur Schweizerischen Zeitschrift für Psychologie und ihre Anwendungen, No. 34. Bern, Switzerland: Hans Huber, [1957?]. Pp. 445. *

2376. BERGER, STANLEY I. *Similarities of Rorschach Records Obtained Through Re-testing Procedures as Indicated by the Ability of Judges to Match Protocols.* Doctor's thesis, University of Kansas (Lawrence, Kan.), 1957.

2377. BOREHAM, J. L. "A Form of Reporting Projective Test Findings." *Rorsch Newsl* 2:7–12 D '57. *

2378. BURNHAM, RHODA K. *The Relationship of Personality to Oral Conditions in Children: An Evaluation by Means of the Rorschach and the Blacky Test.* Doctor's thesis, New York University (New York, N.Y.), 1957. (DA 18:1488)

2379. GEIST, HAROLD. "Emotional Aspects of Dermatitis." *J Clin & Exp Psychopathol* 18:87–93 Mr '57. * (PA 32:4433)

2380. HARRIS, RILDA. "A Comparative Study of Two Groups of Boys, Delinquent and Non-Delinquent, on the Basis of Their Wechsler and Rorschach Test Performances." *B Maritime Psychol Assn* 6:21–8 sp '57. * (PA 33:4295)

2381. HERMAN, JACK L. *Ideational and Motor Correlates of the Rorschach Experience Type.* Doctor's thesis, New York University (New York, N.Y.), 1957. (DA 20:3831)

2382. KALDEGG, A. "A Rorschach Re-test of a Schizophrenic Under Promazine (HCL)." *Rorsch Newsl* 2:3–4 D '57. *

2383. LOW, NATALIE S. *A Rorschach Study of the Parents of Children With Childhood Schizophrenia.* Doctor's thesis, New York University (New York, N.Y.), 1957. (DA 21:240)

2384. MOORE, EARL LEE. *The Concept of "Distanciation" Applied to the Rorschach and Draw-A-Person Techniques.* Doctor's thesis, University of Denver (Denver, Colo.), 1957.

2385. PENNINGTON, HARRY, III. *An Experimental Investigation of Several Card-Concepts, Using the Rorschach Ink Blots as Stimuli.* Master's thesis, University of Texas (Austin, Tex.), 1957.

2386. SAMIS, FRANCIS W. *A Study of the Characteristics of a Group of Mentally Competent Offenders as Revealed by the Rorschach Test.* Master's thesis, University of Alberta (Edmonton, Alta., Canada), 1957.

2387. STERNBERGER, ULRICH; SPITZ, HERMAN; AND GOYNE, JAMES B. "Evaluation of Chlorpromazine and Reserpine Therapy With Follow-Up Study." *J Clin & Exp Psychopathol* 18:258–68 S '57. * (PA 33:1504)

2388. TAKALA, MARTTI; PIHKANEN, TOIVO A.; AND MARKKANEN, TOUKO. *The Effects of Distilled and Brewed Beverages: A Physiological, Neurological, and Psychological Study.* The Finnish Foundation for Alcoholic Studies, No. 4. Stockholm, Sweden: Almqvist & Wiksell, 1957. Pp. 195. * (PA 31:4890)

2389. TRAISMAN, ROBERT NEIL. *A Study of Rorschach Characteristics of Asthmatic Children.* Doctor's thesis, Loyola University (Chicago, Ill.), 1957.

2390. ZEEUW, JOH. DE. "The Administration and Interpretation of the Rorschach Test in Three Phases." *Zeitschrift für Diagnostische Psychologie und Persönlichkeitsforschung* 5(1):5–19 '57. *

2391. ADCOCK, CYRIL J., AND RITCHIE, JAMES E. "Intercultural Use of Rorschach." *Am Anthrop* 60:881–92 O '58. * (PA 33:10152)

2392. ALLEN, ROBERT M., AND GROMAN, WILLIAM. "A Note on Rorschach Test Age Norms." *Zeitschrift für Diagnostische Psychologie und Persönlichkeitsforschung* 6(2):178–80 '58. * (PA 33:10308)

2393. BAGH, D. "An Experimental Study of Rorschach Characteristics of Different Cultural Groups of Rural Bengal." *Indian J Psychol* 33:55–66 Ja–Mr '58. * (PA 35:3320)

2394. BAUGHMAN, E. EARL. "A New Method of Rorschach Inquiry." *J Proj Tech* 22:381–9 D '58. * (PA 34:1333)

2395. BENE, EVA. "A Rorschach Investigation Into the Mothers of Autistic Children." *Brit J Med Psychol* 31:226–7 pt 3 & 4 '58. * (PA 34:1340)

2396. BONDEL, GERTRUDE. *An Investigation Into the Relationship Between the Rorschach Test and the First Dream in Therapy.* Doctor's thesis, New York University (New York, N.Y.), 1958. (DA 19:3018)

2397. BOVA, LOUIS WILLIAM, JR. *Perceptual Rigidity: An Experiment With the Rorschach Test and the Autokinetic Effect.* Doctor's thesis, University of Florida (Gainesville, Fla.), 1958. (DA 19:1112)

2398. CANTER, ARTHUR. "The Effect of Unshaded Bright Colors in the Rorschach Upon the Form-Color Response Balance of Psychotic Patients." *J Proj Tech* 22:390–3 D '58. * (PA 34:1343)

2399. CARR, ARTHUR C. Chap. 4, "The Psychodiagnostic Test Battery: Rationale and Methodology," pp. 28–39. In *Progress in Clinical Psychology, Vol. 3.* Edited by Daniel Brower and Lawrence E. Abt. New York: Grune & Stratton, Inc., 1958. Pp. vi, 249. * (PA 33:8255)

2400. CASTRO, PERLA N. *A Cross Cultural Study of Popular Responses in the Rorschach Test.* Master's thesis, University of Kansas (Lawrence, Kan.), 1958.

2401. CHARNY, ISRAEL W. *Rorschach Areas Designated as "Sex Populars."* Doctor's thesis, University of Rochester (Rochester, N.Y.), 1958.

2402. CURTIS, JEAN McCALLEY. *The Use of the Rorschach Prognostic Rating Scale With Children.* Doctor's thesis, University of California (Los Angeles, Calif.), 1958.

2403. DELAY, J.; PICHOT, P.; LEMPÉRIÈRE, J.; AND PERSE, J. *The Rorschach and the Epileptic Personality.* New York: Logos Press, Inc., 1958. Pp. xx, 265. * (PA 33:8866)

2404. DIAMOND, FLORENCE. *Style and Content in Personality Rigidity.* Doctor's thesis, Claremont Graduate School (Claremont, Calif.), 1958. (DA 20:2901)

2405. EDMONSTON, WILLIAM E., AND GRIFFITH, RICHARD M. "Rorschach Content and Ink Blot Structure." *J Proj Tech* 22:394–7 D '58. * (PA 34:1350)

2406. EIDUSON, BERNICE T. "Artist and Nonartist: A Comparative Study." *J Personality* 26:13–28 Mr '58. * (PA 33:5807)

2407. FA-YU, CHENG; CHU-CHANG, CHEN; AND HSIEN, RIN. "A Personality Analysis of the Ami and Its Three Subgroups by Rorschach Test." *Acta Psychologica Taiwanica* (1):131–43 N '58. *

2408. FISHER, RHODA LEE. "The Effect of a Disturbing Situation Upon the Stability of Various Projective Tests." *Psychol Monogr* 72(14):1–23 '58. * (PA 34:1357)

2409. FISHER, SEYMOUR, AND CLEVELAND, SIDNEY E. *Body Images and Personality.* Princeton, N.J.: D. Van Nostrand Co., Inc., 1958. Pp. xi, 420. * (PA 32:3926)

2410. FOX, JACK. "A Note on Klopfer's Hypothesis About Shading Responses." *J Proj Tech* 22:398 D '58. * (PA 34:1360)

2411. GOLDBERGER, L. *Individual Differences in Effects of Perceptual Isolation as Related to Rorschach Manifestations of the Primary Process.* Doctor's thesis, New York University (New York, N.Y.), 1958. *(DA* 19:1816)

2412. GOLDSTONE, MARTIN H. *The Relationship Between Certain Rorschach Indicators and the Magnitude of Kinesthetic After-Effect.* Doctor's thesis, Yeshiva University (New York, N.Y.), 1958. *(DA* 21:1254)

2413. GOODALL, BEBE J. *Investigation of Rorschach Personality Factors Related to Educational Progress in the Educable Mentally Handicapped Adolescent.* Master's thesis, De Paul University (Chicago, Ill.), 1958.

2414. GRUEN, ARNO. "A New Level of Aspiration Test and an Application of It." *J General Psychol* 59:73–7 Jl '58. * *(PA* 36:2HB73G)

2415. GRUEN, ARNO. "Psychological Testing With the Older Client: A Case of Paresis." *J Proj Tech* 22:26–32 Mr '58. * *(PA* 33:6232)

2416. HABER, WILLIAM B. "Reactions to Loss of Limb: Physiological and Psychological Aspects." *Ann N Y Acad Sci* 74:14–24 S 30 '58. * *(PA* 34:3359)

2417. HAFNER, A. JACK. "Rorschach Test Behavior and Related Variables." *Psychol Rec* 8:7–12 Ja '58. * *(PA* 33:7602)

2418. HAMBY, RONALD. *The Trailmaking Test and Immediately Successive Administrations of the Rorschach Psychodiagnostic Test in the Differentiation and Study of the Effects of Brain Damage.* Master's thesis, University of Kansas (Lawrence, Kan.), 1958.

2419. HAWARD, L. R. C. "Rorschach." *Psychometric Res B* (2):[31–3] Ag '58. *

2420. HEATH, DOUGLAS. "Projective Tests as Measures of Defensive Activity." *J Proj Tech* 22:284–92 S '58. * *(PA* 33:10333)

2421. HOLT, ROBERT R., AND LUBORSKY, LESTER; WITH THE COLLABORATION OF WILLIAM R. MORROW, DAVID RAPAPORT, AND SIBYLLE K. ESCALONA. *Personality Patterns of Psychiatrists: A Study of Methods for Selecting Residents, Vol. 1.* New York: Basic Books, Inc., 1958. Pp. xiv, 386. * *(PA* 33:5751)

2422. HOWIE, MARGARET M. "The Rorschach Test Applied to a Group of Scottish Children." *Rorsch Newsl* 3:14–5 Je '58. *

2423. KADEN, S. *A Formal-Comparative Analysis of the Relationships Between the Structuring of Marital Interaction and Rorschach Blot Stimuli.* Doctor's thesis, Clark University (Worcester, Mass.), 1958. *(DA* 19:1820)

2424. KANTER, V. B., AND WILLIAMS, CELIA. "The Interaction of Emotional and Organic Factors in the Rorschach and T.A.T. Records of a Male Alcoholic Aged 60." *Rorsch Newsl* 3:22–3 D '58. *

2425. KING, GERALD F. "A Theoretical and Experimental Consideration of the Rorschach Human Movement Response." *Psychol Monogr* 72(5):1–23 '58. * *(PA* 33:10338)

2426. LEIDING, WALDEMAR C. *A Comparison of the Content and Sign Approaches in Evaluating a Projective Test Battery and Its Component Tests.* Doctor's thesis, University of Houston (Houston, Tex.), 1958. *(DA* 19:1822)

2427. LEVINE, ABRAHAM. "A Comparative Evaluation of Latent Schizophrenic and Overt Schizophrenic Patients With Respect to Certain Personality Variables." *J Hillside Hosp* 7:131–52 Jl–O '58. * *(PA* 34:3280)

2428. LEVINSON, BORIS M. "Some Aspects of the Personality of the Native-Born White Homeless Man as Revealed by the Rorschach." *Psychiatric Q Sup* 32:278–86 pt 2 '58. * *(PA* 34:3213)

2429. MANUS, GERALD IRWIN. *A Study of the Relationship of Certain Rorschach Content Factors to Successful and Unsuccessful Extra-Mural Adjustment of Hospitalized Schizophrenic Patients.* Doctor's thesis, New York University (New York, N.Y.), 1958. *(DA* 19:2149)

2430. MARKHAM, SYLVIA. "The Dynamics of Post-Partum Pathological Reactions as Revealed in Psychological Tests." *J Hillside Hosp* 7:178–89 Jl–O '58. * *(PA* 34:3011)

2431. MARSZALEK, K. S. "Munroe Check List." *Psychometric Res B* (1):[3–5] My '58. *

2432. MONS, W. E. R. "The Development of the Personality as Seen in the Rorschach." *Rorsch Newsl* 3:32–8 D '58. *

2433. MONS, W. E. R. "The Function of Extreme Types of Personality in Neurosis and Hysteria, and Some Psychoses." *Rorsch Newsl* 3:9–13 Je '58. *

2434. NEWMAN, R. E. "Personality Development in a Primitive 'Adolescent' Group (as Revealed by the Rorschach Technique)." *Zeitschrift für Diagnostische Psychologie und Persönlichkeitsforschung* 6(3):241–53 '58. * *(PA* 34:2779)

2435. PAREIS, EGBERT NELSON. *Inkblot Perception and Personality: An Experimental Departure From the Rorschach Test.* Doctor's thesis, University of Texas (Austin, Tex.), 1958. *(DA* 19:1118)

2436. PERLMAN, STANFORD EUGENE. *Some Correlates of Social Awareness.* Doctor's thesis, Columbia University (New York, N.Y.), 1958. *(DA* 21:242)

2437. PIOTROWSKI, ZYGMUNT A. Chap. 8, "The Psychodiagnostic Test Battery: Clinical Application," pp. 72–85. In *Progress in Clinical Psychology, Vol. 3.* Edited by Daniel Brower and Lawrence E. Abt. New York: Grune & Stratton, Inc., 1958. Pp. vi, 249. * *(PA* 33:8255)

2438. PIOTROWSKI, ZYGMUNT A., AND BRICKLIN, BARRY. "A Long-Term Prognostic Criterion for Schizophrenics Based on Rorschach Data." *Psychiatric Q Sup* 32:315–29 pt 2 '58. * *(PA* 34:3293)

2439. PRENSKY, SAMUEL J. *An Investigation of Some Personality Characteristics of Epileptic and Psychosomatic Patients: An Evaluation of Certain Personality Measures and Reactions to Frustration in Idiopathic Epileptic, Symptomatic Epileptic, and Peptic Ulcer Patients.* Doctor's thesis, New York University (New York, N.Y.), 1958. *(DA* 19:3025)

2440. RIESSMAN, FRANK, AND MILLER, S. M. "Social Class and Projective Tests." *J Proj Tech* 22:432–9 D '58. * *(PA* 34:1268)

2441. ROTHSTEIN, CHARLES, AND COHEN, IRA S. "Hostility and Dependency Conflicts in Peptic Ulcer Patients." *Psychol Rep* 4:555–8 D '58. * *(PA* 34:1856)

2442. RYAN, WILLIAM. *Capacity for Mutual Dependence and Involvement in Group Psychotherapy.* Doctor's thesis, Boston University (Boston, Mass.), 1958. *(DA* 19:1119)

2443. SAFIAN, MURRAY Z. *A Study of Certain Psychological Factors in the Rehabilitation of Potentially Employable Homebound Adults.* Doctor's thesis, New York University (New York, N.Y.), 1958. *(DA* 19:3372)

2444. SCHAFER, ROY. "On the Psychoanalytic Study of Retest Results." *J Proj Tech* 22:102–9 Mr '58. * *(PA* 33:6286)

2445. SCHON, MARTHA, AND BARD, MORTON. "The Effect of Hypophysectomy on Personality in Women With Metastatic Breast Cancer as Revealed by the Rorschach Test." *J Proj Tech* 22:440–5 D '58. * *(PA* 34:1419)

2446. SCOTT, EDWARD M. "A Case of Folie à Deux and Projective Techniques." *J Consult Psychol* 22:90 Ap '58. * *(PA* 35:3636, title only)

2447. SELIG, KALMAN. *Personality Structure as Revealed by the Rorschach Technique of a Group of Children Who Test at or Above 170 I.Q. on the 1937 Revision of the Stanford-Binet Scale (Volumes I–V).* Doctor's thesis, New York University (New York, N.Y.), 1958. *(DA* 19:3373)

2448. SHEEHAN, JOSEPH G. "Projective Studies of Stuttering." *J Speech & Hearing Disorders* 23:18–25 F '58. *

2449. SHERMAN, RUTH LAUBGROSS. *A Study With Projective Techniques of Sociometrically High and Sociometrically Low Children.* Doctor's thesis, University of Maryland (College Park, Md.), 1958. *(DA* 20:767)

2450. SINGER, MARGARET THALER, AND SCHEIN, EDGAR H. "Projective Test Responses of Prisoners of War Following Repatriation." *Psychiatry* 21:375–85 N '58. * *(PA* 34:10113)

2451. SPIVACK, GEORGE; LEVINE, MURRAY; AND SPRIGLE, HERBERT. "Barron M Threshold Values in Emotionally Disturbed Adolescents." *J Proj Tech* 22:446–9 D '58. * *(PA* 34:1423)

2452. STAFFORD-CLARK, D. "Projective Tests and Clinical Judgment." *Rorsch Newsl* 3:4 Je '58. *

2453. STAMPFL, THOMAS G. *Rorschach Prognostic Rating Scale Assessment of Ego Structure in the Children of Psychotic Parents.* Doctor's thesis, Loyola University (Chicago, Ill.), 1958.

2454. STEIN, HARRY. "Age, Physical Disability and Responsivity in Relation to Spontaneous Rotation of Rorschach Cards." *J Proj Tech* 22:450–2 D '58. * *(PA* 34:1424)

2455. SU, HSIANG-YU; CHANG, SIN-HWA; CHANG, SOPHIA; AND HSIAO, SHIH-LANG. "A Study of 'Goitrous Personality' From the Rorschach Responses." English abstract. *Acta Psychologica Taiwanica* (1):103 N '58. * *(PA* 34:3034)

2456. SWENSON, W. M., AND GRIMES, B. P. "Characteristics of Sex Offenders Admitted to a Minnesota State Hospital for Pre-Sentence Psychiatric Investigation." *Psychiatric Q Sup* 32(1):110–23 '58. * *(PA* 34:3250)

2457. TAMKIN, ARTHUR S. "Rorschach Card Rejection by Psychiatric Patients." *J Consult Psychol* 22:441–4 D '58. * *(PA* 33:10784)

2458. TANIGUCHI, MAYUMI; DE VOS, GEORGE; AND MURAKAMI, EIJI. "Identification of Mother and Father Cards on the Rorschach by Japanese Normal and Delinquent Adolescents." *J Proj Tech* 22:453–60 D '58. * *(PA* 34:1428)

2459. TAYLOR, JAMES BENTLEY. *Social Desirability and the MMPI Performance of Schizophrenics.* Doctor's thesis, University of Washington (Seattle, Wash.), 1958. *(DA* 19:1828)

2460. VERNIER, CLAIRE M.; STAFFORD, JOHN W.; AND KRUGMAN, ARNOLD D. "A Factor Analysis of Indices From Four Projective Techniques Associated With Four Different Types of Physical Pathology." *J Consult Psychol* 22:433–7 D '58. * *(PA* 33:9360)

2461. VERRILL, BERNARD VICTOR. *An Investigation of the Concept of Impulsivity.* Doctor's thesis, University of Houston (Houston, Tex.), 1958. *(DA* 19:183)

2462. WENAR, CHARLES. "The Degree of Psychological Disturbance in Handicapped Youth." *Excep Child* 25:7–10+ S '58. * *(PA* 33:10380)

2463. WILLIAMS, JESSIE M. "The Use of the Rorschach in the Study of Personality Development of Cerebral-Palsied Children." *Rorsch Newsl* 3:3–21 D '58. *

2464. WINDER, C. L., AND KANTOR, ROBERT E. "Rorschach Maturity Scores of the Mothers of Schizophrenics." *J Consult Psychol* 22:438–40 D '58. * *(PA* 33:10381)

2465. YOUNG, HARL H. "Relationships Between and Reliability Estimates of New (Holtzman) Ink Blot Variables and

Conventional Rorschach Scoring Categories." *Proc Okla Acad Sci* 38:111–5 D '58. *

2466. ZUCKER, LUISE J. *Ego Structure in Paranoid Schizophrenia.* Springfield, Ill.: Charles C Thomas, Publisher, 1958. Pp. x, 186. * (*PA* 33:1916)

2467. ——. "An Organic-Looking Rorschach Obtained From a Depressed Patient." *Rorsch Newsl* 4:25–7 Je '59. *

2468. ABEL, THEODORA M., AND METRAUX, RHODA. "Sex Differences in a Negro Peasant Community: Montserrat, B.W.I." *J Proj Tech* 23:127–33 Je '59. * (*PA* 35:4755)

2469. ADCOCK, C. J., AND RITCHIE, JAMES E. "Intercultural Use of Rorschach: Rejoinder to Clifton." Letter. *Am Anthrop* 61:1090–2 D '59. *

2470. ADCOCK, C. J., AND RITCHIE, JAMES E. "Rejoinder to Edgerton and Polk." Letter. *Am Anthrop* 61:1093–4 D '59. *

2471. AFFLECK, D. CRAIG, AND MEDNICK, SARNOFF A. "The Use of the Rorschach Test in the Prediction of the Abrupt Terminator in Individual Psychotherapy." *J Consult Psychol* 23:125–8 Ap '59. * (*PA* 34:1328)

2472. AINSWORTH, MARY D., AND KUETHE, JAMES L. "Texture Responses in the Rorschach and in a Sorting Test." *J Proj Tech* 23:391–402 D '59. * (*PA* 35:4900)

2473. ALCOCK, THEODORA, AND TUSTIN, FRANCES. "Personality Disturbance Impairing Educational Ability: The Case of Derek B." *Rorsch Newsl* 4:7–18 D '59. *

2474. AMES, LOUISE BATES. "Further Check on the Diagnostic Validity of the Ames Danger Signals." *J Proj Tech* 23:291–8 S '59. * (*PA* 35:4949)

2475. AMES, LOUISE BATES; MÉTRAUX, RUTH W.; AND WALKER, RICHARD N. *Adolescent Rorschach Responses: Developmental Trends From Ten to Sixteen Years.* New York: Hoeber Medical Division, Harper & Row, Publishers, Inc., 1959. Pp. xiii, 313. * (*PA* 34:1329)

2476. APPELBAUM, STEPHEN. "The Effect of Altered Psychological Atmosphere on Rorschach Responses: A New Supplementary Procedure." *B Menninger Clinic* 23:179–89 S '59. * (*PA* 35:794)

2477. ARNAUD, SARA H. "Some Psychological Characteristics of Children of Multiple Sclerotics." *Psychosom Med* 21:8–22 Ja–F '59. * (*PA* 34:1863)

2478. ARNAUD, SARA H. "A System for Deriving Quantitative Rorschach Measures of Certain Psychological Variables, for Group Comparisons." *J Proj Tech* 23:403–11 D '59. * (*PA* 35:4901)

2479. BARKER, G. B. "Diagnostic Study of a Young Woman, Using Rorschach Tests and Paintings." *Rorsch Newsl* 4:19–26 D '59. *

2480. BASIT, ABDUL. *A Comparative Study of Personality Development in Identical and Fraternal Twins by Means of the Rorschach Method.* Master's thesis, University of Kansas (Lawrence, Kan.), 1959.

2481. BATHURST, G. C. "Some Tentative Inferences From the Rorschach Records of 100 Alcoholics." *Rorsch Newsl* 4: 11–2 Je '59. *

2482. BATHURST, G. C., AND GLATT, M. M. "Some Psychological Reflections on Vulnerability to Alcoholism." *Psychiatria et Neurologia* 138:27–46 '59. *

2483. BAUGHMAN, E. EARL. "The Effect of Inquiry Method on Rorschach Color and Shading Scores." *J Proj Tech* 23:3–7 Mr '59. * (*PA* 34:6002)

2484. BAUGHMAN, E. EARL. "An Experimental Analysis of the Relationship Between Stimulus Structure and Behavior on the Rorschach." *J Proj Tech* 23:134–83 Je '59. * (*PA* 35:4902)

2485. BEACH, LEE. "Rorschach Variables and Vocational Choice." *B Maritime Psychol Assn* 8:28–33 Ap '59. *

2486. BERGER, LESLIE. "Crossvalidation of 'Primary' and 'Reactive' Personality Patterns With Non-Ulcer Surgical Patients." *J Proj Tech* 23:8–11 Mr '59. * (*PA* 34:6004)

2487. BIRCH, HERBERT G., AND DILLER, LEONARD. "Rorschach Signs of 'Organicity': A Physiological Basis for Perceptual Disturbances." *J Proj Tech* 23:184–97 Je '59. * (*PA* 35:4903)

2488. BLECKNER, JANET E. "The Responses of Average and Gifted Students on the Group Rorschach Test." *Calif J Ed Res* 10:200–6 N '59. * (*PA* 34:7831)

2489. BOHM, EWALD. *A Textbook in Rorschach Test Diagnosis for Psychologists, Physicians, and Teachers.* Translated by Anne G. Beck and Samuel J. Beck. New York: Grune & Stratton, Inc., 1959. Pp. xiii, 322. * (*PA* 33:6211)

2490. BOLIN, B. J. "An Investigation of Relationship Between Birth-Duration and Childhood Anxieties." *J Mental Sci* 105:1045–52 O '59. * (*PA* 34:6227)

2491. BOLLE, A. M. *The Personality Structure of Thyroid Patients on the Rorschach Test.* Doctor's thesis, University of Ottawa (Ottawa, Ont., Canada), 1959. (Abstract: *Can Psychologist* 1:112–3)

2492. BRICKLIN, BARRY. *The Prediction of Long Term Follow Up Conditions of Schizophrenic Patients by Means of the Rorschach Test.* Doctor's thesis, Temple University (Philadelphia, Pa.), 1959. (*DA* 20:3373)

2493. BROWN, D. G. "Psychosomatic Correlates in Contact Dermatitis: A Pilot Study." *J Psychosom Res* 4:132–9 D '59. * (*PA* 34:8214)

2494. CAMPBELL, FRANCES A., AND FIDDLEMAN, PAUL B. "The Effect of Examiner Status Upon Rorschach Performance." *J Proj Tech* 23:303–6 S '59. * (*PA* 35:4904)

2495. CHARNY, ISRAEL W. "A Normative Study of Rorschach 'Sex Populars' for Males." *J Proj Tech* 23:12–23 Mr '59. * (*PA* 34:6008)

2496. CLEVELAND, SIDNEY E. "Personality Dynamics in Torticollis." *J Nerv & Mental Dis* 129:150–61 Ag '59. * (*PA* 34:6407)

2497. CLIFTON, JAMES A. "On the Intercultural Use of the Rorschach." Letter. *Am Anthrop* 61:1087–90 D '59. *

2498. COAN, RICHARD W. "Perceptual Aspects of Attributed Movement." *Genetic Psychol Monogr* 59:45–100 F '59. * (*PA* 34:1346)

2499. DANA, RICHARD H. "American Culture and Chinese Personality." *Psychol Newsl* 10:314–21 My–Je '59. * (*PA* 34:1213)

2500. DAVIS, HANNAH SUSAN. *Judgments of Intellectual Level From Various Features of the Rorschach Including Vocabulary.* Doctor's thesis, Columbia University (New York, N.Y.), 1959. (*DA* 20:1436)

2501. EDGERTON, ROBERT B., AND POLK, KENNETH. "Statistical Problems in the Intercultural Use of Rorschach." Letter. *Am Anthrop* 61:1092–3 D '59. *

2502. EISDORFER, CARL. *The Effect of Sensory Decrement Upon Rorschach Performance in a Senescent Population.* Doctor's thesis, New York University (New York, N.Y.), 1959.

2503. ENGEL, CYNTHIA. "The Relationship Between Rorschach Responses and Attitudes Toward Parents." *J Proj Tech* 23:311–4 S '59. * (*PA* 35:4910)

2504. EXNER, JOHN E., JR. "The Influence of Chromatic and Achromatic Color in the Rorschach." *J Proj Tech* 23: 418–25 D '59. * (*PA* 35:4911)

2505. EXNER, JOHN ERNEST, JR. *The Influence of Color in Projective Testing.* Doctor's thesis, Cornell University (Ithaca, N.Y.), 1959. (*DA* 20:754)

2506. EYSENCK, H. J. "Personality Tests: 1950–55," pp. 118–59. In *Recent Progress in Psychiatry, Vol. 3.* Edited by G. W. T. H. Fleming and A. Walk. London: J. & A. Churchill Ltd., 1959. Pp. iv, 397. *

2507. FARBEROW, NORMAN L. "Validity and Methodology in Projective Tests." *J Proj Tech* 23:282–6 S '59. * (*PA* 35:4912)

2508. FEFFER, MELVIN H. "The Cognitive Implications of Role Taking Behavior." *J Personality* 27:152–68 Je '59. * (*PA* 34:4380)

2509. FISHER, SEYMOUR; BOYD, INA; WALKER, DONALD; AND SHEER, DIANNE. "Parents of Schizophrenics, Neurotics, and Normals." *A.M.A. Arch Gen Psychiatry* 1:149–66 Ag '59. * (*PA* 34:6184)

2510. FOLLETT, GEORGE C., JR. *The Comparison of Rorschach Responses Between Superior, Average, and Retarded Children.* Master's thesis, Kent State University (Kent, Ohio), 1959.

2511. FORSYTH, RALPH P. "The Influences of Color, Shading, and Welsh Anxiety Level on Elizur Rorschach Content Test Analyses of Anxiety and Hostility." *J Proj Tech* 23: 207–13 Je '59. * (*PA* 35:4915)

2512. GARDNER, RILFY W.; HOLZMAN, PHILIP S.; KLEIN, GEORGE S.; LINTON, HARRIET B.; AND SPENCE, DONALD P. "Cognitive Control: A Study of Individual Consistencies in Cognitive Behavior." *Psychol Issues* 1(4):1–186 '59. * (*PA* 35:2266)

2513. GLADSTON, ELAINE R., AND HAGUENAUER, GINETTE. "Somatic Preoccupation in a Paranoid Schizophrenic: Mlle. V." *Rorsch Newsl* 4:27–33 D '59. *

2514. GLICKSTEIN, MITCHELL. "A Note on Wittenborn's Factor Analysis of Rorschach Scoring Categories." *J Consult Psychol* 23:69–75 F '59. * (*PA* 34:125)

2515. GORDON, JESSE E. "Rorschach Responses as Verbal Behavior." *J Proj Tech* 23:426–8 D '59. * (*PA* 35:4916)

2516. GROSS, LEONARD R. "Effects of Verbal and Nonverbal Reinforcement in the Rorschach." *J Consult Psychol* 23:66–8 F '59. * (*PA* 34:1368)

2517. GRUEN, WALTER. "Behavioral Correlates of Some Dimensions of the Cognitive Field." *J Personality* 27:169–86 Je '59. * (*PA* 34:3882)

2518. GUILFORD, J. P. *Personality,* pp. 288–98, 309–14. New York: McGraw-Hill Book Co., Inc., 1959. Pp. xiii, 562. *

2519. HEIMAN, N., AND COOPER, S. "An Experiment in Clinical Integration." *J Hillside Hosp* 8:290–7 O '59. * (*PA* 35:4919)

2520. HEIMANN, ROBERT A., AND ROTHNEY, JOHN W. M. "Development and Applications of Projective Techniques." *R Ed Res* 29:73–83 F '50. * (*PA* 34:6021)

2521. HELME, WILLIAM HURD. *A Study of Relationships Between the Rorschach Method and Objective Tests of Interests and Values by Means of Factor Analysis.* Doctor's thesis, New School for Social Research (New York, N.Y.), 1959.

2522. HERTZ, MARGUERITE R. "The Use and Misuse of the Rorschach Method: 1, Variations in Rorschach Procedure." *J Proj Tech* 23:33–48 Mr '59. * (*PA* 34:6022)

2523. JACKSON, PHILIP W., AND GETZELS, JACOB W. "Psychological Health and Classroom Functioning: A Study of Dissatisfaction With School Among Adolescents." *J Ed Psychol* 50:295–300 D '59. * (*PA* 34:8368, 36:1FH05J)

2524. JENSEN, ARTHUR R. "The Reliability of Projective Techniques: Review of the Literature." *Acta Psychologica* 16(1):108–36 '59. * (*PA* 34:5956)

2525. KAHN, MARVIN W. "A Comparison of Personality,

Intelligence, and Social History of Two Criminal Groups." *J Social Psychol* 49:33–40 F '59. * (*PA* 35:5214)

2526. KATAGUCHI, YASUFUMI. "Rorschach Schizophrenic Score (RSS)." *J Proj Tech* 23:214–22 Je '59. * (*PA* 35:4960)

2527. KOENIG, FRANCES G. *A Study of Anxiety in Children With Rheumatic Fever: The Relationship Between Recurrences of Rheumatic Fever and Rorschach Indices of Anxiety in Children.* Doctor's thesis, New York University (New York, N.Y.), 1959. (*DA* 20:1438)

2528. KRASNOFF, ALAN. "Psychological Variables and Human Cancer: A Cross-Validation Study." *Psychosom Med* 21:291–5 Jl–Ag '59. * (*PA* 34:4736)

2529. LANGE, HERBERT. *An Investigation of the Validity of the Rorschach Technique in Predicting Sociability.* Doctor's thesis, Purdue University (Lafayette, Ind.), 1959. (*DA* 20:2920)

2530. LEARMONTH, GEORGE J.; ACKERLY, WILLIAM; AND KAPLAN, MIKE. "Relationships Between Palmar Skin Potential During Stress and Personality Variables." *Psychosom Med* 21:150–7 Mr–Ap '59. * (*PA* 34:1384)

2531. LEDWITH, NETTIE H. *Rorschach Responses of Elementary School Children: A Normative Study.* Pittsburgh, Pa.: University of Pittsburgh Press, 1959. Pp. xi, 185. * (*PA* 34:1385)

2532. LEVINE, DAVID. "Rorschach Genetic-Level and Mental Disorder." *J Proj Tech* 23:436–9 D '59. * (*PA* 35:4925)

2533. LEVINE, MURRAY; SPIVACK, GEORGE; AND WIGHT, BYRON. "The Inhibition Process, Rorschach Human Movement Responses, and Intelligence: Some Further Data." *J Consult Psychol* 23:306–12 Ag '59. * (*PA* 34:4390)

2534. LEVY, LEON H., AND ORR, THOMAS B. "The Social Psychology of Rorschach Validity Research." *J Abn & Social Psychol* 58:79–83 Ja '59. * (*PA* 34:1388)

2535. LINTON, HARRIET, AND GRAHAM, ELAINE. Chap. 4, "Personality Correlates of Persuasibility," pp. 69–101. (*PA* 34:7403) In *Personality and Persuasibility.* Edited by Carl I. Hovland and Irving L. Janis. New Haven, Conn.: Yale University Press, 1959. Pp. xiv, 333. *

2536. LITTLE, KENNETH B. "Connotations of the Rorschach Inkblots." *J Personality* 27:397–406 S '59. * (*PA* 34:6032)

2537. LITTLE, KENNETH B., AND SHNEIDMAN, EDWIN S. "Congruencies Among Interpretations of Psychological Test and Anamnestic Data." *Psychol Monogr* 73(6):1–42 '59. * (*PA* 34:3010)

2538. LOVELAND, NATHENE TURK, AND SINGER, MARGARET THALER. "Projective Test Assessment of the Effects of Sleep Deprivation." *J Proj Tech* 23:323–34 S '59. * (*PA* 34:4928)

2539. LYNN, DAVID B. "Ambiguity and Projection." *Psychol Newsl* 10:289–94 My–Je '59. * (*PA* 34:1393)

2540. MACHOVER, SOLOMON, AND PUZZO, FRANK S. "Clinical and Objective Studies of Personality Variables in Alcoholism: 1, Clinical Investigation of the 'Alcoholic Personality.'" *Q J Studies Alcohol* 20:505–19 S '59. * (*PA* 34:6253)

2541. MACHOVER, SOLOMON, AND PUZZO, FRANK S. "Clinical and Objective Studies of Personality Variables in Alcoholism: 2, Clinical Study of Personality Correlates of Remission From Active Alcoholism." *Q J Studies Alcohol* 20:520–7 S '59. * (*PA* 34:6253)

2542. MACHOVER, SOLOMON; PUZZO, FRANK S.; MACHOVER, KAREN; AND PLUMEAU, FRANCIS. "Clinical and Objective Studies of Personality Variables in Alcoholism: 3, An Objective Study of Homosexuality in Alcoholism." *Q J Studies Alcohol* 20:528–42 S '59. * (*PA* 34:6254)

2543. MCKEEVER, WALTER F., AND GERSTEIN, ALVIN I. "Base Rate Data on Rorschach Card Rejection." *J Clin Psychol* 15:425–7 O '59. * (*PA* 36:1HI25M)

2544. MCREYNOLDS, PAUL, AND WEIDE, MARIAN. "The Prediction and Assessment of Psychological Changes Following Prefrontal Lobotomy." *J Mental Sci* 105:971–8 O '59. * (*PA* 34:6471)

2545. MARKS, JOHN B. "Rorschach Water Responses in Alcoholics: Levels of Content Analysis and Consensual Validation." *J Proj Tech* 23:69–71 Mr '59. * (*PA* 34:6035)

2546. MARTIN, HARRY JEROME, JR. *A Comparison of Sign and Clinical Approaches in Predicting Psychiatric Diagnosis.* Doctor's thesis, University of Houston (Houston, Tex.), 1959. (*DA* 20:3837)

2547. MONS, W. E. R., AND KANTER, V. B. "Use of a 'Blind' Analysis of the Rorschach in the Investigation of an Insurance Compensation Case." *Rorsch Newsl* 4:2–10 Je '59. *

2548. MOYLAN, JOSEPH J. "Stimulus Generalization in Projective Test (Rorschach) Behavior." *J Personality* 27:18–37 Mr '59. * (*PA* 34:3966)

2549. MURSTEIN, BERNARD I., AND WHEELER, JOHN I., JR. "The Projection of Hostility on the Rorschach and Thematic Stories Test." *J Clin Psychol* 15:316–9 Jl '59. * (*PA* 35:3474)

2550. MYDEN, WALTER. "Interpretation and Evaluation of Certain Personality Characteristics Involved in Creative Production." *Percept & Motor Skills* 9:139–58 Je '59. *

2551. NEIGER, STEPHEN. "Frequent Rorschach Responses in the Toronto Area and Their Comparison With Responses From Other Areas." *Ont Hosp Psychol B* 5:10–24 D '59. *

2552. NELSON, MARVEN O.; WOLFSON, WILLIAM; AND LOCASCIO, RALPH. "Sexual Identification in Responses to Rorschach Card III." *J Proj Tech* 23:354–6 S '59. * (*PA* 35:4934)

2553. NIKELLY, A. G. *The Bruner-Postman Hypothesis Theory and Perceptual Responses to Inkblots.* Doctor's thesis, University of Ottawa (Ottawa, Ont., Canada), 1959. (Abstract: *Can Psychologist* 1:115–6)

2554. NUNNERY, MICHAEL Y. "How Useful Are Standardized Psychological Tests in the Selection of School Administrators." *Ed Adm & Sup* 45:349–56 N '59. * (*PA* 35:7092)

2555. OGDON, DONALD P., AND ALLEE, RUTH. "Rorschach Relationships With Intelligence Among Familial Mental Defectives." *Am J Mental Def* 63:889–96 Mr '59. * (*PA* 34:1675)

2556. OTIS, LEON S. "What Does the Rorschach Z Score Reflect?" *J Consult Psychol* 23:373–4 Ag '59. * (*PA* 34:4399)

2557. PARKER, ROLLAND S. *An Investigation of the Content of the Rorschach Human Movement Response Utilizing the Subjects' Associations to Their Own M.* Doctor's thesis, New York University (New York, N.Y.), 1959. (*DA* 20:384)

2558. PENA, CESAREO D. "Influence of Social Desirability Upon Rorschach Content." *J Clin Psychol* 15:313–6 Jl '59. * (*PA* 35:3436)

2559. PEPINSKY, HAROLD B. "A Note on the Rorschach Prognostic Rating Scale." *J Counsel Psychol* 6:160–2 su '59. *

2560. PHILLIPS, LESLIE; KADEN, STANLEY; AND WALDMAN, MARVIN. "Rorschach Indices of Developmental Level." *J Genetic Psychol* 94:267–85 Je '59. *

2561. PIOTROWSKI, ZYGMUNT A. "Test Indication and Contraindications for Adult Therapy: Indications and Contraindications for Adult Therapy: Workshop, 1958." *Am J Orthopsychiatry* 29:60–8 Ja '59. * (*PA* 34:3062)

2562. PIOTROWSKI, ZYGMUNT A., AND LEVINE, DAVID. "A Case Illustrating the Concept of the Alpha Schizophrenic." *J Proj Tech* 23:223–36 Je '59. * (*PA* 35:5256)

2563. PODELL, JEROME E., AND PHILLIPS, LESLIE. "A Developmental Analysis of Cognition as Observed in Dimensions of Rorschach and Objective Test Performance." *J Personality* 27:439–63 D '59. *

2564. PORT, YALE I. *An Investigation of the Effect of Optimal Symptom Alleviation of Parkinson's Disease Upon Certain Aspects of the Personality as Reflected in the Rorschach.* Doctor's thesis, Yeshiva University (New York, N.Y.), 1959.

2565. RABIN, A. I. "A Contribution to the 'Meaning' of Rorschach's Inkblots via the Semantic Differential." *J Consult Psychol* 23:368–72 Ag '59. * (*PA* 34:4403)

2566. RIOCH, MARGARET J., AND LUBIN, ARDIE. "Prognosis of Social Adjustment for Mental Hospital Patients Under Psychotherapy." *J Consult Psychol* 23:313–8 Ag '59. * (*PA* 34:4404)

2567. ROSEN, ALEXANDER C. "A Clinical Evaluation of Eysenck's 'Objective Rorschach.'" *J Clin Psychol* 15:320–1 Jl '59. * (*PA* 35:3477)

2568. RYCHLAK, JOSEPH F. "Forced Associations, Symbolism, and Rorschach Constructs." *J Consult Psychol* 23:455–60 O '59. * (*PA* 34:5978)

2569. SANDLER, JOSEPH. "The Rorschach and the Feeling of Safety." *Rorsch Newsl* 4:2–6 D '59. *

2570. SASLOW, HARRY LEWIS. *Longitudinal Stability of Rorschach Factorial Structure of School-Age Children.* Doctor's thesis, University of Pittsburgh (Pittsburgh, Pa.), 1959. (*DA* 20:3391)

2571. SCHMEIDLER, GERTRUDE RAFFEL; NELSON, MARJORY J.; AND BRISTOL, MARJORIE. "Freshman Rorschachs and College Performance." *Genetic Psychol Monogr* 59:3–43 F '59. * (*PA* 34:1972)

2572. SHANMUGAM, A. V. "A Rorschach Study of Stars and Isolates Among High School Students." *Psychol Studies* 4:35–49 Ja '59. *

2573. SHAPIRO, DAVID. "The Integration of Determinants and Content in Rorschach Interpretation." *J Proj Tech* 23:365–73 S '59. * (*PA* 35:4938)

2574. SHRIFTE, MIRIAM HARRIET. *An Investigation of Relationship Between Underlying Unpleasant Feeling Tensions and Cancer Growth: A Comparative Study of Two Groups of Cancer Patients Differentiated on the Basis of Cancer Course.* Doctor's thesis, New York University (New York, N.Y.), 1959. (*DA* 20:4179)

2575. SILVERMAN, LLOYD H. "A Q-Sort Study of the Validity of Evaluations Made From Projective Techniques." *Psychol Monogr* 73(7):1–28 '59. * (*PA* 34:3030)

2576. SINES, LLOYD K. "The Relative Contribution of Four Kinds of Data to Accuracy in Personality Assessment." *J Consult Psychol* 23:483–92 D '59. * (*PA* 34:6046)

2577. SJOSTEDT, ELSIE MARIE, AND HURWITZ, IRVING. "A Developmental Study of Sexual Functioning by Means of a Cognitive Analysis." *J Proj Tech* 23:237–46 Je '59. * (*PA* 35:5205)

2578. SMITH, C. M., AND HAMILTON, J. "Psychological Factors in the Narcolepsy-Cataplexy Syndrome." *Psychosom Med* 21:40–9 Ja–F '59. * (*PA* 34:1858)

2579. SMITH, LAURENCE C., JR., AND PHILLIPS, LESLIE. "Social Effectiveness and Developmental Level in Adolescence." *J Personality* 27:239–49 Je '59. * (*PA* 34:3898)

2580. SOSKIN, WILLIAM F. "Influence of Four Types of Data on Diagnostic Conceptualization in Psychological Testing." *J Abn & Social Psychol* 58:69–78 Ja '59. * (*PA* 34:1422)

2581. SPIVACK, GEORGE; LEVINE, MURRAY; AND SPRIGLE, HERBERT. "Intelligence Test Performances and the Delay

Functions of the Ego." *J Consult Psychol* 23:428–31 O '59. * (*PA* 34:6049)

2582. SPIVACK, GEORGE; LEVINE, MURRAY; FUSCHILLO, JEAN; AND TRAVERNIER, ANN. "Rorschach Movement Responses and Inhibition Processes in Adolescents." *J Proj Tech* 23: 462–6 D '59. * (*PA* 35:4939)

2583. STONE, JOHN TRUMAN. *An Experimental Investigation of the Effect of Mode of Color Stimulation on Inkblot Response Items.* Doctor's thesis, University of Pittsburgh (Pittsburgh, Pa.), 1959. (*DA* 20:2391)

2584. TABOR, ANTHONY B. *Process Analysis of Rorschach Interpretation.* Doctor's thesis, Loyola University (Chicago, Ill.), 1959.

2585. TAMKIN, ARTHUR S. "Intelligence as a Determinant of Rorschach Card Rejection." *J Clin Psychol* 15:63–4 Ja '59. * (*PA* 34:2740)

2586. TOWBIN, ALAN P. "Hostility in Rorschach Content and Overt Aggressive Behavior." *J Abn & Social Psychol* 58: 312–6 My '59. * (*PA* 34:6052)

2587. TYCKO, MILICENT. "Rorschach Responses at Four Exposure Levels." *Percept & Motor Skills* 9:167–80 Je '59. * (*PA* 38:4331)

2588. VALENTINE, MAX. "Psychometric Testing in Iran." *J Mental Sci* 105:93–107 Ja '59. * (*PA* 34:1065)

2589. WALLER, PATRICIA FOSSUM. *Correlates of Rorschach Shading Scores Obtained With Two Methods of Inquiry.* Doctor's thesis, University of North Carolina (Chapel Hill, N.C.), 1959. (*DA* 20:2912)

2590. WILENIUS, HAROLD. "Rorschach Developmental Level and Social Participation of Chronic Schizophrenics." *J Proj Tech* 23:87–92 Mr '59. * (*PA* 34:6058)

2591. WISHNER, JULIUS. "Factor Analyses of Rorschach Scoring Categories and First Response Times in Normals." *J Consult Psychol* 23:406–13 O '59. * (*PA* 34:5999)

2592. WITTENBORN, J. R. "Some Comments on Confounded Correlations Among Rorschach Scores." *J Consult Psychol* 23:75–7 F '59. * (*PA* 34:187)

2593. WOLF, MARTIN G. *The Rorschach as an Indicator of Intelligence in Seventh Grade Children.* Master's thesis, North Texas State College (Denton, Tex.), 1959.

2594. WOLPIN, MILTON, AND HAMLIN, ROY M. "Effect of Form-Color Incongruity on Responses to Inkblots." *J Clin Psychol* 15:151–5 Ap '59. * (*PA* 34:4947)

2595. ABEL, THEODORA M. "Differential Responses to Projective Testing in a Negro Peasant Community: Montserrat, B.W.I." *Int J Social Psychiatry* 6:218–24 au '60. *

2596. ALCOCK, THEODORA. "Some Personality Characteristics of Asthmatic Children." *Brit J Med Psychol* 33:133–41 pt 2 '60. * (*PA* 35:2671)

2597. ALLEN, ROBERT M., AND LICHTENSTEIN, DON. "The Rorschach and Intelligence: A Note of Caution." *J Genetic Psychol* 97:169–71 S '60. * (*PA* 35:6434)

2598. AMES, LOUISE B.; WITH THE ASSISTANCE OF MARJEAN KREMER. "Longitudinal Survey of Child Rorschach Responses: Older Subjects Ages 10 to 16 Years." *Genetic Psychol Monogr* 62:185–229 Ag '60. * (*PA* 35:6200)

2599. AMES, LOUISE BATES. "Age Changes in the Rorschach Responses of a Group of Elderly Individuals." *J Genetic Psychol* 97:257–85 D '60. * (*PA* 35:6220)

2600. AMES, LOUISE BATES. "Age Changes in the Rorschach Responses of Individual Elderly Subjects." *J Genetic Psychol* 97:287–315 D '60. * (*PA* 35:6221)

2601. AMES, LOUISE BATES. "Constancy of Content in Rorschach Responses." *J Genetic Psychol* 96:145–64 Mr '60. * (*PA* 34:7829)

2602. AMES, LOUISE BATES. "Longitudinal Survey of Child Rorschach Responses: Younger Subjects Two to 10 Years." *Genetic Psychol Monogr* 61:229–89 My '60. * (*PA* 35:6203)

2603. AMMONS, CAROL H., AND AMMONS, R. B. "Rorschach Responses of Individuals Sensitive to Stress Induced by Extreme Perceptual-Motor Conflict." *Psychologia* 3:246–53 D '60. *

2604. ARMON, VIRGINIA. "Some Personality Variables in Overt Female Homosexuality." *J Proj Tech* 24:292–309 S '60. * (*PA* 35:818)

2605. AZIMA, FERN CRAMER, AND KRAL, V. A. "Effects of Blindfolding on Persons During Psychological Testing: A Psychometric Study of Various Age Groups." *Geriatrics* 15: 780–92 N '60. *

2606. BECK, SAMUEL J. *The Rorschach Experiment: Ventures in Blind Diagnosis.* New York: Grune & Stratton, Inc., 1960. Pp. viii, 256. * (*PA* 34:7753)

2607. BOHM, EWALD. Chap. 8, "The Binder Chiaroscuro System and Its Theoretical Basis," pp. 202–22. In *Rorschach Psychology.* Edited by Maria A. Rickers-Ovsiankina. New York: John Wiley & Sons, Inc., 1960. Pp. xvi, 483. * (*PA* 35:2231)

2608. BORELLI, GEORGE LOUIS. *A Study of the Meanings of Rorschach Cards Through Use of the Semantic Differential Technique.* Doctor's thesis, Ohio State University (Columbus, Ohio), 1960. (*DA* 21:3161)

2609. BOWER, PHILIP A.; TESTIN, ROBERT; AND ROBERTS, ALAN. "Rorschach Diagnosis by a Systematic Combining of Content, Thought Process, and Determinant Scales." *Genetic Psychol Monogr* 62:105–83 Ag '60. * (*PA* 35:6203)

2610. BURNAND, G. "A Scale for Assessing Psychosis From the Rorschach." *Psychometric Res B* (6):[5–10] su '60. *

2611. BURNAND, G. "A Scale for Psychosis." *Rorsch Newsl* 5:27–8 Je '60. *

2612. CARRIGAN, PATRICIA M. "Extraversion-Introversion as a Dimension of Personality: A Reappraisal." *Psychol B* 57: 329–60 S '60. * (*PA* 35:4976)

2613. CARSTAIRS, G. M.; PAYNE, R. W.; AND WHITTAKER, S. "Rorschach Responses of Hindus and Bhils." *J Social Psychol* 51:217–27 My '60. * (*PA* 34:7762)

2614. COHEN, IRWIN H. *Adaptive Regression, Dogmatism, and Creativity.* Doctor's thesis, Michigan State University (East Lansing, Mich.), 1960. (*DA* 21:3522)

2615. CROOKES, T. G., AND KELLER, ANNA J. "Rorschach Card Rejection and IQ." *J Clin Psychol* 16:424–6 O '60. * (*PA* 37:3140)

2616. DASTON, PAUL G., AND SAKHEIM, GEORGE A. "Prediction of Successful Suicide From the Rorschach Test, Using a Sign Approach." *J Proj Tech* 24:355–61 D '60. * (*PA* 35: 4952)

2617. DAVIS, A. D. "Some Physiological Correlates of Rorschach Body Image Productions." *J Abn & Social Psychol* 60:432–6 My '60. * (*PA* 35:5035)

2618. DELANY, LLOYD T. *A Comparison of the Individual Rorschach Method and the Group Discussion Rorschach Method as a Diagnostic Device With Delinquent Adolescent Boys: A Study of Certain Personality Characteristics of Delinquent Adolescent Boys as Revealed by Their Responses to the Individual and the Group Discussion Rorschach Method.* Doctor's thesis, New York University (New York, N.Y.), 1960. (*DA* 20:4715)

2619. DINOFF, MICHAEL. "Subject Awareness of Examiner Influence in a Testing Situation." Abstract. *J Consult Psychol* 24:465 O '60. * (*PA* 35:4909)

2620. DRECHSLER, ROBERT J. "Affect-Stimulating Effects of Colors." *J Abn & Social Psychol* 61:323–8 N '60. * (*PA* 36: 2HG23D)

2621. DREGER, RALPH MASON. "The Relation Between Rorschach M and TAT Content Categories as Measures of Creative Productivity in a Representative High-Level Intelligence Population." *J General Psychol* 63:29–33 Jl '60. * (*PA* 35: 6437)

2622. DUDEK, STEPHANIE (ZUPERKO). *Creativity and the Rorschach Human Movement Response.* Doctor's thesis, New York University (New York, N.Y.), 1960.

2623. EIGENBRODE, CHARLES R., AND SCHIPMAN, WILLIAM G. "The Body Image Barrier Concept." *J Abn & Social Psychol* 60:450–2 My '60. * (*PA* 35:5282)

2624. EISDORFER, CARL. "Developmental Level and Sensory Impairment in the Aged." *J Proj Tech* 24:129–32 Je '60. * (*PA* 35:4740)

2625. EISDORFER, CARL. "Rorschach Rigidity and Sensory Decrement in a Senescent Population." *J Gerontol* 15:188–90 Ap '60. * (*PA* 35:6230)

2626. ELSTEIN, ARTHUR. *Behavioral Correlates of the Rorschach Shading Response.* Doctor's thesis, University of Chicago (Chicago, Ill.), 1960.

2627. EYSENCK, H. J. Chap. 7, "The Analysis of Projective Techniques," pp. 271–85. In his *The Structure of Human Personality, Second Edition.* London: Methuen & Co. Ltd., 1960. Pp. xix, 448. *

2628. FAGER, ROBERT E. "Relation of Rorschach Movement and Color Responses to Cognitive Inhibition." Abstract. *J Consult Psychol* 24:276 Je '60. *

2629. FISHER, SEYMOUR. "Right-Left Gradients in Body Image, Body Reactivity, and Perception." *Genetic Psychol Monogr* 61:197–228 My '60. * (*PA* 35:6478)

2630. FONDA, CHARLES P. Chap. 4, "The White-Space Response," pp. 80–105. In *Rorschach Psychology.* Edited by Maria A. Rickers-Ovsiankina. New York: John Wiley & Sons, Inc., 1960. Pp. xvi, 483. * (*PA* 35:2231)

2631. FRIEDMAN, HOWARD. "A Note on the Revised Rorschach Development Scoring System." *J Clin Psychol* 16:52–4 Ja '60. * (*PA* 36:1HC52F)

2632. GILBERT, M. M., AND MARADIE, L. J. "The Differential Diagnosis Between Postconcussion Syndrome and Neuroses by Use of Rorschach Content Analysis." *J Neuropsychiatry* 1:210–2 Mr–Ap '60. *

2633. GOLDMAN, ROSALINE. "Changes in Rorschach Performance and Clinical Improvement in Schizophrenia." *J Consult Psychol* 24:403–7 O '60. * (*PA* 35:4596)

2634. GOTTLIEB, ANN LODGE, AND PARSONS, OSCAR A. "A Coaction Compass Evaluation of Rorschach Determinants in Brain Damaged Individuals." *J Consult Psychol* 24:54–60 F '60. * (*PA* 34:8243)

2635. HAFNER, A. JACK, AND KAPLAN, ARTHUR M. "Hostility Content Analysis of the Rorschach and TAT." *J Proj Tech* 24:137–43 Je '60. * (*PA* 35:4918)

2636. HALPERN, FLORENCE. Chap. 2, "The Rorschach Test With Children," pp. 14–28. In *Projective Techniques With Children.* Edited by Albert I. Rabin and Mary R. Haworth. New York: Grune & Stratton, Inc., 1960. Pp. xiii, 392. * (*PA* 35:2229)

2637. HAMMER, EMANUEL F. "An Exploratory Investigation of the Personalities of Creative Adolescent Students." Discussion by Margaret Naumberg. *Studies Art Ed* 1:42–72 sp '60. *

2638. HARRIS, JESSE G., JR. Chap. 14, "Validity: The Search for a Constant in a Universe of Variables," pp. 380–

439. In *Rorschach Psychology*. Edited by Maria A. Rickers-Ovsiankina. New York: John Wiley & Sons, Inc., 1960. Pp. xvi, 483. * (PA 35:2231)

2639. HEMMENDINGER, LAURENCE. Chap. 3, "Developmental Theory and the Rorschach Method," pp. 58–79. In *Rorschach Psychology*. Edited by Maria A. Rickers-Ovsiankina. New York: John Wiley & Sons, Inc., 1960. Pp. xvi, 483. * (PA 35:2231)

2640. HERTZ, MARGUERITE R. Chap. 2, "The Organization Activity," pp. 25–57. In *Rorschach Psychology*. Edited by Maria A. Rickers-Ovsiankina. New York: John Wiley & Sons, Inc., 1960. Pp. xvi, 483. * (PA 35:2231)

2641. HERTZ, MARGUERITE R. Chap. 3, "The Rorschach in Adolescence," pp. 29–60. In *Projective Techniques With Children*. Edited by Albert I. Rabin and Mary R. Haworth. New York: Grune & Stratton, Inc., 1960. Pp. xiii, 392. * (PA 35:2229)

2642. HERTZ, MARGUERITE R., AND PAOLINO, ALBERT F. "Rorschach Indices of Perceptual and Conceptual Disorganization." *J Proj Tech* 24:370–88 D '60. * (PA 35:4957)

2643. HILKEVITCH, RHEA R. "Social Interactional Processes: A Quantitative Study." *Psychol Rep* 7:195–201 O '60. * (PA 35:2114)

2644. HOLT, ROBERT R. "Cognitive Controls and Primary Processes." *J Psychol Res* 4:105–12 S '60. * (PA 35:4921)

2645. HOLT, ROBERT R., AND HAVEL, JOAN. Chap. 10, "A Method for Assessing Primary and Secondary Process in the Rorschach," pp. 263–315. In *Rorschach Psychology*. Edited by Maria A. Rickers-Ovsiankina. New York: John Wiley & Sons, Inc., 1960. Pp. xvi, 483. * (PA 35:2231) [Revision of reference 2051.]

2646. HOLZBERG, JULES D. Chap. 13, "Reliability Re-examined," pp. 361–79. In *Rorschach Psychology*. Edited by Maria A. Rickers-Ovsiankina. New York: John Wiley & Sons, Inc., 1960. Pp. xvi, 483. * (PA 35:2231)

2647. HOOKER, EVELYN. "The Fable." *J Proj Tech* 24:240–5 S '60. * (PA 35:10)

2648. JUDSON, ABE J., AND MACCASLAND, BARBARA W. "The Effects of Chlorpromazine on Psychological Test Scores." Abstract. *J Consult Psychol* 24:192 Ap '60. * (PA 34:7888)

2649. KADEN, STANLEY E., AND LIPTON, HERBERT. "Rorschach Developmental Scores and Post-Hospital Adjustment of Married Male Schizophrenics." *J Proj Tech* 24:144–7 Je '60. * (PA 35:1136)

2650. KAGAN, JEROME. "The Long Term Stability of Selected Rorschach Responses." *J Consult Psychol* 24:67–73 F '60. * (PA 34:7851)

2651. KAGAN, JEROME; MOSS, HOWARD A.; AND SIGEL, IRVING E. "Conceptual Style and the Use of Affect Labels." *Merrill-Palmer Q* 6:261–78 Jl '60. *

2652. KAHN, MARVIN W. "Psychological Test Study of a Mass Murderer." *J Proj Tech* 24:148–60 Je '60. * (PA 35:5213)

2653. KAHN, ROBERT L., AND FINK, MAX. "Prognostic Value of Rorschach Criteria in Clinical Response to Convulsive Therapy." *J Neuropsychiatry* 1:242–5 My–Je '60. *

2654. KALDEGG, A. "A Note on Tabulating Scores." *Rorsch Newsl* 5:25 D '60. *

2655. KAMANO, DENNIS K. "Symbolic Significance of Rorschach Cards IV and VII." *J Clin Psychol* 16:50–2 Ja '60. * (PA 36:1HG50K)

2656. KANTER, V. B. "Body Image and Psychosomatic Illness." *Rorsch Newsl* 5:2–14 D '60. *

2657. KAPLAN, DONALD MARTIN. *Differences in Attitudes and Personality of "Subject-Oriented" and "Pupil-Oriented" Secondary School Teachers: A Comparative Analysis of Two Groups of Secondary School Teachers With the Minnesota Teacher Attitude Inventory and the Rorschach*. Doctor's thesis, New York University (New York, N.Y.), 1960. (DA 21:2988)

2658. KING, GERALD F. "An Interpersonal Conception of Rorschach Human Movement and Delusional Content." *J Proj Tech* 24:161–3 Je '60. * (PA 35:5248)

2659. KLOPFER, WALTER G.; ALLEN, BERNADENE V.; AND ETTER, DAVID. "Content Diversity on the Rorschach and 'Range of Interests.'" *J Proj Tech* 24:290–1 S '60. * (PA 35:801)

2660. KORCHIN, SHELDON J. Chap. 5, "Form Perception and Ego Functioning," pp. 109–29. In *Rorschach Psychology*. Edited by Maria A. Rickers-Ovsiankina. New York: John Wiley & Sons, Inc., 1960. Pp. xvi, 483. * (PA 35:2231)

2661. KRIMSKY, MARTIN LOUIS. *The Rebirth Fantasy in Catatonic Schizophrenia and Its Implications*. Doctor's thesis, University of Oklahoma (Norman, Okla.), 1960. (DA 21:367)

2662. KUHN, ROLAND. Chap. 11, "Some Problems Concerning the Psychological Implications of Rorschach's Form Interpretation Test," pp. 310–40. In *Rorschach Psychology*. Edited by Maria A. Rickers-Ovsiankina. New York: John Wiley & Sons, Inc., 1960. Pp. xvi, 483. * (PA 35:2231)

2663. KUMAR, PRAMOD. "The Rorschach Test in Manic and Normal Groups." *Indian J Psychol* 35:35–8 pt 1 '60. *

2664. LAPKIN, B. *The Relation of Primary Process Thinking to the Recovery of Subliminal Material*. Doctor's thesis, New York University (New York, N.Y.), 1960. (DA 21:3165)

2665. LEBO, DELL; TOAL, ROBERT; AND BRICK, HARRY. "Rorschach Performance in the Amelioration and Continuation of Observable Anxiety." *J General Psychol* 63:75–80 Jl '60. * (PA 35:6529)

2666. LEBOVITS, BINYAMIN Z.; VISOTSKY, HAROLD M.; AND OSTFELD, ADRIAN M. "Lysergic Acid Diethylamide (LSD) and JB 318: A Comparison of Two Hallucinogens: 2, An Exploratory Study." *Arch Gen Psychiatry* 3:176–87 Ag '60. *

2667. LEDWITH, NETTIE H. *A Rorschach Study of Child Development*. Pittsburgh, Pa.: University of Pittsburgh Press, 1960. Pp. ix, 336. * (PA 35:1998)

2668. LESLEY, EUGENIA LUKAS. *Selected Rorschach Responses of First-Year Students of Dentistry, Engineering, and Law*. Doctor's thesis, University of Denver (Denver, Colo.), 1960.

2669. LESSING, ELISE ELKINS. "Prognostic Value of the Rorschach in a Child Guidance Clinic." *J Proj Tech* 24:310–21 S '60. * (PA 35:965)

2670. LEVINE, ABRAHAM. "Appraising Ego Strength From the Projective Test Battery." *J Hillside Hosp* 9:228–40 Jl '60. *

2671. LEVINE, DAVID. "Rorschach Genetic Level and Psychotic Symptomatology." *J Clin Psychol* 16:164–7 Ap '60. * (PA 36:2HG64L)

2672. LEVITT, EUGENE E., AND GROSZ, HANUS J. "A Comparison of Quantifiable Rorschach Anxiety Indicators in Hypnotically Induced Anxiety and Normal States." *J Consult Psychol* 24:31–4 F '60. * (PA 34:7855)

2673. LEVITT, EUGENE E., AND PERSKY, HAROLD. "Relation of Rorschach Factors and Plasma Hydrocortisone Level in Hypnotically Induced Anxiety." *Psychosom Med* 22:218–23 My–Je '60. * (PA 35:5038)

2674. LEZAK, MURIEL DEUTSCH. *The Conscious Control of Rorschach Responses*. Doctor's thesis, University of Portland (Portland, Ore.), 1960.

2675. McREYNOLDS, PAUL, AND WEIDE, MARIAN. "Psychological Measures as Used to Predict Psychiatric Improvement and to Assess Behavioural Changes Following Prefrontal Lobotomy." *J Mental Sci* 106:256–72 Ja '60. * (PA 35:6530)

2676. MAGNUSSEN, M. G. "Verbal and Nonverbal Reinforcers in the Rorschach Situation." *J Psychol Studies* 11:203–5 My–Je '60. * Slightly condensed reprinting in *J Clin Psychol* 16:167–9 Ap '60. * (PA 36:2HG67M)

2677. MAGNUSSON, DAVID. "Some Personality Tests Applied on Identical Twins." *Scandinavian J Psychol* 1(2):55–61 '60. * (PA 35:6424)

2678. MARSH, LOYAL FRANCIS. *The Meaning of Rorschach Cards IV and VII*. Doctor's thesis, University of Portland (Portland, Ore.), 1960.

2679. MASLING, JOSEPH. "The Influence of Situational and Interpersonal Variables in Projective Testing." *Psychol B* 57:65–85 Ja '60. * (PA 34:7788)

2680. MINER, HORACE M., AND DE VOS, GEORGE. *Oasis and Casbah: Algerian Culture and Personality in Change*. University of Michigan, Museum of Anthropology, Anthropological Papers, No. 15. Ann Arbor, Mich.: the Museum, 1960. Pp. v, 236. *

2681. MOGENSEN, ALAN; FENGER, GJERTRUD; AND LANGE, BENT. *Rorschach on 122 Ten-Year Old Danish Children: A Standardizational and Structural Study: A, The Normative Results*. Psychological Research Report 2A. Risskov, Denmark: Institute of Psychiatry, State Mental Hospital, [1960]. Pp. 54. * (PA 36:4HG49M)

2682. MOLLER, HELLA. *Stuttering, Predelinquent, and Adjusted Boys: A Comparative Analysis of Personality Characteristics as Measured by the WISC and the Rorschach Test*. Doctor's thesis, Boston University (Boston, Mass.), 1960. (DA 21:1461)

2683. MONS, W. E. R. "Group Signs and the Dynamics of the Personality." *Rorsch Newsl* 5:5–7 Je '60. *

2684. MOYLAN, JOSEPH H.; SHAW, JULIE; AND APPLEMAN, WAYNE. "Passive and Aggressive Responses to the Rorschach by Passive-Aggressive Personalities and Paranoid Schizophrenics." *J Proj Tech* 24:17–20 Mr '60. *

2685. MUMMERY, WILLIAM JAMES. *An Investigation of Conformity as It Relates to Ways of Handling Hostility*. Doctor's thesis, University of Oklahoma (Norman, Okla.), 1960. (DA 21:241)

2686. MURPHY, LOIS, AND MURPHY, GARDNER. Chap. 12, "Hermann Rorschach and Personality Research," pp. 341–57. In *Rorschach Psychology*. Edited by Maria A. Rickers-Ovsiankina. New York: John Wiley & Sons, Inc., 1960. Pp. xvi, 483. * (PA 35:2231)

2687. MURSTEIN, BERNARD I. "Factor Analyses of the Rorschach." *J Consult Psychol* 24:262–75 Je '60. * (PA 35:6446)

2688. NEEL, ANN FILINGER. "Inhibition and Perception of Movement on the Rorschach." *J Consult Psychol* 24:224–30 Je '60. * (PA 35:6447)

2689. O'REILLY, P. O., AND HARRISON, K. "Experimentation With an Objective Test Battery." *Can Psychiatric Assn J* 5:108–23 Ap '60. *

2690. PERDUE, WILLIAM CARROLL. *A Comparison of the Rorschach Responses of Two Groups of Murderers Confined in Prison*. Master's thesis, College of William and Mary (Williamsburg, Va.), 1960.

2691. PHARES, E. JERRY; STEWART, LAWRENCE M.; AND FOSTER, JAMES M. "Instruction Variation and Rorschach Performance." *J Proj Tech* 24:28–31 Mr '60. * (PA 35:803)

2692. PINE, FRED, AND HOLT, ROBERT R. "Creativity and Primary Process: A Study of Adaptive Regression." *J Abn & Social Psychol* 61:370–9 N '60. * (PA 36:2HD70P)

2693. PIOTROWSKI, ZYGMUNT A. Chap. 6, "The Movement Score," pp. 130–53. In *Rorschach Psychology.* Edited by Maria A. Rickers-Ovsiankina. New York: John Wiley & Sons, Inc., 1960. Pp. xvi, 483. * (*PA* 35:2231)

2694. PIOTROWSKI, ZYGMUNT A. "The Rorschach Test," pp. 56–67, 116–49. In *The Prediction of Overt Behavior Through the Use of Projective Techniques.* Edited by Arthur C. Carr. Springfield, Ill.: Charles C Thomas, Publisher, 1960. Pp. xiii, 177. * (*PA* 36:2HG77C)

2695. RADER, GORDON E. "Rorschach Productivity and Participation in Group Psychotherapy." *J Clin Psychol* 16:422–4 O '60. * (*PA* 37:3369)

2696. REISMAN, JOHN M. "Types of Movement in Children's Rorschachs." *J Proj Tech* 24:46–8 Mr '60. * (*PA* 35:806)

2697. RICHARDS, THOMAS W. "Personality of Subjects Who Volunteer for Research on a Drug (Mescaline)." *J Proj Tech* 24:424–8 D '60. * (*PA* 35:4554)

2698. RICKERS-OVSIANKINA, MARIA A. Chap. 1, "Synopsis of Psychological Premises Underlying the Rorschach," pp. 3–22. In her *Rorschach Psychology.* New York: John Wiley & Sons, Inc., 1960. Pp. xvi, 483. * (*PA* 35:2231)

2699. RICKERS-OVSIANKINA, MARIA A., Editor. *Rorschach Psychology.* New York: John Wiley & Sons, Inc., 1960. Pp. xvi, 483. * (*PA* 35:2231)

2700. RIKLAN, MANUEL; DILLER, LEONARD; AND WEINER, HERMAN. "Psychological Studies on the Effects of Chemosurgery of the Basal Ganglia in Parkinsonism: 2, Aspects of Personality." *Arch Gen Psychiatry* 3:267–75 S '60. *

2701. ROE, ANNE, AND MIERZWA, JOHN. "The Use of the Rorschach in the Study of Personality and Occupations." *J Proj Tech* 24:282–9 S '60. * (*PA* 35:1301)

2702. ROSEN, EPHRAIM. "Connotative Meanings of Rorschach Inkblots, Responses, and Determinants." *J Personality* 28:413–26 D '60. * (*PA* 35:4936)

2703. ROSNER, STANLEY. "Inquiry: Partial or Total." *J Proj Tech* 24:49–51 Mr '60. * (*PA* 35:807)

2704. RYCHLAK, JOSEPH F., AND GUINOUARD, DONALD. "Rorschach Content, Personality, and Popularity." *J Proj Tech* 24:322–32 S '60. * (*PA* 35:686)

2705. SCHAFER, ROY. "Bodies in Schizophrenic Rorschach Responses." *J Proj Tech* 24:267–81 S '60. * (*PA* 35:1142)

2706. SCHAFER, ROY. "Representations of Perceiving and Acting in Psychological Test Responses," pp. 291–312. (*PA* 35:850) In *Festschrift for Gardner Murphy.* Edited by John G. Peatman and Eugene L. Hartley. New York: Harper & Brothers, 1960. Pp. xi, 411. *

2707. SCHLEIFER, MAXWELL J., AND HIRE, A. WILLIAM. "Stimulus Value of Rorschach Inkblots Expressed as Trait and Affective Characteristics." *J Proj Tech* 24:164–70 Je '60. * (*PA* 35:4937)

2708. SCHMEIDLER, GERTRUDE RAFFEL. "Changing Field Relations of an ESP Experiment," pp. 94–105. (*PA* 35:398) In *Festschrift for Gardner Murphy.* Edited by John G. Peatman and Eugene L. Hartley. New York: Harper & Brothers, 1960. Pp. xi, 411. *

2709. SCHMEIDLER, GERTRUDE RAFFEL. *ESP in Relation to Rorschach Test Evaluation.* Parapsychology Monographs, No. 2. New York: Parapsychology Foundation, Inc., 1960. Pp. iii, 89. *

2710. SCOTT, EDWARD M. "Psychological Examination of Quadruplets." *Psychol Rep* 6:281–2 Ap '60. * (*PA* 35:5080)

2711. SEIDEL, CLAUDENE. "The Relationship Between Klopfer's Rorschach Prognostic Rating Scale and Phillips' Case History Prognostic Rating Scale." *J Consult Psychol* 24:46–9 F '60. * (*PA* 34:862)

2712. SEMEONOFF, BORIS. "Rorschach Concomitants of Self-Description Variables." *Rorsch Newsl* 5:26–34 D '60. *

2713. SHAPIRO, DAVID. Chap. 7, "A Perceptual Understanding of Color Response," pp. 154–201. In *Rorschach Psychology.* Edited by Maria A. Rickers-Ovsiankina. New York: John Wiley & Sons, Inc., 1960. Pp. xvi, 483. * (*PA* 35:2231)

2714. SILVERMAN, LLOYD H., AND SILVERMAN, DORIS K. "Womb Fantasies in Heroin Addiction: A Rorschach Study." *J Proj Tech* 24:52–63 Mr '60. * (*PA* 35:1094)

2715. SINES, J. O. "An Approach to the Study of the Stimulus Significance of the Rorschach Ink Blots." *J Proj Tech* 24:64–6 Mr '60. *

2716. SINGER, JEROME L. Chap. 9, "The Experience Type: Some Behavioral Correlates and Theoretical Implications," pp. 223–59. In *Rorschach Psychology.* Edited by Maria A. Rickers-Ovsiankina. New York: John Wiley & Sons, Inc., 1960. Pp. xvi, 483. * (*PA* 35:2231)

2717. STARER, EMANUEL, AND ROSENBERG, SELIG. "A Multiple Choice Rorschach Technique for Increasing Test Productivity in Chronic Schizophrenics." *J Proj Tech* 24:429–32 D '60. * (*PA* 35:4940)

2718. STEIN, HARRY. "Rotation and Reliability of the Rorschach." *J Proj Tech* 24:171–81 Je '60. * (*PA* 35:4941)

2719. STONE, HERBERT K., AND DELLIS, NICHOLAS P. "An Exploratory Investigation Into the Levels Hypothesis." *J Proj Tech* 24:333–40 S '60. * (*PA* 35:791)

2720. THOMAS, CAROLINE BEDELL. "Characteristics of Smokers Compared With Nonsmokers in a Population of Healthy Young Adults, Including Observations on Family History, Blood Pressure, Heart Rate, Body Weight, Cholesterol and Certain Psychologic Traits." *Ann Internal Med* 53:697–718 O '60. *

2721. TOBIAS, S. *Effects of Reinforcement of Verbal Behavior on Response Changes in a Nonreinforced Situation.* Doctor's thesis, Columbia University (New York, N.Y.), 1960. (*DA* 21:964)

2722. TOLOR, ALEXANDER; GLASS, HARVEY L.; AND MERMELSTEIN, MATTHEW D. "Rorschach Card Rejection as a Correlate of Intelligence in Children." *J Proj Tech* 24:71–4 Mr '60. * (*PA* 35:2250)

2723. TONG, J. E., AND MURPHY, I. C. "Rorschach Indices and Autonomic Stress Reactivity." *J Clin Psychol* 16:324–8 Jl '60. * (*PA* 36:2HN24T)

2724. TOOMEY, LAURA C., AND RICKERS-OVSIANKINA, MARIA A. "Tabular Comparison of Scoring Systems," pp. 441–65. In *Rorschach Psychology.* Edited by Maria A. Rickers-Ovsiankina. New York: John Wiley & Sons, Inc., 1960. Pp. xvi, 483. * (*PA* 35:2231)

2725. VAN DE CASTLE, R. L. "Perceptual Defense in a Binocular-Rivalry Situation." *J Personality* 28:448–62 D '60. * (*PA* 35:5010)

2726. VINSON, DAVID B. "Responses to the Rorschach Test That Identify Schizophrenic Thinking, Feeling, and Behavior." *J Clin & Exp Psychopathol* 21:34–40 Ja–Mr '60. * (*PA* 34:4703)

2727. VON HOLT, HENRY W., JR.; SENGSTAKE, CORD B.; SONODA, BEVERLY C.; AND DRAPER, WILLIAM A. "Orality, Image Fusions and Concept-Formation." *J Proj Tech* 24:194–8 Je '60. * (*PA* 35:4943)

2728. VORHAUS, PAULINE G. "The Hibernating Syndrome." *J Proj Tech* 24:199–210 Je '60. * (*PA* 35:4944)

2729. WALLER, PATRICIA F. "A Comparison of Shading Responses Obtained With Two Rorschach Methodologies From Psychiatric and Nonpsychiatric Subjects." *J Consult Psychol* 24:43–5 F '60. * (*PA* 34:8188)

2730. WALLER, PATRICIA F. "The Relationship Between the Rorschach Shading Response and Other Indices of Anxiety." *J Proj Tech* 24:211–7 Je '60. * (*PA* 35:4945)

2731. WILKINSON, NORMAN W. "A Rorschach Study of 'Olga': A Schizoid Adolescent Girl." *Rorsch Newsl* 5:15–22 D '60. *

2732. WILSON, V. W. "The Use of the Rorschach Method With Asian People." *Austral J Psychol* 12:199–202 D '60. *

2733. WYSOCKI, BOLESLAW A. "A Factorial Study of Rorschach Protocols." *Percept & Motor Skills* 10:105–6 Ap '60. * (*PA* 35:6451)

2734. YAMAHIRO, ROY S., AND GRIFFITH, RICHARD M. "Validity of Two Indices of Sexual Deviancy." *J Clin Psychol* 16:21–4 Ja '60. * (*PA* 36:1HE21Y)

2735. ZAMANSKY, HAROLD S., AND GOLDMAN, ALFRED E. "A Comparison of Two Methods of Analyzing Rorschach Data in Assessing Therapeutic Change." *J Proj Tech* 24:75–82 Mr '60. * (*PA* 35:2234)

2736. ZAX, MELVIN, AND LOISELLE, ROBERT H. "The Influence of Card Order on the Stimulus Value of the Rorschach Inkblots." *J Proj Tech* 24:218–21 Je '60. *

2737. ZAX, MELVIN, AND LOISELLE, ROBERT H. "Stimulus Value of Rorschach Inkblots as Measured by the Semantic Differential." *J Clin Psychol* 16:160–3 Ap '60. * (*PA* 36:2HG60Z)

2738. ZAX, MELVIN, AND STRICKER, GEORGE. "The Effect of a Structured Inquiry on Rorschach Scores." *J Consult Psychol* 24:328–32 Ag '60. * (*PA* 35:2235)

2739. ZAX, MELVIN; LOISELLE, ROBERT H.; AND KARRAS, ATHAN. "Stimulus Characteristics of Rorschach Inkblots as Perceived by a Schizophrenic Sample." *J Proj Tech* 24:439–43 D '60. * (*PA* 35:4948)

2740. ZAX, MELVIN; STRICKER, GEORGE; AND WEISS, JONATHAN H. "Some Effects of Non-Personality Factors on Rorschach Performance." *J Proj Tech* 24:83–93 Mr '60. * (*PA* 35:2236)

2741. ABRAMS, STANLEY. *The Relationship of Repression, Projection and Preference in the Realm of Hostility.* Doctor's thesis, Temple University (Philadelphia, Pa.), 1961. (*DA* 22:635)

2742. ADAMS, HENRY B., AND COOPER, G. DAVID. "Rorschach Response Productivity and Overt Psychiatric Symptomatology." *J Clin Psychol* 17:355–7 O '61. * (*PA* 38:8538)

2743. ALCOCK, THEODORA. "The Reality Basis of Rorschach Interpretation." *Rorsch Newsl* 6:6–11 D '61. *

2744. ANASTASI, ANNE. *Psychological Testing, Second Edition,* pp. 568–73. New York: Macmillan Co., 1961. Pp. xiii, 657. * (*PA* 36:1HA57A)

2745. APPELBAUM, STEPHEN A. "The End of the Test as a Determinant of Response." *B Menninger Clinic* 25:120–8 My '61. * (*PA* 36:4HE20A)

2746. BARCLAY, A., AND HILDEN, ARNOLD H. "Variables Related to Duration of Individual Psychotherapy." *J Proj Tech* 25:268–71 S '61. * (*PA* 36:3IE68B)

2747. BARENDREGT, J. T.; ARIS-DIJKSTRA, M.; DIERCKS, L. M. J.; AND WILDE, G. J. S. Chap. 3, "The Rorschach Test as a Means of Testing the Hypothesis of Psychosomatic Specificity: A Cross Validation Study," pp. 33–52. In *Research in Psychodiagnostics.* Edited by J. T. Barendregt. The Hague, Holland: Mouton & Co., 1961. Pp. vii, 221. *

2748. BEARDSLEY, KATHARINE. "Analysis of Psychological

Tests of Persons Diagnosed Sociopathic Personality Disturbance." *Arch Crim Psychodynam* 4:389–411 su '61. *

2749. BECK, SAMUEL J.; BECK, ANNE G.; LEVITT, EUGENE E.; AND MOLISH, HERMAN B. *Rorschach's Test: 1, Basic Processes, Third Edition.* New York: Grune & Stratton, Inc., 1961. Pp. x, 237. * (*PA* 36:1HG37B)

2750. BENE, EVA. "Anxiety and Emotional Impoverishment in Men Under Stress." *Brit J Med Psychol* 34:281–9 pt 3 & 4 '61. * (*PA* 37:1297)

2751. BERRYMAN, EILEEN. "Poets' Responses to the Rorschach." *J General Psychol* 64:349–58 Ap '61. * (*PA* 36:1HG49B)

2752. BIRCH, HERBERT G., AND BELMONT, IRA. "Functional Levels of Disturbance Manifested by Brain-Damaged (Hemiplegic) Patients as Revealed in Rorschach Responses." *J Nerv & Mental Dis* 132:410–6 My '61. * (*PA* 36:2JF10B)

2753. BLATT, SIDNEY J.; ENGEL, MARY; AND MIRMOW, ESTHER LEE. "When Inquiry Fails." *J Proj Tech* 25:32–7 Mr '61. * (*PA* 36:1HG32B)

2754. BLOOM, BERNARD L., AND ARKOFF, ABE. "Role Playing in Acute and Chronic Schizophrenia." *J Consult Psychol* 25:24–8 F '61. * (*PA* 36:3JQ24B)

2755. BOSGANG, IRWIN. *A Construct Validation Study of the Leveling-Sharpening Cognitive Control by Means of Rorschach Response Behavior.* Doctor's thesis, New York University (New York, N.Y.), 1961. (*DA* 23:698)

2756. BOWYER, RUTH. "A Case of Over-Identification in Childhood Schizophrenia." *Rorsch Newsl* 6:30–2 Je '61. *

2757. BRAMS, JEROME M. "Counselor Characteristics and Effective Communication in Counseling." *J Counsel Psychol* 8:25–30 sp '61. * (*PA* 36:3KI25B)

2758. BRICKLIN, BARRY. "Clinical Use of the n Affiliation Score." *J Proj Tech* 25:277–81 S '61. * (*PA* 36:3HG77B)

2759. BRICKLIN, BARRY, AND GOTTLIEB, SOPHIE G. "The Prediction of Some Aspects of Marital Compatibility by Means of the Rorschach Test." *Psychiatric Q Sup* 35:281–303 pt 2 '61. * (*PA* 37:5297)

2760. BROWN, FRED; CHASE, JANET; AND WINSON, JUDITH. "Studies in Infant Feeding Choices of Primiparae: 2, Comparison of Rorschach Determinants of Accepters and Rejecters of Breast Feeding." *J Proj Tech* 25:412–21 D '61. *

2761. BROWN, THELMA E. "Factors Relating to Turnover Among Veterans Administration Nursing Assistants." *J Clin & Exp Psychopathol* 22:226–34 D '61. *

2762. BURNAND, GORDON. "Further Work on a Scale for Assessing Psychosis From the Rorschach." *Rorsch Newsl* 6:27–9 Je '61. *

2763. BURSTEIN, ALVIN G. "A Note on Time of First Responses in Rorschach Protocols." *J Consult Psychol* 25:549–50 D '61. * (*PA* 37:5023)

2764. CHUNG, BOM MO. "A Factorial Study of Rorschach Protocols." Abstract. *Acta Psychologica* 19:123–4 '61. *

2765. CLIFTON, JAMES A., AND LEVINE, DAVID. *Klamath Personalities: Ten Rorschach Case Studies.* [Lawrence, Kan.: James A. Clifton, University of Kansas], 1961. Pp. iv, 80. *

2766. COBRINIK, LEONARD, AND POPPER, LILY. "Developmental Aspects of Thought Disturbance in Schizophrenic Children: A Rorschach Study." *Am J Orthopsychiat* 31:170–80 Ja '61. * (*PA* 36:1JQ70C)

2767. COHEN, SYDNEY. *An Experimental Investigation of the Validity of Universal Symbolic Significance as Employed in the Content Analysis of the Rorschach Ink Blot Test.* Doctor's thesis, New York University (New York, N.Y.), 1961. (*DA* 23:305)

2768. COLE, DAVID L. "The Prediction of Teaching Performance." *J Ed Res* 54:345–8 My '61. * (*PA* 36:3KM45C)

2769. DAVIS, HANNAH S. "Judgments of Intellectual Level From Various Features of the Rorschach Including Vocabulary." *J Proj Tech* 25:155–7 Je '61. * (*PA* 36:2HG55D)

2770. DAVIS, HAROLD BERNARD. *Some Symbolic Meanings of the Rorschach Inkblots.* Doctor's thesis, Michigan State University (East Lansing, Mich.), 1961. (*DA* 22:4405)

2771. DREIER, JACOB LEON. *An Inverted Factor Analysis of Rorschach Protocols of Neurotic Parents in a Child Guidance Clinic.* Doctor's thesis, Adelphi College (Garden City, N.Y.), 1961.

2772. ECKHARDT, WILLIAM. "Piotrowski's Signs: Organic or Functional?" *J Clin Psychol* 17:36–8 Ja '61. * (*PA* 37:3172)

2773. EXNER, JOHN E., JR. "Achromatic Color in Cards IV and VI of the Rorschach." *J Proj Tech* 25:38–40 Mr '61. * (*PA* 36:1HG38E)

2774. FREED, GRIFFITH OSLER. *A Projective Test Study of Creativity in College Students in Visual Arts.* Doctor's thesis, University of Michigan (Ann Arbor, Mich.), 1961. (*DA* 22:640)

2775. GEISER, ROBERT LEE. *The Psychodiagnostic Efficiency of WAIS and Rorschach Scores: A Discriminant Function Study.* Doctor's thesis, Boston University (Boston, Mass.), 1961. (*DA* 22:915)

2776. GILBERT, MICHAEL M., AND MARADIE, LOUIS J. "The Incidence of Psycopathy in a Group of Prisoners Referred for Psychiatric Evaluation." *Arch Crim Psychodynam* 4:480–8 su '61. * (*PA* 36:2JO80G)

2777. GILL, HARWANT SINGH. *Delay of Response in Problem Solving and Color Response to Rorschach Stimuli.* Doctor's thesis, Boston University (Boston, Mass.), 1961. (*DA* 22:1252)

2778. GLADSTON, ELAINE R., AND AMADO-HAGUENAUER, GINETTE. "Distanciation in Space and Time: A Study in Unstable Hypo-Manic Denial." *Rorsch Newsl* 6:16–26 Je '61. *

2779. GOLDBERGER, LEO. "Reactions to Perceptual Isolation and Rorschach Manifestations of the Primary Process." *J Proj Tech* 25:287–302 S '61. * (*PA* 36:3HJ87G)

2780. GOLDFARB, ALLAN. "Performance Under Stress in Relation to Intellectual Control and Self-Acceptance." *J Consult Psychol* 25:7–12 F '61. * (*PA* 36:3HJ07G)

2781. GOLDMAN, ALFRED E., AND HERMAN, JACK L. "Studies in Vicariousness: The Effect of Immobilization on Rorschach Movement Responses." *J Proj Tech* 25:164–5 Je '61. * (*PA* 36:2HG64G)

2782. GRIB, THOMAS F. *Pattern Analysis of Movement Responses and Location Choices on the Rorschach.* Doctor's thesis, Loyola University (Chicago, Ill.), 1961.

2783. GRIFFITH, RICHARD M. "Rorschach Water Percepts: A Study in Conflicting Results." *Am Psychologist* 16:307–11 Je '61. * (*PA* 36:2JK07G)

2784. HAFNER, A. JACK. "Rorschach Card Stimulus Values for Children." *J Proj Tech* 25:166–9 Je '61. * (*PA* 36:2HG66H)

2785. HAMMER, EMANUEL F. "Emotional Instability and Creativity." *Percept & Motor Skills* 12:102 F '61. * (*PA* 35:6439)

2786–7. HASKELL, ROYAL J., JR. "Relationship Between Aggressive Behavior and Psychological Tests." *J Proj Tech* 25:431–40 D '61. *

2788. HAZARI, ANANDI, AND SINHA, S. N. "Rorschach Ranking Conformity Test: A Revision and an Evaluation." *J Psychol Res* 5:77–9 My '61. * (*PA* 38:8550)

2789. HERTZ, MARGUERITE R. *Frequency Tables for Scoring Rorschach Responses, Fourth Edition.* Cleveland, Ohio: Western Reserve University Press, 1961. Pp. ii, 253. *

2790. HORIUCHI, HARUOY. "A Study of Perceptual Process of Rorschach Cards by Tachistoscopic Method on Movement and Shading Responses." *J Proj Tech* 25:44–53 Mr '61. * (*PA* 36:1HG44H)

2791. JOURARD, SIDNEY M. "Self-Disclosure and Rorschach Productivity." *Percept & Motor Skills* 13:232 O '61. *

2792. KALDEGG, A. "The Case of an Alcoholic—Prognosis and Follow-Up." *Rorsch Newsl* 6:12–9 D '61. *

2793. KIKUCHI, TETSUHIKO. "Rorschach Response and Epileptic Personality." *Tohoku Psychologica Folia* 19(3–4):93–102 '61. *

2794. KIKUCHI, TETSUHIKO; KITAMURA, SEIRŌ; AND ŌYAMA, MASAHIRO. "Rorschach Performance in Alcoholic Intoxication." *Tohoku Psychologica Folia* 20(1–2):45–71 '61. * (*PA* 36:5DK45K)

2795. KIRESUK, THOMAS JACK. *The Effect of Test Sophistication on the Diagnostic Validity of the Minnesota Multiphasic Personality Inventory and the Rorschach With Paranoid Schizophrenics.* Doctor's thesis, University of Minnesota (Minneapolis, Minn.), 1961. (*DA* 22:2875)

2796. KLOPFER, BRUNO, AND BOYER, L. BRYCE. "Notes on the Personality Structure of a North American Indian Shaman: Rorschach Interpretation." *J Proj Tech* 25:170–8 Je '61. * (*PA* 36:2HG70K)

2797. KODMAN, FRANK, JR., AND WATERS, JERRY E. "Rorschach Responses of Children Exhibiting Psychogenic Auditory Symptoms." *J Clin Psychol* 17:305–6 Jl '61. * (*PA* 38:8554)

2798. KUMAR, PRAMOD. "The Rorschach Test in Psychoneurotic and Normal Groups." *Indian J Psychol* 36:169–72 D '61. * (*PA* 37:6741)

2799. KUMAR, PRAMOD. "The Rorschach Test in Some Mental Disorders—Schizophrenic Group." *Psychologia* 4:36–40 Mr '61. *

2800. KUTSCHE, RUDOLPH PAUL, JR. *A Rorschach Comparison of Adult Male Personality in Big Cove, Cherokee, North Carolina, and "Henry's Branch," Kentucky.* Doctor's thesis, University of Pennsylvania (Philadelphia, Pa.), 1961. (*DA* 22:969)

2801. LEAGUE, BETTY JO, AND JACKSON, DOUGLAS N. "Activity and Passivity as Correlates of Field-Independence." *Percept & Motor Skills* 12:291–8 Je '61. * (*PA* 36:2HJ91L)

.2802. LEBEL, RICHARD AIMÉ. *A Study to Measure the Stimulus Value of Color as an Indicator of an Individual's Emotional Relationship to the Environment.* Doctor's thesis, Boston University (Boston, Mass.), 1961. (*DA* 23:152)

2803. LENOUE, DALE; SPILKA, BERNARD; VAN DE CASTLE, ROBERT; AND PRINCE, ALBERT. "Social Desirability and the Group Rorschach." *J Clin Psychol* 17:175–7 Ap '61. * (*PA* 38:1016)

2804. LFSSER, ERWIN. "Popularity of Rorschach Training in the United States." *J Proj Tech* 25:179–83 Je '61. * (*PA* 36:2HG79L)

2805. LINDZEY, GARDNER. *Projective Techniques and Cross-Cultural Research.* New York: Appleton-Century-Crofts, Inc., 1961. Pp. xi, 339. * (*PA* 37:3199)

2806. LIPSHUTZ, DANIEL M. "Some Dynamic Factors in the Problem of Aggression." *Psychiatric Q* 35:78–87 Ja '61. * (*PA* 36:2IF78L)

2807. LOVELAND, NATHENE TURK. "Epileptic Personality and Cognitive Functioning." *J Proj Tech* 25:54–68 Mr '61. * (*PA* 36:1HG54L)

2808. LUCAS, WINAFRED B. "The Effects of Frustration on

the Rorschach Responses of Nine Year Old Children." *J Proj Tech* 25:199–204 Je '61. * (*PA* 36:2FF99L)

2809. MacCasland, Barbara Whittredge. *The Relation of Aggressive Fantasy to Aggressive Behavior in Children.* Doctor's thesis, Syracuse University (Syracuse, N.Y.), 1961. (*DA* 23:300)

2810. McConnell, R. A. "The Discontinuity in Schmeidler's ESP-Rorschach Data." *J Psychol* 52:87–97 Jl '61. * (*PA* 36:2BP87M)

2811. McCully, Robert S. "Human Movement in the Rorschach Materials of a Group of Pre-Adolescent Boys Suffering From Progressive Muscular Loss." *J Proj Tech* 25:205–11 Je '61. * (*PA* 36:2HG05M)

2812. Malmivaara, Katri, and Kolho, Pirkko. "Retesting of Primary School Children With Sceno and Rorschach Tests." *Annales Paediatriae Fenniae* 7(4):251–8 '61. *

2813. Malmivaara, Katri, and Kolho, Pirkko. "Use of the Sceno and the Rorschach Tests in the Study of Personality in Children of Kindergarten Age." *Annales Paediatriae Fenniae* 7(1):44–61 '61. *

2814. Mandler, George; Mandler, Jean M.; Kremen, Irwin; and Sholiton, Robert D. "The Response to Threat: Relations Among Verbal and Physiological Indices." *Psychol Monogr* 75(9):1–22 '61. * (*PA* 36:3HN22M)

2815. Markham, Sylvia. "A Comparative Evaluation of Psychotic and Nonpsychotic Reactions to Childbirth." *Am J Orthopsychiatry* 31:565–78 Jl '61. * (*PA* 36:4JP65M)

2816. Marks, Philip A. "Effects of Texture and Form on the Popular Response to Card VI of the Rorschach." *J Clin Psychol* 17:38–41 Ja '61. * (*PA* 37:3200)

2817. Marsh, Loyal F. "Parental Attitudes as the Basis for Attributing Meaning to Rorschach Cards IV and VII." *J Proj Tech* 25:69–74 Mr '61. * (*PA* 36:1HE69M)

2818. Mayer, Joseph, and Binz, Elizabeth. "Stimulus Values of Rorschach Cards." *J Clin Psychol* 17:186–7 Ap '61. * (*PA* 38:1019)

2819. Meyer, M. L., and Partipilo, Michael A. "Examiner Personality as an Influence on the Rorschach Test." *Psychol Rep* 9:221–2 O '61. *

2820. Meyer, Mortimer M. "The Case of El: Blind Analysis of the Tests of an Unknown Patient." *J Proj Tech* 25:375–82 D '61. *

2821. Nikelly, Arthur G. "'Hypothesis' Theory and Perceptual Responses to Inkblots." *J Proj Tech* 25:75–80 Mr '61. * (*PA* 36:1HG75N)

2822. Pelz, Kurt S.; Ames, Louise B.; and Pike, Frances. "Measurement of Psychologic Function in Geriatric Patients." *J Am Geriatrics Soc* 9:740–54 S '61. *

2823. Perdue, William C. "A Study of the Rorschach Records of Forty-Seven Murderers." *J Social Ther* 7(3):158–67 '61. * (*PA* 36:4JO58P)

2824. Piotrowski, Zygmunt A. "Prediction of Overt Behavior From Projective Test Data." Abstract. *Acta Psychologica* 19:111–4 '61. *

2825. Piotrowski, Zygmunt A., and Bricklin, Barry. "A Second Validation of a Long-Term Rorschach Prognostic Index for Schizophrenic Patients." *J Consult Psychol* 25:123–8 Ap '61. * (*PA* 36:4JQ23P)

2826. Ramer, John Carl. *The Rorschach Barrier Score and Social Behavior.* Doctor's thesis, University of Washington (Seattle, Wash.), 1961. (*DA* 22:4086)

2827. Reisman, John M. "An Interpretation of *m*." Abstract. *J Consult Psychol* 25:367 Ag '61. * (*PA* 37:1273)

2828. Richardson, Charles E. "Health Education or Hypochondriasis." *Am J Pub Health* 51:1561–71 O '61. *

2829. Rigney, Francis J., and Smith, L. Douglas. *The Real Bohemia: A Sociological and Psychological Study of the "Beats."* New York: Basic Books, Inc., 1961. Pp. xxi, 250. * (*PA* 36:1GB50R)

2830. Rossi, Ascanio M., and Neuman, Gerard G. "A Comparative Study of Rorschach Norms: Medical Students." *J Proj Tech* 25:334–8 S '61. * (*PA* 36:3HC34R)

2831. Rychlak, Joseph F., and Guinouard, Donald E. "Symbolic Interpretation of Rorschach Content." Abstract. *J Consult Psychol* 25:370 Ag '61. * (*PA* 37:1275)

2832. Sappenfield, Bert R. "Perception of Masculinity-Femininity in Rorschach Blots and Responses." *J Clin Psychol* 17:373–6 O '61. * (*PA* 38:8569)

2833. Sherman, Murray H., Editor. *A Rorschach Reader.* New York: International Universities Press, Inc., 1961. Pp. xvi, 440. * (*PA* 36:4HG40S)

2834. Speisman, Joseph C., and Singer, Margaret Thaler. "Rorschach Content Correlates in Five Groups With Organic Pathology." *J Proj Tech* 25:356–9 S '61. * (*PA* 36:3HI56S)

2835. Stein, Harry. "An Evaluation of Rorschach Reliability Through the Alternate-Response Method." *J Clin Psychol* 17:241–5 Jl '61. * (*PA* 38:8438)

2836. Symonds, Percival M.; with Arthur R. Jensen. *From Adolescent to Adult*, pp. 119–75, 213–402. New York: Columbia University Press, 1961. Pp. x, 413. * (*PA* 35:2021)

2837. Taulbee, Earl S. "The Relationship Between Rorschach Flexor and Extensor M Responses and the MMPI and Psychotherapy." *J Proj Tech* 25:477–9 D '61. *

2838. Van Pelt, Warren Palmer. *Perceptual-Cognitive Development as Reflected by Rorschach Test Content.* Doctor's thesis, Syracuse University (Syracuse, N.Y.), 1961. (*DA* 23:316)

2839. Wagner, Edwin E. "The Interaction of Aggressive Movement Responses and Anatomy Responses on the Rorschach in Producing Anxiety." *J Proj Tech* 25:212–5 Je '61. * (*PA* 36:2HG12W)

2840. Weiner, Irving B. "Cross-Validation of a Rorschach Checklist Associated With Suicidal Tendencies." *J Consult Psychol* 25:312–5 Ag '61. * (*PA* 37:1734)

2841. Weiner, Irving B. "Three Rorschach Scores Indicative of Schizophrenia." *J Consult Psychol* 25:436–9 O '61. * (*PA* 37:3717)

2842. Wells, St. "The Relationships Between Real and Apparent Movement and Rorschach Form Perception." Abstract. *Acta Psychologica* 19:823–4 '61. *

2843. Williams, Celia, and Boreham, John. "Test and Re-test—Mr. John: Changes in the Rorschach Following Short-Term Psychoanalytically Orientated Psychotherapy." *Rorsch Newsl* 6:3–15 Je '61. *

2844. Williams, Jessie M. "Children Who Break Down in Foster Homes: A Psychological Study of Patterns of Personality Growth in Grossly Deprived Children." *J Child Psychol & Psychiatry* 2:5–20 Je '61. * (*PA* 36:2HG12W)

2845. Zax, Melvin, and Benham, Frank G. "The Stimulus Value of the Rorschach Inkblots as Perceived by Children." *J Proj Tech* 25:233–7 Je '61. * (*PA* 36:2HG33Z)

2846. Zuckerman, Marvin; Levitt, Eugene E.; and Lubin, Bernard. "Concurrent and Construct Validity of Direct and Indirect Measures of Dependency." *J Consult Psychol* 25:316–23 Ag '61. *

2847. Zukowsky, Eugene. *Measuring Primary and Secondary Process Thinking in Schizophrenics and Normals by Means of the Rorschach.* Doctor's thesis, Michigan State University (East Lansing, Mich.), 1961. (*DA* 23:316)

2848. Adams, Henry B., and Cooper, G. David. "Three Measures of Ego Strength and Prognosis for Psychotherapy." *J Clin Psychol* 18:490–4 O '62. * (*PA* 39:5142)

2849. Alimena, Benjamin. "An Experimental Investigation of the Affective Qualities of Rorschach Color, Form and Shading." *J Clin Psychol* 18:107–9 Ja '62. * (*PA* 38:8539)

2850. Appelbaum, Stephen A., and Holzman, Philip S. "The Color-Shading Response and Suicide." *J Proj Tech* 26:155–61 Je '62. * (*PA* 37:3623)

2851. Arnholter, Ethelwyne G. "The Validity of Fisher's Maladjustment and Rigidity Scales as an Indicator of Rehabilitation." *Personnel & Guid J* 40:634–7 Mr '62. * (*PA* 37:1544)

2852. Baldwin, Joan Carroll. *Rorschach Personality Pattern Differences Between Overachievers, Normals and Underachievers at the Fifth Grade Level.* Doctor's thesis, Loyola University (Chicago, Ill.), 1962.

2853. Belmont, Ira, and Birch, Herbert G. "'Productivity' and Mode of Function in the Rorschach Responses of Brain-Damaged Patients." *J Nerv & Mental Dis* 134:456–62 My '62. * (*PA* 37:1652)

2854. Block, William E. "Psychometric Aspects of the Rorschach Technique." *J Proj Tech* 26:162–72 Je '62. * (*PA* 37:3186)

2855. Bloom, Bernard L. "The Rorschach Popular Response Among Hawaiian Schizophrenics." *J Proj Tech* 26:173–81 Je '62. * (*PA* 37:3187)

2856. Brawer, Florence Blum. *The Introversive-Extratensive Dimensions of the Rorschach Technique and Their Relationships to Jungian Typology.* Master's thesis, University of California (Los Angeles, Calif.), 1962.

2857. Bricklin, Barry. "Comment on Adcock and Ritchie's 'Intercultural Use of Rorschach.'" *Am Anthrop* 64:1296–9 D '62. *

2858. Burgemeister, Bessie B. *Psychological Techniques in Neurological Diagnosis.* New York: Hoeber Medical Division, Harper & Row, Publishers, Inc., 1962. Pp. viii, 248. *

2859. Burke, Mary. *The Control of Response Choice on Projective Techniques.* Doctor's thesis, University of Denver (Denver, Colo.), 1962. (*DA* 24:2119)

2860. Burnand, Gordon. "Note on the Main Changes in the 1962 Revision of the Severe Disturbance Scale." *Rorsch Newsl* 7:20 D '62. *

2861. Buss, Arnold H.; Fischer, Herbert; and Simmons, Alvin J. "Aggression and Hostility in Psychiatric Patients." *J Consult Psychol* 26:84–9 F '62. * (*PA* 37:5055)

2862. Caracena, Philip F., and King, Gerald F. "Generality of Individual Differences in Complexity." *J Clin Psychol* 18:234–6 Ap '62. * (*PA* 38:8480)

2863. Caspari, Irene E. "A Rorschach Record of an Adolescent With Severe Reading Difficulties and Some Notes on His Remedial Teaching." *Rorsch Newsl* 7:3–14 Je '62. *

2864. Cleveland, Sidney E., and Johnson, Dale L. "Personality Patterns in Young Males With Coronary Disease." *Psychosom Med* 24:600–10 N–D '62. * (*PA* 37:8204)

2865. Coates, Stephen. "Homosexuality and the Rorschach Test." *Brit J Med Psychol* 35:177–90 pt 2 '62. * (*PA* 37:3612)

2866. Cooper, George David. *Changes in Ego Strength Following Brief Social and Perceptual Deprivation.* Doctor's thesis, Duke University (Durham, N.C.), 1962. (*DA* 23:4742)

2867. Coopersmith. Stanley. "Resources and Strength in Child Personality: Clinical Explorations of Self Esteem," pp. 61–78. (*PA* 37:4730) In *Child and Education.* Proceedings of the XIV International Congress of Applied Psychology, Vol. 3. Copenhagen, Denmark: Munksgaard, Ltd., 1962. Pp. 197. *

2868. Craft, Michael; Fabisch, Walter; Stephenson, Geoffry; Burnand, Gordon; and Kerridge, David. "100 Admissions to a Psychopathic Unit." *J Mental Sci* 108:564-83 S '62. * (*PA* 38:2138)

2869. Crumpton, Evelyn. "Projective Case Study of a True Hermaphrodite." *J Proj Tech* 26:266-75 S '62. * (*PA* 37:3396)

2870. Dana, Richard H. "The Validation of Projective Tests." *J Proj Tech* 26:182-6 Je '62. * (*PA* 37:3189)

2871. Daston, Paul G., and McConnell, Owen L. "Stability of Rorschach Penetration and Barrier Scores Over Time." Abstract. *J Consult Psychol* 26:104 F '62. * (*PA* 37:5024)

2872. DuBrin, Andrew J. "The Rorschach 'Eyes' Hypothesis and Paranoid Schizophrenia." *J Clin Psychol* 18: 468-71 O '62. * (*PA* 39:5197)

2873. Eiduson, Bernice T. *Scientists: Their Psychological World.* New York: Basic Books, Inc., 1962. Pp. xvi, 299. * (*PA* 37:111)

2874. Eisdorfer, Carl. "Changes in Cognitive Functioning in Relation to Intellectual Level in Senescence," pp. 888-96. In *Social and Psychological Aspects of Aging.* Proceedings of the Fifth Congress of the International Association of Gerontology. Edited by Clark Tibbitts and Wilma Donahue. New York: Columbia University Press, 1962. Pp. xviii, 952. *

2875. Epstein, Seymour; Lundborg, Elizabeth; and Kaplan, Bert. "Allocation of Energy and Rorschach Responsivity." *J Clin Psychol* 18:236-8 Ap '62. * (*PA* 38:8547)

2876. Exner, John E., Jr. "The Effect of Color on Productivity in Cards VIII, IX, X of the Rorschach." *J Proj Tech* 26:30-3 Mr '62. * (*PA* 37:3191)

2877. Fisher, Seymour. "Relationship of Rorschach Human Percepts to Projective Descriptions With Self Reference." *J Proj Tech* 26:231-3 Je '62. * (*PA* 37:3193)

2878. Freeman, Frank S. *Theory and Practice of Psychological Testing, Third Edition,* pp. 614-38. New York: Holt, Rinehart & Winston, Inc., 1962. Pp. xix, 697. *

2879. Geertsma, Robert H. "Factor Analysis of Rorschach Scoring Categories for a Population of Normal Subjects." *J Consult Psychol* 26:20-5 F '62. * (*PA* 37:5026)

2880. Geist, Harold. *The Etiology of Idiopathic Epilepsy,* pp. 116-53, 234-55. New York: Exposition Press, 1962. Pp. 297. *

2881. Glymour, Clark; Ammons, C. H.; and Ammons, R. B. "Projective Test Protocols of Students Placing Extreme (High or Low) Value on Intellectual Activity." *Proc Mont Acad Sci* 21:105-12 '62. * (*PA* 37:3195)

2882. Goldfried, Marvin R. "Rorschach Developmental Level and the MMPI as Measures of Severity of Psychological Disturbance." *J Proj Tech* 26:187-92 Je '62. * (*PA* 37:3219)

2883. Goldfried, Marvin R. "Some Normative Data on Rorschach Developmental Level 'Card Pull' in a Psychiatric Population." *J Proj Tech* 26:283-7 S '62. * (*PA* 37:3196)

2884. Gordon, Rosemary. "Fear and Attraction to Death as Shown by Rorschach Material." *Rorsch Newsl* 7:25-34 Je '62. *

2885. Grimm, Elaine R. "Psychological Investigation of Habitual Abortion." *Psychosom Med* 24:369-78 Jl-Ag '62. * (*PA* 37:5427)

2886. Hauser, Russell Jerome. *The Validity of the Formal and Linguistic Aspects of the Rorschach in Predicting Intelligence.* Doctor's thesis, New York University (New York, N.Y.), 1962. (*DA* 24:4303)

2887. Haworth, Mary R. "Responses of Children to a Group Projective Film and to the Rorschach, CAT, Despert Fables and D-A-P." *J Proj Tech* 26:47-60 Mr '62. * (*PA* 37:2893)

2888. Hersch, Charles. "The Cognitive Functioning of the Creative Person: A Development Analysis." *J Proj Tech* 26:193-200 Je '62. * (*PA* 37:3129)

2889. Herzberg, Irene. "The Pre-Psychotic Patient: How Can the Rorschach Test Help in Assessing Whether the Pre-Psychotic Patient Is Likely to Break Down in Treatment?" *Rorsch Newsl* 7:21-40 D '62. *

2890. Hirt, Michael, Editor. *Rorschach Science: Readings in Theory and Method.* New York: Free Press of Glencoe, 1962. Pp. ix, 438. * (*PA* 37:6737)

2891. Howard, Kenneth I. "The Convergent and Discriminant Validation of Ipsative Ratings From Three Projective Instruments." *J Clin Psychol* 18:183-8 Ap '62. * (*PA* 38:8551)

2892. Huzioka, Yosinaru. "Rorschach Test in Farming Villages of North Thailand," pp. 139-273. In *Nature and Life in Southeast Asia, Vol. 2.* Edited by Tatuo Kira and Tadao Umesao. Kyoto, Japan: Fauna and Flora Research Society, 1962. Pp. vii, 276. *

2893. Kettell, Marjorie E. "Rorschach Indicators of Senility in Geriatric Patients," pp. 639-43. In *Social and Psychological Aspects of Aging.* Proceedings of the Fifth Congress of the International Association of Gerontology. Edited by Clark Tibbitts and Wilma Donahue. New York: Columbia University Press, 1962. Pp. xviii, 952. *

2894. Kikuchi, Tetsuhiko; Kitamura, Seiro; and Ōyama, Masahiro. "Rorschach Performance in Alcoholic Intoxication, 2." *Tohoku Psychologica Folia* 21(1-3):19-46 '62-63. * (*PA* 37:7711)

2895. Klopfer, Bruno, and Davidson, Helen H. *The Rorschach Technique: An Introductory Manual.* New York: Harcourt, Brace & World, Inc., 1962. Pp. viii, 245. *

2896. Knoblock, Peter. *An Investigation of Essential Elements of the Reading Process by Means of Standard and Experimental Administrations of the Rorschach Inkblot Test.* Doctor's thesis, University of Michigan (Ann Arbor, Mich.), 1962. (*DA* 23:532)

2897. Korner, Ija N.; Allison, Roger B., Jr.; and Zwanziger, Max D. "Stimulus Size and Rorschach Responses." *J Psychol* 54:491-4 O '62. * (*PA* 37:6740)

2898. Kottenhoff, Heinrich. "Metric Determination of Schizophrenic Dementia." *Psychol Rep* 11:646 D '62. * (*PA* 38:3058)

2899. Kumar, Pramod. "Popular Responses in the Rorschach Test." *Psychologia* 5:161-9 S '62. * (*PA* 38:2717)

2900. Kumar, Pramod. "The Rorschach Test in Depressive and Normal Groups." *Indian J Psychol* 37:89-92 Ja '62. * (*PA* 37:6760)

2901. Levin, Rachel Babin. *The Psychology of Women: An Empirical Test of a Psychoanalytic Construct.* Doctor's thesis, Syracuse University (Syracuse, N.Y.), 1962. (*DA* 24:837)

2902. Levine, David, and Cohen, Jacob. "Symptoms and Ego Strength Measures as Predictors of the Outcome of Hospitalization in Functional Psychoses." *J Consult Psychol* 26: 246-50 Je '62. * (*PA* 38:1304)

2903. Levine, Murray, and Spivack, George. "Human Movement Responses and Verbal Expression in the Rorschach Test." *J Proj Tech* 26:299-304 S '62. * (*PA* 37:3197)

2904. Levitt, Eugene E.; Lubin, Bernard; and Zuckerman, Marvin. "A Simplified Method of Scoring Rorschach Content for Dependency." *J Proj Tech* 26:234-6 Je '62. * (*PA* 37:3198)

2905. Lipsher, David Harold. *Consistency of Clinicians' Judgments Based on MMPI, Rorschach and TAT Protocols.* Doctor's thesis, Stanford University (Stanford, Calif.), 1962. (*DA* 22:4409)

2906. Lucas, Carol. "Frustration and the Perception of Aggressive Animals." *J Consult Psychol* 26:287 Je '62. * (*PA* 38:926)

2907. McCully, Robert S. "Certain Theoretical Considerations in Relation to Borderline Schizophrenia and the Rorschach." *J Proj Tech* 26:404-18 D '62. * (*PA* 37:6742)

2908. Majumdar, Alok Kumar, and Roy, Arunangsu Bikash. "Latent Personality Content of Juvenile Delinquents." *J Psychol Res* 6:4-8 Ja '62. * (*PA* 37:3643)

2909. Malmivaara, Katri, and Kolho, Pirkko. "The Personality of 5- to 7-Year-Old Enuretics in the Light of the Sceno and Rorschach Tests." *Annales Paediatriae Fenniae* 8(3):166-72 '62. *

2910. Malmivaara, Katri, and Kolho, Pirkko. "The Personality of Stuttering Children at the Age of 5-7 Years in the Light of the Sceno and Rorschach Tests." *Annales Paediatriae Fenniae* 8(1):17-23 '62. *

2911. Meketon, Betty W.; Griffith, Richard M.; Taylor, Vivian H.; and Wiedeman, Jane S. "Rorschach Homosexual Signs in Paranoid Schizophrenics." *J Abn & Social Psychol* 65:280-4 O '62. *

2912. Mogar, Robert E. "Anxiety Indices in Human Figure Drawings: A Replication and Extension." Abstract. *J Consult Psychol* 26:108 F '62. * (*PA* 37:4989)

2913. Moos, Rudolf H. "Effects of Training on Students' Test Interpretations." *J Proj Tech* 26:310-7 S '62. * (*PA* 37:3201)

2914. Moskowitz, Samuel. *Concrete and Formal Thought in Personification and Causal Responses in the Rorschach Test.* Doctor's thesis, New York University (New York, N.Y.), 1962. (*DA* 24:2125)

2915. Mueller, A. D. "Pain Study of Paraplegic Patients: The Rorschach Test as an Aid in Predicting Pain Relief by Means of Chordotomy." *Arch Neurol* 7:355-8 O '62. * (*PA* 37:5367)

2916. Neiger, Stephen; Slemon, Alan G.; and Quirk, Douglas A. "The Performance of 'Chronic Schizophrenic' Patients on Piotrowski's Rorschach Sign List for Organic CNS Pathology." *J Proj Tech* 26:419-28 D '62. * (*PA* 37:6763)

2917. Neuringer, Charles. "Manifestations of Anxiety on the Rorschach Test." *J Proj Tech* 26:318-26 S '62. * (*PA* 37:3203)

2918. Orme, J. E. "Rorschach Sex Response in a Psychiatric Population." *J Clin Psychol* 18:303 Jl '62. * (*PA* 39:1867)

2919. Palmer, James O., and Lustgarten, Billie J. "The Prediction of TAT Structure as a Test of Rorschach's Experience-Balance." *J Proj Tech* 26:212-20 Je '62. * (*PA* 37:3204)

2920. Pauker, Jerome D. "Base Rates in the Prediction of Suicide: A Note on Appelbaum's and Holzman's 'The Color-Shading Response and Suicide.'" Reply by Stephen A. Appelbaum and Philip S. Holzman. *J Proj Tech* 26:429-30 D '62. *

2921. Pelz, Kurt; Pike, Frances; and Ames, Louise B. "A Proposed Battery of Childhood Tests for Discriminating Between Different Levels of Intactness of Function in Elderly Subjects." *J Genetic Psychol* 100:23-40 Mr '62. * (*PA* 37:975)

2922. Petersen, Paul A. *A Correlational Investigation Between Rorschach Indices and Independent Ratings of Empathy and Over-Control vs Over-Lability of Feelings.* Master's thesis, De Paul University (Chicago, Ill.), 1962.

2923. Pettifor, R. E. "Personality Studies in Ulcer and Alcoholic Patients." *Med Services J Can* 18:187-90 Mr '62. *

2924. Phelan, J. G. "Projective Techniques in the Selection

of Management Personnel." *J Proj Tech* 26:102–4 Mr '62. *
(*PA* 37:3915)

2925. PINE, FRED. "Creativity and Primary Process: Sample
Variations." *J Nerv & Mental Dis* 134:506–11 Je '62. * (*PA*
37:3205)

2926. PRICE, A. COOPER. "A Rorschach Study of the Development of Personality Structure in White and Negro Children
in a Southeastern Community." *Genetic Psychol Monogr* 65:
3–52 F '62. *

2927. PURCELL, KENNETH; TURNBULL, JOHN W.; AND BERN-
STEIN, LEWIS. "Distinctions Between Subgroups of Asthmatic
Children: Psychological Test and Behavior Rating Compari-
sons." *J Psychosom Res* 6:283–91 O–D '62. * (*PA* 37:8210)

2928. QUIRK, DOUGLAS A.; QUARRINGTON, MARY; NEIGER,
STEPHEN; AND SLEMON, ALAN G. "The Performance of Acute
Psychotic Patients on the Index of Pathological Thinking and
on Selected Signs of Idiosyncrasy on the Rorschach." *J Proj
Tech* 26:431–41 D '62. * (*PA* 37:6745)

2929. RICCIUTI, HENRY. "Development and Application of
Projective Techniques of Personality." *R Ed Res* 32:64–77 F
'62. * (*PA* 37:1274)

2930. ROSENTHAL, MELVIN. "Some Behavioral Correlates of
the Rorschach Experience-Balance." *J Proj Tech* 26:442–6 D
'62. * (*PA* 37:6747)

2931. SATO, ISAO; ŌYAMA, MASAHIRO; KITAMURA, SEIRO;
AND KIKUCHI, TETSUHIKO. "Rorschach Performance Under
Ravona Dosage." *Tohoku Psychologica Folia* 21(1–3):1–17
'62–63. * (*PA* 37:7715)

2932. SEEMAN, WILLIAM, AND MARKS, PHILIP A. "A Study
of Some 'Test Dimensions' Conceptions." *J Proj Tech* 26:
469–73 D '62. * (*PA* 37:6678)

2933. SEMEONOFF, BORIS. "Self-Description as an Instrument in Personality Assessment." *Brit J Med Psychol* 35:165–
75 pt 2 '62. * (*PA* 37:3236)

2934. SILVERMAN, LLOYD H.; LAPKIN, BENJAMIN; AND
ROSENBAUM, IRA S. "Manifestations of Primary Process
Thinking in Schizophrenia." *J Proj Tech* 26:117–27 Mr '62.
* (*PA* 37:3712)

2935. SMITH, THOMAS E. "The Relationship Between Depressive Personality Characteristics and Rorschach Card Preference." *J Consult Psychol* 26:286 Je '62. * (*PA* 38:934)

2936. STARK, STANLEY. "A Note on Time, Intelligence, and
Rorschach Movement Responses." *Percept & Motor Skills* 15:
267–72 O '62. * (*PA* 37:7997)

2937. STEIN, HARRY. "An Analysis of Two Components
Entering Into Rorschach Reliability Values." *J Proj Tech* 26:
474–7 D '62. * (*PA* 37:6748)

2938. SUPER, DONALD E., AND CRITES, JOHN O. *Appraising
Vocational Fitness by Means of Psychological Tests, Revised
Edition*, pp. 560–75. New York: Harper & Brothers, 1962. Pp.
xv, 688. * (*PA* 37:2038)

2939. THOMAS, CAROLINE BEDELL, AND KENDRICK, MIL-
DRED A. "Psychobiological Studies: 1, The Relationship of
Intellectual Productivity as Measured by the Rorschach Test
to Body Weight." *Ann Internal Med* 56:440–7 Mr '62. *

2940. TIZARD, BARBARA. "The Personality of Epileptics: A
Discussion of the Evidence." *Psychol B* 59:196–210 My '62.
* (*PA* 37:3522)

2941. VIITAMAKI, R. OLAVI. *Psychoses in Children: A Psychological Follow-Up Study*. Annals of the Finnish Academy
of Science and Letters, Series B, Vol. 125, Part 2. Helsinki,
Finland: Suomalainen Tiedeakatemia, Academia Scientiarum
Fennica, 1962. Pp. 52. * (*PA* 39:2650)

2942. VINSON, DAVID B., AND GAITZ, CHARLES M. "The
Objective Measurement of Psychobiologic Decline: A Preliminary Report," pp. 578–82. In *Social and Psychological Aspects
of Aging*. Proceedings of the Fifth Congress of the International Association of Gerontology. Edited by Clark Tibbitts
and Wilma Donahue. New York: Columbia University Press,
1962. Pp. xviii, 952. *

2943. WEINER, IRVING B. "Rorschach Tempo as a Schizophrenic Indicator." *Percept & Motor Skills* 15:139–41 Ag '62.
* (*PA* 37:5050)

2944. WISEMAN, RICHARD JOHN. *The Rorschach as a Stim-
ulus for Hypnotic Dreams: A Study of Unconscious Processes*.
Doctor's thesis, Michigan State University (East Lansing,
Mich.), 1962. (*DA* 23:3996)

2945. WOLFENSBERGER, WOLF P.; MILLER, MARTIN B.;
FOSHEE, JAMES G.; AND CROMWELL, RUE L. "Rorschach Cor-
relates of Activity Level in High School Children." *J Consult
Psychol* 26:269–72 Je '62. * (*PA* 38:711)

2946. ZUCKER, LUISE J. "Evaluating Psychopathology of
the Self." *Ann N Y Acad Sci* 96:844–52 Ja 27 '62. * (*PA*
37:6769)

2947. ACKER, CHARLES W. "Personality Concomitants of
Autonomic Balance: 1, Rorschach Measures." *J Proj Tech*
27:12–9 Mr '63. * (*PA* 38:1064)

2948. ACKER, CHARLES W. "Personality Concomitants of
Autonomic Balance: 2, Inventory Measures." *J Proj Tech*
27:20–2 Mr '63. * (*PA* 38:1064)

2949. ADAMS, HENRY B.; COOPER, G. DAVID; AND CARRERA,
RICHARD N. "The Rorschach and the MMPI: A Concurrent
Validity Study." *J Proj Tech* 27:23–34 Mr '63. * (*PA* 38:
976)

2950. ALCOCK, THEODORA. *The Rorschach in Practice*. London: Tavistock Publications (1959) Ltd., 1963. Pp. xii, 252. *

2951. ALCOCK, THEODORA. "The Vulnerable Personality."
Rorsch Newsl 8:2 D '63. *

2952. APPERSON, LOUISE; GOLDSTEIN, ARNOLD D.; AND
WILLIAMS, W. W. "Rorschach Form Level as an Indicator
of Potential in Mentally Retarded Children." *J Clin Psychol*
19:320–2 Jl '63. *

2953. BARNOUW, VICTOR. Chap. 15, "The Rorschach Test,"
pp. 239–59. In his *Culture and Personality*. Homewood, Ill.:
Dorsey Press, Inc., 1963. Pp. xi, 410. *

2954. BARRON, FRANK. Chap. 11, "The Disposition Toward
Originality," pp. 139–52. In *Scientific Creativity: Its Recog-
nition and Development*. Edited by Calvin W. Taylor and
Frank Barron. New York: John Wiley & Sons, Inc., 1963.
Pp. xxiv, 419. * (*PA* 38:2689)

2955. BLATT, SIDNEY J., AND ALLISON, JOEL. "Methodological Considerations in Rorschach Research: The W Response
as an Expression of Abstractive and Integrative Strivings."
J Proj Tech & Pers Assess 27:269–78 S '63. * (*PA* 38:4316)

2956. BLOCK, WILLIAM E. "Sequential Effects in the Presentation of Rorschach Inkblots." *J Clin Psychol* 19:462 O
'63. *

2957. BOYD, RICHARD W. "Cross-Validation of an Objective
Rorschach." *J Clin Psychol* 19:322–3 Jl '63. *

2958. BRICKLIN, BARRY, AND ZELEZNIK, CARTER. "A Psy-
chological Investigation of Selected Ethiopian Adolescents by
Means of the Rorschach and Other Projective Tests." *Hum
Org* 22:291–303 w '63–64. *

2959. BURNAND, GORDON. "Relative Difficulty of Rorschach
Cards and Diagnosis, Personality Defects and Symptoms, Part
1." *Rorsch Newsl* 8:24–30 Je '63. *

2960. BURNAND, GORDON. "Relative Difficulty of Rorschach
Cards and Diagnosis, Personality Defects and Symptoms, Part
2." *Rorsch Newl* 8:27–33 D '63. * (*PA* 38:8544)

2961. CERBUS, GEORGE, AND NICHOLS, ROBERT C. "Personality Variables and Response to Color." *Psychol B* 60:566–75
N '63. * (*PA* 38:4228)

2962. CLEMES, STANLEY; TANOUS, JAMES C.; AND KANTOR,
ROBERT E. "Level of Perceptual Development and Psychosomatic Illness." *J Proj Tech & Pers Assess* 27:279–87 S
'63. * (*PA* 38:4317)

2963. COOLEY, WILLIAM W. "Predicting Choice of a Career
in Scientific Research." *Personnel & Guid J* 42:21–8 S '63. *

2964. DAVIDS, ANTHONY, AND TALMADGE, MAX. "A Study
of Rorschach Signs of Adjustment in Mothers of Institutionalized Emotionally Disturbed Children." *J Proj Tech & Pers
Assess* 27:292–6 S '63. * (*PA* 38:4318)

2965. DAVIDS, ANTHONY, AND TALMADGE, MAX. "Utility of
the Rorschach in Predicting Movement in Psychiatric Casework." *Am J Orthopsychiatry* 33:290–1 Mr '63. *

2966. EBLE, SELMA J.; FERNALD, L. DODGE, JR.; AND GRAZI-
ANO, ANTHONY M. "The Comparability of Quantitative Rorschach and Z-Test Data." *J Proj Tech & Pers Assess* 27:166–
70 Je '63. * (*PA* 38:2692)

2967. EIDUSON, BERNICE T.; MEYER, MORTIMER M.; AND
LUCAS, WINAFRED B. "Contribution of Psychological Testing
of Parents to the Understanding of the Child." *J Proj Tech
& Pers Assess* 27:387–417 D '63. * (*PA* 38:8088)

2968. EISDORFER, CARL. "Rorschach Performance and Intellectual Functioning in the Aged." *J Gerontol* 18:358–63 O
'63. * (*PA* 38:5822)

2969. EISNER, BETTY GROVER. "Some Psychological Differences Beween Fertile and Infertile Women." *J Clin Psychol*
19:391–5 O '63. *

2970. ENDICOTT, NOBLE A., AND ENDICOTT, JEAN. "'Improvement' in Untreated Psychiatric Patients." *Arch Gen
Psychiatry* 9:575–85 D '63. * (*PA* 38:8643)

2971. ENDICOTT, NOBLE A., AND ENDICOTT, JEAN. "Objective Measures of Somatic Preoccupation." *J Nerv & Mental
Dis* 137:427–37 N '63. * (*PA* 38:6356)

2972. ENGEL, MARY. "Psychological Testing of Borderline
Psychotic Children." *Arch Gen Psychiatry* 8:426–34 My '63.
* (*PA* 38:2451)

2973. EVANS, RAY B., AND MARMORSTON, JESSIE. "Psychological Test Signs of Brain Damage in Cerebral Thrombosis."
Psychol Rep 12:915–30 Je '63. * (*PA* 38:6413)

2974. GLESER, GOLDINE C. "Projective Methodologies." *Annual R Psychol* 14:391–422 '63. *

2975. GOFF, REGINA M. "Trait Identification as a Means of
Predicting Academic Goal Attainment." *J Exp Ed* 31:297–302
Mr '63. *

2976. GOLDFRIED, MARVIN R. "The Connotative Meaning of
Some Animal Symbols for College Students." *J Proj Tech* 27:
60–7 Mr '63. * (*PA* 38:1010)

2977. GREBSTEIN, LAWRENCE C. "Relative Accuracy of Actuarial Prediction, Experienced Clinicians, and Graduate Students in a Clinical Judgment Task." *J Consult Psychol* 27:
127–32 Ap '63. * (*PA* 37:8023)

2978. GROSS, SEYMOUR Z. "Critique: Children Who Break
Down in Foster Homes: A Psychological Study of Patterns
of Personality Growth in Grossly Deprived Children." *J Child
Psychol & Psychiatry* 4:61–6 Ap '63. *

2979. HOWARD, KENNETH I. "Ratings of Projective Test
Protocols as a Function of Degree of Inference." *Ed & Psychol Meas* 23:267–75 su '63. * (*PA* 38:1013)

2980. KIKUCHI, TETSUHIKO; SATO, ISAO; AND ŌYAMA,
MASAHIRO. "Types of Alcoholic Alteration of Rorschach Test
Performance: A Case Study." *Tohoku Psychologica Folia*
21(4):97–105 '63. * (*PA* 38:4322)

2981. KIVILUOTO, H. "Trends of Development in Rorschach Responses 1962." *Rorsch Newsl* 8:9–16 D '63. * (*PA* 38:8553)

2982. KURZ, RONALD B. "Relationship Between Time Imagery and Rorschach Human Movement Responses." *J Consult Psychol* 27:273–6 Je '63. * (*PA* 38:1015)

2983. LAUNER, PHILIP T. *The Relationship of Given Interest-Patterns to Certain Aspects of Personality.* Doctor's thesis, New York University (New York, N.Y.), 1963. (*DA* 24:2564)

2984. LEBOWITZ, ANNE. "Patterns of Perceptual and Motor Organization." *J Proj Tech & Pers Assess* 27:302–8 S '63. * (*PA* 38:4502)

2985. LEVINE, MURRAY, AND SPIVACK, GEORGE. "The Rorschach Index of Ideational Repression: Application to Quantitative Sequence Analysis." *J Proj Tech* 27:73–8 Mr '63. * (*PA* 38:1017)

2986. LEVITT, EUGENE E.; BRADY, JOHN PAUL; AND LUBIN, BERNARD. "Correlates of Hypnotizability in Young Women: Anxiety and Dependency." *J Personality* 31:52–7 Mr '63. *

2987. LOISELLE, ROBERT H., AND KLEINSCHMIDT, ANN. "A Comparison of the Stimulus Value of Rorschach Inkblots and Their Percepts." *J Proj Tech & Pers Assess* 27:191–4 Je '63. * (*PA* 38:2719)

2988. LOVELAND, NATHENE T.; WYNNE, LYMAN C.; AND SINGER, MARGARET T. "The Family Rorschach: A New Method for Studying Family Interaction." *Family Process* 2:187–215 S '63. * (*PA* 38:8558)

2989. McCUE, KEMPER W.; ROTHENBERG, DAVID; ALLEN, ROBERT M.; AND JENNINGS, THEODORE W. "Rorschach Variables in Two 'Study of Values' Types." *J General Psychol* 68:169–72 Ja '63. * (*PA* 38:2742)

2990. McCULLY, ROBERT S. "An Interpretation of Projective Findings in a Case of Female Transsexualism." *J Proj Tech & Pers Assess* 27:436–46 D '63. * (*PA* 38:8766)

2991. MATHUR, SHANTA, AND PAIS, CLARA M. "Extratensive and Introversive Experience Balances as Tested by the Rorschach Test and the Sacks Completion Test." *Manas* 10(1):1–13 '63. * (*PA* 38:8559)

2992. MONS, W. E. R. "Nail-Biters and Card-Rejectors." *Rorsch Newsl* 8:11–4 Je '63. *

2993. NEIGER, STEPHEN, AND PAPASTERGIOU, CHRISTOS. "The Relationship Between Depressive Personality Characteristics and Rorschach Card Preference: A Reply to T. E. Smith." Abstract. *J Consult Psychol* 27:463 O '63. *

2994. NICKOLS, JOHN. "Rorschach Z Scores on Disturbed Subjects." *J Consult Psychol* 27:544–5 D '63. * (*PA* 38:8561)

2995. ORME, J. E. "Rorschach Alphabetical and Geometrical Responses." *J Clin Psychol* 19:459–60 O '63. *

2996. OSBORNE, ELSIE L. "Some Problems Associated With School Phobia as Illustrated in the Rorschach Record of a 6 Yr. Old Girl." *Rorsch Newsl* 8:3–10 Je '63. *

2997. OTTEN, MARK W., AND VAN DE CASTLE, R. L. "A Comparison of Set 'A' of the Holtzman Inkblots With the Rorschach by Means of the Semantic Differential." *J Proj Tech & Pers Assess* 27:452–60 D '63. * (*PA* 38:8562)

2998. PALMER, JAMES O. "Alterations in Rorschach's Experience Balance Under Conditions of Food and Sleep Deprivation: A Construct Validation Study." *J Proj Tech & Pers Assess* 27:208–13 Je '63. * (*PA* 38:2723)

2999. PARKER, ROLLAND S. "The Perceiver's Identification of the Figure in the Rorschach Human Movement Response." *J Proj Tech & Pers Assess* 27:214–9 Je '63. * (*PA* 38:2724)

3000. PAUKER, JEROME D. "Relationship of Rorschach Content Categories to Intelligence." *J Proj Tech & Pers Assess* 27:220–1 Je '63. * (*PA* 38:2725)

3001. PIOTROWSKI, ZYGMUNT A. "Use of the Rorschach Test as a Diagnostic Criterion." Letter. *Am Psychologist* 18:621–2 S '63. *

3002. PIOTROWSKI, ZYGMUNT A., AND ROCK, MILTON R.; WITH THE ASSISTANCE OF JOHN J. GRELA. *The Perceptanalytic Executive Scale: A Tool for the Selection of Top Managers.* New York: Grune & Stratton, Inc., 1963. Pp. iv, 220. * (*PA* 38:9357)

3003. POPE, BENJAMIN, AND BARE, CAROLE E. "Rorschach Percepts and Personal Concepts as Semantically Equivalent Members." *Percept & Motor Skills* 17:15–22 Ag '63. * (*PA* 38:8563)

3004. RAMER, JOHN. "The Rorschach Barrier Score and Social Behavior." *J Consult Psychol* 27:525–31 D '63. * (*PA* 38:8564)

3005. RAY, JOSEPH B. "The Meaning of Rorschach White Space Responses." *J Proj Tech & Pers Assess* 27:315–23 S '63. * (*PA* 38:4325)

3006. RICHARDSON, HELEN. "Rorschachs of Adolescent Approved School Girls, Compared With Ames' Normal Adolescents." *Rorsch Newsl* 8:3–8 D '63. * (*PA* 38:8566)

3007. RICKERS-OVSIANKINA, MARIA A.; KNAPP, ROBERT H.; AND McINTIRE, DONALD W. "Factors Affecting the Psychodiagnostic Significance of Color Perception." *J Proj Tech & Pers Assess* 27:461–6 D '63. * (*PA* 38:8567)

3008. ROSS, W. D.; ADSETT, NANCY; GLESER, GOLDINE; JOYCE, C. R. B.; KAPLAN, S. M.; AND TIEGER, M. E. "A Trial of Psychopharmacologic Measurement With Projective Techniques." *J Proj Tech & Pers Assess* 27:222–5 Je '63. *

3009. SAPOLSKY, ALLAN. "An Indicator of Suicidal Ideation on the Rorschach Test." *J Proj Tech & Pers Assess* 27:332–5 S '63. * (*PA* 38:4328)

3010. SCHULMAN, R. E. "Use of the Rorschach Prognostic

Rating Scale in Predicting Movement in Counseling." *J Counsel Psychol* 10:198–9 su '63. *

3011. SEMEONOFF, BORIS. "An Application of Inter-Person Analysis in Personality Assessment." *Brit J Psychol* 54:71–81 F '63. * (*PA* 37:8004)

3012. SILVER, ALBERT W., AND DERR, JOHN. "The Effect of Oral Gratification on Children's Rorschach Scores and Differences Between Examiners." *J Clin Psychol* 19:310–1 Jl '63. *

3013. SILVERMAN, LLOYD H. "On the Relationship Between Aggressive Imagery and Thought Disturbance in Rorschach Responses." *J Proj Tech & Pers Assess* 27:336–44 S '63. * (*PA* 38:4329)

3014. SINGER, MARGARET THALER, AND WYNNE, LYMAN C. "Differentiating Characteristics of Parents of Childhood Schizophrenics, Childhood Neurotics, and Young Adult Schizophrenics." *Am J Psychiatry* 120:234–43 S '63. *

3015. STOKVIS, BERTHOLD, AND BOLTEN, MART P. "Statistical Data on Personality Alterations in Chronic Illness." *Psychol Rep* 13:829 D '63. * (*PA* 38:9114)

3016. TAKAHASHI, S. "Statistical Analysis of Scoring Assumption Employed in the Psychodiagnosis via Group Method of the Rorschach Test." English abstract. *Jap J Psychol* 34:82–3 Je '63. *

3017. TESTIN, ROBERT FRANCIS. *Ego Strength Scale Differences Between Psychotic and Nonpsychotic Inpatients.* Doctor's thesis, Fordham University (New York, N.Y.), 1963. (*DA* 24:839)

3018. THOMAS, CAROLINE BEDELL, AND ROSS, DONALD CLARE. "A New Approach to the Rorschach Test as a Research Tool: 1, Preliminary Note." *B Johns Hopkins Hosp* 112:312–7 Je '63. *

3019. THOMAS, E. LLEWELLYN. "Eye Movements and Fixations During Initial Viewing of Rorschach Cards." *J Proj Tech & Pers Assess* 27:345–53 S '63. * (*PA* 38:4330)

3020. VORHAUS, PAULINE G. "The Ego-Asserting; Ego-Deflating Syndrome." *J Proj Tech & Pers Assess* 27:379–86 D '63. *

3021. VOTH, HAROLD M., AND MAYMAN, MARTIN. "A Dimension of Personality Organization: An Experimental Study of Ego-Closeness–Ego-Distance." *Arch Gen Psychiatry* 8:366–80 Ap '63. * (*PA* 38:2651)

3022. WAGONER, ROBERT A. "The Rorschach Test: A Perceptual or a Grammatical Device?" *Percept & Motor Skills* 17:419–22 O '63. * (*PA* 38:6102)

3023. WALLACE, JOHN, AND SECHREST, LEE. "Frequency Hypothesis and Content Analysis of Projective Techniques." *J Consult Psychol* 27:387–93 O '63. * (*PA* 38:4335)

3024. WEINGOLD, HAROLD P.; WEBSTER, RONALD L.; AND DAWSON, JOSEPH G. "Reinforcing Properties of Selected Rorschach Cards: A Methodological Study." *Percept & Motor Skills* 17:655–8 D '63. * (*PA* 38:5316)

3025. WEST, J. V.; BAUGH, V. S.; AND BAUGH, ANNIE P. "Rorschach and Draw-A-Person Responses of Hypnotized and Nonhypnotized Subjects." *Psychiatric Q* 37:123–7 Ja '63. *

3026. YANG, KUO-SHU; TZUO, HUAN-YUAN; AND WU, CHING-YI. "Rorschach Responses of Normal Chinese Adults: 2, The Popular Responses." *J Social Psychol* 60:175–86 Ag '63. * (*PA* 38:4336)

3027. YEN, YI-SHIU. "The Diagnostic Indicators of Simple Schizophrenia in the Rorschach Test." *Acta Psychologica Taiwanica* (5):52–6 Mr '63. * (*PA* 38:8573)

3028. ZAX, MELVIN; COWEN, EMORY L.; AND PETER, MARY. "A Comparative Study of Novice Nuns and College Females Using the Response Set Approach." *J Abn & Social Psychol* 66:369–75 Ap '63. * (*PA* 37:8005)

3029. ZELIN, MARTIN, AND SECHREST, LEE. "The Validity of the 'Mother' and 'Father' Cards of the Rorschach." *J Proj Tech* 27:114–21 Mr '63. * (*PA* 38:1027)

3030. LEVINE, MURRAY, AND SPIVACK, GEORGE. *The Rorschach Index of Repressive Style.* Springfield, Ill.: Charles C Thomas, Publisher, 1964. Pp. xvi, 164. * (*PA* 39:1747)

RICHARD H. DANA, *Professor of Psychology, University of South Florida, Tampa, Florida.*

In a previous review Shaffer suggested that the Rorschach is no longer a "promising" measuring instrument (see 5:154). More evidence has appeared in specific area reviews of anxiety scores (*2917*), factor analytic studies (*2687*), set and examiner (*2740*), situational and interpersonal variables (*2679*), and the stimulus (*2251*). Psychometric aspects of the Rorschach have been rigorously reexamined (*2854*).

This review will not duplicate specific area reviews and is based on 315 articles, including some dissertations where available, which appeared from 1958 through summer 1963. The literature for even this period is incomplete. However, classification should represent interests: general discussions (6 per cent), validation (40 per cent), stimulus (11 per cent), norms (9 per cent), and modified tests (7 per cent). Since 11 per cent of the studies were not relevant, this leaves a scant 16 per cent for administration, reliability, subject, examiner, and scoring variables, not to mention case studies. Clearly, the emphasis is still on applied research with the exception of sustained concern with stimulus properties of the blots.

When the validity studies are tallied, a similar result. is noted. Criterion-oriented or concurrent, predictive, and congruent designs account for 32, 17, and 20 per cent, respectively. Construct validation has been employed in 18 per cent and the remainder are general discussions. A few years ago it would have made sense to tally positive and negative results for each kind of validation. The lack of replication, systematic or otherwise, or of consensus in definition of variables, and the capricious dilettantism of some investigators, renders such scrutiny empty and mechanical.

No one now doubts that the early research history combined misplaced conviction and methodological naïveté. However, these attitudes are gradually being replaced by a more uniform competence: recent studies are sophisticated methodologically and prone to ask meaningful questions. We still experience the clinician's trust in procedural evidence while psychological science demands empirical justification for the continued daily use of the Rorschach. Nonetheless, in the attempt to provide a factual basis for practice, we invest our methodologies with our preconceptions and our labors are rewarded in the same coin.

Levy and Orr (2534) randomly and reliably selected 40 Rorschach studies and classified them in terms of the researcher's institution, academic or nonacademic, type of validity, criterion or construct, and outcome, favorable or unfavorable. The probability of positive results varies from 70 to 50 per cent for construct validity, and from 34 to 59 per cent for criterion-oriented validity as a function of academic or nonacademic settings, respectively. Where we work tends to focus our biases and dictates not only the research preoccupation but affects the probability of obtaining particular results.

Two blatant discrepancies between methodology and practice continue to be relevant. First, the methodology used to examine the Rorschach asks questions which differ from those asked of the test in clinical practice. The clinician uses scores and nonquantifiable data in combination, common interpretations are abstracted, and finally these interpretations are rationally ordered or contrived in terms of the Rorschacher's frame of reference. Reports are rich in meaning and in testable hypotheses to the extent that the clinician is able to maximize his use of these available cues in the context of a wealth of theoretical data and past experience. And finally the technical skill in putting the report on paper is related to the usefulness of the hypotheses contained therein. In this process there are no unqualified interpretative hypotheses for particular scores or combinations of scores. It has been shown repeatedly that the kind of data is irrelevant in the conceptual diagnostic task (2580).

Our research subculture has stereotyped the kinds of questions which may be legitimately asked. We attempt to relate specific Rorschach variables to external criteria which are about as unreliable as the test scores themselves. The psychologist in a clinical position is often concerned with concurrent validity, typically the prediction of clinical diagnosis. While this effort may be relevant to institutional practice, it rests upon acknowledged disagreement among experts as to the criterion diagnoses. Similarly, predictive validity is often concerned with outcome of psychotherapy. Again there is no acceptable criterion for therapy outcome. Congruent validity asks the question of relationship to another test of either questionable reliability or dubious validity, or both. There is no rational reason to expect successful prediction of an external criterion, except by accident or a combination of situation-determined variables which render cross validation unlikely. Construct validation is also hazardous. One attempts to construct theory with a relatively constricted methodology and in terms of quasi-reliable measures. The result is a plethora of tenuous relationships. For example, even the relatively well established relationships between M, human movement, and inhibition appear to have limited generality (2688).

Further complications result from the now well documented belief that the Rorschach measures a level of personality which is somewhat below the surface behavior (*2719*). No systematic attempt has been made to assess the aspect of validation neglected by Levy and Orr (*2534*), the expectation of differential results when the test is used for different measurement purposes. Additionally, while the preeminence of examiner influence is recognized, such awareness is not reflected in systematic examination of clinician impact upon Rorschach performance, scoring, or interpretation. For example, the examiner and not the specific instructional set is responsible for response differences (*2691*). It is noteworthy that only a very few studies were found in this area.

The second clinical versus research usage discrepancy is that the traditional and formal scores (e.g., Beck and Klopfer) are not genuine psychometric scores but a clinical shorthand (*2687*). This notation is dependent upon the subject's verbal skills which are inhibited or facilitated by social class bias (*2440*). Examiner judgment assesses the "goodness of fit" between a stimulus and a response mediated by verbal behavior (*2854*). Since the examiner's own behavior has directed and reinforced these responses (*2516, 2619, 2676*), the confounding in scores is apparent. The use of these nominal scale products as ordinal or ratio scales has further confused the validity issue. The presence of formal scores has endowed us with a convenient set of ready made variables which are often used instead of psychological thinking. Such scores are often isolated from theory and may not even be representative of the processes being studied (*2444, 2955*).

The purpose of these remarks is to outline a dilemma. We expose faith in the Rorschach and in our own clinical skills by continuing to use it in the face of strong professional admonitions to the contrary. We recognize that adequate use of the test is dependent upon the clinician; a function of training, experience, and unknown personality variables. Simultaneously, there is continual pressure to demonstrate that the test meets the usual psychometric criteria of objectivity, reliability, validity, additivity, scaling procedures, etc., which in fact it does not.

There is a recent and novel tendency to think about the meaning of the Rorschach task, to ask questions and find tentative answers within the context of theory (e.g., *2753*). The vehicles are content categories and composite variables derived as deductions from theory or presented as ways of testing clinical hypotheses. Several kinds of modified scoring variables merit discussion.

Werner is responsible for general developmental theory which has stimulated Rorschach scores (*2639*). Distribution-free measures provide quantification for the genetic level of perceptual behavior and comparisons between normal and deviant patterns of perceptual activity. These scores are of known and adequate reliability (*2560*). These developmental indices are related to personality and behavior variables in a variety of studies (*2255, 2274, 2590*). While there remains doubt as to the diagnostic validity of these scores (*2631*), the meaning of particular responses (e.g., *2582* for M and *2955* for W), and of personality processes (e.g., cognitive function, *2888*) has been enriched.

An elaborate and psychoanalytically derived method of scoring for primary and secondary process analysis has been developed as a research tool (*2645*). The emphasis is on primary process analysis of content in relatively sophisticated adults. Although reliability assessment is difficult, gross estimates of nominal and ordinal variables obtained with trained scorers are satisfactory. Goldberger (*2779*) has explored validation aspects of combined scores for adaptive and maladaptive regression. Cohen (*2614*) has studied artistic creativity in terms of primary process. Pine and Holt (*2692*) have evidence that expression and control of primary processes are independent. Sample differences appear to be relevant (*2925*). While the body of research using this system is still meager, the wealth of conceptually related data available in Rorschach records scored on these variables suggests that classical scoring variables are expendable.

Examples of highly specific scores occur in the work of McReynolds and Weide (*2544, 2675*) and Birch and Belmont (*2752, 2853*). The McReynolds J score from the Concept Evaluation Technique results from the number of agreements with suggested concepts for 50 blot areas. The J score apparently reflects rigor in habits of conceptualization and a low score is related to post lobotomy improvement. Levels of functioning in the response, inquiry, and testing-the-limits, may be distinguished (*2752*). Comparison of traditional and functional level scoring resulted in new information about the consequences of brain injury in left hemiplegic patients. Heath (*2420*) has made a plea for more highly structured stimuli and replication as antidote for the confounding of stimulus characteristics and the assumed manifest or latent stimulus meanings. His own Phrase Association Test for measuring defensive behavior is an example. These studies were selected to represent three degrees of alteration in administration, sources of scoring variables, or a substitute stimulus.

Personality study is stimulated by new scores developed from theory. Each new score gives us something else and not necessarily something new upon which to focus our awareness. As such these are exercises in sensitization similar to those offered by Zubin 25 years ago. The parameters of human complexity and human inventiveness provide wide limits for development of new scores. While the new scores lend hope that the Rorschach dilemma is resolvable, they are test-oriented solutions.

Somewhere in our hasty hope that nomothetic science would provide the empirical basis for Rorschach practice, we have overlooked the obvious. It is clinician and not test which enables personality study. In spite of our persistent attempts to convert the Rorschach into a psychometric instrument, we have failed. At best the test can provide an approximation of another person's reality, a framework for giving our hypotheses the possibility of being tested, and a consistent stimulus to minimize our own biases.

Indeed we have come to the end of an era: preoccupation with the Rorschach as a test. Perhaps the salient issue has been a wish to endow the Rorschach with respectability and a place of honor in psychometrica. This necessarily implies precedence of empirical over procedural evidence, a substitution of academic social sanctions for an understanding that requires neither replication nor statistics. We are limited in our tools for exploring man *qua* man; we do tend to rely on instruments less ambiguous and prone to folly and blind choice than ourselves. The Rorschachiana, empirical and otherwise, has confirmed some antique wisdom and provoked discard of legend about humanness. However, this has been a byproduct, largely of the construct validity studies,

the most sustained systematic replication that the technique has undergone (*2870*).

The Rorschach is being replaced for three sensible reasons: (*a*) limited tests for particular measurement purposes can be given more than a semblance of psychometric purity; (*b*) the Holtzman inkblots have been constructed in such a manner that many of the psychometric cavils are met for more generalized personality study; (*c*) the aura of magic surrounding an unknown and miraculous instrument has been dispelled by empirical studies. In Masling's choice words (*2679*), the x-ray did become a mirror in which we confused our own image with those of test and subject. While there is no ready tranquilizer for our test-oriented anxiety, there is still hope for self-understanding among clinicians. Moreover, for the psychologist who accepts his own inner resources as the instrument for putting together the pieces of someone else's experience, the Rorschach will continue to be a convenient touchstone.

LEONARD D. ERON, *Professor of Psychology, State University of Iowa, Iowa City, Iowa.*

This reviewer will not attempt to survey the voluminous Rorschach literature to date. Previous editions of the yearbook have contained such reviews and the monotonous overall conclusions have been that there is little evidence to support the claims made for the technique by its proponents. The results of research published subsequent to the last edition of the yearbook have not perceptibly altered this grim picture of the reliability and validity of the Rorschach procedure. Yet its use in clinical and educational settings continues unabated. Although it has been suggested that this persistence is nothing more than a demonstration of functional autonomy, it is this reviewer's opinion that the use of the Rorschach method persists because it is a useful tool in personality assessment and often can contribute to an understanding of the individual. At the very least, it is right more often than it is wrong. However, when it is right, it probably is so for the wrong reasons. Although this is unfortunate for those who have been trying to validate the traditional scoring systems, it very likely explains why the Rorschach method works in the clinic but not in research. There is no evidence, e.g., that color and shading responses *per se* have the significance for personality functioning traditionally assigned to them, and location of response has been consistently related to nothing. There is some slight evidence that human movement responses are an index to cognitive inhibition (*2196*) and the ability to inhibit motility (*1444*), although even these minimal claims have not uniformly been replicated (*2688*), and that indefiniteness and inaccuracy of form are indications of impulsivity and poor reality testing (*1257*). However, it is the content of the responses, devaluated by Rorschach himself and long neglected by his followers, that stands up as the lone aspect of the responses that has any stability and relates consistently to outside criteria. In this regard, whatever validity the human movement response and form accuracy have is very likely a function of content.

Rorschach and most of those who have come after him have regarded his procedure as a perceptual task. However, there is little reason to believe that telling an examiner what inkblots look like is a task essentially perceptual in nature. Even if it were, there is certainly no agreement among those doing research in perception that perception is indeed a function of personality. Thus, the so called perceptual determinants of the responses are largely irrelevant and it is as a conceptual task, with content taking its rightful place, that the Rorschach method should reasonably be evaluated. When it is so regarded, attempts at validation have been more successful, as will be noted in the following discussion.

It has been suggested by Zubin (*1826*) that the Rorschach is nothing more or less than a standard interview and should be treated as such by a systematic analysis of the content. In a forthcoming volume,[1] Zubin, Eron, and Schumer present a series of standard scales by which Rorschach responses can be evaluated. Previously, Zubin, Eron, and Sultan (*2155*), utilizing these scales, rated the records of 43 superior individuals and obtained very high interscorer reliability. However, they were also concerned with another kind of reliability which has to do with the subject's consistency of performance. It would be expected that if

an individual perceives in Rorschach space the same way he perceives in real life space, then these characteristic habits of perception would consistently mark his performance. Thus, some degree of agreement should emerge when ratings on one half of an individual's responses are compared with ratings on the other half. Alternative responses were used to divide each of the protocols in half. The authors found that those scales which measured so called perceptual habits, e.g., use of color, form, texture, shading, etc., produced reliabilities so low as to indicate they revealed little that was consistently characteristic of the subjects. However, those scales which measured content factors and ways of thinking had such high reliabilities that they were obviously reflecting consistent trends in the subjects.

The superiority of content scoring in terms of various kinds of reliability has been corroborated by a number of other studies which have used both content and so called perceptual scoring. Ramzy and Pickard (*853*) obtained very high interscorer agreement on Beck's content categories but not on any other scores. Holzberg and Wexler (*966*), using 20 schizophrenic subjects, studied temporal reliability over a three-week period and found correlations for scores at the two different times ranging from −.17 to .95, with reliabilities for content categories, M, and F clustering around .70 and color and shading clustering around .30. Kagan (*2650*), reporting on the long term stability of Rorschach responses (subjects were 37 males and 38 females tested at ages 10, 13, 16, and finally at 35), found only number of responses, human movement, and content showing statistically significant stability.

Since perceptual scoring reveals little that is consistently characteristic of individuals, while content scoring does, it can be concluded that the content of the protocols and not the so called perceptual factors is the basis for whatever success the Rorschach has achieved. However, more is meant by content scoring than Rorschach's simple classification of responses into animal, human, object, etc. Emphasis has often been laid on the dynamic or psychoanalytic aspects of the response and its symbolic referent (*981, 1787, 2051, 2645*). For example, Schafer's volume (*1787*) is devoted mostly to an examination of the total Rorschach situation from a psychoanalytic point of view. The

1 Zubin, Joseph; Eron, Leonard D.; and Schumer, Florence. *An Experimental Approach to Projective Techniques.* New York: John Wiley & Sons, Inc. Scheduled for publication in 1965.

principles, rules of thumb, and skills presented here are based largely on insightful, undoubtedly wise but not necessarily public procedures, since they are derived almost entirely from the author's own clinical experience. In his chapter on thematic analyses, Schafer illustrates his psychoanalytic method of thematic (content) analysis. He cautions the clinician that it is important not to be too "wild" with interpretations which always should be corroborated by turning to other tests to see if the themes recur. The general methods of content analysis which Schafer proposes may be extremely helpful clinically, but they await validation through more advanced methodological and theoretical developments than are now available. Fisher and Cleveland (2409) have developed a content scoring system from a different theoretical point of view, based on constructs relating to body image. Responses may have vulnerable boundaries (scored P-penetration) or nonvulnerable boundaries (scored B-barriers) and this dichotomy is purportedly related to attitudes and feelings the subject has about his own body. These attitudes in turn, it is claimed, reflect personality and diagnostic groupings.

However, in analyzing Rorschach responses in terms of nonperceptual factors, it is not necessary to delve into the symbolic significance of each utterance in order to derive meaningful material for personality description. The subject's verbal productions can be placed into such categories as compulsive thinking, disorganized thinking, or creative thinking; poverty of ideas or fluency; confabulation or clarity; rigidity or flexibility; perplexity or straightforwardness; rejection or compliance. The scales noted above which have been developed by Zubin and his students cover many aspects of the response which are not regarded as perceptual in nature but which tap the quality of the subject's verbalizations and interpretive attitudes. If the Rorschach situation is conceived of as an interview in which the subject is presented with a novel, but standardized, problem solving task, it can be seen that there are many facets of his behavior which can be assessed in a meaningful way for personality interpretation. For example, reliable scales have been developed to assess attitudinal factors (dominance, evaluative attitude, mood, self reference, dehumanization) and thinking proc-

esses (perseveration, elaboration, congruity, communality, definiteness of concept, distance in time and space). It is these attitudes and characteristics of thought which indicate, for example, whether the subject is schizophrenic or normal, just in the same way that the clinical interview might reveal these factors. The advantage of the Rorschach inheres in the fact that it is a standard interview providing a systematic framework for eliciting psychopathological trends. Furthermore, it may elicit these trends in patients who are otherwise not communicative. The inclusive quality of the scales which have been mentioned, in addition to the fact that their reliability and validity are open to public inspection and use, contrast this approach to that utilized by psychoanalytically oriented workers who are concerned with what they claim to be more clinically meaningful and provocative schemes.

Validity studies using content-oriented scoring schemes have met with more success than the standard Rorschach study. McCall (1152), using the Zubin scales, found that psychometrically weighted nonperceptual categories having to do with verbalization of content and thought process related significantly to outcome in psychosurgery, either pre or post operatively or both. The ascendance-submission scale was the most sensitive, although no rationale was provided to explain why those destined for eventual improvement showed a consistent tendency to see more submissive human figures in the Rorschach cards. In the same evaluation of psychosurgery (2300), researchers utilizing these scales found quantitative relationships with anxiety, e.g., the number of movement responses rose and fell with anxiety level (as judged both by a psychiatrist and on the basis of psychological interviewing using anchored scaling devices). The degree of tentativeness or insecurity in giving responses also correlated positively with these ratings of anxiety.

Sen (1030) administered the Rorschach to 100 Indian students who had been living together in England for two years and who also evaluated each other's personalities. The correlations between these evaluations and Beck's scores were nonsignificant. However, when scored for content the correlations ranged from .57 to .66. Sandler and Ackner (1184) factor analyzed the content scores of 50 psychiatric patients. Four factors were obtained whose psychological meaningfulness was ascertained by correlating them with personality evaluations on the basis of psychiatric interview and case history methods. The productivity factor (R) was related to previous productivity in life, to chronicity of symptoms, and to a schizo-affective picture at the time of hospitalization. The anatomy factor was related to an insecure, withdrawn, "previous" personality picture, bad physical health, and an emotional deluded state for the present symptoms. The remaining factors were analyzed in similar fashion.

Watkins and Staufacher (*1461*) provided a series of quantitative indices of deviant verbalizations based on the content of protocols (derived from Rapaport's 13 types of deviant Rorschach responses), and found that such indicators had a reliability of .77 between two raters and that these indices distinguished normals from neurotics and the latter from schizophrenics. Powers and Hamlin (*2283*) replicated this work and further refined Rapaport's deviant response types into four large classes: intellectual disorganization, inappropriate increase or loss of distance, deviant content, and affective response. All four classes could be reliably scored but the first two proved to be the most differentiating. Bower, Testin, and Roberts (*2609*) have developed an extensive series of scales which tap content and thought processes as reflected in Rorschach protocols. These scales were empirically weighted to result in maximum discriminatory power. Although some promising trends were found, further refinement of the scales and cross validation on a new population must be awaited before any overall evaluation of this research can be made.

Elizur (*799*) found that an analysis of content in relation to anxiety and hostility yielded significant interscorer and split-half reliabilities and also related significantly to self ratings as well as ratings made by three judges on the basis of observation of a 45-minute semistructured interview. On the whole, evidence for the validity of Elizur's RCT, obtained in studies by other investigators, has been positive when applied to the records of undergraduates (*1639*), NP patients (*1883*), and adolescents (*1348*), but not so successful when used with children (*2808*).

Rader's (*2214*) results in trying to predict overt aggressive verbal behavior from Ror-

schach content, analyzed by an expanded version of the Elizur method, were more equivocal. His subjects were 38 state prison inmates and his criterion was behavior in therapeutic discussion groups. He found that aggressive content, especially mutilation, was significantly, positively related to aggressive behavior (primarily verbal) although the correlations were not high enough to be used in individual prediction. Towbin (*2586*) also found a significant, positive correlation between assaultive behavior on a VA neuropsychiatric ward and two measures of aggression based on the content of the Rorschach record, one having to do with aggressive comments directed toward the card and one with the actual concepts seen.

Although anxiety and aggression are the primary variables for which content scoring systems have been developed, other variables have also been the object of this type of analysis. DeVos (*1330*) developed a system of scoring Rorschach content for dependency which has been somewhat simplified by Levitt, Lubin, and Zuckerman (*2904*). The latter scheme proved quite reliable even when the scoring was done by non-expert judges and some evidence for construct validity was derived from two replications of a study which showed that dependency scores for volunteers for a hypnosis experiment were significantly greater than for non-volunteers. However, a concurrent measure of validity, relationship of dependency scores to peer ratings of dependency, was less successful (*2846*). Rychlak and Guinouard (*2704*) confirmed their hypothesis, using the Harrower Group Rorschach, that certain limited measures of content (whether human, animal, kind of interaction, or extent of tension indicated) would be related to independent measures of personality (*IPAT High School Personality Questionnaire*) and popularity (sociometric choice). The results of these studies dealing with content and description of thought process are impressive when viewed against the uniformly negative research findings with determinant scores.

In general, Rorschach validation has been directed toward relating either the individual scores or global impressions and holistic configurations to outside criteria. As indicated above, attempts at validating the so called perceptual scores have been almost wholly unsuccessful while correlation of overall impressions of the Rorschach records with ratings, case histories, and behavioral criteria has by and large met with more success. Zamansky and Goldman (2735), for example, have shown that global Rorschach evaluations were much better indicators of actual changes in ward social adjustment (ratings made after completion of various ancillary therapies with a group of male and female hospitalized psychotics) than were 11 quantitative Rorschach indices. Crumpton (2032), in a study of signs of color shock, has shown that although statistical use of the usual signs failed to discriminate records based on an achromatic and a chromatic (standard) Rorschach series in which the judges did not know on which series the records were based, the use of clinical, global ratings of the protocols did result in a statistically significant, valid differentiation of the records.

Corsini, Severson, Tunney, and Uehling (1858) explored the relative validity of a Rorschach checklist (928), and judgments of clinicians in separating "normal" and "abnormal" Rorschach protocols. The normal records were obtained from 50 prison guards, and the abnormal records were obtained from a group of 50 prisoners who had not only committed serious felonies, but had been referred for testing because of a possibility of having "serious personality deviations." All identifying data had been removed from the Rorschach protocols, and prisoners and guards were matched, as far as possible, for age. Inmates of average intelligence and lower middle class status only were used. Subjects were all white. Four psychologists were asked to rank all protocols, from 1 to 100, in terms of adjustment of the subject. Reliability of rankings (interjudge comparisons) was of a relatively low order. But comparison of number of normal protocols placed in the top half of the rankings by the Davidson Rorschach Adjustment Scale and by each of the judges, yielded the finding that global judgments were more accurate. Time spent in the judging process was shown to be positively related to the accuracy of the ranking, it might be noted. The findings do indeed suggest that global, clinical methods are more successful than mechanical checklists, in terms of "separation capacity," but a question should be raised as to whether or not either of these methods could have effectively separated a

more meaningful, better matched group—prisoners with and without "serious personality deviations." Language, content, and general approach to the Rorschach situation might well differ sufficiently between guards and prisoners to yield definite clues, independent of Rorschach scoring itself, as to which subject is likely to come from which group.

Although the relative superiority of global impressions of the Rorschach record over the use of individual scores lends support to the notion that the Rorschach is best evaluated as an interview, it should be pointed out that the record of success even with global evaluations is not totally encouraging and until we find out the basis on which the global evaluations are made, we are no further ahead scientifically or in the ability to teach the technique to others.

Another indication that the Rorschach method is best considered a more or less standardized interview is the accumulated information concerning the examiner-subject interaction (1786, 2740). The quantity and quality of responses elicited by the inkblots are affected to a measurable degree by the individual characteristics and overt behavior of the administrator. The effect of the examiner is further complicated by the purpose of the subject in taking the test. Is he there by order of the court? Is he trying to get a discharge from the army or compensation for injuries? Is he an applicant to a medical school or a junior executive looking for a promotion? Is he an introductory psychology student picking up extra credits by being a subject for a graduate student's experiment? What are the reasons given to the subject by the examiner for taking the test; what are the subject's preconceptions about the procedure and what is his cover story?

Early studies were directed toward showing that when large samples of protocols obtained by different examiners from similar populations were compared, many more differences in scoring categories than could reasonably be expected by chance were found among the examiners even though the same scoring system was used by all (1079, 1224, 1525). Some examiners consistently had more of one kind of response than others. It was apparent that it was necessary to look at the examiners' behavior to determine what accounted for these consistent differences. Later studies indicated that the differences could be explained by variations in instructions given by the examiner (*968, 1111, 2311*); by the sets with which the subjects were provided, whether deliberately or not (*916, 1067, 2050, 2070, 2298, 2619*); by the specific but often subtle reinforcing behaviors of the examiner (*2145, 2516, 2676*); by whether he and the subjects were male or female (*1096, 1767, 1871*); by the difference between them in social class and ethnic group (*2440*); and by the examiner's warmth and friendliness or lack thereof (*1567*). It has been demonstrated that despite instructions to the examiner that he behave otherwise, his basic personality, as judged by others, whether warm and permissive or cold and authoritarian, comes through and affects the response (*982*). Overt and covert hostility and anxiety of the examiner, as independently rated by others, are also related to specific patterns of scores obtained by the subjects (*1606*).

Of all parts of the Rorschach it would seem that it is in the inquiry that the examiner can most directly influence the ultimate scoring of the response. A number of investigators have been concerned about the lack of standard procedure in the inquiry and have demonstrated its effect on the scoring of the responses (*1344, 2483, 2738*). Baughman (*2394*) has suggested a method which he claims achieves more precision and standardization in the inquiry. Essentially it is a paired comparison technique in which the subject is asked to contrast the standard card with six types of modified cards, identical in form to the Rorschach, but systematically varying in color, shading, figure-ground contrast, and complexity of form. By use of a series of standard questions the examiner can determine precisely the influence and relevance of color, shading, etc.

Although his technique has been criticized for being unwieldy and time consuming, the modifications Baughman has introduced seem to represent considerable improvement over standard inquiry procedure. The question of the validity of the scores themselves, however, remains pertinent, with or without the use of Baughman's method. As a case in point, Baughman has indicated that the paired comparison technique should produce significantly more shading responses when the standard and modified inquiries are compared, suggest-

ing the technique affords greater opportunity for more valid, as well as more reliable, indicators of determinants to emerge. However, Waller (*2730*) found that, although the number of shading responses did indeed increase with the modified inquiry, there was no improvement in prediction to three independent measures of anxiety. It would seem that no matter how refined and reliable the measures of shading become, relations to outside criteria won't improve because, as mentioned before, it's neither shading nor texture nor achromatic color but the content that is the most likely aspect of the response that is significant for personality.

The majority of studies cited here present unmistakable evidence of the fact that situational and interpersonal variables influence responses to the Rorschach procedure, thus reinforcing the view that the Rorschach best be analyzed as an interview situation in which the test response and the accompanying behavior of both the examiner and the subject must always be interpreted in the light of the total situation. Because the Rorschach response is susceptible to these influences and is not the foolproof x-ray it was once claimed to be, does not mean it has no value in assessment. These influences are not always sources of error; they can indicate the way the subject—as well as the examiner—approaches a novel problem solving task and how he adapts to it. These behaviors, along with the content produced in the record, are subject to the most rigorous scrutiny. The Zubin scales provide a framework for such an evaluation of the Rorschach. The recommended approach requires a shift in emphasis from the perceptual to the thought content aspects of the Rorschach. It is indeed true that Hermann Rorschach himself turned away from the content of the subject's responses and advocated a perceptual analysis. He stated that the content of the responses yielded little insight into the content of the personality; but he may have been wrong. Or he may have defined content too narrowly. If content is defined as an essential element of the protocol, including verbalization of thought processes and problem solving behavior, and the Rorschach record is treated like any other interview material, the mystery surrounding the expert's interpretation may yet yield to scientific scrutiny, since it is a moot question whether Rorschach experts do not indeed derive most of their insights into personality from a direct or indirect analysis of content and the interaction of the subject with the examiner.

ARTHUR R. JENSEN, *Associate Professor of Educational Psychology, and Associate Research Psychologist, Institute of Human Learning, University of California, Berkeley, California.*

In the 43 years since Hermann Rorschach published the *Psychodiagnostik,* his set of ten carefully chosen inkblots has become the most popular of all psychological tests. A recent survey [1] of hospitals, clinics, guidance centers, and the like, indicates that the Rorschach clearly outstrips all its competitors, both in the number of institutions using the test and in the amount of usage. Furthermore, the curve depicting the increase in popularity of the Rorschach over the past decade is positively accelerated. On the basis of Sundberg's survey we can safely estimate that, at the very least, the Rorschach is administered to a million persons a year in the United States; it consumes on the average approximately five million clinical man-hours (which is 571 years), at a total cost to the clients of approximately 25 million dollars. Thus, in terms of usage the Rorschach is easily the Number One psychological instrument. It has become as closely identified with the clinical psychologist as the stethoscope is with the physician.

The amount of research and publication on the Rorschach is even more impressive. On this count no other test equals it. Over the past decade it has inspired on the average not fewer than three publications per week in the United States alone. The rate of Rorschach publication, also, is positively accelerated. The Rorschach bibliography has already passed 3000.

Of course, it is too much to expect any one person to review and assess in its totality any phenomenon of such fabulous proportions as the Rorschach. *The Fifth Mental Measurements Yearbook* presented very thorough and comprehensive reviews of the most important Rorschach research up to that time, and the conclusions arrived at by these reviewers are

highly representative of the assessments made of the Rorschach in psychological textbooks reviewing much the same material. Put frankly, the consensus of qualified judgment is that the Rorschach is a very poor test and has no practical worth for any of the purposes for which it is recommended by its devotees.

To make his task manageable, the present reviewer has decided to focus attention on the Rorschach literature appearing since *The Fifth Mental Measurements Yearbook,* to determine the degree to which recent research has turned up anything that might in some way alter the negative judgments arrived at by earlier reviewers. Much of the early research on the Rorschach has often been criticized for methodological and statistical inadequacy, but this fortunately can no longer be said of the recent research published in the leading psychological journals. There are now a number of methodologically and statistically sound and sophisticated studies. Even more important, in terms of doing full justice to the Rorschach, is that the good research is now being done by the Rorschachers and projective test experts themselves, often with the full cooperation of their clinical colleagues who are highly experienced in the use of projective techniques. No longer can it be claimed that negative findings are the result of bluenose methodologists of statistics and experimental psychology applying inappropriate criteria to an instrument for which they have no sympathy, no clinical experience, no intuitive feeling, and no talent.

Detailed reviews of recent Rorschach research have been made by Heiman and Rothney (*2520*) and by Ricciuti (*2929*). A book edited by Rickers-Ovsiankina (*2699*) is probably the most important publication in the field in the past several years and contains excellent discussions of Rorschach research by a number of prominent psychologists in the fields of projective techniques, clinical psychology, and personality research. The reader is also referred to the *Annual Review of Psychology* for coverage of the most important contributions; the review by Gleser (*2974*) is especially worthwhile.

RORSCHACH TRAINING. The Rorschach is not just another test which the clinician can learn to use by reading a manual. It is a whole culture, the full acquisition of which depends upon intensive tutorial training, a great deal

1 SUNDBERG, NORMAN D. "The Practice of Psychological Testing in Clinical Services in the United States." *Am Psychologist* 16:79–83 F '61. *

of clinical experience with projective materials, a certain degree of dedicated discipleship, and, perhaps most difficult of all, acclimatization to an atmosphere that is philosophically quite alien to the orientation of modern psychology as it is now taught in the leading American and British universities. In addition, the would-be Rorschacher, if he is to hold his own among the experts, must possess a kind of gift similar to the literary talent of a novelist or biographer, combining a perceptive and intuitive sensitivity to human qualities and the power to express these perceptions in subtle, varied, and complex ways. The Rorschach report of an expert is, if nothing else, a literary work of art. This is the chief criterion of expertness with the Rorschach, for the research has not revealed any significant differences in reliability or validity between beginners in the Rorschach technique and acknowledged masters.

Qualified Rorschachers generally have had at least three semesters, the equivalent of a year and a half, of intensive training in the use of the Rorschach. The first semester is usually devoted merely to learning how to score the test, while the second and third semesters are devoted to interpretation. As is typical of most textbooks on the Rorschach, there is little or no reference to the research literature in most traditional Rorschach courses. At least 100 tests must be administered, scored, and interpreted under the close supervision of an expert before the novice is considered sufficiently qualified to be left on his own. Unfortunately, many clinicians, and especially school psychologists, who use the Rorschach in their daily clinical practice are inadequately trained, with the consequence that their reports have a stereotyped, cookbook quality which can add nothing of clinical value to the understanding of the patient and can often be injudiciously misleading or even harmful. It is the reviewer's impression from reading many psychological reports based on the Rorschach that the acknowledged experts are usually more cautious and wise in their use of the instrument than are clinicians who have had relatively meager training or who are self-taught.

USES OF THE RORSCHACH. The technique has been used with all age levels in clinics, guidance centers, hospitals, schools, and in indus-

try, to assess, diagnose, and describe every aspect of the human personality—cognitive, emotional, and motivational—in both normal and psychiatric subjects. In tabulating the types of interpretive statements made from a single Rorschach protocol (analyzed by Klopfer), Shneidman (2361) concluded that the Rorschach concentrates on the areas of affect, diagnosis, quality of perception, ego capacity, personality mechanisms, sexual thought, and psychosexual level. One is impressed after reading a large number of Rorschach reports that no facet of the human psyche and no aspect of human feeling or behavior is inaccessible to the Rorschach. Certainly it excels all other psychological tests in permitting a richness of personality description that comprehends the entire lexicon of human characteristics. It has even been used to attempt to differentiate children with defective hearing from those with normal hearing (2520). Its chief use, however, remains that of aiding in the formulation of psychiatric diagnosis and prognosis.

The Rorschach has also been used, with questionable success, as a research tool in the investigation of personality and in anthropological and cross-cultural studies. Its contributions in the personality realm have been evaluated by Gardner and Lois Murphy (2686), and Lindzey (2805) has written a comprehensive review of its use in cross-cultural research. Neither the Murphys nor Lindzey credits the Rorschach with substantial contributions to research in these fields.

ADMINISTRATION AND SCORING. The test materials have not changed in 43 years; they are the same 10, bilaterally symmetrical blots originated by Rorschach. The Rorschach culture apparently has assumed that these 10 blots cannot be improved upon and that they alone are a sufficient foundation for building a science of personality diagnosis. The great orthodoxy and appeal to authority in the Rorschach culture is reflected also in the scoring procedures which have changed in only minor details from the method originally laid down by Rorschach.

Incidentally, if the color in the five chromatic blots plays as important a role as the Rorschachers claim for it, then note should be taken of the fact that different editions of the blots differ in color, some being more vivid and others more pastel.

The test takes approximately 45 to 60 minutes to administer, depending upon the productivity of the subject and the thoroughness of the examiner's inquiry and testing of the limits. The procedures are described in detail in all the Rorschach textbooks and are matters on which authorities differ very little.

The scoring of the subject's responses, which generally number between 10 and 30, is a highly technical procedure requiring many hours of practice before it becomes an easy task. The several different scoring systems currently in use are all basically much alike, and once having learned one it is easy to adopt another. The systems of Rorschach and Binder, Rapaport and Schafer, Beck, Piotrowski, Hertz, and Klopfer have been systematically compared in the last chapter of the volume edited by Rickers-Ovsiankina (2724).

RORSCHACH INTERPRETATION. Many elements enter into interpretation. First there are the formal scores, which are generally interpreted in terms of configurations or combinations with other Rorschach scores. Textbooks on interpretation are seldom explicit or precise concerning the quantitative aspects of the Rorschach scores and indices, although the language of the discussion clearly implies quantitative considerations. Reference is made to "a lot of shading responses," "a high M per cent," "long reaction time," "many CF responses," and so on. The exact quantity is rarely specified. Examiners must have had experience with at least 100 protocols before developing some subjective notion of the "norms" of the various scores. There are, however, published norms (e.g., 1300, 1651, 2475), but these are seldom referred to by clinicians, and the leading textbooks on Rorschach interpretation make no use of them. Almost every page of the long-awaited and important book on Rorschach interpretation by Piotrowski (2211) contains typical examples of the interpretations connected with various scores. For example: "There is something uncompromising, inflexible, and daring about those subjects who give c'R (dark shading responses). By contrast, the individual with many cR (light shading responses) prefers to sacrifice....his important goals of external achievement in order to appear less competitive and assertive to the world. If necessary, he surrenders part of his personality rather than antagonize others." These elaborate and subtle interpretations of Rorschach scores are totally unsupported by any kind of research evidence.

But much more than the formal scores enters into the interpretation. The subject's language, the content of his responses, the particular sequence of his responses, his reaction time to each card, the way he handles the cards and turns the cards, every aspect of his behavior during the testing—all are grist for the interpretive mill which grinds extremely fine. The full flavor of this art can be savoured from a number of published Rorschach reports by masters of the technique. The thinking that enters into the interpretation is clearly delineated by Schafer in his excellent text (1787) and in the detailed case analysis presented in the textbook by Phillips and Smith (1588). A highly professional report by Stephanie Dudek, typical of the productions of the most skilled Rorschachers, is to be found in Appendix A of the book by Symonds and Jensen (2836). It is evident that nothing in the Rorschach protocol or in the subject's behavior during the testing is regarded as "noise" in the system—everything is considered significant and interpretable. And the final report of an expert, in its wealth of detail, its subtlety of personality description, breadth of comprehension, and depth of penetration, can often rival the most elaborate characterizations of Marcel Proust or Henry James.

Aside from considerations of reliability and validity, a question must be asked concerning the semantics of the Rorschach report itself. How unambiguously meaningful is the interpretation to a number of different persons reading the final report? Little is factually known about this. It could well be that the Rorschach report is itself projective material for the person to whom the report is referred, serving mainly to bolster his confidence in his own interpretations derived from other sources. The real question is, how much can the report *add* to the psychiatrist's understanding of his patient gained through other means, even assuming it is valid? This we do not know, but the question becomes wholly academic when we take account of the known reliability and validity of Rorschach interpretation.

RELIABILITY. Few other tests provide so many opportunities for the multiplication of error variance as does the Rorschach. We must consider separately the reliability of scoring and of interpretation, the stability of these in time, the internal consistency of scores, and the effect of the interaction of examiners and subjects.

First, it must be pointed out that most of the traditional Rorschach scores have two strikes against them from a psychometric standpoint. In the typical protocol, most of the scoring categories are used relatively infrequently so that their reliability is practically indeterminate. For example, the average frequencies of various Rorschach scores in a sample of 28 nonpsychiatric subjects (*2836*) is Dd = 1.0, S = 0.3, M = 2.9, k = 0.2, K = 0.1, FK = 0.6, FC = 0.9, C = 0.2. The only really large frequencies are R (number of responses) = 22.1, D (large detail) = 12.1, W (whole responses) = 8.0, and F (form) = 7.5. The distributions of these scores are generally very skewed, and the small amount of variation that occurs among the majority of subjects easily falls within the standard error of measurement for most of the scores. By all criteria R (number of responses) has the highest reliability of any of the scores, and by virtue of this it spuriously inflates the reliability of the various index scores into which it enters, such as M%, F%, W%, etc. Most of the combinational scores from the Rorschach, consisting of ratios and differences among the various primary scores, are, of course, even more unsusceptible to a satisfactory demonstration of reliability than are the primary scores.

Another question that is seldom asked is whether the scoring categories themselves have any particular meaning or uniqueness in a psychological sense. That is, are the various movement responses, shading responses, color responses, texture responses, or content of the responses measuring some common factor more or less peculiar to these particular classes of determinants? Factor analyses of the scores indicate that the underlying factors do not coincide at all well with the traditional scoring categories (e.g., *1058*). Correlations between the various movement responses (M, FM, m) on the Rorschach, Behn-Rorschach, and Levy Movement Cards are in the range from .12 to .41 (*2281*), so that if the tendency to perceive movement in ambiguous figures is an important and stable characteristic of individuals, as Rorschach theory would have us believe, it is apparent that the Rorschach is unable to demonstrate reliable individual differences in this trait. That is to say, various M responses seem to be highly stimulus-specific. The various color scoring categories have been brought even more seriously into question by experiments using totally achromatic reproductions of the Rorschach blots. In a review of this research Baughman concluded that "color has little or no effect upon a subject's behavior to the extent that his behavior is represented by the psychogram or similar scoring scales" (*2251*). The 25 studies of this type reviewed by Baughman lead to the conclusion that "the form or shape of the blot is the only relevant dimension. Certainly color does not appear to affect behavior very much, and if color is ineffective shading seems even less likely to be a significant variable." In view of this, how meaningful is an index such as the very important M:sum C ratio, which is said to indicate the subject's "experience-type" measured along the dimension of "introversive-extratensive"? The literature on experience-type is reviewed by Singer (*2716*), who concludes that after 40 years of the Rorschach nothing yet is known concerning the psychometric or statistical characteristics of the very central experience balance ratio of M:sum C.

A word of caution concerning improper estimates of Rorschach reliability: these often consist of reporting the *percentage of agreement* between two or more judges. It should be clear that percentage agreement is not a legitimate measure of reliability and tells us none of the things we want to know when we ask about the reliability of a test. What we want to know is the proportion of variance in the scores that is not error variance. The reliability coefficient tells us this; the percentage agreement does not. The latter measure can often be misleading and should always be discounted as an index of reliability unless other crucial information is also provided. Take the following fictitious example, in which two judges independently sort a sample of 500 protocols in terms of the presence or absence of indicators of a particular syndrome. The judges agree on presence in 491 protocols and on absence in one protocol. The eight on which they disagree are evenly divided into agree-disagree and disagree-agree categories. This percentage agreement is 98 per cent—impressively high. When reliability is obtained in the proper way, however, by determining the correlation between the two judges, the reliability coefficient turns out to be only .19.

The present reviewer has presented a detailed discussion of the reliability of Rorschach scores elsewhere (2524), and a more recent consideration of the whole reliability problem has been presented by Holzberg (2646). Some of the conclusions may be summarized briefly:

Scoring reliability per se has been determined very seldom. The few instances reported in the literature constitute the highest reliabilities to be found for any aspect of the Rorschach. Reliability of scoring depends to a large extent upon the degree of similarity of the training of the scorers and has been reported as ranging from .64 to .91.

Split-half reliability has always been frowned upon by Rorschachers as inappropriate. Nevertheless, split-half estimates have yielded comparatively high reliabilities, ranging in one study (16, 17) from .33 (F+%) to .91 (R), with an average reliability coefficient of .54 (corrected by the Spearman-Brown formula). In another study (21) an odd-even split of the cards for 100 subjects yielded an average reliability for 20 Rorschach scores of .83, with a range from .67 to .97.

Test-retest reliability ranges from about .10 to about .90, depending largely upon the test-retest interval and the particular score. For a two-weeks interval the reliabilities of various scores range between .60 and .80 (2254). The most extensive determination of retest reliability is that of Epstein and others (2179), who gave the Rorschach to 16 college students a total of 10 times over a period of five weeks. The average reliabilities for various response categories ranged from .20 to .56.

Parallel forms reliability has been determined by use of the Behn-Rorschach, a set of similar blots which seem to meet all the psychometric criteria for qualifying as an equivalent form of the Rorschach. For 35 scoring categories the means and standard deviations of the Behn and the Rorschach do not differ significantly in normal and psychiatric populations and the two forms seem to correlate as highly with each other as each correlates with itself. The correlations for various scores range from about zero to .86, with a mean around .60.

Examiner and situational influences have been increasingly recognized in recent research as significant contributors to the variance of Rorschach scores (e.g., 982, 1079, 1525, 1606, 2050). The subject-examiner interaction is certainly one of the most important aspects of the test. The effect of the setting in which the test is taken and the fact that different examiners consistently elicit different amounts of various scored determinants from subjects should make it imperative that future Rorschach studies be based upon a representative sampling of examiners as well as of subjects.

Reliability of interpretation is, of course, the most important matter of all. It may be stated as a general principle that the most crucial reliability is that of the end product of the test, which, in the case of the Rorschach, usually consists of a verbal description of personality characteristics based on a global evaluation of all aspects of the subject's protocol. Contrary to the usual claim of Rorschachers that this global interpretation is more reliable or more valid than any of the elements on which it is based, such as the scores and the various derived combinations and indices, a systematic search of the literature has not turned up a single instance where the overall interpretation was more reliable than the separate elements entering into it. Rorschach textbooks have not presented any evidence of satisfactory reliability of the final product of the test and the reviewer has not been able to find any such evidence in the research literature.

Here are some typical examples of what has been found. Lisanksy (2074) had six highly qualified Rorschachers rate 40 subjects on 10 personality items which they agreed could be confidently assessed from the Rorschach protocol. To make the experiment similar to clinical conditions the Rorschachers were provided also with an abstract of each patient's history. The degree of agreement between the judges was measured by the phi coefficient, which averaged .33. Six other clinicians rated the same traits on the basis of the case history abstracts alone, with an average phi of .31, which is not significantly different from the reliability of the clinicians who were aided by the Rorschach. The interesting point is that the 10 rated personality items were specially selected as being the kinds of questions which the Rorschach, and not particularly the case history, is supposed to be able to answer.

Korner and Westwood (*1913*) had three clinical psychologists, qualified in the use of the Rorschach, sort the protocols of 96 college freshmen into three categories for level of personality adjustment. The average correlation among the three judges was .31.

Datel and Gengerelli (*1863*) found that when 27 Rorschachers were required to match personality interpretations written by each other on the basis of the protocols of six subjects (presented for matching in sets of six), there were more mismatchings than correct matchings. Of the total of 324 discrete matchings, 148 were correct and 176 incorrect. Despite the fact that the subjects from whom the protocols were obtained differed greatly from one another in nosology, etc., the average reliability for the individual clinicians was not significantly greater than zero.

The most careful and methodologically sophisticated study of Rorschach reliability and validity has been carried out by two leading projective test experts, Little and Shneidman (*2537*). The editors of the *Journal of Projective Techniques* chose 12 distinguished Rorschach experts—all eminent teachers and writers in this field—to participate in the study. Rorschach protocols were obtained from 12 patients, three each from the psychotic, neurotic, psychosomatic, and psychiatrically normal diagnostic categories. The Rorschach judges were each provided with one protocol from each of the four categories and asked to perform the following interpretive tasks: assign diagnostic labels, rate the subject for personality adjustment (on a scale from 0 to 8), answer 100 true-false factual items taken from the case histories of the subjects, answer 117 true-false personality items typical of those contained in psychological reports, and perform a Q-sort of 76 items typical of the kinds of statements made in Rorschach interpretations. The reliability estimate of the diagnostic labeling consisted of having four other judges rate degree of similarity of diagnosis among pairs of the Rorschach judges on a 6-point scale (0–5). The mean rating among all the Rorschach judges was 2.50, which led the authors to conclude that "diagnostic labels based upon blind analyses of protocols may be quite wide of the mark and the present analysis

indicates that the judges may not be even shooting at the same target." The method of treating the ratings of maladjustment makes it difficult to obtain an estimate of interrater reliability, but it is interesting that the non-psychiatric patients were rated as considerably more pathological on the basis of their Rorschachs (as well as on three other clinical tests of personality) than when they were rated solely on the basis of anamnestic data. This tendency for Rorschach interpretations to be excessively biased toward the pathological has been well known from earlier studies; a good illustration of the tendency may be found in the Rorschach analyses of 28 nonpsychiatric subjects reported in great detail by Symonds and Jensen (*2836*). The true-false factual and personality items were correlated with outside criteria and therefore will be discussed in the section on validity. The Q-sort yielded the most easily interpretable index of inter-judge reliability. The correlations between the judges' Q-sorts for the 12 patients range from −.13 to .64, with a mean of .31. It is instructive to note that when the Q-sorts of each set of four subjects rated by the same judge are intercorrelated, the mean correlation is .27, which is not significantly different from the *inter*-judge reliability of .31. In other words, at least as much of the variance in Rorschach interpretations is attributable to differences among the interpreters as to differences among the subjects. Little and Shneidman concluded, "Test interpreters tend to make their interpretations in a stereotyped manner independent of the subject."

How well did each interpreter agree with himself? To find out, the investigators had the judges perform the same interpretive tasks on the same protocols just 10 days later and intercorrelated the ratings of the first occasion with those of the second. Only those results which can be reported in terms of a correlation coefficient are reported here. For the factual true-false items the average correlation is .74; for the personality true-false items the mean correlation is .77; for the Q-sorts the correlations range from .26 to .81, with a mean of .61.

Silverman (*2575*) carried out a somewhat more detailed study of Rorschach reliability and validity, using the Q-sort. The judges were selected in terms of amount of training and clinical experience with projective techniques, including the Rorschach. There were 10 noted projective test experts, 10 clinicians with 5 to 8 years of experience in projective testing, and 10 clinicians with fewer than three years of experience in projective testing. The Rorschach, TAT, H-T-P, and the Most Unpleasant Concept test were obtained from 10 adult males undergoing psychotherapy. There were six separate Q-sorts for different areas of interpretation. The 180 Q-sort items were typical of the statements found in Rorschach and projective reports. The reliabilities, as estimated from the correlations among the Q-sorts, were: defenses = .27, motivating needs and affects = .25, character traits = .44, diagnosis and symptoms = .44, interpersonal behavior = .21. The overall reliability was .34. The degree of reliability was unrelated to the amount of experience of the judges: there was no higher agreement among the most experienced clinicians than among the least experienced.

One recent study (*2891*) strongly stacked the cards in favor of maximizing the reliability by selecting seven clinicians who had very similar orientations toward the use and interpretation of psychological tests and 10 subjects who were very heterogeneous in pathology. The clinicians' task was to rank 10 psychological needs as to their relative importance for each of the 10 subjects. The interrater reliability was .12. (When the same task was performed with the TAT and a sentence completion test, the reliabilities were .14 and .30, respectively.)

VALIDITY. Considering the reliability of the Rorschach, its poor validity would seem to be a foregone conclusion. However, though it is axiomatic in psychometric theory that the validity of a test cannot be higher than the square root of its reliability, it has often been claimed that the Rorschach (as well as other projective tests) is exempt from this general rule. Therefore a study of the evidence for the validity of the Rorschach might be worthwhile.

Guilford (*2518*) succinctly reviewed the status of Rorschach validity up to 1959 and came to the following conclusions:

In spite of the widespread popularity and use of the Rorschach ink blots, the reliabilities of scores tend to be relatively low, and validities, although quite varied, are generally near zero. This statement regarding validity applies to use of the instrument in discriminating pathological from normal individuals, for diagnosis of more particular pathologies such as anxiety, for indicating degree of maladjustment in the general population, and for predicting academic and vocational success.

The most recent comprehensive review and discussion of Rorschach validity is by Harris (*2638*). It is the most thoughtful and objective article on this subject the present reviewer has encountered. From his extensive survey, Harris concluded: "By the canons of test analysis, the Rorschach technique as a whole has been shown at present to have neither satisfactory validity nor invalidity." Predicting the future of Rorschach research, Harris states, "There is very little concrete basis for making an optimistic prediction that a review of studies of validity, in which the ten Rorschach cards have served as the sole instrument of investigation, will be any different 25 years from now than they were when reviewed in 1954 by Ainsworth [in *1730*]."

What, specifically, have the most recent studies found?

First, a distinction must be made between experimental and clinical types of validation studies. In experimental studies, particular Rorschach scores (often scores that have been specially derived for the particular study) are in some way tested for their correlation with some non-Rorschach criterion. The criterion may or may not be of clinical relevance. Clinical validation studies, on the other hand, involve a more global use of the Rorschach protocol, typical of its use in clinical practice, with the aim of testing the correlation of the Rorschach with various clinically relevant criteria. Older reviews of Rorschach validity are based predominantly on the experimental type of study. Recent research has concentrated more on the clinical validity of the instrument as it is typically used by clinical psychologists. Many of the experimental type studies have been reviewed by Zubin (*1826*). The fact that some of these studies have reported validity coefficients which, when significant at all, are generally in the range of .20 to .40, cannot be interpreted as supporting the clinical usefulness of the test. Aside from the fact that validity in this range is practically useless for individual assessment, the validated "scores" are often not those used by the clinician or they are used in a different way. Even when the scores do happen to be those that enter into the clinical interpretation of the protocol, such as the M per cent, clinicians seldom heed the experimental findings. It is easy to find statements in current clinical reports that a subject is "creative" on the basis of a high M per cent in his protocol, despite the well known failure of this relationship to be borne out in studies which are seemingly ideal for capturing it (e.g., *539*).

Beck's *z* and *g* scores, characterized as an "organizational factor," are derived scores which have gained popularity in clinical use. These scores are a systematic weighted combination of Rorschach attributes claimed to be indicative of intelligence and efficiency of intellectual functioning. The *g* score does have some validity, showing correlations with psychometrically measured intelligence in the range of .20 to .25 (*2640*).

Another special scoring method has been devised by Holt and Havel (*2645*) to measure degree of adaptive versus maladaptive regressive tendencies. When this index was correlated with 55 items of various behavioral and personality test criteria, 20 of the correlations were significant beyond the .10 level. The mean of the correlations significant beyond the .10 level was .59. Cross validation of such studies generally loses many of the formerly significant correlations, and no such correlations should be accepted without evidence of cross validation. For example, Holt and Havel (*2645*) state concerning the validity of the regression score,

The correlation coefficients are not impressively large, for the most part not even being highly significant, but they are in the right directions. A word of caution, however: Incomplete but largely negative preliminary results from a group of college girls of the same age [as the college men on whom the original correlations were obtained] suggest that these correlations may not hold up in different samples, but may, in some as yet unknown way, be specific to unknown parameters of the present group of college boys.

It seems safe to conclude that experimental studies of particular Rorschach attributes have been able to show statistically significant correlations with other psychological criteria. These correlations have been generally rather low (i.e., between .20 and .40), only rarely exceeding .50, and most such correlations have not stood the test of cross validation.

How valid is the Rorschach when it is used as a clinical instrument by acknowledged experts? Three recent studies, which have taken care to avoid the criticism that the obtained validity coefficients do not represent the validity of the Rorschach when used by experts, are instructive.

The study by Little and Shneidman (*2537*),

which has already been described in the section on reliability, used 12 Rorschach experts who were selected by the editors of the *Journal of Projective Techniques* and whose names are given in the appendix of the published monograph. The Rorschach protocols were obtained from 12 patients equally divided among the psychiatrically normal, neurotic, psychosomatic, and psychotic categories. The various criteria against which validation was attempted were obtained from the pooled judgments of 23 psychiatrists and one psychologist on the basis of a comprehensive psychiatric case history on each patient, obtained by one psychiatrist in 4 to 8 interviews of 1 to 3 hours duration. On a true-false questionnaire of 117 personality items typical of those in Rorschach reports, the correlation between the Rorschach judges and the anamnestic judges ranged from −.20 to .74, with a mean of .37. With a true-false questionnaire of 100 factual items which could be verified from the case history, the Rorschach correlations ranged from −.12 to .42, with a mean of .14. The correlations between a Q-sort of personality items obtained from the Rorschach judges and from the anamnestic judges ranged from −.10 to .47, with a mean of .17. This validity coefficient becomes .21 when corrected for attenuation of the criterion. But as compared with the other psychological tests used in the Little and Shneidman study (*Make A Picture Story, Thematic Apperception Test,* and *Minnesota Multiphasic Personality Inventory*), the Rorschach is not much worse. The MMPI, for example, which made a consistently better showing than any of the projective techniques, had an overall Q-sort validity of .33 (corrected for attenuation).

The study by Silverman (*2575*) described in the section on reliability compared Q-sorts of projective test experts with Q-sorts performed by the therapists of 10 adult males after 35 hours of psychotherapy. There were six Q-sorts made up of typical Rorschach report items covering the areas of defenses, motivating needs and affects, character traits, diagnosis and symptoms, interpersonal behavior, and infancy and childhood perceptions of parental figures. The validity coefficients for these areas range from .12 to .50, with a mean of .29.

On the basis of a preliminary study (*1983*) in which the Rorschach protocol of a patient in psychotherapy was sent to 12 Rorschach experts for independent interpretations, the one expert with the largest percentage of "hits" in agreement with the psychotherapist's knowledge of the patient was selected to perform Rorschach analyses of 28 nonpsychiatric subjects who were also assessed by interviews and other tests. A detailed account of the Rorschach analyses is presented by Symonds and Jensen (*2836*). The Rorschach expert was asked to rank the subjects for overall personality adjustment on the basis of her analysis of the Rorschach protocols. As the criterion two psychologists performed the same task from anamnestic data and from direct impressions gained in several hours of interview with each subject. The correlation between the Rorschach ratings and the criterion, corrected for attenuation, was .34. One could argue that the criterion itself had little validity, but this points up one of the crucial problems of Rorschach interpretation: are the test interpreter and the person to whom the interpretation is addressed both speaking the same language? If not, of what value is the Rorschach report? Most psychiatrists receiving psychological reports based in whole or in part on the Rorschach, it should be remembered, have not been trained in Rorschach interpretation.

The use of the Rorschach in vocational psychology has been reviewed by Super and Crites (*2938*), who conclude that "too little is now known to justify its use in practical counseling or personnel work." Similarly, Ricciuti (*2929*) has concluded a recent review of this subject as follows: "The practical usefulness of projective techniques in predicting educational or industrial criteria continues to be small."

SUMMARY. Research on the Rorschach published since the *Fifth Mental Measurements Yearbook* has not brought forth any substantial evidence that would alter the conclusions of the reviewers in that volume. If anything, recent studies add support to the conclusion that the Rorschach as a clinical instrument has too inadequate reliability and too meagre validity, even in the hands of the most expert, to justify any claims for its practical usefulness. The strong bias toward pathology in Rorschach reports on nonpsychiatric subjects can lead to harmful consequences in nonpsychiatric settings, such as in schools and in industry. Even in cases where harm might not result, one must weigh the scant validity of the test against the fact that of all psychological assessment techniques it is the most time consuming and requires the most extensive training of its practitioners. Many psychologists who have looked into the matter are agreed that the 40 years of massive effort which has been lavished on the Rorschach technique has proven unfruitful, at least so far as the development of a useful psychological test is concerned.

Until proponents of the Rorschach can produce evidence which substantially contradicts this verdict—and thus far such evidence is conspicuously lacking in the Rorschach textbooks—it seems not unreasonable to recommend that the Rorschach be altogether abandoned in clinical practice and that students of clinical psychology not be required to waste their time learning the technique.

The question of why the Rorschach still has so many devotees and continues to be so widely used is quite another problem and is beyond the scope of this review. A satisfactory explanation of the whole amazing phenomenon is a task for future historians of psychology and will probably have to wait upon greater knowledge of the psychology of credulity than we now possess. Meanwhile, the rate of scientific progress in clinical psychology might well be measured by the speed and thoroughness with which it gets over the Rorschach.

For reviews by Samuel J. Beck, H. J. Eysenck, Raymond J. McCall, and Laurance F. Shaffer, see 5:154; for a review by Helen Sargent, see 4:117; for reviews by Morris Krugman and J. R. Wittenborn, see 3:73; for excerpts from related book reviews, see B40, B52, B72–3, B91, B129, B152, B260, B295, B306–7, B344, B398, B409, B452, B526, 5:B32, 5:B34, 5:B40–1, 5:B60, 5:B73, 5:B79, 5:B190, 5:B247–8, 5:B337, 5:B369, 5:B372, 5:B402, 4:118–28, and 3:74–91.

[238]

*Rosenzweig Picture-Frustration Study. Ages 4–13, 14 and over; 1944–60; also called *Rosenzweig P-F Study;* 15 scores: direction of aggression (extrapunitive, intropunitive, impunitive), type of aggression (obstacle-dominance, ego-defense, need-persistence), 9 combinations of the preceding categories; 2 levels; record blank ('48, 1 page) for each level; $5 per 25 tests; $1.25 per 25 record blanks; postage extra; specimen set not available; [15–20] minutes; Saul Rosenzweig; the Author. *

a) FORM FOR CHILDREN. Ages 4–13; 1948–60; 1 form ('48, 7 pages); manual ('48, 53 pages, reprint of *21* below); supplementary data ('60, 29 pages, reprint of

222 below); tentative norms; $1.25 per manual and supplementary data.

b) REVISED FORM FOR ADULTS. Ages 14 and over; 1944–49; 1 form ('48, 7 pages); manual ('47, 48 pages, reprint of *15* below; includes 1949 revised norms); no data on reliability and validity; norms for ages 20–29 only; $1.25 per manual.

REFERENCES

1–77. See 4:129.
78–186. See 5:155.
187. FISHER, SEYMOUR, AND HINDS, EDITH. "The Organization of Hostility Controls in Various Personality Structures." *Genetic Psychol Monogr* 44:3–68 Ag '51. * (*PA* 26:2889)
188. REID, L. LEON. "An Evaluation of the Rosenzweig Picture-Frustration Test." *Proc W Va Acad Sci* 23:170–2 Ap '52. *
189. ANGELINO, HENRY, AND SHEDD, CHARLES L. "Reactions to 'Frustration' of Mentally Retarded Children as Measured by the Rosenzweig P-F Test." Abstract. *Proc Okla Acad Sci* 36:104–5 D '55. *
190. ZUK, GERALD H. "The Influence of Social Context on Impulse and Control Tendencies in Preadolescence." *Genetic Psychol Monogr* 54:117–66 N '56. * (*PA* 33:3464)
191. COONS, MARGERY OLSTEAD. "Rosenzweig Differences in Reaction to Frustration in Children of High, Low, and Middle Sociometric Status." *Group Psychother* 10:60–3 Mr '57. * (*PA* 33:3393)
192. TAKALA, ANNIKA, AND TAKALA, MARTTI. "Finnish Children's Reactions to Frustration in the Rosenzweig Test: An Ethnic and Cultural Comparison." *Nordisk Psykologi* 9(1):43–50 '57. * Also in *Acta Psychologica* 13(1):43–50 '57. * (*PA* 33:1326)
193. TAKALA, MARTTI; PIHKANEN, TOIVO A.; AND MARKKANEN, TOUKO. *The Effects of Distilled and Brewed Beverages: A Physiological, Neurological, and Psychological Study.* The Finnish Foundation for Alcoholic Studies, No. 4. Stockholm, Sweden: Almqvist & Wiksell, 1957. Pp. 195. * (*PA* 31:4890)
194. FRIEDMAN, BERT. *A Study of the Szondi Assumptions of Identification and Counteridentification Utilizing Modified Versions of the Rosenzweig P-F Study on Criminal Groups.* Doctor's thesis, Fordham University (New York, N.Y.), 1958.
195. NORMAN, RALPH D., AND KLEINFELD, GERALD J. "Rosenzweig Picture-Frustration Study Results With Minority Group Juvenile Delinquents." *J Genetic Psychol* 92:61–7 Mr '58. * (*PA* 36:1JO61N)
196. PAREEK, UDAI. "Some Preliminary Data About the Indian Adaptation of Rosenzweig P-F Study (Children's Form)." *Ed & Psychol* 5:105–13 Je '58. * (*PA* 34:1407)
197. PAREEK, UDAI. "Studying Cultural Differences in Personality Development With the Help of Rosenzweig P-F Study." *J All-India Inst Mental Health* 1:113–23 Jl '58. * (*PA* 35:720)
198. PRENSKY, SAMUEL J. *An Investigation of Some Personality Characteristics of Epileptic and Psychosomatic Patients: An Evaluation of Certain Personality Measures and Reactions to Frustration in Idiopathic Epileptic, Symptomatic Epileptic, and Peptic Ulcer Patients.* Doctor's thesis, New York University (New York, N.Y.), 1958. (*DA* 19:3025)
199. PURDOM, GLEN A., JR. *Comparison of Performance of Competent and Incompetent Readers in a State Training School for Delinquent Boys on the WAIS and the Rosenzweig P-F Study.* Doctor's thesis, University of Oregon (Eugene, Ore.), 1958. (*DA* 19:1016)
200. SHEEHAN, JOSEPH G. "Projective Studies of Stuttering." *J Speech & Hearing Disorders* 23:18–25 F '58. *
201. SMITH, MARSHALL L. *Some Effects of Socio-Economic, Age, and Sex Factors on Children's Responses in Adult-Child and Child-Child Situations in the Rosenzweig Picture-Frustration Study.* Master's thesis, Southern Methodist University (Dallas, Tex.), 1958.
202. TAFT, RONALD. "Is the Tolerant Personality Type the Opposite of the Intolerants?" *J Social Psychol* 47:397–405 My '58. * (*PA* 33:8186)
203. BATHURST, G. C., AND GLATT, M. M. "Some Psychological Reflections on Vulnerability to Alcoholism." *Psychiatria et Neurologia* 138:27–46 '59. *
204. HAYASHI, KATSUO; SUMITA, KATSUMI; AND ICHITANI, TSUYOSHI. "A Factorial Study of the Rosenzweig Picture-Frustration Study." *Jap Psychol Res* 1:20–6 N '59. *
205. LANGE, PATRICIA. "Frustration Reactions of Physically Handicapped Children." *Excep Child* 25:355–7 Ap '59. * (*PA* 35:2493)
206. LIPMAN, RONALD S. "Some Test Correlates of Behavioral Aggression in Institutionalized Retardates With Particular Reference to the Rosenzweig Picture-Frustration Study." *Am J Mental Def* 63:1038–45 My '59. * (*PA* 34:4587)
207. McQUEEN, ROBERT, AND PEARSON, WAYNE O. "Stimulus-Word Changes in Picture-Frustration Situations." *Percept & Motor Skills* 9:407–10 D '59. * (*PA* 34:5629)
208. PAREEK, UDAI. "Rosenzweig Picture-Frustration Study —A Review." *Psychol Newsl* 10:98–114 Ja–F '59. * (*PA* 34:1047)
209. PAREEK, UDAI, AND ROSENZWEIG, SAUL. *Manual of the Indian Adaptation of Rosenzweig Picture-Frustration Study (Children's Form).* Delhi, India: Mānasāyan, 1959. Pp. iv, 71. *
210. ROGERS, ARTHUR H., AND PAUL, COLEMAN. "Impunitiveness and Unwitting Self-Evaluation." *J Proj Tech* 23:459–61 D '59. * (*PA* 35:5005)
211. STOLTZ, ROBERT E., AND SMITH, MARSHALL D. "Some Effects of Socio-Economic, Age and Sex Factors on Children's Responses to the Rosenzweig Picture-Frustration Study." *J Clin Psychol* 15:200–3 Ap '59. * (*PA* 35:4725)
212. TRAPP, E. PHILIP. "Threat and Direction of Aggression." *J Clin Psychol* 15:308–10 Jl '59. * (*PA* 35:3513)
213. VINACKE, W. EDGAR. "A Comparison of the Rosenzweig P-F Study and the Brown Interracial Version: Hawaii." *J Social Psychol* 49:161–75 My '59. * (*PA* 34:4232)
214. WILSON, MILTON E., JR. *The Rosenzweig Picture-Frustration Study: An Appraisal of Methodology and Underlying Assumptions.* Master's thesis, Kent State University (Kent, Ohio), 1959.
215. BENNETT, LAWRENCE A., AND RUDOFF, ALVIN. "Changes in Direction of Hostility Related to Incarceration and Treatment." *J Clin Psychol* 16:408–10 O '60. * (*PA* 37:3269)
216. DAVIDS, ANTHONY, AND OLIVER, GERALDINE R. "Fantasy Aggression and Learning in Emotionally Disturbed and Normal Children." *J Proj Tech* 24:124–8 Je '60. * (*PA* 35:1069)
217. GABRIEL, JOHN, AND HERD, JEAN. "Culturally Expected Responses and the Rosenzweig P-F Test, Children's Form." *Austral J Psychol* 12:178–88 D '60. *
218. GOLD, LEO. *Reaction of Male Adolescent Addicts to Frustration as Compared to Two Adolescent Non-Addicted Groups.* Doctor's thesis, New York University (New York, N.Y.), 1960. (*DA* 20:4716)
219. KASWAN, J.; WASMAN, M.; AND FREEDMAN, LAWRENCE ZELIC. "Aggression and the Picture-Frustration Study." *J Consult Psychol* 24:446–52 O '60. * (*PA* 35:4923)
220. PAREEK, UDAI. "Developmental Patterns of Rosenzweig P-F Study Variables in Indian Children." *Manas* 7:19–35 '60. * (*PA* 37:890)
221. PAREEK, UDAI. "An Investigation of the Validity of the Indian Adaptation of the Rosenzweig Picture-Frustration Study (Children's Form)." *Indian J Psychol* 35:71–88 pt 2 '60. * (*PA* 36:4HG71P)
222. ROSENZWEIG, SAUL. Chap. 8, "The Rosenzweig Picture-Frustration Study, Children's Form," pp. 149–76. In *Projective Techniques With Children.* Edited by Albert I. Rabin and Mary R. Haworth. New York: Grune & Stratton, Inc., 1960. Pp. xiii, 392. * (*PA* 35:2229)
223. SHAW, MERVILLE C., AND BLACK, MICHAEL DORIS. "The Reaction to Frustration of Bright High School Underachievers." *Calif J Ed Res* 11:120–4 My '60. * (*PA* 35:7025)
224. SMITH, STANLEY KECK, JR. *A Factor Analytic Study of the Rosenzweig Picture-Frustration Study as a Predictor of Academic Achievement.* Doctor's thesis, Temple University (Philadelphia, Pa.), 1960. (*DA* 22:647)
225. CORKE, PATRICIA PERRY. *A Comparison of Frustration-Aggression Patterns of Negro and White Southern Males and Females.* Doctor's thesis, University of Houston (Houston, Tex.), 1961. (*DA* 22:2870)
226. HARRIGAN, JOHN E.; DOLE, ARTHUR A.; AND VINACKE, W. EDGAR. "A Study of Indignation-Bigotry and Extrapunitiveness in Hawaii." *J Social Psychol* 55:105–12 O '61. * (*PA* 36:4GD05H)
227. MASKIT, MAE LEE. *Management of Aggression in Preadolescent Girls: Its Effects on Certain Aspects of Ego Funtioning.* Doctor's thesis, University of Michigan (Ann Arbor, Mich.), 1961. (*DA* 22:917)
228. MAUSNER, BERNARD. "Situational Effects on a Projective Test." *J Appl Psychol* 45:186–92 Je '61. * (*PA* 36:4HG86M)
229. SWICKARD, DON L., AND SPILKA, BERNARD. "Hostility Expression Among Delinquents of Minority and Majority Groups." *J Consult Psychol* 25:216–20 Je '61. *
230. TRENTINI, G. "A New Method of Validation Applied to Reaffirm the Validity of the Rosenzweig P.F.S." Abstract. *Acta Psychologica* 19(2):121–2 '61. *
231. BREWER, JETTA J. A. *A Comparison of Slightly and Severely Orthopedically Disabled Adults on Rosenzweig's Picture-Frustration Study.* Master's thesis, University of Utah (Salt Lake City, Utah), 1962.
232. CESA-BIANCHI, MARCELLO, AND TRENTINI, GIANCARIO. "A Further Contribution to the Study of Adjustment in Old Age," pp. 623–7. In *Social and Psychological Aspects of Aging.* Proceedings of the Fifth Congress of the International Association of Gerontology. Edited by Clark Tibbitts and Wilma Donahue. New York: Columbia University Press, 1962. Pp. xviii, 952. *
233. CHOROST, SHERWOOD BRUCE. "Parental Child-Rearing Attitudes and Their Correlates in Adolescent Hostility." *Genetic Psychol Monogr* 66:49–90 Ag '62. * (*PA* 37:4743)
234. FOREMAN, MILTON E. "Predicting Behavioral Problems Among Institutionalized Mental Retardates." *Am J Mental Def* 66:580–8 Ja '62. * (*PA* 36:4JI80F)
235. HARVEY, O. J. "Personality Factors in Resolution of Conceptual Incongruities." *Sociometry* 25:336–52 D '62. *

236. KIRSCHNER, R.; McCARY, J. L.; AND MOORE, C. W. "A Comparison of Differences Among Several Religious Groups of Children on Various Measures of the Rosenzweig Picture-Frustration Study." *J Clin Psychol* 18:352–3 Jl '62. * (PA 39:1575)

237. MERCER, MARGARET, AND KYRIAZIS, CHRIST. "Results of the Rosenzweig Picture-Frustration Study for Physically Assaultive Prisoner Mental Patients." Abstract. *J Consult Psychol* 26:490 O '62. *

238. MUTHAYYA, B. C. "An Experimental Validation of the Madras Picture-Frustration Study." *Psychol Studies* 7:10–5 Ja '62. * (PA 37:1206)

239. RAPAPORT, GERALD M., AND MARSHALL, ROBERT J. "The Prediction of Rehabilitative Potential of Stockade Prisoners Using Clinical Psychological Tests." *J Clin Psychol* 18:444–6 O '62. * (PA 39:5087)

240. HERBERT, N., AND TURNBULL, G. H. "Personality Factors and Effective Progress in Teaching." *Ed R* 16:24–31 N '63. *

241. MOORE, MARY E., AND SCHWARTZ, MILTON M. "The Effect of the Sex of the Frustrated Figure on Responses to the Rosenzweig P-F Study." *J Proj Tech & Pers Assess* 27:195–9 Je '63. * (PA 38:2720)

242. NATHAN, PETER E. "Conceptual Ability and Indices of Frustration Tolerance on the Rosenzweig Picture-Frustration Study." *J Proj Tech & Pers Assess* 27:200–7 Je '63. * (PA 38:2639)

243. ROSENZWEIG, SAUL. "Validity of the Rosenzweig Picture-Frustration Study with Felons and Delinquents." *J Consult Psychol* 27:535–6 D '63. *

244. ROSS, W. D.; ADSETT, NANCY; GLESER, GOLDINE; JOYCE, C. R. B.; KAPLAN, S. M.; AND TIEGER, M. E. "A Trial of Psychopharmacologic Measurement With Projective Techniques." *J Proj Tech & Pers Assess* 27:222–5 Je '63. *

245. SUMITA, K.; HAYASHI, K.; ICHITANI, T.; AND YAMAGUCHI, H. "Personality Types as Revealed by the Factorial Pattern of the Rosenzweig Picture-Frustration Study." *Manas* 10(1):25–34 '63. * (PA 38:8508)

246. WEINSTEIN, A. D.; MOORE, C. W.; AND McCARY, J. L. "A Note on Comparison of Differences Between Several Religious Groups of Adults on Various Measures of the Rosenzweig Picture-Frustration Study." *J Clin Psychol* 19:219 Ap '63. * (PA 39:5220)

247. WITTENBORN, J. R., AND PLANTE, MARC. "Patterns of Response to Placebo, Iproniazid and Electroconvulsive Therapy Among Young Depressed Females." *J Nerv & Mental Dis* 137:155–61 Ag '63. *

ÅKE BJERSTEDT, *Professor of Education, University of Lund, Lund, Sweden.*

The purpose of the *Rosenzweig P-F Study* is to enable the investigator to study typical reaction patterns in potentially frustrating situations. Representing an attempt to translate a theory of frustration into operational terms, the instrument has been used (*a*) as a research tool in testing various general theories on frustration tolerance, directions of "aggression," etc. as related to other biosocial variables, and (*b*) for individual diagnostic assessment of frustration-related behavior tendencies.

The P-F Study has certainly not remained unnoticed. About 275 published references were known to the test author in 1962, and considering its widespread international use, there is probably an additional number of articles in more remote sources and in less well-known languages.

In view of this abundance of material it is obviously impossible in this review to give more than scattered attention to the work done. Inasmuch as the manuals now distributed with the test forms present much too little of what is known about the tests, there is a great need for integrative surveys. The best single source

written by the test author is a chapter in a book on projective techniques (*222*), but this covers only the children's version. Among the best general sources by other authors is a 132-page report by Christiansen,[1] but this is written in Norwegian and now somewhat dated.

BASIC THEORY AND TERMINOLOGY. As is well known, subject's responses to cartoon-like drawings of frustrating situations are categorized in a three-by-three system which cross-classifies "types" and "directions" of "aggression." In some earlier texts Rosenzweig used the more neutral term "type of reaction," but in 1960 he explicitly recommended the use of the term "aggression." "Need-persistence" is considered in terms of "constructive aggression" and "ego-defense" in terms of "destructive aggression," while "obstacle-dominance" is described as a type of aggression in which the response is curtailed before either of the other modes can be actuated. The reviewer cannot help finding this overall use of the term "aggression" (already overused in psychology) unnecessarily confusing. Would not more neutral phrases like "direction of activity" (instead of "direction of aggression") and "attention dominance" (instead of "type of aggression") be less misleading?

The test author has apparently had a feeling that the punitive overtones were somewhat too strong in the terminology, for in 1960 he recommended that the term "extrapunitive," earlier used for all outward-oriented reactions, should now refer only to the ego-defensive type of outward-reaction, whereas the obstacle-dominant type should be called "extrapeditive," and the need-persistent type, "extrapersistive." Similar innovations were recommended for the inward reactions ("intropeditive," "intropunitive," and "intropersistive") and the passivity reactions ("impeditive," "impunitive," and "impersistive"). These neologisms seem useful, but no new terms were presented for the more comprehensive concepts earlier called "extrapunitive," "intropunitive," and "impunitive." In a personal communication, however, Rosenzweig has informed the reviewer that he has been using the notations "extra-directed," "intro-directed," and "im-directed" in his oral teaching to refer to the more inclusive categories. Recently these terms have also found

---

[1] CHRISTIANSEN, BJØRN. *Rosenzweigs billed-frustrasjonstest: en diskusjon av dens anvendbarhet belyst ved andres og egne undersøkelser.* Nordisk Psykologi's Monografiserie No. 7. Copenhagen: Einar Munksgaard, 1955. Pp. 132. *

their way into print (*242*). The last mentioned term may be somewhat awkward linguistically in its attempt to retain the "m" from "impunitive," but on the whole this set of words represents a less loaded terminology. In a way, questions of terminology like these are unimportant, as long as operational definitions are clear. On the other hand, surplus meanings evoked by everyday usage or well-known etymology are difficult to get rid of and tend to make interpretational discussions less rigorous than desirable.

Some behavior categories derived by Rosenzweig from the cross-classification tend to be less natural than others. "Obstacle-dominance" apparently was a latecomer in Rosenzweig's theory[2] and seems to fit in best with outward-reaction ("extrapersistive") as long as frustrations are imposed from outside. Finding illustrations of "intropeditive" reactions is, consequently, difficult. No examples of this category are given for 15 out of the 24 situations in the scoring samples from about 500 American child records or in the scoring samples from 1,000 Indian child records for 17 of the situations. Such unevenness makes interpretations and comparisons between the categories more difficult and tends to make the low frequency categories less useful and reliable. It is not quite clear whether this unevenness is a logical or psychological necessity, or if it could be corrected for by another sample of stimulus situations.

Rosenzweig (*53, 243*) is well aware of the problem of level of response, but his awareness has not been followed by any solution to the problem. We do not know whether the subject's reactions mirror (*a*) his overt everyday behavior as observed by others, (*b*) his behavior experienced subjectively but consciously by himself, (*c*) his covert needs, or (*d*) his opinions on how he ought to behave. The only solutions offered are the advice to assume if no other clues are at hand that the overt level has been tapped, and the recommendation to make non-leading inquiry. Neither suggestion is very helpful. The assumption mentioned might be tenable as a gross probability statement in some groups, but it is of very little value for handling of a single case; as to the inquiry, Rosenzweig himself admits that rationalizations may be even more frequent in this phase than in the original testing.

This problem pops up again and again in interpretational discussions. To take only one example: The Group Conformity Rating, derived by comparing each item score with modal responses in the norm group, is usually interpreted as a rough measure of social adjustment. Some empirical data tend to verify this interpretation (*186*). To two investigators (*133*) it was an unexpected finding that delinquents had high conformity scores, depressed extrapunitive scores, and elevated intropunitive scores. In discussing these findings, Rosenzweig points to several possibilities: (*a*) that delinquent subjects in the situation used might have been motivated to put up a good face on their responses (ideal-level response); or (*b*) that their delinquency was of the conformity type (gang conformity, overt response); or (*c*) that their delinquency was inspired by an unconscious sense of guilt (the intropunitive scores reflecting a covert need symptom). Any or all of these hypotheses—covering three different "levels" of behavior—may be correct, but the need for such rationalizations or guesswork *after* testing and without support for any of the alternatives leaves the reader unsatisfied.

For certain general categories of interaction tendencies, Leary[3] has shown that a testing strategy utilizing different methodological approaches at the same time for the mapping of the same categories of behavior may clarify the problem of levels and help for individual diagnosis. Could not such a strategy be a solution also to the problem of levels in the P-F Study? For example, same-category behavior on different methodological levels may indicate behavioral stability over time, whereas different-category behavior on various levels may signal intrapersonal conflict with subsequent changes on the overt level. That different personality types have different degrees of interlevel similarity would then not be a methodological weakness, but, when established by the test battery, a diagnostic indication of importance (*187*). Apparently, Rosenzweig started out long ago with a multi-method instrument but later singled out the more absorbing projective-method part for separate study (*222*). Would it not be good to take up again the more

2 ROSENZWEIG, SAUL. "An Experimental Study of 'Repression' With Special Reference to Need-Persistence and Ego-Defensive Reactions to Frustration." *J Exp Psychol* 32:64–74 Ja '43. *

3 LEARY, TIMOTHY. *Interpersonal Diagnosis of Personality: A Functional Theory and Methodology for Personality Evaluation.* New York: Ronald Press Co., 1957. Pp. xix, 518. *

inclusive approach once envisioned, at least for the purpose of further research? Such a multi-level frustration test, where the P-F type of approach was only one of various approaches, might have been a better guide in the decisions on alternative interpretations in several studies. It might also be a better guide in decisions on whether or not a subject has succeeded in putting up a good face in a personally important test situation. Some investigators (*179, 228*) have seen such situational effects whereas one investigator [4] found the present test fairly resistive to faking.

TEST STIMULI. Each form consists of 24 frustration situations involving two persons. One says something which frustrates the other or helps to describe his frustration. The subject gives the verbal reaction of the other person (the identification figure). Facial features are vague to facilitate projective structuring. There is some indication of low item homogeneity. Few items yield responses in all nine possible categories, and some very one-sidedly attract responses in a particular category. Lack of homogeneity should not be considered too serious in itself in this device (unless it leads to *excessive* lack of differentiation). More important are "situational representativeness" and "subject-category fairness." The situations sampled should be representative of the frustrating situations characteristic of the target population. The author leaves us without information on his exact procedures to ensure such representativeness. Further, various potential subgroups, such as male and female subjects, ought to be given parallel treatment. This is not done for the present instrument. It may be a disproportion representative of the American scene that in the child form a boy has to answer a female adult in a frustrating situation in seven cases whereas only in one case must a girl answer a male adult. Such a disproportion may be acceptable, but it is not acceptable that a girl subject has only 8 same-sex identification figures, whereas a boy has 16 same-sex identification figures. In a similar way the adult form is best adapted to male subjects: there are 16 males as against 6 female identification figures (while 2 cases are somewhat ambiguous). In no case in the adult form does a woman have to answer a man. In sum, it might be of value

to try to construct for research purposes a parallel P-F form with more explicit selection procedures, with more fair sex treatment, and with more strict criteria on response differentiation. Such an instrument might well be more reliable and valid and thus more useful for its intended purpose than the present one.

TEST SITUATION. The test situation was not the same for various age groups in the norm population: the youngest children responded orally, older children wrote their answers and then read them aloud, and adults only wrote their answers. This variation may make for some difficult-to-interpret differences between various groups and be a source of error in developmental studies. Oral responses may increase censorship for some kinds of children, decrease it for others. In a way, oral responses should be the most sensitive indicators of response nature since intonation can give the same word various meanings. This argument would favor using an oral response procedure in all cases. On the other hand, group testing procedures could not then be used. In addition to being more economical, group testing with written answers has the advantage of minimizing influence of the specific investigator-subject relationship which may otherwise be a source of variation not to be overlooked in a situation leaning so heavily on interactional statements, especially where the investigator himself also *reads* the frustrating statements to the subject. More studies of the importance of various ways of presentation would be desirable and should include attempts to use oral stimulus and oral response in a nonpersonal and nonvarying setting, for instance, with the aid of tape recording equipment of the language laboratory type. In such a setting, group testing with identical stimulus situations could be arranged while still maintaining oral responses. In addition, permanent records for more reliable scoring of intonational overtones would be obtained. At present the user has to choose either desirable auditive discrimination together with undesirable interactional variations and undesirable administration costs or desirable minimal interaction variation and desirable time economy together with undesirable lack of spontaneous auditive information. Most users seem to prefer the latter alternative.

Total time is recorded, but no important use seems to be made of this variable. Differential time information, especially stimulus-response

4 TRENTINI, GIANCARIO. *Contributo sperimentale alla validazione del test di Rosenzweig.* Contributi dell' Istituto di Psicologia, Serie 25. Milan, Italy: Società Editrice Vita e Pensiero, 1961. Pp. 20.

interval for specific pictures, might be more interesting (*108*). The tape recording situation recommended above might be a good instrument for studying this possibility further.

Little information is given on how to keep the recommended inquiry free from leading suggestions and after-rationalizations. A certain number of unscorable answers might be better than answers scored from two different interactional situations. (Some answers, easily scored directly from the written text, are not inquired about, while others are scored on the basis of questions in a specific investigator-subject interaction.) The few references to techniques of inquiry in empirical studies lead us to believe that inquiry is usually not used. The reviewer has not been able to locate definite studies on the value of inquiry.

SCORING. Scoring is—at least compared to several other projective techniques—fairly easy and is facilitated by extensive and good scoring samples. These scoring samples would have been still better, however, if the authors had indicated the frequency of various answer categories (the German manual gives better information than the American in this respect) and if the authors had indicated on what kind of answers they considered inquiry essential. It is not clear from the samples if the position of some answers with seemingly strange placement is due to additional information obtained through inquiry. Trend scoring is especially interesting and contributes to one type of operational definition of "frustration tolerance" (*52*). However, a longer series of stimuli, with forced-tempo reactions and with scoring over more than two phases, would perhaps yield more valid data on individual process characteristics. So far most studies have been mainly interested in the sum scores within classification categories, but to this reviewer an extended process analysis is an area of potential importance for future research.

Could other types of scores, not usually used, be of some value? Attempts to assess intensity of reaction would be one possibility, since some categories contain a great variety of reaction intensities not mirrored in the scores. (Cf. Zuk's attempts to derive an "impulsivity" score, *190*.) Scoring over separate stimulus categories would be another possibility: ego-blocking versus superego-blocking, child-adult versus child-child, male-frustrator versus female-frustrator, etc. Some studies (e.g., *171*) indicate

that such subdivisions may be meaningful for certain purposes and that item homogeneity is increased when studied by such a "regional analysis." A third possibility includes inter-role comparisons. Scores expressing discrepancies between various perceived roles, as well as scores expressing discrepancies or similarities between ego role and the perceived roles of others, carry a potential interest (and would start out from separate administrations with the instruction to guess the reactions of specified others).

NORM DATA. As published in the two manuals, norm data are somewhat limited in value and should be considered tentative only. The reviewer does not regret too much that representative national norms were not established; the cost of such samples may outweigh their possible contributions in devices of this type. But more comprehensive and better defined groups would be desirable. The adult sample is limited to ages 20–29 and seems overrepresentative of people with above-average education. The child norms are established on fairly small groups per age level, the lower levels coming from private schools, the higher levels from public schools. No controlling subdivisions for social class, occupation, or intelligence are reported. That intelligence influences situation perception, and hence responses, is indicated in some studies (e.g., *121*). No attempts are made to base conclusions about developmental trends on longitudinal studies. Of course, the fairly limited norm data in the manual are considerably extended in other published reports. Normative information is available for other American groups and for non-American groups, such as French, German, Indian, Italian, and Japanese children. Unfortunately, the scattered normative data have not been integrated and incorporated in the general manuals. If this were done (with additional information on relevant comparative variables) it could mean a better frame of reference for interpretation and, in addition, a starting point for interesting hypotheses on intercultural variations in basic interaction patterns. Tentative work in this direction has been reported from various corners of the world (e.g., *192*).

RELIABILITY. The P-F Study has one foot in the projective-test camp, with its underlying theory of projections on identification figures, and one foot in the psychometric camp, with a scoring technique that emphasizes the quantitative approach. This commendable attempt has the disadvantage to attract criticisms from two frontiers. Some clinically oriented psychologists see the test as too restricted in aim and too simple in interpretational background. On the other hand, psychometrists are sometimes quick to point out flaws in measurement precision in terms of reliability. Interscorer consistency is fairly high according to several studies (e.g., *13*), but could probably be further improved by stimulus revisions, since some items tend to attract far more inconsistencies than others. Internal consistency, on the other hand, is very often found to be low (*115*). If other test utility indicators are high, this one need not be taken too seriously, however. (There is no reason why, for instance, first-half scores should be identical with second-half scores. On the contrary, the analysis of trend, especially, uses score discrepancies between phases for diagnostic purposes.) Parallel test consistency has not attracted much attention, although some study of the interchangeability of the adult and children forms has been made. Retest reliability is more important for the interpretational possibilities than internal consistency, for even though we do not expect interaction tendencies to be free from change, too much change from one time to another will make the test worthless for predictional purposes. Studies of retest data do show the reliability of some scores (such as GCR) to be rather low for individual diagnosis, whereas others are as reliable as could be expected for data of this kind (*25, 111*).

VALIDITY. The question of empirical validity is not given much attention in the manuals, but many studies have contributed to the field. Good surveys of earlier studies are given by Mirmow (*108*) and Rosenzweig (*222*). The evidence is somewhat ambiguous. It would, apparently, seldom be fair to demand a one-to-one correspondence between scores from a test of this type and specific outside criteria. We do not consider this test a short-cut measure of something we have a reliable, but time consuming, measure of somewhere else, which we could use as a prototype in validation studies. Neither is a test of this type a one-purpose prediction tool, for which non-ambiguous data on prediction success could be collected. Instead, it is an instrument based on a theory of individual differentiation in the frustration reaction field and on a number of relevant subhypotheses. If

this instrument could be shown to "behave" according to theoretical expectations, so that we obtain patterns of meaningful correlations and group differences, we would feel that it works. Hence, while not demanding one-to-one correspondences, we desire relational fertility in terms of meaningful result patterns. A large body of data now shows increasing evidence of this type. Interesting findings are reported by Christiansen,[5] Davids and Oliver (*216*), Duhm,[6] Farberow (*43*), French (*44*), Kaswan, Wasman, and Freedman (*219*), Levitt and Lyle (*150*), Rosenzweig and Rosenzweig (*110*), and others. Among the methods used are experiments with artificially induced frustration, which, for example, significantly increased O-D and E scores (*209*). Original approaches for studying validity are presented by Rogers and Paul (*210*) and by Schwartz (*177*). But among many supportive findings, unexpected inconsistencies occur. Obviously, the question of relational fertility is intimately connected with the basic difficulties in terms of level of response and, to some extent perhaps, the problems of stimulus sampling, both discussed above. If these problems could be solved better than they are now, we would have reason to expect a higher degree of consistency in the validity studies.

RECOMMENDATIONS ON CHANGES AND RESEARCH. Summarizing some of the points made above, a list of *desiderata* for future work would include (*a*) revised manuals, incorporating and integrating the now scattered information on norms, reliability, and validity; (*b*) an attempt to construct a parallel instrument including more systematic and sex-fair test stimuli and using a sorting-out process for situations with low differentiating value; (*c*) research on various administration strategies, including oral-nonpersonal presentation; (*d*) studies of whether or not inquiry increases validity of information; and (*e*) research on the basic problem of response level, especially with attempts to construct a multilevel instrument.

RECOMMENDATIONS ON USES. As stated earlier, two main uses have been made of this test: (*a*) individual diagnosis of frustration-related behavior tendencies, and (*b*) research in testing various general theories on frustration

5 CHRISTIANSEN, *op. cit.*
6 DUHM, ERNA. "Die Reaktionen von Problemkindern im Rosenzweig-Picture-Frustration-Test." *Psychologische Rundschau* 10:283–91 O '59. *

tolerance, directions of "aggression," etc., as related to other biosocial variables. What conclusions should be drawn from the comments made above? Apparently, the P-F Study has many features that may evoke criticism, especially from more tough-minded psychometrists. The test stimuli could have been chosen according to a more explicit empirical procedure. The test situation involves uncertainties as to the best strategy. Norms as presented in the manuals should be considered tentative only. Retest reliability is low for some scoring categories. Basic theoretical problems, such as the question of response level, have not been solved.

Especially the last two facts mentioned would lead us to conclude that it should not be used in its present form for individual clinical decisions without intra-case validation from other sources. While the advanced clinician who is keenly aware of its limitations and knows how to supplement its information may sometimes find it of interest in clinical work, this test cannot be generally recommended for routine use or for immediate practical decisions by school psychologists, guidance workers, or teachers. It might be added that this characteristic is shared by most of today's personality devices and that to the reviewer's knowledge there is no competing test designed to study the same specific patterns of behavior that could claim any better standing in this respect.

A fairly specific use might be mentioned in passing. With its attempt to combine projective and psychometric features, it has often been a stimulating starting point for discussions in advanced personality assessment courses. In such a use, some of its difficulties are educationally very fruitful, tending quickly to involve students in basic methodological debate.

The main use of the P-F Study, however, has been and will be for basic research for testing theories on inter-variable relationships in frustration. In addition, it seems to be a good starting point for the further penetration of the theoretical and methodological questions on behavior levels. If successful, attempts to construct a multilevel instrument as recommended above may in time lead us toward a revolution in personality assessment strategy, so that one-level, one-shot instruments are replaced by multilevel approaches. If so, the P-F Study will have the merit of being one of the

first instruments that made this problem—implicit in so much personality testing—explicit and acute. Whatever specific changes the test may undergo in the future, however, the basic methodology—unique as it is—will continue to attract the interest of research workers and clinicians alike. At present, it is without doubt one of the most interesting and research-generating projective devices we have.

For reviews by Richard H. Dana and Bert R. Sappenfield, see 5:155; for reviews by Robert C. Challman and Percival M. Symonds, see 4:129.

[239]

The Rotter Incomplete Sentences Blank. Grades 9–12, 13–16, adults; 1950; 1 form (2 pages); 3 levels; manual (86 pages); manual and standardization data based on college level only; $1.25 per 25 tests; $1.90 per manual; postpaid; specimen set not available; (20–40) minutes; Julian B. Rotter and Janet E. Rafferty (manual); Psychological Corporation. *

REFERENCES

1–6. See 4:130.
7–24. See 5:156.
25. FITZGERALD, BERNARD JOSEPH. *The Relationship of Two Projective Measures to a Sociometric Measure of Dependent Behavior.* Doctor's thesis, Ohio State University (Columbus, Ohio), 1954. (*DA* 20:2380)
26. LENT, ADA. "A Survey of the Problems of Adolescent High School Girls Fourteen to Eighteen Years of Age." *Alberta J Ed Res* 3:127–37 S '57. * (*PA* 33:3415)
27. SCHMITT, JOHN A. *Identifying Maladjusted Youth in a Rural High School—an Investigation of the Usefulness of Rotter's Incomplete Sentences Blank.* Master's thesis, Cornell University (Ithaca, N.Y.), 1957.
28. YOSHPE, SELINA R. *A Validation Study of the Rotter Incomplete Sentences Blank: High School Form.* Master's thesis, Sacramento State College (Sacramento, Calif.), 1957.
29. CHANCE, JUNE ELIZABETH. "Adjustment and Prediction of Others' Behavior." *J Consult Psychol* 22:191–4 Je '58. * (*PA* 35:4977)
30. GUERTIN, WILSON H. "An Analysis of Gross Errors on a Sentence Completion Test." *J Clin Psychol* 15:415–6 O '59. * (*PA* 36:1HC14G)
31. HALE, PETER P. "The Rotter: A Vocational Counselor's Goldmine." *Voc Guid Q* 9:119–20 w '60. *
32. STEPHENS, MARK W. "The Incomplete Sentences Blank: Sources of Variance in Retest Reliability." *J Clin Psychol* 16:331–3 Jl '60. * (*PA* 36:2HC31S)
33. PRENTICE, NORMAN M. "Ethnic Attitudes, Neuroticism, and Culture." *J Social Psychol* 54:75–82 Je '61. * (*PA* 36:2HF75P)
34. BILLARD, RICHARD G. "Comparison of Teacher Ratings of Personality With Results of an Incomplete Sentences Blank." *Personnel & Guid J* 41:58–9 S '62. *
35. DOYLE, FLORENCE ESTHER. *An Analysis of Intercorrelations Among Adjustment Scores Attained by Delinquents on Independent and Experimental Measures Based on the Luker Index.* Doctor's research study No. 1, Colorado State College (Greeley, Colo.), 1962. (*DA* 23:1271)
36. NEWTON, DARWIN RUSSELL. *An Analysis of Intercorrelations Between the Rotter ISB and Other Measures of Adjustment Based on the Luker Index.* Doctor's research study No. 1, Colorado State College (Greeley, Colo.), 1962. (*DA* 22:4272)
37. RENNER, K. EDWARD; MAHER, BRENDAN A.; AND CAMPBELL, DONALD T. "The Validity of a Method for Scoring Sentence-Completion Responses for Anxiety, Dependency, and Hostility." *J Appl Psychol* 46:285–90 Ag '62. * (*PA* 37:3155)
38. THEINER, ERIC C. "The Magnitude of Four Experimental Needs as Expressed by Two Projective Techniques." *J Proj Tech* 26:354–65 S '62. * (*PA* 37:3163)
39. JESSOR, RICHARD; LIVERANT, SHEPHARD; AND OPOCHINSKY, SEYMOUR. "Imbalance in Need Structure and Maladjustment." *J Abn & Social Psychol* 66:271–5 Mr '63. * (*PA* 37:8032)
40. KENNEDY, WALLACE A.; COTTRELL, TED; AND SMITH, AL. "Norms of Gifted Adolescents on the Rotter Incomplete Sentence Blank." *J Clin Psychol* 19:314–5 Jl '63. *
41. WALLACE, JOHN, AND SECHREST, LEE. "Frequency Hypothesis and Content Analysis of Projective Techniques." *J Consult Psychol* 27:387–93 O '63. * (*PA* 38:4335)

For reviews by Charles N. Cofer and William Schofield, see 4:130.

[240]

★The South African Picture Analysis Test. Ages 5–13; 1960, c1959; 8 interpretive categories: condition of hero, environmental pressure, needs, reactions, characteristics of stories (4 categories); individual; 1 form (12 cards, 8 for boys or girls and 2 for boys only and 2 for girls only); manual ('60, c1959, 71 pages); no data on reliability; gld. 24,50 ($6.75) per set of cards and manual; gld. 7,90 ($2.25) per manual purchased separately; postage extra; (60) minutes; B. F. Nel and A. J. K. Pelser; Swets & Zeitlinger. *

S. G. LEE, *Professor of Psychology, University of Leicester, Leicester, England.*

The pictures of this test have been specifically designed to elicit projections from primary school children aged 5–13. The intention is to fill a presumed age gap between the TAT, the *Symonds Picture-Story Test,* and the CAT. The final version adopted to reduce the time taken in administration and scoring consists of 12 pictures.

Before considering the test material and its administration and interpretation in more detail it is informative to consider the theoretical and moral biases of the authors. For, from the statement, "there is a vast difference between the philosophy of life of the American and that of the Continental psychologist, i.e., a pragmatic philosophy of life as against an idealistic rationalistic philosophy of life," we are led on to the "continental" idea of the "person," a "moral being" whose personality is far from representing "the external manifestations of traits or qualities, which develop from the animalistic layers [sic] of the human organism"—this last being the view of "American psychology." The authors in fact identify themselves with the "continental" view: "Under personality is understood the external manifestation of this original and inherent spiritual core of the human existence. It may be pointed out that this conception of personality acquires a more comprehensive and more profound meaning when the human being is also considered as a Creation of God. Owing to the fact that this Creation has a spiritual core and is therefore a 'person,' he does not only build up relations with his fellow man but also and especially with God, his Creator." Again we have: "Man cannot be understood from within himself, but only in his complete existential relation, i.e., in his contact, in his dialogue with the things and human beings around him and with God." In similar vein, and closer to the purposes of the test, we are told that real projection can only take place in an "existential" situation. A protocol produced by the testee in a projective test should be "a story in which no attention is given to its essence but which is the direct emanation of his whole existence. Existence is identical to freedom; freedom to choose the ways and means of self-realization." As a result of all this we are told, later in the text of the manual, "In other words all the characters in the story feel, think and act as the testee does."

If all this means anything useful, and the reviewer does not feel himself metaphysically capable of evaluating it in other than the terms of basic English and scientific enquiry, this test should be literally a marvellous one. The authors state, "Suffice it to say that according to the experience of the authors the SAPAT has the qualities of a suitable projection test." Throughout the manual, minimal empirical support for this statement is adduced by Nel and Pelser. As Mark Twain might have said: "It don't suffice me."

In the devising of the test, "five hundred odd pupils of both sexes" [sic] were asked what their preferences in stories were from a limited list of stories, possibly appropriate, set before them by the authors. Themes ranging from fairy stories to Tarzan stories emerged as preferred. Boys of eight and above were no longer interested in fairy stories. If this is a useful criterion to use in the choice of stimulus pictures it seems odd that in this test for children up to 13, seven of the final twelve stimulus pictures are of pixies, fairies, and similar "wee folk," two are of mice dressed in human clothes, and three are of ordinary human beings. By the authors' own criteria three quarters of the pictures could be more or less inappropriate for the older child. The pictures are crudely drawn and "slanted" in content, in terms of the preconceptions of the authors, e.g., picture 2, which the authors describe as follows: "Mickey Mouse is standing in a room and talking seriously to a little mouse. Behind and against a wall are hanging a sjambok [rhinoceros hide whip—reviewer's translation], a hunting knife and a mounted buck's head. In the background a mother mouse sits knitting, and on the table lies a pair of scissors. * The symbols of punishment (the sjambok), and of castration (the scissors and the knife) might evoke further projections."

Indeed, the authors' analysis of protocols is largely that of *verstehende* psychology, mostly Freudian, with the occasional touch of Jung. They acknowledge that their scheme of interpretation is, in many respects, "based on work previously done by Murray, Rotter, Tomkins, Rapaport, Rosenzweig, Van Lennep, and others." With the possible exception of the last-named, all these would presumably be regarded by the authors as "pragmatic psychologists" interested only in the products of the "animalistic layers" of the human organism. Their following of these is astonishing in that the underlying philosophy of the authors is essentially the existentialism of Jean-Paul Sartre.

It seems to me that there is precious little that is new or useful in this test but much that is bad. Some analysis is given of 63 specimen protocols, three complete records among them. Specimen analysis sheets are given. The easy identification of the "hero" and of the subject's motives is assumed throughout. Some stories are dismissed as "insignificant," others contain "numerous significant projections." In another case, "The stories are unnatural and the pictures are often misunderstood and misinterpreted." No norms are quoted and it is impossible for this reviewer to see how these certainties were arrived at. The authors seem to be ignorant or heedless of the great body of controlled and experimental investigation into the mechanism of projection that has been accumulated in the West over the last 20 years. Instead: "It is presumed that the analyst has a thorough knowledge of the basical [*sic*] theories underlying projection tests."

One additional comment must be made. I can feel nothing but pity for children attending any child guidance clinic whose personalities are assessed in these subjective and biased terms. I wish that there were space in this review to cite the whole of the last complete record given in the manual. Perhaps the beginning and end of this "analysis" will give some idea of the type of judgments arrived at throughout the examples given:

The child is well cared for, mostly happy and feels herself quite adequate. She is full of confidence and able to take care of herself. She is however restless, due to internal stresses of a sexual nature. She is pre-occupied with "sexual" adventures: going to parties, dances, for a walk with a friend, etc. Her needs are therefore those for affiliation, play or exhibition-

ism, always however with a sexual connotation. She is independent, practical and generally happy. Her attitude towards, and intense interest in sexual matters is however of such a cold-blooded nature that there seems to be real danger that she might try experimenting in this direction. * Her exaggerated interest in sexual matters, which is probably accompanied by masturbation, explains the tics as well as her desire to be the centre of attraction.

The authors give no clue as to how they arrived at these "conclusions" from the stories cited. To this reviewer and to other psychologists consulted, few or no sexual themes are discoverable in the stories told by the nine-year-old girl in question, and it might be appropriate to rechristen the SAPAT as "The South African Psychomantic Analysis Test." The *analyses* do, I think, demonstrate clearly the validity of the concept of projection.

JOHANN M. SCHEPERS, *Senior Research Officer, National Institute for Personnel Research, Johannesburg, Republic of South Africa.*

Working at the Child Guidance Clinic of the Faculty of Education, University of Pretoria, the authors felt the need for a projective test of the TAT type, specially suited for use with children in the age range 5–13 years. The *South African Picture Analysis Test* (SAPAT) is their answer to this need.

The construction of the SAPAT raises many important questions and merits our serious consideration.

Every attempt at projective test construction is hampered by the fact that several questions of fundamental importance concerning the construction of the stimulus material have remained unanswered. More often than not some *ad hoc* approach to the matter is followed, with the result that very little is learned in the process. Issues such as the following need to be settled before we can confidently embark on the task of projective test construction: What types of stories will appeal most to children of various age levels? How stable are these preferences when viewed cross-nationally or cross-culturally? What features of the stimulus material facilitate the production of projective responses? Is identification with some central figure necessary for projection? Will the level of projection co-vary with the degree of identification with some central figure? What would happen if the figures depicted in projective material represent an ethnic type dissimilar to that of the testee? Will children readily identify with animal characters? How will children's projections be influenced by bedtime stories about animals if animal characters are used? What is the optimal degree of structuredness of stimulus material for use with children? Should one vary the style of the pictures by having more than one artist? Should one introduce color into the pictures?

The authors have given a detailed account of the various considerations they had in mind when constructing the SAPAT. A commendable feature of their research is the fact that they first tried to establish what types of stories would appeal most to the primary school child. A study involving 500 odd cases showed a wide divergence in the choice of stories, with the result that the authors had to use as wide a range of figures as possible in order to cover the spectrum of interests.

Twenty themes were selected and the pictures drawn by a commercial artist. After an initial investigation using 40 primary school children, eight of the pictures were discarded as relatively unsuitable. Eight pictures were found to be equally suitable for both boys and girls, two were found to be specially suitable for boys and two for girls. Ten pictures were accordingly selected for use with boys and 10 for girls. The authors decided not to reduce the number of pictures to less than 10 because they have found "that there is a definite positive relation between the number of stories analysed and the validity of the interpretation."

The authors claim that in each of the pictures there is one person or figure with whom a child can readily identify. The 12 pictures finally selected are composed as follows: (a) Two pictures where the hero is alone. (b) Two pictures where the hero is with one other person. (c) Three pictures where the hero is in the company of two other people or figures. (d) Four pictures where the hero is in the company of more than two people. (e) Two pictures where the home situation is depicted. (f) One picture where the school situation is represented. (g) One picture where the playground situation is depicted. (h) Three pictures with a sexual connotation. (i) One picture concerning achievement, competition, and exhibitionism.

The authors purposely tried to make the pictures more structured than the usual TAT pictures, because they had found that children tend to lose interest if the themes are vague. They tried to achieve this by having the facial expressions of the characters clearly defined whilst keeping the background fairly neutral. At the same time the authors state that their pictures are polyvalent. It is very difficult to judge this claim because no distribution of themes over the 12 pictures is shown.

The usual TAT instruction is given, but in simpler language. The stories which are produced orally are recorded by the examiner. The test requires less than one hour to administer.

A detailed scheme for the analysis of the protocols is given in the 74-page manual. Eight interpretive categories are presented, four of which relate to the content of the protocols and four to the formal characteristics of the stories. The authors make it clear that the interpretation remains a matter of "verstehen" and that they offer the scheme to compel "the analyst to judge more objectively." Their scheme is comprehensive and might well be used with TAT's generally.

The manual contains numerous illustrative protocols and case histories, together with brief analyses of these protocols. However, no normative material is presented, and one is left with the impression that the test has not yet been extensively applied. No information regarding scorer reliability, test-retest reliability, or validity is given. The psychology of "verstehen" is offered as an apology for this omission.

The authors are at pains to eschew the American approach to personality and projection, and to espouse the Continental approach. American readers might well find the vague metaphysical language of existentialism disturbing. Paradoxically, however, the authors find it necessary to draw heavily on the work of Murray, Tomkins, Rapaport, and others.

The SAPAT is unique in the sense that it is specially suitable for use with primary school children, and as such should fulfil a real need. The dwarf and fairylike characters resemble "real" boys and girls fairly closely and might therefore be of general appeal cross-nationally.

J Proj Tech 24:446 D '60. Wilson H. Guertin. * a constructive contribution * The authors seem to have accomplished their goal of filling the gap between the Childrens Apperception Test (CAT) (animal pictures) and the Symonds Picture Story Test (adolescents). Interest should be optimum for children from about five to twelve years of age. None of the pictures depicts anything culturally unique to Africa and all children are White. Like the CAT each picture is distinctly drawn. It would appear that the clarity of the structure of the stimulus material would decrease the range of different needs that might be projected into a given picture. Thus, ambivalence would probably not be as clearly expressed in responses to the SAPAT cards as to the Symonds or TAT pictures. The manual's introduction concerning differences between European and American conceptions of personality and projection may interest some. However, the final analysis of a protocol by the authors differs in no significant way from American analysis of TAT pictures. The semiobjective scheme for analysis appears to be an eclectic American approach. * Some examples of stories and interpretations are given in the manual. However, the neophyte should not expect to find a scoring and interpretation scheme that dispenses with the intuitive skills of the clinician. The reviewer must admit that the stimuli appear to meet the need for TAT type material for the grade-school child. A sound, objectively-scored projective test would have made a greater methodological contribution, but the clinical value of the TAT method is such that it deserves to be extended to all populations.

[241]

★Structured Doll Play Test. Ages 2–6; 1959–60; family and peer relationships; individual; 2 forms; 3 editions (identical except for test figures): Caucasian, Negroid, Oriental; no data on reliability and validity; $14 per set of all 3 editions including 10 record forms, general manual, and manual of instructions; $10 per Caucasian-figures edition including preceding accessories; $3.50 per 25 record forms; $1 per general manual; $3.50 per manual of instructions; postpaid; (30–45) minutes; David B. Lynn; Test Developments. *
a) [SERIES 1.] 1959; 1 form ['59, 12 cardboard figures and objects and 4 background cards]; manual of instructions ('59, 18 pages); general manual ('59, 25 pages); record form ('59, 10 pages).
b) [SERIES 2.] 1959–60; for research use only; 1 form ['60, 10 cardboard figures and objects and 3 background cards]; manual of instructions ('60, 15 pages); general manual ('60, 4 pages); record form ('59, 8 pages); no norms.

REFERENCES

1. LYNN, DAVID B. "Development and Validation of a Structural Doll Play Test for Children." Q B Ind.ana Univ, Med Center 17:16–7 Ja '55. *
2. LYNN, DAVID B. An Investigation of Hypotheses Basic to a Concept of Relative Intensity of Interaction as Applied to Structural Doll Play Test Responses. Doctor's thesis, Purdue University (Lafayette, Ind.), 1955. (DA 15:869)
3. LYNN, ROSALIE. A Study of the Responses of Four and Six Year Olds to a Structured Doll Play Test. Master's thesis, Purdue University (Lafayette, Ind.), 1955.
4. LYNN, DAVID B. "A Relative Measure of Interaction." J Psychol Studies 11:52–61 N–D '59. * (PA 34:5774)
5. LYNN, DAVID B., AND LYNN, ROSALIE. "The Structured Doll Play Test as a Projective Technique for Use With Children." J Proj Tech 23:335–44 S '59. * (PA 35:4929)
6. LYNN, ROSALIE. Sex Role Preference and Mother-Daughter Fantasies in Young Girls. Doctor's thesis, University of Denver (Denver, Colo.), 1961. (DA 22:4084)

TERENCE MOORE, Research Psychologist and Lecturer, Centre for the Study of Human Development, University of London Institute of Education, London, England.

It is well known that young children readily project their feelings and fantasies about close personal relationships onto dolls, and there are obvious attractions in the idea of exploring these aspects of their personality through a systematically structured technique. Such systematic exploration is clearly indicated for research purposes, and has advantages also in a clinical setting wherever the aim is not, as in free doll play, to ventilate whatever fantasies are uppermost in the child's mind at the moment, but rather to survey in a single interview a wide range of areas in which conflicts commonly arise, or to map out the parts played by father and mother in the child's mental schema of family life. Although not so defined by the author, these appear to be the main functions of Lynn's Structured Doll Play Test.

The 18 situations of Series 1 cover most aspects of the everyday life of a typical preschool child, while Series 2 takes him on to school, to the doctor's, and introduces a "bad animal," thus inviting rather more symbolic fantasy. In nearly every scene the child is first asked to make a choice (either a choice between a more and a less mature object, e.g., a glass and a baby's bottle for the ego doll, or else a choice between the parents) and then encouraged by more open questions to extend his fantasy as he will. The choices are used as a basis for scoring, while the freer fantasy is of more general clinical interest. In order not to limit the fantasy to the chosen parent, each scene is followed by another in which the examiner introduces the non-chosen parent in a somewhat similar role, and asks the subject what will happen. This is ingenious, but is fairly often defeated by a strong-minded child who demands the parent of his own choice in the second scene as well, while some children are anxious to include both parents, suggesting that they place a high valuation on family harmony—an attitude that can easily get obscured by uncritical acceptance of the underlying assumption that a child should choose (and in choosing, prefer or identify with) *either* father *or* mother. Moreover, since the roles (nurturant, authoritarian, depriving, etc.) allotted to father or mother dolls vary fundamentally from scene to scene and from subject to subject, one may wonder how useful it is to add them up. A better case could be made for adding responses indicative of maturity-immaturity, which is at least generally thought of as unidimensional; but are four items an adequate measure of it?

Norms (in the form of percentages of each age-sex group from 2 to 6 years making either possible choice in each item, and summed over items) are presented in a layout that makes comparison of ages and sexes unnecessarily difficult, and Lynn records his impression that his standardization sample of 240 private school children (30 per age-sex group) came from a higher than average socio-economic level and included a disproportionate number of children from broken homes. He claims "construct validity" on the grounds that the scores do differentiate age, sex, and educational groups, and to some extent between children whose fathers are at home and away. This in itself would not seem to bear closely on the value of the scores for individual diagnosis. For this purpose the free material produced in response to the open questions would seem much more useful; and in the reviewer's experience such material is produced in diagnostically useful quantities mainly by older, brighter, and less inhibited children.

The author originally designed the test for children aged 2 to 6, and now finds that it is acceptable with slight verbal modifications for children up to 11. Lower school children will indeed often use dolls for expressing their fantasies quite readily if they are presented in the right way. As regards the lower age limit, while it is possible that choices might be elicited from bright children of 2+, fantasy is rarely articulate enough to provide very rich clinical material much below 4. Nevertheless, this technique does offer the younger child an acceptable and easily comprehended medium through which to express whatever he can and will, either in words or action or both. Given dolls to handle and a few questions to stimulate fantasy, many children are able to respond much more fruitfully than they can to a test such as the CAT, which requires the ability both to construct and to verbalize a story from pictures alone.

The dolls used in this test are of die-cut cardboard and any necessary furniture is printed on cardboard sheets. Besides making for cheapness and portability as compared with more realistic toys, this design is said to reduce tangential manipulation without reducing fantasy content. Although children do seem to identify with these not very attractive cardboard objects, and to express fantasy through them, it is a question whether they are not limited by the rigidity of the board figures and derive less pleasure from handling them than they would from the conventional wire dolls. Having tried both, the reviewer still prefers three-dimensional apparatus. The envelopes supplied as containers, opening at the ends, are not very satisfactory, as they lead to a good deal of fumbling and hunting; or if the contents are emptied out, the child sees more than he is intended to have. A flat box divided into shallow compartments with hinged lids would serve better.

The recording sheet is well drawn up, with small diagrams which remind the examiner of the positions of the dolls and properties for each item and also facilitate recording of the choices made. An improvement found useful by this reviewer in similar work is a list of abbreviations of the commoner types of overt affect, which can be printed for each item and circled as the child's expressions are observed, to capture something of the emotional flavour of each response.

If an adequate picture of the child's outlook on life is required, full account must be taken of the affect expressed around each situation, and to this end, refusals, avoidances, tangential conversation, and spontaneous extension of the play situations are at least as important as the responses proper. But no directions for recording these occur in the manual. Nor is any attempt made to discuss interpretation. One caution should perhaps be issued: since fantasy functions at different levels of realism from child to child, and even from moment to moment in the same child, we must beware of the fallacy of attributing behaviour or attitudes depicted in the play too glibly to the real child and his parents. One interaction of the dolls may represent a wish fulfilment, the next a feared event, a third the reflection of a real life relationship. All will have their significance, but other evidence may well be needed in deciding between the possible interpretations.

In summary, then, this technique does provide a useful projective screen for eliciting fantasy material from young children; it has the advantage over pictorial tests in that it does not require the child to be especially creative or able to order his fantasy in verbal terms; its structure is such that it taps many of the crucial conflict areas, and its combination of choices and open questions gives satisfactory scope for most children. Like all projective techniques, it must be interpreted with tact and caution, and the value of its scoring system still remains to be demonstrated.

ALAN O. ROSS, *Chief Psychologist, Pittsburgh Child Guidance Center, Pittsburgh, Pennsylvania.*

This instrument represents a cross between the *Make A Picture Story* with its cut-out figures and variable background scenes, the Duess-Despert Fables [1] with their structured situational questions, and the little-known but ingenious Miniature Situation Test [2] with its binary choices. This discussion is based primarily on the first of the two forms, i.e., Series I.

The *Structured Doll Play Test,* which its author describes as a "clinically useful doll play projective technique," presents the child with a cardboard doll in 18 family or peer situations. Each situation is verbally structured and pictorially represented and the child is asked to resolve the situation and to play the story out with the cardboard dolls and props. In 12 of the situations the child is asked to make a choice between two alternatives—e.g., between crib and bed, bottle and glass, father and mother, toilet and potty. The remaining 6 situations require the child to say what is taking place or will happen in the scene structured by the examiner.

The following will serve as an example of the test items: A picture of a crib and a bed is placed before the child who is handed a cardboard doll representing his sex with the instructions, "Take the little boy (girl) in your hand. This is the baby crib and this is the bed. Let's pretend that this little boy can sleep in either the baby crib or the bed. You put him to sleep. Lay him down on either the bed or the baby

crib." After the child has made the choice he is asked, "Why is it he sleeps in the bed (baby crib) and not in the baby crib (bed)?" Immediately following this the parent dolls are presented and the child is told, "Now let's pretend the little boy (girl) is in bed and mommy or daddy comes in. Which one comes in, mommy or daddy?" The child is handed the chosen parent and instructed, "Now take mommy (daddy) in your hand and show me and tell me what happens."

The immature wording of many of the questions can be modified when the test is used with older children but even then some of the situations, such as the child being taken to the toilet by one of his parents, would be more suitable for children under six despite the fact that the manual states that the test is "equally useful with children from seven through eleven."

The normative data included in the manual show the percentage of various choices made by 240 children between the ages of 2 and 6. The data presented show an increase in the "maturity" of choices when younger children are compared with older children. The easily checked test-retest reliability of these choices is not reported and it is impossible to determine whether an "immature" choice actually reflects immaturity or, for example, a more active and accessible fantasy life on the part of the younger children. The meaning of any particular response is left to the clinician to interpret, for the author feels that it is premature to publish interpretive guides at the present stage of this test's development, though he promises to publish interpretive hypotheses representing a blend of research and clinical knowledge at a later time.

For research purposes the author offers a mimeographed preliminary scoring manual providing for quantification of 163 response categories. This system is admittedly far too complex for everyday clinical use and the author again promises a brief modification for clinical purposes for some later date. If such a scoring manual could indeed be produced it would represent a true contribution to the field of thematic testing.

In one of the publications describing this test (5) the author makes the observation that "Fortunately, the period in Clinical Psychology is virtually ended when a psychologist can originate a test and place it on the market without supporting research. Some research has been

1 MOSSE, HILDE L. "The Duess Test." *Am J Psychother* 8:251–64 Ap '54. *
2 SANTOSTEFANO, SEBASTIAN. "Miniature Situation Tests as a Way of Interviewing Children." *Merrill-Palmer Q* 8:261–9 O '62. *

completed with the SDP and more is currently under way." There have indeed been a few studies, mostly with earlier or modified forms of the test, but when the manual speaks of "norms and research findings which will be published in the future" it raises the question whether publication of this instrument as a clinically useful projective technique might not have been premature.

The SDP is a cleverly designed device which can facilitate the study of young children in a manner which has more structure and objectivity than the usual thematic picture test, but whether it elicits more or better information than available projective techniques, including the informal and spontaneous doll play interview, remains to be demonstrated.

[242]

Structured-Objective Rorschach Test: Preliminary Edition. Adults; 1958; also called *S-O Rorschach Test;* 15 scores (for deriving 26 traits): whole-blot (W), major details (D), minor details (Dd), white space (S), form resemblance (F), poor form resemblance (F−), human movement (M), animal movement (FM), color and form resemblance (FC), color and poor form resemblance (CF), shading (Fch), animal figure (A), human figure (H), modal responses (P), rare responses (O); IBM; 1 form; 2 editions; preliminary manual (28 pages); separate answer sheets must be used; 10¢ per IBM answer sheet; $1.50 per set of hand scoring stencils; postage extra; scoring service available; (30–50) minutes; Joics B. Stone; California Test Bureau. *

a) ILLUSTRATED EDITION. 1 form (12 pages); $7.50 per test.

b) NON-ILLUSTRATED EDITION. 1 form (23 pages); to be used with slides or cards; $5 per 10 tests; $13 per set of inkblot cards; $12.50 per set of kodaslides; $1 per specimen set without slides or cards, postpaid.

REFERENCES

1. KHAN, LILIAN. *Factor Analysis of Certain Aptitude and Personality Variables.* Doctor's thesis, University of Southern California (Los Angeles, Calif.), 1959. (*DA* 20:2889)
2. ANGELINO, HENRY, AND HALL, RICHARD L. "Temperament Factors in High- and Low-Achieving High School Seniors." *Psychol Rep* 7:518 D '60. * (*PA* 35:2005)
3. HAMPTON, PETER J. "Use of Rorschach Test in Selecting Factory Supervisors." *Personnel J* 39:46-8 Je '60. * (*PA* 35:7190)
4. HOSFORD, PRENTISS McINTYRE. *Characteristics of Science-Talented and Language-Talented Secondary School Students.* Doctor's thesis, University of Georgia (Athens, Ga.), 1961. (*DA* 22:2687)
5. MINK, OSCAR GORTON. *A Study of Certain Cognitive and Conative Factors Affecting Academic Progress in Chemical and Metallurgical Engineering at Cornell University.* Doctor's thesis, Cornell University (Ithaca, N.Y.), 1961. (*DA* 22:2695)
6. HAMMES, JOHN A., AND OSBORNE, R. TRAVIS. "Discrimination of Manifest Anxiety by the Structured-Objective Rorschach Test." *Percept & Motor Skills* 15:59-62 Ag '62. * (*PA* 37:5083)
7. HICKS, JOHN A., AND STONE, JOICS B. "The Identification of Traits Related to Managerial Success." *J Appl Psychol* 46:428-32 D '62. * (*PA* 37:5714)
8. KHAN, LILIAN. "Factor Analysis of Certain Aptitude and Personality Variables." *Indian J Psychol* 37:27-38 Mr '62. * (*PA* 37:6716)
9. LANGER, PHILIP. "Compulsivity and Response Set on the Structured Objective Rorschach Test." *J Clin Psychol* 18:299-302 Jl '62. * (*PA* 39:1862)
10. LANGER, PHILIP. "Social Desirability and Acquiescence on the SORT." *Psychol Rep* 11:531-4 O '62. * (*PA* 37:8018)
11. LAW, DAVID H., AND NORTON, JOSEPH L. "The SORT as a Differentiator Between High and Low Achievers." *J Counsel Psychol* 9:184 su '62. *
12. LITTLE, ELDON LEROY. *SORT Evaluation of Midshipmen in the First Year Naval Reserve Officers' Training Corps Program.* Doctor's thesis, University of Oklahoma (Norman, Okla.), 1962. (*DA* 23:2012)
13. VINSON, DAVID B. "Objectivity in the Assessment of Psychobiologic Decline." *Vita Hum* 4(3):134-42 '62. *
14. LANGER, PHILIP; CARLISLE, ALMA L.; AND HAYES, WILLIAM G. "The Effects of Anxiety and Conformity on the Structured-Objective Rorschach Test (SORT)." *J Clin Psychol* 19:317-9 Jl '63. *
15. LANGER, PHILIP; HAYES, WILLIAM G.; AND SHARP, HEBER C. "Effect of Anxiety and Induced Stress on the Structured-Objective Rorschach Test." *Percept & Motor Skills* 16:573-80 Ap '63. * (*PA* 38:2718)
16. PERRY, MARIAN LOUISE. *The Relationship of Selected Variables to the Success of Camp Counselors.* Doctor's thesis, University of Southern California (Los Angeles, Calif.), 1963. (*DA* 24:613)

JESSE G. HARRIS, JR., *Professor of Psychology and Chairman of the Department, University of Kentucky, Lexington, Kentucky.*

The *Structured-Objective Rorschach Test* is a multiple choice instrument which uses the 10 original inkblots in either an illustrated or non-illustrated booklet form, the latter of which must be accompanied by either the 10 cards or slides for a projector. The SORT requires neither free association nor inquiry, is suitable for individual or group administration, and is objectively scored by means of templates or IBM test scoring machine. The subject is required, by forced choice procedure, to select from each of 10 sets of triads for each card the response which is *"most clearly represented by* the blot or *by some part* of the blot." The concrete, abstract, and mythological noun responses are, in some items, qualified by descriptive adjectives. Each response alternative provides at least two scores and, in some instances, additional scores for content and for statistically determined populars and originals. The scoring format is apparently an eclectic synthesis of several well known scoring systems, including the Beck, Klopfer and Kelley, Schafer, and Harrower-Erickson. The 15 basic raw scores are converted to normalized T scores and, for subsequent interpretation of personality attributes, are read as ratings of "high," "above average," "average," "below average," or "low," from tables of single variables or from the diagonal bands of two-dimensional abacs, when multiple determinants are involved.

The method of analysis is an approximation to the "cookbook" approach for inexperienced technicians, a methodology for which Rorschach enthusiasts, ironically, have long expressed a profound distaste. Although the details of method of derivation and sequential arrangement of response choices are not described clearly either in the manual or in the research literature, the procedure has involved use of Beck's location charts, Harrower-Erickson's tables of frequency of occurrence of responses, and a judgmental arrangement of response combinations. Both tester and researcher must assume a high probability of correspondence between the subject's actual percept and the area of the blot for which the structured response was intended by the author. Mutual contamination of verbal and perceptual free associations is inevitable in this, as in any other, type of multiple choice inkblot test, regardless of the seemingly structured nature of the response alternatives. The manual states that the SORT provides an assessment of temperament patterns for educational-vocational guidance work and for personnel selection, and that it is not intended for clinical use, apparently because it lacks the free associational characteristics of the more commonly used projective techniques.

The instrument seems to possess properties which are usually regarded as highly desirable for a research tool designed for large scale investigation. Although it suffers the usual lack of a suitable alternate form for studies of reliability, the SORT has test-retest reliability coefficients at least equivalent to, and possibly higher than, those of similar tests (medians of 15 scoring variables for two groups reported in the Preliminary Manual of the order, $r = .75$, with a minimum value of $r = .62$). Concurrent validity coefficients are reported for 1,616 telephone company employees as correlations between Rorschach variables and job classification, and for 2,600 college freshmen as correlations between Rorschach variables and grade point average. Tables of mean number of responses are presented for several different occupational groups. Information on construct validity of the instrument is provided in the Preliminary Manual in the form of measures of correspondence between supervisors' ratings and Rorschach ratings.

The SORT has also generated research by other investigators concerned with construct validity, as is reflected in the accompanying list of titles of research articles. Some of the hypotheses in these studies have been sound, and others which have produced negative results may or may not reflect inadequacy of the test instrument. Only further research can de-

termine whether the SORT describes or predicts behavior as accurately as, or more accurately than, conventional personality inventories. Khan (8) has reported, in a factor analytic study, a relative independence of variables on the SORT from those of the *Guilford-Zimmerman Temperament Survey* and of the *Multiple Aptitude Tests,* devised by Segel and Raskin. Although the SORT has now made its formal appearance among the storm-swept islands of Rorschach literature and, of necessity, will be required to generate some impressive research data on validity if it is to advance the cause of inkblot testing, it does seem to possess a set of structural attributes which should permit a rigorous evaluation, on a large scale basis, of fundamental Rorschach hypotheses.

The SORT has the same physical limitations which are inherent in the original set of Rorschach inkblots, but the techniques of collecting, scoring, and interpreting data are sufficiently economical and objective to encourage further research with the instrument, not only in the areas of personnel selection and counseling, but also in more basic studies of perception. With regard to construction of response alternatives and statistical properties of the instrument as a whole, the SORT may prove to have an advantage over the multiple choice Rorschach test, developed by Harrower and Steiner, which is similar in purpose and in application. From the point of view of construction of stimulus materials, however, the SORT may have less to recommend it than the *Holtzman Inkblot Technique,* which employs free association and inquiry and is highly developed statistically. The SORT deserves further exploration at the level of collection and analysis of raw data in a variety of settings. Interpretation of data need not be restricted to a reading of the author's abacs or to an adoption of his first order derivatives of conventional Rorschach hypotheses. Economy of method, it would seem, is sufficient justification for further research with this test on a large scale basis by persons who have convictions about the merits of the inkblot approach to the study of the normal or abnormal personality. One might hope, also, that the author of the SORT would plan and develop a manual to supersede the preliminary edition, reporting all findings, both positive and negative, which have been obtained on samples of large size. Such a request should seem reasonable, if the author is himself convinced of the fundamental worth of the test as an instrument of science.

BORIS SEMEONOFF, *Reader in Psychology, University of Edinburgh, Edinburgh, Scotland.*

Introducing the *Structured-Objective Rorschach Test* (SORT), the author claims that it "combines the subtle features of the widely respected and highly developed Rorschach inkblot projective methodology with the practical group methodology of the objective test." The second of these requirements has certainly been met: the SORT has been admirably produced; instructions, layout, recording and scoring devices, etc. could hardly be bettered. Nevertheless, whether the test can truly be described as "objective" is open to doubt, and its claim to possess the "subtle features" of Rorschach could not be upheld by any but the most naïve user of the original technique.

The test is constructed on the forced-choice principle. The stimuli are the 10 original Rorschach blots, for each of which 10 triads of responses are offered; the instruction is "select the *one* response from each group of three items that you think is *best represented* by the blot or some part of the blot." Every protocol will thus consist of 100 responses, which are analysed to yield 15 "scores." Expressed in Rorschach symbols these are: W, D, Dd, S, F, F−, M, FM, FC, CF, Fch, A, H, P, O. These are mostly self-explanatory, but the following divergences from normal Rorschach practice should be noted: (*a*) All S (space) responses are also scored as W, D, or Dd. (*b*) CF responses are defined as those "involving color and poorly resembling the form of the stimulus." (*c*) Fch covers all responses "involving textural density of gray or shading." (*d*) P indicates "modal" responses, i.e., the responses most commonly chosen from each and every triad. (*e*) O covers many responses which will be recognised by the experienced Rorschach user as not even "rare," let alone *original* in the orthodox sense.

Raw scores are converted to *T*-scores, and these in turn to ratings, on a five-point scale, on each of 26 attributes, either direct from a single "factor," or by means of "abacs" based on a combination of scores on two or more factors. The 26 attributes (in actual fact 30, since one has 5 subvarieties) are grouped under four broad heads: mental functioning (9 items); interests (2); responsiveness (2); and temperament (13).

The rationale for these attributes is said to rely on "basic Rorschach interpretation." In most cases this claim is justified (assuming, at any rate, that the techniques are equivalent), but there are some curious exceptions. Thus, Concentration (a "Mental functioning" variable) and Impulsiveness (a "Temperament" variable) are both derived from a combination of F and F−; examination of the respective abacs indeed reveals that one is the exact inverse of the other. There are also some oddities in terminology, the chief example being Aggressiveness (derived, incidentally, from F and M), which is defined as "the aspiration toward goals by means of well-accepted and morally developed procedures; willingness and desire to work; sense of a mature self-control with social conformity."

The points of criticism so far noted are of course of a minor nature, and it must be added that the manual for the SORT presents reasonably satisfactory reliability and validity data. On construct validity the data may be summed up by saying that in two studies of correspondence between trait ratings of employees by supervisors and on the basis of SORT, a good measure of agreement was obtained in roughly 70 per cent of cases. The author is also careful to state that the SORT is "not intended for clinical use" but is "designed to appraise and analyze vocationally significant temperament traits." In fact, he leans over backward in recommending caution and "the exercise of suspended judgement." In view of all these facts is it unfair to extend criticism on the basis of one or two unusually surprising results?

Probably not, if examination of the underlying causes calls attention to fundamental weaknesses in test construction. To take but a single case: A highly qualified psychologist received a rating of "Low" (actual *T*-score 27, or almost into the lowest 1 per cent *of the general population*) on the attribute Theoretical, defined as "facility for generalizing, capacity for abstraction"—in other words, as near as one can get to Spearman's "g." This rating is derived direct from the W score, and the palpable "incorrectness" of the rating prompted the writer to find out what are, in fact, the available W responses. Scrutiny showed that of the 62 possible W responses, no less than 25 come into categories such as "modernistic painting," "coat of arms," "squashed bug," and others which would almost certainly be regarded as in some way "unfavourable" by users of normal Rorschach. Further examination showed that to achieve a rating of "High" on Theoretical one would have to have used *at least four* of these "unfavourable" responses.

Clearly something is specifically wrong here, but more important is the wider implication that a forced choice technique which assumes that a given response can always be scored in the same way is basically fallacious. To take one further example: the response "X-ray of bony structure" to Card 1 is scored W; the subject quoted above chose this response, but referred it to a D area—which suggests that his W score (and his Theoretical rating) should really have been still further reduced! What the SORT therefore may be doing is not scoring a subject's response objectively, but guessing at what the subject meant and scoring that guess.

Can the SORT, then, be said to be "objective"? Or in more general terms, is a test objective if it is not clear to what question a particular answer has been given? Even if it were possible to frame test items in such a way as to circumvent this difficulty, a still more fundamental objection to equating SORT with Rorschach remains. Reference to Rorschach's original text shows that the object of his "experiment" was to arrive at an understanding of personality through analysis of perception, the subject's spontaneous perception and the ways in which he organizes it—not, as in the case of SORT, the way in which he handles someone else's perceptions. Stone, although conceding that a subject may experience difficulty in choosing between three interpretations all of which seem inappropriate to him, claims that something similar is done in "limits-testing." But normal Rorschach practice keeps spontaneous and forced responses quite separate, whereas in SORT the distinction is irretrievably lost. Again, SORT gives no information about creativity, *genuine* originality, nor any of the truly "subtle features" of the full Rorschach protocol. This surely is throwing the baby out with the bath water. Yet again one must recognize that Stone is aware of this; SORT, he says, "defers to the indi-

vidual protocol which....permits greater usefulness in diagnosis of deviant emotional syndromes." Unfortunately, a previous application of SORT is almost certain to contaminate one's response to normal Rorschach, and it seems a pity to run this risk when other, unrelated means of vocational assessment are available.

J Consult Psychol 23:471–2 O '59. Edward S. Bordin. * The validity of the test seems to rest mainly on two bases: first, its supposed relationship to Rorschach phenomena; second, two empirical studies. Without considerable empirical evidence, there is great room for doubt that responses to the SORT are mainly tapping perceptual phenomena analogous to its prototype. The method of test administration contains no procedures that ensure that the subject has seen the percept that he chooses nor for that matter that he has even looked at the blot. Response sets of various sorts, particularly social desirability stereotypes, are probably greatly enhanced under such circumstances. The manual gives a brief report of two unpublished validity studies. In one, the SORT increased the correlation of high school grade point average with first year grades from .59 to .68, using the best 2 of 15 scores. No cross-validation data are offered. In the other, the SORT variables are correlated with supervisors' ratings in 29 occupational groups. A suggestive but not impressive array of correlations was obtained. Again no cross-validation. This all sums up to the fact that we have here an interesting new experiment in adapting Rorschach testing techniques to the need for large scale testing and objective scoring and interpretation. But it is still *experimental,* and every effort should be made to warn against adopting it for operational use. I do not believe the "Preliminary Edition" in the title or the caution section in the manual, largely irrelevant to this issue, represent sufficient effort to emphasize the fact that this instrument is not ready for operational use.

J Counsel Psychol 6:72–3 sp '59. Laurence Siegel. * The development of an objectively scorable form of the Rorschach test specifically designed for vocational applications will be welcomed in many quarters. The S-O *Rorschach Test* is well-conceived and excellently executed. The manual is a model of clarity and organization. It is likely that the test will be extensively used for executive appraisal in industry, for vocational guidance in schools and for research purposes in countless settings wherein the personnel director, counselor or researcher wants Rorschach-type data for some non-clinical purpose. The attractiveness of the SORT format does, however, necessitate consideration of a problem that may eventually prove to be of some consequence. The fact that this test makes it possible for persons who otherwise would never have considered themselves sufficiently qualified to administer a Rorschach now to do so, means that we may anticipate increased exposure to the Rorschach blots. Persons who have taken the SORT are no longer naive with respect to the specific Rorschach content. Their resultant sophistication may be of import at some future time when they may be required to respond to the Rorschach as an aid to clinical diagnosis. Perhaps an even more serious consideration is the fact that the SORT exposes respondents not only to the Rorschach ink-blot, but also to 30 possible responses to each of these blots. How many (if indeed any) and what kinds of these responses may subsequently be parroted by the previously SORT-tested clinical respondent is a problem that merits additional research.

[243]

*Szondi Test. Ages 4 and over; 1937–61; 8 factors, 4 vectors (each vector is a total of 2 factors) : homosexual, sadistic, sexual vector, epileptic, hysteric, paroxysmal vector, catatonic, paranoic, schizophrenic vector, depressive, manic, contact vector; 1 form; 2 editions: individual, group; no data on reliability; postage extra; Lipot Szondi; Hans Huber. * (United States publisher of English-language manual and distributor of the individual test: Grune & Stratton, Inc.; United States distributor of the group test: Intercontinental Medical Book Corporation.)
a) [INDIVIDUAL] SZONDI TEST. 1937–52; 1 form ('47, 48 pictures); manual ('52, 264 pages, translated by Gertrude All, see 87 below); 10-profile form ('49, 1 page, labeled Form B) ; table of tendency tension ('49, 1 page, labeled Form C) ; record folder ('49, 3 pages, labeled Form A, a combination of Forms B and C); computing form ('47, 1 page, labeled Form D); sexual-social index form ('47, 1 page); Fr. 34 per set of pictures, 20 copies of Form B, and 10 copies of Form A; $11 per set of pictures; Fr. 8 ($3.25) per 50 copies of Form A; Fr. 8 ($3.25) per 100 copies of Form B; Fr. 2.50 per 100 copies of Form D (Grune & Stratton, Inc. sells, at $2 per 50 copies, an IBM answer sheet, labeled Form D, designed by H. P. David, but there are no scoring stencils and no instructions for using the separate answer sheet); Fr. 12 per 100 sexual-social index forms (not available in the U.S.); $14 per manual; must be administered "at least six, preferably ten, times with at least one day intervals between administrations"; (10–15) minutes per administration.
b) THE GROUP SZONDI TEST. 1961; 1 form (12 slides,

pictures identical with the 1947 pictures in the individual form) ; directions for administration (26 pages, containing instructions in English, French, and German) ; 10-profile form (1 page, labeled Form 2, identical with 1949 individual Form B) ; tendency tension quotient computing form (1 page, called form 6) ; record folder (3 pages, called form 1, identical with 1949 individual Form A) ; test behavior record (1 page, called form 5) ; computing form (1 page, called form 7) ; separate answer sheets (called form 3) must be used; Fr. 48 ($12) per set of 10 copies of form 1, 20 copies of Form 2, 100 copies of form 3, 100 copies of form 5, 100 copies of form 6, 10 copies of form 7, scoring templates, and directions; Fr. 52 ($13) per set of slides; 8–10 administrations are recommended with 2 administrations per day suggested; [15–30] minutes per administration; adapted for group administration by A. Friedemann.

REFERENCES

1–64. See 4:134.
65–138. See 5:162.
139. SCOTT, E. *The Szondi Test as a Diagnostic Instrument in Predicting Delinquency.* Doctor's thesis, University of Portland (Portland, Ore.), 1953.
140. ABEL, THEODORA M., AND METRAUX, RHODA. "Sex Differences in a Negro Peasant Community: Montserrat, B.W.I." *J Proj Tech* 23:127–33 Je '59. * (*PA* 35:4755)
141. BLAZSANYIK, J. "Psychological Impotency: A Case Analysis." *Austral J Psychol Res* 1:49–54 O '59. *
142. COULTER, WALTER M. "The Szondi Test and the Prediction of Antisocial Behavior." *J Proj Tech* 23:24–9 Mr '59. * (*PA* 34:6011)
143. HAMILTON, J. T. "A Study of Incidental Stimulus Values in the Szondi Test." *J Clin Psychol* 15:322–4 Jl '59. * (*PA* 35:3468)
144. NOLAN, EDWARD GILLIGAN. *Uniqueness in Monozygotic Twins.* Doctor's thesis, Princeton University (Princeton, N.J.), 1959. (*DA* 21:247)
145. SZONDI, LIPOT; MOSER, ULRICH; AND WEBB, MARVIN W. *The Szondi Test: Its Diagnosis, Prognosis and Treatment.* Philadelphia, Pa.: J. B. Lippincott Co., 1959. Pp. xv, 309. * (*PA* 33:10370)
146. WALDER, HANS. *Drive Structure and Criminality: Criminobiologic Investigations, Revised Edition.* Translated by Marvin W. Webb. Springfield, Ill.: Charles C Thomas, Publisher, 1959. Pp. xvii, 174. *
147. WALDER, HANS. "Crime and Destiny." *Austral J Psychol Res* 2:13–24 sp '60. *
148. BARATZ, STEPHEN S. *A Semantic Analysis of the Szondi Test.* Master's thesis, University of Kansas (Lawrence, Kan.), 1961.
149. BEARDSLEY, KATHARINE. "Analysis of Psychological Tests of Persons Diagnosed Sociopathic Personality Disturbance." *Arch Crim Psychodynam* 4:389–411 su '61. *
150. BEELI, ARMIN. "Some Psychological Aspects of Religious Formation." *Austral J Psychol Res* 2:66–79 au '61. *
151. BLAZSANYIK, J. "Separation Anxiety, Despair and Detachment During Puberty." *Austral J Psychol Res* 2:112–20 au '61. *
152. CONWAY, RONALD. "The Szondi Test: An Elementary Discussion." *Austral J Psychol Res* 2:121–4 au '61. *
153. HOLMQVIST, S. "The Reliability of the Szonditest." Abstract. *Acta Psychologica* 19:120 '61. *
154. LOGAN, JAMES C. "Szondi Profile Changes From Sorrow Arousal." *J Proj Tech* 25:184–92 Je '61. * (*PA* 36: 2HE84L)
155. MOGENSEN, ALAN, AND JUEL-NIELSEN, NIELS. "Factors Influencing the Selection and Rejection of Szondi's Pictures: A Study of Uniovular Twins Brought Up Apart." *Acta Psychiatrica Scandinavica* 37(1):32–6 '61. * (*PA* 36:4HG32M)
156. NOLAN, EDWARD G. "Szondi Test Protocols of Monozygotic and Dizygotic Twin Populations." *J Proj Tech* 25: 471–6 D '61. *
157. RAMFALK, CARL W., AND RUDHE, LENNART. "A Contradicted Hypothesis Related to Szondi's Theory: The Szondi Test as Used on Alcoholics." *Scandinavian J Psychol* 2(2): 100–4 '61. * (*PA* 36:2HI00R)
158. FANCHER, EDWIN C. "A Comparative Study of American and Hungarian Developmental Trends With the Szondi Test." *J Genetic Psychol* 101:229–53 D '62. * (*PA* 37:6467)
159. SEEMAN, WILLIAM, AND MARKS, PHILIP A. "A Study of Some 'Test Dimensions' Conceptions." *J Proj Tech* 26: 469–73 D '62. * (*PA* 37:6678)

For reviews by Ardie Lubin and Albert I. Rabin, see 4:134; for a review by Susan K.

Deri, see 3:100; for excerpts from related book reviews, see B474, B501, 5:B418, and 4:135.

[244]

★**Ten Silhouettes.** Ages 5 and over; 1959–60; individual; 1 form ['60, 10 cards]; directions for administering ['60, 2 pages]; no data on reliability and validity; no norms; 63s. per set of testing materials, postpaid; [45] minutes; B. E. Dockar-Drysdale; the Author. *

REFERENCES

1. DRYSDALE, B. E. DOCKAR. "Notes on the History of the Development of a Projection Technique 'The Silhouettes.'" *Acta Psychologica* 16(3):157–64 '59. * (PA 34:5935)
2. RUDOLPH, RIGMOR. "The Silhouette Test." *Acta Psychologica* 16(1):25–43 '59. * (PA 34:3023)
3. RUDOLPH, RIGMOR. "The Silhouette Test." *Nordisk Psykologi* 11(1):25–44 '59. * (PA 34:1415)
4. SMITH, B. BABINGTON. "Ten Silhouettes: An Account of Perceptual and Procedural Problems Encountered in the Development of a Fresh Projective Technique." *Acta Psychologica* 16(3):165–77 '59. * (PA 34:5983)

[245]

Thematic Apperception Test. Ages 4 and over; 1936–43; commonly known as TAT; individual; 1 form ('43, 20 cards); manual ('43, 20 pages); no data on reliability; $6 per set of testing materials; 50¢ per manual; cash orders postpaid; 100(120) minutes in 2 sessions 1 day apart; Henry A. Murray; Harvard University Press. * (*Bellak TAT Blank.* 1947–51; 1 form ('47, 6 pages); analysis sheet ('47, 2 pages); manual ('51, 10 pages); $1.25 per 10 blanks; $1.75 per 100 analysis sheets; 35¢ per manual; 60¢ per specimen set of 1 blank, 10 analysis sheets, and manual; postpaid; Leopold Bellak; Psychological Corporation. *)

REFERENCES

1–101. See 3:103.
102–299. See 4:136.
300–610. See 5:164.
611. GUREL, L. *Quantitative Differences in Responses to Twenty Stimulus Cards of the Thematic Apperception Test.* Master's thesis, Purdue University (Lafayette, Ind.), 1950.
612. FISHER, SEYMOUR, AND HINDS, EDITH. "The Organization of Hostility Controls in Various Personality Structures." *Genetic Psychol Monogr* 44:3–68 Ag '51. * (PA 26:2889)
613. RAPAPORT, DAVID. "Projective Techniques and the Theory of Thinking." *J Proj Tech* 16:269–75 S '52. * (PA 28:2254)
614. SHANMUGAM, T. E. "Characteristics of Adolescent Girls Fantasy." *J Madras Univ* 22(1):119–28 '52. *
615. SCHNECK, JEROME, AND KLINE, MILTON V. "The H-T-P and TAT Hypnodiagnostic Studies." *Brit J Med Hypnosis* 5:3–15 au '53. *
616. FITZGERALD, BERNARD JOSEPH. *The Relationship of Two Projective Measures to a Sociometric Measure of Dependent Behavior.* Doctor's thesis, Ohio State University (Columbus, Ohio), 1954. (DA 20:2380)
617. HENRY, WILLIAM E. "Trukese T.A.T.'s." Letter. *Am Anthrop* 56:889 O '54. *
618. BARRON, FRANK. "The Disposition Toward Originality." *J Abn & Social Psychol* 51:478–85 N '55. * (PA 31:2533)
619. NORGARB, BRIAN N. "Psychodiagnostic Testing and Hypnosis." *J Clin & Exp Hypnosis* 3:44–8 Ja '55. * (PA 29:8624)
620. BOLTON, RITA J. *A Comparison of the T.A.T. and the Michigan Picture Test With Adolescents.* Master's thesis, Cornell University (Ithaca, N.Y.), 1956.
621. CARTWRIGHT, ROSALIND DYMOND; SEEMAN, JULIUS; AND GRUMMON, DONALD L. "Patterns of Perceived Interpersonal Relations." *Sociometry* 19:166–77 Mr '56. * (PA 31:8009)
622. CAUDILL, WILLIAM, AND DE VOS, GEORGE. "Achievement, Culture and Personality: The Case of the Japanese Americans." *Am Anthrop* 58:1102–26 D '56. *
623. LEARY, TIMOTHY; WITH THE COLLABORATION OF HELEN LANE, ANNE APFELBAUM, MARY DELLA CIOPPA, AND CHARLOTTE KAUFMANN. *Multilevel Measurement of Interpersonal Behavior: A Manual for the Use of the Interpersonal System of Personality.* Berkeley, Calif.: Psychological Consultation Service, 1956. Pp. vii, 110. *
624. ROTHNEY, JOHN W. M., AND HEIMANN, ROBERT A. "Development and Applications of Projective Technics." *R Ed Res* 26:56–71 F '56. * (PA 31:6127)
625. SHNEIDMAN, EDWIN S. Chap. 17; "Some Relationships Between the Rorschach Technique and Other Psychodiagnostic Tests," pp. 595–642. In *Developments in the Rorschach Technique: Volume 2, Fields of Application.* By Bruno Klopfer and others. Yonkers, N.Y.: World Book Co., 1956. Pp. xx, 828. * (PA 30:7202)
626. VENTUR, PIERRE; KRANSDORFF, MORRIS; AND KLINE, MILTON V. "A Differential Study of Emotional Attitudes Toward Hypnosis With Card 12M of the Thematic Apperception Test." *Brit J Med Hypnosis* 8:5–16 w '56–57. *
627. ZUK, GERALD H. "The Influence of Social Context on Impulse and Control Tendencies in Preadolescence." *Genetic Psychol Monogr* 54:117–66 N '56. * (PA 33:3464)
628. GUNDLACH, RALPH. "Research With Projective Techniques." *J Proj Tech* 21:350–4 D '57. *
629. MCNEIL, ELTON B., AND COHLER, J. ROBERT, JR. "The Effect of Personal Needs on Counselors' Perception and Behavior." *Papers Mich Acad Sci Arts & Letters* 42:281–8 pt 2 '57. * (PA 37:6924)
630. TAKALA, MARTTI; PIHKANEN, TOIVO A.; AND MARKKANEN, TOUKO. *The Effects of Distilled and Brewed Beverages: A Physiological, Neurological, and Psychological Study.* The Finnish Foundation for Alcoholic Studies, No. 4. Stockholm, Sweden: Almqvist & Wiksell, 1957. Pp. 195. * (PA 31:4890)
631. "The Personality of Duodenal Ulcer Patients: A Note on Mr. V. B. Kanter's Investigation of T.A.T. Material." *Rorsch Newsl* 3:8 Je '58. *
632. ABEGGLEN, JAMES C. "Personality Factors in Social Mobility: A Study of Occupationally Mobile Businessmen." *Genetic Psychol Monogr* 58:101–59 Ag '58. * (PA 34:990)
633. ANDERSON, DARRELL EDWARD. *Personality Variables and Verbal Conditioning.* Doctor's thesis, University of Nebraska (Lincoln, Neb.), 1958. (DA 19:1811)
634. ATKINSON, JOHN W., EDITOR. *Motives in Fantasy, Action, and Society: A Method of Assessment and Study.* Princeton, N.J.: D. Van Nostrand Co., Inc., 1958. Pp. xv, 873. * (PA 33:758)
635. CALOGERAS, ROY C. "Some Relationships Between Fantasy and Self-Report Behavior." *Genetic Psychol Monogr* 58:273–325 N '58. * (PA 34:2028)
636. CARR, ARTHUR C. Chap. 4, "The Psychodiagnostic Test Battery: Rationale and Methodology," pp. 28–39. In *Progress in Clinical Psychology, Vol. 3.* Edited by Daniel Brower and Lawrence E. Abt. New York: Grune & Stratton, Inc., 1958. Pp. vi, 249. * (PA 33:8255)
637. CLIFFORD, PAUL I. "Emotional Contacts With the External World Manifested by a Selected Group of Highly Creative Chemists and Mathematicians." *Percept & Motor Skills* 8:3–26 Mr '58. * (PA 33:3039)
638. DAVIDS, ANTHONY, AND PILDNER, HENRY, JR. "Comparison of Direct and Projective Methods of Personality Assessment Under Different Conditions of Motivation." *Psychol Monogr* 72(11):1–30 '58. * (PA 33:9937)
639. DILWORTH, TOM, IV. "A Comparison of the Edwards PPS Variables With Some Aspects of the TAT." Abstract. *J Consult Psychol* 22:486 D '58. * (PA 33:10321)
640. DILWORTH, TOM, IV. *A Comparison of the Edwards Personal Preference Schedule Variables With Some Aspects of the Thematic Apperception Test.* Master's thesis, Southern Methodist University (Dallas, Tex.), 1958.
641. EIDUSON, BERNICE T. "Artist and Nonartist: A Comparative Study." *J Personality* 26:13–28 Mr '58. * (PA 33:5807)
642. FISHER, RHODA LEE. "The Effect of a Disturbing Situation Upon the Stability of Various Projective Tests." *Psychol Monogr* 72(14):1–23 '58. * (PA 34:1357)
643. FISHER, SEYMOUR, AND CLEVELAND, SIDNEY E. *Body Images and Personality.* Princeton, N.J.: D. Van Nostrand Co., Inc., 1958. Pp. xi, 420. * (PA 32:3926)
644. GUREL, LEE, AND ULLMANN, LEONARD P. "Quantitative Differences in Response to TAT Cards: The Relationship Between Transcendence Score and Number of Emotional Words." *J Proj Tech* 22:399–401 D '58. * (PA 34:1369)
645. HEATH, DOUGLAS. "Projective Tests as Measures of Defensive Activity." *J Proj Tech* 22:284–92 S '58. * (PA 33:10333)
646. HOKANSON, JACK E., AND GORDON, JESSE E. "The Expression and Inhibition of Hostility in Imaginative and Overt Behavior." *J Abn & Social Psychol* 57:327–33 N '58. * (PA 33:10523)
647. HOLT, ROBERT R., AND LUBORSKY, LESTER; WITH THE COLLABORATION OF WILLIAM R. MORROW, DAVID RAPAPORT, AND SIBYLLE K. ESCALONA. *Personality Patterns of Psychiatrists: A Study of Methods for Selecting Residents, Vol. 1.* New York: Basic Books, Inc., 1958. Pp. xiv, 386. * (PA 33:5751)
648. KANTER, V. B., AND WILLIAMS, CELIA. "The Interaction of Emotional and Organic Factors in the Rorschach and T.A.T. Records of a Male Alcoholic Aged 60." *Rorsch Newsl* 3:12–3 D '58. *
649. LEICHTY, MARY M. *The Absence of the Father During Early Childhood and Its Effect Upon the Oedipal Situation as Reflected in Young Adults.* Doctor's thesis, Michigan State University (East Lansing, Mich.), 1958. (DA 19:1821)
650. LUBIN, BERNARD. *Some Effects of Set and Stimulus Properties on Thematic Apperception Test Stories and on Resulting Clinical Judgment.* Doctor's thesis, Pennsylvania State University (University Park, Pa.), 1958. (DA 19:181)
651. LYLE, J. G., AND GILCHRIST, A. A. "Problems of T.A.T.

Interpretation and the Diagnosis of Delinquent Trends." *Brit J Med Psychol* 31:51–9 pt 1 '58. * *(PA* 33:8371)

652. McCANDLISH, LEO ALEXANDER. *An Investigation of a New Method of T.A.T. Analysis.* Doctor's thesis, Loyola University (Chicago, Ill.), 1958.

653. MARKHAM, SYLVIA. "The Dynamics of Post-Partum Pathological Reactions as Revealed in Psychological Tests." *J Hillside Hosp* 7:178–89 Jl–O '58. * *(PA* 34:3011)

654. NEUGARTEN, BERNICE L., AND GUTMANN, DAVID L. "Age-Sex Roles and Personality in Middle Age: A Thematic Apperception Study." *Psychol Monogr* 72(17):1–33 '58. * *(PA* 33:10103)

655. ROSENFELD, IRWIN JOSEPH. *Mathematical Ability as a Function of Perceptual Field-Dependency and Certain Personality Variables.* Doctor's thesis, University of Oklahoma (Norman, Okla.), 1958. *(DA* 19:880)

656. SAFIAN, MURRAY Z. *A Study of Certain Psychological Factors in the Rehabilitation of Potentially Employable Homebound Adults.* Doctor's thesis, New York University (New York, N.Y.), 1958. *(DA* 19:3372)

657. SANO, KATSUO, AND MAKITA, HITOSHI. "Fundamental Requirements for the Construction of TAT." *Jap Psychol Res* 1:22–34 Jl '58. *

658. SHANMUGAM, T. E. "Sex Delinquent Women and Their Fantasies." *J Psychol Res* 2(2):77–82 '58. * *(PA* 33:6591)

659. SHEEHAN, JOSEPH G. "Projective Studies of Stuttering." *J Speech & Hearing Disorders* 23:18–25 F '58. *

660. SINGER, MARGARET THALER, AND SCHEIN, EDGAR H. "Projective Test Responses of Prisoners of War Following Repatriation." *Psychiatry* 21:375–85 N '58. * *(PA* 33:10113)

661. ZUCKERMAN, MARVIN, AND GROSZ, HANUS J. "Suggestibility and Dependency." Abstract. *J Consult Psychol* 22:328 O '58. * *(PA* 34:1435)

662. BUDNOFF, CHRISTINE K. *Awareness of Identification as a Factor on the TAT: A Proposed Modification of the Administration of the TAT.* Master's thesis, City College of New York (New York, N.Y.), 1959.

663. CLEVELAND, SIDNEY E. "Personality Dynamics in Torticollis." *J Nerv & Mental Dis* 129:150–61 Ag '59. * *(PA* 34:6407)

664. DANA, RICHARD H. "American Culture and Chinese Personality." *Psychol Newsl* 10:314–21 My–Je '59. * *(PA* 34:1213)

665. DANA, RICHARD H. "The Perceptual Organization TAT Score: Number, Order, and Frequency of Components." *J Proj Tech* 23:307–10 S '59. * *(PA* 35:4906)

666. DANA, RICHARD H. "Proposal for Objective Scoring of the TAT." *Percept & Motor Skills* 9:27–43 Mr '59. * *(PA* 34:1347)

667. DANA, RICHARD H., AND CHRISTIANSEN, KENNETH. "Repression and Psychopathology." *J Proj Tech* 23:412–6 D '59. * *(PA* 35:4981)

668. EASTON, JUDITH C. "Some Personality Traits of Underachieving and Achieving High School Students of Superior Ability." *B Maritime Psychol Assn* 8:34–9 Ap '59. * *(PA* 34:4786)

669. FISHER, SEYMOUR; BOYD, INA; WALKER, DONALD; AND SHEER, DIANNE. "Parents of Schizophrenics, Neurotics, and Normals." *A.M.A. Arch Gen Psychiatry* 1:149–66 Ag '59. * *(PA* 34:6184)

670. FOULDS, G. A. "The Relative Stability of Personality Measures Compared With Diagnostic Measures." *J Mental Sci* 105:783–7 Jl '59. * *(PA* 34:6016)

671. GREENWALD, ALAN F. "Affective Complexity and Psychotherapy." *J Proj Tech* 23:429–35 D '59. * *(PA* 35:5070)

672. GUILFORD, J. P. *Personality,* pp. 299–303. New York: McGraw-Hill Book Co., Inc., 1959. Pp. xiii, 562. *

673. HARTMAN, A. A. "Personality Factors in Perceptual Distortion." *J General Psychol* 61:181–8 Jl '59. * *(PA* 35:798)

674. HEIMANN, ROBERT A., AND ROTHNEY, JOHN W. M. "Development and Applications of Projective Techniques." *R Ed Res* 29:73–83 F '59. * *(PA* 34:6021)

675. HENRY, WILLIAM E., AND FARLEY, JANE. "A Study in Validation of the Thematic Apperception Test." *J Proj Tech* 23:273–7 S '59. * *(PA* 35:4920)

676. HENRY, WILLIAM E., AND FARLEY, JANE. "The Validity of the Thematic Apperception Test in the Study of Adolescent Personality." *Psychol Monogr* 73(17):1–40 '59. * *(PA* 35:694)

677. JENSEN, ARTHUR R. "The Reliability of Projective Techniques: Review of the Literature." *Acta Psychologica* 16(1):108–36 '59. * *(PA* 34:5956)

678. KAGAN, JEROME. "The Stability of TAT Fantasy and Stimulus Ambiguity." *J Consult Psychol* 23:266–71 Je '59. * *(PA* 34:4385)

679. KAGAN, JEROME, AND MOSS, HOWARD A. "Stability and Validity of Achievement Fantasy." *J Abn & Social Psychol* 58:357–64 My '59. * *(PA* 34:6027)

680. KOENIG, KATHRYN, AND McKEACHIE, W. J. "Personality and Independent Study." *J Ed Psychol* 50:132–4 Je '59. * *(PA* 35:1201)

681. LEBO, DELL. "An Empirical Approach to Problems Concerning the Diagnostic Value of a Pictureless TAT." *J Proj Tech* 23:107 Mr '59. *

682. LEBO, DELL, AND SHERRY, P. JAMES. "Visual and Vocal Presentation of TAT Descriptions." *J Proj Tech* 23:59–63 Mr '59. *

683. LINDZEY, GARDNER, AND SILVERMAN, MORTON. "Thematic Apperception Test: Techniques of Group Administra-

tion, Sex Differences, and the Role of Verbal Productivity." *J Personality* 27:311–23 S '59. * *(PA* 34:6031)

684. LINDZEY, GARDNER; BRADFORD, JEAN; TEJESSY, CHARLOTTE; AND DAVIDS, ANTHONY. *The Thematic Apperception Test: An Interpretive Lexicon for Clinician and Investigator.* Journal of Clinical Psychology Monograph Supplement No. 12. Brandon, Vt.: Journal of Clinical Psychology, April 1959. Pp. 98. *

685. LITTLE, KENNETH B., AND SHNEIDMAN, EDWIN S. "Congruencies Among Interpretations of Psychological Test and Anamnestic Data." *Psychol Monogr* 73(6):1–42 '59. * *(PA* 34:3010)

686. LYNN, DAVID B. "Ambiguity and Projection." *Psychol Newsl* 10:289–94 My–Je '59. * *(PA* 34:1393)

687. MACBRAYER, CAROLINE TAYLOR. "Relationship Between Story Length and Situational Validity of the TAT." *J Proj Tech* 23:345–50 S '59. * *(PA* 35:4930)

688. MACHOVER, SOLOMON, AND PUZZO, FRANK S. "Clinical and Objective Studies of Personality Variables in Alcoholism: 2, Clinical Study of Personality Correlates of Remission From Active Alcoholism." *Q J Studies Alcohol* 20:520–7 S '59. * *(PA* 34:6253)

689. MADDOX, GEORGE L., AND JENNINGS, AUDREY M. "An Analysis of Fantasy: An Exploratory Study of Social Definitions of Alcohol and Its Use by Means of a Projective Technique." *Q J Studies Alcohol* 20:334–45 Je '59. * *(PA* 34:5852)

690. MAGNUSSON, DAVID. *A Study of Ratings Based on TAT.* Swedish Council for Personnel Administration, Report No. 22. Stockholm, Sweden: Almqvist & Wiksell, 1959. Pp. 176. * *(PA* 34:1394)

691. MOTTO, JOSEPH J. "The TAT in the Counseling Process." *Voc Guid Q* 8:29–37 au '59. *

692. MURSTEIN, BERNARD I., AND WHEELER, JOHN I., JR. "The Projection of Hostility on the Rorschach and Thematic Stories Test." *J Clin Psychol* 15:316–9 Jl '59. * *(PA* 35:3474)

693. NOLAN, EDWARD GILLIGAN. *Uniqueness in Monozygotic Twins.* Doctor's thesis, Princeton University (Princeton, N.J.), 1959. *(DA* 21:247)

694. PECK, ROBERT F. "Measuring the Mental Health of Normal Adults." *Genetic Psychol Monogr* 60:197–255 N '59. * *(PA* 34:5913)

695. PETRAUSKAS, FRANCIS BERNARD. *A TAT and Picture-Frustration Study of Naval Offenders and Nonoffenders.* Doctor's thesis, Loyola University (Chicago, Ill.), 1959.

696. PHARES, E. JERRY. "The Relationship Between TAT Responses and Leaving-the-Field Behavior." *J Clin Psychol* 15:328–30 Jl '59. * *(PA* 35:3475)

697. PILE, EVERETT; MISCHEL, WALTER; AND BERNSTEIN, LEWIS. "A Note on Remoteness of TAT Figures as an Interpretive Concept." *J Consult Psychol* 23:252–5 Je '59. * *(PA* 34:4402)

698. PINE, FRED. "Thematic Drive Content and Creativity." *J Personality* 27:136–51 Je '59. * *(PA* 34:4026)

699. SCODEL, ALVIN; RATOOSH, PHILBURN; AND MINAS, J. SAYER. "Some Personality Correlates of Decision Making Under Conditions of Risk." *Behav Sci* 4:19–28 Ja '59. * *(PA* 34:1057)

700. SEMEONOFF, BORIS. "An Analysis of the Counsellor Personality." *Rorsch Newsl* 4:13–20 Je '59. *

701. SHELDON, M. STEPHEN; COALE, JACK M.; AND COPPLE, ROCKNE. "Concurrent Validity of the 'Warm Teacher Scale.'" *J Ed Psychol* 50:37–40 F '59. * *(PA* 35:2810)

702. SHELLEY, ERNEST L. V. *The Effect of an Organized Counseling Program on the Anti-Social Themes Elicited by the Thematic Apperception Test From Youthful Prison Inmates.* Doctor's thesis, Michigan State University (East Lansing, Mich.), 1959. *(DA* 21:3528)

703. SILVERMAN, LLOYD H. "A Q-Sort Study of the Validity of Evaluations Made From Projective Techniques." *Psychol Monogr* 73(7):1–28 '59. * *(PA* 34:3030)

704. SILVERSTEIN, A. B. "Identification With Same-Sex and Opposite-Sex Figures in Thematic Apperception." *J Proj Tech* 23:73–5 Mr '59. *

705. SOLKOFF, NORMAN. "Effects of a Variation in Instructions and Pictorial Stimuli on Responses to TAT-Like Cards." *J Proj Tech* 23:76–82 Mr '59. *

706. TRICE, HARRISON M. "The Affiliation Motive and Readiness to Join Alcoholics Anonymous." *Q J Studies Alcohol* 20:313–20 Je '59. * *(PA* 34:6283)

707. VIITAMAKI, R. OLAVI. *Psychometric Analysis of the Thematic Apperception Test: With Reference to Personality Structure and School Success in Adolescence.* Annals of the Finnish Academy of Science and Letters, Series B, Vol. 115, Part 2. Helsinki, Finland: Suomalainen Tiedeakatemia, Academiae Scientiarum Fennicae, 1959. Pp. 61. * *(PA* 38:4332)

708. CAINE, T. M. "The Expression of Hostility and Guilt in Melancholic and Paranoid Women." *J Consult Psychol* 24:18–22 F '60. * *(PA* 34:7967)

709. CHOWDHURY, UMA. "An Indian Modification of the Thematic Apperception Test." *J Social Psychol* 51:245–63 My '60. * *(PA* 34:7764)

710. DANA, RICHARD H. "Objective TAT Scores and Personality Characteristics: Perceptual Organization (PO)." *Percept & Motor Skills* 10:154 Ap '60. * *(PA* 35:6436)

711. DANA, RICHARD H., AND GOOCHER, BUELL. "Pessimism Reaffirmed: A Reply to Witkin." *Percept & Motor Skills* 11:243–4 D '60. * *(PA* 35:2206)

712. DAVIDS, ANTHONY, AND DeVAULT, SPENCER. "Use of the TAT and Human Figure Drawings in Research on Personality, Pregnancy, and Perception." *J Proj Tech* 24:362–5 D '60. * (*PA* 35:4872)

713. De VOS, GEORGE. "The Relation of Guilt Toward Parents to Achievement and Arranged Marriage Among the Japanese." *Psychiatry* 23:287–301 Ag '60. * (*PA* 36:4GB87D)

714. DOLLIN, ADELAIDE POLIZZOTTO. *The Effect of Order of Presentation on Perception of TAT Pictures.* Doctor's thesis, University of Connecticut (Storrs, Conn.), 1960. (*DA* 21:1999)

715. DREGER, RALPH MASON. "The Relation Between Rorschach *M* and TAT Content Categories as Measures of Creative Productivity in a Representative High-Level Intelligence Population." *J General Psychol* 63:29–33 Jl '60. * (*PA* 35:6437)

716. FAETH, HAROLD WILLIAM, JR. *The Discrepancy Between Self-Ideal Self Concepts as Needs Projected to Thematic Apperception Test Pictures.* Doctor's thesis, Purdue University (Lafayette, Ind.), 1960. (*DA* 21:1999)

717. FISHER, SEYMOUR, AND FISHER, RHODA LEE. "A Projective Test Analysis of Ethnic Subculture Themes in Families." *J Proj Tech* 24: 366–9 D '60. * (*PA* 35:4760)

718. GARCIA-PALMIERI, RAFAEL A. *Autonomic Response Specificity and Anxiety.* Doctor's thesis, Louisiana State University (Baton Rouge, La.), 1960. (*DA* 21:2364)

719. GOLDSTEIN, MICHAEL J., AND BARTHOL, RICHARD P. "Fantasy Responses to Subliminal Stimuli." *J Abn & Social Psychol* 60:22–6 Ja '60. * (*PA* 34:6932)

720. HAFNER, A. JACK, AND KAPLAN, ARTHUR M. "Hostility Content Analysis of the Rorschach and TAT." *J Proj Tech* 24:137–43 Je '60. * (*PA* 35:4918)

721. HAMMER, EMANUEL F. "An Exploratory Investigation of the Personalities of Creative Adolescent Students." Discussion by Margaret Naumberg. *Studies Art Ed* 1:42–72 sp '60. *

722. HENRY, WILLIAM E. "The Thematic Apperception Test," pp. 18–29, 106–15. In *The Prediction of Overt Behavior Through the Use of Projective Techniques.* Edited by Arthur C. Carr. Springfield, Ill.: Charles C Thomas, Publisher, 1960. Pp. xiii, 177. * (*PA* 36:2HG77C)

723. JOHN, LaVERD. *The Relationship of the Achievement Motives as Projected Into Thematic Apperception Stories to Children's School Achievement.* Doctor's thesis, Utah State University (Logan, Utah), 1960. (*DA* 21:2985)

724. KAGAN, JEROME. Chap. 6, "Thematic Apperceptive Techniques With Children," pp. 105–29. In *Projective Techniques With Children.* Edited by Albert I. Rabin and Mary R. Haworth. New York: Grune & Stratton, Inc., 1960. Pp. xiii, 392. * (*PA* 35:2229)

725. KAGAN, JEROME; MOSS, HOWARD A.; AND SIGEL, IRVING E. "Conceptual Style and the Use of Affect Labels." *Merrill-Palmer Q* 6:261–78 Jl '60. *

726. KAHN, MARVIN W. "Psychological Test Study of a Mass Murderer." *J Proj Tech* 24:148–60 Je '60. * (*PA* 35:5213)

727. KOHN, HUGH. "Some Personality Variables Associated With Binocular Rivalry." *Psychol Rec* 10:9–13 Ja '60. * (*PA* 34:7853)

728. KRUMBEIN, ELIEZER. *Reliability of Techniques for Scoring T.A.T. Responses and Rating Predicted Executive Behavior: A Study of Advertising Agency Executives.* Doctor's thesis, Northwestern University (Evanston, Ill.), 1960. (*DA* 21:1256)

729. LEBO, DELL. "The Development and Employment of VTAT's or Pictureless TAT's." *J Psychol* 50:197–204 O '60. * (*PA* 35:6443)

730. LUBIN, BERNARD. "Some Effects of Set and Stimulus Properties on TAT Stories." *J Proj Tech* 24:11–6 Mr '60. * (*PA* 35:802)

731. MARUI, FUMIO. "A Normative Study on TAT: Chiefly on Emotional Tone, Outcome and Shift." English abstract. *Jap J Psychol* 31:93–4 Jl '60. *

732. MASLING, JOSEPH. "The Influence of Situational and Interpersonal Variables in Projective Testing." *Psychol B* 57:65–85 Ja '60. * (*PA* 34:7788)

733. MUMMERY, WILLIAM JAMES. *An Investigation of Conformity as It Relates to Ways of Handling Hostility.* Doctor's thesis, University of Oklahoma (Norman, Okla.), 1960. (*DA* 21:241)

734. MURSTEIN, BERNARD I. "The Effect of Long-Term Illness of Children on the Emotional Adjustment of Parents." *Child Develop* 31:157–71 Mr '60. *

735. MURSTEIN, BERNARD I. "The Measurement of Ambiguity for Thematic Cards." *J Proj Tech* 24:419–23 D '60. * (*PA* 35:4933)

736. NI, LIAN. "Study on the Concealment of Subjects in Telling Stories on TAT Pictures." *Acta Psychologica Taiwanica* (2):1–6 Mr '60. * (*PA* 38:8560)

737. O'CONNOR, PATRICIA ANN CLAIRE. *The Representation of the Motive to Avoid Failure in Thematic Apperception.* Doctor's thesis, University of Michigan (Ann Arbor, Mich.), 1960. (*DA* 20:4708)

738. PECK, ROBERT F. "Personality Factors in Adjustment to Aging." *Geriatrics* 15:124–30 F '60. * (*PA* 35:4747)

739. PERRY, C. W. "Some Properties of T.A.T. Influencing Response." Abstract. *Austral J Psychol* 12:237–8 D '60. *

740. PINE, FRED. "A Manual for Rating Drive Content in the Thematic Apperception Test." *J Proj Tech* 24:32–45 Mr '60. * (*PA* 35:804)

741. PINE, FRED, AND HOLT, ROBERT R. "Creativity and Primary Process: A Study of Adaptive Regression." *J Abn & Social Psychol* 61:370–9 N '60. * (*PA* 36:2HD70P)

742. RICHARDS, THOMAS W. "Personality of Subjects Who Volunteer for Research on a Drug (Mescaline)." *J Proj Tech* 24:424–8 D '60. * (*PA* 35:4554)

743. ROSEN, JACQUELINE L., AND NEUGARTEN, BERNICE L. "Ego Functions in the Middle and Later Years: A Thematic Apperception Study of Normal Adults." *J Gerontol* 15:62–7 Ja '60. * (*PA* 35:6242)

744. ROSENBLATT, DANIEL. "Responses of Former Soviet Citizens to Selected TAT Cards." *J General Psychol* 62:273–84 Ap '60. * (*PA* 34:7657)

745. SCHAFER, ROY. "Representations of Perceiving and Acting in Psychological Test Responses," pp. 291–312. (*PA* 35:850) In *Festschrift for Gardner Murphy.* Edited by John G. Peatman and Eugene L. Hartley. New York: Harper & Brothers, 1960. Pp. xi, 411. *

746. SCODEL, ALVIN; RATOOSH, PHILBURN; AND MINAS, J. SAYER. "Some Personality Correlates of Decision Making Under Conditions of Risk," pp. 37–49. In *Decisions, Values and Groups: Reports From the First Interdisciplinary Conference in the Behavioral Science Division Held at the University of New Mexico, Vol. I.* Edited by Dorothy Willner. Sponsored by the Air Force Office of Scientific Research. New York: Pergamon Press, 1960. Pp. xxix, 348. * (*PA* 36:5CP48W)

747. SCOTT, EDWARD M. "Psychological Examination of Quadruplets." *Psychol Rep* 6:281–2 Ap '60. * (*PA* 35:5980)

748. SOLKOFF, NORMAN. "Effects of a Variation in Instructions on Responses to TAT Cards." *J Proj Tech* 24:67–70 Mr '60. * (*PA* 35:808)

749. STARR, SHELDON. *The Relationship Between Hostility-Ambiguity of the TAT Cards, Hostile Fantasy, and Hostile Behavior.* Doctor's thesis, Washington State University (Pullman, Wash.), 1960. (*DA* 21:2372)

750. ANASTASI, ANNE. *Psychological Testing, Second Edition,* pp. 573–8. New York: Macmillan Co., 1961. Pp. xiii, 657. * (*PA* 36:1HA57A)

751. BELLAK, LEOPOLD; SALK, LEE; AND ROSENHAN, DAVID. "A Process Study of the Effects of Deprol on Depression: Exemplification of a Method of Psychodynamic Process Study of Psychotropic Drugs." *J Nerv & Mental Dis* 132:531–8 Je '61. *

752. BLENDSTRUP, UFFE, AND NIELSEN, GERHARD S. "Transcendence in the TAT." *Scandinavian J Psychol* 2(2):105–12 '61. * (*PA* 36:2HG05B)

753. BRAYER, RICHARD; CRAIG, GRACE; AND TEICHNER, WARREN. "Scaling Difficulty Values of TAT Cards." *J Proj Tech* 25:272–6 S '61. * (*PA* 36:3HG72B)

754. BRENNER, MARLIN SYDNEY. *The Relationship Between TAT Hostility and Overt Hostile Behavior as a Function of Self Reported Anxiety.* Doctor's thesis, Columbia University (New York, N.Y.), 1961. (*DA* 22:637)

755. CLEVELAND, SIDNEY E. "Personality Patterns Associated With the Professions of Dietitian and Nurse." *J Health & Human Behav* 2:113–24 su '61. * (*PA* 36:3AK13C)

756. CONRAD, WALTER KARR. *Prediction of TAT Imagery From Measures of Arousal.* Doctor's thesis, University of California (Berkeley, Calif.), 1961.

757. CUMMING, ELAINE, AND HENRY, WILLIAM E. *Growing Old: The Process of Disengagement.* New York: Basic Books, Inc., 1961. Pp. xvi, 293. *

758. DANA, RICHARD H., AND MUELLER, DONALD J. "Congruent Validation of a TAT Score: Perceptual Organization." *J Psychol Studies* 12:150–7 Jl '61 [issued Mr '63]. *

759. DAVIDS, ANTHONY; DeVAULT, SPENCER; AND TALMADGE, MAX. "Psychological Study of Emotional Factors in Pregnancy: A Preliminary Report." *Psychosom Med* 23:93–103 Mr–Ap '61. * (*PA* 36:3JU93D)

760. DOLLIN, ADELAIDE, AND REZNIKOFF, MARVIN. "TAT Stories and the Social Desirability Variable." *Percept & Motor Skills* 13:281–2 D '61. *

761. EWALD, HATTIE HOFF. *The Relationship of Scores on the Differential Aptitude Tests to Scholarship in High School and College.* Doctor's thesis, State University of South Dakota (Vermillion, S.D.), 1961. (*DA* 22:880)

762. FESHBACH, SEYMOUR. "The Influence of Drive Arousal and Conflict Upon Fantasy Behavior," pp. 119–40. Discussion by Kenneth Purcell and others, pp. 141–52. In *Contemporary Issues in Thematic Apperceptive Methods.* Edited by Jerome Kagan and Gerald S. Lesser. Springfield, Ill.: Charles C Thomas, Publisher, 1961. Pp. xiv, 328. * (*PA* 36:1HG28K)

763. FINE, REUBEN. "The Case of El: The MAPS Test." *J Proj Tech* 25:383–9 D '61. *

764. FISHER, GARY M., AND SHOTWELL, ANNA M. "Preference Rankings of the Thematic Apperception Test Cards by Adolescent Normals, Delinquents and Mental Retardates." *J Proj Tech* 25:41–3 Mr '61. * (*PA* 36:1HG41F)

765. FORER, BERTRAM R. "The Case of El: Vocational Choice." *J Proj Tech* 25:371–4 D '61. *

766. FORSYTH, RALPH P., AND FAIRWEATHER, GEORGE W. "Psychotherapeutic and Other Hospital Treatment Criteria: The Dilemma." *J Abn & Social Psychol* 62:598–604 My '61. * (*PA* 36:4IE98F)

767. FREED, GRIFFITH OSLER. *A Projective Test Study of*

Creativity in College Students in Visual Arts. Doctor's thesis, University of Michigan (Ann Arbor, Mich.), 1961. (*DA* 22: 640)

768. HAMMER, EMANUEL F. "Emotional Instability and Creativity." *Percept & Motor Skills* 12:102 F '61. * (*PA* 35: 6439)

769. HASKELL, ROYAL J., JR. "Relationship Between Aggressive Behavior and Psychological Tests." *J Proj Tech* 25: 431–40 D '61. *

770. HOLT, ROBERT R. "The Nature of TAT Stories as Cognitive Products: A Psychoanalytic Approach," pp. 3–43. Discussion by Silvan S. Tomkins and others, pp. 44–50. In *Contemporary Issues in Thematic Apperceptive Methods.* Edited by Jerome Kagan and Gerald S. Lesser. Springfield, Ill.: Charles C Thomas, Publisher, 1961. Pp. xiv, 328. * (*PA* 36:1HG28K)

771. KAGAN, JEROME. "Stylistic Variables in Fantasy Behavior: The Ascription of Affect States to Social Stimuli," pp. 196–220. Discussion by Irving E. Sigel and others, pp. 221–8. In *Contemporary Issues in Thematic Apperceptive Methods.* Edited by Jerome Kagan and Gerald S. Lesser. Springfield, Ill.: Charles C Thomas, Publisher, 1961. Pp. xiv, 328. * (*PA* 36:1HG28K)

772. KAGAN, JEROME, AND LESSER, GERALD S., EDITORS. *Contemporary Issues in Thematic Apperceptive Methods.* Springfield, Ill.: Charles C Thomas, Publisher, 1961. Pp. xiv, 328. * (*PA* 36:1HG28K)

773. KAGAN, JEROME, AND MOSS, HOWARD A. "The Availability of Conflictful Ideas: A Neglected Parameter in Assessing Projective Test Responses." *J Personality* 29:217–34 Je '61. * (*PA* 36:4HG17K)

774. KENNY, DOUGLAS T. "A Theoretical and Research Reappraisal of Stimulus Factors in the TAT," pp. 288–310. Discussion by Paul H. Mussen and others, pp. 311–4. In *Contemporary Issues in Thematic Apperceptive Methods.* Edited by Jerome Kagan and Gerald S. Lesser. Springfield, Ill.: Charles C Thomas, Publisher, 1961. Pp. xiv, 328. * (*PA* 36: 1HG28K)

775. LAZARUS, RICHARD S. "A Substitutive-Defensive Conception of Apperceptive Fantasy," pp. 51–71. Discussion by John W. Atkinson and others, pp. 72–82. In *Contemporary Issues in Thematic Apperceptive Methods.* Edited by Jerome Kagan and Gerald S. Lesser. Springfield, Ill.: Charles C Thomas, Publisher, 1961. Pp. xiv, 328. * (*PA* 36:1HG28K)

776. LEIMAN, ALAN HOWARD. *Relationship of TAT Sexual Drive, Sexual Guilt and Sexual Conflict.* Doctor's thesis, University of Massachusetts (Amherst, Mass.), 1961.

777. LINDZEY, GARDNER. *Projective Techniques and Cross-Cultural Research.* New York: Appleton-Century-Crofts, Inc., 1961. Pp. xi, 339. * (*PA* 37:3199)

778. LUBIN, BERNARD. "Judgments of Adjustment From TAT Stories as a Function of Experimentally Altered Sets." *J Consult Psychol* 25:249–52 Je '61. *

779. MacCASLAND, BARBARA WHITTREDGE. *The Relation of Aggressive Fantasy to Aggressive Behavior in Children.* Doctor's thesis, Syracuse University (Syracuse, N.Y.), 1961. (*DA* 23:300)

780. MARKHAM, SYLVIA. "A Comparative Evaluation of Psychotic and Nonpsychotic Reactions to Childbirth." *Am J Orthopsychiatry* 31:565–78 Jl '61. * (*PA* 36:4JP65M)

781. MARQUIS, JOHN NEIL. *Fantasy Measures of Aggressive Behavior.* Doctor's thesis, University of Michigan (Ann Arbor, Mich.), 1961. (*DA* 21:3854)

782. MASKIT, MAE LEE. *Management of Aggression in Preadolescent Girls: Its Effect on Certain Aspects of Ego Functioning.* Doctor's thesis, University of Michigan (Ann Arbor, Mich.), 1961. (*DA* 22:917)

783. MOSS, HOWARD A. "The Influences of Personality and Situational Cautiousness on Conceptual Behavior." *J Abn & Social Psychol* 63:629–35 N '61. * (*PA* 37:1310)

784. MOSS, HOWARD A., AND KAGAN, JEROME. "Stability of Achievement and Recognition Seeking Behaviors From Early Childhood Through Adulthood." *J Abn & Social Psychol* 62: 504–13 My '61. * (*PA* 36:4HJo4M)

785. MULLEN, F. A. "An Inductive Method for Determining Significant Aspects of the Responses of Mentally Handicapped Children to the Thematic Apperception Test and the Michigan Picture Test." Abstract. *Acta Psychologica* 19:861– 2 '61. *

786. MURRAY, HENRY A. "Commentary on the Case of El." *J Proj Tech* 25:404–11 D '61. *

787. MURSTEIN, BERNARD I. "The Role of the Stimulus in the Manifestation of Fantasy," pp. 229–73. Discussion by Gerald S. Lesser and others, pp. 274–87. In *Contemporary Issues in Thematic Apperceptive Methods.* Edited by Jerome Kagan and Gerald S. Lesser. Springfield, Ill.: Charles C Thomas, Publisher, 1961. Pp. xiv, 328. * (*PA* 36:1HG28K)

788. MURSTEIN, BERNARD I.; DAVID, CHARLOTTE; FISHER, DAVID; AND FURTH, HANS G. "The Scaling of the TAT for Hostility by a Variety of Scaling Methods." *J Consult Psychol* 25:497–504 D '61. * (*PA* 37:5029)

789. MUSSEN, PAUL. "Some Antecedents and Consequents of Masculine Sex-Typing in Adolescent Boys." *Psychol Monogr* 75(2):1–24 '61. * (*PA* 36:3FH24M)

790. NAWAS, MUNIR MIKE. *A Longitudinal Study of the Changes in Ego Sufficiency and Complexity From Adolescence to Young Adulthood as Reflected in the TAT.* Doctor's thesis, University of Chicago (Chicago, Ill.), 1961.

791. OLTMAN, RUTH MARIE. *Personality Differences Between Orthopedically Handicapped and Non-Handicapped Persons as Measured by the Thematic Apperception Test.* Doctor's thesis, Western Reserve University (Cleveland, Ohio), 1961.

792. PHARES, E. JERRY. "TAT Performance as a Function of Anxiety and Coping-Avoiding Behavior." *J Consult Psychol* 25:257–9 Je '61. *

793. PIOTROWSKI, ZYGMUNT A. "Prediction of Overt Behavior From Projective Test Data." Abstract. *Acta Psychologica* 19:111–4 '61. *

794. REITMAN, E. EDWARD, AND WILLIAMS, CARL D. "Relationships Between Hope of Success and Fear of Failure, Anxiety, and Need for Achievement." *J Abn & Social Psychol* 62:465–7 Mr '61. * (*PA* 36:4HJ65R)

795. REYHER, JOSEPH, AND SHOEMAKER, DONALD. "A Comparison Between Hypnotically Induced Age Regressions and Waking Stories to TAT Cards: A Preliminary Report." *J Consult Psychol* 25:409–13 O '61. * (*PA* 37:3388)

796. REZNIKOFF, MARVIN. "Social Desirability in TAT Themes." *J Proj Tech* 25:87–9 Mr '61. * (*PA* 36:1HG87R)

797. REZNIKOFF, MARVIN, AND DOLLIN, ADELAIDE. "Social Desirability and the Type of Hostility Expressed on the TAT." *J Clin Psychol* 17:315–7 Jl '61. * (*PA* 38:565)

798. RHUDICK, PAUL J., AND DIBNER, ANDREW S. "Age, Personality, and Health Correlates of Death Concerns in Normal Aged Individuals." *J Gerontol* 16:44–9 Ja '61. * (*PA* 35:6241)

799. RIGNEY, FRANCIS J., AND SMITH, L. DOUGLAS. *The Real Bohemia: A Sociological and Psychological Study of the "Beats."* New York: Basic Books, Inc., 1961. Pp. xxi, 250. * (*PA* 36:1GB50R)

800. ROSENBAUM, MILTON E., AND STANNERS, ROBERT F. "Self-Esteem, Manifest Hostility, and Expression of Hostility." *J Abn & Social Psychol* 63:646–9 N '61. * (*PA* 37: 1317)

801. SECTER, IRVING I. "T.A.T. Card 12M as a Predictor of Hypnotizability." *Am J Clin Hypnosis* 3:179–84 Ja '61. * (*PA* 36:1I179S)

802. SHIPMAN, W. G.; DANOWSKI, T. S.; AND MOSES, D. C., JR. "The Relation of Some Morphological, Physiological, and Genetic Dimensions to the Cattell 16PF and T.A.T. Scales." Abstract. *Acta Psychologica* 19:208–10 '61. *

803. SHNEIDMAN, EDWIN S. "The Logic of El: A Psychological Approach to the Analysis of Test Data." *J Proj Tech* 25:390–403 D '61. *

804. SHNEIDMAN, EDWIN S. "Psycho-logic: A Personality Approach to Patterns of Thinking," pp. 153–90. Discussion by Julian D. Rotter and others, pp. 191–5. In *Contemporary Issues in Thematic Apperceptive Methods.* Edited by Jerome Kagan and Gerald S. Lesser. Springfield, Ill.: Charles C Thomas, Publisher, 1961. Pp. xiv, 328. * (*PA* 36:1HG28K)

805. STRAUSS, F. H. "Analytic Implications of the Test Situation." *Brit J Med Psychol* 34:65–72 pt 1 '61. * (*PA* 36: 2HE65S)

806. TERRILL, JAMES McGUFFIN. *The Relationships Between Level II and Level III in the Interpersonal System of Personality Diagnosis.* Doctor's thesis, Stanford University (Stanford, Calif.), 1961. (*DA* 21:3529)

807. VEROFF, JOSEPH. "Thematic Apperception in a Nationwide Sample Survey," pp. 83–111. Discussion by William E. Henry and others, pp. 112–8. In *Contemporary Issues in Thematic Apperceptive Methods.* Edited by Jerome Kagan and Gerald S. Lesser. Springfield, Ill.: Charles C Thomas, Publisher, 1961. Pp. xiv, 328. * (*PA* 36:1HG28K)

808. WEISSKOPF-JOELSON, EDITH, AND WICH, RICHARD. "An Experiment Concerning the Value of a 'Pictureless TAT.'" *J Proj Tech* 25:360–2 S '61. *

809. WELCH, BRIAN; SCHAFER, ROY; AND DEMBER, CYNTHIA FOX. "TAT Stories of Hypomanic and Depressed Patients." *J Proj Tech* 25:221–32 Je '61. * (*PA* 36:2HI21W)

810. ZUCKERMAN, MARVIN; LEVITT, EUGENE E.; AND LUBIN, BERNARD. "Concurrent and Construct Validity of Direct and Indirect Measures of Dependency." *J Consult Psychol* 25:316–23 Ag '61. *

811. ARNOLD, MAGDA B. "A Screening Test for Candidates for Religious Orders," pp. 1–63. In *Screening Candidates for the Priesthood and Religious Life.* By Magda B. Arnold and others. Chicago, Ill.: Loyola University Press, 1962. Pp. x; 205. *

812. ARNOLD, MAGDA B. *Story Sequence Analysis: A New Method of Measuring Motivation and Predicting Achievement.* New York; Columbia University Press, 1962. Pp. ix, 287. *

813. AVILA, DONALD L., AND LAWSON, JOHN R. "The Thematic Apperception Test as a Diagnostic Tool With Retarded Adults." *Percept & Motor Skills* 15:323–5 O '62. * (*PA* 37: 8015)

814. BURKARD, M. INNOCENTIA. "Discernment of Teacher Characteristics by TAT Sequence Analysis." *J Ed Psychol* 53:279–87 D '62. * (*PA* 37:5677)

815. CLEVELAND, SIDNEY E., AND JOHNSON, DALE L. "Personality Patterns in Young Males With Coronary Disease." *Psychosom Med* 24:600–10 N–D '62. * (*PA* 37:8204)

816. COX, F. N. "An Assessment of Children's Attitudes Towards Parent Figures." *Child Develop* 33:821–30 D '62. * (*PA* 37:6484)

817. COX, F. N. "An Assessment of the Achievement Be-

havior System in Children." *Child Develop* 33:907–16 D '62. * (*PA* 37:6465)

818. CRUMPTON, EVELYN. "Projective Case Study of a True Hermaphrodite." *J Proj Tech* 26:266–75 S '62. * (*PA* 37:3396)

819. DOLLIN, ADELAIDE, AND SAKODA, JAMES M. "The Effect of Order of Presentation on Perception of TAT Pictures." *J Consult Psychol* 26:340–4 Ag '62. * (*PA* 38:4320)

820. EIDUSON, BERNICE T. *Scientists: Their Psychological World.* New York: Basic Books, Inc., 1962. Pp. xvi, 299. * (*PA* 37:111)

821. FIELD, P. B.; MALDONADO-SIERRA, E. D.; WALLACE, S. E.; BODARKY, C. J.; AND COELHO, G. V. "An Other-Directed Fantasy in a Puerto Rican." *J Social Psychol* 58:43–60 O '62. * (*PA* 37:6883)

822. FILMER-BENNETT, GORDON, AND KLOPFER, WALTER G. "Levels of Awareness in Projective Tests." *J Proj Tech* 26: 34–5 Mr '62. * (*PA* 37:3192)

823. FREEMAN, FRANK S. *Theory and Practice of Psychological Testing, Third Edition,* pp. 638–49. New York: Holt, Rinehart & Winston, Inc., 1962. Pp. xix, 697. *

824. GEIST, HAROLD. *The Etiology of Idiopathic Epilepsy,* pp. 153–92, 256–77. New York: Exposition Press, 1962. Pp. 297. *

825. GLYMOUR, CLARK; AMMONS, C. H.; AND AMMONS, R. B. "Projective Test Protocols of Students Placing Extreme (High or Low) Value on Intellectual Activity." *Proc Mont Acad Sci* 21:105–12 '62. * (*PA* 37:3195)

826. GRIMM, ELAINE R. "Psychological Investigation of Habitual Abortion." *Psychosom Med* 24:369–78 Jl–Ag '62. * (*PA* 37:5427)

827. HOGUE, J. PIERRE; OTIS, JAY L.; AND PRIEN, ERICH P. "Assessments of Higher-Level Personnel: 6, Validity of Predictions Based on Projective Techniques." *Personnel Psychol* 15:335–44 au '62. * (*PA* 37:7249)

828. HOWARD, KENNETH I. "The Convergent and Discriminant Validation of Ipsative Ratings From Three Projective Instruments." *J Clin Psychol* 18:183–8 Ap '62. * (*PA* 38:8551)

829. ISMIR, AWAD A. "The Effects of Prior Knowledge of the Thematic Apperception Test on Test Performance." *Psychol Rec* 12:157–64 Ap '62. * (*PA* 37:6738)

830. KRAMER, HARVEY J. *Stimulus Variables in Auditory Projective Testing: 1, An Information Theory Method for Measuring Psychological Ambiguity; 2, Effects of Varying Ambiguity and Type of Content Upon Projection With Blind and Sighted.* AFB Publications, Research Series No. 9. New York: American Foundation for the Blind, Inc., 1962. Pp. 81. * (*PA* 37:5028)

831. LEVITT, EUGENE E.; LUBIN, BERNARD; AND BRADY, JOHN PAUL. "On the Use of TAT Card 12M as an Indicator of Attitude Toward Hypnosis." *Int J Clin & Exp Hypnosis* 10:145–50 Jl '62. * (*PA* 37:5233)

832. LIPSHER, DAVID HAROLD. *Consistency of Clinicians' Judgments Based on MMPI, Rorschach and TAT Protocols.* Doctor's thesis, Stanford University (Stanford, Calif.), 1962. (*DA* 22:4409)

833. McGREEVEY, JAMES C. "Interlevel Disparity and Predictive Efficiency." *J Proj Tech* 26:80–7 Mr '62. * (*PA* 37:3152)

834. McNEIL, ELTON B. "Aggression in Fantasy and Behavior." *J Consult Psychol* 26:232–40 Je '62. * (*PA* 38:1018)

835. MURSTEIN, BERNARD I., AND COLLIER, HERBERT L. "The Role of the TAT in the Measurement of Achievement as a Function of Expectancy." *J Proj Tech* 26:96–101 Mr '62. * (*PA* 37:3202)

836. PALMER, JAMES O., AND LUSTGARTEN, BILLIE J. "The Prediction of TAT Structure as a Test of Rorschach's Experience-Balance." *J Proj Tech* 26:212–20 Je '62. * (*PA* 37:3204)

837. PARTRIDGE, CLOYD RONALD. *The Use of Biographical and Projective Data in Predicting Productivity of Business Machine Salesmen.* Doctor's thesis, Purdue University (Lafayette, Ind.), 1962. (*DA* 23:3980)

838. PHELAN, J. G. "Projective Techniques in the Selection of Management Personnel." *J Proj Tech* 26:102–4 Mr '62. * (*PA* 37:3915)

839. PINE, FRED. "Creativity and Primary Process: Sample Variations." *J Nerv & Mental Dis* 134:506–11 Je '62. * (*PA* 37:3205)

840. PISHKIN, VLADIMIR, AND WOLFGANG, AARON. "Relationship of Empathy to Job Performance in a Psychiatric Setting." *J Clin Psychol* 18:494–7 O '62. * (*PA* 39:5482)

841. RICCIUTI, HENRY. "Development and Application of Projective Techniques of Personality." *R Ed Res* 32:64–77 F '62. * (*PA* 37:1274)

842. ROTHAUS, PAUL. "Problems in the Measurement of Aggression-Anxiety." *J Proj Tech* 26:327–31 S '62. * (*PA* 37:3301)

843. RUBY, WALTER McCLINTOCK, JR. *An Investigation of Differentiating Personality Factors Between Achieving and Low Achieving College Students.* Doctor's thesis, University of Tennessee (Knoxville, Tenn.), 1962. (*DA* 23:3785)

844. SCHAEFER, JUDITH BLAKE. *Stability and Change in Thematic Apperception Test Response From Adolescence to Adulthood.* Doctor's thesis, University of Chicago (Chicago, Ill.), 1962.

845. SEEMAN, WILLIAM, AND MARKS, PHILIP A. "A Study of Some 'Test Dimensions' Conceptions." *J Proj Tech* 26:469–73 D '62. * (*PA* 37:6678)

846. SEMEONOFF, BORIS. "Self-Description as an Instrument in Personality Assessment." *Brit J Med Psychol* 35:165–75 pt 2 '62. * (*PA* 37:3236)

847. SIMMONS, WILLIAM L., AND CHRISTY, EDWARD G. "Verbal Reinforcement of a TAT Theme." *J Proj Tech* 26: 337–41 S '62. * (*PA* 37:2455)

848. SINGER, MARGARET THALER. "A Conceptual Model for Rating Projective Test Responses From Aged Subjects: Relationships Between Test Ratings, Health Status, and Certain Behavioral Features," pp. 644–9. In *Social and Psychological Aspects of Aging.* Proceedings of the Fifth Congress of the International Association of Gerontology. Edited by Clark Tibbitts and Wilma Donahue. New York: Columbia University Press, 1962. Pp. xviii, 952. *

849. SMITH, DONALD C. *Personal and Social Adjustment of Gifted Adolescents.* CEC Research Monograph, Series A, No. 4. Washington, D.C.: Council for Exceptional Children, 1962. Pp. iv, 65. *

850. STRICKER, GEORGE. "The Construction and Partial Validation of an Objectively Scorable Apperception Test." *J Personality* 30:51–62 Mr '62. * (*PA* 38:8507)

851. TEDESCHI, JAMES T., AND KIAN, MOHAMED. "Cross-Cultural Study of the TAT Assessment for Achievement Motivation: Americans and Persians." *J Social Psychol* 58: 227–34 D '62. * (*PA* 37:6551)

852. THEINER, ERIC C. "The Magnitude of Four Experimental Needs as Expressed by Two Projective Techniques." *J Proj Tech* 26:354–65 S '62. * (*PA* 37:3163)

853. TURNER, GEORGE C., AND COLEMAN, JAMES C. "Examiner Influence on Thematic Apperception Test Responses." *J Proj Tech* 26:478–86 D '62. * (*PA* 37:6749)

854. VASSILIOU, VASSO. *Motivational Patterns of Two Clinical Groups as Revealed by TAT Sequence Analysis.* Doctor's thesis, Loyola University (Chicago, Ill.), 1962.

855. WEATHERLEY, DONALD. "Maternal Permissiveness Toward Aggression and Subsequent TAT Aggression." *J Abn & Social Psychol* 65:1–5 Jl '62. * (*PA* 38:4092)

856. WEISS, PETER, AND EMMERICH, WALTER. "Dependency Fantasy and Group Conformity in Ulcer Patients." *J Consult Psychol* 26:61–4 F '62. * (*PA* 37:5540)

857. ABRAMSON, LEONARD S. "A Comparison of an Auditory and a Visual Projective Technique." *J Proj Tech* 27:3–11 Mr '63. * (*PA* 38:1005)

858. BARNOUW, VICTOR. Chap. 16, "The Thematic Apperception Test," pp. 260–75. In his *Culture and Personality.* Homewood, Ill.: Dorsey Press, Inc., 1963. Pp. xi, 410. *

859. BARRON, FRANK. Chap. 11, "The Disposition Toward Originality," pp. 139–52. In *Scientific Creativity: Its Recognition and Development.* Edited by Calvin W. Taylor and Frank Barron. New York: John Wiley & Sons, Inc., 1963. Pp. xxiv, 419. * (*PA* 38:2689)

860. BERG, PAUL SAUL DAVID. *Neurotic and Psychopathic Criminals: Some Measures of Ego Syntonicity, Impulse Socialization and Perceptual Consistency.* Doctor's thesis, Michigan State University (East Lansing, Mich.), 1963. (*DA* 24:2559)

861. BERNSTEIN, LEWIS, AND DANA, RICHARD H. "Effect of Order of Presentation of TAT Cards." *J Consult Psychol* 27:533–5 D '63. * (*PA* 38:8540)

862. BRAMEL, DANA. "Selection of a Target for Defensive Projection." *J Abn & Social Psychol* 66:318–24 Ap '63. * (*PA* 37:8038)

863. BREGER, LOUIS. "Conformity as a Function of the Ability to Express Hostility." *J Personality* 31:247–57 Je '63. *

864. BRITTON, JOSEPH H. "Dimensions of Adjustment of Older Adults." *J Gerontol* 18:60–5 Ja '63. * (*PA* 38:4098)

865. BROWN, L. B., AND HETZEL, B. S. "Stress, Personality and Thyroid Disease." *J Psychosom Res* 7:223–8 D '63. * (*PA* 38:8584)

866. CARTWRIGHT, DESMOND S.; KIRTNER, WILLIAM L.; AND FISKE, DONALD W. "Method Factors in Changes Associated With Psychotherapy." *J Abn & Social Psychol* 66:164–75 F '63. * (*PA* 37:6833)

867. CLEVELAND, SIDNEY E. "Personality Characteristics of Dietitians and Nurses." *J Am Dietetic Assn* 43:104–9 Ag '63. *

868. CONNERS, C. KEITH. "Birth Order and Needs for Affiliation." *J Personality* 31:408–16 S '63. *

869. COOLEY, WILLIAM W. "Predicting Choice of a Career in Scientific Research." *Personnel & Guid J* 42:21–8 S '63. *

870. ENDICOTT, NOBLE A., AND ENDICOTT, JEAN. "'Improvement' in Untreated Psychiatric Patients." *Arch Gen Psychiatry* 9:575–85 D '63. * (*PA* 38:8643)

871. ENDICOTT, NOBLE A., AND ENDICOTT, JEAN. "Objective Measures of Somatic Preoccupation." *J Nerv & Mental Dis* 137:427–37 N '63. * (*PA* 38:6356)

872. ENGEL, MARY. "Psychological Testing of Borderline Psychotic Children." *Arch Gen Psychiatry* 8:426–34 My '63. * (*PA* 38:2451)

873. EPLEY, DAVID, AND RICKS, DAVID R. "Foresight and Hindsight in the TAT." *J Proj Tech* 27:51–9 Mr '63. * (*PA* 38:1008)

874. FISHER, SEYMOUR, AND SEIDNER, RICHARD. "Body Experiences of Schizophrenic, Neurotic and Normal Women." *J Nerv & Mental Dis* 137:252–7 S '63. * (*PA* 38:6358)

875. GILL, WAYNE S. "Interpersonal Affect and Conformity Behavior in Schizophrenics." *J Abn & Social Psychol* 67:502–5 N '63. * (*PA* 38:4602)
876. GLESER, GOLDINE C. "Projective Methodologies." *Annual R Psychol* 14:391–422 '63. *
877. HEDVIG, ELEANOR B. "Stability of Early Recollections and Thematic Apperception Stories." *J Indiv Psychol* 19:49–54 My '63. * (*PA* 38:1011)
878. HOWARD, KENNETH I. "Ratings of Projective Test Protocols as a Function of Degree of Inference." *Ed & Psychol Meas* 23:267–75 su '63. * (*PA* 38:1013)
879. KENNY, DOUGLAS T., AND CHAPPELL, MARGUERITE C. "Anxiety Effects in Thematic Apperception Induced by Homogeneous Visual Stimulation." *J Proj Tech & Pers Assess* 27:297–301 S '63. *
880. LEVITT, EUGENE E., AND LUBIN, BERNARD. "TAT Card '12 MF' and Hypnosis Themes in Females." *Int J Clin & Exp Hypnosis* 11:241–4 O '63. * (*PA* 38:8556)
881. LITTIG, LAWRENCE W. "Effects of Motivation on Probability Preferences." *J Personality* 31:417–27 S '63. *
882. McEVOY, THEODORE LEE. *A Comparison of Suicidal and Nonsuicidal Patients by Means of the Thematic Apperception Test.* Doctor's thesis, University of California (Los Angeles, Calif.), 1963. (*DA* 24:1248)
883. MITCHELL, HOWARD E. "Application of the Kaiser Method to Marital Pairs." *Family Process* 2:265–79 S '63. *
884. MURSTEIN, BERNARD I. "The Relationship of Expectancy of Reward to Achievement Performance on an Arithmetic and Thematic Test." *J Consult Psychol* 27:394–9 O '63. * (*PA* 38:4144)
885. MURSTEIN, BERNARD I. "TAT Hostility and the Buss Hostility Scale." *Percept & Motor Skills* 16:520 Ap '63. * (*PA* 38:2699)
886. MURSTEIN, BERNARD I. *Theory and Research in Projective Techniques (Emphasizing the TAT).* New York: John Wiley & Sons, Inc., 1963. Pp. xiii, 385. * (*PA* 38:6098)
887. MURSTEIN, BERNARD I., AND WIENS, ARTHUR N. "A Factor Analysis of Various Hostility Measures on a Psychiatric Population." *J Proj Tech & Pers Assess* 27:447–51 D '63. * (*PA* 38:8594)
888. NORMAN, RUSSELL P. "Need for Social Approval as Reflected on the TAT." Abstract. *J Consult Psychol* 27:464 O '63. *
889. POSER, ERNEST G., AND LEE, S. GILLMORE. "Thematic Content Associated With Two Gastrointestinal Disorders." *Psychosom Med* 25:162–73 Mr–Ap '63. * (*PA* 38:4505)
890. RYCHLAK, JOSEPH F. "Personality Correlates of Leadership Among First Level Managers." *Psychol Rep* 12:43–52 F '63. * (*PA* 38:2600)
891. SALTZ, GEORGE, AND EPSTEIN, SEYMOUR. "Thematic Hostility and Guilt Responses as Related to Self-Reported Hostility, Guilt, and Conflict." *J Abn & Social Psychol* 67:469–79 N '63. * (*PA* 38:4327)
892. SEMEONOFF, BORIS. "An Application of Inter-Person Analysis in Personality Assessment." *Brit J Psychol* 54:71–81 F '63. * (*PA* 37:8004)
893. SILVER, ALBERT W. "TAT and MMPI Psychopath Deviant Scale Differences Between Delinquent and Nondelinquent Adolescents." Abstract. *J Consult Psychol* 27:370 Ag '63. * (*PA* 38:3032)
894. SINGER, MARGARET THALER, AND WYNNE, LYMAN C. "Differentiating Characteristics of Parents of Childhood Schizophrenics, Childhood Neurotics, and Young Adult Schizophrenics." *Am J Psychiatry* 120:234–43 S '63. *
895. TESTIN, ROBERT FRANCIS. *Ego Strength Scale Differences Between Psychotic and Nonpsychotic Inpatients.* Doctor's thesis, Fordham University (New York, N.Y.), 1963. (*DA* 24:839)
896. WALLACE, JOHN, AND SECHREST, LEE. "Frequency Hypothesis and Content Analysis of Projective Techniques." *J Consult Psychol* 27:387–93 O '63. * (*PA* 38:4335)
897. WYLIE, RUTH C.; SISSON, BOYD D.; AND TAULBEE, EARL. "Intraindividual Consistency in 'Creative' and 'Memory' Stories Written for TAT Pictures." *J Consult Psychol* 27:145–51 Ap '63. * (*PA* 37:8022)

C. J. ADCOCK, *Associate Professor of Psychology, Victoria University of Wellington, Wellington, New Zealand.*

Writing a review of a test like the TAT is rather like the task of the journalist who has to write about Christmas. It has been done so many times before that one feels everything of consequence must have been said and yet the status of the test is not very different from when the last *Mental Measurements Yearbook* was published. The number of papers grows apace but there is still a lack of reassuring validative studies. There are still numerous research projects which have used the test with degrees of success impossible to estimate. There are still enthusiastic clinicians and doubting statisticians. Since there are few important developments in its literature we may usefully discuss some basic issues in a systematic way.

THE RATIONALE OF THE TEST. The basic assumption of the test is that, when called upon to tell a story about a picture, one necessarily gives expression to one's own motives, interests, and anxieties, and provides evidence of one's experiences. That this is true to some extent seems reasonable enough but there remains much doubt as to the degree to which it holds in any particular instance. A character may be described as interested in astronomy, not because the testee has any interest in this subject but because he read a story about such a person recently. Similarly, the testee may provide details of lurid upbringing because he has recently seen an account of this kind of thing and contrasts it with his own sheltered life.

The degree of projection involved in story telling must always be problematical and must be assessed in the light of internal and external evidence. The clinician who has repeatedly met his patient is thus in a much stronger position to interpret the TAT record. He just has more evidence and in particular is in a position to distinguish between behavioural tendencies and compensatory fantasy. Bold deeds and aggressive responses may figure largely in the protocol of a timid introvert and must not be confused with the real life tendencies of an uninhibited extravert.

Such considerations constitute a warning against any mere counting of needs, presses, and the like. This may have good significance when we are concerned with group averages but may be grossly misleading with regard to John Smith. It may, of course, be useful to score Smith's protocol in this way but only as one way of classifying the evidence for further study. No useful conclusion can be arrived at without the insight which develops from long acquaintance with the complexity of determination which enters into story telling of this kind.

The fundamental fact which we have to face with regard to a test of this type is that it is subject to a much wider range of distorting factors than operate with regard to questionnaire tests or even some other projective tests. It is not a matter of individual items being unreliable yet the sum tending to average out the errors but rather the possibility of the test as a whole being distorted to an unknown degree. This fact seems to require that the test be restricted to two major uses: (*a*) a clinical tool which can be supplemented and validated by other clinical procedures; and (*b*) a research tool for the investigation of group differences. Such indeed appears to be the general tendency in practice.

WHAT DOES IT MEASURE? The range of a projective test is determined by the degree of structure of the stimuli. In this case the variety of pictures and the range of responses which can be made to each ensure that there will be a broad coverage. There seems no reason why all the more basic personality factors should not be represented but there is no guarantee that they will and even less certainty that they will be present to a degree to make reliable measurement possible. If you wish to assess a student's knowledge of psychology it may be sufficient to ask him to write an essay on a psychological topic of his own choice but this approach may also fail to give information about many aspects. If you require specific information you must ask specific questions.

An important point about the TAT is that it can provide information about the particular content of the subject's cognitive and affective reference frames. It is one thing to decide that a patient has a severe superego and quite another to be able to say what are the particular requirements laid down by his superego. This is the type of knowledge which this test can often provide as few other tests can. Some would claim that it is a useful instrument to measure the relative strengths of various types of motivation but there is room to doubt its suitability for this purpose. Specially designed instruments of the same type may be useful but the shotgun approach is too unreliable for this purpose. This breadth and lack of specificity, on the other hand, may make it an ideal instrument for picking up specific sources of disturbance in the subject's life. Like King Charles' head these will intrude themselves into the protocol.

We shall take the position that as an indicator of general interests, important current sources of motivation, areas of emotional disturbance, and clues for clinical discussion the test has excellent possibilities, but it is not suitable for providing a profile of personality traits or a reliable measurement of any one trait.

WHAT IS ITS RELIABILITY? This is a thorny problem. Some have sought to measure reliability in terms of interscorer agreement. Apart from the fact that this reliability may be negatively correlated with validity (simply counting words may ensure perfect interscorer agreement but useless scores), it is obvious that the level of reliability will vary according to the system involved. These are legion and no coefficient can be considered except in relation to the particular system concerned. Jensen, in his review of this test in *The Fifth Mental Measurements Yearbook* (5:164) reported 15 estimates of scoring reliability ranging from .54 to .91. The succeeding years have not changed this position. It is obvious that under optimum conditions this is not a serious source of unreliability and that even the lower estimates indicate enough agreement for many research purposes.

But we are concerned not merely with the reliability of the scorer. The test data themselves may lack reliability. This would be indicated either by lack of internal agreement or low retest reliability. On this point too there is little to add to Jensen's report. Only three of the studies listed in *Psychological Abstracts* during the last three years concern themselves with reliability and these deal with specific aspects. The average internal consistency reliability of .13 reported by Jensen seems to call for no revision and indicates a grave need for caution. It is sometimes argued that with a test of this kind internal reliability is not a fair measure, but insofar as summed scores are resorted to, it must be justified by such a criterion.

Retest reliability is seriously contaminated by a tendency to remember and repeat the same stories. To have any significance, different stories must be required and under these circumstances many attempted measures appear to be of doubtful significance. The evidence would seem to indicate that to expect to get reliable measures of more than half a dozen personality aspects would be very optimistic and that to expect such reliability to be greater than would justify group differentiation would be even more optimistic.

HOW VALID IS IT? The data available on reliability do not raise any high expectations with regard to validity. So far as statistical data are concerned, there has been little advance in the last few years. Takahashi [1] found no significant relationship between hostile content of TAT stories and overt aggression. His Hostile Sentence Completion Test, however, scored high with both extreme aggressors and extreme nonaggressors and low with moderates. Possibly a similar ambivalent effect was operating with the TAT but in a less systematic way so that the two opposing tendencies simply cancelled out. Hafner and Kaplan (720) found no significant relationship between the TAT overt and covert scales and Rorschach results. Dreger (715) found no relation between productivity as measured by the Rorschach and TAT. Dana (666) has suggested a new objective scoring system and presents evidence from which he concludes that it is satisfactory for clinical use. In a study of two identical twins, Henry (722) succeeded in identifying the disturbed one but formulated no clear principles for this purpose.

CONCLUSIONS. The aim of a review such as this is largely to inform those unfamiliar with the test so that they can decide about the desirability of using it. For such a person the answer seems plain enough in this case: if you need to consult the review you had better not use the test. It is definitely a test for the sophisticated. For research purposes it may sometimes be the best approach available but it would be wise to look for other suitable tests first. For the clinical psychologist no advice is necessary. He will recognise the test as another vehicle for his use of clinical insight but he may well be warned against developing false confidence based on his subjective impression of reliability. Because one draws the same conclusion from two sources of evidence it may be easy to decide that both are valid.

For reviews by Leonard D. Eron and Arthur R. Jensen, see 5:164; for a review by Arthur L. Benton, see 4:136; for reviews by Arthur L. Benton, Julian B. Rotter, and J. R. Wittenborn, see 3:103 (1 excerpt); for excerpts from related book reviews, see B60, B326, 5:B63, 5:B204, 5:B395, 4:139–41, 3:104, and 3:104a.

1 TAKAHASHI, SHIGEO. "Toei kensa ni yoru jidō no kōgekiteki kōdō no kenkyū." *Jap J Ed Psychol* 8:85–91 '60. (PA 35:2232) Original article not seen; citation based upon the English abstract in *Psychological Abstracts*.

For an excerpt from a review of the Bellak TAT Blank, *see 4:137. For excerpts from reviews of the* Thompson Modification, *see 4:138.*

[246]

*The Tomkins-Horn Picture Arrangement Test.
Ages 10 and over; 1942–59; 1 form ('44, 30 pages); manual ('57, 399 pages, see 5 below); interpretation manual ('59, 191 pages, see 7 below); scoring materials ['57, 63 cards, 100 sheets, punch, board, and instructions, 8 pages, reprinted from manual]; profile ('58, 4 pages); $15 per 50 tests; $25 per set of scoring materials; $4.50 per 100 scoring sheets; $17.50 per 100 profiles; $10 per manual; $5.50 per interpretive manual; postage extra; (30–60) minutes; Silvan S. Tomkins, Daniel Horn, and John B. Miner (manuals); Springer Publishing Co., Inc. *

REFERENCES

1–6. See 5:167.
7. TOMKINS, SILVAN S., AND MINER, JOHN B. *PAT Interpretation: Scope and Technique.* New York: Springer Publishing Co., Inc., 1959. Pp. vii, 184. * (PA 34:1430)
8. MINER, JOHN B. "The Concurrent Validity of the PAT in the Selection of Tabulating Machine Operators." *J Proj Tech* 24:409–18 D '60. * (PA 35:5391)
9. MCCARTER, ROBERT E.; SCHIFFMAN, HAROLD M.; AND TOMKINS, SILVAN S. "Early Recollections as Predictors of Tomkins-Horn Picture Arrangement Test Performance." *J Indiv Psychol* 17:177–80 N '61. *
10. MINER, JOHN B. "The Validity of the PAT in the Selection of Tabulating Machine Operators: An Analysis of Predictive Power." *J Proj Tech* 25:330–3 S '61. * (PA 36:3LD30M)
11. PATE, KENTON DONESE. *The Picture Arrangement Test as Related to Occupational Choice Values.* Doctor's thesis, University of Houston (Houston, Tex.), 1961. (DA 21:3856)
12. MINER, JOHN B. "Personality and Ability Factors in Sales Performance." *J Appl Psychol* 46:6–13 F '62. * (PA 36:5LD06M)
13. HIGASHIMACHI, WILFRED H. "The Construct Validity of the Progressive Matrices as a Measure of Superego Strength in Juvenile Delinquents." *J Consult Psychol* 27:415–9 O '63. * (PA 38:4302)

ROBERT C. NICHOLS, *Program Director, National Merit Scholarship Corporation, Evanston, Illinois.*

The novel method of obtaining objectively recorded projective responses, the extensive standardization, and the elaborate scoring procedure of the *Tomkins-Horn Picture Arrangement Test* (PAT) have been described by previous reviewers (5:167). The test consists of 25 plates, each with three pictures which the subject arranges in one of six possible orders to tell a story. The arrangements are scored for 651 scales which are made manageable by screening out a few extreme scores for interpretation and ignoring the rest.

The PAT scales (called "patterns" or "keys") consist of several arrangements with some common feature. The arrangements to be counted for a given key were selected according to two criteria: content, and frequency of occurrence in a normative group ($n = 1500$). The 156 content areas represented by keys are grouped into 32 general areas of personality (e.g., social restlessness, optimism, superego, etc.). Each of the 156 content scales is scored for from one to six subscales, determined by the frequency with which the scored arrangements were given by the normative group. In addition to the content scales a group of 96 "Conformity" keys were constructed solely on the basis of response frequency. Arrangements falling in eight frequency categories were grouped into keys separately for 12 subgroups of the normative sample based on age, education, and intelligence.

The content keys are quite short; some consist of only two arrangements, and the average is about four per key. Item overlap among the keys is great and some keys are identical with others.

In the suggested interpretation of the various keys it is assumed that personality is expressed quite literally by picture arrangements. For example, the "High General Sociophilia" key (arrangements ending with the hero in the company of other people) is interpreted as "a preference for, or expectation of, being with people rather than being alone when a choice is possible." In a case study in the interpretive manual, a major reason for diagnosing a subject's vocational maladjustment as due to limited opportunities for interpersonal contact on the job was a very high "High General Sociophilia" score. No evidence is offered for the validity of these suggested interpretations, and the experienced clinician may legitimately wonder if in the personality area anything this self-evident can really be true.

The manual reports those keys on which certain diagnostic groups of mental patients obtain extremely high scores more frequently than normals. (Those on which normals obtain higher scores are not reported.) The performance of these diagnostic groups on the various keys does not increase confidence in the proposed interpretations. For example, high scores on the "High General Sociophilia" key are obtained more frequently by paranoid schizophrenics, schizophrenics, and character disorders than by the normative group, and high scores on the "High General Self-confidence" key are obtained more frequently by paranoid schizophrenics, schizophrenics, and manic-depressives than by normals. One wishes that the test authors had presented fewer scales and more evidence bearing on the interpretation of the scales.

The limitations of *a priori* scales have long been recognized by users of personality inventories, yet *a priori* content scales, even without internal consistency analysis, seem to be accepted uncritically by many projective testers, including the authors of the PAT. Scales superior to the present *a priori* keys could probably be constructed for the PAT by criterion keying or other scale construction procedures.

According to the manual, the meaning of a given response is often ambiguous because the response may be given for different reasons by different subjects. It is assumed that infrequently occurring responses have fewer possible causes and are thus more clearly interpretable. For this reason only responses which occur rarely (in less than 5 per cent of normative subjects) are used in the usual interpretation of the PAT. The rare responses considered for interpretation include "pattern rares" (extreme scores on the various keys) and "plate rares" (unusual single arrangements).

No empirical evidence is offered in support of the thesis that rare responses and extreme scores are less ambiguous than more common responses or scores. Evidence is presented, however, which suggests that the rare responses are less reliable in a test-retest situation than more common ones.

In view of the shortage of evidence supporting the assumptions on which the test is constructed and interpreted, one would like to have available a number of studies dealing with the usefulness of the test in a practical assessment situation. This requirement is only minimally satisfied by the PAT. Miner has reported on the use of the PAT in the selection of tabulating machine operators (8) and petroleum dealer salesmen (12). Essentially the same procedure was used in both of these studies. The PAT's and criterion performance (sales records of the salesmen and supervisor's ratings of the machine operators) for a small sample of subjects were studied intensively to derive a single predictive PAT score which was cross validated on the remaining cases (n's of 44 salesmen and 31 machine operators). Validity coefficients for the overall criterion were .57 for salesmen and .72 for machine operators. (The latter correlation is a biserial coefficient which is not appropriate for the essentially dichotomous PAT prediction. Corrected to the more appropriate point-biserial, the validity coefficient is .58.) Both of these studies were concurrent, but in a further study of the tabulating machine operators Miner (*10*) showed that the PAT index predicted performance ratings over an average of seven months with a validity of .61. (The corresponding point-biserial is .45.)

These findings are indeed impressive. Regardless of what one may think of its rationale and method of development, if the PAT can continue to produce such results in other situations and for investigators other than the test authors, it should rightfully take its place among our most valuable assessment devices. However, in view of the theoretical questions raised above, the uncritical acceptance of the PAT is not recommended before these further validation studies are completed.

J Proj Tech 23:474–5 D '59. Leonard P. Ullmann. [Review of the interpretive manual.] The rationale....assumes that the most useful information about a person deals with that individual's distinctive behaviors. The logic of test interpretation thus rests upon the response which is rare or improbable when one compares one subject with all others but which is very frequent for the person under investigation. * With consistency and scientific honesty ....[the earlier book-manual for the test; see 5:167] presents the reasoning and decisions made when constructing a test in which this rationale was followed and in which explicitly no contemporary theory of personality was felt to be powerful enough to determine the test content or interpretation. The result is a stimulating case history in science. While the reader might well disagree with many of the authors' decisions, in supporting his disagreements the reader would have to do some thinking and come to greater understanding of his own position. In view of this background, *PAT Interpretation,* a book of interpretations of PAT protocols, is somewhat disappointing. Some of the reasons for this may be traced to the derivation of the test. With no particular theory of personality, the test has no particular focus or purpose. Any number of scales might have been derived, and indeed a great number of keys are presented. The areas covered by these keys— social orientation, optimism-pessimism, and level of functioning—were, in the authors' words, selected by "prejudice and hunch, both personal and professional." The difficulties in PAT scoring are not reduced by the presence

of three sets of norms: age, I.Q., and education. Since an individual falls into all of these categories, the authors suggest averaging across the three norms to establish the probabilities of the occurrence of a response for an individual. Having isolated the relevant (rare) responses, interpretation becomes the crucial problem. Assuming the validity of the statistical procedures used to designate relevant material, all the examiner knows is that a behavior is rare. At this point the authors assume a commonality of the perception of the stimuli and an equivalence of psychological meaning of identical stimulus orderings. The basis on which interpretation is made therefore is face validity. The strength of the use of protocols presented in *PAT Interpretation* lies in the public specification of how the material to be used was selected and in explicit statement of the probability levels from which inferences were made. That is, a part of the clinician's work, normally done implicitly, is made explicit. However, because of the lack of theory, the write-ups seem, at least to this reviewer, to validate antecedent descriptions of the subjects and to add little to enrich or extend knowledge of these people, or even, at times, to help to describe them as unique individuals. The result is essentially a summation of "signs" of dubious value and arbitrary selection. In summary, *PAT Interpretation* is the fruit of the consistent application of a methodological view point. Following through the sample cases for scoring and interpretation, the clinician will learn something about the most fascinating client he will ever have, himself. In terms of clinical application, an interesting set of stimuli has been added to the tester's armamentarium. While the work done by the authors is more than sufficient to merit a fair trial in the clinic, when dealing with the individual case the amount of time required for scoring, the tenuous validity of the instrument, and the fragmentary nature of the interpretations will probably lead to limited acceptance and use of the PAT.

Occupational Psychol 34:149–50 Ap '60. H. Phillipson. [Review of the manual.] * While the development of the test as described in this volume is clearly a monumental piece of work, admirable in its thinking, design and execution, the psychologist who is experienced in the uses of such techniques as Rorschach and T.A.T. will feel a sense of disappointment at the end product. The individual per-

sonality picture that emerges from the quantitative data is too general and too lacking in
dynamic and causal information, and one is
thrown back on the verbal material, which
though valuable is not likely to be more useful
than the more traditional projective test responses. For the present reviewer it is the lack
of theoretical rationale for the choice of test
material and the interpretation of the responses
that brings the main feelings of dissatisfaction.
For without this we cannot postulate why the
subject behaves as he does with the test material, nor what his behaviour means in terms
of his personality functioning as a whole.

*Personnel & Guid J 38:240–2 N '59. Sidney
E. Cleveland.* [Review of the interpretive manual.] * The thoroughness and detail with which
the authors describe the scoring procedure,
tabulation of scores, and reference to the normative tables make for rather tedious and uninteresting reading. No doubt this is inevitable
in a technical manual of this nature. However,
the reader tends to lose sight of the person
whose test responses are being analyzed while
pursuing the intricacies of the mechanics of interpretation. It is interesting to note that despite all of the attention paid by the authors
to a careful statistical analysis of the frequency
of the various picture arrangement sequences,
a wealth of dynamic material is gained from
simply a clinical appraisal of the subject's free
written responses to each sorting. * The PAT
is an ingenious device which combines the clinical insights offered in a projective technique
with the efficiency of scoring found in a psychometric instrument. For this reason, if no other,
the test should have considerable promise in
research projects involving the testing of large
groups. The modification of projective tests to
suit large scale testing is a promising development and one being applied to an increasing
number of testing devices (for example, The
Holtzman Ink Blot Test, University of Texas).
One can foresee the possibility of administering a battery of group projective tests, including a measure such as the PAT, and emerging
with test data as rewarding as if individual
TAT's and Rorschachs had been obtained. In
summary, the volume *PAT Interpretation* represents a thorough guidebook for those uninitiated but interested in the application of a relatively new addition to the assessment of human
motives and behavior.

*For reviews by Donald W. Fiske, John W.
Gittinger, and Wayne H. Holtzman, see 5:167
(1 excerpt).*

[247]

★**Visual Apperception Test '60.** Ages 12 and over;
1960–62; prevalent mood and clinical diagnosis; 1
form ('60, 14 pages); manual, third edition ('62, 30
pages); $10 per 15 tests and manual; 50¢ per single
copy; $2.50 per manual; postpaid; set of crayons
necessary for administration; [35] minutes; Rafi Z.
Khan; Midwest Psychological Services. *

BERT R. SAPPENFIELD, *Professor of Psychology, Montana State University, Missoula,
Montana.*

The inventor of the VAT '60 makes several
laudatory statements about his test, which, if
eventually confirmed by research and clinical
experience, would place the VAT '60 among
the top ranking clinical instruments of all
time. The test is said to be "a highly sensitive
instrument capable of multilevel functioning
* [It] can guide us into the labyrinths of the
deep psyche, step by step, without groping in
the dark * [It] provides a great insight into
the personality stratification which is of immense help in the psychotherapeutic planning."

The stimuli for the VAT '60 are 12 "plates
consisting of lines randomly drawn under controlled conditions." Each of these plates (with
one exception) has the appearance of a doodle
produced by drawing a continuous line, with
much overlapping and crossing of itself, until
the final product takes on a more or less circular or elliptical shape, containing within itself
many other delineated forms; the twelfth plate
differs from the others in that it has been produced by making fairly square turns and in
that the final gestalt has a more or less rectangular appearance.

The subject is provided with eight crayons
(red, orange, blue, green, yellow, purple,
brown, and black) and told to "color whatever
design, pattern or object" he sees in each plate.
He is permitted to choose the color or colors
to be used in each drawing, and is asked to
give a name to whatever he draws.

The nature of the subject's drawings is purported to be a valid basis for clinical diagnosis.
The manual describes, and gives examples of,
the types of patterns said to be characteristic
of each of 12 different nosological categories
(including normals, neurotics, psychopaths,
and three types of schizophrenics). The validity information is, at best, extremely ambiguous. The author lists the number of patients

in each of eight clinical categories (total $n =$ 149) and states that the patients were compared with 87 "normal" subjects. He immediately concludes, without further description of his procedure, that "the validity coefficient for the above clinical types is .89." Since no operational definition of this "validity coefficient" is provided, the reader comes away with the equivalent of no validity information whatever.

The manual's treatment of retest reliability is also ambiguous; the procedure appears to have involved diagnosis "by three persons specially trained in the interpretation of responses on VAT '60," and a comparison of "diagnoses" of individual patients on the test and retest. In any case, the retest reliability (reported to be .79 for an n of 359) may not be, for a test of this kind, as appropriate as some form of split-half technique.

The names given by the subject to his drawings are purported to have value for thematic interpretation, although the author considers this type of analysis to be at an experimental stage. He gives some examples of this approach, one of which involves the case of a "woman with an unhappy marital relationship [who] perceived [her drawing as] her husband being clubbed by somebody."

What Khan calls "mood measurement" is based on the subject's choice of colors. Khan believes that he has evidence that blue and green indicate cheerful moods, that yellow indicates anxiety, that black and brown indicate depression, that red and orange indicate aggression, and that purple indicates self-control and psychotherapeutic resistance. On the basis of an elaborate tabulation of color choices, the subject's inferred "moods" can be ordered into a hierarchy, which purportedly corresponds to an "emotional stratification"; the predominant "mood" is said to be most manifest in behavior, while the less predominant "moods" are said to be less available for expression. The manual gives one example of this "emotional stratification" and its utilization in psychotherapy, and also describes briefly and incompletely two studies which led Khan to believe in the emotional significance of color choices.

Any critical reader of Khan's manual is likely to be either awed or doubt-ridden by the alleged virtues of the VAT '60. The test would turn out to be a truly remarkable instrument

if it should prove to accomplish what it is stated to accomplish in the way of clinical diagnosis and "mood measurement." The reviewer is inclined to believe that the VAT '60 should not be ignored, that it may eventually be demonstrated to have some, though probably limited, value for personality diagnosis. However, at present, it is likely that the VAT '60 should be used, if at all, only with cautious skepticism.

STANLEY J. SEGAL, *Associate Professor of Psychology, and Director, Student Counseling Center, State University of New York at Buffalo, Buffalo, New York.*

The foreword by Silvano Arieti in the VAT '60 manual forewarns by its tentative endorsement, "Even if we do not accept the early conclusions of the author, concerning his first results and his classification of mental disorders, we must admit that the test is offering a new and valuable approach."

The VAT '60, presenting the subject with 12 plates of lines randomly drawn and asking that he *color* "whatever design, pattern, or object" he sees, is yet another new projective technique, rushed into publication with promises of things to come, but with very little evidence that what is already presented has been carefully constructed, standardized, and evaluated.

Prevalent mood is measured by standardized scoring of the incidence of use of eight colors in the drawings. The manual offers little explanation of: (*a*) The basis for relating particular colors to particular moods. ("Initial studies revealed that the choice of colors by the patients in spontaneous drawing reflected their moods." No studies are described and no bibliographic references are listed.) (*b*) The rationale of the scoring system where the extent of use of a color, that is if it is the only one used, or dominates, or is secondary, is weighted on a 3, 2, 1 basis.

Clinical diagnosis is based on a standardization group of "149 patients of distinct clinical types in whose case the diagnosis was 'finally and firmly' established." The eight groups listed include from 10 to 39 patients and do not include manics, depressives, or organics with the possible exception of "structural epileptics with an IQ range of 37–59." Yet some of the diagnostic illustrations given offer typical patterns of organics. In this area, as with prevalent mood, discussion of interpretation is *not* offered in terms of normative data but rather seems offhand, clinical, intuitive, and frequently overgeneralized. In some instances, a specific case is given with some brief discussion while in others a more general group, for example, "emotionally immature adults," is discussed.

Although there is discussion of testing of children, no age range is mentioned in the manual and there are no data offered about children's reactions to the test. (This is one of the promises for later.)

The author indicates that individuals with an IQ of 34 and up complete the test. There is, however, no analysis offered on the standardization group as to whether IQ affects performance. In those examples given where IQ is noted, the reviewer felt that this might be a significant variable.

Other specific criticism can be raised, but it would seem unnecessary, for the author's report of high correlations with the MMPI suggests that the Multiphasic measures these same variables and offers the test user a more meaningful basis for interpretation. It seems unlikely that there is a good basis for the claim in the manual that the *Visual Apperception Test* differentiates types of schizophrenia since only 23 psychotics classified as simple schizo-

phrenics or delusional psychoses with a limited IQ range are included in the standardization group. Therefore, this claim used as evidence of an advantage of the VAT '60 over the MMPI seems untenable.

For the moment this new projective would seem poorly constructed with limited normative data available and with many questions as to the basis of interpretations offered. Until the author can offer some of the promised data and can approach the task of validation in a more careful and exacting manner, the VAT '60 would seem to offer little of value to the diagnostician.

The publication of this test at its present stage of development is another sad example of clinically oriented people prejudicing the case for the use of projective techniques by adding to the already existing number rather than devoting themselves to testing and improving those presently in wide use. Perhaps a moratorium on the publication of new projectives is needed until the wheat is separated from the chaff of those already in print.

[Other Tests]

For tests not listed above, see the following entries in *Tests in Print:* 325, 333–4, 337–40, 342, 344, 346–7, 359, 364–5, 368–70, 376, 378, 380, 383–4, 391–2, and 394–7; out of print: 343, 354, 386, and 390; status unknown: 330 and 377.

MMY Test Index

THIS chapter presents a classified listing of all tests listed in one or more of the six *Mental Measurements Yearbooks*. The title last used in an MMY is presented for each test along with a listing of the names of persons who have reviewed the test in an MMY, the number of reviews excerpted in an MMY from other sources, and the number of references on the construction, validation and use of the test. The MMY Test Index does not indicate whether a test is currently in print; nor does it list tests published since the 6th MMY; it is a master index to the tests, reviews, excerpts, and references to be found in the first six *Mental Measurements Yearbooks*. Within each classification, tests are listed in alphabetical order. If information is wanted about tests in a particular area, consult the following key to the classification used in the MMY Test Index; if information is wanted about a particular test, consult the title index; if information is wanted about the tests reviewed by a particular person, consult the name index.

KEY TO CLASSIFICATION

ACHIEVEMENT BATTERIES

A1. American School Achievement Tests. For additional information and reviews by Robert H. Bauernfeind and Frank B. Womer, see 6:2; for reviews by J. Raymond Gerberich and Virgil E. Herrick, see 5:1; for a review by Ralph C. Preston of an earlier edition, see 4:1; for reviews by Walter W. Cook and Gordon N. Mackenzie (with Glen Hass), see 3:1. For reviews of subtests, see 5:174 (2 reviews), 5:455 (1 review), 5:456 (2 reviews), and 5:620 (2 reviews).

A2. California Achievement Tests. For additional information and reviews by Jack C. Merwin and Robert D. North, see 6:3 (20 references); for a review by Charles O. Neidt, see 5:2 (10 references); for reviews by Warren G. Findley, Alvin W. Schindler, and J. Harlan Shores of an earlier edition, see 4:2 (8 references); for a review by Paul A. Witty, see 3:15 (3 references); for reviews by C. W. Odell and Hugh B. Wood, see 2:1193 (1 reference); for a review by D. Welty Lefever, see 1:876 (1 excerpt). For reviews of subtests, see 6:251 (1 review), 5:177 (2 reviews), 5:468 (1 review), 4:151 (2 reviews), 4:411 (1 review), 4:530 (2 reviews, 1 excerpt), 2:1292 (2 reviews), 2:1459 (2 reviews), 2:1563 (1 review), 1:893 (1 review), and 1:1110 (2 reviews).

A3. California Basic Skills Tests. For additional information and a review by Robert D. North, see 6:4.

A4. California Tests in Social and Related Sciences. For additional information and a review by David R. Krathwohl, see 5:4; for reviews by Harry D. Berg and J. Raymond Gerberich of an earlier edition, see 4:23.

A5. Canadian Test of General Information (CTGI). For additional information and reviews by J. Douglas Ayers and Robert J. Solomon, see 6:5 (2 references).

A6. Closed High School Placement Test. For additional information and reviews by Marion F. Shaycoft and James R. Hayden, see 6:6; for reviews by William C. Cottle and Robert A. Jones of an earlier form, see 5:15.

A7. Comprehensive Testing Program. For additional information and reviews by Richard Ledgerwood, W. J. Osburn, and Ernest W. Tiegs, see 1:869 (2 references).

A8. Cooperative General Achievement Tests [Revised Series]. For additional information and a review by Willard G. Warrington, see 6:7 (4 references); for a review by Max D. Engelhart, see 5:6 (12 references); for a review by Paul L. Dressel of earlier forms, see 4:5 (9 references); for a review by John V. McQuitty, see 3:3. For reviews of individual tests, see 3:316 (1 review), 3:548 (1 review), and 3:596 (1 review).

A9. Cooperative General Achievement Tests [Survey Series]. For additional information and reviews, see 1:870.

A10. Cooperative General Culture Test. For additional information and a review by Benjamin S. Bloom, see 5:7 (9 references); for a review by John V. McQuitty of earlier forms, see 4:6 (10 references); for reviews by Benjamin S. Bloom and H. T. Morse, see 3:4 (14 references); for reviews by Lavone A. Hanna, Edward S. Jones, and Hilda Taba, see 2:1184 (2 references); for a review by F. S. Beers, see 1:871.

A11. Coordinated Scales of Attainment. For additional information and a review by Alvin W. Schindler, see 4:8; for reviews by Roland L. Beck, Lavone A. Hanna, Gordon N. Mackenzie (with Glen Hass), and C. C. Ross, see 3:6.

A12. Eighth Grade Test. For additional information, see 6:8 (1 reference).

A13. Entrance and Classification Examination for Teachers Colleges: Elementary Test. For additional information, see 2:1185.

A14. Essential High School Content Battery. For additional information and reviews by Herbert S. Conrad, J. Thomas Hastings, and Gordon N. Mackenzie (with A. Harry Passow), see 4:9.

A15. Every Pupil Primary Achievement Test. For additional information and a review by C. C. Ross, see 3:7.

A16. General Scholarship Test for High School Seniors. For additional information, see 6:8a (2 references); for a review by C. C. Ross of an earlier form, see 3:14.

A17. Graduate Record Examination Profile Tests. For additional information and a review by Max D. Engelhart, see 4:10 (5 references).

A18. Graduate Record Examination Tests of General Education. For additional information, see 4:11 (1 reference).

A19. The Graduate Record Examinations: The Area Tests. For additional information and reviews by Paul L. Dressel and Everett B. Sackett, see 6:9 (10 references); for reviews by Benjamin S. Bloom and Frederick B. Davis of earlier forms, see 5:10. For a review of the testing program, see 5:601.

A20. The Gray-Votaw-Rogers General Achievement Tests. For additional information and reviews by Kenneth D. Hopkins, Victor H. Noll, and Ellis Batten Page, see 6:10; for reviews by Warren G. Findley and Douglas E. Scates of an earlier edition, see 5:11 (1 reference); for a review by Oliver F. Anderhalter, see 4:12; for a review by Roland L. Beck, see 3:9 (3 references); for reviews by Joseph E. Moore and C. C. Ross, see 2:1187 (1 reference).

A21. Group Achievement Test: Dominion Tests, 1934 Edition. For additional information, see 5:12.

A22. Group Achievement Tests: Dominion Tests: Niagara Edition. For additional information, see 5:13.

A23. The Harlow Achievement Tests for Texas. For additional information, see 4:13.

A24. The Harlow Battery Achievement Test. For additional information, see 4:14.

A25. High School Classification Examination. For additional information and reviews by Thomas W. Mahan, Jr. and David V. Tiedeman, see 6:11 (1 reference).

A26. High School Fundamentals Evaluation Test. For additional information and reviews by George D. Demos and Jason Millman, see 6:12 (1 reference); for reviews by Victor H. Noll and Verner M. Sims, see 5:14.

A27. Iowa Every-Pupil Tests of Basic Skills. For additional information and reviews by Miriam M. Bryan and Anton Thompson, see 4:15 (4 references); for reviews by Frederic L. Ayer, Gustav J. Froehlich, and Ralph C. Preston, see 3:10 (8 references); for reviews by Harriet M. Barthelmess [Morrison], William A. Brownell, J. Murray Lee, and Charles W. Odell of an earlier edition, see 1:872 (3 references). For reviews of subtests, see 3:334 (2 reviews) and 3:501 (2 reviews).

A28. Iowa High School Content Examination. For additional information and a review by David V. Tiedeman, see 4:16 (4 references); for a review by Maurice E. Troyer, see 3:11 (7 references).

A29. Iowa Tests of Basic Skills. For additional information, see 6:13 (17 references); for reviews by Virgil E. Herrick, G. A. V. Morgan, and H. H. Remmers, see 5:16 (1 excerpt).

A30. The Iowa Tests of Educational Development. For additional information and reviews by El-lis Batten Page and Alexander G. Wesman, see 6:14 (23 references); for reviews by J. Murray Lee and Stephen Wiseman, see 5:17 (9 references); for a review by Eric F. Gardner of earlier forms, see 4:17 (3 references); for reviews by Henry Chauncey, Gustav J. Froehlich, and Lavone A. Hanna, see 3:12. For reviews of separate tests, see 6:579 (1 review), 6:876 (2 reviews), and 6:969 (1 review).

A31. Master Achievement Tests. For additional information and a review by Clifford Woody, see 1:873.

A32. Metropolitan Achievement Tests. For additional information and reviews by Paul L. Dressel, Henry S. Dyer, and Warren G. Findley, see 6:15 (16 references); for a review by Warren G. Findley of an earlier edition, see 4:18 (10 references); see also 3:13 (7 references); for reviews by E. V. Pullias and Hugh B. Wood, see 2:1189 (3 references); for reviews by Jack W. Dunlap, Charles W. Odell, and Richard Ledgerwood, see 1:874. For reviews of subtests, see 6:627 (2 reviews), 6:797 (1 review), 6:877 (2 reviews), 6:970 (2 reviews), 4:416 (1 review), 4:543 (2 reviews), 2:1458.1 (2 reviews), 2:1551 (1 review), 1:892 (2 reviews), and 1:1105 (2 reviews).

A33. Modern School Achievement Tests. For additional information and a review by Charles R. Langmuir, see 4:19; for reviews by William A. Brownell, Herbert S. Conrad, and Herschel T. Manuel of the original edition, see 2:1190 (3 references).

A34. Municipal Battery: National Achievement Tests. For additional information and a review by J. Murray Lee, see 5:18; for a review by Ralph C. Preston, see 4:20; for reviews by A. M. Jordan and Hugh B. Wood, see 2:1191. For reviews of subtests, see 5:790 (1 review), 4:406 (2 reviews), and 4:664 (1 review).

A35. Myers-Ruch High School Progress Test. For additional information and reviews by Harl R. Douglass, August Dvorak, John M. Stalnaker, and Ernest W. Tiegs, see 2:1192.

A36. National Achievement Tests. For additional information, see 6:16; for a review by William E. Coffman, see 5:19.

A37. National Educational Development Tests. For additional information and reviews by Willis W. Clark, Arthur E. Traxler, and Alexander G. Wesman, see 6:17.

A38. National Merit Scholarship Qualifying Test. For additional information and reviews by Dorothy C. Adkins, George K. Bennett, and J. Thomas Hastings, see 6:18 (12 references); for reviews by Benno G. Fricke and Roger T. Lennon of the 1958 test, see 5:20.

A39. Public School Achievement Tests. For additional information, see 6:19 (2 references); for reviews by Herbert S. Conrad and E. V. Pullias, see 2:1194.

A40. Public School Attainment Tests for High School Entrance: Examination of Abilities in Reading, English, and Mathematics. For additional information and a review by Benjamin S. Bloom, see 3:17; for reviews by Harold Gulliksen and C. C. Ross, see 2:1195 (1 reference).

A41. Public School Correlated Attainment Scales. For additional information and reviews by C. W. Odell and Robert K. Speer, see 2:1196 (1 reference, 2 excerpts); for reviews by H. S. Conrad and H. E. Schrammel, see 1:877.

A42. Pupil Record of Educational Progress. For additional information and reviews by George D. Demos and Jack C. Merwin, see 6:20.

A43. SRA Achievement Series. For additional information and a review by Jacob S. Orleans, see 6:21 (3 references); for reviews by Warren G. Findley and Worth R. Jones, see 5:21. For reviews of subtests, see 6:632 (1 review), 6:808 (1 review), 5:200 (2 reviews), 5:483 (2 reviews), 5:649 (2 reviews), and 5:696 (2 reviews).

A44. SRA High School Placement Test. For additional information and reviews by Walter N. Durost and Charles O. Neidt, see 6:22 (3 references); for reviews by Cyril J. Hoyt (with W. Wesley Tennyson) and William W. Turnbull of earlier forms, see 5:22.

A45. Scholastic Achievement Series. For additional information and reviews by J. Stanley Ahmann and Thomas W. Mahan, Jr., see 6:23; for reviews by William E. Coffman and James R. Hayden, see 5:23. For reviews of subtests, see 5:201 (2 reviews) and 5:484 (2 reviews).

A46. Secondary School Admission Tests: General School Ability and Reading Test. For additional information and reviews by Charles O. Neidt and David V. Tiedeman, see 6:24 (1 reference).

A47. Sequential Tests of Educational Progress. For additional information and reviews by Harold Seashore and John E. Stecklein, see 6:25 (6 references); for reviews by Robert W. B. Jackson and Wilbur L. Layton, see 5:24 (1 excerpt). For reviews of individual tests, see 6:292 (2 reviews, 1 excerpt), 6:590 (2 reviews), 6:810 (2 reviews), 6:882 (2 reviews), 6:971 (2 reviews), 5:206 (3 reviews), 5:207 (3 reviews), 5:438 (3 reviews), 5:578 (2 reviews), 5:653 (3 reviews), 5:716 (3 reviews), and 5:792 (3 reviews).

A48. Seven Plus Assessment: The Northumberland Series. For additional information and a review by Stanley D. Nisbet, see 4:24.

A49. Stanford Achievement Test. For additional information and a review by Miriam M. Bryan, see 6:26 (13 references, 1 excerpt); for a review by N. L. Gage of an earlier edition, see 5:25 (19 references); for reviews by Paul R. Hanna (with Claude E. Norcross) and Virgil E. Herrick, see 4:25 (20 references); for reviews by Walter W. Cook and Ralph C. Preston, see 3:18 (34 references). For reviews of subtests, see 5:656 (2 reviews), 5:698 (2 reviews), 5:799 (1 review), 4:419 (1 review), 4:555 (1 review), 4:593 (2 reviews), 3:503 (1 review), and 3:595 (1 review).

A50. Test for High School Entrants: [National Achievement Tests]. For additional information and a review by Jacob S. Orleans, see 5:26; for a review by Benjamin S. Bloom, see 3:19.

A51. Tests of General Educational Development. For additional information and a review by Robert J. Solomon, see 5:27 (39 references); for a review by Gustav J. Froehlich, see 4:26 (27 references); for reviews by Herbert S. Conrad and Warren G. Findley, see 3:20 (11 references). For reviews of individual tests, see 3:122 (1 review) and 3:528 (2 reviews).

A52. Unit Scales of Attainment. For additional information and a review by D. Welty Lefever, see 2:1197 (2 references); for reviews by Herbert S. Conrad and Ethel L. Cornell, see 1:878. For reviews of subtests, see 2:1315 (2 reviews), 2:1463 (2 reviews), 2:1581 (2 reviews), and 1:1115 (1 review).

A53. Wide Range Achievement Test: Reading, Spelling, Arithmetic From Kindergarten to College. For additional information, see 6:27 (15 references); for reviews by Paul Douglas Courtney, Verner M. Sims, and Louis P. Thorpe, see 3:21.

A54. Wisconsin Composite Achievement Test. For additional information and reviews by Ernest W. Tiegs and Maurice E. Troyer, see 3:22 (4 references).

BUSINESS EDUCATION

B1. Business Backgrounds Test. For additional information, see 2:1478 (1 reference, 1 excerpt).

B2. Business Education: National Teacher Examinations. For additional information, see 6:28. For reviews of the testing program, see 6:700 (1 review), 5:538 (3 reviews), and 4:802 (1 review).

B3. Business Education: Teacher Education Examination Program. An inactive form of B2; for additional information, see 6:29. For a review of the testing program, see 5:543; for references to additional reviews, see B2.

B4. Business Fundamentals and General Information Test: National Business Entrance Tests. For additional information, see 6:30; for reviews by Vera M. Amerson and C. C. Upshall of an earlier form, see 3:369. For reviews of the complete battery, see 6:33 (1 review), 5:515 (3 reviews), and 3:396 (1 review).

B5. Business Relations and Occupations: Midwest High School Achievement Examinations. For additional information, see 5:510.

B6. General Business: Every Pupil Scholarship Test. For additional information and a review by Ray G. Price, see 6:31.

B7. General Clerical: Every Pupil Test. For additional information, see 1:937.

B8. General Office Clerical Test (Including Filing): National Business Entrance Tests. For additional information, see 6:32 (1 reference). For reviews of the complete battery, see 6:33 (1 review), 5:515 (3 reviews), and 3:396 (1 review).

B9. General Test of Business Information. For additional information and reviews by Vera M. Amerson and Herbert A. Tonne, see 3:380.

B10. National Business Entrance Tests. For additional information and a review by Melvin R.

Marks, see 6:33 (6 references); for reviews by Edward N. Hay, Jacob S. Orleans, and Wimburn L. Wallace, see 5:515; see also 4:453 (1 reference); for a review by Paul S. Lomax of earlier forms, see 3:396; see also 2:1476 (9 references). For reviews of individual tests, see 6:55 (1 review), 5:514 (1 review), 5:522 (1 review), 5:526 (1 review), 3:368 (2 reviews), 3:369 (2 reviews), 3:379 (2 reviews), 3:384 (1 review), 3:391 (2 reviews), and 3:394 (2 reviews).

B11. Thompson Business Practice Test. For additional information and a review by Herbert A. Tonne, see 1:942.

BOOKKEEPING

B12. Bookkeeping: Every Pupil Scholarship Test. For additional information, see 6:34.

B13. Bookkeeping: Minnesota High School Achievement Examinations. For additional information and a review by Harold L. Royer, see 6:35; for a review by I. David Satlow of an earlier form, see 5:504.

B14. Bookkeeping Test: National Business Entrance Tests. For additional information, see 6:36; for reviews by Harvey A. Andruss and Ray G. Price of an earlier form, see 3:368. For reviews of the complete battery, see 6:33 (1 review), 5:515 (3 reviews), and 3:396 (1 review).

B15. Bookkeeping Test: State High School Tests for Indiana. For additional information, see 3:367.

B16. Breidenbaugh Bookkeeping Tests: Single Proprietorship. For additional information, see 2:1477 (1 excerpt).

B17. Examination in Bookkeeping and Accounting. For additional information and a review by Harvey A. Andruss, see 3:373.

B18. First-Year Bookkeeping: Every Pupil Test. For additional information, see 6:37.

B19. Shemwell-Whitcraft Bookkeeping Test. For additional information and a review by Arnold E. Schneider, see 3:387.

MISCELLANEOUS

B20. Clinton-LeMaster Commercial and Business Law Test. For additional information, see 2:1479.

B21. Commercial Law: Every Pupil Scholarship Test. For additional information, see 6:38.

B22. Dictating Machine Transcription Test: National Clerical Ability Tests. For additional information, see 2:1482.

B23. Examination in Commercial Correspondence—College Level. For additional information and reviews by Orrel E. Little and Herbert A. Tonne, see 3:376.

B24. Filing Test: United-NOMA Business Entrance Tests. For additional information and reviews by Arnold E. Schneider and C. C. Upshall, see 3:379.

B25. Machine Calculation Test: National Business Entrance Tests. For additional informa-

tion, see 6:39; for a review by Dorothy C. Adkins, see 5:514; for a review by Elizabeth Fehrer of an earlier form, see 3:384. For reviews of the complete battery, see 6:33 (1 review), 5:515 (3 reviews), and 3:396 (1 review).

B26. Parke Commercial Law Test. For additional information and a review by Ray G. Price, see 3:385.

B27. Qualifying Test for Ediphone Voice Writing. For additional information, see 2:1488.

SHORTHAND

B28. APT Dictation Test. For additional information, see 6:40.

B29. Byers' First-Year Shorthand Aptitude Tests. For additional information and a review by Edward O. Swanson, see 6:41 (1 reference).

B30. Commercial Education Survey Tests: Junior and Senior Shorthand. For additional information, see 1:936 (2 references, 1 excerpt).

B31. E.R.C. Stenographic Aptitude Test. For additional information and reviews by Philip H. DuBois and Edward A. Rundquist, see 3:372 (1 reference).

B32. Examination in Gregg Shorthand. For additional information and a review by Agnes E. Osborne, see 3:377.

B33. First-Year Shorthand: Every Pupil Test. For additional information, see 6:42.

B34. Hiett Simplified Shorthand Test (Gregg). For additional information and a review by Gale W. Clark, see 5:512.

B35. Hiett Stenography Test (Gregg). For additional information and a review by Agnes E. Osborne, see 3:381.

B36. Personnel Research Institute Test of Shorthand Skills. For additional information and a review by Irol Whitmore Balsley, see 6:43.

B37. Revised Standard Graded Tests for Stenographers. For additional information, see 6:44.

B38. SRA Dictation Skills. For additional information and a review by Harold F. Rothe, see 4:454 (1 reference).

B39. The Seashore-Bennett Stenographic Proficiency Tests: A Standard Recorded Stenographic Worksample. For additional information, see 5:519 (2 references); for a review by Harold F. Rothe, see 4:455 (1 reference); for a review by Ann Brewington, see 3:386.

B40. Shorthand Aptitude Test. For additional information and a review by James Lumsden, see 5:520.

B41. Shorthand Test: Individual Placement Series (Area IV). For additional information, see 6:45.

B42. Shorthand Test: State High School Tests for Indiana. For additional information, see 4:457.

B43. Shorthand II: Every Pupil Test. For additional information, see 4:456.

B44. Stenogauge. For additional information and a review by Beatrice J. Dvorak, see 3:389.

B45. Stenographic Aptitude Test. For additional information and reviews by Philip H. DuBois and Edward A. Rundquist, see 3:390 (1 reference); see also 2:1677 (1 reference).

B46. Stenographic Dictation Test. For additional information, see 6:46.

B47. Stenographic Test: National Business Entrance Tests. For additional information, see 6:47 (1 reference); for a review by Edward B. Greene, see 5:522; for reviews by Ann Brewington and Elizabeth Fehrer of an earlier form, see 3:391. For reviews of the complete battery, see 6:33 (1 review), 5:515 (3 reviews), and 3:396 (1 review).

B48. Test for Stenographic Skill. For additional information and reviews by Reign H. Bittner and Clifford E. Jurgensen, see 4:459.

B49. Test of Dictation Speed. For additional information, see 6:48.

B50. Turse-Durost Shorthand Achievement Test (Gregg). For additional information, see 3:392 (1 excerpt).

B51. Turse Shorthand Aptitude Test. For additional information and a review by Leslie M. Haynes, see 4:460 (5 references); for a review by Philip H. DuBois, see 3:393.

TYPEWRITING

B52. Commercial Education Survey Tests: Junior and Senior Typewriting. For additional information, see 2:1480 (1 excerpt).

B53. Examination in Typewriting. For additional information and a review by E. G. Blackstone, see 3:378.

B54. First-Year Typewriting: Every Pupil Test. For additional information, see 6:49.

B55. Grading Scales for Typewriting Tests. For additional information, see 2:1486 (1 excerpt).

B56. Kauzer Typewriting Test. For additional information and a review by E. G. Blackstone, see 3:382.

B57. Kimberly-Clark Typing Ability Analysis. For additional information, see 5:513 (2 references); for a review by E. G. Blackstone, see 3:383.

B58. [McCann Typing Tests.] For additional information, see 6:50.

B59. SRA Typing Adaptability Test. For additional information and reviews by Gale W. Clark and Edward B. Greene, see 5:518.

B60. SRA Typing Skills. For additional information and reviews by Lawrence W. Erickson and Jacob S. Orleans, see 6:51 (2 references).

B61. The Tapping Test: A Predictor of Typing and Other Tapping Operations. For additional information and reviews by Ray G. Price and Henry Weitz, see 6:52 (2 references).

B62. Test for Typing Skill. For additional information and a review by Bernadine Meyer, see 5:523.

B63. Test of Typing Speed. For additional information, see 6:53.

B64. Typewriting I and II: Every Pupil Scholarship Test. For additional information, see 6:54.

B65. Typewriting Test: National Business Entrance Tests. For additional information and a review by Lawrence W. Erickson, see 6:55 (1 reference); for a review by Clifford E. Jurgensen, see 5:526; for reviews by E. G. Blackstone and Beatrice J. Dvorak of an earlier form, see 3:394. For reviews of the complete battery, see 6:33 (1 review), 5:515 (3 reviews), and 3:396 (1 review).

B66. Typewriting Test: State High School Tests for Indiana. For additional information, see 4:463.

B67. Typewriting II: Every Pupil Test. For additional information, see 1:944.

B68. Typing Test: Individual Placement Series (Area IV). For additional information, see 6:56.

B69. United Students Typewriting Tests. For additional information, see 5:527.

ENGLISH

C1. A.C.E.R. English Usage Tests. For additional information and a review by J. A. Richardson, see 5:173.

C2. Ability for English (Language): Fife Tests of Ability, Test 1. For additional information, see 3:114 (1 reference). For reviews of the complete battery, see 4:713 (1 review) and 3:8 (1 review).

C3. American School Achievement Tests: Part 3, Language and Spelling. For additional information, see 6:248 (1 reference); for reviews by M. A. Brimer and Clarence Derrick, see 5:174. For reviews of the complete battery, see 6:2 (2 reviews), 5:1 (2 reviews), 4:1 (1 review), and 3:1 (2 reviews).

C4. Analytical Survey Test in English Fundamentals. For additional information and reviews by Leonard S. Feldt and Roger A. Richards, see 6:249 (2 references).

C5. Barrett-Ryan English Test. For additional information and a review by Clarence Derrick, see 6:250 (2 references); for a review by J. Raymond Gerberich, see 5:175.

C6. Barrett-Ryan-Schrammel English Test. For additional information and reviews by Leonard S. Feldt and Cleveland A. Thomas, see 5:176 (1 reference); for reviews by G. Frederic Kuder, Robert C. Pooley, and Charles Swain Thomas of the original edition, see 2:1267.

C7. Basic Language Skills: Iowa Every-Pupil Tests of Basic Skills, Test C. For additional information, see 4:150; see also 3:116 (2 references).

For reviews of the complete battery, see 4:15 (2 reviews), 3:10 (3 reviews), and 1:872 (4 reviews).

C8. California Language Test. For additional information and a review by Richard E. Schutz, see 6:251 (1 reference); for reviews by Constance M. McCullough and Winifred L. Post, see 5:177 (3 references); for reviews by Gerald V. Lannholm and Roert C. Pooley of an earlier edition, see 4:151; for reviews by Harry A. Greene and J. Paul Leonard, see 2:1292. For reviews of the complete battery, see 6:3 (2 reviews), 5:2 (1 review), 4:2 (3 reviews), 3:15 (1 review), 2:1193 (2 reviews), and 1:876 (1 review, 1 excerpt).

C9. Canadian Achievement Test in English (CATE). For additional information and a review by Bernard Spolsky, see 6:252 (2 references).

C10. Canadian English Achievement Test (CEAT). For additional information and reviews by J. Douglas Ayers and Bernard Spolsky, see 6:253 (2 references).

C11. The Clapp-Young English Test. For additional information and a review by Gerald V. Lannholm, see 3:117.

C12. Cleveland English Composition and Grammar Test. For additional information and a review by Frank P. De Lay, see 2:1269.

C13. College English Test: National Achievement Tests. For additional information and a review by Osmond E. Palmer, see 5:178; for reviews by Constance M. McCullough and Robert W. Howard, see 2:1269.1.

C14. College Entrance Examination Board Advanced Placement Examination: English. For additional information, see 6:254.

C15. College Placement Test in English. For additional information and a review by Charlotte Croon Davis, see 4:153.

C16. College Preparatory Test in English. For additional information and a review by Charlotte Croon Davis, see 4:154.

C17. Columbia Research Bureau English Test. For additional information and reviews by L. K. Shumaker and Louis C. Zahner, see 2:1270.

C18. Cooperative English Test: Usage, Spelling, and Vocabulary. For additional information and reviews by Margaret F. Lorimer and John M. Stalnaker, see 6:255 (5 references); for reviews by Carleton C. Jones, Jeanette McPherrin, Louis C. Zahner, Henry D. Rinsland, and L. K. Shumaker, see 2:1271 (11 references); for reviews by John M. Stalnaker, Charles S. Thomas, and John H. Thompson of earlier forms, see 1:961.

C19. Cooperative English Tests. For additional information and reviews by Leonard S. Feldt and Margaret F. Lorimer, see 6:256 (52 references, 1 excerpt); see also 5:179 (58 references) and 4:155 (53 references); for reviews by J. Paul Leonard, Edward S. Noyes, and Robert C. Pooley of an earlier edition, see 3:120 (29 references); see also 2:1276 (2 references). For reviews of subtests, see 6:258 (2 reviews), 6:806 (2 reviews), and 3:497 (2 reviews).

C20. Coordinated Scales of Attainment: English. For additional information, see 5:180. For reviews of the complete battery, see 4:8 (1 review) and 3:6 (4 reviews).

C21. Correct English Usage Test. For additional information, see 4:156.

C22. Correctness and Appropriateness of Expression: The Iowa Tests of Educational Development, Test 3. For additional information, see 6:267 (1 reference). For reviews of the complete battery, see 6:14 (2 reviews), 5:17 (2 reviews), 4:17 (1 review), and 3:12 (3 reviews).

C23. Correctness and Effectiveness of Expression: Tests of General Educational Development, Test 1. For additional information, see 5:181; for a review by Charlotte W. Croon [Davis] of the college level, see 3:122. For reviews of the complete battery, see 5:27 (1 review), 4:26 (1 review), and 3:20 (2 reviews).

C24. Cotswold Junior English Ability Test. For additional information and reviews by M. A. Brimer and John C. Daniels, see 5:182.

C25. Cotswold Measurement of Ability: English. For additional information and reviews by M. A. Brimer and S. C. Richardson, see 5:183.

C26. Cross English Test. For additional information and reviews by Roland L. Beck and Edward S. Noyes, see 2:1272 (3 references).

C27. Davis-Schrammel Elementary English Test. For additional information and reviews by Keith Goltry and Rachel Salisbury, see 2:1273.

C28. Diagnostic Tests in English Composition. For additional information and reviews by Harry A. Greene and Jean Hoard, see 2:1274.

C29. "Dingwall" Test in English Usage. For additional information and a review by Robert H. Thouless, see 3:124; for a review by Charles Fox, see 2:1275.

C30. English Classification Test for High Schools and Colleges. For additional information, see 2:1277.

C31. English: Every Pupil Scholarship Test. For additional information, see 6:257 (1 reference).

C32. English Expression: Cooperative English Tests. For additional information and reviews by John C. Sherwood and John M. Stalnaker, see 6:258; for a review by Chester W. Harris of an earlier edition, see 4:155. For reviews of the the complete battery, see 6:256 (2 reviews, 1 excerpt), 4:155 (1 review), and 3:120 (3 reviews).

C33. English Language and Literature: National Teacher Examinations. For additional information and a review by Holland Roberts, see 6:259. For reviews of the testing program, see 6:700 (1 review), 5:538 (3 reviews), and 4:802 (3 reviews).

C34. English Language and Literature: Teacher Education Examination Program. An inactive form of C33; for additional information, see 6:260; for a reference to a review, see C33. For a review of the testing program, see 5:543.

C35. English No. 4, Grammar and Style: Midland Attainment Tests. For additional information, see 1:962.

C36. English Placement Test. For additional information and reviews by Roland L. Beck and Robert W. Howard, see 2:1278 (2 references).

C37. English Placement Test for Iowa Universities and Colleges. For additional information, see 1:958.

C38. English Progress Tests. For additional information, see 6:261; for reviews by Neil Gourlay and Stanley Nisbet, see 5:187.

C39. English Survey Test: Ohio Scholarship Tests: Ohio Senior Survey Tests. For additional information, see 5:188; for reviews by Charlotte W. Croon [Davis] and J. Paul Leonard of the original edition, see 3:125 (1 reference).

C40. English Test (Adv.). For additional information and a review by A. E. G. Pilliner, see 6:262.

C41. English Test (Four-Year Course): Affiliation Testing Program for Catholic Secondary Schools. For additional information and a review by Henry Chauncey, see 6:263. For a review of the complete program, see 6:758.

C42. English Test: Municipal Tests: National Achievement Tests. For additional information, see 5:190. For reviews of the complete battery, see 5:18 (1 review), 4:20 (1 review) and 2:1191 (2 reviews).

C43. English Test: National Achievement Tests. For additional information, see 5:191; for a review by Winifred L. Post, see 4:162; for a review by Harry A. Greene, see 3:126.

C44. English Test 2. For additional information and reviews by Reginald Edwards, S. C. Richardson, and Cleveland A. Thomas, see 5:192.

C45. English Tests 1, 3–13. For additional information and reviews by Stanley Nisbet and H. J. Sants, see 6:264 (1 reference).

C46. English: Thanet Mental Tests. For additional information and a review by C. Ebblewhite Smith, see 2:1279.

C47. English Usage: Every Pupil Test. For additional information, see 6:265 (2 references); for a review by J. R. Gerberich of the 1946 forms, see 3:127.

C48. Entrance and Classification Examination for Teachers Colleges: English Test. For additional information, see 2:1280.

C49. Essentials of English Tests. For additional information and a review by J. Raymond Gerberich, see 6:266; for reviews by Charlotte W. Croon [Davis] and Gerald V. Lannholm, see 3:128 (1 excerpt).

C50. Examination in Business English—High-School Level. For additional information and a review by Orrel E. Little, see 3:375.

C51. Examination in English—College Level. For additional information and a review by John S. Diekhoff, see 3:129.

C52. Examination in English—High-School Level. For additional information and reviews by Holland Roberts and Louis C. Zahner, see 3:130 (4 references).

C53. Grammar: Public School Achievement Tests. For additional information and reviews of the complete battery, see 2:1194.

C54. Greene-Stapp Language Abilities Test. For additional information and reviews by Richard A. Meade and Osmond E. Palmer, see 5:195 (1 reference).

C55. Gregory Diagnostic Tests in Language. For additional information and reviews by Keith Goltry and J. Paul Leonard, see 2:1282.

C56. Hoyum-Schrammel English Essentials Tests. For additional information and reviews by Worth R. Jones and Ruth Strickland, see 5:196.

C57. Iowa Every-Pupil Test in English Correctness. For additional information, see 1:965.

C58. Iowa Grammar Information Test. For additional information and a review by Robert C. Pooley, see 4:164.

C59. Iowa Language Abilities Test. For additional information and a review by Margaret G. McKim, see 4:165.

C60. Iowa Placement Examinations: English Aptitude. For additional information and reviews by Clarence Derrick and W. C. Kvaraceus, see 4:166 (5 references); for a review by Robert C. Pooley, see 3:115 (9 references).

C61. Iowa Placement Examinations: English Training. For additional information and reviews by Clarence Derrick and W. C. Kvaraceus, see 4:167 (5 references); for a review by Robert C. Pooley, see 3:131 (15 references).

C62. Kentucky English Test. For additional information, see 3:132; for a review by Henry D. Rinsland, see 1:966; see also F96.

C63. Language Arts: Minnesota High School Achievement Examinations. For additional information and a review by Marvin D. Glock, see 6:268; for a review by Roger A. Richards of earlier forms, see 5:186.

C64. Language Essentials Tests. For additional information and a review by Harry A. Greene, see 3:133.

C65. Language Perception Test. For additional information, see 6:269.

C66. Language Usage: Public School Achievement Tests. For additional information and reviews of the complete battery, see 2:1194.

C67. Leonard Diagnostic Test in Punctuation and Capitalization. For additional information and a review by Jean Hoard, see 2:1285 (2 references).

C68. Linguistic Awareness Test. For additional information, see 2:1287.

C69. Los Angeles Diagnostic Tests: Language (A Test in Capitalization, Punctuation and Language Usage). For additional information and a review by Gerald V. Lannholm, see 4:168.

C70. Mechanics of Written English: State High School Tests for Indiana. For additional information, see 4:169.

C71. Metropolitan Achievement Tests: High School Language Tests. For additional information, see 6:270. For reviews of the complete battery, see 6:15 (3 reviews), 4:18 (1 review), 2:1189 (2 reviews), and 1:874 (3 reviews).

C72. Modern English Usage Test. For additional information and a review by Holland Roberts, see 5:198; for a review by Walter N. Durost, see 4:170.

C73. Moray House English Tests. For additional information and a review by M. Alan Brimer, see 6:271 (7 references).

C74. Nationwide English Grammar Examination. For additional information, see 6:272.

C75. Nelson's High School English Test. For additional information and reviews by Frank P. De Lay and Jacob S. Orleans, see 2:1290.

C76. The New Purdue Placement Test in English. For additional information and reviews by Gerald V. Lannholm and M. J. Wantman, see 5:199 (5 references); see also 4:173 (9 references).

C77. Novelty Grammar Tests. For additional information, see 6:273.

C78. Objective Test in Grammar. For additional information, see 4:171.

C79. Objective Tests in English. For additional information, see 4:172.

C80. Pressey English Tests for Grades 5 to 8. For additional information, see 2:1291 (2 excerpts).

C81. The Pribble-Dallmann Diagnostic Tests in Elementary Language Skills. For additional information and reviews by William H. Lucio and George D. Spache, see 6:274.

C82. The Pribble-McCrory Diagnostic Tests in Practical English Grammar. For additional information and a review by Clarence Derrick, see 6:275.

C83. The Purdue High School English Test. For additional information and reviews by Charlotte Croon Davis and Benjamin Rosner, see 6:276.

C84. Purdue Placement Test in English. For additional information, see 4:173 (9 references); for revised edition, see C76.

C85. Rinsland-Beck Natural Test of English Usage. For additional information and reviews by John M. Stalnaker and Charles Swain Thomas, see 2:1293 (3 references, 1 excerpt).

C86. SRA Achievement Series: Language Arts. For additional information and a review by Miriam M. Bryan, see 6:277 (1 reference); for reviews by Constance M. McCullough and Winifred L. Post, see 5:200. For reviews of the complete battery, see 6:21 (1 review) and 5:21 (2 reviews).

C87. SRA Language Skills. For additional information, see 3:388c.

C88. Scholastic Achievement Series: English-Spelling. For additional information, see 6:278 (1 reference); for reviews by Geraldine Spaulding and Ruth Strickland, see 5:201. For reviews of the complete battery, see 6:23 (2 reviews) and 5:23 (2 reviews).

C89. The Schonell Diagnostic English Tests. For additional information and reviews by John Cohen and Robert H. Thouless, see 3:135.

C90. Shepherd English Test. For additional information and a review by Ruth D. Churchill, see 3:136 (2 references).

C91. Stanford Achievement Test [Language Arts]. For additional information, see 4:174 (1 reference).

C92. Stanford Achievement Test: Spelling and Language Tests. For additional information, see 6:279. For reviews of the complete battery, see 6:26 (1 review, 1 excerpt), 5:25 (1 review), 4:25 (2 reviews), and 3:18 (2 reviews).

C93. Survey of Language Achievement: California Survey Series. For additional information and a review by Miriam M. Bryan, see 6:280.

C94. Survey Tests of English Usage. For additional information and a review by Holland Roberts, see 6:281 (1 reference).

C95. T. C. English Test. For additional information, see 6:282.

C96. Test of English Usage [California Test Bureau]. For additional information and a review by John C. Sherwood, see 6:283; for a review by Charlotte Croon Davis, see 4:175.

C97. A Test of English Usage [Manasayan]. For additional information, see 6:284.

C98. Test of Language Skill. For additional information, see 6:285.

C99. Tests of Language Usage: Active Vocabulary and Expression: Cooperative Inter-American Tests. For additional information and a review by Walter V. Kaulfers, see 4:176 (3 references).

C100. Tools of Written English: State High School Tests for Indiana. For additional information, see 4:177.

C101. Tressler English Minimum Essentials Tests. For additional information and reviews by Osmond E. Palmer and Roger A. Richards, see 6:286 (1 reference).

C102. 20th Century Test for English. For additional information, see 4:159 and 4:160.

C103. Wisconsin Language Usage Test. For additional information, see 3:138.

COMPOSITION

C104. College Entrance Examination Board Achievement Test: English Composition. For additional information and reviews by Charlotte Croon Davis, Robert C. Pooley, and Holland Roberts, see 6:287 (6 references); see also 5:204 (14 references); for a review by Charlotte Croon Davis (with Frederick B. Davis) of earlier forms, see 4:178 (6 references). For reviews of the testing program, see 6:760 (2 reviews).

C105. College Entrance Examination Board Advanced Placement Examination: English Composition. For additional information and a review by Robert C. Pooley, see 5:205.

C106. College Entrance Examination Board Placement Tests: English Composition Test. For additional information, see 6:288.

C107. College Entrance Examination Board Writing Sample. For additional information and a review by Robert C. Pooley, see 6:289 (2 references). For reviews of the testing program, see 6:760 (2 reviews).

C108. Diagnostic Test of Letter-Writing Ability. For additional information, see 2:1481 (1 excerpt).

C109. Hudelson's Typical Composition Ability Scale. For additional information and a review by Worth J. Osburn, see 4:179 (7 references).

C110. Judging the Effectiveness of Written Composition: Test 3.8. For additional information, see 2:1283 (1 reference).

C111. Nationwide English Composition Examination. For additional information, see 6:290.

C112. Sequential Tests of Educational Progress: Essay Test. For additional information, see 6:291 (3 references); for reviews by John S. Diekhoff, John M. Stalnaker, and Louis C. Zahner, see 5:206. For reviews of the complete battery, see 6:25 (2 reviews) and 5:24 (2 reviews, 1 excerpt).

C113. Sequential Tests of Educational Progress: Writing. For additional information and reviews by Hillel Black and Albert N. Hieronymus, see 6:292 (3 references, 1 excerpt); for reviews by Charlotte Croon Davis, John M. Stalnaker, and Louis C.

Zahner, see 5:207. For reviews of the complete battery, see 6:25 (2 reviews) and 5:24 (2 reviews, 1 excerpt).

C114. Writing Skills Test. For additional information and reviews by William E. Coffman and Osmond E. Palmer, see 6:293.

LITERATURE

C115. Ability to Interpret Literary Materials: The Iowa Tests of Educational Development, Test 7. For additional information, see 6:300 (1 reference). For reviews of the complete battery, see 6:14 (2 reviews), 5:17 (2 reviews), 4:17 (1 review), and 3:12 (3 reviews).

C116. Alphabetical List of 1000 Fiction Authors Classified by Subject and Maturity Level. For additional information, see 2:1294 (1 reference).

C117. American Literature: Every Pupil Scholarship Test. For additional information, see 5:208.

C118. American Literature: Every Pupil Test. For additional information, see 6:294.

C119. Analytical Scales of Attainment in Literature. For additional information and reviews by Carleton C. Jones and Robert K. Speer, see 2:1295.

C120. An Awareness Test in 20th Century Literature. For additional information, see 4:182; for reviews by H. H. Giles and Ann L. Gebhardt, see 2:1296.

C121. Barrett-Ryan Literature Test. For additional information and a review by Chester W. Harris, see 3:139.

C122. Book Review Tests. For additional information, see 6:295.

C123. Carroll Prose Appreciation Test. For additional information and a review by Chester W. Harris, see 3:140 (4 references).

C124. Catholic Book Tests. For additional information, see 6:296.

C125. Center-Durost Literature Acquaintance Test. For additional information and a review by Holland Roberts, see 5:210 (1 reference).

C126. Check List of Novels. For additional information and a review by John S. Diekhoff, see 4:183 (2 references).

C127. Checklist of One Hundred Magazines. For additional information, see 2:1297.

C128. College Entrance Examination Board Advanced Placement Examination: Literature. For additional information and a review by John S. Diekhoff, see 5:211.

C129. Cooperative Literary Acquaintance Test. For additional information, see 3:141 (1 reference); for reviews by Lou LaBrant and Edward S. Noyes, see 2:1298; for reviews by Carleton C. Jones and John H. Thompson, see 1:970.

C130. Cooperative Literary Comprehension and Appreciation Test. For additional information, see 4:184 (1 reference); for a review by Holland Roberts, see 3:142 (3 references).

C131. Cooperative Literary Comprehension Test. For additional information and reviews by Lou LaBrant and Edward A. Tenney, see 2:1299 (3 references); for reviews by Charles Swain Thomas and John H. Thompson, see 1:971.

C132. Davis-Roahen-Schrammel American Literature Test. For additional information, see 6:297; for reviews by Paul B. Diederich and Violet Hughes, see 2:1300.

C133. The Eaton Book-Report System. For additional information and a review by Paul B. Diederich, see 1:972.

C134. The Eaton Literature Tests. For additional information, see 1:978.

C135. Elementary Literature: Every Pupil Scholarship Test. For additional information, see 5:218.

C136. English Literature: Every Pupil Test. For additional information, see 6:298.

C137. English No. 5, Knowledge of Literature: Midland Attainment Tests. For additional information, see 1:973.

C138. English Tests for Outside Reading. For additional information, see 2:1301.

C139. English: Understanding and Appreciation of Poetry: State High School Tests for Indiana. For additional information and a review by Chester W. Harris, see 3:143.

C140. The Graduate Record Examinations Advanced Tests: Literature. For additional information, see 6:299; for a review by Robert C. Pooley of an earlier form, see 5:215. For a review of the testing program, see 5:601.

C141. Interpretation of Literary Materials: Tests of General Educational Development, Test 4. For additional information, see 5:216. For reviews of the complete battery, see 5:27 (1 review), 4:26 (1 review), and 3:20 (2 reviews).

C142. Interpretation of Literature Test: General Education Series. For additional information and reviews by John S. Diekhoff and John M. Stalnaker, see 4:187.

C143. Inventory of Satisfactions Found in Reading Fiction: General Education Series. For additional information and a review by Holland Roberts, see 4:188 (2 references).

C144. Iowa Every-Pupil Test in Reading Comprehension in Literature. For additional information, see 1:975.

C145. The Jones Book-A-Day Tests: For Checking Outside Reading of High School Pupils. For additional information, see 4:189.

C146. Literary Information Test: American Literature: Test 3.5. For additional information, see 2:1288 (1 reference).

C147. Literary Information Test: English Literature: Test 3.4. For additional information, see 2:1289 (1 reference).

C148. Literature Appreciation Tests. For additional information, see 4:190; for a review by Paul B. Diederich, see 1:976.

C149. Literature: Every Pupil Scholarship Test. For additional information, see 6:301.

C150. Literature Questionnaire: The Drama: Test 3.21. For additional information, see 2:1302 (1 reference).

C151. Literature Questionnaire: The Novel: Test 3.2a. For additional information, see 2:1303 (1 reference).

C152. Literature Test: Municipal Tests: National Achievement Tests. For additional information, see 4:191.

C153. Literature Test: National Achievement Tests. For additional information, see 5:219; for reviews by H. H. Giles and Robert C. Pooley, see 2:1304.

C154. The New Eaton Literature Test. For additional information, see 1:978.

C155. Objective Tests in American Anthology. For additional information, see 6:302.

C156. Objective Tests in English Anthology. For additional information, see 6:303.

C157. Objective Tests in English [Perfection Form Co.]. For additional information, see 6:304.

C158. Objective Tests in English [Turner E. Smith & Co.]. For additional information, see 4:194.

C159. Outside Reading Tests for Freshmen and Sophomores. For additional information, see 6:305.

C160. Outside Reading Tests for Junior High Schools. For additional information, see 6:307.

C161. Outside Reading Tests for Juniors and Seniors. For additional information, see 6:306.

C162. Questionnaire on Voluntary Reading: Test 3.31. For additional information, see 2:1305 (1 reference).

C163. Rigg Poetry Judgment Test. For additional information and reviews by John S. Diekhoff and Louis C. Zahner, see 3:146 (2 references).

C164. Stanford Achievement Test [Literature]. For additional information and a review by Winifred L. Post, see 4:195.

C165. Stanford Test of Comprehension of Literature. For additional information and a review by J. Wayne Wrightstone, see 2:1306 (1 reference).

C166. Survey Test in American Literature. For additional information, see 3:147.

C167. Survey Test in English Literature. For additional information and a review by John S. Diekhoff, see 4:196.

C168. Test of Literary Essentials. For additional information, see 4:217.

C169. Tests for the Appreciation of Literature. For additional information and a review by Ann L. Gebhardt, see 2:1307.

C170. Ullman-Clark Test on Classical References and Allusions. For additional information, see 4:197.

SPEECH

C171. The Arizona Articulation Proficiency Scale. For additional information, see 6:307a (2 references).

C172. Bryan-Wilke Scale for Rating Public Speeches. For additional information, see 2:1308.

C173. Forms From Diagnostic Methods in Speech Pathology. For additional information, see 6:308 (1 reference).

C174. The Graduate Record Examinations Advanced Tests: Speech. For additional information, see 6:309 (1 reference). For a review of the testing program, see 5:601.

C175. Guidance Questionnaire for Students of Speech. For additional information, see 3:150 (4 references).

C176. The Houston Test for Language Development. For additional information, see 6:310 (1 reference).

C177. An Integrated Articulation Test for Use With Children With Cerebral Palsy. For additional information, see 6:311 (9 references).

C178. Language Modalities Test for Aphasia. For additional information and a review by T. R. Miles, see 6:312 (1 reference).

C179. Nationwide Speech Examination. For additional information, see 6:313.

C180. Oral English Observation Schedule. For additional information, see 1:1094.

C181. The Orzeck Aphasia Evaluation. For additional information, see 6:313a.

C182. Speech Articulation Test for Young Children. For additional information, see 6:314.

C183. Speech Attitude Scale. For additional information, see 3:151 (2 references).

C184. Speech Experience Inventory. For additional information, see 3:152 (2 references).

C185. Templin-Darley Screening and Diagnostic Tests of Articulation. For additional information, see 6:315 (9 references, 2 excerpts).

C186. Verbal Language Development Scale. For additional information, see 6:316 (7 references).

C187. Weidner-Fensch Speech Screening Test. For additional information and a review by Robert S. Cathcart (with Louise B. Scott), see 5:221.

SPELLING

C188. A.C.E.R. Spelling Test (Form C). For additional information and reviews by J. A. Richardson and D. K. Wheeler, see 5:222.

C189. A.C.E.R. Spelling Tests. For additional information and a review by David H. Russell, see 2:1309 (1 reference).

C190. Ayer Standardized Spelling Test. For additional information and a review by Gus P. Plessas, see 6:317; for a review by Harold H. Bixler, see 4:198 (1 reference).

C191. Buffalo Spelling Scale. For additional information and reviews by John C. Almack and M. E. Broom, see 2:1310; for a review by Henry D. Rinsland, see 1:1158.

C192. Coordinated Scales of Attainment: Spelling. For additional information, see 5:223. For reviews of the complete battery, see 4:8 (1 review) and 3:6 (4 reviews).

C193. Davis-Schrammel Spelling Test. For additional information and a review by Anton Thompson, see 4:199; for reviews by Walter W. Cook and Joseph C. Dewey, see 2:1311 (1 reference).

C194. Gates-Russell Spelling Diagnostic Tests. For additional information, see 6:318; for a review by George Spache, see 4:200 (1 reference); for reviews by John C. Almack and Thomas G. Foran, see 1:1159.

C195. Graded Word Spelling Test. For additional information and a review by John Nisbet, see 5:224.

C196. Group Diagnostic Spelling Test. For additional information, see 6:319.

C197. High School Spelling Test. For additional information and a review by Walter W. Cook, see 2:1312 (2 references).

C198. Kansas Spelling Test. For additional information and reviews by Henry D. Rinsland and Guy M. Wilson, see 3:153.

C199. Kelvin Measurement of Spelling Ability. For additional information, see 1:1160.

C200. Lincoln Diagnostic Spelling Tests. For additional information and a review by Gus P. Plessas, see 6:320 (6 references); for reviews by Walter Scribner Guiler and George Spache of the intermediate and advanced tests, see 4:202-3.

C201. The Morgan Spelling Test for Schools and Colleges. For additional information and a review by Harold H. Bixler, see 4:204.

C202. Morrison-McCall Spelling Scale. For additional information and a review by Anton Thompson, see 4:205 (2 references).

C203. Nationwide Spelling Examination. For additional information, see 6:321.

C204. The New Iowa Spelling Scale. For additional information, see 6:322 (1 reference).

C205. The New Standard High School Spelling Scale. For additional information, see 4:206.

C206. Rich-Engelson Spelling Test. For additional information and a review by Henry D. Rinsland, see 4:207.

C207. Spelling and Vocabulary: Every Pupil Test. For additional information, see 6:323.

C208. [Spelling and Word Meaning Tests]. For additional information, see 6:324.

C209. Spelling Errors Test. For additional information, see 5:228 (1 reference).

C210. Spelling: Every Pupil Scholarship Test. For additional information, see 6:325.

C211. Spelling: Public School Achievement Tests. For additional information and reviews of the complete battery, see 2:1194 (2 reviews).

C212. Spelling: Seven Plus Assessment: Northumberland Series. For additional information, see 4:210. For a review of the complete battery, see 4:24.

C213. Spelling Test for Clerical Workers: [Personal Research Institute Clerical Battery]. For additional information and a review by Harold H. Bixler, see 4:211. For reviews of the complete battery, see 4:729 (2 reviews).

C214. Spelling Test: National Achievement Tests. For additional information and a review by James A. Fitzgerald, see 5:230; for a review by W. J. Osburn, see 1:1161.

C215. Standard Elementary Spelling Scale. For additional information, see 2:1313.1.

C216. Traxler High School Spelling Test. For additional information and a review by Gus P. Plessas, see 6:326; for a review by Henry D. Rinsland, see 4:212.

C217. Unit Scales of Attainment in Spelling. For additional information and reviews by John C. Almack and G. M. Wilson, see 2:1315 (1 reference). For reviews of the complete battery, see 2:1197 (1 review) and 1:878 (2 reviews).

C218. Wellesley Spelling Scale. For additional information and a review by Janet G. Afflerbach, see 5:232 (1 reference); for reviews by Henry D. Rinsland and Guy M. Wilson, see 3:157.

VOCABULARY

C219. A.C.E.R. Word Knowledge Test. For additional information, see 6:327 (1 reference).

C220. American Literacy Test. For additional information and a review by Victor H. Noll, see 6:328.

C221. Bruce Vocabulary Inventory. For additional information, see 6:329.

C222. Clinton General Vocabulary Test for High Schools and Colleges. For additional information and a review by Harold H. Bixler, see 3:158.

C223. Columbia Vocabulary Test. For additional information and reviews by Verner M. Sims and Clifford Woody, see 3:159 (4 references).

C224. Cooperative Vocabulary Test. For additional information, see 4:213 (4 references); for reviews by Edgar Dale and Henry D. Rinsland, see 3:160.

C225. Durost-Center Word Mastery Test. For additional information and a review by George P. Winship, Jr., see 6:330; for a review by A. N. Hieronymus, see 5:233.

C226. English No. 2, Vocabulary: Midland Attainment Tests. For additional information, see 1:980.

C227. English Recognition Vocabulary Test. For additional information and reviews by Paul S. Burnham and Edgar Dale, see 3:161 (12 references); see also 2:1319 (3 references).

C228. General Vocabulary: The Iowa Tests of Educational Development, Test 8. For additional information, see 6:332. For reviews of the complete battery, see 6:14 (2 reviews), 5:17 (2 reviews), 4:17 (1 review), and 3:12 (3 reviews).

C229. Gulick Vocabulary Survey. For additional information and a review by George P. Winship, Jr., see 6:331 (1 reference).

C230. High School Vocabulary Test. For additional information and a review by Harold H. Bixler, see 3:162.

C231. Holborn Vocabulary Test for Young Children. For additional information and a review by C. M. Fleming, see 4:215 (1 reference).

C232. The Inglis Tests of English Vocabulary. For additional information, see 5:234 (3 references); for a review by Henry D. Rinsland, see 3:163 (7 references).

C233. Johnson O'Connor English Vocabulary Worksamples. For additional information, see 6:333 (5 references).

C234. Johnson O'Connor Vocabulary Tests. For additional information, see 6:334.

C235. Kansas Vocabulary Test. For additional information and a review by Harold H. Bixler, see 3:164.

C236. Kennon Test of Literary Vocabulary. For additional information and a review by H. H. Remmers, see 3:165 (1 reference).

C237. Michigan Vocabulary Profile Test. For additional information and a review by David Segel, see 4:216 (7 references) ; for a review by Joseph E. King, see 3:166 (6 references) ; for a review by Herbert A. Landry, see 2:1320 (2 references, 1 excerpt) ; for reviews by John G. Darley, Richard Ledgerwood, John M. Stalnaker, M. R. Trabue, and Arthur E. Traxler of an earlier edition, see 1:1171.

C238. Nationwide English Vocabulary Examination. For additional information, see 6:335.

C239. New Standard Vocabulary Test. For additional information, see 6:336; for reviews by Richard A. Meade and Osmond E. Palmer, see 5:236.

C240. Purdue Industrial Supervisors Word-Meaning Test. For additional information and reviews by Jerome E. Doppelt and Bernadine Meyer, see 5:237 (2 references).

C241. Quick-Scoring Vocabulary Test: Dominion Tests. For additional information and a review by Stephen Hunka, see 6:337.

C242. Schrammel-Wharton Vocabulary Test. For additional information and a review by Arthur E. Traxler, see 2:1321.

C243. Survey Test of Vocabulary. For additional information, see 5:239 (3 references) ; for reviews by Verner M. Sims and Clifford Woody, see 3:167 (1 reference).

C244. A Test of Active Vocabulary. For additional information, see 6:338.

C245. Vocabulary: Every Pupil Scholarship Test. For additional information, see 6:339.

C246. Vocabulary: Parr Skill-Ability Tests. For additional information, see 2:1321.1.

C247. Vocabulary Power Tests. For additional information, see 2:1322.

C248. Vocabulary Test for High School Students and College Freshmen. For additional information, see 6:342a.

C249. Vocabulary Test—GT. For additional information and a review by Robert E. Stake, see 6:342 (6 references).

C250. Vocabulary Test [Management Service Co.]. For additional information, see 6:340.

C251. Vocabulary Test: National Achievement Tests. For additional information, see 5:241 ; for a review by Clifford Woody, see 3:168.

C252. Vocabulary Test [Richardson, Bellows, Henry & Co.]. For additional information, see 6:341.

C253. Wide Range Vocabulary Test. For additional information and a review by Paul S. Burnham, see 3:169 (1 reference).

C254. Word Clue Test. For additional information, see 6:343.

C255. Word Dexterity Test. For additional information, see 4:218; see also 3:170 (2 references).

FINE ARTS

D1. Graduate Record Examinations Advanced Fine Arts Test. For additional information, see 4:219.

D2. Oberlin Test of Music and Art. For additional information, see 6:344.

ART

D3. Art Education: National Teacher Examinations. For additional information and a review by Harold A. Schultz, see 6:345. For reviews of the testing program, see 6:700 (1 review), 5:538 (3 reviews), and 4:802 (1 review).

D4. Graves Design Judgment Test. For additional information and reviews by William B. Michael and Edwin Ziegfeld, see 4:220 (2 references, 1 excerpt).

D5. Horn Art Aptitude Inventory. For additional information and a review by Orville Palmer, see 5:242 ; for a review by Edwin Ziegfeld, see 3:171 (1 reference).

D6. Knauber Art Ability Test. For additional information and a review by Edwin Ziegfeld, see 4:222; for a review by Norman C. Meier, see 2:1323 (4 references).

D7. Knauber Art Vocabulary Test. For additional information and a review by Edwin Ziegfeld, see 4:223 (2 references) ; for reviews by Ray Faulkner and Joseph E. Moore, see 2:1324 (4 references).

D8. McAdory Art Test. For additional information and reviews by Norman C. Meier and Edwin Ziegfeld, see 2:1325 (13 references).

D9. Measuring Scale for Freehand Drawing. For additional information, see 1:896.

D10. The Meier Art Tests. For additional information and a review by Harold A. Schultz of test 2, see 6:346 (8 references) ; for a review by Harold A. Schultz of test 1, see 4:224 (9 references) ; for a review by Edwin Ziegfeld, see 3:172 (4 references) ; for reviews by Paul R. Farnsworth and Aulus Ward Saunders of the original edition of test 1, see 2:1326 (15 references).

D11. Practical Drawing Ability Test: Gibson's Attainment Tests. For additional information, see 1:1036.

D12. Selective Art Aptitude Test. For additional information and a review by Edwin Ziegfeld, see 3:173.

D13. Seven Modern Paintings: Test 3.9. For additional information, see 2:1328.

D14. Tests in Fundamental Abilities of Visual Arts. For additional information and reviews by Ray Faulkner and Aulus Ward Saunders, see 2:1329 (6 references).

MUSIC

D15. Aliferis Music Achievement Test: College Level. For additional information, see 6:347 (5 references); for a review by Herbert D. Wing, see 5:243 (5 references).

D16. Aliferis-Stecklein Music Achievement Test: College Midpoint Level. For additional information and reviews by Paul R. Farnsworth and Herbert D. Wing, see 6:347 (5 references).

D17. Beach Music Test. For additional information and a review by James L. Mursell, see 3:174.

D18. Conrad Instrument-Talent Test. For additional information and a review by Herbert D. Wing, see 5:244.

D19. Diagnostic Tests of Achievement in Music. For additional information and reviews by William S. Larson and Herbert D. Wing, see 4:226.

D20. Drake Musical Aptitude Tests. For additional information and reviews by Robert W. Lundin and James Mainwaring, see 5:245 (1 reference). For references to reviews of a subtest, see D21.

D21. Drake Musical Memory Test: A Test of Musical Talent. For additional information and a review by William S. Larson, see 3:175 (2 references); for reviews by Paul R. Farnsworth and James L. Mursell, see 2:1330 (2 references); see also 1:1083 (1 excerpt). For references to additional reviews, see D20.

D22. Ear Tests in Harmony. For additional information and a review by Jay W. Fay, see 1:1084.

D23. The Farnum Music Notation Test. For additional information and reviews by Kenneth L. Bean and William S. Larson, see 5:246 (1 reference).

D24. The Graduate Record Examinations Advanced Tests: Music. For additional information, see 6:348; for a review by William S. Larson, see 5:247. For a review of the testing program, see 5:601.

D25. Hillbrand Sight-Singing Test. For additional information and a review by Alton O'Steen, see 2:1331 (1 reference).

D26. Jones Music Recognition Test. For additional information and a review by Herbert D. Wing, see 6:349.

D27. Knuth Achievement Tests in Music: For Recognition of Certain Rhythmic and Melodic Aspects. For additional information and a review by Carl E. Seashore, see 2:1332 (1 reference); for reviews by Jay W. Fay and James L. Mursell, see 1:1085.

D28. Kwalwasser-Dykema Music Tests. For additional information and a review by William S. Larson, see 3:176 (29 references).

D29. Kwalwasser Music Talent Test. For additional information and reviews by Paul R. Farnsworth and Kate Hevner Mueller, see 5:248.

D30. Kwalwasser-Ruch Test of Musical Accomplishment. For additional information and reviews by William S. Larson and James L. Mursell, see 2:1333 (1 reference).

D31. Kwalwasser Test of Music Information and Appreciation. For additional information and reviews by Raleigh M. Drake and Karl W. Gehrkens, see 2:1334 (1 reference).

D32. McCauley Examination in Public School Music. For additional information and a review by Alton O'Steen, see 2:1335.

D33. Music Education: National Teacher Examinations. For additional information and a review by William S. Larson, see 6:350. For reviews of the testing program, see 6:700 (1 review), 5:538 (3 reviews), and 4:802 (1 review).

D34. Music Education: Teacher Education Examination Program. An inactive form of D33; for additional information, see 6:351. For a review of the testing program, see 5:543; for references to additional reviews, see D33.

D35. Musical Achievement Test. For additional information and a review by Raleigh M. Drake, see 2:1336.

D36. Musical Appreciation Ability Test: Gibson's Attainment Tests. For additional information, see 1:1086.

D37. Musical Aptitude Test. For additional information and a review by Herbert D. Wing, see 6:352 (2 references); for a review by Robert W. Lundin, see 5:250; for a review by William S. Larson, see 4:228.

D38. Providence Inventory Test in Music. For additional information and reviews by William S. Larson and Clara J. McCauley, see 2:1337.

D39. Seashore Measures of Musical Talents. For additional information and reviews by Kenneth L. Bean and Robert W. Lundin, see 6:353 (13 references); see also 5:251 (9 references); for reviews by John McLeish and Herbert D. Wing of the 1939 revision, see 4:229 (16 references); for reviews by Paul R. Farnsworth, William S. Larson, and James L. Mursell, see 3:177 (46 references); see also 2:1338 (60 references).

D40. Strouse Music Test. For additional information and reviews by Clara J. McCauley and Carl E. Seashore, see 2:1339 (1 reference); for a review by Paul R. Farnsworth, see 1:1087.

D41. Test of Musicality. For additional information and reviews by Paul R. Farnsworth and Kate Hevner Mueller, see 5:252 (1 reference).

D42. Watkins-Farnum Performance Scale: A Standardized Achievement Test for All Band Instruments. For additional information and a review by Herbert D. Wing, see 5:253 (2 references).

D43. Wing Standardised Tests of Musical Intelligence. For additional information and reviews by William S. Larson and Robert W. Lundin, see 6:354 (6 references); see also 5:254 (4 references); for a review by John McLeish of an earlier edition, see 4:230 (6 references).

FOREIGN LANGUAGES

E1. Foreign Language Prognosis Test. For additional information and a review by Wayne D. Fisher (with Bertram B. Masia), see 6:355 (1 reference); for a review by William B. Michael, see 4:232; for a review by Walter V. Kaulfers, see 2:1340 (6 references).

E2. The Graduate School Foreign Language Testing Program. For additional information, see 6:356; for a review of the French test, see 6:377; for a review of the German test, see 6:391.

E3. Iowa Placement Examinations: Foreign Language Aptitude. For additional information and a review by H. E. Brogden, see 3:178 (7 references).

E4. Language Aptitude Test: George Washington University Series. For additional information and a review by H. E. Brogden, see 3:179.

E5. Luria-Orleans Modern Language Prognosis Test. For additional information and a review by Walter V. Kaulfers, see 2:1341 (3 references).

E6. Modern Language Aptitude Test. For additional information and reviews by Wayne D. Fisher (with Bertram B. Masia) and Marion F. Shaycoft, see 6:357 (10 references, 4 excerpts).

ENGLISH

E7. Diagnostic Test for Students of English as a Second Language. For additional information and reviews by Nelson Brooks and Herschel T. Manuel, see 5:255.

E8. English Examinations for Foreign Students. For additional information and reviews by Ralph Bedell, John A. Cox, Jr., and Charles R. Langmuir, see 5:256.

E9. English Language Test for Foreign Students. For additional information and a review by John A. Cox, Jr., see 5:257 (1 reference); for a review by Clarence E. Turner, see 4:234 (2 references).

E10. An English Reading Test for Students of English as a Foreign Language. For additional information and reviews by Ralph Bedell and John A. Cox, Jr., see 5:258.

E11. English Usage Test for Non-Native Speakers of English. For additional information, see 6:358.

E12. Examination in Structure (English as a Foreign Language). For additional information, see 5:260.

E13. Listening Test for Students of English as a Second Language. For additional information, see 6:359.

E14. Michigan Test of English Language Proficiency. For additional information and a review by John B. Carroll, see 6:360.

E15. Oral Rating Form for Rating Language Proficiency in Speaking and Understanding English. For additional information, see 6:361.

E16. Test of Aural Comprehension. For additional information and reviews by Herschel T. Manuel and Clarence E. Turner, see 5:261.

E17. Test of Aural Perception in English for Japanese Students. For additional information, see 6:362.

E18. Test of Aural Perception in English for Latin-American Students. For additional information, see 5:262.

E19. A Vocabulary and Reading Test for Students of English as a Second Language. For additional information, see 6:363.

FRENCH

E20. American Council Alpha French Test. For additional information and reviews by C. E. Ficken and Warren S. Holmes, see 2:1342 (9 references).

E21. American Council Alpha French Test: Aural Comprehension. For additional information and a review by Nelson Brooks, see 2:1343 (3 references).

E22. American Council Beta French Test. For additional information and a review by Bateman Edwards, see 2:1344 (2 references).

E23. American Council French Grammar Test. For additional information and reviews by Harry Heller and Charles Holzwarth, see 2:1345 (5 references).

E24. American Council on Education French Reading Test. For additional information and a review by Charles Holzwarth, see 2:1346 (1 reference); for a review by Nelson Brooks, see 1:984.

E25. Baltimore County French Test. For additional information and reviews by Nelson Brooks and Mary E. Turnbull, see 6:364 (1 reference).

E26. Canadian Achievement Test in French (CATF). For additional information and a review by Mary E. Turnbull, see 6:365 (2 references).

E27. Cohen French Test. For additional information and a review by Mary E. Turnbull, see 4:236.

E28. College Entrance Examination Board Achievement Test: French. For additional information, see 6:366 (4 references); see also 5:263 (2 references); for a review by Walter V. Kaulfers of earlier forms, see 4:237 (7 references). For reviews of the testing program, see 6:760 (2 reviews).

E29. College Entrance Examination Board Achievement Test: French Listening Comprehension. For additional information, see 6:367. For reviews of the testing program, see 6:760 (2 reviews).

E30. College Entrance Examination Board Advanced Placement Examination: French. For additional information, see 6:368 (3 references).

E31. College Entrance Examination Board Placement Tests: French Listening Comprehension Test. For additional information, see 6:369.

E32. College Entrance Examination Board Placement Tests: French Reading Test. For additional information, see 6:370.

E33. Columbia Research Bureau Aural French Test. For additional information and a review by Clarence E. Turner, see 2:1347 (1 reference).

E34. Columbia Research Bureau French Test. For additional information and reviews by Joseph F. Jackson and Laura B. Johnson, see 2:1348 (3 references).

E35. Common Concepts Foreign Language Test: French. For additional information, see 6:371.

E36. Cooperative French Comprehension Test. For additional information and reviews by Joseph F. Jackson and Clarence E. Turner, see 3:180; see also E39.

E37. Cooperative French Listening Comprehension Test. For additional information and reviews by Walter V. Kaulfers and Kathleen N. Perret, see 5:265 (1 reference).

E38. Cooperative French Test. For additional information, see 3:181 (3 references); for reviews by C. E. Ficken, Harry Heller, and Joseph F. Jackson of an earlier form of the advanced level, see 2:1349 (4 references); for reviews by Warren S. Holmes and James B. Tharp of an earlier form of the elementary level, see 2:1350 (6 references); for a review by Nelson Brooks, see 1:985; for a review by Walter V. Kaulfers, see 1:986.

E39. Cooperative French Test: Lower and Higher Levels. For additional information and a review by Elton Hocking, see 4:238 (3 references); for reviews by John H. Meyer and Roland Vinette, see 3:182; for reviews of Part 1, see E36.

E40. Examination in French Grammar. For additional information and a review by Nelson Brooks, see 3:183.

E41. Examination in French Reading Comprehension. For additional information and reviews by Joseph F. Jackson and Clarence E. Turner, see 3:184.

E42. Examination in French Vocabulary. For additional information and a review by Nelson Brooks, see 3:185.

E43. First Year French: State High School Tests for Indiana. For additional information, see 1:987.

E44. First Year French Test. For additional information and reviews by Nelson Brooks and Mary E. Turnbull, see 5:266.

E45. Ford-Hicks French Grammar Completion Tests. For additional information, see 6:372.

E46. French, First Year—Second Semester: State High School Tests for Indiana. For additional information and a review by Clarence E. Turner, see 4:240 (1 reference).

E47. French Grammar Test: Dominion Tests. For additional information and a review by John H. Meyer, see 3:186.

E48. French Life and Culture Test. For additional information and reviews by Bateman Edwards and Clarence E. Turner, see 2:1351 (1 reference).

E49. French I and II: Minnesota High School Achievement Examinations. For additional information, see 6:373; for a review by Mary E. Turnbull of earlier forms, see 5:268; for a review by Elton Hocking, see 4:239.

E50. French Reading Test: Dominion Tests. For additional information and a review by Geraldine Spaulding, see 3:187.

E51. French: Teacher Education Examination Program. For additional information, see 6:374. For a review of the testing program, see 5:543.

E52. French Test (Two-Year Course): Affiliation Testing Program for Catholic Secondary Schools. For additional information and a review by Henry Chauncey, see 6:375. For a review of the complete program, see 6:758.

E53. French Vocabulary Test: Dominion Tests. For additional information and a review by Roland Vinette, see 3:188.

E54. The Graduate Record Examinations Advanced Tests: French. For additional information and a review by Nelson Brooks, see 6:376; for a review by Walter V. Kaulfers, see 5:270. For a review of the testing program, see 5:601.

E55. Graduate School Foreign Language Test: French. For additional information and a review by Clarence E. Turner, see 6:377.

E56. Iowa Placement Examinations: French Training. For additional information and a review by Geraldine Spaulding, see 3:189 (4 references).

E57. Lundeberg-Tharp Audition Test in French. For additional information and a review by Nelson Brooks, see 2:1354 (3 references).

E58. MLA-Cooperative Foreign Language Tests: French. For additional information, see 6:378.

E59. MLA Foreign Language Proficiency Tests for Teachers and Advanced Students: French. For additional information and reviews by Paul Pimsleur and James H. Ricks, Jr., see 6:379 (3 references).

E60. Miller-Davis French Test. For additional information and reviews by Walter V. Kaulfers and James B. Tharp, see 2:1355 (1 reference).

E61. Second Year French: State High School Tests for Indiana. For additional information, see 1:988.

E62. Second Year French Test. For additional information and reviews by Geraldine Spaulding and Clarence E. Turner, see 5:271.

E63. Standard French Test: Vocabulary, Grammar, and Comprehension. For additional information and a review by Laura B. Johnson, see 2:1356 (2 references).

E64. A Standardised French Grammar Test. For additional information, see 6:380 (1 reference); for reviews by Nelson Brooks and Donald G. Burns, see 4:242.

E65. A Standardised French Vocabulary Test. For additional information, see 6:381 (1 reference); for reviews by Nelson Brooks and Donald G. Burns, see 4:243.

GERMAN

E66. AATG German Test. For additional information and reviews by Gilbert C. Kettelkamp and Theodor F. Naumann, see 6:382.

E67. American Council Alpha German Test. For additional information and a review by C. H. Handschin, see 2:1357 (3 references).

E68. American Council on Education German Reading Test. For additional information, see 2:1358; for a review by Curtis C. D. Vail, see 1:999.

E69. College Entrance Examination Board Achievement Test: German. For additional information and a review by Gilbert C. Kettelkamp, see 6:383; for a review by Harold B. Dunkel of an earlier form, see 5:272 (3 references); for a review by Herbert Schueler, see 4:244 (3 references). For reviews of the testing program, see 6:760 (2 reviews).

E70. College Entrance Examination Board Achievement Test: German Listening Comprehension. For additional information and reviews by Harold B. Dunkel and Herbert Schueler, see 6:384 (1 reference). For reviews of the testing program, see 6:760 (2 reviews).

E71. College Entrance Examination Board Advanced Placement Examination: German. For additional information, see 6:385 (5 references); for a review by Herbert Schueler of an earlier form, see 5:273.

E72. College Entrance Examination Board Placement Tests: German Listening Comprehension Test. For additional information, see 6:386.

E73. College Entrance Examination Board Placement Tests: German Reading Test. For additional information, see 6:387.

E74. Columbia Research Bureau German Test. For additional information and a review by Harold B. Dunkel, see 2:1359 (1 reference).

E75. Common Concepts Foreign Language Test: German. For additional information, see 6:388.

E76. Cooperative German Test: Advanced Form. For additional information and a review by Herbert Schueler, see 4:245 (3 references); for a review by Harold B. Dunkel, see 3:190; for a review by C. H. Handschin, see 2:1360 (4 references); for a review by Curtis C. D. Vail, see 1:1000.

E77. Cooperative German Test: Elementary Form. For additional information, see 2:1361; for a review by Curtis C. D. Vail, see 1:1001.

E78. Examination in German Grammar—Lower Level. For additional information and a review by Herbert Schueler, see 3:191.

E79. Examination in German Reading Comprehension—Lower Level. For additional information and a review by Herbert Schueler, see 3:192.

E80. Examination in German Vocabulary—Lower Level. For additional information and a review by Herbert Schueler, see 3:193.

E81. First Year German Test. For additional information and a review by Herbert Schueler, see 5:274.

E82. German: Every Pupil Test. For additional information, see 6:389.

E83. German I and II: Minnesota High School Achievement Examinations. For additional information, see 6:390; for a review by Harold B. Dunkel of earlier forms, see 5:276.

E84. Graduate Record Examinations Advanced German Test. For additional information, see 4:247.

E85. Graduate School Foreign Language Test: German. For additional information and a review by Jack M. Stein, see 6:391.

E86. Lundeberg-Tharp Audition Test in German. For additional information and a review by Harold B. Dunkel, see 3:194.

E87. MLA-Cooperative Foreign Language Tests: German. For additional information, see 6:392.

E88. MLA Foreign Language Proficiency Tests for Teachers and Advanced Students: German. For additional information and reviews by Harold B. Dunkel and Herbert Schueler, see 6:393 (3 references).

GREEK

E89. College Entrance Examination Board Achievement Test: Greek. For additional information, see 6:394; for a review by Konrad Gries of an earlier form, see 5:277. For reviews of the testing program, see 6:760 (2 reviews).

E90. College Entrance Examination Board Placement Tests: Greek Test. For additional information, see 6:395.

HEBREW

E91. College Entrance Examination Board Achievement Test: Hebrew. For additional information, see 6:396. For reviews of the testing program, see 6:760 (2 reviews).

E92. Group Test in Siddur Reading. For additional information, see 3:195.

E93. Hebrew Aptitude Test. For additional information, see 3:196 (1 reference).

E94. Hebrew Intermediate Test. For additional information, see 3:197.

E95. Hebrew Primary Test. For additional information, see 3:198.

E96. Test on the Fundamentals of Hebrew. For additional information, see 6:397.

ITALIAN

E97. College Entrance Examination Board Achievement Test: Italian Listening Comprehension. For additional information, see 6:398. For reviews of the testing program, see 6:760 (2 reviews).

E98. College Entrance Examination Board Achievement Test: Italian Reading and Essay. For additional information, see 6:399. For reviews of the testing program, see 6:760 (2 reviews).

E99. College Entrance Examination Board Placement Tests: Italian Listening Comprehension. For additional information, see 6:400.

E100. College Entrance Examination Board Placement Tests: Italian Test. For additional information, see 6:401.

E101. Cooperative Italian Test. For additional information and a review by Elton Hocking, see 3:199.

E102. Examination in Italian Grammar—Lower Level. For additional information, see 3:200.

E103. Examination in Italian Reading Comprehension—Lower Level. For additional information, see 3:201.

E104. Examination in Italian Vocabulary—Lower Level. For additional information, see 3:202.

E105. MLA-Cooperative Foreign Language Tests: Italian. For additional information, see 6:402.

E106. MLA Foreign Language Proficiency Tests for Teachers and Advanced Students: Italian. For additional information, see 6:403 (3 references).

LATIN

E107. Cicero Test. For additional information and a review by S. D. Atkins, see 2:1363.

E108. College Entrance Examination Board Achievement Test: Latin. For additional information, see 6:404; for a review by Konrad Gries of an earlier form, see 5:280 (1 reference); for a review by Harold B. Dunkel, see 4:250 (2 references). For reviews of the testing program, see 6:760 (2 reviews).

E109. College Entrance Examination Board Advanced Placement Examination: Latin. For additional information, see 6:405.

E110. College Entrance Examination Board Placement Tests: Latin Reading Test. For additional information, see 6:406.

E111. Cooperative Latin Test. For additional information, see 3:204 (1 reference); for reviews by Harold B. Dunkel and John Flagg Gummere of an earlier form of the elementary level, see 2:1365; for a review by S. D. Atkins, see 1:1065; for a review by Norman T. Pratt, Jr. of an earlier form of the advanced level, see 1:1064.

E112. Cooperative Latin Test: Lower and Higher Levels. For additional information and a review by Konrad Gries, see 4:251 (3 references); for a review by C. W. Odell, see 3:205; for a review by Hazel M. Toliver of Part 1, see 3:203.

E113. First- and Second-Year Latin: Every Pupil Test. For additional information, see 6:407.

E114. First Year Latin: Every Pupil Scholarship Test. For additional information, see 6:408.

E115. Godsey Latin Composition Test. For additional information and a review by Konrad Gries, see 4:253 (2 references).

E116. Holtz Vergil Test. For additional information and reviews by W. L. Carr and Norman T. Pratt, Jr., see 2:1366.

E117. Hutchinson Latin Grammar Scale. For additional information and a review by S. D. Atkins, see 2:1367 (2 references).

E118. Iowa Every Pupil Test in Latin Reading Comprehension. For additional information, see 1:1069.

E119. Kansas First Year Latin Test. For additional information, see 5:283; for a review by Hazel M. Toliver of an earlier edition, see 3:206; for a review by John Flagg Gummere, see 2:1368 (1 reference).

E120. Kansas Second Year Latin Test. For additional information and a review by W. C. Kvaraceus, see 4:254; for a review by W. L. Carr, see 2:1369 (1 reference).

E121. Latin I and II: Every Pupil Test. For additional information, see 5:285.

E122. Latin I and II: Minnesota High School Achievement Examinations. For additional information, see 6:409; for a review by Mary E. Turnbull of earlier forms, see 5:286.

E123. Latin Test: State High School Tests for Indiana. For additional information, see 4:252 and 4:257.

E124. Latin Test (Two-Year Course): Affiliation Testing Program for Catholic Secondary Schools. For additional information and a review by Henry Chauncey, see 6:410. For a review of the complete program, see 6:758.

E125. Orleans-Solomon Latin Prognosis Test. For additional information and a review by C. W. Odell, see 3:207.

E126. Powers Diagnostic Latin Test. For additional information and reviews by Paul B. Diederich and Norman T. Pratt, Jr., see 2:1370.

E127. Second Year Latin: Every Pupil Scholarship Test. For additional information, see 6:411.

E128. White Latin Test. For additional information and a review by Konrad Gries, see 4:258 (1 reference).

RUSSIAN

E129. College Entrance Examination Board Achievement Test: Russian. For additional information, see 6:412. For reviews of the testing program, see 6:760 (2 reviews).

E130. College Entrance Examination Board Achievement Test: Russian Listening Comprehension. For additional information, see 6:413. For reviews of the testing program, see 6:760 (2 reviews).

E131. College Entrance Examination Board Placement Tests: Russian Listening Comprehension Test. For additional information, see 6:414.

E132. Graduate School Foreign Language Test: Russian. For additional information, see 6:415.

E133. MLA-Cooperative Foreign Language Tests: Russian. For additional information, see 6:416.

E134. MLA Foreign Language Proficiency Tests for Teachers and Advanced Students: Russian. For additional information and a review by Wayne D. Fisher, see 6:417 (3 references).

SPANISH

E135. American Council Alpha Spanish Test. For additional information and reviews by Lawrence Andrus and Christian O. Arndt, see 2:1371 (4 references).

E136. Baltimore County Spanish Test. For additional information and a review by Mariette Schwarz, see 6:418.

E137. College Entrance Examination Board Achievement Test: Spanish. For additional information, see 6:419 (1 reference); see also 5:287 (1 reference) and 4:259 (3 references). For reviews of the testing program, see 6:760 (2 reviews).

E138. College Entrance Examination Board Achievement Test: Spanish Listening Comprehension. For additional information, see 6:420. For reviews of the testing program, see 6:760 (2 reviews).

E139. College Entrance Examination Board Advanced Placement Examination: Spanish. For additional information, see 6:421 (1 reference).

E140. College Entrance Examination Board Placement Tests: Spanish Listening Comprehension Test. For additional information, see 6:422 (1 reference).

E141. College Entrance Examination Board Placement Tests: Spanish Reading Test. For additional information, see 6:423.

E142. Columbia Research Bureau Spanish Test. For additional information and reviews by James C. Babcock and Harry J. Russell, see 2:1372 (7 references).

E143. Common Concepts Foreign Language Test: Spanish. For additional information, see 6:424.

E144. Cooperative Spanish Test: Elementary and Advanced Forms. For additional information and a review by Christian O. Arndt of the elementary level, see 2:1374; for reviews by Lawrence Andrus and Harry J. Russell of the advanced level, see 2:1373 (3 references); for a review by Walter V. Kaulfers of an earlier form of the elementary level, see 1:1156.

E145. Cooperative Spanish Test: Lower and Higher Levels. For additional information and a review by James B. Tharp, see 4:260 (3 references).

E146. Examination in Spanish Grammar—Lower Level. For additional information and a review by Frederick B. Agard, see 3:208.

E147. Examination in Spanish Reading Comprehension—Lower Level. For additional information and a review by Harry J. Russell, see 3:209.

E148. Examination in Spanish Vocabulary—Lower Level. For additional information, see 3:210.

E149. First Year Spanish Test: State High School Tests for Indiana. For additional information, see 4:261.

E150. Furness Test of Aural Comprehension in Spanish. For additional information, see 4:262; for reviews by Frederick B. Agard and Walter V. Kaulfers, see 3:213.

E151. The Graduate Record Examinations Advanced Tests: Spanish. For additional information, see 6:425. For a review of the testing program, see 5:601.

E152. Iowa Placement Examinations: Spanish Training. For additional information and a review by Harry J. Russell, see 3:212 (2 references).

E153. Kansas First Year Spanish Test. For additional information, see 4:264.

E154. Kansas Second Year Spanish Test. For additional information, see 5:290.

E155. Lundeberg-Tharp Audition Test in Spanish. For additional information and reviews by Frederick B. Agard and Walter V. Kaulfers, see 3:211 (1 excerpt).

E156. MLA-Cooperative Foreign Language Tests: Spanish. For additional information, see 6:426.

E157. MLA Foreign Language Proficiency Tests for Teachers and Advanced Students: Spanish. For additional information and a review by Walter V. Kaulfers, see 6:427 (3 references).

E158. National Spanish Examination. For additional information, see 6:428 (8 references).

E159. Spanish and Latin American Life and Culture. For additional information and a review by Kathleen N. Perret, see 5:291.

E160. Spanish Life and Culture. For additional information and a review by James C. Babcock, see 2:1375; for a review by Walter V. Kaulfers, see 1:1157.

E161. Spanish I and II: Minnesota High School Achievement Examinations. For additional information, see 6:429.

E162. Spanish: Teacher Education Examination Program. For additional information, see 6:430. For a review of the testing program, see 5:543.

E163. Spanish Test (Two-Year Course): Affiliation Testing Program for Catholic Secondary Schools. For additional information and a review by Henry Chauncey, see 6:431. For a review of the complete program, see 6:758.

E164. The Stanford Spanish Tests. For additional information and a review by James B. Tharp, see 4:266.

INTELLIGENCE

GROUP

F1. A.C.E.R. Advanced Test B40. For additional information and a review by C. Sanders, see 5:296 (3 references).

F2. A.C.E.R. Advanced Tests AL and AQ. For additional information and a review by Duncan Howie, see 5:295.

F3. A.C.E.R. Higher Tests. For additional information, see 6:432 (1 reference); for a review by C. Sanders, see 5:297.

F4. A.C.E.R. Intermediate Test A. For additional information, see 6:433.

F5. A.C.E.R. Intermediate Test C. For additional information and a review by James Lumsden, see 5:298 (2 references).

F6. A.C.E.R. Intermediate Test D. For additional information and a review by James Lumsden, see 5:298 (2 references).

F7. A.C.E.R. Junior A Test. For additional information, see 6:434; for a review by R. Winterbourn, see 5:299.

F8. A.C.E.R. Junior B Test. For additional information, see 6:435 (1 reference); for a review by R. Winterbourn, see 5:300.

F9. A.C.E.R. Junior Non-Verbal Test. For additional information and a review by D. A. Pidgeon, see 5:301 (1 reference).

F10. A.C.E.R. Non-Verbal Test. For additional information and a review by F. J. Schonell, see 4:272 (2 references).

F11. A.C.E.R. Test L. For additional information, see 4:273.

F12. A.C.E.R. Test W.N.V. For additional information, see 6:436.

F13. APT Performance Test. For additional information, see 5:302.

F14. Academic Alertness "AA": Individual Placement Series (Area I). For additional information, see 6:437.

F15. Academic Aptitude Test: Non-Verbal Intelligence: Acorn National Aptitude Tests. For additional information, see 5:303; for a review by William B. Schrader, see 4:274.

F16. Academic Aptitude Test: Verbal Intelligence: Acorn National Aptitude Tests. For additional information, see 5:304; for a review by William B. Schrader, see 4:275; for a review by Marion A. Bills, see 3:215.

F17. Adaptability Test. For additional information and a review by John M. Willits, see 5:305 (13 references); for reviews by Anne Anastasi and Marion A. Bills, see 3:216 (3 references).

F18. Advanced Personnel Test. For additional information, see 5:306.

F19. Advanced Test N. For additional information and reviews by A. E. G. Pilliner and C. Sanders, see 5:307.

F20. Akron Classification Test. For additional information and a review by Erwin K. Taylor, see 4:276.

F21. The American College Testing Program Examination. For additional information and reviews by Max D. Engelhart and Warren G. Findley, see 6:1 (14 references, 1 excerpt).

F22. American Council on Education Psychological Examination for College Freshmen. For additional information, see 6:438 (96 references); for reviews by Hanford M. Fowler and William B. Michael, see 5:308 (163 references); see also 4:277 (133 references); for reviews by W. D. Commins and J. P. Guilford of an earlier edition, see 3:217 (95 references); for reviews by Jack W. Dunlap and Robert L. Thorndike, see 2:1377 (48 references); for reviews by Anne Anastasi and David Segel, see 1:1037.

F23. American Council on Education Psychological Examination for High School Students. For additional information and a review by William B. Michael, see 5:309 (1 reference); see also 4:278 (2 references); for a review by Carl I. Hovland of an earlier edition, see 3:218 (7 references); for a review by A. H. Turney, see 2:1378 (2 references); for a review by V. A. C. Henmon, see 1:1038.

F24. American School Intelligence Test. For additional information and reviews by David A. Payne and Frank B. Womer, see 6:439 (1 reference).

F25. Analysis of Relationships. For additional information and reviews by Gustav J. Froehlich and Wimburn L. Wallace, see 6:440 (2 references).

F26. The Army Alpha Examination: First Nebraska Revision. For additional information and a review by Robert G. Demaree (with Louis L. McQuitty), see 4:279 (1 reference); for a review by W. D. Commins, see 1:1039 (1 reference).

F27. Army General Classification Test. For additional information and reviews by Bert A. Goldman and Howard B. Lyman, see 6:441 (5 references); see also 5:310 (17 references); for a review by John T. Dailey, see 4:280 (15 references); see also 3:219 (14 references, 1 excerpt).

F28. Army Group Examination Alpha. For additional information and reviews by John T. Dailey and Willis C. Schaefer, see 4:281 (12 references); see also 3:220 (77 references).

F29. Army Group Examination Alpha: Schrammel-Brannan Revision. For additional information, see 3:220 (77 references); for a review by W. D. Commins, see 1:1040.

F30. Auditory Scale for Group Measurement of General Mental Ability. For additional information, see 1:1041.

F31. [Benge Employment Tests.] For additional information and reviews by Brent Baxter and Marion A. Bills, see 3:221.

F32. Bristol Group Reasoning Tests. For additional information and reviews by Charles Fox and Percival Smith, see 2:1381 (1 reference).

F33. The Business Test. For additional information and reviews by Louis C. Nanassy and James H. Ricks, Jr., see 5:311.

F34. California Analogies and Reasoning Test. For additional information and reviews by John R. Hills and Wimburn L. Wallace, see 6:442 (2 excerpts).

F35. California Capacity Questionnaire. For additional information, see 4:282e; for reviews by Anne Anastasi and Emily T. Burr, see 3:222.

F36. California Short-Form Test of Mental Maturity. For additional information and a review by Julian C. Stanley, see 6:443 (11 references); for a review by Cyril Burt of an earlier edition, see 5:313 (15 references); see also 4:282 (1 excerpt). For reference to reviews of the regular edition, see F37.

F37. California Test of Mental Maturity. For additional information, see 6:444 (30 references); for reviews by Frank S. Freeman and John E. Milholland of an earlier edition, see 5:314 (34 references); see also 4:282 (24 references, 1 excerpt); for a review by Henry E. Garrett, see 3:223 (10 references, 2 excerpts); for reviews by Raymond B. Cattell and F. Kuhlmann, see 2:1384 (5 references, 1 excerpt); for reviews by W. D. Commins, Rudolf Pintner, and

Arthur E. Traxler, see 1:1042 (1 excerpt). For references to reviews of the short form, see F36.

F38. Canadian Academic Aptitude Test. (CAAT). For additional information and reviews by Donald B. Black and George A. Ferguson, see 6:445 (2 references).

F39. Cardall-Miles Test of Mental Alertness. For additional information, see 6:446.

F40. The Carlton Picture Intelligence Test. For additional information and reviews by Elizabeth D. Fraser and S. Rachman, see 6:447.

F41. Carnegie Mental Ability Tests. For additional information and reviews by W. D. Commins and Robert L. Thorndike, see 3:224 (3 references).

F42. Cattell Intelligence Tests. For additional information and a review by I. Macfarlane Smith, see 5:315 (9 references); for a review by Godfrey H. Thomson, see 2:1386 (3 references).

F43. Chicago Non-Verbal Examination. For additional information and a review by Raleigh M. Drake, see 5:316 (10 references); for reviews by Robert G. Bernreuter, Myrtle Luneau Pignatelli, and S. D. Porteus, see 2:1387.

F44. Classification Test 40-A. For additional information and reviews by N. M. Downie and David G. Ryans, see 6:448.

F45. Cole-Vincent Group Intelligence Test for School Entrants. For additional information and a review by Ruth W. Washburn, see 3:226.

F46. College Entrance Examination Board Scholastic Aptitude Test. For additional information and reviews by John E. Bowers and Wayne S. Zimmerman, see 6:449 (79 references); for a review by John T. Dailey of an earlier form, see 5:318 (20 references); for a review by Frederick B. Davis, see 4:285 (22 references).

F47. College Placement Test. For additional information and reviews by Gustav J. Froehlich and David V. Tiedeman, see 5:319.

F48. College Qualification Tests. For additional information and reviews by Ralph F. Berdie and Warren G. Findley, see 6:450 (11 references); for reviews by Gustav J. Froehlich, A. E. G. Pilliner, and David V. Tiedeman, see 5:320.

F49. College Transfer Test. For additional information, see 4:286 (1 reference).

F50. Concept Mastery Test. For additional information, see 6:451 (8 references); for reviews by J. A. Keats and Calvin W. Taylor, see 5:321 (4 references).

F51. Cooperative School and College Ability Tests. For additional information and a review by Russel F. Green, see 6:452 (64 references); for reviews by Frederick B. Davis, Hanford M. Fowler, and Julian C. Stanley, see 5:322 (7 references).

F52. Cotswold Junior Ability Tests. For additional information, see 5:323.

F53. Cotswold Measurement of Mental Ability. For additional information and a review by A. W. Heim, see 5:324.

F54. Culture Fair Intelligence Test. For additional information and reviews by John E. Milholland and Abraham J. Tannenbaum, see 6:453 (15 references); for a review by I. Macfarlane Smith, see 5:343 (11 references); for reviews by Raleigh M. Drake and Gladys C. Schwesinger, see 4:300 (2 references).

F55. Culture-Free Test. For additional information and a review by Raleigh M. Drake, see 4:287; for reviews by L. S. Penrose, Walter C. Shipley, and David Wechsler, see 3:228 (4 references).

F56. The D48 Test. For additional information and reviews by Paul C. Davis and S. S. Dunn, see 6:454 (3 references).

F57. Daneshill Intelligence Test. For additional information and reviews by A. W. Heim and F. W. Warburton, see 5:325.

F58. Davis-Eells Test of General Intelligence or Problem-Solving Ability. For additional information and reviews by Cyril Burt, Raleigh M. Drake, and J. P. Guilford, see 5:326 (36 references).

F59. Dawson Mental Test. For additional information and reviews by Raymond B. Cattell and Percival Smith, see 2:1389; see also 1:1043 (2 excerpts).

F60. Deeside Non-Verbal Reasoning Test: English-Welsh Bilingual Version. For additional information, see 6:455.

F61. Deeside Picture Puzzles. For additional information and reviews by Charlotte E. K. Banks and M. L. Kellmer Pringle, see 5:327.

F62. Detroit Advanced First-Grade Intelligence Test. For additional information and a review by A. M. Jordan, see 2:1392.

F63. Detroit Beginning First-Grade Intelligence Test (Revised). For additional information and a review by Psyche Cattell, see 1:1044 (1 excerpt).

F64. Detroit General Intelligence Examination. For additional information, see 5:328.

F65. [Detroit Intelligence Tests.] For additional information, see 5:329 (9 references); see also 4:288 (2 references); for a review by W. Line, see 2:1393.

F66. The Dominion Group Test of Intelligence. For additional information, see 5:330.

F67. Doppelt Mathematical Reasoning Test. For additional information and a review by W. V. Clemans, see 6:456 (2 references).

F68. Duplex Series of Ability Tests. For additional information and reviews by W. G. Emmett and Stanley D. Nisbet, see 4:289 (2 references, 1 excerpt).

F69. Easel Age Scale. For additional information and reviews by Naomi Stewart and Florence M. Teagarden, see 5:332.

F70. The Essential Intelligence Test. For additional information and a review by R. Winterbourn, see 5:333; for a review by F. W. Warburton, see 4:290.

F71. Figure Reasoning Test: A Non-Verbal Intelligence Test. For additional information and a review by A. W. Heim, see 6:457; for reviews by E. J. G. Bradford and James Maxwell, see 4:291 (1 reference, 1 excerpt).

F72. Fiji Test of General Ability. For additional information, see 2:1395 (2 references).

F73. General Intelligence Test for Africans. For additional information, see 2:1396 (4 references).

F74. General Verbal Practice Tests. For additional information, see 6:458.

F75. Gestalt Continuation Test. For additional information, see 6:459 (3 references).

F76. Gibson's Intelligence Tests. For additional information, see 1:1045.

F77. Glick-Germany Scholastic Aptitude Test. For additional information, see 2:1186.

F78. Goodenough-Harris Drawing Test. For additional information, see 6:460 (43 references); see also 5:335 (34 references); for a review by Naomi Stewart of the original edition, see 4:292 (60 references).

F79. The Graduate Record Examinations Aptitude Test. For additional information and reviews by Robert L. French and Warren W. Willingham, see 6:461 (17 references); for a review by John T. Dailey of an earlier form, see 5:336 (7 references); for reviews by J. P. Guilford and Carl I. Hovland, see 4:293 (2 references). For a review of the testing program, see 5:601.

F80. Group Selective Test No. 1. For additional information and a review by T. R. Miles, see 5:337.

F81. Group Test of Learning Capacity: Dominion Tests. For additional information, see 5:341; for a review by W. G. Emmett, see 4:294 (3 references); for a review by F. T. Tyler, see 3:231.

F82. Group Tests 33 and 33B. For additional information, see 5:339 (9 references); see also 4:295 (2 references).

F83. Group Test 36. For additional information, see 4:296.

F84. Group Test 70. For additional information and a review by George Westby, see 4:297 (5 references).

F85. Group Test 75. For additional information, see 5:338.

F86. Group Test 90A. For additional information and a review by John Liggett, see 5:340.

F87. The Henmon-Nelson Tests of Mental Ability. For additional information and a review by Norman E. Wallen of the college level, see 6:462 (11 references, 1 excerpt); for reviews by D. Welty Lefever and Leona E. Tyler of the other levels, see 5:342 (14 references, 1 excerpt); for a review by H. M. Fowler of an earlier edition, see 4:299 (25 references); for reviews by Anne Anastasi, August Dvorak, Howard Easley, and J. P. Guilford, see 2:1398 (1 excerpt).

F88. Inductive Reasoning Test. For additional information and a review by Charles R. Langmuir, see 3:232.

F89. Intelligence Test: Comprehensive Testing Program. For additional information and a review by W. D. Commins, see 1:869 (2 references).

F90. Inventory No. 2. For additional information, see 6:463.

F91. Jenkins Non-Verbal Test. For additional information, see 5:344 (2 references).

F92. Junior Scholastic Aptitude Test. For additional information and a review by Jerome E. Doppelt, see 6:464 (5 references); see also 5:345 (7 references) and 3:233 (3 references).

F93. Junior School Grading Test. For additional information and a review by E. Patricia Hunt, see 2:1400.

F94. Kelvin Measurement of Ability in Infant Classes. For additional information, see 5:346.

F95. Kelvin Measurement of Mental Ability. For additional information, see 1:1047.

F96. Kentucky Classification Battery. For additional information and a review by David V. Tiedeman of an earlier edition, see 4:301 (1 reference); see also 2:1402 (3 references); for reference to reviews of subtests, see C62 and F97.

F97. Kentucky General Ability Test. For additional information, see 3:234; for a review by Richard Ledgerwood, see 1:1048; see also F96.

F98. The Kingston Test of Intelligence. For additional information and a review by H. J. Sants, see 6:465; for a review by A. W. Heim, see 5:347.

F99. Kingsway Intelligence Tests. For additional information, see 3:235 (1 excerpt); see also 2:1403 (1 excerpt).

F100. Kuhlmann-Anderson Intelligence Tests. For additional information and reviews by William B. Michael and Douglas A. Pidgeon, see 6:466 (11 references, 1 excerpt); see also 5:348 (15 references); for reviews by Henry E. Garrett and David Segel of an earlier edition, see 4:302 (10 references); for reviews by W. G. Emmett and Stanley S. Marzolf, see 3:236 (25 references); for a review by Henry E. Garrett, see 2:1404 (15 references); for reviews by Psyche Cattell, S. A. Courtis, and Austin H. Turney, see 1:1049.

F101. Kuhlmann-Finch Tests. For additional information and reviews by Walter N. Durost, Henry E. Garrett, and Charles O. Neidt, see 5:349 (3 references).

F102. Laycock Mental Ability Test. For additional information and reviews by George A. Ferguson and F. T. Tyler, see 3:237.

F103. The Lorge-Thorndike Intelligence Tests. For additional information, see 6:467 (11 references); for reviews by Frank S. Freeman, John E. Milholland, and D. A. Pidgeon, see 5:350 (6 references).

F104. Lowry-Lucier Reasoning Test Combination. For additional information and reviews by Andrew R. Baggaley and Russel F. Green, see 6:468 (6 references).

F105. Maddox Verbal Reasoning Test. For additional information and reviews by T. R. Miles and A. E. G. Pilliner, see 6:469 (1 excerpt).

F106. Manchester General Ability Test (Senior). For additional information and reviews by A. W. Heim and Arthur B. Royse, see 6:470 (1 reference); for a review by A. E. G. Pilliner of the lower level, see 5:351.

F107. Mental Alertness Test: George Washington University Series. For additional information and a review by J. P. Guilford, see 3:238.

F108. Mill Hill Vocabulary Scale. For additional information and a review by Morton Bortner, see 6:471 (16 references); see also 4:303 (7 references); for a review by David Wechsler, see 3:239 (3 references).

F109. Miller Analogies Test. For additional information and reviews by Lloyd G. Humphreys, William B. Schrader, and Warren W. Willingham, see 6:472 (26 references); for a review by John T. Dailey, see 5:352 (28 references); for reviews by J. P. Guilford and Carl I. Hovland, see 4:304 (16 references).

F110. Mitchell Vocabulary Test. For additional information, see 6:473 (1 reference).

F111. Modified Alpha Examination Form 9. For additional information and a review by Dael Wolfle, see 4:305 (5 references).

F112. [Moray House Intelligence Tests.] For additional information, see 6:474 (13 references); see also 5:353 (2 references); for a review by Patrick Slater of earlier forms, see 3:241 (2 references); for a review by C. Ebblewhite Smith, see 2:1409.

F113. Moray House Picture Test 2. For additional information, see 6:475; for reviews by Gertrude Keir and M. L. Kellmer Pringle of the earlier test, see 4:306 (5 references).

F114. Multi-Mental Scale. For additional information and a review by D. A. Worcester, see 3:242 (8 references).

F115. Multi-Racial Picture Intelligence Tests Suitable for Use in African and Asian Schools. For additional information, see 6:476.

F116. N.B. Group Tests. For additional information, see 6:477.

F117. New Rhode Island Intelligence Test. For additional information and a review by Raymond C. Norris, see 5:354 (6 references).

F118. New South African Group Test. For additional information, see 5:355.

F119. Non-Language Multi-Mental Test. For additional information and a review by Carroll A. Whitmer, see 3:243 (1 reference).

F120. Non-Verbal Reasoning Test. For additional information and reviews by James E. Kennedy and David G. Ryans, see 6:478.

F121. Non-Verbal Tests 1–5. For additional information and reviews by T. R. Miles and John Nisbet, see 6:479 (1 reference); for a review by Cyril A. Rogers, see 5:356 (1 reference); for a review by E. A. Peel of the original edition, see 4:307 (3 references).

F122. Northox Group Intelligence Test. For additional information and a review by E. Patricia Hunt, see 2:1410; see also 1:1050 (1 excerpt).

F123. The Ohio Penal Classification Test. For additional information and a review by Norman Eagle, see 5:358.

F124. Ohio State University Psychological Test. For additional information and a review by Cyril J. Hoyt (with W. Wesley Tennyson), see 5:359 (29 references); for a review by George A. Ferguson, see 4:308 (23 references); for a review by J. P. Guilford, see 3:244 (28 references); for reviews by Louis D. Hartson, Theos A. Langlie, and Rudolf Pintner, see 1:1051.

F125. An Orally Presented Group Test of Intelligence for Juniors. For additional information and a review by Elizabeth D. Fraser, see 5:360 (2 references).

F126. O'Rourke General Classification Test, Senior Grade. For additional information and a review by Marion A. Bills, see 3:246 (3 references).

F127. The "Orton" Intelligence Test, No. 4. For additional information, see 1:1052.

F128. Otis Classification Test. For additional information, see 3:247 (3 references, 1 excerpt).

F129. Otis Employment Tests. For additional information, see 4:310.

F130. Otis General Intelligence Examination: Designed Especially for Business Institutions. For additional information and a review by Frederic Kuder, see 3:248.

F131. Otis Group Intelligence Scale. For additional information and a review by D. Welty Lefever, see 6:480 (44 references).

F132. Otis Quick-Scoring Mental Ability Tests. For additional information, see 6:481 (24 references); for reviews by D. Welty Lefever and Alfred Yates, see 5:362 (33 references); for a review by Frederic Kuder of the earlier forms, see 3:249 (9 references); for reviews by F. Kuhlmann and C. Spearman, see 2:1413; for reviews by Psyche Cattell and R. Pintner, see 1:1053 (2 excerpts).

F133. Otis Self-Administering Tests of Mental Ability. For additional information, see 5:363 (52 references); for a review by Frederic Kuder, see 3:250 (71 references). For the Australian edition, see 2:1412.

F134. PTI-Oral Directions Test. A subtest of F143 which see for a review; for reviews by Charles D. Flory, Irving Lorge, and William W. Turnbull of the original edition, see 3:245.

F135. Pattern Perception Test. For additional information and a review by Alice W. Heim, see 4:312 (3 references).

F136. The Peel Group Tests of Practical Ability. For additional information and a review by George Westby, see 4:313 (2 references).

F137. Perception of Relations Scales. For additional information and a review by Charles D. Flory, see 3:251.

F138. Performance Alertness "PA" (With Pictures): Individual Placement Series (Area 1). For additional information, see 6:482.

F139. Personal Classification Test. For additional information, see 6:483.

F140. Personnel Classification Test [Henderson]. For additional information and reviews by Brent Baxter and John C. Flanagan, see 3:252.

F141. Personnel Research Institute Classification Test. For additional information and reviews by James R. Glennon and Melvin R. Marks, see 6:484 (2 references).

F142. Personnel Research Institute Factory Series Test. For additional information and a review by N. M. Downie, see 6:485.

F143. Personnel Tests for Industry. For additional information and a review by Erwin K. Taylor, see 5:366; for reference to reviews of a subtest, see F134.

F144. Picture Test 1. For additional information, see 6:486; for reviews by Charlotte E. K. Banks and M. L. Kellmer Pringle, see 5:367.

F145. Pintner General Ability Tests: Non-Language Series. For additional information and a review by Carroll A. Whitmer, see 3:254.

F146. Pintner General Ability Tests: Verbal Series. For additional information, see 5:368 (10 references); for reviews by Stanley S. Marzolf and D. A. Worcester, see 3:255 (13 references); see also 2:1416 (3 excerpts).

F147. Pintner Non-Language Primary Mental Test. For additional information and reviews by Psyche Cattell and Carroll A. Whitmer, see 3:256 (6 references).

F148. The Preliminary Scholastic Aptitude Test. For additional information and a review by Wayne S. Zimmerman, see 6:487 (2 references).

F149. [Pressey Classification and Verifying Tests.] For additional information and a review by Walter N. Durost, see 6:488 (11 references).

F150. Primary Verbal Tests. For additional information, see 6:489; for reviews by John Nisbet and F. W. Warburton, see 5:369.

F151. Profion Dealltwriaeth Cyfaddasiad Cymbraeg. For additional information, see 3:257.

F152. Progressive Matrices. For additional information and a review by Morton Bortner, see 6:490 (78 references); see also 5:370 (62 references); for reviews by Charlotte Banks, W. D. Wall, and George Westby, see 4:314 (32 references); for reviews by Walter C. Shipley and David Wechsler of the 1938 edition, see 3:258 (13 references); for a review by T. J. Keating, see 2:1417 (8 references).

F153. Proverbs Test. For additional information and reviews by Eugene L. Gaier and Alfred B. Heilbrun, Jr., see 5:371 (4 references).

F154. Psychological Examination. For additional information and reviews by Howard Easley and D. A. Worcester, see 2:1418; for a review by John C. Flanagan, see 1:1054.

F155. Purdue Non-Language Test. For additional information and reviews by John D. Hundleby and Benjamin Rosner, see 6:491.

F156. Quantitative Evaluative Device. For additional information, see 6:492 (1 reference).

F157. Quick-Scoring Group Test of Learning Capacity: Dominion Tests. For additional information and reviews by Donald B. Black and George A. Ferguson, see 6:493.

F158. Reasoning Tests for Higher Levels of Intelligence. For additional information and a review by Reginald R. Dale, see 5:374.

F159. Revised Alpha Examination, Forms 5 and 7. For additional information and a review by Dael Wolfle, see 4:315 (4 references).

F160. Revised Alpha Examination, Form 6. For additional information and reviews by Edwin R. Henry and Dael Wolfle, see 4:316 (1 reference).

F161. Revised Beta Examination. For additional information and a review by Bert A. Goldman, see 6:494 (13 references); see also 5:375 (14 references); for reviews by Raleigh M. Drake and Walter C. Shipley, see 3:259 (5 references); for reviews by S. D. Porteus and David Wechsler, see 2:1419 (4 references).

F162. Revision of Army Alpha Examination. For additional information and reviews by Edward E. Cureton and Edwin R. Henry, see 4:317 (3 references).

F163. The Ryburn Group Intelligence Tests. For additional information, see 2:1421.

F164. SRA College Classification Tests. For additional information, see 5:376.

F165. SRA Non-Verbal Form. For additional information and a review by W. D. Commins, see 4:318; see also 3:261 (1 excerpt).

F166. SRA Tests of Educational Ability. For additional information and reviews by J. Stanley Ahmann and John E. Horrocks, see 6:495 (1 reference, 1 excerpt); for reviews by Joshua A. Fishman, William B. Michael, and E. A. Peel of the tests for grades 9–12, see 5:377.

F167. [SRA] Tests of General Ability. For additional information and reviews by John E. Horrocks and Richard E. Schutz, see 6:496 (1 excerpt).

F168. SRA Verbal Form. For additional information, see 5:378; for reviews by W. D. Commins and Willis C. Schaefer, see 4:319.

F169. Safran Culture Reduced Intelligence Test. For additional information, see 6:497 (1 reference).

F170. The Scholarship Qualifying Test. For additional information and reviews by Lee J. Cronbach and Roger T. Lennon, see 5:379.

F171. Scholastic Mental Ability Tests. For additional information and reviews by Walter N. Durost and Alexander G. Wesman, see 5:380.

F172. School Aptitude Test: Thanet Mental Tests. For additional information and a review by C. Ebblewhite Smith, see 2:1422.

F173. Schrammel General Ability Test. For additional information, see 6:498; for a review by Henry E. Garrett, see 5:381.

F174. Schubert General Ability Battery. For additional information and a review by William B. Schrader, see 5:382.

F175. Scovill Classification Test. For additional information and reviews by Robert G. Bernreuter and Edward E. Cureton, see 4:320 (1 reference).

F176. Secondary Verbal Tests 1–2. For additional information and a review by Stanley Nisbet of test 1, see 6:499.

F177. Ship Destination Test. For additional information and a review by William B. Schrader, see 6:500 (8 references); for a review by C. J. Adcock, see 5:383.

F178. The Simplex GNV Intelligence Tests. For additional information and a review by Philip M. Levy, see 6:501 (2 references).

F179. The Simplex Group Intelligence Scale. For additional information and a review by James Mainwaring, see 5:385.

F180. [The Simplex Junior Intelligence Tests.] For additional information and a review by Arthur B. Royse, see 5:386 (1 reference); see also 4:322 (2 references).

F181. Sleight Non-Verbal Intelligence Test. For additional information, see 6:502 (1 reference); for reviews by John C. Daniels and M. L. Kellmer Pringle, see 5:387.

F182. The Southend Test of Intelligence. For additional information and a review by James Mainwaring, see 5:388; for a review by Gertrude Keir of the original edition, see 4:323 (1 reference); see also 2:1423 (1 excerpt).

F183. Survey of Mental Maturity: California Survey Series. For additional information and a review by Naomi Stewart, see 6:503.

F184. Terman-McNemar Test of Mental Ability. For additional information, see 4:324 (12 references); for reviews by Carl I. Hovland and Robert L. Thorndike, see 3:263 (25 references); for reviews by Anne Anastasi and Howard Easley of the original edition, see 2:1424 (25 references).

F185. Test of General Knowledge. For additional information, see 2:1425 (1 reference).

F186. Test of Learning Ability. For additional information, see 6:504 (2 references).

F187. Test of Non-Verbal Reasoning. For additional information, see 6:505 (3 references).

F188. Test of Word-Number Ability. For additional information and reviews by I. David Satlow and John M. Willits, see 5:389 (1 reference) ; for a review by Jane Loevinger of an earlier edition, see 4:333.

F189. Tests AH4 and AH5. For additional information and a review by John Liggett, see 6:506; for reviews by George A. Ferguson of Test AH4 and J. A. Keats of Test AH5, see 5:390 (11 references).

F190. Tests of General Ability: Cooperative Inter-American Tests. For additional information, see 6:507; for reviews by Raleigh M. Drake and Walter N. Durost, see 4:325 (8 references).

F191. Thurstone Test of Mental Alertness. For additional information and a review by Joshua A. Fishman, see 5:391; see also 4:326 (3 references) ; for reviews by Anne Anastasi and Emily T. Burr of an earlier edition, see 3:265.

F192. The Tomlinson Junior School Test. For additional information and a review by John C. Daniels, see 5:392.

F193. Unit Scales of Aptitude. For additional information and a review by Herschel T. Manuel, see 2:1428.

F194. V.G.C. Intelligence Indicator. For additional information and a review by George A. Ferguson, see 4:327.

F195. Verbal and Non-Verbal Test 1. For additional information and a review by T. R. Miles, see 5:393.

F196. Verbal Capacity Sampler. For additional information, see 5:394.

F197. Verbal Intelligence Test. For additional information and a review by John P. Foley, Jr., see 5:395; for a review by William B. Schrader, see 4:329.

F198. The Verbal Power Test of Concept Equivalence. For additional information, see 6:508 (3 references).

F199. Verbal Reasoning. For additional information and reviews by James E. Kennedy and David G. Ryans, see 6:509.

F200. Verbal Test (Adv.). For additional information and reviews by J. S. Lawes and John Nisbet, see 6:510.

F201. Verbal Tests 1–2, 4–13. For additional information and a review by Arthur B. Royse, see 6:511 (1 reference).

F202. Vocabulary Tests. For additional information and a review by John Nisbet, see 5:398.

F203. Wesman Personnel Classification Test. For additional information, see 5:399 (8 references) ; for reviews by John C. Flanagan and Erwin K. Taylor, see 4:331 (3 references) ; see also 3:253 (1 excerpt).

F204. The "West Riding" Tests of Mental Ability. For additional information and a review by Ll. Wynn Jones, see 2:1430.

F205. "West Yorkshire" Group Test of Intelligence. For additional information, see 4:332.

F206. The Western Personnel Tests. For additional information and reviews by Lewis E. Albright and Erwin K. Taylor, see 6:512.

F207. Willis-Smith Advanced Mental Test. For additional information and reviews by Harold H. Bixler and F. T. Tyler, see 3:268.

F208. Wonderlic Personnel Test. For additional information and reviews by N. M. Downie and Marvin D. Dunnette, see 6:513 (17 references) ; see also 5:400 (59 references) ; for reviews by H. E. Brodgen, Charles D. Flory, and Irving Lorge, see 3:269 (7 references) ; see also 2:1415 (2 references).

INDIVIDUAL

F209. Alexander Performance Scale: A Performance Scale for the Measurement of Practical Ability. For additional information and a review by H. Gwynne Jones, see 6:514 (3 references) ; for a review by Charles A. Strickland, see 4:334 (4 references) ; for a review by John Cohen, see 3:270 (1 reference, 2 excerpts) ; for a review by J. M. Blackburn, see 2:1376 (3 references).

F210. Arthur Point Scale of Performance Tests. For additional information and a review by William R. Grove, see 4:335 (12 references) ; for reviews by Andrew W. Brown and Carroll A. Whitmer, see 2:1379 (16 references, 1 excerpt) ; see also 3:271 (19 references, 1 excerpt).

F211. California First-Year Mental Scale. For additional information and a review by Florence L. Goodenough, see 2:1382 (1 reference).

F212. California Preschool Mental Scale. For additional information and reviews by B. M. Castner and Florence L. Goodenough, see 2:1383 (1 reference).

F213. Canadian Intelligence Examination. For additional information and a review by Gwen F. Arnold, see 4:336; see also 3:272 (1 reference, 2 excerpts).

F214. Carl Hollow Square Scale. For additional information and a review by Grace H. Kent, see 3:273 (3 references) ; for a review by T. J. Keating, see 2:1385 (2 references).

F215. Cattell Infant Intelligence Scale. For additional information, see 6:515 (22 references) ; for reviews by Florence M. Teagarden and Beth L. Wellman, see 3:281 (1 excerpt).

F216. Children's Picture Information Test. For additional information and reviews by Dorothy Eichorn and T. Ernest Newland, see 6:516 (2 references).

F217. Columbia Mental Maturity Scale. For additional information and reviews by Marshall S. Hiskey and T. Ernest Newland, see 6:517 (22 references) ; see also 5:402 (13 references).

F218. Cornell-Coxe Performance Ability Scale. For additional information and reviews by Francis N. Maxfield and Carroll A. Whitmer, see 2:1388 (3 references).

F219. Crichton Vocabulary Scale. For additional information and a review by Morton Bortner, see 6:518 (1 reference) ; for reviews by Charlotte Banks and W. D. Wall, see 4:337.

F220. Curtis Classification Form. For additional information and a review by Harold G. Seashore, see 4:338.

F221. Dearborn-Anderson Formboards 2 and 2b. For additional information and a review by Grace H. Kent, see 2:1390 (4 references).

F222. Dearborn Formboard 3. For additional information and a review by Grace H. Kent, see 2:1391 (8 references).

F223. Detroit Kindergarten Test. For additional information and reviews by Psyche Cattell and Ruth W. Washburn, see 3:274 (1 reference).

F224. Detroit Tests of Learning Aptitude. For additional information, see 5:403; for a review by F. L. Wells, see 3:275 (1 reference); for reviews by Anne Anastasi and Henry Feinberg of an earlier edition, see 1:1058 (1 excerpt).

F225. Diagnostic Performance Tests. For additional information and a review by H. Gwynne Jones, see 6:519 (1 reference).

F226. English Picture Vocabulary Test. For additional information and reviews by L. B. Birch and Philip M. Levy, see 6:520.

F227. Ferguson Formboards. For additional information and a review by Grace H. Kent, see 2:1394 (12 references).

F228. Full-Range Picture Vocabulary Test. For additional information, see 6:521 (30 references); for reviews by William D. Altus and William M. Cruickshank, see 4:340 (10 references).

F229. Gesell Developmental Schedules. For additional information and a review by Emmy E. Werner, see 6:522 (27 references); see also 4:341 (5 references); for reviews by Nancy Bayley and Florence M. Teagarden, see 3:276 (28 references).

F230. The Griffiths Mental Development Scale for Testing Babies From Birth to Two Years. For additional information and a review by C. B. Hindley, see 6:523 (4 references); for a review by Nancy Bayley, see 5:404 (3 references).

F231. Herring Revision of the Binet-Simon Tests. For additional information and a review by Andrew W. Brown, see 2:1399 (13 references).

F232. The Immediate Test: A Quick Verbal Intelligence Test. For additional information and reviews by Jerome E. Doppelt and Ivan Norman Mensh, see 4:342 (1 reference).

F233. Intelligence Tests for Children. For additional information and reviews by Elizabeth D. Fraser and G. A. V. Morgan, see 5:405 (2 references); see also 4:343 (3 references) and 3:283 (1 excerpt).

F234. Kahn Intelligence Tests. For additional information, see 6:524 (2 references).

F235. Kent Series of Emergency Scales. For additional information and a review by Ivan Norman Mensh, see 4:346 (8 references); for a review by Charles N. Cofer, see 3:284 (26 references).

F236. Kent-Shakow Formboard. For additional information and a review by Milton L. Blum, see 3:660 (11 references); for a review by Lorene Teagarden, see 2:1401 (9 references).

F237. The Leiter Adult Intelligence Scale. For additional information and reviews by Paul C. Davis and Frank B. Jex, see 6:525 (15 references, 1 excerpt); for reviews by Harold A. Delp and Herschel Manuel of the original edition, see 4:350 (4 references, 1 excerpt). For reviews of subtests, see 4:355 (1 review, 1 excerpt), 4:347 (1 excerpt), and 4:348 (1 excerpt).

F238. Leiter International Performance Scale. For additional information and a review by Emmy E. Werner, see 6:526 (10 references); see also 5:408 (17 references); for a review by Gwen F. Arnold, see 4:349 (25 references, 1 excerpt).

F239. Linfert-Hierholzer Scale for Measuring the Mental Development of Infants During the First Year of Life. For additional information and a review by Nancy Bayley, see 3:285 (6 references).

F240. Merrill-Palmer Scale of Mental Tests. For additional information and a review by Marjorie P. Honzik, see 6:527 (16 references); for reviews by Nancy Bayley, B. M. Castner, Florence L. Goodenough, and Florence M. Teagarden, see 2:1406 (13 references).

F241. Minnesota Preschool Scale. For additional information and a review by Marjorie P. Honzik, see 6:528 (3 references); see also 4:351 (2 references); for a review by Beth L. Wellman, see 3:286 (2 references); for reviews by Rachel Stutsman Ball, Nancy Bayley, and Florence M. Teagarden of the original edition, see 2:1407 (3 references).

F242. Modification of the Kent-Shakow Formboard. For additional information, see 2:1408 (3 references).

F243. Nebraska Test of Learning Aptitude. For additional information and a review by William Sloan, see 5:409 (8 references); for a review by Mildred C. Templin of an earlier edition, see 4:353 (1 reference); see also 3:289 (3 references).

F244. Non-Verbal Intelligence Test for Deaf and Hearing Subjects. For additional information and a review by J. S. Lawes, see 6:529 (2 references).

F245. The Northwestern Intelligence Tests: For Measuring Adaptation to the Physical and Social Environment. For additional information and a review by Nancy Bayley, see 5:411; for a review by Mildred C. Templin, see 4:354 (9 references, 1 excerpt).

F246. Ontario School Ability Examination. For additional information and a review by W. Line, see 2:1411 (2 references).

F247. The Passalong Test: A Performance Test of Intelligence. For additional information and reviews by James Drever, T. J. Keating, and Grace H. Kent, see 2:1414 (5 references). For reference to additional reviews, see F209.

F248. Pathways Test. For additional information and a review by George K. Bennett, see 4:355 (1 reference, 1 excerpt).

F249. Peabody Picture Vocabulary Test. For additional information and reviews by Howard B. Lyman and Ellen V. Piers, see 6:530 (21 references).

F250. Performance Tests of Intelligence: A Series of Non-Linguistic Tests for Deaf and Normal Children. For additional information, see 3:290 (2 references).

F251. Pictorial Test of Intelligence. For additional information, see 6:531 (2 references).

F252. Pintner-Paterson Scale of Performance Tests. For additional information and a review by Francis N. Maxfield, see 1:1061 (1 reference).

F253. The Porteus Maze Test. For additional information, see 6:532 (38 references); see also 5:412 (28 references); for reviews by C. M. Louttit and Gladys C. Schwesinger, see 4:356 (56 references).

F254. Preliminary Test of Intelligence: A Brief Test of Adult Intelligence Designed for Psychiatric Examiners. For additional information, see 3:291.

F255. Quick Screening Scale of Mental Development. For additional information and a review by Boyd R. McCandless, see 6:533.

F256. The Quick Test. For additional information and reviews by Boyd R. McCandless and Ellen V. Piers, see 6:534 (3 references).

F257. Slosson Intelligence Test (SIT). For additional information, see 6:535.

F258. Stanford-Binet Intelligence Scale. For additional information and a review by Elizabeth D. Fraser, see 6:536 (110 references, 5 excerpts); for reviews by Mary R. Haworth and Norman D. Sundberg of the second edition, see 5:413 (127 references); for a review by Boyd R. McCandless, see 4:358 (142 references); see also 3:292 (217 references) and 2:1420 (134 references, 3 excerpts); for reviews by Francis N. Maxfield, J. W. M. Rothney, and F. L. Wells, see 1:1062.

F259. Tests of Mental Development. For additional information and reviews by Grace H. Kent, Francis N. Maxfield, Myrtle Luneau Pignatelli, and F. L. Wells, see 2:1426 (1 reference, 2 excerpts).

F260. Van Alstyne Picture Vocabulary Test. For additional information and reviews by Mary R Haworth and Ellen V. Piers, see 6:537 (6 references); for a review by Ruth W. Washburn of the original edition, see 3:296.

F261. Wechsler Adult Intelligence Scale. For additional information, see 6:538 (180 references); for reviews by Nancy Bayley and Wilson H. Guertin, see 5:414 (42 references). For reference to reviews of an earlier edition, see F262.

F262. Wechsler-Bellevue Intelligence Scale. For additional information, see 6:539 (123 references); see also 5:415 (254 references); for reviews by Murray Aborn and William D. Altus, see 4:361 (250 references); for a review by Robert I. Watson, see 3:298 (119 references); for a review by F. L. Wells, see 2:1429 (2 references, 2 excerpts). For reference to reviews of a later edition, see F261.

F263. Wechsler Intelligence Scale for Children. For additional information and a review by Alvin G. Burstein, see 6:540 (155 references); for reviews by Elizabeth D. Fraser, Gerald R. Patterson, and Albert I. Rabin, see 5:416 (111 references); for reviews by James M. Anderson, Harold A. Delp, and Boyd R. McCandless, see 4:363 (22 references, 1 excerpt).

F264. Williams Intelligence Test for Children With Defective Vision. For additional information and a review by T. Ernest Newland, see 6:541 (2 references).

SPECIFIC

F265. Alternate Uses. For additional information, see 6:542 (7 references).

F266. Benton Visual Retention Test. For additional information, see 6:543 (22 references); for a review by Nelson G. Hanawalt, see 5:401 (5 refer-

ences); for reviews by Ivan Norman Mensh, Joseph Newman, and William Schofield of the original edition, see 4:360 (3 references); see also 3:297 (1 excerpt).

F267. Christensen-Guilford Fluency Tests. For additional information and reviews by J. A. Keats and Albert S. Thompson, see 6:544 (4 references).

F268. Closure Flexibility (Concealed Figures). For additional information and a review by Leona E. Tyler, see 6:545 (4 references).

F269. Closure Speed (Gestalt Completion). For additional information and a review by Leona E. Tyler, see 6:546 (3 references).

F270. Consequences. For additional information and a review by Goldine C. Gleser, see 6:547 (13 references).

F271. Decorations. For additional information, see 6:548 (1 reference).

F272. The FR-CR Test. For additional information and a review by William S. Kogan, see 4:339 (1 reference).

F273. Illinois Test of Psycholinguistic Abilities. For additional information, see 6:549 (22 references).

F274. Jensen Alternation Board. For additional information, see 6:550 (2 references).

F275. Kit of Reference Tests for Cognitive Factors. For additional information, see 6:551.

F276. The Leiter Adaptation of Arthur's Stencil Design Test. For additional information, see 4:347 (1 reference, 1 excerpt).

F277. The Leiter Adaptation of the Painted Cube Test. For additional information, see 4:348 (1 reference, 1 excerpt).

F278. Making Objects. For additional information, see 6:552 (1 reference).

F279. Marianne Frostig Developmental Test of Visual Perception. For additional information and reviews by James M. Anderson and Mary C. Austin, see 6:553 (7 references).

F280. Match Problems. For additional information, see 6:554 (7 references).

F281. Nufferno Tests of Speed and Level. For additional information, see 6:555 (4 references); for reviews by John Liggett and E. A. Peel, see 5:357 (3 references).

F282. Perceptual Speed (Identical Forms). For additional information and a review by Leroy Wolins, see 6:556.

F283. Pertinent Questions. For additional information, see 6:557 (3 references).

F284. Possible Jobs. For additional information, see 6:558 (1 reference).

F285. The Rutgers Drawing Test. For additional information, see 6:559 (2 references).

F286. Stencil Design Test. For additional information and a review by Benjamin Balinsky, see 4:359 (4 references); for a review by James M. Anderson, see 3:295.

F287. Subsumed Abilities Test. For additional information and a review by Naomi Stewart, see 6:560.

F288. Time Appreciation Test. For additional information and reviews by E. J. G. Bradford and Charles N. Cofer, see 3:266 (2 references).

F289. Wechsler Memory Scale. For additional information, see 6:561 (9 references); for reviews by Ivan Norman Mensh and Joseph Newman, see 4:364 (6 references); for a review by Kate Levine Kogan, see 3:302 (3 references).

F290. Word Fluency. For additional information and a review by James E. Kennedy, see 6:562.

MATHEMATICS

G1. Ability to Do Quantitative Thinking: The Iowa Tests of Educational Development, Test 4. For additional information and a review by Peter A. Lappan, Jr., see 6:579. For reviews of the complete battery, see 6:14 (2 reviews), 5:17 (2 reviews), 4:17 (1 review), and 3:12 (3 reviews).

G2. Business Mathematics: Every Pupil Scholarship Test. For additional information, see 6:563.

G3. California Mathematics Test. The advanced level of test G131; for additional information, see 6:564 (9 references); for a review by Robert D. North of test G131, see 5:468. For reviews of the complete battery, see 6:3 (2 reviews), 5:2 (1 review), 4:2 (3 reviews), 3:15 (1 review), 2:1193 (2 reviews), and 1:876 (1 review, 1 excerpt).

G4. Canadian Achievement Test in Mathematics (CATM). For additional information and a review by Frances Crook Morrison, see 6:565 (2 references).

G5. Canadian Achievement Test in Technical and Commercial Mathematics (CATTCM). For additional information and a review by Stanley Clark, see 6:566 (2 references).

G6. Canadian Mathematics Achievement Test (CMAT). For additional information and reviews by Stanley Clark and Frances Crook Morrison, see 6:567 (2 references).

G7. College Entrance Examination Board Achievement Test: Advanced Mathematics. For additional information and a review by Saunders Mac Lane, see 6:568 (3 references); see also 5:417 (3 references); for a review by Paul L. Dressel of earlier forms, see 4:367 (4 references). For reviews of the testing program, see 6:760 (2 reviews).

G8. College Entrance Examination Board Achievement Test: Intermediate Mathematics. For additional information and a review by Paul L. Dressel, see 6:569 (1 reference); see also 5:418 (3 references); for a review by Paul J. Blommers of earlier forms, see 4:368 (2 references). For reviews of the testing program, see 6:760 (2 reviews).

G9. College Entrance Examination Board Advanced Placement Examination: Mathematics. For additional information, see 6:570 (4 references); for a review by Paul L. Dressel of an earlier form, see 5:419.

G10. College Entrance Examination Board Placement Tests: Advanced Mathematics Test. An inactive form of test G7; for additional information, see 6:571; for references to reviews, see G7.

G11. College Entrance Examination Board Placement Tests: Intermediate Mathematics Test. An inactive form of test G8; for additional information, see 6:572; for references to reviews, see G8.

G12. Cooperative College Mathematics Test for First-Year Courses. For additional information and reviews by Albert A. Bennett and Nathan Morrison, see 3:304.

G13. Cooperative General Achievement Tests: Test 3, Mathematics. For additional information, see 6:573 (4 references); for a review by John F. Randolph of earlier forms, see 3:316. For reviews of the complete battery, see 6:7 (1 review), 5:6 (1 review), 4:5 (1 review), and 3:3 (1 review).

G14. Cooperative General Mathematics Test for College Students. For additional information and a review by Tomlinson Fort, see 2:1431; for a review by M. W. Richardson, see 1:1071.

G15. Cooperative General Mathematics Test for High School Classes. For additional information and a review by L. B. Kinney, see 2:1432 (1 reference); for a review by Maurice Hartung of an earlier form, see 1:1072.

G16. Cooperative Mathematics Pre-Test for College Students. For additional information and a review by E. P. Starke, see 4:369; for reviews by M. W. Richardson and S. S. Wilks of earlier forms, see 1:1073.

G17. Cooperative Mathematics Tests for Grades 7, 8, and 9. For additional information and a review by Gordon Fifer, see 5:421 (1 reference); see also 4:370 (2 references); for a review by M. L. Hartung of earlier forms, see 3:305 (1 reference); for reviews by Richard M. Drake, Judson W. Foust, and G. M. Ruch, see 2:1433 (2 references).

G18. Cooperative Test in Secondary School Mathematics: Higher Level. For additional information and a review by E. H. C. Hildebrandt, see 3:303.

G19. Davis Test of Functional Competence in Mathematics. For additional information and reviews by Paul L. Dressel and Tom A. Lamke, see 5:422 (2 references).

G20. ERB Mathematics Tests. For additional information, see 6:574 (2 references).

G21. Foust-Schorling Test of Functional Thinking in Mathematics. For additional information and reviews by William Betz and M. L. Hartung, see 3:306 (1 reference, 2 excerpts).

G22. Functional Evaluation in Mathematics. For additional information and a review by Charles S. Ross, see 4:372.

G23. General Mathematical Ability: Tests of General Educational Development, Test 5. For additional information, see 5:426. For reviews of the complete battery, see 5:27 (1 review), 4:26 (1 review), and 3:20 (2 reviews).

G24. General Mathematics: Every Pupil Scholarship Test. For additional information, see 6:575.

G25. General Mathematics: Every Pupil Test. For additional information, see 6:576.

G26. General Mathematics: Minnesota High School Achievement Examinations. For additional information and a review by Gerald L. Ericksen, see 6:577.

G27. Graded Arithmetic-Mathematics Test. For additional information and a review by Stanley Nisbet, see 5:476.

G28. The Graduate Record Examinations Advanced Tests: Mathematics. For additional information and a review by Paul C. Rosenbloom, see 6:578; for a review by Eric F. Gardner of an earlier form, see 5:427 (1 reference). For a review of the testing program, see 5:601.

G29. Iowa Placement Examinations: Mathematics Aptitude. For additional information and reviews by Edmund P. Churchill and Paul L. Dressel, see 3:308 (18 references).

G30. Iowa Placement Examinations: Mathematics Training. For additional information and reviews by Edmund P. Churchill and Paul L. Dressel, see 3:309 (8 references).

G31. Junior High School Mathematics Test: Acorn Achievement Tests. For additional information and a review by Myron F. Rosskopf, see 5:429; for a review by William Betz, see 3:310.

G32. Junior Math Reasoning Test. For additional information, see 6:580.

G33. Kansas Mathematics Test. For additional information and a review by Paul Blommers, see 5:430.

G34. Kentucky Mathematics Test. For additional information, see 3:311; see also F96.

G35. Mathematical Ability Test. For additional information, see 1:1075.

G36. Mathematical Literacy for High School Seniors: A Test of Basic Skills and Abilities: [Ohio Senior Survey Tests]. For additional information, see 5:431.

G37. Mathematics: Every Pupil Test. For additional information, see 6:581.

G38. Mathematics: Minnesota High School Achievement Examinations. For additional information, see 6:582.

G39. Mathematics: National Teacher Examinations. For additional information and a review by Paul Blommers, see 6:583. For reviews of the testing program, see 6:700 (1 review), 5:538 (3 reviews), and 4:802 (1 review).

G40. Mathematics: Teacher Education Examination Program. An inactive form of test G39; for additional information, see 6:584; for a reference to a review, see G39. For a review of the testing program, see 5:543.

G41. Mathematics Test (Adv.). For additional information and a review by Kenneth Lovell, see 6:585.

G42. Mathematics Test: Ohio Senior Survey Tests. For additional information and a review by William G. Mollenkopf, see 3:313.

G43. Mathematics Test 1. For additional information and a review by Jack Wrigley, see 5:436.

G44. Metropolitan Achievement Tests: High School Mathematics Tests. For additional information, see 6:586. For reviews of the complete battery, see 6:15 (3 reviews), 4:18 (1 review), 2:1189 (2 reviews), and 1:874 (3 reviews).

G45. Minimum Essentials for Modern Mathematics. For additional information and a review by Gerald L. Ericksen, see 6:587.

G46. The Morgan Achievement Test in Mathematics for Employee Selection. For additional information and a review by Marion F. Shaycoft, see 5:437.

G47. Portland Prognostic Tests for Mathematics. For additional information and a review by Cyril J. Hoyt, see 6:588 (1 reference).

G48. Problems in Quantitative Thinking. For additional information, see 1:1077.

G49. Purdue Industrial Mathematics Test. For additional information and reviews by Clyde H. Coombs and C. C. Upshall, see 3:314.

G50. The Purdue Mathematics Training Test: Arithmetic and Algebra. For additional information and a review by Lynnette B. Plumlee, see 6:589 (8 references).

G51. Rasmussen General Mathematics Test. For additional information and a review by William G. Mollenkopf, see 3:315 (1 reference).

G52. Sequential Tests of Educational Progress: Mathematics. For additional information and reviews by Arthur Mittman and Douglas A. Pidgeon, see 6:590 (5 references); for reviews by Paul L. Dressel, Gordon Fifer, and Tom A. Lamke, see 5:438. For reviews of the complete battery, see 6:25 (2 reviews) and 5:24 (2 reviews, 1 excerpt).

G53. Snader General Mathematics Test. For additional information, see 5:439; for reviews by Paul J. Blommers and Howard F. Fehr, see 4:378.

G54. Solution of Mathematical Problems. For additional information, see 1:1078.

G55. Survey of Mathematics Achievement: California Survey Series. For additional information and reviews by William R. Crawford and Arthur Mittman, see 6:591.

G56. Survey Test in Mathematics: Cooperative General Achievement Test, Part 3. For additional information and a review by Paul R. Rider, see 2:1434; for reviews by Arnold Dresden, Palmer O. Johnson, M. W. Richardson, and S. S. Wilks, see 1:870.

G57. T.C. Mathematics Test. For additional information, see 6:592.

G58. Test of Mathematical Fundamentals for Grades 7 to 12. For additional information and a review by Frances E. Crook [Morrison], see 5:440.

ALGEBRA

G59. Ability for Algebra: Fife Tests of Ability, Test 3. For additional information and a review by William G. Mollenkopf, see 4:380 (3 references). For reviews of the complete battery, see 4:713 (1 review) and 3:8 (1 review).

G60. Advanced Algebra: Minnesota High School Achievement Examinations. For additional information and reviews by Lynnette B. Plumlee and James P. Rizzo, see 6:593; for a review by Emma Spaney of earlier forms, see 5:442.

G61. Advanced Algebra Test: State High School Tests for Indiana. For additional information, see 4:382.

G62. Algebra: Cooperative Mathematics Tests. For additional information and a review by Paul Blommers, see 6:594.

G63. Algebra Prognosis Test. For additional information and reviews by Paul J. Blommers and William G. Mollenkopf, see 4:383.

G64. Algebra Readiness Test. For additional information and a review by Harold Gulliksen, see 4:384.

G65. Algebra Test for Engineering and Science: National Achievement Tests. For additional information and a review by Peter A. Lappan, Jr., see 6:595.

G66. Blyth Second-Year Algebra Test. For additional information and reviews by Paul Blommers and Myron F. Rosskopf, see 5:443.

G67. Breslich Algebra Survey Test. For additional information and a review by John R. Clark, see 2:1435.

G68. California Algebra Aptitude Test. For additional information, see 5:444; for a review by William G. Mollenkopf, see 4:385; for a review by David Segel, see 3:320.

G69. Columbia Research Bureau Algebra Test. For additional information and a review by Stanley Clark, see 4:386; for reviews by L. B. Kinney and S. S. Wilks, see 2:1436 (1 reference).

G70. Colvin-Schrammel Algebra Test. For additional information and a review by J. H. Minnick, see 2:1437; for a review by Maurice Hartung, see 1:879.

G71. Cooperative Algebra Test: Elementary Algebra Through Quadratics. For additional information and a review by Stanley Clark, see 4:387 (4 references); for a review by W. C. Brenke of earlier forms, see 3:321; for reviews by Harl R. Douglass and Harold Fawcett, see 2:1438; for reviews by William Betz, Helen Walker, and S. S. Wilks, see 1:880.

G72. Cooperative Intermediate Algebra Test: Quadratics and Beyond. For additional information and reviews by Lucien B. Kinney and E. P. Starke, see 4:388 (3 references); for a review by L. B. Plumlee of earlier forms, see 3:322; for reviews by Albert A. Bennett and Earle R. Hedrick, see 2:1439; for reviews by J. O. Hassler and S. S. Wilks, see 1:881.

G73. Cooperative Mathematics Test for College Students: Comprehensive Examination in College Algebra. For additional information and reviews by Albert A. Bennett and Paul R. Rider, see 2:1440 (1 reference); for reviews by Arnold Dresden, Marion W. Richardson, and Henry L. Rietz, see 1:882.

G74. Diagnostic Test in Basic Algebra. For additional information and a review by Stanley Clark, see 5:445.

G75. Elementary Algebra: Every Pupil Test. For additional information, see 6:596.

G76. Elementary Algebra: Minnesota High School Achievement Examinations. For additional information, see 6:597; for a review by Lynnette B. Plumlee of earlier forms, see 5:448.

G77. Elementary Algebra Test: Affiliation Testing Program for Catholic Secondary Schools. For additional information and a review by Henry Chauncey, see 6:598 (2 references). For a review of the complete program, see 6:758.

G78. Examination in College Algebra. For additional information and reviews by Albert A. Bennett and Edmund P. Churchill, see 3:323 (1 reference).

G79. Examination in Elementary Algebra—High-School Level. For additional information and reviews by Richard M. Drake and John A. Long, see 3:324.

G80. Examination in Second-Year Algebra—High-School Level. For additional information and reviews by L. B. Plumlee and Daniel W. Snader, see 3:325.

G81. First Year Algebra: Every Pupil Scholarship Test. For additional information, see 6:599.

G82. First Year Algebra Test: National Achievement Tests. For additional information and a review by Donald L. Meyer, see 6:600.

G83. First Year Algebra Test: State High School Tests for Indiana. For additional information, see 4:391.

G84. Garman-Schrammel Algebra Test. For additional information and reviews by Paul Blommers and E. H. C. Hildebrandt, see 3:326.

G85. Illinois Algebra Test. For additional information and reviews by Stanley Clark and Theodore E. Kellogg, see 5:450.

G86. Iowa Algebra Aptitude Test. For additional information and reviews by Harold Gulliksen and Emma Spaney, see 4:393; for a review by David Segel, see 3:327 (2 references); for reviews by Richard M. Drake and M. W. Richardson of an earlier edition, see 2:1441 (1 reference).

G87. Iowa Every-Pupil Test in Ninth Year Algebra. For additional information and a review by John R. Clark, see 2:1442.

G88. Lankton First-Year Algebra Test. For additional information and a review by Emma Spaney, see 5:451; for a review by Stanley Clark, see 4:394.

G89. Larson-Greene Unit Tests in First-Year Algebra. For additional information, see 4:395.

G90. Lee Test of Algebraic Ability. For additional information and a review by S. S. Wilks, see 2:1443 (1 reference).

G91. Orleans Algebra Prognosis Test. For additional information and reviews by Harold Gulliksen and Emma Spaney, see 4:396 (1 reference); for a review by S. S. Wilks of the original edition, see 2:1444 (4 references).

G92. Seattle Algebra Test. For additional information and reviews by Sheldon S. Myers and Willard G. Warrington, see 6:601 (1 reference); for a review by Albert E. Meder, Jr., see 5:452.

G93. Survey Test in Elementary Algebra. For additional information and reviews by John A. Long and Daniel W. Snader, see 3:328.

G94. Survey Test of Algebraic Aptitude: California Survey Series. For additional information and reviews by Cyril J. Hoyt and Donald L. Meyer, see 6:602.

G95. 20th Century Test for First Year Algebra. For additional information, see 4:392.

G96. The Votaw Algebra Test: Elementary Algebra. For additional information and a review by Kenneth F. McLaughlin, see 6:603; for reviews by Richard M. Drake and Nathan Morrison of earlier forms, see 3:329.

G97. Wisconsin Algebra Test. For additional information, see 3:330.

ARITHMETIC

G98. A.C.E.R. Arithmetic Tests. For additional information, see 4:398.

G99. A.C.E.R. Arithmetic Tests: Standardized for Use in New Zealand. For additional information, see 5:453 (the 2 references for this test are incorrectly placed and are for 5:454).

G100. A.C.E.R. Number Test. For additional information, see 5:454 (2 references for this test are incorrectly placed under 5:453); for a review by Leslie M. Haynes of the original edition, see 4:399.

G101. American Numerical Test. For additional information and reviews by Marvin D. Glock and Richard T. Johnson, see 6:604.

G102. American School Achievement Tests: Arithmetic Readiness. For additional information and a review by Harold E. Moser, see 5:455. For reviews of the complete battery, see 6:2 (2 reviews), 5:1 (2 reviews), 4:1 (1 review), and 3:1 (2 reviews).

G103. American School Achievement Tests: Part 2, Arithmetic. For additional information, see 6:605 (1 reference); for reviews by Joseph Justman and J. Fred Weaver, see 5:456. For reviews of the complete battery, see 6:2 (2 reviews), 5:1 (2 reviews), 4:1 (1 review), and 3:1 (2 reviews).

G104. Analytical Scales of Attainment: Arithmetic. For additional information and reviews by R. L. Morton, W. J. Osburn, and G. M. Wilson, see 2:1447.

G105. Analytical Survey Test in Computational Arithmetic. For additional information and a review by Emma Spaney, see 5:457.

G106. Arithmetic Computation: Public School Achievement Tests. For additional information, see 6:606. For reviews of the complete battery, see 2:1194 (2 reviews).

G107. Arithmetic: Cooperative Mathematics Tests. For additional information and a review by O. F. Anderhalter, see 6:607.

G108. Arithmetic Essentials Test. For additional information and a review by J. Wayne Wrightstone, see 5:458; for reviews by Foster E. Grossnickle and Charles S. Ross of the original edition, see 4:400.

G109. Arithmetic: Every Pupil Scholarship Test. For additional information, see 6:608.

G110. Arithmetic: Every Pupil Test. For additional information, see 6:609.

G111. Arithmetic Fundamentals Test: State High School Tests for Indiana. For additional information, see 4:402.

G112. Arithmetic: Midland Attainment Tests. For additional information and a review by Fred J. Schonell, see 2:1448.

G113. Arithmetic Progress Tests. For additional information, see 6:610; for reviews by William Curr and John Sutherland, see 5:461.

G114. Arithmetic Reasoning [B. V. Moore]. For additional information and a review by Jacob S. Orleans, see 3:331.

G115. Arithmetic Reasoning: Public School Achievement Tests. For additional information, see 6:612. For reviews of the complete battery, see 2:1194 (2 reviews).

G116. Arithmetic Reasoning [Richardson, Bellows, Henry & Co., Inc.]. For additional information, see 6:611.

G117. Arithmetic Reasoning Test: Personnel Research Institute Clerical Battery. For additional information, see 4:403. For reviews of the complete battery, see 4:729 (2 reviews).

G118. Arithmetic: Seven Plus Assessment: Northumberland Series. For additional information, see 4:404. For a review of the complete battery, see 4:24.

G119. Arithmetic Test: Fundamental Operations: Dominion Tests. For additional information and a review by Harry L. Stein, see 5:462; for a review by C. L. Thiele, see 3:332.

G120. Arithmetic Test (Fundamentals and Reasoning): Municipal Tests: National Achievement Tests. For additional information, see 5:463; for reviews by Foster E. Grossnickle and Charles S. Ross, see 4:406. For reviews of the complete battery, see 5:18 (1 review), 4:20 (1 review), and 2:1191 (2 reviews).

G121. Arithmetic Test: National Achievement Tests. For additional information, see 6:613; for reviews by R. L. Morton and Leroy H. Schnell, see 2:1449; for reviews by William A. Brownell and W. J. Osburn, see 1:889.

G122. Arithmetic Tests 1–2, 4–13. For additional information, see 6:614 (1 reference).

G123. Arithmetic: Thanet Mental Tests. For additional information and reviews by Fred J. Schonell and C. Ebblewhite Smith, see 2:1450.

G124. Arithmetical Reasoning Test. For additional information and a review by William L. Schaaf, see 4:407.

G125. Basic Arithmetic Skills: Iowa Every-Pupil Tests of Basic Skills, Test D. For additional information, see 4:408; for reviews by William A. Brownell and Leroy H. Schnell, see 3:334. For reviews of the complete battery, see 4:15 (2 reviews), 3:10 (3 reviews), and 1:872 (4 reviews).

G126. Basic Number Skills Test for Employee Selection. For additional information and reviews by Dorothy C. Adkins and Marion F. Shaycoft, see 5:466.

G127. Basic Skills in Arithmetic Test. For additional information and reviews by Jacob S. Orleans and F. Lynwood Wren, see 3:335.

G128. Bobbs-Merrill Arithmetic Achievement Tests. For additional information, see 6:615.

G129. A Brief Survey of Arithmetic Skills. For additional information and a review by H.. Vernon Price, see 5:467 (1 reference); for reviews by William A. Brownell and Henry Van Engen of the original edition, see 4:409.

G130. [Brueckner Diagnostic Arithmetic Tests.] For additional information and a review by Herbert F. Spitzer, see 4:410.

G131. California Arithmetic Test. A subtest of A2; for additional information, see 6:616 (4 references); for a review by Robert D. North, see 5:468; for a review by Robert L. Burch of an earlier edition, see 4:411; for reviews by C. L. Thiele and Harry Grove Wheat, see 2:1459; for a review by William A. Brownell, see 1:893. For reviews of the complete battery, see 6:3 (2 reviews), 5:2 (1 review), 4:2 (3 reviews), 3:15 (1 review), 2:1193 (2 reviews), and 1:876 (1 review, 1 excerpt).

G132. Cardall Arithmetic Reasoning Test. For additional information, see 6:617; for a review by William L. Schaaf, see 4:407.

G133. Chicago Arithmetic Readiness Test. For additional information and a review by Foster E. Grossnickle, see 3:337 (1 reference).

G134. Chicago Arithmetic Survey Tests. For additional information and reviews by William A. Brownell and Foster E. Grossnickle, see 3:338; see also 2:1453 (1 excerpt).

G135. The Clapp-Young Arithmetic Test. For additional information and a review by Leroy H. Schnell, see 3:339.

G136. Commercial Arithmetic Test: State High School Tests for Indiana. For additional information, see 4:448.

G137. Compass Diagnostic Tests in Arithmetic. For additional information and reviews by William A. Brownell and Foster E. Grossnickle, see 2:1454.

G138. Compass Survey Tests in Arithmetic. For additional information and a review by William A. Brownell, see 2:1455.

G139. Computation Test A/67. For additional information, see 6:618.

G140. Cooperative Commercial Arithmetic Test. For additional information and a review by Bertram Epstein, see 4:449.

G141. Coordinated Scales of Attainment: Arithmetic. For additional information, see 5:469. For reviews of the complete battery, see 4:8 (1 review) and 3:6 (4 reviews).

G142. Cotswold Junior Arithmetic Ability Test. For additional information and reviews by William Curr and George W. Sturrock, see 5:470.

G143. Cotswold Measurement of Ability: Arithmetic. For additional information, see 5:471; for a review by W. L. Sumner, see 4:412.

G144. Diagnostic Arithmetic Tests. For additional information, see 6:619.

G145. Diagnostic Chart for Fundamental Processes in Arithmetic. For additional information and a review by Leo J. Brueckner, see 4:413; for reviews by H. E. Benz and Foster E. Grossnickle, see 2:1456.

G146. Diagnostic Tests and Self-Helps in Arithmetic. For additional information and a review by Harold E. Moser, see 5:472.

G147. Diagnostic Tests in Arithmetic Fundamentals: Dominion Tests. For additional information and a review by John Sutherland, see 5:473; for a review by Leo J. Brueckner of the original edition, see 3:341.

G148. Diagnostic Tests in Money. For additional information and reviews by Kenneth Lovell and G. A. V. Morgan, see 6:620.

G149. Diagnostic Tests in Vulgar Fractions, Decimal Fractions and Percentages. For additional information and a review by Reginald Edwards, see 5:474.

G150. [Essential Arithmetic Tests.] For additional information and reviews by John Cohen and Stephen Wiseman, see 3:342.

G151. Examination in Advanced Arithmetic— High-School Level. For additional information and reviews by Monica M. Hoye and F. Lynwood Wren, see 3:343.

G152. Examination in Business Arithmetic. For additional information, see 3:374.

G153. Gilbert Business Arithmetic. For additional information and a review by William L. Schaaf, see 4:450.

G154. Group Test of Speed and Accuracy in Arithmetic Computation: Dominion Tests. For additional information and reviews by Frances E. Crook [Morrison] and William Harrison Lucow, see 5:477.

G155. Hildreth Arithmetic Achievement Tests. For additional information and reviews by William A. Brownell and Leo J. Brueckner, see 1:890.

G156. Hundred Problem Arithmetic Test. For additional information and a review by William Betz, see 3:344 (2 references, 1 excerpt); for a review by W. J. Osburn of an earlier edition, see 2:1462.

G157. Intermediate Diagnostic Arithmetic Test. For additional information and a review by Stanley Nisbet, see 6:621.

G158. Kansas Arithmetic Test. For additional information and reviews by H. E. Benz and W. J. Osburn, see 2:1457.

G159. Kansas Primary Arithmetic Test. For additional information and reviews by W. J. Osburn and G. M. Ruch, see 2:1458.

G160. Kelvin Measurement of Ability in Arithmetic. For additional information, see 1:891.

G161. Lee-Clark Arithmetic Fundamentals Survey Test: High School Edition. For additional information and reviews by Monica M. Hoye and F. Lynwood Wren, see 3:345.

G162. Los Angeles Diagnostic Tests: Fundamentals of Arithmetic. For additional information, see 6:622.

G163. Los Angeles Diagnostic Tests: Reasoning in Arithmetic. For additional information, see 6:623.

G164. Madden-Peak Arithmetic Computation Test: Evaluation and Adjustment Series. For additional information, see 6:624; for reviews by Theodore E. Kellogg and Albert E. Meder, Jr., see 5:478.

G165. Manchester Mechanical Arithmetic Test (Sen.) 1. For additional information, see 6:625.

G166. Mechanical Arithmetic Tests. For additional information, see 6:626; for reviews by George W. Sturrock and Jack Wrigley, see 5:489.

G167. Metropolitan Achievement Tests: [Arithmetic]. For additional information and reviews by O. F. Anderhalter and E. W. Hamilton, see 6:627 (1 reference) ; for a review by Robert L. Burch of an earlier edition, see 4:416; for reviews by Peter L. Spencer and Harry Grove Wheat, see 2:1458.1; for reviews by Foster E. Grossnickle and Guy M. Wilson, see 1:892. For reviews of the complete battery, see 6:15 (3 reviews), 4:18 (1 review), 2:1189 (2 reviews), and 1:874 (3 reviews).

G168. Milne Arithmetic Test. For additional information, see 5:479.

G169. [Moray House Arithmetic Tests.] For additional information, see 6:628 (9 references) ; for a review by John Cohen of earlier forms, see 3:346.

G170. N.B. Arithmetic Tests. For additional information, see 6:629.

G171. New York Test of Arithmetical Meanings. For additional information and a review by Charles S. Ross, see 5:480.

G172. Number Fact Check Sheet. For additional information and a review by Miriam M. Bryan, see 4:417.

G173. Oral Diagnostic Test in Addition: Analysis of Errors in Addition: Dominion Tests. For additional information and a review by Leo J. Brueckner, see 3:348.

G174. Primary Arithmetic: Every Pupil Scholarship Test. For additional information, see 6:630.

G175. Renfrow Survey Tests of Mathematical Skills and Concepts. For additional information and a review by C. L. Thiele, see 3:349.

G176. Retail Arithmetic Worksample. For additional information and a review by William J. E. Crissy, see 4:418 (1 reference).

G177. Revised Southend Attainment Test in Mechanical Arithmetic. For additional information, see 6:631; for a review by Stephen Wiseman of the original edition, see 3:352.

G178. SRA Achievement Series: Arithmetic. For additional information and a review by E. W. Hamilton, see 6:632 (1 reference) ; for reviews by Robert D. North and J. Fred Weaver, see 5:483. For reviews of the complete battery, see 6:21 (1 review) and 5:21 (2 reviews).

G179. Sangren-Reidy Survey Tests in Arithmetic. For additional information and reviews by Leo J. Brueckner and C. L. Thiele, see 2:1460.

G180. Scale of Problems in Commercial Arithmetic. For additional information, see 2:1489 (3 references, 1 excerpt).

G181. Scholastic Achievement Series: Arithmetic. For additional information, see 6:633; for reviews by Joseph Justman and Charles S. Ross, see 5:484. For reviews of the complete battery, see 6:23 (2 reviews) and 5:23 (2 reviews).

G182. Schonell Diagnostic Arithmetic Tests. For additional information and a review by John Sutherland, see 5:485 (1 reference) ; see also 3:350 (1 reference) ; for a review by C. Ebblewhite Smith of an earlier edition, see 2:1461 (2 references).

G183. Schrammel-Otterstrom Arithmetic Test. For additional information, see 6:634; for a review by William A. Brownell, see 3:351.

G184. Seeing Through Arithmetic Tests. For additional information and a review by William H. Lucio, see 6:635.

G185. Shop Arithmetic Test. For additional information, see 6:636 (2 references).

G186. Speed Addition Test. For additional information, see 1:1081.

G187. The Staffordshire Arithmetic Test. For additional information, see 5:486.

G188. Stanford Achievement Test: Arithmetic Tests. For additional information and a review by C. Alan Riedesel, see 6:637 (7 references) ; for a review by Robert L. Burch of an earlier edition, see 4:419. For reviews of the complete battery, see 6:26 (1 review, 1 excerpt), 5:25 (1 review), 4:25 (2 reviews), and 3:18 (2 reviews).

G189. Survey of Arithmetic Achievement: California Survey Series. For additional information and reviews by C. Alan Riedesel and Harold C. Trimble, see 6:638.

G190. Survey Test of Arithmetic Fundamentals: Dominion Tests. For additional information and a review by Frances E. Crook [Morrison], see 5:488.

G191. Test A/8: Arithmetic. For additional information, see 6:639.

G192. Test in Fundamental Processes in Arithmetic. For additional information, see 1:894.

G193. Test of Arithmetic Fundamentals. For additional information, see 6:640.

G194. Test on Arithmetic Meanings and Vocabulary. For additional information and a review by Foster E. Grossnickle, see 3:353.

G195. The Tiedeman Arithmetical Knowledge and Information Test. For additional information and a review by James H. Ricks, Jr., see 5:490.

G196. Understanding the Meanings in Arithmetic: A Diagnostic Test. For additional information and reviews by Richard T. Johnson and Harold C. Trimble, see 6:641 (2 references).

G197. Unit Scales of Attainment in Arithmetic. For additional information and reviews by W. J. Osburn and Peter L. Spencer, see 2:1463. For reviews of the complete battery, see 2:1197 (1 review) and 1:878 (2 reviews).

G198. The Wirral Mechanical Arithmetic Tests. For additional information and a review by John Sutherland, see 6:642.

G199. Wisconsin Inventory Tests in Arithmetic. For additional information and a review by Leo J. Brueckner, see 2:1464.

G200. Woody-McCall Mixed Fundamentals in Arithmetic. For additional information and a review by William A. Brownell, see 4:421.

CALCULUS

G201. Calculus: Cooperative Mathematics Tests. For additional information, see 6:654.

G202. Examination in Calculus II—Integral Calculus (Following Initial Course Containing No Integration). For additional information and a review by John F. Randolph, see 3:355 (1 reference).

G203. Examination in Differential Calculus. For additional information, see 3:354 (1 reference).

GEOMETRY

G204. Ability for Geometry: Fife Tests of Ability, Test 4. For additional information, see 3:356 (2 references). For reviews of the complete battery, see 4:713 (1 review) and 3:8 (1 review).

G205. Analytic Geometry: Cooperative Mathematics Tests. For additional information, see 6:643.

G206. Becker-Schrammel Plane Geometry. For additional information and reviews by Harold Fawcett and Judson W. Foust, see 2:1465 (1 reference).

G207. Columbia Research Bureau Plane Geometry Test. For additional information and a review by Cyril J. Hoyt (with Theodore E. Kellogg), see 4:422 (1 reference); for reviews by W. Elmer Lancaster and J. H. Minnick, see 2:1466.

G208. Cooperative Plane Geometry Test. For additional information and a review by Cyril J. Hoyt (with Theodore E. Kellogg), see 4:423 (1 reference); for reviews by Harold P. Fawcett and C. O. Oakley of earlier forms, see 3:357; for a review by Leroy H. Schnell, see 2:1467; for reviews by Charles C. Weidemann and S. S. Wilks, see 1:993.

G209. Cooperative Solid Geometry Test. For additional information and reviews by J. O. Hassler and Earle R. Hedrick, see 2:1468.

G210. Diagnostic Test in Basic Geometry. For additional information, see 6:644.

G211. Examination in Analytic Geometry. For additional information and a review by C. O. Oakley, see 3:358 (1 reference).

G212. Examination in Plane Geometry—High-School Level. For additional information and a review by Hale C. Pickett, see 3:359.

G213. Geometry Attainment Test. For additional information and reviews by I. Macfarlane Smith and W. L. Sumner, see 4:424.

G214. Geometry: Cooperative Mathematics Tests. For additional information, see 6:645 (1 reference).

G215. Geometry: Every Pupil Test. For additional information, see 6:646.

G216. Illinois Plane Geometry Test. For additional information and a review by Lynnette B. Plumlee, see 5:491.

G217. Iowa Every-Pupil Test in Plane Geometry. For additional information and a review by J. H. Blackhurst, see 1:994.

G218. Iowa Plane Geometry Aptitude Test. For additional information and a review by Philip H. Du-Bois, see 3:360; for reviews by Edward E. Cureton and Charles C. Weidemann of an earlier edition, see 2:1469.

G219. Lane-Greene Unit Tests in Plane Geometry. For additional information, see 4:426.

G220. Lee Test of Geometric Aptitude. For additional information and reviews by Kenneth F. McLaughlin and Lynnette B. Plumlee, see 6:647 (5 references); for reviews by Edward E. Cureton and Charles C. Weidemann of the original edition, see 2:1470.

G221. Nelson-Richardson Plane Geometry Readiness Test. For additional information, see 1:995.

G222. Orleans Geometry Prognosis Test. For additional information, see 4:427 (2 references); for reviews by Edward E. Cureton and Charles C. Weidemann of the original edition, see 2:1471 (3 references).

G223. Orleans Plane Geometry Achievement Test. For additional information and a review by Harold P. Fawcett, see 3:361.

G224. Plane Geometry: Every Pupil Scholarship Test. For additional information, see 6:648.

G225. Plane Geometry: Minnesota High School Achievement Examinations. For additional information, see 6:649; for a review by Harold P. Fawcett of an earlier form, see 5:495.

G226. Plane Geometry: National Achievement Tests. For additional information, see 6:650.

G227. Plane Geometry Test: Affiliation Testing Program for Catholic Secondary Schools. For additional information and a review by Henry Chauncey, see 6:651. For a review of the complete program, see 6:758.

G228. Plane Geometry Test: State High School Tests for Indiana. For additional information, see 4:429.

G229. Schrammel-Reed Solid Geometry Test. For additional information and a review by H. Vernon Price, see 5:496.

G230. Seattle Plane Geometry Test. For additional information and a review by Harold P. Fawcett, see 5:497.

G231. Shaycoft Plane Geometry Test. For additional information, see 5:498; for reviews by Harold P. Fawcett and Cyril J. Hoyt (with Theodore E. Kellogg), see 4:433.

G232. Solid Geometry: Minnesota High School Achievement Examinations. For additional information, see 6:652.

G233. Solid Geometry: National Achievement Tests. For additional information and a review by Sheldon S. Myers, see 6:653.

G234. Solid Geometry Test: State High School Tests for Indiana. For additional information, see 4:435.

G235. Survey Test in Plane Geometry. For additional information and a review by Harold P. Fawcett, see 4:436.

G236. 20th Century Test for Plane Geometry. For additional information, see 4:430.

G237. The Van Dyke Solid Geometry Test. For additional information, see 4:437.

G238. Wisconsin Geometry Test. For additional information, see 3:362.

MISCELLANEOUS

G239. Structure of the Number System: Cooperative Mathematics Tests. For additional information, see 6:655.

TRIGONOMETRY

G240. American Council Trigonometry Test. For additional information and reviews by J. O. Hassler and G. E. Hawkins, see 2:1473.

G241. Cooperative Plane Trigonometry Test. For additional information, see 4:438; for a review by G. E. Hawkins of an earlier form, see 2:1474 (1 reference); for reviews by J. O. Hassler and S. S. Wilks, see 1:1074.

G242. Examination in Plane Trigonometry. For additional information, see 3:364 (1 reference).

G243. Plane Trigonometry: National Achievement Tests. For additional information, see 6:656.

G244. Rasmussen Trigonometry Test. For additional information and a review by Lynnette B. Plumlee, see 5:501.

G245. Trigonometry: Cooperative Mathematics Tests. For additional information, see 6:657.

G246. Trigonometry: Minnesota High School Achievement Examinations. For additional information, see 6:658.

G247. Trigonometry Test: State High School Tests for Indiana. For additional information, see 4:440.

MISCELLANEOUS

H1. How Well Can You Read Lips? For additional information, see 5:579 (2 references).

H2. Sign-Search Test. For additional information, see 1:1080.

H3. What Do You Know About Photography? For additional information, see 5:580.

AGRICULTURE

H4. Agriculture: Every Pupil Scholarship Test. For additional information, see 6:659.

H.5. Animal Husbandry Test: State High School Tests for Indiana. For additional information, see 3:365.

H6. Clinton-Walker General Farm Mechanics Test. For additional information, see 2:1475.

H7. Farm Shop Tools: Recognition and Use: State High School Tests for Indiana. For additional information and a review by M. Ray Karnes, see 4:441 (1 reference).

H8. Graduate Record Examinations Advanced Agriculture Test. For additional information, see 4:442.

COMPUTATIONAL AND SCORING DEVICES

H9. Age and I.Q. Calculator. For additional information, see 4:464.

H10. The Bowman I.Q. Kalculator. For additional information, see 5:528.

H11. Burnham Correlation Form. For additional information, see 1:946 (1 excerpt).

H12. Chronological Age Computer. For additional information, see 6:660.

H13. The Delp I.Q. Computer. For additional information, see 4:465 (1 excerpt).

H14. Digitek Optical Test Scoring and Document Scanning System. For additional information, see 6:661.

H15. Dominion Table for Converting Mental Age to I.Q. For additional information, see 6:662.

H16. Durost-Walker Correlation Chart: For Machine or Computation. For additional information, see 1:947.

H17. The EB Punch-Key Scoring and Answer Sheet System. For additional information, see 6:663.

H18. [Grade Averaging Charts.] For additional information, see 6:664.

H19. Grade Master. For additional information, see 6:665.

H20. Grade-O-Mat. For additional information, see 6:666.

H21. Hankes' Answer Sheets. For additional information, see 6:667; see also 5:529 (1 reference) and 4:466 (5 references).

H22. IBM Optical Mark Scoring Reader. For additional information, see 6:668.

H23. IBM Test Scoring Machine. For additional information, see 6:669 (3 references); see also 5:530 (15 references); for a review by Arthur E. Traxler, see 3:397 (22 references); for reviews by John G. Darley and H. T. Manuel, see 2:1492 (14 references).

H24. MRC Test Processing Service. For additional information, see 6:670.

H25. Morgan IQ Calculator. For additional information, see 2:1493 (1 excerpt).

H26. The Multiscore Profile Form and Scoring Codes. For additional information, see 4:467.

H27. NCS Digital Test Scoring and Data Processing. For additional information, see 6:671.

H28. Plumb IQ Slide Rule for Use With the Wechsler-Bellevue Intelligence Scale. For additional information, see 4:362 (1 excerpt).

H29. Psychometric Research and Service Chart Showing the Davis Difficulty and Discrimination Indices for Item Analysis. For additional information, see 6:672 (1 excerpt).

H30. The Rapid-Rater. For additional information, see 6:673.

H31. SRA Self-Scorer. For additional information and reviews by James M. Anderson and Arthur E. Traxler, see 4:468 (4 references).

H32. STAR Score Teach Answer Record. For additional information, see 6:674.

H33. Thurstone Scoring Board. For additional information, see 3:398.

H34. The Tweeddale I.Q. Conversion Tables. For additional information, see 4:469.

H35. [V.G.C. Answer Strips and Scoring Sleeves.] For additional information, see 4:470.

COURTSHIP AND MARRIAGE

H36. A Courtship Analysis. For additional information and a review by William R. Reevy, see 6:675.

H37. A Dating Problems Checklist. For additional information and reviews by Clifford R. Adams and Robert A. Harper, see 6:676.

H38. The El Senoussi Multiphasic Marital Inventory. For additional information, see 6:677.

H39. Individual and Marriage Counseling Inventory. For additional information, see 6:678.

H40. The Male Impotence Test. For additional information, see 6:679.

H41. Marital Roles Inventory. For additional information and a review by Robert A. Harper, see 6:680 (3 references).

H42. A Marriage Adjustment Form. For additional information and a review by Lester W. Dearborn, see 6:681 (1 reference).

H43. The Marriage Adjustment Inventory. For additional information and reviews by Clifford R. Adams and Albert Ellis, see 6:682.

H44. The Marriage Adjustment Sentence Completion Survey. For additional information and a review by Albert Ellis, see.6:683.

H45. A Marriage Prediction Schedule. For additional information and a review by Lester W. Dearborn, see 6:684; see also 5:84 (8 references).

H46. Marriage Role Expectation Inventory. For additional information and a review by Robert C. Challman, see 6:685 (6 references).

H47. Otto Pre-Marital Counseling Schedules. For additional information and reviews by Robert C. Challman and William R. Reevy, see 6:686 (2 references).

H48. Sex Knowledge Inventory. For additional information and a review by Clifford R. Adams, see 6:687 (3 references); for a review by Albert Ellis, see 4:488 (1 excerpt).

H49. Sex Knowledge Test. For additional information, see 6:688.

DRIVING AND SAFETY EDUCATION

H50. [American Automobile Association Driver Testing Apparatus.] For additional information, see 4:521.

H51. Auto and Highway Safety Test. For additional information and a review by Harry R. DeSilva, see 2:1521.

H52. Driver Attitude Survey. For additional information, see 6:689.

H53. Examination for Driving Instructors. For additional information, see 4:522.

H54. General Achievement Test in Fire Safety: National Fire Prevention Tests. For additional information, see 4:523.

H55. General First-Aid Test for Senior-High-School Students: National Safety Education Tests. For additional information, see 2:1522.

H56. General Safety Education Test for Junior-High-School Pupils: National Safety Education Tests. For additional information, see 2:1523.

H57. General Test on Traffic and Driving Knowledge. For additional information, see 5:922.

H58. Hannaford Industrial Safety Attitude Scales. For additional information and a review by David O. Herman, see 6:690.

H59. Home Safety Test for High-School Students and Adults: National Safety Education Tests. For additional information, see 2:1524.

H60. An Instructional Test in Safety. For additional information, see 3:457.

H61. Judgment Test on Safe Driving Practices. For additional information and a review by Harry R. DeSilva, see 2:1525 (2 excerpts).

H62. Lauer Driver Reaction Inventory. For additional information, see 5:593 (2 references).

H63. The McGlade Road Test for Use in Driver Licensing, Education and Employment. For additional information, see 6:691 (1 reference).

H64. National Bicycle Tests. For additional information, see 2:1526.

H65. National Test in Driver Education. For additional information, see 6:692.

H66. Rating Scale for Automobile-Driver Skills: The Abercrombie Driver Test. For additional information, see 4:524.

H67. Revere Safety Test. For additional information and reviews by Willard A. Kerr and Harold G. Seashore, see 4:525.

H68. Road Test Check List for Passenger Car Drivers. For additional information, see 5:594.

H69. Rogers-Lauer Driver Rating Inventory. For additional information, see 5:595.

H70. Siebrecht Attitude Scale. For additional information, see 6:693 (3 references).

H71. Student Record in Driver Education. For additional information, see 6:694.

EDUCATION

H72. Academic Freedom Survey. For additional information, see 5:531.

H73. Aptitude Test for Elementary School Teachers-in-Training. For additional information and reviews by Robert M. W. Travers and Edwin Wandt, see 4:792 (2 references, 1 excerpt).

H74. Attitude Toward Student Ratings of Instruction. For additional information, see 5:532.

H75. Barr-Harris Teacher's Performance Record. For additional information, see 4:793.

H76. Brown Rating Profile for Student Teachers and Teachers of Physical Education. For additional information, see 2:1494.

H77. Clinton-Castle Self-Rating Scale for County School Superintendents. For additional information, see 2:1495.

H78. College Efficiency-of-Instruction Index. For additional information, see 2:1496 (1 reference).

H79. College and University Environment Scales (CUES). For additional information, see 6:695 (2 references).

H80. Comprehensive Examination in Secondary Education. For additional information, see 1:953.

H81. Coxe-Orleans Prognosis Test of Teaching Ability. For additional information and reviews by Harl R. Douglass and David G. Ryans, see 3:399 (5 references).

H82. Diagnostic Teacher-Rating Scale. For additional information, see 6:696; for a review by Dorothy M. Clendenen, see 5:534 (5 references); see also 4:795 (2 references).

H83. Educational Aptitude Test: George Washington University Series. For additional information and reviews by A. S. Barr and Harl R. Douglass, see 3:400 (3 references).

H84. Educational Interest Inventory. For additional information, see 5:535.

H85. Exceptional Teacher Service Record. For additional information and reviews by Leo J. Brueckner and Edwin Wandt, see 4:796.

H86. Faculty Morale Scale for Institutional Improvement. For additional information, see 6:697.

H87. The Graduate Record Examinations Advanced Tests: Education. For additional information and a review by D. Welty Lefever, see 6:698 (7 references); for a review by Harry N. Rivlin of an earlier form, see 5:537. For a review of the testing program, see 5:601.

H88. How I Counsel. For additional information and reviews by Clifford P. Froehlich and Milton E. Hahn, see 4:798 (4 references).

H89. How I Teach: Analysis of Teaching Practices. For additional information and reviews by May V. Seagoe and D. A. Worcester, see 4:799 (4 references); for a review by David G. Ryans, see 3:403.

H90. How Teach and Learn in College? For additional information and a review by Dean A. Worcester, see 4:800 (4 references).

H91. Illinois Opinion Inventories. For additional information and a review by Kenneth E. Clark, see 4:52 (1 reference).

H92. Introduction to Education. For additional information, see 1:954.

H93. Minnesota Teacher Attitude Inventory. For additional information, see 6:699 (146 references); for reviews by Dwight L. Arnold and Lee J. Cronbach, see 4:801 (9 references).

H94. Morrison Rating Scale Profile for Teachers. For additional information and a review by Leo J. Brueckner, see 1:955.

H95. National Teacher Examinations. For additional information and a review by Harold Seashore, see 6:700 (5 references); for reviews by William A. Brownell, Walter W. Cook, and Lawrence G. Derthick of earlier forms, see 5:538 (6 references); for a review by Harry N. Rivlin, see 4:802 (43 references). For reviews of individual tests, see 6:259 (1 review), 6:345 (1 review), 6:350 (1 review), 6:583 (1 review), and 6:974 (1 review).

H96. Ohio Teaching Record: Anecdotal Observation Form. For additional information, see 3:402 (1 reference, 1 excerpt).

H97. Pictographic Self Rating Scale. For additional information and reviews by Stanley E. Davis and John D. Krumboltz, see 6:701 (2 references).

H98. A Pupil's Rating Scale of an Instructor. For additional information and a review by James R. Hayden, see 6:702.

H99. Purdue Instructional Television Attitude Scale. For additional information, see 6:703.

H100. The Purdue Instructor Performance Indicator. For additional information and a review by C. Robert Pace, see 6:704 (3 references).

H101. The Purdue Rating Scale for Instruction. For additional information and a review by C. Robert Pace, see 6:705 (5 references); for a review by Kenneth L. Heaton, see 4:803 (26 references).

H102. The Purdue Teacher Morale Inventory. For additional information, see 6:706.

H103. Rating Instrument for the Evaluation of Student Reactions. For additional information, see 2:1497 (2 references).

H104. Rating Instrument for the Evaluation of the Reactions of College Students. For additional information, see 2:1498 (2 references).

H105. Remmlein's School Law Test. For additional information, see 6:707.

H106. SRA Educators Opinion Inventory. For additional information, see 5:540.

H107. Scale for Rating Effective Teacher Behavior. For additional information and reviews by Leo J. Brueckner and Edwin Wandt, see 4:804 (1 reference).

H108. School Practices Questionnaire. For additional information and reviews by Harriet M. Barthelmess [Morrison] and Hilda Taba, see 1:869 (2 references).

H109. A Self Appraisal Scale for Teachers. For additional information, see 5:541.

H110. Sizing Up Your School Subjects. For additional information, see 6:708.

H111. Stanford Educational Aptitudes Test. For additional information and reviews by A. S. Barr and David G. Ryans, see 3:404 (4 references).

H112. Teacher Education Examination Program. For additional information, see 6:709; for a review by Walter W. Cook, see 5:543.

H113. Teacher Opinionaire on Democracy. For additional information and reviews by George W. Hartmann and C. Robert Pace, see 4:805.

H114. Teaching Aptitude Test: George Washington University Series. For additional information and a review by May V. Seagoe, see 4:806; for a review by A. S. Barr, see 3:405 (8 references).

H115. The Teaching Evaluation Record. For additional information, see 5:542.

H116. A Test on Adult Attitudes Toward Children. For additional information and a review by Elizabeth Hagen, see 6:710.

H117. What Would *You* Do? Perplexing Incidents in Human Relations. For additional information, see 5:545.

H118. The Wilson Teacher-Appraisal Scale. For additional information and a review by James R. Hayden, see 6:711.

ETIQUETTE

H119. The Best Thing to Do: A Test of Knowledge of Social Standards. For additional information and a review by Helen Shacter, see 4:471.

H120. Furbay-Schrammel Social Comprehension Test. For additional information and a review by James H. Ricks, Jr., see 4:472 (1 reference).

H121. The New Century Social Conduct Test. For additional information, see 5:547.

H122. Parsons Social Comprehension Test. For additional information, see 5:548.

H123. Test of Etiquette: George Washington University Series. For additional information and a review by James H. Ricks, Jr., see 4:473.

H124. Test of Knowledge of Social Usage. For additional information and a review by Hilda Taba, see 4:474 (1 reference).

H125. Test on Social Usage. For additional information, see 5:549.

HANDWRITING

H126. The American Handwriting Scale. For additional information and a review by Theodore L. Harris, see 6:712.

H127. Ayres Measuring Scale for Handwriting. For additional information, see 5:550; for a review by Worth J. Osburn, see 4:475 (9 references).

H128. Evaluation Scales for Guiding Growth in Handwriting. For additional information and a review by Theodore L. Harris, see 6:713 (2 references).

H129. Normal Handwriting Scale. For additional information and a review by Theodore L. Harris, see 6:714.

H130. The Thorndike Scale for Handwriting of Children. For additional information and a review by Stuart A. Courtis, see 4:477 (4 references).

HEALTH AND PHYSICAL EDUCATION

H131. AAHPER Youth Fitness Test. For additional information, see 6:715 (21 references).

H132. ACH Index of Nutritional Status. For additional information, see 1:1002 (1 reference, 1 excerpt).

H133. Achievement Scales in Physical Education Activities for Boys and Girls in Elementary and Junior High Schools. For additional information, see 1:1003.

H134. Achievement Scales in Physical Education Activities for College Men. For additional information, see 1:1004.

H135. Action-Choice Tests for Competitive Sports Situations. For additional information, see 6:716 (2 references).

H136. Basic Fitness Tests. For additional information, see 6:716a (1 reference).

H137. Belmont Measures of Athletic Performance: Field Hockey Scale. For additional information, see 6:717.

H138. Brewer-Schrammel Health Knowledge and Attitude. For additional information and reviews by John C. Almack and Frederick Rand Rogers, see 2:1499 (1 reference).

H139. Byrd Health Attitude Scale. For additional information and reviews by Mayhew Derryberry and H. H. Remmers, see 3:418 (1 reference, 1 excerpt).

H140. College Health Knowledge Test, Personal Health. For additional information and reviews by James E. Bryan and Peter G. Loret, see 6:718 (4 references); for a review by H. Harrison Clarke, see 4:478.

H141. Cornell Medical Index—Health Questionnaire. For additional information, see 6:719 (31 references).

H142. Cowell Test of Ability to Recognize the Operation of Certain Principles Important to Physical Education. For additional information, see 6:720 (1 reference).

H143. Elementary Health: Every Pupil Scholarship Test. For additional information, see 6:721.

H144. [French Tests for Professional Courses in Knowledge of Sports]: Physical Education Major Examinations. For additional information and a review by H. Harrison Clarke, see 4:480 (2 references).

H145. Gates-Strang Health Knowledge Tests. For additional information and a review by Paul E. Kambly, see 4:481 (2 references); see also 3:419 (1 excerpt); for reviews by Frederick Rand Rogers and A. H. Turney, see 2:1500 (1 excerpt).

H146. Gill-Schrammel Physiology Test. For additional information and a review by Clarence H. Nelson, see 5:554.

H147. The Graduate Record Examinations Advanced Tests: Physical Education. For additional information, see 6:722. For a review of the testing program, see 5:601.

H148. Health and Safety Education Test: National Achievement Tests. For additional information, see 6:724; for a review by Clarence H. Nelson, see 5:555.

H149. Health and Safety Education Test: State High School Tests for Indiana. For additional information, see 3:420.

H150. Health Awareness Test. For additional information and a review by R. Lenox Criswell, see 2:1501 (1 reference, 1 excerpt); for a review by Austin H. Turney, see 1:1006.

H151. Health Behavior Inventory. For additional information and reviews by James E. Bryan and Peter G. Loret, see 6:723.

H152. Health Education and Hygiene: Every Pupil Test. For additional information, see 6:725.

H153. Health Education Test: Knowledge and Application: Acorn National Achievement Tests. For additional information, see 5:557 (1 reference); for reviews by H. H. Remmers and Mabel E. Rugen, see 3:421.

H154. Health Inventories. For additional information and a review by Benjamin Shimberg, see 4:484 (1 reference).

H155. Health Inventory for High School Students. For additional information and reviews by Mayhew Derryberry and Mabel E. Rugen, see 3:422 (1 reference).

H156. Health Knowledge Test for College Freshmen: National Achievement Tests. For additional information and a review by James E. Bryan, see 5:558 (3 references).

H157. Health Practice Inventory. For additional information and a review by James E. Bryan, see 5:559 (2 references); for a review by Thomas Kirk Cureton of the original edition, see 3:423 (2 references).

H158. Health Test: National Achievement Tests. For additional information and a review by Benno G. Fricke, see 5:560; for a review by Jacob S. Orleans, see 4:485.

H159. High School Health: Every Pupil Scholarship Test. For additional information, see 6:726.

H160. Indiana University Motor Fitness Index. For additional information, see 3:424 (4 references).

H161. Kilander Health Knowledge Test. For additional information, see 5:562 (3 references); see also 2:1503 (2 excerpts).

H162. Kilander Nutrition Information Test. For additional information, see 3:425 (1 reference).

H163. Patient's Self-History Form. For additional information, see 4:486.

H164. Personal Health Inventory. For additional information and a review by Willard W. Patty, see 4:487.

H165. Physical Education Achievement Scales for Boys in Secondary Schools. For additional information, see 1:B338 (1 excerpt).

H166. Physical Education: National Teacher Examinations. For additional information, see 6:727. For reviews of the testing program, see 6:700 (1 review), 5:538 (3 reviews), and 4:802 (1 review).

H167. Physical Education: Teacher Education Examination Program. An inactive form of H166; for additional information, see 6:728. For a review of the testing program, see 5:543.

H168. Physical Education Tests. For additional information, see 5:565 (1 reference).

H169. Physical Examination Record. For additional information, see 2:1504 (1 reference).

H170. Smoking Habits Questionnaire. For additional information, see 6:729.

H171. Trusler-Arnett Health Knowledge Test. For additional information and a review by Thomas Kirk Cureton, see 3:426.

H172. Veenker Health Knowledge Test for the Seventh Grade. For additional information, see 6:730 (1 reference).

H173. [Wetzel Grid Charts.] For additional information and a review by Dorothy Eichorn, see 6:731 (26 references); see also 4:489 (9 references).

H174. Width-Weight Tables. For additional information, see 4:490 (1 reference).

H175. [Winsberg Tests: Examinations for Physical Education Major Students.] For additional information, see 5:567.

HOME ECONOMICS

H176. Assisting With Care and Play of Children: State High School Tests for Indiana. For additional information and a review by Helen C. Dawe, see 3:427.

H177. Assisting With Clothing Problems: State High School Tests for Indiana. For additional information, see 3:428.

H178. Child Development: State High School Tests for Indiana. For additional information and a review by Helen C. Dawe, see 3:429.

H179. Clothing: Every Pupil Scholarship Test. For additional information, see 6:732.

H180. Clothing I: State High School Tests for Indiana. For additional information, see 3:430.

H181. Clothing II: State High School Tests for Indiana. For additional information, see 3:431.

H182. Cooperative Test in Foods and Nutrition. For additional information and a review by Robert L. Ebel, see 4:491 (1 reference).

H183. Cooperative Test in Home Management. For additional information, see 4:492 (1 reference).

H184. Cooperative Test in Household Equipment. For additional information and reviews by Faith Madden and Victor H. Noll, see 4:493 (1 reference).

H185. Cooperative Test in Textiles and Clothing. For additional information, see 4:494 (1 reference).

H186. Engle-Stenquist Home Economics Test. For additional information and reviews by Clara M. Brown [Arny] and Hester Chadderdon, see 2:1505.

H187. Foods: Every Pupil Scholarship Test. For additional information, see 6:733.

H188. Foods I, Food Selection and Preparation: State High School Tests for Indiana. For additional information concerning earlier forms, see 4:495; for a review by Hester Chadderdon, see 1:1029.

H189. Foods II, Planning for Family Food Needs: State High School Tests for Indiana. For additional information concerning earlier forms, see 4:496.

H190. Frear-Coxe Clothing Test. For additional information and reviews by Laura B. Hadley and Esther F. Segner, see 2:1507.

H191. General Home Economics: Clothing, Home Relations, and Social Usage: State High School Tests for Indiana. For additional information and a review by Clara M. Brown [Arny], see 1:1030.

H192. General Home Economics: Foods, the House, and Child Development: State High School Tests for Indiana. For additional information and a review by Clara M. Brown [Arny], see 1:1030.

H193. Graduate Record Examinations Advanced Home Economics Test. For additional information, see 4:497.

H194. Helping With Food in the Home: State High School Tests for Indiana. For additional information and a review by Jean D. Amberson, see 4:498.

H195. Helping With the Housekeeping: State High School Tests for Indiana. For additional information and a review by Hester Chadderdon, see 4:499.

H196. Home Care of the Sick Test: State High School Tests for Indiana. For additional information, see 4:500.

H197. Home Economics Education: National Teacher Examinations. For additional information, see 6:734. For reviews of the testing program, see 6:700 (1 review), 5:538 (3 reviews), and 4:802 (1 review).

H198. Homemaking I and II: Every Pupil Scholarship Test. For additional information, see 6:735.

H199. Housing the Family: State High School Tests for Indiana. For additional information and a review by Jean D. Amberson of an earlier form, see 4:501.

H200. Information Test on Foods: Illinois Food Test. For additional information and reviews by Norma A. Albright and Clara M. Brown [Arny], see 2:1508 (1 reference).

H201. Johnson Home Economics Interest Inventory. For additional information and reviews by John D. Black and Leona E. Tyler, see 5:570 (6 references).

H202. Minnesota Check List for Food Preparation and Serving. For additional information, see 5:571; see also 2:1509 (1 reference, 1 excerpt).

H203. Minnesota Food Score Cards. For additional information, see 3:439.

H204. Minnesota House Design and House Furnishing Test. For additional information and a review by Ray Faulkner, see 1:1031 (1 reference).

H205. Nutrition Information. For additional information, see 4:502.

H206. Nutrition Information Test. For additional information, see 3:425 (1 reference).

H207. Scales for Appraising High School Homemaking Programs. For additional information, see 5:572.

H208. Tests in Comprehension of Patterns. For additional information and reviews by Laura B. Hadley and Berenice Mallory, see 2:1510.

H209. Unit Scales of Attainment in Foods and Household Management. For additional information and reviews by Norma A. Albright and Hester Chadderdon, see 2:1511.

INDUSTRIAL ARTS

H210. Achievement Test in Mechanical Drawing. For additional information and a review by Verne C. Fryklund, see 2:1512 (1 reference).

H211. Drawing Aptitude Test. For additional information, see 2:1512.1.

H212. Examination in Mechanical Drawing. For additional information, see 3:440.

H213. Industrial Arts Education: National Teacher Examinations. For additional information, see 6:736. For reviews of the testing program, see 6:700 (1 review), 5:538 (3 reviews), and 4:802 (1 review).

H214. Industrial Arts: Every Pupil Scholarship Test. For additional information, see 6:737.

H215. Industrial Arts: Teacher Education Examination Program. An inactive form of H213; for additional information, see 6:738. For a review of the testing program, see 5:543.

H216. Mechanical Drawing. For additional information and a review by Dean M. Schweickhard, see 2:1513.

H217. Mechanical Drawing Performance Test. For additional information and a review by Emanuel E. Ericson, see 2:1514 (1 reference); see also 1:1034 (1 excerpt).

H218. Mechanical Drawing Test: State High School Tests for Indiana. For additional information and a review by William J. Micheels, see 4:503.

H219. Mechanical Drawing Tests. For additional information and a review by Emanuel E. Ericson, see 2:1515.

H220. Middleton Industrial Arts Test. For additional information and a review by William J. Micheels, see 4:504.

H221. Newkirk-Stoddard Home Mechanics Test. For additional information and a review by Arthur B. Mays, see 2:1516 (1 reference).

H222. Practical Arts: Every Pupil Test. For additional information, see 1:1035.

H223. Standard Test in Fundamental Mechanical Drawing. For additional information and a review by Verne C. Fryklund, see 2:1517.

LISTENING COMPREHENSION

H224. Brown-Carlsen Listening Comprehension Test. For additional information, see 6:739 (9 references); for reviews by E. F. Lindquist and Irving Lorge, see 5:577 (13 references).

H225. Sequential Tests of Educational Progress: Listening. For additional information, see 6:740 (11 references); for reviews by E. F. Lindquist and Irving Lorge, see 5:578. For reviews of the complete battery, see 6:25 (2 reviews) and 5:24 (2 reviews, 1 excerpt).

PHILOSOPHY

H226. The Graduate Record Examinations Advanced Tests: Philosophy. For additional information, see 6:741. For a review of the testing program, see 5:601.

H227. The Graduate Record Examinations Advanced Tests: Scholastic Philosophy. For additional information, see 6:742 (2 references). For a review of the testing program, see 5:601.

PSYCHOLOGY

H228. The Case of Mickey Murphy: A Case-Study Instrument in Evaluation. For additional information and a review by Dwight L. Arnold, see 5:533 (2 references); for a review by Frank S. Freeman of the second edition, see 4:794.

H229. Case Study Tests in Human Growth and Development. For additional information and reviews by Harold E. Jones and Goodwin Watson of the original edition, see 3:406 (3 references).

H230. Comprehensive Examination in Psychology. For additional information and a review by Edith M. Huddleston, see 4:507.

H231. Engle Psychology Test. For additional information and a review by Harold Seashore, see 5:582.

H232. Examination in Elementary Psychology —College Level. For additional information, see 3:401.

H233. The Graduate Record Examinations Advanced Tests: Psychology. For additional information, see 6:743; for a review by Harold Seashore, see 5:583. For a review of the testing program, see 5:601.

H234. Hogan Psychology Test. For additional information and a review by Harold Seashore, see 5:584.

H235. Psychology Test: Every Pupil Scholarship Test. For additional information, see 6:744.

H236. Toothman Test in Elementary Educational Psychology. For additional information and a review by V. A. C. Henmon, see 1:956.

RECORD AND REPORT FORMS

H237. A/9 Cumulative Record Folder. For additional information, see 6:745.

H238. American Council on Education Cumulative Record Folders. For additional information and reviews by Warren R. Baller and Arthur H. Brayfield, see 4:510; for reviews by Herbert A. Toops, see 3:444-5.

H239. Blum-Fieldsteel Development Charts. For additional information, see 5:585 (1 reference).

H240. [California Cumulative Record and Health Insert.] For additional information and a review by Warren R. Baller of the original edition, see 4:511.

H241. The Cassel Developmental Record. For additional information and a review by William E. Henry, see 5:586.

H242. Comprehensive Individual History Record Form for Infancy Through High School. For additional information and reviews by Charles D. Flory and Chauncey M. Louttit, see 1:1116.

H243. Cumulative Guidance Record. For additional information, see 4:512; for revision, see TIP 1305.

H244. Cumulative Personnel Record. For additional information, see 4:513.

H245. Diagnostic Child Study Record. For additional information and reviews by Charles D. Flory, Chauncey M. Louttit, and J. W. M. Rothney, see 1:1117 (2 references).

H246. [Guidance Cumulative Folder and Record Forms.] For additional information, see 6:746.

H247. Hamilton Cumulative Record Folder. For additional information, see 3:447.

H248. Indiana Psychodiagnostic Blank. For additional information, see 2:1518 (3 references).

H249. Ontario School Record System. For additional information, see 6:747.

H250. Permanent Record Card. For additional information, see 4:515 (1 reference).

H251. [Personnel Record Form.] For additional information and a review by Charles D. Flory, see 1:1120.

H252. [Physical Growth Record.] For additional information, see 6:748 (1 reference).

H253. A Pre-School Record Form. For additional information, see 5:587.

H254. Profile Chart for Individual Diagnosis. For additional information, see 1:1121.

H255. [Pupils' Record Cards.] For additional information, see 2:1519 (1 reference).

H256. Secondary-School Record. For additional information, see 4:516 (1 reference); for revision, see TIP 1318.

H257. Standard Profile Chart. For additional information and a review by Charles R. Langmuir, see 3:448.

H258. Supplementary Entrance Interview Schedule. For additional information, see 1:1122.

H259. V.G.C. Anecdotal Record Form. For additional information, see 3:449; for revision, see TIP 1306.

H260. V.G.C. Cumulative Record Folder. For additional information, see 4:517; for revision, see TIP 1307.

H261. V.G.C. Interview Record Form. For additional information, see 3:451; for revision, see TIP 1308.

H262. V.G.C. Student Information Form. For additional information, see 3:452; for revision, see TIP 1309.

RELIGIOUS EDUCATION

H263. Achievement Test for Weekday Afternoon Congregational Schools. For additional information, see 6:750.

H264. Achievement Test in Jewish History. For additional information, see 6:749.

H265. Attitude Inventory [Concordia]. For additional information, see 5:588 (1 reference).

H266. Bible History Tests. For additional information, see 5:589.

H267. Hebrew School Attitude Test. For additional information, see 3:452a.

H268. Jewish Home Environment Test. For additional information, see 3:453.

H269. Jewish Information Test. For additional information, see 4:518.

H270. Opinion Survey. For additional information, see 4:519.

H271. Peters Biblical Knowledge Test. For additional information and a review by Janet G. Afflerbach, see 5:590.

H272. Religion Essentials Test. For additional information, see 3:455 (2 references).

H273. Religion Test for Grades Two and Three. For additional information, see 5:591.

H274. Religion Test for High Schools. For additional information, see 5:592.

H275. Religion Test (Four-Year Course): Affiliation Testing Program for Catholic Secondary Schools. For additional information and a review by Henry Chauncey, see 6:751. For a review of the complete program, see 6:758.

H276. Scholastic Achievement Series: Religion. For additional information, see 6:752. For reviews of the complete battery, see 6:23 (2 reviews) and 5:23 (2 reviews).

H277. Standardized Bible Content Test. For additional information, see 6:753.

H278. Test in Religious Instruction for High School Students. For additional information, see 2:1520.

H279. Test on Biblical Information. For additional information, see 6:754.

H280. Theological School Inventory. For additional information, see 6:755.

H281. Uniform Achievement Tests. For additional information, see 5:278.

H282. Unit Tests on Luther's Catechism. For additional information, see 6:756 (1 reference).

H283. Wilson Tests of Religious Aptitude. For additional information and a review by Goodwin Watson, see 3:456 (1 reference).

SOCIOECONOMIC STATUS

H284. The American Home Scale. For additional information, see 5:596 (2 references); for reviews by Henry S. Maas and Verner M. Sims, see 3:417 (7 references).

H285. The Minnesota Home Status Index: A Scale for Measuring Urban Home Environment. For additional information and a review by Verner M. Sims, see 1:983 (1 reference, 4 excerpts).

H286. Sims SCI Occupational Rating Scale. For additional information and a review by Henry Weitz, see 5:597 (10 references).

H287. The Social Status Scale. For additional information, see 5:598 (7 references).

H288. Socio-Economic Status Scale. For additional information, see 6:757 (1 excerpt).

TEST PROGRAMS

H289. The Affiliation Testing Program for Catholic Secondary Schools. For additional information and a review by Henry Chauncey, see 6:758.

H290. College Board Placement Tests. For additional information, see 6:759.

H291. College Entrance Examination Board Admissions Testing Program. For additional information and reviews by Benno G. Fricke and Dean K. Whitla, see 6:760 (12 references); see also 5:599 (3 references) and 4:526 (9 references). For reviews of individual tests, see 6:287 (3 reviews), 6:289 (1 review), 6:383 (1 review), 6:384 (2 reviews), 6:449 (2 reviews), 6:568 (1 review), 6:569 (1 review), 6:914 (1 review), 6:966 (1 review), 6:967 (1 review), 5:272 (1 review), 5:277 (1 review), 5:280 (1 review), 5:318 (1 review), 5:723 (1 review), 5:742 (1 review), 5:749 (1 review), 5:786 (1 review), 4:178 (1 review), 4:237 (1 review), and 4:367 (1 review).

H292. College Entrance Examination Board Advanced Placement Examinations. For additional information, see 6:761 (5 references). For reviews of individual tests, see 6:893 (1 review), 6:1000 (1 review), 5:205 (1 review), 5:211 (1 review), 5:273 (1 review), 5:419 (1 review), 5:724 (1 review), 5:743 (1 review), 5:750 (1 review), and 5:812 (2 reviews).

H293. Cooperative Inter-American Tests. For additional information and reviews of individual tests, see 4:176 (1 review), 4:325 (2 reviews), 4:557 (2 reviews), 4:576 (1 review), and 4:577 (2 reviews).

H294. The Graduate Record Examinations. For additional information, see 6:762 (1 reference); for a review by Harold Seashore, see 5:601 (12 references); see also 4:527 (24 references). For reviews of individual tests, see 6:9 (2 reviews), 6:376 (1 review), 6:461 (2 reviews), 6:578 (1 review), 6:698 (1 review), 6:919 (1 review), 6:931 (1 review), 6:1021 (1 review), 5:10 (2 reviews), 5:215 (1 review), 5:247 (1 review), 5:270 (1 review), 5:336 (1 review), 5:427 (1 review), 5:537 (1 review), 5:583 (1 review), 5:727 (1 review), 5:754 (1 review), 5:818 (1 review), and 5:835 (1 review).

H295. National Guidance Testing Program. For additional information, see 6:763.

H296. Project Talent Test Battery: A National Inventory of Aptitudes and Abilities. For additional information, see 6:764 (5 references).

H297. [Science Talent Search Program.] For additional information, see 6:765.

MULTI-APTITUDE BATTERIES

I1. Academic Promise Tests. For additional information and reviews by Julian C. Stanley and William W. Turnbull, see 6:766.

I2. Aptitude Tests for Occupations. For additional information and a review by Lloyd G. Humphreys, see 5:891; for a review by Clifford P. Froehlich, see 4:710 (1 excerpt).

I3. Detroit General Aptitudes Examination. For additional information, see 5:603; for reviews by G. Frederic Kuder, Irving Lorge, and John Gray Peatman, see 2:1654.

I4. Differential Ability Tests. For additional information, see 5:604.

I5. Differential Aptitude Tests. For additional information and reviews by J. A. Keats and Richard E. Schutz, see 6:767 (52 references); for reviews by John B. Carroll and Norman Frederiksen, see 5:605 (49 references); for reviews by Harold Bechtoldt, Ralph F. Berdie, and Lloyd G. Humphreys, see 4:711 (28 references); see also 3:620 (1 excerpt).

I6. Differential Test Battery. For additional information, see 6:768; for reviews by E. A. Peel, Donald E. Super, and Philip E. Vernon, see 5:606.

I7. Employee Aptitude Survey. For additional information and reviews by Paul F. Ross and Erwin K. Taylor, see 6:769 (4 references, 1 excerpt); for reviews by Dorothy C. Adkins and S. Rains Wallace, see 5:607.

I8. Factored Aptitude Tests. For additional information and reference to reviews, see 6:774; for a review by Harold P. Bechtoldt, see 5:602; for a review by D. Welty Lefever of an earlier edition, see 4:712 (1 reference, 1 excerpt).

I9. Fife Tests of Ability. For additional information and a review by I. Macfarlane Smith, see 4:713 (3 references); for a review by James Maxwell, see 3:8.

I10. Flanagan Aptitude Classification Tests. For additional information and reviews by Norman Frederiksen and William B. Michael, see 6:770 (7 references); for reviews by Harold P. Bechtoldt, Ralph F. Berdie, and John B. Carroll, see 5:608.

I11. General Aptitude Test Battery. For additional information and reviews by Harold P. Bechtoldt and John B. Carroll, see 6:771 (55 references); for reviews by Andrew L. Comrey, Clifford P. Froehlich, and Lloyd G. Humphreys, see 5:609 (176 references); for reviews by Milton L. Blum, Edward B. Greene, and Howard R. Taylor, see 4:714 (33 references).

I12. The Guilford-Zimmerman Aptitude Survey. For additional information, see 6:772 (17 references); for reviews by Anne Anastasi, Harold Bechtoldt, John B. Carroll, and P. E. Vernon, see 4:715 (15 references).

I13. Holzinger-Crowder Uni-Factor Tests. For additional information and reviews by Anne Anastasi, Benjamin Fruchter, and Philip E. Vernon, see 5:610 (3 references).

I14. The Jastak Test of Potential Ability and Behavior Stability. For additional information and reviews by Anne Anastasi and Benjamin Kleinmuntz, see 6:773 (3 references, 2 excerpts).

I15. Job-Tests Program. For additional information and reviews by William H. Helme and Stanley I. Rubin, see 6:774.

I16. Measurement of Skill: A Battery of Placement Tests for Business, Industrial and Educational Use. For additional information and reviews by Dorothy C. Adkins, Lloyd G. Humphreys, and Joseph E. Moore, see 6:775 (2 references).

I17. The Multi-Aptitude Test. For additional information and a review by H. H. Remmers, see 5:612 (1 reference).

I18. Multiple Aptitude Tests. For additional information and reviews by S. S. Dunn and Leroy Wolins, see 6:776 (8 references, 1 excerpt); for reviews by Ralph F. Berdie and Benjamin Fruchter of the original edition, see 5:613.

I19. N.B. Aptitude Tests (Junior). For additional information, see 6:777.

I20. National Institute for Personnel Research High Level Battery. For additional information, see 6:778 (1 reference).

I21. National Institute for Personnel Research Normal Battery. For additional information, see 6:779.

I22. SRA Primary Mental Abilities. For additional information and a review by John E. Milholland, see 6:780 (50 references); for reviews by Norman Frederiksen and Albert K. Kurtz of an earlier edition, see 5:614 (59 references); for reviews by Anne Anastasi, Ralph F. Berdie, John B. Carroll, Stuart A. Courtis, and P. E. Vernon, see 4:716 (42 references); for reviews by Cyril Burt, Florence L. Goodenough, James R. Hobson, and F. L. Wells, see 3:225 (50 references) and 3:264 (2 references); for reviews by Henry E. Garrett, Truman L. Kelley, C. Spearman, Godfrey H. Thomson, and Robert C. Tryon, see 2:1427 (10 references, 3 excerpts).

I23. [United States Employment Service Special Aptitude Tests.] For additional information, see 4:717.

I24. Vocational Guidance Program. For additional information and a review by Leo Goldman, see 6:781.

I25. Yale Educational Aptitude Test Battery. For additional information and reviews by Anne Anastasi and Ruth Churchill, see 5:615 (4 references); see also 4:718 (7 references).

PERSONALITY

NONPROJECTIVE

J1. A-S Reaction Study: A Scale for Measuring Ascendance-Submission in Personality. For additional information and a review by Warren T. Norman, see 6:57 (11 references); see also 5:28 (15 references); for a review by William U. Snyder, see 3:23 (11 references); for a review by Doncaster G. Humm of the 1928 edition, see 2:1198 (19 references).

J2. A-S Reaction Study: Revision for Business Use. For additional information and a review by Doncaster G. Humm, see 2:1199 (4 references).

J3. Activity Vector Analysis. For additional information and reviews by Lewis E. Albright, Alexander W. Astin, and Winton H. Manning, see 6:58 (21 references); for reviews by Brent Baxter and George K. Bennett, see 5:29 (11 references).

J4. The Adjustment Inventory. For additional information and a review by Forrest L. Vance, see 6:59 (11 references, 1 excerpt); see also 5:30 (26 references); for reviews by Nelson G. Hanawalt and Theodore R. Sarbin, see 4:28 (104 references); for reviews by Raymond B. Cattell, John G. Darley, C. M. Louttit, and Percival M. Symonds of the original Student Form, and reviews by S. J. Beck, J. P. Guilford, and Doncaster G. Humm of the Adult Form, see 2:1200 (15 references, 1 excerpt); for a review by Austin H. Turney of the Student Form, see 1:912.

J5. Adjustment Questionnaire. For additional information, see 5:31.

J6. Affectivity Interview Blank. For additional information and reviews by Morris Krugman and Verner M. Sims, see 4:29 (3 references).

J7. The Alcadd Test. For additional information and a review by Dugal Campbell, see 6:60 (6 references); for reviews by Charles Honzik and Albert L. Hunsicker, see 4:30.

J8. Aspects of Personality. For additional information and reviews by C. M. Louttit and P. E. Vernon, see 2:1201 (4 references); see also 1:913 (1 excerpt).

J9. Attitude-Interest Analysis Test. For additional information, see 6:61 (16 references); for a review by Starke R. Hathaway, see 3:24 (20 references).

J10. Attitude Scales for Measuring the Influence of the Work Relief Program. For additional information, see 2:1203 (1 reference).

J11. Attitudes Toward Child Behavior. For additional information, see 2:1204 (2 references).

J12. Attitudes Toward Industrialization. For additional information and a review by Marvin D. Dunnette, see 6:62.

J13. Attitudes Toward Parental Control of Children. For additional information, see 2:1205 (2 references).

J14. The Ayres Space Test. For additional information and reviews by Alvin G. Burstein and Alfred B. Heilbrun, Jr., see 6:63 (2 references).

J15. BEC Personality Rating Schedule. For additional information and reviews by Francis F. Bradshaw and Theos A. Langlie, see 1:915 (1 reference).

J16. Babcock Test of Mental Efficiency. For additional information, see 6:64 (6 references); for reviews by D. Russell Davis and Seymour G. Klebanoff, see 4:31 (10 references); see also 3:71 (21 references) and 2:1248 (16 references).

J17. [The Baxter Group Tests of Child Feeling.] For additional information, see 4:32 (2 references).

J18. Behavior Cards: A Test-Interview for Delinquent Children. For additional information, see 6:65 (1 reference); for reviews by W. C. Kvaraceus and Simon H. Tulchin, see 3:25 (3 references).

J19. Behavior Description. For additional information, see 1:898.

J20. Behavior Maturity Blank. For additional information, see 2:1209 (2 references).

J21. Behavior Maturity Rating Scale for Nursery School Children. For additional information, see 2:1210.

J22. Behavior Preference Record: What Would You Do? (A Study of Some Home and School Problems). For additional information and reviews by J. Thomas Hastings and Edward Landy, see 5:32 (1 excerpt).

J23. Beliefs About School Life: Test 4.6. For additional information, see 2:1211.

J24. Billett-Starr Youth Problems Inventory. For additional information and reviews by Thomas C. Burgess, J. Thomas Hastings, and Henry Weitz, see 6:66 (1 reference).

J25. Biographical Inventory for Students. For additional information, see 6:67 (6 references).

J26. Bonney-Fessenden Sociograph. For additional information and reviews by Åke Bjerstedt and C. Robert Pace, see 5:33.

J27. A Book About Me. For additional information and a review by Florence M. Teagarden, see 5:34.

J28. Bristol Social-Adjustment Guides. For additional information and reviews by G. A. V. Morgan and M. L. Kellmer Pringle, see 6:68 (13 references, 5 excerpts).

J29. Brown Personality Inventory for Children. For additional information, see 5:36 (10 references); for reviews by S. J. Beck and Carl R. Rogers, see 2:1240 (8 references).

J30. C-R Opinionaire. For additional information and a review by George W. Hartmann, see 4:39 (5 references); for a review by Goodwin Watson, see

2:1212 (5 references); for a review by H. H. Remmers, see 1:899.

J31. Cain-Levine Social Competency Scale. For additional information and a review by Marshall S. Hiskey, see 6:69.

J32. The California Medical Survey (CMS). For additional information, see 6:70.

J33. California Psychological Inventory. For additional information and a review by E. Lowell Kelly, see 6:71 (116 references); for reviews by Lee J. Cronbach and Robert L. Thorndike, see 5:37 (33 references, 1 excerpt).

J34. The California Q-Set: A Q-Sort for Personality Assessment and Psychiatric Research. For additional information and reviews by Allen L. Edwards and David T. Lykken, see 6:72 (2 references, 3 excerpts).

J35. California Test of Personality. For additional information, see 6:73 (49 references); for a review by Verner M. Sims, see 5:38 (93 references); for reviews by Laurance F. Shaffer and Douglas Spencer of the original edition, see 3:26 (24 references, 1 excerpt); for reviews by Raymond B. Cattell, Percival M. Symonds, and P. E. Vernon of the elementary and secondary levels, see 2:1213 (1 excerpt).

J36. Case Inventory. For additional information and reviews by Harold E. Jones and E. G. Williamson, see 2:1214 (1 reference); for a review by Richard Ledgerwood, see 1:916.

J37. The Cassel Group Level of Aspiration Test. For additional information and reviews by W. Grant Dahlstrom, Harrison G. Gough, and J. P. Sutcliffe, see 5:39 (5 references, 2 excerpts).

J38. The Cassel Psychotherapy Progress Record. For additional information and a review by William Schofield, see 6:74.

J39. Character and Inventory Chart. For additional information, see 1:917 (1 excerpt).

J40. Character and Personality Rating Scale. For additional information and a review by Bessie Lee Gambrill, see 2:1215.

J41. The Child Behavior Rating Scale. For additional information, see 6:74a.

J42. Children's Embedded Figures Test. For additional information, see 6:74b (2 references).

J43. The Children's Hypnotic Susceptibility Scale. For additional information and reviews by C. Scott Moss and John G. Watkins, see 6:75 (2 references, 1 excerpt).

J44. Client-Centered Counseling Progress Record. For additional information and a review by William Schofield, see 6:76.

J45. The College Inventory of Academic Adjustment. For additional information and a review by Leonard D. Goodstein, see 6:77 (12 references); for reviews by Lysle W. Croft and Harrison G. Gough, see 4:34 (3 references).

J46. Community Improvement Scale. For additional information and a review by Wimburn L. Wallace, see 5:42.

J47. Concept Formation Test. For additional information, see 6:78 (11 references); for a review by Kate Levine Kogan (with William S. Kogan), see 4:35 (8 references); for a review by O. L. Zangwill, see 3:27 (19 references).

J48. Constant-Choice Perceptual Maze Attitude of Responsibility Test. For additional information, see 6:79.

J49. Cornell Index. For additional information, see 5:43 (7 references); for reviews by Hans J. Eysenck, Nelson G. Hanawalt, and Laurance F. Shaffer, see 4:37 (41 references).

J50. Cornell Word Form 2. For additional information and a review by S. B. Sells, see 6:80 (1 reference); see also 5:44 (11 references).

J51. Cotswold Personality Assessment P.A. 1. For additional information and reviews by Ralph D. Dutch and G. A. V. Morgan, see 6:81 (1 reference).

J52. The Cowan Adolescent Adjustment Analyzer. For additional information, see 4:38 (1 reference); for reviews by Harold H. Abelson and William U. Snyder, see 3:30; for a review by Goodwin Watson of an earlier edition, see 2:1217 (3 references); for a review by Harold E. Jones, see 1:918.

J53. Cowell Personal Distance Scale. For additional information, see 6:82 (3 references).

J54. Cowell Social Behavior Trend Index. For additional information, see 6:83 (2 references).

J55. Cree Questionnaire. For additional information and reviews by Allyn Miles Munger and Theodor F. Naumann, see 6:84.

J56. DF Opinion Survey. For additional information and reviews by Andrew R. Baggaley, John W. French, and Arthur W. Meadows, see 5:45.

J57. Detroit Adjustment Inventory. For additional information and a review by Laurance F. Shaffer, see 5:46 (1 reference); for a review by Albert Ellis of the form for grades 7–12, see 3:31.

J58. Detroit Scale of Behavior Factors. For additional information, see 3:32 (1 reference).

J59. Developmental Potential of Preschool Children. For additional information, see 6:84a (1 reference).

J60. Diagnosis and Treatment of Pupil Maladjustment. For additional information and a review by Laurance F. Shaffer, see 3:34 (2 references).

J61. Diplomacy Test of Empathy. For additional information and reviews by Arthur H. Brayfield and Richard S. Hatch, see 6:85 (1 reference); for a review by Robert L. Thorndike of the earlier test, see 5:99.

J62. Dunlap Academic Preference Blank. For additional information and reviews by Lee J. Cronbach, W. C. Kvaraceus, and Edith I. M. Thomson, see 3:35 (6 references, 1 excerpt).

J63. Dynamic Personality Inventory. For additional information and a review by S. B. Sells, see 6:86 (7 references).

J64. Educational Background Questionnaire. For additional information and a review by Verner M. Sims, see 1:869 (2 references).

J65. Edwards Personal Preference Schedule. For additional information and reviews by John A. Radcliffe and Lawrence J. Stricker, see 6:87 (284 references, 1 excerpt); for reviews by Frank Barron, Åke Bjerstedt, and Donald W. Fiske, see 5:47 (50 references, 2 excerpts).

J66. The Ego Strength Q-Sort Test. For additional information and reviews by Allen L. Edwards and Harrison G. Gough, see 6:88 (3 references).

J67. Embedded Figures Test. For additional information and reviews by Harrison G. Gough and Leona E. Tyler, see 6:89 (24 references) ; see also 5:49 (9 references).

J68. Emo Questionnaire. For additional information and reviews by Bertram D. Cohen and W. Grant Dahlstrom, see 6:90 (1 reference).

J69. The Empathy Test. For additional information and a review by Wallace B. Hall, see 6:91 (9 references) ; for a review by Robert L. Thorndike, see 5:50 (20 references).

J70. [Environment Indexes.] For additional information, see 6:92 (19 references).

J71. Environment Inventory for College and University Students. For additional information and a review by E. G. Williamson, see 2:1218 (1 reference).

J72. Euphorimeter. For additional information, see 3:36 (2 references).

J73. Evaluation Modality Test. For additional information and a review by Wilson H. Guertin, see 5:51.

J74. Every-Day Life: A Scale for the Measure of Three Varieties of Self-Reliance. For additional information and a review by Harold E. Jones, see 4:41 ; for a review by Albert Ellis, see 3:38 (6 references).

J75. Examining for Aphasia: A Manual for the Examination of Aphasia and Related Disturbances. For additional information and a review by T. R. Miles, see 5:52 (3 references, 2 excerpts) ; for a review by D. Russell Davis, see 4:42 (2 excerpts) ; for a review by C. R. Strother, see 3:39 (1 excerpt).

J76. Experience Variables Record: A Clinical Revision. For additional information, see 2:1219 (2 references).

J77. Eysenck Personality Inventory. For additional information and a review by James C. Lingoes, see 6:93 (1 reference).

J78. FIRO-B: [Fundamental Interpersonal Relations Orientation—Behavior]. For additional information, see 6:94 (15 references).

J79. Family Adjustment Test. For additional information and a review by John Elderkin Bell, see 6:95; for a review by Albert Ellis, see 5:53 (6 references).

J80. Famous Sayings. For additional information and reviews by Wesley C. Becker and Robert L. Thorndike, see 6:96 (17 references).

J81. Fatigue Scales Kit. For additional information and a review by Richard S. Barrett, see 6:97 (1 reference).

J82. Fels Parent Behavior Rating Scales. For additional information and a review by Dale B. Harris, see 4:43 (15 references).

J83. The Forty-Eight Item Counseling Evaluation Test. For additional information, see 6:98.

J84. The Freeman Anxiety Neurosis and Psychosomatic Test. For additional information and reviews by Gerald A. Mendelsohn and Robert C. Nichols, see 6:99 (4 references) ; see also 5:55 (3 references).

J85. Friend-Critic Statement. For additional information, see 5:56.

J86. G. C. Personality Development Record. For additional information, see 6:100.

J87. Gardner Behavior Chart. For additional information, see 4:44.

J88. General Goals of Life Inventory: General Education Series. For additional information and reviews by C. Robert Pace and Leona E. Tyler, see 4:45 (10 references).

J89. Generalized Attitude Scales. For reviews by Donald T. Campbell and Kenneth E. Clark, see 4:46 (37 references) ; for reviews by W. D. Commins and Theodore Newcomb, see 2:1202 (9 references) ; for a review by Stephen M. Corey, see 1:897. For a later edition, see J222.

J90. Goldstein-Scheerer Tests of Abstract and Concrete Thinking. For additional information and a review by R. W. Payne, see 6:101 (23 references) ; see also 5:57 (21 references) ; for reviews by Kate Levine Kogan, C. R. Strother (with Ludwig Immergluck), and O. L. Zangwill, see 3:41 (28 references).

J91. Gordon Personal Inventory. For additional information and reviews by Charles F. Dicken and Alfred B. Heilbrun, Jr., see 6:102 (13 references) ; for reviews by Benno G. Fricke and John A. Radcliffe, see 5:58 (1 reference, 2 excerpts).

J92. Gordon Personal Profile. For additional information and reviews by Charles F. Dicken and Alfred B. Heilbrun, Jr., see 6:103 (25 references) ; for reviews by Benno G. Fricke and John A. Radcliffe, see 5:59 (16 references, 1 excerpt).

J93. The Grassi Block Substitution Test: For Measuring Organic Brain Pathology. For additional information, see 5:60 (5 references, 2 excerpts).

J94. The Grayson Perceptualization Test. For additional information and reviews by D. Russell Davis and William Schofield, see 5:61.

J95. Group Cohesiveness: A Study of Group Morale. For additional information and reviews by Eric F. Gardner and Cecil A. Gibb, see 6:104 (1 reference).

J96. Group Dimensions Descriptions Questionnaire. For additional information, see 6:105 (5 references).

J97. Guidance Inventory. For additional information and a review by John W. M. Rothney, see 6:106.

J98. Guilford-Holley L Inventory. For additional information, see 6:107.

J99. The Guilford-Martin Inventory of Factors GAMIN. For additional information, see 6:108 (11 references) ; see also 5:63 (33 references) ; for a review by Hubert E. Brogden, see 4:47 (18 references) ; for a review by H. J. Eysenck, see 3:43 (7 references).

J100. The Guilford-Martin Personnel Inventory. For additional information, see 6:109 (9 references) ; see also 5:64 (27 references) ; for a review by Neil Van Steenberg, see 4:48 (20 references) ; for a review by Benjamin Shimberg, see 3:44 (7 references).

J101. Guilford-Martin Temperament Profile Chart. For additional information and a review by R. A. Brotemarkle, see 3:45.

J102. The Guilford-Zimmerman Temperament Survey. For additional information, see 6:110 (120 references) ; for a review by David R. Saunders, see

5:65 (48 references) ; for reviews by William Stephenson and Neil Van Steenberg, see 4:49 (5 references, 1 excerpt).

J103. Haggerty-Olson-Wickman Behavior Rating Schedules. For additional information and a review by Harold E. Jones, see 2:1222 (8 references).

J104. The Handicap Problems Inventory. For additional information and a review by Dorothy M. Clendenen, see 6:111.

J105. Harvard Group Scale of Hypnotic Susceptibility. For additional information and a review by Seymour Fisher, see 6:112 (4 references).

J106. Heston Personal Adjustment Inventory. For additional information, see 6:113 (14 references) ; see also 5:66 (11 references) ; for reviews by Albert Ellis, Hans J. Eysenck, and E. Lowell Kelly, see 4:50 (2 references, 1 excerpt).

J107. High School Attitude Scale. For additional information, see 6:168; for a review by Lee J. Cronbach, see 3:46.

J108. The Hoffer-Osmond Diagnostic Test (HOD). For additional information and reviews by Maurice Lorr and William Schofield, see 6:114 (6 references).

J109. Holland Vocational Preference Inventory. For additional information and reviews by Robert L. French and H. Bradley Sagen, see 6:115 (13 references).

J110. The Hooper Visual Organization Test. For additional information and reviews by Ralph M. Reitan and Otfried Spreen, see 6:116 (4 references).

J111. Hospital Adjustment Scale. For additional information and a review by Wilson H. Guertin, see 6:117 (3 references) ; for a review by Maurice Lorr, see 5:67 (5 references).

J112. How Well Do You Know Yourself? For additional information and reviews by Lee J. Cronbach and Harrison G. Gough, see 6:118 (2 references, 2 excerpts).

J113. Human Relations Inventory. For additional information, see 6:119 (6 references) ; for reviews by Raymond C. Norris and John A. Radcliffe, see 5:68.

J114. The Humm-Wadsworth Temperament Scale. For additional information and reviews by James R. Glennon and Floyd L. Ruch, see 6:120 (3 references) ; see also 5:69 (20 references) ; for reviews by H. J. Eysenck, H. Meltzer, and Lorenz Misbach of the 1940 edition, see 3:48 (31 references) ; for reviews by Forrest A. Kingsbury and P. E. Vernon, see 2:1223 (13 references) ; for a review by Daniel A. Prescott of an earlier edition, see 1:920.

J115. Hunt-Minnesota Test for Organic Brain Damage. For additional information and a review by Seymour G. Klebanoff, see 4:51 (8 references) ; for reviews by Margaret Ives and O. L. Zangwill, see 3:49 (11 references).

J116. The IPAT Anxiety Scale Questionnaire. For additional information and a review by Jacob Cohen, see 6:121 (23 references) ; for reviews by J. P. Guilford and E. Lowell Kelly, see 5:70 (1 excerpt).

J117. IPAT Children's Personality Questionnaire. For additional information and reviews by Anne Anastasi, Wilbur L. Layton, and Robert D. Wirt, see 6:122 (2 references).

J118. IPAT Contact Personality Factor Test. For additional information, see 6:123 (6 references) ;

for reviews by Cecil D. Johnson and S. B. Sells, see 5:71.

J119. IPAT 8-Parallel-Form Anxiety Battery. For additional information and reviews by Jacob Cohen and Paul M. Kjeldergaard, see 6:124 (4 references).

J120. The IPAT Humor Test of Personality. For additional information and reviews by W. Grant Dahlstrom, Ardie Lubin (with Frank M. Loos), and J. R. Wittenborn, see 4:61 (5 references).

J121. IPAT Music Preference Test of Personality. For additional information and reviews by Kenneth L. Bean and Paul R. Farnsworth, see 6:125 (7 references) ; for a review by Neil J. Van Steenberg, see 5:73 (4 references).

J122. IPAT Neurotic Personality Factor Test. For additional information and reviews by S. B. Sells and William Stephenson, see 5:74.

J123. Information Blank EA: A Questionnaire on Emotional Adjustment. For additional information and a review by Percival M. Symonds, see 3:50; for a review by Stanley G. Dulsky, see 2:1224.

J124. Inpatient Multidimensional Psychiatric Scale (IMPS). For additional information, see 6:126 (26 references).

J125. Institute of Child Study Security Test. For additional information and a review by Laurance F. Shaffer, see 5:75.

J126. Interaction Chronograph. For additional information and a review by Cecil A. Gibb, see 5:76 (20 references) ; see also 3:688 (5 references).

J127. Interaction Process Analysis. For additional information and a review by Cecil A. Gibb, see 5:77 (10 references) ; for a review by Launor F. Carter, see 4:56 (3 references).

J128. Interest Analysis. For additional information and a review by Edward B. Greene, see 3:51.

J129. Interest Index: General Education Series. For additional information, see 4:58 (2 references) ; see also 2:1226 (4 references).

J130. Interest Inventory for Elementary Grades: George Washington University Series. For additional information and reviews by Harold D. Carter and Lee J. Cronbach, see 3:52 (1 reference).

J131. Interest Questionnaire: Games and Sports: Test 8.3. For additional information, see 2:1227.

J132. Interest-Values Inventory. For additional information and reviews by E. Lowell Kelly and Paul E. Meehl, see 3:53 (5 references) ; see also 2:1228 (1 excerpt).

J133. Interests and Activities: Tests 8.2b and 8.2c. For additional information, see 2:1225 (7 references).

J134. Interpersonal Check List. For additional information and a review by P. M. Bentler, see 6:127 (39 references).

J135. Inventory of Affective Tolerance. For additional information and reviews by Paul R. Farnsworth, E. Lowell Kelly, and William U. Snyder, see 3:54 (5 references).

J136. An Inventory of Factors STDCR. For additional information, see 6:128 (17 references) ; see also 5:78 (28 references) ; for a review by Hubert E.

Brogden, see 4:59 (17 references); for a review by H. J. Eysenck, see 3:55 (10 references).

J137. Inventory of Personal-Social Relationships: General Education Series. For additional information and reviews by N. L. Gage and Theodore R. Sarbin, see 4:60 (2 references).

J138. It Scale for Children. For additional information and reviews by Philip L. Harriman and Boyd R. McCandless, see 6:129 (18 references).

J139. JNB Psychograph. For additional information, see 3:56 (1 reference).

J140. Johnson Temperament Analysis. For additional information, see 6:130 (10 references); for a review by Albert Ellis, see 4:62 (6 references); for a review by H. Meltzer, see 3:57.

J141. Jones Personality Rating Scale. For additional information, see 2:1230.

J142. Jr.-Sr. High School Personality Questionnaire. For additional information and reviews by C. J. Adcock and Philip E. Vernon, see 6:131 (17 references); see also 5:72 (4 references).

J143. Jurgensen Classification Inventory. For additional information and reviews by Robert G. Demaree (with Louis L. McQuitty) and William J. E. Crissy, see 4:63 (11 references).

J144. KD Proneness Scale and Check List. For additional information and a review by John W. M. Rothney, see 5:79 (6 references); for reviews by Douglas Courtney and Dale B. Harris, see 4:64.

J145. Kuder Preference Record—Personal. For additional information and reviews by Dorothy M. Clendenen and Wilbur L. Layton, see 6:132 (11 references); for a review by Dwight L. Arnold, see 5:80 (5 references); see also 4:65 (4 references, 1 excerpt).

J146. The Leadership Ability Evaluation. For additional information and reviews by John D. Black and Cecil A. Gibb, see 6:133 (4 references).

J147. The Leadership Q-Sort Test (A Test of Leadership Values). For additional information and reviews by Joel T. Campbell, Cecil A. Gibb, and William Stephenson, see 6:134 (6 references).

J148. Lewerenz-Steinmetz Orientation Test: Concerning Fundamental Aims of Education. For additional information and reviews by Frederic L. Ayer and Roger T. Lennon, see 4:66 (3 references).

J149. Life Adjustment Inventory. For additional information and reviews by John W. M. Rothney and Helen Shacter, see 4:67.

J150. Life Experience Inventory. For additional information and reviews by Dan L. Adler and Douglas T. Kenny, see 5:81 (1 reference).

J151. The MACC Behavioral Adjustment Scale: An Objective Approach to the Evaluation of Behavioral Adjustments of Psychiatric Patients. For additional information and a review by Wilson H. Guertin, see 6:135 (2 references); for a review by Maurice Lorr of an earlier edition, see 5:82.

J152. M-B History Record. For additional information, see 6:136 (2 references).

J153. McCleery Scale of Adolescent Development. For additional information and reviews by Eugene L. Gaier and John E. Horrocks, see 5:83 (1 reference).

J154. The Manson Evaluation. For additional information and a review by Dugal Campbell, see 6:137 (5 references); for reviews by Charles H. Honzik and Albert L. Hunsicker, see 4:68 (4 references).

J155. Maudsley Personality Inventory. For additional information and reviews by Arthur R. Jensen, James C. Lingoes, William Stephenson, and Philip E. Vernon, see 6:138 (120 references, 3 excerpts).

J156. Maxfield-Buchholz Scale of Social Maturity for Use With Preschool Blind Children. For additional information, see 6:139 (2 references).

J157. Memory-For-Designs Test. For additional information and a review by Otfried Spreen, see 6:140 (18 references); see also 4:69 (5 references).

J158. Mental Health Analysis. For additional information and a review by J. Robert Williams, see 6:141 (8 references); for reviews by William E. Coffman, Henry E. Garrett, C. M. Louttit, James Maxwell, and Douglas Spencer of the original edition, see 3:59 (1 excerpt).

J159. Minnesota Counseling Inventory. For additional information and reviews by Norman Frederiksen and John W. M. Rothney, see 6:142 (10 references); see also 5:85 (1 excerpt).

J160. The Minnesota Inventory of Social Attitudes. For additional information and a review by Verner M. Sims, see 4:70 (12 references); for reviews by J. P. Guilford and George W. Hartmann, see 1:900.

J161. Minnesota Multiphasic Personality Inventory. For additional information and reviews by C. J. Adcock and James C. Lingoes, see 6:143 (626 references); for reviews by Albert Ellis and Warren T. Norman, see 5:86 (496 references); for a review by Arthur L. Benton, see 4:71 (211 references); for reviews by Arthur L. Benton, H. J. Eysenck, L. S. Penrose, and Julian B. Rotter, see 3:60 (72 references, 1 excerpt).

J162. Minnesota Personality Scale. For additional information, see 5:87 (22 references); for reviews by Philip Eisenberg and John W. French, see 3:61 (9 references).

J163. Minnesota Rating Scale for Personal Qualities and Abilities. For additional information and a review by Dorothy M. Clendenen, see 5:88 (1 reference).

J164. Minnesota Scale for the Survey of Opinions. For additional information and reviews by H. H. Remmers and Goodwin Watson, see 1:901 (1 reference).

J165. Minnesota T-S-E Inventory. For additional information, see 6:144 (5 references); for reviews by Philip Eisenberg and John W. French, see 3:62 (6 references).

J166. Mooney Problem Check List. For additional information and a review by Thomas C. Burgess, see 6:145 (25 references); see also 5:89 (26 references); for reviews by Harold E. Jones and Morris Krugman, see 4:73 (13 references); for reviews by Ralph C. Bedell and Theodore F. Lentz, see 3:67 (17 references).

J167. The Mother-Child Relationship Evaluation. For additional information and reviews by John Elderkin Bell and Dale B. Harris, see 6:146.

J168. Motivation Analysis Test. For additional information, see 6:146a.

J169. Myers-Briggs Type Indicator. For additional information and reviews by Gerald A. Mendelsohn and Norman D. Sundberg, see 6:147 (10 references, 1 excerpt).

J170. Nebraska Personality Inventory. For additional information and reviews by John C. Flanagan and C. M. Louttit, see 1:922 (1 reference).

J171. The Neuroticism Scale Questionnaire. For additional information and reviews by E. Lowell Kelly and Jerome D. Pauker, see 6:148 (1 reference, 2 excerpts).

J172. Northampton Activity Rating Scale. For additional information, see 4:74.

J173. Objective-Analytic (O-A) Anxiety Battery. For additional information and a review by Harold Borko, see 6:149 (5 references, 1 excerpt).

J174. Objective-Analytic Personality Test Batteries. For additional information and a review by H. J. Eysenck, see 5:90 (6 references).

J175. Occupational Personality Inventory. For additional information, see 2:1232 (3 references).

J176. Ohio Guidance Tests for Elementary Grades. For additional information and reviews by M. H. Elliott and John W. M. Rothney, see 3:63 (8 references).

J177. Omnibus Personality Inventory. For additional information and reviews by Paul M. Kjeldergaard and Norman E. Wallen, see 6:150 (11 references, 1 excerpt).

J178. Opinion, Attitude and Interest Survey. For additional information and reviews by John O. Crites and Harold Webster, see 6:151 (4 references).

J179. Organic Integrity Test. For additional information, see 6:152 (1 reference).

J180. The Orientation Inventory. For additional information and reviews by Richard S. Barrett and H. Bradley Sagen, see 6:153 (2 references).

J181. P.Q. or Personality Quotient Test. For additional information and reviews by Douglas Spencer and Simon H. Tulchin, see 2:1233 (5 references); for reviews by C. M. Louttit and Edmund G. Williamson, see 1:921.

J182. P-S Experience Blank: Psycho-Somatic Inventory. For additional information and reviews by Doncaster G. Humm and Charles I. Mosier, see 2:1234 (2 references).

J183. Parents Rating Scale. For additional information, see 2:1235.

J184. Personal Adaptability Test. For additional information and a review by Harold Webster, see 5:91 (1 reference).

J185. Personal Adjustment Inventory. For additional information and reviews by Norman D. Sundberg and Robert D. Wirt, see 6:154 (6 references); for reviews by Dan L. Adler and Harrison G. Gough, see 5:117 (19 references); for a review by C. M. Louttit, see 2:1258.

J186. The Personal and Social Development Program. For additional information and reviews by Edward Landy and C. Gilbert Wrenn (with Roy D. Lewis), see 5:92.

J187. Personal Audit. For additional information and a review by William Seeman, see 4:75 (3 references); for a review by Percival M. Symonds, see 3:64 (9 references).

J188. Personal Data Scale. For additional information, see 1:1119.

J189. Personal History Record [C. H. Stoelting Co.]. For additional information, see 2:1236 (1 reference).

J190. Personal Index. For additional information and reviews by J. B. Maller and Carl R. Rogers, see 2:1237 (5 references).

J191. The Personal Preference Inventory: Student Form. For additional information and reviews by E. Lowell Kelly and C. M. Louttit, see 4:76.

J192. The Personal Preference Scale. For additional information, see 5:93 (2 references).

J193. Personal Qualities Inventory. For additional information, see 6:155 (1 reference).

J194. Personality and Interest Inventory. For additional information, see 6:156; for a review by Stephen M. Corey, see 2:1238 (3 references); for a review by Jack W. Dunlap, see 1:924.

J195. The Personality Evaluation Form: A Technique for the Organization and Interpretation of Personality Data. For additional information and a review by Dorothy H. Eichorn, see 5:94 (1 excerpt).

J196. Personality Index. For additional information and a review by Benjamin Shimberg, see 3:65.

J197. The Personality Inventory. For additional information and reviews by Wesley C. Becker and Donald J. Veldman, see 6:157 (22 references); see also 5:95 (40 references); for a review by Leona E. Tyler, see 4:77 (188 references); for reviews by Charles I. Mosier and Theodore Newcomb, see 2:1239 (71 references).

J198. Personality Rating Chart for Preschool Children. For additional information, see 2:1241 (1 reference).

J199. Personality Rating Scale. For additional information and a review by Laurance F. Shaffer, see 6:158 (4 references); for reviews by Robert H. Bauernfeind and Dale B. Harris, see 5:41 (18 references).

J200. Personality Rating Scale for Preschool Children. For additional information, see 2:1242 (1 reference).

J201. Personality Record (Revised). For additional information and a review by Verner M. Sims of the original edition, see 4:78 (1 reference).

J202. Personality Schedule. For additional information, see 6:159 (38 references); for a review by J. P. Guilford, see 2:1243 (28 references).

J203. Personality Sketches. For additional information and reviews by Henry E. Garrett and J. P. Guilford, see 1:925.

J204. The Personality Survey. For additional information and reviews by Douglas Courtney and John W. M. Rothney, see 4:79 (2 references).

J205. The Philo-Phobe. For additional information and a review by Parker Davis, Jr., see 3:66 (3 references).

J206. Pictorial Study of Values: Pictorial Allport-Vernon. For additional information and reviews by Andrew R. Baggaley and Harrison G. Gough, see 5:96.

J207. Polyfactorial Study of Personality. For additional information and reviews by Bertram D. Cohen and Donald R. Peterson, see 6:160 (1 excerpt).

J208. Position Response Form and Response Form. For additional information, see 6:161.

J209. The Power of Influence Test. For additional information and reviews by Åke Bjerstedt and Eric F. Gardner, see 6:162 (1 reference).

J210. Practical Policy Test. For additional information, see 5:98 (9 references).

J211. Pre-Counseling Inventory. For additional information and a review by Charles H. Honzik, see 4:80 (1 reference).

J212. The Press Test. For additional information and reviews by William H. Helme and Allyn Miles Munger, see 6:163.

J213. Pressey Interest-Attitude Tests. For additional information and a review by Douglas Spencer, see 2:1243.1 (5 references).

J214. Problem Check List: Form for Rural Young People. For additional information, see 4:81 (2 references).

J215. Problem Check List: Form for Schools of Nursing. For additional information, see 4:82 (1 reference).

J216. A Process for In-School Screening of Children With Emotional Handicaps. For additional information and reviews by Alan O. Ross and J. Robert Williams, see 6:164 (3 references).

J217. Progress Assessment Chart (P-A-C). For additional information, see 6:165.

J218. Psychometric Behavior Checklist. For additional information, see 6:166 (1 reference).

J219. The Psychotic Reaction Profile (PRP): An Inventory of Patient Behavior for Use by Hospital Personnel. For additional information and a review by Wilson H. Guertin, see 6:167 (4 references).

J220. Pupil Adjustment Inventory. For additional information and reviews by Robert H. Bauernfeind and John Pierce-Jones, see 5:100 (1 excerpt).

J221. Pupil Portraits. For additional information and a review by Simon H. Tulchin, see 2:1244 (2 references).

J222. The Purdue Master Attitude Scales. For additional information and a review by Donald T. Campbell, see 6:168. For an earlier edition, see J89.

J223. Purdue Rating Scale for Administrators and Executives. For additional information and reviews by John P. Foley, Jr. and Herbert A. Tonne, see 5:101 (1 reference); for a review by Kenneth L. Heaton, see 4:83 (7 references).

J224. Radio Checklist. For additional information, see 2:1245.

J225. Rating Scale for Pupil Adjustment. For additional information and reviews by William E. Henry and Morris Krugman, see 5:102.

J226. Recreation Inquiry. For additional information and reviews by Theodore F. Lentz and Louis Long, see 3:70 (2 references).

J227. Report Form on Temperament and Social Behavior. For additional information, see 2:1247 (1 reference).

J228. Rutgers Social Attribute Inventory. For additional information and reviews by David B. Orr and John Pierce-Jones, see 6:169.

J229. SAQS Chicago Q Sort. For additional information and reviews by William Stephenson and Clifford H. Swensen, Jr., see 5:103 (2 references).

J230. SRA Junior Inventory. For additional information and a review by Warren R. Baller, see 5:104 (2 excerpts); for a review by Dwight L. Arnold, see 4:90.

J231. SRA Youth Inventory. For additional information and a review by Forrest L. Vance, see 6:170 (12 references, 1 excerpt); see also 5:105 (12 references); for reviews by Kenneth E. Clark and Frank S. Freeman, see 4:91 (7 references).

J232. Scale for Evaluating the School Behavior of Children Ten to Fifteen. For additional information, see 1:926 (1 reference, 1 excerpt).

J233. Scale of Beliefs for Junior High School: Tests 4.4 and 4.5. For additional information, see 2:1251 (1 reference).

J234. Scale of Beliefs: Tests 4.21 and 4.31. For additional information, see 2:1250 (7 references).

J235. A Scale to Measure Attitudes Toward Disabled Persons. For additional information, see 6:171.

J236. The School Inventory. For additional information and a review by Ross W. Matteson, see 4:84 (3 references); for reviews by Robert G. Bernreuter and J. B. Maller, see 2:1252 (4 references).

J237. Schrammel-Gorbutt Personality Adjustment Scale. For additional information and reviews by Raleigh M. Drake and Nelson G. Hanawalt, see 3:92.

J238. The Science Research Temperament Scale. For additional information and reviews by John D. Black and David R. Saunders, see 5:106 (1 reference).

J239. Security-Insecurity Inventory. For additional information and reviews by Nelson G. Hanawalt and Harold Webster, see 5:107 (10 references).

J240. Selective Vocabulary Test. For additional information and a review by James Maxwell, see 4:85 (2 references); for reviews by Jack W. Dunlap and Starke R. Hathaway, see 3:93.

J241. Self-Analysis Inventory. For additional information and reviews by Warren R. Baller and John W. Gustad, see 5:108.

J242. Self-Appraisal Schedule. For additional information, see 1:927 (1 reference).

J243. Self-Interview Inventory. For additional information and reviews by Andrew R. Baggaley and David T. Lykken, see 6:172 (1 reference).

J244. Self-Perception Inventory: An Adjustment Survey With Special Reference to the Speech Situation. For additional information and a review by C. R. Strother, see 5:109.

J245. Sense of Humor Test. For additional information, see 3:94.

J246. The Sherman Mental Impairment Test. For additional information and reviews by D. Russell Davis and William Schofield, see 5:110 (1 reference).

J247. Shipley-Institute of Living Scale for Measuring Intellectual Impairment. For additional information, see 6:173 (13 references); see also 5:111

(23 references); for reviews by E. J. G. Bradford, William A. Hunt, and Margaret Ives, see 3:95 (26 references).

J248. Sixteen Personality Factor Questionnaire. For additional information and a review by Maurice Lorr, see 6:174 (81 references); for a review by C. J. Adcock, see 5:112 (21 references); for reviews by Charles M. Harsh, Ardie Lubin, and J. Richard Wittenborn, see 4:87 (8 references).

J249. Social Attitude Scales. For additional information and reviews by H. H. Remmers and Goodwin Watson, see 1:902.

J250. A Social Competence Inventory for Adults. For additional information and reviews by William J. Eichman and Jerome D. Pauker, see 6:175.

J251. Social Distance Scale. For additional information and a review by Donald T. Campbell, see 4:88 (19 references).

J252. Social Intelligence Test: George Washington University Series. For additional information, see 6:176 (14 references); see also 4:89 (7 references); for reviews by Glen U. Cleeton and Howard R. Taylor, see 3:96 (9 references); for a review by Robert L. Thorndike, see 2:1253 (20 references).

J253. Social Orientation. For additional information and a review by Charles C. Peters, see 1:903.

J254. Social Participation Scale. For additional information, see 5:113.

J255. Social Personality Inventory for College Women. For additional information and a review by Nelson G. Hanawalt, see 3:97 (10 references).

J256. Social Problems: Test 1.42. For additional information, see 2:1254 (1 reference).

J257. Spiral Aftereffect Test. For additional information and reviews by William J. Eichman and Ralph M. Reitan, see 6:177 (43 references).

J258. Stanford Hypnotic Susceptibility Scale. For additional information and reviews by Milton V. Kline and C. Scott Moss, see 6:178 (17 references).

J259. Stanford Profile Scales of Hypnotic Susceptibility. For additional information and reviews by Seymour Fisher and Eugene E. Levitt, see 6:179.

J260. Stern Activities Index. For additional information, see 6:180 (27 references).

J261. Straus Rural Attitudes Profile. For additional information, see 6:181 (1 reference, 1 excerpt).

J262. Student Questionnaire. For additional information and a review by Simon H. Tulchin, see 3:98.

J263. Study of Attitudes Toward the Administration of Justice. For additional information, see 2:1255 (1 reference).

J264. Study of Values: A Scale for Measuring the Dominant Interests in Personality. For additional information and reviews by John D. Hundleby and John A. Radcliffe, see 6:182 (137 references); for a review by N. L. Gage of the second edition, see 5:114 (57 references); for reviews by Harrison G. Gough and William Stephenson, see 4:92 (25 references, 1 excerpt); for a review by Paul E. Meehl of the original edition, see 3:99 (61 references).

J265. Style of Mind Inventory: Trait, Value and Belief Patterns in Greek, Roman and Judeo-Christian Perspectives. For additional information, see 6:183.

J266. Survey of Attitudes and Beliefs. For additional information and reviews by Donald T. Campbell and C. Robert Pace, see 5:116.

J267. Survey of Interpersonal Values. For additional information and reviews by Lee J. Cronbach, Leonard D. Goodstein, and John K. Hemphill, see 6:184 (12 references, 1 excerpt).

J268. Survey of Personal Attitude "SPA" (With Pictures): Individual Placement Series (Area III). For additional information, see 6:185.

J269. Syracuse Scales of Social Relations. For additional information and reviews by Åke Bjerstedt and Donald T. Campbell, see 6:186 (16 references, 1 excerpt).

J270. Teacher's Rating Scales for Pupil Adjustment. For additional information and a review by Bessie Lee Gambrill, see 2:1256.

J271. Temperament and Character Test. For additional information, see 5:115.

J272. Temperament Comparator. For additional information and reviews by Lawrence J. Stricker and Robert L. Thorndike, see 6:187 (1 reference).

J273. Tentative Check List for Determining Attitudes on Fifty Crucial Social, Economic, and Political Problems. For additional information, see 2:1257.

J274. Test for Developmental Age in Girls. For additional information, see 1:1140.

J275. Test of Basic Assumptions. For additional information, see 6:188.

J276. Test of Behavioral Rigidity. For additional information and reviews by Douglas P. Crowne and Benjamin Kleinmuntz, see 6:189 (9 references).

J277. Test of Social Attitudes. For additional information, see 2:1260.

J278. Test of Social Insight. For additional information and reviews by John D. Black and John Pierce-Jones, see 6:190 (4 references, 1 excerpt).

J279. Test of Work Competency and Stability. For additional information, see 6:191 (2 references).

J280. Tests of the Socially Competent Person. For additional information and reviews by Alvin C. Eurich, Warren G. Findley, and Pedro T. Orata, see 2:1259 (1 reference); for reviews by Douglas E. Scates and Hilda Taba, see 1:1154.

J281. Thurstone Temperament Schedule. For additional information, see 6:192 (17 references); for a review by Neil J. Van Steenberg, see 5:118 (12 references); for reviews by Hans J. Eysenck, Charles M. Harsh, and David G. Ryans, see 4:93 (1 excerpt).

J282. Torgerson's Inventories and Record Forms. For additional information and a review by Harold H. Abelson, see 3:105 (1 reference).

J283. Triadal Equated Personality Inventory. For additional information, see 6:193.

J284. Tulane Factors of Liberalism-Conservatism. For additional information and reviews by Donald T. Campbell and C. Robert Pace, see 5:119 (2 references).

J285. V.G.C. Personality Adjustment Indicator. For additional information, see 3:106.

J286. Vineland Social Maturity Scale. For additional information, see 6:194 (20 references); see also 5:120 (15 references); for reviews by William M.

Cruickshank and Florence M. Teagarden, see 4:94 (21 references); for reviews by C. M. Louttit and John W. M. Rothney, see 3:107 (58 references, 1 excerpt); for reviews by Paul H. Furfey, Elaine F. Kinder, and Anna S. Starr of an experimental form, see 1:1143.

J287. The Visual-Verbal Test: A Measure of Conceptual Thinking. For additional information and reviews by R. W. Payne and Donald R. Peterson, see 6:195 (8 references).

J288. WLW Personal Attitude Inventory. For additional information, see 6:196.

J289. Walther Social Attitudes Test. For additional information, see 2:1261.

J290. Washburne Social-Adjustment Inventory. For additional information and a review by William Seeman, see 4:95 (12 references); see also 3:110 (11 references, 2 excerpts) and 2:1262 (4 references); for a review by Daniel A. Prescott of an earlier edition, see 1:928.

J291. A Weighted-Score Likability Rating Scale. For additional information, see 5:121.

J292. Weitzman's Inventory of Social Behavior. For additional information and reviews by Louis Long and Goodwin Watson, see 3:111 (3 references).

J293. Welsh Figure Preference Test. For additional information and a review by Harold Borko, see 6:197 (20 references, 1 excerpt).

J294. The Western Personality Inventory. For additional information, see 6:198; for reviews of the component tests, see 6:60 (1 review), 6:137 (1 review), 4:30 (2 reviews), and 4:68 (2 reviews).

J295. What Do You Think? For additional information and a review by Ralph K. Watkins, see 2:1263 (3 references, 1 excerpt); for a review by Francis D. Curtis, see 1:1139.

J296. What I Like to Do: An Inventory of Children's Interests. For additional information and reviews by John W. M. Rothney and Naomi Stewart, see 5:122 (1 excerpt).

J297. What Should Our Schools Do? A Poll of Public Opinion on the School Program. For additional information, see 2:1264 (1 excerpt).

J298. What Would You Do? A Survey of Student Opinion. For additional information, see 2:1265 (1 reference).

J299. William, Lynde & Williams Analysis of Personal Values. For additional information, see 6:199.

J300. Willoughby Emotional Maturity Scale. For additional information and a review by Lysle W. Croft, see 4:96 (7 references).

J301. Wilson Scales of Stability and Instability. For additional information and reviews by Paul E. Meehl and Katherine W. Wilcox, see 3:112.

J302. Winnetka Scale for Rating School Behavior and Attitudes. For additional information and a review by Harriet M. Barthelmess [Morrison], see 1:929 (2 references).

J303. The Wishes and Fears Inventory. For additional information, see 4:97.

J304. The Wishing Well. For additional information, see 4:98 (1 reference).

J305. Wittenborn Psychiatric Rating Scales. For additional information and reviews by H. J. Eysenck and Maurice Lorr, see 5:123 (15 references, 1 excerpt).

J306. Work Preference Inventory. For additional information, see 4:99; for reviews by Edwin W. Davis, John C. Flanagan, and Gilbert J. Rich, see 3:113.

J307. Wrightstone Scale of Civic Beliefs. For additional information and reviews by Stephen M. Corey and Harold Gulliksen, see 2:1266 (3 references).

J308. Your Activities and Attitudes. For additional information, see 4:100 (4 references, 1 excerpt).

PROJECTIVE

J309. The African T.A.T. For additional information, see 6:200 (1 reference).

J310. Animal Puzzles. For additional information, see 1:1057.

J311. Association Adjustment Inventory. For additional information and reviews by W. Grant Dahlstrom and Bertram R. Forer, see 6:201 (1 excerpt).

J312. The Auditory Apperception Test. For additional information and reviews by Kenneth L. Bean and Clifford H. Swensen, Jr., see 5:124 (3 references).

J313. The Behavioral Complexity Test: A Test for Use in Research. For additional information and a review by John Elderkin Bell, see 6:202 (4 references).

J314. Bender Gestalt Test. For additional information and a review by C. B. Blakemore, see 6:203 (99 references, 1 excerpt); see also 5:172 (118 references); for reviews by Arthur L. Benton and Howard R. White, see 4:144 (34 references); see also 3:108 (8 references).

J315. The Blacky Pictures: A Technique for the Exploration of Personality Dynamics. For additional information and a review by Bert R. Sappenfield, see 6:204 (34 references); for a review by Kenneth R. Newton, see 5:125 (38 references, 1 excerpt); for a review by Albert Ellis, see 4:102 (7 references, 3 excerpts).

J316. Buttons: A Projective Test for Pre-Adolescent and Adolescent Boys and Girls. For additional information, see 6:205.

J317. Children's Apperception Test. For additional information and reviews by Bernard I. Murstein and Robert D. Wirt, see 6:206 (19 references); for reviews by Douglas T. Kenny and Albert I. Rabin, see 5:126 (15 references); for reviews by John E. Bell and L. Joseph Stone, see 4:103 (2 references, 5 excerpts).

J318. Controlled Projection for Children. For additional information and a review by John Liggett, see 6:207; see also 5:127 (8 references, 3 excerpts); for reviews by Arthur L. Benton and Percival M. Symonds of the original edition, see 3:29 (5 excerpts).

J319. Curtis Completion Form. For additional information and reviews by Irwin G. Sarason and Laurance F. Shaffer, see 6:208 (2 references); for a review by Alfred B. Heilbrun, Jr., see 5:128.

J320. The Draw-A-Person. For additional information, see 6:209.

J321. Draw-A-Person Quality Scale. For additional information and a review by Philip L. Harriman, see 5:129 (3 references).

J322. The Drawing-Completion Test: A Projective Technique for the Investigation of Personality. For additional information, see 5:130 (3 references, 4 excerpts).

J323. The Driscoll Play Kit. For additional information, see 6:210 (2 references).

J324. The Eight Card Redrawing Test (8CRT). For additional information, see 6:211 (4 excerpts); for reviews by Cherry Ann Clark and Philip L. Harriman, see 5:131 (6 references, 1 excerpt).

J325. Expressive Movement Chart. For additional information, see 4:104 (2 references).

J326. "F" [Fluency of Association] Test. For additional information and reviews by J. M. Blackburn, P. E. Vernon, and Ll. Wynn Jones, see 2:1220 (10 references, 1 excerpt).

J327. The Family Relations Indicator: A Projective Technique for Investigating Intra-Family Relationships. For additional information and reviews by C. B. Blakemore and Walter Katkovsky, see 6:212 (1 reference).

J328. Family Relations Test: An Objective Technique for Exploring Emotional Attitudes in Children. For additional information and reviews by John E. Bell, Dale B. Harris, and Arthur R. Jensen, see 5:132 (1 reference).

J329. The Five Task Test: A Performance and Projective Test of Emotionality, Motor Skill and Organic Brain Damage. For additional information and reviews by Dorothy H. Eichorn and Bert R. Sappenfield, see 5:133 (1 excerpt).

J330. The Forer Structured Sentence Completion Test. For additional information and reviews by Charles N. Cofer and Percival M. Symonds, see 5:134 (5 references).

J331. The Forer Vocational Survey. For additional information and reviews by Benjamin Balinsky and Charles N. Cofer, see 5:135 (1 excerpt).

J332. Four Picture Test (1930). For additional information and reviews by S. G. Lee and Johann M. Schepers, see 6:213 (3 references); for reviews by John E. Bell, E. J. G. Bradford, and Ephraim Rosen of the original edition, see 4:105 (3 references, 1 excerpt).

J333. Franck Drawing Completion Test. For additional information and a review by Arthur W. Meadows, see 5:136 (5 references).

J334. The Graphomotor Projection Technique. For additional information and a review by Philip L. Harriman, see 5:137 (7 references, 2 excerpts).

J335. The Group Personality Projective Test. For additional information, see 6:214 (7 references).

J336. Group Projection Sketches for the Study of Small Groups. For additional information and a review by Cecil A. Gibb, see 5:138 (1 reference); for reviews by Robert R. Holt and N. W. Morton, see 4:106.

J337. H-T-P: House-Tree-Person Projective Technique. For additional information and a review by Mary R. Haworth, see 6:215 (32 references);

for a review by Philip L. Harriman, see 5:139 (61 references); for reviews by Albert Ellis and Ephraim Rosen, see 4:107 (14 references, 1 excerpt); for reviews by Morris Krugman and Katherine W. Wilcox, see 3:47 (5 references).

J338. The Hand Test. For additional information and a review by Goldine C. Gleser, see 6:216 (6 references, 1 excerpt).

J339. The Holtzman Inkblot Technique. For additional information and reviews by Richard W. Coan, H. J. Eysenck, Bertram R. Forer, and William N. Thetford, see 6:217 (22 references).

J340. Horn-Hellersberg Test. For additional information, see 6:218 (1 reference); for reviews by Philip L. Harriman and T. W. Richards, see 4:108 (5 references).

J341. The Howard Ink Blot Test. For additional information and reviews by Jesse G. Harris, Jr. and Bernard I. Murstein, see 6:219 (1 reference, 1 excerpt); for a review by C. R. Strother, see 5:141 (3 references, 1 excerpt).

J342. The IES Test. For additional information and reviews by Douglas P. Crowne and Walter Katkovsky, see 6:220 (15 references, 1 excerpt).

J343. An Incomplete Sentence Test. For additional information, see 6:221; for a review by Benjamin Balinsky, see 5:142.

J344. The Industrial Sentence Completion Form. For additional information, see 6:222.

J345. The Insight Test: A Verbal Projective Test for Personality Study. For additional information and a review by Richard Jessor, see 5:143 (8 references).

J346. Interpersonal Diagnosis of Personality. For additional information and a review by Jerry S. Wiggins, see 6:223 (10 references); see also 5:144 (11 references).

J347. Kahn Test of Symbol Arrangement. For additional information, see 6:224 (10 references); for reviews by Cherry Ann Clark and Richard Jessor, see 5:145 (16 references, 1 excerpt); for a review by Edward Joseph Shoben, Jr., see 4:110 (2 references).

J348. The Kell-Hoeflin Incomplete Sentence Blank: Youth-Parent Relations. For additional information, see 6:225 (2 references).

J349. Kent-Rosanoff Free Association Test. For additional information and a review by Jerry S. Wiggins, see 6:226 (82 references).

J350. The Lowenfeld Kaleidoblocs. For additional information and reviews by T. R. Miles and George Westby, see 6:227 (3 references).

J351. Lowenfeld Mosaic Test. For additional information and reviews by T. R. Miles and George Westby, see 6:228 (20 references); for a review by C. J. Adcock, see 5:147 (43 references); see also 4:115 (13 references).

J352. Machover Draw-A-Person Test. For additional information and a review by Philip M. Kitay, see 6:229 (84 references); see also 5:148 (39 references); for reviews by Philip L. Harriman and Naomi Stewart, see 4:111 (13 references).

J353. Make a Picture Story. For additional information and a review by Arthur R. Jensen, see 6:230 (10 references); see also 5:149 (19 references); for reviews by Albert I. Rabin and Charles R. Strother, see 4:113 (19 references).

J354. The Michigan Picture Test. For additional information and reviews by William E. Henry and Morris Krugman, see 5:150 (7 references, 2 excerpts).

J355. Miner Sentence Completion Scale. For additional information, see 6:230a (2 references).

J356. Minnesota Percepto-Diagnostic Test. For additional information and reviews by Richard W. Coan and Eugene E. Levitt, see 6:231 (2 references).

J357. Myokinetic Psychodiagnosis (MKP). For additional information and reviews by Philip L. Harriman and Irwin G. Sarason, see 6:232 (10 references).

J358. The Object Relations Technique. For additional information and a review by H. R. Beech, see 6:233 (7 references, 1 excerpt); for a review by George Westby, see 5:151 (6 references).

J359. Pickford Projective Pictures. For additional information and a review by Stanley J. Segal, see 6:234 (5 references, 3 excerpts).

J360. The Picture Impressions: A Projective Technique for Investigating the Patient-Therapist Relationship. For additional information, see 5:152 (1 reference, 1 excerpt).

J361. The Picture World Test. For additional information and a review by Walter Kass, see 5:153 (1 excerpt).

J362. Plot-Completion Test. For additional information and reviews by Robert C. Challman and Percival M. Symonds, see 4:116 (2 references).

J363. Psychiatric Attitudes Battery. For additional information, see 6:235 (10 references).

J364. Rock-A-Bye, Baby: A Group Projective Test for Children. For additional information, see 6:236 (4 references).

J365. Rorschach. For additional information and reviews by Richard H. Dana, Leonard D. Eron, and Arthur R. Jensen, see 6:237 (732 references); for reviews by Samuel J. Beck, H. J. Eysenck, Raymond J. McCall, and Laurance F. Shaffer, see 5:154 (1078 references); for a review by Helen Sargent, see 4:117 (621 references); for reviews by Morris Krugman and J. R. Wittenborn, see 3:73 (451 references); see also 2:1246 (147 references).

J366. Rosenzweig Picture-Frustration Study. For additional information and a review by Åke Bjerstedt, see 6:238 (61 references); for reviews by Richard H. Dana and Bert R. Sappenfield, see 5:155 (109 references); for reviews by Robert C. Challman and Percival M. Symonds, see 4:129 (77 references).

J367. The Rotter Incomplete Sentences Blank. For additional information, see 6:239 (17 references); see also 5:156 (18 references); for reviews by Charles N. Cofer and William Schofield, see 4:130 (6 references, 1 excerpt).

J368. Self Valuation Test. For additional information, see 5:157 (2 references).

J369. Sentence Completions Test. For additional information, see 5:158 (1 reference); for reviews by Charles N. Cofer and Charles R. Strother of an earlier edition, see 4:131 (3 references, 1 excerpt).

J370. The South African Picture Analysis Test. For additional information and reviews by S. G. Lee and Johann M. Schepers, see 6:240 (1 excerpt).

J371. Structured Doll Play Test. For additional information and reviews by Terence Moore and Alan O. Ross, see 6:241 (6 references).

J372. Structured-Objective Rorschach Test. For additional information and reviews by Jesse G. Harris, Jr. and Boris Semeonoff, see 6:242 (16 references, 2 excerpts).

J373. Symbol Elaboration Test. For additional information and a review by Richard H. Dana, see 5:160 (1 reference).

J374. Symonds Picture-Story Test. For additional information and reviews by Walter Kass and Kenneth R. Newton, see 5:161 (2 references); for a review by E. J. G. Bradford, see 4:132 (2 references, 1 excerpt).

J375. Szondi Test. For additional information, see 6:243 (21 references); see also 5:162 (74 references); for reviews by Ardie Lubin and Albert I. Rabin, see 4:134 (64 references); for a review by Susan K. Deri, see 3:100.

J376. Ten Silhouettes. For additional information, see 6:244 (4 references).

J377. A Test of Family Attitudes. For additional information and a review by John E. Bell, see 5:163 (2 references).

J378. Thematic Apperception Test. For additional information and a review by C. J. Adcock, see 6:245 (287 references); for reviews by Leonard D. Eron and Arthur R. Jensen, see 5:164 (311 references); for a review by Arthur L. Benton, see 4:136 (198 references); for reviews by Arthur L. Benton, Julian B. Rotter, and J. R. Wittenborn, see 3:103 (101 references, 1 excerpt).

J379. Thematic Apperception Test for African Subjects. For additional information and a review by Mary D. Ainsworth, see 5:165 (1 reference).

J380. Thematic Apperception Test: Thompson Modification. For additional information and a review by Mary D. Ainsworth, see 5:166 (4 references); see also 4:138 (5 references, 3 excerpts).

J381. The Tomkins-Horn Picture Arrangement Test. For additional information and a review by Robert C. Nichols, see 6:246 (7 references, 3 excerpts); for reviews by Donald W. Fiske, John W. Gittinger, and Wayne H. Holtzman, see 5:167 (6 references, 1 excerpt).

J382. The Toy World Test. For additional information and a review by L. Joseph Stone, see 5:168 (11 references); see also 4:147 (6 references).

J383. The Travis Projective Pictures. For additional information and a review by Edwin S. Shneidman, see 5:169 (1 reference); for a review by Robert R. Holt of the original edition, see 4:142 (3 references).

J384. The Tree Test. For additional information, see 5:170 (2 references).

J385. Twitchell-Allen Three-Dimensional Personality Test. For additional information, see 5:171 (3 references); for a review by Edward Joseph Shoben, Jr., see 4:143.

J386. Visual Apperception Test '60. For additional information and reviews by Bert R. Sappenfield and Stanley J. Segal, see 6:247.

READING

K1. A.C.E.R. Silent Reading Tests, Forms A and B. For additional information and a review by Fred J. Schonell, see 5:616.

K2. A.C.E.R. Silent Reading Tests, Forms C and D. For additional information, see 6:782 (1 reference) ; for reviews by Fred J. Schonell and D. K. Wheeler, see 5:617.

K3. A.C.E.R. Silent Reading Tests: Standardized for Use in New Zealand. For additional information, see 5:618.

K4. Achievement Test in Silent Reading: Dominion Tests. For additional information and reviews by Harry L. Stein and Magdalen D. Vernon, see 5:619; for a review by Henry P. Smith, see 4:529; for a review by Margaret G. McKim, see 3:476.

K5. American School Achievement Tests: Part 1, Reading. For additional information, see 6:783; for reviews by Russell G. Stauffer and Agatha Townsend, see 5:620. For reviews of the complete battery, see 6:2 (2 reviews), 5:1 (2 reviews), 4:1 (1 review), and 3:1 (2 reviews).

K6. American School Reading Tests. For additional information and reviews by Henry S. Dyer and Donald E. P. Smith, see 5:621.

K7. Basic Reading Tests. For additional information, see 1:1096.

K8. The "Brighton" Reading Tests. For additional information and a review by Frederick B. Davis, see 2:1529.

K9. Buffalo Reading Test for Speed and Comprehension. For additional information and reviews by Holland Roberts and William W. Turnbull, see 3:477.

K10. California Reading Test. For additional information, see 6:784 (13 references) ; see also 5:622 (5 references) ; for reviews by John C. Flanagan and James R. Hobson of an earlier edition, see 4:530 (1 excerpt) ; for a review by Frederick B. Davis, see 2:1563; for reviews by Ivan A. Booker and Joseph C. Dewey, see 1:1110. For reviews of the complete battery, see 6:3 (2 reviews) and 5:2 (1 review) ; for reviews of earlier editions, see 4:2 (3 reviews), 3:15 (1 review), 2:1193 (2 reviews), and 1:876 (1 review, 1 excerpt).

K11. Canadian English Achievement Test (CEAT): Part 1, Reading Comprehension. For additional information and reviews of the complete battery, see 6:253 (2 reviews).

K12. Chapman Reading Comprehension Test. For additional information and a review by Russell P. Kropp, see 5:623.

K13. Chicago Reading Tests. For additional information, see 3:478 (1 reference, 1 excerpt) ; for reviews by Robert Lawrence McCaul and W. J. Osburn, see 2:1531.

K14. Commerce Reading Comprehension Test. For additional information, see 5:624.

K15. Comprehension Test for Training College Students. For additional information, see 6:785.

K16. Davis Reading Test. For additional information and reviews by William E. Coffman and Alton L. Raygor, see 6:786 (2 references) ; for a review by Benjamin Rosner of the lower level, see 5:625.

K17. DeVault Primary Reading Test. For additional information and a review by Alice N. Jameson, see 3:479.

K18. Developmental Reading Tests. For additional information and reviews by Edward B. Fry and Agatha Townsend, see 6:787.

K19. Diagnostic Examination of Silent Reading Abilities. For additional information and reviews by Frederick B. Davis, W. E. Hall, and J. B. Stroud, see 3:480 (2 references) ; see also 2:1532 (1 excerpt).

K20. Elementary Reading: Every Pupil Scholarship Test. For additional information, see 6:788.

K21. Elementary Reading: Every Pupil Test. For additional information, see 6:789.

K22. Emporia Silent Reading Test. For additional information and reviews by M. E. Broom and Harriet Barthelmess Morrison, see 2:1534.

K23. English No. 1, Reading Comprehension: Midland Attainment Tests. For additional information, see 1:1101.

K24. Garrison First Year Reading Test. For additional information and a review by Ruth Lowes, see 3:483 (2 references).

K25. Garvey Primary Reading Test. For additional information, see 4:533.

K26. Gates Advanced Primary Reading Tests. For additional information and a review by Kenneth D. Hopkins, see 6:790 (1 reference) ; see also 5:630 (3 references) ; for reviews by Virginia Seavey and George Spache of an earlier edition, see 3:484.

K27. Gates Basic Reading Tests. For additional information and reviews by Albert N. Hieronymus and Arthur E. Traxler, see 6:791 (1 reference) ; for a review by S. S. Dunn, see 5:631 (1 reference) ; for reviews by George Spache, Herbert F. Spitzer, and T. L. Torgerson of an earlier edition, see 3:485 (2 references) ; for reviews by Joseph C. Dewey and James R. Hobson, see 2:1539 (5 references, 1 excerpt).

K28. Gates Primary Reading Tests. For additional information and reviews by William Eller and Coleman Morrison, see 6:792 (1 reference) ; see also 5:632 (2 references) ; for reviews by William S. Gray and George Spache of an earlier edition, see 3:486 (7 references).

K29. Gates Reading Survey. For additional information and reviews by George Spache and Morey J. Wantman, see 6:793 (7 references) ; for reviews by Dorothy E. Holberg and Herbert F. Spitzer of an earlier edition, see 3:487.

K30. General Reading Test: Ohio Senior Survey Tests. For additional information, see 4:534.

K31. Haggerty Reading Examination. For additional information and a review by William S. Gray, see 4:535 (5 references).

K32. High School Reading Test: National Achievement Tests. For additional information and a review by Victor H. Noll, see 5:634; for a review by Holland Roberts, see 4:536; for a review by Robert L. McCaul, see 3:488.

K33. Ingraham-Clark Diagnostic Reading Tests. For additional information and a review by Katherine G. Keneally, see 4:538.

K34. Iowa Silent Reading Tests. For additional information and a review by Worth R. Jones, see 6:794 (40 references); for reviews by Frederick B. Davis and William W. Turnbull, see 3:489 (21 references, 2 excerpts); for reviews by Ivan A. Booker and Holland D. Roberts of an earlier edition, see 2:1547 (6 references).

K35. Kansas Primary Reading Test. For additional information and a review by Nila Banton Smith, see 4:539; for a review by Alice K. Liveright, see 2:1549.

K36. Kelley-Greene Reading Comprehension Test. For additional information and reviews by Russell P. Kropp and Magdalen D. Vernon, see 5:636 (1 reference).

K37. Kelvin Measurement of Reading Ability. For additional information, see 1:1103.

K38. The Kingston Test of Silent Reading. For additional information and reviews by Neil Gourlay and Magdalen D. Vernon, see 5:637.

K39. Lee-Clark Reading Test. For additional information and reviews by Thomas C. Barrett and Coleman Morrison, see 6:795; for a review by Ruth Lowes of the 1943 edition of the primer level, see 3:490.

K40. Los Angeles Elementary Reading Test. For additional information and a review by Henry P. Smith, see 4:541.

K41. Los Angeles Primary Reading Test. For additional information and a review by Nila Banton Smith, see 4:542 (1 reference).

K42. Manchester Reading Comprehension Test (Sen.) 1. For additional information, see 6:796 (1 reference).

K43. Metropolitan Achievement Tests: Reading. For additional information and a review by H. Alan Robinson, see 6:797 (4 references); for reviews by James R. Hobson and Margaret G. McKim of an earlier edition, see 4:543; for a review by D. A. Worcester, see 2:1551; for reviews by Ivan A. Booker and Joseph C. Dewey, see 1:1105. For reviews of the complete battery, see 6:15 (3 reviews), 4:18 (1 review), 2:1189 (2 reviews), and 1:874 (3 reviews).

K44. Minnesota Reading Examination for College Students. For additional information and a review by James M. McCallister, see 3:491 (3 references); for a review by W. C. McCall, see 2:1554 (3 references); for a review by Ruth Strang, see 1:1106.

K45. Monroe's Standardized Silent Reading Test. For additional information and reviews by Charles R. Langmuir and Agatha Townsend, see 6:798 (5 references).

K46. N.B. Silent Reading Tests (Beginners): Reading Comprehension Test. For additional information, see 6:799.

K47. The Nelson-Denny Reading Test: Vocabulary and Paragraph. For additional information and a review by Ivan A. Booker, see 4:544 (17 references); for a review by Hans C. Gordon, see 2:1557 (6 references).

K48. The Nelson-Denny Reading Test: Vocabulary-Comprehension-Rate. For additional information and reviews by David B. Orr and Agatha Townsend, see 6:800 (13 references, 1 excerpt); for references to reviews of an earlier edition, see K47.

K49. Nelson-Lohmann Reading Test. For additional information and a review by Jason Millman, see 6:801.

K50. The Nelson Reading Test. For additional information and a review by H. Alan Robinson, see 6:802; for reference to reviews of an earlier edition, see K51.

K51. The Nelson Silent Reading Test: Vocabulary and Paragraph. For additional information and a review by William D. Sheldon of an earlier edition, see 4:545 (1 reference); for a review by Constance M. McCullough, see 3:492; see also 2:1558 (1 excerpt); for reference to a review of a later edition, see K50.

K52. Primary Reading: Every Pupil Scholarship Test. For additional information, see 6:803.

K53. Primary Reading: Every Pupil Test. For additional information, see 6:804; for reviews by William S. Gray and Virginia Seavey of an earlier form, see 3:493.

K54. Primary Reading Test. For additional information and a review by Ruth Lowes, see 3:494 (1 reference).

K55. Primary Reading Test: Acorn Achievement Tests. For additional information, see 5:642; for a review by Alice N. Jameson, see 3:495.

K56. The Purdue Reading Test. For additional information, see 5:643; for a review by Albert J. Harris, see 3:496.

K57. Reading Comprehension: Cooperative English Tests. For additional information and reviews by W. V. Clemans and W. G. Fleming, see 6:806 (12 references); see also 5:645 (21 references) and 4:547 (20 references); for reviews by Robert Murray Bear and J. B. Stroud of an earlier edition, see 3:497 (15 references); see also 2:1564 (2 references). For reviews of the complete battery, see 6:256 (2 reviews, 1 excerpt) and 3:120 (3 reviews).

K58. Reading Comprehension Test: National Achievement Tests [Crow, Kuhlmann, and Crow]. For additional information, see 5:647.

K59. Reading Comprehension Test: National Achievement Tests [Speer and Smith]. For additional information, see 5:646; for a review by James R. Hobson, see 3:498.

K60. Reading: Public School Achievement Tests. For additional information, see 6:807. For reviews of the complete battery, see 2:1194 (2 reviews).

K61. Reading: Seven Plus Assessment: Northumberland Series. For additional information, see 4:548. For a review of the complete battery, see 4:24.

K62. Reading Test (Comprehension and Speed): Municipal Tests: National Achievement

Tests. For additional information, see 5:648. For reviews of the complete battery, see 5:18 (1 review), 4:20 (1 review), and 2:1191 (2 reviews).

K63. SRA Achievement Series: Reading. For additional information and a review by Edward B. Fry, see 6:808; for reviews by N. Dale Bryant and Clarence Derrick, see 5:649. For reviews of the complete battery, see 6:21 (1 review) and 5:21 (2 reviews).

K64. SRA Reading Record. For additional information and a review by William W. Turnbull, see 4:550 (2 references); for a review by Frances Oralind Triggs, see 3:502 (1 excerpt).

K65. Sangren-Woody Reading Test. For additional information and a review by David H. Russell, see 4:551; for a review by Alice K. Liveright, see 2:1565 (7 references).

K66. Schrammel-Gray High School and College Reading Test. For additional information and reviews by James M. McCallister and Robert L. McCaul, see 3:500 (1 excerpt).

K67. Sentence Reading Test 1. For additional information, see 6:809; for reviews by Reginald R. Dale and Stephen Wiseman, see 5:652.

K68. Sequential Tests of Educational Progress: Reading. For additional information and reviews by Emmett Albert Betts and Paul R. Lohnes, see 6:810 (6 references); for reviews by Eric F. Gardner, James R. Hobson, and Stephen Wiseman, see 5:653. For reviews of the complete battery, see 6:25 (2 reviews) and 5:24 (2 reviews, 1 excerpt).

K69. Shank Tests of Reading Comprehension. For additional information and a review by William D. Sheldon, see 4:553; for a review by James R. Hobson, see 2:1567 (3 references).

K70. Silent Reading Comprehension: Iowa Every-Pupil Tests of Basic Skills, Test A. For additional information, see 4:554; for reviews by James R. Hobson and Constance M. McCullough, see 3:501. For reviews of the complete battery, see 4:15 (2 reviews), 3:10 (3 reviews), and 1:872 (4 reviews).

K71. Silent Reading Tests. For additional information, see 6:811.

K72. Southgate Group Reading Tests. For additional information and reviews by M. L. Kellmer Pringle and Magdalen D. Vernon, see 6:812 (1 excerpt).

K73. Stanford Achievement Test: Reading Tests. For additional information, see 6:813 (1 reference); for reviews by Helen M. Robinson and Agatha Townsend of an earlier edition, see 5:656; for a review by James R. Hobson, see 4:555 (4 references); for a review by Margaret G. McKim, see 3:503. For reviews of the complete battery, see 6:26 (1 review, 1 excerpt), 5:25 (1 review), 4:25 (2 reviews), and 3:18 (2 reviews).

K74. Stone-Webster Test in Beginning Reading. For additional information and a review by Ruth Lowes, see 3:504 (1 reference).

K75. Survey of Primary Reading Development. For additional information and reviews by Thomas C. Barrett and Russell G. Stauffer, see 6:814.

K76. Survey of Reading Achievement: California Survey Series. For additional information and reviews by Clarence Derrick and J. Raymond Gerberich, see 6:815.

K77. Techniques in Reading Comprehension: Every Pupil Test. For additional information, see 6:816; for reviews by Ivan A. Booker and James M. McCallister of earlier forms, see 3:505.

K78. Tests of Reading: Cooperative Inter-American Tests. For additional information, see 6:818 (4 references); for reviews by Jacob S. Orleans and Frederick L. Westover, see 4:557 (4 references).

K79. Thorndike-Lorge Reading Test. For additional information and a review by Ivan A. Booker, see 4:558 (1 reference); for a review by Robert L. McCaul, see 3:506 (1 excerpt).

K80. Traxler High School Reading Test. For additional information and a review by Harold D. Carter, see 4:559 (4 references); for reviews by Alvin C. Eurich, Constance M. McCullough, and C. Gilbert Wrenn, see 2:1578 (2 excerpts).

K81. Traxler Silent Reading Test. For additional information and a review by J. Thomas Hastings, see 4:560 (2 references); for reviews by Robert L. McCaul and Miles A. Tinker, see 2:1579 (3 references, 1 excerpt); for reviews by Frederick B. Davis and Spencer Shank, see 1:1114.

K82. Unit Scales of Attainment in Reading. For additional information and reviews by Ivan A. Booker and J. Wayne Wrightstone, see 2:1581; for a review by Joseph C. Dewey, see 1:1115. For reviews of the complete battery, see 2:1197 (1 review) and 1:878 (2 reviews).

K83. W.A.L. English Comprehension Test. For additional information, see 6:819.

K84. Whipple's High-School and College Reading Test. For additional information and a review by Frederick B. Davis, see 3:507 (3 references).

K85. Williams Primary Reading Test. For additional information, see 5:658; for a review by Alice N. Jameson, see 3:508.

K86. Ypsilanti Reading Test. For additional information, see 2:1583.1.

DIAGNOSTIC

K87. California Phonics Survey. For additional information and a review by Thomas E. Culliton, Jr., see 6:820 (1 reference).

K88. Diagnostic Reading Scales. For additional information and a review by N. Dale Bryant, see 6:821.

K89. Diagnostic Reading Test: Pupil Progress Series. For additional information and a review by Agatha Townsend, see 6:822.

K90. Diagnostic Reading Tests. For additional information and reviews by Albert J. Kingston and B. H. Van Roekel, see 6:823 (21 references); for reviews by Frederick B. Davis, William W. Turnbull, and Henry Weitz, see 4:531 (19 references).

K91. Doren Diagnostic Reading Test of Word Recognition Skills. For additional information and reviews by B. H. Van Roekel and Verna L. Vickery, see 5:659.

K92. Durrell Analysis of Reading Difficulty. For additional information and reviews by James Maxwell and George D. Spache, see 5:660; for a review by Helen M. Robinson, see 4:561 (2 references); for reviews by Guy L. Bond and Miles A. Tinker, see 2:1533; for a review by Marion Monroe [Cox], see 1:1098.

K93. Gates-McKillop Reading Diagnostic Tests. For additional information and reviews by N. Dale Bryant and Gabriel M. Della-Piana, see 6:824 (2 references) ; for a review by George D. Spache of an earlier edition, see 5:662; for a review by Worth J. Osburn, see 4:563 (2 references) ; for a review by T. L. Torgerson, see 3:510 (3 references):

K94. Group Diagnostic Reading Aptitude and Achievement Tests. For additional information, see 6:825.

K95. Hildreth Diagnostic Reading Record. For additional information, see 2:1541.

K96. Individual Reading Test. For additional information and a review by R. W. McCulloch, see 5:663.

K97. McCullough Word-Analysis Tests. For additional information and reviews by Emery P. Bliesmer and Albert J. Harris, see 6:826.

K98. McGuffey Diagnostic Reading Test. For additional information, see 5:664.

K99. OC Diagnostic Syllable Test. For additional information, see 6:827.

K100. Phonics Knowledge Survey. For additional information, see 6:828.

K101. Phonovisual Diagnostic Test. For additional information and reviews by Charles M. Brown and George D. Spache, see 6:829.

K102. Primary Reading Profiles. For additional information and reviews by James R. Hobson and Verna L. Vickery, see 5:665.

K103. Reading Diagnostic Record for High School and College Students. For additional information and reviews by Marvin D. Glock and Donald E. P. Smith, see 5:666; for reviews by Robert Murray Bear and Carolyn M. Welch of the original edition, see 3:509; for a review by Henry D. Rinsland, see 2:1535 (3 excerpts).

K104. Record for Reading Diagnosis. For additional information and a review by Carolyn M. Welch, see 3:512.

K105. Roswell-Chall Auditory Blending Test. For additional information and reviews by Ira E. Aaron and B. H. Van Roekel, see 6:830 (2 references).

K106. Roswell-Chall Diagnostic Reading Test of Word Analysis Skills. For additional information and reviews by Ira E. Aaron and Emmett Albert Betts, see 6:831 (1 reference) ; for a review by Byron H. Van Roekel, see 5:667.

K107. Scholastic Diagnostic Reading Test. For additional information and reviews by Russell G. Stauffer and Arthur E. Traxler, see 5:650.

K108. The Schonell Reading Tests. For additional information and a review by R. W. McCulloch, see 5:651 (4 references) ; for a review by M. L. Kellmer Pringle, see 4:552 (3 references) ; for a review by Edith I. M. Thomson, see 3:499.

K109. Silent Reading Diagnostic Tests: The Developmental Reading Tests. For additional information and reviews by Emery P. Bliesmer and Albert J. Kingston, see 6:832 (1 reference).

K110. The Standard Reading Tests. For additional information and a review by L. B. Birch, see 6:833 (1 reference).

K111. Stanford Diagnostic Phonics Survey. For additional information, see 5:670.

MISCELLANEOUS

K112. Botel Reading Inventory. For additional information and reviews by Ira E. Aaron and Charles M. Brown, see 6:834.

K113. Durrell-Sullivan Reading Capacity and Achievement Tests. For additional information and a review by James Maxwell, see 5:661 (5 references) ; for a review by Helen M. Robinson, see 4:562 (4 references) ; for reviews by William S. Gray and Marion Monroe [Cox] of the original edition, see 1:1099 (1 excerpt).

K114. Functional Readiness Questionnaire for School and College Students. For additional information, see 6:835.

K115. Instructional Reading Tests for the Intermediate Grades. For additional information, see 2:1543.

K116. Inventory of Reading Experiences. For additional information and a review by Albert J. Harris, see 3:511 (2 references).

K117. Learning Methods Test. For additional information and reviews by Thomas E. Culliton, Jr. and William Eller, see 6:836 (1 reference).

K118. The Master Ophthalmograph. For additional information and a review by Miles A. Tinker, see 4:660 (8 references) ; see also 3:470 (15 references) ; for a review by G. T. Buswell of an earlier model, see 2:1559 (2 references, 2 excerpts) ; for reviews by Stella S. Center, David Kopel, Marion Monroe [Cox], Joseph Tiffin, and Miles A. Tinker, see 1:1108 (1 excerpt).

K119. The Reader Rater. For additional information, see 6:837.

K120. The Reading Eye. For additional information and reviews by Arthur S. McDonald and George D. Spache, see 6:838 (3 references).

K121. Reading Versatility Test. For additional information, see 6:839 (1 reference).

K122. SRA Achievement Series: Language Perception. For additional information, see 5:668.

ORAL

K123. Articulation Test With Reading Disability Feature. For additional information and a review by Irving H. Anderson, see 1:1095.

K124. Flash-X Sight Vocabulary Test. For additional information, see 6:841.

K125. Gilmore Oral Reading Test. For additional information and reviews by Lydia A. Duggins and Maynard C. Reynolds, see 5:671 (1 reference).

K126. Gray Oral Reading Test. For additional information and reviews by Emery P. Bliesmer, Albert J. Harris, and Paul R. Lohnes, see 6:842.

K127. Holborn Reading Scale. For additional information and a review by Stanley Nisbet, see 5:635 (1 reference) ; for a review by C. M. Fleming, see 4:537.

K128. Jenkins Oral Reading Test: Individualized Oral Diagnostic Test for Children With Serious Reading Difficulties. For additional information and reviews by Guy L. Bond, David Kopel, and Clarence R. Stone, see 2:1548.

K129 PERSONALITY TESTS AND REVIEWS [1404

K129. Kindergarten-Primary Articulation Test.
For additional information and a review by Irving H.
Anderson, see 1:1104.

K130. Leavell Analytical Oral Reading Test.
For additional information and reviews by Lydia A.
Duggins and Maynard C. Reynolds, see 5:672.

K131. Neale Analysis of Reading Ability. For
additional information and reviews by M. Alan Brimer
and Magdalen D. Vernon, see 6:843 (1 excerpt).

**K132. Oral Diagnostic Test of Word-Analysis
Skills, Primary: Dominion Tests.** For additional
information and a review by S. A. Rayner, see 5:673;
for a review by Nila Banton Smith, see 4:565.

K133. Oral Word Reading Test. For additional
information and reviews by S. A. Rayner and D. K.
Wheeler, see 5:674.

K134. Slosson Oral Reading Test (SORT). For
additional information, see 6:844.

K135. Standardized Oral Reading Check Tests.
For additional information and reviews by David H.
Russell and Clarence R. Stone, see 2:1570 (1 reference).

K136. Standardized Oral Reading Paragraphs.
For additional information and reviews by David Kopel
and Clarence R. Stone, see 2:1571 (7 references).

READINESS

**K137. American School Reading Readiness
Test.** For additional information and reviews by Joan
Bollenbacher and Helen M. Robinson, see 5:675 (3
references); for reviews by David H. Russell and
Paul A. Witty, see 3:513.

**K138. The Anton Brenner Developmental
Gestalt Test of School Readiness.** For additional
information, see 6:844a (8 references).

K139. Betts Ready to Read Tests. For additional
information and reviews by I. H. Anderson, David
Kopel, Marion Monroe [Cox], and Guy Wagner, see
1:1097 (1 reference).

**K140. Binion-Beck Reading Readiness Test for
Kindergarten and First Grade.** For additional in-
formation and reviews by Irving H. Anderson and
Paul A. Witty, see 3:514 (1 reference).

**K141. Classification Test for Beginners in
Reading.** For additional information and reviews by
Marion Monroe Cox and David H. Russell, see 3:515
(2 references).

K142. Gates Reading Readiness Tests. For
additional information, see 6:845 (1 reference); for a
review by F. J. Schonell, see 4:566; for reviews by
Marion Monroe Cox and Paul A. Witty, see 3:516 (3
references); see also 2:1537 (5 references, 2 excerpts).

**K143. Group Test of Reading Readiness: The
Dominion Tests.** For additional information and a
review by N. Dale Bryant, see 5:676.

**K144. The Harrison-Stroud Reading Readiness
Profiles.** For additional information and a review by
S. S. Dunn, see 5:677 (2 references); for a review by
William S. Gray of an earlier edition, see 4:568.

K145. Lee-Clark Reading Readiness Test. For
additional information, see 6:846 (9 references); for
a review by James R. Hobson of an earlier edition, see
5:678; for reviews by Marion Monroe Cox and David
H. Russell, see 3:517.

**K146. Maturity Level for School Entrance and
Reading Readiness.** For additional information, see
6:847; for a review by David H. Russell of the original edition, see 4:572.

K147. Metropolitan Readiness Tests. For additional information and a review by Eric F. Gardner
of an earlier edition, see 4:570 (3 references, 1 excerpt); for a review by Irving H. Anderson, see 3:518
(5 references); for a review by W. J. Osburn, see
2:1552 (10 references).

**K148. Murphy-Durrell Diagnostic Reading
Readiness Test.** For additional information and reviews by Joan Bollenbacher and S. S. Dunn, see 5:679
(2 references); see also 4:571 (2 references).

K149. Reading Aptitude Tests. For additional
information and a review by Irving H. Anderson, see
3:519 (5 references).

K150. Reading Readiness Test. For additional
information and a review by David A. Payne, see
6:849 (1 reference).

K151. Scholastic Reading Readiness Test. For
additional information and a review by David A.
Payne, see 6:850.

K152. Stevens Reading Readiness Test. For
additional information and reviews by Irving H. Anderson and Marion Monroe Cox, see 3:521.

K153. Van Wagenen Reading Readiness Scales.
For additional information and a review by David H.
Russell of Part 2, see 3:520 (4 references).

K154. Watson Reading-Readiness Test. For
additional information, see 6:851.

K155. Webster Reading-Readiness Test. For
additional information, see 5:682.

SPECIAL FIELDS

**K156. Ability to Interpret Reading Materials
in the Natural Sciences: The Iowa Tests of Educational Development, Test 6.** For additional
information, see 6:853. For reviews of the complete
battery, see 6:14 (2 reviews), 5:17 (2 reviews), 4:17
(1 review), and 3:12 (3 reviews).

**K157. Ability to Interpret Reading Materials
in the Social Studies: The Iowa Tests of Educational Development, Test 5.** For additional information, see 6:852. For reviews of the complete battery,
see 6:14 (2 reviews), 5:17 (2 reviews), 4:17 (1 review), and 3:12 (3 reviews).

**K158. Interpretation of Reading Materials in
the Natural Sciences: Tests of General Educational Development, Test 3.** For additional information, see 5:683. For reviews of the complete battery,
see 5:27 (1 review), 4:26 (1 review), and 3:20 (2
reviews).

**K159. Interpretation of Reading Materials in
the Social Studies: Tests of General Educational
Development, Test 2.** For additional information,
see 5:684; for reviews by W. E. Hall and C. Robert
Pace, see 3:528 (1 reference). For reviews of the
complete battery, see 5:27 (1 review), 4:26 (1 review), and 3:20 (2 reviews).

**K160. Lorimer Braille Recognition Test: A
Test of Ability in Reading Braille Contractions.**
For additional information, see 6:854 (1 reference).

K161. Mathematics, Biology, Physical Science. For additional information, see 2:1550.

K162. Purdue Reading Test for Industrial Supervisors. For additional information and reviews by Jerome E. Doppelt and Louis C. Nanassy, see 5:644 (1 reference).

K163. RBH Reading Comprehension Test. For additional information, see 6:817.

K164. Reading Adequacy "READ" Test: Individual Placement Series. For additional information, see 6:805.

K165. Reading Scales in History. For additional information and reviews by Paul Blommers and Albert J. Harris, see 3:530.

K166. Reading Scales in Literature. For additional information, see 3:531.

K167. Reading Scales in Science. For additional information and a review by Ivan A. Booker, see 3:532.

K168. [Robinson-Hall Reading Tests.] For additional information and a review by Robert Murray Bear, see 4:575 (2 references); see also 3:533 (3 references).

K169. Southeastern Problems and Prospects: Social Studies and English. For additional information, see 2:1569.

K170. Tests of Natural Sciences: Vocabulary and Interpretation of Reading Materials: Cooperative Inter-American Tests. For additional information and a review by Clarence H. Nelson, see 4:576 (4 references).

K171. Tests of Social Studies: Vocabulary and Interpretation of Reading Materials: Cooperative Inter-American Tests. For additional information and reviews by Gustav J. Froehlich and Martha E. Layman, see 4:577 (4 references).

K172. Tooze Braille Speed Test: A Test of Basic Ability in Reading Braille. For additional information, see 6:855.

K173. Understanding Communication (Verbal Comprehension). For additional information and reviews by C. E. Jurgensen and Donald E. P. Smith, see 6:840.

SPEED

K174. Chapman-Cook Speed of Reading Test. For additional information and a review by Eason Monroe, see 3:522 (1 reference).

K175. Michigan Speed of Reading Test. For additional information and a review by Eason Monroe, see 3:523 (1 reference); see also 2:1553 (2 references); for reviews by Richard Ledgerwood and M. R. Trabue, see 1:1171.

K176. Minnesota Speed of Reading Test for College Students. For additional information and a review by J. R. Gerberich, see 2:1555 (2 references); for reviews by Frederick B. Davis and Ruth Strang, see 1:1107.

K177. Reading Speed and Comprehension: Ohio Senior Survey Tests. For additional information and reviews by J. B. Stroud and Miles A. Tinker, see 3:524.

K178. Reading Speed Test: National Achievement Test. For additional information and a review by Eason Monroe, see 3:525.

K179. Tinker Speed of Reading Test. For additional information and a review by Leonard S. Feldt, see 5:687.

STUDY SKILLS

K180. Analysis of Controversial Writing: Test 5.31. For additional information, see 2:1527.

K181. Application of Certain Principles of Logical Reasoning: Test 5.12. For additional information, see 2:1528.

K182. Applied Reading for Junior-Senior High School: Every Pupil Test. For additional information and a review by Ivan A. Booker, see 3:534.

K183. Bennett Use of Library Test. For additional information and a review by Louis Shores, see 4:578.

K184. California Study Methods Survey. For additional information and reviews by John D. Krumboltz and Donald E. P. Smith, see 6:857 (2 references, 2 excerpts); see also 5:689 (7 references).

K185. Cooperative Dictionary Test. For additional information and a review by A. N. Hieronymus, see 5:690.

K186. Critical Classification of Magazines and Newspapers. For additional information, see 1:1163.

K187. Critical-Mindedness in the Reading of Fiction: Test 3.7. For additional information, see 2:1530 (1 reference).

K188. Edmiston How to Study Test. For additional information, see 4:580.

K189. Evaluation Aptitude Test. For additional information and reviews by J. Thomas Hastings and Walker H. Hill, see 5:691.

K190. Information Concerning Library Processes. For additional information, see 1:1164.

K191. Interpretation of Data Test: General Education Series. For additional information and reviews by J. Raymond Gerberich and Victor H. Noll, see 4:581 (5 references); for a review by J. Wayne Wrightstone, see 3:535 (4 references); see also 2:1544 (9 references).

K192. Interpretation of Data: Test 2.71. For additional information, see 2:1545 (4 references).

K193. A Library Orientation Test for College Freshmen. For additional information and a review by Morey J. Wantman, see 6:859 (1 reference); for reviews by Janet G. Afflerbach (with Lois Grimes Afflerbach) and J. Wayne Wrightstone, see 5:693.

K194. Library Test for Junior High Schools. For additional information and reviews by Robert A. Davis and Ethel M. Feagley, see 3:536.

K195. Library Usage Test. For additional information and a review by J. Wayne Wrightstone, see 3:537.

K196. Logical Reasoning. For additional information and reviews by Duncan Howie and Charles R. Langmuir, see 5:694 (1 reference).

K197. Logical Reasoning Test: General Education Series. For additional information and a review by Robert L. Ebel, see 4:582 (1 reference); see also 2:1528 (4 references).

K198. Nationwide Library Skills Examination. For additional information, see 6:860.

K199. Nature of Proof: Test 5.22. For additional information, see 2:1556 (3 references).

K200. OC Diagnostic Dictionary Test. For additional information, see 6:861.

K201. Parr Skill-Ability Tests. For additional information, see 2:1559.1.

K202. Peabody Library Information Test. For additional information and a review by Douglas E. Scates, see 3:538 (2 references, 2 excerpts).

K203. Poley Precis Test: A Test by Paragraph Summaries of Reading Comprehension. For additional information and a review by Edward A. Tenney, see 2:1561.

K204. Reading and Construction of Tables and Graphs. For additional information, see 1:1165.

K205. SRA Achievement Series: Work-Study Skills. For additional information, see 6:862; for reviews by Robert L. Ebel and Ruth M. Strang, see 5:696. For reviews of the complete battery, see 6:21 (1 review) and 5:21 (2 reviews).

K206. Senior High School Library and Reference Skills Test. For additional information, see 6:863.

K207. Special Reading Test: Ohio Senior Survey Tests. For additional information and a review by Miles A. Tinker, see 3:539.

K208. Spitzer Study Skills Test. For additional information and a review by Alton L. Raygor, see 6:864 (1 reference); for a review by James Deese, see 5:697.

K209. Stanford Achievement Test: Study Skills. For additional information and reviews by Robert L. Ebel and Ruth M. Strang, see 5:698. For reviews of the complete battery, see 6:26 (1 review, 1 excerpt), 5:25 (1 review), 4:25 (2 reviews), and 3:18 (2 reviews).

K210. Student Skills Inventory. For additional information, see 2:1573 (1 reference).

K211. Study Habits Inventory. For additional information and a review by Douglas E. Scates, see 3:540 (8 references); for reviews by Edward S. Jones and William A. McCall, see 2:1574.

K212. Study Outline Test. For additional information and a review by Harriet Barthelmess Morrison, see 2:1575 (1 reference).

K213. The Study Skills Counseling Evaluation. For additional information and reviews by Stanley E. Davis and W. G. Fleming, see 6:865.

K214. Survey of Study Habits. For additional information and a review by Warren R. Baller, see 4:583 (1 reference).

K215. Survey of Study Habits and Attitudes. For additional information, see 6:856 (12 references); for reviews by James Deese and C. Gilbert Wrenn (with Roy D. Lewis), see 5:688 (14 references).

K216. Test of Critical Thinking. For additional information, see 4:584.

K217. A Test of Study Skills. For additional information and a review by Marvin D. Glock, see 5:699; for a review by Douglas E. Scates, see 3:542.

K218. Test on the Use of Books and Libraries: General Education Series. For additional information and reviews by Henry D. Rinsland and Louis Shores, see 4:585 (1 reference).

K219. A Test on Use of the Dictionary. For additional information, see 6:866.

K220. Tyler-Kimber Study Skills Test. For additional information and reviews by William A. McCall and Rachel Salisbury, see 2:1580 (1 reference); for reviews by Edward S. Jones and C. Gilbert Wrenn, see 1:1166.

K221. The Use of Library and Study Materials. For additional information and a review by Robert Murray Bear, see 4:586 (1 reference); for a review by Ethel M. Feagley, see 3:543.

K222. Use of Sources of Information: The Iowa Tests of Educational Development, Test 9. For additional information, see 6:858. For reviews of the complete battery, see 6:14 (2 reviews), 5:17 (2 reviews), 4:17 (1 review), and 3:12 (3 reviews).

K223. Watson-Glaser Critical Thinking Appraisal. For additional information, see 6:867 (24 references); for reviews by Walker H. Hill and Carl I. Hovland of an earlier edition, see 5:700 (8 references); for a review by Robert H. Thouless, see 3:544 (3 references, 1 excerpt).

K224. Work-Study Skills: Iowa Every-Pupil Tests of Basic Skills, Test B. For additional information, see 4:588; for a review by J. Wayne Wrightstone, see 3:545. For reviews of the complete battery, see 4:15 (2 reviews), 3:10 (3 reviews), and 1:872 (4 reviews).

SCIENCE

L1. Ability for Science: Fife Tests of Ability, Test 2. For additional information, see 3:546 (2 references). For reviews of the complete battery, see 4:713 (1 review) and 3:8 (1 review).

L2. Advanced General Science: Cooperative Science Tests. For additional information, see 6:867a.

L3. Analytical Scales of Attainment in Elementary Science. For additional information and reviews by Francis D. Curtis and Victor H. Noll, see 2:1598; see also 1:1123 (1 excerpt).

L4. Application of Principles in Science: Test 1.3b. For additional information, see 2:1599 (2 references); superseded by L42.

L5. Biology and General Science: National Teacher Examinations. For additional information, see 6:868. For reviews of the testing program, see 6:700 (1 review), 5:538 (3 reviews), and 4:802 (1 review).

L6. Chemistry, Physics and General Science: National Teacher Examinations. For additional information, see 6:869. For reviews of the testing program, see 6:700 (1 review), 5:538 (3 reviews), and 4:802 (1 review).

L7. Cooperative General Achievement Tests: Test 2, Natural Science. For additional information, see 6:870 (4 references); for a review by Palmer O. Johnson of earlier forms, see 3:548. For reviews of the complete battery, see 6:7 (1 review), 5:6 (1 review), 4:5 (1 review), and 3:3 (1 review).

L8. Cooperative General Science Test. For additional information and a review by John S. Richardson, see 4:623 (1 reference); for a review by G. W. Hunter of an earlier form, see 2:1601; for reviews by W. B. Meldrum and Alvin W. Schindler, see 1:1125.

L9. Cooperative General Science Test for College Students. For additional information, see 1:1126.

L10. Cooperative Science Test for Grades 7, 8, and 9. For additional information and a review by R. Will Burnett, see 4:624; for reviews by Hans C. Gordon and Herbert A. Thelen of earlier forms, see 3:571.

L11. Coordinated Scales of Attainment: Science. For additional information, see 5:704. For reviews of the complete battery, see 4:8 (1 review) and 3:6 (4 reviews).

L12. Elementary Science and Health: Every Pupil Test. For additional information, see 6:872.

L13. Elementary Science: Every Pupil Scholarship Test. For additional information, see 6:871.

L14. Elementary Science Test: National Achievement Tests. For additional information and a review by William Harrison Lucow, see 5:707.

L15. Examination in General Science—High-School Level. For additional information and reviews by Hans C. Gordon and Victor H. Noll, see 3:573.

L16. Examination in Senior Science—High-School Level. For additional information and a review by Richard H. Jordan, see 3:574.

L17. General Background in the Natural Sciences: The Iowa Tests of Educational Development, Test 2. For additional information and reviews by Lloyd H. Heidgerd and Jacqueline V. Mallinson, see 6:876 (1 reference). For reviews of the complete battery, see 6:14 (2 reviews), 5:17 (2 reviews), 4:17 (1 review), and 3:12 (3 reviews).

L18. General Science: Cooperative Science Tests. For additional information, see 6:872a.

L19. General Science: Every Pupil Scholarship Test. For additional information, see 6:873.

L20. General Science: Every Pupil Test. For additional information, see 6:874.

L21. General Science: Minnesota High School Achievement Examinations. For additional information, see 6:875.

L22. General Science Test: Gibson's Attainment Tests. For additional information, see 1:1129.

L23. General Science Test: National Achievement Tests. For additional information and a review by Robert M. W. Travers, see 5:712; for reviews by Francis D. Curtis and G. W. Hunter, see 2:1602.

L24. General Science Test: State High School Tests for Indiana. For additional information, see 4:592.

L25. Iowa Every-Pupil Test in General Science. For additional information and a review by Edward E. Cureton, see 1:1131.

L26. McDougal General Science Test. For additional information and reviews by Hans C. Gordon and Herbert A. Thelen, see 3:576.

L27. Metropolitan Achievement Tests: [Science]. For additional information and reviews by William W. Cooley and George G. Mallinson, see 6:877. For reviews of the complete battery, see 6:15 (3 reviews), 4:18 (1 review), 2:1189 (2 reviews), and 1:874 (3 reviews).

L28. Physical Science Aptitude Examination. For additional information and reviews by Jack W. Dunlap and John C. Flanagan, see 3:547.

L29. Physical Science: Teacher Education Examination Program. An inactive form of test L6; for additional information, see 6:878. For a review of the testing program, see 5:543.

L30. Purdue Physical Science Aptitude Test. For additional information and a review by William W. Cooley, see 6:879 (8 references).

L31. Read General Science Test. For additional information, see 5:715 (1 reference); for reviews by Benjamin S. Bloom and John S. Richardson, see 4:628.

L32. Science Applications Test: Gibson's Attainment Tests. For additional information, see 1:1132.

L33. Science Background: A Science Service Test to Identify Potential Scientific and Technical Talent. For additional information, see 6:880.

L34. Science Information Test. For additional information and reviews by Hans C. Gordon and G. W. Hunter, see 2:1603.

L35. Science: Minnesota High School Achievement Examinations. For additional information and reviews by Elizabeth Hagen and Jacqueline V. Mallinson, see 6:881.

L36. Sequential Tests of Educational Progress: Science. For additional information and reviews by John C. Flanagan and George G. Mallinson, see 6:882 (2 references); for reviews by Palmer O. Johnson, Julian C. Stanley (with M. Jacinta Mann), and Robert M. W. Travers, see 5:716. For reviews of the complete battery, see 6:25 (2 reviews) and 5:24 (2 reviews, 1 excerpt).

L37. Stanford Achievement Test: Science. For additional information, see 6:883; for reviews by Bertram Epstein and Paul E. Kambly of an earlier edition, see 4:593. For reviews of the complete battery, see 6:26 (1 review, 1 excerpt), 5:25 (1 review), 4:25 (2 reviews), and 3:18 (2 reviews).

L38. Survey Test in Introductory Science: California Survey Series. For additional information and reviews by Kenneth E. Anderson and Lloyd H. Heidgerd, see 6:884.

L39. Survey Test in Physical Science: California Survey Series. For additional information and a review by Irvin J. Lehmann, see 6:885.

L40. Survey Test in the Natural Sciences: Cooperative General Achievement Test, Part 2. For additional information, see 2:1604; for a review by Palmer O. Johnson, see 1:870.

L41. T. C. General Science Test. For additional information, see 6:886.

L42. Test of Application of Principles in General Science: General Education Series. For additional information and a review by R. Will Burnett, see 4:629 (3 references).

L43. Test of Application of Principles in Physical Science: General Education Series. For additional information and a review by Palmer O. Johnson, see 4:594 (3 references).

L44. Wisconsin General Science Test. For additional information, see 3:577.

BIOLOGY

L45. Application of Principles in Biological Science: Test 1.33A. For additional information, see 2:1584 (2 references).

L46. Biological Science: Teacher Education Examination Program. An inactive form of test L5; for additional information, see 6:887. For a review of the testing program, see 5:543.

L47. Biology: Cooperative Science Tests. For additional information, see 6:887a.

L48. Biology: Every Pupil Scholarship Test. For additional information, see 6:888.

L49. Biology: Every Pupil Test. For additional information, see 6:889.

L50. Biology: Minnesota High School Achievement Examinations. For additional information and a review by Barbara F. Esser, see 6:890.

L51. Biology Test: Affiliation Testing Program for Catholic Secondary Schools. For additional information and a review by Henry Chauncey, see 6:891. For a review of the complete program, see 6:758.

L52. Biology Test: State High School Tests for Indiana. For additional information, see 4:598.

L53. College Entrance Examination Board Achievement Test: Biology. For additional information, see 6:892 (3 references); for a review by Elizabeth Hagen of an earlier form, see 5:723; for a review by Clark W. Horton, see 4:600. For reviews of the testing program, see 6:760 (2 reviews).

L54. College Entrance Examination Board Advanced Placement Examination: Biology. For additional information and a review by Clarence H. Nelson, see 6:893 (1 reference); for a review by Clark W. Horton of an earlier form, see 5:724.

L55. College Entrance Examination Board Placement Tests: Biology. An inactive form of test L53; for additional information, see 6:894.

L56. Cooperative Biology Test. For additional information and a review by Leland P. Johnson, see 4:601; for a review by C. W. Horton of earlier forms, see 3:550 (1 reference); for a review by Ralph W. Tyler, see 2:1585; for reviews by Francis D. Curtis and George W. Hunter, see 1:907.

L57. Cooperative Biology Test: Educational Records Bureau Edition. For additional information, see 6:895; see also 5:725 (1 reference) and 4:602 (2 references).

L58. Cooperative Botany Test. For additional information and a review by F. C. Jean, see 1:908.

L59. Cooperative College Biology Test. For additional information and reviews by Clarence H. Nelson and Joseph J. Schwab, see 3:551.

L60. Cooperative Zoology Test. For additional information and a review by Dael L. Wolfle, see 1:909.

L61. Examination in Biology—College Level. For additional information and a review by C. W. Horton, see 3:552.

L62. Examination in Biology—High-School Level. For additional information and reviews by C. W. Horton and Richard H. Jordan, see 3:553 (1 reference).

L63. Examination in Botany—College Level. For additional information and reviews by C. W. Horton and Clarence H. Nelson, see 3:554.

L64. General Biology Test: National Achievement Tests. For additional information and reviews by Elizabeth Hagen and Clark W. Horton, see 5:726.

L65. The Graduate Record Examinations Advanced Tests: Biology. For additional information, see 6:896; for a review by Clark W. Horton of an earlier form, see 5:727. For a review of the testing program, see 5:601.

L66. Hanes-Benz Biology Test. For additional information and a review by Clark W. Horton, see 2:1586 (1 reference).

L67. Iowa Every-Pupil Test in Biology. For additional information and a review by George W. Hunter, see 1:910.

L68. Nelson Biology Test. For additional information, see 5:728; for reviews by Clark W. Horton and Leland P. Johnson, see 4:605.

L69. Presson Biology Test. For additional information and reviews by Thomas F. Morrison and Dael L. Wolfle, see 2:1587 (2 references).

L70. Ruch-Cossmann Biology Test. For additional information and reviews by Thomas F. Morrison and Dael L. Wolfle, see 2:1588 (3 references).

L71. Semester Test for Biology. For additional information, see 4:599.

L72. Survey Test in Biological Science: California Survey Series. For additional information and reviews by Barbara F. Esser and Clarence H. Nelson, see 6:897.

L73. Test of Application of Principles in Biology: General Education Series. For additional information and reviews by Clark W. Horton and Clarence H. Nelson, see 4:606 (4 references).

L74. Williams Biology Test. For additional information and reviews by Clark W. Horton, Victor H. Noll, and Dael L. Wolfle, see 2:1589 (1 reference).

L75. Wisconsin Biology Test. For additional information, see 3:555.

CHEMISTRY

L76. A.C.S. Cooperative Examination: Biochemistry. For additional information, see 6:898 (2 references, 1 excerpt).

L77. A.C.S. Cooperative Examination for Graduate Placement in Analytical Chemistry. For additional information, see 6:899 (1 reference).

L78. A.C.S. Cooperative Examination for Graduate Placement in Organic Chemistry. For additional information, see 6:900 (1 reference).

L79. A.C.S. Cooperative Examination for Graduate Placement in Physical Chemistry. For additional information, see 6:901 (1 reference).

L80. A.C.S. Cooperative Examination in General Chemistry. For additional information and reviews by J. A. Campbell and William Hered, see 6:902 (3 references, 1 excerpt) ; for reviews by Frank P. Cassaretto and Palmer O. Johnson, see 5:732 (2 references) ; for a review by Kenneth E. Anderson of earlier forms, see 4:610 (1 reference) ; for reviews by Sidney J. French and Florence E. Hooper, see 3:557 (3 references) ; see also 2:1593 (5 references).

L81. A.C.S. Cooperative Examination in Physical Chemistry. For additional information, see 6:904 (1 reference) ; see also 4:612 (1 reference) ; for a review by Alfred S. Brown of an earlier form, see 3:559.

L82. A.C.S. Cooperative Examination: Inorganic Chemistry. For additional information and a review by Frank J. Fornoff, see 6:903 (1 reference, 1 excerpt).

L83. A.C.S. Cooperative Examination in Quantitative Analysis. For additional information, see 6:907 (1 reference) ; see also 5:735 (1 excerpt) ; for reviews by William B. Meldrum and William Rieman III of an earlier form, see 3:563.

L84. [A.C.S. Cooperative Examinations in Organic Chemistry.] For additional information, see 6:905 (4 references, 1 excerpt) ; for a review by Shailer Peterson of an earlier form, see 3:558 (1 reference).

L85. [A.C.S. Cooperative Examinations in Qualitative Analysis.] For additional information, see 6:906 (4 references, 2 excerpts) ; for a review by William Rieman III of earlier forms, see 4:608 (2 references) ; for reviews by William B. Meldrum and William Rieman III, see 3:562.

L86. A.C.S.-N.S.T.A. Cooperative Examination: High School Chemistry. For additional information and reviews by Frank J. Fornoff and William Hered, see 6:908 (5 references, 2 excerpts) ; for reviews by Edward G. Rietz and Willard G. Warrington, see 5:729.

L87. A.C.S.-N.S.T.A. Cooperative Examination: High School Chemistry [Advanced Level]. For additional information and reviews by Frank J. Fornoff and William Hered, see 6:909.

L88. Anderson Chemistry Test. For additional information and a review by Theo. A. Ashford, see 5:737; for a review by William Rieman III, see 4:613.

L89. Chemistry: Cooperative Science Tests. For additional information, see 6:909a.

L90. Chemistry: Every Pupil Scholarship Test. For additional information, see 6:910.

L91. Chemistry: Every Pupil Test. For additional information, see 6:911.

L92. Chemistry: Minnesota High School Achievement Examinations. For additional information, see 6:912; for a review by Edward G. Rietz of earlier forms, see 5:741.

L93. Chemistry Test: Affiliation Testing Program for Catholic Secondary Schools. For additional information and a review by Henry Chauncey, see 6:913. For a review of the complete program, see 6:758.

L94. Chemistry Test: State High School Tests for Indiana. For additional information, see 4:616;

for a review by Fred P. Frutchey of an earlier form, see 1:931.

L95. Clinton-Osborn-Ware General Chemistry Test. For additional information, see 2:1590.

L96. College Entrance Examination Board Achievement Test: Chemistry. For additional information and a review by William Hered, see 6:914 (4 references) ; for a review by Max D. Engelhart, see 5:742 (2 references) ; for a review by Evelyn Raskin, see 4:617 (4 references). For reviews of the testing program, see 6:760 (2 reviews).

L97. College Entrance Examination Board Advanced Placement Examination: Chemistry. For additional information, see 6:915 (1 reference) ; for a review by Theo. A. Ashford of an earlier form, see 5:743.

L98. College Entrance Examination Board Placement Tests: Chemistry Test. An inactive form of test L96; for additional information, see 6:916; for reference to reviews, see L96.

L99. Columbia Research Bureau Chemistry Test. For additional information and a review by Max D. Engelhart, see 2:1591.

L100. Cooperative Chemistry Test. For additional information and reviews by Frank P. Cassaretto and Willard G. Warrington, see 5:744; see also 4:618 (4 references) ; for a review by John H. Daugherty of an earlier form, see 3:561; for reviews by Charles L. Bickel and Louis M. Heil, see 2:1592; for reviews by Edward E. Cureton and W. B. Meldrum, see 1:932.

L101. Cooperative Chemistry Test: Educational Records Bureau Edition. For additional information and a review by Kenneth J. Jones, see 6:917; see also 5:745 (1 reference) and 4:619 (2 references).

L102. Cooperative Chemistry Test: Provisional Form. For additional information and a review by Max D. Engelhart, see 1:933.

L103. Cooperative Objective Tests in Organic Chemistry. For additional information, see 2:1595.

L104. Examination in Chemistry—High-School Level. For additional information and a review by Victor H. Noll, see 3:564 (1 reference).

L105. Examination in General Chemistry—College Level. For additional information and reviews by John H. Daugherty and Florence E. Hooper, see 3:565 (1 reference).

L106. General Chemistry Test: National Achievement Tests. For additional information and a review by J. A. Campbell, see 6:918.

L107. Glenn-Welton Chemistry Achievement Test. For additional information and reviews by Max D. Engelhart, Victor H. Noll, and Eugene A. Waters, see 2:1596 (1 excerpt) ; see also 1:934 (1 excerpt).

L108. The Graduate Record Examinations Advanced Tests: Chemistry. For additional information and a review by Max D. Engelhart, see 6:919. For a review of the testing program, see 5:601.

L109. Intermediate Chemistry Test. For additional information, see 2:1597.

L110. Iowa Placement Examinations: Chemistry Aptitude. For additional information and a review by Kenneth E. Anderson, see 4:621 (5 references) ; for a review by Theodore A. Ashford, see 3:566 (15 references).

L111. Iowa Placement Examinations: Chemistry Training. For additional information and a review by Kenneth E. Anderson, see 4:622 (1 reference); for a review by Theodore A. Ashford, see 3:567 (14 references).

L112. A Junior Chemistry Test. For additional information and reviews by Roy W. Stanhope and Mervyn L. Turner, see 5:747.

L113. Kirkpatrick Chemistry Test. For additional information and a review by Theodore A. Ashford, see 3:568 (1 reference).

L114. Qualitative Analysis Supplement for General Chemistry. For additional information and reviews by Frank P. Cassaretto and Palmer O. Johnson of the complete test, see 5:732 (2 references).

L115. Toledo Chemistry Placement Examination. For additional information and reviews by Kenneth E. Anderson and William R. Crawford, see 6:920 (1 reference).

L116. Wisconsin Achievement Tests: Chemistry. For additional information and a review by Victor H. Noll, see 3:569.

MISCELLANEOUS

L117. Cause and Effect Relationship Test in Science: Scientific Attitudes, Test 2. For additional information and a review by Louis M. Heil, see 2:1600.

L118. Common Science Vocabulary. For additional information, see 1:1124.

L119. Cooperative Geology Test. For additional information, see 3:579.

L120. Examination in Astronomy—College Level. For additional information, see 3:578.

L121. Examination in Meteorology—High-School Level. For additional information, see 3:580.

L122. The Facts About Science. For additional information, see 6:921.

L123. The Graduate Record Examinations Advanced Tests: Geology. For additional information, see 6:922. For a review of the testing program, see 5:601.

L124. Measurement of Observation and Understanding of Physical Phenomena and Life Processes. For additional information, see 4:631.

L125. The New Air World. For additional information, see 4:632.

L126. Scientific Attitudes. For additional information, see 1:1135.

L127. Scientific Methods: Test 1, Controlled Experimentation Test in Science. For additional information, see 1:1136.

L128. Scientific Thinking: Every Pupil Test. For additional information and a review by Victor H. Noll, see 1:1137.

L129. Steps in Problem Solving. For additional information, see 1:1138.

L130. Test of Chemical Comprehension. For additional information, see 6:923.

L131. Test of Reasoning in Conservation. For additional information, see 6:924 (1 reference).

L132. Test on Understanding Science (TOUS). For additional information, see 6:925 (3 references).

PHYSICS

L133. Application of Principles in Physical Science: Test 1.34. For additional information, see 2:1606 (2 references); for revised edition, see L43.

L134. College Entrance Examination Board Achievement Test: Physics. For additional information, see 6:926 (4 references); for a review by Theodore G. Phillips of an earlier form, see 5:749 (2 references); for a review by Palmer O. Johnson, see 4:633 (3 references). For reviews of the testing program, see 6:760 (2 reviews).

L135. College Entrance Examination Board Advanced Placement Examination: Physics. For additional information, see 6:927 (2 references); for a review by Leo Nedelsky of an earlier form, see 5:750.

L136. College Entrance Examination Board Placement Tests: Physics Test. An inactive form of test L134; for additional information, see 6:928.

L137. Columbia Research Bureau Physics Test. For additional information and a review by Eugene A. Waters, see 2:1607 (1 reference).

L138. Cooperative Physics Test. For additional information and a review by Theodore G. Phillips, see 5:751 (1 reference); see also 4:634 (2 references); for a review by G. P. Cahoon of earlier forms, see 3:581; for reviews by Andrew Longacre, Alvin W. Schindler, and Ralph K. Watkins, see 2:1608; for reviews by Ernest E. Bayles and A. W. Hurd, see 1:1088.

L139. Cooperative Physics Test: Educational Records Bureau Edition. For additional information, see 6:929; see also 5:752 (1 reference) and 4:635 (2 references).

L140. Cooperative Physics Tests for College Students. For additional information and a review by Edgar P. Slack, see 3:582 (1 reference); for a review by Alan T. Waterman, see 2:1609 (4 references); for a review by Paul A. Northrop, see 1:1089.

L141. Dunning Physics Test. For additional information and a review by Robert M. W. Travers, see 5:753; for a review by G. P. Cahoon, see 4:636.

L142. Examination in Electricity and Magnetism—College Level. For additional information, see 3:583.

L143. Examination in Electron Tubes and Circuits. For additional information, see 3:584.

L144. Examination in Physics—College Level. For additional information, see 3:586.

L145. Examination in Physics—High-School Level. For additional information and reviews by G. P. Cahoon and Palmer O. Johnson, see 3:585.

L146. Fulmer-Schrammel Physics Test. For additional information and reviews by Palmer O. Johnson and Alvin W. Schindler, see 2:1610.

L147. General Physics Test: National Achievement Tests. For additional information and a review by Theodore G. Phillips, see 6:930.

L148. The Graduate Record Examinations Advanced Tests: Physics. For additional information and a review by Theodore G. Phillips, see 6:931; for a review by Leo Nedelsky of an earlier form, see 5:754. For a review of the testing program, see 5:601.

L149. Hurd Test in High School Physics. For additional information and reviews by Andrew Longacre and Paul A. Northrop, see 2:1611.

L150. Iowa Every-Pupil Test in Physics. For additional information and reviews by Ernest E. Bayles and Archer W. Hurd, see 1:1091.

L151. Iowa Placement Examinations: Physics Aptitude. For additional information and a review by John W. French, see 4:638 (2 references); for a review by Robert M. W. Travers, see 3:587 (4 references).

L152. Iowa Placement Examinations: Physics Training. For additional information and a review by G. P. Cahoon, see 4:639 (2 references).

L153. A Junior Physics Test. For additional information and reviews by Roy W. Stanhope and Mervyn L. Turner, see 5:755.

L154. Physics: Cooperative Science Tests. For additional information, see 6:931a.

L155. Physics: Every Pupil Scholarship Test. For additional information, see 6:932.

L156. Physics: Every Pupil Test. For additional information, see 6:933.

L157. Physics: Minnesota High School Achievement Examinations. For additional information and a review by Irvin J. Lehmann, see 6:934.

L158. Physics Test: State High School Tests for Indiana. For additional information, see 4:642; for a review by A. W. Hurd of an earlier form, see 1:1092.

L159. Physics Test (Traditional and PSSC): Affiliation Testing Program for Catholic Secondary Schools. For additional information and a review by Henry Chauncey, see 6:935. For a review of the complete program, see 6:758.

L160. Tests of the Physical Science Study Committee. For additional information and reviews by George G. Mallinson and Leo Nedelsky, see 6:936 (1 reference).

L161. Torgerson-Rich-Ranney Tests in High School Physics. For additional information and reviews by Palmer O. Johnson and Paul A. Northrop, see 2:1612.

L162. 20th Century Test for Physics. For additional information, see 4:643.

L163. Wisconsin Physics Test. For additional information, see 3:589 (1 reference); for a review by Louis M. Heil, see 2:1613.

SENSORY-MOTOR

M1. Harris Tests of Lateral Dominance. For additional information, see 5:761 (1 reference); for reviews by William G. Peacher and Miles A. Tinker of an earlier edition, see 4:644; see also 3:466 (1 excerpt).

M2. Leavell Hand-Eye Coordinator Tests. For additional information, see 6:937.

M3. Moore Eye-Hand Coordination and Color-Matching Test. For additional information, see 5:872 (1 reference); for reviews by Norman Frederiksen and Jay L. Otis, see 4:750 (6 references).

M4. Pre-Tests of Vision, Hearing, and Motor Coordination. For additional information, see 4:645.

M5. Robbins Speech Sound Discrimination and Verbal Imagery Type Tests. For additional information and a review by Louis M. DiCarlo, see 6:938.

HEARING

M6. ADC Audiometers. For additional information, see 5:762.

M7. Ambco Audiometers. For additional information, see 6:939.

M8. Auditory Discrimination Test. For additional information and a review by Louis M. DiCarlo, see 6:940 (2 references).

M9. Auditory Tests. For additional information, see 6:941 (20 references).

M10. Audivox Audiometers. For additional information and a review by Louis M. DiCarlo, see 6:942.

M11. Beltone Audiometers. For additional information, see 6:943. For comments by Louis M. DiCarlo on screening audiometers in general and specific comments on Model 9-C and three other portable audiometers, see 6:942.

M12. The Children's Auditory Test. For additional information, see 6:944.

M13. Eckstein Audiometers. For additional information, see 6:945.

M14. Grason-Stadler Audiometers. For additional information, see 6:946 (6 references).

M15. Maico Audiometers. For additional information, see 6:947 (2 references); see also 5:763 (4 references). For comments by Louis M. DiCarlo on screening audiometers in general and specific comments on Model MA-2B and three other portable audiometers, see 6:942.

M16. Maico Hearing Impairment Calculator. For additional information, see 6:948.

M17. The Massachusetts Hearing Test. For additional information, see 6:949 (10 references).

M18. New Group Pure Tone Hearing Test. For additional information, see 6:950 (3 references).

M19. [Rush Hughes (PB 50): Phonetically Balanced Lists 5–12.] For additional information, see 6:951 (6 references).

M20. Sonotone Pure-Tone Audiometers. For additional information, see 6:951a.

M21. Stycar Hearing Tests. For additional information, see 6:952.

M22. Tests for the Hearing of Speech by Deaf People. For additional information, see 2:1526.1 (1 reference, 3 excerpts).

M23. Western Electric Audiometer. For additional information, see 3:475 (9 references); replaced by M10.

M24. Zenith Audiometers. For additional information, see 6:953. For comments by Louis M. DiCarlo on screening audiometers in general and specific comments on Model ZA-100-T and three other portable audiometers, see 6:942.

MOTOR

M25. Brace Scale of Motor Ability. For additional information and a review by Anna S. Espenschade, see 5:766 (17 references).

M26. Edmiston Motor Capacity Test. For additional information, see 4:649.

M27. The Lincoln-Oseretsky Motor Development Scale. For additional information and a review by Anna Espenschade, see 5:767 (10 references). For an earlier edition, see M28.

M28. Oseretsky Tests of Motor Proficiency: A Translation From the Portuguese Adaptation. For additional information and a review by Anna Espenschade, see 4:650 (10 references); see also 3:472 (6 references, 1 excerpt). For a revised edition, see M27.

M29. The Rail-Walking Test. For additional information and a review by William Sloan, see 4:652.

M30. V.D.L. Psychomotor Scale for the Measurement of Manual Ability. For additional information and reviews by Anna Espenschade and William Sloan, see 4:653 (1 reference).

VISION

M31. A-B-C Vision Test for Ocular Dominance. For additional information and a review by Miles A. Tinker, see 4:654; see also 3:459 (5 references).

M32. AO H-R-R Pseudoisochromatic Plates. For additional information, see 5:768 (11 references); see also 4:661 (8 references) and 3:473 (9 references, 1 excerpt).

M33. AO School Vision Screening Test. For additional information, see 5:769 (4 references).

M34. AO Sight Screener. For additional information, see 5:770 (8 references); for reviews by Henry A. Imus and F. Nowell Jones, see 3:460 (7 references).

M35. The Atlantic City Eye Test. For additional information, see 6:954 (1 reference).

M36. Burnham-Clark-Munsell Color Memory Test. For additional information, see 5:771 (1 reference).

M37. The Color Aptitude Test. For additional information, see 5:772.

M38. Dvorine Color Discrimination Screening Test. For additional information, see 3:461a (1 reference).

M39. Dvorine Pseudo-Isochromatic Plates. For additional information, see 6:955 (12 references); see also 5:773 (13 references, 3 excerpts); for the original edition, see 3:462 (4 references, 6 excerpts).

M40. Eames Eye Test. For additional information and a review by Helen M. Robinson, see 6:956 (1 reference); for a review by Magdalen D. Vernon, see 5:774 (2 references); see also 3:463 (5 references).

M41. Farnsworth Dichotomous Test for Color Blindness: Panel D-15. For additional information and a review by Elsie Murray, see 4:656 (2 references); see also 3:464 (1 excerpt).

M42. The Farnsworth-Munsell 100-Hue Test for the Examination of Color Discrimination. For additional information, see 5:775 (1 reference); for a review by Elsie Murray, see 4:657 (2 references).

M43. Freeman Acuity-Tester. For additional information, see 5:776.

M44. Freeman Protometer. For additional information, see 5:777.

M45. Glenn Colorule. For additional information, see 4:658 (1 reference).

M46. The Illuminant-Stable Color Vision Test. For additional information, see 5:778 (2 references); for a review by Elsie Murray of the original edition, see 4:659 (2 references).

M47. Inter-Society Color Council Color Aptitude Test. For additional information, see 5:779 (5 references).

M48. Keystone Occupational Telebinocular. For additional information and a review by F. Nowell Jones, see 3:467 (43 references, 1 excerpt).

M49. Keystone Tests of Binocular Skill: An Adaptation of the Gray Oral Reading Check Tests for Use in the Keystone Telebinocular. For additional information, see 6:957 (1 reference).

M50. Keystone Visual Tests. For additional information, see 5:780 (18 references). For reference to reviews of a subtest, see K139.

M51. Massachusetts Vision Test. For additional information, see 5:781 (14 references); see also 3:468 (5 references, 1 excerpt).

M52. New Test for the Detection of Color-blindness. For additional information, see 3:469 (2 excerpts).

M53. New York School Vision Tester. For additional information and a review by Helen M. Robinson, see 6:958 (2 references).

M54. Ortho-Rater. For additional information, see 5:783 (59 references); for reviews by Henry A. Imus and F. Nowell Jones, see 3:471 (30 references).

M55. Perceptual Forms Test. For additional information and a review by Mary C. Austin, see 6:848 (6 references).

M56. Spache Binocular Reading Test. For additional information and a review by Helen M. Robinson, see 6:959; see also 5:784 (4 references); for a review by Albert J. Harris of the upper level, see 3:461 (4 references).

M57. Stycar Vision Test. For additional information, see 6:960.

M58. T/O Vision Testers. For additional information, see 6:961 (1 reference).

M59. Test for Colour-Blindness. For additional information, see 6:962 (58 references).

M60. Test of Color Blindness. For additional information, see 3:474.

SOCIAL STUDIES

N1. American History—Government—Problems of Democracy: Acorn Achievement Tests. For additional information and a review by Richard E. Gross, see 5:785; for a review by Howard R. Anderson, see 3:590.

N2. American School Achievement Tests: Part 4, Social Studies and Science. For additional information, see 6:963. For reviews of the complete battery, see 6:2 (2 reviews), 5:1 (2 reviews), 4:1 (1 review), and 3:1 (2 reviews).

N3. Beard-Erbe Social Science Tests. For additional information and a review by Kenneth E. Gell, see 2:1614; for a review by Edgar B. Wesley, see 1:1144.

N4. Christian Democracy Test (Civics, Sociology, Economics): Affiliation Testing Program for Catholic Secondary Schools. For additional information and a review by Henry Chauncey, see 6:964. For a review of the complete program, see 6:758.

N5. Citizenship: Every Pupil Scholarship Test. For additional information, see 6:965.

N6. College Entrance Examination Board Achievement Test: American History and Social Studies. For additional information and a review by Howard R. Anderson, see 6:966; for a review by Ralph W. Tyler of an earlier form, see 5:786; for a review by Robert L. Thorndike, see 4:662. For reviews of the testing program, see 6:760 (2 reviews).

N7. College Entrance Examination Board Achievement Test: European History and World Cultures. For additional information and a review by David K. Heenan, see 6:967.

N8. Cooperative General Achievement Tests: Test 1, Social Studies. For additional information, see 6:968; see also 4:668 (3 references); for a review by Harry D. Berg of earlier forms, see 3:596. For reviews of the complete battery, see 6:7 (1 review), 5:6 (1 review), 4:5 (1 review), and 3:3 (1 review).

N9. Cooperative Social Studies Test for Grades 7, 8, and 9. For additional information and a review by Hilda Taba, see 4:663; for reviews by Robert A. Davis and Edgar B. Wesley of earlier forms, see 3:592.

N10. Cooperative Test of Social Studies Abilities. For additional information and a review by Roy A. Price, see 2:1615; for a review by Howard R. Anderson, see 1:1146.

N11. The Greig Social Studies Test. For additional information and a review by David R. Krathwohl, see 5:788.

N12. Historical Development and Cultural Change. For additional information, see 1:1147.

N13. History and Civics Test: Municipal Tests: National Achievement Tests. For additional information and a review by Howard R. Anderson, see 5:790; for a review by Harry D. Berg, see 4:664. For reviews of the complete battery, see 5:18 (1 review), 4:20 (1 review), and 2:1191 (2 reviews).

N14. Illinois Teachers College Cooperative Social Science Test. For additional information and a review by Harry D. Berg, see 3:593.

N15. Indiana History. For additional information, see 4:691.

N16. Melbo Social Science Survey Test. For additional information and reviews by Howard R. Anderson and R. M. Tryon, see 2:1616 (2 references); for a review by Alvin C. Eurich, see 1:1150.

N17. Metropolitan Achievement Tests: [Social Studies]. For additional information and reviews by Richard E. Gross and Robert J. Solomon, see 6:970. For reviews of the complete battery, see 6:15 (3 reviews), 4:18 (1 review), 2:1189 (2 reviews), and 1:874 (3 reviews).

N18. Sequential Tests of Educational Progress: Social Studies. For additional information and reviews by Jonathon C. McLendon and Donald W. Oliver, see 6:971 (1 reference); for reviews by Richard E. Gross, S. A. Rayner, and Ralph W. Tyler, see 5:792. For reviews of the complete battery, see 6:25 (2 reviews) and 5:24 (2 reviews, 1 excerpt).

N19. Shearer Social Studies Test. For additional information and a review by Raymond C. Norris, see 5:793 (1 reference).

N20. Social Situation Interview. For additional information, see 1:1152.

N21. Social Studies: Every Pupil Scholarship Test. For additional information, see 6:972.

N22. Social Studies: Minnnesota High School Achievement Examinations. For additional information, see 6:973.

N23. Social Studies: National Teacher Examinations. For additional information and a review by Harry D. Berg, see 6:974. For reviews of the testing program, see 6:700 (1 review), 5:538 (3 reviews), and 4:802 (1 review).

N24. Social Studies: Teacher Education Examination Program. An inactive form of test N23; for additional information, see 6:975; for a reference to a review, see N23. For a review of the testing program, see 5:543.

N25. Social Studies Test: Acorn National Achievement Tests. For additional information and a review by Edgar B. Wesley, see 4:666.

N26. Social Studies Test: National Achievement Tests. For additional information, see 5:798; for a review by Ray G. Wood, see 3:594.

N27. Social Studies 12 (American Problems): Minnesota High School Achievement Examinations. For additional information, see 6:976.

N28. Stanford Achievement Test: Social Studies Test. For additional information, see 6:977; for a review by Harry D. Berg of an earlier edition, see 5:799; for a review by Ray G. Wood, see 3:595. For reviews of the complete battery, see 6:26 (1 review, 1 excerpt), 5:25 (1 review), 4:25 (2 reviews), and 3:18 (2 reviews).

N29. Survey Test in the Social Studies: Cooperative General Achievement Test, Part 1. For additional information and a review by Hilda Taba, see 2:1618; for a review by Harold Gulliksen, see 1:870.

N30. T.C. Social Studies Test. For additional information, see 6:978.

N31. Test of Critical Thinking in the Social Studies: Elementary School Series. For additional information and reviews by Warren G. Findley, Pedro T. Orata, and G. M. Ruch, see 2:1619 (1 excerpt).

N32. Understanding of Basic Social Concepts: The Iowa Tests of Educational Development, Test 1. For additional information and a review by Morey J. Wantman, see 6:969. For reviews of the complete battery, see 6:14 (2 reviews), 5:17 (2 reviews), 4:17 (1 review), and 3:12 (3 reviews).

N33. Wesley Test in Social Terms. For additional information and a review by Howard R. Anderson, see 2:1622 (3 references).

CONTEMPORARY AFFAIRS

N34. Contemporary Affairs: Every Pupil Test. For additional information, see 6:979.

N35. Cooperative Contemporary Affairs Test for College Students. For additional information and reviews by Benjamin S. Bloom and John V. McQuitty, see 4:4 (4 references); for a review by H. T. Morse, see 3:2 (12 references); for a review by Ralph W. Tyler, see 2:1182 (5 references); for a review by Paul M. Limbert, see 1:948.

N36. Cooperative Contemporary Affairs Test for High School Classes. For additional information and reviews by John M. Stalnaker and R. M. Tryon, see 2:1183; for reviews by Howard R. Anderson and J. Wayne Wrightstone, see 1:950.

N37. Cooperative Current Literature and Arts Test for High School Classes. For additional information and reviews by Walter Barnes and H. H. Giles, see 1:949.

N38. Cooperative Test on Foreign Affairs. For additional information and a review by Christine McGuire, see 6:980 (1 reference, 1 excerpt).

N39. Cooperative Test on Recent Social and Scientific Developments. For additional information and a review by Roger T. Lennon, see 4:7 (2 references); for reviews by Ernest W. Tiegs, Ralph W. Tyler, and Edgar B. Wesley, see 3:5.

N40. Current Affairs: Every Pupil Scholarship Test. For additional information, see 6:981.

N41. Iowa Every-Pupil Test in Understanding of Contemporary Affairs. For additional information and a review by Alvin C. Eurich, see 1:951.

N42. Nationwide Current Events Examination. For additional information, see 6:982.

N43. New York Times Current Affairs Test. For additional information, see 6:983.

N44. New York Times Current Affairs Test for Colleges. For additional information, see 6:984.

N45. Newsweek Current News Test. For additional information, see 6:985.

N46. Newsweek NewsQuiz. For additional information, see 6:986.

ECONOMICS

N47. Cooperative Economics Test. For additional information, see 3:597; for a review by Edgar B. Wesley, see 2:1624.

N48. Economics Test: State High School Tests for Indiana. For additional information, see 4:670.

N49. The Graduate Record Examinations Advanced Tests: Economics. For additional information, see 6:987 (1 reference). For a review of the testing program, see 5:601.

N50. Hills Economics Test. For additional information, see 4:673.

N51. Iowa Every-Pupil Test in Economics. For additional information, see 1:1148.

N52. A Standard Achievement Test in Economic Understanding for Secondary Schools. For additional information, see 6:988.

N53. Test of Economic Understanding. For additional information, see 6:989.

N54. 20th Century Test for Economics. For additional information, see 4:671.

GEOGRAPHY

N55. Analytical Scales of Attainment in Geography. For additional information and a review by Ernest C. Witham, see 2:1625.

N56. Brandywine Achievement Test in Geography for Secondary Schools. For additional information, see 6:990.

N57. Coordinated Scales of Attainment: Geography. For additional information, see 5:801. For reviews of the complete battery, see 4:8 (1 review) and 3:6 (4 reviews).

N58. Economic Geography: Midwest High School Achievement Examinations. For additional information concerning earlier forms, see 5:803.

N59. Emporia Geography Test. For additional information and reviews by Edwin H. Reeder and Agatha Townsend, see 3:598.

N60. Fourth Grade Geography Test. For additional information and reviews by Elaine Forsyth [Cook] and Agatha Townsend, see 3:599 (1 reference).

N61. Geography Ability Test: Gibson's Attainment Tests. For additional information, see 1:990.

N62. Geography: Every Pupil Scholarship Test. For additional information, see 6:991.

N63. [Geography]: Every Pupil Test. For additional information, see 6:992.

N64. Geography Test: Municipal Tests: National Achievement Tests. For additional information, see 5:806; for a review by Edwin H. Reeder, see 4:676. For reviews of the complete battery, see 5:18 (1 review), 4:20 (1 review), and 2:1191 (2 reviews).

N65. Geography Test: National Achievement Tests. For additional information, see 4:677; for a review by Elaine Forsyth [Cook], see 3:600.

N66. Modern Geography and Allied Social Studies. For additional information and reviews by Edith M. Huddleston and Edwin H. Reeder, see 4:678.

N67. Physical Geography: Every Pupil Scholarship Test. For additional information, see 6:993.

N68. Survey Test in Geography: California Survey Series. For additional information and a review by Jonathon C. McLendon, see 6:994.

N69. Tate Economic Geography Test. For additional information and a review by Marguerite Uttley, see 3:601.

N70. Wiedefeld-Walther Geography Test. For additional information and a review by Marguerite Uttley, see 3:602; for reviews by Anna Parsek and Marie E. Trost, see 2:1626.

N71. World Geography: Every Pupil Scholarship Test. For additional information, see 6:995.

N72. World Geography Test: Dominion Tests. For additional information and a review by Edwin H. Reeder, see 3:603.

HISTORY

N73. American Council European History Test. For additional information and a review by S. P. McCutchen, see 2:1628.

N74. American History: Every Pupil Scholarship Test. For additional information, see 6:996.

N75. American History: Every Pupil Test. For additional information, see 6:997.

N76. American History Test: Affiliation Testing Program for Catholic Secondary Schools. For additional information and a review by Henry Chauncey, see 6:998. For a review of the complete program, see 6:758.

N77. American History Test: National Achievement Tests. For additional information, see 5:811; for reviews by Jacob S. Orleans and Wallace Taylor, see 2:1630.

N78. American History Test: State High School Tests for Indiana. For additional information, see 4:682.

N79. Analytical Scales of Attainment in American History. For additional information and reviews by Wilbur F. Murra and Margaret Willis, see 2:1631.

N80. Ancient History: Every Pupil Scholarship Test. For additional information, see 6:999.

N81. Bowman United States History Test. For additional information and a review by W. C. McCall (with Grace Graham), see 2:1632.

N82. College Entrance Examination Board Advanced Placement Examination: American History. For additional information and a review by Harry D. Berg, see 6:1000 (1 reference); for reviews by James A. Field, Jr. and Christine McGuire of an earlier form, see 5:812.

N83. College Entrance Examination Board Advanced Placement Examination: European History. For additional information, see 6:1001 (2 references).

N84. Cooperative American History Test. For additional information and reviews by Dorothy C. Adkins and Martha E. Layman, see 4:684 (2 references); see also 3:604 (3 references); for a review by Margaret Willis of an earlier form, see 2:1633; for a review by Edgar B. Wesley, see 1:1014.

N85. Cooperative Ancient History Test. For additional information, see 4:685; for a review by S. P. McCutchen, see 2:1634; for a review by Wilbur F. Murra of an earlier form, see 1:1015.

N86. Cooperative Modern European History Test. For additional information, see 4:686; for a review by Lavone A. Hanna of an earlier form, see 2:1635; for reviews by A. C. Krey and S. P. McCutchen, see 1:1016.

N87. Cooperative Topical Tests in American History. For additional information, see 6:1002.

N88. Cooperative World History Test. For additional information and a review by David K. Heenan, see 5:814; for a review by Kenneth E. Gell of an earlier form, see 2:1636; for a review by R. M. Tryon, see 1:1017.

N89. Coordinated Scales of Attainment: History. For additional information, see 5:815. For reviews of the complete battery, see 4:8 (1 review) and 3:6 (4 reviews).

N90. Crary American History Test. For additional information and a review by Frederick H. Stutz, see 5:816 (2 references); for a review by Edgar B. Wesley, see 4:688.

N91. Cummings World History Test. For additional information, see 5:817 (1 reference); for reviews by Dorothy C. Adkins and Howard R. Anderson, see 4:689.

N92. Ely-King Interpretation Tests in American History. For additional information and reviews by Clinton C. Conrad and Edgar B. Wesley, see 2:1637.

N93. Emporia History Test. For additional information, see 1:1018.

N94. Examination in American History. For additional information and a review by Howard R. Anderson, see 3:607 (1 reference).

N95. Examination in Modern European History. For additional information and a review by Frederick H. Stutz, see 3:608.

N96. Examination in World History—High-School Level. For additional information and reviews by Dorothy C. Adkins and Wallace W. Taylor, see 3:609.

N97. The Graduate Record Examinations Advanced Tests: History. For additional information, see 6:1003; for a review by Robert H. Ferrell of an earlier form, see 5:818. For a review of the testing program, see 5:601.

N98. History: Every Pupil Scholarship Test. For additional information, see 6:1004.

N99. Information Tests in American History. For additional information and a review by Roy A. Price, see 2:1638.

N100. Iowa Every-Pupil Test in United States History. For additional information, see 1:1020.

N101. Iowa Every-Pupil Test in World History. For additional information, see 1:1021.

N102. Kansas American History Test. For additional information and a review by W. H. Cartwright, see 3:610; for a review by Wilbur F. Murra, see 2:1639.

N103. Kansas Modern European History Test. For additional information and a review by Frederick H. Stutz, see 3:611; for a review by Clinton C. Conrad, see 2:1640.

N104. Kansas United States History Test. For additional information, see 6:1005; for reviews by Wayne A. Frederick and John Manning, see 5:820.

N105. Kniss World History Test. For additional information and reviews by Dorothy C. Adkins and Wallace W. Taylor, see 3:612 (2 references, 2 excerpts).

N106. Medieval History: Every Pupil Test. For additional information, see 1:1022.

N107. Modern History: Every Pupil Test. For additional information, see 1:1023.

N108. Objective Tests in American History. For additional information, see 6:1006.

N109. Objective Tests in World History. For additional information, see 6:1007.

N110. Semester Test for American History. For additional information, see 4:683.

N111. Semester Test for High School World History. For additional information, see 4:697.

N112. Social Studies 10 (American History): Minnesota High School Achievement Examinations. For additional information, see 6:1008; for a review by Howard R. Anderson of earlier forms, see 5:810.

N113. Social Studies 11 (World History): Minnesota High School Achievement Examinations. For additional information, see 6:1009.

N114. Survey Test in Introductory American History: California Survey Series. For additional information and a review by Richard E. Gross, see 6:1010.

N115. Survey Test in United States History. For additional information, see 3:613 (16 references).

N116. Taylor-Schrammel World History Test. For additional information and a review by J. R. Gerberich, see 2:1641.

N117. Test of Factual Relations in American History. For additional information and a review by Robert E. Keohane, see 2:1642 (1 reference); for a review by Wilbur F. Murra, see 1:1024.

N118. Understanding of American History. For additional information and a review by Elizabeth C. Adams, see 4:693.

N119. Wisconsin American History Test. For additional information, see 1:1025.

N120. World History: Every Pupil Scholarship Test. For additional information, see 6:1011.

N121. World History: Every Pupil Test. For additional information, see 6:1012.

N122. World History Test: Acorn National Achievement Tests. For additional information and a review by John Manning, see 5:825.

N123. World History Test: Affiliation Testing Program for Catholic Secondary Schools. For additional information and a review by Henry Chauncey, see 6:1013. For a review of the complete program, see 6:758.

N124. World History Test: State High School Tests for Indiana. For additional information, see 4:696.

POLITICAL SCIENCE

N125. American Civics and Government Tests for High Schools and Colleges. For additional information and a review by John H. Haefner, see 6:1013a.

N126. American Government and Citizenship: Every Pupil Test. For additional information, see 6:1014; for a review by Elizabeth C. Adams of the 1951 form, see 4:699.

N127. American Government: Every Pupil Scholarship Test. For additional information, see 6:1015.

N128. Attitude Toward Politicians Scale. For additional information and a review by Donald T. Campbell, see 5:829.

N129. Civic Vocabulary Test. For additional information and a review by I. G. Meddleton, see 5:830 (1 reference).

N130. Civics: Every Pupil Test. For additional information, see 1:1145.

N131. Constitution: Every Pupil Scholarship Test. For additional information, see 6:1016.

N132. Cooperative American Government Test. For additional information and a review by Frederic L. Ayer, see 4:702.

N133. Cooperative Community Affairs Test. For additional information and reviews by W. H. Cartwright, J. R. Gerberich, and Lavone A. Hanna, see 3:591 (1 reference).

N134. Dimond-Pflieger Problems of Democracy Test. For additional information and reviews by John H. Haefner and Douglas E. Scates, see 5:833 (1 reference).

N135. Duke University Political Science Information Test (American Government). For additional information, see 6:1017.

N136. Examination in Civics. For additional information and a review by Roy A. Price, see 3:616 (1 reference).

N137. Examination in Problems of Democracy —High-School Level. For additional information and a review by Lavone A. Hanna, see 3:617 (2 references).

N138. General Knowledge Test of Local, State, and National Government. For additional information and a review by Wayne A. Frederick, see 5:834.

N139. The Graduate Record Examinations Advanced Tests: Government. For additional information, see 6:1018; for a review by Christine McGuire of an earlier form, see 5:835. For a review of the testing program, see 5:601.

N140. Iowa Every-Pupil Test in American Government. For additional information, see 1:1019.

N141. Junior High School Civics Test: State High School Tests for Indiana. For additional information, see 4:704.

N142. The Kansas Constitution Test. For additional information and a review by David K. Heenan, see 5:836.

N143. Mordy-Schrammel Constitution Test. For additional information and a review by W. H. Cartwright, see 3:618.

N144. Mordy-Schrammel Elementary Civics Test. For additional information and a review by C. Robert Pace, see 3:619.

N145. Newspaper Reading Survey: What Do You Read? For additional information and reviews by Frederick H. Stutz and M. J. Wantman, see 5:837.

N146. Patterson Test or Study Exercises on the Constitution of the United States. For additional information, see 5:838.

N147. Patterson Test or Study Exercises on the Declaration of Independence. For additional information, see 5:839.

N148. Patterson's Tests on the Federal Constitution. For additional information, see 4:705.

N149. Peltier-Durost Civics and Citizenship Test. For additional information and reviews by Howard R. Anderson and Christine McGuire, see 6:1019.

N150. Principles of American Citizenship Test. For additional information and reviews by Howard R. Anderson and M. J. Wantman, see 5:841 (1 reference).

N151. Principles of Democracy Test. For additional information and reviews by William C. Bingham and John H. Haefner, see 6:1020.

N152. Senior High School Civics Test: For a One-Semester Course: State High School Tests for Indiana. For additional information, see 4:706.

N153. Senior High School Civics Test: State High School Tests for Indiana. For additional information, see 4:707.

N154. 20th Century Test for Civics. For additional information, see 4:701.

N155. Wesley Test in Political Terms. For additional information and a review by Howard R. Anderson, see 2:1621 (1 reference).

SOCIOLOGY

N156. Black-Schrammel Sociology Test. For additional information, see 4:708.

N157. Contemporary Problems. For additional information and a review by Harry D. Berg, see 5:832.

N158. The Graduate Record Examinations Advanced Tests: Sociology. For additional information and a review by J. Richard Wilmeth, see 6:1021. For a review of the testing program, see 5:601.

N159. Sare-Sanders Sociology Test. For additional information and a review by J. Richard Wilmeth, see 6:1022.

N160. Sociology: Every Pupil Scholarship Test. For additional information, see 5:844.

VOCATIONS

O1. Airman Qualifying Examination. For additional information, see 6:1023 (1 reference).

O2. [Aptitude Inventory.] For additional information and reviews by Leonard W. Ferguson and C. E. Jurgensen, see 6:1024 (1 reference, 1 excerpt).

O3. ETSA Tests. For additional information and reviews by Marvin D. Dunnette and Raymond A. Katzell, see 6:1025.

O4. General Adaptability Battery. For additional information, see 6:1026 (1 reference).

O5. Individual Placement Series. For additional information, see 6:1027.

O6. Personnel Selection and Classification Test. For additional information and reviews by Dorothy C. Adkins, George K. Bennett, and George A. Ferguson, see 3:690.

O7. Screening Tests for Apprentices. For additional information, see 6:1028.

O8. Steward Personnel Tests (Short Form). For additional information and reviews by Leonard V. Gordon and Lyman W. Porter, see 6:1029.

O9. Vocational Aptitude Examination, Type E-A. For additional information and reviews by D. Welty Lefever and Benjamin Shimberg, see 3:695 (1 reference); for reviews by Harold D. Carter and M. R. Trabue of an earlier edition, see 2:1679 (3 references).

CLERICAL

O10. A.C.E.R. Short Clerical Test. For additional information, see 6:1030.

O11. A.C.E.R. Speed and Accuracy Tests. For additional information, see 6:1031 (2 references) ; for a review by D. W. McElwain of an earlier form, see 4:719.

O12. Beginner's Clerical Test. For additional information and reviews by Stephen Hunka and Harry L. Stein, see 6:1032.

O13. Cardall Test of Clerical Perception. For additional information, see 6:1033.

O14. Checking Test. For additional information, see 6:1034.

O15. Classifying Test. For additional information, see 6:1035.

O16. Clerical Aptitude Test: Acorn National Aptitude Tests. For additional information, see 5:847 (1 reference) ; for reviews by Marion A. Bills, Donald G. Paterson, Henry Weitz, and E. F. Wonderlic, see 3:623.

O17. Clerical Perception Test. For additional information and reviews by Edward N. Hay, Raymond A. Katzell, Erwin K. Taylor, and E. F. Wonderlic, see 3:624 (1 excerpt).

O18. Clerical Test D: Extending—Verifying—Checking—Classifying. For additional information and reviews by Donald G. Paterson and John M. Willits, see 3:625.

O19. Clerical Tests 1 and 2. For additional information, see 5:848.

O20. Clerical Tests, Series N. For additional information, see 6:1036.

O21. Clerical Tests, Series V. For additional information, see 6:1037.

O22. Clerical Worker Examination. For additional information, see 6:1038.

O23. Cross Reference Test. For additional information and a review by Philip H. Kriedt, see 6:1039.

O24. Detroit Clerical Aptitudes Examination. For additional information and a review by E. F. Wonderlic, see 3:626 (1 reference) ; for reviews by Irving Lorge and M. W. Richardson of an earlier edition, see 2:1655.

O25. Group Test 20. For additional information and a review by E. G. Chambers, see 4:723 (2 references).

O26. Group Test 25 (Clerical). For additional information and a review by E. G. Chambers, see 4:724 (1 reference).

O27. Hay Tests for Clerical Aptitude. For additional information, see 5:849 (2 references) ; for reviews by Reign H. Bittner and Edward E. Cureton, see 4:725 (8 references).

O28. Martin Office Aptitude Tests. For additional information and reviews by D. Welty Lefever and Ross W. Matteson, see 4:726.

O29. Minnesota Clerical Test. For additional information, see 6:1040 (10 references) ; for a review by Donald E. Super, see 5:850 (46 references) ; for reviews by Thelma Hunt, R. B. Selover, Erwin K. Taylor, and E. F. Wonderlic, see 3:627 (22 references) ; for a review by W. D. Commins, see 2:1664 (18 references).

O30. National Institute of Industrial Psychology Clerical Test (North American Revision). For additional information and a review by Harry L. Stein, see 6:1041 ; for a review by R. B. Selover of the American revision, see 3:628 (4 references) ; for a review by Donald G. Paterson, see 2:1665 (2 references).

O31. Number Checking Test. For additional information, see 6:1042.

O32. Office Skills Achievement Test. For additional information and reviews by Douglas G. Schultz and Paul W. Thayer, see 6:1043.

O33. Office Worker Test. For additional information and reviews by Ray G. Price and Douglas G. Schultz, see 6:1044.

O34. O'Rourke Clerical Aptitude Test, Junior Grade. For additional information, see 5:851 (1 reference) ; for a review by Raymond A. Katzell, see 3:629 (3 references).

O35. Personnel Institute Clerical Tests. For additional information, see 5:852.

O36. Personnel Research Institute Clerical Battery. For additional information and reviews by Louise Witmer Cureton and Albert K. Kurtz, see 4:729. For a review of a subtest, see 4:211.

O37. Psychological Corporation General Clerical Test. For additional information and reviews by Edward E. Cureton and G. A. Satter, see 4:730 (4 references) ; for reviews by Edward N. Hay, Thelma Hunt, Raymond A. Katzell, and E. F. Wonderlic, see 3:630.

O38. Purdue Clerical Adaptability Test. For additional information and reviews by Mary Ellen Oliverio and Donald Spearritt, see 5:853 (2 references) ; for reviews by Edward N. Hay, Joseph E. Moore, and Alec Rodger of the previous edition, see 4:731.

O39. SRA Clerical Aptitudes. For additional information and reviews by Edward N. Hay and G. A. Satter, see 4:732.

O40. The Short Employment Tests. For additional information and a review by Leonard W. Ferguson, see 6:1045 (9 references) ; for a review by P. L. Mellenbruch, see 5:854 (16 references).

O41. Short Tests of Clerical Ability. For additional information and reviews by Philip H. Kriedt and Paul W. Thayer, see 6:1046.

O42. Speed Tabulation Test. For additional information, see 1:1082.

O43. Survey of Clerical Skills (SOCS): Individual Placement Series (Area IV). For additional information, see 6:1047.

O44. Survey of Working Speed and Accuracy. For additional information and reviews by Edward N. Hay, Donald G. Paterson, and Erwin K. Taylor, see 3:631.

O45. Thurstone Examination in Clerical Work. For additional information and reviews by John M. Willits and E. F. Wonderlic, see 3:632 (6 references).

O46. Turse Clerical Aptitudes Test. For additional information and reviews by Robert A. Jones and Donald Spearritt, see 5:855 (1 reference).

O47. V.G.C. Clerical Indicator. For additional information and a review by George A. Ferguson, see 4:735.

INTERESTS

O48. ABC Occupational Inventory. For additional information, see 4:736.

O49. Basic Interest Questionnaire: For Selecting Your Vocation or Avocation. For additional information, see 3:633 (1 excerpt).

O50. Brainard Occupational Preference Inventory. For additional information and a review by William C. Cottle, see 5:856 (2 references); for a review by Elmer D. Hinckley, see 4:737 (1 reference); for reviews by Edwin W. Davis and Herschel T. Manuel, see 3:634 (2 references); for reviews by Jack W. Dunlap and M. R. Trabue of the original edition, see 2:1675 (4 references); for a review by Everett B. Sackett, see 1:1176.

O51. Burke Inventory of Vocational Development. For additional information, see 6:1048.

O52. Career Finder. For additional information and reviews by Arthur C. MacKinney and Charles F. Warnath, see 6:1049.

O53. Career Incentive and Progress Blank. For additional information, see 2:1648.

O54. Chatterji's Non-Language Preference Record. For additional information, see 6:1050.

O55. Cleeton Vocational Interest Inventory. For additional information and reviews by Edward B. Greene, C. A. Oakley, and Arthur E. Traxler, see 3:635 (19 references, 1 excerpt); for reviews by Forrest A. Kingsbury and N. W. Morton, see 2:1682 (1 excerpt); for reviews by Albert S. Thompson, M. R. Trabue, and E. G. Williamson of an earlier edition, see 1:1181.

O56. College Planning Inventory, Senior College Edition. For additional information, see 6:1051.

O57. Curtis Interest Scale. For additional information and reviews by Warren T. Norman and Leona E. Tyler, see 6:1052.

O58. Devon Interest Test. For additional information and reviews by Arthur B. Royse and Alfred Yates, see 5:857 (3 references).

O59. Edmiston Inventory of Interest. For additional information and a review by Arthur E. Traxler, see 4:738 (1 reference).

O60. Fowler-Parmenter Self-Scoring Interest Record. For additional information and reviews by David P. Campbell and John W. French, see 6:1053 (2 references).

O61. The Geist Picture Interest Inventory. For additional information and reviews by Milton E. Hahn and Benjamin Shimberg, see 6:1054 (12 references, 2 excerpts).

O62. Geist Picture Interest Inventory: Deaf Form: Male. For additional information, see 6:1055 (1 reference).

O63. Gordon Occupational Check List. For additional information and reviews by John O. Crites and Kenneth B. Hoyt, see 6:1056.

O64. Gregory Academic Interest Inventory. For additional information and reviews by Paul S. Burnham, Lysle W. Croft, and Herbert A. Toops, see 3:636 (1 reference).

O65. The Guilford-Shneidman-Zimmerman Interest Survey. For additional information and reviews by George K. Bennett and Wilbur L. Layton, see 4:739 (2 references).

O66. The Guilford-Zimmerman Interest Inventory. For additional information and a review by Kenneth B. Hoyt, see 6:1057.

O67. Hackman-Gaither Vocational Interest Inventory. For additional information, see 6:1058 (4 references).

O68. Henderson Analysis of Interest. For additional information and reviews by Wilbur L. Layton and Donald E. Super, see 4:740.

O69. How Well Do You Know Your Interests. For additional information and a review by John R. Hills, see 6:1059 (1 reference, 1 excerpt); for reviews by Jerome E. Doppelt and Henry S. Dyer, see 5:859.

O70. Interest Check List. For additional information, see 5:860; for reviews by Milton L. Blum and Howard R. Taylor of the original edition, see 4:741.

O71. Interest Questionnaire for High School Students. For additional information and a review by Lysle W. Croft, see 3:637 (6 references).

O72. Inventory of Vocational Interests: Acorn National Aptitude Tests. For additional information and a review by John W. French, see 6:1060; for reviews by Marion A. Bills, Edward S. Bordin, Harold D. Carter, and Patrick Slater, see 3:638.

O73. Job Choice Inventory. For additional information, see 6:1061.

O74. Job Qualification Inventory. For additional information and reviews by Ralph F. Berdie and Stanley G. Dulsky, see 3:639 (5 references, 2 excerpts).

O75. Kuder General Interest Survey. For additional information, see 6:1061a.

O76. Kuder Preference Record—Occupational. For additional information and a review by David P. Campbell, see 6:1062 (13 references); for reviews by Edward S. Bordin and John W. Gustad, see 5:862.

O77. Kuder Preference Record—Vocational. For additional information and a review by Martin Katz, see 6:1063 (148 references); for reviews by Clifford P. Froehlich and John Pierce-Jones, see 5:863 (211 references); for reviews by Edward S. Bordin, Harold D. Carter, and H. M. Fowler, see 4:742 (146 references); for reviews by Ralph F. Berdie, E. G. Chambers, and Donald E. Super, see 3:640 (60 references, 1 excerpt); for reviews by A. B. Crawford and Arthur E. Traxler of an earlier edition, see 2:1671 (2 references).

O78. Motivation Indicator. For additional information and reviews by Norman Frederiksen and Arthur E. Traxler, see 3:641 (1 excerpt).

O79. Occupational Interest Blank. For additional information and reviews by Stanley G. Dulsky and J. B. Miner, see 2:1666; for reviews by W. V. Bingham and M. R. Trabue, see 1:1174.

O80. Occupational Interest Blank for Women. For additional information and reviews by Gwendolen Schneidler Dickson and Frances Oralind Triggs, see 3:642 (6 references).

O81. Occupational Interest Inventory. For additional information, see 6:1064 (6 references); for reviews by Martin Katz and Wilbur L. Layton, see

5:864 (20 references) ; for a review by Arthur H. Brayfield of the original edition, see 4:743 (20 references) ; for reviews by Edward S. Bordin and Stanley G. Dulsky, see 3:643.

O82. Occupational Interest Survey (With Pictures): Individual Placement Series (Area II). For additional information, see 6:1065.

O83. Occupational Interests: Self Analysis Scale. For additional information and a review by Stanley G. Dulsky, see 3:644.

O84. Picture Interest Inventory. For additional information and reviews by Ralph F. Berdie and Donald E. Super, see 6:1066 (4 references, 1 excerpt).

O85. Primary Business Interests Test. For additional information, see 6:1067 (2 references) ; for reviews by George K. Bennett, Glen U. Cleeton, and George A. Ferguson, see 3:645.

O86. Qualifications Record. For additional information and reviews by Arthur C. MacKinney and Charles F. Warnath, see 6:1068; see also O52.

O87. Rothwell-Miller Interest Blank. For additional information, see 5:867.

O88. Safran Vocational Interest Test. For additional information, see 6:1069 (1 reference).

O89. Self-Administering Vocational Interest Locator With Work Interest Picture. For additional information and a review by Donald E. Super, see 4:744.

O90. Strong Vocational Interest Blank for Men. For additional information and reviews by Alexander W. Astin and Edward J. Furst, see 6:1070 (189 references) ; see also 5:868 (153 references) ; for reviews by Edward S. Bordin and Elmer D. Hinckley, see 4:747 (98 references) ; see also 3:647 (104 references) ; for reviews by Harold D. Carter, John G. Darley, and N. W. Morton, see 2:1680 (71 references) ; for a review by John G. Darley of an earlier edition, see 1:1178.

O91. Strong Vocational Interest Blank for Women. For additional information, see 6:1071 (12 references) ; see also 5:869 (19 references) ; for a review by Gwendolen Schneidler Dickson, see 3:649 (36 references) ; for a review by Ruth Strang of an earlier edition, see 2:1681 (9 references) ; for a review by John G. Darley, see 1:1179.

O92. Thurstone Interest Schedule. For additional information and reviews by Norman Frederiksen and Donald E. Super, see 4:745 (1 reference).

O93. VALCAN Vocational Interest Profile (VIP). For additional information, see 6:1072.

O94. The Vocational Apperception Test. For additional information and reviews by Benjamin Balinsky and William E. Henry, see 4:146 (1 reference, 1 excerpt).

O95. Vocational Interest Analyses: A Six-Fold Analytical Extension of the Occupational Interest Inventory. For additional information and a review by Wilbur L. Layton, see 5:870 (1 reference) ; for a review by Julian C. Stanley, see 4:746.

O96. Vocational Interest Schedule. For additional information and a review by Donald E. Super, see 3:653 (8 references) ; for a review by J. B. Miner, see 2:1683 (4 references) ; for reviews by Harold D. Carter and N. W. Morton, see 1:1180.

O97. A Vocational Interest Test for College Women. For additional information and a review by Frances Oralind Triggs, see 3:654 (2 references).

O98. Vocational Inventory. For additional information and reviews by Edward S. Bordin, Harold D. Carter, and Donald E. Super, see 3:655 (4 references, 1 excerpt).

O99. Vocational Sentence Completion Blank. For additional information, see 6:1073 (4 references).

O100. William, Lynde & Williams Analysis of Interest. For additional information, see 6:1074.

O101. Young-Estabrooks Scale for Measuring Studiousness by Means of the Strong Vocational Interest Blank for Men. For additional information and a review by Edmund G. Williamson, see 1:904 (4 references).

O102. Your Educational Plans. For additional information and a review by Leo Goldman, see 6:1075 (1 reference, 1 excerpt).

MANUAL DEXTERITY

O102.1. APT Manual Dexterity Test. For additional information, see 6:1076.

O103. Benge HanDexterity Test. For additional information and reviews by C. H. Lawshe, Jr. and Joseph E. Moore, see 3:656.

O104. Benge Two Hand Coordination Test. For additional information and a review by Milton L. Blum, see 3:657.

O105. Crawford Small Parts Dexterity Test. For additional information and a review by Neil D. Warren, see 5:871 (8 references) ; for a review by Raymond A. Katzell, see 4:752 ; for a review by Joseph E. Moore, see 3:667.

O106. Hand-Tool Dexterity Test. For additional information and reviews by C. H. Lawshe, Jr. and Neil D. Warren, see 3:659 (2 references).

O107. Martin Peg Board (Finger Dexterity Test). For additional information, see 4:749.

O108. Mellenbruch Curve-Block Series. For additional information and reviews by William R. Grove and Willard A. Kerr, see 3:662 (1 reference).

O109. Minnesota Rate of Manipulation Test, [1946 Edition]. For additional information, see 6:1077 (24 references) ; for reviews by Edwin E. Ghiselli and John R. Kinzer, see 3:663 (22 references, 1 excerpt) ; for reviews by Lorene Teegarden and Morris S. Viteles, see 2:1662 (4 references).

O110. O'Connor Finger Dexterity Test. For additional information, see 6:1078 (32 references) ; for a review by Morris S. Viteles, see 2:1659 (15 references).

O111. O'Connor Tweezer Dexterity Test. For additional information, see 6:1079 (23 references) ; for a review by Morris S. Viteles, see 2:1678 (13 references).

O112. Pennsylvania Bi-Manual Worksample. For additional information and reviews by Edwin E. Ghiselli, Thomas W. Harrell, Albert Gibson Packard, and Neil D. Warren, see 3:665 (3 references).

O113. Purdue Hand Precision Test. For additional information, see 6:1080 (2 references).

O114. Purdue Pegboard. For additional information, see 6:1081 (15 references) ; for a review by Neil D. Warren, see 5:873 (11 references) ; see also 4:751

(12 references); for reviews by Edwin E. Ghiselli, Thomas W. Harrell, and Albert Gibson Packard, see 3:666 (3 references).

O115. Stromberg Dexterity Test. For additional information and a review by Julian C. Stanley, see 4:755 (1 reference).

MECHANICAL ABILITY

O116. A.C.E.R. Mechanical Comprehension Test. For additional information and reviews by John R. Jennings and Haydn S. Williams, see 5:874 (2 references); for a review by D. W. McElwain, see 4:756.

O117. A.C.E.R. Mechanical Reasoning Test. For additional information, see 6:1082; for reviews by John R. Jennings and Haydn S. Williams, see 5:875.

O118. Chriswell Structural Dexterity Test. For additional information, see 6:1083 (1 reference); for a review by A. Pemberton Johnson, see 5:876.

O119. College Entrance Examination Board Placement Tests: Spatial Relations Test. For additional information, see 6:1084 (4 references).

O120. College Entrance Examination Board Special Aptitude Test in Spatial Relations. For additional information and a review by Robert L. Thorndike, see 4:808.

O121. [Cox Mechanical and Manual Tests.] For additional information and reviews by C. A. Oakley and Alec Rodger, see 2:1652-3 (4 references).

O122. Crawford Spatial Relations Test. For additional information and a review by William R. Grove, see 3:658 (7 references).

O123. [Curtis Object Completion and Space Form Tests.] For additional information and reviews by Richard S. Melton and I. Macfarlane Smith, see 6:1085.

O124. Detroit Mechanical Aptitudes Examination. For additional information and reviews by Lloyd G. Humphreys and Dewey B. Stuit, see 3:668 (4 references); for a review by Irving Lorge, see 2:1656 (1 excerpt).

O125. Dynamicube Test of Power to Visualize. For additional information, see 1:1167.

O126. Flags: A Test of Space Thinking. For additional information and a review by I. Macfarlane Smith, see 6:1086.

O127. Form Relations Group Test. For additional information and a review by A. T. Welford, see 4:757 (10 references).

O128. Girls' Mechanical Assembly Test. For additional information and a review by Richard Ledgerwood, see 1:1032 (2 references).

O129. Group Test 80A. For additional information and reviews by E. G. Chambers and John Liggett, see 5:877.

O130. Group Test 81. For additional information and a review by E. G. Chambers, see 4:758 (5 references).

O131. Hazlehurst Primary Mechanical Ability Tests. For additional information, see 6:1087.

O132. MacQuarrie Test for Mechanical Ability. For additional information, see 4:759 (15 references);

see also 4:760 (1 excerpt); for reviews by John R. Kinzer, C. H. Lawshe, Jr., and Alec Rodger, see 3:661 (43 references).

O133. Mechanical Aptitude Test: Acorn National Aptitude Tests. For additional information, see 5:878; for reviews by Reign H. Bittner, James M. Porter, Jr., and Alec Rodger, see 3:669.

O134. Mechanical Information Questionnaire. For additional information, see 6:1088.

O135. Mechanical Movements: A Test of Mechanical Comprehension. For additional information and a review by William A. Owens, see 6:1089.

O136. Mellenbruch Mechanical Motivation Test. For additional information and reviews by Arthur H. Brayfield and John B. Morris, see 5:879; for reviews by Lloyd G. Humphreys and C. A. Oakley of the original edition, see 3:670.

O137. Minnesota Assembly Test. For additional information and a review by William R. Grove, see 3:671 (11 references).

O138. Minnesota Spatial Relations Test. For additional information and a review by Milton L. Blum, see 3:664 (18 references); for a review by Lorene Teegarden, see 2:1663 (10 references).

O139. Moray House Space Test 2. For additional information and a review by E. Anstey, see 6:1090 (4 references).

O140. Mutilated Cubes Test of Power to Visualize. For additional information, see 1:1173.

O141. N.I.I.P. Squares Test. For additional information and a review by J. F. Clark, see 5:880 (9 references).

O142. O'Connor Wiggly Block. For additional information, see 6:1091 (27 references).

O143. O'Rourke Mechanical Aptitude Test. For additional information, see 5:882; for reviews by Jay L. Otis and George A. Satter, see 3:672 (8 references); for a review by Herbert A. Landry, see 2:1668.

O144. Perceptual Mechanics Test. For additional information and a review by Charles M. Harsh, see 3:673.

O145. Prognostic Test of Mechanical Abilities. For additional information and reviews by Willard A. Kerr and Douglas G. Schultz, see 4:761 (1 reference); see also 3:674 (1 excerpt).

O146. Purdue Mechanical Adaptability Test. For additional information, see 4:762 (6 references); for reviews by Jay L. Otis and Dewey B. Stuit, see 3:676.

O147. Purdue Mechanical Performance Test. For additional information, see 5:883 (1 reference).

O148. Revised Minnesota Paper Form Board Test. For additional information, see 6:1092 (16 references); for a review by D. W. McElwain, see 5:884 (29 references); for reviews by Clifford E. Jurgensen and Raymond A. Katzell, see 4:763 (38 references); for a review by Dewey B. Stuit, see 3:677 (48 references); for a review by Alec Rodger, see 2:1673 (9 references).

O149. SRA Mechanical Aptitudes. For additional information and reviews by Alec Rodger and Douglas G. Schultz, see 4:764.

O150. Spatial Tests 1, 2, and 3. For additional information, see 6:1093 (4 references); for reviews by E. G. Chambers and Charles T. Myers of tests 1 and 2, see 5:885; for a review by E. A. Peel of test 1, see 4:753.

O151. Staticube Test of Power to Visualize. For additional information, see 1:1177.

O152. Stenquist Assembling Test. For additional information and a review by William R. Grove, see 3:679 (10 references).

O153. Stenquist Mechanical Aptitude Test. For additional information and a review by James M. Porter, Jr., see 3:678 (18 references).

O154. Survey of Mechanical Insight. For additional information and a review by Arthur H. Brayfield, see 5:886 (3 references); for reviews by Reign H. Bittner, Jay L. Otis, and Shailer Peterson of the original edition, see 3:680.

O155. Survey of Object Visualization. For additional information and a review by William J. Micheels, see 5:887 (5 references); for reviews by Charles M. Harsh, Clifford E. Jurgensen, Shailer Peterson, and Patrick Slater of the original edition, see 3:681.

O156. Survey of Space Relations Ability. For additional information and a review by D. W. McElwain, see 5:888 (4 references); for reviews by E. G. Chambers, Clifford E. Jurgensen, and James M. Porter, Jr., see 3:682.

O157. Tests of Mechanical Comprehension. For additional information, see 6:1094 (15 references); see also 5:889 (46 references); for a review by N. W. Morton, see 4:766 (28 references); for reviews by Charles M. Harsh, Lloyd G. Humphreys, and George A. Satter, see 3:683 (19 references).

O158. Three-Dimensional Space Test. For additional information, see 6:1095.

O159. Tool Knowledge Test [Australian Council for Educational Research]. For additional information and reviews by J. F. Clark and I. G. Meddleton, see 5:890.

O160. Tool Knowledge Test [Richardson, Bellows, Henry & Co., Inc.]. For additional information, see 6:1096.

O161. Two-Dimensional Space Test. For additional information, see 6:1097.

O162. V.G.C. Object Visualization Indicator. For additional information, see 4:767.

O163. V.G.C. Space Relations Ability Indicator. For additional information, see 4:768.

O164. The Vincent Mechanical Models Test A (Industrial). For additional information and a review by A. T. Welford, see 4:769 (7 references).

O165. Weights and Pulleys: A Test of Intuitive Mechanics. For additional information and a review by William A. Owens, see 6:1098.

MISCELLANEOUS

O166. Adjusted Graphic Analysis Chart. For additional information, see 2:1644 (1 reference).

O167. Admission Test for Graduate Study in Business. For additional information, see 5:910.

O168. Aids to Self-Analysis and Vocational Planning Inventory. For additional information, see 2:1645 (1 reference).

O169. The Biographical Index. For additional information and reviews by John K. Hemphill and Richard S. Melton, see 6:1099.

O170. Breadth of Information. For additional information, see 6:1100.

O171. Business Judgment Test. For additional information, see 6:1101 (4 references); for a review by Edward B. Greene, see 5:893.

O172. Cancellation Test. For additional information and a review by Herbert A. Tonne, see 5:894; for a review by Joseph E. King, see 3:684.

O173. Cardall Test of Practical Judgment. For additional information, see 6:1102 (4 references); see also 4:784 (6 references); for reviews by Glen U. Cleeton and Howard R. Taylor of an earlier edition, see 3:694.

O174. Check List for Self-Guidance in Choosing an Occupation. For additional information, see 2:1649.

O175. Check List of Occupations. For additional information, see 2:1650.

O176. Conference Meeting Rating Scale. For additional information, see 6:1103.

O177. Dartnell Self-Administered Employee Opinion Unit. For additional information and a review by Raymond A. Katzell, see 6:1104.

O178. Employee Opinion Survey. For additional information, see 6:1105.

O179. Entrance Questionnaire and Experience Record. For additional information, see 2:1658 (1 reference).

O180. Guidance Questionnaire. For additional information, see 2:1659.1.

O181. Guidance Summary Form for Use in Vocational and Educational Counseling. For additional information and a review by Norman Frederiksen, see 3:446 (1 excerpt).

O182. Identical Forms. For additional information, see 5:899.

O183. Individual Guidance Record. For additional information, see 2:1660 (1 reference).

O184. Information Blank: For Obtaining Data About Vocational Plans and Problems of High School Students. For additional information, see 1:1169.

O185. The Jenkins Job Attitudes Survey. For additional information, see 6:1106 (1 reference).

O186. Kahn Career Orientation Questionnaire: A Preliminary to Vocational or Educational Counseling, Student Form. For additional information and a review by Arthur E. Traxler, see 4:777.

O187. Kefauver-Hand Guidance Tests and Inventories. For additional information and a review by E. G. Williamson, see 2:1661; for reviews by Harold D. Carter, Gwendolen Schneidler, and M. R. Trabue, see 1:1170 (2 excerpts).

O188. Mathematical and Technical Test. For additional information and reviews by Charles R. Langmuir and F. W. Warburton, see 4:779.

O189. Michigan Adult Profile. For additional information and reviews by Richard Ledgerwood, M. R. Trabue, John G. Darley, John M. Stalnaker, and Arthur E. Traxler, see 1:1171.

O190. Miles Career Evaluation Inventory. For additional information, see 4:780 (1 reference).

O191. Minnesota Occupational Rating Scales and Counseling Profile. For additional information and a review by M. H. Elliott, see 3:689 (5 references).

O192. Occupational Analysis Form. For additional information, see 2:1665.1.

O193. Occupational Orientation Inquiry. For additional information and reviews by John Gray Peatman and C. Gilbert Wrenn, see 2:1667 (1 reference).

O194. The Organization Survey. For additional information, see 6:1107.

O195. Per-Flu-Dex Tests. For additional information and reviews by Andrew L. Comrey and John W. French, see 5:901.

O196. SRA Employee Inventory. For additional information and reviews by Erwin K. Taylor and Albert S. Thompson, see 5:905 (10 references).

O197. A Self-Rating Scale for Leadership Qualifications. For additional information, see 5:906.

O198. Survey of Company Morale: Job Satisfaction Blank No. 12. For additional information and a review by William W. Waite, see 3:693 (1 reference).

O199. The Tear Ballot for Industry. For additional information and a review by Raymond A. Katzell, see 6:1108 (5 references); for a review by Brent Baxter, see 4:783 (4 references).

O200. [Tests A/9 and A/10.] For additional information, see 6:1109.

O201. Vocational Guidance Questionnaire. For additional information, see 2:1679.1.

O202. Whisler Strategy Test. For additional information and reviews by Jean Maier Palormo and Paul F. Ross, see 6:1110 (1 reference).

O203. Work Information Inventory. For additional information, see 6:1111.

SELECTION & RATING FORMS

O204. APT Controlled Interview. For additional information, see 6:1112.

O205. [Biography Forms]: Application-Interview Series. For additional information, see 5:892.

O206. [Cardall Interviewing Aids.] For additional information, see 6:1114.

O207. Career Counseling Personal Data Form. For additional information, see 6:1113.

O208. Diagnostic Interviewer's Guide. For additional information and a review by Albert K. Kurtz, see 6:1115 (2 references); for reviews by Clyde H. Coombs and Douglas H. Fryer, see 3:685.

O209. Employee Evaluation Form for Interviewers. For additional information and reviews by Douglas H. Fryer and C. H. Ruedisili, see 3:686 (2 excerpts).

O210. Employee Merit Report. For additional information, see 4:771.

O211. Employee Performance Appraisal. For additional information and a review by Jean Maier Palormo, see 6:1116.

O212. [Employee Rating and Development Forms.] For additional information and a review by Richard S. Barrett, see 6:1117; for reviews by Harry W. Karn and Floyd L. Ruch, see 4:781.

O213. [Employee Rating Forms.] For additional information, see 6:1118.

O214. [Employee Selection Forms.] For additional information, see 4:772.

O215. [Executive, Industrial, and Sales Personnel Forms.] For additional information and a review by John P. Foley, Jr., see 6:1119 (1 reference); for a review by Floyd L. Ruch, see 4:773.

O216. Hiring Summary Worksheet. For additional information, see 5:898.

O217. Individual Background Survey. For additional information, see 6:1120.

O218. Interview Rating Scale for Prospective Employees. For additional information and reviews by Jay L. Otis and S. Rains Wallace, Jr., see 4:776.

O219. Job Description Questionnaire. For additional information, see 6:1121.

O220. Lawshe-Kephart Personnel Comparison System. For additional information and a review by Reign H. Bittner, see 4:778 (1 reference).

O221. The McQuaig Manpower Selection Series. For additional information, see 6:1122.

O222. Merit Rating Series. For additional information and a review by Seymour Levy, see 6:1123; for a review by Brent Baxter of the original series, see 4:770 (1 reference).

O223. The Nagel Personnel Interviewing and Screening Forms. For additional information, see 6:1124.

O224. The Performance Record. For additional information and reviews by Albert K. Kurtz and Albert S. Thompson, see 5:902 (1 reference).

O225. [Performance Review Forms.] For additional information, see 6:1125.

O226. Personal Data Blank. For additional information and a review by Arthur E. Traxler, see 5:903; for reviews by Edward S. Jones and Donald G. Paterson of an earlier edition, see 2:1669.

O227. Personal History Record [Richardson, Bellows, Henry & Co., Inc.]. For additional information, see 6:1126.

O228. [Personnel Interviewing Forms.] For additional information, see 6:1127.

O229. Rating Form for Use of Interviewers and Oral Examiners. For additional information and a review by Douglas H. Fryer, see 3:691 (2 references); for a review by Ruth Strang, see 2:1672.

O230. [Selection Interview Forms.] For additional information, see 6:1128.

O231. [Stevens-Thurow Personnel Forms.] For additional information, see 6:1129.

SPECIFIC VOCATIONS

O232. Probst Rating System. For additional information and reviews by Milton M. Mandell and Dale Yoder, see 4:785 (2 references).

ACCOUNTING

O233. Accounting Orientation Test: High School Level. For additional information, see 5:907 (2 references).

O234. American Institute of Certified Public Accountants Testing Programs. For additional information, see 5:911 (6 references); see also 4:787 (15 references).

DENTISTRY

O235. Dental Aptitude Testing Program. For additional information, see 5:916 (6 references); see also 4:788 (2 references).

O236. Dental Hygiene Aptitude Testing Program. For additional information, see 5:917.

ENGINEERING

O237. AC Test of Creative Ability. For additional information and reviews by Samuel T. Mayo, Philip R. Merrifield, and Albert S. Thompson, see 6:1130 (1 reference).

O238. College Entrance Examination Board Test in Pre-Engineering Science Comprehension. For additional information, see 4:809.

O239. Engineering Aide Test. For additional information, see 6:1131.

O240. Engineering and Physical Science Aptitude Test. For additional information and a review by John W. French, see 4:810 (6 references); for reviews by Norman Frederiksen and Robert M. W. Travers, see 3:698.

O241. Examination in Advanced Engineering Electronics. For additional information, see 3:407.

O242. Examination in Advanced Radio Engineering—College Level. For additional information, see 3:414.

O243. Examination in Diesel Engineering. For additional information, see 3:408.

O244. Examination in Engineering Drawing. For additional information, see 3:409.

O245. Examination in Engineering Electronics. For additional information, see 3:410.

O246. Examination in Engineering Mechanics. For additional information, see 3:411.

O247. Examination in Fluid Mechanics. For additional information, see 3:412.

O248. Examination in Machine Design. For additional information, see 3:413.

O249. Examination in Strength of Materials. For additional information, see 3:415.

O250. Examination in Surveying. For additional information, see 3:416.

O251. The Graduate Record Examinations Advanced Tests: Engineering. For additional information, see 6:1132. For a review of the testing program, see 5:601.

O252. Minnesota Engineering Analogies Test. For additional information, see 6:1133 (2 references); for reviews by A. Pemberton Johnson and William B. Schrader, see 5:933 (6 references).

O253. National Engineering Aptitude Search Test: The Junior Engineering Technical Society. For additional information, see 6:1134.

O254. The Owens' Creativity Test for Machine Design. For additional information and reviews by Samuel T. Mayo and Philip R. Merrifield, see 6:1135 (1 reference).

O255. Placement Examination in General Engineering Drawing. For additional information, see 1:1175.

O256. Pre-Engineering Ability Test. For additional information and reviews by Jerome E. Doppelt and Dewey B. Stuit, see 4:812 (11 references).

O257. Purdue Creativity Test. For additional information and reviews by Samuel T. Mayo and Philip R. Merrifield, see 6:1136 (2 references).

O258. Stanford Scientific Aptitude Test. For additional information and reviews by Joseph E. Moore and Dewey B. Stuit, see 4:813 (4 references); for a review by A. B. Crawford, see 2:1676 (3 references).

LAW

O259. Iowa Legal Aptitude Test. For additional information and a review by Alexander G. Wesman, see 4:814 (5 references).

O260. Law School Admission Test. For additional information, see 5:928 (7 references); for a review by Alexander G. Wesman, see 4:815 (6 references).

MEDICINE

O261. Medical College Admission Test. For additional information and reviews by Robert L. Ebel and Philip H. DuBois, see 6:1137 (43 references); for a review by Alexander G. Wesman of forms previously published by Educational Testing Service, see 5:932 (4 references); for a review by Morey J. Wantman, see 4:817 (11 references).

O262. Medical School Instructor Attitude Inventory. For additional information, see 6:1138 (1 reference).

O263. Veterinary Aptitude Test. For additional information, see 6:1139 (3 references); see also 5:957 (3 references).

MISCELLANEOUS

O264. Card Punch Operator Aptitude Test. For additional information, see 6:1140 (2 references).

O265. Chemical Operators Selection Test. For additional information, see 6:1141 (1 reference).

O266. The Diebold Personnel Tests. For additional information, see 6:1142.

O267. Firefighter Test. For additional information, see 6:1143.

O268. [Firefighting Promotion Tests.] For additional information, see 6:1144.

O269. Fireman Examination. For additional information, see 6:1145.

O270. Memory and Observation Tests for Policeman. For additional information, see 6:1146.

O271. Mooseheart Graphic Rating Scale for Housemothers and Housefathers. For additional information, see 1:1172.

O272. [NCR Test Battery for Prospective Check-Out Cashiers.] For additional information and a review by David O. Herman, see 6:1147.

O273. P-L-S Journalism Test. For additional information, see 3:149.

O274. Personnel Service Rating Report. For additional information, see 5:939.

O275. Police Performance Rating System. For additional information, see 6:1148.

O276. Police Promotion Examinations. For additional information, see 6:1149.

O277. Policeman Examination. For additional information, see 6:1150.

O278. Policeman Test. For additional information, see 6:1151.

O279. The Potter-Nash Aptitude Test for Lumber Inspectors and Other General Personnel Who Handle Lumber. For additional information, see 6:1152.

O280. Punched Card Machine Operator Aptitude Test. For additional information, see 5:941.

O281. Revised Programmer Aptitude Test. For additional information, see 6:1153 (2 references).

O282. The Store Personnel Test. For additional information and reviews by Raymond A. Katzell and John B. Morris, see 5:954 (1 reference).

O283. Visual Comprehension Test for Detective. For additional information, see 6:1154.

NURSING

O284. Achievement Tests in Nursing. For additional information, see 6:1155.

O285. Achievement Tests in Practical Nursing. For additional information, see 5:909.

O286. Entrance Examination for Schools of Nursing. For additional information, see 6:1156 (2 references).

O287. Entrance Examinations for Schools of Practical Nursing. For additional information, see 5:920.

O288. George Washington University Series Nursing Tests. For additional information, see 4:818 (2 references); see also 3:699 (6 references).

O289. The Gordon-Douglass Fraction Test for Beginning Students of Nursing. For additional information, see 1:1168 (1 excerpt).

O290. NLN Achievement Tests for Basic Professional Nursing. For additional information, see 6:1157 (1 reference).

O291. NLN Achievement Tests for Psychiatric Aides. For additional information, see 6:1158.

O292. NLN Graduate Nurse Examination. For additional information, see 6:1159 (4 references).

O293. NLN Practical Nurse Achievement Tests. For additional information, see 6:1160.

O294. NLN Pre-Admission and Classification Examination. For additional information, see 6:1161 (1 reference).

O295. NLN Pre-Nursing and Guidance Examination. For additional information, see 6:1162 (8 references).

O296. PSB-Entrance Examination for Schools of Practical Nursing. For additional information, see 6:1163.

RESEARCH

O297. Research Personnel Review Form. For additional information, see 6:1164.

O298. Supervisor's Evaluation of Research Personnel. For additional information and a review by John W. French, see 6:1165 (3 references, 1 excerpt).

O299. Surveys of Research Administration and Environment. For additional information, see 6:1166.

O300. Technical Personnel Recruiting Inventory. For additional information, see 6:1167.

SELLING

O301. Aptitude Index Selection Procedure. For additional information, see 6:1168 (1 reference); see also 5:913 (1 reference); for reviews by Donald G. Paterson and Albert S. Thompson of an earlier form, see 4:825 (14 references); see also 2:1646 (5 references).

O302. Aptitudes Associates Test of Sales Aptitude: A Test for Measuring Knowledge of Basic Principles of Selling. For additional information, see 6:1169 (6 references); for reviews by Milton E. Hahn and Donald G. Paterson, see 4:824. For a revised edition, see O317.

O303. Combination Inventory. For additional information, see 6:1170 (1 reference).

O304. The Dealer Inventory. For additional information, see 6:1171.

O305. Detroit Retail Selling Inventory. For additional information and reviews by Milton E. Hahn and Floyd L. Ruch, see 3:697 (2 excerpts).

O306. The Evaluation Record. For additional information, see 6:1172.

O307. Hall Salespower Inventory. For additional information, see 5:924.

O308. Hanes Sales Selection Inventory. For additional information and reviews by William E. Kendall and Albert K. Kurtz, see 6:1173.

O309. Hiring Kit. For additional information, see 4:826.

O310. Information Index. For additional information, see 6:1174 (1 reference); see also 5:927 (3 references).

O311. Interviewer's Impressions—Sales Applicants. For additional information, see 6:1175.

O312. LIAMA Inventory of Job Attitudes. For additional information, see 5:929.

O313. Measure of Consociative Tendency. For additional information, see 5:931.

O314. Personal History. For additional information, see 2:1670 (5 references).

O315. Personnel Institute Hiring Kit. For additional information, see 6:1176 (3 references).

O316. SRA Sales Attitudes Check List. For additional information and a review by John P. Foley, Jr., see 6:1177.

O317. Sales Comprehension Test. For additional information, see 6:1178 (7 references); for a review by Raymond A. Katzell, see 5:947 (10 references); for an earlier edition, see O302.

O318. Sales Employee Inventory. For additional information, see 6:1179.

O319. Sales Motivation Inventory. For additional information and a review by S. Rains Wallace, see 5:948 (2 references).

O320. Sales Personnel Description Form. For additional information and a review by Wayne K. Kirchner, see 6:1180 (2 references).

O321. Sales Questionnaire. For additional information and a review by Robert G. Bernreuter, see 3:703 (1 reference).

O322. The Sales Sentence Completion Blank. For additional information and a review by William E. Kendall, see 6:1181 (1 excerpt).

O323. Sales Situation Test. For additional information, see 4:827 (1 reference).

O324. Steward Basic Factors Inventory. For additional information and reviews by Leonard V. Gordon and Lyman W. Porter, see 6:1182.

O325. Steward Life Insurance Knowledge Test. For additional information, see 5:950.

O326. Steward Occupational Objectives Inventory. For additional information, see 5:951.

O327. Steward Personal Background Inventory. For additional information and reviews by Leonard V. Gordon and Lyman W. Porter, see 6:1183; see also 5:952 (1 reference).

O328. Steward Selection System. For additional information and reviews by Donald G. Paterson and Albert S. Thompson, see 4:828 (2 references); for reviews by Milton E. Hahn and Floyd L. Ruch, see 3:704 (2 references); see also 2:1651 (3 references).

O329. Test for Ability to Sell: George Washington University Series. For additional information, see 4:829; for a review by Floyd L. Ruch, see 3:705.

O330. Test of Sales Judgment. For additional information, see 4:830.

O331. Word Check Forms. For additional information, see 6:1184.

SKILLED TRADES

O332. Automotive Mechanic Test. For additional information, see 6:1185.

O333. The Fiesenheiser Test of Ability to Read Drawings. For additional information and a review by Joseph E. Moore, see 6:1186.

O334. Garage Mechanic Test. For additional information, see 5:573.

O335. Purdue Blueprint Reading Test. For additional information, see 4:782.

O336. Purdue Industrial Training Classification Test. For additional information and reviews by D. Welty Lefever and Charles I. Mosier, see 3:675 (2 references).

O337. Purdue Interview Aids. For additional information and a review by William W. Waite, see 4:775.

O338. Purdue Test for Electricians. For additional information and a review by John W. French, see 3:701.

O339. Purdue Test for Machinists and Machine Operators. For additional information, see 4:816; for a review by William W. Waite, see 3:702.

O340. Purdue Trade Information Test for Sheetmetal Workers. For additional information, see 5:942.

O341. Purdue Trade Information Test in Carpentry. For additional information and a review by P. L. Mellenbruch, see 5:943 (1 reference).

O342. Purdue Trade Information Test in Engine Lathe Operation. For additional information and a review by William J. Micheels, see 5:944.

O343. Purdue Trade Information Test in Welding. For additional information, see 5:945.

O344. Technical Tests. For additional information, see 6:1187.

O345. Written Trade Tests. For additional information, see 6:1188.

SUPERVISION

O346. A Chart for the Rating of a Foreman. For additional information, see 5:915.

O347. How Supervise? For additional information and a review by Joel T. Campbell, see 6:1189 (9 references); see also 5:926 (18 references); for a review by Milton M. Mandell, see 4:774 (8 references); for reviews by D. Welty Lefever, Charles I. Mosier, and C. H. Ruedisili, see 3:687 (5 references).

O348. Leadership Opinion Questionnaire. For additional information and reviews by Jerome E. Doppelt and Wayne K. Kirchner, see 6:1190 (6 references).

O349. Managerial Scale for Enterprise Improvement. For additional information and reviews by Brent Baxter and Edward B. Greene, see 5:930.

O350. Personal Development Record. For additional information, see 6:1191.

O351. Supervisory Index. For additional information and reviews by Arthur H. Brayfield and Albert K. Kurtz, see 6:1192 (1 reference).

O352. Supervisory Inventory on Human Relations. For additional information and a review by Seymour Levy, see 6:1193 (1 reference).

O353. Supervisory Practices Test. For additional information, see 6:1194 (4 references); for reviews by Clifford E. Jurgensen and Mary Ellen Oliverio, see 5:955.

O354. Test of Practical Judgment. For additional information, see 4:784 (6 references); for reviews by Glen U. Cleeton and Howard R. Taylor, see 3:694.

O355. Test of Supervisory Judgment. For additional information, see 6:1195.

O356. WLW Supervisor Survey. For additional information, see 6:1196.

TRANSPORTATION

O357. [American Transit Association Tests.] For additional information, see 5:912; for reviews by

Harold G. Seashore, Morris S. Viteles, and J. V. Waits, see 3:696 (1 reference).

O358. Driver Selection Forms and Tests. For additional information and a review by Joseph E. Moore, see 6:1197; for a review by S. Rains Wallace, Jr., see 4:789.

O359. McGuire Safe Driver Scale and Interview Guide. For additional information and reviews by Willard A. Kerr and D. H. Schuster, see 6:1198 (1 reference).

O360. Road Test Check List for Testing, Selecting, Rating, and Training Coach Operators. For additional information, see 5:946.

O361. Road Test in Traffic for Testing, Selecting, Rating, and Training Truck Drivers. For additional information and a review of the battery, see 6:1197g.

O362. Traffic and Driving Knowledge for Drivers of Motor Trucks. For additional information and a review of the battery, see 6:1197f.

O363. Truck Driver Test. For additional information and reviews by Willard A. Kerr and D. H. Schuster, see 6:1199.

O364. Wilson Driver Selection Test. For additional information and reviews by Willard A. Kerr and D. H. Schuster, see 6:1200.

MMY Book Review Index

THIS chapter is an index to the book review excerpts published in the first six *Mental Measurements Yearbooks* and in *Educational, Psychological, and Personality Tests of 1936*. A few books have been omitted—books in areas no longer considered eligible for inclusion in the book sections of the MMY's; for example, books on interviewing, research methods, social case records, and statistics.

The MMY Book Review Index lists 926 books published over a thirty-one year period, 1933 through 1963, with a few 1964 titles. The Index serves as a guide to the published reviews of books on testing and closely related areas. The primary purpose of the Index is to facilitate, for historical purposes, the retrieval of comments, criticisms, and viewpoints from among the thousands of review excerpts which have been published in the six MMY's and related publications.

The bibliographic information presented for each book has been compiled from the last listing in an MMY. No information is presented regarding prices, present name of publisher, or whether the book is still in print. The names of reviewers are presented along with references to the MMY's containing the reviews.

All but a few of the cross references are to reviews in the first six MMY's; for example, 2:B930 refers to book B930 in the second MMY and 6:B120 refers to book B120 in the sixth MMY. Reviews in three other publications are cited in a few instances: 36:B258 refers to book B258 in *Educational, Psychological, and Personality Tests of 1936;*[1] the complete titles are given in the few instances when references are made to other related publications.[2]

Titles are arranged alphabetically by authors with anonymous titles listed first. Readers may want to skim over the titles looking for books which may be of historical interest to them. Readers may also find the following classified index useful in locating books in a particular area. All the authors and reviewers are listed in the Index of Names; the titles, in the Index of Titles.

[1] BUROS, OSCAR K. *Educational, Psychological, and Personality Tests of 1936: Including a Bibliography and Book Review Digest of Measurement Books and Monographs of 1933–36.* Rutgers University Bulletin, Vol. 14, No. 2A; Studies in Education, No. 11. Highland Park, N.J.: Gryphon Press, August 1937. Pp. 141. Paper. $1.50.
[2] BUROS, OSCAR KRISEN, EDITOR. *The Second Yearbook of Research and Statistical Methodology Books and Reviews.* Highland Park, N.J.: Gryphon Press, 1941. Pp. xx, 383. Out of print.
BUROS, OSCAR KRISEN, EDITOR. *Statistical Methodology Reviews, 1941–50.* New York: John Wiley & Sons, Inc., 1951. Pp. xi, 457. Out of print.

SUBJECT GUIDE TO BOOKS

GENERAL

Bibliographies and reviews: P144–53, P179, P353, P432, P763, P874
Conference proceedings: P3–4, P247, P397, P461–4, P593, P846

General books for: COUNSELORS, P95–6, P320–1, P356, P632, P644, P704–6, P783, P791, P842; LAYMEN, P111, P182, P376, P437, P892, P922; MILITARY PERSONNEL, P25, P855; NURSES, P513, P569; PERSONNEL SPECIALISTS, P26, P106, P250, P252, P374, P522; PHYSICAL EDUCATORS, P120, P190, P352, P781;

P457, P512, P641, P832; SZONDI, P239, P798–9, P871; OTHER TESTS, P24, P28, P47, P86, P92, P113, P126, P159, P240, P299, P305, P391, P423, P439–40, P476, P500, P511, P516, P527, P540, P552, P562, P591, P653, P656, P678, P698, P713, P740, P742–3, P794, P796–7, P833–4, P860
Research monographs: P24, P160, P176, P184, P276, P290, P333, P398, P583, P647, P650, P687, P696, P709, P802, P823, P869, P925
Sociometry: P108–10, P208, P212, P287, P375, P471–2, P595–8, P627–8

VOCATIONS

General: P26, P106, P250, P252, P374, P522, P571, P599, P601, P771, P791, P819

Administrative: P56, P104, P425, P427, P780
Bibliographies: P91, P93–4
Civil service: P105, P186, P445, P636
Clerical: P42, P93, P542
Interests: P98, P165, P187, P225, P324, P790; SVIB, P222, P519, P523–4, P722, P784–5, P898
Job satisfaction: P142, P923
Mechanical: P94, P202
Miscellaneous: P18, P30–1, P57, P97, P178, P271, P273, P349, P445, P491, P539, P547, P584, P629, P643, P773, P812
Ratings: P248, P298, P387, P485, P514, P575, P610, P667, P895, P906, P924
Research monographs: P243, P269, P289, P294–6, P385, P426, P568, P602, P642, P731, P817, P886
Salesman: P161, P226, P358, P702, P777, P888

P1. Army Air Forces Aviation Psychology Program Research Reports, Nos. 1–19. Washington, D.C.: U.S. Government Printing Office, 1947–1948.
For a review by H. J. Eysenck, see 4:B2. For reviews of individual volumes, see P103, P166, P198, P218, P230, P236, P266, P306, P350, P380, P434, P497, P536, P580, P588, P820, and P897.

P2. Attitude Scaling. Publications of the Market Research Society, No. 4. London: Oakwood Press, 1960. Pp. vi, 76.
For a review, see 6:B1.

P3. Conference on Examinations (Vol. II): Under the Auspices of the Carnegie Corporation, the Carnegie Foundation, the International Institute of Teachers College, Columbia University at the Hotel Metropole, Folkestone, England, June 8th to 10th, 1935. Edited by Paul Monroe. New York: Bureau of Publications, the College, 1936. Pp. xviii, 300.
For reviews by A. H. Lass, W. McAndrew, and A. G. Schmidt, see 36:B73.

P4. Editors and Writers Conference on Testing, May 13 and 14, 1958, Princeton, New Jersey. Princeton, N.J.: Educational Testing Service, 1959. Pp. 78.
For a review by Thomas M. Magoon, see 6:B3.

P5. Evaluation of Pupil Progress in Business Education. American Business Education Yearbook, Vol. 17, 1960. Edited by Estelle L. Popham. New York: New York University Campus Stores, 1960. Pp. x, 399.
For a review, see 6:B5.

P6. Intelligence Testing: Its Use in Selection for Secondary Education. Special articles from the *Times Educational Supplement* with two leading articles by P. E. Vernon and letters to the editor. London: Times Publishing Co. Ltd., 1952. Pp. 31.
For a review by C. W. Valentine, see 5:B6.

P7. Mental Testing Number. *Education and Psychology,* Vol. 1, Nos. 4–5. Delhi, India: Education and Psychology, 1954. Pp. ii, 180.
For a review by Boris Semeonoff, see 5:B8.

P8. The Scottish Scholastic Survey, 1953. Publications of the Scottish Council for Research in Education, [No.] 48. London: University of London Press Ltd., 1963. Pp. 218.
For a review by R. R. Dale, see 6:B24.

P9. Studies in Selection Techniques for Admission to Grammar Schools. University of Bristol, Institute of Education, Publication No. 3. London: University of London Press Ltd., 1952. Pp. 68.
For a review, see 5:B12.

P10. The Trend of Scottish Intelligence: A Comparison of the 1947 and 1932 Surveys of the Intelligence of Eleven-Year-Old Pupils. Publications of the Scottish Council for Research in Education [No.] 30. London: University of London Press Ltd., 1949. Pp. xxviii, 151.
For reviews by M. B. Brody, R. C. K. Ensor, L. S. Penrose, R. W. Pickford, Wm. H. Sewell, W. J. Sparrow, Arthur Summerfield, and two others, see 4:B18.

P11. Uppsala Symposium on Psychological Factor Analysis, 17–19 March 1953. Nordisk Psykologi's Monograph Series 3. Stockholm, Sweden: Almqvist & Wiksell, 1953. Pp. 91.
For a review by Godfrey Thomson, see 5:B17.

P12. ABT, LAWRENCE EDWIN, and BELLAK, LEOPOLD, EDITORS. **Projective Psychology: Clinical Approaches to the Total Personality.** New York: Alfred A. Knopf, Inc., 1950. Pp. xvii, 485, xiv.
For reviews by Robert M. Allen, Manford H. Kuhn, Irving Lazar, Alec Rodger, Julian B. Rotter, Helen D. Sargent, Laurance F. Shaffer, and Dorothy Tilden Spoerl, see 4:B20.

P13. ADAMS, GEORGIA SACHS, and TORGERSON, THEODORE L. **Measurement and Evaluation for the Secondary-School Teacher: With Implications for Corrective Procedures.** New York: Dryden Press, Inc., 1956. Pp. xiii, 658.
For reviews by Wm. C. Cottle, Walter F. Johnson, Robert B. Nordberg, and R. Roderick Palmer, see 5:B20.

P14. ADCOCK, C. J. **Factorial Analysis for Non-Mathematicians.** Melbourne, Australia: Melbourne University Press, 1954. Pp. 88.
For reviews by Anne Anastasi, David Duncan, and Arthur Summerfield, see 5:B21.

P15. ADCOCK, C. J. **Intelligence and High Level Achievement.** Victoria University College, Publications in Psychology, No. 1. Wellington, New Zealand: Department of Psychology, Victoria University College, 1952. Pp. 27.
For a review by P. E. Vernon, see 5:B22.

P16. ADKINS, DOROTHY C., and LYERLY, SAMUEL B.; with the assistance of GOLDIE DEMB and DANIEL

W. CAMPBELL. **Factor Analysis of Reasoning Tests.** Chapel Hill, N.C.: University of North Carolina Press, 1952. Pp. iv, 122.
For reviews by Edward E. Cureton and Lyle V. Jones, see 5:B23.

P17. ADKINS, DOROTHY C.; with the assistance of ERNEST S. PRIMOFF, HAROLD L. McADOO, CLAUDE F. BRIDGES, and BERTRAM FORER. **Construction and Analysis of Achievement Tests: The Development of Written and Performance Tests of Achievement for Predicting Job Performance of Public Personnel.** United States Civil Service Commission. Washington, D.C.: U.S. Government Printing Office, 1947. Pp. xvii, 292.
For reviews by E. Anstey, Fred S. Beers, Frederick B. Davis, Henry F. Hubbard, Charles I. Mosier, Laurance F. Shaffer, Dewey B. Stuit, Robert M. W. Travers, and P. E. Vernon, see 4:B22.

P18. AHERN, EILEEN. **Handbook of Personnel Forms and Records.** Research Report No. 16. New York: American Management Association, 1949. Pp. 227.
For reviews by E. Fassberg and Robert W. Pearson, see 4:B23.

P19. AHMANN, J. STANLEY, and GLOCK, MARVIN D. **Evaluating Pupil Growth, Second Edition.** Boston, Mass.: Allyn & Bacon, Inc., 1963. Pp. xi, 640.
For reviews by Sam Duker and John W. M. Rothney of the first edition, see 6:B33.

P20. AHMANN, J. STANLEY; GLOCK, MARVIN D.; and WARDEBERG, HELEN L. **Evaluating Elementary School Pupils.** Boston, Mass.: Allyn & Bacon, Inc., 1960. Pp. xviii, 435.
For a review by Blanche B. Paulson, see 6:B35.

P21. AHMAVAARA, YRJÖ. **On the Unified Factor Theory of Mind.** Annals of the Academia Scientiarum Fennica, Series B, Vol. 106. Helsinki, Finland: Suomalainen Tiedeakatemia, Academia Scientiarum Fennica, 1957. Pp. 176.
For reviews by Rolf Bargmann and Charles Wrigley, see 6:B36.

P22. AHMAVAARA, YRJÖ. **Transformation Analysis of Factorial Data and Other New Analytical Methods of Differential Psychology With Their Application to Thurstone's Basic Studies.** Annals of the Finnish Academy of Science and Letters, Series B, No. 88, Part 2. Helsinki, Finland: Suomalainen Tiedeakatemia, Academia Scientiarum Fennica, 1954. Pp. 150.
For reviews by Henry F. Kaiser (with William B. Michael) and Joseph R. Royce, see 5:B26.

P23. AHMAVAARA, YRJÖ, and MARKKANEN, TOUKO. **The Unified Factor Model: Its Position in Psychometric Theory and Application to Sociological Study.** Finnish Foundation for Alcohol Studies, Alcohol Research in the Northern Countries, Vol. 7. Stockholm, Sweden: Almqvist & Wiksell, 1958. Pp. 188.
For reviews by Rolf Bargmann and Jum C. Nunnally, see 6:B37.

P24. AINSWORTH, MARY D., and AINSWORTH, LEONARD H. **Measuring Security in Personal Adjustment.** Toronto, Canada: University of Toronto Press, 1958. Pp. xiii, 98.
For reviews by H. Phillipson and R. W. Pickford, see 6:B38.

P25. AIR UNIVERSITY, AIR COMMAND AND STAFF SCHOOL. **Evaluation in Air Force Instruction,** Revised Edition: Academic Instructor Course, Vol. II. Maxwell Air Force Base, Ala.: Air University, November 1953. Pp. vi, 90.
For a review by Robert E. Hubbard, see 5:B30.

P26. ALBRIGHT, LEWIS E.; GLENNON, J. R.; and SMITH, WALLACE J. **The Use of Psychological Tests in Industry.** Cleveland, Ohio: Howard Allen, Inc., Publishers, 1963. Pp. 196.
For a review by Wayne K. Kirchner, see 6:B39.

P27. ALCOCK, THEODORA. **The Rorschach in Practice.** London: Tavistock Publications, 1963. Pp. xii, 252.
For reviews by C. H. Ammons and Jessie Francis-Williams, see 6:B40.

P28. ALEXANDER, THERON. **The Adult-Child Interaction Test: A Projective Test for Use in Research.** Monographs of the Society for Research in Child Development, Vol. 27, No. 2, Serial No. 55. Lafayette, Ind.: Child Development Publications, Inc., 1955. Pp. v, 40, plus 8 cards.
For a review by H. Phillipson, see 5:B31.

P29. ALEXANDER, WILLIAM P. **Intelligence, Concrete and Abstract: A Study in Differential Traits.** British Journal of Psychology Monograph Supplements, No. 19. London: Cambridge University Press, 1935. Pp. x, 178.
For reviews by H. E. Garrett, W. Stephenson, and three others, see 1:B293; for a review by W. G. Emmett, see 36:B3.

P30. ALLEN, E. PATRICIA, and SMITH, PERCIVAL. **Selection of Skilled Apprentices for the Engineering Trades: Third Report of Research.** Birmingham, England: City of Birmingham Education Committee, 1939. Pp. iii, 37.
For a review, see 2:B820.

P31. ALLEN, E. PATRICIA, and SMITH, PERCIVAL. **The Value of Vocational Tests as Aids to Choice of Employment.** Birmingham, England: City of Birmingham Education Committee, 1940. Pp. 45.
For a review, see 3:714.

P32. ALLEN, RICHARD D. **Self-Measurement Projects in Group Guidance: A Laboratory Course for Pupils in the Study of Individual Differences.** Inor Group Guidance Series, Vol. III. New York: Inor Publishing Co., 1934. Pp. xvii, 274.
For reviews by R. N. Anderson and A. C. Eurich, see 1:B294; for reviews by John M. Brewer and one other, see 36:B5.

P33. ALLEN, ROBERT M. **Elements of Rorschach Interpretation: With an Extended Bibliography.** New York: International Universities Press, Inc., 1954. Pp. 242.
For reviews by William M. Cruickshank, Fred J. Goldstein, and J. R. Wittenborn, see 5:B32.

P34. ALLEN, ROBERT M. **Guide to Psychological Tests and Measurements, Third Edition.** Coral Gables, Fla.: University of Miami Bookstore, 1960. Pp. i, 68.
For a review by William Coleman of the first edition, see 5:B33.

P35. ALLEN, ROBERT M. **Introduction to the Rorschach Technique: Manual of Administration and Scoring.** New York: International Universities Press, Inc., 1953. Pp. ii, 126.
For reviews by Myrtle Astrachan, Mortimer M. Meyer, and one other, see 5:B34.

P36. ALLEN, ROBERT M. **Personality Assessment Procedures: Psychometric, Projective, and Other**

Approaches. New York: Harper & Row, Publishers, Inc., 1958. Pp. xi, 541.
For reviews by Betty L. Kalis and R. Wirt, see 6:B43.

P37. ALLEN, ROBERT M., and JEFFERSON, THOMAS W. **Psychological Evaluation of the Cerebral Palsied Person: Intellectual, Personality, and Vocational Applications.** Springfield, Ill.: Charles C Thomas, Publisher, 1962. Pp. xiii, 86.
For reviews by Salvatore G. DiMichael, J. A. L. Naughton, and L. Leon Reid, see 6:B44.

P38. ALLEN, WENDELL C. **Cumulative Pupil Records: A Plan for Staff Study and Improvement of Cumulative Pupil Records in Secondary Schools.** New York: Bureau of Publications, Teachers College, Columbia University, 1943. Pp. ix, 69.
For reviews by A. S. Edwards, N. G. Fawcett, Gustav J. Froehlich, and Rebecca C. Tansil, see 3:715.

P39. ALLPORT, GORDON W. **The Use of Personal Documents in Psychological Science.** Social Science Research Council, Bulletin 49. New York: the Council, 1942. Pp. xix, 210.
For reviews by Emory S. Bogardus, Ernest W. Burgess, Peter Hampton, Joseph Lander, David M. Levy, Robert E. Park, Mary C. Van Tuyl, and one other, see 3:716.

P40. ALLPORT, GORDON W., and VERNON, PHILIP E. **Studies in Expressive Movement.** Chapter 10, "Matching Sketches of Personality With Script," by Edwin Powers. New York: Macmillan Co., 1933. Pp. xiii, 269.
For reviews by Herbert Blumer, C. W. Brown, Thos. H. Howells, Dorothea Johannsen, Frank K. Shuttleworth, and one other, see 2:B821.

P41. AMERICAN ASSOCIATION OF EXAMINERS AND ADMINISTRATORS OF EDUCATIONAL PERSONNEL. **Principles and Procedures of Teacher Selection: A Monograph.** Philadelphia, Pa.: the Association, 1952. Pp. viii, 146.
For a review by Harrison F. Heath, see 5:B36.

P42. AMERICAN BANKERS ASSOCIATION, CUSTOMER AND PERSONNEL RELATIONS DEPARTMENT. **Clerical Testing in Banks.** New York: the Association, 1952. Pp. v, 65.
For a review, see 5:B37.

P43. AMERICAN COUNCIL ON EDUCATION. **The Construction and Use of Achievement Examinations: A Manual for Secondary School Teachers.** Edited by Herbert E. Hawkes, E. F. Lindquist, and C. R. Mann. Boston, Mass.: Houghton Mifflin Co., 1936. Pp. x, 497.
For a review by Norman Woelfel, see 2:B822; for reviews by K. E. Gell, G. W. Hartmann, G. F. Kuder, J. S. Orleans, and two others, see 1:B295; for reviews by August Dvorak, A. S. Edwards, E. R. Gabler, W. McAndrew, John L. Stenquist, and four others, see 36:B6.

P44. AMERICAN COUNCIL ON EDUCATION, COMMITTEE ON MEASUREMENT AND EVALUATION. **College Testing: A Guide to Practices and Programs.** Washington, D.C.: the Council, 1959. Pp. x, 190.
For reviews by Joseph C. Heston and Wilbur L. Layton, see 6:B48.

P45. AMERICAN COUNCIL ON EDUCATION, COMMITTEE ON MEASUREMENT AND GUIDANCE. **New Directions for Measurement and Guidance: A Symposium Sponsored by the Committee on Measurement and Guidance.** American Council on Education Studies, Vol. 8; Series I, Reports of Commit-

tees and Conferences, No. 20. Washington, D.C.: the Council, 1944. Pp. vii, 103.
For reviews by Philip W. L. Cox and H. B. McDaniel, see 3:724.

P46. AMERICAN COUNCIL ON EDUCATION, COMMITTEE ON PERSONNEL METHODS. **Measurement and Guidance of College Students.** Baltimore, Md.: Williams & Wilkins Co., 1933. Pp. xi, 199.
For a review by C. M. Rebert, see 1:B298; for reviews by R. W. Cullen, R. H. Hodgkins, E. S. Jones, C. H. Ruedisili, and L. W. Zimmer, see 36:B12.

P47. AMES, LOUISE BATES, and ILG, FRANCES L. **Mosaic Patterns of American Children.** New York: Hoeber Medical Division, Harper & Row, Publishers, Inc., 1962. Pp. xii, 297.
For reviews by Austin E. Grigg, H. R. Schaffer, and Frederic Wertham, see 6:B51.

P48. AMES, LOUISE BATES; LEARNED, JANET; MÉTRAUX, RUTH W.; and WALKER, RICHARD N. **Child Rorschach Responses: Developmental Trends From Two to Ten Years.** New York: Paul B. Hoeber, Inc., 1952. Pp. xv, 310.
For a review by M. L. Aronson, see 5:B40.

P49. AMES, LOUISE BATES; LEARNED, JANET; MÉTRAUX, RUTH W.; and WALKER, RICHARD N. **Rorschach Responses in Old Age.** New York: Paul B. Hoeber, Inc., 1954. Pp. xv, 229.
For reviews by Warner L. Lowe and Mortimer M. Meyer, see 5:B41.

P50. AMES, LOUISE BATES; MÉTRAUX, RUTH W.; and WALKER, RICHARD N. **Adolescent Rorschach Responses: Developmental Trends From Ten to Sixteen Years.** New York: Hoeber Medical Division, Harper & Row, Publishers, Inc., 1959. Pp. xiii, 313.
For reviews by Samuel J. Beck (with Anne G. Beck) and Irwin J. Knopf, see 6:B52.

P51. ANASTASI, ANNE. **Psychological Testing, Second Edition.** New York: Macmillan Co., 1961. Pp. xiii, 657.
For reviews by Frederick G. Brown, Andrew L. Comrey, and Richard E. Schutz, see 6:B53; for reviews by G. A. Foulds, B. Fruchter, Ann Margaret Garner, J. P. Guilford, Florence Mitchell, Merle M. Ohlsen, R. W. Pickford, Alec Rodger, and R. J. Thomson of the first edition, see 5:B42.

P52. ANDERSON, CHARLES C. **Function Fluctuation.** British Journal of Psychology Monograph Supplements, No. 30. London: Cambridge University Press, 1958. Pp. vii, 104.
For reviews by H. J. Eysenck and George A. Ferguson, see 6:B55.

P53. ANDERSON, HAROLD H., and ANDERSON, GLADYS L. **An Introduction to Projective Techniques and Other Devices for Understanding the Dynamics of Human Behavior.** New York: Prentice-Hall, Inc., 1951. Pp. xxv, 720.
For reviews by Arthur Burton, Leslie Phillips, William Schofield, Robert I. Watson, and Walter L. Wilkins, see 5:B44.

P54. ANDERSON, HOWARD R., and LINDQUIST, E. F.; revised by DAVID K. HEENAN, **Selected Test Items in World History, Third Edition.** National Council for the Social Studies, Bulletin No. 9, Third Edition. Washington, D.C.: the Council, 1960. Pp. vi, 93.
For a review by R. J. Purcell of an earlier edition, see 1:B302.

P55. ANDERSON, HOWARD R., and LINDQUIST, E. F.; revised by HARRIET STULL. **Selected Test Items**

in American History, Fifth Edition. National Council for the Social Studies, Bulletin No. 6, Fifth Edition. Washington, D.C.: the Council, 1964. Pp. ii, 126.

For a review by J. Wayne Wrightstone of an earlier edition, see 3:734.

P56. ARBOUS, A. G. **Selection for Industrial Leadership.** London: Oxford University Press, 1953. Pp. xiv, 179.

For reviews by Geoffrey Hutton, Charles E. Scholl, Jr., and P. E. Vernon, see 5:B47.

P57. ARBOUS, A. G. **Tables for Aptitude Testers: The Operating Characteristics of Aptitude Test Batteries.** Johannesburg, South Africa: National Institute for Personnel Research, South African Council for Scientific and Industrial Research, 1952. Pp. iii, 86.

For reviews by E. Elliott, N. F. Holt, Olgierd Porebski, and Robert L. Thorndike, see 5:B48.

P58. ARNOLD, MAGDA B. **Story Sequence Analysis: A New Method of Measuring Motivation and Predicting Achievement.** New York: Columbia University Press, 1962. Pp. ix, 287.

For reviews by George Adelman and A. Kaldegg, see 6:B60.

P59. ARON, BETTY. **A Manual for Analysis of the Thematic Apperception Test: A Method and Technique for Personality Research.** Berkeley, Calif.: Willis E. Berg, 1949. Pp. xiii, 163.

For reviews by Robert R. Holt, Laurance F. Shaffer, and one other, see 4:139.

P60. ARTHUR, GRACE. **A Point Scale of Performance Tests: Vol. I, Clinical Manual, Second Edition.** New York: Commonwealth Fund, 1943. Pp. xi, 64.

For a review by Donald Snedden, see 2:1379.

P61. ARTHUR, GRACE. **A Point Scale of Performance Tests: Volume II, The Process of Standardization.** New York: Commonwealth Fund, 1933. Pp. xi, 106.

For a review, see 2:B830; for reviews by P. L. Boynton, M. R. Emerson, W. Line, F. N. Maxfield, F. C. Shrubsall, F. K. Shuttleworth, and one other, see 1:B304; for a review by E. P. Hunt, see 36:B19.

P62. AULD, FRANK, JR. **The Influence of Social Class on Tests of Personality.** Drew University Bulletin, Vol. 40, No. 4; Drew University Studies No. 5. Madison, N.J.: Drew University, 1952. Pp. 18.

For a review, see 5:B51.

P63. AUSTIN, MARY C.; BUSH, CLIFFORD L.; and HUEBNER, MILDRED H. **Reading Evaluation: Appraisal Techniques for School and Classroom.** New York: Ronald Press Co., 1961. Pp. v, 256.

For a review by Harry T. Hahn, see 6:B62.

P64. AVENT, JOS. E. **Standard Testing Reduced to Its Lowest Terms.** Knoxville, Tenn.: Jos. E. Avent, Publisher, 1936. Pp. xiv, 266.

For reviews by A. G. Schmidt and R. Wallace, see 36:B20.

P65. BABCOCK, HARRIET. **The MacQuarrie Test as a Clinical Instrument: Validity of Vocabulary-MacQuarrie Deviations as a Measure of Abnormal Mental Functioning When Scored in Psychological Units.** Lancaster, Pa.: Science Press, 1950. Pp. vii, 72.

For a review by Laurance F. Shaffer, see 4:760.

P66. BABCOCK, HARRIET. **Time and the Mind: Personal Tempo—The Key to Normal and Pathological Mental Conditions.** Cambridge, Mass.: Sci-Art Publishers, 1941. Pp. 304.

For reviews by Arthur L. Benton, Irving Lorge, G. K. Yacorzynski, and one other, see 3:72.

P67. BAILEY, EDNA W.; LATON, ANITA D.; and BISHOP, ELIZABETH L. **Studying Children in School, Second Edition.** New York: McGraw-Hill Book Co., Inc., 1939. Pp. vii, 182.

For a review by Claire C. Dimmick, see 3:743; for reviews by C. M. Louttit and one other, see 2:B831; for a review of the first edition, see 1:B305.

P68. BAKER, HARRY J., and TRAPHAGEN, VIRGINIA. **The Diagnosis and Treatment of Behavior-Problem Children.** New York: Macmillan Co., 1935. Pp. xiv, 393.

For a review by Edward H. Stullken, see 3:33; for reviews by W. W. Bauer, Marjorie R. Leonard, Frederick L. Patry, and one other, see 2:B835; for reviews by T. W. Brockbank, J. E. Greene, C. M. Louttit, F. N. Maxfield, P. M. Symonds, A. Temple, C. Towle, R. P. Truitt, P. V. Young, and three others, see 1:B306; for reviews by H. H. Anderson, R. S. Cavan, M. A. Durea, H. Heffernan, G. Hildreth (with E. H. Martens), D. E. Johannsen, P. J. Kruse, W. McAndrew, S. H. Pease, W. C. Reckless, A. G. Schmidt, W. Seybrook, F. L. Wells, E. F. Young, and one other, see 36:B24.

P69. BALES, ROBERT F. **Interaction Process Analysis: A Method for the Study of Small Groups.** Cambridge, Mass.: Addison-Wesley Press, Inc., 1950. Pp. xi, 203.

For reviews by Paul B. Foreman, Ernest Greenwood, Howard E. Jensen, Daniel Lerner, Wesley Osterberg, Bruce M. Pringle, Laurance F. Shaffer, Alvin Zander, and one other, see 4:57.

P70. BALL, JOHN C. **Social Deviancy and Adolescent Personality: An Analytical Study With the MMPI.** Lexington, Ky.: University of Kentucky Press, 1962. Pp. xv, 119.

For a review by Louise J. Farnham, see 6:B64.

P71. BALLARD, PHILIP BOSWOOD. **Teaching and Testing English.** London: University of London Press Ltd., 1939. Pp. xi, 167.

For reviews by Albert E. Chapman and two others, see 3:747 and 2:B837.

P72. BARON, DENIS, and BERNARD, HAROLD W. **Evaluation Techniques for Classroom Teachers.** New York: McGraw-Hill Book Co., Inc., 1958. Pp. xi, 297.

For reviews by Dugald S. Arbuckle and Max D. Engelhart, see 5:B56.

P73. BASS, BERNARD M., and BERG, IRWIN A., Editors. **Objective Approaches to Personality Assessment.** Princeton, N.J.: D. Van Nostrand Co., Inc., 1959. Pp. x, 233.

For reviews by W. Grant Dahlstrom, Edwin C. Nevis, and S. B. Sells, see 6:B68.

P74. BAUERNFEIND, ROBERT H. **Building a School Testing Program.** Boston, Mass.: Houghton Mifflin Co., 1963. Pp. xvii, 343.

For reviews by John R. Hills and Donald E. Super, see 6:B69.

P75. BAUGHMAN, M. DALE, Editor. **Pupil Evaluation in the Junior High School: Review of Relevant Literature, Position Papers on Evaluation, Opinions on Aspects of Evaluation and Prevailing Practices in Representative Junior High Schools.** Danville, Ill.: Interstate Printers & Publishers, Inc., 1963. Pp. vii, 80.

For a review by Richard E. Schutz (with James C. Moore), see 6:B70.

P76. BAUMAN, MARY K. **A Manual of Norms for Tests Used in Counseling Blind Persons.** AFB Publications, Research Series, No. 6. New York: American Foundation for the Blind, 1958. Pp. 40.
For a review, see 5:B58.

P77. BAUMAN, MARY K., and HAYES, SAMUEL P. **A Manual for the Psychological Examination of the Adult Blind.** A project of the National Psychological Research Council for the Blind. New York: Psychological Corporation, 1951. Pp. 58.
For a review by Laurance F. Shaffer, see 4:B40.

P78. BAYER, LEONA M., and BAYLEY, NANCY. **Growth Diagnosis: Selected Methods for Interpreting and Predicting Physical Development From One Year to Maturity.** Chicago, Ill.: University of Chicago Press, 1959. Pp. xiv, 241.
For reviews by Edward E. Hunt, Jr. and J. M. Tanner, see 6:B71.

P79. BEAN, KENNETH L. **Construction of Educational and Personnel Tests.** New York: McGraw-Hill Book Co., Inc., 1953. Pp. viii, 231.
For reviews by Philip Rothman and Wayne S. Zimmerman, see 5:B59.

P80. BECK, SAMUEL J. **Introduction to the Rorschach Method: A Manual of Personality Study.** Monograph No. 1 of the American Orthopsychiatric Association. New York: the Association, 1937. Pp. xv, 278.
For reviews by J. D. Benjamin, A. Guirdham, H. H. Jasper, W. Line, C. R. Rogers, C. L. Vaughn, P. E. Vernon, and three others, see 1:B308.

P81. BECK, SAMUEL J. **Personality Structure in Schizophrenia: A Rorschach Investigation in 81 Patients and 64 Controls.** Nervous and Mental Disease Monograph No. 63. New York: Nervous and Mental Disease Monographs, 1938. Pp. 88.
For a review by D. Shakow, see 3:74; for reviews by Joseph L. Abramson, John D. Benjamin, A. Guirdham, Bruno Klopfer, David Lester, W. Line, Maria Rickers-Ovsiankina, P. E. Vernon, and four others, see 2:B841.

P82. BECK, SAMUEL J. **The Rorschach Experiment: Ventures in Blind Diagnosis.** New York: Grune & Stratton, Inc., 1960. Pp. viii, 256.
For reviews by A. Kaldegg, Gertrud M. Kurth, Martin Mayman, and Otfried Spreen, see 6:B72.

P83. BECK, SAMUEL J. **Rorschach's Test: 2, A Variety of Personality Pictures.** New York: Grune & Stratton, Inc., 1945. Pp. xii, 402.
For reviews by Philip Lawrence Harriman, Albert I. Rabin, Saul Rosenzweig, Donald E. Super, Frederic S. Weil, and two others, see 3:76; for reviews by Zygmunt A. Piotrowski and one other of Volumes I and II, see 3:77.

P84. BECK, SAMUEL J. **Rorschach's Test: 3, Advances in Interpretation.** New York: Grune & Stratton, Inc., 1952. Pp. x, 301.
For reviews by Lee J. Cronbach, Herbert Dörken, Jr., William Healy, Mortimer M. Meyer, Helen D. Sargent, B. M. Spinley, David Wechsler, and one other, see 5:B60.

P85. BECK, SAMUEL J.; BECK, ANNE G.; LEVITT, EUGENE E.; and MOLISH, HERMAN B. **Rorschach's Test: 1, Basic Processes, Third Edition.** New York: Grune & Stratton, Inc., 1961. Pp. x, 237.
For reviews by Zygmunt A. Piotrowski, Philip Roos, and Adolf G. Woltmann, see 6:B73; for re-

views by M. R. Harrower-Erickson, Robert M. Lindner, Lawson G. Lowrey, Wendell Muncie, F. W. O'Brien, F. C. Redlich, Saul Rosenzweig, W. D. Wall, Frederic S. Weil, and three others of the first edition, see 3:75; for reviews by Zygmunt A. Piotrowski and one other of Volumes I and II, see 3:77.

P86. BELL, HUGH M. **The Theory and Practice of Personal Counseling: With Special Reference to the Adjustment Inventory.** Stanford University, Calif.: Stanford University Press, 1939. Pp. v, 167.
For reviews by Ruth E. Salley, Austin G. Schmidt, and two others, see 2:B842; for a review by C. S. Kimball of an earlier edition, see 1:B309; for reviews by W. McAndrew, A. G. Schmidt, J. E. Walters, and two others, see 36:B30.

P87. BELL, JOHN ELDERKIN. **Projective Techniques: A Dynamic Approach to the Study of the Personality.** New York: Longmans, Green & Co., Inc., 1948. Pp. xvi, 533.
For reviews by Magda B. Arnold, William G. Barrett, Gotthard Booth, Edward M. L. Burchard, Robert R. Holt, Paul E. Meehl, Joseph Sandler, Pauline Snedden Sears, Laurance F. Shaffer, Arthur Weider, Adolf G. Woltmann, and two others, see 4:B43.

P88. BELLAK, LEOPOLD. **The Thematic Apperception Test and the Children's Apperception Test in Clinical Use.** New York: Grune & Stratton, Inc., 1954. Pp. x, 282.
For reviews by Frank L. Catalano, A. S. Edwards, Max L. Hutt, Douglas M. Kelley, J. G. Lyle, Boris Semeonoff, Laurance F. Shaffer, and Edwin S. Shneidman, see 5:B63.

P89. BENDER, LAURETTA. **A Visual Motor Gestalt Test and Its Clinical Use.** American Orthopsychiatric Association, Research Monographs, No. 3. New York: the Association, 1938. Pp. xi, 176.
For reviews by W. Line and M. A. Rickers-Ovsiankina, see 3:109; for reviews by J. F. Brown, Ernst Fantl, Edward J. Stainbrook, Miles A. Tinker, F. L. Wells, and five others, see 2:B843.

P90. BENGE, EUGENE J. **The Right Career for You: How to Plan for Job Success.** New York: Funk & Wagnalls Co., 1950. Pp. ix, 150.
For a review by Hyman Brandt, see 4:B45.

P91. BENJAMIN, HAZEL C. **Employment Tests in Industry and Business: A Selected, Annotated Bibliography, 1945.** Princeton University, Department of Economics and Social Institutions, Industrial Relations Section, Bibliographic Series, No. 76, Revised. Princeton, N.J.: the Section, 1945. Pp. vii, 46.
For reviews by Louise E. Gettys, T. A. Ryan, and one other, see 3:756.

P92. BENNETT, EDWARD. **Personality Assessment and Diagnosis: A Clinical and Experimental Technique.** New York: Ronald Press Co., 1961. Pp. xiv, 287.
For reviews by John D. Black, Theodore H. Blau, Harold Borko, and Miriam G. Siegel, see 6:B74.

P93. BENNETT, GEORGE K., and CRUIKSHANK, RUTH M. **A Summary of Clerical Tests.** New York: Psychological Corporation, 1949. Pp. vii, 122.
For reviews by Roy N. Anderson, W. J. E. Crissy, Donald E. Super, and one other, see 4:B46.

P94. BENNETT, GEORGE K., and CRUIKSHANK, RUTH M. **A Summary of Manual and Mechanical Ability Tests, Preliminary Form.** New York: Psychological Corporation, 1942. Pp. v, 80.
For reviews by Louise E. Gettys, Forrest H. Kirkpatrick, and one other, see 3:758.

P95. BERDIE, RALPH F.; LAYTON, WILBUR L.; SWANSON, EDWARD O.; and HAGENAH, THEDA. **Testing in Guidance and Counseling.** New York: McGraw-Hill Book Co., Inc., 1963. Pp. xiii, 288.
For reviews by Hugh M. Bell, William C. Cottle, and Donald E. Super, see 6:B76.

P96. BERDIE, RALPH F.; LAYTON, WILBUR L.; SWANSON, EDWARD O.; HAGENAH, THEDA; and MERWIN, JACK C. **Counseling and the Use of Tests: A Manual for the State-Wide Testing Programs of Minnesota, Revised Edition.** Minneapolis, Minn.: University of Minnesota Press, 1962. Pp. xi, 192.
For a review by Thomas M. Magoon of the first edition, see 6:B75.

P97. BERGEN, GARRET L.; SCHNEIDLER, GWENDOLEN; and SHERMAN, LEROY. **Use of Tests in the Adjustment Service.** American Association for Adult Education, Adjustment Service Series, Report 4. New York: the Association, 1935. Pp. 70.
For reviews by H. Clark, A. G. Schmidt, and E. K. Strong, Jr., see 36:B32.

P98. BERMAN, ISABEL R.; DARLEY, JOHN G.; and PATERSON, DONALD G. **Vocational Interest Scales: An Analysis of Three Questionnaires in Relation to Occupational Classification and Employment Status.** University of Minnesota, Bulletins of the Employment Stabilization Research Institute, Vol. 3, No. 5. Minneapolis, Minn.: University of Minnesota Press, 1934. Pp. 35.
For a review by A. B. Crawford, see 1:B311; for a review by A. G. Schmidt, see 36:B33.

P99. BETTS, EMMETT ALBERT. **Data on Visual Sensation and Perception Tests: Part 1, Lateral Imbalance.** Meadville, Pa.: Keystone View Co., 1939. Pp. 27.
For reviews by C. L. Nemzek and Howard E. Tempero, see 2:B844.1.

P100. BETTS, EMMETT ALBERT; with the assistance of ARTHUR W. AYERS. **Data on Visual Sensation and Perception Tests: Part 2, Visual Efficiency.** Meadville, Pa.: Keystone View Co., 1940. Pp. 66.
For a review by William W. Brickman, see 3:761.

P101. BHATIA, C. M. **Performance Tests of Intelligence Under Indian Conditions.** Bombay, India: Oxford University Press, 1955. Pp. xi, 144.
For reviews by A. E. G. Pilliner and one other, see 5:B66.

P102. BIESHEUVEL, S. **African Intelligence.** Johannesburg, South Africa: South African Institute of Race Relations, 1943. Pp. viii, 225.
For a review, see 3:764.

P103. BIJOU, SIDNEY W., Editor. **The Psychological Program in AAF Convalescent Hospitals.** Army Air Forces Aviation Psychology Program Research Reports, Report No. 15. Washington, D.C.: U.S. Government Printing Office, 1947. Pp. viii, 256.
For reviews by George A. Kelly and Laurance F. Shaffer, see 4:B50. For a review of the series, see P1.

P104. BINGHAM, W. V. **Administrative Ability: Its Discovery and Development.** Society for Personnel Administration, Pamphlet No. 1. Washington, D.C.: the Society, 1939. Pp. iii, 17.
For a review, see 2:B845.

P105. BINGHAM, W. V. **Oral Examinations in Civil Service Recruitment: With Special Reference to Experiences in Pennsylvania.** Civil Service Assembly of the United States and Canada, Pamphlet No. 13. Chicago, Ill.: the Assembly, 1939. Pp. 30.

For reviews by James M. Mitchell and D. T. Stanley, see 2:B847.

P106. BINGHAM, WALTER VAN DYKE. **Aptitudes and Aptitude Testing.** New York: Harper & Brothers, 1937. Pp. ix, 390.
For reviews by W. A. Stumpf and three others, see 2:B846; for reviews by E. S. Bogardus, G. Brighouse, S. G. Estes, J. Graham, J. G. Jenkins, A. M. Jordan, H. D. Kitson, D. G. Paterson, E. Slocombe, W. H. Stead, E. L. Stogdill, M. R. Trabue, R. S. Uhrbrock, C. S. Yoakum, and two others, see 1:B313.

P107. BIRNEY, ROBERT C., and TEEVAN, RICHARD C., Editors. **Measuring Human Motivation: An Enduring Problem: Selected Readings.** Princeton, N.J.: D. Van Nostrand Co., Inc., 1962. Pp. ix, 181.
For reviews by Edward Levonian and W. R. Robinson, see 6:B81.

P108. BJERSTEDT, ÅKE. **Glimpses From the World of the School Child: Self and Other Explored in Dyadic Communication.** Sociometric Monograph No. 41. Beacon, N.Y.: Beacon House, Inc., Publishers, 1960. Pp. 131.
For reviews by I. D. Steiner and W. Cody Wilson, see 6:B82.

P109. BJERSTEDT, ÅKE. **Interpretations of Sociometric Choice Status: Studies of Workmate Choices in the School Class and Selected Correlates With Special Emphasis on the Methodology of Preferential Sociometry.** Studia Psychologica et Paedagogica, Series Altera, Investigationes 8. Lund, Sweden: C W K Gleerups, 1956. Pp. 408.
For reviews by A. R. MacKinnon, D. M. Edwards Penfold, and Leslie D. Zeleny, see 5:B69.

P110. BJERSTEDT, ÅKE. **The Methodology of Preferential Sociometry: Selected Trends and Some Contributions.** Sociometry Monographs, No. 37. Beacon, N.Y.: Beacon House, Inc., Publishers, 1956. Pp. 156.
For reviews by Edgar F. Borgatta and Renato Tagiuri, see 5:B70.

P111. BLACK, HILLEL. **They Shall Not Pass.** New York: William Morrow & Co., Inc., 1963. Pp. ix, 342.
For reviews by Joann Chenault, Henry S. Dyer, Charles A. Sukman, and M. H. Trytten, see 6:B83.

P112. BLISS, ELISHA F., JR. **Standardized Tests and Educational Practice.** Brooklyn, N.Y.: the Author, 1940. Pp. 29.
For reviews by Henry D. Rinsland, Austin G. Schmidt, and one other, see 3:768.

P113. BLOCK, JACK. **The Q-Sort Method in Personality Assessment and Psychiatric Research.** Springfield, Ill.: Charles C Thomas, Publisher, 1961. Pp. ix, 161.
For reviews by Samuel J. Beck, Harold Borko, and John E. Exner, Jr., see 6:72.

P114. BLOOM, BENJAMIN S., and PETERS, FRANK R. **The Use of Academic Prediction Scales for Counseling and Selecting College Entrants.** New York: Free Press of Glencoe, 1961. Pp. xiii, 145.
For a review by Donivan J. Watley, see 6:B89.

P115. BLOOM, BENJAMIN S.; ENGELHART, MAX D.; FURST, EDWARD J.; HILL, WALKER H.; and KRATHWOHL, DAVID R. **Taxonomy of Educational Objectives: The Classification of Educational Goals: Handbook I, Cognitive Domain.** New York: Longmans, Green & Co., Inc., 1956. Pp. xiii, 207.
For reviews by William E. Coffman, Henry J. Ehlers, Anthony Nemetz, Julian C. Stanley (with Dale L. Bolton), and one other, see 5:B72.

P116. BLUM, HENRIK L.; PETERS, HENRY B.; and BETTMAN, JEROME W. **Vision Screening for Elementary Schools: The Orinda Study.** Berkeley, Calif.: University of California Press, 1959. Pp. xi, 146.
For a review by Charles R. Stewart, see 6:B90.

P117. BLUM, LUCILLE HOLLANDER; DAVIDSON, HELEN H.; and FIELDSTEEL, NINA D.; with the assistance of LOUIS GETOFF. **A Rorschach Workbook.** New York: International Universities Press, Inc., 1954. Pp. iv, 169.
For reviews by E. Lowell Kelly, Leonard B. Olinger, and one other, see 5:B73.

P118. BOCHNER, RUTH, and HALPERN, FLORENCE. **The Clinical Application of the Rorschach Test, Second Edition.** New York: Grune & Stratton, Inc., 1945. Pp. xi, 331.
For reviews by Vernon Clark, Isabelle V. Kendig, Leslie Phillips, Albert I. Rabin, Donald E. Super, and two others, see 3:79; for reviews by S. J. Beck, Ralph R. Brown, C. J. C. Earl, R. M. Finney, Arthur N. Foxe, Martin Grotjahn, M. R. Harrower-Erickson, Webb Haymaker, Morris Krugman, Lawson G. Lowrey, Edna Mann, Ernest G. Schachtel, W. D. Wall, and five others of the first edition, see 3:78.

P119. BOHM, EWALD. **A Textbook in Rorschach Test Diagnosis for Psychologists, Physicians, and Teachers.** New York: Grune & Stratton, Inc., 1959. Pp. xiii, 322.
For reviews by Daniel G. Brown, Henry P. David, and B. Semeonoff, see 6:B91.

P120. BOVARD, JOHN F.; COZENS, FREDERICK W.; and HAGMAN, E. PATRICIA. **Tests and Measurements in Physical Education, Third Edition.** Philadelphia, Pa.: W. B. Saunders Co., 1949. Pp. xvii, 410.
For reviews by Virginia Peaseley and Evelyn B. Spindler of the second edition, see 2:B848; for reviews by J. E. Caswell, A. G. Schmidt, and one other, see 1:B316.

P121. BOWER, ELI M. **Early Identification of Emotionally Handicapped Children in School.** Springfield, Ill.: Charles C Thomas, Publisher, 1960. Pp. xiii, 120.
For a review by Frederick H. Allen, see 6:B93.

P122. BOWLEY, AGATHA H. **A Study of Factors Influencing the General Development of the Child During Pre-School Years by Means of Record Forms.** British Journal of Psychology Monograph Supplements, Vol. 8, No. 25. London: Cambridge University Press, 1940. Pp. xi, 48.
For reviews by C. Birchenough and Ll. Wynn Jones, see 3:776.

P123. BOYNTON, PAUL L. **Intelligence: Its Manifestations and Measurement.** New York: D. Appleton-Century Co., 1933. Pp. xi, 466.
For reviews by L. N. Yepsen and one other, see 1:B317; for reviews by H. Easley, A. S. Edwards, M. H. Krout, J. B. Miner, R. Pintner, F. M. Schaefer, R. C. Tryon, E. I. F. Williams, L. N. Yepsen, and one other, see 36:B36.

P124. BRADFIELD, JAMES M., and MOREDOCK, H. STEWART. **Measurement and Evaluation in Education: An Introduction to Its Theory and Practice at Both the Elementary and Secondary School Levels.** New York: Macmillan Co., 1957. Pp. xiv, 509.
For reviews by Philip Himelstein and Edith Jay, see 5:B75.

P125. BRERETON, J. L. **The Case for Examinations: An Account of Their Place in Education With Some Proposals for Their Reform.** London: Cambridge University Press, 1944. Pp. viii, 226.
For reviews by C. Birchenough and Vera French, see 3:778.

P126. BRICKLIN, BARRY; PIOTROWSKI, ZYGMUNT A.; and WAGNER, EDWIN E. **The Hand Test: A New Projective Test With Special Reference to the Prediction of Overt Aggressive Behavior.** Springfield, Ill.: Charles C Thomas, Publisher, 1962. Pp. x, 100.
For a review by Irving R. Stone, see 6:216; for a review by Melvin Roman, see 6:B95.

P127. BRIGHAM, CARL C. **Examining Fellowship Applicants: A Report Made to the Social Science Research Council on the Method of Selecting Fellows for First-Year Graduate Study.** Social Science Research Council Bulletin, No. 23. Princeton, N.J.: Princeton University Press, 1935. Pp. 58.
For a review by Carl E. Seashore, see 36:B38.

P128. BRIGHAM, CARL C. **Reading of the Comprehensive Examination in English: An Analysis of the Procedures Followed During the Five Reading Periods From 1929 Through 1933.** College Entrance Examination Board. Princeton, N.J.: Princeton University Press, 1934. Pp. 43.
For reviews by F. P. Frutchey and J. T. Russell, see 36:B39.

P129. BROADLEY, CHARLES V., and BROADLEY, MARGARET E. **Know Your Real Abilities: Understanding and Developing Your Aptitudes.** New York: McGraw-Hill Book Co., Inc., 1948. Pp. vii, 209.
For two reviews, see 4:B59.

P130. BROCKINGTON, W. A. **A Secondary School Entrance Test.** London: Oxford University Press, 1934. Pp. 72.
For a review, see 36:B40.

P131. BROOM, M. E. **Educational Measurements in the Elementary School.** New York: McGraw-Hill Book Co., Inc., 1939. Pp. x, 345.
For reviews by C. M. Fleming, Alice Temple, and one other, see 3:781; for reviews by F. J. Adams, R. L. Bedwell, C. C. Crawford, J. Murray Lee, Worth J. Osburn, Austin G. Schmidt, Eugene Shen, C. W. Webb, and two others, see 2:B850; for a review by R. C. Perry of an earlier edition, see 36:B41.

P132. BROWN, CLARA M. **Evaluation and Investigation in Home Economics.** New York: Appleton-Century-Crofts, Inc., 1941. Pp. xviii, 461.
For reviews by Elizabeth Stevenson and Frances Swineford, see 3:782.

P133. BROWN, WILLIAM, and THOMSON, GODFREY H. **The Essentials of Mental Measurement, Fourth Edition.** London: Cambridge University Press, 1940. Pp. x, 256.
For a review by Albert K. Kurtz, see 3:785.

P134. BRUNSCHWIG, LILY. **Study of Some Personality Aspects of Deaf Children.** Columbia University, Teachers College, Contributions to Education No. 687. New York: Bureau of Publications, the College, 1936. Pp. xi, 143.
For reviews by F. Heider, M. K. Mason, and one other, see 1:B321.

P135. BRUSSEL, JAMES A.; HITCH, KENNETH S.; and PIOTROWSKI, ZYGMUNT A. **A Rorschach Train-**

ing Manual, [Third Edition]. Utica, N.Y.: State Hospitals Press, 1950. Pp. 86.

For reviews by M. M. Genn, Walter Kass, and George A. Ulett, see 4:118.

P136. BRYAN, ROY C. **Pupil Rating of Secondary School Teachers.** Columbia University, Teachers College, Contributions to Education No. 708. New York: Bureau of Publications, the College, 1937. Pp. vi, 96.

For reviews by A. H. Lass, Clarence M. Pruitt, and William A. Smith, see 2:B854; for reviews by P. W. Hutson, R. J. Maaske, W. D. Reeves, H. H. Remmers, A. G. Schmidt, and one other, see 1:B323.

P137. BRYAN, ROY C., and YNTEMA, OTTO. **A Manual on the Evaluation of Student Reactions in Secondary Schools.** Kalamazoo, Mich.: Western State Teachers College, 1939. Pp. ii, 56.

For reviews by Clarence E. Howell, Austin G. Schmidt, Willis L. Uhl, and one other, see 2:B855.

P138. BUEHLER, CHARLOTTE, and HETZER, HILDE-GAARD. **Testing Children's Development From Birth to School Age.** New York: Farrar & Rinehart, Inc., 1935. Pp. xi, 191.

For reviews by T. J. Padshah and two others, see 2:B855.1; for reviews by E. F. Kinder, C. M. Louttit, R. Stutsman, and one other, see 1:B324; for reviews by N. Freeman (with G. T. Buswell), H. Highfield, B. E. Holaday, and one other, see 36:B44.

P139. BUHLER, CHARLOTTE, and LEFEVER, D. WELTY. **A Rorschach Study on the Psychological Characteristics of Alcoholics.** Yale University, Laboratory of Applied Physiology, Memoirs of the Section of Studies on Alcohol, No. 6. New Haven, Conn.: Quarterly Journal of Studies on Alcohol, 1948. Pp. viii, 64.

For reviews by Albert Ax (with Milton Greenblatt), Gotthard Booth, Isabelle V. Kendig, Laura Malkenson, and two others, see 4:120.

P140. BUHLER, CHARLOTTE; BUHLER, KARL; and LEFEVER, D. WELTY. **Development of the Basic Rorschach Score With Manual of Directions.** Rorschach Standardization Studies. No. 1. Los Angeles, Calif.: Charlotte Buhler, 1948. Pp. ix, 190.

For reviews by Goldie Ruth Kaback, Walter Kass, Douglas M. Kelley, Mortimer M. Meyer, Herman Molish, Zygmunt A. Piotrowski, Maria A. Rickers-Ovsiankina, Laurance F. Shaffer, and one other, see 4:119.

P141. BUHLER, CHARLOTTE; LEFEVER, D. WELTY; KALLSTEDT, FRANCIS E.; and PEAK, HORACE M. **Development of the Basic Rorschach Score: Supplementary Monograph.** Los Angeles, Calif.: Rorschach Standardization Study, 1952. Pp. iv, 71.

For reviews by Walter Kass and Ann Magaret, see 5:B79.

P142. BULLOCK, ROBERT P. **Social Factors Related to Job Satisfaction: A Technique for the Measurement of Job Satisfaction.** Ohio State University, Bureau of Business Research, Research Monograph No. 70; Ohio Studies in Personnel. Columbus, Ohio: the Bureau, 1952. Pp. xii, 105.

For a review by L. Lawrence Schultz, see 5:B80.

P143. BURGEMEISTER, BESSIE B. **Psychological Techniques in Neurological Diagnosis.** New York: Hoeber Medical Division, Harper & Row, Publishers, Inc., 1962. Pp. viii, 248.

For a review by Walter G. Klopfer, see 6:B100.

P144. BUROS, OSCAR K. **Classified Index of Tests and Reviews in The Fourth Mental Measure-**
ments Yearbook. Highland Park, N.J.: Gryphon Press, 1953. Pp. 60.

For a review by H. F. Lock, see 5:B82.

P145. BUROS, OSCAR K. **Educational, Psychological, and Personality Tests of 1933 and 1934.** Rutgers University Bulletin, Vol. 11, No. 11; Studies in Education, No. 7. New Brunswick, N.J.: School of Education, Rutgers University, 1935. Pp. 44.

For a review by L. V. Koos, see 36:B45.

P146. BUROS, OSCAR K. **Educational, Psychological, and Personality Tests of 1933, 1934, and 1935.** Rutgers University Bulletin, Vol. 13, No. 1; Studies in Education, No. 9. New Brunswick, N.J.: School of Education, Rutgers University, 1936. Pp. 83.

For two reviews, see 2:B856 and 1:B325; for reviews by H. T. Eaton, N. Fenton, W. J. Gifford, A. G. Schmidt, R. K. Watkins, and four others, see 36:B46.

P147. BUROS, OSCAR K. **Educational, Psychological, and Personality Tests of 1936: Including a Bibliography and Book Review Digest of Measurement Books and Monographs of 1933–36.** Rutgers University Bulletin, Vol. 14, No. 2A; Studies in Education, No. 11. New Brunswick, N.J.: School of Education, Rutgers University, 1937. Pp. 141.

For two reviews, see 2:B857; for reviews by E. L. Abell, D. C. Adkins, H. R. Anderson, P. W. L. Cox, C. A. Gibb, W. J. Gifford, A. M. Jordan, H. D. Kitson E. Lawrence, C. M. Louttit, A. J. Mitrano, F. F. Powers, W. C. Reckless, P. Sandiford, Old Stager, W. Stephenson, A. E. Traxler, J. W. Wrightstone, and six others, see 1:B326.

P148. BUROS, OSCAR KRISEN, Editor. **The 1938 Mental Measurements Yearbook of the School of Education, Rutgers University.** New Brunswick, N.J.: Rutgers University Press, 1938. Pp. xv, 415.

For reviews by M. N. Banerji, S. J. Beck, J. M. Blackburn, Emory S. Bogardus, M. E. Broom, William A. Brownell, Cyril Burt, Turner C. Chandler, Stanley G. Dulsky, Michael B. Dunn, Howard Easley, Alvin C. Eurich, C. A. Gibb, W. J. Gifford, A. R. Gilliland, Carter V. Good, Alice W. Goodman, Ernest E. Hadley, Ruth M. Hubbard, A. M. Jordan, Harry D. Kitson, A. H. Lass, W. Line, John A. Long, M. M. Meyer, Horace T. Morse, Donald H. Nottage, Doris M. Odlum, John Gray Peatman, Francis F. Powers, Henry D. Rinsland, J. W. M. Rothney, Austin G. Schmidt, Richard S. Schultz, Gretchen P. Seiler, R. F. Sharp, C. E. Smith, W. C. Smyser, Wm. Stephenson, Robert H. Thouless, F. L. Wells, Guy M. Wilson, Ll. Wynn Jones, and thirteen others, see 2:B858.

P149. BUROS, OSCAR KRISEN, Editor. **The Nineteen Forty Mental Measurements Yearbook.** Highland Park, N.J.: Gryphon Press, 1941. Pp. xxv, 674.

For reviews by H. P. Maiti, Horace T. Morse, P. E. Vernon, and Vincent Wilking, see 4:B70; for reviews by E. L. Abell, Roger M. Bellows, M. E. Broom, Michael B. Dunn, N. L. Engelhardt, Jr., Warren G. Findley, C. M. Fleming, G. W. T. H. Fleming, Earl R. Gabler, C. A. Gibb, Elizabeth Gifford, David M. Glixon, Carter V. Good, Jessie Graham, Ernest E. Hadley, Kenneth L. Heaton, Nelson B. Henry, Thelma Hunt, Harry D. Kitson, Harold W. Leuenberger, John A. Long, Lawson G. Lowrey, Pedro T. Orata, Frederick L. Patry, D. G. Ryans,

Austin G. Schmidt, J. Conrad Seegers, David Segel, Louise Shores, Edward J. Stainbrook, J. B. Stroud, and seventeen others, see 3:788.

P150. BUROS, OSCAR KRISEN, Editor. **The Third Mental Measurements Yearbook.** Highland Park, N.J.: Gryphon Press, 1949. Pp. xv, 1047.

For reviews by J. Brožek, A. S. Edwards, C. M. Fleming, Earl R. Gabler, D. A. Grant, F. J. Houlahan, A. M. Jordan, Henry Clay Lindgren, Donald G. Paterson, Ralph E. Pickett, William B. Reiner, A. Rodger, Laurance F. Shaffer, E. Donald Sisson, Donald E. Super, D. A. Worcester, and two others, see 4:B71.

P151. BUROS, OSCAR KRISEN, Editor. **The Fourth Mental Measurements Yearbook.** Highland Park, N.J.: Gryphon Press, 1953. Pp. xxv, 1163.

For reviews by Cyril Burt, Arthur P. Coladarci, L. E. Cortis, Lee J. Cronbach, Frederick B. Davis, Robert L. Ebel, Maurice L. Hartung, Jack A. Holmes, Jacob T. Hunt, Irving Lorge, Peter McKellar, Leola E. Neal, Frederick L. Patry, Anne Roe, Frank K. Shuttleworth, O. Glenn Stahl, D. F. Vincent, and two others, see 5:B84.

P152. BUROS, OSCAR KRISEN, Editor. **The Fifth Mental Measurements Yearbook.** Highland Park, N.J.: Gryphon Press, 1959. Pp. xxix, 1292.

For reviews by Charlotte Banks, Irwin A. Berg, Bertram R. Forer, James G. Foshee, Charles R. Langmuir, R. E. Muuss, Harold Seashore, B. Semeonoff, Agatha Townsend, W. D. Wall, R. L. Want, and three others, see 6:B104.

P153. BUROS, OSCAR KRISEN, Editor. **Tests in Print: A Comprehensive Bibliography of Tests for Use in Education, Psychology, and Industry.** Highland Park, N.J.: Gryphon Press, 1961. Pp. xxix, 479.

For reviews by C. M. Fleming, Bertram R. Forer, James Lumsden, William B. Michael, Jum C. Nunnally, Harold Seashore, Raymond J. Steimel, and Frank B. Womer, see 6:B105.

P154. BURPEE, ROYAL HUDDLESTON. **Seven Quickly Administered Tests of Physical Capacity: And Their Use in Detecting Physical Incapacity for Motor Activity in Men and Boys.** Columbia University, Teachers College, Contributions to Education, No. 818. New York: Bureau of Publications, the College, 1940. Pp. vii, 151.

For reviews by Karl W. Bookwalter, Charles C. Cowell, and one other, see 3:789.

P155. BURT, CYRIL. **The Factors of Mind: An Introduction to Factor-Analysis in Psychology.** London: University of London Press Ltd., 1940. Pp. xiv, 509.

For reviews by Anne Anastasi, W. Line, H. T. H. Piaggio, T. Raymont, W. J. H. Sprott, Robert H. Thouless, and one other, see 52 in *Statistical Methodology Reviews, 1941–1950;* for reviews by Godfrey Thomson, Dael Wolfle, and three others, see 48 in *The Second Yearbook of Research and Statistical Methodology Books and Reviews.*

P156. BURT, CYRIL. **Handbook of Tests for Use in Schools, Second Edition.** London: Staples Press Ltd., 1948. Pp. xvi, 110.

For reviews by C. M. Fleming and one other, see 4:B73.

P157. BURT, CYRIL. **Mental and Scholastic Tests, Fourth Edition.** London: Staples Press Ltd., 1962. Pp. xxxi, 549.

For a review by E. R. Jennings, see 6:B106; for three reviews of the second edition, see 4:B74.

P158. CALANDRA, ALEXANDER. **Objective Questions in College Chemistry.** Brooklyn, N.Y.: Chemistry Book Store, 1938. Pp. viii, 151.

For a review by O. M. Smith, see 1:B327.

P159. CALIGOR, LEOPOLD. **A New Approach to Figure Drawing: Based Upon an Interrelated Series of Drawings.** Springfield, Ill.: Charles C Thomas, Publisher, 1957. Pp. xii, 149.

For reviews by Seymour Fisher, Emanuel F. Hammer, Alfred B. Heilbrun, Jr., and one other, see 6:211; for a review by H. C. Gunzburg, see 5:131.

P160. CAPPS, HARRY MARCELLUS. **Vocabulary Changes in Mental Deterioration: The Relationship of Vocabulary Functioning as Measured by a Variety of Word Meaning and Usage Tests to Clinically Estimated Degrees of Mental Deterioration in "Idiopathic" Epilepsy.** Columbia University, Archives of Psychology, No. 242. New York: the University, September 1939. Pp. 81.

For a review, see 2:B858.1.

P161. CAPWELL, DORA F. **Psychological Tests for Retail Store Personnel.** Pittsburgh, Pa.: Research Bureau for Retail Training, University of Pittsburgh, 1949. Pp. 48.

For a review, see 4:B77.

P162. CARKHUFF, ROBERT R. **The MMPI: An Outline for General Clinical and Counseling Use.** Lexington, Ky.: the Author, University of Kentucky, 1961. Pp. vi, 60.

For a review by Thomas M. Magoon, see 6:B113.

P163. CARR, ARTHUR C.; FORER, BERTRAM R.; HENRY, WILLIAM E.; HOOKER, EVELYN; HUTT, MAX L.; and PIOTROWSKI, ZYGMUNT A. **The Prediction of Overt Behavior Through the Use of Projective Techniques.** Springfield, Ill.: Charles C Thomas, Publisher, 1960. Pp. xii, 177.

For reviews by Stephanie Z. Dudek, Thomas W. Richards, and B. Semeonoff, see 6:B116.

P164. CARRUTHERS, ROBERT B. **Building Better English Tests: A Guide for Teachers of English in the Secondary Schools.** Champaign, Ill.: National Council of Teachers of English, 1963. Pp. 32.

For a review by Oscar M. Haugh, see 6:B117.

P165. CARTER, HAROLD D. **Vocational Interests and Job Orientation: A Ten-Year Review.** Applied Psychology Monographs of the American Association for Applied Psychology, No. 2. Stanford, Calif.: Stanford University Press, 1944. Pp. 85.

For a review by Edward B. Greene, see 3:650.

P166. CARTER, LAUNOR F., Editor. **Psychological Research on Navigator Training.** Army Air Forces Aviation Psychology Program Research Reports, Report No. 10. Washington, D.C.: U.S. Government Printing Office, 1947. Pp. ix, 186.

For a review by John L. Kennedy, see 4:B80; for a review, see 3:793. For a review of the series, see P1.

P167. CASSEL, ROBERT H. **The Vineland Adaptation of the Oseretsky Tests.** Training School Bulletin, Supplement to Vol. 46, Nos. 3–4, May–June 1949. Monograph Supplement Series, No. 1. Vineland, N.J.: Training School, [1949]. Pp. 32.

For a review by Laurance F. Shaffer, see 4:651.

P168. CATTELL, PSYCHE. **The Measurement of Intelligence of Infants and Young Children, Revised Edition.** New York: Psychological Corporation, 1960. Pp. 274.

For reviews by Rachel Stutsman Ball, C. M. Louttit, T. L. McCulloch, and Helen Speyer of the first edition, see 3:282.

P169. CATTELL, RAYMOND B. **Description and Measurement of Personality.** Yonkers, N.Y.: World Book Co., 1946. Pp. xx, 602.
For reviews by Josef Brožek, Cyril Burt, A. Chapanis, Robert P. Fischer, J. P. Guilford, Margaret Ives, Roswell H. Johnson, Douglas M. Kelley, W. Line, and one other, see 4:B83; for reviews by H. J. Eysenck, Earl R. Gabler, Ralph M. Stogdill, Godfrey Thomson, and one other, see 3:796.

P170. CATTELL, RAYMOND B. **Factor Analysis: An Introduction and Manual for the Psychologist and Social Scientist.** New York: Harper & Brothers, 1952. Pp. xiii, 462.
For reviews by W. J. E. Crissy, James Deese, A. S. C. Ehrenberg, Edward Elliott, Roy G. Francis, Henry E. Garrett, Dorothy M. Knoell, William B. Michael, Philip E. Vernon, and Charles Wrigley, see 5:B89.

P171. CATTELL, RAYMOND B. **The Fight for Our National Intelligence.** London: P. S. King & Son, Ltd., 1937. Pp. xx, 166.
For three reviews, see 2:B859; for reviews by J. M. Blackburn, E. J. G. Bradford, R. B. Cattell, J. Fisher, E. F. Griffith, F. H. Hankins, W. S. Neff, P. E. Vernon, and five others, see 1:B328.

P172. CATTELL, RAYMOND B. **A Guide to Mental Testing: For Psychological Clinics, Schools, and Industrial Psychologists, Third Edition.** London: University of London Press Ltd., 1953. Pp. xv, 446.
For reviews by Cyril Burt, A. Richardson, and one other, see 5:B90; for reviews by Josef Brožek, C. M. Fleming, and four others of an earlier edition, see 4:B84; for three reviews, see 2:B860; for reviews by J. C. Raven, C. Simmins, and two others, see 1:B329; for reviews by J. M. Blackburn, R. Pintner, and three others, see 36:B48.

P173. CATTELL, RAYMOND B. **An Introduction to Personality Study.** London: Hutchinson's University Library, 1950. Pp. 235.
For reviews by Marjorie Brierley, H. J. Eysenck, J. P. Guilford, W. H. N. Hotopf, Laurance F. Shaffer, P. E. Vernon, and one other, see 4:B85.

P174. CATTELL, RAYMOND B. **Personality: A Systematic Theoretical and Factual Study.** New York: McGraw-Hill Book Co., Inc., 1950. Pp. xii, 689.
For reviews by Richard L. Jenkins, Tamotsu Shibutani, P. E. Vernon, and two others, see 4:B86.

P175. CATTELL, RAYMOND B. **Personality and Motivation Structure and Measurement.** New York: Harcourt, Brace & World, Inc., 1957. Pp. xxv, 948.
For reviews by Irwin A. Berg, A. G. Hammer, Charles Hanley, and S. B. Sells, see 6:B119; for reviews by John Beloff, Edgar M. Haverland, and one other, see 5:B91.

P176. CATTELL, RAYMOND B., and SCHEIER, IVAN H. **The Meaning and Measurement of Neuroticism and Anxiety.** New York: Ronald Press Co., 1961. Pp. ix, 535.
For reviews by H. R. Beech, Raymond B. Cattell, Sanford J. Dean, and H. J. Eysenck, see 6:B120.

P177. CAVAN, RUTH SHONLE; BURGESS, ERNEST W.; HAVIGHURST, ROBERT J.; and GOLDHAMER, HERBERT. **Personal Adjustment in Old Age.** Chicago,

Ill.: Science Research Associates, Inc., 1949. Pp. xiii, 204.
For reviews by Albert R. Chandler and Arthur Chen, see 4:101.

P178. CHAMBERS, E. G. **Psychological Tests for Accident Proneness and Industrial Proficiency.** Privy Council, Medical Research Council Memorandum No. 31. London: H.M. Stationery Office, 1955. Pp. iii, 30.
For a review by Boris Semeonoff, see 5:B92.

P179. CHAMPNEYS, MARY C. **An English Bibliography of Examinations: (1900–1932).** International Institute Examinations Enquiry. London: Macmillan & Co., Ltd., 1934. Pp. xxiv, 141.
For a review, see 1:B330; for reviews by A. E. Chapman, B. D. Wood, and two others, see 36:B50.

P180. CHAPIN, FRANCIS S. **Measurement of Social Status by the Use of the Social Status Scale, 1933.** Minneapolis, Minn.: University of Minnesota Press, 1933. Pp. 16.
For reviews by R. S. Cavan and C. S. Wyand, see 1:B331; for reviews by W. McAndrew and one other, see 36:B51.

P181. CHAPPLE, ELIOT D.; with the collaboration of CONRAD M. ARENSBERG. **Measuring Human Relations: An Introduction to the Study of the Interaction of Individuals.** Genetic Psychology Monographs, Vol. 22, No. 1. Provincetown, Mass.: Journal Press, 1940. Pp. 147.
For a review by Carle C. Zimmerman, see 3:797.

P182. CHAUNCEY, HENRY, and DOBBIN, JOHN E. **Testing: Its Place in Education Today.** New York: Harper & Row, Publishers, Inc., 1963. Pp. xiii, 225.
For reviews by M. H. Trytten and Paul Woodring, see 6:B125.

P183. CHEYDLEUR, FREDERIC D. **Placement Tests in Foreign Languages at the University of Wisconsin: A Forward Step in Education, 1930–1943.** Bulletin of the University of Wisconsin, Serial No. 2686, General Series No. 2470. Madison, Wis.: Bureau of Guidance and Records, the University, 1943. Pp. 39.
For a review by James B. Tharp, see 3:798.

P184. CHITTENDEN, GERTRUDE E. **An Experimental Study in Measuring and Modifying Assertive Behavior in Young Children.** Monographs of the Society for Research in Child Development, Vol. 7, No. 1, Serial No. 31. Washington, D.C.: the Society, 1942. Pp. v, 87.
For a review, see 3:799.

P185. CIOCCO, ANTONIO, and PALMER, CARROLL E. **The Hearing of School Children: A Statistical Study of Audiometric and Clinical Records.** Monographs of the Society for Research in Child Development, Vol. 6, No. 3, Serial No. 29. Washington, D.C.: the Society, 1941. Pp. v, 77.
For two reviews, see 3:800.

P186. CIVIL SERVICE ASSEMBLY OF THE UNITED STATES AND CANADA, COMMITTEE ON ORAL TESTS IN PUBLIC PERSONNEL SELECTION. **Oral Tests in Public Personnel Selection: A Report Submitted to the Civil Service Assembly.** Chicago, Ill.: the Assembly, 1943. Pp. xviii, 174.
For a review by Arthur Burton, see 3:801.

P187. CLARK, KENNETH E. **The Vocational Interests of Nonprofessional Men.** Minneapolis,

Minn.: University of Minnesota Press, 1961. Pp. xi, 129.

For reviews by Robert Callis and Donald E. Super, see 6:B126.

P188. CLARK, RUTH MILLBURN. **A Method of Administering and Evaluating the Thematic Apperception Test in Group Situations.** Genetic Psychology Monographs, Vol. 30, No. 1. Provincetown, Mass.: Journal Press, 1944. Pp. 55.

For a review by Percival M. Symonds, see 3:104.

P189. CLARKE, E. R. **Predictable Accuracy in Examinations.** British Journal of Psychology Monograph Supplements, Vol. 8, No. 24. London: Cambridge University Press, 1940. Pp. xi, 48.

For reviews by Frank Sandon, Ll. Wynn Jones, and one other, see 3:804.

P190. CLARKE, H. HARRISON. **Application of Measurement to Health and Physical Education, Third Edition.** Englewood Cliffs, N.J.: Prentice-Hall, Inc., 1959. Pp. xv, 528.

For a review by C. H. McCloy of an earlier edition, see 4:B92; for a review by A. S. Daniels, see 3:805; for a review by Frederick Rand Rogers, see 3:806.

P191. CLIFTON, JAMES A., and LEVINE, DAVID. **Klamath Personalities: Ten Rorschach Case Studies.** [Lawrence, Kan. James A. Clifton, University of Kansas], 1961. Pp. iv, 80.

For reviews by Roy G. D'Andrade and Sohan Lal Sharma, see 6:B129.

P192. COLLEGE ENTRANCE EXAMINATION BOARD. **Manual of Freshman Class Profiles, 1964 Edition.** New York: the Board, 1964. Pp. xiv, 584.

For a review by Jean Reiss of the 1961 edition, see 6:B136.

P193. COLLEGE ENTRANCE EXAMINATION BOARD, COMMISSION ON ENGLISH. **End-of-Year Examinations in English for College-Bound Students Grades 9–12: Sample Questions in Language, Literature, and Composition; Sample Responses by Students; Evaluations of the Responses.** New York: the Board, 1963. Pp. viii, 193.

For reviews by Edmund J. Farrell and Charles D. O'Connell, see 6:B138.

P194. COMMITTEE OF THE SECONDARY SCHOOL EXAMINATIONS COUNCIL. **Curriculum and Examinations in Secondary Schools: Report of the Committee of the Secondary School Examinations Council Appointed by the President of the Board of Education in 1941.** London: H.M. Stationery Office, 1943. Pp. ix, 152.

For a review by Frank Smith, see 3:911.

P195. CONANT, MARGARET M. **The Construction of a Diagnostic Test for Senior High School Students and College Freshmen.** Columbia University, Teachers College, Contributions to Education, No. 861. New York: Bureau of Publications, the College, 1942. Pp. ix, 156.

For reviews by A. M. Jordan and Miles A. Tinker, see 3:815.

P196. CONRAD, HERBERT S. **A Statistical Study of Ratings on the California Behavior Inventory for Nursery-School Children.** Genetic Psychology Monographs, Vol. 16, No. 1. Worcester, Mass.: Clark University Press, 1934. Pp. 78.

For a review by F. L. Goodenough, see 36:B75.

P197. CONWAY, CLIFFORD B. **The Hearing Abilities of Children in Toronto Public Schools.** University of Toronto, Ontario College of Education,

Department of Educational Research, Bulletin No. 9. Toronto, Canada: the Department, 1937. Pp. 132.

For two reviews, see 2:B872; for reviews by A. G. Schmidt and one other, see 1:B334.

P198. COOK, STUART W., Editor. **Psychological Research on Radar Observer Training.** Army Air Forces Aviation Psychology Program Research Reports, Report No. 12. Washington, D.C.: U.S. Government Printing Office, 1947. Pp. x, 340.

For reviews by C. S. Bridgman and Laurance F. Shaffer, see 4:B99. For a review of the series, see P1.

P199. COOMBS, CLYDE H. **A Theory of Psychological Scaling.** University of Michigan, Engineering Research Institute, Bulletin No. 34. Ann Arbor, Mich.: University of Michigan Press, 1952. Pp. vi, 94.

For reviews by Marvin D. Dunnette, Allen L. Edwards, and Ardie Lubin, see 5:B104.

P200. COOMBS, CLYDE H., and KAO, R. C. **Nonmetric Factor Analysis.** University of Michigan, Engineering Research Institute, Bulletin No. 38. Ann Arbor, Mich.: University of Michigan Press, 1955. Pp. vii, 63.

For a review by Samuel Messick, see 6:B142.

P201. CORNELL, ETHEL L., and COXE, WARREN W. **A Performance Ability Scale: Examination Manual.** Yonkers, N.Y.: World Book Co., 1934. Pp. iv, 88.

For reviews by G. Hildreth, H. C. Mahan, F. N. Maxfield, S. K. Richardson, F. K. Shuttleworth, and three others, see 1:B335; for a review by R. Pintner, see 36:B77.

P202. COX, J. W. **Manual Skill: Its Organization and Development.** London: Cambridge University Press, 1934. Pp. xx, 247.

For two reviews, see 2:B872.1; for reviews by J. M. Blackburn, F. M. Earle, H. E. Garrett, E. B. Greene, A. H. Martin, K. W. Oberlin, T. H. Pear, C. S. Slocombe, P. E. Vernon, and three others, see 1:B336.

P203. COZENS, FREDERICK W. **Achievement Scales in Physical Education Activities for College Men.** Philadelphia, Pa.: Lea & Febiger, 1936. Pp. 118.

For a review by A. G. Schmidt, see 36:B78.

P204. COZENS, FREDERICK W.; TRIEB, MARTIN H.; and NEILSON, NEILS P. **Physical Education Achievement Scales for Boys in Secondary Schools.** New York: A. S. Barnes & Co., 1936. Pp. vi, 155.

For a review by R. E. Sparks, see 1:B338; for reviews by W. McAndrew, B. Oberteuffer, A. G. Schmidt, and one other, see 36:B79.

P205. COZENS, FREDERICK WARREN; CUBBERLEY, HAZEL J.; and NEILSON, NEILS P. **Achievement Scales in Physical Education Activities for Secondary School Girls and College Women.** New York: A. S. Barnes & Co., 1937. Pp. ix, 165.

For reviews by Virginia Blunt, Marie Hartwig, and Wilda Logan, see 2:B873; for reviews by A. G. Schmidt, J. R. Sharman, and one other, see 1:B337.

P206. CRANE, MARIAN M.; FOOTE, FRANKLIN M.; SCOBEE, RICHARD G.; GREEN, EARL L.; and PRICE, BRONSON. **Screening School Children for Visual Defects: Report of a Study Conducted in St. Louis, Missouri, 1948–49.** United States Department of Health, Education, and Welfare, Children's Bureau Publication No. 345. Washington, D.C.: U.S. Government Printing Office, 1954. Pp. iii, 92.

For a review, see 5:B109.

P207. CRAWFORD, ALBERT B., and BURNHAM, PAUL S. **Forecasting College Achievement: A Survey of Aptitude Tests for Higher Education: Part 1, General Considerations in the Measurement of Academic Promise.** New Haven, Conn.: Yale University Press, 1946. Pp. xxi, 291.
For reviews by Herbert A. Carroll, Louis M. Heil, A. W. Heim, James S. Kinder, John Dale Russell, Arthur E. Traxler, Valerie C. Wickhem, and one other, see 3:817.

P208. CRISWELL, JOAN HENNING. **A Sociometric Study of Race Cleavage in the Classroom.** Columbia University, Archives of Psychology, No. 235. New York: the University, 1939. Pp. 82.
For a review by Barbara S. Burks, see 2:B874.

P209. CRONBACH, LEE J. **Essentials of Psychological Testing, Second Edition.** New York: Harper & Row, Publishers, Inc., 1960. Pp. xxi, 650.
For reviews by R. W. Payne, J. A. Radcliffe, and Benjamin Rosner, see 6:B145; for reviews by Alfred L. Baldwin, Madison Bentley, John C. Flanagan, P. Lafitte, Roger T. Lennon, Zygmunt A. Piotrowski, Clare Wright Thompson, Arthur E. Traxler, and Adolf G. Woltmann of the first edition, see 4:B101.

P210. CRONBACH, LEE J., and GLESER, GOLDINE C. **Psychological Tests and Personnel Decisions.** Urbana, Ill.: University of Illinois Press, 1957. Pp. x, 165.
For reviews by H. C. Baker, Jerome E. Doppelt, Richard H. Gaylord, Bert F. Green, Jr., W. R. Norton, and J. A. Radcliffe, see 5:B111.

P211. CUNNINGHAM, K. S., and PRICE, W. T. **Standardization of an Australian Arithmetic Test.** Australian Council for Educational Research, Educational Research Series, No. 21. Melbourne, Australia: Melbourne University Press, 1934. Pp. 115.
For reviews by J. F. Abel and A. P. Braddock, see 36:B80.

P212. [CUNNINGHAM, RUTH.] **How to Construct a Sociogram.** New York: Bureau of Publications, Teachers College, Columbia University, 1947. Pp. iv, 37.
For a review by G. Derwood Baker, see 4:B102.

P213. CURETON, THOMAS KIRK. **Physical Fitness Workbook: A Manual of Conditioning Exercises and Standards, Tests, and Rating Scales for Evaluating Physical Fitness, Third Edition.** St. Louis, Mo.: C. V. Mosby Co., 1947. Pp. xi, 164.
For reviews by S. R. M. Reynolds and Mabel E. Rugen, see 4:B103.

P214. CURETON, THOMAS KIRK; HUFFMAN, WARREN J.; WELSER, LYLE; KIREILIS, RAMON W.; and LATHAM, DARRELL E. **Endurance of Young Men: Analysis of Endurance Exercises and Methods of Evaluating Motor Fitness.** Monographs of the Society for Research in Child Development, Vol. 10, No. 1, Serial No. 40. Washington, D.C.: the Society, 1945. Pp. xxiii, 284.
For a review, see 3:823.

P215. CURETON, THOMAS KIRK, JR.; assisted by FREDERICK W. KASCH, JOHN BROWN, and W. G. Moss. **Physical Fitness Appraisal and Guidance.** St. Louis, Mo.: C. V. Mosby Co., 1947. Pp. 566.
For reviews by Adolphe Abrahams, David B. Dill, S. R. M. Reynolds, Mabel E. Rugen, and one other, see 4:B105.

P216. DAHL, LORAINE ANSON. **Public School Audiometry: Principles and Methods.** Danville, Ill.: Interstate Printers & Publishers, Inc., 1949. Pp. viii, 290.
For reviews by Warren H. Gardner, Miles A. Tinker, and one other, see 4:B106.

P217. DAHLSTROM, W. GRANT, and WELSH, GEORGE SCHLAGER. **An MMPI Handbook: A Guide to Use in Clinical Practice and Research.** Minneapolis, Minn.: University of Minnesota Press, 1960. Pp. xx, 559.
For a review by E. R. Oetting, see 6:B146.

P218. DAILEY, JOHN T., Editor. **Psychological Research on Flight Engineer Training.** Army Air Forces Aviation Psychology Program Research Reports, Report No. 13. Washington, D.C.: U.S. Government Printing Office, 1947. Pp. vii, 227.
For reviews by Laurance F. Shaffer and G. Raymond Stone, see 4:B107. For a review of the series, see P1.

P219. DALE, R. R. **From School to University: A Study With Special Reference to University Entrance.** London: Routledge & Kegan Paul Ltd., 1954. Pp. xi, 258.
For reviews by James Henderson, C. Sanders, and P. E. Vernon, see 5:B113.

P220. DAME, J. FRANK; BRINKMAN, ALBERT R.; and WEAVER, WILBUR E. **Prognosis, Guidance, and Placement in Business Education.** Cincinnati, Ohio: South-Western Publishing Co., 1944. Pp. v, 216.
For a review, see 3:825.

P221. DANIELS, JOHN C. **The Teachers' Handbook of Test Construction, Marking and Records.** London: Crosby Lockwood & Son Ltd., 1949. Pp. 79.
For reviews by C. L. Winters, Jr. and one other, see 4:B108.

P222. DARLEY, JOHN G. **Clinical Aspects and Interpretation of the Strong Vocational Interest Blank.** New York: Psychological Corporation, 1941. Pp. 72.
For reviews by Bertha Peterson Harper and Donald E. Super, see 3:648.

P223. DARLEY, JOHN G. **Promise and Performance: A Study of Ability and Achievement in Higher Education.** Berkeley, Calif.: Center for Study of Higher Education, University of California, 1962. Pp. vii, 191.
For a review by Paul S. Burnham, see 6:B149.

P224. DARLEY, J. G.; ALEXANDER, W. B.; BAILEY, H. W.; COOK, W. W.; EDGERTON, H. A.; and VAUGHN, K. W. **The Use of Tests in College.** American Council on Education Studies, Series 6, Student Personnel Work, No. 9. Washington, D.C.: the Council, 1947. Pp. vii, 82.
For reviews by Arthur H. Brayfield, Wilbur S. Gregory, Milton E. Hahn, Harold B. Pepinsky, Laurance F. Shaffer, and one other, see 4:B109.

P225. DARLEY, JOHN G., and HAGENAH, THEDA. **Vocational Interest Measurement: Theory and Practice.** Minneapolis, Minn.: University of Minnesota Press, 1955. Pp. xvii, 279.
For reviews by Wm. C. Cottle, Barbara A. Kirk, T. A. Ryan, Lawrence H. Stewart, and Donald E. Super, see 5:B115.

P226. DARTNELL CORPORATION. **Tests in Selecting Salesmen.** Special Report, Sales Methods Research, Report No. 518. Chicago, Ill.: Dartnell Corporation, 1945. Pp. ii, 65, 42 inserts.
For a review by Roy N. Anderson, see 3:831.

P227. DAVIES, J. B., and JONES, G. A. **Selection of Children for Secondary Education.** London: George G. Harrap & Co., Ltd., 1936. Pp. 181.

For reviews by A. E. Chapman and one other, see 36:B83.

P228. DAVIS, FRANK G. **Classroom Teacher's Cumulative Pupil Personnel Record.** Lewisburg, Pa.: Royal Stationery Co., 1944. Pp. 150.

For a review, see 3:833.

P229. DAVIS, FREDERICK B. **Utilizing Human Talent: Armed Services Selection and Classification Procedures.** Washington, D.C.: American Council on Education, 1947. Pp. ix, 85.

For reviews by Verne C. Fryklund, Wilbur S. Gregory, John G. Jenkins, and J. M. Stephens, see 4:B111; for a review, see 3:835.

P230. DAVIS, FREDERICK B., Editor. **The AAF Qualifying Examination.** Army Air Forces Aviation Psychology Program Research Reports, Report No. 6. Washington, D.C.: U.S. Government Printing Office, 1947. Pp. xvii, 266.

For reviews by Andrew L. Comrey and Herbert S. Conrad, see 4:B112; for a review, see 3:836. For a review of the series, see P1.

P231. DAVIS, H. McVEY. **Use of State High School Examinations as an Instrument for Judging the Work of Teachers.** Columbia University, Teachers College, Contributions to Education No. 611. New York: Bureau of Publications, the College, 1934. Pp. 101.

For reviews by P. W. L. Cox, J. L. Hupp, and A. G. Schmidt, see 36:B84.

P232. DAWES, ROBERT. **Voice Recording as an Instrument of Therapy and Analysis in the Speech Correction Clinic.** Philadelphia, Pa.: Temple University, 1936. Pp. 62.

For reviews by A. G. Schmidt and J. Tiffin, see 1:B342.

P233. DEARBORN, WALTER F., and ROTHNEY, JOHN W. M.; with the cooperation of HOWARD H. LONG, JOHN M. RATCLIFF, WILLIAM J. CRISSY, HELEN E. DONNELLY, and GRACE McGLINCHEY. **Predicting the Child's Development, Second Edition.** Cambridge, Mass.: Sci-Art Publishers, [1963]. Pp. 368.

For a review by G. T. Kowitz, see 6:B151; for reviews by Cyril Burt, Horace B. English, C. M. Fleming, J. R. Gentry, Harold E. Jones, John Gray Peatman, and Austin G. Schmidt of the first edition, see 3:837.

P234. DEARBORN, WALTER F.; ROTHNEY, JOHN W. M.; and SHUTTLEWORTH, FRANK K. **Data on the Growth of Public School Children: From the Materials of the Harvard Growth Study.** Monographs of the Society for Research in Child Development, Vol. 3, No. 1, Serial No. 14. Washington, D.C.: the Society, 1938. Pp. iii, 136.

For a review, see 3:838; for reviews by Fowler D. Brooks and two others, see 2:B879 and 1:B343.

P235. DEAVER, GEORGE G. **Fundamentals of Physical Examination.** Philadelphia, Pa.: W. B. Saunders Co., 1939. Pp. 299.

For reviews by N. P. Neilson, Austin G. Schmidt, Rachel Weems, and six others, see 2:B880.

P236. DEEMER, WALTER L., JR., Editor. **Records, Analysis, and Test Procedures.** Army Air Forces Aviation Psychology Program Research Reports, Report No. 18. Washington, D.C.: U.S. Government Printing Office, 1947. Pp. ix, 621.

For reviews by E. R. Henry and Laurance F. Shaffer, see 4:B113. For a review of the series, see P1.

P237. DELAY, J.; PICHOT, P.; LEMPÉRIÈRE, J.; and PERSE, J. **The Rorschach and the Epileptic Personality.** New York: Hoeber Medical Division, Harper & Row, Publishers, Inc., 1958. Pp. xx, 265.

For reviews by Theodora Alcock and Benjamin Pope, see 6:B152.

P238. DEMPSTER, J. J. B. **Selection for Secondary Education: A Survey.** London: Methuen & Co. Ltd., 1954. Pp. vii, 128.

For reviews by A. F. Watts and Stephen Wiseman, see 5:B119.

P239. DERI, SUSAN. **Introduction to the Szondi Test: Theory and Practice.** New York: Grune & Stratton, Inc., 1949. Pp. xiv, 354.

For reviews by George K. Bennett, Walter Kass, Joseph P. Lord, B. L. Margolet, Paul E. Meehl, William F. Murphy, Helen D. Sargent, Roy Schafer, and Laurance F. Shaffer, see 4:135.

P240. DE RIDDER, J. C. **The Personality of the Urban African in South Africa: A Thematic Apperception Test Study.** London: Routledge & Kegan Paul Ltd., 1961. Pp. xvi, 180.

For reviews by Leonard W. Doob, S. G. Lee, and Robert A. LeVine, see 6:B153.

P241. DEUTSCHE, JEAN MARQUIS. **The Development of Children's Concepts of Causal Relations.** University of Minnesota, Institute of Child Welfare, Monograph Series, No. 13. Minneapolis, Minn.: University of Minnesota Press, 1937. Pp. x, 104.

For reviews by Harold P. Fawcett, John Irving Lacey, and C. W. Valentine, see 2:B881; for reviews by D. McCarty, W. C. Reckless, A. G. Schmidt, and two others, see 1:B344.

P242. DICKTER, MORRIS RICHARD. **The Relationship Between Scores on the Scholastic Aptitude Test and Marks in Mathematics and Science.** Philadelphia, Pa.: the Author, 1937. Pp. 57.

For a review by A. W. Hurd, see 2:B882.

P243. DODGE, ARTHUR F. **Occupational Ability Patterns.** Columbia University, Teachers College, Contributions to Education No. 658. New York: Bureau of Publications, the College, 1935. Pp. 97.

For reviews by A. G. Schmidt, C. O. Weber, E. G. Williamson, and one other, see 1:B346.

P244. DOLL, EDGAR A. **The Measurement of Social Competence: A Manual for the Vineland Social Maturity Scale.** Minneapolis, Minn.: Educational Test Bureau, 1953. Pp. xviii, 664.

For reviews by John E. Anderson, Wm. M. Cruickshank, Ira Iscoe, Oliver P. Kolstoe, Morris Krugman, Laurance F. Shaffer, and Edwin S. Shneidman, see 5:B121.

P245. DOLLARD, JOHN. **Criteria for the Life History: With Analyses of Six Notable Documents.** Yale University Institute of Human Relations Publications. New Haven, Conn.: Yale University Press, 1935. Pp. 288.

For reviews by Horace M. Kallen, Edwin A. Kirkpatrick, N. D. C. Lewis, Nathaniel Ross, Percival Symonds, and two others, see 2:B884.

P246. DONAHUE, WILMA, and DABELSTEIN, DONALD, Editors. **Psychological Diagnosis and Counseling of the Adult Blind: Selected Papers From the Proceedings of the University of Michigan Conference for the Blind, 1947.** New York:

American Foundation for the Blind, Inc., 1950. Pp. vii, 173.
For a review by Kathryn E. Maxfield, see 4:B118.

P247. DONAHUE, WILMA T.; COOMBS, CLYDE H.; and TRAVERS, ROBERT M. W. **The Measurement of Student Adjustment and Achievement.** Ann Arbor, Mich.: University of Michigan Press, 1949. Pp. xiv, 256.
For reviews by Neal B. Andregg, L. A. Rutledge, and Harold Seashore, see 4:B117.

P248. DOOHER, M. JOSEPH, and MARQUIS, VIVIENNE, Editors. **Rating Employee and Supervisory Performance: A Manual of Merit Rating Techniques.** New York: American Management Association, 1950. Pp. 192.
For reviews by M. Bucklow and J. D. Handyside, see 4:B119.

P249. DOPPELT, JEROME EDWARD. **The Organization of Mental Abilities in the Age Range 13 to 17.** Columbia University, Teachers College, Contributions to Education No. 962. New York: Bureau of Publications, the College, 1950. Pp. x, 86.
For a review, see 4:B120.

P250. DORCUS, ROY M., and JONES, MARGARET HUBBARD. **Handbook of Employee Selection.** New York: McGraw-Hill Book Co., Inc., 1950. Pp. xv, 349.
For reviews by Carol S. Bellows (with Roger M. Bellows), A. S. Edwards, E. W. Fassberg, N. F. Kristy, C. M. Louttit, M. N. Oxlade, Harold F. Rothe, Laurance F. Shaffer, E. Donald Sisson, Joseph Tiffin, and one other, see 4:B121.

P251. DOWNIE, N. M. **Fundamentals of Measurement: Techniques and Practices.** New York: Oxford University Press, 1958. Pp. xi, 413.
For reviews by M. Jacinta Mann and P. E. Vernon, see 6:B156.

P252. DRAKE, CHARLES A. **Personnel Selection by Standard Job Tests.** New York: McGraw-Hill Book Co., Inc., 1942. Pp. ix, 147.
For reviews by Edward N. Hay, Patricia Lee Scharf, C. L. Shartle, and R. S. Uhrbrock, see 3:841.

P253. DRAKE, L. E., and OETTING, E. R. **An MMPI Codebook for Counselors.** Minneapolis, Minn.: University of Minnesota Press, 1959. Pp. vii, 140.
For reviews by Irwin A. Berg, Florian J. Hering, and B. Semeonoff, see 6:B159.

P254. DRESSEL, PAUL, Editor. **Evaluation in the Basic College at Michigan State University.** New York: Harper & Row, Publishers, Inc., 1958. Pp. viii, 248.
For a review by H. Taylor Morse, see 6:B160.

P255. DRESSEL, PAUL L. **Evaluation in Higher Education.** Boston, Mass.: Houghton Mifflin Co., 1961. Pp. xvi, 480.
For reviews by C. E. Ayres and Richard H. Lindeman, see 6:B161.

P256. DRESSEL, PAUL L., Editor. **Evaluation in General Education.** Dubuque, Iowa: Wm. C. Brown Co., 1954. Pp. viii, 333.
For a review by B. Lamar Johnson, see 5:B125.

P257. DRESSEL, PAUL L., and MAYHEW, LEWIS B. **General Education: Explorations in Evaluation: The Final Report of the Cooperative Study of Evaluation in General Education of the American Council on Education.** Washington, D.C.: the Council, 1954. Pp. xxiii, 302.

For reviews by Henry S. Dyer and Edmund G. Williamson, see 5:B127.

P258. DRESSEL, PAUL L., and MAYHEW, LEWIS B., Editors. **Critical Thinking in Social Science.** Dubuque, Iowa: Wm. C. Brown Co., 1954. Pp. viii, 36.
For a review by James M. Wood, Jr., see 5:B128.

P259. DRESSEL, PAUL L., and MAYHEW, LEWIS B., Editors. **Handbook for Theme Analysis.** Dubuque, Iowa: Wm. C. Brown Co., 1954. Pp. v, 78.
For a review by Hobart Burnett, see 5:B129.

P260. DRESSEL, PAUL L., and MAYHEW, LEWIS B., Editors. **Science Reasoning and Understanding.** Dubuque, Iowa: Wm. C. Brown Co., 1954. Pp. viii, 223.
For a review by Jeremy P. Ward, see 5:B130.

P261. DRESSEL, PAUL L., and NELSON, CLARENCE H., Editors. **Questions and Problems in Science: Test Item Folio No. 1.** Princeton, N.J.: Cooperative Test Division, Educational Testing Service, 1956. Pp. xvi, 805.
For a review by Henry J. Ehlers, see 5:B131.

P262. DRESSEL, PAUL L., and SCHMID, JOHN. **An Evaluation of the Tests of General Educational Development.** Washington, D.C.: American Council on Education, 1951. Pp. x, 57.
For a review by H. T. Morse, see 5:B132.

P263. DREVER, J., and COLLINS, M. **Performance Tests of Intelligence: A Series of Non-Linguistic Tests for Deaf and Normal Children, Second Edition.** Edinburgh, Scotland: Oliver & Boyd, 1936. Pp. 56.
For three reviews, see 36:B87.

P264. DRISCOLL, GERTRUDE. **How to Study the Behavior of Children.** Practical Suggestions for Teachers, No. 2. New York: Bureau of Publications, Teachers College, Columbia University, 1941. Pp. ix, 84.
For reviews by Hubert C. Armstrong, Horace B. English, and Austin G. Schmidt, see 3:845.

P265. DRISCOLL, GERTRUDE PORTER. **The Developmental Status of the Preschool Child as a Prognosis of Future Development.** Columbia University, Teachers College, Child Development Monographs, No. 13. New York: Bureau of Publications, the College, 1933. Pp. xiv, 111.
For reviews by Charles D. Flory and Ruth Pearson Koshuk, see 2:B886; for a review by H. B. English, see 36:B88.

P266. DuBois, PHILIP H., Editor. **The Classification Program.** Army Air Forces Aviation Psychology Program Research Reports, Report No. 2. Washington, D.C.: U.S. Government Printing Office, 1947. Pp. xiv, 394.
For reviews by Roger M. Bellows and Laurance F. Shaffer, see 4:B123. For a review of the series, see P1.

P267. du MAS, FRANK M. **Manifest Structure Analysis.** Montana State University Studies, Vol. 3. Missoula, Mont.: Montana State University Press, 1956. Pp. ix, 193.
For reviews by R. B. Ammons, David G. Hays, and Karl F. Schuessler, see 5:B134.

P268. DUROST, WALTER N., and PRESCOTT, GEORGE A. **Essentials of Measurement for Teachers.** New York: Harcourt, Brace & World, Inc., 1962. Pp. vii, 167.

For reviews by Dugald S. Arbuckle, Frederick B. Davis, and Gilbert Sax, see 6:B164.

P269. DVORAK, BEATRICE J. **Differential Occupational Ability Patterns.** University of Minnesota, Bulletin of the Employment Stabilization Research Institute, Vol. 3, No. 8. Minneapolis, Minn.: University of Minnesota Press, 1935. Pp. 46.
For a review by E. K. Strong, Jr., see 1:B348; for a review by A. G. Schmidt, see 36:B90.

P270. DYER, HENRY S., and KING, RICHARD G. **College Board Scores: Their Use and Interpretation, No. 2.** New York: College Entrance Examination Board, 1955. Pp. viii, 192.
For a review by Hubert S. Shaw, see 5:B136.

P271. EARLE, FRANK M. **Psychology and the Choice of a Career.** London: Methuen & Co. Ltd., 1933. Pp. vii, 103.
For reviews by Donald G. Paterson and one other, see 2:B886.1.

P272. EARLE, FRANK M. **Tests of Ability for Secondary School Courses.** Publications of the Scottish Council for Research in Education, No. 10. London: University of London Press Ltd., 1936. Pp. xiii, 138.
For a review, see 1:B349; for reviews by L. W. Jones and one other, see 36:B91.

P273. EARLE, FRANK M., and KILGOUR, J. **A Vocational Guidance Research in Fife.** National Institute of Industrial Psychology, Studies in Vocational Guidance, No. 5. London: the Institute, 1935. Pp. 101.
For a review, see 1:B350.

P274. EASTERN COMMERCIAL TEACHERS ASSOCIATION. **Measuring for Vocational Ability in the Field of Business Education.** Tenth Yearbook. Philadelphia, Pa.: the Association, 1937. Pp. 442.
For reviews by Jessie Graham and one other, see 1:B351.

P275. EBERT, ELIZABETH, and SIMMONS, KATHERINE. **The Brush Foundation Study of Child Growth and Development: 1, Psychometric Tests.** Monographs of the Society for Research in Child Development, Vol. 8, No. 2, Serial No. 35. Washington, D.C.: the Society, 1943. Pp. xiv, 113.
For reviews by S. Brecher, Charles D. Flory, Francis N. Maxfield, Mapheus Smith, Theta Wolf, Henriette Woolf, and two others, see 3:851.

P276. EDWARDS, ALLEN L. **The Social Desirability Variable in Personality Assessment and Research.** New York: Holt, Rinehart & Winston, Inc., 1957. Pp. xv, 108.
For reviews by Samuel Messick and Jerry S. Wiggins, see 6:B167.

P277. EDWARDS, ALLEN L. **Techniques of Attitude Scale Construction.** New York: Appleton-Century-Crofts, Inc., 1957. Pp. xvi, 256.
For reviews by Leonard W. Ferguson, Samuel Messick, and H. H. Remmers, see 5:B138.

P278. EELLS, KENNETH; DAVIS, ALLISON; HAVIGHURST, ROBERT J.; HERRICK, VERGIL E.; and TYLER, RALPH W. **Intelligence and Cultural Differences: A Study of Cultural Learning and Problem-Solving.** Chicago, Ill.: University of Chicago Press, 1951. Pp. xii, 388.
For reviews by Quinn McNemar, S. Stansfeld Sargent, William H. Sewell, and Rachel T. Weddington, see 5:B140.

P279. EISNER, HARRY. **The Classroom Teacher's Estimation of Intelligence and Industry of**

High School Students. Columbia University, Teachers College, Contributions to Education No. 726. New York: Bureau of Publications, the College, 1937. Pp. v, 108.
For a review by A. H. Lass, see 2:B891; for reviews by A. M. Jordan, W. D. Reeves, and A. G. Schmidt, see 1:B353.

P280. ELMGREN, JOHN. **School and Psychology: A Report on the Research Work of the 1946 School Commission, 1948:27.** Göteborg, Sweden: Institute of Psychotechnics, University of Göteborg, 1952. Pp. 342.
For a review, see 5:B141.

P281. EMMETT, W. G. **An Inquiry Into the Prediction of Secondary-School Success.** London: University of London Press Ltd., 1942. Pp. 58.
For reviews by C. Birchenough, Max D. Engelhart, Charles S. Myers, and Ll. Wynn Jones, see 3:870.

P282. EMMETT, W. G. **The Use of Intelligence Tests in the 11+ Transfer Examination.** London: University of London Press Ltd., 1952. Pp. 8.
For a review by C. Birchenough, see 5:B142.

P283. ENGLER, DAVID. **How to Raise Your Child's IQ.** New York: Ballantine Books, Inc., 1961. Pp. 153.
For a review by Edward J. Murray, see 6:B171.

P284. ENGLISH, HORACE B., and RAIMY, VICTOR. **Studying the Individual School Child: A Manual of Guidance.** New York: Henry Holt & Co., 1941. Pp. vii, 131.
For reviews by Rose G. Anderson, Stanley G. Dulsky, Carter V. Good, and Austin G. Schmidt, see 3:871.

P285. ERNEST, JOHN W. **Tests and Testing in Distributive Education.** California State Department of Education, Commission for Vocational Education, Bureau of Business Education, Business Education Publication No. 38. Sacramento, Calif.: the Bureau, 1948. Pp. v, 87.
For a review, see 4:B141.

P286. ESPENSCHADE, ANNA. **Motor Performance in Adolescence: Including the Study of Relationships With Measures of Physical Growth and Maturity.** Monographs of the Society for Research in Child Development, Vol. 5, No. 1, Serial No. 24. Washington, D.C.: the Society, 1940. Pp. viii, 126.
For reviews by Mabel E. Rugen, Austin G. Schmidt, and one other, see 2:B894.

P287. EVANS, K. M. **Sociometry and Education.** London: Routledge & Kegan Paul Ltd., 1962. Pp. vii, 149.
For reviews by W. A. L. Blyth and P. K. Poppleton, see 6:B172.

P288. EVANS, ROBERT O. **Practices, Trends, and Issues in Reporting to Parents on the Welfare of the Child in School: Principles Upon Which an Effective Program May Be Built.** New York: Bureau of Publications, Teachers College, Columbia University, 1938. Pp. vi, 98.
For a review by Charles C. Cowell, see 2:B895.

P289. EYDE, LORRAINE DITTRICH. **Work Values and Background Factors as Predictors of Women's Desire to Work.** Ohio State University, College of Commerce and Administration, Ohio Studies in Personnel, Bureau of Business Research Monograph No. 108. Columbus, Ohio: the Bureau, 1962. Pp. xi, 88.
For a review by Edwin C. Lewis, see 6:B173.

P290. EYSENCK, H. J. **Dimensions of Personality.** A record of research carried out in collaboration with H. T. Himmelweit and W. Linford Rees with the help of M. Desai, W. D. Furneaux, H. Halstead, O. Marum, M. McKinlay, A. Petrie, and P. M. Yap. London: Kegan Paul, Trench, Trubner & Co. Ltd., 1947. Pp. xi, 308.

For reviews by Clifford Allen, C. P. Blacker, Josef Brožek, Raymond Cattell, C. A. Gibb, Isabelle V. Kendig, H. J. A. Rimoldi, Jurgen Ruesch, Louise M. Thompson, Leona E. Tyler, Arthur Weider, and three others, see 4:B143; for a review by P. E. Vernon, see 3:873.

P291. EYSENCK, H. J. **Know Your Own I.Q.** London: Penguin Books, Ltd., 1962. Pp. 192.

For reviews by Max Hamilton and G. R. Roberts, see 6:B174.

P292. EYSENCK, H. J. **The Scientific Study of Personality.** London: Routledge & Kegan Paul Ltd., 1952. Pp. xiii, 320.

For reviews by Dan L. Adler, Cyril Burt, James Drever, Samuel S. Dubin, Boris Semeonoff, and Laurance F. Shaffer, see 5:B143.

P293. EYSENCK, H. J. **The Structure of Human Personality, Second Edition.** London: Methuen & Co. Ltd., 1960. Pp. xix, 448.

For a review by P. E. Vernon, see 6:B175; for reviews by Dan L. Adler, D. Graham, Richard L. Jenkins, Hiram K. Johnson, J. A. Radcliffe, Laurance F. Shaffer, J. D. Uytman, and P. E. Vernon of the first edition, see 5:B144.

P294. FARMER, E., and CHAMBERS, E. G. **The Prognostic Value of Some Psychological Tests.** Medical Research Council, Industrial Health Research Board, Report No. 74. London: H.M. Stationery Office, 1936. Pp. iv, 41.

For a review by M. Shirley, see 1:B355; for a review, see 36:B104.

P295. FARMER, E., and CHAMBERS, E. G. **A Study of Accident Proneness Among Motor Drivers.** Medical Research Council, Industrial Health Board, Report No. 84. London: H.M. Stationery Office, 1939. Pp. iii, 47.

For a review by M. G. Kendall, see 2:B896.

P296. FARMER, E.; CHAMBERS, E. G.; and KIRK, F. J. **Tests for Accident Proneness.** Medical Research Council, Industrial Health Research Board, Report No. 68. London: H.M. Stationery Office, 1933. Pp. iv, 37.

For reviews by A. Bradford Hill and Charles S. Slocombe, see 2:B897.

P297. FARNSWORTH, PAUL RANDOLPH. **Musical Taste: Its Measurement and Cultural Nature.** Stanford University Publications, University Series, Education-Psychology, Vol. 2, No. 1. Stanford, Calif.: Stanford University Press, 1950. Pp. 94.

For reviews by Joseph A. Leeder, Kate Hevner Mueller, R. M. Ogden, V. Howard Talley, and one other, see 4:B144.

P298. FEAR, RICHARD A., and JORDAN, BYRON. **Employee Evaluation Manual for Interviewers.** New York: Psychological Corporation, 1943. Pp. 39.

For reviews by Kenneth Byers and Martin L. Reymert, see 3:686.

P299. FEIN, LEAH GOLD. **The Three-Dimensional Personality Test: Reliability, Validity and Clinical Implications.** New York: International Universities Press, Inc., 1960. Pp. xii, 324.

For reviews by Theodore H. Blau, Austin Grigg, and B. Semeonoff, see 6:B176.

P300. FERGUSON, GEORGE A. **The Reliability of Mental Tests.** London: University of London Press Ltd., 1941. Pp. x, 150.

For reviews by J. W. Jenkins, S. J. F. Philpott, P. Slater, and Simon H. Tulchin, see 3:875.

P301. FERGUSON, LEONARD W. **Personality Measurement.** New York: McGraw-Hill Book Co., Inc., 1952. Pp. xv, 457.

For reviews by H. J. Eysenck, Harrison G. Gough, J. P. Guilford, J. D. Handyside, Laurance F. Shaffer, Frank K. Shuttleworth, and Ross Stagner, see 5:B147.

P302. FILLMORE, EVA A. **Iowa Tests for Young Children.** University of Iowa Studies, New Series, No. 315, Studies in Child Welfare, Vol. 11, No. 4. Iowa City, Iowa: the University, 1936. Pp. 58.

For a review by A. G. Schmidt, see 36:B105.

P303. FINDLEY, WARREN G. **Specialization of Verbal Facility at the College Entrance Level: A Comparative Study of Scientific and Literary Vocabularies.** Columbia University, Teachers College, Contributions to Education No. 567. New York: Bureau of Publications, the College, 1933. Pp. v, 76.

For reviews by J. H. Edds, C. W. Gifford, A. H. Turney, and M. A. Twomey, see 1:B356.

P304. FITT, A. B. **The Stanford-Binet Scale: Its Suitability for New Zealand.** New Zealand Council for Educational Research, Studies in Education Series No. 14. Christchurch, New Zealand: Whitcombe & Tombs Ltd., 1953. Pp. 32.

For a review by C. M. Fleming, see 5:B149.

P305. FLANAGAN, JOHN C. **Factor Analysis in the Study of Personality.** Stanford, Calif.: Stanford University Press, 1935. Pp. 103.

For reviews by W. P. Alexander and one other, see 1:B358; for reviews by H. V. Gaskill, H. P. Hartkemeier, P. Horst, W. Richmond, A. G. Schmidt, F. Swineford (with K. J. Holzinger), and two others, see 36:B108.

P306. FLANAGAN, JOHN C., Editor. **The Aviation Psychology Program in the Army Air Forces.** Army Air Forces Aviation Psychology Program Research Reports, Report No. 1. Washington, D.C.: U.S. Government Printing Office, 1948. Pp. xii, 316.

For reviews by Madison Bentley, Andrew L. Comrey, Lee J. Cronbach, Bertram R. Forer, Lyle H. Lanier, Laurance F. Shaffer, and Dewey B. Stuit, see 4:B147. For a review of the series, see P1.

P307. FLANAGAN, JOHN C.; DAILEY, JOHN T.; SHAYCOFT, MARION F.; GORHAM, WILLIAM A.; ORR, DAVID B.; and GOLDBERG, ISADORE. **Design for a Study of American Youth: 1, The Talents of American Youth.** Boston, Mass.: Houghton Mifflin Co., 1962. Pp. 240.

For reviews by Julian C. Stanley and David V. Tiedeman, see 6:B178.

P308. FLECK, HENRIETTA. **How to Evaluate Students.** Bloomington, Ill.: McKnight & McKnight Publishing Co., 1953. Pp. 85.

For reviews by Lysle W. Croft, Bernard Rabin, and one other, see 5:B150.

P309. FORD, MARY. **The Application of the Rorschach Test to Young Children.** University of Minnesota, Institute of Child Welfare Monograph Series, No. 23. Minneapolis, Minn.: University of Minnesota Press, 1946. Pp. xii, 114.

For reviews by Frances S. Alexander, Helen

Hewitt Arthur, Z. A. Piotrowski, and three others, see 4:121; for reviews by Lee J. Cronbach, C. M. Louttit, L. Joseph Stone, Adolf G. Woltmann, and one other, see 3:80.

P310. FOWLER, FRED M. **Selection of Students for Vocational Training.** Federal Security Agency, United States Office of Education, Vocational Division Bulletin, No. 232; Occupational Information and Guidance Series, No. 13. Washington, D.C.: U.S. Government Printing Office, 1945. Pp. iv, 156.
For a review by Silas Hertzler, see 3:882.

P311. FRANDSEN, ARDEN. **An Eye-Movement Study of Objective Examination Questions.** Genetic Psychology Monographs, Vol. 16, No. 2. Worcester, Mass.: Clark University Press, 1934. Pp. 79–138.
For a review, see 36:B109.

P312. FRANK, LAWRENCE K. **Projective Methods.** Springfield, Ill.: Charles C Thomas, Publisher, 1948. Pp. vii, 86.
For reviews by R. L. Ackoff, Arthur L. Benton, Isabelle V. Kendig, Zygmunt A. Piotrowski, Roy Schafer, Laurance F. Shaffer, Miriam G. Siegel, Bessie Sperry, Arthur Weider, and two others, see 4:B153.

P313. FRANKLIN, ERIK. **Tonality as a Basis for the Study of Musical Talent.** Göteborg, Sweden: Gumperts Förlag, 1956. Pp. 193.
For a review by Carroll C. Pratt, see 5:B156.

P314. FREEMAN, FRANK N. **Mental Tests: Their History, Principles and Applications, Revised Edition.** Boston, Mass.: Houghton Mifflin Co., 1939. Pp. xi, 460.
For reviews by A. G. Bills, M. E. Broom, Stephen M. Corey, A. S. Edwards, Henry E. Garrett, F. Kuhlmann, and two others, see 2:B908.

P315. FREEMAN, FRANK S. **Theory and Practice of Psychological Testing, Third Edition.** New York: Holt, Rinehart & Winston, Inc., 1962. Pp. xix, 697.
For a review by Richard E. Schutz, see 6:B189; for reviews by H. Glenn Ludlow, A. W. Tamminen, Leona E. Tyler, and Wimburn L. Wallace of an earlier edition, see 5:B158; for reviews by Seth Arsenian, M. Bentley, Frederick B. Davis, Miles Murphy, and Laurance F. Shaffer, see 4:B155.

P316. FRENCH, JOHN W. **The Description of Aptitude and Achievement Tests in Terms of Rotated Factors.** Psychometric Monograph No. 5. Chicago, Ill.: University of Chicago Press, 1951. Pp. x, 278.
For a review by Lee J. Cronbach, see 5:B160.

P317. FRIEDENHAIN, PAULA. **Write and Reveal: Interpretation of Handwriting.** London: Peter Owen Ltd., 1959. Pp. 184.
For a review by P. E. Vernon, see 6:B190.

P318. FRIEDMAN, BERTHA B. **Foundations of the Measurement of Values: The Methodology of Location and Quantification.** Columbia University, Teachers College, Contributions to Education, No. 914. New York: Bureau of Publications, the College, 1946. Pp. ix, 227.
For reviews by Ernest J. Chave, Andrew L. Comrey, Louis Guttman, J. B. Stroud, and one other, see 4:B157; for reviews by Elizabeth Duffy and Babette Samelson Whipple, see 3:887.

P319. FRIZZLE, ARNOLD LUTHER. **A Study of Some of the Influences of Regents Requirements and Examinations in French.** Columbia University,

Teachers College, Contributions to Education, No. 964. New York: Bureau of Publications, the College, 1950. Pp. xi, 154.
For a review by James B. Tharp, see 4:B158.

P320. FROEHLICH, CLIFFORD P., and BENSON, ARTHUR L. **Guidance Testing.** Chicago, Ill.: Science Research Associates, Inc., 1948. Pp. viii, 104.
For reviews by Thomas E. Christensen, Milton E. Hahn, Stewart Murray, Harold B. Pepinsky, W. D. Perry, and Laurance F. Shaffer, see 4:B159.

P321. FROEHLICH, CLIFFORD P., and HOYT, KENNETH B. **Guidance Testing and Other Student Appraisal Procedures for Teachers and Counselors, Third Edition.** Chicago, Ill.: Science Research Associates, Inc., 1959. Pp. xviii, 438. [The first edition, *Testing and Counseling in the High School Program,* was by John G. Darley; the second edition, *Studying Students,* was by Clifford P. Froehlich and John G. Darley.]
For reviews by Frank M. Fletcher, Jr., J. T. Hunt, and J. David O'Dea of an earlier edition, see 5:B162; for reviews by Edwin W. Davis, Welty Lefever, and Donald E. Super, see 3:828.

P322. FRUCHTER, BENJAMIN. **Introduction to Factor Analysis.** New York: D. Van Nostrand Co., Inc., 1954. Pp. xii, 280.
For reviews by Ardie Lubin, William B. Michael, D. R. Saunders, and Charles Wrigley, see 5:B164.

P323. FRUMKIN, ROBERT M. **Measurement of Marriage Adjustment.** Washington, D.C.: Public Affairs Press, 1954. Pp. ii, 13.
For a review, see 5:B165.

P324. FRYER, DOUGLAS. **The Measurement of Interests: In Relation to Human Adjustment.** New York: Henry Holt & Co., Inc., 1931. Pp. xxxvi, 488.
For reviews by M. Punnett and two others, see 1:B361.

P325. FUESS, CLAUDE M. **The College Board: Its First Fifty Years.** New York: Columbia University Press, 1950. Pp. vii, 222.
For reviews by J. A. Petch and M. J. White, see 4:B160.

P326. FURST, EDWARD J. **Constructing Evaluation Instruments.** New York: David McKay Co., Inc., 1958. Pp. xv, 334.
For reviews by Elizabeth Hagen and Wimburn L. Wallace, see 6:B193.

P327. GABLE, FELICITA. **Effect of Two Contrasting Forms of Testing Upon Learning.** Johns Hopkins University, Studies in Education, No. 25. Baltimore, Md.: Johns Hopkins Press, 1936. Pp. 33.
For a review by E. L. Welborn, see 1:B362; for reviews by A. G. Schmidt and one other, see 36:B112.

P328. GAGE, N. L. **Scaling and Factorial Design in Opinion Poll Analysis.** Purdue University, Division of Educational Reference, Studies in Higher Education LXI; Further Studies in Attitudes, Series X. Lafayette, Ind.: the Division, 1947. Pp. vi, 84.
For a review by Lessing A. Kahn, see 4:B161.

P329. GALBRAITH, WILLIAM JOHN. **Examinations.** London: John Bale, Sons & Danielson, Ltd., 1936. Pp. 175.
For a review, see 36:B113.

P330. GANS, ROMA. **A Study of Critical Reading Comprehension in the Intermediate Grades.** Columbia University, Teachers College, Contributions

to Education, No. 811. New York: Bureau of Publications, the College, 1940. Pp. vii, 135.
For reviews by Helen M. Carpenter, John J. De Boer, F. Melvyn Lawson, and Miles A. Tinker, see 3:890.

P331. GANSL, IRENE. **Vocabulary: Its Measurement and Growth.** Columbia University, Archives of Psychology, No. 236. New York: the University, 1939. Pp. 52.
For a review by Austin G. Schmidt, see 2:B909.

P332. GARDNER, D. E. M. **Testing Results in the Infant School.** London: Methuen & Co. Ltd., 1942. Pp. ix, 158.
For two reviews, see 3:891.

P333. GARDNER, ERIC F., and THOMPSON, GEORGE G. **Social Relations and Morale in Small Groups.** New York: Appleton-Century-Crofts, Inc., 1956. Pp. xi, 312.
For reviews by Walter H. Crockett and Leon Gorlow, see 5:B169.

P334. GARRETT, HENRY E. **Testing for Teachers.** New York: American Book Co., 1959. Pp. x, 262.
For a review by Samuel T. Mayo, see 6:B195.

P335. GARRETT, HENRY E., and SCHNECK, MATTHEW R. **Psychological Tests, Methods, and Results.** New York: Harper & Brothers, 1933. Pp. x, part 1, 137; part 2, 235.
For reviews by A. H. Martin and one other, see 1:B363; for reviews by F. N. Freeman (with G. T. Buswell), J. G. Jenkins, A. H. Lass, H. C. Mahan, F. M. Schaefer, and M. R. Trabue, see 36:B114.

P336. GATES, A. I.; BOND, G. L.; and RUSSELL, D. H.; assisted by EVA BOND, ANDREW HALPIN, and KATHRYN HORAN. **Methods of Determining Reading Readiness.** New York: Bureau of Publications, Teachers College, Columbia University, 1939. Pp. iv, 55.
For reviews by A. S. Edwards and Austin G. Schmidt, see 2:B911.

P337. GATES, ARTHUR I. **The Improvement of Reading: A Program of Diagnostic and Remedial Methods, Third Edition.** New York: Macmillan Co., 1947. Pp. xxi, 657.
For reviews by Laurance F. Shaffer and Miles A. Tinker, see 4:564.

P338. GAYEN, A. K.; NANDA, P. B.; MATHUR, R. K.; DUARI, P; DUBEY, S. D.; and BHATTACHARYYA, N. **Measurement of Achievement in Mathematics: A Statistical Study on Effectiveness of Board and University Examinations in India.** Report No. 1 of the Research Project on Examinations Sponsored by the Ministry of Education, Government of India, New Delhi. [New Delhi, India: National Council of Educational Research and Training, 1961.] Pp. 246.
For reviews by R. Beard and D. J. Finney, see 6:B197.

P339. GERBERICH, J. RAYMOND. **Specimen Objective Test Items: A Guide to Achievement Test Construction.** New York: Longmans, Green & Co., Inc., 1956. Pp. xi, 436.
For reviews by Robert L. Ebel and John R. Ginther, see 5:B172.

P340. GERBERICH, J. RAYMOND; GREENE, HARRY A.; and JORGENSEN, ALBERT N. **Measurement and Evaluation in the Modern School.** New York: David McKay Co., Inc., 1962. Pp. xviii, 622.
For reviews by Theodore R. Husek, David A.

Payne, and one other, see 6:B200; for reviews by Cyril Burt, Harold F. Cottingham, Walter M. Lifton, and Jack C. Merwin of an earlier edition, see 5:B181-2; for reviews by James B. Burr, Gustav J. Froehlich, Gerald V. Lannholm, Joseph G. Phoenix, Austin G. Schmidt, and William E. Young, see 3:914-5.

P341. GESELL, ARNOLD. **Atlas of Infant Behavior: A Systematic Delineation of the Forms and Early Growth of Human Behavior Patterns, Two Volumes.** New Haven, Conn.: Yale University Press, 1934. Pp. 921.
For reviews by John E. Anderson, G. E. Coghill, and Borden S. Veeder, see 2:B912.

P342. GESELL, ARNOLD, and AMATRUDA, CATHERINE S. **Developmental Diagnosis: Normal and Abnormal Child Development: Clinical Methods and Practical Applications.** New York: Paul B. Hoeber, Inc., 1941. Pp. xiii, 447.
For reviews by Edgar A. Doll, Milton H. Firestone, Arthur N. Foxe, Warren H. Gardner, Carter V. Good, Helen L. Koch, Alfred A. Washburn, Margaret T. Wilson, and three others, see 3:277.

P343. GESELL, ARNOLD, and ILG, FRANCES L.; in collaboration with LOUISE BATES AMES and GLENNA E. BULLIS. **The Child From Five to Ten.** New York: Harper & Brothers, 1946. Pp. xiii, 475.
For a review, see 3:903.

P344. GESELL, ARNOLD, and THOMPSON, HELEN; assisted by CATHERINE STRUNK AMATRUDA. **Infant Behavior: Its Genesis and Growth.** New York: McGraw-Hill Book Co., Inc., 1934. Pp. viii, 343.
For reviews by Margaret Curti, Florence L. Goodenough, Norman L. Munn, George D. Stoddard, C. W. Valentine, and three others, see 2:B915.

P345. GESELL, ARNOLD, and THOMPSON, HELEN; assisted by CATHERINE STRUNK AMATRUDA. **The Psychology of Early Growth: Including Norms of Infant Behavior and a Method of Genetic Analysis.** New York: Macmillan Co., 1938. Pp. ix, 290.
For a review, see 3:280; for reviews by Donald K. Adams, Nancy Bayley, A. S. Edwards, Gertrude Hildreth, Kai Jensen, Ruth Pearson Koshuk, Stanley S. Lamm, Russell G. Leiter, Lillian Malcove, Amalie K. Nelson, John Gray Peatman, Margarethe A. Ribble, Gilbert J. Rich, and one other, see 2:B916.

P346. GESELL, ARNOLD; AMATRUDA, CATHERINE S.; CASTNER, BURTON M.; and THOMPSON, HELEN. **Biographies of Child Development: The Mental Growth Careers of Eighty-Four Infants and Children; A Ten-Year Study from the Clinic of Child Development at Yale University.** New York: Paul B. Hoeber, Inc., 1939. Pp. xvii, 328.
For reviews by W. Line, Elizabeth E. Lord, Livingston Welch, and one other, see 3:278; for reviews by Donald K. Adams, Nancy Bayley, Mary S. Ryan, Mary Shirley, C. W. Valentine, and eight others, see 2:B913.

P347. GESELL, ARNOLD; HALVERSON, HENRY M.; THOMPSON, HELEN; ILG, FRANCES L.; CASTNER, BURTON M.; AMES, LOUISE BATES; and AMATRUDA, CATHERINE S. **The First Five Years of Life: A Guide to the Study of the Preschool Child.** From the Yale Clinic of Child Development. New York: Harper & Brothers, 1940. Pp. xiii, 393.
For reviews by Richard A. Bolt, Ives Hendrick, Aleš Hrdlička, J. W. Jenkins, C. W. Valentine, and three others, see 3:279; for reviews by Orvis C. Irwin, D. G. Ryans, Austin G. Schmidt, Ira S. Wile, and two others, see 2:B914.

P348. GETZELS, JACOB W., and JACKSON, PHILIP W. **Creativity and Intelligence: Explorations With Gifted Students.** New York: John Wiley & Sons, Inc., 1962. Pp. xvii, 293.

For reviews by Frank Barron, Lee J. Cronbach, Richard de Mille (with Philip R. Merrifield), Ariel Mengarini, Victor H. Rosen, and E. Paul Torrance, see 6:B201.

P349. GHISELLI, EDWIN E. **The Measurement of Occupational Aptitude.** University of California Publications in Psychology, Vol. 8, No. 2. Berkeley, Calif.: University of California Press, 1955. Pp. ii, 101–216.

For reviews by Donald L. Grant and Donald E. Super, see 5:B174.

P350. GIBSON, JAMES J., Editor. **Motion Picture Testing and Research.** Army Air Forces Aviation Psychology Program Research Reports, Report No. 7. Washington, D.C.: U.S. Government Printing Office, 1947. Pp. xi, 267.

For reviews by W. C. H. Prentice and Laurance F. Shaffer, see 4:B168. For a review of the series, see P1.

P351. GLASSEY, WILLIAM, and WEEKS, EDWARD J. **The Educational Development of Children: The Teacher's Guide to the Keeping of School Records.** London: University of London Press Ltd., 1950. Pp. xiii, 248.

For reviews by I. E. Campbell, C. M. Fleming, M. A. Mellone, and two others, see 4:B169.

P352. GLASSOW, RUTH B., and BROER, MARION R. **Measuring Achievement in Physical Education.** Philadelphia, Pa.: W. B. Saunders Co., 1938. Pp. 344.

For reviews by Dorothy Beise, Helen L. Bryan, Charles C. Cowell, Evelyn B. Spindler, and two others, see 2:B917; for a review, see 1:B364.

P353. GOHEEN, HOWARD W., and KAVRUCK, SAMUEL. **Selected References on Test Construction, Mental Test Theory, and Statistics, 1929–1949.** United States Civil Service Commission. Washington, D.C.: U.S. Government Printing Office, 1950. Pp. xii, 209.

For reviews by Laurance F. Shaffer and two others, see 4:B170.

P354. GOLDBERG, WOOLF. **The Carnegie Examinations at Temple University: A Study of the Examinations of the Carnegie Foundation in the Teachers College of Temple University.** Philadelphia, Pa.: Temple University, 1938. Pp. vi, 105.

For a review by Austin G. Schmidt, see 2:B918.

P355. GOLDFARB, WILLIAM. **An Investigation of Reaction Time in Older Adults and Its Relationship to Certain Observed Mental Test Patterns.** Columbia University, Teachers College, Contributions to Education, No. 831. New York: Bureau of Publications, the College, 1941. Pp. ix, 76.

For a review by J. R. Gentry, see 3:907.

P356. GOLDMAN, LEO. **Using Tests in Counseling.** New York: Appleton-Century-Crofts, Inc., 1961. Pp. xix, 434.

For reviews by Irwin A. Berg, John O. Crites, and Barbara Kirk, see 6:B205.

P357. GOLDSTEIN, KURT, and SCHEERER, MARTIN. **Abstract and Concrete Behavior: An Experimental Study With Special Tests.** American Psychological Association, Psychological Monographs, Vol. 53, No. 2, Whole No. 239. Washington, D.C.: the Association, Inc., 1941. Pp. vi, 151.

For a review by Austin G. Schmidt, see 3:42.

P358. GOLDWAG, ELLIOTT M. **A Survey on the Use of Psychological Tests in Selecting Salesmen.** New York: National Sales Executives, Inc., 1956. Pp. 64.

For a review by S. Rains Wallace, see 5:B176.

P359. GOOD, PATRICIA KING-ELLISON, and BRANTNER, JOHN P. **The Physician's Guide to the MMPI.** Minneapolis, Minn.: University of Minnesota Press, 1961. Pp. 69.

For a review, see 6:B206.

P360. GOODENOUGH, FLORENCE L. **Mental Testing: Its History, Principles, and Applications.** New York: Rinehart & Co., Inc., 1949. Pp. xxi, 609.

For reviews by Madison Bentley, Josef Brožek, Harold D. Carter, Lee J. Cronbach, Edgar A. Doll, John C. Flanagan, C. M. Fleming, Morris Krugman, Ann Magaret, Leola E. Neal, Wesley Osterberg, Gladys C. Schwesinger, Adolf G. Woltmann, and two others, see 4:B171.

P361. GOODENOUGH, FLORENCE L., and MAURER, KATHARINE M. **The Mental Growth of Children From Two to Fourteen Years: A Study of the Predictive Value of the Minnesota Preschool Scales.** University of Minnesota, Institute of Child Welfare Monograph Series, No. 20. Minneapolis, Minn.: University of Minnesota Press, 1942. Pp. xv, 130.

For reviews by Nancy Bayley, Gustav J. Froehlich, Willard C. Olson, C. W. Valentine, and one other, see 3:287.

P362. GOSLIN, DAVID A. **The Search for Ability: Standardized Testing in Social Perspective.** Volume 1 of a Series on the Social Consequences of Ability Testing. New York: Russell Sage Foundation, 1963. Pp. 204.

For reviews by Alexander W. Astin, J. Beker, and Donald E. Super, see 6:B207.

P363. GOTTSCHALK, LOUIS; KLUCKHOHN, CLYDE; and ANGELL, ROBERT. **The Use of Personal Documents in History, Anthropology, and Sociology.** Prepared for the Committee on Appraisal of Research, Social Science Research Council, Bulletin 53. New York: the Council, 1945. Pp. xiv, 243.

For a review by Arthur F. Jenness, see 3:910.

P364. GOUDE, GUNNAR. **On Fundamental Measurement in Psychology.** Stockholm Studies in Psychology 2. Stockholm, Sweden: Almqvist & Wiksell, 1962. Pp. 176.

For a review by Andrew Comrey, see 6:B208.

P365. GRASSI, JOSEPH R. **The Grassi Block Substitution Test for Measuring Organic Brain Pathology.** Springfield, Ill.: Charles C Thomas, Publisher, 1953. Pp. ix, 75.

For reviews by J. G. McMurray and one other, see 5:60.

P366. GRAY, J. L. **The Nation's Intelligence.** London: C. A. Watts & Co., Ltd., 1936. Pp. v, 154.

For a review, see 2:B919; for reviews by E. C. Rhodes and four others, see 1:B365; for reviews by S. Anthony, J. Brentnall, R. B. Cattell, and two others, see 36:B119.

P367. GRAYBEAL, ELIZABETH. **The Measurement of Outcomes of Physical Education for College Women.** Minneapolis, Minn.: University of Minnesota Press, 1937. Pp. viii, 80.

For reviews by Virginia Peaseley and Evelyn B. Spindler, see 2:B920; for reviews by R. J. Cline and three others, see 1:B366.

P368. GREEN, JOHN A. **Teacher-Made Tests.** New York: Harper & Row, Publishers, Inc., 1963. Pp. ix, 141.
For a review by William S. Graybeal, see 6:B211.

P369. GREENE, EDWARD B. **Measurements of Human Behavior, Revised Edition.** New York: Odyssey Press, 1952. Pp. xxxi, 790.
For reviews by Robert M. Allen, Roger T. Lennon, Evelyn Raskin, and Laurance F. Shaffer, see 5:B179; for reviews by Amos C. Anderson, M. E. Broom, Andrew W. Brown, William J. E. Crissy, Herman Feldman, J. P. Guilford, A. M. Jordan, Robert M. Lindner, Thomas C. McCormick, Julian B. Rotter, Austin G. Schmidt, and J. Gustav White of the first edition, see 3:912.

P370. GREENE, HARRY A., and JORGENSEN, ALBERT N. **The Use and Interpretation of Elementary School Tests.** New York: Longmans, Green & Co., Inc., 1935. Pp. xxviii, 530.
For reviews by A. H. Lass, F. J. Schonell, and one other, see 36:B121.

P371. GREENE, HARRY A., and JORGENSEN, ALBERT N. **The Use and Interpretation of High School Tests.** New York: Longmans, Green & Co., Inc., 1936. Pp. xxvi, 614.
For reviews by L. V. Koos, A. G. Schmidt, E. I. F. Williams, and two others, see 36:B122.

P372. GREULICH, WILLIAM WALTER; DAY, HARRY G.; LACHMAN, SANDER E.; WOLFE, JOHN B.; and SHUTTLEWORTH, FRANK K. **A Handbook of Methods for the Study of Adolescent Children.** Monographs of the Society for Research in Child Development, Vol. 3, No. 2, Serial No. 15. Washington, D.C.: the Society, 1938. Pp. xix, 406.
For a review by Lawson G. Lowrey, see 3:916; for reviews by Fowler D. Brooks, Warren E. Forsythe, F. P. Robinson, Austin G. Schmidt, and six others, see 2:B922.

P373. GRIFFITHS, RUTH. **The Abilities of Babies: A Study in Mental Measurement.** London: University of London Press Ltd., 1954. Pp. x, 229.
For reviews by J. H. Conn, V. Franks, Margaret Martin, and C. W. Valentine, see 5:B184.

P374. GRIMSLEY, G., and WICKERT, F. R. **Psychological Techniques in Personnel Research: A Syllabus and Workbook.** East Lansing, Mich.: Michigan State College Press, 1948. Pp. v, 147.
For a review by Frank J. Harris, see 4:B175.

P375. GRONLUND, NORMAN E. **Sociometry in the Classroom.** New York: Harper & Row, Publishers, Inc., 1959. Pp. xix, 340.
For reviews by K. M. Evans, Britomar J. Handlon, and Renato Tagiuri, see 6:B214.

P376. GROSS, MARTIN L. **The Brain Watchers.** New York: Random House, Inc., 1962. Pp. x, 305.
For reviews by C. H. Ammons (with R. B. Ammons), W. J. E. Crissy, John Dollard, Leo Goldman, and John Nickols (with Marcia Nickols), see 6:B215.

P377. GUILFORD, J. P. **Personality.** New York: McGraw-Hill Book Co., Inc., 1959. Pp. xiii, 562.
For reviews by Ronald Taft and Julius Wishner, see 6:B228.

P378. GUILFORD, J. P. **Psychometric Methods, Second Edition.** New York: McGraw-Hill Book Co., Inc., 1954. Pp. ix, 597.
For reviews by Allen L. Edwards, Bert F. Green, and Roland Harper, see 5:B185; for reviews by W.

R. Ashby, H. A. Edgerton, S. W. Fernberger, H. E. Garrett, F. N. Maxfield, W. Stephenson, and one other of the first edition, see 1:B631; for reviews by J. W. Dunlap, S. J. F. Philpott, A. G. Schmidt, H. Woodrow, and two others, see 36:B124.

P379. GUILFORD, J. P., and MICHAEL, WILLIAM B. **The Prediction of Categories From Measurements: With Applications to Personnel Selection and Clinical Prognosis.** Beverly Hills, Calif.: Sheridan Supply Co., 1949. Pp. v, 55.
For reviews by Hubert E. Brogden and Laurance F. Shaffer, see 141 in *Statistical Methodology Reviews, 1941–1950.*

P380. GUILFORD, J. P., Editor; with the assistance of JOHN I. LACEY. **Printed Classification Tests.** Army Air Forces Aviation Psychology Program Research Reports, Report No. 5. Washington, D.C.: U.S. Government Printing Office, 1947. Pp. xi, 919.
For reviews by Thomas W. Harrell and Laurance F. Shaffer, see 4:B182. For a review of the series, see P1.

P381. GULLIKSEN, HAROLD. **Theory of Mental Tests.** New York: John Wiley & Sons, Inc., 1950. Pp. xix, 486.
For reviews by John B. Carroll, Harold Gulliksen, and Louis Guttman, see 5:B188; for reviews by Robert M. Allen, Kenneth E. Anderson, G. D. Bradshaw, Thomas L. Bransford (with Joseph Lev), John W. Chotlos, Max D. Engelhart, Clifford P. Froehlich, W. E. Hick, Paul Horst, Fred McKinney, Quinn McNemar, John E. Nixon, and Kenneth W. Vaughn, see 4:B183.

P382. GULLIKSEN, HAROLD, and MESSICK, SAMUEL, Editors. **Psychological Scaling: Theory and Applications.** New York: John Wiley & Sons, Inc., 1960. Pp. xvi, 211.
For reviews by J. A. Keats and William B. Michael, see 6:B229.

P383. GURVITZ, MILTON S. **The Dynamics of Psychological Testing: A Formulation and Guide to Independent Clinical Practice.** New York: Grune & Stratton, Inc., 1951. Pp. xvi, 396.
For reviews by Lee J. Cronbach, Stephen Griew, William A. Hunt, Martin Mayman, Bruce Quarrington, and Robert I. Watson, see 5:B189.

P384. HAEUSSERMANN, ELSE. **Development Potential of Preschool Children: An Evaluation of Intellectual, Sensory, and Emotional Functioning.** New York: Grune & Stratton, Inc., 1958. Pp. xvii, 285.
For a review by Charles D. Smock, see 6:B230.

P385. HALLER, ARCHIBALD O., and MILLER, IRWIN W. **The Occupational Aspiration Scale: Theory, Structure and Correlates.** Michigan State University, Agricultural Experiment Station, Department of Sociology and Anthropology, Technical Bulletin 288. East Lansing, Mich.: the Station, 1963. Pp. 132.
For a review by C. Gilbert Wrenn, see 6:B231.

P386. HALPERN, FLORENCE. **A Clinical Approach to Children's Rorschachs.** New York: Grune & Stratton, Inc., 1953. Pp. xv, 270.
For reviews by Dorothy S. Fuller, Lily Gondor, J. Lyle, and one other, see 5:B190.

P387. HALSEY, GEORGE D. **Making and Using Industrial Service Ratings: Practical Suggestions for Measuring and Rating Individual Performance of Executives and Employees Including How to Use These Ratings in Improving Per-**

formance. New York: Harper & Brothers, 1944. Pp. xxii, 149.

For reviews by Charles C. Gibbons, Richard S. Schultz, and O. Glenn Stahl, see 3:918.

P388. HAMALAINEN, ARTHUR EMIL. **An Appraisal of Anecdotal Records.** Columbia University, Teachers College, Contributions to Education, No. 891. New York: Bureau of Publications, the College, 1943. Pp. vii, 87.

For a review by F. S. Beers, see 3:919.

P389. HAMLEY, HERBERT R., Editor. **The Testing of Intelligence.** London: Evans Brothers Ltd., 1935. Pp. 175.

For reviews by G. Rawlings and one other, see 1:B372; for reviews by R. B. Cattell and two others, see 36:B126.

P390. HAMLEY, H. R.; OLIVER, R. A. C.; FIELD, H. E.; and ISAACS, SUSAN. **The Educational Guidance of the School Child: Suggestions on Child Study and Guidance Embodying a Scheme of Pupils' Records.** London: Evans Brothers, Ltd., [1937]. Pp. 122.

For a review, see 2:B924; for reviews by A. Rodger and four others, see 1:B373.

P391. HAMMER, EMANUEL F., Editor. **The Clinical Application of Projective Drawings.** Springfield, Ill.: Charles C Thomas, Publisher, 1958. Pp. xxii, 663.

For reviews by Walter G. Klopfer, R. W. Payne, and Robert I. Yufit, see 6:B232.

P392. HAND, HAROLD C. **What People Think About Their Schools: Values and Methods of Public-Opinion Polling as Applied to School Systems.** Yonkers, N.Y.: World Book Co., 1948. Pp. iv, 219.

For a review by John Withall, see 4:53.

P393. HANFMANN, EUGENIA, and KASANIN, JACOB. **Conceptual Thinking in Schizophrenia.** Nervous and Mental Disease Monograph, No. 67. New York: Nervous and Mental Disease Monographs, 1942. Pp. viii, 115.

For reviews by Oskar Diethelm, Thomas M. French, W. H. Gillespie, K. Goldstein, George W. Hartmann, Meyer Maskin, Wendell Muncie, A. S. Pickford (with R. W. Pickford), Clara Thompson, David G. Wright, and two others, see 3:28.

P394. HARDAWAY, MATHILDE, and MAIER, THOMAS B. **Tests and Measurements in Business Education, Second Edition.** Cincinnati, Ohio: South-Western Publishing Co., 1952. Pp. x, 434.

For reviews by Louise Green, Austin G. Schmidt, and two others of the first edition, see 3:933.

P395. HARDY, MARTHA CRUMPTON, and HOEFER, CAROLYN H. **Healthy Growth: A Study of the Influence of Health Education on Growth and Development of School Children.** Chicago, Ill.: University of Chicago Press, 1936. Pp. xii, 360.

For reviews by Ross L. Allen, Roger T. Lennon, Ruth Strang, and one other, see 2:B925.

P396. HARMAN, HARRY H. **Modern Factor Analysis.** Chicago: University of Chicago Press, 1960. Pp. xvi, 469.

For reviews by Henry F. Kaiser and J. A. Keats, see 6:B233.

P397. HARRIS, CHESTER W., Editor. **Problems in Measuring Change.** Proceedings of a Conference Sponsored by the Committee on Personality Development in Youth of the Social Science Research Council,

1962. Madison, Wis.: University of Wisconsin Press, 1963. Pp. x, 259.

For a review by William W. Cooley, see 6:B235.

P398. HARRIS, HENRY. **The Group Approach to Leadership-Testing.** London: Routledge & Kegan Paul Ltd., 1949. Pp. x, 288.

For reviews by F. C. Bartlett, Bernard M. Bass, John Munro Fraser, S. W. Gillman, R. S. Horne, N. A. B. Wilson, and two others, see 4:B191.

P399. HARRIS, MARY JORDAN. **Review of Methods of Scale and Item Analysis and Their Application to a Level of Living Scale in North Carolina.** North Carolina Agricultural Experiment Station, Progress Report RS-13. Raleigh, N.C.: the Station, 1951. Pp. 31.

For a review by Paul J. Jehlik, see 5:B196.

P400. HARRIS, ROBERT E.; MILLER, JAMES G.; MUENCH, GEORGE A.; STONE, L. JOSEPH; TEUBER, HANS-LUKAS; and ZUBIN, JOSEPH. **Recent Advances in Diagnostic Psychological Testing: A Critical Summary.** Springfield, Ill.: Charles C Thomas, Publisher, 1950. Pp. x, 120.

For reviews by William A. Hunt, R. W. Pickford, and Laurance F. Shaffer, see 4:B192.

P401. HARRISON, M. LUCILLE. **Reading Readiness, Revised Edition.** Boston, Mass.: Houghton Mifflin Co., 1939. Pp. xiii, 255.

For reviews by Emmett Albert Betts, M. E. Broom, Alice Temple, Miles A. Tinker, and one other, see 2:B926; for reviews by A. S. Edwards and three others, see 1:B375; for reviews by E. W. Dolch, W. McAndrew, A. G. Schmidt, A. Temple, and M. A. Tinker, see 36:B127.

P402. HARROWER, M. R., and STEINER, M. E. **Large Scale Rorschach Techniques: A Manual for the Group Rorschach and Multiple Choice Tests, Second Edition.** With contributions by Floyd O. Due, Beatrice A. Wright, and M. Erik Wright. Springfield, Ill.: Charles C Thomas, Publisher, 1951. Pp. xx, 353.

For reviews by Laurance F. Shaffer and one other, see 4:122; for reviews by Robert C. Challman, Bruno Klopfer, Louis A. Lurie, M. F. Ashley Montagu, Z. A. Piotrowski, Fred V. Rockwell, Donald E. Super, and six others of the first edition, see 3:82.

P403. HARROWER, M. R., and STEINER, M. E. **Manual for Psychodiagnostic Inkblots (A Series Parallel to the Rorschach Blots.)** New York: Grune & Stratton, Inc., 1945. Pp. 112.

For reviews by Gotthard Booth, William F. Murphy, Zygmunt A. Piotrowski, and Adolf G. Woltmann, see 3:81.

P404. HARROWER, MOLLY. **Appraising Personality: An Introduction to Projective Techniques, Revised Ediiton.** New York: Franklin Watts, Inc., 1964. Pp. xix, 302.

For reviews by Dan L. Adler, Arthur L. Benton, James M. Cunningham, Lawrence S. Rogers, and one other of the first edition, see 5:B197.

P405. HARROWER, MOLLY. **Personality Change and Development as Measured by the Projective Techniques.** New York: Grune & Stratton, Inc., 1959. Pp. vii, 383.

For reviews by Theodore H. Blau and Sheldon J. Korchin, see 6:B238.

P406. HARROWER, MOLLY; VORHAUS, PAULINE; ROMAN, MELVIN; and BAUMAN, GERALD. **Creative Variations in Projective Techniques.** Springfield, Ill.: Charles C Thomas, Publisher, 1960. Pp. viii, 138.

For a review by Albert I. Rabin, see 6:239.

P407. HART, HORNELL. **Chart for Happiness.** New York: Macmillan Co., 1940. Pp. xi, 198. For reviews by Emory S. Bogardus, J. W. Macmillan, J. L. Moreno, H. Neumann, Dortha Williams Osborn, and Howard Davis Spoerl, see 3:37.

P408. HARTER, RICHARD S., and SMELTZER, C. H. **Self-Instructional Manual in Handling Test Scores.** New York: Henry Holt & Co., 1933. Pp. 58. For a review by J. C. Peterson, see 36:B128.

P409. HARTMANN, GEORGE W. **Measuring Teaching Efficiency Among College Instructors.** Columbia University, Archives of Psychology, No. 154. New York: the University, 1933. Pp. 45. For a review, see 1:B376; for a review by A. G. Schmidt, see 36:B129.

P410. HARTOG, PHILIP. **The Purposes of Examinations: A Symposium.** Reprinted from *The Yearbook of Education 1938.* London: Evans Brothers, Ltd., [1938]. Pp. 146. For reviews by T. N. Siqueira, S. Parker Smith, and one other, see 2:B931.

P411. HARTOG, PHILIP. **Secondary School Examinations and the Curricula of Secondary Schools: With Suggestions for Reform.** London: National Union of Teachers, 1937. Pp. 34. For three reviews, see 2:B927 and 1:B377.

P412. HARTOG, PHILIP, and RHODES, E. C. **An Examination of Examinations: Being a Summary of Investigations on the Comparison of Marks Alloted to Examination Scripts by Independent Examiners and Boards of Examiners, Together With a Section on a Viva Voce Examination.** London: Macmillan & Co., Ltd., 1935. Pp. 81. For reviews by G. F. Bridge, W. C. Burnet, J. F. Duff, and two others, see 2:B928; for reviews by B. A. Howard, A. M. Jordan, and six others, see 1:B378; for reviews by J. D. Russell, F. C. S. Schiller, and two others, see 36:B130.

P413-4. HARTOG, PHILIP, and RHODES, E. C. **The Marks of Examiners: Being a Comparison of Marks Alloted to Examination Scripts by Independent Examiners and Boards of Examiners, Together With a Section on a Viva Voce Examination.** London: Macmillan & Co., Ltd., 1936. Pp. xix, 344. For a review, see 2:B929; for reviews by E. R. Gabler, B. A. Howard, L. W. Jones, and A. M. Jordan, see 1:B379; for reviews by F. A. Cavenaugh, J. F. Duff, M. W. Richardson, D. L. Wolfle, and two others, see 36:B131.

P415. HARTOG, PHILIP; BALLARD, P. B.; GURREY, P.; HAMLEY, H. R.; and SMITH, C. EBBLEWHITE. **The Marking of English Essays: A Report of an Investigation Carried Out by a Sub-Committee of the International Institute Examinations Enquiry Committee.** London: Macmillan & Co., Ltd., 1941. Pp. xv, 165. For reviews by Clarissa C. Bell and P. E. Vernon, see 3:928.

P416. HARTOG, PHILIP; with the assistance of GLADYS ROBERTS. **A Conspectus of Examinations in Great Britain and Northern Ireland.** London: Macmillan & Co., Ltd., 1937. Pp. xiv, 182. For reviews by Earl R. Gabler, E. C. Rhodes, T. N. Siqueira, and one other, see 2:B930; for five reviews, see 1:B380.

P417. HATHAWAY, STARKE R., and MEEHL, PAUL E. **An Atlas for the Clinical Use of the MMPI.** Minneapolis, Minn.: University of Minnesota Press, 1951. Pp. xliv, 799.

For reviews by Clare Wright Thompson and George S. Welsh, see 5:B199; for reviews by Laurance F. Shaffer and one other, see 4:72.

P418. HATHAWAY, STARKE R., and MONACHESI, ELIO D. **An Atlas of Juvenile MMPI Profiles.** Minneapolis, Minn.: University of Minnesota Press, 1961. Pp. xviii, 402. For reviews by Alfred B. Heilbrun, Jr. and Richard L. Jenkins, see 6:B241.

P419. HATHAWAY, STARKE R., and MONACHESI, ELIO D., Editors. **Analyzing and Predicting Juvenile Delinquency With the MMPI.** Minneapolis, Minn.: University of Minnesota Press, 1953. Pp. viii, 153. For reviews by Howard F. Hunt, H. Meltzer, Clarence Schrag, Karl F. Schuessler, and Helen L. Witmer, see 5:B200.

P420. HATTWICK, MELVIN S., and WILLIAMS, H. M. **Measurement of Musical Development, 2.** State University of Iowa Studies, New Series, No. 290. Studies in Child Welfare, Vol. 11, No. 2. Iowa City, Iowa: the University, 1935. Pp. 100. For a review by A. G. Schmidt, see 36:B134.

P421. HAYDEN, HOWARD. **The Evaluation of Education in Barbados: A First Experiment.** Bridgeton, Barbados, B.W.I.: Department of Education, 1945. Pp. ii, 34. For a review, see 3:930.

P422. HAYES, SAMUEL P. **Vocational Aptitude Tests for the Blind.** Perkins Publications, No. 14. Watertown, Mass.: Perkins Institution and Massachusetts School for the Blind, 1946. Pp. 32. For a review by Salvatore G. DiMichael, see 3:932.

P423. HELLERSBERG, ELIZABETH F. **The Individual's Relation to Reality in Our Culture: An Experimental Approach by Means of the Horn-Hellersberg Test.** Springfield, Ill.: Charles C Thomas, Publisher, 1950. Pp. x, 128. For reviews by Alfred Jacobs, Walter Kass, Joseph Katz, E. Lowell Kelly and one other, see 4:109.

P424. HELM, A. W. **The Appraisal of Intelligence.** London: Methuen & Co. Ltd., 1954. Pp. vii, 171. For reviews by Cyril Burt, L. S. Hearnshaw, R. M. Mowbray, and Stephen Wiseman, see 5:B202.

P425. HEMPHILL, JOHN K. **Dimensions of Executive Positions: A Study of the Basic Characteristics of the Positions of Ninety-Three Business Executives.** Ohio State University, College of Commerce and Administration, Ohio Studies in Personnel, Bureau of Business Research Monograph No. 98. Columbus, Ohio: the Bureau, 1960. Pp. xiv, 103. For a review by Harold Borko, see 6:B244.

P426. HEMPHILL, JOHN K. **Group Dimensions: A Manual for Their Measurement.** Ohio State University, Bureau of Business Research, Research Monograph No. 87. Columbus, Ohio: the Bureau, 1956. Pp. xi, 66. For a review by Jay M. Jackson, see 5:B203.

P427. HEMPHILL, JOHN K.; GRIFFITHS, DANIEL E.; and FREDERIKSEN, NORMAN; with the assistance of GLEN STICE, LAURENCE IANNACCONE, WILLIAM COFFIELD, and SYDELL CARLTON. **Administrative Performance and Personality: A Study of the Principal in a Simulated Elementary School.** New York: Bureau of Publications, Teachers College, Columbia University, 1962. Pp. xix, 432. For a review by William E. Kendall, see 6:B245.

P428. HENRY, WILLIAM E. **The Analysis of Fantasy: The Thematic Apperception Technique in the Study of Personality.** New York: John Wiley & Sons, Inc., 1956. Pp. xiii, 305.

For reviews by F. N. Cox, Mortimer M. Meyer, Bert R. Sappenfield, Theodore R. Sarbin, and Frederick A. Zehrer, see 5:B204.

P429. HENRYSSON, STEN. **Applicability of Factor Analysis in the Behavioral Sciences: A Methodological Study.** Stockholm Studies in Educational Psychology 1. Stockholm, Sweden: Almqvist & Wiksell, 1957. Pp. 156.

For reviews by Raymond B. Cattell and Edwin A. Fleishman, see 6:B247.

P430. HIGGINS, MARY XAVIER. **Reducing the Variability of Supervisors' Judgments: An Experimental Study.** Johns Hopkins University Studies in Education, No. 23. Baltimore, Md.: Johns Hopkins Press, 1936. Pp. ix, 69.

For reviews by A. G. Schmidt and one other, see 1:B383.

P431. HILDEN, ARNOLD H. **Table of Heinis Personal Constant Values.** Minneapolis, Minn.: Educational Test Bureau, Inc., 1933. Pp. 28.

For a review, see 36:B135.

P432. HILDRETH, GERTRUDE H. **A Bibliography of Mental Tests and Rating Scales, Second Edition.** New York: Psychological Corporation, 1939. Pp. xxiv, 295.

For reviews by Thelma Hunt and one other, see 2:B937; for reviews by F. N. Freeman and one other of first edition, see 1:B384; for reviews by C. W. Odell, P. J. Rulon, A. G. Schmidt, and two others, see 36:B136.

P433. HIRT, MICHAEL, Editor. **Rorschach Science: Readings in Theory and Method.** New York: Free Press of Glencoe, 1962. Pp. ix, 438.

For reviews by Bernice T. Eiduson and James J. Muller, see 6:B260.

P434. HOBBS, NICHOLAS, Editor. **Psychological Research on Flexible Gunnery Training.** Army Air Forces Aviation Psychology Program Research Reports, Report No. 2. Washington, D.C.: U.S. Government Printing Office, 1947. Pp. viii, 508.

For reviews by W. E. Kappauf, Jr. and Laurance F. Shaffer, see 4:B197. For a review of the series, see P1.

P435. HOCH, PAUL H., and ZUBIN, JOSEPH, Editors. **Relation of Psychological Tests to Psychiatry.** The Proceedings of the Fortieth Annual Meeting of the American Psychopathological Association, Held in New York City, June 1950. New York: Grune & Stratton, Inc., 1951. Pp. viii, 301.

For reviews by Wayne H. Holtzman, B. H. McNeel, and one other, see 5:B210.

P436. HOFFMAN, MOSES N. H. **Measurements of Bilingual Background.** Columbia University, Teachers College, Contributions to Education No. 623. New York: Bureau of Publications, the College, 1934. Pp. 75.

For reviews by P. W. L. Cox, A. G. Schmidt, J. E. Wert, and Clifford Woody, see 36:B137.

P437. HOFFMANN, BANESH. **The Tyranny of Testing.** New York: Crowell-Collier Press, 1962. Pp. 223.

For reviews by Lawrence Beymer and John L. Holland, see 6:B263.

P438. HOHNE, H. H. **Success and Failure in Scientific Faculties of the University of Melbourne.**

Melbourne, Australia: Australian Council for Educational Research, 1955. Pp. vii, 129.

For a review by D. M. Lee, see 5:B211.

P439. HOLSOPPLE, JAMES QUINTER, and MIALE, FLORENCE R. **Sentence Completion: A Projective Method for the Study of Personality.** Springfield, Ill.: Charles C Thomas, Publisher, 1954. Pp. xiii, 179.

For reviews by Leonard B. Olinger, Boris Semeonoff, Edward Joseph Shoben, Jr., and George A. Talland, see 5:B213.

P440. HOLTZMAN, WAYNE H.; THORPE, JOSEPH S.; SWARTZ, JON D.; and HERRON, E. WAYNE. **Inkblot Perception and Personality: Holtzman Inkblot Technique.** Austin, Tex.: University of Texas Press, 1961. Pp. xi, 417.

For reviews by A. Barclay and Norman D. Sundberg, see 6:B264.

P441. HOLZINGER, KARL J., and HARMAN, HARRY H. **Factor Analysis: A Synthesis of Factorial Methods.** Chicago, Ill.: University of Chicago Press, 1941. Pp. xii, 417.

For reviews by C. C. Craig, M. A. Girshick, J. P. Guilford, Margaret Jarman Hagood, Charles M. Harsh, Paul Horst, Harold Hotelling, Truman L. Kelley, and Chester E. Kellogg, see 168 in *Statistical Methodology Reviews, 1941–1950.*

P442. HOLZINGER, KARL J., and SWINEFORD, FRANCES. **A Study in Factor Analysis: The Stability of a Bi-factor Solution.** University of Chicago, Department of Education, Supplementary Educational Monographs, No. 48. Chicago, Ill.: the Department, 1939. Pp. xi, 91.

For reviews by Austin G. Schmidt and A. H. Turney, see 2:B939.

P443. HOLZINGER, KARL J.; assisted by FRANCES SWINEFORD and HARRY HARMAN. **Student Manual of Factor Analysis: An Elementary Exposition of the Bi-factor Method and Its Relation to Multiple-factor Methods.** Chicago, Ill.: Statistical Laboratory, Department of Education, University of Chicago, 1937. Pp. vi, 101.

For reviews by H. Gulliksen and A. H. Turney, see 1:B639.

P444. HOOK, J. N. **How to Write Better Examinations.** College Outline Series. New York: Barnes & Noble, Inc., 1941. Pp. iii, 32.

For a review by Austin G. Schmidt, see 3:940.

P445. HORCHOW, REUBEN. **Machines in Civil Service Recruitment: With Special Reference to Experiences in Ohio.** Civil Service Assembly of the United States and Canada, Pamphlet No. 14. Chicago, Ill.: the Assembly, 1939. Pp. 43.

For reviews by Albert T. Helbing and one other, see 2:B940.

P446. HORST, PAUL; with the collaboration of PAUL WALLIN and LOUIS GUTTMAN; assisted by FRIEDA BRIM WALLIN, JOHN A. CLAUSEN, ROBERT REED, and ERICH ROSENTHAL. **The Prediction of Personal Adjustment: A Survey of Logical Problems and Research Techniques, With Illustrative Application of Problems of Vocational Selection, School Success, Marriage, and Crime.** Social Science Research Council, Bulletin 48. New York: the Council, 1941. Pp. xii, 455.

For reviews by Daniel Horn, Douglas E. Scates, Dewey B. Stuit, Percival M. Symonds, and Erle F. Young, see 3:942.

P447. HORTON, CLARK W. **Achievement Tests in Relation to Teaching Objectives in General Col-**

lege Botany. Botanical Society of America, Bulletin No. 120. Sponsored by the Committee on the Teaching of Botany in American Colleges and Universities. Charleston, Ill.: the Committee, Eastern Illinois State College, 1939. Pp. 71.
For reviews by Elliott R. Downing and Victor C. Smith, see 3:943.

P448. HOWARD, FREDERICK THOMAS. **Complexity of Mental Processes in Science Testing.** Columbia University, Teachers College, Contributions to Education, No. 879. New York: Bureau of Publications, the College, 1943. Pp. v, 54.
For reviews by Miles A. Tinker and one other, see 3:944.

P449. HOWARD, GLENN W. **A Measurement of the Achievement in Motor Skills of College Men in the Game Situation of Basketball.** Columbia University, Teachers College, Contributions to Education No. 733. New York: Bureau of Publications, the College, 1937. Pp. v, 109.
For reviews by J. E. Caswell and A. G. Schmidt, see 1:B387.

P450. HUBBARD, JOHN P., and CLEMANS, WILLIAM V. **Multiple-Choice Examinations in Medicine: A Guide for Examiner and Examinee.** Philadelphia, Pa.: Lea & Febiger, 1961. Pp. 186.
For a review by Peter G. Loret, see 6:B266.

P451. HUDSON, HOLLAND, and VAN GELDER, ROSETTA. **Counseling the Handicapped: A Manual on Aptitudes: Their Discovery and Interpretation.** New York: National Tuberculosis Association, 1940. Pp. x, 55.
For a review by Rose G. Anderson, see 3:947.

P452. HUFF, DARRELL. **Score: The Strategy of Taking Tests.** New York: Appleton-Century, 1961. Pp. ix, 148.
For a review by W. Porter Swift, see 6:B267.

P453. HUMPHREY, CLYDE W., and LAMB, MARION M. **Evaluating and Reporting Student Progress in Business Education.** Federal Security Agency, Office of Education, Vocational Division Bulletin No. 238, Business Education Series No. 17. Washington, D.C.: U.S. Government Printing Office, 1949. Pp. iv, 16.
For a review, see 4:B201.

P454. HUNT, E. P. ALLEN, and SMITH, PERCIVAL. **A Guide to Intelligence and Other Psychological Testing, Revised Edition.** London: Evans Brothers, Ltd., 1947. Pp. 108.
For reviews by M. M. MacTaggart and two others of the first edition, see 1:B392; for reviews by R. Knight and four others, see 36:B141.

P455. HUNT, THELMA. **Measurement in Psychology.** New York: Prentice-Hall, Inc., 1936. Pp. xx, 471.
For reviews by H. Robert Otness and one other, see 2:B964; for reviews by G. H. Hildreth, S. J. F. Philpott, W. C. Trow, H. C. Werner, and one other, see 1:B393; for reviews by H. M. Adams, A. C. Anderson, Q. McNemar, F. N. Maxfield, A. G. Schmidt, and one other, see 36:B140.

P456. HUSÉN, TORSTEN, and HENRICSON, SVEN-ERIC. **Some Principles of Construction of Group Intelligence Tests for Adults: A Report on the Construction and Standardization of the Swedish Induction Test (The I-Test).** Stockholm, Sweden: Almqvist & Wiksell, 1951. Pp. 100.
For a review, see 5:B219.

P457. HUTT, MAX L., and BRISKIN, GERALD J. **The Clinical Use of the Revised Bender-Gestalt Test.** New York: Grune & Stratton, Inc., 1960. Pp. viii, 168.
For reviews by S. Z. Dudek and Clifford H. Swensen, Jr., see 6:B268.

P458. INBAU, FRED E. **Lie Detection and Criminal Interrogation.** Baltimore, Md.: Williams & Wilkins Co., 1942. Pp. vii, 142.
For reviews by Howard F. Hunt, William A Hunt, and one other, see 3:949.

P459. INGLIS, ALEXANDER. **Inglis Intelligence Quotient Values, Second Edition.** Yonkers, N.Y.: World Book Co., 1938. Pp. i, 16.
For a review, see 1:B396.

P460. INSTITUTE FOR ADMINISTRATIVE OFFICERS OF HIGHER INSTITUTIONS. **Tests and Measurements in Higher Education.** Chicago, Ill.: University of Chicago Press, 1936. Pp. viii, 237.
For a review, see 1:B397; for reviews by W. McAndrew, A. G. Schmidt, F. Swineford (with K. J. Holzinger), and one other, see 36:B149.

P461. INVITATIONAL CONFERENCE ON TESTING PROBLEMS. **Exploring Individual Differences: A Report of the 1947 Invitational Conference on Testing Problems, New York City, November 1, 1947.** Henry Chauncey, Chairman. American Council on Education Studies, Vol. 12, Series 1, No. 32. Washington, D.C.: the Council, 1948. Pp. 110.
For a review by Dorothy C. Adkins, see 4:B206.

P462. INVITATIONAL CONFERENCE ON TESTING PROBLEMS. **National Projects in Educational Measurement: A Report of the 1946 Invitational Conference on Testing Problems, New York City, November 2, 1946.** Herschel T. Manuel, Chairman. American Council on Education Studies, Vol. 11, Series 1, No. 28. Washington, D.C.: the Council, 1947. Pp. vii, 80.
For a review by Dorothy C. Adkins, see 4:B205.

P463. INVITATIONAL CONFERENCE ON TESTING PROBLEMS. **Proceedings of the 1950 Invitational Conference on Testing Problems, October 28, 1950.** Robert L. Thorndike, Chairman. Princeton, N.J.: Educational Testing Service, 1951. Pp. 117.
For a review by Laurance F. Shaffer, see 4:B209.

P464. INVITATIONAL CONFERENCE ON TESTING PROBLEMS. **Proceedings of the 1959 Invitational Conference on Testing Problems, October 31, 1959.** Dorothy Adkins Wood, Chairman. Princeton, N.J.: Educational Testing Service, 1960. Pp. 99.
For a review by Thomas M. Magoon, see 6:B270.

P465. JACKSON, JOSEPH FRANCIS, and STALNAKER, JOHN MARSHALL. **Report on the French Examination of June 1938: A Description of the Procedures Used in Preparing and Reading the Examination in French and an Analysis of the Results of the Reading.** New York: College Entrance Examination Board, 1939. Pp. iii, 65.
For a review by Austin G. Schmidt, see 2:B967.

P466. JACKSON, ROBERT W. B., and FERGUSON, GEORGE A. **Studies on the Reliability of Tests.** University of Toronto, Department of Educational Research, Bulletin No. 12. Toronto, Canada: the Department, 1941. Pp. 132.
For reviews by C. Birchenough and Austin G. Schmidt, see 3:952.

P467. JACOBY, H. J. **Analysis of Handwriting: An Introduction Into Scientific Graphology.** London: George Allen & Unwin Ltd., 1939. Pp. 287, 26 plates.

For reviews by Steuart H. Britt, Ernest Jones, William Plomer, P. E. Vernon, and two others, see 3: 953; for reviews by Thea Stein Lewinson, M. J. Mannheim, R. A. S. Paget, E. I. Shanks, and one other, see 2:B969.

P468. JACOBY, H. J. **Self-Knowledge Through Handwriting.** London: J. M. Dent & Sons Ltd., 1941. Pp. xv, 71.
For a review by Austin G. Schmidt, see 3:954.

P469. JALOTA, S. S. **Handbook of Successful Preparation for Examinations.** Lahore, India: Careers, 1937. Pp. ii, 92.
For a review, see 1:B401.

P470. JARVIE, L. L., and ELLINGSON, MARK. **A Handbook on the Anecdotal Behavior Journal.** Chicago, Ill.: University of Chicago Press, 1940. Pp. xii, 71.
For reviews by W. H. Burton, John Carr Duff, Eugene R. Smith, W. C. Smyser, Dewey B. Stuit, and three others, see 3:955.

P471. JENNINGS, HELEN HALL. **Leadership and Isolation: A Study of Personality in Inter-Personal Relations, Second Edition.** New York: Longmans, Green & Co., Inc., 1950. Pp. xvii, 349.
For reviews by Morris Janowitz, Joseph I. Meiers, Donald R. Roberts, Bernard Steinzor, and Renato Tagiuri, see 4:B216; for reviews by Jean M. Arsenian, H. B. English, Robert E. L. Faris, Ben Karpman, Martha L. Lemmon, Clarence Leuba, Ronald Lippitt, Ruth Loveland, H. Meltzer, and Clara Thompson of the first edition, see 3:956.

P472. JENNINGS, HELEN HALL. **Sociometry in Group Relations: A Manual for Teachers, Second Edition.** Washington, D.C.: American Council on Education, 1959. Pp. xi, 105.
For a review by Robert B. Nordberg, see 6:B278; for reviews by Emory S. Bogardus, Louisa P. Holt, Stanton B. Langworthy, and Laurance F. Shaffer of the first edition, see 4:B217.

P473. JENSS, RACHEL M., and SOUTHER, SUSAN P. **Methods of Assessing the Physical Fitness of Children: A Study of Certain Methods Based on Anthropometric, Clinical, and Socioeconomic Observations Made of 713 7-Year-Old White Boys and Girls in New Haven, Conn., Over a Period of 19 or 20 Months During 1934–36.** United States Department of Labor, Children's Bureau, Bureau Publication No. 263. Washington, D.C.: U.S. Government Printing Office, 1940. Pp. vi, 121.
For a review by John R. Miner, see 3:959.

P474. JOHNSON, WENDELL; DARLEY, FREDERIC L.; and SPRIESTERSBACH, D. C. **Diagnostic Methods in Speech Pathology.** New York: Harper & Row, Publishers, Inc., 1963. Pp. xvii, 347.
For a review by Harry Hollien, see 6:B281.

P475. JOINT COMMITTEE OF THE WEST RIDING TEACHERS' ASSOCIATION AND THE WEST YORKSHIRE COUNTY ASSOCIATION OF THE NATIONAL UNION OF TEACHERS. **Special Place Examinations: The Report of an Investigation by a Joint Committee of the West Riding Teachers' Association and the West Yorkshire County Association of the National Union of Teachers, of the Merits and Defects of Some Forms of Special Place Examination.** London: University of London Press Ltd., 1941. Pp. viii, 71.
For reviews by Philip Hartog and C. W. Valentine, see 3:961.

P476. JOLLES, ISAAC. **A Catalogue for the Qualitative Interpretation of the H-T-P.** Beverly Hills, Calif.: Western Psychological Services, 1952. Pp. 97.
For reviews by Wilson H. Guertin and Laurance F. Shaffer, see 5:B234.

P477. JONES, EDWARD S. **Comprehensive Examinations in American Colleges: An Investigation for the Associaton of American Colleges.** New York: Macmillan Co., 1933. Pp. xix, 436.
For two reviews, see 1:B402; for reviews by G. U. Cleeton, W. McAndrew, J. C. Miller, A. G. Schmidt, and B. D. Wood, see 36:B150.

P478. JONES, EDWARD S. **Comprehensive Examinations in the Social Sciences: Comprehensive Examination Questions in History, Economics, Government, Sociology, and Psychology.** Supplement to the December 1933 Bulletin of the Association of American Colleges. New York: the Association, 1933. Pp. 128.
For a review, see 1:B404; for reviews by H. L. Dodge, A. L. Hall-Quest, and two others, see 36:B151.

P479. JONES, FRANK H. **Guide to Examination Success.** Stanmore, England: Barkeley Book Co. Ltd., 1947. Pp. 60.
For a review, see 4:B220.

P480. JONES, HAROLD E. **Development in Adolescence: Approaches to the Study of the Individual.** New York: Appleton-Century-Crofts, Inc., 1943. Pp. xix, 166.
For reviews by Peter Blos, Ruth Shonle Cavan, Henry E. Garrett, Elisabeth R. Geleerd, Robert J. Havighurst, Richard L. Jenkins, Leonard S. Kogan, Frank K. Shuttleworth, Robert W. White, John B. Wolfe, and one other, see 3:962.

P481. JONES, HAROLD E. **Motor Performance and Growth: A Developmental Study of Static Dynamometric Strength.** University of California, Publications in Child Development, Vol. 1, No. 1. Berkeley, Calif.: University of California Press, 1949. Pp. x, 181.
For reviews by Alfred L. Baldwin and Miles A. Tinker, see 4:B221.

P482. JONES, LLOYD MEREDITH. **A Factorial Analysis of Ability in Fundamental Motor Skills.** Columbia University, Teachers College, Contributions to Education No. 665. New York: Bureau of Publications, the College, 1935. Pp. ix, 100.
For a review by A. R. Lauer, see 2:B975.

P483. JORDAN, A. M. **Measurement in Education: An Introduction.** New York: McGraw-Hill Book Co., Inc., 1953. Pp. xi, 533.
For reviews by Mary A. Lanigan and one other, see 5:B238.

P484. JÖRESKOG, K. G. **Statistical Estimation in Factor Analysis: A New Technique and Its Foundation.** Stockholm, Sweden: Almqvist & Wiksell, 1963. Pp. 145.
For a review by M. S. Bartlett, see 6:B283.

P485. JURGENSEN, CLIFFORD E.; LOPEZ, FELIX M., JR.; and RICHARDS, KENNETH E. **Employee Performance Appraisal Re-examined.** Personnel Brief No. 613. Chicago, Ill.: Public Personnel Association, 1961. Pp. 29.
For a review by P. L. Mason, see 6:B284.

P486. KABACK, GOLDIE RUTH. **Vocational Personalities: An Application of the Rorschach Group Method.** Columbia University, Teachers College, Contributions to Education, No. 924. New York:

Bureau of Publications, the College, 1946. Pp. xi, 116.

For a review by Boyd McCandless, see 4:123; for reviews by Max Hertzman and Joseph Zubin, see 3:82a.

P487. KAGAN, JEROME, and LESSER, GERALD S., Editors. **Contemporary Issues in Thematic Apperceptive Methods.** Springfield, Ill.: Charles C Thomas, Publisher, 1961. Pp. xiv, 328.

For reviews by A. Kaldegg, Bernard Landis, and Edith Weisskopf-Joelson, see 6:B285.

P488. KAHN, THEODORE C., and GIFFEN, MARTIN B. **Psychological Techniques in Diagnosis and Evaluation.** Oxford, England: Pergamon Press Ltd., 1960. Pp. xi, 164.

For reviews by Max L. Fogel, Herbert J. Schlesinger, and B. Semeonoff, see 6:B286.

P489. KAMAT, V. V. **Measuring Intelligence of Indian Children, Third Edition.** Bombay, India: Oxford University Press, 1958. Pp. 284.

For a review by George Westby of the second edition, see 5:B240; for reviews by C. M. Fleming and three others of the first edition, see 3:964.

P490. KANDEL, I. L. **Examinations and Their Substitutes in the United States.** Carnegie Foundation for the Advancement of Teaching, Bulletin No. 28. New York: the Foundation, 1936. Pp. xii, 183.

For a review, see 2:B977; for reviews by M. Domitilla, R. H. Eckelberry, P. J. Hartog, A. W. Hurd, and two others, see 1:B405; for reviews by D. A. Robertson, A. G. Schmidt, and two others, see 36:B152.

P491. KANDEL, I. L. **Professional Aptitude Tests in Medicine, Law, and Engineering.** New York: Bureau of Publications, Teachers College, Columbia University, 1940. Pp. x, 78.

For reviews by Roger M. Bellows, Stephen M. Corey, Austin G. Schmidt, and one other, see 3:965.

P492. KATZ, MARTIN. **Selecting an Achievement Test, Second Edition.** Evaluation and Advisory Service Series, No. 3. Princeton, N.J.: Educational Testing Service, 1961. Pp. 32.

For a review by Thomas M. Magoon of the first edition, see 6:B289.

P493. KEELER, LOUIS W. **Results of the Testing Program in the Grass Lake Public School.** University of Michigan, School of Education, Bureau of Educational Reference and Research Bulletin, No. 143. Ann Arbor, Mich.: the School, 1933. Pp. 39.

For reviews by A. G. Schmidt and one other, see 36:B153.

P494. KELLEY, IDA B., and PERKINS, KEITH J. **An Investigation of Teachers' Knowledge of and Attitudes Toward Child and Adolescent Behavior in Everyday School Situations.** Purdue University, Division of Educational Reference, Studies in Higher Education, [No.] 42; Further Studies in Attitudes, Series 4. Lafayette, Ind.: the Division, 1941. Pp. 99.

For a review by Austin G. Schmidt, see 3:966.

P495. KELLEY, TRUMAN L. **Essential Traits of Mental Life: The Purposes and Principles Underlying the Selection and Measurement of Independent Mental Factors Together With Computational Tables.** Harvard University Studies in Education, Vol. 26. Cambridge, Mass.: Harvard University Press, 1935. Pp. x, 145.

For reviews by P. O. Johnson and A. M. Jordan, see 1:B406; for reviews by H. E. Garrett, K. J. Holzinger, A. G. Schmidt, F. Swineford (with K. J. Holzinger), P. V. West, and two others, see 36:B154.

P496. KELLEY, TRUMAN L., and KREY, AUGUST C. **Tests and Measurements in the Social Sciences.** American Historical Association, Report of the Commission on the Social Studies, Part 4. New York: Charles Scribner's Sons, 1934. Pp. xiv, 635.

For reviews by M. Levine and two others, see 1:B407; for reviews by O. K. Buros, A. S. Edwards, W. McAndrew, P. J. Rulon, A. G. Schmidt, H. H. Shoen, R. M. Tryon, and one other, see 36:B155.

P497. KEMP, EDWARD H., and JOHNSON, A. PEMBERTON, Editors. **Psychological Research on Bombardier Training.** Army Air Forces Aviation Psychology Program Research Reports, Report No. 9. Washington, D.C.: U.S. Government Printing Office, 1947. Pp. x, 294.

For a review by Delos D. Wickens, see 4:B226. For a review of the series, see P1.

P498. KENT, GRACE H. **Mental Tests in Clinics for Children.** New York: D. Van Nostrand Co., Inc., 1950. Pp. xii, 180.

For reviews by Helmer R. Myklebust and Laurance F. Shaffer, see 4:B228.

P499. KILGORE, WILLIAM ARLOW. **Identification of Ability to Apply Principles of Physics.** Columbia University, Teachers College, Contributions to Education, No. 840. New York: Bureau of Publications, the College, 1941. Pp. ix, 34.

For a review by Austin G. Schmidt, see 3:970.

P500. KINGET, G. MARIAN. **The Drawing-Completion Test: A Projective Technique for the Investigation of Personality Based on the Wartegg Test Blank.** New York: Grune & Stratton, Inc., 1952. Pp. xv, 238.

For reviews by Fred Brown, John P. Foley, Jr., Goldine C. Gleser, and Walter Kass, see 5:130.

P501. KINTER, MADALINE. **The Measurement of Artistic Abilities: A Survey of Scientific Studies in the Field of Graphic Arts.** New York: Psychological Corporation, 1933. Pp. 90.

For a review by K. A. Preston, see 1:B408; for reviews by R. Pintner, W. G. Whitford, and one other, see 36:B156.

P502. KLINE, LINUS W., and CAREY, GERTRUDE L. **Measuring Scale for Free-Hand Drawing, Part 2, Design and Composition.** Johns Hopkins University, Studies in Education, No. 5. Baltimore, Md.: Johns Hopkins Press, 1933. Pp. 58.

For a review by W. G. Whitford, see 1:B409; for a review by A. G. Schmidt, see 36:B157.

P503. KLOPFER, BRUNO. **The Rorschach Technique: A Manual for a Projective Method of Personality Diagnosis.** With clinical contributions by Douglas McGlashan Kelley. Yonkers, N.Y.: World Book Co., 1946. Pp. xi, 475.

For a review by W. D. Wall, see 3:78; for reviews by S. J. Beck, R. Milton Finney, Philip Lawrence Harriman, Robert E. Harris, M. R. Harrower-Erickson, Morris Krugman, Edna Brand Mann, Claire Myers, Z. A. Piotrowski, Ernest G. Schachtel, Ira S. Wile, and two others, see 3:84.

P504. KLOPFER, BRUNO, and DAVIDSON, HELEN H. **The Rorschach Technique: An Introductory Manual.** New York: Harcourt, Brace & World, Inc., 1962. Pp. viii, 245.

For reviews by Theodora Alcock and Mortimer M. Meyer, see 6:B295.

P505. KLOPFER, BRUNO, and DAVIDSON, HELEN H. **The Rorschach Technique: 1946 Supplement.**

Yonkers, N.Y.: World Book Co., 1946. Pp. 431–75.
For a review, see 3:83.

P506. KLOPFER, BRUNO; AINSWORTH, MARY D.;
KLOPFER, WALTER G.; and HOLT, ROBERT R. **Developments in the Rorschach Technique: Vol. I, Technique and Theory.** Yonkers, N.Y.: World Book Co., 1954. Pp. x, 726.
For reviews by George W. Albee, Lee J. Cronbach, Albert Ellis, J. G. Lyle, Boris Semeonoff, and Edward Joseph Shoben, Jr., see 5:B247.

P507. KLOPFER, BRUNO; with contributions by MARY D. AINSWORTH, DOROTHY V. ANDERSON, GERTRUDE BAKER, HEDDA BOLGAR, JACK FOX, A. IRVING HALLOWELL, EILEEN HIGHAM, SAMUEL KELLMAN, WALTER G. KLOPFER, GERTRUDE MEILI-DWORETZKI, EDWIN S. SHNEIDMAN, ROBERT F. SNOWDEN, MARVIN SPEIGELMAN, MARIE D. STEIN, EVELYN TROUP, and GERTHA WILLIAMS. **Developments in Rorschach Technique: Vol. II, Fields of Application.** Yonkers, N.Y.: World Book Co., 1956. Pp. xx, 828.
For reviews by Theodora Alcock, Samuel J. Beck, Bernard I. Murstein, and B. Semeonoff, see 5:B248.

P508. KLOPFER, WALTER G. **Suggestions for the Systematic Analysis of Rorschach Records.** Los Angeles, Calif.: U.C.L.A. Student's Store, University of California, 1949. Pp. 16.
For a review by Winafred Lucas, see 4:124.

P509. KNIGHT, REX. **Intelligence and Intelligence Tests.** Methuen's Monographs on Philosophy and Psychology. London: Methuen & Co. Ltd., 1933. Pp. ix, 98.
For three reviews, see 1:B410; for reviews by A. E. Chapman, E. Lawrence, and three others, see 36:B158.

P510. KNOTT, VIRGINIA BERGSTRESSER. **Physical Measurement of Young Children: A Study of Anthropometric Reliabilities for Children Three to Six Years of Age.** University of Iowa Studies, Studies in Child Welfare, Vol. 18, No. 3, [New Series] No. 394. Iowa City, Iowa: University of Iowa Press, 1941. Pp. 99.
For a review by Austin G. Schmidt, see 3:976.

P511. KOCH, CHARLES. **The Tree Test: The Tree-Drawing Test as an Aid in Psychodiagnosis.** Berne, Switzerland: Hans Huber, 1952. Pp. 87.
For reviews by Bertram R. Forer and Goldine C. Gleser, see 5:B251.

P512. KOPPITZ, ELIZABETH MUNSTERBERG. **The Bender Gestalt Test for Young Children.** New York: Grune & Stratton, Inc., 1964. Pp. xi, 195.
For a review by C. H. Ammons, see 6:B297.

P513. KRAKOWER, HYMAN. **Tests and Measurements Applied to Nursing Education.** New York: G. P. Putnam's Sons, 1949. Pp. xi, 179.
For reviews by Dorothy Deming, Marguerite C. Holmes, and one other, see 4:B231.

P514. KROEGER, L. J., and BYERS, K. **Reports of Performance: A System of Service Ratings for the California State Civil Service.** Sacramento, Calif.: State Personnel Board, 1939.
For a review by Ward Steward, see 2:B983.2.

P515. KUHLMANN, F. **Tests of Mental Development: A Complete Scale for Individual Examination.** Minneapolis, Minn.: Educational Test Bureau, Inc., 1939. Pp. xi, 314.
For reviews by Gertrude Hildreth and Austin G. Schmidt, see 2:1426.

P516. KUTASH, SAMUEL B., and GEHL, RAYMOND H. **The Graphomotor Projection Technique: Clinical Use and Standardization.** Springfield, Ill.: Charles C Thomas, Publisher, 1954. Pp. xi, 133.
For reviews by Marion Font and H. Phillipson, see 5:137.

P517. KWALWASSER, JACOB. **Exploring the Musical Mind.** New York: Coleman-Ross Co., Inc., 1955. Pp. x, 189.
For reviews by John T. Cowles and Paul R. Farnsworth, see 5:B255.

P518. LADO, ROBERT. **Language Testing: The Construction and Use of Foreign Language Tests: A Teacher's Book.** London: Longmans, Green & Co. Ltd., 1961. Pp. xxiii, 389.
For reviews by H. H. Stern and one other, see 6:B300.

P519. LALEGER, GRACE ELIZABETH. **The Vocational Interests of High School Girls: As Inventoried by the Strong and Manson Blanks.** Columbia University, Teachers College, Contributions to Education, No. 857. New York: Bureau of Publications, the College, 1942. Pp. vii, 102.
For reviews by Arthur F. Dodge and D. Welty Lefever, see 3:981.

P520. LALL, SOHAN. **Mental Measurement: A Survey of Intelligence and Achievement of School Pupils in the United Provinces.** Allahabad, India: Kitabistan, 1948. Pp. 88.
For reviews by Henry E. Garrett and one other, see 4:B236.

P521. LAWLEY, D. N., and MAXWELL, A. E. **Factor Analysis as a Statistical Method.** London: Butterworth & Co. (Publishers) Ltd., 1963. Pp. viii, 117.
For a review by M. G. Kendall, see 6:B303.

P522. LAWSHE, C. H., JR. **Principles of Personnel Testing.** New York: McGraw-Hill Book Co., Inc., 1948. Pp. xi, 227.
For reviews by Harold Fields, Edwin E. Ghiselli, F. E. Hewitt, Clifford E. Jurgensen, Luigi Petrullo, A. J. Wyndham, and one other, see 4:B239.

P523. LAYTON, WILBUR L. **Counseling Use of the Strong Vocational Interest Blank.** Minnesota Studies in Student Personnel Work, No. 8. Minneapolis, Minn.: University of Minnesota Press, 1958. Pp. 40.
For reviews by Robert Callis and Thomas M. Magoon, see 6:B304.

P524. LAYTON, WILBUR L., Editor. **The Strong Vocational Interest Blank: Research and Uses: Papers From the Institute on the Strong Vocational Interest Blank Held at the University of Minnesota in February 1955.** Minnesota Studies in Student Personnel Work, No. 10. Minneapolis, Minn.: University of Minnesota Press, 1960. Pp. viii, 191.
For reviews by Peter F. Merenda and Lawrence H. Stewart, see 6:B305.

P525. LEAHY, ALICE M. **Measurement of Urban Home Environment: Validation and Standardization of the Minnesota Home Status Index.** University of Minnesota, Institute of Child Welfare Monograph Series, No. 11. Minneapolis, Minn.: University of Minnesota Press, 1936. Pp. vii, 70.
For reviews by Stuart C. Dodd, Dorothy Hutchinson, Emily L. Stogdill, and R. Clyde White, see 1:983; for reviews by A. D. McHenry and R. C.

White, see 1:B411; for reviews by W. McAndrew, A. G. Schmidt, and one other, see 36:B162.

P526. LEARNED, WILLIAM S., and WOOD, BEN D. **The Student and His Knowledge: A Report to the Carnegie Foundation on the Results of the High School and College Examinations of 1928, 1930, and 1932.** Carnegie Foundation for the Advancement of Teaching, Bulletin No. 29. New York: the Foundation, 1938. Pp. xx, 406.
For reviews by E. R. Dowling, M. W. Richardson, and Lewis M. Terman, see 2:B988; for reviews by J. Graham, A. G. Schmidt, and one other, see 1:B412.

P527. LEARY, TIMOTHY. **Interpersonal Diagnosis of Personality: A Functional Theory and Methodology for Personality Evaluation.** New York: Ronald Press Co., 1957. Pp. xix, 518.
For reviews by Leon Gorlow, Helen D. Sargent, William C. Schutz, Laurence Siegel, Louis P. Thorpe, and Jeanne Watson, see 5:B261.

P528. LEDWITH, NETTIE H. **Rorschach Responses of Elementary School Children: A Normative Study.** Pittsburgh, Pa.: University of Pittsburgh Press, 1959. Pp. xi, 185.
For reviews by Samuel J. Beck (with Anne G. Beck), Wayne H. Holtzman, and Mortimer M. Meyer, see 6:B306.

P529. LEDWITH, NETTIE H. **A Rorschach Study of Child Development.** Pittsburgh, Pa.: University of Pittsburgh Press, 1960. Pp. ix, 336.
For reviews by Erika Fromm, Bruno Klopfer, and Mortimer M. Meyer, see 6:B307.

P530. LEE, J. MURRAY, and SEGAL, DAVID. **Testing Practices of High School Teachers.** United States Department of the Interior, Office of Education Bulletin, 1936, No. 9. Washington, D.C.: U.S. Government Printing Office, 1936. Pp. 42.
For reviews by W. McAndrew, A. G. Schmidt, and one other, see 36:B164.

P531. LEE, J. MURRAY; assisted by DORIS M. LEE. **A Guide to Measurement in Secondary Schools: A Practical Guide in the Administration, Construction, and Use of Tests and Measurements in Secondary Education.** New York: D. Appleton-Century Co., Inc., 1936. Pp. xv, 514.
For a review, see 1:B413; for reviews by S. Carpenter, L. V. Koos, A. H. Lass, A. G. Schmidt, and two others, see 36:B165.

P532. LEFEVER, D. WELTY, and CARNES, EARL F. **A Workbook in Measurement and Evaluation.** Los Angeles, Calif.: College Book Store, 1956. Pp. ix, 128.
For a review by Max D. Engelhart, see 5:B263.

P533. LEITER, RUSSELL GRAYDON. **The Leiter International Performance Scale: Vol. 1, Directions for the Application and Scoring of the Individual Tests.** Santa Barbara, Calif.: Santa Barbara State College Press, 1940. Pp. ix, 95.
For a review by Henry D. Rinsland, see 2:B989.

P534. LEONARD, EUGENIA A., and TUCKER, ANTHONY C. **The Individual Inventory of Guidance Programs in Secondary Schools: A Study of Present Practices in Selected Schools.** Federal Security Agency, United States Office of Education, Vocational Division Bulletin, No. 215; Occupational Information and Guidance Series, No. 7. Washington, D.C.: U.S. Government Printing Office, 1941. Pp. v, 60.
For a review by Arthur J. Jones, see 3:982.

P535. LEONHARD, DIETZ L. **Consumer Research With Projective Techniques: A Case Report of Theory and Successful Experimentations in Market and Marketing Research.** Shenandoah, Iowa: Ajax Corporation, 1955. Pp. ii, 151.
For a review by Melvin S. Hattwick, see 5:B265.

P536. LEPLEY, WILLIAM M., Editor. **Psychological Research in the Theaters of War.** Army Air Forces Aviation Psychology Program Research Reports, Report No. 17. Washington, D.C.: U.S. Government Printing Office, 1947. Pp. vi, 202.
For reviews by N. H. Pronko and one other, see 4:B243; for a review, see 3:984. For a review of the series, see P1.

P537. LEVINE, EDNA SIMON. **The Psychology of Deafness: Techniques of Appraisal for Rehabilitation.** New York: Columbia University Press, 1960. Pp. xii, 383.
For reviews by Carl W. Fuller and one other, see 6:B309.

P538. LEWINSON, THEA STEIN, and ZUBIN, JOSEPH. **Handwriting Analysis: A Series of Scales for Evaluating the Dynamic Aspects of Handwriting.** New York: King's Crown Press, 1942. Pp. xiii, 147.
For reviews by H. D. Carter, Walter W. Marseille, and four others, see 3:986.

P539. LIBO, LESTER M. **Attitude Prediction in Labor Relations: A Test of "Understanding."** Stanford University, Graduate School of Business, Division of Industrial Relations, Studies in Industrial Relations, No. 10. Stanford, California: the Division, [1948]. Pp. ii, 17.
For a review, see 4:B245.

P540. LIBO, LESTER M. **Measuring Group Cohesiveness.** University of Michigan, Institute for Social Research, Research Center for Group Dynamics, No. 3. Ann Arbor, Mich.: University of Michigan Press, 1953. Pp. ix, 111.
For reviews by Chris Argyris and Ruth Tolman, see 5:B267.

P541. LIEBERS, ARTHUR. **How to Pass Employment Tests.** New York: Arco Publishing Co., Inc., 1959. Pp. ii, 99, 222, plus supplements.
For a review by Lyle D. Schmidt, see 6:B311.

P542. LIFE OFFICE MANAGEMENT ASSOCIATION. **The Application of Psychological Tests to the Selection, Placement, and Transfer of Clerical Employees.** Report No. 6 of the Committee on Tests of the Life Office Management Association. New York: the Association, 1942. Pp. iv, 26.
For a review by Edward N. Hay, see 3:994.

P543. LINCOLN, EDWARD A., and WORKMAN, LINWOOD L. **Testing and the Use of Test Results.** New York: Macmillan Co., 1935. Pp. xi, 317.
For reviews by F. L. Goodenough and one other, see 1:B415; for reviews by F. P. Frutchey, A. H. Lass, W. McAndrew, W. S. Monroe, A. G. Schmidt, G. M. Wilson, and three others, see 36:B167.

P544. LINDQUIST, E. F., Editor. **Educational Measurement.** Washington, D.C.: American Council on Education, 1951. Pp. xix, 819.
For reviews by Cyril Burt, Lloyd G. Humphreys, Julian C. Stanley, and Robert M. W. Travers, see 5:B269; for reviews by Roy M. Hall, F. J. Houlahan, William B. Michael, Laurance F. Shaffer, and one other, see 4:B247.

P545. LINDVALL, C. M. **Testing and Evaluation: An Introduction.** New York: Harcourt, Brace & World, Inc., 1961. Pp. viii, 264.

For a review by Robert H. Bauernfeind, see 6:B312.

P546. LINDZEY, GARDNER. **Projective Techniques and Cross-Cultural Research.** New York: Appleton-Century-Crofts, Inc., 1961. Pp. xi, 339.
For reviews by William E. Henry, Bert Kaplan, and George D. Spindler, see 6:B313.

P547. LOCK, H. F. **The Use of Tests in Selection Procedures.** London: British Institute of Management, 1956. Pp. 26.
For a review by Denis McMahon, see 5:B271.

P548. LOEVINGER, JANE. **Objective Tests as Instruments of Psychological Theory.** Psychological Reports Monograph Supplement 9. Missoula, Mont.: Psychological Reports, 1957. Pp. 635–94.
For a review by Robert M. W. Travers, see 6:B316.

P549. LOMBARDI, MARYELLAN MAHER. **The Inter-Trait Rating Technique.** Columbia University, Teachers College, Contributions to Education, No. 760. New York: Bureau of Publications, the College, 1938. Pp. vii, 99.
For reviews by Margaret Marshall and Francis N. Maxfield, see 3:997; for a review by Margaret Marshall, see 2:B997.

P550. LONG, JOHN A., and SANDIFORD, PETER. **The Validation of Test Items.** University of Toronto, Department of Educational Research, Bulletin No. 3. Toronto, Canada: the Department, 1935. Pp. 126.
For reviews by P. J. Rulon, F. Swineford (with K. J. Holzinger), and one other, see 36:B169.

P551. LORENZ, JENNIE. **Consistency of Auditory Acuity: Or, Variability of Individuals Among Four Tests With the 2A Audiometer.** Sheboygan, Wis.: the Author, 1936. Pp. 162.
For reviews by E. Girden and R. West, see 1:B417.

P552. LOWENFELD, MARGARET. **The Lowenfeld Mosaic Test.** London: Newman Neame Ltd., 1954. Pp. 360.
For reviews by M. Bassett, M. Collins, Lydia Jackson, Morris Krugman, and Laurance F. Shaffer, see 5:B274.

P553. LYMAN, HOWARD B. **Test Scores and What They Mean.** Englewood Cliffs, N.J.: Prentice-Hall, Inc., 1963. Pp. xv, 223.
For reviews by Arthur P. Coladarci, J. O. Crites, and Richard E. Schutz (with James C. Moore), see 6:B318.

P554. MCCALL, WILLIAM A. **Measurement.** New York: Macmillan Co., 1939. Pp. xv, 535.
For reviews by Albert Bailey, Lee J. Cronbach, E. R. Henry, and one other, see 3:1000; for reviews by M. E. Broom, August Dvorak, Max D. Engelhart, Earl R. Gabler, Silas Hertzler, John A. Long, Quinn McNemar, H. T. Manuel, C. W. Odell, Clarence M. Pruitt, Henry D. Rinsland, Austin G. Schmidt, Eugene Shen, Guy M. Wilson, Ll. Wynn Jones, and five others, see 2:B1000.

P555. MCCLELLAND, WILLIAM. **Selection for Secondary Education.** Publications of the Scottish Council for Research in Education, [No.] 19. International Examinations Inquiry. London: University of London Press Ltd., 1942. Pp. xxiv, 264.
For reviews by C. Birchenough, Cyril Burt, and one other, see 3:1002.

P556. MCCLOY, C. H. **Appraising Physical Status: Methods and Norms.** University of Iowa

Studies, New Series, No. 356; Studies in Child Welfare, Vol. 15, No. 2. Iowa City, Iowa: the University, 1938. Pp. 260.
For a review by Weston LaBarre, see 2:B1001.

P557. MCCLOY, CHARLES H. **Appraising Physical Status: The Selection of Measurements.** University of Iowa Studies, New Series, No. 319; Studies in Child Welfare, Vol. 12, No. 2. Iowa City, Iowa: the University, 1936. Pp. 126.
For a review by Weston LaBarre, see 2:B1002; for reviews by A. G. Schmidt and two others, see 36:B171.

P558. MCCLOY, CHARLES HAROLD, and YOUNG, NORMA DOROTHY. **Tests and Measurements in Health and Physical Education, Third Edition.** New York: Appleton-Century-Crofts, Inc., 1954. Pp. xxi, 497.
For a review by Charles H. Keene, see 5:B278; for reviews by Karl W. Bookwalter, Nellie Bussell Cochran, C. D. Giauque, M. Immaculata, Charles H. Keene, Austin G. Schmidt, and two others of the first edition, see 2:B1003.

P559. MACCURDY, HOWARD L. **A Test for Measuring the Physical Capacity of Secondary School Boys.** Yonkers, N.Y.: Senior High School, 1933. Pp. 59.
For a review by J. F. Bovard, see 1:B420.

P560. MACFARLANE, JEAN WALKER. **Methodology of Data Collection and Organization: Studies in Child Guidance, 1.** Monographs of the Society for Research in Child Development, Vol. 3, No. 6, Serial No. 19. Washington, D.C.: the Society, 1938. Pp. vii, 254.
For reviews by Lawson G. Lowrey and one other, see 3:1005.

P561. MACGREGOR, GREGOR. **Achievement Tests in the Primary School: A Comparative Study With American Tests in Life.** Publications of the Scottish Council for Research in Education, No. 6. London: University of London Press Ltd., 1934. Pp. xiii, 136.
For reviews by R. Knight, R. Pintner, Clifford Woody, and one other, see 36:B172.

P562. MACHOVER, KAREN. **Personality Projection in the Drawing of the Human Figure: A Method of Personality Investigation.** Springfield, Ill.: Charles C Thomas, Publisher, 1949. Pp. ix, 183.
For reviews by John E. Bell, Hanna F. Faterson, Robert H. Gault, Irene Hollingsworth, Lillian Wald Kay, Isabelle V. Kendig, Noel Mailloux, Olive Westbrooke Quinn, T. W. Richards, Laurance F. Shaffer, Magdalen D. Vernon, Samuel Waldfogel, John G. Watkins, and one other, see 4:112.

P563. MACHOVER, SOLOMON. **Cultural and Racial Variations in Patterns of Intellect: Performance of Negro and White Criminals on the Bellevue Adult Intelligence Scale.** Columbia University, Teachers College, Contributions to Education, No. 875. New York: Bureau of Publications, the College, 1943. Pp. v, 91.
For reviews by W. Eliasberg, Robert E. L. Faris, and Raymond F. Sletto, see 3:1006.

P564. MCINTOSH, DOUGLAS M. **Promotion From Primary to Secondary Education.** Publications of the Scottish Council for Research in Education XXIX. London: University of London Press Ltd., 1948. Pp. xiv, 152.
For a review, see 4:B254.

P565. McINTOSH, DOUGLAS M.; WALKER, DAVID A.; and MACKAY, DONALD. **The Scaling of Teachers' Marks and Estimates, Revised Edition.** Edinburgh, Scotland: Oliver & Boyd Ltd., 1962. Pp. xii, 182.
For a review by Dormer Ellis, see 6:B322; for reviews by C. M. Fleming and one other of the first edition, see 4:B255.

P566. McINTYRE, G. A. **The Standardization of Intelligence Tests in Australia.** Australian Council for Educational Research, Educational Research Series, No. 54. Melbourne, Australia: Melbourne University Press, 1938. Pp. 82.
For a review, see 2:B1005.

P567. McKOWN, HARRY C. **How to Pass a Written Examination.** New York: McGraw-Hill Book Co., Inc., 1943. Pp. xi, 1962.
For reviews by Benjamin Bloom, A. M. Jordan, Benjamin E. Mallary, Norman J. Powell, and C. A. Stone, see 3:1008.

P568. MACKWORTH, N. H. **Researches on the Measurement of Human Performance.** Medical Research Council, Special Report Series, No. 268. London: H.M. Stationery Office, 1950. Pp. 156.
For reviews by Madison Bentley, Edward Elliott, and H. J. Eysenck, see 4:B256.

P569. McMANUS, R. LOUISE. **Study Guide on Evaluation: Suggestions for Faculty Committees and Other Groups Studying Evaluation in Nursing.** New York: National League of Nursing Education, 1944. Pp. 32.
For a review by Helen W. Munson, see 3:1010.

P570. MACMEEKEN, A. M. **The Intelligence of a Representative Group of Scottish Children.** Publications of the Scottish Council for Research in Education, [No.] 15. International Examinations Inquiry. London: University of London Press Ltd., 1939. Pp. xvi, 144.
For a review by Francis N. Maxfield, see 3:1011; for reviews by Edith O. Mercer and three others, see 2:B1006.

P571. McMURRY, ROBERT N.; ARNOLD, JAMES S.; BROWNE, ROBERT F.; HAMSTRA, R. HOLLIS; MILLER, KATHERINE S.; SHAEFFER, ROBERT E.; and SHAEFFER, RUTH J. **Tested Techniques of Personnel Selection.** Chicago, Ill.: Dartnell Corporation, 1955. Pages not numbered.
For reviews by Edwin R. Henry and Milton M. Mandell, see 5:B281.

P572. McNEMAR, QUINN. **The Revision of the Stanford-Binet Scale: An Analysis of the Standardization Data.** Boston, Mass.: Houghton Mifflin Co., 1942. Pp. ix, 189.
For reviews by Cyril Burt, Ethel L. Cornell, Henry E. Garrett, Forrest H. Kirkpatrick, Francis N. Maxfield, and one other, see 3:293.

P573. MAGNUSON, HENRY W.; GIPE, MELVIN W.; and SHELLHAMMER, THOMAS A. **Evaluating Pupil Progress, 1960 Edition.** California State Department of Education Bulletin, Vol. 29, No. 14. Sacramento, Calif.: the Department, 1960. Pp. vii, 229.
For reviews by Guy W. Buddemeyer and one other of the first edition, see 5:B283.

P574. MAGNUSSON, DAVID. **A Study of Ratings Based on TAT.** Swedish Council for Personnel Administration, Report No. 22. Stockholm, Sweden: Almqvist & Wiksell, 1959. Pp. 176.
For a review by C. H. Ammons, see 6:B326.

P575. MAHLER, WALTER R. **Twenty Years of Merit Rating, 1926–1946: Selected, Annotated and Classified References From Industry, Business, Government, and Education, Experience and Research.** New York: Psychological Corporation, 1947. Pp. viii, 73.
For a review by M. W. Richardson, see 3:1014.

P576. MANUEL, HERSCHEL T. **Taking a Test: How to Do Your Best.** Yonkers, N.Y.: World Book Co., 1956. Pp. ii, 77.
For a review by Marie A. Flesher, see 5:B285.

P577. MARSTON, WILLIAM M. **The Lie Detector Test.** New York: Richard R. Smith, Inc., 1938. Pp. 179.
For a review by Fred E. Inbau, see 3:1018; for reviews by James Hargan, Verne W. Lyon, and Paul W. Tappan, see 2:B1014; for reviews by G. L. Freeman, W. Healy, A. G. Schmidt, and one other, see 1:B426.

P578. MASLOW, PAUL. **The Analysis and Control of Human Experiences: The Individual Seen Through Rorschach, Volumes 1 and 2.** Brooklyn, N.Y.: the Author, 1947. Pp. iii, 233; iv, 195.
For reviews by Alfred R. Lindesmith, W. Donald Ross, and three others, see 4:125; for reviews by Rose Palm and one other, see 3:86; for reviews by Milton H. Erickson, D. R. Miller, William F. Murphy, and one other of an earlier edition, see 3:87; for a review by Milton H. Erickson, see 3:88.

P579. MAURER, KATHARINE M. **Intellectual Status at Maturity as a Criterion for Selecting Items in Preschool Tests.** University of Minnesota, Institute of Child Welfare Monograph Series, No. 21. Minneapolis, Minn.: University of Minnesota Press, 1946. Pp. ix, 166.
For reviews by Nancy Bayley, Lee J. Cronbach, H. J. Eysenck, C. M. Fleming, and Quinn McNemar, see 4:352; for reviews by two others, see 3:288.

P580. MELTON, ARTHUR W., Editor. **Apparatus Tests.** Army Air Forces Aviation Psychology Program Research Reports, Report No. 4. Washington, D.C.: U.S. Government Printing Office, 1947. Pp. xxiv, 1056.
For reviews by Robert H. Seashore and Laurance F. Shaffer, see 4:B267. For a review of the series, see P1.

P581. MENDEL, A. O. **Personality in Handwriting: A Handbook of American Graphology, Second Edition.** New York: Stephen Daye Press, 1958. Pp. 376.
For a review by P. E. Vernon, see 6:B336; for reviews by William H. Brown, Douglas M. Kelley, Z. A. Piotrowski, George E. Reed, Werner Wolff, and three others of the first edition, see 4:B268.

P582. MENZEL, EMIL W. **Suggestions for the Use of New-Type Tests in India, Second Edition.** Bombay: Oxford University Press, 1942. Pp. xiii, 283.
For reviews by H. Maiti and one other of the first edition, see 3:1026; for two reviews, see 2:1017.

P583. MESSICK, SAMUEL, and ROSS, JOHN, Editors. **Measurement in Personality and Cognition.** New York: John Wiley & Sons, Inc., 1962. Pp. xi, 334.
For a review by Walter Mischel, see 6:B337.

P584. METROPOLITAN LIFE INSURANCE COMPANY, POLICYHOLDERS SERVICE BUREAU. **Testing Applicants for Employment.** New York: the Bureau, [1939]. Pp. iv, 32.
For a review, see 2:B1019.

P585. MEYER, JEROME S. **The Handwriting Analyzer.** New York: Simon & Schuster, Inc., 1953. Pp. iii, 103.

For a review, see 5:B290.

P586. MICHEELS, WILLIAM J., and KARNES, M. RAY. **Measuring Educational Achievement.** New York: McGraw-Hill Book Co., Inc., 1950. Pp. vii, 496.

For a review by J. R. Gerberich, see 4:B271.

P587. MICHIGAN STATE COLLEGE, THE BOARD OF EXAMINERS (PAUL L. DRESSEL, Chairman). **Comprehensive Examinations in a Program of General Education.** East Lansing, Mich.: Michigan State College Press, 1949. Pp. ix, 165.

For reviews by Henry Borow, Harold D. Carter, John V. McQuitty, and Herschel T. Manuel, see 4:B272.

P588. MILLER, NEAL E., Editor. **Psychological Research on Pilot Training.** Army Air Forces Aviation Psychology Program Research Reports, Report No. 8. Washington, D.C.: U.S. Government Printing Office, 1947. Pp. xix, 488.

For reviews by J. L. Finan and Laurance F. Shaffer, see 4:B274. For a review of the series, see P1.

P589. MILNE, F. T. **The Use of Scholastic Tests in South African Schools: An Arithmetic Test Standardized on Witwatersrand Pupils.** South African Council for Educational and Social Research, Research Series, No. 2. Pretoria, South Africa: J. L. Van Schaik, Ltd., 1937. Pp. 162.

For a review, see 2:B1020.

P590. MINER, JOHN B. **Intelligence in the United States: A Survey—With Conclusions for Manpower Utilization in Education and Employment.** New York: Springer Publishing Co., Inc., 1957. Pp. xii, 180.

For reviews by Henry E. Garrett, Frank C. J. McGurk, John B. Miner, and Dorothy Ransom, see 6:B342; for reviews by John B. Carroll, Harold Goldstein, A. W. Heim, Howard A. Moss, and one other, see 5:B293.

P591. MIRA Y LOPEZ, EMILIO. **M.K.P.: Myokinetic Psychodiagnosis.** New York: [Hoeber Medical Division, Harper & Row, Publishers, Inc.], 1958. Pp. xx, 186.

For reviews by Sidney J. Blatt and David Wechsler, see 6:B343.

P592. MOGENSEN, ALAN; FENGER, GJERTRUD; and LANGE, BENT. **Rorschach on 122 Ten-Year Old Danish Children: A Standardizational and Structural Study: A, The Normative Results.** Psychological Research Report 2A. Risskov, Denmark: Institute of Psychiatry, State Mental Hospital, [1960]. Pp. 54.

For a review by Max L. Fogel, see 6:B344.

P593. MONROE, PAUL, Editor. **Conference on Examinations: Under the Auspices of the Carnegie Corporation, the Carnegie Foundation, and the International Institute of Teachers College, Columbia University at the Hotel Royal, Dinard, France, September 16 to 19, 1938.** New York: Bureau of Publications, Teachers College, Columbia University, 1939. Pp. xiii, 330.

For reviews by A. P. Braddock, Harold Gulliksen, Samuel R. Laycock, and two others, see 3:1030; for reviews by Stephen M. Corey, Alvin C. Eurich, Wm. Reitz, Austin G. Schmidt, and one other, see 2:B1021.

P594. MONS, W. **Principles and Practice of the Rorschach Personality Test, Second Edition.** London: Faber & Faber Ltd., 1950. Pp. 176.

For reviews by Mary Morrow, Laurance F. Shaffer, and one other, see 4:127; for reviews by Emory S. Bogardus, Edward M. L. Burchard, John Cohen, B. A. Farrell, Peter H. Knapp, Zygmunt A. Piotrowski, Fred V. Rockwell, Laurance F. Shaffer, Eliot Slater, I. K. Waterhouse, and three others of the first edition, see 4:126.

P595. MORENO, J. L. **Who Shall Survive: Foundations of Sociometry, Group Psychotherapy, and Sociodrama, [Revised Edition].** Beacon, N.Y.: Beacon House, Inc., Publishers, 1953. Pp. cxiv, 763.

For reviews by Edgar F. Borgatta, Leon Festinger, Eugene L. Hartley, Earl A. Loomis, Jr., Fred McKinney, R. B. Morton, Mary L. Northway, and Thelma Veness, see 5:B299; for reviews by Irving M. Derby, George A. Lundberg, Gardner Murphy, Winifred Richmond, Gladys C. Schwesinger, and five others of the first edition, see 2:B1022.

P596. MORENO, J. L., Editor. **Sociometry and the Science of Man.** New York: Beacon House, Inc., Publishers, 1956. Pp. viii, 474.

For a review by Ben Willerman, see 5:B300.

P597. MORENO, J. L., Editor. **The Sociometry Reader.** New York: Free Press of Glencoe, 1960. Pp. xxiv, 773.

For reviews by Henry A. Davidson and Nathaniel H. Siegel, see 6:B345.

P598. MORENO, J. L., and JENNINGS, HELEN H. **Sociometric Measurement of Social Configurations Based on Deviation From Chance.** Sociometry Monographs, No. 3. New York: Beacon House, Inc., Publishers, 1945. Pp. 35.

For reviews by Louisa P. Holt and two others, see 4:B279.

P599. MORGAN, HOWARD K. **Industrial Training and Testing.** New York: McGraw-Hill Book Co., Inc., 1945. Pp. x, 225.

For reviews by Arthur F. Dodge, D. R. Miller, Bruce V. Moore, William P. Sears, and Robert E. Smith, see 3:1038.

P600. MORSE, HORACE T., and McCUNE, GEORGE H. **Selected Items for the Testing of Study Skills and Critical Thinking, Fourth Edition.** National Council for the Social Studies, Bulletin No. 15, Fourth Edition. Washington, D.C.: the Council, 1964. Pp. vii, 91.

For reviews by Howard L. Hurwitz and J. Wayne Wrightstone of the first edition, see 3:1039.

P601. MORTON, N. W. **Individual Diagnosis: A Manual for the Employment Office.** McGill University, McGill Social Research Series, No. 6. Montreal, Canada: McGill University, 1937. Pp. xvii, 123.

For a review, see 2:B1023; for reviews by L. Fairley, E. N. Hay, R. S. Shultz, and four others, see 1:B432.

P602. MORTON, NELSON W. **Occupational Abilities: A Study of Unemployed Men.** McGill University, McGill Social Research Series, No. 3. Toronto, Canada: Oxford University Press, 1935. Pp. xxvi, 279.

For a review, see 1:B433; for a review by J. G. Darley and one other, see 36:B182.

P603. MUNROE, RUTH LEARNED. **Prediction of the Adjustment and Academic Performance of College Students by a Modification of the Rorschach Method.** Applied Psychology Monographs of the American Association for Applied Psychology,

No. 7. Stanford, Calif.: Stanford University Press, 1945. Pp. 104.

For reviews by Marion Cowin, Paul E. Meehl, and Donald E. Super, see 3:89.

P604. MURPHY, GARDNER, and LIKERT, RENSIS. **Public Opinion and the Individual: A Psychological Study of Student Attitudes on Public Questions, With a Retest Five Years Later.** New York: Harper & Brothers, 1938. Pp. ix, 316.

For reviews by Emory S. Bogardus, Hadley Cantril, and Elio D. Monachesi, see 2:B1024; for a review by E. Raskin, see 1:B434.

P605. MURPHY, LOIS BARCLAY; with the collaboration of EVELYN BEYER, ANNA HARTOCH, EUGENE LERNER, L. JOSEPH STONE, and TRUDE SCHMIDL-WAEHNER. **Personality in Young Children: Vol. I, Methods for the Study of Personality in Young Children.** New York: Basic Books, Inc., 1956. Pp. xx, 424.

For a review by Frank Barron, see 5:B303.

P606. MURRAY, HENRY A.; and other workers at the Harvard Psychological Clinic. **Explorations in Personality: A Clinical and Experimental Study of Fifty Men of College Age.** New York: Oxford University Press, 1938. Pp. xiv, 761.

For reviews by John Dollard, Livingston Welch, and three others, see 3:1042; for reviews by Edward N. Barnhart, Albert K. Cohen, Kingsley Davis, Carney Landis, Kurt Lewin, W. Line, Henry C. Link, C. M. Louttit, K. A. Menninger, Milton L. Miller, M. F. Ashley Montagu, Kimball Young, and three others, see 2:B1026.

P607. MURSELL, JAMES L. **Psychological Testing, Second Edition.** New York: Longmans, Green & Co., Inc., 1949. Pp. xvi, 488.

For reviews by Frederick B. Davis, W. M. O'Neil, Laurance F. Shaffer, and Samuel Waldfogel, see 4:B283; for reviews by Josef Brožek, W. Grant Dahlstrom, Paul E. Eiserer, Frank N. Freeman, Miles Murphy, Bert R. Sappenfield, William B. Schrader, Laurance F. Shaffer, Clare Wright Thompson, C. H. Wedell, Walter L. Wilkins, and Stanley B. Williams of the first edition, see 4:B282; for a review by William R. Sur, see 3:1043.

P608. NATIONAL COUNCIL OF TEACHERS OF MATHEMATICS. **Evaluation in Mathematics: Twenty-Sixth Yearbook.** Washington, D.C.: the Council, Inc., 1961. Pp. iv, 216.

For a review by Jens L. Lund, see 6:B351.

P609. NATIONAL EDUCATION ASSOCIATION, DEPARTMENT OF ELEMENTARY SCHOOL PRINCIPALS. **Appraising the Elementary-School Program.** Sixteenth Yearbook, The National Elementary Principal, Vol. 16, No. 6. Washington, D.C.: the Association, 1937. Pp. 227–665.

For reviews by W. J. Gifford, J. F. Hosic, and one other, see 1:B436.

P610. NATIONAL INDUSTRIAL CONFERENCE BOARD, INC. **Plans for Rating Employees.** Studies in Personnel Policy, No. 8. New York: the Board, 1938. Pp. 39.

For reviews by Ward Steward and Donald J. Sublette, see 2:B1031.

P611. NATIONAL LEAGUE FOR NURSING. **The Construction and Use of Teacher-Made Tests.** Use of Tests in Schools of Nursing Pamphlet No. 5. New York: the League, Inc., 1957. Pp. vi, 102.

For a review by Thomas M. Magoon, see 5:B313.

P612. NATIONAL SOCIETY FOR THE STUDY OF EDUCATION. **Educational Diagnosis: Thirty-Fourth Yearbook.** Bloomington, Ill.: Public School Publishing Co., 1935. Pp. x, 563.

For reviews by L. J. Brueckner, W. McAndrew, W. J. Osburn, and A. G. Schmidt, see 36:B189.

P613. NATIONAL SOCIETY FOR THE STUDY OF EDUCATION. **The Impact and Improvement of School Testing Programs: Sixty-Second Yearbook, Part 2.** Edited by Warren G. Findley. Chicago, Ill.: University of Chicago Press, 1963. Pp. xii, 304, ciii.

For reviews by Carmen J. Finley and John C. Gowan, see 6:B362.

P614. NATIONAL SOCIETY FOR THE STUDY OF EDUCATION, Committee on "Intelligence: Its Nature and Nurture," GEORGE D. STODDARD, Chairman. **Intelligence: Its Nature and Nurture: Thirty-Ninth Yearbook, Parts 1 and 2.** Bloomington, Ill.: Public School Publishing Co., 1940. Pp. xviii, 471; xviii, 409, xxxvii.

For reviews by A. A. Campbell, Elliott R. Downing, and Gladys C. Schwesinger, see 3:1062; for reviews by Harold H. Bixler and Lois Coffey Mossman, see 2:B1034.

P615. NATIONAL SOCIETY FOR THE STUDY OF EDUCATION, Committee on the Measurement of Understanding, WILLIAM A. BROWNELL, Chairman. **The Measurement of Understanding: The Forty-Fifth Yearbook, Part 1.** Chicago, Ill.: University of Chicago Press, 1946. Pp. xi, 338.

For reviews by Edgar M. Draper (with Alice H. Hayden), Denton L. Geyer, J. Wayne Wrightstone, and one other, see 4:B296; for a review by J. B. Stroud, see 3:1063.

P616. NATIONAL UNION OF TEACHERS. **Transfer From Primary to Secondary Schools.** Report of a Consultative Committee (G. B. Jeffrey, Chairman). London: Evans Brothers, Ltd., 1949. Pp. 189.

For two reviews, see 4:B297.

P617. NEILSON, NEILS P., and COZENS, FREDERICK W. **Achievement Scales in Physical Education Activities: For Boys and Girls in Elementary and Junior High Schools.** New York: A. S. Barnes & Co., 1934. Pp. x, 171.

For reviews by W. H. Lauritsen, J. R. Sharman, and A. L. Strum, see 1:B441; for reviews by L. W. Irwin, C. H. McCloy, A. G. Schmidt, and C. F. Scofield, see 36:B190.

P618. NELSON, M. J. **Handbook of Educational Psychology and Measurement.** New York: Dryden Press, Inc., 1941. Pp. vi, 174.

For reviews by Austin G. Schmidt and one other, see 3:1064.

P619. NELSON, M. J. **Tests and Measurements in Elementary Education.** New York: Dryden Press, Inc., 1939. Pp. 351.

For reviews by Henry D. Rinsland and Austin G. Schmidt, see 2:B1035.

P620. NETZER, ROYAL F. **The Evaluation of a Technique for Measuring Improvement in Oral Composition.** University of Iowa Studies, New Series, No. 367; Studies in Education, Vol. 10, No. 4; Research Studies in Elementary School Language, No. 2. Iowa City, Iowa: the University, 1939. Pp. 48.

For a review by Austin G. Schmidt, see 2:B1036.

P621. NEW YORK PUBLIC SCHOOLS, BUREAU OF REFERENCE, RESEARCH AND STATISTICS, DIVISION OF TESTS AND MEASUREMENTS. **Determining Readiness for Reading.** Educational Research Bulletin of the Bureau of Reference, Research and Statistics, No. 6. New York: the Bureau, 1943. Pp. vi, 49.

For a review by Miles A. Tinker, see 3:1067.

P622. NEWKIRK, LOUIS V., and GREENE, HARRY A. **Tests and Measurements in Industrial Education.** New York: John Wiley & Sons, Inc., 1935. Pp. x, 253.

For reviews by H. Burtt and one other, see 1:B442; for reviews by G. U. Cleeton, W. McAndrew, B. E. Mallary, H. J. Smith, R. C. Woellner, F. W. Ziegenhagen, and three others, see 36:B194.

P623. NEWMAN, FRANCES BURKS. **The Adolescent in Social Groups: Studies in the Observation of Personality.** Applied Psychology Monographs of the American Psychological Association, No. 9. Stanford, Calif.: Stanford University Press, 1946. Pp. 94.

For reviews by Dale B. Harris, Donald E. Super, and one other, see 3:1070.

P624. NICHOLSON, R. J., and GALAMBOS, P. **Performance in G.C.E. (Advanced Level) Examinations and University Examinations.** Hull, England: University of Hull, 1960. Pp. 22.

For a review, see 6:B367.

P625. NOBLE, M. C. S., JR. **Practical Measurements for School Administrators.** Scranton, Pa.: International Textbook Co., 1939. Pp. xix, 330.

For two reviews, see 3:1072; for reviews by Harl R. Douglass, N. L. Engelhardt, Jr., Henry D. Rinsland, and Austin G. Schmidt, see 2:1037.

P626. NOLL, VICTOR H. **Introduction to Educational Measurement.** Boston, Mass.: Houghton Mifflin Co., 1957. Pp. xxi, 437.

For reviews by S. S. Dunn and John B. Morris, see 6:B369; for a review by Samuel T. Mayo, see 5:B321.

P627. NORTHWAY, MARY L. **Appraisal of the Social Development of Children at a Summer Camp.** University of Toronto Studies, Psychology Series, Vol. 5, No. 1. Toronto, Canada: University of Toronto Press, 1940. Pp. 62.

For a review by Joseph Sargent, see 3:1074.

P628. NORTHWAY, MARY L. **A Primer of Sociometry.** Toronto, Canada: University of Toronto Press, 1952. Pp. vii, 48.

For reviews by Helen Hall Jennings and Mary J. Wright, see 5:B322.

P629. NUALLÁIN, C. O. **Personnel Assessment and Selection.** Administrative Procedures: 2. Dublin, Ireland: Institute of Public Administration, 1961. Pp. 32.

For a review, see 6:B370.

P630. NUNNALLY, JUM C., JR. **Tests and Measurements: Assessment and Prediction.** New York: McGraw-Hill Book Co., Inc., 1959. Pp. x, 446.

For reviews by William E. Coffman and Marvin D. Dunnette, see 6:B372.

P631. OSS ASSESSMENT STAFF. **Assessment of Men: Selection of Personnel for the Office of Strategic Services.** New York: Rinehart & Co., Inc., 1948. Pp. xv, 541.

For reviews by Harold E. Burtt, H. J. Eysenck, Cecil A. Gibb, Harold M. Hildreth, William A. Hunt, William Line, D. Macleod, Walter R. Mahler, T. A. Ryan, Donald E. Super, Wilse B. Webb, and F. L. Wells, see 4:B301.

P632. O'CONNOR, JOHNSON. **Psychometrics: A Study of Psychological Measurements.** Cambridge, Mass.: Harvard University Press, 1934. Pp. xxxiv, 292.

For reviews by C. R. Brolyer, F. L. Wells, and one other, see 1:B444; for reviews by R. B. Cattell, H. S. Conrad, E. B. Greene, D. G. Paterson, and two others, see 36:B195.

P633. ODELL, C. W. **How to Improve Classroom Testing, Revised Edition.** Dubuque, Iowa: Wm. C. Brown Co., 1958. Pp. vii, 213.

For reviews by Chester W. Harris and Robert B. Nordberg of the first edition, see 5:B325.

P634. ODENWELLER, ARTHUR LEONARD. **Predicting the Quality of Teaching: The Predictive Value of Certain Traits for Effectiveness in Teaching.** Columbia University, Teachers College, Contributions to Education, No. 676. New York: Bureau of Publications, the College, 1936. Pp. xi, 158.

For a review by Robert W. Richey, see 2:B1039; for reviews by S. M. Corey, A. G. Schmidt, G. M. Wilson, and one other, see 1:B445.

P635. OLIVER, R. A. C. **An Experimental Test in English.** Joint Matriculation Board, Universities of Manchester, Liverpool, Leeds, Sheffield, and Birmingham, Occasional Publication 13. [Manchester, England: Joint Matriculation Board], 1963. Pp. 56.

For a review by James Britton, see 6:B374.

P636. ORDWAY, SAMUEL H., JR., and O'BRIEN, JAMES C. **An Approach to More Objective Oral Tests.** Society for Personnel Administration, Pamphlet No. 2. Washington, D.C.: the Society, 1939. Pp. 31.

For reviews by W. V. Bingham and one other, see 2:B1040.

P637. ORLEANS, JACOB S. **Measurement in Education.** New York: Thomas Nelson & Sons, 1937. Pp. xvi, 11–461.

For a review, see 2:B1040.1; for reviews by A. G. Schmidt and one other, see 1:B446.

P638. OSBORNE, AGNES ELIZABETH. **The Relationship Between Certain Psychological Tests and Shorthand Achievement.** Columbia University, Teachers College, Contributions to Education No. 873. New York: Bureau of Publications, the College, 1943. Pp. vii, 58.

For reviews by Harold E. Burtt and Thelma Hunt, see 3:1083.

P639. OSGOOD, CHARLES E.; SUCI, GEORGE J.; and TANNENBAUM, PERCY H. **The Measurement of Meaning.** Urbana, Ill.: University of Illinois Press, 1957. Pp. vii, 342.

For reviews by Roger W. Brown and Harold Gulliksen, see 6:B380.

P640. PASCAL, G. R., and JENKINS, W. O. **Systematic Observation of Gross Human Behavior.** New York: Grune & Stratton, Inc., 1961. Pp. ix, 126.

For a review by John A. Stern, see 6:B384.

P641. PASCAL, GERALD R., and SUTTELL, BARBARA J. **The Bender-Gestalt Test: Quantification and Validity for Adults.** New York: Grune & Stratton, Inc., 1951. Pp. xiii, 274.

For reviews by J. L. Boreham, J. G. Lyle, and Adolf G. Woltmann, see 5:B330; for reviews by Lee J. Cronbach and two others, see 4:145.

P642. PATERSON, D. G., Editor. **Research Studies in Individual Diagnosis.** University of Minnesota, Bulletin of the Employment Stabilization Research Institute, Vol. 3, No. 4. Minneapolis, Minn.: University of Minnesota Press, 1934. Pp. 55.

For reviews by A. B. Crawford, P. W. Hutson, and A. G. Schmidt, see 36:B202.

P643. PATERSON, DONALD G.; GERKEN, C. D'A.; and HAHN, MILTON E. **Revised Minnesota Occupational Rating Scales.** Minnesota Studies in Student Personnel Work, No. 2. Minneapolis, Minn.: University of Minnesota Press, 1953. Pp. ix, 85.
For a review by Anne Roe, see 5:B331; for a review by M. H. Elliott of the first edition, see 3:689.

P644. PATERSON, DONALD G.; SCHNEIDLER, GWENDOLEN C.; and WILLIAMSON, EDMOND G. **Student Guidance Techniques: A Handbook for Counselors in High Schools and Colleges.** New York: McGraw-Hill Book Co., Inc., 1938. Pp. xviii, 316.
For reviews by D. H. Gardiner, Franklin J. Keller, and Mary Theresa Scudder, see 2:B1042; for reviews by J. E. Corbally, H. A. Edgerton, and E. S. Jones, see 1:B448.

P645. PATTERSON, C. H. **The Wechsler-Bellevue Scales: A Guide for Counselors.** Springfield, Ill.: Charles C Thomas, Publisher, 1953. Pp. viii, 146.
For reviews by Robert K. Robison and Laurance F. Shaffer, see 5:B332.

P646. PEMBERTON, W. A. **Ability, Values, and College Achievement.** University of Delaware Studies in Higher Education, No. 1. Newark, Del.: University of Delaware Bookstore, 1963. Pp. xii, 77.
For a review by Irvin J. Lehmann, see 6:B387.

P647. PERRY, RAYMOND CARVER. **A Group Factor Analysis of the Adjustment Questionnaire.** University of Southern California, Southern California Education Monographs, 1933-34 Series, No. 5. Los Angeles, Calif.: University of Southern California Press, 1934. Pp. xi, 93.
For reviews by G. W. Allport and M. E. Broom, see 2:B1043; for reviews by R. J. Hannelly and one other, see 1:B451.

P648. PETCH, JAMES A. **Fifty Years of Examining: The Joint Matriculation Board, 1903–1953.** London: George G. Harrap & Co., Ltd., 1953. Pp. 226.
For a review by A. C. F. Beales, see 5:B334.

P649. PETERS, ALISON. **How to Pass College Entrance Tests, Third Edition.** New York: Arco Publishing Co., Inc., 1956. Pp. 185.
For reviews by Max D. Engelhart, Clifford W. Hall, and one other of the first edition, see 4:B310.

P650. PETERS, MARY FRIDIANA. **A Comparative Study of Some Measures of Emotional Instability in School Children.** Lafayette, Ind.: St. Francis Community Press, 1939. Pp. xvii, 71.
For a review by Austin G. Schmidt, see 2:B1044.

P651. PHILLIPS, GILBERT E. **The Constancy of the Intelligence Quotient in Subnormal Children.** Publications of the Australian Council for Educational Research, Educational Research Series, No. 60. Melbourne, Australia: Melbourne University Press, 1940. Pp. 86.
For reviews by J. W. Jenkins and two others, see 3:1085.

P652. PHILLIPS, LESLIE, and SMITH, JOSEPH G. **Rorschach Interpretation: Advanced Technique.** New York: Grune & Stratton, Inc., 1953. Pp. xiii, 385.
For reviews by Lee J. Cronbach, Douglas M. Kelley, Ruth A. Neu, and one other, see 5:B337.

P653. PHILLIPSON, HERBERT. **The Object Relations Technique.** London: Tavistock Publications, Ltd., 1955. Pp. x, 224.
For reviews by Ralph Hetherington, G. Keir, Samuel B. Kutash, Denis McMahon, Mortimer M. Meyer, Edwin C. Nevis, S. B. Sells, Boris Semeonoff, and Laurance F. Shaffer, see 5:B338.

P654. PHYSICAL SOCIETY COLOUR GROUP COMMITTEE. **Report on Defective Colour Vision in Industry.** London: Physical Society, 1946. Pp. ii, 52.
For a review by L. C. Martin, see 3:1086.

P655. PICKETT, HALE. **An Analysis of Proofs and Solutions of Exercises Used in Plane Geometry Tests.** Columbia University, Teachers College, Contributions to Education No. 747. New York: Bureau of Publications, the College, 1939. Pp. vii, 120.
For reviews by Elizabeth M. Cooper, Harold Fawcett, H. F. Munch, Austin G. Schmidt, and Joseph J. Urbancek, see 2:B1045.

P656. PICKFORD, R. W.; with the assistance of RUTH BOWYER and JOHN STRUTHERS. **Pickford Projective Pictures.** London: Tavistock Publications, 1963. Pp. xi, 122.
For reviews by R. Hetherington and two others, see 6:234.

P657. PINNEAU, SAMUEL R. **Changes in Intelligence Quotient: Infancy to Maturity: New Insights From the Berkeley Growth Study With Implications for the Stanford-Binet Scales and Applications to Professional Practice.** Boston, Mass.: Houghton Mifflin Co., 1961. Pp. xi, 233.
For reviews by Dale B. Harris and A. B. Silverstein, see 6:B396.

P658. PINTNER, RUDOLF; DRAGOSITZ, ANNA; and KUSHNER, ROSE. **Supplementary Guide for the Revised Stanford-Binet Scale (Form L).** Applied Psychology Monographs of the American Psychological Association, No. 3. Stanford, Calif.: Stanford University Press, 1944. Pp. 135.
For reviews by Earl R. Gabler and Francis N. Maxfield, see 3:294.

P659. PIOTROWSKI, ZYGMUNT A. **Perceptanalysis: A Fundamentally Reworked, Expanded, and Systematized Rorschach Method.** New York: Macmillan Co., 1957. Pp. xix, 505.
For reviews by Bruno Klopfer and Herman B. Molish, see 6:B398; for reviews by Mortimer M. Meyer, B. Semeonoff, and one other, see 5:B340.

P660. PIOTROWSKI, ZYGMUNT A., and ROCK, MILTON, R.; with the assistance of JOHN J. GRELA. **The Perceptanalytic Executive Scale: A Tool for the Selection of Top Managers.** New York: Grune & Stratton, Inc., 1963. Pp. iv, 220.
For a review by John A. Bromer, see 6:B399.

P661. PORTEUS, S. D. **The Porteus Maze Test Manual.** London: George G. Harrap & Co., Ltd., 1952. Pp. 64.
For two reviews, see 5:B342.

P662. PORTEUS, S. D. **Primitive Intelligence and Environment.** New York: Macmillan Co., 1937. Pp. ix, 325.
For reviews by Albert E. Chapman, Martha Gruening, and one other, see 3:1089; for reviews by Samuel J. Beck, Emory S. Bogardus, Kingsley Davis, Homer W. Smith, Clark Wissler, and two others, see 2:B1046; for reviews by A. Anastasi, F. C. Bartlett, D. S. Davidson, F. H. Hankins, O. Klineberg, H. H. Long, C. M. Louttit, A. G. Schmidt, and five others, see 1:B454.

P663. PORTEUS, STANLEY D. **The Maze Test and Clinical Psychology.** Palo Alto, Calif.: Pacific Books, 1959. Pp. vii, 203.
For reviews by J. Drewery, A. James Gregor, and Henry N. Peters, see 6:B400.

P664. PORTEUS, STANLEY D. **Maze Test and Mental Differences.** Vineland, N.J.: Smith Printing & Publishing House, 1933. Pp. ix, 212.
For reviews by R. Pintner and J. W. Tilton, see 1:B453; for reviews by J. H. McFadden, A. G. Schmidt, and C. L. Stone, see 36:B210.

P665. PORTEUS, STANLEY D. **The Maze Test: Recent Advances.** Palo Alto, Calif.: Pacific Books, 1955. Pp. 71.
For a review by Laurance F. Shaffer, see 5:B343.

P666. PORTEUS, STANLEY D. **The Porteus Maze Test and Intelligence.** Palo Alto, Calif.: Pacific Books, 1950. Pp. vi, 194.
For reviews by Madison Bentley, Lee J. Cronbach, Laurance F. Shaffer, and D. A. Worcester, see 4:357.

P667. PROBST, JOHN B. **Measuring and Rating Employee Value.** New York: Ronald Press Co., 1947. Pp. xi, 166.
For reviews by Dorothy C. Adkins and Charles A. Meyer, see 4:786.

P668. PRYOR, HELEN. **Width-Weight Tables: For Boys and Girls from 1 to 16 Years; for Men and Women from 17 to 24 Years.** Stanford, Calif.: Stanford University Press, 1936. Pp. 15.
For reviews by B. France, J. Gregory, F. R. Rogers, and one other, see 1:B455; for reviews by W. McAndrew, H. M. Mitchell, and one other, see 36:B211.

P669. PULLIAS, EARL V. **Variability in Results from New Achievement Tests.** Duke University Research Studies in Education, No. 2. Durham, N.C.: Duke University Press, 1937. Pp. 100.
For a review by Francis P. Robinson, see 2:B1048; for reviews by A. G. Schmidt and J. E. Wert, see 1:B457.

P670. PURNELL, RUSSELL T., and DAVIS, ROBERT A. **Directing Learning by Teacher-Made Tests.** Boulder, Colo.: Bureau of Publications, Extension Division, University of Colorado, 1939. Pp. vii, 92.
For a review by Paul Murphy, see 3:1098; for a review by Henry D. Rinsland, see 2:B1049.

P671. RABIN, ALBERT I., and HAWORTH, MARY R., Editors. **Projective Techniques With Children.** New York: Grune & Stratton, Inc., 1960. Pp. xiii, 392.
For reviews by Walter G. Klopfer, Robert D. Wirt, and one other, see 6:B402.

P672. RABKIN, E. B. **Polychromatic Plates for Color Sense Examination.** Kharkoo, U.S.S.R.: State Medical Publishing Board, 1936. Pp. 40, 20 colored plates.
For a review by M. Collins, see 1:B458.

P673. RAND, HENRY A. **Graphology: A Handbook, Second Edition.** Cambridge, Mass.: Sci-Art Publishers, 1961. Pp. 208.
For reviews by H. J. Eysenck and H. Wallerstein, see 6:B403; for reviews by V. C. Branham, Jules D. Holzberg, Douglas M. Kelley, Joseph Zubin, and one other of the first edition, see 4:B315.

P674. RAPAPORT, DAVID; with the collaboration of MERTON GILL and ROY SCHAFER. **Diagnostic Psychological Testing: The Theory, Statistical Evaluation, and Diagnostic Application of a Battery of Tests, Volumes I and II.** Chicago, Ill.: Year Book Publishers, Inc., 1945, 1946. Pp. xi, 573; xi, 516.
For reviews by D. Kelley, M. J. Langeveld, W. Line, and one other see 4:B316; for reviews by Paul Bergman, Henry E. Garrett, Howard F. Hunt, Morris Krugman, Solomon Machover, C. H. Patterson, and

two others, see 3:1104; for reviews by Andrew W. Brown, Quinn McNemar, and Clare Wright Thompson of Volume I, see 3:1102; for reviews by Robert M. Lindner and D. R. Miller of Volume II, see 3:1103.

P675. RAPAPORT, DAVID; with the collaboration of ROY SCHAFER and MERTON GILL. **Manual of Diagnostic Psychological Testing: 1, Diagnostic Testing of Intelligence and Concept Formation.** Review Series, Vol. 2, No. 2. New York: Josiah Macy, Jr. Foundation, 1944. Pp. xiii, 239.
For a review by Adolf G. Woltmann, see 3:1105.

P676. RAPAPORT, DAVID, and SCHAFER, ROY; with the collaboration of MERTON GILL. **Manual of Diagnostic Psychological Testing: 2, Diagnostic Testing of Personality and Ideational Content.** Review Series, Vol. 3, No. 1. New York: Josiah Macy, Jr. Foundation, 1946. Pp. 105.
For reviews by S. Brecher and one other, see 3:1106.

P677. RASCH, G. **Probabilistic Models for Some Intelligence and Attainment Tests.** Danish Institute for Educational Research, Studies in Mathematical Psychology 1. Copenhagen, Denmark: Danish Science Press, Ltd., 1960. Pp. xiii, 184.
For reviews by Eric F. Gardner and Rosedith Sitgreaves, see 6:B404.

P678. RAVEN, J. C. **Controlled Projection for Children, Second Edition.** London: H. K. Lewis & Co. Ltd., 1951. Pp. 176.
For reviews by Geraldine Pederson-Krag, R. W. Pickford, and one other, see 5:127; for reviews by M. B. Brody, John Cohen, and three others of the first edition, see 3:29.

P679. RAY, JOSEPH J. **Generalizing Ability of Dull, Bright, and Superior Children.** George Peabody College for Teachers, Contribution to Education, No. 175. Nashville, Tenn.: the College, 1936. Pp. xiii, 109.
For a review by M. L. Hartung, see 1:B461.

P680. REAVIS, WILLIAM C., and COOPER, DAN H. **Evaluation of Teacher Merit in City School Systems.** University of Chicago, Department of Education, Supplementary Educational Monographs, No. 59. Chicago, Ill.: University of Chicago Press, 1945. Pp. vi, 138.
For reviews by Leo M. Hauptman and Virgil M. Rogers, see 3:1109.

P681. REDMOND, MARY, and DAVIES, F. R. J. **The Standardization of Two Intelligence Tests.** New Zealand Council for Educational Research, Educational Research Series, No. 14. Wellington, New Zealand: Whitcombe & Tombs Ltd., 1940. Pp. xv, 129.
For a review by Lee J. Cronbach, see 3:1110.

P682. REMMERS, H. H. **Introduction to Opinion and Attitude Measurement.** New York: Harper & Brothers, 1954. Pp. viii, 437.
For reviews by Robert P. Abelson, G. D. Bradshaw, Ralph R. Canter, Sidney S. Goldish, and Donald E. Super, see 5:B349.

P683. REMMERS, H. H., and GAGE, N. L., Editors. **Two Thousand Test Items in American History.** Lafayette, Ind.: State High School Testing Service for Indiana, Division of Educational Reference, Purdue University, 1941. Pp. v, 110.
For a review by Austin G. Schmidt, see 3:1114.

P684. REMMERS, H. H., Editor. **Further Studies in Attitudes, Series 3.** Purdue University, Division of Educational Reference, Studies in Higher Education, [No.] 34. Lafayette, Ind.: the University, 1938. Pp. 151.

For reviews by Lloyd L. Ramseyer and Austin G. Schmidt, see 2:B1050.

P685. REMMERS, H. H.; GAGE, N. L.; and RUMMEL, J. FRANCIS. **A Practical Introduction to Measurement and Evaluation.** New York: Harper & Row, Publishers, Inc., 1960. Pp. xiii, 370.
For reviews by John W. M. Rothney and Robert L. Thorndike, see 6:B406; for a review by William Coleman of an earlier edition, see 5:B350; for reviews by Warren G. Findley, Gustav J. Froehlich, C. L. Murray, and Howard L. Siple, see 3:I112.

P686. REMMERS, HERMAN H., Editor. **Studies in Attitudes: A Contribution to Social-Psychological Research Methods.** Bulletin of Purdue University, Vol. 35, No. 4; Division of Educational Reference, Studies in Higher Education, No. 26. Lafayette, Ind.: the University, 1934. Pp. 112.
For reviews by F. P. Frutchey and one other, see 36:B216.

P687. RICE, MARY BERENICE. **Diagnosis of the Mental Hygiene Problems of College Women by Means of Personality Ratings.** Washington, D.C.: Catholic University of America, 1937. Pp. ix, 71.
For a review by A. G. Schmidt, see 1:B463.

P688. RICHARDSON, C. A. **An Introduction to Mental Measurement and Its Applications.** London: Longmans, Green & Co. Ltd., 1955. Pp. vii, 102.
For reviews by L. B. Birch and P. E. Vernon, see 5:B351.

P689. RICHARDSON, CYRIL A., and STOKES, CHARLES W. **Growth and Variability of Intelligence.** British Journal of Psychology Monograph Supplements, No. 18. London: Cambridge University Press, 1933. Pp. viii, 83.
For a review, see 1:B464; for a review by G. H. Thomson, see 36:B220.

P690. RICHMAN, ELI. **College Admissions Based on S.A.T. Scores, 1962–1963.** [Chelsea, Mass.: the Author, School Department, 1963.] Pp. i, 63.
For a review by Thomas M. Magoon of the first edition, see 6:B407.

P691. RICKERS-OVSIANKINA, MARIA. **Rorschach Scoring Samples: Compiled From Various Sources for Private Circulation, [Revised Edition].** Norton, Mass.: the Author, 1942. Pp. v, 197.
For a review by Zygmunt A. Piotrowski, see 3:89a.

P692. RICKERS-OVSIANKINA, MARIA A., Editor. **Rorschach Psychology.** New York: John Wiley & Sons, Inc., 1960. Pp. xvi, 483.
For reviews by Stephanie Z. Dudek, Erika Fromm, and Laurance F. Shaffer, see 6:B409.

P693. RILEY, MATILDA WHITE; RILEY, JOHN W., JR., and TOBY, JACKSON; in association with MARCIA L. TOBY, RICHARD COHN, HARRY C. BREDEMEIER, MARY MOORE, and PAUL FINE; with contributions by URIEL G. FOA, ROBERT N. FORD, LOUIS GUTTMAN, and SAMUEL A. STOUFFER. **Sociological Studies in Scale Analysis: Applications, Theory, Procedures.** New Brunswick, N.J.: Rutgers University Press, 1954. Pp. xii, 433.
For reviews by H. J. Eysenck and David Gold, see 5:B352.

P694. RINSLAND, HENRY D. **Analysis of Completion Sentences and Arithmetical Problems as Items for Intelligence Tests.** Columbia University, Teachers College, Contributions to Education No. 666. New York: Bureau of Publications, the College, 1935. Pp. 49.

For reviews by H. B. English, J. A. Long, and A. G. Schmidt, see 1:B465; for a review, see 36:B222.

P695. RINSLAND, HENRY DANIEL. **Constructing Tests and Grading in Elementary and High School Subjects.** New York: Prentice-Hall, Inc., 1937. Pp. xvi, 323.
For a review by Gertrude Hildreth, C. W. Odell, and two others, see 2:B1052; for reviews by H. R. Anderson, S. M. Corey, W. J. Gifford, E. F. Lindquist, A. G. Schmidt, G. F. Wells, and two others, see 1:B466.

P696. ROBERTS, KATHERINE ELLIOTT, and FLEMING, VIRGINIA VAN DYNE. **Persistence and Change in Personality Patterns.** Monographs of the Society for Research in Child Development, Vol. 8, No. 3, Serial No. 36. Washington, D.C.: the Society, 1943. Pp. vii, 206.
For reviews by S. Brecher, Morris E. Eson, Jules Masserman, Francis N. Maxfield, Theta Wolf, and two others, see 3:I123.

P697. ROBINSON, HELEN M., Editor. **Evaluation of Reading: Proceedings of the Annual Conference on Reading Held at the University of Chicago, 1958.** Supplementary Educational Monographs, Vol. 20, No. 88. Chicago, Ill.: University of Chicago Press, 1958. Pp. vii, 208.
For a review by Gladys L. Persons, see 6:B411.

P698. ROHDE, AMANDA R. **The Sentence Completion Method: Its Diagnosis and Clinical Application to Mental Disorders.** New York: Ronald Press Co., 1957. Pp. xii, 301.
For a review by Margaret Ives, see 5:B358.

P699. ROMAN, KLARA G. **Handwriting: A Key to Personality.** New York: Pantheon Books, Inc., 1952. Pp. xi, 382.
For reviews by Elizabeth C. Anderson, Deso A. Weiss, and Rose Wolfson, see 5:B360.

P700. RORSCHACH, HERMANN. **Psychodiagnostics: A Diagnostic Test Based on Perception: Including Rorschach's Paper, "The Application of the Form Perception Test" (Published Posthumously by Dr. Emil Oberholzer), Second Edition.** Translation and English edition by Paul Lemkau and Bernard Kronenberg. Edited by W. Morgenthaler. Berne, Switzerland: Verlag Hans Huber, 1942. Pp. 238.
For reviews by Bruno Klopfer and three others, see 3:90.

P701. ROSEN, ALBERT. **Development of MMPI Scales Based on a Reference Group of Psychiatric Patients.** American Psychological Association, Psychological Monographs: General and Applied, Vol. 76, No. 8, Whole No. 527. Washington, D.C.: the Association, Inc., 1962. Pp. 25.
For a review by L. E. Drake, see 6:B414.

P702. ROSENSTEIN, J. L. **The Scientific Selection of Salesmen.** New York: McGraw-Hill Book Co., Inc., 1944. Pp. xii, 259.
For a review by Milton E. Hahn, see 3:I128.

P703. ROSENZWEIG, SAUL; with the collaboration of KATE LEVINE KOGAN. **Psychodiagnosis: An Introduction to Tests in the Clinical Practice of Psychodynamics.** New York: Grune & Stratton, Inc., 1949. Pp. xii, 380.
For reviews by Sibylle Escalona, Frank S. Freeman, Robert R. Holt, Howard F. Hunt, James W. Layman, Wendell Muncie, William F. Murphy, Laurance F. Shaffer, Richard S. Siegal, Alexander Simon,

Nathaniel Thornton, Adolf G. Woltmann, Stanley B. Zuckerman, and one other, see 4:B323.

P704. ROTHNEY, JOHN W. M., and ROENS, BERT A. **Counseling the Individual Student.** New York: William Sloane Associates, Inc., 1949. Pp. vii, 364.
For reviews by Thomas E. Christensen, Henry Clay Lindgren, and Fred McKinney, see 4:B326.

P705. ROTHNEY, JOHN W. M.; DANIELSON, PAUL J.; and HEIMANN, ROBERT A. **Measurement for Guidance.** New York: Harper & Row, Publishers, Inc., 1959. Pp. xiii, 378.
For reviews by J. C. Gowan and Donald E. Super, see 6:B417.

P706. RUCH, GILES M., and SEGEL, DAVID. **Minimum Essentials of the Individual Inventory in Guidance.** United States Department of Interior, Office of Education, Vocational Division Bulletin, No. 202; Occupational Information and Guidance, Series No. 2. Washington, D.C.: U.S. Government Printing Office, 1940. Pp. vi, 83.
For a review by J. Kenneth Mulligan, see 3:1135; for a review by Beatrice Candee, see 2:B1055.

P707. RUNDQUIST, EDWARD A., and SLETTO, RAYMOND F. **Personality in the Depression: A Study of the Measurement of Attitudes.** University of Minnesota, Institute of Child Welfare, Monograph Series, No. 12. Minneapolis, Minn.: University of Minnesota Press, 1936. Pp. xxii, 398.
For reviews by E. J. Chave, G. Murphy, L. F. Shaffer, L. J. Stone, and two others, see 1:B469; for reviews by W. McAndrew, N. W. Morton, A. G. Schmidt, and one other, see 36:B225.

P708. SADLER, MICHAEL. **Essays on Examinations.** International Institute Examinations Enquiry. London: Macmillan & Co., Ltd., 1936. Pp. xii, 168.
For reviews by A. C. Eurich, W. C. Fletcher, A. M. Jordan, W. J. McCallister, and two others, see 1:B470; for reviews by J. F. Abel, E. R. Gabler, and four others, see 36:B226.

P709. SALTER, MARY D. **An Evaluation of Adjustment Based Upon the Concept of Security.** University of Toronto Studies, Child Development Series, No. 18. Toronto, Canada: University of Toronto Press, 1940. Pp. 72.
For a review by C. M. Fleming, see 3:1141.

P710. SANDIFORD, PETER; CAMERON, M. A.; CONWAY, C. B.; and LONG, J. A. **Forecasting Teaching Ability.** University of Toronto, Department of Educational Research, Bulletin No. 8. Toronto, Canada: the Department, 1937. Pp. 93.
For a review, see 3:1142; for reviews by Earl W. Anderson and one other, see 2:B1056; for two reviews, see 1:B471.

P711. SANFORD, R. NEVITT; ADKINS, MARGARET M.; MILLER, R. BRETNEY; and COBB, ELIZABETH A. **Physique, Personality and Scholarship: A Cooperative Study of School Children.** Monographs of the Society for Research in Child Development, Vol. 8, No. 1, Serial No. 34. Washington, D.C.: the Society, 1943. Pp. ix, 705.
For reviews by David V. Tiedeman and one other, see 3:1143.

P712. SARASON, SEYMOUR B. **The Clinical Interaction: With Special Reference to Rorschach.** New York: Harper & Brothers, 1954. Pp. xi, 425.
For reviews by H. J. Eysenck, Leonard D. Goodstein, Mortimer M. Meyer, R. M. Mowbray, Henry C. Schumacher, and Laurance F. Shaffer, see 5:B369.

P713. SARGENT, HELEN D. **The Insight Test: A Verbal Projective Test for Personality Study.** The Menninger Clinic Monograph Series No. 10. New York: Grune & Stratton, Inc., 1953. Pp. xii, 276.
For reviews by Frank L. Catalano, Jules D. Holzberg, Herman B. Molish, Henry H. Morgan, and one other, see 5:B370.

P714. SCHAFER, ROY. **The Clinical Application of Psychological Tests: Diagnostic Summaries and Case Studies.** The Menninger Foundation Monograph Series No. 6. New York: International Universities Press, Inc., 1948. Pp. 346.
For reviews by M. B. Brody, G. A. Foulds, William Guy, Robert R. Holt, Walter Kass, Richard S. Lazarus, Joseph Sandler, Theodore R. Sarbin, Laurance F. Shaffer, Adolf G. Woltmann, and one other, see 4:B332.

P715. SCHAFER, ROY. **Psychoanalytic Interpretation in Rorschach Testing: Theory and Application.** Austen Riggs Foundation Monograph Series, No. 3. New York: Grune & Stratton, Inc., 1954. Pp. xiv, 446.
For reviews by Theodora Alcock, S. J. Beck, Cyril M. Franks, Roy M. Hamlin, J. G. Lyle, and Mortimer M. Meyer, see 5:B372.

P716. SCHENCK, ETHEL A. **Studies of Testing and Teaching in Modern Foreign Languages: Based on Materials Gathered at the University of Wisconsin by the Late Professor Frederic D. Cheydleur.** Madison, Wis.: Dembar Publications, Inc., 1952. Pp. vi, 72.
For a review by Theodore Huebener, see 5:B373.

P717. SCHONELL, FRED J. **Diagnosis of Individual Difficulties in Arithmetic, Second Edition.** Edinburgh, Scotland: Oliver & Boyd Ltd., 1942. Pp. xi, 115.
For a review by C. Ebblewhite Smith of the first edition, see 2:B1058; for three reviews, see 1:B474.

P718. SCHONELL, FRED J., and SCHONELL, F. ELEANOR. **Diagnostic and Attainment Testing: Including a Manual of Tests, Their Nature, Use, Recording and Interpretation.** Edinburgh, Scotland: Oliver & Boyd Ltd., 1950. Pp. viii, 168.
For reviews by C. M. Fleming and K. F. Hirsch, see 4:B335.

P719. SCHROEDER, ELINOR MARIE. **On Measurement of Motor Skills: An Approach Through a Statistical Analysis of Archery Scores.** New York: King's Crown Press, 1945. Pp. xvi, 210.
For reviews by Knight Dunlap and James M. Lynch, see 3:1147.

P720. SCHUTZ, WILLIAM C. **FIRO: A Three-Dimensional Theory of Interpersonal Behavior.** New York: Holt, Rinehart & Winston, Inc., 1958. Pp. xiii, 267.
For reviews by Harold Borko and Jack D. Douglas, see 6:B432.

P721. SCHWARTZ, ALFRED, and TIEDEMAN, STUART C.; with the assistance of DONALD G. WALLACE. **Evaluating Student Progress in the Secondary School.** New York: David McKay Co., Inc., 1957. Pp. xiii, 434.
For a review by Roger T. Lennon, see 6:B433; for reviews by W. H. King and Paul Klohr, see 5:B376.

P722. SCHWEBEL, MILTON. **The Interests of Pharmacists.** New York: King's Crown Press, 1951. Pp. xii, 84.
For reviews by Alan Robinson and Laurance F. Shaffer, see 4:748.

P723. SCHWESINGER, GLADYS C. **Heredity and Environment: Studies in the Genesis of Psychological Characteristics.** Studies in Social Eugenics, [No.] 1. New York: Macmillan Co., 1933. Pp. xi, 484.
For reviews by Charles B. Davenport and Stanley S. Lamm, see 2:B1060; for reviews by L. Bloom, H. E. Chamberlain, C. B. Davenport, M. F. Dunn, F. N. Freeman, N. M. Grier, F. H. Hankins, J. Jastrow, M. Krugman, B. Malzberg, W. S. Miller, G. M. Morant, H. G. Poncher, P. Popenoe, J. Regensburg, F. C. Shrubsall, W. Stephenson, W. A. White, I. S. Wile, R. D. Williams, and six others, see 1:B475; for reviews by B. S. Bosanquet, B. S. Burks, R. W. Cullen, W. McAndrew, J. Meloun, N. L. Munn, C. L. Stone, C. J. Warden, P. V. Young, and two others, see 36:B229.

P724. SCOTT, M. GLADYS, and FRENCH, ESTHER. **Evaluation in Physical Education: Better Teaching Through Testing.** St. Louis, Mo.: C. V. Mosby Co., 1950. Pp. 348.
For a review by C. H. Keene, see 4:B337.

P725. SCOTT BLAIR, G. W. **Measurements of Mind and Matter.** London: Dennis Dobson, 1950. Pp. 116.
For reviews by Orville G. Brim, Jr. and George H. Collier, see 5:B378; for reviews by G. R. Noakes and two others, see 4:B52.

P726. SCOTTISH COUNCIL FOR RESEARCH IN EDUCATION. **Educational and Other Aspects of the 1947 Scottish Mental Survey.** Publications of the Scottish Council for Research in Education [No.] 41. London: University of London Press Ltd., 1958. Pp. xvii, 150.
For a review, see 5:B379.

P727. SCOTTISH COUNCIL FOR RESEARCH IN EDUCATION. **Prognostic Value of University Entrance Examinations in Scotland.** Publications of the Scottish Council for Research in Education, [No.] 9. London: University of London Press Ltd., 1936. Pp. x, 198.
For reviews by J. E. Greene, W. G. Whitman, and one other, see 1:B476; for reviews by A. Dvorak, L. W. Jones, J. D. Russell, and Ben D. Wood, see 36:B230.

P728. SCOTTISH COUNCIL FOR RESEARCH IN EDUCATION. **Social Implications of the 1947 Scottish Mental Survey.** Publications of the Scottish Council for Research in Education No. 35. London: University of London Press Ltd., 1953. Pp. xxiii, 356.
For reviews by Cyril Burt, Alexander Laing, and P. E. Vernon, see 5:B380.

P729. SCOTTISH COUNCIL FOR RESEARCH IN EDUCATION, MENTAL SURVEY COMMITTEE. **The Intelligence of Scottish Children: A National Survey of an Age-Group.** Publications of the Scottish Council for Research in Education, [No.] 5. London: University of London Press Ltd., 1933. Pp. x, 160.
For a review by Cyril Burt, see 2:B1061; for reviews by G. M. Ruch and R. R. Willoughby, see 1:B477; for reviews by F. C. Bartlett, H. B. English, R. Knight, and two others, see 36:B231.

P730. SCOTTISH COUNCIL FOR RESEARCH IN EDUCATION, TERMAN REVISION COMMITTEE. **Modifications Proposed for British Use of the Revised Stanford-Binet Tests of Intelligence in Measuring Intelligence by Lewis M. Terman and Maud A. Merrill.** Published by George G. Harrap & Company, Ltd., 1937. Edinburgh, Scotland: the Council, 1939. Pp. iv, 16, i, 11.
For a review, see 2:B1062.

P731. SEARLES, JOHN R., and LEONARD, J. M. **Experiments in the Mental Testing of Detroit Policemen.** Schools of Public Affairs and Social Work of Wayne University, Report No. 5. Detroit, Mich.: the Bureau, 1936. Pp. vi, 54.
For two reviews, see 2:B1063.

P732. SEGEL, DAVID. **Differential Diagnosis of Ability in School Children.** Baltimore, Md.: Warwick & York, Inc., 1934. Pp. vii, 86.
For a review, see 2:B1065; for a review by H. D. Carter, see 1:B481; for reviews by A. S. Edwards, A. M. Jordan, R. L. Morton, D. E. Scates, and A. H. Turney, see 36:B232.

P733. SEGEL, DAVID. **Intellectual Abilities in the Adolescent Period: Their Growth and Development.** Federal Security Agency, Office of Education, Bulletin 1948, No. 6. Washington, D.C.: U.S. Government Printing Office, 1948. Pp. v, 41.
For reviews by Thomas E. Christensen and Laurance F. Shaffer, see 4:B339.

P734. SEGEL, DAVID. **National and State Cooperative High-School Testing Programs.** United States Department of the Interior, Office of Education, Bulletin 1933, No. 9. Washington, D.C.: U.S. Government Printing Office, 1933. Pp. 47.
For reviews by L. V. Koos and one other, see 36:B234.

P735. SEITZ, J. A. **Variability of Examination Results: A Study of the Public Examinations in Victoria, 1922–1933.** Australian Council for Educational Research, Educational Research Series, No. 43. Melbourne, Australia: Melbourne University Press, 1936. Pp. 55.
For reviews by A. G. Schmidt and one other, see 36:B237.

P736. SELIGSON, HENRY, and SIMON, LEONARD. **Evaluation: A Memorandum for Curriculum Workers.** Board of Education of the City of New York, Bureau of Curriculum Research, Curriculum Research Report. New York: Curriculum Center, the Bureau, [1959]. Pp. iii, 61.
For a review by Berj Harootunian, see 6:B448.

P737. SELOVER, MARGARET; TOWNSEND, AGATHA; JACOBS, ROBERT; and TRAXLER, ARTHUR E. **Introduction to Testing and the Use of Test Results.** Educational Records Bulletin, No. 55. New York: Educational Records Bureau, 1950. Pp. vii, 107.
For reviews by Kenneth E. Anderson and Jules Kolodny, see 4:B342.

P738. SEMEONOFF, BORIS, and TRIST, ERIC. **Diagnostic Performance Tests: A Manual for Use With Adults.** London: Tavistock Publications, 1958. Pp. xvi, 176.
For reviews by Cyril Burt, B. Clarke, and Florence E. MacNeill, see 6:B449. For an additional review, see 6:519.

P739. SEWELL, WILLIAM H. **The Construction and Standardization of a Scale for the Measurement of the Socio-Economic Status of Oklahoma Farm Families.** Oklahoma Agricultural and Mechanical College, Agricultural Experiment Station, Technical Bulletin No. 9. Stillwater, Okla.: the Station, 1940. Pp. 88.
For reviews by Howard R. Cottam and one other, see 3:1152.

P740. SHEEHY, LORETTA MARIA. **A Study of Preadolescents by Means of a Personality Inventory.** Washington, D.C.: Catholic University of America Press, 1938. Pp. x, 76.
For a review by Howard B. English, see 3:1153; for a review by Austin G. Schmidt, see 2:B1069.

P741. SHERMAN, MURRAY H., Editor. **A Rorschach Reader.** New York: International Universities Press, Inc., 1961. Pp. xvi, 440.

For reviews by Max L. Fogel and Philip Roos, see 6:B452.

P742. SHNEIDMAN, EDWIN S. **Manual for the Make A Picture Story Method.** Projective Techniques Monograph No. 2. New York: Society for Projective Techniques and Rorschach Institute, Inc., 1952. Pp. iv, 92.

For reviews by Thelma G. Alper, Hedda Bolgar, Lee J. Cronbach, Samuel B. Kutash, Charles McArthur, E. L. Schott, and Laurance F. Shaffer, see 5:B395.

P743. SHNEIDMAN, EDWIN S. **Schizophrenia and the *MAPS* Test: A Study of Certain Normal Psycho-Social Aspects of Fantasy Production in Schizophrenia as Revealed by Performance on the Make a Picture Story (*MAPS*) Test.** *Genetic Psychol Monogr* 38:145–223 N '48.

For reviews by John E. Bell and Robert R. Holt, see 4:114.

P744. SHNEIDMAN, EDWIN S.; with the collaboration of WALTHER JOEL and KENNETH B. LITTLE. **Thematic Test Analysis.** New York: Grune & Stratton, Inc., 1951. Pp. xi, 320.

For two reviews, see 4:B346.

P745. SHUEY, AUDREY M. **The Testing of Negro Intelligence.** Lynchburg, Va.: J. P. Bell Co., Inc., 1958. Pp. xv, 351.

For reviews by Ina C. Brown, W. L. Cash, Jr., A. E. Maxwell, P. E. Vernon, and Roger K. Williams, see 6:B455; for a review by Anne Anastasi, see 5:B396.

P746. SHUTTLEWORTH, FRANK K. **The Adolescent Period: A Graphic and Pictorial Atlas.** Monographs of the Society for Research in Child Development, Vol. 3, No. 3, Serial No. 16. Washington, D.C.: the Society, 1938. Pp. v, 246.

For a review by Lawson G. Lowrey, see 3:1154; for reviews by Fowler D. Brooks, F. P. Robinson, Mabel E. Rugen, and seven others, see 2:B1071.

P747. SIMMONS, KATHERINE. **The Brush Foundation Study of Child Growth and Development: 2, Physical Growth and Development.** Monographs of the Society for Research in Child Development, Vol. 9, No. 1. Washington, D.C.: the Society, 1943. Pp. xvii, 87.

For reviews by Gustav J. Froehlich and Adolph H. Schultz, see 3:1156.

P748. SIMON, BRIAN. **Intelligence Testing and the Comprehensive School.** London: Lawrence & Wishart Ltd., 1953. Pp. 112.

For reviews by P. E. Vernon and A. F. Watts, see 5:B397.

P749. SINGER, ERIC. **Personality in Handwriting: The Guiding Image in Graphology.** London: Gerald Duckworth & Co. Ltd., 1954. Pp. 120.

For reviews by Lorna M. Simpson and I. M. Stirling, see 5:B399.

P750. SKEET, D. V. **The Child of Eleven: A Brief Survey of Transfer Tests Between Primary and Secondary Schooling.** London: University of London Press Ltd., 1957. Pp. 176.

For a review, see 5:B401.

P751. SLETTO, RAYMOND FRANKLIN. **Construction of Personality Scales by the Criterion of Internal Consistency.** Hanover, N. H.: Sociological Press, 1937. Pp. vii, 92.

For a review by Kimball Young, see 2:B1075; for reviews by J. W. Dunlap, J. P. Guilford, W. C. Reckless, and A. G. Schmidt, see 1:B486.

P752. SMALL, LEONARD. **Rorschach Location and Scoring Manual.** New York: Grune & Stratton, Inc., 1956. Pp. ix, 214.

For reviews by Gertrude Baker and Zanvel A. Liff, see 5:B402.

P753. SMALLWOOD, MARY L. **Historical Study of Examinations and Grading Systems in Early American Universities: A Critical Study of the Original Records of Harvard, William and Mary, Yale, Mount Holyoke, and Michigan From Their Founding to 1900.** Harvard Studies in Education, Vol. 24. Cambridge, Mass.: Harvard University Press, 1935. Pp. 132.

For reviews by Albert B. Crawford, W. McAndrew, J. D. Russell, A. G. Schmidt, and two others, see 36:B239.

P754. SMITH, B. OTHANEL. **Logical Aspects of Educational Measurement.** New York: Columbia University Press, 1938. Pp. x, 182.

For reviews by Alice I. Bryan, Elizabeth H. Ross, and one other, see 3:1158; for reviews by E. L. Abell, Edward E. Cureton, Paul Hounchell, A. M. Jordan, Quinn McNemar, Henry D. Rinsland, Austin G. Schmidt, Eugene Shen, Willis L. Uhl, J. Wayne Wrightstone, and five others, see 2:B1076.

P755. SMITH, C. EBBLEWHITE. **The Construction and Validation of a Group Test of Intelligence Using the Spearman Technique.** University of Toronto, Ontario College of Education, Department of Educational Research, Bulletin No. 5. Toronto, Canada: the Department, 1935. Pp. 56.

For reviews by F. Swineford (with K. J. Holzinger) and one other, see 36:B240.

P756. SMITH, CHRISTINA A. **Mental Testing of Hebridean Children in Gaelic and English.** Publications of the Scottish Council for Research in Education, [No.] 27. London: University of London Press Ltd., 1948. Pp. 42.

For reviews by P. E. Vernon and one other, see 4:B352.

P757. SMITH, EUGENE R., and TYLER, RALPH W. **Appraising and Recording Student Progress.** Adventure in American Education, Vol. III. New York: Harper & Brothers, 1942. Pp. xxiii, 550.

For reviews by Howard R. Anderson, Warren G. Findley, Cyril O. Houle, and A. M. Jordan, see 3:1159.

P758. SMITH, MAX. **The Relationship Between Item Validity and Test Validity.** Columbia University, Teachers College, Contributions to Education No. 621. New York: Bureau of Publications, the College, 1934. Pp. 40.

For a review by J. A. Long, see 1:B487; for reviews by J. W. Dunlap, A. G. Schmidt, J. Wert, and Paul V. West, see 36:B242.

P759. SOBEL, FRANCES. **Teachers' Marks and Objective Tests as Indices of School Adjustment.** Columbia University, Teachers College, Contributions to Education No. 674. New York: Bureau of Publications, the College, 1936. Pp. 74.

For reviews by A. H. Lass and M. R. Trabue, see 1:B488; for reviews by A. G. Schmidt and one other, see 36:B243.

P760. SOLOMON, HERBERT, Editor. **Studies in Item Analysis and Prediction.** Stanford Mathematical Studies in the Social Sciences, No. 6. Stanford, Calif.: Stanford University Press, 1961. Pp. ix, 310.
For reviews by D. M. Lee, Frederic M. Lord, and A. E. Maxwell, see 6:B461.

P761. SONNEMANN, ULRICH. **Handwriting Analysis as a Psychodiagnostic Tool: A Study in General and Clinical Graphology.** New York: Grune & Stratton, Inc., 1950. Pp. x, 276.
For reviews by Elizabeth C. Anderson, Samuel J. Beck, John E. Bell, H. M. Graumann, Laurance F. Shaffer, Nathaniel Thornton, and two others, see 4:B355.

P762. SOUTH, EARL BENNETT. **A Dictionary of Terms Used in Measurements and Guidance.** New York: Psychological Corporation, 1939. Pp. iv, 88.
For reviews by Ross Pollock and one other, see 2:B1078.

P763. SOUTH, EARL BENNETT. **An Index of Periodical Literature on Testing: A Classified Selected Bibliography of Periodical Literature on Educational and Mental Testing, Statistical Method and Personality Measurement, 1921–1936.** New York: Psychological Corporation, 1937. Pp. xiii, 286.
For a review, see 2:B1079; for reviews by C. M. Louttit and A. G. Schmidt, see 1:B489.

P764. SPEARMAN, C., and WYNN JONES, LL. **Human Ability: A Continuation of "The Abilities of Man."** London: Macmillan & Co. Ltd., 1950. Pp. vii, 198.
For reviews by A. D. Harris, A. W. Heim, James Maxwell, B. Semeonoff, Laurance F. Shaffer, P. E. Vernon, and one other, see 4:B356.

P765. SPEARRITT, DONALD. **Listening Comprehension—A Factorial Analysis.** A.C.E.R. Research Series No. 76. Hawthorn, Australia: Australian Council for Educational Research, 1962. Pp. x, 149.
For a review by F. W. Warburton, see 6:B462.

P766. SPENCER, DOUGLAS. **Fulcra of Conflict: A New Approach to Personality Measurement.** Yonkers, N.Y.: World Book Co., 1938. Pp. xii, 306.
For reviews by Jerome S. Bruner, H. E. Chamberlain, and A. N. Foxe, see 3:1164; for reviews by Luton Ackerman, Joseph Chassell, Henry A. Murray, Henry C. Patey, Eunice Acheson Pugh, Carl R. Rogers, J. J. Smith, and Melvin J. Vincent, see 2:B1081.

P767. SPIER, JULIUS. **The Hands of Children: An Introduction to Psycho-Chirology, Second Edition.** London: Routledge & Kegan Paul Ltd., 1955. Pp. xvi, 199.
For a review by R. W. Pickford, see 5:B405.

P768. STANLEY, JULIAN C. **Measurement in Today's Schools, Fourth Revision.** Englewood Cliffs, N.J.: Prentice-Hall, Inc., 1964. Pp. xviii, 414. [C. C. Ross was author of the first two editions.]
For reviews by Lee J. Cronbach and Chester O. Mathews of an earlier edition, see 5:B361; for reviews by Carroll D. Champlin, Walter W. Cook, Frederick B. Davis, Richard M. Drake, and Florence S. Dunlop, see 4:B325; for reviews by Amos C. Anderson, A. S. Edwards, Earl R. Gabler, Robert Y. Walker, and one other, see 3:1131.

P769. STANTON, HAZEL M. **Measurement of Musical Talent: the Eastman Experiment.** University of Iowa Studies, New Series No. 291; Studies in the Psychology of Music, Vol. II. Iowa City, Iowa: the University, 1935. Pp. 140.
For reviews by A. E. Pierce, A. G. Schmidt, and one other, see 36:B246.

P770. STANTON, HAZEL M., and KOERTH, WILHELMINE. **Musical Capacity Measures of Children Repeated After Musical Training.** University of Iowa Studies, New Series No. 259; Series on Aims and Progress of Research, No. 42. Iowa City, Iowa: the University, 1933. Pp. 48.
For reviews by F. N. Freeman (with G. T. Buswell), A. G. Schmidt, and one other, see 36:B247.

P771. STEAD, WILLIAM H.; SHARTLE, CARROLL L.; OTIS, JAY L.; WARD, RAYMOND S.; OSBORNE, HERBERT F.; ENDLER, O. L.; DVORAK, BEATRICE J.; COOPER, JOHN H.; BELLOWS, ROGER M.; and KOLBE, LAVERNE E. **Occupational Counseling Techniques: Their Development and Application.** New York: American Book Co., 1940. Pp. ix, 273.
For reviews by G. E. Bathhurst, Harold E. Burtt, Eleanor Loeb, Ross L. Mooney, Dean M. Schweickhard, and one other, see 3:1166; for a review by Marion M. Lamb, see 2:B1083.

P772. STEIN, MORRIS I. **Thematic Apperception Test: An Introductory Manual for Its Clinical Use With Adults, Second Edition.** Cambridge, Mass.: Addison-Wesley Publishing Co., Inc., 1955. Pp. xviii, 365.
For reviews by Ralph Hetherington, Robert R. Holt, Zygmunt A. Piotrowski, Joseph Sandler, Roy Schafer, Laurance F. Shaffer, and Helen Thompson of the first edition, see 4:140.

P773. STEINER, M. E. **The Psychologist in Industry.** Springfield, Ill.: Charles C Thomas, Publisher, 1949. Pp. vii, 107.
For reviews by M. Bentley, C. E. Jurgensen, Laurance F. Shaffer, B. Steinzor, Frederick A. Zehrer, and two others, see 4:B359.

P774. STEPHENSON, WILLIAM. **The Study of Behavior: Q-Technique and Its Methodology.** Chicago, Ill.: University of Chicago Press, 1953. Pp. ix, 376.
For reviews by Charlotte Banks, Cyril Burt, Lee J. Cronbach (with Goldine C. Gleser), H. J. Eysenck, Bernard Glueck, Quinn McNemar, and William Stephenson, see 5:B408.

P775. STEPHENSON, WILLIAM. **Testing School Children: An Essay in Educational and Social Psychology.** London: Longmans, Green & Co. Ltd., 1949. Pp. 127.
For reviews by Cyril Burt, C. M. Fleming, and two others, see 4:B360.

P776. STERN, GEORGE G.; STEIN, MORRIS I.; and BLOOM, BENJAMIN S. **Methods in Personality Assessment: Human Behavior in Complex Social Situations.** Glencoe, Ill.: Free Press, 1956. Pp. 271.
For reviews by Kenneth R. Hammond, Barbara J. Suttell, F. W. Warburton, and Charles F. Warnath, see 5:B409.

P777. STEWARD, VERNE. **The Use and Value of Special Tests in the Selection of Life Underwriters.** Los Angeles, Calif.: the Author, 1934. Pp. 93.
For a review by R. S. Schultz, see 1:B491.

P778. STODDARD, GEORGE D. **The Meaning of Intelligence.** New York: Macmillan Co., 1943. Pp. ix, 504.
For reviews by Cyril Burt, G. T. Buswell, Herbert S. Conrad, Robert E. L. Faris, Paul R. Farnsworth, Henry E. Garrett, H. H. Goddard, Florence L.

Goodenough, I. Newton Kugelmass, Frances N. Maxfield, M. F. Ashley Montagu, H. B. Reed, and Benjamin R. Simpson, see 3:1168.

P779. STODOLA, QUENTIN. **Making the Classroom Test: A Guide for Teachers, Second Edition.** Evaluation and Advisory Service Series, No. 4. Princeton, N.J.: Educational Testing Service, 1961. Pp. 27.
For a review by Thomas M. Magoon, see 6:B466.

P780. STOGDILL, RALPH M., and COONS, ALVIN E., Editors. **Leader Behavior: Its Description and Measurement.** Ohio State University, Bureau of Business Research, Research Monograph No. 88. Columbus, Ohio: the Bureau, 1957. Pp. xv, 168.
For a review by Robert Fitzpatrick, see 5:B411.

P781. STOTT, LELAND H. **The Longitudinal Study of Individual Development: Techniques for Appraising Developmental Status and Progress.** Detroit, Mich.: Merrill-Palmer School, 1955. Pp. x, 113.
For reviews by Lois Meek Stolz and one other, see 5:B412.

P782. STOUFFER, SAMUEL A.; GUTTMAN, LOUIS; SUCHMAN, EDWARD A.; LAZARSFELD, PAUL F.; STAR, SHIRLEY A.; and CLAUSEN, JOHN A. **Measurement and Prediction.** Studies in Social Psychology in World War II, Vol. 4. Princeton, N.J.: Princeton University Press, 1950. Pp. x, 756.
For reviews by Steuart Henderson Britt, H. J. Eysenck, Daniel Katz, Alfred McClung Lee, Daniel O. Price, Laurance F. Shaffer, and one other, see 4:B361.

P783. STRANG, RUTH. **Counseling Technics in College and Secondary School, Revised Edition.** New York: Harper & Brothers, 1949. Pp. xiii, 302.
For reviews by Iona R. Logie, John M. Stalnaker, and one other, see 4:B362; for reviews by W. H. Cowley, John G. Darley, Carter V. Good, R. W. Husband, Frank Meyerson, and E. V. Pullias of the first edition, see 2:B1088; for reviews by S. A. Hamrin, A. G. Schmidt, E. G. Williamson, and one other, see 1:B493.

P784. STRONG, EDWARD K., JR. **Vocational Interests 18 Years After College.** Minneapolis, Minn.: University of Minnesota Press, 1955. Pp. xiv, 207.
For reviews by E. Gordon Collister, John C. Flanagan, Allen O. Gamble, and Donald E. Super, see 5:B414.

P785. STRONG, EDWARD K., JR. **Vocational Interests of Men and Women.** Stanford, Calif.: Stanford University Press, 1943. Pp. xxix, 746.
For reviews by Harold D. Carter, Stephen M. Corey, John G. Darley, Robert J. Havighurst, G. Frederic Kuder, Charles S. Myers, C. L. Shartle, William H. Stone, Donald E. Super, and one other, see 3:652.

P786. STROUP, FRANCIS. **Measurement in Physical Education: An Introduction to Its Use.** New York: Ronald Press Co., 1957. Pp. xiii, 192.
For a review by L. Joseph Lins, see 5:B416.

P787. STUIT, DEWEY B., Editor. **Personnel Research and Test Development in the Bureau of Naval Personnel.** Princeton, N.J.: Princeton University Press, 1947. Pp. xxiv, 513.
For reviews by John C. Flanagan, Donald Sisson, N. A. B. Wilson, and C. Gilbert Wrenn, see 4:B363.

P788. STUIT, DEWEY B.; DICKSON, GWENDOLEN S.; JORDAN, THOMAS F.; and SCHLOERB, LESTER. **Predicting Success in Professional Schools.** Wash-

ington, D.C.: American Council on Education, 1949. Pp. xii, 187.
For reviews by Barbara A. Kirk, Marjorie McGillicuddy, Laurance F. Shaffer, Ordway Tead, and Walter Watson, see 4:B364.

P789. SULLIVAN, CELESTINE. **A Scale for Measuring Developmental Age in Girls.** Catholic University of America, Studies in Psychology and Psychiatry, Vol. 3, No. 4. Baltimore, Md.: Williams & Wilkins Co., 1934. Pp. vii, 65.
For a review by R. S. Cavan, see 1:B495.

P790. SUPER, DONALD E. **Avocational Interest Patterns: A Study in the Psychology of Avocations.** Stanford, Calif.: Stanford University Press, 1940. Pp. xiv, 148.
For reviews by Emory S. Bogardus, Lysle W. Croft, Thomas M. Harris, Frank J. Kobler, William McGehee, Paul H. Sheats, Stuart M. Stoke, and E. G. Williamson, see 3:1177; for a review by Austin G. Schmidt, see 2:B1089.

P791. SUPER, DONALD E., and CRITES, JOHN O. **Appraising Vocational Fitness by Means of Psychological Tests, Revised Edition.** New York: Harper & Row, Publishers, Inc., 1962. Pp. xv, 688.
For reviews by J. F. Clark and William C. Cottle, see 6:B472; for reviews by J. B. Boyd, Josef Brožek, Mitchell Dreese, Milton Hahn, Bernard J. Muller-Thym, S. A. Nock, Marian Rayburn, R. C. Rogers, William P. Sears, Laurance F. Shaffer, J. R. Wittenborn, and one other of the first edition, see 4:B368.

P792. SUTCLIFFE, A., and CANHAM, J. W. **The Heights and Weights of Boys and Girls.** London: John Murray, 1950. Pp. ix, 84.
For a review by C. M. Fleming, see 4:B369.

P793. SWINEFORD, FRANCES, and HOLZINGER, KARL J. **A Study in Factor Analysis: The Reliability of Bi-Factors and Their Relation to Other Measures.** University of Chicago, Department of Education, Supplementary Educational Monographs, No. 53. Chicago, Ill.: University of Chicago Press, 1942. Pp. xi, 88.
For a review by A. S. Edwards, see 3:1180.

P794. SYMONDS, PERCIVAL M. **Adolescent Fantasy: An Investigation of the Picture-Story Method of Personality Study.** New York: Columbia University Press, 1949. Pp. xii, 397.
For reviews by Helen Arthur, Eva Ruth Balken, Madison Bentley, Robert R. Blake, John A. Grimshaw, F. J. Houlahan, Leo Kanner, Hyman S. Lippman, M. Powell, Laurance F. Shaffer, and one other, see 4:133.

P795. SYMONDS, PERCIVAL M. **Psychological Diagnosis in Social Adjustment: Including an Annotated List of Tests, Questionnaires, and Rating Scales for the Study of Personality and Conduct.** New York: American Book Co., 1934. Pp. ix, 362.
For a review, see 2:B1090; for reviews by P. Blanchard, T. W. Brockbank, J. Regensburg, M. Sherman, and P. V. Young, see 1:B496; for reviews by H. de Fremery, J. Dollard, C. M. Louttit, F. Meyerson, A. G. Schmidt and four others, see 36:B253.

P796. SYMONDS, PERCIVAL M., and JACKSON, CLAUDE E. **Measurement of the Personality Adjustments of High School Pupils.** New York: Bureau of Publications, Teachers College, Columbia University, 1935. Pp. xi, 110.
For reviews by M. Brown, R. S. Cavan, W. H. Cowley, A. G. Schmidt, and E. G. Williamson, see 36:B254.

P797. SYMONDS, PERCIVAL M.; with ARTHUR R. JENSEN. **From Adolescent to Adult.** New York: Columbia University Press, 1961. Pp. x, 413.

For reviews by Dale B. Harris, Merle Ohlsen (with Ray Thompson), and H. H. Stern, see 6:B473.

P798. SZONDI, L. **Experimental Diagnostics of Drives.** New York: Grune & Stratton, Inc., 1952. Pp. x, 254.

For reviews by Henry P. David, Irwin J. Knopf, and Victor C. Raimy, see 5:B418.

P799. SZONDI, LIPOT; MOSER, ULRICH; and WEBB, MARVIN W. **The Szondi Test: In Diagnosis, Prognosis and Treatment.** Philadelphia, Pa.: J. B. Lippincott Co., 1959. Pp. xv, 309.

For reviews by Walter G. Klopfer, Mary Williams, and Robert I. Yufit, see 6:B474.

P800. TABA, HILDA. **Social Sensitivity.** Progressive Education Association, Evaluation in the Eight Year Study, Bulletin No. 6. Columbus, Ohio: the Study, Ohio State University, 1936. Pp. 50.

For a review by Howard E. Wilson, see 36:B255.

P801. TABA, HILDA; BRADY, ELIZABETH HALL; ROBINSON, JOHN T.; and VICKERY, WILLIAM E. **Diagnosing Human Relation Needs.** Washington, D.C.: American Council on Education, 1951. Pp. xi, 155.

For reviews by Douglas D. Blocksma and Joe McPherson, see 5:B419.

P802. TAKALA, MARTTI. **Studies of Psychomotor Personality Tests I.** Annals of the Finnish Academy of Science and Letters, Series B, No. 81, Part 2. Helsinki, Finland: Suomalainen Tiedeakatemia, Academia Scientiarum Fennica, 1953. Pp. 130.

For a review by Peter Venables, see 5:B420.

P803. TANSIL, REBECCA CATHERINE. **The Contributions of Cumulative Personnel Records to a Teacher-Education Program: As Evidenced by Their Use at the State Teachers College at Towson, Maryland.** Columbia University, Teachers College, Contributions to Education No. 764. New York: Bureau of Publications, the College, 1939. Pp. viii, 158.

For reviews by M. E. Bennett, F. C. Landsittel, Harry N. Rivlin, Austin G. Schmidt, and one other, see 2:B1091.

P804. TAYLOR, EDITH MEYER. **Psychological Appraisal of Children With Cerebral Defects.** Cambridge, Mass.: Harvard University Press, 1959. Pp. xvii, 499.

For a review by Alan O. Ross, see 6:B477.

P805. TAYLOR, STANFORD E. **Eye-Movement Photography With the Reading Eye, Second Edition.** Huntington, N. Y.: Educational Developmental Laboratories, Inc., 1960. Pp. 69, 12, iv, 22.

For a review by N. Dale Bryant, see 6:B478.

P806. TELTSCHER, HERRY O. **Handwriting: The Key to Successful Living, Second Edition.** New York: G. P. Putnam's Sons, 1946. Pp. xiii, 301.

For a review by Lee R. Steiner of the first edition, see 3:1181.

P807. TERMAN, LEWIS M., and MERRILL, MAUD A. **Measuring Intelligence: A Guide to the Administration of the New Revised Stanford-Binet Tests of Intelligence.** Boston, Mass.: Houghton Mifflin Co., 1937. Pp. xiv, 461.

For reviews by Cyril Burt, Grace H. Kent, and M. Krugman, see 2:1420; for reviews by C. J. C. Earl and two others, see 2:B1093; for reviews by Cyril Burt, R. B. Cattell, J. C. Flanagan, F. N. Freeman, F. L. Goodenough, E. N. Hay, E. Kawin, A. H.

Martin, Francis N. Maxfield, E. M. Nevill, C. Spearman, A. E. Traxler, P. E. Vernon, and nine others, see 1:B497.

P808. TERMAN, LEWIS M., and MILES, CATHERINE COX; assisted by JACK W. DUNLAP, HAROLD A. EDGERTON, E. LOWELL KELLY, ALBERT K. KURTZ, E. ALICE MCANULTY, QUINN MCNEMAR, MAUD A. MERRILL, FLOYD L. RUCH, and HORACE G. WYATT. **Sex and Personality: Studies in Masculinity and Femininity.** New York: McGraw-Hill Book Co., Inc., 1936. Pp. xii, 600.

For reviews by J. C. Flügel, William V. Silverberg, and Richard S. Uhrbrock, see 2:B1094; for reviews by G. Bryson, G. W. Hartmann, H. McCurdy, G. C. Schwesinger, W. Stephenson, K. Young, and seven others, see 1:B498; for reviews by C. N. Allen, E. B. Reuter, A. G. Schmidt, H. A. Shapiro, M. J. Vincent, D. Wechsler, and two others, see 36:B256.

P809. THOMAS, DOROTHY S.; LOOMIS, ALICE M.; and ARRINGTON, RUTH E. **Observational Studies of Social Behavior, 1.** New Haven, Conn.: the Institute of Human Relations, Yale University, 1933. Pp. xvii, 271.

For reviews by H. E. Chamberlain, C. L. Fry, Sister Mary, M. U. Moore, and C. M. Rebert, see 1:B499; for reviews by I. Knickerbocker, K. Young, and two others, see 36:B257.

P810. THOMAS, FRANK C. **Ability and Knowledge: The Standpoint of the London School.** London: Macmillan & Co., Ltd., 1935. Pp. xx, 338.

For a review by T. N. Siqueira, see 2:B1096; for reviews by R. B. Cattell, J. Drever, C. A. Gibb, and one other, see 1:B500; for reviews by F. Swineford (with K. J. Holzinger), C. W. Valentine, and three others, see 36:B258.

P811. THOMAS, R. MURRAY. **Judging Student Progress, Second Edition.** New York: David McKay Co., Inc., 1960. Pp. x, 518.

For a review by Harold F. Bligh, see 6:B481; for a review by J. Thomas Hastings of the first edition, see 5:B422.

P812. THOMPSON, LORIN ANDREW; assisted by DANIEL C. LAURENCE and ARCHIE ALLARDYCE. **Interview Aids and Trade Questions for Employment Offices.** New York: Harper & Brothers, 1936. Pp. xvii, 173.

For two reviews, see 2:B1097; for reviews by G. L. Bergen and one other, see 1:B501.

P813. THOMSON, GODFREY. **The Factorial Analysis of Human Ability, Fifth Edition.** London: University of London Press Ltd., 1951. Pp. xvi, 383.

For reviews by Cyril Burt, E. G. Chambers, J. P. Guilford, G. E. Metz, Patrick Slater, J. Wishart, and one other, see 2:B1098; for reviews by Cyril Burt, C. M. Fleming, John W. Tukey, Helen M. Walker, J. Wishart, and three others of an earlier edition, see 290 in *Statistical Methodology Reviews, 1941–1950*; for reviews by John C. Flanagan, H. L. Seal, W. Stephenson, and three others, see 288 in *The Second Yearbook of Research and Statistical Methodology Books and Reviews.*

P814. THOMSON, GODFREY. **The Trend of National Intelligence: The Galton Lecture, 1946.** Eugenics Society, Occasional Papers on Eugenics, No. 3. London: Cassell & Co. Ltd., 1947. Pp. 35.

For reviews by C. M. Fleming, C. W. Valentine, and one other, see 4:B378.

P815. THOMSON, GODFREY H. **An Analysis of Performance Test Scores of a Representative**

Group of Scottish Children. Publications of the Scottish Council for Research in Education, [No.] 16, International Examinations Inquiry. London: University of London Press Ltd., 1940. Pp. vii, 58.
For reviews by Miles A. Tinker and two others, see 3:1185; for a review, see 2:B1097.1.

P816. THOMSON, GODFREY H. **The Geometry of Mental Measurement.** London: University of London Press Ltd., 1954. Pp. 60.
For reviews by M. A. Creasy, L. Joseph Lins, E. A. Peel, and Arthur Summerfield, see 5:B423.

P817. THORNDIKE, EDWARD L.; assisted by ELSIE O. BREGMAN, IRVING LORGE, ZAIDA F. METCALFE, ELEANOR E. ROBINSON, and ELLA WOODYARD. **Prediction of Vocational Success.** New York: Commonwealth Fund, 1934. Pp. xxiv, 284.
For reviews by A. P. Braddock, W. H. Brentlinger, C. C. Brigham, M. H. S. Hayes, A. W. Kornhauser, A. H. Martin, J. J. Seidel, E. B. Sullivan, H. A. Toops, G. B. Vold, and two others, see 1:B502.

P818. THORNDIKE, ROBERT L. **The Concepts of Over- and Under-Achievement.** New York: Bureau of Publications, Teachers College, Columbia University, 1963. Pp. ix, 79.
For a review by William W. Farquhar, see 6:B482.

P819. THORNDIKE, ROBERT L. **Personnel Selection: Test and Measurement Techniques.** New York: John Wiley & Sons, Inc., 1949. Pp. viii, 358.
For reviews by Marion R. Bartlett, Ruth Bishop, Frank M. Fletcher, Jr., L. M. Haynes, Albert S. Thompson, and P. E. Vernon, see 4:B379.

P820. THORNDIKE, ROBERT L., Editor. **Research Problems and Techniques.** Army Air Forces Aviation Psychology Program Research Reports, Report No. 3. Washington, D.C.: U.S. Government Printing Office, 1947. Pp. viii, 163.
For a review, see 3:1187. For a review of the series, see P1.

P821. THORNDIKE, ROBERT L., and HAGEN, ELIZABETH. **Measurement and Evaluation in Psychology and Education, Second Edition.** New York: John Wiley & Sons, Inc., 1961. Pp. viii, 602.
For reviews by Ralph F. Berdie, Andrew L. Comrey, and Robert B. Nordberg, see 6:B483; for reviews by Ralph F. Berdie, Paul L. Dressel, Walter N. Durost, J. Lumsden, John E. Milholland, and one other of the first edition, see 5:B424.

P822. THORNE, FREDERICK C. **Principles of Psychological Examining: A Systematic Textbook.** Brandon, Vt.: Journal of Clinical Psychology, 1955. Pp. vii, 494.
For reviews by Paul W. Pruyser, David V. Tiedeman, and J. Richard Wittenborn, see 5:B425.

P823. THORNTON, GEORGE R. **Factor Analysis of Tests Designed to Measure Persistence.** American Psychological Association, Psychological Monographs, Vol. 51, No. 3, Whole No. 229. Evanston, Ill.: the Association, 1939. Pp. 42.
For a review by Austin G. Schmidt, see 2:B1098.1.

P824. THURSTONE, L. L. **The Measurement of Values.** Chicago, Ill.: University of Chicago Press, 1959. Pp. vii, 322.
For a review by H. J. Eysenck, see 6:B486.

P825. THURSTONE, L. L. **Multiple-Factor Analysis: A Development and Expansion of *The Vectors of Mind*.** Chicago, Ill.: University of Chicago Press, 1947. Pp. xix, 535.
For reviews by Cyril Burt, Raymond B. Cattell,

H. J. Eysenck, Paul Hanly Furfey, Louis Guttman, Charles M. Harsh, Paul Horst, D. N. Lawley, Quinn McNemar, J. W. Tukey, and Robert J. Wherry, see 293 in *Statistical Methodology Reviews, 1941–1950;* for reviews by H. C. Beyle, H. E. Garrett, H. F. Gosnell, G. A. Lundberg, and S. S. Wilks of an earlier edition, see 1:B505; for reviews by H. E. Burtt, W. S. Carlson, J. W. Dunlap, F. Swineford (with K. J. Holzinger), and G. H. Thomson (with W. Ledermann), see 36:B263.

P826. THURSTONE, L. L. **Primary Mental Abilities.** Psychometric Society, Psychometric Monograph No. 1. Chicago, Ill.: University of Chicago Press, 1938. Pp. ix, 121.
For reviews by A. B. Crawford and John M. Stalnaker, see 2:1427; for reviews by E. G. Chambers, H. J. Eysenck, Thomas M. French, Henry E. Garrett, Quinn McNemar, W. P. Shofstall, Joseph N. Stonesifer, Joseph Zubin, and one other, see 2:B1099; for reviews by E. N. Hay, G. A. Lundeberg, C. E. Smith, and E. F. Young, see 1:B503.

P827. THURSTONE, L. L. **A Simplified Multiple Factor Method and an Outline of Computations.** Chicago, Ill.: University of Chicago Bookstore, 1933. Pp. 25.
For a review by Raymond Royce Willoughby, see 2:B1101.

P828. THURSTONE, L. L., and THURSTONE, THELMA GWINN. **Factorial Studies of Intelligence.** Psychometric Society, Psychometric Monograph No. 2. Chicago, Ill.: University of Chicago Press, 1941. Pp. v, 94.
For reviews by Austin G. Schmidt and one other, see 3:1189.

P829. THURSTONE, LOUIS L. **The Theory of Multiple Factors.** Ann Arbor, Mich.: Edwards Brothers, Inc., 1933. Pp. vii, 65.
For a review by R. R. Willoughby, see 1:B504; for a review by W. G. Findley, see 36:B262.

P830. TIEGS, ERNEST W. **Tests and Measurements in the Improvement of Learning.** Boston, Mass.: Houghton Mifflin Co., 1939. Pp. xxi, 490.
For reviews by John G. Darley, Harold B. Gores, C. M. Louttit, C. W. Odell, and John B. Whitelaw, see 2:B1102.

P831. TINKELMAN, SHERMAN. **Difficulty Prediction of Test Items.** Columbia University, Teachers College, Contributions to Education, No. 941. New York: Bureau of Publications, the College, 1947. Pp. vii, 55.
For reviews by Fred S. Beers, Charles I. Mosier, Miles A. Tinker, and Carl Wedell, see 4:B383.

P832. TOLOR, ALEXANDER, and SCHULBERG, HERBERT C. **An Evaluation of the Bender-Gestalt Test.** Springfield, Ill.: Charles C Thomas, Publisher, 1963. Pp. xxiii, 229.
For reviews by Read D. Tuddenham and Adolf G. Woltmann, see 6:B487.

P833. TOMKINS, SILVAN S., and MINER, JOHN B. **PAT Interpretation: Scope and Technique.** New York: Springer Publishing Co., Inc., 1959. Pp. vii, 184.
For reviews by Sidney E. Cleveland, H. Phillipson, and Leonard P. Ullmann, see 6:246.

P834. TOMKINS, SILVAN S., and MINER, JOHN B. **The Tomkins-Horn Picture Arrangement Test.** New York: Springer Publishing Co., Inc., 1957. Pp. xvi, 383.
For a review by Leonard D. Goodstein, see 5:167.

P835. TOMKINS, SILVAN S.; with the collaboration of ELIZABETH J. TOMKINS. **The Thematic Apperception Test: The Theory and Technique of Interpretation.** New York: Grune & Stratton, Inc., 1947. Pp. xi, 297.
For reviews by Rudolf Ekstein, Robert R. Holt, R. M. Ogden, Helen Oexle Pierce, Zygmunt A. Piotrowski, Suzanne Reichard, T. W. Richards, Helen Sargent, Stanley B. Williams, Adolf G. Woltmann, Frederick Wyatt, and three others, see 4:141; for a review, see 3:104a.

P836. TORGERSON, THEODORE L., and ADAMS, GEORGIA SACHS. **Measurement and Evaluation for the Elementary-School Teacher: With Implications for Corrective Procedures.** New York: Dryden Press, Inc., 1954. Pp. xiii, 489.
For reviews by Althea Beery and Robert A. Jones, see 5:B429.

P837. TORGERSON, WARREN S. **Theory and Methods of Scaling.** New York: John Wiley & Sons, Inc., 1958. Pp. xiii, 460.
For reviews by S. B. Hammond and Joseph L. Zinnes, see 6:B489.

P838. TRAVERS, ROBERT M. W. **Educational Measurement.** New York: Macmillan Co., 1955. Pp. xix, 420.
For reviews by Robert A. Davis, C. M. Fleming, Leo R. Kennedy, and Edwin Wandt, see 5:B432.

P839. TRAVERS, ROBERT M. W. **How to Make Achievement Tests.** New York: Odyssey Press, 1950. Pp. xi, 180.
For reviews by A. M. Jordan, Herschel T. Manuel, William B. Reiner, and one other, see 4:B386.

P840. TRAXLER, ARTHUR E. **How to Use Cumulative Records: The Manual for the SRA Cumulative Record for Junior and Senior High Schools.** Chicago, Ill.: Science Research Associates, Inc., 1947. Pp. 40.
For a review by Miles A. Tinker, see 4:B388.

P841. TRAXLER, ARTHUR E. **The Nature and Use of Reading Tests.** Educational Records Bulletin, No. 34. New York: Educational Records Bureau, 1941. Pp. 64.
For reviews by G. T. Buswell, W. D. Perry, Austin G. Schmidt, and Ruth Strang, see 3:1199.

P842. TRAXLER, ARTHUR E. **Techniques of Guidance: Tests, Records, and Counseling in a Guidance Program.** New York: Harper & Brothers, 1945. Pp. xv, 394.
For reviews by F. S. Beers, Thomas E. Christensen, Warren G. Findley, Earl R. Gabler, Arthur J. Jones, Henry C. Mills, Alec Rodger, Merrill Roff, and one other, see 3:1200.

P843. TRAXLER, ARTHUR E. **The Use of Test Results in Diagnosis and Instruction in the Tool Subjects, [Third Edition].** Educational Records Bulletin No. 18 (Second Revision). New York: Educational Records Bureau, 1949. Pp. v, 82.
For two reviews of earlier editions, see 3:1201 and 36:B270.

P844. TRAXLER, ARTHUR E. **The Use of Test Results in Secondary Schools.** Educational Records Bulletin No. 25. New York: Educational Records Bureau, 1938. Pp. vi, 108.
For a review by Henry D. Rinsland, see 2:B1109.

P845. TRAXLER, ARTHUR E. **The Use of Tests and Rating Devices in the Appraisal of Personality, Revised Edition.** Educational Records Bul-

letin, No. 23 (Revised). New York: Educational Records Bureau, 1942. Pp. ix, 74.
For reviews by John G. Darley and one other, see 3:1202; for reviews by Anthony J. Mitrano, Carl R. Rogers, Phillip J. Rulon, David Segel, and one other, see 2:B1108; for reviews by A. G. Schmidt and one other, see 1:B508.

P846. TRAXLER, ARTHUR E., Editor. **Measurement and Evaluation in the Improvement of Education: A Report of the Fifteenth Educational Conference, New York City, October 26 and 27, 1950, Held Under the Auspices of the Educational Records Bureau and the American Council on Education.** American Council on Education Studies, Vol. 15; Series I, Reports of Committees and Conferences, No. 46. Washington, D.C.: the Council, 1951. Pp. vi, 141.
For a review by William B. Michael, see 4:B390.

P847. TRAXLER, ARTHUR E.; JACOBS, ROBERT; SELOVER, MARGARET; and TOWNSEND, AGATHA. **Introduction to Testing and the Use of Test Results in Public Schools.** New York: Harper & Brothers, 1953. Pp. xi, 113.
For reviews by Dora E. Damrin, Harry D. Lovelass, Robert B. Nordberg, and Carl H. Waller, see 5:B433.

P848. TROYER, MAURICE E., and PACE, C. ROBERT. **Evaluation in Teacher Education.** Washington, D.C.: American Council on Education, 1944. Pp. xii, 368.
For reviews by Howard R. Anderson, George E. Schlesser, and one other, see 3:1206.

P849. TRYON, CAROLINE McCANN. **Evaluations of Adolescent Personality by Adolescents.** Monographs of the Society for Research in Child Development, Vol. 4, No. 4, Serial No. 23. Washington, D.C.: the Society, 1939. Pp. x, 83.
For reviews by Mabel E. Rugen and Austin G. Schmidt, see 2:B1110.

P850. TRYON, ROBERT CHOATE. **Cluster Analysis: Correlation Profile and Orthometric (Factor) Analysis for the Isolation of Unities in Mind and Personality.** Berkeley, Calif.: Associated Students Store, University of California, 1939. Pp. ix, 122.
For reviews by Austin G. Schmidt and Dael L. Wolfle, see 2:B1111.

P851. TYLER, FRED T. **The Prediciton of Student-Teaching Success From Personality Inventories.** University of California, Publications in Education, Vol. 11, No. 4. Berkeley, Calif.: University of California Press, 1954. Pp. 233-313.
For a review by P. E. Vernon, see 5:B435.

P852. TYLER, LEONA E. **Tests and Measurements.** Englewood Cliffs, N.J.: Prentice-Hall, Inc., 1963. Pp. xi, 116.
For reviews by E. Fisk, C. A. Gibb, and Herbert Zimiles, see 6:B491.

P853. TYLER, RALPH W. **Constructing Achievement Tests.** Reprints from the Educational Research Bulletin. Columbus, Ohio: Bureau of Educational Research, Ohio State University, 1934. Pp. 102.
For a review by C. M. Pruitt, see 1:B509; for reviews by F. N. Freeman (with G. T. Buswell) and A. G. Schmidt, see 36:B272.

P854. ULETT, GEORGE. **Rorschach Introductory Manual: A Primer for the Clinical Psychiatric Worker: With Interpretive Diagram to Permit Clinical Use While Learning the Ink-Blot Tech-**

nique, Second Edition. Beverly Hills, Calif.: Western Psychological Services, 1955. Pp. 49.

For reviews by T. Alcock, Lily H. Gondor, W. Donald Ross, L. Joseph Stone, and two others of the first edition, see 4:128.

P855. UNITED STATES ARMY PERSONNEL RESEARCH OFFICE. **Army Personnel Tests and Measurement.** Department of the Army Pamphlet No. 611-2. Washington, D.C.: Publications Branch, The Adjutant General's Office, Department of the Army, 1962. Pp. iv, 114.

For reviews by Harold E. Burtt, Lee J. Cronbach, Edwin E. Ghiselli, and W. S. Paul of the first edition, see 5:B1.

P856. UNIVERSITY OF MINNESOTA, COMMITTEE ON EDUCATIONAL RESEARCH. **The Effective General College Curriculum as Revealed by Examinations.** Minneapolis, Minn.: University of Minnesota Press, 1937. Pp. xvi, 427.

For reviews by J. E. Bathurst and H. E. Hawkes, see 2:B1112; for reviews by G. R. Koopman, H. H. Punke, A. G. Schmidt, and one other, see 1:B511.

P857. UNIVERSITY OF MINNESOTA, COMMITTEE ON EDUCATIONAL RESEARCH. **Studies in College Examinations: An Experimental Investigation in the Construction and Use of College Examinations.** Minneapolis, Minn.: The Committee, 1934. Pp. vii, 204.

For reviews by C. J. Pruitt and one other, see 1:B512.

P858. VALENTINE, C. W. **Examinations and the Examinee: Some Suggested Reforms.** Birmingham, England: Birmingham Printers, Ltd., 1938. Pp. 39.

For reviews by T. N. Siqueira and one other, see 2:B1113; for reviews by F. Smith and three others, see 1:B513.

P859. VALENTINE, C. W. **Intelligence Tests for Children, Sixth Edition.** London: Methuen & Co. Ltd., 1958. Pp. xiii, 87.

For reviews by John Cohen and one other of an earlier edition, see 4:344; for reviews by E. M. Bartlett, Cyril Burt, S. J. F. Philpott, and one other, see 4:345; for reviews by C. Burt and one other, see 3:283.

P860. VERNIER, CLAIRE MYERS. **Projective Test Productions: 1, Projective Drawings.** New York: Grune & Stratton, Inc., 1952. Pp. viii, 168.

For reviews by A. Jean Brown, Leonard Horowitz, Morris Krugman, and Irene R. Pierce, see 5:B444.

P861. VERNON, P. E. **The Assessment of Psychological Qualities by Verbal Methods: A Survey of Attitude Tests, Rating Scales, and Personality Questionnaires.** Medical Research Council, Industrial Health Research Board, Report No. 83. London: H.M. Stationery Office, 1938. Pp. vi, 124.

For reviews by Paul Horst, B. Babington Smith, and D. T. Stanley, see 2:B1114; for two reviews, see 1:B514.

P862. VERNON, P. E. **Intelligence and Attainment Tests.** London: University of London Press Ltd., 1960. Pp. 207.

For reviews by J. Stanley Ahmann, Carl Bereiter, and Julian C. Stanley, see 6:B495.

P863. VERNON, P. E., Editor. **Secondary School Selection: A British Psychological Society Inquiry.** London: Methuen & Co., Ltd., 1957. Pp. 216.

For a review by F. W. Warburton, see 5:B447.

P864. VERNON, PHILIP E. **The Measurement of Abilities, Second Edition.** London: University of London Press Ltd., 1956. Pp. xii, 276.

For a review by S. B. Sells, see 6:B496; for reviews by A. C. F. Beales, John D. Handyside, D. M. Lee, and Boris Semeonoff, see 5:B445; for reviews by Anne Anastasi, Forrest H. Kirkpatrick, Evelyn Lawrence, Quinn McNemar, Robert H. Thouless, and three others of the first edition, see 3:1219; for reviews by J. I. Cohen, John C. Raven, Alec Rodger, and three others, see 2:B1115.

P865. VERNON, PHILIP E. **Personality Tests and Assessments.** London: Methuen & Co., Ltd., 1953. Pp. xi, 220.

For reviews by Dan L. Adler, Cyril Burt, Florence Macneill, R. M. Mowbray, Alec Rodger, and Laurance F. Shaffer, see 5:B446.

P866. VERNON, PHILIP E. **The Structure of Human Abilities, Second Edition.** London: Methuen & Co. Ltd., 1961. Pp. x, 208.

For reviews by Cyril Burt, Patrick Slater, F. W. Warburton, and two others of the first edition, see 4:B406.

P867. VERNON, PHILIP E., and PARRY, JOHN B. **Personnel Selection in the British Forces.** London: University of London Press Ltd., 1949. Pp. 324.

For reviews by M. B. Brody, Douglas H. Fryer, H. T. Himmelweit, Lester Luborsky, Ben S. Morris, Alec Rodger, Dewey B. Stuit, E. K. Taylor, C. W. Valentine, and one other, see 4:B407.

P868. VICTOR, FRANK. **Handwriting: A Personality Projection.** Springfield, Ill.: Charles C Thomas, Publisher, 1952. Pp. xii, 149.

For reviews by Gerald S. Blum, Julian B. Rotter, Laurance F. Shaffer, and Werner Wolff, see 5:B448.

P869. VIITAMÄKI, R. OLAVI. **Personality Traits Between Puberty and Adolescence: Their Relationships, Development and Constancy With Reference to Their Relation to School Achievement.** Annals of the Academia Scientiarum Fennica, Series B, Vol. 104. Helsinki, Finland: Suomalainen Tiedeakatemia, Academia Scientiarum Fennica, 1956. Pp. 183.

For a review by J. A. Radcliffe, see 6:B499.

P870. WAGONER, LOVISA C. **Observation of Young Children.** New York: McGraw-Hill Book Co., Inc., 1935. Pp. ix, 297.

For reviews by D. McCarthy and one other, see 1:B517; for reviews by A. G. Schmidt and one other, see 36:B275.

P871. WALDER, HANS. **Drive Structure and Criminality: Criminobiologic Investigations, Revised Edition.** Springfield, Ill.: Charles C Thomas, Publisher, 1959. Pp. xvii, 174.

For reviews by F. Ferracuti and Frederic Wertham, see 6:B501.

P872. WALKER, ALICE S. **Pupils' School Records: A Survey of the Nature and Use of Cumulative School Records in England and Wales.** National Foundation for Educational Research in England and Wales, Publication No. 8. London: Newnes Educational Publishing Co., Ltd., 1954. Pp. xviii, 199.

For reviews by R. R. Dale and one other, see 5:B451.

P873. WANDT, EDWIN, and BROWN, GERALD W. **Essentials of Educational Evaluation.** New York: Henry Holt & Co., Inc., 1957. Pp. 125.

For a review by Edith Jay, see 5:B454.

P874. WANG, CHARLES K. A. **An Annotated Bibliography of Mental Tests and Scales, Volumes I and II.** Publications of the College of Education, Catholic University of Peking, No. 1. Peiping, China: Catholic University Press, 1939, 1940. Pp. vi, 725; viii, 698.
For a review, see 3:1223; for reviews by John G. Darley, C. R. Myers, T. L. Torgerson, Guy M. Wilson, and two others of Volume I, see 3:1221; for reviews by A. Jean Brown and John G. Darley of Volume II, see 3:1222.

P875. WARBURTON, F. W. **The Selection of University Students.** Publications of the University of Manchester School of Education, No. 1. Manchester, England: University of Manchester Press, 1952. Pp. vii, 46.
For reviews by A. H. D. Tozer and one other, see 5:B457.

P876. WARNER, W. LLOYD; with MARCHIA MEEKER and KENNETH EELLS. **Social Class in America: A Manual of Procedures for the Measurement of Social Status.** New York: Harper & Row, Publishers, Inc., 1960. Pp. xiii, 298.
For reviews by Harold Goldstein, Manson Van B. Jennings, E. Lowell Kelly, and one other, see 4:B409.

P877. WATERMAN, ALAN TOWER, and STALNAKER, JOHN MARSHALL. **Report on the Physics Examination of June 1938: A Description of the Procedures Used in Preparing and Reading the Examination in Physics and an Analysis of the Results of the Reading.** New York: College Entrance Examination Board, 1939. Pp. iii, 43.
For a review by Austin G. Schmidt, see 2:B1118.

P878. WATKINS, JOHN GOODRICH. **Objective Measurement of Instrumental Performance.** Columbia University, Teachers College, Contributions to Education, No. 860. New York: Bureau of Publications, the College, 1942. Pp. x, 98.
For reviews by Alvin W. Ahrens, Louis Cheslock, Abraham Pepinsky, and M. Emett Wilson, see 3:1228.

P879. WATTS, A. F. **Can We Measure Ability?** London: University of London Press Ltd., 1953. Pp. 80.
For a review, see 5:B459.

P880. WATTS, A. F., and SLATER, PATRICK. **The Allocation of Primary School Leavers to Courses of Secondary Education: First Interim Report.** National Foundation for Educational Research in England and Wales, Publication No. 2. London: Newnes Educational Publishing Co., Ltd., 1950. Pp. 68.
For reviews by M. Brearley, P. E. Vernon, and one other, see 4:B411.

P881. WATTS, A. F.; PIDGEON, D. A.; and YATES, A. **Secondary School Entrance Examinations: A Study of Some of the Factors Influencing Scores in Objective Tests With Particular Reference to Coaching and Practice: Second Interim Report on the Allocation of Primary School Leavers to Courses of Secondary Education.** National Foundation for Educational Research in England and Wales, Publication No. 6. London: Newnes Educational Publishing Co., Ltd., 1952. Pp. 77.
For two reviews, see 5:B460.

P882. WEBB, L. W., and SHOTWELL, ANNA MARKT. **Testing in the Elementary School.** New York: Farrar & Rinehart, Inc., 1939. Pp. xix, 407.
For reviews by C. W. Odell, Austin G. Schmidt, and J. Wayne Wrightstone, see 2:B1119.

P883. WECHSLER, DAVID. **The Measurement and Appraisal of Adult Intelligence, Fourth Edition.** Baltimore, Md.: Williams & Wilkins Co., 1958. Pp. ix, 300.
For reviews by William D. Altus, Philip S. Holzman, and Read D. Tuddenham, see 6:B503; for reviews by Alfred L. Baldwin, Edward E. Cureton, Clinton P. McCord, Emily L. Stogdill, Charles L. Vaughn, and one other of an earlier edition, see 3:299; for reviews by Anne Anastasi, Irving Lorge, B. D. Misselbrook, Winifred Richmond, Henriette Woolf, J. Wayne Wrightstone, and one other, see 3:300; for reviews by Quinn McNemar, Ann Magaret, Irma Stark, C. Hart Westbrook, and one other, see 3:301; for reviews by Grace H. Kent and one other, see 2:1429; for reviews by C. R. Atwell, Walter V. Clarke, Isabelle Kendig, George Lawton, Milton M. Parker, Wm. Reitz, Austin G. Schmidt, Frank K. Shuttleworth, W. A. Varvel, and one other, see 2:B1121.

P884. WECHSLER, DAVID. **The Range of Human Capacities.** Baltimore, Md.: Williams & Wilkins Co., 1935. Pp. ix, 159.
For reviews by Edward Girden, Edward A. Lincoln, Helen Peak, Frank K. Shuttleworth, and six others, see 2:B1122.

P885. WEISENBURG, THEODORE; ROE, ANNE; and McBRIDE, KATHERINE E. **Adult Intelligence: A Psychological Study of Test Performances.** New York: Commonwealth Fund, 1936. Pp. xii, 155.
For reviews by M. R. Fernald, H. M. Johnson, W. Line, D. G. Paterson, and two others, see 1:B519; for reviews by L. W. Jones, J. C. Peterson, A. G. Schmidt, and three others, see 36:B281.

P886. WEISLOGEL, MARY H.; KOLOVOS, ERNEST R.; and RIGBY, MARILYN K. **The Development of a Test for Selecting Research Personnel.** Pittsburgh, Pa.: American Institute for Research, 1950. Pp. vi, 33.
For a review by John G. Darley, see 4:B413.

P887. WEITZMAN, ELLIS, and McNAMARA, WALTER J. **Constructing Classroom Examinations: A Guide for Teachers.** Chicago, Ill.: Science Research Associates, Inc., 1949. Pp. xvi, 153.
For reviews by Walter W. Cook and one other, see 4:B414.

P888. WELCH, JOSEPHINE S., and STONE, C. HAROLD. **How to Build a Merchandise Knowledge Test.** University of Minnesota, Industrial Relations Center, Research and Technical Report 8. Dubuque, Iowa: Wm. C. Brown Co., 1952. Pp. vi, 21.
For a review by Edwin E. Ghiselli, see 5:B465.

P889. WELLMAN, BETH L. **The Intelligence of Preschool Children as Measured by the Merrill-Palmer Scale of Performance Tests.** University of Iowa Studies, Studies in Child Welfare, Vol. 15, No. 3, New Series, No. 361. Iowa City, Iowa: University of Iowa Press, 1938. Pp. 150.
For a review by Barbara S. Burks, see 3:1234; for reviews by S. J. Beck, Barbara S. Burks, W. Line, Austin G. Schmidt, and one other, see 2:B1123.

P890. WELLS, F. L., and RUESCH, JURGEN. **Mental Examiners' Handbook, Revised Edition.** New York: Psychological Corporation, 1945. Pp. vii, 211.
For a review by Paul E. Meehl, see 3:1237; for reviews by Elizabeth Gifford Bull and one other of an earlier edition, see 3:1236.

P891. WELSH, GEORGE SCHLAGER, and DAHLSTROM, W. GRANT, Editors. **Basic Readings on the MMPI**

in Psychology and Medicine. Minneapolis, Minn.: University of Minnesota Press, 1956. Pp. xvii, 656.

For reviews by Irwin A. Berg, Lee J. Cronbach, Charles McArthur, George A. Talland, Richard H. Walters, and Frederick A. Zehrer, see 5:B467.

P892. WERNICK, ROBERT. They've Got Your Number. New York: W. W. Norton & Co., Inc., 1956. Pp. 124.

For reviews by H. J. Sheffield and one other, see 5:B469.

P893. WEST, JOE YOUNG. A Technique for Appraising Certain Observable Behavior of Children in Science in Elementary Schools. Columbia University, Teachers College, Contributions to Education No. 728. New York: Bureau of Publications, the College, 1937. Pp. vii, 118.

For reviews by Clarence M. Pruitt, Mabel E. Rugen, and J. Wayne Wrightstone, see 2:B1124; for reviews by C. M. Pruitt and A. G. Schmidt, see 1:B520.

P894. WHILDE, NOEL E. The Application of Psychological Tests in Schools. London: Blackie & Son Ltd., 1955. Pp. xi, 179.

For reviews by Stephen Wiseman and one other, see 5:B477.

P895. WHISLER, THOMAS L., and HARPER, SHIRLEY F., Editors. Performance Appraisal: Research and Practice. New York: Holt, Rinehart & Winston, Inc., 1962. Pp. xiii, 593.

For a review by Wayne K. Kirchner, see 6:B514.

P896. WHITCRAFT, LESLIE H. Some Influences of the Requirements and Examinations of the College Entrance Examinations of the College Entrance Examination Board on Mathematics in Secondary Schools in the United States. Columbia University, Teachers College, Contributions to Education No. 557. New York: Bureau of Publications, the College, 1933. Pp. 115.

For reviews by V. Sanford and G. M. Wilson, see 1:B522; for reviews by E. R. Breslich and D. F. Van Bramer, see 36:B283.

P897. WICKERT, FREDERIC, Editor. Psychological Research on Problems of Redistribution. Army Air Forces Psychology Program Research Reports, Report No. 14. Washington, D.C.: U.S. Government Printing Office, 1947. Pp. vii, 298.

For reviews by Donald E. Baier and Laurance F. Shaffer, see 4:B419. For a review of the series, see P1.

P898. WIGHTWICK, M. IRENE. Vocational Interest Patterns: A Developmental Study of a Group of College Women. Columbia University, Teachers College, Contributions to Education, No. 900. New York: Bureau of Publications, the College, 1945. Pp. vii, 231.

For reviews by Barbara Mayer Kirchheimer and Isabel K. Wallace, see 3:1240.

P899. WILEY, GEORGE M. The Changing Function of Regents Examinations. University of the State of New York Bulletin, No. 1114. Albany, N.Y.: University of the State of New York Press, 1937. Pp. 29.

For a review by A. G. Schmidt, see 1:B523.

P900. WILLIAMS, G. PERRIE. The Northamptonshire Composition Scale. London: George G. Harrap & Co., Ltd., 1933. Pp. 136.

For reviews by K. R. Cunningham and P. C. Mahalanobis, see 1:B524; for a review, see 36:B284.

P901. WILLIAMS, HAROLD M.; SIEVERS, CLEMENT H.; and HATTWICK, MELVIN S. Measurement of Musical Development. University of Iowa Studies, New Series, No. 243; Studies in Child Welfare, Vol. 7, No. 1. Iowa City, Iowa: the University, 1933. Pp. 192.

For reviews by R. W. Cullen, F. L. Goodenough, J. A. Leeder, and one other, see 36:B285.

P902. WILLIAMSON, E. G. The University Testing Bureau: A Manual of Staff Procedures. University of Minnesota. Minneapolis, Minn.: Engineers Book Store, 1936. Pp. vi, 50.

For a review by W. H. Cowley, see 36:B287.

P903. WING, HERBERT. Tests of Musical Ability and Appreciation: An Investigation Into the Measurement, Distribution, and Development of Musical Capacity. British Journal of Psychology Monograph Supplements, Vol. 8, No. 27. London: Cambridge University Press, 1948. Pp. vii, 88.

For reviews by C. Burt, P. E. Vernon, and three others, see 4:231.

P904. WISEMAN, STEPHEN, Editor. Examinations and English Education. Manchester, England: Manchester University Press, 1961. Pp. xx, 188.

For a review by James Maxwell, see 6:B517.

P905. WOLF, RALPH ROBINSON, JR. Differential Forecasts of Achievement and Their Use in Educational Counseling. American Psychological Association, Psychological Monographs, Vol. 51, No. 1, Whole No. 227. Washington, D.C.: the Association, Inc., 1939. Pp. v, 53.

For a review by Walter W. Cook, see 3:1242; for a review by Austin G. Schmidt, see 2:B1132.

P906. WOLF, WILLIAM B. Merit Rating as a Managerial Tool: A Simplified Approach to Merit Rating. Seattle, Wash.: Bureau of Business Research, College of Business Administration, University of Washington, 1958. Pp. ix, 91.

For a review by B. L. White, see 6:B518.

P907. WOLFF, CHARLOTTE. The Hand in Psychological Diagnosis. London: Methuen & Co. Ltd., 1951. Pp. xv, 218.

For reviews by William A. Hunt, F. K. Taylor, P. H. C. Tibout, and one other, see 5:B480.

P908. WOLFF, CHARLOTTE. The Human Hand. New York: Alfred A. Knopf, Inc., 1942. Pp. xvii, 198, vi, 26 pl.

For reviews by Marjory Brierley, A. N. Foxe, K. Goldstein, Theophile Raphael, and one other, see 3:1243.

P909. WOLFF, WERNER. Diagrams of the Unconscious: Handwriting and Personality in Measurement, Experiment and Analysis. New York: Grune & Stratton, Inc., 1948. Pp. xiv, 423.

For reviews by Paul Bergman, Fred Y. Billingslea, Herbert Boehm, Wladimir Eliasberg, Joseph C. Franklin, Gerald R. Pascal, Laurance F. Shaffer, Joseph Zubin, and two others, see 4:B422.

P910. WOLFF, WERNER. The Expression of Personality: Experimental Depth Psychology. New York: Harper & Brothers, 1943. Pp. xiv, 334.

For reviews by Arthur N. Foxe, Arnold Gesell, Carl M. Herold, Max Meenes, Frank K. Shuttleworth, Percival M. Symonds, Heinz Werner, and two others, see 3:1244.

P911. WOLFF, WERNER. The Personality of the Preschool Child: The Child's Search for His Self. New York: Grune & Stratton, Inc., 1946. Pp. xvi, 341.

For a review, see 3:1245.

P912. WOLFSON, ROSE. **A Study in Handwriting Analysis.** New York: the Author, 1949. Pp. xii, 97. For a review by Laurance F. Shaffer, see 4:B424.

P913. WOMER, FRANK B. **Testing Programs in Michigan Schools.** A study conducted by the Testing and Guidance Committee, Michigan Association of Secondary School Principals. The University of Michigan Official Publication, Vol. 60, No. 137. Ann Arbor, Mich.: Bureau of School Services, the University, 1959. Pp. vii, 62. For a review by Thomas M. Magoon, see 6:B520.

P914. WOOD, BEN D., and HAEFNER, RALPH. **Measuring and Guiding Individual Growth.** New York: Silver Burdett Co., 1948. Pp. viii, 535. For reviews by Gertrude Boyd, William W. Brickman, Burton P. Fowler, Earl R. Gabler, Adah Gould, and Eleanor Volberding, see 4:B425.

P915. WOOD, DOROTHY ADKINS. **Test Construction: Development and Interpretation of Achievement Tests.** Columbus, Ohio: Charles E. Merrill Books, Inc., 1960. Pp. ix, 134. For reviews by Jerome E. Doppelt, Elizabeth Hagen, and one other, see 6:B521.

P916. WOODSIDE, C. W., and WANOUS, S. J. **Bibliography of Tests and Testing in Business Subjects.** Cincinnati, Ohio: South-Western Publishing Co., 1939. Pp. 36. For a review, see 2:B1133.

P917. WOODY, CLIFFORD. **Sophomore Testing Program in the Accredited High Schools of Michigan, 1936.** University of Michigan, School of Education, Bureau of Educational Reference and Research, Bulletin No. 148, Ann Arbor, Mich.: the School, 1936. Pp. 95. For a review by F. P. Frutchey, see 2:B1135; for reviews by A. G. Schmidt and one other, see 36:B290.

P918. WRIGHT, WENDELL W. **Reading Readiness: A Prognostic Study.** Bulletin of the School of Education, Indiana University, Vol. 12, No. 3. Bloomington, Ind.: University Bookstore, 1936. Pp. 46. For a review by A. G. Schmidt, see 1:B527; for reviews by W. McAndrew, K. L. McLaughlin, and two others, see 36:B291.

P919. WRIGHT, WENDELL W. **Visual Outline of Educational Tests and Measurements.** New York: Longmans, Green & Co., Inc., 1937. Pp. iii, 99. For a review by A. G. Schmidt, see 1:B528.

P920. WRIGHTSTONE, J. WAYNE; JUSTMAN, JOSEPH; and ROBBINS, IRVING. **Evaluation in Modern Education.** New York: American Book Co., 1956. Pp. xiii, 481. For a review by James C. Reed, see 5:B483.

P921. WRINKLE, WILLIAM L. **Improving Marking and Reporting Practices in Elementary and Secondary Schools.** New York: Rinehart & Co., Inc., 1947. Pp. v, 120. For reviews by A. S. Edwards, Earl R. Gabler, Warren E. Gauerke, Sara M. Krentzman, Walter L. Wilkins, and Wayne Wrightstone, see 4:B426.

P922. YOUNG, MICHAEL. **The Rise of the Meritocracy 1870–2033: An Essay on Education and Equality.** London: Thames & Hudson, Ltd., 1958. Pp. 160. For a review by Harry Laurent, see 6:B523.

P923. YUZUK, RONALD PAUL. **The Assessment of Employee Morale: A Comparison of Two Measures.** Ohio State University, College of Commerce and Administration, Ohio Studies in Personnel, Bureau of Business Research Monograph No. 99. Columbus, Ohio: the Bureau, 1961. Pp. ix, 67. For a review by V. J. Bentz, see 6:B524.

P924. ZANDER, ALVIN F., Editor. **Performance Appraisals: Effects on Employees and Their Performance.** Ann Arbor, Mich.: Foundation for Research on Human Behavior, 1963. Pp. ii, 64. For a review by Carl J. Kujawski, see 6:B525.

P925. ZUBIN, JOSEPH, and THOMPSON, JANE. **Sorting Tests in Relation to Drug Therapy in Schizophrenia.** New York: New York State Psychiatric Institute, 1941. Pp. v, 23. For a review, see 3:1253.

P926. ZULLIGER, HANS. **Behn-Rorschach Test: Text.** Berne, Switzerland: Hans Huber, 1956. Pp. 200. For reviews by Murray Levine and Horst Rodies, see 6:B526.

P927.[1] ZULLIGER, HANS. **Einführung in den Behn-Rorschach Test.** Berne, Switzerland: Verlag Hans Huber, 1941. Pp. 232. For a review, see 3:91.

---

[1] Because of an unused number (414), the total number of books is 926.

APA-AERA-NCME Standards

IT HAS been a long uphill struggle trying to persuade test authors and publishers to report more adequate data on the construction, use, and validity of their tests. In 1925, a well-known testing specialist and author of numerous tests, Giles M. Ruch, severely criticized test authors and publishers for not providing sufficient information to permit test users and test specialists to choose tests wisely. He urged that action be taken at once to establish working criteria for test construction and that uniform practices in reporting on tests be adopted by all concerned—test users, test authors, and test publishers. Ruch proposed that this information should be preferably reported in the test manuals which he said might well be expanded to one hundred pages.[1] Unfortunately, Ruch's criticisms and suggestions appeared to have little or no effect upon test authors and publishers.

When the *Mental Measurements Yearbooks* began publication in 1938, one of the objectives of the series was to impel test authors and publishers "to provide test users with detailed and accurate information on the construction, validation, uses, and limitations of their tests at the time they are first placed on the market."[2] Some progress toward improving test manuals probably resulted from the publication of the MMY's, but to the editor it seems that it was discouragingly small.

A big step forward was taken in 1954 and 1955 with the publication of two small monographs prepared jointly by three professional organizations in education and psychology:

American Psychological Association, American Educational Research Association, and National Council on Measurements Used in Education. *Technical Recommendations for Psychological Tests and Diagnostic Techniques* was published in 1954.[3] *Technical Recommendations for Achievement Tests* was published in 1955.[4] The scope of these monographs is much narrower than implied by the titles. Both publications would have been more accurately described by titles similar to the title of Ruch's 1925 article, "Minimum Essentials in Reporting Data on Standard Tests." Nevertheless, the Technical Recommendations were rightly acclaimed as a landmark in the history of testing. Very few readers of the Recommendations were aware that these reports appeared twenty-nine years after Ruch had urged that similar publications be prepared "at once." A generation of progress!

The objectives of the Technical Recommendations may be summarized by the following excerpts from the 1954 monograph:

> The test producer....has the task of providing sufficient information about each test so that users will know what reliance can safely be placed on it. * test manuals and associated aids to test usage should be made complete, comprehensible, and unambiguous * *The essential principle that sets the tone for this document is that a test manual should carry information*

[1] RUCH, GILES M. "Minimum Essentials in Reporting Data on Standard Tests." *J Ed Res* 12:349–58 D '25. *
[2] *The 1940 Mental Measurements Yearbook*, p. xviii.
[3] *Technical Recommendations for Psychological Tests and Diagnostic Techniques.* Prepared by a Joint Committee of the American Psychological Association, American Educational Research Association, and National Council on Measurements Used in Education. Supplement to the *Psychological Bulletin*, Vol. 51, No. 2, March 1954. Washington, D.C.: American Psychological Association, Inc., March 1954. Pp. ii, 38. (Reprinted in *Tests in Print*.)
[4] *Technical Recommendations for Achievement Tests.* Prepared by the Committees on Test Standards of the American Educational Research Association and the National Council on Measurements Used in Education. Washington, D.C.: American Educational Research Association, 1955. Pp. 36. (Reprinted in *Tests in Print*.)

sufficient to enable any qualified user to make sound judgments regarding the usefulness and interpretation of the test. This means that certain research is required prior to release of a test for general use by psychologists or school personnel. The results must be reported or summarized in the manual, and the manual must help the reader to interpret these results. A manual is to be judged not merely by its literal truthfulness, but by the impression it leaves with the reader. * It is not appropriate to call for a particular level of validity and reliability, or to otherwise specify the nature of the test. It _is_ appropriate to ask that the manual give the information necessary for the user to decide whether the accuracy, relevance, or standardization of the test makes it suitable for his purposes. These recommendations, then, suggest standards of _test description and reporting_ without stating minimum statistical specifications.

There can be no question but that the Technical Recommendations have had an important influence for the good. As a result, most test authors and publishers are now reporting more adequate information. The improvement in a manual, however, does not mean that the test has necessarily been improved. A test may have a manual which, relative to other tests, does a fairly good job of reporting the information recommended by these reports and yet the test may be worthless. The information presented in the manual must still be evaluated.

Within six or seven years after the publication of the Technical Recommendations, the three cooperating associations set up new committees to revise the reports. The revised report, _Standards for Educational and Psychological Tests and Manuals_,[5] was published in 1966, twelve years after the publication of the first report. The Standards have the same objectives and character as the original reports. Most testing specialists will find themselves in disagreement with some of the proposed standards. Most of the recommendations were supported by all members of the eight-man Committee; but other recommendations represent compromises or majority opinions of the Committee. (The writer was a member of the Committee.) Nevertheless, the report is an important document which should be widely read by test users. In order to make the Standards more easily accessible, they are reprinted here with the permission of the publisher, the American Psychological Association. Certainly, every serious user of _Personality Tests and Reviews_ should consider the APA-AERA-NCME Standards must reading.

[5] _Standards for Educational and Psychological Tests and Manuals._ Prepared by a Joint Committee of the American Psychological Association, American Educational Research Association, and National Council on Measurement in Education. John W. French and William B. Michael, Cochairmen. Washington, D.C.: American Psychological Association, Inc., 1966. Pp. iii, 40.

STANDARDS FOR EDUCATIONAL AND PSYCHOLOGICAL TESTS AND MANUALS

FOREWORD

Standards for Educational and Psychological Tests and Manuals has been approved by the governing bodies of the American Psychological Association (APA), the American Educational Research Association (AERA), and the National Council on Measurement in Education (NCME). The current statement constitutes a revision of two documents: (_a_) _Technical Recommendations for Psychological Tests and Diagnostic Techniques_ which was prepared by a committee of the APA and published in March 1954 by this organization, and (_b_) _Technical Recommendations for Achievement Tests_ which was put together by two committees of the AERA and the National Council on Measurements Used in Education (now known as the National Council on Measurement in Edu-

cation—NCME) and issued under a January 1955, copyright by the National Education Association. An APA committee and a combined AERA-NCME committee were consolidated in late 1963 into one truly joint APA-AERA-NCME committee of eight members that worked as one body in the formulation of the present technical standards.

In the main, the same format and style of presentation have been employed in the new document as in the two earlier reports. Additional details underlying the points of view and positions taken by the joint committee in the preparation of the new version of test standards may be found in the first section titled "Development and Scope of the Standards."

Many of the statements presented in this report reflect substantial revisions of the original statements in the two earlier documents. These revisions have been based on written comments of measurement specialists including test publishers who were invited to submit criticisms on both oral and written comments communicated by participants at several open meetings held at the annual conventions of the three cooperating professional organizations, and on the collaborative efforts of the committee members who participated in numerous formal and informal working sessions.

During the period of preparation which lasted over 5 years, the membership of the APA Committee on Test Standards changed from time to time. Grateful acknowledgment is made to the former members of several APA committees on test standards who made valuable suggestions regarding modifications in the 1954 APA document. In particular, appreciation is expressed to Jane Loevinger, Warren Norman, John T. Cowles, and Edward E. Cureton, among several others whose significant ideas substantially influenced the thinking of the members of the current joint committee. Credit is due Gordon MacDonald Mather, III for work on the index. Finally, thanks are extended to the membership of each of the three participating professional organizations for their continued interest in and support of the work of the committee members.

> John W. French, Cochairman
>   Committee on Test Standards, APA
> William B. Michael, Cochairman
>   Committee on Test Standards, AERA-NCME
> Oscar K. Buros
> Herbert S. Conrad
> Lee J. Cronbach
> Max D. Engelhart
> J. Raymond Gerberich
> Willard G. Warrington

DEVELOPMENT AND SCOPE

This revised statement of technical recommendations, now to be called standards, for psychological and educational tests represents an effort, in purpose and scope, similar to that underlying the preparation of both the *Technical Recommendations for Psychological Tests and Diagnostic Techniques* issued in March 1954 by the American Psychological Association and the *Technical Recommendations for Achievement Tests* prepared through the joint efforts of two committees on test standards of the American Educational Research Association and the National Council on Measurement

in Education and published in January 1955. In view of the similarity in the nature of many (but not all) problems in both educational and psychological measurement, the joint committees representing all of these organizations decided that it was advantageous to issue one set of standards to cover both educational and psychological tests. The basic structure and format of the first report have been retained. However, many of the recommendations and standards have been substantially modified; others have been dropped; a few new ones have been added. Despite changes in psychological points of view in the theoretical and technical phases of educational and psychological measurement, the principal subdivisions for classifying types of standards still appeared to be sufficiently intact in current testing practices to be retained.

Psychological and educational tests are used in arriving at decisions which may have great influence on the ultimate welfare of the persons tested, on educational points of view and practices, and on development and utilization of human resources. Test users, therefore, need to apply high standards of professional judgment in selecting and interpreting tests, and test producers are under obligation to produce tests which can be of the greatest possible service. The test producer, in particular, has the task of providing sufficient information about each test so that the users will know what reliance can safely be placed on it.

Professional workers agree that test manuals and associated aids to test users should be made complete, comprehensive, and unambiguous, and for this reason there have always been informal "test standards." Publishers and authors of tests have adopted standards for themselves, and standards have been proposed in textbooks and other publications. Through application of these standards, the best tests have attained a high degree of quality and usefulness.

Until 1954, however, there was no statement representing a consensus concerning what information is most helpful to the test consumer. In the absence of such a guide, it was inevitable that some tests did appear with less adequate supporting information than did others of the same type, and that facts about a test which some users regarded as indispensable had not been reported because they seemed to the test producer to be relatively unimportant or, perhaps, too revealing of a weakness in the test. The first report was the outcome of an attempt to survey the possible types of information that test producers might make available, to indicate roughly the relative importance of each type of information, and to make recommendations regarding test preparation and publication.

This second report brings the first ones up to date and takes account of 12 years of progress and of the helpful criticisms of many test publishers and users. Questionnaires and letters of inquiry were sent to professional and research workers in the area of educational and psychological measurement, and several open committee meetings and invitational conferences were held. The current report contains many of the suggestions made by scores of interested people —test authors, test publishers, research workers, college teachers of measurement, and public school personnel including counselors, administrators, curriculum coordinators, and teachers. The particular biases of the committee members are obviously present, although a conscientious effort was made to take a position, in use of technical vocabulary and statistical methodology, in harmony with the practices of the majority of research and professional personnel in the field of testing.

In 1966 as well as in 1954, issuing specifications for tests could indeed discourage the development of new types of tests. So many different sorts of tests are needed in present educational and psychological practice that limiting the kind or the specifications would not be sound procedure. Appropriate standardization of tests and manuals, however, need not interfere with innovation. One purpose of the revised recommendations presented here is to assist test producers in bringing out a wide variety of tests that will be suitable for all the different purposes for which tests should be used, and to make those tests as valuable as possible.

Information Standards as a Guide to Producers and Users of Tests

As in the two previous sets of recommendations *the essential* principle underlying this document is that a test manual should carry information sufficient to enable any qualified user to make sound judgments regarding the usefulness and interpretation of the test. This goal means that certain research is required prior to release of a test for general use by psychologists or school personnel. The results should be reported or summarized in the manual, and the manual should help the reader to interpret these results.

A manual is to be judged not merely by its literal truthfulness, but by the impression it leaves with the reader. If the typical professional user is likely to obtain an inaccurate impression of the test from the manual, the manual is poorly written. Ideally, manuals would be tested in the field by comparing the conclusions of a group of typical readers with the judgment of measurement specialists regarding the test. In the absence of such trials, the standards proposed are intended to apply to the spirit and tone of the manual as well as to its literal statements.

A manual must often communicate information to many different groups. Many tests are used by classroom teachers or psychometrists with very limited training in testing. These users will not follow technical discussion or understand detailed statistical information. At the other extreme of the group of readers, the available information about any test should be sufficiently complete for specialists in the area to judge the technical adequacy of the test. Sometimes the more technical information can be presented in a supplementary handbook, but it is most important that there be made available to the person concerned with the test a sound basis for whatever judgments his duties require.

Although it is not appropriate to call for a particular level of validity and reliability, or otherwise to specify the nature of the test, it *is* appropriate to ask that the manual give the information necessary for the user to decide whether the accuracy, relevance, or standardization of the test makes it suitable for his purposes. *These standards of test description and reporting exist without a statement of minimum statistical specifications.*

The aim of the present standards is partly to make the requirements as to information accompanying published tests explicit and conveniently available. In arriving at those requirements, it has been necessary to judge what is presently the reasonable degree of compromise between pressures of cost and time, on the one hand, and the ideal, on the other. The test producer ordinarily spends large sums of money in developing and standardizing a test. Insofar as these recommendations indicate the kind of information that would be most valuable to the people who use tests, test authors and publishers can allocate their funds to gathering and reporting those data. The completion of predictive validity studies related to job criteria, for example, is essential before a vocational interest inventory can be used practically, but they are only a desirable addition for a values inventory and irrelevant for an inventory designed to diagnose mental disorders. These standards, therefore, represent an attempt to state what type of studies should be completed before a test is ready for release to the profession for operational use. They are already reached by many of the better tests.

Tests to Which the Standards Apply

These recommended standards cover not only tests as narrowly defined, but also most *published* devices for diagnosis, prognosis, and evaluation. The standards apply to interest inventories, personality inventories, projective instruments and related clinical techniques, tests of aptitude or ability, and achievement tests— especially those in an educational setting. The same general types of information are needed for all these varieties of tests. General recommendations have been prepared with all these techniques and instruments in mind. Since each type of test presents certain special requirements, additional comments have been made to indicate specific applications of the standards to particular tests or techniques. Many principles of specific importance in measurement of achievement have been cited.

Tests can be arranged according to degree of development. The highest degree of development is needed for tests distributed for use in practical situations where the user is unlikely to carry out validity studies for himself. Such a user must assume that the test does measure what it is presumed to measure on the basis of its title and manual. For instance, if a clerical aptitude measure is used in vocational guidance under the assumption that this will predict success in office jobs, there is very little possibility that the counselor could himself determine the validity of the test for the wide range of office jobs to which his clients might go.

At the other extreme of the continuum are tests in the very beginning stages of their development. At this point, perhaps the investigator is not sure whether his test is measuring any useful variable. Sometimes, because the theory for interpreting the test is undeveloped,

the author can restrict use of the test to situations where he himself knows the persons who will use the test, can personally caution them as to its limitations, and can use the research from these trials as a way of improving the test or the information about it.

Between these tests which are so to speak embryonic and the tests which are released for practical application without local validity studies, are tests released for somewhat restricted use. There are many tests which have been examined sufficiently to indicate that they will probably be useful tools for psychologists, but which are released with the expectation that the user will verify suggested clinical interpretations by studying the subsequent behavior of persons in treatment. Examples are certain tests of spatial ability, and some inventories measuring such traits as introversion.

The present standards apply to devices which are distributed for use as a basis for practical judgments rather than solely for research. Most tests which are made available for use in schools, clinics, and industry are of this practical nature. Tests released for operational use should be prepared with the greatest care. They should be released to the general user only after their developer has gathered information which will permit the users to know for what purpose the test can be trusted. These statements regarding recommended information apply with especial force to tests distributed to users who have only that information which is provided in the test manual and other accessories. In the preparation of the standards, no attention was paid to tests which are privately distributed and circulated only to specially trained users. The standards also do not apply to tests presented in journal articles, unless the articles are intended to fulfill the functions of a manual.

A brief discussion of problems of projective techniques is needed here because of the opinion occasionally voiced that these devices are so unlike other testing procedures that they cannot be judged according to the same standards. Many users of projective devices aim at idiographic analysis of an individual. Since this kind of analytical thinking places heavy reliance on the creative, artistic activity of the clinician, not all of this process can be covered in test standards. That is, the recommendations herein presented are necessarily of a psychometric nature and should not be interpreted as necessarily applying to all users of projective techniques. Nevertheless, proposals for arriving at such unique idiographic interpretations are almost always partially based upon some nomothetic premises, for example, that a Rorschach determinant tends to correlate with a specified internal factor. There is no justification for failure to apply the usual standards in connection with premises of this kind. Therefore, although these devices present unusual problems, the user of projective techniques requires much of the same information that is needed by users of other tests.

Even though the data from projective tests are more often qualitative than quantitative, these devices should be accompanied by appropriate evidence on validity, reliability, and standards of scoring and interpretation. A projective test author need not identify his test's validity by correlating it with any simple criterion. But if he goes so far as to make any generalization about what "most people see" or what "schizophrenics rarely do," he is making an out-and-out statistical claim and should be held to the usual rules for supporting it. Obviously, when quantitative information is asked for in the standards, it is expected to apply where a quantitative kind of claim has been made. If a projective test makes no such claim, a quantitative standard would not be meaningful for it.

On the other hand, clinicians sometimes forget that the words "more," "usual," "typical," and the like are *quantity* words. Any textual discourse containing such words, or any verbal statement describing a correspondence between test performance and personality structure is making a quantitative claim. The only difference between such a verbal statement and a statistical table is the relative exactness of the latter. For this reason, many of the standards apply to aspects of projective instruments for which verbal rather than numerical interpretations are suggested.

Many comments have been made to amplify and illustrate the standards. To avoid the possible charge of showing undue favoritism or negativism toward particular tests or publishers, the Committee decided *not* to mention the names of specific tests as being examples of good or poor practice (as has been done in the first report). Instead, examples of what was judged to be desirable or undesirable practices were taken from existing test manuals in such a manner as not to identify a particular test or publisher. It is hoped that these examples will help to clarify ways in which the standards apply to practical problems concerning interpretation and use of test data.

Three Levels of Standards

Manuals can never give all the information that might be desirable, because of economic limitations. At the same time, restricting this statement of recommendations solely to essential or indispensable information might tend to discourage reporting of additional information. To avoid curtailment of the presentation of information in test manuals, recommendations are grouped in three levels: ESSENTIAL, VERY DESIRABLE, and DESIRABLE. Each proposed requirement is judged in the light of its importance and the feasibility of attaining it.

The statements listed as ESSENTIAL are intended to represent the consensus of present-day thinking concerning what is normally required for operational use of a test. Any test presents some unique problems, and it is undesirable that standards should bind the producer of a novel test to an inappropriate procedure or form of reporting. The ESSENTIAL standards indicate what information will be needed for most tests in their usual applications. When a test producer fails to satisfy this need, he should do so only as a considered judgment. In any single test, there may be some ESSENTIAL standards which do not apply.

If some type of ESSENTIAL information is not available on a given test, it is important to help the reader recognize that the research on the test is incomplete in this respect. A test manual can satisfy all the ESSENTIAL standards by clear statements of what research has been done and by avoidance of misleading statements. It will not be necessary to perform much additional research to satisfy the standards, but only to discuss the test so that the reader fully understands what is known (and unknown) about it.

The category VERY DESIRABLE is used to draw attention to types of information which contribute greatly to the user's understanding of the test. They have not been listed as ESSENTIAL for various reasons. For example, if it is very difficult to acquire information (e.g., long-term follow-up), such information cannot always be expected to accompany the test. However, the information is still very desirable, since many users wish it, but it is not classed as ESSENTIAL so long as its usefulness is debated.

The category DESIRABLE includes information which would be helpful, but less so than the ESSENTIAL and VERY DESIRABLE information. Test users welcome any information of this type the producer offers.

When a test is widely used, the producer has a greater responsibility for investigating it thoroughly and providing more extensive reports than when the test is limited or restricted in its use. The large sale of such tests makes such research financially possible. Therefore, the producer of a popular test can add more of the VERY DESIRABLE and DESIRABLE information in subsequent editions of the manual. For tests having limited sale, it is unreasonable to expect that as much of these two categories of information will be furnished. In making such facts available, the producer performs a service beyond the level that can reasonably be anticipated for most tests at this time.

THE AUDIENCE FOR THESE STANDARDS

These standards are intended to guide test development and reporting. A great deal of the information to be reported about tests is technical, and therefore the wording of the standards is of necessity technical. They should be meaningful to readers who have training approximately equivalent to a level between the master's degree and the doctorate in education or psychology at a superior institution of higher learning. It would be reasonable to expect that for most readers at least two and perhaps three courses in measurement have been taken along with at least two semesters of statistical methods.

One audience for the standards is the authors and publishers who are responsible for test development. The standards should also aid the thinking of test users as well as of advanced students working either in psychology or education. It is not expected that the classroom teacher who has not had a course in tests and measurements will himself use this report. The report should, however, be helpful to directors of research, school psychologists, counselors, supervisors, and administrators who select tests to use for various school purposes.

As an aid to test development, the standards provide a kind of checklist of factors to be considered in designing the standardization and validation of tests. Test authors should refer to these standards in deciding what studies to

perform on their tests and how to report them in their manuals. Test publishers can use the standards in planning revision of their present tests. In considering proposed manuals, publishers can suggest to authors the types of information which need to be gathered in order to make the manual as serviceable as it should be. Because of the possibility of misunderstanding or misinterpretation, it would not be appropriate to state that a test manual "satisfies" or "follows" these standards. There would be no objection to a statement that an author has "attempted to take into account or considered" these standards in preparing the manual.

CAUTIONS TO BE EXERCISED IN USE OF STANDARDS

Almost any test can be useful for some functions and in some situations, but even the best test can have damaging consequences if used inappropriately. Therefore, primary responsibility for improvement of testing rests on the shoulders of test users. These standards should serve to extend the professional training of these users so that they will make better use of the information about tests and the tests themselves. The standards draw attention to recent developments in thinking about tests and test analysis. The report should serve as a reminder regarding features to be considered in choosing tests for a particular program.

It is not inconceivable that many test makers and test publishers could fulfill to a highly adequate degree most of the standards presented and still produce a test that would be virtually worthless from the standpoint of fulfilling its intended or stated objectives. In the instance of educational achievement tests such a risk can be great. Thus one might have access to a carefully standardized achievement test for which both estimates of reliability and comprehensiveness of norms would be judged quite satisfactory; yet the test might fail almost completely to duplicate or to reflect basic instructional objectives or specific outcomes of the teaching-learning process. Too frequently in educational measurement attention is restricted to criterion-related validity. Efforts should also be directed toward both the careful construction of tests around the content and process objectives furnished by a two-way grid and the use of the judgment of curricular specialists concerning what is highly valid in reflecting the desired outcomes of instruction.

Professional thinking about tests is much influenced by test reviews, textbooks on testing, and courses in measurement. These standards may be helpful in improving such aids, for instance, by suggesting features especially significant to examine in a test review. The standards can be a teaching aid in measurement courses. It is important to note that publication of superior information about tests by no means guarantees that tests will be used well. The continual improvement of courses which prepare test users and of leadership in all institutions using tests is a responsibility in which everyone must share.

THE STANDARDS

A. DISSEMINATION OF INFORMATION

The test user needs information to help him select the test that is most adequate for a given purpose, and most of that information must come from the test producer. The practices of authors and publishers in furnishing information have varied. With some tests, the user is offered directions for administering and scoring the test, norms of uncertain origin, and virtually nothing more. In contrast, other tests have manuals that furnish extensive information on their development, their validity and reliability, the bases for their norms, the kinds of interpretations that are appropriate, and the uses for which the tests can best be employed.

A1. When a test is published for operational use, it should be accompanied by a manual (or other published and readily available information) that makes every reasonable effort to follow the recommendations in this report. ESSENTIAL

[Comment: Not all the standards in this report will apply to any one particular test. A standard may be ignored if it is irrelevant in the light of the purpose of the test and the claims made for it, but it may not be ignored merely because it is difficult to meet or has not usually been met by similar tests.]

A1.1. If certain information needed to support interpretations suggested in the manual cannot be presented at the time the manual is published, the manual should satisfy the intent of standard A1 by pointing out the absence and importance of this information. ESSENTIAL

A1.2. Where the information is too extensive to be fully reported in the manual the ESSENTIAL information should be summarized and accompanied by references to other existing sources of information, such as technical supplements, articles, or books. VERY DESIRABLE

[Comment: Some well-known tests provide extensive technical manuals, make further research data available through the American Documentation Institute, or include relevant information in technical books which users are encouraged to consult. In other instances, only the ESSENTIAL information is given in the manual sold with the instrument, along with references to other useful sources.

Publications by persons other than the original author of the test frequently fulfill many functions of a manual. If a book about a test is designed to serve as a manual, its author and publisher have the same responsibility in preparing it as do the author and publisher of a test. Each edition of the manual should cite any highly pertinent works on the test by persons other than the original author. (See A2.1 and B3.3.)]

A1.21. When information about the test is provided by the author or publisher in a separate publication, that publication should meet the same standards of accuracy and freedom from misleading impressions as apply to the manual. ESSENTIAL

A1.22. Promotional material for a test should be accurate and complete and should not give the reader false impressions. ESSENTIAL

[Comment: Materials developed to present tests to prospective customers will, of necessity, mix some of the milder characteristics of commercial advertising with those of professional literature, but publishers must avoid using high-pressure advertising techniques. For example, a brochure describing an achievement battery makes the statement that this test "measures dependably what is being taught today." Such a statement may falsely suggest to the potential user that, without further examination, he can be sure the test is appropriate for his school.]

A2. The test and its manual should be revised at appropriate intervals. While no universal rule can be given, it would appear proper in most circumstances for the publisher to withdraw a test from the market, if the manual is 15 or more years old and no revision can be obtained. (See also C6.71.)

[Comment: Both the technical characteristics and the usefulness of a test change with such things as social conditions, job definitions, educational pressures, and the composition of relevant school populations. For example, changes in the objectives of programs of mathematics that place more emphasis on problem solving, systems development, and logical analysis and less emphasis on mechanical manipulations and computations reduce the value for many purposes of older tests of mathematical ability. Such drastic changes in curricular objectives require drastically revised tests.

Revisions are also important in the area of personality testing. The manual for one widely used instrument in this area has not been revised for nearly 30 years, even though extensive published research challenges statements made in that manual.]

A2.1. Competent studies of the test following its publication, whether the results are favorable or unfavorable to the test, should be taken into account in revised editions of the manual or its supplementary reports. Pertinent studies by investigators other than the test authors and publishers should be included. VERY DESIRABLE

[Comment: Test reviews that express opinions about the test without supplying new data would be included only at the author's discretion, but they should not be quoted out of context or selected so as to give a misleading impression.]

A2.2. When new information obtained by the test author or others indicates significant facts and recommendations presented in the manual to be incorrect, a revised manual should be issued promptly. ESSENTIAL

A2.3. When the test is revised or a new form is issued, the manual should be suitably revised to take changes in the test into account. ESSENTIAL

[Comment: In a new edition of one well-known test, whose directions and scoring procedure were modified, the norms should have been verified or redetermined. Instead, the earlier tables for converting scores to a standard scale were carried over, without change, and without justification, to the new edition.]

A2.31. If a short form of the test is prepared by reducing the number of items or organizing a portion of the test into a separate form, new evidence should be obtained and reported for that shorter test. ESSENTIAL

[Comment: It is especially important to report the standard error of measurement of the test in its shorter form. In addition to data on the error of measurement, new evidence for interpretation is helpful for shortened tests, because placing an item in a new context may alter the responses to it.]

A2.32. When a short form is prepared from a test, the manual should present evidence that the items in the short form represent the items in the long form or measure the same characteristics as the long form. VERY DESIRABLE

A2.4. When a test is issued in revised form the new copyright date should be indicated on both the test and the manual. The nature and extent of the revision and the comparability of data between the old test and the revised test should be explicitly stated. Dates should be given for the collection of new data and the establishment of new norms. ESSENTIAL

[Comment: Too often, a test is reissued with a new copyright date and no other apparent change. It is hard to escape the conclusion that such an updating is no more than an attempt to mislead the purchaser.

One new revision of a long-established achievement test battery illustrates a desirable practice by listing all previous editions and then describing in detail the relation of the new revision to the previous editions.]

B. INTERPRETATION

Responsibility for making inferences as to the meaning and legitimate uses of test results in a particular setting rests with the user, but in making such judgments he is dependent upon the available information about the test.

The manual cannot fully prepare the user for interpretation of any test. He will sometimes have to make judgments that have not been substantiated by the published evidence. Thus the vocational counselor cannot expect to have regression equations available for each job about which he makes tentative predictions from test scores. The clinician must bring general data and theory into his interpretation of data from a personality inventory, because research on no instrument is complete. The degree to which the manual can be expected to prepare the user for accurate interpretation and effective use of the test varies with the type of test and the purpose for which it is used.

B1. The test, the manual, record forms, and other accompanying material should assist users to make correct interpretations of the test results. ESSENTIAL

B1.1. Names given to published tests, and to scores within tests, should be chosen to minimize the risk of misinterpretation by test purchasers and subjects. ESSENTIAL

[Comment: While the names given to research tests may be justified on grounds varying with the circumstances, published tests should be given names that are based on the content or process involved in the test, but which carry no unwarranted suggestion as to the characteristics measured. Such names as "culture-fair," "culture-free," "primary mental abilities," "originality" tests, or "creativity" tests are questionable for published tests, since they suggest interpretations going beyond the demonstrable meaning of the test score.

Provided no adverse effect on the subject can possibly occur, names designed to disguise the purpose of a test from a subject may properly be used. In such a case, the manual (and the publisher's catalogue) should explain the reason for choosing this name and should state the actual purpose of the test.]

B1.11. Devices for identifying interests and personality traits through self-report should be entitled "inventories," "questionnaires," or "checklists," rather than "tests." VERY DESIRABLE

[Comment: Typically the instruments considered here are those that can be "faked" in a desirable direction by alert subjects. In referring to such instruments in textual material, however, the word test may be used to simplify the language even where the word test is properly avoided in the title.]

B1.2. The manual should draw the user's attention to data that need to be taken into special account in the interpretation of test scores. VERY DESIRABLE

[Comment: For example, many college entrance test manuals point out that test scores should be only one of several types of information useful in evaluating the potential of a candidate; they should supplement the high school record, recommendations, and other factors.

One personality assessment manual states that "the psychologist should know the following basic facts: the sex and age of the subject, whether his parents are dead or separated, the ages and sexes of his siblings, his vocational and his marital status."]

B1.3. When case studies are used in the manual to illustrate interpretations of test scores, the examples presented should include some relatively complicated cases where interpretation is somewhat ambiguous. VERY DESIRABLE

[Comment: Test manuals may err by including excessively simplified reports on complex cases or by choosing stereotyped cases that are exceptionally free from complication. Some publishers have found it advantageous to present detailed case studies in separate publications. Such presentations properly emphasize the possible influence of nontest data on case interpretation.]

B1.4. If any systematic error resulting from testing conditions, regional factors, and other things, is likely to enter the test score, the manual should warn the user about it and discuss its probable size and direction. ESSENTIAL

B1.5. The manual should draw attention to, and warn against, any serious error of interpretation that is known to be frequent. ESSENTIAL

[Comment: Some users of general intelligence tests think of the score as a direct measure of inherent native ability; it is desirable for manuals of such tests to caution against this interpretation. For example, they should warn the user of low scores that are often obtained by culturally deprived persons or persons with a poor background in the language of the test.

Manuals for interest indices should make clear and should urge the counselor to stress the fact that interest does not necessarily imply ability and is only one factor to be considered in choosing among occupations.]

B2. The test manual should state implicitly the purposes and applications for which the test is recommended. ESSENTIAL

[Comment: A clear statement of a test's purposes will help prevent the misapplication of test scores. It will alert the user to the kind and extent of evidence he should expect to find in the manual in support of the claims made for the test by the author and publisher. For example, if an achievement test is recommended as a survey test of what students know,

an accurate description of its content is important. If, on the other hand, it is recommended as a diagnostic test or one that predicts performance, data on its relationship with one or more criteria are required. See Section C on validity.]

B2.1. If a test is intended for research use only, and is not distributed for operational use, that fact should be prominently stated in the accompanying materials. ESSENTIAL

[Comment: The term "operational use" refers to making practical decisions about the evaluation or handling of individuals, groups, curricula, therapeutic treatments, and so forth. If the developer of a new device for studying personality, for example, releases his instrument for studies by other investigators before he considers it ready for operational use, it is appropriate to print "distributed for research use only" on the test package or cover of the booklet of directions, and also in any catalogue where it is listed. This serves to caution against premature use of the instrument in guidance or selection.]

B3. The test manual should indicate the qualifications required to administer the test and to interpret it properly. ESSENTIAL

[Comment: The following categorization of tests has been found useful by the American Psychological Association:[1]

Level A. Tests or aids that can adequately be administered, scored, and interpreted with the aid of the manual and a general orientation to the kind of institution or organization in which one is working (e.g., achievement or proficiency tests).

Level B. Tests or aids that require some technical knowledge of test construction and use, and of supporting psychological and educational fields such as statistics, individual differences, psychology of adjustment, personnel psychology, and guidance (e.g., aptitude tests, adjustment inventories applicable to normal populations).

Level C. Tests and aids that require substantial understanding of testing and supporting psychological fields, together with supervised experience in the use of these devices (e.g., projective tests, individual mental tests).

The manual might identify a test according to one of the foregoing levels, or might employ some form of statement more suitable for that test.]

B3.1. The manual should not imply that the test is "self-interpreting," or that it may be interpreted by a person lacking proper training. ESSENTIAL

[Comment: Even in the case of tests described above as belonging to Level A, use and interpretation should not be left to an untrained individual. As described in *Ethical Standards of Psychologists,* Level A tests should be interpreted by persons having at least the general training of "responsible, educated, nonpsychologists such as school principals and business executives."

[1] Ethical Standards for the Distribution of Psychological Tests and Diagnostic Aids. *American Psychologist,* 1950, 5, 620–626, or *Ethical Standards of Psychologists,* Washington, D.C.: American Psychological Association, 1953. This statement also includes descriptions of general levels of training which correspond to the three levels of tests.

The manual should indicate what may be done by untrained persons and what should not be done. One well-known interest test manual, for example, indicates that examinees may perform the mechanics of scoring their own tests but properly stresses that they need the help of a trained teacher or counselor in making interpretations and future plans.]

B3.2. Where a test is recommended for a variety of purposes or types of inference, the manual should indicate the amount of training required for each use. ESSENTIAL

B3.3. The manual should draw the user's attention to the kind of references with which he should become familiar before attempting to interpret the test results. The references might be to books or articles dealing with related psychological theory or with the particular test in question. VERY DESIRABLE

B4. Statements in the manual reporting relationships are by implication quantitative and should be stated as precisely as the data permit. If data to support such statements have not been collected, that fact should be made clear. ESSENTIAL

[Comment: Writers sometimes say, for example, "Spatial ability is required for architectural engineering" or "Bizarre responses may indicate schizophrenic tendencies." Such statements should be made quantitatively adequate. In what proportion of cases giving bizarre responses has schizophrenia been shown to develop? How much has architectural success been found to depend upon spatial ability? Numerical data relating the test scores to definite criteria would provide the needed answers.]

B4.1. When the term "significant" is employed, the manual should make clear whether statistical or practical significance is meant, and what practical significance the statistically significant reliable differences have. ESSENTIAL

B4.2. When the statistical significance of a relationship is reported, the statistical report should be in a form that makes clear the sensitivity or power of the significance test. ESSENTIAL

[Comment: Statistical significance that has no practical significance can often be obtained by using a highly sensitive experiment, for example, by using a very large number of cases. One who uses an insensitive statistical test can falsely conclude that there is no difference. In general, it is more appropriate in reporting test data to state a confidence interval or the likelihood function for the parameter of interest than to report only that the null hypothesis can or cannot be rejected.]

B4.3. The manual should clearly differentiate between an interpretation (a) that is applicable only to average tendencies in a group, and (b) that is applicable to an individual within the group. ESSENTIAL

[Comment: Some tests are sufficiently reliable to provide a relatively stable estimate of a group average, but are not reliable enough to provide a usable individual score or to permit comparisons among individuals.]

B4.4. The manual should state clearly what interpretations are intended for each subscore as well as for the total test. ESSENTIAL (See also C1.2.)

[Comment: Where subscores are obtained only for convenience in scoring the test, and no interpretation is intended, this should be made clear. For some tests, keys are provided for subscores that have possible research use but are not intended to be interpreted; this again should be made clear.]

C. VALIDITY

Validity information indicates the degree to which the test is capable of achieving certain aims. Tests are used for several types of judgment, and for each type of judgment, a different type of investigation is required to establish validity. For purposes of describing the uses for three kinds of validity coefficients, we may distinguish three of the rather numerous aims of testing:

1. *The test user wishes to determine how an individual performs at present in a universe of situations that the test situation is claimed to represent.* For example, most achievement tests used in schools measure the student's performance on a sample of questions intended to represent a certain phase of educational achievement or certain educational objectives.

2. *The test user wishes to forecast an individual's future standing or to estimate an individual's present standing on some variable of particular significance that is different from the test.* For example, an academic aptitude test may forecast grades, or a brief adjustment inventory may estimate what the outcome would be of a careful psychological examination.

3. *The test user wishes to infer the degree to which the individual possesses some hypothetical trait or quality (construct) presumed to be reflected in the test performance.* For example, he wants to know whether the individual stands high on some proposed abstract trait such as "intelligence" or "creativity" that cannot be observed directly. This may be done to learn something about the individual, or it may be done to study the test itself, to study its relationship to other tests, or to develop psychological theory.

Different types of tests are often used for

each of the different aims, but this is not always the case. There is much overlap in types of tests and in the purposes for which they are used. Thus, a vocabulary test might be used (*a*) simply as a measure of present vocabulary, the universe being all the words in the language, (*b*) as a screening device to discriminate present or potential schizophrenics from organics, or (*c*) as a means of making inferences about "intellectual capacity."

To determine how suitable a test is for each of these uses, it is necessary to gather the appropriate sort of validity information. The kind of information to be gathered depends on the aim or aims of testing rather than on the type of test. The three aspects of validity corresponding to the three aims of testing may be named content validity, criterion-related validity, and construct validity.

Content validity is demonstrated by showing how well the content of the test samples the class situations or subject matter about which conclusions are to be drawn. Content validity is especially important for achievement and proficiency measures and for measures of adjustment or social behavior based on observation in selected situations. The manual should justify the claim that the test content represents the assumed universe of tasks, conditions, or processes. A useful way of looking at this universe of tasks or items is to consider it to comprise a *definition* of the achievement to be measured by the test. In the case of an educational achievement test, the content of the test may be regarded as a definition of (or a sampling from a population of) one or more educational objectives. The aptitudes, skills, and knowledges required of the student for successful test performance must be precisely the types of aptitudes, skills, and knowledges that the school wishes to develop in the students and to evaluate in terms of test scores. Thus evaluating the content validity of a test for a particular purpose is the same as subjectively recognizing the adequacy of a definition. This process is actually quite similar to the subjective evaluation of the criterion itself. Unless, however, the aim of an achievement test is specifically to forecast or substitute for some criterion, its correlation with a criterion is *not* a useful evaluation of the test.

Criterion-related validity is demonstrated by comparing the test scores with one or more external variables considered to provide a direct measure of the characteristic or behavior in question. This comparison may take the form of an expectancy table or, most commonly, a correlation relating the test score to a criterion measure. Predictive uses of tests include long-range forecasts of one or more measures of academic achievement, prediction of vocational success, and prediction of reaction to therapy. For such predictive uses the criterion data are collected an appropriate amount of time after the administration of the tests under study. For other purposes the criterion data may be collected concurrently with the test; for example, when one wishes to know whether a testing procedure can take the place of more elaborate procedures for diagnosing personality disorders. A test that is related to one or more concurrent criteria will not necessarily predict status on the same criterion at some later date. Whether the criterion data should be collected concurrently with the testing or at a later time depends on whether the test is recommended for prediction or for assessment of present status.

Construct validity is evaluated by investigating what qualities a test measures, that is, by determining the degree to which certain explanatory concepts or constructs account for performance on the test. To examine construct validity requires a combination of logical and empirical attack. Essentially, studies of construct validity check on the theory underlying the test. The procedure involves three steps. First, the investigator inquires: From this theory, what hypotheses may we make regarding the behavior of persons with high and low scores? Second, he gathers data to test these hypotheses. Third, in light of the evidence, he makes an inference as to whether the theory is adequate to explain the data collected. If the theory fails to account for the data, he should revise the test interpretation, reformulate the theory, or reject the theory altogether. Fresh evidence would be required to demonstrate construct validity for the revised interpretation.

A simple procedure for investigating what a test measures is to correlate it with other tests. We would expect a valid test of numerical reasoning, for example, to correlate more highly with other numerical tests than with clerical perception tests. Another procedure is experimental. If it is hypothesized, for example, that form perception on a certain projective test indicates probable ability to function well under emotional stress, this inference may be checked by placing individuals in an experimental situation producing emotional stress and observing whether their behavior corresponds to the hypothesis.

Construct validity is ordinarily studied when the tester wishes to increase his understanding of the psychological qualities being measured by the test. A validity coefficient relating test to criterion, unless it is established in the context of some theory, yields no information about *why* the correlation is high or low, or about how one might improve the measurement. Construct validity is relevant when the tester accepts no existing measure as a definitive criterion of the quality with which he is concerned (e.g., in measuring a postulated drive such as need for achievement), or when a test will be used in so many diverse decisions that no single criterion applies (e.g., in identifying the ability of Peace Corps trainees to adapt to new cultures). Here the traits or qualities underlying test performance are of central importance. It must be remembered, however, that, without a study of criterion-related validity, a test developed for diagnosis or prediction can be regarded only as experimental.

These three aspects of validity are only conceptually independent, and only rarely is just one of them important in a particular situation. A complete study of a test would normally involve information about all types of validity. A first step in the preparation of a predictive (*criterion-related*) instrument may be to consider what *constructs* are likely to provide a basis for selecting or divising an effective test. Sampling from a *content* universe may also be an early step in producing a test whose use for *prediction* is the ultimate concern. Even after satisfactory *prediction* has been established, information regarding *construct* validity may make the test more useful; it may, for example, provide a basis for identifying situations other than the validating situation where the test is appropriate as a predictor. To analyze *construct* validity, all the knowledge regarding validity would be brought to bear.

The three concepts of validity are pertinent to all kinds of tests. It is the intended use of the test rather than its nature that determines what kind of evidence is required.

Intelligence or scholastic aptitude tests most often use criterion-related validity to show how well they are able to predict academic success in school or college, but the nature of the aptitudes measured is often judged from the content of the items, and the place of the aptitude within the array of human abilities is deduced from correlations with other tests.

For achievement tests, content validity is usually of first importance. For example, a testing agency has a group of subject-matter specialists devise and select test items that they judge to cover the topics and mental processes relevant to the field represented by the test. Similarly, a teacher judges whether the final test in his course covers the kinds of situations about which he has been trying to teach his students certain principles or understandings. The teacher also judges content when he uses a published test, but he can appropriately investigate criterion-related validity by correlating this test with tests he has prepared or with other direct measures of his chief instructional objectives. When the same published achievement test is used for admissions testing, it may reasonably be checked against a later criterion of performance. In any theoretical discussion of what is being measured by the achievement test, a consideration of construct validity is required. Whether the score on a science achievement test, for example, reflects reading ability to a significant degree, and whether it measures understanding of scientific method rather than mere recall of facts are both questions about construct validity.

Development of a personality inventory will usually start with the assembly of items covering content the developer considers meaningful. Such inventories are then likely to be interpreted with the aid of theory; any such interpretation calls for evidence of construct validity. In addition, a personality inventory must have criterion-related validity, if, for example, it is to be used in screening military recruits who may be maladjusted.

Interest measures are usually intended to predict vocational or educational criteria, but many of them are also characterized by logical content and constructs. This makes it more likely that they can provide at least a rough prediction for the very many occupations and activities that exist and for which specific evidence of criterion-related validity has not been obtained.

For projective techniques, construct validity is the most important, although criterion-related validity using criteria collected either concurrently with the testing or afterwards may be pertinent if the instruments are to be used in making diagnostic classifications.

C1. The manual should report the validity of the test for each type of inference for which it is recommended. If its validity for some suggested interpretation has not been investigated, that fact should be made clear. ESSENTIAL

C1.1. Statements in the manual about validity should refer to the validity of particular interpretations or of particular types of decision. ESSENTIAL

[Comment: It is incorrect to use the unqualified phrase "the validity of the test." No test is valid for all purposes or in all situations or for all groups of individuals. Any study of test validity is pertinent to only a few of the possible uses of or inferences from the test scores.

If the test is likely to be used incorrectly for certain areas of decision, the manual should include specific warnings. For example, the manual for a writing skills test states that the test apparently is not sufficiently difficult to discriminate among students "at colleges that have selective admissions."]

C1.2. Wherever interpretation of subscores, score differences, or profiles is suggested, the evidence in the manual justifying such interpretation should be made explicit. ESSENTIAL (Also see B4.4.)

[Comment: One aptitude test manual indicates the difficulties involved in computing the statistical significance of differences between scores in a profile. In an effort to cope with this problem a convenient method of approximating the significance of plotted differences is provided. Cautions and limitations of this type of profile interpretation are suggested.]

C1.21. If the manual for an inventory suggests that the user consider responses to separate items as a basis for personality assessment, it should either present evidence supporting this use or call attention to the absence of such data. The manual should warn the reader that inferences based on responses to single items are subject to extreme error, hence should be used only to direct further inquiry, as, perhaps, in a counseling interview. ESSENTIAL

C2. Item-test correlations should not be presented in the manual as evidence of criterion-related validity, and they should be referred to as item-discrimination indices, not as item-validity coefficients. ESSENTIAL

[Comment: It is, of course, possible to make good use of item-test correlations in reasoning about construct validity. However, such correlations are not, in themselves, indicators of test validity; they are measures of internal consistency.]

Content Validity

C3. If a test performance is to be interpreted as a sample of performance or a definition of performance in some universe of situations, the manual should indicate clearly what universe is represented and how adequate is the sampling. ESSENTIAL

[Comment: Some consideration should be given to the adequacy of sampling from both the appropriate universe of content and the universe of behaviors that the items are intended to represent. For example, the manual of a test of achievement in American history might not only describe the item types used and the coverage of the subject matter, but also should describe to what extent responding to the test items serves as an adequate sample of the examinee's attainment of such skills as critical reading of historical material, including evaluation of evidence, analysis of cause and effect relationships, and whatever other behaviors are considered to be "achievement in American history."]

C3.1. When experts have been asked to judge whether items are an appropriate sample of a universe or are correctly scored, the manual should describe the relevant professional experience and qualifications of the experts and the directions under which they made their judgments. VERY DESIRABLE

C3.11. When the items are selected by experts, the extent of agreement among independent judgments should be reported. DESIRABLE

C3.2. In achievement tests of educational outcomes, the manual should report the classification system used for selecting items. DESIRABLE

[Comment: In a test of a field of knowledge, it is desirable to present a table showing the classification of items with respect to mental content and process categories even though these are necessarily judgmental. One such set of categories is described in the *Taxonomy of Educational Objectives*.

One popular achievement test battery includes an item content outline with suggestions as to how the information in the outline might be used in improving instructions.]

C3.21. Where an achievement test has been prepared according to a two-way topic-by-process outline, that outline should be presented in the manual, with a list of the items identified with each cell of the outline. VERY DESIRABLE

C3.3. Conclusions in the manual based on logical analysis of content should be carefully distinguished from those based on empirical findings. ESSENTIAL

[Comment: Content validity is established by demonstrating that a test represents a particular area. The user cannot judge, from this alone, how well the test permits inferences about any form of behavior other than the test behavior. For example, a vocational interest inventory containing items that represent vocational areas yields important information about content validity, but does nothing to establish that a student's score predicts his satisfaction in a given type of job.]

C3.4. Any statement in the manual of the relation of items to a course of study (or other source of content) should mention the date when the course of study was prepared. ESSENTIAL

[Comment: In achievement testing, it is frequently the practice to identify significant topics for items by a careful sampling from textbooks. Textbooks and courses of study change, however, and the test that was once an excellent sample becomes out-of-date. Therefore, the manual should report such information as the range and median of copyright dates of the textbooks examined or the date at which the experts judged the items to be representative.

One problem checklist lists problems common to students. The manual for this checklist properly reports the date when the list was assembled. With the passage of time, it will be necessary to determine whether student problems have changed, and if so, to change the test accordingly.]

Criterion-Related Validity

C4. All measures of criteria should be described completely and accurately. The manual should comment on the adequacy of the criterion. Whenever feasible, it should draw attention to significant aspects of performance that the criterion measure does not reflect and to irrelevant factors that are likely to affect it. ESSENTIAL

[Comment: Desirable practices are illustrated in a manual for a test designed to measure abstract intelligence. Several validity studies relating this instrument to criteria are reported, some involving concurrent measures and others involving predictions over periods of time. Limitations of the studies are recognized and it is stated that "no one criterion is uniquely appropriate." The value of local norms is stressed and an example of a local expectancy table is provided.

In the case of interest measures, it is sometimes not made clear whether the criterion indicates satisfaction, success, or merely continuance in the activity under examination. When criterion groups include men in a given occupation and when a comparison of such groups is made to men-in-general, the manual should point out the distinction between presence in an occupation and success in it or satisfaction with it.]

C4.1. The manual should report the validity of the test for each criterion about which a recommendation is made. If validity for some recommended interpretation has not been tested, that fact should be made clear. ESSENTIAL

C4.2. For any type of prediction the manual should report test-criterion correlations for a variety of institutions or situations. Where validity studies have been confined to a limited range of situations, the manual should remind the reader of the risks involved in generalizing to other types of situations. ESSENTIAL

[Comment: One manual for an aptitude battery presents a great variety of test-criterion correlations. It states that even though the large amount of test-criterion data presented may be confusing to the user, it is nevertheless necessary since "validity is specific" and must always be interpreted for a particular setting in which "the test user himself must evaluate and integrate all of the data available to him."]

C4.3. Since the criterion measure is a sample of possible criterion data, the agreement of that sample with other similar samples that might have been used as measures of the criterion should be reported. If evidence on this question cannot be given, the author should make this clear and should discuss the probable extent of agreement of the sample with other samples as judged from indirect evidence. VERY DESIRABLE

[Comment: When validity is measured by agreement of the test with psychiatric judgment, for example, the degree of agreement among judges should be described. Where a published achievement test is used to obtain the criterion measures, the form-to-form agreement or the reliability reported by the test's author may be used as a basis for evaluating the criterion, due regard being given to the effect of differences between the present sample of persons and the original sample.]

C4.31. If validity coefficients are corrected for errors of measurement *in the criterion,* the computation of the reliability coefficient of the criterion should be explained, and both corrected and uncorrected coefficients should be reported in the manual. ESSENTIAL

[Comment: Coefficients corrected for errors of measurement in the *test* are not estimates of the criterion validity of the existing test and should not be reported. Corrections for attenuation are very much open to misinterpretation, and if misinterpreted give an unjustifiably favorable picture of the validity of the test. The hazard is illustrated in the manual for an adjustment inventory. The author reports correlations between inventory scores and criterion ratings, and also reports the estimated correlations between "true" inventory and criterion scores. He then comments that the augmented correlations "are as high as those often secured between college aptitude tests and college grades." The comparison is improper, since the test author is comparing his augmented coefficients with uncorrected coefficients for ability tests.]

C4.32. For users who are technically oriented, breakdown of test variance into the following sources is appropriate: variance relevant to the criterion, variance explained as form-to-form or trial-to-trial inconsistency, and a reliable-irrelevant remainder. VERY DESIRABLE

[Comment: Such a breakdown is far less subject to misinterpretation than a "corrected" validity coefficient.]

C4.4. The time elapsing between the test administration and the collection of criterion data should be reported in the manual. If the criterion data are collected over a period of time, beginning and ending data should be included. ESSENTIAL

C4.41. If a test is recommended for long-term predictions, but comparisons with concurrent criteria only are presented, the manual should emphasize that the validity of predictions is undetermined. ESSENTIAL

C4.5. The criterion score should be determined independently of test scores. The manual should describe any precautions taken to avoid contamination of the criterion or should warn the reader of posible contamination. ESSENTIAL

[Comment: When the criterion depends on a judgment, the manual should state whether the test data were available to the rater or were capable of influencing his judgment in any other way. If the test data could have influenced the criterion rating, the user should be warned that the reported validities are likely to be spuriously high.]

C4.6. When the validity of a test is appraised by its agreement with psychiatric diagnoses, the diagnostic terms or categories should be defined specifically and clearly described. VERY DESIRABLE

[Comment: For example, "paranoid schizophrenia, chronic" is preferable as a category to "schizophrenia." Since the types of patients included in specific diagnostic classifications depend to some extent on the point of view of the classifying psychiatrist, an amplified description of each diagnostic category used in the validity study should be presented.]

C4.61. When the validity of a test is appraised by its agreement with psychiatric judgment, the training, experience, and professional status of the psychologist(s) or psychiatrist(s) should be stated, and the nature and extent of his contacts with the patients should be reported. VERY DESIRABLE

C4.7. When the validity of a test for predicting occupational performance is reported, the manual should describe the duties of the workers as well as give their job titles. VERY DESIRABLE (See Comment C5.2.)

C4.71. Where a wide range of duties is subsumed under a given occupational label, the test user should be warned against assuming that only one pattern of interests or abilities is compatible with the occupation. VERY DESIRABLE

[Comment: The manual for one interest inventory rightly points out that, "for any given interest pattern, or combination of patterns, there are jobs at many levels for individuals with a wide range of abilities."]

C4.72. The amount and kind of any schooling or job training received by the subjects between the time of testing and the time of criterion collection should be stated. VERY DESIRABLE

C4.8. When the validity of a test for predicting grades in a course is reported, the reader of the manual should be given a reasonably clear understanding regarding the types of performance required in the course, the nature of instructional method, and the way in which performance is measured. If the test was administered after the course was started, this fact should be specified. ESSENTIAL

C4.9. Local collection of evidence on criterion-related validity is frequently more useful than published data. In such cases the manual should suggest appropriate emphasis on local validity studies, giving advice on how to conduct the studies and how to set up usable expectancy tables or other means for interpreting the results of the studies. VERY DESIRABLE

[Comment: In cases where criteria differ from one locality to another or from one institution to another, no published validity data can serve all localities. For example, the validity of a certain test for predicting grades at a college with a unique kind of curriculum may be quite different from the published validity of the same test that was based on more conventional colleges.]

Criterion-Related Validity Sample

C5. The sample employed in a validity study and the conditions under which testing is done should be consistent with the recommendations made in the manual. They should be described sufficiently for the user to judge whether the reported validity is pertinent to his situation. ESSENTIAL

[Comment: In his effort to provide adequate data on the sample and on the testing conditions, the publisher is often faced with a dilemma. Too much detailed information in a manual may reduce its effectiveness; yet insufficient data do not allow for proper judgments by the competent user. One aptitude test publisher meets this problem by reporting only major findings, indicating that "detailed data are available from the American Documentation Institute."]

C5.1. Basic statistics that should be reported in the manual for the validation sample are measures of central tendency and variability. ESSENTIAL

C5.11. If the test scores that are analyzed have a distribution markedly different from the distribution of the group with whom the test is ordinarily to be used, correlations or other measures of discrimination in the group to whom the test is likely to be given should be estimated. In reporting such estimates, the manual should cite the original coefficient, the distribution characteristics used in making the new estimate, and the statistical procedure. ESSENTIAL

[Comment: An estimate larger than the observed validity coefficient may be needed when the observed coefficient is based on a group of employees or students who have been selected in such a way as to restrict the range of scores on the test. On the other hand, an estimate lower than the observed coefficient will be appropriate for the biserial correlation between a scholastic aptitude test and college success, where the persons distinguished are dropouts (lower end of the continuum) and honor students (upper end of the continuum). As the test will normally be applied to the whole group of entering students, the validity coefficient should reflect the somewhat lower predictive power of the test in that group.]

C5.2. The validity sample should be described in the manual in terms of those variables known to be related to the quality tested, such as age, sex, socioeconomic status, and level of education. Any selective factor determining the composition of the sample should be indicated. ESSENTIAL

[Comment: If a validity study uses patients as subjects, the diagnoses of the patients would usually be important to report. The severity of the diagnosed condition should be stated when feasible. For tests used in industry the occupation and experience of the workers should be described. For educational tests the nature of the community and any selection policy of the school should be reported.]

C5.3. If the validity sample is made up of records accumulated haphazardly or voluntarily submitted by test users, this fact should be stated in the manual, and the test user should be warned that the group is not a systematic or random sample of any specifiable population. Probable selective factors and their presumed influence on test variables should be stated. ESSENTIAL

[Comment: While it is entirely appropriate to include in the manual such phrases as "the author and publisher of this test would welcome additional data derived from its use," it is extremely difficult to judge adequately the quality and representativeness of most of the resulting reports.]

C5.4. The validity of a test should be determined on subjects who are at the age or in the same educational or vocational situation as the persons for whom the test is recommended in practice. Any deviation from this requirement should de described in the manual. ESSENTIAL

[Comment: The validity of tests intended for guidance should generally be determined on subjects tested prior to or near the time when they are making educational or vocational choices.

One interest inventory was standardized at first on men currently employed in the occupation in question.

The ability of these scales to differentiate between occupational groups did not, in and of itself, warrant using the inventory in the counseling of high school or college students. Better evidence was obtained later by administering the inventory to students, determining the nature of their later employment, and then establishing the relation between preoccupational score and later occupation.

If an interest inventory uses a criterion of enrollment or nonenrollment in a certain occupation, the sample used in its validation should include only the range of mental ability appropriate to the occupational group. For example, college students are not suitable subjects with which to estimate the validity of a scale of interest in manual skills, even though some of them later enter manual occupations.]

C5.41. If an ability test is to be used for educational or occupational selection, its validity should be established using subjects who are actual candidates and who are therefore motivated to perform well. If the subjects used in a validity study did not believe that their test scores would be used in making decisions about them, this fact should be made clear. VERY DESIRABLE

C5.5. If the validity of the test is likely to be different for subsamples that can be identified when the test is given, the manual should report the results for each subsample separately or should report that no differences were found. VERY DESIRABLE

[Comment: It is often useful to perform validity studies separately on samples differing in one or more of the common demographic variables. Since subsamples are likely to differ in range, statistical corrections may be necessary to make the results comparable. In such cases a regression equation may be more informative than a correlation coefficient.]

C5.6. In collecting data for a validity study, the person who administers, scores, or interprets the test should have only that information about the examinees that is ordinarily expected to be available in practical use of the test. If there is any possible contamination associated with prior favorable or unfavorable knowledge about the examinees, the manual should discuss its effect on the outcome of the study. ESSENTIAL

[Comment: Whenever knowledge about the examinee may influence test administration or scoring, as it might in the case of individual intelligence tests or projective techniques, the test administrator should not possess knowledge about the examinees that might bias his interpretation of the examinee's responses. Knowing that an examinee is regarded as maladjusted but able may make the person administering an individual test more prone to explore borderline answers or to encourage the examinee when he encounters difficulty. Data collected under such circumstances do not provide an adequate basis for judging the validity of the test by itself.]

Criterion-Related Validity Analysis

C6. Any statistical analysis of criterion-related validity should be reported in the manual in a form from which the reader can determine what confidence is to be placed in judgments or predictions regarding the individual. ESSENTIAL

C6.1. Statistical procedures that are well known and readily interpreted should be preferred in the manual for reporting validity. Any uncommon statistical techniques should be explained, and references to descriptions of them should be given. ESSENTIAL

[Comment: Publishers need not adhere to the commonly used procedures for reporting validity data, but there should be sufficient standard terminology and procedures to allow for adequate judgment by reasonably competent users. One recently developed ability test manual introduces "circular" profiles, "range" and "stability" scores, and other novel statistical procedures so inadequately explained as to give an aura of the bizarre to the entire manual.]

C6.11. A report in the manual or elsewhere concerning the criterion-related validity of tests should ordinarily include: (*a*) one or more correlation coefficients of a familiar type, (*b*) descriptions of the efficiency with which the test separates criterion groups, (*c*) expectancy tables, or (*d*) charts that graphically illustrate the relationship between test and criterion. ESSENTIAL

[Comment: Reports of differences between group means by themselves give inadequate information regarding validity. If variance is large, classification may be inaccurate even if means differ significantly. A description indicating amount of misclassification or overlapping should be included. The emphasis should be on descriptive statistics for individuals; a significance test alone is insufficient.

In general, since manuals are directed to readers who have limited statistical knowledge, every effort should be made to communicate validity information clearly. For instance, a certain manual reports no criterion-related validity data collected over a period of time; yet the case studies presented suggest a degree of validity totally unsupported by the data in the manual.]

C6.12. If a test is suggested for the differential diagnosis of patients, the manual should include evidence of the test's ability to place individuals in diagnostic groups rather than merely to separate diagnosed abnormal cases from the normal population. ESSENTIAL

[Comment: When a test is recommended for the purpose of assigning patients to discrete categories, such statistics as contingency coefficients, phi coefficients, or discriminant functions should be supplemented by a table of misclassification rates giving, for example, the proportion of patients falsely included in a category or falsely excluded from it. Such proportions should be compared with base rates, i.e., the proportions of correct classifications made possible by a mere knowledge of the sizes of the categories.]

C6.2. An overall validity coefficient should be supplemented with a report regarding the regression slope and intercept and the standard error of estimate at different points along the score range. VERY DESIRABLE

[Comment: The required information could be presented in an expectancy table showing the range of possible criterion values for each of several points on the score range.

For a dichotomous criterion, this objective might be achieved by indicating the proportion of hits, misses, and false inclusions at various cutting scores. One reading readiness test, for instance, reports the percentage of failure in primary reading expected among pupils at each level of test score.]

C6.3. When information other than the test scores is known to have an appreciable degree of criterion-related validity and is ordinarily available to the prospective test user, the manual should report the validity of the other information and the resulting multiple correlation when the new test information is combined with it. ESSENTIAL

[Comment: Whether a test should be used for prediction and classification when other information is readily available depends not on the validity of the test but on its "incremental validity," i.e., what it adds to the soundness of the judgment that would otherwise be made.

For a test recommended as a predictor of school achievement, the manual should report how much the test enhances prediction based on the subjects' previous school records. A test is not likely to improve greatly the prediction of college grades when it is highly correlated with past high school grades. Such a test may be used in dealing with pupils coming from scattered high schools, the past records of which are not available or not on a comparable scale, or it may be used to correct statistically the records for different schools to make them comparable.

For a questionnaire intended to predict marital success, delinquency, and similar behavioral variables, the manual should report how much the questionnaire enhances prediction over that provided by base rates developed from demographic variables such as socioeconomic status.]

C6.31. If the validity of a test is demonstrated by comparing groups that differ on the criterion, the manual should report whether and by how much the groups differ on other available variables that are relevant. VERY DESIRABLE

[Comment: Since groups which differ on a criterion may also differ in other respects, the test may be discriminating on a quality other than that intended. Types of mental disorder, for instance, are associated with age, education, and length of time in hospital.

Confounding of this sort should be taken into account when appraising the usefulness of the test for diagnosis.]

C6.4. When a scoring key or the selection of items is based on a tryout sample, the manual should report validity coefficients based on one or more separate cross-validation samples, rather than on the tryout sample or on a larger group of which the tryout sample is a part. ESSENTIAL

C6.5. If the manual recommends certain regression weights for combining scores on the test or for combining the test with other variables, the validity of the composite should be based on a cross-validation sample. VERY DESIRABLE

[Comment: Cross-validation is particularly necessary when the number of predictors entering the study (not the final equation) is greater than four or five and when the sample size is less than 200.]

C6.6. Whenever it is proposed that decisions be based on a complex nonlinear combination of scores, it should be shown that this combination has greater validity than some simpler linear combination. VERY DESIRABLE

[Comment: The use of "moderator variables," for example, is to be recommended only where this produces a clear improvement in validity in a cross-validation sample. Also, when it is proposed that some pattern of scores, for example, high standing in scores on both Variables 2 and 5, is an indicator of success, it is necessary to show that the proportion of successful persons in the group so identified is higher than would be expected from the regression of frequency of success on a linear combination of Scores 2 and 5.]

C6.7. To ensure the continued correct interpretation of scores, the validity of the suggested interpretations should be rechecked periodically and the results reported in subsequent editions of the manual. VERY DESIRABLE

[Comment: Job requirements, conditions of work, and the types of person entering an occupation often change materially with the passage of time. Similarly the meanings of clinical categories, the nature of therapeutic treatment, and the objectives in any school course change. So also will the difficulty and psychological meaning of test items. Hence, the reader should be in a position to judge the extent to which scales are obsolete.

Criterion data for the psychologist scale of a much used interest test were gathered in 1927. Subsequent research showed that these psychologists were no longer representative of the field. The current manual reports the date (1948) of the validating studies for the revised key. With the growth of mathematical psychology on the one hand, and of private clinical practice on the other, this scale may, in certain aspects, again be obsolescent.]

C6.71. If the validity of a suggested test interpretation has not been checked within 15

or 20 years, the test should be withdrawn from general sale and distributed, if at all, only to persons who will conduct their own validity studies. DESIRABLE (See A2.)

[Comment: This standard, as worded, is extremely liberal. Removal of tests from the market and repetition of validity studies have not been common practice. The present liberal standard moves only a short way toward the ideal. It is not necessary to repeat every part of the validation; what is needed is a repetition of those studies that are most likely to have been rendered obsolete.]

Construct Validity

C7. If the author proposes to interpret the test as a measure of a theoretical variable (ability, trait, or attitude), the proposed interpretation should be fully stated. The interpretation of the theoretical construct should be distinguished from interpretations arising under other theories. ESSENTIAL

[Comment: For example, if a test is intended to measure the construct of anxiety, the test author should distinguish his formulation of the construct from any other meanings he can think of and should relate his concept to measures of anxiety discussed in the literature.

The description of a construct may be as simple as the identification of "creativity" with "making many original contributions." Even this definition provides some basis for judging whether or not various pieces of empirical evidence support the proposed interpretation. Ordinarily, however, the test author will have a more elaborate conception. He may wish to rule out such originality as derives only from a large and varied store of information. He may propose explicitly to identify the creative person as one who produces numerous ideas, whether of high or low quality. He may propose to distinguish the ability to criticize ideas from the ability to be "creative." He may go on to hypothesize that the person who shows originality in identifying or describing pictures will also have unconventional preferences in food and clothing. All such characterizations or hypotheses are part of the author's concept of "what the test measures" and are needed in designing and in drawing conclusions from empirical investigations of the psychological interpretation of the construct.]

C7.1. The manual should indicate the extent to which the proposed interpretation has been substantiated and should summarize investigations of the hypotheses derived from the theory. ESSENTIAL

C7.11. Each study investigating a theoretical inference regarding the test should be summarized in a way that covers both the operational procedures of the study and the implications of the results for the theory. VERY DESIRABLE

C7.12. The manual should report correlations between the test and other relevant tests for which the interpretation is relatively clear. VERY DESIRABLE

[Comment: It is desirable, for instance, to know the correlation of an "art aptitude" test for college freshmen with measures of general or verbal ability, and also with measures of skill in drawing, if there are satisfactory measures available. The interpretation of test scores would differ, depending on whether these correlations are high or low.]

C7.13. The manual should report the correlations of the test with other available measures of the same attributes that have been generally accepted. VERY DESIRABLE

[Comment: When a test is advanced as a measure of "general adjustment," its correlations with other measures of this characteristic should be reported. The user can infer, from the size of such correlations, whether generalizations established on the older tests can be expected to hold for the new one.

Or similarly, a new interest test that emphasizes the factorial approach to construct validity should nevertheless report relationships of the new instrument to relevant scales of some well-established interest tests.

If a great many measures of the attributes are available, it is sufficient for the author to compare his test with only a representative selection of other tests.]

C7.2. The manual should report evidence on the extent to which constructs other than those proposed by the author account for variance in scores on the test. VERY DESIRABLE

[Comment: Although it is unreasonable to require a test author to anticipate or to include every counter interpretation in a test manual, he ought to present sufficient data to rule out the counter-hypotheses that are most likely to account for variance in the test scores.]

C7.21. The manual for any specialized test or inventory used in educational selection and guidance should report its correlation with a well-established measure of verbal and quantitative ability in an appropriately representative population. VERY DESIRABLE

[Comment: Verbal and quantitative ability are specified here, because their importance in educational performance is recognized, and numerous tests for these abilities are already available. To be of use, a new test must do more than simply duplicate the measurement of verbal and quantitative ability.]

C7.22. Whenever a test has been included in factorial studies that indicate the proportion of the test variance attributable to widely known reference factors, such information should be presented in the manual. VERY DESIRABLE

C7.23. For any personality measure, evidence should be presented on the extent to which scores are susceptible to an attempt by the examinee to present a false or unduly favorable picture of himself. VERY DESIRABLE (See C5.41.)

C7.24. If a personality questionnaire calls for "yes-no" or "agree-disagree" responses, the manual should report evidence on the degree to which the scores reflect a set to acquiesce. DESIRABLE

[Comment: Appropriate evidence might be the proportion of the total test variance accounted for by variance in the number of "yes" responses to the test, the correlation of the test scores with one or more independent measures of the acquiescence tendency, or a study comparing the test scores to those on a "reversed" test in which each item is worded in the opposite manner.]

C7.25. If a test given with a time limit is to be interpreted as measuring a hypothetical psychological attribute not specifically related to speed, evidence should be present in the manual concerning the effect of speed on the test scores and on their correlation with other variables. ESSENTIAL

[Comment: The most complete evidence on the effect of speed would be the comparison of one form, using the usual time limit, with another form having unlimited time. The correlation of scores at the end of the usual time with scores obtained with extra time on the same trial is of limited meaning, because the two scores are not independent. Less complete evidence would consist of data on the percentage of examinees who attempted the last item or some item very near the end of the test. This evidence is usually satisfactory if the percentage is high, but if the percentage is below about 90, a more penetrating study is needed to show that individual differences on the test do not reflect speed to any great extent.]

C7.26. Where a low correlation or small difference between groups is advanced as evidence *against* some counter-interpretation, the manual should report the confidence interval for the parameter. The manual should also correct for or discuss any errors of measurement that may have lowered the apparent relationship. DESIRABLE

D. RELIABILITY

Reliability refers to the accuracy (consistency and stability) of measurement by a test. Any direct measurement of such consistency obviously calls for a comparison between at least two measurements. (Whereas "accuracy" is a general expression, the terms "consistency" and "stability" are needed to describe, respectively, form-associated and time-associated reliability.) The two measurements may be obtained by *retesting* an individual with the identical test. Aside from practical limitations, retesting is not a theoretically desirable method of determining a reliability coefficient if, as usual, the items that constitute the test are only one of many sets (actual or hypothetical) that might equally well have been used to measure the particular ability or trait. Thus, there is ordinarily no reason to suppose that *one* set of (say) 50 vocabulary items is especially superior (or inferior) to another comparable (equivalent) set of 50. In this case it appears desirable to determine not only the degree of response variation by the subject from one occasion to the next (as is accomplished by the retest method), but also the extent of sampling fluctuation involved in selecting a given set of 50 items. These two objectives are accomplished most commonly by correlating scores on the original set of 50 items with scores by the same subjects on an independent but similar set of 50 items—an "alternate form" of the original 50. If the effect of content-sampling *alone* is sought (without the effects of response variability by the subject), or if it is not practical to undertake testing on two different occasions, a test of 100 items may be administered. Then the test may be divided into two sets of 50 odd-numbered items and 50 even-numbered items; the correlation between scores on the odd and the even sets is a "split-half" or "odd-even" correlation, from which a reliability (consistency) coefficient for the entire test of 100 items may be estimated by the Spearman-Brown formula (involving certain generally reasonable assumptions). Essentially the same type of estimated reliability coefficient may be obtained from item-analysis data through use of the Kuder-Richardson formulas (which involve various assumptions, some more reasonable and exact than others). It should be noted that despite the possible heterogeneity of content, the odd-even correlation between the sets of items may be quite high if the items are easy and if the test is administered with a short time limit. Such odd-even correlations are in a sense spurious, since they merely reflect the expected correlation between two sets of scores each of which is a measure of rate of work. (See D5.2.)

From the preceding discussion, it is clear that *different methods of determining the reliability coefficient take account of different sources of error*. Thus, from one testing to the other, the retest method is affected not only by response variability of the subjects but also by differences in administration (most likely if different persons administer the test on the two occa-

sions). Reliability coefficients based on the single administration of a test ignore response variability and the particular administrative conditions: their effects on scores simply do not appear as errors of measurement. Hence, "reliability coefficient" is a generic term referring to various types of evidence; each type of evidence suggests a different meaning. It is essential that *the method used to derive any reliability coefficient should be clearly described*.

As a generic term reliability refers to many types of evidence, each of which describes the agreement or consistency to be expected among similar observations. Each type of evidence takes into account certain kinds of errors or inconsistencies and not others. The operation of measurement may be viewed as a sample of behavior; in a typical aptitude or achievement test the person is observed on a particular date as he responds to a particular set of questions or stimuli, and his responses are recorded and scored by a particular tester or system. The occasion is a sample from the period of time within which the same general inquiry would be pertinent; some sampling error is involved in selecting any one date of observation. The items that constitute the test are only one of many sets (actual or hypothetical) that might have been used to measure the same ability or trait. The choices of a particular test apparatus, test administrator, observer, or scorer, are also sampling operations. Each such act of sampling has some influence on the test score. It is valuable for the test user to know how much a particular score would be likely to change if any one of these conditions of measurement were altered.

There are various components that may contribute to inconsistency among observations: (*a*) response variation by the subject (due to changes in physiological efficiency, or in such psychological factors as motivation, effort, or mood): these may be especially important in inventories of personality; (*b*) variations in test content or the test situation (in "situational tests" which include interacting persons as part of the situation, this source of variation can be relatively large); (*c*) variations in administration (either through variations in physical factors, such as temperature, noise, or apparatus functioning, or in psychological factors, such as variation in the technique or skill of different test administrators or raters); and (*d*) variations in the process of observation. In addition to these errors of observation, scoring-error variance in test scores reflects variation in the process of scoring responses as well as mistakes in recording, transferring, or reading of scores.

The estimation of clearly labeled components of error variance is the most informative outcome of a reliability study, both for the test developer wishing to improve the reliability of his instrument and for the user desiring to interpret test scores with maximum understanding. The analysis of error variance calls for the use of an appropriate *experimental* design. There are many different multivariate designs that can be used in reliability studies; the choice of design for studying the particular test is to be determined by its intended interpretation and by the practical limitations upon experimentation. In general, where more information can be obtained at little increase in cost, the test developer should obtain and report that information.

Although estimation of clearly labeled components of error variance is the most informative outcome of a reliability study, this approach is not yet prominent in reports on tests. In the more familiar reliability study the investigator obtains two measures and correlates them, or derives a correlation coefficient by applying one of several formulas to part or item scores within a test. Such a correlation is often interpreted as a ratio of "true variance" to "true variance plus error variance." Many different coefficients, each involving its own definition of "true" and "error" variance, may be derived from a multivariate reliability experiment with the presence of controls for such factors as those of content, time, and mode of administration. Hence, any single correlation is subject to considerable misinterpretation unless the investigator makes clear just what sampling errors are considered to be error in the particular coefficient he reports. The correlation between two test forms presented on different days has a different significance from an internal-consistency coefficient, for example, because the latter allocates day-to-day fluctuations in a person's efficiency to the true rather than to the error portion of the score variance.

In the present set of *Standards,* the terminology by which the 1954 *Technical Recommendations* classified coefficients into several types (e.g., coefficient of equivalence) has been discarded. Such a terminological system breaks down as more adequate statistical analyses are applied and methods are more adequately described. Hence it is recommended that test authors work out suitable phrases to convey the meaning of whatever coefficients they report; as an example, the expression, "the stability of measurements by different test forms as determined over a 7-day interval," although lengthy, will be reasonably free from ambiguity.

General Principles

D1. The test manual should report evidence of reliability that permits the reader to judge whether scores are sufficiently dependable for the recommended uses of the test. If any of the necessary evidence has not been collected, the absence of such information should be noted. ESSENTIAL

[Comment: One recently published manual for a mental ability test presents four types of reliability data: test-retest, odd-even, alternate forms, and intercorrelations of parts. It also includes standard error of measurement and confidence bands for deviation IQs.

Another manual states that "the reliabilities reported for . . . are the results of internal analyses based on a single administration of the tests. . . . Correlations between alternate forms and test-retest correlations have not been obtained."]

D1.1. The test manual should furnish, in so far as feasible, a quantitative analysis of the total inconsistency of measurement into its major identifiable components; viz., fluctuations or inconsistency in responses of the subject; inconsistency or heterogeneity within the sample of test content (such as the stimulus items, questions, and situations); inconsistencies in administration of the test; inconsistency among scorers, raters, or units of apparatus; and mechanical errors of scoring. VERY DESIRABLE

[Comment: In general, the desired analysis will not be feasible unless scores are expressed in quantitative, as distinguished from categorical or nonparametric, terms, and unless the design of data collection includes the necessary controls.

With group tests of school achievement, the *principal sources of error* to be evaluated usually include (*a*) inconsistency or heterogeneity within the sample of test content (although, admittedly in an achievement test the content should be just as heterogeneous as the subject matter or the functions that are involved in successful use of knowledge), (*b*) inconsistencies in test administration, and (*c*) inconsistency in responses of the examinee over time; i.e., instability. The collection of data should be designed to permit evaluation of these three factors. In the case of projective tests, fluctuation or inconsistency in the responses of the subject is usually a major source of random error to be evaluated; inconsistency among scorers or raters should also be evaluated.]

D1.2. A measure of reliability or errors of measurement should be reported in the test manual even when a test is recommended solely for empirical prediction of criteria. VERY DE-SIRABLE

[Comment: Such information adds to the user's understanding of the test, since it permits more intelligent application and interpretation than is possible without such information. For certain judgments, such as the potential effect of lengthening the test, information about reliability is required and should be available to the user.]

D1.3. The standards for reliability should apply to every score, subscore, or combination of scores (such as a sum, difference, or quotient) which is recommended by the test manual (either explicitly or implicitly) for other than merely tentative or pilot use. ESSENTIAL

D1.4. For instruments that yield a profile having a low reliability of differences between scores, the manual should explicitly caution the user against casual interpretation of differences between scores, except as a source of tentative information requiring external verification. ESSENTIAL

D1.5. The manual should state the minimum difference between two scores ordinarily required for statistical significance. VERY DESIRABLE

D2. **In the test manual reports on reliability or error of measurement, procedures, and samples should be described sufficiently to permit a user to judge to what extent the evidence is applicable to the person and problems with which he is concerned.** ESSENTIAL

[Comment: The maturity of the group, the variation in the group, and the attitude of the group toward the test should represent normal conditions of test use. For example, the reliability of a test to be used in selecting employees should be determined by testing applicants for positions rather than by testing college students or workers already employed.]

D2.1. The reliability of a school intelligence or achievement test should generally be estimated separately for each of many classes at each of several grade levels within each of several school systems. The mean and standard deviation for each sample should be reported in the test manual, along with its reliability coefficients. VERY DESIRABLE

[Comment: In some instances, there may be advantages to reporting components of variation underlying each of several classificatory variables in a testing situation.

As supplementary information, estimates of reliability for combined samples may be provided. See also C4.32, D1.1, and D3.]

D2.2. The reliability sample should be described in the test manual in terms of any

selective factors related to the variable being measured. ESSENTIAL

D2.21. Demographic information, such as distributions of the subjects with respect to age, sex, socioeconomic level, intellectual level, employment status or history, and minority group membership should be given in the test manual. DESIRABLE

D2.3. If reliability coefficients are corrected for range, both the uncorrected and the corrected coefficients should be reported in the test manual, together with the standard deviation of the group actually tested and the standard deviation assumed for the corrected sample. ESSENTIAL

[Comment: The "assumed" standard deviation should correspond to that in the population for which the test is intended or in which the test is most likely to be used.]

D2.4. When a test is recommended or ordinarily employed to make discriminations within various particular categories of persons, the reliability and error of measurement within that category should be independently investigated and reported in the test manual. ESSENTIAL

[Comment: The mechanical reasoning section of a well-known aptitude test has different reliability for boys and girls. The manual reports the reliability for each sex in each grade.]

D2.41. When reported in the test manual, a reliability analysis for an intelligence or achievement test intended to effect usable differentiation within a single school grade should be based on children within the given grade only, not on a multigrade sample with a wider range of ability. ESSENTIAL

D2.42. The test manual should report whether the error of measurement varies at different score levels. If there is significant change in the error of measurement from level to level, this fact should be reported. VERY DESIRABLE

[Comment: In the manual for one well-known intelligence test, the authors have pointed out that the differences in estimated IQs on two forms of the instrument are much larger for IQs above 100 than for low IQs. Another test of college aptitude reports standard error of measurements for three score levels; at the mean, one standard deviation above the mean, and one standard deviation below the mean.]

D3. Reports of reliability studies should ordinarily be expressed in the test manual in terms of variances for error components (or their square roots) or standard errors of measurement, or product-moment reliability coefficients. ESSENTIAL

[Comment: Test authors and publishers should avoid unconventional statistics unless conventional statistics are definitely inappropriate. If unusual statistical analyses are presented, the explanation should minimize the likelihood of misinterpretation. Any statistic employed should indicate the degree of relationship rather than merely whether an hypothesis of zero relationship can be rejected.]

D3.1. The manual should make clear that measures of reliability do not demonstrate the criterion-related validity of the test. ESSENTIAL

[Comment: Reliabilty is a necessary but not a sufficient condition of validity. Reliability coefficients are pertinent to validity in the negative sense that unreliable scores cannot be valid. But reliable scores are by no means *ipso facto* valid, since validity depends on what interpretation is proposed. Reliability is of special importance in support of, but not in replacement of, the analysis and estimation of content, criterion-related, and construct validity.]

Comparability of Forms

D4. If two forms of a test are published, both forms being intended for possible use with the same subjects, the means and variances of the two forms should be reported in the test manual along with the coefficient of correlation between the two sets of scores. If necessary evidence is not provided, the test manual should warn the reader against assuming comparability. ESSENTIAL

D4.1. Whenever feasible, the test manual should present a summary of item statistics for each form, such as a frequency distribution of item difficulties and of indices of item discrimination. DESIRABLE

D4.2. Whenever the content of the items can be described meaningfully, it is advisable that a comparative analysis of the forms be presented in the test manual to show how similar they are. VERY DESIRABLE

[Comment: In the instance of two forms of an achievement test, a chart or table should be presented. Not only frequency distributions of item statistics but also a tabulation of frequency of items by categories of subject-matter content and of behavioral or instructional objectives should be furnished. The two forms should represent different samples of items within each category. Artificially close similarity between forms which could be attained by matching item for item from form to form is not desirable because it hides real errors of measurement associated with content sampling, and in this case the interitem correlation is a spuriously high estimate of the reliability.]

D4.3. Whenever two sets of performances on a test are correlated to determine comparability and stability, the interval of time between the testings should be specified in the test manual. ESSENTIAL

D4.4. To show comparability over the range of scores, the test manual should present a table showing what raw scores on the two forms occupy the same percentile positions in the population. The data may be obtained from appropriately stratified samples adequately large in relation to the reported size of the standard deviation (stratified on sex and other salient variables). If one sample receives each form, care must be taken to control differential practice and fatigue effects through use of an appropriate design of test administration. DESIRABLE

Internal Consistency

D5. If the test manual suggests that a score is a measure of a generalized, homogeneous trait, evidence of internal consistency should be reported. ESSENTIAL

[Comment: Internal consistency is important if items are viewed as a sample from a relatively homogeneous universe, as in a test of addition with integers, a list of general high school vocabulary, or a test presumed to measure introversion. Nevertheless, measures of internal consistency should not be regarded as a substitute for other measures. When alternate forms are available, alternate-form reliabilities should be reported in preference to but not necessarily to the exclusion of coefficients based on internal analysis.]

D5.1. Estimates of internal consistency should be determined by the split-half methods or methods of the Kuder-Richardson type, if these can properly be used on the data under examination. Any other measure of internal consistency which the author wishes to report in addition should be carefully explained in the test manual. ESSENTIAL

[Comment: There will no doubt be unusual circumstances where special coefficients give added information.]

D5.2. Whenever reliability coefficients based upon internal analysis are reported, the test manual should present evidence that speed of work has a negligible influence on scores. ESSENTIAL

[Comment: If speed is a consequential factor, the internal correlation measures will be too high by an indeterminate amount; in such cases, assuming that alternate forms are not available, the reliability coefficient should be based upon separately timed half tests.]

D5.3. When a test consists of separately scored parts or sections, the correlation between the parts or sections should be reported in the test manual along with relevant means and standard deviations. DESIRABLE

D5.31. If the test manual reports the correlation between a subtest and a total score, it should be pointed out that part of this correlation is artificial. VERY DESIRABLE

D5.4. If several questions within a test are experimentally linked so that the reaction to one question influences the reaction to another, the entire group of questions should be treated preferably as an "item" when data arising from application of the split-half or appropriate analysis-of-variance methods are reported in the test manual. ESSENTIAL

[Comment: In a reading test, several questions about the same paragraph are ordinarily experimentally dependent. All of these questions should be placed in the same half-test in using the split-half method. In the Kuder-Richardson method, the score on the group of questions should be treated as an item score. However, there may be occasions when even if the various questions based on the same paragraph of a reading test are regarded as experimentally linked it would be desirable to obtain an estimate of the reliability of the score in the sense that the derived coefficient must be a measure of the extent to which the items are experimentally linked.]

D5.5. If a test can be divided into sets of items of different content, and if it is desired to estimate its correlation with another test of similarly distributed content, the internal analysis reported in the test manual should be determined by procedures designed for such tests. VERY DESIRABLE

[Comment: One such procedure is the division of the test into "parallel" rather than random half-tests. Another procedure is to apply the Jackson-Ferguson "battery reliability" formula, in which each type of content is treated as a subtest.]

Comparisons over Time

D6. The test manual should indicate to what extent test scores are stable, that is, how nearly constant the scores are likely to be if a test is repeated after time has lapsed. The manual should also describe the effect of any such variation on the usefulness of the test. The time interval to be considered depends on the nature of the test and on what interpretation of the test scores is recommended. ESSENTIAL

[Comment: For most purposes in psychology and education, fluctuations of test scores within a few hours, days, or even months will interfere with measurement. The intention in using educational and psychological tests is to draw conclusions about relatively lasting characteristics of the person tested; hence, instability over trials or observations within a short period is regarded as a source of error variance which lowers reliability. For example, a college entrance test which is administered once is intended to measure

a characteristic of a person that is related to his accomplishments over the first year of college. To the extent that the test scores fluctuate from day to day about the person's average level, they are in error. In some situations, however, where the test is intended as a measure of a changing characteristic, fluctuation over a period of weeks or months is not to be regarded as a defect in the measurement. A reading readiness test used only once for an initial tentative assignment of first-grade pupils among instructional groups is an example. Even for this test, however, stability over a month, perhaps, is required if scores are to serve their intended purpose. In experiments on the effects of drugs, on the other hand, it may be desirable to measure meaningful changes in two sets of test scores that represent a time lapse of only a few minutes.

It seems reasonable to require an assessment of stability for projective techniques and other devices for assessing personality dynamics even though it is recognized in some instances that a low retest stability over a substantial period merely reflects true trait fluctuation and hence indicates desired validity. Clinical practice rarely presumes that the inferences from projective tests are to be applied on the very day the test is given. Realistically, one must recognize that pragmatic decisions are being made from test data which are meaningful only in terms of at least days, and usually weeks or months, of therapy and other procedures following the test administraton. If a certain test result is empirically found to ·be highly unstable from day to day, this evidence casts doubt upon the utility of the test for most purposes even if that fluctuation might be explained by the hypothesis of trait inconstancy.]

D6.1. In any report in the test manual concerning the determination of the stability of scores by repeated testing, alternate forms of the test should have been used to minimize recall of specific answers, especially if the time interval is not long enough to assure forgetting. VERY DESIRABLE

D6.11. Every time the correlation between scores on two halves of a given form or on two alternate forms of a test is reported in the test manual, the split-half coefficient, Spearman-Brown index, or a Kuder-Richardson Formula 20 estimate of consistency should be cited for the given form or for each alternate form along with a coefficient reflecting stability of the scores on each form from one administration to a subsequent administration. VERY DESIRABLE

D6.2. The report in a test manual of a study of consistency over time should state what period of time elapsed between tests and should give the mean and standard deviation of scores at each testing, as well as the correlation. ESSENTIAL

D6.3. If test scores are likely to be retained in a person's record to be consulted as new questions about him arise, the test manual should indicate the length of time following the test during which the score may continue to be used effectively for the recommended purposes. The manual should report evidence regarding the extent to which scores change within and subsequent to this interval. VERY DESIRABLE

[Comment: Since some schools administer general mental tests or interest tests only at intervals of 2 or 3 years, the manual for such tests should report correlations and changes in means and standard deviations between tests administered 1 year apart, 2 years apart, and 3 years apart. From these data the user can learn how rapidly test records become obsolescent with the passage of time.]

D6.31. In reporting on stability, the test manual should describe the relevant experience or education of the group between testings. ESSENTIAL

E. ADMINISTRATION AND SCORING

E1. The directions for administration should be presented in the test manual with sufficient clarity and emphasis that the test user can duplicate, and will be encouraged to duplicate, the administrative conditions under which the norms and the data on reliability and validity were obtained. ESSENTIAL

[Comment: Because persons administering tests in schools sometimes may not follow instructions rigidly and may not understand the need for doing so, it is necessary that the manual be very persuasive on this point.]

E1.1. The directions published in the test manual should be complete enough that persons tested will understand the task in the way the author intended. ESSENTIAL

[Comment: For example, in a personality inventory, it is intended that the subject give the first response that occurs to him. Hence, this expectation should be made clear in the directions read by or to the subject. Directions for interest inventories should specify whether the person is to mark what things he would ideally like to do or whether he is also to consider the possibility that he would have the opportunity and ability to do them. Likewise, the directions should specify whether the person is to mark those things he would like to do or does do *occasionally,* or only those things he would like to do or does do *regularly.*]

E1.12. The directions to the examinee in the test manual should clearly point out critical matters, such as instructions on guessing, time limits, and procedures for marking answer sheets. VERY DESIRABLE

E1.2. If expansion or elaboration of instructions described in the test manual is permitted, the conditions under which they may be done should be clearly stated either in the form of general rules or in terms of giving numerous examples, or both. VERY DESIRABLE

E1.21. If in rare instances the examiner is allowed freedom and judgment in elaborating instructions or giving examples, empirical data should be presented in the test manual regarding the effect of variation in examiner procedures upon scores. If empirical data on the effect of variation in examiner procedures are not available, this fact should be stated explicitly, and the user should be warned that the effects of such variations are unknown. DESIRABLE

E2. The procedures for scoring the test should be presented in the test manual with a maximum of detail and clarity so as to reduce the likelihood of scoring error. ESSENTIAL

E2.1. The test manual should furnish scoring instructions which maximize the accuracy of scoring an objective test by outlining a procedure for checking the obtained scores for computational or clerical errors. VERY DESIRABLE

[Comment: A checking procedure might involve scoring the answer sheets twice, scoring "rights" and "wrongs" separately (at two scoring sessions or by two different scorers), scoring by two independent scorers, spot-checking the accuracy of test scoring, or cross-checking of totals.]

E2.2. Where subjective processes enter into the scoring of a test, evidence on the degree of agreement between independent scorings under operational conditions should be presented in the test manual. If such evidence is not provided, the manual should draw attention to scoring variations as a possible significant source of errors of measurement. VERY DESIRABLE

E2.21. The bases for scoring and the procedures for training the scorers should be presented in the test manual in sufficient detail to permit other scorers to reach the degree of agreement reported in studies of scorer agreement given in the manual. VERY DESIRABLE

E2.22. If persons having various degrees of supervised training are expected to score the test, studies of the interscorer agreement at each skill level should be presented in the test manual. DESIRABLE

E2.3. If the test is designed to use more than one method for the examinee's recording his responses, such as hand-scored answer sheets, machine-scored answer sheets, or entering of responses in the test booklet, the test manual should report data on the degree to which results from these methods are interchangeable. ESSENTIAL

[Comment: The different amounts of time required for responding to items in forms adapted to different scoring methods may affect the reliability or validity of the test or the applicability of the test norms.]

E2.4. If an unusual or complicated scoring system is used, the test manual should indicate the approximate amount of time required to score the test. DESIRABLE

E2.5. The test manual should recommend that "correction for guessing" formulas or multiple-regression analysis should usually be used with multiple-choice and true-false items unless: (*a*) there is either no time limit, or a generous time limit *and* a warning is given by the proctor near the end concerning the amount of time remaining; and (*b*) instructions are unequivocal to mark every item, including *pure guesses*. ESSENTIAL

E2.51. When the test manual indicates that the "correlation for guessing" formula is to be used, examinees should be instructed to make the best choice that they can on items the answers of which they do not know, and to skip an item *only* if an answer would be a *pure guess*. ESSENTIAL

F. SCALES AND NORMS

F1. Scales used for reporting scores should be so carefully described in the test manual as to increase the likelihood of accurate interpretation and the understanding of both the test interpreter and the subject. ESSENTIAL

[Comment: Scales in which the test scores are reported are extremely varied. Both raw and relative scores are used. Scales purporting to represent equal intervals with respect to some external dimension (such as age) are sometimes employed. It is unwise for these recommendations to discourage the development of new scaling methods through insistence on one form of reporting. On the other hand, many different systems are now used which have no logical advantage one over the other. The recommendations below that the number of systems now employed be reduced to a few with which testers can become familiar are not intended to discourage the use of unique scales for special problems. Suggestions concerning preferable scales for general reporting are not intended to restrict use of other scales in research.]

F1.1. Standard scores should in general be used in preference to other derived scores. The system of standard scores should be consistent with the purposes for which the test is intend-

ed, and should be described in detail in the test manual. The reasons for choosing that scale in preference to other scales should also be made clear in the manual. VERY DESIRABLE

[Comment: The most widely used conventions are as follows: for a two-digit standard score, a mean of 50 and standard deviation of 10; for a one-digit standard score, a mean of 5 and a standard deviation of 2 (as in stanines). The foregoing are proposed as ways of standardizing practice among test developers. It is expected that institutions wth established systems will continue to retain them as suited to their purposes. The manual should also specify whether the standard scores are linear transformations of raw scores or normalized.]

F1.2. Whenever it is suggested in the test manual that percentile scores are to be plotted on a profile sheet, the profile sheet should be based on the normal probability scale or some other appropriate nonlinear transformation. VERY DESIRABLE

F1.3. If grade norms are provided, tables for converting scores to standard scores or percentile ranks within each grade should also be provided in the test manual. DESIRABLE

[Comment: At the high school level, norms within courses (e.g., second-year Spanish) may be more appropriate than norms within grades.]

F2. If scales are revised, new forms added, or other changes made, the revised test manual should provide tables of equivalence between the new and the old forms. This provision is particularly important in cases where data are recorded on cumulative records. ESSENTIAL

[Comment: New forms of a test should be equated to *recently determined* standard score scales of other forms in order that the user may be confident that the scores furnished by the new forms are comparable with those of earlier forms.]

F3. Local norms are more important for many uses of tests than are published norms. In such cases the test manual should suggest appropriate emphasis on local norms and describe methods for their calculation. VERY DESIRABLE

[Comment: Local norms furnish types of information different from that furnished by regional or national norms. They are more important for many uses of tests than are published norms. A test manual may advantageously furnish an explanation of how local norms may be established. They may be obtained through utilization of the same procedures as those employed in determination of national norms. For example, when local percentile ranks are obtained, the cumulated frequency ought to include half the frequency of a given raw score if this same circumstance characterizes the tables of national percentiles. Many achievement tests, clinical tests, and tests used for vocational guidance might well present a similar statement. In addition, it should be general practice to explain the preparation of expectancy tables to accompany local norms, as well as to indicate whether the scores are to be used in prediction or in identification of "overachievers" and "underachievers."]

F4. Except where the primary use of a test is to compare individuals with their own local group, norms should be published in the test manual at the time of release of the test for operational use. ESSENTIAL

[Comment: A well-known interest schedule provides a profile of 20 raw scores. Because all fields involve the same number of items, norms are said to be unnecessary. Yet a change in any one group of items would make that category more or less preferred. Hence, to know whether a high score reflects this individual's interests, or only that these items are popular wth everyone, the user must consult a set of norms. Judgment in terms of raw scores could be made only if by some unusual method it could be demonstrated that the items in each category are a representative sample of that field and preferably only when the means and standard deviations are available.]

F4.1. Even though a test is used primarily with local norms, the test manual should give some norms to aid the interpreter who lacks local norms. DESIRABLE

[Comment: One instrument designed to measure employee aptitude stresses the value of local norms but also includes norms based on a wide variety of occupational and educational classifications.]

F5. Norms should be reported in the test manual in terms of standard scores or percentile ranks which reflect the distribution of scores in an appropriate reference group or groups. ESSENTIAL

F5.1. Measures of central tendency and variability of each distribution should be given in the test manual. ESSENTIAL

F5.2. In addition to norms, tables showing what expectation a person with a test score has of attaining or exceeding some relevant criterion score should be given in the test manual whenever possible. Conversion tables translating test scores into proficiency levels should be given whenever possible. Conversion tables translating test scores into proficiency levels should be given when proficiency can be described on a meaningful absolute scale. DESIRABLE

F6. Norms presented in the test manual should refer to defined and clearly described populations. These populations should be the groups to whom users of the test will ordinarily wish to compare the persons tested. ESSENTIAL

[Comment: There should be a description of the detailed method of deriving the norms, the bases for extrapolation of the norms, if any, the methods used to assure comparability of different forms used on different levels and of alternate forms, and the methods employed to determine the comparability of revised and earlier forms. General aptitude tests designed for use with elementary school children might well present norms by grade-groups and by chronological age groups.

For occupational interest inventories, norms based on men who have entered specific occupations should be developed except where cutting scores or regression formulas are provided for predicting occupational criteria. Ultimately, norms should also be developed for groups of students at different ages before they enter occupations.

The manual should point out that a person who has a high degree of interest in a curriculum or occupation, when compared to men-in-general, will generally have a much lower degree of interest when compared with persons actually engaged in that field. Thus a *high* percentile score on a scale reflecting mechanical interest, in which the examinee is compared with men-in-general, may be equivalent to a *low* percentile when the examinee is compared with auto mechanics.]

F6.1. The test manual should report the method of sampling from the population of examinees and should discuss any probable bias in this sampling procedure. ESSENTIAL

F6.11. Norms reported in any test manual should be based on a well-planned sample rather than on data collected primarily on the basis of availability. ESSENTIAL

[Comment: Occupational and educational test norms have often been based on scattered groups of test papers, for authors sometimes have requested that all users mail in results for use in subsequent reports of norms. Distributions so obtained are subject to unknown degrees and types of biases. Hence, the methods for obtaining such samples should be clearly described. Whenever possible, such samples should be stratified and weighted through use of census data to remove some of the bias. Samples which are carefully designed *ab initio* will give more dependable norms than samples chosen in terms of their availability, since stratification in this situation cannot remove all sampling error.]

F6.12. In the instance of achievement tests the adequacy of the normative sample described in the test manual should be judged primarily in terms of the number of schools as well as the number of cases, provided, of course, that the number of students in each school is large enough to reflect the performance associated with certain levels on the stratifying variables. ESSENTIAL

F6.2. The description of the norm group should be sufficiently complete in the test manual that the user can judge whether his sample data fall within the population data represented by the norm group. The description should include number of cases, classified by such relevant variables as age, sex, and educational status. If cluster sampling is employed, the description of the norm group should state the number of separate groups tested. ESSENTIAL

[Comment: Manuals often use too gross a classification system in describing their normative data. For example, one employee aptitude survey instrument provides a variety of normative data for many occupational and educational groupings. However, the lack of information as to sex, age, education, and experience levels within these groupings considerably reduces the usefulness of the norms.]

F6.3. The number of cases on which the norms are based should be reported in the test manual. If cluster sampling is employed, the number and description of the separate groups included in the sample should be cited. ESSENTIAL

F6.31. If the sample on which norms are based is small or otherwise undependable, the user should be cautioned explicitly in the test manual regarding the possible magnitude of errors arising in interpretation of scores. ESSENTIAL

F6.4. The test manual should report whether scores vary for groups differing on age, sex, amount of training, and other equally important variables. ESSENTIAL

F6.5. Norms on subtests or groups of test items should be reported in the test manual only if data on the validity and reliability of such subtests or groups of items are also indicated. ESSENTIAL

[Comment: The test user is justified in assuming that, when norms are given for a part of a test, the author implies the usefulness of them for interpreting pupil performance. The reliability and validities of such scores should be reported to support such uses.]

F6.6. Some profile sheets record, side by side, scores from tests so standardized that for different scores the person is compared to different norm groups. The test manual should recommend profiles of this type for use only when tests are intended to assess or to predict the person's standing in different situations or when he competes with the different groups. Whenever such mixed scales are compared, the fact that the norm groups differ (or may differ) should be made clear on the profile sheet. VERY DESIRABLE

F6.7. The conditions under which normative data were obtained should be reported in the test manual. The conditions of testing, including the cirmumstances under which the sub-

jects took the test, and their levels of motivation, should be reported. ESSENTIAL

[Comment: Some tests are standardized on job-applicant groups; others, on groups which have requested vocational guidance; and still others, on groups which realized that they were experimental subjects. Motivation for taking tests, test-taking attitudes, abilities, and personality characteristics possibly differ in these groups.]

INDEX

Publishers Directory and Index

This directory and index lists all known publishers of personality tests in English-speaking countries for the period 1933 through 1968. Full addresses are reported only for publishers with tests (not necessarily personality) currently in print as of June 1, 1969. References are to entry numbers, not to page numbers. Stars indicate test publishers which issue catalogs devoted entirely or in large part to tests. The directory lists 160 publishers of in print personality tests.

★AVA Publications, Inc., 11 Dorrance St., Providence, R.I. 02903: 2

Acorn Publishing Co. Tests acquired by Psychometric Affiliates.

Addiction Research Center (Att.: Charles Haertzen), National Institute of Mental Health, P.O. Box 2000, Lexington, Ky. 40501: 3

Addison-Wesley Publishing Co., Inc.: *out of print, 327*

American Foundation for the Blind, Inc., 15 West 16th St., New York, N.Y. 10011: 8, 162, 417

★American Guidance Service, Inc., Publishers' Bldg., Circle Pines, Minn. 55014: 281; *out of print, 353*

American Orthopsychiatric Association, Inc., 1790 Broadway, New York, N.Y. 10019: 415

Aptitude Associates, Merrifield, Va. 22116: 5:56 (Since this publisher refused to supply current information about his test or to check the accuracy of the entry prepared, we have not listed the test in the Personality Test Index. The reference here is to the last listing in an MMY.)

Associated Publishers, 355 State St., Los Altos, Calif. 94022: 39

Association Press, 291 Broadway, New York, N.Y. 10007: 191; *out of print, 371*

Audio-Visual Services, Pennsylvania State University, 6 Willard Bldg., University Park, Pa. 16802: 468

★Australian Council for Educational Research, 9 Frederick St., Hawthorn, Vic., Australia, 3122: 181, 252, 281, 432

BADGER Tests Co., Ltd., 17–18 St. Dunstan's Hill, London E.C.2, England: 449–50

Baisden (Joyce B.), 2021 E. Lemon Heights Drive, Santa Ana, Calif. 92705: 488

Baxter Foundation for Research in Education, Inc.: *out of print, 298*

Bealls (J. & P.) Ltd., Gallowgate, Newcastle Upon Tyne, England: 473A

Behavioral Publications, Inc., 2852 Broadway, New York, N.Y. 10025: 14, 45

Bell-Craig, Inc., 41–14 Twenty-Seventh St., Long Island City, N.Y. 11101: 110

★Benge Associates, 357 Lancaster Ave., Haverford, Pa. 19041: *out of print, 328*

Betts (G. L.): *out of print, 337*

Biometrics Laboratory, University of Miami, Coral Gables, Fla. 33124: 41

Biometrics Research, New York State Psychiatric Institute, 722 West 168th St., New York, N.Y. 10032: 53A, 164, 216A, 217; *out of print, 365A*

★Bobbs-Merrill Co., Inc. (The), 4300 West 62nd St., Indianapolis, Ind. 46268: 58, 136, 240 (A subsidiary of Howard W. Sams & Co., Inc.)

Bogardus (Emory S.): *out of print, 381*

Boyle (Mrs. John H.), 1454 Filbert Ave., Chico, Calif. 95926: 244

Briggs (Peter F.), 860 Mayo Bldg., University of Minnesota, Minneapolis, Minn. 55414: 148

★Bruce (Martin M.), Publishers, 340 Oxford Road, New Rochelle, N.Y. 10804: 206, 270, 278, 413, 445

Buck (John): *out of print, 334*

★Bureau of Educational Measurements, Kansas State Teachers College, 1200 Commercial St., Emporia, Kan. 66802: *out of print, 310, 376, 405*

Bureau of Publications. See Teachers College Press.

Butler (Edward), 1355 Hunter Ave., Columbus, Ohio 43201: 144

C.P.S. Inc., P.O. Box 83, Larchmont, N.Y. 10538: 419

★California Test Bureau, Del Monte Research Park, Monterey, Calif. 93940: 18, 29; *out of print, 302, 336, 339* (A division of McGraw-Hill Book Co.)

Campus Publishers, 711 North University Ave., Ann Arbor, Mich. 48108: 222

Campus Stores: *out of print, 494*

Carlile (A. B.), 330 West 44th St., Indianapolis, Ind. 46208: 286

Cassel (Russell N.): *out of print, 337*

Catholic University of America Press (The), 620 Michigan Ave., N.E., Washington, D.C. 20017: 267

★Center for Psychological Service, 1835 Eye St., N.W., Washington, D.C. 20006: 126, 250

Chapple (E. D.) Co., Inc.: *out of print, 326*

Character Research Association, 6251 San Bonita, St. Louis, Mo. 63105: 21

Child Development Laboratories: *out of print, 293*

Child Development Products, Box 388, Fort Lauderdale, Fla. 33302: 94

Child Development Publications, Society for Research in Child Development, Inc.: *out of print, 501*

Child Guidance Clinic, Mooseheart, Ill. 60539: 291

Church Youth Research, Protestant Center, 122 West Franklin, Minneapolis, Minn. 55404: 22

Clarke (Walter V.) Associates, Inc. See AVA Publications, Inc.

Colgate University Testing Service, Hamilton, N.Y. 13346: 195

Colorado State College of Education: *out of print*, 351

Committee on Publications, Harvard Graduate School of Education: *out of print*, 403

Concordia Publishing House, 3558 South Jefferson Ave., St. Louis, Mo. 63118: 211

★Consulting Psychologists Press, Inc., 577 College Ave., Palo Alto, Calif. 94306: 4–5, 15, 23, 27–8, 34, 36–7, 43, 71, 79, 107, 112, 124, 133, 187, 189, 198, 207, 237, 239, 253–4, 269, 283, 287, 464; *out of print*, 384

★Cooperative Test Division, Educational Testing Service, Princeton, N.J. 08540: *out of print*, 320, 329, 333

Cornell University Medical College, 1300 York Ave., Box 88, New York, N.Y. 10021: 49–50

Counselor Recordings and Tests, Box 6184, Acklen Station, Nashville, Tenn. 37212: 266

DE PALMA (Nicholas), Metro Bordeaux Hospital, Nashville, Tenn. 37218: 470

Department of Psychiatry, Children's Hospital Medical Center, 300 Longwood Ave., Boston, Mass. 02115: 481

Department of Research, Stockton State Hospital, 510 East Magnolia St., Stockton, Calif. 95202: 257

Devereux Foundation Press (The), Devon, Pa. 19333: 60–2

Dockar-Drysdale (B. E.), Mulberry Bush School, Standlake, Oxfordshire, England: 482

EDUCATION-Industry Service, 1225 East 60th St., Chicago, Ill. 60637: 141

★Educational & Industrial Testing Service, P.O. Box 7234, San Diego, Calif. 92107: 20, 30–1, 57, 77, 135, 161, 176, 179, 193, 227

Educational Service Co., P.O. Box 1882, Grand Rapids, Mich. 49501: 63, 274

Educational Test Bureau. See American Guidance Service, Inc.

★Educational Testing Service, Princeton, N.J. 08540: 17, 42, 44, 98, 122, 171, 177, 215, 230

★Educators'–Employers' Tests & Services Associates, 120 Detzel Place, Cincinnati, Ohio 45219: 199

8CRT, Box 31, Gracie Station, New York, N.Y. 10028: 425

Evaluation Division, Bureau of Educational Research, Ohio State University: *out of print*, 407

Evaluation in the Eight Year Study, Progressive Education Association: *out of print*, 299, 303, 329–30, 332, 368, 374–5, 385

Executive Analysis Corporation, 76 Beaver St., New York, N.Y. 10005: 113

FAMILY Life Publications, Inc., P.O. Box 6725, College Station, Durham, N.C. 27708: 52, 55, 154, 156, 158–9, 249

Fels Research Institute (The), Yellow Springs, Ohio 45387: 84

Fetler (Daniel), Deer Ridge Drive, Staatsburg, N.Y. 12580: 260

Fiscal Office, State Department of Education, 721 Capitol Mall, Sacramento, Calif. 95814: 215

Florida State University, (Att.: Jay L. Chambers), Tallahassee, Fla. 32306: 463

Follett Educational Corporation, 1010 West Washington Blvd., Chicago, Ill. 60607: 426

Follett Publishing Co. See Follett Educational Corporation.

Fritz (Martin F.), Iowa State University, Ames, Iowa 50010: 210

GALLAGHER (Ralph), 613 North Mountain Ave., Bound Brook, N.J. 08805: 100

Gibson (Robert) & Sons, Glasgow, Ltd., 2 West Regent St., Glasgow C.2, Scotland: 51

Gilbert (Jules R.), Ltd., 3701 Dundas St., West, Toronto 9, Ont., Canada: 110

Gough (Harrison G.), Institute of Personality Assessment and Research, University of California, Berkeley, Calif. 94720: 202

Griffin-Patterson Co., Inc.: *out of print*, 505

Grune & Stratton, Inc., 381 Park Ave. South, New York, N.Y. 10016: 59, 86, 415, 420, 436, 470, 480, 489; *out of print*, 496–7, 500

★Guidance Centre, The College of Education, University of Toronto, 371 Bloor St., West, Toronto 5, Ont., Canada: 88; *out of print*, 397

Gutenberg Press: *out of print*, 300

HALE (E. M.) & CO.: *out of print*, 314

★Harcourt, Brace & World, Inc., 757 Third Ave., New York, N.Y. 10017: 92–3, 470; *out of print*, 294, 304, 315, 321–2, 324, 390, 399, 410

★Harrap (George G.) & Co. Ltd., P.O. Box 70, 182 High Holborn, London W.C.1, England: *out of print*, 377

Harvard University Press, 79 Garden St., Cambridge, Mass. 02138: 484, 486

Hatfield (W. Wilbur): *out of print*, 503

Hellersberg (Elisabeth F.), P.O. Box 104, Harvard, Mass. 01451: 441

Henderson (Robert W.): *out of print*, 409

Henry (William E.), Committee on Human Development, University of Chicago, 5835 South Kimbark Ave., Chicago, Ill. 60637: 435

Hoeber Medical Division, Harper & Row, Publishers, Inc.: *out of print*, 502

★Houghton Mifflin Co., 110 Tremont St., Boston, Mass. 02107: 1, 236, 259; *out of print*, 366

Huber (Hans), Marktgasse 9, 3000 Berne 7, Switzerland: 420, 470, 480, 489

Human Resources Center, Albertson, N.Y. 11507: 235

★Human Sciences Research Council, Private Bag 41, Pretoria, South Africa: *out of print*, 292A

Humm Personnel Consultants, P.O. Box 75938, Sanford Station, Los Angeles, Calif. 90005: 115

IPAT-Southern, Box 3361-A, Birmingham, Ala. 35205: 246

Industrial Psychological Services, Box 9571, Johannesburg, South Africa: 412, 473B

Industrial Psychology, Inc., 515 Madison Ave., New York, N.Y. 10022: 121, 245

★Industrial Relations Center, The University of Chicago, 1225 East 60th St., Chicago, Ill. 60637: 53, 72, 213, 265

Institute for Behavioral Research, 2429 Linden Lane, Silver Spring, Md. 20910: 440

★Institute for Personality and Ability Testing, 1602 Coronado Drive, Champaign, Ill. 61820: 38, 66, 116–21, 136, 136A, 175, 178, 182, 245; *out of print*, 344

Institute of Child Study, University of Toronto, 45 Walmer Road, Toronto, Ont., Canada: 125

Institute of Clinical Analysis, 1000 East Broadway, Glendale, Calif. 91205: 167

Institute of Living, 400 Washington St., Hartford, Conn. 06102: 467

★Institute of Psychological Research, Inc., 34 Fleury St. West, Montreal 12, Que., Canada: 225, 271

Intercontinental Medical Book Corporation, 381 Park Ave., South, New York, N.Y. 10016: 480

Interpersonal Research Institute. See Stephenson (Richard R.).

JOEL (Walther): *out of print*, 301, 348

Jones Teaching Aids, 3442 Avenue C, Council Bluffs, Iowa 51501: 134

Journal of Clinical Psychology, 4 Conant Square, Brandon, Vt. 05733: 442, 457

Jurgensen (Clifford E.): *out of print*, 335

KATZ (Martin M.), Clinical Research Branch, National Institute of Mental Health, Chevy Chase, Md. 20203: 138

Kew (Clifton E.), 245 East 19th St., New York, N.Y. 10003: 99

Kundu (Ramanath), Department of Psychology, University of Calcutta, 92, Acharya Prafulla Chandra Road, Calcutta-9, India: 140

LA RUE Printing Co.: *out of print*, 357

Lawrence (Trudys), 5532 Poplar Blvd., Los Angeles, Calif. 90032: 89

Layton (Wilbur L.), 3604 Ross Road, Ames, Iowa 50010: 183

Lewis (H. K.) & Co. Ltd., 136 Gower St., P.O. Box 66, London W.C.1, England: *out of print*, 495

Lidec, Inc.: *out of print*, 392

MCFARLAND (Ross A.), Harvard School of Public Health, 665 Huntington Ave., Boston, Mass. 02115: 220

McGraw-Hill Book Co., Inc., 330 West 42nd St., New York, N. Y. 10036: 9

Macmillan Co.: *out of print*, 313, 317

Maller (J. B.): *out of print*, 361, 382

Management Service. See Benge Associates.

Mandel (Nathan G.), Department of Corrections, State of Minnesota, St. Paul, Minn. 55101: 151

Medical Research Council, Department of Psychological Medicine, Royal Free Hospital, Lawn Road, London N.W.3, England: 190A

Merrill-Palmer Institute, 71 East Ferry Ave., Detroit, Mich. 48202: 123; *out of print*, 358-9

Merrill-Palmer School. See Merrill-Palmer Institute.

Methuen & Co. Ltd., 36 Essex St., Strand, London W.C.2, England: *out of print*, 504

Midwest Psychological Services, P.O. Box 27072, Minneapolis, Minn. 55427: 491

Miller Associates, 673 Boylston St., Boston, Mass. 02116: 106

Ministry Studies Board, 1717 Massachusetts Ave., N.W., Washington, D.C. 20036: 273

Morrison (James H.), 9804 Woodward, Overland Park, Kansas City, Mo. 66212: 146, 268

NATIONAL Association of Secondary-School Principals, 1201 Sixteenth St., N.W., Washington, D.C. 20036: 200, 258

National Bureau of Educational and Social Research, Department of Higher Education. See Human Sciences Research Council.

National Computer Systems, 1015 South Sixth St., Minneapolis, Minn. 55415: 255-6

National Council of the Churches of Christ, 475 Riverside Drive, New York, N.Y. 10027: 273

★National Foundation for Educational Research in England and Wales, The Mere, Upton Park, Slough, Bucks, England: 65, 81, 128, 150, 259A, 458, 462

Netherlands Institute of Industrial Psychology, Utrecht, Holland: 431

Nijhoff (Martinus), P.O. Box 269, The Hague, Holland: 431

OAIS Testing Program, P.O. Box 388, Ann Arbor, Mich. 48107: 185

Ohio College Association. Tests acquired by Wilbur L. Layton.

Ohio Scholarship Tests: *out of print*, 346

Oliver & Boyd Ltd., Tweeddale Court, 14 High St., Edinburgh 1, Scotland: 427

PACIFIC Books: *out of print*, 354

Park (John C.): *out of print*, 309

Personnel Research Associates, Inc., P.O. Box 2994, Dallas, Tex. 75221: 262

Peters and Associates, 328 Huckleberry Hill Road, Avon, Conn. 06001: 234

Pikunas (Justin), Psychology Department, University of Detroit, Detroit, Mich. 48221: 433

Progressive Education Association. See Evaluation in the Eight Year Study.

Psychodiagnostic Test Co., Box 528, East Lansing, Mich. 48823: 186

Psychodynamic Instruments, Box 1221, Ann Arbor, Mich. 48106: 416

Psychological Consultation Service, 11 Columbia Circle, Berkeley, Calif. 94708: 127, 446

★Psychological Corporation (The), 304 East 45th St., New York, N.Y. 10017: 48, 67, 76, 91, 165-6, 168, 173, 184, 276, 424, 439, 452, 470, 472, 484; *out of print*, 292, 340-1, 345, 347, 363, 369, 373, 394, 408, 493, 495

Psychological Publications, Inc., 5300 Hollywood Blvd., Los Angeles, Calif. 90027: 264

★Psychological Publications Press, 8830 West McNichols Road, Detroit, Mich. 48221: 40, 190, 459, 465

Psychological Research & Development Corporation, 20 Martinique Ave., Tampa, Fla. 33606: 251

Psychological Research Associates, 4 Conant Square, Brandon, Vt. 05733: 125A (A division of Clinical Psychology Publishing Co., Inc.)

Psychological Services Press, 364 Fourteenth St., Oakland, Calif. 94612: 157

Psychological Test Publications, Scamps Court, Pilton St., Barnstaple, Devon, England: 96, 110

Psychological Test Specialists, Box 1441, Missoula, Mont. 59801: 82, 131, 163, 434, 443, 447, 492

★Psychometric Affiliates, Chicago Plaza, Brookport, Ill. 62910: 10, 46, 64, 69, 73-4, 80, 83, 97, 114, 143, 145, 204, 209, 231-2, 238, 241, 279-80; *out of print*, 364

Public School Publishing Co.: for in print tests, see Bobbs-Merrill Co., Inc.; *out of print*, 305, 308, 349, 362

Publications Sales and Distribution, Ohio State University, 2500 Kenny Road, Columbus, Ohio 43210: 132, 214; *out of print*, 365

Pumroy (Donald K.), University of Maryland, College Park, Md. 20742: 160

RKA Publishing Co., 3551 Aurora Circle, Memphis, Tenn. 38111: 212

Reading Laboratory and Clinic, University of Florida, Gainesville, Fla. 32603: 444

★Research Concepts, 1368 East Airport Road, Muskegon, Mich. 49444: 454 (A division of Test Maker, Inc.)

Research Psychologists Press Inc., 13 Greenwich Ave., Goshen, N.Y. 10924: 201

★Richardson, Bellows, Henry & Co., Inc., Suite 209, 1140 Connecticut Ave., N.W., Washington, D.C. 20036: *out of print*, 355

Roche Psychiatric Service Institute, Roche Laboratories, Nutley, N.J. 07110: 169 (A division of Hoffman-La Roche Inc.)

Rosenzweig (Saul), 8029 Washington St., St. Louis, Mo. 63114: 471

Rulon (Philip J.) : *out of print, 297*

SEFA (Publications) Ltd., 240 Holliday St., Birmingham 1, England: 216

S-O Publishers, 1822 Old Canyon Drive, Hacienda Heights, Calif. 91745: 477

Sage Publications, 275 South Beverly Drive, Beverly Hills, Calif. 90212: 109

Scherer (Isidor W.), 231 Wells Road, Palm Beach, Fla. 33480: 180

★Scholastic Testing Service, Inc., 480 Meyer Road, Bensenville, Ill. 60106: 232A, 233

Schubert (Herman J. P.), 500 Klein Road, Buffalo, N.Y. 14221: 423

Sci-Art Publishers, 25 Fenway Dr., Framingham, Mass. 01701: *out of print, 380*

★Science Research Associates, Inc., 259 East Erie St., Chicago, Ill. 60611: 19, 68, 139, 192, 226, 261, 263, 277, 289, 455; *out of print, 350, 389, 411* (A subsidiary of International Business Machines Corporation.)

Sheppard & Enoch Pratt Hospital: *out of print, 318*

★Sheridan Psychological Services, Inc., P.O. Box 837, Beverly Hills, Calif. 90213: 54, 75, 101-4, 129-30, 272; *out of print, 343, 400*

Sheridan Supply Co. See Sheridan Psychological Services, Inc.

Slosson Educational Publications, 140 Pine St., East Aurora, N.Y. 14052: 248

Sound Apperception Test Distributor, 3505 Oakdale, Temple, Tex. 76501: 474

★Springer Publishing Co., Inc., 200 Park Ave., South, New York, N.Y. 10003: 128, 205, 285, 456, 462, 473, 487

Stanford University Press, Stanford, Calif. 94305: *out of print, 404* (Most tests acquired by Consulting Psychologists Press, Inc.)

Steck Co. See Steck-Vaughn Co.

Steck-Vaughn Co., P.O. Box 2028, Austin, Tex. 78767: *out of print, 325*

Stephenson (Richard R.), 2437 Second Ave., San Diego, Calif. 92101: 218

★Stoelting (C. H.) Co., 424 North Homan Ave., Chicago, Ill. 60624: 16, 47, 448; *out of print, 352, 378, 499*

Stogdill (Ralph M.), 3658 Olentangy Blvd., Columbus, Ohio 43214: 11; *out of print, 296*

Stone (LeRoy A.), 1720 Cottonwood St., Grand Forks, N.D. 58201: 108

Sumner (F. C.) : *out of print, 388*

★Swets & Zeitlinger, Keizersgracht 471 and 487, Amsterdam-C, Holland: 475 (The prices and in print status reported for this test may be in error due to the publisher's failure to reply to our repeated requests to check copy.)

TAV Selection System, 12807 Arminta St., North Hollywood, Calif. 91605: 263A

Tabin (Johanna Krout), 162 Park Ave., Glencoe, Ill. 60022: 194, 478 (The prices and in print status reported for these tests may be in error due to the publisher's failure to reply to our repeated requests to check copy.)

Taylor (Martha Pingel), P.O. Box 804, San Antonio, Tex. 78206: 460, 483

★Teachers College Press, Teachers College, Columbia University, 525 West 120th St., New York, N.Y. 10027: 479; *out of print, 306-7, 331, 356, 367, 387, 393, 395, 401-2*

Test Developments, P.O. Box 167, Burlingame, Calif. 94012: 476

Thomas (Charles C), Publisher, 327 East Lawrence Ave., Springfield, Ill. 62703: 451

Torgerson (Theodore L.) : *out of print, 396*

Tri-State Offset Co.: *out of print, 311-2*

Tuttle (Harold S.) : *out of print, 382*

Twitchell-Allen (Doris), 2447 Clybourn Place, Cincinnati, Ohio 45219: 490

★UNIVERSITY Book Store, 360 State St., West Lafayette, Ind. 47906: 105, 223-4

University Counseling Center, University of Maryland, College Park, Md. 20742: 219

University of Chicago Press: *out of print, 360, 391*

University of Denver Bookstores: *out of print, 379*

University of Florida Press: *out of print, 295*

★University of London Press Ltd., Saint Paul's House, Warwick Lane, London E.C.4, England: 20, 77-8, 90, 135, 161, 179, 196; *out of print, 498*

University of Minnesota Press, 2037 University Ave., Southeast, Minneapolis, Minn. 55455: 170, 172; *out of print, 323, 342, 383*

University of Natal Press, P.O. Box 375, Pietermaritzburg, Union of South Africa: 485

University of Nebraska Press: *out of print, 338*

University Publication Sales. See Publication Sales and Distribution.

VALENTINE (C. W.) : *out of print, 370*

Vocational Guidance Centre. See Guidance Centre.

WAGNER (Edwin E.), 76 North Revere Road, Akron, Ohio 44313: 438

Walther (E. Curt) : *out of print, 398*

Washington State University: *out of print, 386*

Webster Publishing Co.: *out of print, 316*

★Western Psychological Services, 12031 Wilshire Blvd., Los Angeles, Calif. 90213: 7, 12-3, 24-6, 32-3, 35, 56, 70, 85, 95, 111, 137, 142, 147, 149, 152-53, 155, 174, 188, 197, 203, 221, 221A, 228, 243, 247, 275, 282, 288, 414-5, 418, 421-2, 428-30, 437-8, 453, 458, 466, 469-70

Wilcox (Paul H.) : *out of print, 319*

William, Lynde & Williams, 113 East Washington St., Painesville, Ohio 44077: 284, 290

Winnetka Educational Press: *out of print, 406*

World Book Co. See Harcourt, Brace & World, Inc.

ZUNG (William W. K.), Duke University Medical Center, Durham, N.C. 27706: 242

Index of Titles

In addition to listing all personality tests known to be in print as of June 1, 1969, this index also includes: (a) all tests which have been listed in a *Mental Measurements Yearbook, Tests in Print,* or *Reading Tests and Reviews;* (b) acronyms for most personality tests and for selected nonpersonality tests; and (c) most books for which review excerpts have been published in an MMY. References are to entry numbers, not to page numbers. Numbers not preceded by a letter refer to personality tests in this monograph. Numbers preceded by a letter between A and O inclusive refer to nonpersonality tests in the MMY Test Index. Numbers preceded by the letter P refer to books in the MMY Book Review Index. Numbers preceded by TIP refer to tests only in *Tests in Print.* Numbers preceded by RTR refer to tests in *Reading Tests and Reviews,* either new reading tests or tests revised since last listed in an MMY. Superseded or nonpreferred titles are followed by a see reference; for example, "see G86" indicates that the indexed title has been superseded by, or is less preferred than, the title reported for test G86. In summary, this is an index to all personality tests known to be in print and to all other tests which have been listed in an MMY, TIP, or RTR.

APT Controlled Interview, O204
APT Dictation Test, B28
APT Manual Dexterity Test, O102.1
APT Performance Test, F13
APT Quick Screening Interview, see O204
[APT Test Batteries], TIP 1819
ARC Inventory, see 3
ARCI, Addiction Research Center Inventory, 3
A-S Reaction Study, 1; Revision for Business Use, 292
ASB, Anxiety Scale for the Blind, 8
ASQ, IPAT Anxiety Scale Questionnaire, 116
ASRS, A-S Reaction Study, 1
AST, Ayres Space Test, 12
AT, Alcadd Test, 7
ATDP Scale, see 235
ATDP, Scale to Measure Attitudes Toward Disabled Persons, 235
ATI, Attitudes Toward Industrialization, 10
ATPCC, Attitudes Toward Parental Control of Children, 11
AULC Interview Rating Form, see E15
AVA, Activity Vector Analysis, 2
AVL, Study of Values, 259
Abercrombie Driver Test, see H66
Abilities of Babies, P373
Ability and Knowledge, P810
Ability for Algebra: Fife Tests of Ability, G59
Ability for English (Language): Fife Tests of Ability, C2
Ability for Geometry: Fife Tests of Ability, G204
Ability for Science: Fife Tests of Ability, L1
Ability to Do Quantitative Thinking: Iowa Tests of Educational Development, G1
Ability to Interpret Literary Materials: Iowa Tests of Educational Development, C115
Ability to Interpret Reading Materials in the Natural Sciences: Iowa Tests of Educational Development, RTR 207, K156
Ability to Interpret Reading Materials in the Social Studies: Iowa Tests of Educational Development, RTR 208, K157
Ability to Learn (Exploratory and Corrective Inventory), TIP 1519
Ability, Values, and College Achievement, P646
Abstract and Concrete Behavior, P357
Abstract Reasoning: Differential Aptitude Tests, I5
Academic Alertness "AA": Individual Placement Series (Area I), F14
Academic Aptitude Test: Non-Verbal Intelligence, F15; Verbal Intelligence, F16
Academic Freedom Survey, H72
Academic Promise Tests, I1
Accounting Orientation Test: High School Level, O233
Achievement Examinations for Secondary Schools. See Minnesota High School Achievement Examinations
Achievement Scales in Physical Education Activities for Boys and Girls in Elementary and Junior High Schools, H133, P617
Achievement Scales in Physical Education Activities for College Men, H134, P203
Achievement Scales in Physical Education Activities for Secondary School Girls and College Women, P205
Achievement Test for Weekday Afternoon Congregational Schools, H263
Achievement Test in Jewish History, H264
Achievement Test in Mechanical Drawing, H210
Achievement Test in Silent Reading: Dominion Tests, RTR 5, K4
Achievement Test of English Usage, see C94

Achievement Tests in Nursing, O284
Achievement Tests in Practical Nursing, O285
Achievement Tests in Relation to Teaching Objectives in General College Botany, P447
Achievement Tests in the Primary School, P561
Acorn Achievement Tests, G31, K55, N1
Acorn National Achievement Tests, H153, N25, N122
Acorn National Aptitude Tests, F15-6, O16, O72, O133
Action-Choice Tests for Competitive Sports Situations, H135
Activities Index, see 255
Activity Rating Scale for Psychiatric Patients, TIP 100
Activity Vector Analysis, 2
Adaptability Test, F17
Addiction Research Center Inventory, 3
Addition Test: Factor N (Number Facility), F275
Adjective Check List, 4
Adjusted Graphic Analysis Chart, O166
Adjustment Inventory, 5
Adjustment Questionnaire, 292A
Administrative Ability, P104
Administrative Performance and Personality, P427
Admission Test for Graduate Study in Business, O167
Adolescent Fantasy, P794
Adolescent in Social Groups, P623
Adolescent Period, P746
Adolescent Rorschach Responses, P50
Adult Basic Reading Inventory, RTR 209
Adult-Child Interaction Test, see 494; P28
Adult 18 O-A Battery, 344a
Adult Intelligence, P885
Adult Test (B40), see F1
Adult 12 O-A Battery, 344b
Adult Version of the Family Relations Test, 81b
Advanced Algebra: Minnesota High School Achievement Examinations, G60
Advanced Algebra Test: State High School Tests for Indiana, G61
Advanced Algebra (II): Final District-State Scholarship Test, TIP 981
Advanced Algebra (II): Preliminary District-State Scholarship Test, TIP 982
Advanced General Science: Cooperative Science Tests, L2
Advanced Perception of Relations Scale, F137
Advanced Personnel Test, F18
Advanced Progressive Matrices, F152
Advanced Test N, F19
Advanced Vocabulary Test: Factor V (Verbal Comprehension), F275
Affectivity Interview Blank, 293
Affiliation Testing Program for Catholic Secondary Schools, H289; separate tests: C41, E52, E124, E163, G77, G227, H275, L51, L93, L159, N4, N76, N123
African Intelligence, P102
African T.A.T., 412
Age and I.Q. Calculator, H9
Agriculture: Every Pupil Scholarship Test, H4
Aids to Self-Analysis and Vocational Planning Inventory, O168
Aids to the Vocational Interview, see O181
Air Force Preference Inventory, TIP 2014
Airman Classification Battery, see O1
Airman Qualifying Examination, O1
Akron Classification Test, F20
Alcadd Test, 7
Alexander Performance Scale, F209
Algebra: Cooperative Mathematics Tests, G62
Algebra Prognosis Test, G63
Algebra Readiness Test, G64

General Science: Midwest High School Achievement Examinations, see L21

General Science: Minnesota High School Achievement Examinations, L21

General Science: Preliminary District-State Scholarship Test, TIP 1558

General Science Scales, TIP 1559

General Science Test for Prospective Nurses, O288

General Science Test: Gibson's Attainment Tests, L22

General Science Test: National Achievement Tests, L23

General Science Test: State High School Tests for Indiana, L24

General Shop Woodworking: Manchester Semester-End Achievement Tests, TIP 1276

General Speech Behavior Rating, C173

General Test N, see F19

General Test of Business Information, B9

General Test on Traffic and Driving Knowledge, H57

General Test T, see F7

General Verbal Practice Tests, F74

General Vocabulary: Iowa Tests of Educational Development, C228

General Voice Quality Examination, C173

Generalized Attitude Scales, see 223

Generalizing Ability of Dull, Bright, and Superior Children, P679

Geography Ability Test: Gibson's Attainment Tests, N61

Geography: Every Pupil Scholarship Test, N62

[Geography]: Every Pupil Test, N63

Geography Test: Municipal Tests: National Achievement Tests, N64

Geography Test: National Achievement Tests, N65

Geometry Attainment Test, G213

Geometry: Cooperative Mathematics Tests, G214

Geometry: Every Pupil Test, G215

Geometry of Mental Measurement, P816

Geometry Survey Test, TIP 1107

George Washington University Series, 126, 250, E4, F107, H83, H114, H123, O329

George Washington University Series Nursing Tests, O288

German: Every Pupil Test, E82

German I and II: Midwest High School Achievement Examinations, see E83

German I and II: Minnesota High School Achievement Examinations, E83

Gesell Developmental Schedules, F229

Gestalt Completion: A Test of Speed of Closure, see F269

Gestalt Completion Test: Factor CS (Speed of Closure), F275

Gestalt Continuation Test, F75

Gestalt Transformation: Factor RE (Semantic Redefinition), F275

Getting Along, 89

Gibson Spiral Maze, 90

Gibson's Attainment Tests, D11, D36, L22, L32, N61

Gibson's Intelligence Test, F76

Gilbert Business Arithmetic, G153

Gill-Schrammel Physiology Test, H146

Gilliland Learning Potential Examination, RTR 152

Gilliland-Shotwell Intelligence Scale, see F245

Gilmore Oral Reading Test, RTR 165, K125

Girls' Mechanical Assembly Test, O128

Gleb-Goldstein Color Sorting Test, 91b

Glenn Colorule, M45

Glenn-Welton Chemistry Achievement Test, L107

Glick-Germany Scholastic Aptitude Test, F77

Glimpses From the World of the School Child, P108

Goal Preference Inventory, TIP 162

Godsey Latin Composition Test, E115

Goldstein-Scheerer Cube Test, 91a

Goldstein-Scheerer Object Sorting Test, 91c

Goldstein-Scheerer Stick Test, 91e

Goldstein-Scheerer Tests of Abstract and Concrete Thinking, 91

Goodenough-Harris Drawing Test, F78

Goodenough Intelligence Test, see F78

Gordon-Douglass Fraction Test for Beginning Students of Nursing, O289

Gordon Occupational Check List, O63

Gordon Personal Inventory, 92

Gordon Personal Profile, 93

Gottschaldt Figures, see F268

[Grade Averaging Charts], H18

Grade Master, H19

Grade-O-Mat, H20

Graded Arithmetic-Mathematics Test, G27

Graded Spelling Test: Standard Reading Tests, RTR 139k, TIP 1452k

Graded Test of Reading Experience: Standard Reading Test, RTR 139l, TIP 1452l

Graded Vocabulary Tests, RTR 166

Graded Word Reading Test: [Burt], RTR 176; [Vernon], RTR 166, TIP 1484

Graded Word Reading Test: Schonell Reading Tests, RTR 136a, TIP 1446a

Graded Word Spelling Test, C195

Grading Scales for Typewriting Tests, B55

Graduate Record Examination Profile Tests, A17

Graduate Record Examination Tests of General Education, A18

Graduate Record Examinations, H294

Graduate Record Examinations Advanced Tests: Agriculture, H8; Biology, L65; Chemistry, L108; Economics, N49; Education, H87; Engineering, O251; Fine Arts, D1; French, E54; Geology, L123; German, E84; Government, N139; History, N97; Home Economics, H193; Literature, C140; Mathematics, G28; Music, D24; Philosophy, H226; Physical Education, H147; Physics, L148; Psychology, H233; Scholastic Philosophy, H227; Sociology, N158; Spanish, E151; Speech, C174

Graduate Record Examinations Aptitude Test, F79

Graduate Record Examinations: The Area Tests, A19

Graduate School Foreign Language Test: French E55; German, E85; Russian, E132

Graduate School Foreign Language Testing Program, E2

Grammar: Public School Achievement Tests, C53

Graphology: A Handbook, P673

Graphomotor Projection Technique, 499, P516

Graphoscopic Scale, 433

Grason-Stadler Audiometers, M14

Grassi Block Substitution Test, 94, P365

Graves Design Judgment Test, D4

Gray Oral Reading Test, RTR 167, K126

Gray-Votaw General Achievement Tests, see A20

Gray-Votaw-Rogers General Achievement Tests, A20

Grayson Perceptualization Test, 95

Greene-Stapp Language Abilities Test, C54

Gregory Academic Interest Inventory, O64

Gregory Diagnostic Tests in Language, C55

Greig Social Studies Test, N11

Grid for Evaluating Physical Fitness in Terms of Physique (Body Build), Development Level and Basal Metabolism, H173

Grid Test of Schizophrenic Thought Disorder, 96

Griffiths Mental Development Scale for Testing Babies From Birth to Two Years, F230

Group Achievement Test: Dominion Tests, A21

Group Achievement Tests: Dominion Tests: Niagara Edition, A22; Diagnostic Paragraph Comprehension, RTR 31

Index of Names

This analytical name index indicates whether a citation refers to authorship of a test review, a personality test, a measurements book, an excerpted review, or a reference dealing with a specific personality test. Thus, *"rev, 5:112"* denotes authorship of a review of personality test 112 reprinted from the 5th MMY; *"rev, F37,"* a review of a nonpersonality test; *"test, 82,"* personality test 82; *"bk, P57,"* book P57; *"exc, 4:138,"* an excepted review reprinted in this volume; *"exc, P462,"* an excerpted book review; *"ref, 47(163),"* reference 163 for test 47; and *"ref, 3:73(568),"* reference 568 for test 73 reprinted from the 3rd MMY. Citations beginning with a letter refer to reviews and excerpts which must be consulted in an MMY.

AALTO, E. E.: *ref,* 6:143(853)

Aaron, I. E.: *rev,* K105–6, K112

Aaron, N. S.: *ref,* 472(60), 484 (1145)

Aarons, W. B.: *ref,* 5:30(120)

Aaronson, B. S.: *ref,* 4(58), 166 (1476, 1561, 2331), 4:71(189), 5:86(730), 5:111(40), 5:172(68, 131), 6:143(854–5, 943, 1049), 6:177(13)

Abate, M.: *ref,* 67(583)

Abbott, C. F.: *ref,* 42(14)

Abbott, E.: *ref,* 6:217(15)

Abbott, G. Van C.: *ref,* 5:154 (1232)

Abbott, P. S.: *ref,* 41(10), 112(10), 124(69), 138(6), 147(7), 221A (18), 285(10), 408(30)

Abbott, R. F.: *ref,* 415(276)

Abbott, W. D.: *ref,* 3:73(294), 3:95(6)

Abdel-Ghaffar, A. S. A. K.: *ref,* 136(23)

Abdel-Meguid, S. G. M.: *ref,* 5:86 (476)

Abe, C.: *ref,* 283(21–2)

Abe, S. K.: *ref,* 442A(121), 6:87 (57), 6:143(813)

Abegglen, J. C.: *ref,* 6:245(632)

Abel, H.: *ref,* 173(111), 6:186(4)

Abel, J. F.: *exc,* P211, P708

Abel, T. M.: *ref,* 450(85), 470 (3066, 3167), 484(955), 3:73 (359, 410–2), 3:103(46), 4:117 (664, 772–3), 5:154(1242, 1470, 1998, 2202), 6:228(64), 6:237 (2468, 2595), 6:243(140)

Abeles, N.: *ref,* 102(73), 103(64), 130(74), 166(1416), 259(290), 464(2)

Abell, E. L.: *exc,* 1:917, 3:35, P147, P149, P754

Abelson, H. H.: *rev,* 3:30, 3:105

Abelson, R. P.: *exc,* P682

Aber, W. E.: *ref,* 5:154(1999)

Abernethy, E. M.: *ref,* 5:30(134), 5:63(42)

Abidin, R. R.: *ref,* 166(2258–9), 447(47–9, 55, 61)

Aborn, M.: *rev,* F262

Abou-Ghorra, I. M.: *ref,* 54(7), 67(462)

Abraham, H. H. L.: *ref,* 67(348), 6:87(223)

Abrahams, A.: *exc,* P215

Abrahams, N.: *ref,* 27(185), 259 (334)

Abrahamsen, D.: *ref,* 5:154(1413, 1761)

Abrams, A.: *ref,* 136(32), 245(180)

Abrams, D. F.: *ref,* 6:73(120)

Abrams, E. N.: *ref,* 4:71(190), 5:154(1829), 5:155(117)

Abrams, J. C.: *ref,* 5:36(16), 5:154 (1830)

Abrams, P.: *ref,* 53(1), 238(3)

Abrams, S.: *ref,* 244(78), 470 (3218), 6:237(2741)

Abramson, H. A.: *ref,* 3:60(14–5, 33), 5:86(477), 5:154(1918), 5:172(95)

Abramson, J. H.: *ref,* 49(47, 52)

Abramson, J. L.: *exc,* P81

Abramson, L. S.: *ref,* 417(1), 4:117 (900, 1067), 6:245(857)

Abramson, Y.: *ref,* 470(3438, 3747)

Abt, L. E.: *bk,* P12; *ref,* 3:73 (551), 4:77(234), 4:89(34), 4:117(626)

Acey, A. E.: *ref,* 27(316)

Achard, F. H.: *ref,* 4:77(141, 181)

Achilles, P. S.: *ref,* 2:1199(2), 3:23(24)

Acker, C. W.: *ref,* 166(1715, 2299), 6:99(6), 6:143(1168), 6:237 (2947–8)

Acker, M. B.: *ref,* 201(3)

Ackerly, W.: *ref,* 6:143(900), 6:237(2530)

Ackerson, L.: *exc,* P766

Ackner, B.: *ref,* 4:117(1184)

Ackoff, R. L.: *exc,* P312

Adair, A. V.: *ref,* 166(1562)

Adam, J.: *ref,* 251(59)

Adams, A.: *ref,* 196(1, 3, 13, 15–6)

Adams, A. A.: *ref,* 6:119(5)

Adams, A. J.: *ref,* 3:73(478, 594), 6:237(2336)

Adams, C. K.: *ref,* 6:87(213)

Adams, C. R.: *rev,* H37, H43, H48; *test,* 192; *ref,* 3:44(5), 3:64(2, 7)

Adams, D. K.: *exc,* P345–6; *ref,* 166(1737, 2381)

Adams, E. B.: *ref,* 4:63(2)

Adams, E. C.: *rev,* N118, N126

Adams, E. L.: *ref,* 3:64(5a)

Adams, F. J.: *test,* 325; *exc,* P131

Adams, G. S.: *bk,* P13, P836

Adams, H. B.: *ref,* 127(72, 80), 144(6), 166(1763, 1948), 470 (3338), 6:143(1169, 1291), 6:237 (2742, 2848, 2949)

Adams, H. E.: *ref,* 4(27), 6:87(95)

Adams, H. L.: *ref,* 4(52, 67), 27 (244, 296), 259(361)

Adams, H. M.: *exc,* P455

Adams, J.: *ref,* 67(539), 166(2002), 5:114(104), 6:182(153)

Adcock, C. J.: *rev,* 5:112, 5:147,

Brodman, K.: *test,* 48–9; *ref,* 49(1–7, 15), 4:37(2, 4–5, 9, 15–6, 21–2, 32, 39), 5:44(1–2)
Brodsky, A. M.: *ref,* 438(14)
Brodsky, S. L.: *ref,* 438(14)
Brodsly, W. J.: *ref,* 447(30), 5:145(6)
Brody, A. B.: *ref,* 4:117(913)
Brody, C. M. H.: *ref,* 5:147(44), 5:154(1855)
Brody, D. S.: *ref,* 4:71(196)
Brody, E. B.: *ref,* 381(36, 40)
Brody, G. F.: *ref,* 160(1–2)
Brody, G. G.: *ref,* 5:154(1495)
Brody, H.: *ref,* 470(3095), 484 (907)
Brody, J. R.: *ref,* 5:154(2072), 5:164(546)
Brody, M. B.: *exc,* 3:29, P10, P714, P867; *ref,* 3:71(22–3)
Broe, J. R.: *ref,* 477(17)
Broedel, J. W.: *ref,* 470(3575)
Broer, M. R.: *bk,* P352
Brogden, H. E.: *rev,* 4:47, 4:59, E3–4, F208; *exc,* P379; *ref,* 4:77 (163), 5:114(93)
Broida, D. C.: *ref,* 5:86(482), 5:154(1670–1), 5:164(432)
Brolyer, C. R.: *exc,* P632
Bromer, J. A.: *exc,* P660; *ref,* 6:87(228)
Bromley, D. B.: *ref,* 47(43)
Bronzaft, A.: *ref,* 6:57(52–3), 6:138(30–1)
Bronzo, A. F.: *ref,* 261(43, 51), 263(2)
Brook, J. G.: *ref,* 49(47)
Brook, R. R.: *ref,* 67(362)
Brooks, E.: *ref,* 4:96(3), 6:159 (44)
Brooks, F. D.: *exc,* P234, P372, P746
Brooks, J. J.: *ref,* 2:1201(4), 2:1222(8), 3:107(42)
Brooks, L. E.: *ref,* 4:51(12)
Brooks, L. M.: *ref,* 4:88(8)
Brooks, M.: *ref,* 127(71), 5:154 (2166, 2255)
Brooks, N.: *rev,* E7, E21, E24–5, E38, E40, E42, E44, E54, E57, E64–5
Brooks, R. D.: *ref,* 259(364)
Broom, M. E.: *rev,* C191, K22; *bk,* P131; *exc,* P148–9, P314, P369, P401, P554, P647; *ref,* 2:1198(6), 2:1253(5, 8)
Broomhead, E.: *ref,* 4:117(612)
Broota, A.: *ref,* 484(1193)
Broota, K. D.: *ref,* 484(989, 1193)
Brosin, H. W.: *ref,* 2:1246(129), 3:73(241), 4:117(679)
Brotemarkle, R. A.: *rev,* 3:45; *ref,* 2:1239(8)
Brothers, W. L.: *ref,* 4:71(197), 6:143(1066)
Brotman, S.: *ref,* 5:86(547)
Broussard, L. J.: *ref,* 463(3–4)
Brouwer, P. J.: *test,* 333; *ref,* 4:60(2)
Brower, D.: *ref,* 3:60(54), 3:73 (556), 3:107(56), 4:28(86), 4:39(9), 4:71(73, 75, 100), 4:117(615, 680, 737), 4:136(121, 253), 5:28(32), 5:44(5)

Brower, E.: *ref,* 4:136(105, 281)
Brower, J. F.: *ref,* 3:107(56)
Brower, J. L.: *ref,* 6:57(55), 6:87(229)
Brown, A. C.: *ref,* 49(24, 63)
Brown, A. F.: *ref,* 6:87(85), 6:182(175)
Brown, A. J.: *exc,* P860, P874
Brown, A. S.: *rev,* L81
Brown, A. W.: *rev,* F210, F231; *exc,* P369, P674; *ref,* 6:103(30)
Brown, B. H.: *ref,* 5:154(2020)
Brown, C.: *ref,* 415(421)
Brown, C. C.: *ref,* 4:117(1097)
Brown, C. M.: *rev,* H186, H191–2, H200, K101, K112; *test,* 170; *bk,* P132; *ref,* 5:88(1)
Brown, C. P.: *ref,* 5:89(36), 5:105(8)
Brown, C. R.: *ref,* 6:129(18)
Brown, C. W.: *exc,* P40
Brown, D. G.: *test,* 131; *exc,* P119; *ref,* 65(8), 130(77), 161 (166), 220(12), 470(3335), 6:129(1–5, 11), 6:229(54), 6:237 (2493)
Brown, D. J.: *ref,* 5(159), 259 (288), 6:87(131), 6:110(96), 6:143(951)
Brown, D. R.: *ref,* 4(2), 5:37(18), 5:114(104), 6:182(153)
Brown, E.: *ref,* 5:154(2141)
Brown, F.: *test,* 305; *exc,* 5:130; *ref,* 321(12), 451(218), 470 (3722), 2:1240(1–6), 5:36(9, 12–3), 5:139(24, 63, 79), 5:148 (17), 5:154(1316, 1496, 1507, 2038, 2055, 2167), 6:215(101), 6:237(2760)
Brown, F. G.: *exc,* P51; *ref,* 166(1579, 1965), 6:142(2, 5–6)
Brown, F. T.: *ref,* 3:73(349)
Brown, G. G.: *ref,* 4:117(935)
Brown, G. I.: *ref,* 15(4–5), 287(25, 27)
Brown, G. J.: *ref,* 67(589)
Brown, G. K.: *ref,* 4:45(5, 7)
Brown, G. W.: *bk,* P873
Brown, H. S.: *ref,* 4:71(76, 101)
Brown, I.: *ref,* 5:57(35), 6:101 (55)
Brown, I. C.: *exc,* P745
Brown, I. D.: *ref,* 289(3)
Brown, J.: *bk,* P215; *ref,* 5:154 (1699)
Brown, J. E.: *ref,* 484(1149), 4:77(113)
Brown, J. F.: *exc,* P89; *ref,* 3:27(9), 3:41(10), 4:129(11)
Brown, J. R.: *ref,* 472(61)
Brown, L. B.: *ref,* 116(55), 161 (217), 166(1580), 451(199), 470(3561), 471(276), 5:154 (2021), 6:245(865)
Brown, L. P.: *ref,* 5:38(81)
Brown, M.: *exc,* P796; *ref,* 166 (2352), 184(54), 4:117(914), 1085)
Brown, M. A.: *test,* 3:102; *ref,* 4:71(198)
Brown, M. B.: *ref,* 67(467), 259 (365)
Brown, M. M.: *ref,* 4:51(14), 4:129(12)

Brown, M. N.: *ref,* 4:71(199), 5:95(274)
Brown, M. R.: *ref,* 259(291)
Brown, P. A.: *ref,* 3:38(5), 6:159(50)
Brown, P. L.: *ref,* 6:143(952)
Brown, R. A.: *ref,* 4(14), 67(528), 166(1702), 470(3552), 6:143 (1176)
Brown, R. D.: *ref,* 184(64)
Brown, R. L.: *ref,* 381(47), 5:155 (129)
Brown, R. R.: *exc,* 3:78; *ref,* 3:73(242, 302), 4:117(681)
Brown, R. W.: *exc,* P639
Brown, S. W.: *ref,* 166(1861)
Brown, T. E.: *ref,* 6:237(2761)
Brown, V. H.: *ref,* 5:63(48)
Brown, W.: *bk,* P133
Brown, W. E.: *test,* 284
Brown, W. H.: *exc,* P581; *ref,* 5:89(41)
Brown, W. T.: *ref,* 4:136(291)
Browne, R. F.: *bk,* P571
Brownell, W. A.: *rev,* A27, A33, G121, G125, G129, G131, G134, G137–8, G155, G183, G200, H95; *bk,* P615; *exc,* P148
Brownsberger, C. N.: *ref,* 166 (1970)
Brownstein, J. B.: *ref,* 29(173)
Broxton, J. A.: *ref,* 4(26)
Brožek, J.: *exc,* P150, P169, P172, P290, P360, P607, P791; *ref,* 166(1418, 1874, 1966), 245(111), 4:71(102–3, 136, 245), 4:129 (18, 28), 5:86(322–3, 548), 5:154(1374)
Bruce, J. M.: *ref,* 5:154(1497)
Bruce, M. M.: *test,* 413, 445; *ref,* 5:65(40), 5:80(8), 5:86(679), 5:95(283, 287–8, 294, 298–9), 5:118(12), 6:143(861), 6:176(37, 39–40, 42–5)
Bruch, C.: *ref,* 4(79)
Bruck, M.: *ref,* 451(140), 6:203 (221), 6:229(90, 110, 128)
Bruder, G.: *ref,* 6:124(2)
Brudo, C. S.: *ref,* 5:154(1498)
Brueckel, J. E.: *ref,* 5:63(26), 5:64(28), 5:78(28)
Brueckner, L. J.: *rev,* G145, G147, G155, G173, G179, G199, H85, H94, H107; *exc,* P612
Bruel, I.: *ref,* 67(688)
Bruell, J. H.: *ref,* 470(3171)
Brumbaugh, R. B.: *ref,* 79(31)
Brunclik, H. L.: *ref,* 166(2445), 472(76), 6:143(1159)
Bruner, H. B.: *test,* 393
Bruner, J. S.: *exc,* P766; *ref,* 3:73(561), 3:99(58), 4:92(71), 4:117(682)
Bruning, C. R.: *ref,* 256(37)
Bruning, H.: *ref,* 6:159(57)
Brunkan, R. J.: *ref,* 4(61)
Brunschwig, L.: *bk,* P134; *ref,* 2:1239(47)
Brussel, J. A.: *bk,* P135; *ref,* 3:73(243–4), 4:117(631)
Bryan, A. I.: *exc,* P754; *ref,* 4:77(98, 142)
Bryan, H. L.: *exc,* P352

Bryan, J. E.: *rev,* H140, H151, H156–7
Bryan, J. H.: *ref,* 27(241, 292), 166(1840, 2049), 6:177(18, 27, 34), 6:143(1117)
Bryan, J. R.: *ref,* 4:28(109), 5:38(63)
Bryan, L. L.: *ref,* 6:143(1258)
Bryan, M. M.: *rev,* A27, A49, C86, C93, G172
Bryan, R. C.: *bk,* P136–7
Bryant, G. P.: *ref,* 245(258)
Bryant, J. E.: *ref,* 48(60), 484(953)
Bryant, N. D.: *rev,* K63, K88, K93, K143; *exc,* P805
Bryn, D.: *ref,* 2:1246(46)
Bryson, G.: *exc,* P808
Buchan, L. G.: *ref,* 477(33)
Bucher, S.: *ref,* 5:164(381)
Buchholz, S.: *test,* 162; *ref,* 6:139(2)
Buck, J. N.: *test,* 203, 334, 437; *ref,* 437(130), 3:47(1–3), 3:56(1), 3:66(1), 4:107(6–8, 10, 13–4, 17–8), 5:139(28, 79)
Buck, R. C.: *ref,* 29(175)
Buckalew, R. J.: *ref,* 6:141(4)
Buckingham, G. E.: *test,* 349; *ref,* 5:91(1)
Buckingham, R. A.: *ref,* 190A(4)
Buckle, D. F.: *ref,* 3:73(303), 4:117(1086), 5:154(1672)
Bucklow, M.: *exc,* P248
Budd, W. C.: *ref,* 6:108(60)
Buddemeyer, G. W.: *exc,* P573
Budnoff, C. K.: *ref,* 6:245(662)
Budoff, M.: *ref,* 6:206(25, 34)
Buechley, R.: *ref,* 5:86(324)
Buehler, C.: *bk,* P138
Buel, W. D.: *ref,* 6:109(63), 6:182(219), 6:192(23)
Buer, C. F.: *ref,* 6:143(815)
Bues, H. W.: *test,* 223; *ref,* 4:46(12)
Buffaloe, W. J.: *ref,* 166(2322)
Bugental, J. F. T.: *ref,* 6:143(783), 6:237(2312)
Buhler, C.: *test,* 197, 428, 466, 488, 6:237; *bk,* P139–41; *ref,* 466(1), 3:60(29), 3:73(304, 444, 557), 3:103(53), 4:117(632, 683–4, 786–7, 915), 4:147(2, 5–6), 5:154(1317, 1499), 5:168(10–3, 15)
Buhler, K.: *test,* 6:237; *bk,* P140; *ref,* 4:117(683)
Buker, S. L.: *ref,* 4:117(865, 1087), 5:154(1318)
Bull, E. G.: *exc,* P890
Bullis, G. E.: *bk,* P343
Bulloch, S. I.: *ref,* 6:145(67)
Bullock, R. P.: *bk,* P142
Bunin, S. M.: *ref,* 6:87(132)
Burch, R. L.: *rev,* G131, G167, G188
Burchard, E. M. L.: *exc,* 4:126, P87; *ref,* 321(13, 16), 2:1246(123), 3:73(486), 3:107(38), 4:94(68), 5:154(1319)
Burchinal, L. G.: *ref,* 341(34, 36), 5:117(16–8), 6:73(124), 6:87(90), 6:154(20)
Burdick, H.: *ref,* 5:164(518)

Burdick, H. A.: *ref,* 471(268), 484(988)
Burdick, J. A.: *ref,* 71(47), 420(7)
Burdick, L. A.: *ref,* 6:174(99a)
Burdock, E. I.: *test,* 164, 285; *ref,* 164(1–2), 285(1–3), 5:86(483), 5:114(111), 6:182(203)
Burdus, J. A.: *ref,* 6:140(11)
Burgart, H. J.: *ref,* 6:157(312)
Burge, E. W.: *ref,* 67(590)
Burgemeister, B. B.: *bk,* P143; *ref,* 3:73(419), 3:99(32), 4:117(1219), 6:237(2858)
Burger, F. E.: *ref,* 3:24(15)
Burgess, E.: *ref,* 5:86(415, 614), 5:95(295), 5:154(1500, 2022), 5:155(119, 161), 5:164(382, 522), 6:77(4, 7)
Burgess, E. W.: *test,* 154, 158, 411; *bk,* P177; *exc,* P39; *ref,* 154(1), 4:100(1), 5:84(1), 6:159(62)
Burgess, F.: *ref,* 408(22)
Burgess, G. G.: *ref,* 5:155(163)
Burgess, T. C.: *rev,* 6:66, 6:145
Burk, H. W.: *ref,* 6:143(1314)
Burk, K. W.: *ref,* 6:174(85)
Burkard, M. I.: *ref,* 6:245(814)
Burke, H. R.: *ref,* 4:28(78), 4:92(66), 4:95(21), 5:38(33)
Burke, K. R.: *ref,* 104(232)
Burke, M.: *ref,* 6:217(10), 6:237(2859)
Burke, R.: *ref,* 6:87(52), 6:94(1), 6:174(34)
Burke, V. B.: *ref,* 4(62)
Burks, B. S.: *exc,* P208, P723, P889
Burks, F. W.: *ref,* 2:1253(18)
Burleson, D. E.: *ref,* 4:144(22)
Burlingame, C. C.: *ref,* 3:95(4)
Burnand, G.: *ref,* 470(3562), 6:68(8), 6:143(1184), 6:237(2610–1, 2762, 2860, 2868, 2959–60)
Burnes, A. J.: *test,* 45; *ref,* 45(1–2)
Burnet, W. C.: *exc,* P412
Burnett, A.: *ref,* 457(8)
Burnett, C. W.: *ref,* 415(422)
Burnett, H.: *exc,* P259
Burnett, R. W.: *rev,* L10, L42
Burnham, C. A.: *ref,* 4:117(788), 4:129(2)
Burnham, P. S.: *rev,* C227, C253, O64; *bk,* P207; *exc,* P223; *ref,* 2:1239(26)
Burnham, R. K.: *ref,* 6:204(51), 6:237(2378)
Burns, D. G.: *rev,* E64–5
Burns, L.: *ref,* 5:38(64)
Burns, N. M.: *ref,* 166(1967)
Burns, W. H.: *ref,* 5:139(78), 6:215(103)
Buros, O. K.: *bk,* P144–53; *exc,* P496
Burpee, R. H.: *bk,* P154
Burr, E. T.: *rev,* F35, F191; *ref,* 4:31(38)
Burr, J. B.: *exc,* P340
Burrall, L.: *ref,* 5:38(86, 95)
Bursch, C. W.: *ref,* 5:86(325)
Bursill, A.: *exc,* 6:138
Burstein, A. G.: *rev,* 6:63, F263; *ref,* 6:237(2763)
Burstein, E.: *ref,* 484(971)

Burt, C.: *rev,* F36, F58, I22; *bk,* P155–7, P413; *exc,* P10, P148, P151, P169, P172, P233, P292, P340, P424, P544, P555, P572, P728–9, P738, P774–5, P778, P807, P813, P825, P859, P865–6, P903
Burton, A.: *exc,* P53, P186; *ref,* 442A(113), 3:60(36, 55), 4:71(153), 4:117(789), 4:136(159)
Burton, J. G.: *ref,* 67(436)
Burton, J. L.: *ref,* 6:127(37)
Burton, M. V.: *ref,* 4:77(182)
Burton, R. V.: *ref,* 104(176)
Burton, W. H.: *exc,* P470
Burtt, H. E.: *exc,* P622, P631, P638, P771, P825, P855
Busbice, J. J.: *ref,* 159(6)
Bush, C. L.: *bk,* P63
Bushey, J. T.: *ref,* 433(1)
Buss, A. H.: *ref,* 6:143(1048), 6:237(2861)
Busse, W.: *ref,* 166(2227–8)
Buswell, G. T.: *rev,* K118; *exc,* P138, P335, P770, P778, P841, P853
Butcher, H. J.: *ref,* 175(1), 245(262), 6:131(16), 6:174(108), 6:182(280)
Butcher, J. N.: *ref,* 166(1581–2, 1756, 1968–9)
Butcher, T.: *ref,* 470(3662)
Butler, A. J.: *ref,* 163(28), 166(1955)
Butler, B. V.: *ref,* 415(408)
Butler, G. A.: *ref,* 484(1194)
Butler, J. R.: *ref,* 4(27), 166(2222)
Butler, M. N.: *test,* 492; *ref,* 4:146(1)
Butler, O. P.: *ref,* 4:136(122)
Butler, R. L.: *ref,* 6:206(29), 6:229(69)
Butler, W. R.: *ref,* 5:77(5)
Butt, D. S.: *ref,* 245(174, 214)
Butt, S. D.: *ref,* 245(175)
Buttenwieser, P.: *ref,* 4:77(88)
Butterfield, E. C.: *ref,* 415(345), 6:143(1177, 1296)
Buttimore, D. J.: *ref,* 353(7), 5:38(32)
Button, A. D.: *ref,* 5:86(615), 5:154(2023)
Butts, H. F.: *ref,* 6:73(163)
Buzby, D. E.: *ref,* 71(73), 442A(174)
Byars, H.: *ref,* 266(29)
Byers, A. P.: *ref,* 67(468, 652)
Byers, K.: *bk,* P514; *exc,* P298
Byrd, E.: *ref,* 5:126(10), 5:172(96, 117), 6:174(40)
Byrne, A. E.: *ref,* 447(45)
Byrne, D.: *ref,* 27(223), 166(1583), 484(944–5, 972), 6:143(1067, 1297)
Byrum, M.: *ref,* 6:143(888)
Bystryn, D.: *ref,* 4(2), 5:37(18)

CABANSKI, S. J.: *ref,* 6:143(816)
Cabe, P. A.: *ref,* 71(72)
Cabeen, C. W.: *ref,* 6:143(1068)
Cabrer, S. M.: *ref,* 6:87(61)
Cacavas, P. D.: *ref,* 6:229(112)

(394), 339(19), 6:143(799), 6:182(158), 6:192(13)

Conkey, R. C.: *ref*, 4:117(927)

Conklin, E. S.: *ref*, 2:1243(16)

Conley, N. L.: *ref*, 259(368), 277 (41)

Conlin, J. E.: *ref*, 415(267)

Conn, J. H.: *exc*, P373

Conner, H. T.: *ref*, 5:86(486)

Conner, J. D.: *ref*, 42(7, 31)

Conners, C. K.: *ref*, 439(48), 6:94 (12), 6:245(868)

Conners, G. A.: *ref*, 5:155(85)

Connolly, F.: *ref*, 166(2071)

Connor, J. P.: *ref*, 415(346)

Connor, W. H.: *ref*, 161(254), 166 (2382), 245(338)

Conrad, C. C.: *rev*, N92, N103

Conrad, D. C.: *ref*, 4:117(1031)

Conrad, H. S.: *rev*, A14, A33, A39, A41, A51–2; *bk*, P196; *exc*, P230, P632, P778; *ref*, 4:37(30), 4:71(113), 4:77(221), 5:69(51), 6:120(65)

Conrad, W. K.: *ref*, 6:245(756)

Consalvi, C.: *ref*, 5:154(2030, 2172)

Constantinides, P. D.: *ref*, 29(199)

Conway, C. B.: *bk*, P197, P710; *ref*, 2:1239(39)

Conway, R.: *ref*, 6:243(152)

Conwell, D. V.: *ref*, 5:86(552)

Coody, B. E.: *ref*, 67(547, 593)

Cook, B. F.: *ref*, 470(3566)

Cook, C. H.: *ref*, 4:35(22)

Cook, D. L.: *ref*, 6:87(185, 296), 6:110(115, 138, 158), 6:143 (1077)

Cook, E. B.: *ref*, 4:71(204)

Cook, E. F.: *rev*, N60, N65

Cook, J. M.: *ref*, 5:59(13), 5:63 (58), 5:64(54), 5:114(132)

Cook, M. M.: *ref*, 455(10)

Cook, P. E.: *ref*, 166(2263), 439 (95), 484(1172)

Cook, P. H.: *ref*, 2:1239(65); 3:73 (246–7, 303), 4:117(616)

Cook, R. A.: *ref*, 94(13), 5:164 (327, 385), 5:166(7), 6:71(97)

Cook, R. L.: *ref*, 67(380)

Cook, S. W.: *bk*, P198

Cook, W. E.: *ref*, 442A(70), 5:139 (53)

Cook, W. W.: *rev*, A1, A49, C193, C197, H95, H112; *bk*, P224; *exc*, P768, P887, P905; *ref*, 5:86(487, 553)

Cooke, J. K.: *ref*, 166(2156-7)

Cooke, J. W. K.: *ref*, 166(1588)

Cooke, M. K.: *ref*, 166(2158)

Cooke, N. B.: *ref*, 477(24)

Cooke, R. M.: *ref*, 166(1589)

Cooke, T. F.: *ref*, 5:65(41)

Cooley, C. E.: *ref*, 116(41)

Cooley, G. M.: *ref*, 259(422)

Cooley, J. C.: *ref*, 6:157(313)

Cooley, W. W.: *rev*, L27, L30; *exc*, P397; *ref*, 6:110(159), 6:182 (256), 6:237(2963), 6:245(869)

Coombs, C. H.: *rev*, G49, O208; *bk*, P199–200, P247

Coombs, R. W.: *ref*, 5:86(554), 5:105(15)

Coons, A. E.: *bk*, P780

Coons, M. O.: *ref*, 6:238(191)

Coons, W. H.: *ref*, 5:57(44), 6:177 (29)

Cooper, A.: *ref*, 470(3162)

Cooper, B.: *ref*, 49(63), 127(48), 166(1513), 324(4)

Cooper, D. H.: *bk*, P680; *ref*, 294 (10), 5:38(29)

Cooper, E. M.: *exc*, P655

Cooper, G. D.: *ref*, 127(72, 80), 144 (6), 166(1763, 1948), 470(3338), 6:143(1169, 1291), 6:237(2742, 2848, 2866, 2949)

Cooper, G. W.: *ref*, 161(139), 253 (19), 470(3339), 484(992)

Cooper, J. G.: *ref*, 4:117(792, 1093), 5:154(1857)

Cooper, J. H.: *bk*, P771

Cooper, J. R.: *ref*, 415(347, 380)

Cooper, L. M.: *test*, 254; *ref*, 37(4, 6), 253(27), 254(4), 6:178(9)

Cooper, M.: *ref*, 5:154(1510)

Cooper, M. N.: *ref*, 5:63(49), 5:64 (47), 5:78(48), 5:86(555)

Cooper, R.: *ref*, 77(24)

Cooper, S.: *ref*, 45(1), 6:237(2519)

Cooperative Study in General Education: *test*, 320, 333; *ref*, 4:45 (4), 4:60(1)

Coopersmith, S.: *ref*, 6:237(2867)

Cope, R. G.: *ref*, 184(46, 65)

Copeland, H. W.: *ref*, 4:77(90)

Copeland, L. P.: *ref*, 4:111(7), 6:229(61)

Copeman, J.: *ref*, 6:87(186)

Coppedge, R. J.: *ref*, 6:174(42)

Coppen, A.: *ref*, 161(168-70), 6:138(92)

Copper, J.: *ref*, 6:216(5)

Coppinger, N. W.: *ref*, 448(111), 6:89(29), 6:96(16), 6:143(1299), 6:215(109)

Copple, R.: *ref*, 6:87(117), 6:143 (925), 6:182(194), 6:245(701)

Corah, N. L.: *ref*, 36(3), 71(48), 166(1590), 451(152), 5:47(37), 6:87(141, 187)

Corah, P. L.: *ref*, 451(152)

Corbally, J. E.: *exc*, P644

Corby, P. G.: *test*, 347

Corey, S. M.: *rev*, 1:897, 2:1238, 2:1266; *exc*, P314, P491, P593, P634, P695, P785

Corke, P. P.: *ref*, 470(3315), 6:238 (225)

Corlis, R.: *ref*, 177(49)

Corlis, R. B.: *ref*, 6:143(963)

Cornelison, A. R.: *ref*, 5:148(47), 5:154(2230), 5:156(23), 5:164 (584)

Cornell, E. L.: *rev*, A52; *bk*, P201; *exc*, P572

Cornell, F. G.: *test*, 402

Cornish, R. L.: *ref*, 27(225)

Cornwell, H. G.: *ref*, 245(216), 259(395)

Coroso, J.: *ref*, 5:65(51), 5:73(4)

Corotto, L. V.: *ref*, 27(169, 179), 124(53), 166(1764), 244(79), 415 (306, 336-7), 6:71(125), 6:143 (1183), 6:203(182, 184, 224)

Corrigan, H. G.: *ref*, 3:73(485)

Corrigan, S. M.: *ref*, 6:143(788)

Corsini, R. J.: *test*, 213, 232; *ref*,

4:71(159), 4:77(194), 5:103(1–2), 5:154(1677, 1858)

Corter, H. M.: *ref*, 5:154(1327), 6:78(29)

Cortis, G. A.: *ref*, 245(331)

Cortis, L. E.: *exc*, P151

Cortner, R. H.: *ref*, 5:154(1859), 5:162(114)

Cosby, B. W.: *ref*, 6:180(19)

Cosentino, F.: *ref*, 4(34)

Cosgrove, A. M.: *ref*, 6:103(32)

Costa, L. D.: *ref*, 166(1765), 6:143 (1300)

Costantini, A.: *ref*, 263(3)

Costanza, V.: *ref*, 6:220(8)

Costello, C. G.: *ref*, 179(3, 5), 5:154(2258), 6:132(15), 6:138 (93)

Costin, F.: *ref*, 4(35)

Cottam, H. R.: *exc*, P739

Cottingham, A.: *ref*, 480(177), 4:136(232, 286), 4:138(4-5)

Cottingham, H. F.: *exc*, P340

Cottle, W. C.: *rev*, A6, O50; *test*, 236; *exc*, P13, P95, P225, P791; *ref*, 27(360), 166(2343), 236(3–6), 4:28(87, 97–9, 110–1), 4:49 (5), 4:71(109, 160–2, 205–7, 250), 5:65(12–3, 20, 29), 5:86 (423, 488–9, 583, 706), 5:89(40)

Cottrell, L. S.: *ref*, 154(1), 5:77 (13), 5:84(1), 6:105(3)

Cottrell, T.: *ref*, 6:239(40)

Cottrell, T. B.: *ref*, 67(432)

Couch, A. S.: *ref*, 6:96(8), 6:143 (893, 964, 1078), 6:174(53), 6:192(18)

Coulson, R. W.: *ref*, 6:71(39), 6:110(64), 6:143(820)

Coulter, W. M.: *ref*, 6:243(142)

Counts, R. M.: *ref*, 4:117(922)

Counts, S.: *ref*, 6:143(1130)

Court, J. H.: *ref*, 245(177)

Courtis, S. A.: *rev*, F100, H130, I22

Courtless, T. F.: *ref*, 484(1228)

Courtney, D.: *rev*, 4:64, 4:79, A53

Coutts, R. L.: *ref*, 6:182(233)

Covey, D. S.: *ref*, 470(3567)

Covington, J. D.: *ref*, 67(364), 259 (309)

Cowan, E. A.: *test*, 310; *ref*, 2:1217 (1)

Cowan, G.: *ref*, 484(1152)

Cowan, V. D.: *ref*, 3:67(2)

Cowden, J. E.: *ref*, 165(45), 245 (332)

Cowden, R. C.: *ref*, 5:38(103), 5:139(55), 5:164(472), 5:172 (97)

Cowell, C. C.: *test*, 311–2; *exc*, P154, P288, P352; *ref*, 6:82(1–2), 6:83(1-2)

Cowen, E. L.: *ref*, 4:28(116), 4:117(1094), 5:38(74), 6:237 (3028)

Cowen, J.: *ref*, 5:155(79)

Cowie, V.: *ref*, 161(170), 6:138 (46a)

Cowin, M.: *exc*, 3:89; *ref*, 3:73 (421)

Cowles, J. T.: *exc*, P517

Cowley, J. J.: *ref*, 5:114(105)

Eck, R. A.: *ref,* 439(62)
Eckelberry, R. H.: *exc,* P490
Eckert, R. E.: *test,* 403
Eckert, R. G.: *ref,* 4:28(37), 4:77(118)
Eckhardt, W.: *ref,* 5:154(1867, 2176), 6:237(2772)
Eckman, K. M.: *ref,* 116(63), 166(2328), 176(23), 439(97), 484(1188)
Edds, J. H.: *exc,* P303
Edelman, S. K.: *ref,* 470(3155)
Edelstein, R. R.: *ref,* 5:164(533)
Edgar, C. L.: *ref,* 5:149(38)
Edgar, M. S.: *ref,* 415(350)
Edgerly, J.: *ref,* 470(3242)
Edgerton, H. A.: *bk,* P224, P808; *exc,* P378, P644; *ref,* 3:24(3)
Edgerton, R. B.: *ref,* 6:237(2501)
Edminster, I. F.: *ref,* 6:143(1241)
Edmiston, R. W.: *ref,* 3:26(17), 5:38(34, 51)
Edmonson, B. W.: *ref,* 5:154(2111)
Edmonson, L. D.: *test,* 284
Edmonston, W. E.: *ref,* 67(402), 6:237(2405)
Edrington, T. C.: *ref,* 6:78(34)
Edson, K. C.: *ref,* 42(4)
Edwards, A. E.: *ref,* 49(28), 6:110(147), 6:173(57)
Educational Testing Service: *test,* 273
Edwards, A. L.: *rev,* 6:72, 6:88; *test,* 67–8; *bk,* P276–7; *exc,* P199, P378; *ref,* 27(186), 67(416), 127(40), 161(142), 166(1607–11, 1772–3, 1987, 2173), 5:47(1), 5:144(9), 6:87(53, 94, 140, 232–3), 6:127(4), 6:143 (800, 972, 1082–5, 1189–93, 1307–8)
Edwards, A. S.: *exc,* P38, P43, P88, P123, P150, P250, P314, P336, P345, P401, P496, P732, P768, P793, P921
Edwards, B.: *rev,* E22, E48
Edwards, E. S.: *ref,* 6:197(8)
Edwards, J. A.: *ref,* 166(1520)
Edwards, R.: *rev,* C44, G149
Eells, K.: *bk,* P278, P876
Efron, H. Y.: *ref,* 470(3343, 3462, 3675)
Efstathiou, A.: *ref,* 251(56)
Egas, E. O.: *ref,* 3:73(423)
Egbert, R. L.: *ref,* 27(357), 5:164 (568)
Egeland, B. R.: *ref,* 415(351, 381)
Egermeier, J. C.: *ref,* 165(12)
Ehlers, H. J.: *exc,* P115, P261
Ehrenberg, A. S. C.: *exc,* P170
Ehrenwald, J.: *ref,* 470(3463)
Ehrhardt, A. A.: *ref,* 415(340)
Ehrle, R. A.: *ref,* 166(1612)
Ehrlich, H. J.: *ref,* 27(278)
Eicher, I. L.: *ref,* 166(1613)
Eichler, H.: *ref,* 5:154(1687), 6:226(75)
Eichler, M.: *ref,* 415(309)
Eichler, R. M.: *ref,* 4:117(934, 1099–1101)
Eichman, W. J.: *rev,* 6:175, 6:177; *ref,* 6:143(874, 1086, 1194)
Eichorn, D. H.: *rev,* 5:94, 5:133, F216, H173

Eichorn, J. R.: *ref,* 137(8)
Eiduson, B. T.: *exc,* P433; *ref,* 6:237(2406, 2873, 2967), 6:245 (641, 820)
Eigenbrode, C. R.: *ref,* 104(185), 451(137), 6:110(112), 6:237 (2623)
Eilbert, L.: *ref,* 5:155(81)
Eimicke, V. W.: *ref,* 4:77(220, 256), 4:89(33, 36), 4:92(80)
Eisdörfer, C.: *ref,* 6:237(2502, 2624–5, 2874, 2968)
Eisele, M. C.: *ref,* 4:49(5)
Eisenberg, H.: *ref,* 166(2379, 2422)
Eisenberg, P.: *rev,* 3:61–2; *ref,* 3:97(1–2, 5), 4:77(124), 6:159 (55–6)
Eisendorfer, A.: *ref,* 3:73(491), 3:103(64)
Eisenman, R.: *ref,* 4(100), 27(362), 111(8, 11), 166(1988, 2142), 470 (3464, 3738)
Eisenson, J.: *test,* 76; *ref,* 5:52(2)
Eisenstein, D.: *ref,* 5:154(1513)
Eiserer, P. E.: *exc,* P607
Eisman, H. D.: *ref,* 470(3344)
Eisner, B. G.: *ref,* 5:154(2177), 6:237(2969)
Eisner, H.: *bk,* P279
Ekberg, K.: *ref,* 470(3355)
Eklund, S.: *ref,* 415(310)
Ekman, P.: *ref,* 166(1483)
Ekstein, R.: *exc,* 4:141; *ref,* 3:103 (79), 4:136(138)
Ekstrom, P. R.: *ref,* 4:48(16)
Elder, S. T.: *ref,* 4(27)
Eldred, S. H.: *ref,* 124(72)
Elias, G.: *test,* 80; *ref,* 5:53(1, 5)
Elias, J. Z.: *ref,* 5:38(75)
Eliasberg, W.: *exc,* P563, P909
Elicker, P. E.: *ref,* 4:78(1)
Eliseo, T. S.: *ref,* 124(45)
Elithorn, A.: *test,* 190A; *ref,* 190A (1–8, 13–4, 17, 23)
Elizur, A.: *ref,* 4:117(799)
Elkan, G.: *ref,* 470(3465)
Elkin, A.: *ref,* 4:71(208)
Elkind, D.: *ref,* 6:89(30), 6:173 (59)
Elkins, E.: *ref,* 5:154(2260)
Elkisch, P.: *ref,* 442A(38), 5:137 (3)
Ellenberger, H.: *ref,* 470(3092)
Eller, W.: *rev,* K28, K117
Ellingson, M.: *bk,* P470
Ellinwood, E. H.: *ref,* 166(2174)
Elliot, J.: *ref,* 5:38(76)
Elliott, D. N.: *ref,* 5:101(8)
Elliott, E.: *exc,* P57, P170, P568
Elliott, H. E.: *ref,* 285(1)
Elliott, J. J.: *ref,* 251(51)
Elliott, L. L.: *ref,* 29(238)
Elliott, M. H.: *rev,* 3:63, O191; *exc,* P643
Elliott, R.: *ref,* 71(38)
Ellis, A.: *rev,* 3:31, 3:38, 4:50, 4:62, 4:102, 4:107, 5:53, 5:86, H43–4, H48; *exc,* P506; *ref,* 3:60 (38), 3:73(562), 4:28(72), 4:37 (30), 4:71(112–3), 4:77(195, 221), 5:69(51), 5:86(425), 5:125 (20), 6:120(65)
Ellis, D.: *exc,* P565
Ellis, D. B.: *ref,* 2:1222(6)

Ellis, F. W.: *ref,* 5:86(394), 6:143 (784)
Ellis, M. W.: *ref,* 165(31)
Ellis, R. W.: *ref,* 4:117(935)
Ellman, G. L.: *ref,* 6:143(1241)
Ells, E. M.: *ref,* 166(2175)
Ellsworth, R. B.: *test,* 147; *ref,* 147(9–10, 12), 6:126(11), 6:135 (1), 6:143(1290a)
Elmadjian, F.: *ref,* 3:73(579)
Elmgren, J.: *bk,* P280
Elmore, T. M.: *ref,* 166(2176), 193(11)
Elms, A. C.: *ref,* 166(1989)
Elonen, A. S.: *ref,* 4:117(697, 1108), 4:134(50), 4:136(262), 6:226(21)
El Senoussi, A.: *test,* 70, 149
Elstein, A. S.: *ref,* 470(3345), 6:237(2626)
Elton, C. F.: *ref,* 184(22, 35–7, 41, 48–51, 66), 472(58), 6:226(55)
Elvekrog, M. O.: *ref,* 166(1614), 6:143(1309)
Elzey, F. F.: *test,* 23; *ref,* 23(2)
Embree, E. D.: *ref,* 415(382)
Embree, R. A.: *ref,* 273(1)
Emch, M.: *ref,* 4:77(100)
Emerson, A. R.: *ref,* 49(17)
Emerson, M. R.: *exc,* P61
Emery, M.: *ref,* 470(3031)
Emfinger, W. E.: *ref,* 29(171), 321 (19)
Emmerich, W.: *ref,* 6:245(856)
Emmett, W. G.: *rev,* F68, F81, F100; *bk,* P281–2; *exc,* P29
Endacott, J. L.: *ref,* 470(3034), 3:73(170, 191, 424), 5:154(1688)
Ende, R. S.: *ref,* 457(17–8)
Endicott, J.: *test,* 53A, 164, 216A, 217, 365A; *ref,* 53A(1), 164 (7–8), 166(1615–6), 470(3243–4), 6:143(1310–1), 6:229(130), 6:237(2970–1), 6:245(870–1)
Endicott, N. A.: *ref,* 166(1615–6, 1990, 2177), 439(66, 83), 470 (3243–4), 6:143(1310–1), 6:229 (130), 6:237(2970–1), 6:245 (870–1)
Endler, N. S.: *ref,* 67(334), 6:87 (192)
Endler, O. L.: *bk,* P771
Ends, E. J.: *ref,* 5:55(3), 5:86 (692)
Endsley, R. C.: *ref,* 131(23)
Engel, B. T.: *ref,* 166(2013)
Engel, C.: *ref,* 6:237(2503)
Engel, I. M.: *ref,* 9(39), 27(279), 166(1991), 432(6, 8), 6:61(36), 6:71(90), 6:143(1195)
Engel, M.: *exc,* 6:68; *ref,* 5:143 (8), 6:237(2753, 2972), 6:245 (872)
Engel, R. G.: *ref,* 27(200)
Engel, W. E.: *ref,* 29(192)
Engelhardt, N. L.: *exc,* P149, P625
Engelhart, M. D.: *rev,* A8, A17, F21, L96, L99, L102, L107–8; *bk,* P115; *exc,* P72, P281, P381, P532, P554, P649
Engelhart, R. S.: *ref,* 166(2111), 6:143(1200)
Engelmann, H. O.: *test,* 74
England, L.: *ref,* 6:138(37)

Farrington, A. D.: *ref,* 6:58(12, 21)
Farrow, B. J.: *ref,* 29(176)
Farwell, E. D.: *ref,* 6:150(5)
Fassberg, E. W.: *exc,* P18, P250
Fassett, K. K.: *ref,* 5:86(290), 5:143(1, 3)
Fast, I.: *ref,* 470(3575), 484(1107)
Faterson, H. F.: *exc,* 4:112; *ref,* 71(59), 442A(120), 3:73(425a), 6:89(28), 6:229(53)
Faucett, E. C.: *ref,* 5:154(2193)
Faulkner, R.: *rev,* D7, D14, H204
Fauls, L. B.: *ref,* 166(1774)
Faunce, P. S.: *ref,* 166(1993, 2350)
Faust, J.: *ref,* 235(14)
Faust, M.: *ref,* 415(353)
Faust, W. L.: *ref,* 415(353)
Faw, V.: *ref,* 166(2351), 4:77(223), 6:143(824)
Fawcett, H. P.: *rev,* G71, G206, G208, G223, G225, G230–1, G235; *exc,* P241, P655
Fawcett, J.: *ref,* 6:127(25)
Fawcett, N. G.: *exc,* P38
Fay, J. W.: *rev,* D22, D27
Fay, P. J.: *ref,* 4:54(1)
Fa-yu, C.: *ref,* 6:237(2407)
Feagley, E. M.: *rev,* K194, K221
Feamster, J. H.: *ref,* 480(160), 5:139(55), 5:164(472), 5:172(97)
Fear, R. A.: *bk,* P298
Fears, E. B.: *ref,* 136(50)
Feather, D. B.: *ref,* 442A(57), 4:71(210)
Feather, N. T.: *ref,* 161(226)
Febinger, G. N.: *ref,* 245(178)
Fecher, I. B.: *ref,* 3:95(18)
Feder, D. D.: *ref,* 2:1200(5), 2:1243(17), 4:77(126)
Feder, Z.: *ref,* 6:143(1204)
Fee, M.: *ref,* 2:1200(2)
Feffer, M. H.: *ref,* 484(1200), 6:230(40), 6:237(2508)
Fehr, H. F.: *rev,* G53
Fehrer, E.: *rev,* B25, B47
Feigenbaum, K.: *ref,* 470(3573)
Feigenbaum, L.: *ref,* 4:134(48), 5:162(99)
Feil, M. H.: *ref,* 4:71(164)
Fein, L. G.: *test,* 490; *bk,* P299; *ref,* 116(29, 64), 472(71), 490(4–5), 4:117(938), 5:171(3)
Feinberg, H.: *rev,* F224
Feinberg, L. B.: *ref,* 235(13)
Feinberg, L. D.: *ref,* 5:154(1691, 1708)
Feinberg, M. R.: *ref,* 48(64), 82(18), 259(336)
Feingold, B. F.: *ref,* 166(2189), 6:143(1197)
Feirstein, A.: *ref,* 470(3576, 3659)
Feiveson, P.: *ref,* 5:38(89)
Feld, S. C.: *ref,* 484(942)
Feldberg, T. M.: *ref,* 3:73(394)
Feldhusen, J. F.: *ref,* 166(2445), 472(76)
Feldman, E. I.: *ref,* 6:143(1226)
Feldman, H.: *exc,* P369
Feldman, I. S.: *ref,* 415(264), 5:172(56)
Feldman, L. P.: *ref,* 5:52(3)
Feldman, M. J.: *test,* 282; *ref,*

4:71(114), 5:47(37), 5:86(301, 333, 426, 744), 5:148(48), 5:154(1692–3), 6:87(141), 6:195(2, 6), 6:229(94)
Feldmann, S. C.: *ref,* 415(270)
Feldstein, S.: *ref,* 48(69)
Feldt, L. S.: *rev,* C4, C6, C19, K179; *ref,* 415(425)
Felleman, C. A.: *ref,* 470(3118)
Felling, J.: *ref,* 442A(173)
Fellner, C.: *ref,* 166(1836)
Fellows, T. T.: *ref,* 27(326)
Felton, J. S.: *ref,* 4:37(33)
Felzer, S. B.: *ref,* 5:65(26), 5:154(1694, 1871)
Fenger, G.: *bk,* P592; *ref,* 6:237(2681)
Fenton, G. W.: *ref,* 161(227)
Fenton, N.: *exc,* P146
Fenwick, J.: *ref,* 415(365)
Fenz, W. D.: *ref,* 166(2352), 6:87(234)
Ferguson, A. B.: *ref,* 4:136(207)
Ferguson, G. A.: *rev,* F38, F102, F124, F157, F189, F194, O6, O47, O85; *bk,* P300, P466; *exc,* P52; *ref,* 3:73(456), 4:117(1103)
Ferguson, J. L.: *ref,* 6:110(54)
Ferguson, J. T.: *test,* 112; *ref,* 5:67(1)
Ferguson, L. W.: *rev,* O2, O40; *bk,* P301; *exc,* P277; *ref,* 342(9), 2:1239(56), 3:99(40)
Ferguson, R. A.: *ref,* 5:154(1336)
Ferguson, R. G.: *ref,* 3:60(39)
Fernald, L. D.: *ref,* 116(55), 161(217), 451(199), 470(3561), 6:237(2966)
Fernald, M. R.: *exc,* P885
Fernald, P. S.: *ref,* 439(34, 67)
Fernberger, S. W.: *exc,* P378
Ferracuti, F.: *exc,* P871
Ferreira, A. H.: *ref,* 484(1103)
Ferreira, A. J.: *ref,* 176(4), 327(32), 484(1091, 1142, 1187)
Ferrell, R. H.: *rev,* N97
Ferriman, M. R.: *ref,* 5:145(15, 18)
Fertman, M. H.: *ref,* 363(15–6)
Feshbach, S.: *ref,* 5:164(479), 6:245(762)
Fessenden, S. A.: *test,* 18
Fessler, M. H.: *ref,* 4:95(18)
Fest, B.: *ref,* 4:117(1186), 4:129(72), 4:136(160, 287)
Festinger, L.: *exc,* P595
Fetler, D.: *test,* 260
Fetterman, J. L.: *ref,* 2:1248(11)
Feurfile, D.: *ref,* 5:154(1248)
Fewell, M.: *ref,* 6:157(302)
Fey, W. F.: *ref,* 5:86(633), 5:111(30)
Ficca, S. C.: *ref,* 4:117(939)
Fick, D. J.: *ref,* 42(18), 5:59(7), 5:86(6)
Fick, R. L.: *ref,* 5:89(37), 5:105(11)
Ficken, C. E.: *rev,* E20, E38
Fiddleman, P. B.: *ref,* 166(1460), 6:237(2494)
Fiebert, M. S.: *ref,* 36(4, 9)
Fiedler, F. E.: *ref,* 442A(15), 484(986)
Fiedler, M. F.: *ref,* 5:154(2037)

Field, H. E.: *bk,* P390
Field, J.: *ref,* 5:172(142)
Field, J. A.: *rev,* N82
Field, J. G.: *ref,* 166(1087), 6:123(6), 6:138(48–9), 6:143(1087)
Field, L. W.: *ref,* 5:125(25)
Field, P. B.: *ref,* 107(5, 9–10), 253(34), 327(25), 6:245(821)
Field, W. F.: *ref,* 5:164(310)
Fielder, D. W.: *ref,* 104(209), 166(1618)
Fielding, B.: *ref,* 5:154(2038)
Fields, H.: *exc,* P522
Fields, S. J.: *ref,* 6:143(825)
Fieldsteel, N. D.: *bk,* P117; *ref,* 470(3247), 5:154(1666)
Fifer, G.: *rev,* G17, G52
Figetakis, N.: *ref,* 416(92)
Figura, C. J.: *ref,* 6:143(1198)
Filella, J.: *ref,* 470(3514)
Fillenbaum, S.: *ref,* 6:143(877, 1088)
Fillmore, E. A.: *bk,* P302
Filmer-Bennett, G. T.: *ref,* 4:117(1104), 5:154(1337, 1872), 6:245(822)
Fils, D. H.: *ref,* 4:110(1), 5:145(3)
Finan, J. L.: *exc,* P588
Finch, F. H.: *ref,* 2:1239(2), 3:71(29)
Finco, A. A.: *ref,* 104(258), 259(399)
Findley, D. G.: *ref,* 67(600)
Findley, W. G.: *rev,* 2:1259, A2, A20, A32, A43, A51, F21, F48, N31; *bk,* P303, P613; *exc,* P149, P685, P757, P829, P842
Fine, B. J.: *ref,* 161(250), 166(1521, 2353), 344(22), 471(307), 484(1201), 5:86(745), 6:143(878, 1089)
Fine, H. J.: *ref,* 470(3151, 3436), 5:77(12), 5:154(1348, 2018), 5:161(3)
Fine, M. J.: *ref,* 125(2–3)
Fine, P.: *bk,* P693
Fine, R.: *ref,* 4:113(4, 18), 4:117(699), 4:136(128, 290), 5:149(23, 30), 5:164(480–1), 6:230(44), 6:245(763)
Finegan, A.: *ref,* 195(13)
Finesinger, J. E.: *ref,* 326(2), 3:73(226), 5:76(11)
Finger, J. A.: *test,* 195; *ref,* 195(4, 7, 10–2)
Fink, D. M.: *ref,* 71(36), 166(1433)
Fink, H. H.: *ref,* 5:145(12), 6:224(19)
Fink, J. H.: *ref,* 166(1443, 1522), 244(62, 64), 451(147, 153), 470(3156, 3192), 484(940, 975)
Fink, M.: *ref,* 124(40), 470(3188), 6:71(91, 131), 6:237(2653)
Fink, M. A.: *ref,* 5:154(1234)
Fink, R. W.: *ref,* 245(219)
Fink, S. L.: *ref,* 6:203(178)
Finkle, R. B.: *ref,* 5:65(32)
Finlay, G. C.: *test,* 324
Finley, C. J.: *exc,* P613
Finley, J. R.: *ref,* 6:110(148)
Finn, J. A.: *ref,* 470(3677)

Goldwyn, R. M.: *ref,* 5:155(133)
Golen, M. E.: *ref,* 433(7)
Golias, G. A.: *ref,* 443(22), 6:206 (26)
Golightly, C.: *ref,* 27(223), 186 (10), 415(420)
Golin, S.: *ref,* 161(228), 166(1793, 2198), 470(3253)
Golle, R.: *ref,* 161(262)
Goltry, K.: *rev,* C27, C55
Gomez, B. J.: *ref,* 77(14, 29)
Gonda, T. A.: *ref,* 166(1633), 5:154 (1695, 1875-6)
Gondor, L. H.: *exc,* 4:128, P386
Gonen, J. Y.: *ref,* 166(2369)
Gonen, Y.: *ref,* 13(56)
Gonik, U.: *ref,* 6:143(1314a)
Gonyea, G. G.: *ref,* 283(14)
Gooch, P. H.: *ref,* 5:36(14)
Goocher, B.: *ref,* 6:89(13, 16), 6: 245(711)
Good, C. V.: *exc,* P148-9, P284, P342, P783
Good, J. A.: *ref,* 419(43), 455(17)
Good, P. K. E.: *bk,* P359; *ref,* 6: 143(1098)
Goodall, B. J.: *ref,* 6:237(2413)
Goodchilds, J. D.: *ref,* 6:143(1373)
Goodenough, D. R.: *ref,* 71(59), 442A(120), 6:74b(1-2), 6:89(20, 28, 32)
Goodenough, E.: *ref,* 5:154(2160)
Goodenough, F. L.: *rev,* F211-2, F240, I22; *bk,* P360-1; *exc,* P196, P344, P543, P778, P807, P901
Goodfellow, C. L.: *ref,* 179(2)
Goodfellow, R. L.: *ref,* 141(2)
Goodling, R. A.: *ref,* 5:65(33), 6: 110(70), 6:143(852)
Goodman, A.: *ref,* 6:89(33), 6:229 (133)
Goodman, A. W.: *exc,* P148; *ref,* 3:107(29)
Goodman, C.: *ref,* 67(603)
Goodman, C. H.: *ref,* 4:77(146)
Goodman, D.: *ref,* 470(3682)
Goodman, H. W.: *ref,* 4:117(803, 953-4)
Goodman, J. G.: *ref,* 245(179)
Goodman, M.: *ref,* 67(419), 442A (58-9), 5:164(333), 6:87(240)
Goodman, M. I.: *ref,* 4:136(263)
Goodner, S.: *ref,* 198(339)
Goodrich, A. H.: *ref,* 67(637), 255 (63)
Goodrich, D. C.: *ref,* 5:155(131), 5:164(440)
Goodrich, D. W.: *ref,* 5:76(22)
Goodstein, L. D.: *rev,* 6:77, 6:184; *exc,* 5:167, P712; *ref,* 4(14), 166 (1741, 2056), 256(36), 5:86(498, 630-1), 5:154(1705, 1883), 5:164 (484), 5:172(98), 6:71(70, 72, 95, 132), 6:87(96, 98, 195-7, 241), 6:143(982-3), 1099-100, 1176, 1232, 1315)
Goodwin, W. L.: *ref,* 136(32), 245 (180), 259(339)
Goosman, E. T.: *test,* 156
Goralski, P. S.: *ref,* 67(420)
Gorbutt, D. G.: *test,* 376
Gordon, C.: *ref,* 49(17)
Gordon, C. E.: *ref,* 27(157)

Gordon, C. M.: *ref,* 65(9)
Gordon, G.: *ref,* 49(61)
Gordon, H. C.: *rev,* K47, L10, L15, L26, L34; *ref,* 3:110(7)
Gordon, H. L.: *ref,* 5:164(334, 394)
Gordon, H. P.: *ref,* 3:61(7), 4:77 (171)
Gordon, I. E.: *ref,* 6:138(57)
Gordon, I. J.: *ref,* 6:87(298), 6: 192(28)
Gordon, J. E.: *ref,* 6:237(2515), 6:245(646)
Gordon, J. H.: *ref,* 259(426)
Gordon, L. V.: *rev,* O8, O324, O327; *test,* 92-3, 173, 261, 263; *ref,* 67(661), 79(34), 261(23, 28-30, 36-8, 45, 54), 263(1), 4:73 (22-4), 5:59(1-4, 9), 5:162(93, 105), 6:184(1, 4)
Gordon, M.: *ref,* 67(425), 127(60)
Gordon, R.: *ref,* 6:237(2884)
Gordon, T.: *ref,* 4:71(167)
Gores, H. B.: *exc,* P830
Gorfein, D. S.: *ref,* 6:119(6)
Gorham, D. R.: *test,* 439-40; *ref,* 91(78), 124(31, 36), 221A(6), 439(35, 41, 50, 73, 85, 98, 101), 440(1-5), 470(3490), 6:217(16)
Gorham, W. A.: *bk,* P307
Gorlow, L.: *exc,* P333, P527; *ref,* 79(24), 259(427), 4:136(249), 5:154(1348), 5:161(3)
Gorman, B. S.: *ref,* 77(41)
Gorman, F. J.: *ref,* 166(2189), 6: 143(1197)
Gorman, J. A.: *ref,* 166(1634)
Gorman, J. R.: *ref,* 6:143(1101), 6:145(70)
Gorman, M. M.: *ref,* 4:115(7)
Gorsuch, R. L.: *ref,* 245(269)
Gortner, S. R.: *ref,* 184(67), 259 (462)
Goshorn, W. M.: *ref,* 4:65(3)
Goslin, D. A.: *bk,* P362
Gosnell, H. F.: *exc,* P825
Goss, A.: *ref,* 67(662-4)
Goss, A. M.: *ref,* 67(544, 604)
Gotham, R. E.: *ref,* 3:110(11), 4: 77(183), 4:95(20)
Gothberg, L. C.: *ref,* 3:103(95)
Gottesfeld, B. H.: *ref,* 5:154(1617)
Gottesman, I. I.: *ref,* 27(281), 166 (1679-80), 6:131(13, 18), 6:143 (984, 1209, 1316)
Gottesman, I. J.: *ref,* 166(2248)
Gottfried, N. W.: *ref,* 67(550), 484(927, 1108)
Gottheil, E.: *ref,* 166(2370), 245 (250)
Gottlieb, A. L.: *ref,* 6:237(2634)
Gottlieb, L. S.: *ref,* 5:154(1864)
Gottlieb, S. G.: *ref,* 5:154(1686), 6:237(2759)
Gottsagen, M. L.: *ref,* 415(383)
Gottsch, L. G.: *ref,* 6:174(64)
Gottschalk, L. A.: *bk,* P363; *ref,* 245(268)
Gottsdanker, J. S.: *ref,* 184(68)
Gottsegen, M. G.: *ref,* 5:120(93)
Goude, G.: *bk,* P364
Goudey, E.: *ref,* 4:136(211)
Gough, H. G.: *rev,* 4:34, 4:92, 5:39, 5:96, 5:117, 6:88-9, 6:118;

test, 4, 27, 34, 202; *exc,* P301; *ref,* 4(6), 27(190-4, 232-3, 282-4, 310, 363-7), 34(2), 166(1395, 1794), 3:60(40, 58), 4:71(115-8, 168-9, 212, 256-9), 4:136(131), 5:37(1-8, 10-1, 13, 20), 5:86 (340-1, 431, 499), 5:107(4), 6: 71(58)
Gough, J. W.: *ref,* 225(3)
Gough, P.: *ref,* 6:178(1)
Gould, A.: *exc,* P914
Gould, E.: *ref,* 166(2125), 244(83), 470(3546)
Gould, G.: *ref,* 3:110(15), 4:28 (80)
Gould, H.: *ref,* 5:30(125), 5:95 (268)
Gould, N. S.: *ref,* 159(4)
Goulding, A. V.: *ref,* 5:145(13)
Goulding, C. W.: *ref,* 5:86(304)
Goulet, L. R.: *ref,* 6:194(113-4)
Gourlay, N.: *rev,* C38, K38
Gouws, D. J.: *ref,* 6:143(1102)
Gowan, J. C.: *exc,* P613, P705; *ref,* 4(3, 79), 5:37(14, 32), 5:65 (28, 52), 5:86(561-2, 632, 746), 5:95(291), 5:114(124, 133, 139), 6:71(35, 59), 6:110(60, 100-1), 6:182(159)
Gowan, M. S.: *ref,* 5:37(14), 5:65 (28), 5:86(562)
Goyne, J. B.: *ref,* 6:237(2387)
Grace, D. P.: *ref,* 166(1635)
Gradel, D. V.: *ref,* 255(41), 256 (39)
Grady, M. J.: *ref,* 255(34)
Graff, F. A.: *ref,* 5:89(55)
Graff, H.: *ref,* 116(42)
Graff, R. L.: *ref,* 127(92)
Graham, A. W.: *ref,* 3:26(21)
Graham, D.: *exc,* P293
Graham, E.: *ref,* 6:237(2535)
Graham, E. E.: *ref,* 5:154(1368)
Graham, F. K.: *test,* 163; *ref,* 4:96 (1-2, 4), 6:140(12)
Graham, G.: *rev,* N81
Graham, H.: *ref,* 3:73(554)
Graham, J.: *exc,* P106, P149, P274, P526
Graham, J. R.: *ref,* 166(1795, 2199)
Graham, L. E.: *ref,* 178(7), 255 (54)
Graham, L. R.: *ref,* 5:86(747)
Graham, S. R.: *ref,* 442A(71, 80), 5:154(1706, 1884), 6:203(171)
Graine, G. N.: *ref,* 5:47(22), 5:155 (172)
Grainer, H. M.: *ref,* 5:154(1885)
Graley, J.: *ref,* 5:154(1692)
Grams, A.: *ref,* 5:148(49)
Grande, P. P.: *ref,* 195(14-5)
Grangaard, G. H.: *ref,* 54(4), 166 (1636)
Granick, S.: *ref,* 41(2), 5:86(432), 5:125(44), 5:148(21), 5:154 (1321)
Grant, B.: *test,* 227
Grant, C. O.: *ref,* 67(366)
Grant, D. A.: *exc,* P150
Grant, D. L.: *exc,* P349; *ref,* 67 (527), 102(77), 472(55, 63), 484 (1161), 5:64(39-40)
Grant, H.: *ref,* 3:60(41), 4:37(10)
Grant, J. D.: *ref,* 4:117(1031)

Grummon, D. L.: *ref,* 5:164(441), 6:245(621)
Grumpelt, H. R.: *ref,* 6:143(1049)
Grunberg, F.: *ref,* 110(13)
Grundig, M. H.: *ref,* 166(2009)
Grupp, S.: *ref,* 27(368)
Grygier, P.: *ref,* 6:86(2)
Grygier, T. G.: *test,* 65; *ref,* 6:86(3–6)
Guba, E. G.: *ref,* 5:47(24), 5:114 (125)
Gudiksen, K. S.: *ref,* 127(87)
Gudobba, R.: *ref,* 166(1742)
Guerin, A. J.: *ref,* 447(41, 51, 55)
Guerino, R.: *ref,* 6:103(40), 6:182 (260)
Guerney, B.: *ref,* 6:59(155), 6:127 (29, 37)
Guerra, J. R.: *ref,* 442A(128)
Guertin, W. H.: *rev,* 5:51, 6:117, 6:135, 6:167, F261; *exc,* 6:240, P476; *ref,* 148(3), 4:107(9), 4:134(26–7, 51–3), 5:67(4), 5:154(1532), 5:162(79), 5:172 (58, 83–5, 100), 6:203(253), 6:239(30)
Guetzkow, H.: *test,* 435; *ref,* 320(11), 5:138(1)
Guidance Centre: *test,* 88
Guido, S. M.: *ref,* 166(1809), 245(182), 415(318), 470(3353), 484(1055)
Guiler, W. S.: *rev,* C200
Guilford, J. P.: *rev,* 1:900, 1:925, 2:1200, 2:1243, 5:70, F22, F58, F79, F87, F107, F109, F124; *test,* 54, 101–4, 130, 272, 343, 3:45; *bk,* P377–80; *exc,* P51, P169, P173, P301, P369, P441, P751, P813; *ref,* 343(1), 2:1239 (38.1), 2:1246(58), 3:43(1–3), 3:55(1–2, 4), 5:63(32, 44, 53–4), 5:64(41, 50–1), 5:78(36, 46, 51–2), 5:86(343), 5:95(276), 5:114(112), 5:154(1224), 6:108 (63), 6:109(57), 6:110(75), 6:120(67), 6:128(63), 6:143 (886), 6:157(306), 6:237(2518), 6:245(672)
Guilford, J. S.: *ref,* 5:63(27, 33), 5:64(29, 33), 5:78(30, 37)
Guilford, M. S.: *ref,* 321(9), 2:1200(6), 2:1237(3), 2:1239 (46)
Guilford, R. B.: *ref,* 343(1), 2:1239(38.1), 3:43(1–3), 3:55 (1–2)
Guinan, J. F.: *ref,* 451(173)
Guinouard, D. E.: *ref,* 6:131(10, 14), 6:141(3), 6:237(2704, 2831)
Guion, R. M.: *ref,* 104(235)
Guirdham, A.: *exc,* P80–1; *ref,* 2:1246(28–9, 48–9)
Gulde, C. J.: *ref,* 3:60(59)
Gulliksen, H.: *rev,* 2:1266, A40, G64, G86, G91, N29; *bk,* P381–2; *exc,* P381, P443, P593, P639
Gullion, M. E.: *ref,* 5:86(433), 6:143(827)
Gulutsan, M.: *ref,* 184(25)
Gumeson, G. G.: *ref,* 67(386), 259(320)
Gummere, J. F.: *rev,* E111, E119

Gunderson, E. K.: *ref,* 442A(16, 21, 47, 60)
Gunderson, E. K. E.: *ref,* 49(53), 79(32–3), 259(400–1), 261(31–3)
Gundlach, R.: *ref,* 6:245(628)
Gunn, R. C.: *ref,* 415(348), 419 (40)
Gunnell, D. C.: *ref,* 5:38(114)
Gunnison, H.: *ref,* 193(2)
Günzburg, H. C.: *test,* 216; *exc,* 5:131; *ref,* 216(1–5), 281(121), 442A(22, 42), 5:139(22)
Gupta, G. C.: *ref,* 104(299), 6:110(139)
Gupta, V. P.: *ref,* 161(195, 210, 252)
Gurel, L.: *ref,* 5:164(537), 6:245 (611, 644)
Gurevitz, S.: *ref,* 4:103(2)
Gurin, G.: *ref,* 484(942)
Gurin, M. G.: *ref,* 5:150(5–6)
Gurrey, P.: *bk,* P415
Gursslin, C.: *ref,* 5:154(1693)
Gurvitz, M. S.: *bk,* P383; *ref,* 442A(43), 470(3072, 3082), 4:111(10), 4:117(1117–8), 5:154 (1352, 1533, 1687, 1691, 1708)
Guskin, S.: *ref,* 5:154(2252)
Gussett, R. L.: *ref,* 185(18)
Gustad, J. W.: *rev,* 5:108, O76; *exc,* 5:47; *ref,* 340(14)
Gustafson, M. C.: *ref,* 6:87(146)
Gustav, A.: *ref,* 3:73(496), 6:87 (147)
Guthrie, G. M.: *ref,* 124(27), 166(2203), 201(7), 259(428), 4:71(213, 243), 5:86(344, 450, 759), 6:143(1317), 6:182(261)
Gutman, B.: *ref,* 442A(44)
Gutman, G. M.: *ref,* 161(196)
Gutmann, D.: *ref,* 484(1105)
Gutmann, D. L.: *ref,* 484(1001, 1013), 6:245(654)
Gutsch, K. U.: *ref,* 175(6), 178(9), 266(22)
Guttentag, M.: *ref,* 470(3351)
Guttman, I.: *ref,* 5:86(705), 6:143 (908)
Guttman, L.: *bk,* P446, P693, P782; *exc,* P318, P381, P825; *ref,* 5:154(1887)
Guy, M.: *ref,* 5:164(401)
Guy, W.: *exc,* P714
Guze, H.: *ref,* 6:215(81)
Guze, S. B.: *ref,* 326(27, 32), 5:76(19–20)
Gynther, M. D.: *ref,* 116(31), 127(76–7, 93), 166(1541, 1639, 1797–8, 2010, 2204–5, 2373), 5:67(5), 6:87(244–5, 313), 6:117(6), 6:126(10), 6:127(26–8, 39), 6:140(19), 6:143(1103–4, 1210–1, 1250, 1318, 1343), 6:177 (12), 6:203(249), 6:223(13, 16), 6:235(9)

HAAN, N.: *ref,* 27(234), 166 (1799), 470(3254)
Haas, K.: *ref,* 6:87(300), 6:143 (1216)
Haas, R. F.: *ref,* 27(196), 200(4)
Haase, R. F.: *ref,* 470(3551, 3583)
Haase, W.: *ref,* 5:154(2046)

Habbe, S.: *ref,* 2:1243(7), 6:159 (34)
Haber, R. N.: *ref,* 6:99(4)
Haber, W. B.: *ref,* 6:237(2416)
Hackbusch, F.: *ref,* 3:73(497), 3:103(69)
Hackett, C. G.: *ref,* 4:91(7)
Hackett, H. R.: *ref,* 27(204), 5:86(564), 6:71(133), 6:143 (987)
Hackfield, A. W.: *ref,* 2:1246(30)
Hackman, J. R.: *ref,* 185(23)
Hackman, R. C.: *ref,* 4:28(39)
Haddox, G.: *ref,* 6:133(1), 6:134 (4–5), 6:190(2), 6:214(5)
Haden, P.: *ref,* 6:101(71)
Hadley, E. E.: *exc,* P148–9
Hadley, J. E.: *test,* 2:1202; *ref,* 4:46(29, 33)
Hadley, J. M.: *ref,* 4:48(11–2)
Hadley, L. B.: *rev,* H190, H208
Hadley, L. S.: *ref,* 3:70(2)
Haefner, D. A.: *ref,* 255(56), 256 (61)
Haefner, J. H.: *rev,* N125, N134, N151
Haefner, R.: *bk,* P914
Haertzen, C. A.: *test,* 3; *ref,* 3(1–15), 104(236), 166(2374), 245 (221), 6:143(887, 991, 1218, 1319), 6:173(60)
Haeussermann, E.: *test,* 59; *bk,* P384; *ref,* 6:84a(1)
Hafner, A. J.: *ref,* 470(3255), 5:154(1888, 2264), 6:237(2417, 2635, 2784), 6:245(720)
Hafner, J. L.: *ref,* 5:86(634)
Hagen, E.: *rev,* H116, L35, L53, L64; *bk,* P821; *exc,* P326, P915
Hagen, J. W.: *ref,* 36(5)
Hagenah, T.: *bk,* P95–6, P225
Haggard, E. A.: *ref,* 195(2), 419(38), 470(3145)
Haggerty, A. D.: *ref,* 5:164(400, 442), 6:229(93)
Haggerty, M. E.: *test,* 321; *ref,* 2:1222(1)
Hagin, R. A.: *ref,* 415(300)
Haglund, C. A.: *ref,* 5:154(1889)
Hagman, E. P.: *bk,* P120
Hagood, M. J.: *exc,* P441
Hague, H. R.: *ref,* 94(11)
Haguenauer, G.: *ref,* 6:237(2513)
Hahn, F.: *ref,* 471(248), 5:154 (1364)
Hahn, H.: *ref,* 458(16), 6:138(29)
Hahn, H. T.: *exc,* P63
Hahn, K.: *ref,* 67(658)
Hahn, M.: *exc,* P791
Hahn, M. E.: *rev,* H88, O61, O302, O305, O328; *test,* 24; *bk,* P643; *exc,* P224, P320, P702; *ref,* 340(13), 3:62(4), 5:30(121), 5:87(10)
Haigh, G. V.: *ref,* 5:144(95)
Haimes, P. E.: *test,* 60
Haimowitz, M. L.: *ref,* 6:237 (2307)
Haimowitz, N. R.: *ref,* 6:237(2307)
Hain, J. D.: *ref,* 27(210), 415(289)
Haines, L. E.: *ref,* 6:87(148), 6:94(7)
Hake, D. T.: *ref,* 4:136(127, 205)
Hakel, M. D.: *ref,* 67(545, 665)

Henrichs, T. F.: *ref,* 166(1465, 1646, 2017), 6:143(1324), 6:229 (56)
Henricson, S. E.: *bk,* P456
Henrikson, L. V.: *ref,* 48(65)
Henry, A. F.: *ref,* 5:164(475)
Henry, D. R.: *ref,* 6:87(273)
Henry, E. M.: *ref,* 5:154(2049-50)
Henry, E. R.: *rev,* F160, F162; *exc,* P236, P554, P571
Henry, J.: *ref,* 3:73(201, 288), 5:154(1538, 1895)
Henry, M.: *ref,* 4:77(107)
Henry, N. B.: *exc,* P149
Henry, P. M.: *ref,* 6:143(1108)
Henry, W. E.: *rev,* 4:146, 5:102, 5:150, H241, O94; *test,* 435; *bk,* P163, P428; *exc,* P546; *ref,* 3: 103(85), 4:117(808), 4:136(104, 163, 266), 5:138(1), 5:164(538, 556, 589), 6:245(617, 675-6, 722, 757, 807)
Henry, Z.: *ref,* 3:73(288)
Henrysson, S.: *bk,* P429
Henschel, B. J. S.: *ref,* 67(426)
Hensley, R.: *ref,* 4:77(145)
Henze, M. V.: *ref,* 289(1)
Heppell, H. K.: *ref,* 4:136(267)
Herbert, M.: *ref,* 471(278), 484 (1054)
Herbert, N.: *ref,* 6:157(321), 6:176 (50), 6:238(240)
Herd, J.: *ref,* 6:238(217)
Herdt, B. F.: *ref,* 470(3587)
Hered, W.: *rev,* L80, L86-7, L96
Herger, J.: *ref,* 451(161)
Hering, F. J.: *exc,* P253
Heriot, J. T.: *ref,* 281(132)
Herman, D. O.: *rev,* H58, O272
Herman, G. N.: *ref,* 5:164(336)
Herman, H.: *exc,* 4:103
Herman, J. L.: *ref,* 5:154(1795), 6:237(2381, 2781)
Herman, L.: *ref,* 124(44), 221A (11)
Herman, P. S.: *ref,* 5:154(1920), 5:164(497)
Hernández, C.: *ref,* 5:104(5)
Herold, C. M.: *exc,* P910
Heron, A.: *ref,* 190A(20)
Herr, E. L.: *ref,* 255(58), 256(22, 40, 52, 62-3)
Herr, V. V.: *ref,* 6:57(50), 6:226 (53)
Herreid, C. F.: *ref,* 166(2018)
Herreid, J. R.: *ref,* 166(2018)
Herrick, C. J.: *ref,* 3:73(224), 3:107(33)
Herrick, V. E.: *rev,* A1, A29, A49; *bk,* P278
Herring, F. H.: *ref,* 166(2405), 169(9)
Herrington, R. N.: *ref,* 6:138(90-1), 6:177(39)
Herrman, L.: *ref,* 236(4)
Herrman, W. L.: *ref,* 236(2)
Herrmann, R. S.: *ref,* 5:154(1961)
Herron, E. W.: *test,* 439; *bk,* P440; *ref,* 161(228), 166(2198), 176 (27), 439(40, 51, 102), 6:217 (7, 11, 13)
Herron, M. K.: *test,* 138
Herron, W. G.: *ref,* 166(1486, 1809), 245(182), 415(318), 443

(16, 26), 470(3175, 3353), 484 (1055), 6:220(5)
Herrscher, B. R.: *ref,* 42(20)
Hersch, C.: *ref,* 5:154(2186), 6:237 (2888)
Hersch, P. D.: *ref,* 4(82), 27(334), 472(64)
Hersen, M.: *ref,* 166(2182)
Hershenson, D. B.: *ref,* 451(204)
Hershenson, J. R.: *ref,* 4:117(809)
Hershey, H.: *ref,* 245(226)
Hertz, H.: *ref,* 2:1246(90, 113)
Hertz, M. R.: *ref,* 470(3197), 2:1246(21, 32-3, 50-1, 65, 68, 91-3, 114-5, 135-7), 3:73(148, 173, 202-7, 259-64, 320-4, 376, 434, 502, 562), 4:117(620, 708-9, 810, 961, 1128-9), 5:154(1255, 1356-8, 1712, 1896), 6:237(2522, 2640-2, 2789)
Hertzberg, O. E.: *ref,* 2:1243(6)
Hertzler, S.: *exc,* P310, P554
Hertzman, M.: *exc,* 3:82a; *ref,* 3:73(265-6, 325-6, 377, 563), 4:117(811), 5:49(2), 5:148(30), 5:154(1713, 1822), 5:164(443, 467)
Herz, M. I.: *ref,* 5:123(8)
Herzberg, F.: *ref,* 5:65(21), 5:86 (347), 5:154(1409)
Herzberg, I.: *ref,* 470(3258), 6:237 (2889)
Herzig, S. A.: *test,* 492; *ref,* 4:146 (1)
Heseltine, G. F.: *ref,* 196(6), 6:138 (101)
Hesler, A. R.: *ref,* 6:159(39)
Heslop, J. R.: *ref,* 47(45)
Hess, D. W.: *ref,* 6:230(42)
Hessel, M. G.: *ref,* 5:154(1359)
Heston, J. C.: *test,* 322; *exc,* P44; *ref,* 363(17), 4:50(1), 4:71(121)
Hetherington, E. L.: *ref,* 54(2), 245 (117)
Hetherington, M.: *ref,* 6:87(292)
Hetherington, R.: *exc,* 4:140, 6:234, 4:140, P653
Hetlinger, D. F.: *ref,* 6:87(199)
Hetrick, W. R.: *ref,* 6:143(1216)
Hetzel, B. S.: *ref,* 6:245(865)
Hetzer, H.: *bk,* P138
Heuckeroth, O.: *ref,* 166(1605)
Heuser, K. D.: *ref,* 3:73(503)
Heusinkveld, E. D.: *ref,* 27(199), 166(1647), 6:71(36)
Hewer, V. H.: *ref,* 5:86(637)
Hewitt, C. C.: *ref,* 3:60(6)
Hewitt, F. E.: *exc,* P522
Hewitt, J. H.: *ref,* 6:143(1217)
Hewlett, J. H. G.: *ref,* 6:64(50), 6:101(61)
Heyder, D. W.: *ref,* 470(3259)
Heymann, G. M.: *ref,* 5:164(486, 539)
Heyns, R. W.: *ref,* 5:164(427)
Heywood, H. L.: *ref,* 263A(1-7, 9-11)
Hibbeler, H. L.: *ref,* 3:60(60)
Hibler, F. W.: *ref,* 3:67(12)
Hick, T. L.: *ref,* 477(25, 27-8, 34)
Hick, W. E.: *exc,* P381
Hickman, N. W.: *ref,* 166(1412), 470(3119)
Hicks, D. J.: *ref,* 6:229(57)

Hicks, E. M.: *ref,* 3:99(18)
Hicks, J. A.: *ref,* 6:110(140), 6:242 (7)
Hieronymus, A. N.: *rev,* C113, C225, K27, K185
Higashimachi, W. H.: *ref,* 6:246 (13)
Higbee, D. S.: *ref,* 6:203(189)
Higginbotham, S. A.: *ref,* 3:73 (293)
Higgins, J.: *ref,* 166(1810), 470 (3489)
Higgins, J. D.: *ref,* 125A(7)
Higgins, M. X.: *bk,* P430
Higgins, N.: *ref,* 71(75)
Higham, E.: *bk,* P507; *ref,* 5:154 (2063), 6:237(2338)
Highfield, H.: *exc,* P138
Hildebrandt, E. H. C.: *rev,* G18, G84
Hilden, A. H.: *bk,* P431; *ref,* 3:73 (504), 4:117(710), 5:154(1684), 5:164(422), 6:237(2746)
Hildreth, G. H.: *test,* 356, 493, 4:131; *bk,* P432; *exc,* 2:1426, P68, P201, P345, P455, P515, P695; *ref,* 2:1238(1-3), 3:73 (435)
Hildreth, H. M.: *exc,* P631
Hildreth, R. A.: *ref,* 6:87(199)
Hildt, M. T.: *ref,* 251(53)
Hiler, E. W.: *ref,* 442A(142), 5:154(1526, 1539, 1703)
Hilgard, E. R.: *test,* 253-4; *ref,* 166 (1811), 253(22, 25), 254(1-2), 6:71(96), 6:112(1), 6:138(102), 6:178(1-2, 5-6, 12, 14)
Hilgard, J. R.: *ref,* 253(26), 254 (3)
Hilgeman, L. M. B.: *ref,* 5:125(9)
Hilkevitch, R. R.: *ref,* 6:237(2643)
Hill, A.: *ref,* 4:77(176)
Hill, A. B.: *exc,* P296
Hill, A. H.: *ref,* 27(285, 335)
Hill, E.: *ref,* 440(1), 6:217(16)
Hill, E. F.: *ref,* 439(71)
Hill, H. E.: *test,* 3; *ref,* 3(2-5), 166(2374), 6:143(887, 991, 1218, 1319), 6:173(60)
Hill, L. K.: *ref,* 447(31-2), 6:224 (25, 27)
Hill, R. E.: *ref,* 27(177, 367), 6:71 (60, 74)
Hill, T. B.: *ref,* 98(6), 6:105(5)
Hill, V. T.: *ref,* 5:162(94, 96, 106)
Hill, W. F.: *test,* 109
Hill, W. H.: *rev,* K189, K223; *bk,* P115
Hill, W. R.: *ref,* 166(1422)
Hillaby, T. G.: *ref,* 451(216)
Hilliard, A. G.: *ref,* 67(387)
Hilliard, J.: *ref,* 5:86(580)
Hillman, C. H.: *ref,* 127(71)
Hills, D. A.: *ref,* 6:71(61)
Hills, J. R.: *rev,* F34, O69; *exc,* P74; *ref,* 6:73(154)
Hiltmann, H.: *test,* 420; *ref,* 470 (3354)
Hilton, A. C.: *ref,* 104(175), 259 (282)
Hilton, T. L.: *ref,* 259(342)
Hilzim, E. S.: *ref,* 4:117(812)
Himelstein, P.: *exc,* P124; *ref,* 166 (1812, 2019, 2212), 6:87(65)

Kahn, L. A.: *exc*, P328
Kahn, M.: *ref*, 484(1059)
Kahn, M. W.: *ref*, 166(1820), 451 (175), 470(3363, 3592), 5:154 (1370), 6:237(2525, 2652), 6:245 (726)
Kahn, P.: *ref*, 470(3593)
Kahn, R. L.: *ref*, 5:154(2055), 6:237(2653)
Kahn, S.: *ref*, 5:154(2056), 6:87 (101)
Kahn, T. C.: *test*, 434, 447; *bk*, P488; *ref*, 434(8), 447(64), 4:110 (2), 5:145(4-5, 9-12, 14, 16-7), 6:214(1, 4), 6:224(19, 21)
Kaiman, B. D.: *ref*, 49(41, 64), 173(99, 114)
Kaiser, H. F.: *exc*, P22, P396; *ref*, 6:110(124-5), 6:174(76), 6:192 (24)
Kaiser, R. L.: *test*, 284
Kakkar, S. B.: *ref*, 173(104), 261 (29, 36-7)
Kaldegg, A.: *exc*, P58, P82, P487; *ref*, 450(92), 470(3265, 3485), 4:117(969, 1132), 4:134(54), 5:127(1, 6), 5:154(1545, 2057-8), 5:172(122), 6:237(2382, 2654, 2792)
Kaldenberg, D. E.: *test*, 10
Kalhorn, J.: *test*, 84; *ref*, 4:43(7, 10, 14), 4:71(84)
Kalil, A. J.: *ref*, 415(411)
Kalin, R.: *ref*, 484(1004, 1059)
Kalinkowitz, B. N.: *ref*, 4:117(715)
Kalis, B. L.: *exc*, P36; *ref*, 6:71 (99a), 6:143(1226a)
Kalish, R. A.: *ref*, 6:113(22)
Kallen, H. M.: *exc*, P245
Kallstedt, F. E.: *bk*, P141; *ref*, 5:154(1317, 1371)
Kalnius, D.: *ref*, 5:164(593)
Kalt, N. C.: *ref*, 184(47)
Kalton, G.: *ref*, 49(63)
Kamano, D. K.: *ref*, 166(2035), 442A(109), 470(3486), 6:87 (308), 6:237(2655)
Kamat, V. V.: *bk*, P489
Kambly, P. E.: *rev*, H145, L37
Kamenetzky, J.: *ref*, 5:155(163)
Kamman, G. R.: *ref*, 470(3081), 3:60(63), 3:73(379, 567), 4:117 (817), 5:86(572), 5:154(1905), 5:164(490), 5:172(102)
Kandel, A.: *ref*, 6:138(108)
Kandel, I. L.: *bk*, P490-1
Kandil, B. A.: *ref*, 5:164(491)
Kaneko, Z.: *ref*, 470(3201), 484 (980)
Kanfer, F. H.: *ref*, 48(58), 166 (1446), 6:143(1227), 6:226(65)
Kania, W.: *ref*, 166(1822)
Kannenberg, K. M.: *ref*, 4:136 (135-6)
Kanner, L.: *exc*, 4:133
Kanter, V. B.: *ref*, 161(149), 470 (3131, 3266), 484(930, 1005), 5:154(1722, 1906), 6:237(2424, 2547, 2656), 6:245(648)
Kantner, L. A.: *ref*, 439(92)
Kantor, R. E.: *ref*, 166(1809), 245(182), 415(318), 470(3353), 484(1055), 4:71(126), 5:154 (1546), 6:237(2464, 2962)

Kanun, C.: *ref*, 5:86(638), 6:143 (995)
Kao, R. C.: *bk*, P200
Kaplan, A. H.: *ref*, 2:1246(86)
Kaplan, A. M.: *ref*, 442A(158), 451(157-9), 6:237(2635), 6:245 (720)
Kaplan, B.: *exc*, P546; *ref*, 470 (3163), 484(950), 5:154(1723, 1907, 2059-60, 2141), 6:237 (2875)
Kaplan, B. E.: *ref*, 125A(7)
Kaplan, D. M.: *ref*, 6:237(2657)
Kaplan, E.: *ref*, 166(1640)
Kaplan, H.: *ref*, 5:164(342)
Kaplan, H. K.: *ref*, 415(268), 6:177 (10)
Kaplan, J. E.: *ref*, 5:86(758), 5:107(10)
Kaplan, M.: *ref*, 6:143(900), 6:237 (2530)
Kaplan, M. F.: *ref*, 4(83), 484 (1060, 1165, 1207)
Kaplan, M. J.: *ref*, 484(919)
Kaplan, M. L.: *ref*, 470(3594), 5:154(1693)
Kaplan, S. M.: *ref*, 6:237(3008), 6:238(244)
Kapoor, K.: *ref*, 178(4, 10), 245 (188)
Kapoor, S. D.: *ref*, 178(10), 245 (154, 189-90), 6:174(103)
Kappauf, W. E.: *exc*, P434
Karabelas, M. J.: *ref*, 6:143(1258)
Karas, S. F.: *ref*, 136(26)
Kardner, A.: *ref*, 3:73(390)
Karen, R. L.: *ref*, 429(9)
Kark, E.: *ref*, 49(31)
Kark, S. L.: *ref*, 49(47)
Karlan, S. C.: *ref*, 3:48(18), 3:73 (512)
Karlin, L.: *ref*, 5:155(121, 138)
Karmel, L. J.: *ref*, 6:143(1110)
Karn, H. W.: *rev*, O212; *ref*, 5:114(96)
Karnes, M. R.: *rev*, H7; *bk*, P586
Karon, B. P.: *ref*, 484(1174), 5:167 (6)
Karp, S. A.: *test*, 36; *ref*, 71(50, 62, 67), 442A(120), 6:74b(1), 6:89(20, 25, 28, 33), 6:229(133)
Karpman, B.: *exc*, P471
Karr, C.: *ref*, 6:87(66, 102, 254)
Karras, A.: *ref*, 6:237(2739)
Karras, E. J.: *ref*, 6:174(45)
Karslake, R. H.: *ref*, 4:46(43)
Karson, S.: *ref*, 38(7), 136(33), 245(279, 339, 346), 5:86(639, 700, 754), 5:112(26, 29), 5:154 (2189), 6:174(46, 56, 71)
Karstendiek, B.: *ref*, 5:50(7), 5:59(6), 5:156(12), 6:176(38)
Karve, B. D.: *ref*, 2:1220(4)
Kasanin, J. S.: *test*, 47; *bk*, P393; *ref*, 3:27(3, 5, 5a, 12, 16)
Kasch, F. W.: *bk*, P215
Kasin, E. D.: *ref*, 4:136(137)
Kaskoff, Y. D.: *ref*, 6:177(14)
Kasl, S.: *ref*, 41(5)
Kaspar, E. A.: *ref*, 256(51)
Kaspar, J. C.: *ref*, 415(331)
Kasper, E. C.: *ref*, 256(41)
Kass, E. H.: *ref*, 166(2207)
Kass, W.: *rev*, 5:153, 5:161; *exc*,

4:109, 4:118-9, 4:135, 5:130, P141, P714; *ref*, 4:136(138), 5:154(1372, 2061)
Kassarjian, H. H.: *ref*, 49(32), 166(2036), 259(379), 6:110(163)
Kassarjian, W. M.: *ref*, 166(2036), 259(379)
Kassebaum, G. G.: *ref*, 6:143(893)
Kaswan, J.: *ref*, 6:238(219)
Kataguchi, Y.: *ref*, 5:154(2190), 6:237(2526)
Katahn, M.: *ref*, 470(3263)
Kates, S. L.: *ref*, 91(79), 442A (46), 4:117(818, 970-2), 5:154 (2221-2, 2270), 5:155(87, 104), 5:172(76), 6:101(64)
Kates, W. W.: *ref*, 6:101(64)
Katkin, E. S.: *ref*, 166(1656, 2037)
Katkovsky, W.: *rev*, 6:212, 6:220; *ref*, 472(63), 484(1161)
Kato, N.: *ref*, 419(47), 470(3536), 484(1137)
Katter, R. V.: *ref*, 6:71(34a), 6:110(57), 6:174(32)
Katz, D.: *exc*, P782; *ref*, 166 (1529)
Katz, G.: *ref*, 124(38)
Katz, I.: *ref*, 6:87(156)
Katz, J.: *exc*, 4:109; *ref*, 166 (2429), 442A(36), 4:117(1133), 4:134(55), 4:136(273)
Katz, L. F.: *ref*, 390(20)
Katz, M.: *rev*, O77, O81; *bk*, P492
Katz, M. M.: *test*, 138; *ref*, 41(9), 124(47, 61-2, 84), 138(1-4, 7, 10), 285(9), 470(3688)
Katz, S. E.: *ref*, 2:1239(17, 31), 2:1243(11), 3:41(2)
Katzell, M. E.: *ref*, 6:87(255), 6:143(1228)
Katzell, R. A.: *rev*, O3, O17, O34, O37, O105, O148, O177, O199, O282, O317; *ref*, 6:87(255), 6:143(1228)
Katzman, R.: *ref*, 166(1765)
Kaufman, A.: *ref*, 484(1073)
Kaufman, J. B.: *ref*, 5:125(12)
Kaufman, L. W.: *ref*, 5:154(1547)
Kaufman, M.: *ref*, 5:86(573), 5:154 (1908)
Kaufman, M. R.: *ref*, 5:154(1918), 5:172(95)
Kaufmann, C.: *ref*, 6:127(2), 6:143 (791), 6:223(12), 6:245(623)
Kaufmann, P.: *ref*, 4:71(217)
Kaul, M. M.: *ref*, 321(20)
Kaulfers, W. V.: *rev*, C99, E1, E5, E28, E37-8, E54, E60, E144, E150, E155, E157, E160
Kaur, R.: *ref*, 239(25)
Kausch, D. F.: *ref*, 166(2345)
Kausler, D. H.: *ref*, 6:67(4-5)
Kavazanjian, T.: *ref*, 470(3082)
Kavruck, S.: *bk*, P353
Kawai, H.: *ref*, 470(3231-2, 3560)
Kawakami, D.: *ref*, 5:86(750)
Kawin, E.: *test*, 391; *exc*, P807
Kay, B.: *ref*, 5:37(25), 6:71(40, 67)
Kay, D. W. K.: *ref*, 166(2150)
Kay, E.: *ref*, 5:148(47), 5:154 (2230), 5:156(23), 5:164(584)
Kay, L. W.: *exc*, 4:112; *ref*, 3:73 (329)

McGregor, J. R.: *ref,* 5:86(551), 5:156(17)
MacGregor, R.: *ref,* 5:154(1581)
McGuire, C.: *rev,* N38, N82, N139, N149; *ref,* 5:164(421), 6:131 (12), 6:180(5)
McGuire, F. L.: *ref,* 166(1849), 5:155(166), 6:132(18), 6:203 (198)
McGuire, R. J.: *ref,* 6:138(78, 107)
McGuirl, D.: *ref,* 6:229(104, 119)
McGurk, E.: *ref,* 4(50), 27(243)
McGurk, F. C. J.: *exc,* P590
McGurk, W. S.: *ref,* 470(3278)
McHale, A.: *ref,* 281(133)
McHenry, A. D.: *exc,* P525
McHenry, T. B.: *ref,* 6:71(112)
Machi, V. S.: *ref,* 5:154(2243)
Machir, D.: *ref,* 439(82)
Machl, M.: *ref,* 470(3276)
Machover, K.: *test,* 451; *bk,* P562; *ref,* 442A(61, 72), 3:73(572), 4:111(1, 4–5, 11–2), 4:117(733), 5:49(2), 5:148(23, 28, 30, 39), 5:154(1822), 5:164(467), 6:143 (905), 6:229(82, 95–6), 6:237 (2542)
Machover, S.: *bk,* P563; *exc,* P674; *ref,* 5:86(299, 358, 445), 5:154(2199), 6:61(28), 6:143 (905), 6:204(61–2), 6:229(80–2), 6:237(2540–2), 6:245(688)
McHugh, A. F.: *ref,* 442A(148), 451(164, 194), 6:215(110), 6:229 (134)
McHugh, G.: *test,* 52, 55
McHugh, R. B.: *ref,* 166(1716), 6:143(1344)
Macindoe, I.: *ref,* 244(85)
McIntire, D. W.: *ref,* 6:237(3007)
McIntosh, D. M.: *bk,* P564–5
McIntyre, C. J.: *ref,* 5:89(32, 42), 5:164(452)
McIntyre, G. A.: *bk,* P566
McIntyre, S.: *ref,* 408(24)
McIver, M. R.: *ref,* 38(8)
Mack, R.: *ref,* 484(1030)
McKain, C. W.: *ref,* 4(38), 269 (10), 477(21)
McKay, B. E.: *ref,* 3:107(8, 17)
Mackay, D.: *bk,* P565
Mackay, E. A.: *ref,* 5:154(1264)
McKay, H. E.: *ref,* 6:87(185), 6:110(115), 6:143(1077)
McKeachie, W. J.: *ref,* 320(11), 484(1213), 6:71(47, 124a), 6:174 (102), 6:245(680)
McKee, J. P.: *ref,* 6:71(78), 6:87 (205)
McKee, N. R.: *ref,* 67(557)
McKeever, W. F.: *ref,* 41(7), 147 (6), 166(1852), 244(70), 6:237 (2543)
McKegney, F. P.: *ref,* 127(94), 166(1853, 2255)
McKellar, P.: *exc,* P151
McKendry, M. S.: *ref,* 6:143 (1317), 6:182(261)
McKenna, F. S.: *ref,* 5:28(42), 5:66(4), 5:78(38)
McKenna, H. V.: *ref,* 6:110(123)
Mackenzie, G. N.: *rev,* A1, A11, A14
McKenzie, J.: *ref,* 5:86(742)

McKenzie, J. D.: *ref,* 166(1677), 6:143(1123)
McKenzie, M. T.: *ref,* 484(952)
McKenzie, R. E.: *ref,* 67(383), 93 (48), 166(2256), 415(278), 451 (154), 470(3194, 3382), 480 (170), 484(976)
McKerracher, D. G.: *ref,* 408(24)
McKerracher, D. W.: *ref,* 77(44)
Mackie, J. B.: *ref,* 163(27)
McKim, M. G.: *rev,* C59, K4, K43, K73
McKinlay, M.: *bk,* P290; *ref,* 3:43 (6), 3:44(6), 3:55(9), 3:73 (559)
McKinley, D. P.: *ref,* 471(253)
McKinley, J. C.: *test,* 166; *ref,* 3:60(1–5, 8, 12), 4:71(130)
MacKinney, A. C.: *rev,* O52, O86; *ref,* 6:109(61), 6:110(105), 6:157(310)
McKinney, E. D.: *ref,* 6:102(2), 6:103(21), 6:110(67)
McKinney, F.: *exc,* P381, P595, P704; *ref,* 2:1243(27), 6:159 (46)
MacKinnon, A. R.: *exc,* P109
MacKinnon, D. W.: *ref,* 4(1, 20), 6:71(105), 6:72(2), 6:143(1124, 1251), 6:147(1, 3), 6:182(223, 240), 6:197(3, 11, 15)
Mackler, B.: *ref,* 71(68)
McKown, H. C.: *bk,* P567
Mackworth, N. H.: *bk,* P568
McLachlan, D. G.: *ref,* 6:143 (1379)
McLain, R. E.: *ref,* 448(92, 109)
Mac Lane, S.: *rev,* G7
McLaughlin, K. F.: *rev,* G96, G220
McLaughlin, K. L.: *exc,* P918
McLaughlin, R. J.: *ref,* 77(32), 255(50), 256(54)
MacLean, A. G.: *ref,* 5:86(446)
McLean, J.: *ref,* 319(3)
MacLean, L. S.: *ref,* 256(69)
McLean, M. J.: *ref,* 6:203(229)
McLean, R. S.: *ref,* 166(2387)
McLeish, J.: *rev,* D39, D43
McLemore, M. H.: *ref,* 104(283)
McLendon, I. R.: *ref,* 346(9)
McLendon, J. C.: *rev,* N18, N68
Macleod, D.: *exc,* P631
McLeod, H.: *ref,* 4:117(984)
McLeod, H. N.: *ref,* 94(12), 6:174 (74), 6:224(22–3)
McLeod, J.: *ref,* 245(149)
McLeod, M. A.: *ref,* 471(266)
McMahan, H. G.: *ref,* 4:134(53)
McMahon, D.: *exc,* P547, P653
McMahon, F. B.: *test,* 85; *ref,* 166 (1854), 470(3383)
McMahon, W. J.: *ref,* 259(350), 322(30)
McManus, R. L.: *bk,* P569
Macmeeken, A. M.: *bk,* P570
McMichael, A. E.: *ref,* 470(3204), 5:154(1768)
McMichael, R. E.: *ref,* 6:125(7)
Macmillan, J. W.: *exc,* 3:37
McMillin, M. R.: *ref,* 104(242), 193(5)
McMorries, J. C.: *ref,* 4:28(29), 4:77(101)
MacMullen, M. R.: *ref,* 3:49(11)

McMurray, J. G.: *exc,* 5:60
McMurry, R. N.: *bk,* P571
McNair, D. M.: *test,* 124; *ref,* 124 (41, 50, 65, 68), 221A(13), 6:94 (13), 6:126(19, 23), 6:180(23), 6:223(20)
McNamara, H. J.: *ref,* 470(3384)
McNamara, L. F.: *ref,* 5:164(475)
McNamara, T. C.: *ref,* 177(54)
McNamara, W. J.: *test,* 341; *bk,* P887; *ref,* 93(53), 342(6, 8), 2:1200(10), 3:61(4–5), 4:28 (36), 4:70(7–8)
MacNaughton, D.: *ref,* 3:73(470)
McNaughton, F. L.: *ref,* 3:73(398, 457), 3:95(12)
McNeal, B. F.: *ref,* 166(1654, 1819)
McNeel, B. H.: *exc,* P435
McNeely, H. E.: *ref,* 5:154(1925)
McNeil, E. B.: *ref,* 80(7), 194(3), 484(931), 5:125(16), 6:143 (806), 6:245(629, 834)
Macneil, V. A.: *ref,* 4:77(253)
MacNeill, F. E.: *exc,* P738, P865
McNemar, O. W.: *ref,* 4:77(259)
McNemar, Q.: *bk,* P572, P808; *exc,* P278, P381, P455, P554, P579, P674, P754, P774, P825–6, P864, P883; *ref,* 3:24(3)
McPeek, B. L.: *ref,* 42(12)
McPhee, W. M.: *ref,* 5:38(79), 5:84(5)
McPherrin, J.: *rev,* C18
McPherson, F. M.: *ref,* 13(55), 161(179)
McPherson, J.: *exc,* P801; *ref,* 166 (1438)
McPherson, M. W.: *ref,* 5:164 (548), 5:172(106)
McQuaid, J.: *ref,* 245(289)
McQuary, J. P.: *ref,* 5:86(359, 578)
MacQueen, J. C.: *ref,* 166(2104)
McQueen, R.: *ref,* 6:238(207)
McQuitty, J. V.: *rev,* A8, A10, N35; *exc,* P587
McQuitty, L. L.: *rev,* 4:63, F26; *ref,* 2:1239(59), 4:77(133, 238)
McReynolds, G. M.: *ref,* 29(216)
McReynolds, P.: *test,* 112, 470; *ref,* 112(14), 166(1678), 470(3500–1), 4:117(837–8, 1091, 1154), 5:67(1), 5:154(1641, 1750), 6:117(7), 6:237(2544, 2675)
MacTaggart, M. M.: *exc,* P454
McWhinnie, H. J.: *ref,* 287(36)
Madaus, G. F.: *ref,* 259(434)
Madden, F.: *rev,* H184
Madden, J. E.: *ref,* 6:143(1125)
Maddock, M. E.: *ref,* 4:144(25)
Maddox, G. L.: *ref,* 6:245(689)
Madison, L.: *ref,* 5:155(105)
Madow, L. W.: *ref,* 3:73(287)
Madsen, C. H.: *ref,* 37(5)
Maehr, M. L.: *ref,* 6:182(241)
Maes, J. L.: *ref,* 416(94), 484(982)
Magaret, A.: *exc,* P141, P360, P883; *ref,* 5:111(28, 31), 5:154 (1389), 5:164(335)
Magaw, D. C.: *ref,* 2:1246(97), 6:102(4), 6:143(906)
Magee, P. C.: *ref,* 104(199)
Maglione, F. D.: *ref,* 235(8)
Magnuson, H. W.: *bk,* P573

Pooley, R. C.: *rev,* C6, C8, C19, C58, C60-1, C104-5, C107, C140, C153

Poor, F. A.: *ref,* 43(18), 67(371)

Pope, B.: *exc,* P237; *ref,* 161(186), 166(1901, 2282), 244(73), 470 (3620), 484(1019, 1131, 1177, 1180), 5:154(2104, 2212), 6:237 (3003)

Popenpoe, P.: *exc,* P723

Popham, E. L.: *bk,* P5

Popham, W. J.: *ref,* 6:77(11-2)

Popper, L.: *ref,* 6:237(2766)

Popplestone, J. A.: *ref,* 451(142), 5:154(1947), 5:172(126), 6:143 (1358), 6:203(186)

Poppleton, P. K.: *exc,* P287

Porch, B. E.: *test,* 207

Porebski, O.: *exc,* P57

Port, Y. I.: *ref,* 6:237(2564)

Portenier, L.: *ref,* 4:28(90), 4:71 (134), 4:77(227), 4:92(70)

Porter, F. S.: *ref,* 3:103(42)

Porter, H. M.: *ref,* 5:154(1272)

Porter, J. B.: *ref,* 67(631)

Porter, J. M.: *rev,* O133, O153, O156

Porter, K. D.: *ref,* 166(1548)

Porter, L. G.: *ref,* 5:65(37)

Porter, L. W.: *rev,* O8, O324, O327

Porter, R. B.: *test,* 38; *ref,* 38(8), 136(28)

Porteus, S. D.: *rev,* F43, F161; *bk,* P661-6; *ref,* 3:73(224), 3:107 (33)

Portnoy, B.: *ref,* 5:155(135)

Poser, E. G.: *ref,* 470(3085), 484 (904), 4:117(849, 914, 1085, 1170), 6:245(889)

Poshek, N. A.: *ref,* 166(2290)

Posner, R.: *ref,* 4:129(68), 4:136 (272), 5:28(41)

Post, F.: *ref,* 415(269), 5:172(120, 142)

Post, W. L.: *rev,* C8, C43, C86, C164

Postel, H.: *exc,* 3:110

Postema, L. J.: *ref,* 166(2283)

Poster, D. C.: *ref,* 6:89(33), 6:229 (133)

Postman, L.: *ref,* 3:99(58), 4:92 (71), 6:182(151)

Potash, H. M.: *ref,* 442A(141)

Poteet, J. A.: *ref,* 415(418)

Pothast, M. D.: *ref,* 5:86(649), 5:154(2105)

Potter, C. S.: *ref,* 4:71(228)

Potter, E. H.: *ref,* 3:73(581, 586)

Potter, H. W.: *ref,* 4:111(6)

Pottharst, K.: *ref,* 4:117(815, 968, 1008)

Poulton, I. A.: *ref,* 470(3395)

Pouncey, A. T.: *ref,* 27(145)

Powell, D. H.: *ref,* 67(383), 93 (48), 415(278), 451(154), 470 (3194), 484(976)

Powell, E. K.: *ref,* 5:125(39)

Powell, J. O.: *ref,* 4:28(99), 4:71 (162, 250)

Powell, K. S.: *ref,* 419(39), 484 (954)

Powell, L.: *ref,* 373(2), 3:107(34)

Powell, M.: *exc,* 4:133; *ref,* 2:1246 (38), 4:28(113)

Powell, M. G.: *ref,* 4:77(228)

Powell, N. J.: *exc,* P567

Powell, R. K.: *ref,* 166(2135)

Powell, V. M.: *ref,* 4:28(74)

Power, R. P.: *ref,* 161(263)

Powers, C. A.: *ref,* 5:148(20)

Powers, E.: *bk,* P40

Powers, F. F.: *exc,* P147-8

Powers, J. H.: *ref,* 166(1495)

Powers, M. E.: *ref,* 6:182(178)

Powers, W. T.: *ref,* 5:154(1948, 2265, 2283), 6:237(2331)

Prabhu, G. G.: *ref,* 470(3621)

Prado, W. M.: *ref,* 244(72, 81, 95), 6:203(201)

Prados, M.: *ref,* 470(3036), 3:73 (392, 582)

Prakash, J.: *ref,* 381(48), 484 (1124)

Prange, A. J.: *ref,* 6:143(968)

Pranis, R. W.: *test,* 265

Prasad, K.: *ref,* 4:117(622, 656)

Pratap, S.: *ref,* 470(3514)

Prater, G. F.: *ref,* 442A(28)

Pratt, B. M.: *ref,* 2:1217(1)

Pratt, C.: *ref,* 5:154(1416-7)

Pratt, C. C.: *exc,* P313

Pratt, M. A.: *ref,* 5:30(130)

Pratt, N. T.: *rev,* E111, E116, E126

Pred, A. L. S.: *ref,* 4:77(255)

Pred, G. D.: *ref,* 4:63(3)

Prelinger, E.: *ref,* 4:134(33)

Prema, P.: *ref,* 470(3471)

Prensky, S. J.: *ref,* 6:237(2439), 6:238(198)

Prentice, N. M.: *ref,* 220(13), 6:239(33)

Prentice, W. C. H.: *exc,* P350

Prescott, D. A.: *rev,* 1:920, 1:928

Prescott, G. A.: *bk,* P268

Presher, C. H.: *ref,* 6:223(13)

Pressey, A. W.: *ref,* 71(65)

Pressey, L. C.: *test,* 363; *ref,* 363 (6-7), 2:1243.1(1)

Pressey, S. L.: *test,* 363, 369; *ref,* 363(6-7), 2:1243.1(1, 3)

Preston, A.: *ref,* 84(17, 21), 6:87 (188)

Preston, C. E.: *ref,* 127(87), 451 (167), 470(3288), 471(272), 484 (1020)

Preston, K. A.: *exc,* P501

Preston, R. C.: *rev,* A1, A27, A34, A49

Price, A. C.: *ref,* 5:154(1590), 6:140(10), 6:177(3, 8), 6:237 (2926)

Price, B.: *bk,* P206

Price, D. O.: *exc,* P782

Price, H.: *ref,* 6:177(42)

Price, H. V.: *rev,* G129, G229

Price, J. R.: *ref,* 166(1496, 2051)

Price, J. W.: *ref,* 6:203(179)

Price, L.: *ref,* 71(45), 176(7)

Price, M. A.: *test,* 214, 365

Price, R. A.: *rev,* N10, N99, N136

Price, R. G.: *rev,* B6, B14, B26, B61, O33

Price, R. H.: *ref,* 470(3133)

Price, R. V.: *ref,* 166(2284)

Price, T. H.: *ref,* 29(230)

Price, W. T.: *bk,* P211

Prickett, F. S.: *ref,* 5:117(13)

Pride, L. F.: *ref,* 116(67)

Prien, E. P.: *ref,* 92(21), 93(57), 261(42), 6:87(231, 249), 6:103 (31), 6:110(136, 141), 6:245 (827)

Prien, R. F.: *ref,* 124(87)

Prieur, M.: *ref,* 3:67(11, 14)

Primoff, E. S.: *bk,* P17

Prince, A.: *ref,* 6:237(2803)

Prince, A. J.: *ref,* 67(397)

Prince, S. D.: *ref,* 4:117(850)

Pringle, B. M.: *exc,* 4:57

Pringle, M. L. K.: *rev,* 6:68, F61, F113, F144, F181, K72, K108; *ref,* 281(127-8), 4:94(78), 6:194 (106)

Prior, J. J.: *ref,* 256(24)

Probst, J. B.: *bk,* P667

Probst, K. A.: *ref,* 3:60(34)

Procter, D.: *ref,* 6:87(106)

Pronko, N. H.: *exc,* P536

Proshansky, H. M.: *ref,* 3:103(33)

Prothro, E. T.: *ref,* 381(25-6), 4:46(46)

Proud, A. P.: *ref,* 5:149(33)

Prudden, G. H.: *ref,* 3:48(20a)

Pruitt, C. J.: *exc,* P857

Pruitt, C. M.: *exc,* P136, P554, P853, P893

Pruitt, R. C.: *ref,* 5:50(7), 5:59 (6), 5:156(12), 6:176(38)

Pruitt, W. A.: *ref,* 470(3289), 6:143(1268)

Pruyser, P. W.: *exc,* P822; *ref,* 5:154(1949)

Pryer, M. W.: *ref,* 147(11), 187(3, 9, 15), 245(146)

Pryor, D. B.: *ref,* 470(3622, 3705)

Pryor, H.: *bk,* P668

Psathas, G.: *ref,* 67(530, 568), 327 (16, 19)

P'simer, C.: *ref,* 6:215(96)

Psychological Research & Development Corporation: *test,* 251

Psychological Research and Development Institute: *test,* 40, 190, 459, 465

Ptacek, J. E.: *ref,* 5:60(3)

Ptasnik, J. A.: *ref,* 166(2420)

Pugh, D. S.: *ref,* 5:154(1765)

Pugh, E. A.: *exc,* P766

Pugh, T. J.: *ref,* 4:92(84)

Pullen, M.: *ref,* 163(29), 415(303)

Pullias, E. V.: *rev,* A32, A39; *bk,* P669; *exc,* P783

Pulos, L.: *ref,* 6:87(272), 6:126 (22), 6:173(56)

Pumroy, D. K.: *test,* 160, 219; *ref,* 160(3), 5:86(765), 6:71 (110), 6:166(1)

Pumroy, S. S.: *ref,* 5:123(11)

Punke, H. H.: *exc,* P856

Punnett, M.: *exc,* P324

Purcell, C. K.: *ref,* 5:86(373), 5:154(1591)

Purcell, J. F.: *ref,* 4(12), 116(26), 277(33)

Purcell, K.: *ref,* 5:154(2284), 5:164 (553, 600), 6:87(97), 6:122(1), 6:131(15), 6:143(1026), 6:237 (2927), 6:245(762)

Purcell, R. J.: *exc,* P54

Purcell, T. D.: *ref,* 67(497)

Roberts, M. R.: *ref,* 6:112(1a), 6:178(13)
Roberts, R.: *ref,* 5:154(2122)
Robertson, D. A.: *exc,* P490
Robertson, M.: *ref,* 439(69), 484 (1162), 4:129(31)
Robertson, M. H.: *ref,* 127(80), 166 (1948), 439(70), 5:147(53)
Robertson, P. C.: *ref,* 6:143(1027)
Robertson, Y.: *ref,* 3:60(43a)
Robey, D. L.: *ref,* 29(184), 302(2)
Robin, A. A.: *ref,* 484(965), 4:117 (1047), 4:136(241-2)
Robinowitz, R.: *ref,* 6:143(1030)
Robins, S.: *ref,* 176(10)
Robinson, A.: *exc,* P722
Robinson, B. W.: *ref,* 166(2086)
Robinson, C. A.: *ref,* 5:38(58)
Robinson, E. E.: *bk,* P817
Robinson, F. P.: *exc,* P372, P669, P746
Robinson, H. A.: *rev,* K43, K50; *ref,* 442A(84, 115)
Robinson, H. M.: *rev,* K73, K92, K113, K137, M40, M53, M56; *bk,* P697
Robinson, H. P.: *ref,* 4:117(1146)
Robinson, J. F.: *ref,* 5:154(2093)
Robinson, J. O.: *ref,* 161(147, 156), 6:138(111)
Robinson, J. T.: *bk,* P801; *ref,* 77 (12)
Robinson, M. E.: *ref,* 6:228(63)
Robinson, M. F.: *ref,* 4:44(2)
Robinson, N. M.: *ref,* 5:172(78)
Robinson, S. A.: *ref,* 416(109, 117)
Robinson, T. R.: *ref,* 6:110(85)
Robinson, W.: *ref,* 6:110(145)
Robinson, W. R.: *exc,* P107
Robison, R. K.: *exc,* P645
Robles, A.: *ref,* 450(82), 470(3292)
Roby, T. B.: *ref,* 54(11), 4:136 (170)
Rochester, D. E.: *ref,* 259(448)
Rochlin, G. N.: *ref,* 3:73(284)
Rochlin, I.: *ref,* 5:154(1420)
Rochman, J. E.: *ref,* 165(22)
Rochwarg, H.: *ref,* 5:154(1776)
Rock, M. L.: *ref,* 5:164(414)
Rock, M. R.: *bk,* P660; *ref,* 6:237 (3002)
Rock, R. W.: *ref,* 256(25)
Rockberger, H.: *ref,* 5:154(1598, 1777)
Rockwell, F. V.: *exc,* 3:82, 4:126; *ref,* 470(3039-41), 3:73(537)
Rodd, W. G.: *ref,* 6:182(192)
Rodell, C.: *ref,* 5:154(1599)
Rodger, A.: *rev,* O38, O121, O132-3, O148-9; *exc,* P12, P51, P150, P390, P842, P864-5, P867
Rodgers, D. A.: *ref,* 27(307), 166 (1886, 2087), 5:154(2218)
Rodgers, F. P.: *ref,* 6:87(115)
Rodies, H.: *exc,* P926
Rodnick, E. H.: *ref,* 3:73(369, 467), 3:103(21, 57), 4:117(701), 4:129(5)
Roe, A.: *bk,* P885; *exc,* P151, P643; *ref,* 470(3061), 484(901), 3:73(538-41), 3:103(74-6), 4:117(623-4, 658, 861-2, 1013, 1177), 4:136(108, 115, 173, 283), 5:154(1275, 1421-3, 1600), 5:164 (315), 6:237(2701)

Roebuck, J.: *ref,* 27(252), 166 (1884)
Roeder, W.: *test,* 209
Roehrig, W. C.: *ref,* 251(47), 5: 154(1601)
Roemer, G. A.: *ref,* 470(3627)
Roemmich, H.: *ref,* 67(633)
Roen, S. R.: *test,* 45; *ref,* 45(1-2)
Roens, B. A.: *bk,* P704
Roessel, F. P.: *ref,* 5:86(527)
Roessler, R.: *ref,* 166(1434, 1506, 1528-9, 1551)
Roff, M.: *exc,* P842; *ref,* 4:43(15)
Roffee, D. T.: *ref,* 6:73(141)
Rogers, A. H.: *ref,* 6:143(919), 6: 238(210)
Rogers, C. A.: *rev,* F121
Rogers, C. R.: *rev,* 2:1237, 2:1240; *test,* 191; *exc,* P80, P766, P845; *ref,* 5:117(1)
Rogers, F. R.: *rev,* H138, H145; *exc,* P190, P668
Rogers, L. S.: *exc,* P404; *ref,* 4:117 (1178), 5:154(1602)
Rogers, M. S.: *ref,* 27(253), 166 (1900), 6:71(138)
Rogers, R. C.: *exc,* P791
Rogers, V. M.: *exc,* P680
Rogers, W. A.: *ref,* 184(58), 259 (449)
Rogge, H. J.: *ref,* 6:143(920)
Rogolsky, M. M.: *ref,* 470(3710)
Rohde, A. R.: *test,* 469; *bk,* P698; *ref,* 4:131(1-2), 5:158(4)
Rohr, M. E.: *ref,* 470(3628)
Rohrer, J. H.: *ref,* 5:154(1226, 1424, 1961, 2111)
Rohrs, D. K.: *ref,* 399(33)
Rohrs, F. W.: *ref,* 161(157)
Roland, W. A.: *ref,* 5:148(32-3)
Rolfe, J. F.: *ref,* 3:110(12), 4:66 (1), 4:77(187)
Roman, K. G.: *bk,* P699
Roman, M.: *bk,* P406; *exc,* P126; *ref,* 470(3655)
Romanella, A. E.: *ref,* 470(3398)
Romano, R. L.: *ref,* 6:223(15)
Rome, H. P.: *ref,* 166(1497-8, 1552, 1722, 1874-5, 1887, 1922), 168(1, 3, 5-6)
Rommel, R. C. S.: *ref,* 6:143(842)
Romney, A. K.: *ref,* 4:88(19)
Romoser, R. C.: *ref,* 245(294)
Ronan, W. W.: *ref,* 103(66), 104 (220)
Roody, S. I.: *test,* 503; *ref,* 4:116 (1-2)
Rook, L. H.: *ref,* 4:117(745), 5: 154(1230)
Rooker, J. L.: *ref,* 484(1178)
Roos, P.: *exc,* P85, P741; *ref,* 6: 203(236)
Root. A. R.: *ref,* 6:159(43)
Rorabaugh, M. E.: *ref,* 5:86(450)
Rorer, L. G.: *ref,* 27(187-8), 67 (418), 166(1525, 1629, 1888-90), 6:143(1360)
Rorschach, H.: *test,* 470; *bk,* P700; *ref,* 2:1246(1), 3:73(285), 5:154 (1778)
Ros, P. de M. M.: *ref,* 5:38(93)
Rosander, A. C.: *test,* 371-2
Rosanes, M. B.: *ref,* 470(3629)
Rosanoff, A. J.: *test,* 448; *ref,* 6:226 (1, 4, 6, 13, 19)

Rosanoff, I. R.: *ref,* 6:226(6, 13)
Roscoe, D. L.: *ref,* 176(20)
Rose, A. A.: *ref,* 4:28(75, 104)
Rose, A. M.: *ref,* 381(21)
Rose, A. W.: *ref,* 470(3045), 484 (898)
Rose, D.: *ref,* 450(82), 470(3292)
Rose, F. H.: *ref,* 4:77(103)
Rose, G.: *ref,* 5:50(15)
Rose, H. A.: *ref,* 184(29, 36-7, 41, 49-51, 66), 472(54, 58)
Rose, R.: *ref,* 166(1538)
Roseborough, M. E.: *ref,* 4:56(3)
Rosen, A.: *bk,* P701; *ref,* 166 (2088), 442A(178), 5:86(377-8, 451, 528, 768), 6:143(843, 921, 1270, 1361), 6:177(15)
Rosen, A. C.: *ref,* 6:143(1031), 6: 237(2567)
Rosen, E.: *rev,* 4:105, 4:107; *exc,* 4:102; *ref,* 470(3255), 4:71(230, 274), 4:117(1179), 5:86(379, 652-3), 5:136(1), 5:154(1425), 6:143(1143-4, 1362), 6:237 (2702)
Rosen, G.: *ref,* 49(70), 471(305)
Rosen, G. P.: *ref,* 3:27(4), 3:41(4)
Rosen, H.: *ref,* 176(27), 439(102), 3:60(13), 6:226(36)
Rosen, I. C.: *ref,* 5:86(380), 5:125 (17), 5:154(1426)
Rosen, J.: *ref,* 67(570, 634), 259 (416, 450)
Rosen, J. C.: *ref,* 15(2), 6:197(5)
Rosen, J. L.: *ref,* 484(1023), 6:245 (743)
Rosen, V. H.: *exc,* P348
Rosenbaum, B. B.: *ref,* 6:159(47)
Rosenbaum, G.: *ref,* 166(2429)
Rosenbaum, I. S.: *ref,* 442A(98), 6:237(2934)
Rosenbaum, M. E.: *ref,* 6:245(800)
Rosenberg, A. M.: *ref,* 415(329), 6:71(112)
Rosenberg, B. G.: *ref,* 166(1920), 305(20-1), 6:87(325), 6:143 (1381), 6:203(215)
Rosenberg, C. M.: *ref,* 67(635), 161(239), 245(305)
Rosenberg, C. Y.: *ref,* 442A(126), 470(3210)
Rosenberg, L.: *test,* 91
Rosenberg, L. A.: *ref,* 415(329), 442A(150), 6:71(111-2), 6:143 (1217)
Rosenberg, L. M.: *ref,* 5:57(31)
Rosenberg, N.: *ref,* 5:63(40, 51), 5:64(37, 49), 5:78(43, 49), 5:95 (284)
Rosenberg, S.: *ref,* 5:154(1427), 6: 237(2717)
Rosenberg, S. J.: *ref,* 3:73(394)
Rosenblatt, B.: *ref,* 5:154(1779, 1798)
Rosenblatt, D.: *ref,* 5:164(587), 6: 245(744)
Rosenblatt, H. S.: *ref,* 38(14)
Rosenblatt, M. S.: *ref,* 6:206(20)
Rosenbloom, P. C.: *rev,* G28
Rosenblum, M. P.: *ref,* 124(55), 6: 126(17), 6:167(3)
Rosenblum, S.: *ref,* 47(42)
Rosenfeld, H. M.: *ref,* 484(1093)
Rosenfeld, I. J.: *ref,* 6:89(12), 6: 229(65), 6:245(655)

Rosenhan, D.: *ref,* 6:71(113), 6:112(2), 6:245(751)
Rosenhan, D. L.: *ref,* 67(452), 107(7)
Rosenstein, A. J.: *ref,* 166(1450)
Rosenstein, J. L.: *bk,* P702
Rosenthal, D.: *ref,* 5:114(121), 5:172(109), 6:138(108)
Rosenthal, E.: *bk,* P446
Rosenthal, F. M.: *ref,* 3:107(31, 43)
Rosenthal, I.: *ref,* 5:90(3), 5:112(20)
Rosenthal, J. C.: *ref,* 193(17)
Rosenthal, M.: *ref,* 5:154(1780), 6:237(2930)
Rosenthal, R.: *ref,* 23(3)
Rosenthal, T. L.: *ref,* 166(1553)
Rosenwald, A. K.: *ref,* 3:26(5), 3:73(585), 4:117(746)
Rosenwald, G. C.: *ref,* 484(1024, 1225)
Rosenzweig, L.: *ref,* 4:129(21), 5:155(110)
Rosenzweig, M.: *ref,* 5:154(1475)
Rosenzweig, M. R.: *ref,* 448(91), 6:226(69)
Rosenzweig, N.: *ref,* 470(3311)
Rosenzweig, S.: *test,* 471; *bk,* P703; *exc,* 3:75–6; *ref,* 471(275, 282, 301–2), 2:1246(39), 3:24(6), 3:60(51), 3:73(395, 542), 3:103(22, 77, 91), 4:71(182), 4:77(241), 4:92(73), 4:117(863), 4:129(1, 4, 9–10, 13, 15, 21, 32, 52–7), 4:136(140, 174–6), 4:147(4), 5:155(110, 125, 169), 6:238(209, 222, 243)
Rosett, H. L.: *ref,* 27(380), 421(5), 448(115)
Rosevear, W. H.: *ref,* 5:154(1792)
Roslow, S.: *test,* 347; *ref,* 347(7–8), 2:1199(4), 2:1233(5), 2:1240(8)
Rosman, B.: *ref,* 91(82)
Rosman, R. R.: *ref,* 166(2089)
Rosner, B.: *rev,* C83, F155, K16; *exc,* P209
Rosner, S.: *ref,* 6:237(2703)
Ross, A. O.: *rev,* 6:164, 6:241; *exc,* P804
Ross, A. T.: *ref,* 5:86(591), 5:154(1962)
Ross, C. C.: *rev,* A11, A15–6, A20, A40; *bk,* P768
Ross, C. S.: *rev,* G22, G108, G120, G171, G181
Ross, D.: *ref,* 5:154(1308), 5:164(376)
Ross, D. C.: *ref,* 439(110), 470(3425, 3711), 6:237(3018)
Ross, D. R.: *ref,* 29(203)
Ross, E. H.: *exc,* P754
Ross, E. N.: *ref,* 471(283)
Ross, G.: *ref,* 5:120(88)
Ross, H. L.: *ref,* 5:154(1781)
Ross, J.: *bk,* P583; *ref,* 27(213), 161(162), 177(36, 45), 6:147(5, 7, 9–10)
Ross, N.: *exc,* P245
Ross, P. F.: *rev,* I7, O202; *ref,* 64(2), 93(52), 269(11)
Ross, R. T.: *ref,* 6:61(26)
Ross, R. W.: *ref,* 4:129(58)
Ross, S.: *ref,* 3:73(399)

Ross, W. D.: *exc,* 4:125, 4:128; *ref,* 245(273), 439(90), 2:1246(146), 3:73(184, 225, 286, 348–9, 396–9, 455–7), 3:95(12), 4:117(603, 1014–5), 5:154(1782), 6:237(3008), 6:238(244)
Rossi, A. M.: *ref,* 177(35), 5:86(676), 6:143(1059), 6:204(72), 6:237(2830)
Rosskopf, M. F.: *rev,* G31, G66
Rossman, J. E.: *ref,* 341(34)
Rostker, L. E.: *ref,* 3:110(13), 4:66(2), 4:77(188)
Roston, R. A.: *ref,* 166(1891)
Rosvold, H. E.: *ref,* 5:154(1782)
Roth, H. S.: *ref,* 166(2288)
Roth, I.: *ref,* 470(3269, 3367)
Roth, R. H.: *ref,* 166(1957, 2145), 442A(165)
Roth, R. M.: *test,* 174; *ref,* 471(303), 6:73(155, 166)
Rothaus, P.: *ref,* 127(97), 166(2291), 235(7), 6:245(842)
Rothe, H. F.: *rev,* B38–9; *exc,* P250
Rothenberg, D.: *ref,* 6:182(266), 6:237(2989)
Rothenberg, H. A.: *ref,* 415(368)
Rothkopf, E. Z.: *ref,* 6:226(70–1)
Rothman, E. P.: *test,* 418
Rothman, I.: *ref,* 166(1476)
Rothman, P.: *exc,* P79
Rothmann, E.: *ref,* 3:73(429a)
Rothney, J. W. M.: *rev,* 3:63, 3:107, 4:67, 4:79, 5:79, 5:122, 6:106, 6:142, F258, H245; *bk,* P233–4, P704–5; *exc,* P19, P148, P685; *ref,* 3:99(15, 19), 6:237(2359, 2520), 6:245(624, 674)
Rothschild, B. H.: *ref,* 470(3211, 3293, 3698)
Rothstein, C.: *ref,* 124(44), 221A(11), 6:237(2441)
Rothstein, R.: *ref,* 439(102), 470(3212)
Rotman, S. R.: *ref,* 166(1706)
Rotter, J. B.: *rev,* 3:60, 3:103; *test,* 144, 472; *exc,* P12, P369, P868; *ref,* 144(1–3), 3:60(62), 3:73(437, 565), 3:103(10, 48, 78, 86), 4:113(18), 4:117(662, 747), 4:130(2–4, 6), 4:136(290), 4:144(12), 5:154(2050), 5:156(11, 13), 6:245(804)
Rottersman, W.: *ref,* 3:73(458)
Rotton, L. B.: *ref,* 42(26)
Roulette, T. G.: *ref,* 5:154(1276)
Roulon, P. J.: *exc,* P496
Routsoni, A.: *ref,* 470(3399)
Rowan, T.: *ref,* 5:155(163)
Rowe, F. B.: *ref,* 166(1414)
Rowe, R.: *ref,* 6:121(19)
Rowell, D.: *ref,* 43(23)
Rowell, J. T.: *ref,* 5:86(587)
Rowland, C.: *test,* 3:101
Rowley, I. F.: *ref,* 145(1)
Rowley, V. N.: *ref,* 166(2104), 6:143(1100, 1271, 1377)
Roy, A. B.: *ref,* 6:237(2908)
Roy, H. L.: *ref,* 3:60(59)
Roy, S.: *ref,* 245(278)
Royal, E. A.: *ref,* 5:139(76)
Royal, R. E.: *ref,* 442A(19), 4:117(1016)
Royce, J. R.: *exc,* P22

Royer, H. L.: *rev,* B13
Royse, A. B.: *rev,* F106, F180, F201, O58
Rozan, G. H.: *ref,* 48(69)
Rozehnal, B. J.: *ref,* 6:130(16)
Rozynko, V. V.: *ref,* 27(233), 166(1794), 6:87(194)
Rubenstein, B. B.: *ref,* 2:1246(115)
Rubin, B.: *ref,* 2:1248(9.1)
Rubin, E. Z.: *ref,* 5:154(2193)
Rubin, H.: *ref,* 4:71(135, 231), 5:86(529), 5:139(40, 50), 5:154(1603)
Rubin, H. K.: *ref,* 4:136(284)
Rubin, S. B.: *ref,* 5:86(315)
Rubin, S. I.: *rev,* I15
Rubin, S. S.: *ref,* 484(1025)
Rubinstein, E. A.: *ref,* 6:126(2–3, 7)
Rubisoff, R.: *ref,* 3:53(5)
Ruble, R. A.: *ref,* 6:71(123)
Ruby, W. M.: *ref,* 6:174(96), 6:245(843)
Ruch, F. L.: *rev,* 6:120, O212, O215, O305, O328–9; *bk,* P808; *ref,* 166(2289), 3:24(3), 3:26(14), 4:77(154)
Ruch, G. M.: *rev,* G17, G159, N31; *bk,* P706; *exc,* P729
Ruch, W. W.: *ref,* 166(2289)
Ruckhaber, C. J.: *ref,* 415(297)
Rudhe, L.: *ref,* 6:243(157)
Rudoff, A.: *ref,* 5:37(23), 6:238(215)
Rudolf, G. de M.: *ref,* 4:94(74–5)
Rudolph, R.: *ref,* 6:244(2–3)
Ruebush, B. K.: *ref,* 439(30), 6:143(1032)
Ruedisili, C. H.: *rev,* O209, O347; *exc,* P46
Ruesch, H. A.: *ref,* 4:117(1002)
Ruesch, J.: *bk,* P890; *exc,* P290; *ref,* 3:73(226)
Ruess, A. L.: *ref,* 5:154(2287), 5:164(601)
Rufe, C. P.: *ref,* 27(226)
Rugen, M. E.: *rev,* H153, H155; *exc,* P213, P215, P286, P746, P849, P893
Ruggles, R.: *ref,* 2:1198(18)
Ruiz, R. A.: *ref,* 166(2234–5, 2290), 244(86, 90)
Rule, E. T.: *ref,* 5:154(1783)
Rulon, P. J.: *test,* 297; *exc,* P432, P550, P845; *ref,* 297(1)
Rumage, C. J.: *ref,* 5:79(4)
Rumbaugh, D. M.: *test,* 30; *ref,* 30(1)
Rummel, J. F.: *bk,* P685
Rumrill, C.: *ref,* 6:143(937)
Rundquist, E. A.: *rev,* B31, B45; *test,* 342; *bk,* P707; *ref,* 342(1)
Runte, R. M.: *ref,* 261(59)
Rupe, J. F.: *ref,* 4:83(5–7)
Rupiper, O. J.: *ref,* 6:110(146), 6:182(244)
Rushton, J.: *ref,* 38(10)
Rusmore, J. T.: *ref,* 5:59(11)
Rusnak, A. W.: *ref,* 470(3461)
Russell, D. H.: *rev,* C189, K65, K135, K137, K141, K145–6, K153; *bk,* P336
Russell, E. W.: *ref,* 470(3630)
Russell, H. J.: *rev,* E142, E144, E147, E152

Saslow, H. L.: *ref,* 5:154(2220), 6:237(2570)

Sassenrath, J. M.: *ref,* 184(70)

Satake, R.: *ref,* 480(180)

Satir, K. R.: *ref,* 136(51)

Satlow, I. D.: *rev,* B13, F188

Sato, I.: *ref,* 6:237(2931, 2980)

Satter, G. A.: *rev,* O37, O39, O143, O157; *ref,* 5:57(42), 5:120(89, 91–2), 5:139(51), 5:172(92)

Satterlee, R. L.: *ref,* 5:117(14)

Sattler, J. M.: *ref,* 470(3403)

Satz, P.: *ref,* 6:87(214)

Saucer, R. T.: *ref,* 6:89(29), 6:96 (16), 6:143(1299), 6:177(5), 6:215(109)

Sauer, R. E.: *ref,* 484(920)

Saugstad, R. G.: *ref,* 5:39(1)

Saunders, A. W.: *rev,* D10, D14

Saunders, D. R.: *rev,* 5:65, 5:106; *test,* 344, 5:112; *exc,* P322; *ref,* 4:87(8), 5:73(2)

Saunders, J. C.: *ref,* 326(29, 33)

Saunders, M. H.: *ref,* 6:215(102), 6:229(106)

Saunders, R.: *ref,* 5:162(67, 118)

Saunders, W. W.: *ref,* 5:162(95, 110)

Sauté, G. DeW.: *ref,* 6:143(922)

Sauté, L.: *ref,* 67(344)

Savage, C.: *ref,* 127(88), 166(1684, 1707, 2092)

Savage, E.: *ref,* 166(1707)

Savage, R. D.: *ref,* 77(21), 161 (158), 166(1964, 2150, 2292), 6:138(80)

Savering, F. R.: *ref,* 415(423)

Sawrey, W. L.: *ref,* 6:143(799), 6:182(158), 6:192(13)

Sawyer, C. R.: *ref,* 116(45)

Sawyer, G. W.: *ref,* 5:155(92)

Sawyer, J.: *ref,* 192(16)

Sawyier, W. G.: *ref,* 484(1026)

Sax, G.: *exc,* P268

Saxe, C. H.: *ref,* 4:136(233), 5:164 (300)

Saxon, S. V.: *ref,* 165(14)

Sayons, K.: *ref,* 5:154(1609)

Sayons, Z.: *ref,* 5:154(1609)

Scagnelli, D. P.: *ref,* 5:123(9)

Scalea, C. J.: *ref,* 6:186(7)

Scales, E. E.: *ref,* 6:87(213a)

Scales, M. B.: *ref,* 5:154(1966)

Scandrette, O. C.: *ref,* 5:38(94), 6:87(275)

Scanlon, J. C.: *ref,* 6:180(9–10)

Scarborough, B. B.: *ref,* 5:66(12)

Scarpitti, F. R.: *ref,* 6:71(89)

Scarr, H. A.: *ref,* 166(1713)

Scarr, S.: *ref,* 4(70–1)

Scates, D. E.: *rev,* 1:1154, A20, K202, K211, K217, N134; *exc,* P446, P732

Schaaf, W. L.: *rev,* G124, G132, G153

Schachtel, A. H.: *ref,* 470(3032), 3:73(288, 400, 461)

Schachtel, E. G.: *exc,* 3:78, 3:84; *ref,* 470(3032, 3516, 3632), 2:1246 (65, 80), 3:73(169, 227, 258, 351–2, 462), 4:117(1025–6, 1185)

Schachtitz, E.: *ref,* 4:130(6)

Schaefer, B. R.: *ref,* 3:99(20)

Schaefer, C. E.: *ref,* 4(87), 15(15, 20), 287(43), 432(9)

Schaefer, E. S.: *ref,* 84(19), 5:154 (1278), 6:126(3, 6)

Schaefer, F. M.: *exc,* P123, P335

Schaefer, J. B.: *ref,* 6:245(844)

Schaefer, W. C.: *rev,* F28, F168

Schaeffer, R. W.: *ref,* 451(168)

Schafer, R.: *bk,* P674–6, P714–5; *exc,* 4:135, 4:140, P312; *ref,* 13 (57), 91(91), 470(3035, 3633, 3707), 484(1224), 3:27(17–8), 3:41(24, 27), 3:71(27–8, 32), 3:73(454, 534–5), 3:103(72–3), 4:31(39), 4:35(25), 4:117(749, 1027), 4:136(142), 5:154(1316, 1432, 1610, 1787, 2115), 5:164 (603), 6:237(2444, 2705–6), 6:245(745, 809)

Schafer, S.: *ref,* 3:103(89), 4:117 (750), 4:136(143)

Schafer, W. E.: *test,* 222

Schaffer, H. R.: *exc,* P47

Schaffer, R. E.: *ref,* 6:177(23)

Schaie, K. W.: *test,* 269, 420; *ref,* 136(22), 269(13), 420(1–2, 4, 6, 8–9), 5:47(6), 6:131(21), 6:189 (1–6, 8)

Schalling, D.: *ref,* 94(14)

Schalock, R. L.: *ref,* 244(97), 245 (240), 471(294)

Schalon, C. L.: *ref,* 266(24)

Schanberger, W. J.: *ref,* 5:147(27)

Schapero, M.: *ref,* 5:65(15)

Scharf, G. C.: *ref,* 259(417)

Scharf, P. L.: *exc,* P252

Scharles, H. G.: *ref,* 67(572)

Schatia, V.: *ref,* 4:117(604)

Schatz, L.: *ref,* 67(338)

Schauble, P. G.: *ref,* 166(2426)

Schaw, L. C.: *ref,* 5:164(556)

Scheckel, R.: *ref,* 471(254)

Scheerer, M.: *test,* 91; *bk,* P357; *ref,* 3:41(9), 5:57(32, 36)

Scheflen, N. A.: *ref,* 5:125(44)

Scheibe, K. E.: *ref,* 4(82), 27 (334), 472(64)

Scheidel, T. M.: *ref,* 259(317), 5:47(12), 5:114(129), 6:87(79), 6:182(172)

Scheier, I. H.: *test,* 116, 118, 178, 182; *bk,* P176; *exc,* 6:148; *ref,* 116(25), 121(4), 182(6), 245 (346), 344(7, 11, 15), 6:121(2, 6, 13), 6:124(1, 4), 6:148(1), 6:149(1–3, 5), 6:174(41, 66)

Schein, E. H.: *ref,* 5:154(2136), 6:143(846), 6:237(2450), 6:245 (660)

Schein, J. D.: *ref,* 6:177(15, 19, 30)

Scheiner, S. B.: *ref,* 470(3661)

Scheinker, J. L.: *ref,* 166(1952–3)

Schell, R. E.: *ref,* 131(25), 166 (2283)

Schellenberg, E. D.: *ref,* 6:203 (237)

Schellenberg, P. E.: *ref,* 6:226(24)

Schenck, E. A.: *bk,* P716

Schendel, J.: *ref,* 27(254)

Schenk, Q. F.: *ref,* 4:88(19)

Schenke, L. W.: *ref,* 5:172(112)

Schepers, J. M.: *rev,* 6:213, 6:240

Scherer, I. W.: *test,* 180; *ref,* 4:31

(41),   4:51(18),   4:117(867), 4:134(15, 61), 5:86(723), 5:111 (35), 5:162(86), 6:194(110)

Scheuerman, E. L.: *ref,* 198(323)

Schiele, B. C.: *ref,* 3:60(9), 4:71 (103, 136), 5:86(471), 6:143 (1282)

Schiele, W.: *ref,* 5:95(262)

Schiff, H. M.: *test,* 344; *ref,* 5:86 (406, 480), 5:154(1480, 1653)

Schiff, S.: *ref,* 470(3528)

Schiffman, D. C.: *ref,* 67(683), 245(352), 266(26), 484(1184, 1235)

Schiffman, H.: *ref,* 177(36), 448 (105, 113), 6:246(9)

Schilder, P.: *ref,* 3:108(3, 6)

Schill, T. R.: *ref,* 166(2093), 416 (110), 471(304)

Schiller, F. C. S.: *exc,* P412

Schiller, M.: *ref,* 6:143(896)

Schimek, J. G.: *ref,* 470(3714)

Schindler, A. W.: *rev,* A2, A11, L8, L138, L146

Schindler, M. Du P.: *ref,* 104(202)

Schipman, W. G.: *ref,* 6:237(2623)

Schiro, F. M.: *ref,* 9(41), 102(80), 166(2293)

Schlaff, A.: *test,* 104; *ref,* 6:110 (76)

Schlag, M.: *ref,* 5:47(3), 5:114 (114)

Schleifer, M. J.: *ref,* 5:154(1900), 6:237(2707)

Schlesinger, H. J.: *exc,* P488; *ref,* 4:117(976, 1138)

Schlesinger, K.: *ref,* 6:143(1197)

Schlesinger, R. J.: *ref,* 470(3391)

Schlesser, G. E.: *test,* 195; *exc,* P848; *ref,* 195(1, 4, 7)

Schletzer, V. M.: *ref,* 166(1494)

Schlicht, W. J.: *ref,* 472(75)

Schloener, C. J.: *ref,* 173(108)

Schloerb, L.: *bk,* P788

Schlosser, J. R.: *ref,* 5:154(1279)

Schlueter, M. P.: *ref,* 29(185)

Schmale, H. T.: *ref,* 4:115(3)

Schmeidler, D.: *ref,* 107(13), 253 (20, 29), 451(187)

Schmeidler, G. R.: *ref,* 416(93), 470(3077), 4:117(868), 4:129 (59), 5:114(99), 5:154(2086), 5:155(81), 6:237(2571, 2708–9)

Schmickel, C. A.: *ref,* 281(132)

Schmid, F. W.: *ref,* 470(3715)

Schmid, J.: *bk,* P262; *ref,* 4:71 (183, 233), 4:73(26, 28), 4:95 (22, 26)

Schmidl, F.: *ref,* 3:73(463, 588), 4:117(607)

Schmidl-Waehner, T.: *bk,* P605; *ref,* 442A(8), 4:117(605)

Schmidt, A. G.: *exc,* 2:1228, 2:1264, 3:42, P3, P64, P68, P86, P97–8, P112, P120, P131, P136–7, P146, P148–9, P197, P203–5, P231–3, P235, P241, P243, P264, P269, P279, P284, P286, P302, P305, P327, P331, P336, P340, P347, P354, P369, P371–2, P378, P394, P401, P409, P420, P430, P432, P436, P442, P444, P449, P455, P460, P465–6, P468, P477, P490–1, P493–6, P499, P502,

Singh, P. N.: *ref,* 6:87(276), 6:182 (245)
Singh, R. K. J.: *ref,* 470(3412)
Singh, S. C. P.: *ref,* 450(98)
Singh, S. D.: *ref,* 161(210), 6:138 (60, 114)
Singh, U. P.: *ref,* 161(211, 240)
Singlestad, R.: *ref,* 165(15)
Sinha, A. K.: *ref,* 104(304), 161 (241, 266), 239(24)
Sinha, A. K. P.: *ref,* 381(35)
Sinha, J. N.: *ref,* 1(65)
Sinha, S. N.: *ref,* 6:237(2788)
Sinkeldam, C.: *ref,* 71(41)
Sinnett, E. R.: *ref,* 5:63(34), 5:125(22), 5:154(1391, 2122), 5:164(352), 6:143(1149, 1275), 6:204(48)
Sinowitz, M.: *ref,* 451(218), 470 (3722)
Siple, H. L.: *exc,* P685; *ref,* 4:117 (754)
Sipprelle, C. N.: *ref,* 5:148(42–3)
Siqueira, T. N.: *exc,* P410, P416, P810, P858
Sirota, L. M.: *ref,* 259(289), 416 (82)
Sisk, H. L.: *ref,* 3:60(70), 3:73 (589–90), 3:103(92)
Siskind, G.: *ref,* 32(6), 6:126(22)
Sisler, G. C.: *ref,* 67(645), 166 (2326), 6:87(326), 6:143(1393)
Sisney, V. V.: *ref,* 127(89)
Sisson, B.: *ref,* 3:99(37), 4:77 (123)
Sisson, B. D.: *ref,* 5:86(724), 5:154(1805, 1973, 2123, 2132), 6:245(897)
Sisson, E. D.: *exc,* P150, P250, P787; *ref,* 3:99(37), 4:77(123)
Sistrunk, F.: *ref,* 67(440), 104 (217), 127(66), 261(21)
Sitgreaves, R.: *exc,* P677
Sitts, M. R.: *ref,* 245(115)
Sivanich, G.: *ref,* 6:143(1037, 1344)
Sivley, R. B.: *ref,* 166(1909)
Sjoberg, B. M.: *ref,* 6:143(1165), 6:178(4)
Sjostedt, E. M.: *ref,* 5:154(1974), 5:167(2), 6:237(2577)
Skaer, M.: *ref,* 2:1217(1)
Skager, R. W.: *ref,* 122(1–2)
Skeath, J. M.: *ref,* 340(15)
Skeen, D.: *ref,* 27(374)
Skeen, D. R.: *test,* 108; *ref,* 472 (75)
Skeet, D. V.: *bk,* P750
Skidmore, R. A.: *ref,* 5:38(79), 5:84(5)
Skiff, S. C.: *ref,* 6:57(47), 6:237 (2302)
Sklar, J.: *ref,* 285(1)
Sklar, M.: *test,* 247; *ref,* 49(28), 91(73), 247(1), 415(274), 470 (3183), 6:110(147), 6:173(57)
Skolnick, A.: *ref,* 484(1133–4)
Skorodin, B.: *ref,* 3:24(10)
Skrincosky, P. C.: *ref,* 5:86(459)
Skrzypek, G. J.: *ref,* 166(2101)
Skurdal, M. A.: *test,* 108; *ref,* 472 (75)
Slack, C. W.: *ref,* 4:136(236)
Slack, E. P.: *rev,* L140

Slack, G. K.: *ref,* 470(3708)
Slade, H. C.: *ref,* 49(61)
Slater, E.: *exc,* 4:126; *ref,* 161 (170), 4:85(2)
Slater, G. R.: *ref,* 41(6), 166 (1663), 439(42), 484(1007)
Slater, P.: *rev,* F112, O72, O155; *test,* 377; *bk,* P880; *exc,* P300, P813, P866; *ref,* 3:95(11, 15), 4:85(1–2), 5:111(26)
Slater, P. E.: *ref,* 166(1713), 6:143 (893, 1276)
Slavinska-Nyles, N.: *ref,* 136(46)
Slawson, P. F.: *ref,* 166(1554)
Slayton, W. G.: *ref,* 116(47), 259 (387)
Sleeper, M. L.: *ref,* 6:63(2)
Slemboski, J.: *ref,* 470(3745)
Slemon, A. G.: *ref,* 470(3389, 3413), 6:237(2916, 2928)
Sletto, R. F.: *test,* 342; *bk,* P707, P751; *exc,* P563; *ref,* 342(1)
Slife, W. G.: *ref,* 6:182(246)
Sloan, T. J.: *ref,* 5:86(769)
Sloan, W.: *rev,* F243, M29–30; *ref,* 3:73(591), 4:107(9), 4:117 (755, 1126), 4:136(265), 5:139 (52)
Sloane, R. B.: *ref,* 161(133, 205, 236)
Slobin, M. S.: *test,* 443; *ref,* 6:220 (1, 3)
Slocombe, C. S.: *exc,* P202, P296
Slocombe, E.: *exc,* P106
Slocombe, E. E.: *ref,* 5:172(93)
Slosson, R. L.: *test,* 248
Slote, W. H.: *ref,* 4:117(1193)
Slusher, H. S.: *ref,* 166(1714)
Slusser, G. H.: *ref,* 67(351)
Slutz, M.: *ref,* 3:103(14)
Smail, D. J.: *ref,* 196(19), 484 (1082, 1135)
Smalheiser, I.: *ref,* 4:117(1212)
Smalheiser, L.: *ref,* 161(161)
Small, I. F.: *ref,* 163(31), 415(354)
Small, J. G.: *ref,* 163(31), 415 (354), 6:143(1276a)
Small, L.: *bk,* P752; *ref,* 5:154 (2124)
Smallenburg, H. W.: *ref,* 3:26(7), 4:58(6)
Smalley, N. S.: *ref,* 127(99)
Smallwood, M. L.: *bk,* P753
Smarr, R. G.: *ref,* 6:177(43)
Smart, R. G.: *ref,* 161(187), 6:60 (6), 6:137(8)
Smathers, S.: *ref,* 6:143(810)
Smee, P. G.: *ref,* 67(677)
Smelser, W.: *ref,* 5:86(772)
Smeltzer, C. H.: *bk,* P408
Smith, A. A.: *ref,* 415(396)
Smith, A. C.: *ref,* 67(454)
Smith, A. H.: *ref,* 67(432), 259 (322), 6:143(1230), 6:239(40)
Smith, A. J.: *ref,* 6:182(162, 173, 216)
Smith, A. P.: *ref,* 165(23)
Smith, B. B.: *exc,* P861; *ref,* 6:244(4)
Smith, B. F.: *ref,* 399(28)
Smith, B. O.: *bk,* P754
Smith, C. A.: *bk,* P756
Smith, C. E.: *rev,* C46, F112, F172, G123, G182; *bk,* P415, P755;

exc, P148, P717, P826; *ref,* 415 (389, 413), 6:203(208, 241, 257)
Smith, C. L.: *ref,* 195(8)
Smith, C. M.: *ref,* 408(24, 27), 6:138(24, 93), 6:143(927), 6:237(2578)
Smith, D. C.: *ref,* 415(398), 6:127 (32), 6:245(849)
Smith, D. D.: *ref,* 5:80(9), 6:103 (27), 6:132(12)
Smith, D. E. P.: *rev,* K6, K103, K173, K184
Smith, D. M.: *ref,* 324(4), 4:117 (876)
Smith, D. W.: *ref,* 5:86(656, 716)
Smith, E.: *ref,* 442A(62)
Smith, E. E.: *ref,* 6:143(928, 1373)
Smith, E. L.: *ref,* 294(13)
Smith, E. R.: *test,* 1:898; *bk,* P757; *exc,* P470; *ref,* 110(26)
Smith, F.: *exc,* P194, P858
Smith, F. J.: *ref,* 5:50(11)
Smith, F. R.: *ref,* 5:65(17)
Smith, G.: *ref,* 5:69(63–4), 6:120 (66)
Smith, G. M.: *ref,* 67(507, 642), 245(205, 308, 317), 4:117(811)
Smith, H. C.: *ref,* 4:89(35), 4:92 (74), 4:117(877), 5:107(5), 6:226(43)
Smith, H. J.: *exc,* P622
Smith, H. N.: *ref,* 2:1243(8)
Smith, H. P.: *rev,* K4, K40; *ref,* 4:28(84)
Smith, H. W.: *exc,* P662
Smith, I. F.: *test,* 46
Smith, I. L.: *ref,* 67(679)
Smith, I. M.: *rev,* F42, F54, G213, I9, O123, O126
Smith, J.: *ref,* 166(2437)
Smith, J. A.: *ref,* 4:136(291)
Smith, J. E.: *ref,* 67(680), 259 (469)
Smith, J. G.: *bk,* P652; *ref,* 5:154 (1588)
Smith, J. H.: *ref,* 3:24(20)
Smith, J. J.: *exc,* P766
Smith, J. M.: *ref,* 4:28(46)
Smith, J. P.: *ref,* 251(55), 415 (326)
Smith, J. R.: *ref,* 5:149(34), 5:154 (2125), 6:143(1374)
Smith, J. T.: *ref,* 29(232)
Smith, L. C.: *ref,* 415(333), 447 (46), 6:194(99), 6:237(2579)
Smith, L. D.: *ref,* 6:71(84), 6:143 (1142), 6:237(2829), 6:245(799)
Smith, L. F.: *ref,* 4:28(50)
Smith, L. J.: *ref,* 5:86(432), 5:148 (21)
Smith, L. M.: *ref,* 5:38(107, 117), 5:117(15, 19), 5:155(155, 186), 6:170(25)
Smith, M.: *bk,* P758; *exc,* P275
Smith, M. A.: *ref,* 425(7)
Smith, M. D.: *ref,* 6:238(211)
Smith, M. E.: *ref,* 484(1109), 6:182(247)
Smith, M. L.: *ref,* 6:238(201)
Smith, M. S.: *ref,* 484(1230)
Smith, N. B.: *rev,* K35, K41, K132; *ref,* 6:177(10)
Smith, N. Van O.: *ref,* 4:61(5)
Smith, O. M.: *exc,* P158

Vroom, A. L.: *ref,* 6:204(68–9)
Vuorinen, V.: *ref,* 496(11)

WAAGE, L.: *ref,* 4:62(4)
Waddell, W.: *ref,* 6:204(70), 6:229 (99)
Wadsworth, B. J.: *ref,* 261(59)
Wadsworth, G. W.: *test,* 3:48; *ref,* 2:1223(1–3), 3:48(14, 16, 22, 23a, 30)
Wadsworth, H. M. M.: *ref,* 5:86 (600)
Waehner, T. S.: *ref,* 442A(10), 3:73(388)
Waggoner, G. H.: *ref,* 6:87(121), 6:182(197)
Wagman, M.: *ref,* 166(2451), 259 (420)
Wagner, C. M.: *ref,* 439(82)
Wagner, E. E.: *test,* 438; *ref,* 104(223), 166(2316), 415(372), 438(9, 11–3, 16), 470(3428, 3540, 3744–5), 6:110(89, 109), 6:121 (14), 6:132(16), 6:216(1–6), 6:237(2839)
Wagner, G.: *rev,* K139
Wagner, M. E.: *test,* 423; *ref,* 5:129(1–3)
Wagner, N. N.: *ref,* 245(247, 315)
Wagner, P.: *ref,* 4:77(217)
Wagner, R. F.: *ref,* 6:143(1162)
Wagoner, L. C.: *bk,* P870
Wagoner, R. A.: *ref,* 470(3314), 6:237(3022)
Wahba, M.: *ref,* 166(1504), 287 (21)
Wahl, C. A.: *ref,* 27(315)
Wahler, H. J.: *ref,* 49(77), 166 (1929, 2452), 244(97), 5:86 (557), 6:143(1163), 6:173(58)
Wahlstrom, L. F.: *ref,* 3:34(2)
Wahlstrom, M. W.: *ref,* 67(517), 484(1089)
Wait, M. E.: *ref,* 451(183)
Waite, R. R.: *ref,* 439(30), 442A (93), 5:36(18), 5:154(2288), 6:143(1032)
Waite, W. W.: *rev,* O198, O337, O339
Waits, J. V.: *rev,* O357
Walberg, H. J.: *ref,* 67(640, 684–5), 259(456, 471–2)
Walch, A. E.: *ref,* 4:71(90)
Walcher, H. R.: *ref,* 192(13)
Walcott, W. O.: *ref,* 470(3105), 484(913), 4:136(185)
Walder, H.: *bk,* P871; *ref,* 6:243 (146–7)
Waldfogel, S.: *exc,* 4:112, P607
Waldman, M.: *ref,* 4:117(1209), 6:237(2560)
Waldrop, R. S.: *ref,* 5:114(101)
Wales, B.: *ref,* 166(2453)
Walike, B. C.: *ref,* 166(2114)
Walker, A. S.: *bk,* P872
Walker, C. E.: *ref,* 166(2317), 472 (68)
Walker, D.: *ref,* 6:237(2509), 6:245(669)
Walker, D. A.: *bk,* P565
Walker, E. L.: *ref,* 3:24(13), 5:154(1345, 1525)
Walker, E. M.: *ref,* 5:38(25)
Walker, F. A.: *ref,* 399(34)
Walker, H.: *rev,* G71

Walker, H. A.: *ref,* 283(20)
Walker, H. E.: *ref,* 185(5)
Walker, H. M.: *exc,* P813
Walker, J. N.: *ref,* 6:87(233), 6:143(1083–5, 1164, 1193, 1287)
Walker, R. E.: *ref,* 161(198), 173 (125), 443(24)
Walker, R. G.: *ref,* 4:113(15, 19), 4:117(764, 1048, 1210), 4:129 (64), 4:134(63), 5:154(1633), 5:155(98), 6:116(3–4)
Walker, R. N.: *bk,* P48–50; *ref,* 470(3222, 3327, 3651), 5:147(55), 5:154(1300, 1476, 1651, 2160), 6:237(2475)
Walker, R. Y.: *exc,* P768
Walker, W. B.: *ref,* 104(175), 259 (282)
Walker, W. J.: *ref,* 256(34)
Walker, W. L.: *ref,* 245(249)
Wall, H. R.: *ref,* 455(12)
Wall, W. D.: *rev,* F152, F219; *exc,* 3:75, 3:78, P152; *ref,* 281 (128)
Wallace, A. F. C.: *ref,* 5:154 (1460)
Wallace, D.: *ref,* 5:155(99)
Wallace, D. G.: *bk,* P721
Wallace, I. K.: *exc,* P898
Wallace, J.: *ref,* 381(50), 442A (136), 484(1139), 6:237(3023), 6:239(41), 6:245(896)
Wallace, J. L.: *ref,* 480(163)
Wallace, R.: *exc,* P64
Wallace, S. E.: *ref,* 6:245(821)
Wallace, S. R.: *rev,* I7, O218, O319, O358; *exc,* P358; *ref,* 4:48 (13), 5:29(7)
Wallace, W. L.: *rev,* 5:42, B10, F25, F34; *exc,* P315, P326
Wallach, M. A.: *ref,* 6:87(91), 6:128(62), 6:143(1041)
Wallach, M. S.: *ref,* 166(1930), 6:143(1387)
Wallen, N. E.: *rev,* 6:150, F87
Wallen, R.: *ref,* 4:117(764), 4:134 (63)
Wallen, R. W.: *ref,* 5:154(1811, 2140), 5:164(561)
Wallen, V.: *ref,* 470(3642)
Waller, C. H.: *exc,* P847
Waller, L. T.: *ref,* 5:89(54)
Waller, P. F.: *ref,* 6:237(2589, 2729–30)
Wallerstein, H.: *exc,* P673
Wallin, F. B.: *bk,* P446
Wallin, P.: *bk,* P446; *ref,* 6:159 (62)
Wallner, J. M.: *ref,* 5:154(1546)
Wallon, E. J.: *ref,* 451(144), 5:155 (182)
Walnut, F.: *ref,* 5:86(536)
Walsh, J.: *ref,* 166(1824), 259 (380), 472(53)
Walsh, J. A.: *ref,* 27(186), 161 (142), 166(1610), 6:143(1307–8)
Walsh, R. P.: *ref,* 147(3), 6:87 (122), 6:115(1)
Walsh, T. M.: *ref,* 82(19), 6:101 (64), 6:143(919)
Walsmith, C. R.: *ref,* 104(254), 259(394), 339(19)
Walsworth, B. M.: *ref,* 3:73(300), 4:77(162), 5:117(3)
Walter, D.: *ref,* 472(50)

Walter, J. I.: *ref,* 177(59)
Walter, P. B.: *ref,* 6:143(851)
Walter, S.: *ref,* 6:71(104), 6:142 (9)
Walter, V. A.: *ref,* 5:156(9, 21)
Walters, A.: *ref,* 4:45(2, 5, 10)
Walters, C. A.: *ref,* 5:154(1634)
Walters, C. E.: *ref,* 6:140(14)
Walters, J.: *ref,* 5:87(27)
Walters, J. E.: *exc,* P86
Walters, R. H.: *exc,* P891; *ref,* 5:154(1635)
Walters, W. M.: *ref,* 166(2398)
Walther, E. C.: *test,* 398
Waltmann, R. H.: *ref,* 166(1931, 2170), 167(1–2)
Walton, A. J.: *ref,* 137(9)
Walton, D.: *ref,* 5:154(1992), 6:138(82), 6:143(934), 6:206 (23)
Walton, D. F.: *ref,* 339(17)
Walton, H. J.: *ref,* 184(61), 245 (354)
Walton, R. E.: *test,* 226, 455; *ref,* 455(8), 5:150(1–2, 4)
Walton, W. E.: *ref,* 4:77(218)
Wambach, H. S.: *ref,* 470(3259), 6:153(1)
Wanderer, Z. W.: *ref,* 451(170, 198)
Wandt, E.: *rev,* H73, H85, H107; *bk,* P873; *exc,* P838
Wang, C.: *ref,* 451(195)
Wang, C. K. A.: *test,* 378; *bk,* P874; *ref,* 378(1), 1:927(1), 2:1198(9), 3:23(21), 3:96(23)
Wang, R. P.: *ref,* 6:237(2319)
Wanner, P. W.: *ref,* 5:148(44)
Wanous, S. J.: *bk,* P916
Wanser, B. R.: *ref,* 6:110(170)
Want, R. L.: *exc,* P152
Wantman, M. J.: *rev,* C76, K29, K193, N32, N145, N150, O261
Wapner, S.: *ref,* 442A(96), 5:49 (2), 5:148(30), 5:154(1822, 2142), 5:164(467)
Warburton, F. W.: *rev,* F57, F70, F150, O188; *bk,* P875; *exc,* P765, P776, P863, P866; *ref,* 6:174(67, 108), 6:182(280)
Warburton, J. W.: *ref,* 13(53)
Warburton, M. A.: *ref,* 4(56), 27 (262)
Ward, A. J.: *ref,* 470(3541)
Ward, B.: *ref,* 49(31)
Ward, G.: *ref,* 6:87(186), 6:96(13)
Ward, J.: *ref,* 6:143(935)
Ward, J. L.: *ref,* 110(27)
Ward, J. P.: *exc,* P260
Ward, L. B.: *ref,* 4:77(160)
Ward, L. C.: *ref,* 4:136(198)
Ward, L. W.: *ref,* 2:1239(38)
Ward, P. L.: *ref,* 6:87(123), 6:132 (13), 6:182(198)
Ward, R. S.: *bk,* P771
Ward, W. D.: *ref,* 67(400), 6:130 (10)
Wardeberg, H. L.: *bk,* P20
Warden, C. J.: *exc,* P723
Wardlow, M. E.: *ref,* 237(8), 346 (13), 5:80(6), 5:89(39), 5:105 (12)
Ware, K. E.: *ref,* 5:154(1240)
Wargo, D. G.: *ref,* 165(47), 166 (2446)

Weiss, A. A.: *ref,* 71(71), 91(84), 470(3217, 3431, 3643–4), 5:154 (2296)

Weiss, A. J.: *ref,* 5(170), 198(334)

Weiss, D. A.: *exc,* P699

Weiss, G.: *ref,* 5:155(127)

Weiss, J. H.: *ref,* 6:237(2740)

Weiss, J. L.: *ref,* 6:204(69)

Weiss, L.: *ref,* 470(3698), 3:23(25)

Weiss, P.: *ref,* 6:87(124), 6:245 (856)

Weiss, R.: *ref,* 42(11), 256(50), 6: 102(6)

Weiss, R. J.: *ref,* 166(1936)

Weiss, R. L.: *ref,* 166(1937), 470 (3215)

Weiss, S. D.: *ref,* 472(72)

Weiss, S. M.: *ref,* 166(1938)

Weiss, W.: *ref,* 5:123(7)

Weissenberg, P.: *ref,* 71(58)

Weisskopf, E. A.: *ref,* 3:73(292), 4:136(243–4, 298), 5:164(373)

Weisskopf-Joelson, E.: *exc,* P487; *ref,* 484(922), 5:126(8), 5:164 (424, 586), 6:206(33), 6:245 (808)

Weissman, H. N.: *ref,* 184(30)

Weissman, S. L.: *ref,* 484(984, 1037)

Weissmann, S.: *ref,* 470(3066), 5: 154(1470)

Weitemeyer, W.: *ref,* 161(262)

Weitman, M.: *ref,* 326(35)

Weitz, H.: *rev,* 6:66, B61, H286, K90, O16; *ref,* 6:143(1280)

Weitzenhoffer, A. M.: *test,* 253–4; *exc,* 6:75; *ref,* 6:110(71), 6:143 (1165), 6:174(38), 6:178(1–2, 4, 10, 17)

Weitzenhoffer, G. B.: *ref,* 6:110 (71), 6:174(38)

Weitzman, E.: *test,* 400; *bk,* P887; *ref,* 3:111(1–3)

Weitzner, M.: *ref,* 67(501, 642), 184(28), 245(317)

Wekstein, L.: *ref,* 3:73(593), 3: 103(101)

Welborn, E. L.: *exc,* P327

Welch, B.: *ref,* 6:245(809)

Welch, C. M.: *rev,* K103–4

Welch, J. S.: *bk,* P888

Welch, L.: *exc,* P346, P606; *ref,* 470(3040–1), 3:73(537), 4:117 (696), 6:57(52–3), 6:138(30–1)

Welch, W. W.: *ref,* 67(640), 259 (456)

Weldon, P. I.: *ref,* 439(81)

Welford, A. T.: *rev,* O127, O164

Welles, H. H.: *ref,* 2:1239(3)

Wellington, J. A.: *ref,* 5:89(50)

Wellisch, E.: *ref,* 4:117(888–91, 1050), 5:154(1814)

Wellman, B. L.: *rev,* F215, F241; *bk,* P889

Wells, F. L.: *rev,* F224, F258–9, F262, I22; *bk,* P890; *exc,* P68 P89, P148, P631–2; *ref,* 198 (322), 470(3035, 3064–5), 2:1246 (42), 3:49(11), 6:226(2–3, 5, 20)

Wells, G. F.: *exc,* P695

Wells, H.: *ref,* 3:103(58)

Wells, H. P.: *ref,* 6:174(39)

Wells, R. V.: *ref,* 342(16)

Wells, S.: *ref,* 4:134(36), 5:154 (2239), 6:237(2842)

Wells, W. D.: *test,* 231

Wells, W. S.: *ref,* 93(54), 104 (226)

Welman, A. J.: *ref,* 489(5)

Welna, C. T.: *ref,* 6:113(20)

Welsch, L. A.: *ref,* 92(25), 259 (457)

Welser, L.: *bk,* P214

Welsh, G. S.: *test,* 15, 166, 287; *bk,* P217, P891; *exc,* P217, P417; *ref,* 4(63), 15(1, 8), 166(1939), 287(31, 38), 415(260), 4:71(146, 189, 280), 5:86(386, 392–3, 669), 6:143(969), 6:197(1–2)

Welsh, R. S.: *ref,* 484(1038)

Weltman, R.: *ref,* 470(3318)

Wenar, C.: *ref,* 5:154(1462), 5: 168(17), 6:237(2462)

Wendland, L. V.: *ref,* 5:155(143), 6:117(8), 6:143(1040)

Wendland, M. M.: *ref,* 266(28)

Wenig, P. W.: *ref,* 5:164(324)

Wenk, E. A.: *ref,* 27(233), 166 (1794)

Wentworth-Rohr, I.: *ref,* 4:117 (1051), 4:136(245)

Wepman, J. M.: *test,* 141; *ref,* 94 (16–8), 141(1, 5–8), 190A(18–9, 22)

Werkman, S. L.: *ref,* 166(2320)

Werner, A. C.: *ref,* 245(250)

Werner, D. S.: *ref,* 102(70)

Werner, E. E.: *rev,* F229, F238; *ref,* 38(11), 281(129, 135), 415 (401), 6:194(97)

Werner, H.: *exc,* P910; *ref,* 442A (96), 3:73(476–7), 5:154(2142)

Werner, H. C.: *exc,* P455

Werner, M.: *ref,* 91(86), 484 (1084)

Werner, S.: *ref,* 4:71(119)

Wernert, C.: *ref,* 484(936)

Wernick, R.: *bk,* P892

Wernimont, P.: *ref,* 27(185), 259 (334)

Wert, J. E.: *exc,* P436, P669, P758

Wertham, F.: *exc,* P47, P871; *ref,* 2:1246(9), 4:115(2, 12), 6:228 (57)

Wertheimer, M.: *ref,* 5:154(1637, 2240), 6:87(124), 6:127(7), 6: 143(836)

Wertheimer, R. R.: *ref,* 5:154 (1638, 1815, 2241)

Werts, C. E.: *ref,* 166(1453, 2005), 470(3160, 3473)

Wertz, C.: *ref,* 6:143(1130)

Weschler, I. R.: *ref,* 4:48(19), 6: 103(24)

Wesley, E.: *ref,* 3:44(4), 3:60(32)

Wesley, E. B.: *rev,* N3, N9, N25, N39, N47, N84, N90, N92

Wesley, E. L.: *ref,* 5:111(33)

Wesley, S. M.: *ref,* 4:31(37), 4: 117(787)

Wesman, A. G.: *rev,* A30, A37, F171, O259–61; *ref,* 5:95(282), 6:159(56)

Wessell, A.: *ref,* 27(219)

Wessman, A. E.: *ref,* 471(255)

West, D. J.: *ref,* 49(65)

West, J. V.: *ref,* 6:229(135), 6:237 (3025)

West, J. Y.: *bk,* P893

West, K. L.: *ref,* 166(2116)

West, L. J.: *ref,* 5:86(471)

West, L. L.: *ref,* 5:86(661)

West, P. M.: *ref,* 5:86(394), 6:143 (784)

West, P. V.: *exc,* P495, P758

West, R.: *exc,* P551

Westberg, W. C.: *ref,* 5:64(43–5)

Westbrook, C. H.: *exc,* P883

Westby, G.: *rev,* 5:151, 6:227–8, F84, F136, F152; *exc,* P489

Westfall, R.: *ref,* 277(36)

Westie, C. M.: *test,* 98; *ref,* 6:105 (1)

Westover, F. L.: *rev,* K78

Westrope, M. R.: *ref,* 5:154(1463, 1639)

Westwood, D.: *ref,* 5:154(1913)

Wetherhorn, M.: *ref,* 5:154(2143)

Wetsel, H.: *ref,* 438(16)

Wetzel, R. J.: *ref,* 470(3184)

Wexberg, E.: *ref,* 3:41(12)

Wexler, M.: *ref,* 442A(24, 52), 4:117(966)

Wexler, N.: *ref,* 448(113)

Wexler, R. M.: *ref,* 4:111(1), 4: 117(733)

Wexner, L. B.: *ref,* 5:86(538)

Weybrew, B. B.: *ref,* 6:87(124a), 6:182(199)

Whaley, D.: *ref,* 163(26)

Wharton, L. H.: *ref,* 5:148(24)

Wharton, M. C.: *ref,* 127(45)

Wheat, H. G.: *rev,* G131, G167

Wheatley, L. A.: *ref,* 3:99(57), 4: 77(202)

Wheeler, D. K.: *rev,* C188, K2, K133

Wheeler, E. T.: *ref,* 3:95(13), 4: 71(91), 4:117(661), 4:136(117), 5:111(29)

Wheeler, J. I.: *ref,* 6:237(2549), 6: 245(692)

Wheeler, M. D.: *ref,* 5:154(1994)

Wheeler, N. C.: *ref,* 4:71(80)

Wheeler, W. M.: *ref,* 4:71(219, 238, 281), 4:117(787, 892–3, 1052), 5:126(15), 5:154(1816, 2144), 6:237(2335)

Wherry, R. J.: *exc,* P825; *ref,* 4:71 (204)

Whetstone, B. D.: *ref,* 261(14, 26), 471(265, 288)

Whilde, N. E.: *bk,* P894

Whipple, B. S.: *exc,* P318

Whipple, C. I.: *ref,* 415(373)

Whipple, G. M.: *ref,* 6:226(9)

Whiskin, F. E.: *ref,* 49(49)

Whisler, L. D.: *test,* 223; *ref,* 2: 1202(6), 2:1243(25), 4:46(40, 42), 5:29(9)

Whisler, R. H.: *ref,* 166(2117)

Whisler, T. L.: *bk,* P895

Whitaker, L.: *ref,* 439(63), 470 (3432), 6:229(108)

Whitcomb, J. C.: *ref,* 104(174)

Whitcomb, M. A.: *ref,* 3:107(54)

Whitcraft, L. H.: *bk,* P896

White, A. A.: *ref,* 166(1399)

White, B. L.: *exc,* P906

White, C.: *ref,* 49(14)

White, C. A.: *ref,* 166(2363)

White, E. B.: *ref,* 166(1730)

White, H. R.: *rev,* 4:144

Young, F. M.: *ref,* 5:60(3), 5:86 (647), 5:164(564)
Young, G. C.: *ref,* 179(10)
Young, H. A.: *ref,* 3:67(16)
Young, H. H.: *ref,* 451(141), 470 (3125), 484(924), 6:217(3), 6:237(2465)
Young, K.: *exc,* P606, P751, P808-9
Young, K. M.: *ref,* 470(3378), 4:117(768)
Young, L. A.: *ref,* 6:143(890, 990)
Young, L. L.: *ref,* 294(10), 3:63 (8), 5:38(29)
Young, M.: *bk,* P922
Young, N.: *ref,* 5:86(474), 5:95 (285)
Young, N. D.: *bk,* P558
Young, N. M.: *ref,* 4:117(1186), 4:129(72), 4:136(287)
Young, P. V.: *exc,* P68, P723, P795
Young, R. A.: *ref,* 3:73(293)
Young, R. C.: *ref,* 166(1945), 6:143 (1394)
Young, R. D.: *ref,* 5:164(425)
Young, R. J.: *ref,* 4:117(767, 1061)
Young, W. E.: *exc,* P340
Younng, J. H.: *test,* 235; *ref,* 235 (10)
Yourshaw, S.: *ref,* 166(2416)
Yu, P. E.: *ref,* 4:77(82), 5:123(9)
Yu, W.: *ref,* 470(3491)
Yudin, L. W.: *ref,* 484(1144)
Yufit, R. I.: *exc,* P391, P799; *ref,* 67(498)
Yuker, H. E.: *test,* 235; *ref,* 235 (10)
Yuzuk, R. P.: *bk,* P923

ZACCARIA, J. S.: *ref,* 67(652), 193(19)
Zacharewicz, M. M.: *ref,* 6:110 (173)
Zadek, M.: *ref,* 5:148(39)
Zahn, T. P.: *ref,* 166(2141)
Zahner, L. C.: *rev,* C17-8, C52, C112-3, C163
Zaidi, S. M. H.: *ref,* 381(53), 471 (289)
Zakolski, F. C.: *ref,* 347(15), 4:28 (107), 4:38(4), 4:77(246), 4:95 (24), 5:38(61), 6:65(4), 6:159 (65)
Zalany, A.: *ref,* 49(31)
Zalman, W. R.: *ref,* 4:77(170, 193)
Zamansky, H. S.: *ref,* 5:164(594), 6:237(2735)
Zander, A.: *exc,* 4:57
Zander, A. F.: *bk,* P924
Zangwill, O. L.: *rev,* 3:27, 3:41, 3:49; *ref,* 3:73(480), 4:117 (1153)

Zaretsky, H. H.: *ref,* 93(58-9), 166(2131)
Zax, M.: *ref,* 470(3379, 3529, 3637, 3685), 484(1050, 1205), 6:108(67), 6:237(2736-40, 2845, 3028)
Zeaman, J. B.: *ref,* 5:86(672)
Zedek, M. E.: *ref,* 6:71(52)
Zehrer, F. A.: *exc,* P428, P773, P891; *ref,* 4:117(1218)
Zeichner, A. M.: *ref,* 5:154(1996, 2151), 5:164(517, 565)
Zeisset, R. M.: *ref,* 166(2124)
Zektick, I. N.: *ref,* 166(2203), 259 (428)
Zelen, S. L.: *ref,* 166(2125), 244 (83), 470(3546), 4:117(1062), 5:38(100), 5:154(1825)
Zeleny, L. D.: *exc,* P109
Zeleny, M. P.: *ref,* 5:86(406, 480), 5:154(1653)
Zeleznik, C.: *ref,* 6:237(2958)
Zeligs, R.: *ref,* 4:88(4-6, 10)
Zelin, M.: *ref,* 6:237(3029)
Zeller, W. W.: *test,* 467; *ref,* 6:235 (1-4)
Zeman, F. D.: *ref,* 5:43(48)
Zenger, J. H.: *ref,* 6:103(24)
Zepelin, H.: *ref,* 49(76), 166(2423)
Zerilli, V. I.: *ref,* 2:1239(37)
Ziegenhagen, F. W.: *exc,* P622
Ziegfeld, E.: *rev,* D4-8, D10, D12; *ref,* 3:62(5)
Ziegler, F. F.: *ref,* 166(1886)
Zielonka, A. W.: *ref,* 245(319)
Zigler, E.: *ref,* 141(3)
Ziller, R. C.: *ref,* 6:143(1046)
Zimerberg, S. M.: *ref,* 27(354), 79(42)
Zimet, C. N.: *ref,* 470(3151, 3436, 3649), 484(1189), 5:77(12), 5:86(673), 5:154(1348, 2152), 5:161(3), 6:143(1047)
Zimiles, H.: *exc,* P852; *ref,* 442A (138)
Zimmer, H.: *ref,* 442A(78, 86)
Zimmer, L. W.: *exc,* P46
Zimmerman, C. C.: *exc,* P181
Zimmerman, F. T.: *ref,* 4:117 (1219)
Zimmerman, I. L.: *ref,* 29(212), 166(1946, 2194), 470(3547), 5:154(1294, 1997)
Zimmerman, J.: *ref,* 442A(9)
Zimmerman, M. A.: *ref,* 6:159(61)
Zimmerman, M. C.: *ref,* 5:154 (1294)
Zimmerman, W. S.: *rev,* F46, F148; *test,* 104; *exc,* P79; *ref,* 176(20), 5:63(53-4), 5:64(50-1), 5:78(51-2)
Zimpfer, D. G.: *ref,* 127(109), 390 (19)

Zingle, S. A.: *ref,* 200(2)
Zinnes, J. L.: *exc,* P837
Ziskind, E.: *ref,* 6:143(784)
Zisson, M. M.: *ref,* 3:73(529)
Zobel, H.: *test,* 124
Zoberi, H.: *ref,* 102(74), 104(188), 54(1), 259(302)
Zolik, E. S.: *ref,* 173(94), 5:172 (67, 160)
Zoob, I.: *ref,* 71(45), 176(7)
Zook, E. A.: *ref,* 6:129(9)
Zoolalian, C. H.: *ref,* 165(29)
Zubek, J. P.: *ref,* 67(582), 166 (2122), 277(43), 470(3545), 6:87 (250), 6:143(1222), 6:192(26)
Zubin, J.: *test,* 285; *bk,* P400, P435, P538, P925; *exc,* 3:82a, P673, P826, P909; *ref,* 166(2376), 285 (2), 470(3437, 3684), 484(1092, 1204), 2:1239(31), 3:27(11), 3:41(14), 3:73(235-6, 358, 597), 4:77(197), 4:117(768, 1063), 5:154(1414, 1454, 1826-7, 2153-5), 6:182(203), 6:237(2300)
Zucker, K. B.: *ref,* 438(18)
Zucker, L. J.: *ref,* 442A(101), 470 (3079), 4:117(663, 769, 898, 1064), 6:228(62, 75), 6:237(2466, 2946)
Zucker, R. A.: *ref,* 166(2126)
Zuckerman, M.: *test,* 176; *ref,* 4 (102), 67(689), 71(45, 80), 116 (63), 166(1560, 2327-9), 176(1-2, 5, 7-10, 21-3, 28), 439(97), 469(7), 484(1188), 5:47(50), 5:155(157), 6:87(84, 125, 222, 265), 6:110(93), 6:127(23), 6:143(942, 949, 1048, 1167), 6:237 (2846, 2904), 6:245(661, 810)
Zuckerman, S. B.: *exc,* P703; *ref,* 4:117(770)
Zuckman, L.: *ref,* 9(37)
Zuercher, M. C.: *ref,* 470(3548)
Zuidema, G. D.: *ref,* 6:204(70), 6:229(99)
Zuk, G. H.: *ref,* 6:194(100), 6:229 (126), 6:237(2372), 6:238(190), 6:245(627)
Zukowsky, E.: *ref,* 6:237(2847)
Zulliger, H.: *test,* 470; *bk,* P926-7; *ref,* 3:73(236a), 4:117(899, 1065-6), 5:154(1643, 2156)
Zung, W. W. K.: *test,* 242; *ref,* 166(1947, 2330), 242(1-2, 5-6)
Zunich, M.: *ref,* 6:145(77)
Zurick, G. T.: *ref,* 136(39)
Zussman, C.: *ref,* 5:154(1280)
Zuwaylif, F. H.: *ref,* 67(533)
Zwaag, L. V.: *ref,* 124(80)
Zwanziger, M. D.: *ref,* 484(985), 6:237(2897)
Zwetschke, E. T.: *ref,* 5:86(475)

Scanning Index to Tests

This Scanning Index is an expanded table of contents to the personality tests listed in the Personality Test Index, the first chapter of this monograph. The title, acronym (except for out of print tests), and entry number are reported for each test along with information as to whether it is a new test not previously listed in an MMY or whether it has been revised or supplemented since last listed in an MMY. Subtests with distinctive titles are also reported for in print tests. Stars indicate new tests and scoring services; asterisks, revised or supplemented tests. Within each of the two categories—nonprojective and projective—in print tests are listed first followed by out of print tests set in smaller type size.

NONPROJECTIVE

OUT OF PRINT